# EXPLANATORY NOTES AND SYMBOLS — *continued*

All "officially recognized" specialties are indicated with language which identifies the approving or certifying authority. Such programs are now in existence in Arizona, Arkansas, California, Florida, Louisiana, Minnesota, New Jersey, New Mexico, North Carolina, South Carolina, Tennessee, Texas and Ontario, Canada.

*Title of public office, company name, government agency, educational institution, etc.,* with which a lawyer is connected is shown in his or her listing.

*Professional Companies, Corporations or Associations:* Chartered, Associated, P.C., P.A., S.C., Inc., Ltd., etc. following the name of an individual lawyer or law firm means that such office is operating as a Professional Company, Corporation or Association under the laws of that jurisdiction.

"‡" devotes all or the greater part of one's time to the affairs of a single client, or is retired, semi-retired or semi-active, or principally engaged in activities other than the practice of law.

"⊙" maintains law offices at more than one place.

"★" with Armed Forces.

"(Pat.)" indicates lawyers who are registered to practice before the U.S. Patent and Trademark Office and who devote a considerable portion of time or duties to Patent, Trademark and other related matters.

"Ⓣ" indicates the rating was established in an admitting jurisdiction other than where the attorney is currently listed.

"BR" indicates a subscriber to the Martindale-Hubbell® Bar Register of Preeminent Lawyers.

# IMPORTANT NOTICES

Martindale-Hubbell has used its best efforts in collecting and preparing material for inclusion in the Martindale-Hubbell® Law Directory but cannot warrant that the information herein is complete or accurate, and does not assume, and hereby disclaims, any liability to any person for any loss or damage caused by errors or omissions in the Martindale-Hubbell® Law Directory whether such errors or omissions result from negligence, accident or any other cause.

Lawyers providing information regarding themselves and their law firms for inclusion in the Martindale-Hubbell® Law Directory are responsible for both the accuracy of the information submitted and compliance with local law and bar regulations.

The information contained in this Directory, including Martindale-Hubbell legal ratings, is intended primarily for the use of lawyers and law firms in the practice of their profession. It may not be used without permission from, and acknowledgement of, Martindale-Hubbell in any advertisement or for any commercial, political or other purpose.

Omission of individual lawyer ratings should not be construed as unfavorable since Martindale-Hubbell does not undertake to develop ratings for every lawyer. In addition, certain lawyers have requested their ratings not be published. In other instances, definitive information has yet to be developed.

Some lawyers and law firms are omitted from the Martindale-Hubbell® Law Directory by request while others are omitted because adequate information is not yet available.

# MARTINDALE-HUBBELL® LAW DIRECTORY

—•—

VOLUME 2

CALIFORNIA
A – R

**MARTINDALE-HUBBELL**
121 Chanlon Road
New Providence, NJ 07974
1-800-526-4902
Email: info@martindale.com
World Wide Web: http://www.martindale.com

Published by Martindale-Hubbell®, a member of the Reed Elsevier plc group

Lou Andreozzi, Publisher
Carol D. Cooper, Vice President, Associate Publisher
Larry Thompson, Vice President, Marketing
Kevin English, Vice President, Sales
Edward J. Roycroft, Vice President, Sales Support
Dean Hollister, Vice President Database Production
Chuck Doscher, Vice President Production
John R. Agel, Vice President, Ratings

Copyright © 1996, 1997 by Reed Elsevier Inc.
All Rights Reserved

Previous Editions
Copyright © 1994, 1995
Reed Elsevier Inc.

Copyright © 1991, 1992, 1993
Reed Publishing (USA) Inc.

Copyright © 1969, 1970, 1971, 1972, 1973, 1974, 1975, 1976, 1977, 1978
1979, 1980, 1981, 1982, 1983, 1984, 1985, 1986, 1987, 1988, 1989, 1990
Martindale-Hubbell, Inc.

*No part of this publication may be reproduced or transmitted in any form or by any means, or stored in any information storage and retrieval system, without prior written permission of Martindale-Hubbell.*

International Standard Book Number: 1-56160-222-1 (Set)

Printed and Bound in the United States of America
by R.R. Donnelley & Sons Company
Chicago, Illinois and Willard, Ohio

MARTINDALE-HUBBELL®, MARTINDALE-HUBBELL PRACTICE PROFILE™,
PRACTICE PROFILES®, AV®, BV®, CV®, LEXIS®, NEXIS® are trademarks
of Reed Elsevier Properties Inc., used under license.

ISBN 1-56160-222-1

# TABLE OF CONTENTS

Explanatory Notes and Symbols ............................................. Inside Front Cover;
Facing Page Inside Front Cover
Important Notices ......................................................... Facing Title Page
Foreword .................................................................. Page V
Martindale-Hubbell Legal Advisory Board ................................... Page VI
User's Guide .............................................................. Page VII
Martindale-Hubbell Ratings ................................................ Page XI
List of Colleges, Universities and Law Schools ............................ Page XIII

## PRACTICE PROFILES BAR ROSTER (Blue Pages)

Alabama, Alaska, Arizona, Arkansas ........................................ Volume 1
California (A — R) ........................................................ Volume 2
California (S — Z), Colorado .............................................. Volume 3
Connecticut, Delaware, District of Columbia, U.S. Government .............. Volume 4
Florida ................................................................... Volume 5
Georgia ................................................................... Volume 6
Guam ...................................................................... Volume 16
Hawaii, Idaho ............................................................. Volume 6
Illinois, Indiana, Iowa ................................................... Volume 7
Kansas, Kentucky, Louisiana, Maine, Maryland .............................. Volume 8
Massachusetts, Michigan ................................................... Volume 9
Minnesota, Mississippi, Missouri, Montana, Nebraska, Nevada, New Hampshire ... Volume 10
New Jersey, New Mexico, New York (Excluding New York City) ................ Volume 11
New York (Bronx, Brooklyn, Manhattan, Queens, Staten Island) .............. Volume 12
North Carolina, North Dakota, Ohio, Oklahoma, Oregon ...................... Volume 13
Pennsylvania .............................................................. Volume 14
Puerto Rico ............................................................... Volume 16
Rhode Island, South Carolina, South Dakota ................................ Volume 14
Tennessee, Texas .......................................................... Volume 15
U.S. Pacific Territories, Utah, Vermont, Virgin Islands, Virginia, Washington,
   West Virginia, Wisconsin, Wyoming ...................................... Volume 16
Corporate Law Departments ................................................. Volume 17

## PATENT AND TRADEMARK PRACTICE PROFILES SECTION (Blue Pages)
(Follows Practice Profiles Bar Roster in each volume)

## PROFESSIONAL BIOGRAPHIES SECTION (White Pages)

Alabama, Alaska, Arizona, Arkansas ........................................ Volume 1
California (A — R) ........................................................ Volume 2
California (S — Z), Colorado .............................................. Volume 3
Connecticut, Delaware, District of Columbia ............................... Volume 4
Florida ................................................................... Volume 5
Georgia ................................................................... Volume 6
Guam ...................................................... Volume 16 and International Volume I
Hawaii, Idaho ............................................................. Volume 6
Illinois, Indiana, Iowa ................................................... Volume 7
Kansas, Kentucky, Louisiana, Maine, Maryland .............................. Volume 8
Massachusetts, Michigan ................................................... Volume 9
Minnesota, Mississippi, Missouri, Montana, Nebraska, Nevada, New Hampshire ... Volume 10
New Jersey, New Mexico, New York (Excluding New York City) ................ Volume 11
New York (Bronx, Brooklyn, Manhattan, Queens, Staten Island) .............. Volume 12
North Carolina, North Dakota, Ohio, Oklahoma, Oregon ...................... Volume 13
Pennsylvania .............................................................. Volume 14
Puerto Rico ............................................... Volume 16 and International Volume II
Rhode Island, South Carolina, South Dakota ................................ Volume 14
Tennessee, Texas .......................................................... Volume 15
U.S. Pacific Territories .................................. Volume 16 and International Volume I
Utah, Vermont ............................................................. Volume 16

# TABLE OF CONTENTS — *continued*

PROFESSIONAL BIOGRAPHIES SECTION (White Pages) — *Continued*
    Virgin Islands .................................................. Volume 16 and International Volume II
    Virginia, Washington, West Virginia, Wisconsin, Wyoming .............................. Volume 16
    State Bar Association Section ................................................... Volume 17
    Corporate Law Departments Section .............................................. Volume 17
    Law School Section .......................................................... Volume 17

SERVICES, SUPPLIERS, CONSULTANTS SECTION (Yellow Pages)
• Including Indexes and List of Categories
    Alabama, Alaska, Arizona, Arkansas .............................................. Volume 1
    California (A — R) ............................................................ Volume 2
    California (S — Z), Colorado ................................................... Volume 3
    Connecticut, Delaware, District of Columbia ...................................... Volume 4
    Florida ..................................................................... Volume 5
    Georgia .................................................................... Volume 6
    Guam .......................................................... Volume 16 and International Volume III
    Hawaii, Idaho ............................................................... Volume 6
    Illinois, Indiana, Iowa ......................................................... Volume 7
    Kansas, Kentucky, Louisiana, Maine, Maryland .................................... Volume 8
    Massachusetts, Michigan ...................................................... Volume 9
    Minnesota, Mississippi, Missouri, Montana, Nebraska, Nevada, New Hampshire ......... Volume 10
    New Jersey, New Mexico, New York (Excluding New York City) ....................... Volume 11
    New York (Bronx, Brooklyn, Manhattan, Queens, Staten Island) ...................... Volume 12
    North Carolina, North Dakota, Ohio, Oklahoma, Oregon ............................. Volume 13
    Pennsylvania ................................................................ Volume 14
    Puerto Rico .................................................... Volume 16 and International Volume III
    Rhode Island, South Carolina, South Dakota ...................................... Volume 14
    Tennessee, Texas ............................................................ Volume 15
    U.S. Pacific Territories ........................................... Volume 16 and International Volume III
    Utah, Vermont .............................................................. Volume 16
    Virgin Islands .................................................. Volume 16 and International Volume III
    Virginia, Washington, West Virginia, Wisconsin, Wyoming .......................... Volume 16

ALPHABETICAL INDEX (United States and Puerto Rico & U.S. Territories)
    Alphabetical Index
    Services, Suppliers, Consultants National Alphabetical Index
    Services, Suppliers, Consultants National Geographical Index

AREAS OF PRACTICE INDEX
    Table of Contents
    Areas of Practice Index

INTERNATIONAL LAW DIRECTORY (3 Volumes)
    Volume I
      Law Firm Associations
      Europe, Asia, Australasia, Middle East & Africa
       • Professional Biographies
    Volume II
      Law Firm Associations
      North America, The Caribbean, Central & South America
       • Professional Biographies
    Volume III
      Law Firm Associations
      Indexes
       • Alphabetical
       • Areas of Practice
        • Canadian Practice Profiles
      Services, Suppliers, Consultants

# FOREWORD

Welcome to the 1997 *Martindale-Hubbell® Law Directory*, the legal community's most widely consulted and most respected directory of lawyers, law firms, and the legal market. The *Law Directory* contains information on virtually every active lawyer and law firm in the U.S. In total, it now covers more than 900,000 lawyers and law firms worldwide.

For over 129 years, Martindale-Hubbell's reputation as the definitive authority for and about the legal profession has been founded on a number of distinctive characteristics: accuracy, reliability, the impartiality of the Ratings system, and the ability to anticipate and respond to the evolving needs of the legal profession. This edition, with its increased international coverage, continues that tradition. In addition, there are other enhancements to the *Martindale-Hubbell Law Directory* that go beyond these printed pages.

As you may already be aware, on June 1, 1996, Martindale-Hubbell launched a new and innovative Internet distribution via **martindale.com**. With this service, Martindale-Hubbell's unique and comprehensive database of lawyers and law firms is now widely available in four formats: print, CD-ROM, online via the LEXIS®-NEXIS® services, and the Internet.

The **martindale.com** World Wide Web site (at http://www.martindale.com) is the cyberspace hub for information about the legal profession, facilitating access and exchange of data about attorneys and law firms. The *Martindale-Hubbell® Lawyer Locator™*, a key part of this Web site, enables users of the World Wide Web to access fully up-to-date information about every lawyer and law firm in the database — at no charge.

The site includes hypertext links that transport visitors from the Martindale-Hubbell attorney listings for a law firm directly to that firm's web site or home page on the Internet, and from those law firm sites back to the Martindale-Hubbell Professional Biographies. The availability of lawyer and law firm information on Martindale-Hubbell's Web site provides lawyers an unprecedented level of professional visibility before millions of businesses, government agencies, libraries, individuals, and other lawyers worldwide.

LEXIS®-NEXIS® continues to offer a vital service to professional researchers who execute an average of 2.5 million searches of the *Law Directory* a year.

As the number of international legal transactions increases, our coverage of international lawyers and law firms has expanded accordingly. The *International Law Directory* now encompasses over 150 countries, and the International Law Digest includes new sections for Vietnam, the Slovak Republic, and Latvia. The Law Digest on the LEXIS®-NEXIS® services enables users to search multiple jurisdictions simultaneously. It's easier than ever to search by specific topics and retrieve relevant cases. This service gives you access to more than 25 Uniform and Model Acts available in the LEXIS® Model Library.

Martindale-Hubbell continues to introduce enhancements which increase the convenience and utility of the database:

A Windows® version of the *Martindale-Hubbell Law Directory on CD-ROM* on the Folio® VIEWS® platform couples the full power of Martindale-Hubbell's database with the ease of one of today's most popular software platforms. Now Windows users can explore *Martindale-Hubbell on CD-ROM* while employing a more intuitive electronic interface: mouse-driven menus and clickable tool bars for every function, easy-to-read displays in the user's choice of fonts, and handy clipboards for cutting and pasting information. A network version of the *Martindale-Hubbell Law Directory on CD-ROM* is now available; many law firms — large and small — provide the database to every desktop computer in their firm.

The 1997 edition of the *Martindale-Hubbell International Arbitration and Dispute Resolution Directory* will be published in May. It is the only resource of its kind to provide those considering litigation alternatives, on a worldwide basis, with concise listings of professionals in dispute resolution.

One final note regarding the Internet. This medium gives you yet another avenue of communication with us; you can now Email your comments, questions, and suggestions to us at **info@martindale.com**.

It is our objective to ensure that Martindale-Hubbell continues to meet the legal community's ever-evolving information needs. We encourage you to contact us with any ideas and suggestions for our products, and thank you for your support.

Lou Andreozzi
Publisher

MARTINDALE-HUBBELL, LEXIS and NEXIS are registered trademarks of Reed Elsevier Properties Inc., used under license. WINDOWS is a registered trademark of the Microsoft Corporation.

# MARTINDALE-HUBBELL®/LEXIS®-NEXIS® LEGAL ADVISORY BOARD

The Martindale-Hubbell/LEXIS-NEXIS Legal Advisory Board was formed to ensure that Martindale-Hubbell and LEXIS-NEXIS are responsive to the constantly changing needs of the legal profession. The following lawyers selected from the private, corporate and international sectors of the profession, as well as the legal academic community, comprise the 1996-1997 Board.

**VINCENT J. APRUZZESE** of Apruzzese, McDermott, Mastro & Murphy, Liberty Corner, NJ. Mr. Apruzzese is a former President of the New Jersey State Bar Association, a former member of the ABA Board of Governors and House of Delegates, and former Chair of the Labor and Employment Law Section of the ABA. Mr. Apruzzese is a Fellow of the American College of Trial Lawyers.

**MARTHA W. BARNETT** of Holland & Knight, Tallahassee, Florida. Ms. Barnett is the Immediate Past Chair of the House of Delegates of the American Bar Association, the first woman lawyer to be so honored, and serves on the ABA's Board of Governors.

**ALLEN E. BRENNECKE** of Harrison, Brennecke, Moore, Sasha & McKibben, Marshaltown, Iowa. Mr. Brennecke has served as a Member of the Board of Directors of the National Judicial College, President of the Iowa State Bar Association, a Member of the ABA House of Delegates since 1975 and its Chair, 1984-1986. His prior service to the ABA also includes four years on the Board of Governors and three years as Chair of the IOLTA Commission. He currently serves on the Board of Editors of the American Bar Association Journal and previously served as Chair from 1989 to 1995.

**BENJAMIN R. CIVILETTI** of Venable, Baetjer, Howard & Civiletti, Baltimore, Maryland. Mr. Civiletti is a former Attorney General of the United States under President Carter, 1979-1981. He has been a Trustee of Johns Hopkins University since 1980. He also serves as Chairman of Venable, Baetjer & Howard. Mr. Civiletti is a Fellow of the American College of Trial Lawyers.

**DOUGLAS B. HENDERSON** is the Founding and Senior Partner of Finnegan, Henderson, Farabow, Garrett & Dunner, Washington, D.C. Mr. Henderson is a Member of the Board of Advisors of The George Washington University Law School, Member of the Advisory Council of the United States Court of Federal Claims, and a Member of the Board of the Federal Circuit Bar Association. He was formerly Chairman of the Patent Division and Member of Council of Patent, Trademark and Copyright Law Section of the American Bar Association. He was the Founder of the Federal Circuit Bar Association, a co-founder of the U.S. Court of Federal Claims Bar Association, and a co-founder of the ITC Trial Lawyers Association.

**THOMAS G. HEINTZMAN, Q.C.,** of McCarthy Tétrault, Toronto, Ontario, is a member of the Canadian Bar Association and a Past President (1994-1995). In addition, he is a member of the International Bar Association and serves as the Canadian Delegate to the IBA Council. He is also a member of the Inter-American Bar Association. Mr. Heintzman is a Fellow of the American College of Trial Lawyers and is Chair of its Canadian Judiciary Committee.

**THOMAS J. KLITGAARD,** fomerly Senior Vice President and General Counsel of Sega of America, Inc., is now in private practice in San Francisco. He is a former Chairman of the California State Bar's Committee on the Maintenance of Professional Competence. Mr. Klitgaard began his legal career as a law clerk to Supreme Court Justice William O. Douglas. From 1963-1985, he was in private practice with the San Francisco law firm of Pillsbury, Madison & Sutro, where he specialized in anti-trust and securities litigation. Since 1979, he has been active in East Asian legal affairs. Fluent in conversational Mandarin Chinese, Mr. Klitgaard is Vice-Chairman of the Shanghai-San Francisco Friendship Committee, and has served as Chairman of the Board of the Chinese Cultural Foundation of San Francisco. He is also a Director of the American Arbitration Association, a Trustee of the University of San Francisco and a member of the Advisory Board for The Southwestern Legal Foundation since 1990.

**RALPH I. LANCASTER, JR.** of Pierce, Atwood, Portland, Maine. Mr. Lancaster is Past-President of the Maine State Bar Association, and a former member of the House of Delegates of the American Bar Association. He has served as Chairman of the Standing Committee on the Federal Judiciary of the ABA. He is a Fellow of the American College of Trial Lawyers of which he was President, 1989-1990.

**JERALYN E. MERRITT,** of Denver, Colorado, is an author and frequent lecturer on criminal defense. She was selected by Chairman Bill McCollum, House Judiciary Committee, Subcommittee on Crime, to present oral and written congressional testimony on federal marijuana sentencing laws on behalf of the National Association of Criminal Defense Lawyers (NACDL) on March 6, 1996, in Washington, D.C. She served as Chair from 1995-1996 while a judicially appointed member of the Standing Committee on the Criminal Justice Act for the United States District Court for the District of Colorado from 1994-1996. Ms. Merritt is currently a member of the Board of Directors and Chair of the Advisory Board for the National Association of Criminal Defense Lawyers, the Director of the Cyberspace Bar Association and a member of the Board of Governors for the American Board of Criminal Lawyers.

**HARRIET E. MIERS,** President of Locke Purnell Rain Harrell, Dallas, Texas, has previously served as President and Director of the State Bar of Texas as well as President and Chairman of the Board of Directors for the Dallas Bar Association. She is currently Chair of the ABA Journal Board of Editors and a member of the House of Delegates for the American Bar Association. Ms. Miers also serves as Chair of the Texas Lottery Commission and as a member of the Board of Directors of the Attorneys Liability Assurance Society.

**WILLIAM G. PAUL** of Crowe & Dunlevy, Oklahoma City, Oklahoma. Mr. Paul is the former Senior Vice President & General Counsel, Phillips Petroleum Company, Bartlesville, Oklahoma. He has served as President of the Oklahoma State Bar Association, President of the National Conference of Bar Presidents, a Member of the American Bar Association, House of Delegates 1975-1995 and is a Fellow in the American College of Trial Lawyers. In February 1995, he was nominated to the Board of Governors of the American Bar Association to serve a three-year term, 1995-1998.

**FERNANDO POMBO,** of Gomez-Acebo & Pombo, Madrid, Spain, has contributed to and authored several publications in the field of international commerce. Currently, he is the International Bar Association Secretary (SGP). Mr. Pombo has been a visiting professor at the Institute on International Legal Studies in Salzburg, Austria since 1985. He is also a former President of LES International and a member of the Spanish Arbitration Court. He is fluent in Spanish, English, French and German.

**ROBERTA COOPER RAMO,** a shareholder of Modrall, Sperling, Roehl, Harris & Sisk in Albuquerque, NM is Immediate Past President of the American Bar Association and currently serves on the ABA Board of Governors. She also served on the Board of the American Bar Retirement Association from 1990-1994 and was Chair of the ABA Council of Section Officers from 1984-1986. She is a former President of the Albuquerque Bar Association (1980) and a member (1988-1994) and President (1991-1993) of the University of New Mexico Board of Regents. Currently, she is a member of the State Bar of Texas, the State Bar of New Mexico, the New Mexico Estate Planning Council, and a Fellow of the American College of Trust and Estate Council. She also serves on the University of Chicago Law School Visiting Committee.

**WM. REECE SMITH, JR.** of Tampa, Florida, is the senior member of Carlton, Fields, Ward, Emmanuel, Smith & Cutler, P.A., a law firm. A Rhodes Scholar at Oxford University, England, he was later president of The Florida Bar (1972-73), the American Bar Association (1980-81), and the International Bar Association (1988-90). He is a Fellow of the American College of Trial Lawyers and the International Academy of Trial Lawyers and serves on the Council of the American Law Institute. He received the American Bar Association's Gold Medal for "exceptionally distinguished service to the cause of American Jurisprudence."

**WALTER H. WHITE, JR.** is Managing Director of Steptoe & Johnson International, in Moscow, Russia, and Partner in Steptoe & Johnson L.L.P. in Washington, D.C. Mr. White served as the Wisconsin Commissioner of Securities, 1988-1991. He is a former member of the ABA House of Delegates, and has served on the Board of Milwaukee Foundation and currently is a board member of the Central-Asian-American Enterprise Fund by appointment of President Clinton.

# USER'S GUIDE

The Martindale-Hubbell® Law Directory now consists of:

- sixteen numbered U.S. volumes (burgundy spine accent). Each volume is separated into three main sections, which have been color-coded for easy access: Practice Profiles (blue pages), Professional Biographies (white pages) and Services, Suppliers, Consultants (yellow pages). In each Section, headings are provided at the top of each page to indicate the section being referenced and to provide a guide to the listings on that page.
- one volume (Volume 17) containing listings for State Bar Association Profiles, Corporate Law Departments and Law Schools (burgundy spine accent)
- one Martindale-Hubbell Alphabetical Index volume (green spine accent)
- one Martindale-Hubbell Areas of Practice Index volume (green spine accent)
- three volumes of the Martindale-Hubbell International Law Directory (blue spine accent), containing listings for lawyers and firms in over 150 countries (including sections for Canada and U.S. lawyers with international interests)
- two Martindale-Hubbell Law Digests for the U.S. (black spine accent)
- one Martindale-Hubbell International Law Digest (black spine accent)

Guam, Puerto Rico, U.S. Pacific Territories and the Virgin Islands can be found both at the end of the U.S. volumes (Volume 16) and in the appropriate sections of the Martindale-Hubbell International Law Directory (see Table of Contents).

# SECTION DESCRIPTIONS

## PRACTICE PROFILES (BLUE PAGES)

Contains rosters for the Bars of the United States. Listings of United States Government Lawyers located in Washington, D.C. are grouped by departments, agencies and commissions, etc. and follow the regular listings for that city in Volume 4.

This Section is alphabetically arranged by state, by city or town, and then by name of attorney or law firm. Contact information for state bar associations appears on the first page of each state.

Listings for individual attorneys include the following information, when available: name, rating if any, year of birth, first year of admission to the Bar, college attended, first degree received, law school attended, first degree received, and where the attorney practices.

A typical individual attorney listing follows:

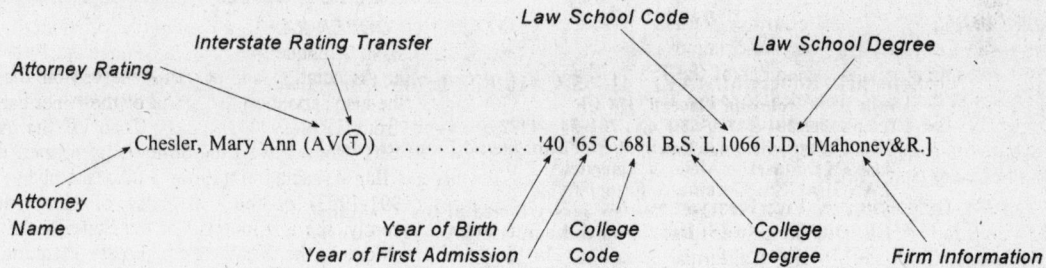

Law firm listings provide name, address and rating information, where available.

A typical law firm listing will appear as follows:

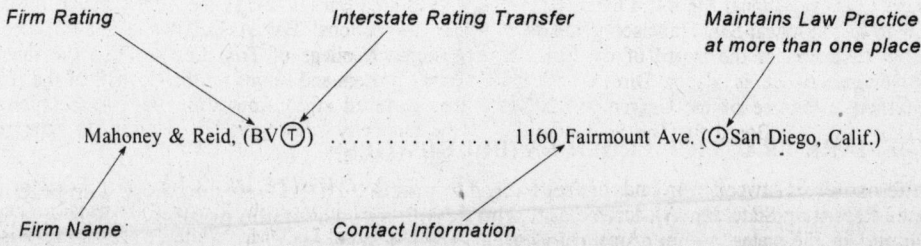

Practice Profiles listings for subscribing attorneys and law firms appear in boldface type and include name, rating (if available), address, firm personnel, statement of practice, representative clients, references, and language proficiency as well as other pertinent information.

Typical Subscriber Full Practice Profiles follow:

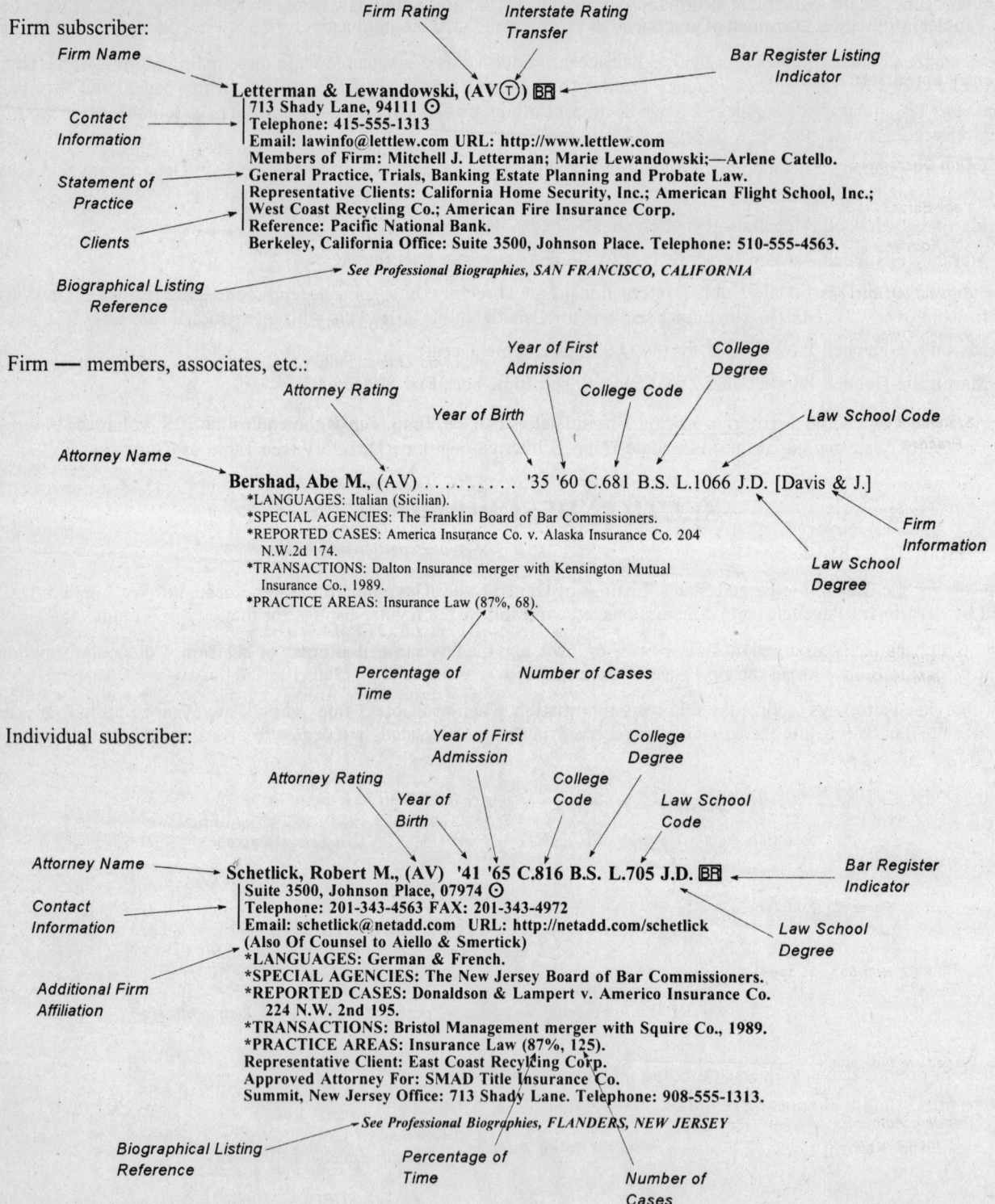

## PATENT AND TRADEMARK PRACTICE PROFILES (BLUE PAGES)

This Section contains the names of subscribing lawyers registered to practice Patent Law and those who practice Trademark Law before The United States Patent and Trademark Office and who devote a considerable portion of their practice or duties to this field of law. It is arranged in the same manner as the Practice Profiles Section.

## PROFESSIONAL BIOGRAPHIES (WHITE PAGES)

The Professional Biographies Section is arranged alphabetically by state, by city or town, and then by name of attorney or law firm. It provides substantial biographical information on individual attorneys within law firms. Entries in this section include the firm name, contact information, statement of practice, firm profile, individual biographical information, representative clients and references.

A typical entry appears as follows:

|  |  |
|---|---|
| Firm Name | ***LETTERMAN & LEWANDOWSKI*** |
| Firm Descriptor | *A Partnership including A Professional Corporation* |
| Year Established | *Established in 1990* |
| Formerly | *Formerly Letterman and Rosta* |
| Contact Information | *731 SHADY LANE* **SAN FRANCISCO, CALIFORNIA 94111** *Telephone: 415-555-1313 FAX: 415-555-7351 Email: lawinfo@lettlew.com URL: http://www.lettlew.com* |
| Branch Office Information | *Berkeley, California Office:* Suite 3500, 110 Johnson Place. Telephone: 510-555-4563. Fax: 510-555-4972. |
| Statement of Practice | *General Practice, Trials, Banking, Finance, Wills, Trusts, Estate Planning and Probate Law.* |
| Firm Profile | *FIRM PROFILE: Letterman & Lewandowski was founded in 1990. The firm encourages continuing professional development and all partners and associates participate in continuing legal education seminars, professional association activities and civic affairs.* |

*MEMBERS OF FIRM*

Individual Biographical Information / Military →
**MITCHELL J. LETTERMAN, (P.C.),** born Summit, New Jersey, January 14, 1939; admitted to bar 1968, California. *Education:* United States Naval Academy (B.S., 1960); Harvard University (J.D., summa cum laude, 1968). Private Pilots License, 1960. *Member:* State Bar of California. [Lt., U.S. Navy, 1961-1964]. **PRACTICE AREAS:** Banking Law (50%); Finance (25%); Wills and Trusts (25%). **Email:** mjletter@lettlew.com.

Percentage of Time / Number of Cases →
**MARIE LEWANDOWSKI,** born Jeanette, Pennsylvania, October 7, 1940; admitted to bar, 1965, California. *Education:* University of California at Berkeley (B.A., summa cum laude, 1962); Hastings College of the Law, University of California (J.D., summa cum laude, 1965). Editor-in-Chief, Hastings Law Journal, 1961-1962. *Member:* Bar Association of San Francisco; State Bar of California. (Also Of Counsel, Rudy & Catello). **LANGUAGES:** Spanish and French. **SPECIAL AGENCIES:** Goodman Zoning Board. **REPORTED CASES:** Bilko Inc. v. Zotser Trucking Co. **TRANSACTIONS:** Aiello Packing merger with Alboum Paper Products. **PRACTICE AREAS:** Estate Planning Law (48%, 78); Probate Law (52%). **Email:** mlewando@lettlew.com.

Associate Indicator → ―――――――

Pending Admission Indicator →
**ARLENE CATELLO,** born San Mateo, California, January 11, 1965; (admission pending). *Education:* Radcliffe College (B.S., cum laude, 1987); Boalt Hall School of Law, University of California (J.D. summa cum laude, 1991). *Email:* acatello@lettlew.com.

*LEGAL SUPPORT PERSONNEL*

Individual Email Address →
**KATHLEEN VECCHIA,** born Summit, New Jersey, August 22, 1962. *Education:* Rutgers University (B.A., 1984). Certified Paralegal, New Jersey, 1984. *Member:* National Association of Paralegals. (Paralegal). **PRACTICE AREAS:** Estates (85%).

Clients →
REPRESENTATIVE CLIENTS: California Home Security, Inc.; American Flight School, Inc.; West Coast Recycling Co.; American Fire Insurance Corp. REFERENCE: Pacific National Bank.

## STATE BAR ASSOCIATION PROFILES (WHITE PAGES)

Volume 17 includes State Bar Association Profiles. These profiles include a brief history, mission statements of the association, names of officers, directors, and key staff personnel, as well as membership and program information.

This section is arranged alphabetically by state.

## CORPORATE LAW DEPARTMENTS (WHITE PAGES)

Corporate Law Department representations are resident in Volume 17. They are arranged alphabetically by name and present information about corporations and corporate attorneys. Typical information supplied includes name, company profile, office location(s) and type of business.

## LAW SCHOOLS (WHITE PAGES)

The Law School Section, in Volume 17, profiles the academic programs, special course offerings and teaching staff of participating schools. Schools choosing not to present complete profiles are also identified.

For each school, the data may include: school name, address, telephone and telecopier numbers; the names, titles and direct dial numbers of key contacts; a substantial description including the history, academic character, resources, special programs and activities of the institution; and a roster of full time faculty with biographical summary information.

This section is arranged alphabetically by law school name.

## SERVICES, SUPPLIERS, CONSULTANTS (YELLOW PAGES)

This Section is arranged alphabetically by state, city or town, category of service provided, and then by company name. Full listing information is given, and over 200 major categories appear in our new three-tiered format provide easy access to needed support services utilized by lawyers and law firms.

National Alphabetical and Geographical Indexes to the cumulative content of the Services, Suppliers, Consultants Indexes by category are provided at the end of the Alphabetical Index Volume.

# USER AIDS

In the front matter, sections are provided to aid in the use of the Directory. "Explanatory Notes and Symbols", found inside the front cover, provide a guide to the various symbols and notations which are utilized in the individual entries. The "List of Colleges, Universities, and Law Schools", found on page XIII provides a comprehensive guide to numeric codes which are used in Practice Profiles listings to indicate academic institutions and law schools attended by individual attorneys.

Page numbers in the 1997 Martindale-Hubbell Law Directory are constructed in the format XXYYYZ, where XX is the state, province or international grouping, YYY is a consecutive page numbering, and Z is a code denoting section.

XX is the standard U.S. state abbreviations; pages listing attorneys under the U.S. Government use the abbreviation "GV". The Law School Section uses the abbreviation "LS". The abbreviation "SB" is used for the State Bar Association Profiles. For International Volumes, the following group abbreviations are used:

- EU (Europe)
- AS (Asia)
- AU (Australasia)
- AF (Middle East & Africa)
- NA (North America & Caribbean)
- CB (The Caribbean)
- CS (Central & South America)

Z may be one of the following:

- P for "Practice Profiles"
- B for "Professional Biographies"
- T for "Patent & Trademark"
- S for "Services, Suppliers, Consultants"

For additional help or explanation, please call Martindale-Hubbell Customer Service, at 1-800-MARTIND(ALE) or in New Jersey, at 908-464-6800.

# MARTINDALE-HUBBELL RATINGS

The first Martindale books were published in 1868, the principal one being Martindale's United States Law Directory and later Martindale's American Law Directory.

In 1930, the publishing rights to Hubbell's Legal Directory were purchased by the Martindale Company and ever since has been known as the Martindale-Hubbell® Law Directory.

Legal Ability and General Recommendation Ratings have appeared in the Directory for over 100 years, with a company imperative to publish fair and accurate ratings for as many lawyers as possible, subscribers and non-subscribers alike. While the vast majority of rating reviews are initiated by the Company, an inquiry will be undertaken upon request. Lawyers, both private and corporate, refer to ratings when forwarding legal matters with confidence in the accuracy of the information presented.

**Legal Ability Ratings are:** "A" (from Very High to Preeminent), "B" (from High to Very High), "C" (from Fair to High).

**General Recommendation Rating is:** "V" (Very High).

Unless a rating is established in both categories, no rating will be published.

Approximately 50,000 Rating reviews are undertaken each year. Of those, 40,000 are done at our own initiative, primarily for lawyers admitted 5, 10, 15, 20 and 25 years. An additional 10,000 are conducted by request and through the efforts of our Field Staff.

Martindale-Hubbell develops its ratings for individual lawyers by soliciting confidential opinions from members of the Bar, including those who themselves have ratings and those who do not. In addition, members of the Judiciary are queried. We encourage all lawyers to participate in the process. Greater participation enhances the accuracy of the system. Respondents to written questionnaires and personal interviews are requested to base their opinions on the following:

## LEGAL ABILITY RATING

Based on the standard of ability for the place or area where the lawyer practices, it takes into consideration experience, nature of practice and qualifications relevant to the profession. Where a lawyer's practice is limited or specialized, rating opinions are made on the basis of performance in those Fields of Law. There are no minimum periods of time in practice required for any rating.

## GENERAL RECOMMENDATION RATING

Embraces faithful adherence to professional standards of conduct and ethics of the legal profession, professional reliability and diligence, and standards relevant to the attorney's discharge of his or her professional responsibilities.

Legal Ability and General Recommendation ratings appearing in the Directory reflect strictly confidential opinions and responses to professionally developed surveys and adhere to meticulously monitored research principles and practices. Martindale-Hubbell does not make any independent evaluation of lawyers, depending exclusively upon the opinions expressed by its confidential sources.

## FIRM RATING

Generally, a law firm will be accorded the rating of its highest rated principal.

Where a lawyer's practice is limited or specialized, the rating recommendations are made on the basis of performance in those particular fields of law. In some instances, lawyers may be asked to submit names of lawyers and judges with whom they have had professional involvement.

Inquiries are then directed to those sources in addition to sources developed by Martindale-Hubbell.

Field Representatives of Martindale-Hubbell visit tens of thousands of law offices on an annual basis. They make oral rating inquiries during these calls and submit written reports for review. Such a review must occur before any rating is established, advanced, lowered or withdrawn.

> *Martindale-Hubbell does not undertake developing ratings for every listed lawyer. The absence of a rating should not be misconstrued. Some lawyers have requested their ratings not be published. In other instances definitive information has not yet been completely developed.*

Ratings are produced for United States lawyers, excluding Guam, Puerto Rico, Virgin Islands, U.S. Pacific and Other Territories.

No subscription or listing in the Martindale-Hubbell® Law Directory is ever solicited or accepted on the promise of publication of a particular rating. No preferential consideration is ever given to any lawyer or law firm.

As a general rule, ratings are transferable within state boundaries. Ratings may be transferred inter-state with the Ⓣ symbol indicating the rating was obtained in another State.

It is company policy to conduct regular periodic reviews of all ratings to insure accuracy. Where supporting opinions are received, appropriate action (such as deleting, raising or lowering a rating) is taken to fulfill our obligation to the users of the Directory.

There is never any payment made to lawyers and judges who participate in Ratings reviews. The process is a cooperative service to the Bar. It has always been Martindale-Hubbell policy to treat all phases of the ratings review process as absolutely confidential. Sources contacted participate with that understanding and under no circumstances will any review materials ever be released.


Note: Please review Important Notices located on facing title page.

# List of Colleges, Universities and Law Schools in the United States

This list is a guide to the numeric school codes found in Practice Profiles Section entries. Not included are all normal schools, junior colleges, institutions which no longer exist, correspondence schools or colleges with very small enrollments. Such unlisted schools are indicated by the numeric codes "999" in listings for U.S. and Canadian attorneys, and "061" for attorneys in other countries.

## A

1. Abilene Christian University
   Abilene, Texas
2. Academy of the New Church
   Bryn Athyn, Pa.
3. Adams State College
   Alamosa, Col.

   Adelbert College
   See No. 930
4. Adelphi University
   Garden City, N.Y.
5. Adrian College
   Adrian, Mich.
6. Agnes Scott College
   Decatur, Ga.

   Agricultural and Mechanical College of Kentucky
   Now University of Kentucky
   See No. 383

   Agricultural & Technical College of North Carolina
   Now North Carolina Agricultural Technical State University
   See No. 548
7. Akron University Law School
   Akron, Ohio
8. Akron, University of
   Formerly Buchtel College
   Akron, Ohio

   Alabama Agricultural and Mechanical University
   See No. 1010
9. Alabama College
   Now Montevallo University
   Montevallo, Ala.
10. Alabama Polytechnic Institute
    Now Auburn University
    Auburn and Montgomery, Ala.
11. Alabama State Teachers College
    Now University of North Alabama
    Florence, Ala.
12. Alabama State Teachers College
    Now Jacksonville State University
    Jacksonville, Ala.
13. Alabama State Teachers College
    Now Livingston University
    Livingston, Ala.
14. Alabama State University
    Formerly Montgomery State College
    Montgomery, Ala.
15. Alabama State Teachers College
    Now Troy State University
    Troy, Ala.
16. Alabama, University of
    Birmingham, Huntsville and Tuscaloosa, Ala.
17. Alaska, University of
    Fairbanks, Anchorage and Juneau, Alaska
18. Albany College
    Portland, Ore.

    Albany Law School of Union College
    See No. 982

    Albert Einstein College of Medicine
    Now Yeshiva University
    See No. 978

    Albertson College of Idaho
    See No. 335
19. Albertus Magnus College
    New Haven, Conn.
20. Albion College
    Albion, Mich.
21. Albright College
    Reading, Pa.

    Albuquerque, University of
    See No. 1143
22. Alcorn A. & M. College
    Alcorn, Miss.
23. Alderson-Broaddus College
    Philippi, W.Va.

    Alfred Holbrook College
    See No. 995
24. Alfred University
    Alfred, N.Y.
25. Allegheny College
    Meadville, Pa.
26. Allen University
    Columbia, S.C.

    Allentown College of St. Francis De Sales
    See No. 1296

    Alliance College
    See No. 1072
27. Alma College
    Alma, Mich.

    Alverno College
    See No. 1352

    American College of Law
    See No. 1240

    American Extension School of Law
    See No. 1007
28. American International College
    Springfield, Mass.
29. American University
    Los Angeles, Cal.
30. American University
    Washington, D.C.
    See also No. 904
31. Amherst College
    Amherst, Mass.

    Anderson College
    See No. 992
32. Andrew Jackson University
    Nashville, Tenn.

    Andrews University
    Formerly Emmanuel Missionary College
    See No. 243

    Angelo State University
    See No. 1096
33. Antioch College
    Yellow Springs, Ohio

    Antioch School of Law
    See No. 1162
34. Appalachian State University
    Boone, N.C.

    Aquinas College
    See No. 1121
35. Arizona State College
    Now Northern Arizona University
    Flagstaff, Ariz.
36. Arizona State University
    Tempe, Ariz.
37. Arizona, University of
    Tucson, Ariz.
38. Arkansas A. & M. College
    Now University of Arkansas at Monticello
    Monticello, Ark.
39. Arkansas A. M. & N. College
    Now University of Arkansas at Pine Bluff
    Pine Bluff, Ark.
40. Arkansas Baptist College
    Little Rock, Ark.
41. Arkansas College
    Batesville, Ark.
42. Arkansas Law School
    Little Rock, Ark.

    Arkansas at Little Rock, University of
    See No. 1243

    Arkansas at Monticello, University of
    Formerly Arkansas A. & M. College
    See No. 38

    Arkansas at Pine Bluff, University of
    Formerly Arkansas A. M. & N College
    See No. 39

    Arkansas Polytechnic University
    Now Arkansas Tech University
    See No. 1125
43. Arkansas State University
    State College (Jonesboro), Ark.
44. Arkansas, State College of
    Now University of Central Arkansas
    Conway, Ark.

    Arkansas Tech University
    See No. 1125
45. Arkansas, University of
    Fayetteville, Ark.

    Arlington State
    Now University of Texas at Arlington
    See No. 1142
46. Armour Institute of Technology
    Now Illinois Institute of Technology
    Chicago, Ill.

    Armstrong College
    See No. 1197

    Armstrong State College
    See No. 1276
47. Asbury College
    Wilmore, Ky.
48. Asheville, University of North Carolina,
    Asheville, N.C.
49. Ashland College
    Ashland, Ohio

    Assumption College
    See No. 1107
50. Athens State College
    Athens, Ala.
51. Atlanta Law School
    Atlanta, Ga.
52. Atlanta University
    Atlanta, Ga.
53. Atlantic Christian College
    Wilson, N.C.
54. Atlantic Union College
    South Lancaster, Mass.

    Auburn University
    Formerly Alabama Polytechnic Institute
    See No. 10

XIII

55. Augsburg College
    Minneapolis, Minn.
    Augusta College
    See No. 1267
    Augusta Law School
    See No. 1277
56. Augustana College
    Sioux Falls, S.D.
57. Augustana College
    Rock Island, Ill.
58. Aurora College
    Aurora, Ill.
59. Austin College
    Sherman, Texas
    Austin Peay State University
    See No. 1081
    Avila College
    See No. 1297
    Azusa Pacific University
    See No. 1232

# B

Babson College
See No. 1155
60. Baker University
    Baldwin City, Kan.
61. Balboa Law College
    Now California Western School of Law
    San Diego, Cal.
62. Baldwin-Wallace College
    Berea, Ohio
63. Ball State University
    Muncie, Ind.
    Baltimore Law School
    Now University of Maryland
    See No. 446
64. Baltimore, University of
    Baltimore, Md.
    Baptist College at Charleston
    See No. 1328
    Barat College
    See No. 991
65. Bard College
    Formerly St. Stephen's College
    Annandale on Hudson, N.Y.
66. Barnard College
    New York, N.Y.
    Barry College
    See No. 1278
67. Bates College
    Lewiston, Me.
    Bates College of Law
    Part of University of Houston
    See No. 326
68. Battle Creek College
    Battle Creek, Mich.
69. Baylor University
    Waco, Texas
70. Beaver College
    Jenkintown, Pa.
71. Belhaven College
    Jackson, Miss.
    Bellarmine College
    See No. 1150
    Belmont Abbey College
    See No. 1126
72. Beloit College
    Beloit, Wis.
    Bemidji State University
    Formerly Minnesota State Teachers College
    See No. 488
73. Benedict College
    Columbia, S.C.
    Benedictine College
    See No. 1182
    Benedictine Heights College
    Formerly Catholic College of Oklahoma for Women
    See No. 126
    Benjamin N. Cardozo School of Law
    Part of Yeshiva University
    See No. 978
    Benjamin Franklin University
    See No. 1279

74. Benjamin Harrison Law School
    Now Indiana University
    Indianapolis, Ind.
    See also No. 347
    Bennett College
    See No. 1298
75. Bennington College
    Bennington, Vt.
    Bentley College
    See No. 1134
76. Benton College of Law
    Saint Louis, Mo.
77. Berea College
    Berea, Ky.
    Berklee College of Music
    See No. 1293
    Bernard M. Baruch College of the City University of New York
    See No. 1138
78. Berry College
    Mount Berry, Ga.
79. Bessie Tift College
    Forsyth, Ga.
    See also No. 99
80. Bethany College
    Lindsborg, Kan.
81. Bethany College
    Bethany, W.Va.
82. Bethany-Nazarene College
    Now Southern Nazarene University
    Bethany, Okla.
83. Bethel College
    North Newton, Kan.
84. Bethel College
    McKenzie, Tenn.
    Bethel College
    Saint Paul, Minn.
    See No. 1144
85. Bethune-Cookman College
    Daytona Beach, Fla.
    Beverly College of Law
    Now Whittier College School of Law
    See No. 1148
    Biddle University
    Now Johnson C. Smith University
    See No. 369
86. Billings Polytechnic Institute
    Now Rocky Mountain College
    Billings, Mont.
    Biola University
    See No. 1259
87. Birmingham School of Law
    Birmingham, Ala.
88. Birmingham-Southern College
    Birmingham, Ala.
    Biscayne College
    Now St. Thomas University
    See No. 1158
89. Bishop College
    Marshall, Texas
    Blackburn College
    See No. 1101
    Black Hills State College
    See No. 1255
    Blackstone School of Law
    See No. 1008
    Bloomfield College
    See No. 1180
    Bloomington Law School
    Now Illinois Wesleyan University
    See No. 340
    Bloomsburg State College
    See No. 646
    Bloomsburg University of Pennsylvania
    Formerly Pennsylvania State Teachers College
    See No. 646
90. Blue Mountain College
    Blue Mountain, Miss.
    Blue Ridge College
    See No. 984
91. Bluffton College
    Bluffton, Ohio
    Boalt Hall School of Law, University of California, Berkeley
    See No. 1066
92. Bob Jones University
    Greenville, S.C.

Boise State University
See No. 1193
93. Boston College
    Newton Centre and Chestnut Hill, Mass.
    Boston State College
    See No. 1149
94. Boston University
    Boston, Mass.
95. Bowdoin College
    Brunswick, Me.
96. Bowling Green College of Commerce
    Part of Western Kentucky University
    Bowling Green, Ky.
97. Bowling Green State University
    Bowling Green, Ohio
98. Bradley University
    Peoria, Ill.
    Brandeis University
    See No. 1036
99. Brenau College
    Gainesville, Ga.
    Brescia College
    See No. 1299
    Briarcliff College
    See No. 1233
    Briar Cliff College
    See No. 985
    Bridgeport, University of
    See No. 1029
100. Bridgewater College
     Bridgewater, Va.
     Bridgewater State College
     Formerly Massachusetts State College, Bridgewater
     See No. 455
101. Brigham Young University
     Provo, Utah
     See also No. 1335
102. Brooklyn College of the City University of New York
     Brooklyn, N.Y.
     Brooklyn Law School
     See No. 1009
     Brothers College
     Now Drew University
     See No. 222
103. Brown University
     Providence, R.I.
     Bryan College
     See No. 946
     Bryant College
     See No. 1145
104. Bryn Mawr College
     Bryn Mawr, Pa.
     Buchtel College
     Now University of Akron
     See No. 8
105. Bucknell University
     Lewisburg, Pa.
106. Buena Vista College
     Storm Lake, Iowa
107. Buffalo, University of
     Now State University of New York at Buffalo
     Buffalo, N.Y.
108. Butler University
     Indianapolis, Ind.

# C

Cabrillo Pacific University
Now National University
See No. 1241
Cabrini College
See No. 1199
Caldwell College
See No. 1343
109. California Associated Colleges
     Los Angeles, Cal.
110. California Christian College
     Fresno, Cal.
     California College of Law
     See No. 1127
111. California Institute of Technology
     Pasadena, Cal.
     California Lutheran College
     Now California Lutheran University
     See No. 1253

# LIST OF COLLEGES

California Maritime Academy
See No. 1250

California Polytechnic State University (San Luis Obispo)
See No. 1074

California State College, Bakersfield
See No. 1212

California State Polytechnic University (Pomona)
See No. 1075

California State University, Chico
Formerly Chico State College
See No. 147

California State University, Dominguez Hills
See No. 1131

California State University, Fresno
Formerly Fresno State College
See No. 267

California State University, Fullerton
See No. 1109

California State University, Hayward
See No. 1073

California State University, Long Beach
See No. 1042

California State University, Los Angeles
See No. 1097

California State University, Northridge
See No. 1077

California State University, Sacramento
See No. 1060

California State University, San Bernardino
See No. 1110

California State University, San Francisco
Now San Francisco State University
See No. 766

California State University, Stanislaus
See No. 1079

California University of Pennsylvania
Formerly Pennsylvania State Teachers College
See No. 647

112. California, University of
Berkeley, Davis, Irvine, Los Angeles, San Francisco, Santa Barbara, Riverside and San Diego, Cal.

*Note: There are four separate and distinct law schools: Berkeley (Boalt Hall), Los Angeles, San Francisco (Hastings College of Law) and Davis. See. No's. 1065 to 1068.*

113. See No. 112
California at Santa Cruz, University of
See No. 1169

California Western School of Law
Formerly Balboa College of Law
See No. 61

California Western University
Now United States International University
See No. 1188

114. Calvin College
Grand Rapids, Mich.

Calvin Coolidge College
See No. 1022

Cameron University
See No. 1300

115. Campbell College
Jackson, Miss.

Campbell University
See No. 1228

Campbell University School of Law
Now Wiggins, Norman A., School of Law
See No. 1345

116. Canisius College
Buffalo, N.Y.

Canterbury College
Formerly Central Normal College
See No. 135

117. Capital University
Columbus, Ohio

Cardozo, Benjamin N., School of Law
Part of Yeshiva University
See No. 978

118. Carleton College
Northfield, Minn.

Carlow College
Formerly Mount Mercy College
See No. 521

119. Carnegie Mellon University
Formerly Carnegie Institute of Technology
Pittsburgh, Pa.

120. Carroll College
Helena, Mont.

121. Carroll College
Waukesha, Wis.

122. Carson-Newman College
Jefferson City, Tenn.

123. Carthage College
Formerly at Carthage, Ill.
Kenosha, Wis.

124. Case Institute of Technology
Now Case Western Reserve University
Cleveland, Ohio
See also No. 930

Case Western Reserve University
Formerly Western Reserve University
See No. 930

Castleton State College
See No. 1330

125. Catawba College
Salisbury, N.C.

126. Catholic College of Oklahoma for Women
Now Benedictine Heights College
Guthrie, Okla.

127. Catholic Sisters College
Now Catholic University of America
Washington, D.C.
See also No. 128

128. Catholic University of America
Washington, D.C.

Catholic University of Puerto Rico
See No. 1087

CBN University
Now Regent University
See No. 1339

129. Cedar Crest College
Allentown, Pa.

130. Cedarville College
Cedarville, Ohio

131. Centenary College
Shreveport, La.

Central Arkansas, University of
Formerly Arkansas, State College of
See No. 44

132. Central College
Pella, Iowa

133. Central College
Now Central Methodist College
Fayette, Mo.

Central Connecticut State College
Formerly Teachers College of Connecticut, The
See No. 829

Central Florida, University of
See No. 1175

Central Methodist College
Formerly Central College
See No. 133

Central Michigan University
See No. 136

134. Central Missouri State University
Formerly Missouri State University
Warrensburg, Mo.

135. Central Normal College
Now Canterbury College
Danville, Ind.

136. Central Michigan University
Mount Pleasant, Mich.

Central Oklahoma, University of
Edmond, Okla.
See No. 1147

Central State University
Wilberforce, Ohio
See No. 1023

Central State University
Now University of Central Oklahoma
Edmond, Okla.
See No. 1147

Central University
Now Centre College of Kentucky
See No. 138

Central Washington University
Formerly Washington State Normal School
See No. 909

137. Central Y.M.C.A. College
Chicago, Ill.

138. Centre College of Kentucky
Formerly Central University
Danville, Ky.

# CLARION STATE COLLEGE

Chadron State College
Formerly Nebraska State Teachers College
See No. 542

Chaminade University of Honolulu
See No. 1069

139. Chapman College
Orange, Cal.

140. Charleston, College of
Charleston, S.C.

141. Charleston Educational Center
Charleston, W.Va.

Charleston, University of
Formerly Morris Harvey College
See No. 516

Chase, Salmon P., College of Law
Part of Northern Kentucky University
See No. 151

Chatham College
Formerly Pennsylvania College for Women
See No. 643

142. Chattanooga College of Law
Chattanooga, Tenn.

143. Chattanooga, University of
Now University of Tennessee at Chattanooga
Chattanooga, Tenn.

Chestnut Hill College
Formerly Mount St. Joseph College
See No. 522

Cheyney State College
See No. 1261

144. Chicago Law School
Formerly Midland University
Chicago, Ill.

Chicago State University
Formerly Chicago Teachers College
See No. 1191

Chicago Teachers University
Now Chicago State University
See No. 1191

145. Chicago, University of
Chicago, Ill.

146. Chicago-Kent College of Law,
Illinois Institute of Technology
Chicago, Ill.

147. Chico State College
Now California State University, Chico
Chico, Cal.

148. Chicora College
Columbia, S.C.

Christian Brothers College
See No. 1034

Christopher Newport College
Formerly Christopher Newport College of the College of William and Mary
See No. 1329

149. Chowan College
Murfreesboro, N.C.

150. Cincinnati, University of
Cincinnati, Ohio

151. Cincinnati Y.M.C.A. Schools
Cincinnati, Ohio
Cincinnati, OH,

152. Citadel, The
Charleston, S.C.

Citrus Belt Law School
See No. 1198

City College of the City University of New York
See No. 563

City University of New York, City College of the
See No. 563

City University of New York, Queens College of the
See No. 994

City University of New York, Hunter College of the
331

City University of New York School of Law, Queens College of the
See No. 1178

153. Claflin College
Orangeburg, S.C.

154. Claremont McKenna College
Claremont, Cal.

Clarion State College
See No. 648

XV

Clarion University of Pennsylvania
Formerly Clarion State College
See No. 648
155. Clark College
Atlanta, Ga.
156. Clark University
Worcester, Mass.
157. Clarke College
Dubuque, Iowa
158. Clarkson University
Formerly Clarkson College of Technology
Potsdam, N.Y.
159. Cleary College
Ypsilanti, Mich.
160. Clemson University
Clemson, S.C.
Cleveland College
Now Case Western Reserve University
See No. 930
Cleveland Marshall College of Law
See No. 1003
161. Cleveland State University
Cleveland, Ohio
Clinch Valley College
Now University of Virginia
See No. 893
162. Coe College
Formerly Western College
Cedar Rapids, Iowa
163. Coker College
Hartsville, S.C.
164. Colby College
Waterville, Me.
165. Colgate University
Hamilton, N.Y.
College of St. Mary of the Springs
See No. 737
166. College of the Holy Names
Now Holy Names College
Oakland, Cal.
167. College Misericordia
Dallas, Pa.
168. College of the Ozarks
Clarksville, Ark.
169. College of the Pacific
Now University of the Pacific
Stockton, Cal.
See also No. 464
College of St. Francis Xavier
See No. 1006
College of Staten Island of the City University
of New York
See No. 1140
170. Colorado College
Colorado Springs, Col.
171. Colorado School of Mines
Golden, Col.
172. Colorado A. & M. College
Now Colorado State University
Fort Collins, Col.
173. Colorado State College
Now University of Northern Colorado
Greeley, Col.
Colorado State University
Formerly Colorado A. & M. College
See No. 172
174. Colorado at Boulder, University of
Boulder, Col.
Colorado at Colorado Springs, University of
See No. 1164
Colorado at Denver, University of
See No. 1165
Colorado Women's College
See No. 1264
175. Colored Agricultural & Normal University
Now Langston University
Langston, Okla.
176. Columbia College
Columbia, S.C.
177. Columbia College of Dubuque
Now Loras College
Dubuque, Iowa
Columbia Union College
Formerly Washington Missionary College
See No. 905
178. Columbia University
New York, N.Y.

Columbian University
Now George Washington University
See No. 273
Columbus College
See No. 1301
179. Columbus College of Law
Now Capital University
Columbus, Ohio
See also No. 117
180. Columbus University
Now Catholic University of America
Washington, D.C.
See also No. 128
181. Concord College
Athens, W.Va.
182. Concordia College
Moorehead, Minn.
183. Connecticut College
New London, Conn.
184. Connecticut, University of
Storrs and Hartford, Conn.
Connecticut, School of Law, University of
Formerly Hartford College of Law
Hartford, Conn.
See No. 306
185. Converse College
Spartanburg, S.C.
186. Cooper Union
New York, N.Y.
187. Cornell College
Mount Vernon, Iowa
188. Cornell University
Ithaca, N.Y.
Corpus Christi State University
See No. 1284
189. Cotner College
Lincoln, Neb.
Convenant College
See No. 1195
190. Creighton University
Omaha, Neb.
191. Culver-Stockton College
Canton, Mo.
Cumberland College
See No. 1302
192. Cumberland School of Law of Samford
University
Formerly part of Cumberland University
(now Cumberland College of Tennessee, at
Lebanon, Tenn.)
Birmingham, Ala.
Curry College
See No. 1303
C. W. Post College
Now Long Island University
See No. 415

# D

Dakota Northwestern University
Formerly North Dakota State College
See No. 584
193. Dakota Wesleyan University
Mitchell, S.D.
Dallas, University of
See No. 1105
194. Dana College
Blair, Neb.
Dana College
Now Rutgers University
Newark, N.J.
See No. 705
195. Daniel Baker College
Brownwood, Texas
196. Daniel W. Voorhees Law School
Terre Haute, Ind.
197. Dartmouth College
Hanover, N.H.
David Lipscomb College
See No. 1064
198. Davidson College
Davidson, N.C.
199. Davis & Elkins College
Elkins, W.Va.
200. Dayton Law School
Dayton, Ohio

201. Dayton, University of
Dayton, Ohio
202. Decorah College for Women
Decorah, Iowa
203. Defiance College
Defiance, Ohio
Delaware Law School of Widener University
Now Widener University School of Law
See No. 1338
204. Delaware State College
Dover, Del.
205. Delaware, University of
Newark, Del.
206. Delta State College
Cleveland, Miss.
207. Denison University
Granville, Ohio
208. Denver, University of
Denver, Col.
209. De Paul University
Chicago, Ill.
210. DePauw University
Greencastle, Ind.
211. Des Moines College of Law
Now Drake University
See also No. 221
212. Detroit City Law School
Now Wayne University
Detroit, Mich.
213. Detroit College of Law
Detroit, Mich.
214. Detroit Institute of Technology
Detroit, Mich.
215. Detroit, University of
Detroit, Mich.
216. Dickinson College
Carlisle, Pa.
Dickinson School of Law
See No. 1017
Dickinson State College
Formerly North Dakota State College
See No. 581
217. Dillard University
New Orleans, La.
District of Columbia, University of
See No. 1280
218. Doane College
Crete, Neb.
219. Dominican College of San Rafael
San Rafael, Cal.
220. Dominican College
Now St. Mary's Dominican College
New Orleans, La.
Dordt College
See No. 1304
Douglass College
Part of Rutgers University
See No. 705
Dowling College
See No. 1192
221. Drake University
Formerly Des Moines College of Law
Des Moines, Iowa
222. Drew University
Formerly Brothers College
Madison, N.J.
223. Drexel University
Philadelphia, Pa.
224. Dropsie University
Philadelphia, Pa.
225. Drury College
Springfield, Mo.
Dubuque College
Now Loras College
See No. 177
226. Dubuque, University of
Dubuque, Iowa
227. Duchesne College
Omaha, Neb.
228. Duke University
Formerly Trinity College of North Carolina
Durham, N.C.
Dunbarton College of the Holy Cross
See No. 1295
229. Duquesne University
Pittsburgh, Pa.

# LIST OF COLLEGES

# GLASSBORO STATE COLLEGE

230. D'Youville College
Buffalo, N.Y.

## E

231. Earlham College
Richmond, Ind.
232. East Carolina University
Greenville, N.C.
East Central Oklahoma State University
Formerly Oklahoma East Central State College
See No. 618
East Stroudsburg University
Formerly Pennsylvania State Teachers College
See No. 649
East Tennessee State University
Formerly Tennessee Teacher's College
See No. 835
East Tennessee Wesleyan University
See No. 143
233. East Texas State University
Commerce, Texas
Eastern College
See No. 1305
Eastern College of Commerce and Law
Now University of Baltimore School of Law
See No. 1002
234. Eastern Illinois University
Charleston, Ill.
235. Eastern Kentucky University
Formerly Kentucky Normal College
Richmond, Ky.
Eastern Mennonite College
See No. 1124
Eastern Michigan University
Formerly Michigan State Normal College
See No. 476
Eastern Montana College
See No. 1235
236. Eastern Nazarene College
Quincy, Mass.
Eastern New Mexico University
See No. 1012
Eastern Oregon College
See No. 1104
Eastern Washington University
Formerly Washington State Normal School
See No. 908
Eckerd College
See No. 1236
Edinboro University of Pennsylvania
Formerly Pennsylvania State Teachers College
See No. 650
237. Elizabethtown College
Elizabethtown, Pa.
238. Elmhurst College
Elmhurst, Ill.
239. Elmira College
Elmira, N.Y.
Elms College
Formerly College of Our Lady of the Elms
See No. 633
240. Elon College
Elon College, N.C.
Embry-Riddle Aeronautical University
See No. 1333
241. Emerson College
Boston, Mass.
242. Emmanuel College
Boston, Mass.
243. Emmanuel Missionary College
Now Andrews University
Berrien Springs, Mich.
244. Emory and Henry College
Emory, Va.
245. Emory University
Formerly Lamar School of Law
Atlanta, Ga.
Empire College School of Law
See No. 1227
Empire State College
Part of State University of New York
See No. 1044
246. Emporia, College of
Emporia, Kan.

Emporia State University
Formerly Kansas State College
See No. 376
Epworth University
Now Oklahoma City University
See No. 616
247. Erskine College
Due West, S.C.
248. Eureka College
Eureka, Ill.
Evangel College
See No. 1359
249. Evansville, University of
Evansville, Ind.
Evergreen State College, The
See No. 1331

## F

Fairfield University
See No. 1030
Fairhaven College
Now Western Washington University
See No. 907
Fairleigh Dickinson University
See No. 1046
250. Fairmont State College
Fairmont, W.Va.
Fairmount College
Now Wichita State University
See No. 942
Fayetteville State University
See No. 1011
251. Fenn College
Now Cleveland State University
Cleveland, Ohio
See also No. 161
252. Ferris State College
Big Rapids, Mich.
253. Findlay College
Findlay, Ohio
254. Fisk University
Nashville, Tenn.
Fitchburg State College
Formerly Massachusetts State College
See No. 456
255. Fletcher School of Law & Diplomacy
Medford, Mass.
256. Flora Macdonald College
Red Springs, N.C.
Florence State University
Now University of North Alabama
See No. 11
257. Florida A. & M. University
Tallahassee, Fla.
Florida Atlantic University
See No. 1086
Florida Institute of Technology
See No. 1210
Florida International University
See No. 1222
258. Florida Southern College
Lakeland, Fla.
259. Florida State University
Tallahassee, Fla.
Florida Technological University
Now University of Central Florida
See No. 1175
260. Florida, University of
Gainesville, Fla.
261. Fontbonne College
St. Louis, Mo.
262. Fordham University
New York, N.Y.
263. Ft. Hays State University
Hays, Kan.
Fort Lewis College
See No. 1262
Framingham State College
Formerly Massachusetts State College
See No. 457
264. Franklin & Marshall College
Lancaster, Pa.
265. Franklin College of Indiana
Franklin, Ind.

Franklin Law School of Capital University
Now Capital University
See No. 117
Franklin Pierce College
See No. 1170
Franklin Pierce Law Center
See No. 1218
Franklin T. Bacchus College
Now Case Western Reserve University
See No. 930
266. Franklin University
Columbus, Ohio
Fremont College
Now Midland Lutheran College
See No. 480
267. Fresno State College
Now California State University, Fresno
Fresno, Cal.
268. Friends University
Wichita, Kan.
Frostburg State College
Formerly Maryland State Teachers College
See No. 443
Fuchsberg Law Center, Touro College, Jacob D.
See No. 1325
269. Furman University
Greenville, S.C.

## G

270. Gallaudet College
Washington, D.C.
Gannon University
See No. 1062
General Motors Institute
See No. 1229
271. Geneva College
Beaver Falls, Pa.
George Fox College
Formerly Pacific College
See No. 635
George Mason University
Formerly George Mason College of the University of Virginia
See No. 1356
George Mason University School of Law
See No. 1209
272. George Peabody College for Teachers
Formerly University of Nashville
Nashville, Tenn.
George, Walter F., Law School
Part of Mercer University
See No. 469
273. George Washington University
Washington, D.C.
274. George Williams College
Downer's Grove, Ill.
275. Georgetown College
Georgetown, Ky.
276. Georgetown University
Washington, D.C.
277. Georgia Institute of Technology
Atlanta, Ga.
278. Georgia College
Milledgeville, Ga.
Georgia Southern College
See No. 1063
Georgia Southwestern College
See No. 1282
Georgia State University
See No. 1059
279. Georgia State Womans College
Now Valdosta State College
Valdosta, Ga.
Georgia Teachers College
Formerly South George Teachers College
See No. 794
280. Georgia, University of
Athens, Ga.
281. Georgian Court College
Lakewood, N.J.
282. Gettysburg College
Gettysburg, Pa.
Glassboro State College
See No. 1116

XVII

Glendale University
See No. 1190
283. Glenville State College
Glenville, W.Va.
Goddard College
See No. 1123
284. Golden Gate University
San Francisco, Cal.
285. Gonzaga University
Spokane, Wash.
286. Good Counsel College
White Plains, N.Y.
287. Gooding College
Wesleyan, Idaho
288. Goshen College
Goshen, Ind.
289. Goucher College
Towson, Md.
Graceland College
See No. 1281
Grambling State University
See No. 1177
Grand Valley State College
See No. 1265
Great Falls, College of
See No. 1306
Greenleaf, Simon, School of Law
See No. 1351
290. Greensboro College
Greensboro, N.C.
291. Greenville College
Greenville, Ill.
292. Greenville Woman's College
Greenville, S.C.
293. Grinnell College
Grinnell, Iowa
294. Grove City College
Grove City, Pa.
295. Guadelupe College
Seguin, Texas
Guam, University of
See No. 1334
296. Guilford College
Guilford College, N.C.
297. Gustavus Adolphus College
St. Peter, Minn.

# H

298. H. Sophie Newcomb Memorial College
New Orleans, La.
299. Hamilton College
Clinton, N.Y.
300. Hamline University
St. Paul, Minn.
301. Hampden-Sydney College
Hampden-Sydney, Va.
Hampshire College
See No. 1307
302. Hampton Institute
Hampton, Va.
303. Hanover College
Hanover, Ind.
304. Hardin-Simmons University
Abilene, Texas
305. Harding University
Searcy, Ark.
Harding, Warren G., College of Law
Now Ohio Northern University
See No. 607
Harpur College
Part of State University of New York at
Binghamton
See No. 1349
306. Hartford College of Law
Now University of Connecticut School of
Law
Hartford, Conn.
307. Harris-Stowe State College
St. Louis, Mo.
Hartford, University of
See No. 1033
308. Hartwick College
Oneonta, N.Y.
309. Harvard University
Cambridge, Mass.

Harvey Mudd College
See No. 1167
310. Hastings College
Hastings, Neb.
Hastings College of the Law, University of
California, San Francisco
See No. 1065
311. Haverford College
Haverford, Pa.
312. Hawaii, University of
Including William S. Richardson School of
Law
Honolulu, Hilo and Manoa, Hawaii
313. Heidelberg College
Tiffin, Ohio
314. Henderson State University
Arkadelphia, Ark.
315. Hendrix College
Conway, Ark.
Herbert H. Lehman College of the City
University of New York
See No. 1160
316. High Point College
High Point, N.C.
317. Hillsdale College
Hillsdale, Mich.
Hillyer College
Now University of Hartford
See No. 1033
318. Hiram College
Hiram, Ohio
319. Hobart and William Smith Colleges
Formerly Hobart College and William Smith
College. Note: These are two separate
schools operating under one name and
sharing faculty and facilities.
Geneva, N.Y.
Hofstra University
See No. 1019
320. Hollins College
Hollins, Va.
321. Holy Cross, College of the
Worcester, Mass.
Holy Names College
Formerly College of the Holy Names
See No. 166
322. Hood College
Frederick, Md.
323. Hope College
Holland, Mich.
324. Houghton College
Houghton, N.Y.
Houston Baptist University
Houston, Texas
See No. 1052
325. Houston College
Now Texas Southern University
Houston, Texas
Houston Law School
See No. 998
326. Houston, University of
Including University of Houston Law Center
Houston, Texas
327. Howard College
Now Samford University
Birmingham, Ala.
328. Howard Payne University
Brownwood, Texas
329. Howard University
Washington, D.C.
330. Humboldt State University
Arcata, Cal.
Humphreys College
See No. 1132
331. Hunter College of the City University of New
York
New York, N.Y.
332. Huntingdon College
Montgomery, Ala.
333. Huntington College
Huntington, Ind.
334. Huron College
Huron, S.D.
Huston-Tillotson College
See No. 1037
Hyannis State College
Formerly Massachusetts State College
See No. 458

# I

335. Idaho, Albertson College of
Caldwell, Idaho
Idaho State University
See No. 1032
336. Idaho, University of
Moscow, Idaho
Illinois Benedictine College
Formerly St. Procopius College
See No. 750
337. Illinois College
Jacksonville, Ill.
Illinois College of Law
Now De Paul University
See No. 209
Illinois Law School
Now De Paul University
See No. 209
338. Illinois State University
Normal, Ill.
Illinois Institute of Technology
See No. 46
339. Illinois, University of
Champaign-Urbana and Chicago, Ill.
340. Illinois Wesleyan University
Bloomington, Ill.
341. Immaculata College
Immaculata, Pa.
342. Immaculate Heart College
Hollywood, Cal.
343. Incarnate Word College
San Antonio, Texas
344. Indiana Central University
Now University of Indianapolis
Indianapolis, Ind.
Indiana Institute of Technology
See No. 1159
345. Indiana University School of Law
Formerly Indiana Law School
Indianapolis, Ind.
346. Indiana State University
Terre Haute, Ind.
347. Indiana University
Bloomington and Indianapolis, Ind.
*(Also maintains campuses at Kokomo, South
Bend, Gary and New Albany, Ind., and jointly
with Purdue University at Indianapolis and Ft.
Wayne, Ind.)*
Indiana University of Pennsylvania
Formerly Pennsylvania State Teachers College
See No. 651
Indiana University School of Law
See No. 1119
Indianapolis, University of
Formerly Indiana Central University
See No. 344
Inter-American University of Puerto Rico
See No. 1088
348. Intermountain Union College
Great Falls, Mont.
International School of Law
See No. 1184
349. International Y.M.C.A. College
Now Springfield College
Springfield, Mass.
Iona College
See No. 1041
350. Iowa State College of A. & M. Arts
Now Iowa State University
Ames, Iowa
351. Iowa State Teachers College
Now University of Northern Iowa
Cedar Falls, Iowa
Iowa State University
Formerly Iowa State College of A. & M. Arts
See No. 350
352. Iowa, University of
Formerly State University of Iowa
Iowa City, Iowa
353. Iowa Wesleyan College
Mt. Pleasant, Iowa
Irvine University
See No. 1225

# LIST OF COLLEGES

354. Ithaca College
Ithaca, N.Y.

## J

355. Jackson State University
Jackson, Miss.
356. Jackson School of Law
Now Mississippi College School of Law
Jackson and Clinton, Miss.

Jacksonville State University
Formerly Alabama State Teachers College
See No. 12

Jacksonville University
See No. 1038

Jacob D. Fuchsberg Law Center, Touro College
See No. 1325

James Madison University
Formerly Virginia State Teachers College
See No. 891

357. James Millikin University
Now Millikin University
Decatur, Ill.
358. Jamestown College
Jamestown, N.D.
359. Jefferson School of Law
Now University of Louisville
Louisville, Ky.
360. Jefferson School of Law
Dallas, Texas

Jersey City State College
Formerly New Jersey State College
See No. 1025

361. John Brown University
Siloam Springs, Ark.
362. John B. Stetson University
Now Stetson University
De Land and St. Petersburg, Fla.
363. John Carroll University
Formerly St. Ignatius College
Cleveland, Ohio

John F. Kennedy University
See No. 1153

364. John Fletcher College
Now Kletzing College
University Park, Iowa

John Jay College of Criminal Justice of the City University of New York
See No. 1139

John Marshall Law School
Atlanta, Ga.
See No. 1000

365. John Marshall Law School
Chicago, Ill.

John Marshall Law School
Jersey City, N.J.
See No. 997

John Marshall Law School
Cleveland, Ohio
See No. 989

366. John Randolph Neal College of Law
Knoxville, Tenn.
367. Johns Hopkins University
Baltimore, Md.
368. Johnson Bible College
Kimberlin Heights, Tenn.
369. Johnson C. Smith University
Formerly Biddle University
Charlotte, N.C.
370. Jones Law School
Montgomery, Ala.

J. Rueben Clark Law School
Now Brigham Young University
See No. 101

371. Judson College
Marion, Ala.
372. Juniata College
Huntingdon, Pa.

## K

373. Kalamazoo College
Kalamazoo, Mich.
374. Kansas City School of Law
Part of University of Missouri at Kansas City
Kansas City, Mo.

Kansas City, University of
Now University of Missouri at Kansas City
See No. 986

Kansas Newman College
See No. 1283

375. Kansas State College of Agriculture and Applied Science
Now Kansas State University
Manhattan, Kan.
376. Kansas State College
Now Emporia State University
Emporia, Kan.
377. Kansas State College
Now Pittsburg State University
Pittsburg, Kan.

Kansas State University
Formerly Kansas State College of Agriculture & Applied Science
See No. 375

378. Kansas, University of
Lawrence, Kan.
379. Kansas Wesleyan University
Salina, Kan.

Kean College of New Jersey
Formerly New Jersey State College
See No. 553

Kearney State College
Now University of Nebraska at Kearney
See No. 543

380. Keene State College
Keene, N.H.
381. Kent State University
Kent, Ohio

Kentucky Normal College
Now Eastern Kentucky University
See No. 235

382. Kentucky State University
Frankfort, Ky.
383. Kentucky, University of
Lexington, Ky.
384. Kentucky Wesleyan College
Owensboro, Ky.
385. Kenyon College
Gambier, Ohio
386. Keuka College
Keuka Park, N.Y.

Kilbride Law School
Now Woodrow Wilson College of Law
See No. 969

387. King College
Bristol, Tenn.

King Hall School of Law, University of California, Davis
Now University of California School of Law, Davis
See No. 1067

King's College
See No. 1113

Kirkland College
Now Hamilton College
See No. 299

Kletzing College
Formerly John Fletcher College
See No. 364

388. Knox College
Galesburg, Ill.
389. Knoxville College
Knoxville, Tenn.

Kutztown University
Formerly Pennsylvania State Teachers College
See No. 652

## L

390. Lafayette College
Easton, Pa.
391. LaGrange College
LaGrange, Ga.
392. Lake Erie College
Painesville, Ohio

Lake Erie Law School
Now Cleveland-Marshall College of Law
Cleveland, Ohio
See No. 1003

393. Lake Forest College
Lake Forest, Ill.

Lake Superior State College
See No. 1285

# LIVINGSTON UNIVERSITY

Lamar School of Law
Now Emory University
See No. 245

Lamar University
See No. 1061

394. Lambuth College
Jackson, Tenn.
395. Lander College
Greenwood, S.C.
396. Lane College
Jackson, Tenn.

Langston University
Formerly Colored Agricultural & Normal University
See No. 175

397. LaSalle University
Philadelphia, Pa.

LaSalle Extension University
See No. 981

La Sierra College
Now Loma Linda University
Arlington, Cal.
See No. 1163

398. La Verne, University of
La Verne, Cal.

Lawrence Institute of Technology
See No. 1217

399. Lawrence University
Appleton, Wis.

Lebanon University
Now Cumberland University

400. Lebanon Valley College
Annville, Pa.
401. Lehigh University
Bethlehem, Pa.
402. Leland College
Baker, La.

Le Moyne College
Syracuse, N.Y.
See No. 1031

403. Le Moyne-Owen College
Memphis, Tenn.
404. Lenoir-Rhyne College
Hickory, N.C.

Lewis and Clark College
See No. 1051

405. Lewis Institute
Now Illinois Institute of Technology
Chicago, Ill.
See also No. 46

Lewis University
See No. 1151

Lewis University Law School
Now Northern Illinois University College of Law
See No. 589

406. Limestone College
Gaffney, S.C.
407. Lincoln College of Indiana
Indianapolis, Ind.
408. Lincoln College of Law
Bakersfield, Cal.

Lincoln College of Law
Springfield, Ill.
See No. 996

409. Lincoln Memorial University
Harrogate, Tenn.

Lincoln University
San Francisco, San Jose and Sacramento, Cal.
See No. 1026

Lincoln University School of Law
Now Lincoln University
St. Louis, Mo.
See No. 410

410. Lincoln University
Jefferson City, Mo.
411. Lincoln University
Lincoln University, Pa.
412. Lindenwood Colleges, The
St. Charles, Mo.
413. Linfield College
McMinnville, Ore.

Little Rock University
Now University of Arkansas at Little Rock
See No. 1243

Livingston University
Formerly Alabama State Teachers College
See No. 13

XIX

414. Livingstone College
    Salisbury, N.C.
Lock Haven University of Pennsylvania
    Formerly Pennsylvania State Teachers College
    See No. 653
Loma Linda University
    See No. 1163
Lone Mountain College
    Formerly San Francisco College for Women
    See No. 764
Long Beach State University
    Now California State University, Long Beach
    See No. 1042
415. Long Island University, C.W. Post Campus of
    Brookville, N.Y.
Long Island University, Brooklyn Campus of
    See No. 1353
Longwood College
    Formerly Virginia State Teachers College
    See No. 889
Loras College
    See No. 177
416. Loretto Heights College
    Denver, Col.
Los Angeles College of Law
    See No. 1251
Los Angeles State College
    Now California State University, Los Angeles
    See No. 1097
417. Louisiana College
    Pineville, La.
418. Louisiana Polytechnic Institute
    Now Louisiana Tech University
    Ruston, La.
419. Louisiana State Normal College
    Now Northwestern State University
    Natchitoches, La.
420. Louisiana State University and A. and M.
    College
    Baton Rouge, La.
Louisiana State University at Alexandria
    See No. 1098
Louisiana State University at New Orleans
    Now University of New Orleans
    See No. 1099
Louisiana State University at Shreveport
    See No. 1237
Louisiana Tech University
    Formerly Louisiana Polytechnic Institute
    See No. 418
421. Louisville, University of
    Formerly Jefferson School of Law
    Louisville, Ky.
Lowell, University of
    Formerly Massachusetts State College
    See No. 459
422. Lowell Technological Institute
    Part of University of Lowell
    Lowell, Mass.
423. Loyola College
    Baltimore, Md.
Loyola Marymount University
    Formerly Loyola College
    See No. 426
424. Loyola University
    Chicago, Ill.
425. Loyola University
    New Orleans, La.
426. Loyola Marymount University
    Los Angeles, Cal.
Lumpkin Law School
    Now University of Georgia
    See No. 280
427. Luther College
    Decorah, Iowa
Lycoming College
    See No. 1047
428. Lynchburg College
    Lynchburg, Va.

# M

429. Macalester College
    St. Paul, Minn.
430. MacMurray College
    Jacksonville, Ill.

Madison, James, University
    Formerly Virginia State Teachers College
    See No. 891
431. Maine, University of
    Orono, Farmington, Fort Kent, Machias and
    Presque Isle, Me.
Maine, University of, School of Law
    See No. 1294
432. Manchester College
    N. Manchester, Ind.
433. Manhattan College
    Riverdale, N.Y.
Manhattanville College
    Formerly Manhattanville College of the
    Sacred Heart
    See No. 706
Mankato State University
    Formerly Minnesota State Teachers College
    See No. 490
Mansfield University
    Formerly Pennsylvania State Teachers College
    See No. 654
Marian College
    See No. 1216
434. Marietta College
    Marietta, Ohio
435. Marion College
    Marion, Ind.
Marist College
    See No. 1266
436. Marquette University
    Milwaukee, Wis.
Mars Hill College
    See No. 1129
437. Marshall University
    Huntington, W.Va.
Marshall-Wythe School of Law
    Now College of William and Mary
    See No. 945
438. Mary Baldwin College
    Staunton, Va.
439. Mary Hardin-Baylor College
    Belton, Texas
440. Mary Manse College
    Toledo, Ohio
Mary Washington College
    Formerly Virginia State Teachers College
    See No. 890
Marycrest College
    See No. 707
441. Marygrove College
    Detroit, Mich.
442. Maryland College for Women
    Lutherville, Md.
443. Maryland State Teachers College
    Now Frostburg State College
    Frostburg, Md.
444. Maryland State Teachers College
    Now Salisbury State University
    Salisbury, Md.
445. Maryland State Teachers College
    Now Towson State University
    Towson, Md.
446. Maryland, University of
    Baltimore and College Park, Md.
447. Marylhurst College
    Oswego, Ore.
448. Marymount College of Kansas
    Salina, Kan.
449. Marymount College
    Tarrytown, N.Y.
Marymount-Manhattan College
    See No. 1135
450. Maryville College
    St. Louis, Mo.
451. Maryville College
    Maryville, Tenn.
452. Marywood College
    Scranton, Pa.
453. Massachusetts Institute of Technology
    Cambridge, Mass.
454. Massachusetts, University of
    Amherst and Boston, Mass.
Massachusetts Maritime Academy
    See No. 1308
455. Massachusetts State College
    Now Bridgewater State College
    Bridgewater, Mass.

456. Massachusetts State College
    Now Fitchburg State College
    Fitchburg, Mass.
457. Massachusetts State College
    Now Framingham State College
    Framingham, Mass.
458. Massachusetts State College
    Now Hyannis State College
    Hyannis, Mass.
459. Massachusetts State College
    Now University of Lowell
    Lowell, Mass.
460. Massachusetts State College
    Now North Adams State College
    North Adams, Mass.
461. Massachusetts State College
    Now Salem State College
    Salem, Mass.
462. Massachusetts State College
    Now Westfield State College
    Westfield, Mass.
463. Massachusetts State College
    Now Worcester State College
    Worcester, Mass.
Massachusetts, University of
    See No. 454
Mayville State College
    Formerly North Dekota State College
    See No. 582
464. McGeorge School of Law
    Part of University of the Pacific
    Sacramento, Cal.
465. McKendree College
    Lebanon, Ill.
466. McMurry College
    Abilene, Texas
McNeese State University
    See No. 1089
467. McPherson College
    McPherson, Kan.
Memphis State University
    See No. 836
Memphis, University of
    See No. 1015
Menlo College
    See No. 1254
468. Mercer Beasley School of Law
    Now Rutgers University
    Newark, N.J.
    See also No. 705
469. Mercer University
    Macon, Ga.
470. Mercyhurst College
    Erie, Pa.
471. Meredith College
    Raleigh, N.C.
Merrimack College
    See No. 1057
Messiah College
    See No. 1053
Methodist College
    See No. 1309
Metropolitan State College
    See No. 1201
472. Miami, University of
    Coral Gables, Fla.
473. Miami University
    Oxford, Ohio
474. Michigan Technological University
    Houghton, Mich.
475. Michigan State University
    E. Lansing, Mich.
476. Michigan State Normal College
    Now Eastern Michigan University
    Ypsilanti, Mich.
477. Michigan, University of
    Ann Arbor, Dearborn and Flint, Mich.
Mid-America Nazarene College
    See No. 1257
Middle Tennessee State University
    Formerly Tennessee State Teachers College
    See No. 837
478. Middlebury College
    Middlebury, Vt.
479. Middlesex University
    Waltham, Mass.

# LIST OF COLLEGES

480. Midland Lutheran College
Formerly Fremont College
Fremont, Neb.

Midland University
Now Chicago Law School
Chicago, Ill.
See No. 144

Mid Valley College of Law
See No. 1221

Midwestern State University
See No. 1050

481. Miles College
Birmingham, Ala.

Millersville University of Pennsylvania
Formerly Pennsylvania State Teachers College
See No. 655

482. Milligan College
Milligan College, Tenn.

Millikin University
Formerly James Millikin University
See No. 357

483. Mills College
Oakland, Cal.

484. Millsaps College
Jackson, Miss.

485. Milton College
Milton, Wis.

486. Milwaukee-Downer College
Milwaukee, Wis.

Milwaukee Law School
Now Marquette University
See No. 436

Minneapolis-Minnesota College of Law
See No. 1018

487. Minnesota College of Law
Now William Mitchell College of Law
Minneapolis, Minn.
See also No. 1035

Minnesota Duluth, University of
Formerly Minnesota State Teachers College
See No. 489

Minnesota Morris, University of
See No. 1207

488. Minnesota State Teachers College
Now Bemidji State University
Bemidji, Minn.

489. Minnesota State Teachers College
Now University of Minnesota Duluth
Duluth, Minn.

490. Minnesota State Teachers College
Now Mankato State University
Mankato, Minn.

491. Minnesota State Teachers College
Now Moorhead State University
Moorhead, Minn.

492. Minnesota State Teachers College
Now St. Cloud State University
St. Cloud, Minn.

493. Minnesota State Teachers College
Now Winona State University
Winona, Minn.

494. Minnesota, University of
Minneapolis and St. Paul, Minn.

Minot State Teachers College
Now Dakota Northwestern University
See No. 584

495. Mission House College & Theological Seminary
Plymouth, Wis.

496. Mississippi College
Clinton, Miss.

Mississippi College of Law
Formerly Jackson School of Law
See No. 356

497. Mississippi State University
State College, Miss.

498. Mississippi State University for Women
Columbus, Miss.

499. Mississippi, University of Southern
Hattiesburg, Miss.

500. Mississippi, University of
University, Miss.

501. Mississippi Woman's College
Now William Carey College
Hattiesburg, Miss.

Missouri School of Mines and Metallurgy
Now University of Missouri
See No. 502

Missouri Southern State College
See No. 1310

Missouri State University
Now Central Missouri State University
See No. 134

502. Missouri, University of
Columbia, Rolla, St. Louis and Kansas City, Mo.

Missouri at Kansas City, University of
See No. 986

Missouri at St. Louis, University of
See No. 1347

503. Missouri Valley College
Marshall, Mo.

Missouri Western State College
See No. 1311

504. Monmouth College
Monmouth, Ill.

Monmouth University
See No. 1108

505. Montana College of Mineral Science and Technology
Butte, Mont.

506. Montana State University
Bozeman, Mont.

507. Montana State Normal College
Now Western Montana College
Dillon, Mont.

508. Montana, University of
Formerly Montana State University
Missoula, Mont.

Montclair State University
Formerly New Jersey State College
See No. 555

Monterey College of Law
See No. 1226

Monterey Institute of International Studies
See No. 1354

Montevallo University
Formerly Alabama College
See No. 9

Montgomery State College
Now Alabama State University
See No. 14

Moorhead State University
Formerly Minnesota State Teachers College
See No. 491

509. Moravian College & Theological Seminary
Bethlehem, Pa.

510. Morehead State University
Morehead, Ky.

511. Morehouse College
Atlanta, Ga.

512. Morgan State University
Baltimore, Md.

513. Morningside College
Formerly University of Northwest
Sioux City, Iowa

514. Morris Brown College
Atlanta, Ga.

515. Morris College
Sumter, S.C.

516. Morris Harvey College
Now University of Charleston
Charleston, W.Va.

517. Mount Angel Seminary
St. Benedict, Ore.

518. Mount Holyoke College
South Hadley, Mass.

519. Mount Mary College
Milwaukee, Wis.

520. Mount Mercy College
Grand Rapids, Mich.

521. Mount Mercy College
Now Carlow College
Pittsburgh, Pa.

522. Mount St. Joseph College
Now Chestnut Hill College
Chestnut Hill, Pa.

523. Mount St. Joseph-on the Ohio, College of
Mount St. Joseph, Ohio

524. Mount St. Mary's College
Emmitsburg, Md.

525. Mount St. Mary's College
Los Angeles, Cal.

526. Mount St. Scholastica College
Atchison, Kan.

527. Mount St. Vincent, College of
Riverdale, N.Y.

528. Mount Union College
Alliance, Ohio

Mt. Vernon School of Law
See No. 1002

529. Muhlenberg College
Allentown, Pa.

530. Mundelein College
Chicago, Ill.

Municipal University of Wichita
Now Wichita State University
See No. 942

531. Murray State University
Murray, Ky.

532. Muskingum College
New Concord, Ohio

# N

533. Nashville Agricultural Normal Institute
Now Tennessee State University
Nashville, Tenn.
See also No. 1220

Nashville School of Law
See No. 1045

Nashville, University of
Now George Peabody College for Teachers
See No. 272

Nashville Y.M.C.A. Night Law School
Now Nashville School of Law
See No. 1045

534. Nassau College
Hempstead, N.Y.

535. Nasson College
Springvale, Me.

536. National College of Education
Formerly Pestalozzi Froebel Teachers College
Evanston, Ill.

National University
San Diego, Cal.
See No. 1241

537. National University
Now George Washington University
Washington, D.C.
See also No. 273

538. Nazareth College
Louisville, Ky.

539. Nazareth College
Nazareth, Mich.

540. Nazareth College of Rochester
Rochester, N.Y.

Nebraska at Kearney, University of
Formerly Kearney State College
See No. 543

Nebraska at Lincoln, University of
See No. 546

Nebraska at Omaha, University of
Formerly Municipal University of Omaha
See No. 627

541. Nebraska Central College
Central City, Neb.

542. Nebraska State Teachers College
Now Chadron State College
Chadron, Neb.

543. Nebraska State Teachers College
Now University of Nebraska at Kearny
Kearney, Neb.

544. Nebraska State Teachers College
Now Peru State College
Peru, Neb.

545. Nebraska State Teachers College
Now Wayne State College
Wayne, Neb.

546. Nebraska at Lincoln, University of
Lincoln, Neb.

547. Nebraska Wesleyan University
Lincoln, Neb.

548. Negro Agriculture & Technical College
Now North Carolina Agricultural & Technical State University
Greensboro, N.C.

549. Nevada, University of
Reno and Las Vegas, Nev.

New College of California
See No. 1230

New College of the University of South Florida
See No. 1275

XXI

Newark State College
Now Kean College of New Jersey
See No. 553

New England College
See No. 1312

New England School of Law
See No. 1202

550. New Hampshire, University of
Durham, N.H.

New Haven, University of
See No. 1156

551. New Jersey College for Women
Now Douglass College of Rutgers University
New Brunswick, N.J.
See also No. 705

New Jersey Institute of Technology
Formerly Newark College of Engineering
See No. 570

552. New Jersey Law School
Now Rutgers University
Newark, N.J.
See also No. 705

New Jersey State College
Jersey City, N.J.
See No. 1025

553. New Jersey State College
Now Kean College of New Jersey
Union, N.J.

554. New Jersey State College
Now Trenton State College
Trenton, N.J.

555. New Jersey State College
Now Montclair State University
Upper Montclair, N.J.

556. New Mexico College of A. & M. Arts
Now New Mexico State University
University Park, N.M.

New Mexico University, Eastern
See No. 1012

557. New Mexico Highlands University
Las Vegas, N.M.

558. New Mexico Institute of Mining & Technology
Socorro, N.M.

559. New Mexico Western College
Now Western New Mexico University
Silver City, N.M.

New Mexico State University
Formerly New Mexico College of A. & M. Arts
See No. 556

560. New Mexico, University of
Albuquerque, N.M.

New Orleans, University of
See No. 1099

561. New River State College
Now West Virginia Institute of Technology
Montgomery, W.Va.

562. New Rochelle, College of
New Rochelle, N.Y.

New School for Social Research
See No. 1313

563. New York, City College of the City University of
New York, N.Y.

New York College of Environmental Science & Forestry, State University of
See No. 565

New York Institute of Technology
See No. 1133

564. New York Law School
New York, N.Y.

565. New York State College of Forestry
Now State University of New York College of Environmental Science & Forestry
Syracuse, N.Y.

566. New York State College for Teachers
Albany, N.Y.

New York State Maritime College
See No. 1044

567. New York State Teachers College
Now State University of New York at Buffalo
Buffalo, N.Y.
See also No. 107

New York at Albany, State University of
Albany, N.Y.
See No. 1044

*Decentralized institution with administrative office at Albany composed of 64 colleges, schools, technical and agricultural institutes located throughout the state.*

New York at Binghamton, State University of
See No. 1349

New York at Buffalo, State University of
See No. 107

New York at Stony Brook, State University of
See No. 1350

568. New York Teachers College
New York, N.Y.

569. New York University
New York, N.Y.

570. Newark College of Engineering
Now New Jersey Institute of Technology
Newark, N.J.

571. Newark, University of
Now Rutgers University
Newark, N.J.
See also No. 705

572. Newberry College
Newberry, S.C.

Newcomb Memorial College, H. Sophie
See No. 298

Newton College
Now Boston College
See No. 93

573. Niagara University
Niagara University, N.Y.

Nicholls State University
See No. 1166

Norfolk State University
See No. 1286

Norman A. Wiggins School of Law
See No. 1345

North Adams State College
Formerly Massachusetts State College
See No. 460

North Alabama, University of
Formerly Alabama State Teachers College
See No. 11

North Carolina Agricultural & Technical State University
Formerly Negro Agriculture & Technical College
See No. 548

574. North Carolina Central University
Durham, N.C.

North Carolina State University
See No. 576

575. North Carolina, University of
Chapel Hill, N.C.

North Carolina, University of
Asheville, N.C.
See No. 48

North Carolina, University of
Charlotte, N.C.
See No. 1128

576. North Carolina State University
Raleigh, N.C.

577. North Carolina, University of, Greensboro, N.C.
Greensboro, N.C.

North Carolina, University of
Wilmington, N.C.
See No. 953

578. North Central College
Naperville, Ill.

579. North Dakota Agricultural College
Now North Dakota State University
Fargo, N.D.

580. North Dakota State Normal & Industrial College
Part of University of North Dakota
Ellendale, N.D.

581. North Dakota State College
Now Dickinson State College
Dickinson, N.D.

582. North Dakota State College
Now Mayville State College
Mayville, N.D.

583. North Dakota State College
Now Valley City State University
Valley City, N.D.

584. North Dakota State College
Now Dakota Northwestern University
Minot, N.D.

North Dakota State University
Formerly North Dakota Agricultural College
See No. 579

585. North Dakota, University of
Grand Forks, N.D.

North Florida, University of
See No. 1287

North Georgia College
See No. 1039

North Park College
See No. 1106

586. North Texas State University
Now University of North Texas
Denton, Texas

Northeast Louisiana University
See No. 1080

587. Northeast Missouri State University
Kirksville, Mo.

Northeastern Illinois University
See No. 1183

Northeastern Oklahoma State University
See No. 1013

588. Northeastern University
Boston, Mass.

Northern Arizona University
Formerly Arizona State College
See No. 35

Northern Colorado, University of
Formerly Colorado State College
See No. 173

589. Northern Illinois University
DeKalb and Glen Ellyn, Ill.

Northern Indiana Law School
Now Valparaiso University
See No. 879

Northern Iowa, University of
Formerly Iowa State Teachers College
See No. 351

Northern Kentucky University
See No. 1161

590. Northern State College
Aberdeen, S.D.

591. Northern Michigan University
Marquette, Mich.

Northern Montana College
See No. 1084

592. Northland College
Ashland, Wis.

Northrop University
See No. 1179

593. Northwest Missouri State University
Maryville, Mo.

594. Northwest Nazarene College
Nampa, Idaho

Northwest, University of
Now Morningside College
See No. 513

Northwestern College
Orange City, Iowa
See No. 1348

595. Northwestern College
Watertown, Wis.

596. Northwestern College of Law
Now Northwestern School of Law
Portland, Ore.

Northwestern Oklahoma State University
Formerly Oklahoma Northwestern State College
See No. 620

Northwestern State University
Formerly Louisiana State Normal College
See No. 419

597. Northwestern University
Evanston, Ill.

598. Norwich University
Northfield, Vt.

599. Notre Dame College
South Euclid, Ohio

600. Notre Dame of Maryland, College of
Baltimore, Md.

601. Notre Dame College of Staten Island
Part of St. Johns University
Staten Island, N.Y.
See also No. 724

# LIST OF COLLEGES

602. Notre Dame, University of
  Notre Dame, Ind.
  Nova University
  See No. 1206

## O

603. Oakland City College
  Oakland City, Ind.
  Oakland College of Law
  See No. 1344
  Oakland University
  See No. 1154
604. Oberlin College
  Oberlin, Ohio
605. Occidental College
  Los Angeles, Cal.
606. Oglethorpe University
  Atlanta, Ga.
  Ohio Dominican College
  Formerly St. Mary of the Springs College
  See No. 737
607. Ohio Northern University
  Ada, Ohio
608. Ohio State University, The
  Columbus, Ohio
609. Ohio Teachers College
  Now The Athenaeum of Ohio
  Cincinnati, Ohio
610. Ohio University
  Athens, Ohio
611. Ohio Wesleyan University
  Delaware, Ohio
612. Oklahoma A. & M. College
  Now Oklahoma State University
  Stillwater, Okla.
613. Oklahoma Baptist University
  Shawnee, Okla.
614. Oklahoma Central State Teachers College
  Now Central State University
  Edmond, Okla.
  See also No. 1147
  Oklahoma Christian College
  See No. 1315
615. Oklahoma City University School of Law
  Formerly Oklahoma City College of Law
  Oklahoma City, Okla.
616. Oklahoma City University
  Formerly Epworth University
  Oklahoma City, Okla.
617. Oklahoma College of Liberal Arts
  Now University of Science and Arts of Oklahoma
  Chickasha, Okla.
618. Oklahoma East Central State College
  Now East Central Oklahoma State University
  Ada, Okla.
619. Oklahoma Northeastern State College
  Now Northeastern Oklahoma State University
  Tahlequah, Okla.
620. Oklahoma Northwestern State College
  Now Northwestern Oklahoma State University
  Alva, Okla.
  Oklahoma Panhandle State University of Agriculture and Applied Sciences
  Formerly Panhandle State College
  See No. 639
621. Oklahoma Southeastern State College
  Now Southeastern Oklahoma State University
  Durant, Okla.
622. Oklahoma Southwestern Institute of Technology
  Now Southwestern Oklahoma State University
  Weatherford, Okla.
  Oklahoma State University
  Formerly Oklahoma A. & M. College
  See No. 612
623. Oklahoma, University of
  Norman, Okla.
  Oklahoma, University of Science and Arts of
  Formerly Oklahoma College of Liberal Arts
  See No. 617
  Old Dominion University
  See No. 1083

624. Olivet Nazarene College
  Kankakee, Ill.
625. Olivet College
  Olivet, Mich.
626. Omaha Law School, Inc., University of
  Omaha, Neb.
627. Omaha, Municipal University of
  Now University of Nebraska at Omaha
  Omaha, Neb.
  Oral Roberts University
  See No. 1288
  Orange State College
  See No. 1076
  Orange University College of Law
  See No. 1117
  Oregon College of Education
  See No. 1181
628. Oregon State University
  Corvallis, Ore.
629. Oregon, University of
  Eugene, Ore.
630. Ottawa University
  Ottawa, Kan.
631. Otterbein College
  Westerville, Ohio
632. Ouachita Baptist University
  Arkadelphia, Ark.
633. Our Lady of the Elms, College of
  Now Elms College
  Chicopee, Mass.
634. Our Lady of the Lake University
  San Antonio, Texas
  Ozarks, School of the
  See No. 1314

## P

Pace University
  See No. 1040
Pacific Coast University
  See No. 1001
635. Pacific College
  Now George Fox College
  Newberg, Ore.
  Pacific Lutheran College
  See No. 1058
636. Pacific Union College
  Angwin, Cal.
637. Pacific University
  Forest Grove, Ore.
  Pacific, University of the
  See No. 464
638. Paine College
  Augusta, Ga.
  Pan American University
  See No. 1219
639. Panhandle State College
  Now Oklahoma Panhandle State University of Agriculture and Applied Sciences
  Goodwell, Okla.
640. Park College
  Parkville, Mo.
641. Parsons College
  Fairfield, Iowa
642. Pasadena College
  Pasadena, Cal.
  Paul M. Hebert Law Center of Louisiana State University
  Now Louisiana State University and A. & M. College
  See No. 420
  Peabody Institute
  Now Vanderbilt University
  See No. 880
  Pembroke College
  Now Brown University
  See No. 103
  Pembroke State University
  See No. 1317
643. Pennsylvania College for Women
  Now Chatham College
  Pittsburgh, Pa.
644. Pennsylvania Military College
  Now Widener University
  Chester, Pa. and Wilmington, Del.
  See also No. 1338

# POMONA COLLEGE

645. Pennsylvania State University
  University Park, Pa.
646. Pennsylvania State Teachers College
  Now Bloomsburg University of Pennsylvania
  Bloomsburg, Pa.
647. Pennsylvania State Teachers College
  Now California University of Pennsylvania
  California, Pa.
648. Pennsylvania State Teachers College
  Now Clarion University of Pennsylvania
  Clarion, Pa.
649. Pennsylvania State Teachers College
  Now East Stroudsburg University
  E. Stroudsburg, Pa.
650. Pennsylvania State Teachers College
  Now Edinboro University of Pennsylvania
  Edinboro, Pa.
651. Pennsylvania State Teachers College
  Now Indiana University of Pennsylvania
  Indiana, Pa.
652. Pennsylvania State Teachers College
  Now Kutztown University
  Kutztown, Pa.
653. Pennsylvania State Teachers College
  Now Lock Haven University of Pennsylvania
  Lock Haven, Pa.
654. Pennsylvania State Teachers College
  Now Mansfield University
  Mansfield, Pa.
655. Pennsylvania State Teachers College
  Now Millersville University of Pennsylvania
  Millersville, Pa.
656. Pennsylvania State Teachers College
  Now Shippensburg University of Pennsylvania
  Shippensburg, Pa.
657. Pennsylvania State Teachers College
  Now Slippery Rock University
  Slippery Rock, Pa.
658. Pennsylvania State Teachers College
  Now West Chester University
  West Chester, Pa.
  Pennsylvania State University
  See No. 645
659. Pennsylvania, University of
  Philadelphia, Pa.
  Peoples College of Law
  See No. 1238
  Pepperdine University
  See No. 990
  Peru State College
  Formerly Nebraska State Teachers College
  See No. 544
660. Pestalozzi Froebel Teachers College
  Now National College of Education
  Chicago, Ill.
  See also No. 536
  Pfeiffer College
  See No. 1318
  Philadelphia College of Textiles and Science
  See No. 1316
661. Philander Smith College
  Little Rock, Ark.
662. Philippines, University of
  Manila, P.I.
663. Phillips University
  Enid, Okla.
  Phoenix, University of
  See No. 1245
664. Piedmont College
  Demorest, Ga.
  Pikeville College
  See No. 1319
  Pittsburg State University
  Formerly Kansas State College
  See No. 377
665. Pittsburgh, University of
  Bradford, Greensburg, Johnstown and Pittsburgh, Pa.
  Pitzer College
  See No. 1168
666. Plymouth State College
  Plymouth, N.H.
667. Polytechnic Institute of New York
  Formerly Polytechnic Institute of Brooklyn
  Brooklyn, N.Y.
668. Pomona College
  Claremont, Cal.

XXIII

669. Portia Law School
Now New England School of Law
Boston, Mass.
See also No. 1202

Portland State University
See No. 1056

670. Portland, University of
Portland, Ore.

Portland University Law School
See No. 431

Potomac School of Law
See No. 1234

671. Prairie View A. and M. University
Prairie View, Texas

672. Pratt Institute
Brooklyn, N.Y.

673. Presbyterian College
Clinton, S.C.

Prescott College
See No. 1346

Princess Anne State College
See No. 1092

674. Princeton University
Princeton, N.J.

675. Principia College, The
Elsah, Ill.

676. Providence College
Providence, R.I.

677. Puerto Rico, University of
Rio Piedras, P.R.

678. Puget Sound, University of
Tacoma, Wash.

Puget Sound School of Law, University of
See No. 1358

679. Purdue University
Lafayette and Hammond, Ind.

*(Also maintains joint campuses with Indiana University at Indianapolis and Ft. Wayne, Ind.)*

# Q

680. Queens College
Charlotte, N.C.

Queens College of the City University of New York
See No. 994

Queens College School of Law of the City University of New York
See No. 1178

Quincy College
See No. 1082

Quinnipiac College
See No. 1252

# R

681. Radcliffe College
Now Affiliated with Harvard University
Cambridge, Mass.

Radford University
Formerly Virginia State Teachers College
See No. 888

Ramapo College
See No. 1269

682. Randolph-Macon College
Ashland, Va.

683. Randolph-Macon Woman's College
Lynchburg, Va.

684. Redlands, University of
Redlands, Cal.

685. Reed College
Portland, Ore.

Regent University
See No. 1339

686. Regis College
Denver, Col.

687. Regis College
Weston, Mass.

688. Rensselaer Polytechnic Institute
Troy, N.Y.

689. Rhode Island College
Providence, R.I.

690. Rhode Island, University of
Kingston, R.I.

Rhodes College
See No. 806

691. Rice University
Houston, Texas

Richardson, William S. School of Law
Part of University of Hawaii
See No. 312

Richmond College of the City University of New York
See No. 1140

Richmond Professional Institute
See No. 1090

692. Richmond, University of
Richmond, Va.

693. Rider University
Lawrenceville, N.J.

694. Ripon College
Ripon, Wis.

695. Roanoke College
Salem, Va.

Robert H. Terrell Law School
See No. 1014

Rochester Institute of Technology
See No. 1213

696. Rochester, University of
Rochester, N.Y.

697. Rockford College
Rockford, Ill.

698. Rockhurst College
Kansas City, Mo.

Rocky Mountain College
Formerly Billings Polytechnic Institute
See No. 86

Roger Williams University School of Law
See No. 1360

699. Rollins College
Winter Park, Fla.

Roosevelt University
See No. 1016

700. Rosary College
River Forest, Ill.

701. Rose-Hulman Institute of Technology
Formerly Rose Polytechnic Institute
Terre Haute, Ind.

702. Rosemont College
Rosemont, Pa.

703. Russell Sage College
Troy, N.Y.

704. Rust College
Holy Springs, Miss.

705. Rutgers University
Camden, Newark and New Brunswick, N.J.

*Note: There are two separate law schools, one at Newark, N.J. (No. 705) and one at Camden, N.J. (No. 1292)*

Rutgers University Law School
Camden, N.J.
See No. 1292

# S

Sacramento College of Law
Now University of the Pacific
See No. 464

Sacramento State College
Now California State University, Sacramento
See No. 1060

706. Sacred Heart, Manhattanville College of the
Now Manhattanville College
Purchase, N.Y.

Sacred Heart College
Now Kansas Newman College
See No. 1283

Sacred Heart University
See No. 1211

Saginaw Valley College
See No. 1249

707. St. Ambrose College
Now St. Ambrose College and Marycrest College
Davenport, Iowa

St. Andrews Presbyterian College
See No. 1130

708. St. Anselm College
Manchester, N.H.

709. St. Augustine's College
Raleigh, N.C.

710. St. Benedict, College of
St. Joseph, Minn.

711. St. Benedict's College
Atchison, Kan.

St. Bernard College
See No. 1244

St. Bernardine of Siena College
Now Siena College
See No. 1021

712. St. Bonaventure University
St. Bonaventure, N.Y.

713. St. Catherine, College of
St. Paul, Minn.

St. Cloud State University
Formerly Minnesota State Teachers College
See No. 492

St. Edward's Seminary
See No. 987

714. St. Edward's University
Austin, Texas

715. St. Elizabeth, College of
Convent Station, N.J.

716. St. Francis College
Brooklyn, N.Y.

717. St. Francis College
Loretto, Pa.

718. St. Francis College
Burlington, Wis.

719. St. Francis, College of
Joliet, Ill.

St. Francis De Sales
Now Allentown College of St. Francis De Sales
See No. 1296

St. Francis Xavier, College of
See No. 1006

720. St. Francis Xavier College for Women
Now St. Xavier College
Chicago, Ill.

721. St. Ignatius College
Now San Francisco, University of
San Francisco, Cal.
See also No. 767

St. Ignatius College
Now John Carroll University
Cleveland, Ohio
See No. 363

St. John Fisher College
See No. 1122

722. St. John's College
Annapolis, Md.

St. John's College (Camarillo)
See No. 1258

St. Johns College (Santa Fe)
See No. 1320

St. John's Seminary
See No. 1263

723. St. John's University
Collegeville, Minn.

724. St. John's University
Jamaica, N.Y.

725. St. Joseph College
W. Hartford, Conn.

St. Joseph's College
East Chicago, Ind.
See No. 1157

St. Joseph's College
Rensselaer, Ind.
See No. 1024

726. St. Joseph's College
Emmitsburg, Md.

727. St. Joseph's College
Princeton, N.J.

728. St. Joseph's University
Philadelphia, Pa.

729. St. Joseph's College & Academy
Adrian, Mich.

730. St. Joseph's College
Standish, Me.

731. St. Joseph's College
Formerly St. Joseph's College for Woman
Brooklyn, N.Y.

732. St. Lawrence University
Canton, N.Y.

St. Lawrence University, Brooklyn Law School of
Now Brooklyn Law School
See No. 1009

# LIST OF COLLEGES

## SOUTHEASTERN MASSACHUSETTS UNIVERSITY

Saint Leo College
See No. 1290
733. St. Louis City College of Law
St. Louis, Mo.
734. St. Louis University
St. Louis, Mo.
735. St. Martin's College
Lacey, Wash.
736. St. Mary College
Leavenworth, Kan.
St. Mary of the Plains College
See No. 1004
737. St. Mary of the Springs College
Now Ohio Dominican College
Columbus, Ohio
738. St. Mary-of-the-Wasatch, College of
Salt Lake City, Utah
739. St. Mary-of-the-Woods College
St. Mary of the Woods, Ind.
740. St. Mary's College of California
Moraga, Cal.
741. St. Mary's College
Notre Dame, Ind.
742. St. Mary's University of Minnesota
Winona, Minn.
St. Mary's College
Orchard Lake, Mich.
See No. 993
St. Mary's College of California
See No. 740
St. Mary's College of Maryland
See No. 1203
St. Mary's Dominican College
Formerly Dominican College
See No. 220
743. St. Mary's Seminary & University
Roland Park, Md.
744. St. Mary's University of San Antonio
San Antonio, Texas
745. St. Michael's College
Winooski, Vt.
746. St. Norbert College
West De Pere, Wis.
747. St. Olaf College
Northfield, Minn.
St. Patrick's College
See No. 1256
748. St. Paul College of Law
Now William Mitchell College of Law
St. Paul, Minn.
See also No. 1035
749. St. Peter's College
Jersey City, N.J.
750. St. Procopius College
Now Illinois Benedictine College
Lisle, Ill.
751. St. Rose, College of
Albany, N.Y.
752. St. Scholastica, College of
Duluth, Minn.
St. Stephen's College
Now Bard College
See No. 65
753. St. Teresa, College of
Winona, Minn.
754. St. Thomas College
Now University of Scranton
Scranton, Pa.
755. St. Thomas, College of
St. Paul, Minn.
St. Thomas, University of
Houston, Texas
See No. 1268
St. Thomas University
Miami, Fla.
See No. 1158
St. Thomas, University of
See No. 1268
756. St. Viator College
Bourbonnais, Ill.
757. St. Vincent College
Latrobe, Pa.
St. Xavier College
Formerly St. Francis Xavier College for Women
Chicago, Ill.
See No. 720

758. Salem College
Winston-Salem, N.C.
759. Salem College
Salem, W.Va.
Salem State College
Formerly Massachusetts State College
See No. 461
Salisbury State University
Formerly Maryland State Teachers College
See No. 444
Salmon P. Chase College of Law
Part of Northern Kentucky University
See No. 151
Samford University
Formerly Howard College
See No. 327
760. Sam Houston State University
Huntsville, Texas
761. Samuel Huston College
Now Huston-Tillotson College
Austin, Texas
See also No. 1037
San Angelo State University
Now Angelo State University
See No. 1096
762. San Antonio Public School of Law
San Antonio, Texas
San Antonio, University of
See No. 983
763. San Diego State University
San Diego, Cal.
San Diego, University of
See No. 1049
San Fernando College of Law
See No. 398
San Fernando Valley State College
Now California State University, Northridge
See No. 1077
San Fernando Valley, University of
See No. 1095
764. San Francisco College for Women
Now Lone Mountain College
San Francisco, Cal.
765. San Francisco Law School
San Francisco, Cal.
San Francisco Law School, University of
See No. 1355
766. San Francisco State University
Formerly California State University
San Francisco, Cal.
767. San Francisco, University of
Formerly St. Ignatius College
San Francisco, Cal.
Sangamon State University
See No. 1247
San Joaquin College of Law
See No. 1189
768. San Jose State University
San Jose, Cal.
San Mateo Law School
See No. 1231
769. Santa Barbara State College
Now University of California at Santa Barbara
Santa Barbara, Cal.
770. Santa Clara, University of
Now Santa Clara University
Santa Clara, Cal.
Santa Fe, College of
See No. 1146
771. Sarah Lawrence College
Bronxville, N.Y.
Savannah State College
See No. 1289
772. Scarritt College for Christian Workers
Nashville, Tenn.
Scranton, University of
Formerly St. Thomas College
See No. 754
773. Scripps College
Claremont, Cal.
Seattle University
See No. 988
Seattle University School of Law
See No. 1358
774. Seattle Pacific University
Seattle, Wash.

775. Selma University
Selma, Ala.
776. Seton Hall University
S. Orange & Newark, N.J.
777. Seton Hill College
Greensburg, Pa.
778. Shaw University
Raleigh, N.C.
Sheffield College of Law
Now Yale University
See No. 976
779. Shepherd College
Shepherdstown, W.Va.
Shimer College
See No. 1100
Shippensburg University of Pennsylvania
Formerly Shippensburg State College
See No. 656
780. Shorter-Flipper-Curry College
Now Shorter College
N. Little Rock, Ark.
781. Shorter College
Rome, Ga.
782. Shurtleff College
Alton, Ill.
Siena College
See No. 1021
783. Simmons College
Boston, Mass.
Simon Greenleaf School of Law
See No. 1351
Simon's Rock of Bard College
See No. 1215
784. Simpson College
Indianola, Iowa
785. Sioux Falls College
Sioux Falls, S.D.
786. Sisters' College of Cleveland
Cleveland, Ohio
787. Skidmore College
Saratoga Springs, N.Y.
Slippery Rock University
Formerly Slippery Rock State College
See No. 657
788. Smith College
Northampton, Mass.
Sonoma State University
See No. 1078
South Alabama, University of
See No. 1091
South Bay University
See No. 1152
789. South Carolina State College
Orangeburg, S.C.
790. South Carolina, University of
Columbia, S.C.
791. South Dakota State University
Brookings, S.D.
792. South Dakota School of Mines and Technology
Rapid City, S.D.
793. South Dakota, University of
Vermillion, S.D.
South Florida, University of
See No. 1111
794. South Georgia Teachers College
Now Georgia Teachers College
Collegeboro, Ga.
795. South Jersey, College of
Now Rutgers University
Camden, N.J.
See also No. 1292
796. South Texas College of Law
Formerly South Texas Colleges of Law and Commerce
Houston, Texas
797. South, University of the
Sewanee, Tenn.
798. Southeast Missouri State University
Cape Girardeau, Mo.
799. Southeastern University
Washington, D.C.
Southeastern Louisiana University
See No. 1055
Southeastern Massachusetts University
See No. 1173

XXV

Southeastern Oklahoma State University
Formerly Oklahoma Southeastern State College
See No. 621

Southern Arkansas University
See No. 1094

Southern California Institute of Law
See No. 1336

800. Southern California, University of
Los Angeles, Cal.

Southern College of Seventh-Day Adventists
See No. 1185

Southern Colorado, University of
See No. 1196

Southern Connecticut State College
See No. 1102

801. Southern Illinois University
Carbondale and Edwardsville, Ill.

Southern Law University
See No. 1005

Southern Maine, University of
See No. 1248

802. Southern Methodist University
Dallas, Texas

Southern Missionary College
Now Southern College of Seventh-Day Adventists
See No. 1185

Southern Mississippi, University of
See No. 499

Southern Nazarene University
Formerly Bethany-Nazarene College
See No. 82

Southern Normal School
Now Western Kentucky University
See No. 929

Southern Oregon State College
See No. 1071

Southern State College
Now Southern Arkansas University
See No. 1094

803. Southern University
Baton Rouge, La.

Southern Utah State College
Now Southern Utah University
See No. 1324

Southwest Baptist University
See No. 1321

804. Southwest Missouri State University
Springfield, Mo.

Southwest State University
See No. 1342

805. Southwest Texas State University
San Marcos, Texas

806. Southwestern at Memphis
Now Rhodes College
Memphis, Tenn.

807. Southwestern College
Winfield, Kan.

808. Southwestern Louisiana, University of
Lafayette, La.

Southwestern Oklahoma State University
Formerly Oklahoma Southwestern Institute of Technology
See No. 622

Southwestern Presbyterian University
Now Rhodes College
See No. 806

809. Southwestern University School of Law
Los Angeles, Cal.

810. Southwestern University
Georgetown, Texas

811. Spelman College
Atlanta, Ga.

Spessard Holland Law Center
Now University of Florida
See No. 260

812. Spring Hill College
Spring Hill, Ala.

Springfield College
Formerly International Y.M.C.A. College
See No. 349

813. Stanford University
Palo Alto, Cal.

Stanislaus State College
Now California State University, Stanislaus
See No. 1079

State Agricultural and Mechanical Institute
Now Alabama Agricultural & Mechanical University
Normal, Ala.
See No. 1010

814. Stephen F. Austin State University
Nacogdoches, Texas

Stephens College
See No. 1322

815. Sterling College
Sterling, Kan.

Stetson University
Formerly John B. Stetson University
See No. 362

Steubenville, University of
See No. 1323

816. Stevens Institute of Technology
Hoboken, N.J.

Stockton State College
See No. 1214

Stonehill College
See No. 1200

817. Stout State College
Now University of Wisconsin-Stout
Menomonie, Wis.

818. Suffolk University
Boston, Mass.

Sulpician Seminary of the Northwest
Formerly St. Edward's Seminary
See No. 987

819. Sul Ross State University
Alpine, Texas

820. Susquehanna University
Selinsgrove, Pa.

821. Swarthmore College
Swarthmore, Pa.

822. Sweet Briar College
Sweet Briar, Va.

823. Syracuse University
Syracuse, N.Y.

# T

824. Talladega College
Talladega, Ala.

825. Tampa, University of
Tampa, Fla.

826. Tarkio College
Tarkio, Mo.

Tarleton State University
See No. 1332

827. Taylor University
Upland, Ind.

T.C. Williams School of Law
Now University of Richmond
See No. 692

828. Teachers College of the City of Boston
Boston, Mass.

829. Teachers College of Connecticut, The
Now Central Connecticut State College
New Britain, Conn.

830. Teachers College of Kansas City
Kansas City, Mo.

831. Temple University
Philadelphia, Pa.

832. Tennessee A. & I. State University
Now Tennessee State University
Nashville, Tenn.

833. Tennessee College for Women
Murfreesboro, Tenn.

834. Tennessee Polytechnic Institute
Now Tennessee Technological University
Cookeville, Tenn.

835. Tennessee State Teachers College
Now East Tennessee State University
Johnson City, Tenn.

836. Memphis State University
Memphis, Tenn.

837. Tennessee State Teachers College
Now Middle Tennessee State University
Murfreesboro, Tenn.

Tennessee State University
Formerly Tennessee A & I State University
See No. 832

Tennessee Technological University
Formerly Tennessee Polytechnic Institute
See No. 834

Tennessee at Chattanooga, University of
Formerly University of Chattanooga
See No. 143

838. Tennessee at Knoxville, University of
Knoxville, Tenn.

Tennessee at Martin, University of
See No. 1204

Tennessee at Memphis, University of
See No. 1205

Tennessee at Nashville, University of
See No. 1220

Tennessee Wesleyan College
See No. 1054

Terrell, Robert H., Law School
See No. 1014

839. Texas A & M University
College Station, Texas

840. Texas Christian University
Fort Worth, Texas

841. Texas College
Tyler, Texas

842. Texas Arts & Industries University
Kingsville, Texas

843. Texas, College of Mines & Metallurgy
Now University of Texas-El Paso
El Paso, Texas

Texas Lutheran College
See No. 1270

Texas Southern University
See No. 325

844. Texas State College for Women
Now Texas Woman's University
Denton, Texas

845. Texas Tech University
Lubbock, Texas

846. Texas, University of
Austin, Texas

Texas at Arlington University of
See No. 1142

Texas, University of, Dallas
See No. 1271

Texas, University of, El Paso
Formerly College of Mines & Metallurgy
See No. 843

Texas, University of, Galveston
See No. 1337

Texas, University of, Houston
See No. 1341

Texas, University of, Permian Basin
See No. 1272

Texas, University of, San Antonio
See No. 1273

Texas, University of, Tyler
See No. 1274

847. Texas Wesleyan College
Fort Worth, Texas

Texas Western College
Now University of Texas-El Paso
See No. 843

Texas Woman's University
Formerly Texas State College for Women
See No. 844

The Athenaeum of Ohio
Formerly Ohio Teachers College
See No. 609

848. Thiel College
Greenville, Pa.

Thomas M. Cooley Law School
See No. 1187

Thomas More College
Formerly Villa Madonna College
See No. 1118

Thurgood Marshall School of Law
Part of Texas Southern University
See No. 325

Tift College
Now Brenan College
See No. 99

849. Tillotson College
Now Huston-Tillotson College
Austin, Texas
See also No. 1037

850. Toledo Teachers College
Toledo, Ohio

851. Toledo, University of
Toledo, Ohio

852. Tougaloo College
Tougaloo, Miss.

# LIST OF COLLEGES

Touro College
See No. 1357

Touro College Jacob D. Fuchsberg Law Center
See No. 1325

Towson State University
Formerly Maryland State Teachers College
See No. 445

853. Transylvania University
Lexington, Ky.

Trenton State College
Formerly New Jersey State College
See No. 554

Trevecca Nazarene College
See No. 1327

854. Tri-State University
Angola, Ind.

855. Trinity College
Hartford, Conn.

856. Trinity College
Washington, D.C.

857. Trinity College
Sioux City, Iowa

858. Trinity College
Burlington, Vt.

Trinity College of North Carolina
Now Duke University
See No. 228

859. Trinity University
San Antonio, Texas

Troy State University
Formerly Alabama State Teachers University
See No. 15

860. Tufts University
Medford, Mass.

861. Tulane University of Louisiana
New Orleans, La.

862. Tulsa, University of
Tulsa, Okla.

863. Tusculum College
Greeneville, Tenn.

864. Tuskegee University
Tuskegee, Ala.

## U

865. Union College
Barbourville, Ky.

866. Union College
Lincoln, Neb.

Union College of Law
Now Northwestern University

867. Union College
Schenectady, N.Y.

868. Union University
Jackson, Tenn.

United States Air Force Academy
See No. 1070

869. United States Coast Guard Academy
New London, Conn.

United States International University
See No. 1188

United States Merchant Marine Academy
Kings Point, N.Y.
See No. 1027

870. United States Military Academy
West Point, N.Y.

871. United States Naval Academy
Annapolis, Md.

United States Naval Postgraduate School
See No. 1242

872. Upper Iowa University
Fayette, Iowa

873. Upsala College
East Orange, N.J.

Urbana College
See No. 1112

874. Ursinus College
Collegeville, Pa.

Ursuline College
Louisville, Ky.
See No. 1150

875. Ursuline College
New Orleans, La.

876. Ursuline College
Cleveland, Ohio

877. Utah State University
Formerly Utah State Agricultural College
Logan, Utah

878. Utah, University of
Salt Lake City, Utah

Utica College of Syracuse University
See No. 1093

## V

Valdosta State College
Formerly Georgia State Woman's College
See No. 279

Valley City State College
Formerly North Dakota State College
See No. 583

Valley University College of Law
See No. 1224

879. Valparaiso University
Formerly Northern Indiana Law School
Valparaiso, Ind.

880. Vanderbilt University
Nashville, Tenn.

Van Norman University
See No. 1114

881. Vassar College
Poughkeepsie, N.Y.

Ventura College of Law
See No. 1186

Vermont Law School
See No. 1194

882. Vermont, University of
Burlington, Vt.

Villa Madonna College
See No. 1118

883. Villa Maria College
Erie, Pa.

884. Villanova University
Villanova, Pa.

Virginia Commonwealth University
Formerly Richmond Professional Institute
See No. 1090

885. Virginia Military Institute
Lexington, Va.

886. Virginia Polytechnic Institute and State University
Blacksburg, Va.

887. Virginia State University
Petersburg (Ettrick), Va.

888. Virginia State Teachers College
Now Radford Unversity
East Radford, Va.

889. Virginia State Teachers College
Now Longwood College
Farmville, Va.

890. Virginia State Teachers College
Now Mary Washington College
Fredericksburg, Va.

891. Virginia State Teachers College
Now James Madison University
Harrisonburg, Va.

892. Virginia Union University
Richmond, Va.

893. Virginia, University of
Charlottesville, Va.

## W

894. Wabash College
Crawfordsville, Ind.

895. Wagner College
Staten Island, N.Y.

896. Wake Forest University
Winston-Salem, N.C.

897. Walla Walla College
College Place, Wash.

Walsh College
See No. 1260

Walter F. George Law School
Part of Mercer University
See No. 469

Warren G. Harding College of Law
Now Ohio Northern University
See No. 607

898. Wartburg College
Waverly, Iowa

## WEST VIRGINIA UNIVERSITY

899. Wartburg Theological Seminary
Dubuque, Iowa

900. Washburn University of Topeka
Topeka, Kan.

901. Washington & Jefferson College
Washington, Pa.

902. Washington & Lee University
Lexington, Va.

903. Washington College
Chestertown, Md.

904. Washington College of Law
(of American University.)
Washington, D.C.
See also No. 30

905. Washington Missionary College
Now Columbia Union College
Takoma Park, D.C.

Washington Square
Now New York University
See No. 569

906. Washington, State College of
Now Washington State University
Pullman, Wash.

907. Washington State Normal School
Now Western Washington University
Bellingham, Wash.

908. Washington State Normal School
Now Eastern Washington University
Cheney, Wash.

909. Washington State Normal School
Now Central Washington University
Ellensburg, Wash.

Washington State University
Formerly State College of Washington
See No. 906

910. Washington University
St. Louis, Mo.

911. Washington, University of
Seattle, Wash.

Wayne State College
Formerly Nebraska State Teachers College
See No. 545

912. Wayne State University
Detroit, Mich.

Wayne University
Formerly Detroit City Law School
See No. 212

913. Waynesburg College
Waynesburg, Pa.

Weber State College
See No. 1085

Webster College
See No. 1291

Webster College of Law
Now Illinois Institute of Technology
See No. 46

914. Wellesley College
Wellesley, Mass.

915. Wells College
Aurora, N.Y.

916. Wesley College
Grand Forks, N.D.

917. Wesleyan College
Macon, Ga.

918. Wesleyan University
Middletown, Conn.

919. West Baden College
West Baden, Ind.

West Chester University
Formerly Pennsylvania State Teachers College
See No. 658

West Florida, University of
See No. 1176

West Georgia College
See No. 1223

920. West Liberty State College
W. Liberty, W.Va.

West Los Angeles, University of
See No. 1136

921. West Texas State University
Canyon, Texas

West Virginia Institute of Technology
Formerly New River State College
See No. 561

922. West Virginia State College
Institute, W.Va.

923. West Virginia University
Morgantown, W.Va.

XXVII

924. West Virginia Wesleyan College
    Buckhannon, W.Va.
925. Western Carolina University
    Cullowhee, N.C.
    Western College
    Now Coe College
    Cedar Rapids, Iowa
    See No. 162
926. Western College
    Oxford, Ohio
    Western Connecticut State University
    See No. 1103
927. Western Illinois University
    Macomb, Ill.
928. Western Maryland College
    Westminster, Md.
929. Western Kentucky University
    Formerly Western Kentucky State College
    Bowling Green, Ky.
    Western Montana College
    Formerly Montana State Normal College
    See No. 507
    Western New England College
    See No. 1048
    Western New Mexico University
    Formerly New Mexico Western College
    See No. 559
    Western Oregon State College
    Formerly Oregon College of Education
    See No. 1181
930. Western Reserve University
    Now Case Western Reserve University
    Cleveland, Ohio
931. Western State College of Colorado
    Gunnison, Col.
932. Western Michigan University
    Kalamazoo, Mich.
    Western State University
    See No. 1137
933. Western Union College
    Now Westmar College
    Le Mars, Iowa
    Western Washington University
    See No. 907
    Westfield State College
    Formerly Massachusetts State College
    See No. 462
    Westhampton College
    Now University of Richmond
    See No. 692
    Westmar College
    Formerly Western Union College
    See No. 933
934. Westminster College
    Fulton, Mo.
935. Westminster College
    New Wilmington, Pa.
    Westminster College
    Salt Lake City, Utah
    See No. 1120
936. Westminster College of Law
    Now University of Denver
    Denver, Col.
    Westmont College
    See No. 1239
    Wharton School
    Now University of Pennsylvania
    See No. 659
937. Wheaton College
    Wheaton, Ill.
938. Wheaton College
    Norton, Mass.
    Wheeling College
    Now Wheeling Jesuit College
    See No. 1115
939. Whitman College
    Walla Walla, Wash.
940. Whittier College
    Whittier, Cal.
    Whittier College School of Law
    See No. 1148
941. Whitworth College
    Spokane, Wash.
942. Wichita State University
    Wichita, Kan.
    Widener University
    Formerly Pennsylvania Military College
    See No. 1338

Wiggins, Norman A., School of Law
    See No. 1345
943. Wilberforce University
    Wilberforce, Ohio
944. Wiley College
    Marshall, Texas
    Wilkes University
    See No. 1028
    William Carey College
    Formerly Mississippi Woman's College
    See No. 501
945. William & Mary, College of
    Williamsburg, Va.
946. William Jennings Bryan College
    Dayton, Tenn.
947. William Jewell College
    Liberty, Mo.
948. William McKinley School of Law
    Canton, Ohio
    William Mitchell College of Law
    See No. 1035
    William Paterson College of New Jersey
    See No. 1174
949. William Penn College
    Oskaloosa, Iowa
950. Willamette University
    Salem, Ore.
    William S. Richardson School of Law
    Part of University of Hawaii
    See No. 312
    William Smith College
    Now Hobart and William Smith Colleges
    See No. 319
951. Williams College
    Williamstown, Mass.
    Williams, T. C., School of Law
    Now University of Richmond
    See No. 692
    Williamsburg, The College in
    See No. 1053
952. Wilmington College
    Wilmington, Ohio
953. Wilmington College
    Now University of North Carolina at Wilmington
    Wilmington, N.C.
954. Wilson College
    Chambersburg, Pa.
    Winona State University
    Formerly Minnesota State Teachers College
    See No. 493
955. Winston-Salem State University
    Winston-Salem, N.C.
956. Winthrop College
    Rock Hill, S.C.
957. Wisconsin-Eau Claire, University of
    Eau Claire, Wis.
    Wisconsin-Green Bay, University of
    See No. 1171
958. Wisconsin-La Crosse, University of
    La Crosse, Wis.
959. Wisconsin-Milwaukee, University of
    Milwaukee, Wis.
960. Wisconsin-Oshkosh, University of
    Oshkosh, Wis.
    Wisconsin-Parkside, University of
    See No. 1172
961. Wisconsin-Platteville, University of
    Platteville, Wis.
962. Wisconsin-River Falls, University of
    River Falls, Wis.
963. Wisconsin-Stevens Point, University of
    Stevens Point, Wis.
    Wisconsin-Stout, University of
    Formerly Stout State College
    See No. 817
964. Wisconsin-Superior, University of
    Superior, Wis.
965. Wisconsin-Whitewater, University of
    Whitewater, Wis.
966. Wisconsin-Madison, University of
    Madison, Wis.
967. Wittenberg University
    Springfield, Ohio
968. Wofford College
    Spartanburg, S.C.

Woodbury University
    See No. 1246
Woodland University
    See No. 1221
969. Woodrow Wilson College of Law
    Formerly Kilbride Law School
    Atlanta, Ga.
970. Wooster, College of
    Wooster, Ohio
971. Worcester Polytechnic Institute
    Worcester, Mass.
    Worcester State College
    Formerly Massachusetts State College
    See No. 463
    Wright State University
    See No. 1208
972. Wyoming, University of
    Laramie, Wyo.

## X

973. Xavier University
    Cincinnati, Ohio
974. Xavier University of Louisiana
    New Orleans, La.

## Y

Y.M.C.A. Law School
    Now Nashville School of Law
    See No. 1045
975. Y.M.C.A. Schools
    Houston, Texas
976. Yale University
    New Haven, Conn.
977. Yankton College
    Yankton, S.D.
978. Yeshiva University
    New York, N.Y.
979. York College
    York, Neb.
    York College of Pennsylvania
    See No. 1326
    York College of the City University of New York
    See No. 1141
980. Youngstown State University
    Youngstown, Ohio

*Institutions Added After the Establishment of This List*

981. LaSalle Extension University
    Chicago, Ill.
982. Albany Law School of Union College
    Albany, N.Y.
983. San Antonio, University of
    San Antonio, Texas
984. Blue Ridge College
    New Windsor, Md.
985. Briar Cliff College
    Sioux City, Iowa
986. Missouri at Kansas City, University of
    Formerly University of Kansas City
    Kansas City, Mo.
987. St. Edward's Seminary
    Now Sulpician Seminary of the Northwest
    Seattle, Wash.
988. Seattle University
    Seattle, Wash.
989. John Marshall Law School
    Now Cleveland Marshall College of Law
    Cleveland, Ohio
    See also No. 1003
990. Pepperdine University
    Los Angeles, Malibu, Anaheim and Santa Ana, Cal.
991. Barat College
    Lake Forest, Ill.
992. Anderson College
    Anderson, Ind.
993. St. Mary's College
    Orchard Lake, Mich.
994. Queens College of the City University of New York
    Flushing, N.Y.

# LIST OF COLLEGES

995. Alfred Holbrook College
  Manchester, Ohio
996. Lincoln College of Law
  Springfield, Ill.
997. John Marshall Law School
  Now Seton Hall University
  Jersey City, N.J.
  See also No. 776
998. Houston Law School
  Houston, Texas
999. Unlisted colleges, etc., see prefatory notice
1000. John Marshall Law School
  Atlanta, Ga.
1001. Pacific Coast University
  Los Angeles, Cal.
1002. Mt. Vernon School of Law
  Now University of Baltimore School of Law
  Baltimore, Md.
1003. Cleveland Marshall College of Law
  Part of Cleveland State University
  Cleveland, Ohio
1004. St. Mary of the Plains College
  Dodge City, Kan.
1005. Southern Law University
  Part of Memphis State University
  Memphis, Tenn.
1006. College of St. Francis Xavier
  New York, N.Y.
1007. American Extension School of Law
  Chicago, Ill.
1008. Blackstone School of Law
  Carrollton, Texas
1009. Brooklyn Law School
  Formerly Brooklyn Law School of St. Lawrence University
  Brooklyn, N.Y.
1010. Alabama Agricultural and Mechanical University
  Formerly State Agricultural and Mechanical Institute
  Normal, Ala.
1011. Fayetteville State University
  Fayetteville, N.C.
1012. Eastern New Mexico University
  Portales, N.M.
1013. Northeastern Oklahoma State University
  Formerly Oklahoma Northeastern State University
  Tahlequah, Okla.
1014. Robert H. Terrell Law School
  Washington, D.C.
1015. Memphis, University of
  Now Memphis State University
  Memphis, Tenn.
1016. Roosevelt University
  Chicago, Ill.
1017. Dickinson School of Law
  Carlisle, Pa.
1018. Minneapolis-Minnesota College of Law
  Now William Mitchell College of Law
  Minneapolis, Minn.
  See also No. 1035
1019. Hofstra University
  Hempstead, N.Y.
1020. Portland University Law School
  Now part of University of Maine
  Portland, Me.
  See also No. 431
1021. Siena College
  Formerly St. Bernardine of Siena College
  Loudonville, N.Y.
1022. Calvin Coolidge College
  Now New England School of Law
  Boston, Mass.
  See also No. 1202
1023. Central State University
  Wilberforce, Ohio
1024. St. Joseph's College
  Rensselaer, Ind.
1025. New Jersey State College
  Now Jersey City State College
  Jersey City, N.J.
1026. Lincoln University
  San Francisco, San Jose and Sacramento, Cal.
1027. United States Merchant Marine Academy
  Kings Point, N.Y.
1028. Wilkes University
  Wilkes-Barre, Pa.
1029. Bridgeport, University of
  Bridgeport, Conn.
1030. Fairfield University
  Fairfield, Conn.
1031. Le Moyne College
  Syracuse, N.Y.
1032. Idaho State University
  Formerly Idaho State College
  Pocatello, Idaho
1033. Hartford, University of
  Formerly Hillyer College
  Hartford, Conn.
1034. Christian Brothers College
  Memphis, Tenn.
1035. William Mitchell College of Law
  St. Paul, Minn.
1036. Brandeis University
  Waltham, Mass.
1037. Huston-Tillotson College
  Austin, Texas
1038. Jacksonville University
  Jacksonville, Fla.
1039. North Georgia College
  Dahlonega, Ga.
1040. Pace University
  New York, Pleasantville and White Plains, N.Y.
1041. Iona College
  New Rochelle, N.Y.
1042. California State University, Long Beach
  Formerly Long Beach State University
  Long Beach, Cal.
1043. Los Angeles State College of Applied Arts and Sciences
  Now California State University, Los Angeles
  Los Angeles, Cal.
  See also No. 1097
1044. New York at Albany, State University of
  Albany, N.Y.
1045. Nashville School of Law
  Nashville, Tenn.
1046. Fairleigh Dickinson University
  Madison, Rutherford and Teaneck, N.J.
1047. Lycoming College
  Williamsport, Pa.
1048. Western New England College
  Springfield, Mass.
1049. San Diego, University of
  San Diego, Cal.
1050. Midwestern State University
  Wichita Falls, Texas
1051. Lewis and Clark College
  Portland, Ore.
1052. Houston Baptist University
  Houston, Texas
1053. Messiah College
  Grantham, Pa.
1054. Tennessee Wesleyan College
  Athens, Tenn.
1055. Southeastern Louisiana College
  Hammond, La.
1056. Portland State University
  Portland, Ore.
1057. Merrimack College
  North Andover, Mass.
1058. Pacific Lutheran University
  Tacoma, Wash.
1059. Georgia State University
  Atlanta, Ga.
1060. California State University, Sacramento
  Formerly Sacramento State College
  Sacramento, Cal.
1061. Lamar University
  Beaumont, Texas
1062. Gannon University
  Erie, Pa.
1063. Georgia Southern College
  Statesboro, Ga.
1064. David Lipscomb College
  Nashville, Tenn.
1065. Hastings College of the Law, University of California
  San Francisco, Cal.
1066. Boalt Hall School of Law, University of California
  Berkeley, Cal.
1067. California School of Law, Davis, University of
  Davis, Cal.
1068. California School of Law, Los Angeles, University of
  Los Angeles, Cal.

# ASSUMPTION COLLEGE

1069. Chaminade University of Honolulu
  Honolulu, Hawaii
1070. United States Air Force Academy
  Colorado Springs, Col.
1071. Southern Oregon State College
  Ashland, Ore.
1072. Alliance College
  Cambridge Springs, Pa.
1073. California State University, Hayward
  Hayward, Cal.
1074. California Polytechnic State University
  San Luis Obispo, Cal.
1075. California State Polytechnic University
  Pomona, Cal.
1076. Orange State College
  Fullerton, Cal.
1077. California State University, Northridge
  Formerly San Fernando Valley State College
  Northridge, Cal.
1078. Sonoma State University
  Rohnert Park, Cal.
1079. California State University, Stanislaus
  Formerly Stanislaus State College
  Turlock, Cal.
1080. Northeast Louisiana University
  Monroe, La.
1081. Austin Peay State University
  Clarksville, Tenn.
1082. Quincy College
  Quincy, Ill.
1083. Old Dominion University
  Norfolk, Va.
1084. Northern Montana College
  Havre, Mont.
1085. Weber State College
  Ogden, Utah
1086. Florida Atlantic University
  Boca Raton, Fla.
1087. Catholic University of Puerto Rico
  Ponce, P.R.
1088. Inter-American University of Puerto Rico
  San Juan, P.R.
1089. McNeese State University
  Lake Charles, La.
1090. Richmond Professional Institute
  Now Virginia Commonwealth University
  Richmond, Va.
1091. South Alabama, University of
  Mobile, Ala.
1092. Princess Anne State College
  Princess Anne, Md.
1093. Utica College of Syracuse University
  Utica, N.Y.
1094. Southern Arkansas University
  Formerly Southern State College
  Magnolia, Ark.
1095. San Fernando Valley, University of
  Now University of La Verne College of Law
  Sepulveda, Cal.
1096. Angelo State University
  Formerly San Angelo State University
  San Angelo, Texas
1097. California State University, Los Angeles
  Formerly Los Angeles State College
  Los Angeles, Cal.
1098. Louisiana State University at Alexandria
  Alexandria, La.
1099. New Orleans, University of
  Formerly Louisiana State University of New Orleans
  New Orleans, La.
1100. Shimer College
  Waukegan, Ill.
1101. Blackburn College
  Carlinville, Ill.
1102. Southern Connecticut State College
  New Haven, Conn.
1103. Western Connecticut State University
  Danbury, Conn.
1104. Eastern Oregon College
  La Grande, Ore.
1105. Dallas, University of
  Irving, Texas
1106. North Park College
  Chicago, Ill.
1107. Assumption College
  Worcester, Mass.

1108. Monmouth University
West Long Branch, N.J.
1109. California State University, Fullerton
Fullerton, Cal.
1110. California State University, San Bernardino
San Bernardino, Cal.
1111. South Florida, University of
Tampa, Fla.
1112. Urbana College
Urbana, Ohio
1113. King's College
Wilkes Barre, Pa.
1114. Van Norman University
Los Angeles, Cal.
1115. Wheeling College
Now Wheeling Jesuit College
Wheeling, W.Va.
1116. Glassboro State College
Glassboro, N.J.
1117. Orange University College of Law
Now Pepperdine School of Law
Santa Ana, Cal.
1118. Villa Madonna College
Now Thomas More College
Covington, Ky.
1119. Indiana University School of Law
Bloomington, Ind.
1120. Westminster College
Salt Lake City, Utah
1121. Aquinas College
Grand Rapids, Mich.
1122. St. John Fisher College
Rochester, N.Y.
1123. Goddard College
Plainfield, Vt.
1124. Eastern Mennonite College
Harrisonburg, Va.
1125. Arkansas Tech University
Formerly Arkansas Polytechnic University
Russellville, Ark.
1126. Belmont Abbey College
Belmont, N.C.
1127. California College of Law
Hollywood and West Covina, Cal.
1128. North Carolina, University of
Charlotte, N.C.
1129. Mars Hill College
Mars Hill, N.C.
1130. St. Andrews Presbyterian College
Laurinburg, N.C.
1131. California State University, Dominguez Hills
Dominguez Hills, Cal.
1132. Humphreys College
Stockton, Cal.
1133. New York Institute of Technology
New York, N.Y.
1134. Bentley College
Waltham, Mass.
1135. Marymount-Manhattan College
New York, N.Y.
1136. West Los Angeles, University of
Culver City, Cal.
1137. Western State University
Fullerton & San Diego, Cal.
1138. Bernard M. Baruch College of the City
University of New York
New York, N.Y.
1139. John Jay College of Criminal Justice of the City
University of New York
New York, N.Y.
1140. College of Staten Island of the City University
of New York
Formerly Richmond College of the City
University of New York
Staten Island, N.Y.
1141. York College of the City University of New
York
Queens, N.Y.
1142. Texas at Arlington, University of
Arlington, Texas
1143. Albuquerque, University of
Albuquerque, N.M.
1144. Bethel College
St. Paul, Minn.
1145. Bryant College
Smithfield, R.I.
1146. Santa Fe, College of
Santa Fe, N.M.

1147. University of Central Oklahoma
Formerly Central State University
Edmond, Okla.
1148. Whittier College School of Law
Formerly Beverly College of Law
Los Angeles, Cal.
1149. Boston State College
Boston, Mass.
1150. Bellarmine College
Formerly Bellarmine Ursuline College
Louisville, Ky.
1151. Lewis University
Lockport, Ill.
1152. South Bay University
Harbor City, Cal.
1153. John F. Kennedy University
Walnut Creek, Cal.
1154. Oakland University
Rochester, Mich.
1155. Babson College
Babson Park, Mass.
1156. New Haven, University of
West Haven, Conn.
1157. St. Joseph College
East Chicago, Ind.
1158. St. Thomas University
Formerly Biscayne College
Miami, Fla.
1159. Indiana Institute of Technology
Fort Wayne, Ind.
1160. Herbert H. Lehman College of the City
University of New York
Bronx, N.Y.
1161. Northern Kentucky University
Highland Heights, Ky.
1162. Antioch School of Law
Washington, D.C.
1163. Loma Linda University
Formerly La Sierra College
Loma Linda, Cal.
1164. University of Colorado at Colorado Springs
Colorado Springs, Col.
1165. University of Colorado at Denver
Denver, Col.
1166. Nicholls State University
Thibodaux, La.
1167. Harvey Mudd College
Claremont, Cal.
1168. Pitzer College
Claremont, Cal.
1169. University of California at Santa Cruz
Santa Cruz, Cal.
1170. Franklin Pierce College
Rindge, N.H.
1171. Wisconsin-Green Bay, University of
Green Bay, Wis.
1172. Wisconsin-Parkside, University of
Kenosha, Wis.
1173. Southeastern Massachusetts University
North Dartmouth, Mass.
1174. William Patterson College of New Jersey
Wayne, N.J.
1175. Central Florida, University of
Formerly Florida Technological University
Orlando, Fla.
1176. West Florida, University of
Pensacola, Fla.
1177. Grambling State University
Grambling, La.
1178. City University of New York School of Law,
Queens College
Flushing, N.Y.
1179. Northrop University
Inglewood, Cal.
1180. Bloomfield College
Bloomfield, N.J.
1181. Oregon College of Education
Now Western Oregon State College
Monmouth, Ore.
1182. Benedictine College
Atchison, Kan.
1183. Northeastern Illinois University
Chicago, Ill.
1184. International School of Law
Now George Mason University School of
Law
Arlington, Va.
1185. Southern College of Seventh-day Adventists
Formerly Southern Missionary College
Collegedale, Tenn.

1186. Ventura College of Law
Ventura, Cal.
1187. Thomas M. Cooley Law School
Lansing, Mich.
1188. United States International University
Formerly California Western University
San Diego, Cal.
1189. San Joaquin, College of Law
Fresno, Cal.
1190. Glendale University
Glendale, Cal.
1191. Chicago State University
Chicago, Ill.
1192. Dowling College
Oakdale, N.Y.
1193. Boise State University
Boise, Idaho
1194. Vermont Law School
South Royalton, Vt.
1195. Covenant College
Lookout Mountain, Tenn.
1196. University of Southern Colorado
Pueblo, Col.
1197. Armstrong College
Berkeley, Cal.
1198. Citrus Belt Law School
Riverside, Cal.
1199. Cabrini College
Radnor, Pa.
1200. Stonehill College
North Easton, Mass.
1201. Metropolitan State College
Denver, Col.
1202. New England School of Law
Boston, Mass.
1203. St. Mary's College of Maryland
St. Mary's City, Md.
1204. Tennessee at Martin, University of
Martin, Tenn.
1205. Tennessee at Memphis, University of
Memphis, Tenn.
1206. Nova University
Fort Lauderdale, Fla.
1207. Minnesota Morris, University of
Morris, Minn.
1208. Wright State University
Dayton, Ohio
1209. George Mason University School of Law
Arlington, Va.
See also No. 1184
1210. Florida Institute of Technology
Melbourne, Fla.
1211. Sacred Heart University
Bridgeport, Conn.
1212. California State College, Bakersfield
Bakersfield, Cal.
1213. Rochester Institute of Technology
Rochester, N.Y.
1214. Stockton State College
Pomona, N.J.
1215. Simon's Rock of Bard College
Great Barrington, Mass.
1216. Marian College
Indianapolis, Ind.
1217. Lawrence Institute of Technology
Southfield, Mich.
1218. Franklin Pierce Law Center
Formerly part of Franklin Pierce College
Concord, N.H.
1219. Pan American University
Edinburg, Texas
1220. Tennessee at Nashville, University of
Formerly Nashville Agricultural Normal
Institute
Nashville, Tenn.
1221. Woodland University
Van Nuys, Cal.
1222. Florida International University
Miami, Fla.
1223. West Georgia College
Carrollton, Ga.
1224. Valley University College of Law
North Hollywood, Cal.
1225. Irvine University
Irvine, Cal.
1226. Monterey College of Law
Monterey, Cal.

# LIST OF COLLEGES

# MONTEREY INSTITUTE OF INTERNATIONAL STUDIES

1227. Empire College School of Law
Santa Rosa, Cal.
1228. Campbell University
Buies Creek, N.C.
1229. General Motors Institute
Flint, Mich.
1230. New College of California
San Francisco, Cal.
1231. San Mateo Law School
San Mateo, Cal.
1232. Azusa Pacific University
Azusa, Cal.
1233. Briarcliff College
Briarcliff Manor, N.Y.
1234. Potomac School of Law
Washington, D.C.
1235. Eastern Montana College
Billings, Mont.
1236. Eckerd College
St. Petersburg, Fla.
1237. Louisiana State University at Shreveport
Shreveport, La.
1238. Peoples College of Law
Los Angeles, Cal.
1239. Westmont College
Santa Barbara, Cal.
1240. American College of Law
Anaheim, Cal.
1241. National University
Formerly Cabrillo Pacific University
San Diego, Cal.
1242. United States Naval Postgraduate School
Monterey, Cal.
1243. Arkansas at Little Rock, University of
Formerly Little Rock University
Little Rock, Ark.
1244. St. Bernard College
St. Bernard, Ala.
1245. Phoenix, University of
Phoenix, Ariz.
1246. Woodbury University
Los Angeles, Cal.
1247. Sangamon State University
Springfield, Ill.
1248. Southern Maine, University of
Portland, Me.
1249. Saginaw Valley College
University Center, Mich.
1250. California Maritime Academy
Vallejo, Cal.
1251. Los Angeles College of Law
Los Angeles, Cal.
1252. Quinnipiac College
Hamden, Conn.
1253. California Lutheran University
Formerly California Lutheran College
Thousand Oaks, Cal.
1254. Menlo College
Menlo Park, Cal.
1255. Black Hills State College
Spearfish, S.D.
1256. St. Patrick's College
Mountain View, Cal.
1257. Mid-American Nazarene College
Olathe, Kan.
1258. St. John's College
Camarillo, Cal.
1259. Biola University
La Mirada, Cal.
1260. Walsh College
Canton, Ohio
1261. Cheyney State College
Cheyney, Pa.
1262. Fort Lewis College
Durango, Col.
1263. St. John's Seminary
Brighton, Mass.
1264. Colorado Women's College
Denver, Col.
1265. Grand Valley State College
Allendale, Mich.
1266. Marist College
Poughkeepsie, N.Y.
1267. Augusta College
Augusta, Ga.
1268. St. Thomas, University of
Houston, Texas
1269. Ramapo College
Mahwah, N.J.
1270. Texas Lutheran College
Seguin, Texas

1271. Texas at Dallas, University of
Richardson, Texas
1272. Texas of the Permian Basin, University of
Odessa, Texas
1273. Texas at San Antonio, University of
San Antonio, Texas
1274. Texas at Tyler, University of
Tyler, Texas
1275. New College of the University of South Florida
Sarasota, Fla.
1276. Armstrong State College
Savannah, Ga.
1277. Augusta Law School
Augusta, Ga.
1278. Barry College
Miami Shores, Fla.
1279. Benjamin Franklin University
Washington, D.C.
1280. District of Columbia, University of
Washington, D.C.
1281. Graceland College
Lamoni, Iowa
1282. Georgia Southwestern College
Americus, Ga.
1283. Kansas Newman College
Formerly Sacred Heart College
Wichita, Kan.
1284. Corpus Christi State University
Corpus Christi, Texas
1285. Lake Superior State College
Sault Ste. Marie, Mich.
1286. Norfolk State University
Norfolk, Va.
1287. North Florida, University of
Jacksonville, Fla.
1288. Oral Roberts University
Tulsa, Okla.
1289. Savannah State College
Savannah, Ga.
1290. Saint Leo College
Saint Leo, Fla.
1291. Webster College
St. Louis, Mo.
1292. Rutgers University Law School
Camden, N.J.

*Note: There are two separate Law Schools. One at Newark, N.J. (No. 705) and one at Camden, N.J. (No. 1292).*

1293. Berklee College of Music
Boston, Mass.
1294. Maine, University of, School of Law
Portland, Me.
1295. Dunbarton College of the Holy Cross
Washington, D.C.
1296. Allentown College of St. Francis De Sales
Formerly St. Francis De Sales
Center Valley, Pa.
1297. Avila College
Kansas City, Mo.
1298. Bennett College
Greensboro, N.C.
1299. Brescia College
Owensboro, Ky.
1300. Cameron University
Lawton, Okla.
1301. Columbus College
Columbus, Ga.
1302. Cumberland College
Williamsburg, Ky.
1303. Curry College
Milton, Mass.
1304. Dordt College
Sioux Center, Iowa
1305. Eastern College
St. Davids, Pa.
1306. Great Falls, College of
Great Falls, Mont.
1307. Hampshire College
Amherst, Mass.
1308. Massachusetts Maritime Academy
Buzzards Bay, Mass.
1309. Methodist College
Fayetteville, N.C.
1310. Missouri Southern State College
Joplin, Mo.
1311. Missouri Western State College
St. Joseph, Mo.
1312. New England College
Henniker, N.H.

1313. New School for Social Research
New York, N.Y.
1314. Ozarks, School of the
Point Lookout, Mo.
1315. Oklahoma Christian College
Oklahoma City, Okla.
1316. Philadelphia College of Textiles and Science
Philadelphia, Pa.
1317. Pembroke State University
Pembroke, N.C.
1318. Pfeiffer College
Misenheimer, N.C.
1319. Pikeville College
Pikeville, Ky.
1320. St. Johns College
Santa Fe, N.M.
1321. Southwest Baptist University
Bolivar, Mo.
1322. Stephens College
Columbia, Mo.
1323. Steubenville, University of
Steubenville, Ohio
1324. Southern Utah University
Formerly Southern Utah State College
Cedar City, Utah
1325. Touro College Jacob D. Fuchsberg Law Center
New York, N.Y.
1326. York College of Pennsylvania
York, Pa.
1327. Trevecca Nazarene College
Nashville, Tenn.
1328. Baptist College at Charleston
Charleston, S.C.
1329. Christopher Newport College
Formerly Christopher Newport College of the
College of William and Mary
Newport News, Va.
1330. Castleton State College
Castleton, Vt.
1331. Evergreen State College, The
Olympia, Wash.
1332. Tarleton State University
Stephenville, Texas
1333. Embry-Riddle Aeronautical University
Daytona Beach, Fla.
1334. Guam University of
Agana, Guam
1335. Brigham Young University
Laie, Hawaii
1336. Southern California Institute of Law
Santa Barbara and Ventura, Cal.
1337. Texas, University of
Galveston, Texas
1338. Widener University
(Including Widener University School of Law,
formerly Delaware Law School)
Chester, Pa. and Wilmington, Del.
1339. Regent University
Formerly CBN University
Virginia Beach, Va.
1340. Salmon P. Chase College of Law
Highland Heights, Ky.
1341. Texas, University of
Houston, Texas
1342. Southwest State University
Marshall, Minn.
1343. Caldwell College
Caldwell, N.J.
1344. Oakland College of Law
Oakland, Cal.
1345. Wiggins, Norman A., School of Law
Formerly Campbell University School of Law
Buies Creek, N.C.
1346. Prescott College
Prescott, Ariz.
1347. Missouri at St. Louis, University of
St. Louis, Mo.
1348. Northwestern College
Orange City, Iowa
1349. New York at Binghamton, State University of
Binghamton, N.Y.
1350. New York at Stony Brook, State University of
Stony Brook, N.Y.
1351. Simon Greenleaf School of Law
Anaheim, Cal.
1352. Alverno College
Milwaukee, Wis.
1353. Long Island University, Brooklyn Campus of
Brooklyn, N.Y.
1354. Monterey Institute of International Studies
Monterey, Cal.

1355. University of San Francisco Law School
San Francisco, Cal.
1356. George Mason University
Formerly George Mason College of The University of Virginia
Fairfax, Va.
1357. Touro College
New York, N.Y.
1358. Seattle University School of Law
Formerly University of Puget Sound School of Law
Tacoma, Wash.
1359. Evangel College
Springfield, Mo.
1360. Roger Williams University School of Law
Bristol, R.I.

## Canadian Colleges, Universities and Law Schools

01. Acadia University
Wolfville, P.E.I.
02. Alberta, University of
Edmonton, Alta.
Assumption University
See No. 030
03. Bishop's University
Lennoxville, Que.
Brandon University
See No. 049
04. British Columbia, Law Society of
Vancouver, B.C.
05. British Columbia, University of
Vancouver, B.C.
Brock University
See No. 081
Calgary, University of
See No. 037
Carleton University
See No. 034
Concordia University
See Nos. 09 and 041
06. Dalhousie University
Halifax, N.S.
(Sir) George Williams University
See No. 041
Guelph, University of
See No. 040
07. King's College, University of
Halifax, N.S.
Lakehead University
See No. 080
Laurentian University of Sudbury
See No. 083
08. Laval University
Quebec, Que.
Lethbridge, University of
See No. 044
09. Loyola College
Now Concordia University
Montreal, Que.
010. MacDonald College
Ste. A. de Bellevue, Que.
011. Manitoba, University of
Winnipeg, Man.
012. McGill University
Montreal, Que.
013. McMaster University
Hamilton, Ont.
Memorial University of Newfoundland
See No. 036
Moncton, University of
See No. 046
014. Montreal, University of
Montreal, Que.
015. Mount Allison University
Sackville, N.B.
016. New Brunswick, University of
Fredericton, N.B.
017. Nova Scotia College of Agriculture
Truro, N.S.

Osgoode Hall
See No. 029
018. Ottawa, University of
Ottawa, Ont.
Prince Edward Island, University of
Quebec Bar Law School
See No. 087
Quebec, University of
See No. 085
019. Queen's University
Kingston, Ont.
Regina, University of
See No. 048
Royal Military College
See No. 032
020. St. Dunstan's University
Charlottetown, P.E.I.
021. St. Francis Xavier University
Antigonish, N.S.
022. St. Joseph's University
St. Joseph, N.B.
St. Mary's University
See No. 042
St. Thomas University
See No. 047
023. Ste. Marie, College of
Montreal, Que.
024. Saskatchewan, University of
Saskatoon, Sask.
Sherbrooke, University of
See No. 086
Simon Fraser University
See No. 043
025. Toronto, University of
Toronto, Ont.
Trent University
See No. 084
026. Upper Canada, Law Society of
Toronto, Ont.
027. Victoria University
Toronto, Ont.
Victoria, University of (B.C.)
See No. 039
Waterloo Lutheran University
Now Wilfred Laurier University
See No. 033
Waterloo University
Now University of Waterloo
See No. 038
028. Western Ontario, University of
London, Ont.
Wilfrid Laurier University
See No. 033
Windsor, University of
See No. 031
Winnipeg, University of
See No. 045
York University
See No. 035
999. Unlisted colleges, etc., see prefatory notice
029. Osgoode Hall
Toronto, Ont.

030. Assumption University
Windsor, Ont.
031. Windsor, University of
Windsor, Ont.
032. Royal Military College
Kingston, Ont.
033. Waterloo Lutheran University
Now Wilfrid Laurier University
Waterloo, Ont.
034. Carleton University
Ottawa, Ont.
035. York University
Toronto, Ont.
036. Memorial University of Newfoundland
St. John's, Nfld.
037. Calgary, University of
Calgary, Alta.
038. Waterloo University
Now University of Waterloo
Waterloo, Ont.
039. Victoria, University of
Victoria, B.C.
040. Guelph, University of
Guelph, Ont.
041. (Sir) George Williams University
Now Concordia University
Montreal, Que.
042. St. Marys University
Halifax, N.S.
043. Simon Fraser University
Burnaby, B.C.
044. Lethbridge, University of
Lethbridge, Alta.
045. Winnipeg, University of
Winnipeg, Man.
046. Moncton, University of
Moncton, N.B.
047. St. Thomas University
Fredericton, N.B.
048. Regina, University of
Regina, Sask.
049. Brandon University
Brandon, Man.
080. Lakehead University
Thunder Bay, Ont.
081. Brock University
St. Catharines, Ont.
082. Prince Edward Island, University of
Charlottetown, P.E.I.
083. Laurentian University of Sudbury
Sudbury, Ont.
084. Trent University
Peterborough, Ont.
085. Quebec, University of
Sainte Foy, Montreal, Trois-Rivieres, Chicoutimi, Hull and Rimouski, Que.
086. Sherbrooke, University of
Sherbrooke, Que.
087. Quebec Bar Law School
Montreal, Que.

## International Universities

050. Cambridge University
Cambridge, England
051. Oxford University
Oxford, England
052. Heidelberg University
Baden, Germany
053. Sorbonne University
Now University of Paris
See also No. 055
London School of Economics
See No. 054
054. London, University of
London, England
055. University of Paris
Paris, France

University of Philippines
See No. 662
Queen's University, The
See No. 068
056. University of Rome
Rome, Italy
057. University of Vienna
Vienna, Austria
058. Trinity College, University of Dublin
Dublin, Ireland
059. Edinburgh University
Edinburgh, Scotland
060. University of Munich
Munich, Germany
061. Unlisted colleges, etc., see prefatory notice

062. National University of Ireland
Dublin, Ireland
063. Royal Military Academy
Sandhurst, England
064. University of Santo Thomas
Manila, P.I.
065. University of Durham
Durham, England
066. Manuel L. Quezon University
Manila, P.I.
067. Stockholm, University of
Stockholm, Sweden
068. Queen's University, The
Belfast, Northern Ireland

# PRACTICE PROFILES BAR ROSTER

---

CALIFORNIA
A — R

# CALIFORNIA

## CAPITAL: SACRAMENTO

State Bar of California
555 Franklin Street
San Francisco, CA 94102-4498
Telephone: 415-561-8200
Fax: 415-561-8228

*Index of Towns and Cities Listed by County*

*Indicates County Seat

**Alameda County**
Alameda
Albany
Berkeley
Castro Valley
Dublin
Emeryville
Fremont
Hayward
Livermore
Newark
* Oakland
Piedmont
Pleasanton
San Leandro
San Lorenzo
Union City

**Alpine County**
Bear Valley
* Markleeville

**Amador County**
Ione
* Jackson
Pine Grove
Pioneer
Plymouth
Sutter Creek
Volcano

**Butte County**
Chico
Durham
Forest Ranch
Gridley
Magalia
* Oroville
Paradise

**Calaveras County**
Altaville
Angels Camp
Arnold
* San Andreas
West Point

**Colusa County**
Arbuckle
* Colusa
Princeton

**Contra Costa County**
Alamo
Antioch
Bethel Island
Brentwood
Byron
Canyon
Clayton
Concord
Crockett
Danville
Diablo
El Cerrito
El Sobrante
Hercules
Kensington
Lafayette
* Martinez

**Contra Costa Co.**—*Continued*
Moraga
Oakley
Orinda
Pinole
Pittsburg
Pleasant Hill
Point Richmond
Richmond
San Pablo
San Ramon
Walnut Creek

**Del Norte County**
* Crescent City

**El Dorado County**
Cameron Park
Coloma
Diamond Springs
El Dorado
El Dorado Hills
Garden Valley
Georgetown
Grizzly Flat
* Placerville
Pollock Pines
Rescue
Shingle Springs
South Lake Tahoe

**Fresno County**
Clovis
Coalinga
Del Rey
Firebaugh
Fowler
* Fresno
Kerman
Kingsburg
Parlier
Piedra
Pinedale
Reedley
Riverdale
Sanger
Selma
Shaver Lake
Tranquillity

**Glenn County**
Orland
* Willows

**Humboldt County**
Arcata
Blue Lake
Cutten
* Eureka
Ferndale
Fortuna
Garberville
Hydesville
Kneeland
McKinleyville
Miranda
Orleans
Trinidad
Willow Creek

**Imperial County**
Brawley
Calexico
* El Centro
Holtville
Imperial
Palo Verde
Seeley
Westmorland

**Inyo County**
Bishop
Darwin
* Independence
Lone Pine

**Kern County**
* Bakersfield
California City
Delano
DiGiorgio
Edwards
Frazier Park
Keene
Kernville
Lake Isabella
Lebec
Mojave
Oildale
Ridgecrest
Rosamond
Shafter
Tehachapi
Tupman
Wasco

**Kings County**
Corcoran
* Hanford
Lemoore

**Lake County**
Clearlake
Cobb
Kelseyville
* Lakeport
Lower Lake
Middletown
Upper Lake

**Lassen County**
McArthur
* Susanville
Westwood

**Los Angeles County**
Acton
Agoura Hills
Agua Dulce
Alhambra
Altadena
Arcadia
Arleta
Artesia
Avalon
Azusa
Baldwin Park
Bel Air
Bell
Bellflower

**Los Angeles Co.**—*Continued*
Bell Gardens
Beverly Hills
Bradbury
Burbank
Calabasas
Canoga Park
Canyon Country
Carson
Century City
Cerritos
Chatsworth
City of Commerce
City of Industry
Claremont
Commerce
Compton
Covina
Culver City
Diamond Bar
Downey
Duarte
Eagle Rock
El Monte
El Segundo
Encino
Flintridge
Gardena
Glendale
Glendora
Granada Hills
Hacienda Heights
Harbor City
Hawaiian Gardens
Hawthorne
Hermosa Beach
Hidden Hills
Hollywood
Huntington Park
Hynes
Inglewood
Irwindale
La Canada Flintridge
La Crescenta
La Habra Heights
Lake Hughes
Lakewood
La Mirada
Lancaster
La Puente
La Verne
Lawndale
Little Rock
Lomita
Long Beach
* Los Angeles
Malibu
Manhattan Beach
Marina Del Rey
Maywood
Mission Hills
Monrovia
Montebello
Monterey Park
Montrose
Newhall
North Hollywood
Northridge
North Sherman Oaks
Norwalk

**Los Angeles Co.**—*Continued*
Pacific Palisades
Pacoima
Palmdale
Palos Verdes Estates
Palos Verdes Peninsula
Panorama City
Paramount
Pasadena
Pico-Rivera
Playa Del Rey
Pomona
Rancho Palos Verdes
Redondo Beach
Reseda
Rolling Hills
Rolling Hills Estates
Rosemead
Rowland Heights
San Dimas
San Fernando
San Gabriel
San Marino
San Pedro
Santa Clarita
Santa Fe Springs
Santa Monica
Saugus
Sepulveda
Sherman Oaks
Sierra Madre
Signal Hill
South El Monte
South Gate
South Pasadena
Studio City
Sunland
Sun Valley
Sylmar
Tarzana
Temple City
Toluca Lake
Topanga
Torrance
Tujunga
Universal City
Valencia
Van Nuys
Venice
Vernon
Walnut
West Chester
West Covina
West Hills
West Hollywood
West Los Angeles
Westwood Village
Whittier
Wilmington
Winnetka
Woodland Hills

**Madera County**
Bass Lake
Chowchilla
Coarsegold
* Madera
North Fork
Oakhurst

CAA1I

## Marin County
- Belvedere-Tiburon
- Bolinas
- Corte Madera
- Dillon Beach
- Fairfax
- Greenbrae
- Inverness
- Kentfield
- Larkspur
- Marshall
- Mill Valley
- Nicasio
- Novato
- Olema
- Point Reyes Station
- Ross
- San Anselmo
- San Geronimo
- San Quentin
- *San Rafael
- Sausalito
- Stinson Beach
- Tiburon

## Mariposa County
- *Mariposa
- Yosemite National Park

## Mendocino County
- Boonville
- Branscomb
- Comptche
- Covelo
- Fort Bragg
- Gualala
- Little River
- Mendocino
- Philo
- Redwood Valley
- *Ukiah
- Westport
- Willits

## Merced County
- Atwater
- Dos Palos
- Gustine
- Los Banos
- *Merced

## Modoc County
- *Alturas

## Mono County
- *Bridgeport
- Coleville
- Mammoth Lakes

## Monterey County
- Big Sur
- Carmel
- Carmel Highlands
- Carmel Valley
- Castroville
- Greenfield
- King City
- Marina
- Monterey
- Moss Landing
- Pacific Grove
- Pebble Beach
- *Salinas
- Seaside

## Napa County
- American Canyon
- Angwin
- Calistoga
- *Napa
- St. Helena
- Yountville

## Nevada County
- Grass Valley
- *Nevada City

*Indicates County Seat

**CAA2I**

## Nevada Co.—Continued
- Penn Valley
- Rough and Ready
- Truckee

## Orange County
- Aliso Viejo
- Anaheim
- Balboa
- Balboa Island
- Brea
- Buena Park
- Capistrano Beach
- Corona Del Mar
- Costa Mesa
- Coto De Caza
- Cypress
- Dana Point
- El Toro
- Fountain Valley
- Fullerton
- Garden Grove
- Huntington Beach
- Irvine
- Laguna Beach
- Laguna Hills
- Laguna Niguel
- La Habra
- Lake Forest
- La Palma
- Los Alamitos
- Mission Viejo
- Monarch Beach
- Newport Beach
- Orange
- Placentia
- Rancho Santa Margarita
- Rossmoor
- San Clemente
- San Juan Capistrano
- *Santa Ana
- Santa Ana Heights
- Seal Beach
- Silverado
- South Laguna
- Stanton
- Sunset Beach
- Trabuco Canyon
- Tustin
- Villa Park
- Westminster
- Yorba Linda

## Placer County
- Applegate
- *Auburn
- Carnelian Bay
- Colfax
- Dutch Flat
- Gold Run
- Granite Bay
- Lincoln
- Loomis
- Meadow Vista
- New Castle
- Olympic Valley
- Rocklin
- Roseville
- Tahoe City
- Tahoe Vista

## Plumas County
- Blairsden
- Graeagle
- Greenville
- Portola
- *Quincy

## Riverside County
- Anza
- Banning
- Beaumont
- Bermuda Dunes
- Big River
- Blythe
- Calimesa

## Riverside Co.—Continued
- Canyon Lake
- Cathedral City
- Coachella
- Corona
- Desert Hot Springs
- Hemet
- Homeland
- Idyllwild
- Indian Wells
- Indio
- Lake Elsinore
- La Quinta
- Moreno Valley
- Mountain Center
- Murrieta
- Norco
- North Palm Springs
- Nuevo
- Palm Desert
- Palm Springs
- Perris
- Rancho California
- Rancho Mirage
- *Riverside
- Sun City
- Sunnymead
- Temecula
- Thousand Palms
- Wildomar

## Sacramento County
- Carmichael
- Citrus Heights
- Elk Grove
- Elverta
- Fair Oaks
- Folsom
- Galt
- Gold River
- Herald
- Mather
- North Highlands
- Orangevale
- Rancho Cordova
- Rancho Murieta
- *Sacramento
- Walnut Grove
- Wilton

## San Benito County
- *Hollister
- San Juan Bautista

## San Bernardino County
- Alta Loma
- Apple Valley
- Barstow
- Big Bear City
- Big Bear Lake
- Bloomington
- Blue Jay
- Cedar Glen
- Chino
- Chino Hills
- Colton
- Crestline
- Cucamonga
- Fawnskin
- Fontana
- Grand Terrace
- Helendale
- Hesperia
- Highland
- Joshua Tree
- Lake Arrowhead
- Loma Linda
- Mentone
- Montclair
- Needles
- Ontario
- Phelan
- Pioneertown
- Rancho Cucamonga
- Redlands
- Rialto

## San Bernardino Co.—Continued
- Running Springs
- *San Bernardino
- Twentynine Palms
- Twin Peaks
- Upland
- Victorville
- Wrightwood
- Yucaipa
- Yucca Valley

## San Diego County
- Alpine
- Bonita
- Bonsall
- Borrego Springs
- Cardiff-By-The-Sea
- Carlsbad
- Chula Vista
- Coronado
- Del Mar
- Dulzura
- El Cajon
- Encinitas
- Escondido
- Fallbrook
- Imperial Beach
- Jamul
- Julian
- La Jolla
- Lake San Marcos
- Lakeside
- La Mesa
- Lemon Grove
- Leucadia
- Mount Laguna
- National City
- Ocean Beach
- Oceanside
- Pauma Valley
- Poway
- Ramona
- Rancho Bernardo
- Rancho La Costa
- Rancho Santa Fe
- *San Diego
- San Luis Rey
- San Marcos
- Santee
- San Ysidro
- Solana Beach
- Spring Valley
- Valley Center
- Vista

## San Francisco County
- *San Francisco

## San Joaquin County
- Escalon
- Lockeford
- Lodi
- Manteca
- Ripon
- *Stockton
- Tracy
- Woodbridge

## San Luis Obispo County
- Arroyo Grande
- Atascadero
- Avila Beach
- Baywood Park
- Cambria
- Cayucos
- Creston
- Grover Beach
- Grover City
- Los Osos
- Morro Bay
- Nipomo
- Paso Robles
- Pismo Beach
- *San Luis Obispo
- Shandon
- Shell Beach

## San Luis Obispo Co.—Continued
- Templeton

## San Mateo County
- Atherton
- Belmont
- Brisbane
- Burlingame
- Colma
- Daly City
- El Granada
- Foster City
- Half Moon Bay
- Hillsborough
- Menlo Park
- Millbrae
- Montara
- Moss Beach
- Pacifica
- Portola Valley
- *Redwood City
- San Bruno
- San Carlos
- San Gregorio
- San Mateo
- South San Francisco
- Woodside

## Santa Barbara County
- Buellton
- Carpinteria
- Goleta
- Guadalupe
- Lompoc
- Los Olivos
- Montecito
- Orcutt
- *Santa Barbara
- Santa Maria
- Santa Ynez
- Solvang
- Summerland

## Santa Clara County
- Campbell
- Cupertino
- Gilroy
- Los Altos
- Los Altos Hills
- Los Gatos
- Milpitas
- Monte Sereno
- Morgan Hill
- Mountain View
- Palo Alto
- Redwood Estates
- *San Jose
- San Martin
- Santa Clara
- Saratoga
- Stanford
- Sunnyvale

## Santa Cruz County
- Aptos
- Ben Lomond
- Boulder Creek
- Brookdale
- Capitola
- La Selva Beach
- *Santa Cruz
- Scotts Valley
- Soquel
- Watsonville

## Shasta County
- Anderson
- Enterprise
- Fall River Mills
- *Redding
- Shasta

## Sierra County
- *Downieville

## COUNTIES, CITIES AND TOWNS

**YUBA COUNTY—MARYSVILLE**

**Siskiyou County**
   Dunsmuir
   Fort Jones
   Hornbrook
   Montague
   Mount Shasta
   Sawyers Bar
   Weed
 * Yreka

**Solano County**
   Benicia
   Dixon
 * Fairfield
   Rio Vista
   Suisun
   Suisun City
   Vacaville
   Vallejo

**Sonoma County**
   Bodega Bay
   Cloverdale
   Cotati
   Forestville
   Geyserville
   Glen Ellen
   Healdsburg
   Kenwood
   Monte Rio
   Occidental
   Penngrove
   Petaluma
   Rio Nido
   Rohnert Park
 * Santa Rosa
   Sebastopol
   Sonoma
   The Sea Ranch
   Windsor

**Stanislaus County**
   Ceres
   Hughson
 * Modesto
   Newman
   Oakdale
   Patterson
   Riverbank
   Turlock

**Sutter County**
   Live Oak
   Robbins
 * Yuba City

**Tehama County**
   Corning
 * Red Bluff

**Trinity County**
 * Weaverville

**Tulare County**
   Dinuba
   Exeter
   Farmersville
   Lindsay
   Porterville
   Springville
   Three Rivers
   Tulare
 * Visalia

**Tuolumne County**
   Groveland
   Jamestown
 * Sonora
   Soulsbyville
   Twain Harte

**Ventura County**
   Camarillo
   Channel Island
   Fillmore
   Moorpark

**Ventura Co.**—*Continued*
   Newbury Park
   Oak Park
   Oak View
   Ojai
   Oxnard
   Port Hueneme
   Santa Paula
   Simi Valley
   Somis
   Thousand Oaks
 * Ventura
   Westlake Village

**Yolo County**
   Davis
   El Macero
   West Sacramento
   Winters
 * Woodland

**Yuba County**
   Brownsville
   Camptonville
 * Marysville

*Indicates County Seat

Perry, Lorraine D.H. .................. '54 '84 C.112 A.B. L.1065 J.D. 1424 Fountain St.
Preville, Eileen, (BV) ...................... '51 '76 C.112 A.B. L.284 J.D. [Preville&W.]
Preville & Wilson, Law Offices of, (AV) ........................ 2223 Santa Clara Ave.
Rasch, Thomas A. ....................... '51 '76 C.112 B.A. L.284 J.D. Mun. Ct. Comr.
Reeves, Bruce C., (BV) .................. '48 '75 C.112 B.A. L.1065 J.D. [Reeves,S.&H.]
Reeves, Seidler & Howell, (BV) ..................................... 2527 Santa Clara Ave.
Ritchie, Peggy J. ......................... '49 '78 C.112 B.A. L.1137 J.D. Soc. Sec. Admr.
Rosenberg, Steven G. ..................... '48 '76 C.112 B.S. L.765 J.D. 512 Westline Dr.
Russum, W. Lance, (BV) .......... '41 '66 C.285 A.B. L.1065 J.D. 2500 Santa Clara Ave.
Scheckman, Howard B. '22 '54
C.339 B.S.M.E. L.29 J.D. Asst. Resident Coun., Univ. of Calif. (Pat.)
Schwarz, Fred ........................... '20 '47 C.911 A.B. L.285 LL.B. 1303 Caroline‡
Seidler, Felix A. ............................................ '41 '74 [Reeves,S.&H.]
Shafer, Warren W. ....................... '27 '57 C&L.494 B.S.L., J.D. 148 Roxburg Lane‡
Silva, Gregory A., (BV) .................. '50 '75 C.112 B.A. L.809 J.D. [Stonehouse&S.]
Silverman, Donald R. ............... '33 '71 C.112 B.S. L.765 J.D. 2223 Santa Clara Ave.
Small, Steven P. ........................ '42 '67 C.112 L.426 LL.B. 2509 Santa Clara Ave.
Stonehouse, James A., (BV) ............ '37 '66 C.112 A.B. L.1065 J.D. [Stonehouse&S.]
Stonehouse & Silva, (BV) ................................................... 512 Westline Dr.
**Sullivan, Thomas P., (P.C.), (AV)** ........ '56 '81 C.768 B.S. L.1065 J.D. [Mendelson&B.]
*PRACTICE AREAS: Commercial; Banking; Real Estate; Construction.
Tanenbaum, Stephen M. ....... '45 '71 C.1138 B.B.A. L.1009 J.D. 1321 Harbor Bay Pkwy.
Thomson, Joe ............................ '13 '47 C.112 B.S. L.284 J.D. 2310 Alameda Ave.
Turman, Audrey M. ................. '56 '90 C.766 B.A. L.464 J.D. 2500 Santa Clara Ave.
White, Gordon B., (BV) ............... '29 '60 C.112 B.A. L.1066 LL.B. 307 Laguna Vi5

**Widenor, Mary H., (AV) '37 '77 C.668 B.A. L.1066 J.D.**
**2223 Santa Clara Avenue Suite B, 94501**
**Telephone: 510-865-2223; 1-800-40 Probate Ex. 135 FAX: 510-865-0375**
**(Certified Specialist Estate Planning, Trust and Probate Law, State Bar of California Board of Legal Specialization).**
**Probate, Estate Planning, Estate and Trust Litigation, Real Property and Business Law.**
***See Professional Biographies, ALAMEDA, CALIFORNIA***

Williams, Stuart S., (A Prof. Corp.) ......... '47 '74 C.1073 B.S. L.1026 J.D. 1319 High St.
Wilson, Thomas W., (AV) ................... '44 '70 C.908 B.A. L.1066 J.D. [Preville&W.]
Yoshida, T. Mae .......... '53 '86 C.112 B.A. L.1065 J.D. Gen. Coun., Boehm and Assocs.
**Young, Samuel P.**, (AV) ................... '43 '69 C.1097 B.A. L.1065 J.D. [Young&Y.]
**Young, Sheila Brutoco** ........................ '45 '86 C.734 B.S. L.284 J.D. [Young&Y.]

**Young & Young, LLP, (AV)**
**1826 Clement Street, 94501⊙**
**Telephone: 510-865-2600**
**URL: http://www.samyoung@ihot.com**
**Samuel P. Young; Sheila Brutoco Young.**
**General Practice including Business Transactions, Major Loan Restructures, Hospital Law, Land Use and Development, Real Estate and Real Estate Syndication.**
**San Francisco, California Office: Three Embarcadero Center, Suite 1160, 94111. Telephone: 415-438-3660. Fax: 415-291-9222.**
***See Professional Biographies, ALAMEDA, CALIFORNIA***

Zukerman, Michael J. '59 '85 C.112 B.A. L.904 J.D.
Secy. & Gen. Coun., Farallon Computing, Inc.

## ALAMO, —, *Contra Costa Co.*

**Barnes, Michael W.** ..................... '57 '91 C.112 A.B. L.284 J.D. [Ⓐ Berding&W.]
**Barton, Scott William** ................... '63 '92 C.1027 B.S. L.770 J.D. [Ⓐ Berding&W.]
**Berding, Tyler P.**, (AV) ................... '44 '74 C.1073 B.A. L.1067 J.D. [Berding&W.]

**Berding & Weil, (AV)**
**3240 Stone Valley Road West, 94507⊙**
**Telephone: 510-838-2090 Facsimile: 510-820-5592**
**URL: http://www.berding-weil.com**
**Members of Firm: Tyler P. Berding; Steving S. Weil; James O. Devereaux; Jeffrey B. Cereghino; Michael J. Hughes; Deon R. Stein (Resident at Rancho Cordova Office); Eugene P. Haydu (Resident at Rancho Cordova Office); Mary Walker Filson; Daniel L. Rottinghaus (Resident at Santa Clara Office). Of Counsel: David M. Birka-White; Randolph M. Paul (Resident at Santa Clara Office). Associates: Michael W. Barnes; Scott William Barton; Joshua Sulter Berezin; David Darroch; John P. Gill; Cori L. Goldstein; Stephanie J. Hayes; Kim I. Hickman; Dana S. Marron; Marilyn J. Stewart; Evan D. Williams (Resident at Rancho Cordova Office).**
**Construction Litigation and Community Association Law. Non-Profit Corporation Law. Appellate Practice.**
**Rancho Cordova, California Office: 2200 Sunrise Boulevard, Suite 220. 95670 Telephone: 916-851-1910. Fax: 916-851-1914.**
**Santa Clara, California Office: 3600 Pruneridge Avenue, Suite 130. 95051 Telephone: 408-556-0220. Fax: 408-556-0224.**
**Fresno, California Office: 516 West Shaw Avenue, Suite 200, 93704. Telephone: 209-221-2556. Fax: 209-221-2558.**
***See Professional Biographies, ALAMO, CALIFORNIA***

**Berezin, Joshua Sulter** ................. '69 '96 C.29 B.A. L.1338 J.D. [Ⓐ Berding&W.]
*LANGUAGES: Spanish.
Bernstein, Richard H. ................... '48 '75 C.169 B.A. L.464 J.D. 934 Escondido Ct.‡

**Birka-White, David M., Law Offices of, (AV) '52 '79 C.112 B.A. L.765 J.D.** BB
**3240 Stone Valley Road West, Suite 102, 94507**
**Telephone: 510-838-2090 Facsimile: 510-820-5592**
**Construction Defects, ABS Plastic Pipe and General Products Liability, Insurance Coverage.**
***See Professional Biographies, ALAMO, CALIFORNIA***

**Cereghino, Jeffrey B.**, (BV) ............. '53 '81 C.446 B.A. L.284 J.D. [Berding&W.]
*LANGUAGES: French.
Cheonis, Ernest G., (BV) ................... '31 '58 C.112 B.A. L.1065 J.D. P.O. Box 318
Clegg, Steven R. '52 '91 C.846 B.A. L.326 J.D.
(adm. in TX; not adm. in CA) Pres., Catrep Corp.
Conhain, Stephen M. '38 '62 C&L.339 A.B., J.D.
(adm. in IL; not adm. in CA) P.O. Box 409
Corley, E. Todd ......................... '35 '71 C.37 B.A. L.1153 J.D. 2257 Granite Ct.‡
Dailey, Thomas A. ............ '33 '63 C.347 B.S. L.1119 LL.B. D & M Development Co.
**Darroch, David** .............................................. '52 '96 C.999 B.A. L.765 J.D. [Ⓐ Berding&W.]
Davis, Walter L., (BV) ................. '54 '81 C.154 B.A. L.767 J.D. 3189 Danville Blvd.
**Devereaux, James O.** ......................... '40 '67 C.215 A.B. L.477 J.D. [Berding&W.]
*REPORTED CASES: Burnham v. Superior Court (1990) 495 U.S. 604, 109 L. Ed 2d 631, 110 S. Ct. 2105; Lauriedale Associates, Ltd. v. Wilson (1992) 7 Cal. App. 4th 1439, 9 Cal. Rptr. 2d 774; Nahrstedt v. Lakeside Village Condominium Association (1994) 8 Cal. 4th 361, 33 Cal. Rptr 2d 63, 878 P 2d 1275.
Filice, Gerald W. ......................... '56 '81 C.740 B.A. L.208 J.D. 3201 Danville Blvd.
**Filson, Mary Walker** ........................ '50 '86 C.801 B.A. L.1066 J.D. [Berding&W.]
Gall, Russell B. ............................ '27 '55 C.1197 L.1026 LL.B. 2837 Litina Court.
**Gill, John P.** ............................... '64 '90 C.770 B.A. L.1065 J.D. [Ⓐ Berding&W.]
**Goldstein, Cori L.** .......................... '63 '92 C.768 B.A. L.770 J.D. [Ⓐ Berding&W.]
Golman, Sidney J. ............................................. '15 '53 L.284 J.D. 65 Holliday Dr.
Hannon, Robt. E. ........................ '29 '53 C.740 L.1065 J.D. 1015 Kirkcrest Ln.‡
**Hayes, Stephanie J.** ......................... '54 '81 C.339 B.A. L.365 J.D. [Ⓐ Berding&W.]
**Hickman, Kim I.** .............................................. '55 '94 L.1153 J.D. [Ⓐ Berding&W.]
**Hughes, Michael J.**, (BV) ................ '47 '74 C.769 B.A. L.1065 J.D. [Berding&W.]⊙

Jennings, Roger W. ........................ '44 '78 C.490 B.S. L.809 J.D. 312 Canterbury Ct.
Johnson, Edward C. A. ........................................ '39 '70 C.494 L.284 J.D. 1530 Liting Dr.
Justin-Reed, Denise L. ....................... '60 '87 C.813 B.A. L.770 J.D. 115 Jennifer Ct.
Lentz, Harold S. ................................ '27 '53 C&L.477 A.B., J.D. 119 Romero Cir.‡
**Marron, Dana S.** .............................. '67 '93 C.94 B.A. L.61 J.D. [Ⓐ Berding&W.]
*LANGUAGES: French.
Mizis, Marvin L. ................................ '38 '64 C.112 B.S. L.813 J.D. 2204 Nelda Way‡
Osterloh, Michael P. ........................ '63 '91 C.101 B.S. L.1049 J.D. 3201 Danville Blvd.
Russell, Lawrence F. ............... '53 '87 C.907 B.A. L.770 J.D. 3240 stone Valley R.d
Scott, Milton B., (BV) ............... '36 '72 C.112 A.B. L.981 LL.B. 3201 Danville Blvd.
Stepkin, Charles .......................... '39 '79 C.597 B.A. L.1066 J.D. 1443 Danville Blvd.
**Stewart, Marilyn J.** .......................... '49 '94 C.112 B.A. L.1153 J.D. [Ⓐ Berding&W.]
Stratmore, Robert D. ......................... '46 '72 C.112 A.B. L.1066 J.D. P.O. Box 232
Sullivan, Michael F. .......................... '52 '77 C&L.884 B.S., J.D. [M.F.Sullivan]
Sullivan, Michael F., A Prof. Corp. ........................................ 3165 Stonegate Dr.
Thiessen, Brian D., Law Offices of, (AV) '39 '67
C.228 A.B. L.1065 J.D. 3201 Danville Blvd., Ste 295
**Weil, Steven S.** ................................ '54 '80 C.1044 B.A. L.767 J.D. [Berding&W.]
*LANGUAGES: French.
Wickersham, James B., (BV) ........ '43 '73 C.1073 B.S. L.765 J.D. 3200A Danville Blvd.

## ALBANY, 16,327, *Alameda Co.*

Anderson, William W., Jr. ................. '44 '79 C.918 B.A. L.813 J.D. 901 Peralta Ave.
Atkinson, S. Earle ....................... '45 '70 C.112 B.S. L.767 J.D. 1045 Key Rt. Blvd.
Bolger, Sally J. ..................... '60 '85 C.1074 B.S. L.1065 J.D. Exec. V.P., Inductran Corp.
Coleman, Robert L. ..................... '45 '75 C.112 A.B. L.1066 J.D. 545 Pierce St.
Crosby, Karen Matcke ................... '— '89 C.1074 B.A. L.770 J.D. 1225 Solano Ave.
Donaldson, Douglas C. .................. '44 '73 C.393 B.A. L.1065 J.D. 627 Spokane Ave.

**Foley McIntosh & Foley, Professional Corporation**
**(See Lafayette)**

Furth, Alan C., (AV) ................... '22 '50 C.112 A.B. L.1066 LL.B. 1225 Solano Ave.
Johns, William F., (BV) ............... '46 '73 C.112 B.A. L.1065 J.D. 1301 Solano Ave.
Johnson, Marjorie R. ................... '25 '74 C.267 A.B. L.284 J.D. 600 San Pablo Ave.‡
Johnson, William A., (BV) ....... '30 '61 C.112 A.B. L.1066 LL.B. 600 San Pablo Ave.‡
Kasten, Sandra J. .......................... '51 '77 C.767 B.A. L.1065 J.D. 1309 Solano Ave.
Kruse, J. Henry, Jr. ..................... '25 '52 C.222 A.B. L.705 LL.B. 801 Stannage Ave.
Lightner, David M. ..................... '38 '64 C.112 A.B. L.1066 LL.B. 920 Tulare Ave.
Murray, Terrance C., (AV) ............. '48 '74 C.1073 B.S. L.767 J.D. 1225 Solano Ave.
Olson, Elaine J., (BV) ................. '48 '76 C.112 B.A. L.1026 J.D. 1316 Solano Ave.
Schoener, Wm. L., (BV) ............. '14 '38 C.112 A.B. L.1066 LL.B. 505 Carmel Ave.
Taft, Geoffrey '43 '71 C.102 B.A. L.446 J.D.
(adm. in MI; not adm. in CA) 831 Carmel Ave.‡
Traer, Robert A. '43 '76 C.118 B.A. L.1067 J.D.
(adm. in CO; not adm. in CA) 845 Jackson St.‡
Watt, Dennis R. ........................ '35 '66 C.112 A.B. L.284 LL.B. 901 Peralta Ave.
Weaver, Eric M. ............................. '56 '84 C.170 B.A. L.767 J.D. P.O. Box 6294
Zimmerman, Stanley R. .................. '28 '79 C.569 B.S. L.408 J.D. 555 Pierce St.

## ALHAMBRA, 82,106, *Los Angeles Co.*

Aguirre, Rudy, (AV) ..................... '52 '79 C.112 B.A. L.1068 J.D. 36 N. Garfield Ave.
Akullian, Arthur J. .................... '49 '79 C.588 B.A. L.1095 J.D. 741 S. Garfield Ave.
Arnberger, Kim, Buxbaum & Choy, (AV)
320 South Garfield, Suite 206 (⊙N.Y., N.Y., Beijing, Los Angeles & San Fran., Ca., Canton, People's Rep. of China, Hong Kong, Xiamen City, Shenzhen, Shanghai)
Augustine, Michael R., (AV) ......... '48 '73 C.112 B.A. L.426 J.D. [Augustine&S.]
Augustine and Seymour, (AV) ............................................. 741 S. Garfield Ave.
Baugham, Lucille H. .................. '47 '81 C.800 B.A. L.1068 J.D. 430 S. Garfield Ave.
Bogh, Richard J. ....................... '51 '78 C.800 B.A. L.426 J.D. 1825 S. 4th St.
Burke, Talmage V., (BV) ................ '17 '43 C&L.800 A.B., LL.B. Mayor [T.V.Burke]
Burke, Talmage V., P.C., (BV) ................................................ 100 N. 1st St.
Byrnes, John S., Jr., (BV) ......... '28 '56 C.112 B.S. L.1068 LL.B. 307 N. Garfield Ave.
Chisholm, James R. ................... '40 '72 C.112 B.S. L.426 J.D. 1000 S. Fremont Ave.
Clewis, Monroe Thomas .......... '44 '85 C.112 B.A. L.426 J.D. 814 N. Monterey St., #6
Coco, Salvatore, (BV) ................. '45 '75 C.999 L.1136 J.D. 100 E. Huntington Dr.
Coleman, Bebette G. ................... '30 '57 C.525 A.B. L.426 LL.B. P.O. Box 6066‡
Corral, Jaime R. ............................................ '38 '71 C.112 L.809 J.D. Supr. Ct. J.
Crow, Lawrence J. ..................... '30 '57 C.618 L.623 LL.B. [L.J.Crow]
Crow, Lawrence J., A Law Corporation ..................................... 1231 S. Garfield Ave.
Culkins, L. William, (BV) ........... '34 '63 C.112 B.S. L.800 LL.B. 1225 N. Granada
DeMarco, Robert J., (AV) '39 '71 C.1097 B.A. L.800 J.D.
100 E. Huntington Dr. Ste. 100
Denton, Wayne C. ..................... '43 '74 C.112 B.A. L.426 J.D. 1231 S. Garfield Ave.
Ellis, Anthony Michael ................ '58 '89 C.112 B.A. L.1068 J.D. Off. of Dist. Atty.
Francis, Merrill W., (BV) ............. '33 '60 C.605 B.A. L.1068 LL.B. [Francis&B.]
Francis & Blanco, (BV) ..................................................... 100 E. Huntington Dr.
Freedland, Arnold I. .................... '45 '71 C.494 B.A. L.878 J.D. 55 S. Raymond Ave.
Gomez, Robert J., Jr. ................ '35 '77 C.1097 B.A. L.426 J.D. One W. Hellman Ave.
**Grant, Alexander M.** ................... '36 '66 C.870 B.S. L.1065 J.D. Brown & Root, Inc.
Greenburg, Samuel A., (BV) ..................... '12 '41 L.809 LL.B. 600 Irving, Ste. 113
Gutierrez, Gabriel A. ................... '37 '65 C&L.770 B.A., J.D. Supr. Ct. J.
Hernandez, Enrique, Jr. ..... '55 '80 C&L.309 A.B., J.D. Pres., Inter-Con Security Systems
Hernandez, Roland A. ......... '57 '83 C&L.309 A.B., J.D. Pres., Interspan Communications
Hunt, Elizabeth .... '61 '87 C.94 B.A. L.309 J.D. Corp. Coun., Inter-Con Security Systems
Ito, Kenji ................................. '09 '36 C&L.911 LL.B. 1901 W. Grand Ave.‡
Kanner, Michael A. .................... '42 '70 C.800 B.A. L.809 J.D. Mun. Ct. J.
Kolstad, Charles K. ................ '53 '80 C.884 B.S. L.602 J.D. [Ⓒ Arnberger,K.B.&C.]⊙
Lee, Timothy F. ....................... '41 '71 C.1097 B.A. L.1095 J.D. 55 S. Raymond Ave.

**Lin, Grace L. '56 '85 L.061 LL.B.**
**2225 West Commonwealth Avenue, Suite 109, 91803**
**Telephone: 818-281-3618 Fax: 818-570-0542**
***PRACTICE AREAS: Civil Litigation; Business Law; Corporate Law; Real Property; Torts.**
**General Civil Litigation, Business, Corporate, Real Property, Immigration and Naturalization.**

Lombardi, Richard B. .................. '46 '72 C.940 B.A. L.1068 J.D. 1 W. Hellman Ave.
Mulcahy, Robert W., (AV) ............. '40 '70 C.93 B.S. L.273 J.D. 320 S. Garfield (Pat.)
O'Brien, Mark M., (BV) ............... '43 '71 C.112 A.B. L.800 J.D. 36 W. Bay State St.
Olson, Wade D. ...................... '48 '73 C&L.585 B.S.B.A., J.D. L.A. Co. Supr. Ct. Comr.
**Parrington, Thomas E.**, (AV) ......... '39 '65 C.813 B.A. L.1066 LL.B. [Tompkins&P.]
*PRACTICE AREAS: Real Estate; Redevelopment; Probate; Trust; Estate Planning.
Penn, Wayne P. ........................ '48 '82 C.1077 B.A. L.1136 J.D. 711 W. Valley Blvd.
Saxton, Roger S. '52 '80 C.930 B.A. L.607 J.D.
(adm. in PA; not adm. in CA) [Ⓒ Arnberger,K.B.&C.]⊙
Seymour, Frederick J., (AV) ........... '48 '76 C.426 B.A. L.1190 LL.B. [Augustine&S.]
Shuai, Yee-Jen ........................ '49 '80 C.061 LL.B. L.1065 J.D. 711 W. Valley Blvd.
**Tompkins, Emmett A., Jr.**, (AV) ......... '35 '61 C.112 B.A. L.1068 LL.B. [Tompkins&P.]
*PRACTICE AREAS: Probate and Trust; Estate Planning.

## ACTON, —, *Los Angeles Co.*

Kelso, Nancy L. ... '44 '72 [Kelso&Y.]
Kelso & Young ... P.O. Box 70
Layton, Larry H., (CV) ... '42 '75 L.1190 LL.B. 3807 W. Sierra Hwy.
Young, Calvin M., III ... '38 '71 C.684 B.A. L.1068 J.D. [Kelso&Y.]

## AGOURA HILLS, 20,390, *Los Angeles Co.*

Allen, Barry M. ... '46 '75 C.1077 B.A. L.1221 J.D. 5699 Kanan Rd.
Anderson, Robert D. ... '48 '79 C.1097 B.A. L.809 J.D. [⊡ Byers&L.]
Baker, R. Brooks ... '30 '72 C.112 B.A. L.426 J.D. P.O. Box 98
Ball, Pyfrom, Yorke, & Associates, Law Offices of
28720 Roadside Dr. (⊙Ventura, Santa Monica)
Bayer, Shelley A. ... '54 '83 C.112 B.A. L.809 J.D. 1237 N. Dubonnet Ct.
Buongiorno, Ernest A. ... '54 '90 C.1174 B.S. L.809 J.D. 160 N. Satinwood Ave.
Byers, Michael W., (AV) ... '43 '71 C.312 B.A. L.809 J.D. [Byers&L.]
Byers & Lyden, A Professional Corporation, (AV) ... 30101 Agoura Ct., Suite 100
Cohen, Ira ... '49 '78 C.415 B.A. L.809 J.D. 5236 Colodny Dr.
Collier, Gerald A., (A Law Corp.) ... '42 '70 C&L.800 B.S., J.D. 5699 Kanan Rd.
Culver, Woody H. ... '47 '79 C.851 B.B.A. L.1095 LL.B. 28215 Agoura Rd.‡
Doheney, Clyde T. ... '46 '76 C.800 B.A. L.1068 J.D. 473 Cresthill Dr.‡
Eichenberg, Tim R. ... '53 '81 C.112 B.A. L.1137 J.D. [Harrison,E.&M.]
Gershon, Lorry F. ... '46 '82 C.37 B.A. L.1095 J.D. 3947 Patrick Henry Pl.
Ginder, Eric R. ... '69 '96 C.800 B.A. L.809 J.D. [⊡ Ball,P.Y.&Assoc.]
Gross, Steven ... '44 '81 C.813 B.A. L.1136 LL.B. 30101 Agoura Ct.
Grossman, Jan, (AV) ... '51 '81 C.112 B.A. L.940 J.D. 5004 Evanwood Ave., Agoura
Harrison, S. Michael ... '50 '78 C.763 B.A. L.1137 J.D. [Harrison,E.&M.]
Harrison, Eichenberg & Murphy ... P.O. Box 640
James, Margo L. ... '51 '77 C.112 B.A. L.1065 J.D. 28726 Aries St.‡

**Karno, Schwartz, Friedman, Shafron & Warren, (AV)**
**A Partnership including Professional Corporations**
**30497 Canwood Street, Suite 102, 91301⊙**
**Telephone: 818-597-7977 Fax: 818-597-7970**
**Earl W. Warren.**
**Real Estate, Tax, Corporate, Business, ERISA, Estate Planning and Probate Law. Litigation.**
**Encino, California Office: Manufacturers Bank Building, Suite 1200, 16255 Ventura Boulevard.**
**Telephone: 818-981-3400; 213-872-1800. Telecopier: 213-872-1278.**
*See Professional Biographies, AGOURA HILLS, CALIFORNIA*

**Koslov & Medlen**
**(See Los Angeles)**

Liakas, Nicolas '46 '73 C.563 A.B. L.262 J.D.
(adm. in NY; not adm. in CA) 5910 Grey Rock Rd.‡
Lindauer, Thayer C. '39 '63 C&L.145 B.A., J.D.
(adm. in AZ; not adm. in CA) 5548 DeVore Ct.‡
Louth, Kevin H. ... '57 '83 C.1077 B.A. L.990 J.D. [⊡ Ball,P.Y.&Assoc.]
Luster, Eleanor ... '16 '65 C.831 B.S.E.D. L.1068 LL.B. 30120 Elizabeth Ct.
Lyddon, Phillip S. ... '32 '58 C.37 B.S.B.A. L.1068 J.D. Gen. Coun., Amer. Bakeries Co.
Lyden, D. Michael, (AV) ... '41 '71 L.809 J.D. [Byers&L.]
Macks, Jonathan L. '54 '80 C&L.884 B.A., J.D.
(adm. in PA; not adm. in CA) 790 Oak Branch Dr.
Mast, Andrea ... '59 '87 C.112 B.A. L.1068 J.D. Coun., ProCentric Computer Servs., Inc.
Matthew, Sandra Medway ... '52 '79 C.112 B.A. L.809 J.D. 358 N. Kanan Rd.
Miller, Mark F. ... '60 '86 C.273 B.A. L.800 J.D. 2317 Waring Dr.
Monroe, David A. ... '47 '73 C&L.608 B.A., J.D. 1312 Dubonnet Ct.
Murphy, Patrick M. ... '56 '83 C.398 B.A. L.990 J.D. [Harrison,E.&M.]
**Owens, James J.** '42 '87 C.740 B.A. L.1186 J.D.
Sr. V.P., Secy., GE Heritage Ins. Grp.
Pyfrom, Gregory C. '47 '77
C.1077 B.A. L.1190 J.D. [Ball,P.Y.&Assoc.] (⊙Santa Monica)
Reitman, Gordon H. ... '40 '68 C.112 B.S. L.1065 J.D. P.O. Box 833

**Schroeder, Rick A. '61 '86 C.966 B.B.A. L.1068 J.D.**
**638 Lindero Canyon Road, Suite 392, 91301**
**Telephone: 818-879-1943 Telecopier: 818-879-5443**
**Email: 73430.2763@compuserve.com**
***PRACTICE AREAS: Bankruptcy; Commercial Litigation; Business.**
**Bankruptcy, Insolvency, Creditors' Rights, Commercial and Business Litigation.**
*See Professional Biographies, AGOURA HILLS, CALIFORNIA*

Schwartz, Richard E. ... '53 '80 C.112 B.A. L.472 J.D. 501 Savona Way

**Scott, Mary B. '59 '91 C.763 B.S. L.1049 J.D.**
**5699 Kanan Road, Suite 339, 91301**
**Telephone: 818-889-9220 Fax: 818-889-9255**
**General Civil Practice, Business Matters including Intellectual Property, Trademark and Copyright, and Libel, Slander and Defamation.**
*See Professional Biographies, AGOURA HILLS, CALIFORNIA*

Siegan, Robert J. ... '50 '76 C.112 L.1095 J.D. 6236 Shadycreek Dr.
Silverman, Lawrence S. ... '49 '75 C.1077 B.A. L.809 J.D. 5514 N. Fairgrange Dr.
Stanton, Marta I. ... '66 '91 C.112 B.A. L.1065 J.D. 494 Savona Wy.
Thornburg, Michael L. ... '57 '82 C.169 B.A. L.569 J.D. 343 Savoy Ct.
Vosguanian, Bruce C. ... '51 '81 C.262 B.S. L.990 J.D. [Vosguanian&V.]
Vosguanian, Rodney N. ... '50 '80 C.262 B.S. L.990 J.D. [Vosguanian&V.]
Vosguanian & Vosguanian ... 28030 Dorothy Dr.
Walsh, Dennis M. ... '52 '82 C.1077 B.A. L.770 J.D. 5737 Kanan Rd.
**Warren, Earl W.**, (AV) ... '40 '66 C.112 B.A. L.1068 LL.B. [Karno,S.F.S.&W.]
*PRACTICE AREAS: Transactional Residential Real Estate Development; Commercial and Industrial Real Estate Development; General Corporate Law; Luxury, Sales and Use Tax Documented Vessels.
Weingart, Ronald C. '41 '72 C.454 B.S.M.E. L.1095 J.D.
3836 Castle View Dr., Augoura
Williamson, Agnes M., (Mrs.) ... '28 '72 C&L.1095 B.A., J.D. 29101 Fountainwood St.‡
Zuckerman, Ellen M. ... '51 '78 C.477 A.B. L.215 J.D. 360 Turin St.

## AGUA DULCE, 900, *Los Angeles Co.*

Alderman, Robert E., Jr. ... '47 '73 C&L.426 B.A., J.D. [R.E.Alderman,Jr.]
Alderman, Robert E., Jr., Prof. Law Corp. ... 33336 Agua Dulce Canyon Rd.
Perry, William T. ... '50 '88 C.112 A.B. L.1148 J.D. 33338 Agua Dulce Canyon Rd.
Vaughan, Ame D. ... '56 '83 C.1042 B.A. L.426 J.D. 13108 Reservoir Ave.

## ALAMEDA, 76,459, *Alameda Co.*

Allen, Jeffrey S. ... '43 '73 C.768 B.S. L.767 J.D. Mun. Ct. J.
Ashford, Charles W. ... '53 '85 C.280 B.A. L.767 J.D. 1330 St. Charles St.
Bacich, Jeffrey V. ... '50 '75 C.112 A.B. L.1065 J.D. 1824 Pearl St.
Bartalini, C. Richard ... '31 '57 C.112 B.A. L.1065 J.D. Ret. Supr. Ct. J.
**Beattie, Gregory L.** ... '54 '80 C.813 A.B. L.309 J.D. [Mendelson&B.]
*PRACTICE AREAS: Technology; Corporate; Securities; Commercial.
Bell, Edward C., (CV) ... '37 '70 1516 Oak St.
Belt, Taylor M. '23 '54 C&L.972 B.S.M.E., J.D.
(adm. in WY; not adm. in CA) 1825 Shoreline Dr.‡
Berg, William L. ... '52 '80 C.112 B.A. L.767 J.D. [W.L.Berg]
Berg, William L., Law Office of ... 2156 Central Ave.
Brewer, John C. ... '53 '78 C.569 B.A. L.477 J.D. 909 Marina Village Pkwy.
Britton, Shawn M. ... '64 '90 C.112 B.A. L.1065 J.D. Taylor & Co.
**Brown, Michael S., (P.C.)**, (AV) ... '52 '78 C.208 B.A. L.426 J.D. [Mendelson&B.]
*PRACTICE AREAS: Real Estate; Commercial; Insurance; Environmental.
Buono, John F., Jr., (AV) ... '42 '67 C.767 B.S. L.1065 J.D. 1630 Park St.
Caspari, William S. ... '52 '85 C.112 B.A. L.1066 J.D. 1320 Harbor Bay Pky.
Caton, Thomas E., (BV) ... '27 '54 C.112 A.B. L.1065 LL.B. 512 Westline Dr.
Cline, Charles P., (CV) ... '48 '76 C.1075 B.A. L.765 J.D. 512 Westline Dr.
Clinton, Janet, (AV) ... '52 '80 C.112 B.A. L.809 J.D. 2425 Webb Ave.
Codiga, Gayle Godfrey, (Mrs.) ... '56 '84 C.112 B.S. L.766 J.D. 1134 Bay St.
Cunningham, Frederick M. ... '16 '50 C.112 A.B. L.1065 J.D. 2410 Otis Dr.
Davis, James B., (P.C.), (AV) ... '29 '56 C.112 B.S. L.1066 J.D. 6 Purcell Dr.
Day, Montie S. ... '41 '77 C.267 B.S. L.1197 J.D. 883 Island Dr.
Deal, Betty Barry ... '21 '55 C.112 A.B. L.1066 J.D. 1201 San Antonio Ave.‡
Dickson, John B., (AV) '37 '69
C.668 B.A. L.1026 J.D. 1040 Marina Village Pkwy, Suite B
Doll, Ronald W. ... '36 '66 C.813 A.B. L.1065 J.D. 2236 Mariner Sq. Dr.
Dooley, Michael J. ... '— '87 C.1169 B.A. L.767 J.D. 70 Justin Cir.

**Dósa, Andrew Alexander, (BV) '58 '84 C.112 A.B. L.767 J.D.**
**2504 Santa Clara Avenue, 94501**
**Telephone: 510-865-1600 FAX: 510-865-7245**
***PRACTICE AREAS: Personal Injury; General Civil Litigation; Litigation; Criminal Law.**
**Personal Injury, General, Civil and Business Litigation. Criminal Law.**
*See Professional Biographies, ALAMEDA, CALIFORNIA*

Drake, Robert W. ... '47 '80 C.112 B.A. L.1065 J.D. 1105 Sherman St.
Duncan, Matthew J., (CV) ... '56 '81 C.112 B.A. L.767 J.D. 1516 Oak St.
Eichhorn, Charles L. ... '50 '81 C.1090 B.A. L.1065 J.D. 19 Thurles Pl.
Ezzy, Marilyn E. ... '52 '84 C.112 B.S. L.770 J.D. 903 Grand St.
Falzone, Gerard A. ... '56 '82 C.112 B.A. L.1066 J.D. 2500 Santa Clara Ave.
Ferro, Thos. L. ... '15 '43 C.770 B.S. L.765 LL.B. 1826 Clement Ave.‡
Fertig, Gary L., (BV) ... '48 '74 C.1073 B.A. L.284 J.D. 2223 Santa Clara Ave.
Fisher, Everett E. ... '13 '37 C.902 A.B. L.150 LL.B. 1361 East Shore Dr.‡
Garber, Alan S., (AV) ... '50 '77 C.608 B.S. L.30 J.D. 1040 Marina Village Pkwy. Ste B
Grappo, Michael A. ... '15 '55 C.608 B.Sc. L.1026 LL.B. P.O. Box 1189‡
Greely, Gail A. ... '54 '79 C.813 A.B. L.178 J.D. 147 Tynebourne Pl.
Groenewold, Glenn ... '31 '55 C&L.174 B.A., J.D. 2263 Pacific Ave.‡
Gruber, Walter F. ... '54 '79 C.1350 B.A. L.588 J.D. 1516 Oak St.
Hanson, John F., Jr. ... '14 '39 C&L.813 A.B., J.D. 2425 Webb Ave.
Haverkamp, James A. ... '48 '81 C.970 B.A. L.1065 J.D. 1040 Marina Village Pky.
**Holloway, Bruce D.** ... '55 '90 C.112 A.B. L.1066 J.D. [⊡ Mendelson&B.]
*LANGUAGES: Norwegian, German, Danish, Swedish, Dutch.
*PRACTICE AREAS: Trademark; Technology; Corporate; Commercial.
Howell, Laurie ... '53 '81 [Reeves,S.&H.]
Iandoli, Claire C. ... '57 '90 C.156 B.A. L.1202 J.D. Calif. State Employees Assn.
Jaber, Edward J. ... '52 '78 C.112 A.B. L.765 J.D. 1216 Regent St.‡
James, John N., (AV) ... '17 '41 C.267 A.B. L.1066 LL.B. 1826 Clement Ave.
Joesting, Linden H. ... '58 '88 C.914 B.A. L.813 J.D. Atty., U.S. Coast Guard★
Johnson, Beverly J. ... '58 '86 C.1073 B.A. L.464 J.D. 2500 Santa Clara Ave.
Johnson, Jean H. '— '79 C.627 B.S.N. L.1026 J.D.
Sr. V.P., Professional Risk Mgmt., Inc.
Keebler, Michael J. ... '46 '75 C.477 A.B. L.912 J.D. 875A Island Dr.
Kennedy, James T., (BV) ... '42 '73 C.768 B.A. L.767 J.D. 2447 Santa Clara Ave.
Kessler, Leslie M., (AV) ... '12 '36 C.112 A.B. L.1066 LL.B. 1000 Harina Village Pkwy.
Kirby, Donald A., (BV) ... '45 '75 C.768 B.S. L.464 J.D. 2325 Clement Ave.
Kofman, Kenneth ... '38 '63 C.112 A.B. L.1066 LL.B. 1080 Jost Lane‡
Korade, Carol A. ... '53 '78 C.1044 B.A. L.809 J.D. City Atty.
Kyle, Mark L. ... '55 '90 C.94 B.A. L.1067 J.D. Operating Engrs. Local Union #3
Lancaster, Clifford R., (BV) ... '51 '76 C.685 B.A. L.1066 J.D. 1826 Clement Ave.

**Leadlove-Plant, Elaine F.B. '49 '89 C.766 L.1153 J.D.**
**909 Marina Village Parkway, Suite 339, 94501**
**Telephone: 510-523-4586**
***PRACTICE AREAS: Banking Litigation (70%); Business Law (10%); Bankruptcy (10%); Consumer Law (10%).**
**Construction Law, Bankruptcy.**
*See Professional Biographies, ALAMEDA, CALIFORNIA*

Lederman, Michael J. ... '63 '89 C.446 A.B. L.945 J.D. U.S. Coast Guard
Lucas, Karin ... '34 '70 C&L.061 2254 Encinal Ave.
**Lyons, Richard A.** ... '49 '82 C.112 B.A. L.1066 J.D. [Mendelson&B.]
*PRACTICE AREAS: Corporate; Partnerships; Securities; Technology.
MacLeod, Donald, (AV) ... '23 '52 L.1065 J.D. 229 Cumberland Ct.
Mahoney, John D., (AV) ... '42 '72 C.740 B.A. L.767 J.D. 1720 Palmera Ct.
Maloney, Patrick J. ... '43 '69 C.918 B.A. L.1065 J.D. [P.J.Maloney]
Maloney, Patrick J., A Professional Corporation ... 2425 Webb Ave.
McCollom, William G. '36 '65 C.309 A.B. L.893 J.D.
(adm. in MO; not adm. in CA) 1137 Camino del Vale‡
McDonald, George E. ... '20 '50 C&L.767 B.A., LL.D. Ret. Mun. J.
**Mendelson, Ralph N., (P.C.)**, (AV) '30 '55 C.494 B.A. L.976 LL.B.
[⊡ Mendelson&B.]
*PRACTICE AREAS: Commercial Law; Banking.

**Mendelson & Brown, (AV)**
**A Partnership including Professional Corporations**
**1040 Marina Village Parkway, Suite B, 94501**
**Telephone: 510-521-1211 FAX: 510-521-7879**
**Email: dm@mendelson-brown.com**
**Members of Firm: Michael S. Brown (P.C.); Thomas P. Sullivan (P.C.); Gregory L. Beattie; Richard A. Lyons. Associates: Bruce D. Holloway. Of Counsel: Ralph N. Mendelson (P.C.).**
**General Civil and Trial Practice. Corporate, Commercial, Real Estate, Labor, Construction, Banking, Environmental, Securities, Technology, Trademark, and Energy.**
**Reference: Alameda First National Bank.**
*See Professional Biographies, ALAMEDA, CALIFORNIA*

Moeller, Walter S. ... '39 '79 C.836 A.B. L.1066 J.D. 1320 Harbor Bay Pkwy.

**Owen & Melbye, A Professional Corporation**
**(See Redwood City)**

**Pedder, William Robert**, (AV) ... '42 '68 C&L.813 A.B., J.D. [W.R.Pedder]

**Pedder, William Robert, A Professional Corporation, (AV)**
**2447 Santa Clara Avenue, Suite 201, 94501**
**Telephone: 510-523-9152 FAX: 510-523-9154**
**William Robert Pedder.**
**General Civil and Trial Practice. Real Estate, Personal Injury, Corporate Business, Estate Planning, Trust and Probate Law.**
*See Professional Biographies, ALAMEDA, CALIFORNIA*

CAA1P

**Tompkins & Parrington, (AV)**
**320 North Garfield Avenue, P.O. Box 589, 91802**
**Telephone: 818-289-3727; 213-283-3107 Telecopier: 818-289-0918**
**Members of Firm: Emmett A. Tompkins, Jr.; Thomas E. Parrington.**
**Probate, Estate Planning, Taxation, Real Estate, Zoning and Business Law.**
**References: Bank of America, Alhambra Branch; Security Pacific National Bank, Alhambra Branch.**
*See Professional Biographies, ALHAMBRA, CALIFORNIA*

Torres, Edward A. ....'52 '83 C.1097 B.S. L.1137 J.D. 200 S. Garfield Ave.
Trapani, John ....'29 '61 L.724 LL.B. 317 W. Main St.
Tripi, Cecelia (Reid) ....'59 '85 C.800 B.A. L.426 J.D. P.O. Box 7306
Valdez, Earl ....'35 '72 C&L.800 B.S., J.D. 940 E. Main St.
Watson, David L. ....'50 '78 C&L.1077 B.A., J.D. 223 E. Valley Blvd.
Wong, Fred A. ....'59 '86 C.1097 B.S. L.800 J.D. 100 E. Huntington Dr.
Wong, Wei C. ....'56 '84 C.112 B.A. L.426 J.D. 716 S. Garfield Ave.
Wood, Roger H. ....'23 '53 C&L.813 B.A., LL.B. Chaplain, Episcopal Home‡

## ALISO VIEJO, 7,612, *Orange Co.*

Buteyn, Debra K. ....'54 '84 C.112 B.A. L.426 J.D. 26 Helmcrest
**Conner, Frank A.**, (BV) ....'53 '79 C&L.101 B.S., J.D. [Wordes,W.G.&C.]
*PRACTICE AREAS: Real Estate and Business Litigation.
Garcia, Anthony M. ....'64 '91 C.112 B.A. L.37 J.D. 95 Argonaut
**Goren, Michael E.** ....'50 '75 C.112 B.A. L.1068 J.D. [Wordes,W.G.&C.]
*PRACTICE AREAS: Commercial Real Estate; Shopping Center Law.
Hylton, Jeffrey M. ....'44 '79 C.36 B.S. L.1137 J.D. 85 Argonaut
Solomon, Lorie G. ....'52 '82 C.1042 B.S. L.809 J.D. 22 Orchestra Ln.
**Wilshin, David B.**, (AV) ....'42 '72 C.871 B.S. L.1068 J.D. [Wordes,W.G.&C.]
*PRACTICE AREAS: Real Estate Law; Business Law; Litigation; International Trade Law.
**Wordes, Richard S.**, (BV) ....'50 '75 C.112 B.A. L.809 J.D. [Wordes,W.G.&C.]
*PRACTICE AREAS: Real Estate; Business Law.

**Wordes, Wilshin, Goren & Conner, (AV)**
**31 Journey Street, Suite 120, 92656-3334**
**Telephone: 714-643-1000 Telecopier: 714-643-2000**
**Email: firm@wwgc.com URL: http://www.wwgc.com**
**Members of Firm: Richard S. Wordes; David B. Wilshin; Michael E. Goren; Frank A. Conner.**
**Real Estate and Business Law, Litigation.**
*See Professional Biographies, ALISO VIEJO, CALIFORNIA*

## ALPINE, 1,570, *San Diego Co.*

Donnell, Kerry M. ....'50 '78 C.112 B.A. L.1137 J.D. 2457 Victoria Cirle
Fisher, Robert T. ....'26 '68 C&L.912 B.S., J.D. P.O. Box 612
Johnson, H. Alan ....'31 '69 C.800 B.E. L.770 J.D. 2640 Starkey Way
Knowlton, Daniel R. ....'49 '77 C.878 B.A. L.1137 J.D. 2128 Arnold Way
Logan, William F., (BV) ....'39 '65 C.112 B.A. L.1065 LL.B. 1347 Tavern Rd.
Royal, Don G. ....'43 '79 C.763 B.A. L.1137 J.D. P.O. Box 1767
Winkelman, Johnny M., (CV) ....'46 '78 C&L.1137 B.S., J.D. 1870 Rancho Judith

## ALTADENA, 42,415, *Los Angeles Co.*

Conroy, Bruce L. ....'40 '75 C.453 B.S. L.426 J.D. P.O. Box 20009‡
Coyne, Jeffrey C., (AV) ....'54 '79 C.112 A.B. L.228 J.D. 2235 Lake Ave.
Flanagan, Michael G. '61 '86
C.627 B.S. L.188 J.D. Dir., Mktg., Southern Calif. Print Corp.
Gargrave, Jeffrey J. ....'49 '80 C.1208 B.A. L.770 J.D. 2506 Lake Ave.
Hatten, Byron M. ....'45 '72 C.605 A.B. L.800 J.D. 2116 E. Altadena Dr.
Herbert, Leon L., II, (BV) ....'37 '64 C&L.800 B.S., J.D. 1246 E. Sunny Oaks Cir.
Lousteau, Kristi ....'53 '79 C.426 B.A. L.809 J.D. 4385 El Prieto Rd.
Maple, Chas. A. ....'22 '52 C.112 B.A. L.309 LL.B. 1639 E. Gaywood Dr.
McKenna, John N., (BV) ....'10 '38 C.112 A.B. L.1066 LL.B. 596 Buena Loma St.
McMullin, Joseph B., (AV) ....'23 '50 C&L.623 A.B., J.D. 2195 Crescent Dr.‡
Middleton, William J. ....'40 '79 115 E. Palm
Nelson, Susan M. ....'53 '81 C.112 B.A. L.426 J.D. 3564 Glenrose Ave.
Shatford, Henry W. ....'18 '47 C.113 B.A. L.800 J.D. Supr. Ct. J.
Sheats, Saml. C. ....'24 '54 C.511 A.B. L.976 LL.B. 5556 Canyon Crest Rd.‡
Wade, Jas. W. ....'21 '55 C&L.813 A.B., LL.B. 2025 Midlotman Dr.‡
White, Terry L. ....'56 '84 C.768 B.A. L.1068 J.D. 2860 Holliston Ave.
Wopschall, Carl E., (AV) ....'16 '40 C&L.800 B.S.B.A., LL.B. 2269 Sinaloa Ave.‡

## ALTA LOMA, —, *San Bernardino Co.*

Bauer, Donald R. ....'46 '77 L.1137 J.D. 8780 19th St.
Inglis, Alan L. ....'45 '83 C&L.174 B.S., J.D. 6610 Post Pl.
Mckay, Charles W. ....'33 '68 C.1042 B.A. L.809 LL.B. 9414 Banyan St.

## ALTAVILLE, —, *Calaveras Co.*

Test, E. Allen, (BV) ....'42 '67 C.112 B.A. L.767 1071 Brunner Hill Dr.

## ALTURAS, * 3,231, *Modoc Co.*

Baker, John P., (AV) ....'41 '70 C.813 A.B. L.1066 J.D. Supr. Ct. J.
Barclay, Francis W., (BV) ....'54 '81 C.112 B.A. L.1065 J.D. 201 S. Court St., Suite A
Barclay, Robert A. ....'34 '61 C.999 L.1065 J.D. Cir. Jus. Ct. J.
Comisky, Hugh E., Jr., (BV) ....'43 '72 C.767 B.A. L.765 J.D. P.O. Box 1249
Dier, Wendy J. ....'68 '94 C.1169 B.A. L.629 J.D. 201 S. Court St.
Sorensen, Ruth ....'— '71 C.477 B.A. L.930 J.D. Co. Coun., Dist. Atty.
Young, Guy M. ....'33 '60 C.112 B.A. L.1068 J.D. Supr. Ct. J.‡

## AMERICAN CANYON, —, *Napa Co.*

Poire, Alfonso L. '63 '90 C.112 B.A. L.1066 J.D.
Gen. Coun., Golden State Lumber, Inc.

## ANAHEIM, 266,406, *Orange Co.*

Abbes, George W. ....'58 '82 C&L.1137 B.S.L., J.D. 12680 Kona Lane
Ambrosi, E. Michael, (BV) ....'45 '78 C.1097 B.S. L.1137 J.D. [E.M.Ambrosi]
Ambrosi, E. Michael, A Professional Corporation, (BV) ....100 S. Anaheim Blvd.
Andersen, Gary Wayne ....'65 '95 C.112 B.A. L.1137 J.D. 222 S. Harbor Blvd.
Ascher, Ralph ....'54 '83 C.102 B.A. L.300 J.D. 2331 W. Lincoln Ave.
**Baker, Kelli L.** ....'65 '91 C.347 B.A. L.589 J.D. [▣ O'Flaherty&B.]
Barber, William L. '48 '74 C.792 B.S.Ch.E. L.426 J.D.
V.P., Sec. & Co. Coun., CalComp
Barker, Ann S. ....'34 '79 C.546 A.B. L.990 J.D. 1720 W. Ball Rd.
**Belgum, Lee T.** ....'53 '78 C.1253 B.A. L.1068 J.D. [▣ O'Flaherty&B.]
Bernstein, Arnold S. ....'37 '64 C.112 B.S. L.800 J.D. 145 S. Barbara Way
Biggs, Mary Gregory, (BV) ....'29 '75 C&L.1137 B.S.L., J.D. 1674 W. Tonia Pl.
Bisson, Randall W. ....'49 '77 C.1109 B.A. L.1137 J.D. 505 S. Euclid Ave.
Bloch, Patricia Kathleen ....'56 '89 C&L.1137 B.S.L., J.D. 222 S. Harbor Blvd.
Blum, Edward F., Jr. ....'43 '80 C.426 B.A. L.1137 J.D. 6951 Country Club Lane
**Boarnet, Barbara S.** ....'66 '92 C.112 B.A. L.426 J.D. [▣ O'Flaherty&B.]
Bolinger, R. Stephen, (BV) ....'47 '84 C.800 B.A. L.1136 J.D. 421 N. Brookhurst St.
Briggs, Robert W., (BV) ....'26 '65 C.326 B.S. L.426 J.D. 558 S. Harbor Blvd.
Bunzel, Elaine K. ....'38 '77 C.477 B.A. L.1137 J.D. 101 E. Lincoln Ave.
Callen, Ralph I., (BV) ....'31 '58 C&L.800 A.B., J.D. 2141-C W. La Palma Ave.
**Catanzarite, Kenneth J.**, (AV) ....'49 '74 C.8 B.S.B.A. L.7 J.D. [Catanzarite]
*PRACTICE AREAS: Business Transactions and Litigation; Federal and State Taxation Law; Securities Law; Employee Benefits Law; Bankruptcy Law.

**Catanzarite Law Corporation, (AV)**
**2331 West Lincoln Avenue, 92801**
**Telephone: 714-520-5544; 800- 326-5544 Fax: 714-520-0680**
**Kenneth J. Catanzarite (Certified Specialist, Taxation Law and Personal and Small Business Bankruptcy, The State Bar of California Board of Legal Specialization).**
**Business Transactions, Federal and State Taxation, Pensions, Employee Benefits, Real Estate, Securities, Estate Planning, Health Care, Labor, Corporate, Business Litigation, Professional Malpractice and Bankruptcy.**
*See Professional Biographies, ANAHEIM, CALIFORNIA*

Celio, Richard C. '50 '82
C.800 B.S. L.1137 J.D. V.P. & Gen. Coun., Carl Karcher Enterprises
Champon, Into Bo ....'— '92 C.800 B.S. L.464 J.D. 1738 W. La Palma Ave.
Chandler, Odra L. ....'15 '53 L.426 LL.B. [Chandler&A.]
Chandler & Armstrong ....1582 Sim Place W.
**Chen, Ernest C.**, (BV) ....'46 '72 C&L.425 B.A., J.D. [O'Flaherty&B.]
*PRACTICE AREAS: Business Litigation.
Cook, D. Martin, (AV) ....'25 '54 C&L.878 B.S., LL.B. 1337 S. Empire St.‡
Corsiglia, Sharon McDaniel ....'47 '73 C.1109 B.A. L.1049 J.D. 2180 W. Crescent Ave.
Coulter, Janet M. ....'52 '82 C.107 B.S.Ed. L.809 J.D. Wkrs. Comp. App. Bd. J.
**Cross, Lisa A.** ....'59 '88 C.112 B.A. L.990 J.D. [O'Flaherty&B.]
Curatola, Neal T. ....'54 '83 C.64 B.A. L.1137 J.D. 2300 E. Katella Ave.
Daniels, Joan C. ....'39 '82 C.1042 B.A. L.1137 J.D. 2400 E. Katella Ave.
Dean-Richardson, Laura L. ....'59 '84 C.112 B.A. L.800 J.D. 1470 N. Hundley St.
de Best, Shirley Ann ....'42 '85 C.950 B.A. L.1137 J.D. 1678 W. Broadway
DeForest, Thomas M. '34 '66 C.813 B.S.C.E. L.1068 LL.B.
V.P., Secy. & Gen. Coun., Fujitsu Bus. Communications of Amer.
DePerine, Gary A., (BV) '49 '75
C.800 B.A. L.990 J.D. 581 S. Weymouth Ct., Anaheim Hills
Doezie, Janice J. ....'50 '87 C.1042 B.A. L.1137 J.D. 2100 S. State College Blvd.
Duffy, John M. ....'52 '91 C.112 B.A. L.665 J.D. 18002 Irvine Blvd
Edwards, J. Bruce ....'53 '79 C&L.1137 B.S.L., J.D. [Edwards&E.]
Edwards, Joseph B., (BV) ....'29 '66 C.999 L.809 LL.B. [Edwards&E.]
Edwards & Edwards, A Prof. Corp., (BV) ....1237 S. Euclid Ave.
Elder, William N., Jr. ....'55 '83 C.112 B.A. L.809 J.D. 2180 W. Crescent Ave.
**Elguindy, Joseph M.** ....'69 '94 C.112 B.A. L.990 J.D. [▣ O'Flaherty&B.]
Ermes, Charles E. ....'24 '63 C.225 A.B. L.502 J.D. 181 S. Old Springs Rd.
Ewenike, Ogbonna ....'57 '88 C.878 B.S. L.1137 J.D. 434 S. Euclid Ave.
Faal, Edi M.O., (Mr.) ....'54 '82 C.1222 B. Sc. L.1137 J.D. 222 S. Harbor Blvd.
**Farano, Charles M.**, (BV) ....'52 '79 C.1079 B.A. L.1137 J.D. [Farano&K.]
*REPORTED CASES: Miller's National Insurance Company vs. Axel's Express (1988) 851 F2d 267; Global Van Lines vs. Superior Court (1983) 144 C.A. 3d 483; Suburban Motors vs. State Farm (1990) 218 C.A. 3d 1354.
*PRACTICE AREAS: Litigation; Trial Practice; Municipal Law; Code Enforcement.
**Farano, Floyd L.**, (AV) ....'27 '55 C.339 B.A. L.365 J.D. [Farano&K.]
*PRACTICE AREAS: Transportation Law; Land Use Law; Development Law; Zoning Law; Politics and Campaign Law.
**Farano, Jeffrey L.** ....'56 '84 C&L.1137 B.S.L., J.D. [Farano&K.]⊙
*PRACTICE AREAS: Transportation Law; Land use and Zoning; Government Contract Law.

**Farano and Kieviet, A Professional Law Corporation, (AV)**
**2100 South State College Boulevard, 92806**
**Telephone: 714-935-2400 Fax: 714-935-2410**
**Floyd L. Farano; Charles M. Farano; Thomas G. Kieviet; Jeffrey L. Farano.**
**General Civil Trial and Appellate Practice, State and Federal Courts. Transportation Law, Government Contract Law, Land Use, Zoning, Development and Real Estate Law, Municipal Law and Code Enforcement, Mobile Home Park Law, Corporate and Business Law, Creditors Rights, Probate and Estate Planning, Medical Malpractice, Insurance and Defense, Criminal Law, Labor Law.**
*See Professional Biographies, ANAHEIM, CALIFORNIA*

Fernandez, Steven P. ....'61 '88 C.112 B.A. L.1068 J.D. 1738 w. La Palma Ave.
Fields, C. Kerry, (BV) ....'51 '76 C.800 B.S. L.770 J.D. 8141 E. Kaiser Blvd.
Findley, Gary S. ....'54 '79 C.605 B.A. L.1148 J.D. 1470 N. Hundley St.
Fiola, Dale M. ....'51 '77 C.112 B.A. L.1179 J.D. [D.M.Fiola]
Fiola, Dale M., Inc. ....1678 W. Bway.
Fischer, Eugene K., Jr. ....'31 '56 C&L.705 B.A., LL.B. 1678 W. Broadway, Suite 209
Fischer, Karen ....'47 '88 C.798 B.S. L.1179 J.D. Coun., Fremont Investment & Loan
Fleming, Richard A., (CV) ....'53 '79 C.1044 B.A. L.1137 J.D. 101 E. Lincoln Ave.
Flynn, Carol J., (AV) ....'— '83 C.1109 B.A. L.1137 J.D. Dep. City Atty.
**Ford, Don R.**, (AV) ....'45 '74 C.1042 B.S.B.A. L.990 J.D. [D.R.Ford]

**Ford, Don R., A Professional Corporation, (AV)**
**8141 East Kaiser Boulevard, Suite 210, 92808-2214**
**Telephone: 714-998-6214 Facsimile: 714-998-6551**
**Don R. Ford.**
**General Civil and Trial Practice. Personal Injury, Business, Probate, Estate Planning and Corporate.**
*See Professional Biographies, ANAHEIM, CALIFORNIA*

Fuller, Alfonso C., Jr. '53 '94 C&L.912 B.S., J.D.
(adm. in MD; not adm. in CA) 571 S. Ave. Faro (Anaheim Hills)
Gady, N. David ....'24 '71 C.665 B.S. L.990 J.D. 2020 W. Lincoln Ave.
**Gilmore, Kevin R.** '64 '88 C.999 L.018 LL.B.
V.P., Bus. Affs., Disney Sports Enterprises, Inc.
Glatzhofer, Gene W., (BV) ....'38 '70 C.1097 B.S. L.809 J.D. 2020 W. Lincoln
Grady, Ryan A. ....'56 '83 C.494 B.A. L.818 J.D. Fron Corp.
Gray, Arthur W., Jr., (AV) ....'28 '53 C.879 B.A. L.1065 J.D. 914 W. Lincoln Ave.
Gray, Joel W. ....'29 '66 C.112 B.A. L.809 J.D. Wkrs. Comp. J.
Gray, Thomas D. ....'60 '85 C.112 B.A. L.1049 J.D. 914 W. Lincoln Ave.
Greenberg, Jules L. '42 '83 C.1077 B.A. L.1137 J.D.
Jud. Wkrs. Comp. App. Bd., Div. of Wkrs. Comp.
Griffin, John A. ....'22 '52 C.800 L.809 LL.B. 795 Peralta Hills Dr.‡
Gwosdof, Peter M., (BV) ....'38 '64 C.1042 A.B. L.1065 J.D. 451 W. Lincoln Ave.
Hannah, Mitchell Blinn ....'58 '88 C.1109 B.A. L.1137 J.D. 2180 W. Crescent Ave.
Hardin, Robert W. ....'27 '60 C.763 A.B. L.809 LL.B. 2127 W. Ball Rd.
Harrison, Kevin F. ....'50 '88 C.112 L.1137 J.D. [Harrison&W.]
Harrison & Woodhouse ....505 S. Villa Real (Anaheim Hills)
Hartnett, Patrick Michael ....'60 '86 C&L.770 B.A., J.D. 801 E. Katella Ave.
**Hatton, Gregory M.** ....'55 '85 C.1169 B.A. L.1049 J.D. [O'Flaherty&B.]
Hendel, Toni L. ....'— '94 C.112 B.A. L.280 J.D. 222 S. Harbor Blvd.
Hervatin, Lisa T. ....'56 '82 C.209 B.A. L.1049 J.D. 780 S. Ruby Ln.
Hoalst, Laura McCarthy ....'57 '81 C.1109 B.A. L.398 J.D. [▣ Winn&S.]
Hogeland-Hannah, Hallie D. ....'64 '92 C.1109 B.A. L.1137 J.D. 2180 W. Cresent Ave.
Holler, Julie L. ....'63 '96 [▣ Winn&S.]
Holoboski, H. Craig ....'45 '74 C.813 A.B. L.1137 J.D. 2141 W. La Palma
Holper, James A., (BV) ....'42 '74 1475 S. State College Blvd.
Howard, Margie E. ....'50 '87 C&L.1137 B.S., J.D. 2166 W. Bdwy., Ste 538

CAA3P

CALIFORNIA—ANAHEIM MARTINDALE-HUBBELL LAW DIRECTORY 1997

Humphries, Erin H. ................., '44 '83 C.999 B.A. L.1001 J.D. 8180 E. Kaiser Blvd.
Hunter, Fred R., (BV) .................................'41 '75 L.1137 J.D. 224 E. Bway.
**Jackson, Erik L.** ....................... '65 '93 C.112 B.A. L.800 J.D. [ⓑ O'Flaherty&B.]
Jarman, Michael R., (AV) .............. '52 '78 C.800 B.S. L.809 J.D. 888 South West St.
Kellogg, LeRoy L. '40 '77 C.336 B.A. L.1137 J.D.
Asst. Supt., Anaheim Union High School Dist.
Kemmerly, Peter A. ....... '52 '78 C.112 B.A. L.990 J.D. V.P. & Editor, Spidell Publishing
Kennedy, William J. ............... '48 '92 C.602 B.A. L.1137 J.D. 100 S. Anaheim Blvd.
Kent, John M., (AV) ......... '15 '54 C.705 B.S. L.800 J.D. 300 S. Harbor Blvd., Ste 704
**Kieviet, Thomas G., (AV)** ...................'54 '79 C.1109 B.A. L.990 J.D. [Farano&K.]
*PRACTICE AREAS: Corporate Law; Business Law; Real Estate Law; Estate Planning Law; Land use and Zoning.
Kim, Erica M. .................................... '— '92 C.188 B.A. L.1068 J.D. [McVey&K.]⊙

**Kinkle, Rodiger and Spriggs, Professional Corporation**
**(See Santa Ana)**

Knefel, Deborah P. ....................... '52 '84 C.1109 B.A. L.1137 J.D. Dep. City Atty.
Kron, Michael ......................... '60 '88 C&L.477 B.B.A., J.D. 434 S. Euclid St.
Kuehn, Robert H. ............. '29 '61 C&L.560 J.D. 400 W. Freedman Way, Suite 800‡
Lais, Ronald E. ............................................'42 '75 C.999 L.1137 J.D. [R.E.Lais]
Lais, Ronald E., Inc., Law Offices of
136 S. Imperial Hwy. (⊙Munich, Germany; Zagreb, Croatia)
Larson, Konrad K., (BV) ......... '39 '65 C.112 A.B. L.1065 LL.B. 914 W. Lincoln Ave.
Lavoie, Robert L., (BV) ....................'51 '78 C.312 B.A. L.1137 J.D. 888 South West St.
Lea, Michael R. ............'51 '82 C&L.1137 B.S.L., J.D. 101 E. Lincoln Ave., Ste. 200
Lehan, William J. ...............................'28 '61 C.999 L.1114 LL.B. 726 S. Knott Ave.
Lobel, Gary D. ..................'57 '82 C.1077 B.A. L.809 J.D. 2544 W. Woodland Dr.
Logan, Mark A., (BV) ................ '47 '73 C.1042 B.A. L.61 J.D. Sr. Asst. City Atty.
Lorand, John C. ..........................................'49 '76 C.801 B.A. L.1137 J.D. [Zinn&L.]
Lowsen, Sharon ...................'— '84 C.1042 B.A. L.1137 J.D. 1842 W. Lincoln Ave.
**Mahoney, Joseph A.** ....................... '51 '78 C.454 B.A. L.809 J.D. [ⓑ O'Flaherty&B.]
*PRACTICE AREAS: Insurance Defense; Products Liability; Medical Malpractice; Aviation.
Mann, Selma J., (BV) ......................'38 '83 C.112 B.A. L.426 J.D. Off. of City Atty.
Martin, Gary R. ..........................................'50 '76 C.1042 B.S. L.1137 J.D. [Martin&S.]
Martin and Stamp, A Professional Corporation, (AV)
8141 E. Kaiser Blvd., Ste., 130 (⊙Long Beach)
Mathews, Robert E. ...........................'51 '77 C.101 B.A. L.990 J.D. P.O. Box 17103
McCaffrey, Roger ........................'53 '78 C.1109 B.A. L.990 J.D. 1678 W. Bway.

**McFarlane, Richard A. '62 '91 C.1109 B.A. L.809 J.D.**
**2323 West Lincoln Avenue Suite 127, P.O. Box 1606, 92801**
**Mailing Address: P.O. Box 1606, Orange, CA 92866**
**Telephone: 714-991-9131 Fax: 714-991-6526**
**Email: richard.mcfarlane@counsel.com**
***LANGUAGES: Afrikaans.**
***PRACTICE AREAS: Bankruptcy; Estate Planning; Corporate Transactions.**
**Bankruptcy, Estate Planning, Corporate Transactions.**
*See Professional Biographies, ANAHEIM, CALIFORNIA*

**McGuire, David F.** '43 '73 C&L.966 B.A., J.D.
(adm. in WI; not adm. in CA) V.P., Law & Litig., Colonial Ins. Co. of Calif.
McMahon, Judith D. '50 '91
C.1042 B.A. L.1137 J.D. Assoc. Coun., Specialty Restaurants Corp.
McVey, David A., (BV) ...........................'48 '74 C.193 B.A. L.665 J.D. [McVey&K.]⊙
McVey & Kim, (BV) ........................................2283 W. Lincoln Ave. (⊙Los Angeles)
Menicucci, Michael J., (BV) ................ '55 '82 C.549 B.A. L.1137 J.D. [Martin&S.]
Michels, Helen A. ........................................... '52 '84 L.1137 J.D. [Michels&W.]
Michels & Weeks ..................................................1475 S. State College Blvd.
Migan, Michael James ............................'52 '81 L.1137 J.D. 2400 E. Katella Ave.
Migliore, Alfonso J. ..........................'45 '90 C&L.800 B.S.L., J.D. 212 N. Helena St.
**Mikhail, Barbara Voigt** '47 '88
C.959 B.A. L.1137 J.D. Assoc. Coun., Colonial Ins. Co. of Calif.
*RESPONSIBILITIES: Insurance Defense Law.
Milker, Mark Steven '51 '81 C.154 B.A. L.1225 J.D.
Dean of Students, Southern Calif. College of Business & Law
Miller, Bruce E. ..................... '48 '83 C.1097 B.S. L.990 J.D. 4501 E. La Palma Ave.
Millers, John E. ....................................'45 '75 C.800 B.S. L.61 J.D. 801 E. Katella Ave.
Moehring, Mary M. '47 '75 C.753 B.A. L.966 J.D.
(adm. in WI; not adm. in CA) 1340 N. Mako Lane
Monaghan, Jeffry D. ..............'45 '75 C.201 B.S. L.990 J.D. 5372 E. Honeywood Lane
Morgan, Alfred, Jr. ..............'42 '78 C.112 B.S.E.E. L.1137 J.D. 520 N. Redwood Dr.
Morris, M. Conway, (BV) '29 '56
C&L.878 B.A., J.D. Moreno Valley Law Ctr. (⊙Moreno Valley)
Moser, Jody Ann ............................'47 '83 C.203 B.A. L.1137 J.D. P.O. Box 17565
Moses, Edward M. ..............'38 '79 C&L.1137 B.S.L., J.D. 2141 West La Palma Ave.
Mowery, Jack H. ........................ '32 '70 C.1097 A.B. L.800 J.D. 1730 W. La Palma
Murphy, Michael L. .....................................'38 '65 C.112 B.A. L.1065 J.D. [Winn&S.]
Nash, Andrew H. ......... '50 '76 C.112 B.S. L.809 J.D. Workers Comp. J., Appeals Brd.
Naumann, Franklin F. ........................'42 '74 C&L.1137 B.S.L., J.D. Dep. City Atty.
Nihill, Peter G. ..................... '19 '61 C.800 B.A. L.1001 LL.B. 2950 W. Lynrose Dr.
Nutto, Francis X. ...................'23 '73 C.477 B.S.E. L.1137 J.D. 621 Jambolaya St.‡
Nygaard, James L. ...................'47 '77 C.990 M.B.A. L.1179 J.D. 134 S. Jeanine Way

**O'Flaherty & Belgum, (AV)**
**222 South Harbor Boulevard, Suite 600, 92805-3701⊙**
**Telephone: 714-533-3373 Fax: 714-533-2607**
**Email: oandb&primenet.com URL: http://www.oandb-law/oandb**
**Resident Partners: Gregory M. Hatton; Ernest C. Chen; Lisa A. Cross. Of Counsel: Lee T. Belgum; C. Snyder Patin. Resident Associates: Kelli L. Baker; Arthur R. Petrie, II; Barbara S. Boarnet; Joseph A. Mahoney; Susan E. Shube; Kathleen McCaffrey Wynen; Donald W. Ormsby; Erik L. Jackson; Joseph M. Elguindy; Stephen Z. Vegh; Michael P. Sandler; Paul D. Slater, Dr.**
**General Civil, Trial and Appellate Practice in State and Federal Courts. Medical and Dental Malpractice, Products Liability, General Insurance Law, Insurance Coverage, Wrongful Termination, Workers' Compensation and Business and Environmental Litigation.**
**Glendale, California Office: 1000 North Central, Suite 300, 91202-2957. Telephone: 818-242-9229. Fax: 818-242-9114.**
**Long Beach, California Office: 100 Oceangate Suite 500, 90802-4312. Telephone: 310-437-0090. Fax: 310-437-5550.**
**Riverside, California Office: 3880 Lemon Street, Suite 450, 92501-3301. Telephone: 909-341-0049. Fax: 909-341-3919.**
**Ventura, California Office: 840 County Square Drive, Suite 200, 93003-5406. Telephone: 805-650-2600. Fax: 805-650-2658.**
*See Professional Biographies, ANAHEIM, CALIFORNIA*

Ordlock, David G. ....................... '55 '82 C.1109 B.A. L.1137 J.D. 5633 E. Vista Del Valle
**Ormsby, Donald W.** ...................... '64 '93 C.112 B.A. L.800 J.D. [ⓑ O'Flaherty&B.]

**Overholt, E. Llewellyn, Jr., (AV) '27 '57 C.605 B.A. L.1066 J.D.**
**Bank of America Building, Suite 802, 300 South Harbor Boulevard, 92805**
**Telephone: 714-776-7500 Fax: 714-776-4284**

(This Listing Continued)

**Overholt, E. Llewellyn, Jr. (Continued)**
**Corporation, Probate, State and Federal Taxation, Estate Planning and Trust Law. Civil Trial Practice in all Courts.**

**Patin, C. Snyder, (AV)** ...........................'30 '75 C.178 B.S. L.1148 J.D. [ⓑ O'Flaherty&B.]
*LANGUAGES: Greek, Latin, French and German.
*REPORTED CASES: Arato v. Avedon, 5 Cal 4th 1172.
*PRACTICE AREAS: Medical Malpractice; Dental Malpractice; Products Liability; Staff Privileges Issues.
Payne, Andrea J. ............................ '66 '94 C.1042 B.A. L.280 J.D. 222 S. Harbor Blvd.
**Petrie, Arthur R., II** ......................... '59 '92 C.112 B.A. L.1137 J.D. [ⓑ O'Flaherty&B.]
Pierce, Ellen Lewis ............ '35 '76 C.1097 B.A. L.809 J.D. Legal Aid Soc. of Orange Co.
Porter, William F., Jr. '44 '69 C.976 B.E.E.E. L.309 LL.B.
(adm. in MA; not adm. in CA; Pat.) Pat. Coun. & Dir., Patents & Lic., CalComp
Posey, Janette R., (BV) ........................ '39 '76 C.1109 M.A. L.1137 J.D. [Posey&P.]
Posey & Posey, (BV) ............................................2180 W. Crescent Ave.
Radus, Sidney L., (AV) ........................................'20 '68 C.473 L.809 J.D. 17625‡
Redden, Edward T. ........'21 '51 C&L.436 B.E.E., LL.B. 2115-E S. Redwood Dr. (Pat.)‡
Richard, Kenneth J. ........................ '58 '88 C.454 B.S. L.1137 J.D. 222 S. Harbor Blvd.
Roberts, Furman, (AV) ........... '29 '55 C.112 A.B. L.1066 LL.B. 2504 E. Paladin Ave.‡

**Rocks, Joanne S., (AV) '42 '72 C.800 B.S. L.426 J.D.**
**Suite 207C Anaheim Hills Professional Center, 6200 East Canyon Rim Road, 92807**
**Telephone: 714-974-2000 Fax: 714-974-2063**
**General Practice. Business, Corporate, Partnership, State, Federal and International Taxation, Real Property and Real Estate Finance Law.**
*See Professional Biographies, ANAHEIM, CALIFORNIA*

Rohrer, George J., Jr., (BV) .................................'31 '69 L.1001 J.D. [Rohrer&H.]⊙
Rohrer & Holtz, A Professional Law Corporation, (BV)
Ste, 100, 401 N. Brookhurst St. (⊙Bellflower)
Ross, Roger S. ......................'46 '85 C&L.1137 B.S., J.D. 401 N. Brookhurst, Ste 100
Roy, Sharmila, (CVⓉ) '46 '85 C.061 B.S. L.37 J.D.
(adm. in AZ; not adm. in CA) Asst. Prof. of Law, Chapman Univ.
Salisbury, Robert D. ..............................................'47 '77 L.1137 J.D. P.O. Box 17399
**Sandler, Michael P.** ............................ '70 '95 C.112 B.A. L.426 J.D. [ⓑ O'Flaherty&B.]
Scheckler, Marc A. .........................................................'55 '89 [ⓑ Winn&S.]
Schweppe, William P. '13 '42 C.733 L.999 LL.B.
(adm. in MO; not adm. in CA) 2653 Stockton Ave.‡
Seals, Linda L. ...........................................'58 '87 C&L.1137 B.S.L., J.D. [Seals&T.]
Seals, Philbert E. ..................................'28 '60 C.927 B.S. L.424 J.D. [ⓑ Seals&T.]
Seals & Tenenbaum ..............................................................2323 W. Lincoln Ave.
**Shube, Susan E.** ............................ '65 '90 C.112 B.A. L.800 J.D. [ⓑ O'Flaherty&B.]
Silverman, Phillip E., (BV) .................... '42 '70 C.999 L.809 J.D. 620 S. Euclid St.
**Simms, Dennis L.** '53 '91 C.961 B.S. L.1035 J.D.
(adm. in MN; not adm. in CA) Reg. Litig. Dir., Colonial Ins. Co. of Calif.
Sims, Ralph L. ........................................... '47 '78 C.1044 B.A. L.1137 J.D. [Winn&S.]
Skudstad, Michael S. ..............................................................'49 '92 2540 W. Ball Rd.
**Slater, Paul D.** .............................'62 '95 C.813 B.S. L.878 J.D. [ⓑ O'Flaherty&B.]
*PRACTICE AREAS: Medical Malpractice Defense.
Slaughter, Malcolm E., (BV) ................ '41 '72 C.473 B.A. L.1137 J.D. Dep. City Atty.
Smith, Clay M. '50 '77 C.101 B.A. L.878 J.D.
Asst. Gen. Coun., Catellus Develop. Corp.
Smith, Guido R. .......................... '51 '76 C.112 B.A. L.802 J.D. 901 S. Marjan St.
Smith, Joseph P. ..............................'56 '83 C.262 B.A. L.273 J.D. Dep. Dist. Atty.
Souders, Terry P. ...............................................'45 '77 C.216 L.1137 J.D. 9512 Ball Rd.
Soukup, William W. ............... '45 '77 C.1109 B.A. L.990 J.D. 8141 E. Kaiser Blvd.
Spina, Frank S. ....................................'45 '85 C.222 B.A. L.1137 J.D. 805 N. Helena St.
Springer, Gerald C. ..........................'34 '79 C.990 B.S. L.1240 J.D. 9251 Greenwich St.‡
Stashik, Anthony G., (BV) .................. '43 '73 C.1113 B.A. L.1068 J.D. Dep. City Atty.
Steinert, Raymond L. ...............'49 '91 C.1042 B.A. L.1137 J.D. 101 E. Lincoln Ave.
Stricklen, Charles W. ..................................'36 '63 C.999 L.809 J.D. 300 S. Harbor
**Stubins, J. David** '57 '84 C.846 B.S. L.245 J.D.
(adm. in GA; not adm. in CA) Reg. Litig. Dir., Colonial Ins. Co. of Calif.
Swift, Charmayne S. ..........................'53 '79 C&L.1137 B.S., J.D. 2756 W. Storybrook Dr.
Tahajian, Gerald Lee, (BV) '41 '70 C&L.267 B.S., J.D.
2283 W. Lincoln Ave. (⊙Los Angeles & Fresno)
Taller, Martin ............................'51 '76 C&L.800 B.A., J.D. 2099 S. State Coll. Blvd.
Tannaz, William J. .........'46 '78 C.705 B.S. L.1095 J.D. V.P. & Legal Coun., MagneTek
Tenenbaum, Jay M. ................................................'59 '88 C.1201 B.S. L.940 J.D. [Seals&T.]
Tice, Jim Travis, (BV) ............. '42 '71 C.1013 B.A. L.208 J.D. 2331 W. Lincoln Ave.
Townley, Donald J., (BV) ..........'35 '62 C.112 B.A. L.1068 J.D. 320 N. Wilshire Ave.
Trad, Phillip G. .....'48 '78 C.1109 B.A. L.1137 J.D. 505 S. Villa Real Dr. (Anaheim Hills)
Trigg, Edward W., Jr. .................................'48 '80 C.112 B.A. L.1137 J.D. P.O. Box 2332
Tulsiak, Dennis C. ......................................... '60 '85 C.976 B.A. L.800 J.D. 801 E. Katella
Van Tubbergen, Faith E. ............'37 '82 C&L.1137 B.S.L., J.D. 2020 W. Lincoln Ave.
Vaughn, Norman '32 '73 C.280 A.B.J. L.1000 J.D.
Sr. Land Agent, Shell Pipeline Corp.
**Vegh, Stephen Z.** ...........................'67 '94 C.112 B.S. L.464 J.D. [ⓑ O'Flaherty&B.]
VeuCasovic, James B. '34 '71 C&L.912 Ph.B., J.D.
(adm. in MI; not adm. in CA) 2331 W. Lincoln Ave.
Von Rueden, Harold C. ............'42 '77 C.494 B.A. L.426 J.D. 121 N. State Coll. Blvd.
Weaver, Stephen A. '52 '78
C.188 A.B. L.309 J.D. Gen. Coun., Specialty Restaurants Corp.
Weeks, Douglas L. ..................................'49 '77 C.801 B.A. L.1137 J.D. [Michels&W.]
Weiss, Edward A. ........................... '48 '75 C.1097 B.S. L.61 J.D. 700 S. MacDuff
White, Jack L., (AV) ........................... '44 '70 C.800 B.A. L.1068 J.D. City Atty.
Wilcox, Winifred L. ................................................................'49 '87 [ⓑ Winn&S.]
Winn, Brian N., (AV) .................................'50 '79 C.112 B.A. L.809 J.D. [Winn&S.]
Winn and Simms, A Professional Corp., (AV) ..........2323 West Lincoln Ave., Suite 101
Winsor, Travis W. .......................'66 '92 C.800 B.S. L.990 J.D. 222 S. Harbor Blvd.
Winters, Michael L. ..................'56 '92 C.896 B.A. L.607 J.D. U.S. Immig & Nat. J.
Wood, Donald E. .............................'27 '64 C.381 B.A. L.809 LL.B. Aim Ins. Co.
Woodhouse, Violet P. ..................................................................'48 '93 [Harrison&W.]
Workman, Brian G. ........................... '48 '83 L.1240 J.D. 520 N. Brookhurst St.
**Wynen, Kathleen McCaffrey** ............'51 '93 C.398 B.S. L.426 J.D. [ⓑ O'Flaherty&B.]
Zimmerman, Robert D. ...................................'35 '60 C&L.813 A.B., J.D. 335 Starfire St.
Zinn, Wayne Michael ........................ '45 '74 C.1042 B.A. L.809 J.D. [Zinn&L.]
Zinn & Lorand ..................................................................8180 E. Kaiser Blvd.

## ANDERSON, 8,299, *Shasta Co.*

Darley, D. Jack, (CV) ........................ '27 '55 C.112 B.A. L.1066 LL.B. 2275 North St.
Kagan, Ronald H. ..............................'50 '76 C.1044 B.A. L.284 J.D. P.O. Box 1168‡
Scott, Curtis, (CV) ..................... '51 '89 C.999 B.A. L.1067 J.D. 2600 Balls Ferry Rd.

## ANGELS CAMP, —, *Calaveras Co.*

Laskin, Franklin Theo. .................. '27 '55 C.197 B.A. L.976 LL.B. 1289 S. Main St.

### ANGWIN, 2,690, *Napa Co.*

Benson, Eva N. ... '49 '88 C.880 M.S.N. L.112 J.D. 1440 Crestmont Dr.
Benton, Elvin L. '25 '68 C.866 B.A. L.904 J.D.
(adm. in MD; not adm. in CA) 543 White Cottage Rd. S.‡
Kopitzke, Henry W. '45 '80 C.1163 B.S. L.336 J.D.
(adm. in ID; not adm. in CA) P.O. Box 885

### ANTIOCH, 62,195, *Contra Costa Co.*

**Beard, Terrence A. '53 '81 C.112 B.A. L.999 J.D.**
**3377 Deer Valley Road, Suite 334, 94509**
**Telephone: 510-778-1060 Fax: 510-778-1207**
***PRACTICE AREAS: Franchising; Sexual Harassment; Personal Injury; Civil Litigation; Business Litigation.**
**Franchising, Sexual Harassment, Personal Injury, Civil Litigation, Business Litigation.**

Begin, John F. ... '21 '49 C.755 L.767 J.D. 1120 San Jose‡
Bundy, Roger L. ... '41 '73 C.112 B.S. L.765 J.D. 300 "H" St.
Coon, Earl F. ... '48 '77 C.112 B.A. L.1067 J.D. 3711 Lone Tree Way‡
Cox, Donald L., Law Office of ... '48 '88 C.1097 B.S. L.1153 J.D. 1709 Taft Ct.
Galstan, William R., (BV) ... '47 '73 C.768 B.A. L.1065 J.D. City Atty.
Gartrell-Solak, Roxanne ... '56 '85 C.173 B.A. L.284 J.D. P.O. Box 4877
Harris, Joel A. ... '63 '90 C.464 B.A. L.770 J.D. 1407 A St.
Hobin, Richard D. ... '49 '77 C.628 B.S. 1011 A St.
Huffaker, Jeffrey D., (BV) ... '52 '79 C.112 B.S. L.1067 J.D. 511 West Third St.
Johnson, Curtis Lee ... '50 '85 C.147 B.A. L.1153 J.D. 3240 Lone Tree Way
McCracken, Sherrie L. ... '49 '86 C.1075 B.S. L.999 J.D. 2938 Delta Fair Blvd.
Miller, George, III ... '45 '72 C.766 A.B. L.1067 J.D. (M.C.)
Orduna, Robert J. ... '55 '80 C.112 B.A. L.221 J.D. 1104 Buchanan Rd.
Pappas, Peter C. ... '45 '78 L.1153 J.D. 2400 Sycamore Dr.
Pegnim, Thomas M. ... '51 '78 C.309 B.A. L.284 J.D. 3105 Lone Tree Way
Stephens, Randy L. ... '47 '85 C.267 L.765 J.D. 511 W. 3rd St.
Thomas, David S., (BV) ... '40 '72 C.766 B.A. L.1067 J.D. 608 W. 2nd St. (©Pioneer)
Tobin, Harold W. ... '22 '49 C&L.767 J.D. 3240 Lone Tree Way
Ulrich, William C., (CV) ... '42 '77 C.668 L.1153 J.D. 2400 Sycamore Dr.
Van Hasselt, George H. ... '46 '69 C.374 B.A. L.1119 J.D. 4733 Knoll Park Cir.

### ANZA, —, *Riverside Co.*

Hix, Elizabeth ... '13 '51 C.622 L.809 J.D. P.O. Box 497

### APPLEGATE, —, *Placer Co.*

Cohen, Matthew L. ... '54 '79 C.112 B.A. L.770 J.D. P.O. Box 728
Macomber, A. Grant ... '38 '65 C.1254 B.S. L.1065 J.D. P.O. Box 248

### APPLE VALLEY, 46,079, *San Bernardino Co.*

Douglass, John E. ... '47 '80 C.1097 B.S. L.1190 J.D. 19951 Ocotillo Way
Gilmore, Robert W. ... '52 '78 C.112 B.A. L.398 J.D. 16430 Olacee Rd.★
Henderson, Paul P., (BV) ... '53 '85 C.1209 B.A. L.990 J.D. 19167 Highway 18
Innenberg, Walter ... '35 '75 C&L.1095 B.A., J.D. 20847 Poppy Rd.
Koppel, Carol S. ... '39 '74 C.1077 B.A. L.1095 J.D. 16976 Comanche Rd.
Lingo, R. Craig, (CV) ... '52 '80 C.793 B.S. L.1137 J.D. 16085 Tuscola Rd.
Moore, James T., (AV) ... '26 '53 C.999 L.809 LL.B. 19977 Chickasaw Rd.
Morgan, Brian John ... '47 '76 C&L.1137 B.S., B.S. [Morgan&N.]
Morgan & Newman ... 19167 Hwy. 18
Newman, John ... '51 '80 C.112 B.A. L.1137 J.D. [Morgan&N.]
Popineau, Debra ... '53 '78 C.999 B.A. L.976 J.D. 18936 Waseca Rd.
St. Charles, Donald B., (BV) ... '24 '61 C.800 B.E. L.809 LL.B. 11619 Ash St.
Turnbow, Charles E., (CV) ... '31 '83 C.970 B.S. L.1127 J.D. 21812 Hwy. 18

### APTOS, 8,704, *Santa Cruz Co.*

Anderson, Robert C., (BV) ... '22 '63 C.112 L.464 J.D. [Anderson&N.]
Anderson & Norton, (BV) ... 8048 Soquel Dr.
Bierbaum, Mary-Margaret, Law Offices of, (CV) '56 '83
C.112 A.B. L.174 J.D. 9057 Soquel Dr., Bldg. A
Blair, Mark, (BV) ... '56 '85 C.679 B.A. L.1068 J.D. 228 Florence Dr.
Britton, Kathryn Howe ... '41 '79 C.112 A.B. L.770 J.D. 3757 Vienna Dr.
Christerson, John A. ... '53 '79 C.1239 B.A. L.1065 J.D. 311 Bonita Dr.
Clarenbach, Sara, (AV) ... '49 '74 C.966 B.A. L.1066 J.D. 9053 Soquel Dr. (©Captitola)
Dorosin, Norman ... '25 '79 C.352 B.A. L.767 J.D. 1800 Via Pacifica‡
Fife, Robert G., (CV) ... '17 '53 C.453 B.S. L.426 LL.B. 6233 Soquel Dr.
Fisher, Thomas J. '50 '75 C.170 B.A. L.378 J.D.
Chf. Coun. & Dir., Opers., Sage Instruments, Inc.
Forshee, F. LaMar ... '12 '38 C&L.477 A.B., J.D. 519 Monterey Dr.‡
Galway, Carlyn Froerer ... '28 '53 C.112 A.B. L.1065 J.D. 406 Ewell Ave.‡
Garrison, Melissa Lyn ... '53 '93 C.1169 B.A. L.1355 J.D. P.O. Box 1811
Gawthrop, Howard E., (BV) ... '11 '37 C.112 A.B. L.1066 LL.B. 8048 Soquel Dr.
Grubb, Earl R. ... '27 '55 C.112 B.S. L.1065 J.D. 117 Via Medici‡
Halterman, Carlin W. ... '16 '71 L.981 LL.B. 300 Quail Run Rd.
Jackson, James A., (AV) ... '37 '64 C.112 B.A. L.1065 LL.B. 202 Florence Dr.
Jacobson, James A. ... '44 '90 C.112 D.D.S. L.770 J.D. 9057 Soquel Dr., Bldg. A
**Kehoe, Dennis J.**, (AV) ... '37 '64 C.770 B.S.C. L.1065 J.D. [D.J.Kehoe]
*REPORTED CASES: Aptos Seascape Corp. v. County of Santa Cruz (1982), 138 CA 3rd 484, 188 CR 191.
*PRACTICE AREAS: Eminent Domain; Land Use; Civil Litigation; Personal Injury.

**Kehoe, Dennis J., A Law Corporation, (AV)** BR
**311 Bonita Drive, 95003**
**Telephone: 408-662-8444 Fax: 408-662-0227**
**Dennis J. Kehoe.**
**Eminent Domain, Land Use, Civil Litigation and Personal Injury Law.**
***See Professional Biographies, APTOS, CALIFORNIA***

Kiesling, Roy, Jr. '34 '59 C.976 B.A. L.846 LL.B.
(adm. in TX; not adm. in CA) 502 Woodhaven Ct.
Klein, Richard A. ... '31 '56 C&L.813 A.B., J.D. 9053 Soquel Dr.
Lesar, A. Keith ... '42 '70 C.813 B.A. L.1066 J.D. 9053 Soquel Dr.
Long, E. Burke, (BV) ... '51 '77 C.112 B.A. L.1049 J.D. P.O. Box 1947
**Mair, Peter K.**, (AV®) '45 '72 C.477 B.A. L.813 J.D.
[Rummonds,W.&M.] (©Seattle, Washington)
*PRACTICE AREAS: Federal Criminal Law (50%, 15); State Criminal Law (20%, 16); Civil Litigation (20%, 10); Administration Law (10%, 3).
Miller, Nancy B. ... '50 '80 C.112 B.S. L.1230 J.D. 311 Bonita Ave.
Norton, Thomas C. ... '52 '82 C.228 B.A. L.284 J.D. [Anderson&N.]
Popin, James T., (CV) ... '37 '65 C.112 B.A. L.1065 LL.B. 2001 Wallace Ave.
Rost, Clayton O. ... '23 '46 C&L.494 B.S.L., J.D. 619 Seacliff Dr. W.‡
**Rummonds, James S.**, (AV) '42 '74 C&L.813 B.A., J.D.
[Rummonds,W.&M.] (©Seattle, Washington)
*LANGUAGES: Spanish.
*PRACTICE AREAS: Legal and Medical Malpractice; Personal Injury Law; Real Estate and Business Litigation.

**Rummonds, Waltz & Mair, (AV)** BR
**311 Bonita Drive, P.O. Box 1870, 95001©**
**Telephone: 408-688-2911**
**Members of Firm: James S. Rummonds; Patrick J. Waltz (Resident, Sacramento Office); Peter K. Mair.**
**General Civil Litigation, Personal Injury, Professional Malpractice, Insurance Law, Wrongful Death, Wrongful Termination and Liability Defense.**
**Sacramento, California Office: 6991 Garden Highway. 95837. Telephone: 916-927-4610.**
***See Professional Biographies, APTOS, CALIFORNIA***

Shaw, Michael C. ... '49 '74 C&L.770 B.A., J.D. Shaw Mgmt.
Stewart, Wm. L. ... '17 '43 C&L.608 A.B., J.D. Ret. Supr. Ct. J.‡
Teale, Donna Mae ... '41 '80 C.636 B.A. L.1095 J.D. P.O. Box 2618
Truce, Walter, (AV) ... '16 '46 C.477 A.B. L.911 LL.B. 135 Via La Jolla‡
Wochos, Lisa E., (BV) ... '51 '79 C.966 B.A. L.770 J.D. P.O. Box 2313
Zang, Robert E., (AV) ... '24 '50 C.878 B.S. L.178 J.D. 1046 Via Malibu‡

### ARBUCKLE, 1,037, *Colusa Co.*

Carrion, Al J. ... '44 '71 C.147 B.A. L.169 J.D. Jus. Ct. J.

### ARCADIA, 48,290, *Los Angeles Co.*

**Albert, Bruce H.** ... '64 '90 C.1044 B.A. L.809 J.D. [Shiney,F.&S.]©
*LANGUAGES: Swedish and German.
*PRACTICE AREAS: Workers' Compensation Defense; Subrogation; Civil Litigation.
Ammon, Larry L. ... '37 '70 C.679 B.S.C.E. L.1127 J.D. 2574 Longanrita Ave.
Anderson, Christopher J. ... '51 '76 C.112 B.S. L.990 J.D. Sr. Coun., The Vons Cos., Inc.
Arkley, Butterfield & Swayne, (BV) ... 33 E. Huntington Dr.
Barnes, Patrick L., (BV) ... '39 '67 C.112 A.B. L.1068 LL.B. 650 W. Duarte Rd.
Bell, Cynthia A., (BV) ... '49 '81 C&L.1137 B.S.L., J.D. Sr. Coun., The Vons Cos., Inc.
Blackburn, John M. ... '37 '79 [Blackburn&M.]
Blackburn and Muslin ... 323 E. Foothill Blvd., #D
Butterfield, Wayne A., (Inc.), (BV) ... '37 '65 C.1075 B.S. L.1068 J.D. [Arkley,B.&S.]
Byrne, Steven P. ... '52 '78 C.1097 B.A. L.809 J.D. 41 E. Foothill Blvd.
Chavez, Lincoln J., (AV) ... '15 '49 C.273 B.A. L.597 J.D. 1636 Oakwood Ave.‡
Chu, Betty Tom '37 '61 C&L.800 B.S., LL.B.
Chmn. of the Bd. & CEO, Trust Svgs. Bk.
Cole, S. Michael ... '52 '77 C&L.911 B.A., J.D. Coun., State Comp. Ins. Fund
Cosso, Dennis G., (BV) ... '44 '70 C.112 B.A. L.426 J.D. [Cosso,P.&W.]
Cosso, Pintarelli & Watchman, Inc., (BV) ... 20 E. Foothill Blvd. Ste., 205
Coughlin, James J., (BV) ... '26 '52 C&L.477 A.B., J.D. 51 E. Foothill Blvd.
Crawford, Dale L. ... '41 '79 C.1097 B.A. L.1190 J.D. 11242 E. Danbury
Daines, Larry M. ... '38 '66 C.101 B.S. L.878 J.D. 5611 Peck Rd.‡
Davidson, Norman ... '46 '73 C.976 B.A. L.893 J.D. 638 W. Duarte Rd.
**de la Loza, Edward T.** ... '66 '91 C.1042 B.A. L.477 J.D. [Shiney,F.&S.]
*LANGUAGES: Spanish.
*PRACTICE AREAS: Workers' Compensation Defense; Civil Litigation.
DiChiaro, Joseph, Jr., (BV) ... '36 '72 C.103 A.B. L.426 J.D. 9626 E. Naomi Ave.
**Fargo, Michael D.**, (AV) ... '54 '83 C.1102 B.A. L.1077 J.D. [Shiney,F.&S.]©
*PRACTICE AREAS: Workers' Compensation Defense; Subrogation; Civil Litigation.
Fierson, Morris '14 '39 C&L.724 B.S., LL.B.
(adm. in NY; not adm. in CA) 1149 Arcadia Ave.‡

**Freeman, David F., (BV) '45 '73 C.112 B.A. L.61 J.D.**
**Suite 685 Towne Centre Building, 150 North Santa Anita Avenue, 91006**
**Telephone: 818-445-7610 Fax: 818-445-2085**
***PRACTICE AREAS: Real Estate Transactions; Litigation.**
**General Civil and Trial Practice. Real Estate and Construction Law.**
**Representative Clients: Arcadia Board of Realtors; Monrovia/Duarte Association of Realtors.**
**Reference: Bank of America N.T. & S.A. (Arcadia).**

Gelber, Louise C., (CV) ... '21 '45 C.112 A.B. L.1066 J.D. 1225 Rancho Rd.
Gottschalk, Ronald N. ... '43 '68 C.477 B.A. L.912 J.D. [R.N.Gottschalk]
Gottschalk, Ronald N., Associates ... 1160 S. Goldenwest Ave.
Graham, Robert A., Jr., (BV) ... '51 '77 C.169 B.A. L.1148 J.D. 41 E. Foothill Blvd.
**Hanrahan, James J.**, (AV) ... '34 '66 C.94 A.B. L.809 J.D. [Helms,H.&M.]
*PRACTICE AREAS: Personal Injury; Worker's Compensation (Plaintiff's).
Hardy, Louis S. '06 '30 C&L.966 LL.B.
(adm. in WI; not adm. in CA) 915 Fairview Ave.‡
Harrison, Maurice E., III '50 '77 C.112 A.B. L.1065 J.D.
Sr. Coun., The Vons Cos., Inc.
Hatchman, Jeffrey W. '53 '87 C.112 B.S. L.426 J.D.
Asst. V.P., New York Life Ins. Co.
Hege, Henry H. ... '22 '51 C&L.813 A.B., J.D. [Hege&R.] ‡
Hege & Rasmussen, (AV) ... 550 W. Duarte Rd.
**Helms, James R., Jr.**, (AV) ... '25 '52 C.797 B.S. L.800 J.D. [Helms,H.&M.]
*PRACTICE AREAS: Estate Planning; Probate; Business; Real Property.

**Helms, Hanrahan & Myers, (AV)** BR
**Suite 685 Towne Centre Building, 150 North Santa Anita Avenue, 91006**
**Telephone: 818-445-1177**
**Email: helmsj@aol.com**
**James R. Helms, Jr. (Certified Specialist, Probate, Estate Planning and Trust Law, The State Bar of California Board of Legal Specialization); James J. Hanrahan; Sterling E. Myers (Certified Specialist, Family Law, The State Bar of California Board of Legal Specialization).**
**General Civil and Trial Practice in all State and Federal Courts. Corporation, Estate Planning, Probate, Personal Injury, Negligence and Family Law.**
**Reference: Bank of America National Trust & Savings Assn. (Arcadia Branch).**
***See Professional Biographies, ARCADIA, CALIFORNIA***

Humble, Arnold, (BV) ... '23 '55 C.112 B.S. L.809 LL.B. 75 N. Santa Anita Ave.
Jackson, Sally Finck ... '54 '80 C.112 B.A. L.809 J.D. 482 W. Longden Ave.
Jenks, Robert E., Jr., (AV) ... '42 '70 C.1077 B.A. L.1068 J.D. 232 W. Leroy Ave.‡
Kasper, Mary M. ... '60 '88 C.112 B.A. L.1068 J.D. The Vons Cos., Inc.
Kazandjieff, Nicola ... '54 '84 C.112 B.A. L.1190 J.D. 301 E. Foothill Blvd.
Keiser, Thomas ... '51 '76 C.800 B.A. L.426 J.D. 550 W. Duarte Rd.
Krishan, Manoj ... '58 '90 C.959 B.B.A. L.809 J.D. 224 S. Santa Anita Ave.
Kurosaki, Glenn M. ... '58 '85 C.605 B.A. L.1068 J.D. [Kurosaki&L.]
Kurosaki & Lin ... 805 West Duarte Rd.
**Legorreta, Genaro, Jr.** ... '64 '91 C.112 B.A. L.1148 J.D. [Shiney,F.&S.]
*LANGUAGES: Spanish.
*PRACTICE AREAS: Workers' Compensation Defense; Subrogation; Civil Litigation.
Leon, Donald E. ... '31 '55 C.112 B.A. L.1068 LL.B. 1030 W. Huntington Dr.
Lieber, Bennett M. ... '48 '78 L.1077 J.D. State Comp. Ins. Fund
Lin, Vincent W. ... '56 '92 C.999 A.B. L.659 J.D. [Kurosaki&L.]
**Mackenzie, Peter Neil** ... '61 '91 C.1077 B.A. L.809 J.D. [Shiney,F.&S.]©
*PRACTICE AREAS: Workers' Compensation Defense; Subrogation.
Malmrose, Earl ... '14 '37 C.877 L.809 LL.B. 1054 Volante Dr.
Martin, Theodore K. ... '26 '56 C.112 B.A. L.1068 J.D. 333 E. Foothill Blvd.
Mathiesen, Stanley A. ... '20 '62 L.981 LL.B. P.O. Box 661243‡
McClain, Deborah L. '53 '76
C.475 B.A. L.912 J.D. Claims Atty., Auto. Club of Southern Calif.
McLee, Edward G. ... '43 '69 C.676 A.B. L.818 J.D. 33 E. Huntington Dr.

Melom, Gail B. '50 '75 C.112 B.A. L.426 J.D. 78 W. Winnie Way
Miller, Michael H. '42 '68 C.629 B.S. L.1065 J.D. City Atty.
Moloney, Nancy P. '49 '76 C&L.770 B.A., J.D. 755 Hampton Rd.
Montpas, James A., (BV) '25 '52 C.642 L.809 LL.B. 385 W. Walnut Ave.‡
Murphy, Timothy J. '46 '80 C.1097 B.A. L.1137 J.D. 700 W. Huntington Dr.
Muslin, Melvin G. '29 '77 C.644 B.A. L.1127 J.D. [Blackburn&M.] ‡
**Myers, Sterling E., (AV)** '47 '72 C&L.800 B.A., J.D. [Helms,H.&M.]
*PRACTICE AREAS: Family Law.
Ntephe, Azike A. '44 '82 C.668 B.A. L.1066 J.D. Staff Coun., State Comp. Ins. Fund
Ogle, Robert D., (AV) '20 '48 C&L.426 LL.B. 1743 Claridge St.‡
Osband, Marvin B. '34 '85 C.112 B.S. L.809 J.D. 701 S. 1st Ave.
Oyer, Clinton C. '13 '38 C&L.378 A.B., LL.B. 481 Oxford Dr.
Paradise, Robt. E., (AV) '07 '29 C&L.813 B.A., J.D. 1144 Rancho Rd.‡
Pintarelli, John C., Jr. '45 '77 C.1097 B.A. L.1148 J.D. [Cosso,P.&W.]
Powell, Kenneth L., (AV) '45 '77 C.1097 B.A. L.1148 J.D. 1245 W. Huntington Dr.
Rasmussen, Leslie D., (AV) '49 '74 C.112 A.B. L.426 J.D. [Hege&R.]
Reeves, R. L. '48 '77 C.800 B.S. L.1137 J.D. 538 W. Naomi Ave.
Rios, Edward E. '39 '79 C.1109 L.1137 J.D. 700 W. Huntington Dr., Suite 200
Rosenstein, Robert B. '54 '79 C.1077 B.A. L.809 J.D. Corp. Coun., BSE Mgmt., Inc.
**Salcedo, Paul J., (AV)** '45 '74 C.1097 B.A. L.1190 J.D. [Shiney,F.&S.]
*LANGUAGES: Spanish.
*PRACTICE AREAS: Workers' Compensation Defense; Subrogation; Civil Litigation; Wrongful Termination.
Saunders, John H. '16 '42 C.112 B.A. L.800 LL.B. 841 San Simeon Rd.‡
Schmitt, Wilfred J., (BV) '23 '47 C.586 B.S. L.190 J.D. 51 E. Foothill Blvd.
**Shiney, Michael E.** '55 '80 C.1097 L.398 J.D. [Shiney,F.&S.]⊙
*PRACTICE AREAS: Workers' Compensation Defense; Subrogation.

**Shiney, Fargo & Salcedo, A Law Corporation, (AV)**
**301 East Foothill Boulevard, Suite 200, 91006⊙**
**Telephone: 818-359-8652 Fax: 818-357-8172**
**Email: cntymsclvr@aol.com**
**Michael E. Shiney; Michael D. Fargo; Paul J. Salcedo;—Bruce H. Albert; Peter Neil Mackenzie; Richard Villasenor; Genaro Legorreta, Jr.; Edward T. de la Loza.**
**Workers' Compensation Insurance Defense, Third Party Subrogation.**
**Sherman Oaks, California Office: 13400 Ventura Boulevard, Second Floor. Telephone: 818-501-8100. Fax: 818-501-3824.**
*See Professional Biographies, ARCADIA, CALIFORNIA*

Smith, Michael A. '39 '94 C.112 B.S. L.398 J.D. [M.A.Smith]
Smith, M.A., APLC 323 E. Foothill Blvd.
Somerville, Lawrence W. '13 '41 C.999 L.273 LL.B.
L.A. County Assessment App. Bd.‡
Swayne, G. Barrett, Jr., (BV) '42 '68 C.154 B.A. L.426 J.D. [Arkley,B.&S.]
Szekunda, Raymond T. '51 '81 C.184 B.A. L.1218 J.D. Coun., State Fund Ins. Comp.
Van Doren, Max E. '29 '57 C.375 B.S. L.378 LL.B. 990 Singing Wood Dr.‡
Verlato, Cletus R., (CV) '27 '70 C.800 L.809 J.D. P.O. Box 660309
**Villasenor, Richard** '57 '89 C.605 B.A. L.1068 J.D. [⊠ Shiney,F.&S.]
*PRACTICE AREAS: Workers Compensation Law; Labor Law.
Wallock, Terrence J. '44 '71
C.112 A.B. L.1068 J.D. Exec. V.P., Gen. Coun., The Vons Cos., Inc.
Watchman, Hal G. '55 '85 C.36 B.S. L.809 J.D. [Cosso,P.&W.]
Wilkins, Ralph M. '— '92 C.891 B.B.A. L.1241 J.D. 125 W. Huntington Dr.
Williams, George L., (CV) '32 '70 C.112 A.B. L.809 LL.B. 33 E. Huntington Dr.
Wilson, Clayton D., (BV) '42 '67 C.426 B.A. L.112 J.D. [Wilson&W.]
Wilson, Elaine D., (BV) '42 '78 C.112 L.1148 J.D. [Wilson&W.]
Wilson, Lawrence L. '29 '55 C&L.546 B.S., J.D. 18 Woodland Lane‡
Wilson & Wilson, (BV) 414 S. 1st Ave.

## ARCATA, 15,197, *Humboldt Co.*

Allen, Ben T. '44 '73 C.763 B.S. L.1049 J.D. Humboldt State Univ.
Blatt, Ira S., (CV) '46 '71 C.685 B.A. L.145 J.D. P.O. Box 1164
Brown, Barrett P. '57 '85 C.763 B.A. L.1049 J.D. 315 Park Ave.‡
Brucker, Daniel T. '13 '39 C&L.569 A.B., J.D.
(adm. in NY; not adm. in CA) 1261 J St.‡
Cissna, Timothy P., (BV) '50 '76 C.330 B.A. L.1065 J.D. [Ferro&C.]
Collins, Kenneth J., (CV) '48 '81 C.1097 B.A. L.426 J.D. 791 8th St.
Ferro, Victor M., (BV) '43 '72 C.1097 B.A. L.1190 J.D. [Ferro&C.]
Ferro & Cissna, (BV) 1448 G Street
Flashman, Martin E. '46 '81 C.1036 B.A. L.569 J.D.
(adm. in NY; not adm. in CA) Prof. of Mathematics, Humboldt State Univ.‡
Friedman, Gilbert B. '35 '64 C.477 B.A. L.309 LL.B. 1735 J St.
Golden, Michael D. '44 '76 C.112 B.A. L.770 J.D. P.O. Box 1000
Gompertz, Steven M. '45 '73 C.309 A.B. L.1066 J.D. 1642 G St.
**Hamer, Chris Johnson, (BV)** '55 '82 C.112 B.A. L.276 J.D. [Stokes,S.R.&H.]
*PRACTICE AREAS: Real Estate; Business; Construction Litigation.
Hannon, Theodore B. '52 '77 C.821 B.A. L.1067 J.D. Gen. Coun., Sierra Pacific Ind.
Harris, Mark P., (CV) '62 '89 C.147 B.S. L.767 J.D. P.O. Box 982
Knapp, J. Jeffrey '42 '68 C&L.477 B.A., J.D. 1193 G St.
Petersen, Thomas C. '— '75 C.330 B.A. L.1049 J.D. P.O. Box 4193
Risling, Mary J., (CV) '54 '79 C.112 B.A. L.1067 J.D. Calif. Indian Legal Servs.
**Rowe, Thomas Dean** '48 '85 C.1169 B.A. L.1065 J.D. [Stokes,S.R.&H.]
*PRACTICE AREAS: Taxation Law; Estate Planning and Probate Law; Business Law.
Rowland, Ronald D. '38 '75 L.999 LL.B. Mun. Ct. J.
Schaub, Victor T., (CV) '43 '73 C.1097 B.A. L.1066 J.D. 791 8th St.
**Stokes, John R., III, (CV)** '48 '75 C.112 A.B. L.464 J.D. [Stokes,S.R.&H.]
*REPORTED CASES: Marriage of Henderson (1990) 225 Cal App 3d 531; County of Humboldt v. Harris (1988) 206 Cal App 3d 857.
*PRACTICE AREAS: Family Law; Criminal Law; General Litigation.
**Stokes, John R., (Inc.), (AV)** '17 '48 C.112 A.B. L.1066 LL.B. [Stokes,S.R.&H.]
*PRACTICE AREAS: Business Law; Estate Planning and Probate Law; Real Property Law.

**Stokes, Steeves, Rowe & Hamer, (AV)**
**A Partnership including a Professional Corporation**
**381 Bayside Road, P.O. Box 1109, 95521-1109**
**Telephone: 707-822-1771 Fax: 707-822-1901**
**Dorothy L. Steeves (1926-1996); John R. Stokes (Inc.); Thomas Dean Rowe; John R. Stokes, III; Chris Johnson Hamer.**
**Real Estate, Construction, Business and General Civil Litigation, Probate and Estate Planning, Business, Real Estate, Taxation, Family, Criminal and Administrative Law.**
*See Professional Biographies, ARCATA, CALIFORNIA*

Tranberg, David E., (BV) '48 '73 C.330 B.A. L.284 J.D. 607 "F" St.
**Watson, W. G., Jr., Law Firm of**
(See Eureka)
Whitledge, Lyle '— '55 C&L.339 B.S., J.D.
(adm. in IL; not adm. in CA) 2001 11th St.‡
Young, John H. '49 '74 C.1060 B.A. L.1065 J.D. 352 9th St.

## ARLETA, —, *Los Angeles Co.*

(Part of the incorporated City of Los Angeles)

Cohen, Sheldon S. '53 '82 C.645 B.S. L.1190 J.D. 9322 Greenbush Ave.
Perplies, Edward V. '54 '81 C.339 B.S. L.1148 J.D. 13615 W. Wentworth St.
Vickers, James R. '43 '77 C.1077 B.A. L.1137 J.D. 14134 Garber St.
Wisner, Bryce D. '20 '56 C.999 L.809 LL.B. P.O. Box 998

## ARNOLD, —, *Calaveras Co.*

Driscoll, Frank B. '38 '89 C.768 B.A. 1004 Highway 4, Suite G
Hutchins, Wells A. '22 '50 2307 Sultana Rd.‡
Kraft, Sandra, (CV) '38 '73 L.1026 LL.B. P.O. Box 2040
Motta, Ronald J., (BV) '33 '60 C.321 B.A. L.770 J.D. P.O. Box 2

## ARROYO GRANDE, 14,378, *San Luis Obispo Co.*

Cook, Darold, (CV) '35 '66 C.704 B.S.M.E. L.770 J.D. 415 El Camino Real
Cool, Stephen N., (BV) '40 '66 C.605 B.A. L.1068 LL.B. 1577 El Camino Real
David, Andrew, (BV) '22 '51 C.112 B.S. L.1066 LL.B. [David&Z.]
David and Zimmerman, (BV) 227 E. Branch St.
del Campo, Robert A., (BV) '37 '70 C.1097 B.A. L.809 J.D. U.S. Dist. Ct. Mag.
Dorrance, Jerry M., (BV) '46 '71 C.112 B.A. L.1065 J.D. [Schweitzer,D.&Assoc.]
**George, Gallo & Sullivan, A Law Corporation**
(See San Luis Obispo)
Giddings, Ron '46 '85 C.112 B.A. L.1051 J.D. 709 Grand
Gould, Ronald I., (BV) '29 '57 C.1043 L.426 J.D. 710 Grand Ave.
Gould, Valerie A. '57 '89 C.1074 B.A. L.769 J.D. 710 Grand Ave.
Gwinn, James E. '24 '53 C.172 L.472 LL.B. 880 Turquoise Dr.‡
Harris, Ronald E. '44 '76 C.1060 B.A. L.1065 J.D. 1190 Grand Ave.
Haynes, Donald W., (BV) '39 '65 C.1077 B.A. L.800 J.D. [Haynes W.S.]⊙
Haynes-Wilkison-Stone, (BV) 1012 Grand Ave. (⊙Santa Maria)
Mackaoui, Linden N. '62 '91 C.1075 B.A. L.284 J.D. 588 Carmella Dr.
McQuown, H. Phillip '24 '63 C.940 B.A. L.800 J.D. 288 Sunrise Dr.‡
Medof, Robert G. '53 '79 C.800 B.A. L.990 J.D. 101 W. Branch St.
Molin, Ernest S. '15 '40 C.477 L.912 LL.B.
(adm. in AZ; not adm. in CA) 378 Sunrise Ter.‡
Olpin, A. Edwin, (BV) '40 '70 C.101 B.S. L.878 J.D. 1012 Grand Ave.
Peters, Glenn E. '24 '62 C.112 B.A. 1587 El Camino Real St.
Pruneda, M. Ilda '46 '80 C.1169 B.A. L.1066 J.D. [⊠ Haynes W.S.]
Schweitzer, Dorrance & Associates, A Prtnshp. incl. A Prof. Corp., (BV)
405 E. Branch St., Suite K (⊙Santa Barbara)
Scott-Graham, Elizabeth, (CV) '43 '79 C.1044 B.A. L.999 J.D. 1012 Grand Ave.
Sinclair, Tana L. '59 '92 C.846 B.J. L.326 J.D. 221 E. Branch St.
Stake, Robert B., III '61 '89 L.999 J.D. 710 Grand Ave.
Stone, Margaret R., (BV) '50 '76 C.813 B.A. L.770 J.D. [Haynes W.S.]⊙
Weilbacher, David P '48 '88 L.999 J.D. 134 Nelson St.
Wilkison, Warren K., (BV) '44 '76 C.112 B.A. L.1068 J.D. [Haynes W.S.]⊙
Zeilenga, Robert P., (CV) '49 '78 C.114 B.A. L.1137 J.D. P.O. Box 166
Zimmerman, Michael E., (CV) '52 '78 C.1074 B.S. L.1137 J.D. [David&Z.]
Zuber, William L. '43 '76 C.608 B.A. L.744 J.D. 709 Grand Ave.

## ARTESIA, 15,464, *Los Angeles Co.*

Manek, Jivraj S. '32 '91 C&L.061 B.A., J.D. 17726 S. Pioneer Blvd.
Patel, Niranjan D. '55 '85 C.061 LL.B. L.309 LL.M. 17127 Pioneer Blvd.
Ringwald, Siegfried C. '26 '77 C.800 B.A. L.1137 J.D. 11428 Artesia Blvd.
Vachhani, Jagdish M. '47 '81 C.061 B.A.B.S. L.1188 J.D. 18173 Pioneer Blvd.

## ATASCADERO, 23,138, *San Luis Obispo Co.*

Ashe, James J., (BV) '21 '54 C.494 L.748 LL.B. 1843 El Camino Real
Casacca, Ernest A. '59 '85 C.477 B.S. L.464 J.D. 5950 Entrada Ave.
Dashjian, Michael B., Law Offices of, (AV) '57 '83
C.112 B.A. L.1066 J.D. 7343 El Camino Real
**Donovan, Maribeth H.** '61 '93 C.654 B.A. L.999 J.D. [⊠ Wright&S.]
**George, Gallo & Sullivan, A Law Corporation**
(See San Luis Obispo)
Harrell, J. Kirby '14 '37 C&L.500 LL.B.
(adm. in MS; not adm. in CA) 4650 Portola Rd.‡
Holtzman, Michael, (AV) '43 '68 C.502 L.910 J.D. 8400 San Gregorio Rd.

**Jones, Robert M., Jr., (CV) '49 '79 C.112 B.A. L.464 J.D.**
**8655 Morro Road, Suite C, 93422**
**Telephone: 805-466-4422 Fax: 805-466-7267**
***PRACTICE AREAS: General Civil Trial Practice; Corporate Litigation.**
**General Civil Trial Practice, Corporate Litigation.**
*See Professional Biographies, ATASCADERO, CALIFORNIA*

**Lilley, Robert B., (BV)** '43 '72 C&L.770 B.A., J.D. [R.B.Lilley]
*PRACTICE AREAS: Civil Litigation (40%); Bodily Injury (40%); Business Law; Real Estate.

**Lilley, Robert B., A Professional Law Corporation, (BV)**
**8740 Pueblo Avenue, Suite B, 93422**
**Telephone: 805-466-3545 Fax: 805-461-5340**
**Robert B. Lilley.**
**General Civil Trial Practice. Construction Disputes, Real Property Disputes, Personal Injury, Wrongful Termination and Sexual Harassment Defense.**

Locke, Jeffrey C. '46 '72 C.210 L.1148 J.D. Pres.
McGurty, Kevin W. '54 '82 C.1079 B.A. L.1065 J.D. 14002 San Antonio Rd.
McNeil, John W. '13 '48 C.112 A.B. L.1001 LL.B. 8765 Sierra Vista Rd.‡
Morlan, Thomas M., (CV) '48 '74 C.112 B.A. L.464 J.D. 7350 El Camino Real
Peterson, David C., (BV) '48 '76 C&L.1137 B.S., J.D. 6955 El Camino Rd.
Rice, Terence R. '45 '71 C.112 A.B. L.178 J.D. 6817 Santa Lucia Ave.‡
Rippen, Eugene '27 '61 C&L.802 B.A., LL.B. P.O. Box 1896
**Sanders, Betty R., (BV)** '34 '79 C&L.999 J.D. [Wright&S.]
Voorhis, Charles B., II, (BV) '31 '64 C.990 B.A. L.608 J.D. 7627 Morro Rd.

**Wood, Frederick J., (BV) '57 '85 C.36 B.S. L.101 J.D.**
**5950 Entrada Avenue, 93422**
**Telephone: 805-466-7404 Fax: 805-466-9098**
**General civil and trial practice with particular emphasis on real estate and construction, mechanic's lien, landlord-tenant, commercial and personal injury matters.**
**Reference: Santa Lucia National Bank (Atascadero).**

**Wright & Sanders, A Law Corporation, (BV)**
**5950 Entrada Avenue, 93422**
**Telephone: 805-466-9026 Fax: 805-466-9098**
**Betty R. Sanders;—Maribeth H. Donovan.**
**General Civil Practice. Probate, Guardianship and Conservatorship and Elder Law. Business and Business Litigation, Solid Waste, Environmental, Labor and Employment Law.**
**Representative Clients: Atascadero News; Wil-Mar Disposal Company, Inc.**
**References: Wells Fargo Bank (Atascadero); Santa Lucia National Bank (Atascadero).**

## ATHERTON, 7,163, *San Mateo Co.*

Archer, Shirley Sugimura '59 '85 C.818 B.A. L.276 J.D. 98 Placitas Ave.
Blough, Marcine A. '52 '80 C.659 B.A. L.188 J.D. Prof. of Law, Menlo Coll.

Burkett, Charles W. ........................'13 '39 C&L.813 B.A., J.D. 2 Belbrook Way‡
Danchuk, Kathleen M. ................ '49 '75 C.788 A.B. L.178 J.D. 11 Maple Leaf Way
Fennell, John F. '24 '53 C&L.190 B.S.C., LL.B.
(adm. in NE; not adm. in CA) 76 Fairoaks Lane‡
Fernandez, William J. ........................'31 '55 C&L.813 A.B., LL.B. 62 De Bell Dr.
Finch, Ronald G. '49 '75 C.976 B.A. L.37 J.D.
(adm. in AZ; not adm. in CA) 302 Fletcher Dr.‡
Gardner, Anne v.d.L. ......................... '35 '59 C&L.813 A.B., LL.B. 286 Selby Ln.
Iwama, Frank A., (AV) ................... '41 '70 C.768 B.S. L.770 J.D. 98 Placitas Ave.
McNertney, William John ...................'32 '55 C&L.352 B.A., J.D. 1 Watkins Ave.
Moore, Daniel K. '14 '40 C.928 B.A. L.276 J.D.
(adm. in DC; not adm. in CA) 95 Middlefield Rd.‡
Rauen, Eugene B. ......................... '28 '56 C&L.813 A.B., LL.B. 232 Oak Grove
Robertson, Donald F. .................... '37 '66 C.112 B.S. L.1065 J.D. 302 Stevick Dr.
Russell, John D. '11 '35 C.813 A.B. L.596 LL.B.
(adm. in OR; not adm. in CA) 1000 El Camino Real‡
Schwab, Robert H., Jr. ................. '12 '35 C.112 L.1065 LL.B. 188 Fair Oaks Lane‡
Short, Catherine W. .................'59 '85 C.999 B.A. L.1066 J.D. 173 Isabella Ave.‡
Trabucco, James J. ........................................'29 '53 C&L.813 A.B., LL.B. 58 Deadora
Walton, Avis G. ............................'22 '45 C&L.813 A.B., LL.B. 397 Fletcher Dr.‡
Washburn, Rodney H. ................ '29 '56 C.112 A.B. L.309 LL.B. 97 Holbrook Lane‡

## ATWATER, 22,282, *Merced Co.*

Boyle, William E., (BVⓉ) '48 '74 C.1086 B.A. L.192 J.D.
(adm. in FL; not adm. in CA) 101 Manzanita Dr.‡
Callahan, Dennis W., (CV) ............. '47 '73.C.267 B.S. L.464 J.D. 800 Bellevue Rd.
Logan, George G. .................................. '35 '63 C&L.800 LL.B. 2669 Alabama Ave.

## AUBURN, * 10,592, *Placer Co.*

Akers, Virginia I. .........................'48 '80 C.768 B.A. L.770 J.D. 1 California St.
**Amara, Dirk R.**, (BV) ........................ '52 '77 C.112 A.B. L.464 J.D. [Amara&K.]
Amara, Sandra R. ......................... '52 '94 C.1026 B.A. L.765 J.D. 160 Cherry Ln.

**Amara & Keller, (BV)**
**160 Cherry Avenue, 95603**
**Telephone: 916-888-1511 Fax: 916-888-1236**
**Dirk R. Amara; Dennis H. Keller.**
**General Civil Trial Practice, Personal Injury, Family and Business Law.**

Aronowitz, Paul S., (BV) ...............'50 '78 C.472 B.G.S. L.767 J.D. [Aronowitz&B.]
Aronowitz & Bordelon, (BV) ............................................ 1293 Lincoln Way

**Auburn Legal Clinic**
**152 Maple Street, Suite E, 95603-5042**
**Telephone: 916-888-1905 Fax: 916-888-1936**
**Christopher R. Collins; Mary Ann Collins.**
**General Civil and Criminal Practice, Family Law, Estate Planning.**
***See Professional Biographies, AUBURN, CALIFORNIA***

**Baldo, Russell P.**, (AV) ............ '46 '73 C.112 A.B. L.464 J.D. [Chamberlain,C.&B.]
*PRACTICE AREAS: Probate Law; Estate Planning Law; Trusts Law; Real Estate Law.
Barker, Robert W., Law Offices of, (AV) '44 '73 C.112 A.B. L.800 J.D.
3265 Fortune Ct.
Barney, G. Lant, Jr. ................................'49 '74 C&L.878 J.D. 110 Maple St.
Beaver, James L. ........................'42 '74 C.446 B.A. L.1067 J.D. 430 Foresthill Ave.
Berg, Mark A., (BV) ........................ '49 '76 C.1077 L.1095 J.D. [Lipschultz&B.]
Bergen, William A. ......................'49 '87 C.1130 B.A. L.809 J.D. 1133 High St.
Bjork-Tjornhom, Karin E. ................. '63 '90 C.429 B.A. L.61 J.D. Dep. Dist. Atty.
Bordelon, Jeffrey F., (BV) .............................'50 '77 L.1026 LL.B. [Aronowitz&B.]
Bowman, Rebecca D., (CV) ...........'55 '85 C.147 B.A. L.464 J.D. 1449 Lincoln Hwy.
Breitkreutz, Carolyn R. ...................'68 '95 C.678 B.A. L.1358 J.D. 3265 Fortune Ct.
Brown, Thomas B. ...............'42 '73 C.267 B.A. L.464 LL.B. 610 Auburn Ravine Rd.
Buckwalter, Kenneth D., (BV) .....'46 '72 C.605 B.A. L.813 J.D. 251 Auburn Ravine Rd.
Bush, Mary J. ..................................'53 '80 C.1060 B.A. L.1067 J.D. Dep. Dist. Atty.
Cameron, Ronald G. ...................'17 '49 C.112 A.B. L.800 LL.B. Ret. Supr. Ct. J.
Carden, Gerald O. ......................'53 '80 C.112 A.B. L.1068 J.D. Sr. Dep. Co. Coun.
**Chamberlain, Paul H.**, (AV) ......'23 '51 C.112 B.S. L.1065 LL.B. [Chamberlain,C.&B.]
*PRACTICE AREAS: Probate Law; Estate Planning Law; Municipal Law; Public Utility Law; Special Districts Law.

**Chamberlain, Chamberlain & Baldo, (AV)**
**The Bank of California Building, P.O. Box 32, 95604**
**Telephone: 916-885-4523 FAX: 916-885-5814**
**Members of Firm: L. L. Chamberlain (1888-1913); T. L. Chamberlain (1913-1975); T. L. Chamberlain, Jr. (1950-1984); Paul H. Chamberlain; Russell P. Baldo.**
**General Civil Practice. Personal Injury, Probate, Estate Planning, Trusts, Real Estate, Corporation, Municipal, Public Utility and Special Districts Law.**
**Local Counsel for: The Bank of California N.A.; Tahoe City P.U.D.; North Tahoe Fire Protection District; Donner Summit P.U.D.; Alpine Springs County Water District; First American Title Insurance Co.**
***See Professional Biographies, AUBURN, CALIFORNIA***

Coffin, Timothy L. .....................'48 '89 C.197 B.A. L.464 J.D. 516 Adriana Place
Cole, Kimberly ..............................'58 '86 C.999 A.A. L.1026 J.D. 164 Maple St.
**Collins, Christopher R.** ....................................'58 '89 C.740 B.A. L.809 J.D. [Auburn]
*PRACTICE AREAS: Criminal; Family Law; General Civil Litigation; Trials; Estate Planning.
**Collins, Mary Ann** .................................'60 '89 C.740 B.S. L.809 J.D. [Auburn]
*PRACTICE AREAS: Criminal Defense; Misdemeanors; Felonies; Juvenile; Family.
Connelly, Brian P. ........................'58 '88 C.112 B.A. L.596 J.D. 3265 Fortune Ct.
**Constantino, Alexander L.**, (BV) .......'56 '86 C.766 B.S. L.464 J.D. [Johanson,K.&C.]
*PRACTICE AREAS: Real Estate; Business Litigation.
Cosgrove, John L. ...........................................'45 '75 C.988 B.C.S. L.464 J.D. Mun. Ct. J.
Couzens, J. Richard ......................'44 '70 C.911 A.B. L.1067 J.D. Ret. Supr. Ct. J.
Couzens, John R. .............................................'10 '36 L.911 LL.B. P.O. Box 4625‡
Daugherty, William ...................'28 '91 C.870 B.S. L.1026 J.D. 11216 Greenbriar Way
Davis, Robert G., (BV) .........................'50 '76 C.800 B.A. L.464 J.D. [Paulsen&D.]
Denison, James R. .......................................'47 '79 C.768 B.A. L.770 J.D. 1223 High St.
Dowis, Joan R. .............................'35 '72 C.1109 L.1137 J.D. Sr. Dep. Co. Coun.
Driscoll, Richard E. ..........................'51 '79 C.285 B.B.A. L.767 J.D. 3265 Fortune Ct.
Dutton, John J., (BV) ......... '30 '59 C.112 A.B. L.1066 LL.B. 1505 Grass Valley Hwy.
Eames, Anthony L., (BV) ........................'41 '71 C.629 B.A. L.1067 J.D. [Norman&E.]
Emery, Gregory S., (CV) ................'52 '80 C.636 B.S. L.1137 J.D. 1223 High St.
Fenocchio, Bradford R., (BV) .................'47 '78 C.1060 B.A. L.1026 J.D. Dist. Atty.
Fitzpatrick, Gary R., (BV) ......................'45 '77 C&L.1137 B.S.L., J.D. 1223 High St.
Garbolino, James D. .....................................'43 '70 C&L.767 B.A., J.D. Supr. Ct. J.
Gong, Daniel Ling, (BV) ........................'55 '83 C.763 B.A. L.767 J.D. Dep. Dist. Atty.
Goodwin, Harrison L., (BV) ..... '42 '75 C.1042 B.A. L.209 J.D. 400 Auburn-Folsom Rd.
Graves, Laurence A. ...............................'27 '70 C.147 L.1065 J.D. 701 High St.
Grisham, Nancy E. Stuart ........... '49 '77 C.813 B.A. L.1065 J.D. Sr. Dep., Co. Coun.
Hamel, Linda L. ...........................'49 '87 C.1163 B.S. L.464 J.D. 610 Auburn Rivne Rd.
Harvey, James Creighton ............'51 '77 C.911 B.A. L.950 J.D. 11899 Edgewood Rd.
Hederman, Albert E., Jr., (AV) ...........'20 '51 C.112 L.284 LL.B. 23775 Chestnut Ct.‡

**Henderson, John P. '59 '86 C.112 B.A. L.464 J.D.**
**251 Auburn Ravine Road, Suite 105, 95603**
**Telephone: 916-889-0304 Fax: 916-885-7559**
***PRACTICE AREAS: Civil Litigation.**
**Business, Real Estate, Personal Injury and Employment Litigation.**
***See Professional Biographies, AUBURN, CALIFORNIA***

Henriques, Allan ..................... '48 '74 C.112 A.B. L.464 J.D. 13620 Lincoln Way
Herman, Donald Charles ..........................................'49 '81 L.1026 J.D. 164 Maple St.
Hoffman, Douglas R. ...........................................'52 '88 L.1026 J.D. 461 Grass Valley Hwy.
Holloway, J. Christopher ....................'49 '74 C&L.767 B.A., J.D. 2422 Linbergh St.
Hymore, Charles ..........................'37 '72 C.966 B.S. L.284 J.D. 12345 Krista Lane
Iversen, Roland E. ......................'28 '56 C.112 B.A. L.1066 LL.B. Dep. Dist. Atty.
Janes, Bertram D. .........................'15 '46 C.112 A.B. L.1066 LL.B. P.O. Box 6209‡
Jeske, Howard L. ........................'17 '52 C.187 B.A. L.464 LL.B. 4035 Eagles Nest‡
**Johanson, Theodore L., (P.C.)**, (AV) ....'33 '70 C.112 B.S. L.464 J.D. [Johanson,K.&C.]
*LANGUAGES: German.
*REPORTED CASES: Tanko v. Dodds 117 Cal App 3d 588, 172 Cal Rptr 829; People v. Ryser 40 C.A. 3d 1, 114 Cal. Rptr 668.
*PRACTICE AREAS: Estate Planning; Trust; Probate; Title Insurance Law.

**Johanson, Koons & Constantino, (AV)**
**A Partnership including Professional Corporations**
**Suite 105, 251 Auburn Ravine Road, 95603**
**Telephone: 916-885-7538 Fax: 916-885-7559**
**Members of Firm: Theodore L. Johanson (P.C.) (Certified Specialist, Probate, Estate Planning and Trust Law, The State Bar of California Board of Legal Specialization); Edward C. Koons (P.C.); Alexander L. Constantino.**
**General Civil Practice. Real Estate, Corporation and Business Law. Title Insurance Defense, Estate Planning, Probate and Trust Law.**
**References: Wells Fargo Bank, N.A.; Valli Bank.**
***See Professional Biographies, AUBURN, CALIFORNIA***

Jones, Michael G. ........................'62 '90 C.112 B.A. L.464 J.D. 3265 Fortune Ct.
Kearney, Frances, (AV) ...................'51 '79 C&L.1049 B.A., J.D. Supr. Ct. Comr.
**Keller, Dennis H.**, (CV) ......................'44 '85 C.629 B.S. L.464 J.D. [Amara&K.]
Kochenderfer, S. Ross, Jr. .......'52 '77 C.169 B.A. L.464 J.D. 12210 Herdal Dr., Suite 11
**Koons, Edward C., (P.C.)**, (CV) .......'52 '78 C.112 B.A. L.464 J.D. [Johanson,K.&C.]
*REPORTED CASES: Vaughn Materials v. Security Pacific National Bank, 1985, 170 Cal App 3d 908.
*PRACTICE AREAS: Real Estate; Business Litigation.
LaBouff, Anthony J. .......................'49 '75 C.112 A.B. L.426 J.D. Chf. Dep. Co. Coun.
Larson, G. Chris, (BV) .....................'43 '72 C.147 L.464 12220 Herdal Dr., Suite 12
Lazar, James S., (BV) ......................'50 '76 C.112 B.A. L.426 J.D. 1515 Lincoln Way
Lee, Wayne C. ...............................'35 '79 C.823 B.E.E. L.981 LL.B. P.O. Box 6139
**Leupp, Thomas A.**, (AV) .......................'52 '78 C.112 B.A. L.464 J.D. [Leupp&W.]
*PRACTICE AREAS: Criminal Defense Law.

**Leupp & Wachob, (AV)**
**149 Court Street, 95603**
**Telephone: 916-888-1100 Fax: 916-888-1821**
**Members of Firm: Thomas A. Leupp (Certified Specialist, Family Law, The State Bar of California Board of Specialization); Charles D. Wachob. Associate: Timothy S. Woodall.**
**General Civil and Trial Practice. Personal Injury, Family, Criminal, Insurance Defense.**
***See Professional Biographies, AUBURN, CALIFORNIA***

Lewis, Douglas A., (BV) ..........................'37 '67 C.999 L.464 360 Nevada St.
Lipschultz, William H., (AV) ..............'29 '65 C.274 B.S. L.365 J.D. [Lipschultz&B.]
Lipschultz & Berg, (AV) ................................................................1515 Lincoln Way
**Lyon, Bruce A.**, (BV) ..................'51 '77 C.169 A.B. L.1065 J.D. [Robinson,R.&L.]
*PRACTICE AREAS: Real Estate Law; Litigation; Business Law; Personal Injury; Probate and Estate Planning.
Mackie, Bette A. '46 '79 C.388 B.A. L.208 J.D.
(adm. in CO; not adm. in CA) 445 Finley St.‡
Marchi, William D. ........................'49 '75 C.112 B.A. L.464 J.D. Dep. Dist. Atty.
Marks, Norine Bobby ..................'58 '85 C.112 B.A. L.1067 J.D. 129 Cary Dr.‡
Maxwell, John E. ...........................'27 '62 C.112 B.A. L.284 J.D. P.O. Box 7605‡
Mayes, Sharon K. ................................'46 '83 L.398 J.D. 19930 Heritage Oak Pl.
Maynard, April D., (AV) ........................'52 '77 C.112 B.A. L.1067 J.D. 149 Ct. St.
Merrilees, Alison York .................'65 '92 C.112 B.A. L.1067 J.D. [Lipschultz&B.]
Mitchell, Jack, (AV) ......................'33 '62 C.267 B.S. L.1068 LL.B. 110 Maple St.
Moglen, Leland ...................'44 '89 C.778 B.A. L.765 J.D. 12367 Torrey Pines Dr.
Nase, Ralph J., (CV) ......................'40 '70 C.1060 B.S. L.464 J.D. 1223 High St.
Nichols, Colleen M. ......................'59 '85 C.147 B.A. L.1067 J.D. Comm. Supr. Ct.
Norman, James K., (AV) ....................'30 '63 C.352 B.A. L.1065 J.D. [Norman&E.]
Norman & Eames, (AV) .............................................................1409 Lincoln Way
North, William M., Jr. '18 '47 C&L.793 J.D.
(adm. in SD; not adm. in CA) 123 Birdsall Ave.‡
Pappalardo, Victor A. ............'62 '91 C.228 A.B. L.477 J.D. Legal Servs. of N. Calif.
Paulsen, John H., (BV) .....................'48 '74 C.800 B.A. L.990 J.D. [Paulsen&D.]
Paulsen & Davis, A Professional Corporation, (BV) ............................ 1147 High St.
Peasley, Rick ..............................'45 '71 C.1077 B.A. L.426 J.D. 110 Maple St.
Penney, Jeffrey S. ..........................'61 '90 C&L.101 B.A., J.D. Dep. Dist. Atty.
Pratt, Gwynne T. ...........................'51 '79 C.1060 L.408 LL.B. Placer Co. Coun.
Quinn, Sharon ...............................'53 '82 C.740 B.A. L.464 J.D. Dep. Dist. Atty.
Roberts, Raymond R., (AV) ...............'20 '48 C&L.426 A.B., LL.B. 430 Kevin Ct.‡
**Robinson, D. R., (P.C.)**, (AV) .........'17 '47 C.112 A.B. L.1066 J.D. [Robinson,R.&L.]
*PRACTICE AREAS: Probate Law; Estate Planning.

**Robinson, Robinson & Lyon, (AV)**
**A Partnership including a Professional Corporation**
**One California Street, 95603**
**Telephone: 916-885-8900 Fax: 916-885-0633**
**Members of Firm: D. R. Robinson (P.C.); Bruce A. Lyon.**
**General Civil Practice. Real Estate, Litigation, Business, Personal Injury, Probate, Estate Planning, and Insurance Defense.**
**Reference: Bank of America, N.A.**
***See Professional Biographies, AUBURN, CALIFORNIA***

Roeder, James L. ..............................'44 '76 C.894 B.A. L.464 J.D. Supr. Ct. J.
Rose, Lyle D. ..........................................'30 '71 C.1060 L.464 J.D. Co. Coun.
Sampson, David A. ...............'56 '87 C.766 B.A. L.767 J.D. Tanman-Konkol-Benton
Schulzke, Ernest F. H. ..................'33 '63 C.101 B.A. L.145 J.D. 1840 Little Creek Rd.
Shafer, David A., (BV) ......................'50 '79 C&L.1137 B.S.L., J.D. 1515 Lincoln Way
Shelley, John E. .........................................'33 '68 C.112 B.A. L.765 J.D. Dist. Atty.
Skidmore, Lawrence E. ..................'61 '88 C.112 B.A. L.464 J.D. 1293 Lincoln Way
Smathers, H. Gary ..............................'46 '83 L.1026 J.D. 400 Auburn Folsom Rd.

**Smits, Stuart Lansing, Law Offices of, (AV) '49 '75 C.861 B.A. L.61 J.D.**
**1515 Lincoln Way, 95603**
**Telephone: 916-887-8585 Fax: 916-889-1711**
***REPORTED CASES: Kuhl v. Sullivan, California Court of Appeal, Third District, 1993 (13 Cal.App. 4th 1589); Lincoln Properties v. Higgins, U.S. District Court, Eastern District of California, 1993 (823 F. Supp. 1528); Hulsey v. Koehler, California Court of Appeal, Third District, 1990 (218**

(This Listing Continued)

CALIFORNIA—AUBURN MARTINDALE-HUBBELL LAW DIRECTORY 1997

**Smits, Stuart Lansing, Law Offices of (Continued)**
**Cal.App.3d 1150); Jenkins v. Tuneup Masters, California Court of Appeal, Third District, 1987 (190 Cal.App.3d); United States v. Johnson, U.S. Court of Appeal, Ninth Circuit, 1981 (660 F.2d 749).**
**Real Estate and Land Use Litigation, Mediation, Environmental Litigation, Select Business Litigation.**
*See Professional Biographies, AUBURN, CALIFORNIA*

Steffan, Richard D., (BV) ....................'46 '78 C.808 B.A. L.464 J.D. 560 Wall St.
Tauman, Leonard K., (BV) ....................'47 '71 C.800 B.A. L.1066 J.D. Co. Pub. Def.
Tindall, Kern E. ....................'20 '50 C.112 A.B. L.1065 J.D. 701 High St.
Tower, William C. ....................'— '76 C.911 B.S.L. L.464 J.D. 216 Belmont Dr.‡
Turley, Richard L. '26 '51 C.81 A.B. L.1119 LL.B.
(adm. in IN; not adm. in CA) 11781 Torrey Pines Dr.‡
Tuttle, Fred P., (BV) ....................'29 '59 C.1060 L.464 LL.B. P.O. Box 247
Urch, Jack W. ....................'20 '50 C.112 B.S. L.1065 J.D. 3315 Wasatch Dr.
Vaughan, Robert, (BV) ....................'59 '90 C.999 L.464 J.D. 110 Maple
**Wachob, Charles D.**, (AV) ....................'52 '78 C.112 A.B. L.1067 J.D. [Leupp&W.]
*PRACTICE AREAS: Personal Injury Law; Insurance Law.
Walker, James A., (CV) ....................'59 '91 C.629 B.S. L.999 J.D. 110 Maple St.
Welch, Howard P. ....................'16 '50 C.906 B.A. L.284 LL.B. P.O. Box 7200‡
Wolfe, Evan A., (BV) ....................'42 '69 C.1042 L.809 LL.B. 110 Maple St.
**Woodall, Timothy S.**, (CV) ....................'56 '84 C.112 B.A. L.1065 J.D. [Leupp&W.]
*PRACTICE AREAS: Insurance Defense Law; Criminal Defense Law; Plaintiffs Personal Injury Law.
Worcester, Nanci R. ....................'47 '81 C.112 B.A. L.809 J.D. 2, 10 Magnolia Ave.
Yonehiro, George ....................'22 '55 C.999 L.365 LL.B. Supr. Ct. J.
Young, Robert A. ....................'40 '72 C.1097 B.A. L.464 J.D. 164 Maple Street
Zimmerman, Barry A. ....................'61 '87 C.112 B.A. L.284 J.D. 2422 Lindbergh St.
Zmrzel, Laurie E. ....................'63 '87 C.1060 B.A. L.464 J.D. 3265 Fortune Ct.

## AVALON, 2,918, *Los Angeles Co.*

Mirich, Peter J., Jr. ....................'51 '78 C.112 B.A. L.426 J.D. Mun. J.
Park, Wendy Putnam ....................'— '82 C.629 L.1137 J.D. P.O. Box 1301

## AVILA BEACH, —, *San Luis Obispo Co.*

Prince, Ralph H. ....................'25 '53 C.381 L.588 LL.B. P.O. Box 2343

## AZUSA, 41,333, *Los Angeles Co.*

Anton, Barry V. ....................'37 '73 C.1097 B.A. L.309 J.D. 371-A N. Barranca Ave.
Brumbaugh, Randall V. ....................'50 '80 C.1060 B.A. L.898 J.D. 375 N. Citrus Ave.
Decker, Willard R., (BV) ....................'16 '49 C.165 A.B. L.426 J.D. 627 N. San Gabriel
Deppe, Robyn A. ....................'43 '89 C.684 B.A. L.426 J.D. 426 N. San Gabriel Ave.
Englund, Philip J. ....................'44 '74 C.768 B.S. L.770 J.D. V.P., Optical Radiation Corp.
Monohan, John C. ....................'45 '89 C.398 B.A. L.1137 J.D. 161 E. Russell St.
Robutz, Mary E., (BV) ....................'21 '72 L.1127 LL.B. 426 N. San Gabriel Ave.
Rosedale, Miles R. ....................'51 '77 C.813 B.A. L.800 J.D. Monrovia Nursery Co.
Schuessler, John S. ....................'47 '79 C.1075 B.A. L.398 LL.B. 426 N. San Gabriel Ave.

## BAKERSFIELD, * 174,820, *Kern Co.*

Abarca, Rosemary ....................'51 '81 C.112 B.A. L.61 J.D. 107 17th St.
Abbott, Keith E. ....................'31 '62 C.273 B.A. L.1066 LL.D. 5900 Burke Wy.
**Abril, Michael S.**, (BV) ....................'60 '86 C.112 B.A. L.800 J.D. [Klein,W.D.G.&M.]
*TRANSACTIONS: Attorney for Bank One, Columbus, N.A. (Indenture Trustee), in Chapter 11 Reorganization of Leisure Technology, Inc.
*PRACTICE AREAS: Bankruptcy; Corporate Reorganizations; Creditors Rights; Corporate and Business Transactions; Real Estate Law.
Alexander, William L. ....................'59 '86 C.763 B.S. L.770 J.D. [Noriega&A.]
**Allard, Victoria R.**, (CV) ....................'63 '91 C.112 B.A. L.763 J.D. [Borton,P.&C.]
*PRACTICE AREAS: Personal Injury and Casualty Defense; Insurance Litigation.
**Anchordoquy, Arnold**, (BV) ....................'48 '73 C.740 B.A. L.464 J.D. [Clifford&B.]
*PRACTICE AREAS: Civil Litigation.
Anderson, Joseph I. ....................'33 '69 C.1074 B.S. L.800 J.D. 5001 E. Commerce Ctr. Dr.
Andreesen, Joel T. ....................'63 '91 C&L.352 J.D. [Etcheverry&N.]
Anspach, Robert J. ....................'36 '62 C.602 B.A. L.1066 LL.B. Supr. Ct. J.
Anthony, E. DeWitt, Jr. '27 '66 C&L.846 B.S., LL.B.
(adm. in TX; not adm. in CA) 8209 Birmingham St.‡
Anthony, James D., (CV) ....................'47 '79 C.36 B.A. L.464 J.D. Pub. Def. Off.
Anton, Thomas J., (Inc.) ....................'44 '73 C.770 B.S. L.464 J.D. [Anton,G.&M.]
Anton, Gordon & Monje, (CV) ....................1600 Truxtun Ave., 3rd Fl.

**Arrache, Clark & Potter, (AV)**
**4800 Easton Drive, Suite 114, 93309-9424**
**Telephone: 805-328-1800**
**Members of Firm: Juan E. Arrache, Jr. (1943-1990); Thomas S. Clark; David B. Potter.**
**General Civil Litigation. Business, Oil and Gas, Commercial, Taxation, Energy, Livestock, Agricultural Real Estate Law and Probate.**
*See Professional Biographies, BAKERSFIELD, CALIFORNIA*

Ash, John D. ....................'51 '79 C.208 B.A. L.896 J.D. Union Oil Co.
Austin, Stephen B., (BV) ....................'45 '71 C.112 B.A. L.1067 J.D. [Austin,T.&S.]
Austin, Thompson & Sims, (BV) ....................2800 "F" St.
**Azemika, Anthony P.** ....................'67 '92 C.766 B.S. L.1065 J.D. [Azemika&A.]
*PRACTICE AREAS: Family Law; Adoptions; Guardianships; Conservatorships.
**Azemika, Nicholas P.** ....................'67 '92 C.766 B.S. L.1065 J.D. [Azemika&A.]
*PRACTICE AREAS: Family Law.

**Azemika & Azemika**
**The Bank of America Tower, 1430 Truxtun Avenue, Suite 707, 93301**
**Telephone: 805-322-8166 Fax: 805-322-8168**
**Anthony P. Azemika; Nicholas P. Azemika.**
**Family Law.**
*See Professional Biographies, BAKERSFIELD, CALIFORNIA*

Baca, Robert T. ....................'25 '56 C.800 L.426 LL.B. Supr. Ct. J.
Baehr, Roy D., (P.C.), (BV) ....................'35 '72 C.267 B.A. L.1065 J.D. [Hanna,B.M.M.&J.]

**Baker, Manock & Jensen, A Professional Corporation**
**(See Fresno)**

Banducci, Janice, (CV) ....................'43 '87 C.112 B.A. L.809 J.D. 1200 Truxtun Ave.
Barmann, Bernard C., Sr., (BV) ....................'32 '74 C.813 B.A. L.763 J.D. Co. Coun.‡
**Barnes, Karen S.**, (CV) ....................'53 '91 C.1212 A.A. L.1241 J.D. [Jenkins,B.&B.]
Barton, Robert A. ....................'62 '88 C.267 B.S. L.1067 J.D. Dep. Dist. Atty.
Bates, Kenneth H., (AV) ....................'16 '40 C.112 A.B. L.1066 LL.B. 1122 Truxtun Ave.‡
Bauer, Nancy D., (CV) ....................'43 '76 C.766 B.A. L.61 J.D. P.O. Box 348
**Beardsley, Craig N.**, (BV) ....................'44 '73 C.112 B.A. L.767 J.D. [Borton,P.&C.]
*PRACTICE AREAS: Personal Injury; Casualty Defense (including Malpractice); Product Liability; Insurance Litigation.
Beaver, H. Dennis ....................'46 '72 C.1077 B.A. L.426 J.D. 1311 L St.
Beckett, Joseph K., Jr. ....................'32 '66 C.171 Geol.E. L.1065 J.D. Dep. Dist. Atty.
Beckman, Peter W., (CV) ....................'52 '78 C.111 B.S. L.629 J.D. 1400 Chester Ave., Ste N

**Benavides, Jose** ....................'56 '82 C.112 B.A. L.1068 J.D. [Klein,W.D.G.&M.]
*LANGUAGES: Spanish.
*PRACTICE AREAS: Products Liability; Employment Law; Major Tort Litigation; Insurance Bad Faith.
Benham, Susan Merrill ....................'53 '79 C.659 B.A. L.1068 J.D. Princ. Atty., Off. of Pub. Def.
Berry, Wm. Todd ....................'59 '94 C.845 B.S. L.999 J.D. 110 S. Montclair St.
Bianchi, Henry E. ....................'21 '50 C.112 A.B. L.1065 J.D. Ret. Supr. Ct. J.
Bianco, D., (AV) ....................'05 '30 L.767 J.D. 261 Hermosa Dr.‡
**Biel, Phillip J.** ....................'67 '92 C.686 B.A. L.990 J.D. [Biel&B.]
*PRACTICE AREAS: Personal Injury and Criminal Defense; Traffic Violation; Commercial Litigation.

**Biel & Brehmer**
**903 H Street, Suite 200, 93304**
**Telephone: 805-322-8113 Fax: 805-322-2575**
**Phillip J. Biel; Charles R. Brehmer.**
**Personal Injury, Criminal Defense and Business Litigation. General Civil Trial Practice.**
*See Professional Biographies, BAKERSFIELD, CALIFORNIA*

**Bisol, Brian E.** ....................'68 '95 C.112 B.A. L.37 J.D. [Borton,P.&C.]
*PRACTICE AREAS: Insurance Defense.
**Bjorn, Teri A.**, (BV) ....................'53 '79 C.352 B.A. L.273 J.D. [Clifford&B.]
*LANGUAGES: French.
*PRACTICE AREAS: Real Estate Law.
Blake, Oscar A. '34 '61 C.912 B.A. L.188 J.D.
(adm. in NY; not adm. in CA) 1200 Discovery Dr.
Blanton, Nancy S., (CV) ....................'53 '85 C.1212 B.A. L.398 J.D. [Blanton&B.]
Blanton, Philip C., (BV) ....................'46 '72 C.976 B.A. L.61 J.D. [Blanton&B.]
Blanton & Blanton, (BV) ....................1200 Truxton Ave.

**Bloom, David B., A Prof. Corp., Law Offices of**
**(See Los Angeles)**

**Borton, Petrini & Conron, (AV)**
**The Borton, Petrini & Conron Building, 1600 Truxtun Avenue, P.O. Box 2026, 93303**
**Telephone: 805-322-3051 Voice Mail: 805-395-6700 Fax: 805-322-4628**
**Email: bpcbak@bpclaw.com**
**Members of Firm: Fred E. Borton (1877-1948); James Petrini (1897-1978); Harry M. Conron (1907-1971); Kenneth D. Pinsent (1953-1984); Richard E. Hitchcock; John F. Petrini; George F. Martin; Stephen M. Dake; Paul Lafranchise; Steven M. Karcher; Mark Alan Jones; Victoria R. Allard. Associates: Craig N. Beardsley; Randall Steven Joyce; Wendy E. Coulston; Greg L. Ferrari; Brian E. Bisol; Tobias A. Dorsey; Richard E. Morton; Andrew C. Thomson; Joe W. Whittington; Elizabeth M. Giesick; Timothy C. Hale; J. David Bournazian; Linda M. Marschang; William H. Cantrell (Resident Member, Newport Beach Office); J. David Petrie (Resident Member, Fresno Office); Daniel L. Ferguson (Resident Member, San Bernardino Office); Rocky K. Copley (Resident Member, San Diego Office); Craig R. McCollum (Resident Member, San Luis Obispo Office); Mark S. Newman (Resident Member, Sacramento Office); James M. McKanna (Resident Member, San Luis Obispo, Office); Richard M. Macias (Resident Member, Los Angeles Office); Dale M. Dorfmeier (Resident Member, Fresno Office); Phillip B. Greer (Resident Member, Newport Beach Office); Robert H. Grove (Resident Member, Ventura Office); Steven M. Shewry (Resident Member, San Diego Office); Robert J. Gundert (Resident Member, San Luis Obispo Office); Randall L. Harr (Resident Member, Redding Office); George J. Hernandez, Jr. (Resident Member, Los Angeles Office); Robert N. Ridenour (Resident Member, Los Angeles Office); Rick D. Hardin (Resident Member, Santa Barbara Office); Paul Kissel (Resident Member, San Diego Office); Carla J. Hartley (Resident Member, San Francisco Office); Sharon G. Pratt (Resident Member, San Jose Office); Bradley A. Post (Resident Member, Modesto Office); Michael J. Macko (Resident Member, Modesto Office); Tracy W. Goldberg (Resident Member, San Bernardino Office); Samuel L. Phillips (Resident Member, Modesto Office); Calvin R. Stead (Resident Member, Santa Rosa Office); Gary C. Harvey (Resident Member, Fresno Office); Michael F. Long (Resident Member, Newport Beach Office); Thomas A. Gifford (Resident Member, Sacramento Office); Thomas J. Stoddard (Resident Member, San Diego Office); Kenneth B. Arthofer (Resident Member, Redding Office); Darlene M. Ball (Resident Member, Visalia Office); Steven G. Gatley (Resident Member, Los Angeles Office); Rosemarie Suazo Lewis (Resident Member, Los Angeles Office); Dennis D. Resh (Resident Associate, Los Angeles Office); R. Stephen Kinnaird (Resident Associate, Santa Barbara Office); Thomas F. Brooks (Resident Member, Ventura Office); Richard E. Korb (Resident Associate, San Francisco Office); Nelson H. Chan (Resident Associate, Sacramento Office); J. Albert Boada (Resident Associate, San Luis Obispo Office); Tuvana B. Jeffrey (Resident Associate, San Francisco Office); Gary A. Bixler (Resident Associate, San Luis Obispo Office); Michael V. Peros (Resident Associate, San Bernardino Office); Christopher Der Manuelian, Jr. (Resident Associate, San Jose Office); Lynne L. Bentley (Resident Member, San Jose Office); Barton C. Merrill (Resident Member, Santa Barbara Office); Marc C. Gessford (Resident Associate, Sacramento Office); Paige M. Hibbert (Resident Member, Sacramento Office); Donald A. Diebold (Resident Associate, Newport Beach Office); William F. Klausner (Resident Member, San Bernardino Office); Arcangelo Clarizio (Resident Associate, Ventura Office); Paul T. McBride (Resident Associate, Newport Beach Office); Mark T. Coffin (Resident Associate, Santa Barbara Office); Michelle L. Van Dyke (Resident Associate, San Diego Office); Steven P. Owen (Resident Associate, Los Angeles Office); Paul C. Clauss (Resident Associate, Santa Rosa Office); Michael J. Boyajian (Resident Associate, Fresno Office); Daniel J. Tekunoff (Resident Associate, Fresno Office); Guy Chirinian (Resident Associate, Los Angeles Office); Sharon P. McAleenan (Resident Associate, Los Angeles Office); Alfred W. Mondorf (Resident Associate, Redding Office); Robert D. Reed (Resident Associate, San Luis Obispo Office); Carol D. Janssen (Resident Associate, San Luis Obispo Office); Eric J. Larson (Resident Associate, San Diego Office); Cari S. Baum (Resident Associate, Newport Beach Office); Carolyn M. Kern (Resident Associate, Newport Beach Office); Joyce M. Stovall (Resident Associate, San Bernardino Office); Kari L. Rutherford (Resident Associate, San Bernardino Office); Barton F. Hoey (Resident Associate, San Luis Obispo Office); Janice K. Lachman (Resident Associate, Sacramento Office); Greg Rubinoff (Resident Associate, Sacramento Office). Of Counsel: Roy J. Gargano; Jere N. Sullivan, Sr.**
**Commercial/Real Estate Litigation, Insurance Law, General Civil Trial and Appellate Practice in State and Federal Courts, Personal Injury and Casualty Defense Litigation, Insurance Bad Faith and Coverage, Labor and Employment, Toxic Torts, Real Estate, Land Use Planning, Zoning, Municipal, Professional Errors and Omissions, Healthcare Provider Malpractice Defense, Products Liability, Oil and Gas, Water, Natural Resources, Environmental, Public Entity, Administrative, Agricultural, Banking, Contracts, Corporations, Partnerships, Taxation, Creditor's Remedies, Bankruptcy, Probate, Estate Planning, Family Law.**
**Representative Clients: Castle and Cooke; Wells Fargo Bank; Pacific Gas & Electric.**
**San Luis Obispo, California Office: 1114 Marsh Street. Telephone: 805-541-4340. Fax: 805-541-4558. Email: bpcslo@bpclaw.com.**
**Visalia, California Office: 206 South Mooney Boulevard, P.O. Box 1028. Telephone: 209-627-5600. Fax: 209-627-4309. Email: bpcvis@bpclaw.com.**
**Fresno, California Office: T. W. Patterson Building, 2014 Tulare Street, Suite 830. Telephone: 209-268-0117. Fax: 209-237-7995. Email: bpcfrs@bpclaw.com.**
**Sacramento, California Office: 2233 Watt Avenue, Suite 290. Telephone: 916-484-3555. Fax: 916-484-3550. Email: bpcsac@bpclaw.com.**
**Santa Barbara, California Office: 211 East Victoria Street, Suite D. Telephone: 805-564-2404. Fax: 805-564-2176. Email: bpcsb@bpclaw.com**
**Los Angeles, California Office: 707 Wilshire Boulevard, Suite 5100. Telephone: 213-624-2869. Fax: 213-489-3930. Email: bpcla@bpclaw.com.**
**San Diego, California Office: John Burnham Building, 610 West Ash Street, 9th Floor. Telephone: 619-232-2424. Fax: 619-531-0794. Email: bpcsd@bpclaw.com.**
**Newport Beach, California Office: 4675 MacArthur Court, Suite 1150. Telephone: 714-752-2333. Fax: 714-752-2854. Email: bpcnb@bpclaw.com.**
**Modesto, California Office: The Turner Building, 900 "H" Street, Suite D. Telephone: 209-576-1701. Fax: 209-527-9753. Email: bpcmod@bpclaw.com.**
**San Francisco, California Office: 111 Pine Street, Suite 730. Telephone: 415-981-4415. Fax: 415-391-5538. Email: bpcsf@bpclaw.com.**
**Redding, California Office: 280 Hemsted Drive, Suite 100. Telephone: 916-222-1530. Fax: 916-222-4498. Email: bpcred@bpclaw.com.**
**San Bernardino, California Office: 290 North "D" Street, Suite 500. Telephone: 909-381-0527. Fax: 909-381-0658. Email: bpcsbdo@bpclaw.com.**
**San Jose, California Office: 2 North Second Street. Telephone: 408-298-3997. Fax: 408-298-3365. Email: bpcsj@bpclaw.com.**
**Ventura, California Office: 1000 Hill Road, Suite 310. Telephone: 805-650-9994. Fax: 805-650-7125. Email: bpcvta@bpclaw.com.**

(This Listing Continued)

**Borton, Petrini & Conron (Continued)**

Santa Rosa, California Office: 50 Santa Rosa Avenue, Suite 300. Telephone: 707-527-9477. Fax: 707-527-9488. Email: bpcsr@bpclaw.com.

*See Professional Biographies, BAKERSFIELD, CALIFORNIA*

**Bournazian, J. David** ................. '69 '96 C.705 B.S. L.1049 J.D. [Ⓐ Borton,P.&C.]
**Bowman, Stacy Henry** ............ '59 '93 C.276 B.S. L.809 J.D. [Ⓐ Klein,W.D.G.&M.]
Boyle, George A., (A Prof. Corp.) ........ '30 '70 C.999 A.B. L.809 J.D. 416 Truxtun Ave.
**Boyle, Stephen H.** ............... '53 '78 C.112 B.A. L.61 J.D. [Clifford&B.]
*PRACTICE AREAS: Estate Planning/Probate Law; Taxation Law; Corporation Law.
Bracy, Carol Ratsamy '56 '80 C.1109 B.A. L.800 J.D.
Dir. of Litigation, Greater Bakersfield Assistance Inc.
Bradshaw, J. Eric, (CV) .............. '58 '85 C.147 B.A. L.61 J.D. [Noriega&A.]
Bradshaw, Richd. W. ............ '27 '55 C.813 A.B. L.1065 J.D. J. Pro Tem, Mun. Ct.‡
**Brady, Mathew M.**, (CV) .............. '60 '88 C.1212 B.A. L.464 J.D. [Jenkins,B.&B.]
Braun, Craig D. ............... '67 '93 C.1109 B.A. L.1067 J.D. 1430 Truxtun Ave.
**Brehmer, Charles R.** ..................... '66 '92 C&L.879 B.A., J.D. [Biel&B.]
*PRACTICE AREAS: Personal Injury; Business Litigation; Casualty Defense.
Brent, Anthony R. .............. '40 '74 C.768 B.A. L.770 J.D. Dep. Pub. Def.
**Brown, James E.**, (AV) .............. '40 '66 C.585 B.S. L.1065 LL.B. [Clifford&B.]
*PRACTICE AREAS: Civil Litigation.
Brownlee, John R. ................ '62 '90 C.35 B.S. L.464 J.D. Dep. Dist. Atty.
**Bruce, William A.**, (BV) .............. '53 '80 C.112 B.A. L.990 J.D. [Klein,W.D.G.&M.]
*PRACTICE AREAS: Civil Litigation; Agri-Business; Product Liability Litigation; Environmental Litigation.
**Brumfield, Lorna Hislop**, (CV) .......... '57 '83 C.1074 B.S. L.464 J.D. [Ⓐ J.B.Hislop]
*PRACTICE AREAS: Insurance Defense; Personal Injury; Civil Litigation; Products Liability; Insurance Law.
**Brumfield, Robert H., III**, (BV) ....... '58 '84 C.1074 B.A. L.464 J.D. [Byrum,H.B.&D.]
*PRACTICE AREAS: Bankruptcy; Corporation Law; Partnership Law; General Civil Litigation; Construction Law.
**Buckles, Rodney G.** '33 '60 C&L.623 B.A., J.D.
(adm. in OK; not adm. in CA) Assoc. Gen. Coun., Occidental Oil & Gas Corp.
*RESPONSIBILITIES: International Oil & Gas.
Buelow, Roger M. ......... '51 '77 C.177 B.A. L.352 J.D. Land Atty., Chevron U.S.A., Inc.
Bulich, Antone S., Jr. ................ '51 '76 C&L.770 B.S., J.D. 3008 Sillect Ave.
Bultman, M. Glenn ........... '14 '40 C.112 A.B. L.1065 J.D. 7218 Meadowbrook Lane‡
**Bunker, Bruce F.**, (AV) .............. '24 '51 C&L.800 J.D. [Ⓒ Klein,W.D.G.&M.]
*PRACTICE AREAS: Business Litigation; Business Planning; Estate Planning; Trusts and Probate; Real Property.
Bunton, Cynda L. ....................... '52 '82 C.330 B.A. L.464 J.D. Dep. Pub. Def.
**Burger, Christopher P.** .............. '52 '92 C.112 B.S. L.999 J.D. [Ⓐ Klein,W.D.G.&M.]
*PRACTICE AREAS: Environmental Law; Administrative Law; Business/Commercial Litigation.

**Burke, John J., Jr. '51 '85 C.112 B.A. L.809 J.D.**
**1600 Truxtun Avenue, Third Floor, 93301**
**Telephone: 805-324-7627**
**Estate Planning, Probate and Elder Law.**

*See Professional Biographies, BAKERSFIELD, CALIFORNIA*

**Burruss, Darrell E.** .................. '43 '73 C.267 B.S. L.284 J.D. Mgr., Chevron Corp.
Butkiewicz, Frank S. ............... '53 '81 C.1044 B.A. L.61 J.D. 1430 Truxtun Ave.

**Butz, Donald F., (BV) '47 '79 C.1079 B.A. L.767 J.D.**
**1402 26th Street, 93301**
**Telephone: 805-327-2367**
**(Certified Specialist, Family Law, The State Bar of California Board of Legal Specialization).**
***PRACTICE AREAS: Family Law.**
**Family Law.**

*See Professional Biographies, BAKERSFIELD, CALIFORNIA*

**Byrum, Kenneth M.**, (BV) ........... '39 '66 C.112 B.S. L.1068 J.D. [Byrum,H.B.&D.]
*PRACTICE AREAS: Real Estate Law; Business and Construction Litigation; Natural Resources Law.

**Byrum, Holland, Brumfield & Dietrich, (AV)**
**5201 California Avenue, Suite 450, 93309**
**Telephone: 805-861-6191 Facsimile: 805-861-6190**
**Kenneth M. Byrum; Kenneth A. Holland; Robert H. Brumfield, III; Christopher M. Dietrich. Associates: Alan B. Harris; Brian M. Ledger.**
**General Civil and Trial Practice in all State and Federal Courts. Administrative Agencies, Business and Tax Planning, Estates Planning, Trusts and Probate, Insolvency, Real Property, Real Property Taxation, Title Insurance, Banking, Construction, Natural Resources, Environmental, Public Health and Personal Injury.**

*See Professional Biographies, BAKERSFIELD, CALIFORNIA*

Campbell, Richard F., III, (AVⓉ) ............ '46 '75 C.45 B.S. L.623 J.D. [Campbell&S.]
Campbell & Steele, (AVⓉ) ........................................ 1401 19th St., Ste., 200
Caraway, William L. .................... '36 '60 C.112 B.A. L.1065 J.D. P.O. Box 320
**Carlovsky, Michael Andrew** ............ '65 '92 C.1074 B.A. L.61 J.D. [Ⓐ E.J.Thomas]
*PRACTICE AREAS: Family Law.
**Carpenter, Edward M.**, (AV) ............ '30 '64 C.813 A.B. L.981 LL.B. [Ⓒ Young W.]
*PRACTICE AREAS: Banking Litigation; Commercial Litigation.
Carrick, Patrick C., (BV) ........................ '49 '74 C&L.800 B.A., J.D. [Griffin C.]
Carton, Peter C., (BV) ..................... '43 '73 C&L.426 B.A., J.D. Carton Law Ctr.
Casas, Estela '55 '90 C.1212 B.A. L.1068 J.D.
Exec. Dir., Greater Bakersfield Legal Asst., Inc.
Caufield, Jeffery .......................... '68 '93 C.112 B.A. L.464 J.D. [Ⓒ Griffin C.]
Chain, Younger, Lemucchi, Cohn, & Stiles, (AV) ..................... 1430 Truxtun Ave.
Chapin, Sidney P. ......................... '40 '72 C.112 A.B. L.1065 J.D. Supr. Ct. J.
**Christiansen, Heather June** ............ '71 '96 C.1169 B.A. L.464 J.D. [Ⓐ E.J.Thomas]
*PRACTICE AREAS: Family Law.
Cicone, Frank J., (BV) ....................... '45 '71 C.940 B.A. L.1066 J.D. [F.J.Cicone]
Cicone, Frank J., Law Corp., (BV) ................................ 5601 Truxtun Ave.
**Clark, Gregory G.** '51 '83 C.101 B.A. L.336 J.D.
(adm. in OK; not adm. in CA) Legal Mgr., Occidental Oil & Gas Corp.
*LANGUAGES: Spanish.
*RESPONSIBILITIES: International Oil and Gas.
**Clark, Thomas S.**, (AV) ..................... '47 '73 C&L.800 B.A., J.D. [Arrache,C.&P.]
*PRACTICE AREAS: Civil Litigation; Real Estate Development; Condemnation.
**Clifford, Stephen T.**, (AV) .............. '40 '66 C.112 B.S. L.1065 LL.B. [Clifford&B.]
*PRACTICE AREAS: Civil Litigation.

**Clifford & Brown, A Professional Corporation, (AV)**
**Suite 900, 1430 Truxtun Avenue, 93301**
**Telephone: 805-322-6023 Fax: 805-322-3508**
**Email: cblaw@lightspeed.net**
**Stephen T. Clifford; James E. Brown; Robert D. Harding; Arnold Anchordoquy; Anthony L. Leggio; Patrick J. Osborn; Michael L. O'Dell; Grover H. Waldon; John R. Szewczyk; Stephen H. Boyle; James B. Wiens; Richard G. Zimmer; Charles D. Melton;—Teri A. Bjorn; Gregory J. Kohler; Stephen P. Wainer; Scott L. Harper; Bill J. Kuenzinger; Beth A. Van Voorhis; Winifred Thomson Hoss; Peter S. Thorne; Mark E. Pafford. Of Counsel: Curtis Darling (Certified Specialist, Taxation Law, The State Bar of California Board of Legal Specialization); Thomas M. Stanton.**
**General Civil Practice in all State and Federal Courts. Civil and Business Litigation, Negligence, Products Liability, Matters of Professional Negligence, Creditor's Rights, Insurance, Estate Planning and Probate, Tax Planning, Land Use, Agriculture, Real Estate, Corporation, Employment, Oil and Gas and Environmental Law.**

(This Listing Continued)

**Clifford & Brown, A Professional Corporation (Continued)**

**Representative Clients: Monsanto Agricultural Products Co.; Chevron, U.S.A.; Atchison, Topeka and Santa Fe Railway Co.; The Travelers Insurance Cos.; Royal Insurance Co.; Aetna Casualty and Surety Co.; Southern California Physicians Insurance Exchange; Goodyear Tire and Rubber Co. References: California Republic Bank (Bakersfield Main Office); Bank of America N. T. & S. A. (Bakersfield Main Office).**

*See Professional Biographies, BAKERSFIELD, CALIFORNIA*

Closs, Louise Toby ............................. '36 '80 C&L.999 B.S.L., J.D. Asst. City Atty.
Clow, Thomas D. ..................... '47 '75 C.112 B.A. L.1137 J.D. Dep. Co. Coun.
Cohn, David K., (BV) .................. '49 '76 C.800 A.B. L.809 J.D. [Chain,Y.L.C.&S.]
Coker, James E. ............. '48 '82 C.766 B.A. L.1049 J.D. Princ. Atty., Co. Pub. Def.
Coley, Roger D., (BV) ...................... '36 '68 C.976 B.A. L.846 LL.B. [Coley,R.D.]
Coley, Roger D., a Professional Corporation, (BV) ................................ 330 H St.
Collins, Charles F., (BV) .................. '52 '82 C.112 B.A. L.770 J.D. Co. Coun. Off.
Compton, James L. ............ '52 '78 C.1212 B.S. L.61 J.D. 5001 E. Commerce Ctr. Dr.
**Conant, Ernest A.**, (AV) ..................... '53 '79 C.1074 B.S. L.990 J.D. [Young W.]
*PRACTICE AREAS: Administrative Law.
Condley, Walter H. ........................ '23 '50 C&L.813 A.B., LL.B. Ret. Supr. Ct. J.
Conklin, Jonathan B. ........................ '60 '85 C.1075 B.S. L.464 J.D. Dep. Dist. Atty.
**Cooper, David J.**, (BV) ........... '45 '71 C.112 B.A. L.1066 LL.B. [Klein,W.D.G.&M.]
*PRACTICE AREAS: Business/Commercial Litigation; Appellate Law; Environmental Law.
Cote-Sanders, Patricia J. '59 '89
C.112 B.A. L.1049 J.D. Staff Coun., State Comp. Ins. Fund
**Coulston, Wendy E.** ..................... '66 '92 C.1109 B.A. L.1137 J.D. [Ⓐ Borton,P.&C.]
*PRACTICE AREAS: Insurance Defense; Medical Malpractice; Civil Litigation.
**Cox, Larry R.**, (BV) .............................. '50 '79 C.37 B.S. L.790 J.D. [Young W.]
*PRACTICE AREAS: Probate Law; Estate Planning; Litigation.
**Crear, Thomas A.**, (BV) ............ '51 '77 C.112 B.A. L.770 J.D. [LeBeau,T.L.M.&C.]
Curran, Arthur H., III, (BV) ............. '42 '69 C.768 B.S. L.1065 J.D. Dep. Co. Atty.
**Dake, Stephen M.**, (BV) ................ '54 '79 C.1074 B.S. L.426 J.D. [Borton,P.&C.]
*PRACTICE AREAS: Taxation; Business Planning; Estate Planning; Corporations; Partnerships.
Daly, Thomas P., Jr., (BV) ................ '17 '47 C.426 B.S. L.800 J.D. P.O. Box 9715‡
**D'Amico, Antonio** '65 '90 C.597 B.S.J. L.209 J.D.
(adm. in IL; not adm. in CA) Coun., Occidental Oil & Gas Corp.
Daniels, Michael O. ................... '46 '81 C.1097 B.S. L.809 J.D. 1000 Truxton Ave.

**Daniels, Baratta & Fine, (AV)**
**A Partnership including a Professional Corporation**
**Suite 400, 5201 California Avenue, 93309⊙**
**Telephone: 805-335-7788 Telecopier: 805-324-3660**
**Mark R. Israel; Spencer A. Schneider.**
**General Civil Trial and Appellate Practice in all State and Federal Courts. Insurance, Products Liability, Tort, Wrongful Termination and Employment Discrimination, Business, Entertainment, Real Estate and Construction Law, Environmental and Toxic Torts**
**Los Angeles, California Office: 1801 Century Park East, 9th. Floor. Telephone: 310-556-7900. Telecopier: 310-556-2807.**

*See Professional Biographies, BAKERSFIELD, CALIFORNIA*

**Darling, Curtis**, (AV) ..................... '18 '49 C.112 B.S. L.813 J.D. [Ⓒ Clifford&B.]
*PRACTICE AREAS: Real Estate Law; Business Law; Tax Planning Law; Corporate Law; Estate Planning.
Davis, Gerald K. ................... '32 '60 C.378 A.B. L.1066 LL.B. Ret. Supr. Ct. J.‡
Davis, Kathe Kates ............................ '55 '80 C.260 B.A. L.259 J.D. [Kates&D.]
Del Pellegrino, Victoria ................... '53 '90 C.102 B.A. L.284 J.D. Dep. Dist. Atty.
**DeNatale, Thomas V., Jr.**, (BV) ..... '49 '75 C.112 B.A. L.1095 J.D. [Klein,W.D.G.&M.]
*PRACTICE AREAS: Business/Commercial Litigation; Real Property Litigation; Eminent Domain Litigation.
Dennis, Terry ............................................ '— '89 L.1132 J.D. 1331 L Street
Denvir, John R. ................. '63 '89 C.800 B.A. L.1049 J.D. 5001 E. Commerce Ctr.
Dessy, Fawn Kennedy, (BV) ............. '54 '79 C.1212 B.A. L.1095 J.D. 1301 "L" St.
Dessy, Ronald Daniel, (CV) ........................................... '— '80 1301 L St.
**Dietrich, Christopher M.**, (BV) ........ '59 '85 C.112 B.A. L.464 J.D. [Byrum,H.B.&D.]
*REPORTED CASES: Estate of Robert Daniels, Deceased, (1991) 228 Cal.App.3d 486.
*PRACTICE AREAS: Estate Planning; Probate; Business Transactions.
Dietrich, Erin ................................ '56 '84 C.549 B.A. L.464 J.D. Co. Pub. Def.
Di Giorgio, Vincent P., (BV) ......... '14 '39 C&L.800 B.S. in B.A., J.D. [V.P.DiGiorgio]

**Di Giorgio, Davis, Klein, Wegis, Duggan & Friedman**
**(See Klein, Wegis, DeNatale, Goldner & Muir)**

Di Giorgio, V.P., Inc., (BV) .................................................. P.O. Box 996
Divelbiss, Bruce A. .............. '46 '76 C.112 B.S.M.E. L.878 J.D. Chf. Dep. Co. Coun.
**Dorsey, Tobias A.** .......................... '67 '93 C.188 B.A. L.1068 J.D. [Ⓐ Borton,P.&C.]
*PRACTICE AREAS: Business Litigation; Constitutional Law; Insurance Defense.
Dotterweich, John P. '63 '88 C.190 B.A. L.1243 J.D.
(adm. in AR; not adm. in CA) Jud. Research Atty., Supr. Ct.
Dowd, Robert E. ....................... '45 '80 C.101 B.A. L.1127 J.D. 930 Truxton Ave.
**Draper, Jack Alden, II**, (BV) ............ '50 '75 C.605 B.A. L.800 J.D. [J.A.Draper]⊙
*LANGUAGES: German, Indonesian, Spanish and Cantonese.

**Draper, Jack A., Law Offices of, (BV)**
**901 Tower Way, Suite 301, 93309⊙**
**Telephone: 805-322-7272 FAX: 805-322-9359**
**Jack Alden Draper II.**
**Environmental, Natural Resources, Employment, Real Estate and International Law, Trials in all Courts.**
**Los Angeles, California Office: 2121 Avenue of the Stars, Suite 1750. Telephone: 805-322-7272. FAX: 805-322-9359.**

*See Professional Biographies, LOS ANGELES, CALIFORNIA*

Drennan, James H. .............................................. '46 '94 L.464 J.D. 1801 18th St.
Duncan, James M. ................................ '55 '92 C.558 B.S. L.464 J.D. [Griffin C.]
Dunn, Philip E., Jr. .......... '51 '77 C.602 B.A. L.398 J.D. 200 New Stine Rd., Suite 195
**Dunphy, Ned E.**, (CV) ........................................ '58 '87 C.025 [Ⓐ Klein,W.D.G.&M.]
*LANGUAGES: Spanish.
*PRACTICE AREAS: Personal Injury; Negligence Litigation; Product Liability.
Edmonston, Craig A., (CV) ................ '59 '87 C.273 B.A. L.1188 J.D. [Noriega&A.]
**Ehrlich, Melvin L.**, (BV) .............. '45 '74 C&L.378 B.S., J.D. [Ⓐ Klein,W.D.G.&M.]
*PRACTICE AREAS: Oil and Gas Law; Environmental Law; Real Estate Law.
Elwell, David A. ........................ '59 '85 C.878 B.A. L.464 J.D. 918 Truxtun Ave.
Errea, Larry A. ..................... '45 '76 C.1212 B.S. L.1148 J.D. 1830 Truxtun Ave.
Etcheverry, Louis P., (BV) ............... '40 '74 C.740 B.S. L.336 J.D. [Etcheverry&N.]
Etcheverry & Noriega, (BV) ............................................. 3300 Truxtun Avenue

**Etienne, Linda, (BV) '54 '78 C&L.420 J.D.**
**4140 Truxtun Avenue, Suite 200, 93309**
**Telephone: 805-633-2341 Fax: 805-321-9016**
***PRACTICE AREAS: General Business Litigation.**
**General Business, Real Estate, Civil Litigation and Appellate Practice in all State and Federal Courts.**

*See Professional Biographies, BAKERSFIELD, CALIFORNIA*

Eyherabide, Dominic P., Jr., (BV) ............... '50 '78 C.112 B.A. L.770 J.D. 1331 L St.
Fachin, Gary M., (BV) ....................... '48 '75 C.112 B.A. L.767 J.D. 110 S. Montclair

CAA9P

CALIFORNIA—BAKERSFIELD MARTINDALE-HUBBELL LAW DIRECTORY 1997

**Fagre, Nathan E.** '55 '86 C&L.309 A.B., J.D.
(adm. in NY; not adm. in CA) Sr. V.P. & Gen. Coun., Occident Oil & Gas Corp.
*RESPONSIBILITIES: International; Energy; Corporate.
Fairman, Robert P., Jr. .............. '54 '92 C.477 B.S. L.1212 J.D. 5201 California Ave.
Falk, Gregory P., (CV) .............. '53 '77 C.1109 B.A. L.426 J.D. [Falk&F.]
Falk, Stephanie H. .............. '55 '85 C.1109 B.A. L.426 J.D. [Falk&F.]
Falk & Falk, (CV) .............. 5001 E. Commerce Ctr. Dr.
Fallgatter, Thomas C., (BV) .............. '46 '73 C.112 B.A. L.1065 J.D. 1605 "G" St.
Farley, Sean E. .............. '64 '91 C.602 B.B.A. L.1049 J.D. 1712 E. St.
**Farr, G. Neil**, (AV) .............. '32 '61 C.112 A.B. L.1065 J.D. [Young W.]
*PRACTICE AREAS: Domestic Relations; Litigation.
Faulkner, James L., (BV) .............. '39 '74 C.766 B.A. L.1190 J.D. [Faulkner&F.]
Faulkner, Kathleen E, (CV) .............. '42 '87 [Faulkner&F.]
Faulkner & Faulkner, (BV) .............. P.O. Box 2810
**Feher, Thomas P.**, (CV) .............. '63 '90 C.763 B.A. L.1049 J.D. [Ⓐ LeBeau,T.L.M.&C.]
*LANGUAGES: Hungarian.
Fekete, Frank J. .............. '44 '69 C.705 A.B. L.309 J.D. Gen. Coun., Schools Legal Servs.
Felice, Lee P. .............. '48 '74 C.770 B.S.C. L.767 J.D. Mun. J.
Ferguson, Michael D. '44 '77 C.855 B.A. L.352 J.D.
(adm. in IA; not adm. in CA) Dir., Mojave Pipeline Co.
**Ferrari, Greg L.** .............. '52 '93 C.1042 B.A. L.1137 J.D. [Ⓐ Borton,P.&C.]
*PRACTICE AREAS: Municipal Law; Estate Planning; Probate; Corporate Law.
Fields, Larry L. .............. '59 '88 C.1212 B.A. L.61 J.D. [Fields&H.]
Fields & Humphrey .............. 2211 17th St.
Fillerup, David J., (CV) .............. '54 '84 C.101 B.A. L.464 J.D. 1801 Oak St.
**Findley, Kevin C.**, (BV) .............. '53 '79 C.502 B.A. L.990 J.D. [Ⓐ Klein,W.D.G.&M.]
*PRACTICE AREAS: Estate Planning; Probate Law; Trust Law; Pension and Profit Sharing Law; ERISA.
**Fisher, Arthur F., (A Professional Corporation)**, (BV) '29 '55
C.793 B.S. L.972 J.D. [Goldberg&F.]
*PRACTICE AREAS: Personal Injury Law; Workers Compensation Law; Business Law.
Foley, Therese M. .............. '51 '76 C.770 B.A. L.1066 J.D. 2721 Drake St.
**Fontes, Marshall S.** .............. '61 '89 C.473 B.S. L.930 J.D. [Ⓐ Robinson,P.&L.]
*PRACTICE AREAS: Civil Litigation.
**Foster, Luke A.** .............. '66 '93 C.112 B.S. L.464 J.D. [Ⓐ Robinson,P.&L.]
*PRACTICE AREAS: Civil Litigation.
Fowler, Peter W. .............. '27 '53 C.967 B.A. L.608 J.D. Workers Comp. J.
Francisco, Kelly Allen, (CV) .............. '52 '79 C.112 A.B. L.1065 J.D. [K.A.Francisco]
Francisco, Kelly Allen, A Professional Corporation, (CV) .............. P.O. Box 2263
Franks, Cynthia J. .............. '59 '84 C.1212 B.A. L.426 J.D. Dep. Dist. Atty.
Frassinelli, Louis E. .............. '42 '74 C.112 M.A. L.426 J.D. 1301 "L" St.
Friedman, Gary T. .............. '43 '69 C.112 B.A. L.1066 J.D. Supr. Ct. J.
Fuller, Peggy S. .............. '54 '80 C.112 B.A. L.809 J.D. P.O. Box 41508
**Gale, Paul A.** .............. '67 '94 C.267 B.A. L.464 J.D. [Ⓐ P.Kavanagh]
*PRACTICE AREAS: Bankruptcy.
**Gall, Todd A.** .............. '68 '95 C.1074 B.A. L.1188 J.D. [Ⓐ Young W.]
*PRACTICE AREAS: Personal Injury Litigation; Business Litigation; Commercial Litigation.
**Ganong, Philip W.**, (BV) .............. '53 '79 C.112 A.B. L.1065 J.D. [Ganong&K.]
*LANGUAGES: German.
*PRACTICE AREAS: Business Litigation; Personal Injury; Oil and Gas Litigation; Wrongful Termination.

**Ganong & Kleier, (BV)**
**924 Truxtun Avenue, 93301**
**Telephone: 805-327-3337 Fax: 805-327-3395**
**Members of Firm: Philip W. Ganong; Timothy L. Kleier.**
**General Civil Trial Practice, Oil & Gas, Personal Injury, Labor and Business Litigation, Medical and Legal Malpractice.**
***See Professional Biographies, BAKERSFIELD, CALIFORNIA***

Garcia, Christine M. .............. '— '91 C.768 B.A. L.1065 J.D. Dep. Dist. Atty.
Garcia, Louis .............. '63 '89 C.846 B.A./B.S. L.1066 J.D. Kern County Dep. Co. Coun.
Gardiner, Robert J., (CV) .............. '30 '78 C.112 B.A. L.1221 J.D. 4219 Glencannon
Gardner, D. Max, (CV) .............. '61 '87 C&L.101 B.A., J.D. 5500 Ming Ave.
**Gargano, Roy J.**, (AV) .............. '17 '46 C.740 J.B.A. L.800 LL.B. [Ⓐ Borton,P.&C.]
Garibaldi, Mark J. .............. '59 '89 C.1049 B.A. L.464 J.D. Dep. Dist. Atty.
**Garrett, Jeannette** '54 '87 C&L.846 B.A., J.D.
(adm. in OK; not adm. in CA) Coun., Chevron U.S.A. Production Co.
Garrett, Sharon K., Law Office of .............. '43 '77 C.1074 B.A. L.1065 J.D. 1601 F St.
Gattuso, Guy J., Jr., (CV) .............. '52 '83 C.717 B.A. L.464 J.D. [Gattuso,K.&W.]
Gattuso, Kukmmer & Worthing, (CV) .............. 5531 Business Park, S.
Geraldine, Hilaire Ann .............. '— '62 C.773 B.A. L.397 P.O. Box 9715
Gianquinto, J. J., (BV) .............. '39 '71 C&L.1095 B.A., LL.B. 1601 "H" St., Suite 206
Gibbons, Earle J. .............. '29 '61 C.112 A.B. L.1068 LL.B. Sr. V.P., Karpe Real Estate Ctr.

**Gibbs, Steven G., (CV) '60 '87 C.1154 B.A. L.464 J.D.**
**Arco Tower, 4550 California Avenue Suite 150, 93309**
**Telephone: 805-633-1144 Fax: 805-636-0703**
**Email: gibbs@lightspeed.net**
***PRACTICE AREAS: Real Estate; Employment; Partnerships; Corporations; General Business Litigation.**
**Real Estate, Construction, Partnerships, Corporations, General Business Litigation, Personal Injury Litigation, Labor and Employment Law.**
***See Professional Biographies, BAKERSFIELD, CALIFORNIA***

Gibson, John D., (CV) .............. '46 '83 C.1212 B.A. L.769 J.D. [Gibson&G.]
Gibson, Katherine O., (CV) .............. '52 '82 C.1212 B.A. L.999 J.D. [Gibson&G.]
Gibson & Gibson, (CV) .............. 10000 Ming Ave.
**Giesick, Elizabeth M.** .............. '66 '96 C.36 B.S. L.1137 J.D. [Ⓐ Borton,P.&C.]
Gildner, Stephen P. .............. '50 '77 C.112 B.A. L.1049 J.D. Supr. Ct. J.
Gill, Susan M., (CV) .............. '58 '83 C.800 A.B. L.426 J.D. Dep. Co. Coun.
Giuffre, Joseph G., (BV) .............. '30 '74 C.999 B.S.L. L.1190 LL.B. 1209 Columbus Ave.
**Giumarra, Cynthia A.** '51 '77 C.346 B.S. L.796 J.D.
Asst. Gen. Coun., Chevron U.S.A. Production Co.
Giumarra, John G., Jr. .... '40 '66 C.112 B.S. L.813 LL.B. V.P., Giumarra Vineyards Corp.
**Goe, Pamela L.** .............. '50 '75 C.112 A.B. L.426 J.D. [Mullen&F.]
Goetz, Catherine E. .............. '53 '86 L.1127 J.D. Dep. Dist. Atty.
**Goldberg, David F.**, (AV) .............. '18 '46 C.800 A.B. L.1066 LL.B. [Goldberg&F.]
*PRACTICE AREAS: Business Law; Probate Law.

**Goldberg & Fisher, (AV)**
**(An Association of Attorneys, Not a Partnership)**
**Commonwealth Building, 3300 Truxtun Avenue, Suite 390, 93301-3145**
**Telephone: 805-327-2231 Fax: 805-327-2397**
**David F. Goldberg; Arthur F. Fisher (A Professional Corporation).**
**General Civil Practice in all State and Federal Courts. Personal Injury, Corporation, Probate, Real Property, Commercial, Bankruptcy.**
**Representative Clients: First Trust Bank; Mazzie Trust; Oil Well Service Co.; Great Wester Builders, Inc.; Casa Moore Entities; Alumax Fabricated Products, Inc.; Bender Oil Operations.**
**Reference: Bank of America.**
***See Professional Biographies, BAKERSFIELD, CALIFORNIA***

**Goldner, Barry L.**, (BV) .............. '57 '82 C.154 B.A. L.1068 J.D. [Klein,W.D.G.&M.]
*REPORTED CASES: American National Bank v. Stanfill (1988) 205 Cal. App. 3d 1089.
*PRACTICE AREAS: Business/Commercial Litigation; Agriculture Litigation; Real Estate Litigation; Construction Litigation.
Goldner, Theresa A., Law Offices of, (BV) '57 '82
C.112 B.A. L.1068 J.D. 5000 Calif, Ave. Ste 202
Gonzalez, Arthur I. .............. '54 '82 C&L.426 B.A., J.D. Dep. Pub. Def.
Goodsell, Gerald W. .............. '29 '59 C.112 B.A. L.1068 LL.B. 2731 Talisman
Gordon, Edward .............. '66 '90 C.112 A.B. L.800 J.D. 5201 Truxtun Ave., 3rd Fl.
Gordon, Franklin D., (CV) .............. '60 '85 C.216 B.A. L.464 J.D. [Anton,G.&M.]
Granger, George W., (BV) .............. '30 '58 C&L.477 B.A., J.D. P.O. Box 9965
Grass, Roger Richard .............. '54 '85 C&L.309 B.A., J.D. Coun., Schools Legal Servs.
Green, Jeffrey .............. '59 '84 C.763 B.A. L.1049 J.D. Dist. Attys. Off.
Green, Lisa S. .............. '58 '83 C.267 B.S. L.763 J.D. Dist. Atty's. Off.
Greer, Lesley Mason .............. '47 '81 C.112 B.A. L.1065 J.D. Sr. Atty., Co. Pub. Def.
Griffin, David R., (BV) .............. '52 '77 C.1212 B.A. L.426 J.D. [Griffin C.]
Griffin Carrick, (BV) .............. 1675 Chester Ave., 4th Fl.
**Griffin-Lazerson, Kelly A.**, (CV) .............. '61 '90 C.112 B.S. L.1148 J.D. [Ⓐ Werdel&S.]
*PRACTICE AREAS: Labor Relations and Employment (Management); Civil Trial and Appellate Practice; Agricultural; Construction Law.
**Grogan, Carol J.** .............. '49 '92 C.608 B.S.Ed. L.1049 J.D. [Ⓐ Klein,W.D.G.&M.]
*PRACTICE AREAS: Business Litigation; Health Care Law.
Halderson, Clark A. '42 '67 C.378 B.A. L.623 J.D.
(adm. in OK; not adm. in CA) 1200 Discovery Dr.
**Hale, Timothy C.** .............. '67 '96 C.1060 B.A. L.878 J.D. [Ⓐ Borton,P.&C.]

**Hall, John C., Law Offices of, (BV) '54 '81 C.112 B.S. L.464 J.D.**
**Suite 114 1200 Truxtun Avenue, 93301**
**Telephone: 805-328-1200 Telecopier: 805-328-1281**
***PRACTICE AREAS: Medical/Pharmaceutical Malpractice Litigation; Product Liability Litigation; Personal Injury Negligence Litigation; Insurance Law.**
**General Trial Practice. Personal Injury, Products Liability, Medical Malpractice, Toxic Tort Litigation, Environmental Law, Business Litigation, Employment Law and Insurance Law.**
***See Professional Biographies, BAKERSFIELD, CALIFORNIA***

**Hall, Laurence C.** .............. '47 '74 C.800 B.A. L.809 J.D. [Ⓐ Klein,W.D.G.&M.]
*PRACTICE AREAS: Products Liability Law; Premises Liability Law; Insurance Law.
**Hamilton, Thomas I.** '48 '75
C.813 B.A. L.800 J.D. Mng. Coun., Occidental Oil & Gas Corp.
Hanna, Brophy, MacLean, McAleer & Jensen, (AV)
200 N. Stine Rd. (⊙San Fran., Fresno, Sacramento, Oakland, Redding, Santa Rosa, Salinas, Stockton & San Bernardino)
**Harding, Robert D.**, (BV) .............. '49 '74 C.112 B.A. L.1065 J.D. [Clifford&B.]
*PRACTICE AREAS: Civil Litigation.
**Harper, Scott L.**, (CV) .............. '61 '91 L.464 J.D. [Ⓐ Clifford&B.]
*PRACTICE AREAS: Civil Litigation.
**Harris, Alan B.** .............. '55 '82 C.112 B.A. L.61 J.D. [Ⓐ Byrum,H.B.&D.]
*PRACTICE AREAS: Civil Litigation; Title Insurance Defense; Real Property Law.
Hartsell, Stephen L. .............. '50 '80 C.154 B.A. L.770 J.D. Coun.
Hartsock, Robert W., (CV) .............. '57 '83 C.932 B.B.A. L.1049 J.D. [McMurtrey&H.]
Haut, Andrew R., (CV) .............. '53 '78 C.1120 B.S. L.990 J.D. 4664 American Ave.
Hays, Dennis R., (BV) '43 '72 C.101 B.S. L.1067 J.D.
V.P., Fin., Centre For Neuro Skills
Heap, Edw. L., (BV) .............. '28 '57 C.999 L.800 LL.B. 4205 Planz Rd.
Heider, Tony K., (BV) .............. '48 '73 C.766 B.A. L.767 J.D. Chf. Dep. Pub. Def.
Henderson, Elizabeth Ann .............. '50 '90 C.768 B.S. L.464 J.D. 1415 18th St.
Henry, Russell B. .............. '18 '46 L.1065 LL.B. Dep. Pub. Def.
Herstam, David N. .............. '42 '70 C.36 B.S. L.37 J.D. Dep. Pub. Def. [Ⓐ Young W.]
**Hicks, Russell B.** .............. '49 '76 C.101 B.A. L.800 J.D. [Ⓐ Young W.]
*LANGUAGES: Spanish.
*REPORTED CASES: Dwyer v. Crocker National Bank, 194 Cal. App. 3d 1418 (2nd Dist. 1987).
*PRACTICE AREAS: Business Law; Business Litigation; Personal Injury Litigation.
Hill, J. Suzanne .............. '51 '83 C.549 B.A. L.990 J.D. Sr. Atty., Atlantic Richfield Co.
Hinds, Leo M. .............. '62 '94 C.1212 B.S. L.999 J.D. 1600 Truxtun Ave.
Hirsch, Gerald S., (CV) .............. '39 '72 C.763 B.A. L.767 J.D. Dep. Pub. Def.

**Hislop, Jack B., (BV) '26 '54 C&L.813 A.B., LL.B.**
**Suite 420, 5201 California Avenue, 93309**
**Telephone: 805-321-9900 FAX: 805-327-0137**
***PRACTICE AREAS: Insurance Defense; Personal Injury; Probate; Products Liability; Insurance Law.**
**Associates: Lorna Hislop Brumfield.**
**Insurance Defense, Personal Injury, Real Property, Probate, Civil Litigation, Products Liability and Insurance Law.**
***See Professional Biographies, BAKERSFIELD, CALIFORNIA***

**Hitchcock, Richard E.**, (AV) .............. '25 '52 C.112 B.A. L.1065 J.D. [Borton,P.&C.]
*PRACTICE AREAS: Commercial/Real Estate Litigation; Personal Injury and Casualty Defense (including Malpractice); Insurance Litigation.
**Holland, Kenneth A.**, (AV) .............. '47 '73 C.112 B.A. L.602 J.D. [Byrum,H.B.&D.]
*REPORTED CASES: United States vs. Turcotte, 515 F.2d 145, (CA 2 1975); States vs. DiMuro, 540 F.2d 503 (CA 1 1976); J. Paul Getty Museum vs. County of Los Angeles, 248 Cal. App. 3d 600 (1980); Rancho La Costa vs. County of San Diego, 111 Cal.App.3d 54, (1980); Pope vs. State Board of Equalization, 146 Cal.App.3d 1132 (1983).
*PRACTICE AREAS: General Civil Litigation; Real Property; Title Insurance Defense; Professional Negligence Defense; Administrative Agencies.
Hoover, Frank A. .............. '47 '72 C.112 B.A. L.1068 J.D. Mun. Ct. J.
Hornback, William A., (CV) .............. '48 '79 C.267 B.S. L.464 J.D. 2229 19th St.
**Hoss, Winifred Thomson**, (BV) .............. '51 '81 C.112 B.S. L.1067 J.D. [Ⓐ Clifford&B.]
*PRACTICE AREAS: Business Transactions; Agricultural Law; Business Formation; Real Estate; Estate Planning.
Houle, Robert E., (CV) .............. '50 '78 C.112 A.B. L.426 J.D. 323 18th St.
Howland, Christian G. .............. '64 '90 C.299 B.A. L.1049 J.D. 1405 Commercial Way
**Howry, Scott D.** .............. '68 '93 C.154 B.A. L.770 J.D. [Ⓐ Young W.]
*PRACTICE AREAS: Business Litigation; Commercial Litigation; Real Estate Litigation; Construction Litigation.
Huffman, David A. .............. '32 '67 C.1060 B.A. L.464 J.D. 3000 Elmhurst Dr.
**Hughes, Joseph D.** .............. '68 '93 C.112 B.A. L.770 J.D. [Ⓐ Kuhs,P.&S.]

**Hugie, Eldon R., (AV) '32 '60 C.877 B.S. L.122 J.D.**
**841 Mohawk Street, Suite 140, 93309**
**Telephone: 805-328-0200 Fax: 805-328-0204**
**State and Federal Taxation, Probate, Estate Planning, Business, Partnership, Trust, Corporate, Agriculture and Real Estate Laws.**
**Representative Clients: Tri-Fanucchi Farms, Inc.; Kern College Land Co.**
**Reference: Valliwide Bank (Bakersfield Main Branch).**
***See Professional Biographies, BAKERSFIELD, CALIFORNIA***

Hulsy, James R., (BV) .............. '49 '79 C.112 B.S. L.1190 J.D. [Hulsy&H.]
Hulsy & Hulsy, (BV) .............. 412 Truxtun Avenue
Humphrey, Kyle J. .............. '57 '85 C.763 B.A. L.1137 J.D. [Fields&H.]
Irby, John R. .............. '45 '78 C.766 B.A. L.408 J.D. Dep. Co. Coun.
**Israel, Mark R.** .............. '62 '86 C.645 B.A. L.1068 J.D. [Daniels,B.&F.]⊙

CAA10P

# PRACTICE PROFILES

# CALIFORNIA—BAKERSFIELD

**Jacobson, Hansen, Najarian & Flewallen, A Professional Corporation**
(See Fresno)

Jagels, Edward R., (BV) .................... '49 '74 C.813 A.B. L.1065 Dist. Atty.
Jameson, Dustin N. .............. '18 '47 C.629 B.S. L.813 LL.B. 208 Fairway Dr.‡
**Jamieson, Krystyna L.,** (CV) ...... '64 '90 C.174 B.A. L.128 J.D. [Ⓐ Klein,W.D.G.&M.]
**Jamieson, Thomas J., Jr.** .......... '63 '93 C.112 B.A. L.464 J.D. [Ⓐ Klein,W.D.G.&M.]
 *PRACTICE AREAS: Business Litigation; Personal Injury.
Jelletich, John D. .................. '27 '53 C.990 L.1065 J.D. Ret. Supr. Ct. J.
**Jenkins, J. Craig,** (BV) ................ '41 '66 C.999 L.809 LL.B. [Jenkins,B.&B.]
**Jenkins, Barnes & Brady,** (BV)
**1675 Chester Avenue, Suite 300, 93301**
Telephone: 805-631-2196 Facsimile: 805-631-2199
Members of the Firm: J. Craig Jenkins; Karen S. Barnes; Mathew B. Brady. Associate: Jennifer A. McGill.
General Civil Practice in all State and Federal Courts, with emphasis in Health Care Law, Professional Liability Defense, Oil and Gas Law, Personal Injury Defense, Public Entity Defense, Civil and Business Litigation, Negligence, Products Liability and Insurance Law.

See Professional Biographies, BAKERSFIELD, CALIFORNIA

Jennison, Patrick E., (A P.C.), (CV) '52 '77 C.112 B.A. L.809 J.D.
 5000 California Ave.
Johnson, Craig E. ................... '61 '89 C&L.101 B.A., J.D. 5330 Office Ctr. Court
**Jones, Mark Alan** ................... '54 '90 C.1272 B.S. L.464 J.D. [Borton,P.&C.]
 *PRACTICE AREAS: Business and Real Estate Litigation; Personal Injury and Casualty Defense Litigation; Medical Malpractice and Professional Negligence Defense Litigation; Oil, Gas and Mineral Law and Litigation; Environmental Law and Litigation.
**Joyce, Bob H.,** (BV) ................. '47 '78 C.112 B.A. L.464 J.D. [LeBeau,T.L.M.&C.]
**Joyce, Randall Steven** ............... '50 '89 C.605 B.A. L.1186 J.D. [Ⓐ Borton,P.&C.]
 *PRACTICE AREAS: Medical Malpractice; Workers' Compensation; Labor/Employment Law; Personal Injury.
Jurich, John A., (AV) ............. '45 '78 C.1077 J.D. L.426 J.D. [Patterson,R.L.G.&J.]
**Kaia, Michael A.,** (BV) ............ '53 '86 C.267 B.S.B.A. L.1189 J.D. [Young W.]
 *PRACTICE AREAS: Real Property Litigation; Contract Litigation.
Karcher, Steven M. ................ '56 '89 C.1073 B.A. L.245 J.D. [Borton,P.&C.]
 *PRACTICE AREAS: Business Litigation; Alternative Dispute Resolution; Bankruptcy and Creditor's Rights; Professional Liability Defense.
Kates, George W., (AV) ................... '22 '49 C&L.260 J.D. [Kates&P.]
Kates & Davis, (AV) ....................... 1700 K St., Ste., 200
Katz, Steven M., (CV) ................. '61 '88 C.112 B.A. L.426 J.D. Dep. Dist. Atty.
**Kavanagh, Patrick, Law Offices of,** (BV) '53 '81 C.823 B.S. L.767 J.D.
**1331 "L" Street, 93301**
Telephone: 805-322-5553 Fax: 805-322-5779
 *PRACTICE AREAS: Bankruptcy; Debtors/Creditors; Trustee Law; Creditors Committees Law.
Associates: Paul A. Gale.
Practice Limited to Bankruptcy Law Including Representation of Debtors, Creditors, Trustees and Creditors Committees.
Reference: California Republic Bank.

See Professional Biographies, BAKERSFIELD, CALIFORNIA

Kelly, John I. ........................ '32 '63 C.871 B.S. L.813 LL.B. Supr. Ct. J.
Kendall, Donald G., (BV) ........... '11 '33 C.813 B.A. L.1065 J.D. P.O. Box 10929
Kennedy, Dawn, (CV) ............... '54 '79 C.1212 B.A. L.1077 J.D. 1000 Truxtun Ave.
Kilpatrick, Michael R., (CV) ........ '56 '82 C&L.1137 B.S.L., J.D. 1700 K St.
**Kimball, Claude P.,** (AV) ............ '39 '66 C.770 B.A. L.1068 LL.B. [Klein,W.D.G.&M.]
 *PRACTICE AREAS: Taxation Law; Business Planning; Acquisitions, Divestitures and Mergers; Estate Planning; Partnership Taxation.
**Kimble, MacMichael & Upton, A Professional Corporation**
(See Fresno)

King, Robert E., (AV) ................. '25 '50 C.934 L.800 J.D. 10000 Ming Ave.
**Kinney, J. Nile,** (BV) ............... '53 '83 C&L.800 B.A., J.D. [LeBeau,T.L.M.&C.]
Kleier, Loren N. ................... '62 '90 C.763 B.A. L.1049 J.D. 1830 Truxtun Ave.
**Kleier, Timothy L.,** (CV) ............ '57 '84 C&L.1049 B.A., J.D. [Ganong&K.]
 *PRACTICE AREAS: Business Litigation; Business and Real Estate Transactions; Construction; Agri Business; Environmental.
Klein, Alan E. .................... '47 '72 C.112 A.B. L.1068 J.D. Mun. Ct. J.
**Klein, Anthony J., (Inc.),** (AV) ... '38 '64 C.813 A.B. L.1066 LL.B. [Klein,W.D.G.&M.]
 *REPORTED CASES: B.P. Alaska Exploration Nahama Weagant Energy Co. (1988) 199 Cal.App. 3d 1240.
 *PRACTICE AREAS: Complex Litigation; Products Liability Litigation; Environmental Litigation; Oil and Gas Litigation; Business Litigation.
**Klein, Wegis, DeNatale, Goldner & Muir, LLP,** (AV) [Ⓑ]
A Partnership including Professional Corporations
(Formerly Di Giorgio, Davis, Klein, Wegis, Duggan & Friedman)
**ARCO Tower, 4550 California Avenue, Second Floor, P.O. Box 11172, 93389-1172**
Telephone: 805-395-1000 Telecopier: 805-326-0418
Email: kwdgm@kwdgm.com
Thomas R. Davis (1920-1990). Members of Firm: Anthony J. Klein (Inc.); Ralph B. Wegis (Inc.); Thomas V. DeNatale, Jr.; Gregory A. Muir; Barry L. Goldner; Jay L. Rosenlieb; David J. Cooper; Claude P. Kimball; William A. Bruce. Associates: Denise Martin; David L. Saine; Laurence C. Hall (Recognized experienced Trial Lawyer in the fields of Trial Law and Products Liability by the California Trial Lawyers Association); William H. Slocumb; Ned E. Dunphy; Barry E. Rosenberg; Kirk S. Tracey; Christopher P. Burger; Kevin C. Findley; Carol J. Grogan; Jose Benavides; Michael S. Abril; Melvin L. Ehrlich; Krystyna L. Jamieson; Stacy Henry Bowman; Thomas J. Jamieson, Jr.; Jeffrey W. Noe. Of Counsel: Bruce F. Bunker.
General Civil Trial and Appellate Practice. Federal Trial Practice, Commercial, Litigation, Bankruptcy, Construction, Eminent Domain, Agriculture, Real Estate, Employment Law, Environmental, ERISA Litigation, Estate Planning, Negligence, Oil and Gas, Pension and Profit Sharing, Probate, Products Liability, Tax.
Representative Clients: Bank of America; Great Western Bank; Mojave Pipeline Co.; Transamerican Title Insurance Co.; Dean Whittier Reynolds, Inc.; California Republic Bank; San Joaquin Bank; Nahama & Weagant Energy Co.; Freymiller Trucking, Inc.; Westinghouse Electric Co.

See Professional Biographies, BAKERSFIELD, CALIFORNIA

Kohler, Andrea S. (Wall), (BV) ........... '64 '89 C.826 B.A. L.990 J.D. Dep. Dist. Atty.
**Kohler, Gregory J.,** (CV) ............ '60 '89 C.1109 B.A. L.990 J.D. [Clifford&B.]
 *LANGUAGES: Spanish.
 *PRACTICE AREAS: Civil Litigation; Insurance Coverage; Insurance Litigation.
Konnoff, Michael S., (BV) ............ '41 '70 C&L.284 B.B.A., J.D. 1308 Chester Ave.
**Koontz, Hal M., Law Offices of,** (BV) '49 '74 C.112 B.A. L.426 J.D.
**2821 "H" Street, 93301**
Telephone: 805-634-1141 Fax: 805-327-1923
(Certified Specialist, Taxation Law, The State Bar of California Board of Legal Specialization).
Estate Planning, Estate Administration, Taxation Law, and Business Transactions.

See Professional Biographies, BAKERSFIELD, CALIFORNIA

Krech, Judith L., (CV) ............... '— '90 C.763 B.A. L.1049 J.D. Dep. Dist. Atty.
Kronick, Robert A., (BV) ............ '53 '84 C.112 B.A. L.464 J.D. 2931 20th St.
**Kuenzinger, Bill J.** ............... '65 '92 C.1079 B.A. L.1187 J.D. [Clifford&B.]
 *PRACTICE AREAS: General Business Planning Law; Litigation.
**Kuhs, Robert G.** .................... '65 '92 C.112 B.A. L.809 J.D. [Kuhs,P.&S.]
**Kuhs, William C.,** (AV) ............... '37 '66 C.112 B.A. L.276 J.D. [Kuhs,P.&S.]
**Kuhs, Parker & Stanton,** (AV)
**Suite 200, 1200 Truxtun Avenue, P.O. Box 2205, 93303**
Telephone: 805-322-4004 FAX: 805-322-2906
Email: kpslaw@maillightspeed//.net

(This Listing Continued)

**Kuhs, Parker & Stanton** (Continued)
William C. Kuhs; James R. Parker, Jr.; David B. Stanton;—Robert G. Kuhs; Joseph D. Hughes. General Civil, Trial and Appellate Practice. Administrative, Construction, Environmental, Municipal, Oil and Gas, Real Property and Water Law.
Reference: Home Savings of America (Bakersfield Main Branch).

See Professional Biographies, BAKERSFIELD, CALIFORNIA

Kummer, Dixon G. ..................... '59 '86 C.101 B.S. L.990 J.D. [Gattuso,K.&W.]
**Kuney, Scott K.,** (BV) ................ '56 '83 C.112 B.A. L.464 J.D. [Young W.]
 *PRACTICE AREAS: Water Rights Law; Eminent Domain.
**Lafranchise, Paul** .................. '50 '78 C.128 B.A. L.280 J.D. [Borton,P.&C.]
 *LANGUAGES: Spanish.
 *PRACTICE AREAS: Labor and Employment (Management).
Lahey, James A., Jr. ................ '60 '86 C.112 B.A. L.464 J.D. 333 Palmer Dr., Suite 200
Lahiri, Indra, (CV) ................... '56 '81 C&L.051 B.A. 1601 F Street, 2nd Fl.
**Lampe, David R.,** (BV) ............... '52 '77 C.1212 B.A. L.770 J.D. [LeBeau,T.L.M.&C.]
Langland, Paul A. .................. '54 '80 C.378 B.A. L.900 J.D. 2500 Beech St.
Lanier, James T., (CV) ................ '35 '71 L.1095 J.D. 1700 N. Chester Ave.
**LeBeau, Bernard G., Jr.,** (BV) ....... '53 '78 C&L.770 B.S.C., J.D. [LeBeau,T.L.M.&C.]
**LeBeau, Thelen, Lampe, McIntosh & Crear,** (AV)
**5001 East Commerce Drive Suite 300, 93309-1667**
Telephone: 805-325-8962 FAX: 805-325-1127
Members of Firm: David R. Lampe; Dennis R. Thelen; Bernard G. LeBeau, Jr.; Thomas S. McIntosh; Thomas A. Crear; J. Nile Kinney; Bob H. Joyce;—W. Steven Shayer; Thomas P. Feher; Kerry L. Lockhart.
Civil Trial Practice in all State and Federal Courts. Insurance, Employment Litigation, Business, Real Estate, Corporate, Partnership, Taxation, Probate, Estate Planning, Commercial, Agricultural, Administrative and Oil and Gas Law.
Representative Clients: Corporate: Federal Land Bank and Production Credit Assn.; Greater Bakersfield Memorial Hospital. Insurance: Ohio Casualty; Farmers Insurance Group; Fireman's Fund Insurance; Atlantic Insurance Co.; Southern California Physicians Insurance Exchange; California Casualty.

See Professional Biographies, BAKERSFIELD, CALIFORNIA

Ledger, Brian M. ..................... '60 '91 C.649 B.S. L.477 J.D. [Ⓐ Byrum,H.B.&D.]
 *PRACTICE AREAS: Environmental Litigation and Regulatory Compliance; Real Property Litigation; Business Litigation.
**Leggio, Anthony L.,** (BV) ............ '52 '77 C.169 B.A. L.464 J.D. [Clifford&B.]
 *PRACTICE AREAS: General Business Planning Law; Litigation.
Lemucchi, Timothy J., (AV) ........... '37 '66 C.813 B.A. L.276 J.D. [Chain,Y.L.C.&S.]
**Leon, David F.** .................... '67 '94 C&L.112 B.S., J.D. [Ⓐ Young W.]
 *PRACTICE AREAS: Business Law.
Leverett, Gerald M., (BV) ............ '45 '71 C.112 B.A. L.846 J.D. 1400 Chester Ave.
Lewis, Michael Bruce ................ '52 '83 C.1212 B.A. L.1077 J.D. Dep. Dist. Atty.
Lewy, Timothy J. .................... '48 '76 C.112 B.A. L.770 J.D. [T.J.Lewy]
Lewy, Timothy J., Inc. ................................... 18400 Hwy. 65
Linford, John B. .................... '56 '88 C.792 B.S. L.623 J.D. 1701 Westwind Dr.
**Lockhart, Kerry L.** ................. '62 '96 C&L.347 B.A., J.D. [Ⓐ LeBeau,T.L.M.&C.]
**Logan, Gary L.,** (BV) ............... '53 '79 C.147 B.A. L.1049 J.D. [Robinson,P.&L.]
 *PRACTICE AREAS: Civil Litigation.
Long, Richard M. .................... '34 '64 C.321 B.S. L.94 LL.B. 3200 21st. St.
Long, Thomas W. .................... '50 '78 C.112 B.A. L.1137 J.D. P.O. Box 80812
Lorenz, Eugene R. ................... '45 '71 C.494 B.A. L.1066 J.D. 1227 Calif. Ave.
Lueje, Anna '62 '91 C.367 B.A. L.477 J.D.
 (adm. in NY; not adm. in CA) Coun., Occidental Oil & Gas Co.
 *LANGUAGES: Italian and Spanish.
 *RESPONSIBILITIES: International Law; International Oil and Gas; Corporate.
Lukehart, Michael C., (BV) ........... '53 '80 C.840 L.809 J.D. Dep. Pub. Def.
Lunardini, Lawrence M. ............. '43 '69 C.602 A.B. L.276 J.D. City Atty.‡
Lund, Jack E. ....................... '22 '52 C.999 L.809 LL.B. 5206 Ojai Dr.‡
**Lynch, Craig M.,** (CV) ............... '58 '82 C&L.426 B.A., J.D. [Lynch&L.]◎
 *PRACTICE AREAS: Civil Litigation; Business Law; Oil and Gas; Real Estate Law.
**Lynch and Lynch,** (AV)
**4800 Eastern Drive, Suite 114, 93309**◎
Telephone: 805-322-8396 Fax: 805-328-0380
Craig M. Lynch.
Civil Litigation, Personal Injury, Negligence and Business Law.
San Fernando, California Office: 501 South Brand Boulevard, Suite 5. Telephone: 818-361-3838. Fax: 818-361-1126.

See Professional Biographies, BAKERSFIELD, CALIFORNIA

Mack, Henry C., Jr., (CV) ............ '31 '60 C&L.813 B.A., LL.B. 1600 Truxtun Ave.
Maclin, Bruce, (BV) ................. '42 '68 C.112 A.B. L.1066 J.D. San Joaquin Bank
**Madison, James D.,** (CV) ............ '43 '72 C.378 B.S. L.426 J.D. [Ⓐ Werdel&S.]
 *PRACTICE AREAS: Appellate Practice; Civil Trial.
Magnus, Melvin Walter, (CV) ........ '11 '40 L.1001 LL.B. 828 Chester Ave.
Maher, Daniel R. ..................... '45 '70 C&L.912 B.A., J.D. 1217 "L" St.
Malahowski, Roy F. '44 '74
 C.508 B.A. L.174 J.D. Greater Bakersfield Legal Assistance, Inc.
Maloney, James J. '51 '88 C.1169 B.A. L.1067 J.D.
 Greater Bakersfield Legal Assistance
Manolakas, George, (BV) ............. '51 '76 C.800 B.S. L.990 J.D. 1430 Truxton Ave.
Marchbanks, Michael L., (AV) ....... '50 '80 C.112 B.A. L.1065 J.D. 8311 E. Brundage Ln.
Marcks, R. Michael .................. '46 '77 C.549 L.1026 LL.B. [Hanna,B.M.M.&J.]
**Marek, Frank E., Jr.** '47 '73 C&L.276 B.S.F.S., J.D.
 (adm. in DC; not adm. in CA) Manag. Coun., Occidental Oil & Gas Corp.
 *RESPONSIBILITIES: International Oil and Gas.
Marino, Laura C. .................... '59 '84 C&L.378 B.A., J.D. Asst. City Atty.
Mark, Ronald H. ..................... '47 '94 C.1131 B.S. L.911 J.D. 10000 Ming Ave.
Marschang, Linda M. ................ '59 '96 C.798 B.S. L.208 J.D. [Ⓐ Borton,P.&C.]
**Martin, Denise** ................... '60 '89 C.112 B.A. L.1065 J.D. [Ⓐ Klein,W.D.G.&M.]
 *PRACTICE AREAS: Products Liability Law; Negligence Litigation; Personal Injury Law.
Martin, George F., (AV) ............. '44 '72 C.1060 B.A. L.1067 J.D. [Borton,P.&C.]
 *PRACTICE AREAS: Commercial/Real Estate Litigation; Personal Injury and Casualty Defense (including Malpractice); Insurance Litigation.
Mayo, Ralph E. '53 '80
 C.1029 B.A. L.1137 J.D. Sr. Coun., Chevron U.S.A. Production Co.
McAtee, Fred S., (BV) ............... '53 '77 C.1212 B.A. L.61 J.D. 1217 "L" St.
McBurnie, Richard G., (BV) .... '49 '74 C.112 B.A. L.1065 J.D. 3761 Bernaro St., Ste. 107
McCarthy, William H. ................ '50 '87 C.813 B.A. L.767 J.D. Dep. Dist. Atty.
**McCartney, N. Thomas,** (BV) ......... '50 '75 C.740 B.A. L.767 J.D. [McCartney&M.]
 *LANGUAGES: Spanish.
 *REPORTED CASES: Clark Equipment Company v. Mastellotto, 87 Cal. App. 3d 88 (1978); American National Bank v. Stanfill, 205 Cal. App. 3d 1089 (1988).
 *PRACTICE AREAS: Business Litigation; Environmental Litigation; Civil Litigation; Personal Injury.
**McCartney & Mercado,** (BV)
**3434 Truxtun Avenue, Suite 280, 93301-3044**
Telephone: 805-327-4147 Telecopier: 805-325-9309
N. Thomas McCartney; Jess A. Mercado.
Business, Civil Trial and Appellate Practice, Business, Insurance, Personal Injury, Real Estate and Commercial Litigation.

(This Listing Continued)

CAA11P

**McCartney & Mercado (Continued)**

**Representative Clients: State Farm Fire and Casualty; Coleman Construction, Inc.; Hartford Accident and Indemnity Co.; Mid State Development Company; Security Pacific National Bank; Reliance United Pacific Surety Managers.**

***See Professional Biographies, BAKERSFIELD, CALIFORNIA***

McCown, Barry L., (CV) . . . '52 '79 C.154 B.A. L.1065 J.D. 5100 Calif. Ave.
**McDermott, Sam** . . . '67 '95 C.1049 L.800 J.D. [A B.L.Price]
**McGill, Jennifer A.** . . . '71 '96 C.112 B.S. L.464 J.D. [A Jenkins,B.&B.]
McGillivray, Len M. . . . '40 '66 C.112 B.S. L.1065 J.D. Supr. Ct. J.
**McIntosh, Thomas S., (BV)** . . . '52 '77 C.906 B.A. L.1049 J.D. [LeBeau,T.L.M.&C.]
McKnight, Benton F., (CV) . . . '60 '85 C.1259 B.S. L.800 J.D. [McKnight,M.M.&M.]
McKnight, Cleve, (CV) . . . '59 '84 C.1259 B.S. L.1065 J.D. [McKnight,M.M.&M.]
McKnight, Eugene W. . . . '22 '55 C.112 L.426 LL.B. 2418 Driller Ave.
McKnight, Ralph L. . . . '24 '56 C.112 B.S. L.1068 LL.B. 305 Truxtun Ave.‡
McKnight, Ralph L., Jr., (BV) . . . '53 '77 C.112 A.B. L.1068 J.D. [McKnight,M.M.&M.]
McKnight, McKnight, McKnight & McKnight, (BV) . . . 305 Truxtun Ave.
McMurtrey, Gene R., (BV) . . . '43 '69 C.426 A.B. L.1065 J.D. [McMurtrey&H.]
McMurtrey & Hartsock, A Professional Corporation, (BV) . . . Suite 100, 2001 22nd Street
McNutt, Charles P. . . . '47 '72 C.112 A.B. L.1067 J.D. Mun. Ct. J.
Meadows, Robert L. . . . '28 '56 C&L.800 A.B., LL.B. 2222 Niles St.
Means, Harvey H., (AV) . . . '23 '53 C.228 L.767 J.D. Mgr., Harry & Ethel West Found.
Mears, Michael P., (BV) . . . '48 '74 C.112 B.A. L.426 J.D. 5500 Ming Ave.
Meier, Bruce N. . . . '41 '67 C.112 B.A. L.1066 J.D. 1801 Panorama Dr.
**Melton, Charles D., (CV)** . . . '62 '87 C.169 B.S. L.1065 J.D. [Clifford&B.]
*PRACTICE AREAS: Commercial Law; Constitutional Law; Creditors' Rights; General Business; Landlord-Tenant.
**Mercado, Jess A., (CV)** . . . '61 '86 C.209 B.A. L.990 J.D. [McCartney&M.]
*LANGUAGES: Spanish and Portuguese.
*PRACTICE AREAS: Insurance; Business; Civil Litigation.
Merenbach, Alice T., (CV) . . . '36 '66 C.112 A.B. L.426 LL.B. P.O. Box 9848
Mettler, Sharon Wallis . . . '48 '73 C.112 B.A. L.1065 J.D. Mun. Ct. J.
Middlebrook, Richard O. . . . '68 '93 C.1253 B.A. L.1067 J.D. 1712 19th St.
**Millar, James E., (CV)** . . . '50 '80 C.112 B.A. L.1065 J.D. [⊡ Young W.]
*PRACTICE AREAS: Personal Injury Law; Labor Law; Workers' Compensation Law; Employment Law Management; Civil Litigation Business.
Miller, Dean J. . . . '51 '86 C.30 B.A. L.990 J.D. 416 Truxtun Ave.
Miller, Michael F. . . . '55 '80 C&L.862 B.S., J.D. 1200 Discovery Dr.
Mitts, Gregory H., (BV) . . . '51 '76 C.1163 L.426 J.D. 1830 Truxtun Ave.
Moffat, Douglas S., (BV) . . . '50 '80 C.112 B.A. L.61 J.D. 1400 Chester Ave.
Monje, Richard A., (CV) . . . '52 '77 C.767 B.A. L.1065 J.D. [Anton,G.&M.]
**Morton, Richard E., (AV)** . . . '40 '72 C.1109 B.A. L.990 J.D. [A Borton,P.&C.]
*PRACTICE AREAS: Insurance Defense; Business Litigation; Construction Defects; Real Property; Environmental Law.
Mosley, Rosa M. . . . '43 '84 C.1097 B.A. L.1137 J.D. 1215 Truxtun
Mueller, Melvin T. . . . '49 '77 C.112 A.B. L.990 J.D. Dep. Pub. Def.
**Muir, Gregory A., (BV)** . . . '50 '82 C.112 B.A. L.767 J.D. [Klein,W.D.G.&M.]
*PRACTICE AREAS: Products Liability Litigation; Personal Injury Negligence Litigation; Psychotherapy Law Litigation.
Mull, Rex R. . . . '26 '54 C.169 A.B. L.813 LL.B. 600 Oleander Ave.
Mullen, Ray T., (CV) . . . '52 '83 L.765 J.D. 1405 Commercial Way

**Mullen & Filippi, (AV)**
**5000 California Avenue Suite 211, 93309⊙**
**Telephone: 805-328-0224**
**Bruce K. Wade; Pamela L. Goe.**
**Insurance Defense, Workers Compensation, Liability and Subrogation.**
**Other California Offices: San Francisco, San Jose, Sacramento, Fresno, Santa Rosa, Long Beach, Salinas, Stockton, Redding, Woodland Hills and Oakland.**

***See Professional Biographies, SAN FRANCISCO, CALIFORNIA***

**Murchison, Bruce K.** '50 '82 C.390 B.A. L.724 J.D.
(adm. in NY; not adm. in CA) Pres., Celeron Corp.
*RESPONSIBILITIES: Corporate Business and Legal.
Murray, Charles E., (BV) . . . '41 '72 C.112 B.A. L.1049 J.D. 2001 22nd St.
Myers, Brett . . . '59 '94 L.1148 J.D. 4909 Stockdale Hwy.
Nairn, John M. . . . '15 '49 C.229 A.B. L.426 LL.B. Ret. Supr. Ct. J.
Nations, Mark L. . . . '54 '81 C&L.101 B.A., J.D. Co. Coun. Off.
Neumeister, William David . . . '51 '80 C.1131 B.A. L.809 J.D. 308 18th St.
**Nichols, Steve W., (BV)** . . . '53 '80 C.877 B.A. L.990 J.D. [Young W.]
*PRACTICE AREAS: Business Litigation; Commercial Litigation; Personal Injury Litigation.
Nickerson, Ralph N. . . . '21 '49 C&L.800 B.S., LL.B. 3701 Harmony Dr.‡
Nisson, Scott H. '52 '77 C&L.831 B.B.A., J.D.
(adm. in PA; not adm. in CA) Gen. Tax Coun., CalResources
**Noe, Jeffrey W.** . . . '67 '93 C.276 A.B. L.112 J.D. [A Klein,W.D.G.&M.]
*PRACTICE AREAS: Labor and Employment Law; Business/Commercial Litigation.
Noland, Peggy . . . '31 '67 C&L.1114 B.S., J.D. Corporate Compliance Consultants, Inc.
Noriega, James E., (BV) . . . '47 '73 C.767 B.A. L.1065 J.D. [Etcheverry&N.]
Noriega, Joseph, (AV) . . . '29 '60 L.800 LL.B. [Noriega&A.]
Noriega, Robert J., (CV) . . . '60 '86 C.1049 B.A. L.1068 J.D. [Noriega&A.]
Noriega & Alexander, (AV) . . . 1801 18th Street
Norris, Arthur B. . . . '64 '91 C.112 B.A. L.426 J.D. Dep. Dist. Atty.
Oberholzer, Richard J. . . . '42 '71 C&L.426 B.S.M.E., J.D. Supr. Ct. J.
**O'Dell, Michael L., (BV)** . . . '55 '80 C.763 A.B. L.1065 J.D. [Clifford&B.]
*PRACTICE AREAS: Civil Litigation; Employment Law.
Olcott, William D., (CV) . . . '48 '88 C.543 B.A. L.546 J.D. 1430 Truxtun Ave., 6th Fl.
Oldaker, Donald . . . '58 '93 C.05 B.A. L.999 J.D. 1801 18th St.
Oldfield, Gerald H. . . . '58 '88 C.1060 B.A. L.1153 J.D. [Yinger&O.]
O'Neil, Gary A., (CV) . . . '42 '77 C.36 B.S. L.1026 J.D. [O'Neil&W.]
O'Neil & Widelock, (CV) . . . 5401 California Avenue, Suite 300 (⊙Los Angeles)
**Osborn, Patrick J., (BV)** . . . '51 '77 C.112 A.B. L.464 J.D. [Clifford&B.]
*PRACTICE AREAS: Civil Litigation.
Owen, Richard D., (CV) '45 '71 C.112 B.S. L.1067 J.D.
Sr. Staff Coun. & Supvr., State Comp. Ins. Fund.
Owens, Mark D., (CV) . . . '59 '84 C.1212 B.A. L.464 J.D. Dep. Pub. Def.
**Pafford, Mark E.** . . . '71 '96 C.990 B.A. L.464 J.D. [A Clifford&B.]
Page, Charles G., III . . . '51 '89 C&L.1137 B.S., J.D. 1315 L St.
**Palmer, William D., (BV)** . . . '43 '69 C.549 B.S. L.1049 J.D. [Robinson,P.&L.]
*PRACTICE AREAS: Civil Litigation; Water Law; Business Law; Public Entity.
Papst, Richard J., (BV) . . . '52 '78 C.36 B.A. L.464 J.D. 1430 Truxton Ave.
**Parker, James R., Jr., (BV)** . . . '47 '74 C.976 B.A. L.1067 J.D. [Kuhs,P.&S.]
Patrick, Kelley D. . . . '62 '92 C&L.1212 J.D. Pub. Def
Patterson, Robert D., (BV) . . . '29 '55 C.112 A.B. L.1066 J.D. 1830 Truxtun Ave.

**Patterson, Ritner, Lockwood, Gartner & Jurich, (AV)**
**A Partnership including Professional Corporations**
**Suite 522, 1415 Eighteenth Street, 93301-5216⊙**
**Telephone: 805-327-4387 FAX: 805-327-9041**
**John A. Jurich;—Marisa S. Vidaurreta.**
**Insurance, Personal Injury, Products Liability, Casualty and Medical Malpractice Law. Trials. Legal Malpractice.**

(This Listing Continued)

**Patterson, Ritner, Lockwood, Gartner & Jurich (Continued)**

**Los Angeles, California Office: Suite 900, 3580 Wilshire Boulevard. Telephone: 213-487-6240.**
**Ventura, California Office: Suite 231, 260 Maple Court. Telephone: 805-644-1061.**
**San Bernardino, California Office: 325 Hospitality Lane, Suite 204. Telephone: 909-885-6063.**

***See Professional Biographies, BAKERSFIELD, CALIFORNIA***

Peake, Alan J., (CV) . . . '60 '88 C.999 L.1186 J.D. [Wall,W.&P.]
Peake, Larry F., (BV) . . . '50 '78 C.112 B.A. L.464 J.D. City Atty. [Wall,W.&P.]
Peden, Jeanne W. . . . '— '82 C.813 A.B. L.61 J.D. P.O. Box 9546
Perkins, Kirk B. . . . '55 '81 C.1212 B.S. L.770 J.D. Dep. Co. Coun.
Perlman, Scott D. . . . '58 '87 C.1078 B.A. L.464 J.D. [Griffin C.]
**Petrini, John F., (AV)** . . . '44 '71 C.112 B.A. L.1067 J.D. [Borton,P.&C.]
*PRACTICE AREAS: Commercial/Real Estate Litigation; Personal Injury and Casualty Defense; Professional E & O; Insurance Litigation; Banking.
Pfister, Charles B. . . . '49 '74 C.591 B.A. L.61 J.D. Mun. Ct. J.
**Pinson, Harley F.** '50 '77
C.112 B.A. L.464 J.D. Mng. Coun., Occidental Oil & Gas Corp.
*RESPONSIBILITIES: Petroleum Resources; International; Contracts.
Pluta, Joseph, (CV) . . . '48 '78 C.103 B.A. L.1049 J.D. 408 18th St.
**Potter, David B., (BV)** . . . '52 '79 C.112 B.A. L.770 J.D. [Arrache,C.&P.]
*PRACTICE AREAS: General Civil Litigation; Collection.
Powelson, Donald L. . . . '48 '76 C.740 B.A. L.767 J.D. [Hanna,B.M.M.&J.]

**Price, Brett L., Law Offices of, (BV) '50 '75 C.112 B.A. L.1067 J.D.**
**Greystone Plaza Building, 841 Mohawk Street, Suite 200, 93309**
**Telephone: 805-323-3400 Fax: 805-323-3957**
**Email: bkfldlaw@aol.com**
**Associate: Sam McDermott.**
**Business and Commercial Law, Litigation, Property Taxation, Bankruptcy, Farm and Ranch Law, Real Estate, Construction Law, Oil and Gas Law.**
**Representative Clients: Kern County; Indepent Pipe and Tubing, Inc.; Century 21 Stroope Realty; Lambourne Travel, Inc.; San Joaquin County; Data Team, Inc.; Ellis Electric; Trico Mechanical, Inc.**

***See Professional Biographies, BAKERSFIELD, CALIFORNIA***

Qadar, Sohaib '65 '90 C.611 B.A. L.150 J.D.
(adm. in OH; not adm. in CA) 1200 Discovery Dr.
Quick, George Wright, (CV) . . . '44 '71 C.766 B.A. L.1065 J.D. 409 17th St.
Raison, Margo A. . . . '60 '88 C.813 A.B. L.426 J.D. Dep. Co. Coun.
Randall, Roger D. . . . '41 '67 C.169 B.A. L.976 LL.B. Supr. Ct. J.
Randolph, Patricia J. . . . '56 '81 C.112 A.B. L.1067 J.D. Co. Coun.
Reedy, John R., (BV) . . . '47 '73 C.1060 B.A. L.1067 J.D. 3434 Truxton Ave.
Reid, Christopher . . . '50 '89 C.112 B.A. L.809 J.D. 6705 Leisure St.
Reid, Dennis N. . . . '28 '61 C&L.145 A.B., J.D. 1415 18th St.
Reynolds, Harry M. . . . '37 '75 C.329 B.S.E.E. L.1068 J.D. 1206 "L" St.
Riebesell, Gary R. . . . '60 '86 C.776 B.A. L.1148 J.D. 1801 Oak St.
Robinson, Glen S. . . . '58 '85 C.112 B.A. L.464 J.D. 1600 Truxtun Ave.
**Robinson, Oliver U., (AV)** . . . '39 '66 C.112 B.A. L.1065 LL.B. [Robinson,P.&L.]
*PRACTICE AREAS: Civil Litigation.

**Robinson, Palmer & Logan, (AV) BB**
**Suite 150, 3434 Truxtun Avenue, 93301**
**Telephone: 805-323-8277 Fax: 805-323-4205**
**Members of Firm: Oliver U. Robinson; William D. Palmer; Gary L. Logan. Associates: Luke A. Foster; Marshall S. Fontes.**
**General Civil and Trial Practice. Insurance Defense, Water Rights, Public, Land Use and Business Law.**

***See Professional Biographies, BAKERSFIELD, CALIFORNIA***

Rodriguez, Daniel, (BV) . . . '53 '80 C.667 B.A. L.112 J.D. 3300 Truxtun Ave.
**Rosenberg, Barry E.** . . . '59 '86 C.102 B.A. L.982 J.D. [A Klein,W.D.G.&M.]
*REPORTED CASES: Hayter Trucking, Inc. v. Shell Western E&P, Inc., (1993) 18 Cal. App. 1; Marques v. Telles Ranch, Inc. (N.D. CA 1995) 11 IER Cases 36.
*PRACTICE AREAS: Labor and Employment Law; Business/Commercial Litigation; Appellate Law; ERISA Litigation.
**Rosenlieb, Jay L., (BV)** . . . '58 '83 C.154 B.A. L.1065 J.D. [Klein,W.D.G.&M.]
*REPORTED CASES: BP Alaska Exploration v. Nahama Weagant Energy Company (1988) 199 Cal. App. 3d 1240.
*PRACTICE AREAS: Employment Litigation; Oil and Gas Litigation.
Rosenstein, Gerald . . . '36 '61 C.188 B.A. L.309 LL.B. 1315 Truxtun Ave.
Rostain, Oliver E. . . . '22 '52 C.112 A.B. L.1065 J.D. 1300 Lymric Way‡
Rudnick, Daniel L., Law Office of, (BV) '57 '83 C.1074 B.S. L.61 J.D.
924 Truxtun Ave.
Rudnick, Philip . . . '32 '61 C&L.800 B.S., J.D. 1400 Easton‡
**Russell, Diane E.** . . . '55 '87 C&L.420 B.S., J.D. Coun., Chevron U.S.A. Production Co.
Russell, Michael D. . . . '46 '78 C.101 B.A. L.426 J.D. 8200 Stockdale Hwy.
Ryals, Sara O'Shields, (BV) . . . '36 '78 C.1365 B.A. L.1137 J.D. Dep. Dist. Atty.
Ryan, J. Colleen Ward . . . '44 '69 C&L.336 B.A., J.D. Dep. Dist. Atty.
Saghatelian, Tommi R. . . . '56 '86 C.267 B.A. L.464 J.D. 2821 H. St.
**Saine, David L., (BV)** . . . '49 '82 C.174 B.A. L.208 J.D. [A Klein,W.D.G.&M.]
*PRACTICE AREAS: Appeals; Appellate Law.
Salehi, Susan J. . . . '51 '91 C.267 B.A. L.999 J.D. 1331 "L" St.
Saltz, Michael Cary '61 '93 C.1248 B.S. L.1194 J.D.
(adm. in PA; not adm. in CA) 1200 Truxtun Ave.
Samples, Frank P. . . . '33 '59 C.10 L.192 LL.B. 1331 L St.
Sanders, Steven L. . . . '57 '83 C.67 B.A. L.1049 J.D. Dep. Co. Coun.
Schlosser, John A. . . . '47 '81 C.273 B.A. L.770 J.D. Sr. Atty., CalResources
**Schneider, Spencer A.** . . . '69 '94 C&L.112 B.A., J.D. [A Daniels,B.&F.]⊙
Schroeter, Thomas F., (BV) . . . '47 '74 C.112 A.B. L.1065 J.D. 254 "H" St.
Scott, Kenneth W. . . . '61 '89 C.169 B.A. L.940 J.D. 1600 Truxtun Ave.
Scully, Cynthia R., (CV) . . . '49 '89 C.1044 B.S. L.1189 J.D. 1301 L Street
Seferovich, Patrick B. '46 '81 C.36 B.A. L.692 J.D.
(adm. in CO; not adm. in CA) 1200 Discovery Dr.
Seidman, Michael L. . . . '47 '78 C.994 B.A. L.1095 J.D. 2104 24th St.
**Self, Robert J., (BV)** . . . '32 '61 C.112 B.S. L.1066 J.D. [Young W.]
*REPORTED CASES: People v. Brock, 57 Cal2d 644 (1962); Keen v. Harling, 61 Cal2d 318 (1964); Runyan v. Pacific Air Industries, 2 Cal3d 304 (1970).
*PRACTICE AREAS: Business Law; Real Property Law; Commercial Litigation.
Shaw, Errol G., (A Professional Corporation), (CV) '40 '70
C.267 B.A. L.1095 J.D. [E.G.S.A.]
Shaw, Errol G., A.P.C., (CV) . . . Suite 6, 330 H Street
**Shayer, W. Steven, (CV)** . . . '60 '85 C.112 B.A. L.990 J.D. [A LeBeau,T.L.M.&C.]
**Shea, Edwin Timothy, III** . . . '53 '77 C.1297 B.A. L.502 J.D. [Werdel&S.]
*PRACTICE AREAS: Labor Relations and Employment (Management); Civil Trial and Appellate Practice; Agricultural; Construction Law.
Shorr, Renee M. Bazar . . . '49 '83 C.36 B.A. L.1095 J.D. 2025 Westwind Dr.
Shumaker, Ronald L. . . . '41 '67 C.1042 B.A. L.1068 LL.B. Dep. Dist. Atty.
Siemon, Bennett . . . '12 '37 C.112 L.809 LL.B. 1743 Glenwood Dr.‡
Simrin, Stanley, (AV) . . . '29 '71 C.102 B.S. L.981 LL.B. 1430 Truxton Ave.
Sims, Ronald S., (CV) . . . '51 '78 C&L.101 B.A., J.D. [Austin,T.&S.]
Sims, William M., (BV) . . . '26 '53 C&L.950 B.A., LL.B. 2225 E St.

**Slocumb, William H.**, (CV) ........ '51 '81 C.112 B.A. L.1137 J.D. [Klein,W.D.G.&M.]
*PRACTICE AREAS: Real Property Law; Land Use and Planning; Products Liability Law; Civil Trial; Defense Litigation.
Smart, Daniel C. ........................'57 '83 C.101 B.S. L.426 J.D. 4140 Truxtun Ave.
Smith, Jay C. .............................. '50 '76 C.112 B.A. L.284 J.D. [Smith&S.]
Smith, Margaret H., (CV) ............................ '50 '91 C.1212 B.A. [Smith&S.]
Smith, Todd Michael ........................ '67 '94 C.112 B.S. L.464 J.D. [Griffin C.]
Smith and Smith, (CV) ............................ 1400 Chester Avenue, Suite R
Snyder, Robert E. ........................ '16 '53 C.112 A.B. L.809 LL.B. 22601 Fast Ct.‡
Somers, John S., (BV) ..................... '59 '84 C.388 B.A. L.813 J.D. Dep. Dist. Atty.
**Songer, Vickie Y.** ......................................'48 '92 L.999 J.D. [Young W.]
*PRACTICE AREAS: Workers' Compensation Law.
Sparks, Thomas D., (BV) .............'45 '73 C.112 B.A. L.767 J.D. Chf. Dep. Dist. Atty.
Sprague, Michael L., (CV) .................. '38 '65 C.112 B.A. L.1065 J.D. 1415 18th St.
Staley, Harry A. ........................................'49 '76 C.569 B.S. L.1049 J.D. Mun. J.
**Stanton, David B.** ............................. '41 '65 C&L.800 B.S.L., LL.B. [Kuhs,P.&S.]
**Stanton, Thomas M.**, (AV) ............ '42 '67 C.112 A.B. L.813 LL.B. [Clifford&B.]
*PRACTICE AREAS: Civil Litigation; Insurance Defense.

**Stanton, Thomas M., (AV) '42 '67 C.112 A.B. L.813 LL.B.**
**1430 Truxtun Avenue, Suite 900, 93301**
**Telephone: 805-861-8655 Fax: 805-322-3508**
***PRACTICE AREAS: Civil Litigation; Insurance Defense.**
**General Civil Practice, Insurance Defense.**
***See Professional Biographies, BAKERSFIELD, CALIFORNIA***

Starr, C. M., II, (BV) ...................... '50 '79 C.169 B.S.C.E. L.464 J.D. Dep. Dist. Atty.
Steele, J. Kelly ........................................'15 '41 L.1065 J.D. Ret. Supr. Ct. J.

**Steele, Patrick J., The Law Offices of, (CV) '57 '82 C.112 B.A. L.1066 J.D.**
**1401 19th Street, Suite 200, 93301**
**Telephone: 805-334-1145**
***PRACTICE AREAS: Commercial Litigation; Real Estate Litigation; Construction Litigation; Environmental Litigation; Trusts and Estates.**
**Commercial Litigation, Real Estate Litigation, Construction Litigation, Environmental Litigation, Trusts and Estates and Wills.**
***See Professional Biographies, BAKERSFIELD, CALIFORNIA***

Stevens, John R., (CV) ..................... '45 '73 C.228 B.A. L.188 J.D. Dep. Dist. Atty.
Stiles, David V., (BV) .................. '50 '76 C.112 B.A. L.1065 J.D. [Chain,Y.L.C.&S.]
Stovall, John F. ........'48 '82 C.112 B.A. L.426 J.D. Gen. Coun., Kern Co. Water Agency
Strom, Lynn M., (CV) .................... '57 '89 C.1060 B.A. L.1067 J.D. Dep. Dist. Atty.
Stuart, James M. ........................................ '42 '69 C.112 A.B. L.1065 J.D. Supr. Ct. J.
**Sullivan, Jere N., Sr.**, (AV) ............... '20 '49 C.31 A.B. L.309 J.D. [Borton,P.&C.]
Sybrandt, Robt. ............................ '22 '45 C&L.800 LL.B. Paul Sybrandt, Inc.
**Szewczyk, John R.**, (CV) ..................... '57 '83 C.112 B.A. L.426 J.D. [Clifford&B.]
*PRACTICE AREAS: Civil Litigation; Employment Law; Landlord/Tenant Appellate Law.
Tafoya, Robert S., (BV) .............. '— '79 C.1060 B.A. L.1065 J.D. 1430 Truxtun Ave.
**Talbot, James S.** '52 '79
C.859 B.A. L.744 J.D. Sr. Coun., Chevron U.S.A. Production Co.
Tauzer, Stephen M. ...................... '45 '71 C.767 B.A. L.1067 J.D. Dep. Dist. Atty.
Taylor, Gail S. ...................... '47 '81 C.1074 B.A. L.769 J.D. 5000 California Ave.
Tello, John A., (BV) ...................... '44 '79 C.1131 B.A. L.112 J.D. 1430 Truxtun Ave.
**Thelen, Dennis R.**, (AV) ...............'53 '78 C&L.770 B.A., J.D. [LeBeau,T.L.M.&C.]
Thomas, Daron J. .............................. '50 '77 C.37 B.S. L.398 J.D. 3801 Standard St.
**Thomas, Edward J.**, (AV) ................... '46 '71 C.489 B.A. L.494 J.D. [E.J.Thomas]
*PRACTICE AREAS: Family Law.
Thomas, J. Richard .................... '23 '50 C.813 A.B. L.1065 J.D. 1601 F St., 2nd Fl.
Thomas, John P. ............................ '27 '59 C.768 B.A. L.464 LL.B. Asst. Pub. Def.

**Thomas, Edward J., A Professional Corporation, (AV)**
**Suite 400, 5201 California Avenue, 93309**
**Telephone: 805-322-1777 Fax: 805-324-3560**
**Email: thomaslaw@lightspeed.net**
**Edward J. Thomas;—Michael Andrew Carlovsky; Heather June Christiansen.**
**Practice Limited to Family Law and Estate Planning.**
***See Professional Biographies, BAKERSFIELD, CALIFORNIA***

Thompson, Melvin J., (CV) ................... '47 '76 C.101 B.A. L.1049 J.D. [Austin,T.&S.]
**Thomson, Andrew C.** .................. '56 '90 C.1212 B.A. L.999 J.D. [Borton,P.&C.]
*PRACTICE AREAS: Insurance Defense; Public Entity Representation and Defense; Business Litigation.
**Thorne, Peter S.** ........................ '68 '96 C.766 B.A. L.1068 J.D. [Clifford&B.]
**Torigiani, Steven M.** ..................... '67 '93 C.1074 B.S. L.464 J.D. [Young W.]
*PRACTICE AREAS: Water Law; Business Law; Litigation.
**Tracey, Kirk S.**, (BV) ............ '59 '89 C.1131 B.A. L.809 J.D. [Klein,W.D.G.&M.]
*PRACTICE AREAS: Business/Commercial Litigation.
Tragish, Murray, (CV) ......... '45 '78 C.831 B.B.A. L.1137 J.D. 1405 Commercial Way
**Tripathi, Ashok K.** '67 '94 C.69 B.A. L.602 J.D.
(adm. in TX; not adm. in CA) Atty., Occidental Oil & Gas Corp.
*RESPONSIBILITIES: International Law.
Turner, Jerold L. .................................. '50 '76 C.112 B.A. L.1224 J.D. Supr. Ct. J.
Twisselman, Kenneth C., II ..................... '53 '77 C.112 B.A. L.1065 J.D. Supr. Ct. J.
Ulman, John M., II ............................ '44 '70 C&L.477 B.A., J.D. Actg. Pub. Def.
Underhill, Thomas H., (BV) ................. '24 '53 C&L.767 B.S., J.D. [T.H.Underhill] ‡
Underhill, Thomas H., A Professional Corporation ........................ 201 El Rio Dr.
Vander Noor, Robert B., (CV) ............. '39 '65 C&L.770 B.S.C., LL.B. 1401 19th St.
Van Meter, George E. ................ '32 '64 C.880 B.A. L.910 LL.B. 7400 El Verano Dr.
**Van Voorhis, Beth A.** .......................... '65 '92 C.132 B.A. L.1065 J.D. [Clifford&B.]
*PRACTICE AREAS: General Business; Real Estate.
Vega, Louie L. ................................... '49 '84 C.112 B.A. L.1068 J.D. Mun. Ct. Comr.
**Vidaurreta, Marisa S.** ............ '65 '90 C.605 B.A. L.273 J.D. [Patterson,R.L.G.&J.]
Voge, Jeri G. ........................... '48 '80 C.1077 B.A. L.1136 J.D. Dep. Dist. Atty.
Vollmer, Deborah A. ..................... '48 '74 C.156 B.A. L.446 J.D. 1706 Chester Ave.
Voth, Darrell H. '48 '75 C.267 B.S. L.464 J.D.
5201 California Ave., Ste., 450 (©Wasco)
**Wade, Bruce K.** ............................. '56 '84 C.112 A.B. L.101 J.D. [Mullen&F.]
**Wainer, Stephen P.**, (CV) .................. '66 '91 C.112 A.B. L.763 J.D. [Clifford&B.]
*PRACTICE AREAS: Civil Litigation.
Walbaum, Gerard E., (CV) ................ '49 '74 C.1075 B.A. L.809 J.D. P.O. Box 1592
**Waldon, Grover H.**, (BV) ................ '58 '83 C.1060 B.S. L.464 J.D. [Clifford&B.]
*PRACTICE AREAS: Civil Litigation; Business.
Wall, John S., (BV) ..................... '53 '78 C.1212 B.A. L.1137 J.D. [Wall,W.&P.]
Wall, Stephen E., (BV) ............................ '16 '51 C.112 L.426 LL.B. [Wall,W.&P.]
Wall, Wall & Peake, A Professional Corporation, (BV) ................... 1601 "F" St.
Wallace, Arthur E. ......................... '38 '64 C.112 B.S. L.1065 J.D. Supr. Ct. J.
Walters, Bryan C., (CV) .................. '62 '91 C.1212 B.A. L.990 J.D. 2328 19th St.
Walton, Lewis R. ........................................ '41 '68 L.1049 J.D. 2701 Rio Vista
Warmerdam, Peter A. ..................... '54 '78 C.169 B.A. L.464 J.D. Dep. Dist. Atty.
Webb, Michael J., (CV) .............. '45 '71 C.112 B.S. L.1067 J.D. 1430 Truxtun Ave.
Weddell, Willard L. .................................. '32 '61 C.999 L.464 LL.B. Pub. Def.
**Wegis, Ralph B., (Inc.)**, (AV) ...... '44 '75 C.1074 B.S. L.1095 J.D. [Klein,W.D.G.&M.]
*PRACTICE AREAS: Products Liability Litigation; Personal Injury Negligence Litigation; Civil Litigation.

Weisman, Donna S. ........................... '56 '81 C.112 B.A. L.810 J.D. Dep. Co. C.
Welchans, Paul A., (BV) ..................... '50 '83 C.589 B.S. L.1068 J.D. 1430 Truxtun A.
**Welsh, Leonard K., (BV) '54 '81 C.101 B.A. L.902 J.D.**
**Ming Office Park, 5500 Ming Avenue, Suite 350, 93309**
**Telephone: 805-835-1122 Fax: 805-835-8918**
**Insolvency, Bankruptcy, Business and Farm Reorganization, Debtor and Creditor Rights and Business Law.**
***See Professional Biographies, BAKERSFIELD, CALIFORNIA***
**Werdel, Charles C.**, (BV) '38 '66 C.112 A.B. L.1065 J.D.
[Werdel&W.] & [Werdel&S]
*PRACTICE AREAS: Business Transactions; Oil and Gas; Taxation; Business and Estate Planning; Estates and Trusts.
**Werdel, Terence J.**, (BV) .................. '42 '70 C.426 B.A. L.1066 J.D. [Werdel&S.]
*PRACTICE AREAS: Corporate; General Business; Estate Planning; Probate; Real Estate.
**Werdel, Thomas H., Jr.**, (AV) '35 '63
C&L.813 A.B., J.D. [Werdel&W.] & [Werdel&S]
*PRACTICE AREAS: Business Transactions; Oil and Gas; Taxation; Business and Estate Planning; Estates and Trusts.

**Werdel & Shea, (BV)**
**5500 Ming Avenue, Suite 140, 93309**
**Telephone: 805-837-8053 Fax: 805-837-2936**
**Members of Firm: Terence J. Werdel; Edwin Timothy Shea, III. Associates: Kelly A. Griffin-Lazerson; James D. Madison. Of Counsel: Thomas H. Werdel, Jr. (Certified Specialist, Taxation Law, The State Bar of California Board of Legal Specialization); Charles C. Werdel.**
**Corporate, Labor Relations and Employment (Management), General Business. Civil Trial and Appellate Practice (State and Federal). Probate and Estate Planning, Oil and Gas, Natural Resources, Real Estate, Agricultural and Construction Law.**
**Reference: Wells Fargo Bank.**

**Werdel & Werdel, (AV)**
**Suite 140, 5500 Ming Avenue, P.O. Box 9415, 93309**
**Telephone: 805-834-5930 Fax: 805-834-3950**
**Members of Firm: Thomas H. Werdel, Jr. (Certified Specialist, Taxation Law, The State Bar of California Board of Legal Specialization); Charles C. Werdel.**
**Business, Business Planning, Commercial Law, Corporations, Partnerships, Taxation, Real Estate, Oil and Gas, Agriculture, Estate Planning, Trusts, Probate and International Business Law.**
**Reference: Home Savings of America (Bakersfield Main Office).**

Westra, Clarence, Jr. ......................... '45 '72 C.112 A.B. L.1067 J.D. Supr. Ct. J.
Wetteroth, Warren C., (AV) ................ '30 '59 C.112 A.B. L.1065 J.D. 1801 Oak St.
White, Richard G. '46 '70 C.309 B.A. L.273 J.D.
(adm. in VA; not adm. in CA) 2201 Tilden Way‡
**Whittington, Joe W.** ............................... '51 '96 L.999 J.D. [Borton,P.&C.]
*PRACTICE AREAS: Employment Law; Construction Law; Civil Litigation.

**Whittington, Michael T., (CV) '58 '84 C&L.770 B.S., J.D.**
**Commonwealth Plaza, 3300 Truxtun Avenue, Suite 390, 93301©**
**Telephone: 805-327-2294 Fax: 805-323-8731**
**Real Estate, Business, General Civil Litigation and Trials.**
**Newport Beach, California Office: 4590 MacArthur, Suite 550, 92660. Telephone: 714-833-2370. Fax: 714-833-0949.**
**Los Gatos, California Office: 15425 Los Gatos Boulevard, Suite 120, 95032. Telephone: 408-369-9655. Fax: 408-369-0355.**
***See Professional Biographies, BAKERSFIELD, CALIFORNIA***

Widelock, Marc D., (CV) ..................... '51 '86 C&L.1137 B.S., J.D. [O'Neil&W.]
Wied, Charles D. ........................... '36 '67 C.763 B.A. L.61 J.D. 615 Calif. Ave.
Wiele, Julie A. ............................. '59 '87 C.210 B.A. L.464 J.D. Dist. Atty. Off.
**Wiens, James B.**, (BV) ..................... '49 '78 C.112 B.A. L.61 J.D. [Clifford&B.]
*PRACTICE AREAS: Estate Planning/Probate Law; General Business; Agricultural Law.
Williams, Robert S., (BV) ................ '51 '76 C.1212 B.S. L.770 J.D. [Williams&W.]
Williams, Robt. L., (BV) ...................... '21 '48 C&L.276 B.A., J.D. [Williams&W.]
Williams, Rod, (BV) ...................... '37 '66 C.766 B.A. L.1065 J.D. [R.Williams]
Williams, Scott R. '53 '80 C&L.585 B.A., J.D.
(adm. in ND; not adm. in CA) Right of Way Specialist, Chevron Pipe Line Co.
Williams, Rod, Law Corp. of, (BV) ...................................... 1309 "L" St.
Williams & Williams, Inc., (BV) ....................................... 1706 Chester Ave.
Wilson, Donn H. ............... '46 '76 C.174 B.S. L.208 J.D. Mgr., Chevron U.S.A. Inc.
Wilson, Edwin W. ......................... '22 '50 C.112 B.S. L.1065 J.D. [E.W.Wilson]
Wilson, Edwin W., Inc., A Prof. Law Corp. ............................ 1112 Truxton Ave.
Wolfe, William Andrew, (CV) .... '59 '91 C.1077 B.S. L.426 J.D. 5001 E. Commerce Ctr.
Woodhead, Frank W., (AV) ........... '09 '36 C.378 B.S. L.426 J.D. 3204 Marnie Lane‡
Woods, Robert D. .................... '46 '73 C&L.1049 B.A., J.D. Chief Dep., Co. Coun.
**Wooldridge, Joseph**, (AV) ............................ '13 '39 C&L.426 J.D. [Young W.]
*PRACTICE AREAS: Personal Injury; Litigation.
Worth, James A. ................................ '62 '90 C.763 B.A. L.61 J.D. [McMurtrey&H.]
Worthing, Michael D., (CV) ............ '54 '80 C.1212 B.A. L.464 J.D. [Gattuso,K.&W.]
Wright, Larry L. ............................ '46 '91 C.612 B.S. L.1212 J.D. P.O. Box 2537
Yinger, Ray A., (BV) ........................ '38 '65 C.112 B.S. L.1068 J.D. [Yinger&O.]
Yinger & Oldfield, (BV) ........................................................ 1600 F St.
**Young, John B.**, (AV) ....................... '13 '37 C.112 A.B. L.1066 J.D. [Young W.]
*PRACTICE AREAS: Probate Law; Estate Planning.
**Young, Michael R.**, (BV) .................. '40 '66 C.112 A.B. L.1065 J.D. [Young W.]
*PRACTICE AREAS: Personal Injury; Probate; Litigation.
Young, Robert M., (CV) ..................... '50 '89 C.112 B.A. L.940 J.D. 1706 Chester Ave.

**Young Wooldridge, Law Offices of, (AV)**
**1800 30th Street, Fourth Floor, 93301**
**Telephone: 805-327-9661 Facsimile: 805-327-1087**
**Members of Firm: Joseph Wooldridge; A. Cameron Paulden (1927-1984); Robert J. Self; G. Neil Farr (Certified Specialist, Family Law, California Board of Specialization); Michael R. Young; Ernest A. Conant; Steve W. Nichols; Larry R. Cox; Scott K. Kuney; Michael A. Kaia. Associates: Russell B. Hicks; Vickie Y. Songer; Steven M. Torigiani; Scott D. Howry; David F. Leon; Todd A. Gall. Of Counsel: John B. Young; Edward M. Carpenter; James E. Millar.**
**General Civil and Trial Practice. Corporation. Condemnation, Oil and Gas, Water Rights, Probate and Estate Planning Law. Agricultural, Bankruptcy, Business, Domestic Relations, Personal Injury and Workers' Compensation.**
**Representative Clients: Arvin-Edison Water Storage District; Motor City Truck Sales and Service.**
**References: Wells Fargo Bank; First Interstate Bank; California Republic Bank.**
***See Professional Biographies, BAKERSFIELD, CALIFORNIA***

Younger, Milton M. ..................... '31 '57 C&L.813 A.B., LL.B. [Chain,Y.L.C.&S.]
**Zimmer, Richard G.**, (CV) ................ '56 '82 C.1213 B.S. L.61 J.D. [Clifford&B.]
*PRACTICE AREAS: Civil Litigation; Business Litigation.

## BALBOA, —, *Orange Co.*

(See Newport Beach)

## BALBOA ISLAND, —, *Orange Co.*

(See Newport Beach)

## BALDWIN PARK, 69,330, *Los Angeles Co.*

Baker, Arthur C. ........................... '11 '40 C.112 A.B. L.1066 LL.B. P.O. Box 717‡
Espinoza, Richard A., (BV) ..................... '42 '77 L.1137 J.D. 4443 Maine Ave.

Espinoza, Rodney J. ....................'56 '85 C.800 B.S. L.1137 J.D. 4443 Maine Ave.
Hadley, Marshall, (BV) .................'26 '55 C&L.800 A.B., LL.B. [Hadley&H.]
Hadley, Milton, (BV) ....................'26 '59 C&L.800 B.A., LL.B. [Hadley&H.] ‡
Hadley & Hadley, (BV) .................................................. 3940 Maine Ave.
Laird, Richard A. ....................'36 '71 C.37 B.S. L.809 LL.B. 3847 Kenmore Ave.
Miller, Douglas G. ....................'45 '78 C.801 B.A. L.398 J.D. 14530 Pacific Ave.

## BANNING, 20,570, *Riverside Co.*

Bergeson, Lester H. ....................'17 '70 C.494 B.B.A. L.800 J.D. 611 La Quinta Dr.‡
Broderick, Phillip R. ....................'41 '67 C.800 B.S. L.1188 J.D. 3088 Ramsey St.‡
Brouillette, Grace C. ....................'47 '84 C.1097 B.S. L.1137 J.D. Dep. Dist. Atty.
Fisher, Alvan H. ....................'13 '37 C.271 A.B. L.665 LL.B. P.O. Box 607‡
Jorgensen, Allen C., (CV) '52 '81 C.112 B.A. L.1049 J.D.
3088 W. Ramsey (⊙Redlands)
Kimbrough, Michael M. ....................'61 '87 C.112 B.A. L.1049 J.D. 385 W. Ramsey St.
McClellan & Wilson .................... 149 North San Gorgonio Avenue (⊙Yucaipa)
Pena, Antonio ....................'26 '77 C.846 B.S.M.E. L.1137 J.D. 1108 S. Riviera Ave.
Peterson, Robert T. ....................'35 '65 C.112 B.A. L.1068 LL.B. Mun. Ct. J.
Pike, Kenneth L. ....................'28 '56 C.940 B.A. L.1068 LL.B. Dep. Dist. Atty.
Weidman, Arnold '12 '44 C&L.378 B.S., LL.B.
(adm. in KS; not adm. in CA) 3222 W. Nicolet St.‡
Wilson, D. Hershel ....................'48 '81 C.305 B.A. L.1137 J.D. [McClellan&W.]⊙

## BARSTOW, 21,472, *San Bernardino Co.*

Arneson, Bruce A., (CV) ....................'49 '76 C.585 B.A. L.1137 J.D. 1107 E. Main St.

**Caldwell & Kennedy, A Professional Corporation**
**(See Victorville)**

Clark, Donald Leland ....................'43 '75 C.1097 B.A. L.1049 J.D. Dep. Dist. Atty.
Dorr, James M. ....................'48 '76 C.475 B.A. L.61 J.D. Mun. Ct. J.

**Hayton Law Corporation**
**(See Victorville)**

Johnson, Alan R. ....................'30 '78 C.347 L.1114 J.D. 316 E. Frederick St.

**Lundberg, Gerald R., The Law Offices of**
**(See Victorville)**

Mahlum, Conrad E. ....................'24 '49 C&L.800 LL.B. U.S. Mag.
Mahlum, Kirtland L. ....................'45 '69 C.112 B.A. L.61 J.D. U.S. Mag. J.
Muncy, Elbert W., Jr. ....................'54 '88 L.1137 J.D. 420 Barstow Rd.
Nielson, LeRoy M., (BV) ....................'32 '73 C.878 B.S. L.1137 J.D. [L.M.Nielson]
Nielson, LeRoy M., Professional Law Corporation, (BV) .................... 304 E. Williams St.
Simmons, LeRoy A. ....................'40 '68 C.101 L.767 J.D. Supr. Ct. J.
Stack, Richard A., (CV) ....................'45 '75 C.763 B.S. L.1049 J.D. 703 E. Main St.
Triplett, Ernest E. ....................'21 '78 C.446 B.S. L.809 J.D. 689 La Quinta Dr.‡
Weber, John F. ....................'57 '91 C.584 B.S. L.61 J.D. 520 Barstow Rd.

**Welebir & McCune, A Professional Law Corporation**
**(See Redlands)**

Yent, Rufus L. ....................'33 '72 C&L.800 B.S.E.E., J.D. Supr. Ct. J.

**Zumbrunn, Lynn E., A Law Corporation**
**(See Victorville)**

## BASS LAKE, 700, *Madera Co.*

Weaver, Gerald C., (AV) ....................'36 '62 C.285 L.1065 J.D. [G.C.Weaver]⊙
Weaver, Gerald C., A Law Corporation, (AV) .................... P.O. Box 594 (⊙San Luis Obispo)

## BAYWOOD PARK, —, *San Luis Obispo Co.*

von Rauner, Vladimir, (CV) ....................'44 '78 C.800 B.S. L.398 J.D. 1281 3rd St.

## BEAUMONT, 9,685, *Riverside Co.*

Fenton, Joanne ....................'— '71 C.273 A.B. L.426 J.D. 1314 Edgar Ave.

## BEL AIR, —, *Los Angeles Co.*

(See Los Angeles)

## BELL, 34,365, *Los Angeles Co.*

Casjens, Carlton B. ....................'25 '54 C.940 B.A. L.809 LL.B. 4663 Gage Ave.‡
Garcia, Anthony R. ....................'51 '82 C.1075 B.A. L.426 J.D. 4723 E. Florence Ave.

## BELLFLOWER, 61,815, *Los Angeles Co.*

Bonazzola, Mark L. ....................'54 '80 C.1042 L.1238 J.D. 16811 Clark
Cooper, Barbara A. ....................'40 '76 L.1137 LL.B. 15556 Bellflower Blvd.
Farina, Joseph A. ....................'21 '67 C.349 B.S. L.1114 LL.B. Mun. Ct. J.
Golz, Helmut ....................'41 '76 C.994 B.A. L.1001 J.D. 16600 Woodruff
Heger, Ellen J. ....................'53 '78 C.102 B.A. L.809 J.D. 9440 Flower St.
Holtz, Richard R. ....................'35 '80 C.1042 B.S. L.1137 J.D. [Rohrer&H.]
Kallins, Nicholas J. ....................'61 '86 C&L.800 B.S., J.D. 15747 S. Woodruff Ave.
Kivo, Robert J. ....................'46 '77 C.264 B.A. L.564 J.D. 67 Flintlock Ln.
Landis, John C. ....................'12 '36 C.310 B.A. L.546 J.D. Ret. Mun. J.
Leavell, Robert F., (BV) ....................'28 '62 9631 Alondra Blvd.
MacKenzie, Lyle M. ....................'32 '66 C.1043 B.A. L.809 LL.B. Mun. Ct. Comr.
Mautino, Philip K. ....................'39 '67 C.112 B.S. L.800 J.D. Mun. J.
Mendoza, Romona Forbes ....................'57 '88 C.322 B.A. L.809 J.D. 10120 Alondra Blvd.
Pohlen, Paul D., Jr. '48 '74 C.154 B.A. L.950 J.D.
(adm. in OR; not adm. in CA) Barbara's Beauty Supplies
Rohrer, George J., Jr., (BV) ....................'31 '69 L.1001 J.D. [Rohrer&H.]⊙
Rohrer & Holtz, A Professional Law Corporation, (BV)
Ste., 103, 9928 E. Flower St. (⊙Anaheim)
Seiden, Steven A. ....................'48 '78 C.560 B.A. L.1095 J.D. 10120 Alondra Blvd.
Songer, Donald J. ....................'29 '62 C.999 L.1001 LL.B. 9631 Alondra Blvd.‡
Sowell, Robert E. ....................'23 '51 C.999 L.800 J.D. P.O. Box 519
Stein, Andrew M., (BV) ....................'54 '78 C.107 B.A. L.1049 J.D. 10120 Alondra Blvd.
Stits, Dana Joseph ....................'63 '92 C.112 B.A. L.813 J.D. [Rohrer&H.]
Swart, Chester A. ....................'29 '85 C.112 B.S. L.1001 J.D. 9847 Belmont St.

## BELL GARDENS, 42,355, *Los Angeles Co.*

Gross, Alan D. ....................'35 '62 C.473 A.B. L.276 LL.B. 6509 Eastern Ave.
Lopez, Luisito L. '39 '75 C&L.061 LL.B.
(adm. in IL; not adm. in CA) 5847 E. Florence Ave.‡

## BELMONT, 24,127, *San Mateo Co.*

Castaneda, Janet Kaiser ....................'43 '84 C.475 B.S. L.678 J.D. 1301 Shoreway Rd. (Pat.)
Gibran-Hesse, M. Ellen ....................'50 '85 C.911 B.S. L.284 J.D. 2970 Hallmark‡
Grathwohl, J. David, (BV) ....................'39 '69 C&L.767 B.S., J.D. 1070 6th Ave.
Graziani, Alfred E., (AV) ....................'11 '36 C&L.767 B.S., LL.B. 1513 Ralston Ave.‡
Gughemetti, Joseph M., (BV) ....................'47 '72 C&L.767 B.S., J.D. P.O. Box 1329
Hatfield, Gene ....................'31 '69 C.843 B.S. L.284 J.D. P.O. Box 66
Herr, Brett W. ....................'57 '86 C.604 B.A. L.309 J.D. Sr. Corp. Coun., Nikon Precision Inc.
Jones, David M. ....................'30 '63 C&L.208 B.S., LL.B. P.O. Box 873
McCallum, Lenell Topol ....................'54 '78 C.112 B.A. L.767 J.D. 1610 Belburn Dr.
Morris, Jackson A., III ....................'42 '76 C.839 B.B.A. L.1231 J.D. 974 Ralston Ave., Suite 2
Rizzo, Ralph A., (BV) ....................'46 '72 C.112 B.A. L.1065 J.D. [Sullivan&R.]
Rosellini, Ildo L., (BV) ....................'23 '52 C.999 L.284 J.D. [Rosellini&W.]
Rosellini & Ward, (BV) .................... 1069 Alameda de las Pulgas St.
Sullivan, Ralph A., (AV) ....................'23 '49 C.560 L.767 LL.B. 9 Korbel Way‡
Sullivan & Rizzo, (BV) .................... 1200 6th Ave.
Tanke, Tony J., (AV) ....................'51 '75 C.958 B.A. L.494 J.D. [Tanke&W.]⊙
Tanke & Willemsen, A Professional Association, (AV) ... 1523 Solana Drive (⊙Palo Alto)
Vallerga, Edw. D., (BV) ....................'18 '53 C.999 L.284 LL.B. P.O. Box AA
Willemsen, Michael A. ....................'37 '63 C&L.813 B.A., LL.B. [Tanke&W.]⊙
Wolfe, Dorothy M., (BV) ....................'21 '74 C.999 L.765 J.D. 2211 Village Ct.

## BELVEDERE-TIBURON, 9,086, *Marin Co.*

Arnold, R. Steven '38 '62 C.103 A.B. L.178 LL.B.
(adm. in NY; not adm. in CA)
Chmn. of the Bd., Pro Sports, Inc., World Telemedia Company
Barrett, Malcolm M., (AV) ....................'24 '51 C&L.813 A.B., J.D. 12 Cove Rd.‡
Blajwas, Harold ....................'40 '70 C.309 B.A. L.477 J.D. 14 Crest Rd.
Blum, Michael G. ....................'42 '70 C.112 B.A. L.767 J.D. 41 Acacia Ave.
Bonelli, Benjamin P. ....................'24 '58 C.188 D.V.M. L.174 LL.B. 56 Peninsula Rd.
Burnham, Albert C., (AVⓉ) '43 '74 C.768 B.S. L.1065 J.D.
(adm. in TN; not adm. in CA) 42 Meadowhill Dr.‡
Cassou, April K. ....................'47 '72 C&L.767 B.A., J.D. 49 Upper North Ter.
Collins, Ernest W., Jr. ....................'42 '67 C.623 B.B.A. L.494 J.D. 4925 Paradise Dr.
Courtney, Jack ....................'24 '55 C.112 B.A. L.800 LL.B. 133 Lyford Dr.

**Curfman, Lawrence E., III, (AV) '40 '63 C.111 B.S. L.309 LL.B.**
**98 Main Street, 94920**
**Telephone: 415-435-8237 Facsimile: 415-435-8375**
***PRACTICE AREAS: Mediation; Arbitration; Discovery Referee.**
**Mediation, Arbitration, Discovery Referee.**

Currie, Allan B. ....................'47 '72 C.770 B.S. L.1065 J.D. P.O. Box 772‡
Dahl, Alrich W. ....................'05 '31 C.813 L.1065 LL.B. 341 Belvedere Avenue‡
Denebeim, James E. ....................'23 '49 C&L.813 A.B., J.D. 206 San Rafael Ave.‡
Doyle, Patricia M. ....................'53 '82 C.914 B.A. L.273 J.D. 115 Avenida Mira Flores
Ehrlich, Philip S., Jr., (AV) ....................'22 '49 C&L.813 B.A., LL.B. 63 Beach Rd.‡
Emerson, Elizabeth L. ....................'14 '72 C.800 A.B. L.284 J.D. 2 Bartel Ct.‡
Ewing, Robert B. ....................'58 '85 C.112 B.A. L.1065 J.D. Town Atty.
FitzGerald, Cynthia ....................'53 '77 C.112 B.A. L.767 J.D. 270 Roundhill Rd.
Fluegelman, Andrew C. '43 '69 C.918 B.A. L.976 LL.B.
Exec. V.P. & Gen. Coun., The Headlands Press, Inc.
Friedman, Michael B., (AV) ....................'39 '66 C.112 A.B. L.793 J.D. P.O. Box 96
Giacomini, Joseph E. ....................'22 '75 C.330 L.1153 LL.B. 1660 Tiburon Blvd.
Gilbert, Cynthia L. ....................'52 '76 C.112 B.A. L.1067 J.D. 10 Beach Rd.
Gilbert, David C. ....................'50 '76 C.112 B.A. L.1067 J.D. 10 Beach Rd.
Gold, Craig Mitchell ....................'55 '89 C.188 B.S. L.284 J.D. Natl. Emer. Servs., Inc.

**Gwatkin, William E., III, (AV) '29 '57 C.970 B.A. L.309 LL.B.**
**20 Harbor Oak Drive #12, P.O. Box 874, 94920**
**Telephone: 415-435-9842**
**Admiralty and Civil Trial and Appellate Practice in Federal and State Courts.**

Hearn, Reginald G., (AV) ....................'13 '39 C.112 A.B. L.765 LL.B. P.O. Box 1086‡
Honchariw, Nicholas J. ....................'47 '72 C&L.309 A.B., J.D. Pres., N.H. Partners
Howard, Jeffrey M. ....................'38 '67 C.608 B.I.E. L.1065 J.D. P.O. Box 409
Hughes, Justin, (AV) ....................'45 '70 C.309 B.A. L.93 J.D. 6 Rolling Hills Rd.‡
Huntington, John B. ....................'37 '68 C.112 A.B. L.1065 J.D. P.O. Box 1006
Johnson, Robert M. ....................'32 '58 C.597 B.A. L.813 J.D. 301 Paradise Dr.
Lauder, Leona L., Law Offices of ....'48 '79 C.477 B.A. L.818 J.D. 6 Mariposa Ct. (Pat.)
Lerner, Esther R. ....................'47 '80 C.260 B.A. L.284 J.D. [Lerner]⊙
Lerner Law Offices ....................104 Main Street, Suite A (⊙San Francisco)
Limbach, Lois R. ....................'32 '82 C.478 B.A. L.1065 J.D. 49 Bellevue‡
Livingston, Lawr., Jr. ....................'18 '47 C.813 A.B. L.976 LL.B. 2311 Mar E. St.‡
Lizza, Tiberio P. ....................'37 '62 C&L.426 B.B.A., J.D. Drawer C‡
Main, William A. ....................'21 '50 C&L.309 B.S., LL.B. 6 W. Shore Rd.‡

**Martinez, George C., (AV) '34 '60 C.766 A.B. L.767 J.D.**
**1610 Tiburon Boulevard, 94920**
**Telephone: 415-789-5086 FAX: 415-789-5088**
**Email: GCMartinez@aol.com**
***REPORTED CASES: Silverthorne v. United States, 400 F. 2d 627 (1968). US v. Hearst 638 F.2d 1190 (1979).**
**Complex White Collar Criminal and Civil Litigation including Real Estate, Business, Transactional and Personal Injury Litigation.**
***See Professional Biographies, BELVEDERE-TIBURON, CALIFORNIA***

McAllister, Kenneth K. ....................'47 '76 C.705 B.A. L.1026 J.D. 2338 Mar East
McKenzie, Scott C. ....................'48 '77 C.112 A.B. L.464 J.D. 4 Tamalpais Rd.
Nemzer, Kenneth P. ....................'40 '69 C.112 A.B. L.309 J.D. 664 Hilary Dr., Tiburon
Neville, J. ....................'61 '87 C.740 B.A. L.767 J.D. 140 St. Thomas Way★
Nielsen, Arlene Merino ....................'44 '77 C.800 B.A. L.1066 J.D. 29 Mark Ter.
Parker, Dvora '40 '81 C.494 B.A. L.1065 J.D.
Dir., Family Law Clinic, Golden Gate Univ., Sch. of Law
Rainis, Richard David ....................'35 '89 C.262 B.S. L.1065 J.D. 78 Marinero Cir.‡
Rankin, Jon P. ....................'55 '81 C.112 B.A. L.809 J.D. 80 Main St.
Rees-Miller, Sheldon J. ....................'46 '78 C.1250 B.S. L.1026 J.D. 10 Bella Vista Ave.
Reuss, Henry S. '12 '36 C.188 A.B. L.309 LL.B.
(adm. in WI; not adm. in CA) 34 Cove Rd.‡
Roland, Maureen W. '47 '72 C.232 B.A. L.472 J.D.
(adm. in FL; not adm. in CA) 170 Trinidad Dr.‡
Rubenstein, Anne Magrath ....................'27 '83 C.145 B.S. L.1065 J.D. 1 Windward Rd.
Savitt, Beverly B. ....................'26 '67 C.119 B.S. L.1066 J.D. 9 Fern Ave.
Schmidt, Eric J. ....................'15 '64 C.112 B.A. L.912 J.D. 534 Silverado Dr.
Severance, Nancy Blank ....................'53 '78 C.183 B.A. L.1066 J.D. 10 Via Paraiso W.
Shadduck, John H. ....................'49 '85 C&L.112 A.B., J.D. 1490 Vistazo W.
Smissaert, John H., (AV) ....................'24 '53 C.813 A.B. L.1065 J.D. 1550 Tiburon Blvd.
Sperry, Leonard M., Jr., (AV) ....................'29 '55 C&L.976 A.A.B., LL.B. 825 Stony Hill Rd.‡
Strunk, June O. ....................'47 '72 C.104 B.A. L.94 J.D. 20 Mark Ter.
ten Doesschate, Paul J. ....................'24 '54 C.112 A.B. L.1065 LL.B. 759 Tiburon Blvd.‡
Weinstein, Richard B., (AV) ....................'36 '64 C.112 B.A. L.1066 LL.B. [R.B.Weinstein]
Weinstein, Richard B., A Prof. Corp., (AV) .................... 1679 Tiburon Blvd.
Wolfe, Bruce F. ....................'42 '77 C.813 A.B. L.1065 J.D. 91 West Shore Rd.

## BENICIA, 24,437, *Solano Co.*

**Barnum, Randal M., Law Offices of, (BV) '58 '83 C.813 B.A. L.1065 J.D.**
**Parkway Executive Center, 2044 Columbus Parkway, 94510⊙**
**Telephone: 707-745-3747 Fax: 707-745-4580**
**Email: RMBLAW@community.net**
**Wrongful Termination, Employment Litigation, Insurance Coverage, Insurance Defense, Personal Injury Law, Alternative Dispute Resolution Services.**
**Walnut Creek, California Office: 319 Lennon Lane, 94598. Telephone: 510-943-2313.**
*See Professional Biographies, BENICIA, CALIFORNIA*

Bianchi, James L. ....'49 '79 C.766 B.A. L.1230 J.D. 130 W. E St.
Bortolazzo, Richard A. ....'44 '71 C.112 A.B. L.1066 J.D. 900 1st St.‡
Denham, Rena ....'56 '82 C.483 B.A. L.767 J.D. 219 Panorama Dr.
Finnell, John W. '16 '47 C&L.16
(adm. in AL; not adm. in CA) 380 W. K St.‡
Friedman, Jerome H. ....'33 '71 C.223 B.S.M.E. L.464 J.D. 839 1st St.
Fulton, Dirk A. ....'54 '79 C.112 A.B. L.1065 J.D. 2044 Columbus Pkwy.
**Gentry, Deborah B.** ....'54 '78 C&L.420 B.S., J.D. Refinery Atty., Exxon Co., U.S.A.
Kerner, Michael P. ....'53 '80 C.33 B.A. L.1051 J.D. [Kerner&W.] (⊙San Francisco)
Kerner & Weppner .... 601 First Street (⊙San Francisco)
King, Christopher K., (BV) ....'52 '78 C.347 A.B. L.1066 J.D. 177 Military E.
Langford, V. Thomas ....'58 '85 C.154 B.A. L.1067 J.D. 905 1st St., 2nd Fl.
Lease, Lawrence M. ....'43 '72 C.696 A.B. L.284 J.D. 926 West K St.
Lofton, Mellanese S. ....'41 '74 C.846 B.A. L.1066 J.D. 110 East "D" St.
Mason, Shawn M. ....'59 '84 C.112 B.A. L.990 J.D. City Atty.
Murphy, George A., Jr. ....'43 '80 L.765 J.D. 130 W.E. St.

**Nolte, Nancy M., (CV) '42 '81 C.147 B.A. L.1067 J.D.**
**159 East D Street, Suite G, 94510⊙**
**Telephone: 707-745-8999**
***PRACTICE AREAS: Family Law; Family Mediation.**
**Family Law, Family Mediation.**
**Fairfield, California Office: 710, Missouri Street, Suite 3. Telephone: 717-425-1058. Fax: 707-425-1059.**
*See Professional Biographies, BENICIA, CALIFORNIA*

Schroth, Robert A., (BV) ....'48 '75 C&L.767 A.B., LL.B. 177 Military E.
Szabo, Peter J. ....'46 '80 C.178 B.S. L.981 LL.B 810 Oxford Way (Pat.)
Taylor, Joanne S. ....'47 '86 C.1073 B.A. L.1153 J.D. 283 East H St.
Weppner, Robert A. ....'51 '80 C.685 B.A. L.596 J.D. [Kerner&W.]
Winters, Mary Ann ....'21 '48 C.697 A.B. L.1066 LL.B. 400 W. "M" St.‡
Winters, Robert K. ....'19 '48 C.112 A.B. L.1066 LL.B. 400 W. "M" St.‡

## BEN LOMOND, —, *Santa Cruz Co.*

Christiansen, Marvin J., (BV) ....'29 '56 C.352 A.B. L.1065 J.D. 8925 Glen Arbor Rd.
Cooper, Daniel E., (BV) ....'29 '54 C.112 L.1065 LL.B. 9666 Highway 9
Mercer, David F. ....'47 '82 730 Eduardo

## BERKELEY, 102,724, *Alameda Co.*

Albuquerque, Manuela, (AV) ....'49 '75 C.061 B.A. L.1065 J.D. City Atty.
Alex, Glenn C. ....'53 '81 C.1169 B.A. L.1067 J.D. 2715 Alcatra 3
**Allen, Margaret J.** ....'52 '84 C.788 B.A. L.284 J.D. [⊠ York&S.]
*PRACTICE AREAS: Bankruptcy; Civil Litigation.
Amatruda, Christine A., (AV) ....'55 '83 C.918 B.A. L.1066 J.D. 1563 Solano Ave., #515
Amberg, Elizabeth Anne ....'48 '77 C.339 B.A. L.46 J.D. 2020 Dwight Way‡
Anderson, Robert P., (AV) ....'43 '79 C.112 B.S. L.765 J.D. [Anderson&D.]
Anderson, Scott, (AV) ....'19 '49 C.312 A.B. L.309 LL.B. 651 The Alameda‡
Anderson & Drossel, (AV) .... 2041 Bancroft Way
Anton, David C. ....'55 '80 C.604 B.A. L.276 J.D. 1950 Addison St.
Appleby, Teri E. ....'52 '78 C.813 B.A. L.800 J.D. 181 Hillcrest Rd.‡
Arding, Jon D. ....'61 '90 C.112 B.A. L.284 J.D. 2171 Shattuck Ave.
Atkins, Robert A., (BV) ....'44 '80 C.563 B.S. L.1066 J.D. 1613 Jaynes St.
Audley, Michael R. ....'62 '87 C.112 B.A. L.1065 J.D. [Audley&A.]
Audley, R. Richard, (AV) ....'37 '63 C.950 B.A. L.1066 J.D. [Audley&A.]
Audley & Audley, (AV) .... 51 Tunnel Rd.
Austin, John Page, (AV) ....'14 '40 C.309 A.B. L.976 LL.B. 66 Southampton Ave.‡
**Austin, Steven K.** ....'56 '81 C.112 B.A. L.1065 J.D. [Buresh,K.J.F.&A.]
*PRACTICE AREAS: Insurance Defense.
Baar, Kenneth K., (BV) ....'47 '74 C.918 B.A. L.1065 J.D. 1331 Milvia St.
Baldwin, Van P. ....'47 '81 C.69 B.B.A. L.1065 J.D. 1950 Addison St.
Barba, Daniel L. ....'62 '92 C.309 A.B. L.1066 J.D. Berkeley Community Law Ctr.
Barber, Bernard B. ....'46 '72 C.112 B.A. L.1066 J.D. Univ. of Calif. at Berkeley
Barber, Robert K. ....'18 '49 C.112 A.B. L.1065 J.D. Ret. Supr. Ct. J.
Barkin, Ronald S., (BV) ....'46 '71 C.112 B.A. L.1066 J.D. 3050 Shattuck Ave.
Barnes, Wallace E., III '— '77 C.103 B.A. L.564 J.D.
(adm. in AZ; not adm. in CA) Berkeley Community Law Center
Barnett, Newell C. ....'11 '35 C.112 A.B. L.1066 LL.B. 3 Rosemont Ave.‡
Barnett, Stephen R. ....'35 '63 C&L.309 A.B., LL.B. Prof. of Law, Univ. of Calif.
Barrett, Donald P. ....'20 '49 C.112 A.B. L.1066 LL.B. 155 Parkside Dr.
Bartells, Jacqueline '15 '50 C&L.911 B.A., J.D.
(adm. in WA; not adm. in CA) Univ. of Calif., Boalt Hall
Barton, Babette B., (AV) ....'30 '55 C.112 B.S. L.1066 LL.B. Prof. of Law, Univ. of Calif.
Baum, James S., (AV) ....'44 '72 C.966 B.S. L.1066 J.D. [Schrag&B.]
Belilove, Saul ....'19 '51 C.103 B.S. L.284 156 Tunnel Rd.‡
Bell, Edward M. ....'17 '43 C.112 L.1065 J.D. 1336 Bayview Pl.
Bellah, Melanie ....'28 '74 C.813 A.B. L.1066 J.D. 10 Mosswood Rd.
Bemesderfer, Karl J. ....'40 '69 C.145 B.A. L.309 LL.B. Pres., KJB Realty Consultants
Bergesen, B. E., III, (AV) ....'34 '67 C.197 A.B. L.976 LL.B. 1990 Berryman St.
Bergman, Robert L., (AV) ....'21 '55 C.112 B.S. L.1065 J.D. 29 Tanglewood Rd.‡
Bergmans, Lois Arnold ....'11 '36 C.112 A.B. L.1066 LL.B. 1320 Addison St.‡
Berland, William S., (AV) ....'43 '69 C.112 B.A. L.1066 J.D. [Ferguson&B.]
**Berliner, Roger A., (AV⊕)** ....'51 '83 C.197 B.A. L.464 J.D. [Brady&B.]⊙
*PRACTICE AREAS: Litigation; Appellate Advocacy; North American Energy Law and Trade; Federal and State Legislation.
Bernal & Rigney, Inc., (AV) .... 2150 Shattuck Ave.
Bisno, Robert H. '51 '78
C.1079 B.A. L.765 LL.B. Chmn. & CEO, Transaction Financial Corp.
Blaine, William L. ....'31 '59 C.208 B.A. L.309 LL.B. Calif. Continuing Educ. of the Bar
Blanchette, Janis LaRoche, (AV) ....'49 '79 C.477 B.A. L.1066 J.D. 2300 Shattuck Ave.
Bobrowski, Paul G. ....'57 '91 C.454 B.S. L.767 J.D. 1563 Solano Ave.
Boedecker, Aviva Shiff '53 '78
C.112 B.A. L.1065 J.D. Dir. of Planned Giving, Univ. of Calif.
**Boer, Gina Dashman** ....'59 '86 C.112 B.A. L.273 J.D. [Buresh,K.J.F.&A.]
*PRACTICE AREAS: Insurance Defense.
Boersch, Martha ....'57 '86 C.629 B.A. L.1066 J.D. Asst. U.S. Atty.
Bond, Charles, (AV) ....'49 '74 C.228 A.B. L.1065 J.D. 821 Bancroft Way (⊙San Fran.)
Bonnell, Fraser A. ....'35 '77 C.112 B.A. L.1066 J.D. 316 Vassar Ave.
Borrus, Michael Glen ....'55 '83 C.674 A.B. L.309 J.D. Univ. of Calif.
Bradley, Bertram ....'32 '59 C.188 A.B. L.597 J.D. 6 Norwood Ave. (Pat.)
Bradley, Rachel ....'— '81 C.813 A.B. L.976 J.D. 1212 Campus Dr.

**Brady & Berliner, (AV⊕)**
**2560 Ninth Street, Suite 316, 94710-2567⊙**
**Telephone: 510-549-6926 Telecopier: 510-649-9793**
**Roger A. Berliner; John W. Jimison (Not admitted in CA).**
**Electricity Restructuring, Administrative Law, Commercial Litigation, Appellate Advocacy, Intergovernmental Affairs, Legislative Practice, Health Policy, International Trade, North American Energy Transactions, Oil and Gas Law and Public Utility Law.**
**References: Canadian Embassy; City of Vernon, California; Polysiocyanurate Insulation Manufacturers Assn.; Watson Cogeneration Co.**
**Washington, D.C. Office: 1225 Nineteenth Street N.W., Suite 800. Telephone: 202-955-6067. Telecopy: 202-822-0109.**
**Los Angeles, California Office: 1875 Century Park East, Suite 700. Telephone: 310-282-6848. Telecopy: 310-282-6841.**
**Sacramento, California Office: 1121 L Street, Suite 606. Telephone: 916-448-7819. Telecopy: 916-448-1140.**
*See Professional Biographies, BERKELEY, CALIFORNIA*

Bresnahan, Terrance M., (BV) ....'35 '61 C.740 B.A. L.767 LL.B. P.O. Box 9084
Briggs, Donald R. '45 '74
C.763 A.B. L.1049 J.D. Resch. Atty., Continuing Educ. of the Bar
Brock, Greg ....'59 '96 C.112 A.B. L.1066 J.D. 1415 Bonita Ave.
Brosnahan, Carol S., (Mrs.) ....'34 '60 C.914 A.B. L.309 LL.B. Mun. Ct. J.
Brown, Maeve Elise '64 '88 C.112 B.A. L.1068 J.D.
Supervising Atty., Berkeley Community Law Ctr.
Brown, Wendy Lea '55 '81 C.103 A.B. L.659 J.D.
Staff Atty., Calif. Continuing Educ. of the Bar
Bruck, Michael R., (BV) ....'49 '74 C.112 B.A. L.1065 J.D. 732 D. Addison St.
Brunn, George ....'24 '51 C&L.813 B.A., J.D. Ret. Mun. Ct. J.
Burcham, Thomas H. ....'36 '62 C.112 A.B. L.1066 J.D. 2320 Shattuck Ave.
**Buresh, Scott, (AV)** ....'51 '76 C.629 B.S. L.464 J.D. [Buresh,K.J.F.&A.]
*PRACTICE AREAS: Insurance Defense.

**Buresh, Kaplan, Jang, Feller & Austin, (AV) BB**
**2298 Durant Avenue, 94704**
**Telephone: 510-548-7474 Fax: 510-548-7488**
**Scott Buresh; Ann S. Kaplan; Alan J. Jang; Fred M. Feller; Steven K. Austin; Gina Dashman Boer; Peggy Chang; Daniel L. Cook; Noël Sidney Plummer.**
**General Civil Appellate and Trial Practice. Insurance Defense, Personal Injury, Business Litigation, Landlord-Tenant, Real Property, Construction and Products Liability.**
*See Professional Biographies, BERKELEY, CALIFORNIA*

**Burnstein, Malcolm S., (AV)** ....'33 '60 C.112 A.B. L.1066 LL.B. [Burnstein&T.]

**Burnstein & Trimbur, (AV)**
**1816 Fifth Street, 94710**
**Telephone: 510-548-5075 FAX: 510-548-5074**
**Members of Firm: Malcolm S. Burnstein; Catherine Trimbur.**
**Civil Litigation in State and Federal Courts. Employment, Family, Custody, Probate and Entertainment Law. Appellate Practice.**
*See Professional Biographies, BERKELEY, CALIFORNIA*

Burton, Stephen D. ....'55 '83 C.112 B.A. L.284 J.D. 1720 Spruce St.
Bushman, Willard M. '37 '66 C.813 B.A. L.1066 LL.B.
Resch. Prog. Atty., Continuing Educ. of the Bar
Buxbaum, Richard M. ....'30 '53 C&L.188 A.B., LL.B. Prof. of Law, Univ. of Calif.
Cahn, Elliot ....'48 '81 C.112 A.B. L.1066 J.D. 3108 Lewiston Ave.
Calderaro, Robert M. ....'56 '84 C.112 A.B. L.1066 J.D. 1676 Dwight Way
Calvert, David W. ....'48 '84 C.188 B.A. L.1230 J.D. [Miller,C.C.&R.]
Calvert, Robert J. ....'27 '54 C&L.813 A.B., LL.B. 1050 Cragmont
Carder, William H., (AV) ....'41 '66 C.112 A.B. L.1066 LL.B. 584 Spruce St.
Caron, David D. '52 '83
C.869 B.S. L.1066 J.D. Prof., Boalt Hall Sch. of Law, Univ. of Calif.
Carroll, William A. ....'25 '53 C.112 A.B. L.309 J.D. Dir., Continuing Educ. of the Bar
Chabasinski, Theodore ....'37 '87 C.563 B.A. L.1230 J.D. 2923 Florence St.
Chamberlain, Michael Alton ....'52 '83 C.1051 B.A. L.767 J.D. Pacific School of Religion
**Chang, Peggy** ....'64 '89 C.766 B.A. L.1066 J.D. [Buresh,K.J.F.&A.]
*LANGUAGES: Mandarin.
*PRACTICE AREAS: Insurance Defense.
Chanin, James B. ....'47 '77 C.112 A.B. L.767 J.D. 3050 Shattuck Ave.
Chapin, John K. ....'46 '71 C.174 B.A. L.846 J.D. Calif. Continuing Educ. of the Bar
Chavez, Kathy Merickel ....'48 '85 C.37 B.A. L.1065 J.D. 1400 Shattuck Ave.
Child, Barbara '38 '77 C.347 B.A. L.7 J.D.
(adm. in OH; not adm. in CA) 2441 Le Conte Ave.‡
Clark, Glenn M. ....'47 '80 C.33 L.1230 J.D. [Miller,C.C.&R.]
Clifford, Denis J. ....'39 '67 C.31 B.A. L.178 LL.B. 2121 Bomar St.
Cohn, Irene P. ....'39 '78 C.331 A.B. L.1065 J.D. Univ. of Calif.
Cohn-Postar, Robert ....'56 '82 C.705 B.A. L.1065 J.D. 739 Allston Way
Cohn-Postar, Susan ....'56 '81 C.112 B.A. L.767 J.D. 739 Allston Way
Cole, Michael P. ....'40 '66 C.629 B.S. L.1066 J.D. 424 Vassar Ave.
Cole, Robert H. '31 '56 C&L.309 A.B., LL.B.
(adm. in DC; not adm. in CA) Univ. of Calif. Law Sch.
Coleston, Howard J., Jr. ....'52 '90 C.112 B.S. L.765 J.D. 2204 Dwight Way
Compton, Linda Anthenien '49 '76
C.112 B.A. L.1065 J.D. Resch. Atty., Continuing Educ. of the Bar
Conger, Julie Mendlow ....'42 '74 C.788 B.S. L.1066 J.D. Mun. Ct. J.
**Connolly, Lizabeth Sara** ....'62 '87 C.1102 B.S. L.262 J.D. [⊠ Methven&Assoc.]
*PRACTICE AREAS: Commercial Litigation; Estate Planning; Taxation.
Cooney, Patricia N. ....'50 '85 C.112 A.B. L.284 J.D. 1108 Fresno Ave.
Corbett, Roger ....'24 '55 C.549 L.767 LL.B. 2205 Shattuck Ave.
Cross, Richard A., (BV) ....'51 '79 C.668 B.A. L.800 J.D. 2150 Shattuck Ave.
Danow, Raymond H. M. ....'12 '48 C.145 A.B. L.765 LL.B. 575 San Luis Rd.‡
Davis, William E. ....'50 '78 C.112 A.B. L.284 J.D. 1760 Solano Ave.

**Dennis-Strathmeyer, Jeffrey A., (AV) '45 '73 C.813 A.B. L.1067 J.D.**
**2300 Shattuck Avenue, Room 308, P.O. Box 533, 94701**
**Telephone: 510-642-8317**
**Email: STRATHJ@CEB.UCOP.EDU**
**(Certified Specialist, Estate Planning, Trust and Probate Law, The State Bar of California Board of Legal Specialization).**
**Estate Planning, Probate, Trust and Related Tax Law.**
*See Professional Biographies, BERKELEY, CALIFORNIA*

Derbin, Robert C., Jr. ....'48 '83 C.215 B.S. L.1026 J.D. 1740 Walnut St.
de Reus, Elizabeth A. ....'— '57 C.352 B.A. L.1066 LL.B. 929 Mendocino Ave.
Diener, S. Robert ....'49 '78 C.659 B.A. L.1230 J.D. 3050 Shattuck Ave.
Dobel, Kathryn E. ....'48 '79 C.766 B.A. L.765 J.D. 2026 Delaware St.
Dolven, Earl P. ....'35 '60 C.966 B.A. L.309 LL.B. 663 Vicente
Dopkin, Steven D. ....'51 '86 C.112 M.A. L.1065 J.D. 2731 Benvenue Ave.
Dorinson, David A. ....'42 '66 C.112 A.B. L.1066 LL.B. 1000 Fresno Ave.
Dromgoole, Armond J., Jr. '46 '78 C.112 A.B. L.1065 J.D.
Research Atty., Calif. Continuing Educ. of the Bar

Drossel, Norlen E., (AV) ....'44 '79 C.112 A.B. L.765 J.D. [Anderson&D.]
Duane, Richard P., (AV) ....'39 '65 C.112 A.B. L.1066 LL.B. [Duane,L.&S.]
Duane, Lyman & Seltzer, (AV) ....2000 Center St.
Duga, Lawrence L. ....'32 '60 C.112 B.A. L.1065 J.D. 857 Neilson St.
Dworin, Christopher D. '50 '75
C.1169 A.B. L.1067 J.D. Calif. Continuing Educ. of the Bar
Edlin, Dorothy M. ....'34 '76 C.685 A.B. L.1065 J.D. 1525 Arch
Edlin, Theodore R. ....'35 '68 C.685 B.A. L.1065 J.D. 612 The Alameda
Elhauge, Einer R. '61 '86 C&L.309 B.A., J.D.
(adm. in PA; not adm. in CA) Prof., Boalt Hall Sch. of Law, Univ. of Calif.
Ellsworth, Robert A. ....'34 '63 C.112 A.B. L.1065 J.D. 2437 Durant Ave.‡
Elmer, Martin James, (BV) ....'51 '79 C.912 B.A. L.284 J.D. 1915 Addison
Elson, Henry M., (BV) ....'26 '53 C.966 A.B. L.1066 J.D. 2000 Center St.
Fathi, David C. ....'62 '89 C.911 B.S. L.1066 J.D. 2222 Martin Luther King Jr. Way
Feller, David E. '16 '41 C&L.309 A.B., LL.B.
(adm. in MA; not adm. in CA) Prof. of Law, Emeritus, Univ. of Calif.
**Feller, Fred M.**, (AV) ....'49 '76 C.668 B.A. L.276 J.D. [Buresh,K.J.F.&A.]
*PRACTICE AREAS: Insurance Defense; Landlord Tenant.
Ferguson, Michael C., (AV) ....'43 '69 C.112 A.B. L.1066 J.D. [Ferguson&B.]
Ferguson & Berland, P.C., (AV) ....1816 5th St.
Fitting, Bruce D. ....'47 '81 C.813 A.B. L.767 J.D. 665 Spruce St.
Fleming, Scott ....'23 '50 C.112 A.B. L.1066 LL.B. 2750 Shasta Rd.‡
Forman, George ....'46 '71 C.112 A.B. L.1066 J.D. 2150 Shattuck Ave.
Freiser, Lawrence M. '42 '66 C.569 B.A. L.1009 J.D.
Calif. Continuing Educ. of the Bar
Frisbie, Richard K., (AV) ....'14 '42 C.112 B.S. L.1066 J.D. 2131 University Ave.
Gaines, Patricia A., (BV) ....'30 '67 C.156 B.A. L.767 J.D. 1440 Acton Crescent
Gale, Barton D. ....'39 '72 C.112 B.A. L.1065 J.D. 3160 College Ave.
Garcia, Jose Joel ....'46 '80 C.112 B.A. L.1066 J.D. Exec. Dir., Univ. of Calif.
Garlin, Victor A. ....'35 '84 C.112 B.A. L.1065 J.D. 1813 Monterey Ave.
Gee, Herbert N.F., (BV) ....'46 '74 C.1097 B.A. L.1066 J.D. 2030 Addison St.
Gelb, Marjorie, (AV) ....'46 '70 C.665 B.A. L.145 J.D. Chf. Coun., City Rent Bd.
**Gibbs, Lawrence A.** ....'52 '80 C.813 B.A. L.1066 J.D. [Grossman&G.]
*PRACTICE AREAS: Criminal and Civil Appeals and Writs.
**Giblin, James A.** ....'41 '69 C.800 B.A. L.1049 J.D. Asst. Pat. Coun., Bayer Corp. (Pat.)

**Gillin, Jacobson, Ellis, Larsen & Doyle**
(See Orinda)

Glatt, Joyce Hiyama ....'49 '78 C.112 B.A. L.767 J.D. 946 San Benito Rd.
Goldmacher, Sheila L. ....'34 '81 C.102 B.A. L.284 J.D. 2341 Parker St.
Goldman, Candace ....'51 '79 C.222 B.A. L.352 J.D. 1652 Euclid Ave.
Goldman, Catherine M. ....'54 '81 C.112 B.A. L.1067 J.D. [Goldman&G.]
Goldman, Eric ....'48 '80 C.685 B.A. L.1067 J.D. [Goldman&G.]
Goldman & Goldman ....2124 Los Angeles Ave.
Goldsmith, Donald W. ....'43 '83 C.309 B.A. L.1066 J.D. 2153 Russell St.
Good, Suzanne E. ....'— '76 Calif. Continuing Educ. of the Bar
Goodwin, Eva S. ....'30 '57 C.604 B.A. L.145 J.D. 919 Shattuck Ave.‡
Gordon, Lawrence H. ....'43 '72 C.563 B.B.A. L.1026 792 Cragmont Ave.
Gordon, Milton H. ....'30 '55 C.112 A.B. L.1066 LL.B. 415 Michigan Ave.‡
Gorelick, Barry P., (BV) ....'59 '85 C.112 A.B. L.284 J.D. 2000 Center St.
Gorman, George C. ....'41 '84 C.188 B.A. L.1066 J.D. 952 The Alameda
Graber, Suzanne E. '40 '66 C.112 B.A. L.1066 LL.B.
Calif. Continuing Educ. of the Bar
Graham, Gordon L. ....'36 '66 C.939 A.B. L.1066 LL.B. 1752 Marin Ave.
Greenberg, Rachel Ada ....'61 '88 C.112 B.A. L.1065 J.D. Continuing Educ. of the Bar
Grimes, J. Stokley, (BV) ....'40 '78 C.112 B.A. L.1065 J.D. 1816 5th St.
**Grossman, Elizabeth R.**, (BV) ....'56 '82 C.112 B.A. L.1065 J.D. [Grossman&G.]
*PRACTICE AREAS: Criminal Trials; Juvenile and Professional Disciplinary Hearings.

**Grossman & Gibbs, (BV)**
**1510 Fourth Street, 94710-1707**
**Telephone: 510-524-4141**
**Members of Firm: Elizabeth R. Grossman; Lawrence A. Gibbs.**
**Criminal Law.**
*See Professional Biographies, BERKELEY, CALIFORNIA*

Grove, Pamela R. ....'50 '78 C.112 B.A. L.1067 J.D. 2827 Regent St.
Gusfield, Ilene L. ....'56 '82 L.1230 LL.B. Berkeley Comm. Law Ctr.
Gutierrez, John E. ....'56 '83 C.966 B.A. L.1066 J.D. 762 Vincente
Hagelstein, Marie ....'— '79 C.999 B.A. L.464 J.D. Calif. Continuing Educ. of the Bar
Hagerty, Lawrence V. ....'15 '45 C.608 A.B. L.309 LL.B. 818 Mendocino Ave.
Halbach, Edward C., Jr. '31 '58 C&L.352 B.A., J.D.
(adm. in IA; not adm. in CA) Prof. of Law, Univ. of Calif.
Halvonik, Paul N., (AV) ....'39 '64 C.112 A.B. L.1066 LL.B. 2600 10th St.
Hammerman, John M., (AV) ....'35 '60 C.659 B.S. L.309 LL.B. 180 Hillcrest Rd.‡
Harper, William S. '63 '92 C.170 B.A. L.174 J.D.
(adm. in CO; not adm. in CA) Berkeley Windsurfing
Harris, Angela ....'61 '88 C.477 B.A. L.145 J.D. Prof., Univ. of Calif., Sch. of Law
Hart, Virginia V. ....'51 '79 C.112 A.B. L.770 J.D. P.O. Box 8342
Harvey, Frederic L., (BV) ....'28 '54 C.112 A.B. L.1066 LL.B. 2832 College Ave.
Hasse, Lizbeth ....'53 '82 C.918 B.A. L.1066 J.D. 2000 Center St. (©San Francisco)
Hauer, Glen L. ....'56 '85 C.1169 B.A. L.1230 J.D. 1626 Channing Way
Hayden, David T. ....'25 '55 C.169 B.A. L.1065 LL.B. 2421 4th St.
Hecht, Henry L. ....'46 '73 C.951 B.A. L.309 J.D. Univ. of Calif. at Berkeley Sch. of Law
Hecker, Cynthia W. ....'46 '72 C.914 B.A. L.309 J.D. 721 Arlington Ave.‡
Herman, Dean M. ....'59 '85 C.659 B.A. L.1066 J.D. 1800 Spruce St.
Hess, C. Victor ....'22 '59 C.112 A.B. L.765 LL.B. 2462 Prince St.
**Hetland, John R.**, (AV) ....'30 '56 C&L.494 B.S.L., J.D. [Hetland&K.]©

**Hetland & Kneeland, A Professional Corporation, (AV)**
**2600 Warring Street, 94704©**
**Telephone: 510-548-5900 Fax: 510-548-0197**
**John R. Hetland.**
**Consultant and expert witness in matters relating to Real Estate and Secured Transactions (Title Insurance, Professional Responsibility, Brokers and Lenders).**
**Orinda, California Office: Hetland & Kneeland. 20 Redcoach Lane. Fax: 510-253-9658.**

Heyman, Ira M. ....'30 '56 C.197 B.A. L.976 LL.B. Univ. of Calif. Sch. of Law
Hill, Margaret R. ....'54 '79 C.112 A.B. L.1066 J.D. 2832 College Ave.
Hill, Richard F., (BV) ....'48 '79 C.112 B.A. L.1066 J.D. 1816 5th St.
Hill, W. J. ....'18 '62 C.976 B.A. L.1066 LL.B. Prof. of Law, Univ. of Calif.

**Himelstein, Mark, (AV) '39 '68 C.347 A.B. L.273 LL.B.**
**2030 Addison Street, Seventh Floor, 94704-1104**
**Telephone: 510-548-2301 Facsimile: 510-848-0266**
***REPORTED CASES: Smith v. Regents, 4 Cal.4th 843, 844 P.2d 500, 16 Cal.Rptr. 2d 181 (1993); Mann v. Alameda County, 85 CA3d 505, 149 Cal.Rptr. 552 (1978); Zumwalt v. Trustees, 33 CA3d 665, 109 Cal.Rptr. 344 (1973); Mabey v. Reagan, 376 F.Supp. 216 (1974); 537 F.2d 1036 (1976); Toney v. Reagan, 326 F.Supp. 1093, 467 F.2d 953, cert. denied, 409 U.S. 1130 (1972).**

(This Listing Continued)



**Himelstein, Mark (Continued)**

**Representation of Business Entities, Nonprofit Organizations and Educational Institutions. Civil Trial Practice, Commercial Transactions, Real Estate, Trusts and Probate.**
*See Professional Biographies, BERKELEY, CALIFORNIA*

Hofmayer, Michael D. '43 '69 C.976 B.A. L.1066 J.D.
Calif. Continuing Educ. of the Bar

**Holmes, Paul W. '54 '81 C&L.101 B.S., J.D.**
**2171 Shattuck Avenue, 94704**
**Telephone: 510-843-5800 Facsimile: 510-843-3999**
**Estate Planning, Probate and Trust Administration.**
*See Professional Biographies, BERKELEY, CALIFORNIA*

Hom, Sharon K. ....'59 '85 C.112 B.A. L.1065 J.D. 1919 Addison St.
Hoogs, William H., (BV) ....'18 '42 C.112 L.1065 LL.B. 1915 Addison St.
Hopkins, Ann ....'58 '87 C.75 B.A. L.1066 J.D. 2030 Addison St.
Houk, Julie M. ....'57 '84 C.436 B.A. L.284 J.D. 3050 Shattuck Ave.
Hsieh, Marina C. '60 '91 C.309 A.B. L.1066 J.D.
(adm. in PA; not adm. in CA) Acting Prof. of Law, Univ. of Calif.
Hubbell, Phyllis L. '44 '75 C.338 B.A. L.339 J.D.
(adm. in IL; not adm. in CA) Starr King Sch. for the Ministry
Hughes, Rodney G. ....'48 '73 C.112 A.B. L.464 J.D. 2320 Ward St.
Hunsberger, David R. ....'47 '87 C.62 B.Mus. L.1066 J.D. 2832 College Ave.
Hunt, Joanna Leigh ....'58 '90 C.112 A.B. L.767 J.D. 535 Arlington Ave.
Irving, Ginny ....'45 '75 C.604 A.B. L.284 J.D. Law Libr., Univ. of Calif.
Jaeger, Lauraine Gold ....'40 '75 C.012 B.Sc. L.765 J.D. 650 Euclid Ave.‡
Jamison, William L. ....'26 '67 C.112 L.765 LL.B. 1660 Tyler St.
Janes, Kathleen Miller ....'47 '85 C.483 B.A. L.767 J.D. Continuing Educ. of the Bar
**Jang, Alan J.**, (BV) ....'53 '78 C.112 B.A. L.284 J.D. [Buresh,K.J.F.&A.]
*PRACTICE AREAS: Insurance Defense.
Jelinek, Donald A., (BV) ....'34 '59 C&L.569 A.B., LL.B. [Jelinek&S.]
Jelinek & Samsel, (BV) ....1919 Addison St.
Jennings, Richard W., (AV) '07 '39
C.640 A.B. L.1066 J.D. Prof. of Law, Emer., Univ. of Calif.‡
Jester, Pamela J. ....'49 '78 C.629 B.S. L.284 J.D. Calif. Continuing Educ. of the Bar
**Jimison, John W.**, (AV©) '46 '75 C.970 B.A. L.276 J.D.
(adm. in VA; not adm. in CA) [Brady&B.] (©Wash., DC)
*LANGUAGES: French, Somali.
Johnson, Elizabeth Marie '49 '78
C.1073 B.A. L.1067 J.D. Resch. Atty., Continuing Educ. of the Bar
Johnson, Phillip E., (AV) ....'40 '66 C.309 A.B. L.145 J.D. Univ. of Calif. Sch. of Law
Jonas, Louis ....'50 '76 C.112 A.B. L.1065 J.D. 698 Cragmont Ave.

**Jordan, Susan B., (AV) '41 '70 C.477 A.B. L.597 J.D.**
**P.O. Box 5805, 94705-0805©**
**Telephone: 510-849-1143 FAX: 510-849-4843**
**Criminal and Civil Trial and Appellate Practice.**
**Ukiah, California Office: 515 S. School Street. Telephone: 707-462-2151. FAX: 707-462-2194.**
*See Professional Biographies, BERKELEY, CALIFORNIA*

Jorde, Thomas M. '47 '75 C&L.976 B.A., J.D.
Prof. of Law, Boalt Hall School of Law, Univ. of Calif.
Joseph, Maria L. ....'57 '82 C.477 B.A. L.767 J.D. 94 The Uplands
Kadish, Sanford H. '21 '48 C.563 B.S. L.178 LL.B.
(adm. in NY; not adm. in CA) Prof. of Law, Emeritus, Univ. of Calif.
Kagan, Robert A. '38 '63 C.309 A.B. L.178 LL.B.
(adm. in NJ; not adm. in CA) Univ. of Calif.
**Kaplan, Ann S.**, (AV) ....'51 '77 C.813 B.A. L.767 J.D. [Buresh,K.J.F.&A.]
*PRACTICE AREAS: Insurance Defense.
Kaplan, Jane R., (BV) ....'51 '79 C.112 B.A. L.767 J.D. 3050 Shattuck Ave.
Karplus, Curtis M. '31 '57
C.188 B.A. L.309 LL.B. Asst. Dir., Continuing Educ. of the Bar
Karshmer, Barbara E. ....'48 '74 C.112 B.A. L.1068 J.D. 2150 Shattuck Ave.
**Katzoff, Kenneth S.**, (BV) ....'56 '82 C.861 B.A. L.767 J.D. [Katzoff&R.]
*PRACTICE AREAS: Civil Litigation; Real Estate Law; Insurance Defense; Insurance Coverage Law; Juvenile Dependency Law.

**Katzoff & Riggs, (AV)**
**3088 Claremont Avenue, 94705©**
**Telephone: 510-597-1990 FAX: 510-597-0295**
**Members of Firm: Robert R. Riggs; Kenneth S. Katzoff. Associates: Jesse D. Palmer.**
**Civil and Criminal Trial Practice, Juvenile Dependency and Appeals. Real Estate and Real Estate Transactions, Construction, Insurance Defense and Insurance Coverage Law, Computer Software Licensing Law.**
**Cobb, California Office: Meadow Springs Shopping Center, P.O. Box 1250. Telephone: 707-928-4600. Fax: 707-928-5075.**
*See Professional Biographies, BERKELEY, CALIFORNIA*

Kaufman, Deborah Ann ....'55 '80 C.999 B.A. L.1065 J.D. 1713 Madera St.
Kay, Herma H. ....'34 '60 C.802 B.A. L.145 J.D. Univ. of Calif. Sch. of Law
Kayne, Marvin S. ....'31 '55 C.597 B.S. L.309 LL.B. Univ. of Calif. Sch. of Law
Keller, Jo Anne Wells ....'42 '78 C.378 B.A. L.1065 J.D. P.O. Box 8032
Kelley, Michael S. ....'43 '69 C.112 B.A. L.1066 523 Santa Barbara Rd.
Kemp, Deborah A. ....'50 '91 C.766 B.A. L.767 J.D. 280 Panoramic Way
Kendall, Deborah ....'51 '77 C.112 B.A. L.284 J.D. P.O. Box 8021
Kennedy, Patrick C. ....'53 '86 C.154 B.S. L.309 J.D. 2714-9th St.‡
Kerman, Peter W. ....'50 '75 C.112 B.A. L.770 J.D. 2030 Addison St., 7th Flr.
Kilb, Linda D. '63 '88 C.112 B.A. L.309 J.D.
Mng. Dir., Disability Rights Educ. & Def. Fund
Kilpatrick, Judith ....'46 '75 C.112 B.A. L.1066 J.D. Calif. Continuing Educ. of the Bar
Kirby, Robert W., Jr. ....'46 '71 C&L.767 B.A., J.D. P.O. Box 911
Klein, Lawrence R. ....'31 '56 C.659 B.S. L.976 LL.B. 3420 Dwight Way‡
Klein, Randi Susan ....'54 '89 C.766 B.A. L.284 J.D. 2625 Alcatraz Ave.
Klein, Ronald H., (AV) ....'33 '62 C.112 A.B. L.1066 LL.B. 1524 Sacramento St.
Knowlton, AnitaChristine ....'50 '78 C.331 B.A. L.1068 J.D. 1707 Parker St.
Koenig, Alan S., (BV) ....'43 '69 C.112 A.B. L.1066 J.D. P.O. Box 1170
Kolling, Alan T. ....'52 '82 C.112 B.A. L.1065 J.D. Asst. Dean of Students, Univ. of Calif.
Kowalski, Joanne M. ....'38 '83 C.477 B.A. L.1230 J.D. 2214 Roosevelt Ave.
Kragen, Adrian A., (AV) ....'07 '34 C.112 A.B. L.1066 J.D. Prof. of Law, Univ. of Calif.‡
Kranz, Paul ....'47 '84 C.1036 B.A. L.1066 J.D. 2560 Ninth St.
Krizack, Marc L. ....'51 '88 C.454 B.A. L.1065 J.D. 2233 Calif. St.
Laflin, James B. ....'52 '79 C.112 B.A. L.767 J.D. 1521 Shattuck Ave.
Larrabee, Philip A. ....'41 '66 C.602 A.B. L.309 LL.B. P.O. Box 832
Launay, Gerard D. ....'53 '78 C.178 B.A. L.1066 J.D. 1674 University Ave.
Lawrence, Charles F. ....'12 '35 L.1066 LL.B. 901 Cragmont Ave.
Lawson, Michael ....'46 '71 C.1073 B.A. L.1067 J.D. City Atty.
Lea, Susan J. ....'50 '78 C.112 A.B. L.1355 J.D. P.O. Box 8088

**Leader-Picone, Malcolm, Law Office of, (BV) '54 '82 C.1169 A.B. L.1066 J.D.**
**P.O. Box 7598, 94707-0598**
Telephone: 510-528-2975 Fax: 510-528-2954
Email: mlp@leader-picone.com URL: http://www.leader-picone.com
*LANGUAGES: Spanish.
*REPORTED CASES: In re Roxford Foods Litigation (E.D.Cal. 1991) 790 F.Supp. 987; Civic Center Square, Inc. v. James Ford (In re Roxford Foods, Inc.) (9th Cir. 1993) 12 F.3d 875; F.D.I.C. v. Jackson-Shaw Partners No. 46, Ltd. (N.D.Cal. 1994) 790 F.Supp. 987.
*PRACTICE AREAS: Commercial Litigation; Bankruptcy; Environmental Law; Employment Discrimination; Real Estate.
Commercial Litigation, Bankruptcy, Environmental Law, Employment Discrimination, Real Estate.
*See Professional Biographies, BERKELEY, CALIFORNIA*

Leavitt, Jack, (BV) '31 '58 C.102 B.A. L.339 LL.B. 1615 Calif. St.
Lee, Harriet Whitman, (BV) '32 '57 C.112 B.A. L.1066 J.D. 1854 Thousand Oaks Blvd.
Lee, Katherine J. '56 '84 C.112 A.B. L.276 J.D. Dep. City Atty.
Lee, Richard D. '35 '61 C.813 B.A. L.976 J.D. Univ. of Calif.
Lee, Timothy J. '48 '73 C.339 B.A. L.145 J.D. Dep. City Atty.
Leighton, Charles J., Jr., (AV) '13 '38 C.112 A.B. L.1066 J.D. 119 Alvarado Rd., Entry B
Lemon, Nancy K.D. '53 '80 C.1169 B.A. L.1066 J.D. 1063 Cragmont Ave.‡
Lempert, David Howard '59 '86 C.976 B.A. L.813 J.D. CEO, Unseen America Projects, Inc.
Leonard, Duane M. '44 '72 C.112 B.A. L.1065 2030 Addison St. 7th Fl.

**Lerman, David A. '63 '91 C.477 A.B. L.809 J.D.**
**2030 Addison Street, 7th Floor, 94704**
Telephone: 510-841-6124 Fax: 510-848-0266
*PRACTICE AREAS: Employment; Whistleblower Litigation; Wrongful Termination; Personal Injury; Federal False Claims.
Labor and Employment Law, Whistleblower Litigation, Wrongful Termination (Plaintiff), Personal Injury, Federal False Claims.
*See Professional Biographies, BERKELEY, CALIFORNIA*

Lesser, Barbara A. '48 '79 C.339 B.A. L.767 J.D. 2397 Shattuck Ave.
Levin, Polly '50 '81 C.112 A.B. L.284 J.D. 2949 Piedmont Ave.
Levin, Robert A. '42 '69 C.1036 B.A. L.659 LL.B. 2039 Shattuck
Levine, Heidi '59 '85 C.112 B.S. L.1065 J.D. 2723 Ashby Place
Levy, Linda B. '— '81 C.813 B.A. L.1065 J.D. (adm. in HI; not adm. in CA) P.O. Box 7678
Levy, Neil M. '43 '67 C.188 A.B. L.145 J.D. 1950 Addison St.
Ligutis, Richard Adam '27 '80 C.145 B.A. L.1065 J.D. 2119 Ashby Ave.‡
Lindheim, Daniel N. '46 '87 C.112 B.A. L.276 J.D. Pres., General Electronics Sys./Diaquest
Loeb, Daniel N., (AV) '37 '61 C.95 A.B. L.309 J.D. [D.N.Loeb]
Loeb, Daniel N., Professional Corporation, (AV) 2030 Addison St.
Longtin, James '36 '63 C.723 L.1049 LL.B. 1143 Hillview Rd.‡
Lorenz, James '38 '65 C&L.309 A.B., LL.B. 16 Hillcrest Ct.‡
Love, Robert '44 '79 C.112 B.A. L.765 J.D. 2427 Durant Ave.
Lowe, Frank A., (BV) '47 '72 C.154 B.A. L.1068 J.D. [Pulich&L.]
Lozenski, James L. '42 '82 C.1073 B.A. L.1197 J.D. 1600 Shattuck Ave.

**Lubman, Stanley B., Law Office of, (AV) '34 '59 C&L.178 A.B., LL.B.**
In Association with Allen & Overy
**1422 Arch Street, 94708**
Telephone: 510-843-8881 Fax: 510-843-8882
Email: slubman@well.com
*LANGUAGES: Modern Chinese; French.
*PRACTICE AREAS: Trade and investment matters involving the People's Republic of China.
General Business Law, International Law, Trade Law and Investment involving the People's Republic of China.
Associated Hong Kong Office: Allen & Overy, 9/F, Three Exchange Square, 8 Connaught Place. Telephone: 852.2840.1282. Fax: 852.2840.0515.
Associated Beijing Office: Allen & Overy, Jing Guang Centre, Suite 3204, Hu Jia Lou, Chao Yang District, 100020, PRC. Telephone: 86-10-65014681. Fax: 86-10-65014682.
Associated London Office: Allen & Overy, One New Change, EC4M 9QQ. Telephone: 44-171-330-3000. Fax: 44-171-330-9999.
*See Professional Biographies, BERKELEY, CALIFORNIA*

**Luten, Susan Burnett, Law Offices of, (AV) '50 '80 C.112 B.A. L.1065 J.D.**
**Suite 401, 2140 Shattuck Avenue, 94704**
Telephone: 510-548-5500 Fax: 510-548-6363
*REPORTED CASES: Marani v. Jackson (1986) 183 Cal App. 3d 695; Davis v. City of Berkeley (1990) 51 Cal. 3d 227; City of Berkeley v. City of Berkeley Rent Stabilization Bd. (1994) 27 Cal.App. 4th 951.
*PRACTICE AREAS: Civil Litigation; Rent Control Law; Appellate Law; Real Estate Law; Expert Witness: Landlord-Tenant.
Litigation, Rent Control Law and Appeals.
*See Professional Biographies, BERKELEY, CALIFORNIA*

Lyman, Edward H., (AV) '43 '69 C.1060 B.A. L.273 J.D. [Duane,L.&S.]
MacEwan, Dorothy D., (Mrs.) '42 '67 C.112 A.B. L.309 LL.B. 1127 Blake St.‡
Mackley, Carter R. '60 '89 C.101 B.S. L.178 J.D. (adm. in NY; not adm. in CA) Univ. of Calif. Sch. of Pub. Health
Magers-Rankin, Deborah K. '49 '83 C.112 A.B. L.1066 J.D. Resch. Atty., Continuing Educ. of the Bar
Mannis, Kent L. '59 '87 C.976 B.A. L.1067 J.D. 2015 Cedar St.
Margolin, Christopher J. '46 '72 C.674 A.B. L.659 J.D. V.P., Gen. Coun. & Secy., XOMA Corp.
Margolin, Steven G. '55 '80 C.976 B.S. L.1066 J.D. 6031 Chabolyn Terr.
Martin, David J., (BV) '29 '54 C.112 B.A. L.1065 J.D. [Martin&M.]
Martin, Stephen B. '44 '76 C.309 A.B. L.284 J.D. 2908 Harper St.
Martin & Martin, (BV) 2171 Shattuck Ave.
Mason, Larry K. '48 '80 C.112 B.A. L.1066 J.D. 2813 Milvia St.
McKeown, David J. '38 '65 C.262 B.S. L.893 LL.B. 3049 Buena Vista Way
McKinley, Joseph A. '20 '48 C.178 B.A. L.37 LL.B. 50 Alvarado Rd.‡
McNeill, Mary B. '54 '85 C.112 B.S. L.1065 J.D. 1604 Solano Ave.
McNulty, John K. '34 '61 C.821 A.B. L.976 LL.B. (adm. in OH; not adm. in CA) Prof. of Law, Univ. of Calif.
Meade, Kenneth A., (BV) '38 '65 C.112 A.B. L.1066 LL.B. 2423 Webster St.
Meade, Nancy Beth '62 '87 C.855 B.A. L.588 J.D. Univ. of Calif.
Melchiskey, Stephen J. '58 '87 C.188 B.S. L.431 J.D. (adm. in ME; not adm. in CA) 1326 Josephine St.‡
**Methven, Bruce E.** '52 '80 C.112 A.B. L.1066 J.D. [Methven&Assoc.]
*PRACTICE AREAS: Computer/Multimedia Law; Business Litigation.

**Methven & Associates**
**2232 Sixth Street, 94710**
Telephone: 510-649-4019 Fax: 510-649-4024
Email: bmethven@aol.com URL: http://members.aol.com/bmethven
Bruce E. Methven. Of Counsel: Frank J. Gilbert; Lizabeth Sara Connolly.

(This Listing Continued)

**Methven & Associates (Continued)**

Computer, Multimedia and Telecommunications Law, Business Advising, Litigation and Arbitration, Copyright, Trademark and Trade Secret Law, Corporate, Partnership and Limited Liability Company Work, Business Leases.
*See Professional Biographies, BERKELEY, CALIFORNIA*

Meyer, Ira H., (AV) '43 '68 C.705 B.A. L.930 J.D. 2832 College Ave.
Micallef, Jane '61 '89 C.477 L.1066 J.D. Exec. Dir., Homeless Action Center
Mikell, Bernard J., Jr. '38 '70 C.299 A.B. L.893 LL.B. 2829 Buena Vista Way
Miller, Allan C., (CV) '44 '72 C&L.477 A.B., J.D. [Miller,C.C.&R.]
Miller, John A. '46 '76 C.576 B.A. L.1065 J.D. V.P., Gen. Coun. & Secy., The Pacific Lumber Co.
Miller, Clark, Calvert and Raimondi, (CV) 2222 Martin Luther King Jr. Way
Millman, Mary D. '41 '77 C.112 B.A. L.284 J.D. 3127 Eton Ave.
Mishkin, Paul J. '27 '50 C&L.178 A.B., LL.B. (adm. in NY; not adm. in CA) Univ. of Calif.
Mitchell, Matthew P., (AV) '32 '61 C.31 B.A. L.1066 LL.B. 151 Alvarado Rd.
**Modersbach, Roger J.** '36 '63 C&L.502 A.B., J.D. (adm. in MO; not adm. in CA) Assoc. Coun., Bayer Corp.
**Molinelli, James P., Jr.** '63 '90 C.770 B.S. L.767 J.D. [[A] York&S.]
Monroe, Gwen M. '25 '62 C.112 A.B. L.767 LL.B. 1087 Keeler Ave.
Montauk, Lance E. '47 '75 C.685 B.A. L.1066 J.D. 3035 Bateman St.‡
Moore, Gregory B. '53 '80 C.112 B.A. L.765 J.D. 597 Santa Clara Ave.
Morgan, Sloane Smith '65 '94 C.918 B.A. L.978 J.D. 1415 McGee Ave.
Morris, Carolyn '50 '80 C.112 B.A. L.284 J.D. 2344 Hilgard
Moses, Martha D '57 '84 C.604 B.A. L.477 J.D. 1941 Rose St.
Moskovitz, Myron, (AV) '38 '65 C.112 B.S. L.1066 LL.B. 2371 Eunice St.
Moy, Kenneth K. '53 '79 C.674 A.B. L.1066 J.D. 2397 Shattuck Ave.
Nakatani, Robert N. '45 '81 C.813 A.B. L.1066 J.D. Calif. Continuing Educ. of the Bar
Naparst, Stan '30 '84 C.563 B.S. L.284 J.D. 1757 Capistrano Ave.
Neal, Lawrence M. '62 '89 C.112 B.S. L.1065 J.D. 1319 Talbot Ave.
Neuman, Richard E. '45 '70 C.178 A.B. L.800 J.D. 1563 Solano Ave.
Nuridin, Khadija '57 '88 C.674 B.A. L.1066 J.D. 2425B Channing Way
Oberlink, James R. '53 '81 C.339 A.B. L.1066 J.D. 1007 Allston Way
Ogg, Wilson Reid '28 '55 C.112 A.B. L.1066 J.D. 1104 Keith Ave.‡
Olken, Robert Max '54 '87 C.112 B.A. L.1067 J.D. Dept. of Toxic Substances Control
Olson, Thomas F. '30 '59 C.352 B.A. L.1066 LL.B. 2320 Shattuck Ave.
Orebic, Matthew J. '59 '86 C.112 B.A. L.1065 J.D. Asst. City Atty.
O'Rourke, Sheila '56 '86 C.813 A.B. L.1066 J.D. Acad. Compl. Affs. Offr., Univ. of California at Berkeley
Oswald, Victoria Kathleen '52 '82 C.1169 B.A. L.1065 J.D. 2224 Blake St.
Outis, Robert R. '45 '74 C.339 B.S. L.276 J.D. [R.R.Outis]
Outis, Robert R., A Professional Corp. 1730A Solano Ave.
Owens, Aletha R., (AV) '33 '64 C.112 A.B. L.284 LL.B. Labor Coun., Berkeley Lab.
**Palmer, Jesse D.** '68 '95 C.112 B.S. L.1065 J.D. [[A] Katzoff&R.]
**Paré, Laura Fisher** '59 '90 C.853 B.A. L.767 J.D. [[A] York&S.]
Parker, Michael L. '35 '61 C.668 B.A. L.309 LL.B. 1700 La Vereda Rd.
Parker, Scott G. '63 '91 C.813 B.A. L.1066 J.D. 109 Panoramic Way
Partridge, Elizabeth W. '17 '44 C.112 B.A. L.1066 LL.B. 12 Hillcrest Ct.‡
Passek, Stephen P. '42 '68 C.976 B.A. L.659 LL.B. 1950 Addison St.
Pearson, Philip E. '48 '78 C.473 B.S. L.767 J.D. 2539 Grant St.
Peyerwold, David L. '54 '82 C.112 B.A. L.1066 J.D. Continuing Educ. of the Bar
Phillips, John H. '51 '77 C.112 B.A. L.1065 J.D. 1776 LeRoy Ave.
Piatt, Norma '56 '81 C.777 B.A. L.1065 J.D. Continuing Educ. of the Bar
Pickus, Bob '46 '78 C.813 B.A. L.284 J.D. Calif. Continuing Educ. of the Bar
Plotz, John R. '48 '76 C.309 A.B. L.1066 J.D. 3027 Regent St.
**Plummer, Noël Sidney** '66 '92 C.976 B.A. L.846 J.D. [Buresh,K.J.F.&A.]
*PRACTICE AREAS: Insurance Defense.
Podren, Cynthia, (AV) '49 '78 C.188 B.A. L.1068 J.D. 2030 Addison St.
Post, Robert C. '47 '79 C.309 A.B. L.976 J.D. Prof. of Law, Univ. of Calif., Boalt Hall
Powers, Richard M. '26 '83 C.112 B.S. L.1197 J.D. 739 Grizzly Peak Blvd.
Prochaska, Patricia A. '63 '89 C.190 B.A. L.273 J.D. 2150 Shattuck Ave.
Pulich, Robin G., (BV) '50 '78 C.112 B.A. L.1065 J.D. [Pulich&L.]
Pulich & Lowe, (BV) 2140 Shattuck Ave.
Pyle, Walter K. '40 '65 C.190 L.424 J.D. 2039 Shattuck
Radisch, Jack B., (BV) '37 '71 C.740 B.A. L.1026 J.D. 602 Santa Barbara St.
Raimondi, Carole '43 '85 C.1078 B.A. L.1230 J.D. [Miller,C.C.&R.]
Ramey, Martha L. '48 '77 C.802 B.A. L.1065 J.D. 1960 Los Angeles Ave.
Rantzman, Jon A. '39 '66 C.188 A.B. L.813 LL.B. Mun. Ct. Comr.
Read, Donald H., (AV) '42 '69 C.112 B.A. L.178 J.D. 982 Santa Barbara Rd. (⊙Oakland & Palo Alto)
Reagan, Bernida M. '54 '79 C.112 B.A. L.1068 J.D. Exec. Dir., Berkeley Community Law Ctr.
Renauer, Albin J. '59 '85 C&L.477 B.A., J.D. Nolo Press
Repa, Barbara Kate '55 '82 C.966 B.A. L.365 J.D. (adm. in IL; not adm. in CA) Legal Editor, Nolo Press
Reuben, Berne, (AV) '47 '77 C.156 B.A. L.1066 J.D. 2222 Martin Luther King, Jr. Way
Rhine, Jennie '39 '70 C.766 B.A. L.1065 J.D. Mun. Ct. J.
Rice, Evelyn F., (AV) '31 '69 C.477 B.S. L.1066 J.D. 2150 Shattuck, Ste. 600
Richardson, Jane '50 '77 C.112 B.A. L.94 LL.B. 732 Neilson St.‡
Rigg, Douglas C. '12 '66 C.112 A.B. L.284 LL.B. 2665 Shasta Rd.‡
**Riggs, Robert R.**, (AV) '58 '83 C.367 B.A. L.813 J.D. [Katzoff&R.]⊙
*LANGUAGES: French and Italian.
*PRACTICE AREAS: Civil Litigation; Construction Law; Computer Software Licensing Law; Real Estate Law; Criminal Law.
Rigney, Robert M., (AV) '22 '48 C.986 A.B. L.477 J.D. [Bernal&R.]
Rivkind, Nina R. '51 '77 C.112 B.A. L.1066 J.D. P.O. Box 5273
Rodin, Ellen E. '43 '80 C.112 A.B. L.1066 J.D. P.O. Box 237
Roeckl, Margaret E. '62 '87 C.696 B.A. L.1065 J.D. 1950 Addison St.
Roland, Thomas V., (BV) '37 '72 C.477 B.S. L.767 J.D. P.O. Box 12217
Roman, Michael W., (AV) '42 '69 C.112 A.B. L.1066 J.D. 1816 5th St.
Rosenthal, Paula '43 '68 C.66 B.A. L.659 LL.B. 1318 Josephine
Ross, Julia, (BV) '40 '77 C.112 B.A. L.284 J.D. 1507 Henry St.
Rothman, Jonathan S. '53 '84 C.112 A.B. L.426 J.D. City Atty. Off.
Rubin, Edward L. '48 '81 C.674 B.A. L.976 J.D. (adm. in NY; not adm. in CA) Prof., Univ. of Calif. Sch. of Law
Ruddy, Sara H. '47 '76 C.604 A.B. L.446 J.D. 2515 Milvia St.
Rumberger, Timothy P. '59 '90 C.937 B.A. L.1065 J.D. 2161 Shattuck Ave.
Ryan, Elizabeth B. '42 '81 C.112 B.A. L.1230 J.D. 1928 Monterey Ave.
Samsel, William M., (BV) '41 '66 C.112 A.B. L.1066 S.J.D. [Jelinek&S.]
Sapirstein, Rhoda L. '31 '73 C.999 B.A. L.284 J.D. 4 Rochdale Way
Sax, Joseph L. '36 '60 C.309 A.B. L.145 J.D. (adm. in DC; not adm. in CA) Prof. of Law, Univ. of Calif.
Schapiro, Susan B. '52 '78 C.339 B.A. L.1066 J.D. 2921 Fulton St.

CAA17P

CALIFORNIA—BERKELEY MARTINDALE-HUBBELL LAW DIRECTORY 1997

Schmid, Minor J., (BV) .......... '22 '52 C.112 A.B. L.1065 J.D. 11 Hill Rd.
Schrag, Thomas F., (AV) .......... '42 '66 C.112 B.A. L.1065 LL.B. [Schrag&B.] ‡
Schrag and Baum, (AV) .......... 280 Panoramic Way
Schwartz, Herbert A. .......... '40 '67 C.145 A.B. L.1065 J.D. 1524 Arch St.
Schwartz, Paul M., (BV) .......... '43 '69 C.112 A.B. L.1068 J.D. 2004 Cedar St.
Scott, Craig H. '41 '69 C.674 B.A. L.1066 J.D.
Resch. Atty., Continuing Educ. of the Bar
Seeman, Paul D. .......... '54 '79 L.1066 J.D. 2124 Kittredge
Selbin, Jeffrey .......... '61 '89 C.477 B.A. L.309 J.D. Berkeley Community Law Ctr.
Seligman, Brad, (AV) .......... '51 '78 C.1078 B.A. L.1065 J.D. 1604 Solano Ave.
Seltzer, Eugene S., (AV) .......... '47 '73 C.112 A.B. L.1065 J.D. [Duane,L.&S.]
Shaked, Nitzhia B. .......... '49 '90 L.061 LL.B. 1038 Sierra St.
Sharee, Eugene .......... '14 '70 C.112 A.B. L.765 J.D. 2550 Dana St.‡
Shaughnessy, Stephen W., (BV) .......... '31 '59 C.352 B.A. L.1066 LL.B. 1215 Walnut Ave.
Shenkin, Ann M. .......... '45 '84 C.112 B.A. L.767 J.D. 38 Oakvale Ave.‡
Sherlin, Mary Johanna .......... '50 '79 C.966 B.A. L.1068 J.D. Continuing Educ. of the Bar‡
Sherman, Richard I., (AV) .......... '42 '74 C.1044 B.A. L.284 J.D. 1916 Los Angeles Ave.
Shore, Erika R. .... '47 '77 C.643 B.A. L.767 J.D. Supvr., Alameda Co. Social Servs. Agcy.
Sigal, Roger H. .......... '56 '88 C.183 B.A. L.1066 J.D. 726 Hilldale
Simpson, James B. '51 '79 C.399 B.A. L.1066 J.D.
Gen. Coun., Western Consortium for Pub. Health
Singer, Joel R. .......... '53 '84 C&L.112 B.S., J.D. 1545 Channin Way
Sinift, Bruce E. .......... '52 '83 C.766 B.A. L.1068 J.D. 1607 Berkeley Way
Smith, Genese Dopson, (BV) .......... '51 '83 C.525 B.S.N. L.426 J.D. 2560 9th St.
Smith, Karen .......... '45 '77 C.112 B.A. L.1066 J.D. 2827 Hillegass Ave.‡
**Smith, Kevin M.** .......... '54 '80 C.112 B.A. L.426 J.D. [York&S.]
*PRACTICE AREAS: General Negligence; Professional Negligence (Medical and Legal); Bad Faith Defense.
Smith, Michael G., (AV) .......... '42 '69 C.976 B.S. L.178 J.D. P.O. Box 7206
Smith, Michael R. '41 '67
C.112 B.A. L.1066 LL.B. Asst. Chanc., Legal Affs., Univ. of Calif.
Smith, Sherry H. .......... '43 '72 C.1097 B.A. L.596 J.D. Calif. Continuing Educ. of the Bar
Soublet, Bruce A. .......... '53 '78 C.112 B.A. L.770 J.D. Dep. City Atty., III
Stack, Bonnie L. .......... '47 '75 C.966 B.A. L.976 J.D. 18 Bridge Rd.
Staring, Diana H. .......... '53 '81 C.112 A.B. L.1066 J.D. 105 Parkside Dr.‡
Steinberg, John, (BV) .......... '51 '76 C.112 B.A. L.767 J.D. P.O. Box 8148
Steinberg, Seymour P., (AV) .......... '08 '32 C.112 L.800 LL.B. 1570 Hawthorne Terr.‡
Steinhauer, R.E. .......... '43 '72 1915 Addison St.
Stevens, Richard B. .......... '37 '67 C.229 B.A. L.767 J.D. Univ. of Calif.
Stolz, Preble .......... '31 '57 C.685 A.B. L.145 J.D. Prof. of Law, Univ. of Calif.
Storr, P. Cecilia .......... '46 '86 C.051 B.A. L.1066 J.D. 3105 Deakin St.
Strauss, Eric W. .......... '39 '68 C.339 B.S. L.1066 J.D. Gen. Mgr., Tin Alloy Co.
Sugarman, Stephen D. .......... '42 '67 C&L.597 B.S.B.A., J.D. Univ. of Calif.
Sugiyama, Jennifer Paul .......... '51 '77 C.112 B.A. L.767 J.D. Univ. of Calif.
Sullivan, Lawrence A. '23 '52 C.800 A.B. L.309 LL.B.
(adm. in MA; not adm. in CA) Prof. of Law, Univ. of Calif.
Sweet, Justin .......... '29 '53 C&L.966 B.A., LL.B. Prof. of Law, Univ. of Calif.
**Tabuena, José A.** .......... '62 '88 C.112 B.A. L.1066 J.D. [York&S.]
Takakuwa, Stephen .......... '50 '80 C.768 B.A. L.1065 J.D. 2 Tunnel Rd.
Talcott, Frederick L. .......... '49 '75 C.910 A.B. L.1065 J.D. 440 Gravatt Dr.
Talcott, Marilyn S. .......... '36 '64 C.273 B.A. L.276 LL.B. 2508 Ridge Rd.
Tardy, Michael K. .......... '42 '70 C.608 B.Sc. L.1066 J.D. 2334 Derby St.
Taylor, William Fayette, (BV) .......... '51 '79 C.629 B.S. L.1067 J.D. 2000 Center St.
Thomas, Lois K. .......... '41 '67 C.112 B.A. L.1066 LL.B. 185 The Uplands
Thomas, Theresa L. .......... '48 '78 C.112 A.B. L.765 J.D. 1825 Marin Ave.
Thompson, James R. .......... '42 '72 C.112 B.S. L.1065 J.D. 54 Tunnel Rd.
Thomson, James S., (AV) .......... '48 '78 C.1042 B.A. L.1137 J.D. P.O. Box 11288
Tindel, Kay E. .......... '52 '81 C.112 B.A. L.1065 J.D. Calif. Continuing Educ. of the Bar
Treadwell, Lujuana W. .......... '41 '77 C.37 B.A. L.1066 J.D. Asst. Dean, Univ. of Calif.
**Trimbur, Catherine** .......... '47 '82 C.112 B.A. L.767 J.D. [Burnstein&T.]
Tussey, Phoebe Jane .......... '51 '85 C.383 B.A. L.846 J.D. 1594 Capistrano Ave.‡
Tussman, David A. .......... '46 '76 C.112 A.B. L.1065 J.D. Pres., Tussman Programs, Inc.
Uradnik, Kathleen Ann '64 '89 C.145 B.A. L.893 J.D.
(adm. in MN; not adm. in CA) 2700 Woolsey St., # 1‡
Valencia, Robert L. .......... '42 '69 C.112 B.S. L.1065 J.D. 2219 Calif. St.
Vanden Heuvel, Kathleen M. .... '51 '86 C.112 A.B. L.1066 J.D. Law Libr., Univ. of Calif.
Vetter, Jan .......... '34 '63 C.112 B.A. L.1068 LL.B. Univ. of Calif.
Voge, Elizabeth Moen .......... '53 '83 C.112 A.B. L.284 J.D. 2039 Shattuck Ave.
Waite, Sarita C. .......... '41 '70 C.112 B.A. L.284 J.D. 1020 Miller‡
Walker, John R. .......... '14 '56 C.061 L.767 9 Wilson Circle‡
Walker, Laurence N. .......... '32 '63 C.112 A.B. L.1066 LL.B. 2922 Forest Ave.
Wasserman, Al .......... '30 '69 C.186 B.C.E. L.767 J.D. O'Brien-Kreitzberg & Assoc., Inc.
Wax, Albert J., (AV) .......... '40 '66 C&L.178 B.A., J.D. 2004 Cedar St.
Wayne, Howard W., (AV) .......... '25 '49 C.112 A.B. L.1066 J.D. 2030 Addison St., 7th Fl.
Weinberg, Joanna K. '46 '72 C.1036 B.A. L.309 J.D.
(adm. in PA; not adm. in CA) 40 Oak Vale Ave.‡
Weininger, Harry D. .......... '33 '89 C.145 B.A. L.1065 J.D. P.O. Box 8214
Weinstein, Craig .......... '46 '79 C.569 B.A. L.1066 J.D. 691 Woodmont Ave.
Weiss, Michael H., Law Offices of, (BV) '38 '67
C&L.477 B.B.A., J.D. 2140 Shattuck Ave.
Weitzman, David M. .......... '37 '65 C.145 B.S. L.273 LL.B. 2026 Delaware St.
Wells, Arthur, Jr., (AV) .......... '37 '63 C.112 B.A. L.1066 J.D. 1171 Cragmont Ave.‡
Westin, Richard J. .......... '41 '70 C.575 A.B. L.1065 J.D. 2614 Telegraph Ave.
Witkin, Gladys S. .......... '15 '54 C.112 B.S. L.1066 LL.B. 2740 Shasta Rd.
Witt, Melvin S. '25 '52 C.112 B.S. L.1065 LL.B.
Editor & Publisher, Calif. Wkrs. Comp. Reporter
Wolinsky, Sidney M., (AV) '36 '61 C.674 B.A. L.976 LL.B.
Disability Rights Advocates
Woods, Michael L. '42 '67
C.845 B.A. L.273 J.D. Resch. Atty., Continuing Educ. of the Bar
Yamasaki, Jean Kim .......... '51 '79 C.72 B.A. L.767 J.D. P.O. Box 10094
Yniguez, Dennis Anthony .......... '49 '83 C.112 M.S.W. L.1066 J.D. 1426 Spruce St.
**York, Jon H.**, (AV) .......... '45 '71 C.668 A.B. L.1066 J.D. [York&S.]

**York & Smith, (AV)**
**2560 9th Street, Suite 218, 94710**
**Telephone: 510-841-1171 Fax: 510-841-1666**
**Members of Firm: Jon H. York; Kevin M. Smith. Associates: Laura Fisher Paré; Margaret J. Allen; James P. Molinelli, Jr.; José A. Tabuena.**
**General Civil Appellate and Trial Practice. Insurance, Personal Injury, Business Litigation, Landlord Tenant, Real Property, Construction and Product Liability.**
*See Professional Biographies, BERKELEY, CALIFORNIA*

Youmans, Alice I. .......... '46 '75 C.477 B.A. L.1065 J.D. Law Libr., Univ. of Calif.
Young, John H. .......... '43 '72 C.309 B.A. L.145 J.D. 2707 Fulton St.
Zamansky, Calvin D. .......... '47 '81 C.608 B.A. L.284 J.D. P.O. Box 209
Zimring, Franklin E. .......... '42 '68 C.912 B.A. L.145 J.D. Univ. of Calif. at Berkeley
Zweben, Robert J., (BV) .......... '45 '71 C.1036 B.A. L.273 J.D. 1730 Solano Ave.

## BERMUDA DUNES, 350, *Riverside Co.*

Jarrett, Joseph W., (AV) .......... '11 '36 C&L.800 A.B., J.D. 78-960 Runaway Bay Dr.‡
Kumler, William L., (AV) .......... '11 '37 C&L.608 A.B., J.D. 79247 Bermuda Dunes Dr.‡
Murphy, George D., Jr. .......... '16 '50 C&L.767 A.B., LL.B. 79890 Ryan Way

## BETHEL ISLAND, 1,398, *Contra Costa Co.*

Walsh, Susan M. .......... '54 '80 C.112 B.A. L.284 J.D. Drawer B

## BEVERLY HILLS, 31,971, *Los Angeles Co.*

**Aagaard, Eric J.** .......... '65 '95 C.36 B.S.M.E. L.990 J.D. [⊠ Trojan]
*PRACTICE AREAS: Patents; Trademarks; Copyrights; Trade Secrets; Intellectual Property Litigation.
Aaronson, Judith B. .......... '20 '52 L.724 LL.B. 161 S. Doheny
**Aberle, Douglas S.** .......... '58 '84 C.112 B.A. L.284 J.D. [Locke,L.R.&A.]
Abrams, Janis .......... '55 '81 C.112 A.B. L.1148 J. D. P.O. Box 18854
Abrams, Stanley .......... '39 '65 C.813 A.B. L.309 LL.B. 712 N. Crescent Dr.
Abronson, William H. .......... '44 '68 C.112 B.S. L.1068 J.D. 433 N. Camden Dr.
**Adam, Frederic J.** .......... '64 '92 C.112 A.B. L.569 J.D. [Hochman,S.&D.]
*LANGUAGES: Swedish, French, German.
*PRACTICE AREAS: Civil and Criminal Tax Litigation; Tax Controversies; Tax; Business; Estate Planning.
Adams, John O. .......... '37 '71 C.912 B.S. L.426 J.D. [Adams&A.]
Adams & Alexander .......... 8383 Wilshire Blvd. (©Pasadena)
Adelman, Milton M., (AV) .......... '07 '30 C&L.339 J.D. 145 S. Wetherly Dr.‡
**Adelman, Robert A.**, (AV) .......... '50 '75 C.112 B.A. L.426 J.D. [R.A.Adelman]
*PRACTICE AREAS: Family Law; Dissolution of Marriage; Spousal and Child Support; Child Custody; Valuation of Marital Assets.
Adelman, Robert J. .......... '46 '72 C.112 A.B. L.1068 J.D. [Adelman&S.]

**Adelman, Robert A., A Law Corporation, (AV)** ⊞
**9454 Wilshire Boulevard Suite PH-29, 90212-2937**
**Telephone: 310-858-1201 Fax: 310-858-6558**
**Robert A. Adelman (Certified Specialist, Family Law, The State Bar of California Board of Legal Specialization).**
**Family Law.**
**Reference: City National Bank.**
*See Professional Biographies, BEVERLY HILLS, CALIFORNIA*

Adelman & Schwartz .......... 9595 Wilshire Blvd., 9th Fl.
Alden, Nick Argaman .......... '38 '82 C.061 L.1095 J.D. 315 S. Beverly Dr.
Alder, C. Michael .......... '67 '92 C&L.420 B.A., J.D. 9601 Wilshire Blvd.
Allan, Ralph E. .......... '35 '75 Med-Tox Assoc., Inc.
Allaria, Marc V. .......... '65 '93 C.1042 B.A. L.809 J.D. 9107 Wilshire Blvd.
**Allen, Albert H.**, (AV) .......... '07 '30 C.339 L.145 LL.B. [Allen&F.]
*PRACTICE AREAS: Real Estate; Probate; Arbitration.

**Allen & Fasman, (AV)**
**Ninth Floor, 9595 Wilshire Boulevard, 90212**
**Telephone: 213-272-8415 Fax: 310-271-4062**
**Members of Firm: Albert H. Allen; Michael J. Fasman.**
**General Civil Practice. Corporate, Real Estate and Probate Law.**
**References: City National Bank (Beverly Hills Main Office); First Interstate Bank (Beverly Hills, California Main Office).**

Alpern, I. Norman .......... '21 '50 C.209 B.A. L.426 LL.B. 188 N. Crescent Dr.‡
Alpern, Jeffrey R. '53 '78 C.823 B.A. L.107 J.D.
(adm. in NY; not adm. in CA) William Morris Agcy., Inc.
Altshuler, Bruce J., (AV) .......... '49 '74 C.112 B.A. L.426 J.D. [Brown,A.&S.]
Altshuler, Leo, (AV) .......... '19 '49 C&L.339 B.S., J.D. [⊡ Brown,A.&S.] ‡

**Amado, Honey Kessler, (BV) '49 '77 C.1042 B.A. L.1137 J.D.**
**261 South Wetherly Drive, 90211**
**Telephone: 310-550-8214 Fax: 310-274-7384**
***REPORTED CASES: In re Marriage of Stephenson (1984) 162 Cal.App.3d 1057. In re Marriage of Gavron (1988) 203 Cal.App.3d 705. Posey v. Leavitt (1991) 229 Cal.App. 1236, 280; People v. DeLeon (1994) 22 Cal. Rep. 4th 1265. In re Marriage of Battenburg (1994) 28 Cal.App.4th 1336. In re Marriage of Hargrave (1995) 36 Cal.App.4th 1313.**
***PRACTICE AREAS: Civil Appeals.**
**Civil Appeals with Emphasis in Family Law.**
*See Professional Biographies, BEVERLY HILLS, CALIFORNIA*

Anderson, Peter W. .......... '46 '73 C.800 A.B. L.426 J.D. 315 S. Beverly Dr.
Anderson, William A. .......... '42 '68 C.276 B.S.F.S. L.309 J.D. [W.A.Anderson]
Anderson, William A., A Professional Law Corporation .......... 405 S. Beverly Dr.
Angela, Barseghian .......... '54 '89 C.112 B.A. L.1137 J.D. 9107 Wilshire Blvd.
Anker, Kurt R., (AV) .......... '19 '53 C.112 B.S. L.809 LL.B. 9201 Wilshire Blvd.‡
**Anteau, Ronald W.**, (AV) .......... '40 '66 C.112 B.A. L.1068 J.D. [Kolodny&A.]
*PRACTICE AREAS: Family Law.
**Antonio, Leah K.** .......... '61 '87 C.860 B.A. L.818 J.D. [Sinclair T.O.&E.]
*PRACTICE AREAS: Entertainment Law; Intellectual Property Law.
Arnold, Larkin, Jr. .......... '42 '72 C.30 B.A. L.329 J.D. 280 S. Beverly Dr.
Aronson, Robert A. .......... '59 '86 C.659 B.A. L.464 J.D. 9595 Wilshire Blvd.
Arshonsky, Richard J. '67 '91 C.210 B.Mus. L.426 J.D.
(adm. in IL; not adm. in CA) Ste., 1250, 9401 Wilshire Blvd.
Atkins, Norman R., (AV) .......... '29 '53 C&L.912 B.A., LL.B. 425 S. Beverly Dr.
**Atwood, A. Rick, Jr.** .......... '65 '91 C.838 B.A. L.880 J.D. [Norminton&W.]
**Aubert, Ronald D.** .......... '36 '66 C.112 A.B. L.1065 J.D. [Turner,G.W.A.&Y.]
Auspitz, James B. .......... '40 '66 C&L.705 A.B., LL.B. 301 N. Canon Dr.
Axelrad, Irving I., (AV) .......... '15 '39 C&L.145 A.B., J.D. Spec. Asst. to Atty. Gen.
Bader, Murray .......... '— '95 9454 Wilshire Blvd., Ste. 313
Bagby, Douglas A., (AV) .......... '45 '72 C.112 A.B. L.1068 LL.B. 121 S. Beverly Dr.
Bailey, Shere R. .......... '62 '91 C.112 B.A. L.1068 J.D. 433 N. Camden Dr.

**Ballesteros, Emma H., Law Office of '— '92 C.1075 M.B.A. L.1137 J.D.**
**433 North Camden Drive, Suite 600, 90210**
**Telephone: 310-288-1829 Fax: 310-273-6329**
***LANGUAGES: Tagalog.**
***PRACTICE AREAS: Estate Planning; Family Law; Civil Litigation; Immigration; Personal Injury.**
**General, Civil and Trial Practice.**
*See Professional Biographies, BEVERLY HILLS, CALIFORNIA*

Barab, Martin J. .......... '45 '71 C.800 B.S. L.426 J.D. [Barab&H.]
Barab & Hart, A Professional Corporation .......... 9606 S. Monica
**Barancik, Stacy J.** .......... '67 '92 C.112 B.A. L.1068 J.D. [⊠ Rosenfeld,M.&S.]
*PRACTICE AREAS: Transactional Entertainment; Film and Television Production.

**Barash, Shula Roth '55 '81 C.112 B.A. L.426 J.D.**
**9454 Wilshire Boulevard, Suite 500, 90212**
**Telephone: 310-247-0636 Fax: 310-275-6647**
***LANGUAGES: Hebrew, French, Spanish and Romanian.**
**Civil and Business Litigation Practice, Sexual Harassment and Wrongful Termination.**

**Barer, Scott I.** .......... '57 '90 C.112 B.A. L.426 J.D. [⊠ Rosenfeld,M.&S.]
*PRACTICE AREAS: Labor and Employment Law; Labor Litigation.

CAA18P

**Barish, Kenneth M.**, (AV) .................'45 '73 C.1077 B.A. L.809 J.D. [Kajan M.&B.]
*PRACTICE AREAS: Tax Controversy; Tax Litigation.
**Barnes, Stephen D.**, (BV) ............ '53 '81 C.800 B.A. L.309 J.D. [Bloom,H.C.D.&K.]
Barnett, Stuart S. ................................'42 '68 C.800 B.A. L.426 J.D. [S.S.Barnett]
Barnett, Stuart S., A Law Corp. ..................................8383 Wilshire Blvd.
Barouh, Albert .....................................'28 '59 C.1043 L.426 LL.B. [Litwin&B.]
**Barrier, Richard G.** '52 '77 C.597 B.A. L.910 J.D.
(adm. in IL; not adm. in CA) Hilton Hotels Corp.
**Barroll, Katherine B.**, (BVⓉ) '57 '77 C.420 B.A. L.790 J.D.
(adm. in LA; not adm. in CA) Sr. Coun., City Natl. Bk.
Barry, Clifford N. ..............................'— '81 C&L.107 B.A., J.D. 8447 Wilshire Blvd.
Barsky, Robert M. ...................'20 '60 C.112 A.B. L.426 LL.B. 8888 Olympic Blvd.
Barson, Marc S. ...............................'64 '93 C.1033 B.S.B.A. L.990 J.D. [L.A.Stark]
Bartlett, Chandler O. ....................'50 '82 C.112 B.S. L.809 J.D. 8665 Wilshire Blvd.
Bartman, Thomas F. .......................'45 '72 C.668 B.A. L.813 J.D. 822 N. Roxbury Dr.
Bates, David Smith ........................'37 '67 C.108 A.B. L.345 J.D. 315 S. Beverly Dr.
Bauer, Martin R. '46 '72 C.563 B.S. L.569 J.D.
(adm. in NY; not adm. in CA) Pres., United Talent Agency
Baum, Leonard P. ............................'28 '51 C.112 L.809 LL.B. 8730 Wilshire Blvd.
**Baum, Michael C.**, (AV) .......................'51 '75 C.112 B.A. L.1068 J.D. [Tucker&B.]
Baumeister, H. Bruce, (AV) ...... '14 '40 C.352 A.B. L.800 LL.B. [Baumeister,Y.D.&H.]
Baumeister, York, Davis & Hunter, (AV) ..........................424 S. Beverly Drive
**Baxa, Diane Wemple** ...........'55 '79 C.1075 B.A. L.800 J.D. Sr. Coun., City Natl. Bk.
*RESPONSIBILITIES: Litigation; Operations; Bank Fraud.
**Beach, Paul B.** ........................'67 '93 C.112 B.A. L.423 J.D. [Gernsbacher&M.]
Bear, Jeffrey L. ......................................'47 '72 C.1077 B.A. L.426 J.D. [Sommer&B.]
Behesnilian, Daniel V. ................'52 '77 C.112 B.A. L.426 J.D. 8665 Wilshire Blvd.
Behrendt, Stephen A. ..................'42 '67 C.668 B.A. L.1068 J.D. 315 S. Beverly Dr.
**Beigel, Herbert**, (AVⓉ) '44 '69 C.1036 B.A. L.659 J.D.
(adm. in DC; not adm. in CA) [Beigel L.R.F.G.&W.]⊙
*PRACTICE AREAS: Securities Litigation; Business and Commercial Litigation; Transactional and Corporate Counseling.

**Beigel Lasky Rifkind Fertik Gelber & White, (AVⓉ)**
**A Partnership including a Professional Corporation**
**9952 Santa Monica Boulevard, 90212⊙**
**Telephone: 310-843-9300 Facsimile: 310-843-0303**
**Herbert Beigel (Not admitted in CA); Michael R. White (Resident);—Mark C. Calahan (Resident); James S. Reed (Resident).**
**Business and Securities Litigation, Toxic Tort, Product Liability and Tax Litigation, Criminal Defense, Corporate and Transactional Matters, Bankruptcy, Estate Planning and International Law, Environmental Law, Contract Litigation and Entertainment Contract Negotiation.**
**Chicago, Illinois Office: 250 South Wacker Drive, Suite 1500. Telephone: 312-466-9444. Fax: 312-466-0347.**
**New York, N.Y. Office: 750 Lexington Avenue, 30th Floor. Telephone: 212-705-5300. Fax: 212-826-1580.**
***See Professional Biographies, BEVERLY HILLS, CALIFORNIA***

**Beletsky, Madge S.**............ '61 '86 C.1349 B.A. L.276 J.D. [Richman,L.M.G.C.F.&P.]
*PRACTICE AREAS: General Corporate; Securities.
**Bell, Louis I., (A Professional Corporation)** '30 '55
C.861 B.A. L.569 LL.B. [Sherman,D.&P.]
Beltran, Steven P. ........................'48 '77 C.1042 B.A. L.1065 J.D. 415 N. Camden Dr.
Bencangey, Ralph ................'41 '69 C.1042 B.A. L.1095 LL.B. 9595 Wilshire Blvd.
Benedek, Peter ......................................'48 '73 C.477 B.A. L.178 J.D. P.O. Box 5514
Berchin, Eugene C. ................'23 '51 C.112 B.A. L.809 LL.B. 2065 San Ysidro Dr.‡
**Bereny, Joshua B.** ...........................'64 '91 C.112 B.A. L.809 J.D. [Wilner,K.&S.]
Berger, David M. ........................'53 '83 C.1246 B.S. L.809 J.D. 405 S. Beverly Dr.
Berger, Jerry S., (A P.C.) ..............'46 '72 C.112 B.A. L.1068 J.D. 9401 Wilshire Blvd.
Berger, Michael Jay, (AV) '57 '81 C.228 B.A. L.1065 J.D.
9454 Wilshire Blvd., 6th Floor
**Bergman, Michael**, (AV) .......'39 '63 C.823 B.A. L.569 LL.B. [Weissmann,W.B.C.&S.]
*PRACTICE AREAS: Litigation; Litigation, Intellectual Property and Entertainment.
**Berkowitz, Jeffrey**, (AV) ...............'54 '80 C.1044 B.S. L.94 J.D. [H.B.California]
*PRACTICE AREAS: U.S. and International Taxation; Estate Planning; General Business; Corporate; Entertainment.
**Berkowitz, Steven**, (BV) ...............'58 '85 C.477 B.A. L.94 J.D. [Glassman,B.&S.]
*PRACTICE AREAS: Civil Litigation; General Litigation; Family Law.
**Berman, Howard Z.** ..........................'62 '86 C&L.800 B.S., J.D. [Ervin,C.&J.]
*PRACTICE AREAS: Corporate Law; Securities Law; Commercial Law; General Business Law.
Berman, Martin B. ....................'19 '49 C.831 B.S. L.809 LL.B. 703 N. Maple Dr.‡
Berman, Richard A. ...................'45 '71 C.800 B.S. L.1049 J.D. 922 N. Beverly Dr.
**Bernfeld, William J.**, (AV) ..........'53 '79 C.112 B.A. L.809 J.D. [Freshman,M.O.C.&K.]
*PRACTICE AREAS: Real Estate; Real Estate Finance; Creditor's Rights; Business Law; Commercial Law.
**Bernhard-Smith, Alison D.**, (BV) '59 '85
C.813 B.A. L.426 J.D. Mng. Coun., City Natl. Bk.
*LANGUAGES: Spanish.
*RESPONSIBILITIES: Bankruptcy (25%); Commercial Law (25%); Creditors Rights (25%); Banking (25%).
Bernstein, Arthur H. '— '87 C.1316 B.S. L.831 J.D.
(adm. in PA; not adm. in CA) Sr. V.P., Producers Entertainment Grp., Ltd.
**Bernstein, Greg S.** ......................'58 '82 C.112 B.A. L.1068 J.D. [Rosenfeld,M.&S.]
*PRACTICE AREAS: Motion Picture Finance/Distribution Law; Entertainment Syndication Law; Business Acquisition Law; General Business Law.
Bernstein, Scott D. .......... '54 '82 C.1044 B.A. L.1136 J.D. 9454 Wilshire Blvd., Ste PH
Berry, Bonnie Eileen ......................................'62 '88 C.674 A.B. L.309 J.D. [Berry&B.]
**Berry, David F.** .......................... '56 '83 C.705 B.A. L.800 J.D. [Nagler&Assoc.]
*REPORTED CASES: Kerins v. Hartley, 27 Cal. App. 4th 1062 (1994); A-Mark Financial v. CIGNA, 34 Cal. App. 4th 1179 (1995).
*PRACTICE AREAS: Appellate Practice; Civil Litigation.
Berry, Gregory A. '56 '80 C.911 B.A. L.659 J.D.
(adm. in PA; not adm. in CA) [Berry&B.]
Berry and Berry ..........................................................8383 Wilshire Blvd.
Bersch, Blanche C., (AV) .............. '34 '69 C.477 B.A. L.1095 J.D. 415 Camden Dr.‡
Bersch, Steven N. .......................'56 '80 C.112 B.S. L.1066 J.D. 20th Century Fox

**Bersin, Peter I. '49 '75 C.385 B.A. L.365 J.D.**
**9454 Wilshire Boulevard, Fifth Floor, 90212**
**Telephone: 310-273-0904 Fax: 310-275-6647**
**Medical Malpractice, Insurance Bad Faith, Civil Trial Law, Product Liability, Wrongful Death.**

Berton, Stuart I., (AV) ............................'40 '65 C.659 B.S. L.813 J.D. [Berton&D.]
Berton & Donaldson, (AV) ..........................................9595 Wilshire Blvd., Ste. 711
Bettin, Frederic .................. '33 '62 C.112 B.A. L.800 J.D. 9903 Santa Monica Blvd.‡

**Biddle, Jonathan W., (AV) '46 '75 C.174 B.A. L.809 J.D.**
**Suite 750 The Wilshire San Vicente Plaza, 8383 Wilshire Boulevard, 90211**
**Telephone: 213-653-4713 Telefax: 213-852-1310**
***PRACTICE AREAS: General Civil Practice before State and Federal Courts; Labor Law; Employment Law.**
**General Civil Practice before State and Federal Courts. Labor and Employment Law.**
**Reference: Bank of America.**
***See Professional Biographies, BEVERLY HILLS, CALIFORNIA***

**Bigby, Darren O.** ......................'69 '94 C&L.800 B.S., J.D. [Freshman,M.O.C.&K.]
*PRACTICE AREAS: Business Litigation.
Bilan, Michael J. ......'42 '67 C.801 B.A. L.477 J.D. Gen. Coun., Mustang Develop. Corp.
Black, Arthur S. ................................'33 '62 C.608 B.A. L.1065 J.D. 9301 Wilshire Blvd.
**Black, Daniel H.** ..........................'51 '77 C.569 B.A. L.273 J.D. [H.B.California]
*PRACTICE AREAS: Entertainment; General Business; Corporate.
**Black, Debra Phillipes** ...............'60 '85 C.228 B.A. L.309 J.D. Hilton Hotels Corp.
Black, Michael R. '48 '73
C.1044 B.A. L.276 LL.B. Sr. V.P., International Creative Mgmt., Inc.
**Blackman, Steven H.** ..........................'55 '80 C.112 B.A. L.309 J.D. [Isaacman,K.&P.]
*PRACTICE AREAS: Employment Law; Entertainment; First Amendment and Business Litigation.
**Blair, Katherine J.** ...................'69 '94 C.112 B.A. L.990 J.D. [Freshman,M.O.C.&K.]
*PRACTICE AREAS: Securities; Corporate; Mergers and Acquisitions.
Blattel, Jesse ......................................'12 '38 C.563 L.1009 LL.B. 1901 San Ysidro Dr.
**Blaufarb, Jonathan K.** .............'57 '84 C.112 B.A. L.1065 J.D. [Bloom,H.C.D.&K.]
Blauschild, Doreen J. '55 '80 C.1046 B.S. L.472 J.D.
Sr. V.P. & Gen. Coun., Southern Calif. Fed. Svgs. & Loan Assn.
Blinderman, Elliott E. ...........................................'31 '76 C.563 B.A. 315 S. Beverly Dr.
**Bloom, Jacob A.**, (AV) ..............'42 '68 C.178 B.A. L.188 LL.B. [Bloom,H.C.D.&K.]
Bloom, Jay S. .............................'53 '78 C.800 B.A. L.1049 J.D. 433 N. Camden Dr.

**Bloom, Hergott, Cook, Diemer & Klein, LLP, (AV)**
**150 South Rodeo Drive Third Floor, 90212**
**Telephone: 310-859-6800 Omnifax: 310-859-2788**
**Members of Firm: Jacob A. Bloom; Alan S. Hergott; Lawrence H. Greaves; Candice S. Hanson; Melanie K. Cook; Tina J. Kahn; Thomas F. Hunter, Jr.; John D. Diemer; Stephen D. Barnes; Stuart M. Rosenthal; Leigh C. Brecheen; Stephen F. Breimer; Deborah L. Klein; Steven L. Brookman; John S. LaViolette; Robyn L. Roth; Richard D. Thompson; Jonathan K. Blaufarb; David B. Feldman. Associates: Roger L. Patton, Jr.; Robert Offer; Thomas B. Collier; David E. Weber; Eric M. Brooks; Michael L. Schenkman.**
**Entertainment Law, General Business, Corporate.**
***See Professional Biographies, BEVERLY HILLS, CALIFORNIA***

**Bloomer, Julianne** .....................'49 '80 C.105 B.S.Ed. L.426 J.D. [Sherman,D.&P.]
*PRACTICE AREAS: Products Liability; Federal and State Complex & Multi District Litigation; Class Actions.
Bloomfield, Karl, (BV) ........................'47 '78 C.831 B.A. L.809 J.D. 280 S. Beverly Dr.⊙
**Blumenfeld, Eli**, (AV) .........................'33 '64 C.112 B.S. L.1068 J.D. [E.Blumenfeld]

**Blumenfeld, Eli, Law Corporation, (AV)**
**433 North Camden Drive, Suite 900, 90210**
**Telephone: 310-205-0800 FAX: 310-888-1120**
**Eli Blumenfeld (Certified Specialist, Taxation Law, The State Bar of California Board of Legal Specialization).**
**Tax Litigation (Civil and Criminal), Tax and Estate Planning.**
**Reference: Union Bank (Century City Office).**
***See Professional Biographies, BEVERLY HILLS, CALIFORNIA***

Blustein, Philip Rubin ..........................'51 '80 C.999 L.1095 J.D. 220 S. Tower Dr.‡
Bodenheimer, Howard S. ................'50 '75 C.112 B.A. L.1049 J.D. 433 N. Camden Dr.
Boffa, Robert C., (AV) ...................'35 '62 C.188 B.S. L.178 LL.B. 9601 Wilshire Blvd.
**Bogen, Judy**, (AV) ........................................'55 '81 C.112 B.A. L.809 J.D. [Jaffe&C.]
*PRACTICE AREAS: Family Law.
Bojeaux, Darian, Ms. .......'47 '79 C.112 B.A. L.426 J.D. 9107 Wilshire Blvd., Penthouse
Bonda, Dana L. .................................................'49 '77 C.281 B.A. L.426 J.D. [Wiley&B.]
**Bonder, Todd W.** ..........................'58 '84 C.659 B.S. L.1068 J.D. [Rosenfeld,M.&S.]
*PRACTICE AREAS: Entertainment Litigation; Intellectual Property Law; Constitutional Law Litigation; General Business Litigation; Construction Litigation.
Bookman, Robert ..........................................'47 '72 C.112 A.B. L.976 J.D. 9830 Wilshire Blvd.
Boothe, Dennis H. ............'50 '79 C.112 B.A. L.426 J.D. 9777 Wilshire Blvd. Ste. 918
**Bordy, Michael J.**, (AV) ..................'52 '86 C.299 B.A. L.800 J.D. [Jacobson,S.&B.]
*PRACTICE AREAS: General Business and Real Estate Transactions; Environmental Law.
Boros, Stuart A. ........................'53 '80 C.112 B.A. L.426 J.D. 9968 W. Wanda Dr.
Borris, Jeffrey '62 '91 C.1077 B.A. L.809 J.D.
(adm. in PA; not adm. in CA) Gen. Coun., Beverly Hills Sports Council
Boswell, J.E. Aeliot ..............................'— '82 C.112 B.A. L.1065 J.D. [Boswell&M.]
Boswell & Munson ................................................................................ Eighth Floor
**Bowers, Mark E.** .......................................'48 '73 C.802 B.B.A. L.846 J.D. [M.E.Bowers]

**Bowers, Mark E., Law Office of**
**9777 Wilshire Boulevard, Suite 512, 90212-1905**
**Telephone: 310-275-3591 Fax: 310-275-4690**
**Email: markebowers@earthlink.com**
**Mark E. Bowers.**
**Tax, Real Estate, Business, Corporate and Securities Law, International Business Transactions.**
***See Professional Biographies, BEVERLY HILLS, CALIFORNIA***

Bowersock, W. Scott, (BV) '36 '67
C.813 B.S. L.1065 LL.B. 8601 Wilshire Blvd., 9th Floor
**Boxwell, Nancy L.** ..........................'63 '91 C.800 B.S. L.1068 J.D. [Gang,T.R.&B.]
*PRACTICE AREAS: General Business; Corporate; Real Estate.
**Boyle, James F.** ..............................'46 '82 C&L.426 B.A., J.D. [Nagler&Assoc.]
*REPORTED CASES: Bowie v. Home Insurance Co., 923 F.2d. 705 (9th Cir. 1991).
*PRACTICE AREAS: Business Litigation.
**Boynton, Esther G.** ..........................'46 '78 C.477 B.A. L.912 J.D. [Schneider,G.&Y.]
**Brachman, Mitchell S.** ....................'61 '87 C.477 A.B. L.904 J.D. [Wilner,K.&S.]
*PRACTICE AREAS: Real Estate; Construction Defect.
Braddock, Isaac H. ........................'49 '77 C.103 A.B. L.880 J.D. 9465 Wilshire Blvd.
Branman, Meyer ..........................'23 '72 C.800 B.S. L.1136 J.D. 280 S. Beverly Dr.
Breakman, Denise M. '52 '76
C.112 B.A. L.426 J.D. 8501 Wilshire Blvd. (⊙Monterey Park)
**Brecheen, Leigh C.** ..........................'55 '79 C.483 B.A. L.36 J.D. [Bloom,H.C.D.&K.]
**Breimer, Stephen F.** ...................'50 '85 C.813 B.A. L.1068 J.D. [Bloom,H.C.D.&K.]
**Brenner, Saul D.** ...........................'62 '87 C.112 A.B. L.309 J.D. [Rosenfeld,M.&S.]
*LANGUAGES: Hebrew, Arabic and Spanish.
*PRACTICE AREAS: Intellectual Property; Entertainment Litigation; General Commercial Litigation; White Collar.
**Briggs, William Joseph, II** ...... '55 '89 C.85 B.A. L.276 J.D. [Richman,L.M.G.C.F.&P.]
*PRACTICE AREAS: Business Litigation; Labor and Employment Law.
Brightman, Allison B. ........................'63 '92 C.112 B.A. L.800 J.D. 9601 Wilshire Blvd.
**Broadbelt, Robert B.** ......................................'59 '84 C.112 A.B. L.800 J.D. [Browne&W.]
**Broadway, Patrick R.** ...............................'65 '90 C&L.575 B.S., J.D. [Rubin&E.]
*PRACTICE AREAS: Insurance Litigation.
Brock, Robert L., (AV) .........................'14 '47 C.112 B.A. L.1251 LL.B. [R.L.Brock] ‡
Brock, Robert L., Inc. ..........................................................................315 S. Beverly Dr.
**Brookey, Brian Kent** ..................'65 '90 C.990 B.A. L.1097 J.D. [Levinson,L.&M.]
*LANGUAGES: German.
*PRACTICE AREAS: Real Estate Litigation; Title Insurance Litigation.
**Brookman, Steven L.** ....................'59 '85 C.165 B.A. L.1066 J.D. [Bloom,H.C.D.&K.]
**Brookman, Stewart S.** ..........'59 '84 C.165 B.A. L.1066 J.D. [Weissmann,W.B.C.&S.]
*PRACTICE AREAS: Entertainment.
**Brooks, Eric M.** ....................'63 '91 C.976 A.B. L.1066 J.D. [Bloom,H.C.D.&K.]
*PRACTICE AREAS: Entertainment Law.
Brooks, W. M. ..............................'24 '50 C.112 B.A. L.800 J.D. 321 S. Beverly Dr.

CAA19P

**Brourman, Phyllis R.,** (AV) '31 '84 C.665 B.S. L.426 J.D.
**315 S. Beverly Drive, Suite 315, 90212-4390**
**Telephone: 310-557-9911; 277-2323 Fax: 310-556-2308**
**(Certified Specialist, Family Law, The State Bar of California Board of Legal Specialization).**
***LANGUAGES: Spanish.**
**Family Law.**
*See Professional Biographies, BEVERLY HILLS, CALIFORNIA*

**Brown, Harold A.,** (AV) ........'52 '76 C.605 B.A. L.1066 J.D. [Gang,T.R.&B.]
*PRACTICE AREAS: Entertainment Law.
**Brown, Hermione K.,** (AV) ........'15 '47 C.914 B.A. L.800 LL.B. [Gang,T.R.&B.]
*PRACTICE AREAS: Estate Planning and Administration; Intellectual Property; Real Estate; General Business.
Brown, Altshuler and Spiro, A Prtnrshp. incl. A Prof. Corp., (AV) .....9301 Wilshire Blvd.
**Browne, Allan,** (AV) ........'38 '64 C.112 B.A. L.800 LL.B. [Browne&W.]
*PRACTICE AREAS: General Civil Trial; Appellate Practice; Unfair Competitive Business Practices.

**Browne & Woods LLP, (AV)**
**450 North Roxbury Drive, 7th Floor, 90210**
**Telephone: 310-274-7100 Telecopier: 310-275-5697**
**Members of Firm: Allan Browne; Edward A. Woods; Marcy Railsback; Benjamin D. Scheibe; Allen B. Grodsky; Peter W. Ross; Robert B. Broadbelt; Jon M. Leader; Michael J. Olecki. Associates: James D. Kozmor; Miles J. Feldman; Ella Marie Martinsen.**
**General Civil Trial and Appellate Practice in all State and Federal Courts with emphasis on Competitive Business Practices, Unfair Competition, Trade Secrets, Business Torts, Defamation, Entertainment Litigation and Insurance Litigation.**
*See Professional Biographies, BEVERLY HILLS, CALIFORNIA*

**Browning, Roger A.,** (AV) ........'40 '66 C.112 B.S. L.1066 J.D. [Glassman,B.&S.]
*PRACTICE AREAS: Business Transactional Matters; Civil and Criminal Tax Matters; Corporate and Partnership Planning; Real Estate; Income Taxation.
Browning, Shelley ........'52 '87 C.112 B.A. L.800 J.D. 9595 Wilshire Blvd.
Brussel, Leo B. ........'54 '84 C.112 B.A. L.426 J.D. [Lichterman,T.&B.]
Brustin, Gary C. ........'49 '76 C.800 B.A. L.1065 J.D. 8383 Wilshire
Brynan, Jeffrey ........'52 '76 C.800 B.S. L.426 J.D. 9430 Olympic Blvd.
Buda, Ian Stewart ........'47 '80 C.1224 B.S.L. L.1127 J.D. 9460 Wilshire Blvd.
Bunnage, M. Alan, (AV) ........'36 '61 C.112 B.A. L.1068 LL.B. 8383 Wilshire Blvd.
**Burger, Mitchell I.** ........'61 '89 C.659 B.S. L.262 J.D. [⊡ Schneider,G.&Y.]
**Burk, Arnold D.** ........'32 '55 C&L.178 A.B., J.D. [⊡ Gang,T.R.&B.] ‡
**Burke, P. John** ........'52 '78 C.800 B.A. L.809 J.D. [⊡ Rosenfeld,M.&S.]
*PRACTICE AREAS: Media Finance; Commercial Transactions; Real Estate Law; International Law.
Burrows, Matthew J. '65 '92 C.112 B.S. L.426 J.D.
Assoc., Bus. Affs., William Morris Agcy., Inc.
Burton, Richard J. ........'33 '68 C.800 B.S. L.809 LL.B. [⊡ Mathon&R.]
Bury, Christopher A. '54 '85
C.602 B.B.A. L.990 J.D. Coun. & Corp. Secy., El Camino Mgmt. Co.
Butler, Terrence L., Law Offices of ....'47 '84 C.608 B.S. L.809 J.D. 8306 Wilshire Blvd.
Byrne, Donald R. ........'27 '60 C.424 A.B. L.276 J.D. 9301 Wilshire Blvd.
Byrne, Thomas M. ........'51 '79 C.426 B.A. L.1136 J.D. 425 S. Beverly Dr.
**Byrnes, Stacey M.** ........'58 '85 C.945 B.A. L.1066 J.D. [Rosenfeld,M.&S.]
*PRACTICE AREAS: Entertainment Litigation.
Caballero, Richard, (BV) ........'30 '57 C&L.569 B.A., LL.B. 280 S. Beverly Dr.
**Calahan, Mark C.** ........'59 '92 C.705 B.A. L.426 J.D. [⊡ Beigel L.R.F.G.&W.]
*PRACTICE AREAS: Business and Civil Litigation; Securities Litigation.
**Calaway, Kathleen A.** ........'52 '86 L.1136 J.D. [Schwartz,W.&W.]
*PRACTICE AREAS: Civil and Business Litigation.
Calaway, Martin Curtis ........'25 '56 C.112 B.S. L.1068 LL.B 425 S. Beverly Hills
Cambria, Paul J., Jr., (AV⊙) '47 '73 C.1044 A.B. L.851 J.D.
(adm. in NY; not adm. in CA) [Lipsitz,G.F.R.S.&C.] (⊙Buffalo, NY)
**Cameron, D. Steve** ........'49 '74 C&L.800 B.A., J.D. [Leonard,D.&S.]
*PRACTICE AREAS: Business and Real Estate Litigation.
**Camp, Tom R.,** (AV) ........'54 '79 C.546 B.S. L.813 J.D. [Gang,T.R.&B.]
*PRACTICE AREAS: General Business; Corporate; Entertainment Law; Real Estate.
**Campbell, Jennifer L.** ........'62 '91 C.940 B.A. L.1065 J.D. [⊡ Rosenfeld,M.&S.]
*PRACTICE AREAS: Estate Planning and Administration.
Campos, Roel C. ........'49 '79 C.1070 B.S. L.309 J.D. 9601 Wilshire Blvd.
Canter, David S. ........'62 '89 C.112 A.B. L.809 J.D. 315 S. Beverly Dr.
Canter, Robert S., (BV) ........'34 '60 C.37 B.S. L.1068 LL.B. 315 S. Beverly Dr.
Caplan, David L. ........'46 '71 C.645 B.A. L.30 J.D. 918 Whittier Dr.
**Capogrosso, Eric G.** ........'50 '79 C.308 B.A. L.1148 J.D. [Jacoby&C.]
*PRACTICE AREAS: Labor and Employment Law.
**Cardozo, Benjamin S.** ........'42 '79 C.112 B.A. L.800 J.D. [Stone&H.]
*REPORTED CASES: Mercury Insurance vs. Checkerboard Pizza 15 Cal. Rptr 657 (1993).
*PRACTICE AREAS: Insurance Bad Faith; Insurance coverage; Business Litigation; Tort Litigation.
Carlin, Gerald S. '40 '67 C.1036 B.A. L.818 LL.B.
(adm. in MA; not adm. in CA) [S.M.Gage]
**Carman, David A.** ........'62 '90 C.385 B.A. L.823 J.D. [⊡ Glassman,B.&S.]
*PRACTICE AREAS: Civil Litigation; General Litigation.
Carpenter, M. Michael, (AV) '36 '64 C&L.446 B.S., LL.B.
V.P. & Dir., Intell. Prop., Western Atlas, Inc. (Pat.)
Carroll, James A., Jr. ........'57 '87 C.339 B.A. L.809 J.D. 433 N. Camden Dr., Ste 400
Carsola, Anthony T. ........'22 '50 C.112 B.A. L.426 LL.B. 425 S. Beverly Dr.
Caruso, Paul, (AV) ........'20 '53 C.732 B.A. L.180 LL.B. 425 S. Beverly Dr.
Caruso, Paul Carey, (BV) ........'51 '80 C.800 B.A. L.1148 J.D. 425 S. Beverly Dr.
Casden, Henry C. ........'44 '71 C.112 B.A. L.1049 J.D. The Casden Co.
**Case, Thomas H.** ........'57 '84 C.976 B.A. L.800 J.D. [⊡ Nagler&Assoc.]
Castelblanco, Eric E. ........'63 '91 C.426 B.S. L.309 J.D. 202 S. LaCienega Blvd., Ste 218
Chakmakis, George, Jr. ........'66 '92 C.112 B.A. L.809 J.D. 9595 Wilshire Blvd.

**Chaleff & English**
**(See Santa Monica)**

Chalfin, Michael R. ........'41 '66 C.112 L.809 LL.B. [Rosen&C.]

**Challgren, Michael L. '59 '88 C.112 B.A. L.426 J.D.**
**433 North Camden Drive, 90210**
**Telephone: 310-372-6600**
***REPORTED CASES: 8 Cal.App. 4th 1039 (1992).**
**General Civil Law, Trial Law, Appellate Practice in all State and Federal Courts, Admiralty Law, Business Law, Entertainment Law, Environmental Law, General Liability and Insurance Law.**

**Charlton, Charles P., Law Offices of '48 '86 C.112 B.A. L.1137 J.D.**
**9454 Wilshire Boulevard, Suite 500, 90212-2908**
**Telephone: 310-471-5365 Fax: 310-471-5374**
**Email: cpclaw@aol.com**
**Personal Injury, Wrongful Death, Products Liability, Civil Trial Practice, Medical Malpractice and Appellate Practice.**
*See Professional Biographies, BEVERLY HILLS, CALIFORNIA*

Chasin, Thomas H. ........'37 '64 C.112 A.B. L.1068 LL.B. 9124 Janice Pl.
Chaskin, Richard M. ........'53 '81 C.426 B.B.A. L.1095 J.D. 8383 Wilshire Blvd.

**Chernick, Dina B. '57 '83 C.659 A.B. L.1065 J.D.**
**Suite 150, 369 South Doheny Drive, 90211**
**Telephone: 310-275-3520**

(This Listing Continued)

**Chernick, Dina B. (Continued)**
**General Business Transactions, Estate Planning, Probate and Trust Administration.**
*See Professional Biographies, BEVERLY HILLS, CALIFORNIA*

Childs, Roland A., (AV) ........'25 '59 C.112 B.S. L.1068 J.D. 9601 Wilshire Blvd. 4th Fl.
**Chizever, Gerald M.** ........'43 '68 C&L.273 B.B.A., J.D. [Richman,L.M.G.C.F.&P.]
*PRACTICE AREAS: Corporate Law; Business Law; Partnership Law.
Cholodenko, Michael A. ........'50 '76 C.112 B.S. L.950 J.D. 9301 Wilshire Blvd.
Christenfeld, Stuart H. '43 '70
C.112 A.B. L.1068 J.D. V.P., Bus. Affs., William Morris Agcy., Inc.
**Christensen, Maren J.,** (AV) ........'43 '76 C.112 B.A. L.800 J.D. [Rosenfeld,M.&S.]
*PRACTICE AREAS: Intellectual Property and General Entertainment Litigation; Copyright Law; Trademark Law; General Entertainment Law.
**Christmas, Kenneth C., Jr.** ........'63 '91 C.813 B.A. L.976 J.D. [Hansen,J.T.&H.]
*PRACTICE AREAS: Entertainment Law; Motion Picture Law; Music Law; Television Law.
Chroman, Nathan L., (AV) ........'29 '57 C.112 L.426 9171 Wilshire Blvd.
Chronis, Phillip, (AV) ........'33 '62 C.999 L.800 J.D. 301 North Canon Dr.
Chu, John Y. ........'30 '67 C.636 B.A. L.426 J.D. City Natl. Bk.
**Chudd, Reeve E.,** (AV) ........'51 '80 C.659 B.A. L.800 J.D. [Ervin,C.&J.]
*PRACTICE AREAS: Taxation Law; Estate Planning Law.
Cibener, Joel A. ........'33 '58 C.563 B.A. L.178 LL.B. 301 N. Canon Dr.
**Ciccarelli, John K.** ........'58 '88 C.259 L.1148 J.D. [⊡ Vorzimer,G.M.&E.]
*PRACTICE AREAS: Insurance Coverage; Civil Litigation.
**Clemens, Bruce A., (A Professional Corporation),** (AV) '46 '74
C.475 A.B. L.1068 J.D. [Jaffe&C.]
*PRACTICE AREAS: Family Law.
Clemens, Michael J., (AV) ........'20 '52 C.871 B.S. L.426 J.D. 433 N. Camden Dr.
Coate, Charles M. ........'63 '89 C.473 B.S. L.608 J.D. 9606 Santa Monica Blvd.
**Coates, Timothy T.** ........'57 '83 C.800 B.A. L.1068 J.D. [Greines,M.S.&R.]
*PRACTICE AREAS: Appellate Law.
Cobert, Harriette I. ........'— '79 C.1097 B.A. L.940 J.D. 433 N. Camden Dr.

**Codikow & Carroll, P.C.**
**(See Los Angeles)**

Coghlan, Theresa A. ........'64 '90 C.273 B.A. L.262 J.D. 9401 Wilshire Blvd.
Cohen, Bert Harold ........'45 '74 C.674 A.B. L.800 J.D. 400 S. Beverly Dr.
Cohen, Gilda R. ........'28 '57 C.1009 L.809 LL.B. 415 N. Camden Dr.
Cohen, Jeffrey Allan ........'43 '68 C.112 B.A. L.426 J.D. 315 S. Beverly Dr.
Cohen, Kenneth L. '44 '69 C.563 B.B.A. L.930 J.D.
(adm. in OH; not adm. in CA) Western Atlas, Inc.
Cohen, Paul Ian ........'60 '87 C.800 B.S. L.426 J.D. 9454 Wilshire Blvd.‡
Cohen, Stephen R. ........'47 '74 C.1154 B.A. L.426 J.D. 8671 Wilshire Blvd. Ste 711
**Cohen, William S.** ........'28 '53 C.569 B.S. L.1009 LL.B. [Isaacman,K.&P.]
*PRACTICE AREAS: Taxation Law; Estate Planning Law; Probate Administration; Corporate Law.
Colden, David, (AV) ........'53 '79 C.668 B.A. L.800 J.D. [Colden&M.]
Colden & Mckuin, LLP, (AV) ........141 El Camino Dr.
Cole, Bruce A. '47 '76 C.112 A.B. L.767 J.D.
Exec. V.P. & Gen. Coun., J.B. Oxford Holdings, Inc.
**Cole, L. David** ........'37 '62 C.821 B.A. L.178 LL.B. [L.D.Cole]

**Cole, L. David, A Law Corporation**
**433 North Camden Drive, 12th Floor, 90210**
**Telephone: 310-205-2080 FAX: 310-275-5409**
**L. David Cole.**
**Real Property Law, General Business and Corporate Law.**
*See Professional Biographies, BEVERLY HILLS, CALIFORNIA*

**Coleman, Stan,** (AV) ........'44 '70 C.188 A.B. L.178 J.D. [Weissmann,W.B.C.&S.]
*PRACTICE AREAS: Entertainment Law; New Technologies; Media.
**Collier, Thomas B.** ........'66 '93 C.575 B.A. L.145 J.D. [⊡ Bloom,H.C.D.&K.]
**Colligan, Brian M.** ........'61 '88 C&L.276 B.S.B.A., J.D. [Richman,L.M.G.C.F.&P.]
*PRACTICE AREAS: Commercial Litigation; Entertainment Litigation.
**Collins, Douglas L.** ........'54 '82 C&L.846 B.A., J.D. Sr. Coun., City Natl. Bk.
*LANGUAGES: Spanish.
*RESPONSIBILITIES: Real Estate; Commercial Lending; Environmental Law.
Colman-Schwimmer, Arlene, (AV) ........'40 '64 C.102 B.A. L.1009 J.D. [Arlene C.-S.]⊙
Colman-Schwimmer, Arlene, A Professional Corporation, (AV)
9595 Wilshire Blvd. (⊙Los Angeles, Laguna Beach)
**Connet, L. Rae** ........'57 '91 C.112 B.S. L.426 J.D. [⊡ Trojan]
*PRACTICE AREAS: Complex Intellectual Property Litigation; Trademarks; Patents; Trade Secrets; Related Business Torts.
**Conway, Michael J.** ........'70 '95 C.112 B.A. L.426 J.D. [⊡ Lurie&Z.]
Cook, D. Durand ........'49 '69 C.1163 B.S. L.61 J.D. [Cook&L.]
**Cook, Melanie K.,** (AV) ........'53 '79 C.112 B.S. L.1068 J.D. [Bloom,H.C.D.&K.]
Cook & Linden, A Professional Corporation ........8383 Wilshire Blvd.
**Cooper, Allan B.,** (AV) ........'49 '74 C.112 A.B. L.1068 J.D. [Ervin,C.&J.]
*REPORTED CASES: Han v. U.S., 944 F.2d 526; Worldwide Church of God, Inc. v. State of California, 623 F.2d 613; Wright v. Schock, 571 F.Supp. 642; Lambert v. Commonwealth Land Title Ins. Co., 53 Cal.3d 1072; Isaac v. A&B Loan Company, Inc., 201 Cal.App.3d 307.
*PRACTICE AREAS: Real Property Litigation; Title and Land Use Litigation; Competitive Business Practices; Legal Malpractice.
**Cooper, Bari J.** ........'64 '90 C&L.273 B.B.A., J.D. [⊡ Ervin,C.&J.]
*PRACTICE AREAS: Real Property Law; Entertainment Law.
Cooper, Michelle ........'55 '80 C.112 B.A. L.426 J.D. [⊡ Mathon&R.]
**Cooper, Richard H.** ........'42 '66 C.112 B.A. L.1068 J.D. [Freshman,M.O.C.&K.]
*PRACTICE AREAS: Complex Litigation; Creditors' Rights; Securities Litigation; Alternative Dispute Resolution; Administrative Hearings and Appeals.
Cooper, Robert S. ........'46 '72 C.1077 B.A. L.1068 J.D. Cooper Design & Construction
**Coopersmith, Stephen,** (BV) ........'41 '70 C.112 B.A. L.1095 LL.B. [⊡ Wilner,K.&S.]
*PRACTICE AREAS: Insurance Defense; Construction Law; Civil Litigation.
Cort, Lee M. ........'54 '79 C.103 A.B. L.813 J.D. 9601 Wilshire Blvd.
**Cotugno, Lee W.,** (AV) ........'51 '77 C.494 B.A. L.1066 J.D. [Kalisch,C.&R.]
**Craigie, Patricia Task** ........'66 '93 C.1077 B.A. L.426 J.D. [⊡ Freshman,M.O.C.&K.]
*PRACTICE AREAS: Business Litigation; Employment Law; Bankruptcy.
**Cranmore, Floyd W.** ........'58 '86 C.623 B.S. L.608 J.D. [⊡ Wilner,K.&S.]
*REPORTED CASES: Hood vs. City of Los Angeles, 804 F.Supp. 65 (C.D. Cal. 1992).
Crawford, Debra Vaniman ........'57 '84 C.112 B.A. L.809 J.D. 424 S. Beverly Dr.
**Cresap, Vicki L.** ........'50 '90 C.112 B.A. L.426 J.D. [⊡ Turner,G.W.A.&Y.]
*PRACTICE AREAS: Business Litigation.
Crowley, Francis L., Jr. '31 '55 C&L.276 B.S., LL.B.
V.P. & Assoc. Gen. Coun., Western Atlas, Inc.
Csiszar, Paul L. ........'57 '86 L.426 J.D. 9300 Wilshire Blvd.
Cwiklo, David P. ........'57 '84 C.436 B.A. L.809 J.D. 8383 Wilshire Blvd.
Daley, Marcia L. ........'60 '90 C&L.426 B.A., J.D. 8501 Wilshire Blvd.
**Dan, Michael A. K.,** (AV) ........'44 '70 C&L.1068 B.A., J.D. [Sherman,D.&P.]
*REPORTED CASES: Doering v. SAS; Harris v. Irish Truck Lines.
*PRACTICE AREAS: Plaintiff Personal Injury; Product Liability; Medical Malpractice; Obstetrical/Neonatal Malpractice; Pharmaceutical.
Daniels, Michael D., (AV) ........'45 '69 C&L.37 B.S., J.D. [M.D.Daniels]
Daniels, Michael D., A Prof. Corp., (AV) ........9440 Santa Monica Blvd., Penthouse
Danziger, Max H., (AV) ........'43 '72 C.1077 B.A. L.1095 J.D. 9777 Wilshire Blvd.

CAA20P

**Dapeer, Kenneth B.** ....................'50 '76 C.1077 B.S. L.1095 J.D. [Dapeer,R.&L.]⊙

**Dapeer, Rosenblit & Litvak, LLP, (AV) BR**
**9460 Wilshire Boulevard, Fifth Floor, 90212⊙**
**Telephone: 310-203-8200; 310-777-6676 Fax: 310-203-8213; 310-777-6675**
**William Litvak; Steven H. Rosenblit; Kenneth B. Dapeer.**
**Business and Real Estate Litigation, Commercial and Corporate Law, including Creditors Rights Law and Commercial Collections, Professional Liability Litigation, Municipal Law and Land Use Law, Civil Trial Practice.**
**Metropolitan Cities Office: 2770 East Slauson Avenue, P.O. Box 2067, Huntington Park, 90255. Telephone: 213-587-5221. Fax: 213-587-4190.**

*See Professional Biographies, BEVERLY HILLS, CALIFORNIA*

Daugherty, David W. '60 '85 C.976 B.A. L.309 J.D.
V.P., Bus. & Legal Affs., Polygram Filmed Entertainment
**Davenport, Michael S.** ....................'65 '91 C.966 B.S. L.809 J.D. [G.A.Yates]
*PRACTICE AREAS: Products Liability; Tort; Police Misconduct; Premises Liability; Civil Litigation.
David, John E. ....................'46 '74 C.36 B.S.B.A. L.1068 J.D. 280 S. Beverly Dr.
**Davidoff, Richard C.**, (AV) ....................'48 '78 C.966 B.A. L.1065 J.D. [Davidoff&D.]
**Davidoff, Susan K.** ....................'50 '79 C.966 B.A. L.1065 J.D. [Davidoff&D.]

**Davidoff & Davidoff, (AV)**
**Suite 888, 433 North Camden Drive, 90210**
**Telephone: 310-274-2883 Telecopier: 310-274-2761**
**Members of Firm: Richard C. Davidoff; Susan K. Davidoff.**
**General, Civil Trial and Appellate Practice in all State and Federal Courts. Business, Commercial, Estate and Probate Litigation.**

*See Professional Biographies, BEVERLY HILLS, CALIFORNIA*

Davidson, Jeffrey L., (AV) '49 '73
C.112 B.A. L.1065 J.D. 9100 Wilshire Blvd., 8th Fl., East Twr.
Davidson, Shirley ....................'— '72 C.102 B.A. L.809 J.D. 810 N. Linden Dr.
Davis, M. Stephen ....................'40 '67 C.112 B.S. L.809 LL.B. [Davis&D.]
Davis, Milton ....................'07 '31 C&L.800 A.B., J.D. [Davis&D.]
Davis & Davis ....................315 S. Beverly Dr.
Dawson, Norma Ann ....................'50 '79 C.645 B.A. L.477 J.D. 11077 Palms Blvd.
Daza, Raul ....................'35 '74 C.061 B.B.A. L.662 LL.B. [Shephard&D.]
**Dean, Donna M.** ....................'65 '96 C.112 B.A. L.1068 J.D. [Lurie&Z.]
**Deane, Jeffrey W.** ....................'61 '87 C.112 B.A. L.284 J.D. [Ⓐ Wilner,K.&S.]
*PRACTICE AREAS: Litigation; Product Liability; Attorney Malpractice; Premises Liability.
DeGeorge, Rex K. ....................'38 '65 C.474 B.S. L.1065 LL.B. 13318 Mulholland Dr.
Dekom, Peter J., (AV) ....................'46 '73 C.976 A.B. L.1068 J.D. 150 S. Rodeo Dr.
Del Rio, Nelson L. ....................'60 '88 C.911 B.A. L.309 J.D. Pres.
De Marco, Joseph M. '60 '85 C.446 B.A. L.809 J.D.
V.P., Legal Affs., Twentieth Century Fox Film Corp.
**Denton, Robert W.** ....................'51 '84 C.798 B.A. L.494 J.D. [Lurie&Z.]
**DeRoy, George**, (AV) ....................'26 '51 C.112 B.A. L.800 LL.B. [© Hochman,S.&D.]
*PRACTICE AREAS: Corporate and Business Litigation; Accounting and Legal Malpractice Defense.
DeWitt, Clyde F. ....................'48 '73 C.999 B.S.E.E. L.326 J.D. [Weston,S.G.&D.]
**Dexheimer, James P.** ....................'50 '83 C&L.1136 B.A., J.D. [Ⓐ Wilner,K.&S.]
*PRACTICE AREAS: Civil Practice; Insurance Defense.
Dezes, B. George ....................'57 '83 C.446 B.A. L.990 J.D. 9201 Wilshire Blvd.
Diaz, Frances L. ....................'55 '92 L.1179 J.D. 8306 Wilshire Blvd.
Dichter, Philip J. ....................'50 '75 C.112 B.A. L.1065 J.D. [Dichter,S.&K.]
Dichter, Spector & Karpel, (AV) ....................9777 Wilshire Blvd.
**Dicker, Kevin S.** ....................'69 '95 C.860 B.A. L.800 J.D. [Ⓐ Leonard,D.&S.]
*PRACTICE AREAS: Business Litigation; Entertainment Law.
**Dicker, Lee T.** ....................'45 '71 C.352 B.A. L.1066 J.D. [Leonard,D.&S.]
*PRACTICE AREAS: Business and Real Estate Transactions and Litigation; Probate Litigation.
Dickerson, William R., (AV) ....................'28 '59 C.1097 B.A. L.1068 J.D. 813 N. Doheny Dr.
**Diemer, John D.** ....................'53 '80 C.112 B.A. L.1068 J.D. [Bloom,H.C.D.&K.]
Dillon, Gregory R. '22 '49 C.238 L.209 LL.B.
(adm. in IL; not adm. in CA) 9336 Civic Ctr. Dr.
Dintzer, Daniel L. ....................'39 '65 C.112 A.B. L.1068 LL.B. 424 S. Beverly Dr.
**Disner, Eliot G.**, (AV) ....................'47 '72 C.477 B.A. L.309 J.D. [Ervin,C.&J.]
*PRACTICE AREAS: Antitrust and Trade Regulation; Complex Business Litigation.
Dizenfeld, David G. ....................'49 '75 C.800 A.B. L.1068 J.D. P.O. Box 3472
Dolgin, Aaron ....................'58 '81 C.1183 B.A. L.426 J.D. 9300 Wilshire Blvd., Ste., 300
Donaldson, Michael C., (AV) ....................'39 '67 C.260 B.S. L.1066 J.D. [Berton&D.]
Doodan, Michael M. '46 '77 C.276 A.B. L.966 J.D.
Sr. V.P., Legal Affs. & Asst. Gen. Coun., Twentieth Century Fox Film Corp.
Dorn, Carl H. ....................'40 '72 C.112 A.B. L.426 J.D. P.O. Box 2711‡
Doumani, Roy, (AV) ....................'35 '61 C.112 B.S. L.800 J.D. World Trade Bk.
**Drucker, Joelle M.** ....................'67 '94 C.112 B.A. L.767 J.D. [Ⓐ Ervin,C.&J.]
*PRACTICE AREAS: Estate Planning; Probate; ERISA.
**Duboff, Allan B.** ....................'58 '84 C.112 B.A. L.659 J.D. [Richman,L.M.G.C.F.&P.]
Dubrow, Robert R. ....................'23 '51 C&L.813 A.B., J.D. 121 S. Bev. Dr.
Ducey, Mitchell F. ....'55 '91 C&L.575 B.A., J.D. 9100 Wilshire Blvd., 8th Fl., East Twr.
Duke, R. Stephen ....................'40 '69 C&L.910 B.S.B.A., J.D. 8665 Wilshire Blvd.

**Dunaetz, Nancy L., (AV) '58 '82 C.112 B.A. L.809 J.D.**
**415 North Camden Drive, Suite 200, 90210**
**Telephone: 310-278-9977 Fax: 310-278-9145**
**Practice Limited to Family Law.**

Dunitz, Sydney J., (AV) ....................'17 '41 C.477 A.B. L.309 LL.B. 9454 Wilshire Blvd.
**Dutton, Carey J.** ........'43 '79 C.174 B.A. L.940 J.D. V.P. & Coun., Hilton Hotels Corp.
**Dymant, Karen Lyn** ....................'69 '94 C.659 B.A. L.477 J.D. [Ⓐ Ervin,C.&J.]
*LANGUAGES: French, Italian, Spanish.
*PRACTICE AREAS: Business and Securities Law.
**Eandi, David R.** ....................'49 '75 C.112 B.A. L.1068 J.D. [Ervin,C.&J.]
*PRACTICE AREAS: Corporate Law; Securities Law; Mergers and Acquisitions Law; General Business Law.
**Ecoff, Lawrence C.** ....................'64 '89 C.112 B.A. L.426 J.D. [Vorzimer,G.M.&E.]
*REPORTED CASES: People vs. Kevin Merritt, 19 Cal. App. 4th 1573 (1993).
*PRACTICE AREAS: White Collar; Criminal Defense; Complex Business Litigation; Appeals.
**Edwards, Mark L.** ....................'59 '85 C.347 B.S. L.426 J.D. [Heller&E.]
*PRACTICE AREAS: Complex Business Litigation; Real Estate; Insurance and Corporate Law.
Eenigenburg, John M. ....................'53 '92 C&L.1097 B.A., J.D. 360 N. Bedford Ave.
Ehrmann, Sanford M., (AV) '29 '56
C.112 B.S. L.1068 LL.B. 9606 Santa Monica Blvd., 3rd Fl.
**Eidel, Michael Lee** ....................'60 '85 C&L.188 B.S., J.D. [Weissmann,W.B.C.&S.]
*LANGUAGES: French.
*PRACTICE AREAS: General Civil Litigation; Contracts; Entertainment; Sports Law; Real Estate.
Einhorn, Avery H., (AV) ....................'54 '78 C.978 B.A. L.705 J.D. 405 S. Beverly Dr.
Eisenberg, David ....................'41 '68 301 N. Canon Dr.
Ellis, David M. ....................'60 '85 C.691 B.A. L.846 J.D. 9601 Wilshire Blvd.
Ellis, Richard N. ....................'33 '60 C.112 B.S. L.1068 J.D. 9864 Wilshire Blvd.
**Ellyn, Heidi H.** ....................'63 '93 C.112 B.A. L.990 J.D. [Wilner,K.&S.]
**Emanuel, Craig A.** ....................'59 '86 C&L.061 [Sinclair T.O.&E.]
Emery, Myron D., P.C., (AV) '27 '57
C.813 A.B. L.208 LL.B. 9100 Wilshire Blvd. 17th Fl. W. Tower
Engel, Alison G. ....................'63 '89 C.66 B.A. L.597 J.D. 9595 Wilshire Blvd., Ste., 810
Engelhardt, Ruth J., (Mrs.) ....................'21 '59 L.809 William Morris Agcy., Inc.
Englund, Craig W. ....................'55 '80 C.668 B.A. L.1068 J.D. 8383 Wilshire Blvd.

**Enright, Judith A. '46 '77 C.112 B.A. L.809 J.D.**
**9100 Wilshire Boulevard Seventh Floor - West Tower, 90212**
**Telephone: 310-274-1830 Facsimile: 310-274-2330**
***REPORTED CASES: Estate of Trynin (1989) 49 Cal.3d 868.**
***PRACTICE AREAS: Non-Profit Corporation Law; Conservatorship; Elder Abuse; Mental Health Law; Employment Law.**
**Associate: Julie A. Ocheltree.**
**General Civil Litigation in all Federal and State Courts and Administrative Tribunals.**

*See Professional Biographies, BEVERLY HILLS, CALIFORNIA*

**Enriquez, Paul M.**, (AV) ......'47 '73 C.800 B.S. L.1068 J.D. [Richman,L.M.G.C.F.&P.]
*PRACTICE AREAS: Real Estate Law; Business Planning; Securities Law; Environmental and Land Use Law.
**Epstein, Ira S.**, (AV) ....................'32 '56 C&L.546 B.S., J.D. [© Weissmann,W.B.C.&S.]
Epstein, Jeffrey M., & Associates, (AV) '47 '82
C.112 B.A. L.1148 J.D. 8383 Wilshire Blvd., Ste 214
Epstein, Steven F. ....................'46 '79 C.112 B.A. L.809 J.D. 415 N. Camden Dr.

**Ervin, Cohen & Jessup LLP, (AV)**
**A Limited Liability Partnership including Professional Corporations**
**9401 Wilshire Boulevard, 90212-2974**
**Telephone: 310-273-6333 Facsimile: 310-859-2325**
**Email: ErvinCohenJessup@counsel.com**
**Members of Firm: John W. Ervin (1917-1982); W. Edgar Jessup, Jr.; Melvin S. Spears; Bertram K. Massing; Marvin H. Lewis; David P. Kassoy; Gary J. Freedman (P.C.); Lee I. Silver; Roger J. Holt; Eliot G. Disner; Allan B. Cooper; John A. Meyers; David R. Eandi; Gary Q. Michel (A P.C.); Joan B. Velazquez; E. A. (Stacey) Olliff III; Thomas F. R. Garvin; Robert M. Waxman; Reeve E. Chudd; Kenneth A. Luer; Philip Starr; Barry J. MacNaughton; Jacob D. Lee; Kelly O. Scott. Associates: Sylvia D. Lautsch; Howard Z. Berman; Layton L. Pace; Mark T. Kawa; Darcy L. Simon; Bari J. Cooper; Chung Jay Won; Ellen S. Kornblum; Kevin K. Haah; Joelle M. Drucker; Elizabeth E. Webb; Michelle Lee Flores; Karen Lyn Dymant.**
**Federal and State Taxation, Business, Corporation, Securities and Real Estate Law. General Business and Commercial Litigation in all State and Federal Trial and Appellate Courts with emphasis on Unfair Competition, Business Torts, Intellectual Property, Trademarks, Trade Secrets and Insurance Coverage and Litigation. Environmental Law, Probate, Estate Planning and Trusts, Insolvency and Creditors' Rights Law, Health Care and Entertainment Law.**
**Reference: Bank of California, N.A. (Beverly Hills).**

*See Professional Biographies, BEVERLY HILLS, CALIFORNIA*

Esensten, Robert L. ....................'49 '75 C.800 B.S. L.809 J.D. [R.L.Esensten]
Esensten, Robert L., A Professional Law Corporation ....................9454 Wilshire Blvd.
Eskander, Mark B. ....................'50 '78 C.1077 B.A. L.1095 J.D. 8447 Wilshire Blvd.
Estabrook, Steven H. '52 '77
C.1109 B.A. L.1065 J.D. Assoc. Dir., Litig., Western Atlas, Inc.
Estep, Ruth L. ....................'52 '79 C.1075 B.A. L.1148 J.D. 170 S. Beverly Dr.
**Evall, Mitchell** ....................'56 '80 C.1036 A.B. L.178 J.D. [Weissmann,W.B.C.&S.]
*PRACTICE AREAS: Real Property Law.
**Evanns, Joseph R.**, (AV) ...'38 '69 C.800 B.S. L.1068 J.D. [Evanns&W.] (See Pat. Sect.)
*REPORTED CASES: Mayview v. Rodstein, 620 F.2d 1347 (9th Cir. 1980), (Patent); Kamar International Inc. v. Russ Berrie & Co., Inc., 657 F.2d 1059 (9th Cir. 1981) (copyright); Hollingsworth Solderless Terminal Co. v. Turley, 622 F.2d 1324 (9th Cir. 1980) (Trade Secret).

**Evanns & Walsh, (AV)**
**Suite 206, 119 North San Vicente Boulevard, 90211**
**Telephone: 310-273-0938; 310-855-0872 Cable Address: "Jorev" Telecopier: 213-651-3027**
**Joseph R. Evanns; Edward C. Walsh (1912-1994).**
**Patent, Copyright, Trademark and Unfair Competition Law. Trials and Appeals in State and Federal Trial and Appellate Courts; proceedings before the United States Patent and Trademark Office and Copyright Office and before the International Trade Commission.**

*See Professional Biographies, BEVERLY HILLS, CALIFORNIA*

Factor, Max, III, (AV) ....................'45 '70 C.309 B.A. L.976 J.D. [M.Factor III]
Factor, Max, III, P.C., (AV) ....................345 N. Maple Dr., Ste., 294
Fadel, Lynda Wolfson ....................'52 '87 C.659 B.A. L.472 J.D. 1018 Summit Dr.
Fagel, Bruce G. ....................'46 '82 C.339 B.A. L.1148 J.D. 445 S. Beverly Dr.

**Fain, Harry M., (AV) '18 '46 C.112 A.B. L.800 J.D. BR**
**121 South Beverly Drive, 90212**
**Telephone: 310-275-5132; 213-272-7807 Fax: 310-271-5269**
***REPORTED CASES: "Marriage of Frick 181 CA3 997 226CR 766," Linsk vs. Linsk, 70 Cal. 2d 272,449 pac. 2d 760.**
**Practice Limited to Family Law.**
**Reference: City National Bank (Beverly Hills Main Office).**

*See Professional Biographies, BEVERLY HILLS, CALIFORNIA*

Falk, Murray H., (AV) ......'29 '59 C.976 B.A. L.893 LL.B. 9595 Wilshire Blvd., Ste 800
Farran, Nelson J. ....................'36 '65 C.912 B.S. L.800 LL.B. 9595 Wilshire Blvd.
**Fasman, Michael J.**, (AV) ....................'09 '31 C.999 L.209 J.D. [Allen&F.]
*PRACTICE AREAS: Real Estate; Probate; Taxation.
**Fayne, Steven E.**, (AV) ....................'44 '71 C.381 B.A. L.178 J.D. [Rosenfeld,M.&S.]
*PRACTICE AREAS: Entertainment Law; Media Finance.
Fechter, Allison Weiner ....................'63 '87 C.66 B.A. L.800 J.D. 9601 Wilshire Blvd.
Feder, Robert S., (AV) ......'15 '40 C&L.800 A.B., LL.B. 9665 Wilshire Blvd., Ste., 210
Federman, Barbara B., (AV) ....................'44 '85 C.112 B.A. L.1136 J.D. 9454 Wilshire Blvd.
Feig, Eric J. ....................'66 '91 C.569 B.A. L.262 J.D. [Berton&D.]
Fein, Bonnie L. ....................'49 '82 C.800 B.A. L.1136 J.D. Arka Properties Grp.
**Feldman, David B.** ....................'59 '90 C.112 B.S. L.1066 J.D. [Bloom,H.C.D.&K.]
Feldman, Eddy S. ....................'20 '41 L.209 LL.B. P.O. Box 2188
**Feldman, Miles J.** ....................'65 '94 C.112 B.A. L.1066 J.D. [Browne&W.]
**Feldman, Orrin M.** ....................'54 '79 C&L.569 A.B., J.D. [Ⓐ Rosenfeld,M.&S.]
*PRACTICE AREAS: Employee Benefits; Taxation; Pension.
Fenimore, George W. '21 '48 C.597 B.S. L.309 J.D.
(adm. in MI; not adm. in CA) 360 N. Crescent Dr.
Fennel, Scott W. ....................'63 '89 C.1 B.A. L.990 J.D. Ste. 700, 9601 Wilshire Blvd.
Fenster, Alan, (AV) ....................'40 '66 C.112 B.S. L.1066 LL.B. 9777 Wilshire Blvd.
**Fenster, Fred A.**, (AV) ....................'46 '72 C&L.800 B.A., J.D. [H.B.California]
*PRACTICE AREAS: Civil Litigation; General Business.
Fenster, Stephen M., (AV) ....................'38 '64 C.112 A.B. L.1068 LL.B. [Polston,S.H.&F.]
**Ferguson, Thomas C.** '— '59 C&L.880 B.A., J.D.
(adm. in IL; not adm. in CA) [© Inman,S.N.&S.]
Fermin, Maria Luisa (Marisa) '60 '86 C.766 B.A. L.1065 J.D.
9601 Wilshire Blvd. 4th Fl.
**Feyder, Robert E.** ....................'61 '87 C.813 A.B. L.1068 J.D. [Ⓐ Freshman,M.O.C.&K.]
Field, Jeffrey H. ....................'59 '87 C.1036 B.A. L.1066 J.D. William Morris Agcy., Inc.
**Fields, Craig M.**, (AV) ....................'56 '82 C.112 A.B. L.1068 J.D. [Glickfeld,F.&J.]

**Fields, Michael S. '39 '69 C.768 B.S. L.809 LL.B.**
**Village on Cañon, Promenade Suite 220, 301 North Cañon Drive, 90210⊙**
**Telephone: 310-273-1209 Fax: 310-273-8229**
***PRACTICE AREAS: Torts and Litigation.**
**Practice limited to Personal Injury Litigation, Professional Malpractice, Product Liability, Vehicular Accidents, Construction Accidents and Insurance Company Bad Faith Actions.**
**Reference: Wells Fargo Bank.**
**Cerritos, California Office: 11554 South Street, Suite 2. Telephone: 310-860-6601.**

*See Professional Biographies, BEVERLY HILLS, CALIFORNIA*

CAA21P

Fields, T. Elizabeth Fields '65 '93 C.276 B.S.F.S. L.1148 J.D. 270 N. Canon Dr., 3rd Fl.
Fimberg, Stanley R., (AV) '34 '61 C.112 A.B. L.1068 LL.B. 9777 Wilshire Blvd.

**Fine, Jack D., (AV) '33 '58 C&L.813 A.B., J.D.**
**424 South Beverly Drive, 90212**
**Telephone: 310-553-8533 FAX: 310-203-9853**
***PRACTICE AREAS: Civil Litigation; General Practice.**
**General Civil Practice, Civil litigation, Contracts, Business Litigation and Commercial Litigation, Probate, Trust, and Estate Planning, Landlord-Tenant, Personal Injury, Arbitration and Mediation.**
*See Professional Biographies, BEVERLY HILLS, CALIFORNIA*

Finestone, Alan E. '46 '75 C.1077 B.S. L.809 J.D. 8383 Wilshire Blvd.
Fink, Mendel E. '22 '61 C.112 B.S. L.800 LL.B. 348 S. Elm Dr.

**Finkel, Charles M. '50 '81 C.472 B.A. L.1148 J.D.**
**Suite 919, 8383 Wilshire Boulevard, 90211**
**Telephone: 213-655-9989 FAX: 213-655-7865**
**Email: CharlesMFinkel@msn.com**
**Aviation Law, Personal Injury and Wrongful Death.**
*See Professional Biographies, BEVERLY HILLS, CALIFORNIA*

Finn, Aubrey I. '14 '37 C&L.809 B.A., LL.B. 433 N. Camden Dr.‡
Finsilver, Iris J. '48 '86 C.1154 B.A. L.213 J.D. 9595 Wilshire Blvd.
Firestone, Howard L. '31 '54 C.8 B.A. L.608 LL.B. 9454 Wilshire Blvd.
Firestone, Randall S. '53 '79 C.112 B.A. L.1065 J.D. 8383 Wilshire Blvd.
Fischbach, Joseph S. '51 '76 C.800 B.A. L.426 J.D. 9595 Wilshire Blvd.
Fischer, Barry '— '86 C.102 B.A. L.1179 J.D. 9777 Wilshire Blvd.
Fischer, Murray D., (BV) '42 '72 C.077 B.S. L.1136 J.D. 405 S. Beverly Dr.
**Fischer, Neil B.** '36 '61 C.966 B.B.A. L.597 J.D. [Isaacman,K.&P.]
*PRACTICE AREAS: Entertainment; Corporate; Securities; Financing.

**Fishbein, Gary, Law Offices of, (AV) '49 '80 C.1077 B.A. L.1136 J.D.**
**9454 Wilshire Boulevard, Suite 203, 90212**
**Telephone: 310-887-6190 Fax: 310-887-6193**
***PRACTICE AREAS: Family Law.**
**Associate: Cheri L. Wood.**
**Family Law.**
*See Professional Biographies, BEVERLY HILLS, CALIFORNIA*

**Fisher, David R.** '60 '85 C.1044 B.A. L.276 J.D. [Herzog,F.&G.]
Fisher, Derrick, (AV) '45 '78 L.061 LL.B. 9601 Wilshire Blvd.
Fisher, Eugene '31 '68 C.499 L.809 LL.B. 120 El Camino Dr.
Fisher, R. Kevin '62 '90 C.838 B.S. L.880 J.D. 9201 Wilshire Blvd.
**Fishkin, Daniel L.** '53 '88 C.102 B.A. L.1009 J.D. [Hansen,J.T.&H.]
*PRACTICE AREAS: Entertainment Law; Television Law; Copyrights.
**Fishman, Lois R.** '50 '94 C.976 B.A. L.276 J.D. [⊠ Rosenfeld,M.&S.]
*LANGUAGES: Spanish and French.
*PRACTICE AREAS: Copyright; Trademark; Litigation; Intellectual Property; Entertainment.
Fitzgerald, Paul J., (AV) '37 '64 C&L.494 B.A., J.D. 424 S. Beverly Dr.
**Fiur, Kevin S.** '66 '91 C&L.846 B.A., J.D. (adm. in TX; not adm. in CA) [⊠ Rosenfeld,M.&S.]
*PRACTICE AREAS: Litigation; Entertainment Litigation.
Flader, David Matthew '60 '85 C.800 B.S. L.426 J.D. 211 Spalding Dr.
Flanagan, Dayna A. Kalins '49 '76 C.112 B.A. L.426 J.D. Pres., Steven Bochco Productions
Flate, Ronald A. '37 '67 C.966 B.S. L.61 J.D. 9300 Wilshire Blvd.
Flax, Larry S., (AV) '42 '68 C.911 B.A. L.800 J.D. California Pizza Kitchen, Inc.
**Fleer, Keith G.** '43 '67 C.30 B.A. L.904 J.D. [⊠ Sinclair T.O.&E.]
Flesch, Michael B., (BV) '47 '73 C.112 B.A. L.1068 J.D. 714 N. Foothill Rd.
**Florence, Kenneth J.**, (AV) '43 '74 C.940 B.A. L.1065 J.D. [Swerdlow,F.&S.]
*PRACTICE AREAS: Management, Labor and Employment Law.
**Flores, Michelle Lee** '68 '93 C.37 B.A. L.1068 [⊠ Ervin,C.&J.]
*PRACTICE AREAS: Business Litigation; Labor and Employment Law.

**Flores, Yvonne Magdalena, Law Offices of '47 '90 C.1060 B.A. L.1165 J.D.**
**9454 Wilshire Boulevard, PH, 90212**
**Telephone: 310-271-0149 Facsimile: 310-271-0469**
***LANGUAGES: Spanish and French.**
**Workers Compensation Defense.**
**Representative Client: Century National Insurance Company.**

**Flynn, Michael C.** '55 '81 C.347 B.A. L.228 J.D. [Rubin&E.]
*PRACTICE AREAS: Business and Commercial Litigation; Real Estate Litigation; Insurance and Insurance Coverage Litigation.
Forbess, John D., (AV) '49 '75 C.31 A.B. L.365 J.D. 9595 Wilshire Blvd.
Forrester, Perry M. '52 '79 C.1109 B.A. L.426 J.D. 9460 Wilshire Blvd. #830
Forrester, Wendy '48 '85 C.1077 B.A. L.809 J.D. 8383 Wilshire Blvd.
Fox, Gerson I. '27 '58 C.800 B.S. 337 S. Roxbury Dr.
Fraade, Richard D. '43 '70 C.112 B.A. L.1009 J.D. 9100 Wilshire Blvd.
Fraade, Robert D. '49 '78 C.415 B.A. L.1137 J.D. 9100 Wilshire Blvd.
Fraider, M. D., (BV) '11 '44 C.800 A.B. L.426 LL.B. 258 McCarty Dr.

**Frandzel & Share, A Law Corporation**
**(See Los Angeles)**

Frank, Carolyn J. '30 '72 C.1097 B.A. L.426 J.D. 8447 Wilshire Blvd.
Frankel, Susan P. '51 '76 618 N. Oakhurst Dr.‡
**Franzen, Don Erik**, (AV) '49 '75 C&L.800 B.A., J.D. [Funsten&F.]
*LANGUAGES: Spanish and Italian.
*REPORTED CASES: (Partial): Nourafchan v. Miner, 169 Cal.App.3d 746, 215 Cal.Rptr. 450 (1985); Tamarind Lithography Workshop, Inc. v. Sanders, 143 Cal.App.3d 571, 168 Cal.Rptr. 409 (1983); Cain v. Air Cargo, Inc., 599 F.2d 316 (9th Cir. 1979).
*PRACTICE AREAS: Entertainment Law; Business Law; Civil Litigation.
Frasier, Berton S. '38 '63 L.426 LL.B. 315 S. Beverly Dr.
**Freedman, Gary J., (P.C.)**, (AV) '42 '68 C.339 A.B. L.1065 J.D. [Ervin,C.&J.]
*PRACTICE AREAS: Corporate Securities Law; Real Property Law; International Law.
**Freimuth, Robert S.** '59 '87 C.966 B.A. L.309 J.D. [Isaacman,K.&P.]
*LANGUAGES: French.
*PRACTICE AREAS: First Amendment; Copyright.
Freis, Joel H. '36 '71 C.813 B.A. L.1148 J.D. 137 El Camino Dr.

**Freshman, Marantz, Orlanski, Cooper & Klein, A Law Corporation, (AV)**
**Eighth Floor, East Tower, 9100 Wilshire Boulevard, 90212**
**Telephone: 310-273-1870 Telecopier: 310-274-8293**
**Philip F. Marantz; Leib Orlanski; Richard H. Cooper; Mark Alexander Klein; Paul W. Sweeney, Jr.; William J. Bernfeld; Thomas J. Poletti;—Robert E. Feyder; Mark J. Kelson; Patricia Task Craigie; Susan B. Kalman (Resident); Christopher J. Kondon; Katherine J. Blair; James K. Lee; Darren O. Bigby; Deborah M. Sturman.**
**General Civil Trial and Appellate Practice. Banking, Corporate, Securities, Commercial, Employment, Real Estate, Real Estate Lending, Sports Law and Creditors Rights.**
*See Professional Biographies, BEVERLY HILLS, CALIFORNIA*

Freudenheim, Harold R. '43 '68 C.30 B.A. L.94 J.D. 9777 Wilshire Blvd. Ste. 918
**Friedman, Abby B.** '46 '90 C.36 B.A. L.1136 J.D. [Friedman&F.]
*PRACTICE AREAS: Civil and Commercial Litigation; Family Law.

**Friedman, Barry A.**, (AV) '41 '66 C.339 B.S. L.597 J.D. [Richman,L.M.G.C.F.&P.]
*PRACTICE AREAS: Business Planning; Securities Law; Real Estate Law; Entertainment Law.
Friedman, David C. '59 '84 C.112 B.A. L.1066 J.D. 9348 Civil Ctr. Dr., Ste 200
**Friedman, Edward** '49 '75 C.668 B.A. L.426 J.D. [Turner,G.W.A.&Y.]
*PRACTICE AREAS: Business Litigation; Real Estate Law; Mediation; Arbitration.
**Friedman, Ira M.**, (AV) '46 '75 C.36 B.S. L.1026 J.D. [Friedman&F.]
*REPORTED CASES: In Re the Marriage of Allison (1979) 99 Cal. App. 3d 993, 168 Cal Rptr 160; In Re the Marriage of Gavron (1988) 203 Cal. App. 3d 705, 250 Cal Rptr 148.
*PRACTICE AREAS: Family Law; Civil and Commercial Litigation.
Friedman, Lester J., (A Prof. Corp.), (AV) '51 '77 C.112 B.A. L.809 J.D. 9777 Wilshire Blvd.

**Friedman, Robert J., (AV) '46 '72 C.112 B.A. L.800 J.D.**
**8648 Wilshire Boulevard, 90211**
**Telephone: 310-659-5757; 213-655-8861 Fax: 310-659-7773**
**(Certified Specialist, Family Law, The State Bar of California Board of Legal Specialization).**
***PRACTICE AREAS: Family Law; Dissolution of Marriage Law; Prenuptial Agreements.**
**Family Law.**
*See Professional Biographies, BEVERLY HILLS, CALIFORNIA*

**Friedman & Friedman, (AV)**
**9454 Wilshire Boulevard, Suite 313, 90212-2904**
**Telephone: 310-273-2800 Fax: 310-273-3642**
**Ira M. Friedman (Certified Specialist, Family Law, The State Bar of California Board of Legal Specialization); Abby B. Friedman.**
**General Civil and Trial Practice. Family Law.**
*See Professional Biographies, BEVERLY HILLS, CALIFORNIA*

Frome, Bruce M. '38 '91 C.011 B.S. L.1136 J.D. [Frome&F.]
Frome, Laurelle L. '52 '91 C.112 B.A. L.1136 J.D. [Frome&F.]
Frome & Frome P.O. Box 15157
**Fruchtman, Cynthia E.** '58 '86 C.597 B.A. L.146 J.D. [Richman,L.M.G.C.F.&P.]
**Frydrych, Jack A.** '48 '73 C.1077 B.A. L.910 J.D. [Frydrych&W.]
*PRACTICE AREAS: Business Planning; Employment Law; Intellectual Property.

**Frydrych & Webster, Inc.**
**9777 Wilshire Boulevard, Suite 1018, 90212**
**Telephone: 310-274-0643 Telecopier: 310-274-5485**
**Jack A. Frydrych; J. Michael Webster;—Richard L. Sprunger; Gary R. Linder (Not admitted in CA); Stephanie H. Izen.**
**Business Planning involving Corporations, Partnerships and Taxation, Civil Litigation, Family Law, Estate Planning, Commercial Law, Real Estate, Transactional Matters and Labor Relations.**
*See Professional Biographies, BEVERLY HILLS, CALIFORNIA*

**Funsten, Peter L.** '51 '78 C.112 A.B. L.1065 J.D. [Funsten&F.]
*LANGUAGES: Italian.
*PRACTICE AREAS: Taxation; Business; Entertainment Law.

**Funsten & Franzen, (AV)**
**An Association of Law Corporations**
**9595 Wilshire Boulevard, Suite 305, 90212-2500**
**Telephone: 310-273-3221 and 310-785-1710 Fax: 310-273-3229 and 310-785-1720**
**Peter L. Funsten; Don Erik Franzen. Of Counsel: James H. Lehr.**
**Business, Entertainment and Tax Law. Civil Litigation (State and Federal).**
*See Professional Biographies, BEVERLY HILLS, CALIFORNIA*

**Fuster, Kathleen Dority, (P.C.)** '60 '85 C.705 B.A. L.659 J.D. [Norminton&W.]
Gabler, Ronald G. '46 '73 C.645 B.A. L.276 J.D. 9606 Santa Monica Blvd., 2nd Fl.
**Gabriel, Joseph M.** '60 '85 C.339 B.A. L.424 J.D. [⊠ Rosenfeld,M.&S.]
*PRACTICE AREAS: Entertainment Litigation; Intellectual Property; Defamation; First Amendment; Business Litigation.
Gage, Sanford M., (AV) '34 '59 C.112 B.S. L.1068 J.D. [S.M.Gage]
Gage, Sanford M., A Professional Corporation, (AV) 9454 Wilshire Blvd., 5th Fl.
**Galka, Renee A.** '68 '92 C.674 A.B. L.1068 J.D. [⊠ Rosenfeld,M.&S.]
*PRACTICE AREAS: Entertainment; Entertainment Industry Transactions; Film Productions; Television Productions; Motion Picture Law.
Galperin, Ron '63 '94 C.910 B.A. L.426 J.D. 8306 Wilshire Blvd.
**Gamble, Kristin** '71 '96 C.112 B.S. L.1068 J.D. [⊠ Jacoby&C.]
**Gambourian, Ashkhen A.** '66 '91 C.112 B.S. L.1148 J.D. [⊠ Inman,S.N.&S.]
*LANGUAGES: Armenian, French, Russian and Turkish.
*PRACTICE AREAS: Immigration.
Gandhi, Indra M. '40 '75 C&L.061 B.Sc., LL.B. 8383 Wilshire Blvd.
**Gang, Martin**, (AV) '01 '27 C.309 B.A. L.1066 J.D. [⊠ Gang,T.R.&B.] ‡

**Gang, Tyre, Ramer & Brown, Inc., (AV)**
**132 South Rodeo Drive, 90212-2403**
**Telephone: 310-777-4800 Fax: 310-777-4801**
**Norman R. Tyre; Hermione K. Brown; Payson Wolff (1921-1995); Bruce M. Ramer; Charles A. Scott; Donald S. Passman; Harold A. Brown; Tom R. Camp; Lawrence D. Rose; Jeffrey M. Mandell; Kevin S. Marks; Gregg Harrison; Fred D. Toczek; Nancy L. Boxwell; Steven G. Krone; Barbara Silberbusch. Of Counsel: Martin Gang (Retired, 1995); Arnold D. Burk (Retired, 1995).**
**Entertainment and Communications Industries Law and Related Services.**
**References: Bank of America (Los Angeles Main Office, also Hollywood Main Office); City National Bank (Beverly Hills Main Office).**
*See Professional Biographies, BEVERLY HILLS, CALIFORNIA*

Gans, Robert H., (AV) '24 '71 C.597 B.M.M.D. L.981 LL.B. 433 N. Camden Dr.

**Gantz, Emmett J., Law Office of, (AV) '43 '73 C.339 B.S. L.426 J.D.**
**Suite 208, 280 South Beverly Drive, 90212**
**Telephone: 213-879-7866; 310-276-3800 Fax: 310-275-5087**
***PRACTICE AREAS: Professional Liability Law; Products Liability Law; Medical Malpractice; Insurance Bad Faith Law; Personal Injury Law.**
**—Barry P. Kaye.**
**Professional Liability, Products Liability, Medical Malpractice, Insurance Bad Faith, Complex Civil Litigation and Personal Injury. Civil Trial and Appellate Practice.**
*See Professional Biographies, BEVERLY HILLS, CALIFORNIA*

**Garber, Ronald D.** '53 '79 C.597 B.A. L.851 J.D. [⊠ Richman,L.M.G.C.F.&P.]
*PRACTICE AREAS: Real Estate.
**Garber, Steven M.** '65 '91 C.1077 B.A. L.940 J.D. [Vorzimer,G.M.&E.]
*PRACTICE AREAS: Complex Business Litigation; Real Estate; Corporations and Partnerships; Insurance Coverage; General Civil Practice.
Garrou, G. Randall '50 '76 C.339 B.S. L.878 J.D. [Weston,S.G.&D.]
**Garvin, Thomas F. R.**, (AV) '55 '79 C.426 B.A. L.1065 J.D. [Ervin,C.&J.]
*PRACTICE AREAS: Taxation Law; Entertainment Law; International Business Law; International Trust and Estate Planning.
**Gasmer, Harlee M.** '60 '85 C.112 B.A. L.426 J.D. [Kolodny&A.]
*PRACTICE AREAS: Family Law.
Gasperian, Garee T. '58 '88 C.112 B.A. L.1065 J.D. 9401 Wilshire Blvd.
Gautreau, Paul N. '53 '79 C.112 B.A. L.464 J.D. 280 S. Beverly Dr.
Gelfand, Gary B., (AV) '49 '74 C.800 B.A. L.1049 J.D. [Gelfand&G.] (⊙Las Vegas & Reno, NV)
Gelfand, Herbert M., (AV) '31 '56 C.112 L.426 J.D. 9171 Wilshire Blvd.
Gelfand, Judith Ann, (AV) '44 '70 C.813 A.B. L.1068 J.D. [Gelfand&G.]
Gelfand and Gelfand, A Law Corporation, (AV) 161 S. Doheny Dr.
General Counsel Services, A Professional Law Corporation, (AV) 9606 Santa Monica Blvd., 3rd Fl. (⊙Oakland)

Genow, Richard M. .................... '63 '89 C.112 B.A. L.309 J.D. 450 N. Roxbury Dr.
George, George A. ........................ '27 '52 C.800 B.S. L.472 LL.B. P.O. Box 1445‡
George, Joseph A. ........................ '36 '66 C.201 L.809 LL.B. P.O. Box 1418‡
George, Michael S. ..................... '46 '80 C.112 B.A. L.809 J.D. 9107 Wilshire Blvd.
**Gernsbacher, David L.** ............... '53 '79 C.112 B.A. L.800 J.D. [Gernsbacher&M.]

**Gernsbacher & McGarrigle**
**9100 Wilshire Boulevard East Tower, Suite 710, 90212**
**Telephone: 310-281-0100 Telecopier: 310-281-0755**
**Members of Firm: David L. Gernsbacher; Patrick C. McGarrigle; Paul B. Beach.**
**Real Estate Transactions; Financing, Management and Litigation; Business Litigation; Corporate and General Civil Litigation; Entertainment Litigation; Federal and State Court Appeals.**
*See Professional Biographies, BEVERLY HILLS, CALIFORNIA*

Gersh, David H., (AV) ................ '48 '73 C.597 B.S. L.1068 J.D. 232 N. Canon Dr.
Gersh, Jeffrey F. ..................... '53 '79 C.1077 B.S. L.1148 J.D. [Zimmerman,R.&G.]
**Gerstenfeld, Gerald F.**, (AV) ........ '31 '53 C&L.597 B.S.L., J.D. [Turner,G.W.A.&Y.]
*PRACTICE AREAS: Estate Planning Law; Probate Law; Trust Law; Real Estate Law; Business Law.
Gertenstein, Brian ..................... '63 '88 L.029 LL.B. 9150 Wilshire Blvd., Ste., 300
Getzels, Morris S. ........................ '51 '76 C.569 B.A. L.1068 J.D. [Malat,M.&G.]
Ghafouri, Noble N. ............... '50 '82 C.800 B.S. L.1179 J.D. 433 N. Camden Dr. #PH
Gianopulos, James N. '52 '77 C.94 B.A. L.262 J.D.
(adm. in NY; not adm. in CA) 1022 Tower Rd.‡
Gibson, Hugh J., (AV) ............. '46 '72 C.058 B.A. L.309 LL.M. 9107 Wilshire Blvd.
Gilbert, Gary L., (AV) ......... '46 '72 C.800 A.B. L.1068 J.D. 150 S. Rodeo Dr., 3rd Fl.
Gilbert, Harvey S., (AV) .................. '41 '67 C.112 B.S. L.1068 J.D. [Gross&G.]
Gilbert, Nat ................. '31 '61 C.800 B.S. L.809 J.D. 9430 Olympic Blvd., Ste., 400
Gindi, Alan J. ............................ '59 '85 C.112 A.B. L.569 J.D. 8665 Wilshire Blvd.
Gindi, Barbara P. ....................... '60 '86 C.994 B.A. L.978 J.D. 8665 Wilshire Blvd.
**Gindi, Elie J.** ......................... '50 '78 C.174 B.A. L.809 J.D. [R.W.Hirsh&Assoc.]
Gindi, Jack E. ............................. '23 '48 C&L.477 J.D. 721 N. Alpine Dr.‡
**Ginise, Russell T.** ....................... '63 '89 C.112 B.A. L.990 J.D. [Stern&G.]
*PRACTICE AREAS: Business Litigation; Employment Law.
Ginsburg, Roland E., (AV) ............ '23 '50 C&L.477 B.A., LL.B. 9454 Wilshire Blvd.
Ginzburg, Alexander Roman ........... '64 '93 C.911 B.S.E.E. L.1148 J.D. [J.Shemaria]
Glaser, Herbert, (AV) ............. '27 '52 C.112 A.B. L.309 J.D. 9595 Wilshire Blvd.‡
Glass, Morris M. ...................................... '24 '50 C.112 L.800 LL.B. P.O. Box 705
**Glassman, Anthony M.**, (AV) ......... '39 '66 C.800 B.A. L.1066 J.D. [Glassman,B.&S.]
*REPORTED CASES: Ward v. News Group, 733 F.Supp. 83 USDC 1990); Tamarind Lithography Workshop, Inc. v. Sanders, 143 Cal.App.3d 571, 193 Cal.Rptr. 409 (1983); Koch v. Goldway, 817 F.2d 507 (9th Cir. 1987).
*PRACTICE AREAS: Defamation; Invasion of Privacy; Misappropriation; Copyright; Entertainment Litigation.

**Glassman, Browning & Saltsman, Inc., (AV)**
**Suite 204, 360 North Bedford Drive, 90210**
**Telephone: 310-278-5100 Fax: 310-271-6041**
**Roger A. Browning; Anthony M. Glassman; Jane D. Saltsman; Amy Osran Jacobs; Barbara Tarlow;—Lori A. Nielsen; David A. Carman; Steven Berkowitz; Kathryn L. Turpin. Of Counsel: Barbara Irshay Zipperman.**
**Civil and Criminal Litigation in all State and Federal Trial and Appellate Courts. Defamation and Invasion of Privacy, Family Law, Estate, Trust and Income Tax Planning, Probate, Corporate, Entertainment, Personal Injury, Malpractice Litigation, Real Estate and General Business Law.**
*See Professional Biographies, BEVERLY HILLS, CALIFORNIA*

**Glavin, William P., IV** ................ '65 '88 C.578 B.A. L.990 J.D. [Kolodny&A.]
*REPORTED CASES: McGinley v. Herman, 1996 Daily Journal, D.A.R. 13509.
*PRACTICE AREAS: Family Law; Juvenile Dependency; Trial Practice.
Glazer, Diane Pregerson, (Mrs.) ..... '25 '51 C.112 B.A. L.800 LL.B. 720 N. Foothill Rd.‡
Gleicher, Gary E., (AV) ............... '48 '74 C.800 B.A. L.809 J.D. 315 S. Beverly Dr.
**Glickfeld, Michael L.**, (AV) ........... '44 '70 C.112 B.A. L.1068 J.D. [Glickfeld,F.&J.]

**Glickfeld, Fields & Jaffe, A Professional Corporation, (AV)**
**9460 Wilshire Boulevard, Fifth Floor, 90212-2711**
**Telephone: 310-550-7222 Fax: 310-550-6222**
**Michael L. Glickfeld; Craig M. Fields; Judianne Jaffe. Of Counsel: Lawrence M. Jacobson.**
**Civil Trial and Appellate Practice in State and Federal Courts, with emphasis on Business, Entertainment and Intellectual Property, Real Estate and Construction, Antitrust, Banking, Bankruptcy, Probate and Securities Litigation.**
**Reference: First Los Angeles Bank (Century City Main Branch).**
*See Professional Biographies, BEVERLY HILLS, CALIFORNIA*

Glickman, Albert B. ............... '33 '60 C.112 B.A. L.1068 LL.B. 9864 Wilshire Blvd.‡
Glickman, David R., (AV) ............. '32 '57 C.990 B.A. L.1068 LL.B. [Glickman&G.]
Glickman, Steven C. ...................... '57 '82 C.112 B.A. L.1068 J.D. [Glickman&G.]
Glickman & Glickman, A Law Corp., (AV) ................................ 9460 Wilshire Blvd.
**Glucksman, William J.** .................... '51 '76 C.112 B.A. L.809 J.D. [Kolodny&A.]
*REPORTED CASES: Kroopf vs. Guffey, 183 L.A. 3d. 1351, 228 C.R. 807, 1986.

**Godfrey, Cyrus V. '49 '75 C.112 B.A. L.1067 J.D.**
**360 North Bedford Drive, Suite 204, 90210**
**Telephone: 310-278-8871 Fax: 310-271-6041**
**Entertainment Litigation.**
*See Professional Biographies, BEVERLY HILLS, CALIFORNIA*

Gold, Chas. I. ....................................... '16 '42 C.112 B.A. L.809 211 Spalding Dr.‡
Gold, Harold, (AV) ......................... '16 '48 C.112 B.S. L.494 J.D. 144 S. Beverly Dr.
Gold, Jack, (AV) ................................... '10 '39 C.112 A.B. L.494 J.D. [Gold&G.]
Gold, Norma S. .................. '46 '84 C.1044 B.A. L.809 J.D. Lawyers for Family Support
Gold and Gold, (AV) ........................................ Ste. 300, 144 S. Beverly Dr.
**Goldberg, Alan** ............................... '55 '80 C.112 B.A. L.426 J.D. [Wilner,K.&S.]
**Goldberg, Alan N.**, (AV) ........................ '58 '83 C.36 B.S. L.990 J.D. [Stern&G.]
*PRACTICE AREAS: Business and Civil Litigation.
Goldberg, Alex ................................................. '— '51 C.809 9454 Wilshire Blvd.
Goldberg, Bruce E. ........................ '59 '90 C.311 B.A. L.112 J.D. 226 N. Clark Dr.
Goldberg, Donald S. ................. '40 '71 C.1077 B.A. L.1095 J.D. 817 Monte Leon Dr.
**Goldberg, Larry** ....... '47 '74 C.112 B.A. L.426 J.D. [Schneider,G.&Y.] (Pasadena)
Goldberg, Lawrence ................... '59 '84 C.188 B.S. L.1068 J.D. 9601 Wilshire Blvd.
**Goldberg, Wendy A.** ............................ '46 '80 C.766 B.A. L.426 J.D. [Wilner,K.&S.]

**Golden, Eugene, (AV) '29 '53 C&L.846 B.B.A., LL.B.**
**9595 Wilshire Boulevard, Suite 900, 90212-2509**
**Telephone: 310-275-9040 Fax: 310-271-4062**
**General Civil Practice, Litigation, Corporation, Business, Real Property, Trust, Probate, Will Contests and Personal Injury.**
*See Professional Biographies, BEVERLY HILLS, CALIFORNIA*

Golden, Roger N. ......................... '48 '74 C.112 B.A. L.1068 J.D. 9300 Wilshire Blvd.
Goldman, Jeffrey A. ...................... '48 '83 C.112 B.A. L.398 J.D. 8383 Wilshire Blvd
Goldman, Robyn S. ............ '54 '78 C.112 B.A. L.1068 J.D. William Morris Agcy., Inc.
Goldner, Justin L., (AV) ........................... '31 '57 C&L.966 B.B.A., J.D. [J.L.Goldner]
Goldner, Justin L., A Professional Corporation, (AV) ........ 9595 Wilshire Blvd., Ste. 800
**Goldring, Fred E.** ......................... '57 '83 C.228 A.B. L.472 J.D. [Hansen,J.T.&H.]
*PRACTICE AREAS: Entertainment Law; Music Recording Law; Copyright Law.
**Goldsmith, Marc H.** .......................... '53 '83 C.1169 A.B. L.494 J.D. [Wilner,K.&S.]

Goldsmith, Marvin, (AV) ........................ '31 '60 C&L.800 B.S., J.D. 229 S. Clark Dr.
Goldstein, Cary W. .......................... '52 '79 C.112 B.A. L.1095 J.D. 8363 Wilshire Blvd.
Goldstein, Howard W. ................ '64 '93 C.1077 B.A. L.1148 J.D. 8306 Wilshire Blvd.

**Goldstein, Susan T., (AV) '54 '78 C.184 B.A. L.851 J.D.**
**9401 Wilshire Boulevard, Suite 1100, 90212**
**Telephone: 310-724-5380 Fax: 310-274-8351**
**Practice limited to Family Law.**
*See Professional Biographies, BEVERLY HILLS, CALIFORNIA*

Goldszer, Ronald Isaac ............ '59 '85 C.1138 B.B.A. L.990 J.D. 8601 Wilshire Blvd.
Gole, Gary M. ........................................ '50 '76 C.1049 B.S. L.1095 J.D. [Tilem&G.]
Gomer, Murray ........................... '21 '51 C.112 B.S. L.426 LL.B. 315 S. Beverly Dr.
Goodfried, Kenneth B. '45 '72
C.112 B.A. L.1065 J.D. 315 S. Beverly Hills Dr., Penthouse
Goodwin, Warren M., (AV) ....... '20 '49 C.112 B.A. L.800 LL.B. 8383 Wilshire Blvd.‡
Gopin, Albert Jacob, (BV) '39 '75 C.339 B.S.M.E. L.426 J.D.
8601 Wilshire Blvd., 8th Fl.
**Gorbis, Boris Z.** .......... '50 '80 C.061 B.S. L.1066 J.D. [Gorbis&L.] (San Francisco)

**Gorbis & Liberty**
**Great Western Center, Suite 800, 8484 Wilshire Boulevard, 90211-3220**
**Telephone: 310-652-0100; 213-651-1600 Fax: 213-651-1778**
**Email: Gorbis_Liberty@juno.com**
**Boris Z. Gorbis; Arthur R. Liberty.**
**General Civil Practice before State and Federal Courts. Personal Injury, Business Transactions in Russia and Ukraine, Products Liability, Business Transactions and Litigation. Corporation and Real Estate Law. Trials and Appeals.**
**Reference: City National Bank.**
**San Francisco, California Office: 500 Sansome Street, Suite 200. Telephone: 415-982-8298. Facsimile: 415-982-3052.**
**San Diego, California Office: 3545 Camino Del Rio South, Suite E. Telephone: 619-563-1832. Facsimile: 619-563-1854.**

Gordon, Frieda, (AV) ........................................ '50 '84 C.999 L.809 J.D. [Gordon]
Gordon, Monte S. ....................... '31 '72 C.475 B.A. L.1077 J.D. 8383 Wilshire Blvd.
Gordon, Paul, (AV) ............................ '15 '38 C.642 L.809 LL.B. 968 No. Alpine Dr.‡
Gordon, Richard H. ........................ '47 '73 C.966 B.A. L.1068 J.D. 9777 Wilshire Blvd.
Gordon Law Offices, (AV) ............................................ Ste., 400, 433 N. Camden Dr.
Gorin, Howard J. ........................ '41 '68 C.112 L.809 LL.B. 433 N. Camden Dr.
Gottlieb, Daniel M. ............ '40 '66 C.800 B.S. L.1066 LL.B. 435 N. Bedford Dr.‡
Gottlieb, Robert J. ........................................ '20 '49 C.800 L.809 617 N. Maple Dr.
**Graber, David F.** ........................ '62 '87 C.112 B.A. L.309 J.D. [Rosenfeld,M.&S.]
*LANGUAGES: French and German.
*PRACTICE AREAS: Entertainment Litigation; Business Litigation.
Graff, Pnina R. '51 '81 C.339 B.A. L.146 J.D.
(adm. in IL; not adm. in CA) 8500 Wilshire Blvd.
Grancell, Sherman, (AV) ............ '10 '33 C.112 B.A. L.800 LL.B. 1469 Carla Ridge‡
Grant, David A. ................. '56 '81 C.112 B.A. L.1067 J.D. Exec. V.P., Fox Bdcstg. Co.
Grant, Harvey F., (AV) ............ '29 '55 C.112 B.A. L.1068 LL.B. 8383 Wilshire Blvd.
Grant, Ronald J., (AV) ...................... '43 '74 C&L.1095 B.A., J.D. [Tilles,W.K.&G.]
**Grayson, Michael A.**, (AV) ............ '43 '68 C.112 B.S. L.1068 J.D. [Herzog,F.&G.]
*PRACTICE AREAS: Corporate; Finance; Real Estate Law; Hospitality, Leisure; Entertainment.
**Grayson, Todd I.** ................................ '69 '93 C.800 B.S. L.809 J.D. [Herzog,F.&G.]
*PRACTICE AREAS: Corporate Law; Real Estate; Commercial Litigation.
**Greaves, Lawrence H.** ............... '51 '77 C.309 A.B. L.846 J.D. [Bloom,H.C.D.&K.]
**Grebow, Arthur**, (AV) ................... '42 '68 C.178 B.A. L.188 J.D. [Grebow,M.P.&Y.]
*REPORTED CASES: Rubin v. Green (1993) 4 Cal.4th 1187; Westbrook v. Fairchild (1992) 7 Cal.App.4th 889; Estate of Zucker (1990) 218 Cal.App.3d 1198; John F. Mutall and Associates, Inc. v. Cloutier (1987) 194 Cal.App.3d 1049; Westbrook v. Superior Court (1986) 176 Cal.App.3d 703.
*PRACTICE AREAS: Business Litigation; Probate Litigation; Insurance Defense Litigation; Mobilehome Park Defense Litigation.

**Grebow, Maruyama, Prinster & Yee, (AV)**
**131 South Rodeo Drive, Suite 250, 90212**
**Telephone: 310-247-7550 Fax: 310-247-7552**
**Arthur Grebow; William K. Maruyama; Patrick K. Prinster; William S. Yee. Associate: Julie H. Rubin.**
**Corporate and Real Estate Transactions, Commercial and Tort Litigation, Mobilehome Park Law, Premises Liability and Insurance Defense Litigation.**
*See Professional Biographies, BEVERLY HILLS, CALIFORNIA*

Green, G. Richard, (AV) ........................ '49 '74 C.1077 B.A. L.464 J.D. [Manns&G.]
Green, Harland N., (AV) ...................... '30 '55 C.112 B.S. L.1068 J.D. [H.N.Green]
Green, Jeff H. ........................ '56 '90 C&L.378 B.A., J.D. 8383 wilshire Blvd., Suite 214
Green, Mark A. ....... '30 '60 C.112 B.S. L.1068 LL.B. 9606 Santa Monica Blvd., 2nd. Fl.
Green, Norman E. ................................ '30 '53 C.150 L.831 LL.B. P.O. Box 3718
Green, Harland N., P.C., (AV) ................................................ 270 N. Canon Dr.
**Greenberg, Bernard A.**, (AV) .... '31 '59 C.112 B.S. L.1068 LL.B. [Rosenfeld,M.&S.]
*PRACTICE AREAS: Estate Planning Law; Tax Planning; Business Aspects of Entertainment Law.
Greenberg, Gail B. ............ '60 '85 C.813 B.A. L.1068 J.D. City National Bank, Legal Dept.
Greenberg, Morton L. ...................................... '33 '61 C.112 B.A. L.800 J.D. [Mathon&R.]
**Greenberg, Ronald M.**, (AV) ...... '39 '65 C.477 A.B. L.813 LL.B. [Rosenfeld,M.&S.]
*PRACTICE AREAS: Civil Litigation; Arbitration; Appellate Practice; Products Liability; Alternative Dispute.
**Greenberger, Feris M., (Ms.)** ........ '56 '80 C.800 A.B. L.1068 J.D. [Greines,M.S.&R.]
*PRACTICE AREAS: Appellate Law.
**Greene, Bruce R.**, (AV) ....... '52 '76 C.659 B.S. L.1068 J.D. [Richman,L.M.G.C.F.&P.]
Greene, Dennis V. ......................... '48 '85 C.1070 B.S. L.990 J.D. 9454 Wilshire Blvd.
Greenfield, Samuel ................................... '13 '36 L.809 LL.B. Ret. Supr. Ct. J.
Greenhill, Roy E., Jr. ........... '64 '91 C.269 B.A. L.976 J.D. 9601 Wilshire Blvd. 4th Fl.
Greenspahn, Jill, (AV) ...................... '48 '75 C.112 B.A. L.1068 J.D. 433 N. Camden Dr.
Greenstein, Earl H. ....................... '29 '56 C.763 B.A. L.1068 LL.B. 161 S. Doheny Dr.
Greenwald, Jeffrey L. ......................... '57 '81 C.112 B.A. L.1136 J.D. [Greenwald&G.]
Greenwald, Thomas H., (AV) ................ '27 '51 C.112 L.809 LL.B. [Greenwald&G.]
Greenwald & Greenwald, (AV) .................................................. 8730 Wilshire Blvd.
Greer, Edward F. ............................... '51 '77 C.112 B.S. L.426 J.D. P.O. Box 751‡

**Greer, Randall E. '49 '74 C.800 B.S. L.426 J.D.**
**9430 Olympic Boulevard, Suite 400, 90212-4552**
**Telephone: 310-551-1232 Fax: 310-551-4926**
***PRACTICE AREAS: Civil Trial; Business; Commercial; Real Estate Law.**
**General Civil Trial, Business, Commercial, and Real Estate Law.**
*See Professional Biographies, BEVERLY HILLS, CALIFORNIA*

**Greines, Irving H.**, (AV) .............. '41 '67 C.112 B.S. L.1068 J.D. [Greines,M.S.&R.]
*PRACTICE AREAS: Appellate practice, including related trial court practice.

**Greines, Martin, Stein & Richland, (AV)**
**Suite 544, 9601 Wilshire Boulevard, 90210**
**Telephone: 310-859-7811 Telecopier: 310-276-5261**
**Members of Firm: Alan G. Martin (1948-1990); Irving H. Greines; Martin Stein; Kent L. Richland; Marc J. Poster; Robin Meadow; Timothy T. Coates; Feris M. Greenberger (Ms.); Barbara W. Ravitz; Robert A. Olson. Associates: Carolyn Oill; Sheila S. Kato; Alison M. Turner; Randel L. Ledesma; Barry M. Wolf; Brian J. Wright; Jennifer L. King; Edward Laucks Xanders. Of Counsel: Barbara S. Perry.**

(This Listing Continued)

CAA23P

**Greines, Martin, Stein & Richland (Continued)**
Appellate, Law and Motion and Related Practice in State and Federal Courts.
Reference: City National Bank (Beverly Hills Branch).
*See Professional Biographies, BEVERLY HILLS, CALIFORNIA*

**Grey, Erin L.** .......... '70 '94 C.1136 B.A. L.809 J.D. [▣ Kolodny&A.]
*PRACTICE AREAS: Family Law.
**Grodin, Alan L.** .......... '43 '67 C.645 B.S. L.569 LL.B. [Weissmann,W.B.C.&S.]
*PRACTICE AREAS: Entertainment.
**Grodsky, Allen B.** .......... '59 '83 C.112 B.A. L.1066 J.D. [Browne&W.]
Groothuis, Martin J. '38 '64
C.299 B.A. L.178 LL.B. Sr. V.P., International Creative Mgmt., Inc.
**Gross, J. Nicholas** .......... '60 '88 C.111 B.S. L.426 J.D. [▣ Trojan] (See Pat. Sect.)
*LANGUAGES: Greek.
*PRACTICE AREAS: Intellectual Property; High Technology Litigation.
Gross, Jared E. .......... '57 '86 C.112 B.A. L.770 J.D. [J.Gross]
Gross, Kenneth L., (AV) .......... '42 '66 C.659 B.S.E. L.884 J.D. [Gross&G.]
Gross & Gilbert, (AV) .......... Ste., 515, 9777 Wilshire Blvd.
Gross, Jared, Law Offices of .......... 8447 Wilshire Blvd.
Grover, Daniel J. .......... '57 '85 C.112 A.B. L.800 J.D. Creative Artists Agcy., Inc.
Gruen, Ronald M. .......... '36 '67 C.831 B.S. L.809 LL.B. 9171 Wilshire Blvd.
**Gubman, David S., (A Professional Corporation)**, (AV) '50 '75
C.813 B.A. L.309 J.D. [Leonard,D.&S.]
*PRACTICE AREAS: Commercial, Real Estate and Bankruptcy Court Litigation.
**Gullen, David J., (P.C.)**, (AV) .... '42 '68 C.93 A.B. L.276 J.D. [Weissmann,W.B.C.&S.]
*PRACTICE AREAS: Federal & State Income Tax; Federal Estate Tax; State Inheritance Tax; Business Transactions; Trademark Licensing.
**Gunshor, Brian** .......... '49 '74 C.659 B.S. L.569 J.D. [B.G.California]

**Gunshor, Brian, Inc., A Calif. Law Corp.**
**Post Office Box 7429, 90212-7429**
Telephone: 310-273-2704; 818-906-0050 Telefacsimile: 310-273-2706; 818-906-0067
Email: bgunshor@IX.netcom.com URL: http://www.gunshorlaw.com
Brian Gunshor.
Complex Civil Litigation and Trial, Arbitration and Alternative Dispute Resolution Practice in all State and Federal Courts and Administrative Agencies involving Contract Disputes, Business Torts, Unfair Competition, Trade Secrets, Intra-Corporate and Partnership Disputes, Probate Contests, Securities, Real Estate, and Commercial Fraud, Insurance Coverage and Interpleader, and Conservatorships. Negotiation and Drafting of Contractual and Related Documents for Business Transactions, including Corporate, Partnership and Sole Proprietorship Business Planning, Formation, Operations, Venture Capital Finance, Acquisitions and Dispositions and Personal Affairs; Investment Risk Counselling and Preventive Law. Serving as Neutral Arbitrator, Mediator or Case Evaluator in Complex Business and Commercial Disputes.
*See Professional Biographies, BEVERLY HILLS, CALIFORNIA*

Gutman, Alan S. .......... '60 '87 C.569 B.A. L.809 J.D. 433 N. Camden Dr.
Gutsue, Nicholas C. .......... '40 '74 C.1246 B.S. L.1136 J.D. 3201 Benedict Canyon Dr.
**Haah, Kevin K.** .......... '65 '92 C.112 B.A. L.188 J.D. [▣ Ervin,C.&J.]
*LANGUAGES: Korean.
*PRACTICE AREAS: Bankruptcy; Creditors' Rights; Business Reorganization.
Hack, Charles H. .......... '45 '90 C.112 B.S. L.1068 J.D. 433 N. Camden
Haddad, Jos. .......... '23 '50 C.299 L.146 LL.B. P.O. Box 570
**Haft, Jonathan D.** .......... '56 '82 C&L.178 B.A., J.D. [Hansen,J.T.&H.]
*PRACTICE AREAS: Entertainment Industry Law.
**Hait, Lawrence W.** .......... '42 '70 C.112 B.A. L.1068 J.D. [Stern&G.]
*PRACTICE AREAS: Business Litigation; Personal Injury Law; Family Law; General Corporate Law.
**Hallam, Kirk M.** .......... '56 '82 C.112 B.A. L.309 J.D. [Rosenfeld,M.&S.]
*PRACTICE AREAS: Entertainment Law; Copyright and Trademark; Unfair Competition.
Halpern, Steven J., (AV) .......... '50 '79 C.112 B.A. L.564 J.D. 440 Martin Ln.
Halverson, Philip J. .......... '40 '71 C.112 B.S. L.767 J.D. 9595 Wilshire Blvd.
Hamar, Maria Rivas '58 '82 C&L.472 B.A., J.D.
(adm. in FL; not adm. in CA) 2437 Briarcrest Rd.
Hamar, Richard A. .......... '45 '70 C.112 B.A. L.472 J.D. 2437 Briar Crest Rd.

**Hamburg, Hanover, Edwards & Martin**
(See Los Angeles)

Hammerman, Janet M. .......... '37 '79 C.112 B.A. L.1148 J.D. 1347 Braeridge Dr.‡
**Handel, William W.** .......... '51 '79 C.1077 B.A. L.1148 J.D. [▣ Vorzimer,G.M.&E.]
*LANGUAGES: Spanish.
*PRACTICE AREAS: Surrogacy Law; Civil Litigation.
Handman, Stanley H. .......... '24 '51 C.563 B.B.A. L.309 J.D. 10160 Cielo Dr.
**Hanna, Michael J.** .......... '44 '74 C.1042 B.A. L.464 J.D. [Turner,G.W.A.&Y.]
**Hansen, Molly C.** .......... '59 '90 C.1097 B.A. L.800 J.D. [▣ Rosenfeld,M.&S.]
*PRACTICE AREAS: Estate Planning; Trust and Probate Administration; Charitable Organizations.
**Hansen, Thomas M.**, (AV) .......... '49 '78 C.112 B.A. L.800 J.D. [Hansen,J.T.&H.]
*PRACTICE AREAS: Entertainment Law; Motion Picture Law; Television Law; Copyright Law.

**Hansen, Jacobson, Teller & Hoberman, (AV)**
**450 North Roxbury 8th Floor, 90210**
Telephone: 310-271-8777 Telecopier: 310-276-8310
Email: la@hjth.com
Walter S. Teller; Craig A. Jacobson; Thomas M. Hansen; Thomas H. Hoberman; Stephen P. Warren; Jeanne M. Newman; Thomas B. McGuire, Jr.; Fred E. Goldring; Kenneth B. Hertz; Jason C. Sloane; Kenneth C. Christmas, Jr.; Kenneth M. Richman; Donald W. Steele; Jonathan D. Haft; Seth Lichtenstein; Daniel L. Fishkin.
Entertainment, Motion Picture, Television, Music and Copyright Law.
*See Professional Biographies, BEVERLY HILLS, CALIFORNIA*

**Hanson, Candice S.** .......... '53 '78 C.05 L.029 LL.B. [Bloom,H.C.D.&K.]
**Hardwick, Craig D.** .......... '59 '85 C.112 B.A. L.800 J.D. [Richman,L.M.G.C.F.&P.]
*PRACTICE AREAS: Real Estate Law; Corporate Law; Commercial Transactions.
Harris, Irving M. .......... '10 '35 C&L.800 B.A., LL.B. 525 Leslie Ln.
Harris, Jimmie .......... '45 '72 C.339 B.S. L.1066 J.D. Vidal Sassoon of Calif.
**Harrison, Gregg** .......... '46 '71 C.112 A.B. L.309 J.D. [▣ Gang,T.R.&B.]
*PRACTICE AREAS: Entertainment Law.
Harrison, Mary Anne '44 '69 C.800 B.A. L.1066 J.D.
Sr. V.P. & Assoc. Gen. Coun., Twentieth Century Fox Film Corp.
Harsell, Maralee D. .......... '23 '68 C.112 A.B. L.809 LL.B. 141 S. Lindon Dr.
Hart, Daniel A. .......... '56 '81 C.37 B.A. L.1068 J.D. [Barab&H.]
**Hart, Joseph F.**, (AV) .......... '52 '78 C.112 A.B. L.1068 J.D. [Weinstein&H.]
*PRACTICE AREAS: Litigation; Entertainment Law.
Hart, Richd. C. .......... '14 '36 C.800 L.809 LL.B. 424 S. Bev. Dr.
Haskins, Linda E. '50 '78 C.846 B.A. L.326
(adm. in TX; not adm. in CA) 9777 Wilshire Blvd.‡
Hason, Michael J. '49 '81 C.976 B.A. L.724 J.D.
(adm. in NY; not adm. in CA) 435 N. Palm Dr., Apt. 302‡
Haughton, Charles D. .......... '46 '71 C.477 A.B. L.284 J.D. P.O. Box 2246
Hayes, Hume & Petas, (AV) .......... 9460 Wilshire Blvd.
**Hebert, Peter M.** .......... '60 '85 C.911 B.A. L.602 J.D. [Levinson,L.&M.]
*PRACTICE AREAS: Real Estate; Commercial Litigation; Banking.
Hecht, Robert .......... '06 '37 L.809 415 S. Spalding Dr.‡
Hecker, Ronald A., (AV) '39 '66
C&L.112 B.A., J.D. 9100 Wilshire Blvd., 8th Floor., E. Tower

**Heenan Blaikie, A Calif. Prof. Corp., (AV)**
**Suite 1100, 9401 Wilshire Boulevard, 90212-2924**
Telephone: 310-275-3600 Telecopier: 310-724-8340
Jeffrey Berkowitz; Daniel H. Black; Fred A. Fenster; Daniel B. Leon; Jody Simon; Deborah F. Sirias; B.J. Yankowitz; Scott B. Zolke.
U.S. and International Entertainment, Corporate, General Business, Commercial, Litigation, Intellectual Property, Securities, Banking and Finance, Tax, Estate Planning and Real Estate.
Affiliated With: Heenan Blaikie of Canada.
*See Professional Biographies, BEVERLY HILLS, CALIFORNIA*

Helfer, Jeffrey S. .......... '57 '85 C.446 B.S. L.809 J.D. 9903 Santa Monica Blvd.
**Heller, Lawrence E.**, (AV) .......... '48 '76 C.172 B.S. L.365 J.D. [Heller&E.]
*PRACTICE AREAS: Complex Business Litigation; Real Estate; Constitutional and Employment Law.
Heller, Robert M. .......... '47 '73 C&L.94 B.A., J.D. 9401 Wilshire Blvd, Ste. 800

**Heller & Edwards, (AV)**
**9454 Wilshire Boulevard, Suite 500, 90212-2982**
Telephone: 310-550-8833 Fax: 310-858-6637
Members of Firm: Lawrence E. Heller; Mark L. Edwards.
General Civil Trial and Appellate Practice in all State and Federal Courts.
*See Professional Biographies, BEVERLY HILLS, CALIFORNIA*

Henderson, James R. .......... '34 '71 C.839 B.S. L.426 J.D. [Henderson&M.]
Henderson & Myers .......... 9399 Wilshire Blvd.
**Hergott, Alan S.** .......... '50 '75 C.477 A.B. L.597 J.D. [Bloom,H.C.D.&K.]
**Hermes, Peter T.**, (BV) .......... '48 '74 C.426 B.S. L.809 J.D. [▣ Kolodny&A.]
*PRACTICE AREAS: Family Law.

**Hersh, Neal R., (AV) '51 '76 C.112 B.A. L.809 J.D.**
**9150 Wilshire Boulevard, Suite 209, 90212**
Telephone: 310-786-1910 Fax: 310-786-1917
*PRACTICE AREAS: Family Law.
Family and Divorce Law. Mediation Practice.
*See Professional Biographies, BEVERLY HILLS, CALIFORNIA*

Hertz, Harvey S. .......... '34 '64 C.174 B.S.E.E. L.273 LL.B. 9777 Wilshire Blvd. (Pat.)
**Hertz, Kenneth B.** .......... '59 '84 C.112 B.S. L.1068 J.D. [Hansen,J.T.&H.]
*PRACTICE AREAS: Entertainment Law; Music Recording Law; Copyright Law.
Hertzberg, Harold J., (AV) .......... '22 '59 C.112 B.S. L.1068 LL.B. 9601 Wilshire Blvd.
**Herzog, James P.**, (AV) .......... '42 '68 C.112 A.B. L.1068 J.D. [Herzog,F.&G.]
Herzog, Rochelle A. .......... '— '85 C.102 B.A. L.1068 J.D. 9107 Wilshire Blvd.

**Herzog, Fisher & Grayson, A Law Corporation, (AV) ▣**
**9460 Wilshire Boulevard Fifth Floor, 90212**
Telephone: 310-278-4300 Fax: 310-278-5430
James P. Herzog; David R. Fisher; Michael A. Grayson;—Pamela M. Rosenthal; Eric M. Rosin. Of Counsel: Todd I. Grayson.
Business and Corporate Law, Business and Commercial Litigation, Administrative Law, Health Care Law, Civil Appeals, Real Estate and Entertainment Law.
*See Professional Biographies, BEVERLY HILLS, CALIFORNIA*

Hicks, David, (AV) .......... '43 '72 C.768 A.B. L.1067 J.D. [General C.]⊙
**Hiles, Russel D.** .......... '42 '74 C.1075 B.S. L.61 J.D. [Stone&H.]
*PRACTICE AREAS: Tort Defense Law.
**Hill, Ranlyn Tilley** .......... '65 '91 C.112 B.A. L.426 J.D. [▣ Reuben&N.]
*PRACTICE AREAS: Employment; Construction; Administrative Law; Non Profit Entities; Intellectual Property Litigation.
Hillman, Stuart S., (AV) .......... '26 '52 C.339 L.800 LL.B. 1852 Noel Pl.‡
Hirsch, Alvin, (AV) .......... '16 '40 C.999 L.146 J.D. 9171 Wilshire Blvd.

**Hirsh, Robert W., & Associates, (AV) '56 '82 C.1044 B.A. L.94 J.D.**
**9100 Wilshire Boulevard, Seventh Floor, West, 90212**
Telephone: 310-275-7800; Fax: 310-274-2330
Of Counsel: Elie J. Gindi. Associate: Shalom Rubanowitz.
Business, Real Estate, Banking, Bankruptcy, Corporate, Entertainment, Apparel Industry and Health Care Law.
*See Professional Biographies, BEVERLY HILLS, CALIFORNIA*

Hirshland, David L. .......... '53 '90 C.103 A.B. L.1068 LL.D. 9601 Wilshire Blvd.
**Hite, Nora J.** .......... '58 '95 C.990 B.S. L.1137 J.D. [▣ Wilner,K.&S.]
**Hoberman, Thomas H.**, (AV) .......... '50 '75 C.112 B.A. L.809 J.D. [Hansen,J.T.&H.]
*PRACTICE AREAS: Entertainment Law.
**Hochman, Bruce I.**, (AV) .......... '29 '52 C.112 B.A. L.1068 LL.B. [Hochman,S.&D.]
*PRACTICE AREAS: Criminal and Civil Tax Controversy and Tax Litigation (Federal and State).

**Hochman, Salkin and DeRoy, A Professional Corporation, (AV) ▣**
**9150 Wilshire Boulevard Suite 300, 90212-3414**
Telephone: 310-281-3200; 273-1181 Fax: 310-859-1430
Bruce I. Hochman (Certified Specialist, Criminal and Taxation Law, The State Bar of California Board of Legal Specialization); Avram Salkin (Certified Specialist, Taxation Law, The State Bar of California Board of Legal Specialization); Charles P. Rettig (Certified Specialist, Taxation Law, The State Bar of California Board of Legal Specialization); Dennis Perez; Steven R. Toscher. Of Counsel: George DeRoy;—Stuart A. Simon; Michael W. Popoff; Frederic J. Adam.
Federal and State Taxation and Corporation Law. Civil and Criminal Tax Litigation and Tax Controversies, Business and Real Estate Transactions, Probate, Civil Forfeitures.
Reference: Union Bank of California.
*See Professional Biographies, BEVERLY HILLS, CALIFORNIA*

Hodgen, Philip D. W. .......... '56 '82 C.154 B.A. L.1068 J.D. 433 N. Camden Dr., Ste., 400
Hoffman, Kris '41 '69 C&L.813 B.S., J.D.
Pres. & Gen. Coun., Albert Glickman & Assocs.
**Hogan, Steven L.**, (AV) .......... '53 '78 C.112 B.A. L.800 J.D. [Lurie&Z.]
**Holley, Susan E.** .......... '61 '91 C.112 B.A. L.813 J.D. [▣ Rosenfeld,M.&S.]
*PRACTICE AREAS: Labor and Employment Law; Labor Litigation; Trade Secrets; Trademark; Copyright Litigation.
**Holmes, Henry W.**, (AV) .......... '43 '70 C.112 B.A. L.1066 J.D. [Weissmann,W.B.C.&S.]
*PRACTICE AREAS: Entertainment; Sports Law.
Holmes, Janet K. .......... '49 '90 C&L.352 B.A., J.D. 9107 Wilshire Blvd.
Holmes, Jeffery D. .......... '55 '81 C.174 B.A. L.1067 J.D. Skouras Pictures Inc.
**Holt, Roger J.** .......... '46 '72 C.112 B.A. L.309 J.D. [Ervin,C.&J.]
*PRACTICE AREAS: Environmental Law.
**Homampour, Arash** .......... '67 '93 C.800 B.S. L.809 J.D. [Rondeau&H.]
Hooker, Alan C. .......... '41 '68 C&L.976 B.A., LL.B. Sec. Coun., Western Atlas, Inc.
Hookstratten, Jon C. .......... '58 '84 C.800 B.S. L.809 J.D. 9536 Wilshire Blvd.
**Hornbeck, John W.** .......... '40 '67 C.197 B.A. L.477 LL.B. [▣ Sherman,D.&P.]⊙
*PRACTICE AREAS: Complex & MDL Litigation; Pharmaceutical and Medical Device Cases.
Horner, Robert B. .......... '48 '76 C.1120 B.A. L.426 J.D. 270 N. Canon Dr., 3rd Fl.
Horton, June C. '57 '83
C.518 B.A. L.800 J.D. V.P., Bus. Affs., William Morris Agcy., Inc.
Horvitz, Sidney E. .......... '16 '39 C.339 L.209 J.D. 8601 Wilshire Blvd., 9th Fl.

**Horwin, Leonard, Law Offices of, (AV) '13 '36 C.112 B.A. L.976 LL.B.**
**121 South Beverly Drive, 90212**
Telephone: 310-275-5132 Los Angeles: 213-272-7807 Fax: 310-275-7216
*LANGUAGES: Spanish, German.
General Civil and Trial Practice. Business, Family, Estate Planning, Trust, Real Property and International Law.
References: Bank of America National Trust & Savings Assn. (Beverly & Wilshire Branch, Beverly Hills, California); Merrill Lynch (Beverly Hills, Office).
*See Professional Biographies, BEVERLY HILLS, CALIFORNIA*

Housman, Robert A. ................... '52 '77 C.112 B.S. L.1049 J.D. 702 N. Bedford Dr.
**Howard, Edwin J.** ..................... '55 '88 C.112 B.A. L.1148 J.D. [Wilner,K.&S.]
Howard, Harvey A., (AV) .............. '31 '55 C&L.477 B.A., J.D. 9595 Wilshire Blvd.
Hume, Richard S., (A Professional Corporation), (AV) '35 '63
C.112 B.A. L.1068 LL.B. [Hayes,H.&P.]
Huncke, John G. ....................... '— '80 C.602 B.S. L.800 J.D. 9100 Wilshire Blvd.
**Hunter, Thomas F., Jr.** .............. '51 '82 C.326 B.A. L.846 J.D. [Bloom,H.C.D.&K.]
Hurvitz, Yardenna .......... '48 '77 C.966 B.A. L.1230 J.D. 433 N. Camden Dr., 12th Fl.
Hutchinson, Robert B. ............ '43 '70 C.339 B.S.B.A. L.1065 J.D. 9454 Wilshire Blvd.

**Ingham, Samuel D., III, (AV) '52 '75 C.112 A.B. L.1068 J.D.**
**Suite 830, 8383 Wilshire Boulevard, 90211-2407**
**Telephone: 213-651-5980 FAX: 213-651-5725**
**Email: sdiesq@aol.com**
**(Certified Specialist, Probate, Estate Planning and Trust Law).**
**Estate Planning, Trusts, Probate, Guardianship and Conservatorship, Oil and Gas and Real Estate Law.**

***See Professional Biographies, BEVERLY HILLS, CALIFORNIA***

**Inman, Lucy Noble** ............. '61 '90 C.576 B.A. L.575 J.D. [Weissmann,W.B.C.&S.]
*PRACTICE AREAS: Litigation.
**Inman, Maurice C., Jr.**, (AV) ............ '31 '57 C.112 B.S. L.309 J.D. [Inman,S.N.&S.]

**Inman, Steinberg, Nye & Stone, APC, (AV)**
**(Formally Inman, Weisz & Steinberg, APC)**
**9720 Wilshire Boulevard, Penthouse, 90212**
**Telephone: 310-274-7111 Fax: 310-274-8889**
**Matthew S. Steinberg; Maurice C. Inman, Jr.; Gary A. Nye; Lincoln Stone;—Veronica Maya Jeffers (Not admitted in CA); Patrick S. Rodriguez; Regina O. Reyes; Melanie K. Lowery; Ashkhen A. Gambourian; Gary W. Park. Of Counsel: Andrew J. Weisz; Thomas C. Ferguson (Not admitted in CA); Jeffrey D. Lewis.**
**General Business Law with an emphasis on Business, Real Estate, Intellectual Property, Employment, and Insurance Litigation in Federal and State Courts, Immigration Law, Estate Planning, Trust Administration, Probate and Corporate Law.**

***See Professional Biographies, BEVERLY HILLS, CALIFORNIA***

Insel, A. Perry ......................... '08 '33 C.563 B.S.S. L.178 LL.B 301 N. Canon Dr.‡
**Isaacman, Alan L.**, (AV) ............... '42 '68 C.645 B.S. L.309 J.D. [Isaacman,K.&P.]
*PRACTICE AREAS: Civil Litigation; Defamation; Copyright; Entertainment; Employment.

**Isaacman, Kaufman & Painter, (AV)**
**8484 Wilshire Boulevard, Suite 850, 90211**
**Telephone: 213-782-7700 Fax: 213-782-7744**
**Alan L. Isaacman; Brian Kaufman; Michael A. Painter; Steven H. Blackman; William S. Cohen (Certified Specialist, Taxation Law, The State Bar of California Board of Legal Specialization); Neil B. Fischer; Robert S. Freimuth.**
**Civil Litigation, Entertainment, Tax, Employment and Business Litigation. Business and Real Estate Transactions. Intellectual Property Matters.**

***See Professional Biographies, BEVERLY HILLS, CALIFORNIA***

Isaacs, Joan R. ......................... '49 '77 C.773 A.B. L.426 J.D. 8383 Wilshire Blvd.
Israel, Wm. G., (AV) ....................... '16 '41 C&L.911 B.A., J.D. [Lever,A.&I.]
Itkin, Mark A. ................. '53 '79 C.112 B.A. L.1066 J.D. William Morris Agcy., Inc.
Itzkowitz, Jay ................ '60 '86 C.309 A.B. L.1292 J.D. V.P., Legal Affs., Fox Inc.
**Izen, Stephanie H.** ..................... '67 '93 C.112 B.A. L.426 J.D. [Frydrych&W.]
**Jacobs, Amy Osran** ..................... '58 '83 C.350 B.S. L.339 J.D. [Glassman,B.&S.]
*PRACTICE AREAS: Estate Planning; Taxation Law; Corporate Planning; General Business.
**Jacobsen, Lisa Marie** ............... '62 '89 C.112 B.A. L.1068 J.D. [Rosenfeld,M.&S.]
*PRACTICE AREAS: Labor Litigation; Labor, Employment Law and Litigation.
**Jacobsen, Marybeth** ................... '55 '82 C&L.339 B.A., J.D. [Rosenfeld,M.&S.]
*LANGUAGES: Spanish.
*REPORTED CASES: W.R. Grace and Co. vs. Continental Casualty Co. et. al., and Carey Canada, Inc. vs. California Union Insurance Co. et. al.
*PRACTICE AREAS: Insurance Coverage and Defense Law.
Jacobson, Burton C., (AV) ............ '31 '57 C.184 B.A. L.426 LL.B. 424 S. Beverly Dr.
**Jacobson, Craig A.**, (AV) ............... '52 '79 C.103 B.A. L.273 J.D. [Hansen,J.T.&H.]
*PRACTICE AREAS: Entertainment Law; Motion Picture Law; Television Law; Copyright Law.
**Jacobson, Lawrence H., (A P.C.)**, (AV) .... '43 '68 C.112 L.1068 J.D. [Jacobson,S.&B.]
*PRACTICE AREAS: General Business; Real Estate Transactions; Finance Law; Estate Planning.

**Jacobson, Sanders & Bordy, LLP, (AV)**
**A Partnership including a Professional Corporation**
**9777 Wilshire Boulevard, Suite 718, 90212-1907**
**Telephone: 310-777-7488**
**Members of Firm: Lawrence H. Jacobson (A P.C.); Michael J. Bordy; Michael R. E. Sanders. Of Counsel: David S. White; Patricia B. Kolber.**
**Business Litigation and Transactions, Real Estate, Probate and Trust Litigation, Tax and Estate Planning.**

***See Professional Biographies, BEVERLY HILLS, CALIFORNIA***

**Jacoby, Aaron H.** ......................... '60 '88 C.1169 B.A. L.767 J.D. [Jacoby&C.]
*LANGUAGES: French, Italian.
*SPECIAL AGENCIES: California Public Utilities Commission; Federal Energy Regulatory Commission; California New Motor Vehicle Board.
*PRACTICE AREAS: Business Litigation; Administrative Law and Litigation; Crude Oil Regulatory Matters; Environmental Compliance Litigation; Land Use.

**Jacoby & Capogrosso**
**9100 Wilshire Boulevard 7th Floor-West Tower, 90212**
**Telephone: 310-274-8301 Fax: 310-274-9910**
**Members of Firm: Aaron H. Jacoby; Eric G. Capogrosso. Associate: Kristin Gamble.**
**Busines Litigation, Labor and Employment Law.**

***See Professional Biographies, BEVERLY HILLS, CALIFORNIA***

**Jaffe, Daniel J., (A Professional Corporation)**, (AV) '37 '62
C.477 B.B.A. L.1068 J.D. [Jaffe&C.]
*PRACTICE AREAS: Family Law.
Jaffe, Jay, (AV) ........................ '47 '72 C.800 A.B. L.809 J.D. 433 N. Camden Dr.
**Jaffe, Judianne**, (AV) ................... '51 '76 C.112 A.B. L.800 J.D. [Glickfeld,F.&J.]

**Jaffe & Clemens, (AV)**
**A Partnership including Professional Corporations**
**Suite 1000, 433 North Camden Drive, 90210**
**Telephone: 310-550-7477 Telecopier: 310-271-8313**
**Daniel J. Jaffe (A Professional Corporation) (Certified Specialist, Family Law, The State Bar of California Board of Legal Specialization); Bruce A. Clemens (A Professional Corporation) (Certified Specialist, Family Law, The State Bar of California Board of Legal Specialization); William S. Ryden (Certified Specialist, Family Law, The State Bar of California Board of Legal Specialization). Associates: Judy Bogen (Certified Specialist, Family Law, California Board of Legal Specialization); David M. Luboff (Certified Specialist, Family Law, The State Bar of California Board of Legal Specialization); Mark L. Levinson; Gretchen Wellman Taylor (Certified Specialist, Family Law, The State Bar of California Board of Legal Specialization); Richard Mackay (Not admitted in CA); Cynthia S. Monaco (On Leave).**
**Practice Limited to Family Law.**

***See Professional Biographies, BEVERLY HILLS, CALIFORNIA***

Jampol, Alan R., (AV) ..................... '47 '72 C.112 B.A. L.1068 J.D. [Ward,K.&J.]
Janger, Jerome, (AV) ................... '33 '62 C.846 B.A. L.800 LL.B. 138 S. Lasky Dr.
Janian, Armen ...................... '50 '82 C.800 B.S. L.1127 J.D. 9401 Wilshire Blvd.

Jason, Judith N. .......................... '56 '81 C.112 B.A. L.309 J.D. 227 S. Bedford Dr.
Jeffers, Susannah Lee '56 '90
C.937 B.A. L.861 J.D. Dir. Bus. & Legal Affs., World Intl. Network
**Jeffers, Veronica Maya** '— '88 C.914 B.A. L.309 J.D.
(adm. in AZ; not adm. in CA) [Inman,S.N.&S.]
Jensen, Geo. J. .............................. '12 '39 C&L.352 B.A., J.D. 1450 Bella Ave.
**Jessup, W. Edgar, Jr.**, (AV) ................ '22 '50 C.103 B.S. L.800 J.D. [Ervin,C.&J.]
*PRACTICE AREAS: Corporate; Taxation; Business Law.
Johnson, David C. ..................... '42 '68 C.112 B.A. L.477 J.D. 9336 Civic Ctr. Dr.
**Johnson, J. Stacie** ................... '59 '84 C.112 A.B. L.1068 J.D. [Nagler&Assoc.]
*PRACTICE AREAS: Business Litigation; Real Estate.
**Jones, Cameron** .................. '67 '92 C.188 A.B. L.309 J.D. [Rosenfeld,M.&S.]
*PRACTICE AREAS: Entertainment Law; New Media Technologies; Intellectual Property.
Jones, H. Bradley, (AV) ............... '20 '45 C&L.309 A.B., LL.B. 9595 Wilshire Blvd.
**Jones, Melanie Grant** ......... '65 '92 C.811 B.A. L.178 J.D. [Weissmann,W.B.C.&S.]
*LANGUAGES: French.
Juniper, Ronald L. ................ '33 '58 C&L.629 B.S., J.D. 8383 Wilshire Blvd. (Pat.)

**Kabrins, Ronald M., (AV) '38 '64 C.112 B.S. L.1068 LL.B.**
**Suite 1250, 9401 Wilshire Boulevard, 90212**
**Telephone: 310-550-8076 Fax: 310-859-3949**
**(Certified Specialist, Taxation Law, The State Bar of California Board of Legal Specialization).**
**Taxation, Estate Planning, Trust and Estate Administration.**

***See Professional Biographies, BEVERLY HILLS, CALIFORNIA***

Kagan, Stuart A., (AV) ................ '33 '60 C&L.800 B.S., LL.B. 8383 Wilshire Blvd.
Kahan, Kenneth L. ................... '59 '83 C.112 B.A. L.1068 J.D. 9864 Wilshire Blvd.

**Kahn, Stephen R. '47 '73 C.112 B.A. L.426 J.D.**
**9150 Wilshire Boulevard, Suite 209, 90212-3429**
**Telephone: 310-246-9227 Fax: 310-246-9656**
**Civil and Criminal Litigation, Family Law and Employment Law.**

***See Professional Biographies, BEVERLY HILLS, CALIFORNIA***

**Kahn, Tina J.** ...................... '54 '82 C.112 B.A. L.597 J.D. [Bloom,H.C.D.&K.]
Kairys, Charles ......................... '40 '70 C.1097 B.S. L.809 J.D. [Kairys,L.W.&K.]
Kairys, Lippman, Weisel & Kipper, (AV) ............................ 8648 Wilshire Blvd.
**Kajan, Elliott H.**, (AV) ................ '38 '65 C.608 B.S. L.1003 J.D. [Kajan M.&B.]
*PRACTICE AREAS: Tax Controversy Law; Tax Litigation.

**Kajan Mather and Barish, A Professional Corporation, (AV)**
**Suite 805, 9777 Wilshire Boulevard, 90212**
**Telephone: 310-278-6080 Fax: 310-278-4805**
**Email: EHKKOTAX@PACBELL.NET**
**Elliott H. Kajan; Steven R. Mather; Kenneth M. Barish.**
**Civil and Criminal Tax Controversy and Tax Litigation.**

***See Professional Biographies, BEVERLY HILLS, CALIFORNIA***

**Kalisch, Mark**, (AV) ............................ '52 '78 C&L.061 B.A. [Kalisch,C.&R.]
*LANGUAGES: German and French.

**Kalisch, Cotugno & Rust, (AV)**
**Penthouse Suite, 9606 Santa Monica Boulevard, 90210**
**Telephone: 310-274-6683 Telecopier: 310-859-7743**
**Mark Kalisch; Lee W. Cotugno; Richard N. Rust. Of Counsel: James S. Rountree; Kathleen G. Smith.**
**General Civil Trial and Appellate Practice in State and Federal Courts, including Business, Real Property, Banking, Insurance, Title Insurance, Entertainment, Commercial, Corporate, Transactional and Personal Injury Litigation.**

***See Professional Biographies, BEVERLY HILLS, CALIFORNIA***

**Kalm, Linda A.** .................. '63 '88 C.813 B.A. L.569 J.D. [Weissmann,W.B.C.&S.]
*PRACTICE AREAS: Corporate Law; Real Estate Law.

**Kalman, Newton, (AV) '20 '51 C.563 B.S. L.309 LL.B.**
**Suite 414, 9454 Wilshire Boulevard, 90212**
**Telephone: 310-274-6971 Fax: 310-275-1386**
***PRACTICE AREAS: Estate Planning; Probate Law; Business Litigation; Personal Injury; Products Liability.**
**Probate, Estate Planning, and General Practice.**
**Reference: First Interstate Bank, Beverly Hills.**

**Kalman, Susan B.** .............. '62 '93 C.860 B.A. L.818 J.D. [Freshman,M.O.C.&K.]
*LANGUAGES: German, Spanish.
*PRACTICE AREAS: Corporate; Corporate Securities.
**Kamarck, Mitchell D.** ................ '60 '87 C.165 B.A. L.188 J.D. [Rosenfeld,M.&S.]
*PRACTICE AREAS: New Media Technologies; Copyright, Trademark and Trade Secrets Litigation; General Business Litigation; Products Liability Litigation.
Kamins, Morton L. ......................... '42 '68 C.112 B.A. L.1068 J.D. P.O. Box 2652
**Kane, Harris J.** ..................... '62 '86 C.112 B.A. L.1068 J.D. [Rosenfeld,M.&S.]
*PRACTICE AREAS: Entertainment Litigation; Business Litigation.
Kantor, Eli M. ........................ '51 '76 C.112 B.A. L.426 J.D. 9595 Wilshire Blvd.
Kaplan, Howard A. ............... '30 '56 C.112 B.S. L.1068 LL.B. 8484 Wilshire Blvd.
Kaplan, Joshua ........................ '46 '70 C.800 B.A. L.426 J.D. 9171 Wilshire Blvd.
Karfiol, Judith Rachel ........... '48 '92 C.800 B.A. L.809 J.D. 9606 Santa Monica Blvd.
**Karl, Donald E.** ......................... '49 '76 C.477 B.S. L.309 J.D. [Rosenfeld,M.&S.]
*PRACTICE AREAS: Corporate Law; Mergers and Acquisitions Law; New Media Technologies; International Law.
Karnes, David A. ............ '57 '85 C.309 B.A. L.1066 J.D. 9601 Wilshire Blvd., 4th Fl.
Karp, Steven D. ...................... '50 '75 C.112 B.A. L.1095 J.D. 9107 Wilshire Blvd.
Karpel, Donald E., (AV) ................ '49 '74 C.112 B.A. L.1049 J.D. [Dichter,S.&K.]
Karpeles, Eli J. ...................... '49 '82 C.1077 B.S. L.426 J.D. 9150 Wilshire Blvd.
**Kartiganer, Lawrence S.**, (AV) ...... '34 '59 C.309 A.B. L.569 LL.B. [Rosenfeld,M.&S.]
*PRACTICE AREAS: Entertainment Law; Music Law; Tax Law.
Karton, David S., (AV) ....................... '46 '72 C.112 B.A. L.1068 J.D. [D.S.Karton]
Karton, David S., A Law Corporation, (AV) .......... 433 North Camden Drive, Suite 888
Karubian, Guitta ........................... '47 '75 C.112 L.809 J.D. 9100 Wilshire Blvd.

**Kass, Gail D., (AV) '50 '75 C.112 A.B. L.1068 J.D.**
**228 South Beverly Drive, 90212-3880**
**Telephone: 310-273-0393 Fax: 310-273-2663**
**Estate Planning, Probate, Trust Law and Taxation Law.**

***See Professional Biographies, BEVERLY HILLS, CALIFORNIA***

**Kassoy, David P.**, (AV) ..................... '35 '64 C.178 A.B. L.309 LL.B. [Ervin,C.&J.]
*PRACTICE AREAS: Commercial Real Property Development Law.
**Katleman, Steven** ............. '54 '80 C.112 A.B. L.1065 J.D. [Weissmann,W.B.C.&S.]
*PRACTICE AREAS: Entertainment Law.
**Kato, Sheila S.** ..................... '47 '73 C.312 A.B. L.1066 J.D. [Greines,M.S.&R.]
*PRACTICE AREAS: Appellate Law.
Katzman, Jerome F. .................. '37 '64 C.112 B.A. L.1068 LL.B. 151 El Camino Dr.
Kaufler, Philip ..................... '52 '78 C.800 A.B. L.426 J.D. 8383 Wilshire Blvd.
**Kaufman, Brian** ........................ '45 '71 C.112 B.S. L.800 J.D. [Isaacman,K.&P.]
*PRACTICE AREAS: Civil Litigation; Business Law; Real Estate; Litigation.
Kaufman, Michael A. C. ............... '44 '69 C.112 B.A. L.1068 J.D. 716 N. Palm Dr.
**Kaufman, Robert S.**, (AV) ............... '37 '64 C.112 B.A. L.809 J.D. [Kaufman&Y.]
*PRACTICE AREAS: Family Law; Trial Practice.
Kaufman, Sidney W. ........................ '10 '34 C&L.800 A.B., J.D. 318 N. Maple Dr.‡

**Kaufman & Young, A Professional Corporation, (AV)**
**121 South Beverly Drive, 90212-3002**
**Telephone: 310-275-5132 Los Angeles: 213-272-7807 Fax: 310-275-2919**
**Robert S. Kaufman; Kenneth M. Young; Marcy L. Kenerson; Scott K. Robinson. Of Counsel: Lance S. Spiegel.**
**Family Law and Trial Practice in all State and Federal Courts.**
**Reference: City National Bank (Beverly Hills Main Office Branch).**
*See Professional Biographies, BEVERLY HILLS, CALIFORNIA*

Kavaller, Miles L., (AV) .................... '47 '72 C&L.107 B.A., J.D. [M.L.Kavaller]

**Kavaller, Miles L., A Professional Law Corporation, (AV)**
**Suite 315, 315 South Beverly Drive, 90212**
**Telephone: 310-277-2323 Fax: 310-556-2308**
**Email: MKavaller@themall.net URL: http://www.LA-Freight.com/Kavaller.htm**
**Miles L. Kavaller.**
**General Civil and Trial Practice in all Courts. Transporation Law.**
**Reference: City National Bank (6th & Olive Branch).**
*See Professional Biographies, BEVERLY HILLS, CALIFORNIA*

**Kawa, Mark T.** .................................. '62 '88 C.112 A.B. L.800 J.D. [Ⓐ Ervin,C.&J.]
*PRACTICE AREAS: Intellectual Property; Real Property Litigation; Banking Law.
Kay, Bart ........................................ '43 '71 C.1077 B.A. L.1095 J.D. 270 N. Canon Dr.
**Kaye, Barry P.** ...................................... '60 '86 C.112 B.A. L.426 J.D. [E.J.Gantz]
*PRACTICE AREAS: Products Liability; Premises Liability; Personal Injury; General Civil Litigation.
**Kelley, Kyle P.** ............... '70 '95 C.705 B.A. L.1148 J.D. [Richman,L.M.G.C.F.&P.]
*PRACTICE AREAS: Business Litigation; Labor Litigation; Entertainment Litigation.
Kelly, Patrick ...................... '68 '93 C.31 B.A. L.309 J.D. 9601 Wilshire Blvd. 4th Fl.
**Kelson, Mark J.** ...................... '59 '91 C.1077 B.S. L.426 J.D. [Ⓐ Freshman,M.O.C.&K.]
*PRACTICE AREAS: Corporate; Corporate Securities.
Kenegos, Joan E. ......................... '54 '80 C.112 B.A. L.809 J.D. 8501 Wilshire Blvd.
**Kenerson, Marcy L.** ........................ '64 '93 C.1097 B.A. L.426 J.D. [Kaufman&Y.]
*PRACTICE AREAS: Family Law; Trial Practice.
Kenis, Stephen M. '38 '63
C.112 B.S. L.1066 LL.B. Mng. Dir., William Morris Agcy., Inc.
Kenny, Charles D. ............ '45 '71 C.1030 A.B. L.128 J.D. 400 N. Roxbury Dr., 5th Fl.
Kent, Leon E., (AV) .................... '15 '38 C.197 A.B. L.976 LL.B. 318 N. Maple Dr.‡
**Kern, Howard J.** ............... '60 '87 C.705 B.A. L.978 J.D. [Richman,L.M.G.C.F.&P.]
Kessler, Arnold H., (P.C.), (AV) '31 '57
C.112 B.A. L.426 LL.B. Ste. 700, 9601 Wilshire Blvd.
**Kessler, Gary S.** .................................. '55 '80 C.112 A.B. L.426 J.D. [Ⓐ Wilner,K.&S.]
**Kessler, Suzanne H.** ................... '64 '94 C.103 A.B. L.813 J.D. [Ⓐ Rosenfeld,M.&S.]
*PRACTICE AREAS: Entertainment; Intellectual Property.
Khastoo, Shapour S. .................. '47 '88 C.112 B.S. L.940 J.D. 9401 Wilshire Blvd.
Kiesel, Paul R., (A Prof. Corp.) ........ '60 '85 C.183 B.A. L.940 J.D. 8501 Wilshire Blvd.
Kime, Robert C. ....... '45 '79 C.63 B.S. L.326 J.D. Assoc. Tax Coun., Western Atlas, Inc.
King, Frank G. ........................ '36 '64 C.112 B.S. L.426 LL.B. 424 S. Beverly Dr.
**King, Jennifer L.** ................................ '62 '88 C&L.813 B.A., J.D. [Ⓐ Greines,M.S.&R.]
*PRACTICE AREAS: Appellate.
Kipper, Robert, (AV) ....................... '48 '74 C.112 B.A. L.800 J.D. [Kipper,R.N.]
Kipper, Robert N., Professional Corporation, (AV) ..................... 8648 Wilshire Blvd.
Kirby, Bruce S. '50 '80 C&L.879 B.A., J.D.
(adm. in NY; not adm. in CA) 270 N. Canon Dr.‡
**Kirios, Alan G., (Law Corporation), (AV) '45 '73**
C.860 B.A. L.94 J.D. [Weissmann,W.B.C.&S.]
*PRACTICE AREAS: Taxation; Estate Planning; Foreign Investment in U.S.
Kite, Richard L. ...... '34 '59 C.112 B.S. L.1068 J.D. 1031 Cove Way

**Kleeman, Dena A., Law Office of, (AV) '54 '83 C.918 B.A. L.813 J.D.**
**499 North Canon Drive, Suite 200, 90210-4248**
**Telephone: 310-247-0727 Fax: 310-273-3030**
**(Certified Specialist, Family Law, The State Bar of California Board of Legal Specialization).**
***PRACTICE AREAS: Family Law; Estate Planning; Guardianship.**
**Of Counsel: Ruth S. Kremen.**
**Family Law.**
*See Professional Biographies, BEVERLY HILLS, CALIFORNIA*

**Klein, Deborah L.** ..................... '60 '85 C.112 B.S. L.800 J.D. [Bloom,H.C.D.&K.]
Klein, Jill ....................................... '54 '79 C.813 A.B. L.800 J.D. 144 S. Crescent Dr.
**Klein, Mark Alexander** .......... '47 '72 C.112 A.B. L.1065 J.D. [Freshman,M.O.C.&K.]
*PRACTICE AREAS: Securities; Corporate Law; Mergers and Acquisitions.
**Klein, Walter,** (AV) ........................ '37 '63 C.112 B.S. L.426 LL.B. [Wilner,K.&S.]
Kleinman, Lisa F. ..................... '64 '91 C.112 B.A. L.426 J.D. 9465 Wilshire Blvd.
Kline, Robert A., (AV) ............... '44 '71 C&L.178 A.B., J.D. 9606 Santa Monica Blvd.
Klugman, Laurence S., (AV) ............ '34 '61 C.112 L.800 LL.B. 9401 Wilshire Blvd.
Koenig, Robert H., (AV) ....................... '27 '54 C.112 B.A. L.813 J.D. [R.H.Koenig]
Koenig, Robert H., Law Corporation, (AV) ................................... 9595 Wilshire Blvd.
**Koepke, Jens B.** ............... '65 '90 C.839 B.A. L.1068 J.D. [Richman,L.M.G.C.F.&P.]
*LANGUAGES: German.
*PRACTICE AREAS: Commercial; Personal Injury Litigation; First Amendment; Intellectual Property.
Koffman, Gregory S. ................. '58 '82 C.800 B.S. L.426 J.D. [Rosenberg&K.]

**Kohn, Gary P. '58 '84 C.1044 B.A. L.245 J.D.**
**9601 Wilshire Boulevard, Suite 828, 90210**
**Telephone: 310-205-0870 Fax: 310-205-0187**
**Email: GPKOHN@aol.com**
**Entertainment, Sports, Music and Corporate Law.**
*See Professional Biographies, BEVERLY HILLS, CALIFORNIA*

Kohn, Leonard C. ............................ '37 '71 C.645 B.A. L.809 J.D. 433 N. Camden Dr.
**Kolber, Patricia B.** ..................... '61 '86 C.112 B.A. L.464 J.D. [Ⓒ Jacobson,S.&B.]
*LANGUAGES: French and Spanish.
**Kolodny, Stephen A.,** (AV) ............................ '40 '66 C&L.94 B.A., LL.B. [Kolodny&A.]

**Kolodny & Anteau, (AV)**
**9100 Wilshire Boulevard Suite 900, 90212**
**Telephone: 310-271-5533 FAX: 310-271-3918**
**Members of Firm: Stephen A. Kolodny (Certified Specialist, Family Law, The State Bar of California Board of Legal Specialization); Ronald W. Anteau (Certified Specialist, Family Law, The State Bar of California Board of Legal Specialization); Harlee M. Gasmer;—William P. Glavin IV; William J. Glucksman; Lauren S. Petkin; Peter T. Hermes; Terry Levich Ross; Erin L. Grey.**
**Practice Limited to Family Law, Domestic Torts, Juvenile Dependency; Paternity; Palimony.**
**Reference: Wells Fargo Bank, Los Angeles, CA.**
*See Professional Biographies, BEVERLY HILLS, CALIFORNIA*

**Kondon, Christopher J.** ......... '66 '94 C.174 B.A. L.426 J.D. [Ⓐ Freshman,M.O.C.&K.]
*PRACTICE AREAS: Business Litigation; Bankruptcy.
Kopald, Jere S., (AV) ............................. '22 '47 C&L.800 A.B., J.D. [Kopald&K.]
Kopald, Steven D., (BV) ...................... '50 '76 C.800 B.S. L.1095 J.D. [Kopald&K.]
Kopald & Kopald, (AV) ........................................................ 8888 Olympic Blvd.
**Kornblum, Ellen S.** ........................ '57 '92 C.112 B.S. L.426 J.D. [Ⓐ Ervin,C.&J.]
*PRACTICE AREAS: General Business Litigation; Bankruptcy Law.
Kornfeld, Joel T. ........................... '59 '84 C.112 B.A. L.1065 J.D. [Ⓐ Ward,K.&J.]
Korobkin, Leonard, A Professional Corporation, (AV) '32 '59
C&L.178 B.A., LL.B. 315 S. Beverly Dr.

Kosloff, Michael L. ......................... '45 '77 C.665 B.A. L.1137 J.D. [M.L.Kosloff]
Kosloff, Michael L., P.C. ........................................................ 9601 Wilshire Blvd.
**Kossoff, Kenneth W.** .................... '58 '83 C.112 A.B. L.228 J.D. [Schneider,G.&Y.]
**Kozmor, James D.** ............................ '68 '93 C.178 A.B. L.1068 J.D. [Ⓐ Browne&W.]
Krakauer, H. Lawrence .............. '50 '77 C.705 B.A. L.1049 J.D. 8447 Wilshire Blvd.
Kramer, Eileen ....................... '45 '80 C.800 B.A. L.1136 J.D. 8601 Wilshire Blvd.

**Kramer, Steven M., & Associates '50 '76 C&L.831 B.A., J.D.**
**9606 Santa Monica Boulevard Second Floor, 90210⊙**
**Telephone: Telephone: 310-519-5708 Telecopier: 310-550-8982**
***REPORTED CASES: Lightning Lube v. Witco Corp.; Danny Kresky Ent. v. Magid, 716 F2d 206 (3d Cir 1983); Danny Kresky Ent. v. Magid 716 F2d 216 (3d Cir 1983); Lightning Lube Ins. v. Witco Corp. 4F3d 1153 (3d Cir 1993); Fineman v. Armstrong World Industries, Inc. 980 F2d 171 (3d Cir. 1992).**
***PRACTICE AREAS: Complex Business Litigation; Antitrust; Securities; Entertainment.**
**Complex Business Litigation, Antitrust, Securities, Entertainment.**
**New York, New York Office: City Spire, 150 West 56th Street, 65th Floor, 10019. Telephone: 212-586-0707. Telecopier: 212-586-0104.**
**Wayne, New Jersey Office: Gateway 80 Office Park, 30 Galesi Drive, Suite 201, 07470. Telephone: 201-785-0143. Telecopier: 201-785-3380.**
*See Professional Biographies, BEVERLY HILLS, CALIFORNIA*

Kray, Dorothy J. ............... '32 '62 C.608 B.A. L.800 LL.B. 505 S. Beverly Dr., #1047
**Kremen, Ruth S.** .......................... '54 '83 C.31 B.A. L.276 J.D. [Ⓒ D.A.Kleeman]
*PRACTICE AREAS: Civil Litigation; Business Law; Family Law.
Krentzman, Paul L., (AV) '34 '60 C.918 B.A. L.1068 J.D.
Penthouse, 9454 wilshire Blvd.
Kreshek, Saul S., (AV) ................. '36 '61 C&L.800 B.S., LL.B. 9300 Wilshire Blvd.
Kroll, Gerald L., (AV) ...................... '50 '75 C.273 B.A. L.1068 J.D. [Ⓐ Ward,K.&J.]
**Krone, Steven G.** .......................... '64 '94 C.800 A.B. L.145 J.D. [Ⓐ Gang,T.R.&B.]
*PRACTICE AREAS: Entertainment Law.
Krueger, Paul M. ..................... '56 '83 C.491 B.A. L.1068 J.D. 8447 Wilshire Blvd.

**Krzyminski, James M., (AV) '54 '79 C.347 B.S. L.813 J.D.**
**345 North Maple Drive, Suite 294, 90210**
**Telephone: 310-777-7481 FAX: 310-777-8754**
**Email: jimkrzymin@aol.com**
**Business, Corporation, Real Estate, Federal and State Taxation, Estate Planning, Trust and Probate Law.**
**Reference: City National Bank, Olympic Plaza Office.**
*See Professional Biographies, BEVERLY HILLS, CALIFORNIA*

Kuhn, Ernest ....... '25 '56 C.800 B.S. L.426 LL.B. 9201 Wilshire Blvd. (⊙Los Angeles)
Kuklin, Jeffrey P. .................. '35 '62 C.176 A.B. L.178 J.D. William Morris Agcy., Inc.
Kulla, Norman S., (AV) ................. '47 '72 C.112 B.A. L.1067 J.D. [Ⓒ Tilles,W.K.&G.]
Kurtz, Philip M. .................................. '31 '57 C.112 B.S. L.1068 LL.B. [P.M.Kurtz]
Kurtz, Philip M., A Law Corp. ................................................ 8601 Wilshire Blvd.
Kurtzman, Raymond .... '27 '54 C.112 B.S. L.800 LL.B. V.P., Creative Artists Agcy., Inc.
Lack, Fred S., Jr., (P.C.), (AV) .......... '21 '50 C.472 L.800 J.D. 1716 Chevy Chase Dr.‡
Lambros, P. Basil, (BV) ............. '24 '52 C.800 B.F.S. L.809 J.D. 8383 Wilshire Blvd.
Landau, Bruce G., (BV) ................. '48 '76 C.205 B.S. L.1148 J.D. [Rosky,L.S.&S.]
**Lansberg, Justin J.** ........................ '64 '89 C.813 B.A. L.800 J.D. [Ⓐ Stern&G.]
*PRACTICE AREAS: Business and Real Estate Litigation; Personal Injury Law.
Larson, William L. ................... '58 '85 C.1109 B.S. L.1148 J.D. 8501 Wilshire Blvd.
Lau, Linda Wong .......... '— '88 C.112 B.A. L.1068 J.D. 9720 Wilshire Blvd., Penthouse
**Lautsch, Sylvia D.** ........................ '57 '82 C.813 A.B. L.1066 J.D. [Ⓐ Ervin,C.&J.]
*PRACTICE AREAS: Commercial Real Property Development Law.
Lavine, Ruth J., (AV) ........................... '20 '44 C&L.800 A.B., J.D. 121 S. Beverly Dr.
**LaViolette, John S.** ..................... '57 '86 C.976 B.A. L.800 J.D. [Bloom,H.C.D.&K.]
Lawrence, Greg ............................ '53 '78 C.112 B.A. L.809 J.D. [Lawrence&L.]
**Lawrence, John A.** ............ '51 '76 C.605 B.A. L.1068 J.D. [Richman,L.M.G.C.F.&P.]
*PRACTICE AREAS: Labor Law; Litigation.
Lawrence, Sull ........................... '21 '48 C.610 B.A. L.930 LL.B. [Lawrence&L.]
Lawrence & Lawrence ................................................... 9454 Wilshire Blvd.
**Lawson, Teri E.** ......................... '60 '87 C.1168 B.A. L.309 J.D. [Ⓐ Wilner,K.&S.]
Leader, Arnold L. ................................ '18 '42 C.112 L.1001 LL.B. [Leader&L.]
**Leader, Jon M.** .............................. '61 '87 C.861 B.A. L.273 J.D. [Browne&W.]
Leader, Sylvia M. ................................ '21 '43 C.113 L.1001 LL.B. [Leader&L.]
Leader & Leader, A Professional Corp. ...................................... 8920 Wilshire Blvd.
Leavitt, David Keene, (AV) '30 '54 C&L.813 A.B., J.D.
9454 Wilshire Blvd., Penthouse
**Lebo, William C., Jr.** '44 '69 C&L.880 B.A., J.D.
(adm. in NY; not adm. in CA) Sr. V.P. & Gen. Coun., Hilton Hotels Corp.
Lederer, Eugene G., (AV) .............. '33 '62 C.37 B.S. L.1068 J.D. 455 S. Bedford Dr.
**Ledesma, Randel L.** ................. '59 '84 C.668 B.A. L.800 J.D. [Ⓐ Greines,M.S.&R.]
*PRACTICE AREAS: Appellate Law.
Lee, Frank ............ '58 '86 C.1077 B.S. L.426 J.D. Schwartz, Kales Accountancy Corp.
**Lee, Jacob D.** ................................. '59 '86 C.112 B.A. L.1065 J.D. [Ervin,C.&J.]
*LANGUAGES: Korean.
*PRACTICE AREAS: Banking; General Business Litigation; Insurance Coverage; Surety and Fidelity Litigation; Bank Loans and Foreclosures.
**Lee, James K.** ....................... '63 '92 C.477 B.A. L.494 J.D. [Ⓐ Freshman,M.O.C.&K.]
*LANGUAGES: Korean.
*PRACTICE AREAS: Commercial Litigation; Real Estate Litigation; Securities Litigation.
Lee, Kimuel W. '61 '89 C.420 Psych. L.990 J.D.
421 N. Rodeo Dr. (⊙Baton Rouge, LA.)
Leeds, Craig B., (AV) ................. '52 '77 C.112 B.A. L.809 J.D. [Zimmerman,R.&G.]
Leff, Ernest, (AV) ..................................... '24 '50 C.184 B.A. L.569 LL.B. [E.Leff]
Leff, Ernest, A Professional Corporation, (AV) ........................ 433 N. Camden Dr.
Lefkowitz, David ................. '60 '86 C.1036 B.A. L.569 J.D. 2121 Ave. of the Stars
**Legget, Marc A.** ............................. '61 '87 C.1077 B.A. L.1065 J.D. [Ⓐ Stone&H.]

**Lehr, James H. '53 '79 C.674 A.B. L.809 J.D.**
**9595 Wilshire Boulevard, Suite 305, 90212**
**Telephone: 310-553-8080 Fax: 310-550-7244**
***REPORTED CASES: Shell Oil Co. v. Nelson Oil Co., Inc., 627 F.2d 228 (T.E.C.A. 1980), cert. den. 449 U.S. 1022; Mobile Oil Corporation v. Rissi (1982) 138 Cal.App. 3d 256, 187 Cal. Rptr. 845; Schroeder v. TWA, Inc., 702 F.2d 189 (9th Cir. 1983); Davis v. Gilf Oil Corp., 572 F. Supp. 1393 (C.D. Cal. 1983); Prestin v. Mobile Oil Corp., 741 F.2d 268 (9th Cir. 1984).**
***PRACTICE AREAS: Litigation; Banking Law; Unfair Competition Law.**
**Business Litigation, Banking Law.**
*See Professional Biographies, BEVERLY HILLS, CALIFORNIA*

**Leichenger, David B. '59 '83 C.112 A.B. L.1065 J.D.**
**8383 Wilshire Boulevard, Suite 750, 90211**
**Telephone: 310-858-3588 Telecopier: 213-655-0525**
**General Civil Litigation before State and Federal Courts.**

Leichter, Alexandra, (AV) ............. '47 '72 C.112 B.A. L.426 J.D. 8665 Wilshire Blvd.
Leichtman, Lauren '49 '77 C.1077 B.A. L.809 J.D.
Levine & Leichtman, Capital Partners
**Lemerman, Barbara S.** ......... '50 '77 C.112 B.A. L.800 J.D. [Richman,L.M.G.C.F.&P.]
*PRACTICE AREAS: Business Planning; Securities Law; Real Estate Law.

**Leon, Daniel B.** ........................ '59 '86 C.800 B.S. L.597 J.D. [H.B.California]
*PRACTICE AREAS: Real Estate; General Business; Corporate; Commercial.
Leonard, Arthur F. ........................ '40 '72 C.800 B.S. L.809 J.D. 175 N. Swall Dr.
**Leonard, Richard C., (A Professional Corporation),** (AV) '46 '71 C.112 B.A. L.1066 J.D. [Leonard,D.&S.]
*PRACTICE AREAS: Business, Real Estate, Entertainment and Copyright Litigation.

**Leonard, Dicker & Schreiber, (AV)**
A Partnership including Professional Corporations
**Suite 400, 9430 Olympic Boulevard, 90212**
Telephone: 310-551-1987 FAX: 310-277-8050
James P. Schreiber (A Professional Corporation); Lee T. Dicker; Richard C. Leonard (A Professional Corporation); David S. Gubman (A Professional Corporation). Associates: Michael R. Rogers; David N. Schultz; Steven A. Schuman; Jack M. Snyder; Kevin S. Dicker. Of Counsel: Gunther H. Schiff (P.C.); D. Steve Cameron; David J. Leonard.
Business and Real Estate Litigation, Entertainment and Copyright Litigation, Estate and Trust Litigation Bankruptcy Litigation and Appellate Practice in State and Federal Courts, Business, Real Estate, Entertainment, Commercial and Corporate Law, Estate Planning, Family Law.
*See Professional Biographies, BEVERLY HILLS, CALIFORNIA*

Lerman, Steven A. ........................ '48 '72 C&L.260 B.A., J.D. 9100 Wilshire Blvd.
Leslie & Rubin ........................ 124 Lasky Dr.
Lever, Anker & Israel, (AV) ........................ 9201 Wilshire Blvd.
Levin, Lionel P. ........................ '48 '74 C.223 B.S. L.884 J.D. [Levin&M.]
Levin & Margolin ........................ 8484 Wilshire Blvd.
Levine, Arthur E. ........................ '51 '83 C.112 B.A. L.178 J.D. 345 N. Maple Ave.
Levine, Peter K. ........................ '53 '79 C.705 A.B. L.982 J.D. 8601 Wilshire Blvd.
Levine, Shelley E. ........................ '57 '81 C&L.112 B.A., J.D. 9601 Wilshire Blvd.
Levine, William G., (P.C.), (AV) ........................ '39 '65 C.674 A.B. L.309 J.D. [Levine&M.]
Levine & Miller, (AV) ........................ 415 N. Camden Dr.

**Levine & Unger, (AV)**
**9454 Wilshire Boulevard-Penthouse, 90212-2937**
Telephone: 310-273-3555 Fax: 310-278-5002
Email: lenunger@earthlink.net
Members of Firm: Leonard Unger; Sid B. Levine (1912-1995).
General Civil and Trial Practice. Corporation, Real Estate, Estate Planning, Probate and Taxation.
Reference: City National Bank (Beverly Hills Main Office)
*See Professional Biographies, BEVERLY HILLS, CALIFORNIA*

**Levinson, Burton S.,** (AV) ........................ '31 '62 C.1043 L.809 J.D. [Levinson,L.&M.]
*PRACTICE AREAS: Title Insurance Law; Real Property Law; Commercial Transactions.
**Levinson, Mark L.,** (AV) ........................ '46 '71 C.1077 B.A. L.800 J.D. [Jaffe&C.]
*PRACTICE AREAS: Family Law.

**Levinson, Lieberman & Maas, A Professional Corporation, (AV)**
**Suite 1250, 9401 Wilshire Boulevard, 90212**
Telephone: 310-550-0500 Telecopier: 310-859-3949
Burton S. Levinson; Lawrence R. Lieberman; Francis S. Maas; Nancy E. Marcus; Peter M. Hebert; Brian Kent Brookey.
General Real Estate and Commercial Practice. Civil Litigation.
Approved Attorneys for: Safeco Title Insurance Co.; First American Title Co.; Title Insurance Company of Minnesota.
Reference: City National Bank (Beverly Hills Office).
*See Professional Biographies, BEVERLY HILLS, CALIFORNIA*

**Levitan, Lynn R.** ........................ '68 '93 C.446 B.A. L.64 J.D. [[A] Vorzimer,G.M.&E.]
*LANGUAGES: Spanish and Sign Language.
*PRACTICE AREAS: Civil Litigation; Real Estate; Entertainment Litigation.
**Levitch, Burt,** (AV) ........................ '53 '80 C.309 A.B. L.569 J.D. [Rosenfeld,M.&S.]
*PRACTICE AREAS: Trusts and Estates; Estate Administration; Estate Planning; Trust Administration; Charitable Trusts and Foundations.
Levitt, Jay T. ........................ '58 '83 C.112 B.A. L.1065 J.D. 8383 Wilshire Blvd.
Levy, Jack ........................ '37 '68 C.4 B.B.A. L.800 J.D. [J.Levy]
Levy, Marjorie A. ........................ '45 '88 C.569 B.S. L.809 J.D. 348 S. Palm Dr.
Levy, Robert '58 '93 C.94 B.A. L.1148 J.D. (adm. in PA; not adm. in CA) 9901 Durant Dr., F‡
Levy, Robert S. ........................ '56 '81 C.112 B.A. L.1148 J.D. 433 N. Camden Dr.
Levy, Jack, Inc. ........................ 8383 Wilshire Blvd.
Lewin, Rodney T. ........................ '50 '76 C.112 A.B. L.809 J.D. 8685 Wilshire Blvd.
**Lewis, Jeffrey D.,** (AV) ........................ '49 '74 C.800 B.A. L.1066 LL.B. [[B] Inman,S.N.&S.]
*PRACTICE AREAS: Estate Planning; Trust Administration; Corporation Law; Business Transactions; Real Estate.
Lewis, Kimberly D. ........................ '61 '88 C.112 B.S. L.426 J.D. [[A] Ward,K.&J.]
**Lewis, Marvin H.,** (AV) ........................ '29 '62 C.112 B.S. L.767 J.D. [Ervin,C.&J.]
*PRACTICE AREAS: Taxation Law; Estate Planning Law; Trust and Probate Law.
**Lewis-Heard, Joan E.** ........................ '61 '86 C.860 B.S. L.112 J.D. [[A] Nagler&Assoc.]
*REPORTED CASES: Royal Neckwear Co., Inc. v. Century City, Inc., 205 Cal.App.3d 1146 (1988).
*PRACTICE AREAS: Business Litigation.
**Liberty, Arthur R.** ........ '58 '83 C.112 B.A. L.426 J.D. [Gorbis&L.] (⊙San Diego, CA)
Libo, David J. ........................ '56 '81 C.860 B.A. L.800 J.D. [[A] Steiner&L.]
Licht, David G. ........................ '24 '50 C&L.37 LL.B. 9171 Wilshire Blvd.
Licht, Roger H. ........................ '59 '78 C.813 A.B. L.1065 J.D. 9171 Wilshire Blvd.
**Lichtenstein, Seth** ........................ '51 '86 C.33 B.A. L.329 J.D. [Hansen,J.T.&H.]
Lichter, George S. ........................ '51 '93 C.112 B.A. L.813 J.D. 9601 Wilshire Blvd. 4th Fl.
Lichterman, Stuart F. ........................ '41 '67 C.800 B.S. L.1065 LL.B. [Lichterman,T.&B.]
Lichterman, Traister & Brussel ........................ 8383 Wilshire Blvd.
Lidman, Daniel H., (BV) ........................ '45 '71 C.823 A.B. L.93 J.D. 9777 Wilshire Blvd.
Lieberman, Glenn B. ........................ '55 '83 C.112 B.A. L.809 J.D. 433 N. Camden Dr.
**Lieberman, Lawrence R.,** (AV) ........ '45 '72 C.112 B.S. L.1068 J.D. [Levinson,L.&M.]
*LANGUAGES: German and Greek.
*REPORTED CASES: Whiteside v. United States of America, 833 F.2d 820 (9th Cir. 1987); Cortese v. United States of America, 782 F.2d 845 (9th Cir. 1986); Republic Bank v. Nelson, 761 F.2d 1320 (9th Cir. 1985); Share v. Air Properties G., Inc., 536 F.2d 279 (9th Cir. 1976); Wright v. Schock, 571 F.Supp. 642 (N.D. Cal. 1983).
*PRACTICE AREAS: Real Property Litigation; Commercial Litigation; Defense of Bad Faith Insurance Claims; Securities Litigation; Anti-Trust Litigation.
Lifton, Stacy D. ........................ '64 '90 C.112 A.B. L.1067 J.D. Coun., Fox Inc.
Lifton, Stanley S., (BV) ........................ '37 '63 C.112 A.B. L.800 J.D. 8601 Wilshire Blvd.
Lind, Harvey J. ........................ '49 '75 C.112 B.A. L.1095 J.D. 502 N. Alpine Dr.
Linder, Barbara J. ........................ '54 '79 C&L.800 B.A., J.D. 305 S. Almont Dr.
**Linder, Gary R.** '54 '86 C.978 B.A. L.597 J.D. (adm. in IL; not adm. in CA) [[A] Frydrych&W.]
*LANGUAGES: Hebrew.
*PRACTICE AREAS: Corporate Law; Real Estate Law; Environmental Law.
**Lipofsky, Louis A., (A Professional Corporation),** (AV) '38 '63 C.112 B.S. L.1066 LL.B. [Lipofsky&R.]
*PRACTICE AREAS: Real Estate; Business Litigation; Land Security Transactions; Real Estate Development; Commercial Law.

**Lipofsky & Ruben, (AV)**
A Partnership including a Professional Corporation
**Suite 708, 8383 Wilshire Boulevard, 90211-2408**
Telephone: 213-653-2004 Telecopier: 213-653-6228
Members of Firm: Louis A. Lipofsky (A Professional Corporation); Joel D. Ruben. Associates: Mark L. Share.

(This Listing Continued)

**Lipofsky & Ruben (Continued)**
General Civil and Trial Practice. Real Estate and Business Litigation, Land Security Transactions, Real Estate Development and Commercial Law.
*See Professional Biographies, BEVERLY HILLS, CALIFORNIA*

Lippman, Harry S., (AV) ........................ '41 '69 C&L.494 B.A., J.D. [Kairys,L.W.&K.]
Lipsitz, Green, Fahringer, Roll, Salisbury & Cambria LLP, (AV⊙) 365 N. Bedford Dr., Suite 204 (⊙Alden, N.Y.C., East Aurora & Buffalo NY)
Lipson, Warren M. ........................ '37 '63 C.112 B.S. L.1066 LL.B. 8530 Wilsire Blvd.
Lipton, Jack P. ........ '52 '89 C.112 B.A. L.37 J.D. 9100 Wilshire Blvd., 8th Fl., East Twr.
**Litvak, William,** (AV) ........................ '55 '79 C.112 B.A. L.1188 J.D. [Dapeer,R.&L.]
*PRACTICE AREAS: Business and Real Estate Litigation; Commercial and Corporate Litigation; Professional Liability—Legal Malpractice; Accounting Malpractice; Insurance Malpractice.
Litwin, Louis L. ........................ '29 '57 C.112 B.A. L.426 LL.B. [Litwin&B.]
Litwin & Barouh ........................ 9100 Wilshire Blvd.
Litz, Paul J. ........................ '41 '68 C.112 B.S. L.1068 J.D. 8906 W. Olympic Blvd.
**Locke, Berry D.,** (AV) ........................ '27 '54 C&L.800 B.A., LL.B. [Locke,L.R.&A.]

**Locke, Locke, Rudman & Aberle, (AV)**
**332 South Beverly Drive, 90212**
Telephone: 310-553-0602 Los Angeles: 213-879-3973
Members of Firm: Martin S. Locke (1929-1988); Berry D. Locke; Barry M. Rudman; Douglas S. Aberle.
General Civil and Trial Practice in all State and Federal Courts and Securities Law.
Reference: First Charter Bank, Beverly Hills, CA.
*See Professional Biographies, BEVERLY HILLS, CALIFORNIA*

Lodmer, Sheldon I. ........................ '45 '71 C.800 B.A. L.426 J.D. [S.I.Lodmer]
Lodmer, Sheldon I., A Professional Corporation ........................ 449 S. Beverly Dr.
Logue, Eric R. ........................ '52 '80 C.763 B.S. L.1137 J.D. 9016 Wilshire Blvd.
Long, Melanie D. ........................ '70 '94 C.112 B.A. L.800 J.D. [[A] Weston,S.G.&D.]
Looby, James V. ........................ '47 '78 C.309 A.B. L.809 J.D. 9150 Wilshire Blvd.
**Lorch, Gary J.,** (BV) ........................ '60 '85 C.112 B.A. L.1065 J.D. [[A] Tucker&B.]
Lord, Jackson Vincent ........................ '45 '80 C.942 L.1221 J.D. 8601 Wilshire Blvd.
Losiewicz, Walter C. '51 '78 C.690 B.A. L.1202 J.D. 8693 Wilshire Blvd. (⊙Quincy, Mass.)
Lotta, Michael A. ........................ '55 '80 C&L.426 B.S., J.D. 301 N. Canon Dr.
Lowe, Jeffrey A. ........................ '53 '92 C.112 B.A. L.1179 J.D. 8383 Wilshire Blvd.
Lowenstein, Aaron '— '37 C.145 B.Ph. L.477 LL.B. (adm. in MI; not adm. in CA) 705 Walden Dr.‡
Lowenstein, Joseph R., (AV) ........................ '36 '62 C.339 B.S. L.597 J.D. [J.R.Lowenstein]
Lowenstein, Joseph R., P.C., (AV) ........................ 705 Walden Dr.
**Lowery, Melanie K.** ........................ '69 '94 C.112 B.A. L.800 J.D. [[A] Inman,S.N.&S.]
*PRACTICE AREAS: Business Litigation; Entertainment and Business Transactions; Intellectual Property.
Lowry, Bruce D. ........................ '50 '76 C.112 B.A. L.1068 J.D. 258 S. Beverly Dr.
Lowy, Steven R. ........................ '51 '77 C.112 B.S. L.809 J.D. 8444 Wilshire Blvd., 8th Fl.
**Luboff, David M.,** (AV) ........................ '54 '79 C.112 B.A. L.1068 J.D. [[A] Jaffe&C.]
*REPORTED CASES: Trimble v. Steinfeldt (1986) 178 Cal.App.3d 646, 224 Cal. Rptr. 195; Yates v. Pollock (1987) 194 Cal.App.3d 195, 239 Cal.Rptr. 383.
*PRACTICE AREAS: Family Law; Appellate Litigation.
**Luer, Kenneth A.** ........................ '50 '80 C.692 B.A. L.893 J.D. [Ervin,C.&J.]
*PRACTICE AREAS: Corporate Law; Securities Law; General Business Law.
**Lund, Eric James,** (AV) ........ '59 '83 C.813 B.A. L.800 J.D. [Lund&L.] (⊙Los Angeles)
*LANGUAGES: French and Farsi.
*PRACTICE AREAS: Estate Planning; Trust and Probate Law.
**Lund, James L.,** (AV) ........................ '26 '55 C.800 B.A. L.809 J.D. [Lund&L.]
*LANGUAGES: French.
*PRACTICE AREAS: International Law; Engineering; Construction Law.

**Lund & Lund, (AV)**
**9595 Wilshire Boulevard, 90212**
Telephone: 310-273-2555 FAX: 310-271-4062
James L. Lund; Eric James Lund.
International Law. Engineering, Construction, Business, Commercial, Real Estate and Corporation Law. Civil Trial and Appellate Practice.
*See Professional Biographies, BEVERLY HILLS, CALIFORNIA*

Lunsman, Lisa A. ........................ '56 '89 C.112 B.A.Econ. L.1136 J.D. 8383 Wilshire Blvd
**Lurie, Bruce J.,** (AV) ........................ '45 '70 C.339 B.S. L.569 J.D. [Lurie&Z.]
Lurie, Myra B. ........................ '53 '79 C.1077 B.A. L.426 J.D. 9300 Wilshire Blvd., Ste., 300

**Lurie & Zepeda, A Professional Corporation, (AV)**
**Suite 800, 9107 Wilshire Boulevard, 90210**
Telephone: 310-274-8700 Fax: 310-274-2798
Email: luriezep@ix.netcom.com
Bruce J. Lurie; Andrew W. Zepeda; Kurt L. Schmalz; Robert W. Denton;—Steven L. Hogan; Ole R. Sandberg;—L. Kimberly Pepper; Brendan F. Macaulay; Michael J. Conway; Donna M. Dean.
Business Litigation, Construction and Real Estate Litigation. Corporate and Securities Litigation, Banking Litigation, Creditors Rights, Landlord and Tenant, Corporate, Partnership, Antitrust, Intellectual Property, Professional Malpractice, State and Federal Civil Trial and Appellate Practice, Entertainment and Aviation. Diplomatic and Foreign Sovereign Immunity. International Child Custody Litigation.
*See Professional Biographies, BEVERLY HILLS, CALIFORNIA*

Lyman, Herbert A. ........................ '34 '70 C.97 B.S. L.1095 J.D. 9454 Wilshire Blvd.
**Maas, Francis S.,** (AV) ........................ '44 '70 C.112 A.B. L.800 J.D. [Levinson,L.&M.]
*LANGUAGES: German.
*PRACTICE AREAS: Real Property Law; Business Law.
**Macaulay, Brendan F.** ........................ '67 '92 C.940 B.A. L.228 J.D. [[A] Lurie&Z.]
*LANGUAGES: Spanish.
**Mackay, Richard,** (BV⊙) '42 '72 C.103 A.B. L.705 J.D. (adm. in NY; not adm. in CA) [[A] Jaffe&C.]
*PRACTICE AREAS: Family Law.
**MacNaughton, Barry J.** ........................ '57 '82 C.859 B.A. L.846 J.D. [Ervin,C.&J.]
*PRACTICE AREAS: Business and Commercial Litigation; Real Property Litigation with an emphasis on Environmental and Construction Matters; Insurance Coverage Disputes; Antitrust; Trade Secrets.
Mahler, Gary L. ........................ '46 '72 C.112 B.A. L.809 J.D. P.O. Box 1379
Maillian, LeAnne Elizabeth ........................ '52 '78 C.769 B.A. L.426 J.D. 9454 Wilshire Blvd.
Maio, Juliana ........................ '53 '78 C.112 B.A. L.1065 J.D. 120 S. El Camino Dr.
Malamed, Kenneth D. ........................ '43 '67 C.112 B.S. L.1068 J.D. 345 N. Maple Dr.
Malat, Gerald A., (AV) ........................ '34 '60 C.112 B.S. L.800 LL.B. [Malat,M.&G.]
Malat, Melvin H., (AV) ........................ '34 '60 C.112 B.S. L.800 LL.B. [Malat,M.&G.]
Malat, Malat & Getzels, (AV) ........................ 301 N. Canon Dr.
Mallicoat, Robt. R. ........................ '23 '54 C.112 B.A. L.800 J.D. 321 S. Beverly Dr.
**Malone, Patrick M.** ........................ '64 '93 C.112 B.S. L.426 J.D. [[A] Wilner,K.&S.]
**Mandavia, Anjani** ........................ '56 '80 C.813 A.B. L.1066 J.D. [Weissmann,W.B.C.&S.]
*PRACTICE AREAS: Civil Litigation.
Mandel, Bruce A. ........................ '62 '90 C.112 B.A. L.398 J.D. 9150 Wilshire Blvd.
Mandel, Joel L. ........................ '58 '83 C.103 B.A. L.1066 J.D. [Mandel&Mand.]
Mandel, Robert A. ........................ '56 '82 C.112 B.A. L.426 J.D. [Mandel&Mand.]
Mandel & Mandel ........................ 9100 Wilshire Blvd.
**Mandell, Jeffrey M.** ........................ '52 '78 C.966 B.A. L.477 J.D. [[A] Gang,T.R.&B.]
*PRACTICE AREAS: Entertainment Law.
Manicom, A. Dale ........................ '44 '79 C.475 B.S.M.E. L.1137 J.D. [[B] Weston,S.G.&D.]

**Mann, Richard L.** ............ '44 '75 C.813 B.A. L.426 J.D. [Richman,L.M.G.C.F.&P.]
*PRACTICE AREAS: Labor Relations Law; Employment Law.
**Mann, Travis** .................... '67 '93 C.802 B.B.A. L.1068 J.D. [⊠ Rosenfeld,M.&S.]
*PRACTICE AREAS: Entertainment.
Manns, Robert S., (AV) .................. '41 '67 C.112 L.809 LL.B. [Manns&G.]
Manns, William, (AV) .................. '07 '33 C.800 L.809 LL.B. 9665 Wilshire Blvd.‡
Manns & Green, (AV) .................................. 9665 Wilshire Blvd.
**Marantz, Philip F., (AV)** ........ '34 '58 C&L.800 B.S.L., LL.B. [Freshman,M.O.C.&K.]
*PRACTICE AREAS: Business Law; Commercial Law; Real Estate Finance; Secured Lending; Sports Law.
**Marcus, Nancy E.** .................. '62 '87 C.845 B.A. L.846 J.D. [Levinson,L.&M.]
*PRACTICE AREAS: Title Insurance Defense Litigation; Real Estate Law.
Marder, Michael ....................... '50 '76 C.1077 L.1221 J.D. 8447 Wilshire Blvd.
Marell, Leslie Sharon .................. '50 '76 C.112 B.A. L.1095 J.D. 433 S. Palm Dr.
Marell, Phyllis S. ..................... '26 '49 C.112 B.A. L.724 LL.B. 433 S. Palm Dr.
Margolese, Vana P. .................. '46 '79 C.586 B.S. L.1095 J.D. 9401 Wilshire Blvd.
Margolin, Elyse R. ..................... '— '76 C.800 B.A. L.809 J.D. [Levin&M.]
Margolis, Gerald A. .................. '29 '55 C&L.112 B.S., LL.B. 9595 Wilshire Blvd.
**Mariz, Darrell J.** .................. '67 '93 C.112 B.A. L.861 J.D. [⊠ Wilner,K.&S.]
Mark, Douglas Stuart ................. '59 '85 C.966 B.A. L.767 J.D. 8900 Wilshire Blvd.
Marker, Richard A .................... '61 '86 C.800 B.S. L.990 J.D. 9665 Wilshire Blvd.
Markman, Ronald A. .................. '36 '79 C.112 B.A. L.1136 J.D. P.O. Box 1272
Marks, J. David ...................... '34 '57 C&L.477 A.B., LL.B. 830 Wilshire Blvd.‡
**Marks, Kevin S.** ................... '57 '82 C.813 A.B. L.1066 J.D. [⊠ Gang,T.R.&B.]
*PRACTICE AREAS: Entertainment Law; Intellectual Property.
Marks, Ronald S. ..................... '45 '70 C.800 B.A. L.1068 J.D. 400 S. Beverly Dr.

**Marpet, Stephen C., (AV) '41 '67 C.112 B.S. L.1065 LL.B.**
**9454 Wilshire Boulevard Suite 313, 90212**
**Telephone: 310-274-6971 Fax: 310-273-3642**
**Email: SCMRUN@aol.com**
**General Civil and Trial Practice in all State and Federal Courts. Corporate, Business, Entertainment, Products Liability. Malpractice and Personal Injury Law. Employment.**
***See Professional Biographies, BEVERLY HILLS, CALIFORNIA***

**Marsh, Cheryl L.** '50 '86 C.112 B.A. L.809 J.D.
V.P. & Corp. Secy., Hilton Hotels Corp.
Martino, Fred J., (AV) ................ '16 '40 C&L.426 LL.B. 424 S. Beverly Dr.
**Martinsen, Ella Marie** ............... '69 '94 C.112 B.A. L.1068 J.D. [Browne&W.]
*PRACTICE AREAS: Civil Litigation.
**Maruyama, William K.** ............... '62 '88 C.112 B.A. L.464 J.D. [Grebow,M.P.&Y.]
*LANGUAGES: Japanese.
*PRACTICE AREAS: Commercial/Corporate Litigation; Tort Insurance Defense Litigation; Product Liability; Probate Litigation; Bankruptcy Litigation.
**Masserman, Dean** .................. '63 '88 C.1049 B.A. L.809 J.D. [Vorzimer,G.M.&E.]
*LANGUAGES: Spanish.
*PRACTICE AREAS: Premises Liability Defense; Criminal Defense Litigation; Civil Litigation.
**Massing, Bertram K., (AV)** ........... '33 '61 C.112 B.S. L.800 J.D. [Ervin,C.&J.]
*PRACTICE AREAS: Corporate Law; Securities Law; Mergers and Acquisitions Law.
**Mather, Steven R.** .................. '57 '82 C&L.352 B.B.A., J.D. [Kajan M.&B.]
*PRACTICE AREAS: Tax Controversy; Tax Litigation.
Mathon, Benjamin D., (AV) ............ '20 '47 C.966 B.A. L.976 LL.B. [⊠ Mathon&R.]
Mathon & Rosensweig, A Law Corporation, (AV) ........ Ste. 300, 9300 Wilshire Blvd.
Mayorga, Scott L. .................... '43 '71 C.178 A.B. L.800 J.D. 200 North Robertson Blvd.
**Mazur, Linda Wight, (AV)** ......... '59 '84 C.668 B.A. L.1068 J.D. [Turner,G.W.A.&Y.]
*PRACTICE AREAS: Probate; Estate Planning; Trust Law; Intellectual Property; Entertainment Law.
McCarthy, Neil D., (AV) ............... '17 '41 C.813 A.B. L.800 LL.B. 424 S. Beverly Dr.
McCullough, William H. ............... '46 '82 C.999 B.M. L.1148 J.D. 412 S. Bedford Dr.
**McGarrigle, Patrick C.** .............. '65 '90 C.178 B.A. L.809 J.D. [Gernsbacher&M.]
**McGuire, Thomas B., Jr.** ............ '53 '83 C.112 B.A. L.1066 J.D. [Hansen,J.T.&H.]
*PRACTICE AREAS: Entertainment Law; Motion Picture Law; Television Law; Copyright Law.
McKesson, Winston K., (BV) ......... '57 '82 C.426 B.A. L.1068 J.D. 315 S. Beverly Dr.
McKuin, Joel .......................... '68 '93 C.867 B.A. L.309 J.D. [Colden&M.]
McLean, Warner H. ................... '36 '68 C.446 B.S. L.213 J.D. 9336 Civic Ctr. Dr.
**Mcpherson, Brian H.** ............... '64 '92 C.154 B.A. L.424 J.D. [⊠ Rosenfeld,M.&S.]
*PRACTICE AREAS: Music; Film; Multimedia.
McWhirk, Robert L. ................... '46 '72 C.112 A.B. L.1067 J.D. 1278 Angelo Dr.
**Meadow, Robin, (AV)** ............... '47 '72 C.112 B.A. L.1066 J.D. [Greines,M.S.&R.]
*PRACTICE AREAS: Appellate Law.
Mednick, Arnold W., (BV) ............ '56 '79 C.112 B.A. L.1065 J.D. 8306 Wilshire Blvd.
Meisel, Brian Paul .................... '52 '79 C.112 B.A. L.1355 J.D. 8827 W. Olympic Blvd.
Mellas, Nicholas C. .................. '30 '56 C.112 B.A. L.1068 LL.B. 8383 Wilshire Blvd.
**Mendelsohn, David H., Ltd.**, (AV⊙) '13 '35 C&L.145 Ph.B., J.D.
(adm. in IL; not adm. in CA) [⊠ Richman,L.M.G.C.F.&P.]
**Mercado, Doreen M.** ................. '58 '91 C.112 B.A. L.426 J.D. [⊠ Stone&H.]

**Merrifield, Lewis B., III, (AV) '39 '68 C.112 A.B. L.800 J.D.**
**270 North Canon Drive Suite 1281, 90210-5323**
**Telephone: 310-274-0693**
**Securities Law.**
**Reference: City National Bank (Pershing Square Office, Los Angeles).**
***See Professional Biographies, BEVERLY HILLS, CALIFORNIA***

Merritt, Brent S. ..................... '48 '72 C.1077 B.S. L.1049 J.D. 415 N. Camden Dr.
**Meyer, Kenneth H.** ................. '43 '70 C.112 B.S. L.1068 J.D. [⊠ Sinclair T.O.&E.]
**Meyer, Marvin B., (AV)** .............. '24 '49 C.800 L.309 J.D. [Rosenfeld,M.&S.]
*PRACTICE AREAS: Entertainment Law.
**Meyers, John A.** .................... '46 '74 C.112 A.B. L.1068 LL.B. [Ervin,C.&J.]
*PRACTICE AREAS: Healthcare; Business; Real Estate.
Meyers, Maurice D. ................... '39 '70 C.763 B.S. L.426 J.D. P.O. Box 5123
**Michel, Gary Q., (A P.C.), (AV)** ......... '51 '75 C.112 B.A. L.1068 J.D. [Ervin,C.&J.]
*PRACTICE AREAS: Health Care; Corporate; Taxation; Real Property Law.
Michel, Herbert L., Jr. ................ '49 '74 C.112 B.A. L.1049 J.D. [H.L.Michel,Jr.]⊙
Michel, Herbert L., Jr., A Professional Law Corporation
9595 Wilshire Blvd. (⊙Las Vegas, NV)
Middleton, Lorraine A. ................ '61 '89 C.800 A.B. L.426 J.D. [⊠ Mathon&R.]
**Miercort, David B.** ................. '67 '94 C.103 B.A. L.178 J.D. [Weissmann,W.B.C.&S.]
*PRACTICE AREAS: Motion Picture and Television Law; Entertainment Contracts; Copyright Law.
Miller, Jerry, (A Professional Corporation), (AV) '37 '63
C&L.800 B.S., LL.B. [Schulman&M.]
Miller, Melvin W. ..................... '25 '49 C.911 L.800 J.D. 9595 Wilshire Blvd., 9th Fl.
**Miller, Michael B.** .................. '60 '87 C.705 B.A. L.569 J.D. [Sherman,N.&M.]
*PRACTICE AREAS: Corporate Transactions; Contracts; Partnerships and Joint Ventures; Labor and Franchising.

**Miller, Mitchell R., (AV) '46 '77 C.475 B.A. L.831 J.D.**
**315 South Beverly Drive, Suite 501, 90212**
**Telephone: 310-277-1848 Fax: 310-551-1929**
**Email: MitchMllr@aol.com**
***REPORTED CASES: Boykin v. Cobin, 30 Cal. Rptr. 428, (1994) appeal dismissed 41 Cal. Rptr. 2d. 219 (1995); Lomma Linda Community Hospital v. Shalala, 907 F. Supp. 1399 (U.S.D.C. Cent. Dist. Ca. 1995).**
***PRACTICE AREAS: Taxation; Estate Planning; Administrative Law.**

(This Listing Continued)

**Miller, Mitchell R. (Continued)**
**Taxation Law, Administrative Law and Estate Planning Law.**
***See Professional Biographies, BEVERLY HILLS, CALIFORNIA***

**Miller, Ovvie, (AV)** ................. '35 '62 C.112 B.A. L.309 J.D. [Rosenfeld,M.&S.]
*PRACTICE AREAS: Family Law; Divorce Law; Civil Trials; Child Custody; Pre-Nuptials.
Miller, Sheldon E., (P.C.), (AV) ........... '43 '69 C.112 B.A. L.1068 J.D. [Levine&M.]
Milliken, Jerry S. .................... '39 '70 C.800 B.A. L.1095 J.D. 9150 Wilshire Blvd.
**Mills, Tobin A.** ..................... '58 '83 C.112 B.A. L.426 J.D. Coun., City Natl. Bk.
*RESPONSIBILITIES: Banking Law; Real Estate (Property) Law; Trust Law.
Minnihan, John K. ................... '36 '78 C.1097 B.S. L.398 J.D. V.P., Earl Scheib, Inc.
Mishkind, Ira L. ..................... '38 '66 C.37 B.S. L.800 J.D. [I.L.Mishkind]
Mishkind, Ira L., A Law Corporation ............................ 9701 Wilshire Blvd.
**Miskinyar, Hedieh** ................. '69 '95 C.112 B.A. L.800 J.D. [⊠ Rondeau&H.]
*LANGUAGES: Farsi.
**Monaco, Cynthia S., (BV)** ............ '50 '76 C.1077 B.A. L.809 J.D. [Jaffe&C.]
*PRACTICE AREAS: Family Law.
**Monos, Margaret** ................... '64 '90 C.112 B.A. L.800 J.D. [⊠ Stone&H.]
Monroe, Irwin R. ..................... '33 '62 C.112 A.B. L.1065 J.D. 9201 W. Olympic Blvd.
Monroe, Linda F. ................ '47 '76 C.1168 B.A. L.426 J.D. V.P., Universal Properties, Inc.
Moreno, Lawrence J., (AV) ............. '31 '60 C.112 B.A. L.1068 J.D. 348 S. Doheny Dr.
Morganstern, Richard, (AV) ...... '41 '66 C.688 B.S.E.E. L.188 J.D. [R.Morganstern] (Pat.)
Morganstern, Richard, Prof. Corp., Law Offices of, (AV) ........ 9595 Wilshire Blvd. (Pat.)
Morris, Michael D. ................... '51 '76 C.347 A.B. L.229 J.D. 120 S. El Camino Dr.
**Morris, Steven A.** ................. '60 '86 C.1077 B.S. L.809 J.D. [⊠ Turner,G.W.A.&Y.]
*PRACTICE AREAS: Business Law; Real Estate Litigation; Construction Litigation.
Morrison, Andrew D. .................. '59 '89 C.1169 B.A. L.426 J.D. [Ross&M.]
Moss, Allen S. ....................... '27 '79 C.46 B.S.E.E. L.1148 J.D. 8383 Wilshire Blvd.

**Mosten & Tuffias**
**(See Los Angeles)**

Mulryan, Lawrence E., (AV) '37 '63
C.763 A.B. L.1065 LL.B. Exec. Dir., Calif. Ins. Guar. Assocs.
**Murphy, James M. A., (AV)** ........... '45 '75 C&L.309 A.B., J.D. [⊠ Rosenfeld,M.&S.]
*PRACTICE AREAS: Employee Benefits; Tax; Estate Planning.
Myers, Howard D. ..................... '42 '68 C.1077 B.A. L.1065 J.D. [Henderson&M.]
Myers, John W. ...................... '11 '36 C.813 B.A. L.309 LL.B. 718 N. Rodeo Dr.‡
Nagel, Stuart ....... '53 '79 C.102 B.A. L.1095 J.D. 9201 Wilshire B.vd. (⊙Port Hueneme)
**Nagin, Jeffrey L., (AV)** .............. '33 '60 C.112 B.A. L.309 LL.B. [Rosenfeld,M.&S.]
*PRACTICE AREAS: Real Estate Law; General Business Law; Copyright Law.

**Nagler, George I., Law Offices of, (AV) '36 '70 C.05 B.Com. L.309 J.D.**
**9777 Wilshire Boulevard, Suite 1009, 90212-1901**
**Telephone: 310-278-0034 Telecopier: 310-859-7890**
***PRACTICE AREAS: Real Estate; Business Law; Corporate Law; Estate Planning; Wills. Business Law, Real Estate & Probate.**
***See Professional Biographies, BEVERLY HILLS, CALIFORNIA***

Nagler, Gina ....................... '67 '93 C.112 B.A. L.284 J.D. 9595 Wilshire Blvd., Ste. 510
**Nagler, Lawrence H., (AV)** ........... '40 '66 C.112 B.A. L.1068 J.D. [Nagler&Assoc.]
*REPORTED CASES: Aragon Haas v. Family Security Insurance Services, 231 Cal. App. 3d 232, 282 Cal. Rptr. 233 (1991); Mirkin v. Wasserman, et al. 227 Cal.App. 3d 1537, 278 Cal. Rptr. 729 (1991); Mirkin v. Wasserman, et al., 5 Cal. 4th 1082, 23 Cal.Rptr. 2d 101 (California Supreme Court 1993); Employers Insurance of Wausau and Federal Insurance Co. v. Musick, Peeler & Garrett, Peat, Marwick, Main & Co. 954 F.2d 575 (9th Cir. 1992); Musick, Peeler & Garrett, et al., v. Employers Insurance of Wausau, et al., 113 S.Ct. 2085, 124 L.Ed.2d 194, 61 U.S.L.W. 4520 (United States Supreme Court, 1993).
*PRACTICE AREAS: Business Litigation.

**Nagler & Associates, (AV)**
**9595 Wilshire Boulevard, Suite 510, 90212-2505**
**Telephone: 310-273-2666 Facsimile: 310-550-7956**
**Email: info@nagler.com**
**Lawrence H. Nagler;—Robert Michael Zabb; James F. Boyle; Susan D. Praskin; Joan E. Lewis-Heard; Thomas H. Case; David F. Berry; J. Stacie Johnson.**
**Complex Multi-Party Litigation Practice in State and Federal Courts.**
***See Professional Biographies, BEVERLY HILLS, CALIFORNIA***

Narvid, Doris B. ...................... '19 '49 C.112 A.B. L.284 LL.B. 272 Lasky Dr.‡
Nasatir, Leonard D., (AV) ............. '29 '54 C.112 A.B. L.800 J.D. 8383 Wilshire Blvd.
**Nathanson, Ken** .................... '51 '77 C.154 B.A. L.1148 J.D. [Sherman,N.&M.]
*PRACTICE AREAS: Real Estate Law; Commercial Acquisition; Contracts.
Nebel, E. Allen, (AV) ................. '30 '55 C.112 B.S. L.1068 LL.B. [Nebel&N.] ‡
Nebel, Jeffrey L. ..................... '62 '87 C.112 B.A. L.1068 J.D. [Nebel&N.]
Nebel, Kenneth W., (AV) ........... '34 '60 C.112 B.S. L.1068 LL.B. 8665 Wilshire Blvd.
Nebel and Nebel ...................................................... 8665 Wilshire Blvd.
**Nelson, Marilyn H.** .................. '45 '88 C.112 B.A. L.809 J.D. [Zukor&N.]
*PRACTICE AREAS: Personal Injury Litigation.

**Nemschoff, Louise, (AV) '50 '75 C.309 B.A. L.976 J.D.**
**433 North Camden Drive, Suite 1200, 90210**
**Telephone: 310-274-4627 FAX: 310-274-5039**
**Entertainment, Copyright and Trademark Law. International Law.**
***See Professional Biographies, BEVERLY HILLS, CALIFORNIA***

Nesbitt, Paul B., (AV) ....... '48 '75 C.800 B.A. L.426 J.D. Ste. 700, 9601 Wilshire Blvd.
Nesis, Joseph J. ................. '26 '56 C.659 B.S. L.569 J.D. 9401 Wilshire Blvd.
Newman, Gerald R. ........................................... '45 '72 P.O. Box 6387
**Newman, Jeanne M.** ................ '54 '80 C.183 B.A. L.800 J.D. [Hansen,J.T.&H.]
*PRACTICE AREAS: Entertainment Law; Motion Picture Law; Television Law; Copyright Law.
Newman, John P., (AV) ............... '48 '74 C.276 A.B. L.800 J.D. 415 N. Camden Dr.
Newman, Stephen M. ................... '40 '65 C&L.846 A.B., LL.B. P.O. Box 745
Newson, Neil C. ............... '40 '68 C.112 B.S. L.809 LL.B. [N.C.Newson&Assoc.]
Newson, Neil C., & Associates, P.C. ................................ 9465 Wilshire Blvd.

**Nicholas, Frederick M., (AV) '20 '52 C&L.800 A.B., J.D.**
**Second Floor, 9300 Wilshire Boulevard, 90212**
**Telephone: 310-273-3077; 271-5176 Fax: 310-276-5632**
**Business and Real Estate Law.**
**Reference: Union Bank (Beverly Hills, California Regional Main Office).**
***See Professional Biographies, BEVERLY HILLS, CALIFORNIA***

Nicolaysen, Gregory, (BV) ............. '56 '81 C.197 B.A. L.978 J.D. [G.Nicolaysen]
*REPORTED CASES: United States v. Javier Vasquez-Valasco, 15 F.3d 833 (9th Cir. 1994); United States v. Richard Miller, 984 F.2d 1028 (9th Cir 1993); Federal Trade Commission v. Figgie International, 1990 WL507421; RRX Industries vs. Lab. Con, Inc., 772 F.2d 543 (9th Cir. 1985).
*PRACTICE AREAS: Federal Criminal Trial and Appellate Practice; Criminal Law; White Collar Defense.

**Nicolaysen, Gregory, A Professional Corporation, (BV)**
**8530 Wilshire Boulevard, Suite 404, 90211**
**Telephone: 310-397-0737 Fax: 310-397-1001**
**Email: greg@ac.net URL: http://www.afda.org**
**Gregory Nicolaysen.**
**Federal Criminal Defense, White Collar Defense.**
***See Professional Biographies, BEVERLY HILLS, CALIFORNIA***

CAA28P

**Nielsen, Lori A.** ........ '63 '88 C.877 B.S. L.878 J.D. [Ⓐ Glassman,B.&S.]
*PRACTICE AREAS: Civil Litigation; Appellate Practice.
Nixon, Timothy K. ........ '44 '76 C.1042 B.A. L.1137 J.D. 9595 Wilshire Blvd.
**Norminton, Thomas M., (P.C.), (AV)** '48 '73 C.112 A.B. L.1066 J.D. [Norminton&W.]

**Norminton & Wiita, (AV)** BB
**A Partnership of Professional Corporations**
**433 North Camden Drive Twelfth Floor, 90210**
**Telephone: 310-288-5900 Facsimile: 310-288-5901**
**Email: norminton@aol.com**
**Thomas M. Norminton (P.C.); Douglas P. Wiita (P.C.); Kathleen Dority Fuster (P.C.).; A. Rick Atwood, Jr.**
**Civil, Trial and Appellate.**
*See Professional Biographies, BEVERLY HILLS, CALIFORNIA*

**Novack, Barry, (AV) '43 '73 C.800 B.S.M.E. L.426 J.D.**
**Suite 830, 8383 Wilshire Boulevard, 90211**
**Telephone: 213-852-1030 Fax: 213-655-9655**
**Personal Injury, Wrongful Death Matters, Tort Actions.**
**Reference: City National Bank, Beverly Hills, California.**
*See Professional Biographies, BEVERLY HILLS, CALIFORNIA*

**Novicoff, Michael L.** ........ '60 '85 C.112 B.A. L.309 J.D. [Reuben&N.]
*PRACTICE AREAS: Business; Real Estate; Entertainment Litigation; International Commercial Disputes; Intellectual Property.
Nownejad, Cyrus S. ........ '30 '63 C.112 B.S. L.1065 J.D. 433 N. Camden Dr. (Pat.)
Nuce, G. Russell '64 '91 C.896 B.A. L.245 J.D.
(adm. in NY; not adm. in CA) 9348 civil Ctr. Dr. Ste 300
Nussbaum, Keith ........ '68 '94 C.30 B.A. L.1049 J.D. Ste. 700, 9601 Wilshire Blvd.
**Nye, Gary A.** ........ '61 '86 C.112 B.A. L.426 J.D. [Inman,S.N.&S.]
*PRACTICE AREAS: Commercial Litigation; Employment Law; Intellectual Property; Insurance.
**Ocheltree, Julie A.** ........ '61 '95 C.1109 B.A. L.809 J.D. [Ⓐ J.A.Enright]
Oda, Helen N. ........ '48 '74 C.112 B.A. L.426 J.D. 129 N. Carson Rd.
**Oei, Perry P.** ........ '62 '87 C.767 B.A. L.112 J.D. Coun., City Natl. Bk.
**Offer, Robert** ........ '64 '92 C.860 B.S. L.1068 J.D. [Ⓐ Bloom,H.C.D.&K.]
Ogletree, John L. ........ '49 '91 C.326 B.S. L.990 J.D. 280 S. Beverly Hill Dr.
**Oill, Carolyn** ........ '57 '87 C.597 B.A. L.809 J.D. [Ⓐ Greines,M.S.&R.]
*PRACTICE AREAS: Appellate Law.
**Olecki, Michael J.** ........ '59 '88 C.311 B.A. L.893 J.D. [Browne&W.]
**Olesiuk, Walter W. J.** ........ '50 '77 C&L.061 B.A. [Sinclair T.O.&E.]
Olinick, Martin ........ '44 '68 C.569 B.S. L.564 J.D. RCA Records

**Oliphant, Jeffrey, (AV) '55 '81 C.112 A.B. L.1068 J.D.**
**9300 Wilshire Boulevard, Suite 200, 90212**
**Telephone: 310-273-3077 Fax: 310-276-5632**
**Real Estate and Business Law.**
**Representative Client: The Hapsmith Co.**
**References: Union Bank, Beverly Hills, Regional Office; Canadian Imperial Bank of Commerce, Los Angeles.**

**Olliff, E. A. (Stacey), III, (AV)** ........ '55 '78 C.1175 B.A. L.309 J.D. [Ervin,C.&J.]
*PRACTICE AREAS: Corporate Law; Commercial Law; Real Property Law.
**Olson, Robert A.** ........ '57 '83 C&L.813 A.B., J.D. [Greines,M.S.&R.]
*PRACTICE AREAS: Appellate Law; Insurance Coverage.
**Opri, Debra A.** ........ '60 '89 C.569 B.F.A. L.1148 J.D. [D.A.Opri]

**Opri, Debra A., A Professional Corporation**
**8383 Wilshire Boulevard Suite 830, 90211**
**Telephone: 213-658-6774 Facsimile: 213-658-5160**
**Debra A. Opri.**
**Civil Litigation. Business and Commercial Law. Entertainment Law. Personal Injury Law.**
*See Professional Biographies, BEVERLY HILLS, CALIFORNIA*

**Orlanski, Leib, (AV)** ........ '42 '68 C.1097 B.A. L.800 J.D. [Freshman,M.O.C.&K.]
*PRACTICE AREAS: Securities; Leveraged Buyouts; Technology Business Startups; Venture Capital.
Osser, A. Irving ........ '33 '69 C.1097 B.A. L.1095 J.D. 9100 Wilshire Blvd.
Osser, Jeffrey S. ........ '59 '87 C.112 B.A. L.1136 J.D. 9100 Wilshire Blvd.
Ostrow, Jack M. ........ '21 '48 C.112 B.S. L.426 J.D. 9601 Wilshire Blvd.
Ostrow, Joseph ........ '25 '51 C.112 B.A. L.424 LL.B. 9903 Santa Monica Blvd.
**Pace, Layton L.** ........ '57 '87 C.911 B.A. L.1065 J.D. [Ⓐ Ervin,C.&J.]
*PRACTICE AREAS: Taxation Law; Corporate Law.
Paddor, Richard S. ........ '52 '79 C.861 B.S. L.365 J.D. 8500 Wilshire Blvd.
Padnick, Glenn A. ........ '47 '73 C&L.309 A.B., J.D. Castle Rock Entertainment
**Painter, Michael A., (AV)** ........ '39 '69 C.112 B.S. L.426 J.D. [Isaacman,K.&P.] (Pat.)
*PRACTICE AREAS: Customs Matters; Domestic and Foreign Patents, Trademark and Copyright Prosecution and Litigation; Related Unfair Competition Matters.
**Pan, Nina L.** ........ '69 '94 C.112 B.A. L.276 J.D. [Ⓐ Rosenfeld,M.&S.]
*PRACTICE AREAS: Labor and Employment; Litigation.
Panter, Gerald M. ........ '40 '64 C.393 B.A. L.597 J.D. 433 N. Camden Dr.
**Pappas, Diane H.** ........ '55 '82 L.809 J.D. [Ⓐ Turner,G.W.A.&Y.]
*LANGUAGES: Spanish, Portuguese and Greek.
*PRACTICE AREAS: Real Estate; Business Law.
**Park, Gary W.** ........ '66 '94 C.112 B.A. L.426 J.D. [Ⓐ Inman,S.N.&S.]
*PRACTICE AREAS: Business Litigation; Franchise Litigation; Consumer Finance; Creditors' Rights; Bankruptcy.
Parsi, Sam ........ '66 '91 C.112 B.A. L.426 [Ⓐ Steiner&L.]
**Passman, Donald S., (AV)** ........ '45 '71 C.846 B.A. L.309 J.D. [Gang,T.R.&B.]
*PRACTICE AREAS: Entertainment Law.
Pattiz, Henry A., (AV) ........ '41 '67 C.659 B.S. L.309 J.D. 9304 Civic Center Dr.
**Patton, Roger L., Jr.** ........ '63 '88 C.976 B.A. L.309 J.D. [Ⓐ Bloom,H.C.D.&K.] ‡
Pearlson, Albert, (BV) ........ '12 '34 L.809 LL.B. 8530 Wilshire Blvd.
Pearlson, Herbert D., (BV) ........ '22 '46 C.113 B.A. L.800 LL.B. 8530 Wilshire Blvd.
**Pearson, Nigel G.** ........ '50 '85 L.054 [Sinclair T.O.&E.]
Pedersen, Anne D. ........ '68 '93 C.112 B.A. L.426 J.D. International Creative Mgmt., Inc.
**Pepper, L. Kimberly** ........ '64 '89 C.10 B.F.A. L.809 J.D. [Ⓐ Lurie&Z.]
Pepper, Murray S. ........ '34 '60 C.112 B.A. L.800 LL.B. Pres., Home Silk Shop, Inc.
**Perez, Dennis** ........ '56 '82 C.763 A.B. L.1068 J.D. [Hochman,S.&D.]
*PRACTICE AREAS: Civil and Criminal Tax Litigation and Tax Controversy Law (Federal and State).
Perez, James T. ........ '59 '89 C.112 B.A. L.398 J.D. [Ⓐ Steiner&L.]
Perkal, Lee ........ '26 '51 C.112 B.A. L.426 9107 Wilshire Blvd.
**Perry, Barbara S.** ........ '38 '68 C.112 B.A. L.426 J.D. [Ⓒ Greines,M.S.&R.]
*PRACTICE AREAS: Appellate Law.
Petermann, Conrad D. ........ '39 '72 C.800 B.S. L.1068 J.D. 8306 Wilshire Blvd.
**Petkin, Lauren S.** ........ '58 '87 C.112 B.S. L.800 J.D. [Ⓐ Kolodny&A.]
*PRACTICE AREAS: Family Law.
**Petoyan, Marcus A.** ........ '56 '83 C.112 B.A. L.809 J.D. [Ⓐ Sherman,D.&P.]
Petrey, Karl R. '47 '76 C.335 B.A. L.1065 J.D.
V.P. & Gen. Coun., Shapell Industries, Inc.
**Phillips, Jerry S.** ........ '40 '66 C.112 B.A. L.1068 J.D. [Richman,L.M.G.C.F.&P.]
*PRACTICE AREAS: Business; Commercial; Probate; Real Estate; Securities.
Phillips, Kenneth Morgan ........ '51 '76 C.112 B.A. L.1068 J.D. 415 N. Camden Dr.
Phillips, Milton A. ........ '31 '62 C.1246 B.A. L.809 LL.B. 8693 Wilshire Blvd.
Phillips, Susan L. ........ '57 '92 C.1075 B.S. L.809 J.D. 9601 Wilshire Blvd., Ste 700

Picard, Clifford J. '48 '75 C.767 A.B. L.1066 J.D.
(adm. in NJ; not adm. in CA) Bogner, Picard & Finkelstein
Pick, David, (AV) ........ '19 '41 L.209 LL.B. [D.Pick]
Pick, David, Law Corporation, (AV) ........ 9454 Wilshire Blvd.
Pierce, David A. ........ '67 '92 C.1349 B.A. L.188 J.D. 421 S. Beverly Dr.
**Pierson, Travis Paul** ........ '69 '95 C.951 B.A. L.112 J.D. [Reuben&N.]
*PRACTICE AREAS: Entertainment Law; Employment Law; Civil Litigation.
Pine, Robert M. ........ '48 '75 C&L.629 B.A., J.D. [Ⓐ R.L.Esensten]
Pinzon, Marlene Gerdts ........ '46 '80 C.112 B.A. L.767 J.D. 9701 Wilshire Blvd.
Pitt, Alan S., (AV) ........ '35 '62 C.112 B.S. L.1068 J.D. 415 N. Camden Dr.
**Pleatman, Amy R.** ........ '58 '86 C.112 B.A. L.1148 J.D. [Ⓐ Swerdlow,F.&S.]
Podrug, Junius T. ........ '— '75 C.1060 B.A. L.464 J.D. 8484 Wilshire Blvd.
**Poletti, Thomas J.** ........ '57 '82 C.276 B.S.F.S. L.770 J.D. [Freshman,M.O.C.&K.]
*PRACTICE AREAS: Corporate Securities; Intellectual Property.
Polston, Schwartz, Hamilton & Fenster, (AV) ........ 9440 Santa Monica Blvd.
Pop, Jeffrey S. ........ '47 '72 C.112 B.S. L.61 J.D. 9107 Wilshire Blvd.
**Popoff, Michael W.** ........ '53 '80 C.800 B.A. L.1066 J.D. [Hochman,S.&D.]
*PRACTICE AREAS: Civil and Criminal Tax Controversy (Federal and State).
**Popowitz, Neil M.** ........ '63 '89 C.112 B.A. L.426 J.D. [Ⓐ Wilner,K.&S.]
*PRACTICE AREAS: Litigation.
Pops, Gerald M. ........ '36 '62 C.112 B.A. L.1066 LL.B. 145 S. Maple Dr.★
**Portanova, Victor E., (AV)** ........ '44 '72 C.197 A.B. L.262 J.D. [V.E.Portanova]

**Portanova, Victor E., A Law Corporation, (AV)**
**601 North Foothill Road, P.O. Box 17419, 90209-3419**
**Telephone: 310-273-5691 Fax: 310-285-0895**
**Email: vportano@counsel.com**
**Victor E. Portanova (Certified Specialist, Taxation Law, California Board of Legal Specialization).**
**Taxation, Corporation, Pension and Estate Planning Law.**
*See Professional Biographies, BEVERLY HILLS, CALIFORNIA*

Porter, Adam M. ........ '68 '94 C.112 B.A. L.990 J.D. P.O. Box 11033 (ⓞWash., D.C.)
**Portugal, Natt** ........ '52 '79 C.112 B.A. L.809 J.D. [Sherman,D.&P.]
**Poster, Marc J.** ........ '45 '71 C.813 B.A. L.1068 J.D. [Greines,M.S.&R.]
*PRACTICE AREAS: Appellate Law.
**Praskin, Susan D.** ........ '57 '85 C.1044 B.A. L.809 J.D. [Nagler&Assoc.]
*LANGUAGES: French.
*PRACTICE AREAS: Business Litigation.
Price, Clarence L. ........ '27 '58 C&L.923 B.S., LL.B. 360 N. Crescent Dr.
Price, Stephen M. ........ '32 '59 C.102 B.A. L.309 LL.B. 9454 Wilshire Blvd.
**Prinster, Patrick K.** ........ '52 '79 C.101 B.A. L.464 J.D. [Grebow,M.P.&Y.]
*LANGUAGES: Spanish.
*PRACTICE AREAS: Real Estate Transactions; Corporate Transactions; General Business; Securities.
Pritikin, Daniel W. ........ '65 '91 C.112 B.A. L.426 J.D. 9478 Cherokee Lane
Pulis, Gregory M. ........ '52 '78 C.197 A.B. L.893 J.D. Creative Artists Agcy., Inc.
**Pyles, Dortha Larene** ........ '49 '76 L.1148 J.D. [Ⓐ Turner,G.W.A.&Y.]
Rabineau, Larry, (P.C.) ........ '42 '71 C.112 B.A. L.426 J.D. 8501 Wilshire Blvd.
Rademacher, Mark H. '52 '77 C.112 B.S. L.1148 J.D.
315 S. Beverly Hills Dr., Penthouse
Rahe, S. Syd ........ '44 '69 C.112 B.S. L.1065 J.D. 315 S. Beverly Dr.
**Railsback, Marcy** ........ '52 '78 C.763 B.A. L.1065 J.D. [Browne&W.]
**Ramer, Bruce M., (AV)** ........ '33 '59 C.674 B.A. L.309 LL.B. [Gang,T.R.&B.]
*PRACTICE AREAS: Entertainment Law.
Randolph, Valerie Robin '62 '87 C.623 B.A. L.893 J.D.
Dir, Bus. & Legal Affs., Polygram Filmed Entertainment
Ranucci, Robert John ........ '64 '91 C.154 B.A. L.800 J.D. [Ranucci&R.]
Ranucci & Ranucci ........ 9665 Wilshire Blvd.
Rapke, Eileen F. ........ '54 '84 C.112 B.A. L.846 J.D. Creative Artists Agcy., Inc.

**Rasch, Howard L. '41 '71 C.112 A.B. L.809 J.D.**
**9454 Wilshire Boulevard Penthouse Suite, 90212-2937**
**Telephone: 310-247-2298 Fax: 310-247-8214**
***PRACTICE AREAS: Family Law; Business Litigation; General Civil Litigation.**
**Family Law, Adoptions, Domestic Violence, Cohabitation Agreements, Pre-Nuptial Agreements, Child Custody, Spousal Support, International Family Law, General Civil Litigation and Business Litigation.**
*See Professional Biographies, BEVERLY HILLS, CALIFORNIA*

**Rathbun, Sandy K.** ........ '59 '88 C.375 B.S. L.597 J.D. [Swerdlow,F.&S.]
*PRACTICE AREAS: Management, Labor and Employment Law.
**Raucher, Stephen L.** ........ '67 '92 C.112 B.A. L.1066 J.D. [Ⓐ Reuben&N.]
*PRACTICE AREAS: Commercial Litigation; Environmental Litigation; Entertainment Litigation.
**Ravitz, Barbara W., (AV)** ........ '45 '79 C.112 B.A. L.1068 J.D. [Greines,M.S.&R.]
*PRACTICE AREAS: Appellate Law.
Reed, David R., (BV) ........ '47 '74 C.112 B.A. L.284 J.D. 8530 Wilshire Blvd.
**Reed, James S.** ........ '64 '92 C.602 B.B.A. L.1068 J.D. [Ⓐ Beigel L.R.F.G.&W.]
*PRACTICE AREAS: Business Litigation; Tort Litigation; Securities Litigation; Professional Malpractice Litigation; Bankruptcy Litigation.
Reed, Karen ........ '50 '88 C.1077 L.398 J.D. 424 S. Beverly Dr.
Reed, Raymond C. ........ '52 '83 C.178 B.A. L.1148 J.D. 433 N. Camden Dr.
Reed, Robert ........ '69 '95 C.112 B.A. L.809 J.D. 9107 Wilshire Blvd.
**Rees, William B.** '37 '62 C.976 A.B. L.477 LL.B.
V.P. & Asst. Gen. Coun., Hilton Hotels Corp.
Regolo, Attilio M., Jr. ........ '59 '89 C.183 B.A. L.1148 J.D. [A.M.Regolo,Jr.]
Regolo, Attilio M., Jr., A Professional Law Corp. ........ 8730 Wilshire Blvd.
Reich, Bernard, (AV) ........ '14 '37 C&L.569 B.S., LL.B. 9454 Wilshire Blvd.
Reich, Gloria '52 '78 C.994 B.A. L.1019 J.D.
V.P., Business Affs., William Morris Agcy., Inc.
Reiss, Saul ........ '46 '71 C.112 A.B. L.1068 J.D. 280 S. Beverly Dr.
Renick, A. L. ........ '25 '53 C.223 B.S. L.569 LL.B. 315 S. Beverly Dr.
**Rettig, Charles P., (AV)** ........ '56 '81 C.112 B.A. L.990 J.D. [Hochman,S.&D.]
*PRACTICE AREAS: Civil and Criminal Tax Litigation; Tax Controversies; Federal Tax Controversies; Tax Planning; Business Planning.
**Reuben, Timothy D.** ........ '55 '80 C&L.309 B.A., J.D. [Reuben&N.]
*PRACTICE AREAS: Business; Real Estate; Entertainment Litigation; Intellectual Property; Unfair Competition.

**Reuben & Novicoff**
**(An Association including Timothy D. Reuben, Inc., A Professional Corporation)**
**9601 Wilshire Boulevard, Suite 644, 90210-5270**
**Telephone: 310-777-1990 Fax: 310-777-1989**
**Email: Attorney initials @rnlaw.com**
**Timothy D. Reuben; Michael L. Novicoff;—Stephen L. Raucher; Ranlyn Tilley Hill; David Z. Ribakoff; Travis Paul Pierson.**
**Business Litigation, including Real Estate, Entertainment, International Commercial Disputes, Intellectual Property, Securities, Complex Civil Matters, Bankruptcy, Insurance, Environmental.**
*See Professional Biographies, BEVERLY HILLS, CALIFORNIA*

**Reyes, Regina O.** ........ '60 '95 C.276 B.S.F.S. L.999 J.D. [Ⓐ Inman,S.N.&S.]
**Ribakoff, David Z.** ........ '66 '92 C.1077 B.A. L.1065 J.D. [Ⓐ Reuben&N.]
*LANGUAGES: Hebrew.
*PRACTICE AREAS: Employment; Insurance; Entertainment Litigation; Intellectual Property.
Rice, Brian E. ........ '60 '85 C.112 B.A. L.813 J.D. 433 N. Camden Dr.

CALIFORNIA—BEVERLY HILLS MARTINDALE-HUBBELL LAW DIRECTORY 1997

**Richland, Kent L.**, (AV) .......... '46 '72 C.112 A.B. L.1068 J.D. [Greines,M.S.&R.]
*PRACTICE AREAS: Appellate Law.
**Richman, Fredric N.**, (AV) '37 '60 C.339 B.A. L.209 LL.B. [Richman,L.M.G.C.F.&P.]
**Richman, Kenneth M.** .......... '68 '93 C&L.309 A.B., J.D. [Hansen,J.T.&H.]
*PRACTICE AREAS: Entertainment Law; Motion Picture Law; Television Law; Copyright Law.
Richman, Roger B. '44 '70 C.528 B.A. L.880 J.D. (adm. in NY; not adm. in CA) Pres., The Roger Richman Agcy., Inc.

**Richman, Lawrence, Mann, Greene, Chizever, Friedman & Phillips, A Professional Corporation, (AV)**
**Penthouse, 9601 Wilshire Boulevard, 90210-5270©**
**Telephone: 310-274-8300 Telecopier: 310-274-2831**
**Fredric N. Richman; John A. Lawrence; Richard L. Mann; Bruce R. Greene; Gerald M. Chizever; Barry A. Friedman; Jerry S. Phillips; Allan B. Duboff; Paul M. Enriquez; Cynthia E. Fruchtman; Madge S. Beletsky; William Joseph Briggs, II; Brian M. Colligan; Craig D. Hardwick; Kyle P. Kelley; Howard J. Kern; Jens B. Koepke; Barbara S. Lemerman. Of Counsel: Ronald D. Garber; Raymond S. Kaplan; Gary P. Kohn; David H. Mendelsohn, Ltd. (Not admitted in CA); Richard B. Skolnick (Certified Specialist, Taxation Law, The State Bar of California Board of Legal Specialization). Marin County Office: Kenneth C. Greene.**
**Transactional Business, Securities, Labor, Entertainment, Real Estate and Environmental Law. Litigation in all Courts.**
**Marin County Office: Suite 250, 300 Drakes Landing Road, Greenbrae, California 94904. Telephone: 415-925-0700. Telecopier: 415-925-1293.**
*See Professional Biographies, BEVERLY HILLS, CALIFORNIA*

Ring, Laurence .......... '41 '67 C.645 B.S. L.831 J.D. 9465 Wilshire Blvd.
Roach, Dennis A., (A Professional Corporation) '47 '72 C.800 B.A. L.1068 J.D. 8900 Wilshire Blvd.
**Robbins, Michael A.** .......... '52 '78 C.763 A.B. L.1068 J.D. [Rosenfeld,M.&S.]
*LANGUAGES: Spanish.
*PRACTICE AREAS: Labor Litigation and Labor and Employment Law.
Roberts, Gary D. .......... '59 '85 C.840 B.A. L.846 J.D. Fox Inc.
Roberts, Norman L. .......... '35 '59 C&L.285 LL.B. Sr. V.P., Western Atlas, Inc.
**Robertson, Mark A.** .......... '59 '91 C.112 B.A. L.800 J.D. Hilton Hotels Corp.
*LANGUAGES: Arabic, Portuguese, French, Spanish.
Robin, Jeffrey S. .......... '45 '71 C.800 A.B. L.426 J.D. William Morris Agcy., Inc.
**Robinson, Ronald R.** .......... '42 '72 C.1097 B.A. L.597 J.D. [Rosenfeld,M.&S.]
*PRACTICE AREAS: Insurance Coverage Law; Environmental Law; Asbestos and Toxic Tort Claim Coverage Law; Litigation; Insurance Defense Litigation.
**Robinson, Scott K.** .......... '62 '88 C.112 B.A. L.36 J.D. [Kaufman&Y.]
*PRACTICE AREAS: Family Law; Civil Litigation; Business; Corporate Law; Secured Transactions.
**Robledo, Angela D.** .......... '63 '89 C.1074 B.S. L.1067 J.D. [Ⓐ Stone&H.]
Rodov, Valentina .......... '45 '85 L.1136 J.D. 315 S. Beverly Dr.
**Rodriguez, Patrick S.** .......... '61 '90 C.800 B.A. L.426 J.D. [Inman,S.N.&S.]
Rogal, Bert L. .......... '35 '78 C.119 B.F.A L.1136 J.D. 9301 Wilshire Blvd.
**Rogers, Michael R.** .......... '43 '69 C.426 B.A. L.1049 J.D. [Ⓐ Leonard,D.&S.]
*PRACTICE AREAS: Business and Real Estate Transactions and Litigation.
**Román, Marissa J.** .......... '68 '93 C.674 A.B. L.813 J.D. [Ⓐ Rosenfeld,M.&S.]
*PRACTICE AREAS: Financial Institutions; Corporate; Securities; Real Estate; Media Finance.
**Rondeau, Charles R.** .......... '66 '93 C.176 A.B. L.809 J.D. [Rondeau&H.]
*LANGUAGES: French, German and Russian.

**Rondeau & Homampour, A Professional Law Corporation**
**8383 Wilshire Boulevard, Suite 830, 90211-2407**
**Telephone: 213-658-8077 Fax: 213-658-8477**
**Charles R. Rondeau; Arash Homampour;—Hedieh Miskinyar.**
**Federal and State Litigation, Taxation, Bankruptcy, Entertainment Law.**
*See Professional Biographies, BEVERLY HILLS, CALIFORNIA*

Roney, Buffy Lyn .......... '53 '78 L.1148 J.D. 101 N. Robertson Blvd.
**Rose, Lawrence D.** .......... '55 '84 C.112 B.A. L.800 J.D. [Gang,T.R.&B.]
*PRACTICE AREAS: Entertainment Law.
Rose, Mark I. .......... '49 '74 C.112 B.A. L.809 J.D. 9440 Santa Monica Blvd.
Rose, Norman D., (Inc.), (AV) '29 '56 C.112 B.S. L.1068 J.D. 9440 Santa Monica Blvd.
Roseman, Steven A. .......... '59 '83 C.1036 B.A. L.659 J.D. 9401 Wilshire Blvd.
Rosen, Aaron .......... '35 '69 C.563 B.Ch.E. L.800 J.D. 433 N. Camden Dr.
Rosen, Robin L. .......... '59 '87 C.1036 B.A. L.273 J.D. Sr. V.P., FoxVideo Intl.
Rosen & Chalfin .......... 8383 Wilshire Blvd. (©Woodland Hills)
Rosenberg, Burton I. .......... '40 '66 C.999 L.809 LL.B. 315 S. Beverly Dr.
Rosenberg, Mark S. .......... '58 '86 C.881 A.B. L.813 J.D. 433 N. Camden Dr.
Rosenberg, Noah D. .......... '50 '80 C.966 B.A. L.426 J.D. 9454 Wilshire Blvd.
Rosenberg, Robert I., (AV) .......... '44 '70 C&L.800 B.S., J.D. 9777 Wilshire Blvd.
Rosenberg, Ronald G. .......... '57 '83 C.800 B.A. L.426 J.D. [Rosenberg&K.]
Rosenberg, S. R. .......... '25 '75 C.563 B.Ch.E. L.1148 J.D. 2075 N. Beverly Dr. (Pat.)
Rosenberg & Koffman .......... 9401 Wilshire Blvd., Ste., 800
Rosenblatt, Howard C. .......... '48 '75 C.112 B.A. L.285 J.D. [Ⓐ J.L.Goldner]
**Rosenblit, Steven H.** .......... '51 '76 C.112 B.S. L.1095 J.D. [Dapeer,R.&L.]©
**Rosenfeld, Michael**, (AV) .......... '42 '68 C.112 B.A. L.1068 J.D. [Ⓒ Rosenfeld,M.&S.]
*PRACTICE AREAS: Entertainment Law.
Rosenfeld, Ronald A., (AV) .......... '38 '65 C.112 B.S.E. L.800 J.D. [Zimmerman,R.&G.]

**Rosenfeld, Meyer & Susman, LLP, (AV)**
**Fourth Floor, First Interstate Bank Building, 9601 Wilshire Boulevard, 90210-5288**
**Telephone: 310-858-7700 Telecopier: 310-271-6430**
**Members of Firm: Donald T. Rosenfeld (1917-1986); Marvin B. Meyer; Allen E. Susman; Jeffrey L. Nagin; Lawrence S. Kartiganer; David D. Wexler; Robert H. Thau; Mel Ziontz; Steven E. Fayne; Maren J. Christensen; Donald E. Karl; Ovvie Miller; William M. Ross; Kirk M. Hallam; James L. Seal; Kathryn A. Young; Ronald R. Robinson; Michael A. Robbins; William J. Skrzyniarz; Todd W. Bonder; Stacey M. Byrnes; David C. Ulich; Jeffrey L. Shumway; Harris J. Kane; David F. Graber; Burt Levitch; Greg S. Bernstein; Mitchell D. Kamarck; Bruce Telles; Lisa Marie Jacobsen; Peter Spelman; Paul S. White. Associates: Scott I. Barer; Ray Tamaddon; Susan E. Holley; Renee A. Galka; Stacy J. Barancik; D. Thomas Triggs; Brian H. Mcpherson; Suzanne H. Kessler; Darren M. Trattner; Orrin M. Feldman; Molly C. Hansen; Travis Mann; Lois R. Fishman; Saul D. Brenner; Jennifer L. Campbell; Marissa J. Román; Cameron Jones; Nina L. Pan; Kevin S. Fiur (Not admitted in CA). Of Counsel: Michael Rosenfeld; James M. A. Murphy; Bernard A. Greenberg; Ronald M. Greenberg; P. John Burke; Marybeth Jacobsen; Joseph M. Gabriel.**
**General Civil, Trial and Appellate Practice in all State and Federal Courts. Banking and Savings and Loan Law, Copyright, Corporate, Employee Benefits, Entertainment (Motion Picture, Television and Music) Transactions, Errors and Omission Clearance, Estate Planning, Family Law, Insurance Coverage and Defense Litigation, International Business Law, Labor and Employment Law, Motion Picture Financing, New Media Technologies, Real Estate, Real Property, Securities, Succession Planning, Taxation (Federal, State and International), Trademark, Trusts and Probate, Unfair Competition, Intellectual Property and Media Finance.**
*See Professional Biographies, BEVERLY HILLS, CALIFORNIA*

Rosensweig, William, (AV) .......... '30 '56 C&L.800 B.S., J.D. [Mathon&R.]
**Rosenthal, Pamela M.** .......... '64 '91 C.659 B.A. L.800 J.D. [Ⓐ Herzog,F.&G.]
**Rosenthal, Stuart M.** .......... '57 '85 C.112 B.A. L.1068 J.D. [Bloom,H.C.D.&K.]
**Rosin, Eric M.** .......... '67 '94 C.976 B.A. L.800 J.D. [Ⓐ Herzog,F.&G.]
Rosky, Burton S., (AV) .......... '27 '54 C.112 B.S. L.426 J.D. [Rosky,L.S.&S.]
Rosky, Landau, Stahl and Sheehy, (AV) .......... 8383 Wilshire Boulevard
Ross, Al .......... '36 '70 C.475 B.S. L.809 J.D. 9903 Santa Monica Blvd., Ste 135
Ross, Gary B. .......... '59 '85 C.112 B.A. L.800 J.D. [Ross&M.]
Ross, Leonard M. .......... '44 '69 C.112 B.S. L.1068 J.D. Pres., Rossco, Inc.
Ross, Melvyn Jay, (AV) .......... '39 '65 C.112 B.A. L.1068 LL.B. 9401 Wilshire Blvd.
**Ross, Peter W.** .......... '58 '83 C.118 B.A. L.813 J.D. [Browne&W.]
**Ross, Terry Levich** .......... '64 '90 C.112 B.A. L.1065 J.D. [Ⓐ Kolodny&A.]
*PRACTICE AREAS: Family Law Practice.
**Ross, William M.** .......... '57 '81 C.112 A.B. L.309 J.D. [Rosenfeld,M.&S.]
*PRACTICE AREAS: Business Law; Securities Law; Mergers and Acquisitions.
Ross & Morrison .......... 9440 Santa Monica Blvd., Suite 515
Rossi, Wendy .......... '57 '84 C.1097 B.S. L.426 9777 Wilshire Blvd. Ste. 918
**Roth, Robyn L.** .......... '64 '89 C.112 B.A. L.309 J.D. [Bloom,H.C.D.&K.]
Rothstein, Thomas D. .......... '51 '77 C.112 B.A. L.1068 J.D. 9595 Wilshire Blvd.
**Rountree, James S.** .......... '48 '82 C.112 A.B. L.1068 J.D. [Ⓒ Kalisch,C.&R.]
**Rubanowitz, Shalom** .......... '66 '95 C.1357 B.A. L.705 J.D. [Ⓐ R.W.Hirsh&Assoc.]
**Ruben, Joel D.**, (AV) .......... '49 '77 C.112 B.A. L.1067 J.D. [Lipofsky&R.]
*PRACTICE AREAS: Real Estate and Business Litigation; Commercial Law; Competitive Business Practices; Environmental Law.
Rubin, Barry S. .......... '33 '58 C.102 B.A. L.178 LL.B. [Leslie&R.]
Rubin, Charles G. .......... '40 '66 C.1043 B.A. L.1068 LL.B. Mun. Ct. J.
**Rubin, Julie H.** .......... '64 '90 C.112 B.A. L.426 J.D. [Ⓐ Grebow,M.P.&Y.]
*PRACTICE AREAS: Real Estate Litigation; Business Litigation; Probate Litigation; Mobilehome Park Defense Litigation.
**Rubin, Sheldon**, (AV) .......... '36 '60 C&L.339 B.S., J.D. [Rubin&E.]©
*PRACTICE AREAS: Real Estate Law; Insurance Law; Title Insurance Law.

**Rubin & Egan, P.C., (AV)**
**Suite 801, 9665 Wilshire Boulevard, 90212©**
**Telephone: 310-785-1700 Telecopier: 310-785-1701**
**John J. Eagan (1913-1982); Sheldon Rubin; Robert Ryan; Michael C. Flynn; Keith J. Turner; Patrick R. Broadway.**
**Civil Practice. State and Federal Litigation. Controversies and Disputes involving Insurance, Real Property, and Commercial Matters. Insurance Controversies including Insurance Bad Faith, Title Insurance, Property Insurance, Professional Liability Insurance, Directors and Officers Insurance, Suretyship, Subrogation, Mortgage Guaranty Insurance and Reinsurance. Real Property Controversies including Financing, Title, Foreclosure, Construction, Lien, Easement, Legal Description, Specific Performance and Escrow.**
**San Francisco, California Office: Suite 1900, 601 California Street. Telephone: 415-434-4946. Telecopier: 415-362-1179.**
*See Professional Biographies, BEVERLY HILLS, CALIFORNIA*

Rubinfier, Jon B. .......... '53 '80 C.112 A.B. L.1048 J.D. 9454 Wilshire Blvd.
Rubins, Harold, (AV) .......... '22 '48 C.113 B.S. L.426 LL.B. 463 S. Elm Dr.
Rudd, Lawrence .......... '49 '90 C.966 B.S. L.309 J.D. [Gelfand&G.]
**Rudman, Barry M.** .......... '45 '71 C.112 B.A. L.426 J.D. [Locke,L.R.&A.]
Rudnick, Claire .......... '62 '87 C.112 B.A. L.426 J.D. 618 N. Rodeo Dr.
Ruman, I. Richard, (AV) .......... '38 '63 C.112 B.S. L.1066 LL.B. 9401 Wilshire Blvd.
Rumer, Mary Jean .......... '57 '81 C.742 B.A. L.426 J.D. 9601 Wilshire Blvd.
Russell, Irwin E. .......... '26 '49 C.659 B.S. L.309 J.D. 433 N. Camden Dr.
**Rust, Richard N.**, (AV) .......... '52 '77 C.813 B.A. L.1068 J.D. [Kalisch,C.&R.]
Ryan, Mary Lee .......... '54 '85 C.104 A.B. L.569 J.D. 9809 Easton Dr.
**Ryan, Robert** .......... '56 '83 C.1307 B.A. L.904 J.D. [Ⓐ Rubin&E.]
*PRACTICE AREAS: Insurance Coverage Litigation; Real Estate Law; Title Insurance; Business Litigation.
**Ryden, William S.**, (AV) .......... '52 '80 C.154 B.A. L.809 J.D. [Jaffe&C.]
*PRACTICE AREAS: Family Law.
Rydstrom, Richard I. .......... '58 '85 C.415 B.S. L.1137 J.D. P.O. Box 7934
**Ryu, Thomas J.** .......... '65 '91 C.112 B.A. L.940 J.D. [Ⓒ Vorzimer,G.M.&E.]
*LANGUAGES: Korean.
*PRACTICE AREAS: Construction; Professional Malpractice; Premises Liability.
**Sabich-Robison, Katharine** .......... '68 '96 C.813 B.A. L.112 J.D. [Weissmann,W.B.C.&S.]
*LANGUAGES: French, Spanish and Latin.
*PRACTICE AREAS: Litigation.
Sacks, Samuel .......... '08 '31 C.563 L.724 LL.B. 211 S. Spalding Dr.
Salka, Fern Topas, (AV) .......... '48 '75 C.112 B.A. L.426 J.D. 9595 Wilshire Blvd., Ste 900
**Salkin, Avram**, (AV) .......... '35 '60 C.112 B.S. L.1066 LL.B. [Hochman,S.&D.]
*PRACTICE AREAS: Civil and Criminal Tax Controversy; Individual Business and Corporate Tax Planning; Business and Real Estate Transactions; Tax, Business and Estate Planning; Probate.
**Salkow, Alan M., (A Professional Corporation)**, (AV) '41 '68 C.112 B.A. L.809 LL.B. [Sherman,D.&P.]
**Saltsman, Jane D.**, (AV) .......... '50 '74 C.112 B.A. L.1066 J.D. [Glassman,B.&S.]
*PRACTICE AREAS: Family Law; General Civil Litigation.
Saltzman, Mark Elliott .......... '57 '91 C.112 B.A. L.809 J.D. 8730 Wilshire Blvd.
**Sanchez, Millicent N.** .......... '54 '81 C.312 B.A. L.1068 J.D. [Swerdlow,F.&S.]
*PRACTICE AREAS: Management, Labor and Employment Law.
**Sandberg, Ole R.** .......... '43 '84 C&L.061 B.A., J.D. [Lurie&Z.]
*LANGUAGES: Norwegian, French, German, Swedish and Danish.
**Sanders, Michael R. E.**, (BV) .......... '46 '87 C.878 B.A. L.339 J.D. [Jacobson,S.&B.]
*LANGUAGES: Japanese.
*PRACTICE AREAS: Taxation (International, Federal and State); Transactional Business Planning; Antitrust; Antitrust.
Sands, Ada P., (BV) .......... '34 '79 C.763 B.A. L.809 J.D. 9606 Santa Monica, 3rd Fl.
Sarno, Robert A., (A Professional Corporation) '42 '71 C.112 B.A. L.1068 J.D. [Weston,S.G.&D.]
Satzman, Barry, (AV) .......... '32 '56 C.102 A.B. L.178 LL.B. 8306 Wilshire Blvd.‡
Scandura, Steven P. .......... '— '91 C&L.112 A.B., J.D. 315 S. Beverly Dr.
Schaefer, Susan G., (AV) .......... '44 '69 C.112 B.A. L.1068 J.D. 9601 Wilshire Blvd.
**Schaffer, David L.** .......... '49 '75 C.112 B.A. L.472 J.D. [Ⓐ Stone&H.]
*PRACTICE AREAS: Insurance Coverage and Bad Faith; Tort Prosecution and Defense.
Schainker, Howard A., (BV©) '42 '70 C.623 A.B. L.45 J.D. (adm. in MO; not adm. in CA) 433 N. Camden Dr.‡
**Scheibe, Benjamin D.** .......... '56 '81 C.112 A.B. L.1068 J.D. [Browne&W.]
Schenk, Harry .......... '49 '76 C.112 B.A. L.767 J.D. 424 S. Beverly Dr.
**Schenkman, Michael L.** .......... '65 '90 C.813 B.A. L.1066 J.D. [Ⓐ Bloom,H.C.D.&K.]
*PRACTICE AREAS: Entertainment Law.
Schermer, Sam .......... '25 '54 C.112 L.426 J.D. [S.Schermer] ‡
Schermer, Sam, A Professional Corp. .......... 245 Spalding Dr.
Schiff, Gunther H., (AV) .......... '27 '52 C&L.276 B.S.F.S., J.D. [G.H.Schiff]
Schiff, Gunther H., A Professional Corporation, (AV) .......... 9430 Olympic, Suite 400
Schkolnick, Barry M. '58 '84 C.821 B.A. L.569 J.D. (adm. in NY; not adm. in CA) 456 S. Roxbury Dr.
Schlesinger, Arnold .......... '47 '70 C.112 L.1068 LL.B. 9595 Wilshire Blvd., 9th Fl.
Schlom, Barry R. .......... '53 '77 C.112 A.B. L.426 J.D. [Polston,S.H.&F.]
**Schmalz, Kurt L.** .......... '56 '83 C&L.880 B.A., J.D. [Lurie&Z.]
**Schmerzler, Andrew J.** .......... '64 '89 C.659 B.A. L.1068 J.D. [Ⓐ Weissmann,W.B.C.&S.]
*PRACTICE AREAS: Corporate Law; Real Estate.
**Schnaid, Stacy Norene** .......... '66 '92 C.112 B.A. L.426 J.D. [Ⓐ Schneider,G.&Y.]
*LANGUAGES: French.
**Schneider, Stephen A.**, (AV) .......... '40 '66 C.112 B.A. L.1068 LL.B. [Schneider,G.&Y.]

**Schneider, Goldberg & Yuen, A Law Corporation, (AV)**
**9100 Wilshire Boulevard Seventh Floor-West Tower, 90212**
**Telephone: 310-274-8201 FAX: 310-274-2330**
**Stephen A. Schneider; Kenneth W. Kossoff;—Stacy Norene Schnaid; Mitchell I. Burger. Of Counsel: Larry Goldberg; Esther G. Boynton.**

(This Listing Continued)

**Schneider, Goldberg & Yuen, A Law Corporation (Continued)**
**General, Civil and Trial Practice in State and Federal Courts. Corporation, Partnership, Business, Real Property, Securities, Business Reorganization, Creditor's Rights, Bankruptcy, Sports and Entertainment, Trademark, Copyright, Estate Planning, Probate and Trust Law.**
***See Professional Biographies, BEVERLY HILLS, CALIFORNIA***

Schoen, Lucille L. .................... '26 '72 C.102 B.A. L.1136 J.D. 264 S. Camden St.‡
**Schreiber, James P., (A Professional Corporation),** (AV) '42 '66
C.112 B.A. L.1066 LL.B. [Leonard,D.&S.]
*PRACTICE AREAS: Entertainment and Copyright Law; Business Transactions and Entertainment, Copyright and Business Litigation; Family Law.
Schulman, Barry A., (AV) ................ '36 '65 C.208 A.B. L.1065 J.D. [Schulman&M.]
Schulman, Richard A. .......... '36 '63 C.112 B.S. L.800 LL.B. 9440 Santa Monica Blvd.

**Schulman, J. Brin**
**(See Los Angeles)**

Schulman & Miller, (AV) ........................................9440 Santa Monica Blvd.
Schultz, Audrey L. .......................... '57 '81 C.102 B.A. L.569 J.D. P.O. Box 2597
**Schultz, David N.** .......................... '58 '86 C.674 A.B. L.309 J.D. [Ⓐ Leonard,D.&S.]
*LANGUAGES: Hebrew.
*PRACTICE AREAS: Business and Entertainment Litigation.
**Schuman, Steven A.** .................. '62 '89 C.112 B.A. L.1068 J.D. [Ⓐ Leonard,D.&S.]
*PRACTICE AREAS: Business and Real Estate Litigation.
**Schwartz, Bruce Edward,** (AV) ..... '47 '74 C.1077 B.A. L.1049 J.D. [Schwartz,W.&W.]
*PRACTICE AREAS: Business; Corporate; Civil Litigation; Insurance Litigation; Probate Litigation.
Schwartz, Kenneth M., (AV) ....... '16 '50 C.930 B.B.A. L.809 LL.B. 141 S. Linden Dr.‡
Schwartz, Michael E., (AV) .......... '38 '64 C.112 B.S. L.1068 LL.B. [Polston,S.H.&F.]
Schwartz, Peter M., and Associates ... '47 '74 C.1077 B.A. L.1049 J.D. 120 S. Doheny Dr.
Schwartz, Robert J. '13 '37 C.659 B.S. L.309 LL.B.
(adm. in NY; not adm. in CA) 1114 Calle Vista‡

**Schwartz, Wisot & Wilson, LLP, (AV)** BB
**Suite 315, 315 South Beverly Drive, 90212**
**Telephone: 310-277-2323 Fax: 310-556-2308**
**Bruce Edward Schwartz; Valerie Wisot; John D. Wilson; Kathleen A. Calaway. Of Counsel: Paula Reddish Zinnemann.**
**General Civil and Trial Practice in all State and Federal Courts. Business Corporate, Civil Litigation, Real Property Transactions, Litigation and Title Insurance, Probate Litigation, Construction Litigation.**
**Reference: Great Western Bank (Century City Office, Los Angeles, California)**
***See Professional Biographies, BEVERLY HILLS, CALIFORNIA***

Schwartzer, Lenard E., (AVⓅ) '50 '74 C.569 B.S. L.982 J.D.
161 S. Doheny Dr. (ⓄLas Vegas & Reno, Nev.)
**Scott, Charles A.,** (AV) ................ '32 '57 C.112 A.B. L.309 LL.B. [Gang,T.R.&B.]
*PRACTICE AREAS: Entertainment Law.
**Scott, Kelly O.** ........................................ '61 '87 C.112 B.A. L.800 J.D. [Ervin,C.&J.]
*PRACTICE AREAS: Commercial Litigation; Entertainment Law; Employment Law.
Scotti, Neil A. ........................... '50 '77 C&L.276 B.A., J.D. 137 S. El Camino Dr.
**Seal, James L.,** (AV) ................ '45 '71 C.150 B.B.A. L.309 J.D. [Rosenfeld,M.&S.]
*PRACTICE AREAS: General Business Litigation; Antitrust and Trade Regulation; Insurance Coverage and Defense Litigation.
Segal, Lawrence ...................... '56 '81 C.659 B.A. L.276 J.D. 433 N. Camden Dr.
Segura, Jacob N. ...................... '55 '80 C.112 B.A. L.1068 J.D. 315 S. Beverly Dr.
Selwyn, Marc ......................... '60 '86 C.813 B.A. L.569 J.D. 300 N. Swall Dr.

**Senkfor, Burton Mark '49 '74 C.112 B.A. L.1068 J.D.**
**9100 Wilshire Boulevard Seventh Floor - West Tower, 90212**
**Telephone: 310-274-8771**
***REPORTED CASES: Spencer v. Older, 133 Cal.App.3d 95 (1982) (corporate control); Mara v. Farmers Group, Inc., 271 Cal.Rptr. 620 (1990) (insurance coverage); First City National Bank and Trust Company v. Zellner, 782 F.Supp. 232 (S.D.N.Y. 1992); Joint Venture Asset Acquisition v. Zellner, 808 F.Supp. 289 (S.D.N.Y. 1992) (banking).**
**Complex Business Litigation and Arbitration in all State and Federal Courts, involving Securities, Intra-Corporate and Partnership Disputes, Corporate Control and Proxies, Lender Liability and Banking, Unfair Competition, Insurance Bad Faith, Real Estate, Construction, Entertainment, Copyright, Contracts and General Business and Corporate Practice.**
***See Professional Biographies, BEVERLY HILLS, CALIFORNIA***

Seri-Levi, Ehud '55 '89 C&L.061 LL.B.
9401 Wilshire Blvd., Ste. 1250 (ⓄTel Aviv, Isaraeł)
**Serpico, Joseph R.** ........................ '51 '77 C.1077 B.S. L.809 J.D. [Wilner,K.&S.]
Shacter, David M., (AV) ........ '41 '69 C.025 B.A. L.809 J.D. 8383 Wilshire Blvd.
Shafer, Bernard W. ............... '12 '35 C.563 B.S. L.1009 LL.B. 424 S. Beverly Dr.
Shaffer, Douglas D. ............ '57 '84 C.608 B.S. L.990 J.D. 9454 Wilshire Blvd., 5th Fl.
Shane, Jeffrey A. ............. '52 '79 C.112 B.A. L.426 J.D. 9th Fl., 9595 Wilshire Blvd.
Shapiro, Michael R. ..................... '40 '65 C.112 A.B. L.800 J.D. [M.R.Shapiro]
Shapiro, Ralph J., (AV) ............ '31 '59 C.112 B.S. L.1068 J.D. 433 N. Camden Dr.
Shapiro, Michael R., P.C. .................................................... 124 S. Lasky Dr.
**Share, Mark L.** ........................ '64 '90 C.685 B.A. L.596 J.D. [Ⓐ Lipofsky&R.]
*PRACTICE AREAS: Real Estate; Business Litigation.
Sharmat, James L. '58 '90 C.1169 B.A. L.426 J.D.
Dir. of Bus. & Legal Affs., Solomon Intl. Enterprises

**Shaw, William A., (AV) '43 '69 C.221 B.S. L.352 J.D.**
**425 South Beverly Drive, 90212**
**Telephone: 310-556-2155**
**Civil Trial Practice in State and Federal Courts. Personal Injury, Real Estate Syndication and Entertainment Law.**
**Reference: Trans World Bank.**
***See Professional Biographies, BEVERLY HILLS, CALIFORNIA***

**Sheehan, Richard H., Jr.,** (AV) '43 '67
C&L.273 B.A., J.D. Sr. V.P. & Gen. Coun., City Natl. Bk.
*RESPONSIBILITIES: Corporate and Securities; Banking and Finance; Real Estate Law; Bankruptcy.
Sheehy, Paul R. ........................ '63 '90 C.349 B.S. L.940 J.D. [Rosky,L.S.&S.]
Sheinbein, Robert A., (BV) ....... '54 '78 C.188 B.S. L.1049 J.D. 9440 Santa Monica Blvd.
Sheinbein, Roger B. .................. '49 '76 C.800 B.A. L.426 J.D. 9454 Wilshire Blvd.
Shekarchian, Haleh ..................... '66 '92 C.112 B.A. L.1148 J.D. [H.Shekarchian]
Shekarchian, Haleh, A Prof. Corp. ....................................9440 Santa Monica Blvd.
Shemaria, Joseph, (AV) ........................ '44 '70 C.37 B.A. L.1068 J.D. [J.Shemaria]
Shemaria, Joseph, Law Offices of, (AV) .................... 415 N. Camden Dr., Ste. 202
**Shenian, Datev K.** ........................ '67 '93 C&L.112 B.A., J.D. [Ⓐ Vorzimer,G.M.&E.]
*LANGUAGES: Armenian.
*PRACTICE AREAS: General Civil Litigation; Real Estate; Appeals.
Shephard & Daza ............................................................... P.O. Box 10358
**Sherman, Arthur,** (AV) ................ '31 '53 C.999 A.A. L.426 J.D. [Sherman,D.&P.]
*REPORTED CASES: Darling v. Caterpillar Tractor, 1959, California Supreme Court; Miller v. U.S.; Gelbardt v. U.S., United States Supreme Court; Paris Air Crash; PSA Air Crash.
*PRACTICE AREAS: Plaintiff's Personal Injury; Product Liability Law; Complex and MDL Litigation; Pharmaceutical; Medical Device.
**Sherman, Richard Lloyd** .............. '57 '82 C.800 B.A. L.1068 J.D. [Sherman,N.&M.]
*PRACTICE AREAS: Contracts; Wrongful Termination; Commercial Landlord-Tenant Disputes; Real Estate; International Trading.

**Sherman, Dan & Portugal, A Professional Corporation, (AV)**
**Suite 550, 9454 Wilshire Boulevard, 90212**
**Telephone: 310-275-5077 Fax: 310-276-5871**
**Arthur Sherman; Michael A. K. Dan; Alan M. Salkow (A Professional Corporation); Natt Portugal;—Jonathan S. Weber; Marcus A. Petoyan. Of Counsel: John W. Hornbeck; Julianne Bloomer; Louis I. Bell (A Professional Corporation).**
**Practice Limited to Personal Injury, Products Liability, Malpractice, Environment, and Aviation Law, Mass Tort Litigation.**
**Reference: Mitsui Manufacturers Bank.**
***See Professional Biographies, BEVERLY HILLS, CALIFORNIA***

**Sherman, Nathanson & Miller, A Professional Corporation**
**9454 Wilshire Boulevard, Suite 820, 90212**
**Telephone: 310-246-0321 Facsimile: 310-246-0305**
**Richard Lloyd Sherman; Ken Nathanson; Michael B. Miller.**
**Commercial Litigation, Corporate and Partnership Law, Real Estate, Commercial and Financial Transactions, Contracts, Wrongful Termination, Sexual Harassment, Landlord-Tenant, Personal Injury, Intellectual Disputes and Alternative Dispute Resolution.**
***See Professional Biographies, BEVERLY HILLS, CALIFORNIA***

Shimer, Gloria K., (AV) ................ '32 '58 C.112 B.S. L.1068 J.D. 144 S. Beverly Dr.
Shimer, Irving A. ............................ '31 '58 C.112 B.A. L.1068 J.D. Supr. Ct. J.
Shire, Harold R. ....................... '10 '37 C.990 M.B.A. L.809 J.D. P.O. Box 1352‡
Shore, Marc L. ......................... '51 '87 C.112 B.A. L.1136 J.D. 345 S. McCarty Dr.
**Shumway, Jeffrey L.** ................ '57 '87 C.112 B.A. L.800 J.D. [Rosenfeld,M.&S.]
*PRACTICE AREAS: Entertainment Law.
Siegel, Gil T. ............................................ '45 '70 C.112 B.S. L.426 J.D. [G.T.Siegel]
**Siegel, Leonard,** (AV) ................................ '50 '74 C.112 B.A. L.426 J.D. [Wilner,K.&S.]
Siegel, Gil Todd, A Prof. Corp. ........................................ 123 N. San Vincente Blvd.
Sierra, Edward .............................. '54 '79 C.800 B.S.B.A. L.426 J.D. 8383 Wilshire Blvd.
Sifuentes, Loretta S. ......... '37 '72 C.112 B.A. L.1068 J.D. V.P. & Gen. Coun., LMI Ltd.

**Sigelman, Paul S., (AV) '42 '67 C&L.494 B.A., J.D.**
**9595 Wilshire Boulevard, Suite 900, 90212**
**Telephone: 310-278-8011 Fax: 310-278-2254**
**Email: PSLF@jovanet.com**
**Civil Trial, Business, Real Estate and Injury Practice.**
***See Professional Biographies, BEVERLY HILLS, CALIFORNIA***

**Silberbusch, Barbara** .................................. '66 '95 L.061 J.D. [Ⓐ Gang,T.R.&B.]
*LANGUAGES: Dutch, German.
*PRACTICE AREAS: Entertainment Law; Estate Planning.
Silver, Jack B. ........................ '31 '61 C.1043 B.A. L.800 J.D. 415 N. Camden Dr.
**Silver, Lee L.,** (AV) .............................. '43 '69 C.112 A.B. L.1068 J.D. [Ervin,C.&J.]
*PRACTICE AREAS: Real Property Law.
Silverman, Bernard .................... '26 '55 C.112 B.S. L.1068 LL.B. 345 N. Maple Dt.
Silverman, Gary ..................... '53 '79 C.1019 B.A. L.809 J.D. 9465 Wilshire Blvd.
**Silverman, Ronald J., (P.C.),** (AV) '46 '73
C.645 B.A. L.273 J.D. [Weissmann,W.B.C.&S.]
*PRACTICE AREAS: Civil Litigation.
**Simon, Darcy L.** ................................ '63 '90 C.103 A.B. L.1068 J.D. [Ⓐ Ervin,C.&J.]
*PRACTICE AREAS: Corporate and Securities Law.
**Simon, Jody** ............................................ '53 '83 C.771 B.A. L.178 J.D. [H.B.California]
*PRACTICE AREAS: Entertainment; Intellectual Property.
Simon, Mace Stephen .................... '51 '76 C.112 B.A. L.809 J.D. 118 S. Beverly Dr.
Simon, Stephen B., (A Prof. Corp.) .... '52 '79 C.475 B.A. L.213 J.D. 8383 Wilshire Blvd.
**Simon, Stuart A.** .................................. '54 '78 C.1077 B.A. L.426 J.D. [Ⓐ Hochman,S.&D.]
Simpson, Robert J. .................... '58 '89 C.1077 B.A. L.809 J.D. 8383 Wilshire Blvd.
**Sinclair, Nigel,** (AV) ................... '48 '81 C.050 M.A. L.178 LL.M. [Sinclair T.O.&E.]

**Sinclair Tenenbaum Olesiuk & Emanuel, (AV)**
**The Ice House, 9348 Civic Center Drive, Suite 200, 90210**
**Telephone: 310-777-7777 Fax: 310-777-7778**
**Leah K. Antonio; Craig A. Emanuel; Walter W. J. Olesiuk; Nigel G. Pearson; Nigel Sinclair; Irwin J. Tenenbaum;—Janet L. Stott; Roberta Marlene Wolff. Of Counsel: Keith G. Fleer; Kenneth H. Meyer.**
**Entertainment, Domestic and International Business, Corporate and Finance.**
***See Professional Biographies, BEVERLY HILLS, CALIFORNIA***

Sires, Bruce D., (AV) .......................... '48 '72 C.112 A.B. L.1065 J.D. [B.D.Sires]
Sires, Bruce D., Prof. Corp., (AV) ...............................................9595 Wilshire Blvd.
**Sirias, Deborah F.** ............................ '56 '82 C.800 A.B. L.809 J.D. [H.B.California]
*LANGUAGES: Spanish, French and Italian.
*PRACTICE AREAS: Civil Litigation.
Sklar, Gary Martin ........................ '44 '81 C.912 B.F.A. L.213 J.D. 424 S. Beverly Dr.
**Skolnick, Richard B.** ............ '44 '69 C.112 A.B. L.1066 J.D. [Ⓒ Richman,L.M.G.C.F.&P.]
*PRACTICE AREAS: Taxation Law; Business Planning Law.
**Skrzyniarz, William J.,** (AV) ......... '56 '86 C.309 A.B. L.813 J.D. [Rosenfeld,M.&S.]
*PRACTICE AREAS: Entertainment Transactions; Motion Picture; New Media Technologies; Theme Parks, Special Effects, Television and Music.
Slade, Robert E. '41 '65 C&L.966 B.A., LL.B.
(adm. in WI; not adm. in CA) V.P., Mgr., Personal Tr., First Interstate Bk. of Calif.
Slavitt, David W., (AV) ............... '31 '56 C.112 B.S. L.1068 J.D. 721 N. Beverly Dr.‡
**Sloane, Jason C.** .............................. '63 '88 C.112 B.S. L.1068 J.D. [Hansen,J.T.&H.]
*PRACTICE AREAS: Entertainment Law; Motion Picture Law; Television Law; Copyright Law.
Small, Lawrence A. ................... '39 '65 C.112 B.S. L.1065 LL.B. 9595 Wilshire Blvd.
Smitas, David A. ........ '52 '78 C.1044 B.S. L.809 J.D. Gen. Coun., Apollo Pictures, Inc.
Smith, Arthur ......................... '26 '53 C&L.309 A.B., LL.B. 8888 Olympic Blvd.‡
**Smith, David S.,** (AV) ...................................... '17 '43 C.112 A.B. L.423 J.D. [Smith&S.]
Smith, Dennis D. ....................... '50 '75 C.112 B.A. L.809 J.D. 321 S. Beverly Dr.
**Smith, Kathleen G.** .................... '47 '81 C.320 B.A. L.800 J.D. [Ⓒ Kalisch,C.&R.]
*PRACTICE AREAS: Litigation.
**Smith, Lee S.** ........................................ '56 '81 C.112 B.A. L.426 J.D. [Smith&S.]
**Smith, M. Hue, III** '41 '66 C&L.880 B.A., LL.B.
(adm. in TN; not adm. in CA) V.P. & Coun., Hilton Hotels Corp.
Smith, Ronald S. ..................................... '46 '71 C.1097 B.A. L.169 J.D. [R.S.Smith]
Smith, Ronald S., A Law Corporation ...............................8383 Wilshire Blvd.

**Smith & Smith, (AV)**
**121 South Beverly Drive, 90212**
**Telephone: 310-275-5132 Los Angeles: 213-272-7807**
**David S. Smith; Lee S. Smith.**
**Civil and Trial Practice in all State and Federal Courts. Corporation, Partnership, Real Property, Construction, Administrative, Estate Planning, Trust, Probate, Entertainment, Family and Personal Injury Law.**
***See Professional Biographies, BEVERLY HILLS, CALIFORNIA***

Snelson, Gary E. ....................... '47 '79 C.800 A.B. L.1127 J.D. 8383 Wilshire Blvd.
**Snoke, Laura J.** ..................................... '49 '81 C.1077 B.A. L.426 J.D. [Wilner,K.&S.]
**Snyder, Jack M.** ............................ '67 '93 C&L.112 B.A., J.D. [Ⓐ Leonard,D.&S.]
*PRACTICE AREAS: Business; Real Estate Litigation.
Sobel, Michael D. ........................ '45 '72 C.1246 B.S. L.809 J.D. 431 N. Doheny Dr.
Sokol, Stacy L., Mr. '54 '84
C.813 B.A. L.1068 J.D. 9100 Wilshire Blvd., 8th Floor E. Tower

**Solomon, Stephen E.**
(See Los Angeles)
Soloway, Steven A. ............ '60 '86 C.228 B.A. L.94 J.D. Gen. Coun., Dove Audio, Inc.
Sommer, Paul R. ......................'47 '76 C.1077 B.A. L.1148 J.D. [Sommer&B.]⊙
Sommer, Seymour D., (AV) .......... '16 '40 C.112 B.A. L.800 J.D. 9777 Wilshire Blvd.
Sommer and Bear ..............................Ste. 512, 9777 Wilshire Blvd. (⊙Encino)
Soriano-Vesagas, Maria Rita ...........'63 '90 C&L.061 B.S., LL.B. 8383 Wilshire Blvd.
Sosnick, Ernest ......................'44 '71 C.800 B.S. L.912 J.D. 8306 Wilshire Blvd.
Soussan, Gerard J. ......................'49 '79 C&L.061 M.B.A., J.D. 9595 Wilshire Blvd.
**Spears, Melvin S.**, (AV) ............................ '27 '52 C.112 L.800 J.D. [Ervin,C.&J.]
*PRACTICE AREAS: Taxation Law; Estate Planning Law; Probate Law.
Spector, Bennett A. ..................... '47 '72 C&L.260 B.S.B.A., J.D. [Dichter,S.&K.]
Spector, J. Paul, (BV) ........... '27 '63 C.112 L.809 LL.B. 9300 Wilshire Blvd. Ste. 300
**Spelman, Peter** ................................ '46 '87 C.966 L.426 J.D. [Rosenfeld,M.&S.]
*PRACTICE AREAS: Family Law: Litigation and Mediation of Family Law Disputes; Civil Litigation.
**Spence, Arthur G.** .... '44 '70 C.112 B.A. L.1068 J.D. Assoc. Gen. Coun., City Natl. Bk.
*RESPONSIBILITIES: Litigation; Bankruptcy; Loan Workouts; Banking Law.
**Spiegel, Lance S.**, (AV) ......................... '45 '72 C&L.800 B.A., J.D. [⊠ Kaufman&Y.]
*PRACTICE AREAS: Family Law; Trial Practice.
**Spielberger, Andrew J.** ........................'59 '85 C.861 B.A. L.464 J.D. [⊠ B.D.Witzer]
*LANGUAGES: French.
*PRACTICE AREAS: Personal Injury; Construction Defect; Entertainment; Business Litigation.

**Spieller, Kent A. '51 '80 C.112 B.A. L.1065 J.D.**
**8383 Wilshire Boulevard, Suite 549, 90211**
**Telephone: 310-859-8080; 213-655-7505 Fax: 213-651-5742**
***LANGUAGES: Spanish, French and German.**
**Government Relations, Technology Transfer, Health Care Law, Land Use Regulation, Waste/Energy.**
*See Professional Biographies, BEVERLY HILLS, CALIFORNIA*

Spinella, Stephen A. ....... '51 '85 C.555 B.A. L.809 J.D. 9665 Wilshire Blvd., Suite 1000
Spiro, Ira, (AV) .....................................'49 '75 C.813 B.A. L.1066 J.D. [Brown,A.&S.]
Spiro, Randy, (AV) .............................'54 '78 C.112 B.A. L.426 J.D. [Brown,A.&S.]
**Sprunger, Richard L.** ........................'49 '76 C&L.800 A.B., J.D. [⊠ Frydrych&W.]
*PRACTICE AREAS: General Corporate; Partnerships; Real Estate Law; Real Estate Finance; Land Use.
Sroloff, Sheldon ................'50 '76 C.112 B.A. L.1068 J.D. Creative Artists Agcy., Inc.
Stahl, Alberta P. .................................'37 '86 C.112 B.S. L.1136 J.D. [Rosky,L.S.&S.]
Stahl, Hortense, (AV) ......................'— '36 C&L.597 B.A., J.D. 622 N. Walden Dr.‡
Stahler, Elliot J. .................'49 '78 C.1028 B.A. L.1137 J.D. 8383 Wilshire Blvd.
Stark, Leland Alan, (AV) ......................'43 '72 C.112 A.B. L.1068 J.D. [L.A.Stark]
Stark, Leland Alan, A Law Corporation, (AV) ...............Ste., 204 9454 Wilshire Blvd.
Starkey, Robert L., (AV) ..............'21 '49 C.112 A.B. L.426 J.D. 9844 Wanda Pk. Dr.‡
**Starr, Philip** ..........................................'49 '82 C.1044 B.A. L.1068 J.D. [Ervin,C.&J.]
Steel, Shawn ..................................'46 '78 C.1077 B.A. L.1179 J.D. 8383 Wilshire Blvd.
**Steele, Donald W.** .................................. '60 '86 C&L.846 B.S., J.D. [Hansen,J.T.&H.]
*PRACTICE AREAS: Motion Picture/Television Law; Copyright Law; Intellectual Property Law.
Stegman, Richard W. .............................'37 '60 C.800 B.S. L.809 LL.B. P.O. Box 10812
Stein, Amy L. ...........................'64 '89 C.112 B.A. L.280 J.D. 437 N. Oakhurst Dr.
Stein, Jay J., (AV) .....................'09 '33 C.145 Ph.B. L.800 J.D. 9454 Wilshire Blvd.
Stein, Judith O. ..........................................'— '62 C&L.800 A.B., J.D. Mun. Ct. J.
**Stein, Martin** ..............................'40 '66 C.112 A.B. L.1068 J.D. [Greines,M.S.&R.]
*PRACTICE AREAS: Appellate Law.
Steinberg, Frederic ................................'37 '62 C&L.800 B.S., LL.B. 415 N. Camden Dr.
Steinberg, Herbert ...................................................'41 '70 415 N. Camden Dr.
**Steinberg, Lawrence B.** ........'57 '81 C.976 B.A. L.309 J.D. [⊠ Weissmann,W.B.C.&S.]
*REPORTED CASES: Levin v. Knight, 780 F.2d 786 (9th Cir. 1986); Rosenthal v. Fonda, 862 F.2d 1398 (9th Cir. 1988); Christensen v. United States District Court, 844 F.2d 694 (9th Cir. 1988); In re Tia Carrere, 64 B.R. 156 (Bankr. C.D. Cal. 1986).
*PRACTICE AREAS: Commercial, Real Estate and Entertainment Litigation.
**Steinberg, Matthew S.**, (AV) ..........'53 '78 C.112 B.A. L.1049 J.D. [Inman,S.N.&S.]
*REPORTED CASES: Atari Corporation v. Ernst & Whinney, 970 F.2d 641 (9th Cir. 1992). Air Sea Forwarders v. Air Asia Company, Ltd., 880 F.2d 176 (9th Cir. 1989). Coopers & Lybrand v. Superior Court, 212 Cal.App.3d 524, 260 Cal.Rptr. 713 (1989).
*PRACTICE AREAS: Civil Litigation; Trial and Appeals in State and Federal Courts.
Steinberg, Steven P. .........................'47 '75 C.209 B.A. L.365 J.D. 9107 Wilshire Blvd.
Steinberg, Ted L., (AV) ....................'43 '69 C&L.575 B.A., J.D. [Steinberg,T.L.] ‡
Steinberg, Ted L., A Professional Corporation .........................13931 Mulholland Dr.
Steinberger, Jeffrey W., (AV) ..................'47 '79 C&L.1136 B.S., J.D. [J.W.Steinberger]
Steinberger, Jeffrey W., A P.C., (AV) ...............................................8383 Wilshire Blvd.
Steiner, Leonard .........'51 '77 C.1044 B.A. L.564 J.D. [Steiner&L.] (⊙New York, N.Y.)
Steiner, Neil S. ..........................'47 '81 C.563 B.B.A. L.1148 J.D. 433 N. Camden Dr.
Steiner & Libo, Professional Corporation ............................................433 N. Camden Dr.
Stempel, Oscar S. .....................'35 '69 C.563 B.A. L.1148 J.D. 8601 Wilshire Blvd.
Sterchi, Karen L. ......'57 '88 C.347 B.M.E. L.602 J.D. Twentieth Century Fox Film Corp.
**Stern, Ellis R.**, (AV) .................................'46 '74 C.1046 B.A. L.861 J.D. [Stern&G.]
*PRACTICE AREAS: Taxation Law; Trusts Law; Estates Law; Business Transactions; Real Property Transactions.
**Stern, Todd M.** ................'63 '88 C.339 B.S. L.1068 J.D. [Weissmann,W.B.C.&S.]
*PRACTICE AREAS: Entertainment Law.

**Stern & Goldberg, (AV)**
**9150 Wilshire Boulevard, Suite 100, 90212**
**Telephone: 213-272-2711; 310-278-8686 Fax: 310-278-5248**
**Ellis R. Stern (Certified Specialist: Taxation Law; Probate, Estate Planning and Trust Law, California Board of Legal Specialization); Alan N. Goldberg (Certified Specialist, Taxation Law, The State Bar of California Board of Legal Specialization); Russell T. Ginise. Associate: Justin J. Lansberg. Of Counsel: Lawrence W. Hait.**
**General Business Law with emphasis in Business Litigation, Real Estate, Corporate, Taxation, Probate and Estate Planning.**
*See Professional Biographies, BEVERLY HILLS, CALIFORNIA*

Stewart, Charles B., Jr. ......................'31 '59 C&L.329 B.S., LL.B. P.O. Box 3775
Stillwater, Sandra .........................'42 '72 C.112 A.B. L.1068 J.D. 424 S. Beverly Dr.
Stone, Douglas R. ...................'60 '86 C.188 B.S. L.1066 J.D. 10029 Westwanda Dr.
**Stone, Lincoln** ..............................'60 '86 C.426 B.A. L.602 J.D. [Inman,S.N.&S.]
**Stone, Richard A.**, (AV) .........................'27 '55 C.112 B.S. L.426 J.D. [Stone&H.]
*PRACTICE AREAS: Real Estate Law; Business Law; Complex Litigation.

**Stone & Hiles, (AV) ⊞**
**9440 Santa Monica Boulevard, Penthouse, 90210**
**Telephone: 310-274-8749 Telecopier: 310-550-0483**
**Email: stonehil@he.net URL: http://www.he.net/~stonehil**
**Members of Firm: Richard A. Stone; Russel D. Hiles; Benjamin S. Cardozo. Associates: Marc A. Legget; Doreen M. Mercado; Margaret Monos; Angela D. Robledo; David L. Schaffer; Heather L. Weakley; Robert D. Stubblefield.**
**General Civil Practice in State and Federal Courts. Civil, Business, Probate, and Corporate Litigation, Tort, Real Estate, Insurance, Personal Injury and Toxic Tort Law.**
*See Professional Biographies, BEVERLY HILLS, CALIFORNIA*

**Stott, Janet L.** ..........................'48 '76 C.681 B.A. L.93 J.D. [⊠ Sinclair T.O.&E.]
*PRACTICE AREAS: Entertainment Law.
Strasser, Averill J. ...................'42 '75 C.112 B.S. L.1136 J.D. 319 S. Robertson Blvd.
Straugh, Deanna K. .................'59 '85 C.112 B.A. L.464 J.D. 8665 Wilshire Blvd.
**Stubblefield, Robert D.** ......................'68 '96 C.112 B.A. L.208 J.D. [⊠ Stone&H.]

**Sturman, Deborah M.** ..........................'— '95 C.999 L.1068 J.D. [⊠ Freshman,M.O.C.&K.]
*PRACTICE AREAS: Securities.
Sugarman, Ronald S. ..........'41 '83 C.800 B.A. L.809 J.D. 433 N. Camden Rd., 12th Fl.

**Supnik, Paul D., (AV) '47 '72 C.112 B.S. L.1065 J.D. ⊞**
**Suite 1200 Wells Fargo Bank Building, 433 North Camden Drive, 90210**
**Telephone: 310-205-2050 Telex: 292416 Facsimile: 310-205-2011**
**Email: ps@supnik.com URL: http://www.supnik.com**
***REPORTED CASES: Brewer v. Hustler Magazine Inc., 749 F.2d 527 (9th Cir. 1984); Poe v. Missing Persons, 745 F. 2d 1238 (9th Cir. 1984).**
**Domestic and International Copyright and Trademark Law, Motion Picture, Television, Publishing, Media and General Entertainment Law, Multimedia and Internet Law. Licensing, Related Litigation.**
*See Professional Biographies, BEVERLY HILLS, CALIFORNIA*

**Susman, Allen E.**, (AV) ....................'19 '47 C&L.309 A.B., J.D. [Rosenfeld,M.&S.]
*PRACTICE AREAS: Litigation; Antitrust Law; Entertainment Law.
Sutton, Ronald T. ...............'36 '64 C.145 B.A. L.1068 LL.B. 291 S. La Cienega Blvd.
Swanson, Walter L. '32 '65 C.999 L.1065 LL.B.
V.P., Legal Affs., Twentieth Century Fox Film Corp.
**Sweeney, Paul W., Jr.** ..............'50 '75 C.800 B.S. L.178 J.D. [Freshman,M.O.C.&K.]
*PRACTICE AREAS: Commercial Litigation; Real Estate Litigation; Banking Litigation; Creditor's Rights; Employment Litigation.
Swerdlow, Edith L. ..........................'21 '46 C.331 B.A. L.178 LL.B. 617 N. Linden Dr.
Swerdlow, Harry B., (AV) ...............'18 '44 C.563 A.B. L.178 LL.B. 345 N. Maple Dr.
Swerdlow, Jonathan A. ....................'55 '81 C.813 B.A. L.800 J.D. 345 N. Maple Dr.
**Swerdlow, Seymour**, (AV) ..........'38 '63 C.186 B.C.E. L.569 LL.B. [Swerdlow,F.&S.]
*PRACTICE AREAS: Management, Labor and Employment Law.

**Swerdlow, Florence & Sanchez, A Law Corporation, (AV) ⊞**
**Suite 828, 9401 Wilshire Boulevard, 90212**
**Telephone: 310-201-4700 Fax: 310-273-8680**
**Email: lucihamilton@compuserve.com**
**Seymour Swerdlow; Kenneth J. Florence; Millicent N. Sanchez; Sandy K. Rathbun; Rosario M. Tobias; Amy R. Pleatman.**
**Management, Labor and Employment Law.**
*See Professional Biographies, BEVERLY HILLS, CALIFORNIA*

**Szymanski, Robert M.** ..........'68 '95 C.112 A.B. L.309 J.D. [Weissmann,W.B.C.&S.]
*PRACTICE AREAS: Entertainment Law; Media Law.
Tabachnick, Neal K. ..................'54 '83 C.33 B.A. L.426 J.D. 9601 Wilshire Blvd. 4th Fl.
Tabibi, Nico N. ...........'67 '93 C.112 B.A. L.1035 J.D. 9454 Wilshire Blvd., Penthouse
**Taksar, Jodi Zucker** ....................................'58 '85 C.112 B.A. L.809 J.D. [Wilner,K.&S.]
**Tamaddon, Ray** ......................................'63 '89 C.95 A.B. L.94 J.D. [⊠ Rosenfeld,M.&S.]
*LANGUAGES: Farsi.
*PRACTICE AREAS: Insurance Law; General Business; Appellate Practice; Environmental Law.

**Tardiff, David C., Law Offices of '34 '63 C.112 B.A. L.1068 LL.B.**
**8888 Olympic Boulevard, 90211**
**Telephone: 310-247-8237 Facsimile: 310-271-8196**
**Email: 76020.1167@COMPUSERVE.COM**
***PRACTICE AREAS: Civil RICO; Criminal Law; Personal Injury; Products Liability; Medical Malpractice.**
**Personal Injury and Criminal Law.**
*See Professional Biographies, BEVERLY HILLS, CALIFORNIA*

**Tarlow, Barbara** .......................'44 '86 C.94 B.A. L.426 J.D. [Glassman,B.&S.]
*PRACTICE AREAS: Defamation and Invasion of Privacy; Defense of Media Torts; Civil Litigation.
Taschner, Dana B., (AV⊕) '60 '88 C.800 B.A. L.312 J.D.
[D.B.Taschner] (⊙Dallas, TX)
Taschner, Dana B., P.C., (AV⊕) ......9454 Wilshire Boulevard, Suite 550 (⊙Dallas, TX.)
Taus, Irachmil B., II ................................................................'39 '69 P.O. Box 3307
**Taylor, Gretchen Wellman**, (AV) ............'45 '79 C.426 B.A. L.809 J.D. [⊠ Jaffe&C.]
*LANGUAGES: Spanish, French.
*PRACTICE AREAS: Family Law.
Telerant, Michael M. ..................'37 '78 C.94 B.A. L.1136 J.D. 400 S. Beverly Dr.
**Teller, Walter S.**, (AV) ...........................'45 '78 C.188 A.B. L.1066 J.D. [Hansen,J.T.&H.]
*PRACTICE AREAS: Entertainment Law; Motion Picture Law; Television Law; Copyright Law.
**Telles, Bruce** ..............................................'54 '87 C.94 B.A. L.93 J.D. [Rosenfeld,M.&S.]
*LANGUAGES: Portuguese.
*PRACTICE AREAS: Civil Litigation; Insurance Coverage Law; Environmental Law; Intellectual Property.
**Tenenbaum, Irwin J.**, (AV) .....................'39 '64 C&L.659 B.S.E., LL.B. [Sinclair T.O.&E.]
Tenzer, David S. ......................'51 '76 C.1169 A.B. L.1067 J.D. 9830 Wilshire Blvd.
Thaler, Howard L., (AV) ..................'31 '59 C.112 B.A. L.800 J.D. 9401 Wilshire Blvd.
Thaler, John H. .............................'64 '90 C.112 B.A. L.1049 J.D. 9401 Wilshire Blvd.
**Thau, Robert H.**, (AV) ........................'39 '65 C.112 B.A. L.309 LL.B. [Rosenfeld,M.&S.]
*PRACTICE AREAS: Commercial Law; Entertainment Litigation; Family Law.
Thomas, William H. ...................................'55 '85 C.823 B.S. L.809 J.D. [W.H.Thomas]
Thomas, William H., A P.L.C. ......................................................8501 Wilshire Blvd.
Thompson, Larry A. .....................'44 '68 C&L.500 B.B.A., J.D. 345 N. Maple Dr.
**Thompson, Richard D.** ...................'55 '80 C.309 A.B. L.813 J.D. [Bloom,H.C.D.&K.]
**Tigerman, Bert Z.**, (AV) ...................'29 '54 C&L.597 B.S., J.D. [⊠ Turner,G.W.A.&Y.]
*PRACTICE AREAS: Probate Law; Real Property Law; Business Litigation.
Tilem, Joseph N., (AV) ..............................'27 '53 C.112 A.B. L.1068 LL.B. [Tilem&G.]
Tilem & Gole, (AV) ...............................................................9454 Wilshire Blvd.
Tilles, Mandy, (AV) ...........................'44 '70 C.112 B.A. L.1068 J.D. [Tilles,W.K.&G.]
Tilles, Webb, Kulla & Grant, A Law Corporation, (AV)
433 North Camden Drive, Suite 1010
**Tobias, Rosario M.** ...................'56 '88 C.112 A.B. L.1068 J.D. [Swerdlow,F.&S.]
*LANGUAGES: Spanish.
**Toczek, Fred D.** ................................'64 '89 C.112 B.A. L.800 J.D. [⊠ Gang,T.R.&B.]
*PRACTICE AREAS: Entertainment Law.
Tolt, Nikki ....................................'55 '83 C.112 B.A. L.426 J.D. 9024 W. Olympic Blvd.
Tordjmann, Dom ...................'62 '89 C.976 A.B. L.800 J.D. 9507 Santa Monica Blvd.
Tortu, William, (AV) ........ '50 '75 C.659 B.A. L.273 J.D. 270 N. Canyon Dr., 3rd Floor
**Toscher, Steven R.** .........................'53 '79 C.549 B.A.B.A. L.1049 J.D. [Hochman,S.&D.]
*PRACTICE AREAS: Civil and Criminal Tax Litigation and Tax Controversy (Federal and State).
Trabolsi, Ilene E. ..........................'46 '82 C.477 B.A. L.1068 J.D. 345 N. Maple Dr.
Traister, F. Brad ..............................................'42 '70 L.1095 LL.B. [Lichterman,T.&B.]
**Trattner, Darren M.** ...............'68 '94 C.112 B.A. L.1066 J.D. [⊠ Rosenfeld,M.&S.]
*LANGUAGES: French.
Traub, Henry L. .............................................'10 '32 C&L.800 B.A., LL.B. P.O. Box 1345‡

**Triffo, Eve, (AV) '— '74 C.1044 B.A. L.1068 J.D.**
**9300 Wilshire Boulevard, Suite 200, 90212**
**Telephone: 310-278-7556 Fax: 310-276-5632**
***PRACTICE AREAS: Bankruptcy; Business Litigation; Health Care Litigation; Appellate. Bankruptcy, Business Litigation, Health, Civil Law, Appellate Law.**
*See Professional Biographies, BEVERLY HILLS, CALIFORNIA*

**Triggs, D. Thomas** .........................'67 '93 C&L.990 B.A., J.D. [⊠ Rosenfeld,M.&S.]
*LANGUAGES: Spanish.
*PRACTICE AREAS: Corporate; Securities; Intellectual Property; Entertainment.
Tringali, Donald J. ..............'58 '82 C.112 A.B. L.309 J.D. 9601 Wilshire Blvd. 4th Fl.

CAA32P

**Trojan, R. Joseph** ................'61 '88 C.800 B.S. L.426 J.D. [Trojan] (See Pat. Sect.)
*PRACTICE AREAS: Patent and Trademark Litigation and Prosecution; Intellectual Property Licensing; Copyright; Trade Secrets.

**Trojan Law Offices**
**Wells Fargo Bank Building, 433 North Camden Drive Fourth Floor, 90210**
**Telephone: 310-281-1662 Telecopier: 310-281-1664**
**Email: trojanlaw@aol.com**
**R. Joseph Trojan. Associate: Eric J. Aagaard. Of Counsel: J. Nicholas Gross; L. Rae Connet. Patent and Trademark Litigation.**

*See Professional Biographies, BEVERLY HILLS, CALIFORNIA*

Trope, Michael L. '51 '87
C.800 B.A. L.426 J.D. 9606 Santa Monica Blvd. (©Los Angeles)
Trugman, Richard S. ....................'42 '66 C.112 L.809 LL.B. 9350 Wilshire Blvd.
Tschopik, Kathryn ....................'— '77 C.112 A.B. L.1066 J.D. 228 S. Beverly Dr.
**Tucker, Kaye E.** ....................'51 '76 C.112 B.A. L.426 J.D. [Tucker&B.]

**Tucker & Baum, (AV)**
**228 South Beverly Drive, 90212**
**Telephone: 310-246-6600 Telecopier: 310-246-6622**
**Kaye E. Tucker; Michael C. Baum. Associates: Gary J. Lorch.**
**General Commercial and Business Practice. Civil Litigation, Commercial, Arbitration, Real Estate, Corporate, Copyright and Family Law.**

*See Professional Biographies, BEVERLY HILLS, CALIFORNIA*

**Turkel, Robert** ............'44 '75 C.800 B.A. L.426 J.D. Sr. Trust Coun., City Natl. Bk.
**Turner, Alison M.** ..............'40 '84 C.681 A.B. L.1068 J.D. [⊠ Greines,M.S.&R.]
*PRACTICE AREAS: Appellate Law.
**Turner, Keith J.** ....................'64 '91 C.966 B.A. L.146 J.D. [⊠ Rubin&E.]
*PRACTICE AREAS: Business Litigation; Title Insurance Law; Real Property; Insurance Coverage.
**Turner, Rubin M.**, (AV) ...............'37 '61 C.112 B.A. L.1068 J.D. [Turner,G.W.A.&Y.]
*PRACTICE AREAS: Real Estate Law; Construction Law; Corporate Law; International Law; Business Law.

**Turner, Gerstenfeld, Wilk, Aubert & Young, LLP, (AV)**
**Formerly Turner, Gerstenfeld, Wilk & Tigerman**
**Suite 510, 8383 Wilshire Boulevard, 90211**
**Telephone: 213-653-3900 Facsimile: 213-653-3021**
**Members of Firm: Rubin M. Turner; Gerald F. Gerstenfeld; Barry R. Wilk; Ronald D. Aubert; Steven E. Young; Edward Friedman; Michael J. Hanna; Linda Wight Mazur. Associates: Dortha Larene Pyles; Steven A. Morris; Diane H. Pappas; Vicki L. Cresap. Of Counsel: Bert Z. Tigerman.**
**General Civil Practice. Civil Litigation, Real Estate, Construction, Probate, Tax, Estate Planning and Family, Franchise, Entertainment, Intellectual Property, Cellular Communication, International, Corporation and Business Law.**

*See Professional Biographies, BEVERLY HILLS, CALIFORNIA*

**Turpin, Kathryn L.** ....................'55 '80 C&L.846 B.A., J.D. [⊠ Glassman,B.&S.]
*PRACTICE AREAS: Business Transactional; Corporate Planning; Taxation Law; General Business; Partnership Planning.
**Tyre, Norman R.**, (AV) ...............'10 '33 C.813 B.A. L.309 LL.B. [Gang,T.R.&B.]
*PRACTICE AREAS: Entertainment Law; Real Estate; General Business.
**Ulich, David C.** ....................'59 '84 C.311 B.A. L.1068 J.D. [Rosenfeld,M.&S.]
*LANGUAGES: German and French.
*PRACTICE AREAS: Taxation Law; Corporate Law; Tax-Exempt Organizations; Charitable Trusts and Foundations; Amateur Sports Law.
Ullman, Michael D., (AV) ...............'49 '73 C.112 L.426 J.D. 8383 Wilshire Blvd.
**Ulloa, Denise D.** ..............'60 '96 C.024 B.Ed. L.940 J.D. [⊠ Vorzimer,G.M.&E.]
*LANGUAGES: French.
*PRACTICE AREAS: Entertainment Law; Civil Litigation.
**Unger, Leonard**, (AV) ...............'47 '71 C.112 B.A. L.1066 J.D. [Levine&U.]
*PRACTICE AREAS: Civil Trial; Corporate; Real Estate; Estate Planning; Probate.
Unger, Steven H. ....................'58 '85 C.30 B.S. L.1148 J.D. 8383 Wilshire Blvd.
Usow, Jason S. ....................'54 '79 C.966 B.A. L.436 J.D. [J.S.Usow]
Usow, Jason S., A Prof. Corp. .................... 433 N. Camden Dr.
Vaughan, Larry B. ...........'39 '68 C.679 B.S.E.E. L.347 J.D. 9606 Santa Monica Blvd.
**Velazquez, Joan B.**, (AV) ...............'50 '78 C.1029 B.S. L.800 J.D. [Ervin,C.&J.]
*PRACTICE AREAS: Finance Taxation Law; Real Property Law; Environmental Law; Business and Securities Law.
Victor, Robert E., (AV) ...............'29 '53 C.994 L.724 LL.B. 722 N. Walden Dr.
Vidibor, Sheldon, (Inc.) ...............'33 '64 C.1016 B.S.C. L.800 J.D. 8804 Charleville Blvd.
Vokulich, Richard M. .... '— '85 C.569 B.S. L.426 J.D. V.P., Bus. Affs., Fox Bdcstg. Co.
**Vorzimer, Andrew W.** ...............'63 '88 C.472 B.A. L.1148 J.D. [Vorzimer,G.M.&E.]
*REPORTED CASES: North River Insurance Co. v American Home Assurance Co., 210 Cal. App. 3d 108 (1989).
*PRACTICE AREAS: Complex Business Litigation; General Civil Litigation; Appeals; Entertainment.

**Vorzimer, Garber, Masserman & Ecoff, A Professional Corporation**
**8383 Wilshire Boulevard Suite 750, 90211**
**Telephone: 213-782-1400 Facsimile: 213-782-1850**
**Email: vgm8383@earthlink.net URL: http://members.aol.com/vgm8383/vgmhome.htm**
**Andrew W. Vorzimer; Steven M. Garber; Dean Masserman; Lawrence C. Ecoff;—Datev K. Shenian; Denise D. Ulloa; Lynn R. Levitan. Of Counsel: William W. Handel; John K. Ciccarelli; Thomas J. Ryu.**
**General Civil, Trial and Appellate Practice in all State and Federal Courts and Administrative Agencies. Business Litigation, Corporate, Real Estate, Criminal Defense, Insurance Coverage, Entertainment, Wrongful Termination and Discrimination, Unfair Competition, Constitutional and Civil Rights Litigation.**

*See Professional Biographies, BEVERLY HILLS, CALIFORNIA*

**Wake, Charles K., Law Offices of '51 '78 C.1169 B.A. L.1066 J.D.**
**8484 Wilshire Boulevard, Suite 850, 90211-3227**
**Telephone: 213-782-7730 Fax: 213-782-0177**
***REPORTED CASES: Arista Films v. Gilford Securities.**
**Entertainment Law, Business Litigation, Employment Law.**

*See Professional Biographies, BEVERLY HILLS, CALIFORNIA*

**Waldman, Julie B.** ............'67 '92 C.103 B.A. L.800 J.D. [⊠ Weissmann,W.B.C.&S.]
*PRACTICE AREAS: Entertainment; Business Litigation.
Waldman, Mark ...............'51 '75 C.831 A.B. L.1068 J.D. 9606 Santa Monica Blvd.
Walker, Joan F. ....................'45 '79 C.881 A.B. L.1234 J.D. Dep. Dist. Atty.
**Wallace, Edward E.** ....................'53 '79 C.147 B.A. L.1065 J.D. [Wilner,K.&S.]
Wallach, Michael J. '54 '75 C.1138 B.B.A. L.818 J.D.
(adm. in NY; not adm. in CA) 9465 Wilshire Blvd.
Wallet, Andrew M. ....................'53 '80 C.102 B.A. L.1179 J.D. 405 S. Beverly Dr.
Walther, Mark '60 '86 C&L.112 B.A., J.D.
(adm. in HI; not adm. in CA) V.P. & Coun., National Partnership Investments Corp.
Walton, Shauná S. ...............'43 '78 C&L.101 B.A., J.D. Ste. 700, 9601 Wilshire Blvd.
Wander, Perry C. ...............'55 '82 C.770 A.B. L.1095 J.D. 9777 Wilshire Blvd.
Ward, Dean M. ....................'51 '77 C.112 B.A. L.426 J.D. [Ward,K.&J.]
Ward, Joel M. ....................'34 '63 C.209 B.S. L.146 J.D. 8383 Wilshire Blvd.
Ward, Rika van Dam ....................'52 '77 C.668 B.A. L.426 J.D. [Ward,K.&J.]
Ward, Kroll & Jampol, A Law Corporation, (AV) .......... 9107 Wilshire Blvd., Ste., 400
**Ware, Thomas M., II** ....................'64 '89 C.549 B.A. L.426 J.D. [⊠ Wilner,K.&S.]
Warren, Arthur D. ....................'33 '75 C.112 B.A. L.426 J.D. 9777 Wilshire Blvd.
Warren, Edie Wittick, (BV) ...............'40 '83 C.112 B.A. L.1137 J.D. [⊠ Arlene C.-S.]
Warren, Joel ....................'42 '81 C.112 B.S.L. L.1136 J.D. 8447 Wilshire Blvd.

**Warren, Stephen P.** ....................'60 '85 C.197 B.A. L.309 J.D. [Hansen,J.T.&H.]
*PRACTICE AREAS: Entertainment Law; Motion Picture Law; Television Law; Copyright Law.
Watson, Thomas Bernard ...............'69 '95 C.309 A.B. L.276 J.D. [⊠ M.Factor III]
**Waxman, Robert M.** ....................'53 '79 C.800 B.A. L.1068 J.D. [Ervin,C.&J.]
*PRACTICE AREAS: Partnership Problems and Dissolutions; Real Property Law; Unfair Competition; Business Tort Litigation.
**Weakley, Heather L.** ....................'68 '95 C.763 B.A. L.809 J.D. [⊠ Stone&H.]
**Webb, Elizabeth E.** ....................'55 '92 C.347 A.B. L.800 J.D. [⊠ Ervin,C.&J.]
*PRACTICE AREAS: Business Litigation.
Webb, Stephen P., (AV) ...............'46 '71 C.1077 B.A. L.1049 J.D. [Tilles,W.K.&G.]
**Weber, David E.** ...............'60 '86 C.813 A.B. L.800 J.D. [⊠ Bloom,H.C.D.&K.]
**Weber, Jonathan S.** ...............'57 '83 C.1044 B.A. L.1148 J.D. [⊠ Sherman,D.&P.]
Weber, Robert D. ...............'67 '92 C.339 B.A. L.146 J.D. 9665 Wilshire Blvd.
**Webster, J. Michael** ....................'47 '74 C.1077 B.A. L.426 J.D. [Frydrych&W.]
*PRACTICE AREAS: Products Liability Law; Business Litigation; Family Law.
Wegner, Steven D. .........'48 '73 C.990 B.A. L.800 J.D. 9100 Wilshire Blvd., 7th Fl. W.

**Weiner, Richard S. '40 '66 C.208 B.S.B.A. L.800 J.D.**
**315 South Beverly Drive, Suite 315, 90212-4309**
**Telephone: 310-277-2323 (Evening Voice Mail EXT. 293) Evening: 310-277-2378 Fax: 310-277-0776**
**Real Estate, Mobile Home Law, Wills and Trusts, Probate, Corporate Law. Mediation.**

**Weinstein, Jerome E., (P.C.)**, (AV) ......'35 '60 C.94 A.B. L.309 LL.B. [Weinstein&H.]
*PRACTICE AREAS: Entertainment Law; Copyright; Corporate Law.
Weinstein, Stanley R., (AV) ...............'32 '60 C.112 B.S. L.1068 J.D. [Weinstein&W.]

**Weinstein and Hart, (AV)**
**A Partnership including a Professional Corporation**
**Imperial Bank Building, 9777 Wilshire Boulevard, Suite 1009, 90212-1901**
**Telephone: 310-274-7157 Fax: 310-274-1437**
**Email: joehartlaw@aol.com**
**Members of Firm: Jerome E. Weinstein (P.C.); Joseph F. Hart.**
**General Civil and Trial Practice in all State and Federal Courts. Entertainment, Copyright, Corporate and Commercial Law.**

*See Professional Biographies, BEVERLY HILLS, CALIFORNIA*

Weinstein & Weinstein, (AV) .................... 9454 Wilshire Blvd., 6th Fl.
Weisel, Marc M. ....................'44 '74 [Kairys,L.W.&K.]
Weisman, Steven S., (AV) ...............'13 '38 C&L.800 B.A., J.D. Ret. Supr. Ct. J.
Weisman, Walter L. ...............'35 '60 C&L.813 A.B., J.D. 300 N. Small Dr.
Weiss, Eugene J. ....................'40 '69 C.1097 B.A. L.426 J.D. 9595 Wilshire Blvd.
Weiss, Michael J. '65 '92 C.831 B.A. L.1338 J.D.
(adm. in PA; not adm. in CA) United Talent Agency
Weissman, Kenneth A. ......'58 '82 C.164 B.A. L.800 J.D. 8601 Wilshire Blvd, Ste., 900
**Weissmann, Eric, (P.C.)**, (AV) '30 '55
C.112 B.A. L.1068 LL.B. [Weissmann,W.B.C.&S.]
*LANGUAGES: French, German and Spanish.
*PRACTICE AREAS: Entertainment Law (Representing Directors); International Transactions.

**Weissmann, Wolff, Bergman, Coleman & Silverman, (AV)**
**A Law Partnership including Professional Corporations**
**9665 Wilshire Boulevard, Suite 900, 90212-2316**
**Telephone: 310-858-7888 Facsimile: 310-550-7191**
**Email: WWBCS@EARTHLINK.NET**
**Members of Firm: Michael Bergman; Stewart S. Brookman; Stan Coleman; Michael Lee Eidel; Mitchell Evall; Alan L. Grodin; David J. Gullen (P.C.); Henry W. Holmes; Linda A. Kalm; Steven Katleman; Alan G. Kirios (Law Corporation); Anjani Mandavia; Ronald J. Silverman (P.C.); Todd M. Stern; Eric Weissmann (P.C.); Daniel H. Wolff. Associates: Lucy Noble Inman; Melanie Grant Jones; David B. Miercort; Katharine Sabich-Robison; Andrew J. Schmerzler; Robert M. Szymanski; Julie B. Waldman. Of Counsel: Ira S. Epstein; Lawrence B. Steinberg.**
**General Civil, Trial and Appellate Practice in all Courts. Entertainment, Motion Picture, Television, Cable, Copyright, Real Estate, Corporate and Securities Law, Taxation, Estate Planning and Probate.**

*See Professional Biographies, BEVERLY HILLS, CALIFORNIA*

**Weisz, Andrew J.** ....................'25 '52 C.563 B.S. L.800 J.D. [⊠ Inman,S.N.&S.]
Weisz, Edward ....................'50 '79 C.994 B.A. L.472 J.D. 8383 Wilshire Blvd.
Wender, Fern Z. ....................'48 '87 C.66 B.A. L.809 J.D. 9107 Wilshire Blvd.
Werber, Clifford L. '58 '84 C.112 A.B. L.426 J.D.
Sr. V.P., Bus. Affs., Twentieth Century Fox Film Corp.
Weston, John H., (A Professional Corporation), (AV) '44 '70
C.112 B.A. L.1068 J.D. [Weston,S.G.&D.]
Weston, Richard G.N. ....................'48 '79 C.112 B.A. L.145 J.D. 433 N. Camden Dr.
Weston, Sarno, Garrou & DeWitt, (AV) .................... 433 North Camden Drive
**Wexler, David D.**, (AV) ...............'39 '63 C&L.966 B.S., LL.B. [Rosenfeld,M.&S.]
*PRACTICE AREAS: Corporate Law; Securities Law; Health Law; General Business Law.
Wexler, Jonathan E. ....................'44 '79 C.112 B.A. L.809 J.D. 9107 Wilshire Blvd.
**White, Bryan S.** ....................'56 '81 C.112 A.B. L.228 J.D. Hilton Hotels Corp.
**White, David S.**, (AV) ...............'50 '77 C.156 B.A. L.1067 J.D. [⊠ Jacobson,S.&B.]
*PRACTICE AREAS: Real Estate; Business and Entertainment Litigation; Alternate Dispute Resolution; Arbitration.
White, Elizabeth A. .....'56 '81 C.112 B.A. L.426 J.D. Twentieth Century Fox Film Corp.
**White, Michael R.** ...............'54 '79 C.976 B.A. L.1066 J.D. [Beigel L.R.F.G.&W.]
*PRACTICE AREAS: Litigation; Business Litigation; Environmental Law; Entertainment Litigation; Employment Litigation.
White, Neil P. ....................'57 '86 C.37 B.S. L.767 J.D. Crossroads Develop. Corp.
**White, Paul S.** ....................'62 '90 C.101 B.A. L.878 J.D. [Rosenfeld,M.&S.]
*PRACTICE AREAS: Insurance Coverage Law; Insurance Defense Law; Civil Litigation; Environmental Law; Intellectual Property Law.
White, Stanley Z. ....................'35 '84 C.229 B.S. L.1228 J.D. 8500 Wilshire Blvd.
Wiegand, Jane S. ..........'— '72 C.112 B.A. L.1049 J.D. 9720 Wilshire Blvd., Penthouse
Wiener, Martin S. ....................'30 '78 C.569 B.S. L.1095 J.D. 9465 Wilshire Blvd.
Wiener, Neal T. ....................'44 '71 C.112 B.A. L.426 J.D. 9100 Wilshire Blvd.
Wiesel, Bernard P. ....................'53 '77 C.423 B.A. L.46 J.D. 405 S. Beverly Dr.
**Wiita, Douglas P., (P.C.)** ...............'46 '77 C.560 B.A. L.464 J.D. [Norminton&W.]
Wildman, Herman ....................'12 '35 C.563 L.724 LL.B. 260 S. La Peer Dr.
Wiley, Thomas J. ....................'49 '77 C.705 B.A. L.1137 J.D. [Wiley&B.]
Wiley and Bonda, P.C. .................... 9538 Brighton Way
**Wilion, Allan E., Inc.** ...............'50 '74 C.112 B.A. L.426 J.D. [⊠ Wilner,K.&S.]
**Wilk, Barry R.**, (AV) ...............'30 '55 C.339 B.S. L.597 J.D. [Turner,G.W.A.&Y.]
*PRACTICE AREAS: Real Estate Law; Business Law; Family Law.
Williams, Andrew S. ....................'69 '95 C.112 B.A. L.809 J.D. [⊠ Ward,K.&J.]
Williams, Elizabeth A. '68 '92 C&L.260 B.A., J.D.
(adm. in FL; not adm. in CA) 9750 W. Olympic Blvd.

**Williams, Arnold F.**
**(See Los Angeles)**

Willinger, Jay S. ....................'49 '76 C.563 B.S. L.809 J.D. 424 S. Beverly Dr.
**Wilner, Samuel**, (AV) ...............'48 '74 C.112 B.A. L.426 J.D. [Wilner,K.&S.]

**Wilner, Klein & Siegel, A Professional Corporation, (AV)**
**Suite 700, 9601 Wilshire Boulevard, 90210©**
**Telephone: 213-272-8631; 310-550-4595 Facsimile: 213-272-4339**
**Walter Klein; Samuel Wilner; Leonard Siegel; Laura J. Snoke; Wendy A. Goldberg; Jodi Zucker Taksar; Edward E. Wallace; Alan Goldberg; Joseph R. Serpico;—Gary S. Kessler; Marc H. Gold**

(This Listing Continued)

**Wilner, Klein & Siegel, A Professional Corporation (Continued)**
**smith; Floyd W. Cranmore; Teri E. Lawson; Edwin J. Howard; Thomas M. Ware, II; Joshua B. Bereny; James P. Dexheimer; Eric S. Blum (Resident, Brea Office); Patrick M. Malone; Nora J. Hite; Mitchell S. Brachman; Stephen Coopersmith; Neil M. Popowitz; Jeffrey W. Deane; Steven J. Parker (Resident, Brea Office); Heidi H. Ellyn; Darrell J. Mariz. Of Counsel: Allan E. Wilion, Inc.; Richard B. Kott (Resident, Brea Office); Michael J. Grobaty (Resident, Brea Office).**
**General Civil and Trial Practice in all State and Federal Courts. Admiralty and General Maritime Law. Real Property, Corporate, Community Association Law, Insurance, Federal Employers Liability Act and Professional Liability Law.**
**Reference: Mitsui Manufacturers Bank.**
**Brea, California Office: 3230 East Imperial Highway, Suite 309. Telephone: 714-579-2600. Facsimile: 714-579-2549.**

*See Professional Biographies, BEVERLY HILLS, CALIFORNIA*

**Wilson, John D.** ........ '53 '80 C.966 B.S. L.1136 J.D. [Schwartz,W.&W.]
*PRACTICE AREAS: Real Property Litigation; Business Litigation; Escrow and Title Insurance Litigation; Construction Litigation.
Wilson, Lauren W. ........ '54 '81 C.783 B.S. L.426 J.D. 9454 Wilshire Blvd.
Winkelman, Peter M. ........ '29 '54 C.112 B.A. L.800 J.D. 9595 Wilshire Blvd.
Winn, Paul B. ........ '31 '70 C&L.800 B.S.L., J.D. 9336 Civic Ctr. Dr.
Winston, Carol Grosman ........ '41 '84 C.705 A.B. L.1136 J.D. 315 S. Beverly Dr.
Winston, Seymour R., (AV) ........ '26 '51 C.112 A.B. L.309 J.D. 315 S. Beverly Dr.
Winthrop, John '47 '72 C.976 A.B. L.846 J.D.
Pres. & CEO, Winthrop Investment Properties
Winthrop, Marilyn M. ........ '44 '72 C&L.800 B.A., J.D. 1055 Shadow Hill Way
**Wisot, Valerie** ........ '47 '83 C.112 B.A. L.1136 J.D. [Schwartz,W.&W.]
*PRACTICE AREAS: Real Property Transactions; Commercial; Business Law.

**Wisotsky, Linda N., (BV) '43 '74 C.800 B.S. L.1148 J.D.**
**Penthouse, 9454 Wilshire Boulevard, 90212**
**Telephone: 310-273-3737**
**Practice Limited to Family Law.**

Witmeyer, Eric John ........ '54 '80 C&L.861 B.A., J.D. 9601 Wilshire Blvd., 4th Fl.

**Witz, Allen Barry '41 '67 C.1016 B.S.B.A. L.424 J.D.**
**505 South Beverly Drive, Suite 1066**
**Telephone: 310-581-4030 Fax: 310-275-3187**
**(Not admitted in CA).**
**Securities and Finance.**

*See Professional Biographies, BEVERLY HILLS, CALIFORNIA*

**Witzer, Brian D., (AV) '53 '77 C&L.831 B.S., J.D.**
**301 North Canon Drive, Suite 210, 90210-4704**
**Telephone: 310-777-5999 Fax: 310-777-5988**
**Associates: Andrew J. Spielberger.**
**Personal Injury, Premises Liability, Insurance Bad Faith, Professional Negligence with emphasis on Medical Malpractice, Wrongful Termination, Entertainment/Copyright Infringement and Criminal Law.**

*See Professional Biographies, BEVERLY HILLS, CALIFORNIA*

**Wolf, Barry M.** ........ '50 '77 C.1349 B.A. L.276 J.D. [Greines,M.S.&R.]
*PRACTICE AREAS: Appellate Law.
Wolf, Paul A. ........ '27 '56 C&L.800 A.B., LL.B. 332 S. Beverly Dr.
Wolf, Robert S. ........ '28 '52 C&L.800 B.S., LL.B. P.O. Box 3487
Wolfe, Gary S. ........ '55 '82 C.112 B.A. L.426 J.D. 9100 Wilshire Blvd.
**Wolfe, Warren I., (AV)** ........ '37 '63 C.112 B.S. L.426 J.D. [W.I.Wolfe]
*REPORTED CASES: Cossack v. City of Los Angeles, 11 Cal.3d 726 (1974); In re Birch, 10 Cal.3d 314 (1973); Reinbold v. Santa Monica, 63 Cal.App.3d 433 (1977); State of California v. La Rue, 409 U.S. 109 (1972).

**Wolfe, Warren I., A Prof. Corp., Law Offices of, (AV)**
**9401 Wilshire Boulevard, 10th Floor, 90212**
**Telephone: 310-277-5000 FAX: 310-278-4144**
**Warren I. Wolfe.**
**Alternative Dispute Resolution, Managed Health Care, Insurance Coverage and High Technology Law.**

**Wolff, Daniel H., (AV)** ........ '37 '65 C.910 B.A. L.309 LL.B. [Weissmann,W.B.C.&S.]
*PRACTICE AREAS: Corporate Law.
**Wolff, Roberta Marlene** ........ '59 '88 C.976 B.A. L.800 J.D. [Sinclair T.O.&E.]
*PRACTICE AREAS: Corporate; Intellectual Property.
**Won, Chung Jay** ........ '64 '90 C.477 B.A. L.1068 J.D. [Ervin,C.&J.]
*LANGUAGES: Korean.
*PRACTICE AREAS: Banking Law; General Business Law.
**Wood, Cheri L.** ........ '60 '95 C.112 B.A. L.426 J.D. [G.Fishbein]
*PRACTICE AREAS: Family Law.
Woodruff, Cynthia A. ........ '60 '87 C.147 B.A. L.770 J.D. 9401 Wilshire Blvd.
**Woods, Edward A., (AV)** ........ '46 '72 C.112 B.A. L.1068 J.D. [Browne&W.]
**Wright, Brian J.** ........ '61 '93 C.309 B.A. L.112 J.D. [Greines,M.S.&R.]
*LANGUAGES: Spanish.
*PRACTICE AREAS: Appellate Law.
Wyshak, Lillian Worthing, (AV) ........ '28 '56 C.112 B.S. L.800 J.D. 8907 Wilshire Blvd.
Wyshak, Robert H., (AV) ........ '23 '47 C&L.309 A.B., J.D. 8907 Wilshire Blvd.
**Xanders, Edward Laucks** ........ '63 '90 C.228 B.A. L.896 J.D. [Greines,M.S.&R.]
*PRACTICE AREAS: Appellate Practice.
**Yankowitz, B.J.** ........ '55 '81 C.112 B.A. L.800 J.D. [H.B.California]
*PRACTICE AREAS: Corporate Law; Securities; Banking and Financial Transactions.
Yanover, Michael I. '63 '89 C&L.025 LL.B.
The Ice House, 9348 Civic Cntr. Dr., Ste., 200
**Yates, Gregory A.** ........ '47 '72 C&L.793 B.A., J.D. [G.A.Yates]
*PRACTICE AREAS: Product Liability; Tort; Public Entity; Civil Litigation; Trial Practice.

**Yates, Gregory A., A Prof. Corp., Law Offices of**
**Glendale Federal Building, Suite 850, 9454 Wilshire Boulevard, 90212**
**Telephone: 310-858-6944 Fax: 310-858-7586**
**Gregory A. Yates (Member of California Trial Lawyers Association, with recognized experience in the fields of Product Liability, Trial Lawyer and General Personal Injury);—Michael S. Davenport.**
**Personal Injury and Products Liability, Civil Litigation.**

*See Professional Biographies, BEVERLY HILLS, CALIFORNIA*

**Yee, William S.** ........ '64 '89 C.605 A.B. L.464 J.D. [Grebow,M.P.&Y.]
*LANGUAGES: Chinese.
*PRACTICE AREAS: Business and Tort Litigation.
Yeldell, Eric B. .... '— '79 C.1097 B.S. L.1068 J.D. Sr. V.P., Legal Affs., Fox Bdcstg. Co.
Yetter, Larry L. ........ '38 '64 C.653 B.S.Ed. L.851 J.D. Sr. Coun., Western Atlas, Inc.
Yoshitake, Alan T. ........ '60 '86 C.800 B.S. L.569 J.D. 315 S. Beverly Dr.
Youner, Bruce D. ........ '46 '72 C.94 B.S. L.724 J.D. The Mortgage Capital Grp.
**Young, Kathryn A.** ........ '52 '80 C.112 B.A. L.1066 J.D. [Rosenfeld,M.&S.]
*PRACTICE AREAS: Business Litigation; Entertainment Litigation; Criminal Defense Litigation.
**Young, Kenneth M., (AV)** ........ '38 '65 C.112 B.S. L.1068 LL.B. [Kaufman&Y.]
*PRACTICE AREAS: Family Law; Trial Practice.
**Young, Steven E.** ........ '48 '74 C.112 B.A. L.800 J.D. [Turner,G.W.A.&Y.]
*PRACTICE AREAS: Business Litigation; Entertainment Law; Real Estate Law.
Younger, Cathy D. ........ '49 '77 C.112 B.A. L.809 J.D. Western Atlas, Inc.

**Zabb, Robert Michael** ........ '53 '80 C.976 B.A. L.178 J.D. [Nagler&Assoc.]
*REPORTED CASES: Employers Insurance of Wausau and Federal Insurance Co. v. Musick, Peeler & Garrett, Peat, Marwick, Main & Co. 954 F.2d 575 (9th Cir. 1992); Musick, Peeler & Garrett, et al., v. Employers Insurance of Wausau, et al., 113 S.Ct. 2085, 124 L.Ed. 194, 61 U.S.L.W. 4520 (United States Supreme Court 1993); Employers Insurance of Wausau and Federal Insurance Co. v. Musick, Peeler & Garrett et al., 871 F.Supp. 381 (1994).
*PRACTICE AREAS: Business Litigation.
Zack, Gerald L. ........ '48 '86 C.800 B.S.B.A. L.1136 J.D. 9350 Wilshire Blvd.
Zebrowski-Heller, Kathy '50 '77 C&L.966 B.A., J.D.
Pres., Contract Lawyer Placement, The Lawyers Network, Inc.
Zelner, Barry S. ........ '51 '76 C.800 B.A. L.809 J.D. 9777 Wilshire Blvd.
**Zepeda, Andrew W., (AV)** ........ '57 '82 C.1121 B.A. L.602 J.D. [Lurie&Z.]
Zerin, Milton, A Professional Corporation, (AV) '24 '51
C&L.800 B.S., LL.B. 9595 Wilshire Blvd.
Zifkin, Walter ........ '36 '62 C.112 A.B. L.800 LL.B. William Morris Agcy., Inc.
Ziman, Richard S., (AV) ........ '42 '68 C&L.800 A.B., J.D. Arden Realty Grp., Inc.
Zimmerman, Gary L., (AV) ........ '37 '65 C&L.800 B.S., LL.B. [Zimmerman,R.&G.]
Zimmerman, Susan B. ........ '47 '76 C.881 B.A. L.1065 J.D. 703 N. Palm Dr.
Zimmerman, Rosenfeld & Gersh, (AV) ........ Ste. 300, 9107 Wilshire Blvd.
**Zinnemann, Paula Reddish** ........ '36 '83 L.1136 J.D. [Schwartz,W.&W.]
*PRACTICE AREAS: Real Property Law.
**Ziontz, Mel, (AV)** ........ '42 '68 C.112 A.B. L.1068 J.D. [Rosenfeld,M.&S.]
*PRACTICE AREAS: Business Law; Corporate Law; Mergers and Acquisitions Law; Securities Law; Corporate Financings.
Ziontz, Natalie C. ........ '61 '86 C.112 A.B. L.1067 J.D. 9401 Wilshire Blvd.
**Zipperman, Barbara Irshay** ........ '51 '78 C.1077 B.A. L.1095 J.D. [Glassman,B.&S.]
*PRACTICE AREAS: Family Law; Probate Law.
Zohar, Lior Z. ........ '69 '94 C.477 B.A. L.112 J.D. 9601 Wilshire Blvd.
Zoline, Joseph T. '12 '35 C&L.145 Ph.B., J.D.
(adm. in IL; not adm. in CA) 624 N. Canon Dr.‡
**Zolke, Scott B.** ........ '54 '80 C.277 B.S. L.472 J.D. [H.B.California]
*PRACTICE AREAS: Entertainment; Intellectual Property; Civil Litigation.
Zorne, Lee, Law Offices of ........ '19 '69 C.662 B.A. L.809 J.D. 139 S. Beverly Dr.
**Zukor, Abram C., (AV)** ........ '46 '74 C.37 B.S. L.809 J.D. [Zukor&N.]
*PRACTICE AREAS: Personal Injury Litigation.

**Zukor & Nelson, A Professional Law Corporation, (AV)**
**9665 Wilshire Boulevard, Suite 505, 90212**
**Telephone: 310-274-0846 Fax: 310-278-4862**
**Abram C. Zukor; Marilyn H. Nelson.**
**Personal Injury Litigation.**

*See Professional Biographies, BEVERLY HILLS, CALIFORNIA*

Zyskind, Morris ........ '47 '76 C.102 B.S. L.426 J.D. 8383 Wilshire Blvd.

## BIG BEAR CITY, —, *San Bernardino Co.*

**Caldwell & Kennedy, A Professional Corporation**
**(See Victorville)**

Gallagher, Hugh J., III ........ '38 '72 C.981 B.A. L.1026 J.D. P.O. Box 403
Mueller, Gene A. ........ '37 '65 C.352 B.A. L.1065 J.D. 1000 Eagle Mt. Dr.

**Zimmerman, Anne Scanlon '56 '80 C.800 B.A. L.426 J.D.**
**895 Needles Lane, P.O. Box 2458, 92314**
**Telephone: 909-585-6485 Fax: 909-585-6485**
**Email: 74051.432@compuserve.com**
***PRACTICE AREAS: Real Estate; Construction; Family Law; Debtor Collections; Appellate.**
**Business, Family Law, Real Estate, Bankruptcy and Civil Litigation.**

*See Professional Biographies, BIG BEAR CITY, CALIFORNIA*

## BIG BEAR LAKE, 5,351, *San Bernardino Co.*

Beardsley, Alvin W., (BV) ........ '30 '62 C.1060 L.464 LL.B. City Atty.
DeGriselles, Daniel G., (CV) '50 '82 C&L.101 B.A., J.D.
41945 Big Bear Blvd., Suite 227
Drake, Robert S. ........ '35 '72 C.1075 B.S. L.398 J.D. Mun. J.
Erdmier, William W. ........ '43 '72 C.801 B.A. L.1137 J.D. P.O. Box 6942
**McIntire, Christopher D., (CV)** ........ '59 '85 C&L.426 B.A., J.D. [McIntire]
*REPORTED CASES: People ex rel Dept of Transportation v, Jenkins (1996) 44 Cal. App.4th 306; Pacific Scene, Inc. v. Penasquitos, Inc. (1988) 46 Cal.3d 407; Yamaha Motor Co. v. Paseman (1989) 210 Cal.App.3d 958; Markley v. Superior Court (1992) 5 Cal.App.4th 738; People v. Jackson (1991) 1 Cal.App.4th 697.
*PRACTICE AREAS: Real Property Litigation; Personal Injury (Plaintiff and Defendant); Business and Government Tort; Insurance; Products Liability.
**McIntire, Michael V.** ........ '35 '64 C.602 B.S.C.E. L.966 J.D. [McIntire]
*SPECIAL AGENCIES: Consultant, U.S. Environmental Protection Agency, 1973-1975. Consultant, U.S. Land Law Review Commission under contract with Rocky Mountain Mineral Law Foundation, 1968-1970.
*REPORTED CASES: People ex rel Dept. of Transportation v, Jenkins (1996) 44 Cal. App.4th 306; Markley v. Superior Court (1992) 5 Cal.App.4th 738; Hartenstine v. Superior Court (1987) 196 Cal.App.3d 206; Graydon v. Pasadena Redevelopment Agency (1980) 104 Cal.App.3d 631 (trial attorney); Hawthorne Redevelopment Agency v. Friedman (1977) 76 Cal.App.3d 188.
*PRACTICE AREAS: Real Property Litigation; Eminent Domain; Inverse Condemnation; Business Litigation; Governmental Tort Litigation.

**McIntire Law Corporation, (CV)**
**41191 Big Bear Boulevard, P.O. Box 1647, 92315**
**Telephone: 909-866-7697/866-8772 Fax: 909-866-8307**
**Michael V. McIntire; Christopher D. McIntire.**
**General Civil Litigation (trial and appeal), emphasizing Real Property, Eminent Domain and Inverse Condemnation, Business and Commercial (contract and tort), Personal Injury (plaintiff and defense), Insurance Coverage and Bad Faith, Products Liability.**

*See Professional Biographies, BIG BEAR LAKE, CALIFORNIA*

Parde, Kristianna M. ........ '64 '91 C.800 B.S., B.A. L.426 J.D. P.O. Box 6217
Skaggs, Darcy A. ........ '14 '67 C.36 A.B. L.800 J.D. P.O. Box 130677‡
Wynn, Gary M., (BV) ........ '43 '74 C.1075 B.S. L.61 J.D. P.O. Box 1652

**Zumbrunn, Lynn E., A Law Corporation**
**(See Victorville)**

## BIG RIVER, —, *Riverside Co.*

Spelman, J. Francis ........ '23 '62 C.999 L.809 LL.B. P.O. Box 6728‡
Willette, Wayne C. ........ '50 '76 C.1190 B.S.L. L.1137 J.D. P.O. Box 2506

## BIG SUR, —, *Monterey Co.*

Raines, Paula M. '51 '77 C.491 B.A. L.383 J.D.
(adm. in KY; not adm. in CA) Esalen Institute‡

## BISHOP, 3,475, *Inyo Co.*

**Alther, Dorothy** ........ '57 '85 C.793 B.A. L.588 J.D. [D.Buchanan]

**Buchanan, Douglas, (AV) '41 '75 C.549 B.A. L.464 J.D.**
**459 West Line Street, P.O. Box 846, 93515**
**Telephone: 619-873-4211 Fax: 619-873-4637**
***REPORTED CASES: Jacobson v. Glidden, 84 Cal. App. 3d 748 (1978).**
***PRACTICE AREAS: Criminal; Probate; Estate Planning; Civil Litigation; Probate Law.**

(This Listing Continued)

**Buchanan, Douglas (Continued)**
Associates: Mark A. Radoff. Of Counsel: Dorothy Alther.
General and Trial Practice. Criminal and Civil Litigation, Probate and Commercial Law, Bankruptcy.
References: Dean Witter Reynolds, Bishop; Monument National Bank, Bishop; Union Bank, Bishop.
*See Professional Biographies, BISHOP, CALIFORNIA*

Camphouse, John G. ........'46 '72 C.188 B.A. L.800 J.D. Pres., Motivation Develop., Inc.
Fowles, Frank H., (CV) ..................... '32 '61 C.112 A.B. L.1065 LL.B. Pub. Def.
**Hardy, Thomas L., (BV) '61 '87 C.154 B.A. L.1068 J.D.**
**645 West Line Street, P.O. Box 547, 93515**
Telephone: 619-873-8010 Fax: 619-873-8011
Email: 74663.731@compuserve.com
*REPORTED CASES: In Re Cicely L. (1994) 28 Cal App. 4th 1697.
*PRACTICE AREAS: Civil Litigation; Appeals; Criminal and Juvenile Law; Business; Real Estate. Litigation and Criminal Defense.
*See Professional Biographies, BISHOP, CALIFORNIA*

James, Gregory L. ...................'47 '73 C.112 A.B. L.1068 J.D. Dir., Co. Water Dept.
Kratz, Bryson M. ...............'31 '62 C.112 B.A. L.809 LL.B. 400 E. Yaney (⊙Pasadena)
**Maillet, Arthur J., Jr., (CV) '46 '78 C.642 B.A. L.284 J.D.**
**106 South Main Street, Suite 200, P.O. Box 485, 93515**
Telephone: 619-872-1101 Fax: 619-872-2781
General Civil and Criminal Practice Litigation with emphasis on Criminal, Family, Bankruptcy, Probate, Mining, Personal Injury, Real Estate and Indian Law.
*See Professional Biographies, BISHOP, CALIFORNIA*

Mc Daniel, W. Garfield ............'18 '55 C.966 B.B.A. L.1068 PH.D. 621 W. Line St.‡
Olson, Richard E., Jr. ..................'46 '74 C.474 B.S. L.588 J.D. 287-A Academy St.
**Radoff, Mark A.** ...........................'59 '85 C.112 B.A. L.464 J.D. [D.Buchanan]
Richardson, Noll A. ......................'42 '77 C.939 B.A. L.1148 J.D. 287 Academy St.
Stout, Dean T. ..............................'53 '77 C.678 B.A. L.1148 J.D. Asst. Dist. Atty.
Summers, Verne ............................'14 '41 C&L.800 A.B., LL.B. Ret. Supr. Ct. J.‡
**Tracy, Peter E., Law Office of, (BV) '46 '76 C.197 A.B. L.982 J.D.**
**The Bank Building, 106 South Main Street, Suite 200, P.O. Box 485, 93514**
Telephone: 619-872-1101 Fax: 619-872-2781
*REPORTED CASES: McClatchy Newspapers vs. Superior Court (1983-1984 Grand Jury for Fresno County) (1988) 44 C3d 1162, 245 C.R.; People v. Mason (1981) 124 CA 3d 346, 177 C.R. 284.
General Civil and Criminal Practice. Litigation, Personal Injury, Real Estate, Business, Bankruptcy, Probate, Mining and Indian Affairs Law.
References: City of Bishop; Town of Mammoth Lakes.
*See Professional Biographies, BISHOP, CALIFORNIA*

## BLAIRSDEN, —, *Plumas Co.*
Graybill, Lloyd C. ................................ '17 '41 C.264 A.B. L.1017 LL.B. P.O. Box 477

## BLOOMINGTON, 11,957, *San Bernardino Co.*
La Barge, Claralou Ahlen, (CV) ..........'32 '82 C.473 B.S. L.398 J.D. 18410 Hawthorne
Massey, Robert R. ................................'39 '76 C.101 B.A. L.398 J.D. P.O. Box 1320
Taggart, Timothy L. ..........................'50 '76 C.1075 B.A. L.398 J.D. 11750 Cedar Ave.

## BLUE JAY, —, *San Bernardino Co.*
Kastner, Jeffrey L. ..............'42 '68 C.112 B.S. L.1068 J.D. 27180 Hwy. 189, Suite 5
McVay, William R. ................................'28 '63 C.910 A.B. L.800 J.D. P.O. Box 4625
O'Connor, John P. .........................'29 '55 C.112 A.B. L.1066 LL.B. P.O. Box 1729‡
Poston, Carolyn Jo Boeka '48 '82 C.543 B.A. L.546 J.D.
(adm. in NE; not adm. in CA) Co. Law Libr.

## BLUE LAKE, 1,235, *Humboldt Co.*
Platz, Richard S., (CV) ................................. '42 '67 C.597 B.A. L.1066 J.D. City Atty.

## BLYTHE, 8,428, *Riverside Co.*
Cormell, Shaffer T. ..............................'62 '91 C.999 L.1351 J.D. 1130 W. Hobsonway
Dean, Shari L. ..........................................'48 '76 C.112 B.S. L.1153 J.D. Dep. Pub. Def.
Finch, Steven ...........................'48 '78 C&L.1137 B.S.L., J.D. 213 E. Hobson Way
Garst, Robert K. ....................................'33 '61 C.112 B.S. L.1066 LL.B. Supr. Ct. J.
Lorden, Ronald G., (BV) ....................'43 '71 C.112 B.A. L.426 J.D. 16120 Riviera Dr.
Noroian, Edith M. .......................................'26 '75 C.112 L.990 J.D. P.O. Box 730
Swambat, Margaret P. ..................'34 '87 C&L.1241 B.B.A., J.D. Dep. Dist. Atty.

## BODEGA BAY, —, *Sonoma Co.*
Fernwood, Raymond F. .......................................'20 '54 C&L.767 LL.B. P.O. Box 487
Lewis, David C. .......................'38 '73 C.112 M.E. L.1067 J.D. 1860 Whaleship Rd.‡
Simmons, Kathie J. ........................'49 '87 C.1077 B.S. L.1227 J.D. 1580 Eastshore Dr.

## BOLINAS, —, *Marin Co.*
Begley, John C. ....................................... '42 '67 C.197 A.B. L.188 LL.B. P.O. Box 236‡
Kayfetz, Paul D. ...................'43 '72 C.112 A.B. L.1066 J.D. Pres., Paul Kayfetz, Inc.
Le Mieux, Dotty E. ................................................'— '87 C.454 L.1230 J.D. P.O. Box 531
Littlefield, Margaret Joan ......................'45 '83 C.112 A.B. L.1065 J.D. P.O. Box 337
Satris, Michael ....................................'50 '75 C.112 B.A. L.1066 J.D. P.O. Box 337
Siedman, Jack ......................................'44 '70 C.112 A.B. L.1065 J.D. P.O. Box 37

## BONITA, —, *San Diego Co.*
Barnes, Brent O. ......................................'37 '76 C&L.1137 B.S., J.D. 4045 Bonita Rd.
Cazares, Carlos A. ...........................'29 '66 C.763 B.S. L.1049 J.D. 5838 Central Ave.‡
Davis, Curtis Wilburn, (BV) ............'41 '68 C&L.477 A.B., J.D. 5687 Sweetwater Rd.
Dolan, Dwain K. ..................................'40 '76 C&L.1049 B.S., J.D. 3339 Winnetka Dr.
Hildahl, George E., (BV) ..............'29 '75 C.729 B.A. L.1137 J.D. 3345 Rio Vista Dr.
Killacky, Kevin M. ..........................'45 '77 C.424 B.S. L.1049 J.D. 4364 Bonita Rd.
Little, Daniel M. ..............................'53 '86 C.932 B.S. L.1137 J.D. 145 Willow St.
Lohrey, Thomas E., Jr. '32 '57 C&L.902 B.S., LL.B.
(adm. in VA; not adm. in CA) 5821 Shadow Canyon Way‡
Malcolm, Lawrence D. ..............'36 '67 C.800 B.S. L.426 J.D. 4609 Schaumberg Pl.
Ortiz, Marian Kent ...........................'58 '85 C.201 B.A. L.602 J.D. 2839 Degen Dr.‡
Parsons, David E. ..........................'38 '79 C.608 M.D. L.1137 J.D. 5777 Pray St.‡
Phillips, Lawrence ..........................'25 '52 C.999 L.767 LL.B. 3855 Corral Cyn Rd.‡
Powell, George W. '29 '59 C.546 B.S. L.208 J.D.
(adm. in CO; not adm. in CA) 3118 Casa Bonita Dr.‡
Taylor, William H., (AV) ..................'31 '62 C.475 B.A. L.178 LL.B. P.O. Box 130
Williams, George A. '25 '51 C&L.352 B.A., J.D.
(adm. in IA; not adm. in CA) 5104 Glen Verde Dr.‡

## BONSALL, —, *San Diego Co.*
McCabe, Wayne L., (BV) ......................'38 '71 C.800 B.S. L.809 J.D. P.O. Box 569
Stickney, Herbert H. '18 '48 C.610 B.S. L.260 J.D.
(adm. in FL; not adm. in CA) P.O. Box 397‡
Zorb, George A. ..........................'51 '76 C.800 B.S. L.426 J.D. 7867 W. Lilac Rd.

## BOONVILLE, —, *Mendocino Co.*
Rose, Geraldine H. ........................'45 '81 C.1073 B.A. L.1153 J.D. P.O. Box 624‡

## BORREGO SPRINGS, —, *San Diego Co.*
Avery, Dennis S., (BV) ..............................'40 '71 C&L.61 B.A., J.D. P.O. Box 540
Floyd, Curtis L. ...........................'23 '52 C.112 A.B. L.1065 J.D. P.O. Box 2267
**Hurley, Emmet D., Jr., (AV) '23 '52 C.276 B.S.S. L.309 J.D.**
**1442 Yaqui Road, P.O. Drawer 2240, 92004**
Telephone: 619-767-5318
General, Civil Practice. Estate Planning, Trust Administration, Corporate, Real Property, Probate and Financial Litigation (selected cases).

Turner, Harold H., (AV) ..........................'26 '52 C.330 L.1065 LL.B. P.O. Box 1126‡

## BOULDER CREEK, 1,806, *Santa Cruz Co.*
Hayes, Jack A. ................ '14 '39 C.112 A.B. L.1066 LL.B. 245 Boulder Brook Drive‡

## BRADBURY, 829, *Los Angeles Co.*
McAnally, Carolyn S. ..................'39 '79 C.112 B.S. L.1127 J.D. 710 Braewood Dr.
Walsh, Adele, (AV) ...............................'15 '42 C&L.813 LL.B. 215 Barranca Rd.

## BRANSCOMB, —, *Mendocino Co.*
McHenry-Kurk, Amaryllis Verne ............ '47 '79 C.940 B.A. L.809 J.D. P.O. Box 234

## BRAWLEY, 18,923, *Imperial Co.*
Altamirano, Diane Bradford, (BV) ........ '48 '77 C.112 B.A. L.426 J.D. [Boggust,Z.&A.]
Bell, Maryanne ........................................'62 '90 C.112 B.A. L.1049 J.D. 104 W. "I" St.
Benson, John R. ............................'38 '65 C.813 B.S. L.1068 LL.B. 426 W. G St.‡
Boggust, Jack .............................'24 '51 C.112 B.S. L.1065 J.D. [Boggust,Z.&A.] ‡
Boggust, Zimmerman & Altamirano, (BV) ........................................ 202 E St.
Fifield, Harold W. ......................'51 '76 C.800 B.A. L.1068 J.D. Suite 108, 229 Main St.
Horton, Knox, Carter & Foote, (AV) ...........................195 South Second Street
Krutzsch, Andrew S., (P.C.), (BV) ..................'45 '72 C.112 B.A. L.61 J.D. 104 W. "I" St.
Pate, Teri D. .................................'59 '88 C.1074 B.S. L.1137 J.D. 396 Allen St.
Schmitt, Joseph, (BV) ..........................'23 '51 C.347 B.S. L.813 LL.B. U.S. Mag.
Sullivan, Orville W. ..............................'24 '63 C.112 L.144 LL.B. Mun. Ct. J.
Wheeler, Mercedes Z. ................'41 '81 C.763 B.A. L.1137 J.D. [Horton,K.C.&F.]
Zimmerman, Joseph W., Jr. .............................'43 '74 C.763 A.B. L.1049 J.D. Mun. J.

## BREA, 32,873, *Orange Co.*
Abbamonto, George X. '16 '40 C&L.209 LL.B.
(adm. in IL; not adm. in CA) 1226 Harbor Lake Ave.‡
Alhandy, Marlene Amera ...............'— '91 C.940 B.A. L.1137 J.D. 525 Dogwood Ct.
Allain, Melissa M. ...............'52 '83 C.426 B.A. L.309 J.D. Asst. Coun., Unocal Corp.
Anthony, Thomas E. ..................'48 '80 C.101 B.S. L.1137 J.D. 690 S. Brea Blvd.
**Arczynski, Andrew V.**, (BV) ......'48 '78 C.1109 B.A. L.1137 J.D. [Markman,A.H.C.&S.]
*PRACTICE AREAS: Municipal; Redevelopment; Housing Law; Municipal Litigation; Public Works.
Bachor, James E. ..........................................'55 '86 C&L.1137 B.S., J.D. [Carroll,G.&B.]
Baker, Dan N. .............'35 '72 C.69 B.A. L.800 J.D. V.P. & C.O.O., Travelers Inns
Bartlett, John A. ............................'34 '66 C&L.174 B.S., J.D. 500 S. Kraemer Blvd.
Bergquist, Alison E. .............'61 '87 C.1074 B.A. L.1137 J.D. 417 S. Associated Rd.
Blum, Eric S. ......................................'— '92 C.659 B.A. L.800 J.D. [▣ Wilner,K.&S.]
Bollington, John R., (AV) ..........'35 '65 C.665 B.A. L.800 LL.B. [▣ Bollington,L.&C.]
Bollington, Lounsbury and Chase ......................................... 1800 E. Imperial Hwy.
Brandon, S. Mark ..................'59 '85 C.112 B.A. L.1049 J.D. [Bollington,L.&C.]
Buegler, Paul W. ..................................'35 '68 C.585 B.S.B.A. L.1035 J.D. Biola Coll.
Carpello, Joseph, (BV) .......................'53 '79 C.1111 B.A. L.1137 J.D. [Carpello,W.H.&S.]
Carpello, Wishart, Hall & Smith, (BV) ....................................324 S. Brea Blvd.
Carroll, James R. ...........................................................'47 '72 [Carroll,G.&B.]
Carroll, Gilbert & Bachor, A Prof. Law Corp. ..................................711 S. Brea Blvd.
Chase, Eric C. ...........................'59 '85 C&L.1137 B.S.L., J.D. [Bollington,L.&C.]
Chavira, Natividad F. ......................'42 '75 C.L.426 J.D. Unocal Corp.
Corson, George E., IV ..........................'64 '91 C.446 B.A. L.1137 J.D. 3 Pointe Dr.
Crim, Walter W., Jr. ...............'39 '78 C.801 B.S. L.1136 J.D. Asst. Coun., Unocal Corp.
**Curley, William P., III** ..........'57 '86 C.1075 B.S. L.1137 J.D. [Markman,A.H.C.&S.]
*PRACTICE AREAS: Municipal; Housing; Redevelopment Law; Fairs and Exposition Law.
Diaz, Heriberto ..................'58 '87 C.800 B.A. L.426 J.D. 1 Civil Ctr. Cir.
Dickey, Gene A. '52 '81 C.870 B.S. L.494 J.D.
(adm. in MN; not adm. in CA) American Suzuki Motor Corporation
Dixon, Brendan M. ..............................'45 '71 C.339 B.A. L.1066 J.D. Unocal Corp.
**Dolan, John Patrick**, (BV) ...........................'49 '78 C.1109 B.A. L.1137 J.D. [Dolan]
*PRACTICE AREAS: Criminal Defense Law.

**Dolan Law Offices, (BV)**
**Three Pointe Drive Suite 302, 92821**
Telephone: 714-257-3400 Fax: 714-257-3424
John Patrick Dolan. Associates: Stephanie M. Goetze-Kuhns.
Criminal Law.
*See Professional Biographies, BREA, CALIFORNIA*

Dooley, Richard L. ......................'60 '94 C.330 B.S. L.1137 J.D. 711 S. Brea Blvd.
Ericson, Sydney K. ..........................................'42 '72 L.1137 J.D. 110 W. Fir
Ettensohn, Richard L. ..............'55 '79 C&L.339 B.A., J.D. Asst. Coun., Unocal Corp.
Finkle, Yale S. '44 '74 C.277 B.Ch.E. L.846 J.D.
(adm. in TX; not adm. in CA; Pat.) Hartley Research Ctr.
Flores, Dorann W. ....................'49 '77 C.464 B.A. L.426 J.D. 2164 E. Clear Springs Rd.
**Fox, D. Craig** ..........................'52 '81 C.1109 B.A. L.1137 J.D. [Markman,A.H.C.&S.]
*PRACTICE AREAS: Municipal Law and Litigation.
Foy, Susan Farris .......................'62 '90 C.112 B.A. L.426 J.D. 743 S. Brea Blvd
Frieman, Shlomo ......... '48 '75 C.705 B.S.B.A. L.564 J.D. Hartley Research Ctr. (Pat.)
Garcia, Thomas K., (BV) ........................'50 '76 C.740 B.A. L.1137 J.D. 3 Pointe Dr.
Garland, E. Jane ..........................'42 '88 C.1042 B.A. L.1137 J.D. [Carpello,W.H.&S.]
Gilbert, Guy J. ..........................................'49 '80 C.1042 B.A. L.1137 J.D. [Carroll,G.&B.]
**Goetze-Kuhns, Stephanie M.** ...........................'64 '91 C.112 B.A. L.809 J.D. [▣ Dolan]
*PRACTICE AREAS: Criminal Defense Law; Estate Planning.
Grobaty, Michael J. .........................'61 '86 C&L.426 B.A., J.D. [▣ Wilner,K.&S.]
Hall, Dean W., (BV) ......................'49 '77 C.112 B.S. L.398 J.D. [Carpello,W.H.&S.]
**Hanson, Ralph D.**, (BV) ..............'52 '80 C.1109 B.A. L.61 J.D. [Markman,A.H.C.&S.]
*PRACTICE AREAS: Municipal; Redevelopment; Land Use Law; Municipal Litigation.
Hiler, Bonnie J. ......................................'50 '91 C&L.1137 B.S.L., J.D. 1698 Greenbriar Ln.
**Hill, Boyd L.** ...........................'60 '89 C.101 B.S. L.893 J.D. [▣ Markman,A.H.C.&S.]
*LANGUAGES: Italian.
*PRACTICE AREAS: Water; Environmental; Real Estate; Construction; Commercial.
Isles, Ronald E. ............................................'38 '86 L.1137 J.D. 595 W. Lambert Rd.
Jacobson, William O. ..........'41 '82 C.563 B.S. L.1137 J.D. Hartley Research Ctr. (Pat.)
Johnston, Linda Osgood .........'49 '80 C.645 B.A. L.229 J.D. Asst. Coun., Unocal Corp.
Jones, Leslie R., (BV) ............................'39 '72 C.800 L.809 J.D. 390 N. Brea Blvd.
Jones, Richard D., (BV) ..........................'49 '74 C.940 B.A. L.464 J.D. City Atty.
Kane, John A. ...........................'55 '79 C.1167 B.S. L.800 J.D. Hartley Research Ctr. (Pat.)
Kemp, Julia A. ...........................'51 '90 C.112 B.A. L.1137 J.D. #1 Civic Cntr. Cir.
Klengler, Joan Leslie ......................'42 '77 C.1171 L.809 J.D. 1800 E. Imperial Hwy.

CAA35P

Kott, Richard B. ....'57 '84 C.684 B.S. L.1137 J.D. [⊡ Wilner,K.&S.]
Krutzsch, Stephen G. ....'50 '77 C.800 B.A. L.990 J.D. Mng. Atty., Hartford Ins. Co.
Lawton, Robert P. ....'26 '51 C.426 L.809 LL.B. 110 W. Fir St.‡
Ledford, Lynn M. ....'61 '86 C.101 B.A. L.1137 J.D. 595 W. Lambert Rd.
Lounsbury, Steven R. ....'50 '79 C.112 B.A. L.1136 J.D. [Bollington,L.&C.]
Mabinton, Loretta I. ....'60 '84 L.061 LL.B. Asst. Coun., Unocal Corp.
**Markman, James L., (AV)** ....'43 '69 C.97 A.B. L.188 J.D. [Markman,A.H.C.&S.]
*PRACTICE AREAS: Municipal; Redevelopment; Water Law.

**Markman, Arczynski, Hanson, Curley & Slough, A Professional Corporation, (AV)**
**Second Floor, Number One Civic Center Circle, P.O. Box 1059, 92822-1059⊙**
Telephone: 714-990-0901; 310-691-3811
Email: MARCZYNSKI@AOL.COM
James L. Markman; Andrew V. Arczynski; Ralph D. Hanson; William P. Curley, III; Marsha G. Slough (Resident, Rancho Cucamonga Office);—D. Craig Fox; Pamela P. King (Resident, Rancho Cucamonga Office); Daren E. Hengesbach (Resident, Rancho Cucamonga Office); Boyd L. Hill.
Municipal, Redevelopment, Water Rights, Real Property, Condemnation, School and Corporation Law. Civil Litigation.
Reference: Southern California Bank (Brea Branch).
Rancho Cucamonga, California Office: 9113 Foothill Boulevard, Suite 200. Telephone: 909-381-0218; 909-980-2742.

*See Professional Biographies, BREA, CALIFORNIA*

Martinez, Ernest R. ....'42 '86 C.990 B.A. L.1137 J.D. Three Pointe Dr.‡
McCay, John F. ....'48 '77 C.112 B.A. L.809 J.D. [Bollington,L.&C.]
McFadden, Edward A. ....'20 '55 L.464 LL.B. 2591 Sand Pebble Lane‡
Melas, Anthony G. ....'46 '71 C&L.597 B.A., J.D. Asst. Coun., Unocal Corp.
Monticue, Deborah Y. ....'— '84 C.112 B.A. L.1068 J.D. Asst. Tax Coun., Unocal Corp.
Mozqueda, Maricela B. ....'— '89 C.1097 B.S. L.1066 J.D. Asst. Coun., Unocal Corp.
O'Brien, Gerard W. ....'56 '91 C.102 B.A. L.1137 J.D. 235 S. Flower Ave.
Orff, George A. ....'44 '78 C.585 B.S.I.E. L.990 J.D. 803 W. Park Crest
Parker, Steven J. ....'64 '89 C.112 B.A. L.1049 J.D. [⊡ Wilner,K.&S.]
Pearson, April V. ....'60 '87 C.1042 B.A. L.990 J.D. Asst. Div. Coun., Unocal Corp.
Peck, Susan Lee ....'64 '91 C.112 B.A. L.426 J.D. Coun., Hartford Ins. Co.
Peniche, Laurel A. ....'59 '88 C.1109 B.A. L.1137 J.D. 1700 Greenbriar Ln.
Radin, David ....'23 '55 C.999 L.809 LL.B. 241 Buttonwood Dr.
Razzano, Vincent J. ....'58 '89 C.823 B.A. L.1137 J.D. Three Pointe Dr.
Reichman, Mark C. ....'66 '93 C.112 B.A. L.1137 J.D. [⊡ Carpello,W.H.&S.]
Salovesh, Charles E. ....'35 '75 C.981 LL.B L.1137 J.D. 565 Candlewood St.‡
Schroeder, John ....'54 '80 C.1075 B.A. L.1049 J.D. 145 S. State Coll.
Slaven, James J. ....'28 '82 C.1258 B.A. L.1137 J.D. 420 Puente St. S.
Smith, John H., III ....'53 '85 C&L.1137 B.S., J.D. [Carpello,W.H.&S.]
Smith, Kendall B. ....'43 '78 C.808 B.S.M.E. L.809 J.D. Asst. Coun., Unocal Corp.
Stoddart, Ronald L. ....'43 '74 C.1075 B.S. L.809 J.D. 1698 Greenbriar Ln.
Taylor, Joel B. ....'29 '80 C.627 B.G.E. L.1137 J.D. 238 S. Orange Ave.‡
Thompson, Alan H. ....'41 '75 C.906 L.398 J.D. Hartley Research Ctr. (Pat.)
Van Camp, Allen C. ....'61 '86 C.1042 B.A. L.285 J.D. [Bollington,L.&C.]
Whelan, Ellen A. ....'60 '85 C.428 B.S. L.724 J.D. Asst. Coun., Unocal Corp.
Wilner, Klein & Siegel, A Professional Corporation, (AV)
3230 E. Imperial Hwy., Ste. 309 (⊙Beverly Hills)
Wirzbicki, Gregory F. ....'46 '72 C.971 B.S. L.426 J.D. Hartley Research Ctr. (Pat.)
Wishart, Barry J., (BV) ....'42 '82 C.101 B.S. L.1137 J.D. [Carpello,W.H.&S.]
Yost, Thomas A. ....'50 '90 C.154 B.A. L.1137 J.D. Legal Dir., Mercury Ins.
Zizzo, Joyce A. ....'56 '87 L.365 J.D. Asst. Coun., Unocal Corp.

## BRENTWOOD, 7,563, *Contra Costa Co.*

Bates, Philip R., (AV) '48 '73
C.112 B.A. L.1065 J.D. COO & Gen. Coun., Hal Porter Homes
Becnel, Christopher A. ....'56 '82 C.1073 B.S. L.770 J.D. 8425 Brentwood Blvd.
Laughlin, R. Gordon, (BV) ....'29 '56 C.763 A.B. L.800 J.D. 11693 San Vicente Blvd.
Rixon, W. Blair ....'08 '35 C.112 A.B. L.1065 J.D. Ret. Mun. Ct. J.
Siino, Horace J., (CV) ....'41 '67 C.768 B.S. L.1065 J.D. 7960 Brentwood Blvd.
Zimmerman, Scott K. ....'45 '75 C&L.878 B.S., J.D. P.O. Box 1120

## BRIDGEPORT, * 240, *Mono Co.*

Denton, N. Edward ....'26 '54 C.549 A.B. L.767 LL.B. Supr. Ct. J.
Eller, Stanley L. ....'49 '74 C.763 A.B. L.1049 J.D. Co. Dist. Atty.
McCarroll, Neil, II ....'44 '69 C&L.800 B.S.L., J.D. Asst. Co. Coun. & Risk Mgr.

## BRISBANE, 2,952, *San Mateo Co.*

Bednar, Walter R. '11 '39 C&L.190 B.S.C., LL.B.
(adm. in NE; not adm. in CA) 8 Margaret Rd.‡
**Girard, Ann Olson** ....'59 '85 C.112 A.B. L.1065 J.D. Corp. Coun., Hitachi America, Ltd.
**Howarth, Steven P.** '57 '81
C.1074 B.S. L.1065 J.D. Western Reg. Coun., Hitachi America, Ltd.
**James, Howard P.** '48 '74 C.855 B.A. L.659 J.D.
(adm. in CT; not adm. in CA) Assoc. Gen. Coun., Hitachi America, Ltd.

## BROOKDALE, —, *Santa Cruz Co.*

Shallcross, Gary Clayton ....'47 '92 C.112 B.A. L.1226 J.D. P.O. Box 311

## BROWNSVILLE, —, *Yuba Co.*

Chapman, Colleen D. ....'52 '77 C.339 B.A. L.426 J.D. P.O. Box 427‡
Guthormsen, Douglas H. ....'47 '93 L.408 J.D. 9138 La Forte Rd.

## BUELLTON, —, *Santa Barbara Co.*

Davidge, Dean G. ....'43 '78 C.154 B.A. L.408 J.D. V.P., SSI Electro-Tech., Inc.

## BUENA PARK, 68,784, *Orange Co.*

Armendariz, Richard C. ....'36 '71 Off. of Appeals
**Black, William Rea** ....'52 '88 C.208 B.S.B.A. L.1137 J.D. Gen. Coun., Sunclipse, Inc.
*LANGUAGES: Spanish.
*RESPONSIBILITIES: Business Law; Corporate Law; Securities Law; Bankruptcy; Litigation.
Fadden, Jerome H. ....'29 '69 6782 Stanton Ave., E.
**Farris, William E., (BV) '29 '60 C&L.502 A.B., J.D.**
**7242 Orangethorpe Avenue, 90620**
Telephone: 714-521-7200 Fax: 714-521-1940
*PRACTICE AREAS: Probate Law; General Business Law; Domestic Relations Law.
General Civil and Criminal Trial Practice. Corporation, Probate, Business and Real Estate Law.
Reference: Frontier Bank.

Fonte, Anthony N., (BV) ....'32 '59 C.381 B.A. L.608 J.D. 5681 Beach Blvd.
Gardner, Michael R. ....'46 '83 C.1109 B.A. L.1137 J.D. 8332 Commonwealth Ave.
Higgins, Lee E. ....'24 '51 C.88 B.A. L.276 LL.B. 6280 Manchester .
Horton, Arletha Ruth ....'34 '61 C.1042 B.A. L.800 LL.B. Off. of Appeals
**Johnson, Byron J.** '44 '77 C.591 B.S. L.1187 J.D.
(adm. in MI; not adm. in CA) V.P. & Gen. Coun., Nutrilite Products, Inc.
King, Jack F. ....'25 '72 C.229 B.A. L.981 LL.B. 8460 Waverly Dr.

Lauritzen, John A. '38 '66
C.112 B.A. L.800 LL.B. Chmn. of the Bd., Stewart/Walker Co.‡
Leland, John S. ....'30 '72 C.208 B.S. L.1001 J.D. 5600 Beach Blvd.
Longenecker, Joel V. ....'33 '68 C.1060 B.A. L.169 J.D. P.O. Box 5076
Lu, David W. C. ....'47 '83 C.628 B.S. L.1137 J.D. Gen. Coun., Yamaha Corp. of Amer.
Plett, Robin J., (Mr.) ....'49 '78 C.668 B.A. L.1137 J.D. Park Auto Glass‡
Roberts, Eugene F. '23 '53 C.187 B.A. L.893 LL.B.
(adm. in IA; not adm. in CA) 5571 Fox Hills Ave.‡
Ross, James G. ....'27 '54 C.475 B.A. L.477 J.D. Knotts Berry Farm
Smiley, George S., Jr., (BV) ....'30 '63 C.352 B.S.C. L.284 J.D. 5681 Beach Blvd.
Stewart, John H. ....'45 '72 C.1097 B.A. L.426 J.D. P.O. Box 5076
Taylor, Robert G. ....'46 '78 L.1137 LL.B. 8081 Stanton Ave.
Tourino, Sherry L. ....'44 '78 8081 Stanton Ave.
Waller, John J., (AV) ....'24 '51 C&L.309 B.A., J.D. 5591 Monticello Ave.‡
Winkler, Ronald C. '45 '72 C.112 B.S. L.1066 J.D.
Pers. Rel. Atty., J.C. Penney Co., Inc.
Zierott, Rex R. '27 '55 C&L.878 B.S., LL.B.
(adm. in UT; not adm. in CA) 4930 Somerset St.‡
Zitny, John J. ....'30 '56 C&L.800 B.A., J.D. 8081 Stanton Ave.

## BURBANK, 93,643, *Los Angeles Co.*

Adelstein, David ....'57 '82 C.319 L.464 J.D. [Taylor,R.B.&G.]
**Aherne, Brian W., & Associates, (AV) '43 '75 C.800 B.S. L.809 J.D.**
**3727 West Magnolia Boulevard, #814, 91510-7711**
Telephone: 818-255-1019 Email: buzzstar@aol.com
Email: BWAherne@juno.com
Personal Injury Defense, Trials, and General Civil Practice.

Ajalat, Gregory M. ....'65 '90 C.112 B.A. L.426 J.D. 3800 Alameda Ave.
Ajalat, Sol P. ....'32 '63 C.112 B.S. L.1068 J.D. 3800 Alameda Ave.
Ajalat, Stephen P. ....'62 '92 C.1077 B.A. L.1137 J.D. 3800 Alameda Ave.
**Aledort, Eric S.** '62 '89 C.881 A.B. L.276 J.D.
(adm. in NY; not adm. in CA) Atty., Walt Disney Pictures and Television
*RESPONSIBILITIES: Entertainment; Intellectual Property/Computers; Internet Online Services.
**Alexander, Wayne Taichi** '54 '75 C.1044 B.A. L.107 J.D.
(adm. in NY; not adm. in CA) V.P.-Coun., Japan Legal Affs., The Walt Disney Co.
*LANGUAGES: Japanese.
*RESPONSIBILITIES: Licensing; Intellectual Property; International.
Allen, James ....'47 '76 C.112 A.B. L.464 J.D. 150 E. Olive Ave.
**Altmeyer, Felicia A.** '55 '80 C.896 B.A. L.273 J.D.
(adm. in DC; not adm. in CA) V.P., W. Coast Develop., The Walt Disney Co.
*LANGUAGES: German and French.
**Altschul, David E., (AV)** '47 '74 C.31 B.A. L.976 J.D.
Vice Chmn. & Gen. Coun., Warner Bros. Records Inc.
Amendola, Anthony J. '62 '87
C.188 B.S. L.813 J.D. V.P., Sr. Employment Coun., Warner Bros.
**Amidon, Robert B.** ....'46 '77 C.871 B.S. L.276 J.D. [R.B.Amidon]
*LANGUAGES: French.
*REPORTED CASES: In Re: Investigation Before Feb., 1977, Lynchburg Grand Jury 1977, United States Court of Appeals, Virginia 563 F.2d 652; In Re: U.S. 1978, United States Court of Appeals, Virginia 588 F. 2d 56; U.S. v. Whitehead 1980, United States Court of Appeals, Virginia 5 Fed. R. Evid Serv. 1046.

**Amidon, Robert B., A Law Corporation**
**3900 West Alameda Avenue, Suite 1700, 91505-4316**
Telephone: 818-972-1800
Robert B. Amidon.
Civil and Criminal Litigation, Commercial Law, Business Law, Employment Law, White Collar Criminal Defense Law.

*See Professional Biographies, BURBANK, CALIFORNIA*

**Antonoplis, Robert A.** '56 '88
C.112 B.S. L.426 J.D. Sr. Coun., Envir., The Walt Disney Co.
Ashley, Mary L. ....'48 '89 C.1273 B.S. L.1049 J.D. 111 N. 1st St.‡
**Austin, Erin Gertrude** '66 '92 C.273 B.B.A. L.309 J.D.
Asst. Gen. Coun., Warner Bros. Records, Inc.
**Bardwil, Steven C.** '51 '77 C.112 B.A. L.426 J.D.
Sr. V.P., Legal Affs., Walt Disney Pictures and Television
**Barkow, Joel Mark** '61 '87 C.475 B.S. L.879 J.D.
Coun., Labor Rel., Walt Disney Pictures & Television
**Basalari, Anthony G.** '61 '87 C&L.276 B.S., J.D.
Exec. Coun., W. Coast Develop., The Walt Disney Co.
Bauer, Philip W. ....'41 '84 C.1097 B.S. L.809 J.D. 2028 N. Valley St.
**Bernstein, Lori** '65 '91 C.94 B.S. L.426 J.D.
Sr. Atty., Walt Disney Pictures and Television
*RESPONSIBILITIES: Entertainment.
**Biebel, Mary J.** '52 '86 C&L.800 B.S., J.D.
V.P., & Assoc. Gen. Coun., Theatrical, Warner Bros.

**Blanchard, John R. '62 '96 C.1163 B.A. L.809 J.D.**
**290 East Verdugo Avenue, Suite 20, 91502-1346**
Telephone: 818-295-6955 Fax: 818-295-6955
General Civil Litigation, Business Litigation and Transactions, Personal Injury, Criminal Defense and Family Law.

*See Professional Biographies, BURBANK, CALIFORNIA*

Bliss, Shirlee L. ....'49 '81 C.768 B.A. L.1238 J.D. 290 E. Verdugo Ave.
Bohannon-Gaunty, Karen ....'57 '82 C.112 B.A. L.1067 J.D. Columbia Plaza
Bond, Michael J. ....'50 '77 C.112 B.A. L.1049 J.D. 441 N. Pass Ave.
**Boon, Robert** ....'54 '79 C.112 B.A. L.426 J.D. [Marrone R.F.&F.]
*PRACTICE AREAS: Products Liability; Professional Liability; Insurance Defense; Personal Injury; Construction.
**Bowman, Ann Katherine** '63 '92
C.502 B.J. L.803 J.D. Atty., Walt Disney Pictures & Television
*RESPONSIBILITIES: Entertainment.

**Bowne, Robert R., (AV) '44 '76 C.1077 B.A. L.809 J.D.**
**Suite 500, 245 East Olive Avenue, 91502**
Telephone: 818-846-5515 Fax: 818-846-5511
General Civil Practice. Probate, Estate Planning and Family Law.

Boylan, Nelson Ross, (BV) ....'52 '77 C.800 B.A. L.809 J.D. 3420 N. San Fernando Blvd.
**Brandis, Bernardine** '53 '78 C.112 B.A. L.1068 J.D.
Exec. V.P., Motion Pictures, Walt Disney Pictures and Television
Brandt, Norman C. ....'18 '45 C.679 B.S. L.1119 LL.B. 530 E. Tufts Ave.
**Breen, Kevin W.** '52 '81 C&L.893 B.A., J.D.
Sr. V.P., Bus. & Legal Affs., Walt Disney Pictures and Television
Bregman, Herbert M. ....'26 '57 C.112 A.B. L.426 LL.B. 308 W. Verdugo Ave.‡
Brock, James C. '44 '70 C.260 B.S. L.362 J.D.
(adm. in FL; not adm. in CA) NBC, Inc.
Brook, Harold N. ....'56 '82 C.112 B.A. L.426 J.D. Sr. V.P., Bus. Affs., NBC, Inc.
**Brown, Denise Gorges** '58 '85
C.801 B.S. L.734 J.D. Coun., Walt Disney Pictures and Television

PRACTICE PROFILES CALIFORNIA—BURBANK

**Brown, Frederick W.** '55 '85 C.112 A.B. L.976 J.D.
V.P., Bus. & Legal Affs., Warner Bros. Records Inc.
Bures, Joseph E. '36 '67 C.608 B.A. L.69 LL.B.
(adm. in NY; not adm. in CA) Sr. V.P., Bus. Affs., NBC, Inc.
Bush, Robert A. .......................... '48 '75 C.112 B.A. L.1068 J.D. [Taylor,R.B.&G.]
Call, Revis T., (AV) .......................... '21 '60 C.999 L.809 LL.B. 1612 W. Olive Ave.‡
Calvert, C. Tok .......................... '53 '78 C.477 A.B. L.800 J.D. Warner Bros., Inc.
Candido, John C. .......................... '33 '63 C.426 L.809 LL.B. 1219 1/2 N. Lincoln St.
Cangilos, John J. .......................... '50 '76 C.321 A.B. L.569 J.D. Columbia Plaza
Cappocchi, Raymond A. .......................... '47 '87 L.398 J.D. 931 E. Verdugo Ave.
Capps, Kendall Earl .......................... '22 '81 C.112 B.A. L.1095 J.D. 714 N. Buena Vista St.
**Carter, Bruce** .......................... '58 '89 C.790 B.S. L.426 J.D. Sr. Coun., The Walt Disney Co.
**Carter, Douglas A.** '60 '85 C.813 B.A. L.1068 J.D.
V.P., Bus. Affs., Walt Disney Pictures and Television
Carter, H. Bruce .......................... '58 '89 C.800 B.S. L.426 J.D. Sr. Coun., The Walt Disney Co.
Cedro, Alfred M. .......................... '51 '79 C.1077 B.A. L.1095 J.D. 301 E. Olive Ave.
**Chapman, Brett Robert** '— '87 C.1077 B.S. L.809 J.D.
Sr. V.P., Bus. & Legal Affs., Walt Disney Pictures & Television
**Chilton, Katherine** .......... '59 '85 C&L.352 B.B.A., J.D. Sr. Litig. Coun., Warner Bros.
Cipriano, Robert F. .......................... '43 '80 C.1097 B.S. L.1095 J.D. 3117 N. Naomi St.
**Clair, Richard F. X.** '— '82 C.674 A.B. L.800 J.D.
V.P. & Coun., The Walt Disney Co.
**Clark, Carolyn L.** '61 '87
C.112 A.B. L.800 J.D. Atty., Walt Disney Pictures and Television
*RESPONSIBILITIES: Entertainment.
Cohen, Robert B. .......................... '52 '79 C.273 B.A. L.796 J.D. Columbia Plaza E.
**Cohen, Valerie A.** '56 '82 C.478 B.A. L.309 J.D.
(adm. in NY; not adm. in CA) Sr. V.P. & Asst. Gen. Coun., The Walt Disney Co.
Connolly, Patricia J. .......................... '53 '78 C.112 B.A. L.1065 J.D. Warner Bros., Inc.
**Conroy, Kristin McQueen** '65 '90
C.668 B.A. L.800 J.D. Atty., Walt Disney Pictures and Television
*RESPONSIBILITIES: Contracts; Entertainment; Marketing.
**Coombs, J. Andrew** .......... '58 '86 C.019 B.A. L.06 LL.B. Sr. Coun., Walt Disney Co.
*LANGUAGES: French.
*RESPONSIBILITIES: Intellectual Property/Computers; Litigation.
**Cooper, Judith Diane** '57 '86
C.1077 B.A. L.426 J.D. V.P. & Sr. Employ. Coun., Warner Bros.
Corshen, Nancy L. '63 '88 C.112 B.A. L.1066 J.D.
Dir., Bus. Affs., Warner Home Video
Costan, Charlotte E. .......................... '36 '84 C.1077 B.A. L.426 J.D. P.O. Box 3083
Cotrel, Thomas P. .......................... '59 '85 C.605 A.B. L.809 J.D. 927 W. Olive Ave.
Crane, Donald H. .......................... '52 '78 C.112 B.A. L.426 J.D. [Leary&C.]
**Cunningham, Robert D.** '49 '75 C.605 B.A. L.1068 J.D.
Sr. V.P. & Gen. Coun., Secy., Walt Disney Pictures and Television
Cutler, Jeffrey L. .......... '54 '81 C.766 B.A. L.809 J.D. 3500 W. Olive Ave., Ste., 1100
**Daitch, Jeffrey A.** '62 '89 C.1044 B.A. L.569 J.D.
(adm. in NY; not adm. in CA) Atty., Walt Disney Pictures & Television
*RESPONSIBILITIES: Entertainment.
**Davine, Howard M.** '56 '82 C.012 B.A. L.426 J.D.
V.P., Network T.V., Bus. Affs., Walt Disney Pictures & Television
*RESPONSIBILITIES: Entertainment; Contracts.
Dazé, D. Timothy .......................... '49 '77 C.426 B.B.A. L.1221 J.D. 3000 N. Clybourn Ave.
**De Franzo, Dennis P.** .......................... '52 '76 C.112 B.A. L.1086 J.D. [Ⓐ Marrone R.F.&F.]
de la Peña, Richard '51 '77
C.800 A.B. L.1066 J.D. Gen. Coun. & Secy., Lockheed Fin. Corp.
**Denenholz, Judy Rimelspach** '52 '77 C.800 B.A. L.1066 J.D.
V.P., Dom. & Intl. Anti-Piracy, Walt Disney Pictures & Television
Depew, David A. .......................... '41 '72 C.1097 L.1008 LL.B. 1446 N. Rose St.‡
**DeRoy, Cathy** .......... '55 '79 C.800 B.A. L.1068 J.D. Sr. Coun., The Walt Disney Co.
*RESPONSIBILITIES: Contracts; General Business; Licensing.
**Detchemendy, Deanna Wollam** '65 '90 C.1077 B.A. L.800 J.D.
Coun., Walt Disney Co.
*RESPONSIBILITIES: Real Estate.
DeVan, Jon W. .......................... '48 '77 C.1077 B.S. L.809 J.D. 1612 W. Olive Ave.
**Devine, Tod A.** .......... '60 '90 C.112 B.S.E.E. L.800 J.D. Coun., Walt Disney Co.
*RESPONSIBILITIES: Contracts; Intellectual Property/Computers; Licensing.
Dickinson, Eugene B. .......................... '28 '65 C.999 B.809 LL.B. [E.B.Dickinson]
Dickinson, Peter S. .......................... '60 '89 C.569 B.A. L.1065 J.D. [Ⓐ Taylor,R.B.&G.]
Dickinson, Eugene B., Inc. .......................... 3312 N. Lamer St.
Doggett, James D., (AV) .......................... '29 '54 C.112 B.A. L.1068 LL.B. 111 N. First St.‡
Downes, J. Kevin .......................... '45 '70 C.454 B.A. L.276 J.D. 1321 W. Burbank Blvd.
**Duke, Alan** '51 '76 C.112 B.A. L.809 J.D.
Sr. V.P., Bus. & Legal Affs., Walt Disney Pictures & Television
*LANGUAGES: French.
*RESPONSIBILITIES: Entertainment.
**Duncan, Patricia** '58 '84
C.668 B.A. L.1066 J.D. Litig. Coun., National Broadcasting Co., Inc.
Edgerton, Lynne T. '47 '72 C&L.880 B.A., J.D.
(adm. in TN; not adm. in CA) V.P., Calstart Advanced Transportation Technologies‡
**Egerton, Anne H.** '54 '80 C.605 B.A. L.1066 J.D.
V.P. & Sr. Litig. Coun., National Broadcasting Co., Inc.
**Ellington, Gary D.** .......................... '52 '90 C.1356 B.A. L.809 J.D. [Ⓐ Marrone R.F.&F.]
**Enzer, Julie** '65 '91 C.112 B.A. L.1065 J.D.
Coun., Consumer Prods., The Walt Disney Co.
*RESPONSIBILITIES: Music.
Ewen, Elaine S. .......................... '42 '81 C.800 A.B. L.426 J.D. [Rawlinson&E.]
**Farren, Merritt D.** '60 '85 C.813 A.B. L.1066 J.D.
V.P., Bus. & Legal Affs., Walt Disney Pictures and Televsion
**Fee, Douglas** .......................... '50 '84 C.1109 B.A. L.45 J.D. [Marrone R.F.&F.]
*REPORTED CASES: Brigante v. Hung, 20 Cal.App.4th 1569, 25 Cal.Rptr.2d 354 (Cal.App. 2 Dist., Dec 14, 1993) (NO. BO48731); Andrea N. v. Laurelwood Hosp., 16 Cal.Rptr.2d 894, Previously published at 13 Cal.App.4th 1492; 18 Cal.App.4th 1698, (See Rules 976, 977, 979 Cal. Rules of Ct.), (Cal.App. 2 Dist., Mar 03, 1993 (NO. BO47221); Stallman v. Bell, 235 Cal.App.3d 740, 286 Cal.Rptr. 755 (Cal.App. 2 Dist., Oct 28, 1991) (NO BO5O327); American Star Ins. Co. v. Insurance Co. of The West, 232 Cal.App.3d 1320, 284 Cal.Rptr. 45 (Cal.App. 4 Dist., Jul 30, 1991) (NO. GOO9430).
*PRACTICE AREAS: Appeals; Insurance; Complex Litigation.
**Feldman, Sherri M.** '59 '84
C.260 B.S. L.724 J.D. Atty., Walt Disney Pictures & Television
*RESPONSIBILITIES: Entertainment.
**Fernea, Laila** .......... '62 '89 C.1168 B.A. L.846 J.D. Coun., The Walt Disney Co.
**Floyd, Christopher S.** '66 '90
C.597 B.A. L.276 J.D. Atty., Walt Disney Pictures and Television
**Fossier, Mary Barnett** '59 '84 C.112 A.B. L.1067 J.D.
Sr. Coun., The Walt Disney Co.
**Foster, Thomas A.** .......................... '47 '73 C.940 B.A. L.1068 J.D. [Marrone R.F.&F.]
*PRACTICE AREAS: Products Liability; Professional Liability; Insurance Defense; Personal Injury; Construction.
**Frederick, J. Alan** .......................... '49 '74 C.112 B.A. L.1068 J.D. [Marrone R.F.&F.]
*REPORTED CASES: Wechsler v. Home Savings & Loan Association (1976) 57 Cal. App. 3d 563; Aetna Casualty & Surety Co. v. Superior Court (1980) 114 Cal. App. 3d 49; Wynn v. Monterey Club (1980) 111 Cal. App. 3d 789; Alameda Tank Co. v. Starkist Foods, Inc.; C.I. Engineers & Constructors Inc. v. Johnson & Turner Painting Co. (1983) 140 Cal. App. 3d 1011.
*PRACTICE AREAS: Products Liability; Professional Liability; Insurance Defense; Personal Injury; Construction.
Friedman, Wallace, (BV) .......................... '25 '63 L.809 LL.B. 301 E. Olive Ave.
**Furie, Daniel I.** ... '58 '83 C.813 A.B. L.800 J.D. V.P., Theater & Business, Warner Bros.
**Gans, Susan L.** '54 '79
C.918 B.A. L.178 J.D. Sr. Atty., Walt Disney Pictures & Television
*LANGUAGES: French.
*RESPONSIBILITIES: Contracts; Entertainment.
Geffner, James, (A Professional Corporation) '44 '70 C.1077 B.A. L.426 J.D.
[J.Geffner]
Geffner, Leo, (AV) .......................... '28 '53 C.112 A.B. L.1066 LL.B. [Taylor,R.B.&G.]
Geffner, James, (A Professional Corporation) .......................... 3500 W. Olive Ave.
Gehan, Bernard J. '39 '67 C&L.262 B.S., LL.B.
(adm. in NY; not adm. in CA) NBC, Inc.
**Gendron, Jay W.** '57 '84
C.602 B.A. L.228 J.D. V.P., Legal Affs., Warner Bros. Television
**Gerse, Steven W.** '56 '83 C.879 B.A. L.339 J.D.
V.P., Bus. & Legal Affs., Walt Disney Pictures and Television
*RESPONSIBILITIES: Entertainment.
Gieselman, Walter B., (AV) .......... '08 '35 C.112 B.A. L.800 LL.B. 800 N. Bel Aire Dr.‡
Gilbert, Jon C. '53 '79 C.112 B.A. L.990 J.D.
Sr. V.P., Studio Servs. & Admn., Warner Bros., Inc.
Gilboa, Tsach I. '57 '88 C.831 B.S. L.940 J.D.
Dir., Television, Bus. & Legal Affs., The Walt Disney Co.
Gold, Stanley P., (AV) '42 '68
C.112 A.B. L.800 J.D. Pres. & CEO, Shamrock Holdings, Inc.
**Goldberg, Karen B.** .......................... '85 '95 C.112 B.A. L.809 J.D. [Marrone R.F.&F.]
*LANGUAGES: Spanish.
Goldman, Karen L. .......................... '65 '89 [Goldman&R.]
Goldman & Ross .......................... 3800 W. Alameda Ave.
**Goldstein, Mark** '54 '78 C.309 A.B. L.800 J.D.
Sr. V.P., Bus. & Legal Affs., Warner Bros. Records Inc.
**Gonzalez, Raymond G.** '62 '87 C.674 A.B. L.813 J.D.
Dir., Bus. & Legal Affs., Warner Bros. Records Inc.
**Gordon, Lawrence M.** .......... '61 '90 C.30 B.A. L.94 J.D. Coun., Warner Home Video
Gorlick, Saml., (AV) .......................... '09 '35 C.188 A.B. L.823 LL.B. 730 Andover Dr.‡
Gottlieb, Ira L. .......................... '55 '81 C.178 B.A. L.1292 J.D. [Taylor,R.B.&G.]
**Grace, Manuel G.** '57 '83 C.602 B.A. L.178 J.D.
(adm. in NY; not adm. in CA) V.P., Coun., Envir., The Walt Disney Co.
*RESPONSIBILITIES: Environmental Law (100%).
Grandy, Donna F. .......... '61 '85 C.112 B.A. L.861 J.D. V.P., Dic Entertainment, L.P.
**Gray, Laurie Davis** '— '81 C.1350 B.A. L.1019 J.D.
(adm. in NY; not adm. in CA)
Dir. of Int'l Bus. & Legal Affs., Warner Bros. Int'l Theatres
Green, Paul H. .......................... '55 '82 C.112 B.A. L.426 J.D. 500 S. Buena Vista St.
Gubler, Marion E. .......................... '30 '60 C&L.878 B.S., J.D. Mun. Ct. J.
Hahn, Helene .......................... '— '75 C.1019 B.A. L.426 J.D. 500 S. Buena Vista St.
**Handlin, Jay S.** '59 '86 C.1036 B.A. L.309 J.D.
(adm. in NY; not adm. in CA) Sr. Coun., Walt Disney Co.
*RESPONSIBILITIES: Litigation.
Hanket, Dominic J., (BV⊙) '47 '76 C.608 B.A. L.117 J.D.
(adm. in OH; not adm. in CA) Asst. Gen. Coun., Lockheed Martin Corp.
**Hanlon, Colleen M.** '58 '83 C.475 B.A. L.477 J.D.
Coun., West Coast, National Broadcasting Co., Inc.
**Harris, Lauryn** .......................... '66 '90 C.1349 B.S. L.569 J.D. Coun., The Walt Disney Co.
*RESPONSIBILITIES: Acquisition/Mergers; General Corporate; Securities/Finance.
Hart, Richard Thomas .......................... '59 '83 C.994 B.A. L.564 J.D. 4000 Warner Blvd.
**Hartman, Andrea R.** '59 '84
C.112 A.B. L.309 J.D. Litig. Coun., National Broadcasting Co., Inc.
**Hausfater, Jere R.** '50 '77 C.94 B.A. L.809 J.D.
Sr. V.P., Acquisitions & Bus. Affs., Walt Disney Pictures & Television
**Hedstrom, Scottye** '53 '79 C.945 B.A. L.893 J.D.
V.P., Network Television & Bus. Affs., Walt Disney Pictures & Television
Heimann, Gerhard M. .......................... '29 '65 L.809 1516 N. San Fernando Blvd.
Helfand, Michael T. '66 '91 C.30 B.A. L.813 J.D.
Dir., Legal & Bus. Affs., Dic Entertainment, L.P.
Hogan, William Hughes .......... '37 '93 C.185 M.A. L.1148 J.D. 1311 Morningside Dr.
**Holland, Nancy E.** .......... '51 '76 C.477 B.A. L.309 J.D. Sr. Coun., The Walt Disney Co.
**Holtzman, Scott R.** '52 '80 C.273 B.A. L.276 J.D.
Sr. V.P., Music, Walt Disney Pictures and Television
*RESPONSIBILITIES: Contracts; Copyright and Trademark; Entertainment.
Horan, John C. .......................... '16 '76 3037 Jolley Dr.
**Horn, Michael A.** .......................... '62 '90 C.112 A.B. L.276 J.D. Coun., Walt Disney Co.
*LANGUAGES: French.
*RESPONSIBILITIES: General Business; General Corporate; Licensing.
Hovsepian, Nora .......................... '63 '89 C.112 B.A. L.398 J.D. 3900 W. Alameda Ave.
**Hoyt, Virginia** '58 '85 C.188 B.S. L.893 J.D.
V.P., Labor Rel. Coun., Walt Disney Pictures and Television
Hunter, John M. .......................... '47 '74 C.1079 B.A. L.464 J.D. Mobil Oil Corp.
Jackson, David A. .......... '44 '68 C.475 B.A. L.912 J.D. 3907 W. Alameda Ave., 2nd Fl.
Jacobson, Kenneth H. .......................... '46 '75 C.800 B.S. L.1136 J.D. 3500 W. Oliver Ave.
Jussim, Jared '35 '61 C.563 L.309 LL.B.
Exec. V.P., Columbia Pictures Entertainment, Inc.
Kalkin, Alan S. .......................... '33 '60 C.945 A.B. L.692 LL.B. Mun. Ct. J.
**Kane, Michele C.** '50 '80 C.1044 B.A. L.145 J.D.
V.P.-Coun., Tech. Law, The Walt Disney Co.
**Kaplan, Lawrence J.**, (AV) '52 '78 C.1169 B.A. L.588 J.D.
Sr. V.P. & Gen. Mgr., Walt Disney Pictures & Television
Katz-White, Rebecca .......................... '65 '90 C&L.813 A.B., J.D. [Ⓐ Taylor,R.B.&G.]
Keeler, Ronald F. .......... '38 '64 C.378 B.S. L.1068 J.D. Pres., Lockheed Fed. Credit Union
Keister, Jean C. .......................... '31 '67 C.999 L.809 1321 W. Burbank Blvd.
**Kellams, Barbara DiFiglio** '48 '78 C.801 B.S. L.424 J.D.
(adm. in IL; not adm. in CA) Exec. Coun., Employee Benefits, The Walt Disney Co.
**Kelley, D. Robbin** '66 '92 C.881 B.A. L.426 J.D.
Atty., Live Stage Plays, Walt Disney Pictures & Television
*RESPONSIBILITIES: Entertainment; Contracts.

**Kellogg, Carol D. '62 '88 C&L.398 B.A., J.D.**
**290 East Verdugo Avenue, Suite 209, 91502-1340⊙**
**Telephone: 818-843-6890 Fax: 818-559-5576**
**(Also Of Counsel to L. Edmund Kellogg).**
**Personal Injury Law. General Civil Practice.**
**Reference: Sterling Bank, Burbank.**

(This Listing Continued)

CAA37P

**Kellogg, Carol D. (Continued)**

**San Clemente, California Office: 118 Avenida Victoria, Suite C. Telephone: 818-843-6890.**

***See Professional Biographies, BURBANK, CALIFORNIA***

Kellogg, L. Edmund, (AV) ... '35 '70 C.602 B.A. L.1114 J.D. [L.E.Kellogg]⊙
Kellogg, L. Edmund, A Professional Corporation, (AV)
290 E. Verdugo Ave., Ste., 201 (⊙San Clemente)
**Kenchelian, Mark L.** '53 '82 C.112 A.B. L.1066 J.D.
V.P., Bus. & Legal Affs., T.V. Animation, Walt Disney Pictures & Television
**Kent, Charles E.** '43 '68 C.447 B.A. L.945 J.D.
(adm. in VA; not adm. in CA) V.P., Bus. Affs., Walt Disney Pictures and Television
**Kim, James** ... '63 '93 C.347 B.S. L.800 J.D. Coun., Tech. Law, The Walt Disney Co.
*RESPONSIBILITIES: Contracts; Intellectual Property/Computers; Licensing.
**Kim, Judy Ann** '61 '87 C.518 B.A. L.178 J.D.
Dir., Legal Affs., Warner Bros. Consumer Products
**King, Marsha K.** '— '84 C.800 B.A. L.309 J.D.
Sr. V.P., Bus. Affs. & Gen. Coun., Warner Home Video
**Kirsh, Pamela** ... '60 '90 C.339 B.S. L.426 J.D. Asst. Gen. Coun., Warner Bros.
**Kishner, Joanna S.** ... '64 '89 C.154 B.A. L.1068 J.D. Sr. Employ. Coun., Warner Bros.
**Klatsky, Gabrielle** '64 '89 C&L.061 B.A., LL.B.
V.P.-Bus. & Legal Affs., Live Stage Plays, Walt Disney Pictures and Television
**Klein, Susan L.** ... '58 '84 C.813 A.B. L.1066 J.D. Exec. Coun., The Walt Disney Co.
Klengler, Ingolf, (AV) ... '50 '78 C.994 B.A. L.809 J.D. 1434 N. Maple St.‡
**Kletzky, Daniel S.** ... '47 '75 C.331 B.A. L.564 J.D. 4000 Warner Blvd.
**Knobloch, Iris Nataly** ... '63 '90 L.061 J.D. European Coun., Warner Bros.
Kohanski, Joseph A. ... '56 '89 C.659 B.A. L.609 J.D. [Taylor,R.B.&G.]
**Krask, Sylvia Jo** '60 '88 C.112 B.A. L.1148 J.D.
Dir., Music Bus. & Legal Affs., Walt Disney Pictures and Television
**Krauss, James L.** '51 '83 C&L.309 A.B., J.D.
V.P., Bus. & Legal Affs., Walt Disney Pictures and Television
*LANGUAGES: French, German.
Kropp, Robert, Jr. ... '46 '74 C.668 B.A. L.800 J.D. [Taylor,R.B.&G.]
**Kuperberg, Frederick** '41 '67 C.112 B.A. L.1068 J.D.
Sr. V.P., Bus. & Legal Affs., Walt Disney Pictures and Television
Kurrasch, Anne L. ... '52 '78 C.813 B.A. L.800 J.D. NBC, Inc.
Lackman, Barbara A. ... '56 '82 C&L.012 B.A., LL.B. Gen. Labor Atty., NBC, Inc.
Ladley, Candace K., (AV) '49 '78
C.1077 B.S. L.809 J.D. 303 N. Glenoaks (⊙Port Orchard, WA)
**Lai, Suet F.** ... '61 '86 C&L.569 B.S., J.D. Exec. Coun., The Walt Disney Co.
*LANGUAGES: Cantonese.
Lamere, Richard C. '50 '75 C.339 B.S. L.365 J.D.
(adm. in IL; not adm. in CA) Lawyer's Mut. Ins. Co.
Landau, Brenda R. ... '65 '92 C.112 B.A. L.569 J.D. 1079 E. Cypress Ave.
**Lawler, Mary** ... '53 '93 C.1042 B.S.W. L.809 J.D. Atty., Warner Bros. Television
**Lazarus, Bruce J.** '53 '90 C.472 B.A. L.809 J.D.
(adm. in NY; not adm. in CA)
Dir., Bus. & Legal Affs., Live Stage Plays, Walt Disney Pictures and Television
*RESPONSIBILITIES: Contracts; Entertainment.
**Leaf, Matthew A.** '68 '93
C.659 B.A. L.800 J.D. Asst. Gen. Coun.- Theatrical, Warner Bros.
Leary, Gary L., (AV) ... '35 '61 C.112 B.A. L.1068 LL.B. [Leary&C.]
Leary & Crane, (AV) ... 4100 West Alameda 3rd Floor
**Lee, Leeton H.** ... '56 '88 C.990 B.S. L.426 J.D. Coun., The Walt Disney Co.
*LANGUAGES: Chinese, Spanish, and French.
*RESPONSIBILITIES: Lease Law; Construction Law; Advertising Law; Marketing Law; Labor Law.
Lee, Paulette W. '47 '76 C.112 B.A. L.809 J.D.
Asst. Gen. Coun., Lockheed Air Terminal, Inc.
**Lee, Peter Y.** ... '66 '93 C&L.112 B.A., J.D. [🄱 Marrone R.F.&F.]
*LANGUAGES: Korean.
*PRACTICE AREAS: Civil Litigation.
Lefkowitz, James J. ... '59 '84 C&L.477 B.B.A., J.D. 500 S. Buena Vista St.
**Leitman, Wendy** ... '56 '85 L.1148 J.D. Exec. Coun., The Walt Disney Co.
Lemberger, Kenneth ... '46 '73 C.994 B.A. L.569 J.D. Columbia Pictures
**Lepow, Gloria S.** ... '64 '89 C&L.846 B.A., J.D. Sr. Coun., The Walt Disney Co.
**Levin, Linda** '63 '90 C&L.262 B.S., J.D.
(adm. in NY; not adm. in CA) Coun., Walt Disney Co.
*RESPONSIBILITIES: Contracts; Licensing.
**Levine, Paul Samuel** ... '54 '82 C.09 B.Comm. L.800 J.D. 4000 Warner Blvd.
**Levinson, Jodi** ... '— '85 Dir., Bus. Affs., Warner Bros.
Lewis, Margaret H. '36 '78 C.473 B.A. L.1095 J.D.
Pres. & CEO, The Burbank Fed. Credit Union
**Lezcano, Abel Michael** '66 '93
C.597 B.S. L.800 J.D. Atty., Walt Disney Pictures & Television
*LANGUAGES: Spanish.
*RESPONSIBILITIES: Entertainment; Contracts; General Business.
**Liberatore, Lisa Winfield** '60 '86
C.112 B.A. L.800 J.D. Atty., Walt Disney Pictures and Television
*LANGUAGES: French, Spanish, Italian, Arabic and Portuguese.
*RESPONSIBILITIES: Entertainment.
Lieberman, David W. '37 '61 C.659 B.S. Econ. L.569 LL.B.
(adm. in NY; not adm. in CA) Pres., Triple Check Income Tax Serv.
**Lieblein, Mark S.** '63 '90 C.976 B.A. L.569 J.D.
Dir., Bus. & Legal Affs., Walt Disney Pictures and Television
*RESPONSIBILITIES: Entertainment; Intellectual Property/Computers; Licensing.
**Lin, Tricia T.** ... '65 '91 C.95 B.A. L.880 J.D. Atty., Walt Disney Pictures and Television
*LANGUAGES: Chinese (Mandarin).
*RESPONSIBILITIES: Intellectual Property; Multimedia Law.
**Litvack, Sanford M.** '36 '59 C.184 B.A. L.276 LL.B.
(adm. in VA; not adm. in CA)
Sr. Exec. V.P. & Chf. Corp. Opers., Gen. Coun., The Walt Disney Co.
*SPECIAL AGENCIES: Bet Tzedek (Board of Directors); Los Angeles Urban League.
**Lo, Clifford** '68 '94 C.976 B.A. L.93 J.D.
(adm. in MA; not adm. in CA) Atty., Walt Disney Pictures and Television
*LANGUAGES: French, German and Italian.
*RESPONSIBILITIES: Copyright and Trademark; Entertainment; International.
Longeretta, A. Thomas '32 '57 C&L.823 B.S., LL.B.
(adm. in NY; not adm. in CA) Group Legal Consultants of Calif., Inc.
**Loock, Kathryn M.** ... '58 '93 C.800 B.A. L.809 J.D. [🄱 Marrone R.F.&F.]
Lopez, Miriam ... '61 '87 C.674 A.B. L.477 J.D. [Taylor,R.B.&G.]
Lopez, Nelida E.M. ... '51 '88 C.061 B.A. L.1238 J.D. P.O. Box 4222
**Loskamp, Alvin N.**, (AV) ... '34 '69 C.813 B.S. L.426 J.D. [A.N.Loskamp]

**Loskamp, Alvin N., A Law Corporation, (AV)** 🄱🄱
**290 East Verdugo Avenue, Suite 103, 91502**
**Telephone: 818-846-9000 Fax: 818-843-1441**
**Alvin N. Loskamp.**
**Estate Planning, Revocable Living Trusts, Wills, Probate, Asset Protection, Business Entities, Business Trusts and Corporate Law.**

(This Listing Continued)

**Loskamp, Alvin N., A Law Corporation (Continued)**

**References: Wells Fargo Bank, Glenoaks Branch, Burbank; Highland Savings & Loan, Burbank.**

***See Professional Biographies, BURBANK, CALIFORNIA***

**Loughery, Don** '50 '78 C.112 B.A. L.426 J.D.
Sr. V.P.-Bus. Affs., Walt Disney Pictures and Television
*RESPONSIBILITIES: Entertainment.
Lowry, Susan Steinhorn ... '56 '93 C.1169 L.398 J.D. [🄱 Taylor,R.B.&G.]
Luppi, Michael D., (BV) ... '46 '73 C.112 A.B. L.1068 J.D. 352 Amherst Dr., #D
Lurie, Leslie K. ... '60 '84 C.112 B.A. L.1068 J.D. NBC, Inc.
**Maatta, John D., Jr.** ... '52 '78 C.767 A.B. L.1065 J.D. V.P. & Sr. Atty., Warner Bros.
Mackey, Robert A. ... '28 '55 C.169 A.B. L.1066 J.D. 4000 Warner Blvd.
**Maloney, Michael B.** '61 '87 C.339 B.A. L.976 J.D.
V.P., Legal Affs., Walt Disney Pictures & Television
Manente, Angelo J. ... '49 '77 C.740 B.A. L.1095 J.D. 2829 N. Glenoaks Blvd.
Maney, Thomas M. ... '39 '69 C.112 B.A. L.1068 J.D. 1701 W. Verdugo Ave.
**Margolis, Lisa** '54 '78 C.568 B.A. L.94 J.D.
Dir, Bus. & Legal Affs., Music, Warner Bros.
**Marrone, Phillip R.**, (AV) ... '43 '70 C.1097 B.A. L.426 J.D. [Marrone R.F.&F.]
*REPORTED CASES: Him v. Superior Court, (1986) 228 Cal. Rptr. 839, 184 Cal. App. 3d 35; Olson v. Arnett, (1989) 169 Cal. Rptr. 629, 113 Cal. App. 3d 59; Waite v. Godfrey, (1980) 163 Cal. Rptr. 106 Cal. App. 760; Transit Casualty Co. v. Giffin (1974) 116 Cal. Rptr. 110, Cal. App. 3d 489.
*PRACTICE AREAS: Insurance Defense; Product Liability; Business Litigation; Personal Injury; Construction.

**Marrone Robinson Frederick & Foster, Professional Corporation, (AV)** 🄱🄱
**111 North First Street, Suite 300, 91502-1851**
**Telephone: 818-841-1144 Fax: 818-841-0746**
**Phillip R. Marrone; Jay Robinson; J. Alan Frederick; Thomas A. Foster; Robert Boon;—Dennis P. De Franzo; Gary D. Ellington; Scot G. Sandoval; Kathryn M. Loock; Peter Y. Lee; James Fitzgerald Robinson; John F. Schilling; Katherine P. Shannon; Karen B. Goldberg; Donald M. Stone; Douglas Fee.**
**General Civil and Trial Practice in all State and Federal Courts. Corporation, Business, Insurance and Probate Law.**
**Representative Clients: Collier-Keyworth Co.; Columbia Pictures Industries, Inc.; Fireman's Insurance of Washington, D.C.; Holiday Inn, Inc.; MCA; Inc.; National Continental Insurance Co.; Textron, Inc.**

***See Professional Biographies, BURBANK, CALIFORNIA***

**Martinez, Elisa M.** ... '57 '82 C.813 B.A. L.112 J.D. Sr. Coun., The Walt Disney Co.
*RESPONSIBILITIES: Litigation; Personal Injury; Products Liability.
Martinez, Marla A. ... '51 '78 C.800 B.A. L.1049 J.D. 303 S. Kenneth Rd.
McGilchrist, Neville ... '56 '81 C.636 B.S. L.990 J.D. 441 E. San Jose Ave.
**McLean, Thomas P.** '65 '91 C.112 B.A. L.813 J.D.
Atty., Bus. & Legal Affs., Warner Bros. Records Inc.
**McNicoll, Elizabeth Carmen** '57 '82 C.860 B.A. L.276 J.D.
Dir. Music Bus. & Legal Affs., Walt Disney Pictures & Television
*LANGUAGES: Spanish.
*RESPONSIBILITIES: Contracts; Entertainment; Director, Law Department.
**Megery, Laurie Burstein** '65 '91 C.112 B.A. L.426 J.D.
Dir., Bus. Affs., Walt Disney Pictures and Television
*RESPONSIBILITIES: Entertainment.
**Meisel, Gary J.** ... '53 '77 C&L.309 B.A., J.D. Sr. V.P., Warner Bros.
**Meyers, Howard D.** '66 '91
C.112 B.A. L.309 J.D. Asst. Gen. Coun., Theatrical, Warner Bros.
**Miele, Ronald W.** '56 '84 C.1213 B.S. L.284 J.D.
V.P., Legal & Bus. Affs., Intl. T.V. Distrib., Warner Bros.
Miller, James R. ... '42 '68 C.823 A.B. L.724 J.D. Exec. V.P., Warner Bros., Inc.
**Miller, Mark A.** ... '57 '84 C.112 B.S. L.976 J.D. 4000 Warner Blvd.
Min, Kelly L. '63 '88 C.813 B.A. L.1066 J.D.
Sr. Coun., Warner Bros. Studios Facilities
**Minnett, Constance B.** '54 '77 C.773 B.A. L.426 J.D.
V.P. & Gen. Coun., Warner Bros. Distributing, Warner Bros.
Moiseeff, Gregory '30 '58 C.112 B.A. L.1065
Gen. Coun., Matthews Studio Equipment Grp.
**Monahan, John B., Jr.** '59 '87 C.112 B.A. L.1065 J.D.
Dir., Dom. & Intl. Anti-Piracy, Walt Disney Pictures & Television
*RESPONSIBILITIES: Intellectual Property Law (100%).
Monette, Steven L ... '60 '87 C&L.426 B.A., J.D. Dep. City Atty.
**Montan, Nils V.** '49 '79
C.188 B.A. L.30 J.D. V.P. & Sr. Intell. Prop. Coun., Warner Bros.
**Moore, Michele Adrienne** '48 '74
C.254 B.A. L.309 J.D. Asst. Gen. Coun., Theatrical, Warner Bros.
**Muhl, Phillip E.** '57 '83 C.1077 B.A. L.893 J.D.
Sr. V.P., Bus. Legal Affs., Walt Disney Pictures & Television
*LANGUAGES: Spanish.
Murphy, Michael C. ... '54 '81 C.426 B.A. L.809 J.D. 3800 W. Alameda Ave.
Murphy, Thomas C. ... '15 '48 C&L.426 LL.B. Supr. Ct. J.
**Mykytyn, Irene M.** ... '58 '83 C.800 B.S. L.1065 J.D. V.P., Coun., The Walt Disney Co.
Nagler, Jeffrey D. '58 '83 C.1349 B.S. L.112 J.D.
V.P., Legal & Bus. Affs., Warner Bros. Studios Facilities
Nathan, Richard A. ... '50 '78 C&L.800 B.A., J.D. NBC, Inc.
**Nelson, Dale Ellen** ... '59 '84 C.966 B.A. L.767 J.D. Sr. Coun., Intell. Prop., Warner Bros.
Nix, Beverly A. '51 '79
C.1097 B.A. L.809 J.D. Sr. V.P., Bus. Affs., Warner Bros. Television
**Noddings, Sarah E.** '— '75
C.705 B.A. L.776 J.D. V.P., Legal Affs., Warner Bros. Television
**Nolan, Peter F.** '43 '68 C&L.276 A.B., J.D.
V.P. & Asst. Gen. Coun., The Walt Disney Co.
**Nowak, Edward J.** '48 '75 C&L.178 A.B., J.D.
Sr. V.P. & Asst. Gen. Coun., The Walt Disney Co.
Olson, Paula M. '54 '91 C.651 B.A. L.809 J.D.
V.P., National Assn. of Broadcast Employees & Technicians
O'Neill, John E., Jr. '41 '76 C.895 B.S. L.776 J.D.
(adm. in NJ; not adm. in CA) V.P., Opers., NBC, Inc.
Oppenheim, Maurice H. ... '32 '60 C.477 B.A. L.145 J.D. 2941 Remy Pl.
Oppenheim, Patricia G. ... '24 '58 C.605 L.809 LL.B. 2941 Remy Pl.‡
Osen, Frank S. '54 '79 C.112 A.B. L.426 J.D.
Sr. V.P. & Gen. Coun., Summit Health Ltd.
Osher, Robert M. ... '59 '84 C.800 A.B. L.276 J.D. 500 S. Buena Vista St.
**Oswald, Christina Metcalf** '62 '89
C.861 B.F.A. L.1066 J.D. Sr. Coun., The Walt Disney Co.
**Parks, Ken** ... '54 '83 C.1044 B.S. L.767 J.D. 4000 Warner Blvd.
Parrille, Anthony P. ... '39 '69 C.426 B.B.A. L.1114 J.D. 1321 W. Burbank Blvd.
**Paule, Jeffrey** '49 '75 C.1060 B.S. L.464 J.D.
V.P., Network TV Legal Affs., Walt Disney Co.
Payne, Gregory Banks '54 '79 C.197 A.B. L.813 J.D.
(adm. in NY; not adm. in CA) Sr. V.P., Legal & Bus. Affs., Dic Entertainment, L.P.
Pearson, Stanley G., (AV) ... '08 '32 C.112 A.B. L.1066 J.D. 511 Via Providencia‡

PRACTICE PROFILES CALIFORNIA—BURLINGAME

Pena, Steven J. ..................'54 '81 C.1169 B.A. L.276 J.D. Gen. Coun., Warner Bros.
Pfizenmayer, Frank J. '36 '62
C.728 A.B. L.659 LL.B. Assoc. Gen. Coun., ARA Services Inc.
Polesetsky, Matthew P. ...............'68 '94 C.311 B.A. L.1066 J.D. [Ⓐ Taylor,R.B.&G.]
**Pope, Clara A. "Zazi"** '59 '87
C.821 B.A. L.309 J.D. V.P. & Sr. Litig. Coun., Warner Bros.
Powers, William F. ...................'19 '48 C&L.477 A.B., LL.B. 1231 Paseo Redondo
**Presser, Sheldon W.** '48 '73
C.112 B.A. L.1068 J.D. Sr. V.P. & Dep. Gen. Coun., Warner Bros.
Proctor, Marlan A., Jr., (AV) ................'43 '68 C.684 A.B. L.800 J.D. [Proctor&P.]
Proctor and Proctor, (AV) ........................................3320 W. Victory Blvd.
Quinonez, Jesus ...........................'56 '82 C.112 B.A. L.1068 J.D. [Taylor,R.B.&G.]
**Raphael, Alan H.** ....... '43 '68 C.188 B.S. L.569 J.D. Sr. V.P., Indus. Rel., Warner Bros.
Rawlinson, Joseph E. .............'15 '59 C.878 B.S. L.426 J.D. 4001 W. Alameda Ave.
Rawlinson, Rex J. ...........................'48 '74 C.800 B.A. L.426 J.D. [Rawlinson&E.]
Rawlinson & Ewen, Inc. ...........................................4001 W. Alameda Ave.
**Read, David** ..........................'52 '82 C&L.061 B.A., PH.D. Sr. Atty., Warner Bros.
Reich, Julie A. ...........................'62 '87 C.339 B.S. L.597 J.D. 4000 Warner Blvd.
Reichman, Neil ..... '48 '74 C.645 B.A. L.8 J.D. Gen. Coun., Lockheed Air Terminal, Inc.
**Rich, Tracy S.** '49 '74 C.112 B.A. L.1067 J.D.
Sr. Coun., West Coast, National Broadcasting Co., Inc.
**Riggs, Conrad A.** '63 '89 C.112 B.S. L.597 J.D.
Dir. Bus. Affs., Walt Disney Pictures & Television
*LANGUAGES: Italian.
*RESPONSIBILITIES: Entertainment.
Riley, Mary F. ...........................'57 '85 C.518 A.B. L.990 J.D. City Atty. Off.
Rivera, Diana C. ...................'58 '83 C.188 B.A. L.813 J.D. 500 S. Buena Vista St.
**Robinson, Claire** '49 '82 C.629 B.A. L.1065 J.D.
V.P. & Coun., Intell. Prop. Law, The Walt Disney Co.
**Robinson, James Fitzgerald** ........'66 '94 C.112 B.A. L.464 J.D. [Ⓐ Marrone R.F.&F.]
**Robinson, Jay**, (AV) ...............'46 '72 C.1109 B.A. L.1068 J.D. [Marrone R.F.&F.]
*PRACTICE AREAS: Products Liability; Professional Liability; Insurance Defense; Personal Injury; Construction.
Rocke, John C., (BV) ....................'50 '77 C.112 A.B. L.1067 J.D. Dep. Pub. Def.
Rogan, Mary Goode ...................'15 '39 C.19 A.B. L.976 LL.B. Ret. Supr. Ct. J.
Rogan, Richard R., (AV) ..............'14 '40 C.112 A.B. L.976 LL.B. 919 Grinnell Dr.‡
Romley, David ....................'51 '78 C&L.426 B.A., J.D. 303 N. Glenoaks Blvd.
**Rone, David B.** '62 '88 C.860 B.A. L.597 J.D.
(adm. in IL; not adm. in CA) V.P., Bus. Affs., Walt Disney Pictures & Television
Root, James G. ..........................'58 '88 C.170 B.A. L.602 J.D. Dep. City Atty.
**Rosen, Adam W.** ..................'66 '91 C.1036 B.A. L.1068 J.D. Atty., Warner Bros.
**Rosenfeld, Michael** '62 '94
C.674 A.B. L.1148 J.D. Coun., Immigration, The Walt Disney Co.
*RESPONSIBILITIES: Contracts; Litigation; Immigration.
Ross, Lauren ...............................'56 '82 C.1077 B.A. L.276 J.D. [Goldman&R.]
Roth, Jay D., (AV) ......................'46 '71 C.882 B.A. L.94 J.D. [Taylor,R.B.&G.]
Rowland, William A. .....................'39 '82 C.1077 B.A. L.426 J.D. 1216 Alta Paseo
Rudkin, Sven C. ...................'55 '83 C.154 B.A. L.1190 J.D. 601 S. Glendaks Blvd.
**Safenowitz, Howard B.** '58 '84 C.696 B.A. L.94 J.D.
V.P., Bus. Affs., Walt Disney Pictures & Television
**Sandoval, Scot G.** ......................'67 '93 C.174 B.S. L.61 J.D. [Ⓐ Marrone R.F.&F.]
Sannita, Terry J. ...............'46 '76 C.347 B.A. L.767 J.D. Aviation Power Supply, Inc.
**Santaniello, Joseph M.** '43 '73 C.321 B.S. L.309 J.D.
(adm. in NY; not adm. in CA) Sr. V.P., Asst. Gen. Coun., The Walt Disney Co.
**Sattinger, Jack M.**, (AV) ............'26 '54 C.112 B.S. L.1068 J.D. V.P., Warner Bros.
**Saxe, Alan J.** ........... '56 '81 C.1044 B.S. L.1049 J.D. V.P., Labor Rel., Warner Bros.
Schacter, David M. ....................'41 '68 C.1077 B.A. L.1095 J.D. Supr. Ct. J.
**Schilling, John F.** ...........'40 '73 C.350 B.S.A.E. L.426 M.S.A.E. [Ⓐ Marrone R.F.&F.]
Schlaak, Ann L. .......................'38 '82 C.966 B.S. L.1153 J.D. 600 E. Olive Ave.
**Schlesinger, Richard C.** '61 '86 C.966 B.A. L.309 J.D.
Dir.-Legal Affs., Walt Disney Pictures & Television
Schlessel, Peter H. '61 '86 C.867 B.S. L.659 J.D.
(adm. in NY; not adm. in CA) V.P., Columbia Tristar Home Video
Schmidt, Stephen C. ....................'48 '75 C&L.1095 B.S., J.D. 211 W. Alameda Ave.
**Schulman, John A.**, (AV) '46 '72
C.976 A.B. L.1066 J.D. Exec. V.P. & Gen. Coun., Warner Bros.
Scott, Juli Christine, (BV) ........'53 '78 C.1077 B.A. L.1095 J.D. Chief Asst. City Atty.
Scott, Lucinda C. ..........................'— '80 C.25 B.A. L.800 J.D. Columbia Plaza
Scott, Philip J., (BV) ...........................'27 '69 L.1095 LL.B. 301 E. Olive Ave.
Seidel, George H., Jr. ..........'50 '77 C.112 B.A. L.1068 J.D. 1317 N. San Fernando Blvd.
**Shaeffer, Erika Solti** '50 '90 C.1042 B.A. L.770 J.D.
V.P., Bus. Affs., Walt Disney Pictures & Television
*LANGUAGES: Hungarian, German, French, Russian.
Shanklin, Dennis L., (BV) ............'44 '72 C.999 L.878 J.D. Comr., Burbank Mun. Ct.
**Shannon, Katherine P.** ................'69 '95 C.112 B.A. L.464 J.D. [Marrone R.F.&F.]
Shapiro, Joe ........................'46 '72 C.659 B.A. L.309 J.D. 500 S. Buena Vista St.‡
Sheahan, Daniel R., (A Law Corp.), (BV) '33 '59
C&L.215 Ph.B., LL.B. 3800 W. Alameda Ave.
**Shuster, Marci** ........'66 '92 C.1111 B.A. L.472 J.D. Atty., Warner Bros. Records Inc.
Sidell, Donald B. ..........................'42 '75 C.800 B.A. L.1095 J.D. 2304 N. Reese Pl.
**Silver, Andrea Feldman** '61 '87 C.112 B.S. L.188 J.D.
Dir, Bus. & Legal Affs., Walt Disney Pictures & Television
**Silverman, Jody** '69 '94 C.477 B.A. L.990 J.D.
Atty., Feature Animation, Walt Disney Pictures & Television
*RESPONSIBILITIES: Contracts; Entertainment.
**Silverman, Marshall M.** '45 '77 C.415 B.A. L.1009 J.D.
(adm. in NY; not adm. in CA) V.P. & Assoc. Gen. Coun., Warner Bros.
**Simon, Gary R.** '49 '75 C.823 B.S. L.262 J.D.
(adm. in NY; not adm. in CA) V.P., Legal Affs., Warner Bros. Consumer Prods.
**Smokler, Sandra K.**........'60 '85 C&L.472 B.A., J.D. Assoc. Gen. Coun., Warner Bros.
Spielholz, Marcia ........................'57 '81 C.569 B.F.A. L.276 J.D. Columbia Plaza
**Stager, Paul** '29 '56 C.611 B.A. L.608 J.D.
Sr. V.P. & Studio Gen. Coun., Warner Bros. Television
**Stark, Mei-lan E. W.** '67 '94 C.940 B.A. L.976 J.D.
(adm. in GA; not adm. in CA) Coun., Walt Disney Co.
*RESPONSIBILITIES: Trademarks.
Starleaf, David C., (BV) ........................................'46 '76 3046 N. Buena Vista St.
Stefano, Vincent, Jr., (AV) ..........'38 '65 C.800 B.S. L.426 J.D. 1612 West Olive Ave.
Stevenson, Terry B., (BV) ...........'49 '76 C.1077 B.A. L.426 J.D. Sen. Asst. City Atty.
Stewart, Richard F., (BV) .................'30 '74 C.112 B.A. L.1095 J.D. [R.F.Stewart]
Stewart, Richard F., A Professional Corporation, (BV) ...................240 S. Lincoln St.
**Stone, Donald M.** ......................'43 '72 C.112 B.A. L.426 J.D. [Marrone R.F.&F.]
*LANGUAGES: French.
*PRACTICE AREAS: Tort Litigation; Real Estate Litigation; Real Estate Transactional.
**Stone, Katherine Grunwald** '60 '86 C.473 B.S. L.201 J.D.
V.P., Bus. Affs., Walt Disney Pictures & Television

**Streicker, Richard Daniel** '52 '78 C.477 B.A. L.309 J.D.
Sr. V.P., Bus. & Legal Affs., E. Coast, Warner Bros. Records Inc.
**Sullivan, Theresa M.** '64 '92
C.1049 B.A. L.426 J.D. Dir., Walt Disney Pictures & Television
*RESPONSIBILITIES: Contracts; Cable.
Sullivan, Timothy J. ..............................................'48 '79 C.36 B.A. NBC, Inc.
**Sunderland, Craig G.** '59 '85
C.800 B.A. L.426 J.D. Sr. Atty., Walt Disney Pictures & Television
**Sunderland, Jeremy H.** ....'63 '90 C.800 B.A. L.426 J.D. Atty., Warner Bros. Television
Sutton, Robert W. ..............'21 '49 C.165 A.B. L.309 LL.B. 414 W. Spazier Ave.
Sweeney, Daniel J. ...................'48 '77 C.128 B.A. L.809 J.D. 290 E. Verdugo Ave.‡
Tabah, Theodore S., A Prof. Corp., (BV) .........'27 '54 C&L.800 B.S., LL.B. [T.S.Tabah]
Tabah, Theodore S., A Prof. Corp., (BV) ......................................4405 Riverside Dr.
Tate, Larry I. ........................'35 '63 C.532 B.A. L.477 LL.B. 1046 E. Fairmount Rd.
Taylor, Carson, (AV) ........'46 '71 C.31 B.A. L.228 J.D. 3500 W. Olive Ave., Ste. 1100
**Taylor, Ruth Anne** '61 '87 C.800 B.A. L.564 J.D.
Assoc. Gen. Coun., Warner Bros. Records Inc.
Taylor, Roth, Bush & Geffner, A Law Corporation, (AV)
Suite 1100, 3500 W. Olive Ave.
**Tenen-Aoki, Elise A.** ....'61 '88 C.860 B.A. L.904 J.D. Intell. Prop. Coun., Warner Bros.
Tenzer, Michael A. .....'54 '80 C.763 B.A. L.61 J.D. V.P., Bus. Affs., NBC Entertainment
Therien, Roger W. '53 '79
C.112 B.A. L.770 J.D. Gen. Coun. & Sr. V.P., Gateway Title Co.
**Thompson, David K.** '49 '81 C.276 B.S.F.S. L.178 J.D.
Sr. V.P. & Asst. Gen. Coun., The Walt Disney Co.
Thompson, Donald M. ........'63 '88 C.1365 B.A. L.94 J.D. Asst. Gen. Coun., UniHealth
Thompson, Jeffrey D. ......'57 '81 C.770 B.S.C. L.800 J.D. Assoc. Gen. Coun., UniHealth
Thorpe, Jack A. '18 '44 C&L.190 Ph.B., LL.B.
(adm. in NE; not adm. in CA) Exec. V.P., Burbank Bd. of Realtors
Tracy, Mark E. ...........................'43 '77 C.800 B.A. L.1068 J.D. P.O. Box 1338‡
Vallier, Averil D. ..................'37 '65 C&L.352 B.A., J.D. 1072 E. Orange Grove Ave.
Van Buren, Culver, (AV) ...............................'13 '45 C&L.800 J.D. 301 E. Olive Ave.
**Vipperman, Ramona M.** ...'55 '79 C.800 B.A. L.1068 J.D. Coun., The Walt Disney Co.
*REPORTED CASES: Attorney for Amicus Curiae - Serrano v. Priest.
**Vogel, Jay M.** '63 '88 C.145 B.A. L.1068 J.D.
Sr. Coun., W. Coast Develop., Walt Disney Co.
*RESPONSIBILITIES: Leasing; Real Estate.
Walch, Victor L., (AV) ..........................'34 '67 C.878 B.S. L.273 J.D. 711 Wilson Ct.
Walker, Darrell E. ............................'54 '82 C.940 B.A. L.813 J.D. Columbia Plaza
**Weiss, Russell G.** '68 '94
C.112 B.A. L.426 J.D. Atty., Walt Disney Pictures and Television
*LANGUAGES: Spanish.
*RESPONSIBILITIES: Contracts; Copyright and Trademark; Multimedia and Internet Law.
Weiss, Suzanne T. '46 '83 C.569 B.F.A. L.564 J.D.
(adm. in NY; not adm. in CA) 434 E. Elmwood
Wente, David O. ....'37 '62 C&L.352 B.A., LL.B. Asst. Div. Coun., Lockheed Fin. Corp.
Wernick, Jeffrey M. '53 '79
C.107 B.A. L.569 J.D. Exec. V.P. & COO, Dic Entertainment, L.P.
**Whalen, Maureen T.** '52 '78 C&L.567 B.A., J.D.
V.P., Bus. Legal Affs., Walt Disney Pictures & Television
**Whitson, Gwen H.** '53 '78 C.668 B.A. L.1068 J.D.
Sr. V.P. & Gen. Coun., Distribution, Warner Bros.
Widman, Michael J. ......................'60 '87 C&L.569 B.A., J.D. 500 S. Buena Vista St.
Wilks, Wayne W. ........................'44 '71 C&L.426 B.A., J.D. 918 E. Harvard Rd.
**Williams, Jeremy N.**, (AV) '45 '74 C.31 B.A. L.309 J.D.
Sr. V.P. & Gen. Coun., Theatrical, Warner Bros.

**Williams, Arnold F.**
(See Los Angeles)

Wilner, Alan D. ...........................'51 '83 C.912 B.A. L.1095 J.D. [A.D.Wilner]
Wilner, Alan D., A P.C. ............................................4405 W. Riverside Dr., #100
**Wilske, Lisa J.** '60 '87 C.911 B.A. L.990 J.D.
Coun., Walt Disney Pictures & Television
*RESPONSIBILITIES: Antitrust; Copyright and Trademark; Trade Regulations.
Wilson, Howard D., (AV) ..............'46 '71 C.1077 B.S. L.802 J.D. 245 E. Olive Ave.
Wise, Helena Sunny, (BV) .....'54 '79 C.112 B.A. L.426 J.D. 1100 N Hollywood Way #A
**Wolf, Renee I.** ..........................'62 '87 C.112 A.B. L.1065 J.D. Sr. Atty., Warner Bros.
**Wright, Paige W.** '68 '94 C.597 B.A. L.145 J.D.
(adm. in IL; not adm. in CA) Atty., Walt Disney Pictures & Television
*RESPONSIBILITIES: Entertainment.
**Yanow, Julie B.** ... '59 '86 C.112 B.A. L.1068 J.D. V.P. & Sr. Empl. Coun., Warner Bros.
**Yellin, Jacob M.** ........'51 '81 C.102 B.A. L.770 J.D. V.P., Coun., The Walt Disney Co.
**Young, Rachel D.** .........'53 '78 C.813 B.A. L.1066 J.D. Atty., Warner Bros. Television
**Zajic, Keith C.** .........'50 '75 C.800 B.S. L.1067 J.D. Sr. V.P., Bus. Affs., Warner Bros.
Zander, James H. ...................'47 '72 C.112 L.823 J.D. 3500 W. Olive Ave.
**Zucker, Michael S.** '57 '82
C.966 B.S. L.1068 J.D. Atty., Walt Disney Pictures & Television
*RESPONSIBILITIES: Entertainment.
Zuckerman, Barbara J. '48 '75
C.800 B.A. L.426 J.D. V.P., Legal Affs., Warner Bros. Television
**Zweig, Jonathan E.** '64 '89 C.855 B.A. L.880 J.D.
(adm. in IL; not adm. in CA) Atty., Walt Disney Pictures & Television
*RESPONSIBILITIES: Entertainment.

## BURLINGAME, 26,801, *San Mateo Co.*

Abraham, Alexander K., (AV) ........'49 '79 C.312 B.A. L.1049 J.D. 500 Airport Blvd.
Alfonso, Carlos H., (BV) ............'50 '76 C.766 B.A. L.1065 J.D. 1801 Murchison Dr.
Andersen, Adam A. .....................'60 '85 C.945 B.A. L.904 J.D. Bay Area Cellular
**Andersen, Lage E.**, (AV) ...............'50 '77 C.597 B.S. L.813 J.D. [Carr,M.I.T.&H.]
*PRACTICE AREAS: Taxation Law.
**Anderson, Steven D.** ..........................'60 '88 C.112 A.B. L.1066 J.D. [Carr,M.I.T.&H.]
*PRACTICE AREAS: Probate Law; Trust Law; Estate Planning Law; Tax Planning Law.
Antone, Gregory J. ...........................'49 '74 C.112 A.B. L.1065 J.D. [G.J.Antone]
Antone, Gregory J., A Professional Corporation ............1200 Howard Ave., Ste., 201
Bailey, Bruce A., (AV) ...................................'31 '56 C&L.813 B.A., J.D. [B.A.Bailey]
Bailey, Elizabeth H., (BV) .......................'54 '82 C.766 B.A. L.284 J.D. [B.A.Bailey]
Bailey, Bruce Albion, A Professional Law Corporation, (AV) .........1800 Trousdale Dr.
Ballout, Haitham Edward ................'61 '90 C.768 B.S. L.284 J.D. 1290 Howard Ave.
Barnett, Stephen R. ...................'35 '66 C&L.309 A.B., LL.B. 840 Malcolm Rd.
**Bartel, Keith P.**, (AV) ...................'50 '78 C.112 B.A. L.767 J.D. [Carr,M.I.T.&H.]
*PRACTICE AREAS: Probate Litigation; Health Care Litigation.
Beggs, Edward L., (AV) ....................'11 '36 C.813 L.1065 J.D. 2609 Martinez Dr.‡
Beglin, Philip J. ...............'54 '80 C.112 A.B. L.1065 J.D. 1799 Old Bayshore Hway.
Berenstein, Joyce L., (BV) ...................'46 '83 C.766 B.A. L.765 J.D. [Chase,B.&M.]

CAA39P

**Berenstein, Sidney, (AV) '42 '67 C.768 B.S. L.767 J.D.**
**700 Airport Boulevard, Suite 450, 94010**
**Telephone: 415-548-1171 FAX: 415-548-0565**
**Commercial Litigation, Collection and Landlord/Tenant.**

**Berger, Matthew I.** ... '50 '79 C.112 B.A. L.629 J.D. [Corporate]
Bergeron, Joseph E., (BV) ... '40 '69 C.712 B.B.A. L.1066 J.D. Sup.Ct. Judge
Bitter, Gehart L. ... '21 '51 C.284 L.1026 LL.B. 2673 Martinez Dr.
Blackman, Clifford A. '49 '76
C.1019 B.A. L.765 J.D. 1800 Trousdale Dr. (⊙Redwood City)
**Blood, James F.** ... '59 '88 C.101 B.A. L.273 J.D. [Carr,M.I.T.&H.]
*PRACTICE AREAS: General Corporate Law; Business Law.
**Book, Norman I., Jr.**, (AV) ... '39 '65 C.668 B.A. L.813 J.D. [Carr,M.I.T.&H.]
*PRACTICE AREAS: General Corporate Law; Real Estate Law; Tax Law.
Brown, Abraham R. ... '66 '91 C.674 B.A. L.813 J.D. 1860 El Camino Real
**Brown, Marion L.**, (AV) ... '38 '67 C.602 B.B.A. L.813 J.D. [Carr,M.I.T.&H.]
*PRACTICE AREAS: Estate Planning Law; Trust Law; Probate Law; Business Law.
Bruss, Robert J. ... '40 '67 C.597 B.S. L.1065 J.D. P.O. Box 129
**Burlingame, Todd L.** ... '58 '86 C.112 B.A. L.1065 J.D. [⊠ Carr,M.I.T.&H.]
Burrall, Susan D. ... '63 '90 C.531 B.S. L.838 J.D. 1805 Easton Dr.
**Byers, David J.**, (BV) ... '51 '78 C.339 B.A. L.1066 J.D. [McCracken&B.]
*PRACTICE AREAS: Public Utility; Condemnation; Land Use; Real Estate; Real Estate Litigation.
Camerlengo, George F., (BV) ... '45 '71 C.884 A.B. L.765 J.D. 500 Airport Blvd.
Caplan, William V. ... '32 '58 C.112 B.A. L.309 LL.B. 1315 Burlingame Ave.
Carr, David C, (AV) ... '55 '86 C.112 B.A. L.426 J.D. 216 Park Rd.
**Carr, David C.**, (AV) ... '31 '61 C&L.813 A.B., J.D. [⊠ Carr,M.I.T.&H.] ‡
**Carr, Luther M.**, (AV) ... '06 '29 C&L.221 A.B., J.D. [⊠ Carr,M.I.T.&H.] ‡

**Carr, McClellan, Ingersoll, Thompson & Horn, Professional Corporation, (AV)**
**216 Park Road, P.O. Box 513, 94011-0513⊙**
**Telephone: 415-342-9600 Telecopier: 415-342-7685**
**Email: cmith@cmithlaw.com**
**E. H. Cosgriff (1880-1947); J. Ed McClellan (1895-1985); Robert R. Thompson (1921-1995); Norman I. Book, Jr.; Robert A. Nebrig; Marion L. Brown (Certified Specialist, Taxation Law and Probate, Estate Planning and Trust Law, The State Bar of California Board of Legal Specialization); L. Michael Telleen; Lage E. Andersen (Certified Specialist, Taxation Law, The State Bar of California Board of Legal Specialization); Keith P. Bartel; Mark A. Cassanego; Laurence M. May; Michael J. McQuaid; Penelope Creasey Greenberg; James R. Cody (Certified Specialist, Estate Planning, Trust and Probate Law, The State Bar of California Board of Legal Specialization).; Edward J. Willig, III; Sarah J. DiBoise; W. George Wailes; Carol B. Schwartz; Lori A. Lutzker; Moira C. Walsh; Jeremy W. Katz; Lisa Hayhurst Stalteri; Elizabeth A. Franklin; Steven D. Anderson (Certified Specialist, Estate Planning, Trust and Probate Law, The State Bar of California Board of Legal Specialization); James F. Blood. Senior Counsel: Denny S. Roja;—Todd L. Burlingame; Michele G. Dulsky; Michael D. Liberty; Wendy L. MacIlwaine; Terese M. Raddie. Chairman Emeritus: Albert J. Horn. Of Counsel: Luther M. Carr (Retired); Frank B. Ingersoll, Jr. (Retired); Cyrus J. McMillan (Retired); David C. Carr (Retired).**
**General Civil and Trial Practice. Corporation, Hospital and Health Care, Labor and Employment, Bankruptcy, Creditors Rights, Commercial, International Business, Tax, Real Estate, Estate Planning and Probate Law.**
**San Francisco, California Office: Suite 1120, Four Embarcadero Center. Telephone: 415-362-1400. Telecopier: 415-362-5149.**

*See Professional Biographies, BURLINGAME, CALIFORNIA*

**Cassanego, Mark A.**, (AV) ... '53 '79 C.770 B.S. L.1066 J.D. [Carr,M.I.T.&H.]
*PRACTICE AREAS: General Corporate Law; Business Law; Securities Law.
Chabot, Joseph E., (AV) ... '50 '82 C.112 B.A. L.1066 J.D. 433 Airport Blvd.
Chase, Charles E., (BV) ... '34 '65 C.215 B.S. L.1065 J.D. [Chase,B.&M.]
Chase, Steven A., (BV) ... '46 '72 C.112 A.B. L.1065 J.D. 1818 Gilbreth Rd.
Chase, Berenstein and Murray, (BV) ... 700 Airport Blvd.
Chayt, Julie I. ... '66 '94 C.188 B.A. L.1065 J.D. 216 Park Rd.

**Church, Mark M.**
**(See Millbrae)**

Clements, Jordan W., (BV) ... '57 '82 C&L.101 B.A., J.D. 216 Park Rd.
**Cody, James R.**, (AV) ... '55 '82 C.976 B.A. L.1065 J.D. [Carr,M.I.T.&H.]
*PRACTICE AREAS: Probate Law; Trust Law; Estate Planning Law; Tax Planning Law.
Cohen, Henry, (AV) ... '28 '62 C.768 A.B. L.1066 J.D. [Cohen&J.]
Cohen and Jacobson, (AV) ... 577 Airport Blvd.
Coit, Laurence '49 '81
C.1250 B.S.M.E. L.770 J.D. Electric Power Research Institute, Inc. (Pat.)
Coleman, Jerome F., (BV) ... '37 '62 C.147 B.A. L.1066 LL.B. City Atty.
Comfort, Michael G., (BV) ... '51 '77 C.767 B.A. L.1026 J.D. 1799 Old Bayshore Hwy.
Connolly, Hugh F., (AV) ... '28 '59 C&L.262 A.B., LL.B. 850 Woodside way
Constantino, Paul J., (BV) ... '44 '75 [Kubota,C.&H.]
Cook, Quentin L., (AV) ... '40 '66 C.877 B.S. L.813 J.D. 216 Park Rd.

**Corporate Law Group, The, (AV)**
**Waterfront Plaza, Suite 120, 500 Airport Boulevard, 94010-1914**
**Telephone: 415-349-8000 Fax: 415-349-8099**
**Email: mail@tclg.com URL: http://www.tclg.com**
**Paul David Marotta; Matthew I. Berger; Kristen Roellig; William J. Moran.**
**Corporate, Finance, Securities, Mergers and Acquisitions, Business Transactions, Licensing and Technology Law, Partnerships and Limited Liability Companies, International Law, Trademarks and Copyrights.**

*See Professional Biographies, BURLINGAME, CALIFORNIA*

**Cotchett, Joseph W.**, (AV) ... '39 '65 C.1074 B.S. L.1065 LL.B. [Cotchett&P.]⊙

**Cotchett & Pitre, (AV)**
**San Francisco Airport Office Center, Suite 200, 840 Malcolm Road, 94010⊙**
**Telephone: 415-697-6000**
**Email: CandPLegal@aol.com**
**Members of Firm: Joseph W. Cotchett; Frank M. Pitre; Bruce L. Simon; Marie Seth Weiner; Nancy Leavitt Fineman. Associates: Virginia Ellen Hewitt; Jack P. Hug; Steven C. Keller; Gregg M. MacMillan; Niall P. McCarthy; Mark C. Molumphy; Marilynn Tham. Of Counsel: Alfred V. Contarino; Mark P. Friedlander, Jr.**
**Practice limited to Tort Law, Environmental, Products Liability, Securities, Antitrust and Commercial Litigation. General Trial and Appellate Practice.**
**Reference: Peninsula Bank of Commerce, Millbrae.**
**Los Angeles, California Office: Suite 1100, 12100 Wilshire Boulevard. Telephone: 310-826-4211.**
**Affiliated Office: Friedlander & Friedlander, P.C., 2018 Clarendon Boulevard, Arlington, Virginia 22201. Telephone: 703-525-6750.**

*See Professional Biographies, BURLINGAME, CALIFORNIA*

**Cray, Barbara Ann, (AV) '54 '79 C.914 B.A. L.1065 J.D.**
**800 Airport Boulevard, Suite 504, 94010**
**Telephone: 415-375-1220 Fax: 415-375-1410**
***PRACTICE AREAS: Lender Liability; Bankruptcy; Creditors Remedies; Real Property; Commercial Code Litigation.**
**Associate: Eleanor T. Miranda.**
**Financial Institutions, Lender Liability, Bankruptcy, Creditors Remedies, Real Property, Unfair Business Practices, Commercial Code and Commercial Litigation.**

*See Professional Biographies, BURLINGAME, CALIFORNIA*

Cvengros, James M., (BV) ... '43 '69 C.1060 B.A. L.1065 J.D. 533 Airport Blvd.
**Delbon, David A.** ... '62 '88 C.112 B.A. L.767 J.D. [Winters,K.&D.]
Demanes, Floyd A., (AV) ... '21 '50 C&L.339 J.D. [B.A.Bailey]

**DiBoise, Sarah J.** ... '56 '82 C.813 B.A. L.1066 J.D. [Carr,M.I.T.&H.]
*PRACTICE AREAS: Hospital & Health Care Law.
Divine, Richard H. '52 '78 C.597 B.S. L.596 J.D.
(adm. in OR; not adm. in CA) V.P., Engg., Contract Surety Consultants Inc.
Doherty, Colleen ... '42 '81 C.629 B.A. L.767 J.D. 1424 Chapin Ave.
Domholt, Richard '46 '76
C.112 A.B. L.1065 J.D. Sr. Contract Admr., Air Line Pilots Assn.
DuComb, Anthony W. '49 '76 C.1030 B.A. L.128 J.D.
(adm. in DC; not adm. in CA) U.S. Postal Serv.
**Dulsky, Michele G.** ... '60 '92 C.112 B.A. L.1049 J.D. [⊠ Carr,M.I.T.&H.]
Dumpis, Juris, (BV) ... '50 '83 C.112 B.A. L.765 J.D. 407 Primrose Rd.
Eibert, Mark Donald ... '56 '82 C.477 B.A. L.813 J.D. 840 Malcolm Rd.
**Enslow, Thomas A.** ... '57 '96 C.966 B.S. L.1066 J.D. [McCracken&B.]
Faber, John J. ... '27 '52 C&L.770 B.S., LL.B. 1245 Drake Ave.‡
Ferdows, Sam ... '62 '93 C.112 B.S. L.765 J.D. P.O. Box 117351
**Fineman, Nancy Leavitt** ... '60 '86 C.112 A.B. L.1066 J.D. [Cotchett&P.]
**Fitzgerald, Christine C.** ... '62 '87 C.770 B.A. L.464 J.D. [⊠ H.H.Fitzgerald]
*PRACTICE AREAS: Eminent Domain Litigation; General Redevelopment; Housing Authority Counseling.
**Fitzgerald, Herman H.**, (AV) ... '32 '62 C&L.851 B.B.A., J.D. [H.H.Fitzgerald]
*PRACTICE AREAS: Eminent Domain Litigation; General Redevelopment Counseling.
Fitzgerald, John L. ... '61 '86 C.602 B.A. L.770 J.D. 840 Malcomb Rd.

**Fitzgerald, Herman H., A Prof. Corp., Law Offices of, (AV)**
**Suite 302, 345 Lorton Avenue, 94010**
**Telephone: 415-348-5195 Fax: 415-348-3518**
**Herman H. Fitzgerald;—Christine C. Fitzgerald.**
**Eminent Domain Litigation, General Redevelopment and Housing Authority Counseling.**

*See Professional Biographies, BURLINGAME, CALIFORNIA*

Fogarty, Janet E. ... '50 '92 C&L.767 B.S., J.D. 433 Airport Blvd. #319
Foote, W. Penn ... '43 '71 C&L.800 A.B., J.D. Corp. Coun., Calif. Teachers Assn.
Francone, Stephanie ... '59 '81 C.768 B.A. L.1065 J.D. 1422 Bellevue Ave., Apt. 504
**Franklin, Elizabeth A.** ... '61 '88 C.112 B.A. L.1065 J.D. [Carr,M.I.T.&H.]
*PRACTICE AREAS: Labor Law; Employment Law.
Fried, Darryl S., (CV) ... '49 '75 C.1077 B.A. L.767 J.D. 1860 El Camino Real
Galasi, Ronald S. ... '46 '73 C.112 B.A. L.1065 J.D. 1633 Old Bayshore Hwy
Garvin, Charles E. '52 '81 C&L.309 B.A., J.D.
(adm. in DC; not adm. in CA) Chmn. of the Bd., Telescan Corp.
Geller, Joseph D., A Professional Corporation, (BV) '28 '52
C.472 L.94 LL.B. 1799 Old Bayshore Hwy.
Gilmartin, Robert A. ... '47 '72 C.112 B.A. L.1065 J.D. 48 Park Rd.
Glafkides, Katherine ... '58 '83 C.112 B.S. L.1065 J.D. 20 Valdivia Ct.
Godinez-Phillips, Doris '46 '82
C.766 B.A. L.1066 J.D. Dep. Chf. Field Coun., U.S. Postal Serv.
Goldman, Craig A. ... '60 '85 C.813 A.B. L.1068 J.D. Burlingame School Dist.
Gradstein, Marc ... '46 '73 C.696 A.B. L.569 J.D. 1204 Burlingame Ave.
Green, Robert L. ... '31 '57 C&L.813 A.B., LL.B. 400 Primrose Rd.
**Greenberg, Penelope Creasey**, (BV) ... '43 '80 C.813 B.A. L.1066 J.D. [Carr,M.I.T.&H.]
*PRACTICE AREAS: Hospital Law; Health Care Law; Municipal Law.
Greenberg-Kinne, Susan, (BV) '59 '84 C.154 B.A. L.1065 J.D.
1799 Old Bayshore Hwy.
Gregorio, Arlen ... '31 '55 C&L.813 B.A., LL.B. Princ., Gregorio, Haldeman & Piazza
Gurwitz, Michael L. ... '47 '81 C.453 B.S. L.284 J.D. 1557 Westmoor Rd.
Guttas, Charles K. ... '52 '79 C.112 A.B. L.464 J.D. 2901 Adeline Dr.
Hamblin, Jos. M. ... '20 '52 C&L.767 B.S., LL.B. 2998 Mariposa Dr.‡
**Hewitt, Virginia Ellen** ... '69 '94 C.575 B.A. L.178 J.D. [⊠ Cotchett&P.]
Hoffman, Rudolph A. ... '35 '66 C.112 A.B. L.767 LL.B. P.O. Box 1873
Holt, Douglas W., (BV) ... '46 '72 C.112 B.A. L.1066 J.D. 1800 Trousdale
**Horn, Albert J.**, (AV) ... '26 '52 C&L.813 A.B., J.D. [Carr,M.I.T.&H.]
*PRACTICE AREAS: Probate Law; Trust Law; Estate Planning Law; Tax Planning Law.
Hortop, Robert Andrew '47 '89 C.477 B.A. L.770 J.D.
V.P., Legal Servs., Mills-Peninsula Health Sys.
**Hug, Jack P.** ... '38 '66 C.870 B.S. L.1066 LL.B. [⊠ Cotchett&P.]
Huguenin, A. Eugene, Jr. '43 '70 C&L.911 B.A., J.D.
Staff Coun., Calif. Teachers Assn.
**Ingersoll, Frank B., Jr.**, (AV) ... '12 '39 C&L.813 A.B., J.D. [⊠ Carr,M.I.T.&H.] ‡
Jackson, Aaron S., (BV) ... '21 '53 C.846 L.767 J.D. 1204 Burlingame Ave.
Jacobson, Lawrence A., (AV) ... '48 '73 C.285 B.A. L.767 J.D. [Cohen&J.]
Johnson, C. Judith ... '41 '82 C.6 B.A. L.767 J.D. 500 Airport Blvd.
Johnson, M. Perry, Jr. ... '43 '69 C.909 B.A. L.45 J.D. Chf. Field Coun; U.S. Postal Serv.
Jones, Fred A. ... '28 '61 C.911 B.A. L.284 LL.B. 411 Calif. Dr.
Jones, William R. ... '44 '76 C.112 A.B. L.426 J.D. 1534 Plaza Lane
Karp, Randall H. ... '51 '82 C.112 B.A. L.1137 J.D. 977 El Camino Real
**Katz, Jeremy W.**, (AV) ... '52 '85 C.112 B.A. L.1065 J.D. [Carr,M.I.T.&H.]⊙
*PRACTICE AREAS: Bankruptcy Law; Insolvency Law.
**Keller, Steven C.** ... '55 '80 C.800 B.A. L.178 J.D. [⊠ Cotchett&P.]
Kim, Chung Nan ... '— '78 P.O. Box 117313
Kingston, Emily J. '62 '87 C.882 B.A. L.1194 J.D.
(adm. in WY; not adm. in CA) 777 El Camino Real No. 14‡
**Krug, John S.**, (AV) ... '50 '76 C.813 B.S. L.284 J.D. [Winters,K.&D.]
Kubota, Noell K., (BV) ... '43 '77 C.312 B.A. L.1065 J.D. [Kubota,C.&H.]
Kubota, Constantino & Hartnett, (BV) ... 433 Airport Blvd.
Lamdan, Leonard K. ... '10 '34 C.563 L.803 1469 Bellevue Ave., Apt. 802‡
Liberman, Eric ... '56 '81 C.165 B.A. L.1065 J.D. 1801 Murchison Dr.
**Liberty, Michael D.** ... '57 '88 C.112 A.B. L.464 J.D. [⊠ Carr,M.I.T.&H.]
**Lutzker, Lori A.** ... '61 '86 C.645 B.A. L.813 J.D. [Carr,M.I.T.&H.]
*PRACTICE AREAS: Civil Litigation.
Lynch, Jeremiah J., (BV) ... '39 '66 C.770 B.A. L.1065 J.D. 1601 Bayshore Hwy. #311
**MacIlwaine, Wendy L.** ... '67 '93 C.597 B.A. L.273 J.D. [⊠ Carr,M.I.T.&H.]
**MacMillan, Gregg M.** ... '70 '95 C.112 B.A. L.770 J.D. [⊠ Cotchett&P.]
Maguire, Frederick B., Jr., (BV) ... '36 '61 C&L.770 B.S., LL.B. 1800 Trousdale Dr.
Marder, Robert S. ... '34 '60 C.823 B.A. L.309 J.D. Admin. Law J., Unemp. Ins. App. Bd.
**Marotta, Paul David**, (BV) ... '57 '83 C.800 B.A. L.990 J.D. [Corporate]
**May, Laurence M.**, (AV) ... '51 '76 C.112 A.B. L.770 J.D. [Carr,M.I.T.&H.]⊙
*PRACTICE AREAS: Real Estate Transactions; Financing Law.
**McCarthy, Niall P.** ... '67 '92 C.112 B.A. L.770 J.D. [⊠ Cotchett&P.]
**McCracken, Michael D.**, (BV) ... '45 '72 C.546 B.A. L.813 J.D. [McCracken&B.]
*PRACTICE AREAS: Land Use; Real Estate; Administrative Law; Real Estate Litigation; Broker Liability.

**McCracken & Byers, (BV)**
**840 Malcolm Road, Suite 100, 94010**
**Telephone: 415-259-5979 Fax: 415-259-5975**
**Members of Firm: Michael D. McCracken; David J. Byers; Thomas A. Enslow.**
**Civil Litigation and Trial Practice. Land Use, Land Development, Zoning, Real Estate, Environmental, Condemnation, Public Utility, Property Tax and Administrative Law.**

*See Professional Biographies, BURLINGAME, CALIFORNIA*

McKay, Gerald R., (AV) ... '45 '72 C&L.494 B.A., J.D. P.O. Box 406
McKim, David M., (BV) ... '52 '77 C.112 A.B. L.770 J.D. 216 Park Rd.

CAA40P

McMillan, Cyrus J., (AV) .... '21 '47 C&L.770 A.B., J.D. [▣ Carr,M.I.T.&H.] ‡
**McQuaid, Michael J.**, (AV) .... '54 '80 C.112 A.B. L.770 J.D. [Carr,M.I.T.&H.]⊙
*PRACTICE AREAS: Bankruptcy Law; Insolvency Law.

**Miller, Russell H., Law Office of '52 '83 C.112 B.A. L.1065 J.D.**
**Matthew Bender & Co., 20 Park Road, Suite E, 94010-4443**
**Telephone: 415-401-8735 Fax: 415-401-8739**
**Email: MILLPESS@WORLDNET.ATT.NET**
***SPECIAL AGENCIES: California Fair Political Practices Commission.**
**Campaign and Election Law Enforcement Campaign, Lobby and Ethics Law Compliance, Estate Planning for Unmarried Individuals and Couples, Real Estate Transactions.**
*See Professional Biographies, BURLINGAME, CALIFORNIA*

**Miranda, Eleanor T.** .... '54 '88 C.800 B.A. L.1068 J.D. [▣ B.A.Cray]
*PRACTICE AREAS: Creditors Remedies; Bankruptcy.
**Molumphy, Mark C.** .... '66 '93 C.112 B.A. L.767 J.D. [▣ Cotchett&P.]
Montgomery, John A. .... '11 '42 C&L.659 B.S., J.D. 185 Los Robles Dr.
**Moran, William J.**, (AV) .... '41 '66 C.262 B.A. L.976 J.D. [Corporate]
Morison, Melinda Chalich '61 '88 C.147 B.A. L.767 J.D.
216 Park Road (⊙San Francisco)
Murray, Lisa R. .... '62 '87 C.94 B.A. L.767 J.D. [Chase,B.&M.]
Musante, Janis R., (BV) .... '43 '78 C.112 B.A. L.765 J.D. 1800 Trousdale Ave.
Mussman, Carol Lynne .... '57 '82 C.104 A.B. L.228 J.D. 216 Park Rd.
**Nagle, William L.**, (AV) .... '48 '74 C.813 B.A. L.767 J.D. [Winters,K.&D.]
Nance, William M. .... '44 '76 C.766 B.A. L.765 J.D. P.O. Box 1188
**Nastari, Jerry E.** .... '59 '90 C.1060 B.A. L.770 J.D. [Winters,K.&D.]
**Nebrig, Robert A.**, (AV) .... '38 '66 C.378 B.A. L.813 J.D. [Carr,M.I.T.&H.]
*PRACTICE AREAS: Civil Litigation; International Transactions.
**Noll, Cheryl A.** .... '62 '88 C.1074 B.A. L.1049 J.D. [Winters,K.&D.]
*PRACTICE AREAS: Insurance Defense; General Practice.
Nykodym, Joseph M. .... '63 '94 C.112 B.A. L.767 J.D. 840 Malcolm Rd.
Ocheltree, Richard L. .... '31 '59 C&L.309 A.B., LL.B. 1446 Floribunda Ave.‡
O'Mahoney, P.J. Benedict .... '60 '88 C.766 B.A. L.770 J.D. 615 Port Dr.
Pagano, William F., (BV) .... '47 '73 C.813 A.B. L.770 J.D. 1424 Chapin Ave.
Parker, Andrew D. .... '48 '88 C.999 B.A. L.765 J.D. 875 Mahler Rd.
Pereira, Mira L. .... '55 '81 C.766 B.A. L.809 J.D. 1411 Montero Ave.
Peros, Nicholas J. .... '46 '80 C.112 B.S. L.1026 J.D. 1105 Cabrillo Ave.
Phillips, Richard L., (BV) .... '44 '71 C.763 B.A. L.1026 J.D. 407 Primrose Rd.
**Pitre, Frank M.**, (AV) .... '55 '81 C&L.767 B.S., J.D. [Cotchett&P.]⊙
Price, Michael B., (BV) .... '45 '72 C.768 B.S. L.1065 J.D. 1290 Howard Ave.
**Raddie, Terese M.**, (BV) .... '58 '84 C.950 B.A. L.284 J.D. [▣ Carr,M.I.T.&H.]
Robbins, Karen R. .... '58 '83 C.668 B.A. L.770 J.D. 2105 Poppy Dr.
**Roellig, Kristen** .... '65 '94 C.112 B.A. L.284 J.D. [Corporate]
**Roja, Denny S.** .... '46 '89 C.061 B.S. L.262 J.D. [▣ Carr,M.I.T.&H.]
*PRACTICE AREAS: Corporate and General Business Law; Mergers and Acquisitions; Securities Law.
Rosner, Marc .... '64 '89 C.813 B.A. L.1065 J.D. 840 Malcolm Rd.
Scharf, Eric J. .... '55 '79 C.1044 B.A. L.1292 J.D. U.S. Postal Serv.
Schutzman, Edward I. .... '44 '74 C.912 B.S. L.477 J.D. 1290 Old Bayshore Hwy.
Schwalm, Charles F. .... '12 '37 C.197 L.150 LL.B. City Mgr.
**Schwartz, Carol B.** .... '45 '82 C.483 B.A. L.1065 J.D. [Carr,M.I.T.&H.]
*PRACTICE AREAS: Real Estate Law.
Sembenini, Robyn Mary-Anuhea '61 '91
C.312 B.A. L.1065 J.D. Staff Atty., U.S. Postal Serv.
Shomer, Evyn L. .... '58 '89 C.107 B.A. L.284 J.D. Lenscrafters, Inc.
Showen, Robert H., (AV) .... '32 '55 C.813 B.A. L.802 LL.B. 1290 Howard Ave.
Siguenza, Joseph J. .... '52 '80 C.770 B.S. L.990 J.D. 1799 Old Bayshore Hwy.
**Simon, Bruce L.**, (AV) .... '53 '80 C.112 A.B. L.1065 J.D. [Cotchett&P.]
**Stalteri, Lisa Hayhurst** .... '63 '87 C.154 B.A. L.1065 J.D. [Carr,M.I.T.&H.]
*PRACTICE AREAS: Real Estate Law; Environmental Law.
Stayner, Anthony G. .... '55 '83 C.112 A.B. L.1066 J.D. 808 Howard Ave.
Stillman, Francis J., (BV) .... '38 '65 C&L.813 B.A., J.D. 1601 Bayshore Hwy.
Taylor, Marian C. .... '48 '90 L.809 J.D. V.P., E.W. Blanch Co.
**Telleen, L. Michael**, (AV) .... '47 '73 C.118 B.A. L.813 J.D. [Carr,M.I.T.&H.]
*PRACTICE AREAS: General Corporate Law; Business Law.
**Tham, Marilynn** .... '65 '95 C.610 B.B.A. L.767 J.D. [▣ Cotchett&P.]
Vlahos, Eugene A. .... '48 '78 C.112 B.S. L.765 J.D. [Vlahos&V.]
Vlahos, John B., (AV) .... '35 '70 C&L.767 B.A., J.D. [Vlahos&V.]
Vlahos & Vlahos, (AV) .... 533 S. Airport Blvd.

**Voltz, Charles E., (AV) '34 '63 C.597 B.S. L.477 J.D.**
**1290 Howard Avenue, Suite 333, 94010**
**Telephone: 415-342-4491 FAX: 415-342-4441**
**Email: law@voltz.com URL: http://www.voltz.com**
**Labor and Employment Law for Employers, Alternative Dispute Resolution, Mediations and Arbitrations.**
*See Professional Biographies, BURLINGAME, CALIFORNIA*

Vorsatz, Mark L. .... '54 '79 C.813 A.B. L.1065 J.D. 1601 Bayshore Hwy.
**Wailes, W. George**, (AV) .... '54 '81 C.112 B.A. L.1067 J.D. [Carr,M.I.T.&H.]⊙
*PRACTICE AREAS: Civil Litigation; ERISA Litigation; Bankruptcy Litigation.
**Walsh, Moira C.** .... '62 '87 C.112 B.A. L.273 J.D. [Carr,M.I.T.&H.]⊙
*PRACTICE AREAS: Bankruptcy Law; Insolvency Law.
Weinberg, Arden K. .... '— '67 C.112 A.B. L.284 J.D. 1800 Trousdale Dr.
**Weiner, Marie Seth**, (AV) .... '59 '83 C.767 B.S. L.1065 J.D. [Cotchett&P.]
Weiss, Susan L. .... '65 '92 C.112 B.A. L.1065 J.D. 1652 Albemarle Way
Weitzer, Steven J. .... '61 '86 C&L.464 B.S., J.D. Mutual Protec. Tr.
Westerberg, Kent .... '62 '88 C&L.05 LL.B. 216 Park Rd.
Wilder, Deborah E. G. .... '56 '81 C.112 B.A. L.1051 J.D. [Wilder,D.&Assoc.]
Wilder, Deborah & Associates .... 433 Airport Blvd.
**Willig, Edward J., III** .... '59 '84 C.813 A.B. L.1066 J.D. [Carr,M.I.T.&H.]
*PRACTICE AREAS: Corporate and General Business Law; Healthcare Law.
**Winters, Daniel W.**, (AV) .... '47 '72 C.210 B.A. L.339 J.D. [Winters,K.&D.]

**Winters, Krug & Delbon, (AV) ▣**
**345 Lorton Avenue, Suite 204, 94010-4116**
**Telephone: 415-579-1422 Fax: 415-579-1852**
**Members of Firm: William L. Nagle; John S. Krug; Daniel W. Winters; David A. Delbon; Cheryl A. Noll; Jerry E. Nastari; David F. Zucca.**
**General Civil and Trial Practice, including Insurance Law, General and Product Liability, Aviation Law, Construction Law, Environmental and Toxic Tort Claims.**
**Representative Clients: State Farm Mutual Automobile Insurance Co.; State Farm Fire & Casualty Co.; Fireman's Fund Insurance Cos.; California State Automobile Assn.; Tokio Marine Management Co.; Chubb Group of Insurance Cos.; Argonaut Insurance Co.; Aviation Office of America; City of Burlingame; City of Half Moon Bay.**
*See Professional Biographies, BURLINGAME, CALIFORNIA*

Wrinkle, Robert S., (BV) .... '36 '66 C.112 A.B. L.1065 J.D. 1601 Bayshore Hwy. #301
**Zucca, David F.** .... '65 '91 C.1060 B.A. L.1067 J.D. [Winters,K.&D.]

## BYRON, —, *Contra Costa Co.*

Worrell, Charles M., (CV) .... '31 '72 4980 North Point

## CALABASAS, —, *Los Angeles Co.*

(Part of the incorporated City of Los Angeles)

Adams, Jack V. .... '17 '40 C&L.597 B.S.L., LL.B. 22242 Cairnloch St.
Anatole, Michael H. .... '53 '91 C.1077 B.A. L.990 J.D. [▣ Murphy&G.]
Apelian, Mark D. .... '60 '90 C.1077 B.S. L.398 J.D. [▣ Effres&B.]
Baker, Mark E. .... '60 '84 C&L.1190 B.S.L., J.D. 23801 Calabasas Rd.
**Berg, Ronald S.**, (BV) .... '52 '76 C.112 B.A. L.809 J.D. [Berg&B.]
*PRACTICE AREAS: Real Property Transactions; Business/Corporate Transactions; Litigation-Business/Corporate/Real Property; Entertainment.

**Berg and Berg, (BV)**
**P.O. Box 8817, 91372-8817**
**Telephone: 818-883-9905 Facsimile: 818-883-9913**
**Email: RSBERGLA@AOL.COM**
**Ronald S. Berg.**
**General Transactional Law, Mergers and Acquisitions, Real Estate and Business Litigation and Entertainment Law.**
**Reference: Western Bank, Santa Monica, California.**
*See Professional Biographies, CALABASAS, CALIFORNIA*

Berger, Mark J. .... '51 '76 C.112 B.A. L.800 J.D. 24947 Lorena Dr.
Bland, Daniel D. .... '47 '83 C.516 B.A. L.426 J.D. 23548 Calabasas Rd.
**Boehm, Joel T.** '46 '72 C&L.190 B.S.B.A., J.D.
(adm. in NY; not adm. in CA) [Sabo&G.]
*PRACTICE AREAS: Municipal Law; Public Finance.
Brand, Richard L. .... '34 '65 C.112 B.A. L.426 J.D. Comr., L.A. Jud. Dist. Ct.
Brundo, Kathleen Lee .... '64 '91 C.112 B.A. L.809 J.D. 24007 Ventura Blvd.
Bryman, Andrew C. .... '53 '81 C.645 B.A. L.1190 J.D. [Effres&B.]
Buckley, James R. .... '58 '86 C.696 B.S.Ch.E. L.800 J.D. Corp. Coun., Lockheed Corp.
**Chahine, Linda** .... '61 '91 C.980 B.S. L.161 J.D. [▣ Sabo&G.]
*PRACTICE AREAS: Redevelopment; Municipal Law; Real Estate; Litigation.
Christenson, David M. .... '43 '72 C.112 A.B. L.1068 J.D. Corp. Coun., Lockheed Corp.
Cohen, William N. .... '42 '72 C.1077 B.A. L.426 J.D. V.P., Valley Crest Landscape, Inc.
**Crump, Alexis G.** .... '62 '88 C.112 A.B. L.276 J.D. [Sabo&G.]
*PRACTICE AREAS: Public Finance Law; Redevelopment Law; Real Estate Law; Civil Litigation.
Datzker, Leigh A. .... '55 '82 C.1077 B.A. L.1095 J.D. [Murphy&G.]
Davis, Robert J. .... '42 '69 C.112 B.S. L.1065 J.D. 4407 Alta Tupelo Dr.
**de Bortnowsky, Andreas G.** .... '57 '85 C.112 B.A. L.809 J.D. [Sabo&G.]
*PRACTICE AREAS: Real Estate Law; Redevelopment Law; Municipal Law; Military Base Closures.
**Diamond, Jeffrey D.**, (AV) .... '53 '78 C.112 B.A. L.426 J.D. [J.D.Diamond]
*REPORTED CASES: Preis v. American Indemnity Company (1990) 220 Cal.App.3d 752.
*PRACTICE AREAS: Insurance Coverage; Insurance Litigation; Civil Litigation; Appellate.

**Diamond, Jeffrey D., A Professional Corporation, (AV)**
**5010 North Parkway Calabasas, Suite 200, 91302-1483**
**Telephone: 818-225-5035 Fax: 818-225-5032**
**Jeffrey D. Diamond.**
**Insurance Coverage, Civil Litigation.**
*See Professional Biographies, CALABASAS, CALIFORNIA*

Doyle, Paul A., Jr. .... '33 '71 C.112 B.S. L.1095 J.D. 5000 Parkway Calabasas
Ebner, Stephen A. .... '49 '83 C.705 B.A. L.1136 J.D. 4766 Park Granada
Effres, Steven B. .... '58 '83 C.1316 B.S. L.426 J.D. [Effres&B.]
Effres & Bryman, A Prof. Corp. .... 5000 Pkwy. Calabasas
Eller, Jay J. .... '29 '54 C.112 B.A. L.800 LL.B. [J.J.Eller]
Eller, Jay J., Inc. .... 4505 Las Virgenes Rd.
Fabos, Suzanna .... '55 '80 C&L.851 B.B.A., J.D. Corp. Coun., Lockheed Corp.
Feldstern, Daniel B. .... '55 '84 C.605 B.A. L.809 J.D. 23373 Park Hacienda
Fischl, Debra Sholl .... '54 '80 C.1097 B.A. L.809 J.D. 5000 N. Pkwy. Calabasas
Fishenfeld, Moses H. .... '47 '76 C.1077 B.S. L.1095 J.D. 3640 Paseo Primario
Floyd, John B. .... '50 '78 C.988 B.Ed. L.809 J.D. 23801 Calabasas Rd.
Fox, Howard .... '54 '85 C.1077 B.A. L.426 J.D. 5146 Douglas Fir Rd.
Garcia, Robert, Jr. .... '59 '90 C.112 B.A. L.990 J.D. 5000 N. Pkwy. Calabasas Dr.
**Gitlin, Gary M.**, (AV) .... '51 '76 C.112 B.A. L.1148 J.D. [G.M.Gitlin]
*PRACTICE AREAS: Real Estate and Business Law and Litigation; Corporate Law.

**Gitlin, Gary M., A Professional Law Corporation, (AV)**
**Suite 110, 23945 Calabasas Road, 91302**
**Telephone: 818-591-3757 Telefax: 818-591-2779**
**Gary M. Gitlin.**
**General Civil Practice. Real Estate, Business, Civil Litigation and related causes.**
*See Professional Biographies, CALABASAS, CALIFORNIA*

Glassman, A. J. .... '63 '95 C.763 B.A. L.398 J.D. [▣ Effres&B.]
Glazer, Mark S. .... '53 '82 C.112 B.A. L.809 J.D. 23622 Calabasas Rd.
Gold, Howard .... '48 '78 C.112 B.A. L.809 J.D. [Murphy&G.]
Gold, Ronald .... '45 '72 C.112 B.A. L.426 J.D. [Murphy&G.]
Gore, Donald E. .... '36 '72 C&L.1137 B.S., J.D. Corp. Coun., Lockheed Corp.
Graditor, Susan Blay .... '55 '81 C.112 B.A. L.1095 J.D. 4437 Tedregal Ct.
Grapp, Wesley G. '18 '44 C.585 Ph.B. L.190 J.D.
(adm. in NE; not adm. in CA) 4240 Bon Homme Rd.‡
Graziano, Joseph P. .... '64 '89 C.676 B.S. L.990 J.D. [Lyden&G.]
**Green, Charles R.** .... '50 '76 C.112 B.A. L.1068 J.D. [Sabo&G.]
*PRACTICE AREAS: Redevelopment; Eminent Domain; Environmental Law; Inverse Condemnation; Litigation.
Greenberg, Raymond A. .... '43 '69 C.37 B.A. L.800 J.D. 23622 Calabasas Rd.
Greene, Harold L., (AV) .... '36 '63 C.112 A.B. L.1068 J.D. 23622 Calabasas Rd.
Gusman, Robert C. '31 '57 C.569 B.A. L.188 J.D.
V.P., Asst. Gen. Coun. & Asst. Secy., Lockheed Corp.
Haines, Todd F. .... '63 '89 C.1049 B.A. L.464 J.D. 23622 Calabasas Rd.
Hampton, Albert, (AV) .... '25 '49 C.421 A.B. L.800 LL.B. The Settlement Company
Harrison, Michael D. .... '51 '77 C.112 A.B. L.1068 J.D. [▣ Murphy&G.]
Heng, Stephanie L. .... '42 '89 C.399 B.A. L.809 J.D. 25600 Maynard Dr.
Hurvitz, Ralph A. .... '38 '65 C&L.94 A.B., LL.B. Sr. Corp. Coun., Lockheed Corp.
Imai, Keiichiro '20 '51 C&L.477 B.S.E., J.D.
Asst. Corp. Pat. Coun., Lockheed Corp. (Pat.)
Kahn, Robert A. .... '53 '80 C.112 B.A. L.426 J.D. 5000 N. Pkwy. Calabasas
Kaplan, David G. .... '44 '82 C.339 B.S. L.426 J.D. 4215 Lost Spring Dr.
Kates, Roy A., (BV) .... '33 '57 C.112 B.A. L.1068 LL.B. 23501 Park Sorrento
Kinney, Kerry M., (AV) .... '52 '77 C.990 B.A. L.800 J.D. 5000 Parkway Calabasas
Klein, Gordon L. .... '56 '80 C&L.477 B.B.A., J.D. 24724 Calle Conejo‡
Knox, Richard E. W. .... '49 '80 C.112 B.A. L.809 J.D. 23586 Calabasas Rd.
Kodish, Martin H. .... '47 '72 C&L.608 B.A., J.D. 4766 Park Granada, Loft
Kolin, Henry .... '15 '62 C.563 B.S. L.229 J.D. 26124 Roymor Dr. (Pat.)
Larson, Gregory L., (AV) .... '47 '74 C.112 B.A. L.426 J.D. 5000 Pkwy. Calabasas
Lavin, Marvin M. .... '20 '75 C.145 B.S. L.426 J.D. 4748 Park Granada‡
Loring, Charles A. .... '15 '38 C.684 LL.D. L.1065 J.D. Ret. Supr. Ct. J.
Lyden, Christine C. .... '58 '83 C.112 B.A. L.464 J.D. [Lyden&G.]
Lyden & Graziano .... 4764 Park Granada
Marks, Richard D. .... '51 '76 C.112 B.A. L.809 J.D. [R.D.Marks]
Marks, Richard D., Professional Corporation .... 23901 Calabasas Rd.

CAA41P

CALIFORNIA—CALABASAS MARTINDALE-HUBBELL LAW DIRECTORY 1997

Marshall, Carol R. .... ’53 ’80 V.P., Secy. & Asst. Gen. Coun., Lockheed Corp.
Matorin, Sidney R. .... ’31 ’70 C.112 B.S. L.1095 J.D. 23901 Calabasas Rd.
Mellen, Chase, III .... ’43 ’75 C.309 A.B. L.1068 J.D. 23945 Calabasas Rd.
Moore, Brian M. .... ’51 ’77 C.1077 B.A. L.426 J.D. 23501 Park Sorrento
Murphy, John J., Jr., (AV) .... ’23 ’49 C.716 B.A. L.724 J.D. [Murphy&G.]
Murphy & Gold, A Professional Corporation, (AV) .... 5146 Douglas Fir Rd.
Nassi, Albert T. ’50 ’76 C.112 B.S.B.A. L.809 J.D.
CEO & Gen. Coun., Nassi Group, The
Nolan, John J., Jr., (BV) .... ’25 ’55 C.426 L.809 LL.B. 4766 Park Granada, #101
O’Reilly, David .... ’31 ’72 C.1042 B.S.E.E. L.276 J.D. 23632 Calabasas Rd. (Pat.)
**Patterson, Robert L.** .... ’61 ’89 C.112 B.A. L.426 J.D. [Ⓐ Sabo&G.]
*PRACTICE AREAS: Business Law; Municipal Law; Homeowner Association Law.
**Pilot, Edward W.** .... ’63 ’88 C.861 B.S.M. L.426 J.D. [Ⓐ Sabo&G.]
*PRACTICE AREAS: Civil Litigation; Municipal Law; Redevelopment Law; Real Estate Law; Environmental Law.
**Quintanilla, Steven B.** .... ’58 ’92 C&L.112 B.A., J.D. [Sabo&G.]⊙
*PRACTICE AREAS: Eminent Domain; Inverse Condemnation; Civil Litigation.
Recchuite, Martin C. ’43 ’68 C.831 B.A. L.477 J.D.
Asst. Treas., Ins. & Risk Mgmt., Atlantic Richfield Co.
Reiss, Stephen J. .... ’47 ’73 C.1077 B.S. L.1049 J.D. 4766 Park Granada
Riddle, Lawson, (AV) .... ’29 ’58 C.629 B.S. L.1065 J.D. 5000 Pkwy. Calabasas‡
Roberts, Donzil D. .... ’34 ’84 C.679 B.S.E.E. L.1095 J.D. [Murphy&G.]
Rosenberg, Florence P. .... ’22 ’46 C.563 L.724 LL.B. 3753 Calle Jazmin
Roth, Barry Stuart .... ’39 ’82 C.1077 B.A. L.1148 J.D. 5608 Las Virgenes Rd.
**Sabo, Timothy J.**, (AV) .... ’47 ’77 C.980 B.M.E. L.208 J.D. [Sabo&G.]
*PRACTICE AREAS: Redevelopment Law; Public Finance Law.

**Sabo & Green, A Professional Corporation, (AV)**
**23801 Calabasas Road, Suite 1015, 91302-1547⊙**
**Telephone: 818-704-0195 Fax: 818-704-4729**
**Timothy J. Sabo; Charles R. Green; Andreas G. de Bortnowsky; Alexis G. Crump; Joel T. Boehm (Not admitted in CA);—Edward W. Pilot; Linda Chahine; Gale Schlesinger; Steven B. Quintanilla; Robert L. Patterson.**
**Municipal Law, Public Finance, Real Estate, Redevelopment, Condemnation, Litigation and Military Base Closures.**
**San Bernardino, California Office: 201 North "E" Street, Suite 206. 92401-1507. Telephone: 909-383-9373. Fax: 909-383-9378.**
**Cathedral City, California Office: 35-325 Date Palm Drive, Suite 150, 92234. Telephone: 619-770-0873. Fax: 619-770-1724.**

***See Professional Biographies, CALABASAS, CALIFORNIA***

Sacks, Belinda Jeri Mason ’67 ’93 C.1044 B.A. L.823 J.D.
(adm. in PA; not adm. in CA) 25890 Chalmers Pl.
Sank, Arnold M. ’30 ’59 C.563 B.B.A. L.1009 LL.B.
(adm. in NY; not adm. in CA) 4403 Park Alisal‡
Saroian, Stephen A. .... ’32 ’69 C.999 B.S. L.1095 J.D. P.O. Box 8399
**Schlesinger, Gale** .... ’58 ’89 C.112 B.A. L.208 J.D. [Ⓐ Sabo&G.]
*PRACTICE AREAS: Municipal Law; Redevelopment Law.
Schwartz, Rick L. .... ’51 ’77 C.1077 B.A. L.61 J.D. 25422 Colette Way
Seccombe, Clinton F., Jr. .... ’18 ’77 C.112 L.1095 J.D. 4030 Park Melinda
Selan, Robert E. .... ’54 ’80 C.800 B.A. L.426 J.D. 23801 Calabasas Rd.
Shelters, Mary K. .... ’49 ’79 C.330 B.A. L.623 J.D. 4764 Park Granada
Shifman, Ronald Jey .... ’58 ’84 C&L.339 B.S., J.D. 24849 Avenida Asoleada
Sibilia, Robert .... ’58 ’86 C.184 B.A. L.940 J.D. 5000 Pkwy. Calabasas
Soben, Howard D. ’42 ’78 C.705 B.A. L.776 J.D.
(adm. in NJ; not adm. in CA) 22223 Via Leonardo‡
Sokol, Michael .... ’54 ’92 C.112 L.398 J.D. 23801 Calabasas Rd.
Steinfeld, Reid L. .... ’53 ’79 C.112 B.A. L.398 J.D. Coun., Grant & Weber
Steinhorn, Alex .... ’24 ’51 C&L.64 J.D. 22725 DeKalb Dr.‡
Sullivan, William A. .... ’38 ’67 C.813 A.B. L.770 J.D. Corp. Coun., Lockheed Corp.
Tanita, Allen K. .... ’51 ’76 C.95 B.A. L.464 J.D. 23801 Calabasas Rd.
Tarlow, Richard G. .... ’44 ’76 C.1077 B.A. L.809 J.D. 23632 Calabasas Rd.
Tierney, Timothy T. .... ’43 ’71 C.1097 B.S. L.426 J.D. 22521 Blueridge Ct.

**Tisser, Doron M., (AV) ’55 ’81 C.112 B.A. L.809 J.D.**
**23622 Calabasas Road, Suite 121, 91302-1553**
**Telephone: 818-222-9085 Fax: 818-222-9087**
**Email: dmtisser@pacificnet.net**
**(Certified Specialist, Probate, Estate Planning and Trust Law, Taxation Law, The State Bar of California Board of Legal Specialization).**
**Estate Planning, Probate and Trust Law, Trust Administration, Estate and Gift Tax Planning, Business Secession Planning, Taxation, Business Law, Corporations and Partnerships.**

***See Professional Biographies, CALABASAS, CALIFORNIA***

Vaccarello, Gerald L. .... ’39 ’74 C.1077 B.S. L.1095 J.D. 24671 Calle Largo
Vinson, William T. ’43 ’70 C.1070 B.S. L.1068 J.D.
V.P. & Gen. Coun., Lockheed Corp.
Vorgitch, George S. .... ’32 ’73 L.1095 J.D. 23501 Park Sorrento
Wagner, Stephen H. ’35 ’63
C.112 B.S. L.800 LL.B. Corp. Coun., Tax & Intl., Lockheed Corp.
Weiss, Stephen M. .... ’47 ’83 C.339 B.A. L.1136 J.D. 23777 Mulholland Hwy.

**Windsor, Susan L., Law Offices of ’57 ’89 L.398 J.D.**
**23901 Calabasas Road Suite 2001, 91302-1542**
**Telephone: 818-223-8282 Facsimile: 818-223-8937**
**Probate, Estate Planning, Probate and Trust Litigation, Guardianships and Conservatorships, General Business, Trust Administrations.**

Woloz, Robert A., (BV) .... ’44 ’70 C.1077 B.A. L.1068 J.D. 5146 Douglas Fir Rd.
Young, Marilyn J. .... ’37 ’79 C.398 B.A. L.1095 J.D. 4500 Park Monaco‡
Zavidow, Patricia Reid .... ’35 ’88 C.112 B.A. L.809 J.D. 5010 N. Parkway Calabasas
Zentil, Dennis P. .... ’47 ’76 C.1042 L.1179 J.D. 23901 Calabasas Rd.

## CALEXICO, 18,633, *Imperial Co.*

Jones, Charles E. .... ’34 ’68 C.763 B.S. L.1049 J.D. Mun. Ct. J.
Ruiz de Chavez, Oscar Arturo .... ’48 ’83 L.1137 J.D. 430 Mary Ave.

## CALIFORNIA CITY, 5,955, *Kern Co.*

Jones, Danny R., (AV) .... ’25 ’49 C&L.800 J.D. P.O. Box 2700‡

## CALIMESA, —, *Riverside Co.*

McKnight, J. Wallace .... ’18 ’50 C&L.878 J.D. 1090 Donna Lane‡

## CALISTOGA, 4,468, *Napa Co.*

Brown, Ira A., Jr. .... ’30 ’56 C.210 A.B. L.477 J.D. Supr. Ct. J.
D’Anneo, Andrew H. .... ’29 ’57 C&L.813 A.B., J.D. 1085 Dunaweal Ln.
Fouts, John D. .... ’47 ’75 C.309 B.A. L.1066 J.D. 3400 Mt. Home Ranch Rd.
Gladstein, John .... ’43 ’70 C.112 B.A. L.284 J.D. 3975 Mt. Home Ranch Rd.
Gordon, Marilynn Z. .... ’38 ’90 C.112 A.B. L.1065 1006 Bale Lane
Gowen, Terence H., (CV) .... ’30 ’72 C.767 B.S. L.284 J.D. 3140 Old Toll Rd.
Jones, Judith A., (CV) .... ’45 ’78 C.518 L.1227 J.D. 1314 Washington
Knickerbocker, Calvin A., (BV) .... ’45 ’72 C.112 A.B. L.1065 3257 Hwy. 128

Miller, Harry C. .... ’20 ’53 C&L.813 B.S., LL.B. P.O. Box 713
Montalbano, Dennis V. .... ’65 ’92 C.1365 B.A. L.1065 J.D. P.O. Box 225
Owens, Stephen W. .... ’49 ’78 C.112 A.B. L.767 J.D. 1220 Washington St.
von Pohle, Janice S. .... ’31 ’79 C.636 B.A. L.1137 J.D. 1381 Tucker Rd.

## CAMARILLO, 52,303, *Ventura Co.*

**Barker, John C.** .... ’56 ’92 C.951 B.A. L.1065 J.D. [Wood&Assoc.]
*PRACTICE AREAS: Insurance; Business Litigation.
Berninger, George R. .... ’38 ’79 C.679 B.S. L.1186 J.D. 1850 La Ramada Dr.
Bonner, William J. .... ’23 ’73 C.644 B.S.E.E. L.981 LL.B. 5365 Holly Ridge Dr.‡
Boyes, William L. .... ’15 ’53 C.267 A.B. L.284 LL.B. 1626 Shorline St.‡

**Burke, Williams & Sorensen, (AV)**
**A Partnership including a Professional Corporation**
**Suite 1, 2310 Ponderosa Drive, 93010⊙**
**Telephone: 805-987-3468**
**Email: bws@bwslaw.com URL: http://www.bwslaw.com**
**Resident Attorneys: J. Robert Flandrick; Brian A. Pierik; Cheryl J. Kane; Don G. Kircher; Mary Redus Gayle.**
**General Civil and Trial Practice in all State and Federal Courts. Securities, Corporate, Taxation, Insurance and Commercial Law. Municipal and Public Agency Representation. Local Government Financing, Taxation and Assessments. Community Redevelopment, Eminent Domain, Environmental and Land Use Law. Employee Benefit Plans, Probate and Estate Planning. Health Care, Medical Research, College and University and Non-Profit Organization Law, Employment and Personnel Law. Tort, Workers Compensation and Insurance Defense.**
**Los Angeles, California Office: 611 West Sixth Street, 25th Floor. Telephone: 213-236-0600.**
**Orange County Office: 3200 Park Center Drive, Suite 750, Costa Mesa, California. Telephone: 714-545-5559.**

***See Professional Biographies, CAMARILLO, CALIFORNIA***

Camarena, Timothy .... ’54 ’81 C.112 B.A. L.464 J.D. 360 Mobil Ave.
Carlson, Jerome Gaylord ’46 ’82 C.990 B.S. L.616 J.D.
(adm. in OK; not adm. in CA) 2561 Corte Olmo‡
Carlson, Ralph W., Jr. ’36 ’76 C.475 B.A. L.209 J.D.
(adm. in IL; not adm. in CA) Arco Solar, Inc.
Churchman, Glenn E., (BV) .... ’38 ’65 C.768 B.S. L.112 LL.B. 340 Rosewood Ave.
Cohen, Grace E., (BV) .... ’33 ’79 C.738 L.1186 J.D. [Cohen&C.]
Cohen and Cohen, A Law Corporation, (BV) .... 445 Rosewood Ave.
Connolly, William M. .... ’48 ’86 C.1077 B.S. L.426 J.D. Pacific Green Care
Darnall, Karen .... ’51 ’90 C.560 B.S. L.1336 J.D. 1000 Paseo Camarillo
Dempsey, Lynn Althaus .... ’42 ’76 C.112 A.B. L.426 J.D. 947 Camino Concordia‡
Edsall, David Edward, (BV) .... ’54 ’79 C.112 B.S. L.1137 J.D. 2301 Daily Dr.
**Flandrick, J. Robert**, (AV) .... ’28 ’56 C&L.800 B.S., J.D. [Burke,W.&S.] (⊙Costa Mesa)
*PRACTICE AREAS: Municipal Law; Eminent Domain Law; Redevelopment Law.
Fox, Alfred L. .... ’11 ’34 C.813 B.A. L.800 LL.B. 37212 Village
**Gayle, Mary Redus** .... ’29 ’80 C.157 B.A. L.426 J.D. [Burke,W.&S.]
Gose, Gregory R., (BV) .... ’54 ’79 C.605 A.B. L.1068 J.D. 1200 Paseo Camarillo
Habeck, Rollyn J., (CV) .... ’34 ’66 C.112 B.S. L.809 LL.B. P.O. Box 143
Halvorson, Eric H. .... ’49 ’76 C.92 B.S. L.228 J.D. Salem Communications Corp.
Hoffman, Paula P. .... ’56 ’84 C.878 B.A. L.990 J.D. 766 Valley Vista Dr.
Holliday, Randall H. .... ’49 ’74 C&L.259 B.A., J.D. Div. Coun., Abex/NWL Aerospace
Howard, Mary M. .... ’50 ’80 L.1186 J.D. 99 Pancho Rd.
**Jeppson, H. Roy**, (AV) .... ’38 ’64 C.112 B.S. L.1068 J.D. [H.R.Jeppson]

**Jeppson, H. Roy, A Professional Corporation, (AV)** BR
**1100 Paseo Camarillo, 93010**
**Telephone: 805-482-3322 FAX: 805-482-6672**
**Email: roy@vcol.net**
**H. Roy Jeppson;—Robyn F. Stalk.**
**Business Litigation in State and Federal Courts. Corporate, Tax, Real Estate, Government Contracts, Labor and Employment, and Estate Planning.**

***See Professional Biographies, CAMARILLO, CALIFORNIA***

Johnson, JoAnn .... ’— ’93 C.1077 L.1186 816 Camarillo Springs Rd.
Kahn, Raymond Lee, (AV) .... ’17 ’40 C&L.800 B.A., LL.B. 1124 Belleza St.‡
**Kane, Cheryl J.** .... ’46 ’79 C.112 B.A. L.809 J.D. [Burke,W.&S.]
*PRACTICE AREAS: Municipal Law; Land Use Law; Environmental Law; Labor Law.
Katler, Deborah M. .... ’50 ’87 C.999 B.A.Mus. L.809 J.D. 10500 Presilla Rd.
**Kircher, Don G.** .... ’33 ’61 C.605 B.A. L.426 J.D. [Burke,W.&S.]
Knight, Donald G. .... ’33 ’58 C&L.260 B.S.B.A., J.D. 1407 Sierra Madre Dr.
Korell, Steven W. .... ’48 ’77 C.1097 B.A. L.809 J.D. Sr. Coun., Unisys Corp.
Kunisaki, Ronald H. .... ’57 ’83 C.112 B.A. L.273 J.D. 77 Fulton St.
Lauten, John H., (AV) .... ’13 ’38 C.112 A.B. L.1066 LL.B. 20214 Village 20‡
Lent, Deborah T. .... ’61 ’85 C.800 B.S. L.1065 J.D. 1531 Calle Aurora
Levinson, Elinor B. .... ’40 ’68 C.112 A.B. L.145 J.D. Dep. Pub. Def.
Lund, Douglas R. ’30 ’65 C.878 B.A. L.724 LL.B.
(adm. in NY; not adm. in CA) 5780 Recodo Way‡

**Malley, Thomas E., (BV) ’44 ’70 C.524 B.S. L.1065 J.D.**
**1200 Paseo Camarillo, Suite 295, 93010**
**Telephone: 805-482-2199**
**Civil Trial Practice in State Courts. Real Property, Corporations, Estate Planning, Probate, Wrongful Termination.**

***See Professional Biographies, CAMARILLO, CALIFORNIA***

McConville, Theresa L., (CV) .... ’49 ’79 C.1190 B.S. L.1186 J.D. 340 Rosewood Ave.
Milhaupt, Thomas J. .... ’58 ’86 C.966 B.B.A. L.800 J.D. [Cohen&C.]
Morgan, John G., (BV) .... ’44 ’74 C.267 B.A. L.426 J.D. [J.G.Morgan]
Morgan, John G., A Professional Corporation, (BV) .... 1000 Paseo Camarillo
Pease, T. Dale, (CV) .... ’34 ’74 L.1095 J.D. 445 Rosewood Ave.
Pesola, Virginia R. .... ’47 ’81 C.1171 B.A. L.426 J.D. 2310 Ponderosa Dr.
**Pierik, Brian A.** .... ’49 ’74 C&L.426 B.A., J.D. [Burke,W.&S.]
*PRACTICE AREAS: Municipal Litigation; Environmental Law; Business Litigation; Insurance Defense Law; Labor Law.
Pontrelli, Michael A., (AV) .... ’29 ’62 C.800 B.A. L.809 LL.B. P.O. Box 945‡
Pugh, Francis L., (BV) .... ’34 ’80 C.10 B.S. L.1186 J.D. 2460 Ponderosa Dr., N., #A110
Reynolds, James A. .... ’39 ’77 C.267 B.S. L.1186 J.D. 2310 E. Ponderosa Dr.
**Rice, Elizabeth M.** .... ’52 ’85 C.94 B.S. L.1065 J.D. [Wood&Assoc.] ‡
*PRACTICE AREAS: Business.
Robertson, Roger E. .... ’19 ’52 C.453 B.S. L.273 J.D. 305El Tuaca Ct.‡
Rolfe, Bennett, A Professional Corporation, (BV) ’38 ’65
C.112 A.B. L.1068 LL.B. 2310 E. Ponderosa Dr.
Rose, Simon L. .... ’10 ’35 L.809 LL.B. 42067 Village St.‡
Roy, Robert P. ’50 ’77 C.112 B.A. L.1188 J.D.
Pres. & Gen. Coun., Ventura Co. Agricultural Assn.
Ruffner, Ben F. .... ’22 ’50 C.112 A.B. L.1066 LL.B. 265 Geneive Cir.‡
Rush, Linda C. .... ’58 ’86 C.112 B.A. L.1186 J.D. 6810 Aviano Dr.
Schochet, Sherman .... ’25 ’69 C.563 B.B.A. L.564 LL.B. 29201 Village 29
Schulner, Lawrence M. .... ’38 ’64 [L.M.Schulner&Assoc.]
Schulner, L. M., & Associates .... 360 Mobil Ave.
Seldeen, Richard .... ’37 ’63 C.732 B.S. L.1009 LL.B. 222 Romona Pl.
Shaw, Robert L., (AV) .... ’19 ’59 C.861 B.A. L.813 LL.B. 3119 Old Coach Rd.‡

Sherman, Milton N. ... '12 '37 L.809 J.D. 32106 Village Lane‡
Shunway, Douglas M. ... '30 '57 C&L.813 A.B., LL.B. 881 Avenida Acaso‡
Staker, Kevin G., (BV) ... '54 '80 C.101 B.A. L.878 J.D. 1200 Paseo Camarillo
**Stalk, Robyn F.** ... '56 '87 C.1077 B.A. L.809 J.D. [A] H.R.Jeppson]
Strand, Edna B. ... '18 '79 L.1136 J.D. 85 Maxine Dr.
Sussman, Richd. C. ... '16 '49 L.426 24143 Village 24
Tumbleson, Mark W., (BV) ... '26 '55 C.112 A.B. L.1068 J.D. 11415 Highridge Ct.
**Tyler, Paul B.** ... '66 '96 C&L.990 B.A., J.D. [Wood&Assoc.]
*PRACTICE AREAS: Insurance; Business Litigation.
Van Conas, Kendall A. ... '66 '92 C.112 B.A. L.809 J.D. [Cohen&C.]
Waldo, Robert S., (BV) ... '35 '67 C.502 B.A. L.1065 J.D. 2301 Daily Dr.
Wasylyshyn, John B. '59 '84 C&L.477 B.A., J.D.
(adm. in NH; not adm. in CA) 1603 Edgemont Dr.‡
Watling, Charles P. ... '53 '83 C.154 B.A. L.770 J.D. 281 Crestview Ave.
White, Timothy D. ... '49 '87 C.767 B.S.B.A. L.809 J.D. 400 Mobil Ave.
Wilkinson, Katherine B. ... '61 '86 C.674 B.A. L.800 J.D. 3202 Calle de Debesa‡
Windom, Gary, (BV) ... '50 '75 C.112 B.A. L.436 J.D. 1373 Oakhurst Ct.
Wolf, James ... '13 '35 C&L.910 J.D. 42210 Village-42
Wolpert, Mason G., (BV) ... '43 '73 C.1042 B.A. L.990 J.D. 450 Rosewood Ave.
**Wood, David E.** ... '57 '85 C.951 B.A. L.1065 J.D. [Wood&Assoc.]
*PRACTICE AREAS: Insurance; Business Litigation.

**Wood & Associates, L.L.P.**
**751 Daily Drive, Suite 250, 93010**
**Telephone: 805-484-3940 Fax: 805-484-2319**
**Email: dew@wood-associates.com URL: http://www.wood-associates.com**
**David E. Wood; Elizabeth M. Rice; Paul B. Tyler; John C. Barker.**
**Insurance and Business Litigation.**
*See Professional Biographies, CAMARILLO, CALIFORNIA*

## CAMBRIA, 1,716, *San Luis Obispo Co.*

Brauer, Donald E. ... '45 '75 C.339 B.S. L.809 J.D. 5030 Grove St.
Hope, Roger Charles, (BV) ... '20 '51 C.273 L.426 LL.B. 2066 Spencer St.
Kalshan, Vernon A. ... '40 '71 C.46 B.S. L.1065 J.D. 440 Kerwin
Kocs, Frank E., (CV) ... '45 '77 C.990 B.S. L.1136 J.D. 780 Main St. (⊙Paso Robles)
Lippold, Rod Earl, (AV) ... '30 '55 C.813 B.A. L.800 J.D. 419 Weymouth
McGurrin, Thomas M., (AV) ... '28 '53 C.999 L.809 J.D. 6410 Santa Rosa Creek Rd.‡
Stotter, James, II ... '29 '54 C&L.976 B.A., LL.B. 1595 Cardiff Dr., 2nd Fl.‡

## CAMERON PARK, —, *El Dorado Co.*

Adams, John V. (Jack), (BV⊙) '32 '62 C&L.880 B.A., J.D.
(adm. in TN; not adm. in CA) 2640 Cambridge Rd., Apt. 117-J‡
**Becker, David C.** ... '57 '83 C.1097 B.A. L.464 J.D. [Becker&R.]
*PRACTICE AREAS: Personal Injury (50%, 100); Real Estate (30%, 100); Business Law (20%, 50).

**Becker & Runkle, (CV)**
**3161 Cameron Park Drive, Suite 225, 95682**
**Telephone: 916-676-6464 Fax: 916-676-5805**
**Members of Firm: David C. Becker; Roger A. Runkle; Rick Mayer.**
**Personal Injury, Real Estate, Business, Corporate, Commercial, Family and Civil Litigation.**
*See Professional Biographies, CAMERON PARK, CALIFORNIA*

Bouillon, Edwin J., Jr. ... '38 '72 C.999 L.464 J.D. 3037 Cambridge Rd., #A
Bradley-Jungemann, Janet ... '54 '82 C.112 B.A. L.464 J.D. 3361 Caballero Ct.‡
**Brooks, Nelson Keith**, (CV) '48 '82
C.770 B.A. L.1065 J.D. [Laurie,M.&W.] (⊙Placerville)
*REPORTED CASES: Lonestar v. Mono County (1986) 639 F. Supp. 1439; Lilly v. USAA (1990) 217 Cad 1396.
*PRACTICE AREAS: Business; Real Estate; Personal Injury Litigation; Employment; Civil Rights Litigation.
Cumming, Richard C. ... '25 '56 C.112 L.809 J.D. 3720 Devon Ct.‡
Davis, Denny R. ... '41 '73 3081 Boeing Rd.
Finen, C. Michael ... '49 '77 C.330 B.A. L.61 J.D. 3461 Robin Lane
Gaffaney, William R., (BV) ... '45 '82 C.1097 B.A. L.464 J.D. 4120 Cameron Park Dr.
Gorman, Stephen B. ... '37 '67 C.112 L.800 J.D. 1010 Camerado Dr.
Guthrie, Gale C. ... '37 '69 C.813 A.B. L.1065 J.D. [Guthrie&G.]
Guthrie, Karen B., (BV) ... '38 '76 C.112 B.S. L.464 J.D. [Guthrie&G.]
Guthrie & Guthrie, (BV) ... 3461 Robin Ln.
Hayward, Scott B. ... '59 '88 C.800 B.A. L.464 J.D. 3461 Robin Lane
Kaufman, Nathan L. ... '49 '80 C.800 B.A. L.464 J.D. 3226 Woodleigh Lane
Kerner, Douglas K. ... '57 '83 C.112 A.B. L.800 J.D. 5180 Cameron Rd.
Kozak, Peter Joseph ... '62 '88 C.112 B.A. L.1067 J.D. Assoc. Atty.
**Laurie, Robert A.**, (BV) ... '46 '75 C.112 B.A. L.464 J.D. [Laurie,M.&W.] (⊙Placerville)
*PRACTICE AREAS: Government Land Use; Business; Real Estate.

**Laurie, Maloney & Wheatley, (AV)**
**3420 Coach Lane, Suite 15, 95682⊙**
**Telephone: 916-677-0245 Fax: 916-677-4802**
**Members of Firm: Robert A. Laurie; Brian E. Maloney; Robert M. Wheatley (Resident Partner, Sacramento County (Folsom) Office); Nelson Keith Brooks; Richard D. Sopp.**
**Land Use, Business, Real Estate, Banking, Estate Planning, Municipal, Employment and Construction Law, Civil and Personal Injury Litigation, Franchising.**
**Placerville (El Dorado County), California Office: 345 Placerville Drive. Telephone: 916-622-7769.**
**Folsom (Sacramento County), California Office: 1004 River Rock Drive, Suite 245. Telephone: 916-988-3857.**
*See Professional Biographies, CAMERON PARK, CALIFORNIA*

**Maloney, Brian E.**, (BV) '50 '76 C.112 A.B. L.464 J.D.
[Laurie,M.&W.] (⊙Placerville)
*PRACTICE AREAS: Real Estate; Business Law; Estate Planning.

**Mason, Jackson H., Jr., (BV) '44 '69 C&L.112 A.B., J.D.**
**Point Loma Center, 3161 Cameron Park Drive, Suite 209, 95682⊙**
**Telephone: 916-677-6877 FAX: 916-677-2824**
**Estate Planning, Wills and Trusts, Probate, Business, Corporate and Commercial Law Practice.**
**Campbell, California Office: Pruneyard Towers II, 1999 South Bascom Avenue, Suite 700. Telephone: 408-371-1011.**
*See Professional Biographies, CAMERON PARK, CALIFORNIA*

**Mayer, Rick** ... '56 '93 C.1060 B.S. L.999 J.D. [Becker&R.]
*PRACTICE AREAS: Personal Injury; Real Estate; Business Law.
Miller, Walter J. ... '33 '68 C.884 B.M.E. L.1068 J.D. 1361 Cameron Pk. Dr. Ste 225
Rademacher, Robert B., (CV) ... '58 '86 C.169 B.A. L.1065 J.D. 3222 Royal Dr.
Remy, William Thomas ... '43 '75 C.1073 B.A. L.464 J.D. 3330 Cameron Park Dr.
Roberts, Pamela ... '51 '81 C.1074 B.A. L.1065 J.D. 3420 Coach Lane
Roeca, Douglas R. ... '52 '77 C.112 B.A. L.1065 J.D. 3294 Royal Dr.
**Runkle, Roger A.**, (CV) ... '61 '86 C.112 B.A. L.464 J.D. [Becker&R.]
*PRACTICE AREAS: Family Law (65%, 200); Personal Injury (35%, 30).
Sebben, Linda S. '50 '91 C.112 B.A. L.464 J.D.
Sr. Atty. & Corp. Coun., Kensington Estate Servs.
Smith, Thomas A. ... '50 '75 C.1097 B.S. L.464 J.D. Mun. Ct. J.
Snyder, G. Joseph, (BV) ... '39 '72 C.267 B.S. L.1065 J.D. P.O. Box 316
**Sopp, Richard D.**, (CV) ... '58 '86 C&L.101 B.A., J.D. [Laurie,M.&W.] (⊙Placerville)
*PRACTICE AREAS: Franchising; Business; Real Estate; Litigation.
Sutherland, Susan L. ... '47 '76 C.112 B.A. L.464 J.D. 4120 Cameron Park Dr.
Teal, Kimberly Perry ... '57 '83 C.1060 B.a. L.464 J.D. 3281 Woodleigh Lane

## CAMPBELL, 36,048, *Santa Clara Co.*

**Adleson, Phillip M.**, (AV) ... '49 '76 C.1077 B.A. L.770 J.D. [Adleson,H.&K.]
*REPORTED CASES: I. E. Associates v. Safeco Title Ins. Co. (1985) 39 Cal.3d 281, 216 Cal.Rptr. 438; Anderson v. Heart Fed. Sav. & Loan (1989) 208 Cal.App.3d 202, 256 Cal.Rptr. 180; In Re BFP (1994) 114 S.Ct. 1757, 62 U.S.L.W. 4359.
*PRACTICE AREAS: Lending/Mortgage Brokering; Real/Personal Property Foreclosures; Real Estate Lending/Civil Litigation; Real Property Sales/Exchanges.

**Adleson, Hess & Kelly, (AV)**
**577 Salmar Avenue, Second Floor, 95008**
**Telephone: 408-341-0234 Telecopier: 408-341-0250**
**Email: pjkelly1@ix.netcom.com**
**Phillip M. Adleson; Randy M. Hess; Patric J. Kelly; Duane W. Shewaga; Steven B. Haley; David M. Trapani; Quentin F. Mommaerts.**
**Real Estate and Foreclosure Matters, Creditor Bankruptcy Representation, Insurance Coverage for Policy Holders.**
*See Professional Biographies, CAMPBELL, CALIFORNIA*

Aldape, Alina A.C.E. ... '52 '77 C&L.813 B.A., J.D. U.S. Chamber of Com.
Alphonse, Harold T., (BV) ... '31 '61 C&L.770 B.S., LL.B. 1901 S. Bascom Ave.
**Birmingham, Hobart McK.**, (AV) '44 '71 C.674 A.B. L.477 J.D.
Sr. Dir., Apple Computer, Inc (Apple Americas)
Bozzo, George L. ... '31 '70 C.475 B.A. L.809 J.D. 2155 S. Bascom Ave.
Branch, Aldo P. O. ... '58 '85 C.768 B.S. L.770 J.D. 2105 S. Bascom Ave.
Brewer, Lisa A. ... '54 '87 C.766 B.A. L.1065 J.D. Coun., Apple Computer, Inc.
Brown, Diane M., (BV) ... '49 '82 C.112 B.A. L.770 J.D. 1999 S. Bascom Ave.
Castello, Raymond V., (BV) ... '39 '65 C.768 B.S. L.813 J.D. 1790 S. Winchester Blvd.
Chavez, Theodore R., (AV) ... '44 '72 C.767 L.1026 J.D. 19999 S. Bascom Ave. Ste 820
Christensen, Barbara B. ... '42 '80 C.1268 B.A. L.770 J.D. 577 Salmar Ave.
Doherty, John E. ... '48 '80 C.851 B.A. L.1137 J.D. 1550 S. Bascom Ave.
Dolwig, Richard J., Jr., (AV) ... '44 '70 C.911 B.A. L.770 J.D. 1475 S. Bascom Ave.
Edgemon, Charles F. ... '34 '72 C.560 B.A., M.A. L.770 J.D. 3001 S. Winchester Blvd.‡
Erickson, Mark A., (AV) ... '52 '79 C.347 B.S. L.770 J.D. 1475 S. Bascom Ave.
Eugenios, Demetrious ... '47 '72 C.768 B.A. L.1067 J.D. 1475 S. Bascom Ave.
Fairbanks, Jack G., (BV) ... '32 '64 C.768 B.A. L.1026 J.D. 3001 S. Winchester Blvd.
Finch, David R., (AV) ... '33 '59 C.768 A.B. L.1065 J.D. 1999 S. Bascom Ave.

**Fukasawa, John K., Jr., (AV) '43 '74 C.1239 B.A. L.770 J.D.**
**The Pruneyard, Tower I, 1901 South Bascom Avenue, Suite 1240, 95008-2212**
**Telephone: 408-371-5980 FAX: 405-371-5984**
**(Certified Specialist, Family Law, The State Bar of California Board of Legal Specialization).**

Furman, James, (A P.C.) ... '45 '76 C.1044 B.A. L.464 J.D. P.O. Box 110460
Garson, Katherine A. ... '65 '91 C.605 A.B. L.770 J.D. 1925 S. Winchester Blvd.
Gerhardt, John S., (BV) ... '37 '64 C&L.770 LL.B. 1901 S. Bascom Ave.
Hagen, William C. ... '37 '75 C.1077 B.A. L.770 J.D. 53 Shereen Pl.
**Haley, Steven B.**, (BV) ... '50 '76 C.768 B.A. L.770 J.D. [A] Adleson,H.&K.]
*REPORTED CASES: Trustors Security Service v. Title Recon Tracking et al. (1996) 56 Cal.Rptr.2d 793.
*PRACTICE AREAS: Real Property Litigation (65%); Bankruptcy Law and Secured Creditors (25%); Real Property Transactions (5%); General Civil (5%).
Hannon, T. Patrick, (BV) ... '48 '74 C&L.770 B.A., J.D. 1901 S. Bascom Ave.
Hao, James P. ... '61 '91 C.838 B.S.E.E. L.421 J.D. 2105 S. Bascom Ave. (Pat.)
Harris, William J., Jr. ... '23 '52 C.112 B.A. L.1065 J.D. Ret. Supr. Ct. J.
Harward, Jon P., (BV) ... '35 '63 C.1032 B.A. L.1065 LL.B. 1901 S. Bascom Ave.
Heffner, Edward W., Jr. ... '60 '85 C&L.770 B.S.C., J.D. 2105 S. Bascom Ave.
**Hess, Randy M.**, (AV) ... '55 '79 C.36 B.S. L.770 J.D. [Adleson,H.&K.]
*REPORTED CASES: Wong v. State Compensation Ins. Fund (1993) 12 Cal.App.4th 686; La Jolla Beach & Tennis Club v. Industrial Indemnity Co. (1994) 9 Cal.4th 27; Apte v. Japra, Inc., — F.3d—, 96 Daily Journal D.A.R. 11960 (9th Cir. 1996); Lesser v. State Farm Ins. Co., 1996 WL 339854 (C.D.Cal. 1996); Gillespie v. Hartford Inc. Co. Midwest, 1996 WL 61155 (N.D.Cal. 1996).
*PRACTICE AREAS: Insurance Coverage/Bad Faith (90%, 100); Personal Injury (10%, 25).
Hoffman, David S. ... '58 '90 C.549 B.A. L.770 J.D. [A] D.R.Sylva]
Hofvendahl, Russell L., (AV) ... '21 '48 C.768 A.B. L.813 LL.B. 1901 S. Bascom Ave.
**Homer, Lloyd W.**, (AV) ... '33 '65 C.112 B.S. L.767 J.D. [Homer&P.] ‡

**Homer & Phillips, A Law Corporation, (AV)**
**Suite 1010 The Pruneyard Towers II, 1999 South Bascom Avenue, 95008**
**Telephone: 408-377-3901 Fax: 408-377-2971**
**Lloyd W. Homer (Retired); Geoffrey W. Phillips (Certified Specialist, Probate, Estate Planning and Trust Law, The State Bar of California Board of Legal Specialization).**
**Estate Planning, Probate, Taxation and Trust Law.**
*See Professional Biographies, CAMPBELL, CALIFORNIA*

Hughes, Scott D. ... '56 '86 C.878 B.S. L.285 J.D. 577 Salmar Ave.
Izor, Paul H., (BV) ... '49 '82 C.238 B.A. L.1026 J.D. 1999 S. Bascom Ave., Suite 510
Jensen, Linda M. ... '45 '87 C.768 B.A. L.770 J.D. 1999 S. Bascom Ave.‡
Johnson, Marion M. ... '34 '83 C.768 B.A. L.770 J.D. 1475 S. Bascom Ave.
Kasolas, George C., (BV) ... '38 '72 C.768 B.S. L.1026 J.D. 1901 S. Bascom Ave., #1220
**Kelly, Patric J.**, (AV) ... '51 '76 C.1073 B.A. L.770 J.D. [Adleson,H.&K.]
*REPORTED CASES: Abdallah v. United Savings Bank 43 Cal.App.4th 1101 (1996); I. E. Associates v. Safeco Title Ins. Co. (1985) 216 Cal.Rptr. 438, 39 Cal.3d 281-amicus; In re Apte, 180 B.R. 223 (9th Cir.BAP (Cal.) 1995); In re McFadyen, 145 B.R. 657 (E.D.Cal. 1992); In re BFP, 114 S.Ct. 1757, (U.S., Supreme Court 1994)-amicus.
*PRACTICE AREAS: Creditor Bankruptcy Law (75%); Real Estate Litigation (20%); Civil and Commercial Litigation (5%).
Key, David S. ... '58 '85 C.112 B.A. L.546 J.D. 176 N. Milton Ave.
Kitsuse, Mari L. ... '55 '79 C.339 B.A. L.770 J.D. [Louie&K.]
La Croix, Edward R., (BV) ... '26 '61 C.610 B.S. L.770 LL.B. 1500 E. Hamilton Ave.
Lefevre, Nicholas R. ... '51 '78 C.30 B.A. L.276 J.D. 51 E. Campbell Ave.
Levinson, Benjamin R. ... '58 '84 C.112 B.A. L.770 J.D. 577 Salmar Ave.
Louie, Calvin S., (CV) ... '53 '80 C.9999 B.A. L.1065 J.D. [Louie&K.]
Louie & Kitsuse, (CV) ... 1475 S. Bascom Ave.
Mahan, William D., (AV) ... '49 '80 C.112 B.A. L.770 J.D. 1550 S. Bascom Ave.
Maino, Roger L., (BV) ... '34 '64 C&L.770 B.S., LL.B. 730 Camden Ave.
Marr, Judith A. ... '54 '80 C.375 B.S. L.770 J.D. 470 Vandell Way
Mason, Jackson H., Jr., (BV) '44 '69
C&L.112 A.B., J.D. 1999 S. Bascom Ave. (⊙Cameron Park)
Maynard, Douglas S. ... '52 '79 C.1169 B.A. L.770 J.D. 1475 S. Bascom Ave.
McDonald, Edward C., Jr. ... '59 '85 C.112 A.B. L.770 J.D. 577 Salmar Ave., 2nd Fl.
**Mommaerts, Quentin F.**, (BV) ... '53 '79 C.1169 B.S. L.770 J.D. [A] Adleson,H.&K.]
*PRACTICE AREAS: Insurance Coverage (90%); Personal Injury Litigation (5%); General Civil Litigation (5%).
Moore, Rob ... '61 '89 C.813 B.A. L.800 J.D. W. Leslie Pelio & Assocs.
Murabito, Anthony C. ... '65 '92 C&L.770 B.S.E.E., J.D. 2105 S. Bascom Ave. (Pat.)
Nealon, Robert J. '17 '60 C&L.276 B.S.S., J.D.
(adm. in DC; not adm. in CA) 3983 W. Rincon Ave.‡
Nino, Dennis M., (BV) ... '46 '73 C.768 B.A. L.770 J.D. 1390 Stevens Ct.
Orozco, Margarita Lopez, (BV) ... '45 '79 C.112 B.A. L.1067 J.D. [Orozco&W.]

Orozco & Willoughby, (AV) ........ 1550 S. Bascom Ave.
O'Shaughnessy, Patrick M., (BV) .... '55 '82 C.767 B.S. L.765 J.D. 1550 S. Bascom Ave.
Petris, Nicholas C. ........ '23 '49 C.112 A.B. L.813 LL.B. 1901 S. Bascom Ave.‡
**Phillips, Geoffrey W.**, (AV) ........ '59 '87 C&L.770 B.S.C., J.D. [Homer&P.]
*PRACTICE AREAS: Estate Planning; Probate; Taxation and Trust Law.
Pickard, Richard R. '53 '79 C.951 B.A. L.945 J.D.
V.P., Gen. Coun. & Secy., Zilog, Inc.
Rashkin, Michael D. ........ '45 '70 C.102 B.A. L.724 J.D. 120 Dot Ave.
Rocha, Denise M. ........ '54 '80 C.112 B.A. L.1067 J.D. Sr. Coun., Apple Computer, Inc.
Rogers, John M. ........ '18 '71 C.823 A.B. L.981 LL.B. Prof., San Jose State Univ.
Sams, William F. ........ '44 '76 C.610 B.B.A. L.770 J.D.
Sanguinetti, Richard B., (BV) ........ '32 '60 C&L.770 B.S., LL.B. 1500 E. Hamilton Ave.
Savas, Theodore Peter ........ '58 '86 C.351 B.A. L.352 J.D. 1475 S. Bascom Ave.
Scholz, Alan W. ........ '53 '82 C.659 B.S. L.284 J.D. 694 Birch Dr.
Schunk, Joli M. ........ '63 '88 C.770 B.S. L.1065 J.D. 1834 White Oaks Ct.
Seaman, Christopher A. ........ '63 '90 C.112 A.B. L.1067 J.D. [D.R.Sylva]
**Shewaga, Duane W.**, (BV) ........ '58 '84 C.768 B.A. L.770 J.D. [▣ Adleson,H.&K.]
*REPORTED CASES: Abdallah v. United Savings Bank (1995) 943 Cal.App.4th 1101; Wong v. State Compensation Insurance Fund (1993) 12 Cal.App.4th 686; In re Nelson (1988) 91 BRW 904; In re Apte, (1996) WL551443 (9th Cir. 1996); In re BFP, (1994) 114 S.Ct. 1757.
*PRACTICE AREAS: Real Property Secured Transactions (35%); Insurance Coverage (50%); Bankruptcy (15%).
Stone, Richard S. '44 '74 C.477 B.A. L.1065 J.D.
Exec. V.P. & Gen. Coun., Peelle Financial Corp.
Sutton, Lawrence T., (BV) ........ '22 '52 C.768 L.770 LL.B. 1901 S. Bascom Ave.
Sylva, David R., (AV) ........ '36 '64 C.768 A.B. L.770 LL.B. [▣ D.R.Sylva]
Sylva, Nancy Burke ........ '40 '94 C.768 B.A. L.770 J.D. [▣ D.R.Sylva]
Sylva, David R., A Prof. Corp., Law Offices of, (AV)
1925 S. Winchester Blvd., Ste. 204
Syphers, Janet, (BV) ........ '45 '78 C.112 A.B. L.770 J.D. 1550 S. Bascom Ave.
Temmerman, Robert E., Jr., (AV) ........ '52 '80 C.93 A.B. L.770 J.D. 1550 S. Bascom Ave.
Tennant, Robert J., (BV) ........ '39 '65 C.768 B.A. L.1066 J.D. 1790 S. Winchester Blvd.
**Trapani, David M.** ........ '62 '87 C&L.770 B.S., J.D. [▣ Adleson,H.&K.]
*PRACTICE AREAS: Plaintiffs Personal Injury (60%, 35); Insurance Coverage (25%, 10); General Civil Litigation (15%, 5).
Tucci, Carl ........ '43 '83 C.768 B.A. L.770 J.D. 136 Memory Lane
Vasil, John G., (AV) ........ '30 '63 C.645 A.B. L.1065 J.D. 1901 S. Bascom Ave.
Vogelgesang, John J., (BV) ........ '34 '69 C.698 B.S. L.502 LL.B. 1901 S. Bascom Ave.
von Dioszeghy, Adam, (BV) ........ '38 '71 C&L.813 A.B., J.D. 1901 S. Bascom Ave.
Walsh, Kevin M. ........ '61 '87 C.112 B.A. L.1065 J.D. 1733 Dell Ave.
Walsh, Michael S. ........ '— '86 C.770 B.S. L.285 J.D. 1475 So. Bascom Ave.
Watson, William E., (AV) '21 '50
C.112 B.S. L.770 LL.B. 1901 S. Bascom Ave., Room 1200
Willoughby, John V., (AV) ........ '52 '78 C.1073 B.A. L.1067 J.D. [Orozco&W.]
Wolen, David H. ........ '45 '81 C.569 B.E. L.770 J.D. ESL Inc.
Zavodnick, Steven D. ........ '62 '88 C.112 A.B. L.770 J.D. [S.D.Zavodnick]
Zavodnick, Steven D., A Professional Law Corporation ..... 1999 S. Bascom Ave., Ste. 700

## CAMPTONVILLE, —, *Yuba Co.*

Buchter, John S. ........ '41 '77 C.330 B.S. L.464 J.D. P.O. Box 282

## CANOGA PARK, —, *Los Angeles Co.*

(Part of the incorporated City of Los Angeles)

Adams, B. J. ........ '30 '72 C.623 B.B.A. L.1095 J.D. 24614 Kittridge St.
Bovshow, Aaron G. ........ '36 '71 C.112 B.S. L.1148 J.D. P.O. Box 7956
Butta, Matthew C. ........ '33 '63 C.423 B.S. L.1068 J.D. 7919 De Soto Ave.‡
**Casey, James J., Jr.** ........ '66 '93 C.554 B.A. L.1148 J.D. [▣ De Simone&Assoc.]
Cohen, Michael N. ........ '63 '88 C.763 B.A. L.1049 J.D. 21515 Vanowen St.
Curry, Gerald E. ........ '50 '77 C.1077 B.A. L.1148 J.D. 21515 Vanowen St.
Dalton, Cynthia Lynn ........ '61 '92 C.1077 B.A. L.426 J.D. [▣ Tropio&M.]
Dambach, John L., (AV) ........ '28 '58 C.112 B.S. L.1068 LL.B. 7106 Owensmouth Ave.‡
**De Simone, Gerald**, (AV) ........ '59 '84 C.1019 B.A. L.990 J.D. [De Simone&Assoc.]
*REPORTED CASES: Southland v. Superior Court; Jurado v. Toys "R" Us, Inc.; Thomas v. Intermedics Orthopedics, Inc.

**De Simone & Associates, (AV)**
**6928 Owensmouth Avenue Second Floor, P.O. Box 352, 91305**
**Telephone: 818-715-7171 Facsimile: 818-715-9843**
**Gerald De Simone; James J. Casey, Jr. Of Counsel: Daniel J. Salomon.**
**Litigation, Premises Liability, Products Liability, Personal Injury, Torts, Insurance, Insurance Defense, Medical Malpractice, Labor and Employment, Alternative Dispute Resolution.**
***See Professional Biographies, CANOGA PARK, CALIFORNIA***

Egermeier, R. P. ........ '27 '77 C.623 B.S.E. L.397 LL.B. 22354 Malden St.‡
Erbeznik, Frank A. '23 '59 C.608 A.B. L.1003 LL.B.
(adm. in OH; not adm. in CA) 6500 Sausalito Ave.‡
Faner, Walter W., (AV) ........ '18 '50 C&L.800 B.S., LL.B. [W.W.Faner]
Faner, Walter W., A Law Corporation, (AV) ........ 7240 Remmet Ave.
Farrar, Joan L. ........ '30 '79 C.112 B.A. L.1136 J.D. 23331 Vanowen St.
Fest, Stuart W., (AV) ........ '44 '74 C.112 B.S. L.1095 J.D. [Fest&W.]
Fest & Williams, (AV) ........ 6928 Owensmouth
Field, Harry B. ..... '47 '75 C.422 B.S. L.64 J.D. Sr. Intell. Prop. Coun., Rocketdyne (Pat.)
Findling, Martin ........ '32 '65 C&L.912 B.A., LL.B. 7108 Desoto Ave.
Gaulton, David J. ........ '51 '76 C.705 B.A. L.276 J.D. Pres., LAMWEST
Geretz, Victor O. ........ '24 '50 C.145 S.B. L.309 LL.B. 6848 Shoup Ave.‡
Gerrity, Harry J. ........ '38 '75 C.209 A.B. L.365 J.D. 8387 Sale Ave.
Gordon, Felix F. '12 '36 C.424 A.B. L.209 J.D.
(adm. in IL; not adm. in CA) 6410 Pat. Ave.‡
Gray, Dana K. ........ '65 '92 C.426 B.A. L.1148 J.D. 21515 Vanowen St.
Gridley, Cynthia L. ........ '55 '88 C.1033 B.A. L.1148 J.D. 22159 Sherman Way
Haroldsen, Orvil O. ........ '31 '73 C.878 B.S.M.E. L.426 J.D. 7156 Kilty Ave.
Hill, Brockton D. ...... '58 '86 C.172 B.A. L.1068 J.D. Assoc. Coun., Coast Fed. Bk., FSB
Jaeger, Susan R. ........ '62 '89 21515 Vanowen St.
Juhas, Carol Adele '62 '89 C.1109 B.A. L.426 J.D.
Asst. V.P., & Assoc. Coun., Coast Fed. Bk., FSB
Kamerian, Van ........ '68 '95 L.809 J.D. 7132 Owensmouth Ave.
Kogen, Barbara C. ........ '51 '78 C.112 B.A. L.426 J.D. 23217 Keswick St.
Landstrom, Mark R. '52 '79 C.800 B.A. L.61 J.D.
V.P. & Asst. Gen. Coun., Coast Fed. Bk., FSB
Law, Richard S. ........ '43 '73 C.1077 B.A. L.1095 LL.B. 20316 Gresham St.
Leonardo, Mark J. ........ '60 '85 C.549 B.S. L.990 J.D. 6928 Owensmouth Ave.
McNamara, Leo F. ........ '28 '69 L.1095 LL.B. 6426 Ellenview, West Hills
Miller, Arthur E. ........ '27 '70 C.800 B.E. L.1095 J.D. 19939 Hatton St.
Moran, Alyson T. ........ '67 '92 C.112 B.A. L.990 J.D. 6928 Owensmouth Ave.
Morgan, Carolyn Y. .... '46 '79 C.329 B.S. L.1068 J.D. Assoc. Coun., Coast Fed. Bk., FSB
Morlan, Michael N. ........ '61 '86 C.147 B.S. L.990 J.D. [Tropio&M.]
Niles, Edwin K., (AV) ........ '24 '58 L.809 6928 Owensmouth Ave., 2nd Fl.
Olsen, Geoffrey G. '51 '76
C.1077 B.S. L.1148 J.D. Assoc. Gen. Coun., Coast Fed. Bk., FSB
Olsen, Scott D. ........ '63 '92 C.37 B.S. L.1206 J.D. 7132 Owensmith Ave.
Potter, Clyde H., Jr., (AV) '22 '52 C&L.800 B.S., J.D.
6928 Owens Mouth Ave., 2nd Fl.‡
Rathbun, Richard ........ '14 '42 C.112 B.A. L.1066 LL.B. 7124 Helmsdale Rd.‡
Robbins, Sanford L. ........ '42 '76 C.1077 B.S. L.1095 J.D. App. Offr., I.R.S.
Rosenfeld, Manfred ........ '27 '56 C.112 A.B. L.809 LL.B. 73 Flintlock Ln.
Ross, Ira J. ........ '39 '67 C.174 B.A. L.1165 J.D. Gen. Coun., Federated Industries, Inc.
Ross, James R., (AV) ........ '44 '74 C.1097 B.A. L.809 J.D. 1146 N. Central Ave.
**Salomon, Daniel J.** ........ '50 '75 C.800 B.A. L.1068 J.D. [▣ De Simone&Assoc.]
Shafron, Mark H. ........ '52 '77 C.1077 B.S. L.1095 J.D. 23676 Elkwood St., West Hills
Simmons, Ronnie M. ........ '40 '77 C.446 B.S. L.809 J.D. 23808 Northwoods View Rd.‡
Smith, Andrew P. ........ '44 '73 C.999 L.1095 J.D. 7437 Topanga Canyon Blvd.
Stober, Ralph K. ........ '29 '56 C.112 M.B.A. L.1068 LL.B. 7140 Topanga Canyon Blvd.
Suttle, Robert E. ........ '43 '70 C.684 B.A. L.112 J.D. 7355 Topanga Canyon Blvd.
Tebelius, Dean Ervin ........ '50 '88 C.1079 B.A. L.1148 J.D. 19725 Sherman Way
Treiman, Jaak ........ '43 '68 C&L.800 A.B., J.D. 21515 Vanowen St.
Tropio, Scott T. ........ '57 '83 C.36 B.S. L.990 J.D. [Tropio&M.]
Tropio & Morlan ........ 6928 Owensmouth Ave. 2nd Fl.
Wallman, Barry J. '57 '82 C.800 B.S. L.809 J.D.
(adm. in IL; not adm. in CA) West Hills Family Practice Med. Grp.‡
Wane, Marc P. '55 '83 C.112 B.A. L.809 J.D.
V.P. & Asst. Gen. Coun., Coast Fed. Bk., FSB
Wheeler, Leslie W. ........ '23 '59 C.560 B.S. L.813 J.D. 7626 Pomelo Dr.‡
Whiteman, Ronald George ........ '47 '77 C.1077 L.1095 J.D. 7437 Topanga Cyn Blvd.
Williams, Garry W., (AV) ........ '45 '74 C.1077 B.A. L.809 J.D. [Fest&W.]

## CANYON, 200, *Contra Costa Co.*

Gotelli, Diane R. ........ '41 '81 C.112 B.A. L.1153 J.D. 115 Pinehurst Rd.‡

## CANYON COUNTRY, —, *Los Angeles Co.*

Eidson, Richard L. ........ '35 '81 C.605 B.A. L.1095 J.D. 15911 Condor Ridge Dr.
Eliasberg, Kenneth C., (AV) '32 '57
C.800 B.A. L.569 J.D. 15800 Live Oak Springs Canyon Rd.
Soman, Peter A. ........ '56 '89 L.398 J.D. 27257 1/2 Camp Plenty Rd.
Ziegler, Thomas Mathew ........ '53 '82 C.763 B.A. L.1137 J.D. 27257 1/2 Camp Plenty

## CANYON LAKE, —, *Riverside Co.*

Eastman, Lynn R., (Mr.) ........ '23 '63 C.684 B.A. L.1001 LL.B. 31341 Emperor Dr.‡
Graff, Steven L. ........ '43 '68 C.640 B.A. L.502 J.D. [S.L.Graff]
Graff, Steven L., Inc. ........ 31523 R.R. Canyon Rd.
Ritsema, George W. ........ '39 '79 C.477 B.S.E. L.1225 J.D. 22344 Whirlaway Ct.
van Rensburg, Ramona M. ........ '57 '88 C&L.061 B.J.P., LL.B. 30217 Skippers Way

## CAPISTRANO BEACH, 4,149, *Orange Co.*

**Eramo, Martin P., (BV) '52 '78 C.454 B.A. L.1137 J.D.**
**34700 Coast Highway, Suite 205, 92624**
**Telephone: 714-240-4425 Fax: 714-240-7881**
**Business, Construction, Real Estate, Landlord, Tenant and Collections.**
***See Professional Biographies, CAPISTRANO BEACH, CALIFORNIA***

Guirado, Edward J. ........ '05 '32 C.940 B.A. L.800 J.D. Ret. Supr. Ct. J.
Hall, Richard M., (BV) ........ '17 '44 C.809 L.1001 LL.B. 26872 Calle Hermosa
Roose, B. J. ........ '24 '49 C&L.800 A.B., J.D. 34693 B Camino Capistrano‡
Rupp, Nancy M., (BV) ........ '44 '83 C&L.1137 B.A., J.D. 26872 Calle Hermosa
Somerville, Don E., (BV) ........ '46 '79 C.1109 B.A. L.1137 J.D. 26872 Calle Hermosa

## CAPITOLA, 10,171, *Santa Cruz Co.*

Alexander, J. L. '14 '38 C&L.145 B.A., J.D.
(adm. in IL; not adm. in CA) 300 Plum St.‡
Brown, Thomas N., (BV) ........ '44 '80 C.696 B.A. L.770 J.D. 331 Capitola Ave.
Clarenbach, Sara, (AV) ........ '49 '74 C.966 B.A. L.1066 J.D. 331 Capitola Ave. (⊙Aptos)
Coolidge, Harry C., (BV) ........ '40 '65 C&L.950 B.A., J.D. 1260 41st. Ave.
Cummins, Richd. E. ........ '25 '52 C&L.966 B.S., LL.B. P.O. Box 948 (Pat.)
Farley, Judson T. ........ '51 '78 C.112 B.A. L.770 J.D. 830 Bay Ave.
House, Wanda ........ '53 '80 C&L.16 B.S., J.D. 314 Capitola Ave.
Katz, Robert Jay, (AV) ........ '52 '78 C.696 B.A. L.770 J.D. [Katz&L.]
Katz & Lapides, A Prof. Corp., (AV) ........ 314 Capitola Ave.
Lapides, Leola, (BV) ........ '53 '78 C.112 B.A. L.770 J.D. [Katz&L.]
Leinen, John D. '37 '65 C&L.208 B.S.B.A., J.D.
(adm. in CO; not adm. in CA) P.O. Box 415‡
Marcus, Howard S., (BV) ........ '41 '66 C.1019 B.A. L.1009 J.D. 331 Capitola Ave.
McGuire, Valerie A., (CV) ........ '45 '81 C.112 B.A. L.1066 J.D. 870 Park Ave.
McSpadden, John H. ........ '54 '84 C&L.912 B.A., J.D. 314 Capitola Ave.
Millenacker, Mark A. ........ '51 '77 C.602 B.A. L.770 J.D. 314 Capitola Ave.
Moore, Thomas M. ........ '31 '59 C.112 B.A. L.1065 J.D. 930 Rosedale Ave.‡
Romero, A. Lewis ........ '23 '60 C.560 B.S. L.1026 LL.B. P.O. Box 1092‡
Sanford, Paul S. ........ '56 '96 C.183 B.A. L.1226 J.D. 1405 Prospect Ave.
Schwartz, Donald C. ........ '54 '86 C.147 B.S. L.276 J.D. P.O. Box 965
Vandenberg, David N. ........ '51 '82 C.1169 B.A. L.61 J.D. 516 Del Monte Ave.

## CARDIFF-BY-THE-SEA, 5,724, *San Diego Co.*

Angus, Steven M., (BV) ........ '43 '74 C.668 L.61 LL.B. 2611 S. Hway. 101
Babcock, Bruce R., (CV) ........ '52 '79 L.1137 J.D. P.O. Box 1023
Baum, Gary S., (CV) ........ '48 '83 C.1108 B.S. L.1137 J.D. 2051 San Elijo Ave.
**Carlson, Roy L., Jr.** ........ '58 '86 C.112 B.A. L.1137 J.D. [Milberg&D.]
*REPORTED CASES: In re Consolidated Pioneer Mortgage, 178 B.R. 222 (9th Cir. BAP 1995); In re Casey, 193 B.R. 942, 1996 WL 137293 (Bkrptcy. S.D., Cal. 1996).
*PRACTICE AREAS: Bankruptcy; Corporate Reorganization; Creditors Rights; Business Litigation.
**Coughlin, Sean C.** ........ '66 '93 C.1049 B.A. L.61 J.D. [Milberg&D.]
*PRACTICE AREAS: Creditor's Rights; Bankruptcy; Business and Real Estate Litigation; Commercial Litigation.
**DePhillips, Russell M.**, (BV) ........ '49 '80 C.589 B.S. L.61 J.D. [Milberg&D.]
*REPORTED CASES: In re Dix, 140 B.R. 997 (Bankr. S.D. Cal. 1992).
*PRACTICE AREAS: Bankruptcy; Corporate Reorganization; Creditors Rights; Business and Real Property Matters; Commercial Litigation.
Diaz, Victoria S. ........ '46 '75 C.608 B.S. L.813 J.D. P.O. Box 934
Frank, Jeanine A. ........ '37 '90 C.1097 B.S. L.1066 J.D. 1346 Summit Ave.
Gadsby, C. Norman, (BV) ........ '45 '71 C.112 B.A. L.1065 J.D. 2533 S. Hwy. 101
Galuppo, Louis A. ........ '57 '89 C.763 B.S. L.61 J.D. 120 Birmingham Dr.
Goldstein, Michael, (AV) ........ '48 '80 C.259 B.S. L.1049 J.D. 120 Birmingham Dr.
Hallen, C. Bradley, (BV) ........ '44 '71 C.763 B.A. L.1065 J.D. 2533 South Hwy. 101
Ignell, David E. ........ '60 '87 C.950 B.S. L.1049 J.D. 2163 Newcastle Ave.
Katkov, Howard I., (BV) ........ '50 '76 C.549 B.A. L.1188 J.D. 2163 Newcastle Ave.
Kimball, John W., (AV) ........ '29 '55 C.768 A.B. L.800 J.D. 1327 Justin Rd.‡
Kurz, Andrew A., (AV) ........ '49 '74 C.112 B.A. L.1068 J.D. 120 Birmingham Dr.

Martin, James H. .................. '46 '79 C.37 B.S. L.1137 J.D. 2356 Montgomery Ave.

**McGovern, John Patrick, (AV) '57 '84 C.112 B.A. L.1067 J.D.**
**2533 South Highway 101, Suite 280, 92007**
**Telephone: 619-944-9941 Facsimile: 619-943-0494**
**Email: JPMcGESQ@AOL.COM**
**Business, Corporate and Real Estate, Intellectual Property, Commercial Litigation, Construction Law and Mechanics Liens, Employment Litigation and Personal Injury.**
*See Professional Biographies, CARDIFF-BY-THE-SEA, CALIFORNIA*

**McNulty, Timothy G.** ........................ '66 '92 C.769 B.A. L.61 J.D. [Milberg&D.]
*LANGUAGES: Spanish.
*PRACTICE AREAS: Civil Litigation; Personal Injury; Maritime Law; Products Liability; Insurance Law.
**Milberg, Frederic J.**, (BV) .................. '49 '76 C.823 B.A. L.284 J.D. [Milberg&D.]
*LANGUAGES: Spanish.
*PRACTICE AREAS: Personal Injury; Products Liability; Workers Compensation; Securities Law.

**Milberg & DePhillips, Professional Corporation, (BV)**
**2163 Newcastle Avenue, Suite 200, 92007**
**Telephone: 619-943-7103 Telecopier: 619-943-6750**
**Frederic J. Milberg; Russell M. DePhillips; William A. Skoog, Jr.; Roy L. Carlson, Jr.; Timothy G. McNulty; Sean C. Coughlin; Kent L. Sharp.**
**General Civil Practice. Business, Corporation, Real Property, Bankruptcy, Commercial, Personal Injury, Products Liability, Workers Compensation and Securities Law. Trials and Appeals.**
*See Professional Biographies, CARDIFF-BY-THE-SEA, CALIFORNIA*

Putnam, M. Warren .................... '39 '74 C.339 B.A. L.1068 J.D. 1309 Cornish Dr.‡
Sankary, Jerry H. ........................ '50 '76 C.800 B.S. L.1049 J.D. P.O. Box 935
**Sharp, Kent L.** ........................... '67 '95 C.763 B.A. L.61 J.D. [Milberg&D.]
*PRACTICE AREAS: Business; Litigation; Creditor's Rights; Bankruptcy; Personal Injury.
**Skoog, William A., Jr.** .................... '54 '84 C.763 B.A. L.61 J.D. [Milberg&D.]
*LANGUAGES: Spanish.
*PRACTICE AREAS: Personal Injury; Products Liability; Workers Compensation; General Civil Litigation; Maritime Law.
Spaid, Noel W., (Ms) ............. '42 '79 C.823 B.S. L.1137 J.D. 2514 Manchester Ave.
Stern, Peter C. '52 '81 C.273 B.A. L.1218 J.D.
(adm. in VT; not adm. in CA) 1232 Rueenstein Ave.‡
Wellcome, Page, (AV) ........................ '32 '59 C.813 A.B. L.508 J.D. [Wellcome]
Wellcome Cardiff-By-The-Sea Law Offices, (AV) ........... 160 Chesterfield Dr., Ste., 1
White, Daniel J. ............................ '59 '86 C.112 B.A. L.61 J.D. 2533 S. Hwy. 101
Wilson, Craig R. .................... '52 '77 C.999 B.A. L.767 J.D. 1564 Rubenstein Ave.

## CARLSBAD, 63,126, *San Diego Co.*

Allen, John Lawrence ............'47 '73 C.1077 B.A. L.809 J.D. 1925 Palomar Oaks Way
Alvord, James C. ...................... '44 '90 C.966 B.S. L.1137 J.D. 5963 La Place Ct.
Armstrong, J. Michael ............. '50 '77 C.768 B.A. L.1137 J.D. 2035 Corte Del Nogal
Balaker, Victor T., (BV) .................. '43 '72 C.433 B.A. L.767 J.D. 2646 Madison St.
**Ballance, Lori D.** ........................ '60 '88 C.1049 B.A. L.1065 J.D. [Gatzke,M.&D.]
Bandemer, Otto H., (BV) ............................. '31 '54 C&L.209 J.D. 2720 Jefferson St.
Barberio, R. J. ......................... '51 '79 C.112 B.A. L.1137 J.D. 2755 Jefferson St.
Beall, James W. ........................ '51 '76 C.107 B.A. L.990 J.D. 2755 Jefferson St.
Behymer, Lynn A., (CV) .............. '36 '82 C.309 A.B. L.1049 J.D. 2745 Jefferson St.
Berlin, Michael D., (BV) ................ '49 '74 C.597 B.A. L.665 J.D. 2777 Jefferson St.
Bertino, Peter A. ........................ '34 '59 C&L.813 A.B., J.D. 3655 Adams St.‡
Besecker, Ruth A., (BV) ..........'50 '82 C.30 B.A. L.1137 J.D. Benchmark Pacific, Inc.
Borg, Rickard L., (CV) ............. '45 '74 C.766 B.A. L.1137 J.D. 2755 Jefferson St.
Bost, John C., (BV) .................. '44 '73 C.763 B.S. L.1065 J.D. 7216 Durango Cir.
Bottomley, James C., (BV) .......... '48 '75 C.813 B.A. L.1065 J.D. 5963 La Place Ct.
Bowen, Duane C. ........................ '22 '50 C.277 B.S. L.145 J.D. 2551 State St. (Pat.)
**Brahms, David Michael** .................... '38 '63 C&L.309 A.B., LL.B. [Brahms&D.]
*PRACTICE AREAS: Military Law; Criminal Law; Personal Injury; Employment Law; Federal Law.

**Brahms & Duxbury**
**800 Grand Avenue, Suite C-14, 92008**
**Telephone: 619-434-4433 Fax: 619-434-1223**
**Marc A. Duxbury; David Michael Brahms.**
**General Civil and Criminal Trial Practice in all Courts. Military Law, Bankruptcy, Personal Injury, Criminal and Divorce Law.**
**Reference: Bank of America.**
*See Professional Biographies, CARLSBAD, CALIFORNIA*

**Broughton, Sharon A., The Law Offices of '45 '89 C.347 A.B. L.800 J.D.**
**2755 Jefferson Street, Suite 203, 92008**
**Telephone: 619-720-9780 Fax: 619-434-6832**
**Email: 105137.26@compuserve.com**
**Business and Civil Litigation with emphasis on Breach of Contract and Insurance Bad Faith. Representation of Corporations, Small Businesses, Partnerships and Limited Liability Companies. Bankruptcy, Preparation of Wills and Trusts.**
*See Professional Biographies, CARLSBAD, CALIFORNIA*

**Brown, Floyd R.** ............................ '35 '62 C.101 B.S. L.1068 J.D. [Brown&P.]
*PRACTICE AREAS: Business Law (25%); Securities Litigation (25%); Cable T.V. (20%); Corporate Law (20%); Insurance Law (10%).

**Brown and Pearson, P.C.**
**5963 La Place Court, Suite 114, 92008**
**Telephone: 619-438-5998 Facsimile: 619-438-7587**
**Floyd R. Brown; Chrissa N. Corday.**
**Civil Litigation in all Courts with special emphasis in Securities and Construction Litigation, Insurance Law, Plaintiff Issues, Representation of Bonding Companies and Governmental Agencies.**
*See Professional Biographies, CARLSBAD, CALIFORNIA*

Burke, Daniel V., (BV) ........ '51 '77 C.339 B.A. L.284 J.D. 2755 Jefferson St., Suite 1
Carroll, C. Daniel, (BV) ............ '56 '82 C.1079 B.A. L.1049 J.D. [McCann&C.]
Caruana, Mark V. ......................'53 '83 C&L.1049 B.A., J.D. 2646 Madison St.
**Cataldo, Mary V.J.** ...................... '53 '94 C.37 B.A. L.1137 J.D. [A Lodge&H.]
*PRACTICE AREAS: Civil Litigation.
Catterlin, Charles F. .................'28 '58 C.800 B.A. L.1065 J.D. 6965 El Camino Real
Chow, Frank S., (AV) '33 '67 C.1316 B.S. L.776 J.D.
(adm. in NJ; not adm. in CA; Pat.) Chf. Pat. Coun., Ontogen Corporation
Copley, Ralph D., Jr. .................. '24 '51 C.171 P.E. L.208 LL.B. 2335 Rue Des Chateaux
**Corday, Chrissa N.** ....................... '60 '86 C.36 B.S. L.1049 J.D. [A Brown&P.]
*REPORTED CASES: Campbel v. Superior Court, 44 Cal.App. 4th 1308.
*PRACTICE AREAS: Civil Litigation; Mechanics Lien Remedies; Surety and Fidelity Bond Law.
Cornwell, Wm. David '60 '86 C.860 B.A. L.276 J.D.
(adm. in NY; not adm. in CA) 5909 Sea Otter Place
Correll, Craig O. ....................... '53 '80 C.112 A.B. L.284 J.D. 2729 Forest Pk.
**Cowen, Gretchen** ................... '68 '93 C.1324 B.S. L.1188 J.D. [A Rushall&M.]
*PRACTICE AREAS: Securities/Transactional and Employment Law.
Crebbin, Anthony M. '52 '77 C.698 A.B. L.734 J.D.
(adm. in MO; not adm. in CA) 916 Rosemary★
Dahlbo, Robert M. ................ '45 '71 C.947 B.A. L.477 J.D. 2141 Palomar Airport Rd.
Dahlgaard, Patricia L., (CV) '44 '85
C.351 B.A. L.1049 J.D. 2111 Palomar Airport Rd. #270
Dale, William J., (AV) .............. '33 '63 C.25 B.A. L.659 LL.B. 2776 Loker Ave. W.

**Deak, Tom** ............................. '67 '96 C.911 B.A. L.629 J.D. [A Gatzke,M.&D.]
Dennis, Robert D. '49 '77 C.878 B.S. L.101 J.D.
(adm. in UT; not adm. in CA) 7521 Esfera St.
DeVito, Robin A., (BV) ................ '57 '83 C.112 B.A. L.61 J.D. 1015 Chestnut Ave.
**Dillon, Mark J.**, (BV) ..................... '55 '83 C.1109 B.A. L.61 J.D. [Gatzke,M.&D.]
Duquette, Richard, (BV) ............ '56 '83 C.112 B.A. L.1137 J.D. 1015 Chestnut Ave.
**Duxbury, Marc A.** ......................... '62 '89 C.1074 B.A. L.61 J.D. [Brahms&D.]
*PRACTICE AREAS: Civil; Criminal; Bankruptcy; Personal Injury; Divorce Law.
Dye, Donald H., (AV) '42 '68 C.112 B.A. L.1068 J.D.
Pres., COO & Gen. Coun., Callaway Golf Co.
**Ebersole, David A.** ........................... '56 '85 C.588 B.S. L.61 J.D. [Weil&W.]
*REPORTED CASES: Flojo Int'l v. Cassleben (1992) 4 Cal. App. 4th 713 Commercial Contract.
*PRACTICE AREAS: Business; Commercial; Landlord and Tenant; Real Estate; Civil Litigation.
Equitz, Howard C. '32 '55 C&L.436 B.S., J.D.
(adm. in WI; not adm. in CA) 3020 Azahar Ct.‡
Farley, James S., (AV) .................. '49 '75 C.112 A.B. L.1188 J.D. 5963 LaPlace Ct.
Fay, Dennis E. ..................... '56 '87 C.112 B.A. L.61 J.D. 701 Palomar Airport Rd.
**Fletcher, William R., (A P.C.)**, (AV) ....... '49 '75 C.763 B.A. L.1049 J.D. [Fletcher&P.]
*REPORTED CASES: People v. Nixon (1982) 131 Cal.App.3d 687; Johnson v. Superior Court (1984) 163 Cal.App.3d 85; Copley Press, Inc. v. Superior Court (1991) 228 Cal.App.3d 77.
*PRACTICE AREAS: Criminal Law.

**Fletcher & Patton, (AV)**
**A Partnership of Professional Corporations**
**2777 Jefferson Street, Suite 200, P.O. Box 4598, 92018-4598**
**Telephone: 619-434-4130 Facsimile: 619-434-0288**
**Email: pattonlaw@aol.com**
**William R. Fletcher (A P.C.) (Certified Specialist, Criminal Law, The State Bar of California Board of Legal Specialization); C. Bradley Patton (A P.C.) (Certified Specialist, Criminal Law, The State Bar of California Board of Legal Specialization).**
**Criminal Defense Litigation in all State and Federal Courts, Felonies and Misdemeanors, Drug Crimes, Violent Crimes, Theft, Sex Crimes, D.U.I. and Administrative Hearings.**
*See Professional Biographies, CARLSBAD, CALIFORNIA*

Freed, William J. .............................. '52 '89 C.763 B.S. L.61 J.D. 3042 Harding St.
**Gatzke, Michael Scott**, (AV) ............... '45 '73 C.112 B.A. L.1068 J.D. [Gatzke,M.&D.]

**Gatzke, Mispagel & Dillon, (AV)** BB
**A Partnership including a Professional Law Corporation**
**Suite 200, 1921 Palomar Oaks Way, P.O. Box 1636, 92009**
**Telephone: 619-431-9501 Fax: 619-431-9512**
**Members of Firm: Michael Scott Gatzke; Mark F. Mispagel; Mark J. Dillon; Lori D. Ballance.**
**Associates: David P. Hubbard; Kristin Beth White; Stephen F. Tee; Tom Deak.**
**Litigation in all State and Federal Courts. General Civil Litigation, Aviation, Governmental, Environmental, Zoning, Planning and Land Use, Administrative, Construction and Real Estate Law.**
*See Professional Biographies, CARLSBAD, CALIFORNIA*

Gibson, Diane H. ......................... '61 '86 C.273 B.A. L.1049 J.D. [Ravreby,S.&G.]
Gilmore, Edward Lee, (A Prof. Corp.), (AV) '24 '52
C.923 A.B. L.273 J.D. 2724 Waterbury Way‡
Gleason Huss, Karen L., (BV) ....'50 '89 C.763 B.A., M.P.A. L.1049 J.D. 1739 Sorrel Ct.
Gniatkowski, Thomas E., (BV) ......... '46 '72 C.724 B.B.A. L.426 J.D. 2777 Jefferson St.
Grant, John K. ................................ '58 '90 C.940 B.A. L.1137 J.D. 785 Grand Ave.
Greber, Forest .................................. '23 '50 C&L.37 LL.B. 7140 Lantana Terrace‡
Grether, Henry M., Jr. '20 '49 C&L.878 B.A., J.D.
(adm. in NE; not adm. in CA) 2508 La Costa Ave.‡
Griffin, William L., Jr. '50 '75 C.35 B.S. L.500 J.D.
(adm. in MS; not adm. in CA) P.O. Box 9040
Grochowiak, Edward A. .................... '39 '77 C.339 B.A. L.1241 J.D. 7176 Tern Pl.
Grosse, Margaret A. '64 '90 C.678 B.A. L.61 J.D.
V.P. & Corp. Coun., Russell W. Grosse Development Co., Inc.
Grosse, Russell W., (BV) '35 '61
C.154 A.B. L.813 LL.B. Pres., Russell W. Grosse Develop. Co.
Gutkin, Jerome S., (CV⊙) '39 '67 C&L.597 B.A., J.D.
(adm. in AZ; not adm. in CA) 6906 Mimosa Dr.‡
Haack, Mark E. ...........'55 '82 C.426 B.A. L.809 J.D. Tax Atty., Cairns, Haack & Co.
Haiman, Mark L. .......................... '41 '65 C.563 B.B.A. L.178 LL.B. 4018 Isle Dr.
**Heller, Richard A.**, (AV) ..................... '49 '75 C.112 A.B. L.1049 J.D. [Lodge&H.]
*PRACTICE AREAS: Business Litigation; Estate Litigation.
**Hilbert, John F.** ................................ '57 '82 C.112 B.A. L.1049 J.D. [Weil&W.]
Hirata, Karen Jeffries ..................... '50 '88 C.1099 B.S. L.1137 J.D. Dep. City Atty.

**Hoffmann, Patricia D. '63 '90 C.570 B.S. L.61 J.D.**
**2131 Palomar Airport Road, Suite 300, 92009**
**Telephone: 619-729-1234 Fax: 619-431-1223**
***PRACTICE AREAS: General Practice.**
**Wills, Trusts, Durable Powers of Attorney, Probate and Probate Litigation, Corporations (Set-Up, Dissolution and Maintenance), Contracts and Business Law.**
*See Professional Biographies, CARLSBAD, CALIFORNIA*

**Hollis & Mauerman**
**7720 B El Camino Real, Suite 174, 92009⊙**
**Telephone: 619-942-9404 Facsimile: 619-942-9403**
**Email: mtmlpm@IX.netcom.com**
**Mark T. Mauerman.**
**Civil Litigation in all State and Federal Courts. Securities, Corporate and Business Transactions, Taxation.**
**Santa Ana, California Office: 2677 North Main Street, Suite 930. Telephone: 714-835-4100. Facsimile: 714-972-4926.**
*See Professional Biographies, CARLSBAD, CALIFORNIA*

**Hubbard, David P.** ....................... '62 '90 C.1169 B.A. L.1066 J.D. [A Gatzke,M.&D.]
Hunter, Harold J. ........................ '27 '75 C&L.1137 B.S., J.D. 2958 Madison St.

**Hyatt, Richard V., Law Office of, (BV) '46 '76 C.763 B.A. L.1137 J.D.**
**Suite 130, 7220 Avenida Encinas, 92009**
**Telephone: 619-438-3088 Telecopier: 619-438-1443**
**Email: rvhesq@aol.com**
**(Certified Family Law Specialist, California Board of Legal Specialization, 1991).**
**Practice limited to Dissolution of Marriage and related proceedings.**
**Representative Client: San Dieguito Boys & Girls Club.**
*See Professional Biographies, CARLSBAD, CALIFORNIA*

Jelovich, Taryn M. ......................... '61 '89 C.25 B.S. L.1137 J.D. 7305 Black Swan Pl.
Jimenez, John, (BV) ...................... '51 '76 C.112 B.A. L.1066 J.D. P.O. Box 1762
Johnson, Michael S. ....................... '51 '83 C.546 B.S. L.61 J.D. 3482 Roosevelt St.
Jonas, Fred ..................................... '25 '55 C.112 B.S. L.1068 J.D. 2065 Caleta Ct.
Judd, T. Conrad .......................... '27 '57 C.101 B.A. L.878 LL.B. 5962 La Place Ct.
Kakadelas, Kim James ........... '53 '82 C.101 B.A. L.809 J.D. 5962 La Pl. Ct., Ste. 200
Kelso, Robert C. '16 '42 C.339 L.365 J.D.
(adm. in IL; not adm. in CA) 4745 Gateshead Rd.‡
Kendall, Kevin S. '64 '91 C.338 B.S. L.477 J.D.
Corp. Coun., The Upper Deck Company
Kosse, Robert B. ........................ '39 '72 C.494 B.S. L.426 J.D. 4585 Sunnyhill Dr.
Kueny, Jay V. ............................ '36 '71 C.36 L.990 J.D. Jay Kueny Electrical

CAA45P

CALIFORNIA—CARLSBAD MARTINDALE-HUBBELL LAW DIRECTORY 1997

Landrum, Lee W. ....................'23 '50 C&L.800 B.S., LL.B. 6965 El Camino Real
Leach, Rob G., (BV) ....................'62 '87 C&L.1049 B.A., J.D. [Reiss&L.]
Lee, Lawrence D., Jr. '27 '63 C.112 A.B. L.800 J.D.
Prof., Calif. Western School of Law
L'Heureux, Stephen M., (BV) '44 '70 C.188 B.S. L.1065 J.D.
2111 Palomar Airport Rd.
**Lodge, Dorothy T.** ....................'12 '39 C.668 B.A. L.800 LL.B. [Lodge&H.] ‡
**Lodge, Eric T., (P.C.), (AV)** ....................'43 '69 C.855 A.B. L.800 J.D. [Lodge&H.]☉
*PRACTICE AREAS: Estate Planning; Probate and Trust Law; Corporate Law.

**Lodge & Heller, (AV)**
**A Partnership including a Professional Corporation**
**1901 Camino Vida Roble, Suite 110, 92008☉**
**Telephone: 619-931-9700 Fax: 619-931-1155**
**Members of Firm: Eric T. Lodge (P.C.) (Certified Specialist, Probate, Estate Planning and Trust Law, The State Bar of California Board of Legal Specialization).; Richard A. Heller; Dorothy T. Lodge (Retired);—Mary V.J. Cataldo; Harriet Avner Waanders (Certified Specialist, Estate Planning, Trust and Probate Law, The State Bar of California Board of Legal Specialization).**
**General Civil and Commercial Trial Practice. Corporate, Real Estate, Construction, Estate Planning, Probate, Trust and Governmental and Land Use Law.**
**Pauma Valley, California Office: The Pauma Building, Suite 403, 16160 Highway 76, P.O. Box 600. Telephone: 619-749-3199.**
*See Professional Biographies, CARLSBAD, CALIFORNIA*

Lynch, Donald W. ....................'28 '57 C&L.37 A.B., J.D. 3260 Dorema Dr.‡
Macgurn, Richard B., (BV) ....................'53 '77 C.154 B.A. L.1049 J.D. 1015 Chestnut Ave.
**Mauerman, Mark T.** ....................'54 '80 C.684 B.S. L.950 J.D. [Hollis&M.]
*LANGUAGES: German.
*PRACTICE AREAS: Corporate; Business Transactions; Securities; Taxation.
McCann, Kevin E., (BV) ....................'52 '79 C.628 B.S. L.1137 J.D. [McCann&C.]
McCann & Carroll, (BV) ....................2890 Pio Pico Dr.
McCracken, Steven C., (AV) ....................'50 '75 C.112 B.A. L.893 J.D. Callaway Golf Co.
McDonald, John P. ....................'40 '71 C.999 L.990 J.D. 2111 Palomar Airport Dr.
**McGeever, Eileen L., (AV)** ....................'48 '74 C.112 B.A. L.1068 J.D. [Rushall&M.]
*PRACTICE AREAS: Securities; Commercial Litigation; Employment Litigation.
McGrath, Thomas H. ....................'32 '86 C.884 B.Ch.E. L.1137 J.D. 2237 Levante St.
McKenzie, David L., (BV) ....................'48 '73 C.112 B.A. L.1049 J.D. 4325 Hillside Dr.
McKenzie, Monica M. '— '82 C.1165 B.S. L.208 J.D.
(adm. in CO; not adm. in CA) Gen. Coun. & Secy., Ashworth, Inc.
Mikhael, Simon ....................'52 '89 C.1040 M.B.A. L.61 J.D. 3150 El Camino Real
Miller, Joseph G. '21 '48 C&L.569 B.A., LL.B.
(adm. in OH; not adm. in CA) 16 Greenview‡

**Mills, George P., (BV) '45 '78 C.668 B.A. L.1009 J.D.**
**2755 Jefferson Street, Suite 205, 92008**
**Telephone: 619-434-8688 Fax: 619-434-6832**
**(Certified Specialist, Family Law, The State Bar of California Board of Legal Specialization).**
***PRACTICE AREAS: Family Law; Mediation; Bankruptcy Law; Guardianships.**
**Practice limited primarily to Family Law. Practice also includes Family Mediation, Bankruptcy and Guardianships.**
*See Professional Biographies, CARLSBAD, CALIFORNIA*

**Mispagel, Mark F.** ....................'42 '75 C.426 B.A. L.464 J.D. [Gatzke,M.&D.]
Mix, Thomas A., (A P.C.), (BV) '41 '74 C.1049 B.A. L.1137 J.D.
5055 Avenida Encinas
Moore, David R., (BV) ....................'53 '80 C.800 B.A. L.61 J.D. [Moore&S.]
Moore, Stephen J., (BV) ....................'52 '82 C.695 L.1137 J.D. 1015 Chestnut Ave.
Moore and Skiljan, (BV) ....................7700 El Camino Real
Moran, Laurel J. ....................'63 '91 C.752 B.A. L.61 J.D. 2755 Jefferson St.
Moriarty, Paul M. ....................'20 '77 C.178 B.A. L.273 J.D. 2958 Madison St.
Moselle, Gary W. ........'42 '71 C.112 B.A. L.1066 J.D. Gen. Coun., Craftsman Book Co.
Murphey, John J., (BV) ....................'36 '67 C.401 B.S. L.8 J.D. 701 Palomar Airport Rd. (Pat.)
Nares, Thomas D. ....................'53 '86 L.1137 J.D. 2777 Jefferson St.
Nassif, David W. '54 '79 C&L.893 B.S., J.D.
(adm. in IL; not adm. in CA) 1360 Corvidae St.
Nelson, D. Marshall, (AV) ....................'44 '70 C.112 B.A. L.1068 J.D. 5340 Los Robles Dr.
Nelson-Laduca, Laurel M. ....................'45 '88 C.494 B.A. L.1241 J.D. 2777 Jefferson St.
Newman, Donald G. ....................'46 '71 C.1024 B.A. L.424 J.D. 2520 Luciernaga St.
Palay, Susan Bartell ....................'49 '88 C.347 B.S. L.1049 J.D. 2385 Camino Vida Roble
Parkinson, Janet L. ....................'61 '86 C.112 B.S. L.990 J.D. 701 Palomar Airport Rd.
**Patton, C. Bradley, (A P.C.), (AV)** ....................'49 '75 C.800 B.S. L.61 J.D. [Fletcher&P.]
*PRACTICE AREAS: Criminal Law.
Patton, Shelley A., (BV) ....................'51 '77 C.494 B.S. L.1049 J.D. 2777 Jefferson St.
Peck, Anthony, (BV) ....................'51 '78 C.1042 B.A. L.1137 J.D. 2551 State St.
Pierce, Paul E., Jr. ....................'49 '82 C.1077 B.A. L.426 J.D. 2131 Palomar Airport Rd.
Platt, Richard L. '57 '83 C&L.966 B.A., J.D.
1st V.P. & Dep. Reg. Coun., Prudential Secs. Inc.
Proctor, Marcia Mace ....................'47 '82 C.112 A.B. L.426 J.D. 2779 Arland Rd.
Prowse, Stanley D., (BV) '45 '74 C.976 B.A. L.309 J.D.
2385 Camino Vida Roble Ste 101
Pultz, William C., (AV) ....................'40 '76 C.207 B.A. L.1137 J.D. 1921 Palomar Oaks Way
Pynes, Benjamin E., Jr. ....................'31 '63 C.112 B.S. L.1068 J.D. 7682 El Camino Real
Radosh, Richard M. ....................'49 '74 C.112 B.A. L.767 J.D. 7220 Avenida Encinas
Rau, Jack L. ....................'10 '35 C.800 L.809 LL.B. 7514 Jerez Ct.‡
Ravreby, Richard R., (BV) ....................'51 '77 C.477 B.A. L.221 J.D. [Ravreby,S.&G.]
Ravreby, Shaner & Gibson, (BV) ....................2755 Jefferson St., Ste 200
Regan, Penelope A. '37 '83 C.1073 B.A. L.209 J.D.
(adm. in IL; not adm. in CA) 2709 Unicornio St.‡
Reiss, R. Robert, (BV) ....................'54 '85 C.475 B.A. L.1137 J.D. [Reiss&L.]
Reiss & Leach, (BV) ....................2011 Palomar Airport Rd.
Rich, Alan S., (BV) ....................'46 '71 C.1075 B.S. L.1068 J.D. [Rich,S.&S.]
Rich, Sussman & Shipley, A Professional Corporation, (AV) .... 2141 Palomar Airport Rd.
Rocco, Matthew P. ....................'60 '86 C.1312 B.A. L.1137 J.D. 2777 Jefferson St., #200
Rudolf, Donald R., II ....................'41 '66 C.282 A.B. L.893 J.D. Asst. City Atty.
**Rushall, Bruce J., (AV)** ....................'46 '74 C.112 B.S. L.1068 J.D. [Rushall&M.]
*PRACTICE AREAS: Securities Law; Corporation Law; Real Property Law.

**Rushall & McGeever, A Professional Law Corporation, (AV)**
**Suite 200, Graham International Plaza, 2111 Palomar Airport Road, 92009**
**Telephone: 619-438-6855 Fax: 619-438-3026**
**Bruce J. Rushall; Eileen L. McGeever; Gretchen Cowen.**
**Securities, Corporation, Real Property, Employment and Commercial Litigation. Trial and Appellate Practice.**
*See Professional Biographies, CARLSBAD, CALIFORNIA*

Sauer, William N., Jr., (AV) ....................'39 '65 C.934 A.B. L.1065 LL.B. P.O. Box 1185
Sax, Richard L., (BV) '50 '78 C.112 B.A. L.1049 J.D.
2192 Palomar Airport Rd., 2nd Fl.
Schlehuber, Clarence H. ....................'36 '62 C.602 B.S. L.1035 J.D. 2720 Jefferson St.
Schneider, Linda K. ....................'56 '81 C.494 B.A. L.809 J.D. 701 Palomar Airport Rd.
Scholl, Verne C., (CV) ....................'42 '71 C.112 B.A. L.477 J.D. 5751 Palmer Way
Schwartz, Norman A. '43 '68 C.36 B.A. L.37 J.D.
(adm. in AZ; not adm. in CA) 7720B El Camino Real
Schwenk, James R. '49 '78 C.871 B.S. L.30 J.D.
(adm. in DC; not adm. in CA) 2613 Viaeco St.★
Severson, Jack O. '23 '53 C.583 L.585 LL.B.
(adm. in ND; not adm. in CA) 4815 Flying Cloud Way‡
Sexton, Nancy S. ....................'56 '91 C.112 M.A. L.1241 J.D. 3036 Ave. Christina
Shaner, Constance H., (BV) ....................'55 '80 C.112 B.A. L.1049 J.D. [Ravreby,S.&G.]
Shipley, Robert L. ....................'58 '83 C.112 B.A. L.1067 J.D. [Rich,S.&S.]
Skiljan, Jeff M., (P.C.), (BV) ....................'50 '78 C.768 B.A. L.1049 J.D. [Moore&S.]
Steward, Harry D., (AV) ....................'22 '50 C&L.800 LL.B. 7941 Represa Cir.‡
Storrow, Louis A. ....................'54 '88 C.569 B.A. L.818 J.D. 5963 La Place Ct.
Sussman, Andrew J., (AV) ....................'51 '77 C.94 B.A. L.472 J.D. [Rich,S.&S.]
Swirsky, Paul S., (BV) ....................'23 '49 C.326 B.S. L.846 LL.B. 785 Grand
**Tee, Stephen F.** ....................'69 '94 C.112 B.A. L.1049 J.D. [A Gatzke,M.&D.]
Thomas, Ivor F. ....................'23 '58 C.453 B.S. L.800 J.D. 2945 Harding St.
Thompson, David R., (AV) ....................'43 '72 C.061 B.S. L.1188 J.D. 580 Beech Ave.
Tiesen, Frank G., (BV) ....................'40 '67 C.768 B.A. L.1188 J.D. 1921 Palomar Oaks Way
Tubbs, Henry W., III ....................'51 '81 C.112 B.A. L.1049 J.D. P.O. Box 561
Tygart, Robert M., (BV) ....................'52 '81 C&L.1137 B.S.L., J.D. 2541 State St.
Vales, Robert B. ....................'42 '81 C.1060 B.A. L.1136 J.D. 1200 Elm Ave.‡
**Waanders, Harriet Avner, (BV)** ....................'47 '82 C.994 B.A. L.1049 J.D. [A Lodge&H.]
*PRACTICE AREAS: Estate Planning Law; Probate and Trust Law.
Wagner, Bruce V., (AV) ....................'31 '64 C.436 B.S. L.1049 LL.B. 3990 Gloria Lane‡
**Weil, Paul M., (AV)** ....................'27 '59 C.112 B.A. L.809 J.D. [Weil&W.]
*PRACTICE AREAS: Real Estate; Business; Commercial; Banking; Civil Litigation.

**Weil & Wright, (AV)**
**1921 Palomar Oaks Way, Suite 301, 92008**
**Telephone: 619-438-1214 Telefax: 619-438-2666**
**Paul M. Weil; Archie T. Wright III; David A. Ebersole; John F. Hilbert.**
**General Civil, Trial and Appellate Practice. Banking, Corporate, Commercial, Real Estate, Creditor Rights and Property Taxation.**
*See Professional Biographies, CARLSBAD, CALIFORNIA*

Wellman, Kathleen D., (BV) ....................'49 '74 C&L.1049 B.A., J.D. P.O. Box 1670
White, K. Martin, (BV) ....................'51 '79 C.1049 B.A.B.S. L.1068 J.D. P.O. Box 1826
**White, Kristin Beth** ....................'65 '92 C.112 B.S. L.1065 J.D. [A Gatzke,M.&D.]
Williamson, Lance ....................'42 '83 C.37 A.B. L.1068 J.D. P.O. Box 4012
Wininger, E. David, (BV) ....................'39 '70 C.999 B.B.A. L.1127 J.D. 2910 Jefferson St.
Winter, James D. ....................'56 '92 C.1241 B.B.A. L.1137 J.D. 7045 Partridge Pl.
Wischkaemper, Michael, Law Offices, (AV) '46 '71
C.668 B.A. L.813 J.D. 2111 Palmar Airport Rd.
Wood, R. Thomas, (BV) ....................'42 '69 C.112 B.A. L.1049 J.D. 325 Carlsbad Village Dr.
**Wright, Archie T., III, (AV)** ....................'46 '74 C.228 B.A. L.188 J.D. [Weil&W.]
*REPORTED CASES: Main & VonKarman Assoc. v. County of Orange (1994) 23 Cal. App. 4th 337 Property Taxes.
*PRACTICE AREAS: Real Estate and Business Transactions; Property Taxation.
Wyman, William A., (BV) ....................'46 '79 C.999 B.S. L.1137 J.D. 5741 Palmer Way
Yearsley, Elliot N. ....................'26 '53 C.112 L.1065 J.D. 6968 Sandpiper Pl.‡
Yerkes, Donald E. ....................'37 '72 C.112 A.B. L.1049 J.D. 2942 Harding St.

## CARMEL, 4,239, *Monterey Co.*

Anderson, Roy E. ....................'18 '50 C.112 B.S. L.813 25215 Stewart Place
Andre, Steven J. ....................'59 '87 C.112 A.B. L.1065 J.D. 26540 Carmel Rancho Blvd.
Anello, Peter ....................'17 '48 C&L.770 B.S., LL.B. P.O. Box 218‡
Beare, Robin E. ....................'47 '84 C.112 A.B. L.1226 J.D. 26465 Carmel Rancho Blvd.
Brand, Thomas J. ....................'46 '74 C.112 B.A. L.1065 J.D. P.O. Box 222966‡
Brenan, Henton S. ....................'11 '35 C&L.813 B.A., LL.B. P.O. Box 3982‡
Brittain, James M. '22 '50 C.390 L.659 LL.B.
(adm. in PA; not adm. in CA) 254 Del Mesa‡
**Buck, Robert B., (BV)** ....................'45 '71 C.197 B.A. L.1065 J.D. [Heisinger,B.M.&R.]
*PRACTICE AREAS: Real Estate Development and Transactions; General Business; Trusts; Estates; Charitable Foundations.
Burd, John S., (AV) ....................'16 '46 C.112 A.B. L.893 LL.B. 277 Del Mesa Carmel‡
**Campbell, Christopher, (BV)** .... '48 '73 C.112 B.A. L.1066 J.D. [A Heisinger,B.M.&R.]
Campbell, Gordon ....................'10 '37 C.813 B.A. L.629 LL.B. P.O. Box AJ‡
Conard, Lynn A. '58 '83 C.612 B.S. L.862 J.D.
(adm. in OK; not adm. in CA) Landmark, Inc.
Condren, Willis D. ....................'22 '78 C.174 B.S. L.1226 J.D. P.O. Box 22205
Corson, Robt. M. ....................'14 '40 C.112 B.A. L.1066 LL.B. 8545 Carmel Valley Rd.‡
**Creely, Andrew E.** ....................'57 '85 C.112 B.A. L.1065 J.D. [Oldfield&C.]
*PRACTICE AREAS: Corporations; Taxation; Estate Planning; Real Estate and Business Transactions.
Crosby, Alexander C. ....................'36 '84 C.112 B.S. L.1266 J.D. P.O. Box 6316‡
Davies, Phyllis ....................'— '79 C.347 M.A. L.1226 J.D. P.O. Box 279
Dupere, Richard A. '35 '66 C.1036 B.A. L.910 J.D.
(adm. in MO; not adm. in CA) 7092 Valley Greens Circle‡
Eisler, Riane, (Mrs.) ....................'31 '66 C.112 B.A. L.1068 LL.B. 25700 Shafter Way
**Fisher, Kevin W.** ....................'62 '88 C.623 B.A. L.309 J.D. [A Heisinger,B.M.&R.]
Fisher, William E. ....................'17 '47 C.188 C.E. L.309 LL.B. Dolores & Sixth St.‡
Fitzgerald, Michael J. '43 '68 C&L.37 B.S., J.D.
(adm. in CO; not adm. in CA) P.O. Box 1150
**Freeman, Donald G., (BV)** ....................'42 '71 C.763 B.A. L.1095 J.D. [Perry&F.]
*REPORTED CASES: Ewing v. City of Carmel-by-the-Sea 234 Cal. App. 3d 1579 (1992).
Friedland, Jed P. ....................'58 '87 C.65 B.A. L.767 J.D. 3855 Via Nona Marie, Ste. 205
Gore, George ....................'12 '38 C&L.309 B.S., LL.B. P.O. Box 4515‡
Gray, Eric S. '32 '59 C&L.569 B.A., LL.B.
(adm. in NY; not adm. in CA) P.O. Box S 3253‡
**Green, Nancy W., (BV)** ....................'31 '79 C.1074 B.S. L.1065 J.D. [Stewart,G.&M.]
*PRACTICE AREAS: Estate Planning and Probate; Trusts; Will Contests; Family Law; Taxation.

**Guest, Kelley, (AV Ⓣ) '48 '73 C.846 B.B.A. L.1066 J.D.**
**26435 Carmel Rancho Boulevard, P.O. Box 221578, 93922**
**Telephone: 408-624-6800 Facsimile: 408-624-6731**
***PRACTICE AREAS: Business; Computer Law and Technology Transactions.**
**Intellectual Property, Business Law, Computer Law and Technology Transactions.**
*See Professional Biographies, CARMEL, CALIFORNIA*

Guinan, Thomas J. '32 '63 C.502 B.S.Pet.E. L.986 J.D.
(adm. in KS; not adm. in CA) P.O. Box S-3162‡
Haas, Vernon W. ....................'23 '74 C.999 B.E. L.981 LL.B. P.O. Box 6424
Hannon, John P. ....................'58 '83 C.740 B.S. L.767 J.D. 27880 Dorris Dr., Suite 110
Harrah, Eugene ....................'10 '33 L.809 P.O. Box 2128‡

**Hawley, Thomas Hart, (AV) '44 '70 C&L.813 B.A., LL.B.**
**San Carlos between 7th & 8th, P.O. Box 805, 93921**
**Telephone: 408-624-5339 Fax: 408-624-5839**
**(Certified Specialist, Estate Planning, Trust and Probate Law, The State Bar of California Board of Legal Specialization).**
**Estate Planning, Probate and Trust.**
*See Professional Biographies, CARMEL, CALIFORNIA*

**Heisinger, James G., Jr.**, (BV) '52 '79 C.1169 B.A. L.1051 J.D. [Heisinger,B.M.&R.]
*PRACTICE AREAS: Administrative Agency; Trial Practice involving Environmental and Land Use Matters; Real Estate Transactions; Trusts; Estates.

**Heisinger, Buck, Morris & Rose, A Professional Corporation, (AV)**
**Dolores and Sixth Streets, P.O. Box 5427, 93921**
**Telephone: 408-624-3891 Fax: 408-625-0145**
**Email: hbmandr@aol.com**
**James G. Heisinger, Jr.; Robert B. Buck; Sidney M. Morris (Certified Specialist, Estate Planning, Trust and Probate Law, The State Bar of California Board of Legal Specialization); Gerard A. Rose;—Christopher Campbell; Kevin W. Fisher.**
**General Civil and Trial Practice. Corporations and Partnerships. Real Estate. Estate Planning, Probate, Trusts and Estates.**
**Reference: Wells Fargo Bank.**
*See Professional Biographies, CARMEL, CALIFORNIA*

Henderson, Forrest E. '23 '49 C&L.585 B.S.C., LL.B.
(adm. in ND; not adm. in CA) 25704 Tierra Grande‡
Hendrick, David R. '31 '86 C.502 B.S. L.1226 J.D. P.O. Box 221622
Herron, Donald F. '30 '54 C&L.285 LL.B.
(adm. in WA; not adm. in CA) P.O. Box 5636‡
Hoegstedt, Kingsley T. '19 '49 C.112 A.B. L.426 J.D. 3536 Greenfield Pl.‡
Holber, Ida '51 '91 L.1226 J.D. 25963 Carmel Knolls Dr.
Holk, Eric N. '51 '88 C.1042 B.A. L.1226 J.D. 3785 Via Nona Marie Ste. 105
Holtom, Gregory L. '54 '79 C.426 B.A. L.770 J.D. 27880 Dorris Dr.
**Horan, Lloyd, Karachale, Dyer, Schwartz, Law & Cook, Incorporated**
**(See Monterey)**
Julber, Eric, (AV) '25 '51 C.112 A.B. L.426 LL.B. 100 Dolores St.
Kahn, Stephen B. '10 '36 C.629 B.S. L.838 LL.B.
(adm. in OR; not adm. in CA) 26320 Scenic Rd.‡
Kaufmann, Arthur M. '48 '84 L.1226 J.D. P.O. Box 139
Kilzer, Barry M. '48 '77 C.602 B.B.A. L.809 J.D. 26225 Carmel Rancho Blvd.‡
Kuykendall, Ronald F. '43 '68 C.845 B.B.A. L.744 J.D.
(adm. in TX; not adm. in CA) Fox & Carskadon
Liebman, Robert Franz '30 '52 C.170 L.107 J.D.
(adm. in NY; not adm. in CA) P.O. Box 7077‡
Marsden, Warren P. '11 '36 C&L.911 LL.B. Del Mesa Carmel‡
Massel, Mark S. '10 '34 C&L.569 M.A., J.D.
(adm. in IL; not adm. in CA) P.O. Box 222231‡
**McGowan, Anne D.**, (CV) '38 '79 C.521 B.S. L.990 J.D. [Stewart,G.&M.]
*SPECIAL AGENCIES: District Counsel, Monterey Peninsula Regional Park District.
*REPORTED CASES: Sobeck v. B & R Investments (1989) 215 Cal.App. 861, 264 Cal.RPTR.156.
*PRACTICE AREAS: Estates Planning; Environmental Law; Government; Real Property; Small Business.
McHarry, Charles P. '12 '36 C.813 A.B. L.1066 177 Del Mesa Carmel‡
McMahan, Michael L., (BV) '42 '72 C.813 A.B. L.1066 J.D. 100 Clocktower Pl.
**McPhail, Ian D.**, (AV) '34 '63 C.050 B.A. L.1066 LL.B. [I.D.McPhail]⊙
*PRACTICE AREAS: Estate Planning; Estate Settlement including Probate.

**McPhail, Ian D., A Professional Corporation, (AV)**
**Villa Carmel, Suite 4, Mission at Fourth, P.O. Box 2734, 93921⊙**
**Telephone: 408-625-4135 Telecopier: 408-625-4155**
**Ian D. McPhail.**
**Estate Planning, Living Trusts, Trust and Probate Law. Gift and Estate Taxation.**
**References: Comerica Bank; Home Savings; Coast Commercial Bank.**
**Santa Cruz, California Office: 331 Soquel Avenue, 95062. Telephone: 408-427-2363. Telecopier: 408-427-0511.**
*See Professional Biographies, CARMEL, CALIFORNIA*

Menken, John F., (CV) '42 '70 C.813 A.B. L.1065 J.D. P.O. Box 563
Monning, William W., (BV) '51 '76 C.112 A.B. L.767 J.D. P.O. Box 844
Morganstern, Martin D., (AV) '36 '63 C.569 A.B. L.309 LL.B.
7026 Valley Greens Circle
**Morris, Sidney M.**, (AV) '44 '70 C.421 B.A. L.383 J.D. [Heisinger,B.M.&R.]
*PRACTICE AREAS: Trust Law; Probate; Estate Planning.
Mullally, David S. '48 '76
C.112 B.A. L.1137 J.D. Ocean Ave. between Lincoln & Delores
Nash, Thomas V. '48 '84 L.1226 J.D. S.W. Mission & 4th
Oberg, Philip A., (CV) '18 '59 C.276 B.S. L.767 LL.B. P.O. Box 1351
**Oldfield, Douglas W.**, (BV) '55 '81 C.112 A.B. L.1065 J.D. [Oldfield&C.]
*PRACTICE AREAS: Business Litigation; Securities Litigation and Arbitration; Real Estate; Trust Law; Partnerships and Corporations.

**Oldfield & Creely, (BV)**
**26619 Carmel Center Place, Suite 202, 93923**
**Telephone: 408-625-3900 Fax: 408-625-6043**
**Douglas W. Oldfield; Andrew E. Creely.**
**Business Litigation, Securities Litigation and Arbitration. Real Estate, Partnership, Corporation, Trust Law and Estate Planning.**
**Reference: Bank of America.**
*See Professional Biographies, CARMEL, CALIFORNIA*

Perkins, Robert, (BV) '50 '77 C.36 B.S. L.1226 J.D. 27570 Mooncrest Dr.‡

**Perry and Freeman, (BV)**
**San Carlos Between 7th & 8th, P.O. Box 805, 93921**
**Telephone: 408-624-5339 Fax: 408-624-5839**
**Email: cityatty@ix.netcom.com**
**Thomas K. Perry (1904-1971); Donald G. Freeman.**
**Civil and Trial Practice. Estate Planning, Probate, Real Property, Business, Environmental, Land Use and Planning, Municipal.**
*See Professional Biographies, CARMEL, CALIFORNIA*

Poole, George A., Jr. '31 '64 C.976 A.B. L.813 LL.B. 4105 Segunda Dr.
Quinn, Wallace C. '46 '71 C.893 B.A. L.861 J.D.
(adm. in LA; not adm. in CA) 6330 Brookdale Dr.‡
Reiser, Thomas F. '36 '69 C.1066 B.S. L.767 J.D. P.O. Box 101‡
Robbins, Elizabeth Field '— '77 C.37 B.A. L.1095 J.D. 2940 Ribera Rd.
**Rose, Gerard A.**, (AV) '46 '73 C&L.770 B.A., J.D. [Heisinger,B.M.&R.]
*PRACTICE AREAS: Trial and Appellate Practice involving General Business; Real Estate; Insurance; Construction Disputes; Oil and Gas Law.
Royster, Carey W., (CV) '31 '64 C.766 A.B. L.276 LL.B. P.O. Box 1645
St. Angelo, Denise C. '51 '79 C.112 A.B. L.36 J.D.
(adm. in AZ; not adm. in CA) 26045 Dougherty Pl.‡
Shevelson, J. Courtney '46 '73 C.976 B.A. L.477 J.D. P.O. Box 223609
Silver, Lori '54 '81 C.112 B.A. L.1065 J.D. P.O. Box 5427
Starr, Mark I., (CV) '33 '61 C.197 A.B. L.284 LL.B. P.O. Box 1645
**Stewart, William Kirk**, (BV) '17 '43 C.112 A.B. L.309 LL.B. [Stewart,G.&M.]
*PRACTICE AREAS: Real Estate; Estate Planning; Probate.

**Stewart, Green & McGowan, (BV)**
**26415 Carmel Rancho Boulevard, 93923**
**Telephone: 408-624-6473 Fax: 408-624-6639**
**Members of Firm: William Kirk Stewart; Nancy W. Green; Anne D. McGowan.**
**Probate, Estate Planning, Taxation, Real Estate, Family and Civil Trial Litigation.**
*See Professional Biographies, CARMEL, CALIFORNIA*

Tersol, Teresa A. '51 '80 C.1169 B.A. L.1067 J.D. P.O. Box 3722
Thompson, Richard '58 '86 C.112 A.B. L.1226 J.D. P.O. Box 3016
**Turner, Scott C., (AV) '48 '78 C.112 A.B. L.800 J.D.**
**P.O. Box 1671, 93921⊙**
**Telephone: 408-626-5626 FAX: 408-626-5634**
**Insurance Claims and Litigation regarding Insurance Coverage of Construction Disputes.**
**Pasadena, California Office: 301 North Lake Avenue, Suite 700. Telephone: 818-440-1822 FAX: 818-440-9409.**
*See Professional Biographies, CARMEL, CALIFORNIA*

Varga, S. Gary '46 '71 C.608 B.S. L.228 J.D. 26613 Carmel Center Pl.
Wallace, Susan Davis '49 '72 C.770 B.S. L.1065 J.D. P.O. Box 3957
Warren, John L. '50 '76 C.999 L.1026 LL.B. P.O. Box 552
Wheeler, William M., Jr. '13 '38 C.976 B.A. L.1066 LL.B. P.O. Box 1493
Yount, Michael E. '51 '77 C&L.623 B.B.A., J.D.
(adm. in OK; not adm. in CA) P.O. Box 22631‡

## CARMEL HIGHLANDS, 900, *Monterey Co.*

Logan, Donald M. '22 '52 C.813 A.B. L.767 LL.B. 230 Peter Pan Rd.‡
Madden, William J. '26 '56 C.870 B.S. L.174 LL.B.
(adm. in CO; not adm. in CA) 137 Boyd Way‡

## CARMEL VALLEY, 3,026, *Monterey Co.*

Bates, David T. '47 '76 C.674 B.A. L.813 J.D. Pres., Robert Talbott, Inc.
Boone, Lucinda C. '50 '76 C.483 B.A. L.1065 J.D. 11630 McCarthy Rd.
Hunter, Nancy A. '39 '67 C.174 B.S. L.276 J.D. 12050 Carola Dr.‡
Machado, E. L. '13 '37 L.1065 J.D. Ret. Supr. Ct. J.‡
Owens, Gerald T. '27 '50 C&L.846 B.A., LL.B.
(adm. in TX; not adm. in CA) 32 Los Robles Dr.‡

## CARMICHAEL, 37,625, *Sacramento Co.*

Ambrose, G. Louis '35 '66 C.767 B.S. L.464 5020 Keane Dr.
Backus, A. Richard '25 '51 C.20 B.A. L.477 LL.B. 2147 Hillcrest Way‡
Beckman, Paul E. '23 '50 C.352 B.A. L.813 J.D. 4304 Kilcher Ct.‡
Binsacca, Victor G., Jr. '38 '65 C.112 B.S. L.1066 J.D. 4864 Sherlock Way
Bleau, Richard E. '32 '78 C.134 B.A. L.793 J.D.
(adm. in SD; not adm. in CA) 6330 Hilltop Dr.‡
Bofinger, Theodore F. '24 '54 C.766 A.B. L.767 J.D. Admin. Law Judge, Ret.‡
Brundage, Kenneth E. '28 '58 C.1043 B.S. L.426 LL.B. P.O. Box 478
Carlson, Robt. F. '28 '53 C.740 A.B. L.1065 J.D. 2120 Lambeth Way‡
Connor, Edward J., Jr. '28 '53 C&L.339 B.S., LL.B. 1209 Macaulay Circle‡
Crawford, Nancy D., (CV) '53 '82 C.112 B.S. L.464 J.D. 6826 Rappahannock Way
Cudlip, Robert E. '— '87 C.112 B.A. L.1049 J.D. U.S. Treasury Dept.
Dormeyer, David C. '23 '54 C.112 L.464 LL.B. 4748 Bellue St.‡
Enriquez, M. Armando '39 '79 C.843 B.S.E.E. L.1026 J.D. Calif. Legal Ctr.
Francke, Joseph T. '44 '79
C.602 A.B. L.464 J.D. Exec. Dir., Calif. 1st Amendment Coalition
Frey, Nancy J. '40 '86 C.112 B.S. L.464 J.D. [Mandell K.&F.]
Gercovich, Lawr. E. '27 '53 C&L.767 B.S., LL.B. State Controllers Off.
Gerdes, Richard S. '39 '74 C.112 A.B. L.464 J.D. 5740 Windmill Way
Gilbert, Shira K. '62 '88 C.339 B.A. L.1065 J.D. 1300 Gary Way
Goldsmith, Geo. W. '20 '55 C.494 L.464 J.D. 2700 Leoleta Way‡
Gurney, Leanne '43 '79 C.608 B.A. L.464 J.D. P.O. Box 1905
Halpenny, Diana D. '51 '80
C.1078 B.A. L.464 J.D. Gen. Coun., San Juan Unified School Dist.
Heintz, Peter, (BV) '27 '63 C.972 L.464 J.D. P.O. Box 889
Henderson, Joseph S. '46 '90 C.623 B.A. L.464 J.D. Amer. Providers Ins. Serv.
**Hilliard, Kenneth J. '51 '82 C.1060 B.A. L.464 J.D.**
**6620 Madison Avenue, Suite A, 95608**
**Telephone: 916-962-0657 FAX: 916-967-6014**
**Email: goldpan@ns.net**
***PRACTICE AREAS: Family Law; Bankruptcy Law.**
**Guardianship, Juvenile and Criminal Law.**
**Reference: Bank of America.**

Hodgson, Timothy E. '54 '83 C.112 B.A. L.464 J.D. [Hodgson&S.]
Hodgson and Straight 5441 Fair Oaks Blvd.
Hoffman, Robert, (BV) '24 '57 C.267 A.B. 84 River Knoll Pl.‡
Hursh, Gary E., (BV) '46 '72 C.37 B.A. L.464 J.D. 6855 Fair Oaks Blvd.
Hursh, Jack E., (AV) '08 '33 C.112 B.A. L.1065 J.D. 5065 Martin Way‡
James, Robert W. '22 '50 C.112 B.A. L.1066 LL.B. Coun., Dept. of Water Res.‡
Leas, Mark Charles '57 '86 C.1060 B.A. L.464 J.D. 5441 Fair Oaks Blvd.
Lerner, Stanley G. '28 '56 C.112 A.B. L.1066 LL.B. P.O. Box 1218
Levy, Leonard M. '11 '39 C.112 B.S. L.284 LL.B. 5630 Frontier Way‡
Lewicki, Elizabeth Krystyna '52 '76 C.813 B.A. L.309 J.D. 4054 Crabtree Ct.
LoPresti, Stephen Philip '58 '88 C.999 A.S. L.1026 J.D. P.O. Box 547
Luoma, Laurie K. '20 '51 C.906 L.472 LL.B.
(adm. in FL; not adm. in CA) Ret. Admn. Law J., Dept. of Int.
Mandell, Stephan A. '50 '80 C.112 A.B. L.464 J.D. [Mandell K.&F.]
Mandell King & Frey 5125 Marconi Ave.
McKenzie, Donald C. '45 '72 C.112 A.B. L.1065 J.D. 6527 Grant Ave.
O'Connor, Leo M., (AV) '24 '53 C&L.767 B.S., LL.B. P.O. Box 1399
O'Neil, William J., Jr. '23 '52 C.597 B.A. L.767 LL.B. 4420 Jasper Ct.‡
Porterfield, Alan R. '27 '55 L.770 LL.B. 6125 Minton Ct.
Quandt, Robert G. '18 '70 L.464 J.D. 3013 Stanton Cir.
Rains, Senator Omer L., (AV) '41 '66 C.112 B.A. L.1066 J.D. 6408 Orange Hill
Reinnoldt, Donald H. '29 '55 C&L.800 B.S., J.D. 6489 Perrin Way‡
Roof, R. Michael '54 '81 C.608 B.A. L.464 J.D. 1213 Beard Way
Scallon, Garth L., (AV) '21 '54 C.112 B.S. L.1066 J.D. 6705 Lakeview Dr.
Shearer, John C. '32 '64 C.502 B.S. L.464 J.D. Adm. Law J., Unemploy. Ins App. Bd.
Shore, David M. '50 '77 C.1060 L.1026 LL.B. 5839 Manzanita Ave.
Smurr, Peter H. '26 '56 C.112 A.B. L.1065 5738 Marconi Ave.
Stassinos, Gail '49 '87 C.766 B.A. L.1067 J.D. 5740 Windmill Way
Steiner, Rudolph M. '25 '50 C&L.508 J.D.
(adm. in MT; not adm. in CA) 5307 El Camino Ave.‡
Straight, Catherine Ashley '46 '85 C.1060 B.S. L.464 J.D. [Hodgson&S.]
Summers, A. Kent, (BV) '43 '78 C.1060 B.A. L.464 J.D. 1597 Menlo Ave.
Taplin, Dennis M. '44 '75 C.506 B.S. L.464 J.D. 2761 Calif. Ave.
Telfer, Jill P. '63 '89 C.112 B.A. L.990 J.D. 5441 Fair Oaks Blvd. Ste. C-4
**Ullrich, Donald W., Jr. '52 '85 C.112 B.A. L.464 J.D.**
**8037 Fair Oaks Boulevard, Suite 113, 95608**
**Telephone: 916-944-8184 Fax: 916-944-8186**
**Email: dwulaw@cwnet.com**
**Bankruptcy, Business, Commercial, Corporations, Finance, Intellectual Property, Investments, International Transactions, Real Estate, Securities, Taxation, Trusts and Estates Law.**
*See Professional Biographies, CARMICHAEL, CALIFORNIA*

Vanderlaan, Marcus, (BV) '22 '50 C.112 A.B. L.1066 J.D. 5820 Landis Ave.

CAA47P

Wallner, Thomas ... '23 '53 C.770 A.B. L.1065 J.D. 4337 Prospect Dr.‡

## CARNELIAN BAY, —, *Placer Co.*

Collins, Elizabeth Margaret ... '64 '89 C&L.446 B.A., J.D. P.O. Box 732

## CARPINTERIA, 13,747, *Santa Barbara Co.*

Bright, Gary M., (CV) ... '51 '77 C.112 B.A. L.1049 J.D. [Bright&P.]
Bright & Powell, (CV) ... 4299 Carpinteria Ave., 2nd Fl.
Erwin, Richard E., (AV) ... '16 '43 C.101 L.809 J.D. 6099F Jacaranda Way‡
Fassett, Melissa J. ... '59 '83 C&L.560 B.A., J.D. 1055 B. Cindy Ln.
Harding, Jeffrey, (BV) ... '44 '71 C.112 B.A. L.1065 J.D. 6650 Casitas Pass Rd.

**Ives, Kirwan & Dibble, A Professional Corporation, (AV)**
**5210 Carpinteria Avenue, P.O. Box 360, 93013⊙**
**Telephone: 805-684-7641 FAX: 805-684-9649**
**Thomas P. Minehan; James M. McFaul; Jerry E. McLinn.**
**Major Insurance Company Clients: American Mutual Insurance Co.; Utica Mutual Insurance Co.**
**Los Angeles, California Office: The Biltmore Court, Fourth Floor, 520 South Grand Avenue. Telephone: 213-627-0113. FAX: 213-627-1547.**
**Orange-San Diego County Office: 101 Pacifica, Suite 250, Irvine, California, 92718. Telephone: 714-450-8900. FAX: 714-450-8908.**
**San Bernardino-Riverside Office: 777 Tahquitz Way, Suite 23, Palm Springs, California. Telephone: 619-778-2611. FAX: 619-778-2612.**

***See Professional Biographies, CARPINTERIA, CALIFORNIA***

Jackson, Toni L. ... '46 '90 C&L.1186 J.D. Staff Coun., Benton Oil & Gas Co.
Jaffe, Arnold S. ... '45 '71 C.112 B.A. L.800 J.D. 1786 Ocean Oaks Rd.
Kvistad, Barbara N. ... '59 '85 C.112 B.A. L.464 J.D. 1745 Ocean Oaks Rd.
Maloney, Robert E. ... '14 '38 C.383 A.B. L.150 J.D. 5540 Calle Jon‡
**McFaul, James M.** ... '51 '78 C.112 B.A. L.426 J.D. [Ives,K.&D.]
**McLinn, Jerry E.** ... '39 '77 C.608 B.S.E.E. L.61 J.D. [Ives,K.&D.]
**Minehan, Thomas P.** ... '44 '75 C.770 B.A. L.809 J.D. [Ives,K.&D.]
Nelson, John R., (BV) ... '55 '80 C.169 B.A. L.426 J.D. 1160 Eugenia Pl.
Poppic, George T., Jr. ... '48 '76 C.426 B.A. L.36 J.D. P.O. Box 778
Powell, Charles L., (CV) ... '51 '79 C.112 B.A. L.1186 J.D. [Bright&P.]
Smigel, Scott B. ... '53 '78 C.112 B.A. L.809 J.D. 4271 Del Mar Ave.
Tobyansen, Marie A. Rodarte, (CV) '41 '83 C.112 B.A. L.1336 J.D.
5320 Carpintena Ave.
Vedder, Phillip ... '— '75 L.284 J.D. 2020 Lillingston Cany Rd.‡
Westwater, Douglas S. ... '45 '71 C.597 A.B. L.800 J.D. Power Research Co.

## CARSON, 83,995, *Los Angeles Co.*

Aguila, Guillermo M. ... '46 '82 C&L.061 A.B., LL.B. 23517 S. Main St.
Barnett, Donald J. '41 '66 C.477 B.A. L.309 LL.B.
Prof. & Chair, Dept. of Acctg. & Law, Calif. State Univ. Dominguez Hills
Carter, Bernice L. ... '— '80 C.1097 M.A. L.1001 J.D. 20715 S. Avalon Blvd.
Cowan, Paul I. ... '51 '76 C.1077 B.A. L.809 J.D. [Janoff,K.&C.]
Frazier, Bradley ... '54 '81 C.911 B.A. L.1068 J.D. Gen. Coun., Watson Land Co.
Ginns, Harvey, (BV) ... '36 '68 C.1036 L.809 LL.B. 450 Carson Plz. Dr.
Graham, Cynthia U. '53 '83 C.880 B.E. L.326 J.D.
(adm. in TX; not adm. in CA) P.O. Box 6249‡
Heiser, James S. ... '56 '80 C.893 B.A. L.813 J.D. V.P. & Gen. Coun., Ducommun Inc.
Janoff, Walter D. ... '42 '67 C.112 B.A. L.426 LL.B. [Janoff,K.&C.]
Janoff, Karpel & Cowan ... 302 E. Carson St.
Jones, Sandra L. ... '— '92 C.112 B.A. L.999 J.D. Coun., Imaginary Man Prod.
Joyce, James D. ... '36 '80 C.966 B.S. L.1153 J.D. Shell Oil Co.
Karpel, Jerome J. ... '45 '71 C.112 B.A. L.1068 J.D. [Janoff,K.&C.]
Lingan, Victor Rirao ... '35 '85 C.016 A.A. L.061 LL.B. 316 W. Carson St.
Mire, Stephanie P. ... '59 '92 C.1042 B.A. L.1049 J.D. Dpty. Dist. Atty.
Posinoff, Eli J., (AV) ... '38 '71 C.112 B.S. L.809 J.D. [Posinoff&R.]
Posinoff & Rowe, (AV) ... One Civic Plaza
Rowe, Lloyd B., (AV) ... '47 '76 L.1152 J.D. [Posinoff&R.] ‡
Sanders, Johnnie M. ... '43 '79 C.1097 B.A. L.1179 J.D. 547 E. Cassidy St.
Singleton, Donald L. '60 '91 C.1168 B.A. L.426 J.D.
(adm. in PA; not adm. in CA) 17540 Rainsbury Ave.
Waks, Michael D., (BV) ... '56 '82 C.1044 B.A. L.809 J.D. One Civic Plaza

## CASTRO VALLEY, 44,760, *Alameda Co.*

Ahern, William H., (AV) ... '23 '53 C.770 B.S. L.767 LL.B. 3553 Castro Valley Blvd.
Blaha, Jerome A. ... '43 '73 C.112 B.A. L.1065 J.D. [Blaha&H.]⊙
Blaha & Hartford, A Professional Corporation ... 2807 Castro Valley Blvd. (⊙Pleasanton)
Borris, Robert C., Jr., (BV) ... '51 '79 C.1073 B.A. L.284 J.D. 20200 Redwood Rd.
Byers, Robert K. ... '31 '60 C.112 B.A. L.1066 J.D. Ret. Supr. Ct. J.
Duman, Fred M., (BV) ... '32 '61 C.94 A.B. L.1066 J.D. 2807 Castro Valley Blvd.
Fernandez, Yolanda B. ... '51 '91 C.424 B.A. L.878 J.D. 21855 Redwood Rd.
Fisher, Charles M., (BV) ... '43 '73 C.1073 B.A. L.1065 J.D. 20980 Redwood Rd.
Frost, Robert M., (BV) ... '47 '74 C.768 B.S. L.770 J.D. 20980 Redwood Rd.
Gibbons, Toni L. ... '46 '79 C.412 B.A. L.765 J.D. 5045 August Ct.
Goldwasser, Donald B. ... '28 '74 19002 Stanton Ave.
Hannon, John F. ... '55 '86 C.1073 B.A. L.284 J.D. [Hannon&L.]
Hannon & Lisoni ... 20416 San Miguel Ave.
Held, Gary K. ... '52 '80 C.112 B.A. L.1068 J.D. 3501 Village Dr.
Jacobs, Steven L, (BV) ... '48 '77 C.1073 B.A. L.1026 J.D. 3053 Castro Valley Blvd.
Kramer, Kenneth A. ... '44 '67 C.188 B.A. L.569 J.D. 20200 Redwood Rd.
Lichtig, Howard S., (BV) ... '49 '76 C.309 B.A. L.1197 J.D. 21855 Redwood Rd.
Lisoni, Antoinette M. ... '54 '86 C.740 B.A. L.284 J.D. [Hannon&L.]
Livanos, Peter E., Jr., (BV) ... '37 '63 C.112 A.B. L.1065 J.D. 20235 Redwood Rd.

**Meyerhoff, Peter S. '48 '74 C.112 A.B. L.1067 J.D.**
**20235 Redwood Road, 94546**
**Telephone: 510-538-1116 Fax: 510-538-1208**
***REPORTED CASES: Gerhardt v. Olsen (San Mateo, California, 1979).**
***PRACTICE AREAS: Personal Injury (35%, 75); Family Law (25%, 75); Divorce (25%, 100); Criminal (15%, 50).**
**Personal Injury, Family Law, Divorce, Criminal.**

***See Professional Biographies, CASTRO VALLEY, CALIFORNIA***

Mooney, Robert P., (BV) ... '25 '51 C.1256 A.B. L.767 LL.B. 3553 Castro Valley Blvd.
Moore, B. G., (BV) ... '22 '52 L.1065 J.D. 20880 Redwood Rd.
Partridge, James Syme ... '59 '88 C.101 B.F.A. L.1065 J.D. 3209 Castro Valley Blvd.
Poniatowski, Mark D., (BV) '57 '86
C.477 B.B.A. L.770 J.D. 2811 Castro Valley Blvd. (⊙Oakland)
Porter, John C., (BV) ... '46 '72 C.112 B.A. L.1066 J.D. 20980 Redwood Rd.
Rodriguez, J. Bryan, (BV) ... '56 '81 C.112 B.A. L.464 J.D. 3553 Castro Valley Blvd.
Roff, Michael B. ... '47 '83 C.999 B.F.A. L.1230 J.D. 20907 Manter Rd.
Smart, Edward S. ... '52 '78 C.112 A.B. L.765 J.D. Dep. Prob. Offr.
Smith, Ernest B. ... '31 '66 C.112 A.B. L.767 LL.B. 4217 Forest Glen Pl.
Spielberg, Matthew M., (BV) ... '51 '76 C.112 A.B. L.950 J.D. 21855 Redwood Rd.
West, Alan D. ... '49 '82 C.172 B.A. L.1026 J.D. 24715 Palomaras Rd.
Woidtke, Jay A., (BV) ... '54 '78 C.112 A.B. L.770 J.D. 20320 Redwood Rd.
Wright, Raymond G., (BV) ... '49 '78 C.1077 B.A. L.1197 J.D. 20980 Redwood Rd.

## CASTROVILLE, 4,396, *Monterey Co.*

Del Piero, Marc J. '53 '80 C&L.770 B.A., J.D.
Chmn., Monterey Co. Bd. of Supervisors

## CATHEDRAL CITY, 30,085, *Riverside Co.*

Ankeny, Clayton J. '16 '39 C&L.546 A.B.
(adm. in NE; not adm. in CA) 68-680 Dinah Shore Dr.‡
Becker, Robert F. ... '52 '80 C.793 B.S. L.1137 J.D. 68769 First St.
Berg, Bernard A. ... '29 '53 C.112 L.1065 J.D. 68697 Calle Tolosa‡
Briggs, Allen R. ... '32 '57 C.912 L.213 J.D. City Atty.
Dahlstrum, Jack A., (AV) ... '28 '58 C.990 B.S. L.426 J.D. P.O. Box 1209‡
Dorius, J. Scott ... '51 '80 C.112 B.A. L.1049 J.D. Watt Industries
Munoz-Muro, Patricia Segura ... '56 '87 C.112 B.A. L.398 J.D. 68-828 Ramon Rd.
Muro, Magdaleno C. ... '51 '86 C.763 B.A. L.398 J.D. 68-828 Ramon Rd.
Paul, Vivian ... '25 '49 C.472 A.B. L.800 LL.B. 69864 Via del Norte
**Quintanilla, Steven B.** ... '58 '92 C&L.112 B.A., J.D. [Sabo&G.]⊙
*PRACTICE AREAS: Eminent Domain; Inverse Condemnation; Civil Litigation.

**Sabo & Green, A Professional Corporation, (AV)**
**35-325 Date Palm Drive, Suite 150, 92234⊙**
**Telephone: 619-770-0873 Fax: 619-770-1724**
**Steven B. Quintanilla.**
**Municipal Law, Public Finance, Real Estate, Redevelopment, Condemnation, Litigation and Military Base Closures.**
**San Bernardino, California Office: 201 North "E" Street, Suite 206, 92401-1507. Telephone: 909-383-9373. Fax: 909-383-9378.**
**Calabasas, California Office: 23801 Calabasas Road, Suite 1015, 91302-1547. Telephone: 818-704-0195. Fax: 818-704-4729.**

***See Professional Biographies, CATHEDRAL CITY, CALIFORNIA***

## CAYUCOS, 1,772, *San Luis Obispo Co.*

McConnell, Lloyd L. ... '37 '88 C.628 B.S. L.999 J.D. 20 15th St.‡
Michie, Doug ... '55 '81 C.112 B.S. L.990 J.D. 690 S. Ocean Ave.
Pearson, A. Hugo, (AV) ... '21 '49 C.57 A.B. L.813 J.D. 148 N. Ocean Ave.
Sexton, James C. ... '40 '77 C&L.800 A.B., J.D. 1 N. Ocean

## CEDAR GLEN, —, *San Bernardino Co.*

Batman, Donald V. ... '34 '64 C.112 L.981 LL.B. P.O. Box 866
Dickson, Delavan Jon ... '55 '81 C.330 B.A. L.1068 J.D. P.O. Box 1

## CENTURY CITY, —, *Los Angeles Co.*

(See Los Angeles)

## CERES, 26,314, *Stanislaus Co.*

Johnson, Carl O. ... '07 '32 L.464 LL.B. 4100 Service Rd.‡
Schneider, Richard L. ... '29 '84 C.1079 B.A. L.1132 J.D. P.O. Box 2660
Sullivan, Mark Tod ... '58 '87 C&L.912 B.A., J.D. 3008 McCord Way
Tosaw, Richard T. ... '25 '51 C.190 B.S.L. L.208 LL.B. P.O. Box 939‡

## CERRITOS, 53,240, *Los Angeles Co.*

**Adams, B. Kimberly** ... '64 '92 C.299 B.A. L.426 J.D. [Ⓐ Atkinson,A.L.R.&R.]
*PRACTICE AREAS: Business Litigation.
**Andelson, Steven J.**, (AV) ... '44 '71 C.112 B.A. L.1067 J.D. [Atkinson,A.L.R.&R.]
*PRACTICE AREAS: School Law; Labor Law; Employment Law; Employment Discrimination Law.
Arlandson, John R. '44 '69 C&L.494 B.A., J.D.
(adm. in MN; not adm. in CA) Coast Indus. Supply Co.
**Atkinson, Steven D.**, (AV) ... '47 '72 C&L.260 B.A., J.D. [Atkinson,A.L.R.&R.]
*PRACTICE AREAS: Employment Law; Construction Law.

**Atkinson, Andelson, Loya, Ruud & Romo, A Professional Corporation, (AV)**
**13304 East Alondra Boulevard, 90703-2263⊙**
**Telephone: 310-404-4444; 714-826-5480 Telecopier: 310-404-8905 Email: AALRR@KINCYB.COM**
**Email: Info@aalrr.com URL: http://www.aalrr.com**
**Steven D. Atkinson; Steven J. Andelson; Paul M. Loya (Resident, Pleasanton Office); Ronald C. Ruud (Resident, San Bernardino Office); James C. Romo; Eugene F. McMenamin; Thomas W. Kovacich; Peter J. Lucey (Resident, Pleasanton Office); Davis D. Thompson; James H. Palmer; Karen E. Gilyard; James Baca; Robert L. Wenzel; Marilou F. Mirkovich; Roy R. Newman; Warren S. Kinsler; Sherry G. Gordon (Resident, San Bernardino Office);—Winlock W. Miller (Resident, San Bernardino Office); Elizabeth B. Hearey (Resident, Pleasanton Office); Hector E. Salitrero; Helen Ryan Frazer (Certified Specialist, Personal and Small Business Bankruptcy Law, The State Bar of California Board of Legal Specialization); Asa E. Reaves; Janice J. Hein (Resident, Pleasanton Office); Angela K. Kreta (Resident, Pleasanton Office); Tina L. Kannarr; Barbara S. Van Ligten; Felicia C. Curran (Resident, Pleasanton Office); Patrick A. Gunn (Resident, Pleasanton Office); Chesley D. Quaide (Resident, Pleasanton Office); Thomas A. Lenz; Kenneth S. Levy; Robert L. Sammis; Ann K. Smith; Terry T. Tao; Karen T. Meyers; Davina F. Harden; B. Kimberly Adams; Todd A. Goluba (Resident, Pleasanton Office); Marleen Lee Sacks (Resident, Pleasanton Office); Donald S. Field; Howard J. Fulfrost (Resident, San Bernardino Office); Robert R. Roginson; Christine D. Lovely (Resident, Pleasanton Office). Of Counsel: James T. Winkler; Nancy Long Cole.**
**Labor Relations representing Management. School Law. Construction and Real Estate Law. Civil Litigation. Corporate, Securities and Tax Law. Estate Planning Law.**
**Representative Clients: Associated Builders & Contractors; California Landscape and Irrigation Council; Huntington National Bank; Over 200 of the State of California School Districts.**
**Reference: Huntington National Bank.**
**Pleasanton, California Office: The Atrium. 5776 Stoneridge Mall Road, Suite 200. 94588. Telephone: 510-227-9200. Telecopier: 510-227-9202.**
**San Bernardino, California Office: 348 West Hospitality Lane, Suite 202. 92408. Telephone: 909-888-4165. Telecopier: 909-884-4118.**

***See Professional Biographies, CERRITOS, CALIFORNIA***

**Baca, James** ... '57 '84 C.940 B.A. L.1068 J.D. [Atkinson,A.L.R.&R.]
*PRACTICE AREAS: School Law; Labor Law; Employment Law; Employment Discrimination Law.
Bailey, William L. ... '38 '74 C.1042 B.A. L.426 J.D. 13142 E. Palm Pl.
Booker, Herbert W. ... '49 '73 C.207 B.A. L.477 J.D. Asst. U.S. Atty
Buynak, D. Michael ... '43 '91 C.475 B.A. L.1137 J.D. Staff Coun., State Comp. Ins. Fund

**Chan, Gary K. '57 '93 C.1097 B.S. L.426 J.D.**
**10945 South Street, Suite 106A, 90703**
**Telephone: 562-402-7338 Fax: 562-402-8958**
**Email: gkchan@earthlink.net**
***PRACTICE AREAS: Estate Planning; Trusts; Trust Administration; Probate; U.S. and International Taxation.**
**Probate, Conservatorship, Trusts and Trusts Administration, Estate Planning, U.S. and International Taxation, Business Planning and Formation and Immigration Law.**

***See Professional Biographies, CERRITOS, CALIFORNIA***

Chiang, Max C. ... '54 '87 L.464 J.D. 11540 South St.
**Cole, Nancy Long** ... '52 '76 C.112 B.A. L.1049 J.D. [Ⓒ Atkinson,A.L.R.&R.]
*PRACTICE AREAS: Civil Litigation.
**Field, Donald S.** ... '67 '93 C.112 B.A. L.809 J.D. [Ⓐ Atkinson,A.L.R.&R.]
*PRACTICE AREAS: Taxation; Corporate; Business; Real Estate; Estate Planning.
Fields, Michael S. ... '39 '69 C.768 B.S. L.809 LL.B. 11554 South St. (⊙Beverly Hills)

CAA48P

**Frazer, Helen Ryan**, (AV) ....... '55 '80 C.800 B.A. L.809 J.D. [A Atkinson,A.L.R.&R.]
*PRACTICE AREAS: Bankruptcy Law; Banking Law; Commercial Law.
**Gilyard, Karen E.** ............... '58 '83 C.112 B.A. L.1068 J.D. [Atkinson,A.L.R.&R.]
*PRACTICE AREAS: School Law; Labor Law; Employment Law; Employment Discrimination Law; Eminent Domain.
**Harden, Davina F.** ................ '66 '91 C.684 B.A. L.1065 [A Atkinson,A.L.R.&R.]
*PRACTICE AREAS: School Law; Public Sector; Government Law; Labor and Employment Law; Redevelopment.
Houston, Patricia A. '60 '84 C.1042 B.A. L.426 J.D.
Staff Coun., State Comp. Ins. Fund
Huang, David M. .......................... '40 '79 L.061 LL.M. 18000 Studebaker Rd.
Johnson, Georgiana Rosenkranz ....'66 '93 C.605 B.A. L.426 J.D. 13304 E. Alondra Blvd.
**Kannarr, Tina L.** ................ '61 '86 C.800 B.A. L.945 J.D. [A Atkinson,A.L.R.&R.]
*PRACTICE AREAS: Public School Employment and Labor Law; Public Education Law; Employment Discrimination Law; Litigation.
**Kinsler, Warren S.** ................ '55 '82 C.112 A.B. L.426 J.D. [Atkinson,A.L.R.&R.]
*PRACTICE AREAS: Education Law; Labor Law.
**Kovacich, Thomas W.** .............. '53 '80 C.112 B.A. L.426 J.D. [Atkinson,A.L.R.&R.]
*PRACTICE AREAS: Management Labor Relations; Public Works; Construction Law.
Kumagai, Wesley S. ...........'54 '81 C.668 B.A. L.112 J.D. Isuzu Motors of Amer. Inc.
Law, John P. ..............'57 '89 C.1109 B.A. L.1137 J.D. Coun.,State Comp. Ins. Fund
**Lenz, Thomas A.** .............. '63 '88 C.436 B.A. L.420 J.D. [A Atkinson,A.L.R.&R.]
*PRACTICE AREAS: Labor Relations and Employment Law for Management.
**Levy, Kenneth S.** ............... '63 '90 C.112 B.A. L.94 J.D. [A Atkinson,A.L.R.&R.]
*PRACTICE AREAS: School Law; Public Works; Land Use; Construction Litigation; Environmental Law.
Madula, Hyelita '47 '87 L.1137 J.D.
(adm. in IN; not adm. in CA) 17303 Stark Ave.‡
Maradiegue, Jorge B. ............... '43 '82 C.1109 B.A. L.464 J.D. 13079 Artesia Blvd.
**McMenamin, Eugene F.**, (AV) ........'49 '76 C&L.262 B.A., J.D. [Atkinson,A.L.R.&R.]
*PRACTICE AREAS: Civil Litigation; Labor Relations Law; Management Law; Construction Default; Delay Claims.
**Meyers, Karen T.** ............... '66 '91 C.477 B.A. L.276 J.D. [A Atkinson,A.L.R.&R.]
*PRACTICE AREAS: School Law; Municipal Law; Labor and Employment Law.
**Mirkovich, Marilou F.** ...........'58 '85 C.684 B.S. L.426 J.D. [A Atkinson,A.L.R.&R.]
*PRACTICE AREAS: Labor Relations Law; Employment Law.
Morehouse, Walter H. ............. '32 '64 C.259 B.S. L.472 J.D. 16954 Sierra Vista Way
**Newman, Roy R.** ............... '62 '86 C.684 B.A. L.426 J.D. [A Atkinson,A.L.R.&R.]
*PRACTICE AREAS: Business Litigation; Construction Law; Employment Law; School Law.
Ochoa, Gloria Megino '45 '76 C.112 B.S. L.1067 J.D.
(adm. in XX; not adm. in CA) 12326 Hedda Dr.
**Palmer, James H.** ................ '48 '79 C.475 B.A. L.990 J.D. [Atkinson,A.L.R.&R.]
*PRACTICE AREAS: Civil Law; Business Litigation.
Patterson, Paul S., (BV) ............'41 '77 C.1042 B.A. L.1137 J.D. 13737 Artesia Blvd.
**Reaves, Asa E.** ................ '34 '80 C.1097 B.A. L.1136 J.D. [A Atkinson,A.L.R.&R.]
*PRACTICE AREAS: Administrative Law; Labor Law.
**Roginson, Robert R.** ............. '67 '96 C.276 B.A. L.426 J.D. [A Atkinson,A.L.R.&R.]
*PRACTICE AREAS: Labor and Employment Law; Employment Litigation.
**Romo, James C.**, (AV) .............. '51 '76 C.763 A.B. L.1068 J.D. [Atkinson,A.L.R.&R.]
*PRACTICE AREAS: Labor Law (Public and Private Sector); School Law; Employment Law, Public and Private (Representing Management).
**Salitrero, Hector E.** ........... '51 '77 C.426 B.A. L.1068 J.D. [A Atkinson,A.L.R.&R.]
*LANGUAGES: Spanish.
*PRACTICE AREAS: Employment Law; Litigation.
**Sammis, Robert L.** ............ '59 '90 C.1042 B.S. L.1190 J.D. [A Atkinson,A.L.R.&R.]
*PRACTICE AREAS: Labor Law; Employment Law; Education Law.
Schuur, Michael L., (BV) ...........'52 '79 C.1042 B.A. L.1137 J.D. 11010 Artesia Blvd.
**Smith, Ann K.** ................... '64 '90 C.112 B.A. L.602 J.D. [A Atkinson,A.L.R.&R.]
*PRACTICE AREAS: Civil Litigation; Labor Law.
**Tao, Terry T.** .................... '64 '91 C.112 A.B. L.426 J.D. [A Atkinson,A.L.R.&R.]
*PRACTICE AREAS: Construction Litigation; Land Use; Environmental Law; Public Contracts; Procurement Law.
**Thompson, Davis D.** ............. '49 '76 C.770 B.A. L.1068 J.D. [Atkinson,A.L.R.&R.]
*PRACTICE AREAS: Corporate and Commercial Law; Corporate and Public Finance; Tax and Estate Planning; Real Estate Law.

**Treister, Robert B., (BV) '39 '68 C.112 B.A. L.1068 J.D.**
**16400 Greenlake Lane, 90703-2065**
**Telephone: 310-924-4427**
**Personal Injury, Family Law, Bankruptcy, Medical Malpractice.**

**Van Ligten, Barbara S.** ......... '61 '87 C.112 B.A. L.426 J.D. [A Atkinson,A.L.R.&R.]
*PRACTICE AREAS: Labor Law; Business Litigation.
**Wenzel, Robert L.** ............... '44 '81 C.123 B.A. L.1137 J.D. [Atkinson,A.L.R.&R.]
*PRACTICE AREAS: Employment Law; Management Law.

**Wieder, Catherine Grant '48 '82 C.1044 B.A. L.1068 J.D.**
**13017 Artesia Boulevard Suite D-120, 90703-1365**
**Telephone: 310-404-4039 Fax: 310-404-4109**
**Email: cgrant@netcom.com**
***LANGUAGES: Spanish.**
***PRACTICE AREAS: Civil Practice (100%).**
**Family Law, Probate and Estate Planning, Wills and Trusts, Conservatorships and Guardianships, Social Security, Disability, SSI, Commercial Law, Collections.**

**Winkler, James T.** ................'46 '72 C.37 B.S. L.1065 J.D. [C Atkinson,A.L.R.&R.]
*PRACTICE AREAS: Labor Relations Law; Management Law.

## CHANNEL ISLAND, —, *Ventura Co.*

Marcus, Bradley D., (AV) ............. '33 '62 C.112 B.A. L.809 LL.B. 4137 Ocean Dr.‡

## CHATSWORTH, —, *Los Angeles Co.*

(Part of the incorporated City of Los Angeles)

Adams, Stephen F. ........... '42 '72 C.874 B.A. L.896 J.D. Sr. V.P. & Secy., Aristar, Inc.
Arevalo, Jaime ...............'63 '89 C.112 B.A. L.1066 J.D. Coun., Great Western Bk.
Arnold, Stanley R., (A P.C.), (AV) '32 '56
C&L.813 A.B., J.D. 9520 Topenga Canyon Blvd.
Ashoorian, Hamid J. ............................................ '57 '91 19812 Lassen St.
Baker, Susan E. '54 '85 C.16 B.S.N. L.370 J.D.
(adm. in AL; not adm. in CA) 22265 Horizon Pl.‡
Brubaker, Richard Alan .............'59 '88 C.645 B.A. L.809 J.D. 21053 Devonshire St.
Clough, Larry Haakon .............'47 '79 C.800 B.A. L.1095 J.D. 21758 Devonshire St.
Cohen, Jack Martin, (BV) ..............'50 '76 C.112 B.A. L.1095 J.D. 20471 Nashville
Cotton, Harold ..................'23 '79 C.1077 M.A. L.1095 J.D. 10437 Larwin Avenue‡
Coughran, L. Craig ................'25 '68 C.1246 A.B. L.1095 LL.B. 19812 Lassen St.
Croner, Charles R. ............................ '21 '76 C.446 B.S. L.1095 J.D. [Croner&C.]
Croner, Melissa A. ........................'56 '81 C.1077 B.S. L.1095 J.D. [Croner&C.]
Croner & Croner ............................................................ 21405 Devonshire St.
Demain, Sanford R. .............'29 '57 C.472 B.B.A. L.1068 LL.B. 21704 Devonshire St.
Eckerling, Herbert ...................'37 '74 C.112 B.S. L.1095 J.D. 20336 Coraline Cir.
Ellis, Harlow J. ........................'27 '67 C.1066 B.S. L.809 LL.B. 19930 Lassen St.
Erikson, J. Lance '42 '69 C.112 B.A. L.1065 J.D.
Exec. V.P., Secy. & Gen. Coun., Great Western Fin. Corp.

Friedman, Michael S. '56 '84 C.112 B.A. L.809 J.D.
(adm. in IL; not adm. in CA) E/W Electronics
Friedmann, Steven C. ........... '61 '89 C.112 B.A. L.809 J.D. Coun., Great Western Bk.
Gabler, Mark J. ........................ '— '78 C.1077 B.S.M.E. L.1095 J.D. 20443 Nashville St.
Garrett, Joseph R., II ............ '58 '89 C.112 B.A. L.767 J.D. Coun., Great Western Bk.
George, Irene S. ..................'61 '87 C.586 B.A. L.990 J.D. Coun., Great Western Bk.
George, Victor E. ............................'54 '79 C.1097 B.A. L.990 J.D. Mng. Atty., F.D.I.C.
Greenbaum, Richard E. ...............'47 '79 C.1077 B.S. L.1065 J.D. Ace Hy Sales Corp.
Gudin, Donald P. ........................................ '31 '70 L.1095 LL.B. 21220 Devonshire St.
Herzog, Julie A. .....................'60 '84 C.112 B.A. L.800 J.D. 23170 Valley Circle Blvd.
Howard, Richard G. ..........................'37 '71 C.1077 L.1095 J.D. 9142 Independence Ave.
Jensen, Leslie F., (BV) ...........'55 '80 C.169 B.A. L.464 J.D. Coun., Great Western Bk.
Kemmel, William A., Jr. '30 '60 C.111 B.S., M.S. L.273 LL.B.
V.P., Secy. & Gen. Coun., Syncor Intl. Corp. (Pat.)
Klein, Jeffrey S. ........................ '53 '80 C.154 B.A. L.813 J.D. Pres., Los Angeles Times
Lenenberg, Mark D. ............................'52 '77 C.112 A.B. L.1068 J.D. P.O. Box 4466
Lesser, Thomas M. ............................'43 '70 C.605 B.A. L.1095 J.D. 19947 Vintage St.
Levy, Daniel C. B. '30 '57 L.05 LL.B.
(adm. in TN; not adm. in CA) 22452 Lassen St.‡
**MacDonald, Reina M.** .... '60 '87 C.048 B.A. L.018 LL.B. Gen. Coun., NMB (USA) Inc.
McKnight, Tina D. ...........'57 '85 C.112 B.A. L.800 J.D. Sr. Coun., Great Western Bk.
Mercado, Raymond J. ........'42 '76 C.763 B.A. L.1049 J.D. Sr. Coun., Great Western Bk.
Mizrahi, Marlene ............................................ '45 '72 Sr. Coun., Great Western Bk.
Morse, Amy ........................'54 '80 C.112 B.A. L.770 J.D. Coun., Great Western Bk.
Nelson, Nancy J. .............'51 '80 C.473 B.S. L.426 J.D. Sr. Coun., Great Western Bk.
Plotkin, Harris I. ............................'32 '55 C&L.986 B.A., LL.B. 20953 Devonshire St.
Posner, Howard ............................'56 '80 C.112 B.A. L.1068 J.D. 20645 Mayall St.

**Powers, William F., Jr., (AV) '45 '71 C.112 B.A. L.426 J.D.**
**Devonshire Professional Building, 20933 Devonshire Street, Suite 102, 91311**
**Telephone: 818-773-9800 Fax: 818-773-1130**
***LANGUAGES: French; Spanish.**
**Real Estate, Business Litigation, Commercial Law, Commercial Landlord-Tenant, Construction Law, Transactional and Litigation Focus.**
***See Professional Biographies, CHATSWORTH, CALIFORNIA***

Rembaum, George J. .......................'25 '51 C&L.477 A.B., LL.B. 10120-2 Larwin Ave.
Russell, Paul E. ..............................'37 '77 C.112 A.B. L.426 J.D. Great Western Bank
Schiffman, Joel A. '53 '79 C.112 B.A. L.464 J.D.
1st V.P. & Assoc. Gen. Coun., Great Western Bk.
Schoenherr, Jeffrey T. ............... '48 '78 C.475 B.S. L.1190 J.D. 20933 Devonshire St.
Schulze, Max H. '39 '67
C.347 B.S. L.276 LL.B. V.P. & Gen. Coun., MCRB Serv. Bur., Inc.
Shinderman, William .........'59 '84 C.112 B.A. L.426 J.D. Sr. Coun., Great Western Bk.
Siff, Marshall S. ........................ '20 '56 C.309 A.B. L.809 LL.B. 10650 Desplain Pl.
Sigman, Isiah '13 '40 C&L.966 B.S., LL.B.
(adm. in WI; not adm. in CA) 20451 Bermuda St.‡
Sledd, Charles M. '48 '74 C.604 B.A. L.767 J.D.
1st V.P. & Assoc. Gen. Coun., Great Western Bk.
Stashevsky, Yury ........................'59 '86 C&L.347 B.S., J.D. Coun., Great Western Bk.
Stein, Theodore O., Jr. ............................'48 '73 C.800 B.A. L.426 J.D. 21358 Nordhoff
Swinney, Richard B. '48 '74 C.629 B.S. L.426 J.D.
1st V.P. & Assoc. Gen. Coun., Great Western Bk.
Towbin, David P. ............... '59 '88 C.1077 B.S. L.426 J.D. Coun., Great Western Bk.
Turbow, Orrin H. .......................'48 '78 C.1077 B.A. L.1095 J.D. 10755 Cozycroft Ave.
Vallens, Brent Edward, Law Offices of '54 '80
C.1077 B.A. L.809 J.D. 20941 Devonshire St.
Vogel, Andrea ...................'62 '87 C.103 A.B. L.145 J.D. Coun., Great Western Bk.
Wankovsky, Edward J. .............'51 '76 C.1097 B.S. L.809 J.D. 31049 Devonshire St.
Watts, Cynthia G. '62 '88 C.976 B.A. L.309 J.D.
V.P., Gen. Coun. & Corp. Secy., Leslie's Poolmart
Weisberg, Michael P. ........................'66 '90 C.112 B.A. L.276 J.D. 21200 Lassen St.

## CHICO, 40,079, *Butte Co.*

Aisthorpe, Robert W. ............................'35 '63 C.112 B.S. L.1065 J.D. 548 Bway.‡
**Alpert, Bruce S.** ................................'51 '77 C.112 B.A. L.809 J.D. [C Craig&S.]
*PRACTICE AREAS: Insurance Defense; Business Litigation; General Business; Real Estate.
Baker, Ken, (CV) ..............................'43 '73 C.635 B.S. L.464 J.D. P.O. Box 1640
**Bakke, Randy L.**, (BV) ......... '50 '77 C.330 B.A. L.464 J.D. [McKernan,L.B.B.&B.]⊙
Baumbach, Larry L., (BV) .............'41 '72 C.636 B.S. L.464 J.D. 686 Rio Lindo Ave.
Bennett, James T. ...........................'50 '84 C.112 B.A. L.464 J.D. 645 Normal Ave.
**Benson, Stephen E.**, (BV) ..... '46 '79 C.636 B.A. L.1137 J.D. [McKernan,L.B.B.&B.]⊙
*REPORTED CASES: Reed v. King (1983) 145C.A.3d 261, 193C.R.130.
Bertoni, Stephanie A. ...........................'57 '92 C.1042 B.A. L.999 J.D. 593 East Ave.
**Bodney, John A.**, (BV) ..........'48 '77 C.629 B.S. L.464 J.D. [McKernan,L.B.B.&B.]⊙
Boehm, Robert G. ......................................'40 '66 C.429 B.A. L.494 LL.B. City Atty.
Brislain, Gregory J., (Inc.), (BV) ...........'47 '72 C.112 B.A. L.1067 J.D. [Brislain&O.]
Brislain & O'Neil, (BV) ...............................................20 Independence Cir.
Brooks, Lorie .......................................'60 '90 C.112 B.S. L.999 J.D. 28 Hanover Ln.
**Brown, W. Z. Jefferson**, (AV) ................'42 '66 C.668 B.A. L.309 J.D. [Price,B.&H.]
*PRACTICE AREAS: Business Law; Real Estate and Agricultural Law; Estate Planning Law; Construction Law.
**Buckley, Larry S.** ............................ '59 '96 C.147 B.S. L.285 J.D. [A Leonard&L.]
*PRACTICE AREAS: Medical Malpractice; Employment Law; Contract Law.
**Burchett, Alan E.**, (AV) ..............'43 '69 C.112 B.S. L.1065 J.D. [Stewart,H.B.S.&M.]
*PRACTICE AREAS: Business Law; Real Estate Law; Probate Law.
Burghardt, John L., (BV) .............'46 '76 C.1073 B.S. L.284 J.D. 1350 E. Lassen Ave.
Burness, Robert E., Jr., (AV) ...........'23 '50 C.112 A.B. L.767 J.D. 16 Lakewood Way
Bush, Michael R. .......................'41 '74 C.766 B.A. L.1065 J.D. Chico Area Legal Servs.
Bussey, Douglas M., (BV) ............'49 '75 C.147 B.A. L.1068 J.D. 1361 The Esplanade
Cameron, Dane A., (BV) ........................'50 '80 C.147 B.A. L.284 J.D. 341 Flume St.

**Carter, John Jeffery, Law Office, (BV) '51 '78 C.276 B.S. L.770 J.D.**
**426 Broadway, Suite 308, P.O. Box 3606, 95927-3606**
**Telephone: 916-342-6196 Fax: 916-342-6195**
**Email: JJZephyr@aol.com**
***PRACTICE AREAS: Business; Corporation; Partnership Law; Real Property; Local Government.**
**Business Transactions and Litigation, Contracts, Corporation, Local Government Law, Employment Law, Partnerships, Real Estate, Land Use and Water Law.**
***See Professional Biographies, CHICO, CALIFORNIA***

**Christensen, Nels A.**, (AV) ............... '40 '66 C&L.813 A.B., J.D. [Christensen&S.]

**Christensen & Schwarz, (AV)**
**45 Main Street, P.O. Box 676, 95927**
**Telephone: 916-343-5875 Fax: 916-343-6454**
**Members of Firm: Nels A. Christensen; John D. Schwarz, Jr.**
**General Civil and Trial Practice. Probate, Corporation, Real Estate, Insurance, Title Insurance, Escrow and Business Law.**
***See Professional Biographies, CHICO, CALIFORNIA***

CAA49P

Cooke, James M. .................................. '29 '58 C.679 B.S. L.1065 J.D. P.O. Box 791
Cornell, Kendal E., (CV) ............. '43 '72 C.284 B.A. L.464 J.D. 686 Rio Lindo Ave.
**Crabtree, Richard L.** .............................. '59 '90 C.112 B.A. L.1067 J.D. [Craig&S.]
*PRACTICE AREAS: Litigation; Employment Law; Environmental.
**Craig, Maynard C., (AV)** .................... '32 '60 C.112 A.B. L.1065 J.D. [Craig&S.]
*PRACTICE AREAS: Insurance Defense; Business Litigation; corporate.

**Craig and Shepherd, (AV)** BB
**Suite 1, 1367 East Lassen Avenue, P.O. Box 658, 95927-0658**
**Telephone: 916-893-3700 Fax: 916-893-1579**
**Members of Firm: Maynard C. Craig; Michael T. Shepherd. Associates: Bruce S. Alpert; Richard L. Crabtree.**
**Civil and Trial Practice including Business, Insurance Defense, Employment Discrimination and Wrongful Termination, Probate, Professional Liability, Corporate and Criminal Law.**
***See Professional Biographies, CHICO, CALIFORNIA***

Davis, Grady M. ..................... '51 '80 C.147 B.A. L.1153 J.D. 242 Broadway, 3rd Fl.
Delorenzo, Teodora C. ..... '54 '80 C.147 B.A. L.1230 J.D. Prof., Calif. State Univ., Chico
Driscol, Alfred W., III, (CV) ..................... '48 '74 C.147 B.A. L.1049 J.D. 1339 Esplanade
Edgar, Thomas E. ..................................... '45 '76 C.112 B.S. L.464 J.D. 682 E. 7th Ave.
**Farnsworth, James C., (CV)** .......... '57 '83 C.112 A.B. L.464 J.D. [Peters,F.R.F.&H.]
*PRACTICE AREAS: Insurance Defense; Personal Injury Law; Property Damage Law; Workers Compensation Law; Products Liability Law.
Felder, John Mark .......................... '54 '87 C.649 B.A. L.464 J.D. 3120 Cohasset Rd.
Forland, Denny R. ......................... '53 '78 C.636 B.S. L.464 J.D. 2261 St. George Ln.
Fuller, Brad L. ........................'56 '83 C.112 B.A.Pol.Sci. L.1065 J.D. 330 W. Fifth St.
Fuller, David R., (AV) ........................'32 '56 C.112 A.B. L.1066 J.D. 414 Salem St.
Fuqua, Morey W., (BV) ......................'39 '72 C.768 B.S. L.1065 J.D. [Matthews,F.&P.]
Gardener, Susan G. ........................ '46 '77 C.112 B.A. L.464 J.D. 870 Manzanuta Ct.
Gould, Ginger L. C., (BV) .....................'47 '72 C.112 B.A. L.1066 J.D. 1334 Bruce St.
**Habib, Mark A., (BV)** ........................ '52 '90 C.111 B.A. L.990 J.D. [Peters,F.R.F.&H.]
*PRACTICE AREAS: Insurance Defense; Personal Injury Law; Property Damage Law; Real Property Law; Civil Litigation.
Hait, Les, (CV) ........................................'43 '72 C.112 B.A. L.1066 J.D. 762 East Ave.
**Halsey, F. Dennis, (BV)** ....................... '44 '75 C.147 B.A. L.1065 J.D. [Price,B.&H.]
*PRACTICE AREAS: Civil Litigation; Insurance Defense; Public Entity Defense.
Hardin, Richard D., (BV) ............... '48 '74 C.147 B.S. L.464 J.D. 7 Williamsburg Ln.
Harp, Robert D. ........................... '60 '85 C.112 B.S. L.770 J.D. 1350 E. Lassen Ave.
Harriman, Richard L., (CV) ...................'44 '75 C.813 B.A. L.1067 J.D. 643 Flume St.
Harris, Neil A. ........................'47 '86 C.147 B.S. L.1065 J.D. 1530 Humboldt Rd.
Hays, Michael O., (CV) .................. '44 '79 C.112 A.B. L.284 J.D. 1362 The Esplanade
Henderson, David ............................ '69 '95 C.1253 B.A. L.464 J.D. [Henderson&H.]
Henderson, Kimberly ...................... '67 '95 C.766 B.A. L.464 J.D. [Henderson&H.]
Henderson & Henderson .................................................... 641 Flume St.
Henry, Paul J. .............................................. '26 '52 L.809 LL.B. [P.J.Henry]
Henry, Paul J., Inc. ................................................... 1604 Meadow Rd.
Herzog, Walter W...................'31 '83 C.339 B.S.E.E. L.981 LL.B. 2925 Burnap Ave.
Hicks, Tom K. ........................ '62 '92 C.112 B.A. L.1189 J.D. 55 Independence
Holcombe, Andrew T. '53 '78
C.861 B.A. L.1049 J.D. Staff Atty., Legal Servs. of N. Calif.
Hoptowit, Dennis R. ......................... '47 '74 C.1235 B.A. L.813 J.D. 1339 Esplanade
Houghton, M. Brooks, (CV) ......... '42 '68 C.147 A.B. L.1065 J.D. 1362 The Esplanade
Hubbard, Lynn, III, (BV) ............. '40 '76 C&L.1137 B.A., B.L. 12 Williamsburg Ln.
**Humpherys, Keith S., (AV)** ..........'29 '61 C.101 B.S. L.273 J.D. [Stewart,H.B.S.&M.]
*PRACTICE AREAS: Personal Injury Law; Probate Law; Business Law.
Jacobs, Douglas Bram, (CV) .....................'53 '78 C.966 B.A. L.464 J.D. 593 E. Ave.
Johnson, John ........................'43 '82 C.767 B.A. L.1026 J.D. 341 Flume St.
Johnson, Robert P. ....................'15 '49 C.870 B.S. L.893 LL.B. 2193 North Ave.
Jones, Gilbert F., (Law Corporation), (BV) '31 '61
C.147 A.B. L.1066 J.D. 1350 E. Lassen Ave.
Keene, Richard J. ............... '57 '89 C.147 B.A. L.999 J.D. 1550 Humboldt Rd., Ste. 1
Kelleher, Timothy M., (BV) ..................'46 '72 C.112 B.S. L.1066 J.D. [Kelleher&O.]
Kelleher & Olivera, (BV) .................................................. 350 E. First St.
Kelly, Thomas W., Law Corporation, (BV) '42 '69 C.147 A.B. L.1065 J.D.
350 E. 1st St.
Kenkel, Jerry J., (AV) ............................'45 '73 C.770 B.A. L.767 J.D. [Latimer&K.]
Kennedy, David W., (CV) ........... '51 '81 C.330 B.A. L.1049 J.D. 1550 Humboldt Rd.
Korber, Jeffrey W. ...................... '50 '77 C.1169 B.A. L.284 J.D. 1550 Humboldt Rd.
Kutz, Robert B., (BV) ....................'22 '49 C.112 L.1065 J.D. 1000 The Esplanade
**Lanam, John D., (BV)** ......... '35 '64 C.147 A.B. L.1066 J.D. [McKernan,L.B.B.&B.]⊙
Latimer, Dennis M., (BV) .......................'45 '71 C.770 B.A. L.464 J.D. [Latimer&K.]
Latimer & Kenkel, A Professional Corporation, (AV) ......................... 330 Wall St.
LeClerc, Michel C., (BV) .............. '62 '89 C.1060 B.A. L.629 J.D. 307 W. 12th Ave.
Ledgerwood, Thomas K., (CV) .................'55 '84 C.147 B.A. L.284 J.D. 762 E. Ave.
Lenzi, Albert J., Jr., (BV) .............................. '55 '79 C.424 B.A. L.464 J.D. [Zink&L.]

**Leonard & Lyde, (AV)** BB
**A Partnership including Professional Corporations**
**1600 Humboldt Road, Suite 1, 95927**⊙
**Telephone: 916-345-3494 Fax: 916-345-0460**
**Raymond A. Leonard (1961-1981); C. Keith Lyde (Inc.); Dorsett Marc Lyde. Associates: Sharon A. Stone; Maria Lathrop Winter; Larry S. Buckley.**
**General Civil and Trial Practice. Medical Law, Business, Probate, Insurance.**
**Oroville, California Office: 1453 Huntoon Street. Telephone: 916-533-2662. Fax: 916-533-3843.**
***See Professional Biographies, CHICO, CALIFORNIA***

Leverenz, Carl B., (BV) .................. '40 '66 C.147 A.B. L.1066 J.D. [C.B.Leverenz]
Leverenz, Carl B., A Professional Corporation, (BV) ......................... 515 Wall St.
Lieberman, Alan S., (BV) '45 '69
C.145 A.B. L.569 J.D. Mng. Atty., Legal Servs. of Northern Calif.
Luvaas, John L., Jr. .................. '43 '69 C.629 B.A. L.1066 J.D. Mediation Law Ctr.
**Lyde, C. Keith, (Inc.), (AV)** ............................. '21 '50 L.1065 J.D. [Leonard&L.]
**Lyde, Dorsett Marc, (CV)** ............... '54 '88 C.605 B.A. L.1049 J.D. [Leonard&L.]
*PRACTICE AREAS: Professional Liability Defense; Insurance Defense Liability; Business Law; Health Care Law; Personal Injury.
Marsh, Harry M., (AV) ..........................'48 '73 C.147 B.A. L.1067 J.D. [Marsh&M.]
Marsh & Marsh, (AV) ..................................................... Ste 6, 3120 Cohasset Rd.
Marshall, Roger V., (BV) ............ '41 '71 C.147 B.S. L.464 J.D. 1350 E. Lassen Ave.

**Matson, Richard S., (CV) '51 '77 C.112 B.A. L.464 J.D.**
**The Silberstein Building, 426 Broadway, Suite 305, P.O. Box 4141, 95927-4141**
**Telephone: 916-342-5396 Fax: 916-342-5395**
**Email: rsmatson@maxinet.com**
***PRACTICE AREAS: Contracts; Acquisitions; Corporations; Partnerships; Real Property.**
**Corporate, Partnership, Business, Contracts, Acquisitions, Real Property, Probate, Wills, Trusts, Estate Planning, Trademarks and Franchise Law.**
***See Professional Biographies, CHICO, CALIFORNIA***

Matthews, Charles D., Jr., (BV) ............. '23 '55 C.147 L.1065 J.D. [Matthews,F.&P.]
Matthews, Fuqua & Puritz, (BV) ........................................ 30 Constitution Dr.

**McCampbell, Daniel J., (BV) '58 '84 C.147 B.A. L.464 J.D.**
**2607 The Esplanade, 95926**
**Telephone: 916-893-1141 Fax: Available Upon Request**
**Bankruptcy (Debtor and Creditor), Business and Agricultural Reorganization and Business Law.**
***See Professional Biographies, CHICO, CALIFORNIA***

McCampbell, Thomas, (AV) ......... '32 '56 C.147 A.B. L.1066 J.D. 2607 The Esplanade
McGie, Elizabeth, (CV) ................. '57 '86 C.147 B.A. L.174 J.D. 910 Oleander Ave.
McHugh, Martin S. ..........................'59 '84 C.740 B.S. L.464 J.D. 350 E. 1st St.
**McKenna, James P., (BV)** ............ '63 '89 C.147 B.A. L.767 J.D. [Ⓐ Peters,F.R.F.&H.]
*PRACTICE AREAS: Premises Liability Law; Personal Injury Law; Civil Litigation; Property Damage.
**McKernan, Roy, (AV)** '24 '53
C.147 A.B. L.1066 J.D. [McKernan,L.B.B.&B.] (⊙Paradise)‡

**McKernan, Lanam, Bakke, Benson & Bodney, (BV)**
**445 Normal Avenue, P.O. Box 3496, 95927**⊙
**Telephone: 916-891-0247 Fax: 916-891-1704**
**Email: mlbbbchico@aol.com**
**Members: Roy McKernan (Retired); John D. Lanam; Randy L. Bakke (Certified Specialist, Family Law, The State Bar of California Board of Legal Specialization); Stephen E. Benson; John A. Bodney.**
**General Civil Practice. Trusts, Probate, Real Estate, Estate Planning, Personal Injury, Medical Malpractice, Legal Malpractice and Bad Faith Law, Corporate Law and Trials.**
**Paradise, California Office: 732 Fir Street, P.O. Box 550. Telephone: 916-877-4961. Fax: 916-877-8163**
***See Professional Biographies, CHICO, CALIFORNIA***

Merlo, A. John ........................ '22 '51 C.112 A.B. L.1065 J.D. 645 Normal Ave.
**Merritt, Harley A., (BV)** ................ '43 '72 C.112 L.1026 LL.B. [Peters,F.R.F.&H.]
*PRACTICE AREAS: Workers Compensation; Personal Injury; Defense.
Millar, Robert L. .................... '52 '79 C.147 B.A. L.1137 J.D. 1600 Humboldt Rd.
Miller, Valerie, (CV) .......................... '56 '81 C&L.770 B.A., J.D. [Persons&M.]
**Molin, Richard J., (AV)** ............ '46 '75 C.766 B.A. L.464 J.D. [Stewart,H.B.S.&M.]
*PRACTICE AREAS: Personal Injury Litigation; Public Entity Defense; Wrongful Termination Defense.
Moran, Michael, (CV) ..................... '44 '76 C.636 B.A. L.1026 J.D. 686 Rio Lindo Ave.
Morony, Jean ................................ '12 '36 C.813 M.A. L.1065 J.D. Ret. Supr. Ct. J.‡
Nickel, Kenneth W. ..............................'53 '89 C.1281 B.A. L.999 J.D. [Wagner&N.]
Olivera, Elizabeth Ufkes ................ '54 '85 C.112 B.A. L.1065 J.D. [Kelleher&O.]
O'Neil, Monica C. ............................... '60 '90 C.262 B.A. L.990 J.D. [Brislain&O.]
Ortner, Eric R., (CV) .............. '52 '81 C.636 B.A. L.1137 J.D. 15 Williamsburg Ln.
Owens, James M. ............ '51 '78 C.623 B.A. L.1137 J.D. Assoc. Prof., Calif. State Univ.
Passmore, Lynda G. ................................ '48 '91 C.147 L.999 J.D. Dep. Dist. Atty.
Peitz, Ruth A. ................................'55 '79 C.480 B.A. L.546 J.D. 2259 North Ave.
Persons, Paul T., (CV) ......... '51 '78 C.147 B.A. L.1230 J.D. 1834 Arroyo Canyon Rd.
Persons, Robert K., (CV) .......................'54 '81 C.1169 B.A. L.770 J.D. [Persons&M.]
Persons & Miller, (CV) .................................................... 1209 The Esplanade
**Peters, Jerome D., Jr., (AV)** ........... '14 '39 C&L.813 A.B., LL.B. [Peters,F.R.F.&H.]
*PRACTICE AREAS: Estate Planning; Probate; Business Law; Water Law; Real Estate Law.

**Peters, Fuller, Rush, Farnsworth & Habib, (AV)** BB
**414 Salem Street, P.O. Box 3509, 95928**
**Telephone: 916-342-3593 FAX: 916-342-4272**
**Members of Firm: Jerome D. Peters, Jr.; David H. Rush; James C. Farnsworth; Mark A. Habib. Associates: James P. McKenna; Harley A. Merritt.**
**General Civil and Trial Practice in all State and Federal Courts. Insurance Defense, Real Property. Estate Planning and Administration, Business and Commercial Law, Workers Compensation.**
**Local Counsel: Pacific Gas & Electric Co.; Southern Pacific Co.; Helena Chemical Co.; California Water Service Co. Insurance Companies: Great American Insurance Co.; Industrial Indemnity; Lloyds of London; Zurich Insurance Co.; U.S.F. & G.; Progressive Insurance Co.**
***See Professional Biographies, CHICO, CALIFORNIA***

Peterson, Todd M., (BV) ....... '49 '74 C.813 B.A. L.477 J.D. 669 Palmetto Ave., Suite F
Potter, Dirk .......................................'54 '82 C.147 B.A. L.1067 J.D. 515 Wall St.
**Price, Philip B., (BV)** ............................'35 '62 C&L.770 B.S., J.D. [Price,B.&H.]
*PRACTICE AREAS: Civil Litigation; Insurance Defense; Public Entity Defense.

**Price, Brown & Halsey, (AV)**
**466 Vallombrosa Avenue, P.O. Box 1420, 95927**
**Telephone: 916-343-4412 Fax: 916-343-7251**
**Grayson Price (1902-1988); Philip B. Price; W. Z. Jefferson Brown; F. Dennis Halsey. Associates: Linda M. Schulken.**
**General Civil and Trial Practice. Business, Insurance and Public Entity Defense, Real Property and Probate Law.**
**Representative Clients: City of Chico (Self Insured); Maryland Casualty; County of Siskiyou (Self Insured); Canadian Indemnity Co.; Lassen Land Co.; Allstate Insurance Co.; Continental Insurance Group; Chubb/Pacific Indemnity Co.; County of Butte; Bidwell Title & Escrow Co.**
***See Professional Biographies, CHICO, CALIFORNIA***

Puritz, Lawrence A., (CV) ............. '50 '78 C.147 B.A. L.1137 J.D. [Matthews,F.&P.]
Reed, Ronald A. ......................'34 '85 C.767 B.S. L.464 J.D. 2864 State Hwy. 32
Reed, Stephen C., (CV) ............. '48 '74 C.940 B.A. L.1049 J.D. Work Injury Law Ctr.
**Rich, Fuidge, Morris & Iverson, Inc.**
**(See Marysville)**

Riley, Stephen F. ............................ '56 '88 C.112 B.A. L.1066 J.D. [Ⓐ Matthews,F.&P.]
**Rush, David H., (AV)** ..................... '38 '66 C.691 B.A. L.1066 J.D. [Peters,F.R.F.&H.]
*PRACTICE AREAS: Insurance Defense; Personal Injury Law; Property Damage Law; Real Estate Law; Products Liability Law.
Rutherford, Ann H. .................................'42 '67 C.112 B.A. L.1065 J.D. Mun. J.
Sabersky, Cynthia ..........................'50 '87 C.112 L.397 J.D. 466 Vallombrosa Ave.
**Sandelman, Raymond L., (BV)** ..... '53 '77 C.112 A.B. L.770 J.D. [Stewart,H.B.S.&M.]
*PRACTICE AREAS: Commercial Litigation; Real Estate Litigation; Probate Litigation.
Schooling, John W., (AV) ............ '40 '67 C.112 A.B. L.1066 J.D. 1530 Humboldt Rd.
**Schulken, Linda M.** ............................. '57 '95 C.147 B.S. L.999 J.D. [Ⓐ Price,B.&H.]
**Schwarz, John D., Jr., (BV)** ............'56 '84 C.147 B.A. L.1065 J.D. [Christensen&S.]
**Shepherd, Michael T., (BV)** ...................... '46 '74 C.112 B.A. L.1065 J.D. [Craig&S.]
*PRACTICE AREAS: Insurance Defense; Business Litigation.
Sibary, Scott ..................................'53 '80 C.112 A.B. L.1066 J.D. Prof., Calif. State Univ.
Skow, Charles A. ....................'28 '56 C.174 B.A. L.981 LL.B. 1212 Glenwood Ave.‡
Stapleton, Steven M. ....... '52 '79 C.147 B.A. L.408 J.D. 1600 Humboldt Rd. (⊙Oroville)
Stevens, Darrell W. .............................................. '38 '66 C.766 L.284 J.D. Mun. Ct. J.
**Stewart, Ronald E., (AV)** .......... '39 '68 C.147 B.A. L.1066 J.D. [Stewart,H.B.S.&M.]
*PRACTICE AREAS: Personal Injury Law; Medical Malpractice; Business Litigation; Trial Practice; Public Entity Defense.

**Stewart, Humpherys, Burchett, Sandelman & Molin, (AV)** BB
**Suite 6, 3120 Cohasset Road, P.O. Box 720, 95927**
**Telephone: 916-891-6111 Telecopier: 916-894-2103**
**Email: shbsm@sunset.net**
**Members of Firm: Ronald E. Stewart; Keith S. Humpherys; Alan E. Burchett; Raymond L. Sandelman; Richard J. Molin; Carol J. Tener; Stephen P. Trover.**
**General Civil and Trial Practice, Probate, Estate Planning, Corporation, Real Estate, Personal Injury, Business Law, Construction, Education Law, Public Entity, Employment Law, Insurance Law, Municipal Law, Public Entity Defense, Wrongful Termination Defense.**
**Representative Clients: North State National Bank; Northern California Federal Land Bank; Northern California Production Credit Assn.; Drake Homes, Avag, Inc.; Meeks Building Center; Land's End Real Estate, Inc.**
***See Professional Biographies, CHICO, CALIFORNIA***

Stuart, William H., III ................'48 '74 C.674 B.S.E. L.813 J.D. 12 Williamsburg Ln.
**Tener, Carol J.** ....................'43 '77 C.147 B.A. L.1137 J.D. [Stewart,H.B.S.&M.]
*PRACTICE AREAS: Education Law; Employment Law.
Thompson, James J., (BV) ............'48 '74 C.154 B.A. L.464 J.D. 1350 E. Lassen Ave.
Tochterman, Mendel B. ............................'17 '50 C.147 L.1065 J.D. 341 Bway
**Trover, Stephen P.**, (BV) ............'54 '89 C.147 B.A. L.464 J.D. [Stewart,H.B.S.&M.]
*PRACTICE AREAS: Commercial Litigation; Construction Litigation; Real Estate Law.
Tuck-Smith, Cheryl L., (CV) .........'— '88 C.972 B.A. L.999 J.D. 2725 The Esplanade

**Volpe, William S., (BV) '49 '74 C.112 A.B. L.1067 J.D.**
**466 Vallombrosa Avenue, 95926**
**Telephone: 916-343-4414 Facsimile: 916-343-7251**
***REPORTED CASES: Ely v. Gray (1990) 224 Cal. App. 3rd 1257; Filmore v. Irvine (1983) 146 Cal. App. 3d 649.**
**Business, Commercial, Corporation, Real Estate, Construction, Debtor/Creditor, Probate, Wills, Trusts and Estates.**
***See Professional Biographies, CHICO, CALIFORNIA***

Wagner, Jeffrey D. ...............................'57 '90 C.147 B.A. L.464 J.D. [Wagner&N.]
Wagner & Nickel ............................................................... Drawer 3589
**Ward, William A.**, (AV) ...................'38 '65 C.112 B.A. L.1068 J.D. [W.A.Ward]

**Ward, William A., A Professional Corporation, (AV)**
**9 Williamsburg Lane Stonebridge Professional Village, 95926**
**Telephone: 916-342-2225 Fax: 916-342-7920**
**William A. Ward.**
**General Civil and Trial Practice, Real Estate, Business, Probate, Corporation, Personal Injury.**
***See Professional Biographies, CHICO, CALIFORNIA***

Willis, F. L. (Larry), Jr., (CV) ...............'43 '72 C.147 A.B. L.464 J.D. [Willis&W.]
Willis, Frank L. ...............................'16 '54 C.112 M.A. L.426 LL.B. 1362 Esplanade‡
Willis & Willis, (CV) .......................................................1362 Esplanade
Wilson, Gary Edward .........'— '78 C.147 B.A. L.1137 J.D. 1600 Humboldt Rd., Suite 4
**Winter, Maria Lathrop** ....................'67 '94 C.112 B.A. L.1240 J.D. [Leonard&L.]
*PRACTICE AREAS: Medical Malpractice; Employment Law.
**Zellmer, Joseph F., III**, (BV) ..................'57 '83 C.112 B.A. L.1065 J.D. [Zellmer]
*PRACTICE AREAS: Real Estate; Business Law; Litigation; Zoning, Planning and Land Use; Commercial Law.

**Zellmer Law Group, (BV)**
**1660 Humboldt Road, Suite 6, 95928**
**Telephone: 916-345-6789 Fax: 916-345-6836**
**Email: zellmo@aol.com**
**Joseph F. Zellmer, III.**
**Real Estate, Business Law, Litigation, Zoning, Planning and Land Use, Commercial Law.**
***See Professional Biographies, CHICO, CALIFORNIA***

Zink, Joseph D. "J.D.", (Inc.), (BV) ...........'41 '73 C.147 B.A. L.1067 J.D. [Zink&L.]
Zink & Lenzi, (BV) ..........................................................20 Independence Cir.

## CHINO, 59,682, *San Bernardino Co.*

Alix, Peter A., (CV) ................'42 '73 C.112 B.A. L.809 J.D. 11760 S. Central Ave.
Assuras, Dennis M., (BV) ............'37 '79 C.339 B.A. L.1137 J.D. 13141 Central Ave.
**Bautista, A. Marquez**, (AV) ...............................'34 '56 C&L.767 J.D. [Leach,M.&B.]⊙
*LANGUAGES: Spanish and Filipino.
*PRACTICE AREAS: Products Liability; Business Litigation; Real Estate Litigation; Environmental Law.
Belmudes, Dennis S. ....................'60 '87 C.112 B.A. L.1137 J.D. 12490 Central Ave.
Bryson, Christiana G. '43 '68
C&L.800 A.B., J.D. V.P. & Gen. Coun., Pacific States Cas. Co.
**Connolly, John C.** ...................'42 '77 C.724 B.A. L.1137 J.D. [Leach,M.&B.]⊙
Darden, William C. ......................'35 '73 C&L.1137 B.S., J.D. 12934 Central Ave.
Demchuk, Eugene A., (BV) .............'33 '63 C.999 B.A. L.800 J.D. [Demchuk,R.&H.]
Demchuk, Robbins & Holdaway, A Professional Corporation, (BV)
13139 Central Avenue
Determan, John D., (AV) '33 '62 C.800 B.E.E. L.1068 J.D.
Chmn. of the Bd. & CEO, Provena Foods Inc.
Edwards, John .........................'42 '77 C.628 B.S. L.1137 J.D. 13141 Central D
Elbertse, Johanna M. ....................'33 '87 C.02 B.Sc. L.1137 J.D. 5780 S. Estern Ct.
Elizalde-Daly, Michele M., (BV) ..........'56 '81 C.112 A.B. L.1066 J.D. Dep. Dist. Atty.
Ephross, Lee E. ...............................'38 '81 C.94 B.S. L.1137 J.D. P.O. Box 806
Gutierrez, Jimmy L., (BV) ......'47 '74 C.668 B.A. L.1068 J.D. City Atty. [J.L.Gutierrez]
Gutierrez, Jimmy L., A Prof. Corp., (BV) ..................................12616 Central Ave.
Holdaway, Richard E., (CV) ......................'54 '81 C&L.101 B.A., J.D. [Demchuk,R.&H.]
Ilg, Carl H. ..................'32 '68 C.570 B.S.M. L.1001 J.D. 16218 Valley Spring Rd.‡
Johnson, Douglas Allan ....................'57 '85 C.398 B.A. L.1137 J.D. 4195 Chino Hills
LaCues, Jerry A., (CV) ...............'50 '77 C.1110 B.A. L.809 J.D. 12606 Central Ave.
**Leach, David G.**, (AV) ................'36 '60 C.912 A.B. L.213 LL.B. [Leach,M.&B.]⊙
*PRACTICE AREAS: Insurance Defense; Civil Litigation; Construction Defects; Medical Malpractice; Workers Compensation.

**Leach, McGreevy & Bautista, (AV)**
**13643 Fifth Street, 91710⊙**
**Telephone: 909-590-2224**
**David G. Leach; Richard E. McGreevy; A. Marquez Bautista;—John C. Connolly.**
**Insurance Defense and Civil Litigation, Wrongful Termination and Maritime Law, Construction Defects, Medical Malpractice, Workers Compensation, Environmental Law.**
**San Francisco, California Office: 1735 Pacific Avenue. Telephone: 415-775-4455. Telefax: 415-775-7435.**
***See Professional Biographies, CHINO, CALIFORNIA***

Martinez, G.J. ..........................'39 '83 C.351 B.A. L.398 J.D. 12555 Central Ave.‡
**McGreevy, Richard E.**, (AV) ...........'46 '76 C.766 B.S. L.767 J.D. [Leach,M.&B.]⊙
*PRACTICE AREAS: Insurance Defense; Civil Litigation; Construction Defects; Medical Malpractice; Workers Compensation.
Morales, William J. ..........................'53 '82 C.1075 B.S. L.800 J.D. 12530 10th St.
Petersen, Mark E. '61 '87 C.1042 B.S. L.1137 J.D.
2545 Chino Hills Pkwy., Chino Hills
Radcliffe, William L. ..............................'58 '83 C.763 L.1137 J.D. 14726 Ramona
Rankin, James A. '52 '79 C.1042 B.S. L.1137 J.D.
16301 Oak Tree Crossing, Chino Hills
Reher, Robley C., (CV) ......................'16 '41 C.112 A.B. L.1065 J.D. P.O. Box 517
Robbins, Diane E., (BV) .................'57 '82 C.668 B.A. L.464 J.D. [Demchuk,R.&H.]
Roberts, John Alden ......................'55 '86 C&L.398 B.A., J.D. 15267 Murray Ave.
Segura, Ralph M. ......................'37 '67 C.763 A.B. L.1066 J.D. 13054 Rimrock Ave.

**Van Wagner, Ellen, Law Offices of, (AV) '42 '84 C.37 B.A. L.398 J.D.**
**12490 Central Avenue, Suite 104, 91710**
**Telephone: 909-902-1210 Fax: 909-902-1215**
**(Certified Specialist, Workers Compensation Law, The State Bar of California Board of Legal Specialization).**
***REPORTED CASES: Barrett Mobil Home Transport v. Bittle; Duroy v. Glass Door; Serrano V. Butler Paper.**
***PRACTICE AREAS: Worker's Compensation Law.**
**Workers Compensation Law.**
***See Professional Biographies, CHINO, CALIFORNIA***

Welborn, John A., (BV) ..........................'19 '55 L.809 LL.B. 15111 Pipe Line Ave.
Youngquist, Raymond C. ...........................'34 '64 C.1097 B.A. L.800 J.D. Mun. J.

## CHINO HILLS, —, *San Bernardino Co.*

Ofner, William B. ...................'29 '66 C.1043 A.B. L.426 LL.B. 13229 Setting Sun Ct.

## CHOWCHILLA, 5,930, *Madera Co.*

Crocker, M. D. .............................'15 '40 C.267 A.B. L.1066 LL.B. U.S. Sr. Dist. J.
DeGroot, John W., Jr. ...............................'47 '74 C.766 B.A. L.1065 J.D. Jus. Ct. J.

## CHULA VISTA, 135,163, *San Diego Co.*

Abbott, Malvina E.J. ...........................'43 '75 C.188 B.S. L.1137 J.D. Dep. Pub. Def.
**Allen, David R.**, (AV) ............................'42 '69 C.813 A.B. L.800 J.D. [Atherton&A.]
*PRACTICE AREAS: Estate Planning; Trust and Probate Law; Corporate Law; Real Estate Law.
Arroyo, Richard F., (BV) ................'53 '80 C.763 B.S. L.1067 J.D. 203 Church Ave.
**Atherton, Keith**, (AV) ....................'12 '38 C.763 A.B. L.477 J.D. [Atherton&A.] ‡
*PRACTICE AREAS: Estate Planning Law; Probate Law.

**Atherton & Allen, (AV)** BB
**210 Towne Centre Professional Building, 345 "F" Street, 91910**
**Telephone: 619-420-6869**
**Members of Firm: Harvey H. Atherton (1881-1972); Keith Atherton (Retired); David R. Allen (Certified Specialist, Estate Planning, Trust and Probate Law, The State Bar of California Board of Legal Specialization).**
**General Civil Practice. Estate Planning, Probate, Corporate and Real Estate Law.**
***See Professional Biographies, CHULA VISTA, CALIFORNIA***

Backes, Ronald J. ........................'30 '77 C.962 B.S. L.1137 J.D. 534 Poinsettia St.‡
Baker, William J. ...........................'62 '92 C.763 B.A. L.1068 J.D. 786 3rd Ave.
Barnes, Steven W. ..............'47 '91 C.112 B.A. L.589 J.D. 539 Telegraph Canyon Rd.
Bauer and Schltz, A Prof. Corp., (BV) ........................................3130 Bonita Rd.
Bendickson, Gerald L., (BV) ..........'14 '50 C.494 B.B.A. L.61 J.D. 160 Montebello St.
Bhayani, Minaz A. ...............................'56 '89 C.705 B.S. L.61 J.D. Dep. Dist. Atty.
**Billingslea, William, Jr.** '40 '71
C.608 B.S. L.1066 J.D. Corp. Coun. & Asst. Secy., Rohr, Inc.
*RESPONSIBILITIES: Environmental Law; Securities; Finance.
Blakely, John M., (BV) ......................'53 '79 C.763 L.1137 J.D. 515 Glover Ave.
Borunda, Ernest ..........................................................'44 '72 Mun. Ct. J.
Bowman, Garry J., (BV) ........................'44 '69 C&L.477 B.B.A., J.D. [G.J.Bowman]
Bowman, Garry J., A Professional Corporation, (BV) ...............Ste. E, 629 3rd Ave.
Boyer, Albert C. ..........................'14 '40 C.112 B.A. L.1066 J.D. 51 Minot Ave.‡
Bryan, John J. ..............................'11 '38 C.112 A.B. L.1066 LL.B. 948 Club View‡
Campbell, Merideth L., Jr ..................'42 '71 C.763 A.B. L.1049 J.D. 226 Church Ave.
Cannon, William S. .................................................'46 '73 C&L.61 B.A., J.D. Mun. Ct. J.
Carriedo, Carlos R., (BV) .......................'47 '73 C.602 B.A. L.1066 J.D. 637 3rd Ave.
Cazares, Roy B. .................................'42 '73 C.763 A.B. L.309 J.D. Mun. Ct. J.
Contreras, Raymond M. ......................'53 '80 C.605 A.B. L.1049 J.D. 721 3rd Ave.
Daley, William D., (BV) ............................'48 '75 C.763 B.A. L.1137 J.D. 535 H St.
Duberg, James S., (BV) ..........................'51 '77 C.112 B.A. L.464 J.D. 727 Third Ave.
Duggan, Marsha M. ..............................'51 '86 C.1109 B.A. L.1137 J.D. Dep. Pub. Def.
Evert, Sharla Leigh .............................'61 '95 C.763 B.A. L.128 J.D. Dep. Dist. Atty.
Falkenborg, Marguerite, (BV) ..................'30 '55 C.112 B.A. L.800 LL.B. 727 3rd Ave.
Fernandez, Frank D. ........................'41 '77 C.112 B.S.E.E. L.1137 J.D. 213 Church Ave.
**Ferrone, Frank A.** ..........'33 '71 C.1041 B.B.A. L.1008 LL.B. Labor Coun., Rohr, Inc.
*RESPONSIBILITIES: Labor and Employment; Wrongful Termination; ERISA; Discrimination; Sexual Harassment.
Finlay, Susan P. ...............................'39 '72 C.823 B.S. L.1049 J.D. Mun. Ct. J.
Fritsch, Ruth M., (AV) ...................'53 '79 C.454 B.A. L.1049 J.D. Asst. City Atty.
**Geerdes, Franklin**, (AV) ....................................'32 '66 L.981 LL.B. [Geerdes&G.]
*PRACTICE AREAS: Civil Litigation; Securities Investor Litigation; Surety Law; Real Estate Law; Environmental Waste Law.
**Geerdes, Mary Elizabeth** ....................'47 '94 C.560 B.S.N. L.999 J.D. [Geerdes&G.]

**Geerdes & Geerdes, (AV)**
**210 Towne Centre Professional Building, 345 "F" Street, 91910**
**Telephone: 619-420-6560**
**Members of Firm: Franklin Geerdes; Mary Elizabeth Geerdes.**
**Civil Litigation, Securities Investor Litigation, Surety Law, Real Estate, Environmental Waste and Corporate Maintenance.**
***See Professional Biographies, CHULA VISTA, CALIFORNIA***

Googins, Glen R. ...........................'63 '88 C.197 A.B. L.1066 J.D. Dep. City Atty.
Green, Michael A., (BV) ........................'46 '75 C.309 B.A. L.1049 J.D. 535 "H" St.
Gustafson, Robert T. ...............................'36 '60 C&L.494 B.S., J.D. 226 Church Ave.
Hendrix, Thomas C. ...............................'38 '68 C.112 B.S. L.1065 J.D. Mun. Ct. J.
Hoysa, Walter A. '09 '36 C&L.209 LL.B.
(adm. in IL; not adm. in CA) 280 "K" St., #13‡
**Irving, Robert J., Jr.** ........... '55 '82 C.813 B.A. L.309 J.D. Admin. Coun., Rohr, Inc.
*RESPONSIBILITIES: Corporate Law; Intellectual Property.
Jeffus, Allen W., (BV) ..........................'38 '72 C.263 B.A. L.1132 J.D. 815 3rd Ave.
Johns, Arthur J. ...................................'29 '53 C&L.597 B.S., J.D. 721 3rd Ave.‡
Kaarsberg-Handrus, Marianne ....................'35 '77 C.763 B.A. L.1137 J.D. 341 J St.
Kingston, John B., (BV) .......'37 '67 C.433 B.B.A. L.61 J.D. 680 Telegraph Canyon Rd.
**Krasne, Albert S.** ..............'45 '72 C.569 B.S. L.1009 J.D. Bus. Coun., Rohr, Inc.
*RESPONSIBILITIES: Contracts.
Kugler, Manuel L. .........................'22 '51 C.112 A.B. L.1065 LL.B. Ret. Mun. Ct. J.
Legler, Paul W., (BV) ................................'41 '72 C.763 B.A. L.1049 J.D. [Legler&T.]
Legler & Tomlinson, (BV) ..........................................................231 4th Ave.
Longo, Charles A., (BV) ....................'49 '78 C.454 B.A. L.1137 J.D. 2053 Port Cardiff
Loughman, John P. ............................'40 '83 C.509 B.A. L.1137 J.D. 637 Third Ave.
Love, Bruce W., (BV) ..............................'45 '72 C.763 B.A. L.1049 J.D. [B.W.Love]
Love, Bruce W., A P.C., (BV) ......................................................231 4th Ave.
**Madsen, Richard W.** '38 '64
C.549 B.A. L.236 LL.B. V.P., Gen. Coun. & Secy., Rohr, Inc.
*RESPONSIBILITIES: Securities; Finance; Environmental; Contracts; Corporate Law.
Marquez, Alfred C. ...........................'22 '50 C&L.37 B.S., LL.B. U.S. Sr. Dist. J.
Mason, Dolores H. '28 '74 C.645 B.S. L.904 J.D.
(adm. in VA; not adm. in CA) 368 Anita St.‡
McDougall, Dennis S., (BV) ..............'42 '75 C.800 B.S. L.1137 J.D. P.O. Box 120482
McGrath, Patrick E. ............................'57 '91 C.871 B.S. L.1049 J.D. Deputy Dist. Atty.
McGreevy, Paul F. ...................'30 '89 C.831 Ed.D. L.1049 J.D. 937 Buena Vista Way
McGuigan, William M., (BV) ...............'39 '77 C.174 B.S. L.1049 J.D. 815 Third Ave.
McKinnon, Edward W. ..............................'23 '73 C&L.1137 B.S., J.D. 1220 3rd Ave.
Montegna, Anthony Roy .......................'50 '85 C.238 L.1095 J.D. 237 Church Ave.
Montegna, Joseph A., II ....................'52 '85 C.999 B.S.L. L.1127 J.D. 815 3rd Ave.
Morell, Frank T., (CV) ..........................'44 '78 C.560 B.S. L.1137 J.D. 651 3rd Ave.
Moreno, Andres ...................................................'49 '84 L.1137 J.D. 786 3rd Ave.
O'Leary, Joseph V., (BV) ..........................'40 '74 C.763 B.A. L.61 J.D. 535 H St.
Osuna, Jesse .....................................'18 '65 C.763 L.61 LL.B. 461 Berland Way‡
Painter, Susan A. .......................'46 '79 C.763 B.A. L.1137 J.D. 704 Gretchen Rd.‡

CALIFORNIA—CHULA VISTA | MARTINDALE-HUBBELL LAW DIRECTORY 1997

Pappas, Gus, (BV) ........................ '26 '64 C.61 B.B.A. L.1049 203 Church Ave.
Paskowitz, Michael A. ........................ '53 '82 C.184 B.A. L.1137 J.D. 640 Port Dunbar
Petterson, James D., (BV) ........... '39 '70 C.999 B.A. L.809 J.D. 539 Telegraph Canyon Rd.
Planas, Luis M. '28 '82 C.061 M.C.E. L.1241 J.D.
(adm. in IN; not adm. in CA) 527 Third Ave.
Pullen, Ronald J., (CV) ........................ '48 '77 L.1137 LL.B. 355 "K" St.
Radford, Michael J., (BV) ........................ '50 '79 C.112 B.A. L.1066 J.D. 470 3rd Ave.
Ramirez, Suzanne Marie ........................ '50 '82 C.1169 B.A. L.464 J.D. 139 Fifth Ave.
Reed, Clifton E., (BV) ........................ '35 '69 C.1016 B.S.B.A. L.1065 J.D. 229 F St.
Roark, Michael J., (BV) ............. '41 '68 C.763 B.S. L.1065 J.D. [Firm of M.J.Roark]
Roark, Michael J., A Prof. Corp., Law Firm of, (BV) ........................ 231 4th Ave.
Rodriguez, Jesus ........................ '51 '76 C&L.1049 B.A., J.D. Supr. Ct. J.
Santana, M. Teresa ........................ '58 '90 C.112 B.A. L.1049 J.D. Dep. Dist. Atty.
Schlesinger, Patrick J. '34 '61 C.623 B.S.E.E. L.862 J.D.
(adm. in OK; not adm. in CA) Foot of H St.‡
Schultz, George J., (BV) ........................ '51 '76 C.388 B.A. L.1049 J.D. [Bauer&S.]
Scott, Terry J. ........................ '43 '73 C.940 B.A. L.1065 J.D. Mun. Ct. J.

**Serrano, John H., (AV) '50 '77 C.112 B.A. L.800 J.D.**
**Suite 311, 4045 Bonita Road, 91902⊙**
**Telephone: 619-267-7300**
**Email: jserr13006@aol.com**
***LANGUAGES: Spanish and French.**
**Civil and Criminal Trial Practice. Criminal Law, Personal Injury, Negligence, and Civil Rights.**
**Yuma Arizona Office: 221 West Second Street, 85364. Telephone: 520-329-7185.**
*See Professional Biographies, CHULA VISTA, CALIFORNIA*

Shorkey, John E. ....... '49 '86 C.37 B.S.B.A. L.861 J.D. Exec. V.P., Assemble In Mexico
Slovinsky, Gustavo B. ........................ '54 '81 C.589 B.A. L.801 J.D. [Slovinsky&S.]
Slovinsky, Mary P. ........................ '59 '88 C&L.1241 B.S.L., J.D. [Slovinsky&S.]
Slovinsky and Slovinsky ........................ 310 "I" Street
Starks, Anthony Charles, (CV) ............. '44 '81 C.431 B.A. L.1137 J.D. 765 3rd Ave.
Stene, Jean S. ........................ '31 '83 L.1137 J.D. 815 3rd Ave.
Stone, John H. ............. '29 '61 C.477 B.A. L.1065 J.D. 774 Monserate Ave.‡
Stone, Todd R., (BV) ........................ '51 '77 C.763 B.A. L.1065 J.D. 629 3rd Ave.
Thompson, John G. ........................ '18 '47 C.763 A.B. L.813 LL.B. 288 F St.
Thornburg, Jon C. ........................ '— '93 L.1241 J.D. 231 4th Ave.
Tomlinson, Thomas M., (BV) ........................ '48 '74 C.1188 B.A. L.61 J.D. [Legler&T.]
Ulovec, Thomas J., (BV) ........................ '52 '78 C&L.1049 B.A., J.D. 815 3rd Ave.
Urias, Victor E. ........................ '20 '50 L.61 LL.B. 765 3rd Ave.
Williamson, Donna M. '60 '90 C.588 B.S. L.770 J.D.
Sweetwater Union High Sch. Dist.
Willoughby, Floyd M., (BV) ........................ '34 '72 C.61 B.A. L.1049 J.D. 227 3rd Ave.
**Wilson, David R.** ........................ '55 '92 C&L.1241 B.B.A., J.D. Sr. Atty., Rohr, Inc.
*RESPONSIBILITIES: Contract Law.
Young, Robert H. ........................ '27 '82 C&L.1137 B.S.L., J.D. 691 Gilbert Pl.‡

## CITRUS HEIGHTS, 21,760, *Sacramento Co.*

Allen, Ronald L. ........................ '45 '77 C.1060 B.S. L.1026 J.D. P.O. Box 7051
Allred, T. Anderson ........................ '58 '90 C.101 B.A. L.464 J.D. [Brekke&A.]
Angerer, John M. ........................ '54 '81 C.169 B.A. L.464 J.D. [Brekke&A.]
Anthony, Thomas W., Jr., (BV) ......... '48 '78 C.870 B.S. L.464 J.D. 7803 Madison Ave.
Baer, Earl L. ........................ '26 '50 C.623 B.A. L.966 LL.B. 8350 Auburn Blvd.
Boyd, George, (BV) ........................ '46 '75 C.1060 B.S. L.464 J.D. 7509 Madison Ave.
Brakowiecki, Lester E. ........................ '35 '78 C.381 L.1026 LL.B. P.O. Box 100
Brekke, George O. ........................ '31 '56 C&L.585 B.S., LL.B. [Brekke&A.]
Brekke & Angerer ........................ 7011 Sylvan Rd.
Budwin, Donna T., (BV) ........................ '50 '85 C.999 A.A. L.1132 J.D. 7509 Madison Ave.
Bunnell, James F., II ............. '43 '74 C.112 A.B. L.1065 J.D. 6817 Lake Cove Lane
Burchett, Warren F. ........................ '21 '65 L.464 LL.B. 7772 Old Auburn Rd.
Cooke, Thomas J. ........................ '45 '80 C.262 B.A. L.464 J.D. P.O. Box 1406
Fuchigami, Walter N. '23 '53 C.173 A.B. L.273 J.D.
(adm. in CO; not adm. in CA) 7035 La Costa Ln.‡
Hamilton, Jas. W. ........................ '23 '52 L.61 LL.B. 7681 Watson Way‡
Heaman, Michael A. ........................ '39 '69 C.112 B.A. L.61 J.D. American Housing Corp.
Henderson, J. Collinsworth ............. '47 '80 C.905 B.A. L.990 J.D. 7610 Auburn Blvd.
Lininger, Thomas D. ........................ '64 '90 C.381 B.A. L.464 J.D. 7803 Madison Ave.
Mandich, George D. ........................ '30 '62 C.1060 B.A. L.1065 J.D. 6318 Nachez Ct.‡
Mattson, Elvin J. '31 '63 C.851 B.B.A. L.912 J.D.
(adm. in MI; not adm. in CA) 8351 Carrick Ct.‡
Melee, Paul J. ........................ '28 '58 C.605 L.1065 J.D. P.O. Box 318
Quirk, James ........................ '31 '68 L.464 J.D. 5435 Ventana Pl.
Raymond, Frank H. ........................ '— '78 C.1060 M.B.A. L.464 J.D. 7803 Madison Ave.
Ripani, Joseph A., Jr. ........................ '53 '79 C&L.1137 B.S.L., J.D. 5530 Birdcage St.
Rountree, Robert W. ........................ '41 '76 C.112 A.B. L.464 J.D. 6949 Burnham Dr.
Shepherd, William N., (BV) ........................ '41 '67 C&L.900 B.A., J.D. 7509 Madison Ave.
Sims, John E. ............. '42 '72 C.172 B.A. L.809 J.D. American Housing Corp.
Wilson, David A., (CV) ........................ '30 '62 C.112 B.S. L.464 LL.B. 7666 Wachtel Way
Yount, George H., (BV) ........................ '39 '82 C.383 B.A. L.1026 J.D. 5530 Bridcage St.

## CITY OF COMMERCE, —, *Los Angeles Co.*

(See Commerce)

## CITY OF INDUSTRY, 664, *Los Angeles Co.*

Chen, Judith S.C. ........................ '— '86 C.061 B.L. L.1137 J.D. 17800 Castleton St.
**Churchill, James A.** ...... '35 '61 C.674 A.B. L.309 LL.B. Gen. Coun., Wilsey Foods, Inc.
*RESPONSIBILITIES: General Corporate; Mergers and Acquisitions; Securities.
Cox, George W., (BV) ........ '45 '71 C.112 B.S. L.464 J.D. 13181 Crossroads Pkwy., N.

**Crawford & Bangs**
**(See West Covina)**

**Egger & Hallett, Professional Law Corporation, (AV)**
**13200 Crossroads Parkway, North, Suite 400, 91746⊙**
**Telephone: 310-695-4951 Fax: 310-695-9647**
**Eugene R. Hallett (Certified Specialist, Workers' Compensation Law, The State Bar of California Board of Legal Specialization); Bruce S. Emerick.**
**Workers Compensation Defense and Wills and Probate Law.**
**San Bernardino, California Office: 325 West Hospitality Lane, Suite 300, P.O. Box 5009. Telephone: 909-890-0403. Fax: 909-890-0503.**
**Yorba Linda, California Office: 22800 Savi Ranch Parkway, Suite 218. Telephone: 714-974-6299. Fax: 714-974-7215.**
**San Diego, California Office: 600 B Street, Suite 2200. Telephone: 619-236-9377. Fax: 619-236-1329.**
**Salinas, California Office: 158 Central Avenue, Suite 3. Telephone: 408-771-1414. Fax: 408-771-1408.**
**Pleasant Hill, California Office: 3478 Buskirk Avenue, Suite 1025. Telephone: 510-746-7187. Fax: 510-937-1611.**
*See Professional Biographies, SAN BERNARDINO, CALIFORNIA*

**Emerick, Bruce S.**, (CV) '49 '81 C.112 B.A. L.398 J.D.
[Egger&H.] (⊙San Bernardino)
*PRACTICE AREAS: Workers Compensation Defense.
**Hallett, Eugene R.**, (AV) ........................ '47 '77 C.112 B.S. L.1137 J.D. [Egger&H.]⊙
*PRACTICE AREAS: Workers Compensation Defense.
**Lee, Douglas J.** '46 '76 C.846 B.B.A. L.1137 J.D.
Dir. Legal Servs., Wilsey Foods, Inc.
*RESPONSIBILITIES: General Corporate; Employment.
Silverman, Stuart A. ........................ '51 '76 C.112 B.A. L.809 J.D. 13300 E. Nelson Ave.
Sirick, James P. ........................ '51 '90 C.112 B.A. L.1137 J.D. 13200 Crossroads Pkwy. N.
Wine, Michael ........................ '48 '73 C.1169 B.A. L.1068 J.D. P.O. Box 91564

## CLAREMONT, 32,503, *Los Angeles Co.*

**Allard, Shelton & O'Connor, (AV)**
**319 Harvard Avenue, 91711-4746**
**Telephone: 909-626-1041 Facsimile: 909-625-5781**
**Members of Firm: Joseph A. Allard, Jr. (1887-1968); Maurice O'Connor (1911-1987); Leonard A. Shelton (1911-1994); Keith A. Johnson; Keith S. Walker; Gary C. Wunderlin; Carol B. Tanenbaum.**
**Of Counsel: Donald K. Byrne.**
**General Civil and Trial Practice in all State and Federal Courts. Corporation, Non-Profit Organizations, Municipal, Real Estate, Taxation, Family Law, Estate Planning, Trust and Probate Law.**
**Reference: Bank of America National Trust & Savings Assn. (Pomona, California, Main Office).**
*See Professional Biographies, CLAREMONT, CALIFORNIA*

Allen, Jerry B. ........................ '44 '82 C.154 Ph. D. L.426 J.D. 237 W. Fourth St.
Ansell, Edward O., (AV) '26 '55 C.966 B.S.E.E. L.273 J.D.
449 W. Willamette Lane (Pat.)
**Arkin, Sharon J.** ........................ '52 '91 C.112 B.S. L.1137 J.D. [Ⓐ Shernoff,B.&D.]
*PRACTICE AREAS: Insurance Bad Faith.
Arter, Margaret H. Wade ........................ '29 '90 C.347 B.S. L.398 J.D. P.O. Box 106
Baldonado, Sandra N., (BV) ........................ '35 '84 C.788 B.A. L.1148 J.D. [Stafford&B.]
**Barta, Theresa J.** ........................ '63 '90 C.1109 B.A. L.426 J.D. [Ⓐ Shernoff,B.&D.]
*PRACTICE AREAS: Insurance Bad Faith.
**Benson, Mark E.** ........................ '52 '86 C.1077 B.A. L.426 J.D. [Shernoff,B.&D.]
*PRACTICE AREAS: Insurance Bad Faith; Insurance Coverage; Appellate Practice.
**Bidart, Michael J., (P.C.)**, (BV) ........ '50 '74 C.1075 B.S. L.990 J.D. [Shernoff,B.&D.]
*LANGUAGES: Basque.
*PRACTICE AREAS: Insurance Bad Faith.
Blickenstaff, Kenneth C., (BV) ............... '50 '77 C.668 B.A. L.426 J.D. P.O. Box 99
**Boileau, E. Burdette**, (AV) ......... '12 '37 C.668 A.B. L.1066 LL.B. [Nichols S.B.&K.]
*PRACTICE AREAS: Trust and Probate Administration; Estate Planning.
**Bollinger, Donald E.**, (AV) ............. '41 '68 C.605 A.B. L.209 J.D. [Nichols S.B.&K.]
*PRACTICE AREAS: Eminent Domain; Zoning and Land Use; Civil Litigation; Real Estate.
Bostwick, James R., Jr. ............. '48 '73 C.999 B.A. L.1049 J.D. 976 W. Foothill Blvd.
**Boyd, Aaron Ray** ............... '57 '90 C.1075 B.A. L.398 J.D. [Ⓐ Dryden,M.S.K.&W.]
*PRACTICE AREAS: Civil Litigation-Emphasizing Defense of Trucking Companies; ERISA; Products Liability; Premises Liability; Construction Defect.
**Brayton, Thomas C.**, (AV) ............ '41 '68 C.1097 A.B. L.1068 J.D. [Jones,M.B.&S.]
*PRACTICE AREAS: Family Law.
**Brown, Steven J.** ............... '60 '95 C.1075 B.S. L.398 J.D. [Ⓐ Dryden,M.S.K.&W.]
*PRACTICE AREAS: Products Liability; Premises Liability; Construction Defect; General Negligence.
**Buxbaum, David A.**, (AV) .............. '— '70 C.605 B.A. L.1068 J.D. [Buxbaum&C.]⊙
*PRACTICE AREAS: Business Banking; Estate Planning; Commercial; Real Estate.

**Buxbaum & Chakmak, A Law Corporation, (AV)**
**414 Yale Avenue, 91711⊙**
**Telephone: 909-621-4707 Fax: 909-621-7112**
**David A. Buxbaum; John Chakmak; Charles L. Zetterberg; Betty O. Yamashiro;—John P. Howland; Joan Penfil.**
**Business, Commercial, Banking, Insurance Coverage (Coverage & Defense) Corporate, Real Estate, Bankruptcy (Creditors' Rights), Estate Planning, Administrative Law and Family Law, Trials in all State and Federal Courts.**
**Newport Beach, California Office: 5160 Campus Drive. Telephone: 714-833-3107. Fax: 714-833-2466.**
*See Professional Biographies, CLAREMONT, CALIFORNIA*

**Byrne, Donald K.**, (AV) ............. '24 '57 C.502 B.A. L.809 LL.B. [Ⓒ Allard,S.&O.]
*PRACTICE AREAS: Civil Litigation; Municipal Law.
**Chakmak, John**, (BV) ................ '45 '71 C.813 B.A. L.1068 J.D. [Buxbaum&C.]⊙
*PRACTICE AREAS: Civil Litigation; Insurance; Commercial; Banking.
Chamness, Christopher L. ...... '50 '81 C.668 B.A. L.809 J.D. 101 Spring St. (⊙Modesto)
**Childs, Mary** ........................ '60 '88 C.1077 B.S. L.1136 J.D. [Dryden,M.S.K.&W.]
*PRACTICE AREAS: Construction Defect; Products Liability; Professional Liability; General Negligence; Premises Liability.
**Darras, Frank N.**, (AV) .............. '54 '87 C.1365 B.S. L.1137 J.D. [Shernoff,B.&D.]
*LANGUAGES: Greek.
*PRACTICE AREAS: Insurance Bad Faith.
Dennis, William E., (BV) ................ '34 '62 C.684 B.A. L.1068 LL.B. 237 W. 4th St.
**Dillon, Timothy P.** ................ '56 '82 C.1044 B.S. L.945 J.D. [Ⓐ Shernoff,B.&D.]
*PRACTICE AREAS: Insurance Bad Faith.

**Dryden, Margoles, Schimaneck, Kelly & Wait, A Law Corporation, (AV)**
**341 West First Street, 91711⊙**
**Telephone: 909-621-5672 Fax: 909-399-0645**
**Thomas B. Wait (Managing Partner); Mary Childs;—Aaron Ray Boyd; Steven J. Brown; Shawn E. McMenomy; A. Kerry Stack.**
**General Civil and Trial Practice. Medical Legal, Product Liability, Insurance, Aviation and Environmental Law.**
**San Francisco, California Office: Suite 2600, One California Street. Telephone: 415-362 -6715.**
*See Professional Biographies, CLAREMONT, CALIFORNIA*

**Echeverria, Ricardo** ................ '68 '93 C.1074 B.S. L.770 J.D. [Ⓐ Shernoff,B.&D.]
*LANGUAGES: Basque.
*PRACTICE AREAS: Insurance Bad Faith.
Elber, George A. ................... '16 '37 C&L.178 B.S., LL.B. 148 E. Chestnut Hill Pl.
Elliott, Ward E. Y. '37 '64 C.309 A.B. L.893 LL.B.
(adm. in VA; not adm. in CA) Prof., Claremont McKenna College

**Ferguson, C. Robert, (AV) '38 '66 C&L.800 B.A., J.D.** BR
**237 West Fourth Street, 91711**
**Telephone: 909-482-0782; 818-795-4181 Fax: 909-624-7291**
**Civil Trial and Appellate Practice. Corporate, Business and Commercial Law. Business, Environmental and Redevelopment Litigation.**

Fessler, John ........................ '50 '79 C&L.426 B.A., J.D. 341 W. First St.
**Fisher, Evangeline L.** ................ '67 '95 C.605 B.A. L.770 J.D. [Ⓐ Shernoff,B.&D.]
*PRACTICE AREAS: Insurance Bad Faith.
Flannery, Kathleen Berwind, (BV) .......... '49 '77 C.668 B.A. L.800 J.D. P.O. Box 358
Gault, Harold S. ................ '41 '79 C.46 B.S.I.E. L.398 J.D. 2549 N. Mt. Ave. (Pat.)
Ginsburg, Roger A., (BV) ........ '38 '74 C.112 B.A. L.464 J.D. 114 N. Indian Hill Blvd.
Gottuso, Josephine M. ............ '27 '73 C.1037 B.A. L.398 J.D. 145 N. Indian Hill Blvd.

**Gray, Paul Bryan, (AV) '38 '70 C.1042 B.A. L.1065 J.D.**
**341 West First Street, 91711**
**Telephone: 909-624-6259 FAX: 909-624-2359**
***LANGUAGES: Spanish.**
**Civil Trials. Corporations, Real Estate, Banking and Criminal Law.**

Hafif, Herbert, (AV) ........................ '29 '56 C.668 B.A. L.800 J.D. [H.Hafif]⊙

Hafif, Herbert, A Professional Corporation, (AV)
269 W. Bonita Ave. (©Newport Beach)
Hamilton, Lisa Oglesby ................ '56 '84 C.684 B.A. L.1148 J.D. 112 Harvard Ave.
Hansen, Debora Schall ..................... '56 '82 C.174 B.A. L.398 J.D. 269 W. Bonita
Harrison, Robin T. ........... '41 '78 C.628 B.S.M.E. L.398 J.D. 1275 N. Indian Hill Blvd.

**Herbold, Carl F., (AV) '40 '68 C.197 A.B. L.976 LL.B.**
**201 West Fourth Street, 91711**
**Telephone: 909-625-6305 FAX: 909-625-3870**
***LANGUAGES: Spanish, Portuguese and French.**
***PRACTICE AREAS: General Business; Non-Profit Corporations; Health Care; Employment. General Civil Litigation, General Commercial Law, Business Law, Corporate Law, Non Profit Organizations, Employment Law including, Sexual Harassment, Wrongful Termination, Discrimination and Tax Law.**
***See Professional Biographies, CLAREMONT, CALIFORNIA***

Holmes, Stuart A., (BV) ......................................... '41 '79 L.1198 J.D. 250 W. 1st St.
Howington, Joseph W., (BV) .................'51 '79 C.1109 B.A. L 1137 J.D. 150 1st St.
**Howland, John P.** ........................ '41 '67 C.197 B.A. L.659 LL.B. [Ⓐ Buxbaum&C.]©
*PRACTICE AREAS: Estate Planning; Corporate; Business; Bankruptcy (Creditors Rights).
**Johnson, Keith A.**, (BV) ................... '50 '74 C.1163 B.S. L.893 J.D. [Allard,S.&O.]
*PRACTICE AREAS: Taxation Law; Business and Non-Profit Organization Law; Real Estate Law.
**Jones, Stephen C.**, (AV) ............... '44 '69 C.426 B.B.A. L.1068 J.D. [Jones,M.B.&S.]
*PRACTICE AREAS: Corporate Law; Business Law; Probate Law; Estate Planning Law; Taxation Law.

**Jones, Mahoney, Brayton & Soll, (AV)**
**150 West First Street, Suite 280, 91711**
**Telephone: 909-399-9977 Fax: 909-399-5959**
**Members of Firm: Stephen C. Jones; Thomas C. Brayton (Certified Specialist, Family Law, The State Bar of California Board of Legal Specialization); Paul M. Mahoney; Richard A. Soll.**
**General Civil and Trial Practice in State and Federal Courts. Business, Construction, Corporation, Insurance, Civil Litigation, Estate Planning, Probate, Taxation, Real Property and Family Law.**
***See Professional Biographies, CLAREMONT, CALIFORNIA***

Kast, Leslie A. ....................... '26 '56 C&L.585 B.S.C., J.D. 976 W. Foothill Blvd.
Keller, James J. ........................................ '41 '78 L.1190 LL.B. 2058 N. Mills Ave.
Kendall, Thomas E. ............................ '67 '92 C.668 B.A. L.770 J.D. P.O. Box 877
**Kostoff, James R.**, (AV) ................'32 '57 C.668 A.B. L.1068 J.D. [Nichols S.B.&K.]
*PRACTICE AREAS: Corporation; Tax Exempt Organization; Estate Planning; Trust and Probate Administration; Eminent Domain.
Loberman, Harry ................. '24 '77 C.477 B.S. L.398 J.D. 876 Occidental Dr. (Pat.)
Lytle, Patricia M. ........................................ '46 '81 L.1137 J.D. 269 W. Bonita Ave.
MacBride, Thomas H. ............................................................ '44 '74 2349 Tulsa
Maddux, John C., (CV) '46 '79
C.1097 B.S. L.1137 J.D. 212 Yale Ave. (©Rancho Cucamonga)
**Mahoney, Paul M.**, (AV) ............... '42 '69 C.112 A.B. L.1068 J.D. [Jones,M.B.&S.]
*REPORTED CASES: Southwest Concrete Products v. Gosh Construction Corp., 51 Cal.3d 701 (1990); American International Group, Inc. v. Superior Court, 234 Cal.App.3d 749 (1991); Horeczko v. State Board of Registration, 232 Cal.App.3d 1352 (1991); Sutake v. Orange County Federal Credit Union, 186 Cal.App.3d 140 (1986); Deckert v. County of Riverdale, 115 Cal.App.3d 85 (1981).
*PRACTICE AREAS: Civil Litigation; Personal Injury Law; Government Contract Construction Litigation; Bad Faith Law; Medical Malpractice.
Matsumura, Michele M. ...................... '68 '93 C.464 B.S. L.112 J.D. 341 W. First St.

**McCarthy, John C., (AV) '23 '53 C.800 B.S. L.1068 J.D. ⓑⓥ**
**401 Harvard Avenue, 91711**
**Telephone: 909-621-4984 Telecopier: 909-621-5757**
**(Also Member, Morrisons, McCarthy & Moore, in Whitefish, Montana).**
**Practice limited to Punitive Damage, Labor, Employment law including Wrongful Discharge, Discrimination, Insurance and Commercial Bad Faith Cases (Plaintiff Only).**
***See Professional Biographies, CLAREMONT, CALIFORNIA***

McGowan, Phillip ................................................. '48 '76 602 Silverdale Dr.‡
**McMenomy, Shawn E.** ........... '59 '90 C.1097 B.S. L.329 J.D. [Ⓐ Dryden,M.S.K.&W.]
*PRACTICE AREAS: Products Liability; Premises Liability; Construction Defect; General Negligence.
Moore, Darrell E. .................. '33 '63 C.940 B.A. L.426 LL.B. 250 W. 1st St., #200‡
Morrisons, McCarthy & Moore, (AV) .................. 401 Harvard Avenue (©Whitefish, Mt.)

**Muckle, Melanie Julian '59 '87 C.813 B.A. L.477 J.D.**
**146 West Butler Court, 91711**
**Telephone: 909-625-8432 Fax: 909-625-2771**
**Environmental Law, Litigation.**
***See Professional Biographies, CLAREMONT, CALIFORNIA***

**Nichols Stead Boileau & Kostoff, A Professional Corporation, (AV)**
**Foothill Independent Bank Building, Second Floor, 223 West Foothill Boulevard, 91711**
**Telephone: 909-398-7000 Fax: 909-398-1000**
**Charles R. Stead (1901-1968); Donald P. Nichols (1901-1978); E. Burdette Boileau (Retired); James R. Kostoff; Donald E. Bollinger; Michael D. Smith; M. Daniel Saylor; Forrest F. Wolfe.**
**General Civil and Trial Practice, State and Federal Courts. Business, Corporation, Tax Exempt Organizations, Insurance, Estate Planning, Probate, Taxation and Real Property Law.**

Novell, Raymond A., (BV) ................. '42 '75 C.1097 B.S. L.809 J.D. 250 W. 1st St.
O'Brien, Mike F. .................. '60 '89 C.120 B.A./B.S. L.398 J.D. 121 N. Harvard Ave.
Odgers, Stephen L. ........................................ '44 '69 C&L.602 B.B.A., J.D. [S.L.Odgers]
Odgers, Stephen L., P.C. ..................................................................... 414 Yale Ave.
Ousley, Bernard V., (AV) ...........'32 '62 C.910 B.S. L.1049 J.D. 140 W. Foothill Blvd.
Peacock, Anthony A. '59 '89 C.02 B.A. L.029 LL.B.
(adm. in ON; not adm. in CA) 1121 Cambridge Ave.
**Penfil, Joan** ..................................'38 '85 C.477 B.A. L.1137 J.D. [Ⓐ Buxbaum&C.]©
*PRACTICE AREAS: Family Law.
Pollard, Christine L. ........................'53 '84 C.668 B.A. L.426 J.D. 675 Foothill Blvd.
Price, Robert B. ..............................'55 '82 C&L.1137 B.S.L., J.D. 1664 N. Shaw Pl.
Reed, Thomas L. ................................................ '49 '85 L.209 J.D. 415 W. Foothill
Richardson, Mary F. .................................. '46 '84 C.999 L.1137 J.D. 201 W. 4th St.
Ross, Mariellen ............'52 '80 C.1109 B.A. L.398 J.D. 223 W. Foothill Blvd., 2nd Fl.
**Ruggero, Rebecca G.** ..................'64 '93 C.352 B.A. L.398 J.D. [Ⓐ Shernoff,B.&D.]
*PRACTICE AREAS: Insurance Bad Faith.
**Saylor, M. Daniel** .............................'54 '80 C.1109 B.A. L.398 J.D. [Nichols S.B.&K.]
*PRACTICE AREAS: Trust and Probate Administration; Estate Planning; Conservatorships.
Schall, Debora ................................ '56 '82 C.174 B.A. L.398 J.D. 269 W. Bonita Ave.
Seapy, Marjorie A. ..................'43 '89 C.684 B.A. L.398 J.D. 226 W. Foothill Blvd.
Shaw, Theresa C., (BV) .............'42 '76 C.1077 B.A. L.1148 J.D. 140 W. Foothill Blvd.
**Shernoff, William M., (P.C.)**, (AV) '37 '62
C.472 B.B.A. L.966 J.D. [Shernoff,B.&D.] (©Palm Desert)
*PRACTICE AREAS: Insurance Bad Faith.

**Shernoff, Bidart & Darras, (AV)**
**A Partnership including Professional Corporations**
**600 South Indian Hill Boulevard, 91711-5498©**
**Telephone: 909-621-4935 Fax: 909-625-6915**
**Members of Firm: William M. Shernoff (P.C.); Michael J. Bidart (P.C.); Frank N. Darras. Associates: Sharon J. Arkin; Theresa J. Barta; Timothy P. Dillon; Ricardo Echeverria; Rebecca G. Ruggero; Evangeline L. Fisher; Mark E. Benson.**

(This Listing Continued)

**Shernoff, Bidart & Darras (Continued)**
**Practice Limited to Plaintiff's Insurance Bad Faith, Automobile Insurance, Fire Insurance, Commercial Liability Insurance, Homeowners Insurance, Accident and Health Insurance, Catastrophic Personal Injury, Wrongful Death, Wrongful Termination, Lender's Liability and Consumer Law Litigation.**
**Laguna Beach, California Office: 130 Cleo Street. Phone: 714-494-6714. Fax: 714-497-0825.**
**Palm Desert, California Office: 73-111 El Paseo, Suite 208. Telephone: 619-568-9944.**
***See Professional Biographies, CLAREMONT, CALIFORNIA***

Simonson, Karen J., (AV) ................. '54 '79 C.681 A.B. L.569 J.D. [Taylor,S.&W.]
**Smith, Michael D.**, (AV) ............ '44 '72 C.1075 B.S. L.1065 J.D. [Nichols S.B.&K.]
*PRACTICE AREAS: Litigation; Estate Planning; Business; Real Estate; Employment Law.
**Soll, Richard A.** ........................... '49 '75 C.112 A.B. L.1068 J.D. [Jones,M.B.&S.]
*PRACTICE AREAS: Civil Litigation; Construction Law; Corporate Law; Real Estate Litigation; Appellate Practice.
**Stack, A. Kerry** .................'56 '87 C.112 B.A. L.1137 J.D. [Ⓐ Dryden,M.S.K.&W.]
*PRACTICE AREAS: Products Liability; Premises Liability; Tort Litigation; Construction Defect; Negligence.
Stafford, Robert A., (AV) ................. '18 '42 C.312 B.A. L.976 LL.B. [Stafford&B.]
Stafford & Baldonado, (AV) ........................................................... 414 Yale Ave.
Stoneman, James P., II ............. '52 '80 C.1109 B.A. L.398 J.D. 100 W. Foothill Blvd.
**Tanenbaum, Carol B.**, (AV) ............... '35 '76 C.103 B.A. L.930 J.D. [Allard,S.&O.]
*PRACTICE AREAS: Civil Litigation; Municipal Law; Probate Law.
Taylor, James D. '47 '74 C.276 B.S.B.A. L.912 J.D.
(adm. in MI; not adm. in CA) Claremont McKenna College‡
Taylor, Marshall W., (AV) .......................'44 '75 C&L.309 B.A., J.D. [Taylor,S.&W.]
Taylor, Simonson & Winter, (AV) ........................................ 144 N. Indian Hill Blvd.
Teran, Carlos M. .................................................. '15 '49 C&L.800 J.D. Ret. Supr. Ct. J
Trozpek, Robin Weeks, (CV) ................ '49 '84 C.773 B.A. L.1068 J.D. 237 W. Fourth St.
Tuckerman, Richard J., (BV) ... '31 '62 C.569 B.S. L.1065 LL.B. 395 S. Indian Hill Blvd.

**Tulac, John W., (AV) '52 '77 C.1075 B.S. L.426 J.D. ⓑⓥ**
**401 Harvard Avenue, 91711**
**Telephone: 909-445-1100 Fax: 909-445-1104**
**Email: jwtulac@ix.netcom.com**
**International Business Law, International Trade Law, General Business and Corporate Law, Foreign Investment in the United States, International Arbitration, Mediation and Litigation, Business Litigation. Professional Mediator and Arbitrator.**
**Reference: Marine National Bank, Irvine.**
***See Professional Biographies, CLAREMONT, CALIFORNIA***

Tully, Marian Haycock ........................... '52 '81 L.1049 J.D. 600 S. Indian Hill Blvd.
Valvo, Victoria M. .................................. '55 '85 L.1137 J.D. 600 S. Indian Hill Dr.

**Vera, Ronald T. '46 '74 C.475 B.S. L.1068 J.D.**
**Foothill Independent Bank Building, 223 West Foothill Boulevard, 2nd Floor, 91711**
**Telephone: 909-624-2941 Fax: 909-398-1000**
***PRACTICE AREAS: Municipal Law; Education Law; Environmental Law; Litigation.**
**General Civil Trial Practice in all State and Federal Courts. Public Agency, Education, Environmental Law and Municipal Law.**
***See Professional Biographies, CLAREMONT, CALIFORNIA***

Vesey, Thomas A. ................................... '34 '76 C.608 L.1127 J.D. 250 W. 1st St.
Wafel, Ira M. ......................................... '58 '85 C.112 B.A. L.208 J.D. 4052 Garey Ave.
**Wait, Thomas B.** .......................'50 '78 C.207 B.A. L.767 J.D. [Dryden,M.S.K.&W.]
*PRACTICE AREAS: Products Liability; Construction Defect; Negligence; Professional Liability; Bad Faith.
**Walker, Keith S.**, (AV) .................. '52 '76 C.1109 B.A. L.1065 J.D. [Allard,S.&O.]
*PRACTICE AREAS: Estate Planning Law; Probate Law; Trusts Law.
Wells, Bernardine C. ............................................ '26 '79 L.1127 J.D. 2945 Rockmont Ave.‡
**Wilkinson, Conrad M.** .......................'37 '76 C.112 B.S. L.1221 J.D. [Wilkinson&W.]
**Wilkinson, Patricia Jo**, (AV) ............ '40 '74 C.112 A.B. L.426 J.D. [Wilkinson&W.]

**Wilkinson & Wilkinson, (AV)**
**341 West First Street, 91711**
**Telephone: 909-482-1555 Fax: 909-482-1557**
**Patricia Jo Wilkinson (Certified Specialist, Estate Planning, Trust and Probate Law, The State Bar of California Board of Legal Specialization); Conrad M. Wilkinson.**
**Estate Planning, Trusts, Probate and Elder Care Law.**
***See Professional Biographies, CLAREMONT, CALIFORNIA***

Winter, Marc J., (AV) .......................... '53 '78 C.413 B.A. L.950 J.D. [Taylor,S.&W.]
**Wolfe, Forrest F.** ..............................'59 '86 C.112 B.A. L.1065 J.D. [Nichols S.B.&K.]
*PRACTICE AREAS: Taxation Law; Estate Planning Law; Trust and Probate Administration Law; Corporate Law; Tax Exempt Organization Law.
**Wunderlin, Gary C.**, (BV) .................. '47 '76 C.932 A.B. L.838 J.D. [Allard,S.&O.]
*PRACTICE AREAS: Civil Litigation; Family Law.
**Yamashiro, Betty O.** ....................... '— '85 C.312 B.Ed. L.1137 J.D. [Buxbaum&C.]©
*PRACTICE AREAS: Banking; Bankruptcy; Creditors Rights; Civil Litigation.
**Zetterberg, Charles L.**, (AV) ......... '43 '71 C.918 B.A. L.178 LL.B. [Buxbaum&C.]©
*PRACTICE AREAS: Civil Litigation; Insurance; Real Estate; Business.
**Zetterberg, Stephen I.**, (AV) ........... '16 '42 C.668 A.B. L.976 LL.B. [Zetterberg&K.]
*PRACTICE AREAS: Trusts; Wills; Estate Planning; Civil Litigation.

**Zetterberg & King, (AV)**
**319 Harvard Avenue, 91711©**
**Telephone: 909-621-2971 Fax: 909-625-5781**
**Stephen I. Zetterberg; Alice M. King (Quincy, California Office).**
**General Civil and Trial Practice in all State and Federal Courts. Wills, Probate, Trusts and Estate Planning Law, Civil Litigation.**
**Quincy, California Office: P.O. Box 3926. Telephone: 916-283-0325. Fax: 916-283-5205.**
***See Professional Biographies, CLAREMONT, CALIFORNIA***

## CLAYTON, 7,317, *Contra Costa Co.*

Calrow, Paul E. '22 '51 C.494 B.S. L.273 LL.B.
(adm. in DC; not adm. in CA) 211 Round House Pl.‡
Chilson, Christopher A. ............... '45 '92 C.1060 B.S. L.284 J.D. Two El Molino Dr.
Cunan, Richard C. ................................ '35 '73 C.112 B.A. L.284 J.D. 620 Julpun Loop
Haydon, Keith L., Jr. ......................................... '47 '75 C.1109 L.1137 J.D. 1542 Ohara Ct.
Strader, G. A. ............................ '19 '46 C.112 A.B. L.1066 J.D. 1809 Yolanda Cir.‡
Wilson, Harry K. '27 '53 C.112 A.B. L.309 LL.B.
(adm. in MA; not adm. in CA) 5116 Keller Ridge Dr.‡

## CLEARLAKE, 11,804, *Lake Co.*

Freeborn, Richard L., (BV) ................................'38 '65 C.112 B.S. L.1065 J.D. Mun. Ct. J.
Stockum, Francis C. ................................ '26 '66 C.1197 B.B.A. L.767 LL.B. P.O. Box 4867

## CLOVERDALE, 4,924, *Sonoma Co.*

Campbell, Anderson, Casey, Sink & Johnson, A Prof. Corp., The Law Offices of, (AV)
112 W. First St.
DeMartini, James F., (CV) .................. '49 '77 C.112 B.A. L.809 J.D. 115 W. 1st St.
Sink, Thomas Reed ............... '59 '84 C.813 A.B. L.767 J.D. [Campbell,A.C.S.&J.]©
Ward, Timothy J., (BV) ........................ '47 '72 C.112 B.A. L.1065 J.D. 108 Roan Ct.

## CLOVIS, 50,323, *Fresno Co.*

Bergstrom, Robert Q. ................... '42 '66 C&L.972 B.A., J.D. 180 W. Bullard Ave.

CALIFORNIA—CLOVIS MARTINDALE-HUBBELL LAW DIRECTORY 1997

**Bolen, Fransen & Boostrom LLP, (AV)**
**414 Pollasky Avenue, 93612⊙**
**Telephone: 209-226-8177 Fax: 209-322-6778**
**Kenneth J. Fransen.**
**General Business, Banking, Creditor's Rights, Corporate, Real Estate and Taxation Law, Agricultural and Water Rights Law, Estate Planning and Probate Law.**
**Fresno, California Office: Suite 430, East Tower, Guarantee Financial Center, 1322 East Shaw Avenue. Telephone: 209-266-8177. Fax: 209-227-4971.**
***See Professional Biographies, CLOVIS, CALIFORNIA***

Born, Timothy, (BV) ....................'46 '73 C.602 B.B.A. L.1068 J.D. 657 Scott Ave.
Courtney, Ralston L., (CV) ............'31 '61 C.169 A.B. L.770 LL.B. 1500 Villa, #109
Cribbs, Robert O. .............................'40 '74 C.651 B.S. L.1137 J.D. [Ninnis&C.]
Dornay, Val J. ..........................'42 '73 C.1075 B.S. L.1137 J.D. 200 W. Bullard
**Fransen, Kenneth J.**, (AV) .............'52 '77 C.267 B.A. L.1068 J.D. [Bolen,F.&B.]⊙
*PRACTICE AREAS: Agricultural and Water Law; Business Law; Real Estate; Trusts and Estates.
Hubbell, Marlene A. .............'65 '92 C.267 B.S. L.1189 J.D. 456 Clovis Ave., Suite 4
James, Paul S. .................'44 '74 C.1085 B.S. L.1189 J.D. 964 Pollasky Ave.,
Jeknavorian, Garbis C. ............................'28 '55 L.966 LL.B. 9584 E. Mesa Ave.
Kern, Karen L. ..........................'53 '80 C.267 B.A. L.1189 J.D. 2099 Vartikian‡
Ninnis, William R., (BV) .........................'32 '63 C.766 A.B. L.1065 J.D. [Ninnis&C.]
Ninnis & Cribbs, (BV) ............................................. 3120 Willow Ave.
Pape, Jeffrey B., (BV) ......................'57 '82 C.513 B.S. L.352 J.D. 657 Scott Ave.
Quatraro, Mio D. ...........................'— '74 C.169 B.A. L.1189 J.D. 455A Pollasky
Routhier, Denise A. .....................'53 '77 C.768 A.B. L.1065 J.D. 5514 N. Amber‡
Ruth-Heffelbower, Duane F. ......'49 '74 C.375 B.A. L.284 J.D. 1450 Tollhouse Rd., #105
Schmidt, Sarah A., (BV) ..................'63 '88 C.1074 B.S. L.1189 J.D. 456 Clovis Ave.
Siggers, E. Gregory ...................'44 '72 C.604 B.A. L.537 J.D. 11413 E. Shaw Ave.
Simmons, Robert J. ...............................'47 '87 L.1189 J.D. 190 W. Menlo Ave.
Spjute, Kent R. ..................'54 '88 C.878 B.S. L.1226 J.D. 206 W. El Paso Ave.
Tatro, Todd R. ..........................'58 '86 C.267 B.S. L.464 J.D. 3120 Willow Ave.
Williams, Patricia L. ......................'50 '93 C.267 B.A. L.1189 J.D. 456 Clovis Ave.
Woodruff, A. C. '34 '69 C.197 B.A. L.945 J.D.
(adm. in VA; not adm. in CA) P.O. Box 159‡

## COACHELLA, 16,896, *Riverside Co.*

Caronna, Anthony C, (BV) ..............'60 '88 C.800 B.S. L.1148 J.D. [A.C.Caronna]⊙
Caronna, Anthony C., P.C., (BV) ............................. 1623 6th Street (⊙Rancho Mirage)
Manning, Guy, (BV) .......'60 '88 C.549 B.S. L.398 J.D. 1623 6th St. (⊙Rancho Mirage)

## COALINGA, 8,212, *Fresno Co.*

Frame, Ted R., (P.C.), (BV) ...................'29 '53 C&L.813 A.B., LL.B. [Frame&M.]
Frame & Matsumoto, A Prtnrshp. incl. A Prof. Corp., (BV) ........... 201 Washington St.
Leckman, Henry T., (BV) ......................'24 '50 C.813 B.A. L.1065 J.D. City Atty.
Matsumoto, Russell ..........................'54 '78 C.112 A.B. L.1065 J.D. [Frame&M.]

## COARSEGOLD, —, *Madera Co.*

Emerick, William F. ....... '26 '54 C.112 B.S. L.426 LL.B. 28791 Long Hollow Court So.

## COBB, 1,477, *Lake Co.*

**Katzoff & Riggs, (AV)**
**Meadow Springs Shopping Center, P.O. Box 1250, 95426⊙**
**Telephone: 707-928-4600 Fax: 707-928-5075**
**Robert R. Riggs.**
**Civil and Criminal Trial Practice, Juvenile Dependency and Appeals. Real Estate and Real Estate Transactions, Construction, Insurance Defense and Insurance Coverage Law, Computer Software Licensing Law.**
**Berkeley California Office: 3088 Claremont Avenue. Telephone: 510-597-1990. Fax: 510-597-0295.**
***See Professional Biographies, COBB, CALIFORNIA***

**Riggs, Robert R.**, (AV) ....................'58 '83 C.367 B.A. L.813 J.D. [Katzoff&R.]⊙
*LANGUAGES: French and Italian.
*PRACTICE AREAS: Civil Litigation; Construction Law; Computer Software Licensing Law; Real Estate Law; Criminal Law.

## COLEVILLE, —, *Mono Co.*

Blizzard, Athena Pappas '61 '90 C.362 B.A. L.904 J.D.
(adm. in FL; not adm. in CA) 208B Vittori Ct.‡

## COLFAX, 1,306, *Placer Co.*

Bardellini, Perry E. ................ '20 '47 C.112 A.B. L.1065 J.D. 18649 Sky Blue Ct.‡
Dunipace, Thomas M. ...................................... '49 '81 C.631 B.A. L.464 J.D. City Atty.
Hinshaw, Charlene M. ...........................'53 '88 C.1109 B.A. L.800 J.D. P.O. Box 779
Holmes, Peter R., (AV) .............................'23 '53 C.147 L.1065 J.D. P.O. Box 1251‡
Smith, Charles T. ........................'10 '35 C.113 A.B. L.800 LL.B. P.O. Box 961‡
Welch, Kenneth T., (BV) ..........................'33 '74 L.1001 J.D. 9 South Main St.

## COLMA, 1,103, *San Mateo Co.*

Hunt, Daniel G. ....................'48 '74 C.112 B.A. L.1067 J.D. Serramonte Ford, Inc.

## COLOMA, —, *El Dorado Co.*

Murphy, Thomas J. ........................ '19 '49 C.174 B.S. L.878 J.D. 7200 Amoloc Lane‡

## COLTON, 40,213, *San Bernardino Co.*

Andrews, Harry G. ..........................................'29 '55 C.112 L.1065 LL.B. P.O. Box 494
Biggs, Julie Hayward ....................'46 '78 C&L.800 A.B., J.D. 650 N. LaCadera Dr.
Herbert, Frances G. ..................'60 '85 C.112 B.A. L.464 J.D. Inland Cos. Reg. Ctr.
Hutton, Lawrence A., (AV) ..................'13 '38 C&L.37 B.A., J.D. 655 N.La Cadena Dr.
Matheson, Ronald G. ........................'51 '77 C.147 B.A. L.1137 J.D. P.O. Box 828
Mitchell, William G., (CV) ...................'46 '75 C.999 L.1137 LL.B. P.O. Box 1341
Von Pahlen-Federoff, Gerold ....................................'44 '71 1515 Mohave Dr.
Williams, William R. ...........'14 '42 C.112 A.B. L.426 LL.B. 23028 Grand Terrace Rd.

## COLUSA, * 4,934, *Colusa Co.*

Abel, S. William ..............................'44 '73 C.1074 B.S. L.426 J.D. Supr. Ct. J.
Ash, Carol Kinder .........................'55 '82 C.1163 B.A. L.950 J.D. Dep. Dist. Atty.
Bates, David L. ..........................'46 '82 C.1078 B.A. L.1227 J.D. Dep. Dist. Atty.
Clark, Robert D., (BV) ........................'35 '66 C.112 B.S. L.767 LL.B. [Clark&N.]
Clark & Nelson, (BV) ....................................................521 Market Street
Fisher, Wm. L., (BV) .....................'19 '51 C.025 B.A. L.767 LL.B. 547 Market St.
Hubbard, Ernest T., Sr., (AV) ...............'24 '54 C.674 A.B. L.1065 J.D. 101 Third St.
Lindquist, Peter N. ........................'57 '90 C.1085 B.S. L.878 J.D. 101 3rd St.
**Littlejohn, Donald W. (Bill)**, (AV) ................'21 '49 C&L.767 J.D. [Littlejohn&W.]
**Littlejohn, Florence Westfall**, (BV) ................'— '56 L.464 J.D. [Littlejohn&W.]

**Littlejohn & Westfall, (AV)**
**519 Jay Street, P.O. Box 927, 95932**
**Telephone: 916-458-4944 Fax: 916-458-5805**
**Members of Firm: Donald W. (Bill) Littlejohn; Florence Westfall Littlejohn.**

(This Listing Continued)



**Littlejohn & Westfall (Continued)**
**General Civil and Criminal Trial Practice, Probate, Real Estate, Corporation, Estate Planning, Tax, Environmental, Agri-Business, Oil and Gas Leases and Entertainment Law.**
**Reference: Feather River State Bank, Wells Fargo.**

**Mehr, Tedd A. '60 '88 C.147 B.A. L.1137 J.D.**
**249 5th Street, P.O. Box 1286, 95932**
**Telephone: 916-458-5481 Fax: 916-458-5482**
***PRACTICE AREAS: General Civil and Criminal Litigation; Business; Real Property; Governmental Law; Family Law.**
**General Civil and Trial Practice in all Courts. Business, Real Property, Governmental Law, Criminal Law and Family Law.**
***See Professional Biographies, COLUSA, CALIFORNIA***

Nelson, David R. ...............................'51 '76 C.112 B.A. L.770 J.D. [Clark&N.]
Patton, Richard E. .................................'20 '48 C.113 L.1065 J.D. Ret. Supr. Ct. J.
Poyner, John R., (CV) ..........................'50 '79 C.766 L.1026 LL.B. Dist. Atty. Off.

**Rich, Fuidge, Morris & Iverson, Inc.**
**(See Marysville)**

Ruminson, Lorie Ann ........................................................ '58 '87 651 Market St.
Steele, Charles F. '10 '34 C.951 A.B. L.309 LL.B.
(adm. in NY; not adm. in CA) 1845 Wilson Ave.‡
Steidlmayer, Leo, (BV) .........................'46 '72 C.770 B.S. L.1067 J.D. 659 Jay St.
Tiernan, John H. ......................................'43 '81 C.147 B.A. L.464 J.D. Mun. J.
Wilsey, Harold R., Jr., (BV) ......................'25 '52 C.999 L.767 LL.B. 200 6th St.
Yerxa, Charles T., Jr. ..........................'57 '87 C.813 B.A. L.770 J.D. 521 Market St.

## COMMERCE, 12,135, *Los Angeles Co.*

Beck, Dennis S. ........................'48 '74 C.813 A.B. L.1068 J.D. Pres., Flavurence Corp.
Brennan, David F. ...............................'51 '79 C.1077 B.A. L.809 J.D. 500 Citadel Dr.
Farman, Richard D. ...............'35 '64 C&L.813 A.B., LL.B. 6055 E. Washington Blvd.
Gliaudys, George J., Jr. ....................'44 '69 C.800 B.A. L.426 J.D. Spec. Asst., Dist. Atty.
Regan, Christopher P. ........................'58 '83 C.112 B.A. L.426 J.D. 5701 Eastern Ave.
Rockett, Thomas E., III ...............'61 '86 C.763 B.S. L.1095 J.D. 5701 S. Eastern Ave.
Webster, H.M., III .............................'48 '76 C.112 B.A. L.809 J.D. Dep. Dist. Atty.
Wilson, Howard L. '23 '50 C&L.421 LL.B.
(adm. in KY; not adm. in CA) Treas., Kurtz, Richards, Wilson & Co., Inc.‡

## COMPTCHE, —, *Mendocino Co.*

Mackie, M. L. Harrison ......................'39 '79 C.112 B.A. L.767 J.D. P.O. Box 331

## COMPTON, 90,454, *Los Angeles Co.*

Alhadeff, Elliott E., (AV) ................'38 '66 C.112 B.S. L.1068 LL.B. Dep. Dist. Atty.
**Bell, Wayne S.** ...............'54 '80 C.112 B.A. L.426 J.D. Sr. Coun., Ralphs Grocery Co.
*RESPONSIBILITIES: General Business Law; Corporate Law.
Blair, Clarence E. ..................'29 '57 C.174 B.A. L.936 LL.B. 491 W. Compton Blvd.
Brown, Irma J. ...................................................'48 '75 C&L.426 B.A., J.D. Co. J.
Clark, William D. .............................'51 '88 C.1175 B.S. L.1148 J.D. Dep. Dist. Atty.
Demoff, Melvin L. ...................'49 '80 C.1042 B.S. L.1136 J.D. 1055 W. Victoria St.
Escalante, Mary Ann ..............................'61 '87 C.763 B.S. L.426 J.D. Dep. Dist. Atty.
Filer, Kelvin D. ..................'55 '80 C.1169 B.A. L.1066 J.D. 363 W. Compton Blvd.‡
Granville, Stanley B. ...................'53 '79 C.178 B.A. L.813 J.D. 213 S. Acacia Ave.
**Gray, Jan Charles** '47 '72 C.112 B.A. L.309 J.D.
Sr. V.P., Gen. Coun. & Secy., Ralphs Grocery Co.
*RESPONSIBILITIES: Corporate Law; Securities Law; General Business Law.
Hall, Henry J. ...........................................'51 '76 C.800 A.B. L.426 J.D. Dep. Pub. Def.
Hill, Hugo E. .............................................'25 '71 C.112 B.A. L.1148 J.D. Mun. Ct. J.
Hughes, Tommy L. .....................'49 '76 C.766 B.A. L.1065 J.D. 406 W. Tichenor St.
Johnson, Jerry E. ...................................................'42 '73 L.990 J.D. Mun. Ct. J.
Jones, Morris B. ...........................................'36 '81 C.1097 B.S. L.1136 J.D. Mun. J.
Joyce, Maureen C. .................'36 '75 C.350 B.A. L.999 J.D. 851 W. Compton Blvd.
Kimbell, Alphonso .........................'50 '76 C.1042 B.A. L.426 J.D. 2160 Lucien St.
Lamon, Dana, (Mr.) ........................'52 '78 C.976 B.A. L.800 J.D. 2015 E. 131st St.
Newman, Jane E. .........................................'62 '88 C&L.112 B.A., J.D. Dep. Pub. Def.
Nishinaka, Robert S. ........................'54 '79 C.813 A.B. L.800 J.D. Dep. Dist. Atty.
Ortega, John R. ..................'35 '70 C.763 A.B. L.1114 J.D. Southern Calif. Law Ctr.
Pellegrino, Dominick F. ...............'33 '67 C.112 A.B. L.800 J.D. 3039 E. Las Hermanas
Pryor, Roger J., (BV) .................'14 '41 C.813 A.B. L.477 J.D. 544 W. Rosecarns Ave.
Ramirez, Maria .......................................'65 '90 C&L.426 B.A., J.D. Dep. Dist. Atty.
Simpson, Thomas R. ...........................'42 '67 C.1042 A.B. L.1066 J.D. Superior Ct. J.
Sloan, Sharon Nader ..................'50 '74 C.475 B.A. L.213 J.D. Ralphs Grocery Co.
Southey, Byron M. '38 '79 C.1042 L.999 J.D.
(adm. in GA; not adm. in CA) 19009 Laurel Park‡
Suzukawa, Steven C. .....................'54 '79 C.112 B.A. L.1068 J.D. Dep. Dist. Atty.
**Travis, William H.** ............'48 '73 C&L.112 B.S., J.D. Sr. Coun., Ralphs Grocery Co.
*RESPONSIBILITIES: Real Estate Law.
Vannorsdall, Hope A. ........................'58 '87 C.112 B.A. L.990 J.D. Dep. Pub. Def.

## CONCORD, 111,348, *Contra Costa Co.*

Adams, Dale C., (BV) ..................'41 '70 C.112 B.A. L.1065 J.D. [Boatwright,A.&B.]
Allen, D. LaBruce ......................'63 '94 C.112 B.A. L.464 J.D. 1320 Willow Pass Rd.
**Andersen, Craig F.**, (BV) ....................'49 '74 C.911 B.A. L.464 J.D. [Andersen&B.]
*PRACTICE AREAS: Construction Law; Land Use.

**Andersen & Bonnifield, (BV)**
**1355 Willow Way, Suite 255, P.O. Box 5926, 94520**
**Telephone: 510-602-1400 Fax: 510-825-0143**
**Email: AandB@AandB.com**
**Members of Firm: Craig F. Andersen; Robert M. Bonnifield. Associates: Madeline L. Buty; Sean A. Cottle; J. Keiko Kobayashi; Kenneth H. Lee.**
**General Civil and Trial Practice in State and Federal Courts. Construction, Financial Institutions, Commercial, Negligence, Real Estate, Corporation, Toxic Torts and Insurance Defense.**
**Reference: Concord Commercial Bank, Concord.**
***See Professional Biographies, CONCORD, CALIFORNIA***

Anderson, Bryce C., (AV) ..............'45 '71 C.112 B.A. L.1065 J.D. 1985 Bonifacio St.
Badal, Charles E. ......................'33 '72 C.477 B.A. L.1153 J.D. 1200 Concord Ave.
Bechelli, F. Joseph, Jr., (BV) ...........'42 '75 C.871 B.S. L.284 J.D. [Boatwright,A.&B.]
Beckner, Rita A. ................'55 '83 C.112 A.B. L.284 J.D. Sr. Consultant, The Wyatt Co.
Berkowitz, Patricia ..........................'45 '77 C.1075 B.S. L.1153 J.D. [Child S.C.]
Betts, William J., (BV) .................'19 '50 C.494 B.A. L.1065 J.D. 1665 Galindo St.‡
Bird, Clyde D., Jr. .................'24 '47 C.112 A.B. L.1066 LL.B. 5291 Concord Blvd.
Blumstein, Stuart I. ...................'52 '85 C.766 B.A. L.464 J.D. Dep. Pub. Def.
Boatwright, Daniel E., (BV) ..........................'30 '60 C.112 A.B. L.1066 J.D. Sen.
Boatwright, Adams & Bechelli, (BV) ............................................1738 Grant St.

**Bobetsky, William B., (BV) '52 '78 C.1044 B.S. L.1137 J.D.**
**2204 Concord Boulevard, 94520**
**Telephone: 510-685-2440**
***PRACTICE AREAS: Family Law; Personal Injury Law; Probate Law; Wills.**

(This Listing Continued)

**Bobetsky, William B. (Continued)**
**Family Law.**
***See Professional Biographies, CONCORD, CALIFORNIA***

Boehme, Mark Thomas ..................'55 '86 C.1056 B.S. L.464 J.D. Asst. City Atty.
**Bonnifield, Robert M.**, (BV) ..................'47 '74 C.768 B.S. L.464 J.D. [Andersen&B.]
*PRACTICE AREAS: Toxic Tort; Construction Defense.
**Bovée, Scott A.** ..................'55 '86 C.112 A.B. L.950 J.D. [Caudle,W.P.&B.]
*PRACTICE AREAS: Insurance Defense; Defense Litigation; Environmental Law; Hazardous Waste; Toxic Substances.
Bows, Harry I. ..................'21 '48 C.999 L.426 LL.B. 3465 Zion Place‡
Brand, Jonathan M. ..................'55 '86 C.1078 B.A. L.1153 J.D. 1800 Sutter St.
Bryant, H. Paul ..................'61 '86 C.112 B.A. L.426 J.D. 2151 Salvio St.
Buchanan, Candace L., (BV) ..................'48 '79 C.112 A.B. L.1065 J.D. 1985 Bonifacio St.
Burak, Blackie, (BV) ..................'43 '72 C.397 B.A. L.767 J.D. [Burak&B.]
Burak & Berg, (BV) ..................1320 Willow Pass Rd (©San Francisco)
Burke, Robert ..................'44 '75 C.304 B.A. L.284 J.D. Dep. Dist. Atty.
**Buty, Madeline L.** ..................'67 '91 C.112 B.A. L.770 J.D. [Ⓐ Andersen&B.]
*PRACTICE AREAS: Toxic Tort Litigation; Products Liability Defense; Construction Litigation Defense.
Callahan, Christine D. ..................'51 '77 C.147 B.A. L.1137 J.D. 2204 Concord Blvd.
Cantwell, Lawrence W. ..................'52 '83 C.112 B.A. L.284 J.D. 3231 Mount Court
**Caudle, John P.**, (AV) ..................'43 '69 C.112 A.B. L.1066 J.D. [Caudle,W.P.&B.]
*PRACTICE AREAS: Insurance Defense; Defense Litigation; Medical Malpractice Defense; Products Liability; Insurance Bad Faith.

**Caudle, Welch, Politeo & Bovée, LLP, (AV)**
**1390 Willow Pass Road, Suite 200, 94520©**
**Telephone: 510-688-8800 Fax: 510-688-8801**
**Email: CWPB@aol.comm**
**John P. Caudle; Michael R. Welch; Deanne B. Politeo; Scott A. Bovée.**
**Automobile/Bodily Injury, Construction Defect Litigation, Discrimination Defense, General Business Litigation, Governmental Entity Defense, Insurance Bad Faith Defense, Appellate Work, Mediations, Arbitrations, Homeowners Liability, Landlord/Tenant, Insurance Coverage, Premises Liability, Products Liability, Professional Malpractice Defense, Toxic Substances Litigation, Wrongful Termination and Legal Opinions.**
**Oakland, California Office: 383 Fourth Street, Suite 201. Telephone: 510-433-9300. Fax: 510-433-9301.**
***See Professional Biographies, CONCORD, CALIFORNIA***

Child Support Collections Legal Center, Inc. .................. Suite 460, 2401 Stanwell Drive
Chisholm, Jack F. ..................'38 '71 C.838 B.S. L.213 J.D. 1430 Willow Pass Rd.
**Coke, Laurel D.** ..................'39 '76 C.945 B.A. L.284 J.D. [Coke&C.]
*PRACTICE AREAS: Personal Injury.
**Coke, Michael E.**, (BV) ..................'38 '69 C.025 B.A. L.284 J.D. [Coke&C.]
*PRACTICE AREAS: Personal Injury.

**Coke & Coke, (BV)**
**1485 Enea Court, Suite G-1450, 94520**
**Telephone: 510-825-4600 Fax: 510-688-0325**
**Michael E. Coke; Laurel D. Coke.**
**Personal Injury.**
***See Professional Biographies, CONCORD, CALIFORNIA***

**Cottle, Sean A.** ..................'64 '90 C.385 B.A. L.861 J.D. [Ⓐ Andersen&B.]
*PRACTICE AREAS: Construction Law; Tort Litigation Defense.
Couick, Shirley B. ..................'33 '92 C.1073 B.A. L.1153 J.D. 2045 Mt. Diablo St.
DeMarco, Peri ..................'60 '89 L.1153 J.D. 1800 Sutter St.
DeMaria, Anthony J., (AV) ..................'44 '70 C.112 A.B. L.1067 J.D. [Filice&D.]
Diaz, Gloria S. ..................'66 '91 C.774 B.A. L.464 J.D. 2300 Clayton Rd.
Disney, James H. ..................'30 '64 C&L.767 B.S., LL.B. 3325 Clayton Rd.‡
Donohue, Brian C. ..................'47 '78 C.262 B.A. L.1179 J.D. 2151 Salvio St.
Donovan, Stephen H. ..................'49 '84 C.285 B.A. L.1153 J.D. [McCray,R.&D.]©
Edmunds, Louis L., Jr. ..................'19 '53 C.112 A.B. L.1065 J.D. Ret. Mun. J.
Ehrich, Lynda Kay ..................'53 '89 C.494 B.S. L.300 J.D. 1850 Gateway Blvd.
Elder, Richard E., Jr. ..................'43 '70 C.766 A.B. L.1067 J.D. 3107 Clayton Rd.
Evans, Janet L., (AV) ..................'50 '75 C.112 A.B. L.1065 J.D. 4415 Cowell Rd.
Ferns, Barry W., (AV) ..................'51 '77 C.1077 B.A. L.1095 J.D. [Ferns&F.]©
Ferns, Laurel A., (BV) ..................'51 '80 C.1077 B.A. L.398 J.D. [Ferns&F.]
Ferns & Ferns, (AV) ..................2300 Clayton Rd. (©Passadena)
Fetto, John A. ..................'52 '87 C.112 B.A. L.1065 J.D. 1200 Concord Ave.
Figur, Lawrence J. '44 '69 C&L.472 B.B.A., J.D.
(adm. in FL; not adm. in CA) 1440 Whitman Rd.‡
Filice & DeMaria, (AV) .................. 1130 Burnett Ave.
Finch, Judith A. ..................'36 '84 C.4366 B.S. L.1153 J.D. 3325 Clayton Rd.
Fishbach, Kenneth J. ..................'45 '73 C.103 B.A. L.1066 J.D. PPH Homequity
Frisch, Frank R. ..................'42 '67 C.112 B.A. L.1065 J.D. 2150 East St.
Gaeta, Joseph D. ..................'22 '55 C&L.1026 LL.B. 1410 Monument Blvd.
Garaventa, John J., (BV) ..................'51 '78 C.766 B.A. L.1153 J.D. P.O. Box 965
Gardner, Douglas Lee ..................'53 '85 C.147 B.S. L.1153 J.D. 1738 Grant St.
Garrison, Julie Ann ....'60 '85 C.112 A.B. L.1066 J.D. Gen. Coun., Concord General Inc.
**Gayda, Michael D.** ..................'54 '79 C.659 B.S. L.94 J.D. Asst. Gen. Coun., Tosco Co.
Germain, Keith V. ..................'50 '77 C.112 B.A. L.273 J.D. V.P., Bk. of America
Glen, Bennett R. ..................'58 '87 C.112 B.A. L.464 J.D. 1200 Concord Ave.
Goforth, Michael D., (BV) ..................'51 '79 C.112 B.A. L.1137 J.D. [Goforth&L.]
Goforth and Lucas, (BV) ..................2300 Clayton Rd.
Gonsalves, Martin T., (CV) ..................'58 '83 C.1060 B.A. L.1065 J.D. 1738 Grant St.
Grant, Irven L., Jr. ..................'43 '76 C.740 B.A. L.765 J.D. 1738 Grant St.
Henry, Kathleen Marie ..................'49 '75 C.112 B.A. L.284 J.D. 2280 Diamond Blvd.
Hodge, James B. ..................'52 '78 C.976 B.A. L.893 J.D. Mid Bay Pacific Cos. Ltd.
**Hooy, Robert J.**, (BV) ..................'58 '85 C.112 B.A. L.767 J.D. [Hooy&H.]
**Hooy, William J.**, (BV) ..................'31 '57 C.112 B.A. L.1066 LL.B. [Hooy&H.]

**Hooy & Hooy, A Professional Law Corporation, (BV)**
**3125 Clayton Road, Second Floor, 94519**
**Telephone: 510-798-0426 Fax: 510-798-0458**
**William J. Hooy; Robert J. Hooy.**
**General Civil and Trial Practice in all State and Federal Courts. Corporate, Real Estate, Computer, Intellectual Property, Environmental, Construction, Business, Employment Discrimination and Wrongful Termination, Personal Injury, Workers Compensation, Estate Planning and Probate.**

Huddleston, John P. ..................'25 '72 L.1153 LL.B. 3325 Clayton Rd.‡
Ingram, Barbara L. ..................'50 '92 C.1073 B.S. L.284 J.D. [Ⓐ McCray,R.&D.]
Jewett, Harold W., III ..................'56 '82 C.112 B.A. L.770 J.D. Dep. Dist. Atty.
Johnson Stott, Lory S. ..................'46 '89 C.475 B.A. L.284 J.D. 2905 Salvio
Jumper, Carol Gresko ..................'53 '84 C.999 B.S. L.1065 J.D. 4324 Chelsea Way
Kadel, Edward E., Jr. ...'45 '71 C.112 B.A. L.1065 J.D. Human Res. Mgr., Chevron Corp.
**Kobayashi, J. Keiko** ..................'67 '95 C.112 B.A. L.1148 J.D. [Ⓐ Andersen&B.]
*PRACTICE AREAS: Tort Litigation Defense.
Kopel, Stuart M. ..................'48 '85 C.158 B.S. L.1153 J.D. 1200 Concord Ave.
Lamar, Douglas George ..................'48 '81 C.112 B.A. L.284 J.D. 2001 Salvio St.
Lanoue, Betty J. ..................'28 '53 C.719 A.B. L.209 J.D. 1229 Sherlock Way
Lawton, Larry ..................'42 '71 C.972 B.S. L.228 J.D. 1200 Concord Ave.

**Lee, Kenneth H.** ..................'66 '94 C.112 B.A. L.823 J.D. [Ⓐ Andersen&B.]
*PRACTICE AREAS: Insurance Defense; Construction Law.
LeVeque, Paul D. ..................'54 '80 C.477 L.1153 J.D. Unit Mgr., Wausau Ins. Co.

**Liddle, Donald J., Law Office of, (BV) '37 '73 C.859 B.S. L.878 J.D.**
**1985 Bonifacio Street, Suite 102, 94520**
**Telephone: 510-685-9000 Fax: 510-685-6722**
**(Certified Specialist, Family Law, The State Bar of California Board of Legal Specialization).**
***PRACTICE AREAS: Family Law; Probate.**
**Family Law.**
***See Professional Biographies, CONCORD, CALIFORNIA***

Liu, Barry R. ..................'43 '82 C.112 D.D.S. L.765 J.D. 2937 Salvio St.
Lucas, Christopher R., (BV) ..................'51 '80 C.112 B.A. L.284 J.D. [Goforth&L.]
MacDonald, Gordon C. '54 '82 C.508 B.A. L.285 J.D.
(adm. in MT; not adm. in CA) F.B.I.
Marianos, Ward N. ..................'27 '60 C.45 B.S. L.425 J.D. 1723 Curletto Dr.‡

**McCabe, Michael, (AV) '39 '64 C&L.767 A.B., J.D.**
**903 Ridge Drive, 94518©**
**Telephone: 510-687-3450 Fax: 510-687-3450**
**Email: mccabe@tpi.net**
***PRACTICE AREAS: Mediator.**
**Mediation.**
**San Francisco, California Office: 50 California Street, Suite 1500. Telephone: 415-392-3450.**
***See Professional Biographies, CONCORD, CALIFORNIA***

McCray, Rowland & Donovan ..................P.O. Box 271583 (©Dublin)
McFarland, James E. ..................'22 '63 C.330 A.B. L.1066 LL.B. 1925 Carzino St.‡
Meaden, John A., III, (BV) ..................'47 '74 C.477 B.S.M.E. L.1065 J.D. 2151 Salvio St.
Morrison, Craig William ..................'63 '90 C.112 B.A. L.1067 J.D. 3125 Clayton Rd.
Moyal, Maurice S. ..................'30 '72 C.112 B.S. L.1153 J.D. [M.S.Moyal]
Moyal, Maurice S., A Professional Law Corporation ..................1899 Clayton Rd.
Mullin, Ronald K., The Law Offices of, (CV) '49 '78
C.740 B.A. L.464 J.D. 1320 Willow Pass Rd., Ste 240
Murphy, Terence M., (BV) ..................'48 '74 C.767 B.A. L.765 J.D. 2280 Diamond Blvd.
Nathans, Marcel W. ..................'22 '81 C.112 Ph.D. L.1153 J.D. 3325 Clayton Rd.‡
Nolan, Holly P. ..................'65 '94 C.112 B.A. L.1355 J.D. 2300 Clayton Rd.
O'Hara, J. Brian ..................'22 '71 C.869 B.S. L.1065 J.D. 1380 Sumac Cir.‡
Oliver, Michael J. ..................'39 '68 C.768 B.A. L.1066 J.D. 1320 Willow Pass Rd.
Orlebeke, W. Ronald, Law Offices of, (BV) '34 '66 C&L.950 B.A., J.D.
3330 Clayton Rd.
Papathemetrios, Constantine ........'41 '76 C.959 B.S. L.64 J.D. 1108 Fair Weather Circle
Pavao, Jeanne C. '60 '85 C.112 B.A. L.770 J.D.
Corp. Coun., Albert D. Seeno Construction Co.
Peterson, Mark A. ..................'44 '70 C.494 B.A. L.309 J.D. 4712 Russo Ct.
Platt, Pamela J ..................'59 '87 C.1073 B.A. L.1153 J.D. 1320 Willow Pass Rd., Ste 240
**Politeo, Deanne B.** ..................'58 '84 C.112 B.A. L.1065 J.D. [Caudle,W.P.&B.]
*PRACTICE AREAS: Insurance Defense; Defense Litigation; Environmental Law; Toxic Substances; Construction Defects.
Pynn, Verne H. ..................'22 '56 L.284 4318 Leewood Pl.‡
Quinton, Alice A. ..................'70 '94 C.112 B.A. L.1188 J.D. [Ⓐ Ferns&F.]
Reardon, Maureen P. ..................'47 '88 C.112 B.A. L.770 J.D. 2151 Salvio St.
Resner, Robert D. ..................'43 '81 1130 Burnett Ave.
Riley, Dennis J. ..................'45 '91 C.36 B.S. L.1153 J.D. 1800 Sutter St.
Ring, Eileen ..................'46 '79 C.627 B.S. L.765 J.D. 1851 Harrison St.
Rogers, Walter D. ..................'38 '64 C.112 B.S. L.1066 J.D. Mun. Ct. J.
Rossi, Robert J., (BV) '35 '65 C.645 B.S.E.E. L.276 J.D.
Sr. V.P. & Gen. Coun., Albert D. Seeno Construction Co.
Rubendall, William M. ..................'49 '78 C.112 B.A. L.1197 J.D. 2045 Mount Diablo St.
Ryan, Dan G. ..................'49 '76 C.1109 B.A. L.1137 J.D. 1850 Gateway Blvd.
Ryan, Michael James ..................'51 '88 C.147 B.S. L.1153 J.D. 1800 Sutter St.
Safine, Stuart A., (CV) ..................'41 '69 C.766 B.A. L.284 J.D. 1850 Gateway Blvd.
Schaefer, Nicholas E. ..................'54 '84 C.173 B.S. L.174 J.D. 1738 Grant St.
Scranton, Michael ..................'40 '67 C.112 B.S. L.1066 J.D. 1200 Concord Ave.
Seibert, Hal F., (BV) ..................'44 '70 C.1077 B.S. L.1065 J.D. 1200 Concord Ave.‡
Silvester, Richard D. ..................'44 '71 C.101 L.878 J.D. 1738 Grant St.
Simons, Mark B. ..................'46 '70 C.477 B.A. L.145 J.D. Mun. Ct. J.
Snethen, Barbara ..................'51 '77 C.350 B.S. L.221 J.D. 2600 Stanwell Dr.

**Starr, John M., (BV) '36 '70 C.169 B.A. L.284 J.D.**
**1985 Bonifacio Street, Suite 102, 94520-2264**
**Telephone: 510-685-9000 Fax: 510-685-6722**
***PRACTICE AREAS: Personal Injury Law; Real Estate Law; Business Law.**
**General Civil and Trial Practice. Personal Injury, Professional Liability, Real Estate, Criminal and Business Litigation.**
**Reference: Bank of America (Clayton Valley Branch).**

Stevens, Mitchell A., (BV) ..................'41 '70 C.228 B.A. L.276 J.D. 1320 Willow Pass Rd.
Stewart, Hallie E. ..................'43 '78 C.260 B.A. L.1197 J.D. Systron Donner Inertial Div.
Vickers, Robert L. ..................'18 '49 C&L.861 LL.B. 811 Ridge Dr.
Walker, Donald R., (BV) ..................'23 '52 C.330 L.1065 LL.B. 1866 Las Ramblas
**Warantz, Elissa** ..................'55 '85 C.477 A.B. L.1065 J.D. Corp. Coun., Tosco Co.
Ward, Jeffrey R. ..................'64 '91 C.112 B.A. L.464 J.D. [Ⓐ Ferns&F.]
**Welch, Michael R.**, (AV) ..................'54 '80 C.112 B.A. L.990 J.D. [Caudle,W.P.&B.]©
*PRACTICE AREAS: Insurance Defense; Defense Litigation; Products Liability.
Willbrand, John C., (BV) ..................'46 '75 C.309 B.A. L.1066 J.D. 2280 Diamond Blvd.
Williscroft, Beverly R. ..................'45 '77 C.800 B.A. L.1153 J.D. 3018 Willow Pass Rd.
Woolard, Deirdre J. '50 '82 C.846 B.S. L.744 J.D.
(adm. in TX; not adm. in CA) 1362 Meadow Glen Way‡
Yesk, Michael J. ..................'61 '87 C.112 A.B. L.767 J.D. 5164 Muirfield Lane

## CORCORAN, 13,364, *Kings Co.*

Nordstrom, Michael N. ..................'57 '82 C.1074 B.S. L.770 J.D. 1100 Whitley Ave.

## CORNING, 5,870, *Tehama Co.*

Rodgers, David A., (BV) ..................'53 '79 C.147 B.A. L.464 J.D. 480 Solano St.

## CORONA, 76,095, *Riverside Co.*

**Bainer, Roland C.**, (BV) ..................'45 '74 C.1163 B.A. L.61 J.D. [Clayson,M.&Y.]
*PRACTICE AREAS: Civil Trial Practice; Personal Injury Law; Business Litigation.
**Barnett, Sallie** ..................'59 '85 C&L.801 B.S., J.D. [Clayson,M.&Y.]
*PRACTICE AREAS: Corporate Law; Business Law; Civil Litigation.
**Brenner, Scott Carleton** ..................'61 '93 C.999 B.S. L.1148 J.D. [Ⓐ Clayson,M.&Y.]
Carter, Charles H., (BV) ..................'17 '46 C&L.972 LL.B. 1025 S. Main St. (©Perris)
Charles, Carim '59 '87 C.563 B.S. L.1068 J.D.
(adm. in PA; not adm. in CA) 2621 Green River Rd.

**Clayson, Mann & Yaeger, A Professional Law Corporation, (AV)** 🅱🅱
**Clayson Law Building, 601 South Main Street, P.O. Box 1447, 91718-1447**
**Telephone: 909-737-1910 Riverside: 909-689-7241 Fax: 909-737-4384**
**Walter S. Clayson (1887-1972); E. Spurgeon Rothrock (1918-1979); Roy H. Mann; Derrill E. Yaeger; Gary K. Rosenzweig (Certified Specialist, Estate Planning, Trust and Probate Law, The State Bar of**

(This Listing Continued)

**Clayson, Mann & Yaeger, A Professional Law Corporation (Continued)**

**California Board of Legal Specialization); Elisabeth Sichel (Certified Specialist, Family Law, The State Bar of California, Board of Legal Specialization); Kent A. Hansen; Roland C. Bainer; David R. Saunders; Sallie Barnett;—Scott Carleton Brenner.**
**General Civil and Trial Practice. Appellate Practice. Probate, Estate Planning, Taxation, Corporation, Real Estate, Employment, Municipal and Water Law, Family Law.**
**Counsel for: Citizens Business Bank; Lee Lake Municipal Water District; Palo Verde Irrigation District; Loma Linda University.**
**Local Counsel: Minnesota Mining & Manufacturing Co.; Western Waste Industries.**
*See Professional Biographies, CORONA, CALIFORNIA*

Coudures, John M. ....... '16 '39 L.1065 LL.B. 1025 S. Main St.‡
Courtney, Norman P., (CV) ....... '22 '49 C.605 L.800 J.D. 424 E. 6th St.
Egli, Carol Hayes ....... '27 '79 C.353 B.S. L.990 J.D. 9383 Stone Canyon Rd.
Evans, Evan G., (BV) ....... '38 '70 C.800 B.S. L.1067 J.D. 601 S. Main St.
Fair, Joshua D. '58 '83 C&L.1288 B.A., J.D.
(adm. in OK; not adm. in CA) 824 Fullerton★
Fisher, Richard I. ....... '44 '76 C.608 B.S. L.1137 J.D. 1152 Neatherly Circle
Fuzak, Arthur W. ....... '23 '55 C.597 B.S.L. L.1068 J.D. Pres., Kimstock, Inc. (Pat.)
**Hansen, Kent A.** ....... '53 '79 C.1163 B.A. L.950 J.D. [Clayson,M.&Y.]
*PRACTICE AREAS: Employment Law; Corporate Law; Business Law.
Harris, Trester S., Jr. ....... '48 '74 C.112 B.A. L.990 J.D. 20430 Corona St.
Holstrom, Dayn A. ....... '58 '90 C&L.1137 B.S.L., J.D. 1307 W. 6th St.
James, Myron B., (BV) ....... '25 '63 C.347 B.S. L.1068 J.D. 1011 Victoria Ave.‡
Kocourek, Kenneth C. ....... '47 '74 C.1042 B.A. L.426 J.D. 541 N. Main St.
Last, Walter J. ....... '40 '69 C.112 L.1114 J.D. 888 Serfas Club Dr.
Liddy, Dan P. ....... '50 '79 219 E. Third St.
Liddy, Joseph P., (BV) ....... '22 '62 C.800 B.A. L.1001 LL.B. 219 E. Third St.
Lind, Robert L. ....... '46 '76 C.112 B.S. L.1137 J.D. Comr. of Consol. Ct. of Riverside Co.
Ludlow, Thos. H., Jr. ....... '24 '52 C.33 L.365 LL.B. [Ludlow&P.]
Ludlow & Price ....... P.O. Box 1028
**Mann, Roy H., (AV)** ....... '23 '51 C.112 A.B. L.800 J.D. [Clayson,M.&Y.]
*PRACTICE AREAS: Business Transactions; Water Rights.
Miller, Nancy E. ....... '52 '85 C.112 B.A. L.809 J.D. 422 Corona Mall
Mohoroski, John E. ....... '31 '63 C.96 B.S. L.426 J.D. 424 E. 6th St.
Parks, Daniel L. ....... '51 '83 C.1075 B.S.C.E. L.1137 J.D. Dep. Dir. Utility Servs. of Corona
Pedneau, Mary Jean ....... '57 '86 C.1097 B.S. L.426 J.D. 2280 Wardlow Circle
Pendleton, Charles F. ....... '22 '49 C.106 B.A. L.800 J.D. Ret. Mun. Ct. J.
Pershing, Richard W. S. ....... '57 '90 C.1163 B.A. L.1137 J.D. 202 Stan Reynolds Pkwy.
Politiski, Gregory J. ....... '35 '71 C.800 B.S. L.809 J.D. 2908 E. Brunswick Cr.
Price, Padgett Coventry ....... '48 '84 C.112 B.A. L.1137 J.D. [Ludlow&P.]
Proksel, William W., (BV) ....... '29 '58 C.190 B.S. L.767 LL.B. 4061 Mount Sernata Cir.
**Rosenzweig, Gary K.** ....... '51 '77 C.893 B.A. L.174 J.D. [Clayson,M.&Y.]
*PRACTICE AREAS: Probate Law; Trust Administration Law; Estate Planning Law.
**Saunders, David R.** ....... '55 '83 C.684 B.A. L.770 J.D. [Clayson,M.&Y.]
*PRACTICE AREAS: Real Property Development Law; Land Use Law; Administrative Law.
Scott, Robert E. ....... '49 '75 C.800 A.B. L.990 J.D. 125 Business Center Dr.
Seidler, Arthur R., (AV) ....... '22 '52 C&L.800 B.S., J.D. [⊠ K.A.Seidler]
Seidler, Kurt A., (BV) ....... '53 '78 C.112 B.A. L.1049 J.D. [K.A.Seidler]
Seidler, Kurt A., Law Offices, (BV) ....... 1007 Victoria Ave.
**Sichel, Elisabeth, (BV)** ....... '54 '79 C.112 B.A. L.1068 J.D. [Clayson,M.&Y.]
*PRACTICE AREAS: Family Law.
Thatcher, Pamela A., Law Offices of, (BV) '59 '83
C.398 B.A. L.426 J.D. 2280 Wardlow Circle
Uhl, Brian W. ....... '52 '77 C.1042 B.A. L.990 J.D. 400 S. Ramona
Williams, Cornelis R. '41 '82 C.803 B.A. L.861 J.D.
(adm. in LA; not adm. in CA) P.O. Box 2800‡
Wilson, Sandy A. ....... '46 '80 L.1137 J.D. P.O. Box 1298
**Yaeger, Derrill E., (BV)** ....... '27 '64 C.999 B.A. L.800 J.D. [Clayson,M.&Y.]
*PRACTICE AREAS: Real Property Development Law; Land Use Law.

## CORONA DEL MAR, —, *Orange Co.*

Bain, Beverly ....... '43 '87 C.347 M.S. L.1137 J.D. 3500 East Coast Hwy.
Black, Hugh L. '42 '68 C.970 B.A. L.930 J.D.
(adm. in OH; not adm. in CA) 900 Sea Lane
Blais, Beverly A., (BV) ....... '— '76 C.800 B.S. L.426 J.D. 1111 Bayside Dr.
Brooke, Eve Lynn ....... '— '89 C.1042 B.A. L.1137 J.D. Pres., Orange Co. Univ. Press
Budlong, Dale H. ....... '27 '59 C.1027 B.S. L.800 J.D. 2525 Ocean Blvd.‡
Carlton, Lucyann O'Donnell ....... '49 '75 C.605 B.A. L.426 J.D. 6 Rocky Point Rd.
Carter, Brian ....... '25 '69 C.352 B.S.E.E. L.990 J.D. 4732 Cortland Dr.‡
Christensen, Thomas E. ....... '50 '75 C&L.800 B.S., J.D. 3334 E. Coast Hwy.
Cooper, Jay P. ....... '26 '53 C&L.665 B.A., LL.B. 4 Atoll Dr.‡
Cyril, William ....... '21 '75 C.112 B.S. L.1136 J.D. 948 Gardenia Way‡
Durst, Lee H., (BV) ....... '49 '76 C.1249 B.A. L.29 J.D. 2121 E. Coast Hway.
Ensign, James G., (BV) ....... '32 '66 C.605 A.B. L.1065 J.D. 215 Milford Dr.
Flores, Edward R. ....... '64 '90 C.549 B.A. L.37 J.D. 308 Jasmine Ave.
Freeman, Alan P. ....... '48 '77 C.684 B.A. L.990 J.D. 441 Isabella Ter‡
Fritz, Barbara Ann ....... '— '86 C.1163 B.S. L.1137 J.D. 3500 E. Coast Hwy.
Giordano, Roy S., (AV) ....... '17 '53 C.112 B.A. L.1066 LL.B. 626 Seaward Rd.‡
Gold, Julia Royall ....... '— '63 C.112 L.426 J.D. 2601 Way Ln.‡
Herman, Michael R. ....... '37 '74 C.569 B.Sc. L.809 J.D. 427 Narcissus Ave.
Herzog, Patricia, (AV) ....... '22 '57 C.846 B.A. L.981 287 Evenino Canyon Rd.‡
Hinch, Diane B. ....... '50 '85 C.061 B.Ed. L.1137 J.D. 2600 E. Coast Hwy.‡
Hougan, Evelyn M. ....... '18 '54 C.112 M.A. L.809 LL.B. 704 Poinsettia Ave.‡
Humbert, Richard B., (AV) ....... '24 '53 C.869 B.S. L.309 LL.B. 1921 Galatea Ter.‡
Keeland, Robert L. '12 '36 L.846 LL.B.
(adm. in TX; not adm. in CA) 22 Beachcomber Dr.‡
Kline, Frederick W., Jr. ....... '49 '80 C&L.1137 B.S.L., J.D. 923 Goldenrod Ave.
Kroopf, Thomas A., (BV) ....... '53 '78 C.112 B.A. L.800 J.D. 4 Sandbar Dr.
Kwatek, Irwin L. ....... '39 '68 C.4 B.B.A. L.262 J.D. 209 Iris Ave.
Landeros, Jose G. ....... '58 '87 C.112 B.A. L.174 J.D. 2121 E. Coast Hwy.
Leshner, Zane '42 '68 C.932 B.S. L.836 J.D.
(adm. in TN; not adm. in CA) 228 Orchid Ave.‡
Lumsdon, Thomas G., (BV) ....... '35 '60 C.668 B.A. L.1066 LL.B. 457 Cabrillo Terr.
Marvel, James K., (AV) '47 '73 C&L.352 B.A., J.D.
1111 Bayside Dr. (©Tucson, AZ; Phoenix, AZ)
McClintock, Stephen H. ....... '41 '67 C.597 B.A. L.813 LL.B. 18 Mission Bay Dr.‡
Obrien, James B., (AV) ....... '58 '85 C.311 A.B. L.800 J.D. Atty. Gen.
Pickart, Gail P. ....... '39 '74 C.791 B.S.C.E. L.990 J.D. 7 San Mateo Way
Pitkin, John M. ....... '46 '71 C.188 B.A. L.569 J.D. 2121 East Coast Hwy.
Ressa, Mark ....... '53 '79 C.1154 B.A. L.1148 J.D. 606 Marcissus Ave.
Richter, Jill A. ....... '50 '78 C.770 B.A. L.1137 J.D. 137 Milford Dr.
Ross, Sheldon E., (BV) ....... '20 '49 C&L.930 A.B., LL.B. 3625 Catamaran Dr.
Shapiro, Paul W. ....... '50 '77 C.999 B.A. L.878 J.D. 3500 E. Coast Hwy.
**Shaw, Gerald M., (AV)** ....... '48 '74 C&L.800 B.S., J.D. [G.M.Shaw]

**Shaw, Gerald M., A Professional Corporation, (AV)**
**1111 Bayside Drive, Suite 270, 92625**
**Telephone: 714-759-5600 Telefax: 714-759-5656**
**Gerald M. Shaw.**
**General Civil Litigation in all State and Federal Courts, Insurance Law, General Tort Litigation, Personal Injury.**
**References: Marine National Bank, Irvine; Western Financial Savings Bank, Irvine.**
*See Professional Biographies, CORONA DEL MAR, CALIFORNIA*

Soden, Mark A. ....... '16 '49 C.966 B.S. L.800 LL.B. Ret. Supr. Ct. J.‡
Tanton, Joyce R. ....... '16 '42 C&L.800 A.B., J.D. 9 Jetty Dr. Jasmine Creek‡
Turpit, W. James ....... '14 '39 C.228 A.B. L.546 LL.B. 30 Jetty Dr.‡
Votaw, Elinor J., (AV) ....... '26 '79 C.172 B.S. L.1137 J.D. 703 Larkspur
Woodward, J. Christopher, (BV) ....... '51 '76 C.112 A.B. L.990 J.D. 1111 Bayside Dr.

## CORONADO, 26,540, *San Diego Co.*

Alfieris, George S. ....... '25 '61 C.878 B.A. L.911 J.D. P.O. Box 180548‡
Barker, James T. '23 '54 C.878 B.S. L.276 LL.B.
(adm. in DC; not adm. in CA) 1780 Avenida del Mundo‡
Barkhurst, William J., (BV) ....... '46 '74 C.147 B.A. L.1049 J.D. 1330 Orange Ave.
Barnes, Deborah Hawkins ....... '50 '81 C.143 B.A. L.838 J.D. 760 Country Club Lane‡
Binder, Timothy R. '49 '77 C.112 B.A. L.1049 J.D.
Vice Chmn. & Corp. Gen. Coun., Hotel Del Coronado Corp.
Boatwright, Camille G. ....... '57 '83 C.813 B.A. L.990 J.D. 1624 Cajon Pl.
Chin, Ronald J. ....... '— '85 C.766 B.S. L.61 J.D. [Rose,M.F.&C.]
Clancy, Benjamin B. '54 '87 C.454 B.A. L.836 J.D.
(adm. in GA; not adm. in CA) U.S. Navy, J. Advocate Gen. Corps★
DeBarr, John R. '20 '52 C.105 A.B. L.273 J.D.
(adm. in PA; not adm. in CA) 51 Spinnakar Way
Dorman, "R" "H" ....... '22 '78 C.446 B.S. L.1137 J.D. 850 Pomona Ave.‡
Downey, Jeremiah J. ....... '40 '84 C.285 B.A. L.1137 J.D. 1330 Orange Ave.
Downey, Mary C., (CV) ....... '42 '84 C.120 B.A. L.1137 J.D. 1330 Orange Ave.
Elliott, Norman, (AV) ....... '23 '50 C.605 B.A. L.800 LL.B. 330 Eighth St.
Feinberg, Louis '09 '36 C.569 L.1009
(adm. in NY; not adm. in CA) 1417 2nd St.‡
Florek, Sara E. ....... '43 '78 C.1157 B.A. L.879 J.D. P.O. Box 180757
Fout, George D. ....... '50 '81 C.112 B.A. L.1067 J.D. [Rose,M.F.&C.]
Gazzo, Raymond J. ....... '45 '70 C.350 B.S. L.190 J.D. 1265 Alameda Blvd.
Geddes, Roger A., (BV) '55 '83 C.119 B.S. L.1049 J.D.
V.P. & Assoc. Gen. Coun., Hotel Del Coronado Corp.
Gill, Elizabeth S. ....... '38 '80 C.378 B.A. L.1137 J.D. 1001 "B" Ave., Ste. 301
Goss, Harry T. '29 '53 L.37 LL.B.
(adm. in AZ; not adm. in CA) 1720 Avenida Del Mundo‡
Greenbaum, Joseph A. ....... '54 '81 C.705 B.A. L.61 J.D. 747 Margarita Ave.
Hafey, Robert E. ....... '29 '63 C&L.878 B.S., J.D. 273 Alameda Blvd.
Haig, Clyde A. '65 '92 C.197 B.A. L.902 J.D.
(adm. in PA; not adm. in CA) P.O. Box 747★
Handel, Susan ....... '55 '86 L.1137 J.D. 1720 Avenida Del Mundo
Hansen, Kathleen, (BV) ....... '57 '82 C&L.1049 B.A., J.D. [K.Hansen]
Hansen, Kathleen (Cuffaro), (BV) ....... 1112 First Street, Suite 109
Hart, James A. '14 '47 C.262 B.S. L.276 J.D.
(adm. in NE; not adm. in CA) 1417 2nd St.‡
Himelstein, Mandel E. ....... '33 '59 C&L.597 B.S., J.D. 1001 B Ave.
Hiscock, William C., (AV) ....... '25 '52 C&L.477 A.B., J.D. 416 Glorietta Blvd.
Hughes, Van V., (BV) ....... '35 '75 C.763 B.S. L.1137 J.D. 35 Green Turtle Rd.
Kopp, John W., Jr. ....... '45 '89 C.871 B.S. L.1241 J.D. 1330 Orange Ave.
Kremen, Seymour S. ....... '19 '73 C.563 B.Sc. L.1137 J.D. 1770 Avenida Del Mundo St.
Landres, Linda Grey, (BV) '46 '72 C.681 A.B. L.94 J.D.
Sr. V.P. & Gen. Coun., Hotel Del Coronado Corp.
Longley-Cook, Barbara A. ....... '42 '80 C.188 M.S. L.770 J.D. 312 F Ave.
Mark, William M. ....... '11 '37 C.867 A.B. L.178 LL.B. 1155 Star Park, E.‡
McLennan, William R. ....... '51 '77 C.597 B.S.J. L.770 J.D. 1034 Loma
Nagler, Karen M. ....... '46 '77 C.112 B.A. L.1137 J.D. 733 Alameda Blvd.
Novick, David J. '28 '61 C.35 B.S. L.37 LL.B.
(adm. in AZ; not adm. in CA) 1122 F Ave.‡
O'Connor, J. Robt. ....... '16 '53 C.763 L.61 LL.B. Ret. Mun. Ct. J.
Plumb, Robert T., II ....... '51 '79 C.335 B.A. L.1137 J.D. 1300 Orange Ave., Suite 300
Prager, Albert U., (AV) ....... '36 '66 C.112 B.S. L.1068 J.D. 724 1st St.
Randolph, William D. ....... '22 '50 C&L.339 B.S., J.D. 53 Green Turtle Rd.‡
Redding, Robert M. '31 '57 C&L.950 B.A., J.D.
(adm. in OR; not adm. in CA) 1018 Adella Ave.‡
Reniche, Allan J., (AV) ....... '31 '59 C&L.339 A.B., J.D. 51 Trinidad Bend
Riley, James E. '26 '52 C.918 A.B. L.976 LL.B.
(adm. in CT; not adm. in CA) 1820 Avenida del Mundo‡
Rockwell, Frank A., (BV) ....... '27 '70 C.112 B.S. L.1049 J.D. 819 1st St.‡
Rose, Munns, Fout and Chin ....... 1014 Park Pl.
Sellars, Bayard B. '24 '56 C.112 L.228 LL.B.
(adm. in NC; not adm. in CA) 943 1/2 F Ave.‡
**Sherman, Sharon Lynn, (AV)** ....... '51 '77 C.112 B.A. L.1049 J.D. [S.L.Sherman]

**Sherman, Sharon Lynn, A Professional Corporation, (AV)**
**1109 Eighth Street, 92118-2217**
**Telephone: 619-435-2282 Fax: 619-435-6417**
**Sharon Lynn Sherman.**
**General Civil Practice. Business Law, Probate, Estate Planning and Family Law.**
**Reference: Bank of Coronado.**
*See Professional Biographies, CORONADO, CALIFORNIA*

Standley, John J. ....... '51 '82 C.174 B.A. L.1137 J.D. 1013 4th St.
Storum, Lea S. ....... '63 '88 C.112 B.A. L.1065 J.D. 1112 Flora Ave.
Swinton, Richard B. ....... '50 '75 C.684 A.B. L.61 J.D. Coun., Wraith Enterprises
Szumowski, David M., (BV) ....... '45 '73 C.692 B.A. L.208 J.D. 946 B.Ave.
Tabin, Leonardo ....... '54 '83 C.767 B.A. L.1049 J.D. 75 Half Moon Bnd
Vienna, Kevin R. '51 '81 C.871 B.S. L.945 J.D.
(adm. in VA; not adm. in CA) 211 F Ave.★
Vomhof, Marion '56 '93 C&L.537 B.B.A., J.D.
Asst. V.P. & Asst. Coun., Hotel Del Coronado Corp.
Von Wantoch, Harvey ....... '27 '76 C.597 B.Sc. L.1137 J.D. 444 Glorietta Blvd.‡
White, Donald B., (AV) ....... '15 '40 C.112 A.B. L.1066 LL.B. 936-H Ave.‡
Zafis, Andrew J. ....... '25 '50 C&L.966 B.S., J.D. 1125 Loma Ave.
Zember, Lisa Marie ....... '64 '89 C.1119 B.A. L.1049 J.D. 150 Carob Way

## CORTE MADERA, 8,272, *Marin Co.*

Andrews, Susan A. '54 '80 C.385 A.B. L.880 J.D.
(adm. in MI; not adm. in CA) 49 Hickory Ave.‡
Axelrod, Peter, (BV) ....... '48 '73 C.112 A.B. L.1066 J.D. [Reid,A.R.K.&M.]
Beck, Georgetta ....... '55 '81 C.1213 B.S. L.284 J.D. [Miller&B.]
Carlile, Maria L. ....... '46 '71 C.813 B.A. L.1066 J.D. Coun. & V.P., Comdisco, Inc.

Chang, Helen Y. ........................'61 '86 C.846 B.A. L.802 J.D. 770 Tamalpais Dr.
Cohen, Judith H. B., (BV) ...........'42 '79 C.597 A.B. L.284 J.D. 21 Tamal Vista Blvd.
Connolly, John, IV '49 '76 C&L.221 B.F.A., J.D.
(adm. in IA; not adm. in CA) Pres., Connolly Bros. Realty Grp., Inc.
Coplin, Holly L. .........................'— '83 C.112 B.A. L.1065 J.D. 46 Sonora Way.
Dovbish, Alfred ..................'32 '64 C.800 B.A. L.809 LL.B. 21 Tamal Vista Blvd.
Doyle, J. Bradford, (BVⓉ) '45 '75 C.988 B.A. L.800 J.D.
(adm. in XX; not adm. in CA) 233 Upland Circle‡

**Fawcett, F. Conger, (AV) '34 '63 C&L.309 A.B., LL.B.**
**240 Tamal Vista Boulevard, Suite 163, 94925⊙**
**Telephone: 415-945-0995 Facsimile: 415-945-0996**
**(Also Of Counsel, Graham & James, San Francisco).**
***SPECIAL AGENCIES: Federal Maritime Commission; Bureau of Alcohol, Tobacco and Firearms.**
***REPORTED CASES: Miranda v. Arizona, 384 U.S. 436 (1966).**
***PRACTICE AREAS: Business; Securities; Alcoholic Beverage; Maritime Regulation.**
**General Practice, with emphasis on Corporate, Business and Securities, Alcoholic Beverage and Maritime Regulatory Law.**
***See Professional Biographies, CORTE MADERA, CALIFORNIA***

Fisher, Robin A. .................. '57 '84 C.623 B.S. L.862 J.D. 373 Corte Madera Ave.
Glantz, Richard M. ..............'45 '70 C.563 B.B.A. L.823 J.D. 21 Tamal Vista Blvd.

**Gordon, Robert E., (AV) '32 '60 C.112 A.B. L.1066 J.D.**
**Suite 840, 5725 Paradise Drive, 94925**
**Telephone: 415-924-1112 Fax: 415-924-7013**
**Copyright, Entertainment, Music and Recording, Motion Picture, Video, Television, Publishing and Unfair Competition Law.**
***See Professional Biographies, CORTE MADERA, CALIFORNIA***

Gross, Geoffrey E. '50 '78 C.276 B.S.B.A. L.861 J.D.
(adm. in NY; not adm. in CA) Coun. & Asst. V.P., Comdisco, Inc.
Guthrie, James W. ......................'44 '71 C.284 B.S. L.1065 J.D. 100 Tamal Plaza
Hart, Darryl A. ..........................'38 '66 C.112 A.B. L.1066 J.D. 25 Rocklyn Ct.
Hernand, Warren L. .................... '36 '65 C.1077 B.A. L.426 J.D. 770 Tamalpais Dr.
Johnson, Leslie H. '11 '36 L.362 LL.B.
(adm. in WA; not adm. in CA) 135 Golden Hinde Passage‡
Kearney, Frederick T. ...................'47 '73 C.766 B.A. L.284 J.D. [Reid,A.R.K.&M.]
McCormack-Healy, Virginia C. ........ '48 '79 C.112 A.B. L.1067 J.D. [Reid,A.R.K.&M.]
Miller, Andrew H. ................... '44 '92 C.46 B.S. L.284 J.D. 136 Mariner Green Ct.
Miller and Beck ..................................417 Sausalito St. (⊙San Francisco)

**Niederreuther, Thomas E. '61 '87 L.765 J.D.**
**5633 Paradise Drive, 94925**
**Telephone: 415-927-4535 Fax: 415-927-7672**
***LANGUAGES: German.**
**Civil Litigation Practice including Personal Injury, Business, Contracts, Real Estate, Lender Liability, Insurance Coverage and Bad Faith, Fraud and R.I.C.O.**
***See Professional Biographies, CORTE MADERA, CALIFORNIA***

**Philipps, Charles J., (AV) '43 '69 C.112 B.A. L.426 J.D.**
**300 Tamal Plaza Drive Suite 250, 94925**
**Telephone: 415-927-9449 Fax: 415-927-0660**
**Associates: Teresa L. Polk.**
**Fidelity and Surety, Construction Litigation and Contract Law. General Civil and Trial Practice.**
***See Professional Biographies, CORTE MADERA, CALIFORNIA***

**Polk, Teresa L.**, (BV) ..................... '54 '83 C.112 B.A. L.1065 J.D. [Ⓐ C.J.Philipps]
Portman, Mark E., (BV) ......................'51 '77 C.608 B.A. L.930 J.D. P.O. Box 548
Reid, Neil D., (AV) ......................'25 '57 C.112 B.A. L.767 J.D. [Reid,A.R.K.&M.] ‡
Reid, Axelrod, Ruane, Kearney & McCormack, A Prof. Corp., (AV) .... 770 Tamalpais Dr.
Ricci, Vincent L. ............... '45 '71 C.813 A.B. L.1066 J.D. Sr. V.P., Comdisco, Inc.
Ruane, Martin T., Jr., (AV) ................ '30 '59 C.767 B.S. L.765 LL.B. [Reid,A.R.K.&M.]
Sarokin, Rebecca '59 '85 C.705 B.A. L.273 J.D.
(adm. in NY; not adm. in CA) 37 Golden Hinde Passage‡
Snyder, William A., Jr., (AVⓉ) ..............'40 '64 C.367 A.B. L.446 LL.B. 722 Robin Dr.
Stewart, Robert W., (BV) ...........'43 '71 C.494 B.A. L.446 J.D. 21 Tamal Vista Blvd.
Sutro, Denis O. ..........................'48 '74 C.813 B.A. L.1065 J.D. 493 Montecito Dr.
Warner, John G., (AV) ................. '41 '66 C&L.608 B.A., LL.B. 21 Tamal Vista Blvd.
Whelan, D. Nicholas ..................'43 '87 C.172 B.S. L.1186 J.D. 478 Montecito Dr.
Wiener, Lewis R. '41 '66
C.882 B.A. L.569 LL.B. 5710 Paradise Dr. Ste. 6 (⊙San Francisco)
Worth, Karen V. ..........................'47 '81 C.766 B.A. L.284 J.D. 21 Tamal Vista Blvd.
Yount, David W., (AV) .........'45 '75 C.766 B.A. L.767 J.D. 300 Tamal Plz., Suite 280

## COSTA MESA, 96,357, *Orange Co.*

Aarons, Julius ................................'34 '58 C.569 B.A. L.178 LL.B. [Aarons&A.]
Aarons, Vilma M., (BV) ................'— '74 C.178 B.S. L.990 J.D. 2790 Harbor Blvd.
Aarons & Aarons, Inc. .............................................2790 Harbor Blvd.
**Adel, Robert Elliot, II** ...................... '62 '93 C.112 B.A. L.1066 [Ⓐ Rutan&T.]
*PRACTICE AREAS: Securities Litigation; Real Estate Litigation; Business Litigation; Civil Trial; Construction.
**Alani, Douglas D.** .........................'53 '87 C.112 B.A. L.809 J.D. [Buckner,A.&Y.]
*PRACTICE AREAS: Commercial Lease Litigation.
**Albert, Fredric I.** ..................'61 '87 C.645 B.A. L.851 J.D. [Ⓒ Sheppard,M.R.&H.]
*PRACTICE AREAS: Civil and Business Litigation; White Collar Criminal Defense.
**Albert, Theodor C.**, (AV) .............. '53 '78 C.813 B.A. L.1068 J.D. [Albert,W.&G.]
*PRACTICE AREAS: Bankruptcy; Commercial Litigation.

**Albert, Weiland & Golden, (AV) BR**
**Center Tower, 650 Town Center Drive, Suite 1350, 92626**
**Telephone: 714-966-10000 FAX: 714-966-1002**
**Email: awglawyers@aol.com**
**Theodor C. Albert; Michael J. Weiland; Jeffrey I. Golden; Jennifer Ann Golison; Evan D. Smiley; Lei Lei Wang Ekvall; Philip E. Strok.**
**Bankruptcy Matters Including the Representation of Creditors, Debtors and Trustees, and Real Estate Including Subdivision Development, Commercial Leasing, Financing, Loan Workouts, Receiverships and Foreclosures.**
***See Professional Biographies, COSTA MESA, CALIFORNIA***

**Aleshire, David J.** ..........................'50 '75 C.813 B.A. L.1068 J.D. [Rutan&T.]
*PRACTICE AREAS: Labor and Employment; Environmental; Construction; Municipal and Zoning; Land Use Law.
**Allen, David B.** ..........................'70 '96 C&L.976 B.A., J.D. [Ⓐ Latham&W.]
**Allen, Terry Jon** ......................'46 '91 C.871 B.S. L.1068 J.D. [Ⓐ Paul,H.J.&W.]
**Allen, Thomas W.**, (AV) ...................'37 '70 C.1109 B.A. L.770 J.D. [Burke,W.&S.]
*PRACTICE AREAS: Municipal Law.
**Allison, Steven D.** ................... '68 '94 C.1053 B.A. L.276 J.D. [Ⓐ Paul,H.J.&W.]
Anapoell, Steven T. ...................................................'63 '89 611 Anton Blvd.
**Anderson, Annette L.** ....................'57 '81 C&L.1137 B.S.L., J.D. [Ricks&A.]
*PRACTICE AREAS: Civil Litigation; Wrongful Termination; Employment and Discrimination Law.
**Anderson, Jon D.**, (AV) .....................'52 '77 C.911 B.A. L.101 J.D. [Latham&W.]
Angulo, Zaida T. ........................ '64 '90 C.112 B.A. L.1065 J.D. 3080 Bristol St.
**Anielski, Tracy L.** ............................ '58 '89 L.1137 J.D. [Ⓐ Ginsburg,S.O.&R.]

**Aplin, Thomas P., (BV) '60 '85 C.684 B.A. L.464 J.D.**
**535 Anton Boulevard, Suite 800, 92626**
**Telephone: 714-546-4608 Facsimile: 714-546-4614**
**Civil Litigation, Emphasizing Landlord/Tenant, Real Property, Construction and Business.**
***See Professional Biographies, COSTA MESA, CALIFORNIA***

Aprahamian, Richard J., (AV) .......... '37 '72 C.800 B.S. L.426 J.D. [Aprahamian&D.]
Aprahamian & Ducote, A Professional Corporation, (AV) ...............611 Anton Blvd.
**Archer, Cindy Thomas** ...................... '— '90 L.276 J.D. [Ⓐ Sheppard,M.R.&H.]
*PRACTICE AREAS: Financial Institutions Litigation.
**Ashley, Jennifer Penoyer** ............. '70 '95 C&L.477 A.B., J.D. [Ⓐ Pillsbury M.&S.]
**Ashman, Phillip** .........................'62 '89 C.112 B.A. L.802 J.D. [Ⓒ Graham&J.]
*PRACTICE AREAS: Creditors' Rights; Bankruptcy; Business Litigation.
**Babbush, Randall M.** ......................'56 '81 C.112 B.A. L.1065 J.D. [Rutan&T.]
*PRACTICE AREAS: Real Estate.
**Bahr, Byron J.** ..................'62 '87 C.147 B.S. L.1067 J.D. [Ⓐ Cooksey,H.M.&T.]
*PRACTICE AREAS: Business and Commercial Litigation; Creditor Bankruptcy Litigation.
**Balfour, Ralph E.**, (AV) ................'44 '69 C&L.800 A.B., J.D. [Balfour M.M.&O.]
*PRACTICE AREAS: Corporate Law; Business Law; Transactional Law; Mergers and Acquisitions; Real Property.

**Balfour MacDonald Mijuskovic & Olmsted, A Professional Corporation, (AV)**
**Suite 1110, 3200 Park Center Drive, 92626**
**Telephone: 714-546-2400 Fax: 714-546-5008**
**Ralph E. Balfour; James B. MacDonald (Certified Specialist, Estate Planning, Trust and Probate Law, The State Bar of California Board of Legal Specialization); Ruth Mijuskovic; R. Wayne Olmsted.**
**Corporate and Business Practice. Estates and Trust Planning and Administration. Litigation in all Federal and State Courts. Mergers and Acquisitions. Real Property.**
***See Professional Biographies, COSTA MESA, CALIFORNIA***

**Bangerter, Steven R.** .............. '61 '93 C.36 B.A. L.1137 J.D. [Ⓐ Cooksey,H.M.&T.]
*PRACTICE AREAS: Litigation; Insurance Defense Law.
**Barbarosh, Craig A.** ............... '67 '92 C.112 B.A. L.464 J.D. [Ⓐ Pillsbury M.&S.]
**Barby, David W.** ............................ '56 '84 C&L.659 B.S., J.D. [Latham&W.]
Barnes, Angel .................................'44 '83 C.1131 L.426 J.D. 611 Anton Blvd.
**Bartel, Marvin I.** ......................'52 '82 C.174 B.A. L.809 J.D. [Pillsbury M.&S.]
Barwick, Curt C. ............................ '54 '83 C.112 B.A. L.1065 J.D. 3070 Bristol
**Basombrio, Juan C.** ...................... '64 '89 C.326 B.A. L.347 J.D. [Ⓐ Dorsey&W.]
*LANGUAGES: Spanish.
*PRACTICE AREAS: Business Litigation; Corporate Law; International Law.
Battaile, Frank W. ........................'50 '90 C.112 B.S. L.1065 J.D. 695 Town Ctr. Dr.
**Beall, Robert S.** .....................'61 '87 C.112 B.A. L.800 J.D. [Sheppard,M.R.&H.]
*PRACTICE AREAS: Financial Institutions Litigation, Shareholders and Partnership Dispute Litigation.
**Beard, David S.** ........................'66 '96 C.1049 B.S. L.36 J.D. [Ⓐ Larsen&Assoc.]
*PRACTICE AREAS: Corporations; Real Property; Federal and State Taxation.
Becker, Peter J. '37 '62 C.184 B.A. L.276 J.D.
(adm. in CT; not adm. in CA) Pres.& CEO, Amer. Consulting Grp.
**Becket, Thomas L.** .................. '51 '76 C.800 B.S. L.1065 J.D. [Pillsbury M.&S.]
**Beckington, Mark R.** ............ '57 '86 C.112 B.A. L.1065 J.D. [Ⓐ Drummy K.W.&G.]
*PRACTICE AREAS: Litigation.
**Beeson, Jonn R.** ............................ '69 '96 C.112 B.S. L.659 J.D. [Ⓐ Latham&W.]
**Behrens, Russell G., (P.C.)**, (AV) .............'36 '61 L.800 J.D. [McCormick,K.&B.]
*PRACTICE AREAS: Public Law; Water Law; Real Property; Construction Law; Environmental Law.
**Bellows, Roger L.** ......................... '55 '80 C.627 B.A. L.190 J.D. [Lewis,D.B.&B.]
*PRACTICE AREAS: Litigation-Business and Personal Injury.
**Bellucci, Doreen R.** '62 '86
C.813 A.B. L.112 J.D. Corp. Coun., Apria Healthcare Grp., Inc.
*RESPONSIBILITIES: Healthcare; Real Estate; Corporate.
Beneville, Edward S., III ........................ '66 '91 C.1109 B.A. L.37 J.D. 2191 Canyon
Bent, Paul '44 '78 C.112 B.A. L.809 J.D.
Gen. Coun., GoodSmith & Co., Inc (⊙New York, N.Y.)
**Bentley, Joseph I.**, (AV) ...........................'40 '69 C.101 A.B. L.145 J.D. [Latham&W.]
Benvenuti, Martha Frances ............. '28 '78 C.597 B.Mus. L.990 J.D. 474 E. 17th St.
Bergland, David P., (AV) ...............'35 '70 C.112 B.A. L.800 J.D. 1773 Bahama Pl.‡
**Biel, William R.**, (AV) ..............................'32 '61 C.112 B.S. L.1068 LL.B. [Rutan&T.]
*PRACTICE AREAS: Commercial; Real Estate.
Bilava, Arthur J., (CV) ...................................'19 '52 C.800 L.426 LL.B. 478 Ogle Kst.
Blackwood, David M. '60 '86
C&L.188 B.A., J.D. Gen. Coun., Canon Computer Systems, Inc.
Blakely, P. Arnsen ........................ '39 '71 C.800 B.A. L.809 J.D. [Davis,S.B.&G.]
**Blakely, Roger W., Jr.**, (AV) '35 '70
C.188 B.M.E. L.426 J.D. [Blakely,S.T.&Z.] (See Pat. Sect.)

**Blakely, Sokoloff, Taylor & Zafman, (AV)**
**A Limited Liability Partnership**
**Suite 850, 611 Anton Boulevard, 92626⊙**
**Telephone: 714-557-3800 Facsimile: 714-557-3347**
**Email: BSTZ_mail@bstz.com URL: http://www.bstz.com**
**Members of Firm: Roger W. Blakely, Jr.†; Ben J. Yorks;—William W. Schaal; Sunny Tamaoki; Kimberley G. Nobles; Kent M. Chen; Thinh V. Nguyen; Babak Redjaian.**
**Intellectual Property Law including Patents, Trademarks, Copyrights, Related Prosecution and Litigation.**
**Los Angeles, California Office: 7th Floor, 12400 Wilshire Boulevard. Telephone: 310-207-3800. Facsimile: 310-820-5988.**
**Sunnyvale, California Office: 1279 Oakmead Parkway. Telephone: 408-720-8598. Facsimile: 408-720-9397.**
**Lake Oswego, Oregon Office: Suite 101, 5285 SW Meadows Road. Telephone: 503-684-6200. Facsimile: 503-684-3245.**
**†Indicates A Law Corporation.**
***See Professional Biographies, COSTA MESA, CALIFORNIA***

**Bohm, James G.** .........................'62 '87 C.112 B.A. L.990 J.D. [Lewis,D.B.&B.]
**Bohn, Brent R.** ......................... '66 '91 C.112 B.A. L.426 J.D. [Ⓐ Paul,H.J.&W.]
**Bollero, Barbara L.** ............... '53 '81 C.339 B.A. L.846 J.D. [Ⓐ Cooksey,H.M.&T.]
*PRACTICE AREAS: Litigation; Personal Injury; Insurance Defense Law.
**Bond, Julia L.** ..........................'67 '93 C.788 B.A. L.1068 J.D. [Ⓐ Rutan&T.]
*PRACTICE AREAS: Municipal and Zoning; Personal Injury; Land Use Law.
**Bonn, Elizabeth Currin** .................... '56 '84 C.37 B.S. L.990 J.D. [Ⓐ Booth,M.&S.]
**Boon, Danny R.** .................. '66 '95 C.839 B.B.A. L.796 J.D. [Ⓐ Larsen&Assoc.]
*PRACTICE AREAS: Estate Planning; Probate; Federal and State Taxation.

**Booth, Mitchel & Strange, (AV)**
**3080 Bristol Street, Suite 550, P.O. Box 5046, 92628-5046⊙**
**Telephone: 714-641-0217 Fax: 714-957-0411**
**Members of Firm: Michael T. Lowe (Resident); Walter B. Hill, Jr. (Resident); Robert H. Briggs (Resident); David R. Kipper; Marla Lamedman Kelley (Resident); Paul R. Howell; Craig E. Guenther (Resident); David L. Hughes (Resident); James G. Stanley (Resident). Associates: Elizabeth Currin Bonn (Resident); Stacie L. Brandt (Resident); David F. McPherson (Resident); Scott S. Mizen (Resident); Sean T. Osborn (Resident); Laila Morcos Santana (Resident).**
**General Civil and Commercial Trial Practice in all State and Federal Courts. Construction, Professional Liability, Environmental, Corporation, Real Property, Savings and Loan, Tax, Insurance, Surety, Estate Planning, Trust and Probate Law.**
**Representative Clients: See listing at Los Angeles, California.**
**Los Angeles, California Office: 3435 Wilshire Boulevard, 30th Floor. Telephone: 213-738-0100. Fax: 213-380-3308.**

(This Listing Continued)

CAA57P

**Booth, Mitchel & Strange (Continued)**

**San Diego, California Office: 550 West "C" Street. Suite 1560. Telephone: 619-238-7620. Fax: 619-238-7625.**

***See Professional Biographies, COSTA MESA, CALIFORNIA***

**Borges, Evan C.** ... '60 '87 C.112 B.A. L.976 J.D. [McIntyre B.&B.]
*PRACTICE AREAS: Litigation.
**Bosko, David M.**, (AV) ... '40 '65 C&L.813 B.S., J.D. [Sheppard,M.R.&H.]
*PRACTICE AREAS: Corporate Law; Mergers and Acquisitions; Securities Law.
**Bowen, Leslie S.** ... '66 '95 C.36 B.S. L.1137 J.D. [🄰 Lewis,D.B.&B.]
**Bower, Robert S.**, (AV) ... '47 '76 C.951 B.A. L.1065 J.D. [Rutan&T.]
*PRACTICE AREAS: Civil Rights; Environmental; Municipal and Zoning; Civil Trial.
**Boyer, David D.** ... '60 '85 C.97 B.S. L.16 J.D. [🄰 McCormick,K.&B.]
*PRACTICE AREAS: Litigation in the areas of Public Law, Real Property and Land Use Planning; Water Law; Business; Commercial Practices and Transactions; Insurance Coverage.
**Braasch, Debra L.** ... '59 '83 C.112 B.S. L.800 J.D. [🄰 Murtaugh,M.M.&N.]
Brady, Richard D. ... '60 '85 C.800 B.S. L.276 J.D. 650 Town Center Dr.
**Brandt, Stacie L.** ... '57 '93 C.188 B.S. L.1049 J.D. [🄰 Booth,M.&S.]
**Braun, Maryls K.** ... '66 '92 C.800 B.S. L.464 J.D. [🄰 Murtaugh,M.M.&N.]
**Braun, Robert C.**, (AV) ... '45 '71 C.800 B.A. L.1066 J.D. [Rutan&T.]
*PRACTICE AREAS: Civil Trial.
**Brazil, F. Kevin** ... '61 '87 C.1042 B.S. L.1067 J.D. [Rutan&T.]
*PRACTICE AREAS: Real Estate; Environmental; Land Use Law; Construction.
**Break, Robert K.**, (AV) ... '48 '75 C.154 B.A. L.178 J.D. [Latham&W.]
**Briggs, Glenn L.** ... '68 '94 C.112 B.A. L.1066 J.D. [🄰 Paul,H.J.&W.]
**Briggs, Robert H.**, (BV) ... '49 '77 C.101 B.A. L.990 J.D. [Booth,M.&S.]
Brinton, Arman L., (BV) ... '45 '85 C.1042 B.A. L.1137 J.D. 3333 Fairview Rd.
**Brockington, Thomas G.** ... '55 '80 C.813 A.B. L.1066 J.D. [Rutan&T.]
*PRACTICE AREAS: Business; Securities.
**Brogan, James P.** ... '65 '91 C.802 B.S.E.E. L.326 J.D. [🄰 Lyon&L.] (See Pat. Sect.)
*PRACTICE AREAS: Patent, Trademark, Copyright, Unfair Competition; Intellectual Property.
Brooke, Shirley J. ... '27 '77 C.569 B.S. L.990 J.D. 409 Flower St.‡
**Brower, Steven**, (AV) ... '54 '80 C.112 A.B. L.1068 J.D. [🄲 Ginsburg,S.O.&R.]
Brown, Angela K. ... '66 '95 C.1041 B.A. L.1068 J.D. 695 Town Ctr. Dr.
Brown, J. Robert ... '41 '77 C.546 B.S. L.1136 J.D. 389 Bayview Ter.
Brown, Jeffrey R. ... '68 '95 C.112 B.A. L.1065 J.D. 611 Anton Blvd.
**Brown, Michael Wayne** '60 '85
C.1109 B.A. L.990 J.D. Corp. Coun., Apria Healthcare Grp., Inc.
*RESPONSIBILITIES: Healthcare Fraud and Abuse; Healthcare Transactions; Healthcare Regulation; Acquisition.
**Browning, John R.** ... '66 '92 C.112 B.A. L.464 J.D. [🄰 Murtaugh,M.M.&N.]
**Bryant, Robert P.** ... '68 '93 C.426 B.A. L.1066 J.D. [🄰 Paul,H.J.&W.]
**Buck, Richard E.** ... '55 '85 C.112 B.A. L.900 J.D. [🄰 Cooksey,H.M.&T.]
*PRACTICE AREAS: Litigation; Insurance Law; Insurance Defense.
**Buckner, William D.** ... '56 '82 C.800 B.A. L.426 J.D. [Buckner,A.&Y.]
*PRACTICE AREAS: Real Estate Law; Real Estate Finance; Mortgage Based Financing.

**Buckner, Alani & Young**
**3146 Redhill Avenue, Suite 200, 92626**
**Telephone: 714-432-0990 Fax: 714-432-0352**
**William D. Buckner; Douglas D. Alani; Matthew S. Duncan; Brett L. Hayes. Of Counsel: Michael J. Mirkovich.**
**Commercial Real Estate.**

***See Professional Biographies, COSTA MESA, CALIFORNIA***

Bunney, Susan D. ... '52 '87 C.763 B.A. L.1137 J.D. 3090 Bristol St.
**Burek, Lawrence M.** ... '50 '87 C.999 B.A. L.990 J.D. [🄰 Drummy K.W.&G.]
*PRACTICE AREAS: Civil Litigation; General Business; Real Estate Law; Commercial Litigation.
**Burge, Robert R.**, (AV) ... '35 '61 C.467 B.S. L.1066 J.D. [🄲 Paul,H.J.&W.]
**Burger, Carolyn C.** ... '69 '94 C.309 B.A. L.659 J.D. [Pillsbury M.&S.]
**Burke, Daniel W.** ... '67 '94 C.112 B.A. L.813 J.D. [🄰 Latham&W.]
Burke, Earle Wm., (AV) ... '14 '38 L.999 LL.B. 181 The Masters Circle‡

**Burke, Williams & Sorensen, (AV)**
**A Partnership including a Professional Corporation**
**3200 Park Center Drive, Suite 750, 92626⊙**
**Telephone: 714-545-5559**
**Email: bws@bwslaw.com URL: http://www.bwslaw.com**
**Resident Attorneys: J. Robert Flandrick; Leland C. Dolley; Jerry M. Patterson; Thomas C. Wood; Thomas W. Allen; Gregory G. Diaz; Bryan Cameron LeRoy.**
**General Civil and Trial Practice in all State and Federal Courts. Securities, Corporate, Taxation, Insurance and Commercial Law. Municipal and Public Agency Representation. Local Government Financing, Taxation and Assessments. Community Redevelopment, Eminent Domain, Environmental and Land Use Law. Employee Benefit Plans, Probate and Estate Planning. Health Care, Medical Research, College and University and Non-Profit Organization Law, Employment and Personnel Law. Tort, Workers Compensation and Insurance Defense.**
**Los Angeles, California Office: 611 West Sixth Street, 25th Floor. Telephone: 213-236-0600.**
**Ventura County Office: 2310 Ponderosa Drive, Suite 1, Camarillo, California. Telephone: 805-987-3468.**

***See Professional Biographies, COSTA MESA, CALIFORNIA***

**Burns, George S.** ... '60 '86 C.800 B.A. L.426 J.D. [McIntyre B.&B.]
*REPORTED CASES: MDFC Loan Corp. v. Greenbrier, et al, 21 Cal.App. 4th 1045 (1994).
*PRACTICE AREAS: Litigation.
Burns, John P. ... '57 '84 C.436 B.A. L.880 J.D. 3070 Bristol St.
**Bushnell, Laura I.** ... '67 '94 C.813 A.B. L.276 J.D. [🄰 Latham&W.]
**Callari, Andrew C.** ... '62 '90 C.1044 B.A. L.188 J.D. [🄰 Pillsbury M.&S.]
Campbell, Caldwell R., (AV) ... '41 '68 C.112 B.A. L.426 J.D. [Day&C.]
Candlish, Richard W. '53 '82 C.1042 B.A. L.1137 J.D.
Staff Coun., State Comp. Ins. Fund
**Caplan, William J.**, (AV) ... '53 '78 C.112 B.A. L.1068 J.D. [Rutan&T.]
*PRACTICE AREAS: Real Estate Litigation; Commercial Landlord-Tenant Litigation; Earth Movement Litigation; Civil Trial.
**Cappel, Timothy R.**, (AV) ... '49 '76 C.502 B.S. L.228 J.D. [Cappel]
*REPORTED CASES: British Airways Board vs. The Port Authority of New York, 564 F.2d 1002 (2nd Cir. 1977); Browne vs. McDonnell Douglas Corporation, 504 F.Supp. 514 (N.D. Cal. 1980); Eldridge vs. Tymshare, Inc., 186 Cal.App.3d 767 (6th App Dist. 1986).

**Cappel Law Offices, (AV)**
**Center Tower * Suite 1950, 650 Town Center Drive, 92626-1925**
**Telephone: 714-850-1900 Facsimile: 714-850-1902**
**Timothy R. Cappel.**
**General Civil, Trial and Appellate Practice in all State and Federal Courts. Commercial, Corporation and Corporate Financing, Real Estate, and Technology Law.**

***See Professional Biographies, COSTA MESA, CALIFORNIA***

**Cardoza, Adele K.** ... '59 '87 C.112 B.S. L.1066 J.D. [🄰 Latham&W.]
**Cardoza, Steven W.** ... '61 '87 C.112 B.S. L.1066 J.D. [Sheppard,M.R.&H.]
*PRACTICE AREAS: Finance and Banking Law; Commercial Law; Problem Loan Workouts.
**Carlozzi, Mark J.** ... '63 '93 C.228 B.S.E.E. L.426 J.D. [🄰 Lyon&L.]
*PRACTICE AREAS: Patent, Trademark, Copyright; Unfair Competition, Trade Secret; Intellectual Property.
**Carlson, Kara S.** ... '70 '95 C.1077 B.A. L.1065 J.D. [🄰 Rutan&T.]
*PRACTICE AREAS: Public Law.

**Carroll, Patrick D.**, (AV) '49 '77 C.112 B.A. L.426 J.D.
**650 Town Center Drive, Suite 750, 92626-1925**
**Telephone: 714-479-1948 Fax: 714-534-3869**
**Email: carroll:567@aol.com**
***PRACTICE AREAS: Complex Litigation; Contract Law; Land Use Law; Landlord and Tenant Law; Civil Trial.**
**General Civil Trial Practice in all State and Federal Courts. Real Estate (Residential and Commercial), Contract Law, Land Use Law, Landlord-Tenant, Civil Trials and Real Estate Litigation.**

**Carruth, Joseph D.**, (AV) ... '42 '68 C.813 B.A. L.1066 J.D. [Rutan&T.]
*PRACTICE AREAS: Business; Tax Law.
**Case, Brian S.** ... '58 '84 C.112 B.A. L.990 J.D. [Case&Assoc.]
*REPORTED CASES: Wright v. USPS, 29 Fed 3rd. 1426, 1994 (Subcontractor's right to pursue federal agency for equitable lien right to payment where prime contractor and surety are insolvent).
*PRACTICE AREAS: Construction Litigation; Business Litigation and Transactions; Real Property Law; Surety and Insurance Law.
**Case, Phillip Andrew** ... '65 '96 C.139 B.A. L.1137 J.D. [Case&Assoc.]

**Case & Associates**
**The Center Tower, 650 Town Center Drive, Suite 550, 92626**
**Telephone: 714-540-3636 Fax: 714-540-3680**
**Brian S. Case. Associates: F. Albert Ibrahim; D. Michael Clauss; Phillip Andrew Case.**
**Construction and Business Litigation, Real Property Law, Surety and Insurance Law.**

***See Professional Biographies, COSTA MESA, CALIFORNIA***

**Casey, Justine Mary** ... '62 '89 C.763 B.S. L.426 J.D. [🄰 Sheppard,M.R.&H.]
**Casey, Wayne J.** ... '55 '81 C.433 B.A. L.800 J.D. [Casey&R.]
*PRACTICE AREAS: Estate Planning; Charitable Giving; Probate; Wills and Trust Law; Administration.

**Casey & Richards**
**3200 Park Center Drive, Tenth Floor, 92626**
**Telephone: 714-850-4575 Facsimile: 714-850-4577**
**Members of Firm: Wayne J. Casey; Marc H. Richards.**
**Estate Planning, Charitable Giving, Probate, Wills and Trust Law and Administration.**

***See Professional Biographies, COSTA MESA, CALIFORNIA***

**Cernius, William J.** ... '60 '85 C.800 B.A. L.1065 J.D. [Latham&W.]
**Chapman, Christofer R.** ... '60 '91 C.636 B.A. L.809 J.D. [🄰 Cooksey,H.M.&T.]
*LANGUAGES: Spanish.
*PRACTICE AREAS: Litigation; Personal Injury; Insurance Defense Law.

**Chapman & Glucksman, A Professional Corporation**
**(See Los Angeles)**

Charness, michelle A. ... '— '95 C.112 B.A. L.426 J.D. 535 Anton Blvd.
Chase, Irving M. ... '52 '79 C.1077 B.A. L.1095 J.D. 129 W. Wilson St.
**Chen, Kent M.** ... '65 '94 C.494 B.E.E. L.569 J.D. [🄰 Blakely,S.T.&Z.] (See Pat. Sect.)
Chesley, William H. ... '51 '84 C&L.1137 B.S., J.D. P.O. Box 10547
**Chodzko, James E.**, (AV) ... '51 '77 C.940 B.A. L.61 J.D. [McInnis,F.R.&S.]⊙
Christensen, Peter T. ... '67 '93 C.112 B.S. L.1066 J.D. 650 Town Center Dr.
**Chuang, Deborah J.** ... '71 '95 C.228 B.A. L.1066 J.D. [🄰 Rutan&T.]
**Clark, Gene R.** ... '— '91 C&L.101 B.A., J.D. [🄰 Sheppard,M.R.&H.]
*PRACTICE AREAS: Real Estate, Banking and Finance Law.
Clark, Paul S. ... '56 '82 C.105 B.A. L.273 J.D. 695 Town Ctr. Dr.
**Clauss, D. Michael** ... '57 '89 C.712 B.S. L.1137 J.D. [🄰 Case&Assoc.]
*PRACTICE AREAS: Business; Construction Law; Mechanics Lien Law; Real Estate; Commercial.
**Clune, John O.** ... '68 '95 C.1049 B.A. L.1065 J.D. [🄰 McCormick,K.&B.]
*LANGUAGES: Spanish.

**Cohen, Martin M., Law Offices of, (AV) '40 '65 C.831 B.S. L.880 J.D.**
**3200 Park Center Drive, Suite 610, 92626-1908**
**Telephone: 714-549-1499 Fax: 714-549-8970**
**Corporate, Partnership, Business Law, Litigation, Wills and Trusts, Probate, Federal Tax, State and Local Tax and International Law.**

***See Professional Biographies, COSTA MESA, CALIFORNIA***

**Cohen, Neal Matthew** ... '64 '96 C.112 L.426 J.D. [🄰 Lyon&L.]
*PRACTICE AREAS: Patent.
**Coleman, Steven M.** ... '68 '94 C.112 B.A. L.1065 J.D. [🄰 Rutan&T.]
*PRACTICE AREAS: Municipal Law; Litigation; Land Use Law.
**Collins, Sue Lee** ... '68 '95 C.112 B.A. L.1068 J.D. [🄰 Rutan&T.]
*PRACTICE AREAS: Business.
Connally, Michael W. ... '57 '81 C&L.426 B.A., J.D. [Lewis,D.B.&B.]
Cooke, Stephen D. ... '58 '85 C.112 A.B. L.1068 J.D. [Paul,H.J.&W.]
**Cooksey, David R.**, (AV) ... '46 '72 C.112 B.A. L.1065 J.D. [Cooksey,H.M.&T.]
*PRACTICE AREAS: Litigation; Personal Injury; Insurance Defense Law.

**Cooksey, Howard, Martin & Toolen, A Professional Corporation, (AV)**
**535 Anton Boulevard, 10th Floor, 92626-1947**
**Telephone: 714-431-1100 Telecopier: 714-431-1119**
**Marven E. Howard; James M. Martin; David R. Cooksey; Robert L. Toolen; Kim P. Gage; Patrick J. Duffy; Philip M. Woog;—Jon A. Hammerbeck; Leroy Einspahr; Byron J. Bahr; Barbara L. Bollero; Lawrence E. Lannon; Christopher J. Henderson; Lawrence H. Miller; Maria De Luna; Moina C. Shiv; Joseph M. Parker; Steven R. Bangerter; Randall P. Mroczynski; Thomas F. Zimmerman; Gregory R. Warnagieris; Christofer R. Chapman; Bradley T. Davis; John A. Marlo, III; Brian R. Van Marter; Richard E. Buck; Michael J. Macie; Theresa H. Lazorisak; C. Brad Johnson; David W. Seal; Griffith H. Hayes.**
**General Civil and Trial Practice in all Courts. Personal Injury, General Liability Insurance, Defense Litigation, Commercial Law, Business Litigation, Creditor-Bankruptcy Law, Corporate, Insurance, Probate, Estate Planning, Real Estate, Antitrust Law and Employment Law.**
**Reference: Eldorado Bank, Tustin, California.**

***See Professional Biographies, COSTA MESA, CALIFORNIA***

**Cooper, Scott B.** ... '69 '94 C.112 B.A. L.145 J.D. [🄰 Latham&W.]

**Coopersmith, Henry J., (AV) '43 '69 C.1073 B.S. L.1066 J.D.** BV
**611 Anton Boulevard, Suite 1110, 92626**
**Telephone: 714-433-7340 Fax: 714-436-6109**
**(Certified Specialist, Taxation Law and Estate Planning, Trust and Probate Law, State Bar of California Board of Legal Specialization).**
**Probate Law, Tax, Estate Planning, Wills and Trusts, Real Estate and Corporate Law and Limited Liability Companies.**

***See Professional Biographies, COSTA MESA, CALIFORNIA***

**Cornwell, Mary L.** ... '62 '87 C&L.800 B.S., J.D. [🄲 Paul,H.J.&W.]
**Correia, Charles A.** ... '52 '79 C.112 A.B. L.800 J.D. [🄰 Ely,F.&H.]
*LANGUAGES: French.
*PRACTICE AREAS: Insurance Defense; Insurance Fraud.
**Cosgrove, David B.**, (AV) ... '59 '84 C.973 H.A.B. L.608 J.D. [Rutan&T.]
*PRACTICE AREAS: Eminent Domain; Water; Municipal Law.
**Coulombe, Ronald B.**, (AV) ... '50 '79 C.1042 B.A. L.426 J.D. [Coulombe&K.]
*REPORTED CASES: Margaret Van Luven v. Rooney Pace, Inc, 195 Cal.App.3d 1201 (1987); BFP v. Resolution Trust Corporation, 114 S.Ct. 1757 (1994).
*PRACTICE AREAS: Civil Trial; Business; Real Estate; Title Insurance; Securities.

**Coulombe & Kottke, A Professional Corporation, (AV)** BV
**Comerica Bank Tower, 611 Anton Boulevard, Suite 1260, 92626**
**Telephone: 714-540-1234 Fax: 714-754-0808; 714-754-0707**
**Email: c-k@coulombe.com**
**Ronald B. Coulombe; Jon S. Kottke. Counsel: Roy B. Woolsey.**

(This Listing Continued)

**Coulombe & Kottke, A Professional Corporation (Continued)**

Civil Litigation in all State and Federal Courts. Bankruptcy Litigation, Appeals, Business, Insurance Coverage and Bad Faith, Real Estate, Title Insurance, Securities, Construction, Commercial, Collections, Landlord-Tenant.

*See Professional Biographies, COSTA MESA, CALIFORNIA*

**Covelman, Joel David** ............. '56 '81 C.154 B.A. L.880 J.D. [Ⓐ Ginsburg,S.O.&R.]
Cover, W. Curtis, Jr. ..................... '42 '70 C.645 B.S. L.426 J.D. 695 Town Ctr. Dr.
**Cox, Charles W., II** ..................... '62 '92 C.871 B.S. L.477 J.D. [Ⓐ Latham&W.]
Craig, William B. ................................ '31 '54 C&L.190 J.D. 575 Anton Blvd.
**Crane, Thomas J.**, (AV) ..................... '57 '82 C.197 A.B. L.276 J.D. [Rutan&T.]
*PRACTICE AREAS: Business; Computer; Commercial; Securities.
**Creasey, Lori** ......................... '57 '84 C.112 B.A. L.809 J.D. [Ⓐ Lewis,D.B.&B.]
**Cruz, John G.** ............................ '51 '79 C.1109 B.A. L.477 J.D. [Daehnke&C.]
*PRACTICE AREAS: Business; Corporate; Real Estate Law; Transactional Law & Lenders.
**Curnutt, Richard A.**, (AV) ............... '39 '65 C.668 B.A. L.1068 LL.B. [Rutan&T.]
*PRACTICE AREAS: Real Estate.
**Currie, Robert E.**, (AV) ................. '37 '67 C.871 B.S. L.309 LL.B. [Latham&W.]
**Currier, Charles L.**, (BV) ............ '49 '74 C.112 B.A. L.1049 J.D. [McInnis,F.R.&S.]
*PRACTICE AREAS: Real Estate; Loan Workouts; Real Estate Litigation; Commercial Litigation.
**Curtis, Kenneth W.** ............ '63 '88 C.1042 B.S. L.424 J.D. [Ⓐ Drummy K.W.&G.]
*PRACTICE AREAS: Civil Litigation with emphasis on Business and Real Estate Law; Lender Liability; Public and Private Works Construction.
**Daehnke, Kevin J.** ......................... '58 '84 C.36 B.A. L.800 J.D. [Daehnke&C.]
*PRACTICE AREAS: Environmental Law.

**Daehnke & Cruz**
**Great Western Bank Tower, 3200 Park Center Drive Suite 800, 92626**
Telephone: 714-557-8255 Fax: 714-557-9344
Members of Firm: Kevin J. Daehnke; John G. Cruz; William J. Moran. Associates: Maureen R. Graves; Gillian Stein. Of Counsel: Steven W. Kerekes; Russell J. Thomas, Jr.
Environmental Law, Corporate Law, Real Estate Law, Commercial Law, Labor Law, Civil Litigation.

*See Professional Biographies, COSTA MESA, CALIFORNIA*

**Dahl, Milford W., Jr.**, (AV) ................ '40 '65 C.112 B.S. L.1065 J.D. [Rutan&T.]
*PRACTICE AREAS: Civil Trial.
**Dallas, Evridiki (Vicki)**, (AV) ................ '52 '79 C.1222 B.A. L.260 J.D. [Rutan&T.]
*PRACTICE AREAS: Business; Securities; Tax Law.
Dana, David T., III, (AV) ... '37 '62 C.674 A.B. L.976 LL.B. 611 Anton Blvd., Ste., 720‡
**Daniels, James W.**, (AV) ................... '45 '71 C.103 A.B. L.145 J.D. [Latham&W.]
**Danz, Barbara R.** .................... '46 '92 C.881 B.A. L.800 J.D. [Ⓐ Paul,H.J.&W.]
**Dassoff, Glenn D.**, (AV) .................. '54 '80 C.800 B.S. L.1066 J.D. [Paul,H.J.&W.]
**Daucher, Brian M.** ................. '69 '94 C.197 A.B. L.228 J.D. [Ⓐ Sheppard,M.R.&H.]
Davidson, Cary, (AV) ............................ '54 '78 C.154 B.A. L.145 J.D. [Reed&D.]⊙
**Davidson, Janet Toll**, (AV) ..................... '39 '78 C.188 L.426 J.D. [Paul,H.J.&W.]
**Davis, Bradley T.** ................ '66 '93 C&L.1137 B.A., J.D. [Ⓐ Cooksey,H.M.&T.]
*LANGUAGES: Korean.
*PRACTICE AREAS: Litigation; Insurance Defense Law.
Davis, Joseph R. .............. '44 '75 C.426 B.S. L.1137 J.D. 2845 Mesa Verde Dr. E.
Davis, Samuelson, Blakely & Goldberg, LLP, (AV) ............ 535 Anton Blvd., Ste., 800
**Dawes, Daniel L.**, (BV) ............ '46 '74 C.112 B.S. L.1068 J.D. [Ⓒ Graham&J.] (Pat.)
*PRACTICE AREAS: Patent; Trademark; Copyright.
**Day, Alexandra M.** ..................... '52 '90 C.813 B.A. L.800 J.D. [Ⓐ Robins,K.M.&C.]
*LANGUAGES: French.
*PRACTICE AREAS: Product Liability Law; Tort and Personal Injury; General Civil Litigation.
Day, Rowland W., II, (BV) ........................ '55 '83 C.1109 B.S. L.1148 J.D. [Day&C.]
Day & Campbell, (AV) ............................................................ 3070 Bristol
**De Frenza, Marcello F.** ............ '63 '88 C.1097 B.S. L.800 J.D. [Ⓒ Pillsbury M.&S.]
deFries, Hiriam A. ............ '41 '77 C.172 B.S. L.1137 J.D. 3465 Santa Clara Circle
**Della Grotta, John F.** ........................ '53 '78 C.800 B.A. L.990 J.D. [Paul,H.J.&W.]
**De Luna, Maria** ................... '— '91 C.800 B.S. L.112 J.D. [Ⓐ Cooksey,H.M.&T.]
*LANGUAGES: Spanish.
*PRACTICE AREAS: Business; Corporate Law; Real Estate; NAFTA.
**Demetre, Dean A.**, (AV) ........... '55 '80 C.112 B.A. L.1068 J.D. [Sheppard,M.R.&H.]
*PRACTICE AREAS: Finance and Banking Law; Commercial Law; Problem Loan Workouts.
**Demmler, Carol Landis** ..................... '63 '89 C.117 B.A. L.608 J.D. [Ⓐ Rutan&T.]
*PRACTICE AREAS: Management, Labor and Employment Law.
**Dennington, Douglas J.** ..................... '67 '94 C.1074 B.S. L.990 J.D. [Ⓐ Rutan&T.]
*PRACTICE AREAS: Public Law.
**Diaz, Gregory G.** ......................... '62 '91 C.1042 B.A. L.1137 J.D. [Ⓐ Burke,W.&S.]
*PRACTICE AREAS: Municipal and Public Law.

**Dickinson, Steven L. '58 '81 C.112 B.A. L.1068 J.D.**
**Suite 1920, 650 Town Center Drive, 92626**
Telephone: 714-662-1600 Fax: 714-754-0444
Email: dassoc@chelsea.ios.com
*PRACTICE AREAS: Commercial Litigation; Intellectual Property Law; Insurance Policy Holders Law; Coverage Litigation.
Insurance Coverage, General Corporate, Intellectual Property Litigation and General Civil and Appellate Litigation in all State and Federal Courts.

*See Professional Biographies, COSTA MESA, CALIFORNIA*

Dill, Jeffrey ................ '61 '92 C.923 B.S. L.1137 J.D. Asst. Coun., 76 Products Co.
**DiPinto, Lawrence J.** .............. '64 '90 C.605 A.B. L.126 J.D. [Ⓐ Murtaugh,M.M.&N.]
**Djang, Edward B.**, (AV) ........................ '37 '76 C.905 B.A. L.30 J.D. [Graham&J.]
*LANGUAGES: Mandarin Chinese.
*PRACTICE AREAS: International Commercial Transactions; Real Estate; Intrastructure; Project Finance.
**Dolley, Leland C.** ........................... '35 '68 C.800 A.B. L.1049 J.D. [Burke,W.&S.]
*PRACTICE AREAS: Public Law; Municipal Law; Redevelopment Law; Municipal Finance Law; Municipal Planning and Environmental Law.
**Donnelly, Jean M.** ........................ '55 '81 C.321 A.B. L.276 J.D. [Ⓒ Latham&W.]
**Donnelly, John Kirk** ............... '67 '95 C.945 B.A. L.1049 J.D. [Murtaugh,M.M.&N.]
**Donovan, Mary A.** ........................ '68 '94 C.112 B.A. L.1068 J.D. [Ⓐ Latham&W.]
**Dorman-Davis, Jessica S.** .............. '48 '86 C.1042 B.A. L.800 J.D. [Ⓐ Paul,H.J.&W.]

**Dorsey & Whitney LLP, (AVⓉ)**
**Center Tower, 650 Town Center Drive, Suite 1850, P.O. Box 5066, 92626**⊙
Telephone: 714-662-7300
Member of Firm: Donald A. Kaul (Not admitted in CA); Jeffrey L Sikkema; Dennis Wong. Associates: Juan C. Basombrio; Nancy B. Smith (Not admitted in CA); Paul Nathan Tauger.
Banking and Commercial, Corporate Finance, Employee Benefits, Environmental, Estate Planning and Administration, Foreign Trade, Health Law, Government and Regulatory Affairs, Intellectual Property, International, Labor and Employment Law, Litigation, Real Estate, Tax, and Municipal and Public Authority Financing.
Representative Clients: First Bank National Assn. (Formerly First National Bank of Minneapolis); The McKnight Foundation; Deluxe Corp.; Mayo Clinic.
Minneapolis, Minnesota Office: 220 South 6th Street, 55402. Telephone: 612-340-2600. Cable Address: "Dorow" Telex: 290605. Answer-back "Dorsey Law MPS".
Rochester, Minnesota Office: 201 First Avenue, S.W., Suite 340, 55902. Telephone: 507-288-3156.
Des Moines, Iowa Office: 801 Grand, Suite 3900, 50309. Telephone: 515-283-1000.
New York, New York Office: 250 Park Avenue, 10177. Telephone: 212-415-9200.
Washington, D.C. Office: Suite 200, 1330 Connecticut Avenue, N.W., 20036. Telephone: 202-452-6900.
Brussels, Belgium Office: 35 Square De Meeûs 1000. Telephone: 011-32-2-504-4611.
London, England Office: 3 Gracechurch Street, EC3V OAT. Telephone: 011-44-171-929-3334.
Billings, Montana Office: 1200 First Interstate Center, 401 North 31st Street, P.O. Box 7188, 59103. Telephone: 406-252-3800.

(This Listing Continued)

**Dorsey & Whitney LLP (Continued)**

Great Falls, Montana Office: 507 Davidson Building, 8 Third Street North, P.O. Box 1566, 59401. Telephone: 406-727-3632.
Missoula, Montana Office: 127 East Front Street, Suite 310, 59802. Telephone: 406-721-6025.
Denver, Colorado Office: 370 Seventeenth Street, Republic Plaza Building, Suite 4400, 80202-5644. Telephone: 303-629-3400.
Salt Lake City, Utah Office: First Interstate Plaza, 170 South Main Street, Suite 925, 84101. Telephone: 801-350-3581.
Fargo, North Dakota Office: Dakota Center, 51 North Broadway, Suite 402, P.O. Box 1344, 58107-1344. Telephone: 701-235-6000.
Seattle, Washington Office: Second and Seneca Building, 1191 Second Avenue, Suite 1440, 98101. Telephone: 206-654-5400.
Hong Kong Office: Suite 4003, Two Exchange Square, 8 Connaught Place, Central Hong Kong. Telephone: 011-852-252-65000. Fax: 011-852-252-43000.

*See Professional Biographies, COSTA MESA, CALIFORNIA*

**Dowling, James B.** ......................................... '47 '78 C.959 B.A. L.990 J.D. [P.E.Whalen]
Downer, John M., (BV) ........................ '42 '67 C.454 B.A. L.94 J.D. 3200 Park Ctr. Dr.
**Draper, Paul D.** ................................ '47 '90 C.768 B.A. L.1065 J.D. [Draper&W.]
*LANGUAGES: Mandarin.
*PRACTICE AREAS: Business Litigation; Property Tax Appeals; Employers Rights; Employees Rights; Real Estate Litigation.

**Draper & Walsh**
**3420 Bristol Street, #225, 92626**
Telephone: 714-557-9874 Fax: 714-557-9908
Paul D. Draper; Michael J. Walsh.
Litigation, General Business Litigation.

*See Professional Biographies, COSTA MESA, CALIFORNIA*

**Droste, Alan J.**, (BV) ................. '56 '82 C.339 B.S. L.1066 J.D. [Pillsbury M.&S.]
**Drummy, Stephen C.**, (AV) ........ '38 '66 C.112 B.S. L.1068 J.D. [Drummy K.W.&G.]
*PRACTICE AREAS: Commercial and Real Estate Litigation.

**Drummy King White & Gire, A Professional Corporation, (AV)**
**3200 Park Center Drive, Suite 1000, 92626**
Telephone: 714-850-1800 Fax: 714-850-4500
Stephen C. Drummy; John P. King, Jr.; Alan I. White; Charles W. Parret; Leroy M. Gire; Michael G. Joerger; Geoffrey S. Payne; Jeffrey M. Richard; Lisa A. Stepanski; Kenneth W. Curtis; Alan A. Greenberg;—Mark R. Beckington; Lawrence M. Burek; Karen Smith French; John D. Ott; Leigh Otsuka.
General Civil Practice, Litigation in all State and Federal Courts. Trial and Appellate Practice, Business, Real Estate, Public and Private Works Construction Law, Financial Institution Liability, Labor Law Matters, Commercial Litigation, Corporate Mergers and Acquisitions, Partnerships, Joint Ventures, Licensing, Securities Offerings, Sale and Leasings of Real Property.

*See Professional Biographies, COSTA MESA, CALIFORNIA*

Duarte, James M. ................... '58 '84 C.112 B.A. L.1067 J.D. 650 Town Center Dr.
**Dubin, Eric J.** ........................ '66 '92 C.37 B.S. L.61 J.D. [Ⓐ Murtaugh,M.M.&N.]
**Dubow, Tod R.** ......................... '64 '91 C.112 B.A. L.990 J.D. [Ⓐ Robins,K.M.&C.]
*PRACTICE AREAS: Commercial Litigation; Products Liability.
DuCote, Harold A., Jr. ..................................... '43 '70 C&L.347 B.S., J.D. [Aprahamian&D.]
**Duffy, Patrick J.**, (AV) ................... '38 '66 C.36 B.S. L.37 LL.B. [Cooksey,H.M.&T.]
*PRACTICE AREAS: Litigation; Personal Injury; Insurance Defense Law; Employment Litigation.
Duggins, Karen Imbernino .... '64 '91 C.154 B.A. L.767 J.D. 650 Town Center Dr., 4th Fl.
Duke, Gerstel, Shearer & Bregante, LLP, (AV) ........ 3200 Park Center Drive, Suite 1000
**Duncan, Matthew S.** ...................... '53 '84 C.112 B.A. L.809 J.D. [Buckner,A.&Y.]
**Dundas, Natalie Sibbald** ................. '71 '96 C.028 B.A. L.276 J.D. [Ⓐ Rutan&T.]
**Dunlavey, Dean G.** ......................... '58 '84 C.309 A.B. L.1066 J.D. [Ⓒ Latham&W.]
**Dunn, Eric L.** ................................ '62 '95 C.801 B.S. L.1137 J.D. [Ⓐ Rutan&T.]
*PRACTICE AREAS: Public Law.
Dunn, Joseph L. ........................ '58 '83 C.755 B.A. L.494 J.D. 600 Anton Blvd.
Dunn, Michael T. ....................... '48 '85 C.940 B.A. L.1137 J.D. 2755 Gannet Dr.
**Earley, Ronit D.** ....................... '71 '95 C.112 B.A. L.178 J.D. [Ⓐ Latham&W.]
**Easton, Brian W.** ................................ '68 '95 C&L.101 B.S., J.D. [W.D.Easton]
*PRACTICE AREAS: Torts; Personal Injury; Litigation; Medical Malpractice.

**Easton, W. Douglas, Law Offices of, (AV) '42 '71 C.101 A.B. L.1066 J.D.** ⒷⒷ
**3200 Park Center Drive, Suite 1000, 92626**
Telephone: 714-850-4590 Fax: 714-850-4500
*LANGUAGES: Finnish.
*PRACTICE AREAS: Personal Injury Law; Medical Malpractice Law; Legal Malpractice Law; Products Liability Law; Insurance Bad Faith.
—Anderson L. Washburn; Russel W. Jones; Brian W. Easton.
Civil Litigation in Personal Injury, Medical Malpractice, Products Liability and Legal Malpractice.

*See Professional Biographies, COSTA MESA, CALIFORNIA*

**Edwards, Troy A.** ..................... '62 '90 C.763 B.S. L.1049 J.D. [Ⓐ Lewis,D.B.&B.]
**Einspahr, Leroy** .................... '46 '85 C.112 B.S. L.1137 J.D. [Ⓒ Cooksey,H.M.&T.]
*PRACTICE AREAS: Litigation; Personal Injury; Insurance Defense; Domestic Relations Law.
**Ekvall, Lei Lei Wang** ..................... '65 '92 C.112 B.S. L.800 J.D. [Ⓐ Albert,W.&G.]
*LANGUAGES: Chinese.
*PRACTICE AREAS: Bankruptcy; Litigation.
**Ellis, Stephen A.**, (BV) ....................... '57 '85 C.1042 B.A. L.1068 J.D. [Rutan&T.]
*PRACTICE AREAS: Real Estate; Construction; Civil Trial.
Ellsworth, Anthony K. ............................ '35 '74 C.1077 B.A. L.426 J.D. 2900 Bristol St.
Ellsworth, Todd A. ............ '62 '88 C.800 B.A. L.990 J.D. 2900 Bristol St., Suite J105
**Ely, Thomas W.**, (AV) ....................... '42 '73 C.1077 B.A. L.990 J.D. [Ely,F.&H.]
*PRACTICE AREAS: Products Liability Law; Negligence Law.

**Ely, Fritz & Hogan, (AV)** ⒷⒷ
**3100 Bristol Street #200, 92626**
Telephone: 714-556-1480 Telecopier: 714-556-2863
Members of Firm: Thomas W. Ely; James H. Fritz; Michael G. Hogan; Jerome D. Rybarczyk;—Charles A. Correia; Ronald F. Templer; Allen D. MacNeil. Of Counsel: Gerald W. Mouzis.
General Civil Practice in all State and Federal Courts. Products Liability, Construction, Insurance and General Negligence, Toxic Tort Defense, Aviation Law, Insurance Fraud.

*See Professional Biographies, COSTA MESA, CALIFORNIA*

**Engel, Jason O.** ............................ '62 '87 C.378 B.S. L.477 J.D. [Ⓒ Paul,H.J.&W.]
**Enright, Madelyn A.** ................... '55 '83 C.763 B.A. L.426 J.D. [Murtaugh,M.M.&N.]
*PRACTICE AREAS: Construction Litigation; Personal Injury Law; Insurance Defense Law; General Civil Trial.
Epp, Timothy Lee ............ '58 '93 C.350 B.S.I.E. L.112 J.D. 3200 Park Ctr. Dr. (Pat.)
**Faber, Malinda A.** ............................ '68 '93 C.112 B.A. L.800 J.D. [Ⓐ Paul,H.J.&W.]
**Farrell, Joseph B.** ............................ '63 '88 C.645 B.A. L.884 J.D. [Latham&W.]
*PRACTICE AREAS: Employment Law; Public Accommodations; Housing Discrimination; Litigation.
**Farrell, Sean P.** ............................ '67 '96 C.112 B.A. L.1065 J.D. [Ⓐ Rutan&T.]
*LANGUAGES: Spanish, French and Portuguese.
*PRACTICE AREAS: Civil Litigation.

**Feldhake, Robert J., Law Offices of, (AV) '54 '79 C.57 B.A. L.209 J.D.** ⒷⒷ
**Plaza Tower, Suite 1730, 600 Anton Boulevard, 92626-7124**⊙
Telephone: 714-438-3885 Fax: 714-438-3888
*PRACTICE AREAS: Litigation; General Business Law.
Associates: Gary W. Dolinski (Resident, San Diego Office); Lorinda B. Harris.
Litigation. General Business-Corporate Law.
San Diego, California Office: 501 West Broadway, Suite 1600, Koll Center, 92101. Telephone: 619-235-9443. Facsimile: 619-235-9449.

*See Professional Biographies, COSTA MESA, CALIFORNIA*

Fell, Sheila, (AV) ... '— '80 C.483 R.N. L.1137 J.D. 3185-B Airway Ave.
**Fiacco, Violet F.** ... '49 '88 C.1042 B.S. L.426 J.D. [Ⓐ Paul,H.J.&W.]
Field, Scott F. ... '56 '82 C.112 A.B. L.1068 J.D. 3200 Park Ctr. Dr.
**Finkelstein, Mark A.** ... '68 '94 C.112 B.A. L.800 J.D. [Ⓐ Latham&W.]
Fiore, Albert A., (BV) ... '49 '75 C.1042 B.A. L.770 J.D. 3200 Bristol St.
Fitzmaurice, Victor E. ... '39 '78 C.112 B.S. L.426 J.D. Asst. Coun., 76 Products Co.

**Fitzpatrick, Cella, Harper & Scinto**
**650 Town Center Drive, Suite 1800, 92626⊙**
**Telephone: 714-540-8700 Facsimile: 714-540-9823**
**Resident Partner: Michael K. O'Neill. Resident Associates: Mark J. Itri; Paul A. Pysher; Joseph G. Swan; Nandu A. Talwalkar.**
**Intellectual Property Practice. Patent, Trademark, Copyright, Trade Secret, Unfair Competition, Computer, Licensing, Antitrust and International Trade Law. Trials and Appeals in Federal and State Courts and Administrative Agencies.**
**New York, N.Y. Office: 277 Park Avenue. Telephone: 212-758-2400. International-Telex: FCHS 236262. Cable Address: "Fitzcel New York". Facsimile: 212-758-2982.**
**Washington, D.C. Office: 1001 Pennsylvania Avenue, N.W. Telephone: 202-347-8100. Facsimile: 202-347-8136.**

***See Professional Biographies, COSTA MESA, CALIFORNIA***

**Flanagan, Kelly M.** ... '64 '89 C.112 B.A. L.426 J.D. [Ⓐ Lewis,D.B.&B.]
**Flandrick, J. Robert**, (AV) ... '28 '56 C&L.800 B.S., J.D. [Burke,W.&S.] (⊙Camarillo)
*PRACTICE AREAS: Municipal Law; Eminent Domain Law; Redevelopment Law.
**Flattum, David C.** ... '64 '90 C.800 B.A. L.976 J.D. [Ⓐ Latham&W.]
Flores, Cirilo ... '48 '76 C.426 B.A. L.813 J.D. P.O. Box 3276
**Flynn, Mark S.** ... '53 '84 C.112 B.A. L.1068 J.D. [Ⓐ McCauley&Assoc.]
*REPORTED CASES: National Solar Equipment Owners' Assn. v. Grumman Corp., 235 Cal.App.3d 1273 (1991); Three Valleys Municipal Water District v. E. F. Hutton & Co., Inc., 925 F.2d 1136 (9th Cir. 1991); Knapp v. Gomez, (1991 Transfer Binder) Fed. Sec.L.Rep. (CCH) paragraphs 96, 166, at 90, 918 (S.D.Cal. June 25, 1991).
*PRACTICE AREAS: Securities Litigation.
Fondler, Howard ... '35 '72 C.112 B.S. L.809 J.D. 628 W. 19th St.
Fong, Alison M. Profeta ... '60 '86 C.1212 B.A. L.464 J.D. 611 Anton Blvd.
Forbath, Kathleen M. ... '59 '84 C.426 B.A. L.1068 J.D. 611 Anton Blvd.
**Forbes, Laura A.** ... '63 '90 C.112 B.A. L.800 J.D. [Ⓐ Paul,H.J.&W.]
**Forsyth, Marcia A.**, (AV) ... '51 '77 C.112 B.A. L.1068 J.D. [Rutan&T.]
*PRACTICE AREAS: Commercial; Business; Real Estate; Construction.
Fouste, James E. ... '48 '77 C.112 B.A. L.990 J.D. 650 Town Ctr. Dr.
**Fowler, Charles Calvin** '64 '94 C.112 B.S.B.E. L.1068 J.D. [Ⓐ Lyon&L.] (See Pat. Sect.)
*PRACTICE AREAS: Patent, Trademark, Copyright; Intellectual Property.
**Francis, Thomas E.** ... '62 '87 C.112 B.A. L.464 J.D. [Ⓐ Lewis,D.B.&B.]
Franklin, Selim S. ... '30 '57 C.668 B.A. L.813 J.D. Ret. Mun. Ct. J.
**Fraser, James M.** ... '54 '81 C.112 B.A. L.1137 J.D. [P.E.Whalen]
**Frazier, Mark B.**, (AV) ... '56 '82 C.605 A.B. L.800 J.D. [Rutan&T.]
*PRACTICE AREAS: Environmental Counseling and Litigation (Liability for Contamination and Cost Recovery); Business Litigation; Unfair Competition; Trade Secrets; Real Property Litigation (Secured Transactions and Seismic Liability).
**Freeman, Corrine M.** ... '64 '91 C.912 B.S. L.800 J.D. [Ⓐ Lyon&L.] (See Pat. Sect.)
*PRACTICE AREAS: Intellectual Property.
**French, Karen Smith** ... '65 '91 C.276 B.S.B.A. L.665 J.D. [Ⓐ Drummy K.W.&G.]
*PRACTICE AREAS: Business and Corporate Law.
Friedemann, F. K., (AV) ... '31 '56 C.879 B.A. L.800 LL.B. 650 Town Center Dr.
**Frieden, Clifford E.**, (AV) ... '49 '74 C.112 B.A. L.1066 J.D. [Rutan&T.]
*PRACTICE AREAS: Civil Trial; Commercial.
**Fritz, James H.** ... '45 '74 C.339 B.S.E.E. L.426 J.D. [Ely,F.&H.] (Pat.)
*PRACTICE AREAS: Aviation Law; Products Liability Law; Construction Law; Negligence Law; Patent Litigation.
Frost, Oakley C., (AV) ... '35 '58 C&L.228 A.B., LL.B. [Ⓐ Menke,F.&C.]
**Fullman, Jay D.** ... '56 '80 C.990 B.A. L.800 J.D. [Ⓒ Murtaugh,M.M.&N.]
*PRACTICE AREAS: Real Property Law; Construction Litigation; Franchise Law.
**Gage, Kim P.**, (BV) ... '53 '78 C.112 B.A. L.61 J.D. [Cooksey,H.M.&T.]
*PRACTICE AREAS: Business and Commercial Litigation; Creditor Bankruptcy Litigation.
Galey, Robert L. ... '59 '88 C.800 B.A. L.1137 J.D. 611 Anton Blvd.
Galosic, Joseph M. ... '62 '87 C.800 B.A. L.990 J.D. [Davis,S.B.&G.]
Garber, Paul E., (BV) ... '34 '61 C.800 B.A. L.426 J.D. 3185 Airway Avenue-B
**Garibaldi, David J., III**, (AV) ... '53 '78 C.112 B.A. L.1068 J.D. [Ⓒ Rutan&T.]
*PRACTICE AREAS: Probate and Estate Planning.
**Garner, Scott B.** ... '66 '91 C.813 A.B. L.309 J.D. [Ⓐ Latham&W.]
Garrett, Gerald A., Law Offices of, (AV) '37 '65 C.154 B.S.B.A. L.800 J.D. 3150 Bristol St., Ste 240
**Garrett, John C.**, (AV) ... '39 '66 C.813 B.A. L.1065 J.D. [Pillsbury M.&S.]
**Gay, William T.** ... '57 '83 C&L.911 B.A., J.D. [McIntyre B.&B.]
*LANGUAGES: Japanese.
*PRACTICE AREAS: Corporate; Finance; Real Estate; High Technology; International Transactions.
Gazin, Michael H., (AV) ... '49 '74 C.768 B.A. L.770 J.D. [Obrien,G.&P.]
Gelber, Joseph A. ... '51 '78 C.1077 B.A. L.809 J.D. 600 Anton Blvd.
Gensler, Howard ... '57 '83 C.112 B.A. L.1066 J.D. 496 Traverse Dr.
**Gerard, Robert J., Jr.** ... '55 '87 C.1108 B.A. L.1049 J.D. [Ⓒ Pillsbury M.&S.]
**Geriak, James W., (A Professional Corporation)**, (AV) '34 '60 C.688 B.Ch.E. L.276 J.D. [Lyon&L.] (See Pat. Sect.)
*PRACTICE AREAS: Patent, Trademark, Trade Regulation, Unfair Competition, Antitrust; Intellectual Property.
**Giampolo, Charles H.**, (BV) ... '56 '82 C.555 B.A. L.809 J.D. [C.H.Giampolo]
*PRACTICE AREAS: Sales and Secured Commercial Transactions; Contract Law; Enforcement of Judgement Law; Collection Law.

**Giampolo, Charles H., A Prof. Corp., Law Offices of, (BV)**
**Imperial Bank Tower, 695 Town Center Drive Suite 1450, Fourteenth Floor, 92626**
**Telephone: 714-979-9044 Fax: 714-979-9047**
**Charles H. Giampolo.**
**Languages: French and Italian**
**Corporate Law; Sales and Secured Commercial Transactions; Contract Law; Business Law; Enforcement of Judgments; Collections.**

***See Professional Biographies, COSTA MESA, CALIFORNIA***

**Ginsburg, Stephan, Oringher & Richman, P.C., (AV)**
**535 Anton Boulevard Suite 800, 92626-1902⊙**
**Telephone: 714-241-0420 Fax: 714-241-0622**
**Of Counsel: Steven Brower; Gary S. Mobley; Sterling A. Smith;—Tracy L. Anielski; Joel David Covelman; Keyvan Samini.**
**General Civil Practice, General Business Litigation, Health Care Law, Corporate and Business Transactions, Professional Liability Defense, Employment Litigation, Coverage Litigation, Intellectual Property Litigation, White Collar Criminal Defense, Real Estate Litigation, Product Liability, Securities Fraud and RICO Defense, Consumer Credit Litigation, Copyright, Trademark, Antitrust and Unfair Competition Law.**
**Los Angeles, California Office: 10100 Santa Monica Boulevard, Eighth Floor, 90067-4012. Telephone: 310-557-2009. Fax: 310-551-0283.**

***See Professional Biographies, COSTA MESA, CALIFORNIA***

**Giovannone, John J.** ... '50 '75 C.674 A.B. L.1065 J.D. [Sheppard,M.R.&H.]
*PRACTICE AREAS: Commodities Law; Securities Law; Life Sciences.

**Gire, Leroy M.**, (AV) ... '38 '64 C.112 B.S. L.1068 LL.B. [Drummy K.W.&G.]
*PRACTICE AREAS: Public and Private Works Construction; Bid Disputes; Contract Formation and Interpretation; Preparing and Defending against Claims arising during construction; Litigation and ADR Procedures.
**Glass, Geoffrey T.** ... '54 '80 C.31 B.A. L.893 J.D. [Robins,K.M.&C.]
*PRACTICE AREAS: Insurance Litigation; Commercial Litigation.
Glasser, Frederick L. ... '59 '84 C.112 B.A. L.800 J.D. 3090 Bristol St.
**Godshall, Randolph B.**, (AV) ... '52 '79 C.976 B.A. L.1066 J.D. [Sheppard,M.R.&H.]
*PRACTICE AREAS: Litigation; Estate Planning; Probate Law; Trust Law.
Goff, Robert K., (A Professional Corporation) '59 '85 C.763 B.S. L.1049 J.D. [Duke,G.S.&B.]⊙
Goldberg, Gerald N. ... '33 '65 C.994 B.A. L.724 J.D. [Davis,S.B.&G.]
**Golden, Jeffrey I.** ... '62 '87 C.112 B.A. L.800 J.D. [Albert,W.&G.]
*PRACTICE AREAS: Insolvency and Litigation.
**Goldfarb, Jeffrey A.** ... '60 '86 C.112 A.B. L.1065 J.D. [Rutan&T.]
*PRACTICE AREAS: Land Use Law; Municipal and Zoning; Civil Rights.
**Golison, Jennifer Ann** ... '64 '89 C.426 B.A. L.602 J.D. [Ⓐ Albert,W.&G.]
*LANGUAGES: French.
*PRACTICE AREAS: Insolvency; Trustee Representation; General Business Litigation.
**Goodin, Karen C.** ... '63 '91 C.800 A.B. L.1066 J.D. [Ⓐ Riordan&M.]
*PRACTICE AREAS: General Corporate; Securities.
**Goon, Steven John** ... '68 '94 C.112 B.A. L.1065 J.D. [Ⓐ Rutan&T.]
*PRACTICE AREAS: Construction; Civil Trial; Business Litigation.

**Graham & James LLP, (AV)**
**650 Town Center Drive, 6th Floor, 92626⊙**
**Telephone: 714-751-8800 Cable Address: "Chalgray Newport Beach" Telex: 4722041 Telecopier: 714-751-8808**
**Email: jscott@gj.com URL: http://www.gj.com**
**Resident Partners: Edward B. Djang; James A. McQueen; W. James Scott, Jr.; Kevin K. Takeuchi; Richard K. Zepfel; Mark A. Ziemba. Of Counsel: Daniel L. Dawes; Gregg P. Martino. Special Counsel: Phillip Ashman. Resident Associates: Laura A. Homan; Kenneth B. Julian; Brian A. Kumamoto; Sandra Lau; Karl Sandoval.**
**General Practice including Litigation in State and Federal Courts. Corporation, Commercial, Intellectual Property, International Business, Labor, Real Estate, Tax, Environmental, Bankruptcy.**
**Other offices located in: San Francisco, Los Angeles, Palo Alto, Sacramento and Fresno, California; Washington, D.C.; Seattle, Washington; New York, New York; Milan, Italy; Beijing, China; Tokyo, Japan; London, England; Dusseldorf, Germany.**
**Associated Offices: Deacons Graham & James, Hong Kong, Sydney, Melbourne, Brisbane, Perth and Canberra, Australia.**
**Affiliated Offices: Deacons Graham & James, Hanoi and Ho Chi Minh City, Vietnam; Taipei, Taiwan and Bangkok, Thailand; In association with Dewi Soeharto & Rekan, Jakarta, Indonesia; Graham & James in affiliation with Taylor Joynson Garrett, London, England, Bucharest, Romania and Brussels, Belgium; Mishare M. Al-Ghazali & Partners, Safat, Kuwait; Law Firm of Salah Al-Hejailan, Jeddah and Riyadh, Saudi Arabia.**

***See Professional Biographies, COSTA MESA, CALIFORNIA***

**Graves, Geoffrey A.** ... '69 '94 C.800 B.A. L.1049 J.D. [Ⓐ Murtaugh,M.M.&N.]
**Graves, Maureen R.** ... '57 '90 C.188 B.A. L.569 J.D. [Ⓐ Daehnke&C.]
*LANGUAGES: Spanish and Mandarin Chinese.
*PRACTICE AREAS: Litigation; Special Education Law.
**Green, Mary M.** ... '55 '80 C&L.800 B.A., J.D. [Rutan&T.]
*PRACTICE AREAS: Real Estate; Environmental.
**Green, Oliver F.**, (AV) ... '24 '51 C.309 A.B. L.659 J.D. [Ⓒ Paul,H.J.&W.]
**Greenberg, Alan A.** ... '64 '89 C.188 A.B. L.94 J.D. [Drummy K.W.&G.]
*PRACTICE AREAS: Civil Litigation with emphasis on General Business Law; Real Estate Law; Commercial Litigation; Bankruptcy Litigation.
**Greenberg, Bart** ... '63 '89 C.112 B.A. L.1066 J.D. [Ⓐ Riordan&M.]
*PRACTICE AREAS: Business and Finance.
**Greene, Allison A.** ... '68 '95 C.976 B.A. L.309 J.D. [Ⓐ Lewis,D.B.&B.]
Gregor, Vanessa J. ... '67 '92 C&L.990 B.A., J.D. 3200 Park Ctr. Dr., Ste 610
Grier, James F. ... '49 '77 C.112 B.A. L.1240 J.D. 925 Mackenzie
**Guenther, Craig E.** ... '60 '86 C.1109 B.A. L.426 J.D. [Booth,M.&S.]
**Guilford, Andrew J.**, (AV) ... '50 '75 C.112 A.B. L.1068 J.D. [Sheppard,M.R.&H.]
*PRACTICE AREAS: Business Trial Law, Appellate Practice, Arbitration Law.
Gunchick, Jeffrey T. ... '55 '85 C.209 B.S.C. L.851 J.D. Assoc. Coun., US Facilities Corp.
Haeussler, Richard L. ... '41 '67 C.112 B.S. L.802 J.D. 3151 Airway Ave.
**Halkowich, Harry A.** ... '45 '75 C.705 B.S. L.990 J.D. [Murtaugh,M.M.&N.]
*PRACTICE AREAS: Business Law; Franchising; Real Estate; Commercial Litigation.
Hall, H. Jack, (BV) ... '23 '50 C.350 B.S. L.477 J.D. 1859 Tahiti Dr.
**Hamilton, James W.**, (AV) ... '32 '60 C&L.813 A.B., LL.B. [Ⓒ Paul,H.J.&W.]
**Hammerbeck, Jon A.** ... '55 '81 C.112 B.A. L.800 J.D. [Ⓐ Cooksey,H.M.&T.]
*PRACTICE AREAS: Litigation; Personal Injury; Insurance Defense Law.
**Hampel, Leonard A., Jr.**, (AV) ... '39 '65 C.112 B.A. L.1068 LL.B. [Rutan&T.]
*PRACTICE AREAS: Civil Trial; Land Use Law; Environmental.
**Hanson, Andrew P.** ... '68 '95 C.101 B.A. L.228 J.D. [Ⓐ Paul,H.J.&W.]
**Harbottle, S. Daniel** ... '57 '91 C.679 B.A. L.347 J.D. [Ⓐ Rutan&T.]
*PRACTICE AREAS: General Practice; Land Use Law; Environmental; Civil Trial.
Hargrave, Allison C. ... '68 '91 C.880 B.A. L.861 J.D. 695 Town Ctr. Dr.
**Harker, Jay D.** ... '66 '93 C.101 B.S. L.1066 J.D. [Ⓐ Lewis,D.B.&B.]
Harlan, Robert W., (P.C.), (BV) ... '39 '67 C.768 B.A. L.1065 J.D. 650 Town Ctr.
**Harris, Lorinda B.** ... '68 '95 C.112 B.A. L.1049 J.D. [Ⓐ R.J.Feldhake]
*LANGUAGES: German.
*PRACTICE AREAS: Business Litigation.
**Harrison, Lien Ski** ... '45 '87 C.112 B.A. L.1137 J.D. [Rutan&T.]
*PRACTICE AREAS: Education Law; Public Sector; Labor Law; Municipal; Administrative.
**Hartley, Teresa M.** ... '53 '91 C.36 B.A. L.1137 J.D. [Hartley&M.]
*PRACTICE AREAS: Workers Compensation; Family Law.

**Hartley & Mazarei**
**Plaza Tower, 600 Anton Boulevard, Suite 1250, 92626**
**Telephone: 714-444-0777 Facsimile: 714-444-1229**
**Members of Firm: Teresa M. Hartley; Rayehe Mazarei.**
**Workers Compensation, Family Law, Immigration and Transactional Business Law, Corporate Law.**

***See Professional Biographies, COSTA MESA, CALIFORNIA***

**Hay, Howard C.**, (AV) ... '44 '70 C.228 B.A. L.477 J.D. [Paul,H.J.&W.]
**Hayes, Brett L.** ... '69 '96 C.880 B.S. L.426 J.D. [Buckner,A.&Y.]
*PRACTICE AREAS: Corporate Law; Real Estate Law; Litigation.
**Hayes, Griffith H.**, (BV) ... '57 '85 C.112 B.A. L.61 J.D. [Ⓐ Cooksey,H.M.&T.]
*PRACTICE AREAS: Construction Defect Litigation; Personal Injury Litigation.
Helfand, Robert F. ... '50 '76 C.705 B.A. L.1338 J.D. 650 Town Center Dr.
**Henderson, Christopher J.** ... '63 '88 C.36 B.A. L.1049 J.D. [Ⓐ Cooksey,H.M.&T.]
*PRACTICE AREAS: Business Litigation; Personal Injury; Insurance Defense Law.
**Henderson, Heather Anne** ... '61 '92 C.1109 B.S. L.940 J.D. [Ⓐ Lewis,D.B.&B.]
**Henderson, Michael S.** ... '70 '95 C.636 B.S. L.464 J.D. [Ⓐ Robins,K.M.&C.]
*PRACTICE AREAS: Insurance; Litigation.
**Henry, Paula F.** ... '51 '88 C.999 B.S.N. L.809 J.D. [Ⓐ Lewis,D.B.&B.]
Hess, Edward W., Jr., (BV) ... '52 '78 C.112 B.A. L.426 J.D. 650 Town Center Dr.
**Hesse, Helen E.** ... '47 '88 C.112 B.A. L.1137 J.D. [Ⓐ Lewis,D.B.&B.]
**Heuser, Gregory M.** ... '46 '90 C.770 B.S. L.1137 J.D. [Ⓐ Murtaugh,M.M.&N.]
**Hickman, Donald P.**, (AV) ... '46 '74 C.966 B.S. L.1065 J.D. [Pillsbury M.&S.]
**Hidalgo, Richard Paul** ... '67 '95 C.846 B.A. L.1049 J.D. [Murtaugh,M.M.&N.]
**Hill, Walter B., Jr.**, (AV) ... '43 '77 C.605 B.A. L.809 J.D. [Booth,M.&S.]

**Himmelstein, Mark S.**, (BV) ........'57 '82 C.228 B.A. L.464 J.D. [Murtaugh,M.M.&N.]
*PRACTICE AREAS: Construction Litigation; Professional Malpractice; General Civil Trial.
Hittner, Bernard J. ........................'54 '80 C.813 B.S. L.426 J.D. 245 Fischer Ave.
**Hochner, David H.** ........................'48 '82 C.1040 B.A. L.1067 J.D. [Ⓐ Rutan&T.]
*PRACTICE AREAS: General Practice; Civil Trial; Business; Construction; Real Estate.
**Hodel, Matthew A.**, (AV) ..............'55 '80 C.1074 B.A. L.1065 J.D. [Paul,H.J.&W.]
**Hogan, Michael G.** ..............................'46 '76 C.679 B.S. L.345 J.D. [Ely,F.&H.]
*PRACTICE AREAS: Products Liability Law; Negligence Law.
**Holcombe, Robert S.** '42 '68 C.674 A.B. L.178 J.D.
(adm. in NY; not adm. in CA) V.P., Secy. & Gen. Coun., Apria Healthcare Grp., Inc.
**Holt, David C.** ..........................'61 '88 C.112 B.S. L.1049 J.D. [Ⓐ Murtaugh,M.M.&N.]
**Homan, Laura A.** ..........................'65 '90 C.861 B.A. L.990 J.D. [Ⓐ Graham&J.]
**Hood, Michael A.**, (AV) ........................'49 '76 C.800 A.B. L.1068 J.D. [Paul,H.J.&W.]
Horan, William C. ..........................'41 '75 C.1042 B.S. L.1137 J.D. 2706 Harbor Blvd.
Hornak, Maria A. ..................................................'— '79 P.O. Box 1950‡
**Hornak, Michael T.**, (AV) ..................'53 '78 C.976 B.A. L.1068 J.D. [Rutan&T.]
*PRACTICE AREAS: Officers, Directors, Fiduciary Litigation and Counseling; Computer and Proprietary Rights Litigation and Licensing; Unfair Competition; Business Litigation; Trademark.
Hovatter, Eric M. ..................'59 '92 C.763 B.S. L.1188 J.D. 3205 Minnesota Ave.
**Howard, Bruce P.** ..........................'53 '84 C.976 B.A. L.309 J.D. [Latham&W.]
**Howard, Marven E.**, (AV) ..........'32 '64 C.112 B.S. L.809 J.D. [Cooksey,H.M.&T.]
*PRACTICE AREAS: Probate; Trusts; Estate Planning Law.
Howell, Debby L. ..........................'55 '81 C.502 B.S. L.734 J.D. 611 Anton Blvd.
**Howell, Paul R.**, (BVⓉ) '48 '77 C.878 B.S. L.678 J.D.
[Booth,M.&S.] (⊙San Diego, CA)
**Howell, Richard K.** ..........................'64 '89 C.112 B.A. L.1066 J.D. [Ⓐ Rutan&T.]
*PRACTICE AREAS: General Practice; Civil Trial; Sports and Entertainment.
Hubbell, Jonathan '46 '78 C.311 B.A. L.464 J.D.
Asst. Gen. Coun., Prudential Real Estate Affiliates, Inc.
Huckenpahler, Robert H., (BV) .......'29 '57 C.221 B.A. L.426 LL.B. 2970 Harbor Blvd.
**Hughes, David L.** ..........................'49 '86 C.101 B.S. L.464 J.D. [Booth,M.&S.]
**Hultman, Madonna L.** ..............'67 '92 C.1044 B.A. L.107 J.D. [Ⓐ Lewis,D.B.&B.]
Hundley, Henry R. ..........................'23 '50 C.437 L.273 LL.B. 3359 Nevada Ave.‡
**Hurlbut, John B., Jr.**, (AV) ...................'39 '65 C&L.813 B.A., J.D. [Rutan&T.]
*PRACTICE AREAS: Real Estate Litigation; Civil Trial.
**Hyden, Cary K.** ..........................'57 '84 C.1105 B.A. L.846 J.D. [Latham&W.]
**Hyland, Charles J.** ....................'61 '88 C.112 B.A. L.1049 J.D. [Ⓐ Lewis,D.B.&B.]
**Ibrahim, F. Albert** ..........................'61 '88 C.97 B.A. L.990 J.D. [Ⓐ Case&Assoc.]
*LANGUAGES: French and Arabic.
*PRACTICE AREAS: Civil Trial Practice; Construction Defects/Claims; Business General Litigation; Real Estate Litigation.
**Immell, Michael W.**, (AV) ..................'38 '65 C.813 B.A. L.1068 J.D. [Rutan&T.]
*PRACTICE AREAS: Real Estate.
**Isenberg, David E.** ......................'60 '86 C.112 B.A. L.1068 J.D. [Lewis,D.B.&B.]
**Itri, Mark J.** ..... '63 '90 C.94 B.S.E.E. L.818 J.D. [Ⓐ Fitzpatrick,C.H.&S.] (See Pat. Sect.)
**Jansen, Allan W.**, (AV) ....... '48 '78 C.339 B.S. L.365 J.D. [Lyon&L.] (See Pat. Sect.)
*PRACTICE AREAS: Patent, Trademark, Copyright, Unfair Competition.
Jaskulski, Alfred A. ..........................'27 '70 C.588 L.990 J.D. 2706 Harbor Blvd.
**Jeffries, Countess Pease** ..................'45 '77 C.329 B.S.E.E. L.309 J.D. [Jeffries A.]
*LANGUAGES: Spanish and Farsi.
*PRACTICE AREAS: Commercial Litigation; Collections; Subrogation.

**Jeffries Advocates Law Offices**
**485 East 17th Street, Suite 390, 92627**
**Telephone: 714-722-0055 Fax: 714-722-8416**
**Email: JeffAdvLaw@aol.com**
**Countess Pease Jeffries.**
**Enforcement of Judgments, Commercial Litigation, Collections, Subrogation.**
***See Professional Biographies, COSTA MESA, CALIFORNIA***

**Jenkins, Fred A.** ..........................'69 '96 C.309 B.A. L.1065 J.D. [Ⓐ Rutan&T.]
**Jenson, M. Katherine** ..........................'58 '83 C.161 B.A. L.608 J.D. [Rutan&T.]
*PRACTICE AREAS: Civil Rights; Municipal and Zoning; Land Use Law; Appellate Practice.
**Joerger, Michael G.** ..................'54 '81 C.1109 A.B. L.426 J.D. [Drummy K.W.&G.]
*PRACTICE AREAS: Civil Litigation with emphasis on Labor, Business and Construction Law.
**Johnson, Beverly A.** ..........................'— '93 L.800 J.D. [Ⓐ Sheppard,M.R.&H.]
*PRACTICE AREAS: Litigation.
**Johnson, C. Brad** ..................'58 '88 C.101 B.S. L.878 J.D. [Ⓐ Cooksey,H.M.&T.]
*PRACTICE AREAS: Real Estate; Corporate; Business Litigation.
**Johnson, Jarret L.** ..........................'67 '93 C.612 B.S. L.426 J.D. [Ⓐ Paul,H.J.&W.]
**Johnson, Robert A.** ................'66 '91 C&L.352 B.B.A., J.D. [Ⓐ McCormick,K.&B.]
*PRACTICE AREAS: Business Litigation; Civil Litigation; Water Law; Real Property Law; Condemnation.
**Johnson, Scott G.** ..................'59 '86 C.493 B.S. L.1035 J.D. [Robins,K.M.&C.]
*PRACTICE AREAS: Insurance Litigation; Commercial Litigation; General Litigation.
**Johnson, Wayne Robert** ................'64 '96 C.579 B.S. L.585 J.D. [Ⓐ Larsen&Assoc.]
*PRACTICE AREAS: Corporations; Mergers and Acquisitions; State and Federal Taxation; Litigation; Commercial.
Jolly, Cameron M. ................'64 '87 C&L.1137 B.S.L., J.D. Ste 510, 575 Anton Blvd.
**Jones, Alan M.** ..........................'47 '80 C.1201 B.S. L.284 J.D. [Robins,K.M.&C.]
*PRACTICE AREAS: Personal Injury Law; Insurance Litigation; Construction Litigation.
Jones, Clare R. ..........................'65 '91 C.112 B.A. L.426 J.D. [McClay&A.]
**Jones, H. Gilbert**, (AV) ..................'27 '57 C.976 B.E. L.1068 J.D. [Lewis,D.B.&B.]
**Jones, Russel W.** ..........................'66 '94 C.101 B.A. L.462 J.D. [Ⓐ W.D.Easton]
*LANGUAGES: Spanish.
*PRACTICE AREAS: Personal Injury; Medical Malpractice; Business Litigation.
**Julian, Kenneth B.** ..........................'65 '90 C.112 B.A. L.1065 J.D. [Ⓐ Graham&J.]
*PRACTICE AREAS: Litigation.
Justice, M. Flynn, III ..........................'63 '89 C&L.878 B.S., J.D. 2995 Redhill Ave.
**Kacer, Jayne Taylor** ..........................'51 '85 C.768 B.A. L.426 J.D. [Rutan&T.]
*PRACTICE AREAS: Complex Litigation; Title Insurance Litigation; Product Liability; Civil Trial.
Kaplan, Kenneth M., (AV) '47 '72 C.605 A.B. L.813 J.D.
Plaza Towr., 600 Anton Blvd.
**Kappos, John C.** ..........................'63 '94 C&L.112 B.S., J.D. [Ⓐ Lyon&L.]
*PRACTICE AREAS: Patent, Trademark, Copyright; Intellectual Property.
**Kaul, Donald A.**, (AVⓉ) '35 '62 C.608 B.M.E. L.273 J.D.
(adm. in DC; not adm. in CA; Pat.) [Dorsey&W.]
*PRACTICE AREAS: Trademark; Copyright; Litigation.
Keene, Galvin R. ..........................'17 '45 C&L.477 B.A., J.D. 1750 Whittier‡
**Kelley, Marla Lamedman** ..................'58 '83 C.112 B.A. L.426 J.D. [Booth,M.&S.]
**Kerekes, Steven W.** ..................'58 '83 C.228 A.B. L.800 J.D. [Ⓒ Daehnke&C.]
*LANGUAGES: French.
*PRACTICE AREAS: Commercial Litigation; Real Estate Law.
**Kidman, Arthur G., (P.C.)**, (AV) ....'46 '74 C.906 B.A. L.145 J.D. [McCormick,K.&B.]
*PRACTICE AREAS: Public Law; Water Law; Environmental Law.
**Kilger, Kraig C.** ..........................'66 '92 C.112 B.A. L.1067 J.D. [Ⓐ Rutan&T.]
*PRACTICE AREAS: Real Estate; Business; Banking.
**Kim, Catherine J.** ..........................'70 '95 C.154 B.A. L.1049 J.D. [Ⓐ Lewis,D.B.&B.]
Kinder, Wuerfel & Cholakian, A Professional Corporation, (AV)
3400 Ave. of The Arts (⊙San Francisco & Santa Rosa)
**King, John P., Jr.**, (AV) ............'44 '69 C.605 A.B. L.1066 J.D. [Drummy K.W.&G.]
*PRACTICE AREAS: Corporate Law; Corporate Acquisitions Law; Securities Law.

**King, Julie Vigil** ..........................'71 '96 C.112 B.A. L.990 J.D. [Ⓐ Latham&W.]
King, Lisa R. ..........................'65 '92 C.112 B.A. L.464 J.D. 3080 Bristol St.
King, Thomas C., (BV) ..............'32 '65 C.112 B.S. L.1065 J.D. 1756 Orange Ave.
**Kipper, David R.** ..............'52 '82 C.112 B.A. L.1049 J.D. [Booth,M.&S.] (⊙L.A.)
**Klatte, Ernest W., III**, (AV) ..............'56 '84 C.112 B.A. L.1067 J.D. [Rutan&T.]
*LANGUAGES: French.
*PRACTICE AREAS: Labor Law; Employment Law.
**Klotz, Robert L.**, (BV) ..............'44 '77 C.813 B.A. L.911 J.D. [Pillsbury M.&S.]
**Knutson, Stephanie H.** ..............'71 '96 C.112 B.A. L.1065 J.D. [Ⓐ Latham&W.]
Koch, Arthur L., Jr. ..............'60 '87 C.1109 B.A. L.1137 J.D. 611 Anton Blvd.
**Kohn, Philip D.**, (AV) ..........................'53 '79 C.1109 B.A. L.1065 J.D. [Rutan&T.]
*PRACTICE AREAS: Constitutional Law; Environmental; Land Use Law; Municipal and Zoning.
Kopchick, Kimberly M. ..............'63 '89 C.732 B.A. L.990 J.D. 611 Anton Blvd.
**Kottke, Jon S.**, (AV) ..............'55 '81 C.112 B.A. L.426 J.D. [Coulombe&K.]
*PRACTICE AREAS: Collections; Enforcement of Judgments; Prejudgment Attachment Proceedings; Commercial; Civil Trial.
**Kozak, Harry T.** ..............'40 '90 C.1097 B.A. L.809 J.D. [Ⓐ Lewis,D.B.&B.]
Kramer, Brian J. ..............'68 '95 C.378 B.A. L.477 J.D. 600 Town Ctr.
**Krasnoff, Brad D.** ..............'60 '86 C.112 B.A. L.1068 J.D. [Lewis,D.B.&B.]
*REPORTED CASES: In re Kruger, 77 Bankr. 785 (Bk. C.D. Cal. 1987).
Kroesche, John E. ..............'54 '80 C.878 B.A. L.101 J.D. P.O. Box 2066
**Kuiper, David L.** ..............'60 '93 C.823 B.S. L.800 J.D. [Ⓐ Latham&W.]
**Kumamoto, Brian A.** ..............'66 '91 C.112 B.A. L.188 J.D. [Ⓐ Graham&J.]
*PRACTICE AREAS: Insolvency; Business Litigation.
**Kuperberg, Joel D.**, (AV) ..............'54 '79 C.668 B.A. L.1068 J.D. [Rutan&T.]
*PRACTICE AREAS: Environmental; Municipal and Zoning; Civil Trial; Land Use Law.
**Labate, Greg S.** .............. '64 '90 C.197 B.A. L.1078 J.D. [Ⓐ Sheppard,M.R.&H.]
Lady, Jeffrey L. ..............'64 '95 C.999 B.A. L.1049 J.D. 3080 Bristol St.
**LaFourcade, Lisa M.** ..............'65 '92 C.684 B.S. L.800 J.D. [Ⓐ Paul,H.J.&W.]
**Lancaster, Michael J.**, (AV) ..............'52 '80 L.1137 J.D. [Lewis,D.B.&B.]
**Lannon, Lawrence E.** ..............'43 '88 C.103 B.S. L.426 J.D. [Ⓐ Cooksey,H.M.&T.]
*PRACTICE AREAS: Litigation; Personal Injury; Insurance Defense Law.
**Lanphar, Anne Nelson**, (AV) ..............'52 '77 C.1109 B.A. L.1065 J.D. [Rutan&T.]
*PRACTICE AREAS: Municipal and Zoning; Real Estate.
**Lape, Gary M.**, (BV) ..............'53 '78 C.276 A.B. L.1067 J.D. [Lewis,D.B.&B.]
**Larsen, David C., (P.C.)**, (AV) ..............'46 '73 C.367 L.878 J.D. [Rutan&T.]
*PRACTICE AREAS: Employment Benefits; Workers' Compensation; Labor and Employment; Construction; Civil Rights.
**Larsen, Gerald L.** ..............'49 '90 C.1077 B.S. L.260 LL.M. [Larsen&Assoc.]
*PRACTICE AREAS: Federal and State Taxation; Probate; Estate Planning; Partnerships; Corporate Law.

**Larsen & Associates**
**3200 Park Center Drive, Suite 720, 92626**
**Telephone: 714-540-1770 Fax: 714-540-1020**
**Gerald L. Larsen. Associates: David S. Beard; Wayne Robert Johnson; Danny R. Boon.**
**Federal and State Taxations, Probate, Estate Planning, Corporations, Mergers and Acquisitions, Real Estate Property, Tax and Commercial Litigation.**
***See Professional Biographies, COSTA MESA, CALIFORNIA***

**Laskin & Graham**
(See Glendale)

**Latham & Watkins, (AV)**
**Suite 2000, 650 Town Center Drive, 92626-1918⊙**
**Telephone: 714-540-1235 Telecopier: 714-755-8290**
**URL: http://www.lw.com**
**Resident Partners: Joseph A. Wheelock Jr.; Robert E. Currie; Alan W. Pettis; Joseph I. Bentley; James W. Daniels; Morris A. Thurston; Jeffrey T. Pero; Bruce A. Tester; Robert K. Break; Jon D. Anderson; Patrick T. Seaver; Gregory P. Lindstrom; Bruce P. Howard; Mary K. Westbrook; Kenneth A. Wolfson; Cary K. Hyden; David W. Barby; Glenda Sanders; Peter J. Wilson; Joseph B. Farrell; William J. Cernius; Linda Schilling. Resident Of Counsel: John R. Stahr; Jean M. Donnelly; Regina M. Schlatter; Andrea L. Mersel; Dean G. Dunlavey. Resident Associates: Adele K. Cardoza; David C. Meckler; David C. Flattum; R. Brian Timmons; Scott B. Garner; Charles W. Cox, II; Charles K. Ruck; Paul N. Singarella; Andrea S. Matiauda; Daniel A. Thomson; David L. Kuiper; Daniel W. Burke; Laura I. Bushnell; R. Scott Shean; Mark A. Finkelstein; Mary A. Donovan; David Pitman; Scott B. Cooper; Jamie L. Wine; Ronit D. Earley; Joseph M. Yaffe; Mark W. Seneca; David B. Allen; Jonn R. Beeson; Julie Vigil King; Stephanie H. Knutson; Gregory M. Saylin; Clay Shevlin; Stephen J. Venuto.**
**General Practice.**
**Los Angeles, California Office: 633 West Fifth Street, Suite 4000. Telephone: 213-485-1234.**
**San Diego, California Office: Suite 2100, 701 B Street. Telephone: 619-236-1234.**
**San Francisco, California Office: 505 Montgomery Street, Suite 1900. Telephone: 415-391-0600.**
**Washington, D.C. Office: Suite 1300, 1001 Pennsylvania Avenue, N.W. Telephone: 202-637-2200.**
**Chicago, Illinois Office: Suite 5800 Sears Tower. Telephone: 312-876-7700.**
**Newark, New Jersey Office: One Newark Center. Telephone: 201-639-1234. Fax: 201-639-7298.**
**New York, N.Y. Office: Suite 1000, 885 Third Avenue. Telephone: 212-906-1200.**
**London, England Office: One Angel Court, EC2R 7HJ. Telephone: +-44-171-374 4444. Telecopier: +-44-171-374 4460.**
**Moscow, Russia Office: Suite C200, 113/1 Leninsky Prospeckt, 117198. Telephone: +-7 503 956-5555. Fax: +-7 503 956-5556.**
**Hong Kong Office: 11th Floor Central Building, Number One Pedder Street, Central Hong Kong. Telephone: 011-852-2841-7779. Fax: 011-852-2841-7749.**
**Tokyo, Japan Office: Infini Akasaka, 8-7-15 Akasaka, Minato-Ku, Tokyo 107, Japan. Telephone: 011 81 3 3423-3970. Fax: 011 81 3 3423 3971.**
***See Professional Biographies, COSTA MESA, CALIFORNIA***

**Lau, Sandra** ..............'70 '95 C.112 B.A. L.426 J.D. [Ⓐ Graham&J.]
Laz, Creighton B., (AV) ..............'51 '83 C.339 B.S. L.809 J.D. Gr. Western Bk. Bldg.
**Lazorisak, Theresa H.** ..............'65 '89 C.800 B.A. L.1065 J.D. [Ⓐ Cooksey,H.M.&T.]
**Lee, Jenny** ..............'67 '91 C.112 B.S. L.1068 J.D. [Ⓐ Robins,K.M.&C.]
*LANGUAGES: Mandarin, Cantonese.
*PRACTICE AREAS: Litigation; Professional Liability; Real Estate; Casualty.
Lee, Yong Tsun ..............'52 '78 C.999 B.S.L. L.1240 J.D. 628 W. 19th St.
**Lemen, Robert T.** ..............'55 '80 C.112 B.A. L.1068 J.D. [Murtaugh,M.M.&N.]
*PRACTICE AREAS: Tort Litigation; Business Litigation; Environmental Litigation; General Civil Trial.
**LeRoy, Bryan Cameron** ..............'65 '95 C.112 B.A. L.1065 J.D. [Ⓐ Burke,W.&S.]
*PRACTICE AREAS: Municipal Law.
**Leslie, Scott N.** ..............'60 '86 C.1109 B.A. L.800 J.D. [Ⓒ Paul,H.J.&W.]
**Levin, Elaine R.** ..............'57 '86 C.813 A.B. L.146 J.D. [Riordan&M.]
Levine, Ronald E. ..............'49 '76 C.813 B.S. L.477 J.D. 575 Anton Blvd., Ste. 300
**Lewis, Robert F., (P.C.)**, (AV) ..............'36 '62 C.112 B.A. L.1068 J.D. [Lewis,D.B.&B.]⊙

**Lewis, D'Amato, Brisbois & Bisgaard, (AV)**
**A Partnership including Professional Corporations**
**650 Town Center Drive, Suite 1400, 92626⊙**
**Telephone: 714-545-9200**
**Partners: Robert F. Lewis (P.C.); Donald A. Ruston; Keith D. Taylor; Gary M. Lape; Nancy E. Zeltzer; Lee A. Wood; Thomas E. Francis; H. Gilbert Jones; Michael W. Connally; Annie Verdries; James G. Bohm; Scott W. Monson; Michael C. Olson; David E. Isenberg; Brad D. Krasnoff; Michael J. Lancaster; Roger L. Bellows. Resident Associates: Leslie S. Bowen; Lori Creasey; Troy A. Edwards; Kelly M. Flanagan; Allison A. Greene; Jay D. Harker; Heather Anne Henderson (Resident); Paula F. Henry; Helen E. Hesse; Madonna L. Hultman; Charles J. Hyland; Catherine J. Kim; Harry T. Kozak.**
**General Practice.**
**Los Angeles, California Office: Suite 1200, 221 North Figueroa Street. Telephone: 213-250-1800. Fax: 213-250-7900.**
**San Diego, California Office: 550 West "C" Street, Suite 800. Telephone: 619-233-1006. Fax: 619-434-0882.**

(This Listing Continued)

CALIFORNIA—COSTA MESA MARTINDALE-HUBBELL LAW DIRECTORY 1997

**Lewis, D'Amato, Brisbois & Bisgaard (Continued)**

San Francisco, California Office: 601 California Street, Suite 1900. Telephone: 415-362-2580. Fax: 415-434-0882.
San Bernardino, California Office: 650 E. Hospitality Lane, Suite 600. Telephone: 714-387-1130. Fax: 714-387-1138.
Sacramento, California Office: 2500 Venture Oaks, 95833. Telephone: 916-564-5400. Fax: 916-564-5444.
Affiliated Offices:
Jakarta, Indonesia Affiliated Office: Mulya Lubis and Partners, Wisma Bank Dharmala, 16th Floor, Jendral, Sudirman, Kav. 28, Jakarta 12920, Indonesia. Telephone: (62)(21) 521-1931/521-1932. Facsimile: (62)(21) 521-1930.
Bangkok, Thailand Affiliated Office: Kanung & Partners Law Offices, Raintree Office Garden, 272 Japanese School Lane, Rama IX Road, Bangkok 10310, Thailand. Telephone: (662) 319-7571/319-7574. Facsimile: (662) 319-6372.

*See Professional Biographies, COSTA MESA, CALIFORNIA*

**Li, Anward** .... '67 '93 C.112 B.S. L.426 J.D. [A Rutan&T.]
*LANGUAGES: Mandarin Chinese.
*PRACTICE AREAS: Public Law; Land Use; Litigation.
**Liljestrom, Brent R.** .... '56 '81 C.112 B.A. L.1068 J.D. [Sheppard,M.R.&H.]
*PRACTICE AREAS: Real Estate Law; Real Estate Finance Law; Tax Exempt Bond Financing.
Lincoln, Jack, (AV) .... '22 '53 C.112 L.809 LL.B. 1879 Maui Circle‡
**Lindstrom, Gregory P.**, (AV) .... '53 '78 C.112 A.B. L.145 J.D. [Latham&W.]
**Linhoff, William P., Jr.**, (AV) .... '46 '74 C.494 B.A. L.174 J.D. [Robins,K.M.&C.]
*PRACTICE AREAS: Insurance Litigation; General Litigation.
Linquist, Cindy R. '55 '87 C.173 B.A. L.378 J.D.
(adm. in CO; not adm. in CA) 3131 Bristol St.‡
Lippold, Brian E. .... '57 '83 C.800 A.B. L.809 J.D. 234 E. 17th St.
**Litfin, Todd Owen** .... '65 '95 C.309 A.B. L.1068 J.D. [A Rutan&T.]
*PRACTICE AREAS: Public Law; Civil Litigation.
Litman, Todd M. .... '60 '86 C.1109 B.A. L.1049 J.D. 650 Town Center Dr.
Liu, Larry J.H. .... '68 '95 C.112 B.A. L.602 J.D. 600 Anton Blvd.
Long, Harrison K. .... '46 '76 C.378 B.A. L.1137 J.D. 611 Anton
**Lope, Susan** .... '66 '95 C.1042 B.A. L.809 J.D. [A Robins,K.M.&C.]
*PRACTICE AREAS: General Civil Litigation; Business; Employment Law.
**Loss, James W.** .... '53 '80 C.674 A.B. L.976 J.D. [Riordan&M.]
**Lowder, Vincent D.** .... '66 '94 C.112 B.A. L.426 J.D. [A Paul,H.J.&W.]
**Lowe, Michael T.** .... '43 '70 C&L.878 B.S., J.D. [Booth,M.&S.]
Lubeck, Daniel J. .... '62 '89 C.112 B.A. L.800 J.D. 3070 Bristol St.
**Lund, Tammy Horton** .... '62 '86 C.112 B.A. L.426 J.D. [P.E.Whalen]
Lynn, Jann M. .... '46 '86 C.339 A.B. L.426 J.D. 3200 Park Ctr. Dr.

**Lyon & Lyon LLP, (AV)**
A Limited Liability Partnership Including Professional Corporations
**Suite 1200, 3200 Park Center Drive, 92626⊙**
Telephone: 714-751-6606 Fax: 714-751-8209
Email: lyon@lyonlyon.com URL: http://www.lyonlyon.com
Resident Partners: James W. Geriak (A Professional Corporation); Robert M. Taylor, Jr.; Samuel B. Stone (A Professional Corporation); Allan W. Jansen; David B. Murphy. Resident Associates: Kurt T. Mulville; James P. Brogan; Corrine M. Freeman; Mark J. Carlozzi; Kenneth S. Roberts; John C. Kappos; Charles Calvin Fowler; James K. Sakaguchi; Neal Matthew Cohen.
Intellectual Property Law including Patent, Trademark, Copyright, Trade Regulation, Unfair Competition and Antitrust Law. Litigation.
Los Angeles, California Office: First Interstate World Center, 47th Floor, 633 West Fifth Street. Telephone: 213-489-1600.
San Jose, California Office: Suite 1150, 303 Almaden Boulevard. Telephone: 408-993-1555.
La Jolla, California Office: Suite 600, 4250 Executive Square. Telephone: 619-552-8400.

*See Professional Biographies, COSTA MESA, CALIFORNIA*

**MacDonald, James B.**, (AV) .... '42 '67 C.112 A.B. L.1066 J.D. [Balfour M.M.&O.]
*REPORTED CASES: Kistler v. Vasi, 71 C. 2d 261; Ryman v. American National Insurance Co., 5C. 3d 620.
*PRACTICE AREAS: Estate and Trust Planning and Administration.
**Macie, Michael J.** .... '66 '92 C.1049 B.A. L.770 J.D. [A Cooksey,H.M.&T.]
*PRACTICE AREAS: Construction Defect Litigation; Construction Injury; Products Liability.
**MacNeil, Allen D.** .... '63 '94 C.112 B.A. L.426 J.D. [A Ely,F.&H.]
*PRACTICE AREAS: General Civil Defense; Insurance Fraud.
**Maga, Joseph Louis, III** .... '66 '92 C.112 B.A. L.800 J.D. [A Rutan&T.]
*PRACTICE AREAS: Real Estate.
Maguire, Michael P., (AV) .... '52 '77 C.112 B.A. L.426 J.D. 611 Anton Blvd.
**Maldonado, Kirk F.**, (BV) .... '50 '78 C.627 B.A. L.190 J.D. [Riordan&M.]
**Malo, Aaron J.** .... '69 '95 C.813 A.B. L.1065 J.D. [A Sheppard,M.R.&H.]
*PRACTICE AREAS: Bankruptcy; Business Litigation.
Mancini, Joseph .... '41 '84 C.1109 B.A. L.1137 J.D. [A Davis,S.B.&G.]
Mansur-Brown, Patricia M. '56 '83 C.112 B.A. L.1137 J.D.
Asst. Gen. Coun., Prudential Real Estate Affiliates, Inc.
**Marlo, John A., III** .... '66 '94 C.800 B.S. L.1137 J.D. [A Cooksey,H.M.&T.]
*PRACTICE AREAS: Litigation; Insurance Defense; Construction Defect Litigation.
**Marsella, Gregory E.** '63 '88
C.112 B.A. L.426 J.D. Corp. Coun., Apria Healthcare Grp., Inc.
**Marticorena, William M.**, (AV) .... '52 '77 C.426 B.A. L.309 J.D. [Rutan&T.]
*PRACTICE AREAS: Civil Trial; Communications; Municipal Bond.
**Martin, Alan H.** .... '61 '87 C&L.893 B.A., J.D. [Sheppard,M.R.&H.]
*PRACTICE AREAS: Bankruptcy Law, Banking Law, Finance Law.
**Martin, James M.**, (AV) .... '44 '71 C.800 B.S. L.228 J.D. [Cooksey,H.M.&T.]
*REPORTED CASES: Humphries Investments, Inc. v. Walsh, (1988) 202 Cal.App.3d 766.
*PRACTICE AREAS: Real Estate; Business; Corporate Law.
**Martinez, Peter W.** .... '65 '91 C.1049 B.A. L.813 J.D. [A Pillsbury M.&S.]
**Martino, Gregg P.**, (AV) .... '52 '78 C.112 B.A. L.1068 J.D. [C Graham&J.]
*PRACTICE AREAS: Litigation; Real Estate (Property) Law.
**Martyn, Elizabeth L.** .... '51 '81 C.112 B.A. L.1068 J.D. [Rutan&T.]
*LANGUAGES: Spanish and French.
*PRACTICE AREAS: Municipal Law; Solid Waste; Land Use Law; Environmental.
**Marx, Paul Frederic**, (AV) .... '31 '57 C.800 B.A. L.309 LL.B. [Rutan&T.]
*PRACTICE AREAS: Probate and Estate Planning; Tax Law.
**Matiauda, Andrea S.** .... '66 '93 C.228 B.A. L.1068 J.D. [A Latham&W.]
**Matsui, Susan S.** .... '65 '93 C.112 B.A. L.800 J.D. [A Sheppard,M.R.&H.]
*LANGUAGES: Japanese.
May, Sally Estes .... '58 '83 C.112 B.A. L.426 J.D. Dep. City Atty.
**Mazarei, Rayehe** .... '66 '91 C.112 B.A. L.1137 J.D. [Hartley&M.]
*LANGUAGES: Farsi.
*PRACTICE AREAS: Immigration Law; Transactional Business Law; Corporate Law.
**McCalla, Patrick D.** .... '63 '89 C.36 B.S. L.800 J.D. [A Rutan&T.]
*PRACTICE AREAS: Banking; Environmental; Construction; Real Estate.
McCarthy, Bonnie L. .... '43 '79 C.1163 B.S. L.398 J.D. 3185-B Airway Ave.
**McCauley, John J.**, (AV) .... '49 '80 C.112 B.A. L.309 J.D. [McCauley&Assoc.]
*REPORTED CASES: Jenkins v. Tuneup Masters, 190 Cal. App. 3d 1, 235 Cal. Rptr. 214 (Cal. App. 3d Dist., 1987) review denied (June 17, 1987); US Aluminum Corporation/Texas v. Alumax, Inc., 831 F. 2d 878 (9th Cir. 1987), cert. denied, 488 U.S. 822, 109 S. Ct 68, 102 L. Ed. 2d 45 (1988); Lund v. Albrecht, 936 F. 2d 459 (9th Cir. 1991).
*PRACTICE AREAS: Trial and Appellate.

**McCauley & Associates, LLP, (AV)** [BB]
**611 Anton Boulevard, Suite 1260, 92626**
Telephone: 714-438-9108 Fax: 714-957-3718

(This Listing Continued)

CAA62P

**McCauley & Associates, LLP (Continued)**

Members of Firm: John J. McCauley;—Mark S. Flynn.
Trial and Appellate Practice in all State and Federal Courts and Arbitration Tribunals, with emphasis on Complex Business Disputes.

*See Professional Biographies, COSTA MESA, CALIFORNIA*

McClay, John B. .... '53 '80 C.112 B.S. L.990 J.D. [McClay&A.]
McClay & Alani, A Professional Law Corporation .... 3146 Red Hill Ave.
McClendon, Frank L., Jr. .... '36 '61 C&L.846 B.S., J.D. 151 Kalmus Dr.
**McCormick, Homer L. (Mike), Jr., (P.C.)**, (AV) '28 '61
C.768 A.B. L.1065 J.D. [McCormick,K.&B.]
*PRACTICE AREAS: Real Estate Law; Property Tax Law; Civil Litigation; Condemnation Law.

**McCormick, Kidman & Behrens, LLP, (AV)** [BB]
A Partnership of Professional Corporations
**Imperial Bank Building, 695 Town Center Drive Suite 1400, 92626-1924**
Telephone: 714-755-3100 Fax: 714-755-3110; 1-800-755-3125
Email: mkb1@ix.netcom.com
Members of Firm: Homer L. (Mike) McCormick, Jr., (P.C.); Arthur G. Kidman (P.C.); Russell G. Behrens (P.C.); Suzanne M. Tague (P.C.); Janet R. Morningstar (P.C.); Keith E. McCullough (P.C.). Associates: David D. Boyer; Robert A. Johnson; John O. Clune; Bradley D. Pierce.
General Civil Practice and Litigation in all State and Federal Courts. Environmental Law, Water Law, Special Districts, Municipal Law, Real Property, Real Estate Transactions and Real Estate Finance, Estate Planning and Probate, Land Use, (including CEQA Compliance), Natural Resources (including Oil and Gas Matters), Property Tax Matters, and Condemnation Actions.

*See Professional Biographies, COSTA MESA, CALIFORNIA*

**McCortney, Ryan D.** '59 '87
C.605 A.B. L.800 J.D. [Sheppard,M.R.&H.] (⊙Los Angeles)
*PRACTICE AREAS: Labor and Employment Law.
**McCullough, Keith E., (P.C.)** .... '62 '89 C.101 B.A. L.966 J.D. [McCormick,K.&B.]
*LANGUAGES: German.
*PRACTICE AREAS: Business Litigation; Water Law; Real Property Law; Condemnation.

**McInnis, Fitzgerald, Rees & Sharkey, A Professional Corporation, (AV)**
**650 Town Center Drive, Suite 1240, 92626⊙**
Telephone: 714-513-2209 Fax: 714-513-2210
James E. Chodzko; James J. Reynolds; Gibson E. Pratt; Charles L. Currier.
Professional Liability, Including Medical, Dental, Legal, Accounting, Architectural and Engineering, Business Litigation, Products Liability, Construction and Soils Erosion Litigation, Hospital Liability, Automobile, Aviation and Public Carrier Liability and Insurance Litigation, Including Bad Faith Liability, Employment Law, Environmental Law, Financial Institutions, Banking and Asset Management Litigation, Transactional and Real Estate.
San Diego, California Office: 1230 Columbia Street, Suite 800. Telephone: 619-236-1711. Fax: 619-236-0387.

*See Professional Biographies, COSTA MESA, CALIFORNIA*

**McIntyre, Joel F.**, (AV) .... '38 '63 C.813 A.B. L.1068 J.D. [McIntyre B.&B.]
*PRACTICE AREAS: Corporate Law; Real Estate; Securities; Business Law.

**McIntyre Borges & Burns LLP, (AV)**
**3070 Bristol Street, Suite 450, 92626**
Telephone: 714-545-7835 Fax: 714-545-7524
Email: wtgay@ix.netcom.com URL: http://www.mcilaw.com
Members of Firm: Joel F. McIntyre; Evan C. Borges; George S. Burns; William T. Gay; Victoria E. Moss; Stefanie L. Miller.
Corporate, Corporate Finance, Securities, Real Estate, General Business and Energy. Civil Litigation in all Federal and State Courts.

*See Professional Biographies, COSTA MESA, CALIFORNIA*

**McKinnon, Michael G.** .... '68 '94 C.188 B.S. L.990 J.D. [A Riordan&M.]
*LANGUAGES: Spanish.
*PRACTICE AREAS: Corporate; Securities.
**McPherson, David F.** .... '69 '94 C.800 B.S. L.809 J.D. [A Booth,M.&S.]
**McQueen, James A.** .... '52 '84 C&L.800 B.S., J.D. [Graham&J.]
*PRACTICE AREAS: Business Litigation; Eminent Domain Law.
**Meckler, David C.** .... '63 '89 C.112 B.A. L.800 J.D. [A Latham&W.]
**Melzer, Layne H.** .... '61 '87 C.1077 B.A. L.1067 J.D. [Rutan&T.]
*PRACTICE AREAS: Municipal and Zoning; Environmental; Civil Trial; Land Use Law.
Menke, Dennis V., (AV) .... '35 '63 C&L.966 B.A., LL.B. [Menke,F.&C.]
Menke, Fahrney & Carroll, A Professional Corporation, (AV)
650 Town Center Dr., Ste. 1250
**Menkes, Susan W.** .... '52 '79 C.853 A.B. L.426 J.D. [C Murtaugh,M.M.&N.]
**Mersel, Andrea L.** .... '63 '87 C.659 B.S. L.1066 J.D. [C Latham&W.]
Meyer, Keith, (BV) .... '27 '79 C.627 B.G.S. L.1137 J.D. [Meyer&Assoc.]
Meyer, Paul Seth, (AV) .... '47 '72 C.112 B.A. L.1068 J.D. 695 Town Center Dr.
**Meyer, Richard E.** .... '37 '63 C&L.800 A.B., J.D. [Murtaugh,M.M.&N.]
*PRACTICE AREAS: Products Liability Law; Catastrophic Personal Injury Law; Premises Liability Law; Governmental Entity Defense Law; Insurance Bad Faith Law.
Meyer & Associates, A Professional Law Corporation, (BV) .... 3185 Airway Ave., Ste. B
**Mijuskovic, Ruth** .... '43 '77 C.114 B.A. L.801 J.D. [Balfour M.M.&O.]
*PRACTICE AREAS: Corporate Law; Securities; Business Law; Transactional Law; Real Property.
**Miller, Bradford H., (A Professional Corporation)**, (AV) '50 '75
C.112 B.A. L.1068 J.D. [Murtaugh,M.M.&N.]
*PRACTICE AREAS: Insurance Coverage/Bad Faith Law; Professional Errors and Omissions Law; Personal Injury Litigation.
**Miller, Lawrence H.** .... '51 '89 C.139 B.A. L.1137 J.D. [A Cooksey,H.M.&T.]
*LANGUAGES: German.
*PRACTICE AREAS: Business and Commercial Litigation; Creditor Bankruptcy Litigation.
**Miller, Marci Lerner** .... '67 '92 C.154 B.A. L.569 J.D. [A Pillsbury M.&S.]
*LANGUAGES: French.
**Miller, Scott R.** .... '64 '95 C.112 B.A. L.426 J.D. [A Paul,H.J.&W.]
**Miller, Stefanie L.** .... '67 '95 C.575 B.A. L.770 J.D. [A McIntyre B.&B.]
*LANGUAGES: French.
*PRACTICE AREAS: Litigation.
**Miller, Thomas A.** .... '52 '78 C.999 B.A. L.477 J.D. [Robins,K.M.&C.]
*PRACTICE AREAS: Business Litigation; Cable Television Law; Employment Law.
**Miller-Romero, Jeanne** .... '65 '95 C.112 B.A. L.1067 J.D. [A Riordan&M.]
*PRACTICE AREAS: Corporate Securities.
Mills, Colen A. .... '18 '72 L.1137 LL.B. Coun., Claims Litig., State Farm Ins. Co.
**Mirkovich, Michael J.** .... '51 '83 C.112 B.A. L.1137 J.D. [C Buckner,A.&Y.]
*PRACTICE AREAS: Commercial Real Estate Law; Real Estate Law.
Mixon, Dean A., (AV) .... '41 '76 C.691 B.A. L.1137 J.D. [Weinfeld&M.]
**Mizen, Scott S.** .... '64 '90 C.339 B.S. L.990 J.D. [A Booth,M.&S.]
**Mobley, Gary S.**, (AV) .... '49 '76 C.112 B.A. L.767 J.D. [C Ginsburg,S.O.&R.]
*PRACTICE AREAS: Civil Trial.
**Monson, Scott W.** .... '56 '83 C.800 B.A. L.426 J.D. [Lewis,D.B.&B.]
**Montevideo, Richard** .... '59 '84 C&L.608 B.S., J.D. [Rutan&T.]
*PRACTICE AREAS: Environmental Law; Cost Recovery; Toxic Tort Litigation; Municipal and Zoning.
Moore, Fredericka Lynne .... '63 '92 C.1042 B.A. L.999 J.D. 3200 Park Cntr. Dr., 9th Fl.
**Moore, James R., (P.C.)**, (AV) .... '27 '57 C.477 A.B. L.813 LL.B. [Rutan&T.]
*PRACTICE AREAS: Real Estate.
**Moran, William J.** .... '53 '78 C.262 B.A. L.976 J.D. [Daehnke&C.]
*LANGUAGES: French.
*PRACTICE AREAS: employment Law; Environmental Litigation; Business Litigation; Appeals.
Morello, Arthur P., Jr., (AV) .... '52 '76 C.800 A.B. L.1066 J.D. 3420 Bristol St.

**Morningstar, Janet R., (P.C.)** ... '56 '81 C.668 B.A. L.800 J.D. [McCormick,K.&B.]
*REPORTED CASES: Biddle v. Superior Court (1985) 170 CalApp3d 135; Brydon v. East Bay Mun. Utility Dist. (1994) 24 CalApp4th 178 (as amicus curiae).
*PRACTICE AREAS: Public Law; Water Law; Real Property Law.
**Morris, James L.**, (AV) ... '52 '78 C.228 B.A. L.276 J.D. [Rutan&T.]
*PRACTICE AREAS: Labor and Employment Law (Management).
Morris, James L., Jr. ... '38 '92 C&L.1137 B.S., J.D. [Rasch&M.]
**Morrow, Donald L.**, (AV) ... '51 '75 C&L.800 A.B., J.D. [Paul,H.J.&W.]
**Mortensen, Stan A.** ... '67 '94 C&L.101 B.A., J.D. [Ⓐ Robins,K.M.&C.]
*LANGUAGES: Spanish.
*PRACTICE AREAS: Insurance Law; Litigation; General Civil Practice; Product Liability Law.
Mosher, Raymond J., (BV) ... '37 '70 C.999 B.A. L.809 J.D. [R.J.Mosher]
Mosher, Raymond J., A Professional Corporation, Law Offices of, (BV)
2664 Newport Blvd.
Moss, Frank, (AV) ... '29 '65 C.763 A.B. L.800 J.D. 1756 Orange Ave.
**Moss, Victoria E.** ... '64 '90 C.763 B.S. L.1049 J.D. [McIntyre B.&B.]
*PRACTICE AREAS: Litigation.
**Mouzis, Gerald W.** ... '53 '80 C.800 B.A. L.809 J.D. [Ⓒ Ely,F.&H.]
*PRACTICE AREAS: Civil Litigation; Products Liability; Construction Defect/Land Subsidence; Real Estate Litigation; Business Litigation and Transactional Matters.
**Mroczynski, Randall P.** ... '63 '91 C.770 B.A. L.464 J.D. [Ⓐ Cooksey,H.M.&T.]
*PRACTICE AREAS: Business and Commercial Litigation; Creditor Bankruptcy Litigation.
**Muldowney, Steven M.** ... '63 '95 C.103 B.A. L.1067 J.D. [Ⓐ Rutan&T.]
*PRACTICE AREAS: Civil Trial.
**Mulville, Kurt T.** ... '62 '90 C.112 B.S. L.426 J.D. [Ⓐ Lyon&L.] (See Pat. Sect.)
*PRACTICE AREAS: Intellectual Property.
**Muñoz, A. Patrick** ... '64 '89 C.112 B.A. L.426 J.D. [Ⓐ Rutan&T.]
*PRACTICE AREAS: Land Use Law; Municipal and Zoning; Civil Trial.
Muramoto, Mika Y. ... '59 '85 C&L.800 B.S., J.D. 1095 Sea Bluff Dr.
Murphy, Christopher J. ... '64 '90 C.112 B.A. L.464 J.D. 3185 B Airway Ave.
**Murphy, David B.** ... '56 '82 C.112 B.A. L.1066 J.D. [Lyon&L.] (See Pat. Sect.)
*SPECIAL AGENCIES: Section 337 Investigations in the International Trade Commission.
*PRACTICE AREAS: Patent, Software Protection; Intellectual Property.
**Murphy, James A., IV** ... '44 '78 C.112 B.A. L.1137 J.D. [Murtaugh,M.M.&N.]
*PRACTICE AREAS: Labor and Employment Counseling and Litigation.
**Murtaugh, Michael J., (A Professional Corporation)**, (AV) '47 '73
C.150 B.A. L.1068 J.D. [Murtaugh,M.M.&N.]
*PRACTICE AREAS: Construction Litigation; Employment Law; Insurance Law; General Civil Trial.

**Murtaugh, Miller, Meyer & Nelson, (AV)**
**A Partnership including Professional Corporations**
**3200 Park Center Drive, 9th Floor, P.O. Box 5023, 92628-5023**
**Telephone: 714-513-6800 Facsimile: 714-513-6899**
**Michael J. Murtaugh (A Professional Corporation); Bradford H. Miller (A Professional Corporation); Michael J. Nelson; Robert T. Lemen; Mark S. Himmelstein; Harry A. Halkowich; Madelyn A. Enright; James A. Murphy, IV; Lawrence A. Treglia, Jr.;—Debra L. Braasch; Thomas J. Skane; David C. Holt; Lawrence J. DiPinto; Debra L. Reilly; Susan Westover; Gregory M. Heuser; Carrie E. Phelan; Maryls K. Braun; John R. Browning; Eric J. Dubin; Geoffrey A. Graves; Tamara Dadd Smith; John Kirk Donnelly; Richard Paul Hidalgo. Of Counsel: Susan W. Menkes; Jay D. Fullman; Richard E. Meyer.**
**General Civil and Trial Practice in all State and Federal Courts. Insurance, Personal Injury, Employment, Professional Liability, Environmental, Business, Franchising, Construction and Commercial Law.**
**Representative Clients: Continental Insurance Cos. (Continental Loss Adjusting Services); Design Professionals Insurance Co.**
**Reference: Wells Fargo Bank.**

***See Professional Biographies, COSTA MESA, CALIFORNIA***

**Nelson, Michael J.**, (AV) ... '53 '79 C.800 B.S. L.990 J.D. [Murtaugh,M.M.&N.]
*PRACTICE AREAS: Construction Litigation and related claims; General Civil Trial.
**Nguyen, Thinh V.** ... '54 '96 C.112 B.S.E.E. L.809 J.D. [Ⓐ Blakely,S.T.&Z.]
**Nichols, Steven A.** ... '52 '80 C.1042 B.A. L.800 J.D. [Rutan&T.]
*PRACTICE AREAS: Business Litigation.
Noble, John R. ... '53 '79 C.1109 B.A. L.1137 J.D. 3140 Redhill Ave.
**Nobles, Kimberley G.** '60 '92
C.608 B.S.E.E. L.800 J.D. [Ⓐ Blakely,S.T.&Z.] (See Pat. Sect.)
**Nock, Steven C.** ... '55 '80 C.201 B.A. L.309 J.D. [Ⓒ Sheppard,M.R.&H.]
Obrien, James W., (AV) ... '27 '53 C.800 B.S. L.1065 LL.B. [Obrien,G.&P.]
**O'Brien, Sean A.** ... '61 '88 C.112 B.A. L.1066 J.D. [Ⓒ Paul,H.J.&W.]
Obrien, Gazin & Peterson, (AV) ... 611 Anton Blvd.
**Oderman, Jeffrey M., (P.C.)**, (AV) ... '49 '75 C.112 B.A. L.813 J.D. [Rutan&T.]
*PRACTICE AREAS: Land Use Law; Real Estate; Municipal and Zoning.
Oldmen, Frank A. ... '29 '72 C.1246 B.B.A. L.990 J.D. P.O. Box 11350‡
**Olmsted, R. Wayne**, (BV) ... '39 '83 C.494 B.S.B.A. L.1068 J.D. [Balfour M.M.&O.]
*PRACTICE AREAS: Business Law; Employment Law; Litigation; Landlord and Tenant Law; Mechanics Lien Law.
**Olson, Michael C.** ... '54 '80 C.475 B.S. L.912 J.D. [Lewis,D.B.&B.]
*PRACTICE AREAS: Insurance Defense Law; Professional Malpractice Law; Construction Defect Law.
**O'Neill, Michael K.** '55 '86
C.816 B.S. L.564 J.D. [Ⓐ Fitzpatrick,C.H.&S.] (See Pat. Sect.)
**Osborn, Sean T.** ... '58 '84 C.800 B.S. L.464 J.D. [Ⓐ Booth,M.&S.]
**Ostergar, Allen C., III** ... '66 '93 C.101 B.A. L.464 J.D. [Ⓐ Rutan&T.]
*LANGUAGES: Portuguese.
*PRACTICE AREAS: Civil Trial.
**Otsuka, Leigh** ... '68 '94 C.800 B.A. L.426 J.D. [Ⓐ Drummy K.W.&G.]
*PRACTICE AREAS: Litigation.
**Ott, John D.** ... '64 '92 C.1109 B.A. L.692 J.D. [Drummy K.W.&G.]
*PRACTICE AREAS: Construction Litigation; Products Liability; Real Estate Litigation; Financial Institutions Representation; Employment.
**Owen, Robert** ... '61 '86 C.668 B.A. L.426 J.D. [Rutan&T.]
*PRACTICE AREAS: Municipal and Zoning; General Practice; Construction; Land Use Law.
**Parker, Joseph M.** ... '66 '92 C.1042 B.A. L.1049 J.D. [Ⓐ Cooksey,H.M.&T.]
*PRACTICE AREAS: Litigation; Insurance Defense Law; Personal Injury; Employment Litigation.
Parker, Michael L. ... '63 '88 C.112 B.A. L.464 J.D. 3080 Bristol St.
**Parret, Charles W.**, (AV) ... '50 '77 C.112 B.S. L.800 J.D. [Drummy K.W.&G.]
*PRACTICE AREAS: Civil Litigation with emphasis on Business and Real Estate Law.
**Patterson, Jerry M.**, (AV) ... '34 '67 C.1042 A.B. L.1068 J.D. [Burke,W.&S.]
*PRACTICE AREAS: Municipal Law; Planning and Zoning Law.
**Paul, Lee G.**, (AV) ... '07 '33 C.95 B.A. L.309 J.D. [Ⓒ Paul,H.J.&W.]

**Paul, Hastings, Janofsky & Walker LLP, (AV)** BR
**A Limited Liability Partnership including Professional Corporations**
**Firm Established in 1951; Office in 1974**
**Seventeenth Floor, 695 Town Center Drive, 92626-1924⊙**
**Telephone: 714-668-6200 Fax: 714-979-1921**
**Email: info@PHJW.com URL: http://www.phjw.com**
**Counsel: Oliver F. Green; Lee G. Paul. Members of Firm: Stephen D. Cooke; Glenn D. Dassoff; Janet Toll Davidson; John F. Della Grotta; Howard C. Hay; Matthew A. Hodel; Michael A. Hood; Donald L. Morrow; Douglas A. Schaaf; William J. Simpson; Peter J. Tennyson; John E. Trinnaman (Certified Specialist in Estate Planning, Trust and Probate Law, The State Bar of California Board of Legal Specialization). Senior Counsel: Robert R. Burge; James W. Hamilton. Of Counsel: Mary L. Cornwell; Jason O. Engel; Scott N. Leslie; Sean A. O'Brien; Darla L. Yancey. Associates: Terry Jon Allen; Steven D. Allison; Brent R. Bohn; Glenn L. Briggs; Robert P. Bryant; Barbara R. Danz; Jessica S. Dorman-Davis; Malinda A. Faber; Violet F. Fiacco; Laura A. Forbes; Andrew P. Hanson; Jarret L. Johnson; Lisa M. LaFourcade; Vincent D. Lowder; Scott R. Miller; John B. Stephens.**
**General Practice.**

(This Listing Continued)

**Paul, Hastings, Janofsky & Walker LLP (Continued)**

**Los Angeles, California Office: Twenty-Third Floor, 555 South Flower Street. Telephone: 213-683-6000.**
**Washington, D.C. Office: Tenth Floor, 1299 Pennsylvania Avenue, N.W. Telephone: 202-508-9500.**
**Atlanta, Georgia Office: 24th Floor, 600 Peachtree Street, N.E. Telephone: 404-815-2400.**
**Santa Monica, California Office: Fifth Floor, 1299 Ocean Avenue. Telephone: 310-319-3300.**
**Stamford, Connecticut Office: Ninth Floor, 1055 Washington Boulevard. Telephone: 203-961-7400.**
**New York, New York Office: 31st Floor, 399 Park Avenue. Telephone: 212-318-6000.**
**Tokyo, Japan Office: Ark Mori Building, 30th Floor, 12-32 Akasaka, P.O. Box 577, 1-Chome, Minato-Ku. Telephone: (03) 3586-4711.**

***See Professional Biographies, COSTA MESA, CALIFORNIA***

**Payne, Geoffrey S.** ... '57 '87 C.1109 B.A. L.426 J.D. [Drummy K.W.&G.]
*PRACTICE AREAS: Commercial Real Property; Corporate Finance; Leases; Lending and Secured Transactions.
Perks, Benjamin W. '42 '67 C.207 B.A. L.150 J.D.
(adm. in OH; not adm. in CA) Price Waterhouse
**Pero, Jeffrey T.** ... '46 '72 C.602 B.A. L.569 J.D. [Latham&W.]
Petersen, Gregory G. ... '48 '77 C.999 L.1137 J.D. 3185 Airway Ave.
Petersen, Michael J. '52 '77 C.963 B.S. L.494 J.D.
V.P. & Gen. Coun., Prudential Real Estate Affiliates, Inc.
Peterson, Gary A. ... '62 '90 C.763 B.S.M.E. L.1137 J.D. 3200 Park Cntr. Dr., 9th Fl.
Peterson, R. Thomas, (AV) ... '48 '73 C.767 B.S. L.1068 J.D. [Obrien,G.&P.]
**Pettis, Alan W.**, (AV) ... '40 '67 C&L.846 B.A., LL.B. [Latham&W.]
**Phelan, Carrie E.** ... '65 '90 C&L.426 B.S., J.D. [Ⓐ Murtaugh,M.M.&N.]
Phelps, Aaron K., (AV) ... '18 '42 C.853 B.A. L.623 J.D. 611 Anton Blvd., Ste., 720‡
Phillips, Lisa Lopin ... '64 '90 C.773 B.A. L.1049 J.D. [Ⓐ Davis,S.B.&G.]
**Pierce, Bradley D.** ... '65 '94 C.139 B.S. L.426 J.D. [Ⓐ McCormick,K.&B.]
*PRACTICE AREAS: Business Litigation; Real Property and Environmental Law; Condemnation.
Pierce, Christina J. ... '45 '76 C.895 B.S. L.1148 J.D. 3090 Bristol St.
Pikulin, David ... '63 '90 C.763 A.B. L.1049 J.D. 3080 Bristol St.

**Pillsbury Madison & Sutro LLP, (AV)**
**Plaza Tower, 600 Anton Boulevard Suite 1100, 92626⊙**
**Telephone: 714-436-6800 Fax: 714-662-6999**
**Members of Firm: Marvin I. Bartel; Thomas L. Becket; Alan J. Droste; John C. Garrett; Donald P. Hickman; Robert L. Klotz; Richard S. Ruben; Henry R. Stiepel. Senior Counsel: Marcello F. De Frenza; Robert J. Gerard, Jr. Associates: Jennifer Penoyer Ashley; Craig A. Barbarosh; Carolyn C. Burger; Andrew C. Callari; Peter W. Martinez; Marci Lerner Miller; William N. Scarff, Jr.; Christopher J. Seiber.**
**General Civil Practice and Litigation in all State and Federal Courts. Business: Banking and Corporate Finance; Commercial Transactions/Energy; Corporate, Securities and Technologies; Creditors' Rights and Bankruptcy; Employee Benefits; Employment and Labor Relations; Environment, Health & Safety; Estate Planning; Finance and Commercial Transactions; Food and Beverage Regulation; Health Care; Political Law; Real Estate; Tax (domestic and international); and Telecommunications. Litigation: Alternative Dispute Resolution; Antitrust/Trade Regulation; Appellate; Banking/Financial Institutions; Commercial Disputes; Construction/Real Estate; Creditors' Rights, Bankruptcy and Insurance Insolvency; Energy Matters; Employment/Equal Opportunity; Environmental/Land Use; ERISA; Insurance; Intellectual Property; Maritime/Admiralty; Media/Entertainment/Sports; Securities; Tort/Product Liability; and White Collar Defense. Intellectual Property: Aesthetic Design & Trade Dress Protection; Biotechnology; Computer Law; Copyright Law; Intellectual Property Audits and Strategic Planning; International Trade Commission; Licensing and Technology Transfer; Procurement of Property Rights; Patent Prosecution; Trade Secrets and Unfair Competition; Trademark Law; Interference Practice; Mechanical/Biomed/Aeronautical; and Physics/Optics.**
**Los Angeles, California Office: Citicorp Plaza, 725 South Figueroa Street, Suite 1200, 90017. Telephone: 213-488-7100. Fax: 213-629-1033.**
**Silicon Valley Office: 2700 San Hill Road, Menlo Park, 94025. Telephone: 415-233-4500. Fax: 415-233-4545.**
**New York, New York Office: 520 Madison Avenue, 40th Floor, 10022. Telephone: 212-328-4810. Fax: 212-328-4824.**
**Sacramento, California Office: 400 Capitol Mall, Suite 1700, 95814. Telephone: 916-329-4700. Fax: 916-441-3583.**
**San Diego, California Office: 101 West Broadway, Suite 1800, 92101. Telephone: 619-234-5000. Fax: 619-236-1995.**
**San Francisco, California Office: 235 Montgomery Street, 94104. Telephone: 415-983-1000. Fax: 415-983-1200.**
**Washington, D C. Office: 1100 New York Avenue, N.W., Ninth Floor, 20005. Telephone: 202-861-3000. Fax: 202-822-0944.**
**Hong Kong Office: 6/7 Asia Pacific Finance Tower, Citibank Plaza, 3 Garden Road, Central. Telephone: 011-852-2509-7100. Fax: 011-852-2509-7188.**
**Tokyo, Japan Office: Pillsbury Madison & Sutro, Gaikokuho Jimu Bengoshi Jimusho, 5th Floor, Samon Eleven Building, 3-1, Samon-cho, Shinjuku-ku, Tokyo 160 Japan. Telephone: 800-729-9830; 011-813-3354-3531. Fax: 011-813-3354-3534.**

***See Professional Biographies, COSTA MESA, CALIFORNIA***

**Pitman, David** ... '53 '94 C&L.061 B.S., LL.B. [Ⓐ Latham&W.]
**Pose, Marlene** ... '71 '96 C.112 B.A. L.1065 J.D. [Ⓐ Rutan&T.]
*LANGUAGES: Spanish.
**Pratt, Gibson E.** ... '45 '72 C.37 B.A. L.61 J.D. [McInnis,F.R.&S.]
*PRACTICE AREAS: Banking and Asset Management Litigation; Professional Liability Litigation; Commercial Litigation; Real Estate Litigation.
**Pysher, Paul A.** '67 '94 C.688 B.S.E.E. L.94 J.D.
[Ⓐ Fitzpatrick,C.H.&S.] (See Pat. Sect.)
Quevedo, George A. ... '49 '78 C.112 B.A. L.767 J.D. 666 Baker St.
Quigley, John P. ... '34 '63 C&L.477 B.S., J.D. 939 Arbor St.
Quinn, Lisa M. ... '58 '87 C.112 B.A. L.880 J.D. 3151 Airway Ave.
**Rafferty, Paul F.** ... '59 '87 C.397 B.S. L.1292 J.D. [Ⓒ Sheppard,M.R.&H.]
*PRACTICE AREAS: Corporate and Real Estate Litigation.
Raileanu, Ina ... '66 '91 C.112 B.A. L.1065 J.D. 611 Anton Blvd.
Rasch, Albert J., Jr. ... '44 '88 C.645 B.S. L.1137 J.D. [Rasch&M.]
Rasch and Morris ... 575 Anton Blvd., 3rd Fl.
Rasner, Bruce E. ... '45 '74 C.1046 B.S. L.990 J.D. 650 Town Ctr. Dr.
**Redjaian, Babak** ... '67 '96 C.1042 B.S.E.E. L.809 J.D. [Ⓐ Blakely,S.T.&Z.]
Reed, Dana W., (Mr.), (AV) ... '44 '75 C.999 L.426 J.D. [Reed&D.]⊙
Reed & Davidson, (AV) ... 3151 Airway Ave. (⊙Los Angeles)
**Reilly, Debra L.** ... '62 '90 C.101 B.S. L.1049 J.D. [Ⓐ Murtaugh,M.M.&N.]
**Reveal, Ernest I., III**, (AV) ... '48 '73 C.188 B.A. L.477 J.D. [Robins,K.M.&C.]
*PRACTICE AREAS: Business Litigation.
**Reynolds, James J.**, (AV) ... '52 '83 C.763 B.A. L.61 J.D. [McInnis,F.R.&S.]⊙
**Richard, Jeffrey M.**, (BV) ... '57 '82 C.112 A.B. L.1066 J.D. [Drummy K.W.&G.]
*PRACTICE AREAS: Civil Litigation with emphasis on Business and Real Estate Law.
**Richards, Marc H.** ... '60 '85 C.154 B.A. L.178 J.D. [Casey&R.]
*PRACTICE AREAS: Estate Planning; Charitable Giving; Probate; Wills and Trust Law; Administration.
**Ricks, Cecil E., Jr.**, (AV) ... '39 '64 C.112 B.A. L.1068 J.D. [Ricks&A.]
*PRACTICE AREAS: Civil Litigation; Wrongful Termination; Employment and Discrimination Law.

**Ricks & Anderson, A Law Corporation, (AV)** BR
**3200 Park Center Drive, Suite 1155, 92626-4413**
**Telephone: 714-966-9190**
**Cecil E. Ricks, Jr.; Annette L. Anderson.**
**General Civil Litigation and Appellate Practice. Wrongful Termination, Employment and Discrimination Law.**

***See Professional Biographies, COSTA MESA, CALIFORNIA***

CALIFORNIA—COSTA MESA

MARTINDALE-HUBBELL LAW DIRECTORY 1997

**Riordan & McKinzie, A Professional Law Corporation, (AV)**
**695 Town Center Drive, Suite 1500, 92626⊙**
**Telephone: 714-433-2900 FAX: 714-549-3244**
**Martin J. Thompson; Kirk F. Maldonado; James W. Loss; Michael P. Whalen; Elaine R. Levin;—James H. Shnell; Bart Greenberg; Karen C. Goodin; Michael G. McKinnon; Jeanne Miller-Romero.**
**General Civil and Trial Practice in all State and Federal Courts. Corporation, Corporate Securities, Real Estate, Antitrust, Patent, Trademark, Copyright and Unfair Competition Law. Taxation, Estate Planning, Trust and Probate Law.**
**Reference: Citibank, 333 S. Grand Ave., Los Angeles, Calif.**
**Los Angeles, California Office: California Plaza, 29th Floor, 300 South Grand Avenue. Telephone: 213-629-4824. FAX: 213-229-8550.**
**Westlake Village, California Office: 5743 Corsa Avenue, Suite 116. Telephones: 818-706-1800; 805-496-4688. FAX: 818-706-2956.**

*See Professional Biographies, COSTA MESA, CALIFORNIA*

**Risley, Robert L.**, (AV) . . . . . . . . . . . . . . . . . .'30 '57 C.502 B.S. L.378 J.D. [Risley&Assoc.]

**Risley & Associates, (AV)** BR
**Suite 225, 3420 Bristol Street, 92626**
**Telephone: 714-557-9712 Fax: 714-557-9908**
**Email: Harviell@aol.com**
**Robert L. Risley (Certified Specialist, Taxation Law, The State Bar of California Board of Legal Specialization).**
**Taxation, Estate Planning, Probate, Real Estate Law, Asset Protection and General Business.**
**Reference: Sanwa Bank, South Coast Office, Santa Ana; First American Trust Co., Newport Beach.**

*See Professional Biographies, COSTA MESA, CALIFORNIA*

Rivas, Sandra . . . . . . . . . . . . . . . . . . . . . '59 '85 C&L.800 B.S., J.D. 6310 San Vicente Blvd.

**Rivin, Ira G., (P.C.)**, (AV) . . . . . . . . . . . . . . . . . .'48 '74 C.112 A.B. L.1066 J.D. [Rutan&T.]
*PRACTICE AREAS: Real Estate; Commercial; Civil Trial.

**Roberts, Kenneth S.** . . . '63 '93 C.886 B.S.M.E. L.1049 J.D. [A Lyon&L.] (See Pat. Sect.)
*PRACTICE AREAS: Patent, Trademark, Copyright; Trade Secret; Intellectual Property.

Roberts, Larry J. . . . . . . . . . . . . . . . . . . . . . . .'46 '71 C.957 B.A. L.309 J.D. 3185 Airway Ave.

**Robins, Kaplan, Miller & Ciresi, (AV)**
**600 Anton Boulevard, Suite 1600, 92626-7147⊙**
**Telephone: 714-540-6200 Fax: 714-545-6915**
**Members of Firm: Geoffrey T. Glass; Scott G. Johnson; Alan M. Jones; William P. Linhoff, Jr.; Thomas A. Miller; Ernest I. Reveal, III; Patrick E. Shipstead. Associates: Alexandra M. Day; Tod R. Dubow; Michael S. Henderson; Jenny Lee; Susan Lope; Stan A. Mortensen; Robert J. Terry; Holly A. H. Williams; Shatara R. Wright.**
**Trials and Appeals in all Federal and State Courts. Administrative, Antitrust, Appellate, Banking, Bankruptcy and Reorganization, Construction, Communications, Corporate, Employment and Employee Benefits, Environmental, Estate Planning and Probate, Franchising, Finance, Health, Insurance Law, Intellectual Property, International Litigation and Trade, Medical Malpractice, Personal Injury, Products Liability, Real Estate, Securities, Tax, Transportation.**
**Atlanta, Georgia Office: 2600 One Atlanta Plaza, 950 East Paces Ferry Road NE. Telephone: 404-233-1114. Fax: 404-233-1267.**
**Boston, Massachusetts Office: Suite 2200, 222 Berkeley Street. Telephone: 617-267-2300. Fax: 617-267-8288.**
**Chicago, Illinois Office: Suite 1400, 55 West Wacker Drive. Telephone: 312-782-9200. Fax: 312-782-7756.**
**Los Angeles, California Office: 2049 Century Park East, Suite 3700. Telephone: 310-552-0130. Fax: 310-229-5800.**
**Minneapolis, Minnesota Office: 2800 LaSalle Plaza, 800 LaSalle Avenue. Telephone: 612-349-8500. Fax: 612-339-4181.**
**San Francisco, California Office: Suite 2700, 444 Market Street. Telephone: 415-399-1800. Fax: 415-391-1968.**
**Washington, D.C. Office: Suite 1200, 1801 K Street, N.W. Telephone: 202-775-0725. Fax: 202-223-8604.**

*See Professional Biographies, COSTA MESA, CALIFORNIA*

**Roosje, Harry A.** '61 '88 C.188 B.A. L.569 J.D.
Assoc. Gen. Coun., ICN Pharmaceuticals, Inc.

**Rose, Jeffrey W., (AV) '62 '87 C.228 A.B. L.1068 J.D.**
**Center Tower, 650 Town Center Drive, Suite 1930, 92626**
**Telephone: 714-751-9215 FAX: 714-754-0444**
**Email: jrose000@counsel.com**
***PRACTICE AREAS: Intellectual Property; Business Litigation; High Technology Law; Insurance Coverage Law.**
**Intellectual Property, Copyrights, Trademarks, Trade Secrets, Multimedia Licensing, Litigation and General Business.**

*See Professional Biographies, COSTA MESA, CALIFORNIA*

**Ross, Matthew K.** . . . . . . . . . . . . . . . . . . . . . . . .'59 '85 C.112 B.A. L.1066 J.D. [Rutan&T.]
*PRACTICE AREAS: Civil Trial; Appellate Practice.

**Ruben, Richard S.**, (AV) . . . . . . . . . . . . . '50 '75 C.800 B.S. L.1068 J.D. [Pillsbury M.&S.]

**Rubin, Michael D.**, (AV) . . . . . . . . . . . . . . . . . . . . . .'48 '74 C&L.477 B.A., J.D. [Rutan&T.]
*PRACTICE AREAS: Civil Trial; Real Estate; Municipal and Zoning; Land Use Law; Environmental.

**Ruck, Charles K.** . . . . . . . . . . . . . . . . . . . . . . .'67 '93 C.112 B.A. L.477 J.D. [A Latham&W.]

**Rudolph, George C.**, (AV) '51 '76 C.800 B.A. L.1065 J.D.
[Rudolph] (⊙Santa Monica)

**Rudolph Law Group, The, A Professional Corporation, (AV)** BR
**3200 Park Center Drive, Suite 1370, 92626**
**Telephone: 714-545-7272; 714-757-7272 Fax: 714-545-7273**
**George C. Rudolph.**
**General Trial and Appellate Practice in State and Federal Courts, including General Business and Commercial Litigation, Real Estate Litigation, Product Liability, Intellectual Property, Trade Secrets and Unfair Competition, Environmental, Employment and Partnership, Corporate and Trust Disputes.**

*See Professional Biographies, COSTA MESA, CALIFORNIA*

Rupp, Stephen V., (A Professional Corporation) '46 '76
C.1078 B.A. L.1049 J.D. [Duke,G.S.&B.] (⊙San Diego)

**Ruston, Donald A.**, (AV) . . . . . . . . . . . . . . .'29 '55 C.990 B.A. L.1068 J.D. [Lewis,D.B.&B.]

**Rutan & Tucker, LLP, (AV)** BR
**A Partnership including Professional Corporations**
**611 Anton Boulevard, Suite 1400, P.O. Box 1950, 92626**
**Telephone: 714-641-5100; 213-625-7586 Telecopier: 714-546-9035**
**Email: rutan&tucker@mcimail.com URL: http://www.rutan.com**
**Members of Firm: James R. Moore (P.C.); Paul Frederic Marx (Certified Specialist, Taxation Law, The State Bar of California Board of Legal Specialization); William R. Biel; Richard A. Curnutt; Leonard A. Hampel, Jr.; John B. Hurlbut, Jr.; Michael W. Immell; Milford W. Dahl, Jr.; Theodore I. Wallace, Jr., (P.C.); Richard P. Sims; Robert C. Braun; Edward D. Sybesma, Jr., (P.C.); Thomas S. Salinger (P.C.); David C. Larsen (P.C.); Clifford E. Frieden; Michael D. Rubin; Ira G. Rivin (P.C.); Jeffrey M. Oderman (P.C.); Joseph D. Carruth; Stan Wolcott (P.C.); Robert S. Bower; David J. Aleshire; Marcia A. Forsyth; William M. Marticorena; James L. Morris; Anne Nelson Lanphar; William J. Caplan; Michael T. Hornak; Philip D. Kohn; Joel D. Kuperberg; Steven A. Nichols; Thomas G. Brockington; William W. Wynder; Evridiki (Vicki) Dallas; Randall M. Babbush; Mary M. Green; Thomas J. Crane; Mark B. Frazier; M. Katherine Jenson; Duke Wahlquist; Richard Montevideo; Lori Sarner Smith; Ernest W. Klatte III; Elizabeth L. Martyn; Kim D. Thompson; Jayne Taylor Kacer; David B. Cosgrove; Hans Van Ligten; Stephen A. Ellis; Matthew K. Ross; Jeffrey Wertheimer; Robert Owen; Adam N. Volkert; Jeffrey A. Goldfarb; F. Kevin Brazil; Layne H. Melzer; Lien Ski Harrison. Associates: Michael K. Slattery; Debra Dunn Steel; David H. Hochner; Elise K. Traynum; Dan Slater; James S. Weisz; Carol Landis Demmler; Patrick D. McCalla; Richard K. Howell; A. Patrick Muñoz; Paul J. Sievers; S. Daniel Harbottle; Joseph Louis Maga III; Kraig C. Kilger; Scott R. Santagata; Sandra J. Young; Allen C. Ostergar III; Julia L. Bond; Jennifer White-Sperling; Robert Elliot Adel II; Anward Li; Steven M. Coleman; Steven John Goon; Douglas J. Dennington; Kara S. Carlson; Sue Lee Collins; Eric L. Dunn; Todd Owen Litfin; Steven M.**

(This Listing Continued)

**Rutan & Tucker, LLP (Continued)**

**Muldowney; Deborah J. Chuang; Natalie Sibbald Dundas; Sean P. Farrell; Fred A. Jenkins; Marlene Pose; April Lee Walter; Karen E. Walter. Of Counsel: Garvin F. Shallenberger; David J. Garibaldi III (Certified Specialist, Probate, Estate Planning and Trust Law, The State Bar of California Board of Legal Specialization).**
**General Civil and Trial Practice in all State and Federal Courts. Municipal Law, Real Estate, Corporate, Securities, Employment and Labor Relations (Management and Public Sector), Taxation, Estate Planning, Trust and Probate, Environmental and Land Use Law, Municipal Finance, Water Rights, Education Law, Bankruptcy and Creditors Rights.**

*See Professional Biographies, COSTA MESA, CALIFORNIA*

**Rybarczyk, Jerome D.** . . . . . . . . . . . . . . . . . . . . . . . .'54 '82 C&L.884 B.A., J.D. [Ely,F.&H.]
*PRACTICE AREAS: Products Liability Law; Insurance Defense; Business Litigation; General Civil Litigation.

Sachrison, Eric W. . . . . . . . . '65 '91 C.112 B.A. L.61 J.D. [A Duke,G.S.&B.] (⊙San Diego)

**Sakaguchi, James K.** . . . . . . . . . . . . . . . . . . . '64 '95 C.112 B.S.E. L.1068 J.D. [A Lyon&L.]
*PRACTICE AREAS: Intellectual Property.

**Salinger, Thomas S., (P.C.)**, (AV) . . . . . . . . . . .'45 '72 C.188 B.A. L.1066 J.D. [Rutan&T.]
*PRACTICE AREAS: Construction; Real Estate; Title Insurance; Financial Institutions.

**Samini, Keyvan** . . . . . . . . . . . . . . . . . . . .'66 '93 C.966 B.S. L.608 J.D. [A Ginsburg,S.O.&R.]

Samuelson, Mitchell, (A L.C.), (AV) . . . . . . . . .'36 '60 C&L.94 A.B., J.D. [Davis,S.B.&G.]

**Sanders, Glenda** . . . . . . . . . . . . . . . . . . . . . . '56 '86 C&L.061 B.A., LL.B. [Latham&W.]

**Sandoval, Karl** . . . . . . . . . . . . . . . . . . . . . . . .'67 '93 C.112 B.A. L.1066 J.D. [A Graham&J.]
*PRACTICE AREAS: Civil and Appellate Litigation.

**Santagata, Scott R.** . . . . . . . . . . . . . . . . . . . . . '67 '92 C.763 B.S. L.1066 J.D. [A Rutan&T.]
*PRACTICE AREAS: Business; Securities.

**Santana, Laila Morcos** . . . . . . . . . . . . . . . . . '65 '91 C&L.990 B.A., J.D. [A Booth,M.&S.]

Santucci, Danny C., (AV) . . . . '47 '72 C.112 B.A. L.1066 J.D. 1011 Brioso Ave., Ste., 111

**Saunders, Lara A.** . . . . . . . . . . . . . '69 '94 C.112 B.A. L.1066 J.D. [A Sheppard,M.R.&H.]

**Saylin, Gregory M.** . . . . . . . . . . . . . . . . . . . . . .'68 '96 C.771 B.A. L.880 J.D. [A Latham&W.]

**Scarff, William N., Jr.** . . . . . . . . . . . . . . '58 '91 C.608 B.A. L.800 J.D. [A Pillsbury M.&S.]

**Schaaf, Douglas A.** . . . . . . . . . . . . . . . . . . . '55 '81 C.746 B.B.A. L.602 J.D. [Paul,H.J.&W.]

**Schaal, William W.** '64 '92
C.112 B.S.E.E. L.426 J.D. [A Blakely,S.T.&Z.] (See Pat. Sect.)

Scheer, Jerry A. . . . . . . . . . . . . . . . . . . . . . . . . '39 '68 C.763 B.A. L.61 J.D. Asst. City Atty.

**Schilling, Linda** . . . . . . . . . . . . . . . . . . . . . . . .'60 '88 C.112 B.A. L.1067 J.D. [Latham&W.]

**Schlatter, Regina M.** . . . . . . . . . . . . . . . . . . . . .'57 '87 C&L.477 B.A., J.D. [C Latham&W.]

Schulman, Alexander R. . . . . . . . . . . . . . . . . . . .'47 '80 C&L.999 J.D. 275 E. 18th St., Apt. 9

**Schulman, Marshall M.**, (AV) . . . . . . . . . . . . . . . .'27 '53 C.112 L.426 J.D. [Schulman&M.]
*PRACTICE AREAS: Criminal Law.

**Schulman & McMillan, Incorporated, (AV)** BR
**3200 Park Center Drive, Suite 600, 92626-7148**
**Telephone: 714-434-9596 Telecopier: 714-434-1823**
**Marshall M. Schulman (Certified Specialist, Criminal Law, The State Bar of California Board of Legal Specialization).**
**Criminal Trial Practice in all State and Federal Courts.**

*See Professional Biographies, COSTA MESA, CALIFORNIA*

Schumacher, Frederick R. . . . . . . . . . . . . . . . . .'30 '57 C.674 A.B. L.188 LL.B. 650 Town Ctr.

Schwarz, Bradley K., (CV) . . . . . . . . . .'18 '53 C.112 A.B. L.1065 J.D. 1786 Newport Blvd.

**Scott, W. James, Jr.** . . . . . . . . . . . . . . . . . . . . .'46 '72 C.197 B.A. L.800 J.D. [Graham&J.]
*PRACTICE AREAS: Corporate Law; Business Law.

**Seal, David W.** . . . . . . . . . . . . . . . . . . '64 '95 C.1042 B.A. L.1137 J.D. [A Cooksey,H.M.&T.]
*PRACTICE AREAS: Construction Defect; Insurance Defense; Litigation.

**Seaver, Patrick T.** . . . . . . . . . . . . . . . . . . . . . . .'50 '78 C.976 B.A. L.813 J.D. [Latham&W.]

Sebade, Donald H. . . . . . . . '31 '70 C.273 B.A. L.990 J.D. Claim Coun., State Farm Ins. Co.

**Seiber, Christopher J.** . . . . . . . . . . . . . . . '69 '94 C.668 B.A. L.846 J.D. [A Pillsbury M.&S.]
*PRACTICE AREAS: Municipal Law; Natural Resources; Public Law Litigation; Land Use.

**Seneca, Mark W.** . . . . . . . . . . . . . . . . . . . . . . '67 '96 C.101 B.S. L.813 J.D. [A Latham&W.]

**Shallenberger, Garvin F.**, (AV) . . . . . . . . . . .'21 '49 C.508 A.B. L.1066 J.D. [C Rutan&T.]

**Shean, R. Scott** . . . . . . . . . . . . . . . . . . . . . . . .'69 '94 C.951 B.A. L.1068 J.D. [A Latham&W.]

Shelley, Gerald N. . . . . . . . . . . . . . . . . . . . . .'48 '74 C.1042 B.S. L.990 J.D. 650 Town Ctr. Dr.

**Sheppard, Mullin, Richter & Hampton LLP, (AV)**
**A Limited Liability Partnership including Professional Corporations**
**650 Town Center Drive, 4th Floor, 92626⊙**
**Telephone: 714-513-5100 Telecopier: 714-513-5130**
**Email: info@smrh.com URL: http://www.smrh.com**
**Members of Firm: Robert S. Beall; David M. Bosko; Steven W. Cardoza; Dean A. Demetre; John J. Giovannone; Randolph B. Godshall; Andrew J. Guilford; Brent R. Liljestrom; Alan H. Martin; Ryan D. McCortney; John R. Simon†; R. Marshall Tanner; Finley L. Taylor†; Perry Joseph Viscounty. Special Counsel: Fredric I. Albert; Steven C. Nock; Paul F. Rafferty. Associates: Cindy Thomas Archer; Justine Mary Casey; Gene R. Clark; Brian M. Daucher; Beverly A. Johnson; Greg S. Labate; Aaron J. Malo; Susan S. Matsui; Lara A. Saunders; Michael D. Stewart; Tawnya R. Wojciechowski.**
**General Civil Trial and Appellate Practice in all State and Federal Courts; Financial Institutions Law; Commercial Law; Banking; Bankruptcy and Reorganization; Corporate; Securities; Antitrust; Intellectual Property; Unfair Competition; Labor and Employment; Pension and Employee Benefits; Federal, State and Local Taxation; Real Estate; Land Use; Environmental; White Collar Criminal Defense; International Business; Administrative; Probate; Trust; and Estate Planning.**
**Los Angeles, California Office: Forty-Eighth Floor, 333 South Hope Street. Telephone: 213-620-1780. Telecopier: 213-620-1398. Cable Address: "Sheplaw". Home Page Address: http://www.smrh.com.**
**San Francisco, California Office: Seventeenth Floor, Four Embarcadero Center. Telephone: 415-434-9100. Telecopier: 415-434-3947. Telex: 19-4424. Home Page Address: http://www.smrh.com.**
**San Diego, California Office: Nineteenth Floor, 501 West Broadway. Telephone: 619-338-6500. Telecopier: 619-234-3815. Telex: 19-4424. Home Page Address: http://www.smrh.com.**
**†Professional Corporation**

*See Professional Biographies, COSTA MESA, CALIFORNIA*

**Shevlin, Clay** . . . . . . . . . . . . . . . . . . . . . . . . .'61 '96 C.464 B.S. L.1066 J.D. [A Latham&W.]

**Shipstead, Patrick E.**, (AV) . . . . . . . . . . . .'48 '76 C.309 A.B. L.477 J.D. [Robins,K.M.&C.]
*PRACTICE AREAS: Insurance Litigation; Personal Injury Law; Mass Tort; Commercial Litigation.

**Shiv, Moina C.** . . . . . . . . . . . . . . . . . . . . '58 '87 C&L.061 B.S., LL.B. [A Cooksey,H.M.&T.]
*LANGUAGES: Spanish and Hindi.
*PRACTICE AREAS: Personal Injury; Insurance Defense Law; Litigation; Coverage Law.

**Shnell, James H.** . . . . . . . . . . . . . . . . . . . . . . '50 '81 C.813 A.B. L.1066 J.D. [A Riordan&M.]
*PRACTICE AREAS: Corporate; Mergers and Acquisitions; Financings.

**Sievers, Paul J.** . . . . . . . . . . . . . . . . . . . . . . . . . .'61 '91 C.112 B.A. L.426 J.D. [A Rutan&T.]
*PRACTICE AREAS: Bankruptcy; Commercial; Real Estate; Civil Trial.

Siglin, I. Steven, Jr. . . . . . . . . . . . . . . . . . . . . . . . . . .'48 '73 C.679 B.A. L.276 J.D. [I.S.Siglin]

Siglin, I. Steven, A P.C. . . . . . . . . . . . . . . . . . . . . . . . . . . . . . . . . . . . . . .650 Town Center Dr.

**Sikkema, Jeffrey L** . . . . . . . . . . . . . . . . . . . . . . '55 '83 C.477 B.A. L.309 J.D. [Dorsey&W.]
*PRACTICE AREAS: Litigation.

**Simon, John R.**, (AV) . . . . . . . . . . . '39 '65 C.112 B.S. L.1066 LL.B. [Sheppard,M.R.&H.]
*PRACTICE AREAS: Real Property Law; Partnership Law; Real Estate Development Law.

**Simpson, William J.**, (AV) . . . . . . . . . . . . . . . . .'54 '79 C&L.893 B.A., J.D. [Paul,H.J.&W.]

**Sims, Richard P.**, (AV) . . . . . . . . . . . . . . . . . . . .'41 '69 C.763 B.S. L.178 LL.B. [Rutan&T.]
*PRACTICE AREAS: Real Estate.

**Singarella, Paul N.** . . . . . . . . . . . . . . . . . . . . . .'58 '91 C.918 B.A. L.800 J.D. [A Latham&W.]

**Skane, Thomas J.** . . . . . . . . . . . . . . . .'59 '84 C.112 B.A. L.426 J.D. [A Murtaugh,M.M.&N.]
*PRACTICE AREAS: Construction; Personal Injury Litigation; Insurance Coverage/Bad Faith.

**Skelly, Alan L.** . . . . . . . . . . . . . . . . . . . . . . . . '55 '87 C.1109 A.B. L.1137 J.D. [P.E.Whalen]

Skok, W. Thomas . . . . '48 '84 C.1047 B.A. L.1137 J.D. Dep. Gen. Coun., 76 Products Co.

**Slater, Dan** . . . . . . . . . . . . . . . . . . . . . . . . . . . .'49 '88 C.464 B.A. L.1066 J.D. [A Rutan&T.]
*PRACTICE AREAS: Land Use Law; Redevelopment Law; Municipal and Zoning.

CAA64P

**Slattery, Michael K.** ........................ '55 '82 C.674 B.A. L.800 J.D. [A Rutan&T.]
*LANGUAGES: French, Italian, Spanish, Swedish.
*PRACTICE AREAS: Bankruptcy; Financial Institution Insolvency; Commercial.

**Slayback, Paul C., (BV) '37 '73 C.475 B.S. L.477 J.D.**
**950 South Coast Drive, Suite 130, 92626**
**Telephone: 714-761-1516 Fax: 714-751-1044**
***PRACTICE AREAS: Personal Injury.**
**Personal Injury.**
***See Professional Biographies, COSTA MESA, CALIFORNIA***

**Smiley, Evan D.** ........................ '66 '92 C.1077 B.S. L.464 J.D. [A Albert,W.&G.]
*PRACTICE AREAS: Bankruptcy; Insolvency; Litigation.
**Smith, Lori Sarner** ........................ '56 '84 C.1056 B.S. L.1067 J.D. [Rutan&T.]
*PRACTICE AREAS: Real Estate; Bankruptcy.
Smith, Mark A. ..........'59 '91 C.172 B.S. Eng. L.1137 J.D. Asst. Coun., 76 Products Co.
**Smith, Nancy B.** '59 '90 C.174 B.A. L.1035 J.D.
(adm. in MN; not adm. in CA) [A Dorsey&W.]
*PRACTICE AREAS: Litigation.
**Smith, Sterling A.** ........................ '50 '78 C.1060 B.A. L.464 J.D. [C Ginsburg,S.O.&R.]
*PRACTICE AREAS: Civil Trial; Real Estate; Taxation.
**Smith, Tamara Dadd** ............'68 '94 C.16 B.A. L.990 J.D. [A Murtaugh,M.M.&N.]
*LANGUAGES: French.
Snyder, Bryan R., (A Professional Corporation) '60 '86
C.112 B.A. L.1049 J.D. [Duke,G.S.&B.] (©San Diego)
Speers, Roland R., (AV) ....... '33 '59 C.112 B.A. L.1068 J.D. 611 Anton Blvd., Ste., 720
**Stahr, John R.**, (AV) ........................ '32 '61 C.813 A.B. L.309 LL.B. [C Latham&W.]
**Stanley, James G.** ........................ '62 '88 C.1042 B.S.C.E. L.464 J.D. [Booth,M.&S.]
Starrels, Andrew J. '60 '85
C.112 A.B. L.188 J.D. Asst. Gen. Coun., ITT Real Estate Servs.
**Steel, Debra Dunn** ........................'55 '80 C.112 B.A. L.1068 J.D. [A Rutan&T.]
*PRACTICE AREAS: Real Estate Litigation; Lease Litigation; Financial Institution Litigation.
**Stein, Gillian** ........................'54 '78 L.061 [A Daehnke&C.]
*PRACTICE AREAS: Special Education; Environmental.
**Stepanski, Lisa A.** ................ '59 '86 C.990 B.S. L.276 J.D. [A Drummy K.W.&G.]
*PRACTICE AREAS: Civil Litigation with emphasis on Business Law.
**Stephens, John B.** ........................'63 '89 C.1075 B.S. L.1067 J.D. [A Paul,H.J.&W.]

**Stern, Neubauer, Greenwald & Pauly, A Professional Corporation**
**(See Santa Monica)**

Stewart, Joanne I '56 '87 C.800 B.A. L.1137 J.D.
(adm. in MT; not adm. in CA) 1162 Kingston St.‡
**Stewart, Michael D.** ........................ '— '92 L.1065 J.D. [A Sheppard,M.R.&H.]
*PRACTICE AREAS: Business Litigation; Creditor Bankruptcy Law.
**Stiepel, Henry R.** ........................ '56 '81 C.112 A.B. L.800 J.D. [Pillsbury M.&S.]
Stinstrom, Richard ........................'57 '89 C.893 B.A. L.426 J.D. 3333 Fairview Rd.
**Stone, Samuel B., (A Professional Corporation)**, (AV) '34 '60
C.886 B.S.E.E. L.273 J.D. [Lyon&L.] (See Pat. Sect.)
*PRACTICE AREAS: Patent, Trademark, Copyright; Intellectual Property.
Stoner, Barbara Fox '52 '84 C.112 B.A. L.809 J.D.
Assoc. Gen. Coun., US Facilities Corp.
**Strok, Philip E.** ........................ '— '93 C.1075 B.S. L.809 J.D. [A Albert,W.&G.]
**Swan, Joseph G.** '63 '93 C.107 B.S. L.178 J.D.
[A Fitzpatrick,C.H.&S.] (See Pat. Sect.)
Swanson, Mary J. ........................ '55 '81 C.112 B.A. L.1065 J.D. 611 Anton Blvd.
**Sybesma, Edward D., Jr., (P.C.)**, (AV) ....... '47 '72 C.347 B.S. L.477 J.D. [Rutan&T.]
*PRACTICE AREAS: Antitrust; Business; Civil Trial; Trademark, Copyright, Unfair Competition; Computer.
**Tague, Suzanne M., (P.C.)**, (BV) .....'52 '77 C.112 B.A. L.990 J.D. [McCormick,K.&B.]
*PRACTICE AREAS: Probate Law; Estate Planning Law; Administration of Class Actions; Adjunct Public Agency Representation.
**Takeuchi, Kevin K.** ........................'55 '82 C.112 B.A. L.1065 J.D. [Graham&J.]
*LANGUAGES: Japanese.
*PRACTICE AREAS: Litigation; Corporate Law; Japanese Business.
**Talwalkar, Nandu A.** '70 '96
C.339 B.S.E.E. L.800 J.D. [A Fitzpatrick,C.H.&S.] (See Pat. Sect.)
**Tamaoki, Sunny** ........................ '65 '93 C.112 B.S. L.426 J.D. [A Blakely,S.T.&Z.]
**Tanner, R. Marshall** .............. '46 '77 C.101 B.A. L.1068 J.D. [Sheppard,M.R.&H.]
**Tauger, Paul Nathan** ........................ '53 '92 C.454 B.A. L.426 J.D. [A Dorsey&W.]
*PRACTICE AREAS: Intellectual Property Litigation; Business Litigation.
**Taylor, Finley L.**, (AV) ..............'45 '71 C.112 B.A. L.880 J.D. [Sheppard,M.R.&H.]
*PRACTICE AREAS: Business Litigation.
**Taylor, Keith D.** ........................'52 '80 C.1109 B.A. L.1049 J.D. [Lewis,D.B.&B.]
**Taylor, Robert M., Jr.**, (AV) '34 '60
C.645 B.S.E.E. L.276 LL.B. [Lyon&L.] (See Pat. Sect.)
*PRACTICE AREAS: Patent; Intellectual Property.
**Templer, Ronald F.** ........................ '63 '89 C.800 B.S. L.990 J.D. [A Ely,F.&H.]
*PRACTICE AREAS: Products Liability; Insurance Defense; Insurance Fraud; Business Litigation; General Civil Litigation.
**Tennyson, Peter J.**, (AV) ................ '46 '75 C.679 B.A. L.893 J.D. [Paul,H.J.&W.]
**Terry, Robert J.** ........................ '66 '96 C.339 B.S. L.494 J.D. [A Robins,K.M.&C.]
*PRACTICE AREAS: Litigation.
**Tester, Bruce A.**, (AV) ........................ '41 '72 C.350 B.S. L.813 J.D. [Latham&W.]

**Thaler, Alan V., (AV) '55 '81 C.112 A.B. L.426 J.D.**
**Center Tower, Suite 1900, 650 Town Center Drive, 92626-1925**
**Telephone: 714-545-3485 Facsimile: 714-755-8290**
**Email: thalerlaw@juno.com**
***LANGUAGES: French and German.**
**General Civil Litigation. Creditor's Rights and Bankruptcy Litigation. Arts and Entertainment.**
***See Professional Biographies, COSTA MESA, CALIFORNIA***

Thibault, Richard D. ..............'42 '84 C&L.1137 B.S., J.D. 1555 Mesa Verde Dr. E.
**Thomas, Russell J., Jr.** ........................'42 '67 C&L.309 A.B., LL.B. [C Daehnke&C.]
*PRACTICE AREAS: Litigation; Employment Law.
Thomas, Timothy R. .............'45 '70 C&L.339 B.S., J.D. Gen. Coun., 76 Products Co.
**Thompson, Kim D.** ........................'60 '85 C.35 B.S. L.800 J.D. [Rutan&T.]
*PRACTICE AREAS: Real Estate Transactions; Tax-deferred Exchanges; Environmental Law; Commercial Leasing; Americans with Disabilities Act.
Thompson, Mark A. ........................ '64 '90 C.587 B.A. L.352 J.D. 611 Anton Blvd.
**Thompson, Martin J.** ........................ '48 '73 C.112 A.B. L.1066 J.D. [Riordan&M.]
**Thomson, Daniel A.** ........................ '64 '93 C&L.101 B.S., J.D. [A Latham&W.]
**Thurston, Morris A.**, (AV) ........................'43 '71 C.101 B.A. L.309 J.D. [Latham&W.]
**Timmons, R. Brian** ........................'63 '91 C.228 A.B. L.309 J.D. [A Latham&W.]
**Toolen, Robert L.**, (AV) .............. '48 '74 C.112 B.A. L.809 J.D. [Cooksey,H.M.&T.]
*REPORTED CASES: Jeffrey E. v. Central Baptist Church, (1988) 197 Cal.App.3d 718.
*PRACTICE AREAS: Litigation; Insurance Law; Insurance Defense Litigation.
Torgerson, Noel K., (BV) ........................'48 '75 C.37 B.A. L.800 J.D. [Davis,S.B.&G.]
Tosti, Joseph M. ........................ '55 '80 C.112 B.A. L.426 J.D. 695 Town Center Dr.
Trachtman, Benjamin R. ....... '62 '88 C.1109 B.A. L.426 J.D. 3200 Park Cntr. Dr., 9th Fl.
**Traynum, Elise K.** ........................'49 '87 C.1110 B.A. L.1065 J.D. [A Rutan&T.]
*PRACTICE AREAS: Educational Law; Land Use Law; Public Law.

**Treglia, Lawrence A., Jr.** ..........'60 '86 C.763 B.A. L.464 J.D. [A Murtaugh,M.M.&N.]
*PRACTICE AREAS: Construction Litigation.
**Trinnaman, John E.**, (AV) ........................ '42 '70 C.178 B.A. L.893 J.D. [Paul,H.J.&W.]
Tripi, Kevin M. ........................ '59 '84 C&L.107 B.S., J.D. 3200 Pk. Cntr. Dr., Ste., 1000
Upton, John H. ........................ '62 '88 C.112 B.A. L.426 J.D. 575 Anton Blvd.
Vail, Edwin H., Jr. ........................ '34 '62 C&L.800 B.S., LL.B. 949 S. Coast Dr.
Vanderford, Madelene P. ........................'59 '85 C.800 B.S. L.426 J.D. 600 Anton Blvd.
Vanderpool, Douglas Brent .............. '60 '92 C.112 B.A. L.1065 J.D. 611 Anton Blvd.
**Van Ligten, Hans** ........................ '59 '85 C.112 B.A. L.426 J.D. [Rutan&T.]
*PRACTICE AREAS: Municipal and Zoning; Environmental; Land Use Law; Civil Rights.
**Van Marter, Brian R.** ............ '66 '93 C.1109 B.A. L.1148 J.D. [A Cooksey,H.M.&T.]
*PRACTICE AREAS: Litigation; Construction Defect; Insurance Defense Law.
Velasco, Jose A. '54 '80 C.426 B.A. L.1068 J.D.
Sr. V.P., Secy. & Gen. Coun., US Facilities Corp.
**Venuto, Stephen J.** ........................'71 '96 C.112 B.A. L.188 J.D. [A Latham&W.]
**Verdries, Annie** ........................ '49 '79 C&L.398 B.A., J.D. [Lewis,D.B.&B.]
*LANGUAGES: Dutch.
Vereker, Daniel A. ........................'43 '77 C&L.1137 B.S.L., J.D. 2790 Habor Blvd.
**Viscounty, Perry Joseph** .............. '62 '87 C&L.800 B.S., J.D. [Sheppard,M.R.&H.]
*PRACTICE AREAS: Litigation; Intellectual Property Law.
**Volkert, Adam N.** ........................'61 '86 C.813 A.B. L.597 J.D. [Rutan&T.]
*PRACTICE AREAS: Real Estate Transactions; Commercial and Industrial Leasing; Environmental; Construction.
**Wahlquist, Duke** ........................ '56 '82 C.878 B.S. L.1068 J.D. [Rutan&T.]
*PRACTICE AREAS: Appellate Practice; Civil Trial.
**Wallace, Theodore I., Jr., (P.C.)**, (AV) ......... '37 '62 C&L.309 B.A., J.D. [Rutan&T.]
*PRACTICE AREAS: Civil Trial.
**Walsh, Michael J.** ........................ '67 '91 C.1109 B.A. L.800 J.D. [Draper&W.]
*PRACTICE AREAS: Mechanics Liens; Construction Litigation; Business Litigation; Real Estate Litigation; Commercial Collections.
**Walter, April Lee** ........................ '71 '96 C.1042 B.S. L.426 J.D. [A Rutan&T.]
**Walter, Karen E.** ........................ '71 '96 C&L.813 B.A., J.D. [A Rutan&T.]
*LANGUAGES: Spanish and French.
*PRACTICE AREAS: Public Law.
Warffuel, Heidi Lynn ........................'57 '89 C.1239 B.A. L.1137 J.D. 611 Anton Blvd.
**Warnagieris, Gregory R.** ............'57 '92 C.112 B.S. L.426 J.D. [A Cooksey,H.M.&T.]
*PRACTICE AREAS: Litigation; Insurance Defense Law; Personal Injury.
**Washburn, Anderson L.** ........................ '56 '88 C&L.101 B.A., J.D. [A W.D.Easton]
*LANGUAGES: Spanish.
Washington, Frank G. '47 '75 C.188 B.S. L.976 J.D.
(adm. in DC; not adm. in CA) V.P., Times Mirror Videotex Servs.
Watkins, Paul K., (AV) ........................'46 '73 C&L.800 A.B., J.D. [Davis,S.B.&G.]
**Watt, David C.** '52 '82 C.763 B.S. L.1137 J.D.
Exec. V.P., Gen. Coun. & Corp. Secy., ICN Pharmaceuticals, Inc.
Wayman, Kenneth L., (AV) ...... '43 '72 C.800 B.A. L.990 J.D. 2845 Mesa Verde Dr. E.
**Weiland, Michael J.**, (AV) ........................ '52 '80 C.112 B.A. L.426 J.D. [Albert,W.&G.]
Weinfeld, David A., (AV) .............. '40 '75 C.563 B.M.E. L.990 J.D. [Weinfeld&M.]
Weinfeld & Mixon, A Law Corporation, (AV) ............Suite 510, 575 Anton Boulevard
**Weisz, James S.**, (CV©) ........................'61 '88 C.846 B.B.A. L.893 J.D. [A Rutan&T.]
*PRACTICE AREAS: Individual and Corporate Taxation; Business Law; Securities Law; Estate Planning and Administration; Trademark, Copyright and Unfair Competition.
Wenkart, Ronald D. ........................ '51 '77 C.1077 B.A. L.1095 J.D. Dept. of Educa.
**Wertheimer, Jeffrey** ........................ '57 '85 C.597 B.A. L.930 J.D. [Rutan&T.]
*PRACTICE AREAS: Civil Rights; Labor and Employment; General Practice.
**Westbrook, Mary K.**, (AV) ........................ '55 '80 C.285 B.S. L.813 J.D. [Latham&W.]
**Westover, Susan** ........................'62 '90 C.93 B.A. L.1049 J.D. [A Murtaugh,M.M.&N.]
*PRACTICE AREAS: Labor and Employment Law; Business Litigation; Civil Appeals.
**Whalen, Michael P.** ........................'54 '81 C.674 A.B. L.309 J.D. [Riordan&M.]
*LANGUAGES: German.
**Whalen, Patrick E.**, (AV) ........................'45 '73 C&L.770 B.A., J.D. [P.E.Whalen]

**Whalen, Patrick E., Law Offices of, (AV)**
**3090 Bristol Street, Suite 650, 92626**
**Telephone: 714-435-6600 Fax: 714-435-6690**
**Staff Counsel American International Companies: Managing Attorney: Patrick E. Whalen. Senior Trial Attorneys: James B. Dowling; James M. Fraser; Tammy Horton Lund; Alan L. Skelly.**
**Products Liability, Professional Liability, Premises Liability, Workers' Compensation and Auto.**
***See Professional Biographies, COSTA MESA, CALIFORNIA***

**Wheelock, Joseph A., Jr.**, (AV) .......... '39 '65 C.951 A.B. L.309 LL.B. [Latham&W.]
**White, Alan I.**, (AV) ........................'45 '71 C.454 A.B. L.276 J.D. [Drummy K.W.&G.]
*PRACTICE AREAS: Civil litigation with emphasis on General Business Law; Real Estate Law; Commercial Litigation; Bankruptcy Litigation.
**White-Sperling, Jennifer** ........................'59 '93 C.112 B.A. L.1065 J.D. [A Rutan&T.]
*PRACTICE AREAS: Civil Trial; Land Use Law; Labor and Employment; Municipal and Zoning.
**Williams, Holly A. H.** ..............'66 '91 C.426 B.A. L.1207 J.D. [A Robins,K.M.&C.]
*LANGUAGES: Spanish.
*PRACTICE AREAS: Litigation; General Civil Business.
Williams, J. Scott ........................ '43 '80 3465 Santa Clara Cir.
**Wilson, Peter J.** ........................'53 '86 C&L.061 B.Com., LL.B. [Latham&W.]
**Wine, Jamie L.** ........................'70 '95 C.401 B.A. L.309 J.D. [A Latham&W.]
**Wojciechowski, Tawnya R.** ....... '65 '95 C.1042 B.A. L.809 J.D. [A Sheppard,M.R.&H.]
*PRACTICE AREAS: Intellectual Property; Civil Litigation.
**Wolcott, Stan, (P.C.)**, (AV) ........................ '46 '73 C.173 B.A. L.1066 J.D. [Rutan&T.]
*PRACTICE AREAS: Municipal Finance; Bond and Underwriter Counsel.
Wold, Darryl R., (AV) ........................'41 '67 C.154 B.A. L.813 J.D. [C Reed&D.]
**Wolfson, Kenneth A.** ........................'57 '82 C.150 B.B.A. L.846 J.D. [Latham&W.]
**Wong, Dennis** ........................ '52 '78 C.112 B.A. L.767 J.D. [Dorsey&W.]
*PRACTICE AREAS: Public Finance; Banking.
**Wood, Lee A.**, (BV) ........................'44 '73 C.446 L.809 J.D. [Lewis,D.B.&B.]
Wood, Paul Kevin ........................ '64 '90 C.990 B.A. L.800 J.D. 611 Anton Blvd.
**Wood, Thomas C.**, (AV) ........................'40 '69 C.112 B.A. L.1065 J.D. [Burke,W.&S.]
*PRACTICE AREAS: Land Use Law; Governmental Law.
**Woog, Philip M.**, (AV) ............ '57 '88 C.1109 B.A. L.1137 J.D. [Cooksey,H.M.&T.]
*PRACTICE AREAS: Litigation; Personal Injury; Insurance Defense Law; Construction Litigation; Insurance Coverage.
**Woolsey, Roy B.**, (BV) ........................'17 '42 C.112 B.A. L.800 J.D. [C Coulombe&K.]
*REPORTED CASES: BFP v. Resolution Trust Corporation, 114 S.Ct. 1757 (1994).
Wright, Maurice E. ........................ '26 '51 C.36 L.37 LL.B. 2790 Harbor Blvd.
**Wright, Shatara R.** ........................'70 '96 C.329 B.A. L.597 J.D. [A Robins,K.M.&C.]
*PRACTICE AREAS: Litigation.
Wuerfel, Mark D., (AV) ........................'50 '77 C.732 B.A. L.1065 J.D. [Kinder,W.&C.]©
Wykidal, Gary, (BV) ........................'54 '80 C.1097 B.S. L.1148 J.D. 245 Fischer Ave.
**Wynder, William W.**, (AV) ........................ '48 '78 C.878 B.S. L.990 J.D. [Rutan&T.]
*PRACTICE AREAS: Appellate Practice; Civil Trial; Municipal and Zoning; Civil Rights; Labor and Employment.
**Yaffe, Joseph M.** ........................'69 '94 C.178 A.B. L.1067 J.D. [A Latham&W.]
**Yancey, Darla L.** ........................'60 '87 C.1042 B.S. L.800 J.D. [C Paul,H.J.&W.]
Yocum, Cheryl L. ........................'62 '87 C.547 B.S. L.546 J.D. 3100 Bristol St.
**Yorks, Ben J.** ........'59 '87 C.10 B.S.M.E. L.326 J.D. [Blakely,S.T.&Z.] (See Pat. Sect.)
**Young, Sandra J.** ........................ '66 '93 C.518 A.B. L.1068 J.D. [A Rutan&T.]
*PRACTICE AREAS: Labor and Employment.

CAA65P

Zeltzer, Nancy E. ....................................'51 '78 C&L.1137 B.S., J.D. [Lewis,D.B.&B.]
**Zepfel, Richard K.**, (BV) ....................'60 '85 C.112 B.A. L.800 J.D. [Graham&J.]
*PRACTICE AREAS: Employment Law; Business Law.
**Ziemba, Mark A.**, (AV) ....................'58 '83 C.112 B.A. L.464 J.D. [Graham&J.]
*PRACTICE AREAS: State and Federal Taxation Law; Corporate Law; Mergers and Acquisitions Law; Tax Litigation; Estate Planning Law.
**Zimmerman, Thomas F.** .......... '67 '93 C.112 B.A. L.940 J.D. [⊠ Cooksey,H.M.&T.]
*PRACTICE AREAS: Litigation; Construction Defect; Personal Injury; Insurance Defense Law.

## COTATI, 5,714, *Sonoma Co.*

Barrett, James M., (BV) ................ '44 '71 C.767 B.A. L.169 LL.B. [Cantor,B.&W.]
Cantor, Jay A., (CV) .................. '38 '66 C.766 A.B. L.1065 LL.B. [Cantor,B.&W.]
Cantor, Barrett & Wheeldin, (BV) ............................................ 45 Henry St.
Haselwood, Hilda P. ............ '— '50 C.102 B.A. L.262 J.D. 8047 Old Redwood Hwy.
Jukes, Mavis ................................'47 '79 C.112 B.A. L.284 J.D. 392 Eucalyptus Ave.
Schiller, Steve William ............... '61 '87 C.1074 B.S. L.426 J.D. 590 W. Cotati Ave.
Wheeldin, Anthony ............................................ '49 '79 [Cantor,B.&W.]

## COTO DE ÇAZA, 2,853, *Orange Co.*

Klein, Barnard F. ...................... '34 '66 C.679 B.S. L.800 LL.B. 31852 Apuesto Wy.
Stevens, Howard J. .................... '44 '80 C.112 B.A. L.1137 J.D. 5 Avenida Daroca

## COVELO, —, *Mendocino Co.*

Combest, Ronald R. .............................. '40 '77 C.800 B.S. L.426 J.D. Jus. Ct. J.

## COVINA, 43,207, *Los Angeles Co.*

Alexander, Sherril L. ........................ '43 '89 C.174 B.S. L.1137 J.D. [⊠ D.C.Solinger]
Annis, Allen D., (BV) ....... '39 '78 C.1097 B.A. L.1190 LL.B. 338 W. Badillo St. Ste A.
Artis, Larry R., (BV) ................................................ '38 '73 642 S. 2nd Ave.
Barnes, H. Robert ...........................'24 '54 C.665 B.S. L.229 LL.B. 547 W. Puente St.‡
Blatt, Meyer, (BV) ........................ '28 '67 C.569 A.B. L.800 J.D. P.O. Box 352‡
Blatt, Rosalind ....................... '30 '68 L.800 J.D. 19760 Golden Bough Dr.‡
Boss, Donald Edwin ...............'64 '90 C.990 B.A. L.228 J.D. 908 S. Village Oaks Dr.
Brajkovich, Steven, (BV) ........ '53 '78 C.1075 B.A. L.398 J.D. 957 S. Village Oaks Dr.
Carmichael, David P. ..................... '49 '79 C.112 A.B. L.398 J.D. 554 E. Badillo St.

**Chrisman, Robert A., (AV) '31 '62 C.1075 B.S. L.846 J.D.**
**Suite 200, 908 South Village Oaks Drive, 91724-3605**
**Telephone: 818-967-0526 Fax: 818-967-5904**
**(Certified Specialist, Family Law, The State Bar of California Board of Legal Specialization).**
**Family Law.**
***See Professional Biographies, COVINA, CALIFORNIA***

Christian, Hurschell D. ................ '42 '71 C.1097 B.A. L.426 J.D. [Jacobsohn,C.&S.]
Clem, Susan C., (BV) ................ '49 '84 C.1097 B.A. L.1137 J.D. 1041 W. Badillo St.
Collins, Harold L. ...........'50 '76 C.1097 B.S. L.809 J.D. 957 Village Oaks Dr., 2nd Fl.
Cristiano, Eugene F., (BV) ..........'58 '83 C.112 B.A. L.809 J.D. 750 Terrado Pl., Ste. 241
Croak, Thomas E., Sr., (BV) ................ '25 '63 C.154 A.B. L.809 J.D. P.O. Box 4181‡
Crow, Carol A. ...............................'55 '85 C.1075 B.S. L.398 J.D. 114 N. 2nd Ave.
Davison, Jay H. ..........................'35 '67 C.1071 B.S. L.1114 J.D. 599 S. Barranca St.
DePietro, Deborah, (BV) ........ '51 '78 C.1044 B.A. L.1221 J.D. 908 S. Village Oaks Dr.
Desport, Cheree D. ................. '57 '83 C.1074 B.A. L.1137 J.D. 5124 Arroway Ave.
Diaz, Richard H. ........................ '37 '78 C.1246 B.B.A. L.1190 LL.B. 262 W Badillo St.
**Dollison, Allan L.** ........................... '66 '95 C.1109 B.A. L.1137 J.D. [A.Dollison]
*LANGUAGES: German.
*PRACTICE AREAS: Civil Litigation; Personal Injury; Landlord/Tenant; Real Estate; Criminal Defense.

**Dollison, Allan, Law Offices of**
**917 South Village Oaks Drive, 2nd Floor, 91724**
**Telephone: 818-339-8947 Fax: 818-339-8678**
**Email: bcorg1979@aol.com**
**Allan L. Dollison.**
**General Civil Litigation, Business, LandLord-Tenant, Real Estate, Criminal, Personal Injury, Family Law.**
***See Professional Biographies, COVINA, CALIFORNIA***

Dominic, Donald Louis '41 '90
C.339 B.S.E.E. L.398 J.D. V.P., Contracts, Sargent Fletcher Co.
**Doonan, Daniel J.**, (BV) .........................'38 '74 C.1075 B.S. L.426 J.D. [D.J.Doonan]
*PRACTICE AREAS: Civil and Business Litigation; Real Estate; Products Liability; Personal Injury; Negligence.

**Doonan, Daniel J., Inc., A Prof. Corp., Law Offices of, (BV)**
**935 West Badillo Street Suite 200, 91722-4110**
**Telephone: 818-332-5090 Telecopier: 818-332-5190**
**Email: DDOONAN@WOW.COM**
**Daniel J. Doonan; Suzanne K. Nalley.**
**Personal Injury, Products Liability, Negligence, Business, Real Estate, Creditors' Rights and Collections. Wills, Trusts and Estate Planning, Malicious Prosecution.**
***See Professional Biographies, COVINA, CALIFORNIA***

Ellena, John C. ........................... '36 '66 C.102 B.A. L.569 J.D. 750 Terrado Plaza
**Ensberg, Stephen E.** .............................'52 '81 C.112 B.A. L.800 J.D. [R.E.Weiss]
*PRACTICE AREAS: Business, Commercial and Real Estate Litigation.
Erickson, Howard C., (AV) ......... '16 '44 C.112 A.B. L.1066 LL.B. 461 N. Grand Ave.
Faith, J. Randall, (AV) ............... '46 '72 C.605 B.A. L.309 J.D. 908 Village Oaks Dr.
Filene, Roger J. ................ '43 '72 C.112 B.A. L.1136 J.D. 303 W. San Bernardino Rd.
Fredericks, Thomas R. ................. '46 '71 C.475 B.S. L.213 J.D. Coun., Kmart Corp.
Garvey, Francis J., (AV) ..................... '13 '35 C&L.424 J.D. 700 Orangewood Dr.‡
Gornik, Gerald A. ............... '57 '86 C.1109 B.A. L.398 J.D. 957 S. Village Oaks Dr.
Green, James E. ................ '29 '63 C.839 B.S.E.E. L.426 LL.B. 1020 N. La Breda

**Guzman, John J. '57 '89 C&L.1137 B.S.L., J.D.**
**917 South Village Oaks Drive Second Floor, 91724**
**Telephone: 818-339-8947 Fax: 818-339-8678**
**Family Law including Dissolutions, Paternity, Adoptions, Child Custody Modifications, Child Support Modifications, Spousal Support, Grandparents Visitation Rights, Personal Injury, Criminal and Civil Law in all California State Courts.**
***See Professional Biographies, COVINA, CALIFORNIA***

Jacobsohn, Christian & Stewart, Law Corp. ........................... 642 S. Second Ave
**Kawa, Margaret F.** .................. '51 '80 C.1169 B.A. L.800 J.D. [Newman,N.&K.]
*PRACTICE AREAS: General Civil Litigation.
Kerckhoff, Anton W., (AV) ......... '30 '58 C.770 B.S. L.1068 LL.B. 118 North 2nd Ave.
Keyfauver, Roger L. .............. '35 '72 L.990 J.D. Pres., Total Lighting Concepts, Inc.
King, Nolan F. ................ '42 '80 C&L.1127 B.S.L., J.D. 338 W. Badillo St., Suite A
**Klingerman, Cris A.**, (BV) .................. '52 '78 C.1097 B.S. L.398 J.D. [R.E.Weiss]
*PRACTICE AREAS: Real Estate; Corporation and Mortgage Law.
Knudson, James A. .......................... '38 '69 C.800 L.1117 J.D. 660 Shoppers Ln.

**Krafft, M. Sue, Law Offices of, (BV) '38 '85 C&L.1137 B.L., J.D.**
**342 West Badillo, 91723**
**Telephone: 818-331-7241 Telecopier: 818-967-6456**
**Email: mskrafft@earthlink.net URL: http://www.krafft.com/legal**
***PRACTICE AREAS: Estate Planning; Probate Law; Real Property; Corporate Law.**

(This Listing Continued)

**Krafft, M. Sue, Law Offices of (Continued)**
**Probate Law, Conservatorship/Guardianship Law, Estate Planning, Real Estate Law, Corporate Law.**
***See Professional Biographies, COVINA, CALIFORNIA***

**Lee, James T.** ........................................ '56 '83 C.475 B.A. L.990 J.D. [R.E.Weiss]
*PRACTICE AREAS: Bankruptcy Law; Real Estate Law; Commercial Law.
Lewis, Valerie B. ...................... '53 '79 C.182 B.A. L.879 J.D. 4516 N. Delay Ave.
Loya, Thomas A., (BV) ................... '53 '82 C.112 B.A. L.1137 J.D. P.O. Box 2254
Maiocco, Val A. ........................... '44 '79 C.728 B.S. L.1137 J.D. P.O. Box 4844
**McAlpin, V. J.**, (AV) .......................... '25 '60 C.801 L.809 LL.B. [McAlpin&N.]
*PRACTICE AREAS: Workers Compensation (50%); Personal Injury (40%); Probate (10%).

**McAlpin & Northwood, A Professional Corporation, (AV)**
**211 South Citrus Avenue, 91723**
**Telephone: 818-331-6376 Fax: 818-339-2450**
**V. J. McAlpin; Inez Northwood.**
**General Civil and Trial Practice. Probate, Living Trusts, Negligence, Family, Workers Compensation, Corporation, Real Estate, Criminal and Personal Injury Law.**
***See Professional Biographies, COVINA, CALIFORNIA***

McBride, Dale R. ..........................'58 '84 C.1365 B.A. L.61 J.D. 223 East Rowland St.
McCormick, George L. ..............'20 '54 C&L.800 A.B., J.D. 908 S. Village Oaks Dr.‡
McCortney, Carroll A., (BV) ........... '31 '66 C.477 A.B. L.809 LL.B. 118 N. 2nd Ave.
McKay, Kirk L. ......................... '41 '77 C.1097 B.S. L.464 J.D. 554 E. Badillo St.

**McMeekin, Daniel G., (BV) '53 '80 C.1097 B.A. L.398 J.D.**
**Old Covina Bank Building, 101 North Citrus, Suite 3A, 91723**
**Telephone: 818-331-0458 Fax: 818-331-4618**
***PRACTICE AREAS: Family Law; Real Estate; Personal Injury; Probate; Criminal Law.**
**General Civil and Criminal Litigation in all State and Federal Courts, Family Law, Real Estate.**
***See Professional Biographies, COVINA, CALIFORNIA***

**Medina, Marian Hamilton** ........... '49 '91 C.1168 B.A. L.398 J.D. [Newman,N.&K.]
*PRACTICE AREAS: Family Law.

**Meeks, Heber S. '52 '86 C.878 B.A. L.61 J.D.**
**P.O. Box 2505, 91722-8505**
**Telephone: 818-332-3754**
***LANGUAGES: Japanese.**
***PRACTICE AREAS: Personal Injury Law (30%, 20); Domestic Relations Law (30%, 20); Real Estate (20%, 5); Bankruptcy Law (20%, 20).**
**Bankruptcy, Family Law, Personal Injury, Construction Litigation, Civil Trial.**
***See Professional Biographies, COVINA, CALIFORNIA***

**Miller, Thomas J., Law Offices of, (BV) '42 '79 C.1079 B.A. L.426 J.D.**
**412 North Barranca Avenue, 91723**
**Telephone: 818-974-8111 Fax: 818-974-8114**
***PRACTICE AREAS: Medical Malpractice; Personal Injury; Wrongful Death; Criminal Law.**
**General Civil Litigation, Medical Malpractice, Personal Injury and Criminal Law.**
***See Professional Biographies, COVINA, CALIFORNIA***

Mulville, Harold J., (BV) ................'51 '82 C.1109 B.A. L.1137 J.D. P.O. Box 4755
Murri, Evan L. ............................'48 '80 C.101 B.A. L.426 J.D. 917 Village Oaks Dr.
Nakatani, Glenn M. ........................ '49 '75 C.112 B.A. L.284 J.D. 554 E. Badillo St.
**Nalley, Suzanne K.** ............................ '50 '92 C&L.1109 B.S., J.D. [D.J.Doonan]
*PRACTICE AREAS: Real Estate; Creditors Rights; Products Liability; Personal Injury; Negligence.
**Nelson, Steven J.** ........................ '56 '81 C.112 B.S. L.800 J.D. [Newman,N.&K.]
*PRACTICE AREAS: Personal Injury; Real Estate.
**Newman, Michael P.**, (AV) ............ '31 '62 C.569 B.A. L.309 J.D. [Newman,N.&K.]
*PRACTICE AREAS: Probate; Estate Planning.

**Newman, Nelson & Kawa, Inc., (AV)**
**908 South Village Oaks Drive, P.O. Box 1227, 91722**
**Telephone: 818-331-2283 Fax: 818-331-2206**
**Michael P. Newman; Steven J. Nelson; Margaret F. Kawa; Marian Hamilton Medina.**
**General Civil and Trial Practice. Estate Planning and Probate, Negligence, Real Estate and Family Law. General Corporate and Business Practice.**
**Representative Clients: Ameritec Corp.; Orange Line Oil Co.; Occidental Mortgage Corp.; Glass Incorporated International; Hassen Real Estate Partnership; Southland Gunite Inc.; Information Concepts, Inc.;**
**Reference: California State Bank, Corporate Headquarters, Covina, CA.**

**Northwood, Inez**, (BV) ......................... '— '77 C.1075 B.A. L.398 J.D. [McAlpin&N.]
*PRACTICE AREAS: Family Law (90%); Real Estate (5%); Probate (5%).
O'Brien, John M. ..................... '51 '77 C.1075 B.A. L.990 J.D. 258 E. Badillo
Olinski, Thomas J. .................... '62 '94 C.1075 B.S. L.809 J.D. 342 W. Radillo
Olson, Mark D. ......................'56 '81 C.1075 B.S. L.1137 J.D. 410 W. Badillo St.
Osko, Eugene ..........................'41 '72 C.1097 B.A. L.426 J.D. 223 E. Rowland St.
Owenby, Ruth L. ......................... '39 '80 C&L.29 B.S., J.D. 1041 W. Badillo St.
**Pacheco, Gayle Elaine** .................. '52 '93 C.684 B.S. L.1137 J.D. [Pacheco&P.]
*LANGUAGES: Spanish.
*PRACTICE AREAS: Civil Litigation; Bankruptcy Law; Personal Injury; Family Law; International Business Transactions.
**Pacheco, Robert**, (BV) .................. '34 '73 C.1042 B.S. L.1137 J.D. [Pacheco&P.]
*LANGUAGES: Spanish.
*PRACTICE AREAS: Real Estate; Probate Law; Corporate Law; Personal Injury; Wrongful Termination.

**Pacheco & Pacheco, (BV)**
**957 South Village Oaks Drive 1st Floor, 91724-3617**
**Telephone: 818-967-9002 Fax: 818-967-7835**
**Robert Pacheco; Gayle Elaine Pacheco.**
**Real Estate, Corporate Law, Probate Law, Personal Injury, Wrongful Termination.**

Parker, William O. ....................'21 '59 C.800 B.E. L.426 LL.B. 646 E. Camellia Dr.‡
Peckham, Verne E., (BV) .............. '16 '65 C.800 A.B. L.809 LL.B. 118 N. 2nd. Ave.

**Perez, Albert, Jr. '61 '90 C.112 B.S. L.1137 J.D.**
**917 South Village Oaks Drive, Second Floor, 91724**
**Telephone: 818-339-9484 Fax: 818-915-3301**
***PRACTICE AREAS: Criminal; Civil Litigation; Trial Work.**
**Civil and Criminal Litigation.**
***See Professional Biographies, COVINA, CALIFORNIA***

Radcliffe, John A., (AV) ................ '27 '62 C.966 B.A. L.145 J.D. P.O. Box 4491‡
Reed, Glenn D., (BV) ....................... '28 '55 C.112 B.A. L.809 B.L. 118 N. 2nd St.
Seese, Harry P., (BV) .................. '32 '73 C&L.426 B.B.A., J.D. 108 W. College St.
Shallito, Vivian Teresa ...............'51 '82 C.112 B.A. L.1137 J.D. 927 E. Covina Blvd.
Shing-Haw Teng, Shawn ....................................... '58 '91 L.061 LL.B. P.O. Box 2727
Shwachman, Ben ......................... '37 '76 C.339 B.S. L.426 J.D. 230 W. College‡
Smith, Daryl L. ......................... '51 '77 C.800 B.S. L.426 J.D. 1338 Center Court Dr.
Soderwall, Loren H. ....................... '29 '86 C.774 B.A. L.1137 J.D. P.O. Box 1227
Solinger, David C., (BV) ................ '50 '77 C.1097 B.A. L.809 J.D. [D.C.Solinger]
Solinger, David C., A Prof. Law Corp., (BV) ................................ 716 N. Citrus Ave.
Standifer, Daniel S., (BV) .............. '47 '73 C&L.770 B.S.C., J.D. 100 S. Citrus Ave.
Stapleton, Kevin ......................... '48 '78 C.990 B.A. L.1179 J.D. [Stapleton&S.]
Stapleton, Victoria Prusas ................'51 '80 C.112 B.A. L.1068 J.D. [Stapleton&S.]
Stapleton & Stapleton .................................................. 401 E. Rowland St.
Stewart, John F. ........................'52 '77 C.940 B.A. L.426 J.D. [Jacobsohn,C.&S.]

Taslitz, Jerome, (AV) .................................. '36 '62 C&L.966 B.S., J.D. [J.Taslitz]
Taslitz, Jerome, A Prof. Law Corp., (AV) ........................ 917 S. Village Oaks Dr.
**Treder, Edward A.** ........................ '59 '84 C.1075 B.S. L.990 J.D. [R.E.Weiss]
*PRACTICE AREAS: Real Estate; Corporation and Mortgage Law.
Vargas, Edward E. ..................... '57 '88 C.800 B.A. L.809 J.D. 724 E. Chester Rd.
Warren, Kelly ............................ '55 '81 C.112 B.A. L.464 J.D. 550 E. Badillo St.
**Weiss, Robert E.**, (AV) ................................... '28 '59 L.809 LL.B. [R.E.Weiss]
*PRACTICE AREAS: Real Estate; Corporation and Mortgage Law.

**Weiss, Robert E., Incorporated, (AV)**
**920 Village Oaks Drive, 91724**
**Telephone: 818-967-4302 Telecopier: 818-967-9216**
**Robert E. Weiss; Cris A. Klingerman; Edward A. Treder; Stephen E. Ensberg; James T. Lee.**
**Real Estate, Corporation and Mortgage Law.**
**Reference: Sanwa Bank.**
***See Professional Biographies, COVINA, CALIFORNIA***

## CRESCENT CITY, * 4,380, *Del Norte Co.*

Burlake, John M. ......................................... '33 '65 C.154 B.A. L.809 J.D. 520 J St.
**Cochran, Robert F.**, (CV) ................... '46 '75 C.112 B.A. L.464 J.D. [Cochran&F.]
Cochran & Follett, (BV) .................................................................. 888 4th St.
Cornell, William A., (CV) .................. '52 '81 C.208 B.A. L.1137 J.D. 450 "H" St.
de Solenni, Mario E. ............................... '39 '67 C.425 B.S. L.800 J.D. 384 G St.
Doehle, Christine A. ........................ '62 '91 C.629 B.S. L.911 J.D. 625 F St., #B
Easton, Thomas .......................... '35 '83 C&L.629 B.S., J.D. 1335 Pebble Beach Dr.
**Follett, William H.**, (BV) .................. '50 '79 C.267 B.A. L.464 J.D. [Cochran&F.]
Henion, Dohn R., (CV) ..................... '54 '80 C.1079 B.A. L.1132 J.D. 879 J St

**Janssen, Malloy, Marchi, Needham & Morrison**
**(See Eureka)**

Levy, Jonathan H. .......................... '58 '92 C.766 B.A. L.999 J.D. 873 2nd St.
Liddicote, Harry, Jr. ................. '35 '73 C.763 B.S. L.1137 J.D. Chf. Dep. Dist. Atty.
Mehr, Ethan ............................... '51 '79 C.208 B.A. L.284 J.D. 550 H St.

**Mitchell, Brisso, Delaney & Vrieze**
**(See Eureka)**

Owen, Thomas S. ...................... '46 '74 C.172 B.A. L.813 J.D. 1745 Del Mar Rd.‡

**Roberts, Hill, Calligan, Bragg, Feeney & Angell**
**(See Eureka)**

Weir, Robert W., Jr. ......................... '44 '69 C.112 B.A. L.846 J.D. Supr. Ct. J.

## CRESTLINE, 3,509, *San Bernardino Co.*

Feldman, David ................................ '21 '50 C.347 L.564 LL.B. Dist. Atty. Off.
Miller, Olga A., (BV) ............................. '15 '65 C.999 L.809 LL.B. 607 Alder Rd.
Wilson, John F. ........................... '50 '81 C.1131 B.A. L.809 J.D. P.O. Box 2670

## CRESTON, —, *San Luis Obispo Co.*

Robinson, Eileen, (AV) ............. '57 '82 C.112 B.A. L.990 J.D. 9400 Huer Huero Rd.
Schneider, Judith A., (BV) ........................ '44 '79 L.1065 J.D. P.O. Box 320

## CROCKETT, —, *Contra Costa Co.*

Medeiros, Leonel D. ................... '42 '82 C.767 B.A. L.284 J.D. 124 Duperu Dr.
Trippe, Hillery Bolt '56 '81 C.112 B.A. L.1066 J.D.
Asst. Gen. Coun. & Govt. Affs. Offr., Calif. & Hawaiian Sugar Co.

## CUCAMONGA, —, *San Bernardino Co.*

(See Rancho Cucamonga)

## CULVER CITY, 38,793, *Los Angeles Co.*

Allen, Luis E. ........... '59 '85 C.800 B.S. L.813 J.D. V.P., Legal Affs., TriStar Pictures
Allen, Robert L. ........................ '37 '74 C.112 B.S. L.809 J.D. 400 Corporate Point
Arkin and Weissman, Law Offices, (BV) .......................... Ste. 301, 9696 Culver Blvd.
Astle, Jas., Jr. .......................................... '11 '52 L.426 LL.B. 11100 Washington Bldg.
Barkin, Gary M. ............................ '64 '93 C&L.309 A.B., J.D. Columbia Pictures
Baughan, Edward W. ................... '50 '86 C.1042 B.S. L.1136 J.D. [Gajewski&B.]
Baumgarten, Lara Sanders .......... '67 '92 C.112 B.A. L.426 J.D. Coun., TriStar Pictures

**Beehler & Pavitt, (AV)**
**Suite 330, 100 Corporate Pointe, 90230**
**Telephone: 310-215-3183 Facsimile: 310-215-3248 Groups 3, 2 & 1 Cable Address: "Interpat," Los Angeles**
**Email: BPLAWYER@AOL.COM**
**Members of Firm: Vernon D. Beehler (1904-1989); William H. Pavitt, Jr.; Mario A. Martella.**
**Associates: Natan Epstein; Robert Jacobs.**
**Patent, Trademark and Copyright Law. Unfair Competition Law. Trial Practice in the Federal Courts.**
**References: Alliance Bank.**
***See Professional Biographies, CULVER CITY, CALIFORNIA***

Berke, Beth '53 '79 C.112 B.A. L.1068 J.D.
Exec. V.P., Legal Div. & Dep. Gen. Coun., Sony Pictures Entertainment, Inc.
**Bernstein, Joan S.** ......................... '65 '90 C.1036 B.A. L.990 J.D. [Ⓐ Sacks,R.&Z.]
*PRACTICE AREAS: Workers Compensation Defense.
Berry, Jan A '55 '87 C.36 B.S. L.426 J.D.
Asst. Gen. Coun., Sony Pictures Entertainment, Inc.
Blau, Eddie E. ............................ '64 '90 C.112 B.A. L.426 J.D. 11869 Teale St.
Bonelli, John G., (AV) ....................................... '21 '56 C.999 L.809 LL.B. [Bonelli&B.]
Bonelli, William Jeffrey ........................ '58 '88 C.112 B.A. L.1137 J.D. [Bonelli&B.]
Bonelli & Bonelli, (AV) ........................................ Ste. 380, 300 Corporate Pt. (Fox Hills)
Bonini, Jean F. '48 '80 C.724 B.B.A. L.1049 J.D.
V.P., Labor Relations, Sony Pictures Entertainment, Inc.
Boone, Gregory K. '53 '77
C.800 A.B. L.1068 J.D. Sr. V.P., TV Legal Affs., Columbia Pictures
Boss, Maria Kathleen ............ '44 '74 C.112 A.B. L.1065 J.D. Prof., Calif. State Univ.
Boyd, Dann W., (BV) ................. '46 '76 C.813 A.B. L.426 J.D. 6319 W. Slauson Ave.
Brockman, Mitchell M. ........................ '15 '54 C.597 L.809 5102 Wilderness Lane
Bruenell, Deborah Derow '55 '85
C.66 A.B. L.813 J.D. V.P., Legal Affs., Columbia Pictures
Bunge, Shelly K. '63 '89 C.35 B.S. L.178 J.D.
Dir., Mus. Bus. Affs., Sony Pictures Entertainment, Inc.
Carl, Linda Rae ................ '52 '90 C.1109 B.A. L.940 J.D. Corp. Atty., GranCare, Inc.
Carr, Nanci K. ............. '60 '90 C.63 B.S. L.809 J.D. Sony Pictures Entertainment, Inc.
Cherness, Harold I. ..................................... '22 '49 C.112 B.A. L.800 LL.B. Mun. Ct. J.
Clough, Roger L. ..................................................... '40 '67 C.33 B.A. L.145 J.D. I.R.S.
Cohen, Ellen B. ......................... '61 '85 C.1036 B.A. L.245 J.D. 9336 W. Washington Blvd.
Cohen, Jeffrey S. ........................ '48 '75 C.1077 B.A. L.1148 J.D. 9696 Culver Blvd.
Cohen, Philip M. '50 '89 C.569 B.A. L.424 J.D.
Asst. Gen. Coun., Sony Pictures Entertainment, Inc.
**Comstock, Horace B.**, (AV) ....................... '19 '51 C&L.800 J.D. [Comstock&S.] ‡

**Comstock & Sharpe, Inc., (BV)**
**11100 Washington Boulevard, 90232**
**Telephone: 310-559-8820; 870-1420 Facsimile: 213-870-1421**
**Richard Sharpe; Horace B. Comstock (Deceased).**
**Estate Planning and Probate, Family Law, Real Estate and Business, General Civil and Personal Injury and Corporate Law.**
***See Professional Biographies, CULVER CITY, CALIFORNIA***

**Coombs, Ronald E.**, (AV) ...................... '41 '69 C&L.61 B.S., J.D. [Coombs&C.]

**Coombs & Coombs, (AV)**
**11100 Washington Boulevard, 90232**
**Telephone: 310-559-8616 Fax: 310-559-8648**
**Ronald E. Coombs.**
**Probate and Estate Planning. Wills and Trusts.**
**References: Bank of America, Los Angeles; Sanwa Bank California; Culver National Bank; Chamber of Commerce, Culver City.**

Coulter, Paul E. ..................... '55 '83 C.645 B.S. L.809 J.D. 6319 W. Slauson Ave.
Cousins, David Alan ....................................... '48 '90 C.1060 B.S. P.O. Box 1022
Culpepper, Gary D. ..................... '49 '76 Sr. Coun., Sony Pictures Entertainment, Inc.
Denkert, Darcie A. '52 '77 C.999 B.A. L.564 J.D.
(adm. in NY; not adm. in CA) Sr. V.P., MGM/UA Communications Co.
Dicker, Brian S. ...................... '52 '82 C.112 B.S. L.1136 J.D. 5000 Overland Ave.
Dicker, Clifford S., (AV) ................................ '26 '63 L.309 5000 Overland Ave.
Duitsman, Robert L. .................. '56 '84 C.800 B.A. L.809 J.D. 5601 Slauson Ave.
Duitsman, Roger G., (AV) ......................... '26 '52 C&L.800 LL.B. 6318 Wooster Ave.‡
Dwyer, Dennis M. ......................... '56 '83 C.112 B.A. L.426 J.D. 300 Corporate Pt.
**Epstein, Natan** ........... '47 '74 C.112 B.A. L.1068 J.D. [Ⓐ Beehler&P.] (See Pat. Sect.)
*LANGUAGES: Spanish.
*PRACTICE AREAS: Intellectual Property Law; Federal Practice.

**Fate, Michael, (AV) '48 '73 C.112 B.A. L.1068 J.D.**
**11100 Washington Boulevard, 90232-3988**
**Telephone: 310-838-1151 Fax: 310-559-8648**
**Business, Real Estate Litigation, Commercial and Corporate Law.**
**References: Culver National Bank, Culver City, CA; First Federal Savings Bank of California, Culver City, CA Branch; Culver City Chamber of Commerce, Culver City, CA.**

Finkel, Jamie ........................... '60 '85 C.112 B.A. L.464 J.D. 4200 Vinton Ave.
Fox, Brad M. ........................... '54 '79 C.763 B.A. L.426 J.D. 10555 Virginia Ave.
Freedman, Horace N., (AV) ............. '21 '56 C.112 B.S. L.800 J.D. 5457 Blanco Way
Freedman, Joseph ........................................................ '63 '89 C.112 L.1065 [Witkin&F.]
Fried, Seymour ......................................... '23 '51 C.999 L.809 LL.B. Mun. Ct. Comr.
Fuchs, Jacqueline L. ................... '59 '92 C.112 B.A. L.309 J.D. Columbia Pictures
Fukunaga, John O. ....... '63 '89 C.112 B.A. L.1068 J.D. Sony Pictures Entertainment, Inc.
Gajewski, Karen A. ........................ '56 '84 C.477 B.A. L.1136 J.D. [Gajewski&B.]
Gajewski & Baughan ...................................................... 9696 Culver Blvd., Ste 301
Gasick, Mary E. ................................ '66 '92 C.339 B.S. L.990 J.D. [Murphy&B.]
Glasser, David M. ........................................................................ '53 '78 [Greenspan&G.]
Gold, Rosalind D. ......................... '56 '82 C.668 B.A. L.309 J.D. 9905 Farragut Dr.
Goldman, Andrew J. ................ '61 '91 C.790 B.A. L.426 J.D. Dep. Alternate Pub. Def.
Goldstein, Charles-Terry ......... '51 '76 C.112 B.A. L.1095 J.D. 10837 Washington Blvd.
**Gollub, Lorraine C.**, (AV) ................................ '30 '53 C.102 L.1009 LL.B. [Gollub&G.]
*REPORTED CASES: In re Rabie 40 Cal. App. 3rd 917 (1974), 115 Cal. R. 594; Everett v. Everett 150 Cal. App. 3rd 1053 (1984) 201 Cal. Rptr. 351; Trope v. Katz, 11 Cal. 4th 274, Cal.Rptr. 2d, P.2d (Oct., 1995).
*PRACTICE AREAS: Marital Dissolution Law; Paternity; Child Custody; Cohabitation; Grandparents Rights and Mediation.

**Gollub & Golsan, (AV)**
**5839 Green Valley Circle, Suite 100, 90230**
**Telephone: 310-342-2818 Fax: 310-342-2825**
**Lorraine C. Gollub (Certified Specialist, Family Law, The State Bar of California Board of Legal Specialization); Maryanne Golsan.**
**Family and Matrimonial Law.**
***See Professional Biographies, CULVER CITY, CALIFORNIA***

**Golsan, Maryanne** ......................................... '51 '93 C.112 L.809 J.D. [Gollub&G.]
*LANGUAGES: French.
*PRACTICE AREAS: Family Law; Probate.
Greenberg, Herbert L. .......................... '43 '71 C.112 B.A. L.1068 J.D. P.O. Box 5445
Greenspan, Robert M., (BV) ........................................ '49 '73 L.809 J.D. [Greenspan&G.]
Greenspan & Glasser, (BV) ........................................................... 400 Corporate Pt.
Gross, Donald R. '26 '52 C.415 B.S. L.1009 J.D.
(adm. in NY; not adm. in CA) 5134 Maytime Ln.‡
Gross, Edgar F., (AV) ................ '31 '57 C.112 B.A. L.309 LL.B. 9696 Culver Blvd.
Grossman, Joel M. '50 '80 C.659 B.A. L.1068 J.D.
Exec. V.P. & Dep. Gen. Coun., Sony Pictures Entertainment, Inc.
Harmon, Carole Helfert '48 '75 C.347 B.A. L.809 J.D.
V.P., Legal Affs., MGM/UA Communications Co.
Heim, Maggie, (AV) '53 '85 C.788 B.A. L.1068 J.D.
Litig. Coun., Sony Pictures Entertainment, Inc.
Hendricks, Charles R. ................. '52 '80 C.1077 B.A. L.284 J.D. 4145 S. Sepulueda
Holliday, Karen L. .................... '46 '78 C.1042 B.A. L.112 J.D. 6319 Slauson Ave.
Holmes, Robert E. '43 '70 C&L.569 B.A., J.D.
(adm. in NY; not adm. in CA)
Exec. V.P.; SPE Music Grp., Sony Pictures Entertainment, Inc.
Hormel, Richard A. ............................ '56 '82 C.262 B.A. L.362 J.D. [Murphy&B.]
Jacobi, Ronald N. '47 '72 C.831 B.A. L.569 J.D.
Sr. V.P. & Gen. Coun., Sony Pictures Entertainment, Inc.
**Jacobs, Robert** ......... '56 '81 C.454 B.B.A. L.472 J.D. [Ⓐ Beehler&P.] (See Pat. Sect.)
*PRACTICE AREAS: Intellectual Property Law; Federal Practice.
Johnson, Lorraine B. '52 '79 C.1042 B.A. L.426 J.D.
V.P., Corp. Legal Affs., Lorimar-Telepictures Corp.
Jones, Mary K. ......................... '50 '82 C.37 B.S.B.A. L.809 J.D. 9696 Culver Blvd.
Josey, William E. ....... '47 '73 C.846 B.S. L.326 J.D. MGM/UA Telecommunications Inc.
Kass, Sandra S. ....................... '51 '75 C.112 B.A. L.1068 J.D. 5721 W. Slauson Ave.
Kay, Kelly W. '54 '83 C.810 B.A. L.178 J.D.
Sr. Coun., Sony Pictures Entertainment, Inc.
Keel, Alice R. ........................................ '— '64 C.999 L.981 LL.B. P.O. Box 91
Kendall, John R. ....................... '50 '76 C.1077 B.S. L.426 J.D. 9600 Lucerne Ave.
Kerner, Jordan R. ............ '50 '77 C.813 A.B. L.1065 J.D. Pres., The Avnet/Kerner Co.
Klosner, Marylyn K. ............. '56 '83 C.999 B.A. L.61 J.D. 400 Corporate Pt., Ste. 800
Kohn, Michael Eliot '61 '86
C.264 B.A. L.94 J.D. Sr. Coun., Sony Pictures Entertainment, Inc.
Kohorn, Larry S. ......... '56 '84 C.976 B.A. L.1068 J.D. Sony Pictures Entertainment, Inc.
Kramer, Andrew J. ............ '67 '91 C.112 B.A. L.809 J.D. Sony Pictures, Triumph Films
Kricun, Stuart L. ....... '56 '81 C.178 B.A. L.569 J.D. MGM/UA Telecommunications Inc.
Lang, Robert B. ..................... '46 '77 C.112 B.A. L.464 J.D. 7309 Summertime Lane‡
**Lea, Arlene C.** ........................................ '55 '90 C&L.1137 B.A., J.D. [Ⓐ Sacks,R.&Z.]
*PRACTICE AREAS: Workers Compensation Defense.
Lehrman, June R. .................. '58 '85 C.976 B.A. L.477 J.D. 11171 Fairbanks Way
Lund, Daniel ............................................................. '41 '70 12115 Hammack St.‡

CAA67P

CALIFORNIA—CULVER CITY MARTINDALE-HUBBELL LAW DIRECTORY 1997

Maragos, Diana ........ '43 '82 C.169 L.1148 J.D. [D.Maragos]
Maragos, Diana, A Professional Corporation ........ 5601 W. Slauson Ave.
**Martella, Mario A.**, (AV) '31 '60
C.262 B.S.Chem. L.276 LL.B. [Beehler&P.] (See Pat. Sect.)
*PRACTICE AREAS: Intellectual Property Law; Federal Practice.
Matlago, John T. ........ '17 '55 C.150 B.S. L.809 LL.B. 100 Corporate Pointe (Pat.)
Matra, John A. ........ '68 '94 C.800 B.S. L.1065 J.D. 8559 Higuera St.
Mayer, Patricia F. '52 '78 C.1036 B.A. L.800 J.D.
Consultant, Labor Rel., Sony Pictures Entertainment, Inc.
McBride, John C., Jr. '55 '84 C.061 M.A. L.724 J.D.
(adm. in NY; not adm. in CA) V.P., Legal Affs., Sony Pictures Entertainment, Inc.
McMahon, John B. '57 '86 C.112 B.S. L.800 J.D.
V.P., Intl. Legal Affs., Sony Pictures Entertainment, Inc.
McMullen, Hugh S. ........ '47 '72 C.309 A.B. L.813 J.D. 5815 Doverwood Dr.
Melville, Andrea J. ........ '60 '85 C.112 B.A. L.800 J.D. Sony Pictures Entertainment, Inc.
Messina, Michael P. '55 '82 C.813 B.A. L.990 J.D.
V.P., Labor Rel., Sony Pictures Entertainment, Inc.
Meyer, Murray ........ '45 '87 C.041 B.A. L.940 J.D. 4258 Overland Ave.
Miller, Larry E. ........ '52 '77 C.112 A.B. L.61 J.D. V.P., Louis G. Miller, Inc.
Minor, Joseph H., (AV) ........ '26 '67 C.112 L.809 J.D. 5008 Showboat Pl.
Mitchell, Brian David '56 '86 C.426 B.A. L.809 J.D.
Reg. Dir., Litigation Sciences, Inc.‡
Morris, Sandra H. '50 '78
C.112 B.A. L.61 J.D. Dir., Lorimar-Telepictures Productions Corp.
Mueller, Roni G. '55 '82 C.112 B.A. L.426 J.D.
Legal Coun., Lorimar-Telepictures Corp.
Murphy and Beane ... 5901 Green Valley Circle (⊙Boston, Mass. & New London, Conn.)
Murrell, Jean K. '61 '88
C.674 A.B. L.800 J.D. Sr. Coun., Sony Pictures Entertainment, Inc.
Myers, James H. ........ '50 '76 C.940 B.A. L.426 J.D. 5185 Dawes Ave.‡
Myers, Patsy Nanna ........ '30 '76 L.1136 J.D. Alternate Def. Coun.
Nollette, Dennis R., (AV⊙) '51 '75
C.911 B.A. L.276 J.D. V.P., Sony Pictures Entertainment, Inc.
O'Hare, Mary V. ........ '— '73 C&L.813 B.A., J.D. V.P., Legal Affs., Columbia Pictures
Paroda, David J., Jr. ........ '52 '91 C.1131 B.S. L.1136 J.D. 9696 Culver Blvd.
**Pavitt, William H., Jr.**, (AV) '16 '39 C&L.178 A.B., LL.B.
[Beehler&P.] (See Pat. Sect.)
*PRACTICE AREAS: Intellectual Property Law; Federal Practice.
Pedowitz, Mark A. '53 '79 C.697 B.A. L.365 J.D.
Sr. V.P., Telephone Bus. Affs., MGM/UA Communications Co.
Phillipson, John ........ '57 '85 C.112 B.A. L.629 J.D. 5107 Raintree Cir.
Platt, William L. ........ '49 '77 L.800 J.D. 400 Corporate Pt., Ste. 800
Powell, Jacqueline ........ '33 '73 10609 Flaxton St.
Presburger, Paul ........ '62 '87 C.112 B.A. L.659 J.D. Sony Pictures Entertainment, Inc.
Putnam, M. Maila ........ '49 '81 C.678 B.A. L.1051 J.D. 6319 W. Slauson Ave.
Ramos, Kiki ........ '61 '87 C.668 B.A. L.309 J.D. Columbia Pictures
Redlich, Edward '58 '85 C.309 B.A. L.569 LL.B.
(adm. in NY; not adm. in CA) MGM/UA Telecommunications Inc.
**Rivera, Oscar J.**, (AV) ........ '48 '78 C.1077 B.A. L.1136 J.D. [Sacks,R.&Z.]
*PRACTICE AREAS: Workers Compensation Defense.
Robbins, Lance Jay ........ '47 '72 C.112 A.B. L.1066 J.D. P.O. Box 1386
Rogers, Steve '58 '84 C.597 B.A., M.M. L.309 J.D.
Asst. Gen. Coun., Columbia Pictures
Rosenblum, Bruce ....'58 '82 C.800 B.S. L.1068 J.D. V.P., Bus. Affs., Lorimar Television
**Sacks, Zachary H., (P.C.)**, (AV) ........ '35 '63 C.976 B.A. L.178 LL.B. [Sacks,R.&Z.]
*PRACTICE AREAS: Workers Compensation Defense.

**Sacks, Rivera & Zolonz, (AV)**
**A Law Partnership including a Professional Corporation**
**400 Corporate Pointe, Suite 800, 90230**
**Telephone: 310-216-7778 Facsimile: 310-216-9552**
**Email: sackslaw@ATTMail.com**
**Zachary H. Sacks (P.C.) (Certified Specialist, Workers' Compensation Law, The State Bar of California Board of Legal Specialization); Oscar J. Rivera (Certified Specialist, Workers Compensation Law, The State Bar of California Board of Legal Specialization); Jeffrey A. Zolonz (Certified Specialist, Workers' Compensation Law, The State Bar of California Board of Legal Specialization).**
**Associates: Arlene C. Lea; Joan S. Bernstein.**
**Workers Compensation Defense, Subrogation.**

Sallus, Gerald M. ........ '27 '77 C.188 B.E.E. L.1137 J.D. 5004 Rainbows End‡
Schachter, Theodore L. '54 '81 C.860 B.A. L.178 J.D.
(adm. in NY; not adm. in CA) V.P., Bus. Affs., MGM/UA Communications Co.
Schaeffer, Paul Michael, (AV) '47 '72
C.645 B.S. L.659 J.D. Exec. V.P., Sony Pictures Entertainment, Inc.
Schultz, Michele P. ... '— '82 C.188 A.B. L.976 J.D. Asst. Gen. Coun., Columbia Pictures
Schwab, Carol A. ........ '55 '85 C.112 A.B. L.1065 J.D. Dep. City Atty.
Seehusen, Paul G. ........ '30 '61 C.350 B.S.C.E. L.426 LL.B. 10667 Cranks Rd.‡
Shaby, John P. ........ '46 '71 C.800 L.809 J.D. 12063 W. Jefferson Blvd.
**Sharpe, Richard**, (BV) ........ '37 '72 C.431 B.A. L.809 J.D. [Comstock&S.]
Singer, Carol B. ........ '51 '79 C.112 B.A. L.426 J.D. 300 Corporate Pointe
Singer, Mitchell F. '55 '85 C.1077 B.S. L.1049 J.D.
Asst. Gen. Coun., Columbia Pictures
Sinser Rolla, Sabrina '64 '90 C.112 B.A. L.800 J.D.
Asst. Gen. Coun., Goldrich & Kest Industries
Solis, Scott B. ........ '59 '87 C.691 B.A. L.770 J.D. 400 Corporate Pt.
Solmon, Vicki R. '44 '80 C.025 B.A. L.426 J.D.
Assoc. Gen. Coun., Sony Pictures Entertainment, Inc.
Solomon, Kristin Olson ........ '55 '84 C.783 B.A. L.982 J.D. 400 Corporate Pt.
Spaulding, Matthew F. ........ '58 '83 C.112 B.A. L.426 J.D. 9696 Culver Blvd.
Spivak, Kenin M. ........ '57 '81 C&L.178 A.B., J.D. MGM/UA Telecommunications Inc.
Stephens, Larry R. '48 '75 C.197 B.A. L.309 J.D.
V.P., Legal Affs. & Asst. Gen. Coun., Sony Pictures Entertainment, Inc.
Stone, Henry S. ........ '46 '76 C.260 B.S. L.990 J.D. [Stone,H.S.]
Stone, Henry S., A Professional Corporation ........ 2643 Fairfax Ave.
Stovall, Harry J. ........ '19 '63 L.809 LL.B. State Compensation Ins. Fund
Tangalakis, Dan J. ........ '23 '50 C.267 L.800 LL.B. 4262 Overland Ave.
Tangalakis, Phillip L., (BV) ........ '49 '77 C.800 A.B. L.1095 J.D. 4262 Overland Ave.
Tellem, Nancy R. ..... '52 '78 C.112 A.B. L.1065 J.D. V.P., Bus. Affs., Lorimar Television
Toll, Roger W. .....'50 '76 C.668 B.A. L.309 J.D. Sr. V.P., Legal Affs., Columbia Pictures
Verbit, Larry E. ........ '52 '87 C.1090 B.F.A. L.809 J.D. Sr. Coun., Westwood One, Inc.
Viebrock, Michael E. '49 '79
C.1077 B.A. L.464 J.D. V.P., Legal & Bus. Affs., Columbia Pictures

**Wall, Thomas Edward, (AV) '49 '77 C.847 B.A. L.1095 J.D.**
**12063 Jefferson Boulevard, 90230**
**Telephone: 310-827-4452 Fax: 310-827-1747**

(This Listing Continued)

**Wall, Thomas Edward (Continued)**
***REPORTED CASES: Brandt v. State Farm, 693 Fed. Supp. 877 (1988); Henchman v. Estate of Sapin, 203 Cal. Rptr. 712 (1983); Nationwide v. Munoz, 245 Cal. Rptr. 324 (1988); People v. Knight, 239 Cal. Rptr. 413 (1987); Bradley v. State Farm, 260 Cal. Rptr. 470 (1989).**
***PRACTICE AREAS: Personal Injury Law; Litigation; Insurance Law.**
**Personal Injury, Civil Trials and Appeals, Insurance Defense Disputes, Child Abuse Law, Alternative Dispute Resolution.**

***See Professional Biographies, CULVER CITY, CALIFORNIA***

Wasney, Cynthia ........ '53 '82 C.813 B.A. L.94 J.D. Columbia Pictures
Weinman, Ann L. ........ '36 '80 C.112 B.A. L.426 J.D. 8210 Raintree Cir.
Weinstein, Gary M. ........ '52 '80 C.1044 B.A. L.1095 J.D. 4258 Overland Ave.
Weiss, Cary B. ........ '43 '71 C.112 B.A. L.464 J.D. Alternate Def. Coun.
Weiss, Eric R. '58 '85 C.705 B.A. L.273 J.D.
(adm. in NY; not adm. in CA) V.P., Bus. & Legal Affs., Westwood One, Inc.
Weissman, Andrew N., (BV) ........ '50 '76 C.1077 B.A. L.426 J.D. [Arkin&W.]
Witkin, Richard G. ........ '50 '75 C.172 B.S. L.1068 J.D. [Witkin&F.]
Witkin & Freedman ........ 9696 Culver Blvd.
Wolfson, Stephen A. ........ '31 '76 C.25 B.A. L.1136 J.D. 11949 W. Jefferson Blvd.
Wright, David Chandler, (AV) '43 '70
C.821 B.S. L.145 J.D. Pres., Sierra Investment Mgmt., Inc.
Wright, Pamela J. ........ '63 '93 C.119 B.A. L.665 J.D. 4117 Overland Ave.
Wyman, Mark L. ..... '55 '80 C.668 B.A. L.800 J.D. V.P., Legal Affs., Columbia Pictures
Wynne, Robert J., (AV) '42 '67 C.112 B.S. L.1068 J.D.
Exec. V.P., Corp. & Legal Affs., Sony Pictures Entertainment, Inc.
Zalma, Barry, Inc., (AV) ........ '42 '72 C.154 B.A. L.1136 J.D. [B.Zalma]
Zalma, Barry, Inc., (AV) ........ 4441 Sepulveda Blvd.
**Zolonz, Jeffrey A.** ........ '51 '76 C.800 B.S. L.1148 J.D. [Sacks,R.&Z.]
*PRACTICE AREAS: Workmen's Compensation Defense.

## CUPERTINO, 40,263, *Santa Clara Co.*

Aaker, Mark Andrew '57 '88
C.813 M.S. L.770 J.D. Pat. Coun., Apple Computer, Inc. (Pat.)
**Abdalah, Richard K.**, (BV) ........ '48 '74 C.112 B.A. L.770 J.D. [Jackson&A.]
*PRACTICE AREAS: Real Estate Law; Business Law; Municipal Law; Employment Law; Civil Litigation.
Angioletti, Thomas J., III '66 '93
C.112 B.A. L.893 J.D. Trademark Coun., Apple Computer, Inc.
Assad, Michael J. '59 '82
C.608 B.A. L.607 J.D. Human Res. Coun., Apple Computer, Inc.
Barocchi, Lindy F. ........ '47 '88 C.483 B.A. L.1065 J.D. 20111 Stevens Creek Blvd.
Beckman, Victor R. '28 '55 C.966 B.S.E.E. L.273 LL.B.
(adm. in DC; not adm. in CA; Pat.) 10311 Cherry Tree Ln.
Belani, Jagdish G. ........ '53 '82 C.061 B.Tech. L.770 J.D. 7707 Seeber Ct.
Bohner, Hal J. ........ '47 '76 C.1167 B.S. L.767 J.D. Measurex Corp. (Pat.)
Braisted, Sharon Hochberg ........ '60 '86 C.914 B.A. L.800 J.D. 10601 S. DeAnza Blvd.
Brazil, Lynn E. ........ '52 '79 C.112 B.A. L.770 J.D. 7450 Barnhart Pl.‡
Calhoun, W. Crisler '47 '76
C.385 A.B. L.280 J.D. Sr. Mng. Coun., Tandem Computers Inc.
Campbell, Patrick J. '56 '87 C.705 B.A. L.1202 J.D.
(adm. in NY; not adm. in CA) Investment Oper. Mgr., Tandem Computers Inc.
Cannady, Cynthia C. ........ '51 '76 C.813 B.A. L.309 J.D. V.P., Apple Computer, Inc.
Carlson, Lloyd A., (AV) '20 '45 C.112 A.B. L.1066 J.D.
23300 Via Esplendor, Villa 51‡
Carmichael, Paul D. '34 '59 C.119 B.S.E.E. L.980 LL.B.
(adm. in NY; not adm. in CA; Pat.)
Acting Gen. Coun. & Dir. Patents & Trademarks, Apple Computer, Inc.
Chargin, Victor A., Jr. ........ '21 '48 C.770 B.S. L.1065 J.D. 7409 Prospect Rd.
Chen, Audrey W. ........ '59 '86 C.061 LL.B. L.312 J.D. 20395 Pacifica Dr.
Chow, Joyce C. ....'62 '87 C.483 B.A. L.1066 J.D. Products Coun., Apple Computer, Inc.
Cohan, Gary J. .... '40 '66 C.569 A.B. L.309 LL.B. Dir. of Law, Tandem Computers, Inc.
Cooper, Kim Martens '58 '83 C.112 B.A. L.426 J.D.
Dir. Products, Apple Computer, Inc.
Cosca, Cecilia E. ....'45 '77 C.843 A.B. L.276 J.D. Products Coun., Apple Computer, Inc.
Coward, John H., (BV) ........ '50 '76 C.169 B.A. L.464 J.D. 20395 Pacifica Dr.
Damico, Chester, Jr. ........ '10 '34 C&L.770 Ph.B., LL.B. 22181 McClellan Rd.‡
Farrington, David G. '56 '83 C.112 B.A. L.1065 J.D.
Dir. Products, Apple Computer, Inc.
Ferris, Dakin Neville ........ '60 '89 C.454 B.A. L.1065 J.D. Symantec Corp.
Fithian, Leslie Ann ..... '59 '85 C&L.813 B.A., J.D. Dir., Products, Apple Computer, Inc.
**Fitzsimmons, Tina** '60 '86 C.112 B.A. L.1065 J.D.
Atty., Corp. Legal Dept., Hewlett-Packard Co.
Gard, Vernon R. '59 '90
C&L.770 B.S.E.E.C.S., J.D. Pat. Coun., Apple Computer, Inc. (Pat.)
Gilbert, Douglas M. ........ '43 '72 C.112 B.S.E.E. L.770 J.D. 11000 Wolfe Rd. (Pat.)
Grayson, Ralph L. '21 '50 C.44 L.1005 LL.B.
(adm. in TN; not adm. in CA) 10380 Farallone Dr.‡
**Haggard, Alan H.** '51 '78 C.98 B.S.E.E. L.1003 J.D.
(adm. in OH; not adm. in CA) Reg. Coun., Hewlett-Packard Co.
Hansen, Nadine R. ........ '47 '86 C.768 B.A. L.770 J.D. 20571 Scofield Dr.
Hart, Patricia E. '46 '81 C.112 B.A. L.464 J.D.
Grp. Coun. & Asst. Secy., Tandem Computers Inc.
Heckman, Sheryl ........ '55 '80 C.879 B.A. L.1065 J.D. 10549 San Felipe Rd.
Helms, Susan J., (AV) '46 '75 C&L.800 B.A., J.D.
Dir. Litig. & Human Res., Apple Computer, Inc.

**Hertzberg, Linda A. '53 '94 C.112 B.A. L.1026 J.D.**
**20370 Town Center Lane, Suite 125, 95014**
**Telephone: 408-255-4900 Fax: 408-255-4906**
**Email: lindahertz@aol.com**
**Workers Compensation Defense.**

***See Professional Biographies, CUPERTINO, CALIFORNIA***

Hoffman, Curtis B. ........ '61 '89 C&L.101 B.S., J.D. 20480 Pacifica Dr.
Hoffman, James C., (CV) ........ '31 '60 C.877 B.S. L.813 J.D. 20480 Pacifica Dr.
Hoffman, Steven D., (BV) ...... '51 '79 C.112 B.A. L.1095 J.D. 20370 Town Center Lane
Hogin, Robert D. ........ '53 '80 C.112 B.A. L.770 J.D. 10680 S. De Anza Blvd.
Horowitz, Bruce A. '59 '90 C.1044 B.S. L.813 J.D.
Products Coun., Apple Computer, Inc.
Houser, Cheryl ......'56 '82 C.800 B.A. L.809 J.D. Products Coun., Apple Computer, Inc.
Hsiang, Jean N. ........ '56 '85 C.061 B.A. L.352 J.D. 10601 S. De Anza Blvd.
**Jackson, James E.**, (BV) ........ '34 '59 C.502 A.B. L.208 J.D. [Jackson&A.]
*REPORTED CASES: Oki America v. Microtech International.
*PRACTICE AREAS: Estate and Business Planning; Real Estate Law; Charitable Trusts; Non-Profit Organizations.

**Jackson & Abdalah, A Professional Corporation, (BV)**
**10455 Torre Avenue, 95014**
**Telephone: 408-252-5211 Fax: 408-996-7045**
**James E. Jackson; Richard K. Abdalah.**

(This Listing Continued)

**Jackson & Abdalah, A Professional Corporation (Continued)**
**General Civil and Trial Practice. Real Estate, Construction Law, Estate Planning, Probate, State and Federal Taxation Law, Corporate, Charitable Organizations, Charitable Trusts, Business, Partnerships, Start-Up Firms, Employment.**
***See Professional Biographies, CUPERTINO, CALIFORNIA***

Jeffers, William A., (BV) '49 '75
C.911 B.A. L.1065 J.D. 10011 N. Foothill Blvd., Ste. 110
**Jelinch, Frank A.**, (AV) .......................'43 '69 C.768 B.A. L.1066 J.D. [Jelinch&R.]
*REPORTED CASES: Hironymous v. Allison, 893 S.W. 2d 578 (Tex.App. Corpus Christi 1994); Wanland v. Los Gatos Lodge, Inc. (1991) 230 C.A. 3d 1507, 281 C.R. 890.
*PRACTICE AREAS: Personal Injury; Employment Law; Construction Law; Subrogation; Civil Litigation.

**Jelinch & Rendler, A Professional Corporation, (AV)**
**Suite 560, 20863 Stevens Creek Boulevard, 95014**
**Telephone: 408-366-6300 Fax: 408-252-3936**
**Frank A. Jelinch; Devereaux Rendler.**
**General Civil and Trial Practice. Personal Injury, Products Liability, Employment Law, Real Property and Business Law, Construction Law, Subrogation Law, Environmental, Insurance.**
**Reference: Security Pacific National Bank (Cupertino Branch).**
***See Professional Biographies, CUPERTINO, CALIFORNIA***

Jette, Robert A., Jr. ............. '51 '80 C.770 B.S. L.990 J.D. 19925 Stevens Creek Blvd.
Kessel, Jacqueline B. ................................ '47 '92 L.990 J.D. 10455 Torre Ave.
**Kilian, Charles T., (AV) '45 '71 C.605 L.477 J.D.**
**10320 S. De Anza Boulevard, Suite 1-D, 95014**
**Telephone: 408-777-3403 Fax: 408-777-3401**
***PRACTICE AREAS: Municipal Law; Local Government Law; Estate and Business Planning; Real Estate Law; Probate.**
**Civil Practice. Real Property, Municipal, Land Use, Zoning and Administrative Law.**
***See Professional Biographies, CUPERTINO, CALIFORNIA***

Larwood, David J. ... '52 '87 C.111 B.S. L.1066 J.D. Sr. Pat. Coun., Apple Computer, Inc.
LaVally, Michelle A., (AV) '52 '79 C.112 B.A. L.770 J.D.
Gen. Coun., Americas Div., Tandem Computers, Inc.
**Lee, Denise A.** .......'61 '90 C.112 B.S. L.1068 J.D. Pat. Atty., Hewlett-Packard Co. (Pat.)
Linden, Jonathan M. '62 '90 C.103 A.B. L.813 J.D.
Products Coun., Apple Computer, Inc.
Liu, Richard C. '57 '92 C.813 M.S.E.E. L.999 J.D.
Pat. Coun., Apple Computer, Inc. (Pat.)
Longinotti, John E. ..............................'14 '38 L.1065 J.D. 23500 Cristo Rey Dr.‡
Lowe, Larry C., (AV) '57 '83
C.112 A.B. L.1065 J.D. Products Coun., Apple Computer, Inc.

**MacAllister, Alice J., (BV) '45 '80 C.645 B.A. L.770 J.D.**
**20395 Pacifica Drive, Suite 103, 95014**
**Telephone: 408-255-4995 Facsimile: 408-255-1036**
**(Certified Specialist, Probate, Estate Planning and Trust Law, The State Bar of California Board of Legal Specialization).**
***REPORTED CASES: Precise Metals (York Fabrication, Inc.); Wood Tech Industries; Columbia Printing; Pearson Ventures, Inc.; Pfandl Metals, Inc.**
***PRACTICE AREAS: Estate Planning; Probate and Trust Law; Elder Law; Conservatorships; Real Estate.**
**Estate Planning, Probate, Conservatorships, Corporate, Business, Partnerships, Technology Law and Elder Law.**
***See Professional Biographies, CUPERTINO, CALIFORNIA***

Maddigan, Richard J., (BV) ........... '46 '72 C.112 A.B. L.1066 J.D. 20395 Pacifica Dr.
Mantovani, Elinora S. '48 '80 C.1097 B.A. L.1066 J.D.
Sr. Coun., Real Estate, Envir., Health & Safety, Apple Computer, Inc.
Mather, Maria W. ....................'43 '76 C.312 B.A. L.770 J.D. Hewlett-Packard Co.
McCarthy, Susan B. ....................'49 '76 C.454 A.B. L.770 J.D. 1121 Yorkshire Dr.
**Mendenhall, Roberta K.** ... '37 '78 C.589 L.410 LL.B. Reg. Coun., Hewlett-Packard Co.
Miller, James G., (BV) ........................ '46 '78 C.976 B.A. L.770 J.D. 20395 Pacifica Dr.
Miller, Philip .... '48 '74 C.112 A.B. L.569 J.D. Assoc. Dir., Tax, Tandem Computers Inc.
Moore, Kenneth C., (CV) .............. '52 '76 C.169 B.A. L.464 J.D. 20395 Pacifica Dr.
Morgan, James R. '46 '73 C.101 B.S. L.878 J.D.
V.P. & Gen. Coun., NFT Ventures, Inc.
Mulford, Elizabeth B., (BV) ............ '— '72 C.813 B.A. L.597 J.D. 10455 Torre Ave.
O'Meara, Patrick J., (AV⓪) '47 '77 C.957 B.S. L.1035 J.D.
(adm. in MN; not adm. in CA) 871 Lily Ave.
Ortler, Lisabeth ................'61 '92 C.431 B.S. L.770 J.D. 19672 Stevens Creek Blvd.
Park, Theodore S. '43 '74 C.112 B.S. L.1067 J.D.
Mng. Tech. Coun., Tandem Computers Inc. (Pat.)
Parry, Josephine T. '— '75 C.768 B.S. L.1065 J.D.
V.P., Gen. Coun. & Secy., Tandem Computers Inc.

**Pitcaithley, Bruce E. '54 '86 C.112 B.A. L.1026 J.D.**
**20370 Town Center Lane, Suite 125, 95014**
**Telephone: 408-255-4900 Fax: 408-255-4906**
**(Certified Specialist, Workers' Compensation Law, The State Bar of California Board of Legal Specialization).**
***PRACTICE AREAS: Workers Compensation Defense Law; Insurance Defense Law; Subrogation Law.**
**Workers' Compensation, Insurance Defense and Subrogation.**
***See Professional Biographies, CUPERTINO, CALIFORNIA***

**Plettner, David A.** '62 '93 C.966 B.S.E.E. L.1035 J.D.
(adm. in MN; not adm. in CA; Pat.) Atty., Corp. Legal Dept., Hewlett-Packard Co.
Preefer, Jeffrey J., P.C. ...........'48 '75 C.813 B.A. L.1068 J.D. 10440 S. de Anza Blvd.
Rasmussen, Mark A. ...... '57 '81 C&L.352 B.B.A., J.D. Tax Coun., Apple Computer, Inc.
Rauch, Harold L. .................. '26 '64 C.1097 A.A. L.1026 LL.B. 21142 Patriot Way
**Rendler, Devereaux** ....................................'59 '85 C&L.770 B.A., J.D. [Jelinch&R.]
*LANGUAGES: German.
*REPORTED CASES: Joseph Gallo v. Superior Court (Sherry) App. 6th Dist. 1988) 246 Cal. Rptr. 587, 200 C.A. 3d 1375, Modified.
*PRACTICE AREAS: Personal Injury Law; Employment Law; Subrogation; Civil Litigation; Insurance Law.
Rodriguez, James J., (BV) .............. '46 '78 C.112 B.A. L.770 J.D. 10455 Torre Ave.
Rosenbloom, Oscar A. '43 '76
C.867 B.A. L.813 J.D. Products Coun., Apple Computer, Inc.
Rudd, Stephen S., (BV) ................... '45 '72 C.154 B.A. L.813 J.D. 10455 Torre Ave.
Rychlik, Robert W., (BV) ...................'35 '71 C.473 B.S. L.813 J.D. [R.W.Rychlik]
Rychlik, Robert W., P.C., (BV) ..........................................10455 Torre Ave.
Scott, Edward W., IV '61 '88
C.846 B.A. L.770 J.D. Pat. Coun., Apple Computer, Inc. (Pat.)
Simon, Nancy R. '60 '91 C.350 B.S.E.E. L.802 J.D.
(adm. in TX; not adm. in CA; Pat.) Pat. Coun., Apple Computer, Inc.

**Skjerven, Morrill, MacPherson, Franklin & Friel LLP**
**(See San Jose)**

Slavik, Leigh Flesher '57 '84
C.813 B.A. L.1065 J.D. Sr. Products Coun., Apple Computer, Inc.
Stahler, Cathy A. ..............................'42 '91 L.999 J.D. 20370 Town Ctr. Lane
Svalya, Phillip G., (Inc.), (BV) ............'43 '74 C.871 B.S. L.770 J.D. 10455 Torre Ave.
Tauber, David ........ '52 '77 C.112 B.A. L.770 J.D. Corp. Coun., Tandem Computers Inc.
Thorner, Susan L. ....... '48 '75 C.1036 B.A. L.309 J.D. Dir. Corp., Apple Computer, Inc.
Tichane, David .......'53 '79 C.604 A.B. L.569 J.D. Tech. Coun., Tandem Computers, Inc.
Torrey, Leon E., III ....................'45 '73 C.311 B.A. L.770 J.D. 10400 Johnson Ave.
Tuttelman, David M. ..........................'50 '77 C.112 B.A. L.1067 J.D. 325 S. First St.

**Uelmen, Martha A., Law Office of, (AV) '43 '87 C.276 B.S.N. L.426 J.D.**
**20111 Stevens Creek Boulevard, Suite 245, 95014-2345**
**Telephone: 408-996-7007 Facsimile: 408-996-3977**
**Family Law, Civil and Family Law Mediation, Arbitration and Special Master.**

Van Dyke, Lindell H., (AV) .......'54 '78 C.339 B.A. L.813 J.D. 10600 N. De Anza Blvd.
Wani, Suvil Sean ....'66 '94 C.112 B.A. L.770 J.D. Products Coun., Apple Computer, Inc.
Wong, Jeffrey H. ..........................'53 '83 C.1239 A.B. L.770 J.D. P.O. Box 2068
Workman, Helene Plotka '62 '90 C.188 B.A. L.245 J.D.
(adm. in MA; not adm. in CA) Pat. Coun., Apple Computer, Inc.
Wyss, R. John, Jr. '51 '77 C.1109 B.A. L.770 J.D.
Corp. Envir. Admin., Siemens Components, Inc.

## CUTTEN, 1,516, *Humboldt Co.*

Kraft, Eleanor M. ..........................'36 '61 C&L.188 B.A., LL.B. P.O. Box 225

## CYPRESS, 42,655, *Orange Co.*

Barbera, Ronald D. ......................... '50 '77 C.112 B.A. L.990 J.D. 9451 Grindlay
**Baumeister, Bryan H.** ........ '60 '85 C.112 B.A. L.1065 J.D. McDonnell Douglas Corp.
Bemis, Gary A. ............ '50 '80 C.1131 B.A. L.1137 J.D. 5400 Orange Ave., #200B
Benson, Allison K. '60 '87 C.1109 B.A. L.800 J.D.
Corp. Atty., McDonnell Douglas Corp.
Borges, Bernita S. (Susan) ................'44 '78 C&L.1137 B.S., J.D. 9461 Grindlay St.
Browning, Patrick L. '54 '88 C&L.1137 B.S., J.D.
V.P., Opers., Emblem Develop. Corp.
Byrd, Marcia K. ................'65 '94 C.8399 B.S. L.990 J.D. McDonnell Douglas Corp.
**Cohen, David L.** .......... '58 '84 C.107 B.A. L.94 J.D. Coun., McDonnell Douglas Corp.
**Davis, Wanda** ....'— '89 C.170 B.A. L.1068 J.D. Sr. Coun., Mitsubishi Elec. Amer., Inc.
Duffy, Paula V. '48 '84 C.1350 B.S. L.724 J.D.
(adm. in NJ; not adm. in CA) Sr. Coun., Sony Electronics, Inc.
Ellerton, Don R., Jr. ..................'27 '63 C&L.878 B.S.L., J.D. 4355 Avinida Carmel
**Fischer, Kristi** '55 '93 C.1097 B.A. L.426 J.D.
Coun., Mitsubishi Motor Sales of America
*RESPONSIBILITIES: Products Liability; Warranty Law.
Frazier, Robert E. ........................ '26 '58 C.999 L.809 LL.B. 10222 Janice Lynn St.
**Gleberman, Ellen J.** '54 '79 C.604 A.B. L.904 J.D.
V.P. & Gen. Coun., Mitsubishi Motor Sales of America, Inc.
Goodrich, Max E. .................'36 '76 C.1042 B.A. L.1137 J.D. 4108 Avenida Sevilla
Green, Douglas R. ......................... '57 '90 C.1042 B.A. L.426 J.D. 5762 Lincoln Ave.
Haymer, Matthew A. '55 '81
C.112 B.A. L.809 J.D. Asst. Gen. Coun., McDonnell Douglas Corp.
**Kanoskie, Judith A.** '59 '85 C.112 B.A. L.800 J.D.
Mng. Coun., Mitsubishi Motor Sales of America, Inc.
Katz, Cherol B. ...........................................'57 '89 C.112 B.A. L.1137 J.D. Prof. of Law
Kehrli, David ........................'50 '92 C.657 B.A. L.1137 J.D. 9981 Madrid Circle
Knudson, Patricia A. ....... '51 '92 C.97 B.S. L.809 J.D. Coun., McDonnell Douglas Corp.
Lacy, Thomas C. ............................ '28 '75 C.112 B.S. L.1008 LL.B. 5295 Vista Real
Leeds, Scott J. '60 '86 C.16 B.S. L.902 J.D.
(adm. in AL; not adm. in CA) 10775 Business Ctr. Dr. Ste. 206-1
**Little, Richard J.** '— '78 C.436 M.A. L.1068 J.D.
Asst. Gen. Coun. & Asst. Secy., Mitsubishi Elec. Amer., Inc.
Madden, John W. .......................................'21 '51 C.999 L.800 J.D. 10081 Saltair Dr.‡
McElroy, John P. '55 '82 C.1042 B.A. L.1068 J.D.
Mitsubishi Motor Sales of Amer., Inc.
McGlamery, Barbara L. '61 '89
C.1059 B.B.A. L.1148 J.D. Corp. Coun., Yamaha Motor Corp.
McIntyre, Donald T. ..........................'49 '87 C.805 B.S. L.1137 J.D. [Rainboldt&M.]
**Metzinger, Philip J.** '48 '74 C.769 B.A. L.1065 LL.B.
Mng. Coun., Mitsubishi Motor Sales of America, Inc.
**Olschwang, Alan P.** '— '66 C&L.339 B.S., J.D.
Exec. V.P., Gen. Coun. & Secy., Mitsubishi Elec. Amer., Inc.
*RESPONSIBILITIES: Management of Department; Commercial; Contract; Litigation.
Pasquinelli, Joseph ........................ '32 '75 C.999 L.1001 J.D. 5327 Vista Del Mar
Plewes, S. Frank ..................'46 '81 C.659 A.B. L.813 J.D. McDonnell Douglas Corp.
Rainboldt, James A. .......................'54 '81 C.1259 B.S. L.1137 J.D. [Rainboldt&M.]
Rainboldt & McIntyre ..............................................................6101 Ball Rd.
Rich, John L. ..................................'32 '60 C.679 B.S. L.208 J.D. 4162 Dover Circle‡
Rosenbloom, Peter C. ...'56 '81 C.1036 B.A. L.659 J.D. Coun., McDonnell Douglas Corp.
**Roude, Carl L.** '61 '86 C.1044 B.A. L.94 J.D.
Sr. Coun., Mitsubishi Motor Sales of Amer., Inc.
*RESPONSIBILITIES: Real Estate Law; Environmental; General Corporate; Anti-Trust.
Sayen, Joanne Vails '61 '90 C.104 A.B. L.276 J.D.
(adm. in NY; not adm. in CA) 5944 Mildred Ave.‡
Sherman, Hope R. ........ '63 '89 C.659 B.A. L.1292 J.D. Gen. Coun., PacifiCare of Calif.
Teutsch, Miriam .........................'50 '85 C.112 A.B. L.426 J.D. 10775 Business Ctr. Dr.
**Turner, Roger C.** '42 '75 C.942 B.S.M.E. L.421 J.D.
Asst. Gen. Coun., Mitsubishi Elec. Amer., Inc. (Pat.)
*RESPONSIBILITIES: Intellectual Property; Contracts; General Corporate.
Webster, Victoria ............. '51 '84 C.642 B.A. L.809 J.D. Coun., Yamaha Motor Corp.
**Westhoff, Douglas J.** '56 '81 C.112 B.S. L.809 J.D.
Mng. Coun., Mitsubishi Motor Sales of America, Inc.
Wong, Kathleen H .........'57 '87 C.668 B.A. L.426 J.D. Coun., McDonnell Douglas Corp.

## DALY CITY, 92,311, *San Mateo Co.*

Agcaoili, Avelino C. '24 '83 C.061 M.B.A. L.662 LL.B.
(adm. in NY; not adm. in CA) 554 Westmoor Ave.
Agcaoili, Paz M. '25 '85 L.662 LL.B.
(adm. in NY; not adm. in CA) 554 Westmoor Ave.
Appleton, Hartley R., (BV) ........................'10 '39 L.765 LL.B. 6717 Mission St.

**Bigeleisen, David Michael '48 '75 C.188 A.B. L.1049 J.D.**
**2171 Junipero Serra Boulevard Seventh Floor, 94104**
**Telephone: 415-755-1414**
***LANGUAGES: Spanish, French, German and Samoan.**
***REPORTED CASES: People v. Meredith, 29 C. 3d 682 (1981).**
**Criminal Defense and Personal Injury. General Civil Trial Practice.**
***See Professional Biographies, DALY CITY, CALIFORNIA***

Blum, Frank B., Jr., (BV) ...................... '43 '71 C.766 B.A. L.284 J.D. [F.B.Blum,Jr.]
Blum, Frank B., Jr., Law Offices of, (BV) ...................................950 John Daly Blvd.
Bonney, Leon J. ......................... '55 '83 C.766 B.A. L.1065 J.D. 301 Crocker Ave.

Brennan, John J. .... '46 '73 C.767 B.A. L.284 J.D. 89 Portola Ave.
Cohen, Gregg .... '62 '91 C.767 B.S. L.1049 J.D. 756 Larchmont Dr.
Duggan, Virginia S. .... '28 '65 C.766 A.B. L.765 LL.B. 297 Del Prado Dr.
Eaton, Kingsley B. .... '25 '52 C&L.911 B.A., J.D. 12 Cliffside Dr.‡

**Fox, Shjeflo, Wohl & Newkold, (BV)**
**Limited Liability Partnership**
**Westlake Building, 375 South Mayfair Avenue, Suite 292, 94015⊙**
**Telephone: 415-994-3044 Fax: 415-994-9323**
**Steven C. Wohl.**
**General Civil, Trial and Appellate Practice. Business, Corporation, Real Estate, Construction, Family, Insurance, Toxic Tort Defense, Products Liability, Drug Liability, Personal Injury, Criminal, Estate Planning, Trust and Probate Law.**
**San Mateo, California Office: Home Savings Building, 1730 South El Camino Real, Sixth Floor. Telephone: 415-341-2900. Fax: 415-341-2258.**

*See Professional Biographies, DALY CITY, CALIFORNIA*

Friedenberg, David J., (BV) .... '26 '54 C.112 B.S. L.1065 J.D. 2171 Junipero Serra Blvd.
Galinsky, Marshall S. .... '39 '68 C.696 B.A. L.188 J.D. 333 Gellert Blvd.
Guralnick, Steven .... '37 '63 C.170 A.B. L.1065 J.D. 375 S. Mayfair Ave.
Hamblin, Rodney H., (AV) .... '22 '51 C&L.767 B.S., LL.B. 61 Lake Forest Dr.‡
Hiester, Thomas L. .... '42 '77 C.312 B.A. L.767 J.D. 6801 Mission St.
Howard, Lytle, Petersen and Mah .... 2171 Junipero Serra Blvd. (⊙Foster City)
Hunniecutt, Robert L. .... '46 '76 C.1060 B.A. L.1026 J.D. 34 Santa Ana Ave.
Hupf, Paul M., (AV) .... '21 '49 C.116 A.B. L.767 J.D. [Hupf&M.]
Hupf & Morgan, (AV) .... 7316 Mission St.
Jackson, Robert G. .... '66 '94 C.112 B.A. L.1065 J.D. [[A] Howard,L.P.&M.]
Kyriakis, Victor G., (BV) .... '35 '64 C.813 B.A. L.1065 LL.B. 375 S. Mayfair Ave.
Lytle, Brett S. .... '58 '85 C.352 B.B.A. L.285 J.D. [Howard,L.P.&M.]
Mah, Donald '58 '88 C.05 B.A. L.285 J.D.
(adm. in WA; not adm. in CA) [Howard,L.P.&M.]
Mittler, Harvey D., (BV) .... '42 '71 C.112 A.B. L.1065 J.D. 6798 Mission St.
Molyneaux, Edward L., III .... '58 '85 C.813 B.A. L.1066 J.D. 7080 Mission St.
Morgan, Tara M., (BV) .... '54 '79 C&L.767 B.A., J.D. [Hupf&M.]
Nuris, Thomas A., (BV) .... '53 '78 C.767 B.A. L.1065 J.D. 2171 Junipero Serra Blvd.
Rothstein, Alan R. .... '41 '71 C.112 B.A. L.767 J.D. 333 Gellert Blvd. (⊙Sun Valley)
Sange, Peter C. .... '51 '77 C.112 B.A. L.1065 J.D. Jacoby & Meyers Law Off.
Saroyan, Cyril M. .... '11 '37 C.813 B.A. L.1065 LL.B. 60 Westline Dr.‡
Schumacher, William J. .... '37 '66 C.766 A.B. L.767 J.D. 160 Werner Ave.
Sheridan, Robert, (AV) .... '40 '67 C.895 A.B. L.569 LL.B. 2171 Junipero Serra Blvd.
Shihadeh, Jameel M. .... '61 '95 L.765 J.D. 333 Gellert Blvd.
Spar, Harold S. .... '41 '70 C.766 B.A. L.1026 J.D. 6798 Mission St.
Steinheimer, Vickie L. .... '42 '79 C.041 B.A. L.767 J.D. 6801 Mission St.
Warnes, John T. .... '47 '85 C.602 B.A. L.1065 J.D. 371 Imperial Way
Weinberger, Robert F., (BV) .... '29 '61 C.112 A.B. L.765 LL.B. 49 Creston Ave.
Weldon, Aubrey W.A. .... '45 '84 C.1097 B.A. L.1065 J.D. 213 Knowles Ave.
**Wohl, Steven C.**, (BV) .... '52 '77 C.112 A.B. L.765 J.D. [Fox,S.W.&N.]⊙
*PRACTICE AREAS: Family Law; Criminal Law; Personal Injury.
Xavier, Angela M. .... '58 '93 C.766 B.A. L.900 J.D. P.O. Box 3002

## DANA POINT, 31,896, *Orange Co.*

Bardet, John J., (AV) .... '31 '63 C.112 B.S. L.1068 LL.B. 9 Costa Del Sol
Bergman, Daniel C. '43 '76
C.763 B.S. L.1049 J.D. Pres. & CFO, Pyrite Canyon Group, Inc.
Bowers, Stacey L. '66 '92 C.665 B.S. L.208 J.D.
(adm. in CO; not adm. in CA) [[A] Hand&H.]
Champlin, Betty Jane .... '47 '74 C.970 B.A. L.1065 J.D. 33832 Barcelon Pl.
Green, William W. .... '50 '77 C.112 B.A. L.398 J.D. 24265 De Leon Dr.
Hand, Jehu .... '56 '84 C.101 B.A. L.569 J.D. [Hand&H.]
Hand & Hand, A Law Corporation .... 24901 Dana Point Harbor Dr.
Kristjanson, Johann D. .... '36 '74 C.101 B.S. L.169 J.D. P.O. Box 777
Lawlor, William F., III .... '42 '72 C.839 B.S. L.744 LL.B. 33242 Palo Alto
Majdick, Michael J. .... '54 '91 C.112 B.S. L.1137 J.D. 34144 Pacific Coast Hwy.
McGrath, Harold F. .... '33 '72 C.1042 B.S. L.1137 J.D. 23806 Cassandra Bay
Mitchell, Dale C., (BV) .... '29 '66 C.267 B.A. L.765 LL.B. 32971 Christina Dr.
Morris, Margaret J. .... '22 '49 C.347 A.B. L.597 J.D. 102 Monarch Bay‡
Morris, Robert S., (AV) .... '17 '48 C.388 A.B. L.597 J.D. 102 Monarch Bay‡
Neale, Matthew E. .... '47 '77 C.1042 B.S.L. L.1198 J.D. 34188 Coast Hwy.
O'Neil, Frank D. .... '22 '47 C&L.813 A.B., LL.B. 25615 Bridgewater Lane‡
Roberts, Edward E. .... '27 '72 C.839 B.S.E.E. L.990 J.D. P.O. Box 3206 (Pat.)
Rosen, Bruce D., (AV) .... '53 '79 C.112 B.A. L.1137 J.D. 24701 La Plaza Dr.
Rosen, Stanley L., (A P.C.), (BV) '27 '53
C.569 B.A. L.188 LL.B. 34179 Golden Lantern St.
Sall, Robert K., (A Prof. Corp.), (BV) .... '53 '78 C.112 A.B. L.1065 J.D. [R.K.Sall]
Sall, Robert K., A Professional Corporation, (BV) .... 33971 Selva Rd.
Saltus, Cheryl A. .... '48 '78 L.1152 J.D. 34148 Pacific Coast Hwy., #A
Scallon, Hugh J., (BV) .... '34 '62 C&L.966 B.B.A., LL.B. 34177 Pacific Coast Hwy.
Shaw, James T., III .... '51 '81 C.623 B.B.A. L.1048 J.D. [J.T.Shaw]
Shaw, James T., The Law Offices of .... 33971 Selva Rd.
Shotton, Janet A. .... '34 '88 C.1245 B.S. L.1137 J.D. 34184 Coast Hwy.
Simmons, Edward W. .... '48 '77 C.1188 B.A. L.1067 J.D. Capistrano Hosp.
Smolowitz, Sindee M. .... '52 '87 C.102 B.S. L.1184 J.D. 33971 Selva Rd.
Taylor, Ronald R. .... '55 '86 C.800 B.S.B.A. L.1137 J.D. 24672 San Juan Ave.
Thompson, Wendell R. .... '19 '47 C.112 A.B. L.477 LL.B. 33622-A Dana Vista Drive‡
Walsh, Nina G. .... '24 '68 C.112 A.B. L.767 LL.B. 34051 El Contento Dr.
West, Charles W. .... '50 '83 C.112 B.S. L.1137 J.D. Co. Dir. of Real Estate
Wittman, William A., (AV) .... '08 '36 C&L.800 A.B. 88 Monarch Bay‡

## DANVILLE, 31,306, *Contra Costa Co.*

Amarant, John R. .... '48 '74 C.740 B.A. L.770 J.D. P.O. Box 1225
**Armstrong, Mark L.**, (AV) .... '51 '78 C.112 B.A. L.284 J.D. [Gagen,M.M.&A.]
*REPORTED CASES: DeVita v. County of Napa (1993) 28 Cal.Rptr.2d 794.
*PRACTICE AREAS: Land Use; Municipal and Environmental Law.
Bean, Ronald K. .... '39 '74 L.1137 LL.B. 10 Harmony Ct.
Begun, Darryn .... '65 '91 C&L.112 B.A., J.D. 263 Greenbrook Dr.
Behring, David E. .... '55 '81 C.674 A.B. L.472 J.D. Exec. V.P., Blackhawk Corp.
Bernstein, Johanna A. .... '52 '86 C.627 B.A. L.1065 J.D. P.O. Box 3093
**Brown, Steven L., Jr.** .... '64 '94 C&L.101 B.A., J.D. [Craddick,C.&C.]
*LANGUAGES: Swedish.
**Candland, D. Stuart**, (AV) .... '42 '71 C.101 B.A. L.1066 J.D. [Craddick,C.&C.]
*LANGUAGES: Spanish.
**Carter, Michael W.**, (BV) .... '55 '83 C.112 B.A. L.1065 J.D. [Gagen,M.M.&A.]
*PRACTICE AREAS: Family Law.
Cochrane, Michael J. .... '58 '85 C.260 B.S. L.910 J.D. 939 Hartz Way
**Conneely, Maureen A.** .... '54 '91 L.1153 J.D. [[A] Frankel&G.]
*PRACTICE AREAS: Business; Employment Law.
**Conti, Richard J.**, (AV) .... '44 '71 C.112 B.S. L.1065 J.D. [Craddick,C.&C.]
**Conti, Victor J.**, (BV) .... '56 '84 C.766 B.S. L.767 J.D. [Gagen,M.M.&A.]
*PRACTICE AREAS: Real Estate Law; Construction Law; Business Law; Civil Litigation.

**Coombs, Linn K.**, (BV) .... '45 '71 C.813 B.A. L.1068 J.D. [Gagen,M.M.&A.]
*PRACTICE AREAS: Estate Planning Law; Wills Law; Trusts Law.
**Craddick, Judy S.**, (BV) .... '— '80 C.421 L.1153 J.D. [Craddick,C.&C.]
**Craddick, Marrs A.**, (AV) .... '28 '59 C.112 B.A. L.1066 J.D. [Craddick,C.&C.]

**Craddick, Candland & Conti, Professional Corporation, (AV) [BR]**
**Danville-San Ramon Medical Center, 915 San Ramon Valley Boulevard, Suite 260, 94526-0810**
**Telephone: 510-838-1100 Fax: 510-743-0729**
**Marrs A. Craddick; D. Stuart Candland; Richard J. Conti; Judy S. Craddick; Robert W. Hodges; W. David Walker; Robert W. Lamson;—Phillip J. Maddux; Jean Louise Perry; Michael J. Garvin; Diane C. Miller; Steven L. Brown, Jr.**
**General Civil and Trial Practice in all State and Federal Courts. Insurance, Malpractice and Business Litigation.**

*See Professional Biographies, DANVILLE, CALIFORNIA*

Craft, Judith J. '41 '83 C.845 B.A. L.1003 J.D.
(adm. in OH; not adm. in CA) 1254 Vailwood Dr.‡
Crichton, James W. .... '24 '76 C.446 B.A. L.284 J.D. 3831 Cottonwood Dr.‡
**Curtin, Patricia E.** .... '62 '87 C.147 B.A. L.464 J.D. [Gagen,M.M.&A.]
*PRACTICE AREAS: Land Use Law; Environmental Law.
DeBene, Linda A., (AV) .... '47 '71 C&L.362 B.A., J.D. [L.DeBene]
DeBene, Linda, P.L.C., (AV) .... 4135 Blackhawk Plz. Cir.
Devito, Francis M. '23 '71 C.705 B.S. L.776 J.D.
(adm. in NJ; not adm. in CA) 3902 Cottonwood Dr.‡
Dister, Robert E. '53 '80 C.477 B.S. L.1066 J.D.
Admin. Dir., Institute for Contemporary Onanism
Elliott, Dru S., (Ms.) .... '54 '78 C&L.1137 B.S.L., J.D. 1900 So. Forest Hill Pl.‡
Field, Harlene I. .... '50 '75 C.112 A.B. L.1065 J.D. 72 Lomitas Rd.
Ford, George D., (BV) .... '38 '71 C.766 B.A. L.1065 J.D. 407 La Quinta Ct.
**Frankel, Richard A.**, (AV) .... '46 '82 C.112 B.A. L.1153 J.D. [Frankel&G.]
*PRACTICE AREAS: Business; Employment Law; Civil Litigation; Alternative Dispute Resolution.

**Frankel & Goldware, (AV)**
**375 Diablo Road Suite 200, 94526**
**Telephone: 510-820-8712 Fax: 510-831-0155**
**Email: Frankel@Danvillelaw.com URL: http://www.Danvillelaw.com**
**Members of Firm: Richard A. Frankel; Stuart I. Goldware. Associates: Maureen A. Conneely; Marcia Jensen Lassiter.**
**Business Law, Litigation, Employment, Real Property, Family Law, Personal Injury, Estate Planning and Alternative Dispute Resolution.**

*See Professional Biographies, DANVILLE, CALIFORNIA*

**Gagen, William E., Jr.**, (AV) .... '43 '69 C.276 A.B. L.1066 J.D. [Gagen,M.M.&A.]
*PRACTICE AREAS: Criminal Trial Practice; Personal Injury Law; Civil Litigation.

**Gagen, McCoy, McMahon & Armstrong, A Professional Corporation, (AV)**
**279 Front Street, P.O. Box 218, 94526⊙**
**Telephone: 510-837-0585 Fax: 510-838-5985**
**William E. Gagen, Jr. (Member of California Trial Lawyers Association, with recognized experience in the fields of Trial Lawyer and General Personal Injury) (Certified Specialist, Criminal Law, The State Bar of California Board of Legal Specialization); Gregory L. McCoy; Patrick J. McMahon; Mark L. Armstrong; Linn K. Coombs (Certified Specialist, Probate, Estate Planning and Trust Law, California Board of Legal Specialization); Stephen W. Thomas; Charles A. Koss; Michael J. Markowitz (Certified Specialist, Criminal Law, The State Bar of California Board of Legal Specialization); Michael W. Carter (Certified Specialist, Family Law, The State Bar of California Board of Legal Specialization); Richard C. Raines; Victor J. Conti; Barbara Duvall Jewell; Robert M. Fanucci; Allan C. Moore; Patricia E. Curtin; Stephen T. Buehl;—Alexander L. Schmid; Daniel A. Muller.**
**General Civil and Criminal Trial Practice, Insurance, Financial, Family, Real Estate, Corporation Law, Estate Planning, Wine Industry Regulatory Matters and Tax Law.**
**Napa, California Office: 1001 Second Street, Suite 315. Telephone: 707-224-8396. Fax: 707-224-5817.**

*See Professional Biographies, DANVILLE, CALIFORNIA*

Galbreath, Robert V. .... '26 '56 C.339 B.S.C.E. L.980 LL.B. 10 Ray Ct.‡
**Garvin, Michael J.** .... '62 '88 C.602 B.A. L.1067 J.D. [[A] Craddick,C.&C.]
**Goldware, Stuart I.**, (BV) .... '50 '77 C.112 A.B. L.426 J.D. [Frankel&G.]
*PRACTICE AREAS: Civil Litigation; Estate Planning/Probate; Alternative Dispute Resolution.
Gray, Stephanie .... '39 '84 C.112 A.B. L.1153 J.D. 375 Diablo Rd.
Harkins, Daniel S. .... '54 '81 C.112 B.A. L.284 J.D. [Harkins&S.]
Harkins & Sargent, (BV) .... 375 Diablo Rd.
Heer, Valeri J. .... '57 '87 87 Hillmont‡
Henze, Thomas E., (AV) .... '33 '59 C.112 A.B. L.1065 J.D. 375 Diablo Rd.
**Hodges, Robert W.**, (BV) .... '49 '80 C.766 B.A. L.1065 J.D. [Craddick,C.&C.]
Huennekens, Deborah Legome .... '64 '91 C.800 B.S. L.93 J.D. 95 Tuscany Way‡
Huovinen, H. Alan, (CV) .... '44 '72 C.147 B.A. L.464 J.D. 811 San Ramon Valley Blvd.
**Jewell, Barbara Duvall**, (BV) .... '47 '81 C.846 B.A. L.426 J.D. [Gagen,M.M.&A.]
*PRACTICE AREAS: Real Estate Litigation; Insurance Coverage Law; Design Professional Defense; Defective Construction.
Kartozian, William F. .... '38 '63 C.813 B.A. L.309 J.D. 318 Diablo Rd.
Klinkner, James A. .... '41 '70 C.112 B.S. L.1065 J.D. 383 Diablo Rd.
Koning, Kirk E. .... '50 '75 C.628 B.S.I.E. L.1065 J.D. 368 Borca Dr.
**Koss, Charles A.** .... '52 '81 C.959 B.B.A. L.1066 J.D. [Gagen,M.M.&A.]
*PRACTICE AREAS: Financial Law; Employment Law; Corporate Law.
Kubicki, Richard R. '25 '52 C&L.215 LL.B.
(adm. in MI; not adm. in CA) 291 Elsie Dr.‡
**Lamson, Robert W.** .... '51 '76 C.813 A.B. L.1066 J.D. [Craddick,C.&C.]
Langthorn, Edward A. .... '37 '70 C.1179 B.S.E.E. L.284 J.D. 338 W. El Pintado Rd.‡
**Lassiter, Marcia Jensen** .... '47 '89 C.267 B.A. L.284 J.D. [[A] Frankel&G.]
*PRACTICE AREAS: Family Law.
Law, Carole A. .... '44 '77 C.763 B.A. L.767 J.D. 279 Front St.
**Maddux, Phillip J.**, (AV) .... '44 '70 C.112 A.B. L.1066 J.D. [[A] Craddick,C.&C.]
Maly, Bonnie C. .... '47 '78 C.846 B.A. L.284 J.D. [[A] L.DeBene]
Marek, Cynthia Love .... '59 '85 C.112 A.B. L.1066 J.D. 62 Stonington Ct.‡
**Markowitz, Michael J.**, (BV) .... '51 '82 C.1044 B.S. L.284 J.D. [Gagen,M.M.&A.]
*PRACTICE AREAS: Criminal Trial Practice (State and Federal Courts); Juvenile Law; Personal Injury Law; General Trial Practice.
**McCoy, Gregory L.**, (AV) .... '49 '74 C.154 B.A. L.1066 J.D. [Gagen,M.M.&A.]
*PRACTICE AREAS: Financial Law; Real Estate Law; Business Law.
**McMahon, Patrick J.**, (AV) .... '42 '74 C.766 B.A. L.93 J.D. [Gagen,M.M.&A.]
*PRACTICE AREAS: General Civil Trial Practice; Business Law.
**Miller, Diane C.** .... '64 '89 C.112 B.A. L.767 J.D. [[A] Craddick,C.&C.]
Mock, Sandra Ford .... '44 '89 C.1060 L.1153 J.D. 375 Diablo Rd.
**Moore, Allan C.**, (BV) .... '54 '79 C.112 B.A. L.1049 J.D. [[A] Gagen,M.M.&A.]
*PRACTICE AREAS: Land Use Law.
**Muller, Daniel A.** .... '66 '94 C&L.112 B.A.;B.S., J.D. [[A] Gagen,M.M.&A.]
*PRACTICE AREAS: Land Use; Environmental Law; Criminal Law.
Nelson, Michael D., (AV) .... '44 '72 C.336 B.S. L.1137 J.D. 939 Hartz Way (Pat.)
Nolting, Leonard L. .... '26 '69 C.1073 A.B. L.284 J.D. 233 W. Prospect Ave.‡
O'Connor, Daniel J. .... '45 '75 C.473 B.A. L.608 J.D. P.O. Box 847
**Perry, Jean Louise** .... '50 '88 C.112 B.A. L.767 J.D. [[A] Craddick,C.&C.]
**Raines, Richard C.**, (AV) .... '46 '74 C.112 B.A. L.1065 J.D. [Gagen,M.M.&A.]
*REPORTED CASES: Green v. Mt. Diablo Hospital District, 207 Cal.App.3d 63; Conrad v. Ball Corporation, 24 Cal.App.4th 439.
*PRACTICE AREAS: Civil Litigation; Real Estate; Employment; Construction.
Rassier, John T. .... '46 '72 C.911 B.A. L.767 J.D. Rassier Properties

Rupprecht, Michael W., (BV) .......... '48 '74 C.475 B.S. L.284 J.D.,MBA 279 Front St.
Ryan, Theresa W. .......................'47 '79 C.188 B.A. L.93 J.D. 1848 Piedras Circle
Sargent, Dolores S., (BV) ................. '49 '84 C.1135 B.A. L.284 J.D. [Harkins&S.]
**Schmid, Alexander L.** ..................'52 '80 C.33 B.A. L.284 J.D. [⊠ Gagen,M.M.&A.]
*LANGUAGES: French and Spanish.
*PRACTICE AREAS: Tax Law; Estate Planning; Probate Law.
Siders, Barry L. ..........................'43 '73 C.112 A.B. L.1065 J.D. 931 Hartz Way
Singh, Mohinder ..........................'28 '75 C.112 M.B.A. L.1066 J.D. 822 Hartz Way
Stephens, Victor L. '35 '61 C&L.502 A.B., LL.B.
(adm. in MO; not adm. in CA) 183 Golden RidgeRd.‡
Suberlak, Patrice Primiano '51 '79 C.700 B.A. L.424 J.D.
(adm. in IL; not adm. in CA) 67 Oak Ridge Ct.‡
Sullivan, Robert J., (BV) ................... '52 '83 C.1211 B.S. L.284 J.D. [R.Sullivan]⊙
Sullivan, Robert, Law Offices of, (BV) ......375 Diablo Rd., Ste. 200 (⊙Westport, Conn.)
Thiel, Adrian ..............................'14 '40 C.813 A.B. L.309 J.D. P.O. Box 686‡
**Thomas, Stephen W., (AV)** ............'49 '76 C.112 A.B. L.284 J.D. [Gagen,M.M.&A.]
*PRACTICE AREAS: Real Estate Law; Real Property Construction Law; Administration Law; Civil Litigation.
Wagda, Joseph A., Jr. ............ '43 '76 C.262 B.S. L.1292 J.D. 547 Blackhawk Club Dr.
**Walker, W. David** ...................... '48 '76 C.112 B.A. L.284 J.D. [Craddick,C.&C.]
Welch, Gerald R., (BV) ................ '46 '76 C.1239 B.A. L.1065 J.D. 939 Hartz Way
Willman, Hubert B. '33 '62 C.698 B.S. L.502 J.D.
(adm. in MO; not adm. in CA) 4405 Deer Ridge Rd.
Yanello, Ralph .......................'41 '72 C.112 B.A. L.1065 J.D. 210 Kingswood Ct.

## DARWIN, 55, *Inyo Co.*

Palazzo, Robert P., (AV) ......... '52 '76 C.112 B.A. L.800 J.D. 230 S. Main St. (⊙L.A.)

## DAVIS, 46,209, *Yolo Co.*

Alcauskas, Richard T., (BV) ............ '44 '74 C.169 B.A. L.464 J.D. 1109 Kennedy Pl.
Ayer, John D. ....... '36 '68 C&L.421 B.A., J.D. Prof. of Law, Univ. of Calif. Sch. of Law
Baron, Roger '38 '63
(adm. in NY; not adm. in CA) Univ. of Calif. Sch. of Law
Barrett, Edward L., Jr., (AV) '17 '41
C.877 B.S. L.1066 LL.B. Dean, Univ. of Calif. Law School
Bartosic, Florian '26 '56 C.999 B.A. L.945 B.C.L.
(adm. in VA; not adm. in CA) Dean & Prof. of Law, Univ. of Calif.
Beede, Christine Z. ....................'56 '92 C.112 B.A. L.1067 J.D. 1712 Picasso Ave.
Beede, John M. ...........................................'23 '61 C.767 L.1026 LL.B. [Beede&B.]
Beede, Rodney J., (CV) .......................'50 '77 C.763 B.A. L.1137 J.D. [Beede&B.]
Beede & Beede, (CV) ........................................................................ 603 G Street
Bernhard, Antonia Eve '45 '82 C.112 B.A. L.1067 J.D.
Asst. Dean for Student Affs., Univ. of Calif. Sch. of Law
Black, Robert N., (BV) ..........................'46 '76 C.112 B.A. L.1067 J.D. 750 F St.
Bradley, Edwin J. ...................'29 '55 C.524 L.276 LL.B. Prof. of Law, Univ. of Cal.
Bruch, Carol S. ............. '41 '73 C.1100 A.B. L.1066 J.D. Prof. of Law, Univ. of Calif.
Callaway, James A., Jr., (BV) ............... '35 '61 C.112 B.A. L.1066 LL.B. 401 2nd St.
Clifton, Gail .........................'45 '78 C.846 B.A. L.1067 J.D. 1019 Stanford Dr.
Coder, Michael G., (BV) ................................................... '48 '74 P.O. Box 4607
Cole, Robert M. ..................................'19 '42 C.112 B.S. L.1066 LL.B. [Cole&C.]
Cole, Stephen N. ..................................'47 '72 C.629 B.S. L.1067 J.D. [Cole&C.]
Cole & Cole ...................................................................... P.O. Box 73800
Cook, Roberta Mendonca .................. '42 '76 C.147 B.A. L.464 J.D. 423 "F" St.
Davis, R. Keenan .................'50 '79 C.101 B.A. L.464 J.D. 3411 Monte Vista Ave.
De Hope, Joseph J., Jr., (BV) ............ '51 '77 C.112 B.A. L.464 J.D. 2008 Matisse St.
Dobris, Joel C. '40 '66 C.976 B.A. L.494 LL.B.
(adm. in NY; not adm. in CA) Prof. of Law, Univ. of Calif. Sch. of Law
Doremus, Holly '59 '91 C.855 B.Sc. L.1066 J.D.
(adm. in OR; not adm. in CA) 207 E. 8th St.‡
Durfee, Glenn .......................................... '47 '73 C.860 A.B. L.145 J.D. 216 F St.
Dykstra, Daniel J. '16 '48 C.962 B.S. L.966 LL.B.
(adm. in WI; not adm. in CA) Prof. of Law, Univ. of Calif.
Feeney, Floyd F. '33 '60 C.198 B.S. L.569 LL.B.
(adm. in NC; not adm. in CA) Univ. of Calif.
Fessler, Daniel William '41 '66 C&L.276 B.S., LL.B.
(adm. in WY; not adm. in CA) Univ. of Calif.
Forbes, Stanley R. '47 '75 C.800 A.B. L.880 J.D.
(adm. in VA; not adm. in CA) 1106 Redwood Ln.‡
Forest, Adam .................................... '60 '87 C.112 B.A. L.1049 J.D. 805 9th St.
Frankel, George Robert ........'56 '85 C.112 B.S. L.976 J.D. Prof. of Law, Univ. of Calif.
Frankel, Merrill A., (BV) ...............'48 '77 C.112 A.B. L.1067 J.D. 1712 Picasso Ave.
Frankel, Thomas H., (AV) ................ '41 '66 C.174 B.A. L.1066 LL.B. [T.H.Frankel]
Frankel, Thomas H., Inc., (AV) ............................................................... 102 E St.
Franks, Robert G. '45 '71 C&L.508 B.A., J.D.
(adm. in MT; not adm. in CA)
Acting V. Chancellor, Student Affairs, Univ. of Calif. Davis★
French, Susan F. '43 '67 C.813 B.A. L.911 J.D.
(adm. in WA; not adm. in CA) Univ. of Calif. Law Sch.
Fried, Leslie B. ...........................................'55 '84 C.112 B.A. L.1068 J.D. 328 A St.
Friedman, Janet, (AV) .............. '43 '69 C.112 B.A. L.1066 J.D. 2400 Bombadil Lane
**Fullerton, Alexandra P.** ..................'67 '94 C.112 B.S. L.1065 J.D. [⊠ J.G.Poulos]
*PRACTICE AREAS: Family Law; Probate; Estate Planning.

**Gambatese, Roger L., (AV) '36 '61 C.976 B.S. L.477 J.D.**
**510 Fourth Street, 95616**
**Telephone: 916-756-8300 Fax: 916-756-9165**
**(Certified Specialist, Estate Planning, Trust and Probate Law, The State Bar of California Board of Legal Specialization).**
**Estate Planning, Trust and Probate Law.**
*See Professional Biographies, DAVIS, CALIFORNIA*

Giannoni, Anthony R., (BV) ................... '45 '71 C.770 B.S. L.1067 J.D. 429 F St.
Gifford, Jean C. .......................'47 '90 C.1044 B.A. L.284 J.D. 1637 Baywood Lane
Glennon, Michael J. '47 '73 C.755 B.A. L.494 J.D.
(adm. in MN; not adm. in CA) Prof. of Law, Univ. of Calif.
Goodpaster, Gary S. '37 '65
C.347 B.A. L.1119 J.D. Prof. of Law, Univ. of Calif., Sch. of Law
Grayden, Margaret Miller ................'61 '93 C.914 B.A. L.1067 J.D. P.O. Box 74245
Grossman, George S. .......................'38 '66 C.145 B.A. L.813 LL.B. Univ. of Calif.
Guarino, Richard ........................'47 '72 C.112 A.B. L.1067 J.D. Rt. 2, Box 2139
Halko, Lisa L. ..........................'60 '90 C.454 B.A. L.1068 J.D. P.O. Box 74022
Hamilton, M. J. ....'39 '75 C.30 PhD. L.1067 J.D. Asst. Dean, Sch. of Law, Univ. of Calif.
Hardy, Alison .............................'61 '88 C.813 B.A. L.1068 J.D. P.O. Box 4745

**Harrington, Michael J. '55 '89 C.112 B.A. L.273 J.D.**
**423 E Street, 95616**
**Telephone: 916-759-8440 Fax: 916-759-8476**
**Email: avialaw@wheel.dcn.davis.ca.us**
***PRACTICE AREAS: Airplane Crash Litigation; Aviation Law; Administrative Hearings and Appeals (Aviation).**
**Airplane Crash Litigation, Aviation Law and Administrative Hearings and Appeals (Aviation).**
*See Professional Biographies, DAVIS, CALIFORNIA*

Hegle, Charlotte Marie .................'57 '87 C.1060 B.A. L.464 J.D. 3326 Victoria Pl.

**Henderson, Mark G., (BV) '54 '81 C.169 B.A. L.464 J.D.**
**429 F Street, Suite 9, 95616-4150**
**Telephone: 916-757-1793 Fax: 916-757-1796**
**(Certified Specialist, Estate Planning, Trust and Probate Law, The State Bar of California Board of Legal Specialization).**
***REPORTED CASES: Archer v. Sybert (1985) 167 Cal. App. 3d 722.**
**Estate Planning, Trusts and Probate, Civil Litigation, Business and Real Estate.**
*See Professional Biographies, DAVIS, CALIFORNIA*

Hogan, James E. '30 '56 C.424 A.B. L.276 LL.B.
(adm. in DC; not adm. in CA) Prof. of Law, Univ. of Calif.
Hoyt, Margaret E. ...........................'27 '53 C.112 A.B. L.1066 J.D. 231 "G" St.
Imwinkelried, Edward J. .... '46 '70 C&L.767 B.A., J.D. Prof., Univ. of Calif. Sch. of Law
Jacobson, A. Ben ......................... '20 '52 C.112 B.S. L.1066 LL.B. 2511 Seville Ct.
Johnson, Joel T. ..................................'44 '72 C.813 B.A. L.309 J.D. Univ. of Calif.
Jones, Emma C. ................. '46 '73 C.766 B.A. L.326 J.D. Law Prof., Univ. of Calif.
Jordan, Ellen R. '43 '72 C.188 B.A. L.178 J.D.
(adm. in MD; not adm. in CA) Prof. of Law, Univ. of Calif., Davis‡
Judd, David J. ............................... '49 '84 C.112 B.A. L.999 J.D. 2108 Loyola Dr.
Juenger, Friedrich K. '30 '62 C.477 M.C.L. L.178 LL.B.
(adm. in NY; not adm. in CA) Prof. of Law, Univ. of Calif., King Hall
Kass, Jan Carmikle ................... '61 '90 C.112 B.S. L.1067 J.D. 2760 Ottowa Ave.
Kopper, William D., (BV) ..........................'48 '80 C.145 B.A. L.1067 J.D. 417 E St.
Kubey, Craig H. ................................'49 '75 C.112 A.B. L.1067 J.D. 313 Hidalgo Pl.
Lassen, Elizabeth '59 '83 C.446 B.S. L.64 J.D.
(adm. in MD; not adm. in CA; Pat.) Calgene
Lawson, Grace A. ...................'41 '80 C.112 A.B. L.464 J.D. 813 Sierra Madre Way
Levitt, Thomas C. ......................'54 '79 C.1067 B.S.Ch.E. L.1065 J.D. 200 "B" St.
Lewis, Alfred J. '35 '65 C&L.831 A.B., J.D.
(adm. in PA; not adm. in CA) Univ. of Calif.
Loiseaux, Pierre R. '25 '50 L.94 LL.B.
(adm. in MA; not adm. in CA) Univ. of Calif.
Love, Jean C. '43 '68 C&L.966 B.A., J.D.
(adm. in WI; not adm. in CA) Univ. of Calif.
Mazelis, Noreen B. ........................... '44 '73 C.112 B.A. L.1067 J.D. 437 "F" St.
Michaud, Laurie Ashley ............'— '89 C.1074 B.A. L.1067 J.D. 1005 Hacienda Ave.
Morris, Robert T. .............................. '49 '80 C.112 A.B. L.464 J.D. 46 Walnut Ln.
Murphy, Millard A. ........................'47 '86 C.1078 B.A. L.1066 J.D. P.O. Box 4745
Oakley, John B. ..................................'47 '72 C.112 B.A. L.976 J.D. Univ. of Calif.
Peirce, John R. ........................... '45 '71 C.339 B.A. L.1066 J.D. 424 Alvarado
Perschbacher, Rex R. '46 '72 C.813 A.B. L.1066 J.D.
Assoc. Dean & Prof. of Law, Univ. of Calif. Sch. of Law
Peter, Donna J. ........................................ '60 '87 C.112 B.S. L.464 J.D. 510 4th St.

**Peterson, Michael R. '54 '81 C&L.800 A.B., J.D.**
**510 Fourth Street, 95616-4125**
**Telephone: 916-756-8300 Fax: 916-756-9165**
**Business and Real Estate Law. Estate Planning, Trusts and Probate.**
*See Professional Biographies, DAVIS, CALIFORNIA*

**Poulos, Joan G. '36 '63 C.378 B.S. L.1065 J.D.**
**1723 Oak Avenue, 95616**
**Telephone: 916-753-4450 Facsimile: 916-753-9457**
***PRACTICE AREAS: Family Law; Real Estate Law; General Civil Litigation; Wills and Trusts; Labor.**
**Associate: Alexandra P. Fullerton.**
**Family Law, Real Estate Law, General Civil Litigation, Wills and Trusts, Labor.**
*See Professional Biographies, DAVIS, CALIFORNIA*

Poulos, John W. ............. '37 '63 C.813 A.B. L.1065 J.D. Prof. of Law, Univ. of Calif.
Pritchard, William R. '24 '57 C.375 D.V.M. L.345 J.D.
(adm. in IL; not adm. in CA) Univ. of Calif.
Rabin, Edward H. ...................'37 '59 C&L.178 A.B., J.D. Prof. of Law, Univ. of Calif.
Ramey, Felicenne H. ....... '— '73 C.645 B.S. L.1067 J.D. Prof. of Law, Calif. State Univ.

**Rosenberg, David, Law Offices of, (AV) '46 '74 C.1074 B.S. L.1067 J.D.**
**503 Third Street, 95616**
**Telephone: 916-750-3000 Telefax: 916-758-4411**
***PRACTICE AREAS: General Civil Law; Trial Practice (State and Federal Courts); Administrative and Government Law; Business Litigation.**
**General Civil Law, Trial Practice (State and Federal Courts), Administrative and Government Law, Business Litigation, Real Estate Litigation.**
*See Professional Biographies, DAVIS, CALIFORNIA*

Sargeant, Kimball J. P. ................................'53 '78 C&L.285 B.A., J.D. 510 4th St.
Saunders, Janet .............................'45 '76 C.102 B.A. L.284 J.D. 2504 Regis Dr.
Smith, James F. ..................................'42 '68 C.36 B.S. L.1066 J.D. Univ. of Calif.
Soika, John J. ........................ '44 '75 C.178 B.A. L.1067 J.D. 637 Portsmouth Ave.
Strohl, Thomas M., (CV) ..................'31 '81 C.679 B.S. L.464 J.D. 1209 W. 8th St.
Taylor, Warren K. ...................'20 '49 C.112 B.S. L.1066 LL.B. 27338 Willowbank Rd.‡
Terlecky, Theodore N. ...................'41 '71 C.980 B.A. L.1067 J.D. 1525 Lemon Lane‡
Theg, Jill Miller '56 '81 C.821 B.A. L.259 J.D.
(adm. in FL; not adm. in CA) 1130 Salamanca Ct.‡
Thorme, Melissa A. ......... '63 '90 C.1074 B.S. L.112 J.D. Coun., Larry Walker Assocs.
Troupe, Edwina L. ............................'59 '92 C.37 B.S. L.1067 J.D. 3050 Donato Ln.
Truskol, Michael F. ........................'44 '72 C.426 B.A. L.1067 J.D. 3620 Chiles Rd.
Uriu, Akiko Lynne ...........................................'36 '81 C.112 B.S. L.1026 J.D. [A.L.Uriu]
Uriu, Akiko Lynne, A Prof. Corp. ...................................................... 901 Kent Dr.
Weetman, David M. ..................'40 '66 C.763 A.B. L.1065 LL.B. 642 Villanova Dr.‡

**Wells, Stanley H., (AV) '31 '72 L.464 J.D.**
**510 Fourth Street, 95616**
**Telephone: 916-758-1990 Fax: 916-758-1181**
**Email: shwells@den.davis.ca.us**
***PRACTICE AREAS: Estate Planning; Probate Law; Trust Law; Business Law for the Small Business Person.**
**Estate Planning, Trust, Probate Law, Probate Litigation, Civil Practice, Taxation, Business and Real Estate.**
*See Professional Biographies, DAVIS, CALIFORNIA*

West, Martha S. '46 '74 C.1036 B.A. L.1119 J.D.
(adm. in IN; not adm. in CA) Prof., Univ. of Calif. Sch. of Law, Davis
White, Bill D. ................................................'22 '69 L.464 J.D. 1007 Villanova Dr.

White, Kathleen M. .... '54 '85 C.228 A.B. L.800 J.D. 730 N. Campus Way
Whitworth, Charles R. .... '29 '83 C.112 B.S. L.464 J.D. 411 Schaiser Ave.
Wilson, Jeanne M. '51 '76 C.464 B.A. L.800 J.D.
Dir., Student Jud. Affs., Univ. of Calif.
Wimer, Kenneth E. .... '39 '78 L.408 J.D. 604 Third St.
Wolf, Arnold J., (AV) .... '47 '71 510 4th St.
Wolf, Arnold J., (AV) .... '47 '71 C&L.659 B.A., J.D. 510 4th St.
Wolk, Bruce '46 '75 C.33 B.S. L.309 J.D.
(adm. in DC; not adm. in CA) Dean, Univ. of Calif. Sch. of Law
Worrell, R. Joan .... '44 '85 C.112 B.A. L.1067 J.D. P.O. Box 4353
Wright, James G. .... '47 '72 C.112 B.A. L.1067 J.D. P.O. Box 1091
Wydick, Richard C. .... '37 '62 C.951 B.A. L.813 LL.B. Prof. of Law, Univ. of Calif.

## DELANO, 22,762, *Kern Co.*

Hourigan, John T., (BV) .... '21 '49 C.321 A.B. L.426 LL.B. 921 13th Ave.
Montgomery, J. Robert, Jr., (CV) .... '40 '67 C.813 A.B. L.1068 J.D. 1201 Jefferson St.
Parsons, Kit .... '47 '73 C.623 B.A. L.1067 J.D. 1012 Jefferson
Salvucci, Susan D. (Johnson) '49 '84
L.1148 J.D. Gen. Coun., Anthony Welded Prods., Inc.
Smith, M. Dwain .... '26 '63 C.622 A.B. L.770 LL.B. P.O. Box 398‡

## DEL MAR, 4,860, *San Diego Co.*

Anglin, Richard L., Jr., (AV) .... '45 '81 C.124 B.S.C.E. L.426 J.D. [Anglin&G.]
Anglin & Giaccherini, (AV) .... 3558 Voyager Circle
Askey, David H., (BV) .... '37 '71 C.174 B.A. L.1241 J.D. 1442 Camino Del Mar
Ayers, Robert S. .... '59 '88 C.1188 B.A. L.1137 J.D. [Frank&A.]
Baldwin, John K. .... '33 '60 C&L.800 B.A., LL.B. 901 Highland Ave.
Becker, John C. .... '45 '72 C.763 B.S. L.1065 J.D. 14872 De la Valle Pl.
Best, Thomas G. .... '48 '72 C&L.500 B.B.A., J.D. 13707 Ruette Le Parc, Unit B‡
Blake, John J., (BV) .... '46 '71 C.602 A.B. L.597 J.D. 1330 Camino del Mar
Borevitz, Ben A., (AV) .... '38 '63 C.112 B.A. L.1066 J.D. 294 Torrey Pines Terrace‡
Charos, Glenn W., (CV) .... '56 '84 C.1173 B.S.L. L.1137 J.D. 3790 Via de la Valle
Comstock, Michael J. .... '53 '89 C.1241 B.B.A. L.1137 J.D. P.O. Box 1093
Cook, Melissa W. .... '62 '88 C.446 B.A. L.30 J.D. [Kissane&C.]
Corn, Jonathan Charles .... '64 '91 C.477 B.A. L.276 J.D. 110 15th St.
Couto, Drew J. .... '59 '86 C.112 B.A. L.990 J.D. P.O. Box 2608
Donaldson, Lorraine M. '45 '84 C.1057 B.S. L.1170 J.D.
(adm. in ME; not adm. in CA; Pat.) 298 Surf View Court
Doolittle, Glenn A., Jr. .... '53 '81 C.846 B.A. L.280 J.D. 1155 Camino Del Mar #120
Ecker, Arthur S., (AV) .... '27 '52 C&L.309 A.B., LL.B. 1232 Crest Rd.
Forbes, Douglas .... '64 '91 C.112 B.A. L.1049 J.D. 4518 Vista de la Tierre
Frank, Robert D., (AV) .... '49 '75 C.347 B.A. L.862 J.D. [Frank&A.]
Frank & Ayers, (AV) .... 1104 Camino Del Mar
Fullerton, Jolene D. .... '62 '86 C.1111 B.A. L.273 J.D. 3790 Via de la Valle
Gamer, Peter P., (AV) .... '38 '67 C.112 B.A. L.309 J.D. [Gamer,P.P.] (⊙San Diego)
Gamer, Peter P., P.C., (AV) .... 3790 Via De La Valle
Giaccherini, Thomas N. .... '56 '81 C.103 A.B. L.184 J.D. [Anglin&G.] (Pat.)
Gigler, James R., (BV) .... '42 '70 C.112 B.A. L.1049 J.D. 1011 Camino Del Mar
Gobar, Neal J. .... '30 '55 C.112 A.B. L.1066 LL.B. 258 19th St.‡
Golden, King, Jr. .... '46 '75 C.112 B.A. L.893 J.D. 12802 Via Nestore
Hahn, Wolfgang F. .... '48 '74 C.763 B.A. L.61 J.D. 280 Torrey Pints Ter.
Hauser, Thomas W., (AV) .... '36 '60 C&L.477 B.B.A., J.D. P.O. Box 2430
Hawkins, Jenny W. .... '38 '77 C.575 A.B. L.1137 J.D. 1330 Camino Del Mar
Hubbard, Roderick R. .... '43 '69 C.112 A.B. L.1065 J.D. 877 Avocado Place‡
Huiskamp, John S., (BV) .... '39 '64 C.674 A.B. L.228 LL.B. 366 Luzon Ave.‡
Kennedy, James H. .... '46 '72 C.763 B.A. L.800 J.D. 707 Hoska
Kennerly, B. Franklin, IV .... '27 '77 C.012 B.Com. L.029 2058 Carmel Valley Rd.
Kissane, Matthew T., (AV) .... '42 '67 C&L.285 B.B.A., J.D. [Kissane&C.]
Kissane & Cook, A Professional Corporation, (AV)
12865 Caminito Pointe Del Mar Way
Lutz, Gregory .... '60 '86 C.25 B.A. L.1137 J.D. 1307 Stratford Ct.
Maas, Earl H., Jr. .... '30 '58 C&L.426 B.S., J.D. Ret. Supr. Ct. J.
McQuillen, Michael T. .... '36 '76 C.688 B.Che. L.1137 J.D. 961 American Way‡
Miller, G. Scott, (BV) .... '16 '50 C.112 B.S. L.1065 J.D. 12745 Via Felino
Osborn, Duncan F. .... '49 '77 C.35 B.S. L.37 J.D. 343 9th St.
Osborne, Diana T. .... '42 '74 C.788 B.A. L.284 J.D. P.O. Box 2121
Porter, Margaret B. .... '— '33 C.881 A.B. L.178 LL.B. 2589 Via Pisa‡
Ross, Marshall .... '12 '35 C&L.800 B.A., J.D. 1620 Luneta Dr.‡
Sankary, Morris .... '26 '51 C.112 B.A. L.800 LL.B. [Sankary&S.]
Sankary & Sankary .... 4518 Vista De La Tierra
Sindell, Joseph M. '15 '40 C&L.930 A.B., J.D.
(adm. in OH; not adm. in CA) 1095 Klish Way‡
Sistos, Roberta R. .... '54 '92 C.763 B.S. L.1049 J.D. [A Kissane&C.]
Smigielski, Mary Ann .... '68 '93 C&L.1049 B.A., J.D. 12702 Via Cortina
Smith, Gene E., (AV) .... '22 '51 C&L.800 LL.B. P.O. Box RFD Box M2
Smith, Stanley D., (AV) .... '35 '65 C.112 L.809 LL.B. 211 23rd. St.‡
Smith, Tricia A., (BV) .... '46 '71 C.112 B.A. L.597 J.D. 1330 Camino del Mar
Spalding, Mark J. .... '61 '86 C.154 B.A. L.426 J.D. 140 12th St.
Winkler, David J. .... '53 '78 C.860 B.S. L.1049 J.D. Del Mar Partnership, Inc.‡
Yesson, Katherine A. .... '61 '87 C.112 B.A. L.1049 J.D. 1104 Camino Del Mar

## DEL REY, 1,661, *Fresno Co.*

Metzler, Dennis K., (AV) .... '40 '66 C&L.800 A.B., LL.B. P.O. Box 509‡
Viau, Floyd R. B. .... '27 '54 C.112 L.1065 LL.B. 6679 South Del Rey Ave.‡
Viau, Lawrence E., Jr. .... '22 '50 C.112 A.B. L.1065 J.D. 10088 E. Lincoln‡

## DESERT HOT SPRINGS, 11,648, *Riverside Co.*

Wells, Arthur R., Sr. .... '19 '69 C.262 L.1095 LL.B. 73400 Rask Rd.

## DIABLO, —, *Contra Costa Co.*

Cole, Dale Sondel .... '53 '80 C.112 B.A. L.800 J.D. P.O. Box 721

## DIAMOND BAR, 53,672, *Los Angeles Co.*

Alvarez, Lazaro .... '37 '82 C.1109 B.A. L.1137 J.D. 556 N. Diamond Bar Blvd.
Bandy, Thomas E. .... '49 '78 C.37 B.S. L.398 J.D. [Bandy&B.]
Bandy, Valerie J. .... '52 '78 C.1253 B.A. L.398 J.D. [Bandy&B.]
Bandy & Bandy .... 20709 Golden Springs Dr.
Flamenbaum, Bruce .... '47 '82 C.1192 B.S. L.809 J.D. 3333 S. Brea Canyon Rd.
Glad, Amy L. '57 '91 C.813 B.A. L.464 J.D.
Exec. V.P., Bldg. Industry Assn. of S. Calif., Inc.
Glickstein-Hernandez, R. Lynne '54 '86 C.347 B.S. L.1137 J.D.
22632 Golden Springs Dr.
Hassan, J. Marvin '51 '80 C.800 B.A. L.329 J.D.
(adm. in PA; not adm. in CA) 21433 Bella Pine Dr.‡
Hemming, Michael J., (BV) '48 '77
C.1097 B.A.Econ. L.1137 J.D. 556 N. Diamond Bar Blvd.
Hernandez, David, Jr. .... '59 '86 C.1042 B.S. L.1137 J.D. [Hernandez&S.]
Hernandez and Schapiro .... 22632 Golden Springs Dr.
Hopson, Stirling J. .... '59 '92 C.800 B.S.L. L.29 J.D. 3333 Brea Canyon Rd.
Horcher, Paul V. .... '51 '78 C.1075 B.A. L.398 J.D. Legis., Calif. State Assembly
Kane, Karen J. .... '57 '92 C&L.1137 B.S.L., J.D. 2380 Diamond Bar Blvd.
MacBride, Dexter D. '17 '39 C.945 L.192 J.D.
(adm. in VA; not adm. in CA) 435 Willapa Lane‡
Madrid, Eduardo M., (A Prof. Law Corp.) '50 '78
C.1131 B.A. L.1240 J.D. 556 N. Diamond Bar Blvd.
Martin, Elmer Dean, III, (AV) .... '43 '68 C.602 B.B.A. L.966 J.D. [E.D.Martin III]⊙
Martin, Elmer Dean, III, A Professional Corporation, (AV)
1081 Grand Ave., Suite G (⊙Los Angeles)
Mednick, Allen D. .... '42 '67 C.563 B.A. L.273 J.D. Sr. Dep. Dist. Pros.
Meza, Daniel Garcia .... '55 '83 C.112 B.A. L.809 J.D. 556 N. Diamond Bar Blvd.
Phillips, Loren C. .... '32 '72 C.800 B.A. L.1127 J.D. 1930 Brea Canyon Rd.
Poirier, G. R. .... '23 '63 C.861 B.S.E. L.800 J.D. 23923 Sunset Crossing Rd.‡
Rios, Delilah Knox, (BV) .... '54 '79 C&L.1137 B.S.L., J.D. 22640 E Golden Springs
Schapiro, Mark Edward .... '60 '87 C.98 B.S. L.1137 J.D. [Hernandez&S.]
Sernel, Elliott R. '55 '85 C.112 B.A. L.809 J.D.
Sr. Dep. Dist. Coun., South Coast Air Quality Mgmt. Dist.
Waters, John J., Jr. .... '52 '85 C.767 B.A. L.464 J.D. 1930 S. Brea Canyon Rd.
Wayland, Land .... '42 '68 C.605 A.B. L.800 J.D. 304 Ballena Dr.
Welsh, R. Michael '57 '91 C.801 B.S. L.1148 J.D.
(adm. in PA; not adm. in CA) P.O. Box 4502★
Wiese, Kurt R. .... '55 '84 C.861 B.S. L.37 J.D. Sr. Dep. Dist. Pros.

## DIAMOND SPRINGS, —, *El Dorado Co.*

Crowell, William F. .... '47 '72 C.112 A.B. L.1065 J.D. 1110 Pleasant Valley Rd.
Sperber, Timothy P. .... '40 '82 L.464 J.D. 540 Main St.

## DiGIORGIO, —, *Kern Co.*

Maciel, Ronald J. .... '43 '74 C.112 B.S. L.426 J.D. Jus. Ct. J.

## DILLON BEACH, 500, *Marin Co.*

Yee, Marilyn .... '53 '80 C.112 A.B. L.1065 J.D. P.O. Box 184

## DINUBA, 12,743, *Tulare Co.*

Ataide, Randy M. '57 '86 C.267 B.A. L.1189 J.D.
Corp. Coun., Laemmlen Orchards Inc.
Cowper, Peter M., (CV) .... '48 '88 C.330 B.A. L.1189 J.D. [A McKinney,W.&S.]⊙
Drew, Stephen .... '47 '72 C&L.767 B.A., J.D. Mun. J.
McKinney, Russell R., (AV) .... '42 '68 C.813 B.A. L.1065 J.D. [McKinney,W.&S.]⊙
McKinney, Wainwright & Saul-Olson, (AV) .... 531 N. Alta Ave., Suite C (⊙Visalia)
Saul-Olson, Randi, (BV) .... '53 '83 C.112 B.A. L.426 J.D. [McKinney,W.&S.]⊙
Stouffer, C. William, (BV) .... '31 '74 [A McKinney,W.&S.]⊙
Wainwright, James A., (BV) .... '43 '76 C.763 A.B. L.1026 J.D. [McKinney,W.&S.]⊙

## DIXON, 10,401, *Solano Co.*

Bernheim, William S. .... '48 '73 C.112 B.S. L.1067 J.D. [Bernheim,G.L.&M.]
Bernheim, Gutierrez, Levin & McCready .... 255 N. Lincoln St.
Gutierrez, Carlos R. .... '57 '85 C.1060 B.A. L.464 J.D. [Bernheim,G.L.&M.]
Levin, Roy C. .... '46 '91 C.766 B.S.E. L.464 J.D. [Bernheim,G.L.&M.]
Lum, Margaret Chan .... '29 '80 C.813 B.S. L.464 J.D. 232 E. "A" St.
MacDonald, Dougal C. .... '40 '66 C.813 B.A. L.976 LL.B. 1140 Pitt School Rd.
McCready, Doris .... '53 '90 [Bernheim,G.L.&M.]
Moe, Ronald E., (BV) .... '39 '66 C.768 B.S. L.464 J.D. 805 N. Lincoln St.
O'Donnell, Hugh, (BV) .... '19 '73 L.464 J.D. 1340 Blackberry Ct.
Randall, Kenneth D. '37 '63 C&L.336 B.A., LL.B.
(adm. in ID; not adm. in CA) 985 Sommer Dr.★
Schafer, Sally A. .... '57 '94 C.767 B.S. L.464 J.D. 255 N. Lincoln St.

## DOS PALOS, 4,196, *Merced Co.*

**Keene, Thomas J.**, (CV) .... '51 '77 C.112 B.A. L.1068 J.D. [C Linneman,B.T.V.&V.]
*REPORTED CASES: Doloris Villa v. Superior Court of Merced County, 124 CA 3d 1063 177 CR 752. People v. Mansfield 200 CA 3d 316 245 CR 572.
*PRACTICE AREAS: Municipal Law; Municipal Finance Law; Bond Law; Special Districts Law.

**Linneman, Burgess, Telles, Van Atta & Vierra, (AV)**
**1820 Marguerite Street, P.O. Box 156, 93620⊙**
**Telephone: 209-392-2141 Fax: 209-392-3964**
**Email: drathmann@aol.com**
**Members of Firm: Carl E. Van Atta; Diane V. Rathmann. Of Counsel: Jess P. Telles, Jr.; Thomas J. Keene.**
**General Civil and Trial Practice. Water District and Rights Law. Real Property, Probate, Negligence, Products Liability, Agricultural Law and Personal Injury.**
**Reference: The Bank of America National Trust and Savings Assn.**
**Merced, California Office: 312 West 19th Street, P.O. Box 2263. Telephone: 209-723-2137. Fax: 209-723-0899.**
**Los Banos, California Office: 654 K Street, P.O. Box 1364. Telephone: 209-826-4911. FAX: 209-826-4766. E-Mail: 1btvv@aol.com.**

***See Professional Biographies, DOS PALOS, CALIFORNIA***

**Rathmann, Diane V.** .... '47 '79 C.813 B.A. L.1068 J.D. [Linneman,B.T.V.&V.]
*LANGUAGES: Spanish.
*PRACTICE AREAS: Water Law; California Water District Law; Agricultural Law; Probate Law.
**Telles, Jess P., Jr.**, (BV) .... '20 '47 C.770 B.S. L.813 J.D. [C Linneman,B.T.V.&V.]
*PRACTICE AREAS: Water Law; California Water District Law; Agricultural Law.
**Van Atta, Carl E.**, (AV) .... '19 '49 C.813 B.A. L.767 J.D. [Linneman,B.T.V.&V.]
*PRACTICE AREAS: Personal Injury Litigation; Probate Law; Agricultural Law.

## DOWNEY, 91,444, *Los Angeles Co.*

Aguirre, Rodolfo A. .... '53 '81 C.112 B.A. L.809 J.D. Dep. Dist. Atty.
**Ahrens, Michele S.**, (BV) .... '53 '82 C.1097 B.A. L.426 J.D. [Tredway,L.&D.]
*REPORTED CASES: Novar Corp. v. Bureau of Collections (1984) 160 Cal. App. 3d 1, 206 Cal. Rptr. 287.
*PRACTICE AREAS: Civil Litigation; Employment Law.
Amacher, Robert P., (BV) .... '29 '54 C&L.629 B.S., LL.B. [Amacher,G.Y.&L.]
Amacher, Going, Yetur & Lin, (BV) .... 9050 Telegraph Rd.
Angotti, Gary L. .... '44 '77 C.347 B.S. L.809 J.D. 10841 Paramount Blvd.
Ardis & Lehn, (BV) .... Suite J, 9530 East Imperial Highway
Bear, Henry L., (AV) .... '17 '39 L.986 J.D. [Bear,K.R.&G.]
Bear, Kotob, Ruby & Gross, (AV) .... 10841 Paramount Boulevard
Beckman, Joel J., (BV) .... '55 '82 C.1109 B.A. L.809 J.D. 8141 E. 2nd St.
Beemer, Paul A. .... '49 '77 C.1167 B.S. L.426 J.D. P.O. Box 2205
Benger, Daniel E. .... '39 '75 C.1042 A.B. L.990 J.D. 9701 Lakewood Blvd.
Birnie, Wm. H. .... '24 '52 C&L.800 B.S., J.D. 10441 Julius Ave.‡
Brazelton, Robert S., (AV) .... '29 '59 C&L.426 B.A., J.D. 10029 Birchdale Ave.
Carfrae, Dorothy L., (BV) .... '50 '81 C.1109 B.A. L.1137 J.D. 7340 E. Florence
Castagno, Joseph D. .... '59 '83 C&L.426 B.A., J.D. 10841 Paramount Blvd.
Celio, Michael D. .... '57 '87 C.112 B.A. L.426 J.D. 9844 Paramount Blvd.
Cort, William G. .... '43 '72 C.112 A.B. L.1068 J.D. [A Amacher,G.Y.&L.]

Cristea, Alexandru Andy '45 '90 C.999 L.061 J.D.
(adm. in LA; not adm. in CA) 9291 Pico Vista Rd.
Davies, John ....................'57 '89 C.623 B.A. L.1137 J.D. 8607 Imperial Hgwy
Dunnum, Priscilla McKinney, (BV) .....'21 '48 C.972 L.426 J.D. 11017 Paramount Blvd.
Eichinger, David C. '38 '64 C&L.966 B.S.M.E., J.D.
(adm. in WI; not adm. in CA) Dir., Contracts & Pricing, Rockwell Intl. Corp.
Emerson, Leon ....................'25 '52 C.426 L.809 J.D. 9701 Lakewood‡
Enlow, Franklin H. ....................'11 '63 C&L.809 10447 Julius Ave.‡
Ferris, Frank R., (CV) ....................'25 '55 L.809 8238 E. 3rd St.
Flan, Jeffrey V. ....................'48 '82 L.1008 LL.B. P.O. Box 39790

**Flanders, Gilbert L., (AV) '35 '65 C.1049 L.809 J.D.**
**11510 South Downey Avenue, P.O. Box 670, 90241**
Telephone: 310-923-9238
*LANGUAGES: Spanish and Italian.
General Civil and Criminal Trial Practice. Personal Injury, Workers Compensation, Corporate, Family and Probate Law.
*See Professional Biographies, DOWNEY, CALIFORNIA*

Flesh, Robert T. .....'50 '79 C.800 B.S. L.426 J.D. Sr. V.P. & Gen. Coun., Thrifty Oil Co.
Freedman, Arthur S. ....................'30 '55 C.112 A.B. L.1068 LL.B. 9050 Telegraph Rd.
Gaines, Paul, Jr., (CV) ....................'25 '54 C.605 L.1065 J.D. 8238 E. 3rd St.
Garcia, Eugene G. ....................'19 '53 C.8 L.809 LL.B. 9928 Lareina‡
Gasdia, Brian F., (BV) ....................'56 '82 C.800 B.S. L.426 J.D. [Gasdia&G.]
Gasdia, Frank R., (AV) ....................'19 '52 L.809 [Gasdia&G.]
Gasdia & Gasdia, A Professional Corporation, (AV) ....................8135 Florence Ave.
Genesta, George, (BV) ....................'50 '75 7340 E. Florence Ave.
Gillespie, James P., (BV) .........'26 '54 C.608 B.A. L.276 LL.B. 12139 Paramount Blvd.
Going, James D., III ....................'42 '86 [Amacher,G.Y.&L.]
**Gold, Daniel R.** ....................'61 '93 C.112 B.A. L.464 J.D. [Tredway,L.&D.]
*PRACTICE AREAS: Civil Litigation; Family Law.
Grant, Ann Ruth ....................'17 '40 C&L.966 B.A., J.D. 8607 Imperial Hwy.
Gray, Steven W. ....................'47 '80 C.800 L.1179 J.D. 9521 Dalen St.‡
Green, Gary B. ....................'46 '76 C.1077 B.S. L.1095 J.D. 7902 6th St.
Hall, Ronald M., (BV) ....................'53 '78 C.1074 B.A. L.398 J.D. 8020 2nd St.
Hoagland, Grant T. ............'49 '79 C.1042 B.A. L.1137 J.D. 8135 Florence Ave., #203
Hoffman, Steven J. ....................'47 '72 C.1097 B.A. L.1049 J.D. 8301 Florence Ave.
Hohn, Bruce A., (BV) ....................'46 '77 C.1190 B.S.L. 12139 Paramount Blvd.
Hughes, Gregg B. ....................'50 '76 C.1077 B.A. L.809 J.D. 8141 2nd St.
Jacobs, Donald R., (BV) .......'32 '61 C.112 B.A. L.1068 LL.B. 10841 Paramount Blvd.‡
Johnson, Charles L. ....................'41 '75 C.1042 B.A. L.426 J.D. Dep. Prob. Officer
**Kinley, Matthew L.** ....................'62 '89 C.112 B.A. L.426 J.D. [Tredway,L.&D.]
*PRACTICE AREAS: Civil Litigation.
Knoll, James M., (BV) ....................'36 '72 C.800 L.1001 J.D. 9701 Lakewood Blvd.
Kotob, Robert I., (BV) ....................'30 '69 C.112 B.S. L.426 J.D. [Bear,K.R.&G.]
Kramer, Connie S. ....................'47 '81 C.1042 B.A. L.169 J.D. 12047 Paramount Blvd.
Lago, Peter L., (BV) ....................'48 '77 C.800 B.S. L.1148 J.D. 12651 Lakewood Blvd.
La Pan, Richard A., (BV) ....................'38 '69 L.809 J.D. 8135 E. Florence Ave.
Lehn, Richard M., (BV) ....................'38 '69 C.966 B.S. L.426 J.D. [Ardis&L.]
Leland, Judith S. ....................'43 '67 C.145 B.A. L.597 J.D. 8345 Firestone Blvd.
Leonard, Richard A., (AV) ........'42 '78 C.990 B.S. L.1221 J.D. 12139 Paramount Blvd.
•**Lieberman, Gary** ....................'64 '90 C.112 B.A. L.426 J.D. [Tredway,L.&D.]
*PRACTICE AREAS: Civil Litigation; Corporate Law.
Lin, George Chao-I ....................'64 '91 C.112 B.A. L.629 J.D. [Amacher,G.Y.&L.]
Linehan, David C. ........'31 '61 C.31 B.A. L.893 J.D. Admn. Law J., Soc. Sec. Adm.
Lopez, Gilbert M., (AV) ............'50 '77 C.800 A.B. L.426 J.D. 7340 E. Florence Ave.
**Lumsdaine, Joseph A.**, (BV) ............'50 '76 C.112 A.B. L.1066 J.D. [Tredway,L.&D.]
*PRACTICE AREAS: Civil Litigation.
Machado, Ramon Rafael, Jr. ..........'66 '94 C.1222 B.S. L.770 J.D. 7959 Irwingrove Dr.
McKibbin, David W., (BV) ....................'29 '58 C&L.629 B.S., J.D. 9025A E. Florence Ave.

**Miller, Paul H.**
(See Santa Fe Springs)

**Molyneux, Sharisse E.** ....................'61 '92 C&L.800 B.S., J.D. [Tredway,L.&D.]
Monkarsh, Ralph M., (BV) .........'25 '53 C.112 B.A. L.800 J.D. 9701 Lakewood Blvd.
Moore, Jerry F. ....................'34 '64 C.1042 B.A. L.800 LL.B. Supr. Ct. Comr.
Neice, William L. ....................'34 '67 C.767 B.S. L.1127 LL.B. 6459 Dos Rios Rd.
Newcomb, Karen A. ...............'48 '94 C.122 B.A. L.1137 J.D. 10901 Paramount Blvd.
Paul, Roy L. ....................'49 '78 C.800 B.A. L.1137 J.D. Mun. J.
Perkins, David W. ....................'35 '77 C.800 B.S. L.1137 J.D. Mun. Ct. J.
Perkins, Kenneth W., Jr. ...........'44 '72 C.1042 B.A. L.1137 J.D. 10945 Rio Hondo Dr.
Perrizo, Mark J., (BV) ....................'49 '75 C&L.770 B.S.C., J.D. [Wilson,W.&P.]
Ratcliffe, Edwin P., (BV) '39 '72 C.768 B.S. L.1067 J.D.
9900 Lakewood Blvd., Suite 105
Rosen, Irving E., (BV) ....................'26 '50 C.867 B.A. L.982 LL.B. 8221 E. Third St.
Sahagun, Raul A., (BV) ....................'54 '79 C.426 B.A. L.1068 J.D. 8301 E. Florence Ave.
Salyer, Richard D. ....................'54 '79 C.112 B.A. L.990 J.D. 8350 Florence Ave.
Sanger, Floyd C., Jr. ....................'31 '57 C&L.800 B.S., LL.B. P.O. Box 1398
Sassover, Moshe J. ................'55 '79 C.424 B.A. L.966 J.D. 10000 Lakewood Blvd.

**Schauf, Carolyn J., (CV) '46 '86 L.1137 J.D.**
**8301 East Florence Avenue Suite 305, 90240-3970**
Telephone: 310-861-4575 FAX: 310-869-0615
*PRACTICE AREAS: Family Law; Estate Planning Law; Bankruptcy Law.
Family Law, Adoptions, Estate Planning, Probate, Debtor and Bankruptcy Law.
*See Professional Biographies, DOWNEY, CALIFORNIA*

Sloan, Carolyn Dunnum .........'47 '87 C.1109 B.A. L.1137 J.D. 11017 Paramount Blvd.
**Smith, Elwayne E.**, (AV) ....................'21 '49 C.846 B.B.A. L.800 J.D. [E.E.Smith]

**Smith, Elwayne E., Inc., (AV)**
**8130 Florence Avenue, P.O. Box 129, 90241-0129**
Telephone: 310-923-9757 FAX: 310-869-9649
Elwayne E. Smith.
Practice Limited to Wills, Living Trusts and Probate Law.
References: Downey National Bank, Downey, California; Bank of America, Downey, California.

Solton, Robert T., (BV) ........'35 '61 C.112 A.B. L.1068 LL.B. 10841 Paramount Blvd.
Torkington, Anne Beytin ......'44 '85 C.112 B.A. L.1068 J.D. Admin. Law J., OHA/SSA
**Tredway, Harold T.** ....................'19 '55 C.807 B.A. L.426 LL.B. [Tredway,L.&D.]⊙

**Tredway, Lumsdaine & Doyle, LLP, (AV)**
**10841 Paramount Boulevard, 90241-3397⊙**
Telephone: 310-923-0971; 714-750-0141 Telecopier: 310-869-4607
Members of Firm: Joseph A. Lumsdaine; Mark C. Doyle (Resident, Irvine Office); Jeffrey B. Singer (Resident at Irvine Office); Michele S. Ahrens; Cheri A. Kadotani (Resident, Irvine Office); Michael A. Lanphere (Resident, Irvine Office); Harold T. Tredway (Retired); Matthew L. Kinley; Lynn L. Walker (1951-1994); Gary Lieberman; Daniel R. Gold; Sharisse E. Molyneux; Joseph A. Maleki (Resident, Irvine Office). Of Counsel: David A. Pasqualini (Resident, Irvine Office).
General Civil Trial Practice, Business, Corporate, Securities, Financial Institutions, Real Estate, Personal Injury, Employment, Environmental Law, Taxation, Probate, Estate Planning, and Family Law.
Reference: Southern California Bank.

(This Listing Continued)

**Tredway, Lumsdaine & Doyle, LLP (Continued)**
Irvine, California Office: Suite 1000, 1920 Main Street. Telephone: 714-756-0684. Telecopier: 714-756-0596.
*See Professional Biographies, DOWNEY, CALIFORNIA*

Vaters, G. Nicholas, Jr., (BV) ....................'46 '71 C.940 B.A. L.1049 J.D. 8141 E. 2nd St.
Vleerick, Howard E., (BV) ....................'21 '52 C&L.809 J.D. 8221 E. 3rd St.
Warner, Susanna A., (BV) ..........'53 '84 C.1109 B.A. L.990 J.D. 9701 Lakwood Blvd.
Wilbur, John H., (BV) ....................'26 '63 L.809 J.D. 9701 Lakewood Blvd., Suite 100
Wilson, Daniel Joseph, (CV) ....................'57 '82 C&L.426 B.A., J.D. [Wilson,W.&P.]
Wilson, Donald L. ....................'— '60 C.426 B.S. L.809 LL.B. Mun. Ct. J.
Wilson, William P., (BV) ....................'23 '50 C&L.426 [Wilson,W.&P.]
Wilson, Wilson & Perizo, (BV) ....................10901 Paramount Blvd.
Yetur, Sreedhar Reddy ....................'52 '92 C.1075 M.S. L.1137 J.D. [Amacher,G.Y.&L.]

## DOWNIEVILLE, * 768, *Sierra Co.*

Littrell, Reginald ....................'33 '64 C.911 L.284 LL.B. Supr. Ct. J.
Pangman, William W. ....................'44 '70 C.605 B.A. L.800 J.D. Co. Coun.

## DUARTE, 20,688, *Los Angeles Co.*

Douglas, Pamela L. ....................'50 '89 C.1097 L.426 J.D. 2617 Sunnydale
Farra, George K. ..............'62 '95 C.061 B.S. L.426 J.D. Geotechnical Claims Servs.
Ritchie, Harold A. ....................'12 '36 C.668 B.A. L.800 LL.B. Micro-OHM Corp.
White, Nicholas John ....................'58 '88 C.1163 B.A. L.800 J.D. I.R.S.

## DUBLIN, 23,229, *Alameda Co.*

Armstrong, James M., (CV) '43 '72
C.766 B.A. L.1065 J.D. V.P., Mauzev Enterprizes, Inc.
Ashford, Bruce W. ....................'46 '72 C.1066 B.A. L.1065 J.D. 7172 Regional St.
Brinker, W. Ren ée '69 '95 C.477 L.215 J.D.
(adm. in MI; not adm. in CA) U.S. Bur. of Prison, Dept. of Jus.
Broughton, Terence D., (CV) ....................'54 '84 7080 Donlon Way
Campanile, Cynthia, (BV) ....................'56 '82 C.112 A.B. L.1065 J.D. [Cheng&C.]
Campbell, Jeffrey C. '60 '86 C&L.900 B.A., J.D.
(adm. in KS; not adm. in CA) U.S. Bur. of Prisons, Dept. of Jus.
Chamberlin, John T. ....................'58 '86 C.112 A.B. L.1153 J.D. 11501 Dublin Blvd.
Cheng, Rosemeri E., (BV) ....................'46 '77 C.629 B.A. L.770 J.D. [Cheng&C.]
Cheng and Campanile, (BV) ....................7033 Village Parkway
Cox, Jim W. ....................'47 '81 C.112 A.B. L.284 J.D. P.O. Box 2205
Devane, Joseph F., (BV) .....'33 '59 C.321 A.B. L.276 J.D. 7080 Donlon Way, Suite 122
Donovan, Stephen H. ....................'49 '84 C.285 B.A. L.1153 J.D. [McCray,R.&D.]⊙
Guthrie, John A. ....................'63 '90 C.927 B.A. L.365 J.D. 6670 Amador Plaza Rd.
Harrington, John '22 '51 C.546 B.S. L.190 LL.B.
(adm. in NE; not adm. in CA) 7392 Shadow Pl.‡
Henderlong, Karla D. ....................'55 '81 C.112 B.A. L.809 J.D. 6400 Village Pkwy.
Lane, Harry M. ....................'44 '78 C.112 B.S. L.1065 J.D. P.O. Box 2823
Leonard, John ....................'53 '80 C.201 B.A. L.607 J.D. 7027 Dublin Blvd.
MacLean, Shian ....................'42 '88 C.659 B.A. L.1153 J.D. 7027 Dublin Blvd.
McCarthy, Brian M., (BV) ....................'47 '72 C.273 B.A. L.1065 7027 Dublin Blvd.
McCray, Rowland & Donovan ....................11960 Silvergate Dr. (⊙Walnut Creek)
Penn, Harlan W. '50 '77 C.587 B.S. L.502 J.D.
(adm. in MO; not adm. in CA) Dept. of Just., Bur. of Prisons
Sette, Joseph M., (CV) .......'65 '90 C.112 B.A. L.464 J.D. 11501 Dublin Blvd. Suite 200
**Willcoxon, Michael**, (AV) '48 '77
C.112 B.A. L.1066 J.D. Gen. Coun., Desilva Gates Construction
*RESPONSIBILITIES: Construction Law; Real Estate Law; General Business and Corporate Law.

## DULZURA, —, *San Diego Co.*

Aronson, Gary D. ....................'54 '82 C.112 B.A. L.1068 J.D. Sunrise Lodge

## DUNSMUIR, 2,129, *Siskiyou Co.*

Jones, Howard E. ....................'21 '52 C.112 A.B. L.1066 J.D. Ret. Jus. Ct. J.

## DURHAM, 3,096, *Butte Co.*

Durrant, Morris ....................'13 '40 C.878 B.A. L.1066 LL.B. P.O. Box 576

## DUTCH FLAT, —, *Placer Co.*

Stamm, Janice Lorraine ....................'42 '85 C.112 B.A. L.940 J.D. P.O. Box 296‡

## EAGLE ROCK, —, *Los Angeles Co.*

(See Los Angeles)

## EDWARDS, 10,331, *Kern Co.*

Mathews, John C. '39 '64 C&L.838 LL.B.
(adm. in TN; not adm. in CA) NASA
Sloup, George P. '45 '71 C.339 B.A. L.209 J.D.
(adm. in IL; not adm. in CA) NASA

## EL CAJON, 88,693, *San Diego Co.*

Aguiar, Antone L. ....................'44 '77 C.101 B.S. L.1137 J.D. 2552 Katherine St.
**Allred, Chris J.**, (BV) ............'53 '82 C.35 B.A. L.61 J.D. [Borgerding,P.B.G.W.&A.]
*LANGUAGES: Spanish.
*PRACTICE AREAS: Civil; Real Property; Bankruptcy; Litigation; Collection.
Allton, Charles R. ....................'35 '76 C.631 B.A. L.1137 J.D. 471 W. Chase Ave.
Alspaugh, Doris Y. '31 '59 C&L.986 B.A., LL.B.
(adm. in KS; not adm. in CA) 5973 Stallion Oaks Rd.‡
Alspaugh, George A., (BV) ..........'30 '54 C.947 A.B. L.986 LL.B. 275 E. Douglas Ave.
Alspaugh, George A., Jr. ............'69 '95 C.112 B.A. L.1049 J.D. 275 E. Douglas Ave.
Ambler, Ronald D., (BV) ....................'36 '72 C.763 B.S. L.1049 J.D. 275 Douglas
Anderson, Robert G. ....................'44 '77 C.763 B.S. L.1137 J.D. 11880 Fuerte Dr.
Atcheson, George S., II ....................'47 '74 C.1236 B.A. L.260 J.D. 1162 Decker St.
Austin, Albert J., (BV) ....................'55 '82 C.763 B.A. L.61 J.D. [Austin&A.]
Austin & Austin, (BV) ....................275 E. Douglas Ave.
Bacal, Dan, (BV) ....................'52 '77 C&L.608 B.A., J.D. 275 E. Douglas
Baptiste, Anne K. ....................'53 '88 C.229 B.S. L.1049 J.D. 2503 Singing Vista Way
Barranco, Elizabeth A., (BV) '60 '84
C.276 B.S.F.S. L.1049 J.D. 9624 Chocolate Summit Dr.
Barrett, Robert J. '40 '68 C&L.190 B.A., J.D.
(adm. in NE; not adm. in CA) 1751 Summer Place Dr.‡
Bearden, Margaret F., (BV) ..........'31 '84 C.763 B.A. L.1137 J.D. 152 West Park Ave.
Beebee, M. Dawn ....................'57 '85 C&L.1137 B.S.L., J.D. Off. of Pub. Def.
Bein, Richard H. ....................'32 '61 C.340 Ph.B. L.112 J.D. Ret. Mun. J.
Bianchini, Victor E. ....................'38 '64 C.763 A.B. L.1049 J.D. Mun. Ct. J.
Blanchette, David J. ....................'47 '79 C.112 B.S. L.1068 J.D. 11675 Vernette Ct.
**Boehmer, Steven E.** ....................'61 '89 C.768 B.S. L.1049 J.D. [McDougal,L.E.&G.]
*PRACTICE AREAS: Business Litigation; Construction Defect Litigation; Personal Injury.

CAA73P

CALIFORNIA—EL CAJON MARTINDALE-HUBBELL LAW DIRECTORY 1997

**Borgerding, C. Albert**, (AV) ..... '35 '62 C&L.770 B.S., J.D. [Borgerding,P.B.G.W.&A.]
*PRACTICE AREAS: Probate; Estate Planning; Real Property.

**Borgerding, Peterson, Burnell, Glauser, Waters & Allred, A Professional Corporation, (AV)**
**222 West Madison Avenue, 92020-3406**
**Telephone: 619-440-5242 Fax: 619-442-0198**
**Email: ECLAW6@AOL.COM**
**C. Albert Borgerding; Richard M. Peterson; William L. Burnell; Gary S. Glauser; Chris J. Allred; David W. Waters.**
**General Civil Litigation. Bankruptcy, Insolvency, Corporation, Business, Administrative, Collection, Probate, Trust, Personal Injury, Family, Criminal and Real Estate Law, Workers' Compensation, Social Security.**
*See Professional Biographies, EL CAJON, CALIFORNIA*

**Boucek, Leah M.** ................. '— '95 C.999 B.A. L.1188 J.D. [McDougal,L.E.&G.]
*PRACTICE AREAS: Family Law.
Bowers, Robert G., (BV) ...........'39 '79 C.763 B.S. L.1241 J.D. 693 S. Magnolia Ave.
Brainard, Larrie R. ................................ '42 '69 C.112 B.A. L.61 J.D. Mun. Ct. J.
Brown, Allen C., (BV) ...........'43 '70 C.61 B.B.A. L.1241 J.D. 270 East Douglas Ave.
Bryans, Joseph W., (AV) ....... '38 '64 C.1049 B.B.A. L.1065 J.D. 350 S. Magnolia Ave.

**Buchenau, Thomas M., (BV) '50 '77 C.855 B.A. L.1049 J.D.**
**275 East Douglas Avenue, Suite 108, 92020-4546**
**Telephone: 619-441-1100 Fax: 619-579-5761**
**Email: tmbuchenau@earthlink.net**
***PRACTICE AREAS: Business Law; Real Estate Law; Family Law.**
**Business Litigation, Corporate Law, Real Estate Law including Residential, Commercial Transactions and Commercial Leasing. Family Law, Probate, Estate Planning and Administration, Trusts, Civil Arbitration and Divorce Mediation.**
*See Professional Biographies, EL CAJON, CALIFORNIA*

**Burnell, William L.**, (AV) ....... '49 '74 C&L.931 B.S., J.D. [Borgerding,P.B.G.W.&A.]
*PRACTICE AREAS: Criminal; Workers Compensation; Personal Injury; Social Security Disability (SSI).
Burns, Dennis D., (BV) ...................... '54 '79 C.1188 B.A. L.61 J.D. 250 E. Douglas
Campanella, Burt D., (BV) ............... '41 '71 C.690 B.S. L.1049 J.D. 251 E. Main St.
Carmody, Jerry L., (BV) ................. '52 '83 C.1262 B.S. L.1137 J.D. [Carmody&W.]
Carmody & Welch, (BV) ................................................. 2494 Fletcher Parkway
Castonguay, Thomas J., (BV) ...........'43 '79 C.763 B.A. L.1241 J.D. 353 E. Park Ave.
Catlin, Ann Blakefield ................. '33 '88 C.1241 B.A. L.61 J.D. 440 Highland Ave.
Clowney, Frank S., III, (BV) ..............'52 '78 C.112 B.A. L.1049 J.D. 1110 N. 2nd St.
Cole, Scott, (BV) ........................'50 '78 C.107 B.A. L.1049 J.D. 416 S. Magnolia Ave.
Colt, Rolf P. ...................................'38 '77 C.763 B.A. L.1049 J.D. 1231 N. 2nd St.
Conaway, C. Dan, (AV) ...........'42 '75 C.813 B.A. L.1049 J.D. 411 S. Magnolia Ave.
Conaway, Robert E. ...............'20 '51 C.169 A.B. L.1065 J.D. 4953 Sunrise Hills Dr.‡
Conway, James G. ...................... '46 '80 C.707 B.A. L.1049 J.D. 270 E. Douglas Ave.
Cookson, Patricia K. .......................................... '53 '79 C.381 B.A. L.989 J.D. Mun. Ct. J.
Costantino, Ralph S., (BV) ......... '35 '73 C.763 B.A. L.1049 J.D. 275 E. Douglas Ave.
Crabtree, E. Hodge, (BV) ...............'42 '69 C.763 A.B. L.61 J.D. 269 E. Lexington Ave.
Cretton, George R. ............ '41 '91 C.1188 B.A. L.1137 J.D. 411-413 S. Magnolia Ave.
Curto, James R., (BV) ..................'20 '63 C.28 B.A. L.1049 LL.B. 2494 Fletcher Pkwy.
Davis, Gordon P. .........................................'59 '86 C.763 B.A. L.61 J.D. Dep. Dist. Atty.
deCamara, Donald M., (BV) ............ '49 '76 C.174 B.S. L.597 J.D. 205 Claydelle Ave.
Dodge, Michael H. ............................ '— '81 C.768 M.P.A. L.61 J.D. 250 E. Douglas
Dolan, Valerie J. ........................................................'59 '88 L.1137 J.D. 168 Rea Ave.
Dunk, John C. S. ..................................'62 '91 C.1049 B.B.A. L.990 J.D. 1734 Naranca Ave.
**Eckis, Stephen M.**, (AV) ........... '48 '73 C.668 B.A. L.1065 J.D. [McDougal,L.E.&G.]
*REPORTED CASES: Barnes v. Personnel Dept. of the city of El Cajon (1978); 87 Cal. App.3d 502; City of Poway v. City of San Diego (1991) 229 Cal.App.3d 847.
*PRACTICE AREAS: Probate Law; Estate Planning Law; Municipal Law.
Edmunds, Alan V. ....................... '48 '76 C.472 B.A. L.1137 J.D. 1014 Broadway
**Erickson, Rex R.** ....................... '66 '92 C&L.378 B.A., J.D. [McDougal,L.E.&G.]
*PRACTICE AREAS: Business Litigation; Personal Injury; Employment Law.
Farrell, John ......................................... '40 '73 C.999 L.1137 LL.B. 168 Rea Ave.
Flickinger, James R. .................................'40 '68 C&L.37 B.S., J.D. 2002 Chardon Ln.

**Frant, Ronald M., (AV) '52 '77 C.112 B.A. L.1049 J.D.**
**1754 Navaja Road, 92020**
**Telephone: 619-440-6073 Fax: 619-440-6013**
**Email: R1754@aol.com**
***LANGUAGES: Spanish.**
***PRACTICE AREAS: General Civil; Criminal.**
**Consultations; Referrals in all Areas of Law.**

Gaidula, Joseph C., (BV) ..................... '38 '70 C.645 B.S. L.61 J.D. P.O. Box 13414
Gallagher, Thomas S. ....................'40 '66 C&L.426 B.A., LL.B. 521 W. Bradley Ave.
Garmo, Freddy ..............................'69 '95 C.477 B.A. L.215 J.D. 275 E. Douglas Ave.
Gilham, G. Anthony, (BV) ..........'42 '70 C.763 B.A. L.1049 J.D. 275 E. Douglas Ave.
**Glauser, Gary S.**, (AV) .......'45 '77 C.101 B.A. L.1137 J.D. [Borgerding,P.B.G.W.&A.]
*LANGUAGES: Spanish.
*PRACTICE AREAS: Family.
Graves, Ralph W. ..........................................'21 '50 C&L.352 LL.B. 505 N. Mollison‡
Greenberg, Ronald E., (BV) .....................'31 '58 C.763 B.A. L.1068 LL.B. 455 Bdwy.
Gregory, James J. ................................'59 '86 C&L.1049 B.A., J.D. 353 E. Park Ave.
Griffin, Andrew H., III ..............................'56 '83 C.970 B.A. L.1137 J.D. [Griffin&G.]
Griffin, Michelle Martin, (BV) ...............'54 '79 C.604 B.A. L.1137 J.D. [Griffin&G.]
Griffin & Griffin, (BV) ...................................................... 275 East Douglas Avenue
**Grindle, Daniel W.**, (AV) .......... '47 '74 C.112 B.A. L.1049 J.D. [McDougal,L.E.&G.]
*PRACTICE AREAS: Business Law; Commercial and Business Litigation; Corporate Law; Real Estate Law.
Hart, Eric D. ...................................'51 '76 C.684 B.A. L.1049 J.D. 717 Denise Ln.‡
Hatcher, William J. ..........................'51 '77 C.763 B.A. L.1137 J.D. 353 E. Park Ave.
Hepperly, Foster J. ........... '46 '77 C.1074 B.S. L.1137 J.D. 1908 Windmill View Rd.‡
Huguenor, Susan D. ................................ '47 '74 C.504 B.A. L.61 J.D. Mun. Ct. J.
Ingalls, Hayden W. .............................................'12 '61 L.1049 LL.B. 13655 Hwy. 8‡
Isaacs, Patricia A. ........................................'39 '78 L.1241 J.D. P.O. Box 20828
Jallins, Richard David .................'57 '88 C.112 B.A. L.1188 J.D. 11857 Via Hacienda
Jandura, Jeffrey M. ...................................'49 '81 C.585 B.A. L.221 J.D. [Ⓐ Lambert&R.]
Jarboe, John C., (BV) ................ '38 '72 C.763 B.A. L.1049 J.D. 275 E. Douglas Ave.
Johnson, Duane D. ..................................'33 '84 C.793 B.A. L.1137 J.D. 152 W. Park Ave.
Kaplan, Howard B. '43 '68 C&L.912 B.A., J.D.
(adm. in MI; not adm. in CA) 2435 Colinas Ct.‡
Klein, Carl J. ................................'28 '51 C.1016 B.A. L.209 J.D. 2533 Wind River Rd.‡
Kohler, Roy ............................................... '35 '93 L.1241 J.D. 270 E. Douglas Ave.
Kraft, George W., Jr., (BV) ..............'26 '62 C.763 B.A. L.61 J.D. 275 E. Douglas Ave.
Kuerbis, Lawrence, Jr., (BV) ............. '36 '66 C.763 B.S. L.1065 LL.B. 275 E. Douglas
Lambert, Stephen F., (BV) ...................'48 '84 C.1188 B.S.L. L.1137 J.D. [Lambert&R.]
Lambert and Rogers, (BV) ............................................................ 164 West Park Ave.
Larkin, Daniel P. ...................................'46 '74 C.134 B.S. L.1137 J.D. 266 S. Magnolia
Lefebvre, George A., (BV) ............'29 '66 C.608 B.S. L.1049 J.D. 203 N. Johnson Ave.
Leonard, Sharyn M., (BV) ........................... '48 '75 C&L.188 A.B., J.D. Dep. Pub. Def.
Lester, Danny B. ...................................... '41 '88 C.988 B.A. L.1049 J.D. Dep. Pub. Def.
Lockwood, Russell D., (BV) .........'56 '82 C.768 B.S. L.1049 J.D. 275 E. Douglas Ave.

**Love, S. Michael**, (AV) ..................'43 '72 C.37 B.S. L.1188 J.D. [McDougal,L.E.&G.]
*PRACTICE AREAS: Family Law.
Luedtke, Jill W. ..........................'56 '83 C.260 B.S. L.862 J.D. 1233-2 Green Garden Dr.
Manley, David W., (CV) .................... '38 '74 C.763 A.B. L.1137 J.D. 535 Broadway
Margolis, Gideon ...................................'51 '89 C.728 B.S.Mgt. L.1137 J.D. P.O. Box 12376
Marienau, Kathryn E. D. ...........'58 '88 C.446 B.A. L.1137 J.D. Research Atty., Mun. Ct.
Marsh, Edward E., Jr., (BV) ................... '26 '56 C.112 L.1065 J.D. 505 N. Mollison
McCabe, Michael R. .......................... '63 '88 C.602 B.A. L.763 J.D. 222 W. Madison Ave.
McCall-Austin, Maureen ............................... '56 '83 C.93 B.A. L.61 J.D. [Austin&A.]
**McDougal, Lynn R.**, (AV) .......... '32 '59 C.378 B.A. L.174 J.D. [McDougal,L.E.&G.]
*REPORTED CASES: San Marcos Water Dist. v. San Marcos Unified School Dist. (1985) 171 Cal. App. 3d 223; San Marcos Water Dist. v. San Marcos Unified School Dist. (1986) 42 C. 3d 154; San Marcos Water Dist. v. San Marcos Unified School Dist. (1987) 190 Cal. App. 3d 1083; Estate of Maniscalco v. Cenplex Corp. (1992) 9 Cal.App.4th 520.
*PRACTICE AREAS: Municipal Law; Business Law; Real Property Law.

**McDougal, Love, Eckis & Grindle, A Professional Corporation, (AV)**
**460 North Magnolia Avenue, P.O. Drawer 1466, 92022-1466**
**Telephone: 619-440-4444 FAX: 619-440-4907**
**C. Rupert Linley (1905-1973); Lynn R. McDougal; S. Michael Love (Certified Specialist, Family Law, The State Bar of California Board of Legal Specialization); Stephen M. Eckis; Daniel W. Grindle; Tamara A. Smith; Steven E. Boehmer; Leah M. Boucek; Rex R. Erickson; Glenn N. Sabine.**
**General Civil and Trial Practice in all State and Federal Courts. Corporation, Probate, Personal Injury, Real Estate, Administrative and Municipal Law.**
**Representative Clients: City of El Cajon; City of Poway; City of Imperial Beach; City of La Mesa; Asphalt, Inc.; El Cajon Re-development Agency; American Valley Bank; The Californian Newspaper.**
**Reference: Scripps Bank.**
*See Professional Biographies, EL CAJON, CALIFORNIA*

McGrath, William J., Jr. ...................... '48 '73 C.770 B.A. L.1049 J.D. Mun. Ct. J.
McKinley, Jon ...............................'48 '75 C.763 B.S. L.1049 J.D. 2494 Fletcher Pkwy.
McLean, Donald F., Jr., (BV) ......................'34 '63 C.871 L.61 LL.B. [McLean&M.]
McLean, Gloria Scheid ........................ '45 '70 C.770 B.A. L.1066 J.D. [McLean&M.]
McLean & McLean, (BV) .............................................................1740 Vakas Dr.
Merkel, Barbara Lynn '62 '87 C.950 B.A. L.1049 J.D.
Research Atty. to City Atty's. Off.
Mietzel, Ann M., (BV) .................... '46 '78 C.763 B.A. L.1049 J.D. 2392 Tampa Ave.
Mietzel, James J., (BV) .................... '42 '77 C.763 B.A. L.1049 J.D. 2392 Tampa Ave.
Miller, Maureen Shellooe .............'53 '78 C.767 B.A. L.765 J.D. 460 N. Magnolia St.
Mills, M. Dale, Jr., (BV) ........................'49 '76 C.1075 B.S. L.1049 J.D. 270 E. Douglas
Morrison, Randal R. ....................'47 '86 C.877 B.S. L.464 J.D. 460 N. Magnolia Ave.
Moss, Gerald R. ................................. '45 '77 C.831 B.S. L.1137 J.D. [G.R.Moss]
Moss, Gerald R., A P.C. ................................................................ P.O. Box 12289
Muller, Lewis C. ........................ '47 '77 C.37 B.S. L.1049 J.D. 1586 Fayette St.
Murphy, Thomas R. ............................ '36 '66 C.112 B.A. L.1066 J.D. Mun. Ct. J.
Murray, Colin H. ............................ '66 '92 C&L.276 A.B., J.D. Dep. Dist. Atty.
Newton, Gilbert E., (BV) ....... '33 '61 C.112 A.B. L.1068 LL.B. 133 W. Lexington Ave.
Newton, Wayne Tyler ...................'47 '86 C.763 B.S. L.1241 J.D. 270 E. Douglas Ave.
Patton, Lawrence A., (AV) .....'21 '50 C&L.339 B.S., LL.B. 1522 Shadwow Vista Way‡
Peck, F. Amos. .........................'19 '75 C.809 L.1137 LL.B. 269 E. Lexington Ave.‡
Peters, Gerald E. ...................... '40 '72 C.679 B.S. L.1049 J.D. 2480 Coinas Paseo‡
**Peterson, Richard M.**, (BV) '42 '72 C.473 B.A. L.1049 J.D.
[Borgerding,P.B.G.W.&A.]
*PRACTICE AREAS: Domestic; Personal Injury.

**Petze, John E., (BV) '53 '85 C.112 B.A. L.1049 J.D.**
**411 South Magnolia, 92020**
**Telephone: 619-441-9404 Telecopier: 619-441-9406**
***PRACTICE AREAS: Insurance Defense; Product Defect; Personal Injury; Construction Site Accidents; Contract Litigation.**
**Insurance Defense, Product Defect, Personal Injury, Construction Site Accidents, Contract Litigation, Business Formations, Civil Litigation.**
*See Professional Biographies, EL CAJON, CALIFORNIA*

Phipps, Blaine R., (BV) .................'42 '72 C.172 B.S. L.1049 J.D. 415 Prescott Ave.
Pike, Russell R., (BV) ...........'34 '65 C.763 B.S. L.1065 LL.B. 275 E. Douglas Ave.
Prazen, Raymond R. ..................................'49 '74 C.339 B.S. L.46 J.D. 1014 Broadway
Price, L. Forrest ...........................'35 '65 C.112 A.B. L.1049 J.D. 353 E. Park Ave.
Provence, Ross C., (AV) ........................ '38 '63 C.1067 L.61 LL.B. [Provence&P.]
Provence & Provence, (AV) ..................................................411 W. Madison Ave.
Purviance, Farris C., III ..................................'52 '89 C&L.1241 B.A., J.D. [Purviance&P.]
Purviance, Lorraine .................................'50 '90 C&L.1241 B.B.A., J.D. [Purviance&P.]
Purviance & Purviance ............................................................ 1283 E. Main St.
Rankin, Robert W. ........... '52 '83 C.252 B.S.B.A. L.1137 J.D. Resch. Atty., Mun. Ct.
Rhodes, Douglas Keith ................. '36 '89 C.950 B.A. L.1137 J.D. Dep. Pub. Def.
Riggs, Elizabeth Ann ..................................'42 '74 C.1298 B.A. L.1292 J.D. Mun. Ct. J.
Riley, Marilyn R. .................................'45 '79 C.112 B.A. L.1049 J.D. 1683 Lisbon Lane
Robinson, Russell K., (BV) ........ '44 '73 C.1109 B.A. L.1049 J.D. 275 E. Douglas Ave.
Rogers, Michael Dean .............................'54 '86 C.475 B.A. L.61 J.D. [Lambert&R.]
Runde, James R. ..........................'50 '86 C.763 A.B. L.1049 J.D. 502 La Sombra Dr.
**Sabine, Glenn N.** .......................'61 '91 C.763 B.A. L.608 J.D. [Ⓐ McDougal,L.E.&G.]
*PRACTICE AREAS: Municipal; Public Law; Land Use Law; Environmental Law.
Sample, Beth A., (AV) ........................ '39 '79 C.63 L.1137 J.D. 275 E. Douglas Ave.
Schmidt, Nancy Jane ....................................'32 '81 L.1137 J.D. 4909 States Way
Silvers, Eleanor Cohen, (BV) ............. '40 '82 C.112 L.1137 J.D. 270 E. Douglas Ave.
Smith, Donald W. ......................................'23 '53 C&L.767 LL.B. Ret. Supr. Ct. J.
**Smith, Tamara A.**, (AV) ......................'48 '84 C.763 L.1137 J.D. [McDougal,L.E.&G.]
*PRACTICE AREAS: Municipal Law; Real Property; Land Use.
Smith-Trafzer, Lee Ann .......'57 '85 C.906 B.A. L.1049 J.D. 411-413 Magnolia Ave., S.
Spaulding, Roger H. ........................ '36 '64 C.112 A.B. L.1066 LL.B. Dept. Pub. Def.
Spilger, Michael ..........................'48 '76 C.763 B.S. L.1049 J.D. 2143 Brookhurst Dr.
Stevens, Robert W., (BV) ................. '29 '63 C.589 B.S. L.1049 J.D. 2638 Navajo Rd.
Stormoen, Ron A. ........................'58 '86 C.763 A.B. L.1049 J.D. 1084 Nidrah St.
Thacher, Penne L., (AV) ............. '48 '74 C.112 B.A. L.1049 J.D. 411 S. Magnolia Ave.
Vandersyde, Arthur ......................... '16 '47 C&L.339 B.S., J.D. 1608 Spanish Oak Pl.‡
Vigdor, Lawrence A., (BV) ........'33 '67 C.475 B.A. L.1188 J.D. 269 E. Lexington Ave.
**Waters, David W.**, (BV) ............'42 '71 C.61 B.S. L.1049 J.D. [Borgerding,P.B.G.W.&A.]
*PRACTICE AREAS: Civil Litigation; Real Property; Business; Commercial Transactions.
Welch, William R., (BV) ........................'49 '76 C.940 B.A. L.1188 J.D. [Carmody&W.]
Wenbourne, Thomas E., (BV) ............'50 '75 C&L.1188 B.A., J.D. 275 E. Douglas Ave.
Winkel, George A. .......................'45 '82 C.763 B.A. L.1137 J.D. 206 Van Houten Ave.

## EL CENTRO, * 31,384, *Imperial Co.*

**Anderholt, L. Brooks** ................ '54 '87 C.999 B.S. L.1137 J.D. [Anderholt,W.&Z.]
*LANGUAGES: Spanish.
*PRACTICE AREAS: Insurance Law; Agricultural Law.

**Anderholt, Walker & Zimmermann**
**654 Main Street, 92243**
**Telephone: 619-352-1311 Facsimile: 619-353-3410**
**Members of Firm: L. Brooks Anderholt; Steven M. Walker; Ann Marie Zimmermann.**

(This Listing Continued)

**Anderholt, Walker & Zimmermann (Continued)**

**General Civil and Trial Practice in all State and Federal Courts. Insurance Law, Collection, Business, Corporation, Real Property, Bankruptcy, Personal Injury, Probate, Commercial Transactions and Agriculture Law.**

*See Professional Biographies, EL CENTRO, CALIFORNIA*

Anderson, Russell R. .................... '31 '74 C.959 B.B.A. L.1137 J.D. Dep. Co. Coun.
Baker, Arthur W., Jr. .................... '45 '71 C.763 B.S. L.1065 J.D. 1797 Sandalwood
**Barrington, Thomas V.** ............ '53 '83 C.112 B.A. L.809 J.D. [A Horton,K.C.&F.]
*PRACTICE AREAS: Insurance Defense Litigation; Eminent Domain Law; Business Litigation.
Benitez, Roger T., (BV) .................... '50 '79 C.763 B.A. L.1137 J.D. [Heim&B.]
**Bermudez Montenegro, Ruth** ........ '67 '93 C.648 B.A. L.112 J.D. [A Horton,K.C.&F.]
*LANGUAGES: Spanish.
*PRACTICE AREAS: Education Law; Corporate Law; Civil Litigation.
Bohlander, Richard W., (BV) .............. '48 '76 C.112 B.A. L.1137 J.D. 380 N. 8th St.
Bowlan, Billy D. .......................................... '34 '86 L.1137 J.D. 770 Main St.
**Breeze, John W.**, (BV) .................... '49 '75 C.112 B.A. L.1137 J.D. [Plourd&B.]
*PRACTICE AREAS: Criminal Law; Medical Malpractice; General Civil Litigation; Wrongful Death; Personal Injury.
Brown, Marjorie E. R. ...................................... '37 '81 C&L.061 Dep. Co. Coun.
**Caldwell, Clifford C.**, (BV) .................. '47 '73 C.112 B.A. L.1068 J.D. [Pinney&C.]
*LANGUAGES: Spanish.
*PRACTICE AREAS: Estate Planning; Probate; Real Property Taxes.
Campbell, D. M. ........................ '13 '38 C.37 A.B. L.813 J.D. 711 Len Rey Ave.‡
**Carter, John Penn, III**, (BV) ........... '42 '67 C.763 A.B. L.61 J.D. [Horton,K.C.&F.]
*PRACTICE AREAS: Water Law; Governmental Law; Agricultural Law.
Chaille, L. Harold ............................ '18 '49 C.477 A.B. L.426 LL.B. Supr. Ct. J.
Contreras, Matias R. ........................... '46 '73 C.112 B.A. L.800 J.D. Mun. Ct. J.
**Cotugno, Michael C.** ........................ '71 '96 C.160 B.S. L.61 J.D. [A Ewing&J.]
*PRACTICE AREAS: Business Planning; Estate Planning; Environmental Law.
Daly, Joseph C., Jr. ......................... '41 '71 C.763 B.S. L.1049 J.D. 770 Main St.
Darrow, James L. .......................................... '46 '72 C&L.426 B.A., J.D. City Atty.
Dawson, Larry ................................ '55 '81 C.37 B.S. L.61 J.D. 444 S. 8th St. Ste. C-1
Donnelly, Donal B. ........................... '54 '81 C.112 B.A. L.1049 J.D. Dist. Atty. Off.
Driskill, Mitchell A. ............................ '58 '91 C.187 B.A. L.1137 J.D. 1221 State St.
**Ellis, Bradley S.** .................... '59 '92 C.112 B.S. L.1049 J.D. [A Horton,K.C.&F.]
*PRACTICE AREAS: Business Litigation; Health Care Law; Creditor's Rights.
**Engstrand, Paul D.**, (AV) ........... '19 '48 C.80 A.B. L.1066 LL.B. [C Horton,K.C.&F.]
Espinosa, Robert A. .................. '42 '73 L.1137 LL.B. 1041 State St. (⊙Santa Ana)
**Ewing, William J.**, (AV) ...................................... '25 '52 L.1065 J.D. [Ewing&J.]
*PRACTICE AREAS: Estate Planning Law; Probate Law; Real Property Law.

**Ewing & Johnson, A Professional Law Corporation, (AV) BB**
**636 State Street, P.O. Box 2568, 92244**
**Telephone: 619-352-6371 Telecopier: 619-353-5355**
**William J. Ewing; Charles G. Johnson; James K. Graves;—Michael C. Cotugno.**
**General Business, Tax and Trial Practice. Agriculture, Business, Commercial, Corporation, Geothermal and Alternative Energy, Estate Planning and Probate, Finance, Real Property and Taxation (State and Federal) Law.**
**Representative Clients: Bonanza Farms, Inc.; Kandal Insurance Agency; Imperial Printers; Robert Hawk Farming; Foss Accountancy Corp.; T. C. Worthy Cash & Carry, Inc.; Val Rock, Inc.; Southland Geotechnical; I.V. Radiology Group; Phillips Cattle Co.**

*See Professional Biographies, EL CENTRO, CALIFORNIA*

**Foote, Orlando B., III**, (AV) ............... '34 '61 C&L.813 A.B., J.D. [Horton,K.C.&F.]
*PRACTICE AREAS: Personal Injury Law; Construction Defect Litigation.
Fries, Thomas M., (BV) ............................. '34 '71 C.267 A.B. L.1137 J.D. Co. Coun.
**Garber, Jeffrey M.** .................... '61 '87 C.705 B.A. L.61 J.D. [A Horton,K.C.&F.]
*PRACTICE AREAS: Litigation (Personal Injury); Construction; Industrial Defect; Insurance; Government.
Garcia, John R. ............. '53 '79 C.112 B.A. L.1049 J.D. 380 N. 8th St. (⊙San Diego)
**Gerber, Neil**, (AV) ................. '49 '75 C.1044 B.A. L.1065 J.D. [Sutherland&G.]
*LANGUAGES: Spanish.
*REPORTED CASES: Aguirre v. Drewry Chemical Co. 162 CA3d 187; 208 CR 390 (1984); Singh v. County of Imperial Board of Retirement System 41 Cal. App. 4th 1180; 49 Cal. Rptr.2d. 220 (1996).
*PRACTICE AREAS: Business Law; Real Property Law.
Glover, Nancy J. .......................... '39 '88 C.763 B.A. L.1137 J.D. Dep. Co. Coun.
Goldberger, Peter C. ........... '48 '75 C.112 B.A. L.1049 J.D. 1224 State St. (⊙La Jolla)
**Graves, James K.** ........................... '54 '83 C.112 B.A. L.1066 J.D. [Ewing&J.]
*PRACTICE AREAS: Business Law; Tax Law; Real Property Law.

**Gray Cary Ware & Freidenrich, A Professional Corporation, (AV) BB**
**Gray Cary Established in 1927**
**Ware & Freidenrich Established in 1969**
**1224 State Street, P.O. Box 2890, 92244⊙**
**Telephone: 619-353-6140 Telecopier: 619-353-6228**
**Email: info@gcwf.com URL: http://www.gcwf.com**
**Jay W. Jeffcoat; Merrill F. Storms, Jr.**
**Languages: Spanish, German, French, Italian and Swedish.**
**General Civil and Trial Practice in all State and Federal Courts and Administrative Agencies. Admiralty, Agribusiness, Antitrust, Aviation, Banking, Bankruptcy and Insolvency, Business, Commercial, Computer Law, Compensation and Benefits, Condemnation, Construction, Copyright and Trademark, Corporation, Corporate Securities, Customs, Eminent Domain, Employment Counseling and Litigation, Environmental, Estate Planning, Family Law, Fidelity and Surety, Government Contracts, Hospital and Health Care, Immigration and Naturalization, Insurance, International Business and Litigation, Publishing, Labor, Land Use, Libel, Negligence, News Media, Pension and Profit Sharing, Privacy, Private Foundation, Probate, Products Liability, Professional Malpractice, Railroad, Real Property, Federal and State Securities, Taxation, Telecommunications, Trade Regulation, Unfair Competition, Wills and Trusts.**
**Representative Clients: American Bankers Life; Asgrow Seed; Boise Cascade; California State Automobile Assn.; Helena Chemical Co.; Hospital Council of San Diego and Imperial Counties; Imperial Valley Press/Brawley News; Unocal; Valley Independent Bank.**
**San Diego, California Office: 401 "B" Street, Suite 1700. Telephone: 619-699-2700.**
**San Diego/Golden Triangle, California Office: 4365 Executive Drive, Suite 1600, 92121. Telephone: 619-677-1400. Fax: 619-677-1477.**
**Palo Alto, California Office: 400 Hamilton Avenue. Telephone: 415-328-6561.**
**La Jolla, California Office: Suite 575, 1200 Prospect Street. Telephone: 619-454-9101.**

*See Professional Biographies, EL CENTRO, CALIFORNIA*

Greaves, Thomas F., (AV) ..................... '27 '56 C.605 B.A. L.276 J.D. 636 State St.
Harmon, James H. ..................................... '40 '66 C&L.800 B.A., J.D. Supr. Ct. J.
Hecht, Richard L., (AV) '32 '61 C.800 B.S. L.426 LL.B.
445 Bwy. (⊙Mexicali, Baja, CA)
Heim, Thomas M., (BV) .................. '34 '64 C.665 B.S.M.E. L.1049 J.D. [Heim&B.]
Heim & Benitez, (BV) ........................................................... 1221 State St.
Holbrook, George L. ......................... '46 '87 C.112 B.A. L.1137 J.D. Dep. Dist. Atty.

**Horton, Knox, Carter & Foote, (AV) BB**
**Suite 101 Law Building, 895 Broadway, 92243⊙**
**Telephone: 619-352-2821 Telefax: 619-352-8540**
**Email: hkcf@QUIX.net**
**Members of Firm: Harry W. Horton (1892-1966); James H. Carter (1918-1978); Orlando B. Foote, III; John Penn Carter, III; Frank A. Oswalt, III; Dennis H. Morita; Philip J. Krum, Jr. (Certified Specialist, Estate Planning, Trust and Probate Law, The State Bar of California Board of Legal Specialization); Mercedes Z. Wheeler (Resident, Brawley Office). Associates: Thomas V. Barrington; Bradley S. Ellis; Patrick M. Pace; Ruth Bermudez Montenegro; Jeffrey M. Garber; Mathew M. McCormick. Of Counsel: Paul D. Engstrand.**

(This Listing Continued)

**Horton, Knox, Carter & Foote (Continued)**

**General Civil and Trial Practice in all State and Federal Courts. Water Rights, Corporation, Insurance, Taxation, Governmental, Real Property and Probate Law.**
**Representative Clients: Automobile Club of Southern Calif.; Imperial Irrigation District; Southern Pacific Co.; Reliance Insurance Co.; Surplus Lines Adjusting Co.; Pioneer Memorial Hospital District; City of Imperial; San Diego Gas & Electric Co.; Chevron U.S.A.; Bixby Land Co.**
**Brawley, California Office: 195 South Second Street. Telephone: 619-344-2360. Fax: 619-344-9778.**

*See Professional Biographies, EL CENTRO, CALIFORNIA*

**Ilagan, Mark L.** ....................................... '65 '95 C.94 B.S.B.A. L.61 J.D. [A Plourd&B.]
*PRACTICE AREAS: Criminal; Family.
**Jeffcoat, Jay W.**, (AV) ... '45 '71 C.112 B.A. L.1068 J.D. [Gray C.W.&F.] (⊙San Diego)
*PRACTICE AREAS: Commercial and Environmental Litigation; Toxic Tort and Product Liability; Agricultural Law.
**Johnson, Charles G.**, (BV) ........................ '50 '76 C.1188 B.A. L.61 J.D. [Ewing&J.]
*LANGUAGES: Spanish.
*PRACTICE AREAS: Business Law; Corporate Law; Real Property Law.
Jones, Jeffrey B. ............................................... '61 '86 C&L.1137 B.S.L., J.D. [Jones&J.]
Jones, Jimmie B. ............................................... '37 '86 C&L.1137 B.A., J.D. [Jones&J.]
Jones & Jones ............................................................................ 444 S. 8th St.
Kimball, Fielding ..................................... '13 '39 C.878 L.273 LL.B. 1236 Pepper Dr.‡
Knox, Reginald L., Jr., (AV) .................. '16 '41 C.112 A.B. L.813 J.D. 776 Sandalwood‡
**Krum, Philip J., Jr.**, (BV) ...................... '49 '76 C&L.763 B.A., J.D. [Horton,K.C.&F.]
*PRACTICE AREAS: Probate Law; Estate Planning Law.
LaBrucherie, Roger A. ................................ '45 '73 C&L.813 B.A., J.D. 1605 Cypress St.‡
LaBrucherie, Timothy J. ............................. '46 '74 C.800 B.S. L.813 J.D. P.O. Box 1420‡
Lafleur, Judith ............... '58 '92 C.666 B.A. L.93 J.D. 1609 Barbara Worth Dr., Ste. 110
Lehnhardt, William E. .................... '31 '59 C.684 B.A. L.1068 LL.B. Ret. Supr. Ct. J.
Lenderman, John F., Jr. .............................. '48 '78 C.205 B.A. L.1137 J.D. P.O. Box 2540
MacCartee, T. Douglas, (CV) .............. '44 '77 C.37 B.S. L.1137 J.D. Dep. Dist. Atty.
Macklin, William F., (CV) ........................ '48 '78 C.763 B.A. L.61 J.D. 1407 Main St.
Marcus, David E., (BV) ............................ '— '74 C.112 B.A. L.426 J.D. P.O. Box 3130
**McCormick, Mathew M.** .............. '66 '96 C.112 B.A. L.999 J.D. [A Horton,K.C.&F.]
*PRACTICE AREAS: Business Law; Taxation; Probate; Estate Planning; Real Property Law.
Monahan, Richard ............................................................... '49 '78 Dep. Co. Coun.
Moore, James D., (BV) ............................ '44 '74 C.112 A.B. L.809 J.D. 1450 Bway.
**Morita, Dennis H.**, (BV) .................. '53 '78 C.112 A.B. L.426 J.D. [Horton,K.C.&F.]
*PRACTICE AREAS: Public Law; Defense Litigation.
**Oswalt, Frank A., III**, (BV) ............ '44 '74 C.112 B.A. L.1049 J.D. [Horton,K.C.&F.]
*PRACTICE AREAS: Business Law; Insurance Defense Litigation.
**Pace, Patrick M.** ....................... '53 '80 C.101 B.A. L.1051 J.D. [Horton,K.C.&F.]
*LANGUAGES: Spanish.
*PRACTICE AREAS: Corporations Law; Business Law; Probate Law; Trust Law.
Pettis, Ronald E., (BV) ........................ '39 '70 C.336 B.A. L.1066 J.D. 1224 State St.
Pierson, Judith Yeager, (BV) ........................ '49 '79 C.112 B.A. L.1186 J.D. [Yeager&P.]
**Pinney, Charles A., Jr.**, (AV) ..................... '19 '58 C.112 A.B. L.813 J.D. [C Pinney&C.]

**Pinney & Caldwell, A P.C., (BV)**
**444 South Eighth Street, P.O. Box 710, 92244**
**Telephone: 619-352-7800 Telefax: 619-352-7809**
**Clifford C. Caldwell;—Marvin Lynn Wilson. Of Counsel: Charles A. Pinney, Jr.**
**General Practice in all State and Federal Courts. Federal and State Tax Law. Estate Planning, Probate, Real Property, Insurance, Negligence and Corporation Law.**
**Representative Clients: Singing Hills Country Club; Disabled American Veterans, Department of California.**

*See Professional Biographies, EL CENTRO, CALIFORNIA*

**Plourd and Breeze, A Professional Corporation, (BV)**
**1005 State Street, P.O. Box 99, 92244-0099**
**Telephone: 619-352-3130 Fax: 619-352-4763**
**Lewis A. Plourd (1925-1978); John W. Breeze;—Mark L. Ilagan.**
**General Civil and Criminal Trial Practice. Personal Injury, Medical Malpractice, Business, Taxation, Criminal, Family and Bankruptcy Law. Trials and Appeals.**

*See Professional Biographies, EL CENTRO, CALIFORNIA*

Richardson, Anne C., (BV) .................. '43 '82 C.1365 B.S. L.878 J.D. 1224 State St.
Rider, Charles P. ............................... '38 '88 C.63 B.S. L.1132 J.D. Dep. Pub. Def.
Rutten, Randy J. ................................... '54 '81 C.112 B.S. L.1137 J.D. [A Yeager&P.]
**Samra, Ravinder** ........................... '53 '83 C.112 B.S. L.1137 J.D. [Sutherland&G.]
*REPORTED CASES: SKF Farms v. Superior Court, 153 CA3d 902; 200 CR 497 (1984).
*PRACTICE AREAS: Business Law; Real Property Law; Tax Law; International Law.
Scoville, Donald L., (CV) .................. '41 '71 C.763 B.S. L.1049 J.D. 1005 State St.
Smith, Larry E. ........................ '33 '79 C&L.1049 B.A., J.D. Asst. Dist. Atty.
Stender, Christopher '65 '90 C.107 B.A. L.823 J.D.
(adm. in CT; not adm. in CA) U.S. Dept. of Jus.
Storey, Thomas W., (BV) ...................................... '49 '77 797 Main St., Ste., B
**Storms, Merrill F., Jr.**, (BV) '48 '77
C.1110 B.A. L.1066 J.D. [Gray C.W.&F.] (⊙San Diego)
*PRACTICE AREAS: Employment Law; Construction Litigation.
Strickland, Richard F., (CV) ................ '43 '74 C.763 B.S. L.61 J.D. 1005 State St.
**Sutherland, Lowell F.**, (AV) ........... '39 '66 C.763 A.B. L.1065 J.D. [Sutherland&G.]
*REPORTED CASES: Zinn v. Fred R. Bright Co., Inc.; 9 CA3d 188; 87 CR 736 (1969); Salton Bay Marina, Inc. v. Imperial Irrigation District; 172 CA3d 914.
*PRACTICE AREAS: Personal Injury Law; Business Law; Eminent Domain Litigation.

**Sutherland & Gerber, A Professional Corporation, (AV) BB**
**Suite 7 The Imperial Building, 300 South Imperial Avenue, 92243**
**Telephone: 619-353-4444 Telefax: 619-352-2533**
**Lowell F. Sutherland (Member of California Trial Lawyers Association, with recognized experience in the fields of Trial Lawyer, General Personal Injury and Product Liability); Neil Gerber; Ravinder Samra.**
**General Civil and Trial Practice in all Courts. Personal Injury, Eminent Domain, Products Liability, Crop Damage, Agricultural, Business and Commercial Law.**

*See Professional Biographies, EL CENTRO, CALIFORNIA*

Townsend, Edward J. .......................... '29 '79 C.652 B.S. L.1137 J.D. P.O. Box 1262
**Walker, Steven M.** ....................... '53 '83 C.911 B.A. L.1049 J.D. [Anderholt,W.&Z.]
*PRACTICE AREAS: Civil Litigation; Governmental Defense; Local Government Law; Labor and Employment Law.
Weis, John F., (CV) ......................... '47 '78 C.906 B.A. L.1137 J.D. Dep. Dist. Atty.
Wien, Henry .................................. '28 '53 C.112 B.A. L.1066 LL.B. Supr. Ct. J.‡
**Wilson, Marvin Lynn** ...................... '38 '88 C.112 B.S. L.1137 J.D. [A Pinney&C.]
*PRACTICE AREAS: Estate Planning; Probate.
Yeager, Joanne L. ................................ '49 '77 C.112 B.A. L.1198 J.D. Co. Coun.
Yeager and Pierson, (BV) ............................................................. 1030 Bway.
**Zimmermann, Ann Marie** .............. '63 '91 C.477 A.B. L.1049 J.D. [Anderholt,W.&Z.]
*PRACTICE AREAS: Probate; Collections; Real Estate; Bankruptcy; Civil Litigation.

## EL CERRITO, 22,869, *Contra Costa Co.*

Black, Cheryl K., (BV) ........................... '51 '80 C.112 B.A. L.1065 J.D. [Black,B.&L.]
Black, Brown and Lanier, (BV) ....................................... 10329 San Pablo Ave.
Brilliant, Robert M. ..................... '30 '59 C.112 A.B. L.1065 J.D. 10567 San Pablo Ave.
Brown, David A. ................................ '56 '80 C.112 A.B. L.1065 J.D. [Black,B.&L.]
Burton, Blair F., (BV) .......................... '20 '50 C.112 B.A. L.1066 LL.B. P.O. Box 413

CALIFORNIA—EL CERRITO MARTINDALE-HUBBELL LAW DIRECTORY 1997

Cambron, Catherine A. ... '59 '91 C.821 B.A. L.1065 J.D. 6827 Snowdon Ave.‡
Carlson, Richard A. ... '35 '78 C.112 B.A. L.1066 J.D. 891 Shevlin Dr.
Carpenter, Arthur N. ... '54 '84 C.330 B.A. L.284 J.D. 7760 Stockton Ave.
Dunn, John J. ... '22 '55 C.112 A.B. L.1065 J.D. 6927 Waldo Ave.‡
Epstein, Roxanne J. ... '60 '89 C.112 B.A. L.284 J.D. P.O. Box 101
Falconer, Donald P., (AV) ... '20 '47 C.112 A.B. L.1066 LL.B. 1226 King Dr.‡
Faussner, Robert E. ... '46 '75 C.494 B.A. L.1065 J.D. 10116 San Pablo Ave.
Foster, W. Paul, (BV) ... '38 '67 C.112 A.B. L.1066 LL.B. 5500 Ludwig Ave.
Jenssen, Leif H. ... '45 '71 C.112 B.A. L.767 J.D. 6407 Fairmount Ave.
Kesler, William E. ... '20 '56 L.1026 LL.B. 725 Kearney St.‡
Langer, Morry D. ... '46 '72 C.112 B.A. L.1065 J.D. 229 Plaza Prof. Bldg.
Lanier, Barbara L., (BV) ... '46 '80 C.911 B.A. L.1065 J.D. [Black,B.&L.]
Lawlor, Eugene K., (AV) ... '16 '47 C.112 L.767 J.D. 8410 Betty Ln.‡
Low, John M. ... '31 '79 C.112 A.B. L.1197 J.D. 7132 Mound St.
Lowen, Claude L. ... '37 '63 C.112 B.S. L.1066 J.D. P.O. Box 833‡
Mandl, Nicolette ... '30 '75 C.112 B.A. L.284 J.D. 901 Avis Dr.
Marks, F. Raymond, (AV) ... '27 '52 C.910 A.B. L.145 J.D. 714 Lexington Ave.
Miner, F. William ... '36 '76 C.767 B.S. L.1197 J.D. 7408 Park Vista
Morgan, Elinore C. ... '25 '57 C.766 L.1065 J.D. 6726 Glen Mawr Ave.‡
Murray, Lora Lucas ... '43 '91 L.1153 J.D. 6311 Fairmount Ave.
Pinto, Craig A. ... '53 '81 C.112 A.B. L.1066 J.D. 6431 Fairmouns Ave.
Power, Dale J. ... '45 '71 C.112 B.A. L.1066 J.D. Nation's Foodservice, Inc.
Reimer, Stephen W. ... '52 '80 C.966 B.S. L.273 J.D. 11072 San Pablo Ave.
Riggs, Gerald E. ... '39 '66 C.112 A.B. L.1065 J.D. P.O. Box 1595
Smith, Jas. B. ... '18 '46 C.767 L.1065 J.D. 516 Balra Dr.
Snyder, Lydia L. ... '20 '55 C.112 A.B. L.1066 LL.B. 2660 Tamapais Ave.‡
Weigand, Clarke M. ... '13 '38 C.112 A.B. L.1066 LL.B. 927 Pomona Ave.
White, T.J., Jr. '53 '82 C.836 B.B.A. L.208 J.D.
(adm. in CO; not adm. in CA) P.O. Box 836‡
Wilson, Chas. E. ... '15 '50 C.982 A.B. L.178 LL.B. 1159 King Ct.

## EL DORADO, —, *El Dorado Co.*

Bedient, Steve L., (BV) ... '46 '76 C.972 B.S. L.464 J.D. 5845 Motherlode Dr.

## EL DORADO HILLS, —, *El Dorado Co.*

Bivens, Harry R. ... '54 '90 C.838 B.S.C.E. L.464 J.D. 2541 Highland Hills Dr.
Bricker, Gary R. ... '49 '82 C.1060 L.464 J.D. 2222 Francisco Dr.
Clemons, Timothy C. ... '51 '77 C.1060 B.A. L.1026 J.D. 4989 Golden Foothill Pky.
Fisher, William J. ... '47 '73 C.93 B.S. L.776 J.D. 981 Governor Dr.
Gibbs, Julia P., (AV) ... '57 '81 C.770 B.S. L.1068 J.D. 991 Governor Dr.
Gore, George R. ... '43 '89 C.502 B.S. L.464 J.D. 1241 Hawks Flight Ct.
Haug, Wayne H. ... '38 '82 L.1026 LL.B. 3720 Mesa Verdes Dr.
Irvine, Randy C. ... '49 '81 C.27 B.S. L.464 J.D. 3238 Ridgeview Dr.
Kallan, Gerald S., (AV) ... '43 '74 C.112 A.B. L.765 J.D. [G.Kallan]
Kallan, Gerald, Law Office of, (AV) ... 2428 Loch Way
Mongan, Edgar J., Jr. ... '23 '72 C.309 B.A. L.464 LL.B. 3506 Patterson Way
Muse, Mary T. ... '50 '78 C.938 B.A. L.464 J.D. 991 Governor Dr.
Noel, Mary K. ... '51 '77 C.1042 B.A. L.426 J.D. 1982 Shelby Cir.
Parise, John S., (BV) ... '26 '71 C.800 A.B. L.1001 LL.B. 1314 Camden Pl.‡
Ramirez, David M. ... '50 '76 C&L.813 B.A., J.D. 4993 Golden Foothill Pkwy.
Ryan, Stephen A. ... '53 '80 C.112 B.A. L.464 J.D. 629 Powers Dr.
Sanchez, Luis P. ... '54 '83 C.1097 B.A. L.464 J.D. 2222 Francisco Dr.
Somogyi, Elaine ... '47 '81 C.72 B.A. L.365 J.D. 3843 Langdon Ct.
Spaulding, Donald O. ... '58 '87 C.605 A.B. L.809 J.D. 4995 Golden Foothill Pkwy.
Visger, Melvin J. ... '54 '88 C.169 B.A. L.1137 J.D. 4995 Golden Foothill Pkwy.

## EL GRANADA, 1,473, *San Mateo Co.*

Chapralis, Janice A. ... '54 '79 C.766 B.A. L.767 J.D. 321 El Granada Blvd.
Damer, Nicholas R. ... '46 '72 C&L.767 A.B., J.D. 30 Ave. Portola, 3rd Fl.

## ELK GROVE, 3,721, *Sacramento Co.*

Bates, Joan M., (CV) ... '34 '80 C.1060 B.A. L.1137 J.D. 8788 Elk Grove Blvd.
Berger, Emil ... '25 '53 C.1060 L.767 LL.B. 9450 Laguna Lake Way‡
Braun, Charles A. ... '63 '91 C.893 B.A. L.945 J.D. 6431 Shasta Creek Way
Dean, Carolyn L. ... '49 '84 C.1060 B.A. L.464 J.D. P.O. Box 1088‡
Farina, Ann Perrin ... '47 '87 C.623 B.A. L.770 J.D. 8788 Elk Grove Blvd.
Goldberg, Carol Moon ... '60 '86 C.834 B.S. L.910 J.D. 4806 Mapleplain Ave.
Henke, James P., (CV) ... '47 '74 C.1060 B.S. L.464 J.D. J., City Municipal Ct.
**Kinney, Jacqueline R.** '61 '90
C.957 B.A. L.128 J.D. Coun., Citizens Utilities Co. of Calif.
Lang, Daniel R., (CV) ... '40 '77 C.597 B.S. L.464 J.D. 9915 Grant Line Rd.
Mahon, Dale W., (BV) ... '40 '70 C.1060 B.S. L.464 J.D. 9951 Grant Line Rd.
Mathiowetz, Thomas M. ... '47 '82 C.492 B.A. L.1026 J.D. 9070 Elk Grove
McKeen, Steven D. ... '58 '88 C.1060 B.A. L.464 J.D. P.O. Box 1055
Melluish, Ronald L. ... '54 '87 C.101 B.S. L.464 J.D. 6506 Cartera Ct.
Morris, John R. ... '38 '67 C.169 A.B. L.464 J.D. 8788 Elk Grove Blvd.
Okwudsa, Chisorom Uba ... '64 '88 C.14 B.S. L.370 J.D. 9390 Cedarview Way
Pinasco, Luana A. ... '45 '75 L.464 J.D. 10320 Upton Ct.‡
**Snider, Barbara L.** '— '87
C.112 B.A. L.1065 J.D. Assoc. Gen. Coun., Citizens Utility Co.
Verneuille, Jo Lynne ... '51 '91 C.1060 B.S. L.1067 J.D. 4434 Shenango Way
Winchell, James W., (BV) '33 '59 C.740 B.A. L.128 LL.B.
Sr. Staff Coun., Calif. Water Resources Control Bd.
Zaremberg, Allen S., (BV) ... '48 '78 C.645 B.S. L.464 J.D. 9220 Purto Bella Way

## EL MACERO, 600, *Yolo Co.*

Arhelger, Robert M. ... '39 '69 C.339 B.A. L.813 J.D. 44132 S. El Macero Dr.‡
Bobby, Charles H. ... '21 '53 C.112 L.1065 LL.B. P.O. Box 2126‡
Rogers, Eugene L., Jr., (BV) ... '19 '60 C.1060 B.A. L.464 LL.B. P.O. Box 2514
Wengel, Susan M. ... '48 '76 C&L.546 B.S., J.D. 27075 E. El Macero Dr.
Wong, Suey Y. ... '49 '73 C.112 B.S. L.426 J.D. 44897 N. El Macero Dr.

## EL MONTE, 106,209, *Los Angeles Co.*

Abrams, Martin L., (BV) ... '22 '52 C.112 B.A. L.800 J.D. [M.L.Abrams]
Abrams, Martin L., A Law Corp., (BV) ... 11350 E. Valley Blvd.
**Aguilera, Daniel P.** ... '54 '83 C.112 B.A. L.426 J.D. [⊠ G.Bacio]
Alcala, Susanna ... '63 '91 C.769 B.A. L.940 J.D. Dep. City Atty.
Amerine, Carrie S. '60 '85 C.1253 B.A. L.800 J.D.
Assoc. Gen. Coun., NavCom Def. Electronics Inc.
Applebaum, Jerome M. ... '30 '72 C.112 L.1136 J.D. 11706 E. Ramona Blvd.
Applebaum, Sandra J. '59 '85 C.1097 B.A. L.809 J.D.
11706 E. Ramona Blvd., Suite 209
Aranguren, H. Irene ... '53 '92 C.767 B.S. L.1136 J.D. 3205 Santa Anita Ave.

**Bacio, Gary A, Law Offices of '59 '88 C.112 B.A. L.426 J.D.**
**El Monte Executive Plaza, 11100 Valley Boulevard, Suite 216, 91731**
**Telephone: 818-452-8010 Facsimile: 818-452-1533**
***PRACTICE AREAS: Insurance Defense Law (65%); Personal Injury Law (20%); Business Law (10%); Wrongful Termination-Employment at Will (5%).**
**Of Counsel: Daniel P. Aguilera.**
**General Civil Litigation, Defense of Premises, Products and Auto Liability Claims.**

***See Professional Biographies, EL MONTE, CALIFORNIA***

Carroll, Frederick A., (AV) ... '11 '35 C&L.835 A.B., J.D. 11001 E. Valley Blvd.
Cichy, Marvin J., (BV) ... '40 '74 C.1042 B.A. L.1137 J.D. Asst. City Atty.
Diaz, Rudolph A. ... '42 '72 C.1042 B.S. L.800 J.D. Mun. Ct. J.
Donovan, Lawrence P., III '47 '91
C.763 B.S. L.1137 J.D. Corp. Coun., Crown City Plating Co.
Galisky, Albert J. ... '31 '67 C.273 A.B. L.426 LL.B. 4399 Santa Anita Ave.
Gately, Francis A., Jr. ... '41 '72 C&L.426 B.A., J.D. Mun. Ct. J.
Gondek, David F. ... '51 '81 C.112 B.A. L.426 J.D. City Atty.
Hernandez, Richard F. '45 '77
C.843 B.A. L.398 J.D. 2364 Peck Rd. (⊙W Covina & S Gate)
Jacobson, William L. ... '34 '71 C.605 L.809 J.D. 2364 Peck Rd.
Lawson, John F. ... '44 '79 C.336 B.S.F. L.1190 J.D. Off. of City Atty.
Leech, D. Wayne ... '56 '81 C.1075 B.S. L.1137 J.D. [Moseley&L.]
Leech, Ralph J., (BV) ... '33 '77 C.642 B.S. L.1136 J.D. [Moseley&L.]
Long, George Edwin, (BV) ... '32 '64 C.642 A.A. L.809 J.D. 11738 Valley Blvd.
McCardle, Arthur A. '26 '54 C&L.800 B.S., LL.B.
Chmn. of the Bd., Calif. Drilling & Blasting Co., Inc.
McNulty, J. Gordon ... '24 '61 C.018 B.A. L.426 Mun. Ct. J.‡
Midgley, James W. '47 '71 C.930 B.A. L.273 J.D.
V.P., Gen. Coun. & Corp. Secy., NavCom Def. Electronics Inc.
**Montgomery, Michael B.**, (AV) '36 '63 C.112 B.S. L.800 J.D.
[M.B.Montgomery] (⊙Ft. Lauderdale & Ocala)
*LANGUAGES: Spanish.

**Montgomery, Michael B., A Law Corporation, (AV) BR**
**10501 Valley Boulevard, Suite 121, 91731⊙**
**Telephone: 818-452-1222 Fax: 818-452-8323**
**Michael B. Montgomery.**
**Civil and Trial Practice in State and Federal Courts. Eminent Domain, Municipal Bond, Community Development, Municipal and Real Property Law, Gaming Law.**
**Reference: Bank of America (San Marino Branch).**
**Ft. Lauderdale, Florida Office: Justice Building, 524 S. Andrews Avenue, Suite 320 N. Telephone: 954-522-9441. Fax: 954-522-2076.**

***See Professional Biographies, EL MONTE, CALIFORNIA***

Moseley, E. Clarke, (BV) ... '48 '74 C.112 B.A. L.169 J.D. [Moseley&L.]
Moseley & Leech, (BV) ... 11001 East Valley Mall
Redeker, Henry K ... '60 '88 C.1075 B.A. L.800 J.D. 11428 Lower Azusa Rd.
Reinhold, Lawrence James '56 '89
C.17 B.B.A. L.192 J.D. Southern Calif. Laborers Tr. Fund
Rios, Ralph R., (BV) ... '46 '78 C.112 B.A. L.800 J.D. 11401 E. Valley Blvd.
Roberts, Melville N. ... '39 '79 C.37 B.S.E.E. L.1095 J.D. NavCom Def. Electronics Inc.
Rodriguez, Jose A. ... '48 '74 C.112 B.A. L.800 J.D. 11234 Valley Blvd.
Ryan, Timothy J. '49 '76
C.602 B.A. L.809 J.D. Gen. Coun., San Gabriel Valley Water Co.
Spicer, Anthony J. ... '29 '78 C.057 L.1136 J.D. V.P. & Gen. Coun., Clayton Mfg. Co.
Van Dusen, Richard W. ... '45 '75 C.139 B.A. L.809 J.D. Mun. Ct. J.
Venegas, John F. ... '43 '84 C.525 M.S. L.1097 J.D. 11500 Hallwood Dr.
Ward, Milburn R., Jr. ... '32 '74 C.1042 B.S. L.809 J.D. 11401 E. Valley Blvd.
Whitehead, Michael L. '48 '77
C.1077 B.A. L.1136 J.D. Pres., San Gabriel Valley Water Co.
Younger, Michael L. ... '46 '71 C.940 B.A. L.1068 J.D. Coun., TransGo, Inc.

## EL SEGUNDO, 15,223, *Los Angeles Co.*

Abert, Karl J. ... '32 '65 C.426 B.S. L.1068 LL.B. 2000 E. Imperial Hwy.
Andrews, Barry S. ... '53 '80 C.602 B.A. L.426 J.D. Dep. Gen. Coun., Unocal Corp.
Baggett, Don A., Law Offices of, (AV) '51 '76
C.1042 B.A. L.809 J.D. 2250 Imperial Hgwy.
Baker, John G. '42 '72 C.128 B.A. L.800 J.D.
Gen. Coun., U.S. Mgrs. Realty, Inc./Brickstone Cos.
Berberian, Aram ... '40 '75 L.809 J.D. [Schimmenti&B.]
Blair, Janyce K.I. ... '42 '82 C.475 B.A. L.284 J.D. [Bleckman&B.]
Blakesley, Leonard E., Jr. '41 '67 C&L.339 A.B., J.D.
Sr. V.P., Gen. Coun. & Secy., Continental Develop. Corp.
Bleckman, Martin J. ... '29 '56 C.112 B.A. L.1068 LL.B. [Bleckman&B.]
Bleckman and Blair ... 302 W. Grand Ave., Ocean Plz.
Boak, Stephen A. ... '52 '80 C.25 L.1131 J.D. 1625 E. Maple Ave., Apt. 6
Breitwisch, Corilynn ... '54 '89 C.959 B.S. L.966 J.D. Dep. Dist. Atty.
Burke, William J. '47 '82 C.870 B.S. L.597 J.D.
Dir., Contracts, The Aerospace Corporation (Pat.)
**Burtis, Jill E.** ... '62 '89 C.112 B.A. L.1066 J.D. Sr. Atty., Mattel, Inc.
*RESPONSIBILITIES: Litigation.
Caimi, August W. ... '56 '83 C.309 A.B. L.94 J.D. 1407 E. Sycamore Ave.
**Codon, Dennis P.** '48 '77 C.101 B.A. L.809 J.D.
V.P., Chf. Legal Offr. & Gen. Coun., Unocal Corp.
Crichton, Roni Michele ... '56 '82 C.813 B.A. L.1065 J.D. Xerox Corp.
**Cummings, William Leamon** ... '54 '86 C.145 B.A. L.426 J.D. [McGarry&L.]
*PRACTICE AREAS: Personal Injury; Insurance Coverage; Bad Faith; Probate; Bankruptcy.
Cunha, Robert E. ... '34 '72 C.112 B.S. L.426 J.D. Xerox Corp.
Dewez, Brigitte M. '56 '84 C.061 L.309 LL.M.
Dep. Gen. Coun. & Corp. Secy., Unocal Corp.
Drury, Edward Anthony '53 '80 C.112 B.S. L.1067 J.D.
V.P., Tax/Legal & Corp. Secy., Standard Brands Paint Co.
**Fisk, Hayward D.** '43 '68 C&L.378 B.S., J.D.
(adm. in KS; not adm. in CA) V.P., Gen. Coun. & Secy., Computer Sciences Corp.
**Fowler, David L.** ... '52 '82 C.870 B.S. L.276 J.D. Sr. Staff Coun., Hughes Aircraft Co.
Friery, John J., Jr. ... '46 '71 C&L.262 A.B., J.D. 2000 E. Imperial Hwy.
Gambaro, Ernest U. '38 '75 C.679 L.426
V.P., Gen. Coun. & Secy., Infonet Servs. Corp.
Greenup, Campbell H. '53 '81 C.112 A.B. L.1065 J.D.
Sr. V.P., Develop. & Mktg., Kilroy Industries
**Hallock, Kurt D.** '53 '81
C.976 B.A. L.569 J.D. Asst. Gen. Coun., Computer Sciences Corp.
*RESPONSIBILITIES: Outsourcing Transactions.
**Hartley, Stephen L.** '51 '76 C.112 A.B. L.800 J.D.
V.P. & Asst. Gen. Coun., Mattel, Inc.
*RESPONSIBILITIES: Corporate Law; Advertising; Product Liability; ERISA.
Horwitz, Gary B. ... '60 '88 C.112 B.A. L.800 J.D. Mattel, Inc.
Householder, Joseph A. ... '55 '84 C.800 B.S. L.426 J.D. V.P., Tax., Unocal Corp.
Jackson-Bryant, Roni ... '62 '87 C&L.659 B.S., J.D. 2230 E. Imperial Hwy.

Jessup, Mary ........................ '— '77 C.788 B.A. L.1190 J.D. Depty. Dist. Atty.
**Johnson, Stephen E.** '54 '85 C.685 B.A. L.800 J.D.
Asst. Gen. Coun. & Asst. Secy., Computer Sciences Corp.
**Kahng, Arlene C** '— '85
C.339 B.A. L.597 J.D. Asst. Legal Coun., Hughes Communications
**Kolakosky, Mary Brann** '— '80 C.1077 B.A. L.1148 J.D.
Coun., The Aerospace Corp.
**Laufenberg, Daniel D.** .................. '58 '83 C.813 A.B. L.426 J.D. [McGarry&L.]
*PRACTICE AREAS: Probate and Estate Planning; Wills and Trusts; Taxation; Personal Injury; Insurance Law.
**Laufenberg, Jeffrey J.**, (AV) ............ '55 '80 C&L.426 B.B.A., J.D. [McGarry&L.]
*PRACTICE AREAS: Personal Injury Defense; Products Liability; Insurance Law; Commercial Litigation; Real Estate.
**Louttit, Gordon J.** '47 '72 C.112 B.A. L.1068 J.D.
V.P., Gen. Coun. & Secy., The Aerospace Corp.
Mansour, N. Ned .......................... '48 '73 C.800 B.S. L.1049 J.D. Mattel, Inc.
Markley, Paul R. ................. '54 '80 C.546 B.S. L.221 J.D. 222 N. Sepulveda Blvd.
Masenga, Robert V., (AV) .......... '49 '74 C.602 B.A. L.426 J.D. 300 N. Sepulveda Blvd.
**Matthews, Robert Donald** .... '48 '78 L.770 J.D. Asst. Gen. Coun., The Aerospace Corp.
McCall, Robert H. ............................ '57 '85 C.48 B.A. L.1049 J.D. 402 Standard St.
McDaniel, Marshall L., (AV) .............. '24 '50 C&L.813 B.A., LL.B. [McDaniel&M.]
McDaniel & McDaniel, (AV) ................................................ 2250 E. Imperial Hwy.
McDowell, Hobart K., III ............ '52 '77 C.813 B.A. L.1068 J.D. 302 W. Grand Ave.
**McGarry, James J.**, (AV) .................. '53 '80 C&L.426 B.B.A., J.D. [McGarry&L.]
*PRACTICE AREAS: Personal Injury Defense; Products Liability; Insurance Law.

**McGarry & Laufenberg, (AV)** BB
**300 North Sepulveda Boulevard, Suite 2294, 90245**
**Telephone: 310-335-1780 Fax: 310-335-1790**
**Members of Firm: James J. McGarry; Jeffrey J. Laufenberg; William Leamon Cummings. Associates: Daniel D. Laufenberg; John E. Zegel.**
**Personal Injury Defense and Insurance Law, Probate and Estate Planning, Wills and Trusts, Taxation, Business and Commercial Litigation.**
***See Professional Biographies, EL SEGUNDO, CALIFORNIA***

McKay, Evans Joseph ................................ '41 '76 C.560 B.A. L.347 J.D. Mattel Toys
**McShane, Michele L.** .................. '53 '81 C&L.831 B.A., J.D. Sr. Atty., Mattel, Inc.
*LANGUAGES: German.
*RESPONSIBILITIES: Contracts Law; Intellectual Property.
Miller, David A. '53 '79
C.103 B.A. L.178 J.D. V.P., U.S. Mgrs. Realty, Inc./Brickstone Cos.

**Miller, Howard B., (AV) '37 '61 C.990 B.A. L.145 J.D.** BB
**2101 Rosecrans Avenue, Suite 5252, 90245**
**Telephone: 310-607-0003 Fax: 310-607-0005**
**Email: hbm@netcom.com**
**Mediation and Arbitration, Civil Trials, Appellate, Intellectual Property, Patents, Copyright, Trademarks, Trade Secrets, Venture Capitol, Real Estate, Bankruptcy.**
**Reference: Wells Fargo Bank (Beverly Hills).**
***See Professional Biographies, EL SEGUNDO, CALIFORNIA***

Mitchell, Melton L. ................................ '53 '79 L.1136 J.D. 2250 Imperial Hgwy
Moran, Cathy Carlson '51 '79 C.518 B.A. L.893 J.D.
(adm. in DC; not adm. in CA)
Exec. V.P., Policy & Legal Affs., Western League of Svgs. Institute
**Mrofka, Kristine E.** '51 '81
C.112 B.A. L.426 J.D. Asst. Legal Coun., Hughes Communications
Munson, Craig E. ....................... '57 '89 C.112 B.A. L.1137 J.D. 2381 Rosecrans Ave.
**Nocket, M. Keith** ........... '51 '82 C.426 B.A. L.1095 J.D. Coun., Hughes Aircraft Co.
**Normile, Robert J.** '59 '86 C.262 B.A. L.569 J.D.
V.P. & Asst. Gen. Coun., Mattel, Inc.
**Ohashi, John E.** ......................... '55 '81 C.112 B.A. L.1067 J.D. [Ohashi&P.]⊙
*REPORTED CASES: Reid vs. Moskovitz 208 Cal. App. 3d 29 (1989).
*PRACTICE AREAS: Business Law; Corporate Law; Real Estate; Employment Law; Federal and State Securities.

**Ohashi & Priver, (AV)**
**222 N. Sepulveda Boulevard 20th Floor, 90245**⊙
**Telephone: 310-364-5215 Facsimile: 310-364-5217**
**Mark S. Priver; John E. Ohashi.**
**Business and Corporate Law. Real Estate, Federal and State Securities, Commerical and Tax Litigation.**
**Pasadena, California Office: 215 North Marengo Avenue. Suite 225. 91101. Telephone: 818-584-1107. Facsimile: 818-356-7414.**
***See Professional Biographies, EL SEGUNDO, CALIFORNIA***

Perkins, Ray H. '37 '70 C.839 B.S.M.E. L.326 J.D.
(adm. in TX; not adm. in CA) 200 N. Nash St.‡
**Priver, Mark S.**, (AV) ..................... '55 '82 C.1169 B.A. L.1148 J.D. [Ohashi&P.]⊙
*PRACTICE AREAS: Business Litigation; Commercial Litigation; Tax Litigation.
Propp, William W. ............... '56 '81 C.277 B.S. L.280 J.D. Coun., Xerox Corp. (Pat.)
**Purcell, Kenneth J.**, (AV) '39 '65
C.813 B.A. L.1068 J.D. Sr. Coun., Computer Sciences Corp.
Raizes, Sheldon F. '36 '61 C.560 B.S. L.273 LL.B.
(adm. in VA; not adm. in CA; Pat.) Xerox Corp.
Richardson, Judith L. '58 '82 C.347 A.B. L.145 J.D.
(adm. in IL; not adm. in CA) U.S. Air Force Space & Missile Systems Ctr.
Ronne, Robert R., (AV) ..................... '55 '80 C.112 A.B. L.809 J.D. 840 Apollo St.
**Rosales, Richard A.** .......... '54 '79 C.112 B.A. L.1137 J.D. Coun., Hughes Aircraft Co.
Rose, Alex J. ......................... '55 '80 C.112 B.A. L.809 J.D. Continental Develop. Corp.
Rudnicki, Andrew M. P. ................. '52 '79 C.112 B.A. L.464 J.D. 2381 Rosecrans Ave.
Schimmenti, John J., (BV) ............... '38 '63 C.178 B.A. L.276 J.D. [Schimmenti&B.]
Schimmenti & Berberian, (BV) ........................................................ 426 Main St.
**Seraydarian, Paul** ......... '57 '82 C.276 B.S.F.S. L.800 J.D. Coun., Hughes Aircraft Co.
Siegel, G. Roger ................................ '46 '73 C.112 B.S. L.809 J.D. 937 Limita
Sindel, Rosario Herrera ........ '66 '89 C.1077 B.A. L.800 J.D. Asst. Coun., Unocal Corp.
Smith, Barry Paul ..................... '43 '68 C.158 B.S.E.E. L.1009 J.D. Xerox Corp. (Pat.)
**Smith, Leland P.** .............................. '63 '89 C.31 B.A. L.800 J.D. Mattel, Inc.
**Smolker, Jennifer Ann** '46 '77 C.112 B.A. L.1136 J.D.
Group V.P., Hughes Aircraft Co.
Strategos, Gena C. ....................... '62 '89 C&L.800 B.A., J.D. 2250 Imperial Hgwy.
Strathman, Charles O., Jr. '43 '79
C.112 B.A. L.1068 J.D. Sr. Dep. Gen. Coun., Unocal Corp.
**Sullivan, Daniel F.** .................. '40 '73 C&L.36 B.S., J.D. Sr. Atty., Mattel, Inc. (Pat.)
*RESPONSIBILITIES: Intellectual Property; Patents, Trademarks and Copyrights; Litigation; Licensing; Contracts.
Taylor, Maureen C. .......................... '40 '91 C.1077 B.A. L.1136 J.D. P.O. Box 998
**Tollefsen, Scott B.** '53 '79 C&L.893 B.A., J.D.
(adm. in OH; not adm. in CA) Hughes Aircraft Co.
Trask, Amy J. ....................... '61 '85 C.112 B.A. L.800 J.D. The Oakland Raiders
Treffert, Thomas L. '59 '94
C.1016 B.S. L.1068 J.D. Corp. Coun., Computer Science Corp.

Veasey, Glenda, (AV) ............... '58 '81 C.1131 B.S. L.800 J.D. 2381 Rosecrans Ave.
**Vesco, John A.** ................ '50 '86 C.112 B.A. L.1137 J.D. Coun., The Aerospace Corp.
Viot, Sheryl Sutherland '57 '84 C.112 B.A. L.329 J.D.
(adm. in PA; not adm. in CA) Asst. Coun., U.S. Dept. of Defense
Wai, Bonnie Y. .......................... '62 '87 C.112 L.1068 J.D. 2250 Imperial Hgwy.
Walsleben, Herbert P., Jr. ......... '35 '70 C.840 B.A. L.426 J.D. Employ. Assistance Prog.
Weiss, Jordan P. ......................... '52 '77 C.260 B.S.B.A. L.245 J.D. Unocal Corp.
Westfall, Lawrence S. ............. '37 '62 C.674 A.B. L.309 J.D. Sr. Coun., Unocal Corp.
Willis, Judy A. ......................................... '49 '79 C.829 B.A. L.93 J.D. Mattel, Inc.
Zahner, Harold E. ......................... '41 '67 C.798 B.S.B.A. L.734 J.D. Unocal Corp.
**Zegel, John E.** ........................ '57 '84 C.1019 B.B.A. L.809 J.D. [A McGarry&L.]
*PRACTICE AREAS: Personal Injury Defense; Products Liability; Insurance Law; Construction Defects.

## EL SOBRANTE, 5,000, *Contra Costa Co.*

Darling, Robert F. '44 '72 C.674 A.B. L.976 LL.B.
(adm. in NY; not adm. in CA) Sr. V.P. & Gen. Coun., Wells Fargo Leasing Corp.
Hall, Randolph Warren .................. '47 '78 C.813 B.A. L.309 J.D. 145 Nitey Nite Lane
Holdrich, Larry F., (BV) ............ '33 '63 C.112 B.A. L.1065 LL.B. 5069 Appian Way
Homec, Martin ........................... '48 '79 C.112 B.A. L.765 J.D. 1030 Jasmine Way
Klobas, Paul T. ............... '47 '74 C.1073 B.A. L.1153 J.D. 4515 San Pablo Dam Rd.
Mansdorf, Paul J. ....................... '64 '88 C.112 B.A. L.1065 J.D. 4980 Appian Way
Schoenleber, Cheryl ................... '50 '84 C.354 B.A. L.1065 J.D. 5069 Appian Way
Sharp, Robt. N., (BV) .......... '26 '54 C.112 A.B. L.1066 LL.B. 3875 San Pablo Dam Rd.
Shelby, Thomas G., (BV) ................ '35 '67 C.112 B.A. L.765 J.D. 307 Del Valle Cir.
Spunaugle, Vaughn E. .................. '51 '80 C.1193 B.A. L.1137 J.D. 4980 Appian Way

## EL TORO, 8,654, *Orange Co.*

Brodkin, Alan L., (BV) ..................... '53 '79 C.1042 B.A. L.1137 J.D. 22932 El Toro Rd.
Carlisle, Carolyn K. ............................ '56 '83 C.918 B.A. L.976 J.D. 15 Eldorado
Feldman, Steven J. ............................ '47 '74 C.112 B.A. L.426 J.D. 22942 El Toro Rd.
Gyves, Alison C. ........................ '65 '94 C.112 B.A. L.1137 J.D. 23704 S. ElTorp Rd.
Harvey, John M., (A Professional Corporation) '30 '73
C.08 B.A. L.1136 J.D. Landscape Specialists, Inc.
Hobbs, Victor E. ............................... '34 '78 C.273 B.A. L.1137 J.D. 23161 Tulip St.
Kumagai, Tom T. .............................. '27 '74 C.878 B.S. L.1137 J.D. P.O. Box 1257
Lewis, Sueanne C. .......................... '32 '58 C.1022 L.669 J.D. P.O. Box 5022-286‡
Marks, Kenneth G. ........................ '56 '81 C.37 B.A. L.61 J.D. 22942 El Toro Rd.
McMaster, Jean ................................. '36 '86 C.24 B.A. L.1137 J.D. P.O. Box 405
Parker, Beatrice C. ............................. '48 '77 C.690 B.S. L.990 J.D. [Parker&P.]
Parker, Robert C. ............................... '45 '77 C.690 B.S. L.1240 J.D. [Parker&P.]
Parker & Parker ........................................................................... 22272 Parkwood
Robinson, Harold H., III .......... '39 '66 C.169 B.A. L.1065 J.D. Certified Portfolios, Inc.
Skinner, David V. ....................... '60 '86 C.800 B.S. L.809 J.D. 22974 El Toro Rd.
Swatez, Harold H., A Prof. Corp. ........................... '29 '65 L.809 P.O. Box 5022
Thacker, Bob E. ............................ '49 '78 C.679 B.S. L.1137 J.D. P.O. Box 367

## ELVERTA, —, *Sacramento Co.*

Whalen, Oakley R. ....................... '33 '83 C.1060 B.A. L.1026 J.D. 300 Charles Ave.

## EMERYVILLE, 5,740, *Alameda Co.*

Assaf, Philip D., (AV) .................... '24 '52 C.309 A.B. L.813 J.D. [Sturgis,N.B.&A.]
Atkins, Ralph L., (BV©) '42 '67 C.708 A.B. L.184 J.D.
(adm. in CT; not adm. in CA) 6363 Christie Ave.‡
**Becherer, Patrick J.**, (AV) .......... '43 '72 C.894 A.B. L.477 J.D. [Becherer B.M.K.&S.]
*PRACTICE AREAS: Litigation.

**Becherer Beers Murphy Kannett & Schweitzer, (AV)**
**2200 Powell Street, Suite 805, 94608**
**Telephone: 510-658-3600 Fax: 510-658-1151**
**URL: http://www.bechererbeers.com**
**Members of Firm: Patrick J. Becherer; John L. Beers; Mark S. Kannett; Timothy J. Murphy; Lori A. Schweitzer. Associates: Kirsten Komoroske; Susan Stockdale; Sarah Valentine.**
**Civil Trial and Litigation.**
***See Professional Biographies, EMERYVILLE, CALIFORNIA***

Becker, Jennifer A. ........................ '59 '85 C.112 B.A. L.1065 J.D. [Starnes B.W.]
**Beers, John L.**, (AV) ............. '51 '76 C.813 B.A. L.1068 J.D. [Becherer B.M.K.&S.]
*PRACTICE AREAS: Employment Litigation.
Belcher, Claudia M. .............. '48 '82 C.112 B.A. L.1066 J.D. Sr. Coun., Chiron Corp.
Biddle, Michael Gerald .............................. '60 '88 C.112 A.B. L.284 J.D. City Atty.
Blackburn, Robert P. '56 '82
C.930 B.S. L.29 J.D. V.P. & Chf. Pat. Coun., Chiron Corp. (Pat.)
Bradley Krant, Susan ............... '62 '87 C.605 A.B. L.1065 J.D. Legal Strategies Group
Brucker, H. Michael, (AV) ........ '37 '65 C.112 B.S.E.E. L.765 J.D. 5855 Doyle St. (Pat.)
Brunsell, Robert ........................ '31 '60 C.112 A.B. L.1066 LL.B. [Sturgis,N.B.&A.]
**Cahn, Timothy R.** ............................ '62 '92 C.935 B.A. L.309 J.D. [Strategies]
**Campbell, Marvin N.** '60 '87 C.103 B.A. L.1066 J.D.
Assoc. Gen. Coun., GE Capital Computer Leasing
Cannady, Walter J., (BV) .............. '42 '70 C.1073 B.A. L.1026 J.D. 2200 Powell St.
Carl, Daniel R. ............. '52 '78 C.813 B.A. L.1065 J.D. Assoc. Gen. Coun., SYBASE, Inc.
Chuh, Teresa D., (AV) .... '54 '80 C.112 B.A. L.1065 J.D. Sr. Corp. Coun., SYBASE, Inc.
Clevenger, Jack D. ...................................... '21 '49 C.684 L.800 LL.B. 4 Captain Dr.
Collins, Amy L. Tsui '48 '82 C.494 B.A. L.1035 J.D.
(adm. in MN; not adm. in CA) Sr. Div. Pat. Coun., Chiron Corp.
Craig, H. Theodore, (BV) ............................ '33 '62 C&L.813 A.B., J.D. [Craig,H.T.]
Craig, H. Theodore, III, Inc., (BV) ................................................ 2200 Powell St.
Crawford, Joseph L. ................. '53 '83 C.801 B.S. L.284 J.D. 5 Commodore Dr.
Dezurick, Bradford Lawrence .......... '64 '92 C.763 B.A. L.765 J.D. [Dezurick,E.&H.]
Dezurick, Paul A., (AV) ............... '42 '68 C&L.767 B.S., J.D. [Dezurick,E.&H.]
Dezurick, Edginton & Harrington, LLP, (AV) ...................................... 6400 Hollis St.
Dobrovolny, Janet Lee ................. '51 '79 C.813 B.A. L.1065 J.D. 2000 Powell St.
Edginton, John A., (AV) ............... '35 '64 C.112 B.A. L.1066 J.D. [Dezurick,E.&H.]
**Floum, Joshua R.** ........................................ '58 '83 C.112 A.B. L.309 J.D. [Strategies]
*PRACTICE AREAS: Antitrust, Intellectual Property, International Trade and Wildlife Litigation.
**Frank, Karen S.** ...................................... '51 '87 C.183 B.A. L.1065 J.D. [Strategies]
**Gilchrist, Gregory S.** ...................................... '58 '83 C&L.477 B.A., J.D. [Strategies]
Glickstein, Robert J. ........................ '46 '72 C.659 B.A. L.569 J.D. 2000 Powell St.
Goldman, Kenneth M. ....... '60 '89 C.309 A.B. L.1068 J.D. Div. Pat. Coun., Chiron Corp.
**Goldsmith, Peter H.**, (AV) ............................ '52 '79 C.976 B.A. L.1066 J.D. [Strategies]
Gorlin, Robert J. ............ '58 '85 C.800 B.S. L.1065 J.D. Sr. Corp. Coun., SYBASE, Inc.
Gould, Alan J. ................................... '29 '54 C.823 L.982 LL.B. 1155 Park Ave.
Gram, Thomas J., (AV) ............................ '44 '70 C.860 B.A. L.569 J.D. The Martin Grp.
Green, William G., (AV) ........ '44 '75 C.976 B.A. L.276 J.D. Gen. Coun., Chiron Corp.
Harper, Gregory Lee ........................ '49 '82 C.339 B.S.B.A. L.1065 J.D. 1420 45th St.
Harrington, Kathleen ........................ '57 '84 C.112 A.B. L.767 J.D. [Dezurick,E.&H.]
Hoover, Jessica M. ......... '57 '83 C.112 A.B. L.976 J.D. Div. Corp Coun., Chiron Corp.
Hunt, Daniel W. ......... '61 '90 C.174 B.A. L.1066 J.D. Corp. Coun., Chiron Corp.
**Johnson, Vincent L.** ...................................... '58 '83 C.674 B.A. L.1066 J.D. [Strategies]

CAA77P

CALIFORNIA—EMERYVILLE MARTINDALE-HUBBELL LAW DIRECTORY 1997

**Kannett, Mark S.**, (AV) .......... '51 '82 C.174 B.A. L.1065 J.D. [Becherer B.M.K.&S.]
*PRACTICE AREAS: Litigation; Professional Liability; Insurance Coverage; Bad Faith Litigation; Environmental Law.
Keating, Laurie Bartlett '53 '79
C.112 A.B. L.1065 J.D. V.P., Gen. Coun. & Secy., SYBASE, Inc.
**Kirmssé, Leigh A.** .......................... '58 '92 C.768 B.A. L.426 J.D. [Strategies]
*PRACTICE AREAS: Complex Litigation; Intellectual Property; Insurance and Products Liability.

**Koller, Lynn Anderson, Law Offices of**
**(See Oakland)**

**Komoroske, Kirsten** ............ '66 '92 C.112 B.A. L.770 J.D. [▣ Becherer B.M.K.&S.]
Kruse, Norman J. ............................ '49 '93 C.112 B.S. L.284 J.D. Chiron Corp. (Pat.)

**Legal Strategies Group, (AV) ▣**
**5905 Christie Avenue, 94608**
**Telephone: 510-450-9600 Fax: 510-450-9601**
**URL: http://www.legalstrategies.com/lsgdemoindex3.html**
**Timothy R. Cahn; Joshua R. Floum; Karen S. Frank; Gregory S. Gilchrist; Peter H. Goldsmith; Vincent L. Johnson; Leigh A. Kirmssé; Louise E. Ma; Heather A. Young. Of Counsel: Robert J. Vizas.**
**Litigation, Alternative Dispute Resolution, Pre-litigation Counseling, and Intellectual Property Counseling, Licensing and Prosecution.**
***See Professional Biographies, EMERYVILLE, CALIFORNIA***

Locke, W. O. .......................... '25 '51 C.911 B.A. L.813 J.D. 2 Commodore Dr.
Long, David A., (AV) ..................... '31 '60 C.112 B.A. L.1066 J.D. 2200 Powell St.
**Ma, Louise E.**, (AV) ........................ '52 '78 C.112 B.A. L.767 J.D. [Strategies]
Martell, Patrick J. ..........'52 '77 C.454 B.A. L.276 J.D. Sr. Corp. Coun., SYBASE, Inc.
McClung, Barbara G ......... '54 '87 C.112 B.A. L.659 J.D. Div. Pat. Coun., Chiron Corp.
McGarrigle, Philip L., Jr. '54 '83
C.550 B.A. L.770 J.D. Div. Pat. Coun., Chiron Corp. (Pat.)
McGrath, Geraldine ................. '49 '82 C.766 B.A. L.765 J.D. Gen. Coun., IA Corp.
Montante, Claudia W. .....'50 '80 C.813 B.A. L.1066 J.D. Div. Corp. Coun., Chiron Corp.
**Murphy, Timothy J.**, (AV) ........ '47 '72 C.813 A.B. L.174 J.D. [Becherer B.M.K.&S.]
*PRACTICE AREAS: Commercial Litigation; Employment Litigation.
Ness, Edwin N. ...................... '13 '55 C.112 A.B. L.1065 LL.B. [Sturgis,N.B.&A.]
Plunkett, Michael O. '40 '67 C.10 B.S. L.260 J.D.
(adm. in FL; not adm. in CA) 6 Captain Dr.‡
Price, Borden B. ................................. '16 '50 C.112 A.B. L.1066 J.D. [B.B.Price]
Price, Borden B., A Prof. Law Corp. .................................6363 Christie Ave.
Ravazzini, Terry J., (BV) ................... '41 '71 C.767 B.S. L.765 J.D. [T.J.Ravazzini]
Ravazzini, Terry J., A Prof. Corp., (BV) ......................................2200 Powell St.
Reaves, Martina E., (AV) ................ '49 '81 C.1071 B.S. L.1230 J.D. 4300 Horton St.
Runnion, Jack C. ........................... '31 '59 C.112 B.S. L.1066 J.D. 2200 Powell St.
Savereide, Paul B. '60 '92 C.747 B.A. L.494 J.D.
(adm. in MN; not adm. in CA; Pat.) Pat. Coun., Chiron Corp.
**Schweitzer, Lori A.**, (BV) ....... '56 '82 C.1044 B.A. L.1065 J.D. [Becherer B.M.K.&S.]
*PRACTICE AREAS: Product Liability Litigation; Insurance Coverage and Bad Faith Litigation.

**Seltzer, James Jay, (AV) '48 '72 C.112 A.B. L.426 J.D.**
**Watergate Towers, Tenth Floor, 2200 Powell Street, 94608**
**Telephone: 510-596-2500 Telecopier: 510-596-2519**
**Email: medlawline@aol.com**
***LANGUAGES: French and Japanese.**
***PRACTICE AREAS: Administrative Law; Criminal Law; Military Law; Medicare; Medicaid. Administrative Law.**
***See Professional Biographies, EMERYVILLE, CALIFORNIA***

Sitkin, Peter E. ................... '40 '64 C.188 B.A. L.178 J.D. 2000 Powell St., Ste.1650
Staple, Peter D. .......'51 '81 C&L.813 B.A., J.D. V.P. & Assoc. Gen. Coun., Chiron Corp.
Starnes, Tanya, (AV) ............................ '53 '77 C.1061 B.A. L.767 J.D. [Starnes B.W.]
Starnes • Becker • White, (AV) ........................................ 4300 Horton St. Ste. 15
**Stockdale, Susan** .............. '65 '92 C.174 B.A. L.770 J.D. [▣ Becherer B.M.K.&S.]
Stratton, Jane L. '41 '78
C.1042 B.A. L.1065 J.D. V.P. & Assoc. Gen. Coun., Chiron Corp.
Sturgis, Ness, Brunsell & Assaf, A Prof. Corp., (AV) .....................2000 Powell St.
Teichmann, David L. '56 '82
C.855 B.A. L.312 J.D. Dir., European Legal Affs., SYBASE, Inc.
**Valentine, Sarah** ................ '61 '92 C.788 B.A. L.818 J.D. [▣ Becherer B.M.K.&S.]
**Vizas, Robert J.**, (AV) ....................... '47 '73 C.477 B.A. L.976 J.D. [▣ Strategies]
White, Arthur G. ........................................ '48 '81 C.37 L.1230 LL.B. [Starnes B.W.]
**Young, Heather A.** ............................. '65 '91 C&L.893 B.A., J.D. [Strategies]
*PRACTICE AREAS: Intellectual Property; Antitrust; Complex Litigation; Appellate.

## ENCINITAS, 55,386, *San Diego Co.*

Allen, Elizabeth L., (BV) .............. '42 '80 C.188 B.A. L.1137 J.D. 4401 Manchester Ave.
Ambrose, Christopher R. '61 '87
C.112 B.A. L.1049 J.D. 227 N. El Camino Real (⊙Portland, OR)
Axelrod, Barry E., (AV) ................ '46 '72 C.112 A.B. L.1068 J.D. 2236 Encinitas Blvd.
Barber, Ann H., (BV) ............'52 '78 C.112 B.A. L.464 J.D. 323 N. Willowspring Dr.
Brown, Arthur L. ..................... '26 '53 C.976 B.A. L.178 LL.B. 2236 Encinitas Blvd.
Brown, Bradley L., (BV) ........... '57 '85 C.950 B.A. L.1049 J.D. 4401 Manchester Ave.
Caligiuri, Debra N. ........................'54 '91 C.763 B.A. L.1137 J.D. 619 S. Vulcan Ave.
**Crickmore, Jerald D.** ....................... '54 '85 C.101 B.A. L.1049 J.D. [Larsen&C.]
*LANGUAGES: Spanish.
*PRACTICE AREAS: Fiduciary Services; Probate and Estate Planning; Transactions; Collections.
Day, Gregory S., (BV) ....... '50 '76 C.347 B.A. L.61 J.D. 120 Birmingham Dr., Ste. 200
DiRe, Daniel M. ...................... '56 '82 C.506 B.S. L.508 J.D. 1862 Avienda Josepha
Dowling, James W. '12 '51 C&L.569 B.S., LL.B.
(adm. in NY; not adm. in CA) 480 S. El Camino Real‡
duPont, Charles E., Jr. ............'45 '74 C.976 B.A. L.174 J.D. 1203 Caminito Graziela
Eden, Lawrence E. ................'41 '66 C.1031 A.B. L.188 J.D. 227 N. El Camino Real

**Forrester, Kevin K., (BV) '57 '87 C.112 B.A. L.1049 J.D.**
**4403 Manchester Avenue, Suite 205, 92024-7903**
**Telephone: 619-944-1918 Fax: 619-944-3517**
**Email: kkf@cts.com**
***SPECIAL AGENCIES: Associate, William B. Enright American Inn of Court, 1992.**
**Real Estate and Business Law, Sports Law, Alternative Dispute Resolution.**
***See Professional Biographies, ENCINITAS, CALIFORNIA***

Freedman, Simon J. ............................ '56 '81 C.339 B.A. L.209 J.D. [Peters&F.]
Gage, Benjamin S., (BV) ............'49 '79 C.112 B.A. L.1136 J.D. 1331 Encinitas Blvd
Greene, Jennifer A. '53 '81 C.72 B.A. L.838 J.D.
(adm. in MA; not adm. in CA) 1410 Santa Fe Dr.
Griffith, Russell E. ................... '58 '85 C.473 A.B. L.61 J.D. 1991 Village Park Way
Hack, Phillip L. ........................'57 '83 C.610 B.S. L.851 J.D. 120 Witham Rd.
Hansen, John W., Jr. ................'45 '79 C.937 B.S. L.146 J.D. 1331 Encinitas Blvd.
Harris, Michael G., (BV) .................'49 '77 C.999 B.A. L.1137 J.D. [Root&H.]
Hersh, Alan S. .................................. '47 '74 C&L.446 B.A., J.D. 133 Beachtree Dr.
Hjelt, Stephen E., (BV) ............ '47 '72 C.112 A.B. L.1068 J.D. 2236 Encinitas Blvd.
Jensen, Walker A. '17 '42 C&L.597 B.S., J.D.
(adm. in IL; not adm. in CA) 1247 Saxony Rd.‡

Johnson, Craig H. ...........'52 '79 C.101 B.A. L.464 J.D. [Packard,P.&J.] (⊙Palo Alto)
Kochsmeiser, Susan E. ..................... '56 '83 C.112 B.A. L.1065 J.D. 174 Beechtree
Kovalsky, Robert M. ................'58 '86 C.112 B.A. L.1049 J.D. 4405 Manchester Ave.
**Larsen, Christopher**, (AV) ................ '51 '77 C.101 B.A. L.273 J.D. [Larsen&C.]
*LANGUAGES: German.
*REPORTED CASES: Bryte v. La Mesa (1989) 207 Cal.App.3d 687, 255 Cal. Rptr. 64.
*PRACTICE AREAS: Civil Litigation; Public Agency.

**Larsen & Crickmore, A Professional Association, (AV)**
**655 Second Street, 92024-3507**
**Telephone: 619-634-2800 Facsimile: 619-634-2569**
**Email: clarsen@ix.netcom.com**
**Christopher Larsen; Jerald D. Crickmore.**
**Civil Litigation, Fiduciary Services, Public Agency, Probate, Estate Planning, Collections.**
***See Professional Biographies, ENCINITAS, CALIFORNIA***

Lloyd, Michael D. ................ '41 '72 C.813 A.B. L.61 J.D. 3615 Fortuna Ranch Rd.
**Marvin, Charles, III**, (AV) ............... '38 '68 C.31 B.A. L.1066 J.D. [C.Marvin III]
*PRACTICE AREAS: Real Property; Corporate Law; Business Law; Partnerships; Limited Liability Companies.

**Marvin, Charles, III, A Professional Corporation, (AV)**
**120 Birmingham Drive, Suite 200, 92024**
**Telephone: 619-944-0123 Fax: 619-942-6176**
**Charles Marvin III.**
**Real Property, Corporate, Business, Partnership and Limited Liability Companies.**
***See Professional Biographies, ENCINITAS, CALIFORNIA***

McMeans, Paul E., (AV) ..........'52 '78 C.112 B.S. L.770 J.D. 1570 Pacific Ranch Dr.
Miller, Merwyn J., (BV) ............... '47 '74 C.112 B.A. L.61 J.D. 191 Calle Magdalena
Miller, Russell L. ................'51 '87 C.1188 B.A. L.1137 J.D. 4405 Manchester Ave.
Mindlin, Suzanne H. ................................................ '46 '96 4403 Manchester Ave.
**Mitchell, Don W.**, (AV) ...................... '28 '57 C&L.174 B.S., J.D. [Mitchell&M.]
*PRACTICE AREAS: Estate Planning; Probate.

**Mitchell and Murrell, (AV)**
**655 Second Street, 92024**
**Telephone: 619-753-6327 FAX: 619-753-6325**
**Don W. Mitchell; Gregory L. Murrell.**
**Estate Planning, Probate, Trust Law, Business Law and Taxation.**
**Reference: Bank of America National Trust & Savings Assn., Encinitas Branch.**
***See Professional Biographies, ENCINITAS, CALIFORNIA***

**Murrell, Gregory L.**, (BV) ..................'42 '78 C.628 B.S. L.61 J.D. [Mitchell&M.]
*PRACTICE AREAS: Estate Planning; Probate; Trust Law; Tax Law.
Nemeth, Valerie A. ...................'54 '79 C.112 B.A. L.1148 J.D. 619 S. Vulcan Ave.
Novack, Jeffrey N., (CV) ...........'57 '85 C.112 B.A. L.1188 J.D. 187 Calle Magdalena
Packard, Packard & Johnson, A Professional Corporation, (AV)
655 Second Avenue (⊙Palo Alto, CA & Salt Lake City, UT)
Page, Mary K. ............................'60 '86 C.1349 B.A. L.1067 J.D. 807 Nardo Rd.
Parker, Keenan A. ................ '53 '89 C.1077 B.A. L.940 J.D. 191 Calle Magdalena
Peters, David M. ......................................... '58 '87 C.990 B.A. L.1065 J.D. [Peters&F.]
Peters & Freedman ..........................................................191 Calle Magdalena
Phelps, Betty Lee, (AV) ....................'30 '70 C.763 B.A. L.1049 J.D. 471 Delage Ct.‡
Phelps, G. William ......................'22 '70 C.763 B.A. L.1008 LL.B. 471 Delage Ct.‡
Pines, Michael T. ................................'57 '89 C.112 B.A. L.1065 J.D. 732 N. Hwy. 101
Poole, Laurie S. .......................'65 '90 C.112 B.A. L.1049 J.D. 191 Calle Magdalena
Ravreby, Ellen W., (BV) ............ '52 '77 C.477 B.A. L.1049 J.D. 179 Via Del Cerrito
Reinschreiber, M. Robert, Jr. ........... '53 '78 C.966 B.A. L.1049 J.D. 1309 Ahlrich Ave.
Robertson, Paul F. '52 '86 C.94 A.B. L.1049 J.D.
Statistician, U.S. Navy Pers. Resch. & Devel. Ctr.
Rogers, Marilyn L. '39 '80 C.576 B.A. L.93 J.D.
(adm. in MA; not adm. in CA) 1106 Second St.‡
Root, Stephen G., (P.C.), (AV) ....................'49 '75 C.668 B.A. L.94 J.D. [Root&H.]
Root & Harris, (AV) ......................................................... 4405 Manchester Ave.
Rosen, Steven M., (AV) ......... '36 '68 C.112 B.S. L.800 J.D. 3226 Country Rose Circle
Sacorafas, Nick '31 '57 C.912 B.A. L.213 J.D.
(adm. in MI; not adm. in CA) Pres., Nationwide Properties Co.
Sager, Melvin S. ...................'31 '59 C.912 B.S. L.966 LL.B. 679 Camino El Dorado
Schmitt, Edward D. ..........................'65 '92 C.1044 B.A. L.61 J.D. 396 N. Hwy. 101
Singer, Michael D. .....................'58 '84 C.766 B.A. L.1065 J.D. 1252 Neptune Ave.
Smith, Jerome R., (BV) ................ '51 '77 C.228 B.A. L.245 J.D. 801 Woodside Lane
Sullivan, Arthur V., Jr. ......................'21 '50 C&L.273 LL.B. 1275 Green Orchard Pl.‡
Taylor, John Michael, (BV) ..........'54 '82 C.112 B.A. L.1137 J.D. 4403 Manchester Ave.
Tutoli, Michele A., (BV) ....... '51 '78 C.276 A.B. L.1009 J.D. 157 Rancho Santa Fe Rd.
Wagner, Thomas A. ............................'39 '66 C.36 B.A. L.767 J.D. 240 LaMesa St.‡
Wallenius, Rena, (BV) .................'55 '79 C.787 B.A. L.1049 J.D. 3364 Country Rose Cir.
Weiss, Nancy E. ....................'59 '91 C.350 B.S. L.1065 J.D. 132 N. El Camino Real
Wilkey, Roscoe S. ..................................'27 '54 C&L.813 A.B., J.D. Ret. Supr. Ct. J.‡
Williams, Michael E., (BV) ........'55 '80 C.112 B.A. L.1049 J.D. 4405 Manchester Ave.
Woolf, Simpson M. '19 '52 C.878 B.S. L.744 LL.B.
(adm. in TX; not adm. in CA) 245 Sunset Dr.‡

## ENCINO, —, *Los Angeles Co.*

(Part of the incorporated City of Los Angeles)

**Aaronson, Arthur**, (AV) .................. '49 '75 C.112 B.A. L.800 J.D. [Aaronson&A.]
*LANGUAGES: Italian.
*PRACTICE AREAS: Business Law; Real Estate; Probate; Civil Litigation; Corporation.
**Aaronson, Edward D.**, (AV) ............. '46 '72 C.112 B.A. L.560 J.D. [Aaronson&A.]
*PRACTICE AREAS: Retail and Commercial Leasing; Real Estate.
Aaronson, Mitchell, (AV) ............ '20 '48 C.494 B.A. L.309 J.D. 16133 Ventura Blvd.

**Aaronson & Aaronson, (AV) ▣**
**16133 Ventura Boulevard, Suite 1080, 91436**
**Telephone: 818-783-3858; 818-783-0444 Fax: 818-783-3873; 818-783-3825**
**Members of Firm: Edward D. Aaronson; Arthur Aaronson. Associates: Steven J. Berman.**
**General Civil and Trial Practice. Commercial and Industrial Leasing, Corporation, Business, Real Property, Family, Entertainment, Partnership, Pension and Profit Sharing, State and Federal Taxation, Estate Planning, Trust and Probate Law.**
***See Professional Biographies, ENCINO, CALIFORNIA***

Abraham, Michael A. .................. '63 '87 C.112 B.A. L.1065 J.D. [▣ Rosenthal&S.]
Abramowitz, Philip D., (AV) ........ '53 '78 C.1077 B.A. L.809 J.D. 15910 Ventura Blvd.

**Abrams, Arnold B. '37 '66 C.477 A.B. L.150 J.D.**
**16055 Ventura Boulevard, Penthouse 1205, 91436**
**Telephone: 818-907-5600 Fax: 818-783-5600**

(This Listing Continued)

**Abrams, Arnold B. (Continued)**
***REPORTED CASES: Isakos Shipping and Trading, SA v. Juniper Garden Town Homes Ltd. Scv 254044-printed in Ca. 2d U.S. Supreme Court.**
***PRACTICE AREAS: Personal Injury; Medical Malpractice; Real Estate; Workers Compensation. Personal Injury, Medical Malpractice, Real Estate and Workers Compensation.**

Abrams, Francine H. .............. '33 '81 C.1077 B.A. L.1095 J.D. 16661 Ventura Blvd.
Abrams, Judd Steven '58 '85 C.763 B.S. L.990 J.D. Gen. Coun., Abrams Construction Co.
Abramson, David H. .......... '47 '79 C.1077 B.A. L.1136 J.D. [▣ J.R.Zeesman&Assoc.]
Aftergood, G. Greg, (BV) ..... '46 '72 C.112 B.S. L.1068 J.D. 15915 Ventura Blvd., PH 1
Agay, Richard D., (AV) '32 '57 C.112 B.S. L.1068 LL.B. 16661 Ventura Blvd., Penthouse
Aheroni, Elliott L., (BV) ...................'45 '71 C&L.1095 B.A., J.D. 16311 Ventura Blvd.
Alexander, Arthur B., (AV) '41 '67 C.112 L.809 J.D. 16830 Ventura Blvd. (⊙Tucson, AZ)
Allen, Lawrence .............. '30 '71 C.930 L.1095 LL.B. 16501 Ventura Blvd., Ste. 601
Alper, David M. ...................'49 '77 C.112 B.A. L.1068 J.D. 16200 Quemada Rd.
**Alperstein, Glenn M.**, (AV) ..... '35 '60 C.112 B.S.B.A. L.1066 LL.B. [Gillin,S.A.G.&S.]
*PRACTICE AREAS: Estate Gift Planning; Taxation Law; Trust Law; Elder Law; Conservatorships.
**Alpert, Lee Kanon**, (AV) .................. '46 '72 C.800 B.S. L.426 J.D. [Alpert,B.&G.]
*PRACTICE AREAS: Arbitration and Mediation; Business and Civil Litigation; Commercial and Construction Law; Family Law; Governmental Relations Law.

**Alpert, Barr and Gross, A Professional Law Corporation, (AV) ▣**
**Encino Office Park I, Suite 300, 6345 Balboa Boulevard, 91316-1523**
**Telephone: 818-881-5000 Fax: 818-881-1150**
**Lee Kanon Alpert; Gary L. Barr; Lisa W. Glazener; Mark P. Gross; Mark S. Blackman; Michael N. Balikian; Judith R. Simon; Jack S. Mack. Of Counsel: Charles M. Hughes; Leonard S. Levy (A Professional Corporation).**
**General Civil Trial and Appellate Practice. Business, Corporate, Banking, Estate Planning and Administration, Family Law, Arbitration and Mediation, Mobile Home Residency Law, and Governmental Relations and Administrative Hearings.**
***See Professional Biographies, ENCINO, CALIFORNIA***

Alschuler, Norman W. .................... '22 '49 C.112 L.800 J.D. 15720 Ventura Blvd.
**Altman, Rex L.**, (AV) ..................... '50 '86 C.112 B.A. L.1136 J.D. [Altman&S.]
*PRACTICE AREAS: Workers Compensation Defense; Commercial collections.

**Altman & Schoemaker, (AV)**
**16255 Ventura Boulevard, Suite 1110, 91436**
**Telephone: 818-995-0080 FAX: 818-995-3419**
**Email: altman.a&s@mcimail.com URL: http://www.debtcollection.com**
**Members of Firm: Rex L. Altman; Charles Schoemaker, Jr. Associates: M. Christina Ramirez; Daniel J. Ysabal.**
**General Civil and Workers Compensation Defense. Trial and Appellate Practice, Commerical Collection and Enforcement of Judgements. Products Liability and Personal Injury.**
***See Professional Biographies, ENCINO, CALIFORNIA***

Andersen, Crossan R. '43 '71 C.197 A.B. L.94 J.D. Legal Dir., Motion Picture Assn. of Amer., Inc.
**Anker, Samuel H.**, (AV) .................... '44 '72 C.1077 B.A. L.1095 J.D. [Anker&H.]
*PRACTICE AREAS: Real Property Law; Transactional and Business Law; Mergers and Acquisitions.

**Anker & Hymes, A Law Corporation, (AV)**
**Suite 1200, 16311 Ventura Boulevard, 91436-2144**
**Telephone: 818-501-5800 Telecopier: 818-501-4019**
**Samuel H. Anker; Larry S. Hymes;—Jonathan L. Rosenbloom. Of Counsel: Douglas K. Schreiber; Daniel B. Spitzer.**
**Business, Corporate and Partnership Matters, Mergers and Acquisitions, Real Estate, Taxation, Estate Planning, Probate and Civil Litigation.**
**Reference: First Los Angeles Bank; Western Bank.**
***See Professional Biographies, ENCINO, CALIFORNIA***

Antler, Helayne '56 '81 C.569 B.A. L.724 J.D. V.P., Legal Affs., Alliance of Motion Picture & Television Producers
Appel, Barry M. .................... '54 '80 C.112 B.A. L.809 J.D. 16830 Ventura Blvd.
Appell, Melvin C., (AV) ................................ '34 '64 15760 Ventura Blvd.‡
Arak, Ronald M. ................................................. '47 '72 15760 Ventura Blvd.
Ash, Paul V. ........................... '66 '91 C.112 B.A. L.990 J.D. [▣ Stein,H.L.&Y.]
Avesar, Josef ............... '53 '82 C.112 B.A. L.809 J.D. 15760 Ventura Blvd., 16th Fl.
Ayvazi, Rafik .......................... '51 '86 C.588 M.S. L.1190 J.D. 15915 Ventura Blvd.
Azran, David A. ....................... '57 '85 C.605 B.A. L.426 J.D. 16311 Ventura Blvd.
Baghdassarian, Stepan W. ........... '61 '89 C.112 B.A. L.1148 J.D. 16000 Ventura Blvd.
**Balikian, Michael N.** ............... '57 '83 C.37 B.S.B.A. L.464 J.D. [▣ Alpert,B.&G.]
*PRACTICE AREAS: Estate Planning; Transactional and Business Law; Trust and Estate Administration.
Baltaxe, George, (AV) ...................... '32 '58 C.882 B.A. L.309 LL.B. [Baltaxe&B.]
Baltaxe, Michael F. ............................ '58 '87 C.112 B.A. L.426 J.D. [Baltaxe&B.]
Baltaxe & Baltaxe, (AV) ............................................... 15821 Ventura Blvd.
Bardwil, Richard B. ................... '22 '52 C.800 B.S. L.1001 LL.B. 5265 Genesta Ave.
Barg, David L. .......................... '41 '67 C.112 B.S. L.1068 J.D. [D.L.Barg]
Barg, David L., A Prof. Corp. .......................................... 16830 Ventura Blvd.
**Barr, Gary L.**, (AV) ..................... '53 '77 C.112 B.A. L.809 J.D. [Alpert,B.&G.]
*PRACTICE AREAS: Civil Litigation; Commercial Trial Litigation; Creditors Rights in Bankruptcy.
Barton, Sidney ........................... '15 '40 C.472 L.705 LL.B. 16962 Cotter Pl.
Bass, Gerald, (BV) ............................. '47 '75 C.1077 B.A. L.1095 J.D. [G.Bass]
**Bass, Robert D.**, (AV) ..................... '47 '74 C.112 B.A. L.1068 J.D. [Greenberg&B.]
*PRACTICE AREAS: Bankruptcy and Insolvency Related Matters.
Bass, Gerald, A Law Corporation, (BV) .................................. 15760 Venture Blvd.

**Bassin, Michael Robert**
**(See Los Angeles)**

Bauducco, Paul C. .......... '58 '85 C.112 B.A. L.990 J.D. 11th Flr., 16633 Ventura Blvd.

**Baum, David H., The Law Offices of, (AV) '53 '78 C.1036 B.A. L.426 J.D.**
**16255 Ventura Boulevard, Suite 704, 91436-2312**
**Telephone: 818-501-8355 Fax: 818-501-8465**
**URL: http://www.adoptlaw.com**
**Adoption, Probate, Family Law.**
***See Professional Biographies, ENCINO, CALIFORNIA***

Beardsley, Alan J. ..................... '56 '81 C.112 B.A. L.569 J.D. 16000 Ventura Blvd.
Bellin, Joseph L. ............................... '25 '53 C.112 A.B. P.O. Box 16152‡
Benson, Gordon S. ..................... '46 '72 C.112 B.A. L.426 J.D. 16830 Ventura Blvd.
**Bentler, Joan Ellen** '56 '81 C.112 A.B. L.426 J.D. National Automatic Merchandising Assn.
Bentley, Roger, (AV) ................. '22 '49 C&L.597 J.D. 16501 Ventura Blvd., Ste 300
Berger, Richard H., (AV) ................. '36 '62 C.112 B.S. L.1068 LL.B. [R.H.Berger]
Berger, Richard H., A Law Corp., (AV) ...................................... 16311 Ventura Blvd.
Berkley, Alyse G. .................... '54 '80 C.1077 B.A. L.809 J.D. 15910 Ventura Blvd.
Berkovitz and Schilit ........................... 16830 Ventura Blvd. (⊙Woodland Hills)
Berman, Martin M., (AV) ............... '34 '63 C&L.800 B.Ch.E., LL.B. [Berman&W.]⊙
**Berman, Steven J.** .................... '57 '85 C.1077 B.A. L.1137 J.D. [Aaronson&A.]
Berman & Weiss, (AV) 16055 Ventura Blvd., Suite 900 (⊙Palm Springs and Palm Desert)
**Bernsley, Mark**, (AV) ........................... '53 '79 C.1044 B.S. L.569 J.D. [M.Bernsley]
*SPECIAL AGENCIES: Staff Attorney, Office of Chief Counsel, Internal Revenue Service, Los Angeles District Counsel's Office (1978-1979).
*REPORTED CASES: Scar v. Commissioner, 814 F.2d 1363 (9th Cir. 1987).

**Bernsley, Mark, A Prof. Corp., Law Offices of, (AV)**
**First Financial Plaza, 16830 Ventura Boulevard, Suite 336, 91436**
**Telephone: 818-981-1776; 310-479-1776 Fax: 818-981-0156**
**Mark Bernsley.**
**Federal and State Tax Controversies. Civil and Criminal Tax Litigation. Business Transactions and Planning. Sales and Acquisitions of Closely Held Business.**

Bernstein, Barry S. ................... '53 '78 C.112 B.A. L.426 J.D. 16133 Ventura Blvd.
Berry, Dennis J. ....................... '52 '78 C.112 B.A. L.1095 J.D. 16133 Ventura Blvd.
Billick, William, (AV) '43 '72 C.309 B.A. L.813 J.D. Gen. Coun., Motion Picture Assoc. of Amer., Inc.
Binder, Barry R. ..................... '42 '72 C.112 B.S. L.1148 J.D. 16000 Ventura Blvd.
Birgel, Andreas, Jr., (BV) ........... '43 '76 C.1097 B.S. L.1095 J.D. 16000 Ventura Blvd.
**Black, Leonard D.**, (BV) .................. '39 '69 C.1077 B.S. L.426 J.D. [L.D.Black]
*PRACTICE AREAS: Business Litigation; Tort Litigation; Real Estate Litigation; Family Law.

**Black, Leonard D., A Professional Corporation, (BV)**
**16311 Ventura Boulevard, Suite 1260, 91436-2152**
**Telephone: 818-986-5680 Facsimile: 818-995-3422**
**Leonard D. Black.**
**Civil Litigation in all State and Federal Courts, including Business, Partnership, Educational Institutions, Construction, Real Property, Commercial, Tort and Significant Family Law Matters.**
***See Professional Biographies, ENCINO, CALIFORNIA***

**Blackman, Mark S.** ........................ '60 '85 C.112 B.A. L.426 J.D. [Alpert,B.&G.]
*PRACTICE AREAS: Bankruptcy/Creditors Rights; Business Law and General Litigation; Real Estate Litigation; Mobilehome Financing and Mobilehome Park Law.

**Blake, Barry A., (BV) '46 '76 C.1077 B.A. L.1095 J.D.**
**15760 Ventura Boulevard, Suite 700, 91436**
**Telephone: 818-990-1457 Fax: 818-990-4006**
**General Civil, Trial Practice in all California State and Federal Courts. Personal Injury, Wrongful Death, Landlord and Tenant and Creditor-Debtor Law.**
**Reference: Bank of America (Tarzana Branch).**
***See Professional Biographies, ENCINO, CALIFORNIA***

Blank, Eleanor, (A P.C.), (BV) ..... '39 '78 C.1077 B.A. L.1095 J.D. 16311 Ventura Blvd.
Bledstein, I. Mark, (BV) ................................................. '46 '71 [Bledstein&L.]
Bledstein & Lauber, (BV) ..................................................... 15915 Ventura Blvd.
Bleier, Elizabeth Ann ............... '45 '78 C.912 B.S. L.1148 J.D. 16130 Ventura Blvd.
**Blinder, Robert D.** ..................... '57 '85 C.112 B.S. L.809 J.D. [▣ Goldstein,G.&S.]
*PRACTICE AREAS: Workers Compensation Defense.
Blitstein, Lee A. ....................... '60 '89 C.1077 B.A. L.809 J.D. 15821 Ventura Blvd.
Blundo, Frank G., (BV) ............. '48 '78 C.602 A.B. L.1221 J.D. 15760 Ventura Blvd.

**Boldra & Klueger**
**(See Los Angeles)**

Bond, Dennis M. ........................... '38 '68 C.605 B.A. L.800 J.D. P.O. Box 261127‡
Bonin, Franklin A. ....................... '45 '72 C&L.262 B.S., J.D. 5758 Jamieson Ave.
Bookman, Lawrence E., (AV) ........................................ '45 '74 16501 Ventura Blvd.
Borenstein, Morton Philip ........... '43 '70 C.112 B.A. L.426 J.D. 16133 Ventura Blvd.
**Borska, Elliot F.** ........................ '54 '83 C.30 B.A. L.809 J.D. [Pearlman,B.&W.]
*PRACTICE AREAS: Workers Compensation Defense; Subrogation; Liability Defense; Employment Litigation.
Boyd, Kurt ......................................... '53 '79 C.112 B.S. L.809 J.D. [Boyd&E.]
Boyd & Ericksen ............................................................... 6345 Balboa Blvd.
Brand, Abraham ....................... '36 '76 C.112 B.S. L.1148 J.D. 3744 Montuso Pl.
Bratter, Jack E., A Law Corporation, (AV) '32 '61 C.112 B.S. L.1068 J.D. 16255 Ventura Blvd.
Braufman, James R. ................. '52 '78 C.112 B.A. L.990 J.D. 15915 Ventura Blvd.
Breen, Susan K. .................. '47 '91 C.1077 L.398 J.D. 15910 Ventura Blvd., 12th Fl.
Bregman, Joseph P., (AV) .................. '34 '64 C&L.912 A.B., J.D. 16133 Ventura Blvd.
Bregman, Theodore G., (BV) .............. '37 '70 C.605 B.A. L.1095 J.D. [T.G.Bregman]
Bregman, Theodore G., A Law Corp., (BV) ...................................... 16311 Ventura Blvd.
Brent, Philip D. .............................. '28 '52 C.563 B.B.A. L.569 J.D. [P.D.Brent]
**Brent, Robert L., (A Professional Corporation)**, (AV) '32 '67 C.112 B.S. L.800 J.D. [▣ Lewitt,H.H.S.M.&H.]
*PRACTICE AREAS: Arbitration.
Brent, Philip D., Professional Corporation ..................................... 16000 Ventura Blvd.
Brifman, Mark A., (BV) ............ '44 '77 C.1042 B.A. L.1068 J.D. 16133 Ventura Blvd.
Brimble, Philip J., (AV) ............ '50 '76 C.112 B.A. L.1068 J.D. 16000 Ventura Blvd.
Broker, Kenneth S. .................. '50 '76 C.1077 B.S. L.809 J.D. 16133 Ventura Blvd.
Bronson, Phillip I. ..................... '37 '63 C.112 A.B. L.1068 LL.B. 16530 Ventura Blvd.
**Brown, Dean S.** ........................ '63 '90 C.112 B.A. L.1148 J.D. [Pearlman,B.&W.]
*PRACTICE AREAS: Workers Compensation.
Brown, Jerry K. ....................... '42 '69 C.112 B.S. L.1068 J.D. 15915 Ventura Blvd.
**Brown, Michael D.**, (AV) ................ '46 '74 C.1109 B.A. L.809 J.D. [▣ Elliot,L.L.&S.]
*PRACTICE AREAS: Insurance Defense; Medical Malpractice Defense.
Brown, Roberta, (AV) .................. '42 '79 C.1019 B.A. L.776 J.D. 15760 Ventura Blvd.

**Brown, Edward R.**
**(See Oxnard)**

Brutzkus, Mark D. ............................ '59 '87 C.339 B.S. L.209 J.D. 16830 Ventura
Burge, John R. ........................... '65 '94 C.475 B.S. L.426 J.D. 16000 Ventura Blvd.
Burge, Robert L. ....................... '38 '72 C.112 B.S. L.1095 J.D. 15760 Ventura Blvd.
Burstein, Herbert ..................... '40 '66 C.563 B.A. L.1009 J.D. 16000 Ventura Blvd.
Calabria, Donald J. .................................................. '43 '69 16133 Ventura Blvd.
**Calvert, Camille** .......................... '65 '91 C&L.846 B.A., J.D. [▣ Stone&R.]
*PRACTICE AREAS: Insurance Defense Litigation; Premises Liability; Civil Appeals and Writs.
Camacho, Andy M. ............................ '39 '74 C.1097 B.A. L.809 4545 Encino Ave.
Camhi, Howard I. ...................... '62 '90 C.426 B.S. L.809 J.D. 16000 Ventura Blvd.
Candaux, David L. ........................ '48 '75 C.988 L.1095 J.D. 16133 Ventura Blvd.
Caplow, Sheldon R., (BV) .................... '24 '52 C.112 B.S. L.800 J.D. [S.R.Caplow]
Caplow, Sheldon R., Inc., A Prof. Corp., (BV) ............................ 15760 Ventura Blvd.
Carlson, Robert J. ................... '47 '75 C.1077 B.A. L.1095 J.D. 16133 Ventura Blvd.
Carlucci, Joseph Robert .................... '69 '94 C.112 B.A. L.426 J.D. [▣ Stein,H.L.&Y.]
Caton, Gilbert C., (BV) ..................... '41 '64 C&L.800 B.S.L., J.D. 16633 Ventura Blvd.
**Cecil, Thomas** ........................ '55 '83 C.800 B.A. L.770 J.D. [▣ Lewitt,H.H.S.M.&H.]
*PRACTICE AREAS: Personal Injury; Products Liability Law; Insurance Litigation.
Chegwidden, Jack L. .......................... '47 '75 C.1077 B.S. L.426 J.D. [J.L.Chegwidden]
Chegwidden, Jack L., A Professional Corporation ........................ 16830 Ventura Blvd.
Cheney, Brent G. ...................... '70 '95 C.800 B.S. L.861 J.D. 16501 Ventura Blvd.
Cheren, David H. ..................... '38 '69 C.112 B.A. L.999 J.D. 15915 Ventura Blvd.
Chernick, Wade J. .................. '60 '86 C.1077 B.A. L.426 J.D. 15760 Ventura Blvd.
Chesler, Mark ......................... '50 '77 C.112 B.A. L.426 J.D. 16530 Ventura Blvd.
Chesney, Stephen L. ........................... '59 '83 C.1077 B.S. L.426 J.D. [▣ Rosenthal&S.]
Chizever, Caroline .................... '46 '81 L.1095 J.D. Prof. of Law, Univ. of La Verne

CAA79P

CALIFORNIA—ENCINO MARTINDALE-HUBBELL LAW DIRECTORY 1997

Cobert, Joseph Maxwell, (A Professional Corporation) '47 '72
C.976 B.A. L.1065 J.D. [J.M.Cobert]
Cobert, Joseph M., A Professional Corporation ........................ 16027 Ventura Blvd.
**Cohen, Felise L.** .......................... '60 '91 C.1077 L.398 J.D. [ K.W.Dean]
*PRACTICE AREAS: Premises, Auto and Products.
Cohen, Harris L. .................. '59 '85 C.112 B.A. L.426 J.D. 5305 Andasol Ave.
Cohen, Joanne Polvy ........... '48 '79 C.112 B.A. L.1095 J.D. Chubb Group of Ins. Cos.
**Cohn, Richard A., (P.C.)** .......... '46 '71 C.1036 B.A. L.178 J.D. [ Karno,S.F.S.&W.]
*PRACTICE AREAS: Taxation; Estate Planning; Business Law.
Collins, Michael J. ................... '47 '75 C.1077 B.S. L.809 J.D. 16133 Ventura Blvd.
Collins, William E. ................ '44 '71 C.1077 B.A. L.426 J.D. 16133 Ventura Blvd.
**Condon, Patrick** ....................... '48 '89 C.373 B.A. L.1066 J.D. [Levinson&K.]
*PRACTICE AREAS: Appellate; Labor; Litigation; Law and Motion.
Connell, Fiona M. ................................ '66 '90 L.054 LL.B. 16501 Ventura Blvd.
**Connor, Ted A.** '62 '87
C.602 B.A. L.1049 J.D. [ Kolod&W.] (San Diego and Santa Ana)
Cooperman, Miles R. ............... '50 '75 C.112 B.A. L.990 J.D. 16000 Ventura Blvd.
Counter, J. Nicholas, III, (AV) '40 '67 C.174 B.S.E.E. L.813 J.D.
Pres., Alliance of Motion Picture & Television Producers
Cox, James E., (BV) .................. '46 '79 C.112 B.A. L.1148 J.D. 16130 Ventura Blvd.
**Crockett, William E.** ..................... '51 '82 C.893 B.A. L.910 J.D. [Greenberg&B.]
*PRACTICE AREAS: Real Estate Litigation; Business Litigation; Commercial Litigation.
Cunial, Gary D., (BV) .................. '37 '70 C.112 B.S. L.1095 J.D. 16530 Ventura Blvd.
**Dallinger, Timothy G.** ........................ '46 '72 C.112 B.A. L.800 J.D. [Marino&D.]
*PRACTICE AREAS: Business Acquisitions; Condominium and Homeowner Associations; Corporate, Business, Commercial and Property Transactional matters; Business, Commercial and Property Litigation matters.
Damiano, Dennis A. ........................ '45 '70 C&L.260 B.A., J.D. 16000 Ventura Blvd.
Daniels, Victor Joseph ................................ '55 '87 L.054 LL.B. 15760 Ventura Blvd.
Darvey, Frederick Lee ............ '41 '70 C.1077 B.A. L.1095 J.D. 15760 Ventura Blvd.
Davis, Greg ...................................... '62 '96 C.645 B.S. L.398 J.D. 16161 Ventura Blvd.
Daymude, Michael R. ............... '49 '74 C.112 A.B. L.1068 J.D. 16000 Ventura Blvd.

**Dean, Kristi Weiler, Law Offices of, (AV) '58 '84 C.267 B.S. L.990 J.D.**
**Suite 230, 6345 Balboa Boulevard, 91316**
**Telephone: 818-774-2131 FAX: 818-774-2141**
**Associates: Felise L. Cohen; Raymond J. Feinberg; Ryan M. Herron.**
**Civil Litigation including Personal Injury, Products Broker and Agent EEO Liability, Medical and Dental Malpractice, Insurance, Premises Liability, Business Litigation Defense and Construction Law.**
**Representative Clients: Topa Insurance; JMB Realty Corp.; The Bekins Co.; AMFAC Resorts; Schifrin, Gagnon and Dickey; AIMS; Alexsis Risk Management, Inc.; Golden Bear Insurance Co.**
*See Professional Biographies, ENCINO, CALIFORNIA*

Dem, Stephen P. .............................. '45 '72 C.1077 B.A. L.1095 J.D. 15915 Ventura Blvd.
Demarest, John A. ................................. '60 '86 C.907 B.A. L.809 J.D. [ Stein,H.L.&Y.]
Dembicer, Melissa E. ........ '59 '92 C.800 B.A. L.809 J.D. 15910 Ventura Blvd., 12th Fl.
deMontesquiou, Paul A., (BV) ........... '52 '78 C.800 A.B. L.1065 J.D. [McCulloch&d.]
Desimone, Salvatore ................ '45 '76 C.1097 B.A. L.1137 J.D. 16530 Ventura Blvd.
Deutsch, Eadie F. ......... '21 '49 C.597 B.S. L.426 LL.B. Prof. of Law, Univ. of La Verne
Deutsch, Lawrence H. .............................. '31 '57 C&L.800 J.D. 16161 Ventura Blvd.
Diamond, Donald ............. '29 '56 C.477 B.S. L.912 LL.B. 16133 Ventura Blvd. (Pat.)
Doberman, Jeffrey J. ............... '53 '79 C.1077 B.A. L.1136 J.D. 16133 Ventura Blvd.
Doctrow, Sherman, (AV) ............ '33 '59 C.112 B.A. L.1068 J.D. 16255 Ventura Blvd.
Donner, Michael ........................... '36 '61 C.4 B.A. L.569 LL.B. 16311 Ventura Blvd.
Dorcy, R. Wayne ......................... '56 '85 C.1077 B.A. L.426 J.D. 15501 Millbank St.
**Dorenfeld, David K.** ..................... '62 '89 C.1077 B.A. L.1148 J.D. [Staitman,S.&T.]
*PRACTICE AREAS: Insurance Defense; Insurance Coverage; General Civil Litigation; Bad Faith; Construction Defect.
Dresben, Fred C. .................... '50 '77 C.1077 B.A. L.1095 J.D. 16133 Ventura Blvd.
Dymond, Alan L. .............................. '34 '76 C.061 L.1095 J.D. 16830 Ventura Blvd.
Edelberg, Sherwin C. .......................... '36 '61 C.1016 L.144 J.D. 15915 Ventura Blvd.
Edwards, James C. '54 '86
C.112 B.A. L.1148 J.D. Asst. Gen. Coun., Western Gen. Ins. Co.
Edzant, Barry L. .................... '61 '89 C.1077 B.A. L.426 J.D. 16633 Ventura Blvd.
Edzant, Jack ............................................................ '27 '68 L.1095 J.D. [J.Edzant]
Edzant, Jack, Law Offices of, A Professional Law Corporation ........ 16633 Ventura Blvd.
Ehrlich, Abraham ................................ '22 '71 C.112 L.1095 J.D. 16501 Ventura Blvd.
Eisenhart, Gary N. .............................. '48 '75 C.102 B.S. L.724 J.D. 6345 Balboa Blvd.
Eisenman, James M. ................ '52 '78 C.112 A.B. L.1068 J.D. 16000 Ventura Blvd.
Eisner, Donald A. ................ '43 '88 C.923 Ph.D. L.1136 J.D. 16133 Ventura Blvd.
Elken, Cassandra S. ............................ '58 '84 C.454 B.A. L.1202 J.D. [Weissman&W.]
Elkins, Staci E. ..................... '66 '91 C.112 B.A. L.1068 J.D. 5200 White Oak
**Elliot, D. Scott** .................... '52 '77 C.1077 B.A. L.809 J.D. [Elliot,L.L.&S.]
*PRACTICE AREAS: Insurance Defense; Medical Malpractice Defense.

**Elliot, Lamb, Leibl & Snyder, (AV)**
**16501 Ventura Boulevard Suite 301, 91436**
**Telephone: 818-380-0123; 310-553-5767 Fax: 818-380-0124**
**Michael V. Lamb; Michael R. Snyder; Loren S. Leibl; D. Scott Elliot; Rebecca J. Hogue;—Linda Ostrin; Jason J. Scupine; Michael J. Van Dyke; Cindy A. Shapiro. Of Counsel: Michael D. Brown.**
**Civil Litigation. Insurance Defense and Medical Malpractice Defense.**
**Redlands, California Office: 101 East Redlands Boulevard, Suite 285, 92373. Telephone: 909-792-8861. Fax: 909-798-6997.**
**Orange County Office: 333 South Anita Drive, Suite 660, Orange, California, 92668. Telephone: 714-978-6255. Facsimile: 714-978-9087.**
*See Professional Biographies, ENCINO, CALIFORNIA*

Ellis, David L., (A Prof. Law Corp.), (AV) '42 '68
C.999 L.809 LL.B. 15760 Ventura Blvd.
Ericksen, Gaylen C. ......................... '46 '78 C.352 B.A. L.1136 J.D. [Boyd&E.]
Ezra, Robert .............................................. '47 '76 C.209 B.S. L.426 J.D. [R.Ezra]
Ezra, Robert, A Professional Corporation ................................ 16830 Ventura Blvd.
Fabrick, Myrna T. ......................... '39 '91 C.112 B.A. L.426 J.D. 17980 Medley Dr.
Fair, Stephen C. ..................... '45 '72 C.112 B.A. L.426 J.D. 16055 Ventura Blvd.
Fassberg, Wendy J. .................. '56 '79 C.112 B.A. L.426 J.D. 17514 Venturn Blvd.
Feder, Harvey L. .................. '35 '61 C.112 A.B. L.1068 LL.B. 16133 Ventura Blvd.
Feinberg, Allan S. ................. '49 '75 C.112 B.S. L.1068 J.D. 16000 Ventura Blvd.
**Feinberg, Raymond J.** ........................ '51 '81 C.94 B.A. L.990 J.D. [ K.W.Dean]
*PRACTICE AREAS: Medical Negligence; Premises Auto and Products; Construction.
Feinberg, William A., (AV) .................... '30 '53 C.999 L.426 J.D. [Feinberg,G.&W.]
Feinberg, Gottlieb & Waller, a Professional Corporation, (AV) ........ 15760 Ventura Blvd.
Felding, Daniel G., Jr. ................. '50 '75 C.1077 B.S. L.809 J.D. 15760 Ventura Blvd.

**Feldman, Stephen M., Law Offices of '50 '75 C.800 B.S. L.809 J.D.**
**15915 Ventura Boulevard Suite 201, 91436**
**Telephone: 818-907-0334 Fax: 818-907-9056**
***PRACTICE AREAS: Business Litigation; Corporate Law; Franchising Law; Probate and Estate Planning; Real Estate Transactions.**
(This Listing Continued)



**Feldman, Stephen M., Law Offices of (Continued)**
**Business Litigation, Business, Personal Injury, Real Estate, Probate/Estate Planning, Business Transactions. Franchising.**

Feldun, Joseph L., (AV) ............... '54 '82 C.800 B.A. L.809 J.D. 15910 Ventura Blvd.
**Felton, James R.** ........................... '63 '88 C.1036 B.A. L.1068 J.D. [Greenberg&B.]
*PRACTICE AREAS: Commercial and Real Estate Litigation; Bankruptcy and Insolvency Related Matters.
**Fensten, Allan M.** ......................... '57 '85 C.112 B.A. L.61 J.D. [ Goldstein,G.&S.]
*PRACTICE AREAS: Workers Compensation.
Fenton, Milton ...................... '22 '49 C.112 B.A. L.800 J.D. 15760 Ventura Blvd.‡
Fenton, Robert L. ................................ '49 '73 C.1042 B.A. L.426 J.D. [Fenton&F.]
Fenton & Fenton .............................................................. 15760 Ventura Blvd.
Ferrone, John A. ............................................................ '65 '92 [ Sparagna&S.]
Ferrone, Paul F. ............................................................ '63 '95 [ Sparagna&S.]
Fichter, Vin A. ..................... '44 '72 C.629 B.S. L.1068 J.D. 16830 Ventura Blvd.
Fields, Howard M., (AV) ..................... '51 '76 C.112 B.A. L.809 J.D. [Fields&F.]
Fields, Janet ............................................ '56 '85 C.1078 B.A. L.1227 J.D. [Fields&F.]
Fields & Fields, (AV) ........................................................ 15821 Ventura Blvd.
Fink, Steven B. ..................... '51 '77 C.112 B.A. L.809 J.D. 16701 Ashley Oaks
Finkel, Robert Louis, (BV) .... '30 '55 C.813 B.S. L.1068 J.D. 16055 Ventura Blvd. (Pat.)
Finley, George W. ................... '47 '73 C.112 B.A. L.1068 J.D. 16000 Ventura Blvd.
Finn, Raymond S. ................ '36 '62 C.112 B.S. L.1068 LL.B. 15760 Ventura Blvd.
Flam, Rick M., (AV) .............................. '46 '72 C&L.800 B.A., J.D. 16000 Ventura Blvd.
Flame, Philip, (AV) .................. '42 '68 C.112 B.A. L.1068 J.D. 15821 Ventura Blvd.
Fleischman, Harold S., (AV) ........ '42 '68 C.112 B.A. L.1068 J.D. 15915 Ventura Blvd.
Flier, Theodore S. ..................... '27 '53 C.102 L.1009 LL.B. 15821 Ventura Blvd.
**Florence, Barry G.** ......................... '53 '81 C.426 B.S. L.1136 J.D. [Shelden,K.R.&F.]
Fogelman, Gerald L., (BV) ......... '48 '73 C.1077 B.A. L.809 J.D. 16133 Ventura Blvd.
Fonstein, Harold, (AV) .............. '27 '58 C.800 B.S. L.809 LL.B. 16133 Ventura Blvd.
Forer, Herbert L., (AV) ..................... '30 '63 C.102 L.426 J.D. 16710 Alginet Place‡
Foster, Richard M, ............................. '51 '80 C&L.1077 J.D. 16055 Ventura Blvd.
Frailich, Stephen M., (P.C.) ................ '52 '80 C.494 B.A. L.1095 J.D. [Frailich&G.]
Frailich & Green, A Ptrnshp. incl. Prof. Law Corp. ...................... 16255 Ventura Blvd.
Frakes, Robert J. .................. '39 '67 C.1077 B.A. L.426 LL.B. 16055 Ventura Blvd.
Francis, J. Patrick, (AV) .... '25 '62 C.800 A.B. L.426 LL.B. 15915 Ventura Blvd., Pthse 1
Frank, Robert J. ..................... '48 '78 C.831 B.A. L.809 J.D. 18075 Ventura Blvd.
Franklin, Roger A. ................. '41 '67 C.112 B.A. L.426 LL.B. 16000 Ventura Blvd.
Frantz, Barbara A. ................. '52 '77 C.112 B.A. L.1049 J.D. 16133 Ventura Blvd.
Freed, Fredric J., (AV) ............. '34 '63 C&L.659 B.S.Ec., LL.B. 3538 Caribeth Dr.‡
Freeman, Lawrence P. ............................ '46 '71 C.1097 B.A. L.426 J.D. [Freeman&F.]
Freeman & Freeman .......................................................... 16027 Ventura Blvd.

**Fried, Alexander '56 '80 C.112 A.B. L.309 J.D.**
**16027 Ventura, Suite 450, 91436-2437**
**Telephone: 818-380-0025 FAX: 818-382-3445**
**Email: alexfried@earthlink.net**
**Estate Planning, Probate and Tax Law, Business Transactions.**

Fried, Dennis W. ............................. '51 '93 C.1097 B.A. L.398 J.D. [ Rosenthal&S.]
**Friedman, Kenneth L., (A Professional Corporation)** '51 '76
C.112 B.A. L.1068 J.D. [Karno,S.F.S.&W.]
Friedman, Wallace ................ '31 '68 C.1097 A.B. L.1095 J.D. 16255 Ventura Blvd.
Frolich, John N. ........................ '15 '37 C&L.724 B.S., LL.B. 16501 Ventura Blvd.
Gach, Andrew C. ................... '47 '74 C.112 A.B. L.1068 J.D. 16000 Ventura Blvd.
Gaines, Kenneth S. .............................. '45 '71 C.112 B.S L.1065 J.D. [K.S.Gaines]
Gaines, Kenneth S., A Prof. Corp. ........................................ 16501 Ventura Blvd.
**Galanti, David M.** ........................... '54 '84 C.597 B.S.J. L.1119 J.D. [ Spile&S.]
*PRACTICE AREAS: Insurance Coverage; Insurance Bad Faith; Litigation; Insurance Defense; Appellate Practice.
Galen, Jeffrey Michael ............. '58 '88 C.1077 B.A. L.1136 J.D. 16255 Ventura Blvd.
**Galer, Deborah K.** ......................... '60 '85 C.800 B.A. L.426 J.D. [ Staitman,S.&T.]
*PRACTICE AREAS: Civil Litigation.
Gantman, Morton, (AV) ........................ '34 '60 C.112 B.A. L.800 J.D. [Gantman&G.]
Gantman, Seymour, (AV) ...................... '34 '60 C.112 B.A. L.800 J.D. [Gantman&G.]
Gantman & Gantman, (AV) ................................................ 16133 Ventura Blvd.
Garry, Lee A. .............. '39 '65 C.112 B.S. L.800 LL.B. 16530 Ventura Blvd., Ste 208
Gart, Ronald A. ..................................... '54 '83 C.112 B.S.B.A. L.398 J.D. [Warden&G.]
**Garwacki, Ray D., Jr.** ....................... '55 '81 C.940 B.A. L.990 J.D. [Hemar,R.&G.]
*PRACTICE AREAS: Creditors Rights; Banking; Equipment Leasing; Bankruptcy and Secured Transactions.
Geffen, David G. ............... '58 '87 C.94 B.S. L.426 J.D. 16027 Ventura Blvd., #420
Georges, Carol M. ....................... '— '90 C.112 M.A. L.426 J.D. 16133 Ventura Blvd.
Geren, David K. ..................... '48 '74 C.112 B.A. L.809 J.D. 15760 Ventura Blvd.
Geren, Jeffrey L. ..................... '50 '77 C.112 B.A. L.1095 J.D. 15915 Ventura Blvd.
**Gertler, Tamar D.** ..................... '67 '94 C.1036 B.A. L.990 J.D. [Gillin,S.A.G.&S.]
*PRACTICE AREAS: Estate Planning; Probate; Conservatorships; Tax Planning.
Gerwer, Carole Gordon, (AV) ....... '41 '79 C.112 B.A. L.1095 J.D. 16000 Ventura Blvd.
Gessin, Joel B. ...................... '47 '79 C.768 B.A. L.809 J.D. 16200 Ventura Blvd.
Geyer, Mark M., (A Prof. Law Corp.) ................ '50 '75 L.809 J.D. 16027 Ventura Blvd.

**Gibson, John A. C. '44 '90 C.846 M.A. L.273 J.D.**
**16000 Ventura Boulevard, Suite 1010, 91436**
**Telephone: 818-382-6480 FAX: 818-382-6482**
***LANGUAGES: French, German.**
***PRACTICE AREAS: Corporate; Regulatory; Administrative; Alcoholic Beverage.**
**Alcoholic Beverage Licensing and Compliance, General Business and Corporate.**
*See Professional Biographies, ENCINO, CALIFORNIA*

**Gillin, Scott, Alperstein, Glantz & Simon, A Law Corporation. (AV)**
**15760 Ventura Boulevard, Suite 1520, 91436-3002**
**Telephone: 818-501-3100 Fax: 818-377-3600**
**Nathan E. Gillin (1908-1996); S. Dell Scott; Glenn M. Alperstein; Jack C. Glantz; Joel M. Simon; Michael I. Glantz; Tamar D. Gertler.**
**Business Law, Corporate Law, Contract Law, Litigation, Estate Gift Planning, Taxation Law, Trust Law, Elder Law, Estate Planning, Probate, Commercial and Family Law.**

Glantz, Fred G., (BV) ............... '39 '66 C.112 B.A. L.426 J.D. 16133 Ventura Blvd.
**Glantz, Jack C.**, (AV) .................. '37 '62 C.112 B.S. L.1068 J.D. [Gillin,S.A.G.&S.]
*PRACTICE AREAS: Estate Planning, Probate & Trust Law (70%, 400); Taxation Law (25%, 175); General Corporate Law (5%, 150).
**Glantz, Michael I.** ..................... '62 '87 C.112 B.S. L.1068 J.D. [Gillin,S.A.G.&S.]
Glanz, Alfred ...................... '47 '80 C.1077 B.A. L.1095 J.D. 16530 Ventura Blvd.
Glass, Michael J. .................................. '56 '82 C.112 B.A. L.426 J.D. [Stein,H.L.&Y.]
**Glazener, Lisa W.**, (AV) ...................... '53 '78 C.813 B.A. L.426 J.D. [Alpert,B.&G.]
*PRACTICE AREAS: Civil Trial Law; Appellate Practice.
Glushon, Eugene E., (BV) ................ '27 '53 C.112 B.A. L.800 J.D. 16149 Huston St.
Goeckner, Gregory Paul '55 '82 C.339 B.S. L.976 J.D.
Dep. Dir. & Spec. Coun., Motion Picture Assn.
Goichman, William A. .............. '31 '55 C.831 B.S. L.659 LL.B. 16161 Ventura Blvd.
Gold, Arnold Barry, (AV) ............................ '44 '72 C.1077 B.A. L.1095 J.D. [A.B.Gold]
Gold, Arnold Barry, A P.C., (AV) .......................................... 15821 Ventura Blvd.
Golden, Alan R., (BV) ........... '38 '64 C.112 B.S. L.1068 LL.B. 16830 Ventura Blvd.

**Goldfarb, Sturman & Averbach**
(See Los Angeles)

Goldin, Howard S., (AV) ............ '21 '44 C.113 A.B. L.800 5353-B White Oak Ave.‡
**Goldman, Amy L.** ........................ '— '88 C.112 B.A. L.426 J.D. [Plotkin,R.&N.]
*PRACTICE AREAS: Bankruptcy Law; Insolvency Law; Receivership Law.
Goldman, Gene C. ................ '48 '78 C.415 B.A. L.1095 J.D. 18075 Ventura Blvd.

**Goldman, Martin B.**
(See Pasadena)

Goldsborough, Nicholas Ridgely ...... '60 '88 C.893 B.A. L.1148 J.D. 16951 Esquira Pl.‡
Goldsobel, Donald G., (BV) ......... '38 '63 C.30 B.S. L.904 LL.B. 15915 Ventura Blvd.
Goldstein, Elise E. .................. '52 '78 C.112 B.A. L.809 J.D. 16000 Ventura Blvd.
Goldstein, Jerold V. ............... '41 '66 C.112 B.A. L.1068 LL.B. 16133 Ventura Blvd.
Goldstein, Murray ...................... '19 '50 C.112 L.809 LL.B. 16000 Ventura Blvd.
Goldstein, Richard, (A P.C.), (BV) '39 '69 C.800 B.A. L.1095 LL.B.
15915 Ventura Blvd.
**Goldstein, Robert H.** ................. '42 '67 C.112 B.A. L.1068 LL.B. [Goldstein,G.&S.]
Goldstein, William I., (BV) '42 '67
C.1077 B.A. L.1068 J.D. 15760 Ventura Blvd., 16th Fl.

**Goldstein, Gurvitz & Silver, (AV)**
**15821 Ventura Boulevard, Suite 600, 91436-2915**
**Telephone: 818-788-3220 Telefax: 818-788-9328**
**Robert H. Goldstein; Ron F. Gurvitz; Scott Z. Silver;—David F. Marlowe; Ronald H. Stillman; Scott D. Miller; Robert D. Blinder; Edwina J. Heine; Allan M. Fensten; Jessica Lille Lemoine; Cathryn R. Pine; Heather Bergerson Weiss.**
**Workers Compensation Defense, Defense of General Civil Liability, Wrongful Termination, Employment Discrimination, Claims under the American Disabilities Act.**
**Representative Clients: Kockheed-Martin Co.; Paramount Pictures Corp.; Time Warner Entertainment Co.; Kaiser Foundation Hospitals; Nordstrom Inc.**

Golstein, Brad I ......................... '56 '84 C.112 A.B. L.1068 J.D. 17522 Collins St.
Goodfriend, Mark E. ....... '53 '81 C.112 A.B. L.1066 J.D. [Krane&S.] (©Woodland Hills)
Goodfriend, Norman L., Jr. ........... '45 '78 C.162 B.A. L.1095 J.D. 16661 Ventura Blvd.
**Goodman, Andrew**, (AV) ............... '59 '84 C.1168 B.A. L.426 J.D. [Greenberg&B.]
*PRACTICE AREAS: Commercial Litigation; Real Estate Litigation; Bankruptcy; Insolvency Related Matters.
Goodman, Diane M. .......................... '58 '84 L.1095 J.D. 15915 Ventura Blvd.
Goolsby, Michael L. .............. '66 '92 C.112 B.A. L.1065 J.D. Chubb Group of Ins. Cos.
**Gordon, Samuel W.**, (AV) ............. '46 '72 C.112 B.A. L.426 J.D. [Hemar,R.&G.]
*PRACTICE AREAS: Creditors Rights; Banking; Equipment Leasing; Bankruptcy and Secured Transactions.
Gottlieb, Mark S. ........................ '49 '77 C.112 B.A. L.809 J.D. [Feinberg,G.&W.]
**Grad, Laleaque** '70 '95 C&L.112 B.A., J.D.
[Ⓐ Kolod&W.] (©San Diego and Santa Ana)
Graham, Lewis W. ....... '26 '53 C.339 B.S.M.E. L.365 M.P.L. 16000 Ventura Blvd. (Pat.)
Graham, Michael R. ............................................ '41 '74 L.981 LL.B. 17652 Rancho St.
Gratz, Mitchell J., (AV) ................... '30 '56 C.813 A.B. L.174 LL.B. [M.J.Gratz]
Gratz, Mitchell J., Law Corp., (AV) ........................................ 16055 Ventura Blvd.
Green, Alvin B., (AV) ........................................ '29 '61 C.800 L.809 LL.B. [Green&K.]
Green, Harry B., (AV) ................... '42 '72 C.36 B.A. L.809 J.D. 16055 Ventura Blvd.‡
Green, Stephen S., (P.C.) ......................... '46 '72 C.912 B.S. L.213 J.D. [Frailich&G.]
Green & Krupp, (AV) .............................................. 16601 Ventura Blvd., Fl. 4
**Greenberg, Arthur A.**, (AV) ............. '51 '76 C.112 A.B. L.426 J.D. [Greenberg&B.]

**Greenberg & Bass, (AV)**
**16000 Ventura Boulevard Suite 1000, 91436-2730**
**Telephone: 818-382-6200**
**Members of Firm: Arthur A. Greenberg; Robert D. Bass; William E. Crockett; Gary K. Salomons; Andrew Goodman; James R. Felton; Harold Gutenberg.**
**General Practice.**
*See Professional Biographies, ENCINO, CALIFORNIA*

**Greenup, Geoffrey H.** ................. '54 '82 C.112 B.A. L.426 J.D. [Pearlman,B.&W.]
*TRANSACTIONS: Moran v. Bradford Bldg. Maintenance.
*PRACTICE AREAS: Workers Compensation Law; Criminal Victim Restitution.
Greenwald, Philip C. ............. '34 '63 C.112 B.S. L.1068 LL.B. 16147 Royal Oak Rd.
Gregory, James D. ........................... '49 '75 C.112 B.A. L.800 J.D. [J.D.Gregory]
Gregory, James D., A Professional Corporation .............................. 6345 Balboa Blvd.
**Greiner, Rodger S.** .................... '61 '89 C.1111 B.A. L.990 J.D. [Ⓐ Staitman,S.&T.]
*PRACTICE AREAS: Insurance Defense; Insurance Coverage; Personal Injury; Product Liability; Premises Liability.
Greinetz, Earl T. '30 '54 C&L.208 B.A., LL.B.
(adm. in CO; not adm. in CA) 16901 Escalon Dr.‡
Grenert, Gerald T., (AV) ............ '30 '55 C.682 B.A. L.705 J.D. 16133 Ventura Blvd.
Griffin, Susanne A. .................. '47 '87 C.112 B.A. L.809 J.D. 15915 Ventura Blvd.
**Gross, Mark P.** ........................................ '60 '85 C&L.260 B.S., J.D. [Alpert,B.&G.]
*PRACTICE AREAS: Family Law.

**Grossman, Allan F., (AV) '32 '56 C.597 B.S.L. L.800 LL.B.**
**Suite 304 Encino Law Center, 15915 Ventura Boulevard, 91436**
**Telephone: 818-990-8200 FAX: 818-990-4616**
**Trial and Appellate Practice in State and Federal Courts.**
**Reference: First Los Angeles Bank, Woodland Hills.**
*See Professional Biographies, ENCINO, CALIFORNIA*

Grubb, Stephen ........................... '19 '50 C.543 L.273 LL.B. 15840 Ventura Blvd.
Gruen, Lisa Parel ...................... '60 '84 C.477 B.A. L.912 J.D. [Ⓐ Stein,H.L.&Y.]
**Gurvitz, Ron F.**, (AV) .................... '54 '80 C.112 B.A. L.809 J.D. [Goldstein,G.&S.]
*PRACTICE AREAS: Tort Law (40%); WOrkers Compensation Law (50%); Wrongful Termination-Employment at Will (10%).
**Gutenberg, Harold** ...................... '32 '72 C.912 A.B. L.809 J.D. [Greenberg&B.]
Gyger, Robert G. ........................... '21 '53 C.800 L.809 LL.B. 4326 Coronet Dr.‡
Haberman, Stanley E., (AV) ............ '33 '58 C.112 B.S. L.800 LL.B. 3730 Westfall Dr.
Hackman, Jonathan I. ............. '47 '75 C.1169 B.A. L.426 J.D. 16133 Ventura Blvd.
**Hackman, Michael**, (AV) ......... '41 '68 C.918 B.A. L.1068 J.D. [Lewitt,H.H.S.M.&H.]
*PRACTICE AREAS: Taxation; Business Law; Estate Planning; Health Care.
Halem, Sydney ......................... '19 '64 C.102 A.B. L.800 J.D. 16953 Cotter Pl.‡
Hall, John Wendell ................ '49 '80 C.221 B.A. L.990 J.D. 6345 Balboa Blvd.
**Hamilton, David S.** ................. '55 '80 C.112 B.A. L.426 J.D. [Ⓒ Lewitt,H.H.S.M.&H.]
*PRACTICE AREAS: Business Law; Securities Law.
**Handy, Thomas E.**, (AV) .......... '43 '73 C.112 B.A. L.1049 J.D. [Ⓐ Pearlman,B.&W.]
*PRACTICE AREAS: Workers Compensation.
**Harlan, Barry T.**, (AV) ........... '43 '68 C.112 B.A. L.426 J.D. [Lewitt,H.H.S.M.&H.]
*PRACTICE AREAS: Family Law; Business Litigation.
Harvey, Arthur ...................... '29 '53 C.188 B.S. L.569 LL.B. 5243 Yarmouth Ave.
Hatkoff, Bruce A. ........................... '50 '75 C.1044 B.A. L.809 J.D. [B.A.Hatkoff]
Hatkoff, Bruce A., A Law Corporation ........................................ 16633 Ventura Blvd.
Hausman, Jeffrey M., (AV) ................ '48 '73 C.112 B.A. L.426 J.D. [Hausman&S.]
Hausman & Sosa, (AV) .............................................................. 16530 Ventura Blvd.
Hawley, Mark S. .................. '53 '80 C.112 A.B. L.1068 J.D. 16530 Ventura Blvd.
**Heald, Daniel A., IV** ...................... '58 '84 C.154 B.A. L.464 J.D. [Hemar,R.&G.]

**Healy, Kevin J.** '62 '92
C.1036 B.A. L.61 J.D. [Ⓐ Kolod&W.] (©San Diego and Santa Ana)
**Heine, Edwina J.** ........................................ '49 '82 L.398 J.D. [Ⓐ Goldstein,G.&S.]
*PRACTICE AREAS: Workers Compensation (100%).
**Heller, Stephen H.**, (AV) ....................... '47 '74 C.112 B.A. L.61 J.D. [S.H.Heller]

**Heller, Stephen H., A Professional Corporation, (AV)** BB
**16830 Ventura Boulevard, Suite B, 91436-1714**
**Telephone: 818-995-4646**
**Stephen H. Heller.**
**Personal Injury Litigation.**
*See Professional Biographies, ENCINO, CALIFORNIA*

**Hemar, Richard P.**, (BV) ................ '44 '70 C.112 B.S. L.1068 J.D. [Hemar,R.&G.]
*LANGUAGES: Polish.
*PRACTICE AREAS: Creditors Rights; Banking; Equipment Leasing; Bankruptcy and Secured Transactions.

**Hemar, Rousso & Garwacki, (AV)**
**15910 Ventura Boulevard, 12th Floor, 91436-2829**
**Telephone: 818-501-3800 FAX: 818-501-2985**
**Members of Firm: Richard P. Hemar; Martin J. Rousso; Ray D. Garwacki, Jr.; Stephen E. Jenkins; Daniel A. Heald, IV; Samuel W. Gordon.**
**Commercial Litigation, Creditors Rights, Banking, Equipment Leasing, Bankruptcy and Secured Transactions.**
**Reference: City National Bank (Westwood Office).**
*See Professional Biographies, ENCINO, CALIFORNIA*

**Herron, Ryan M.** ................................ '67 '94 C.112 B.A. L.802 J.D. [Ⓐ K.W.Dean]
*PRACTICE AREAS: Construction.
Hiestand, Herbert H., Jr., (AV) ........... '29 '59 C.112 B.S. L.1068 LL.B. [Hiestand&B.]
Hiestand & Brandt, Inc., (AV) ........................................................ 5440 Louise Ave.
Hiller, Michael D., (Inc.), (BV) ..................... '38 '62 C&L.800 LL.B. 16055 Ventura Blvd.
Hiller, Simon R. .......................................... '44 '73 C.112 B.A. L.426 J.D. Dep. Dist. Atty.
Hirschman, Robert .............................. '38 '66 C.1077 B.S. L.1065 J.D. 15821 Ventura Blvd.

**Hodges, Clinton M., (AV) '37 '75 C.1056 B.A. L.1148 J.D.**
**16830 Ventura Boulevard, Suite 506, 91436**
**Telephone: 818-990-0707 FAX: 818-990-0425**
***REPORTED CASES: Barme v. Wood, (1984) 37 Cal.3d 174, 207 Cal. Rptr. 816; Kramer v. Cedu Foundation (1979) 93 Cal.App.3d 1, 155 Cal. Rptr. 522; Marathon Steel Company v. Tilley Steel, Inc., (1977) 66 Cal.App.3d 413, 136 Cal. Rptr. 73; Kelly v. Trans Globe Travel (1976) 60 Cal.App.3d 195, 131 Cal. Rptr. 488.**
**Civil Litigation, Personal Injury Defense.**

**Hoefflin, Richard M.**, (AV) ....... '49 '74 C.1077 B.S. L.426 J.D. [Lewitt,H.H.S.M.&H.]
*PRACTICE AREAS: Business Litigation; Real Estate Law; Estate Planning.

**Hoffman, Norman J., Inc., A Professional Corporation**
(See Los Angeles)

Hoffmann, James E., (AV) ......... '51 '80 C.172 B.A. L.1095 J.D. 15821 Ventura Blvd.

**Hoffmann, James W. E.**
(See Los Angeles)

**Hogan, Cynthia Elkins** ............. '60 '86 C.1077 B.S. L.809 J.D. [Ⓐ Pearlman,B.&W.]
*PRACTICE AREAS: Employment Law Management.
**Hogue, Rebecca J.** ........................ '54 '84 C.112 B.A. L.1137 J.D. [Elliot,L.L.&S.]©
*PRACTICE AREAS: Insurance Defense; Medical Malpractice Defense.
Holler, Blake M. ...................... '61 '90 C.112 B.A. L.809 J.D. 16830 Ventura Blvd.

**Horvitz & Levy**
(See Los Angeles)

Huffer, John C. .......... '32 '57 C.473 A.B. L.851 LL.B. Prof. of Law, Univ. of La Verne
**Hughes, Charles M.** .................... '18 '47 C.112 B.A. L.800 LL.B. [Ⓒ Alpert,B.&G.]

**Hughes, J. Michael, (AV) '42 '67 C&L.1049 B.A., J.D.**
**Suite 700, 15760 Ventura Boulevard, 91436**
**Telephone: 818-905-7301 Facsimile: 818-907-6848**
**General Civil Trial and Appellate Practice in all State and Federal Courts. Real Estate, General Business, Corporate, Health Care and Probate Law.**
*See Professional Biographies, ENCINO, CALIFORNIA*

**Hyman, Andrew W.**
(See Los Angeles)

**Hymes, Larry S.**, (AV) ........................ '53 '77 C.112 B.S. L.1049 J.D. [Anker&H.]
*PRACTICE AREAS: Trusts; Probate and Estate Planning; Corporate; Tax Law.
Iezza, Nick I. ...................................... '61 '87 C.112 B.A. L.990 J.D. [Spiwak&I.]
Jelin, Beth Maloney ................................ '53 '81 C.705 A.B. L.1292 J.D. [Jelin&J.]
Jelin, Frederick T. ..................................... '48 '82 C.705 B.A. L.1292 J.D. [Jelin&J.]
Jelin & Jelin ........................................................................... 16350 Ventura Blvd.
**Jenkins, Stephen E.** ......................... '55 '81 C.1042 B.S. L.1137 J.D. [Hemar,R.&G.]
Jinnah, Al. H. ...................................... '39 '81 C.061 L.028 LL.B. [Jinnah&J.]
Jinnah, Leila E. ......................................... '46 '89 C.788 B.A. L.398 J.D. [Jinnah&J.]
Jinnah and Jinnah ........................................................................ 5435 Balboa Blvd.
Johnson, Kenneth A. ...................................... '42 '75 L.1221 J.D. 16055 Ventura Blvd.
Johnson, Paul H. .......... '37 '66 C.426 B.S. L.809 LL.B. 15760 Ventura Blvd., 16th Fl.
Johnston, Thomas V. ........................ '49 '78 C.309 A.B. L.1066 J.D. [T.V.Johnston]
Johnston, Thomas V., P.C. ....................................... 15915 Ventura Blvd., Penthouse Two
Jordan, James F. ................... '50 '77 C.1077 B.A. L.1095 J.D. 16133 Ventura Blvd.
Joyce, Stephen M. ................ '45 '76 C.339 B.S. L.1095 J.D. 16530 Ventura Blvd.
Kahanowitch, Richard ........................ '53 '81 C.112 B.A. L.1137 J.D. [Zimmerman&K.]
Kahn, William J. ................... '66 '90 C.112 B.A. L.426 J.D. 16133 Ventura Blvd.
**Kammer, Kevin David** ............ '59 '86 C.1077 B.A. L.426 J.D. [Ⓐ Karno,S.F.S.&W.]
Kamran, Kia ............................... '68 '96 C.1077 B.S. L.809 J.D. 5048 Gloria Ave.
Kaplan, Dina Coster ................... '55 '80 C.035 B.A. L.1095 J.D. 16133 Ventura Blvd.
**Kaplan, Steven G.** ............................ '62 '88 C.112 B.A. L.426 J.D. [Levinson&K.]
*PRACTICE AREAS: Business and Real Estate Litigation; Business Transactions and Consulting; Medical Practice Law; Acquisitions and Sales.
Kaplon, Joseph J., (AV) ........... '49 '74 C.112 A.B. L.1068 J.D. [Wohlner K.P.V.&Y.]
Karch, Morris N. .......................................... '20 '50 C.911 L.880 LL.B. [M.N.Karch]
Karch, Morris N., A Professional Corporation ................................ 15915 Ventura Blvd.
Karlsen, M. Alfred, (Prof. Corp.), (AV) '38 '66
C.768 A.B. L.1066 LL.B. 16530 Ventura Blvd.
**Karno, Norton S., (A Professional Corporation)**, (AV) '36 '61
C.112 B.S. L.800 J.D. [Karno,S.F.S.&W.]

**Karno, Schwartz, Friedman, Shafron & Warren, (AV)**
**A Partnership including Professional Corporations**
**Manufacturers Bank Building, Suite 1200, 16255 Ventura Boulevard, 91436©**
**Telephone: 818-981-3400; 213-872-1800 Telecopier: 213-872-1278**
**Marshall N. Schwartz (Retired); Norton S. Karno (A Professional Corporation); Kenneth L. Friedman (A Professional Corporation); Shelly Jay Shafron (A Professional Corporation); Earl W. Warren (Resident, Agoura Hills Office);—Kevin David Kammer; Richard A. Cohn (P.C.).**
**Real Estate, Tax, Corporate, Business, ERISA, Estate Planning and Probate Law. Litigation.**
**Agoura Hills, California Office: 30497 Canwood Street, Suite 102. Telephone: 818-597-7977. Telecopier: 818-597-7970.**
*See Professional Biographies, ENCINO, CALIFORNIA*

CAA81P

**Karp, David I.**, (AV) ... '54 '79 C.112 B.A. L.426 J.D. [▣ Spile&S.] (⊙Van Nuys)
*PRACTICE AREAS: Real Estate Litigation; Business Litigation; Commercial Litigation.
Kassan, Alan E. ... '57 '84 C.112 B.A. L.1049 J.D. [Kassan&K.]
Kassan, Melvin E. ... '26 '52 C&L.800 A.B., LL.B. [Kassan&K.]
Kassan & Kassan ... 15915 Ventura Blvd.
Kasztelewicz, Jolanta A. ... '46 '91 C.112 B.A. L.809 J.D. 16530 Ventura Blvd.
Katz, Alan A. ... '42 '68 C&L.800 B.S., J.D. [A.A.Katz]
Katz, Richard M. ... '51 '79 C.1077 B.A. L.1148 J.D. [Berman&W.]⊙
Katz, Alan A., A Professional Law Corporation ... 16633 Ventura Blvd.
Kaufman, Albert I. ... '36 '67 C&L.1095 B.A., J.D. 17609 Ventura Blvd.
Kazan, Kenneth ... '56 '81 C.1077 B.A. L.809 J.D. 16133 Ventura Blvd.
Keeshan, John J. ... '17 '51 C.724 B.S. L.426 LL.B. 17300 Quesan Pl.‡
Kenner, David E., (AV) ... '41 '68 16000 Ventura Blvd., 5th Fl.
Kent, Melissa E. ... '64 '90 C.112 B.A. L.464 J.D. 17748 Alonzo Pl.
Kent, Richard M. ... '51 '76 C.608 B.A. L.809 J.D. 15910 Ventura Blvd.
Kingsley, George R. ... '40 '65 C&L.112 B.S., LL.B. 16133 Ventura Blvd.
Kippen, Harold, (BV) ... '28 '55 C&L.477 B.A., LL.B. 15915 Ventura Blvd., Penthouse 1
Kistler, Wm. F. ... '18 '50 C.37 B.S. L.426 LL.B. 4517 Woodley Ave.‡
Klein, Stanley D. ... '30 '63 C.112 B.A. L.800 LL.B. 4604 Hurford Terr.
**Kolod, Scott M.** '57 '82
C.347 B.S. L.1049 J.D. [Kolod&W.] (⊙San Diego and Santa Ana)
*LANGUAGES: Spanish and French.
*REPORTED CASES: Stonewall Ins. Co. v. City of Palos Verdes Estates, 46 Cal. App. 4th 1810 (1996); Jefferson-Pilot Life Ins. Co. v. Krafka, 50 Cal. App. 4th 190 (1996).

**Kolod & Wager**
**16000 Ventura Boulevard, Fifth Floor, 91436⊙**
**Telephone: 818-788-4348 Fax: 818-788-4349**
**Email: kol-wag@pacbell.net**
**Scott M. Kolod; Jerome Wager. Associates: Ted A. Connor; Holly Nolan; Stephen A. Lindsley; Kevin J. Healy; Laleaque Grad.**
**General Civil, Trial and Appellate Practice in State and Federal Court, emphasizing Insurance Coverage and Bad Faith, Construction Defect and Real Property, Professional Liability, General Tort Liability Defense, Products Liability and Environmental Impairment.**
**Orange County, California Office: 1551 North Tustin Avenue, Suite 195, Santa Ana, 92701. Telephone: 714-543-9300. Fax: 714-543-9400.**
**San Diego, California Office: 16476 Bernardo Center Drive, Suite 100, 92128. Telephone: 619-675-7006. Fax: 619-675-1023.**
**Sonoma, California Office: 589 First Street West, 95476. Telephone: 415-398-1092. Fax: 415-398-6009.**
*See Professional Biographies, ENCINO, CALIFORNIA*

Korn, Dana M. ... '47 '74 C.1097 B.A. L.809 J.D. P.O. Box 17355
Kornswiet, Robert L. ... '52 '77 C.1077 B.A. L.770 J.D. 5435 Balboa Blvd.
Kovalsky, Martin S. ... '62 '92 C.1042 B.A. L.1049 J.D. [▣ Fields&F.]
Krall, Shelley H. ... '50 '86 C.788 B.A. L.1068 J.D. 5311 Genesta Ave.
Krane, Samuel, (AV) ... '41 '66 C.679 B.S. L.800 LL.B. [Krane&S.]
Krane & Smith, (AV) ... 16255 Venture Blvd.
Krausz, Paul D. ... '57 '85 C.112 B.A. L.800 J.D. 15915 Ventura Blvd.
**Kravetz, Dana A.** ... '70 '95 C.112 B.A. L.809 J.D. [Levinson&K.]
*PRACTICE AREAS: Business Litigation; General Civil Litigation; Sports Law.
**Krivis, Jeffrey L.**, (AV) ... '56 '80 C.768 B.A. L.809 J.D. [Spile&S.]
*PRACTICE AREAS: Real Estate; Employment; Insurance; Mediation; Arbitration.

**Krivis, Spile & Siegal, LLP**
**(See Spile & Siegal, LLP)**

Kropach, William J., (AV) ... '42 '72 C.112 B.S. L.1068 J.D. 6345 Balboa Blvd.
Krumm, Stephen H., (BV) ... '49 '74 16055 Ventura Blvd.
Krupp, Gerald, (BV) ... '29 '55 C.112 B.S. L.1068 LL.B. [Green&K.]
**Kulchin, Sydney**, (AV) ... '33 '61 C.112 B.A. L.426 LL.B. [Shelden,K.R.&F.]
Kuritzkes, Beth M. ... '58 '83 C.659 B.A. L.178 J.D. 15613 Woodvale Rd.
Kurtz, Jeffrey S. ... '49 '74 C.112 B.A. L.809 J.D. 16000 Ventura Blvd.

**Kurtz, Steven N., Law Offices of '58 '86 C.763 B.A. L.464 J.D.**
**15760 Ventura Boulevard, 16th Floor, 91436**
**Telephone: 818-981-0974 Telecopier: 818-981-0984**
**Email: skurtz3630@aol.com**
***REPORTED CASES: In re ZZZZ Best Carpet Cleaning Co., Inc., 921 F. 2d 968 (9th Cir. 1990).**
**Business and Commercial Litigation, Bankruptcy, Corporate and Personal Reorganization, Debtor-Creditor Matters and Business Law.**
*See Professional Biographies, ENCINO, CALIFORNIA*

Kwawer, Allen J., (BV) ... '32 '71 C.563 B.S.M.E. L.999 J.D. 15760 Ventura Blvd.
Labin, Paul D. ... '44 '70 C.112 B.A. L.309 J.D. 4930 Valjean Ave.
Lackey, Douglas K. ... '57 '82 C.112 B.A. L.426 J.D. [Zimmerman&K.]
Lake, Don, (AV) ... '46 '72 C.800 B.A. L.426 J.D. [Lake&L.]
Lake & Levine, (AV) ... 6345 Balboa Blvd.
Lakritz, Alfred J. ... '34 '61 C.112 A.B. L.1066 LL.B. 16055 Ventura Blvd.
**Lamb, Michael V.** ... '52 '79 C.477 B.A. L.990 J.D. [Elliot,L.L.&S.]⊙
*PRACTICE AREAS: Insurance Defense; Medical Malpractice Defense.
Lambert, Earle, (AV) ... '37 '62 C.436 B.S. L.966 LL.B. 16133 Ventura Blvd., Ste 965
Lane, Carl J., (AV) ... '32 '59 C&L.339 B.A., LL.B. 16255 Ventura Blvd.
Lantz, Rick P. ... '43 '70 C.475 B.A. L.809 J.D. 5435 Balboa Blvd.
Lappen, Robin D. ... '54 '79 C.112 B.A. L.1068 J.D. 16121 High Valley Pl.
Lappen, William A. ... '54 '80 C.174 B.A. L.1068 J.D. 16121 High Valley Pl.
Lasser, Donald M. ... '32 '57 C&L.339 A.B., LL.B. 15821 Ventura Blvd.
Latt, Miriam Lavenda, (BV) ... '40 '76 C.112 L.1095 J.D. 17000 Ventura Blvd.
Lau, Kenneth B. ... '66 '91 C.154 B.A. L.800 J.D. 15910 Ventura Blvd., 12th Fl.
Lavin, Todd Elliot ... '55 '81 C.112 B.A. L.1148 J.D. [T.E.Lavin]
Lavin, Todd Elliot, A Prof. Corp. ... 16530 Ventura Blvd.
Lazaran, Mary A. ... '61 '89 C.1042 B.S. L.1137 J.D. 15910 Ventura Blvd., 12th Fl.
Lazarus, Leonard Harvey, (AV) ... '42 '69 C.415 B.S. L.564 LL.B. 5435 Balboa Blvd.
Lebby, Richard A., (AV) ... '52 '79 C.112 B.A. L.809 J.D. 16830 Ventura Blvd.
Lederer, David C. ... '50 '85 C.342 B.A. L.426 J.D. 5435 Balboa Blvd.
**Leff, Andrew L.** ... '60 '86 [▣ Spile&S.]
*PRACTICE AREAS: Real Estate Litigation; Tort Litigation.
**Leibl, Loren S.**, (AV) ... '53 '83 C.1042 B.A. L.809 J.D. [Elliot,L.L.&S.]⊙
*PRACTICE AREAS: Insurance Defense; Medical Malpractice Defense.
**Lemoine, Jessica Lille** ... '60 '87 C.1077 B.S. L.990 J.D. [▣ Goldstein,G.&S.]
*PRACTICE AREAS: Insurance Defense (95%); Subrogation (5%).
Lerner, Leonard D. ... '54 '80 C.112 B.A. L.809 J.D. [L.D.Lerner]
Lerner, Leonard D., A P.C. ... 16000 Ventura Blvd.
Lester, Richard M. ... '37 '82 C.999 L.1190 J.D. 15910 Ventura Blvd.
**Leuthold, Richard R.**, (BV) ... '40 '67 C&L.494 B.S., J.D. [▣ Spile&S.]
*REPORTED CASES: Krasley v. Superior Court (1980) 101 CA 3rd 425; Fleming v. Ray-Suzuki (1990) 225 CA 3rd 574; Kazanjian v. Rancho Estates, Ltd (1991) 235 CA 3rd 1621.
*PRACTICE AREAS: Business Litigation; Real Estate Litigation; Professional Negligence.
Levin, Robert S. ... '54 '82 C.36 B.S. L.809 J.D. 15821 Ventura Blvd.
Levine, Allan L., (AV) ... '26 '59 C.424 L.809 LL.B. 5460 White Oak Ave.
Levine, Howard S. ... '49 '74 C.1097 B.S. L.809 J.D. [Lake&L.]
Levine, Lawrence D. ... '41 '67 C.1043 B.A. L.1068 LL.B. 16311 Ventura Blvd.
Levine, Robert E. ... '47 '73 C.112 B.A. L.426 J.D. [Stein,H.L.&Y.]

**Levinson, Carrie A.** ... '59 '85 C.112 B.A. L.1065 J.D. [▣ Lewitt,H.H.S.M.&H.]
*PRACTICE AREAS: Litigation.
**Levinson, Robert A.**, (AV) ... '53 '78 C.800 B.S. L.1068 J.D. [Levinson&K.]
*PRACTICE AREAS: Business and Real Estate Litigation; Employment Law for Management.

**Levinson & Kaplan, A Professional Corporation, (AV)**
**16027 Ventura Boulevard, Suite 450, 91436**
**Telephone: 818-382-3450 Facsimile: 818-382-3445**
**Email: levkaplaw@aol.com URL: http://www.levkaplaw.com**
**Robert A. Levinson; Steven G. Kaplan; Patrick Condon; Dana A. Kravetz.**
**Business Litigation, Real Estate Litigation, Employment Law and General Business Transactions.**
*See Professional Biographies, ENCINO, CALIFORNIA*

Levitt, Stanley D. ... '56 '83 C.800 B.S. L.990 J.D. Pres., CalWind Resources, Inc.
**Levy, Leonard S., (A Professional Corporation)** '48 '73
C.112 B.A. L.426 J.D. [▣ Alpert,B.&G.]
*PRACTICE AREAS: Business Law; Insurance Law; Surety and Fidelity Law; Business, Insurance and Real Estate Litigation.
Levy, Steven E. ... '47 '76 C.912 B.S. L.1095 J.D. 15910 Ventura Blvd.
LeWinter, Anthony A., (AV) ... '52 '76 C.112 B.A. L.309 J.D. [LeWinter&R.]
LeWinter & Rosman, A Professional Corporation, (AV) ... Ste. 600, 16255 Ventura Blvd.
**Lewitt, Leon**, (AV) ... '37 '64 C.608 B.S.B.A. L.1049 J.D. [Lewitt,H.H.S.M.&H.]
*PRACTICE AREAS: Mergers and Acquisitions; Business Law; Resolution of Business Disputes.
**Lewitt, Maurice** ... '31 '54 C.381 B.S. L.608 J.D. [▣ Lewitt,H.H.S.M.&H.]
*PRACTICE AREAS: Business Law; Mergers and Acquisitions; Health Care; Arbitration and Mediation.

**Lewitt, Hackman, Hoefflin, Shapiro, Marshall & Harlan, A Law Corporation, (AV)**
**Eleventh Floor, 16633 Ventura Boulevard, 91436**
**Telephone: 818-990-2120 Telecopier: 818-981-4764**
**Email: lhhsmh@aol.com**
**Leon Lewitt; Michael Hackman (Certified Specialist, Taxation Law, The State Bar of California Board of Legal Specialization); Richard M. Hoefflin; Andrew L. Shapiro; John B. Marshall; Barry T. Harlan (Certified Specialist, Family Law, The State Bar of California Board of Legal Specialization);— Thomas Cecil; Carrie A. Levinson; Michelle S. Robins; Hedwig C. Swanson; Keith Todd Zimmet. Of Counsel: Robert L. Brent (A Professional Corporation); David S. Hamilton; Maurice Lewitt.**
**Business, Corporate, Partnership and Securities Law including Syndications, Mergers and Acquisitions and Public Offerings. Real Estate, Taxation, Domestic Relations, Estate Planning, Probate, Personal Injury and Insurance Regulatory Law and related Civil Litigation and Administrative Law. Health Care and Hospital Law.**
*See Professional Biographies, ENCINO, CALIFORNIA*

Lieber, Stanley ... '48 '73 C.1077 B.A. L.809 J.D. 16027 Ventura Blvd.
Lieberman, Lawrence M. ... '29 '55 C.112 B.A. L.1068 J.D. 16055 Ventura Blvd.
Lin, Edward T. ... '65 '93 C.112 B.A. L.423 J.D. 101 E. Redlands Blvd.
**Lindsley, Stephen A.** '63 '90
C&L.1049 B.A., J.D. [▣ Kolod&W.] (⊙San Diego and Santa Ana)

**Lindvig, Clifford L., (AV) '32 '65 C.800 A.B. L.1065 LL.B.**
**16133 Ventura Boulevard, Suite 585, 91436**
**Telephone: 818-784-1450 Fax: 818-382-9982**
***PRACTICE AREAS: Personal Injury; Medical Malpractice; Products Liability; Tort.**
**Personal Injury, Medical Malpractice, Products Liability, Tort.**

Lipman, Gilbert G. ... '38 '65 C.112 B.S. L.809 J.D. 15821 Ventura Blvd.
Lobl, Richard T., (BV) ... '42 '82 C.273 B.A. L.1137 J.D. 16133 Ventura Blvd.
Lodgen, Edward D. ... '65 '91 C.112 B.A. L.426 J.D. 16633 Ventura Blvd.
Lombardini, Carol A. '54 '79 C.145 B.A. L.813 J.D.
Sr. V.P. & Legal Affs., Alliance of Motion Picture & Television Producers
Long, Hal D. ... '43 '70 C.763 B.S. L.61 J.D. 16830 Ventura Blvd.
Lopata, Stanley S. ... '36 '65 C.174 B.A. L.208 J.D. Ste 700, 15760 Ventura Blvd.
Lorant, Etan Z. ... '55 '83 C.112 B.A. L.809 J.D. 16530 Ventura Blvd.
Lucien, Donald S. ... '39 '81 L.1077 J.D. 16133 Ventura Blvd.
Lynch, Terri G., Law Offices of, (BV) '39 '74
C.1097 B.A. L.1095 J.D. 16255 Ventura Blvd.
**Mack, Jack S.** ... '54 '94 C.1097 B.A. L.809 J.D. [▣ Alpert,B.&G.]
*PRACTICE AREAS: Family Law; Civil Litigation.
Magidsohn, Herman E. ... '36 '71 C.477 A.B. L.809 J.D. 15720 Ventura Blvd.
Magit, George ... '29 '54 C&L.424 J.D. 16830 Ventura Blvd.
Mallut, Daniel ... '46 '87 C.1077 B.S. L.1148 J.D. Western Gen. Ins. Co.
Mamann, David ... '58 '87 C.035 B.A. L.809 J.D. 16830 Ventura Blvd.
Mann, Leo L. ... '24 '53 L.1001 LL.B. 16453 Refugio‡
Mann, Stanley B. ... '48 '73 C.1077 B.A. L.1049 J.D. 16055 Ventura Blvd.
**Marino, J. Anthony, (A Professional Corporation)**, (AV) '41 '71
C.119 B.S.E.E. L.800 J.D. [Marino&D.]
*PRACTICE AREAS: Probate and Trust Law; Estate and Business Planning; Common Interest Ownership Law; Business, Commercial and Property Litigation matters.

**Marino & Dallinger, (AV)**
**An Association including a Professional Corporation**
**17835 Ventura Boulevard, Suite 209, 91316**
**Telephone: 818-774-3636 FAX: 818-774-3635**
**J. Anthony Marino (A Professional Corporation); Timothy G. Dallinger.**
**General Civil and Trial Practice in State and Federal Courts, with practice Limited to Business, Corporate, Partnership, Property, Insurance, Condominium, Probate, Estate Planning, Trust and Tax Law.**

Mark, Daniel S. ... '31 '58 C.116 A.B. L.276 LL.B. 3213 Fond Dr.
**Marlowe, David F.** ... '50 '78 C.241 B.S. L.1095 J.D. [▣ Goldstein,G.&S.]
*PRACTICE AREAS: Workers Compensation (100%, 70).
**Marshall, John B.**, (AV) ... '45 '70 C.800 A.B. L.1066 J.D. [Lewitt,H.H.S.M.&H.]
*PRACTICE AREAS: Real Estate; Environmental; Business; Securities; Commercial Finance Law.
Marshall, Wayne S. ... '51 '78 C.1077 B.A. L.61 J.D. [W.S.Marshall]
Marshall, Wayne S., A Professional Law Corporation ... 16501 Ventura Blvd.
Mavridis, James, (AV) ... '25 '56 C.981 L.809 LL.B. 15760 Ventura Blvd., 16th Fl.‡
**McAndrew, Stephen F.** ... '62 '90 C.112 B.A. L.809 J.D. [Plotkin,R.&N.]
*PRACTICE AREAS: Litigation.
McConnell, Pamela R. ... '53 '78 C.518 A.B. L.426 J.D. Univ. of La Verne
McCulloch, Robert J. ... '52 '79 [McCulloch&d.]
McCulloch & deMontesquiou, (BV) ... 15821 Ventura Boulevard, Suite 545
McGovern, William '34 '59 C.674 A.B. L.309 LL.B.
(adm. in IL; not adm. in CA) 17319 Magnolia Blvd.‡
McGowan, Robert J., (BV) ... '15 '40 C&L.494 B.S., LL.B. 16255 Ventura Blvd.
**McGuire, Richard S.** ... '55 '85 C&L.101 B.S., J.D. [▣ Stone&R.]
*PRACTICE AREAS: Civil Litigation; Premises Liability; Insurance Defense.
McKarus, Douglas G. ... '44 '70 C.112 B.S. L.426 J.D. 15910 Ventura Blvd.
McLaughlin, Janet S. ... '53 '79 C.860 A.B. L.94 J.D. 16130 Ventura Blvd.
McMahon, Bruce K. ... '54 '81 C.112 B.A. L.990 J.D. 6345 Balboa Blvd.
Medin, Fran E. ... '61 '90 C.994 B.A. L.426 J.D. 16661 Ventura Blvd.
Medof, Carol J. ... '49 '79 C.112 B.A. L.809 J.D. 15900 Woodvale Rd.
Melnik, Todd L. ... '62 '87 C.608 B.S. L.950 J.D. 16000 Ventura Blvd.
Meo, Matthew, (BV) ... '37 '65 [Rudofsky&M.]
Metz, Jordon ... '67 '93 C&L.260 B.A., J.D. 15915 Ventura Blvd.
**Michelman, Ronald E.** ... '46 '73 C&L.1095 B.A., J.D. [Michelman&M.]
*PRACTICE AREAS: Bankruptcy; Insolvency; Mergers and Acquisitions.

**Michelman & Michelman, Inc., P.L.C.**
**17071 Ventura Boulevard Suite 206, 91316**
**Telephone: 818-906-7373 Fax: 818-906-7237**
**Ronald E. Michelman.**
**Bankruptcy, Insolvency, Mergers and Acquisitions.**

Mickelson, Charles A. .......................... '41 '75 C.966 B.S. L.426 J.D. [Mickelson&P.]
Mickelson & Pavone .......................................... 16055 Ventura Blvd.
**Miller, Kenneth, (AV) '52 '77 C.1077 B.A. L.1068 J.D.**
**16027 Ventura Boulevard, Suite 420, 91436**
**Telephone: 818-386-0555 Fax: 818-386-0569**
**Email: wizard@sure.net**
***PRACTICE AREAS: Title Insurance; Real Property; Civil Litigation.**
**Title Insurance, Real Property, Civil Litigation.**
**Representative Clients: Commonwealth Land & Title Insurance Co.; Transamerica Title Insurance Co.; Southland Title Co.; Chicago Title Insurance Co.**
*See Professional Biographies, ENCINO, CALIFORNIA*

Miller, Scott C. '56 '81 C.990 B.A. L.930 J.D.
(adm. in OH; not adm. in CA) 18014 Burbank Blvd.‡
**Miller, Scott D.** ........................ '50 '75 C.800 B.S. L.112 J.D. [A Goldstein,G.&S.]
Miller, Steven ........................ '47 '80 C.1246 B.S. L.1221 J.D. 16133 Ventura Blvd.
Miller, Steven L. ........................ '56 '82 C.1077 B.S. L.1137 J.D. 16133 Ventura Blvd.
**Miller, Irwin R. (Rob)**
**(See Oxnard)**
Mink, Michael S., (AV) ....... '42 '68 C.823 B.A. L.800 J.D. 6345 Balboa Blvd. Ste., 300
Minkoff, Barbara B. ..... '42 '86 C.645 B.S. L.1136 J.D. 16255 Ventura Blvd., Ste., 1110
Minkow, Bernard A., (A Law Corporation), (AV) '37 '63
C.347 B.S. L.813 J.D. 16830 Ventura Blvd.
Mitchell, Nadine ........................ '53 '88 C.420 B.A. L.990 J.D. [A Stein,H.L.&Y.]
Moreton, Keith W. ........................ '48 '72 C.497 B.S. L.500 J.D. 15760 Ventura Blvd.
**Moretti, Olga M.** ........................ '50 '94 C.1097 b.a. L.809 J.D. [C Spile&S.]
*PRACTICE AREAS: Real Estate; Construction.
Morris, Norman P. ........................ '52 '79 C.112 A.B. L.1065 J.D. 16954 Cotter Pl.
Morton, Chris R. ........................ '46 '78 C.1077 B.A. L.1095 J.D. 16311 Ventura Blvd.
Most, Milton L. ........................ '17 '52 C.112 A.B. L.426 J.D. 17634 Palora St.‡
Mulally, Thomas R. ........................ '57 '84 C.994 B.A. L.1148 J.D. [Szabo,S.&M.]
Muller, Frederick P. ............ '48 '73 C.112 B.S. L.1068 J.D. 15915 Ventura Blvd. #203
Murray, Steven W. ........................ '41 '68 C.112 B.A. L.800 J.D. 16055 Ventura Blvd.
Nadel, Robert M. ........................ '47 '73 C&L.1190 B.S.L., LL.B. 16311 Ventura Blvd.
**Nahmias, Alan I.**, (AV) ........................ '61 '86 C.800 B.A. L.426 J.D. [Plotkin,R.&N.]
*PRACTICE AREAS: Bankruptcy and Insolvency Law; Real Estate (Property) Law; Commercial Business Litigation.
**Nolan, Holly** '62 '89 C.684 B.A. L.1049 J.D.
[A Kolod&W.] (⊙San Diego and Santa Ana)
Norton, Todd A. ........................ '64 '89 C.112 B.A. L.770 J.D. [Norton&N.]
Norton & Norton, LLP ........................ 16027 Ventura Blvd., Ste. 203
Notrica, Lewis E. ........................ '25 '53 L.809 LL.B. 16133 Ventura Blvd.
Novak, Mark S., (AV) ........ '35 '61 C.339 A.B. L.1066 LL.B. 16830 Ventura Blvd.
Nuth, Timothy E. ........................ '61 '87 C.347 B.A. L.276 J.D. 16130 Ventura Blvd.
**Oldman & Cooley, L.L.P.**
**(See Los Angeles)**
Oppenheim, Scott D. ........................ '54 '80 C.112 B.S. L.809 J.D. 16055 Ventura Blvd.
**Ostrin, Linda** ........................ '48 '78 C.1077 B.S. L.398 J.D. [A Elliot,L.L.&S.]
*PRACTICE AREAS: Insurance Defense; Medical Malpractice Defense.
Pack-Rayman, Nancy ........................ '51 '88 C.1044 B.S. L.1068 J.D. [Saleman&P.]
Padrino, James Lee ....... '— '93 C.1042 B.A. L.1148 J.D. 15910 Ventura Blvd., 12th Fl.
Palty, Joseph L. ........................ '26 '70 C.809 B.C.S. L.1095 LL.B. 16633 Ventura Blvd.
Palty, Robert L. ........................ '52 '78 C.1077 B.A. L.1095 J.D. 16633 Ventura Blvd.
Paris, Sanford P. ........................ '37 '64 C.112 B.S. L.809 LL.B. 16501 Ventura Blvd.‡
Parker, Alison J. ........................ '57 '81 C.813 A.B. L.309 J.D. 4938 Libbitt Ave.
Parker, Joel S. ........................ '48 '76 C.112 B.A. L.809 J.D. 16000 Ventura Blvd.
Patnoi, Stanley G. ........................ '51 '77 C.112 B.A. L.1148 J.D. 15910 Ventura Blvd.
Paul, Jerry Neil ........................ '54 '80 C.1077 B.S. L.398 J.D. 16830 Ventura Blvd.
Pavone, Thomas S., Jr. ........................ '51 '79 C.999 L.1221 J.D. [Mickelson&P.]
**Pearlman, Barry S.** ........................ '56 '81 C.112 B.A. L.809 J.D. [Pearlman,B.&W.]
*SPECIAL AGENCIES: National Association of Insurance Fraud Investigators.
*PRACTICE AREAS: Workers Compensation Defense; Subrogation; Employment Litigation; Employer Liability Defense; Liability Defense.

**Pearlman, Borska & Wax**
**15910 Ventura Boulevard, Eighteenth Floor, 91436**
**Telephone: 818-501-4343 Fax: 818-386-5700**
**Barry S. Pearlman; Elliot F. Borska; Steven H. Wax; Geoffrey H. Greenup; Dean S. Brown. Associates: Louis Peter Trygar; Thomas E. Handy (Certified Specialist, Workers' Compensation Law The State Bar of California Board of Legal Specialization); Cynthia Elkins Hogan.**
**Employment Litigation, Workers Compensation Defense, Liability Defense, Subrogation, Insurance Coverage, Special Investigation Claims.**
*See Professional Biographies, ENCINO, CALIFORNIA*

Pearson, Joyce J. ........................ '50 '87 C.259 B.A. L.809 J.D. 16830 Ventura Blvd.
Pellegrino, Richard B. ........................ '57 '84 C&L.426 B.S., J.D. 1576 Ventora Blvd.
Peretz, Ralph L. ........................ '43 '70 C.994 B.A. L.107 J.D. 15915 Ventura Blvd.
Perlo, Ezekiel P. ........................ '40 '65 C.112 B.A. L.1068 J.D. 16133 Ventura Blvd.
Perlstein, Edwin ........................ '26 '53 C.563 B.B.A. L.1009 J.D. 4322 Grimes Pl.
**Peters, Gerald P.** ........................ '52 '81 C.339 B.A. L.1068 J.D. [A Staitman,S.&T.]
*PRACTICE AREAS: Insurance Defense; General Civil Litigation; Appellate.
Phillips, Gail V. ........................ '53 '80 C.1097 B.A. L.1065 J.D. 15821 Ventura Blvd.
Phillips, Mark C. ....... '57 '83 C.800 B.S. L.426 J.D. Legal Coun., Trizec Properties, Inc.
Phillips, Ralph M. ........................ '48 '75 C.112 B.A. L.61 J.D. [Wohlner K.P.V.&Y.]
**Pine, Cathryn R.** ........................ '64 '90 C.112 B.A. L.809 J.D. [A Goldstein,G.&S.]
*PRACTICE AREAS: Workers' Compensation; Family Law.
Plat, Ben, (BV) ........................ '33 '66 C.112 B.S. L.809 LL.B. 15915 Ventura Blvd.
Plotin, Richard S. ........................ '43 '69 C.112 B.A. L.426 J.D. 16633 Ventura Blvd.
**Plotkin, Gary A.**, (AV) ........................ '38 '63 C.477 B.B.A. L.912 LL.B. [Plotkin,R.&N.]
*PRACTICE AREAS: Business; Real Estate; Bankruptcy; Receivership Law.

**Plotkin, Rapoport & Nahmias, A Professional Corporation, (AV)**
**16633 Ventura Boulevard, Suite 800, 91436-1836**
**Telephone: 818-906-1600; 213-879-9481 Telecopier: 818-907-9261**
**Gary A. Plotkin; Russell H. Rapoport; Alan I. Nahmias; Amy L. Goldman; Stephen F. McAndrew.**
**General Business, Commercial and Real Estate Litigation, Bankruptcy and Receivership Law.**

Pollock, David, (AV) ........................ '10 '37 3626 Crownridge Dr.
**Porvin, Terry** ........................ '61 '89 C.477 B.G.S. L.940 J.D. [A Shelden,K.R.&F.]
Posner, Joseph, (AV) ........................ '41 '74 C.112 B.S. L.426 J.D. [J.Posner]
Posner, Joseph, Inc., (AV) ........................ 16311 Ventura Blvd.
Price, Joan M. ........................ '— '81 C.994 B.A. L.1065 J.D. 16311 Ventura Blvd.
Price, Stuart M. ........................ '64 '90 C.1036 B.A. L.1068 J.D. 15760 Ventura Blvd.
Prince, Arnold E., (AV) ........................ '37 '67 C.705 B.S. L.800 J.D. 3850 Kim Lane‡
Radoff, Franklin ........................ '43 '70 C&L.1095 B.S., J.D. 5145 Yarmouth
Raff, William F. ........................ '34 '59 C&L.813 B.A., J.D. 16200 Ventura Blvd.
**Ramirez, M. Christina** ........................ '49 '85 C.1042 B.A. L.1068 J.D. [Altman&S.]
*PRACTICE AREAS: Workers Compensation Defense; Collections.
Rand, Michael J. ........................ '46 '76 C.112 B.A. L.1095 J.D. 15760 Ventura Blvd.
**Rapoport, Russell H.**, (BV) ........................ '48 '73 C.112 B.A. L.809 J.D. [Plotkin,R.&N.]
*PRACTICE AREAS: Banking Law; Commercial Litigation.
Rauch, Rhonda L. ........................ '63 '91 C.1077 B.A. L.398 J.D. [Tinero&R.]
Raznick, Linda Diamond '51 '77 C.112 B.A. L.1148 J.D.
Editor-In-Chf., Rutter Grp., The
Reichman, Jeffrey S. ....... '53 '77 C.112 B.A. L.1095 J.D. 22120 Clarendon St., Ste. 200
Rentzer, Robert D. ........................ '39 '67 L.809 LL.B. 5445 Balboa Blvd.
Rimer, Neal M. ........................ '52 '76 C.1077 B.S. L.1148 J.D. 16055 Ventura Blvd.
**Rivera, Mario R.** ........................ '61 '89 C.494 B.A. L.808 J.D. [A Shelden,K.R.&F.]
*LANGUAGES: Spanish.
**Robins, Michelle S.** ............ '64 '89 C.112 B.A. L.1065 J.D. [A Lewitt,H.H.S.M.&H.]
*PRACTICE AREAS: Litigation; Family Law; Hospital Law; Personal Injury Law.
Robman, Louis ........................ '44 '75 C.1042 B.A. [Robman&S.]
Robman & Seeley, (AV) ........................ 15760 Ventura Blvd., 16th Fl.
Rocklin, David B '61 '87 C.347 B.A. L.146 J.D.
(adm. in IL; not adm. in CA) Claims Exam., Chubb Group of Ins. Cos.
Rodman, Kenneth B. '49 '76
C.112 B.A. L.809 J.D. 16530 Ventura Blvd. (⊙Westlake Village)
Rogers, John B. ........................ '63 '89 C.446 B.A. L.61 J.D. 15910 Ventura Blvd., 12th Fl.
Romans, Marjorie G. ........................ '— '71 L.1148 J.D. 5124 Encino Ave.
**Rosen, Arnold L.** ........................ '38 '71 C.705 B.A. L.1077 J.D. [Shelden,K.R.&F.]
**Rosenblatt, Ira H.**, (AV) ........................ '63 '89 C.112 B.A. L.464 J.D. [Stone&R.]
*PRACTICE AREAS: Insurance Defense Litigation; Construction Defect; Employment Litigation; Civil Litigation; Business Transactional.

**Rosenbloom, Alvin D., Law Offices of, (AV) '31 '55 C&L.597 B.S.L., J.D.**
**16311 Ventura Boulevard, Suite 1200, 91436-2144**
**Telephone: 818-379-7010 Telecopier: 818-990-9705**
***PRACTICE AREAS: Title Insurance; Secured Real Property Financing Transactions; Real Estate Law; General Civil, Trial and Appellate Practice.**

**Rosenbloom, Jonathan L.** ........................ '63 '91 C.112 A.B. L.597 J.D. [A Anker&H.]
*REPORTED CASES: Waisbren v. Peppercorn Productions, Inc., 41 Cal. App. 4th 246, 48 Cal. Rptr 2d 437 (1995).
*PRACTICE AREAS: Business Law; Business Litigation.
Rosenfield, Sheldon, (BV) ........................ '35 '63 C.999 L.809 LL.B. 16530 Ventura Blvd.
Rosenstock, Dennis I. ........................ '49 '76 C.1077 B.A. L.1136 J.D. 16311 Ventura Blvd.
Rosenthal, Morton D. ........................ '34 '71 C.569 B.S. L.1095 J.D. 15915 Ventura Blvd.
Rosenthal, Richard M., (BV) ........................ '51 '77 C.112 B.A. L.398 J.D. [Rosenthal&S.]
Rosenthal and Smith, (AV) ........................ Ste., 330, 6345 Balboa Blvd.
Rosman, Richard D. ........................ '53 '78 C.112 B.A. L.309 J.D. [LeWinter&R.]
Ross, Alan D., (AV) ........................ '29 '55 C.112 B.A. L.1066 J.D. [A.D.Ross]
Ross, Jason H. ........................ '32 '60 C.112 B.S. L.1068 LL.B. 15821 Ventura Blvd.
Ross, Laurence ........................ '67 '92 C.112 B.A. L.426 J.D. 16633 Ventura Blvd.
Ross, Loren A. ........................ '49 '79 C.112 B.A. L.1148 J.D. 16055 Ventura Blvd.
Ross, Michael A. ........................ '47 '72 C.112 L.426 J.D. V.P. & Gen. Coun., Larwin Co.
Ross, Alan D., Law Corp., (AV) ........................ 17530 Ventura Blvd.
Roth, Raoul Y. ........................ '34 '70 C.839 B.A. L.1095 J.D. 16530 Ventura Blvd.
Rothberg, David A. ........................ '39 '65 C.347 A.B. L.1119 LL.B. 16830 Ventura Blvd.
Rothberg, Myron B., (AV) ........................ '38 '64 C.112 B.S. L.1068 J.D. 16530 Ventura Blvd.
Rothfarb, Fred ........................ '23 '54 C.102 A.B. L.178 LL.B. 5732 Babbitt Ave.
Rotsten, Michael ........................ '42 '70 L.809 J.D. 16133 Ventura Blvd.
**Rousso, Martin J.**, (AV) ........................ '45 '77 C.1097 B.S. L.1095 J.D. [Hemar,R.&G.]
*PRACTICE AREAS: Creditors Rights; Banking; Equipment Leasing; Bankruptcy and Secured Transactions.
Rubel, Gregory A. ........................ '68 '95 C.112 B.A. L.426 J.D. 15915 Ventum Blvd.
Rubin, Frank D. ........................ '47 '74 C.112 B.A. L.426 J.D. 4838 Petit Ave.
Rubin, Marshall L. ........................ '45 '70 C.112 B.A. L.284 J.D. 16255 Ventura Blvd.
Ruch, Lawrence S. ........................ '40 '67 C.156 A.B. L.94 LL.B. [Smith&R.]
Rudofsky, Jack L., (AV) ........................ '32 '58 C.102 B.A. L.1009 LL.B. [Rudofsky&M.]
Rudofsky & Meo, (AV) ........................ 16255 Ventura Blvd.
Rummel, Blake A. ........................ '64 '90 C.112 B.A. L.809 J.D. P.O. Box 18161
Rutter, William A., (AV) ........................ '28 '55 C.112 B.A. L.800 J.D. Pres., Rutter Grp., The
Sack, Henry ........................ '49 '77 C.763 A.B. L.809 J.D. 16255 Ventura Blvd.
St. John-Zegel, Cynthia ........ '59 '84 C.990 B. A. L.809 J.D. Chubb Group of Ins. Cos.
Saleman, Michael N. ........................ '55 '80 C.112 B.A. L.1148 J.D. [Saleman&P.]
Saleman & Pack-Rayman, Law Offices of ........................ 16530 Ventura Blvd.
Salica, William J. ........................ '46 '72 L.724 J.D. 16027 Ventura Blvd.
**Salomons, Gary K.** ........................ '61 '86 C.1077 B.S. L.800 J.D. [Greenberg&B.]
*PRACTICE AREAS: Commercial Litigation; Creditor Rights; Gaming Law.
Saltzburg, Joel ........................ '39 '75 C.112 B.S. L.1095 J.D. 18022 Medley Dr.
Salute, Eugene M., (BV) ........................ '38 '65 C.112 B.S. L.1065 LL.B. 16055 Ventura Blvd.
Samuels, Lawrence C. ........................ '31 '76 L.809 J.D. 15760 Ventura Blvd.
Sanders, Marshall C., (BV) ........................ '43 '71 C.36 B.S. L.809 J.D. 16530 Ventura Blvd.
Sarak, Cynthia Marie ........................ '62 '94 C.1169 B.A. L.990 J.D. [A Stein,H.L.&Y.]
Sarkin, Allan J. ........................ '48 '82 C.112 L.1190 J.D. 15720 Ventura Blvd.
Sarko, Alexander M., (CV) ........................ '36 '66 C.477 M.S.E. L.800 J.D. 15910 Ventura Blvd.
Sauler, Max A. ........................ '48 '74 C.1077 B.A. L.809 J.D. 16000 Ventura Blvd., Suite 701
Savate, Rose D. ........................ '25 '68 C&L.1095 B.A., J.D. Dep. City Atty.
Scharf, Robert Lee ........................ '20 '49 L.424 J.D. P.O. Box 260123
Schenkel, Evan B. ........................ '51 '76 C.1077 B.A. L.800 J.D. [E.B.Schenkel]
Schenkel, Evan B., A Prof. Corp. ........................ 15760 Ventura Blvd., 7th Fl.
Schiff, Lorin A. ........................ '54 '80 C.112 B.A. L.426 J.D. 4811 Andasol Ave.
Schilit, Menachem ........................ '50 '75 C.112 B.A. L.426 J.D. [Berkovitz&S.]
**Schoemaker, Charles, Jr.**, (AV) ........................ '51 '78 C.705 B.A. L.1136 J.D. [Altman&S.]
*REPORTED CASES: Cervantes v. Great American Ins. Co. (1983) 140 CA3d 763; Schlick v. Comco Management, Inc. (1987) 196 CA3d 974.
*PRACTICE AREAS: Personal Injury Law; Products Liability Law; Government Tort Liability; Subrogation Law; Commercial Collection.
**Schreiber, Douglas K.** ........................ '53 '78 C.800 B.S. L.426 J.D. [C Anker&H.]
*REPORTED CASES: Waisbren v. Peppercorn Productions Inc., (1995) 41 Cal.App.4th 246 48 Cal. Rptr. 2d 437; Lewame vs. Franchise Tax Board (1994) 9 Cal.4th 263, 36 Cal. Rptr.2d 563 Amicus Curiae.
*PRACTICE AREAS: Business; Real Estate; Litigation.

**Schreiber, Mark '49 '84 C.685 B.A. L.596 J.D.**
**16501 Ventura Boulevard Suite 401, 91436-2068**
**Telephone: 818-789-2577 Fax: 818-789-3391**
***REPORTED CASES: Klein v. Bia Hotel Corp. 41 Cal.App.4th 1133, Cal.Rptr.2d (1996).**
**Associate: Rebecca Lynn Smith.**
**Personal Injury, Elder Abuse, and Wrongful Death Defense, Copyright, Trademark, Medical Malpractice.**
*See Professional Biographies, ENCINO, CALIFORNIA*

Schuller, Henri R. ........................ '47 '80 L.398 J.D. 15760 Ventura Blvd.
Schultz, Alan Jule ........................ '45 '78 C.831 B.A. L.999 J.D. [A.J.Schultz]
Schultz, Alan Jule, A Law Corporation ........................ 16133 Ventura Blvd., PH A
Schwab, Helen Lorraine ............ '57 '83 C.839 B.A. L.464 J.D. 16055 Ventura Blvd.

CALIFORNIA—ENCINO MARTINDALE-HUBBELL LAW DIRECTORY 1997

Schwam, Bernard R. .................. '44 '75 C.1077 B.A. L.809 J.D. 16133 Ventura Blvd.
Schwartz, David S., (AV) ........... '28 '60 C.112 B.A. L.426 J.D. 15821 Ventura Blvd.
Schwartz, Glen H., (A Law Corp.), (AV) '49 '74 C&L.800 B.A., J.D. 16130 Ventura Blvd.
**Schwartz, Marshall N.**, (BV) ..... '45 '71 C.1077 B.S. L.1068 J.D. [Karno,S.F.S.&W.] ‡
Schwartz, Neil F. .................. '51 '77 C.112 B.A. L.1095 J.D. 15915 Ventura Blvd.
Schwartz, Richard A. ............... '52 '79 C.1019 B.A. L.1148 J.D. 17609 Ventura Blvd.
Schwartz, Ross T., (P.C.) ............. '49 '76 C.112 A.B. L.273 J.D. 17008 Escalon Dr.
**Scott, S. Dell**, (AV) ........................ '21 '48 C&L.145 A.B., J.D. [Gillin,S.A.G.&S.]
*LANGUAGES: German.
*PRACTICE AREAS: Business Law; Corporate Law; Contract Law; Litigation (15%); Construction Law (5%).
**Scupine, Jason J.** ..................... '65 '90 C.112 B.A. L.426 J.D. [Elliot,L.L.&S.]
*PRACTICE AREAS: Insurance Defense; Medical Malpractice Defense.
Seaman, Elizabeth Hobson '57 '83 C.860 B.A. L.494 J.D. (adm. in NY; not adm. in CA) 5147 Newcastle Ave.‡
Seeley, Ronald J., (AV) .................. '51 '77 C.112 B.A. L.1065 J.D. [Robman&S.]
Selwyn, Herbert E. ........................ '25 '50 C.112 L.800 J.D. 15432 Milbank
Seuthe, Kathy B. .................... '59 '85 C.112 B.A. L.426 J.D. 16133 Ventura Blvd.
**Shafron, Shelly Jay, (A Professional Corporation)**, (AV) '50 '75 C.800 B.A. L.426 J.D. [Karno,S.F.S.&W.]
Shandler, Carole C. ................... '57 '83 C.112 B.A. L.800 J.D. 16055 Ventura Blvd.
**Shapiro, Andrew L.**, (AV) ......... '47 '72 C.1077 B.A. L.426 J.D. [Lewitt,H.H.S.M.&H.]
*PRACTICE AREAS: Personal Injury Law; Products Liability Litigation.
**Shapiro, Cindy A.** .................... '66 '94 C.112 B.A.B.S. L.426 J.D. [Elliot,L.L.&S.]
*PRACTICE AREAS: Insurance Defense; Medical Malpractice Defense.
Shapiro, Daniel K. .......................... '67 '93 C&L.800 B.A., J.D. 16000 Ventura Blvd.
Shapiro, Marc S. ........................... '65 '91 C.659 B.A. L.1049 J.D. [Stein,H.L.&Y.]
Shapiro, Stephen N. .................. '50 '76 C.112 B.A. L.1221 J.D. 16830 Ventura Blvd.
Sharf, Mark M. ........................ '65 '88 C.659 B.S. L.1066 J.D. 16830 Ventura Blvd.
Shatzkin, Morton L. .............. '38 '64 C.563 B.B.A. L.1009 LL.B. 16055 Ventura Blvd.
Sheehy, Maureen E. ..................... '44 '79 C.112 Ph.D. L.426 J.D. P.O. Box 18843
**Shelden, Aaron E.**, (AV) .................. '30 '56 C&L.477 B.A., J.D. [Shelden,K.R.&F.]

**Shelden, Kulchin, Rosen & Florence, (AV)**
**16130 Ventura Boulevard Suite 650, 91436-2590**
**Telephone: 818-783-1664 Fax: 818-783-0610**
**Email: SKF4LAW@AOL.COM**
**Members of Firm: Aaron E. Shelden; Sydney Kulchin; Arnold L. Rosen; Barry G. Florence. Associates: Howard D. Silver; Terry Porvin; Mario R. Rivera.**
**General Civil and Trial Practice in all Courts. Insurance Defense, Personal Injury and Family Law.**
*See Professional Biographies, ENCINO, CALIFORNIA*

Sherman, Jay, (AV) ......... '51 '77 C.1042 B.A. L.426 J.D. 16601 Ventura Blvd., 4th Fl.
Sherman, Loren D., II ............... '52 '85 C.1077 B.S. L.940 J.D. 16133 Ventura Blvd.
Shoosmith, John F., Jr. ........................ '48 '73 C&L.776 B.A., J.D. 15840 Ventura Blvd.
Shulman, Shulman & Siegel ......... 16055 Ventura Blvd. (⊙Beverly Hills & Hydesville)
Sidman, Bernard ......................... '50 '83 C.061 LL.B. 16530 Ventura Blvd.
**Siegal, Floyd J.**, (AV) ..................... '52 '78 C.763 B.A. L.426 J.D. [Spile&S.]
*PRACTICE AREAS: Real Estate; Insurance Defense; Professional Liability; Employment; Appellate.
Siegel, Dee Miller ..................... '40 '80 C.112 B.A. L.1095 J.D. [Shulman,S.&S.]
Siegel, Edwin B. ..................... '38 '64 C.112 B.A. L.426 LL.B. 16000 Ventura Blvd.
Silk, Kenneth R. ........................ '37 '62 C&L.800 B.A., LL.B. 16311 Ventura Blvd.
**Silver, Howard D.** ........................... '54 '79 C.36 B.S. L.930 J.D. [Shelden,K.R.&F.]
**Silver, Scott Z.** ..................... '50 '76 C.1042 B.A. L.1137 J.D. [Goldstein,G.&S.]
**Simon, Joel M.**, (AV) .................. '46 '78 C.1077 B.A. L.1148 J.D. [Gillin,S.A.G.&S.]
*PRACTICE AREAS: Corporate Law; Commercial Law; Litigation; Family Law.
**Simon, Judith R.** ............................ '37 '90 C.112 B.S. L.809 J.D. [Alpert,B.&G.]
*PRACTICE AREAS: Family Law.
Simon, Ralph .......................... '27 '77 C.112 L.1095 J.D. 16255 Ventura Blvd.
Sinasohn, John M. ...................... '28 '78 L.1190 LL.B. 18075 Ventura Blvd.
Sisskind, Harvey A. ............ '29 '57 C.112 B.S. L.1068 LL.B. 4249 Bonavita Dr.
Slavin, Robert E. .................. '57 '87 C.1077 B.A. L.1184 J.D. 17609 Ventura Blvd.
Small, Leon ............................ '48 '75 C.112 B.A. L.426 J.D. [L.Small]
Small, Leon, A P.C. ................................................ 16530 Ventura Blvd.
Smith, Edward H. ..................... '46 '75 C.475 B.A. L.809 J.D. [Smith&R.]
Smith, Jerome B., (AV) ............... '51 '76 C.112 B.A. L.770 J.D. [Rosenthal&S.]
Smith, Marc ........................... '51 '76 C.563 B.B.A. L.1095 J.D. [Krane&S.]
**Smith, Rebecca Lynn** .................. '— '95 C.112 B.S. L.809 J.D. [M.Schreiber]
Smith, Selma Moidel, (Mrs.) ............ '19 '43 C.113 L.1001 LL.B. 5272 Lindley Ave.‡
Smith & Ruch ........................................................ 17003 Ventura Blvd.
**Snyder, Bradley A.** ..................... '57 '83 C.112 B.A. L.426 J.D. [Staitman,S.&T.]
*PRACTICE AREAS: Insurance Defense; Insurance Coverage; Personal Injury; Medical Malpractice; Product Liability.
Snyder, Lee Ann ....................... '47 '82 C.628 B.A. L.426 J.D. 5055 Amestoy Ave.
**Snyder, Michael R.** ................. '58 '84 C.1042 B.A. L.1137 J.D. [Elliot,L.L.&S.]⊙
*PRACTICE AREAS: Insurance Defense; Medical Malpractice Defense.
**Soibelman, Adam J.** ..................... '64 '90 C.1077 B.A. L.464 J.D. [Stone&R.]
*SPECIAL AGENCIES: Judge, Regional Client Counseling Competition, Pepperdine University, 1993, 1994, 1995.
*PRACTICE AREAS: Construction Defect; Insurance Defense; Business Litigation.

**Solner, Michael C., (AV) '42 '72 C.800 B.F.S. L.426 J.D.**
**16000 Ventura Boulevard, Suite 500, 91436**
**Telephone: 818-995-6052 FAX: 818-995-0407**
***LANGUAGES: Spanish.**
**Estate Planning, Trust and Probate Law, Civil Litigation, Professional Negligence, Business, White Collar Criminal Litigation, Elder Law.**
*See Professional Biographies, ENCINO, CALIFORNIA*

Sommer, Paul R. ...................... '47 '76 C.1077 B.A. L.1148 J.D. [Sommer&B.]⊙
Sommer and Bear ....................... 15760 Ventura Blvd. (⊙Beverly Hills)

**Sommers, Hubert R., (AV) '30 '60 C.502 B.S.B.A. L.800 J.D.**
**Suite 1228, 16055 Ventura Boulevard, 91436**
**Telephone: 818-789-0465 FAX: 818-990-6304**
**General Civil and Trial Practice in all State Courts. Corporation, Real Estate, Probate, Negligence and Family Law.**
**Reference: City National Bank, Encino Office.**
*See Professional Biographies, ENCINO, CALIFORNIA*

Sosa, Carlos E. ........................... '55 '80 C&L.426 B.A., J.D. [Hausman&S.]
Sowers, Donald G. ................ '53 '86 C.999 A.S. L.809 J.D. [Takakjian&S.]⊙
Sparagna, Diana Biafora .............. '52 '78 C.800 B.A. L.1095 J.D. [Sparagna&S.]
Sparagna, Francis A., Jr. ............. '51 '77 C.197 B.A. L.809 J.D. [Sparagna&S.]
Sparagna and Sparagna ............................................... 5435 Balboa Blvd.
Spencer, Eric A., (AV) ................. '49 '79 C.1077 B.A. L.1148 J.D. [Szabo,S.&M.]
Sperber, David S., (AV) ............ '39 '65 C.112 A.B. L.1068 LL.B. 15910 Ventura Blvd.
Sperber, Lawrence J., (BV) ............ '44 '73 C&L.1095 B.A., J.D. 15760 Ventura Blvd.
**Spile, Steven D.** ............................ '55 '82 C.112 B.A. L.800 J.D. [Spile&S.]
*PRACTICE AREAS: Real Estate; Insurance Defense; Professional Liability; Alternative Dispute Resolution; Risk Management.

**Spile & Siegal, LLP, (AV)**
**Formerly, Krivis, Spile and Siegal, LLP**
**16501 Ventura Boulevard Suite 610, 91436**
**Telephone: 818-784-6899 Facsimile: 818-784-0176**
**Email: fsiegal@counsel.com**
**Steven D. Spile; Floyd J. Siegal. Associates: Andrew L. Leff; Michael P West. Of Counsel: David I. Karp; Jeffrey L. Krivis; Olga M. Moretti; David M. Galanti; Richard R. Leuthold.**
**Insurance Defense, Real Estate, Professional Liability, Employment Law, Criminal Defense and Alternative Dispute Resolution.**
*See Professional Biographies, ENCINO, CALIFORNIA*

**Spitzer, Daniel B.** ........................... '53 '85 C.112 B.A. L.1068 J.D. [Anker&H.]
*LANGUAGES: Hebrew and Yiddish.
*REPORTED CASES: In re Bosse, 122 B. R. 410 (Bkrptcy. C.D. Cal. 1990); Okrand v. City of Los Angeles, 207 Cal. App.3d 566, 254 Cal. Rptr. 913 (1989).
*PRACTICE AREAS: Business Litigation; Real Estate; Bankruptcy and Insolvency; Condominium Law; Legal Malpractice.
Spiwak, Lisa E. ............................. '61 '87 C.1168 B.A. L.809 J.D. [Spiwak&I.]
Spiwak & Iezza ........................................................ 16133 Ventura Blvd.
Stack, William S., (BV) ............. '24 '57 C&L.426 B.Sc., LL.B. 16255 Ventura Blvd.
**Staitman, Jack M.**, (AV) ................. '31 '60 C.112 B.A. L.800 J.D. [Staitman,S.&T.]
*PRACTICE AREAS: Insurance Defense; Insurance Coverage; Legal Malpractice; General Civil Litigation.

**Staitman, Snyder & Tannenbaum, (AV)**
**Suite 1401, 16633 Ventura Boulevard, 91436-1840**
**Telephone: 818-981-5300; 213-872-3530 FAX: 818-981-7104**
**Jack M. Staitman; Bradley A. Snyder; Jack J. Tannenbaum; David K. Dorenfeld;—Rodger S. Greiner; Gerald P. Peters; Deborah K. Galer.**
**General Civil, Trial, Appellate Practice. Insurance Law; Litigation; Personal Injury, Products Liability, Premises Liability, Medical Malpractice, Legal Malpractice, Corporate Real Estate, Commercial and General Business.**
*See Professional Biographies, ENCINO, CALIFORNIA*

Stanley, Lowen H. ....................... '20 '69 C.201 L.809 LL.B. 17125 Nance St.‡
Stanley, Richard B. ................ '50 '76 C.112 B.S. L.1148 J.D. 15760 Ventura Blvd.

**Stanton Law Corporation**
**(See Los Angeles)**

Star, Robert R. ..................... '46 '76 C.1077 B.S. L.1095 J.D. 16133 Ventura Blvd.

**Stavin, Richard A., and Associates '49 '75 C.1046 B.A. L.564 J.D.**
**15760 Ventura Boulevard, Suite 1600, 91436**⊙
**Telephone: 818-385-1144 Fax: 818-385-1149**
**Business and Fraud Litigation, Insurance Defense, Unfair Competition, Wrongful Termination, Discrimination Litigation.**
**Representative Clients: State Farm Insurance Co.; Allstate Insurance Co.; Farmers Insurance Group; California Casualty Group; Metro-Goldwyn Mayer, Inc.; Sizzler International, Inc.; AVI Entertainment Group, Inc.; Metropolitan Property Casualty Insurance Co.; Mercury Insurance Group; Unigard Insurance Co.; Financial Indemnity Co.; Royal Insurance Co.**
**Los Angeles, California Office: 1840 Century Park East, Suite 800. Telephone: 310-553-1144.**
*See Professional Biographies, ENCINO, CALIFORNIA*

Steelman, Henry ..................... '50 '75 C.112 B.A. L.809 J.D. 16000 Ventura Blvd.
Stein, Andrew D., (AV) ................ '39 '64 C.800 A.B. L.426 LL.B. [Stein,H.L.&Y.]
**Stein, Michael M.**, (AV) ...................... '41 '67 C.112 B.S. L.309 J.D. [M.M.Stein]
Stein, Hanger, Levine & Young, A Professional Corporation, (AV) 16501 Ventura Blvd., Ste., 300

**Stein, Michael M., Inc., (AV)**
**17609 Ventura Boulevard, Suite 201, 91316**
**Telephone: 818-788-2700 Fax: 818-788-2788**
**Email: MMSTEININC@AOL.COM**
**Michael M. Stein.**
**Real Estate, Taxation, Corporate, Securities, Business Litigation.**
*See Professional Biographies, ENCINO, CALIFORNIA*

Steinberg, Jody ............................ '65 '90 C.569 B.S. L.990 J.D. [Stein,H.L.&Y.]
Steiniger, Michael G. ............. '42 '67 C.112 B.A. L.1068 LL.B. 16530 Ventura Blvd.
Steinman, Jeffrey Q. ................ '53 '79 C.319 B.A. L.1019 J.D. 16830 Ventura Blvd.
Steinschriber, Frank ................ '48 '75 C.112 B.A. L.809 J.D. 15840 Ventura Blvd.
Stern, Fredrick H., (AV) ............. '47 '73 C.112 B.A. L.1068 J.D. 16830 Ventura Blvd.
Stern, Jerry R., (AV) .................. '39 '66 C.112 B.S. L.426 J.D. 16830 Ventura Blvd.
Stern, Michelle L. ..................... '56 '86 C.1036 B.A. L.800 J.D. 17404 Ventura Blvd.
**Stillman, Ronald H.**, (AV) ........... '47 '74 C.1077 B.A. L.809 J.D. [Goldstein,G.&S.]
*PRACTICE AREAS: Workers Compensation.
Stitz, David D. ....................... '44 '70 C.1077 B.A. L.800 J.D. 16055 Ventura Blvd.
Stone, Donald L. ..................... '30 '66 C.999 L.809 LL.M. 16133 Ventura Blvd.
**Stone, Gregory E.**, (AV) ..................... '63 '89 C.37 B.A. L.809 J.D. [Stone&R.]
*PRACTICE AREAS: Civil Litigation; Premises Liability; Security Guard Liability; Insurance Defense; Municipality Defense.
Stone, Stanley H. ............................ '39 '65 C&L.912 A.B., J.D. [Stone&S.]
Stone, Steven H. ............................ '63 '88 C.112 B.A. L.426 J.D. [Stone&S.]

**Stone & Rosenblatt, A Professional Corporation, (AV)**
**16133 Ventura Boulevard Suite 855, 91436**
**Telephone: 818-789-2232 Fax: 818-789-2269**
**Ira H. Rosenblatt; Gregory E. Stone;—Camille Calvert; Richard S. McGuire; Adam J. Soibelman.**
**Insurance Defense Litigation, Premises Liability Defense, Construction Defect, Municipality Defense, Products, Employment, Corporate and Commercial Transactions.**
*See Professional Biographies, ENCINO, CALIFORNIA*

Stone & Stone ...................................... 15821 Ventura Blvd., Ste. 675
Stratton, Larry ................... '58 '84 C.1042 B.A. L.1148 J.D. 16633 Ventura Blvd.
Sturman, David, (AV) ................ '54 '79 C.605 B.A. L.426 J.D. 16530 Ventura Blvd.
**Swanson, Hedwig C.** ............... '50 '86 C.025 B.A. L.426 J.D. [Lewitt,H.H.S.M.&H.]
*PRACTICE AREAS: Personal Injury Law; Products Liability Law.
Switzer, Craig A. ............ '62 '88 C.436 B.A. L.809 J.D. 15910 Ventura Blvd., 12th Fl.
Sykulski, George H. ........ '42 '67 C.696 B.A. L.1066 J.D. 16027 Ventura Blvd., Ste 460
Szabo, Lawrence J., (AV) .................. '47 '74 C.112 B.A. L.809 J.D. [Szabo,S.&M.]
Szabo, Spencer & Mulally, A Professional Corporation, (AV) ........ 15910 Ventura Blvd.
Takakjian, Paul, (BV) '53 '79 C.112 B.A. L.426 J.D. [Takakjian&S.] (⊙L.A., Oxnard & Orange)
Takakjian & Sowers, (BV) 16501 Ventura Blvd. (⊙Los Angeles, Oxnard, Orange, Pasadena & Long Beach)
Tanchuk, Ila M. ..................... '45 '84 C.112 B.A. L.809 J.D. 16133 Ventura Blvd.
**Tannenbaum, Jack J.**, (AV) ............ '42 '67 C.112 B.A. L.426 LL.B. [Staitman,S.&T.]
*PRACTICE AREAS: Personal Injury Defense; Trial Attorney.
Tasoff, Diane E. ...................... '60 '87 C.112 B.A. L.426 J.D. 16255 Ventura Blvd.
**Tasoff, Lloyd A.** ............................ '15 '38 C.563 B.S. L.1009 LL.B. [Tasoff&T.]
*PRACTICE AREAS: Immigration Law (100%).
**Tasoff, Richard J.**, (AV) ..................... '56 '82 C.112 B.S. L.800 J.D. [Tasoff&T.]
*PRACTICE AREAS: Immigration; Naturalization; Business Immigration; Contracts; Corporate.
**Tasoff, Ron Jeffrey**, (AV) .................. '50 '75 C.112 A.B. L.426 J.D. [Tasoff&T.]
*PRACTICE AREAS: Immigration; Naturalization; Business Immigration; Contracts; Corporate.

**Tasoff and Tasoff, (AV)**
**16255 Ventura Boulevard, Suite 1000, 91436-2302**
**Telephone: 818-788-8900 Fax: 818-788-5900**
**Email: 73032.135@compuserve.com URL: http://www.oaksnet.com/tasoff**

(This Listing Continued)

**Tasoff and Tasoff (Continued)**

**Members of Firm: Lloyd A. Tasoff; Ron Jeffrey Tasoff (Certified Specialist, Immigration and Nationality Law, The State Bar of California Board of Legal Specialization); Richard J. Tasoff (Certified Specialist, Immigration and Nationality Law, The State Bar of California Board of Legal Specialization).**
**Immigration, Naturalization, Business Immigration, Contracts, Corporate, Employer Sanctions.**

Temkin, Vicki L. .................. '48 '82 C.1077 B.A. L.1095 J.D. 15915 Ventura Blvd.
Terry, Baker O., Jr. ..................'51 '76 C.813 A.B. L.1066 J.D. P.O. Box 261128‡
Thabit, Bruce A., (BV) ........... '33 '63 C.437 A.B. L.809 LL.B. 16144 High Valley Pl.
Thaler, Elizabeth K. ....................'59 '83 C.112 B.A. L.464 J.D. 16659 Addison St.
Theofanis, George M., (AV) '53 '84 C.1044 B.A. L.809 J.D.
16601 Ventura Blvd., 4th Fl.
Thomas, Jill A. ............ '50 '80 C.342 B.A. L.809 J.D. 11th Flr., 16633 Ventura Blvd.
Thompson, Jack A., (BV) ................ '33 '72 C.800 B.S. L.1095 J.D. [J.A.Thompson]
Thompson, Jack A., Inc., (BV) ........................................16133 Ventura Blvd.
Thomulka, Russell J. ..................'46 '74 C&L.1095 B.A., J.D. 16530 Ventura Blvd.
Tinero, Ellen-Jo Friedman ...................'60 '89 C.112 B.S. L.1136 J.D. [Tinero&R.]
Tinero and Rauch ........................................................15915 Ventura Blvd.
Tobin, Robert C. '62 '92 C.1077 B.A. L.398 J.D.
House Coun., Republic Indemnity Co. of Amer.
Todd, Loraine ....................... '51 '87 C.112 B.A. L.426 J.D. 16027 Ventura Blvd.
Tollefson, Donald G., (BV) ................. '25 '52 C.112 L.800 LL.B. 17978 Boris Dr.
Torem, Ron ...............................'61 '88 C.1077 B.S. L.990 J.D. 16501 Ventura Blvd.
Treitel, Emanuel ......................'30 '58 C.112 B.S. L.809 J.D. 4792 Park Encino Lane
**Trygar, Louis Peter** ....................'59 '87 C.705 B.A. L.809 J.D. [▣ Pearlman,B.&W.]
*LANGUAGES: French.
*PRACTICE AREAS: Workers Compensation Law; Subrogation.
Tyler, Kenneth C. .......................... '18 '42 C&L.494 J.D. 15760 Ventura Blvd.
Tyler, Terry L. ................ '45 '71 C.112 B.A. L.1068 J.D. 3926 Ballina Canyon Rd.‡
Uhrman, Walter M., (BV) ............... '41 '66 C.674 A.B. L.813 LL.B. 15450 Milbank St.
Vallier, Robt., (AV) ....................'24 '50 C.813 A.B. L.809 LL.B. 15720 Ventura Blvd.
Van Camp, Dale ................................................'48 '89 L.398 J.D. P.O. Box 17675
**Van Dyke, Michael J.** .................. '67 '93 C.770 B.S. L.423 J.D. [▣ Elliot,L.L.&S.]
*PRACTICE AREAS: Insurance Defense; Medical Malpractice Defense.
Vickman, Leon L., (AV) ..................'32 '79 C.111 B.S.E.E. L.426 J.D. [L.L.Vickman]
Vickman, Leon L., A Law Corp., (AV) ...................................16255 Ventura Blvd.

**Victor, Robert M. '66 '91 C.874 B.A. L.990 J.D.**
**16255 Ventura Boulevard, Suite 212, 91436**
**Telephone: 818-385-3744 FAX: 818-385-0410**
**Email: rvictor@themall.net**
**Business Litigation, Personal Injury, Medical Malpractice, Product Liability, Family Law, Adoption, Corporate, Contracts and Collections.**
***See Professional Biographies, ENCINO, CALIFORNIA***

**Vogel, Pearl Franklin, (AV) '37 '69 L.398 J.D.**
**15760 Ventura Boulevard, Suite 700, 91436-3046**
**Telephone: 818-986-6696 Fax: 818-986-3110**
***LANGUAGES: Spanish and Yiddish.**
***PRACTICE AREAS: Family Law (90%); Mediation; Arbitration.**
**Family Law and Mediation.**
***See Professional Biographies, ENCINO, CALIFORNIA***

Wabby, Walter J. ........................ '53 '79 C.229 B.A. L.1095 J.D. 15910 Ventura Blvd.
**Wager, Jerome** ................................. '57 '82 C.112 B.A. L.1049 J.D. [Kolod&W.]⊙
Walch, Joseph ...................................................'41 '73 16000 Ventura Blvd.
Waller, Marshall W., II, (AV) ...........'55 '81 C.1074 B.A. L.426 J.D. [Feinberg,G.&W.]
Walsh, Cheryl Hardt ........................ '65 '91 C.1077 B.S. L.426 J.D. [▣ Stein,H.L.&Y.]
Warden, Thomas H., (BV) .................... '43 '71 C&L.1095 B.A., J.D. [Warden&G.]
Warden and Gart, (BV) ..................................................16255 Ventura Blvd.
Waterman, Michael A. .............. '50 '77 C.112 B.A. L.809 J.D. 17000 Ventura Blvd.
Watnick, Lewis, (AV) ................................ '29 '52 C.215 L.426 LL.D. 5445 Balboa Blvd.
**Wax, Steven H.** ............................ '50 '76 C.1077 B.A. L.809 J.D. [Pearlman,B.&W.]
*PRACTICE AREAS: Workers Compensation.
Waxman, H. Stuart ................................'47 '86 C.549 B.A. L.809 J.D. [▣ Fields&F.]
Wayne, Eric J. .......................... '61 '88 C.112 B.A. L.809 J.D. 15821 Ventura Blvd.
Weinstein, Gerald A. .................'22 '60 C.339 B.S. L.800 LL.B. 15915 Ventura Blvd.‡
Weis, Gary A. .............................'54 '93 C.1155 B.S. L.398 J.D. 16633 Ventura Blvd.
Weisberg, L. Steven .......................................... '48 '76 L.999 J.D. 16161 Ventura Blvd.
**Weiss, Heather Bergerson** ..........'67 '92 C.773 B.A. L.1148 J.D. [▣ Goldstein,G.&S.]
*PRACTICE AREAS: Workers' Compensation.
Weiss, Robert Peter '57 '84
C.1349 B.A. L.904 J.D. 16133 Ventura Blvd., Penthouse Suite A
Weiss, Ronald, (P.C.) ................ '43 '69 C.112 B.A. L.800 J.D. 15910 Ventura Blvd.
Weissman, Robert A., (AV) .............. '50 '75 C.112 B.A. L.809 J.D. [Weissman&W.]
Weissman & Weissman, A Professional Law Corporation, (AV) ...... 16130 Ventura Blvd.
**West, Michael P** ............................... '68 '94 C.305 B.A. L.990 J.D. [▣ Spile&S.]
West, Steven M., (BV) ............ '51 '77 C&L.1136 B.S.L., J.D. 16830 Ventura Blvd.
Widre, Sheryl ............................'64 '89 C.112 B.A. L.1148 J.D. 5704 Ostrom Ave.
Wiener, Herb, (Prof. Corp.), (AV) '22 '47
C.112 B.A. L.800 LL.B. 4141 Hayvenhurst Ave.
Wilson, Ralph, (AV) .............. '14 '38 C.563 B.S.S. L.800 LL.B. 16633 Ventura Blvd.
Wilton, Ronald D. .....................'57 '81 C.112 B.A. L.426 J.D. 16055 Ventura Blvd.
Winer, Marshall M. ......................'37 '66 C.930 B.B.A. L.62 J.D. 15915 Ventura Blvd.
Witt, Gerald A. ............................'42 '67 C.602 B.B.A. L.800 J.D. 15760 Ventura Blvd.
Wittlin, Irwin M. ............ '62 '86 C.112 B.A. L.426 J.D. 15910 Ventura Blvd., 12th Fl.
Wohl, Laurence B. .......................'46 '72 C.112 B.S. L.1067 J.D. 16311 Ventura Blvd.
Wohlner, Jeffrey S. .................... '43 '69 C.352 B.A. L.190 J.D. [Wohlner K.P.V.&Y.]
Wohlner Kaplon Phillips Vogel & Young, (AV) .......................15760 Ventura Blvd.
Wolf, Mervyn H., (AV) ...........'39 '68 C.112 B.A. L.1095 LL.B. 15760 Ventura Blvd.
Worthington, Michael F. .............'47 '77 C.112 B.A. L.1095 J.D. 15760 Ventura Blvd.
Wright, Gordon S. ........................'48 '74 C.112 A.B. L.174 J.D. 15760 Ventura Blvd.
Wynn, Arthur ........................'30 '74 C.1190 B.S. L.999 LL.B. 18075 Ventura Blvd.
Wynn, Marvin ............................'33 '79 C.112 B.A. L.1095 J.D. 18075 Ventura Blvd.
Yallen, Robert B. '57 '85
C.1077 B.S. L.809 J.D. Exec. V.P. & Gen. Coun., Intermedia Co.
Yam, Gerald B. ..........................'28 '55 C.563 B.B.A. L.569 LL.B. 6345 Balboa Blvd.
Yardum, LeVone A., (AV) ..................'21 '53 C.800 L.569 LL.B. 15915 Ventura Blvd.
Yaspan, Robert M. ...................... '46 '72 C.145 A.B. L.800 J.D. 16000 Ventura Blvd.
Yellin, Jeffrey C. ....................................... '49 '79 L.1221 J.D. 17525 Ventura Blvd.
**Young, Kenneth P.** ..........................................'50 '78 [Wohlner K.P.V.&Y.]
**Ysabal, Daniel J.** ..............................'54 '86 C.426 B.A. L.1190 J.D. [Altman&S.]
*PRACTICE AREAS: Workers Compensation Defense; Collections.
Yusim, Milton, (AV) ...................'30 '55 C&L.800 A.B., LL.B. 16501 Ventura Blvd.
Zand, Steve S. .........................'61 '89 C.1077 B.S.C. L.398 J.D. 16027 Ventura Blvd.
Zebberman, Shep A., Law Offices of '59 '91
C.684 B.S.B.A. L.398 J.D. 15760 Ventura Blvd., Suite 1520
Zeesman, Jeffrey R., (BV) ............'47 '79 C.1097 B.S. L.1136 J.D. [J.R.Zeesman&Assoc.]
Zeesman, Jeffrey Reid, & Associates, (BV) .............................16250 Ventura Blvd.
Zeff, Michael D. ........................ '52 '77 C.112 B.A. L.809 J.D. 16027 Ventura Blvd.
Zimmerman, Brian F., (BV) ...........'53 '78 C.1077 B.A. L.426 J.D. [Zimmerman&K.]
Zimmerman & Kahanowitch, (BV) .........................................16000 Ventura Blvd.
**Zimmet, Keith Todd** ............ '61 '87 C.1077 B.S. L.800 J.D. [▣ Lewitt,H.H.S.M.&H.]
*PRACTICE AREAS: Real Estate; Business; Banking; Commercial Finance Law.
Zumwalt, William J., (AV) ......'27 '53 C.94 A.B. L.93 J.D. 16000 Ventura Blvd., 5th Fl.

## ENTERPRISE, 11,486, *Shasta Co.*

Sheppard, Stennett ................ '13 '38 C.813 B.A. L.1066 LL.B. 2680 Reservoir Ln.‡

## ESCALON, 4,437, *San Joaquin Co.*

Naraghi, Wendell J. ............... '42 '67 C.112 B.A. L.165 J.D. H&N Develop. Co., Inc.

## ESCONDIDO, 108,635, *San Diego Co.*

Allen, Noel M. .............. '42 '77 C.871 B.S. L.1049 J.D. 326 E. Grand (⊙San Diego)
**Altona, Erick R.** ............................'59 '85 C.112 B.A. L.1067 J.D. [Lounsbery,F.A.&P.]
*PRACTICE AREAS: Business; Real Estate; Commercial; Corporation; Federal and State Securities.
Anderson, Mark A. ............................'54 '81 C.112 B.A. L.1049 J.D. 205 W. 5th Ave.
Ballun, George '27 '76 C.999 PH.D L.861 J.D.
(adm. in LA; not adm. in CA) 1310 Portola Ave.‡
Barkin, David R., (A P.C.), (BV) .........'48 '76 C.763 B.S. L.1137 J.D. 221 W. Crest St.
**Bartlett, Bradley A.**, (BV) ..............'51 '80 C.112 B.A. L.1049 J.D. [Bartlett K.&L.]

**Bartlett Kirch & Lievers, (BV)**
**221 West Crest Street Suite 200, 92025-1728**
**Telephone: 619-738-9789 Fax: 619-738-8733**
**Members of Firm: Bradley A. Bartlett; Jacques J. Kirch; Gregory Y. Lievers.**
**Personal Injury, Real Estate, Employment Law and Insurance Litigation.**
***See Professional Biographies, ESCONDIDO, CALIFORNIA***

Battle, Anne Glann ................. '55 '85 C.10 B.S. L.836 J.D. 555 W. Country Club Ln.‡
Beall-Templin, Diane, (CV) ......................'47 '73 C&L.107 B.S., J.D. 1016 Circle Dr.
Bell, V. Parker, (BV) ........................ '47 '73 C.112 B.S. L.1049 J.D. 2434 Vineyard Ave.
Beloud, Robert G., (AV) .......... '10 '33 C.477 L.213 LL.B. 29695 Circle R Greens Dr.‡
Black, Karen E., (BV) ........... '38 '83 C.763 B.S. L.1049 J.D. 144 E. Washington Ave.
Borecky, Tamara S. ..................'61 '88 C.1163 B.S. L.426 J.D. 311 Cypress Crest Ter.
Boyer, Richard E., (BVⓣ) '44 '72 C.627 B.G.S. L.1294 J.D.
(adm. in NH; not adm. in CA) 1905 Cortez Ave.‡
**Bright, David S.**, (AV) .......................'49 '74 C.112 B.A. L.1049 J.D. [White&B.]⊙
*PRACTICE AREAS: Real Estate; Civil Litigation.
**Brown, Michelle J.** ........................ '59 '86 C.112 B.A. L.464 J.D. [▣ Lounsbery,F.A.&P.]
*PRACTICE AREAS: Real Estate; Estate Planning; Business; Government Relations.
Bruno, Louis G. ............................................ '52 '88 C.1097 B.S. L.1137 J.D. [L.G.Bruno]
Bruno, Louis G., P.C. .......................................................................456 E. Grand Ave.
Bunce, Art, (BV) ................ '48 '73 C.674 A.B. L.1068 J.D. 430 N. Cedar St., Suite H
Cahill, Lynn J., A Professional Law Corporation, (BV) '45 '78
C.132 B.A. L.1049 J.D. P.O. Box 463907
Carey, Charles G., (BV) ......................'31 '65 C.757 B.A. L.1049 J.D. 225 E. 3rd Ave.
Carl, Scott E. ......................'53 '75 C&L.1188 B.A., LL.B. 1820 S. Escondido Blvd.‡
**Carlin, Ira S.**, (AV) .............................................'36 '65 C&L.178 A.B., LL.B. [I.S.Carlin]
*PRACTICE AREAS: Civil Litigation; Probate; Corporate; Business; Real Property.

**Carlin, Ira S., A Professional Corporation, (AV)**
**235 East Fourth Avenue, 92025**
**Telephone: 619-741-8111 Fax: 619-741-4073**
**Ira S. Carlin.**
**Corporation, Business, Probate and Real Property Law. General Civil and Trial Practice in all State and Federal Courts. Debt Collection and Enforcement of Judgments.**
**Reference: Rancho Santa Fe National Bank (Escondido Office).**
***See Professional Biographies, ESCONDIDO, CALIFORNIA***

Carss, D. Bradley ...............................'48 '77 C.1077 B.S. L.1095 J.D. 3811 Foxley Dr.
Chapman, David R., (BV) ...........................'47 '77 C.685 B.A. L.04 LL.B. City Atty.
Clark, Lorin R. ............................'58 '92 C.763 B.S. L.800 J.D. P.O. Box 460550
Cleary, Patricia L., (BV) .....................'46 '80 C.908 B.S. L.1137 J.D. 350 E. Grand Ave.

**Cole, Dorothy A., (AV) '39 '74 L.1137 J.D. ▣▣**
**Town View Professional Centre, 215 South Hickory Street, Suite 224, 92025-4361**
**Telephone: 619-745-6313**
**(Certified Specialist, Probate, Estate Planning and Trust Law, The State Bar of California Board of Legal Specialization).**
**Estate Planning, Wills, Trusts and Probate Law.**
***See Professional Biographies, ESCONDIDO, CALIFORNIA***

Conkey, Patrick B. ......................'47 '76 C.112 B.A. L.809 J.D. 135 W. Mission Ave.
Connole, James W. ...........................'29 '75 C.763 L.999 J.D. 2948 Verda Ave.‡
Cornelius, Quincy B., (BV) .........'48 '78 C.172 B.S. L.410 J.D. 311 E. Washington Ave.
**Cronin, Daniel J.**, (AV) ........................................'45 '73 L.1137 J.D. [Cronin&C.]
*PRACTICE AREAS: Personal Injury Law; Criminal Law; Business Law; Probate Law.
**Cronin, John O'Shea** ....................................'61 '88 L.1137 B.S.L. [Cronin&C.]
*PRACTICE AREAS: Trial Law; Civil Practice; Criminal Law; Personal Injury; Probate.

**Cronin & Cronin, (AV)**
**225 East Third Avenue, 92025-4203**
**Telephone: 619-745-8103 Fax: 619-739-0911**
**Members of Firm: Daniel F. Cronin (1922-1976); Daniel J. Cronin; John O'Shea Cronin.**
**Business and Commercial Litigation, Personal Injury Litigation with Emphasis in Accident and Injury, Criminal Defense, including matters involving White Collar Crimes, Major Felonies, Misdemeanors, Drug Trafficking, D.W.I, Domestic Violence, Probate Proceedings.**
***See Professional Biographies, ESCONDIDO, CALIFORNIA***

Dean, Peter L., (AV) ......................'39 '73 C.628 B.S. L.767 J.D. 120 Woodward Ave.
Dietrich, D. David, (BV) .............................................— '81 L.1137 J.D. [Dietrich&G.]
Dietrich and Gilmore, (BV) ...................................................239 E. 4th Ave. (⊙San Diego)
Doering, Vivian Velichkoff ........................'30 '89 C.763 M.A. L.1049 J.D. [Doering D.]
Doering Diversified, Ltd. ..................................................................P.O. Box 2968
Dowd, Edward C., (BV) ...................................'34 '63 C.209 B.A. L.1049 J.D. [E.C.Dowd]
Dowd, Edward C., A Prof. Corp., (BV) .............................................225 E. Third Ave.
Edwards, Stacy L. ..........................'62 '95 C&L.1137 B.S., J.D. 144 E. Washington Ave.
Epp, Jeffrey R., (AV) ...................................'59 '84 C&L.972 B.A., J.D. Asst. City Atty.
Feltscher, Jack ..............................................'52 '78 C.563 B.A. L.285 J.D. 1425 Victoria Glenn
**Ferguson, David W.**, (AV) ...........'48 '73 C.112 B.A. L.1068 J.D. [Lounsbery,F.A.&P.]
*PRACTICE AREAS: Local Government Transactions; Public Franchises; Public Contracts; Land Use; Development.
Fischer, Barbara G. ........................................ '42 '89 C.273 B.A. L.61 J.D. 239 E. 4th Ave.
**Fitzpatrick, Curtis M.**, (AV) ..... '28 '64 C.763 A.B. L.1049 J.D. [▣ Lounsbery,F.A.&P.]
*PRACTICE AREAS: Municipal Government; Municipal Financing; Land Use and Planning; Municipal Franchising; Municipal Sports Enterprise.
Fleming, Graham K., (BV) .........'28 '60 C.317 A.B. L.1066 J.D. 605 East Valley Pkwy.
Forrest-Hoadley, Linda, (BV) ...................'56 '83 C.112 B.A. L.1049 J.D. [Hoadley&F.]
Foster, Robert P. .......................'24 '54 C.246 A.B. L.800 LL.B. 3915 Sierra Linda Dr.‡

CAA85P

CALIFORNIA—ESCONDIDO MARTINDALE-HUBBELL LAW DIRECTORY 1997

**Friedrichs, Michael A.** . . . . . . . '64 '95 C.112 B.A. L.1137 J.D. [▣ White&B.]
*PRACTICE AREAS: Civil Litigation.
Gallagher, Thomas P. . . . . . . . '15 '72 C.999 L.809 J.D. 28386 Cavalier Ct.‡
Galyean, Thomas E., (BV) . . . . . . '45 '75 C.112 B.A. L.61 J.D. [Galyean,T.&W.]
Galyean, Talley & Wood, (BV) . . . . . . . 739 E. Pennsylvania Ave.
Garrett, Roy B., (BV) . . . . . . '43 '70 C.763 B.A. L.1049 J.D. 225 E. 3rd Ave.
Goldfeder, Judd . . . . . . . '34 '59 L.800 LL.B. 333 S. Ivy St.
Gorman, Frank M. . . . . . . '21 '48 C.309 A.B. L.930 LL.B. 1729 E. Grand Ave.
Gorman, Thomas F. . . . . . . '22 '73 C&L.1137 B.S., J.D. 137 W. Vermont‡
Halvorson, William J. . . . . . '47 '90 C.999 B.A. L.1065 J.D. 215 S. Hickory
Hanneken, D. V. . . . . . '14 '55 C.061 L.809 J.D. 18941 Starvation Mtn. Rd.
Hoadley, Philip M., Jr., (BV) . . . . . '46 '81 C.763 B.A. L.1049 J.D. [Hoadley&F.]
Hoadley & Forrest, (BV) . . . . . . . 345 W. 9th Ave.
Hudson, Richard B. . . . . . . '43 '89 C.871 B.S. L.1049 J.D. [▣ Jensen&R.]

**Jaques, Bruce D., Jr., (BV) '51 '79 C.813 A.B. L.228 J.D.**
**1520 Encino Drive, 92025**
**Telephone: 619-741-7352 Fax: 619-489-1670**
***REPORTED CASES: Considime Co. v. Shadle, Hunt & Hagar, 187 Cal. App. 3d 760; 232 Cal Rptr 25 (1986).**
**Business Litigation, Business Related Matters, Arbitration, Mediation, Computer Law, Banking, Real Estate Acquisitions and Sales.**
***See Professional Biographies, ESCONDIDO, CALIFORNIA***

Jensen, Jon A., (BV) . . . . . . '46 '74 C.763 B.S. L.61 J.D. [Jensen&R.]
Jensen & Roth, (BV) . . . . . . . 451 Escondido Blvd.
Johnson, Henry P., (BV) . . . . . '28 '57 C.112 B.A. L.1066 J.D. 830 E. Grand Ave.
Jones, Lynne Thompson . . . . . . '61 '91 L.1241 J.D. 333 S. Juniper St.
Joyner, Conrad F., Jr. . . . . . '56 '89 C.763 B.A. L.1241 J.D. 205 W. 5th Ave.
Keim, Judy G. . . . . . . '48 '89 C.651 B.S. L.61 J.D. 1637 E. Valley Pkwy.
Kinch, Allan B. . . . . . '37 '76 C.35 B.S. L.1137 J.D. 507 S. Escondido Blvd.
**Kirch, Jacques J.** . . . . . . '59 '89 C.112 B.A. L.464 J.D. [Bartlett K.&L.]
Kreep, Gary G., (CV) . . . . '50 '75 C.112 B.A. L.1049 J.D. Exec. Dir., U.S. Jus. Foundation
Larmer, Robert C., (BV) . . . . '29 '70 C.112 B.S. L.1049 J.D. 1766 S. Escondido Blvd.
Larsen, Constance . . . . . . '56 '86 C.1193 B.B.A. L.336 J.D. P.O. Box 460147
**LePla, Charles A.** . . . . . '63 '94 C.1074 B.S. L.1049 J.D. [▣ Lounsbery,F.A.&P.]
*PRACTICE AREAS: Land Use; Development; Public Contracts and Franchises.
**Lievers, Gregory Y.**, (BV) . . . . . '57 '83 C.112 B.A. L.800 J.D. [Bartlett K.&L.]
Lisi, Joseph M., (BV) . . . . . . '35 '64 C&L.813 A.B., J.D. 225 E. 3rd Ave.
LoGatto, Anthony F. '15 '55 C.262 M.S.S.S. L.724 J.D.
(adm. in NY; not adm. in CA) 2334 Sunset Dr.‡
Lopardo, Fiorenzo V. . . . . . '20 '49 C.602 A.B. L.309 LL.B. Supr. Ct. J.
Loper, H. William, (BV) . . . . . '49 '74 C.800 B.A. L.1049 J.D. 504 W. Mission Ave.
Lorenz, Walter H. . . . . . '19 '76 C.667 B.M.E. L.1240 J.D. 256 Tampico Glen
**Lounsbery, Daniel** . . . . . '66 '96 C.1358 B.A. L.1049 J.D. [▣ Lounsbery,F.A.&P.]
*PRACTICE AREAS: General Litigation; Land Use; Municipal; Administrative.
**Lounsbery, Kenneth H.**, (AV) . . . . '40 '66 C.945 B.A. L.61 J.D. [Lounsbery,F.A.&P.]
*PRACTICE AREAS: Municipal; Public Finance; Redevelopment; Land Use; Construction.

**Lounsbery, Ferguson, Altona & Peak, LLP, (AV)**
**613 West Valley Parkway, Suite 345, 92025-2552**
**Telephone: 619-743-1201 Facsimile: 619-743-9926**
**Email: LFAPllp@aol.com**
**Kenneth H. Lounsbery; David W. Ferguson; Erick R. Altona; Helen Holmes Peak;—Michelle J. Brown; Kevin P. Sullivan; Charles A. LePla; Daniel Lounsbery. Of Counsel: Garth O. Reid, Jr. (Certified Specialist, Taxation Law, The State Bar of California, Board of Legal Specialization); Curtis M. Fitzpatrick.**
**General Civil and Trial Practice in all State and Federal Courts. Administrative, Banking, Business, Commercial, Construction, Corporation, Eminent Domain, Employment Law, Environmental, Estate Planning, Government Relations, High Tech, Land Use, Municipal, Probate, Public Contracts and Franchises, Public Finance, Real Property, Redevelopment, Federal and State Securities, Tax, Wills and Trust.**
***See Professional Biographies, ESCONDIDO, CALIFORNIA***

Lovenworth, Susan H. . . . . . '41 '89 C.472 B.Ed. L.1137 J.D. 225 East Third Ave.

**Lund, James E., (BV) '51 '79 C&L.101 B.A., J.D.**
**249 East Fourth Avenue, 92025**
**Telephone: 619-747-7800 FAX: 619-489-8423**
**Corporate, Business, Real Property and Entertainment Law. Commercial and Business. Trial Practice in all State and Federal Courts, including Debt Collection and Creditor Bankruptcy Law.**
***See Professional Biographies, ESCONDIDO, CALIFORNIA***

Mainschein, Brian K. . . . . . . '69 '94 C.112 B.A. L.61 J.D. [▣ Jensen&R.]
Marks, Paul D., (BV) . . . . . . '43 '69 C.112 B.A. L.1068 J.D. 345 W. 9th Ave.
Mayian, Stephen M. '36 '76 C.871 B.S. L.146 J.D.
(adm. in IL; not adm. in CA) 3346 Bernardo Ln.‡
**McGauley, Jennifer M.** . . . . . . '61 '91 C.330 B.A. L.1137 J.D. [▣ White&B.]
Meyer, Gordon G., (BV) . . . . . . '47 '72 C.35 B.S. L.61 J.D. 225 E. 3rd Ave.
Miller, Dudley E. . . . . . '21 '49 C.112 B.S. L.767 J.D. 29062 Rocky Point Way‡
Miller, Kenneth H., (AV) . . . . . '47 '73 C.1077 B.S. L.61 J.D. 1766 S. Escondido Blvd.
Mills, Richard E., (AV) . . . . . . '43 '70 C.112 A.B. L.1068 J.D. [R.E.Mills]
Mills, Richard E., P.C., (AV) . . . . . . . 120 W. Woodward
Milner, Anita Cheek, Mrs. . . . . . '36 '86 C.763 M.A. L.61 J.D. 910 Milane Lane‡
Monguia, Anna Rose . . . . . . '51 '87 C.112 B.A. L.1068 J.D. [Monguia&M.]
Monguia, Manuel, (CV) . . . . . . '49 '75 C.112 B.A. L.1068 J.D. [Monguia&M.]
Monguia & Monguia, (CV) . . . . . . . 1523 E. Valley Pkwy.
Nachand, Charles D., III, (BV) . . . . '50 '76 C.112 B.A. L.1049 J.D. 447 S. Escondido Blvd.
Nicholas, Jerry W. . . . . . . '48 '78 C.763 B.A. L.1137 J.D. P.O. Box 121
Nichols, Cathleen Brown . . . . . . '59 '87 C.112 B.A. L.1049 J.D. 139 E. 3rd Ave.
**Ortlieb, Randolph W.** . . . . . . '60 '87 C.668 B.A. L.910 J.D. [White&B.]
*LANGUAGES: Spanish.
*PRACTICE AREAS: Commercial Collections; Real Estate Litigation; Estate Planning; Construction Litigation.
Parrott, Andrew J., (CV) . . . . . . '50 '83 C.628 B.S. L.950 J.D. P.O. Box 461166
**Peak, Helen Holmes** . . . . . . '57 '83 C.813 B.A. L.464 J.D. [Lounsbery,F.A.&P.]
*PRACTICE AREAS: Environmental; Land Use; Municipal; Public Contracts; Real Property.
Pfeiffer, Michael R. . . . . . . '60 '86 C.690 B.S. L.1049 J.D. Realty Income Corp.
Prince, Sharon E. . . . . . . '47 '81 C.763 A.B. L.1049 J.D. 1130 E. Penna. Ave.
**Rayner, Leigh A.**, (BV) . . . . . . '52 '85 L.1137 J.D. [White&B.]
*PRACTICE AREAS: Personal Injury; Business Litigation.
**Reid, Garth O., Jr.**, (AV) '44 '75
C.336 B.S. L.1065 J.D. [G.O.Reid,Jr.] & [▣ Lounsbery,F.A.&P.]

**Reid, Garth O., Jr., A Professional Law Corporation, (AV)** ▣
**319 East Second Avenue, 92025**
**Telephone: 619-746-6420**
**Garth O. Reid, Jr. (Certified Specialist, Taxation Law, The State Bar of California, Board of Legal Specialization).**
**Taxation, Corporations, Estate Planning, Trusts, Business and Commercial Law.**
***See Professional Biographies, ESCONDIDO, CALIFORNIA***

Renshaw, Charles C., II, (AV) . . . . . '28 '65 C.208 B.A. L.1049 J.D. 139 E. 3rd Ave.
Rockwell, Wm. H. '19 '50 C.477 A.B. L.178 LL.B.
(adm. in NY; not adm. in CA) 205 Tampico Glen‡
**Roden, Robert**, (AV) . . . . . . '36 '66 C.147 B.A. L.1065 LL.B. [Roden&T.]
*PRACTICE AREAS: Negligence Law; Wrongful Death Law; Product Liability Law.

**Roden and Thompson, (AV)**
**225 East Third Avenue, 92025**
**Telephone: 619-745-1484 Facsimile: 619-739-0911**
**Members of Firm: Robert Roden; Frank M. Thompson.**
**Trial Practice. Personal Injury, Wrongful Death, Insurance and Products Liability Law.**
**Reference: North County Bank (Escondido Branch).**
***See Professional Biographies, ESCONDIDO, CALIFORNIA***

Romney, Clyde A., (AV) . . . . . . '43 '71 C.813 B.A. L.878 J.D. [Romney&S.]
Romney & Sterling, (AV) . . . . . . . 235 W. 5th Ave., Ste. D
Rosin, Nat, (AV) . . . . . . '09 '34 C&L.800 B.S.B.A., LL.B. 10057 W. Lilac Rd.‡
Roth, James M. . . . . . . '59 '87 C.645 B.A. L.61 J.D. [Jensen&R.]
Schurmann, Anna M. . . . . . '45 '79 C.766 B.A. L.1137 J.D. 1509 Tutela Hts.‡
Sernaker, Gary A., (BV) '53 '78 C.831 B.A. L.1049 J.D.
402 S. Juniper St. (⊙San Diego)
Shores, James L. . . . . . . '39 '78 C.763 A.B. L.1049 J.D. 1892 Villa Del Dios Glen
Singer, Lisa R. . . . . . . '— '90 C&L.112 B.A., J.D. Gen. Coun., Cush Automotive Grp.
Sorman, Cynthia M. . . . . . . '52 '85 C.763 B.A. L.1049 J.D. 2025 Juniper St.
Statile, William J., (A Prof. Law Corp.) '49 '76 C.112 B.A. L.1137 J.D.
530 W. 2nd Ave.

**Sterling, Randall C. '58 '88 C.990 B.S. L.1241 J.D.**
**225 East Third Avenue, 92025-4203**
**Telephone: 619-738-1622 Facsimile: 619-738-4511**
**General Civil Trial Practice.**
***See Professional Biographies, ESCONDIDO, CALIFORNIA***

Stone, Roy C. . . . . . . '41 '77 C.608 B.A. L.1049 J.D. 10324 Meadow Glen Way E.
**Sullivan, Kevin P.** . . . . . . '62 '90 C.112 B.S. L.1019 J.D. [▣ Lounsbery,F.A.&P.]
*REPORTED CASES: Industrial Clearinghouse, Inc. v. Browning Manufacturing, 953 F.2d 1004 (5th Cir. 1992).
*PRACTICE AREAS: Business Litigation; Employment Law; Municipal Law.
Taliaferro, Russell G. . . . . . . '19 '51 C.426 L.809 LL.B. 1066 Memory Lane‡
Talley, James W., (BV) . . . . . . '46 '72 C&L.61 B.S., J.D. [Galyean,T.&W.]
Tanner, Russell G. . . . . . '26 '72 C.763 B.A. L.1049 J.D. 1130 Pennsylvania Ave. E.
Templin, Wayne . . . . . . '53 '87 C.763 B.S. L.1137 J.D. 350 W. 9th Ave.
**Thompson, Frank M.**, (BV) . . . . . . '51 '81 C.1109 B.A. L.61 J.D. [Roden&T.]
*PRACTICE AREAS: Negligence Law; Wrongful Death Law; Product Liability Law.
Van Derhoff, Richard . . . . . . '53 '80 C.1038 B.S. L.1049 J.D. 58 La Calma
Van Dusen, Charles A. . . . . . '51 '80 C.763 B.A. L.61 J.D. 1910 Privado Glen
Veldkamp, Arnold L. '58 '83 C.1304 B.A. L.352 J.D.
Corp. Coun., Superior Ready Mix Concrete, L.P.
Von Drak, Rick, (CV) . . . . . . '51 '77 C.37 B.A. L.1137 J.D. 530 W. 2nd Ave.
Wenzel, John M., (BV) . . . . . . '40 '65 C.763 B.S. L.1065 J.D. 400 N. Bway.
Wheelock, William D. . . . . . '63 '89 C.112 B.A. L.767 J.D. [Romney&S.]
**White, Bruce H.**, (A P.C.), (AV) . . . . . '33 '66 C.940 B.A. L.61 J.D. [White&B.]⊙
*PRACTICE AREAS: Real Estate.

**White and Bright, A Professional Corporation, (AV)**
**355 West Grand Avenue Second Floor, 92025⊙**
**Telephone: 619-747-3200 Fax: 619-747-5574**
**Email: WHITEBRIGH@aol.com**
**David S. Bright; Leigh A. Rayner; Bruce H. White (A P.C.); Randolph W. Ortlieb; Jennifer M. McGauley; Michael A. Friedrichs.**
**General Civil Litigation, Real Estate, Insurance Defense, Business, Environmental, Estate Planning, Construction Defect and Personal Injury Law.**
**References: First Interstate Bank, Escondido Main Branch; North County Bank.**
**Long Beach, California Office: 3780 Kilroy Airport Way, Suite 200. Telephone: 310-490-3120. Fax: 310-981-7353.**
***See Professional Biographies, ESCONDIDO, CALIFORNIA***

Williams, David E. . . . . . . '49 '75 C.800 B.A. L.1049 J.D. 205 W. 5th Ave.
Wolanin, William E. . . . . . . '47 '78 C.475 B.S. L.215 J.D. 135 W. Mission
Wolcott, Raymond O. '12 '37 C&L.494 B.A., J.D.
(adm. in MN; not adm. in CA) 1861 Cortez Ave.‡
Wood, Robert Clayton, (BV) . . . . . . . '43 '77 [Galyean,T.&W.]
Zimmer, Clifford '25 '50 C.611 L.209 LL.B.
(adm. in IL; not adm. in CA) 1428 Via Valente‡

## EUREKA, * 27,025, *Humboldt Co.*

Alley, Roy L. . . . . . . . '19 '54 C.627 A.B. L.813 J.D. 905 F St., #1‡
Anderson, John M., (BV) . . . . . . '43 '74 C.401 B.A. L.61 J.D. [McClendon&A.]
**Angell, Ronald F.**, (AV) . . . . . '42 '67 C.112 B.A. L.1066 J.D. [Roberts,H.C.B.F.&A.]
*PRACTICE AREAS: General Business; Real Property; Municipal Law.
Arnot, Philip M. . . . . . . '37 '64 C.330 A.B. L.1026 LL.B. 307 N St.

**Barnum, William F., (BV) '54 '79 C.330 B.A. L.464 J.D.**
**2103 Myrtle Avenue, P.O. Box 173, 95502**
**Telephone: 707-442-6405 Fax: 707-442-1507**
**Transactional Real Estate, Environmental Law, Land Use Law, Construction and Development Law, Timber and Logging.**
***See Professional Biographies, EUREKA, CALIFORNIA***

Bartlett, James B., (BV) . . . . . . '53 '78 C.330 B.A. L.767 J.D. 1018 7th St.
**Becker, Thomas J.**, (BV) . . . . . . '39 '64 C.812 B.S. L.260 J.D. [Harland]
*PRACTICE AREAS: Civil Litigation; Real Property Law; Administrative Law.
Beeler, Deanna G. . . . . . . '42 '75 C.569 A.B. L.1066 J.D. 517 3rd St.
**Bicknell, Donald W.**, (BV) . . . . . . '49 '74 C.347 A.B. L.976 J.D. [Dalton&B.]
*PRACTICE AREAS: Family Law; Bankruptcy; Civil Litigation.
Boyd, Deborah A. . . . . . . '61 '88 C.1032 B.A. L.800 J.D. 937 6th St.
**Bragg, William R.**, (AV) . . . . . '50 '76 C.1027 B.S. L.1065 J.D. [Roberts,H.C.B.F.&A.]
*PRACTICE AREAS: Insurance Defense and Civil Litigation; Defense of Major Felonies and White-collar Crimes.
Braun, John R. . . . . . . '30 '56 C.330 B.A. L.1066 LL.B. 3005 G St.
**Brisso, Paul A.**, (AV) . . . . . '52 '78 C.330 B.A. L.464 J.D. [Mitchell,B.D.&V.]
*REPORTED CASES: Harrison v. Co. of Del Norte (1985) 168 Cal. App. 3d 1; Herring v. Peterson (1981) 116 Cal. App. 3d 608.
*PRACTICE AREAS: General Civil Litigation; Personal Injury; Construction; Wrongful Termination; Products Liability.
Brown, J. Michael . . . . . . . '40 '65 C&L.767 J.D. Supr. Ct. J.
Buck, Bruce . . . . . . . '54 '85 C.330 B.A. L.464 J.D. Dep. Dist. Atty.
Buffington, John E. . . . . . . '41 '69 C.1027 B.S. L.1065 J.D. Supr. Ct. J.
**Calligan, Michael D.**, (BV) . . . . '38 '65 C.112 A.B. L.1066 J.D. [Roberts,H.C.B.F.&A.]
*PRACTICE AREAS: Insurance Defense and Defense of Municipal Liability Claims.
Cardoza, Max S., (BV) . . . . . . '56 '81 C.112 A.B. L.1066 J.D. Dep. Dist. Atty.
**Carson, William H., Jr.**, (AV) . . . . . '40 '70 C.339 B.S. L.1066 J.D. [Huber&G.]
Cogen, Robert S., (BV) . . . . . . '35 '61 C&L.800 B.S., J.D. P.O. Box 593
Connell, William C., (BV) . . . . . . '35 '61 C.72 B.A. L.813 J.D. Pub. Def.
Conry, Leonard M. . . . . . . '22 '52 C.330 L.767 J.D. 504 I St.

CAA86P

Cook, John D., (CV) .......... '28 '55 C.768 L.1065 J.D. 1190 Vista Dr.
Cooper, John W., Jr. .......... '23 '71 C.999 B.M.S. L.1026 J.D. 515 "J" St.‡
Corbett, Victor M., (AV) .......... '29 '57 C.549 B.S. L.1066 J.D. 3955 V St.‡
Cox, Edward L., II .......... '47 '77 C.330 B.A. L.464 J.D. 517 3rd St.‡
Crane, David J. .......... '41 '71 C.330 A.B. L.767 J.D. 369 8th St.
**Crowley, Michael J.**, (BV) .......... '56 '82 C.93 L.767 J.D. [Zwerdling&C.]
*PRACTICE AREAS: Plaintiff Trial Practice; Personal Injury Law; Employment Litigation; Civil Rights.
Cumming, John W., (BV) .......... '50 '75 C.112 A.B. L.273 J.D. 517 3rd St.
**Dalton, John M.**, (BV) .......... '28 '57 C.112 B.A. L.1066 J.D. [Dalton&B.]
*PRACTICE AREAS: Family Law; Civil Litigation; Probate.

**Dalton & Bicknell, (BV)**
**732 Fifth Street, Suite H, P.O. Box 24, 95502-0024**
**Telephone: 707-443-0878 Fax: 707-443-2429**
**Members of Firm: John M. Dalton (Certified Specialist, Family Law, The State Bar of California Board of Legal Specialization); Donald W. Bicknell (Certified Specialist, Family Law, The State Bar of California Board of Legal Specialization).**
**Family Law, Personal Injury, Probate, Business and Bankruptcy Law.**
**Reference: Humboldt National Bank.**
*See Professional Biographies, EUREKA, CALIFORNIA*

Daly, Richard G. .......... '33 '59 C&L.878 B.S., LL.B. 123 "F" St.
Davis, John C., (BV) .......... '47 '72 C.766 B.A. L.1065 J.D. [Davis&P.]
**Davis, William O.** .......... '48 '88 C.1169 B.A. L.464 J.D. [A Dun&M.]
*PRACTICE AREAS: Mining Reclamation; CEQA; Environmental Law; General Practice; Business Law.
Davis & Poovey, Inc., (BV) .......... 937 6th St.
**Delaney, Nancy K.**, (BV) .......... '50 '76 C.330 A.B. L.1065 J.D. [Mitchell,B.D.&V.]
*PRACTICE AREAS: General Civil Litigation; Estate Planning and Probate; Personal Injury; Civil Rights; Public Entity Defense.

**Dibble, David P., (AV) '50 '77 C.611 B.A. L.192 J.D.**
**628 H Street, 95501**
**Telephone: 707-444-9330**
***PRACTICE AREAS: Personal Injury; Products Liability; Professional Liability; Insurance Bad Faith; Commercial Litigation.**
**General Civil and Trial Practice in all State and Federal Courts. Personal Injury, Products Liability, Professional Liability and Insurance Bad Faith Law. Commercial Litigation.**
*See Professional Biographies, EUREKA, CALIFORNIA*

Diehl, Duke B., (BV) .......... '46 '72 C.999 B.A. L.1066 J.D. 1010 7th St.
**Dun, David H.**, (BV) .......... '49 '76 C.911 B.A. L.678 J.D. [Dun&M.]
*PRACTICE AREAS: Environmental; Business; Timber; General Civil Litigation.

**Dun & Martinek, (BV)**
**730 7th Street Suite B, P.O. Box 1266, 95501-1142**
**Telephone: 707-442-3791 Fax: 707-442-9251**
**Members of Firm: David H. Dun; David E. Martinek. Associates: William O. Davis; James A. Zito.**
**General Civil Trial Practice, Timber Law, Business Law.**
**Representative Client: Sierra Pacific Industries; General Growth; Eel River Saw Mills; Barnum Timber; Security National Partners; City of Rio Dell.**

Edson, Judith L., (BV) .......... '45 '72 C.112 B.A. L.1065 J.D. 1026 3rd St.
Eichenbeg, Gena Rae, (CV) .......... '47 '82 C.330 B.A. L.1067 J.D. 517 Third St.
Eitzen, Lawrence O., (BV) .......... '44 '69 C.477 A.B. L.608 J.D. 816 3rd St.
**Endres, C. Todd** .......... '64 '90 C.112 B.A. L.464 J.D. [Mitchell,B.D.&V.]
**Evans, Cherie L.** .......... '70 '95 C.1074 B.A. L.990 J.D. [A Mitchell,B.D.&V.]
Falor, Tamara Claire .......... '59 '86 C.330 B.A. L.464 J.D. Co. Coun.
Farmer, Terry R., (BV) .......... '44 '71 C.1060 B.A. L.494 J.D. Dist. Atty.
**Feeney, John T.**, (BV) .......... '53 '80 C.112 B.A. L.426 J.D. [Roberts,H.C.B.F.&A.]
*PRACTICE AREAS: Real Estate; Business; Probate; Estate and Trusts.
Ferroggiaro, William F., Jr. .......... '35 '63 C&L.767 B.S., LL.B. Supr. Ct. J.
Flower, James W., (CV) .......... '53 '84 C.766 B.A. L.1065 J.D. Dep. Pub. Def.
Floyd, Bradford C., (CV) .......... '58 '88 C.877 B.A. L.629 J.D. [Mathews&K.]
Forward, John F., II .......... '17 '54 C.763 L.981 LL.B. 1623 Swanson Ln.‡
**Gans, Russell Scott** .......... '69 '96 C.740 L.629 J.D. [A Mitchell,B.D.&V.]
*PRACTICE AREAS: Insurance Defense; Civil Rights.
**Gold, Julia S.** .......... '64 '94 C.112 B.S. L.1051 J.D. [A Harland]
*PRACTICE AREAS: Estate Planning; Probate Law; Tax Law.
**Goodwin, G. Edward**, (AV) .......... '18 '40 C.330 L.1065 J.D. [C Huber&G.] ‡
Ham, John A., (CV) .......... '47 '79 C.1071 B.S. L.1137 J.D. 1731 Third St.
Hanson, Rory A., (BV) .......... '48 '73 C.330 B.A. L.464 J.D. 305 K St.
**Harland, Gerald R.**, (AV) .......... '22 '51 C.826 A.B. L.813 J.D. [Harland] (©Fortuna)
*PRACTICE AREAS: Estate Planning Law; Real Property Law; Probate Law; Business Law.

**Harland Law Firm, (AV)**
**622 H Street, 95501©**
**Telephone: 707-444-9281 Fax: 707-445-2961**
**Members of Firm: Gerald R. Harland; Richard A. Smith; David C. Moore (Certified Specialist, Family Law, The State Bar of California Board of Legal Specialization); Thomas J. Becker; William T. Kay, Jr.; John W. Warren; Geri Anne Johnson. Associate: Julia S. Gold.**
**General Trial and Appellate Practice. Family, Probate, Estate Planning, Timber and Logging, Corporation, Personal Injury, Administrative, Construction, Labor, Education, Business and Real Property Law.**
**Fortuna, California Office: 954 Main Street. Telephone: 707-725-4426. Fax: 707-725-5738.**
*See Professional Biographies, EUREKA, CALIFORNIA*

**Herb, Hans W., Law Offices of**
**(See Santa Rosa)**

Hervey, Linda F., (BV) .......... '57 '83 C.330 B.A. L.1049 J.D. 715 I Street
**Hill, Michael J.**, (BV) .......... '38 '66 C.330 A.B. L.1066 J.D. [Roberts,H.C.B.F.&A.]
*PRACTICE AREAS: Civil and Insurance Defense; Defense of Environmental and Hazardous Waste Claims.
**Hinrichs, Joyce D.**, (BV) .......... '58 '83 C.169 B.A. L.464 J.D. [Firm of W.G.Watson,Jr.]

**Huber & Goodwin, (AV)**
**Huber-Goodwin Building, 550 "I" Street, P.O. Box 23, 95502-0023**
**Telephone: 707-443-4573 Fax: 707-443-7182 Email: prior@humboldt1.com**
**Email: carson@humboldt1.com**
**Members of Firm: Milton L. Huber (1914-1994); G. Edward Goodwin (Retired); Dayton D. Murray, Jr. (1923-1981); Norman C. Cissna (1923-1989); Robert D. Prior; William H. Carson, Jr.**
**General Civil and Trial Practice. Corporation, Small Business, Probate, Estate Planning, Administrative, Personal Injury, Workers Compensation, Forestry, Agricultural, Commercial, Real Property and Environmental Law.**
**Representative Clients: D & B Cattle Co. (livestock); Simpson Timber Co.; Miller & Rellim Redwood Cos.; The Pacific Lumber Co.; Western Self Insurance Service (Workers Compensation); Hilfiker Pipe Co.**
*See Professional Biographies, EUREKA, CALIFORNIA*

Huskey, Christina J., (CV) .......... '63 '90 C.801 B.A. L.112 J.D. Depty. Def.
**Janssen, Clayton R.**, (AV) .......... '25 '52 C&L.813 B.A., J.D. [Janssen,M.M.N.&M.]
*PRACTICE AREAS: Products Liability; Personal Injury; Professional Liability; Medical Malpractice Defense; Real Estate Litigation.

**Janssen, Malloy, Marchi, Needham & Morrison, (AV)**
**730 Fifth Street, P.O. Drawer 1288, 95501**
**Telephone: 707-445-2071 Fax: 707-445-8305**
**Members of Firm: Clayton R. Janssen; Nicholas R. Marchi; Michael F. Malloy; Michael W. Morrison; W. Timothy Needham. Associates: Catherine M. Koshkin.**
(This Listing Continued)

**Janssen, Malloy, Marchi, Needham & Morrison (Continued)**
**General Civil and Business Litigation. Products Liability, Negligence and Professional Liability. Insurance, Bankruptcy (Creditor). Medical Malpractice Defense. Insurance Coverage Litigation. General Personal Injury Litigation. Real Estate Litigation.**
**Counsel for: Clinic Mutual Insurance Co.; TRW, Inc.; U.S. Bank; The Travelers Insurance Co.; General Hospital; Pacific Bell; Reichhold Chemicals, Inc.; Safeco Insurance Companies of America; Lawyers Mutual Insurance Co.**
*See Professional Biographies, EUREKA, CALIFORNIA*

**Johnson, Geri Anne**, (CV) .......... '52 '80 C.147 B.A. L.284 J.D. [Harland]
*PRACTICE AREAS: Appellate Law; Business Law; Corporate Law; Employment Law.
Karjola, Leon A., (CV) .......... '47 '76 C.909 B.A. L.1137 J.D. [Traverse&K.]
**Kay, William T., Jr.**, (BV) .......... '44 '74 C.988 B.A. L.1049 J.D. [Harland]
*PRACTICE AREAS: General Civil Litigation; Personal Injury Law.
Kluck, Laurence Allan, (BV) .......... '48 '86 C.330 B.A. L.464 J.D. [Mathews&K.]
**Koshkin, Catherine M.**, (BV) .......... '54 '90 C.260 B.A. L.464 J.D. [Janssen,M.M.N.&M.]
*PRACTICE AREAS: Bankruptcy; Real Estate Litigation; Business.
Kutz, Robert W. .......... '46 '76 C.112 A.B. L.464 J.D. Wker's. Comp. J.
Lough, James P. .......... '52 '79 C.1109 B.A. L.809 J.D. County Coun., Co. of Humboldt
Lyons, Jon H. .......... '44 '73 C.763 B.A. L.1049 J.D. 203 F St.
**Malloy, Michael F.**, (AV) .......... '49 '74 C.740 B.A. L.1065 J.D. [Janssen,M.M.N.&M.]
*PRACTICE AREAS: Bankruptcy; Business Litigation; Estate Planning; Probate.
Mantle, Gregory E., (CV) .......... '47 '76 C&L.767 B.A., J.D. 203 F St.
**Marchi, Nicholas R.**, (BV) .......... '49 '74 C&L.629 B.S., J.D. [Janssen,M.M.N.&M.]
*PRACTICE AREAS: Professional Liability; Insurance; Medical Malpractice Defense; Insurance Coverage.
**Martinek, David E.**, (BV) .......... '57 '82 C.112 B.A. L.800 J.D. [Dun&M.]
*PRACTICE AREAS: Real Estate; Business Law; General Litigation.
Mathews, Francis B., (AV) .......... '23 '48 C.112 A.B. L.1066 LL.B. [Mathews&K.]
Mathews & Kluck, (AV) .......... 100 "M" St.
McClaran, Joe, (BV) .......... '24 '50 C.336 B.A. L.597 J.D. 555 H. St.
McClendon, William R., III, (BV) .......... '43 '73 C.112 B.A. L.1049 J.D. [McClendon&A.]
McClendon & Anderson, Inc., (BV) .......... 1500 4th St.
McGee, Gerry W. .......... '42 '72 C.1250 B.S. L.464 J.D. 924 5th St.
McKittrick, James R. .......... '32 '57 C.330 L.1065 J.D. 2231 Wycliff Ln.
Miles, Marilyn B., (BV) .......... '— '80 C.768 B.A. L.1067 J.D. Calif. Indian Legal Servs.
**Mitchell, Clifford B.**, (AV) .......... '27 '53 C&L.813 A.B., J.D. [Mitchell,B.D.&V.]
*PRACTICE AREAS: Insurance Defense.
**Mitchell, William F.** .......... '56 '92 C.605 B.A. L.770 J.D. [A Mitchell,B.D.&V.]

**Mitchell, Brisso, Delaney & Vrieze, (AV)**
**814 Seventh Street, P.O. Drawer 1008, 95502**
**Telephone: 707-443-5643 Fax: 707-444-9586**
**Members of Firm: Clifford B. Mitchell; Nancy K. Delaney; Paul A. Brisso; John M. Vrieze; C. Todd Endres. Associates: William F. Mitchell; Cherie L. Evans; Russell Scott Gans. Retired Partner: Robert C. Dedekam.**
**General Civil and Trial Practice in all Courts. Probate, Insurance, Corporation, Real Property, Timber and Logging Law.**
**Representative Clients: Louisiana-Pacific Corp.; City of Eureka; Housing Authority; St. Joseph Health Systems; California Automobile Assn.; K Mart; Hertz Corp.; Walmart; StairMaster Sports/ Medical Products, Inc.; Montgomery Ward.**
*See Professional Biographies, EUREKA, CALIFORNIA*

**Moore, David C.**, (BV) .......... '43 '69 C&L.884 B.S., J.D. [Harland]
*PRACTICE AREAS: Civil Litigation; Family Law.
Morris, William H. .......... '33 '82 C.477 B.S.E. L.999 J.D. 224 E. Harris
Morrison, Jackson E. .......... '44 '74 C.674 A.B. L.1065 J.D. 710 I St.
Morrison, James K., (BV) .......... '31 '60 C&L.813 A.B., J.D. [Morrison&M.]
Morrison, John R. .......... '33 '67 C.813 A.B. L.1097 J.D. Mun. Ct. J.
**Morrison, Michael W.**, (BV) .......... '50 '76 C.147 B.A. L.1065 J.D. [Janssen,M.M.N.&M.]
*PRACTICE AREAS: Products Liability; Professional Liability; Medical Malpractice Defense; Personal Injury; Real Estate Litigation.
Morrison & Morrison, (BV) .......... 233 K St.
Murphy, Patrick Timothy, (BV) .......... '32 '57 C&L.602 B.S., J.D. 6700 North Highway 101
Myers, Larry S., (CV) .......... '46 '74 C.477 B.A. L.912 J.D. 732 5th St.
**Needham, W. Timothy**, (BV) .......... '53 '80 C.330 B.A. L.1067 J.D. [Janssen,M.M.N.&M.]
*PRACTICE AREAS: Products Liability; Professional Liability; Insurance; Personal Injury; Insurance Coverage.
Nicklas, Philip M. .......... '46 '74 C.330 B.A. L.1065 J.D. 417 2nd St.
Nord, Larry B., (BV) .......... '41 '66 C.768 B.A. L.1065 J.D. U.S. Mag.
Parshall, Roger A. .......... '55 '83 C.330 B.A. L.770 J.D. Off. of Pub. Def.
Parsons, Edward E., (BV) .......... '43 '72 C.112 A.B. L.1065 J.D. P.O. Box 9
Pavlich, Roman E., (CV) .......... '35 '69 C.112 B.A. L.1026 LL.B. [Scott,S.R.&P.]
Pentoney, Howard A. .......... '25 '52 C.846 L.1065 LL.B. 3231 Dolbeer St.‡
**Perlman, Randy S.** .......... '60 '87 C.1040 B.A. L.61 J.D. [Roberts,H.C.B.F.&A.]
*PRACTICE AREAS: General Civil and Business Litigation; Insurance Defense.
Poovey, James D., (BV) .......... '53 '78 C.112 B.S. L.1049 J.D. [Davis&P.]
**Prior, Robert D.**, (BV) .......... '32 '57 C&L.813 A.B., J.D. [Huber&G.]
Profant-Turner, Elaine .......... '— '85 C.763 L.1188 J.D. 924 Fifth St.
Quinn, John L., (CV) .......... '31 '58 C.770 B.S.C. L.1065 J.D. 515 J St.
Rael, Gregory L., (BV) .......... '50 '76 C&L.813 B.A., J.D. 1026 3rd St.

**Rawles, Hinkle, Carter, Behnke & Oglesby**
**(See Ukiah)**

Reinholtsen, Dale A., (BV) .......... '47 '72 C.330 B.A. L.1067 J.D. Mun.J.
**Roberts, Donald B.**, (AV) .......... '39 '66 C.112 A.B. L.1066 J.D. [Roberts,H.C.B.F.&A.]
*PRACTICE AREAS: Insurance Defense; Professional Liability; General Business and Construction Litigation.

**Roberts, Hill, Calligan, Bragg, Feeney & Angell, (AV)**
**434 Seventh Street, P.O. Box 1248, 95501-1803**
**Telephone: 707-442-2927 95502-1248 Fax: 707-443-2747**
**Members of Firm: Donald B. Roberts; Michael J. Hill; Michael D. Calligan; William R. Bragg; John T. Feeney; Ronald F. Angell; Randy S. Perlman;—Paul John Warner; Lisa A. Russ.**
**Insurance Defense, Personal Injury and General Civil and Trial Practice and Professional Liability Litigation, Timber and Logging, Construction Contracts and Litigation. Business, Corporation, Probate, and Real Estate Law.**
**Representative Clients: Payless Drug Stores; Fidelity National Title Co.; Allstate Insurance; The City of Eureka; Farmers Insurance Group; Industrial Indemnity Co.; State Farm Fire & Casualty.**
*See Professional Biographies, EUREKA, CALIFORNIA*

Robinson, Michael K., (CV) .......... '54 '80 C.112 A.B. L.284 J.D. [Scott,S.R.&P.]
Rosenberg, Stephen J., (CV) .......... '46 '72 C.330 B.S. L.1065 J.D. 517 3rd St.
**Russ, Lisa A.** .......... '67 '94 C.112 B.A. L.464 J.D. [A Roberts,H.C.B.F.&A.]
Sanders, Neal I., (CV) .......... '51 '79 C.1188 B.A. L.464 J.D. [N.I.Sanders]
Sanders, Neal I., Law Office of, (CV) .......... 123 F St.
Sandquist, John A. .......... '36 '79 C.1042 B.A. L.809 J.D. 1739 3rd. St.
Scott, Jeremiah R., Jr., (CV) .......... '36 '64 C.934 A.B. L.770 J.D. [Scott,S.R.&P.]
Scott, Scott, Robinson & Pavlich, (CV) .......... 1118 6th St.
Sisneros, Patrick D. '38 '76 C.426 B.B.A. L.809 J.D.
Assoc. Gen. Coun., School & College Legal Servs.
Smith, Jacob J., (CV) .......... '47 '74 C.668 B.A. L.569 J.D. Redwood Legal Assist.
**Smith, Richard A.**, (AV) .......... '45 '70 C.112 A.B. L.426 J.D. [Harland]
*PRACTICE AREAS: Business Law; Banking Law; Timber Law; Bankruptcy Law.

CAA87P

CALIFORNIA—EUREKA MARTINDALE-HUBBELL LAW DIRECTORY 1997

Spadoni, Gino, Jr. ........................'45 '72 C.330 B.A. L.1065 J.D. P.O. Box 3297‡
Steinberg, James J., (BV) ..................'50 '76 C.367 B.A. L.1065 J.D. Asst. Pub. Def.
Steward, Lorna L., (CV) ...................................'44 '91 L.1230 J.D. 724 M St.

**Stokes, Steeves, Rowe & Hamer**
(See Arcata)

Thomas, Charles M., Jr. ..........................'12 '39 C.629 L.596 LL.B. Ret. Supr. Ct. J.
Traverse, Edward F., (BV) ..................'22 '51 C.330 B.A. L.767 LL.B. [Traverse&K.]
Traverse & Karjola, (BV) ..................................................732 5th St., Suite E.
Turner, Jan, (CV) '53 '85
C.112 A.B. L.1067 J.D. Housing Atty., Redwood Legal Assistance
**Vrieze, John M.**, (BV) ..................'52 '84 C.472 B.S. L.629 J.D. [Mitchell,B.D.&V.]
*PRACTICE AREAS: General Civil Litigation; Personal Injury; Civil Rights; Public Entity Defense.
**Warner, Paul John**, (CV) ....... '62 '92 C.1060 B.A. L.464 J.D. [🄰 Roberts,H.C.B.F.&A.]
*PRACTICE AREAS: Civil Litigation; Business Litigation; Insurance Defense.
**Warren, John W.**, (BV) ..........................'42 '69 C.330 A.B. L.767 J.D. [Harland]
*PRACTICE AREAS: Business Law; Estate Planning Law; Probate Law; Maritime Law.
**Watson, Philip G.**, (BV) .........'56 '83 C.330 B.A. L.767 J.D. [Firm of W.G.Watson,Jr.]
**Watson, Stephen G.**, (BV) ......'56 '83 C.330 B.A. L.1065 J.D. [Firm of W.G.Watson,Jr.]
Watson, W. Bruce ..........................................'47 '79 C.1060 B.A. L.464 J.D. Mun J.

**Watson, W. G., Jr., Law Firm of, (AV)**
**715 I Street, P.O. Box 1021, 95501**
**Telephone: 707-444-3071 Fax: 707-444-2313**
**Members of Firm: William G. Watson, Jr. (1918-1996); Stephen G. Watson; Philip G. Watson; Joyce D. Hinrichs.**
**General Civil and Criminal Trial Practice, Personal Injury, Negligence, Insurance, Real Estate, Estate Planning, Probate Law, Arbitration, Mediation.**
**Reference: Bank of America.**
*See Professional Biographies, EUREKA, CALIFORNIA*

Wilkinson, Donald H. .............................'14 '40 C.112 A.B. L.1066 LL.B. Ret. Supr. Ct. J.
Wilson, Christopher G., (BV) ......................'57 '84 C.1074 B.A. L.629 J.D. 100 H St.
Woodworth, Allan James, (CV) ............'51 '86 C.330 B.A. L.464 J.D. Dep. Dist. Atty.
**Zito, James A.** .........................................'52 '80 C.112 B.A. L.1188 J.D. [🄰 Dun&M.]
*PRACTICE AREAS: Construction Law; Personal Injury; Business Litigation.
**Zwerdling, Zachary E.**, (AV) .............'51 '76 C.813 B.A. L.770 J.D. [Zwerdling&C.]
*PRACTICE AREAS: Plaintiff Trial Practice; Personal Injury Law; Employment Litigation; Civil Rights.

**Zwerdling & Crowley, (AV)**
**123 F Street, Suite C, P.O. Box 3477, 95501**
**Telephone: 707-445-9628 Fax: 707-443-0442**
**Zachary E. Zwerdling (Member of Consumer Attorneys of California, with recognized experience in the field of General Personal Injury, and as a Trial Lawyer); Michael J. Crowley (Member of Consumer Attorneys of California, with recognized experience in the field of General Personal Injury, and as a Trial Lawyer).**
**Plaintiff Personal Injury Litigation, Employment Litigation and Civil Rights Litigation.**
*See Professional Biographies, EUREKA, CALIFORNIA*

## EXETER, 7,276, *Tulare Co.*

Helgesen, Eric G., (CV) ..............................'46 '79 C.112 B.S. L.1189 J.D. 125 S. B St.
McKenzie, Freddie, (Mrs.) ........................'21 '72 C.1054 L.1132 J.D. P.O. Box 466‡
Spott, Curtis M., (BV) ...........................'38 '74 C.768 B.S. L.1137 J.D. 401 E. Maple St.
Stevenson, Robert, (BV) ..............................................'16 '46 L.284 J.D. P.O. Box 466‡
Wichowski, Loretta J., (CV) .........................'43 '82 L.1189 J.D. P.O. Box 876

## FAIRFAX, 6,931, *Marin Co.*

Birenbaum, David B., (AV) ...................'29 '57 C.112 A.B. L.284 LL.B. P.O. Box 670‡
Harvey, Reed E. ......................................'57 '92 C.128 B.F.A. L.262 J.D. 14 Deuce Ct.
Hug, Gerald I. ........................................'39 '77 C.999 L.1153 J.D. 42 Bolinas Rd.
King, Diana P. ......................................'32 '77 C.112 B.A. L.1066 J.D. 99 Bothin Rd.
Kunkel, Stephen F. ...................'44 '70 C.976 B.A. L.813 J.D. 113 Live Oak Ave.‡
Platt, Robert D. ...........................................'33 '61 C&L.309 A.B., LL.B. 36 Wimbledon Ln.
Sandler, John R. '45 '72 C.563 B.A. L.1009 J.D.
(adm. in ME; not adm. in CA) 3200 Sir Frances Drake‡
Terzian, Sandra ..........................................'36 '67 C.112 A.B. L.1066 J.D. 60 Stevens St.

## FAIRFIELD, * 77,211, *Solano Co.*

Ambrose, Thomas A., (BV) ........'45 '75 C.112 B.A. L.767 J.D. 1590 Webster St., Ste. A
Amen, Charles A. ...........................'52 '82 C.869 B.S. L.1065 J.D. Dep. Dist. Atty.
Atkinson, William R. ..............................'54 '79 C.763 B.A. L.426 J.D. [Coffer&A.]
**Babcock, Katherine M.** .............................'53 '83 C.770 B.A. L.1065 J.D. [Lucas&L.]
*PRACTICE AREAS: General Practice; Insurance Defense; Construction Law; Civil Litigation.
Bakkerud, Constance I. ...........................'39 '83 C.766 B.A. L.1065 J.D. Dep. Pub. Def.
**Bangle, Raymond, III**, (CV) ...........'49 '82 C.112 B.A. L.1067 J.D. [Keitges,B.&O.]⊙
*PRACTICE AREAS: General Insurance Defense; Insurance Coverage; Governmental Entity Defense; Construction Litigation; Medical Malpractice.
**Barnett, Robert E.**, (AV) ..............................'43 '69 C.605 B.A. L.1066 J.D. [Barnett M.]
*PRACTICE AREAS: Personal Injury Law.

**Barnett • Mattice, (AV)** 🄱🄱
**An Association of Sole Practitioners**
**712 Empire Street, 94533**
**Telephone: 707-425-0671 Fax: 707-425-4255**
**Robert E. Barnett (Member of California Trial Lawyers Association, with recognized experience in the fields of Trial Lawyer and General Personal Injury); Michael C. Mattice.**
**Personal Injury and Family Law.**
*See Professional Biographies, FAIRFIELD, CALIFORNIA*

Becksted, Dennis P., (BV) ............................'39 '65 C&L.37 B.A., LL.B. [Whiting&B.]
Bender, Alan Ronald '54 '80 C.910 A.B. L.228 J.D.
(adm. in NY; not adm. in CA) V.P. & Gen. Coun., General Cellular Corp.
Bennett, Scott R., (BV) ..............................'55 '84 C&L.101 B.A., J.D. [Wells,C.&C.]
Bernstein, Robert G. ........................'44 '73 C.112 B.A. L.1067 J.D. 702 Empire St.
Bittle, Timothy A. ...........'56 '83 C.999 B.A. L.464 J.D. Gen. Coun, B & L Properties
**Borges, Guy D.**, (BV) ..............'56 '83 C.112 B.A. L.1049 J.D. [McNamara,H.D.M.&N.]
*PRACTICE AREAS: Insurance Defense.
Bowers, Robert S. .................................'59 '87 C.415 B.A. L.276 J.D. [Jackson&B.]
Brewer, George W. ...............................'24 '52 C&L.767 LL.B. 600 Union Ave.
Brookner, Marvin A. .............................'45 '70 C.103 B.A. L.273 J.D. Pub. Def.
Bunting, Dennis W., (BV) .......................'46 '73 C&L.1067 A.B., J.D. Co. Coun.
Burton, Billy B. ..........................'21 '50 C.942 A.B. L.472 LL.B. Asst. Co. Coun.
Call, R. Dayton, (BV) ..........................'49 '77 C.112 B.A. L.101 J.D. [Wells,C.&C.]
**Carringer, Christine A.** ........................'54 '87 C.645 B.A. L.464 J.D. [🄰 Knox R.]
*PRACTICE AREAS: Civil Trial; Insurance Defense.
**Caulfield, Richard Hyland**, (AV) ...'46 '72 C.112 A.B. L.1067 J.D. [Caulfield,D.&D.]⊙
*PRACTICE AREAS: Business Litigation; Public Entity Defense; Products Liability.

**Caulfield, Davies & Donahue, (AV)**
**Fairfield West Plaza, 1455 Oliver Road, Suite 130, 94533⊙**
**Telephone: 707-426-0223**
**Members of Firm: Richard Hyland Caulfield; Robert E. Davies; James R. Donahue.**
**General Civil Trial, Coverage and Appellate Practice, Negligence, Professional Liability, Automotive, Products Liability, Aviation, Insurance and General Business.**

(This Listing Continued)

**Caulfield, Davies & Donahue (Continued)**
**Sacramento, California Office: 3500 American River Drive, 1st Floor. Telephone: 916-487-7700.**
*See Professional Biographies, FAIRFIELD, CALIFORNIA*

Chikowski, Brian T. .............................'50 '78 C.705 B.A. L.284 J.D. 744 Empire St.
Clark, Thomas C., (CV) ..........................'51 '79 C.112 A.B. L.101 J.D. [Wells,C.&C.]
Clawson, Steven R. ..................................'60 '87 C&L.101 B.S., J.D. [Wells,C.&C.]
Coan, J. Paul ...........................................'37 '64 C.112 A.B. L.1065 J.D. Supr. Ct. Ref.
Coffer, John M. ........................................'53 '79 C.112 A.B. L.61 J.D. [Coffer&A.]
Coffer & Atkinson ...........................................................................737 Jefferson St.

**Coyle, John M., Law Offices of '46 '72 C.911 B.A. L.1065 J.D.**
**639 Kentucky Street, Suite 210, 94533**
**Telephone: 707-422-7300 Fax: 707-422-2637**
***PRACTICE AREAS: Business; Real Estate; Family Law; Personal Injury; Land Use.**
**General Civil Litigation including Business, Real Estate, Family Law, Personal Injury and Land Use Law.**
*See Professional Biographies, FAIRFIELD, CALIFORNIA*

**Davies, Robert E.**, (BV) ...............'52 '82 C.1060 B.A. L.464 J.D. [Caulfield,D.&D.]⊙
*PRACTICE AREAS: Product Liability; Aviation; Construction; Personal Injury.
Dekker, Laura A. ............................'63 '90 C.112 B.A. L.767 J.D. Dep. Dist. Atty.
DeRonde, Glen A. ...............................'53 '78 C.112 B.A. L.1049 J.D. [DeRonde&D.]
DeRonde, John A., Jr. ...........................'47 '74 C.112 B.A. L.464 J.D. [DeRonde&D.]
DeRonde & DeRonde ........................................................................ 460 Union Ave.
**Diffenderfer, William J.**, (BV) '57 '83 C.112 B.A. L.629 J.D.
[McNamara,H.D.M.&N.]
*PRACTICE AREAS: Insurance Defense.
**Donahue, James R.**, (BV) ...............'57 '82 C.740 B.S. L.464 J.D. [Caulfield,D.&D.]⊙
*REPORTED CASES: Ohio Casualty Ins. Co. v. Hartford Accident and Indemnity Co. (1983) 148 Cal. App. 3d 641; California Teachers Assn. v. Cory (1984) 155 Cal. App. 3d 494; Weaver v. Bishop (1988) 206 Cal. App. 3d 1351.
*PRACTICE AREAS: Trials; Personal Injury; Property Damage; Business Litigation; Professional Liability.
Driscoll, David J. .................................'42 '73 C.708 B.A. L.945 J.D. Dep. Dist. Atty.
Dunnell, Adey May, (BV) ...............................'22 '48 C.549 A.B. L.813 J.D. P.O. Box G
Duree, Terry Alan, (BV) ..................'48 '74 C.766 B.A. L.464 J.D. 710 Missouri St.
Ely, Dwight C. .........................................'32 '59 C.112 A.B. L.1066 J.D. Supr. Ct. Dept. 5
Epley-McKenna, Linda K. ..................'55 '82 C.1060 B.A. L.1153 J.D. Dep. Pub. Def.

**Favaro, Lavezzo, Gill, Caretti & Heppell, A Professional Corporation**
(See Vallejo)

**Finkas, R. Anthony**, (AV) ...........'46 '73 C.768 B.A. L.1067 J.D. [Honeychurch&F.]
*PRACTICE AREAS: Criminal Defense; Personal Injury; Felonies; Misdemeanors; Sexual Abuse.
Firpo, Peter A. ....................................'48 '74 C.112 B.A. L.260 J.D. Dep. Pub. Def.
Foos, David P. .................................'52 '78 C.112 A.B. L.1065 J.D. Off. of Pub. Def.
Forve, Frank F. ...................................'19 '50 C.390 A.B. L.276 J.D. 3184 Serra Way‡
Frederick, Laurie ...............................'61 '89 C.685 B.A. L.767 J.D. Dep. Pub. Def.
Furtek, Frank S. ................................'59 '83 C.112 A.B. L.464 J.D. Co. Coun.Off.
Garrett, Ramona J. ..........................'52 '80 C.770 B.A. L.1067 J.D. Chief Dep. Dist. Atty.
**Gaw, David B.**, (BV) ...............'45 '71 C.174 A.B. L.1065 J.D. [Gaw,V.S.M.&M.]⊙
*PRACTICE AREAS: Estate Planning Law; Trust and Probate Law; Elder Law.

**Gaw, Van Male, Smith, Myers & Miroglio, A Professional Law Corporation, (AV)**
**Corporate Plaza, 1261 Travis Boulevard, Suite 350, 94533-4801⊙**
**Telephone: 707-425-1250 Fax: 707-425-1255**
**URL: http://www.gvmsmm.com**
**David B. Gaw (Certified Specialist, Probate, Estate Planning and Trust Law, State Bar of California, Board of Legal Specialization); Nicholas R. Van Male; Wyman G. Smith, III; Bruce A. Myers; Bruce A. Miroglio; S. Scott Reynolds. Of Counsel: Mark A. Hyjek.**
**Business and Corporate Law, Real Estate, Estate Planning and Probate Administration, Family Law, Criminal Law, Corporate and Personal Taxation, Pension and Profit Sharing and Alcohol Beverage Law. General Civil Trial Practice in all State and Federal Courts. Personal Injury, Land Use, Planning and Local Government Law.**
**Napa, California Office: 944 Main Street. Telephone: 707-252-9000. Telecopier: 707-252-0792.**
*See Professional Biographies, FAIRFIELD, CALIFORNIA*

Geiger, Mark O. ...............................'51 '78 C.172 B.S. L.464 J.D. Dep. Dist. Atty.
Gnoss, Kenneth J. ..........................'52 '84 C.990 B.A. L.1137 J.D. Dep. Dist. Atty.
Gonzalez, Criselda B. .......................'56 '88 C.768 B.A. L.767 J.D. Dep. Dist. Atty.
Gordinier, Marilyn Low ............'48 '82 C.112 A.B. L.1153 J.D. Chf. Dep. Dist. Atty.
Gordinier, Thomas H. ....................'35 '68 C.763 A.B. L.999 J.D. Dep. Co. Coun.
Greeley, Carole Speckels ............'42 '74 C.791 B.S. L.813 J.D. 521 Americano Way
Greene, Kerry E. .............................'67 '94 C.347 B.A. L.597 J.D. 1261 Travis Blvd.
Haas, Thomas G., (BV) .......................'44 '70 C.112 A.B. L.1066 J.D. City Atty.

**Hagler & Nelson**
(See Vacaville)

**Harper, Jeffrey A.**, (AV) ........................'47 '78 C.112 B.A. L.1065 J.D. [Knox R.]
*PRACTICE AREAS: Civil Trial and Insurance Defense.
Harris, Richard M. ..................................'37 '64 C.976 B.A. L.1066 J.D. Supr. Ct. J.
Harrison, William C. ...............................'41 '66 C.112 B.S. L.1065 J.D. Supr. Ct. J.
Highsmith, James A., (BV) ................'43 '73 C.906 B.A. L.767 J.D. Dep. Dist. Atty.

**Hillman, M. Kendall, Law Offices of, (BV) '60 '86 C.112 B.A. L.800 J.D.**
**740 Texas Street, Suite 304, 94533**
**Telephone: 707-427-7377 Facsimile: 707-427-7370**
**Email: mkhlaw@aol.com**
**Trust and Estate Tax Planning, Probate, Real Estate, Business Sales and Acquisitions, and Land Use Planning.**
*See Professional Biographies, FAIRFIELD, CALIFORNIA*

**Hodson & Mullin**
(See Vacaville)

Holland, Ronald W. ...............................'53 '80 C.112 A.B. L.284 J.D. [Holland]
Holland Law Offices ..........................................................1600 Travis Blvd.
**Honeychurch, Denis A.**, (BV) .........'46 '72 C.112 B.A. L.1065 J.D. [Honeychurch&F.]
*PRACTICE AREAS: Criminal Defense; Felonies; Homicide; Misdemeanors; Sexual Abuse.

**Honeychurch and Finkas, (AV)**
**Suite C, 823 Jefferson Street, 94533**
**Telephone: 707-429-3111 Fax: 707-429-4302**
**Members of Firm: Denis A. Honeychurch (Certified Specialist, Criminal Law, The State Bar of California Board of Legal Specialization); R. Anthony Finkas.**
**Criminal and Civil Trial Practice. Criminal Defense and Personal Injury Law.**
*See Professional Biographies, FAIRFIELD, CALIFORNIA*

Hornsby, David Thomas .....................'65 '92 C.112 B.S. L.770 J.D. 744 Empire St.
Hughes, Richard L., (BV) .................'60 '87 C.1071 B.S. L.862 J.D. 744 Empire St.
**Hyjek, Mark A.**, (BV) '52 '77 C.169 B.A. L.61 J.D.
[🄰 Gaw,V.S.M.&M.] (⊙Fair Oaks)
*PRACTICE AREAS: Estate Planning; Elder Law.
Ichikawa, Garry T., (BV) ..................'47 '76 C.112 B.A. L.1067 J.D. 825 Webster St.
Jackson, Christopher M., (CV) ...............'54 '80 C.800 A.B. L.990 J.D. [Jackson&B.]
Jackson & Bowers, (CV) ..............................................................740 Texas St.

Joyce, Sharon K. '50 '81 C.801 B.A. L.1067 J.D. Off. of Co. Coun.
Keener, Douglas N. '48 '83 C.1060 B.S. L.284 J.D. Chf. Dep. Dist. Atty.
**Keitges, Cyril A., Jr.**, (AV) '35 '62 C&L.770 B.S., LL.B. [Keitges,B.&O.]⊙
*PRACTICE AREAS: Ski and Sports Injury Litigation; Medical Malpractice; Insurance Fraud; Arbitration and Mediation Services; General Insurance Defense Matters.

**Keitges, Bangle & Owensby, A Professional Law Corporation, (AV)**
**1261 Travis Boulevard, Suite 270, 94533⊙**
Telephone: 707-422-1301 Fax: 707-427-6677
Cyril A. Keitges, Jr.; Raymond Bangle, III; Tracy Owensby; Jill H. Latchaw.
Governmental Entity and Insurance Defense, Insurance Coverage, Insurance Fraud, Ski and Sports Injury Litigation, Medical Malpractice, Products, Commercial and Construction. Liability, ADR Services.
Sacramento, California Office: 2150 River Plaza Drive, Suite 205. 95833. Telephone: 916-568-3400. Fax: 916-568-3404.
*See Professional Biographies, FAIRFIELD, CALIFORNIA*

Kinnicutt, Harry S. '51 '77 C.763 B.S. L.1066 J.D. Supr. Ct. J.
**Knight, Wayne A. '42 '79 C.101 B.A. L.408 J.D.**
**1550 Webster Street, Suite C, 94533**
Telephone: 707-422-5411 Fax: 707-422-0174
*PRACTICE AREAS: Personal Injury; Family Law; Business Law; Bankruptcy; Probate.
General Civil, Personal Injury, Business, Bankruptcy, Family Law, Real Estate.
*See Professional Biographies, FAIRFIELD, CALIFORNIA*

Knox, Daniel B. '46 '75 C.1060 B.A. L.1065 J.D. 2761 Seminole Dr.‡
**Knox Ricksen, LLP, (AV)**
**Corporate Plaza, Suite 300, 1261 Travis Boulevard, 94533⊙**
Telephone: 707-426-3313 Fax: 707-426-0426
Members of Firm: William C. Robbins, III; Jeffrey A. Harper; R. Patrick Snook. Associates: Christine A. Carringer; Dennis Earl Raglin.
General Civil and Trial Practice. Corporate, Real Estate, Land Use, Urban Development and Environmental Law, Taxation, Estate Planning, Probate, Insurance and Medical Liability Defense Practice.
Oakland, California Office: Suite 1700, 1999 Harrison Street. Telephone: 510-893-1000. Fax: 510-446-1946.
San Jose, Santa Clara County, California Office: 100 Park Center Plaza, Suite 560, 95113. Telephone: 408-295-2828. Fax: 408-295-6868.
*See Professional Biographies, FAIRFIELD, CALIFORNIA*

Kobrin, Kenneth '52 '77 C.112 B.A. L.464 J.D. Dep. Dist. Atty.
Kosid, Janet E. '50 '75 C.966 B.A. L.767 J.D. Dep. Dist. Atty.
Lando, Robert E. '46 '76 C.112 B.A. L.1066 J.D. 3411 Kenwood Ct.‡
Lang, James P., (BV) '23 '68 C.999 L.809 LL.B. Dep. Pub. Def.
**Latchaw, Jill H.** '56 '87 C.112 B.A. L.1153 J.D. [Keitges,B.&O.]⊙
*PRACTICE AREAS: Insurance Defense (Personal Injury); Insurance Coverage; Construction Defects; Real Estate Errors and Omissions.
Laughlin, James W. '57 '84 C.112 B.A. L.1067 J.D. Dep. Co. Coun.
Lowe, David William, (BV) '35 '62 C.112 A.B. L.1066 J.D. 740 Texas St.
**Lucas, F. Richard**, (AV) '33 '61 C.770 B.S. L.813 J.D. [Lucas&L.]
*PRACTICE AREAS: General Practice; Civil Litigation; Insurance; Public Entity Defense.
**Lucas, Matthew R.** '65 '90 C.813 A.B. L.1068 J.D. [Lucas&L.]
*LANGUAGES: Italian.
*PRACTICE AREAS: General Practice; Personal Injury; Insurance Defense Law; Civil Litigation; Probate and Estate Planning.

**Lucas & Lucas, (AV)**
**547 Jefferson Street, Suite A, 94533**
Telephone: 707-438-0210
Members of Firm: F. Richard Lucas; Matthew R. Lucas; Katherine M. Babcock.
General Civil and Trial Practice. Insurance Defense, Negligence, Real Estate, Probate, Family and Corporate Law. Mediation and Arbitration Law.
Representative Clients: Farmers' Insurance Group; County of Solano; Fairfield Daily Republic; Geico Insurance Co.; City of Fairfield; City of Dixon; City of Rio Vista.
*See Professional Biographies, FAIRFIELD, CALIFORNIA*

Magalski, Richard A. '60 '89 C.112 B.A. L.1049 J.D. 744 Empire St.
**Mattice, Michael C.**, (BV) '48 '77 C.112 A.B. L.1065 J.D. [Barnett M.]
*PRACTICE AREAS: Personal Injury Law; Family Law.
McCaslin, Neal P., (BV) '20 '60 L.284 LL.B. Dist. Atty.

**McNamara, Houston, Dodge, McClure & Ney, (AV)**
**639 Kentucky Avenue, Suite 110, 94533-5530⊙**
Telephone: 707-427-3998 Fax: 707-427-0268
Members of Firm: Guy D. Borges (Resident); William J. Diffenderfer (Resident). Associates: Kathleen A. Nelson (Resident); Donald A. Odell (Resident).
General Civil Trial Practice in all State and Federal Courts. Corporation, Insurance and Professional Liability Law.
Walnut Creek, California Office: 1211 Newell Avenue, Second Floor, P.O. Box 5288. Telephone: 510-939-5330. Facsimile: 510-939-0203.
*See Professional Biographies, FAIRFIELD, CALIFORNIA*

**McPherson, William H., (AV) '22 '52 C&L.813 A.B., J.D. [BB]**
**825 Webster Street, 94533**
Telephone: 707-422-7706 Fax: 707-425-9331
(Certified Specialist, Family Law, The State Bar of California Board of Legal Specialization).
*REPORTED CASES: IRMO Martinez (1984) 156 CA3 20; IRMO Hebbring (1989) 207 CA3 1260; IRMO Watt (1989) 214 CA 340.
*PRACTICE AREAS: Family Law; Mediation Law; Arbitration Law; Family Law Appeals; Probate Law.
Family, Probate, Arbitration and Mediation. Family Law Appellate.
*See Professional Biographies, FAIRFIELD, CALIFORNIA*

Meyerherm, Charles H. '20 '52 C.999 D.C. L.464 LL.B. Dep. Dist. Atty.
Miranda, Anthony M. '48 '76 C.766 B.A. L.1066 J.D. 690 E. Tabor
**Miroglio, Bruce A.**, (CV) '57 '82 C.112 B.A. L.464 J.D. [Gaw,V.S.M.&M.]⊙
*REPORTED CASES: Vianna v. Doctors' Management Co. (1994) 27 Cal.App.4th 1186.
*PRACTICE AREAS: Civil Litigation; Personal Injury Law; Medical Malpractice Defense; Probate Litigation; Employment Litigation.
Moelk, James F. '36 '63 C.767 B.S. L.1065 J.D. 600 Union Ave.
**Moller, Pascha R.** '70 '96 C&L.112 B.A., J.D. [A N.M.Nolte]
*PRACTICE AREAS: Family Law; Mediation; Child Advocacy.
Morris, Mary J. '— '88 L.408 J.D. 1049 Union Ave.
**Myers, Bruce A.** '51 '81 C.112 B.S. L.464 J.D. [Gaw,V.S.M.&M.]⊙
*PRACTICE AREAS: Taxation Law; Business Transactions; Pension Law; Profit Sharing Law.
Nail, Mike '40 '67 C.1142 B.A. L.1065 J.D. Judge Superior Ct.
Neilson, John F. '47 '77 C.112 B.A. L.310 J.D. Dep. Pub. Def.
**Nelson, Kathleen A.** '63 '92 C.907 B.A. L.770 J.D. [A McNamara,H.D.M.&N.]
*LANGUAGES: Spanish.
*PRACTICE AREAS: Insurance Defense.
Newman, Barry K. '55 '82 C.112 B.A. L.1067 J.D. 740 W. Texas St.
Nielson, John F. '47 '77 C.112 B.A. L.1065 J.D. Asst. Pub. Def.

**Nolte, Nancy M., (CV) '42 '81 C.147 B.A. L.1067 J.D.**
**710 Missouri Street, Suite 3, 94533⊙**
Telephone: 707-425-1058 FAX: 707-425-1059
(Certified Specialist, Family Law, The State Bar of California Board of Legal Specialization).
*PRACTICE AREAS: Family Law; Family Mediation.

(This Listing Continued)

**Nolte, Nancy M. (Continued)**
Associate: Pascha R. Moller.
Family Law, Family Mediation.
Benicia, California Office: 159 East D Street, Suite G. Telephone: 707-745-8999.
*See Professional Biographies, FAIRFIELD, CALIFORNIA*

Nurik, Jeffrey H. '52 '81 C.999 M.A. L.767 J.D. 801 Jefferson St.
**Odell, Donald A.** '60 '94 C.569 B.A. L.464 J.D. [A McNamara,H.D.M.&N.]
*PRACTICE AREAS: Insurance Defense.
O'Hanlon, Jerry M. '35 '67 C.174 B.A. L.767 J.D. Dep. Pub. Def.
Oldwin, Leonard E., Jr. '53 '87 C.925 B.S. L.464 J.D. 740 W. Texas St.
**Owensby, Tracy** '62 '87 C.1060 B.A. L.1067 J.D. [Keitges,B.&O.]⊙
*PRACTICE AREAS: Insurance Fraud; Auto and Homeowners Litigation; Amusement and Recreation Litigation; Construction Defect and Accident Liability.
Parker, Darryl '54 '80 C.262 B.A. L.1066 J.D. 3475 Quincey Ct.
Pascalli, Lewis G. '42 '83 C.749 B.S. L.1153 J.D. 1949 Victoria Ct.
Paulson, David W., (BV) '47 '72 C.597 B.A. L.94 J.D. Dist. Atty.
Pisani, Otto C. '40 '66 C.112 A.B. L.1065 LL.B. Dep. Pub. Def.
**Policar, Raymond**, (BV) '52 '78 C.169 B.A. L.464 J.D.
Asst. V.P. & Western Div. Coun., ORIX Credit Alliance, Inc.
Power, David Edwin '49 '75 C.112 B.A. L.770 J.D. Mun. Ct. Judge
**Raglin, Dennis Earl** '70 '95 C.112 B.A. L.1067 J.D. [A Knox R.]
*PRACTICE AREAS: Insurance Defense.
Rees, Garrison C., Jr., (CV) '50 '82 C.112 B.A. L.767 J.D. 744 Empire St.
**Reynolds, S. Scott** '49 '76 C.813 B.A. L.464 J.D. [Gaw,V.S.M.&M.]
*PRACTICE AREAS: Estate Planning; Trust Administration; Business Law; Corporate Law; Tax Law.
**Robbins, William C., III**, (AV) '41 '66 C.976 B.A. L.1066 LL.B. [Knox R.]⊙
*PRACTICE AREAS: Real Estate Law; Land Use Planning Law; Estate Planning Law.
Rodriguez, Cynthia A. '57 '82 C&L.190 B.A., J.D. 356 Begonia Blvd.
Rubay, Donnell M. '57 '82 C.112 A.B. L.1068 J.D. 2942 Miller Dr.

**Ryan, S. Katelin '46 '88 C.447 B.A. L.1065 J.D.**
**1143 Missouri Street, 94533⊙**
Telephone: 707-425-6023 Fax: 707-425-3468
*PRACTICE AREAS: Civil Litigation; Employment Law; Insurance Law.
General Civil Litigation, Employment Law, Insurance Law.
Napa, California Office: 1370 Trancas Street, Suite 338. Telephone: 707-224- 2322.
*See Professional Biographies, FAIRFIELD, CALIFORNIA*

Schoenke, Lawrence M. '53 '80 C.766 B.A. L.767 J.D. 1125 Missouri St.
Seltzer, David S. '49 '77 C.473 B.A. L.1065 J.D. Dep. Pub. Def.
**Smith, Wyman G., III**, (BV) '50 '76 C.174 B.A. L.464 J.D. [Gaw,V.S.M.&M.]⊙
*PRACTICE AREAS: Business; Corporate; Real Estate Transactions.
**Snook, R. Patrick** '58 '87 C.112 B.A. L.1065 J.D. [Knox R.]
*PRACTICE AREAS: Civil Trial; Insurance Defense; Insurance Coverage.
Soley, Frederick G. '54 '81 C.1073 B.A. L.1065 J.D. Dep. Pub. Def.
Stackhouse, Susan G. '54 '90 C.264 B.A. L.978 J.D. Dep. Pub. Def.
Stanley, E. Glynn, Jr., (BV) '48 '74 C&L.767 B.A., J.D. 728 Texas St.
Strickland, Patricia C. '44 '84 C.770 L.1226 J.D. Dist. Atty.
Sweeney, Christopher W. '64 '89 C.740 B.A. L.284 J.D. 740 Texas St.
Talley, David Allen '60 '90 C.1042 B.A. L.112 J.D. 2801 Waterman Blvd.
Tamayo, Stephen C. '55 '85 C.1060 B.A. L.1065 J.D. Dep. Pub. Def.
Tirrell, Marc K., (CV) '52 '79 C.1154 B.A. L.61 J.D. 639 Kentucky St., Ste., 210
Uldall, Eric R. '45 '71 C&L.767 J.D. Mun. J.
Van Dorn, Frederic E. '10 '34 C&L.477 A.B., J.D. 2175 Monterey Dr.‡
**Van Male, Nicholas R.**, (AV) '38 '71 C.112 A.B. L.1067 J.D. [Gaw,V.S.M.&M.]⊙
*PRACTICE AREAS: Civil Litigation; Family Law; Land Use Planning Law.
Villarreal, Luis M. '49 '75 C.843 B.A. L.765 J.D. Mun. Ct. J.
Walsh, Timothy J. '46 '76 C.1078 B.A. L.1153 J.D. 1319 Travis Blvd.
Wells, E. Gordon, Jr., (BV) '35 '67 C.101 B.S. L.1068 J.D. [Wells,C.&C.]
Wells, Call & Clark, A Prof. Corp., (BV) 1710 Pennsylvania Ave.
Whitaker, Richard A., (CV) '43 '73 C.112 A.B. L.1067 J.D. 460 Union Ave.
Whiting, Sidney E., III, (BV) '38 '65 C.170 B.A. L.174 J.D. [Whiting&B.]
Whiting & Becksted, (BV) 547-D Jefferson St.
Wyeth, Harry B., III '41 '66 C.813 A.B. L.1066 LL.B. Dep. Co. Coun.

## FAIR OAKS, 11,256, *Sacramento Co.*

Ash, Robert W. '42 '75 L.1132 J.D. P.O. Box 979
Bakes, William H. '22 '49 C.629 B.S. L.336 LL.B. 4614 Chicago Ave.‡
Baldwin, Norman D., (BV) '10 '46 C.184 M.A. L.813 J.D. [Wells&B.]
Barbieri, J. Michael, (CV) '49 '80 C&L.1137 B.S.L., J.D. [Giffen&B.]
Bernard, William E., P.C., (BV) '52 '79 C.549 B.A. L.464 J.D. [W.E.Bernard]
Bernard, William E., P.C., (BV) 5330 Primrose Dr.
Brown, Leon F. '22 '50 C&L.546 B.A., J.D.
(adm. in NE; not adm. in CA) 3802 Fair Hill Rd.‡
Browning, James R. '48 '78 C.147 B.A. L.1095 J.D. 10224 Fair Oaks Blvd.
Daggs, Douglas M. '38 '74 C.1026 B.S. 10014 Fair Oaks Blvd.
Davey, Benjamin L. '43 '88 C.36 B.S. L.408 J.D. 5150 Sunrise Blvd.
Dismukes, Jim B., (BV) '46 '76 C.1060 B.S. L.464 J.D. 7728 Lemon St.
Foran, John Francis, (AV) '08 '34 C.112 L.426 J.D. 8842 Winding Way, Apt. 201‡
Fraley, Philip K. '43 '82 C.267 B.S. L.1026 J.D. 5330 Primrose Dr.
Garner, Gerald W. '35 '81 C.147 A.B. L.464 J.D. 5132 Nihoa Ct.
Giffen, John A. '47 '81 C.101 B.S. L.464 J.D. [Giffen&B.]
Giffen & Barbieri, Inc., (CV) 5150 Sunrise Blvd.
Gilbert, Kim Eileen '47 '74 C.112 B.A. L.464 J.D. 8784 Bluff Lane
Hanelt, Fred '39 '67 C.768 A.B. L.767 J.D. 4709 Papaya Dr.
Hart-Nibbrig, Leonard C. '63 '90 C.112 B.A. L.659 J.D. 4944 Tommar Dr.
Hornor, Boyd E. (John), III '37 '65 C.674 A.B. L.893 J.D. 9700 Fair Oaks Blvd.
Hyatt, W. Roland, Jr. '41 '82 C.1060 B.A. L.464 J.D. 7341 Winding Way
Hyjek, Mark A., (BV) '52 '77 C.169 B.A. L.61 J.D. 9801 Fair Oaks Blvd. (⊙Fairfield)
Latzer, Donald H. '51 '77 C.1077 B.A. L.765 J.D. 7840 Madison Ave.
Llewellyn, David L., Jr. '45 '76 C.946 B.A. L.1068 J.D. 4880 SanJuan Ave.
Luther, Florence J., (BV) '28 '64 C.999 L.464 J.D. [Luther&L.]
Luther & Luther, A Professional Corporation, (BV) 11101 Fair Oaks Blvd.
McCoy, Deborah '50 '80 C.112 B.A. L.464 J.D. 4443 Andrew Alan Ln.
McGuire, Thomas K., (AV) '32 '66 C.112 B.A. L.1066 LL.B. 4217 Curragh Oaks Ln.
McKenzie, Alfred B. '31 '57 C.311 A.B. L.1066 LL.B. [McKenzie&D.]
McKenzie & Dalby 10224 Fair Oaks Blvd.
Mullen, Beth '40 '86 C.999 L.408 J.D. 5263 Rimwood Dr.
Ongerth, Richard H. '46 '77 C.112 B.S. L.464 J.D. 10030 Fair Oaks Blvd.
Parquette, Jack R., (BV) '34 '78 C.174 L.408 LL.B. 10014 Fair Oaks Blvd.
Petrozzi, Paul J. '30 '66 C.602 B.S. L.464 LL.B. 4919 Hollycrest Wy.‡
Plexico, William '36 '80 L.1026 J.D. 5150 Sunrise Blvd.
Price, Angel Ann '— '94 C.1320 B.A. L.999 J.D. 4944 Tommar Dr.
Raun, Michael C. '43 '87 L.1026 J.D. 5150 Sunrise Blvd.
Regan, Nancy A., (CV) '49 '75 C.112 A.B. L.1065 J.D. 5060 Sunrise Blvd.
Reynolds, Gary S. '17 '53 C.732 L.273 LL.B. 5714 Hoffman Ln.
Riave, Lionel L. '23 '57 C.112 A.B. L.1066 LL.B. 8719 Lake Nimbus Dr.‡

Rogers, John D. '— '77 C.112 A.B. L.464 7840 Madison Ave.
Samuel, Carl R. '41 '75 C.1097 B.A. L.809 J.D. [Samuel,S.&S.]
Samuel, Jean '42 '81 C.1097 B.S. L.1026 J.D. [Samuel,S.&S.]
Samuel, Peter F. '46 '76 C.1097 B.A. L.1148 J.D. [Samuel,S.&S.]
Samuel, Robert F. '48 '86 C.1097 B.A. L.1026 J.D. [Samuel,S.&S.]
Samuel, Shafie & Samuel 5050 Sunrise Blvd.
Steinmann, Michael A. '48 '83 C.966 B.A. L.1068 J.D.
(adm. in AK; not adm. in CA) Steinmann Grayson Smylie
Sutter, Steve D. '51 '76 C.112 B.S. L.770 J.D. P.O. Box 5292
Tibbitts, Lewis W. '30 '58 C&L.966 B.S.E.E., LL.B. 8156 Pollard
Valerio, David A. '46 '88 C.999 B.A. L.1026 J.D. 8920 Sunset Ave.
Ward, Vincent D., Jr. '43 '79 L.464 J.D. 11140 Fair Oaks Blvd.
Wells, John Jay, (BV) '14 '45 C.112 A.B. L.178 J.D. [Wells&B.]
Wells & Baldwin, (BV) 8844 Bluff Lane
Williams, Hollis '39 '74 L.1026 LL.B. [Williams&Y.]
Williams, Hollis R. '22 '53 C.262 B.S. L.564 LL.B. [Williams&S.]
Williams & Shedd 10014 Fair Oaks Blvd.
Williams & Yeo 10014 Fair Oaks Blvd.
Yeo, James R. '41 '71 C.169 L.464 J.D. [Williams&Y.]
Yungling, Deane J., (CV) '41 '72 C.1060 B.A. L.464 J.D. 5191 Rimwood Dr.
Zamboni, Joyce E. '46 '87 C.1060 B.A. L.464 J.D. 533 Primrose Dr., Ste. 225

## FALLBROOK, 6,945, *San Diego Co.*

Burgoon, Samuel M. '31 '74 C.223 B.S.E.E. L.1136 J.D. 133 Alva Lane
Busch, Henry M. '12 '39 C.605 B.A. L.1065 J.D. 2436 Gird Rd.‡
Butler, Patrick C. '48 '78 C.339 B.A. L.472 J.D.
(adm. in FL; not adm. in CA) 1322 Friends Way‡
Clodig, John B., (BV) '43 '73 [J.B.Clodig]
Clodig, John B., Inc., A Prof. Corp., (BV) 1308 El Nido Dr.

**Crawford, John W., (BV) '47 '77 C.605 B.A. L.1065 J.D.**
**205 West Alvarado Street, 92028**
**Telephone: 619-728-5799 Facsimile: 619-728-5715**
**General Civil and Trial Practice. Real Property, Business, Estate Planning, Probate and Conservatorship Law.**

Croswell, Kevin J., (BV) '49 '76 C.112 B.A. L.61 J.D. 210 E. Fig St., Suite 101

**Donart, James G., (BV) '48 '74 C.813 A.B. L.800 J.D.**
**Suite 20, 300 North Main Street, 92028**
**Telephone: 619-728-6670 FAX: 619-728-9792**
**Wills, Trusts, Estate Planning and Probate Law, Serving San Diego and Riverside Counties.**
**Representative Clients: Union Bank; Northern Trust of California N.A.**
***See Professional Biographies, FALLBROOK, CALIFORNIA***

Duni, Rollin F. '11 '35 L.809 LL.B. 3896 Ladera Vista Rd.‡
Fitzwater, G. Morgan, (AV) '14 '56 C&L.426 990 Rainbow Crest Rd.‡
Gehring, Robert W. '40 '66 C.309 B.A. L.178 J.D. 156 Palacio Norte
Gordon, Ralph R. '15 '39 C.405 L.146 LL.B. 3291 Canonita Dr.‡
Hawkins, Richard M. '23 '47 C.613 L.192 LL.B. 2923 Nuestra
Jackson, Robert W., (BV) '56 '85 C.112 B.A. L.990 J.D. 205 W. Alvarado St.
James, Robert H., (P.C.), (BV) '41 '70 C.690 B.A. L.1049 J.D. [Sachse,J.&L.]
Jennings, Gerald M., Jr. '45 '85 C.169 B.A. L.809 J.D. RR 6 Box 14
Keefe, Richard W., (AV) '23 '65 C.46 B.S.M.E. L.365 J.D. 1439 Knoll Pk. Ln.‡
Leehey, Paul W., (BV) '54 '80 C.426 B.A. L.1049 J.D. 205 W. Alvarado St.
Lopardo, Stephen V., (BV) '54 '78 C.602 B.A. L.1049 J.D. [Sachse,J.&L.]
McDaniel, Rankin H., III '47 '75 C.766 B.A. L.1137 P.O. Box 2588
McNeil, Mary F. '30 '78 C.1131 B.A. L.809 J.D. 1304 Aves Ln.
Medoff, M. Craig '19 '52 C.659 B.S. L.309 LL.B. 5 Golden Meadow Ln.‡
Newton, Johnnie Lee '47 '78 C&L.1049 B.A., J.D. 460 Rancho Camino★

**Reddingius, R. P., (BV) '20 '51 C.112 B.A. L.1065 J.D.**
**566 East Alvarado Street, 92028⊙**
**Telephone: 619-723-6604 FAX: 619-728-0210**
**Wills, Trusts, Probate, Estate Planning, Elder Law and Conservatorships.**
**Pasadena, California Office: 225 South Lake Avenue. Suite 1100 91101. Telephone: 818-795-2117; 213-681-5043. Fax: 818-304-9652.**

Sachse, James & Lopardo, (BV) 205 W. Alvarado St.
Shannon, William V., Jr., (BV) '36 '64 C.668 A.B. L.800 140 W. Hawthorne St.
Sides, Clay R. '61 '86 C.112 B.A. L.1049 J.D. 4120 Arboles Dr.
Smith, Andrew V., (BV) '19 '51 C&L.800 B.A., J.D. 435 Rancho Camino St.
Stephen-Porter, Loren A. '54 '88 C.1109 B.A. L.1241 J.D. 475 Stephens Port
Steres, Michael E. '49 '74 C.154 B.A. L.309 J.D. 35062 Rice Cyn Rd.
Stevens, Russell L. '17 '49 L.174 LL.B. 949 Riverview Dr.‡
Teasdall, Harry Ervin, (BV) '18 '55 L.397 LL.B. 300 N. Main St.
Tiday, Ronald L., (AV) '12 '39 C&L.800 LL.B. 3525 Northcliff Dr.‡
Wheeler, Stephen L., (BV) '41 '66 C.605 A.B. L.1065 J.D. 566 E. Alvarado St.
Zoller, Deborah L. '53 '89 C.1110 B.A. L.398 J.D. 566 E. Alvarado St.

## FALL RIVER MILLS, —, *Shasta Co.*

Holmer, Ray T., Jr. '37 '78 C.112 L.765 J.D. P.O. Box 178

## FARMERSVILLE, 6,235, *Tulare Co.*

Baldwin, Calvin E., (AV) '27 '53 C&L.813 A.B., J.D. Edgewood Orchards‡

## FAWNSKIN, —, *San Bernardino Co.*

Littrell, Lawrence R. '27 '66 C.800 B.S. L.809 LL.B. P.O. Box 116‡
Wheeler, W. David '55 '81 C.112 B.A. L.800 J.D. P.O. Box 448

## FELTON, 2,062, *Santa Cruz Co.*

Muni, Steven D. '51 '77 C.976 B.A. L.61 J.D. 6361 Ashley St.

## FERNDALE, 1,331, *Humboldt Co.*

Hofstetter, Marilynn K. '28 '53 C.504 A.B. L.1066 LL.B. P.O. Box 393‡

## FILLMORE, 11,992, *Ventura Co.*

Brady, Donald S. '31 '56 C.813 B.A. L.426 J.D. Pres., Don-Mar Financial Co.
Kern, Joseph P. D., (BV) '33 '61 C&L.770 B.S.C., LL.B. 448 Sespe Ave.
McNamara, John J., (BV) '51 '77 C&L.1049 B.A., J.D. 459 Main St.
Quici, Christopher L. '63 '91 C.112 B.A. L.769 J.D. 830 Santa Clara Ave.
Scoles, John F., (BV) '41 '72 C.628 B.S. L.464 J.D. 540 Sespe Ave.

## FIREBAUGH, 4,429, *Fresno Co.*

Scott, Dennis R. '30 '60 C.112 A.B. L.1066 LL.B. Co. J.

## FLINTRIDGE, —, *Los Angeles Co.*

(See La Canada Flintridge)

## FOLSOM, 29,802, *Sacramento Co.*

Armbrust, John C. '47 '85 C.754 B.S. L.345 J.D.
(adm. in IN; not adm. in CA) Amfac Electric Supply
Asbury, Charles M., (BV) '34 '69 L.464 J.D. P.O. Box 910
Fait, Sharon G. '42 '76 C.990 B.A. L.464 J.D. 305 Scott St.‡
Fowler, Donald D. '62 '90 C.1060 B.A. L.1026 J.D. 404 Natoma St.
Frese, Glenn C. '44 '71 C.112 B.A. L.1066 J.D. 81 Blue Ravine Rd.
Gibson, Guy G., Jr., (BV) '37 '72 C.1060 B.S. L.464 J.D. [G.G.Gibson,Jr.]⊙
Gibson, Guy G., Jr., A Prof. Corp., Law Offices of, (BV)
404 Natoma St. (⊙West Sacramento)

**Laurie, Maloney & Wheatley, (AV)**
**1004 River Rock Drive, Suite 245, 95630⊙**
**Telephone: 916-988-3857**
**Resident Partner: Robert M. Wheatley.**
**Land Use, Business, Real Estate, Banking, Estate Planning, Municipal, Employment and Construction Law, Personal Injury and Civil Litigation, Franchising.**
**Cameron Park (El Dorado County), California Office: 3420 Coach Lane, Suite 15. Telephone: 916-677-0245. Fax: 916-677-4802.**
**Placerville (El Dorado County), California Office: 345 Placerville Drive. Telephone: 916-622-7769.**
***See Professional Biographies, FOLSOM, CALIFORNIA***

Logan, Robert M. '60 '89 C.636 B.S. L.408 J.D. 404 Natoma St.
McShane, Joanne T. '58 '87 C.770 B.S. L.464 J.D. 150 Black Powder Cir.
Reiken, Paul D. '51 '82 C.259 B.S. L.464 J.D. 555 Oakdale St.
Rudolph, Steven P. '57 '86 C.869 B.S. L.464 J.D. Asst. City Atty.
Seabridge, William B., (BV) '50 '79 C.1042 B.A. L.464 J.D. 110 Blue Ravine Rd.
**Wheatley, Robert M., (AV)** '43 '69 C.813 A.B. L.1065 J.D. [Laurie,M.&W.]
*PRACTICE AREAS: Banking Law; Automobile Dealership Law; Construction Law.
Zal, Cyrus '47 '75 C.112 A.B. L.893 J.D. 102 Mainsail Ct.

## FONTANA, 87,535, *San Bernardino Co.*

Caldwell, Sharon Lee Stine '54 '82 C.1274 B.B.A. L.802 J.D. Dep. Dist. Atty.
Cuthbert, William J., (BV) '32 '62 C&L.800 LL.B. [W.J.Cuthbert]
Cuthbert, William J., Inc., (BV) 9161 Sierra Ave., Ste. 201
Denny, Joyce '— '78 C.605 B.A. L.809 J.D. 8229 Reseda Ave.
Diggs, Weldon, (AV) '43 '69 C.684 B.A. L.1068 J.D. 9161 Sierra Ave.
DuPuis, Daniel G., (BV) '48 '78 L.1198 LL.B. Dep. Pub. Def.
Falkenthal, Robert J. '52 '89 C&L.1137 B.S., J.D. 8414 Sierra Ave.
Glazier, Louis O. '32 '69 C.36 B.S. L.809 LL.B. Mun. J.
Harris, Wendell V., (BV) '14 '47 C.273 A.B. L.280 LL.B. 10973 Catawba Ave.
Kempe-Olinger, Elisabeth '54 '83 C.1110 B.A. L.1137 J.D. 9349 Sierra Ave.
Morris, Philip M. '36 '71 C.684 B.A. L.426 J.D. Mun. Ct. J.
Olio, Louis '22 '49 C.999 L.800 LL.B. 8374 Nuevo Ave.‡
**Rager, John M., (BV)** '41 '66 C.763 B.A. L.1065 J.D. [J.M.Rager]

**Rager, John M., Law Offices of, (BV)**
**8413 Sierra Avenue, Suite A, 92335**
**Telephone: 909-822-4445 Fax: 909-822-6539**
**Henry F. Rager (1914-1980); John M. Rager.**
**Probate Law, Family Law and Estate Planning.**
***See Professional Biographies, FONTANA, CALIFORNIA***

Stewart, Stephen Carl '51 '84 L.1148 J.D. 9161 Sierra Ave.

## FOREST RANCH, —, *Butte Co.*

Watkins, Loy H., (BV) '38 '76 C&L.1137 B.S.L., J.D. 15522 Nopel Ave.

## FORESTVILLE, —, *Sonoma Co.*

Cole, Richard G. '53 '80 C.1078 B.A. L.770 J.D. 6700 Berryhill Ct.
Formaker, William J. '44 '70 C.966 B.S. L.1065 J.D. 10155 Old River Rd.
Lovett, Sarah L. '31 '79 C.112 Ed.D. L.765 J.D. 6909 Nolan Rd.‡
Nestle, Manuel E. '29 '56 C.112 A.B. L.1066 LL.B. P.O. Box 129
Woods, Martin M. '55 '85 C.769 B.A. L.1227 J.D. 6600 Front St. (⊙Santa Rosa)

## FORT BRAGG, 6,078, *Mendocino Co.*

Antler, Steven J. '41 '65 C.309 A.B. L.178 LL.B. [Antler&R.]
Antler & Rainie 136 Oak St.
Bainbridge, Ellen A. '22 '63 C.112 L.1132 31775 Pudding Creek Rd.‡
Bainbridge, Robt. '21 '50 C.112 A.B. L.1065 J.D. 31775 Pudding Creek Rd.‡
Cardiff, Mary '17 '61 C.590 B.S. P.O. Box 661‡
Gobbi, Mark W '61 '87 C.276 B.S. L.1067 J.D. 31200 Country Rd
Godeke, Dan A., (CV) '37 '76 C.801 A.B. L.734 J.D. 703 N. Main St.
Hanson, Jane Ann '49 '75 C.112 A.B. L.1067 J.D. 26361 Blueberry Hill Rd.
Heeb, Robert H., (CV) '27 '56 C.401 B.S. L.188 LL.B. Jus. Ct. J.
Hersh-Sinsel, Eleanor A. '38 '75 C.1246 B.S. L.1136 J.D. 22851 Hwy. 1, N.‡
Kronfeld, Bart P., (CV) '48 '73 C.477 A.B. L.1065 J.D. 310 S. Main St.

**Larson, James L., (AV) '41 '66 C.112 A.B. L.1065 LL.B.**
**311 North McPherson Street, P.O. Box 1369, 95437**
**Telephone: 707-964-6327 Fax: 707-964-7559**
**Email: jlarson@mcn.org**
**(Certified Specialist, Estate Planning, Trust and Probate Law, The State Bar of California Board of Legal Specialization).**
**Estate Planning, Trust and Probate Law.**
**Reference: Savings Bank of Mendocino County, Fort Bragg Branch.**
***See Professional Biographies, FORT BRAGG, CALIFORNIA***

Lehan, Jonathan M. '47 '72 C.1109 B.A. L.61 J.D. Mun. J.
Lonergan, Thomas C., (BV) '33 '59 C.766 A.B. L.1065 J.D. City Atty.
Margulis, Phyllis '26 '59 L.981 LL.B. 32075 Westwood Dr.‡
Petersen, F. Gregory, (BV) '47 '73 C.112 B.A. L.464 J.D. Hwy. 1 S.
Petersen, Robert C., (AV) '34 '59 C.766 A.B. L.1065 J.D. 1102 S. Main St.
Rainie, James C. '48 '74 C.197 A.B. L.813 J.D. [Antler&R.]

**Rawles, Hinkle, Carter, Behnke & Oglesby**
**(See Ukiah)**

**Ruprecht, John J., (AV) '40 '66 C.154 B.A. L.813 J.D.**
**32670 Highway Twenty at South Harbor Drive, P.O. Box 1445, 95437**
**Telephone: 707-964-2973 FAX: 707-964-9255**
***PRACTICE AREAS: Personal Injury; Real Estate.**
**Civil Litigation. Personal Injury, Real Estate and Business Law.**
**A list of Representative Clients will be furnished upon request.**
***See Professional Biographies, FORT BRAGG, CALIFORNIA***

## FORT JONES, 639, *Siskiyou Co.*

Crow, Jerry O. '52 '79 C.763 B.S. L.1186 J.D. 2923 Kidder Creek Rd.

## FORTUNA, 8,788, *Humboldt Co.*

Adams, John B. '41 '66 C.813 B.A. L.1066 J.D. 2295 School St.★
Banducci, Dominic D. '31 '76 C.770 B.S. L.767 Mun. J.

CAA90P

Bender, Cheryl ........................................'45 '78 L.1001 J.D. 652 Main St.
Borntrager, Ezra Eli ............................ '48 '79 C.134 B.A. L.502 J.D. P.O. Box 323
Cooper, Herman '10 '32 L.552 LL.B.
(adm. in NJ; not adm. in CA) 2025 Scenic Dr.‡
Crlenjak, Jack, (CV) ..................'42 '80 C.768 B.A. L.770 J.D. 1100 Main St., Ste. C
**Harland, Gerald R.**, (AV) .......... '22 '51 C.826 A.B. L.813 J.D. [Harland] (ⓒEureka)
*PRACTICE AREAS: Estate Planning Law; Real Property Law; Probate Law; Business Law.

**Harland Law Firm, (AV)**
**954 Main Street, 95540ⓒ**
**Telephone: 707-725-4426 Fax: 707-725-5738**
**Member of Firm: Gerald R. Harland.**
**General Trial and Appellate Practice. Family, Probate, Estate Planning, Timber and Logging, Corporation, Personal Injury, Administrative, Construction, Labor, Education, Business and Real Property Law.**
**References: The Bank of America (Fortuna Branch); U.S. Bank, Eureka, California.**
**Eureka, California Office: 622 H Street. Telephone: 707-444-9281. Fax: 707-445-2961.**
***See Professional Biographies, FORTUNA, CALIFORNIA***

Kruse, Harold C. ............................ '10 '34 C&L.879 A.B., LL.B. 3418 Church St.
Little, Theodore J. ..........................'— '42 C.597 B.S. L.813 J.D. P.O. Box 381‡
Mahan, Collis P. ............................. '15 '43 C.330 A.B. L.1065 J.D. 836 15th St.‡
Stone, Sam L., (BV) ......................... '38 '66 C&L.767 B.S., LL.B. 1330 Main St.
Zigler, Robert A., (CV) .................... '51 '77 C.446 B.A. L.629 J.D. 662 Main St.

## FOSTER CITY, 28,176, *San Mateo Co.*

Akers, Charles O. ............................ '46 '75 C.976 B.S. L.1065 J.D. P.O. Box 4219‡
Barnett, James J. ........................ '58 '84 C&L.813 B.A., J.D. Story Book Heirlooms
Bellesorte, Kathleen M. ......................... '49 '89 L.765 J.D. 555 Pilgrim Dr.
Biernat, James D., (BV) ........ '48 '77 C.770 B.A. L.1065 J.D. Chf. Atty., Safeco Ins. Co.
**Bortner, Scott R.** .... '60 '93 C.188 A.B. L.770 J.D. Coun., PE Applied Biosystems (Pat.)
Creighton, Geoffrey M. '55 '84 C.813 B.A. L.477 J.D.
SOFTBANK Expositions and Conference Co., L.P.
Cunningham, Barbara Lewis ............. '40 '80 C.768 B.A. L.284 J.D. 825 Grenada Ln.
Davis, Peter E. ..................... '45 '70 C.169 B.A. L.1065 J.D. Metropolitan Life Ins.
De Vries, Paul L., (BV) ................ '27 '59 C.723 L.284 J.D. 770 Santa Maria Lane
Fulton, Dennis C. ..................... '37 '70 C.393 B.A. L.284 J.D. 1000 Flying Fish St.‡
Glithero, John C., Jr. ............ '23 '58 C.763 A.B. L.1065 J.D. 635 MainersIsland Blvd.
Greenberg, Arthur '15 '60 C&L.986 B.A., LL.B.
(adm. in MO; not adm. in CA) 120 Trimaran Ct.‡
Gruenberg, Max F. ........................ '15 '41 C.309 M.B.A. L.813 J.D. 1014 Gull Ave.
Harris, Michael T. ................... '39 '67 C.882 B.A. L.284 LL.B. 255 Port Royal Ave.
Hensley, Max D. ....................... '46 '74 C.966 B.S. L.273 J.D. 358 Lakeside Dr. (Pat.)
Hildebrand, James A., (BV) .............. '30 '54 C&L.477 A.B., J.D. 1188 Essex Lane‡
Howard, Lytle, Petersen and Mah .................... 1065 E. Hillsdale Blvd. (ⓒDaly City)
Hudson, Nanette S. .................. '51 '76 C.112 B.A. L.767 J.D. 393 Vintage Park Dr.
Jarchow, Stephen P. '51 '76 C&L.966 B.B.A., J.D.
(adm. in WI; not adm. in CA) Lincoln Property Co.
Kirby, Kathleen M., (BV) ................ '48 '82 C.999 L.765 J.D. 393 Vintage Park Dr.
Kratter, Leslie M. ........................ '45 '72 C&L.813 B.A., J.D. 950 Tower Lane
Lee, William P. ........................ '51 '79 C.112 B.A. L.1065 J.D. 858 Peary Lane
Meyer, Jeannie J. ......................... '43 '68 C&L.494 B.A., J.D. 1441 Halibut St.
Miloglav, Gary D. ........................ '46 '79 C.112 A.B. L.1197 J.D. 331 Cutter St.
Morgan, C. Dennis ..................... '43 '73 C.1163 B.A. L.284 J.D. 519 Saint Vincent Ln.
Moyce, David M. .... '58 '87 C.112 B.A. L.1066 J.D. Gen. Coun., Lyon's Restaurants, Inc.
Nemer, Elaine F. ......................... '23 '54 C.112 A.B. L.767 LL.B. 911 Lido Ln.
Perkowitz, William T. ................... '54 '82 C.801 B.A. L.424 J.D. 803 Comet Dr.
Perry, Mark L. '55 '80 C.112 A.B. L.1067 J.D.
V.P. & Gen. Coun., Gilead Sciences, Inc.
Petersen, William J. ................ '58 '83 C.367 B.A. L.767 J.D. [Howard,L.P.&M.]
Pollock, Edward M. .................. '50 '81 C.112 B.A. L.1065 J.D. 101 Lincoln Ctr. Dr.
**Pond, Stanley E., (BV) '51 '77 C.112 B.A. L.1065 J.D.**
**563 Pilgrim Drive, Suite D, 94404**
**Telephone: 415-341-0400 Facsimile: 415-578-9278**
***PRACTICE AREAS: Insurance Defense; Products Liability; Drug Liability; Collections; Personal Injury.**
**General Civil Trial and Appellate Practice. Business, Collections, Real Estate, Insurance, Toxic Tort Defense, Products Liability, Drug Liability, Personal Injury.**
***See Professional Biographies, FOSTER CITY, CALIFORNIA***

Potasz, Frank J. ....................... '31 '59 C.767 B.S. L.1065 J.D. 1330 Schooner St.
Robin, Alan J. ........................ '49 '75 C.821 B.A. L.569 J.D. 101 Lincoln Ctr. Dr.
Sammet, James L. ..................... '34 '60 C&L.813 B.S., LL.B. 730 Nina Lane‡
Schlaepfer, Joan F. '32 '81 C.945 B.S. L.659 J.D.
(adm. in PA; not adm. in CA) 1463 Marlin Ave.‡
Seiger, Joseph R. ..................... '42 '68 C.665 A.B. L.477 J.D. Vintage Properties
Smith, Bryant M. ..................... '34 '59 C&L.813 A.B., LL.B. 605 Gloucester Ln.
**Smith, Joseph H.** '44 '84 C.37 B.S. L.770 J.D.
Div. V.P., Intell. Prop., PE Applied Biosystems (Pat.)
Squeri, Doris Ann ..................... '58 '85 C.112 B.A. L.770 J.D. 393 Vintage Dr.
**Thibault, Harry G.** '39 '74 C.474 B.S. L.1000 J.D.
(adm. in IL; not adm. in CA; Pat.) Sr. Atty., PE Applied Biosystems
Townsley, Aleck ................... '33 '77 C.766 B.A. L.1231 J.D. 1829 Beach Park Blvd.
Utterback, William F. ................. '43 '77 C&L.608 B.A., J.D. 710 Bounty Dr.
Zimmerer, Joseph J. '51 '78 C.190 B.A. L.276 J.D.
Assoc. Coun., Metropolitan Life Ins.

## FOUNTAIN VALLEY, 53,691, *Orange Co.*

Andrews, Thomas E., (BV) ......... '40 '67 C.1042 B.S. L.1068 LL.B. 10055 Slater Ave.
Anthony, Patricia L., (AV) .................. '39 '78 C&L.1137 B.S.L., J.D. [P.L.Anthony]
Anthony, Patricia L., A Prof. Law Corp., (AV) ......................... 18627 Brookhurst St.
Bame, Jerome M., (AV) ............... '34 '61 C&L.608 B.S., J.D. 10055 Slater Ave., Ste. 250
Blair, Paul R. ..................... '39 '79 C.770 B.A. L.1137 J.D. 17679 San Simeon
**Bloomenstein, Adam H.** '61 '86
C.793 B.A. L.273 J.D. Sr. Coun., Hyundai Motor America
Brady, Marcia P. ..................... '64 '89 C.69 B.A. L.990 J.D. 18556 Santa Tomara
Brown, Richard Scott '46 '72
C.150 B.B.A. L.228 J.D. Assoc. V.P. & Corp. Coun., FHP Intl. Corp.
Burton, Richard H. ..................... '18 '57 C.768 B.A. L.981 LL.B. Safeco Ins. Co.
Bush, K. Dale, (AV) .................... '33 '59 C.132 B.A. L.800 J.D. [Bush,B.&L.]
Bush, Michael P. ..................... '63 '92 C.800 B.S. L.464 J.D. 10061 Talbert Ave.
Bush, Phillip L., (BV) ................... '36 '62 C.132 B.A. L.352 J.D. [Bush,B.&L.]
Bush, Bush & Larsen, (AV) ........................................ 10061 Talbert Ave.
Carter, Kenneth B. ............... '50 '81 C&L.101 B.S., J.D. Corp. Coun., FHP Intl. Corp.
Croteau, Francis L. ................. '34 '75 C.667 B.M.E. L.1137 J.D. 10055 Slater Ave.
**Eisen, Ruth I.** .......... '60 '85 C.145 B.A. L.188 J.D. Mng. Coun., Hyundai Motor America
**Flannery, W. Gerald, Jr.** '57 '82 C.21 B.A. L.884 J.D.
Asst. Gen. Coun. & Dir., Prod. Liab., Hyundai Motor America
Foll, Ronald E. '58 '85 C.636 B.A. L.1065 J.D.
Chf. Legal Offr., Ins. Div., FHP Intl. Corp.
Franklin, Nick, (BV) '43 '69 C.556 B.A. L.273 J.D.
(adm. in NM; not adm. in CA) Sr. V.P., Pub. Affs., FHP, Inc.
Fritch, Roger A. ..................... '36 '75 C.98 B.F.A. L.1137 J.D. 10221 Slater Ave.
**Fuerbringer, Elizabeth M.** '63 '94
C.1253 B.A. L.809 J.D. Coun., Hyundai Motor America
Goeree, Joyce E. ................. '63 '88 C.112 B.A. L.426 J.D. 8810 Hummingbird Ave.
Hammatt, Meryle G. ................. '— '85 C.1042 B.A. L.1137 J.D. 17550 Brookhurst St.
Hoskins, Lorine A., (BV) ............... '34 '76 C.800 B.A. L.1137 J.D. 10055 Slater Ave.
Iba, Lynn E. .................. '57 '83 C.1042 B.S. L.800 J.D. Corp. Coun., FHP Intl. Corp.
**Ide, Clark F.**, (BV) '36 '62 C.112 A.B. L.1066 LL.B.
Gen. Coun., Orange Co. Water Dist.
June, Roy E. ....................... '22 '52 C&L.508 B.A., LL.B. 18176 Muirwood Ct.‡
Kelly, James J. ...................... '44 '73 C.549 L.464 J.D. 18127 Brookhurst St.
Knego, Thomas C. ............. '59 '86 C.1109 B.S. L.61 J.D. Corp. Coun., FHP Intl. Corp.
**Krahelski, Michael A.** '56 '81 C.112 A.B. L.1068 J.D.
V.P. & Gen. Coun., Hyundai Motor Finance Co.
Lam, L. Andre ...................... '54 '90 C.612 B.S. L.862 J.D. 10221 Slater Ave.
Larsen, Lloyd M., (BV) ................. '35 '63 C&L.1035 B.S.L., LL.B. [Bush,B.&L.]
Lindsay, Edward L. ............ '34 '76 C.37 B.S.B.A. L.426 J.D. 8715 Rogue River Ave.
Monson, Kevin E., (AV) ................... '54 '79 C&L.101 B.S., J.D. P.O. Box 8644
Mordkin, Arnold P., (BV) .................. '37 '63 C&L.800 A.B., J.D. 17050 Bushard St.
Namanny, Patrick Norman ............ '53 '80 C.147 B.A. L.1137 J.D. 18520 Morongo St.
Nix, Peter V., Inc., (BV) ............ '40 '73 C.679 B.S.E.E. L.990 J.D. 16480 Harbor Blvd.
Nolde, Virgil G., Jr. ................ '55 '83 C.1075 B.A. L.1148 J.D. 17550 Brookhurst St.
**O'Neill, Finbarr J.** '52 '77
C.178 A.B. L.262 J.D. V.P. & Gen. Coun., Hyundai Motor America
Parry, Richard O., (AV) ................ '50 '77 C.208 B.A. L.426 J.D. 10550 Talbert Ave.
Peek, Lon E. ........................ '43 '90 C.1155 B.S. L.1137 J.D. 18837 Brookhurst St.
Phillips, Russell D., Jr. ........ '62 '88 C.801 B.A. L.910 J.D. Corp. Coun., FHP Intl. Corp.
Reed, Marjorie E. ............................................. '— '72 10055 Slater Ave.
Robinson, Ira L. ............ '38 '67 C.892 B.A. L.893 J.D. Corp. Coun., FHP Intl. Corp.
Rohfeld, Michael D. ............. '56 '83 C.1131 B.A. L.1137 J.D. 17550 Brookhurst St.
Rosen, Glenn M. .................. '51 '77 C.112 B.A. L.809 J.D. 17550 Brookhurst St.
Rosenfield, Paul W. ............. '52 '80 C.1109 B.A. L.1240 J.D. 17550 Brookhurst St.
Rutyna, Edward J. ................. '60 '86 C.93 B.A. L.273 J.D. 10061 Talbert Ave.
Saavedra, Richard .................. '41 '72 C.1097 B.S. L.809 J.D. 10055 Slater Ave.
Sjaarda, Donald S., (BV) ............. '51 '79 C.627 B.S. L.990 J.D. [D.S.Sjaarda]
Sjaarda, Donald S., A Prof. Corp., (BV) ................................ 18837 Brookhurst St.
Smith, Jerry J. ................ '36 '73 C.513 B.S. L.1137 9043 Carson River Dr.
Smith, Michael F. ............ '56 '83 C.1109 J.D. L.1137 J.D. 17150 New Hope St.
Stone, Alfred E. ..................... '23 '66 C.800 B.S. L.809 LL.B. Safeco Ins. Co.
Sundvold, Stephen J. ............ '47 '72 C.1109 B.A. L.1049 J.D. 17550 Brookhurst St.
Trela, Brian P. .................. '58 '86 C.112 B.A. L.1137 J.D. 16480 Harbor Blvd.
**Vanderford, Thomas N., Jr.** '60 '85
C.112 B.A. L.426 J.D. Sr. Coun., Hyundai Motor America
Weinstock, Michael J. '40 '67 C.659 B.A. L.276 LL.B.
Sr. V.P., Gen. Coun. & Secy., FHP Intl. Corp.
Wianecki, Richard James ............ '54 '80 C.112 A.B. L.426 J.D. 17550 Brookhurst St.
Wyckoff, Richard D. '49 '83 C.550 B.S. L.1068 J.D.
Assoc. Corp. Coun., FHP Intl. Corp.
Yoshinaga, Diane J. .............. '64 '90 C.1042 B.A. L.1137 J.D. 16480 Harbor Blvd.
Yule, Roger T. ................ '31 '82 C.679 B.S.M.E. L.1137 J.D. 17550 Brookhurst St.
Zukerman, Roy C., (BV) ................ '32 '65 C.999 L.809 J.D. P.O. Box 8305

## FOWLER, 3,208, *Fresno Co.*

Renge, Howard, (BV) ................. '19 '53 C.112 A.B. L.262 LL.B. 211 E. Merced St.
Uchiyama, Mikio, (BV) ............... '22 '45 C.112 B.A. L.846 LL.B. 313 E. Merced St.

## FRAZIER PARK, 1,167, *Kern Co.*

Olsen, Shirley H. ............................ '27 '51 C&L.800 B.A., LL.B. P.O. Box 6537
Pearce, Sam F. ............................. '23 '56 C&L.911 B.A., J.D. Pine Mt. Club
Shartsis, Loretta Sue '43 '83
C.112 B.A. L.1148 J.D. 16229 Pine Valley Ln., Ste.1, Pine Mountain
Wallace, Vicky ...................... '37 '66 C&L.347 B.S., J.D. 3200 Mt. Pinos Way

## FREMONT, 173,339, *Alameda Co.*

Adams, Paul F. ........... '54 '82 C.870 B.S.E. L.1065 J.D. Pres., Millennium Automation
Aiello, Paula ............ '54 '86 C.112 B.A. L.1065 J.D. 39120 Argonaut Way, No. 276
Albert, Eugene W., (AVⓣ) '58 '83 C.846 B.A. L.802 J.D.
(adm. in TX; not adm. in CA) Spectra Labs., Inc.
Alexander, Sue, (CV) ............... '51 '83 C.768 B.A. L.284 J.D. 39650 Liberty St.
Alpers, Steven J., (BV) .................. '52 '77 C.112 B.A. L.770 J.D. [S.J.Alpers]
Alpers, Steven J., A Professional Corporation, (BV) ........................ 39210 State St.
Argue, Sharon ..................... '63 '90 C.112 B.A. L.770 J.D. 47460 Fremont Blvd.
Arguello, Larry K., (BV) ........... '50 '79 C.768 B.A. L.767 J.D. 39055 Hastings St.
Avera, Fred E., (AV) ....................... '18 '56 C.999 L.981 LL.B. 41752 Chiltern‡
Bagley, Philip H. ..................... '08 '37 C&L.813 A.B., LL.B. 4938 Eggers Dr.‡
Batchelder, Gerald F., (BV) ............ '51 '76 C.1073 B.A. L.770 J.D. [G.F.Batchelder]
Batchelder, Gerald F., A Prof. Corp., (BV) .......................... 39510 Paseo Padre Pkwy.
Beaman, Judith L. ................ '49 '82 C.766 B.A. L.284 J.D. 34325 Windsong Terr.
Bell, Barbara J. ..................... '67 '93 C.112 A.B. L.770 J.D. [Bell,S.&F.]
Bell, Bruce M., (BV) .................. '32 '61 C.112 A.B. L.1065 J.D. [Bell,S.&F.]
Bell, Taylor M. ..................... '62 '88 C.112 B.A. L.1066 J.D. [Bell,S.&F.]
Bell, Sheppard & Faria, A Professional Corporation, (AV) ........ 43213 Mission Boulevard
Bennett, Gary R., (BV) ................. '39 '77 C.768 B.A. L.1137 J.D. [G.R.Bennett]
Bennett, Gary R., A Prof. Corp., (BV) ..................................... 39210 State St.
**Benya, Robert D.**, (BV) ....... '31 '61 C.823 B.S. L.1065 LL.B. [Quaresma,B.H.C.O.&N.]
*PRACTICE AREAS: Personal Injury Law; Products Liability Law; Insurance Law.
Blawie, James L. ..................... '28 '56 C.184 B.A. L.145 J.D. P.O. Box 1102
Bradley, Burke W., Jr., (AV) .... '43 '70 C.768 B.A. L.767 J.D. 39465 Paseo Padre Pkwy.
Brosnan, Pegeen .................. '53 '78 C.966 B.A. L.436 J.D. 45185 Onondaga Dr.
Butterfield, Mark W., (BV) ...... '56 '82 C.1254 B.S. L.770 J.D. 39510 Paseo Padre Pkwy.
Camacho, Robert P., (BV) ... '49 '78 C.1073 B.A. L.1067 J.D. 39120 Argonaut Way, #444
Canaday, Gerald, (BV) .............. '30 '65 C.112 A.B. L.765 LL.B. 40481 Andora Ct.
**Carey, Susan M.** '54 '84 C.112 B.S. L.1065 J.D.
Sr. Coun., New United Motor Manufacturing, Inc.
*RESPONSIBILITIES: Business Law; Trade Law; Corporate Law.
Carpenter, Bruce W., (BV) .............. '39 '73 C.1073 B.A. L.770 J.D. 39210 State St.
Chien-Hale, Elizabeth '61 '94 C.112 B.S. L.312 J.D.
(adm. in HI; not adm. in CA) 105 Durillo Ct.
Chudgar, Praful S. ................... '40 '92 C&L.061 M.A., LL.B. 38800 Hastings St.
Cohen, Mark P., (BV) .......... '55 '82 C.102 B.A. L.284 J.D. 39510 Paseo Padre Pkway.
Collins, Kirk L., (BV) ............... '55 '80 C.112 B.A. L.284 J.D. 3100 Mowry Ave.

CALIFORNIA—FREMONT MARTINDALE-HUBBELL LAW DIRECTORY 1997

**Connich, Michael J.**, (BV) ..... '40 '66 C.767 B.A. L.1065 J.D. [Quaresma,B.H.C.O.&N.]
*PRACTICE AREAS: Probate Law; Family Law; Personal Injury Law; Estate Planning.
Creighton, Patricia A. '54 '90 C.1044 B.A. L.284 J.D.
Corp. Coun., CCS Planning and Engineering, Inc.
Dietrich, Gregory R. .................... '58 '90 C&L.546 B.S., J.D. [Ⓐ Lanferman,F.&H.]
Dietrich, Sheri Passer ................ '64 '90 C.966 B.A. L.546 J.D. 47460 Fremont Blvd.
Dimino, Robert A., (BV) ...... '43 '75 C.563 B.E.E. L.765 J.D. 39510 Paseo Padre Pkwy.
Drahos, Leslie Acerra ........................ '55 '83 C.823 B.S. L.472 J.D. 2483 Euclid Pl.‡
Drollman, Donald W., (BV) ...... '29 '60 C.173 B.A. L.950 J.D. Ste. 209, 39210 State St.
Durham, Patricia A. ...... '44 '74 C.604 B.A. L.1066 J.D. V.P. & Gen. Coun., Qantel Corp.
Edwards, Bob L. ........................ '26 '54 C.112 A.B. L.767 J.D. 40207 Blanchard St.
Eike, Douglas D. ................ '51 '82 C.1073 B.A. L.770 J.D. 39055 Hastings St. Ste. 203
Faria, Joseph R., Jr., (BV) .......................... '49 '74 C&L.770 B.A., J.D. [Bell,S.&F.]
Feder, Daniel L. .................... '62 '87 C.659 B.A. L.1068 J.D. [Ⓐ Lanferman,F.&H.]
Fisher, James I., (BV) ..................... '51 '80 C.423 B.A. L.767 J.D. [Lanferman,F.&H.]
**Fox, Craig S.**, (BV) ..................... '55 '80 C.112 A.B. L.1065 J.D. [King,S.M.&F.]
*PRACTICE AREAS: Commercial, Construction and Real Estate Litigation.
Frost, Raymond E., (BV) ....... '50 '78 C.768 B.A. L.1095 J.D. 39510 Paseo Padre Pkwy.
Fudenna, Keith H. .............................. '49 '74 C.112 B.S. L.1065 J.D. Mun. Ct. Comr.
**Gonsalves, Linda M.**, (BV) ............. '55 '82 C.768 B.A. L.770 J.D. [Gonsalves&K.]
*PRACTICE AREAS: Commercial Law; Real Estate Law; Taxation Law; Estate Planning Law; Probate Law.

**Gonsalves & Kozachenko, (AV)**
**47460 Fremont Boulevard, 94538**
**Telephone: 510-770-3900 Fax: 510-657-9876**
**Linda M. Gonsalves; Paul Kozachenko. Associates: Jan O'Neal; Stephen F. Heller; Daniel Preddy. Of Counsel: Alan L. Reeves; Mary E. Jansing (Former Partner, Logan & Jansing, San Jose, California).**
**General Commercial and Civil Litigation, Real Estate, Land Use and Construction, Corporate, Partnership, Securities, Environmental Compliance and Remediation, Bankruptcy and Creditor's Rights, Intellectual Property and Trade Secrets, Employment Law, Taxation, Estate Planning and Probate Law, Family Law.**
***See Professional Biographies, FREMONT, CALIFORNIA***

Gonzales, James E. ........................ '46 '74 C.1077 B.A. L.1068 J.D. Dep. City Atty.
Gordon, Dan W., (BV) ....................... '55 '81 C.1073 B.A. L.770 J.D. [Bell,S.&F.]
Graaskamp, George W., (BV) ... '30 '60 C.112 B.S. L.1066 J.D. 39510 Paseo Padre Pkwy.
Grimmer, Dan C., (AV) ............. '47 '73 C.112 B.A. L.1065 J.D. 39055 Hastings St.
**Hall, H. Robert**, (AV) ............. '34 '65 C.267 A.B. L.813 J.D. [Quaresma,B.H.C.O.&N.]
*PRACTICE AREAS: Family Law; Business Law.
Harris, Franklin ......................... '20 '67 C.740 B.S. L.284 LL.B. 37177 Fremont Blvd.
Hashimoto, Gail M., (BV) ............ '57 '85 C.813 A.B. L.1065 J.D. [Lanferman,F.&H.]
Hasson, Robert Bruce ................ '46 '90 C.1073 B.A. L.1153 J.D. 39650 Liberty St.
Haun, Marvin G., (AV) ........................ '28 '59 C.169 A.B. L.1065 J.D. Mun. Ct. J.
Heer, Naranjan S. "Jack", (BV) ......... '31 '62 C.112 B.S. L.1066 J.D. 4242 Garland Dr.‡
**Heller, Stephen F.** ......................... '48 '83 C&L.813 A.B., J.D. [Ⓐ Gonsalves&K.]
*PRACTICE AREAS: Business Law; Business Litigation.
Hewitt, C. Lee, (CV) ............ '52 '82 C.768 B.A. L.765 J.D. 39510 Pasco Padre Pkwy.
Hirsch, Mark L., (BV) ...................................... '54 '84 1544 Washington Blvd.

**Hollabaugh, James M., (BV) '43 '75 C.197 A.B. L.284 J.D.**
**General Motors Building, Suite 2410, 39465 Paseo Padre Parkway, 94538**
**Telephone: 510-651-6100**
**Criminal, Trial and Appellate, Commercial Traffic and Personal Injury Law.**
***See Professional Biographies, FREMONT, CALIFORNIA***

Hyman, Morris ................................... '21 '53 C&L.813 LL.B. Bank of Fremont
Jacobs, Shirley D., (BV) .......................................... '43 '78 3100 Moway Ave.
**Jansing, Mary E.**, (BV) ..................... '42 '82 C.768 B.A. L.770 J.D. [Ⓐ Gonsalves&K.]
*REPORTED CASES: In Re Airbeds, Inc., 92 B.R., 419, 9th Cir. BAP, 1988; Pring vs. Commissioner of Internal Revenue, 57 T.C.M. 958, 1989, CCH; Westfall vs. Commissioner of Internal Revenue, 56 T.C.M. 66, 1988, CCH; Borders vs. Commissioner of Internal Revenue, 52 T.C.M. 617, 1986, CCH.
*PRACTICE AREAS: Bankruptcy; Taxes in Bankruptcy.
Jay, Joseph W., Jr. ............................ '28 '55 L.1026 LL.B. Mun. Ct. J.
Jenzen, Thomas M. .................... '48 '79 C.477 B.S.E.E. L.464 J.D. 483 Merlot Dr.
Kanninen, Michael L. .................. '39 '72 C.145 A.B. L.1065 J.D. Mun. Ct. Comm.
Keller, Richard O. ....................................... '42 '67 C.1365 A.B. L.245 J.D. Mun. Ct. J.
Kendrick, Carolyn, (BV) ............. '43 '67 C.605 B.A. L.1065 J.D. 41333 Roberts Ave.
Kensinger, Loren L. ............. '42 '87 C.1042 B.A. L.284 J.D. 39510 Paseo Padre Pkwy.
**King, Bernard M.**, (AV) .................... '28 '53 C.112 B.S. L.1066 J.D. [King,S.M.&F.]
*PRACTICE AREAS: Real Estate Law; Estate Planning Law; Corporate Law.

**King, Snell, Mildwurm & Fox, A Professional Corporation, (AV)**
**39650 Liberty Street, Suite 420, 94538**
**Telephone: 510-770-5770 Fax: 510-651-8043**
**LeRoy A. Broun (1905-1981); Allen G. Norris (1901-1978); Bernard M. King; James C. Snell; Alan W. Mildwurm; Craig S. Fox.**
**General Civil and Trial Practice. Real Estate, Construction, Landslide and Subsidence, Estate Planning, Probate, Corporate, Criminal and Family Law. Personal Injury and Business Litigation. Arbitration and Mediation Law.**
**Representative Clients: Alandale Construction Co.; Niles Electric Co.; Fremont Paving Co., Inc.; Central Chevrolet Co.**
**Reference: Comerica Bank.**
***See Professional Biographies, FREMONT, CALIFORNIA***

Kitta, John N., (CV) .......................... '51 '76 C&L.770 B.S.C., J.D. 39500 Stevenson Pl.
Knowlton, Richard K. ............... '20 '52 C.293 A.B. L.813 LL.B. 40471 Andorra Ct.‡
**Kozachenko, Paul**, (AV) ..................... '58 '82 C.813 B.A. L.770 J.D. [Gonsalves&K.]
*LANGUAGES: Russian.
*PRACTICE AREAS: Real Estate Law; Business Law; Litigation.
Lanferman, David P., (BV) ........... '51 '76 C.112 B.A. L.1065 J.D. [Lanferman,F.&H.]
Lanferman, Fisher & Hashimoto, (BV) ................................ 3100 Mowry, Ste., 300
LaPedis, Michyle A. ............... '62 '87 C.112 B.A. L.1065 J.D. [Ⓐ Lanferman,F.&H.]
Lenhart, Sarah J. '48 '78 C.203 B.A. L.851 J.D.
(adm. in OH; not adm. in CA) 472 Posada Way‡
Levine, Harvey E., (AV) ................. '46 '74 C.112 B.A. L.1065 J.D. City Atty. Off.
Lopus, Lyle L., (BV) .................. '43 '70 C&L.477 B.A., J.D. 39700 Civic Center Dr.
Lutz, Paulette B. Garcia ..................... '57 '83 C.112 B.S. L.464 J.D. Dep. City Atty.
McClanahan, Max L. '50 '79 C.375 B.A. L.878 J.D.
(adm. in MO; not adm. in CA) 38648 Kimbro St.‡
McElwain, Lester S. ........................ '10 '34 C&L.813 B.A., J.D. 4557 Mayfield Ct.‡
McKay, Richard D., (BV) ..................... '33 '78 C.112 B.A. L.1065 J.D. [Willett&M.] ‡
**McKenzie, K. Kelly** '58 '88 C.101 B.A. L.1065 J.D.
Sr. Coun., New United Motor Manufacturing, Inc.
*LANGUAGES: Japanese.
*RESPONSIBILITIES: Products Liability; Premises Liability; Commercial Litigation.
McMorrow, John B., (A P.C.), (BV) ........ '49 '76 C&L.770 B.A., J.D. [McMorrow&S.]
McMorrow & Scholz, (BV) ..................................... Suite 250, 39650 Liberty Street

**Mezzetti, Leon J., Jr., (BV) '51 '76 C.112 A.B. L.770 J.D.**
**Commercial Bank of Fremont Building, 39510 Paseo Padre Parkway, Suite 190, 94538**
**Telephone: 510-791-1836 Fax: 510-796-1624**

(This Listing Continued)

CAA92P

**Mezzetti, Leon J., Jr. (Continued)**
***LANGUAGES: Spanish, Italian and German.**
**Trucking Violations, Criminal Law, Family Law, Evictions, General Civil Practice.**
***See Professional Biographies, FREMONT, CALIFORNIA***

**Mildwurm, Alan W.**, (BV) ................. '52 '78 C&L.767 B.A., J.D. [King,S.M.&F.]
*PRACTICE AREAS: Family Law; General Civil Law; Criminal Law.
Miller, Kathleen A. '57 '83 C.767 B.A. L.284 J.D.
Gen. Coun., Asst. V.P. & Asst. Secy., The Men's Wearhouse, Inc.
Morris, Floyd ........................ '54 '89 C.112 B.A. L.770 J.D. 39055 Hasting St., Ste. 203
Murray, James J. ..................... '45 '75 C.768 B.S. L.770 J.D. 39827 San Moreno Ct.
Naylor, Brian T. .............. '49 '75 C.262 A.B. L.178 J.D. V.P. & Gen. Coun., Qantel Corp.
**Nixon, Thomas J.**, (BV) ........ '59 '84 C.768 B.S. L.770 J.D. [Quaresma,B.H.C.O.&N.]
*PRACTICE AREAS: Corporate Law; Criminal Law; Family Law.
**O'Hara, David M.**, (AV) ... '40 '70 C.98 B.S.C.E. L.1065 J.D. [Quaresma,B.H.C.O.&N.]
*REPORTED CASES: New Haven v. Taco Bell 24 Cal.App.4th 1973.
*PRACTICE AREAS: Public Agency Law; Eminent Domain; Real Estate Law.
**O'Neal, Jan** ....................................... '54 '87 C.112 A.B. L.770 J.D. [Ⓐ Gonsalves&K.]
*PRACTICE AREAS: Business Law; Real Estate Law; Trademark.
Orlick, Jonathan B. '57 '84 C.1111 B.S.E.S. L.1206 J.D.
(adm. in FL; not adm. in CA; Pat.) 39650 Liberty St., 3rd Fl.
Owyang, Albert D. ................... '48 '76 C.766 B.A. L.1067 J.D. 4708 Amiens Ave.
Pacheco, Kathleen A. ....... '63 '92 C.768 B.A. L.770 J.D. Corp. Coun., H&H Bail Bonds
Petersen, Nancy ........................ '57 '89 C.790 B.A. L.284 J.D. 39199 Paseo Padre Pkwy.
**Pineda, Patricia Salas** '51 '77 C.483 B.A. L.1066 J.D.
V.P. Legal Envir. & Govt. Affs. & Corp. Secy., New United Motor Manufacturing, Inc.
*LANGUAGES: Spanish.
*RESPONSIBILITIES: Environmental Law; Corporate Law; Business Law; Tax Law.
Platt, George A. '43 '79 C.33 B.A. L.1066 J.D.
(adm. in OR; not adm. in CA) 1150 Durillo Ct.
**Potts, James Watson, III** '62 '93 C.1060 B.A. L.284 J.D.
Coun., New United Motor Manufacturing, Inc.
*RESPONSIBILITIES: Labor and Employment Law.
**Preddy, Daniel** ............................ '60 '92 C.766 B.A. L.284 J.D. [Ⓐ Gonsalves&K.]
*PRACTICE AREAS: Family Law; Bankruptcy; Probate/Estate Planning.

**Quaresma, Benya, Hall, Connich, O'Hara and Nixon, (AV)**
**Suite 140, 2201 Walnut Avenue, 94538**
**Telephone: 510-793-6400 Fax: 510-793-2086**
**Members of Firm: E. A. Quaresma (1907-1985); Robert D. Ellis (1932-1987); Robert D. Benya; H. Robert Hall (Certified Specialist, Family Law, The State Bar of California Board of Legal Specialization); Michael J. Connich (Certified Specialist, Family Law, The State Bar of California Board of Legal Specialization); David M. O'Hara; Thomas J. Nixon.**
**General Civil Trial Practice in all Courts. Corporation, Real Estate, Eminent Domain, Public Agency, Criminal, Probate, Personal Injury and Family Law.**
**Representative Clients: Kraftile Co.; Union Sanitary District; Future Construction Co.; New Haven United School District School Building Corp.; Livermore Valley Joint Unified School District Educational Facilities Corp.; Weibel, Inc.**
***See Professional Biographies, FREMONT, CALIFORNIA***

Rahmes, Todd W. .......... '56 '89 C&L.477 B.A., J.D. Assoc. Coun., Cirrus Logic, Inc.
Reade, Lynne, (Ms.), (BV) ............. '27 '75 C.1097 B.A. L.426 J.D. 3610 Dunbar Ct.‡
**Reeves, Alan L.** ................................ '43 '81 C.061 B.A. L.813 J.D. [Ⓐ Gonsalves&K.]
*PRACTICE AREAS: Litigation.

**Rifkind & Fuerch, A Professional Corporation**
**(See Hayward)**

Roesler, Oscar R. ............................... '56 '86 C.112 B.A. L.770 J.D. 152 Anza St.
Rogers, S. Taggart ........................ '43 '79 C.813 B.S. L.1153 J.D. 653 Festivo Ct.
Sanders, A. Lee ................. '40 '67 C.1042 B.A. L.1066 LL.B. 43363 Banda Terrace
Satterford, Robert B. ............... '46 '75 C.112 A.B. L.1065 J.D. 45500 Fremont Blvd.
Scholz, Fred J. .......................... '56 '87 C.112 B.A. L.1153 J.D. [McMorrow&S.]
Schwab, Joseph E. ............................... '30 '67 C.112 L.766 4057 Murray Common
Schynert, Mark A. ................... '52 '78 C.112 A.B. L.1067 J.D. 35912 Vivian Pl.
Severson, Lawrence L. ........ '46 '71 C.101 B.A. L.1065 J.D. 39111 Paseo Pkwy., #316
Sheppard, Harry R., (AV) .................... '36 '66 C.165 B.A. L.1065 J.D. [Bell,S.&F.]
**Sherrod, J. Thomas**, (AV) ................. '38 '64 C.112 B.A. L.1066 LL.B. [J.T.Sherrod]

**Sherrod, J. Thomas, A Professional Corporation, (AV)**
**39199 Paseo Padre Parkway, 94538**
**Telephone: 510-796-4444 FAX: 510-791-1639**
**J. Thomas Sherrod.**
**Criminal and Administrative Law, with emphasis on Drug and Alcohol Driving Offenses. Civil Trial Matters.**
***See Professional Biographies, FREMONT, CALIFORNIA***

**Skjerven, Morrill, MacPherson, Franklin & Friel LLP**
**(See San Jose)**

Smith, Cary S. ........................ '56 '82 C.620 B.A. L.846 J.D. 38883 Riverbank Terr.
Smith, Gregory Scott .................. '62 '92 C.112 B.S. L.767 J.D. [Ⓐ Lanferman,F.&H.]
**Snell, James C.**, (BV) .................... '37 '66 C.112 B.S. L.1066 LL.B. [King,S.M.&F.]
*PRACTICE AREAS: Commercial Litigation; Construction Law.
Snow, Charles B., (BV) ...................... '24 '52 C.112 L.1065 J.D. 39210 State St.
Snow, Raymond M., (BV) ................ '42 '70 C.502 Ch.E. L.767 J.D. 39210 State St.
Sperske, Joseph A. ................................ '44 '74 C.1097 B.S. L.284 J.D. [J.A.Sperske]
Sperske, Joseph A., P.C. ......................................................... P.O. Box 7565
Sprague, Allen E., (AV) ............. '35 '61 C.112 A.B. L.1066 LL.B. 3264 Bruce Dr.‡
Squires, Donald B. ................................ '47 '77 C.112 B.A. L.464 J.D. Mun. Ct. J.
Stenersen, Doris R. ......................... '19 '73 C.999 L.1026 LL.B. 3913 Stenersen La.‡
Thomason, Valarie J. ................. '— '82 C.1073 B.S. L.1065 J.D. 39111 Paseo Padre Pky
Trump, John V., (AV) ........................ '36 '65 C.112 B.A. L.1066 J.D. [Trump&L.]ⓞ
Trump & Lewis, (AV) ...................................... 39300 Civic Center Dr. (ⓞSan Fran.)
Venti, Gail ........................ '38 '87 C.112 M.A. L.1066 J.D. 47000 Warm Springs Blvd.
Von Till, Stephen F., (AV) ..................... '45 '70 C.475 B.A. L.339 J.D. 152 Anza St.
Walton, Paul N. ................... '62 '89 C.94 B.A. L.426 J.D. 39791 Paseo Padre Pkwy.
Westendorf, Harald, (BV) ........ '54 '79 C.768 B.A. L.770 J.D. 39510 Paseo Padre Pkwy.
Willett, Louis J., (BV) .......................... '43 '69 C.767 A.B. L.1065 J.D. [Willett&M.]
Willett & McKay, A Professional Corporation, (BV) ........................ 3100 Mowry Ave.
Yamashiro, Donna S. ................. '60 '87 C.112 B.A. L.1067 J.D. 3247 Alder Ave.

## FRESNO, * 354,202, *Fresno Co.*

**Aaron, Richard M.**, (AV) .............. '54 '79 C.800 B.S. L.1065 J.D. [Dowling,A.&K.]
*PRACTICE AREAS: Business Transactions; Acquisitions and Sales of Businesses; Real Estate Law; Estate Planning Law.
Abrams, F. John ................................. '56 '91 C.912 B.B.A. L.213 J.D. 5260 N. Palm
Abrams, Ivan S. ....................................... '47 '75 C&L.665 B.A., J.D. Asst. U.S. Atty.
Adams, Eugene L., (BV) ....................... '22 '49 C&L.813 A.B., LL.B. 1350 "O" St.
**Agrall, Tracy A.**, (BV) ..................... '56 '81 C.267 B.A. L.990 J.D. [Wild,C.&T.]
*PRACTICE AREAS: Employment and Business Law.
Aguirre, L. Kim ............................... '53 '78 C.668 B.A. L.426 J.D. [Gromis&A.]
Aharonian, Richard A. ............ '67 '93 C.112 B.A. L.426 J.D. 10 River Park Pl. East
**Ahronian, Jeffrey R.** ......................... '— '96 C.267 B.S. L.646 J.D. [Ⓐ Baker,M.&J.]

Alabart, Javier A. ..............'56 '82 C.267 B.A. L.352 J.D. 6067 N. Fresno St., Ste. 101
Albrechtson, Albert S., III, (BVⓉ) ........'58 '83 C.1069 B.S. L.312 J.D. 5100 N. 6th St.
Alderson, David R. ..................... '60 '94 C.267 B.A. L.1189 J.D. 7108 N. Fresno St.
**Aldridge, Melanie J.** ........................'63 '91 C.267 B.A. L.112 J.D. [▣ G.W.Sawyers]
**Alikian, Shawn H.** .....................................'70 '96 C&L.112 B.A., JD [▣ Lang,R.&P.]
**Allen, Meredith E.** ....................'71 '96 C.1182 B.A. L.112 J.D. [▣ Kimble,M.&U.]
Altounian, Gregory L. ...............'56 '88 C.800 B.A. L.1137 J.D. 2019 N. Gateway Blvd.
Anderson, Angela Joan ............'45 '75 C.273 B.A. L.990 J.D. 6686 N. Nottingham Ct.
Anderson, Gregory V. .............................'62 '88 C&L.352 B.S., J.D. Dep. Dist. Atty.
Anderson, William D., (BV) .............'46 '74 C.346 B.S. L.767 J.D. [Eldridge,A.&W.]
Arambula, Juan ..................................'52 '81 C.309 L.1066 J.D. 623 E. Cambridge
**Arax, Brian M.**, (BV) .......... '58 '83 C.112 B.A. L.800 J.D. [McCormick,B.S.W.&C.]
Arkelian, Edward .......................................'30 '80 C.800 L.981 1295 E. Browning Ave.‡
Armo, Lance .........................................'63 '95 C.267 B.S. L.1189 J.D. 327 "N" St.

**Aron, Murray M., (AV) '45 '74 C.102 B.A. L.1065 J.D.**
**1396 West Herndon, Suite 106, 93711**
**Telephone: 209-449-7601**
**Civil Litigation, Insurance Defense, Personal Injury, Products Liability, Insurance Coverage Litigation, Appeals.**
***See Professional Biographies, FRESNO, CALIFORNIA***

Artenian, Lawrence M. ......'53 '82 C.309 B.A. L.767 J.D. Prof., San Joaquin Coll. of Law
**Asperger, Donald P.**, (BV) ..............'55 '80 C.112 A.B. L.1066 J.D. [Musick,P.&G.]
*PRACTICE AREAS: Business Transactions; Corporate Law; Estate Planning; Securities Regulation.
Asperger, Lisa E. .......... '55 '83 C.112 B.S. L.1067 J.D. Sr. Atty., Ct. of App., 5th Dist.
**Asperger, Paul**, (AV) ..............'28 '53 C.112 A.B. L.1066 J.D. [Thomas,S.J.R.&A.] ‡
Aspinwall, Timothy J. .......................................'60 '87 C.878 B.A. L.880 J.D. Co. Pub. Def.
**Auchard, Paul**, (AV) ......................'49 '74 C.267 B.A. L.1065 J.D. [Chinello,A.S.&S.]
*PRACTICE AREAS: Insurance Defense; Professional Malpractice; Insurance Coverage; School Liability; Products Liability.
**Aune, Richard E., (Inc.)**, (BV) ............'50 '77 C.763 B.A. L.464 J.D. [Dietrich,G.&J.]
*PRACTICE AREAS: Employee Benefits Law.
Austin, Gary S. ...............................................'50 '76 C.267 B.A. L.1189 J.D. Supr. Ct. J.
**Avery, Steven D.** ..................'64 '94 C.267 B.S. L.1189 J.D. [▣ Marderosian,S.&O.]
*PRACTICE AREAS: Insurance Defense; Bad Faith; Personal Injury.
Ayres, Lawrence E., (CV) ............'40 '76 C.1060 B.A. L.464 J.D. 1233 W. Shaw Ave.
Azevedo, Darlene Marie ...........'49 '76 C.112 A.B. L.284 J.D. 5200 N. Palm, Ste., 211
Bacigalupi, Dale E. .......................'52 '81 C&L.101 B.A., J.D. [Christensen,B.&B.]
Bacon, Daniel A., (BV) ..................................'49 '75 C.267 B.A. L.809 J.D. 906 N St.
Bagdasarian, Gary G. ............. '49 '76 C.813 B.S. L.770 J.D. 2019 N. Gateway Blvd.
Baida, Robert H. ........................................'26 '52 C.112 L.1065 J.D. Asst. City Manager
Bailey, Howard W. .........................'17 '42 C&L.352 B.A., J.D. 3795 N. Fresno St.
Baker, Bethany R. ........ '62 '88 C.267 B.A. L.1189 J.D. Sr. Atty.,Calif. State Ct. of Appl.
**Baker, John H.**, (AV) ..........................'30 '55 C.267 A.B. L.1065 J.D. [Baker,M.&J.]
*PRACTICE AREAS: Civil Trial Practice; Business and Commercial Litigation; Professional Liability Defense.
**Baker, K. Poncho** ...........................'60 '91 C.985 B.S. L.1065 J.D. [▣ Sagaser,H.F.&J.]

**Baker, Manock & Jensen, A Professional Corporation, (AV)** BB
**5260 North Palm, Suite 421, 93704**
**Telephone: 209-432-5400 Fax: 209-432-5620**
**John H. Baker; Kendall L. Manock; Douglas B. Jensen; Donald R. Fischbach; Robert G. Fishman; Howard M. Zidenberg; John L. B. Smith; George L. Strasser; Joseph M. Marchini; Craig A. Houghton; Andrew R. Weiss; Mark W. Snauffer; James E. Shekoyan; Carl R. Refuerzo; John G. Michael; Christopher L. Campbell; Robert D. Wilkinson; Jeffrey A. Jaech; David M. Camenson; Lisa M. Martin; Gayle D. Hearst; Glenn J. Holder; Mark B. Canepa; William S. Barcus; Douglas M. Larsen; Michael W. Goldring; Randall J. Krause;—Michele A. Engnath; William M. White; Kathleen A. Meehan; Gary B. Wells; Richard S. Salinas; Richard A. Ryan; David E. Holland; Glen F. Dorgan; Charles K. Manock; Glenn A. Rowley; Matthew Earl Hoffman; Colleen Schulthies; James M. Cipolla; Mark E. Crone; Paul B. Mello; Kristine R. Cerro; Lisa A. Travis; Jeffrey R. Ahronian. Of Counsel: Michelle T. Tutelian; Leonard I. Meyers; James E. Ganulin.**
**General Civil and Trial Practice. Environmental, Agricultural, Bankruptcy, Cooperative, Corporation, Medical and Malpractice Legal, Taxation, Probate and Estate Planning, Real Estate, Water Rights, Family/Domestic Relations, Oil and Gas Law, Employment, and Intellectual Property.**
**Representative Clients: Bank of America NT&SA; Challenge Dairy Products, Inc.; Fresno Metropolitan Flood Control District; Metropolitan Life Insurance Co.; Norcal Mutual Insurance Co.; Wells Fargo Bank, N.A.; Sun-Maid Growers of California.**
***See Professional Biographies, FRESNO, CALIFORNIA***

Bakker, Laura J. ........................................'50 '88 C.112 B.S. L.999 J.D. Dep. Co. Coun. IV
Balderama, Olga A. .........................................'68 '93 C.69 B.A. L.112 J.D. 377 W. Fallbrook
**Baldwin, Kenneth A.** ........... '62 '87 C.112 B.A. L.1067 J.D. [McCormick,B.S.W.&C.]
**Ball, Michael F.**, (BV) ........... '60 '84 C.472 A.B. L.339 J.D. [McCormick,B.S.W.&C.]
**Baradat, Daniel R.**, (AV) ..........................'50 '76 C.740 B.A. L.767 J.D. [Baradat&E.]
*PRACTICE AREAS: Personal Injury Law; Legal and Medical Malpractice; Insurance Bad Faith Law.

**Baradat & Edwards, (AV)**
**6592 North First Street, 93710**
**Telephone: 209-431-5366 Fax: 209-431-1702**
**Members of Firm: David G. Edwards; Daniel R. Baradat.**
**Practice Limited to Plaintiff's Civil Trial Litigation in all Courts, Personal Injury, Products Liability, Wrongful Death, Professional Negligence and Insurance Law.**
***See Professional Biographies, FRESNO, CALIFORNIA***

**Barcus, William S.** ...........................'63 '89 C.1074 B.S. L.1049 J.D. [Baker,M.&J.]
*PRACTICE AREAS: Business Litigation; Real Property Litigation.
Barker, John A. ........ '45 '81 C.267 B.A. L.999 J.D. 2030 Fresno St., 8th Fl. (⊙Madera)
Barnard, Robt. M. ...................................................'13 '38 C.267 L.813 Ret. Mun. J.
Barrett, Charles M., (BV) ............'55 '80 C.766 B.A. L.1065 J.D. 1745 E. Bullard Ave.
Barrus, John E. .............................'54 '85 C&L.101 B.A., J.D. [Christensen,B.&B.]
**Barsamian, Ronald H.** .......................'53 '78 C.112 A.B. L.61 J.D. [Barsamian&S.]
*REPORTED CASES: Maggio, Inc. v. United Farm Workers of America, AFL-CIO, 227 Cal.App.3d 847, 278 Cal.Reptr. 250 (1991), review denied, cert. denied 112 S.Ct. 187.
*PRACTICE AREAS: Labor Law; Labor Negotiations; Employment Law; Agricultural Law; Commercial Litigation.

**Barsamian & Saqui, A Professional Corporation**
**1141 West Shaw Avenue, Suite 104, 93711-3704**
**Telephone: 209-248-2360 Telex: 209-248-2370**
**Ronald H. Barsamian; Michael C. Saqui; Patrick S. Moody;—E. Mark Hanna.**
**Labor and Employment Law (Representing Management), including Wrongful Discharge, Employment Discrimination, Sexual Harassment, Employment Tort Actions, Labor Relations and Negotiations, Union Avoidance, OSHA and related employee injuries, Unemployment, Immigration, Wage and Hour, Drug and Alcohol Detection and Prevention, Agricultural Labor Relations, ERISA and Employee Benefits, Human Resources, Commercial Litigation, PACA and Transportation Claims.**
***See Professional Biographies, FRESNO, CALIFORNIA***

Barsotti, Todd B., (BV) ....................'63 '90 C.464 B.A. L.1189 J.D. [Emerson&Y.]
**Barstow, James H.**, (AV) '20 '45 C.112 A.B. L.1066 LL.B.
[McCormick,B.S.W.&C.] ‡
**Baxter, Todd W.** ..................'58 '91 C.966 B.S. L.546 J.D. [McCormick,B.S.W.&C.]
**Bayer, Kenneth S.** ...........................'56 '81 C.112 B.A. L.1068 J.D. [McCollum&B.]
*LANGUAGES: German.
*REPORTED CASES: McIntosh v. Aubry 14 Cal App 4th 1576; San Diego County v. Superior Court 176 Cal App 3d 1009.
*PRACTICE AREAS: Bankruptcy; Business Litigation; Health Care.
Beck, Dennis L. ....................................................'47 '72 C&L.945 B.A., J.D. U.S. Mag.
**Bedoyan, Hagop T.**, (BV) .........................'60 '87 C.112 B.A. L.464 J.D. [Bedoyan]
*LANGUAGES: Armenian.

**Bedoyan Law Offices, (BV)**
**2499 West Shaw Avenue, Suite 103, 93711**
**Telephone: 209-228-6166 FAX: 209-229-3525**
**Hagop T. Bedoyan.**
**Bankruptcy and insolvency Law with emphasis on the reorganization of small to medium businesses and farms.**
***See Professional Biographies, FRESNO, CALIFORNIA***

Bedrosian, Gary P. ....................'50 '78 C.112 B.A. L.999 J.D. Bedrosian Bldg. Supply
**Behrens, Jerome M.**, (BV) .........'44 '74 C.112 B.A. L.1065 J.D. [Lozano S.S.W.&B.]
*LANGUAGES: French.
*REPORTED CASES: Tripp v. Swoap (1976) 17 Cal. 3d 671; McClatchy Newspapers v. Superior Court (1988) 44 Cal. 3d 1162; Morgan Hill Unified S.D. v. Kaufman & Broad (1992) 9 Cal. App. 4th 464; Anderson v. Superior Court (1995) 11 Cal. 4th 1152.
*PRACTICE AREAS: Business; Real Property; Eminent Domain; Environmental Law; General Civil Litigation.
Belardinelli, Richard A., (BV) ..............'46 '75 C.267 B.S. L.464 J.D. [Georgeson&B.]
**Bell, James M.**, (AV) ...............'37 '66 C.112 B.S. L.1066 LL.B. [Caswell,B.H.B.&G.]
*PRACTICE AREAS: Taxation; Real Estate; Estate Planning; Business Transactions.
**Beltramo, Mario Louis, Jr.**, (AV) '47 '72
C.767 B.A. L.602 J.D. [McCormick,B.S.W.&C.]
Benck, Ernest A., Jr. ................ '47 '83 C.267 B.A. L.770 J.D. Sr. Atty., Ct. of Appeal
Bennett, Barry J., (AV) ...............................'43 '69 C.696 A.B. L.569 J.D. [Bennett&S.]
Bennett, Catherine Adams, (BV) ... '46 '76 C.112 B.A. L.1148 J.D. 499 W. Shaw, Ste. 116
**Bennett, Shelline Kay** ..............'65 '93 C.267 B.A. L.1065 J.D. [▣ Littler,M.F.T.&M.]
Bennett & Sharpe, A Professional Corporation, (AV) .......................2300 Tulare St.
Bensing, Daniel E. '55 '80 C.188 B.S. L.276 J.D.
(adm. in DC; not adm. in CA) Asst. U.S. Atty.
Bent, David Hewes, (BV) ..... '47 '76 C.205 B.S. L.1065 J.D. 5200 N. Palm Ave, Ste. 201

**Berding & Weil, (AV)**
**516 West Shaw Avenue, Suite 200, 93704⊙**
**Telephone: 209-221-2556 Fax: 209-221-2558**
**Michael J. Hughes.**
**Construction Litigation and Community Association Law. Non-Profit Corporation Law. Appellate Practice.**
**Alamo, California Office: 3420 Stone Valley Road West. Telephone: 510-838-2090. Fax: 510-820-5592.**
**Rancho Cordova, California Office: 2200 Sunrise Boulevard, Suite 220. 95670 Telephone: 916-851-1910. Fax: 916-851-1914.**
**Santa Clara, California Office: 3600 Pruneridge Avenue, Suite 130. 95051 Telephone: 408-556-0220. Fax: 408-556-0224.**
***See Professional Biographies, FRESNO, CALIFORNIA***

Berg, Otto E., (AV) ............'18 '49 C.267 A.B. L.1066 LL.B. 1180 E. Shaw, STE., 214
**Berger, Bruce J.** .........................'57 '88 C.267 B.S. L.1148 J.D. [▣ Stammer,M.B.&B.]
*PRACTICE AREAS: Health Law; Taxation.
**Bergin, Robert E.**, (BV) ..................'44 '74 C.750 B.S. L.1065 J.D. [Kimble,M.&U.]
*PRACTICE AREAS: Corporate and Business Law; Taxation Law; Probate, Trusts and Estate Planning; ERISA Law.
**Berman, Richard P.**, (BV) .....................'46 '73 C.112 B.A. L.1065 J.D. [Nuttall B.]
*PRACTICE AREAS: Criminal Law; White Collar Criminal Defense; Sexual Assault Law; Drug Traffic Offenses; Homicides.

**Berryman, Albert J., (AV) '47 '72 C.602 A.B. L.767 J.D.**
**5088 North Fruit, Suite 102, 93711**
**Telephone: 209-248-4840 Facsimile: 209-248-4833**
**Agricultural Law, Commercial Law, Bankruptcy (Creditors), Banking Law.**
***See Professional Biographies, FRESNO, CALIFORNIA***

**Bessinger, John L. "Sam"** ....................'48 '76 C.877 B.S. L.1095 J.D. [▣ Mullen&F.]
**Bethel, Gary W.**, (BV) '55 '85
C.800 B.A. L.464 J.D. [Littler,M.F.T.&M.] (⊙Santa Maria)
**Betts, James B.** ..............................................'57 '83 C.1049 B.A. L.770 J.D. [Musick,P.&G.]
*PRACTICE AREAS: Litigation; Labor and Employment.

**Bickel, Bruce D., (AV) '52 '77 C.684 B.A. L.1065 J.D.** BB
**470 E. Herndon Avenue, Suite 203, 93720-2929**
**Telephone: 209-435-7575 Facsimile: 209-435-1735**
**Email: brucebickel@earthlink.net**
**(Certified Specialist, Estate Planning, Trust and Probate Law, The State Bar of California Board of Legal Specialization).**
**Business and Estate Planning, Trust Administration and Probate Law.**
***See Professional Biographies, FRESNO, CALIFORNIA***

**Biggs, Jan M., (AV) '48 '74 C.267 B.A. L.464 J.D.**
**1233 West Shaw Avenue, Suite 102, 93711**
**Telephone: 209-221-0200 Fax: 209-221-7997**
**General Civil Trial Practice. Personal Injury Litigation, Insurance Defense Coverage and Business Litigation.**
***See Professional Biographies, FRESNO, CALIFORNIA***

Biglow, Michael J. ....................'45 '71 C.267 B.A. L.1066 J.D. 857 E. Shields Ave.
Birch, Raquel ......................................'58 '92 C.878 B.S. L.464 J.D. 5 River Park Pl. E.
**Black, Donald S.**, (BV) ......... '54 '80 C.478 A.B. L.770 J.D. [McCormick,B.S.W.&C.]
*PRACTICE AREAS: Real Estate Litigation including Brokers and Agents Liability; Creditors Rights and Remedies; Trust and Probate Litigation.
Blackstone, Carl H. ..............................'56 '83 C.112 A.B. L.629 J.D. 1130 "O" St.
**Blanco, Salvador M.**, (BV) ...............'58 '88 C.267 B.A. L.1189 J.D. [Blanco,T.&P.]
*LANGUAGES: Spanish.
*PRACTICE AREAS: Corporate Law; Real Estate Law; Taxation; Trademark Law; International Transactions.

**Blanco, Tomassian & Pimentel, (BV)**
**A Professional Partnership**
**3419 West Shaw Avenue, 93711**
**Telephone: 209-277-7300 Facsimile: 209-277-7350**
**Members of the Firm: Salvador M. Blanco; Gerald M. Tomassian; Paul J. Pimentel; David D. Goss.**
**General Practice, Civil Litigation, Family Domestic Relations, Business, Mergers and Acquisitions, Corporate, Partnership, Limited Liability Companies, Real Estate Transactions, Taxation, Probate and Estate Planning, Intellectual Property Rights, Franchising and Licensing, Software Licensing, Financing Law, International Law, Foreign Investment, Special Expertise in the In-Bond Maquiladora Industry, Customs, Municipal Finance, Government Affairs, Legislative, Administrative Lobbying and Public Administrative Law.**
***See Professional Biographies, FRESNO, CALIFORNIA***

Blanks, Betty E. ...............................'48 '89 C.861 B.A. L.425 J.D. 2300 Tulare St.
Blickenstaff, Dale A., (BV) ...............'41 '67 C.267 B.A. L.61 J.D. 5151 N.Palm Ave.

**Blue, Robert E., (BV) '52 '78 C.101 B.S. L.378 J.D.**
**1180 East Shaw Avenue, Suite 214, 93710-7812**
**Telephone: 209-228-8196 Facsimile: 209-228-0327**
***PRACTICE AREAS: Bankruptcy (Creditors) Law; Business Law; Probate Law.**

(This Listing Continued)

CAA93P

**Blue, Robert E. (Continued)**
Creditor Bankruptcy, and Creditors Rights Litigation.
*See Professional Biographies, FRESNO, CALIFORNIA*

**Bluhm, Mary Ann**, (BV) ........... '52 '78 C.267 B.A. L.1189 J.D. [⊡ Kimble,M.&U.]
*LANGUAGES: French and Armenian.
*REPORTED CASES: Kaljian v. Menezes (1995) 36 Cal.App.4th 573.
*PRACTICE AREAS: Appellate Practice; Business Litigation; Estate Planning; Probate.
**Blumberg, Stephen M.**, (AV) .......... '30 '59 C.813 B.A. L.1068 J.D. [Blumberg,S.&I.]
*PRACTICE AREAS: Professional Malpractice Defense and Real Estate Litigation.

**Blumberg, Seng & Ikeda, A Professional Corporation, (AV)**
**10 River Park Place East, Suite 220, 93720-1531**
Telephone: 209-434-6484 Fax: 209-434-8240
Stephen M. Blumberg; Michael J. Seng; Dale Ikeda; Gary L. Green; Elise M. Shebelut-Krause; Michael P. Slater;—Michelle E. Kunkel; Nancy J. Stegall (Law Clerk).
General Trial Practice in all Courts. Professional Malpractice Defense, Real Estate, Defense of Financial and Title Companies, Personal Injury.
Reference: Regency Bank.
*See Professional Biographies, FRESNO, CALIFORNIA*

**Boehm, Thomas**, (BV) .............. '48 '75 C.546 B.S. L.190 J.D. [Frampton,H.W.&B.]
**Boggs, Celene M.E.** .............. '69 '94 C.728 B.S. L.1065 J.D. [⊡ Stammer,M.B.&B.]
*PRACTICE AREAS: Negligence Law; Litigation.
**Bolen, Hal H., II**, (AV) .................. '49 '76 C.267 B.S. L.1067 J.D. [Bolen,F.&B.]
*PRACTICE AREAS: Business Law; Real Estate; Taxation.

**Bolen, Fransen & Boostrom LLP, (AV)**
**Suite 430, East Tower Guarantee Financial Center, 1322 East Shaw Avenue, 93710⊙**
Telephone: 209-226-8177 Fax: 209-227-4971
Partners: Hal H. Bolen II; Kenneth J. Fransen. Senior Attorney: Jeffrey A. Russell. Associates: Virginia Miller Pedreira. Of Counsel: Donna Boostrom.
General Business, Banking, Creditors' Rights, Corporate, Real Estate and Taxation Law. Agricultural and Water Rights Law. Estate Planning and Probate Law.
Clovis, California Office: 414 Pollasky Avenue. Telephone: 209-226-8177. Fax: 209-322-6778.
*See Professional Biographies, FRESNO, CALIFORNIA*

Bonett, Linda M. ..................... '54 '80 C.267 B.A. L.1189 J.D. 1322 E. Shaw Ave.
**Boostrom, Donna**, (BV) ............... '52 '82 C.494 B.A. L.1065 J.D. [⊡ Bolen,F.&B.]
*PRACTICE AREAS: Banks and Banking; Real Estate.

**Borton, Petrini & Conron, (AV)**
**T. W. Patterson Building, Suite 830, 2014 Tulare Street, 93721⊙**
Telephone: 209-268-0117 Fax: 209-237-7995
Email: bpcfrs@bpclaw.com
Members of Firm: J. David Petrie; Dale M. Dorfmeier; Gary C. Harvey. Associates: Michael J. Boyajian; Daniel J. Tekunoff.
Commercial/Real Estate Litigation, Insurance Law, General Civil Trial and Appellate Practice in State and Federal Courts, Personal Injury and Casualty Defense Litigation, Insurance Bad Faith and Coverage, Labor and Employment, Toxic Torts, Real Estate, Land Use Planning, Zoning, Municipal, Professional Errors and Omissions, Healthcare Provider Malpractice Defense, Products Liability, Oil and Gas, Water, Natural Resources, Environmental, Public Entity, Administrative, Agricultural, Banking, Contracts, Corporations, Partnerships, Taxation, Creditor's Remedies, Bankruptcy, Probate, Estate Planning, Family Law.
Bakersfield, California Office: The Borton, Petrini & Conron Building, 1600 Truxtun Avenue, P.O. Box 2026. Telephone: 805-322-3051. Fax: 805-322-4628. Email: bpcbak@bpclaw.com.
San Luis Obispo, California Office: 1114 Marsh Street. Telephone: 805-541-4340. Fax: 805-541-4558. Email: bpcslo@bpclaw.com.
Visalia, California Office: 206 South Mooney Boulevard, P.O. Box 1028. Telephone: 209-627-5600. Fax: 209-627-4309. Email: bpcvis@bpclaw.com.
Sacramento, California Office: 2233 Watt Avenue, Suite 290. Telephone: 916-484-3555. Fax: 916-484-3550. Email: bpcsac@bpclaw.com.
Santa Barbara, California Office: 211 East Victoria Street, Suite D. Telephone: 805-564-2404. Fax: 805-564-2176. Email: bpcsb@bpclaw.com
Los Angeles, California Office: 707 Wilshire Boulevard, Suite 5100. Telephone: 213-624-2869. Fax: 213-489-3930. Email: bpcla@bpclaw.com.
San Diego, California Office: John Burnham Building, 610 West Ash Street, 9th Floor. Telephone: 619-232-2424. Fax: 619-531-0794. Email: bpcsd@bpclaw.com.
Newport Beach, California Office: 4675 MacArthur Court, Suite 1150. Telephone: 714-752-2333. Fax: 714-752-2854. Email: bpcnb@bpclaw.com.
Modesto, California Office: The Turner Building, 900 "H" Street, Suite D. Telephone: 209-576-1701. Fax: 209-527-9753. Email: bpcmod@bpclaw.com.
San Francisco, California Office: 111 Pine Street, Suite 730. Telephone: 415-981-4415. Fax: 415-391-5538. Email: bpcsf@bpclaw.com.
Redding, California Office: 280 Hemsted Drive, Suite 100. Telephone: 916-222-1530. Fax: 916-222-4498. Email: bpcred@bpclaw.com.
San Bernardino, California Office: 290 North "D" Street, Suite 500. Telephone: 909-381-0527. Fax: 909-381-0658. Email: bpcsbdo@bpclaw.com.
San Jose, California Office: 2 North Second Street. Telephone: 408-298-3997. Fax: 408-298-3365. Email: bpcsj@bpclaw.com.
Ventura, California Office: 1000 Hill Road, Suite 310. Telephone: 805-650-9994. Fax: 805-650-7125. Email: bpcvta@bpclaw.com.
Santa Rosa, California Office: 50 Santa Rosa Avenue, Suite 300. Telephone: 707-527-9477. Fax: 707-527-9488. Email: bpcsr@bpclaw.com.
*See Professional Biographies, FRESNO, CALIFORNIA*

Bosquez-Flores, Linda ........................ '56 '88 C&L.999 A.S., J.D. [Cole,F.B.&C.]
**Boswell, Jeffrey G.**, (AV) .................. '49 '76 C&L.101 B.S., J.D. [Kimble,M.&U.]
*LANGUAGES: Niuean.
*PRACTICE AREAS: Banking Law; Real Estate Law; Secured Lending; Insolvency Law.
Boulger, Richard V. .................. '14 '40 C.585 L.273 LL.B. 4852 N. Bengston Ave.‡
**Boyajian, Michael J.** .................... '58 '87 C.330 B.S. L.809 J.D. [⊡ Borton,P.&C.]
*PRACTICE AREAS: Insurance Defense; Personal Injury; Premises Liability.
Boyajian, Thomas M. .................... '44 '75 C.267 L.284 J.D. 2100 Tulare St.
**Bradley, Peter S.** .................. '59 '83 C.112 A.B. L.1068 J.D. [Doyle,P.&B.]
*REPORTED CASES: Published Opinion: Serian Brothers, Inc. v. Agri Sun Nursery (1994) 25 Cal.App. 4th 306.
*PRACTICE AREAS: Civil Litigation; Employment Law; Business Litigation.
**Branch, Robert William** .............. '60 '91 C.112 B.S. L.629 J.D. [⊡ Kimble,M.&U.]
Brashear, James T. ................ '34 '89 C.1131 B.A. L.426 J.D. 2030 Fresno St., 8th Fl.
**Brewer, C. William**, (AV) ............ '45 '76 C.871 B.S. L.1189 J.D. [Motschiedler,M.&W.]
*PRACTICE AREAS: Real Estate Law/Land Use Development; Civil Litigation; Eminent Domain Law; Inverse Condemnation Law; Regulatory Takings Law.
Bromberg, Dennis M. ..................... '47 '79 C.112 A.B. L.809 J.D. 2300 Tulare St.
Brooks, Wayne A. '28 '53 C.707 B.A. L.352 J.D.
Prof. of Bus. Law, Emeritus, Calif. State Univ.‡
**Brown, Bruce M.**, (BV) .................. '52 '77 C.112 A.B. L.1065 J.D. [Wild,C.&T.]
*SPECIAL AGENCIES: Agribusiness Committee of the Business Law Section of the State Bar of California.
*PRACTICE AREAS: Real Estate; Finance; Agricultural Law.
**Brown, Carl L.**, (BV) .......................... '44 '77 C.999 L.1189 J.D. [Brown&P.]
*PRACTICE AREAS: Insurance Defense; Plaintiff Personal Injury; Product Liability; Construction Litigation.
Brown, Chris Marie ............... '51 '79 C.352 B.A. L.1162 J.D. 1538 W. Sussex Way‡
**Brown, Christopher A.** ............... '60 '89 C.605 B.A. L.770 J.D. [Dowling,A.&K.]
*PRACTICE AREAS: Business Transactions; Real Estate Law; Environmental Law; Land Use Law; Construction Law.
Brown, George A. .................... '17 '48 C.112 B.S. L.813 J.D. Ret. Jus., Ct. of App.

**Brown & Peel, (BV)**
**6760 North West Avenue, Suite 104, 93711**
Telephone: 209-431-1300 Facsimile: 209-431-1442
URL: http://www.rhomberg.com/b&p
Carl L. Brown; James W. Peel;—R. Ernest Montanari, III.
General Civil Trial Practice in State and Federal Courts. Negligence Law, Professional Malpractice, Product Liability, Public Entities Defense, Employment Law, Construction Litigation, Coverage Opinions and Declaratory Relief Actions, Professional Errors and Omissions and Insurance Law.
*See Professional Biographies, FRESNO, CALIFORNIA*

Brungess, Julia Ann .......... '53 '82 C.267 B.S. L.1189 J.D. 5200 N. Palm Ave., Ste. 301
**Buchanan, Timothy J.** ..................... '54 '81 C.112 B.A. L.770 J.D. [Dietrich,G.&J.]
*PRACTICE AREAS: Unfair Competition; Business Litigation; Media and Employment Law; Securities; ERISA Litigation.
Buda, Michael A. ......................... '52 '86 C.36 B.S. L.823 J.D. 1690 West Shaw
Buettner, Michael M. ..................... '55 '84 C.112 A.B. L.1067 J.D. 4747 N. 1st St.
Bumanglag, George ...................... '48 '73 C.1075 B.S. L.1065 J.D. 2500 Merced St.
Bunch, Brad L. ............................ '44 '70 C.763 B.A. L.1049 J.D. 1520 E. Shaw‡
Bunting, Peter B. ............... '49 '86 C.267 B.A. L.1189 J.D. 2501 W. Shaw, Ste. 119
**Burnside, James D., III**, (BV) ...... '51 '77 C.112 A.B. L.770 J.D. [Caswell,B.H.B.&G.]
*PRACTICE AREAS: Construction; Real Estate; Business Litigation; Employment.

**Burt, Karen A., (BV) '54 '84 C.1042 B.A. L.464 J.D.**
**2499 West Shaw Avenue, Suite 103, P.O. Box 9429, 93792-9429**
Telephone: 209-228-6172 Fax: 209-229-3525
Landlord Tenant Law including Commercial and Residential, Common Interest Development Law, Contract Leasing and Real Estate.
*See Professional Biographies, FRESNO, CALIFORNIA*

Burtner, Ann ......................... '56 '81 C.976 B.A. L.800 J.D. Dep. Pub. Def.
Busick, Mark B ..................... '60 '88 C.267 B.S. L.1189 J.D. 1233 W. Shaw Ave.
**Bussing, Heather** ...................... '62 '87 C&L.378 B.A., J.D. [⊡ Musick,P.&G.]
*PRACTICE AREAS: Professional Liability Defense; Labor and Employment Litigation; Commercial and Business Litigation.
Butler, R. Frank, (BV) ..................... '44 '73 C.267 B.S. L.1067 J.D. 1327 N St.
Byers, Garrick A. .................... '49 '79 C.1078 B.A. L.1162 J.D. Dep. Pub. Def.
Byrne, Terrence J. .................... '47 '74 C.767 B.S. L.1065 J.D. [Hanna,B.M.M.&J.]
**Byron, Deborah A.**, (BV) .... '51 '82 C.267 B.A. L.1189 J.D. [⊡ McCormick,B.S.W.&C.]
*PRACTICE AREAS: Employment Law.
Caeton, Anthony D. ............................ '34 '67 C.112 L.800 J.D. Supr. Ct. J.
Calvert, Cynthia S. ...................................... '47 '77 1137 E. Bremer Ave.
**Camenson, David M.**, (BV) ............. '56 '85 C.112 B.A. L.1119 J.D. [Baker,M.&J.]
*PRACTICE AREAS: Business Transactions; Retirement Planning; Intellectual Property; Income Tax; Employment Taxes.

**Campagne, Thomas E. '50 '75 C.770 B.S. L.1189 J.D.**
**Airport Office Center, 1685 North Helm Avenue, 93727**
Telephone: 209-255-1637 Fax: 209-252-9617
Representing Employers in the Public, Private and Agricultural sectors regarding Labor Relations Law and Employment Discrimination and Wrongful Termination Law, Civil Trial and Appellate Practice in all State and Federal Courts, Commercial and Business Litigation, Real Property, Financial and Business Transactions and Agricultural Business Law.
*See Professional Biographies, FRESNO, CALIFORNIA*

**Campbell, Christopher L.**, (BV) ........... '55 '84 C.766 B.A. L.1066 J.D. [Baker,M.&J.]
*SPECIAL AGENCIES: Federal Bureau of Reclamation.
*TRANSACTIONS: Financing Water Transfers.
*PRACTICE AREAS: Agriculture (Financing and Water Rights) Law (75%); Planning and Zoning.
Campbell, Michael A. .......... '50 '75 C.383 B.A. L.259 J.D. Sr. Atty., Calif. Ct. of App.
**Campos, Michael A.**, (BV) '39 '75
C.267 B.S.C.E. L.464 J.D. [Graham&J.] (⊙Sacramento)
*LANGUAGES: Spanish.
*PRACTICE AREAS: Environmental Law; Toxic Tort; Water Law; Natural Resources Law.
Canepa, Marianne L. .................... '60 '88 C.112 B.A. L.1065 J.D. 2300 Tulare St.
**Canepa, Mark B.**, (CV) ................ '59 '89 C.766 B.A. L.1065 J.D. [Baker,M.&J.]
*PRACTICE AREAS: Medical Malpractice Defense; Civil Litigation.
Caples, Patrick W. ..................... '51 '80 C.1109 B.A. L.1148 J.D. Dep. Dist. Atty.

**Capozzi, Anthony P., (AV) '45 '71 C.107 B.A. L.851 J.D.**
**1233 West Shaw Avenue, Suite 102, 93711**
Telephone: 209-221-0200 Facsimile: 209-221-7997
*PRACTICE AREAS: Civil Litigation; Civil Rights; Criminal Law; Appellate Practice; Criminal Tax Audits.
Trial and Appellate Practice Specializing in State and Federal Criminal Defense Litigation. Personal Injury, Tax Litigation, Tax Fraud and IRS/Collections.
*See Professional Biographies, FRESNO, CALIFORNIA*

Caprioglio, Paul E., (A Prof. Corp.), (BV) ....... '46 '72 C.267 A.B. L.464 J.D. 1327 N St.
**Carr, Alyson A.** ............ '72 '96 C.767 B.A. L.1064 J.D. [⊡ McCormick,B.S.W.&C.]
*PRACTICE AREAS: Insurance Coverage; Bad Faith Defense.
**Carrigan, C. Michael** .......................... '60 '92 C&L.1189 PT, J.D/ [Myers&O.]
Carroll, Dorothy A. ................. '66 '93 C.1097 B.A. L.1189 J.D. [⊡ D.J.St. Louis]
Carroll, Peter H., III, (AV⊙) ............ '52 '78 C.112 A.B. L.744 J.D. Asst. U.S. Trustee
**Carroll, Stephen E.**, (BV) ..... '58 '84 C.770 B.A. L.1068 J.D. [McCormick,B.S.W.&C.]
**Carruth, Lowell T.**, (AV) ..... '38 '63 C.813 A.B. L.1066 LL.B. [McCormick,B.S.W.&C.]
Carter, George A., (BV) .................. '28 '59 C.112 B.A. L.1066 LL.B. [G.A.Carter]
Carter, J. Montgomery .............. '24 '53 C.267 A.B. L.767 LL.B. 1039 E. Yale Ave.‡
**Carter, Robert G.**, (AV) ................ '27 '55 C.112 B.A. L.1068 LL.B. [Wild,C.&T.]
*PRACTICE AREAS: Business and Commercial Law.
Carter, George A., A Professional Corporation, (BV) ......... 1476 W. Shaw Ave., Rm. C
Cartier, Richard M. .................. '50 '81 C.1258 B.A. L.1132 J.D. 1120 "T" St.
Castelazo, Thomas A., (BV) ............ '40 '65 C&L.770 B.A., LL.B. 1648 W. Robinwood
**Caswell, G. Thomas, Jr.**, (AV) .... '31 '59 C.267 A.B. L.813 LL.B. [Caswell,B.H.B.&G.]
*PRACTICE AREAS: Real Estate; Business Transaction; Land Use; Estate Planning.

**Caswell, Bell, Hillison, Burnside & Greer, L.L.P., (AV)**
**5200 North Palm Avenue, Suite 211, 93704**
Telephone: 209-225-6550 Fax: 209-225-7912
Members of Firm: G. Thomas Caswell, Jr.; James M. Bell (Certified Specialist, Taxation Law, The State Bar of California Board of Legal Specialization); Robert K. Hillison; James D. Burnside, III; Russell D. Greer; Robert A. Werth; Randolf Krbechek; Beth Maxwell Stratton. Of Counsel: J. Russell Hose; O. James Woodward III.
Business Litigation, Real Estate, Business Law, Construction, Creditors' Rights, Bankruptcy, Corporate, Taxation, Employment Law, Estate Planning and Probate.
*See Professional Biographies, FRESNO, CALIFORNIA*

**Cercone, Sue Ann**, (CV) .......... '55 '89 C.172 B.A. L.1189 J.D. [Marderosian,S.&O.]
*PRACTICE AREAS: Insurance Defense; Bad Faith; Personal Injury.
**Cerna, Catherine J.** ............ '61 '95 C.112 B.A. L.1065 J.D. [⊡ Sagaser,H.F.&J.]
*PRACTICE AREAS: Business and Employment Litigation.
**Cerro, Kristine R.** ................. '56 '95 C.112 B.A. L.1189 J.D. [⊡ Baker,M.&J.]
*PRACTICE AREAS: Medical Malpractice Defense; Health Care Law.
Chambers, Paul T., (A Professional Corporation), (AV) '45 '70
C.267 A.B. L.1067 J.D. [Crossland,C.C.L.&K.]
Chandler, Stuart R., (BV) .................. '54 '79 C.154 B.A. L.950 J.D. [S.R.Chandler]
Chandler, Stuart R., A Prof. Corp., (BV) ................................ 4222 W. Alamos

Chatoian, Edward B., (BV) ................'48 '75 C.906 B.S. L.767 J.D. 2607 Fresno St.
Chester, Bruce C. ......................... '47 '74 C.267 B.S. L.426 J.D. [B.C.Chester]
Chester, Bruce C., Inc. ........................................6073 N. Fresno
**Chielpegian, Elliott D.**, (AV) ........... '35 '61 C&L.770 B.S., LL.B. [E.D.Chielpegian]
*PRACTICE AREAS: Personal Injury Law; Civil Litigation.

**Chielpegian, Elliott D., A Prof. Corp., Law Offices of, (AV)**
**Fig Garden Financial Center, 5200 North Palm Avenue Suite 201, 93704**
**Telephone: 209-225-5370 Facsimile: 209-244-6931**
**Elliott D. Chielpegian.**
**Civil Trial Practice. Personal Injury, Business Litigation and Real Property.**

**Chinello, Auchard, Stewart & Strong, A Professional Corporation, (AV)**
**7341 North First Street, Suite 106, P.O. Box 26270, 93729-6270**
**Telephone: 209-432-0991 Fax: 209-432-1025**
**John D. Chinello, Sr. (1896-1985); John D. Chinello, Jr. (1930-1991); Paul Auchard; Malcolm H. Stewart; Richard C. Strong;—Roberta Rowe. Counsel Emeritus: John M. Shelton.**
**General Civil and Trial Practice in all State and Federal Courts. Insurance Defense, Insurance Coverage, Personal Injury, Railroad, Probate, General Business, Real Estate, Condominium, Construction and Corporate Law, Agriculture, School and Public Entity Law.**

**Chittick, Hilary A.**, (BV) ........... '53 '79 C.112 B.A. L.1065 J.D. [Thomas,S.J.R.&A.]
*LANGUAGES: Spanish.
*PRACTICE AREAS: Civil Litigation; Business Litigation; Federal Criminal Defense.
Choi, Alice H. ......................... '67 '93 C&L.112 B.A., J.D. 5250 N. Palm Ave.
Christensen, Alan D. ................... '16 '40 C.112 A.B. L.1066 LL.B. Ret. U.S. Mag.
Christensen, Craig G., (BV) ........ '46 '75 C.101 B.A. L.880 J.D. [Christensen,B.&B.]⊙
Christensen, Eric C. .....................'54 '83 C.267 B.A. L.1189 J.D. Dep. Pub. Def.
Christensen, Bacigalupi & Barrus, (BV) ............... 7112 N. Fresno St. (⊙Sacramento)
Christiansen, James H. .......... '44 '70 C.112 A.B. L.1066 J.D. Princ. Atty., Ct. of App.
Church, Rayma ........................ '57 '91 C.267 B.S. L.1189 J.D. [Emerson&Y.]
Ciano, Darrel J. ......................... '54 '85 C.267 B.S. L.1189 J.D. 770 E. Shaw
**Cipolla, James M.** ....................'51 '94 C.770 B.S.C. L.1189 J.D. [🄰 Baker,M.&J.]
*PRACTICE AREAS: Real Property Transaction; Receiverships.
Ciummo, Richard A., (CV) ....... '53 '79 C.763 A.B. L.1067 J.D. 2030 Fresno St., 8th Fl.
**Clark, Steven C.** ................. '66 '95 C.267 B.A. L.1189 J.D. [Marderosian,S.&O.]
*PRACTICE AREAS: Insurance Defense; Bad Faith; Environmental Law; Personal Injury.
Clason, Jeffrey D. ................'50 '80 C.267 B.A. L.1137 J.D. [🄰 Christensen,B.&B.]
**Clegg, Trevor C.**, (BV) .......... '47 '74 C.1169 A.B. L.813 J.D. [🄲 Frampton,H.W.&B.]
*REPORTED CASES: In re Marriage of Andreen (1978) 76 Cal. App. 3d 667, 143 Cal. Rptr. 94; In re Torrez (9th Cir. BAP 1986) 63 B.R. 751,.
*PRACTICE AREAS: Bankruptcy; Civil Litigation; Appellate Practice; Insurance Coverage; ERISA Litigation.
Cloud, Stephen R. .................. '44 '69 C.267 B.S. L.1049 J.D. V.P., R.V. Cloud Co.
Codde, Diane L. ............................'— '82 C.215 B.S. L.1132 J.D. 2100 Tulare St.
**Coe, Deborah A.** ................. '51 '91 C.267 A.A. L.1189 J.D. [🄰 Parichan,R.C.&H.]
*PRACTICE AREAS: Products Liability; Personal Injury Defense.
Cole, Curtis A., (AV) ........................'33 '58 C&L.770 B.S., LL.B. [Cole,F.B.&C.]
Cole, Leah R. ............................'59 '92 C.770 B.S. L.1189 J.D. [Cole,F.B.&C.]
Cole, Fisher, Bosquez-Flores & Cole, A Prof. Corp., (AV) ............... 2445 Capital St.
**Coleman, Mark W.**, (CV) ..................'56 '84 C.112 B.A. L.1189 J.D. [Nuttall B.]
*PRACTICE AREAS: Personal Injury Law; Plaintiffs Trial Practice; Criminal Defense Trial Practice (with emphasis on Defense of Federal Prosecutions).
**Coleman, William H.**, (BV) .................'52 '77 C.37 B.S. L.464 J.D. [Coleman&H.]
*PRACTICE AREAS: Taxation; Estate Planning; Probate and Trust; Corporate and Business; Transactions.

**Coleman & Horowitt, (BV)**
**499 West Shaw, Suite 116, 93704**
**Telephone: 209-248-4820 Facsimile: 209-248-4830**
**Members of Firm: William H. Coleman; Darryl J. Horowitt; Lucille Goins Dimmick.**
**General Civil and Trial Practice. Commercial Litigation, Corporation Law, Business, Trust, Taxation, Probate and Estate Planning, Construction, Real Estate, Banking, Appellate Advocacy, Casualty Insurance Defense, Insurance Coverage, Environmental Claims and Commercial Collections.**

***See Professional Biographies, FRESNO, CALIFORNIA***

Cook, Noelle S. ........................'53 '81 L.1189 J.D. 9260 N. Green Meadows Ln.
Cook, Russell D., (BV) ...............'54 '80 C.267 B.S. L.1189 J.D. 6770 N. West Ave.
Coolidge, Katherine A. ...........'48 '79 C.793 B.A. L.1189 J.D. 5250 N. Palm, Ste., 402
**Cooper, Joseph D.**, (CV) ................'60 '89 C.112 B.S. L.1189 J.D. [Cooper&H.]⊙
*PRACTICE AREAS: Personal Injury Defense; Business Litigation; Insurance Coverage; Crop Loss; Product Liability.

**Cooper & Hoppe, (BV)**
**2444 Main Street, Suite 125, 93721-2734⊙**
**Telephone: 209-442-1650 Fax: 209-442-1659**
**Joseph D. Cooper; Theodore W. Hoppe.**
**State and Federal General Civil and Trial Practice. Insurance Defense, Business Litigation, Business Transactions, Insurance Coverage, Estate Planning and Personal Injury. Sports and Entertainment Representation.**
**Monterey, California Office: 1088 Cass Street, 93940. Telephone: 408-649-0330.**

***See Professional Biographies, FRESNO, CALIFORNIA***

Corey, Carol S., (BV) ..................... '46 '87 C.908 B.A. L.1189 J.D. [Emerson&Y.]
**Cornwell, Stephen R.**, (AV) ....'42 '67 C.768 B.S. L.1066 J.D. [McCormick,B.S.W.&C.]
*PRACTICE AREAS: Trial Practice; Products Liability; Engineering; Electricity; Chemistry.
**Corona, Adolfo M.** .................... '59 '86 C.112 A.B. L.1066 J.D. [Dowling,A.&K.]
*LANGUAGES: Spanish.
*PRACTICE AREAS: Business Litigation; Construction Law; Creditors Remedies; Creditor Bankruptcy Litigation; Insurance Coverage.
Costanzo, Neal E. .......................'56 '86 C.267 B.S. L.464 J.D. 7108 N. Fresno St.
**Cothran, Joy D.** .............'51 '95 C.1074 B.S. L.990 J.D. [🄰 McCormick,B.S.W.&C.]
*LANGUAGES: Spanish and French.
*PRACTICE AREAS: Insurance Coverage; Business Litigation.
Cowin, William L., (CV) ........'43 '75 C.267 B.A. L.1189 J.D. 2150 Tulare St., 2nd Flr.
Cox, Ray N., (BV) ....................'45 '72 C.112 A.B. L.1065 J.D. 1849 N. Helm Ave.
Coyle, Robert E. .........................'30 '56 C.267 A.B. L.1065 J.D. U.S. Sr. Dist. Ct.
**Coyle, Sylvia Halkousis** ................ '60 '85 C.289 A.B. L.64 J.D. [Kimble,M.&U.]
*LANGUAGES: French and Greek.
*PRACTICE AREAS: Health Care Law; Corporate Law; Business Law.
Craddock, Nancy Anne ..................'53 '79 C.1154 B.A. L.1187 J.D. Dep. Dist. Atty.
Creede, Frank J., Jr. .............................'25 '51 C.813 A.B. L.767 LL.B. Supr. Ct. J.
**Creede, Mark L.**, (BV) ......................'59 '87 C.1074 B.S. L.767 J.D. [Lang,R.&P.]
*PRACTICE AREAS: Construction Law; Commercial Litigation.
Cremer Noxon, Darci ......................'46 '72 C.763 A.B. L.1065 J.D. Co. Pub. Def.
Criego, Franz A., (BV) ... '50 '81 C.1097 B.A. L.1179 J.D. Def. Coun., Co. Pub. Def. Off.
**Crone, Mark E.** ........................ '65 '95 C.855 B.A. L.770 J.D. [🄰 Baker,M.&J.]
Cronin, Phillip S., (BV) ............................'38 '72 C.988 B.A. L.1065 J.D. Co. Coun.

**Crossland, Robert D., Law Offices of, (AV) '44 '72 C.267 B.A. L.1065 J.D.**
**5200 North Palm Avenue, Suite 209, 93704-2228⊙**
**Telephone: 209-229-6534 Fax: 209-229-2665**
**Estate Planning, Partnership, Tax, Probate, Taxation, Corporate and Partnership Law.**
**San Mateo, California Office: 177 Bovet Road, Suite 600. Telephone: 415-341-1556. Fax: 415-341-1395.**

***See Professional Biographies, FRESNO, CALIFORNIA***

Crossland, Robert S., (AV) ...........'11 '35 C.267 L.1065 J.D. [Crossland,C.C.L.&K.] ‡
Crossland, Crossland, Chambers, Lastreto & Knudson, (AV)
1180 E. Shaw Ave. Ste., 214 (⊙San Mateo)
**Crossman, Richard C.**, (AV) ........'41 '71 C.267 B.A. L.1065 J.D. [Parichan,R.C.&H.]
*PRACTICE AREAS: Insurance Defense and Coverage; Products Liability; Business; Environmental and General Litigation.
Cullers, Mark E. ........................... '58 '86 C.112 B.A. L.273 J.D. Asst. U.S. Atty.
**Culver, Kristi R.** .................... '63 '88 C.147 B.A. L.464 J.D. [🄰 Sagaser,H.F.&J.]
Culy, Michael D., (CV) ....................'39 '70 C.1060 L.464 J.D. 2350 W. Shaw Ave.
Cummings, Steven ................'52 '90 C.1077 B.A. L.809 J.D. 2030 Fresno St., 8th Fl.
Cunningham & Lansden, (BV)
600 W. Shaw, #120 (⊙Simi Valley, Victorville, Lancaster, Oxnard, Modesto & Sacramento)
**Czeshinski, Michael J.**, (BV) ...... '62 '88 C&L.966 B.S., J.D. [McCormick,B.S.W.&C.]
*PRACTICE AREAS: Professional Errors and Omissions; Civil Litigation.
**Dahl, William A.**, (AV) ............. '47 '72 C.976 A.B. L.813 J.D. [McGregor,D.S.&K.]
*REPORTED CASES: Menefee v. County of Fresno (Brewer-Kalar) 163 C.A. 3d 1175.
*PRACTICE AREAS: Estate Planning Law; Real Estate Law; Water Law; Environmental Law.
Dail, Joseph G., Jr. '32 '55 C&L.575 B.S., J.D.
(adm. in NC; not adm. in CA) Adm. Law J., Dept. of Health & Human Servs.
Daniel, Jack ......... '49 '85 C.058 A.B. L.326 J.D. Litig. Dir., Central Calif. Legal Servs.
Davis, Craig A. ....................'62 '88 C.267 B.S. L.1189 J.D. 575 E. Alluvial Ave.
**Davis, Jeffrey Pierce** ...................'55 '93 C.494 B.S. L.1189 J.D. [🄰 Forrest&M.]
*PRACTICE AREAS: General Civil and Business Litigation; Employment Law; Real Property.
Dawson, John .................. '54 '81 C.605 A.B. L.1049 J.D. 2409 Merced St., Ste 4
Deal, Leonard E., (BV) ...... '44 '70 C.112 B.S. L.1067 J.D. 2660 W. Shaw Ave., Ste 100
Dechant, George M., Jr. ................ '58 '91 C.988 B.S. L.911 J.D. 2445 Capitol St.
**Decker, Jason A.** .............'70 '96 C.112 B.S. L.464 J.D. [🄰 McCormick,B.S.W.&C.]
DeFendis, Matthew D. '60 '86 C.112 A.B. L.426 J.D.
Gen. Coun., DiBuduo & DeFendis Insurance Group
De Goede, Dale A., (BV) .................'52 '80 C.112 B.A. L.770 J.D. [McCallum&D.]
de Goede, Mary Beth ........................'51 '80 C.112 B.A. L.770 J.D. [Stroup&d.]
**DeMaria, Anthony N.** ....... '69 '95 C.112 B.A. L.1049 J.D. [🄰 McCormick,B.S.W.&C.]
*PRACTICE AREAS: Insurance Defense; Bad Faith; Insurance Coverage; Business Litigation.
**Demsey, James O.**, (AV) .......... '38 '65 C.112 B.S. L.1066 J.D. [Thomas,S.J.R.&A.]
*PRACTICE AREAS: Real Estate Transactions; Business Transactions; State and Local Taxation Law.
Denning, Stephen M. ................ '50 '78 C.112 B.A. L.1189 J.D. 6073 N. Fresno St.
Derryberry, Reggie, (CV) ...................'42 '85 C.378 L.1189 J.D. 5250 N. Palm Ave.
DeSantis, Kathleen K. ...............'50 '83 C.525 B.S. L.1065 J.D. Sr. Atty., Ct. of App.
Dibiaso, Nickolas J. '43 '69 C.770 A.B. L.1066 J.D.
Assoc. Justice, Ct. of Appeal, 5th Appellate Dist.
**Dietrich, Richard W., (Inc.)**, (AV) .... '30 '59 C.112 A.B. L.1066 LL.B. [Dietrich,G.&J.]
*PRACTICE AREAS: Estate Planning; Pension Planning; Business Transactions.

**Dietrich, Glasrud & Jones, (AV)**
**An Association of Attorneys including Law Corporations**
**5250 North Palm Avenue, Suite 402, 93704**
**Telephone: 209-435-5250 Facsimile: 209-435-8776**
**Richard W. Dietrich (Inc.) (Certified Specialist, Taxation Law, The State Bar of California Board of Legal Specialization); Donald H. Glasrud (Inc.); Vreeland O. Jones (Inc.) (Certified Specialist, Taxation Law, The State Bar of California Board of Legal Specialization); Robert A. Mallek Jr. (Inc.) (Certified Specialist, Taxation Law, The State Bar of California Board of Legal Specialization); Richard E. Aune (Inc.); Timothy J. Buchanan; Bruce A. Owdom; Thomas W. Isaac; Christopher E. Seymour;—Douglas D. Schorling; Leslie G. Miessner.**
**Business Litigation, Unfair Competition and Appellate Practice. Media Law, Environmental Litigation, Corporate, Business, Creditor Bankruptcy, Pension and Profit Sharing, Taxation, Real Property, ERISA Litigation, Health Care, Probate and Estate Planning.**

***See Professional Biographies, FRESNO, CALIFORNIA***

DiMaggio, Diana ........................ '51 '82 C.983 L.809 J.D. 3623 N. Virginia Ln.
**Dimmick, Lucille Goins** ............... '49 '94 C.999 A.S. L.1189 J.D. [🄰 Coleman&H.]
*PRACTICE AREAS: Business Litigation; Commercial Litigation; Real Estate; Construction Law; Commercial Collections.
Disney, Susan E. ........................'40 '74 C.1077 B.A. L.1136 J.D. Admin. Law J.
**Docker, W. F.**, (BV) ........... '49 '77 C.813 B.A. L.770 J.D. [McCormick,B.S.W.&C.]
*PRACTICE AREAS: Health Care; Estate Planning; Business and Agricultural Transactions.
Docker, William F., (AV) .......... '18 '47 C&L.813 A.B., LL.B. 5691 Columbia Dr. S.‡
Dodd, Lesa M. ................. '64 '89 C.154 B.A. L.112 J.D. Sr. Atty., Dist. Appl. Ct.
**Doerksen, Charles L.** ........................'61 '88 C.267 B.Sc. L.05 J.D. [Lang,R.&P.]
*PRACTICE AREAS: Civil Litigation.
Donabed, James M., (BV) .............. '49 '79 C.267 B.A. L.1189 J.D. 2300 Tulare St.
Donaldson, Larry A., (CV) .............. '41 '75 C.267 B.A. L.1189 J.D. Dep. City Atty.
Donegan, James S., Sr. ..........................'34 '73 C.112 L.1137 2010 N. Fine Ave.
Donovan, James L. ............... '50 '76 C.770 B.S. L.678 J.D. Admin. Law J., CUIAB
Donovan, Timothy M., (BV) ...............'64 '89 C.112 B.A. L.990 J.D. Dist. Atty. Off.
**Dorfmeier, Dale M.**, (BV) ..............'49 '77 C.267 B.A. L.1189 J.D. [Borton,P.&C.]
*PRACTICE AREAS: Insurance Defense; Crop Loss.
**Dorgan, Glen F.** ...................... '66 '92 C.267 B.A. L.629 J.D. [🄰 Baker,M.&J.]
Dorian, Brett ...........................'34 '63 C.766 A.B. L.1066 J.D. U.S. Bkrptcy. J.
**Dowling, Michael D.**, (AV) .......... '42 '67 C.813 A.B. L.1065 J.D. [Dowling,A.&K.]
*PRACTICE AREAS: Corporate Law; Business Transactions; Business Organization; Taxation Law; Estate Planning.
**Dowling, Michael P.** ......................'67 '95 C.267 B.A. L.285 J.D. [Dowling,A.&K.]
*PRACTICE AREAS: Business Transactions; Probate and Trust Litigation; Estate Planning; Corporations; Creditor's Remedies.

**Dowling, Aaron & Keeler, Incorporated, (AV) BR**
**Suite 200, 6051 North Fresno Street, 93710**
**Telephone: 209-432-4500 Fax: 209-432-4590**
**Email: dowling-law.com**
**Michael D. Dowling (Certified Specialist, Taxation Law, The State Bar of California Board of Legal Specialization); Richard M. Aaron (Certified Specialist, Estate Planning, Trust and Probate Law, The State Bar of California Board of Legal Specialization); Bruce S. Fraser; William J. Keeler, Jr. (Certified Specialist, Estate Planning, Trust and Probate Law, The State Bar of California Board of Legal Specialization); John C. Ganahl; Adolfo M. Corona; Philip David Kopp; Rene Lastreto, II; Francine Marie Kanne; Christopher A. Brown;—Richard E. Heatter; James C. Sherwood; Michael P. Dowling; Daniel T. Fitzpatrick; Mark D. Kruthers. Of Counsel: Daniel K. Whitehurst; Morris M. Sherr (Certified Specialist, Taxation Law, The State Bar of California Board of Legal Specialization); Blaine Pettitt.**
**Civil Trial and Appellate Practice, State and Federal Courts. Corporation, Banking, Creditor's Rights, Bankruptcy, Securities, Real Estate, Estate Planning, Probate, Taxation, Pension, Agricultural, Administrative, Government, Health Care, Insurance, Labor and Employment, Family Law and Sports Law.**
**Reference: Wells Fargo Bank (Main).**

***See Professional Biographies, FRESNO, CALIFORNIA***

**Doyle, David Douglas** ........................ '54 '81 C.426 B.A. L.464 J.D. [Doyle,P.&B.]
*REPORTED CASES: Southern Pacific Land Co. v. Westlake Farms, Inc., et al., (1987) 188 Cal.App. 3d 807 (233 Cal.Rptr. 794); Selma Pressure Treating Co. v. Osmose Wood Pressuring, Inc. (1990) 221 Cal.App. 1601 (271 Cal.Rptr. 596).
*PRACTICE AREAS: Civil Litigation; Environmental Law; Employment Law; Business Law; Appellate Practice.

**Doyle, Penner & Bradley**
**5250 North Palm Avenue, Suite 401, 93704**
**Telephone: 209-261-9321 Fax: 209-261-9320**

(This Listing Continued)

**CAA95P**

**Doyle, Penner & Bradley (Continued)**
**David Douglas Doyle; Randall M. Penner; Peter S. Bradley.**
**Civil Trial and Appellate Practice in all Courts with Emphasis on Federal Practice and Business, Environmental, Employment and Products Liability Litigation, Environmental Law, Employment Law, Products Liability, Corporate Law, Construction Law, Patent, Trademark and Copyright Law.**
*See Professional Biographies, FRESNO, CALIFORNIA*

Drandell, Harry M. ... '57 '83 C.112 B.A. L.464 J.D. 2333 Merced St.
Driscoll, James D. ... '31 '66 C.267 B.A., M.A. L.464 J.D. 7178 N. Jackson‡
**Drolshagen, John A.**, (BV) ... '55 '82 C.112 B.A. L.770 J.D. [McCormick,B.S.W.&C.]
*PRACTICE AREAS: Environmental, Product Liability; Professional Malpractice.
Duffy, John F. ... '44 '77 C.112 B.S. L.1221 J.D. P.O. Box 27140
**Duffy, Roberta J.** ... '57 '87 C.267 B.S. L.1189 J.D. [Sandell&Y.]
*PRACTICE AREAS: Insurance Defense; Litigation; Personal Injury; Appellate Practice; Insurance.
Duncan, Ronda Mae ... '55 '82 C.267 B.S. L.1189 J.D. Dep. Dist. Atty.
Dunn, Cassandra ... '32 '64 C.273 L.1132 LL.B. 7490 N. Charles Ave.
Dunne, Raymond W. ... '51 '76 C.694 B.A. L.436 J.D. 1725 N. Fine Ave.
**Durbin, D. Greg**, (BV) ... '53 '78 C.112 A.B. L.1065 J.D. [McCormick,B.S.W.&C.]
*PRACTICE AREAS: Real Estate, Commercial and Water Litigation.
Dwelle, Dorsey K., (AV) ... '15 '40 C.267 B.A. L.1065 J.D. [Dwelle&D.]
Dwelle & Dwelle, (AV) ... 3707 E. Iowa Ave.
**Eanni, Carmen A.**, (AV) ... '34 '64 C.766 B.A. L.1065 J.D. [Miles,S.&E.]
*PRACTICE AREAS: Personal Injury (Plaintiff) Law; Litigation; Crop Damage; Agricultural Law.
Edelman, Mark '51 '83 C&L.893 B.A., J.D.
(adm. in VA; not adm. in CA) Asst. U.S. Atty.

**Edginton, Ruthanne '59 '88 C.267 B.S. L.1189 J.D.**
**6435 North Palm Avenue, Suite 106, 93704**
**Telephone: 209-439-3600 Fax: 209-439-5699**
***PRACTICE AREAS: Family Law; Criminal Law; Personal Injury.**
**Family Law, Criminal Law, Personal Injury.**
*See Professional Biographies, FRESNO, CALIFORNIA*

Edman, Leland M. ... '22 '53 C.267 A.B. L.1065 J.D. 1650 W. Browning Ave.‡
**Edwards, David G.**, (BV) ... '55 '82 C.267 B.A. L.770 J.D. [Baradat&E.]
*PRACTICE AREAS: Personal Injury Law; Professional Negligence Law.
Eisinger, Jeffrey W. ... '56 '83 C.608 B.A. L.809 J.D. U.S. Small Bus. Admin.
Eldridge, Anderson & Weakley, (BV) ... 1540 E. Shaw Ave.
**Eleazarian, John P.**, (AV) ... '51 '79 C.112 A.B. L.1068 J.D. [Kimble,M.&U.]
*PRACTICE AREAS: Bankruptcy Law; Reorganization Law; Commercial Law.
Elia, Jim T., (BV) ... '45 '78 C.267 B.A. L.1132 J.D. 2300 Tulare St.
**Eliason, Robert G.**, (CV) ... '53 '82 C.112 B.A. L.1065 J.D. [Parichan,R.C.&H.]
*PRACTICE AREAS: Products Liability Law; Consumer Warranty Defense Law.
Ellis, Robert E. ... '49 '76 C.267 B.A. L.1189 J.D. Dep. Dist. Atty.
Ellison, Wayne R. ... '48 '76 Dep. Dist. Atty.
**Emerich, David R.**, (BV) ... '48 '73 C.684 B.A. L.1049 J.D. [Emerich P.&F.]
*PRACTICE AREAS: White Collar Defense; Business Litigation; Agricultural Law.

**Emerich Pedreira & Fike, A Professional Corporation, (BV)**
**5220 North Palm Avenue, 93704-2209**
**Telephone: 209-431-1008 Facsimile: 209-431-1022**
**David R. Emerich; Thomas A. Pedreira; David A. Fike.**
**Health Care Law, Business Litigation and Transactions, White Collar Defense, Agricultural Law, Municipal Law, Real Estate and Construction Law.**
*See Professional Biographies, FRESNO, CALIFORNIA*

Emerson, James D., (AV) ... '41 '68 C.912 B.S. L.477 J.D. [Emerson&Y.]
Emerson & Yrulegui, (AV) ... 2680 W. Shaw Lane
**Engnath, Michele A.** ... '63 '89 C&L.861 B.A., J.D. [▣ Baker,M.&J.]
*PRACTICE AREAS: Business and Agribusiness Litigation; Bankruptcy.
Enmark, M. Nelson, (BV) ... '37 '62 C.112 B.A. L.1066 LL.B. [M.N.Enmark]
Enmark M. Nelson, Inc., (BV) ... 3447 W. Shaw Ave.
Enright, Patrick L. ... '56 '84 C.645 B.S. L.464 J.D. 7108 N. Fresno St.

**Ericksen, Arbuthnot, Kilduff, Day & Lindstrom, Inc., (AV)**
**2440 West Shaw Avenue, Suite 101, 93711-3300**☉
**Telephone: 209-449-2600 Fax: 209-449-2603**
**Melvin K. Rube; R. Marc Stamper; Michael D. Ott.**
**General Civil, Trial and Appellate Practice in all State and Federal Courts. Corporate, Probate and Insurance Law.**
**Oakland, California Office: 530 Water Street, Port Building, Suite 720. Telephone: 510-832-7770. Fax: 510-832-0102.**
**San Francisco, California Office: 260 California Street, Suite 1100. Telephone: 415-362-7126. Fax: 415-362-6401.**
**Sacramento, California Office: 100 Howe Avenue, Suite 240N. Telephone: 916-483-5181. Fax: 916-483-7558.**
**San Jose, California Office: 152 North Third Street, Suite 700. Telephone: 408-286-0880. Fax: 408-286-0337.**
**Walnut Creek, California Office: 2700 Ygnacio Valley Road, Suite 280. Telephone: 510-947-1702. Fax: 510-947-4921.**
**Riverside, California Office: 1770 Iowa Avenue, Suite 210. Telephone: 909-682-3246. Fax: 909-682-4013.**
**Los Angeles, California Office: 835 Wilshire Boulevard, Suite 500. Telephone: 213-489-4411. Fax: 213-489-4332.**
*See Professional Biographies, FRESNO, CALIFORNIA*

**Esraelian, Robyn L.**, (BV) ... '55 '80 C.267 B.S. L.464 J.D. [Richardson,J.&E.]
*PRACTICE AREAS: Probate; Estate Planning; Corporate; Real Property Law.
Evans, Carl P. ... '22 '51 C&L.767 LL.B. Mun. Ct. J.
**Evans, David A.** ... '70 '96 C&L.112 B.A., J.D. [▣ McCormick,B.S.W.&C.]
*PRACTICE AREAS: Insurance Coverage.
**Everett, Reid H.**, (BV) ... '54 '81 C&L.101 B.A., J.D. [Perkins,M.&E.]
*LANGUAGES: German.
*PRACTICE AREAS: Agricultural Law; Real Property Law; Commercial Law; Secured Transactions; Creditors Rights.

**Ewell, A. Ben, Jr., (AV) '41 '66 C.473 B.A. L.1065 J.D.**
**516 West Shaw Avenue, Suite 200, 93704**
**Telephone: 209-221-2576 FAX: 209-221-2579**
**Water Supply, Water Rights and Regulatory Matters.**

**Fagen, Peter K.**, (CV) ... '60 '89 C.351 B.A. L.352 J.D. [Lozano S.S.W.&B.]
*PRACTICE AREAS: Insurance; Civil Rights; Labor and Employment; Public Agency Law.
Fain, Gregory T. ... '60 '86 C.147 B.S. L.464 J.D. Dep. Dist. Atty.
Faller, Carl M., Jr., (BV) ... '52 '76 C.990 B.A. L.426 J.D. Chf., U.S. Atty. Off.
Fannon, Michael ... '58 '93 C.537 B.B.A. L.464 J.D. 2115 Kern St.
Fanucchi, Edward D. ... '68 '95 C.267 B.S. L.1189 J.D. [▣ Quinlan,K.&F.]
Fanucchi, Edward L., (BV) ... '36 '67 C.267 A.B. L.1065 J.D. [Quinlan,K.&F.]
**Fernow, James B.** ... '68 '93 C&L.37 P.S., J.D. [▣ Lozano S.S.W.&B.]
**Fields, Michael R.** ... '69 '96 C.763 B.S. L.1049 J.D. [▣ McCormick,B.S.W.&C.]
*PRACTICE AREAS: General Litigation; Wrongful Termination; Third Party Insurance Defense.
**Fike, David A.**, (BV) ... '53 '80 C.112 B.A. L.61 J.D. [Emerich P.&F.]
*REPORTED CASES: Nelson v. City of Selma 881 F. 2d 836 (9th Cir. 1989).
*PRACTICE AREAS: Business Litigation; Municipal Law; Real Estate Law; Construction Law.
**Fipps, Roger E.**, (AV) ... '29 '57 C.112 A.B. L.1066 J.D. [Thomas,S.J.R.&A.]
*PRACTICE AREAS: Trusts and Estates; Estate Planning; Estate and Gift Taxation.

**Fischbach, Donald R.**, (AV) ... '47 '72 C.1074 B.S. L.1065 J.D. [Baker,M.&J.]
*PRACTICE AREAS: Litigation; Medical Malpractice Defense and Personal Injury.
Fisher, C. Jeffrey ... '46 '76 C.763 B.S. L.1065 J.D. [Cole,F.B.&C.]
Fisher, Clifford D. '56 '81 C.908 B.A. L.285 J.D.
(adm. in WA; not adm. in CA) 2326 Fresno St.‡
Fisher, Sheri M. ... '53 '91 C.267 B.S. L.1189 J.D. 3817 E. Swift Ave.
**Fishman, Robert G.**, (AV) ... '45 '70 C.473 B.A. L.1119 J.D. [Baker,M.&J.]
*LANGUAGES: German.
*PRACTICE AREAS: Taxation and Real Estate (60%).
Fiske, William S., (BV) ... '42 '69 C.112 B.A. L.1065 J.D. 1060 Fulton Mall
Fitch, John ... '32 '63 C.605 A.B. L.1066 J.D. Supr. Ct. J.
FitzGibbon, Geoffrey Scott '59 '89 C.112 B.A. L.1067 J.D.
Atty. Advsr. Spec. Asst. U.S. Atty., Small Bus. Admn.
**Fitzpatrick, Daniel T.** ... '58 '94 C.267 B.S. L.464 J.D. [Dowling,A.&K.]
*PRACTICE AREAS: Inverse Condemnation; Real Estate; Business Transactions; Labor Law; Probate and Trust Law.
**Flanigan, Philip M.** ... '59 '86 C.267 B.S. L.990 J.D. [McCormick,B.S.W.&C.]
*PRACTICE AREAS: Commercial Litigation; Insurance Coverage and Insurance Bad Faith.
Fletcher, Norman L. S. ... '37 '68 C.267 B.A. L.1065 J.D. [Fletcher&F.]
Fletcher & Fogderude, Inc. ... 5412 N. Palm
**Flewallen, David O.**, (BV) ... '49 '79 C.112 A.B. L.770 J.D. [Jacobson,H.N.&F.]
*PRACTICE AREAS: Insurance Defense Law.
Flierl, David E. '40 '67 C&L.107 B.S., LL.B.
Adm. Law J., Dept. of Health & Human Servs.
Flierl, Patricia Leary ... '35 '62 C.681 A.B. L.107 J.D. State Comp. Ins. Fund
**Floyd, Gregory A.** ... '69 '94 C.112 B.A. L.1065 J.D. [▣ McCormick,B.S.W.&C.]
*PRACTICE AREAS: Insurance Coverage and Bad Faith.
Fogderude, Eric K. ... '47 '76 C.267 B.S. L.464 J.D. [Fletcher&F.]
**Forbes, Donald R.**, (BV) ... '51 '78 C.112 B.A. L.1189 J.D. [Helon&M.]
*PRACTICE AREAS: Civil Litigation; Personal Injury.
Forbes, William E., (BV) ... '23 '52 C.267 A.B. L.1065 J.D. 135 W. Shaw
Ford, Richard T. ... '30 '59 C.267 B.A. L.1065 LL.B. U.S. Bkrptcy. J.
Forestiere, Nicholas P. ... '59 '86 C.1074 B.A. L.464 J.D. 5021 W. Shaw Ave.‡
**Forrest, Theodore R., Jr.**, (BV) ... '50 '77 C.619 B.S. L.1189 J.D. [Forrest&M.]
*PRACTICE AREAS: Business Litigation; Insurance Law; General Civil Trial and Appellate Practice; Unfair Competition; Labor and Employment Law.

**Forrest & McLaughlin, A Professional Corporation, (BV)**
**6790 North West Avenue, Suite 104, 93711**
**Mailing Address: P.O. Box 3317, Pinedale, California 93650-3317**
**Telephone: 209-261-9100 Telecopier: 209-261-9406**
**Theodore R. Forrest, Jr.; William T. McLaughlin, II;—Ronald A. Henderson; Kenton J. Klassen; James F. McBrearty; Steven D. Huff; Timothy R. Sullivan; Jerrald K. Pickering; Jeffrey Pierce Davis; Barbara S. Huff.**
**Business Law and Litigation, Insurance Law and Defense, General Civil Trial and Appellate Practice, Tax Law, Bankruptcy (Creditors); Landlord-Tenant Law, Administrative Law, Labor and Employment Law, Real Property Law, International Law; Business Planning, Corporate and Partnership Law, Commercial Law, Public Finance, Construction Law, Finance Law, Advertising Law, Agricultural Law, Environmental Law, Estate Planning and Probate, Unfair Competition, and Trade Secrets.**
*See Professional Biographies, FRESNO, CALIFORNIA*

Fortier, Terry D. ... '39 '76 C.767 B.S. L.1132 J.D. 3449 W. Franklin Ave.
**Foster, Daniel R.** ... '68 '95 C.1097 B.A. L.339 J.D. [▣ Kimble,M.&U.]
*PRACTICE AREAS: Business Litigation; Corporate Law.
Fourchy, Patrick L., (CV) ... '63 '90 C.112 B.A. L.770 J.D. 3716 N. 1st St.
**Frampton, Mary Louise**, (AV) ... '46 '72 C.103 B.A. L.309 J.D. [Frampton,H.W.&B.]
*PRACTICE AREAS: Labor and Employment Law; Civil Rights; Constitutional.

**Frampton, Hoppe, Williams & Boehm, A Professional Association, (AV)**
**Suite 110, Civic Center Square, 2444 Main Street, 93721-2256**
**Telephone: 209-486-5730**
**Mary Louise Frampton; Robert D. Hoppe; Thomas Boehm; Scott W. Williams. Of Counsel: James M. Kaprielian; Trevor C. Clegg; Kevin G. Little.**
**General Civil and Trial Practice in State and Federal Courts. Civil Appellate Practice, Personal Injury, Business and Commercial Transactions and Litigation, Bankruptcy, Antitrust, Commercial Landlord/Tenant, Criminal Defense, Environmental Law, Water Rights, Civil Rights, Equal Employment, Labor and Employment, ERISA and Health Care Law, Constitutional, Military, Negligence, Administrative.**
*See Professional Biographies, FRESNO, CALIFORNIA*

Francis, Burton J. ... '55 '84 C.112 B.A. L.284 J.D. Dep. Dist. Atty.
**Fransen, Kenneth J.**, (AV) ... '52 '77 C.267 B.A. L.1068 J.D. [Bolen,F.&B.]☉
*PRACTICE AREAS: Agricultural and Water Law; Business Law; Real Estate; Trusts and Estates.
**Franson, Donald R., Jr.**, (AV) ... '52 '78 C.112 A.B. L.1065 J.D. [Sagaser,H.F.&J.]
*REPORTED CASES: All-West Design, Inc. v. Boozer (1986); 183 Cal. App. 3d 1499, 228 Cal. Rptr. 736; Rose v. City of Coalinga (1987), 190 Ca. App. 3d 1627, 236 Cal. Rptr. 124; Stokes v. Dole Nut Co. (1995) 41 Cal.App. 4th 285; San Benito Foods v. Director of the Dept. of Food and Agricultural, State of Calif. (1996) 96 DAR 14097.
*PRACTICE AREAS: Agricultural Law; Business Litigation; Crop Damage Law; Lender Liability; Employment Litigation.
**Fraser, Bruce S.**, (BV) ... '52 '78 C.330 A.B. L.823 J.D. [Dowling,A.&K.]
*PRACTICE AREAS: Pension and Profit Sharing Law; Employee Benefits Law; Corporate Law; Qualified Domestic Relations Orders; Equipment Leasing Law.
Freed, Robert G., (BV) ... '43 '79 C.267 B.A. L.1132 J.D. Chf. Asst. Dist. Atty.
**French, G. Dana**, (BV) ... '51 '77 C.156 B.A. L.851 J.D. [Wild,C.&T.]
*PRACTICE AREAS: Business Transactions; Estate Planning; Tax; Real Estate; Corporations.
Frey, Richard W. ... '44 '72 C.267 B.A. L.1065 J.D. Sr. Dep. Dist. Atty.
Frye, Michael S. ... '62 '92 C.1288 B.A. L.464 J.D. 1260 Fulton Mall
**Gaab, Kimberly A.** ... '67 '93 C.112 B.S. L.1066 J.D. [Sagaser,H.F.&J.]
**Gabriele, Beverly A.** ... '49 '77 C.375 B.S. L.1097 J.D. [Mullen&F.]
Gadebusch, Rolf V. ... '26 '51 C&L.215 LL.B. 1624 W. Stuart‡
**Galtman, Richard B.** ... '63 '88 C.397 B.S. L.94 J.D. [▣ Lozano S.S.W.&B.]
*PRACTICE AREAS: Labor Law; Employment Law; ERISA; Agricultural Law; PACA Trust Enforcement.
Gamoian, Lisa M. ... '58 '86 C.267 B.S. L.1065 J.D. Dep. Dist Atty.
**Ganahl, John C.**, (BV) ... '44 '70 C.602 B.B.A. L.1067 J.D. [Dowling,A.&K.]
*PRACTICE AREAS: Business Transactions; Securities Law; Acquisition, Sale and Financing of Businesses; Health Care Law.
**Ganulin, James E.** ... '34 '60 C.112 B.S. L.1066 LL.B. [▣ Baker,M.&J.]
*PRACTICE AREAS: Water and Public Agency Law; Administrative Matters.
Garland, John F. ... '54 '85 C.109 B.A. L.1189 J.D. 1713 Tulare St.
Garvin, John ... '— '93 C.831 B.A. L.61 J.D. 2030 Fresno St., 8th Fl.

**Gates, Glen E., (BV) '52 '79 C.173 B.A. L.1189 J.D.**
**575 East Alluvial, Suite 105, 93720**
**Telephone: 209-432-0283 Facsimile: 209-432-6321**
***PRACTICE AREAS: Business Litigation; Bankruptcy Litigation; Personal Injury; Family Law.**
**Business Litigation, Creditor Representation in Bankruptcy Court and Family Law and Personal Injury.**
*See Professional Biographies, FRESNO, CALIFORNIA*

**Gauthier, Thomas E.** ... '70 '96 C&L.112 B.A., J.D. [▣ Lang,R.&P.]
Gee, Leroy V. ... '65 '90 C.112 B.A. L.352 J.D. Central Calif. Legal Servs.
Gelegan, John ... '14 '55 L.1007 LL.B. 5658 N. Nantucket‡
**Genda, Judd A.** ... '70 '96 C&L.966 B.A., J.D. [▣ McCormick,B.S.W.&C.]
*PRACTICE AREAS: Insurance Coverage; Bad Faith Litigation.

Gentile, Gary P. ...................... '51 '79 C.740 B.A. L.1137 J.D. [Hanna,B.M.M.&J.]
George, Cynthia F. '47 '79 C.112 B.A.M.A. L.1068 J.D.
Admin. Law J., State Unemploy. Ins. App. Bd.
Georgeson, C. Russell, (AV) ............ '47 '72 C.636 B.A. L.1067 J.D. [Georgeson&B.]
Georgeson & Belardinelli, (AV) ........................................ 575 E. Locust
**Georgouses, Thomas J.**, (BV) ....... '62 '90 C.267 B.S. L.1189 J.D. [Stammer,M.B.&B.]
*PRACTICE AREAS: Insurance Defense; Premises Liability; Professional Liability.
Gibson, Joyce ............ '30 '72 C.112 B.A. L.1132 J.D. 2511 W. Lake Van Ness Cir.
**Gilmore, David M.**, (BV) ........... '58 '82 C.112 A.B. L.464 J.D. [Thomas,S.J.R.&A.]
*REPORTED CASES: Estate of Berdrow (1992) 5 Cal. App. 4th 637; Mosesian v. Pennwalt Corp. (1987) 191 Cal. App. 3d 851; Producers Cotton Oil Co. v. Amstar Corp. (1988) 197 Cal. App. 3d 638.
*PRACTICE AREAS: Litigation; Appellate Practice; Business Law; Securities Litigation; Commercial Law.
Giovacchini, Robert A., (BV) .................. '50 '80 C.770 B.S. L.1189 J.D. 616 P. St.
Giovacchini, Thomas M., (BV) ........ '48 '78 C.770 B.A. L.1189 J.D. 700 E. Shaw Ave.
**Glasrud, Donald H., (Inc.)**, (AV) ........ '42 '69 C.267 A.B. L.1066 J.D. [Dietrich,G.&J.]
*PRACTICE AREAS: Unfair Competition; Media Law; Business and Construction Litigation.
Glassman, Robert B. ......................... '41 '68 C.446 B.S. L.64 J.D. Britz, Inc.
Goldberg, Michael, (BV) ......................... '47 '72 C.112 B.A. L.1068 J.D. 925 N. St.
**Goldring, Michael W.**, (BV) ............. '59 '89 C.800 B.S. L.1189 J.D. [Baker,M.&J.]
*PRACTICE AREAS: Real Property (Secured Transactions, Workouts); Intellectual Property; Health Care Law.
**Gollmer, Larry C.**, (BV) ............ '45 '71 C.112 B.A. L.800 J.D. [Parichan,R.C.&H.]
*PRACTICE AREAS: Corporate Law; Business Law; Probate Law.
Gomes, Gene M. .............................. '46 '72 C.267 B.A. L.464 J.D. Supr. Ct. J.
**Goodrich, Christine A.** ............ '58 '83 C.112 B.A. L.1068 J.D. [Lozano S.S.W.&B.]
*REPORTED CASES: American National Bank v. Peacock (1985) 165 Cal. App. 3d 1206.
*PRACTICE AREAS: Business Litigation; Creditors' Rights; Creditor Bankruptcy.
Goodwin, Hugh W. ..................... '21 '49 C.329 A.B. L.309 LL.B. Ret. Mun. Ct. J.

**Gordon, Dean B. '49 '74 C.1169 B.A. L.112 J.D.**
**1530 East Shaw Avenue, Suite 120, 93710**
**Telephone: 209-221-7777 Fax: 209-221-6812**
**Email: gordondb@lightspeed.net**
***PRACTICE AREAS: Personal Injury; Consumer Law; Juvenile; Criminal Defense.**
**Personal Injury, Consumer Law, Juvenile, Criminal Defense.**
*See Professional Biographies, FRESNO, CALIFORNIA*

**Gordon, Douglas L.** ..................... '61 '93 C.896 B.A. L.1065 J.D. [A Miles,S.&E.]
*PRACTICE AREAS: Plaintiffs Personal Injury Law and related Litigation.
**Gorman, Patrick J.** ............................ '61 '87 C.267 B.S. L.770 J.D. [Wild,C.&T.]
*PRACTICE AREAS: Construction and Business Litigation.
**Goss, David D.** ........................ '47 '95 C.1077 B.S. L.426 J.D. [B Blanco,T.&P.]
*PRACTICE AREAS: Corporate Law; Taxation; Estate Planning; Civil Litigation.
Gottlieb, David A. ........................ '62 '87 C.112 B.A. L.767 J.D. 2030 Fresno St.

**Graham & James LLP, (AV)**
**6051 North Fresno Street, Suite 200, 93710⊙**
**Telephone: 209-449-1400 Telecopier: 209-449-1454**
**Email: mcampos@gj.com URL: http://www.gj.com**
**Michael A. Campos. Resident Associate: Lee N. Smith.**
**Environmental, Toxic Tort, Water Law, Natural Resources Law and Litigation.**
**Other offices located in: San Francisco, Los Angeles, Orange County, Palo Alto and Sacramento, California; Seattle, Washington; Washington, D.C.; New York, New York; Milan, Italy; Beijing, China; Tokyo, Japan; London, England; Dusseldorf, Germany.**
**Associated Offices: Deacons Graham & James, Hong Kong, Sydney, Melbourne, Brisbane, Perth and Canberra, Australia.**
**Affiliated Offices: Deacons Graham & James, Hanoi and Ho Chi Minh City, Vietnam; Taipei, Taiwan and Bangkok, Thailand; In association with Dewi Soeharto & Rekan, Jakarta, Indonesia; Graham & James in affiliation with Taylor Joynson Garrett, London, England, Bucharest, Romania and Brussels, Belgium; Mishare M. Al-Ghazali & Partners, Safat, Kuwait; Law Firm of Salah, Al-Hejailan, Jeddah and Riyadh, Saudi Arabia.**
*See Professional Biographies, FRESNO, CALIFORNIA*

Green, Eric G. ............................ '45 '78 C.766 B.A. L.1189 J.D. Dep. Dist. Atty.
**Green, Gary L.** ....................... '60 '86 C.508 B.A. L.285 J.D. [Blumberg,S.&I.] ‡
*PRACTICE AREAS: Professional Malpractice Defense; Civil Litigation.
Green, H. Wayne ............................ '50 '78 C.878 B.S. L.464 J.D. 5070 N. 6th St.
**Greer, Russell D.** .................. '56 '81 C.267 B.S. L.800 J.D. [Caswell,B.H.B.&G.]
*PRACTICE AREAS: Insolvency; General Business; Real Estate; Estate Planning; Agricultural Law.
Gregory, Jas. V., (AV) ................ '26 '55 C.261 A.B. L.1065 J.D. 1318 E. Shaw Ave.
Grenfell, George A., Jr. ... '41 '70 C.740 B.S. L.1132 J.D. Asst. Dist. Atty., Co. of Fresno
**Griffin, Douglas E.** ..................... '58 '93 C.768 B.A. L.770 J.D. [A Lang,R.&P.]
*PRACTICE AREAS: Civil Litigation; Taxation; Probate and Estate Planning.
Gromis, David P. ........................ '50 '77 C.267 B.A. L.765 J.D. [Gromis&A.]
Gromis & Aguirre ................................................. 6700 N. First St.
Grunwald, Barbara Booth ............. '58 '83 C.547 B.A. L.813 J.D. Dep. Co. Coun.
**Guarino, Thomas P.** ........................... '60 '89 C.1330 B.A. L.45 J.D. [Myers&O.]
Gunderson, Blake J. .................. '56 '84 C.112 A.B. L.284 J.D. Dep. Dist. Atty.
Gunner, Kevin D. ........... '56 '87 C.267 B.S. L.1189 J.D. 1322 E. Shaw Ave., Ste. 400
Gysler, Randolph L. ............ '42 '79 C.608 Ph.D. L.1189 J.D. 842 E. Whitedove Lane
Haas, Douglas E., (BV) .............. '53 '82 C.911 B.A. L.1189 J.D. Sr. Dep. Dist. Atty.
Hager, Paul R., (BV) ............................ '43 '76 C.147 B.A. L.1189 J.D. [Hager,T.&M.]
Hager, Trippel & Macy, (BV) ........................................ 1322 E. Shaw Ave.
Hale, Garvin W. ............... '17 '52 C.378 A.B. L.770 LL.B. 4836 E. Belmont Ave.
Hamilton, David A., (BV) ...................... '53 '82 C&L.1137 B.S., J.D. Dep. Co. Coun.
Hamilton, Jeffrey Y., Jr. ................ '64 '93 C.1074 B.S. L.770 J.D. 5 River Pk. Pl. E.
Hamlin, Charles F. ........... '19 '46 C&L.893 B.A., LL.B. Ret. Asso. Jus., Ct. App.‡
Hamlin, W. Kent, (CV) ............. '55 '87 C.813 B.A. L.1065 J.D. 5 River Park Pl., E.
Hammerschmidt, Jeffrey T., (CV) ....... '60 '87 C.587 B.S. L.502 J.D. 5 River Park Pl. E.
**Hammond, Wesley J.** ......................... '55 '94 C.112 A.B. L.1189 J.D. [A Wild,C.&T.]
*PRACTICE AREAS: Real Estate Law.
Hancock, William F., Jr. .............. '52 '78 C.267 B.S. L.1189 J.D. 575 E. Locust Ave.
**Hanna, E. Mark** ........................ '65 '94 C.999 B.S. L.61 J.D. [A Barsamian&S.]
*PRACTICE AREAS: Labor Law; Employment Law; Agriculture Law; Workers' Compensation Discrimination.
Hanna, Brophy, MacLean, McAleer & Jensen, (AV)
6715 N. Palm Ave. (⊙San Fran., Sacramento, Oakland, Redding, Bakersfield, Santa Rosa, Salinas, Stockton & San Bernardino)
**Hansard, Wade M.**, (BV) ....... '51 '77 C.267 B.S. L.1065 J.D. [McCormick,B.S.W.&C.]
*PRACTICE AREAS: Representing Insurers in coverage Disputes and Bad Faith Litigation; Agent Errors and Omissions; Complex Litigation.
**Hansen, Kevin D.**, (BV) ........ '57 '85 C.267 B.S. L.1189 J.D. [McCormick,B.S.W.&C.]
*PRACTICE AREAS: First and Third Party Insurance Fraud; Bad Faith Law and Defense; First Party Insurance Coverage and Litigation; Arson, Tort and Insurance Defense; Product and Premises Liability Defense.
**Hansen, Leith B.**, (CV) .............. '56 '83 C.685 B.A. L.911 J.D. [Jacobson,H.N.&F.]
*REPORTED CASES: Governing Board of the Eldorado Union High School District v. Commission on Professional Competence, 1985, 171 Cal. App. 3d 324, 217 Cal. Rptr. 457; Lopez v. Sikkema, 229 CA 3d 780, 221 Cal Rpt. 840.
*PRACTICE AREAS: Insurance Defense Law; Insurance Coverage Law; Insurance Subrogation, Interpleader and Appeals.
**Hansen, Stephen A.**, (BV) .............. '43 '74 C.112 A.B. L.767 J.D. [Musick,P.&G.]
*PRACTICE AREAS: Healthcare; Hospitals; Corporate Law.

Hargrove, Richard H., (BV) ........... '37 '65 C.378 B.A. L.813 LL.B. 7108 N. Fresno St.
Harlow, Loren J. .................... '47 '82 C.679 B.S.C.E. L.1189 J.D. 6329 N. Benedict
Haron, Rodney C. ............................ '45 '74 C.267 B.S. L.1189 J.D. 1330 L St.
Harper, George E. ...................... '58 '87 C.267 B.A. L.464 J.D. 7555 N. Del Mar
Harralson, Daniel L., (CV) ...................... '51 '83 L.1189 J.D. 726 W. Barstow Ave.
Harrell, Arlan La Monte ........ '61 '92 C.112 A.B. L.1067 J.D. 5200 N. Palm Ave., 4th Fl.
**Harriman, Richard L.** ..................... '44 '75 C.813 B.A. L.112 J.D. [Wild,C.&T.]
*LANGUAGES: French.
Harris, Elaine J. ..................... '19 '73 C.267 B.A. L.1065 J.D. 1331 Lucerne Lane‡
**Harris, Richard A.**, (BV) .................. '47 '72 C.267 B.A. L.284 J.D. [Wild,C.&T.]
*PRACTICE AREAS: Tax; Family Law; Civil and Criminal Litigation.
Harris, Thomas A. ................. '39 '65 C.800 A.B. L.813 LL.B. Asso. Jus., Ct. of App.

**Hart, Katherine L., (BV) '42 '77 C.878 B.A. L.1189 J.D.**
**800 "M" Street, 93721**
**Telephone: 209-268-4021 Fax: 209-268-5446**
***LANGUAGES: French.**
***PRACTICE AREAS: Criminal Law; Labor and Employment.**
**Criminal Defense and Labor and Employment Law.**
*See Professional Biographies, FRESNO, CALIFORNIA*

Harter, Patricia S. ................................ '46 '95 L.1189 J.D. [A Quinlan,K.&F.]
**Harvey, Gary C.** ........................ '56 '88 C.999 B.A. L.1148 J.D. [Borton,P.&C.]
*PRACTICE AREAS: Insurance Defense; Construction Defect.
**Harvey, Ima Jean**, (BV) ................. '27 '75 C.112 L.1189 J.D. [Parichan,R.C.&H.]
*PRACTICE AREAS: Corporate; Business; Property; Agri-Business; Estate Planning.
**Hatmaker, Susan King** ................ '68 '94 C.267 B.S. L.464 J.D. [A Kimble,M.&U.]
*PRACTICE AREAS: Business Litigation; Employment Defense.
Haught, Rex A. ......... '55 '84 C.1232 B.A. L.464 J.D. Asst. V.P., Chicago Title Ins. Co.
Havlisch, Hal B. ............................ '46 '73 C.267 B.A. L.1132 J.D. 191 W. Shaw
Hayden, Geoffrey L. ...................... '46 '76 C.267 B.S. L.1132 J.D. Dep. City Atty.
**Hays, James N.**, (AV) ................. '25 '51 C&L.813 A.B., LL.B. [Stammer,M.B.&B.]
*PRACTICE AREAS: Products Liability Law; Insurance Coverage Law; Real Estate; Professional Liability; Construction Litigation.
**Hearst, Gayle D.** ...................... '62 '86 C.267 B.S. L.1067 J.D. [Baker,M.&J.]
*PRACTICE AREAS: Business Litigation; Medical Malpractice Defense and Construction Litigation.
**Heatter, Richard E.**, (CV) .......... '44 '89 C.724 B.A. L.1189 J.D. [A Dowling,A.&K.]
*PRACTICE AREAS: Business Litigation; Employment Litigation; Insurance Defense; Intellectual Property.
Heilbut, Philip R. ............................ '30 '80 C.878 L.1132 J.D. 4542 E. Vassar
Heller, Donald R. ........................................ '19 '50 L.800 LL.B. 3242 E. Swift‡
**Helon, Marvin E.**, (AV) ...................... '20 '48 C.629 B.S. L.813 J.D. [Helon&M.]
*PRACTICE AREAS: Estate Planning; Probate; Business Law; Municipal Law.
**Helon, Marvin T.**, (AV) ...................... '53 '78 C.267 B.A. L.1189 J.D. [Helon&M.]
*PRACTICE AREAS: Business Law; Real Estate Law; Estate Planning; Trusts; Probate.

**Helon & Manfredo, (AV)**
**Suite 180, 1318 East Shaw Avenue, 93710**
**Telephone: 209-226-4420 Fax: 209-226-1524**
**Email: helonman@ix.netcom.com**
**Members of Firm: Donald F. Manfredo (Retired); Marvin E. Helon; Marvin T. Helon; John M. McDaniel; Donald R. Forbes; Nicholas Louis Lucich, Jr. (Certified Specialist, Estate Planning, Trust and Probate Law, The State Bar of California Board of Legal Specialization).**
**General Civil and Trial Practice. Agribusiness, Business, Corporate and Real Estate Law. Probate, Trusts and Estate Planning, Personal Injury, Family Law, Domestic Relations and Municipal Law.**
*See Professional Biographies, FRESNO, CALIFORNIA*

**Hendershott, Gregory A.** .......... '66 '95 C.477 B.A. L.629 J.D. [A Littler,M.F.T.&M.]
Henderson, Richard C. '56 '82
C.940 B.A. L.1148 J.D. 1951 W. Gateway Blvd. (⊙Los Angeles)
**Henderson, Ronald A.**, (BV) ............ '50 '80 C.267 B.A. L.1189 J.D. [A Forrest&M.]
*PRACTICE AREAS: Tax Law; Business Planning; Corporate and Partnership Law; Commercial Law; Real Property.
Henry, Jerry E., (BV) ........................ '41 '74 C.768 B.A. L.1189 J.D. [J.E.Henry]⊙
Henry, Stephen R. ................... '36 '69 C.169 B.A. L.1132 J.D. Supr. Ct. J.
Henry, Jerry E., Inc., (BV) ........................................ 2445 Capitol St. (⊙Kerman)
Herbert, Edwin L. '50 '75 C.602 B.A. L.608 J.D.
(adm. in OH; not adm. in CA) Exec. V.P. & Gen. Coun., Vallicorp Holdings, Inc.
**Hertz, Michael T.**, (AV) ...................... '44 '71 C.668 B.S. L.309 J.D. [Lang,R.&P.]
*PRACTICE AREAS: Bankruptcy Law; Debtor-Creditor Practice.
Heslin, Thomas ......................... '49 '77 C&L.767 B.A., J.D. 6715 N. Palm Ave.
**Heyman, Kent F.**, (AV) ................ '55 '80 C.267 B.A. L.464 J.D. [Heyman,K.&M.]
*PRACTICE AREAS: Agricultural Law; Airline Labor Law; Employment Litigation; Telecommunications Law.

**Heyman, Kerkorian & Magarian, (AV)**
**6425 North Palm Avenue, Suite 104, 93704**
**Telephone: 209-261-9300 Fax: 209-261-9305**
**Kent F. Heyman; John G. Kerkorian; Mark D. Magarian. Associate: Brady K. McGuinness. Of Counsel: Donald J. Magarian.**
**Civil Litigation, Employment Law and Family Law.**
*See Professional Biographies, FRESNO, CALIFORNIA*

**Hiber, Edwin H., (AV) '23 '50 C.350 B.Sc. L.546 J.D.**
**108 East Terrace, 93704**
**Telephone: 209-227-9095**
***PRACTICE AREAS: Real Estate; Construction Law; Business Litigation.**
**General Civil and Trial Practice, State and Federal Courts. Corporation, Business, Real Property, Construction and Probate Law.**

Hill, Floyd S., (BV) .................. '30 '61 C.267 A.B. L.770 J.D. 5151 N. Palm Ave.
Hill, Rachel W. ...................... '63 '90 C.1350 B.A. L.602 J.D. 5 River Pk. Pl. E.
**Hillison, Robert K.**, (AV) ........ '39 '65 C.112 B.A. L.1068 LL.B. [Caswell,B.H.B.&G.]
*PRACTICE AREAS: Business, Real Estate and Commercial Litigation; Real Estate.
Hinkly, Paul R., (BV) ...................... '48 '78 C.628 B.S. L.1189 J.D. Dep. Pub. Def.
**Hipp, Spencer H.** ........................ '47 '79 C.311 B.A. L.464 J.D. [Littler,M.F.T.&M.]
Hiyama, Dean Harvo ..................... '56 '81 C.267 B.S. L.426 J.D. 1060 Fulton Mall
Hoar, Leonard C., Jr. .................. '29 '67 C.813 B.A. L.1132 J.D. 3948 E. Gettysburg‡
Hobson, Mary L., (AVⓉ) '49 '80 C&L.986 B.B.A., J.D.
(adm. in MO; not adm. in CA) V.P., Admin. & Gen. Coun., Cal Emblem Labels, Inc.
Hoffman, Bert C., Jr., (BV) .......... '39 '70 C.1109 B.A. L.1049 J.D. 230 W. Hubert Ct.
**Hoffman, Matthew Earl** ................ '68 '94 C.112 B.S. L.1065 J.D. [A Baker,M.&J.]
*PRACTICE AREAS: Business; Taxation.
**Hogan, Michael J.**, (AV) ................ '48 '75 C&L.767 B.A., J.D. [Littler,M.F.T.&M.]
**Holder, Glenn J.**, (BV) ........................ '50 '88 C.770 B.S. L.1189 J.D. [Baker,M.&J.]
*PRACTICE AREAS: Environmental Law; Employment Law; Civil Litigation; Bankruptcy.
**Holford, Maureen P.** ............................ '51 '92 L.1189 J.D. [A Parichan,R.C.&H.]
*PRACTICE AREAS: Products Liability; Insurance Defense.
**Holland, David E.** ........................ '68 '92 C&L.1067 B.A., J.D. [A Baker,M.&J.]
*PRACTICE AREAS: Agribusiness; Real Property; Reclamation; Water Law; Public Agency Law.
Holtz, Thomas L., Jr. ................... '65 '92 C.473 B.A. L.347 J.D. 5 River Pk. Pl. E.
Home, W. Stuart, II, (CV) ............. '37 '66 C.112 B.A. L.1065 J.D. 1221 Van Ness Ave.
Homola, James R. ................... '46 '74 C.1042 B.A. L.1049 J.D. 2950 Mariposa St.
Hooper, Elvoyce ........................ '42 '75 C.112 B.A. L.426 J.D. Dep. Dist. Atty.

CAA97P

CALIFORNIA—FRESNO MARTINDALE-HUBBELL LAW DIRECTORY 1997

**Hoppe, Robert D.**, (BV) ............ '41 '74 C.911 B.A. L.950 J.D. [Frampton,H.W.&B.]
*PRACTICE AREAS: Business and Agricultural Litigation; Criminal Defense.
**Hoppe, Theodore W.**, (BV) ............... '63 '88 C.859 B.A. L.546 J.D. [Cooper&H.]⊙
*PRACTICE AREAS: Insurance Coverage; Personal Injury Defense; Business Litigation.
**Horowitt, Darryl J.** ..................... '56 '81 C.1042 A.B. L.1137 J.D. [Coleman&H.]
*REPORTED CASES: In Re UFW (1989) 15 ALRB 10.
*PRACTICE AREAS: Business Litigation; Commercial Litigation; Real Estate Litigation; Construction Litigation; Banking Litigation.
Horwitz, Clint H. ............ '56 '82 C.112 A.B. L.809 J.D. Sen. Atty., State Ct. of Appl.
**Hose, J. Russell** .................. '47 '72 C.112 B.A. L.809 J.D. [Ⓒ Caswell,B.H.B.&G.]
*LANGUAGES: Spanish.
*PRACTICE AREAS: Business Transactions; Real Estate Transactions; Agricultural Law (Water PACA); Debtor/Creditor Transactions.
**Houghton, Craig A.**, (BV) ............... '54 '79 C.763 B.A. L.1065 J.D. [Baker,M.&J.]
*PRACTICE AREAS: Corporate Partnership and Real Estate Tax Planning; Federal and State Tax Litigation; Mergers and Acquisitions.
Howe, Earnest, (CV) ...................................... '39 '73 2491 W. Shaw Ave.

**Hrdlicka, Steven R., & Associates, (CV) '58 '85 C.267 B.A. L.1189 J.D.**
**2115 Kern, Suite 206, 93721**
**Telephone: 209-485-1453 Fax: 209-485-2356**
**Landlord-Tenant, Collection, Adoption.**
***See Professional Biographies, FRESNO, CALIFORNIA***

**Huff, Barbara S.** ............................ '48 '90 C.768 B.A. L.1049 J.D. [Ⓐ Forrest&M.]
*PRACTICE AREAS: Civil Litigation; Employment Law.
**Huff, Steven D.** ......................... '50 '90 C.1056 B.A. L.1049 J.D. [Ⓐ Forrest&M.]
*PRACTICE AREAS: Business Litigation; General Civil Trial and Appellate Practice; Insurance Law and Defense; Finance Law; Business Transactions.
**Hughes, Michael J.**, (BV) ............. '47 '74 C.769 B.A. L.1065 J.D. [Berding&W.]⊙
Humpal, LeRoy C. ................. '37 '67 C.350 B.S. L.1065 J.D. 2017 N. Gateway Blvd.
Humphry, Steven K., (CV) .......... '50 '77 C.220 B.A. L.1065 J.D. 10 River Pk. Pl. E.
Hunt, Edward W., (BV) .................. '42 '74 C.267 B.S. L.1189 J.D. Dist. Atty.

**Hurley, James M., (BV) '55 '80 C.169 B.A. L.800 J.D.**
**1396 West Herndon, Suite 106, 93711**
**Telephone: 209-449-7601 Facsimile: 209-449-7605**
**Civil Litigation, Insurance Defense, Personal Injury, and Products Liability.**
***See Professional Biographies, FRESNO, CALIFORNIA***

**Huss, Gary L.**, (BV) ........................ '47 '73 C.768 B.A. L.770 J.D. [Wild,C.&T.]
*SPECIAL AGENCIES: State Bar Commission on Criminal Law Specialization.
*PRACTICE AREAS: White Collar Criminal Defense; Department of Motor Vehicles Litigation; General Business Litigation; Agricultural Litigation; Administrative Licensing Litigation.
Hutchings, Chrys A. .................... '64 '92 C.788 A.B. L.94 J.D. 5260 N. Palm Ave.
Ice, G. Brooks ......................... '11 '52 C.768 A.B. L.1065 J.D. Ret. Supr. Ct. J.
**Ichishta, Kristin L.** .......... '69 '94 C.112 B.A. L.770 J.D. [Ⓐ McCormick,B.S.W.&C.]
*PRACTICE AREAS: Insurance Coverage; Bad Faith; Insurance Defense.

**Idiart, Michael G., (BV) '50 '75 C.740 B.A. L.1067 J.D.**
**2333 Merced Street, 93721**
**Telephone: 209-442-0634 FAX: 209-233-6947**
**(Certified Specialist, Criminal Law, The State Bar of California Board of Legal Specialization).**
***LANGUAGES: Spanish.**
**Criminal Defense and Personal Injury.**
***See Professional Biographies, FRESNO, CALIFORNIA***

Igoa, Joseph A. ................ '46 '72 C.767 B.A. L.1065 J.D. 3585 W. Beechwood Ave.
**Ikeda, Dale**, (BV) ...................... '51 '76 C.813 B.A. L.1067 J.D. [Blumberg,S.&I.]
*PRACTICE AREAS: Business Law; Real Estate Law; Professional Malpractice Defense.
**Irwin, William P.**, (AV) .......... '27 '54 C.228 A.B. L.813 LL.B. Pres., Golf West Cos.
*RESPONSIBILITIES: Golf Course Development; Real Estate Development Law; Business Law; Probate Law; Estate Planning.
**Isaac, Thomas W.** ..................... '52 '80 C.267 B.A. L.61 J.D. [Dietrich,G.&J.]
*PRACTICE AREAS: Bankruptcy (Creditors) Law; Commercial Litigation; Savings and Loan Law; Title Insurance; Escrow Law.
Ishikawa, Jin ........................... '15 '41 C.112 B.A. L.1066 LL.B. 1433 Kern St.
Ishikawa, Robert ........................ '51 '79 C.800 B.A. L.809 J.D. 2300 Tulare St.
Jackson, Caroline V. ................... '54 '90 C.1073 B.S. L.765 J.D. 6715 N. Palm Ave.
Jackson, Donald A., (AV) .................. '36 '62 C.37 B.S. L.813 J.D. [Jackson P.&N.]
Jackson Phillips & Nahigian, A Professional Corporation, (AV)
246 West Shaw Avenue, Suite 100
**Jacobson, Lee M.**, (BV) ............. '55 '80 C.112 B.A. L.770 J.D. [Jacobson,H.N.&F.]
*REPORTED CASES: Haldeman v. Boise Cascade, 176 Cal. App. 3d 230 221 Cal. RPTR 412 (1985).
*PRACTICE AREAS: Civil Litigation; Insurance Defense Law.

**Jacobson, Hansen, Najarian & Flewallen, A Professional Corporation, (BV)**
**6715 North Palm Avenue Suite 201, 93704-1073**
**Telephone: 209-448-0400 Telephone: 209-448-0123**
**Lee M. Jacobson; Leith B. Hansen; Jube J. Najarian; David O. Flewallen; Keith C. Rickelman.**
**Civil Litigation emphasizing Insurance Defense.**
**Representative Clients: Allstate Insurance Co.; American Specialty Insurance Co.; Atlantic Mutual Insurance Co.; Circle K Corp.; Condor Insurance Co.; Farmers Insurance Exchange; Financial Indemnity Co.; Fireman's Fund Insurance Co.; GAB Business Services: Hartford Insurance Co.**
***See Professional Biographies, FRESNO, CALIFORNIA***

**Jaech, Jeffrey A.**, (BV) .................. '53 '77 C.906 B.A. L.1066 J.D. [Baker,M.&J.]
*PRACTICE AREAS: Probate and Trust Administration; Estate Planning; White-collar Criminal.
**Jamison, Daniel O.**, (AV) .............. '52 '77 C.112 A.B. L.1067 J.D. [Sagaser,H.F.&J.]
*REPORTED CASES: Madera Community Hospital v. County of Madera, 155 Cal. App. 3d 136 (1984); Turpin v. Sortini, 31 Cal. 3d 220 (1982); Mateo-Woodburn v. Fresno Community Hospital 221 Cal. App. 3d 1169 (1990); Paredes v. County of Fresno 203 Cal. App. 3d 1 (1988).
*PRACTICE AREAS: Hospital Law; Health Care Law; Antitrust Law; Real Estate; Business Litigation.
**Jamison, Oliver M.**, (AV) ........... '16 '41 C&L.813 A.B., J.D. [Thomas,S.J.R.&A.] ‡
Jay, Philip M. ............................. '52 '79 C.1131 B.A. L.61 J.D. Dist. Coun.
**Jenkins, David R.**, (BV) .......... '55 '80 C.740 B.A. L.1067 J.D. [Motschiedler,M.&W.]
*PRACTICE AREAS: Bankruptcy Law; Debtor/Creditor Practice.
**Jensen, Douglas B.**, (AV) .................... '43 '67 C&L.813 A.B., J.D. [Baker,M.&J.]
*LANGUAGES: Spanish.
*PRACTICE AREAS: Water Law; Real Estate; Water Law (50%); Real Estate (30%).
Jensen, Rick E. ..................... '49 '75 C.112 B.A. L.1065 J.D. 7295 N. Sequoia Dr.
Johnsen, Walter C. ...................................... '49 '74 L.1189 2333 Merced St.
Johnson, Bruce B., Jr. .................... '62 '89 C.267 B.S. L.1067 J.D. Dep. Co. Coun.
**Johnson, Carey H.**, (AV) ............. '42 '67 C&L.767 B.S., LL.B. [Stammer,M.B.&B.]
*PRACTICE AREAS: Medical Malpractice; Civil Trial Practice; Personal Injury Law; Insurance Defense.
Johnson, Jack D. ................. '48 '75 C.267 B.A. L.1189 J.D. 6358 N. Poplar Ave.‡
Johnson, John J. ..................... '33 '74 C.1042 B.S. L.1137 J.D. P.O. Box 5314
Johnson, Leslie A. .................... '67 '95 C.37 B.A. L.378 J.D. 5 River Pk. Pl. E.
Johnson, Roger A. ................... '61 '91 C.1310 B.A. L.378 J.D. 5 River Pk. Pl. E.
Johnston, Guy W. .................. '27 '64 C&L.285 B.B.Ad., J.D. 1255 W. Shaw Ave.
Jones, Franklin P. ........................ '35 '65 C.674 A.B. L.1066 LL.B. Supr. Ct. J.
Jones, Ida Mae ........ '53 '78 C.190 B.S. L.569 J.D. Prof. of Bus. Law, Calif. State Univ.
**Jones, Jerry D.** .......................... '51 '76 C.267 B.A. L.602 J.D. [Stammer,M.B.&B.]
*PRACTICE AREAS: Professional Liability; Health Care Law; Business Litigation; Products Liability; Criminal Law.

**Jones, Robert L., Jr., (Inc.)**, (BV) .... '47 '72 C.169 B.A. L.1067 J.D. [Richardson,J.&E.]
*PRACTICE AREAS: Taxation; Probate and Estate Planning; Corporate; Pension and Profit Sharing; Real Property.
**Jones, Timothy**, (BV) .......... '59 '85 C.267 B.S. L.1049 J.D. [McCormick,B.S.W.&C.]
*PRACTICE AREAS: Environmental Litigation.
**Jones, Vreeland O., (Inc.)**, (AV) ......... '45 '76 C.282 B.A. L.464 J.D. [Dietrich,G.&J.]
*PRACTICE AREAS: Business Transactions; Health Care Law; Real Estate Law.
Jordan, William J. ..................... '47 '77 C.768 B.A. L.464 J.D. State Comp. Ins. Fund
**Jory, Jay V.**, (AV) ............................ '46 '72 C.112 B.A. L.1067 J.D. [Jory,P.W.&S.]
*PRACTICE AREAS: Labor (Management) Law; Employment Law; Labor Negotiations; Wage and Hour Law; Employment Discrimination Law.

**Jory, Peterson, Watkins & Smith, (AV) BB**
**555 West Shaw, Suite C-1, P.O. Box 5394, 93755**
**Telephone: 209-225-6700 Telecopier: 209-225-3416**
**Members of Firm: Jay V. Jory; John E. Peterson; Cal B. Watkins, Jr.; Michael Jens F. Smith; Marcia A. Ross; William M. Woolman. Associates: John J. Stander; Jeff W. Reisig; Carla M. McCormack; Matthew D. Ruyak.**
**Civil Trial and Appellate Practice in all State and Federal Courts. Commercial Litigation, Labor Relations Law, Agricultural Labor, Equal Employment, Wage and Hour, Wrongful Discharge Law and Insurance Coverage Litigation.**
**Reference: Valliwide Bank.**
***See Professional Biographies, FRESNO, CALIFORNIA***

Joy, Maurice E. ............................ '45 '73 C.267 B.S. L.284 J.D. 1221 Van Ness
**Jurkovich, Michael J.** ..................... '55 '90 C.267 B.S. L.1189 J.D. [Kimble,M.&U.]
*REPORTED CASES: Kruser v. Bank of America NT & SA (1991) 230 Cal.App.3d 741.
*PRACTICE AREAS: General Business Litigation; Construction Law.
Kalemkarian, David C., (BV) ............. '62 '89 C.267 B.S. L.1066 J.D. 371 E. Bullard
Kalemkarian, Stephen A., (Inc.), (AV) ... '31 '68 C.267 A.B. L.1066 LL.B. 371 E. Bullard
Kalfayan, Garo .......................... '56 '83 C.112 B.S. L.1068 J.D. Prof., Calif. State Univ.
Kandler, Edward R. .................. '49 '81 C.766 B.A. L.1067 J.D. Off. of U.S. Trustee
**Kane, Jeffrey P.**, (AV) .................. '51 '77 C.112 A.B. L.1068 J.D. [Kane,M.&M.]
*PRACTICE AREAS: Business Transactions; Corporate Law; Taxation Law; Trusts, Estate Planning and Probate Law; Real Estate Transactions.
Kane, Stephen J. ................................ '52 '76 C.602 B.A. L.1065 J.D. Supr. Ct. J.

**Kane, McClean & Mengshol, (AV)**
**1530 East Shaw Avenue, Suite 118, 93710**
**Telephone: 209-227-7200 Fax: 209-227-4527**
**Members of Firm: John G. Mengshol; Steven M. McClean; Jeffrey P. Kane.**
**General Civil, Trial and Appellate Practice, all Courts. Taxation (Federal and State). Corporation, Commercial, Securities, Trusts, Probate and Estate Planning and Real Estate Law.**
***See Professional Biographies, FRESNO, CALIFORNIA***

**Kanne, Francine Marie**, (BV) .......... '54 '88 C.267 A.S. L.1189 J.D. [Dowling,A.&K.]
*PRACTICE AREAS: Insurance Defense; Environmental; Business Litigation.
**Kaprielian, James M.** ............. '55 '82 C.112 B.A. L.464 J.D. [Ⓒ Frampton,H.W.&B.]
*PRACTICE AREAS: Business and Agricultural Litigation; Business and Real Estate Transaction.
Karr, F. John, (BV) ................................ '28 '55 C.112 L.1065 J.D. 5151 N. Palm Ave.
**Kaufmann, Bertram T.** ................ '62 '90 C.1333 B.S. L.1066 J.D. [Wild,C.&T.]
*PRACTICE AREAS: Agribusiness; Aviation; Business Transactions; Commercial Law; Real Property.
Kay, Kenneth Dean ..................... '53 '80 C.267 B.S. L.464 J.D. 7740 N. Fresno St.
**Keeler, William J., Jr.**, (AV) .......... '48 '73 C.602 B.A. L.800 J.D. [Dowling,A.&K.]
*PRACTICE AREAS: Estate Planning Law; Probate and Trust Law; Estate Litigation.
Keeling, Daniel L. ......................... '50 '80 C.1079 B.A. L.1067 J.D. 1330 E. Shaw Ave.
Keeling, Roy D. ........................ '48 '77 C.267 B.A. L.464 J.D. [McMurchie,F.B.W.&L.]
**Kelley, Bruce W.** ............ '64 '93 C.627 B.A. L.546 J.D. [Ⓐ McCormick,B.S.W.&C.]
*LANGUAGES: Spanish.
*PRACTICE AREAS: Tort, Copyright and Water Law.
Kelley, H. Lloyd, III '40 '67 C.734 B.S. L.802 LL.B.
(adm. in TX; not adm. in CA) 900 Civic Ctr., Bldg. III‡
Kelso, Walter P., Jr., (BV) .................. '33 '61 C.267 A.B. L.813 J.D. [W.P.Kelso Jr.]
Kelso, Walter P., Jr. Inc., (BV) ............................................ 1665 W. Shaw
Kemp, Deborah J. '51 '81 C&L.260 B.A., J.D.
(adm. in FL; not adm. in CA) Calif. State Univ.
Kemp-Williams, Margaret E., (BV) ............. '48 '83 C.139 B.A. L.966 J.D. 1705 L St.

**Kenkel, Lawrence B. '49 '80 C.150 B.S.C.E. L.734 J.D.**
**West Shaw Financial Park, 2499 West Shaw Avenue, Suite 103, P.O. Box 9429, 93792-9429**
**Telephone: 209-228-6171 Fax: 209-229-3525**
**Bankruptcy Law and Debtor/Creditor Relations**
***See Professional Biographies, FRESNO, CALIFORNIA***

Keppler, Mark J. '57 '84 C.1044 B.S. L.966 J.D.
(adm. in WI; not adm. in CA) California State Univ.
Kerkorian, Gary ................................ '30 '58 C.813 B.A. L.276 J.D. Supr. Ct. J.
**Kerkorian, John G.**, (BV) ................. '62 '88 C.813 A.B. L.36 J.D. [Heyman,K.&M.]
*PRACTICE AREAS: Professional Malpractice Defense; Business Litigation; Employment Litigation.
Kern, Richard J., (BV) ............ '52 '78 C.740 B.A. L.765 J.D. 8483 N. Millbrook Ave.
Kern, Sue E. .......................... '51 '90 C.1350 B.A. L.564 J.D. Resch. Atty., Supr. Ct.
Kershaw, Michael, (BV) ................. '23 '52 C.267 B.A. L.1065 LL.B. [Quinlan,K.&F.]
Kessler, Wilbur K. ........................ '26 '53 C.112 B.A. L.1065 J.D. Ret. Supr. Ct. J.
Keyes, D. Dwayne ........................................ '32 '63 C.940 B.A. L.767 Supr. Ct. J.
Kimball, Robert L., (BV) ............ '35 '63 C.112 B.S. L.1066 LL.B. 1233 W. Shaw Ave.

**Kimble, MacMichael & Upton, A Professional Corporation, (AV) BB**
**Fig Garden Financial Center, 5260 North Palm Avenue, Suite 221, P.O. Box 9489, 93792-9489**
**Telephone: 209-435-5500 Telecopier: 209-435-1500**
**Email: kmu@primenet.com**
**Joseph C. Kimble (1910-1972); Thomas A. MacMichael (1920-1990); Jon Wallace Upton; Robert E. Bergin (Certified Specialist, Taxation Law, The State Bar of California Board of Legal Specialization); Jeffrey G. Boswell; Steven D. McGee; Robert E. Ward (Certified Specialist, Taxation Law, The State Bar of California Board of Legal Specialization); John P. Eleazarian; Robert H. Scribner; Michael E. Moss; Mark D. Miller; Michael F. Tatham; W. Richard Lee; D. Tyler Tharpe; Sylvia Halkousis Coyle; S. Brett Sutton; Michael J. Jurkovich;—Douglas V. Thornton; Robert William Branch; Donald J. Pool; Susan King Hatmaker; Lawrence J. Salisbury; Daniel R. Foster; Meredith E. Allen. Of Counsel: Mary Ann Bluhm.**
**Civil, Trial and Appellate Practice in all Courts with Emphasis in Business, Construction and Environmental Litigation, Real Estate, Bank Securities, Lender and Creditors Rights, Bankruptcy, Secured Lending, Banking, Federal and State Income, Gift and Estate Tax, Securities, Antitrust, Corporation and Probate and Estate Planning, Patent, Trademark and Copyright, Water Rights, Environmental Law, Employee Benefits Law, Products Liability Defense, ERISA Litigation, Employment Defense, Administrative and Health Care Law.**
***See Professional Biographies, FRESNO, CALIFORNIA***

Kinney, Ernest S., (BV) ................ '44 '75 C.267 B.A. L.1189 J.D. 1060 Fulton Mall
Kinzel, Anne .............................. '56 '87 C.112 B.A. L.1189 J.D. Dep. Co. Coun.
Kiraly, John Z. ....................... '29 '65 C.267 A.B. L.1132 4527 E. Cortland Ave.‡
**Klassen, Kenton J.** ..................... '60 '86 C.112 A.B. L.1065 J.D. [Ⓐ Forrest&M.]
*PRACTICE AREAS: Business Litigation; Insurance Law and Defense; Landlord-Tenant Law; Environmental Law; General Civil Trial Practice.
Klawitter, Jason W. ..................... '69 '95 C.154 B.A. L.770 J.D. 5250 N. Palm Ave.
Klein, Robert N. ...................... '45 '74 C&L.813 B.A., J.D. 6790 N. West Ave.‡

**Klingenberger, Daniel K.** ........ '56 '87 C.190 B.S.B.A. L.464 J.D. [Littler,M.F.T.&M.]
**Klug, Kenneth M.**, (AV) .......... '47 '73 C.112 A.B. L.1065 J.D. [McGregor,D.S.&K.]
*PRACTICE AREAS: Probate Law; Estate Planning Law; Trust Administration Law.
Knowles, David E. ........................ '56 '85 C.267 B.A. L.990 J.D. Dep. Dist. Atty.
**Knudsen, Stephen T.**, (BV) ........ '47 '73 C.154 B.A. L.1066 LL.B. [Parichan,R.C.&H.]
*PRACTICE AREAS: Insurance Defense Law; Products Liability Law.
**Knudson, David N.**, (BV) ............... '51 '81 C.766 B.A. L.1065 J.D. [D.N.Knudson]
*PRACTICE AREAS: Estate Planning; Probate; Taxation and Corporate Law.

**Knudson, David N., A Professional Corporation, (BV)**
**East Shaw Court, 1180 East Shaw, Suite 214, 93710-7812**
**Telephone: 209-228-8196 Facsimile: 209-228-0327**
**David N. Knudson (Certified Specialist, Probate, Estate Planning and Trust Law, The State Bar of California Board of Legal Specialization).**
**Estate Planning, Probate and Trust Law.**
***See Professional Biographies, FRESNO, CALIFORNIA***

Koczanowicz, Martin David ..................... '56 '87 C.763 L.398 J.D. Dep. City Atty.
Koligian, Robert, Jr. ..................... '51 '76 C.813 B.A. L.464 J.D. 1100 W. Shaw Ave.
Kolligian, Leo S., (BV) .......... '17 '41 C.267 B.A. L.1066 LL.B. 1100 W. Shaw Ave.‡
**Kopp, Philip David**, (AV) ........... '50 '79 C.1253 B.A. L.1068 J.D. [Dowling,A.&K.]
*PRACTICE AREAS: Business as Commercial Litigation; Water Rights; Environmental Litigation; Intellectual Property Litigation.
Kopsinis, John N. .......................... '36 '69 C.806 B.A. L.1026 LL.B. 2913 Tulare St.
Korotie, Donna Marie ... '28 '85 C.267 A.A. L.1189 LL.D. Law Clk. to U.S. Sr. Dist. Ct.J.
**Kraft, Gary B.** ..................... '66 '96 C&L.37 B.A., J.D. [Ⓐ McCormick,B.S.W.&C.]
*PRACTICE AREAS: Business Litigation; Insurance Defense.
**Krause, Randall J.**, (BV) ................ '61 '87 C.114 B.A. L.1065 J.D. [Baker,M.&J.]
*PRACTICE AREAS: Environmental - Regulatory; Environmental - Litigation.
Kravitz, Judy N. ......................... '52 '77 C.1044 B.A. L.1066 J.D. 1551 E. Shaw Ave.
**Krazan, Tamanee A** ...................... '53 '86 C.267 B.A. L.1189 J.D. [Ⓐ Mullen&F.]
*PRACTICE AREAS: Workers' Compensation Law.
**Krbechek, Randolf**, (BV) ........... '61 '89 C.494 B.A. L.945 J.D. [Caswell,B.H.B.&G.]
*REPORTED CASES: Estate of Berdrow (1992) 5 Cal. App. 4th 637; CTC Food International, Inc. v. PG&E (1992) 45 Cal. Public Utilities Comm. 2d 66 (CPUC).
*PRACTICE AREAS: Business Law; Contracts; Uniform Commercial Code; Real Estate; Business Litigation.
Krebs, John ...................................... '26 '57 C.112 B.A. L.1065 J.D. 1383 W. Sample‡
Krieg, William M., (BV) ........................ '48 '75 C.267 B.A. L.464 J.D. 1330 "L" St.
Krum, Eugene W. .................................. '31 '65 C.267 B.S. L.765 LL.B. Supr. Ct. J.
Krum, Richard W. ........................ '53 '80 C.1075 B.A. L.770 J.D. [Hanna,B.M.M.&J.]
**Kruthers, Mark D.** ..................... '69 '95 C.112 B.A. L.770 J.D. [Ⓐ Dowling,A.&K.]
*PRACTICE AREAS: Business Litigation; Insurance Defense; Environmental Litigation.
**Kunkel, Michelle E.** ........................ '68 '93 C.112 B.A. L.770 J.D. [Ⓐ Blumberg,S.&I.]
*PRACTICE AREAS: Professional Malpractice Defense; Civil Litigation.
Kuwamoto, Arthur T. ........................ '52 '78 C.112 A.B. L.1067 J.D. [Hanna,B.M.M.&J.]
Ladd, Dorin J. ........................ '39 '69 C.267 B.S. L.1065 J.D. Chief Dep. Dist. Atty.
**LaFollette, James E.**, (AV) ....... '28 '59 C.267 A.B. L.1065 J.D. [Ⓑ Thomas,S.J.R.&A.]
*PRACTICE AREAS: Business Litigation; Products Liability Litigation; Appellate Practice.
Lagrand, Charles D. ........................ '43 '75 C.112 B.S. L.990 J.D. Dep. Dist. Atty.
Lambe, James P., (BV) ..................... '52 '77 C.477 A.B. L.339 J.D. Dep. Pub. Def.
**Landen, Robert K.** ........... '62 '90 C.945 B.A. L.966 J.D. [Ⓐ McCormick,B.S.W.&C.]
*PRACTICE AREAS: Insurance Coverage.
**Lang, Frank H.**, (AV) ..................... '36 '62 C.267 B.A. L.1066 LL.B. [Lang,R.&P.]
*PRACTICE AREAS: Insolvency Law; Debtor Creditor Practice.

**Lang, Richert & Patch, A Professional Corporation, (AV) BR**
**Fig Garden Financial Center, 5200 North Palm Avenue, 4th Floor, P.O. Box 40012, 93755**
**Telephone: 209-228-6700 Fax: 209-228-6727**
**Frank H. Lang; William T. Richert (1937-1993); Robert L. Patch, II; Val W. Saldaña; Douglas E. Noll; Michael T. Hertz; Victoria J. Salisch; Bradley A. Silva; Charles Trudrung Taylor; Mark L. Creede; Peter N. Zeitler; Charles L. Doerksen;—Laurie L. Quigley; Douglas E. Griffin; Nabil E. Zumout; Shawn H. Alikian; Thomas E. Gauthier.**
**General Civil and Trial Practice in all Courts. Appeals. Business, Corporation, Bankruptcy, Insolvency, Construction, Real Property, Probate and Estate Planning, Trusts, Personal Injury and Insurance Law.**
**References: Wells Fargo Bank (Fresno Main Office).**
***See Professional Biographies, FRESNO, CALIFORNIA***

Lange, Paul M. '40 '66 C.597 B.S.B.A. L.494 J.D.
(adm. in MN; not adm. in CA) Calif. State Univ.
**Larsen, Douglas M.** ........................ '61 '89 C&L.101 B.A., J.D. [Baker,M.&J.]
*LANGUAGES: French.
*PRACTICE AREAS: Employment Compliance and Litigation; False Claims Act Litigation.
La Rue, Annette .............................. '24 '53 C.267 A.B. L.1065 J.D. Ret. Mun. J.
Lash, Michael E. .............................. '56 '82 C.426 B.A. L.284 J.D. P.O. Box 6282
**Lastreto, Rene, II**, (BV) .................. '56 '81 C.878 B.S. L.767 J.D. [Dowling,A.&K.]
*PRACTICE AREAS: Creditors Rights; Commercial Litigation; Bankruptcy Law; Civil Litigation.
Lawrence, Cynthia G. .................... '64 '90 C.112 B.A. L.464 J.D. 5 River Pk. Pl. E.
Leary, Regina D., (BV) .................. '— '74 C.174 B.A. L.770 J.D. Sr. Dep. Dist. Atty.
Leath, Tom J., (BV) ................................. '43 '74 L.770 J.D. 6067 N. Fresno St.
Lee, Brian D. ........................ '57 '84 C.112 B.A. L.464 J.D. [McMurchie,F.B.W.&L.]
Lee, John Penn ........................ '41 '65 C.902 B.A. L.893 LL.B. 5151 N. Palm Ave.
**Lee, W. Richard**, (BV) ...................... '50 '85 C.800 B.S. L.1189 J.D. [Kimble,M.&U.]
*REPORTED CASES: Represented Creditors Committee - In Re. Montgomery Drilling Co. 121 B.R. 34 (E.D. Cal. 1990); In Re Powerburst Corp., 154 B.R. 307 (E.D. Cal. 1993); Represented Debtor - In Re. Torrez 827 F.2d 1299 (9th Cir. 1987).
*PRACTICE AREAS: Bankruptcy Law; Commercial Law; Real Estate Foreclosures and Receiverships; Construction Law.
Lehman, Kenneth A. ..................... '50 '76 C.112 B.S. L.61 J.D. Lehman's Mfg. Co., Inc.
**Lehman, Michael E.** ........................ '56 '88 C.267 B.A. L.1003 J.D. [Myers&O.]
Leichty, Bruce ........................... '54 '87 C.288 B.A. L.1066 J.D. 407 S. Clovis
**Leifer, William H.**, (BV) ................ '48 '74 C.112 B.A. L.1065 J.D. [Wild,C.&T.]
*SPECIAL AGENCIES: Commissioner, Fresno City Housing Authority.
*PRACTICE AREAS: Landlord/Tenant; Health Insurance; Civil Litigation.
**Lempel, J. Steven**, (BV) ........................ '45 '71 C.659 B.S. L.276 J.D. [J.S.Lempel]

**Lempel, J. Steven, Professional Law Corporation, (BV)**
**800 "M" Street, 93721**
**Telephone: 209-268-4021 Fax: 209-268-5446**
**J. Steven Lempel.**
**Real Property, Eminent Domain, Land Use, and Municipal Law Litigation and Transactions.**
**Representative Client: Fresno County Employee Credit Union.**
**Reference: Fresno County Employee Credit Union.**
***See Professional Biographies, FRESNO, CALIFORNIA***

**Leonard, John A.**, (BV) ........... '60 '89 C&L.546 B.S., J.D. [McCormick,B.S.W.&C.]
Lescoulie, Donald P. ..................... '50 '78 C.112 B.A. L.1136 J.D. 575 E. Alluvial Ave.
Lester, Mark W. ........................... '54 '80 C.112 B.A. L.1065 J.D. Dep. Dist. Atty.
**Levie, Joan Jacobs** ......... '39 '95 C.1019 B.A. L.1189 J.D. [Ⓐ McCormick,B.S.W.&C.]
*PRACTICE AREAS: Insurance Defense; Civil Litigation; Appeals.
Levis, W. Kent, Jr. ........................ '41 '70 C.267 B.A. L.1049 J.D. Mun. Ct. Judge

**Levitt, Donald R.** ...................................... '55 '81 C.154 B.A. L.61 J.D. [D.R.Levitt]
*PRACTICE AREAS: Commercial Debt Collection; Family Law/Matrimonial Disputes; Bankruptcy; Criminal Defense.

**Levitt, Donald R., Inc.**
**3585 West Beechwood Avenue, Suite 103, 93711**
**Telephone: 209-447-1182; 800-347-9634 Fax: 209-439-4633**
**Donald R. Levitt.**
**Commercial Debt Collection, Family Law, Matrimonial Disputes, Bankruptcy and Criminal Defense.**
***See Professional Biographies, FRESNO, CALIFORNIA***

Levy, Herbert I. .............................. '52 '77 C.112 B.A. L.464 J.D. Supr. Ct. J.
Levy, Stanton M., (BV) ...................... '22 '50 C.267 A.B. L.813 LL.B. [S.M.Levy]
Levy, Stanton M., Law Corporation, (BV) ........................ 7337 North First St.
Liggett, Peggy S., (BV) .............. '40 '77 C.766 B.A. L.1189 J.D. 2300 Tulare Ave.
Lind, Ruth P. ........................................ '39 '86 L.1189 J.D. 1322 E. Shaw
**Lindenau, Larry B.** ..................... '67 '92 C&L.101 B.S., J.D. [Ⓐ Perkins,M.&E.]
*PRACTICE AREAS: Business Law; Corporate Law; Real Estate Law; Estate Planning; Probate.

**Linneman, Burgess, Telles, Van Atta & Vierra**
**(See Merced)**

**Lintott, Karen E.** ........... '66 '95 C.800 B.A. L.1049 J.D. [Ⓐ McCormick,B.S.W.&C.]
*PRACTICE AREAS: Insurance Defense; General Litigation; Family Law.
Litman, Roger K., (BV) ................. '47 '73 C.112 B.A. L.1049 J.D. 2300 Tulare St.
**Little, Kevin G.** ...................... '66 '90 C&L.309 B.A., J.D. [Frampton,H.W.&B.]

**Littler, Mendelson, Fastiff, Tichy & Mathiason, A Professional Corporation, (AV)**
**1690 West Shaw, Suite 201, 93711⊙**
**Telephone: 209-431-8300 Facsimile: 209-431-8329**
**URL: http://www.littler.com**
**Michael J. Hogan; Spencer H. Hipp; Gary W. Bethel; Gregory J. Smith; Daniel K. Klingenberger;—Shelline Kay Bennett; Deborah L. Martin; Gregory A. Hendershott.**
**Offices located in: California — Bakersfield, Long Beach, Los Angeles, Menlo Park, Oakland, Sacramento, San Diego, San Francisco, San Jose, Santa Maria, Santa Rosa and Stockton; Denver, Colorado; Washington, D.C.; Atlanta, Georgia; Baltimore, Maryland; Reno and Las Vegas, Nevada (a partnership with the Law Offices of Hicks & Walt); Morristown, New Jersey; New York, New York; and Dallas and Houston, Texas.**
***See Professional Biographies, FRESNO, CALIFORNIA***

**Lloyd, Wendy S.**, (BV) .......... '62 '88 C.112 B.A. L.45 J.D. [McCormick,B.S.W.&C.]
Lodge, Jeffrey James ........................ '64 '91 C.793 B.S. L.546 J.D. Dept. of Jus.
Logoluso, Timothy V., (CV) .................. '59 '87 C.267 B.S. L.1189 J.D. [J.E.Henry]
Long Brown, Patricia ............... '52 '92 C.1169 B.A. L.978 J.D. [Ⓐ Cunningham&L.]
Loomis, John E., (AV) ...... '24 '50 C&L.813 A.B., J.D. 1221 Van Ness Ave., Suite 310‡
**Lopez, Amy L.** ............. '60 '96 C.464 B.A. L.1189 J.D. [Ⓐ McCormick,B.S.W.&C.]
*PRACTICE AREAS: Tort Litigation; Business Litigation.
Lopez, Gilbert D. ............................ '26 '55 C.999 L.809 LL.B. 2014 Tulare St.
Louie, Jay R. ..................... '50 '75 C.112 B.A. L.426 J.D. Pres., Louie Foods Intl.

**Lozano Smith Smith Woliver & Behrens, A Professional Corporation, (AV)**
**2444 Main Street, Suite 260, 93721⊙**
**Telephone: 209-445-1352 Fax: 209-233-5013**
**Max Edward Robinson (Retired); Louis T. Lozano (Resident, Monterey Office); Diana K. Smith (Resident, San Rafael Office); Michael E. Smith (Resident); Sandra Woliver (Managing Shareholder) (Resident San Rafael Office); Thomas J. Riggs (Resident); Jerome M. Behrens (Resident, Fresno); Christine A. Goodrich (Resident); Loren A. Carjulia (Resident, San Rafael Office); Ellen M. Jahn (Resident, Monterey Office); Peter K. Fagen (Resident);—Nancy Lu Klein (Resident, San Rafael Office); David J. Wolfe (Resident); Harold M. Freiman (Resident, Monterey); Eric E. Hill (Resident, San Rafael Office); Christopher D. Keeler (Resident, Monterey Office); Jan E. Tomsky (Resident, San Rafael Office); Eileen M. O'Hare; Ruth E. Mendyk; Karen Segar Salty (Resident, Monterey Office); Trevin E. Sims; Susan Landon Marks (Resident, San Rafael Office); Richard B. Galtman; James B. Fernow. Of Counsel: Paul R. DeLay (Resident, Monterey Office); Patricia Andreen (Resident, San Luis Obispo); Judd L. Jordan (Resident, Monterey Office).**
**Education, Labor and Employment, Civil Rights and Disability, Local Government, Land Use, Eminent Domain, Public Finance, Business and Insurance Litigation.**
**Representative Clients: Mendocino Community College District; Norwalk-LaMirada Unified School District; Palo Alto Unified School District; City of Clovis; City of Fresno; Visalia Unified School District.**
**San Rafael, California Office: 1010 B Street, Suite 200. Telephone: 415-459-3008. Fax: 415-456-3826.**
**Monterey, California Office: One Harris Court, Building A, Suite 200. Telephone: 408-646-1501. Fax: 408-646-1801.**
**San Luis Obispo, California Office: 987 Osos Street. Telephone: 805-549-9541. Fax: 805-549-0740.**
***See Professional Biographies, FRESNO, CALIFORNIA***

**Lucich, Nicholas Louis, Jr.**, (AV) .......... '50 '76 C.112 A.B. L.1065 J.D. [Helon&M.]
*PRACTICE AREAS: Estate Planning; Probate and Trusts; Business Transactions.
Lund, Judith L., (BV) ........................ '39 '78 C.267 B.A. L.1189 J.D. 6435 N. Palm
Lundgren, Craig N. ..................... '59 '90 C&L.112 B.A., J.D. 2300 Tulane St.
Luppino, James R., (BV) ................ '35 '65 C.267 B.S. L.1066 J.D. 1322 W. Show
Lushbough, K. Diane ................ '— '88 C.267 A.A. L.1189 J.D. 7108 N. Fresno St.
Lusk, Martha Uber ........................ '48 '79 C.36 B.A. L.61 J.D. 7636 N. Ingram Ave.
**Lynch, Karen L.** ..................... '58 '92 C.267 B.A. L.546 J.D. [Ⓐ Parichan,R.C.&H.]
*PRACTICE AREAS: Insurance Defense; Products Liability; Federal Appeals.
**Lyons, Daniel P.**, (BV) ......... '53 '80 C.147 B.S. L.1067 J.D. [McCormick,B.S.W.&C.]
MacArthur, J. Douglas, (BV) ............ '42 '71 C.477 B.S. L.1067 J.D. [MacArthur&N.]
MacArthur & Neilson, (BV) ........................................ 2610 West Shaw Ave.
Mach, Philip L. ........................ '49 '78 C.112 B.A. L.1189 J.D. 575 E. Locust
Macy, Harry E., (BV) ........................ '48 '78 C.267 B.A. L.765 J.D. [Hager,T.&M.]
Maddy, Kenneth L., (BV) ........................ '34 '63 C.267 B.S. L.1068 J.D. Sen.
Madsen, Sharon L. ............ '52 '91 C.267 B.S. L.1189 J.D. 5200 N. Palm Ave., Ste 301
**Magarian, Donald J.**, (BV) ............ '33 '64 C.267 A.B. L.1065 J.D. [Ⓑ Heyman,K.&M.]
*PRACTICE AREAS: Family Law.
**Magarian, Mark D.** ........................ '66 '93 C.800 B.S. L.284 J.D. [Heyman,K.&M.]
*PRACTICE AREAS: Business Litigation; Employment Litigation; Labor Law Counseling.
**Magill, Timothy V.**, (BV) ...................... '52 '78 C.1073 B.A. L.1189 J.D. [Magill]

**Magill Law Offices, (BV)**
**2377 West Shaw-104, 93711**
**Telephone: 209-229-3333 Fax: 209-229-4234**
**Timothy V. Magill.**
**Personal Injury, Wrongful Death, Insurance Bad Faith, Trial Practice. Appellate Practice.**
***See Professional Biographies, FRESNO, CALIFORNIA***

**Maglio, Gerald J.**, (AV) .................... '42 '71 C.267 A.B. L.1066 J.D. [Miles,S.&E.]
*PRACTICE AREAS: Personal Injury (Plaintiff) Law and related Litigation.
**Magness, Marcus Don** ............ '65 '90 C.012 B.Eng. L.623 J.D. [Ⓐ Thomas,S.J.R.&A.]
*PRACTICE AREAS: Taxation; Real Property; Business Litigation.
**Maler, Nancy A.** ........................ '62 '92 C.112 B.A. L.1067 J.D. [Sagaser,H.F.&J.]
**Mallek, Robert A., Jr. (Inc.)**, (BV) ....... '47 '78 C.813 B.A. L.464 J.D. [Dietrich,G.&J.]
*PRACTICE AREAS: Business Transactions; Bank Workout Law; Corporate Tax; Estate Planning Law.
**Mallery, Michael P.**, (BV) ........... '59 '84 C.112 B.A. L.464 J.D. [Stammer,M.B.&B.]
*PRACTICE AREAS: Professional Liability; Health Care Law; Discrimination (Employee and Housing); Business Litigation.
**Manfredo, Donald F.**, (BV) .................... '20 '51 C.267 L.1065 J.D. [Helon&M.] ‡
**Mann, Jerry H.**, (BV) ..................... '54 '80 C.112 B.A. L.426 J.D. [Perkins,M.&E.]
*PRACTICE AREAS: Civil Trial; Construction; Business; Employment; Bond Law.
**Manock, Charles K.** ................ '63 '92 C.112 Pol. Sci. L.464 J.D. [Ⓐ Baker,M.&J.]

CAA99P

**Manock, Kendall L.**, (AV) ............... '30 '55 C.267 A.B. L.1066 J.D. [Baker,M.&J.]
*PRACTICE AREAS: Agriculture Law including Farmer Cooperatives; Water Law.
Marcelli, Dominic E. ...................... '52 '76 C&L.770 B.S., J.D. 6715 N. Palm Ave.
**Marchini, Joseph M.**, (AV) .............. '53 '78 C.767 B.A. L.1065 J.D. [Baker,M.&J.]
*LANGUAGES: Italian.
*PRACTICE AREAS: Business Litigation; Insolvency; Agribusiness.
**Marderosian, Michael G.**, (AV) .... '50 '77 C.112 B.A. L.1189 J.D. [Marderosian,S.&O.]
*PRACTICE AREAS: Insurance Defense; Bad Faith; Personal Injury; Business Litigation; Employment Litigation.

**Marderosian, Swanson & Oren, A Professional Corporation, (AV)**
**1260 Fulton Mall, 93721-1783**
**Telephone: 209-441-7991 Facsimile: 209-441-8170**
**C. Sam Titus (1957-1990); Michael G. Marderosian; James W. Swanson; Eric P. Oren; Brett L. Runyon; Alan M. Simpson; Warren R. Paboojian; Sue Ann Cercone;—Steven D. Avery; Steven C. Clark.**
**Insurance Defense including Products Liability Defense, Insurance Bad Faith Defense and Personal Injury Law.**

*See Professional Biographies, FRESNO, CALIFORNIA*

Mardikian, Robt. Z. ........................ '33 '58 C.267 B.A. L.1065 J.D. Ret. Supr. Ct. J.
Margosian, Michael J., (BV) ........ '53 '78 C.267 B.S. L.464 J.D. 1221 Van Ness Ave.
Mariani-Pitalo, Elizabeth E. ............... '60 '88 C.845 B.B.A. L.464 J.D. 2444 Main St.
Marouk, Edward V., (CV) ................... '25 '58 C.267 B.A. L.1065 J.D. 5151 N. Palm
Martin, Bryan G. ........................... '58 '89 C.763 B.A. L.464 J.D. 1725 N. Fine Ave.
**Martin, Deborah L.** .............. '68 '94 C.1049 B.A. L.1065 J.D. [Ⓐ Littler,M.F.T.&M.]
**Martin, Lisa M.** ......................... '57 '82 C.267 B.A. L.1067 J.D. [Baker,M.&J.]
*PRACTICE AREAS: Business Litigation; Medical Malpractice Defense; White Collar Criminal Defense; Wrongful Termination.
Martin, Robert L. ...... '29 '59 C.999 L.1026 LL.B. Assoc. Jus., Ct. of App.-5th App. Dist.
**Martinez, Reynold M.** ........ '71 '96 C.112 B.S. L.1065 J.D. [Ⓐ McCormick,B.S.W.&C.]
*PRACTICE AREAS: Insurance Coverage.
**Martucci, Patrick M.** ......... '67 '93 C.112 B.A. L.770 J.D. [Ⓐ McCormick,B.S.W.&C.]
**Mason, Gregory S.**, (BV) ...... '61 '90 C.763 A.B. L.1049 J.D. [McCormick,B.S.W.&C.]
*PRACTICE AREAS: Civil Litigation; Products Liability; Professional Liability Defense.
Mather, Allen F. ........................ '22 '53 C.165 B.A. L.309 LL.B. 5962 E. Hamilton
Mattson-Markell, Patricia ............... '50 '87 C.1060 B.A. L.1189 J.D. 2135 Fresno St.

**Matychowiak, Thomas C., (BV) '43 '77 C.169 B.A. L.464 J.D.**
**4321 N. West Avenue, Suite 101, 93705**
**Telephone: 209-221-6303 Fax: 209-225-1731**
**Email: tmatycho@ix.netcom.com**
**Civil Trial Practice. Insurance and Casualty Law.**

*See Professional Biographies, FRESNO, CALIFORNIA*

**Maul, Frank D.**, (BV) ............... '50 '75 C.267 B.A. L.1065 J.D. [Stammer,M.B.&B.]
*PRACTICE AREAS: Products Liability Law; Insurance Coverage; Professional Liability; Personal Injury Law; Construction Litigation.
May, Wallace G., (BV) ....................... '14 '39 C.267 L.1065 LL.B. 1738 N. Farris
**Mayfield, Lori R.** ......................... '63 '94 C.907 BA L.1189 J.D. [Myers&O.]
Mazzela, Timothy W. ..................... '61 '93 C.267 B.A. L.1189 J.D. 6780 West Ave.
**McAuliffe, Barbara A.** ........... '58 '89 C.420 B.S. L.1049 J.D. [Motschiedler,M.&W.]
*PRACTICE AREAS: Business Litigation; Construction Law; Employment Law.
**McBrearty, James F.**, (CV) ............. '52 '89 C.728 B.A. L.1189 J.D. [Ⓐ Forrest&M.]
*PRACTICE AREAS: Insurance Defense; Business Litigation; Personal Injury.
McCallum, Scott N., (BV) .................. '54 '81 C.267 B.S. L.809 J.D. [McCallum&D.]
McCallum and De Goede, (BV) ........................................ 1322 E. Shaw Ave.
McCann, John P. '46 '75 C.1105 B.A. L.744 J.D.
(adm. in TX; not adm. in CA) 6750 N. Knoll Ave.‡
**McClean, Steven M.**, (AV) ..................... '51 '77 C.112 A.B. L.1065 J.D. [Kane,M.&M.]
*REPORTED CASES: Producers Cotton Oil v. Amstar Corp. (1988) 197 Cal.App.3d 638 (242 Cal.Rptr. 941) 5 U.C.C. R. Serv. 2d (Callaghan) 32.
*PRACTICE AREAS: Civil Litigation; Antitrust; Trade Secret; Unfair Competition; Real Estate Litigation.
McCollum, Tim D. '37 '65 C&L.575 B.S., LL.B.
(adm. in NC; not adm. in CA) 1520 E. Shaw Ave.
**McCollum, Timothy D., (A.P.C.)**, (AV) .... '38 '76 C&L.1190 B.S., J.D. [McCollum&B.]
*REPORTED CASES: Baar v. Tigerman and the American Arbitration Association (1983) 140 Cal.App.3d 979, 189 Cal.Rptr. 834, cited: 41 ALR 4th 1004, 1013; ALR 3d 815 supp.; Domke, Commercial Arbitration 23:01, et seq.; 67 Marquette L.R. Fall 1983; 21 Cal West L.R. 564, 1985.
*PRACTICE AREAS: Unfair Competition Law; International Law; Business Torts; Environmental Law.

**McCollum and Bunch, A Professional Corporation, (AV)**
**1520 East Shaw Avenue, Suite 103, 93710**
**Telephone: 209-222-4400 FAX: 209-222-3544**
**Timothy D. McCollum (A.P.C.); Kenneth S. Bayer;—Joseph A. Weber.**
**Advertising and Marketing, Agencies and Distributorships, Antitrust and Trade Regulation, Appellate Practice, Business Law, Civil Practice, Complex and Multi-District Litigation, Contracts, Copyrights, Corporate Law, Environmental Law, Franchises and Franchising, Intellectual Property, International Law, Leases and Leasing, Litigation, Racketeer Influence and Corrupt Organizations, Real Estate and Real Property, Tax Matters, Health Care, ERISA, Construction, UCC and Securities.**
**References: United California Bank (Olympic and Purdue, Los Angeles); Security Pacific Bank.**

*See Professional Biographies, FRESNO, CALIFORNIA*

**McCormack, Carla M.** .................. '69 '94 C.218 B.A. L.1066 J.D. [Jory,P.W.&S.]
*PRACTICE AREAS: Civil Litigation; Business Law; Real Estate.

**McCormick, Barstow, Sheppard, Wayte & Carruth LLP, (AV)**
**Five River Park Place East, 93720-1501⊙**
**Mailing Address: P.O. Box 28912, 93729-8912**
**Telephone: 209-433-1300 Fax: 209-433-2300**
**Richard A. McCormick (1915-1981); Stephen Barnett (1931-1988); Dudley W. Sheppard (Retired); James H. Barstow (Retired). Members of Firm: Lawrence E. Wayte; Lowell T. Carruth; James H. Perkins (Certified Specialist, Probate, Estate Planning and Trust Law, The State Bar of California Board of Legal Specialization); Stephen R. Cornwell; Andrew W. Wright; Mario Louis Beltramo, Jr.; Michael G. Woods; James P. Wagoner; Steven G. Rau; Gordon M. Park; Wade M. Hansard; W. F. Docker; Justus C. Spillner; Hilton A. Ryder; D. Greg Durbin; Marshall C. Whitney; Donald S. Black; Daniel P. Lyons; Riley C. Walter; Michael L. Wilhelm; John A. Drolshagen; Brian M. Arax; Walter W. Whelan; Michael F. Ball; Stephen E. Carroll; James H. Wilkins; Timothy Jones; Kevin D. Hansen; Philip M. Flanigan; Matthew K. Hawkins, Resident, Modesto Office); Kenneth A. Baldwin; David R. McNamara; Timothy L. Thompson; Wendy S. Lloyd; Michael J. Czeshinski; John A. Leonard; Gregory S. Mason; Mart B. Oller, IV; Paul J. O'Rourke, Jr.; Todd W. Baxter. Associates: Robert K. Landen; Kurt F. Vote; Blake A. Meyen; Julie A. Noble; Bruce W. Kelley; Patrick M. Martucci; John M. Dunn (Resident, Modesto Office); Gregory A. Floyd; Dirk B. Paloutzian; David T. Wilson; Scott M. Reddie; Kristin L. Ichishta; Karen E. Lintott; Anthony N. DeMaria; Peter L.D. Simon; Stephanie A. Schrandt; David A. Evans; Lisa A. Sondergaard; Edmund H. Mizumoto; Amy L. Lopez; Joy D. Cothran; Joan Jacobs Levie; Michael R. Fields; Jason A. Decker; Alyson A. Carr; Judd A. Genda; Gary B. Kraft; Chris Scheithauer; Sean P. Reis; Reynold M. Martinez. Of Counsel: Deborah A. Byron.**
**General Civil and Trial Practice. Agricultural and Water Law, Banking Law, Bankruptcy and Reorganization, Civil Rights Litigation, Civil Practice, Commodities Law, Condemnation Law, Construction Law, Corporate Law, Employment Law, Environmental Law, Estate Planning, Family Law, Franchise Law, Health Care Law, Insurance Law Legal Malpractice, Medical Malpractice, Municipal Law, Probate, Public Entity, Real Estate Agent Malpractice, Real Estate Law, Securities and Taxation Law.**
**Counsel for: Aetna Life & Casualty Co.; California State Automobile Assn.; Firemen's Fund Insurance Co.; Kings River State Bank; Hartford Accident & Indemnity Co.; Kemper Insurance Group; The Travelers Insurance Co.; United Pacific/Reliance Insurance Co.**
**Modesto, California Office: Centre Plaza Office Tower, 1150 Ninth Street, Suite 1510. Telephone: 209-524-1100. Fax: 209-524-1188.**

*See Professional Biographies, FRESNO, CALIFORNIA*

McCracken, Terri L. ....................... '61 '91 C.267 B.S. L.999 J.D. 3855 N. West
McCully, Brian J., (BV) ................ '52 '77 C.267 B.A. L.1065 J.D. Fresno City Coll.
**McDaniel, John M.**, (BV) .................. '51 '76 C.813 B.A. L.770 J.D. [Helon&M.]
*PRACTICE AREAS: Family Law; Domestic.
McDermott, Wm. J., (BV) ........ '26 '54 C.267 A.B. L.1066 LL.B. 726 W. Barstow Ave.

**McFarland, Pamela J. '— '86 L.1189 J.D.**
**600 West Shaw Avenue, Suite 210, 93704**
**Telephone: 209-225-8895 Fax: 209-225-5908**
***PRACTICE AREAS: Family Law; Domestic Relations; Child Custody.**
**Family Law, Domestic Relations and Child Custody.**

*See Professional Biographies, FRESNO, CALIFORNIA*

McFeeters, John D., Jr., (BV) ....... '31 '56 C.267 A.B. L.1066 LL.B. 6670 N. West Ave.
**McGee, Steven D.**, (BV) .................. '50 '76 C.276 B.S. L.1049 J.D. [Kimble,M.&U.]
*PRACTICE AREAS: Construction Law; Commercial Litigation.
McGinnis, Michael Joseph .............. '41 '73 C.267 B.A. L.1049 J.D. 1111 Fulton Mall
McGraw, Vincent J. ............................ '46 '76 C&L.426 B.A., J.D. Mun. Ct. J.
**McGregor, John J.**, (AV) .......... '46 '72 C.767 A.B. L.1065 J.D. [McGregor,D.S.&K.]
*REPORTED CASES: Zaninovich v. Commissioner 616 F2d 429; Giannini Packing Corp. v. Commissioner 83 TC 526; Salwasser v. Commissioner, 1991-466.
*PRACTICE AREAS: Tax Planning; Tax Litigation; Business Transactions.

**McGregor, Dahl, Sullivan & Klug, (AV)**
**7080 North Whitney Avenue, Suite 105, 93720-0154**
**Telephone: 209-322-9292 FAX: 209-322-9191**
**William A. Dahl; Kenneth M. Klug (Certified Specialist, Probate, Estate Planning and Trust Law, The State Bar of California Board of Legal Specialization).; John J. McGregor (Certified Specialist, Taxation Law, The State Bar of California Board of Legal Specialization); Robert L. Sullivan, Jr. (Certified Specialist, Taxation Law and Estate Planning, Trust and Probate Law, The State of California Board of Legal Specialization).**
**Estate Planning, Trust and Estate Administration, Taxation, Business Transactions, Real Estate, Water and Environmental Law.**

*See Professional Biographies, FRESNO, CALIFORNIA*

**McGuinness, Brady K.** ................ '67 '94 C.267 B.S. L.770 J.D. [Ⓐ Heyman,K.&M.]
*PRACTICE AREAS: Business Litigation; Business Organizations; Contracts; Employment Law.
**McKelvey, James A.** ............ '40 '66 C.267 B.S. L.1066 J.D. [Motschiedler,M.&W.]
*PRACTICE AREAS: Real Estate Law.
**McKnight, Kathleen A.** ............ '51 '82 C.426 B.A. L.1049 J.D. [Ⓐ Musick,P.&G.]
*PRACTICE AREAS: Health Care Law; Hospital Law.
**McLaughlin, William T., II**, (BV) ..... '56 '84 C.999 B.A.B.S. L.1065 J.D. [Forrest&M.]
*PRACTICE AREAS: General Civil Practice; Insurance Law and Defense; Business Law; Partnership Law; Employment Law.
McMurchie, Foley, Brandenburger, Weill & Lenahan, (AV)
2444 Main St. (⊙Sacramento)
McNair, Michele M. ................. '50 '78 C.267 B.S. L.1189 J.D. 6435 N. Palm Ave.
**McNamara, David R.**, (CV) ..... '62 '87 C.960 B.S. L.966 J.D. [McCormick,B.S.W.&C.]
*PRACTICE AREAS: Commercial Litigation; Employment; Real Estate.

**McPike, William R. '51 '80 C.267 B.A. L.1132 J.D.**
**4270 N. Blackstone Avenue, Suite 315, 93726**
**Telephone: 209-224-6363 Facsimile: 209-224-3239**
**Email: Mcpike@pacbell.net**
***PRACTICE AREAS: Personal Injury Law (50); Bankruptcy Law (40); Real Property Law (300); Creditor-Debtor (150); Probate-Estate Law (20).**
**Associate: Judith Tuttle.**
**Civil Trial Practice. Unlawful Detainers, Bankruptcy Filings, Personal Injury, Estate Planning, Probate, Collections, Offshore Banking and Asset Protection.**

*See Professional Biographies, FRESNO, CALIFORNIA*

**McQuillan, Steven M.**, (BV) .......... '56 '82 C.147 B.A. L.770 J.D. [Parichan,R.C.&H.]
*LANGUAGES: German.
*PRACTICE AREAS: Insurance Defense and Coverage; ERISA Litigation; Environmental Litigation.
McWilliams, Keith N. ................ '61 '87 C.112 A.B. L.1065 J.D. Dist. Atty.'s Office
**Meehan, Kathleen A.** .................. '53 '85 C.740 B.A. L.1067 J.D. [Ⓐ Baker,M.&J.]
*PRACTICE AREAS: Business Litigation; Securities Litigation.
Meek, Todd Dean .... '62 '89 C.267 B.A. L.1189 J.D. National Amer. Life Ins. Co. of Ca.
Mele, James J. ........................... '50 '76 C.112 A.B. L.1189 J.D. 7337 N. 1st St.
Melikian, Kenneth J., (BV) ................ '52 '77 C.197 A.B. L.800 J.D. Asst. U.S. Atty.
**Mello, Paul B.** .......................... '69 '95 C&L.112 B.A., J.D. [Ⓐ Baker,M.&J.]
*PRACTICE AREAS: Business Litigation; Employment Law.
Mendoza, Moses M. ......................... '63 '93 C.81 B.A. L.1189 J.D. 2444 Main St.
**Mendyk, Ruth E.** ................. '66 '92 C.747 B.A L.546 J.D. [Ⓐ Lozano S.S.W.&B.]
Mendyk, Stephen A., (BV) ............ '60 '89 C&L.546 B.M.E., J.D. Off. of Dist. Atty.
**Mengshol, John G.**, (BV) ................ '37 '66 C.112 B.S. L.1066 J.D. [Kane,M.&M.]
*PRACTICE AREAS: Business Transactions; Corporate Law; Taxation Law; Trusts, Estate Planning and Probate Law; Real Estate Transactions.
Merritt, John W. ............. '51 '76 C.426 B.B.A. L.1049 J.D. Chief Dep. County Coun.
Metcalf, L. Drew ........................... '67 '94 C&L.36 B.S., J.D. 5 River Pk. Pl. E.
Meux, Peter C., (CV) .................. '46 '82 C.267 B.S.B.A. L.1132 J.D. [Meux&M.]
Meux & Meux, (CV) ................................................ 1060 Fulton Mall
**Meyen, Blake A.** ............ '67 '93 C&L.378 B.G.S., J.D. [Ⓐ McCormick,B.S.W.&C.]
*PRACTICE AREAS: Creditor-Debtor; Bankruptcy; Receiverships; Agricultural Law; General Business Transactions.
**Meyers, Leonard I.**, (AV) ................ '18 '41 C.267 L.1065 LL.B. [Ⓒ Baker,M.&J.]
**Michael, John G.**, (BV) ................. '54 '82 C.1077 B.S. L.1067 J.D. [Baker,M.&J.]
*PRACTICE AREAS: Business and Real Estate; Commercial Law; Litigation.
**Michaelides, Phillip G.**, (BV) ...... '52 '77 C.800 B.S. L.770 J.D. [Motschiedler,M.&W.]
*PRACTICE AREAS: Real Property Transactions; Real Property Finance; Business Transactions.
**Miessner, Leslie G.** .................. '65 '92 C.112 B.A. L.1067 J.D. [Ⓐ Dietrich,G.&J.]
*PRACTICE AREAS: Business Transactions; Health Care Law; Taxation.
Milam, Jeffrey L. '54 '80 C.893 B.A. L.945 J.D.
(adm. in VA; not adm. in CA) 1713 Tulare St.

**Miles, Sears & Eanni, A Professional Corporation, (AV)** BB
**2844 Fresno Street, P.O. Box 1432, 93716**
**Telephone: 209-486-5200 Fax: 209-486-5240**
**Wm. M. Miles (1909-1991); Robert E. Sears (1918-1992); Carmen A. Eanni (Member of California Trial Lawyers Association, with recognized experience in the fields of Trial Lawyer, General Personal Injury, Product Liability and Professional Negligence); Richard C. Watters; Gerald J. Maglio; William J. Seiler; Douglas L. Gordon.**
**Practice limited to Plaintiff's Civil Litigation, Personal Injury, Product Liability and Wrongful Death.**

*See Professional Biographies, FRESNO, CALIFORNIA*

Miller, Keith A. .................. '25 '58 C.267 B.A. L.765 J.D. 3099 W. Roberts Ave.
**Miller, Mark D.**, (BV) ............... '58 '84 C.420 B.S. L.770 J.D. [Kimble,M.&U.]
*REPORTED CASES: Rhône-Poulenc Agrochime S.A. v. Biagro Western Sales, Inc., 35 U.S.P.Q.2d 1203 (E.D.Cal. 1994).
*PRACTICE AREAS: Patent, Trademark and Copyright Law; Commercial Litigation.
Mills, Carol D. .................... '55 '79 C.112 B.A. L.464 J.D. Dept. of Justice
Milnes, Michael A., (BV) ........ '35 '66 C.766 B.A. L.284 LL.B. 1320 W. Herndon Ave.
Milrod, Patience, (BV) .................. '53 '77 C.112 A.B. L.1067 J.D. [Milrod&P.]
Milrod & Phillips, (BV) ........................................ 844 N. Van Ness Ave.

**Missirlian, John H., (BV) '50 '75 C.112 B.A. L.809 J.D.**
**6435 North Palm Avenue, Suite 106, 93704**
**Telephone: 209-439-3600 Fax: 209-439-5699**
**Email: missirlian@world.net.att.net**
**Business, Business Transactions, Taxation, Probate and Estate Planning, Real Estate and Commercial Law.**

*See Professional Biographies, FRESNO, CALIFORNIA*

**Mizumoto, Edmund H.** ........ '66 '95 C.367 B.A. L.597 J.D. [A McCormick,B.S.W.&C.]
*LANGUAGES: Japanese and Spanish.
*PRACTICE AREAS: Insurance Defense Litigation; Business Litigation.
Mohan, Rose E. .................... '48 '92 C.980 B.S. L.1189 J.D. 499 W. Shaw
**Montanari, R. Ernest, III** ................ '62 '91 C.267 B.S. L.1189 J.D. [A Brown&P.]
*PRACTICE AREAS: Insurance Defense; Subrogation; Personal Injury.
**Moody, Patrick S.** .................... '64 '91 C.260 B.A. L.61 J.D. [Barsamian&S.]
*PRACTICE AREAS: Labor Law; Employment Law; Commercial Litigation.
Moore, John P. .................... '39 '69 C.768 B.A. L.1065 J.D. 1107 R St.
Morris, John W., Jr., (BV) ............ '39 '72 C.267 B.S. L.765 J.D. [Mushines&M.]
Morris, Peter C., (BV) .................... '26 '51 C&L.813 A.B., J.D. [Zins&M.]
**Morris, Richard L.** .................... '46 '78 C.112 B.S. L.1068 J.D. [Mullen&F.]
Morse, Carolyn M. .................... '46 '76 C.112 A.B. L.464 J.D. 6435 N. Palm Ave.
**Mortensen, Craig M.**, (BV) ............ '53 '80 C&L.101 B.S., J.D. [Stammer,M.B.&B.]
*LANGUAGES: Japanese.
*PRACTICE AREAS: Water Law; Personal Injury Law; Medical Malpractice.
Mosley, Marian J., (CV) .................... '29 '80 C.267 B.A. L.1132 J.D. 800 "M" St.‡
**Moss, Michael E.**, (BV) .................... '49 '74 C.112 B.A. L.800 J.D. [Kimble,M.&U.]
*PRACTICE AREAS: Construction Law; Employment and Employee Benefits Law; Real Estate Law.
**Motschiedler, J. Carl**, (AV) ...... '42 '69 C.267 B.S. L.1066 J.D. [Motschiedler,M.&W.]
*PRACTICE AREAS: Land Use Development; Real Property; Business Law; Finance.

**Motschiedler, Michaelides & Wishon, (AV)**
**1690 West Shaw Avenue Suite 200, 93711**
**Telephone: 209-439-4000 Telecopier: 209-439-5654**
**J. Carl Motschiedler; Phillip G. Michaelides; A. Emory Wishon, III; James A. McKelvey; C. William Brewer; Myron F. Smith; David R. Jenkins; Russell K. Ryan; Barbara A. McAuliffe.**
**Civil Trial Litigation in all State and Federal Courts, Construction, Environmental, Real Estate, Real Property, Finance, Banking, Land Use Planning, Business Transactions, Corporate, Partnership, Probate and Estate Planning, Administrative, Government, Commercial Litigation, Agricultural Law, Bankruptcy, Insolvency and Employment Law.**
**Reference: First Interstate Bank (Main Office).**

*See Professional Biographies, FRESNO, CALIFORNIA*

Motsenbocker, Gary L., (CV) ............ '40 '85 C.267 B.A. L.1132 J.D. 1060 Fulton Mall

**Mugridge, David R., Law Offices of, (BV) '49 '86 C.061 B.A. L.1189 J.D.**
**2100 Tulare Street, Suite 505, 93721-2111**
**Telephone: 209-264-2688 Fax: 209-264-2683**
***LANGUAGES: Spanish.**
**Criminal Law, Special Circumstance. Homicide Defense, Personal Injury and Appellate Practice.**

**Mullen & Filippi, (AV)**
**6715 North Palm Avenue, Suite 108, 93704⊙**
**Telephone: 209-449-8170**
**Members of Firm: Richard L. Morris (Certified Specialist, Workers Compensation Law, The State Bar of California Board of Legal Specialization); Beverly A. Gabriele; Sarah A. Sharp. Associates: E.W. Rick Wenzel; John L. "Sam" Bessinger; Jane Woodcock; Tamanee A Krazan.**
**Insurance Defense, Workers Compensation, Liability and Subrogation.**
**Other California Offices: San Francisco, San Jose, Sacramento, Santa Rosa, Salinas, Stockton, Long Beach, Bakersfield, Redding, Woodland Hills and Oakland**

*See Professional Biographies, SAN FRANCISCO, CALIFORNIA*

Mushines, Dominic P., P.C., (BV) ......... '34 '71 C.267 B.S. L.1132 J.D. [Mushines&M.]
Mushines & Morris, (BV) .................... 4321 N. West Ave.

**Musick, Peeler & Garrett LLP, (AV)**
**6041 North First Street, 93710-5444⊙**
**Telephone: 209-228-1000 Facsimile: 209-447-4670**
**Members of Firm: Donald P. Asperger; James B. Betts; Stephen A. Hansen; Janet L. Wright. Associates: Heather Bussing; Kathleen A. McKnight.**
**General Practice. Trial and Appellate Practice. Corporation, Securities and Antitrust Law. Healthcare, Hospital, College and University Law. Insurance, Excess, Reinsurance and Coverage. Labor, Real Estate, Land Use, Environmental, Eminent Domain, Oil and Gas and Mining Law. Taxation, Trust, Probate, Estate Planning, Bankruptcy and Pension and Profit Sharing.**
**Los Angeles, California Office: Suite 2000, One Wilshire Boulevard. Telephone: 213-629-7600. Facsimile: 213-624-1376.**
**San Diego, California Office: 1900 Home Savings Tower, 225 Broadway. Telephone: 619-231-2500. Facsimile: 619-231-1234.**
**San Francisco, California Office: Suite 1300, Steuart Street Tower, One Market Plaza. Telephone: 415-281-2000. Facsimile: 415-281-2010.**
**Sacramento, California Office: Wells Fargo Center, Suite 1280, 400 Capitol Mall. Telephone: 916-557-8300. Facsimile: 916-442-8629.**
**Irvine, California Office: 2603 Main Street, Suite 1025. Telephone: 714-852-5122. Facsimile: 714-852-5128.**

*See Professional Biographies, FRESNO, CALIFORNIA*

**Myers, Gregory L.**, (BV) .................... '47 '80 C.267 L.1189 J.D. [Myers&O.]
Myers, R. Rich .................... '46 '80 C.1097 B.A. L.398 J.D. 555 W. Shaw Ave.

**Myers & Overstreet, A Professional Corporation, (BV)**
**1130 East Shaw Avenue, Suite 200, 93710-1592**
**Telephone: 209-222-1005 Fax: 209-222-0702**
**URL: http://www.MyersAndOverstreet.com**
**Gregory L. Myers; David M. Overstreet, IV; Michael E. Lehman; Thomas P. Guarino; Harvie Ruth Schnitzer; C. Michael Carrigan; Barbara L. Scharton; Lori R. Mayfield.**
**General Civil and Trial Practice in State and Federal Courts. Insurance Litigation, including Defense, Bad Faith and Coverage, Construction Litigation, Business Litigation, Civil Rights Litigation, Public Entity Defense, Employment Law, including Discrimination and Americans with Disabilities Act (ADA) Litigation, Environmental Law, including Toxic Tort Litigation, and Products Liability.**

*See Professional Biographies, FRESNO, CALIFORNIA*

Nagel, J. J., (AV) .................... '13 '42 C.267 B.A. L.1065 LL.B. [Nagel&N.]
Nagel, John T., (A Professional Corporation), (BV) '45 '71
C.267 B.A. L.1065 J.D. [Nagel&N.]
Nagel & Nagel, (AV) .................... 1233 W. Shaw Ave.
Nahigian, Archie H., Jr. .............. '53 '79 C&L.276 B.A., J.D. 5260 N. Palm, Ste., 421
Nahigian, Eliot S., (BV) .................... '50 '79 C.267 B.S. L.426 J.D. [Jackson P.&N.]
**Najarian, Jube J.**, (BV) ............ '56 '81 C.267 B.A. L.1049 J.D. [Jacobson,H.N.&F.]
*PRACTICE AREAS: Insurance Defense Law; Civil Litigation; Insurance Coverage Law; Agents and Broker's Errors and Omissions.
Neilson, Bruce A. .................... '54 '81 C&L.878 B.S., J.D. [MacArthur&N.]
Neudek, Dennis A. .................... '44 '78 L.1132 J.D. Dep. Dist. Atty.
Neufeld, Donald Otto, (BV) ....... '51 '77 C.1163 B.A. L.800 J.D. [A Christensen,B.&B.]
Newman, John M., (BV) .................... '37 '74 C.267 B.S. L.1189 J.D. 1396 W. Herndon
Nibler, Timothy R., (Incorporated), (BV) '38 '67 C.670 B.B.A. L.464 J.D.
575 E. Alluvial
Nichols, Woodrow Edgar, Jr., (CV) ...... '47 '89 C.267 B.A. L.1189 J.D. 2333 Merced St.
Nielsen, Donald W. .................... '58 '90 C&L.1137 B.S., J.D. 2300 Tulare St.
Nilmeier, Lisa Jorgensen '59 '87 C.267 B.S. L.1189 J.D.
Legal Coun./ Gen. Mgr., Sanger Telecasters, Inc.
Nitz, Melvin W. .................... '19 '52 C&L.966 B.S., LL.B. 2706 W. Ashlan Ave.‡
Nix, Barry F., (CV) .................... '— '77 C.267 L.1132 J.D. 1713 Tulare St.
**Noble, Julie A.** .................... '66 '93 C.061 B.A. L.763 J.D. [A McCormick,B.S.W.&C.]
**Noll, Douglas E.**, (BV) .................... '50 '77 C.197 B.A. L.464 J.D. [Lang,R.&P.]
*PRACTICE AREAS: Complex Civil Litigation.
Norgaard, Philip J., (BV) ............ '45 '78 C.877 B.S. L.1132 J.D, 2220 Tulare, Ste. 500
**Nuttall, Roger T., (Inc.)**, (AV) ............ '39 '69 C.766 B.A. L.1065 J.D. [Nuttall B.]
*REPORTED CASES: Robert Owen Stewart vs. The Justice Court for Avenal Judicial District of Kings County, 74 CA 3d 607; 141 Cal.Rptr. 589.
*PRACTICE AREAS: Accident and Personal Injury; Plaintiff's Trial Practice; Criminal Trial Practice; White Collar Criminal Defense; Professional Disciplinary Matters.

**Nuttall Berman Attorneys, (AV) BB**
**A Partnership including a Professional Corporation**
**2333 Merced Street, 93721**
**Telephone: 209-233-2333 Fax: 209-233-6947**
**Email: dfndr@cybergate.com**
**Members of Firm: Roger T. Nuttall (Inc.); Richard P. Berman. Associates: Mark W. Coleman.**
**Criminal Trial and Appellate Practice and Plaintiffs Personal Injury Law.**

*See Professional Biographies, FRESNO, CALIFORNIA*

Obata, Keigo .................... '36 '72 C.112 B.A. L.426 J.D. 6067 N. Fresno St.
Oberto, Sheila K. .................... '56 '85 C&L.800 B.S., J.D. Fed. Cthse., 1130 O St.
O'Brien, Daniel P. .................... '42 '74 C.763 A.B. L.809 J.D. [Hanna,B.M.M.&J.]
O'Donovan, Verla R., (CV) .............. '50 '88 C.1060 B.A. L.1226 J.D. Dep. Dist. Atty.
Oeser, Edwin A., (BV) .................... '47 '72 C.112 A.B. L.1067 J.D. Asst. City Atty.‡
Ohanesian, Ara .................... '26 '53 C.267 B.A. L.1066 LL.B. 1060 Fulton Mall
**O'Hare, Eileen M.** .................... '60 '92 C.768 B.A. L.1068 J.D. [Lozano S.S.W.&B.]
*REPORTED CASES: In Re: Estate of Wernicke 16 Cal. App. 4th 1069; Hill v. City of Long Beach 33 Cal. App. 4th 1684; Anderson v. Superior Court 11 Cal. 4th 1152.
*PRACTICE AREAS: Employment Litigation; complex Business Litigation; General Civil Litigation.
Oliver, Robert H. .................... '43 '73 C.267 B.S. L.284 J.D. Mun. Ct. J.
**Oller, Mart B., IV** .............. '65 '90 C.112 B.S. L.1067 J.D. [McCormick,B.S.W.&C.]
Olsen, David A. .................... '43 '75 C.605 B.A. L.800 J.D. 5070 W. Sixth, #185
Olson, Richard L., (BV) ............ '30 '60 C.112 A.B. L.1066 LL.B. 325 W. Shields Ave.
O'Neill, Lawrence J. .................... '52 '79 C.112 A.B. L.1065 J.D. Supr. Ct. J.
O'Neill, Patricia B. .................... '52 '96 C.267 B.S. L.1189 J.D. 3455 W. Shaw
Ontiveros, Janel Tritch .............. '58 '84 C.267 B.S. L.800 J.D. Resch. Atty., Mun. Ct.
Ophelia, Dianne R., (BV) .................... '51 '77 C.267 B.S. L.1189 J.D. 800 "M" St.
Oren, Charles D., (BV) .................... '53 '82 C.267 B.S. L.1137 J.D. [Oren&O.]
Oren, Donald E., (BV) .................... '23 '50 C&L.793 LL.B. [Oren&O.]
**Oren, Eric P.**, (BV) .................... '56 '82 C.112 B.A. L.1137 J.D. [Marderosian,S.&O.]
*PRACTICE AREAS: Insurance Defense; Bad Faith; Personal Injury.
Oren & Oren, Inc., (BV) .................... 470 E. Herndon Ave.

**Ormond, John K., Law Office of '49 '79 C.112 B.A. L.1068 J.D.**
**5151 North Palm, Suite 10, P.O. Box 28532, 93729-8532**
**Telephone: 209-221-8100 Fax: 209-226-8024**
***PRACTICE AREAS: Personal Injury (Plaintiff and Defense); Products Liability; Construction Disputes; Defamation; Agents and Brokers Liability.**
**Personal Injury (Plaintiff and Defense), Products Liability, Construction Disputes, Defamation, Agents and Brokers Liability.**

*See Professional Biographies, FRESNO, CALIFORNIA*

Ornellas, Robert J. '43 '73 C.768 B.S. L.464 J.D.
Sr. V.P., Gen. Coun. & Secy., National Amer. Life Ins. Co. of Ca.
**O'Rourke, Paul J., Jr.** .......... '64 '89 C.112 B.A. L.426 J.D. [McCormick,B.S.W.&C.]
**Ott, Michael D.** .................... '48 '75 C.112 B.A. L.352 J.D. [Ericksen,A.K.D.&L.]
**Overstreet, David M., IV**, (BV) .............. '55 '82 C.267 B.S. L.1189 J.D. [Myers&O.]
**Owdom, Bruce A.** .................... '48 '77 C.770 B.A. L.1189 J.D. [Dietrich,G.&J.]
*PRACTICE AREAS: Business; Construction; Real Property and Environmental Litigation.
**Paboojian, Warren R.**, (BV) ....... '57 '87 C.112 B.A. L.1189 J.D. [Marderosian,S.&O.]
*PRACTICE AREAS: Insurance Defense; Bad Faith; Personal Injury; Business Litigation; Wrongful Termination.
Padgett, Anne '65 '94 C.1060 B.A. L.596 J.D.
(adm. in OR; not adm. in CA) 3294 E. Dakota Ave.‡
**Paganetti, Steven E.**, (BV) .................... '51 '79 C.463 B.A. L.1189 J.D. [Wild,C.&T.]
*PRACTICE AREAS: Trials, Business and Environmental Litigation.
Paige, James V. .................... '11 '39 C.267 B.A. L.1065 J.D. Ret. Mun. J.‡
**Palmer, Samuel C., III**, (AV) ............ '34 '59 C.813 A.B. L.426 J.D. [Thomas,S.J.R.&A.]
*PRACTICE AREAS: Business Litigation.
**Paloutzian, Dirk B.** .............. '69 '94 C&L.112 B.A., J.D. [A McCormick,B.S.W.&C.]
*PRACTICE AREAS: Insurance Coverage; Insurance Defense.
Papadakis, Victor N. .................... '47 '72 C.267 B.A. L.770 J.D. Mun. Ct. J.
Papanickolas, John M. .................... '64 '91 C.112 B.S. L.1065 J.D. 5260 N. Palm
**Parichan, Harold A.**, (AV) ............ '23 '49 C.112 B.S. L.813 J.D. [Parichan,R.C.&H.]
*PRACTICE AREAS: Products Liability Law.

**Parichan, Renberg, Crossman & Harvey, Law Corporation, (AV) BB**
**Suite 130, 2350 West Shaw Avenue, P.O. Box 9950, 93794-0950**
**Telephone: 209-431-6300 Fax: 209-432-1018**
**Harold A. Parichan; Charles L. Renberg; Richard C. Crossman; Ima Jean Harvey; Stephen T. Knudsen; Larry C. Gollmer; Robert G. Eliason; Steven M. McQuillan;—Deborah A. Coe; Maureen P. Holford; Karen L. Lynch; Michael L. Renberg.**
**Civil Litigation. Insurance Defense, Personal Injury, Products Liability, Business, Corporate, Probate and Estate Planning, Agricultural Law, Environmental Law.**
**Reference: Bank of America, Commercial Banking Office, Fresno, California.**

*See Professional Biographies, FRESNO, CALIFORNIA*

**Park, Gordon M.**, (BV) ...... '51 '76 C.1042 B.A. L.1068 J.D. [McCormick,B.S.W.&C.]
Parks, James Edward, (BV) .............. '46 '76 C.267 B.S. L.309 J.D. 7720 N. Fresno St.
Parr, Kent C., (CV) .................... '57 '83 C.249 B.A. L.345 J.D. 246 W. Shaw Ave.
Pasculli, Mark A. .............. '62 '94 C.267 B.S. L.1189 J.D. Chamlian Enterprises, Inc.
Pascuzzi, Harry .................... '51 '86 C.267 B.S. L.1189 J.D. 3455 W. Shaw Ave.
**Patch, Robert L., II**, (AV) .............. '43 '72 C.267 B.A. L.1067 J.D. [Lang,R.&P.]
*PRACTICE AREAS: Personal Injury Law; Medical Malpractice; Construction Litigation.
Pearson, David S. .................... '66 '91 C.549 B.S. L.1065 J.D. 5628 W. Tenaya
Pearson, Janice L. ........ '49 '75 C.112 B.A. L.1066 J.D. Dean, San Joaquin Coll. of Law
**Pedreira, Thomas A.**, (BV) .................... '55 '82 C.813 B.A. L.464 J.D. [Emerich P.&F.]
*LANGUAGES: Italian.
*PRACTICE AREAS: Health Care Law; Business Transactions; Agricultural Law.
**Pedreira, Virginia Miller**, (BV) .......... '61 '88 C.347 B.A. L.800 J.D. [A Bolen,F.&B.]
*PRACTICE AREAS: Real Estate; Business Law.
**Peel, James W.** .................... '59 '86 C.267 B.S. L.1189 J.D. [Brown&P.]
*PRACTICE AREAS: Insurance Defense; Subrogation; Business Litigation; Personal Injury.
Peloian, James H., (BV) .............. '54 '79 C.267 B.S. L.1065 J.D. 4991 E. McKinley
Pena, Rosendo, Jr. .................... '55 '80 C.267 B.A. L.1068 J.D. 6103 N. First
**Penner, Randall M.** .................... '53 '81 C.999 B.A. L.1189 J.D. [Doyle,P.&B.]
*REPORTED CASES: Felix v. Asai (1987) 192 Cal.App.3d 926, 237 Cal.Rptr. 718; Smith v. Royal Ins. Co. (1986) 186 Cal.App.3d 239, 230 Cal.Rptr. 495; Jimenez v. Pacific Western Construction Co. (1986) 185 Cal.App.3d. 102, 229 Cal.Rptr. 575.
*PRACTICE AREAS: Civil Litigation; Products Liability; Personal Injury; Appellate Practice.
**Perkins, James H.**, (AV) .......... '28 '54 C&L.813 A.B., J.D. [McCormick,B.S.W.&C.]

CAA101P

CALIFORNIA—FRESNO MARTINDALE-HUBBELL LAW DIRECTORY 1997

**Perkins, Jan T.**, (BV) ....................'46 '73 C.101 B.A. L.878 J.D. [Perkins,M.&E.]
*LANGUAGES: Japanese.
*PRACTICE AREAS: Real Estate; Business Organization; Taxation Law; Probate; Estate Planning.

**Perkins, Mann & Everett, (BV)**
**2222 West Shaw, Suite 202, 93711-3407**
**Telephone: 209-447-5700 Facsimile: 209-447-5600**
**Jan T. Perkins; Jerry H. Mann; Reid H. Everett. Associate: Larry B. Lindenau.**
**General Civil and Trial Practice in State and Federal Courts. Agricultural Matters, Business, Corporation, Federal and State Taxation, Probate and Estate Planning, Real Estate, Securities Law, Commercial Law, Creditors Rights, Construction Law, Bond Law and Water Law.**
***See Professional Biographies, FRESNO, CALIFORNIA***

**Peterson, John E.**, (AV) ................ '41 '71 C.918 A.B. L.1066 J.D. [Jory,P.W.&S.]
*PRACTICE AREAS: Unfair Competition Law; Real Property; Business Dissolutions; Banking; Construction Defect Litigation.
Peterson, Royce G. .............. '47 '76 C.878 B.A. L.1049 J.D. 3335 W. Fremont Ave.
Petilla, Rudy ..........................................'40 '83 C.999 B.B.A. L.1197 J.D. 2115 Kern St.
**Petrie, J. David**, (BV) ...................'55 '80 C.169 B.S. L.464 J.D. [Borton,P.&C.]
*PRACTICE AREAS: Insurance Defense; Medical Malpractice.
Petrucelli, James Michael, (CV) ...... '49 '89 C.267 B.S. L.1189 J.D. 2350 W. Shaw Ave.
**Pettitt, Blaine** ........................ '16 '42 C.267 B.A. L.1065 J.D. [[C] Dowling,A.&K.]
Phebus, Earla J., (CV) ........................'41 '87 C.508 B.A. L.1189 J.D. [Emerson&Y.]
Phillips, Carolyn Del ...................................'53 '82 C.243 B.A. L.1230 J.D. [Milrod&P.]
Phillips, John W. ......................................'60 '90 C.267 B.S. L.61 J.D. [Jackson P.&N.]
**Phillips, Robert K.** ..............................'58 '86 C.37 B.A. L.602 J.D. [Phillips&S.]⊙
*REPORTED CASES: Creditors' Collection Service v. Hanzell Vineyards, Ltd., 5 Cal. App. 4th Supp. 1 (1992); State Farm Fire and Casualty Company v. Yu Kiyo, Ltd., et al., 870 Fed. Supp. 292 (1994); Edwards v. A.L. Lease & Co. (1st Dist., Div. 5) 46 Cal. App. 4th 1029 (1996).

**Phillips & Spallas, LLP**
**Maubridge Building, 2344 Tulare Street, 93721⊙**
**Telephone: 209-237-8805 Fax: 209-237-8812**
**Robert K. Phillips.**
**General Civil Trial Practice in all State and Federal Courts.**
**San Francisco Office: 225 Bush Street, 16th Floor. 94104. Telephone: 415-439-8870. Fax: 415-439-8822.**
**San Luis Obispo Office: 972 Santa Rosa Street. 93401. Telephone: 805-544-4875. Fax: 805-544-4877.**
***See Professional Biographies, FRESNO, CALIFORNIA***

Piacente, Robert V. ...................................................'64 '92 1725 N. Fine Ave.
**Pickering, Jerrald K.** .......................'56 '82 C.169 B.A. L.464 J.D. [[A] Forrest&M.]
*PRACTICE AREAS: Insurance Law and Defense; Business Litigation; International Law; Construction Law; Labor and Employment Law.
Pilegard, Cris A. ..................................'50 '76 C.112 B.A. L.1065 J.D. 1068 "G" St.‡
**Pimentel, Paul J.** ............................'60 '86 C.112 B.A. L.464 J.D. [Blanco,T.&P.]
*PRACTICE AREAS: Municipal Tort Defense; Business Litigation; Personal Injury; Medical Malpractice; Products Liability.
Pinion, G. Bryan, (CV) ..................'49 '80 C.112 B.A. L.464 J.D. 1221 Van Ness Ave.
Pinkerton, Jean ...................................................'47 '91 L.1189 J.D. 1120 T St.
Pitalo, J. Michael .................................'60 '88 C.112 A.B. L.464 J.D. 2444 Main St.

**Pogoloff, Donald D. '48 '72 C.112 B.A. L.1049 J.D.**
**2650 West Shaw Avenue, Suite 103, 93711**
**Telephone: 209-432-2650 Telefax: 209-432-2653**
**Mental Health Law, Health Care, Hospital Law and Non-Profit Organizations.**
***See Professional Biographies, FRESNO, CALIFORNIA***

Polglase, Janice E. ...........................'59 '89 C.267 B.S. L.1049 J.D. 6253 N Palm Ave
**Pool, Donald J.** ..........................'65 '93 C.1074 B.S. L.800 J.D. [[A] Kimble,M.&U.]
*PRACTICE AREAS: Commercial Litigation; Bankruptcy; Real Property; Collections; Receiverships.
Pope, Amy Lee ...................................'65 '91 C.112 B.A. L.1049 J.D. Dep. Dist. Atty.
Popovich, Milo .................................'13 '38 C.267 L.1065 J.D. 5836 E. Club View Dr.‡
Powell, Hanno T. ...........................'58 '87 C.1075 B.S. L.1049 J.D. 723 W. Shaw Ave.
Prenovost, John F. '51 '79 C.36 B.S. L.1137 J.D.
V.P. & Reg. Coun., First Amer. Title Ins. Co.
Pretzer, Janelle E., (CV) ......................'65 '90 C.267 B.S. L.464 J.D. Off. of Co. Coun.
Price, Edward Dean ........................'19 '49 C.112 A.B. L.1066 LL.B. Sr. U.S. Dist. J.‡
Price, Michael T. ..............................'62 '89 C.267 B.S. L.770 J.D. 1060 Fulton Mall
Proudian, Melissa A. .........................'61 '92 C.267 B.A. L.1065 J.D. 1551 E. Shaw
Putnam, Ralph L. ..........................................'46 '75 C.267 B.A. L.1189 J.D. Mun. J.
Quaschnick, James L. ..........................'33 '65 C.267 A.B. L.1065 LL.B. Supr. Ct. J.
**Quigley, Laurie L.** ............................'66 '91 C.112 B.A. L.1065 J.D. [[A] Lang,R.&P.]
*PRACTICE AREAS: Business Litigation; Construction Law; Personal Injury; Medical Malpractice.
Quinlan, W. Scott .............................'51 '81 C.267 B.A. L.1189 J.D. 2333 Merced St.
Quinlan, William A., (AV) ..............'26 '52 C.112 B.A. L.1065 J.D. [Quinlan,K.&F.]
Quinlan, Kershaw & Fanucchi, (AV) ......................................2409 Merced St.
Ramirez, Frank T. ...............................'52 '78 C.267 B.S. L.1066 J.D. 6103 N. First
Ramsey, Linda L. ............'63 '88 C.477 B.A. L.767 J.D. 5250 N. Palm Ave., Suite 201
Ratzlaff, Ruth E. .................................'50 '79 C.999 B.A. L.284 J.D. 5151 N. Palm
**Rau, Steven G.**, (AV) ..........'50 '75 C.112 B.A. L.1067 J.D. [McCormick,B.S.W.&C.]
*PRACTICE AREAS: Real Estate Development and Finance; General Business.
Rector, Donald F. ........'35 '65 C.188 A.B. L.767 LL.B. Adm. Law J., Social Sec. Admn.
**Reddie, Scott M.** ..............'68 '94 C.112 B.A. L.990 J.D. [[A] McCormick,B.S.W.&C.]
*PRACTICE AREAS: Business Workouts; Bankruptcy Reorganizations; Creditors Remedies.
Reed, Charles L., (BV) .....................'44 '75 C.36 B.S. L.770 J.D. 5151 N. Palm Ave.
Reed, John L. ......................................'54 '80 C.37 L.1186 J.D. Dep. Pub. Def.
**Refuerzo, Carl R.**, (BV) ......................'57 '82 C.112 A.B. L.1066 J.D. [Baker,M.&J.]
*PRACTICE AREAS: Agriculture; Business; Real Estate and Water Law.
Refuerzo, Sharon M. ............... '56 '83 C.1077 B.A. L.767 J.D. Staff Atty., Ct. of App.
Register, G. June, (BV) ........................'30 '72 C.999 L.1132 LL.B. 1120 "T" St.
Reid, Jeffrey M., (BV) .................'59 '84 C.154 B.A. L.1066 J.D. 5 River Park Pl. E.
Reinhardt, LeRoy J., (BV) ..............'24 '50 C.267 A.B. L.813 J.D. 1500 W. Shaw Ave.
**Reis, Sean P.** ...................'71 '96 C.112 B.A. L.705 J.D. [[A] McCormick,B.S.W.&C.]
*LANGUAGES: Spanish.
*PRACTICE AREAS: Insurance Coverage; Bad Faith Litigation.
**Reisig, Jeff W.** ...........................................'69 '96 C.112 L.464 J.D. [Jory,P.W.&S.]
*PRACTICE AREAS: Business Litigation; Employment Litigation.
Reitz-Braze, Patrice ........................'52 '78 C.267 B.S. L.1132 J.D. 2030 Fresno St.
**Renberg, Charles L.**, (AV) ..........'32 '63 C.112 B.A. L.1065 J.D. [Parichan,R.C.&H.]
*PRACTICE AREAS: Insurance Defense Law and Coverage; Environmental; Products Liability and Litigation.
**Renberg, Michael L.** ................'62 '88 C.112 B.A. L.767 J.D. [[A] Parichan,R.C.&H.]
*PRACTICE AREAS: Environmental Law; Insurance Law.
Renge, Lawson K. ..........................'45 '71 C.112 A.B. L.284 J.D. 1330 L St.
Revvill, Jack Carson ............ '56 '91 C.1042 B.A. L.1067 J.D. 1350 Van Ness Ave.
Reynolds, Russell W. '54 '88
C.1074 B.S. L.1189 J.D. V.P. & Coun., Vallicorp Holdings, Inc.
Rice, Dawrence W., Jr. ..................'56 '86 C.1070 B.S. L.464 J.D. Dep. Dist. Atty.

**Richardson, Jones & Esraelian, (BV)**
**A Partnership including a Professional Corporation**
**2660 West Shaw, Suite 100, 93711**
**Telephone: 209-449-1028 Fax: 209-449-8744**

(This Listing Continued)

**Richardson, Jones & Esraelian (Continued)**

**Members of Firm: Baxter K. Richardson (1921-1992); Robert L. Jones, Jr., (Inc.); Robyn L. Esraelian.**
**Taxation, Probate and Estate Planning. General Corporate Practice. Pension and Profit Sharing, Real Property Law.**
**Reference: Bank of Fresno.**
***See Professional Biographies, FRESNO, CALIFORNIA***

Richtel, Melvin M., (BV) ......................'47 '73 C.112 B.A. L.1068 J.D. [Richtel&S.]
Richtel & Smith, (BV) ..........................................................2547 W. Shaw Ave.
**Rickelman, Keith C.** ...............'58 '88 C.339 B.S. L.1137 J.D. [Jacobson,H.N.&F.]
*PRACTICE AREAS: Civil Litigation; Insurance Defense Law.
**Riggs, Thomas J.**, (BV) ...............'44 '74 C.763 B.S. L.1049 J.D. [Lozano S.S.W.&B.]
*REPORTED CASES: U.S. v. Fresno Unified School District (1976) 412 F. Supp. 392 (1979) 592 D.2d 1088; Rosato v. Superior Court (1975) 51 Cal. App. 3d 190; Drum v. Fresno County Dept. of Public Works (1983) 144 Cal. App. 3d 777; Fig Gordon Park No. 2 Assn. v. LAFCO (1984) 162 Cal. App. 3d 336.
*PRACTICE AREAS: Municipal Law; Local Government; Land Use; Eminent Domain.
Riley, Laura J. ....................'61 '88 C.112 B.A. L.285 J.D. Research Atty., Supr. Ct.
Rindlisbacher, Curtis D. ......................'59 '89 C.101 B.A. L.64 J.D. [Thomas&R.]
Robbins, Robert B., (BV) .....................'31 '61 C&L.800 B.S., J.D. [R.B.Robbins]
Robbins, Robert B., P.C., (BV) ......................................................5151 N. Palm
Roberson, Clifford E. .............'37 '67 C.502 B.A. L.904 J.D. Calif. State Univ.
Roberts, David E. ...............................'39 '71 C.1056 B.S. L.464 J.D. P.O. Box 11242
Roberts, Gregory J. ...................'61 '89 C&L.878 B.S., J.D. [[A] Christensen,B.&B.]
**Robinson, Max Edward**, (AV) ...... '32 '58 C&L.45 B.A., LL.B. [[C] Lozano S.S.W.&B.]
Robinson, Paul M. ..........................'46 '80 C.267 B.A. L.112 J.D. Research Atty.
Rockas, Chris E. .......................'30 '55 C.112 A.B. L.1066 LL.B. 929 "L" St.‡
Rodriguez, Armando O. .................'29 '65 C.267 B.A. L.1026 LL.B. Mun. Ct. J.
Roney, Gerard F. .........................'46 '76 C.768 B.A. L.1065 J.D. 8461 N. 8th St.
Rooney, Kevin P. ...........................'55 '80 C.188 B.S. L.245 J.D. Asst. U.S. Atty.

**Rosati, Robert J., (CV) '54 '83 C.1044 B.A. L.1065 J.D.**
**800 M Street, 93721**
**Telephone: 209-268-4021 Facsimile: 209-268-5446**
**Civil Trial and Appellate Practice in all Courts, Business Litigation, Insurance Coverage and Litigation, Labor and Employment, Personal Injury, Environmental and Land Use.**
***See Professional Biographies, FRESNO, CALIFORNIA***

Ross, Audrey Ann '60 '89 C.906 B.A. L.678 J.D.
(adm. in WA; not adm. in CA) 7793 E. Saginaw Way
**Ross, Marcia A.** ...............................'44 '92 C.112 A.B. L.464 J.D. [Jory,P.W.&S.]
*PRACTICE AREAS: Labor (Management) Law; Employment Discrimination Law; Sexual Harassment; Wage and Hour Law; Occupational Safety and Health.
Rountree, L. Clarke, (BV) ..........'43 '72 C.169 A.B. L.1067 J.D. 2505B W. Shaw Ave.
Rowe, Michael E. ...........................'56 '83 C.347 A.B. L.602 J.D. 2300 Tulare St.
**Rowe, Roberta** .......................'53 '96 C.1076 B.S. L.1189 J.D. [Chinello,A.S.&S.]
*PRACTICE AREAS: Insurance Defense.
Rowell, David L. ..................'48 '91 C.1044 A.S.N. L.464 J.D. 1530 East Shaw Ave.

**Rowley, Daniel W. '55 '83 C.768 B.A. L.809 J.D.**
**Guarantee Financial Center, 1320 East Shaw Avenue, Suite 126, 93710**
**Telephone: 209-244-6940 Facsimile: 209-244-6950**
***PRACTICE AREAS: Commercial Litigation; Business Litigation; Employment Litigation. Commercial, Business and Employment Law Litigation, Civil Appeals and Writs.**
***See Professional Biographies, FRESNO, CALIFORNIA***

**Rowley, Glenn A.** ...........................'56 '94 C&L.101 B.A., J.D. [[A] Baker,M.&J.]
*LANGUAGES: French and Japanese.
**Rube, Melvin K.**, (BV) ...........'50 '78 C.112 B.A. L.1132 J.D. [Ericksen,A.K.D.&L.]
*PRACTICE AREAS: Personal Injury Defense; Wills/Probate.
Runner, John F. ....................'14 '48 C.112 A.B. L.813 LL.B. 1132 S. Park Cir. Dr.‡
**Runyon, Brett L.**, (CV) ..........'59 '88 C.267 B.S. L.1189 J.D. [Marderosian,S.&O.]
*PRACTICE AREAS: Insurance Defense; Bad Faith; Personal Injury; Construction Law; Libel Slander.
Russell, Daniel P., (BV) .................'49 '73 C.112 B.A. L.1067 J.D. 555 W. Shaw
**Russell, Jeffrey A.** ........................'59 '86 C.945 B.B.A. L.569 J.D. [Bolen,F.&B.]
*PRACTICE AREAS: Agricultural Law; Business Law; Real Estate.
**Russell, T. Newton**, (AV) .............'18 '43 C&L.813 A.B., J.D. [[C] Thomas,S.J.R.&A.]
*PRACTICE AREAS: Estate Planning Law; Probate Law; Trust Administration Law.

**Rustigian, Darrel R., (CV) '58 '85 C.267 B.A. L.767 J.D.**
**545 East Alluvial Avenue, Suite 107, 93720**
**Telephone: 209-438-8732 Fax: 209-438-7219**
***PRACTICE AREAS: Business Law; Personal Injury.**
**Personal Injury, Civil Litigation, Real Estate and Business Law.**
***See Professional Biographies, FRESNO, CALIFORNIA***

**Ruyak, Matthew D.** ..........................'69 '96 C.94 B.A. L.1065 J.D. [[A] Jory,P.W.&S.]
**Ryan, Richard A.** ....................'58 '91 C&L.36 B.S.C.E., J.D. [[A] Baker,M.&J.]
*PRACTICE AREAS: Patent, Trademark, Copyright and Unfair Competition Law; Litigation.
**Ryan, Russell K.**, (BV) ...........'61 '89 C.101 B.S. L.1066 J.D. [Motschiedler,M.&W.]
*PRACTICE AREAS: Labor and Employment Law; Business and Employment Litigation; Real Estate Law; Unfair Competition; Appellate Practice.
**Ryder, Hilton A.**, (AV) ..........'40 '72 C.350 B.S. L.770 J.D. [McCormick,B.S.W.&C.]
*PRACTICE AREAS: Bankruptcy and Insolvency Workouts.
**Sagaser, Howard A.**, (AV) ............'50 '76 C.1074 B.S. L.1065 J.D. [Sagaser,H.F.&J.]
*REPORTED CASES: Holcomb v. Bingham Toyota, 871 F.2d 109 (1989); J.R. Norton Co. Inc. v. Agricultural Labor Relations Board, 26 Cal. 3d 1, 160 Cal. Rptr. 710 (Amicus) (1979); Joe A. Freitas & Sons v. Food Packers, Processors and Warehousemen Local 865, International Brotherhood of Teamsters, 164 Cal. App. 3d 1210, 211 Cal. Rptr. 157 (1985); Quinn Company, 273 NLRB No. 107, 118 LRRM 1239 (1984); Harris Farms, Inc. v. Superior Court of Fresno County, 285 Cal. Rptr. 659, 234 Cal. App. 3d 415 (1991).
*PRACTICE AREAS: Labor (Management) Law; Labor Negotiations; Agricultural Law; Civil Rights Law; Employment Discrimination Law.

**Sagaser, Hansen, Franson & Jamison, A Professional Corporation, (AV) [BB]**
**2445 Capitol Street, Second Floor, P.O. Box 1632, 93717-1632**
**Telephone: 209-233-4800 Fax: 209-233-9330**
**Eric K. Hansen (1952-1996); Howard A. Sagaser; Donald R. Franson, Jr.; Daniel O. Jamison; Nancy A. Maler; Kimberly A. Gaab; Patti L. Williams; K. Poncho Baker; Kristi R. Culver; Catherine J. Cerna.**
**Civil Trial and Appellate Practice in all State and Federal Courts. Commercial, Agricultural and Employment Litigation, Labor Relations Law (Management). Agricultural Labor, Equal Employment, Wage and Hour, Wrongful Discharge Law and Litigation and Health Care Litigation.**
***See Professional Biographies, FRESNO, CALIFORNIA***

Sage, John A. ...........................'24 '54 C.112 B.S. L.813 LL.B. 2555 W. Bluff Ave.‡
St. Louis, David J., (BV) ....................'39 '67 C.267 B.A. L.1065 J.D. [D.J.St. Louis]
St. Louis, David J., Inc., A Professional Corporation, (BV) ..............575 East Alluvial
Salazar, Steven F. ..........................'56 '87 C.267 B.A. L.1189 J.D. 6535 N. Palm Ave.
**Saldaña, Val W.**, (AV) .....................'51 '77 C.267 B.A. L.1067 J.D. [Lang,R.&P.]
*PRACTICE AREAS: Construction Litigation; Insurance Law; Financial Litigation; Lender Liability Litigation.
**Salinas, Richard S.** .......................'66 '91 C.1212 B.A. L.1067 J.D. [[A] Baker,M.&J.]
*PRACTICE AREAS: Medical Malpractice Defense; Business Litigation.
**Salisbury, Lawrence J.** ............'69 '95 C.1060 B.A. L.1067 J.D. [[A] Kimble,M.&U.]
*PRACTICE AREAS: Business Litigation.

CAA102P

**Salisch, Victoria J.**, (BV) .......... '42 '72 C.112 L.464 J.D. [Lang,R.&P.]
*PRACTICE AREAS: Real Property Law; Development and Finance; Business Law.
Salisch & Salisch, A Professional Law Corporation .......... 3459 W. Shaw Ave.
Sample, René L. .......... '63 '88 C.267 B.S. L.1189 J.D. 5 River Pk. Pl. E.
Sanchez, James C., (CV) .......... '59 '84 C.990 B.A. L.1065 J.D. Asst. City Atty.‡
Sanchez, James J. .......... '50 '76 C.267 L.1189 J.D. 2444 Main St.

**Sandell & Young, (BV)**
**An Association of Attorneys including a Professional Corporation**
**Suite B, 929 "L" Street, 93721-2699**
**Telephone: 209-445-1500 Fax: 209-445-1509**
**Harold D. Sandell (Inc.) (1927-1991); William M. Young (Inc.); Roberta J. Duffy.**
**General Civil and Trial Practice. Insurance Defense, Casualty, Surety, Personal Injury, Negligence, Probate and Estate Planning, Insurance, Appellate Practice, Products Liability, Premises Liability and Probate Law.**
**Representative Clients: California Casualty Indemnity Exchange; Armed Forces Cooperative Insurance Corp.; Fireman's Fund American Insurance Cos.; Allstate Insurance; The Hartford Insurance Group; United Services Automobile Assn.; Hanover Insurance Group; United Pacific/Reliance Insurance Cos.**
*See Professional Biographies, FRESNO, CALIFORNIA*

Sannar, Thomas C. .......... '42 '72 C.112 A.B. L.464 J.D. 5340 N. Fresno St.‡
Sanoian, Joanne .......... '50 '82 C.267 B.S. L.1189 J.D. 800 "M" St.
**Saqui, Michael C.** .......... '63 '90 C.436 B.A. L.61 J.D. [Barsamian&S.]
*PRACTICE AREAS: Labor Law; Labor Negotiations; Employment Law; Construction; Transportation.
Sarkisian, Edward, Jr. .......... '40 '66 C.267 B.A. L.1066 LL.B. Mun. Ct. J.
Savala, Rudy L., (CV) .......... '30 '66 C.267 B.S. L.767 LL.B. 313 N. Blackstone Ave.
Savrnoch, John T. .......... '63 '90 C.436 B.S. L.966 J.D. 5 River Park Pl. E.

**Sawyers, Gary W., (AV) '55 '80 C.112 B.A. L.1068 J.D.**
**1180 East Shaw Avenue Suite 214, 93710-7812**
**Telephone: 209-228-8190 Facsimile: 209-225-8955**
**Email: gsawyers@aol.com**
**—Melanie J. Aldridge.**
**Water Law, Water Rights, Agricultural Matters, Public Agency Representation, Business Law and Real Estate Transactions.**
*See Professional Biographies, FRESNO, CALIFORNIA*

**Scharton, Barbara L.** .......... '61 '93 L.1189 J.D. [Myers&O.]
**Scheithauer, Chris** .......... '71 '96 C&L.800 B.A., J.D. [⊡ McCormick,B.S.W.&C.]
*PRACTICE AREAS: Business Litigation; Insurance Defense.
**Schmalle, Robert C.** .......... '60 '91 C.999 A.A. L.1189 J.D. [⊡ Wild,C.&T.]
*PRACTICE AREAS: Business Litigation; Environmental Law; Entertainment Law (Music).
Schneider, Stephen J. .......... '44 '71 C.330 A.B. L.1065 J.D. 2444 Main St.
**Schnitzer, Harvie Ruth** .......... '65 '92 C.267 B.A. L.284 J.D. [Myers&O.]
**Schorling, Douglas D.**, (BV) .......... '55 '80 C.267 B.A. L.1067 J.D. [⊡ Dietrich,G.&J.]
*PRACTICE AREAS: Business Transactions; Health Care Law; Probate Law.
**Schrandt, Stephanie A.** .......... '69 '95 C&L.378 B.S.J., J.D. [⊡ McCormick,B.S.W.&C.]
*PRACTICE AREAS: Civil Litigation.
Schreiber, Lenore .......... '42 '68 C&L.273 A.B., J.D. 925 N. St.
**Schulthies, Colleen** .......... '56 '94 C.101 B.A. L.878 J.D. [⊡ Baker,M.&J.]
Sciandra, Salvatore, (AV) .......... '46 '73 C.1097 B.A. L.1049 J.D. 2300 Tulare St.
**Scribner, Robert H.**, (AV) .......... '48 '73 C.112 A.B. L.1065 J.D. [Kimble,M.&U.]
*REPORTED CASES: Wisenburg v. Molina (1976) 58 Cal.App.3d 478.
*PRACTICE AREAS: Business Litigation; Real Property Law.
**Seiler, William J.**, (BV) .......... '47 '75 C.147 B.A. L.1067 J.D. [Miles,S.&E.]
*PRACTICE AREAS: Plaintiffs Personal Injury Law and Related Litigation.
Sena, Barbara A. .......... '38 '63 C&L.209 B.A., J.D. 1713 Tulare St.
**Seng, Michael J.**, (AV) .......... '47 '75 C&L.838 B.S., J.D. [Blumberg,S.&I.]
*PRACTICE AREAS: Professional Malpractice Defense; Lender Liability Defense; General Litigation.
Sepulveda, Victor .......... '35 '69 C.809 L.1148 J.D. P.O. Box 28307
Serimian, Marlon .......... '65 '94 C.800 B.S. L.464 J.D. [⊡ Jackson P.&N.]
Servatius, Kathleen A. .......... '62 '87 C.1031 B.A. L.112 J.D. U.S. Atty. Off.

**Setrakian, Philip S. '47 '74 C.112 B.A. L.464 J.D.**
**2350 West Shaw Avenue, Suite 106, 93711**
**Telephone: 209-439-7000 Fax: 209-439-7087**
**Personal Injury, Plaintiff, Criminal Defense, Adult, Juvenile, Federal and State.**
*See Professional Biographies, FRESNO, CALIFORNIA*

**Seymour, Christopher E.** .......... '60 '86 C.1074 B.A. L.426 J.D. [Dietrich,G.&J.]
*PRACTICE AREAS: Business; Construction and Design Professionals Malpractice; Litigation.
Shahbazian, Steven L., (BV) .......... '49 '74 C.267 B.A. L.1068 J.D. 906 "N" St.
Shapiro, Myron .......... '40 '72 C&L.1095 B.A., J.D. Chf. Dep. Dist. Atty.
**Sharp, Sarah A.** .......... '43 '88 C.267 B.A. L.800 J.D. [Mullen&F.]
Sharpe, Thomas M., (BV) .......... '46 '83 C.267 B.A. L.1189 J.D. [Bennett&S.]
**Shebelut-Krause, Elise M.** .......... '62 '87 C.800 B.S. L.1065 J.D. [Blumberg,S.&I.]
*PRACTICE AREAS: Employment Law; Business Litigation; Professional Malpractice Defense; Agricultural Law.
**Shekoyan, James E.**, (AV) .......... '40 '66 C.813 A.B. L.1065 J.D. [Baker,M.&J.]
*PRACTICE AREAS: Estate Planning and Probate Law; Business and Real Estate Transactions.
**Shelton, John M.**, (AV) .......... '31 '57 C.267 A.B. L.1065 J.D. [⊡ Chinello,A.S.&S.]
Shepard, James I. '42 '68 C.352 B.A. L.208 J.D.
(adm. in IA; not adm. in CA) 2682 W. Dovewood Lane‡
Shepard, James S., (BV) .......... '32 '60 C.267 A.B. L.1066 LL.B. 191 W. Shaw Ave.
**Sheppard, Dudley W.**, (AV) '07 '32
C.112 A.B. L.1066 LL.B. [⊡ McCormick,B.S.W.&C.] ‡
**Sherr, Morris M.**, (AV) .......... '30 '56 C.768 B.A. L.1065 J.D. [⊡ Dowling,A.&K.]
*PRACTICE AREAS: Taxation; Estate Planning; Probate; Business Law; Real Estate.
**Sherwood, James C.**, (CV) .......... '65 '90 C.1073 B.S. L.1049 J.D. [⊡ Dowling,A.&K.]
*PRACTICE AREAS: Employment Litigation; Construction Law; Business Litigation; Insurance Defense; Labor Law.
**Shewan, Scott R.**, (BV) .......... '58 '83 C.999 B.A. L.178 J.D. [Thomas,S.J.R.&A.]
*PRACTICE AREAS: Civil Litigation; Securities Arbitration.
Shields, H. R. Hal, (CV) .......... '42 '72 C.267 A.B. L.1065 J.D. 770 E. Shaw Ave.
Shinaver, Gary M., (BV) .......... '55 '83 C.267 B.A. L.61 J.D. Sr. Def. Atty., Pub. Def. Off.
Shipley, William L., Jr., (CV) .......... '61 '88 C.112 B.A. L.1184 J.D. Off. of U.S. Atty.
**Silva, Bradley A.**, (BV) .......... '58 '83 C.267 B.S. L.770 J.D. [Lang,R.&P.]
*PRACTICE AREAS: Construction Litigation; Commercial Law; Agriculture Law; Railroad Law Practice.
Silva, Phillip A. .......... '49 '75 C.267 B.S. L.1065 J.D. Ref., Juv. Ct.
**Simon, Peter L.D.** .......... '68 '95 C.112 B.A. L.770 J.D. [⊡ McCormick,B.S.W.&C.]
*PRACTICE AREAS: Business Litigation; Environmental Litigation; Intellectual Property Litigation.
Simonian, Jeffrey D., (CV) .......... '59 '85 C.267 B.S. L.280 J.D. 1381 E. Decatur
**Simpson, Alan M.**, (CV) .......... '55 '86 C.267 B.A. L.1189 J.D. [Marderosian,S.&O.]
*PRACTICE AREAS: Insurance Defense; Bad Faith; Personal Injury.
**Sims, Trevin E.** .......... '68 '93 C.1288 B.S. L.112 J.D. [⊡ Lozano S.S.W.&B.]
*PRACTICE AREAS: Litigation; Education Law.
Sirabian, John, (A P.C.), (CV) .......... '37 '77 C.1016 B.S. L.1132 J.D. 1665 W. Shaw Ave.
Sisk, Curtis B. .......... '42 '75 L.1221 J.D. 2300 Tulare St.
**Slater, Michael P.**, (CV) .......... '63 '90 C.112 B.A. L.1049 J.D. [Blumberg,S.&I.]
*PRACTICE AREAS: Civil Litigation; Professional Malpractice Defense.
Slinkard, Theodore L., (BV) .......... '27 '61 C.267 L.1065 J.D. 2017 N. Gateway
**Small, Charles E.**, (AV) .......... '28 '57 C.112 B.S. L.1068 J.D. [⊡ Thomas,S.J.R.&A.]
Smith, Gary A., (CV) .......... '45 '77 C.97 B.A. L.1189 J.D. 3455 W. Shaw Ave.
Smith, Gregory J., (BV) .......... '60 '84 C.1060 B.S. L.464 J.D. 1690 W. Shaw
**Smith, Gregory J.** .......... '60 '86 C.1060 B.S. L.464 J.D. [Littler,M.F.T.&M.]
**Smith, John L. B.**, (BV) .......... '45 '75 C.870 B.S. L.1065 J.D. [Baker,M.&J.]
*PRACTICE AREAS: Environmental and Business Litigation.
**Smith, Lee N.** .......... '59 '88 C.103 A.B. L.878 J.D. [⊡ Graham&J.] (⊙Sacramento)
**Smith, M. Bruce** .......... '56 '81 C.112 B.A. L.1065 J.D. [Stammer,M.B.&B.]
*PRACTICE AREAS: Insurance Defense; Employment Discrimination; Sexual Harassment; Criminal Law.
**Smith, Michael E.**, (BV) .......... '54 '80 C.154 B.A. L.1067 J.D. [Lozano S.S.W.&B.]
*REPORTED CASES: Clarence Dilts v. Cantua Elementary School District (1987) 189 Cal. App. 3d 27, 234 Cal. Rptr. 612; Belanger v. Madera Unified School District (9th Cir. 1992) 963 F. 2d 248.
*PRACTICE AREAS: Local Government; School Law; Labor Law; Employment Law; Contract Law.
**Smith, Michael Jens F.**, (BV) .......... '55 '83 C.112 B.A. L.1065 J.D. [Jory,P.W.&S.]
*PRACTICE AREAS: Insurance Coverage; Business Litigation; Employment Litigation.
**Smith, Myron F.**, (BV) .......... '47 '76 C.502 B.A. L.464 J.D. [Motschiedler,M.&W.]
*PRACTICE AREAS: Business Law; Construction Litigation; Insurance Coverage Litigation.
Smith, Ralph C., (BV) .......... '47 '79 C.101 B.A. L.464 J.D. 690 E. Bullard Ave.
Smith, Ransome M., (BV) .......... '33 '59 C.267 B.A. L.1065 LL.B. 6435 N. Palm
Smith, Sheila M. .......... '43 '83 C.267 B.S. L.464 J.D. Dep. City Atty.
Smith, Stephen A., (BV) .......... '49 '77 C.768 B.A. L.464 J.D. [S.A.Smith]
Smith, Steven J., (BV) .......... '50 '78 C.101 B.A. L.464 J.D. 2425 W. Shaw Ave.
Smith, T. Bruce .......... '23 '51 C&L.800 B.S., LL.B. Gen. Coun., United Faith Found.
Smith, Ted A. .......... '64 '92 C.375 B.S. L.378 J.D. 5 River Pk. Pl. E.
Smith, William J., (BV) .......... '46 '73 C.112 B.A. L.1068 J.D. [Richtel&S.]
Smith, Stephen A., A P.C., (BV) .......... 2030 Fresno St.
Smoke, G. Arthur, Jr., (CV) .......... '52 '80 C.169 B.A. L.1132 J.D. 10 River Park Pl., E.
**Snauffer, Mark W.**, (BV) .......... '53 '77 C.112 A.B. L.1068 J.D. [Baker,M.&J.]
*PRACTICE AREAS: Civil Litigation; Product Liability; Professional Liability Defense.
**Snell, William N.**, (AV) .......... '16 '40 C&L.813 A.B., J.D. [⊡ Thomas,S.J.R.&A.]
*REPORTED CASES: Brown v. Halbert, 271 Cal. App. 2d 252; 38 ALR 3d 718.
*PRACTICE AREAS: Corporate Law; Business Law; Products Liability; Securities.
Snyder, LeRoy, Jr., (AV) .......... '25 '50 C.999 L.800 J.D. 1180 East Shaw Ave.
Socha, Stephen E. .......... '53 '79 C.103 A.B. L.94 J.D. Sr. Staff Atty., Calif. Ct. Of App.
Soley, Judith Leslie, (Inc.), (AV) .......... '45 '71 C.112 A.B. L.1066 J.D. 925 "N" St.
Sonder, Tami Suzanne .......... '44 '70 C.112 A.B. L.1065 J.D. Dep. Dist. Atty.
**Sondergaard, Lisa A.** .......... '69 '96 C.800 B.A. L.1189 J.D. [⊡ McCormick,B.S.W.&C.]
*PRACTICE AREAS: Insurance; General Civil Litigation.
Spaulding, Jill .......... '48 '74 C.813 B.A. L.1065 J.D. 2037 W. Bullard
**Spillner, Justus C.**, (BV) .......... '50 '75 C.1073 B.A. L.1049 J.D. [McCormick,B.S.W.&C.]

**Stammer, McKnight, Barnum & Bailey, (AV)** ⊡
**2540 West Shaw Lane, Suite 110, P.O. Box 9789, 93794-9789**
**Telephone: 209-449-0571 Fax: 209-432-2619**
**W. H. Stammer (1891-1969); James K. Barnum (1918-1987); Dean A. Bailey (1924-1995); Galen McKnight (1904-1991); James N. Hays; Carey H. Johnson; Frank D. Maul; Craig M. Mortensen; Jerry D. Jones; Michael P. Mallery; M. Bruce Smith; Thomas J. Georgouses. Associates: Steven R. Stoker; M. Jaqueline Yates; Bruce J. Berger; Celene M.E. Boggs.**
**General Civil and Trial Practice. Insurance, Water Rights Law.**
**Representative Clients: Pacific Bell; Chevron, U.S.A.; Fresno Irrigation District; The Travelers Insurance Group; State Farm Insurance Cos.;**
**Reference: Bank of America National Trust & Savings Assn. (Fresno Main Office).**
*See Professional Biographies, FRESNO, CALIFORNIA*

**Stamper, R. Marc** .......... '61 '87 C.112 B.A. L.1049 J.D. [Ericksen,A.K.D.&L.]
*PRACTICE AREAS: Insurance Defense; Business Litigation; Plaintiff Personal Injury.
**Stander, John J.** .......... '67 '93 C.569 B.A. L.767 J.D. [⊡ Jory,P.W.&S.]
Stefano, Marc A. .......... '32 '69 C.147 L.1132 J.D. 3855 N. West
**Stegall, Nancy J.** .......... '52 '96 C.112 L.999 J.D. [⊡ Blumberg,S.&I.]
*PRACTICE AREAS: Professional Malpractice; Business Litigation.
Stephenson, Leland D. .......... '40 '66 C&L.813 A.B., J.D. 2344 Tulare St.
Stepp, Craig Alan, (CV) .......... '52 '87 C.101 B.S. L.1189 J.D. 443 E. Shields Ave.
Stevenson, Daniel G. .......... '34 '86 C.684 B.A. L.1226 J.D. 1725 N. Fine Ave.
**Stewart, Malcolm H.**, (BV) .......... '43 '78 C.24 B.A. L.1189 J.D. [Chinello,A.S.&S.]
*PRACTICE AREAS: Insurance Defense; Civil Litigation.
Stewart, Mary A., (CV) .......... '51 '82 C.112 A.B. L.1189 J.D. 2440 W. Shaw Ave.
**Stoker, Steven R.** .......... '63 '91 C&L.101 B.A., J.D. [⊡ Stammer,M.B.&B.]
*LANGUAGES: Spanish.
*PRACTICE AREAS: Negligence Law; Litigation; Construction Law; Business Litigation; Health Care Law.
Stone, William A. .......... '39 '65 C&L.813 A.B., J.D. Assoc. Jus., Ct. of App.
**Strasser, George L.**, (BV) .......... '50 '75 C.147 B.A. L.1066 J.D. [Baker,M.&J.]
*PRACTICE AREAS: Business Litigation including Toxics (30%); Medical Malpractice Defense (70%).
**Stratton, Beth Maxwell**, (BV) .......... '63 '88 C.112 B.A. L.1049 J.D. [Caswell,B.H.B.&G.]
*LANGUAGES: Spanish.
*PRACTICE AREAS: Business and Commercial Litigation; Real Estate Litigation; Creditor's Rights; Collections.
Strawn, Thomas C., III .......... '66 '91 C.880 B.A. L.37 J.D. 5 River Park Pl. E.
**Strong, Richard C.**, (BV) .......... '54 '79 C.813 A.B. L.94 J.D. [Chinello,A.S.&S.]
*PRACTICE AREAS: Real Estate; Land Development; Business; Transactions.
Stroup, Robert W. .......... '41 '75 C.768 B.S. L.770 J.D. [Stroup&d.]
Stroup & de Goede .......... 1725 N. Fine Ave.
Stutsman, Judith A. .......... '48 '81 C.267 B.S. L.770 J.D. Soc. Sec. Admin
**Sullivan, Robert L., Jr.**, (AV) .......... '42 '68 C.112 B.S. L.767 J.D. [McGregor,D.S.&K.]
*PRACTICE AREAS: Estate and Tax Planning Law; Trust and Estate Administration Law; Taxation Law.
**Sullivan, Timothy R.** .......... '60 '87 C&L.502 B.A., J.D. [⊡ Forrest&M.]
*PRACTICE AREAS: Insurance Coverage; Bad Faith Litigation; General Civil Trial and Appellate Practice; Business Litigation.
**Sutton, S. Brett** .......... '63 '89 C&L.990 B.A., J.D. [Kimble,M.&U.]
*REPORTED CASES: United States v. Thornburg, 835 F.Supp. 543 (E.D.Cal. 1993).
*PRACTICE AREAS: Commercial Litigation; Real Estate Litigation; Products Liability Defense; Civil Litigation; Trial Practice.
**Swanson, James W.**, (BV) .......... '46 '77 C.267 B.S. L.1189 J.D. [Marderosian,S.&O.]
*PRACTICE AREAS: Insurance Defense; Bad Faith; Personal Injury.
Symes, Deborah M. .......... '51 '77 C.112 A.B. L.1065 J.D. Staff Atty., Ct. of App.
Tahajian, Gerald Lee, (BV) '41 '70 C.267 B.S. L.767 J.D.
4321 N. West Ave. (⊙Los Angeles & Anaheim)
Tangeman, Daniel J. .......... '66 '94 C.937 B.A. L.309 J.D. 5260 N. Palm
Taniguchi, Kenneth K. .......... '51 '81 C.112 B.S. L.809 J.D. Dep. Pub. Def.
Tarr, James G. .......... '27 '61 C.602 B.S.M.E. L.1068 LL.B. Wkrs. Comp. J.
Tatarian, Brian I., (BV) .......... '53 '79 C&L.1137 B.S., J.D. 1221 Van Ness Ave.
**Tatham, Michael F.**, (BV) .......... '58 '85 C.267 B.S. L.990 J.D. [Kimble,M.&U.]
*PRACTICE AREAS: Corporate Law; Real Estate Law; Secured Lending; Insolvency Law.
Tavlian, Philip E. .......... '53 '80 C.267 B.A. L.1189 J.D. Sr. Atty., Ct. of App.
**Taylor, Angela E.** .......... '70 '95 C.112 B.A. L.770 J.D. [⊡ Thomas,S.J.R.&A.]
**Taylor, Charles Trudrung** .......... '54 '86 C.267 B.A. L.770 J.D. [Lang,R.&P.]
*PRACTICE AREAS: Employment Law; Federal Civil Practice; Insurance Law.
Taylor, D. Mitchell, (CV) .......... '54 '83 C.267 B.S. L.1189 J.D. 2350 W. Shaw Ave.
Tedesco, Branden J. .......... '65 '91 C.112 A.B. L.1065 J.D. 5260 N.Palm, Ste., 421
**Tekunoff, Daniel J.** .......... '65 '92 C.112 B.A. L.425 J.D. [⊡ Borton,P.&C.]
*PRACTICE AREAS: Insurance Defense; Bankruptcy; Landlord Tenant.
Templeton, Russell E., (BV) .......... '47 '72 C.112 B.A. L.1067 J.D. 7720 N. Fresno St.
Terry, Anthony L. .......... '46 '76 C.101 B.A. L.1137 J.D. [A.L.Terry]
Terry, Anthony L., A Prof. Corp. .......... 906 "N" St.

**Tharpe, D. Tyler**, (BV) . . . . . . . . . . '59 '85 C.267 B.A. L.464 J.D. [Kimble,M.&U.]
*REPORTED CASES: Mateo-woodburn v. Fresno County Hosp. (1990) 221 Cal.App3d 1169; Rosenfeld Construction Company, Inc. v. Superior Court (1991) 235 Cal.App.3d 566; United States v. Thornburg; 835 F.Supp. 543 (E.D.Cal. 1993); Rhône-Poulenc Agrochime S.A. v. Biagro Western Sales, Inc., 35 U.S.P.Q.2d. 1203 (E.D.Cal. 1994).
*PRACTICE AREAS: Commercial Litigation; Employee Benefits Litigation; Intellectual Property Litigation; Appellate Practice.
Thaxter, James F. . . . . . . . . . . '33 '60 C.267 A.B. L.1065 J.D. Assoc. Jus., App. Ct.
Thomas, Wayne H., Jr., (BV) . . . . . . '44 '72 C.112 B.A. L.1067 J.D. 2660 W. Shaw
Thomas, Wm. Lanier . . . . . . . . . . '53 '79 C.1239 B.A. L.802 J.D. [Thomas&R.]
Thomas & Rindlisbacher . . . . . . . . . . 4949 N. Crystal St.

**Thomas, Snell, Jamison, Russell and Asperger, A Professional Corporation, (AV)**
**2445 Capitol Street, P.O. Box 1461, 93716**
**Telephone: 209-442-0600; 800-559-9009 Telecopier: 209-442-5078**
**Email: tsnell@cybergate.com**
**Howard B. Thomas (1912-1993); Fenton Williamson, Jr. (1926-1993); Roger E. Fipps; Samuel C. Palmer, III; James O. Demsey; Robert J. Tyler; Gerald D. Vinnard; E. Robert Wright; David M. Gilmore; Russell O. Wood; Scott R. Shewan; Hilary A. Chittick. Of Counsel: William N. Snell; T. Newton Russell; Charles E. Small; James E. LaFollette. Retired: Paul Asperger (Retired); Oliver M. Jamison (Retired);—Marcus Don Magness; Angela E. Taylor.**
**Civil Trial and Appellate Practice, all State and Federal Courts. Taxation (Federal and State). Corporation, Securities, Probate and Estate Planning, Labor and Employment, Condominium, Real Estate, Administrative, Environmental, Natural Resources, Creditors' Rights and Government Law.**
**Representative Clients: California Table Grape Commission; Gottschalk's, Inc.**
**Local Counsel for: Metropolitan Life Insurance Co.; PPG Industries; The Vendo Co.**
*See Professional Biographies, FRESNO, CALIFORNIA*

Thompson, Eckhart A. . . . . . . . . . '13 '38 C.267 A.B. L.813 J.D. U.S. Bkrptcy. J.
Thompson, Mark J. . . . . . . . . . '47 '78 C.101 B.A. L.1137 J.D. P.O. Box 711
**Thompson, Timothy L.**, (BV) '62 '88 C.1163 B.S. L.770 J.D. [McCormick,B.S.W.&C.]
*PRACTICE AREAS: Commerical Litigation.
Thompson, Wiley Y. . . . . . . . . '12 '45 C.267 L.284 LL.B. 1024 S. Sunnyside Ave.‡
Thornhill, William T., (BV) . . . . . . '42 '72 C.267 B.A. L.61 J.D. [W.T.Thornhill]
Thornhill, William T., A P.C., (BV) . . . . . . . . . . 124 W. Shaw Ave.
**Thornton, Douglas V.** . . . . . . . '63 '91 C.267 B.A. L.101 J.D. [Kimble,M.&U.]
*PRACTICE AREAS: Environmental Litigation; Business Litigation; Real Estate Law.
Thuesen, Donald C., (AV) . . . . . . '31 '59 C.267 L.1065 J.D. 411 E. Holland Ave.‡
Tirapelle, Leon E., (BV) . . . . . . '50 '75 C.112 A.B. L.464 J.D. 1795 N. Fine Ave.
**Tomassian, Gerald M.**, (BV) . . . . . '61 '88 C.800 B.A. L.1065 J.D. [Blanco,T.&P.]
*LANGUAGES: French.
*PRACTICE AREAS: Business and Real Estate Litigation; Family Law; General Civil Litigation.
**Travis, Lisa A.** . . . . . . . . '— '96 C.1075 B.A. L.1065 J.D. [Baker,M.&J.]
*LANGUAGES: Spanish.
Treisman, Douglas Owen . . . . . . . '60 '87 C.477 A.B. L.770 J.D. Dep. Dist. Atty.
Treviso, Edith W. . . . . . . . . '58 '84 C.112 B.A. L.284 J.D. Dep. Dist. Atty.
Trippel, Craig D. . . . . . . . . . . '50 '80 L.1189 J.D. [Hager,T.&M.]
Tritt, Deloise E. . . . . . . . . . '54 '90 C.267 B.S. L.1189 J.D. [Tritt&T.]
Tritt, James F. . . . . . . . . . '46 '73 C.813 B.S. L.1068 J.D. [Tritt&T.]
Tritt & Tritt . . . . . . . . . . 1540 E. Shaw Ave., Ste. 115
Turner, Patrick A., (BV) . . . . . . '36 '63 C.267 B.S. L.1065 J.D. 5151 N. Palm
Tusan, Thomas J., (BV) . . . . . . '46 '72 C.267 B.A. L.1065 J.D. 1233 W. Shaw
**Tutelian, Michelle T.** . . . . . . . '55 '87 C.800 B.A. L.464 J.D. [Baker,M.&J.]
*PRACTICE AREAS: Real Property.
Tuttle, Ernest H., (BV) . . . . . . '45 '72 C.267 A.B. L.1065 J.D. 351 E. Barstow Ave.
Tuttle, G. Martin, (BV) . . . . . '61 '87 C.1074 B.S. L.464 J.D. 5260 N. Palm, Ste., 421
**Tuttle, Judith** . . . . . . . . . '50 '95 L.1189 J.D. [W.R.McPike]
*PRACTICE AREAS: Civil Litigation; Unlawful Detainers; BankruptcyChapter 7 and 13; Family Trusts.
**Tyler, Robert J.**, (BV) . . . . . . '38 '63 C.763 A.B. L.813 J.D. [Thomas,S.J.R.&A.]
*PRACTICE AREAS: Estate Planning; Probate; Reclamation Law; Taxation Law.
Uhd, Gary E., (BV) . . . . . . . '50 '78 C.112 B.A. L.809 J.D. 4681 W. Holland Ave.
**Upton, Jon Wallace**, (AV) . . . . . . '39 '70 C.267 B.A. L.1065 J.D. [Kimble,M.&U.]
*REPORTED CASES: Gott v. U.S. (1970) 432 F.2d 45; In Re Estate of Murphy (1971) 16 Cal.App.3d 564; Catalano, Inc. v. Target Sales, Inc. (1980) 446 U.S. 643; Danzig v. Grynberg (1984) 161 Cal.App.3d 1128; Mateo-Woodburn v. Fresno Community Hosp. (1990) 221 Cal.App.3d 1169.
*PRACTICE AREAS: Federal Court Litigation; Corporate Law; Securities Law; Antitrust Law.
Uremovic, Joseph A., (BV) '47 '76 C.1074 B.S. L.770 J.D. 5250 N. Palm Ave., Suite 201
Urrizola, Lisa Marie . . . . . . . '60 '87 C.112 A.B. L.1189 J.D. Co. Prosecutor
Vajretti, Jolene A. . . . . . . . '49 '76 C.112 B.A. L.326 J.D. Bloomsaver, Ltd.
Valdez, Edward C. . . . . . . . . '44 '74 C.267 L.1132 B.L. 2140 Merced St.
Valdez, John C. . . . . . . . . . '56 '95 C&L.112 B.A., J.D. 2444 Main St.
Van Beek, James G. . . . . . . . '68 '95 C.154 B.A. L.112 J.D. 5260 N. Palm
Van Dusen, Harvey A. . . . . . . . . '16 '70 L.1132 J.D. 5678 N. Millbrook‡
**VanRozeboom, Russell G.**, (BV) . . . . . '48 '74 C.112 L.1132 LL.B [Wild,C.&T.]
*PRACTICE AREAS: Business and Agricultural Litigation; Insurance Policy Interpretation; General Civil Litigation.
Vartabedian, Steven M. . . . . . '50 '75 C.267 B.A. L.770 J.D. Assoc. Jus. Ct. of App.
Vartan, Robert V. C. . . . . . . '46 '73 C.112 B.A. L.464 J.D. 5588 N. Palm Ave.
Vasquez, Louis M. . . . . . . . . '— '85 C.267 B.S. L.1068 J.D. Dep. Dist. Atty.
Vehrs, Roger K. . . . . . . . . . '43 '76 L.1189 J.D. 2300 Tulare St.
**Vinnard, Gerald D.**, (BV) . . . . . '44 '70 C.267 B.S. L.309 J.D. [Thomas,S.J.R.&A.]
*PRACTICE AREAS: Bankruptcy Law; Business Litigation; Real Estate.
Voris, Ann Hardgrove . . . . . . . '52 '81 C.174 B.S. L.284 J.D. Asst. Fed. Def.
**Vote, Kurt F.** . . . . . . . . '67 '92 C.112 B.S. L.800 J.D. [McCormick,B.S.W.&C.]
*PRACTICE AREAS: Business Litigation; Environmental and Construction Defect Litigation.
**Wagner, Bryan N.**, (BV) . . . . . . '56 '84 C.197 B.A. L.464 J.D. [Wagner&W.]
*PRACTICE AREAS: General Business Law; Real Estate; Land Use; Taxation; Corporate Law.
**Wagner, James F.** . . . . . . . . '29 '55 C.112 B.S. L.1066 J.D. [Wagner&W.]
*PRACTICE AREAS: Trusts and Estates; Probate; Business Law.
Wagner, Jas F. . . . . . . . . '29 '55 C.112 A.B. L.1066 LL.B. 1322 E. Shaw Ave.
**Wagner, Matthew C.** . . . . . . . '62 '89 C.197 B.A. L.1068 J.D. [Wagner&W.]
*PRACTICE AREAS: Trusts and Estates; Probate; Business Law; Taxation Litigation.
Wagner, Nicholas John Paul, (CV) '58 '83 C.720 B.A. L.602 J.D. 1111 E. Herndon Ave.

**Wagner & Wagner, A Professional Corporation, (BV)**
**1322 East Shaw Avenue, Suite 340, 93710**
**Telephone: 209-224-0871 Telecopier: 209-224-0885**
**Bryan N. Wagner; James F. Wagner; Matthew C. Wagner.**
**Estate Planning, Trusts and Probate Law. General Business including Partnerships, Corporation, Complex Business Transactions, Real Estate and Related Tax Issues.**
*See Professional Biographies, FRESNO, CALIFORNIA*

**Wagoner, James P.**, (AV) . . . . '48 '73 C.740 B.A. L.770 J.D. [McCormick,B.S.W.&C.]
Wahab, Muslim, (P.C.), (BV) . . . . . '33 '80 C.267 B.S. L.765 J.D. [Hanna,B.M.M.&J.]
Wahlberg, Arthur C. . . . . . . '13 '38 C.267 B.A. L.1065 J.D. 5050 N. Van Ness Blvd.‡
Wall, Jeffrey L. . . . . . . . . . '47 '73 C.813 B.A. L.1067 J.D. 720 E. Bullard Ave.
**Walter, Riley C.**, (AV) . . . . . '51 '80 C.1074 B.A. L.1137 J.D. [McCormick,B.S.W.&C.]
*PRACTICE AREAS: Bankruptcy, Business Reorganization and Agricultural Law.
Wanger, Oliver W. . . . . . . . . '40 '67 C.800 B.S. L.1066 LL.B. U.S. Dist. J.

**Ward, Robert E.**, (BV) . . . . . . . '48 '77 C.336 B.S. L.1049 J.D. [Kimble,M.&U.]
*PRACTICE AREAS: Health Care Law; Taxation Law; Corporate Law.
Wasson, James E., (BV) . . . . . . . '43 '75 C.267 B.A. L.1189 J.D. [J.E.Wasson]
Wasson, James E., Inc., (BV) . . . . . . . . . . 5151 N. Palm Ave.
Waterman, James B., (CV) . . . . . '27 '57 C.267 A.B. L.1065 J.D. 5723 N. Flora
Waterman, Patrick B. . . . . . . '46 '77 C.112 B.A. L.1137 J.D. Dep. Dist. Atty.
**Watkins, Cal B., Jr.** . . . . . . . . '50 '76 C&L.846 B.A., J.D. [Jory,P.W.&S.]
*PRACTICE AREAS: Labor (Management) Law; Employment Law; Labor Negotiations; Employment Discrimination Law; Sexual Harassment.
Watkins, Howard K. . . . . . . . '47 '73 C.112 A.B. L.1065 J.D. Sr. Dep. Co. Coun.
**Watters, Richard C.**, (AV) . . . . . . '47 '74 C.267 B.S. L.770 J.D. [Miles,S.&E.]
*PRACTICE AREAS: Personal Injury (Plaintiff) Law; Litigation.
**Wayte, Lawrence E.**, (AV) . . . . '36 '62 C.813 A.B. L.1065 J.D. [McCormick,B.S.W.&C.]
Weakley, James D., (BV) . . . . . . '50 '78 C.1078 B.A. L.1189 J.D. [Eldridge,A.&W.]
**Weber, Joseph A.** . . . . . . . . '63 '91 C.112 B.A. L.1065 J.D. [McCollum&B.]
*PRACTICE AREAS: Corporate; Contract; Environmental; Real Estate; Land Use.
Webster, Stephen W. . . . . . . '45 '69 C&L.502 B.A., J.D. Workers Comp. App. Bd. J.
Weisberg, Jacob M. . . . . . . . . . . '45 '71 2300 Tulare St.
**Weiss, Andrew R.**, (AV) . . . . . . '55 '80 C.1109 B.A. L.1067 J.D. [Baker,M.&J.]
*PRACTICE AREAS: Employment Litigation; Medical Malpractice Defense.
Weiss, Jack . . . . . . . . . . '39 '90 C.112 B.A. L.765 J.D. Dep. Pub. Def.
Wells, David J. . . . . . . . '60 '86 C.267 B.S. L.464 J.D. 10 River Park Place East
**Wells, Gary B.** . . . . . . . . '63 '91 C.1032 B.B.A. L.101 J.D. [Baker,M.&J.]
*PRACTICE AREAS: Estate and Tax Planning; Family Law; Business Litigation.
**Wenzel, E.W. Rick** . . . . . . . . '44 '91 C.229 B.S. L.999 J.D. [Mullen&F.]
**Werth, Robert A.** . . . . . . . . '56 '89 C.768 B.S. L.464 J.D. [Caswell,B.H.B.&G.]
*PRACTICE AREAS: Litigation; Business Law; Real Estate Law.
**Whelan, Walter W.**, (BV) . . . . '57 '82 C.813 B.A. L.1068 J.D. [McCormick,B.S.W.&C.]
*LANGUAGES: Spanish and French.
*PRACTICE AREAS: Commercial Litigation; Employment Litigation.
White, Harry E., III . . . . . . . '47 '85 C.267 B.A. L.464 J.D. 7636 N. Ingram Ave.
**White, William M.**, (BV) . . . . . . '64 '91 C.502 B.S. L.1065 J.D. [Baker,M.&J.]
*PRACTICE AREAS: Professional Liability Defense; Business Litigation.
**Whitehurst, Daniel K.**, (BV) . . . . '48 '72 C.740 A.B. L.1065 J.D. [Dowling,A.&K.]
Whitfield, Michael K. . . . . . . . '60 '89 C.112 B.A. L.1066 J.D. 2344 Tulare St.
**Whitney, Marshall C.**, (AV) . . . '51 '78 C.112 B.A. L.1065 J.D. [McCormick,B.S.W.&C.]
*PRACTICE AREAS: Legal and Accounting Malpractice Defense; Business and Commercial Litigation; Construction Law.
Wieland, Charles A., (CV) . . . . . '52 '83 C.556 B.A. L.1189 J.D. Bennett & Sharpe, Inc.

**Wild, Carter & Tipton, A Professional Corporation, (AV)**
**246 West Shaw Avenue, P.O. Box 16339, 93755-6339**
**Telephone: 209-224-2131 Telecopier: 209-224-8462**
**Mount K. Wild (1890-1959); M. Gordon Wild (1922-1972); Arthur L. Blank (1906-1983); Jack M. Tipton (1933-1990); M. Bruce Wild (1946-1990); Robert G. Carter; Bruce M. Brown; William H. Leifer; G. Dana French; Richard A. Harris; Russell G. VanRozeboom; Tracy A. Agrall; Gary L. Huss; Patrick J. Gorman; Steven E. Paganetti; Robert C. Schmalle; Bertram T. Kaufmann; Wesley J. Hammond. Of Counsel: Richard L. Harriman.**
**General Civil, Trial and Appellate Practice. Business, Real Estate, Corporation, Construction, Banking, Environmental, Agriculture, Insurance, Trademark, Probate and Estate Planning, Oil and Gas, Taxation, Bankruptcy and Employment Law.**
**Local Counsel for: Merrill, Lynch, Pierce, Fenner & Smith.**
**References: Bank of America National Trust & Savings Assn.; Regency Bank (Branches at Fresno, California).**
*See Professional Biographies, FRESNO, CALIFORNIA*

**Wilhelm, Michael L.** . . . . . . '55 '81 C.1212 B.S. L.1068 J.D. [McCormick,B.S.W.&C.]
Wilkie, James G. . . . . . . . . '30 '77 C.267 L.1132 J.D. 2222 W. Shaw Ave.‡
Wilkie, Joan B., (CV) . . . . . . . . . '32 '80 L.1132 J.D. 1530 E. Shaw Ave.
**Wilkins, James H.**, (BV) . . . . . '58 '84 C&L.36 B.S., J.D. [McCormick,B.S.W.&C.]
**Wilkinson, Robert D.** . . . . . . . '53 '81 C.147 B.A. L.1067 J.D. [Baker,M.&J.]
*LANGUAGES: Spanish.
*PRACTICE AREAS: Business Litigation; Civil, Criminal and Medical Malpractice Defense.

**Williams, Adrian S., (BV) '36 '61 C.477 B.A. L.912 J.D.**
**1665 West Shaw, Suite 108, 93711**
**Telephone: 209-226-7767 Facsimile: 209-224-4960**
**Email: Available Upon Request**
***REPORTED CASES: Dettman v. Fresno Madera Production Credit Assn. B.A.P. No. EC-87-1203 Docket #88-15197; Christensen v. EMC BAP. No. EC-932082.**
***PRACTICE AREAS: Bankruptcy Reorganization (Chapter 11 & 12); Debtors and Creditors; Bankruptcy-Chapter 7 Insolvencies; Real Property Law; Small Business and Corporate Law. Business Law (Debtors and Creditors), Bankruptcy, Farming (Debtors and Creditors) and Real Property.**
*See Professional Biographies, FRESNO, CALIFORNIA*

Williams, Albert A. '10 '32 C.912 L.213 (adm. in MI; not adm. in CA) 5086 N. Forkner Ave.‡
**Williams, Patti L.** . . . . . . . . '62 '92 C&L.112 B.A., J.D. [Sagaser,H.F.&J.]
Williams, Robert G. . . . . . . . '46 '75 C.267 B.S. L.1189 J.D. 1432 Divisadero
**Williams, Scott W.**, (BV) . . . . . '48 '74 C.813 B.A. L.93 J.D. [Frampton,H.W.&B.]
*PRACTICE AREAS: Employment Law; Labor Law; Civil Rights Law; Education Law; Disability Rights.
Williams, Warren L., (BV) . . . . '41 '71 C.267 B.A. L.61 J.D. Gen. Coun., Gottschalks Inc.
Williford, Glen E. . . . . . . . . '61 '91 C.112 B.A. L.1189 J.D. 140 W. Celeste
Willoughby, Hugh, (BV) . . . . . . '48 '73 C.267 B.A. L.1068 J.D. 1530 E. Shaw Ave.
**Wilson, David T.** . . . . . . . '62 '94 C&L.37 B.S., J.D. [McCormick,B.S.W.&C.]
*LANGUAGES: Spanish.
*PRACTICE AREAS: Health Care; Real Estate; Corporate; Business; Political Law.
Winslow, Jeanne L. . . . . . . . '52 '78 C.112 A.B. L.1065 J.D. 5897 Rancho Dr. E.‡
**Wishon, A. Emory, III**, (AV) . . . . . '45 '80 C.103 A.B. L.813 J.D. [Motschiedler,M.&W.]
*PRACTICE AREAS: Real Property Law; Business Law; Partnership; Corporate Law; Probate.
Witherow, James P. . . . . . . . . '52 '88 C.267 B.A. L.1189 J.D. [Emerson&Y.]
**Wolfe, David J.** . . . . . . . . '62 '88 C.94 B.A. L.464 J.D. [Lozano S.S.W.&B.]
*REPORTED CASES: Kaufman & Broad South Bay v. Morgan Hill Unified School Dist. (1992) 9 Cal. App. 4th 464.
*PRACTICE AREAS: Municipal Law; Zoning and Land Use; Municipal Code Enforcement; Appellate Practice.
**Wood, Russell O.**, (BV) . . . . . . '57 '83 C.267 A.B. L.1066 J.D. [Thomas,S.J.R.&A.]
*PRACTICE AREAS: Real Estate; Trusts and Estates; Business and Financing Transactions.
**Woodcock, Jane** . . . . . . . . . '53 '92 C.999 L.1189 J.D. [Mullen&F.]
*PRACTICE AREAS: Workers Compensation Defense.
**Woods, Michael G.**, (AV) . . . . . '48 '73 C.267 B.A. L.1067 J.D. [McCormick,B.S.W.&C.]
*PRACTICE AREAS: Trial Practice, Employment (Chairman of Employment Law Practice Group); Defense of Public Entities; Civil Rights; Products Liability.
**Woodward, O. James, III** . . . . . '35 '65 C.112 B.A. L.1066 J.D. [Caswell,B.H.B.&G.]
*PRACTICE AREAS: Real Estate; Business Transactions.
Woolf, E. Terrence, (BV) . . . . . . . . . . . '48 '73 1327 "N" St.
**Woolman, William M.** . . . . . . . '62 '89 C.668 B.A. L.1068 J.D. [Jory,P.W.&S.]
*PRACTICE AREAS: Commercial Litigation; Construction Litigation; Employment Litigation; Bankruptcy; Creditor Litigation.
**Worrel, Richard M.**, (AV) . . . . . '13 '42 C.267 A.B. L.999 LL.B. [Worrel&W.] ‡
**Worrel, Rodney K.**, (AV) '43 '72 C.267 B.A. L.1067 J.D. [Worrel&W.] (See Pat. Sect.)

**Worrel & Worrel, (AV)** BB
**Suite 130, Civic Center Square, 2444 Main Street, 93721-1984**
**Telephone: 209-486-4526 Fax: 209-486-6948**
**Richard M. Worrel (1913-1995); Rodney K. Worrel.**
**Domestic and Foreign Patent, Trademark and Copyright and Related Intellectual Property Law. Trials in all Federal Courts.**
**Representative Clients: Bank of America; California State University, Fresno; California State University, Bakersfield; Duncan Enterprises; Fresno Pacific College; J. G. Boswell Co.; The Vendo Co.; City of Visalia.**
*See Professional Biographies, FRESNO, CALIFORNIA*

**Wright, Andrew W.**, (AV) ...... '46 '72 C.154 B.A. L.813 J.D. [McCormick,B.S.W.&C.]
**Wright, E. Robert**, (AV) ............ '44 '72 C.112 B.S. L.309 J.D. [Thomas,S.J.R.&A.]
*REPORTED CASES: California v. Bergland, 483 F. Supp. 465 (E.D. Cal. 1980), aff'd, 690 F.2d 753 (9th Cir. 1982); City of South Lake Tahoe v. California Tahoe Regional Planning Agency, 625 F.2d 231 (9th Cir. 1980), cert. denied, 101 S. Ct. 619 (1980); Horn v. County of Ventura, 24 Cal. 3d 605 (1979).
*PRACTICE AREAS: Civil Litigation; Environmental Litigation.
**Wright, Janet L.**, (AV) .................. '46 '72 C.112 B.A. L.800 J.D. [Musick,P.&G.]
*PRACTICE AREAS: Estate Planning and Administration; Agricultural Law; Taxation; Tax Exempt Entities; General Business Law.
Wuthrich, Daniel S. ............................ '58 '91 C.801 B.S. L.69 J.D. 5 River Pk. Pl. E.
Wyatt, Veldonna Tullis, Ms. ........................................ '37 '87 1702 E. Bullard Ave.
Wyckoff, Robert L. ............ '27 '52 C.999 B.A. L.174 LL.B. 552 N. Temperance Ave.
**Yates, M. Jaqueline** .............. '63 '92 C.267 B.A. L.1189 J.D. [A Stammer,M.B.&B.]
*PRACTICE AREAS: Insurance Defense; Professional Liability; Family Law; Children's Rights.
Yengoyan, Alan ....................... '43 '71 C.267 B.A. L.284 J.D. Sr. Dep. Dist. Atty.
Young, Kevin ................... '48 '79 C.768 B.A. L.1132 J.D. U.S. Small Bus. Admn.
Young, Robert L., (CV) ................ '31 '60 C.112 A.B. L.809 LL.B. 1111 Fulton Mall
**Young, William M., (Inc.)**, (BV) .......... '31 '59 C.112 A.B. L.1065 J.D. [Sandell&Y.]
*PRACTICE AREAS: Litigation; Insurance Defense; Personal Injury; Products Liability; Premises Liability.
Yrulegui, Richard J., (BV) ...................... '47 '72 C.267 A.B. L.464 J.D. [Emerson&Y.]
Zachritz, Linda J. ........................ '58 '86 C.267 B.A. L.1189 J.D. 1111 Fulton Mall
**Zeitler, Peter N.**, (BV) ....................... '56 '82 C.20 B.A. L.477 J.D. [Lang,R.&P.]
*PRACTICE AREAS: Business Law; Health Law.
Zerga, David E. .......................... '48 '76 C.112 B.A. L.770 J.D. P.O. Box 28280‡
**Zidenberg, Howard M.**, (BV) ............ '49 '74 C.112 B.A. L.1068 J.D. [Baker,M.&J.]
*PRACTICE AREAS: Litigation; Medical Malpractice Defense.
Zins, Leonard J., (BV) ......................... '21 '48 C.31 A.B. L.309 LL.B. [Zins&M.]
Zins & Morris, (BV) .................................................................. 1111 Fulton Mall
Zobrosky, Ann E. '61 '87 C.210 B.A. L.1119 J.D.
(adm. in IN; not adm. in CA) Soc. Sec. Admn.
**Zumout, Nabil E.** .......................... '67 '93 C.1169 B.A. L.770 J.D. [A Lang,R.&P.]
*PRACTICE AREAS: Commercial Litigation; Bankruptcy; Business Reorganization.
Zupp, Robert R., (CV) ......... '41 '84 C.880 Ph.D. L.1189 J.D. 5308 N. Briarwood Ave.
Zuzuarregui, Rene F. ........................ '51 '89 C.37 B.S. L.770 J.D. [A Quinlan,K.&F.]
Zylka, John P. .......................... '27 '55 C.972 B.S. L.174 J.D. 2670 W Shaw Ave.‡

## FULLERTON, 114,144, *Orange Co.*

**Ackerman, Richard C.**, (AV) ........ '42 '68 C.112 A.B. L.1065 J.D. [Ackerman,M.&B.]
*PRACTICE AREAS: General Civil Practice and Litigation in all State and Federal Courts; Business; Real Property; Corporation; Partnership.

**Ackerman, Mordock & Bowen, A Professional Corporation, (AV)**
**Suite 640, 2600 East Nutwood Avenue, 92831**
**Telephone: 714-992-2600**
**Email: acmobo@ix.netcom.com**
**Gary E. Mordock; Daniel C. Bowen; Richard C. Ackerman.**
**General Civil Practice and Litigation in all State and Federal Courts. Business, Real Property, Corporation, Partnership, Family, Personal Injury, Estate Planning, Trust and Probate Law.**
**Reference: Wells Fargo (Fullerton Branch).**

Aguirre, Cory Anthony, (BV) ........ '52 '78 C.112 B.A. L.770 J.D. 1235 N. Harbor Blvd.
Aguirre, Frederick P., (BV) '46 '74 C.800 B.A. L.1068 J.D.
446 E. Commonwealth Ave.
Ahle, Patrick M. ............................ '57 '89 C.1042 B.S. L.1137 J.D. Asst. City Atty.
Aldrich, William P. ................ '49 '77 C.112 B.A. L.809 J.D. 1501 E. Chapman Ave.
Anderson, Theodore A. ........ '50 '76 C.105 A.B. L.1137 J.D. 2260 N. State College Blvd.
**Ballard, J. Larry**, (AV) ................ '37 '64 C.112 B.S. L.800 J.D. [Ballard,W.B.&E.]
*PRACTICE AREAS: Estate Planning Law; Real Estate Law; Transactional Law.
Ballard, Steven G., (BV) ............... '54 '84 C.1109 B.A. L.1137 J.D. 1440 N. Harbor Blvd.

**Ballard, Wimer, Brockett & Edwards, (AV)**
**An Association of Attorneys**
**Suite 200, 1235 North Harbor Boulevard, 92632**
**Telephone: 714-871-1132 Facsimile: 714-871-5620**
**J. Larry Ballard (Certified Specialist, Taxation Law and Probate, Estate Planning and Trust Law, The State Bar of California Board of Legal Specialization); Warren B. Wimer; Lee H. Brockett (Certified Specialist, Taxation Law, The State Bar of California Board of Legal Specialization); Thomas C. Edwards; Richard S. Price II; Christopher J. Koorstad; Sara Stewart Bergstrom; Randall J. Friend.**
**Business, Civil and Trial Practice in all State and Federal Courts. Corporate, Mergers and Acquisitions, Antitrust, Unfair Trade Practices, Probate, Estate Planning, Taxation and Real Estate Law, Earth Movement and Construction Defect, Family Law, Custody, Support, UCCJA Matters.**
**Reference: California State Bank (Anaheim, California Office).**
*See Professional Biographies, FULLERTON, CALIFORNIA*

Baugh, George L. ................. '52 '81 C.112 B.A. L.1065 J.D. 2201 E. Chapman Ave.
Bean, Robert L., (BV) .................. '32 '69 C.1042 L.990 J.D. 206 W. Wilshire Ave.
Beaver, Victoria E. ....................... '53 '80 C.1109 B.A. L.1137 J.D. 1018 Dolores Dr.
Becker, Erick J. ........................ '64 '88 C.112 B.A. L.1066 J.D. 2021 Skyline Dr.
Behn, Richard E. ........................ '40 '70 C.999 L.1137 LL.B. Presiding J., Mun. Ct.
**Bergstrom, Sara Stewart** .............. '37 '86 C.112 B.A. L.1137 J.D. [Ballard,W.B.&E.]
*PRACTICE AREAS: Family Law; Elder Law; Probate; Guardianship; Conservatorships.
Berkley, Benjamin H. ............... '52 '78 C.4 B.A. L.1137 J.D. 1235 N. Harbor Blvd.
Black, S. Norman ............... '16 '79 C.16 B.S. L.1137 J.D. 810 E. Commonwealth Ave.
Blake, Donald F. ............ '40 '68 C&L.878 B.A., J.D. Admin. Law J., Unemp. Ins. App.
Boas, Maxwell S. .... '19 '41 C.563 B.S. L.732 LL.B. Dean, Western State Univ. Law Sch.
Boles, Carla L. ..................... '67 '94 C.800 B.S. L.1137 J.D. 2501 E. Chapman Ave.
**Bowen, Daniel C.**, (AV) ............... '44 '72 C.174 B.A. L.284 J.D. [Ackerman,M.&B.]
*PRACTICE AREAS: General Civil Practice and Litigation in all State and Federal Courts; Business; Real Property; Corporation; Partnership.
**Brockett, Lee H.**, (AV) .................. '46 '72 C.605 A.B. L.61 J.D. [Ballard,W.B.&E.]
*PRACTICE AREAS: Taxation Law; Estate Planning Law; Real Estate; Pension Law; Transactional Law.
Bruenning, Daniel G. ................ '52 '88 C.960 B.S. L.1137 J.D. 1501 E. Chapman Ave.
**Brunette, Steven E.** .... '49 '76 C&L.426 B.S., J.D. Asst. Gen. Coun., Hunt-Wesson, Inc.
*RESPONSIBILITIES: Corporate Law; Litigation; Labor Law; Environmental Law; Transactional Law.
Burg, Brian Neil ..................... '48 '84 C.800 A.B. L.1137 J.D. 2201 E. Chapman Ave.

**Bush, William M., (AV) '41 '67 C.813 A.B. L.1065 J.D.**
**110 East Wilshire Avenue, Suite 210, 92632-1998**
**Telephone: 714-992-0800 Fax: 714-879-5811**
**Email: wmbushesq@aol.com**
**(Certified Specialist, Family Law, The State Bar of California Board of Legal Specialization). Practice limited to Family Law, Litigation and Mediation.**
*See Professional Biographies, FULLERTON, CALIFORNIA*

Cameron, Ronald Brooks, (BV) .................. '27 '73 C.930 L.990 J.D. [Cameron&H.]
Cameron & Hoffman, (BV) ............................................. 806 West Valencia Mesa Drive
Carden, Lester L., Jr., (AV) ........... '18 '49 C.813 B.A. L.208 LL.B. 667 Catalina Rd.‡
Carroll, Della J. ........................ '30 '80 C.1110 B.A. L.1137 J.D. 1025 N. Stanford Ave.
Chaffee, Douglas B., (BV) ..................... '43 '69 C.684 B.A. L.597 J.D. [Chaffee&M.]
Chaffee & Marshall, A Prof. Corp., (BV) ........................................ 141 W. Wilshire St.
**Christensen, Robert N.**, (AV) ............... '29 '56 C.999 L.1065 J.D. [Christensen&S.]
*PRACTICE AREAS: Personal Injury Law.
Christensen, Stanley B., (BV) ......... '15 '53 C.813 A.B. L.426 LL.B. 1457 E. Chapman

**Christensen & Stout, (AV)**
**211 East Imperial, Suite 203, 92635**
**Telephone: 714-992-4860 Fax: 714-992-2336**
**Members of Firm: Robert N. Christensen; Richard S. Stout.**
**General Civil and Trial Practice in all State and Federal Courts. Negligence, Personal Injury, Insurance, Litigation, Wrongful Death, Aviation and Products Liability Law.**

Cicino, Helen M. ... '64 '89 C.800 B.A. L.426 J.D. Staff Atty., Beckman Instruments, Inc.
**Clark, Amy Ahrendt** '58 '84
C.896 B.A. L.597 J.D. Assoc. Gen. Coun., Hunt-Wesson, Inc.
*RESPONSIBILITIES: Employment Law; Equal Employment Opportunity/Affirmative Action; Litigation.
Clarke, Allen C. ....................... '35 '64 C.770 B.S.C. L.1066 LL.B. [Hanessian&C.]
Cofer, Patricia K. '50 '81 C.134 B.S. L.986 J.D.
Assoc. Coun., Beckman Instruments, Inc.
Cohen, Arthur J. .......................... '42 '72 C.645 B.S. L.426 J.D. 1235 N. Harbor Blvd.
Comstock, Thomas A., (BV) ........... '23 '59 C&L.178 A.B., J.D. 1440 N. Harbor Blvd.‡
Comstock, Joye & Krawiec, (BV) ........................................ 1440 N. Harbor Blvd.
Cook, James ................................ '22 '55 C.1032 B.A. L.878 J.D. 1452 Skyline Dr.
Cote, Richard P. ..................... '28 '76 C.708 B.A. L.1137 J.D. 2008 Calle Candela
**Curran, Richard J.**, (AV) ..................... '42 '73 C.1042 B.A. L.800 J.D. [Curran&W.]
*PRACTICE AREAS: Criminal Law.

**Curran and Watson, (AV)** BB
**Suite 290, 1235 North Harbor Boulevard, 92632**
**Telephone: 714-871-1138 Facsimile: 714-871-5620**
**Members of Firm: Richard J. Curran; William G. Watson.**
**General Criminal Trial Practice in all State and Federal Courts. Administrative and Family Law.**
*See Professional Biographies, FULLERTON, CALIFORNIA*

Daggett, Steven B., (BV) ................ '33 '66 C.112 B.S. L.1065 J.D. 615 Del Rio Way
Dahle, Sheila R. ......................... '53 '81 C.1109 B.A. L.1137 J.D. 2752 Via Hacienda
Dannemeyer, William E. ........................ '29 '53 C.879 A.B. L.1065 J.D. (M.C.)
Davis, William W. '32 '69
C.910 B.S. L.426 J.D. Asst. Gen. Coun., Beckman Instruments, Inc.
Denney, Roger K., (BV) ............ '32 '65 C.112 B.A. L.1068 J.D. 1440 N. Harbor Blvd.
DeSales, Stephan A., (AV) .................. '45 '71 C.1049 B.A. L.602 J.D. [S.A.DeSales]
DeSales, Stephan A., A Professional Law Corporation, (AV) ........ 2201 E. Chapman Ave.
De Witt, Victor ......................................... '38 '72 L.990 J.D. 1440 N. Harbor Blvd.
Dickson, Karen V.E. ........ '60 '89 C.1109 B.A. L.1137 J.D. 810 E. CommonwealthAve.
Dolan, William A., (BV) ..................... '36 '63 C.426 B.S. L.809 J.D. [W.A.Dolan]
Dolan, William A., Law Offices of, Inc., (BV) ............................ 1400 North Brea Boulevard
Doti, Frank J. .......... '43 '69 C.339 B.S. L.146 J.D. Prof., Western State College of Law
Eagan, Marc T., (BV) ................ '51 '78 C.112 B.A. L.1137 J.D. 1235 N. Harbor Blvd.
**Edwards, Thomas C.**, (AV) ........... '46 '72 C.112 B.A. L.273 J.D. [Ballard,W.B.&E.]
*PRACTICE AREAS: Real Estate; Business Law.
Eldredge, Barbara B. '26 '50 C&L.150 B.A., LL.B.
(adm. in OH; not adm. in CA) Secy. & Treas., T.H. Eldredge, Inc.
**Elenbaas, Thomas E.**, (AV) ............ '52 '77 C.1109 B.S.L. L.1137 J.D. [Elenbaas&S.]
*PRACTICE AREAS: Landlord Tenant; Employment Law; Real Estate; Civil Litigation; Business Litigation.

**Elenbaas & Schoeman, (AV)** BB
**Suite 235, 1370 N. Brea Boulevard, 92635**
**Telephone: 714-871-7100 Fax: 714-871-7142**
**Thomas E. Elenbaas; Cara Hagan Schoeman.**
**General Civil and Trial practice in all State and Federal Courts, Landlord/ Tenant, Business and Corporate Law, Employment Law and Construction Law.**
*See Professional Biographies, FULLERTON, CALIFORNIA*

Engelskirchen, Howard H. '38 '65
C.605 B.A. L.1066 LL.B. Prof., Western State Univ. Coll. of Law
Farrar, Bruce R., (AV) ...................... '39 '71 C.800 L.990 440 E. Commonwealth Ave.
Faust, Jack '32 '64 C.994 B.A. L.1009 J.D.
Prof. of Law, Western State Univ., Coll. of Law
Foster, Elinor J. ................... '35 '83 C.588 B.A. L.1137 J.D. 1953 E. Chapman Ave.
Fox, R. K., (BV) ............................ '34 '65 C.309 A.B. L.813 J.D. City Atty.
**Friend, Randall J.** ............................ '60 '86 C.1109 B.A. L.61 J.D. [Ballard,W.B.&E.]
*PRACTICE AREAS: Taxation Law; Real Estate Law; Construction Defect; Business Law.
Frizell, Samuel '33 '65 C.3 B.A. L.1065 J.D.
Prof., Western State Univ., College of Law‡
Fuller, Marjorie G., (AV) ................ '38 '74 C.477 A.B. L.800 J.D. 110 E. Wilshire Ave.
Gallagher, Phyllis M., (BV) '37 '77 C.1109 B.A. L.426 J.D.
2266 N. State College Blvd.
Garber, Leonard, (AV) .......... '29 '52 C&L.569 B.A., LL.B. 1400 North Harbor Blvd.‡
Gelfer, Florine ................ '25 '76 C.112 B.A. L.1137 J.D. 3008 E. Arlington Ave.
Gervase, Janice E. ............................ '48 '77 C.418 B.A. L.1137 J.D. 1370 Brea Bl.
Gigliotti, Joseph J. .................. '60 '89 C.763 B.A. L.1049 J.D. 434 E. Chapman Ave.
Goldman, F. Elliot ................ '55 '80 C&L.1137 B.S.L., J.D. 1440 North Harbor Blvd.

**Goldstein, Edward D., (AV) '27 '53 C&L.477 A.B., J.D.**
**Suite 305, 110 East Wilshire Avenue, 92632**
**Telephone: 714-525-5055 Telecopier: 714-525-6654**
***PRACTICE AREAS: Health Care; Business; Corporate Law.**
**Corporation, Health Care and Business Law.**
*See Professional Biographies, FULLERTON, CALIFORNIA*

Gordinier, Anne Mitchell ......... '53 '78 C.770 B.A. L.1065 J.D. 1645 W. Valencia Dr.‡
Grant, Arnold '40 '67 C.16 B.S. L.273 J.D.
Asst. Gen. Coun., Beckman Instruments, Inc. (Pat.)
Gregg, Aaron C., (BV) ............ '53 '77 C.1109 B.A. L.1137 J.D. 110 E. Wilshire Ave.
Hall, Moses S. ............................................ '57 '92 2555 E. Chapman Ave.
Hampson, Gary T. '50 '79 C.1074 B.S. L.426 J.D.
Assoc. Coun., Beckman Instruments, Inc. (Pat.)
Hanessian, Edward J. ...................... '39 '65 C.112 A.B. L.1066 [Hanessian&C.]
Hanessian & Clarke ............................................................ 1440 N. Harbor Blvd.
Hara, Max, (BV) ........................ '34 '64 C.642 L.800 LL.B. P.O. Box 5729
Harder, Paul R. '35 '62 C.701 B.S.E.E. L.273 LL.B.
Asst. Gen. Coun., Beckman Instruments, Inc. (Pat.)
**Haseman, Paul B.** .............. '45 '74 C.870 B.S. L.893 J.D. Coun., Hughes Aircraft Co.
Henry, Janis C. '48 '88 C.112 B.A. L.1137 J.D.
Sr. Staff Atty., Beckman Instruments, Inc.
Hoffman, Juanita C., (BV) .................. '37 '74 C&L.990 B.S., J.D. [Cameron&H.]

CAA105P

Johnson, Michael L. '44 '79 C.94 A.B. L.1137 J.D. 1245 N. Gilbert
Jones, Gordon G. '34 '77 C.350 B.S.I.E. L.1137 J.D. 2911 Wellesley Ct.‡
Jovanovich, Alex '50 '76 C.013 B.A. L.031 LL.B. 2600 E. Nutwood Ave.
Joye, John M., (BV) '26 '54 C&L.178 B.S., J.D. [Comstock,J.&K.]
Kane, Carl L., (AV) '32 '60 C.276 B.S. L.800 LL.B. 505 E. Commonwealth Ave.‡
Kelly, James Anthony '46 '76 C.1049 B.S. L.1137 J.D. 1440 N. Harbor Blvd.
Kelly, John F. '40 '76 C.426 B.A. L.1137 J.D. 1370 Brea Blvd.
Kolstad, Richard S., (CV) '26 '54 C&L.800 B.S., J.D. 1370 N. Brea Blvd.
**Koorstad, Christopher J.** '56 '82 C.1109 B.A. L.1067 J.D. [Ballard,W.B.&E.]
*LANGUAGES: Spanish.
*PRACTICE AREAS: Business Law; Real Estate Litigation; Unfair Competition Law; Wrongful Termination Law.
Koppel, Glenn S. '47 '71 C.563 B.A. L.309 J.D. Prof., Western State Coll. of Law
Krawiec, Martin '34 '62 C.188 B.S. L.273 J.D. [Comstock,J.&K.]
Launer, Chaffee & Schulman, (BV) Suite 250, 2600 E. Nutwood Ave.
Lee, Nilane A., (A Professional Corporation) '35 '81
C.314 B.S.E. L.1137 J.D. P.O. Box 6336‡
Leeper, Norman B., (BV) '36 '71 C.626 B.A. L.990 J.D. 1457 E. Chapman Ave.
Leonard, G. Thomas '43 '81 L.1137 J.D. 1235 N. Harbor
Lev, Lester L., (AV) '06 '29 C&L.911 LL.B. 511 Riviera Ct.‡
Levine, Arthur Joel '55 '89 C.112 B.A. L.1137 J.D. 2555 E. Chapman Ave.
Lofstedt, Ben E., (CV) '40 '74 C.426 B.S.E.E. L.1137 J.D. Atty., Christian Law Ctr.
Lofstedt, Sally R. '46 '82 C.112 B.A. L.1137 J.D. Atty., Christian Law Ctr.
Macdonald, James B., (BV) '36 '62 C&L.878 J.D. 2600 E. Nutwood
Mackel, Marilyn H. '45 '77 C.1298 B.A. L.276 J.D.
Assoc. Prof., Western State Univ. College of Law
Markman, Kenneth R. '64 '91 C.112 B.A. L.426 J.D. 1275 N. Berkeley Ave.
Marshall, Paulette A., (BV) '49 '78 C.684 B.A. L.1137 J.D. [Chaffee&M.]
Mason, Frederick T., (AV) '30 '55 C.112 B.A. L.1066 J.D. [F.T.Mason]
Mason, Frederick T., Inc., (AV) 2600 East Nutwood Avenue, Suite 250
Matlock, Bruce '45 '73 C.763 B.A. L.809 J.D. 1501 E. Orangethorpe Ave.
May, William H. '42 '73 C.886 B.S. L.893 LL.B.
V.P., Gen. Coun. & Secy., Beckman Instruments, Inc. (Pat.)
McCabe, Shirley A. '50 '92 C.1042 B.A. L.1137 J.D. 1021 W. Bastanchury Rd.
McCall, John E. '21 '79 C.171 B.S.E. L.990 J.D. 513 Rosarita Dr.
McCallum, Catherine '53 '80 C.1109 B.A. L.1137 J.D. 3304 E. Yorba Linda Blvd.
**McCann, Raymond C.** '51 '79 C.870 B.S. L.893 J.D. Corp. Atty., Hughes Aircraft Co.
McGurk, Allen C. '13 '38 C&L.339 B.S., LL.B. 1250 N. Placentia Ave.‡
McIntyre, Daniel W. '54 '83 C.589 B.S. L.339 J.D.
Law Prof., Western State University Coll. of Law
McOwen, John W. '32 '58 C&L.276 B.S., J.D. Mun. Ct. J.
Merhab, Elizabeth J., (AV) '39 '76 C.112 B.S.L. L.1137 J.D. V.P., The Eadington Cos.
**Miede, Norman K.H.** '55 '80
C.813 A.B. L.1065 J.D. Assoc. Gen. Coun., Hunt-Wesson, Inc.
*RESPONSIBILITIES: Purchasing; International; Research and Development; Finance; Traffic and Distribution.
Miller, Linda Lancet '48 '73 C.112 B.A. L.1049 J.D. Mun. Ct. J.

**Moerbeek, Stanley L., (BV) '51 '80 C.1109 B.A. L.426 J.D.**
**1370 North Brea Boulevard, Suite 210, 92835-4128**
**Telephone: 714-773-5396 FAX: 714-773-5837**
**Real Estate, Civil Litigation, Personal Injury, Business Representation, Collections and Estates and Estate Litigation.**
***See Professional Biographies, FULLERTON, CALIFORNIA***

**Mordock, Gary E.**, (BV) '37 '65 C.813 B.A. L.1066 J.D. [Ackerman,M.&B.]
*PRACTICE AREAS: General Civil Practice and Litigation in all State and Federal Courts; Business; Real Property; Corporation; Partnership.
Morris, Edward N. '43 '68 C.339 L.209 LL.B. 1440 N. Harbor Blvd.
Mullenix, Cynthia L. '— '82 C.112 B.A. L.1137 J.D. Hunt-Wesson, Inc.
Myers, C. Ray, (AV) '39 '73 C.277 L.990 J.D. P.O. Box 294
Neal, Susan F. '40 '85 C&L.1137 B.S.L., J.D. 2501 E. Chapman Ave.
Nelson, John C. '49 '76 C.1109 B.A. L.809 J.D. 1440 N. Harbor

**Nixon, Rosemary, (AV) '37 '78 C.112 B.A. L.1137 J.D.**
**Suite 240, 1235 North Harbor Boulevard, 92632**
**Telephone: 714-773-1938 Fax: 714-773-0986**
**Email: MISSBRUIN@aol.com**
**Family Law, Support & Custody, Bankruptcy and Probate Law and Trust.**
***See Professional Biographies, FULLERTON, CALIFORNIA***

Nuzum, Carolyn J. '46 '81 L.1137 J.D. 4345 W. Artesia Ave.
**Osaki, Kerry G.**, (BV) '53 '78 C.769 B.A. L.426 J.D. [Wheatley O.&Assoc.]⊙
*PRACTICE AREAS: Construction Law; Contracts/Corporations; Insurance Defense and Collections.
Palazzo, John T. '53 '80 C.1109 B.A. L.1049 J.D. 801 E. Commonwealth Ave.
Parker, Ronald G., (BV) '48 '78 C.1075 B.S. L.1137 J.D. 1235 N. Harbor Blvd.
Parkin, Eric G. '63 '90 L.1336 J.D. 2500 W. Orangethorpe
Parkin, Gregory L. '37 '73 C.1109 B.A. L.1137 J.D. 2500 W. Orangethorpe
Parsons, Rodney H., (BV) '47 '75 C.112 B.A. L.1068 J.D. [R.H.Parsons]
Parsons, Rodney H., A Professional Corporation, (BV) 285 Imperial Hwy.
Patno, Judy M. '55 '82 C.560 B.A. L.1049 J.D. 2461 E. Orangethorpe Ave., Suite 228
Perez, James O. '26 '56 C&L.800 B.S., LL.B. 1415 Shadow Ln.‡
Pittman, Juan A. '64 '92 C.329 B.A. L.273 J.D. 1311 S. Highland Ave.
**Price, Richard S., II**, (BV) '57 '82 C.112 B.A. L.1067 J.D. [Ballard,W.B.&E.]
*REPORTED CASES: In Re: Arm (1994) 175 B.R. 349.
*PRACTICE AREAS: Real Estate and Business Litigation; Collections; Real Estate Law.
Prickett, Gregory L. '56 '82 C.800 B.A. L.809 J.D. Mun. J.
Radensky, Joseph H., (BV) '31 '57
C.112 A.B. L.1065 J.D. Prof., Western State Univ. College of Law
Rallis, Kirk Dean '62 '92 C.800 B.A. L.793 J.D. 285 E. Imperial Hwy.
Ray, Gary R. '61 '88 C.112 B.A. L.1065 J.D. 1117 W. Valley View Dr.
Reyes, Elena, (AV) '54 '77 C.139 B.A. L.1137 J.D. 1440 N. Harbor Blvd.
Roberts, Mark Scott, (AV) '51 '80 C.990 B.A. L.1137 J.D. [M.S.Roberts&Assoc.]
Roberts, Mark Scott, and Associates, A Prof. Law Corp., (AV) 1440 N. Harbor Blvd.
Rose, Jack A., (AV) '28 '62 C.112 B.S. L.1068 J.D. 933 Oakwood Ave.‡
Ross, Linda K. '46 '88 C.766 B.A. L.1137 J.D. 1440 N. Harbor Blvd.
**Ryan, Patrick M.**, (AV) '37 '61
C.716 B.A. L.884 J.D. V.P. & Gen. Coun., Hunt Wesson, Inc.
Rylance, Robert G., (BV) '35 '71 C.112 B.A. L.990 J.D. 1400 N. Brea Blvd.
Schack, Michael L. '61 '87 C.1044 B.A. L.809 J.D. 545 N. Lincoln Ave.
Schmid, Wm. Randall '45 '79 C.154 B.A. L.1137 J.D. 2545 E. Chapman Ave.
**Schoeman, Cara Hagan** '62 '90 C.800 B.S. L.1137 J.D. [Elenbaas&S.]
*PRACTICE AREAS: Civil Litigation; Business Law; Landlord Tenant; Real Estate; Construction Law.
Schonfeld, David S. '61 '92 C.130 B.A. L.1137 J.D. 1235 N. Harbor Blvd.
Schulman, David H., (BV) '51 '76 C.1077 B.A. L.990 J.D. [Launer,C.&S.]
Schulte, Frederick W. '12 '38 C.20 A.B. L.213 LL.B. USF & G Co.
Scott, Raymond D. '51 '83 C.1042 B.A. L.426 J.D. 2600 E. Nutwood Ave.
Seldeen, Bruce A. '37 '90 C.668 B.A. L.1137 J.D. P.O. Box 5434
Sherlin, Jacquelyn S. '47 '77 C.330 B.A. L.398 J.D. 680 N. Langsdorf Dr.
Siegel, Trudy S. '48 '79 C.339 B.S. L.426 J.D. Western State Univ. Coll. of Law
Singer, Carla M. '47 '79 C.112 B.A. L.1136 J.D. Mun. Ct. J.
Snyder, O. Keith '25 '65 C.1042 B.A. L.809 LL.B. Western State Univ. Coll. of Law
Somaia, Sunil R. '66 '92 C.999 B.A. L.1137 J.D. 1235 N. Harbor Blvd., #200
Sorokin, Jack E. '50 '75 C.112 A.B. L.1068 J.D.
Assoc. Coun., Beckman Instruments, Inc.

**Stearman, James A., (BV) '51 '77 C.112 B.A. L.990 J.D.**
**Suite 200, 1235 North Harbor Boulevard, 92632**
**Telephone: 714-871-1132; 870-8501 Facsimile: 714-871-5620**
***REPORTED CASES: Ross v. City of Yorba Linda (1991); Calif. Ct. of Appeal-4th Dist. 1 C.A. 4th 954, 2 Cal. Rptr. 2d 638 (Zoning Law-Writ of Mandate).**
**General Civil Trial Practice. Collections, Real Estate, Business, Corporate and Partnership Law.**
**Representative Client: Caesar's Palace.**
***See Professional Biographies, FULLERTON, CALIFORNIA***

Steinmeyer, Robert J. '21 '50 C.546 B.S.E.E. L.273 J.D. 609 Lemon Hill Terr. (Pat.)‡
**Stout, Richard S.**, (BV) '57 '82 C.705 B.A. L.990 J.D. [Christensen&S.]
*PRACTICE AREAS: Personal Injury Law.
Strangman, Ida M. '54 '91 C.800 B.A. L.1049 J.D.
(adm. in TX; not adm. in CA) Pres., Strangman Exploration Co.
Sturm, Edward W., IV '54 '87 C.823 B.S. L.1137 J.D. 137 W. Chapman Ave.
Sunday, Richard J., (BV) '33 '69 C.569 B.S. L.990 J.D. 1440 N. Harbor
Thompson, Jack C. '27 '71 C&L.1137 B.S., J.D. 222 N. Berkeley Ave.
Von Esch, Mark F., (BV) '56 '81 C.1163 B.A. L.990 J.D. 810 E. Commonwealth Ave.
Wada, Robert S. '55 '82 C.112 B.A. L.1137 J.D. 410 W. Amerige Ave.
Walder, Jeannette M. '— '77 C&L.146 B.S., J.D. 1901 W. Malvern (Pat.)
Ward, Robert E., (AV) '23 '50 C&L.966 B.A., J.D. 454 Pinehurst Ct.‡
Warnisher, Raymond A. '18 '50 C.312 B.A. L.209 J.D. 1343 W. Valencia St.
**Watson, William G.**, (AV) '47 '72 C&L.800 B.S., J.D. [Curran&W.]
*PRACTICE AREAS: Criminal Law; Family Law.
Weiss, John A. '53 '80 C&L.800 A.B., J.D. Assoc. Coun., Beckman Instruments, Inc.
Weiss, Roland B. '18 '40 C.582 L.585 J.D.
(adm. in ND; not adm. in CA) 3018 Sunnywood Dr.‡

**Wheatley Osaki & Associates, (BV)**
**2600 East Nutwood Avenue, Suite 101, 92831**⊙
**Telephone: 714-992-6300 FAX: 714-441-1652**
**Jeff R. Wheatley (1927-1994); Kerry G. Osaki.**
**Construction Law, Insurance Defense, Civil Litigation and Collections.**
**Long Beach, California Office: 3780 Kilroy Airport Way, Suite 200, 90806. Telephone: 1-800-422-2090.**
***See Professional Biographies, FULLERTON, CALIFORNIA***

Wilbur, Marcia B. '33 '73
C.267 B.A. L.990 J.D. Dean, Western State Univ. College of Law
Williams, Cleveland R. '40 '75 C.679 B.S. L.1340 J.D.
(adm. in OH; not adm. in CA; Pat.) 1506 N. Sycamore
Wilson, Marcus S. '59 '84 C&L.800 B.S., J.D. Prof. of Law, Fullerton College
**Wimer, Warren B.**, (AV) '39 '67 C.446 B.S. L.426 J.D. [Ballard,W.B.&E.]
*PRACTICE AREAS: Earth Movement; Construction Defects; Real Estate; Business Litigation; Mergers, Acquisitions and Business Purchases.
Wolf, Jerrold M., (BV) '39 '68 C.1077 B.A. L.1095 J.D. 40E. Commonwealth, 2nd Fl.
Wolf, Michael J. '50 '76 C.1042 B.A. L.990 J.D. 1309 W. Valencia Dr.

## GALT, 8,889, *Sacramento Co.*

Allen, Jana L. '62 '92 C.1060 B.A. L.112 J.D. 230 Lapwing Ln.
Dobson, William D. '24 '59 C.864 B.S. L.1065 J.D. 413 Maple St.
Hill, Devoron K. '56 '84 C.1060 B.A. L.999 J.D. 816 C St.

**Neumiller & Beardslee, A Professional Corporation**
**(See Stockton)**

Osgood, Jerry W. '35 '89 C.497 B.S. L.549 J.D.
(adm. in NV; not adm. in CA) 140 Partridge Dr.‡
Skipper-Dotta, Rhonda '64 '89 C.112 B.A. L.464 J.D. 27551 N. Sowles Rd.

## GARBERVILLE, —, *Humboldt Co.*

Fasic, Robert T. '40 '66 C&L.608 B.A., LL.B.
(adm. in IL; not adm. in CA) Pres., Heartwood Institute, Ltd.
Ingold, Douglas A. '40 '69 C.801 B.A. L.339 J.D. 780A Redwood Dr.
Scher, Leslie E., (BV) '46 '72
C.112 B.A. L.1065 J.D. 293 Sprowel Creek Rd. (⊙Sunnyvale)
Sonenshein, Joel A., (CV) '49 '84 C.112 B.A. L.588 J.D. P.O. Box 780

## GARDENA, 49,847, *Los Angeles Co.*

**Colton, Kevin M.** '55 '80 C.112 B.A. L.1068 J.D. Sr. Coun., Nissan N. Amer., Inc.
Davidson, Donald H., (AV) '20 '49 C.502 A.B. L.426 LL.B. [Davidson,R.&H.]
Davidson, Russ & Harris, (AV) 1875 W. Redondo Beach Blvd.
Davis, Thomas '40 '77 C.1042 B.S. L.426 J.D. 18321 S. Western Ave.
Diamond, James A. '57 '85 C.763 B.S. L.1137 J.D. [Davidson,R.&H.]
Dunn, Stanley L. '27 '52 C.112 L.1065 J.D. 1239 W. 130th St.‡
Fairfield, Joseph W. '07 '33 C.563 L.1009 LL.B. 17700 S. Figueroa St.
Fairfield, Robert A. '44 '76 C.800 B.A. L.990 J.D. 17700 S. Figueroa St.
Gibbs, Thomas E., Jr. '43 '70 C.1070 B.S. L.800 J.D. 879 W. 190th St.‡
**Gibson, Lisa M.** '56 '87 C.973 B.S. L.213 J.D.
(adm. in MI; not adm. in CA) Sr. Coun., Nissan N. Amer., Inc.
Harris, Tedd B., Jr., (BV) '38 '68 C&L.800 B.S.L., J.D. [Davidson,R.&H.]
Hiraide, Toshiro, (AV) '22 '57 C.800 B.A. L.809 J.D. 1875 W. Redondo Beach Blvd.
Izumi, Lance Takeo '58 '85 C.112 B.A. L.800 J.D.
(adm. in NE; not adm. in CA) 1708 W. Compton Blvd.‡
Karger, Michael J. '48 '75 C.1349 B.A. L.107 J.D. City Atty.
Kuwahara, Buddy H. '26 '69 C.312 B.A. L.809 LL.B. 813 W. 169th Pl.‡
Maruya, Geo. E. '27 '52 C&L.800 J.D. 1331 W. Gardena Blvd.
Matsumoto, Ellen Mariko '58 '89 C.1169 B.A. L.1065 J.D. 16012 S. Western Ave.
Naruse, James K., (BV) '28 '54 C.112 B.S. L.800 J.D. 1212 W. Gardena Blvd., Ste. C
**Pitterle, Peter T.** '46 '82 C.436 B.A. L.597 J.D. Sr. Coun., Nissan N. Amer., Inc.
Reyes, David K. '57 '83 C.884 B.S.Ec. L.276 J.D.
(adm. in DC; not adm. in CA) Pres., Harbor Distributing Company of California
Russ, Edmond J., (AV) '28 '55 C&L.112 B.S., J.D. [Davidson,R.&H.]
**Ryan, Charles A.** '49 '74 C.755 B.A. L.424 J.D. Sr. Coun., Nissan N. Amer., Inc.
Sandoval, Antonio Z. '39 '80 C.1097 B.S. L.1065 J.D. 346 E. 228th St.
Smith, Mark J. '53 '78 C.1168 B.A. L.1065 J.D. V.P., Coronet Mfg. Co.
Solomon, Scott A. '60 '85 C.339 B.S. L.1068 J.D. Ortho Mattress, Inc.
Steese, Steven M. '55 '80 C.763 B.A. L.1095 J.D. 879 W. 190th St.
Taylor, Douglas R., (BV) '38 '64 C&L.800 B.S., J.D. Pres., Del Mar Die Casting Co.
Towns, Jeffrey B. '59 '85 C.1077 B.A. L.1136 J.D. 15823 S. Western Ave.
Watai, George, (BV) '26 '60 C.800 B.S. L.426 LL.B. 1247 W. 141 St.
**Whalen, William J.** '52 '83
C.215 B.S. L.127 J.D. Asst. Gen. Coun., Nissan N. Amer., Inc.
Wrenn, R. Barry '44 '75 C.886 B.S. L.990 J.D. V.P., Gen. Coun. & Secy., HITCO

## GARDEN GROVE, 143,050, *Orange Co.*

Anderson, B. Ray ... '33 '63 C.101 B.S. L.273 J.D. 300 Plz. Alicante
Block, Gerald, (BV) ... '35 '61 C.112 A.B. L.426 LL.B. 12620 Brookhurst St.
Brown, Roosevelt ... '48 '76 C&L.1137 B.S.L., J.D. 12342 Harbor Blvd.
Bush, Gerald V. ... '41 '78 C.1097 B.S. L.809 J.D. 5702 Daniel Webster Circle
Del Bene, Charles A. '36 '63 C.980 B.A. L.607 LL.B.
(adm. in OH; not adm. in CA) 9302 Stanford Ave.‡
Dunnington, Eugene E., (BV) ... '25 '74 C.112 L.990 J.D. [E.E.Dunnington]
Dunnington, Eugene E., Law Offices of, A Professional Corp., (BV) ... 12399 Lewis St.
Famularo, Robert P. ... '52 '78 C.1042 B.A. L.1137 J.D. 12832 Valley View
Graef, Russell W. ... '44 '72 C.1042 A.B. L.800 J.D. 12900 Garden Grove Blvd.
Gumbinger, Frank E. ... '43 '72 C.800 B.S. L.426 J.D. 6122 Killarney Ave.

**Hayward, Ernest L., (BV) '43 '75 C.1109 B.A. L.809 J.D.**
**12371 Lewis Street Suite 102, 92840-4687**
**Telephone: 714-750-1414 Fax: 714-750-7743**
**Probate and Probate Litigation. Guardianship, Conservatorship and Conservatorship Litigation.**
**Reference: Bank of America.**

***See Professional Biographies, GARDEN GROVE, CALIFORNIA***

Hendry, John F. ... '43 '78 C&L.623 B.S., J.D. 12387 Lewis St.
Horodyski, Joseph B., III ... '58 '83 C.605 A.B. L.245 J.D. 12966 Euclid
Hynes, Thomas J. ... '53 '81 C.197 A.B. L.893 J.D. 13921 Seaboard Cir.
Kroopnick, Meyer N. ... '15 '61 C.112 A.B. L.602 LL.B. 9811 Beverly Ln.
Lauterer, Eric, (BV) ... '35 '62 C&L.800 B.S., J.D. City Atty.
Levin, Dorothy ... '23 '63 C.930 L.1001 LL.B. [Levin&L.]
Levin, Nancy ... '52 '77 C.112 B.A. L.809 J.D. [Levin&L.]
Levin & Levin ... 5249 Lampson Ave.
LeVine, J. Eric ... '51 '78 C.763 L.1137 J.D. 12666 Brookhurst St.
Loukides, Mark ... '57 '86 C.1109 B.A. L.1137 J.D. 9681 Garden Grove Blvd.
Madison, Patina A. ... '51 '92 C.1042 B.A. L.1137 J.D. 12371 Lewis St.
Moriarty, Leo J., Jr. ... '54 '89 C&L.1137 B.S., J.D. 12387 Lewis St.
Neal, James E., (BV) ... '37 '65 C.1042 B.S. L.1065 J.D. 12632 Gilbert St.‡
Park, Jay H. ... '56 '85 C.1097 B.S. L.1137 J.D. 12966 Euclid St.
Patel, Arun S. ... '58 '84 C.823 B.S. L.1068 J.D. 13171 Wilson St.
Pool, Willard R., (AV) ... '13 '38 C.112 A.B. L.1066 LL.B. 12550 Brookhurst St.
Rogers, Darwin L. ... '19 '53 C.143 B.B.A. L.880 LL.B. 10671 Overman‡
Slimmer, Kenneth H., (BV) ... '29 '57 C&L.208 B.S., J.D. 6761 Killarney Ave.
Smolin, Stan, (BV) ... '36 '72 P.O. Box 5128
Todd, Charles J. ... '47 '72 C.894 A.B. L.880 J.D. [C.J.Todd]
Todd, Charles J., Prof. Corp. ... 12211 Salerno St.
Venezia, Thomas L. ... '40 '77 C.768 B.S. L.1137 J.D. 9301 Shannon Ave.
Wolfsen, Thomas H. ... '42 '67 C.999 B.A. L.1068 J.D. 12419 Lewis St.
Woodard, Benny M. ... '28 '72 C.1042 B.S. L.1001 J.D. 12966 Euclid
Zawila, William L. ... '43 '74 C.768 B.S. L.1137 J.D. 12550 Brookhurst St.

## GARDEN VALLEY, 900, *El Dorado Co.*

Pechner, Freda D. ... '53 '78 C.1077 B.A. L.809 J.D. 4661 Marshall Rd.

## GEORGETOWN, —, *El Dorado Co.*

Roseman, Abigail L. ... '50 '78 C.966 B.A. L.809 J.D. Shannon Knox House, 2nd Fl.

## GEYSERVILLE, —, *Sonoma Co.*

Carney, Ann S. ... '49 '78 C.347 B.S. L.209 J.D. 410 Colony Rd.
Carreras, Gerald F. ... '26 '53 C&L.767 B.S., LL.B. 22700 Walling Rd.
Kline, Thomas E. ... '51 '92 C.475 B.A. L.213 J.D. P.O. Box 945

## GILROY, 31,487, *Santa Clara Co.*

Alvarez, John A. ... '43 '84 C.112 B.S. L.770 J.D. 8352 Church St.
Barreto, Julie Kai ... '55 '81 C.112 A.B. L.284 J.D. Calif. Rural Legal Assistance
Braff-Guajardo, Ellen L. ... '55 '81 C.112 A.B. L.1068 J.D. Calif. Rural Leg. Assistance
Cunningham, Brian D. ... '42 '72 C.112 B.S. L.770 J.D. Pres., Cunningham Capital Corp.
Filice, John M., Jr., (BV) ... '43 '69 C.770 B.S.C. L.1066 J.D. 7888 Wren Ave.
Fortino, Andrea L. ... '62 '91 C.1974 B.A. L.1226 J.D. 7770 Filice Dr.
Gonzales, Richard M. ... '50 '78 C.112 B.A. L.285 J.D. 7539 Eigleberry
Gonzalez, Milton F. ... '54 '81 C.112 B.A. L.770 J.D. 8339 Church St.
Harrison, Joan A., (BV) ... '30 '55 C&L.813 A.B., LL.B. [Harrison&H.]
Harrison, Richard S., (BV) ... '29 '55 C.112 A.B. L.1066 LL.B. [Harrison&H.]
Harrison & Harrison, (BV) ... 178 2nd St.
Hofer, Dennis J., (CV) ... '44 '72 C.267 B.A. L.770 J.D. 7415 Eigleberry St.
Jacobs, Bruce M., (BV) ... '26 '53 C.112 A.B. L.767 J.D. [Jacobs&M.]
Jacobs & McDonald, (BV) ... 7995 Princevalle St., Suite 5

**Macias, Ernest R. '— '85 C.763 B.S. L.1137 J.D.**
**8339 Church Street, Suite 107, 95020**
**Telephone: 408-848-5091**
**Email: ernesto2@netcapenavigator.briefexchange.com**
**General Civil Business Practice. Personal Injury, Contract Business Law and Entertainment Law (Music Only), Sexual Harassment and Employer Compliance Law.**

McDonald, Kenneth E., (BV) ... '42 '71 C.112 B.A. L.770 J.D. [Jacobs&M.]
McNulty, Peter J., (AV) ... '54 '79 C.882 B.A. L.93 J.D. 8352 Church St. (⊙Los Angeles)
Schiltz, Ronald L. '45 '76 C.627 B.S. L.190 J.D.
(adm. in NE; not adm. in CA) Corporate Pension Consultants
Thompson, Joseph P., (BV) ... '46 '79 C.768 B.A. L.770 J.D. 8339 Church St.
Van Clark, Cheryl J. ... '— '92 C.112 B.A. L.352 J.D. 8339 Church St.

## GLENDALE, 180,038, *Los Angeles Co.*

**Acierno, Joseph M.** ... '61 '93 C&L.190 B.S., J.D. [[A] O'Flaherty&B.]
*PRACTICE AREAS: Medical Malpractice Defense.
Aden, Kelly L. ... '60 '87 C.1109 B.A. L.1065 J.D. 500 N. Brand Blvd.
**Adler, William J.** ... '59 '86 C.602 B.B.A. L.426 J.D. [Styskal,W.&M.]
*PRACTICE AREAS: General Corporate, Commercial and Consumer Law; Insurance; Computer; Credit Union Law.
Agemian, Varoujan V. ... '58 '85 C.800 B.A. L.809 J.D. 505 N. Brand Blvd.
Aguilar, Michael ... '42 '77 C.1075 B.S.E.E. L.809 J.D. 3508 Angelus Ave.

**Aherne, Brian W., & Associates**
**(See Burbank)**

Aiken, Vincent J. ... '09 '32 C.569 L.1009 LL.B. 500 N. Brand Blvd.
Albaum, Joseph H. '19 '42 C&L.597 B.S., J.D.
(adm. in IL; not adm. in CA) 1408 1/2 Valley View Rd.‡
**Alden, Mary C.** ... '56 '81 C&L.800 B.A., J.D. Assoc. Gen. Coun., Heller Intl. Corp.
Alexander, Leon J., (AV) ... '24 '51 C.102 B.A. L.976 J.D. 2682 Kennington Dr.‡
**Allan, Joan H.**, (AV) ... '44 '79 C.97 B.A. L.809 J.D. [O'Rourke,A.&F.]
*PRACTICE AREAS: Personal Injury; Family Law; Business Litigation.
**Allen, Tom M.** (BV) ... '46 '77 C&L.1137 B.S.L., J.D. [[A] Hemer,B.&C.]⊙
*PRACTICE AREAS: Medical Malpractice Defense.
**Anderson, Jarrett S.**, (AV) ... '36 '61 C.877 B.S. L.800 J.D. [Melby&A.]
*PRACTICE AREAS: Civil Litigation; Family Law.
Anderson, Martin R. ... '46 '74 C.1109 B.A. L.1137 J.D. 130 N. Brand Blvd.
Applegate, E. Timothy '34 '62
C&L.608 B.S., LL.B. Sr. V.P. & Gen. Coun., Forest Lawn Co.
Applegate, Kenneth H. ... '53 '82 C.605 A.B. L.464 J.D. P.O. Box 4208
**Arkuss, David A.** ... '54 '79 C.696 B.A. L.809 J.D. [[A] Hemer,B.&C.]
*PRACTICE AREAS: Medical Malpractice Defense.
Arnold, Michael J. ... '54 '88 C.800 B.M. L.809 J.D. 101 N. Brand Blvd., Suite 600
**Aronson, Craig D.** ... '56 '82 C.197 B.A. L.145 J.D. [Hagenbaugh&M.]
*PRACTICE AREAS: Coverage; Bad Faith; Advertising Injury; Business Litigation.
**Ashton, Eric A.**, (AV) ... '31 '59 C&L.800 B.S., J.D. [Edwards,E.&A.]
*PRACTICE AREAS: Estate Planning; Probate and Trust Law; General Business; Tax Planning.
**Ashton, Eric Andrew** ... '64 '90 C.112 A.B. L.800 J.D. [Edwards,E.&A.]
*PRACTICE AREAS: Estate Planning; Taxation; Real Estate Transactions.
Baker, Dennis J. ... '57 '84 C.112 B.A. L.284 J.D. [Zonni,G.&T.]
Baker, Robert P. ... '49 '83 C.112 B.A. L.398 J.D. 550 N. Brand Blvd.
**Baker, Sheldon S.**, (AV) ... '36 '62 C.705 B.A. L.813 J.D. [Baker,O.L.&D.]

**Baker, Olson, LeCroy & Danielian, A Law Corporation, (AV)** [BR]
**144 North Brand Boulevard, P.O. Box 29062, 91209-9062**
**Telephone: 818-502-5600 Facsimile: 818-241-2653**
**Sheldon S. Baker (Certified Specialist, Taxation Law, The State Bar of California Board of Legal Specialization); Eric Olson; Charles L. LeCroy, III (Certified Specialist, Taxation Law, The State Bar of California Board of Legal Specialization); Arsen Danielian;—Michael S. Simon. Of Counsel: John J. Jacobson.**
**General Civil and Trial Practice in all State and Federal Courts. Federal and State Tax, Corporation, Partnership, Real Estate, Trust, Estate Planning, Probate, General Business Law, Immigration and Naturalization. Business and Probate Litigation.**

***See Professional Biographies, GLENDALE, CALIFORNIA***

**Baldwin, Ernest R.**, (AV) ... '25 '58 C.475 B.S. L.1068 LL.B. [[C] Gill&B.]
*PRACTICE AREAS: Corporate; Business; Transactions; Estate Planning.
**Ball, James H.** '42 '73 C.502 A.B. L.734 J.D.
(adm. in MO; not adm. in CA) Sr. V.P. & Gen. Coun., Nestle USA, Inc.
Bando, Lillian F. ... '48 '85 C&L.112 A.B., J.D. 801 N. Brand Blvd.
Barish, Herbert M., (AV) ... '40 '66 C.112 B.S. L.1068 LL.B. 1007 S. Central Ave.
**Barkus, Ramune E.** ... '49 '79 C.991 B.A. L.809 J.D. [Hemer,B.&C.]⊙
*LANGUAGES: Lithuanian and French.
*PRACTICE AREAS: Medical Malpractice Defense.
**Barrera, Raymond R.** '65 '93 C.112 B.A. L.770 J.D.
Assoc. Coun., First Amer. Title Ins. Co. of L.A.
**Barry, Stephen** ... '53 '79 C.813 B.A. L.1068 J.D. [[A] Hagenbaugh&M.]
Bartholomew, Barry, (AV) ... '50 '79 C.208 B.S.B.A. L.809 J.D. 701 N. Brand Blvd.
Basquin, Philip W. ... '46 '76 C.197 A.B. L.1119 J.D. 100 W. Broadway
**Baumeister, Anastasia** ... '— '90 C.112 A.B. L.767 J.D. [[A] Knapp,P.&C.]
Bautista, Henrico T. ... '61 '87 C.605 A.B. L.1067 J.D. 535 N. Brand Blvd.
Bavaro, Joe Nick ... '36 '72 C&L.1190 B.S.L., J.D. 740 E. Wilson Ave.
Beam, Susan ... '56 '81 C.773 B.A. L.426 J.D. [Beam&H.]
Beam & Hummel ... 801 N. Brand Blvd.
Beaver, Clayton J., Jr. ... '40 '71 C.602 B.A. L.426 J.D. [C.J.Beaver,Jr.]
Beaver, Clayton J., Jr., Law Offices of ... 529 Hahn Ave.
**Becker, Brian L.** ... '59 '84 C.900 B.A. L.378 J.D. [[A] Bright&B.]
*PRACTICE AREAS: Business Litigation.
**Belgum, Stephen L.**, (BV) ... '43 '72 C.940 B.A. L.800 J.D. [O'Flaherty&B.]
*PRACTICE AREAS: Trials.
**Bell, David I.** ... '54 '79 C.112 B.S. L.809 J.D. [Knapp,P.&C.]
**Benben, Pamela A.** ... '55 '81 C.1044 B.A. L.426 J.D. [[A] O'Flaherty&B.]
*REPORTED CASES: Ramos v. Valley Vista Hosp., 234 Cal.Rptr. 608, Ordered Not Published, (Rule 976, Cal. Rules of Ct.) (Cal.App. 2 Dist., Jan 30, 1987) (NO CIV. B019781, CIV. B016746); Grant v. Avis Rent A Car System, Inc., 158 Cal.App.3d 813, 204 Cal.Rptr. 869 (Cal.App. 2 Dist., Jul 26, 1984) (NO. B004006).
**Benjamin, Earl M.**, (AV) ... '52 '79 C.610 A.B. L.1049 J.D. [Benjamin,L.&B.]
**Benjamin, Robert N.**, (AV) ... '46 '79 C.1077 B.S. L.809 J.D. [Benjamin,L.&B.]
*PRACTICE AREAS: Entertainment Law; Licensing; Business Litigation; Insurance Bad Faith.
**Benjamin, Tavi B.** ... '66 '93 C.1099 B.A. L.426 J.D. [Benjamin,L.&B.]
*PRACTICE AREAS: Entertainment; General Business.

**Benjamin, Lugosi & Benjamin, LLP, (AV)**
**520 North Central Avenue, Suite 800, 91203-1919**
**Telephone: 818-502-8400 Fax: 818-956-1099**
**Email: INFO@BENJILULAW.COM**
**Bela G. Lugosi; Robert N. Benjamin; Earl M. Benjamin; Mark W. Yocca; Frank Lupo; Tavi B. Benjamin.**
**Entertainment Law, Licensing, Rights of Publicity and Privacy, General, Civil and Business Litigation including Bad Faith.**
**Representative Clients: Comedy 111 Productions, Inc.; Classic Characters Entertainment Group; Republic Indemnity Company of America; Pacific Rim, Assurance Co.**

***See Professional Biographies, GLENDALE, CALIFORNIA***

Bennett, Ray C. ... '32 '60 C.813 B.A. L.1068 J.D. 1007 S. Central Ave.
Bennett, Richard A. ... '40 '74 C.477 B.S.E.E. L.1148 J.D. 1229 Geneva St.
Berg, Arthur Paul, (AV) ... '47 '73 C.112 B.A. L.1068 J.D. [A.P.Berg]
Berg, Arthur Paul, P.C., (AV) ... 1635 Wabasso Way
**Berg-Wilion, Elayne C.** '51 '75 C.112 B.A. L.426 J.D.
Assoc. Gen. Coun. & Asst. Secy., IHOP Corp.
*RESPONSIBILITIES: Corporate Law.
Berger, Richard L., (AV) ... '31 '59 C&L.813 A.B., J.D. 205 E. Broadway
Berglund, John R. ... '65 '92 C.605 A.B. L.800 J.D. 144 N. Glendale Ave.
Berjikian, Vicken Ohannes ... '53 '83 C.061 B.A. L.1179 J.D. 1535 E. Colorado St.
**Bernstein-Hahn, Adrienne R.** ... '61 '88 C.112 B.A. L.426 J.D. [[A] Calendo,P.S.&D.]
*LANGUAGES: Spanish and French.
*PRACTICE AREAS: Civil Litigation; Insurance Defense.
Bitticks, Robert R. ... '44 '72 C.112 B.S. L.426 J.D. 550 N. Brand Blvd.
Blake, Stuart B. ... '56 '81 C.401 B.S. L.1206 J.D. 31 Baskin-Robbins Pl.
Blakemore, Catherine J. ... '52 '77 C.112 B.A. L.426 J.D. Protec. & Advocacy, Inc.
Blane, Lyle L., (BV) ... '31 '63 C.911 A.B. L.1068 LL.B. P.O. Box 1867
Bogdon, Donald L. ... '57 '83 C.112 B.A. L.800 J.D. 1551 Hillcrest Ave.
Bohlen, Charles E., Jr. ... '47 '73 C.309 B.A. L.976 J.D. 372 Brockmont Dr.
Boller, David B., (AV) ... '28 '59 C.112 B.A. L.1068 J.D. 550 N. Brand Blvd., 7th Fl.
**Booth, Douglas M.**, (AV) ... '44 '75 C&L.1137 B.S., J.D. [Flanagan,B.U.&M.]⊙
*PRACTICE AREAS: Personal Injury.
**Boucher, Craig** '46 '76
C.112 B.A. L.1137 J.D. Sr. V.P., First Amer. Title Ins. Co. of L.A.
Boukidis, Constantine M., Law Offices of '59 '85
C.597 B.A. L.426 J.D. 144 N. Glendale Ave., Ste. 101
**Boyle, Suzanne** ... '49 '89 C.525 B.A. L.1137 J.D. [[A] O'Flaherty&B.]
Bradford, Eugene C. ... '54 '84 C.740 B.A. L.426 J.D. 100 W. Broadway
Bramson, Janet Kay ... '53 '78 C&L.861 B.A., J.D. Sm. Bus. Admin.
**Brandt, Jeffrey P.**, (AV) ... '53 '78 C.112 B.A. L.1066 J.D. [Edwards,E.&A.]
*PRACTICE AREAS: Estate Planning; Probate and Trust Law.
Brar, Vikram ... '62 '92 C.668 B.A. L.1068 J.D. 144 N. Glendale Ave.
Brault, Patrick J. ... '64 '90 [Santochi,F.&G.]

CAA107P

CALIFORNIA—GLENDALE MARTINDALE-HUBBELL LAW DIRECTORY 1997

Breckenridge, Paul G., Jr. ...'27 '53 C&L.813 A.B., LL.B. Ret. Supr. Ct. J.
**Brees, Benjamin M.** ...'50 '90 C.602 B.A. L.398 J.D. [A Thomas&P.]
*PRACTICE AREAS: Civil Litigation.
Bregman, Gary H. ...'48 '84 C.112 B.A. L.809 J.D. Coun., Old Republic Title Co.
**Bright, James S.**, (AV) ...'49 '75 C.800 B.S. L.426 J.D. [Bright&B.]
*PRACTICE AREAS: Business Litigation; Oil and Gas; Environmental.
**Bright, Maureen J.** ...'50 '78 C.800 B.S. L.426 J.D. [Bright&B.]
*PRACTICE AREAS: Business Litigation; Environmental.

**Bright and Brown, (AV)**
**550 North Brand Boulevard, Suite 2100, 91203**
**Telephone: 818-243-2121; 213-489-1414 Facsimile: 818-243-3225**
**James S. Bright; Gregory C. Brown; Maureen J. Bright; John Quirk; Brian L. Becker. Associates: Anthony S. Brill; Doris A. Mendenhall.**
**Business Litigation, Oil, Gas and Energy Law and Environmental Law.**
*See Professional Biographies, GLENDALE, CALIFORNIA*

**Brill, Anthony S.** ...'63 '90 C.112 B.A. L.800 J.D. [A Bright&B.]
*PRACTICE AREAS: Business Litigation; Oil and Gas; Environmental.
**Brink, John H., (P.C.)**, (AV) ...'33 '57 C&L.426 LL.B. [Irsfeld,I.&Y.]
*PRACTICE AREAS: Business Law; Real Property Law; Estate Planning.
**Brown, Gregory C.**, (AV) ...'51 '76 C.273 B.A. L.1068 J.D. [Bright&B.]
*PRACTICE AREAS: Business Litigation; Oil and Gas; Environmental.
Brown, John E. ...'19 '72 C.800 B.S. L.1127 J.D. 416 E. Bway
Brunton, James E., Law Office of, (BV) '30 '61
C.174 B.S. L.208 LL.B. 700 N. Brand St., Ste 1190 (Pat.)
Bunt, Richard A. ...'58 '92 C&L.37 B.A., J.D. 500 N. Brand Blvd.
**Burkin, Mary Ann** ...'49 '92 C.800 B.A. L.426 J.D. [A Calendo,P.S.&D.]
*PRACTICE AREAS: Civil Litigation; Insurance Defense.
Burlison, Robert C., Jr. ...'53 '81 C.321 B.A. L.990 J.D. [Burlison&L.]
Burlison & Luostari ...520 N. Central Ave., Suite 740
**Burns-Haindel, Jeanne** ...'57 '87 C&L.800 B.A., J.D. [A Greenwald,H.&M.]
*PRACTICE AREAS: Probate Law; Estate Planning Law; Real Property; Corporation Law; Business Law.
**Bush, Keri Lynn** ...'63 '92 C.169 B.S. L.464 J.D. [A Hagenbaugh&M.]
Butchko, John T. ...'37 '62 C&L.800 B.S.L., LL.B. 1208 Bruce Ave.‡
**Byer, Valerie K.** ...'49 '90 C.800 B.A. L.426 J.D. [Melby&A.]
*PRACTICE AREAS: Civil Litigation; Family Law.
Cabanillas, Rayda C. ...'51 '89 C.19 B.A. L.809 J.D. 516 Burchett St.
Calabro, Alfred A., (BV) ...'25 '52 C.999 L.809 J.D. [Calabro,C.&C.]
Calabro, Anthony J. ...'24 '51 C.800 L.999 LL.B. 124 S. Isabel St.‡
Calabro, Daniel F. ...'33 '58 C.112 A.B. L.1068 LL.B. Mun. Ct. Comr.
Calabro, Edward H., (BV) ...'27 '52 C.999 L.809 LL.B. [Calabro,C.&C.]
Calabro, Calabro & Calabro, (BV) ...124 S. Isabel St.
**Calendo, Stephen P.**, (BV) ...'57 '82 C.36 B.S. L.990 J.D. [Calendo,P.S.&D.]
*PRACTICE AREAS: Civil Litigation; Insurance Defense.

**Calendo, Puckett, Sheedy & DiCorrado, (AV)**
**701 North Brand Boulevard, Suite 300, 91203**
**Telephone: 818-549-1935 Facsimile: 818-549-0337**
**Members of Firm: Stephen P. Calendo; Kim B. Puckett (Mr.); Christopher M. Sheedy; Richard A. DiCorrado; Christopher E. Dwyer. Associates: Patricia Ariana DuPre; Adrienne R. Bernstein-Hahn; Brian C. O'Hara; Mary Ann Burkin; Mark L. Russakow; James L. Meier; Michael J. Riley; Gregory M. Cribbs.**
**General Defense Litigation in all Courts and Tribunals. Personal Injury, Premises Liability, Products Liability, Property Damage and Virtually every type of Tort Claim.**
*See Professional Biographies, GLENDALE, CALIFORNIA*

Calkins, Kenneth E. ...'31 '82 C.843 B.A. L.1190 J.D. 520 E. Wilson Ave.
Calleton, Theodore E., (AV) ...'34 '63 C.976 B.A. L.178 LL.B. [Calleton&M.]
Calleton & Merritt, (AV) ...500 N Brand Blvd.
Callister, Douglas L., (AV) ...'39 '64 C.101 B.S. L.800 J.D. [Callister&C.]
Callister, Paul D. ...'64 '91 C.101 B.A. L.188 J.D. 700 N. Brand Blvd.
Callister, Stephen R. ...'60 '88 C&L.101 B.A., J.D. 700 N. Brand Blvd.
Callister, Tad R., (AV) ...'45 '72 C.101 B.S. L.1068 J.D. [Callister&C.]
Callister & Callister, (AV) ...700 N. Brand Blvd.
Camastra, Ralph A. ...'53 '79 C.724 B.A. L.1137 J.D. [Zonni,G.&T.]
Camfield, Roland E., Jr. ...'32 '61 C.911 B.A. L.174 LL.B. [Camfield&C.]
Camfield & Christopher ...801 N. Brand Blvd.
Cannella, Marie R. ...'44 '84 C.1077 B.S. L.1190 J.D. 1613 E. Glenoaks Blvd.
**Carey, Patrick** ...'61 '93 C.1042 B.A. L.426 J.D. [A Ott&H.]
*PRACTICE AREAS: Financial Institutions; Employment; Labor.
Carlson, Kenneth H. ...'52 '80 C.112 A.B. L.426 J.D. 700 N. Central Ave.
Carlyle, Huston T. ...'15 '42 C&L.800 B.A., LL.B. P.O. Box 4379
**Carmack, John M.**, (AV) ...'37 '64 C.112 B.S. L.1068 LL.B. [Gill&B.]
*PRACTICE AREAS: Corporate; Business; Transactions; Estate Planning.
**Carnegie, Alan J.** ...'58 '85 C&L.37 B.A., J.D. [A Knapp,P.&C.]
Carpenter, Charles H., (AV) ...'38 '66 C.112 B.A. L.1065 J.D. 730 Omar St.
Carroll, Norman E. ...'16 '46 L.426 J.D. 1631 Parway Dr.‡
**Caswell, Kathleen S.** '49 '85
C.112 B.A. L.1148 J.D. Corp. Coun., Baskin-Robbins USA, Co.
*RESPONSIBILITIES: Franchising; Real Estate; Food Labeling; Advertising.
Cate, Clifford C., (AV) ...'28 '57 C.668 B.A. L.800 J.D. 401 N. Brand Blvd.
Chadwick, William J., (AV) ...'48 '73 C.732 B.A. L.880 J.D. 1015 Grandview Ave.
Chan, Estella S. ...'46 '76 C.012 B.S. L.426 J.D. 4706 Via Colina
Chappell, Alan ...'54 '79 L.1095 J.D. 535 N. Brand Blvd.
Cheng, Kathryn ...'36 '74 C.112 A.B. L.800 J.D. 1309 Beaudry Blvd.
**Chesnut, Kristen L.** ...'48 '90 C.740 B.A. L.284 J.D. [Hemer,B.&C.]⊙
*PRACTICE AREAS: Medical Malpractice Defense.
Chesnut, Nadine L. ...'54 '90 C.1077 B.A. L.809 J.D. 516 Burchett St.
Chorbajian, Vatche ...'61 '88 C.1077 B.A. L.1137 J.D. 550 N. Brand Blvd.
**Chou, Yu-Feng (Frances)** ...'63 '90 L.1065 J.D. [Knapp,P.&C.]
*LANGUAGES: Chinese (Mandarin).
Christopher, Jeffrey P. ...'50 '78 C.800 B.S. L.809 J.D. [Camfield&C.]
Chun, Darrell J. ...'53 '83 C.800 B.A. L.809 J.D. [Santochi,F.&G.]
Ciccozzi, Michael J. ...'63 '88 C.1113 B.S. L.809 J.D. 6055 Washington Blvd.
**Cisneros, Michael Anthony**, (BV) ...'56 '82 C.800 B.A. L.990 J.D. [Laskin&G.]
*LANGUAGES: Spanish.
*PRACTICE AREAS: Bankruptcy; Commercial Litigation; Creditors' Rights.
**Clark, Bradley C.** ...'55 '83 C.684 B.S. L.999 J.D. [Hemer,B.&C.]⊙
*PRACTICE AREAS: Medical Malpractice Defense.
Clark, Robert C., (AV) ...'34 '61 C.1043 B.S. L.800 J.D. [Clark&S.]
Clark & Smith, (AV) ...1156 N. Brand Blvd.
**Clarke, Laurence R.**, (AV) ...'44 '72 C.1097 L.809 J.D. [B Knapp,P.&C.] ‡
**Clayton, Wayne D.** ...'59 '88 C.685 B.A. L.426 J.D. [Ott&H.]
*PRACTICE AREAS: Employment Law; Labor Law; Wrongful Termination.
**Cochran, Brian D.**, (AV) ...'46 '74 C.112 B.A. L.809 J.D. [B Edwards,E.&A.]
*PRACTICE AREAS: Insurance; Business and Commercial Litigation.
**Cohen, Clifford R.** ...'60 '85 C.112 A.B. L.1065 J.D. [Knapp,P.&C.]
**Cohn, Racey** ...'49 '84 C.347 B.A. L.1148 J.D. Sr. Coun., Heller Intl. Corp.
Colaneri, Marie E. ...'33 '74 C.690 B.A. L.1148 J.D. 100 W. Broadway
Cole, R. Rosser ...'39 '68 C&L.846 B.B.A., J.D. 200 N. Maryland Ave.
Cooper, Bernard ...'41 '67 C.112 A.B. L.800 J.D. 230 N. Maryland Ave.

**Cooper-Folb, Gail S.** ...'58 '83 C.112 B.A. L.1068 J.D. [Knapp,P.&C.]
*LANGUAGES: French.
Cordier, David A. ...'47 '83 C.1097 B.S. L.426 535 N. Brand Blvd., Ste. 401
Corey, Dana R. ...'61 '88 C.768 B.S. L.770 J.D. 130 N. Brand Blvd.
Crane, Gary M., (BV) ...'40 '65 C.506 B.S. L.597 J.D. 517 E. Wilson Ave.
**Creamer, Steven E.** ...'65 '94 C.112 B.A. L.426 J.D. [Knapp,P.&C.]
**Cribbs, Gregory M.** ...'65 '95 C.112 B.A. L.1049 J.D. [A Calendo,P.S.&D.]
*PRACTICE AREAS: Civil Litigation; Insurance Defense.
Croft, Janice Claire ...'47 '72 C.112 B.A. L.61 J.D. Mun. Ct. J.
**Croutch, Todd E.** ...'63 '89 C.763 B.S. L.426 J.D. [A O'Flaherty&B.]
*REPORTED CASES: Stevenson v. Superior Court (1996) 42 Cal. App. 4th 1288.
*PRACTICE AREAS: Employment; General Liability; Product Liability Defense Litigation.
**Cutler, Timothy K.** ...'59 '88 C.1109 B.A. L.426 J.D. [Knapp,P.&C.]
**Czajkowskyj, Cyril** ...'51 '78 C.597 B.A. L.767 J.D. [Knapp,P.&C.]
Dabbah, Gary D. ...'59 '87 C.112 B.A. L.1148 J.D. [Zonni,G.&T.]
Dailey, Lawrence ...'53 '80 C.602 B.A. L.809 J.D. 701 N. Brand Blvd.
**Danielian, Arsen** ...'54 '85 C.061 LL.B. L.398 J.D. [Baker,O.L.&D.]
*LANGUAGES: Armenian and Persian (Farsi).
Daniels, Hermine ...'41 '78 C.766 B.A. L.809 J.D. 700 N. Brand Blvd.
**Danis, Michael T.** ...'59 '84 C.1075 B.A. L.1068 J.D. [A Flanagan,B.U.&M.]
*PRACTICE AREAS: Personal Injury.
Darian, Charles ...'30 '80 L.1136 J.D. 144 N. Glendale Ave.
Davidson, Suzanne Mouron '63 '88 C.112 B.A. L.1068 J.D.
Corp. Coun., Forest Lawn Co.
Davis, Jonathan F. ...'51 '75 C.112 B.A. L.1065 J.D. Ste. 840, 800 N. Brand Blvd.
**Deaktor, Michael W.** ...'57 '86 C.36 B.S. L.990 J.D. [Melby&A.]
*PRACTICE AREAS: Probate and Estate Planning.
DeBeau, Betty J., (BV) ...'33 '74 L.1190 517 E. Wilson Ave.
**DeGomez, John P.** ...'45 '81 C.1077 B.A. L.999 J.D. [A Thomas&P.]
*PRACTICE AREAS: Civil Litigation.
Del Mar, Debra G. '56 '91 C.990 B.S. L.809 J.D.
Mgr., Architectural & Engg. Div., Walt Disney Imagineering
Deni, Joseph D., II ...'57 '85 C.1154 B.A. L.800 J.D. 500 N. Brand Blvd.
DeNicholas, Jeffrey J. ...'56 '83 C.112 B.A. L.464 J.D. [Zonni,G.&T.]
**Denney, Richard J., Jr.** ...'39 '65 C.813 B.S. L.309 J.D. [Denney&O.]
*PRACTICE AREAS: Environmental; Litigation.

**Denney & Oths**
**130 North Brand Boulevard Fourth Floor, 91203**
**Telephone: 818-500-9030 Fax: 818-500-8079**
**Email: 71361@compuserve.com**
**Richard J. Denney, Jr.; Eleanor F. Oths. Of Counsel: Joseph J. O'Malley.**
**Environmental Law and Litigation.**
*See Professional Biographies, GLENDALE, CALIFORNIA*

**DeRose, Julie M.** ...'57 '91 C.188 B.S. L.426 J.D. [A Hagenbaugh&M.]
Devereaux, N. Paul ...'45 '72 C.112 A.B. L.1068 J.D. V.P., Nestle USA, Inc.
**DiCorrado, Richard A.**, (AV) ...'57 '85 C.705 B.A. L.990 J.D. [Calendo,P.S.&D.]
*PRACTICE AREAS: Civil Litigation; Insurance Defense.
DiJulio, R. David, (AV) ...'46 '83 C.223 B.S. L.809 J.D. [DiJulio&K.]
DiJulio & King, (AV) ...501 N. Central Ave.
Di Mauro, Marcello M. ...'46 '74 C.768 B.A. L.1065 J.D. 640 Solway St.
**Donahue, Craig R.**, (AV) ...'51 '77 C.112 A.B. L.426 J.D. [Thomas&P.]
*PRACTICE AREAS: Civil Litigation; Medical Malpractice; Insurance Defense.
**DuPre, Patricia Ariana** ...'49 '85 C.1097 L.809 J.D. [A Calendo,P.S.&D.]
*LANGUAGES: Italian.
*PRACTICE AREAS: Civil Litigation; Insurance Defense.
Dwork, Joel ...'42 '70 C.112 B.A. L.1049 J.D. Sr. Assoc. Coun., Glendale Fed. Bk., FSB
**Dwyer, Christopher E.**, (BV) ...'60 '87 C.112 B.A. L.809 J.D. [Calendo,P.S.&D.]
*PRACTICE AREAS: Civil Litigation; Insurance Defense.
Early, Alexander R. ...'17 '46 C.188 A.B. L.309 LL.B. Ret. Supr. Ct. J.‡
**Ebelhar, Melinda W.** ...'57 '83 C.605 A.B. L.1066 J.D. [Hagenbaugh&M.]
*PRACTICE AREAS: Appellate Practice; Insurance Coverage; General Litigation.
Edelstein, Gerald A. ...'42 '67 C.112 B.S. L.1068 J.D. 330 N. Brand Blvd.
**Edwards, John U.**, (AV) ...'19 '46 C.112 B.A. L.1066 LL.B. [Edwards,E.&A.]
*PRACTICE AREAS: Probate and Estate Planning; General Business; Civil Litigation.
**Edwards, Mark U.**, (AV) ...'21 '52 C.112 B.A. L.1065 J.D. [Edwards,E.&A.]
*PRACTICE AREAS: Family Law; Personal Injury and Property Damage Litigation.

**Edwards, Edwards & Ashton, A Professional Corporation, (AV)**
**Suite 500 Wells Fargo Bank Building, 420 North Brand Boulevard, 91203**
**Telephone: 818-247-7380 Los Angeles: 213-245-9451 FAX: 818-247-7025**
**John U. Edwards; Mark U. Edwards (Certified Specialist, Family Law, The State Bar of California Board of Legal Specialization); Eric A. Ashton; Jeffrey P. Brandt; Wilbur Gin; Donna M. Encinas; Eric Andrew Ashton. Of Counsel: Brian D. Cochran.**
**General Civil and Trial Practice. Wills, Trusts, Probate, Estate Planning, Taxation, Corporations, Business, Commercial, Real Property, Family and Personal Injury Law.**
**References: Bank of America; Central Bank of Glendale.**
*See Professional Biographies, GLENDALE, CALIFORNIA*

Eichler, Gregg Alastair ...'48 '77 C.768 B.A. L.464 J.D. 550 N. Brand Ave.
Eldred, Richard E., (AV) ...'35 '68 C.1032 B.S. L.800 J.D. [Eldred&G.]
Eldred & Gantus, (AV) ...Ste. 2150, 550 N. Brand Blvd.
Elias, Diane J. ...'47 '92 C.273 B.A. L.809 J.D. 3705 La Crescenta Ave.
Eller, James R., Jr. '47 '75 C.178 B.A. L.228 J.D.
Corp. Coun. & Secy., Glendale Fed. Bk., FSB
**Encinas, Donna M.** ...'61 '89 C.112 B.A. L.809 J.D. [Edwards,E.&A.]
*PRACTICE AREAS: Family Law.
Etmekjian, Garbis D. ...'56 '90 C.1097 B.A. L.809 J.D. 416 E. Bway.
**Etzwiler, Rhonda L.** ...'62 '90 C.8 B.S.N. L.61 J.D. [A Hagenbaugh&M.]
*PRACTICE AREAS: Medical Malpractice Defense Law.
Evans, Darlene G. ...'— '88 C.1097 B.A. L.809 J.D. 100 W. Broadway
Evans, Godfrey B. '54 '81 C.112 A.B. L.426 J.D.
Exec. V.P., Gen. Coun. & Corp. Secy., Fidelity Fed. Bk.
Everakes, Howard C. '50 '76 C.766 B.A. L.809 J.D.
Exec. V.P. & Gen. Coun., Glendale Fed. Bk., FSB
**Ewing, Malcolm C.** ...'42 '73 C.951 B.A. L.426 J.D. Sr. Coun., Nestle USA, Inc.
Farley, Keith W. ...'62 '87 C&L.190 B.S.B.A., J.D. 500 N. Brand Blvd.
Fedirko, Judith E. ...'51 '83 C.645 B.A. L.1095 J.D. [Knights&S.]
**Feldman, Richard S.** ...'53 '79 C.112 B.A. L.1068 J.D. Sr. Coun., Nestle USA, Inc.
*RESPONSIBILITIES: Real Property; Commercial Transactions.
**Ferioli, William T.** ...'51 '77 C.1074 B.S. L.1049 J.D. Sr. Coun., Nestle USA, Inc.
Fernhoff, Mary Ellen ...'51 '77 C.112 A.B. L.800 J.D. Pub. Storage Inc.
Fields, Larry H., (AV) ...'47 '74 C.1077 B.A. L.809 J.D. [Zonni,G.&T.]
Fimea, Victoria E. '61 '88 C.35 B.S. L.904 J.D.
(adm. in AZ; not adm. in CA) 500 N. Brand Blvd.
Fink, Richard A., (AV) '40 '72
C&L.813 A.B., J.D. Sr. Exec. V.P., Glendale Fed. Bk., FSB
Fisher, Mary-Lynne, (AV) ...'50 '76 C.112 B.A. L.1068 J.D. 801 N. Brand Blvd.
**Flanagan, J. Michael**, (AV) ...'41 '70 C&L.800 B.S., J.D. [Flanagan,B.U.&M.]⊙
*PRACTICE AREAS: Criminal Law; Personal Injury Law.

CAA108P

**Flanagan, Booth, Unger & Moses, (AV) BR**
**1156 North Brand Boulevard, 91202-2582⊙**
**Telephone: 818-244-8694 Fax: 818-244-1852**
**Members of Firm: J. Michael Flanagan; Douglas M. Booth; Charles J. Unger; J. Barry Moses. Associates: Michael T. Danis; James A. Grover.**
**General Civil and Trial Practice in all Courts. Criminal, Driving While Intoxicated and Personal Injury Law.**
**Santa Ana, California Office: 1851 East First Street, Suite 805. 92705. Telephone: 714-835-2607. Fax: 714-835-4825.**

*See Professional Biographies, GLENDALE, CALIFORNIA*

Flett, John G., (AV) .......... '28 '57 C.112 A.B. L.1068 LL.B. 961 Pebbleshire Rd.‡
Flory, Frederick A. .......... '37 '75 C.800 B.S. L.1095 J.D. 100 W. Broadway
**Fong, Roderick D.** .......... '56 '89 C.112 B.A. L.426 J.D. [O'Rourke,A.&F.]
*PRACTICE AREAS: Corporate; Business Litigation; Probate; Construction.
Fonnet, William P., (BV) .......... '40 '75 C.112 A.B. L.426 J.D. 550 N. Brand Blvd.
Fox, Frederick I. '36 '67 C.763 A.B. L.1066 LL.B.
Sr. V.P. & Sr. Coun., Fidelity Fed. Bk.
Francis, William A., (BV) .......... '42 '69 C&L.800 B.A., J.D. 100 W. Bway.
**Fraser, Stephen C.** .......... '56 '91 C.388 B.A. L.809 J.D. [A O'Flaherty&B.]
**Freeman, Gwen** .......... '56 '81 C&L.893 B.A., J.D. [Knapp,P.&C.]
**Freeman, John P.** .......... '61 '91 C.112 B.A. L.809 J.D. [A Hemer,B.&C.]
*PRACTICE AREAS: Medical Malpractice Defense.
**Freixes, Graciela L.**, (BV) .......... '55 '81 C.1077 B.A. L.426 J.D. [A Hagenbaugh&M.]
*LANGUAGES: Spanish.
Freytag, Marilyn V., (AV) .......... '26 '60 C.112 A.B. L.1068 J.D. 205 E. Bway.
Furzer, Joyce Helock .......... '55 '83 C.112 B.A. L.426 J.D. 701 N. Brand Blvd.
**Gammell, Barry R.** .......... '49 '82 C.1075 B.S. L.1137 J.D. [Knapp,P.&C.]
*PRACTICE AREAS: Insurance Coverage Litigation.
Gangi, Robert C. .......... '62 '87 C.112 B.A. L.426 J.D. Gangi Builders, Inc.
Gantus, John M. .......... '48 '73 C.1097 B.A. L.1049 J.D. [Eldred&G.]
**Garcia, Steven Ray** .......... '57 '83 C.154 B.A. L.1068 J.D. [Knapp,P.&C.]
Garrett, Terese L. .......... '31 '53 C&L.508 J.D. 31 Baskin-Robbins Pl.
Gatto, Isolde Plendl .......... '— '88 C.1077 B.A. L.809 J.D. 700 N. Central Ave.
Gavriel, Michelle R. .......... '65 '90 C.112 B.A. L.426 J.D. 411 N. Central Ave.
Genovese, Judith A., (AV) '48 '74
C.770 B.A. L.1065 J.D. Gen. Coun. & Legal Mgr., MCBA, Inc.
Gibson, Terry R. .......... '49 '79 C.178 B.A. L.1068 J.D. U. S. Small Bus. Admin.

**Gill and Baldwin, (AV) BR**
**130 North Brand Boulevard Fourth Floor, 91203**
**Telephone: 818-500-7755; 213-245-3131 Fax: 818-242-4305**
**Members of Firm: Samuel S. Gill (1912-1965); John M. Carmack; Joseph C. Malpasuto; Kirk S. MacDonald. Of Counsel: Ernest R. Baldwin.**
**General Civil and Trial Practice in all State and Federal Courts. Public Contract and Construction Law, Tax and Administrative Law, Estate Planning and Probate.**
**Representative Clients: Kasler Corp.; Bireley Foundation.**
**Reference: American West Bank.**

*See Professional Biographies, GLENDALE, CALIFORNIA*

Gille, Christine D. .......... '51 '89 C.112 B.A. L.809 J.D. 205 E. Broadway
**Gilsleider, Glenn K.** .......... '61 '86 C.112 A.B. L.990 J.D. [Knapp,P.&C.]
**Gin, Wilbur**, (AV) .......... '55 '80 C.112 B.A. L.1068 J.D. [Edwards,E.&A.]
*PRACTICE AREAS: Real Estate Transactions; General Business and Corporate; Estate Planning.
Goethals, Richard B., (AV) .......... '24 '49 C.169 B.A. L.800 LL.B. 1436 Virginia
Goldberg, David, (AV) .......... '49 '74 C.94 A.B. L.1066 J.D. Pub. Storage Inc.
Goldstein, Ira L. .......... '57 '82 C.1169 B.A. L.426 J.D. 712 E. Broadway
Goldstein, Lynne S. .......... '59 '85 C.112 B.A. L.1068 J.D. 525 N. Brand Blvd.
Gonzalez, Donald J. .......... '27 '61 C.112 B.A. L.284 [Samuelsen,G.V.&S.]
**Gonzalez, Richard I.** .......... '67 '91 C.1110 B.A. L.990 J.D. [A Hemer,B.&C.]⊙
*PRACTICE AREAS: Medical Malpractice Defense.
Gooding, Alan Paul .......... '26 '70 C.221 B.A. L.809 J.D. 700 N. Brand Blvd.
Goodman, Deanne H. .......... '— '87 C.800 Ph.D. L.809 J.D. 631 W. Broadway
Gorham, Wayne K. .......... '22 '60 L.810 LL.B. 801 N. Brand Blvd.
**Gorney, David I.** .......... '— '81 C.112 B.A. L.809 J.D. [A Knapp,P.&C.]
**Graham, Arnold K.**, (AV) .......... '44 '70 C.375 B.A. L.1068 J.D. [Laskin&G.]
*PRACTICE AREAS: Litigation; Eminent Domain; Inverse Condemnation; Land Use Law; Zoning and Planning.
Grant, Michael R .......... '58 '87 C.112 B.A. L.809 J.D. City Atty.'s Off.
Grayson, Myrna N. .......... '30 '74 L.1190 LL.B. 205 E. Bdwy.
Green, John W. .......... '45 '73 C.813 B.A. L.770 J.D. 701 N. Brand Blvd.
**Green, Norman H., (P.C.)** .......... '52 '79 C.112 A.B. L.1068 J.D. [Irsfeld,I.&Y.]
*PRACTICE AREAS: Taxation Law; Business Law; Estate Planning and Probate Law.

**Greenwald, Hoffman & Meyer, (AV) BR**
**500 North Brand Boulevard, Suite 920, 91203-1904**
**Telephone: 818-507-8100; 213-381-1131 Fax: 818-507-8484**
**Members of Firm: Guy Preston Greenwald, Jr. (1914-1984); Donald M. Hoffman; Lawrence F. Meyer; Raul M. Montes. Associates: Jeanne Burns-Haindel.**
**General Civil Trial and Appellate Practice. Probate, Trust, Estate Planning, Real Property, Environmental, Condominium, Corporation, Banking, Business and Family Law.**
**References: Bank of America (Los Angeles and Pasadena Trust Offices); Northern Trust of California (Headquarters Office); Bank of America (Glendale Main Branch).**

*See Professional Biographies, GLENDALE, CALIFORNIA*

Greer, Ralph S. .......... '31 '69 C.870 B.S. L.273 J.D. 1945 W. Glenoaks Blvd.
Gregorian, Rima .......... '56 '85 C.914 B.A. L.94 J.D. 520 E. Broadway
**Grover, James A.** .......... '59 '88 C.112 B.A. L.770 J.D. [A Flanagan,B.U.&M.]
*PRACTICE AREAS: Criminal; Personal Injury Law.
**Grover, Maria A.** .......... '62 '87 C&L.770 B.S., J.D. [Knapp,P.&C.]
Gruber, Daniel S. .......... '58 '84 C.112 B.A. L.426 J.D. [Gruber&K.]
Gruber & Kantor .......... 500 N. Brand Blvd., Ste. 1030
Gruen, Randy D. .......... '56 '82 C.260 B.A. L.809 J.D. U.S. Small Bus. Admn.
Guckenberger, Frederick T., (AV) .......... '32 '57 C.976 A.B. L.150 J.D. 700 N. Brand Blvd.
Gustitus, Darlene J. .......... '46 '80 C.352 B.S. L.1136 J.D. 1111 N. Brand Blvd.
**Habeeb, Mark** .......... '66 '95 C&L.990 B.S., J.D. [A Hagenbaugh&M.]
*LANGUAGES: German.
*PRACTICE AREAS: Medical Malpractice.
**Haber, David C.**, (AV) .......... '41 '72 C.154 B.A. L.426 J.D. [Knapp,P.&C.]

**Hagenbaugh & Murphy, (AV) BR**
**A Partnership including Professional Corporations**
**700 North Central Avenue, Suite 500, 91203⊙**
**Telephone: 818-240-2600 Fax: 818-240-1253**
**Email: hmurphy@interserv.com URL: http://www.seamless.com/hm/**
**Van A. Hagenbaugh (1914-1980); Sigurd E. Murphy (1903-1976); William D. Stewart (A P.C.); John J. Tary (A P.C.); Raymond R. Moore (A P.C.); Neil R. Gunny (Resident, Orange County Office); Alan R. Zuckerman; David L. Winter; Mary E. Porter; Daniel A. Leipold (Resident, Orange County Office); Craig D. Aronson; Paul G. Szumiak; Robert F. Donohue (Resident, Orange County Office); Katharine L. Spaniac (Resident, San Bernardino Office); Alan H. Boon (Resident, Orange County Office); Jamie B. Skebba;—Raymond T. Gail (Resident, San Bernardino Office); Kirk G. Neiberger; Meredith A. Musicant; David M. Chute (Resident, Orange County Office); Luanne Walsh; Rhonda L. Etzwiler; Steven M. Schuetze; Thomas J. Heatly; Matthew R. Rungaitis; Stephen Barry; Julie M. DeRose; Randal A. Whitecotton (Resident, San Bernardino Office); Cathy L. Shipe (Resident, Orange**

(This Listing Continued)

**Hagenbaugh & Murphy (Continued)**

**County Office); Keri Lynn Bush; Michael A. Tonya; Laura C. McLennan; Graciela L. Freixes; Melinda W. Ebelhar; Kirk N. Sullivan; Gary P. Simonian; Mark Habeeb; Howard J. Hirsch (Resident, Orange County Office); Michelle Mann.**
**General Civil and Trial Practice in all State and Federal Courts. Insurance, Casualty, Life, Health, Accident and Disability Insurance, Malpractice, Surety and Aviation Law, Employment Law, Business Litigation (including Commercial and Advertising Disputes), Trademark and Copyright Litigation and Workers Compensation Subrogation.**
**Representative Clients: Farmers Insurance Group; Truck Insurance Exchange; Fire Insurance Exchange.**
**Orange County, California Office: 701 South Parker Street, Suite 8200, Orange. Telephone: 714-835-5406. Fax: 714-835-5949.**
**San Bernardino, California Office: 301 Vanderbilt Way, Suite 220. Telephone: 909-884-5331. FAX: 909-889-1250.**

*See Professional Biographies, GLENDALE, CALIFORNIA*

**Hairapetian, Shahen** .......... '59 '83 C.112 B.A. L.209 J.D. [Knapp,P.&C.]
*LANGUAGES: Armenian and Russian.
Hall, Allen F. '10 '40 C.108 B.A. L.347 LL.B.
(adm. in IN; not adm. in CA) 367 Cumberland Rd.‡
Halliday, Joanne A. .......... '61 '87 C.112 B.A. L.809 J.D. Pub. Storage Inc.
Halversen, George C., (AV) .......... '33 '63 C.597 B.S. L.1068 J.D. 216 S. Louise St.
Hanson, Donald E., Jr., (BV) .......... '45 '74 C.628 B.S. L.426 J.D. 600 W, Broadway
Harkins, Kimberly K. .......... '59 '94 C.838 B.A. L.61 J.D. 700 N. Center Ave., Suite 500
**Harris, Stephen M.** .......... '56 '83 C.911 B.A. L.209 J.D. [Knapp,P.&C.]
Harwood, Thomas M. .......... '50 '80 C.354 B.S. L.1190 J.D. 701 N. Brand Blvd.
Hass, Sarah .......... '55 '79 C.563 B.S. L.569 J.D. Pub. Storage Inc.
Have, Andrew C. .......... '56 '90 C.1074 B.S.I.E. L.1137 J.D. 216 S. Louise St.
Healy, Mary Ann .......... '35 '81 C.525 B.A. L.940 J.D. 700 N. Central Ave.
Hearn, Frederick W., (BV) .......... '32 '62 C.188 L.880 LL.B. [Hearn,F.W.]
Hearn, Frederick W., (A Prof. Corp.), (BV) .......... 501 N. Central Ave.
**Heatly, Thomas J.** .......... '52 '90 C.763 B.A. L.1049 J.D. [A Hagenbaugh&M.]
Hedrick, Thomas J. .......... '41 '81 C&L.1137 B.S.L., J.D. [Zonni,G.&T.]
Helphand, Richard J., (BV) .......... '43 '71 C.112 B.A. L.809 J.D. [Helphand&R.]
Helphand & Rich, (AV) .......... 535 N. Brand Blvd.
**Hemer, Ralph S.**, (AV) .......... '31 '62 L.809 LL.B. [Hemer,B.&C.]⊙
*LANGUAGES: German.

**Hemer, Barkus & Clark, (AV) BR**
**550 North Brand Boulevard, Suite 1800, P.O. Box 293, 91202⊙**
**Telephone: 818-241-8999 Fax: 818-241-2014**
**Email: Kallwyr@aol.com**
**Ralph S. Hemer; Ramune E. Barkus; Bradley C. Clark. Associates: Cathy L. Patrenos; Laurence Y. Wong; Kristen L. Chesnut; John P. Freeman; David A. Arkuss; Tom M Allen; Richard I. Gonzalez; Joann G. Housman; Jack Rosenbaum.**
**Civil Trial and Appellate Practice. Medical and Legal Professional Liability, Products Liability, Negligence and Insurance Law.**
**Reference: Sterling Bank.**
**Ontario, California Office: 3401 Centrelake Drive, Suite 400. Telephone: 714-467-0660. Fax: 909-390-3628.**

*See Professional Biographies, GLENDALE, CALIFORNIA*

Hendry, John A. .......... '50 '77 C.763 B.A. L.809 J.D. 801 N. Brand Blvd.
Heron, Carol Ellen .......... '49 '88 C.145 B.A. L.1148 J.D. [C.E.Heron&Assoc.]⊙
Heron, Carol E., & Associates, A Prof Law Corp. .......... 550 N. Broad Ave. (⊙Tarzana)
Hershfield, Alan L. .......... '— '79 L.1136 100 W. Broadway
Hertz, William F., II, (BV) .......... '48 '73 C.112 B.A. L.1049 J.D. [Yanz&H.]
Hescheles, Norma .......... '44 '81 L.398 J.D. [A Zonni,G.&T.]
Hicklin, Stephen T. '62 '88
C.1109 B.A. L.1067 J.D. Assoc. Coun., Glendale Fed. Bk., FSB
**Higgins, John J.** .......... '59 '87 C.475 B.A. L.990 J.D. [Knapp,P.&C.]⊙
**Hill, James K.** .......... '50 '89 L.398 J.D. [MacCarley&R.]
**Hill, John W.**, (AV) .......... '35 '68 C.339 B.S. L.809 J.D. [J.Hill&Assoc.]⊙
*PRACTICE AREAS: Civil Litigation; Toxic Torts; Insurance Defense; Medical Malpractice; Products Liability.

**Hill, John, & Associates, (AV)**
**801 North Brand Boulevard, Suite 240, 91203⊙**
**Telephone: 818-552-2400 Fax: 818-552-4444**
**John W. Hill.**
**General Civil Litigation. Insurance Defense, Products Liability, Toxic Torts, Environmental, Medical Malpractice, Government Liability, Warranty Action, Real Estate, Corporate and Construction Law, Wills and Trusts, Banking.**
**Torrance, California Office: 2050 West 190th Street, Suite 200. Telephone: 310-782-2500. Fax: 310-782-0200.**

*See Professional Biographies, GLENDALE, CALIFORNIA*

Hirsch, Linda J. .......... '56 '81 C.1060 B.A. L.464 J.D. 537 Spencer St.‡
Hodder, Kenneth G. .......... '58 '83 C&L.309 A.B., J.D. The Salvation Army
**Hodge, Timothy A.** .......... '56 '85 C.1077 B.A. L.809 J.D. [A Thomas&P.]⊙
*PRACTICE AREAS: Civil Litigation.
**Hoffman, Donald M.**, (AV) .......... '35 '61 C.112 B.S. L.1068 LL.B. [Greenwald,H.&M.]
*PRACTICE AREAS: Probate Law; Estate Planning Law; Real Property Law; Corporation Law; Business Law.
Hollander, Jeanie Fiskin '62 '87
C.154 B.A. L.813 J.D. Assoc. Coun., Glendale Fed. Bk., FSB
Holle, Marilyn L. .......... '40 '74 C.112 B.A. L.1068 J.D. Protec. & Advocacy, Inc.
Holmes, Deborah M. .......... '53 '92 C.1077 B.A. L.809 J.D. 144 Glendale Ave.
Holmes, Herbert A., Jr. .......... '27 '64 C.454 L.809 J.D. 225 W. Broadway
Holmes, Robert K., (AV) .......... '47 '75 C.800 B.A. L.809 J.D. 1111 N. Brand Blvd.
**Homsey, Philip R., II** .......... '48 '76 C.312 B.A. L.464 J.D. [Knapp,P.&C.]
**Horowitz, Craig A.** .......... '61 '86 C.103 B.A. L.1068 J.D. [Ott&H.]
*PRACTICE AREAS: Employment Law; Labor Law; Wrongful Termination.
**Housman, Joann G.** .......... '57 '87 C.230 B.S. L.809 J.D. [A Hemer,B.&C.]
Howard, Scott H., (AV) .......... '50 '76 C.800 B.S. L.809 J.D. City Atty.
**Hsu, James L.** .......... '68 '94 C.112 B.A. L.1068 J.D. [Knapp,P.&C.]
Huffman, Clair S. .......... '30 '70 C.763 B.S.E. L.426 J.D. 516 Burchett St.
Hummel, Brian G. .......... '58 '83 C.339 B.A. L.770 J.D. [Beam&H.]
Humphrey, Dianne .......... '46 '83 C.1131 B.A. L.1068 J.D. 31 Baskin-Robbins Pl.
**Hurevitz, Linda B.** .......... '50 '86 C.273 B.A. L.999 J.D. [A Thomas&P.]
*PRACTICE AREAS: Civil Litigation.
**Hutton, Greta T.** .......... '— '82 C.813 B.A. L.178 J.D. [Knapp,P.&C.]
Hutton, Richard A., (AV) .......... '45 '71 C.112 B.A. L.1068 J.D. 801 N. Brand Blvd.
**Ibara, Lynn I.** .......... '53 '84 C.312 B.A. L.112 J.D. [Laskin&G.]
*LANGUAGES: Hawaiian.
*PRACTICE AREAS: Eminent Domain; Real Property Litigation; Municipal Law; General Civil Practice.
Irel, Monica L. .......... '59 '88 C.112 B.A. L.800 J.D. 1000 N. Central
**Irsfeld, James B., Jr.**, (AV) .......... '12 '36 C.813 A.B. L.800 LL.B. [C Irsfeld,I.&Y.] ‡
*PRACTICE AREAS: Probate Law; Trusts Law; Estate Planning Law.
**Irsfeld, Peter J., (P.C.)**, (AV) .......... '39 '66 C.813 B.S. L.1068 LL.B. [Irsfeld,I.&Y.]
*PRACTICE AREAS: Bankruptcy (Creditor) Law; Debt Collection Law; Civil Litigation.

**Irsfeld, Irsfeld & Younger LLP, (AV) BR**
**A Partnership including Professional Corporations**
**Suite 900, 100 West Broadway, 91210-1296**
**Telephone: 818-242-6859 Fax: 818-240-7728**
**Email: 104736.1745@compuserver.com**
**Members of Firm: James B. Irsfeld (1880-1966); Kenneth C. Younger (1922-1996); John H. Brink (P.C.); Peter J. Irsfeld (P.C.); James J. Waldorf (P.C.); C. Phillip Jackson (P.C.); Norman H. Green (P.C.); Kathryn E. Van Houten. Associates: Peter C. Wright; Diane L. Walker. Retired: James B. Irsfeld, Jr.**
**General Civil, Business and Real Estate Litigation and Arbitration in all State and Federal Courts. Corporations, Securities, Commercial, Municipal, Estate Planning, Real Property, Personal Injury Litigation, Taxation, Probate, Eminent Domain, Construction Law, Bankruptcy (Creditor) and Debt Collection.**
**Representative Clients: Lear Sieglar, Inc.; Chrysler Credit Corp.**
**References: First Interstate Bank (Glendale Main Office); Bank of Hollywood.**

***See Professional Biographies, GLENDALE, CALIFORNIA***

**Jackson, C. Phillip, (P.C.)**, (AV) '48 '74 C.112 B.A. L.426 J.D. [Irsfeld,I.&Y.]
*PRACTICE AREAS: Construction Law; Business Law; Real Estate; Litigation; Arbitration Law.
Jackson-Davis, Calvin Orlando '58 '89 C.1362 B.S. L.329 J.D.
(adm. in DC; not adm. in CA) Atty., U.S. Small Business Admn.
**Jacobson, John J.** '50 '81 C.1077 B.S. L.1068 J.D. [© Baker,O.L.&D.]
Jagger, Bruce A., (AV) '35 '62 C.560 B.S. L.273 J.D. P.O. Box 2900 (Pat.)
James, Helen Dorroh '34 '68 C.05 L.809 J.D. P.O. Box 11026‡
Jamgotchian, Betty A., (BV) '50 '75 C.800 B.A. L.809 J.D. 100 N Brand Blvd.
Jamison, Max K., (AV) '18 '45
C.112 A.B. L.1065 J.D. V.P. & Gen. Coun., Atlantic Oil Co.
**Jardini, André E.**, (BV) '51 '76 C.602 B.A. L.1065 J.D. [Knapp,P.&C.]
**Jobe, Meredith**, (AV) '56 '81 C.1163 B.A. L.800 J.D. [Jobe&S.]
*PRACTICE AREAS: Real Estate; Estate Planning; Corporations; Nonprofit Organizations.

**Jobe & Stoterau, (AV)**
**330 North Brand Boulevard, Suite 590, 91203**
**Telephone: 818-246-7413 FAX: 818-246-7414**
**Email: 76324.1372@compuserve.com**
**Meredith Jobe; H. Peter Stoterau.**
**Real Estate, Estate Planning, Corporate Law and Nonprofit Organizations.**

***See Professional Biographies, GLENDALE, CALIFORNIA***

Jones, Arthur T., (BV) '26 '49 C&L.800 J.D. [Jones&J.]⊙
Jones, W. Montgomery, (BV) '29 '52 L.426 LL.B. [Jones&J.]⊙
Jones and Jones, (BV) 712 E. Bway. (⊙Monterey)
Jordan, David C. '46 '76 C.276 B.A. L.426 J.D. 411 N. Central Ave.
Kahdeman, Richard J. '46 '72 C.502 B.A. L.910 J.D. Ste. 840, 800 N. Brand Blvd.
Kalin, Joseph R. '35 '62 C.1043 B.A. L.809 LL.B. Supr. Ct. J.
Kantor, Glenn R. '57 '84 C.112 B.A. L.800 J.D. [Gruber&K.]
Kaplan, Kenneth Joseph '67 '92 C.668 B.A. L.464 J.D. [Santochi,F.&G.]
Karayan, John E., (BV) '51 '77 C.112 B.A. L.800 J.D. 1153 Old Phillips Rd.
Karpf, Spencer L. '47 '79
C.1097 B.A. L.1068 J.D. Pres., Software Mgmt. Consultants, Inc.
**Kassabian, Paul R.** '66 '95 C.605 B.A. L.1068 J.D. [Knapp,P.&C.]
*PRACTICE AREAS: Appellate; Insurance Coverage; Probate.
Kay, Larry Alan '47 '73 C.966 B.A. L.1068 J.D. 525 N. Brand Blvd.
Kazanjian, Phillip '45 '79 C.800 B.A. L.1026 J.D. [Kazanjian&M.]
Kazanjian & Martinetti 520 E. Wilson Ave.
Keenan, P. Dennis, (AV) '40 '65 C&L.800 B.S.L., LL.B. 300 W. Glenoaks Blvd.
Keidel, Leslie Ann '53 '84 C.763 B.A. L.809 J.D. 550 N. Brand Blvd.
**Kelley, Thomas M.** '48 '76
C.546 B.A. L.1137 J.D. Pres., First Amer. Title Ins. Co. of L.A.
**Kelley, Troy X.** '64 '89 C.112 A.B. L.107 J.D.
Sr. V.P. & Gen. Coun., First Amer. Title Co. of L.A.
Kennedy, Thomas J., (A P.L.C.), (AV) '40 '69 C&L.426 B.B.A., J.D.
505 E. Wilson Ave.
Ketchum, William M. '52 '80 C.464 B.A. L.800 J.D. 411 N. Central Ave., Suite 605
**Keuper, Janet L.** '60 '87 C.768 B.A. L.990 J.D. [A Thomas&P.]
*PRACTICE AREAS: Civil Litigation.
Kightlinger, Harry J. '27 '58 C.112 B.S. L.809 LL.B. 1827 W. Mountain Ave.
King, David P., (BV) '58 '84 C.838 B.A. L.145 J.D. [DiJulio&K.]
King, William J., (BV) '47 '76 C.1097 B.S. L.809 J.D. 700 N. Central Ave.
Kiriakidis, Lisa E. '56 '86 C.800 B.A. L.809 J.D. 1111 N. Brand Blvd.
Klahs, Donald R., (AV) '45 '76 C.1042 B.A. L.809 J.D. 550 N. Brand Blvd.
**Klein, Alfred** '46 '72 C.477 B.A. L.1066 J.D. [Klein&R.]
*REPORTED CASES: Monard v. FDIC 62 F. 3d 1169.

**Klein & Rosenbaum**
**121 West Lexington Drive, Fifth Floor, 91203**
**Telephone: 818-243-1366 Fax: 818-246-5780**
**Alfred Klein; David E. Rosenbaum.**
**Practice emphasizing: Representing Management and Plaintiffs in Labor and Employment Law including appearances before State and Federal Agencies and Courts.**
**Representative Clients: Pennoyer-Dodge Co.; The Hedman Co.; Reinhold Industries; Gilmore Envelope Corp.; Bon Appetit Danish, Inc.; Hair Club for Men; Family Restaurants, Inc.; Health Care Partners; Molding Corporation of America; HXM Terminals Transport, Inc.**

***See Professional Biographies, GLENDALE, CALIFORNIA***

Klug, Margaret A. '58 '85 C.990 B.A. L.426 J.D. 800 N. Brand Blvd.
**Knapp, Ryan C.**, (AV) '33 '59 C&L.494 B.S.L., LL.B. [Knapp,P.&C.] ‡
*PRACTICE AREAS: Insurance Law; Employment Disputes Law; Products Liability Law.

**Knapp, Petersen & Clarke, A Professional Corporation, (AV)**
**500 North Brand Boulevard, 20th Floor, 91203-1904⊙**
**Telephone: 818-547-5000; 213-245-9400 Telecopier: 818-547-5329**
**Ryan C. Knapp (Retired, 1992); Laurence R. Clarke (Retired); Donald C. Petersen; David C. Haber; Kevin J. Stack; André E. Jardini; Peter J. Senuty; David I. Bell; Cynthia A. Trangsrud; Gwen Freeman; Stephen C. Pasarow; Nancy Menzies Vaessen (Resident, Palm Springs Office); James M. Phillippi; Nancy L. Newman; K. Stephen Tang; Stephen M. Harris; Clifford R. Cohen; Shahen Hairapetian (Certified Specialist, Taxation Law, The State Bar of California, Board of Legal Specialization); Glenn K. Gilsleider; John J. Higgins; William J. Rohr (Resident, Palm Springs Office); Philip R. Homsey, II; Alexander Levy; Steven Ray Garcia; Cyril Czajkowskyj; Jo Ann Montoya; Maria A. Grover; Constance G. Zanglis; Mara L. Weber; Gail S. Cooper-Folb; Daphne B. Subar; Diron M. Ohanian; Timothy K. Cutler; Kristina Ann Tenner; Mitchell B. Ludwig; Alan J. Carnegie; Penny L. Wheat; Yu-Feng (Frances) Chou; Catherine A. Gayer (Resident, Palm Springs Office); Antoinette S. Waller; Greta T. Hutton; Barry R. Gammell; David I. Gorney; Anastasia Baumeister; Daniel T. Mosier; Steven E. Creamer; James L. Hsu; Claire Wong; Debbie S. Harris Sherman (Resident, Palm Springs Office); Paul R. Kassabian; Phillip T. S. Tukia.**
**General Civil, Trial and Appellate Practice in all State and Federal Courts, Arbitration Tribunals and Administrative Agencies. General Insurance, Professional Liability, Product Liability, Environmental, Corporate and General Business, State, Federal and Local Taxation, Real Estate, Escrow Errors and Omissions Defense, Construction and Land Use, Construction Defect Litigation, Estate Planning, Probate, Labor and Employment, Administrative and Regulatory Insurance Law and Title Banking.**
**Reference: Wells Fargo Bank (Glendale, California).**
**Palm Springs, California Office: 960 East Tahquitz Canyon Way, Suite 101. Telephone: 619-325-8500. Telecopier: 619-325-2454.**

***See Professional Biographies, GLENDALE, CALIFORNIA***

Knights, Gregory P., (AV) '46 '76 C.112 B.A. L.1065 J.D. [Knights&S.]
Knights & Summer, (AV) 1007 S. Central Ave., Ste. 204
Koll, Roger '51 '78 C.1077 B.A. L.1095 J.D. 700 N. Central Ave.
Konstantouros, George P. '56 '92 C.800 B.S. L.1065 J.D. 516 Burchett St.
Kopczynski, Jeffrey A. '55 '81 C.121 B.A. L.990 J.D. 447 Burchett St.
Koyama, Julie K. '68 '92 C.112 B.A. L.464 J.D. 550 N. Brand Blvd.
Krause, Jeanine H. '45 '82 C.713 B.A. L.426 J.D. 700 N. Central Ave.
Kucher, Leon '— '80 124 S. Isabel St.
Kupper, Samuel Y. '39 '83 C.1097 B.A. L.426 J.D. 1550 Puebla Dr.
Laichas, James N. '23 '64 C.1016 B.A. L.800 LL.B. 420 N. Louise St.
**Lalafarian, Daniel** '— '81 C.1097 B.A. L.1137 J.D. [Messina,L.&M.]
Lang, Catherine B., (BV) '33 '78 C.243 B.A. L.1221 J.D. 401 N. Brand Blvd.
**Laskin, Richard**, (AV) '33 '59 C.1043 B.A. L.1068 J.D. [© Laskin&G.]
*PRACTICE AREAS: Eminent Domain; Inverse Condemnation; Municipal Law; Real Property; General Civil Litigation.

**Laskin & Graham, (AV) BR**
**Suite 840, 800 North Brand Boulevard, 91203**
**Telephone: 213-665-6955; 818-547-4800; 714-957-3031 Telecopier: 818-547-3100**
**Of Counsel: Richard Laskin. Members of Firm: Arnold K. Graham; Susan L. Vaage; John S. Peterson; Michael Anthony Cisneros; Gregson M. Perry; Lynn I. Ibara.**
**General Civil and Trial Practice in all State and Federal Courts, Eminent Domain, Municipal Law, Environmental Law, Real Property Damage, Employment Law, Construction Law, Land Use, Insurance Law, Professional Liability, Banking, Leasing, Bankruptcy, Financial Institutions Law, Commercial Documentation, Business Law and Litigation.**

***See Professional Biographies, GLENDALE, CALIFORNIA***

Lavender, Carol K. '48 '77 C.112 B.A. L.809 J.D. 525 N. Brand Blvd.
**LeCroy, Charles L., III** '53 '78 C.112 B.A. L.1067 J.D. [Baker,O.L.&D.]
Leech, Colleen A. '63 '93 C.426 B.A. L.809 J.D. 101 N. Brand Blvd., Suite 600
Lenahan, Gregg T. '58 '87 C.112 B.A. L.809 J.D. [Santochi,F.&G.]
Leonard, Sandra C. '40 '82 C.94 B.S. L.1190 J.D. 144 N. Glendale Ave.
**Levy, Alexander** '46 '74 C.112 B.A. L.809 J.D. [Knapp,P.&C.]
Libertucci, Linda M. '53 '91 C.1044 B.S. L.809 J.D. 500 N. Brand Blvd.
**Liddell, Patrick A.**, (AV) '45 '78 C.1077 B.S. L.1095 J.D. [Melby&A.]
*PRACTICE AREAS: Business; Real estate.
Linde, Julian J. '32 '58 C&L.477 B.B.A., LL.B. Protec. & Advocacy, Inc.
**Lister, David E.**, (AV) '42 '72 C.352 B.A. L.813 J.D. [Lister&M.]
*PRACTICE AREAS: Workers Compensation Defense; Disability Discrimination Defense.

**Lister & Martin, (AV)**
**700 North Brand Boulevard, Suite 630, 91203**
**Telephone: 818-551-6444 Fax: 818-242-3816**
**Members of Firm: David E. Lister; John C. Martin. Associates: Ross H. Palfreyman.**
**Practice Limited to Representation of Employers in Workers Compensation, Employment Disability Discrimination Claims (State and Federal), Personnel Relations, Labor and Employment, Wrongful Termination and Sexual Harassment.**
**Reference: Glendale Federal Bank.**

Lombino, Charles D. '55 '80 C.597 B.A. L.1068 J.D. [C.D.Lombino]
Lombino, Charles D., A Professional Corporation 706 W. Bway.
Lotito, L. Anne '— '83 C.1050 B.A. L.426 J.D. 100 W. Bway.
Loughry, Lois M. '50 '81 C.1057 B.A. L.818 J.D.
(adm. in MA; not adm. in CA) 3291 Kirham Dr.‡
Louie, Benjamin '35 '63 C.800 B.A. L.1114 LL.B. 1425 Imperial Dr.
**Louis, Bonnie R.**, (BV) '46 '78 C.1097 B.S. L.809 J.D. [Thomas&P.]
*PRACTICE AREAS: Accounting; Malpractice; Civil Litigation; Personal Injury; Medical Malpractice.
**Lovejoy, Jerry L.** '53 '78 C.197 B.A. L.309 J.D.
V.P. & Gen. Coun., Baskin-Robbins USA, Co.
*RESPONSIBILITIES: General Corporate; Franchising; Employment Law.
Lucett, Gregory J. '52 '82 C.767 B.A. L.765 J.D. 700 N. Central
**Ludwig, Mitchell B.** '59 '84 C.1019 B.B.A. L.809 J.D. [Knapp,P.&C.]
**Lugosi, Bela G.**, (AV) '38 '64 C&L.800 B.S., LL.B. [Benjamin,L.&B.]
*PRACTICE AREAS: Business Litigation; Entertainment Law; Alternative Dispute Resolution.
Luostari, Walter R. '51 '80 C.494 B.S. L.990 J.D. [Burlison&L.]
Lupica, Cynthia A. '57 '84 C.302 B.A. L.809 J.D. [Zonni,G.&T.]
**Lupo, Frank** '55 '86 C.1169 B.A. L.426 J.D. [Benjamin,L.&B.]
*PRACTICE AREAS: Entertainment Law; Licensing; Business Litigation; Insurance Coverage; Insurance Bad Faith.
Lutz, Robert Charles '22 '52 C.112 A.B. L.1065 J.D. 521 Mesa Lila Rd.‡
**MacCarley, Mark**, (AV) '51 '75 C.1077 B.A. L.426 J.D. [MacCarley&R.]
*PRACTICE AREAS: Real Estate (50%); Litigation (50%).

**MacCarley & Rosen, Professional Law Corporation, (AV)**
**800 North Brand Boulevard, Suite 840, 91203**
**Telephone: 818-241-5800**
**Mark MacCarley; Walter K. Rosen; James K. Hill.**
**General Practice.**

**MacDonald, Kirk S.**, (AV) '48 '82 C.800 B.S.C.E. L.1137 J.D. [Gill&B.]
*PRACTICE AREAS: Construction Litigation; Mediation; Arbitration.
Magee, Luanne M. '61 '87 C.607 B.S. L.990 J.D. 550 N. Brand Blvd., Ste. 1800
Malmquist, Ralph D., (AV) '38 '65 C.1077 L.1068 [Zonni,G.&T.]
**Malpasuto, Joseph C.**, (AV) '38 '75 C.169 B.A. L.1095 J.D. [Gill&B.]
*PRACTICE AREAS: Construction Litigation; Mediation; Arbitrator.
Mandell, Robert G. '38 '65 C.800 B.S. L.1068 LL.B. 1750 El Rito Ave.
Manheim, David I. '66 '94 C.112 B.A. L.809 J.D. 1000 N. Central
**Mann, Michelle** '67 '93 C.1077 B.A. L.464 J.D. [A Hagenbaugh&M.]
**Manning, Mary VanOsdel** '52 '81 C.112 B.A. L.809 J.D. [Messina,L.&M.]
Mantle, Douglas L. '50 '76 C.112 B.A. L.800 J.D. 516 Burchett St.
Manzano, Frank R., (AV) '26 '67 C.800 B.P.A. L.809 LL.B. 3786 La Crescenta Ave.
Marshall, E. Bonnie '44 '83 C.383 B.A. L.990 P.O. Box 29019
Marshall, John W. '18 '51 C.800 B.E. L.426 LL.B. 2123 Bonita Dr.‡
Martel, Louis V. '37 '71 C.668 L.809 J.D. Fremont Comp. Ins. Co.
**Marti-Colon, Noelia** '48 '73 C.677 B.A. L.178 LL.B. Sr. Coun., Nestle USA, Inc.
*LANGUAGES: Spanish.
*REPORTED CASES: U.S.I. Properties Corp. v. EPA (D.P.R.), 16 ERC 1408 (1981).
*RESPONSIBILITIES: Environmental Law.
**Martin, John C.**, (AV) '44 '70 C.112 B.A. L.426 J.D. [Lister&M.]
*LANGUAGES: Spanish.
*PRACTICE AREAS: Workers Compensation Defense; Disability Discrimination Defense.
Martin, John H. '18 '43 C.504 B.S. L.145 J.D. 1611 Arboles Dr.
Martinez, Peter L. '59 '91 C.330 B.A. L.464 J.D. 1314 W. Glenoaks Blvd.
Marvasti, Farzaneh '63 '91 C.1136 B.S. L.809 J.D.
Assoc. Coun., Glendale Fed. Bk., FSB
Matlin, Janice A. '— '86 C.112 B.A. L.990 J.D. 701 N. Brand Blvd.
Matti, Michelle E. '— '87 C.800 B.S. L.426 J.D. 210 N. Central Ave.
Matulionis, Margis J. '43 '83 C.011 B.A. L.426 J.D. 512 E. Wilson Ave.
**Maxwell, Barbara L., (BV) '28 '76 C.813 B.A. L.1190 J.D.**
**205 East Broadway, 91205**
**Telephone: 818-500-9989**
***PRACTICE AREAS: Family Law (95%, 60); Estate Planning (5%, 12).**
**Family Law.**

Mayer, Leon, (A L.C.), (AV) '26 '53 C.112 A.B. L.800 LL.B. 225 W. Bway.
McClure, Neal E. '26 '53 C.112 B.S. L.800 J.D. 1633 Oakengate Dr.‡

McCormick, Donald W. .... '54 '81 C.880 B.A. L.861 J.D. 550 N. Brand Blvd.
**McCormick, Kevin M.** .... '58 '84 C.1097 B.A. L.426 J.D. [Ⓐ Thomas&P.]⊙
*PRACTICE AREAS: Civil Litigation.
McCumber, Marilyn P. .... '45 '79 C.112 B.A. L.426 J.D. 130 N. Brand Blvd., 4th Fl.
**McDonald, Rosemary A.** '55 '85
C.800 B.A. L.426 J.D. Corp. Coun., Baskin-Robbins USA, Co.
*RESPONSIBILITIES: Franchising; Real Estate; Trademarks; Marketing.
McGarry, John J., Jr. .... '47 '72 C.712 B.A. L.229 J.D. U.S. Small Bus. Admn.
McGrath, James R. .... '26 '58 C.018 A.B. L.426 J.D. 1253 N. Cedar St.
McGregor, J. Keith .... '31 '61 C.101 B.S. L.1114 LL.B. 220 S. Kenwood Ave.
McKenna, Candice J. .... '58 '87 C.938 L.1068 516 Burchett St.
**McLain, Richard W.**, (AV) .... '38 '69 C&L.426 B.A., J.D. [R.W.McLain]

**McLain, Richard W., A Professional Corporation, (AV)**
**700 North Brand Boulevard, Suite 630, 91203**
**Telephone: 818-549-3930 Fax: 818-549-3939**
**Richard W. McLain; Charles H. Stokes. Of Counsel: D. F. Sacino.**
**Trial and Appellate Practice in all State and Federal Courts, Insurance Law, Bad Faith Defense, Negligence, Products Liability, Casualty and Fire Insurance Law, Professional Negligence, Landslide and Subsidence Law, Environmental Law, Professional Liability, Municipalities and Public Entities, Excess and Surplus Lines.**
*See Professional Biographies, GLENDALE, CALIFORNIA*

**McLennan, Laura C.** .... '57 '86 C.339 B.S.N. L.424 J.D. [Ⓐ Hagenbaugh&M.]
*LANGUAGES: Spanish.
McNamara, Jane M. .... '62 '91 C.549 B.S. L.426 J.D. 701 N. Brand Blvd.
**Mead, David E.** .... '65 '91 C.112 B.A. L.426 J.D. [Ⓐ O'Flaherty&B.]
**Meier, James L.** .... '67 '93 C.347 B.S. L.209 J.D. [Ⓐ Calendo,P.S.&D.]
*PRACTICE AREAS: Civil Litigation; Insurance Defense.
**Melby, Henry**, (AV) .... '19 '48 C.112 B.A. L.800 J.D. [Melby&A.]
*PRACTICE AREAS: Probate; Estate Planning.
**Melby, Randall**, (AV) .... '50 '77 C.1188 B.A. L.61 J.D. [Melby&A.]
*PRACTICE AREAS: Probate and Estate Planning.

**Melby & Anderson, (AV)**
**Fifth Floor, 121 West Lexington Drive, 91203**
**Telephone: 818-246-5644 Los Angeles: 213-245-2606 Fax: 818-246-5780**
**Members of Firm: Henry Melby; Jarrett S. Anderson; Randall Melby; Patrick A. Liddell; Michael W. Deaktor; Valerie K. Byer.**
**General Civil and Trial Practice in State Courts. Trials and Appeals. Probate, Estate Planning, Real Property, Business, Corporation Litigation, Family Law, Water Rights, Municipal Law and Banking.**
**Representative Clients: Glendale Motor Car Dealers Assn.; Crescenta County Water District; Foothill Municipal Water District; R. A. Fisher Medical Equipment.**
**Reference: Wells Fargo Bank, all Glendale Calif. Main Offices.**
*See Professional Biographies, GLENDALE, CALIFORNIA*

**Melchione, Joseph S.**, (AV) .... '48 '74 C.112 B.A. L.1067 J.D. [Styskal,W.&M.]
*SPECIAL AGENCIES: California Department of Corporations Commissioner's Credit Union Advisory Committee.
*PRACTICE AREAS: General Corporate, Commercial and Consumer Law; Insurance; Computer; Credit Union Law.
**Mendenhall, Doris A.** .... '56 '94 C.813 A.B. L.112 J.D. [Ⓐ Bright&B.]
*PRACTICE AREAS: Business Litigation; Environmental.
**Menhennet, Janine R.** .... '66 '92 C.112 B.A. L.426 J.D. [Ⓐ Ott&H.]
*PRACTICE AREAS: Employment; Financial Institutions; Labor; Business Litigation.
Merritt, Valerie J., (AV) .... '47 '77 C.605 A.B. L.1068 J.D. [Calleton&M.]
Meshot, Peter A., (BV) .... '55 '84 C.1169 B.A. L.284 J.D. [Sacino B.&H.]⊙
**Messina, Nina R.** .... '44 '80 C.112 B.A. L.809 J.D. [Messina,L.&M.]

**Messina, Lalafarian & Manning**
**Suite 1670 550 North Brand Boulevard, 91203-1900**
**Telephone: 818-242-5250 FAX: 818-242-4828**
**Nina R. Messina; Daniel Lalafarian; Mary VanOsdel Manning; William P. Ryan.**
**General Liability Defense, Products Liability, Insurance Defense, Insurance Coverage.**
*See Professional Biographies, GLENDALE, CALIFORNIA*

**Meyer, Lawrence F.**, (AV) .... '47 '72 C.800 A.B. L.602 J.D. [Greenwald,H.&M.]
*PRACTICE AREAS: Probate Law; Estate Planning Law; Real Property Law; Corporation Law; Business Law.
Michon, Eleanor Joan, (BV) .... '35 '77 C.1097 B.A. L.809 J.D. 144 N. Glendale Ave.
**Middlebrook, Theresa W.**, (AV) .... '53 '79 C.112 B.A. L.809 J.D. [Wagner&M.]
Miller, Julie A. .... '61 '90 C.112 B.A. L.398 J.D. 800 N. Brand Blvd.‡
**Minami, Ken R.** '60 '87 C.112 B.A. L.426 J.D.
Corp. Coun., Baskin-Robbins USA, Co.
*RESPONSIBILITIES: Franchising; International; Real Estate.
Molfetta, William M. .... '49 '78 C.994 B.A. L.1095 J.D. [Molfetta,R.&W.]
Molfetta, Raymond & Wiedner, (AV) .... 100 W. Broadway
**Montes, Raul M.** .... '56 '81 C.112 B.S. L.1068 J.D. [Greenwald,H.&M.]
*LANGUAGES: Spanish.
*PRACTICE AREAS: General Civil Litigation; Environmental; Real Property Law; Probate Law; Estate Planning Law.
**Montoya, Jo Ann** .... '62 '87 C.112 B.A. L.1065 J.D. [Knapp,P.&C.]
Mooradian, Zorik .... '57 '88 C.1097 B.S. L.398 J.D. 550 N. Brand Blvd.
**Moore, Raymond R., (A P.C.)**, (AV) '43 '69 C.1077 A.B. L.800 J.D.
[Hagenbaugh&M.]
Moorhead, Carlos J. .... '22 '49 C.112 A.B. L.800 J.D. (M.C.)
Morita, Joyce H. .... '46 '85 C.112 B.A. L.426 J.D. 505 N. Louise St.
Morrissey, Clarence J. '24 '63 C.597 M.S. L.365 LL.B.
(adm. in IL; not adm. in CA; Pat.) 1155 N. Brand, #801‡
**Moses, J. Barry** .... '53 '84 C&L.1137 B.S., J.D. [Flanagan,B.U.&M.]
*PRACTICE AREAS: Personal Injury.
**Mosier, Daniel T.** .... '58 '87 C.1169 B.A. L.809 J.D. [Knapp,P.&C.]
*LANGUAGES: Spanish.
Moulton, Robert T., (AV) .... '32 '60 C.1043 B.A. L.426 LL.B. 220 S. Kenwood St.
Mouradian, Viken Samuel .... '60 '86 C.112 B.A. L.800 J.D. 550 N. Brand Blvd.
Movius, Michael J., (BV) .... '45 '74 C.1077 B.A. L.999 J.D. 447 Burchett St.
Mozingo & Vincent .... 1131 Esmeralda Dr.
Murphey, Richard J. .... '54 '82 C.705 B.A. L.990 J.D. [Burlison&L.]
**Musicant, Meredith A.** .... '59 '86 C.605 A.B. L.1067 J.D. [Ⓐ Hagenbaugh&M.]
Najarian, Ara .... '60 '86 C.605 A.B. L.800 J.D. [Najarian&V.]
Najarian & Virgilio .... 550 N. Brand Blvd.
Nameth, Frederick J., (AV) .... '43 '69 C.112 A.B. L.1049 J.D. [Nameth,F.J.]
Nameth, Frederick James, A Professional Law Corp., (AV) .... 415 E. Bway.
Nardoni, Daniel A. .... '50 '80 C.999 B.S. L.1190 J.D. 144 N. Glendale Ave.
Neelley, Allen L., (AV) .... '36 '62 C.813 A.B. L.800 J.D. 101 N. Brand Blvd., 6th Fl.
Neft, Bruce B. .... '47 '76 C.1077 B.A. L.1190 J.D. P.O. Box 29034
Neiberg, Samuel I. '31 '60 C.20 A.B. L.597 J.D.
V.P., Gen. Coun. & Secy., Pacific Compensation Ins. Co.
**Neiberger, Kirk G.** .... '52 '80 C.1042 B.A. L.1137 J.D. [Ⓐ Hagenbaugh&M.]
Nelson, Eric A., (BV) .... '38 '68 C.800 B.A. L.809 LL.B. Ste. 308, 535 N. Brand Blvd.
**Newman, Nancy L.** .... '55 '82 C.112 B.A. L.809 J.D. [Knapp,P.&C.]
Nuanes, Dorothy Higgins .... '54 '84 C.813 A.B. L.426 J.D. 100 W. Broadway
**O'Flaherty, Michael A.**, (AV) .... '47 '73 C.112 B.A. L.800 J.D. [O'Flaherty&B.]

**O'Flaherty & Belgum, (AV)**
**1000 North Central, Suite 300, 91202-2957**⊙
**Telephone: 818-242-9229 Fax: 818-242-9114**
**Email: oandb&primenet.com URL: http://www.oandb-law/oandb**
**Members of Firm: Michael A. O'Flaherty (Resident, Glendale Office); Stephen L. Belgum (Resident, Glendale Office); Todd C. Theodora (Resident, Long Beach Office); John J. Weber (Resident, Long Beach Office); Gregory M. Hatton (Resident, Orange County Office); Lynn E. Ovando (Resident, Long Beach Office); Stephen L. Schumm (Resident, Long Beach Office); Ernest C. Chen (Resident, Orange County Office); Lisa A. Cross (Resident, Orange County Office); Nancy G. Wanski (Resident, Glendale Office); Lee M. Thies (Resident, Riverside Office); Kristen J. Heim (Resident, Long Beach Office); Mike Martinez (Resident, Ventura Office). Of Counsel: Lee T. Belgum (Resident, Orange County Office); C. Snyder Patin (Resident, Anaheim Office). Associates: Pamela A. Benben (Resident, Glendale Office); Robert M. Dato (Resident, Long Beach Office); Donna R. Evans (Resident, Long Beach Office); Suzanne Boyle (Resident, Glendale Office); Sharon A. Brahms (Resident, Long Beach Office); Todd E. Croutch (Resident, Glendale Office); D. Elizabeth Nash (Resident, Riverside Office); Stephen C. Fraser (Resident, Glendale Office); Johanna A. Schleuter (Resident, Long Beach Office); Cheryl P. Nessel (Resident, Long Beach Office); Ronald A. Chavez (Resident, Long Beach Office); Alexander M. Watson (Resident, Glendale Office); Kelli L. Baker (Resident, Orange County Office); David E. Mead (Resident, Glendale Office); Arthur R. Petrie, II (Resident, Orange County Office); Barbara S. Boarnet (Resident, Orange County Office); Joseph A. Mahoney (Resident, Orange County Office); Kathleen E. Barnett (Resident, Long Beach Office); Susan E. Shube (Resident, Orange County Office); Daniel K. Dik (Resident, Long Beach Office); Debra L. Denton (Resident, Long Beach Office); Sheryl A. Ragen (Resident, Glendale Office); Joseph M. Acierno (Resident, Glendale Office); Kathleen M. Wynen (Resident, Orange County Office); Donald W. Ormsby (Resident, Orange County Office); Erik L. Jackson (Resident, Orange County Office); Joseph M. ElgGuindy (Resident, Orange County Office); Richard G. Kolostian, Jr (Resident, Long Beach Office); Mark H. Shpall (Resident, Glendale Office); Stephen Z. Vegh (Resident, Orange County Office); William D. Hardy (Resident, Long Beach Office); Peter S. Kravitz (Resident, Long Beach Office); Cynthia D. Rogers; Marcel R. Pidoux (Resident, Glendale Office); Brian P. Barrow (Resident, Long Beach Office); Michael P. Sandler (Resident, Anaheim Office); Paul D. Slater, Dr.**
**General Civil, Trial and Appellate Practice in State and Federal Courts. Medical and Dental Malpractice, Products Liability, General Insurance Law, Insurance Coverage, Wrongful Termination, Workers' Compensation, Business and Environmental Litigation.**
**Long Beach, California Office: 100 Oceangate, Suite 500, 90802-4312. Telephone: 310-437-0090. Fax: 310-437-5550.**
**Orange County, California Office: 222 South Harbor Boulevard, Suite 600, Anaheim, CA 92805-3701. Telephone: 714-533-3373. Fax: 714-533-2607.**
**Riverside, California Office: 3880 Lemon Street, Suite 450, 92501-3301. Telephone: 909-341-0049. Fax: 909-341-3919.**
**Ventura, California Office: 840 County Square Drive, Suite 200, 93003-5406. Telephone: 805-650-2600. Fax: 805-650-2658.**
*See Professional Biographies, GLENDALE, CALIFORNIA*

**Ohanian, Diron M.** .... '65 '91 C.112 B.A. L.800 J.D. [Knapp,P.&C.]
**O'Hara, Brian C.** .... '55 '88 C.112 B.A. L.426 J.D. [Ⓐ Calendo,P.S.&D.]
*PRACTICE AREAS: Civil Litigation; Insurance Defense Law.
**Olson, Eric**, (AV) .... '40 '66 C.668 B.A. L.309 J.D. [Baker,O.L.&D.]
*PRACTICE AREAS: Business Law; Real Property; Commercial; Business Litigation; Probate Litigation.
**O'Malley, Joseph J.**, (AV) .... '23 '56 C.754 B.A. L.276 J.D. [Ⓒ Denney&O.]
*PRACTICE AREAS: Corporate Litigation; Antitrust; Environmental.
Orosz, Donald G., (AV) .... '43 '69 C.197 B.A. L.1066 J.D. 505 E. Wilson Ave.
**O'Rourke, Denis M.**, (AV) .... '39 '68 C.1043 B.S. L.800 J.D. [O'Rourke,A.&F.]
*PRACTICE AREAS: Complex Civil Litigation; Construction; Real Estate Litigation.
**O'Rourke, Denise Michelle** .... '65 '92 C.800 B.A. L.1148 J.D. [Ⓐ O'Rourke,A.&F.]
*PRACTICE AREAS: General Civil Litigation; Entertainment Law; Business Litigation; Municipal Litigation.

**O'Rourke, Allan & Fong, (AV)** [BR]
**3rd Floor, 104 North Belmont, P.O. Box 10220, 91209-3220**
**Telephone: 818-247-4303 Fax: 818-247-1451**
**Members of Firm: Denis M. O'Rourke; Joan H. Allan; Roderick D. Fong. Associates: Denise Michelle O'Rourke.**
**General Civil and Trial Practice in all State and Federal Courts. Real Estate, Construction, Business, Probate, Personal Injury, Family Law and Negligence Law, Entertainment Law.**
**References: Verdugo Banking Co. (Glendale, California); Community Bank (Glendale, California).**
*See Professional Biographies, GLENDALE, CALIFORNIA*

Osborn, Donald R. .... '29 '58 C.871 B.S. L.813 LL.B. 1918 Montecito Dr.
Oshima, Kathryn Phillips .... '48 '77 C.234 L.1095 J.D. P.O. Box 5538
**Oths, Eleanor F.** .... '64 '89 C&L.347 B.A., J.D. [Denney&O.]
*LANGUAGES: French.
*PRACTICE AREAS: Environmental; Litigation.
**Ott, Thomas H.**, (AV) .... '47 '79 C.1075 B.S. L.809 J.D. [Ott&H.]
*PRACTICE AREAS: Labor; Employment; Credit Union; Insurance Coverage.

**Ott & Horowitz, A Professional Corporation, (AV)** [BR]
**700 North Central Avenue, 8th Floor, Suite 850, 91203**
**Telephone: 818-242-3100 Fax: 818-242-3102**
**Email: ohlaw@aol.com**
**Thomas H. Ott; Craig A. Horowitz; Wayne D. Clayton;—Steven H. Taylor; Janine R. Menhennet; Patrick Carey.**
**General Civil, Trial and Appellate Practice in State and Federal Courts and Arbitration Tribunals, Commercial Litigation, Labor, Real Estate and Corporate.**
*See Professional Biographies, GLENDALE, CALIFORNIA*

**Pagliuso, James J., (AV) '45 '71 C.112 B.A. L.1068 J.D.**
**801 North Brand Boulevard Suite 320, 91203**
**Telephone: 818-244-2253; 213-744-1330 Fax: 818-547-0283**
**Negligence Law. Trials and Appeals, Medical Malpractice and Products Liability Law.**
**Reference: Bank of America, West Glenoaks Branch.**
*See Professional Biographies, GLENDALE, CALIFORNIA*

Palfi, Csaba .... '49 '80 C.1077 B.A. L.1137 J.D. 500 N. Brand Blvd.
**Palfreyman, Ross H.** .... '54 '82 C.1324 B.A. L.800 J.D. [Ⓐ Lister&M.]
*LANGUAGES: Thai.
*PRACTICE AREAS: Workers Compensation Defense; Disability Discrimination Defense.
Parkin, David S., (AV) .... '40 '69 C.101 B.S. L.878 J.D. 1100 San Luis Rey
Parra, Phillip A. .... '55 '83 C.112 B.A. L.1137 J.D. 100 W. Broadway
**Pasarow, Stephen C.** .... '52 '80 C.112 B.A. L.809 J.D. [Knapp,P.&C.]
**Patrenos, Cathy L.** .... '53 '89 C.999 B.S. L.1198 J.D. [Ⓐ Hemer,B.&C.]
*PRACTICE AREAS: Medical Malpractice Defense.
Paulson, Ross W. .... '59 '84 C.585 B.S.B.A. L.494 J.D. 100 W. Broadway
**Pearson, Bruce A.** .... '63 '92 C.339 B.A. L.809 J.D. [Styskal,W.&M.]
*LANGUAGES: Russian.
*PRACTICE AREAS: General Corporate, Commercial and Consumer Law; Insurance; Computer; Credit Union Law.
Penchef, Esther .... '16 '60 C.97 B.S. L.809 LL.B. 105 W. Kenneth Rd.
Perez, Vicente S. .... '45 '91 L.999 L.L.B. 100 N. Brand Blvd.
**Perry, Gregson M.** .... '61 '86 C.112 B.A. L.464 J.D. [Laskin&G.]
*PRACTICE AREAS: Eminent Domain; Condemnation; Real Property; Municipal Law; General Civil Practice.
Peter, Jeffrey C. .... '53 '82 C.222 B.A. L.990 J.D. 550 N. Brand Blvd.
**Petersen, Donald C.**, (AV) .... '34 '60 C&L.494 B.S.L., LL.B. [Knapp,P.&C.]
Peterson, Duane .... '27 '58 C.112 B.A. L.1066 1235 N. Brand Blvd.
**Peterson, John S.**, (AV) .... '56 '81 C.112 A.B. L.1068 J.D. [Laskin&G.]
*PRACTICE AREAS: Litigation; Eminent Domain; Inverse Condemnation; Land Use Law; Zoning and Planning.
Peterson, Lynn P. .... '49 '82 L.1148 J.D. 130 N. Brand
**Pfeiffer, Christine M.** .... '49 '81 C.1077 B.S. L.809 J.D. Sr. Coun., Nestle USA, Inc.

CALIFORNIA—GLENDALE MARTINDALE-HUBBELL LAW DIRECTORY 1997

**Phillippi, James M.** ....'53 '81 C.1078 B.A. L.426 J.D. [Knapp,P.&C.]
Piccola, Stephen ....'49 '76 C.1077 B.A. L.426 J.D. [Zonni,G.&T.]
**Pidoux, Marcel R.** ....'67 '93 C&L.800 B.A., J.D. [A O'Flaherty&B.]
*LANGUAGES: Spanish.
*PRACTICE AREAS: Medical Malpractice Defense.
Pingel, Heidi L. ....'59 '87 C.112 B.A. L.893 J.D. 550 N. Brand Blvd., Ste 1800
Plunkett, Harry L. ....'14 '61 C.339 B.S. L.809 J.D. 628 E. Colorado
Popko, John S. ....'52 '83 C.112 B.A. L.1137 J.D. 700 N. Central Ave.
**Porter, Mary E.**, (AV) ....'46 '77 C.1042 A.B. L.426 J.D. [Hagenbaugh&M.]
Poston, Daniel D. ....'53 '79 C.813 A.B. L.426 J.D. P.O. Box 11355
Powers, Stephen R., Jr. ....'21 '49 C&L.426 A.B., LL.B. 248 W. Loraine St.‡
**Price, Lawrence E.**, (AV) ....'42 '73 C.1061 B.S.E.E. L.426 J.D. [Thomas&P.]
*PRACTICE AREAS: Product Liability; Construction; Civil Litigation; Personal Injury; Medical Malpractice.
**Puckett, Kim B., (Mr.)**, (AV) ....'53 '79 C.347 B.A. L.426 J.D. [Calendo,P.S.&D.]
*PRACTICE AREAS: Civil Litigation; Insurance Defense.
Putnam, Michael R. ....'49 '75 C.112 B.A. L.426 J.D. I.R.S.
**Quirk, John** ....'49 '79 C.1077 B.A. L.426 J.D. [Bright&B.]
*PRACTICE AREAS: Oil and Gas Transactions and Title; Land Use Regulation and Permitting.
**Ragen, Sheryl A.** ....'63 '92 C.525 B.A. L.426 J.D. [A O'Flaherty&B.]
Ray, Gerson ....'06 '28 L.809 LL.B. 515 Kenwood St.‡
Reed, Glenn E. ....'44 '73 C.549 B.S. L.426 J.D. 550 N. Brand Blvd., 17th Fl.
Reed, Loyd W., (AV) ....'29 '59 C&L.800 A.B., LL.B. 2716 E. Glenoaks Blvd.
Regan, James C. ....'47 '81 C.276 A.B. L.93 J.D. 501 N. Central Ave.
Rein, Steven ....'44 '70 C.112 B.A. L.426 J.D. 416 E. Broadway
Remboldt, Darwin R. '48 '76 C.1163 B.A. L.950 J.D.
V.P., Glendale Adventist Med. Ctr.
Remery, William R. ....'51 '79 C&L.107 B.A., J.D. 1955 W. Glenoaks Blvd.
Rich, Donald E., (AV) ....'49 '78 C.927 B.A. L.1221 J.D. [Helphand&R.]
Rich, Susan D. ....'62 '89 C.94 B.A. L.823 J.D. 550 N. Brand Blvd., Ste., 2100
Richardson, Kemp A. ....'60 '84 C.684 B.A. L.426 J.D. 101 N. Brand Blvd., #1900
Riehl, Victor M. ....'43 '75 C.707 B.A. L.61 J.D. V.P. & Gen. Coun., Librascope Corp.
**Riley, Michael J.** ....'66 '94 C.112 B.A. L.426 J.D. [A Calendo,P.S.&D.]
*PRACTICE AREAS: Civil Litigation; Insurance Defense.
Robinson, Stephen P. ....'50 '87 C.813 B.S. L.911 J.D. 1514 Roca Dr.
Rodriguez, Manuel H. ....'30 '66 C.112 B.A. L.426 LL.B. 1223 Howard
Roeschlaub, Ronald C., (AV) ....'13 '40 C.112 B.A. L.309 LL.B. 327 W. Arden Ave.‡
Rogan, James E. ....'57 '84 C.112 B.A. L.1068 J.D. Mun. J.
**Rogers, Cynthia D.** ....'59 '95 C.147 B.A. L.940 J.D. [A O'Flaherty&B.] (©Ventura)
Rosen, Jesse N., (AV) ....'— '80 C.112 B.A. L.426 J.D. 100 W. Broadway
**Rosen, Walter K.**, (AV) ....'22 '82 C.309 B.S. L.426 J.D. [MacCarley&R.]
*PRACTICE AREAS: Probate, Estate Planning and Trust Law; Litigation to Elder Abuse.
**Rosenbaum, David E.** ....'42 '67 C&L.502 B.A., J.D. [Klein&R.]
*PRACTICE AREAS: Labor and Employment; OSHA and Environmental; Government Contracts.
**Rosenbaum, Jack** ....'— '96 C.659 B.A. L.884 J.D. [A Hemer,B.&C.]
*PRACTICE AREAS: Medical Malpractice Defense.
Ross, W. Barrett ....'51 '76 C.800 B.S. L.809 J.D. 318 Mesa Lila Rd.
Rosten, Philip M., (AV) ....'38 '66 C.309 A.B. L.1066 LL.B. 144 N. Glendale Ave.
Rotkin, Arnold Louis ....'50 '78 C.339 B.A. L.597 J.D. 516 Burchett St.
**Rungaitis, Matthew R.** ....'64 '90 C.494 B.I.S. L.464 J.D. [A Hagenbaugh&M.]
**Russakow, Mark L.** ....'67 '92 C.112 B.A. L.426 J.D. [A Calendo,P.S.&D.]
*PRACTICE AREAS: Civil Litigation; Insurance Defense.
Russell, Crystal A., (AV) ....'42 '73 C&L.36 B.A., J.D. 500 N. Brand Blvd.
Rustin, Peter B. ....'56 '82 C.183 B.A. L.30 J.D. 130 N. Brand Blvd
**Ryan, William P.** ....'— '89 C.1077 B.A. L.398 J.D. [Messina,L.&M.]
**Sacino, D. F.** ....'30 '62 C.800 A.B. L.809 LL.B. [R.W.McLain]©
*LANGUAGES: Spanish and Italian.
Sacino Bertolino & Hallissy, A Professional Corporation, (BV)
700 N. Brand Blvd. (©Sacramento)
Sackett, Bruce A. ....'39 '75 C.940 B.A. L.1148 J.D. 100 West Broadway
Sainburg, Robert P. ....'60 '92 C.112 B.A. L.426 J.D. 550 N. Brand Blvd.
Samuelsen, Gonzalez, Valenzuela & Sorkow, (AV) .... 100 W. Broadway (©San Pedro)
**Sanders, Robert H.** '46 '71 C&L.36 B.S., J.D.
V.P. & Dep. Gen. Coun., Nestle USA, Inc.
Sandoval, Robert J. ....'50 '77 C.1097 B.A. L.464 J.D. 401 Cumberland Rd.
**Sanne, Christian E.** ....'53 '82 C.112 B.A. L.809 J.D. [A Thomas&P.]
*PRACTICE AREAS: Civil Litigation.
Santochi, Victor W., (AV) ....'53 '78 C.112 B.A. L.809 J.D. [Santochi,F.&G.]
Santochi, Fitzer & Gable, (AV) ....505 N. Brand Blvd. (©Irvine)
Schad, Michael A. ....'51 '83 C.475 B.S. L.1136 J.D. [Zonni,G.&T.]
Schad, William O., (AV) ....'36 '65 C.426 B.S. L.809 LL.B. 628 E. Colorado St.
Scher, Gregory B. ....'61 '88 C.312 B.A. L.1067 J.D. 500 N. Brand Blvd.
Schetina, Elizabeth D. ....'61 '87 C.773 B.A. L.1066 J.D. 1151 N. Jackson St.
Schissell, Gerald Z. ....'34 '76 C.112 B.A. L.1224 J.D. 130 N. Brand Blvd.
Schneider, William J., Jr. ....'30 '76 C.800 B.S.E.E. L.426 J.D. 514 Naranja Dr. (Pat.)
Schock, John P., (BV) ....'41 '72 C.1097 B.A. L.426 J.D. [Schock&S.]
Schock, Margaret ....'— '70 C.112 B.A. L.426 J.D. [Schock&S.]
Schock & Schock, A Law Corp., (BV) ....144 N. Glendale Ave.
Schub, Ralph E. ....'43 '69 C.339 A.B. L.1068 J.D. 516 Burchett St.
Schuck, Dennis H., (AV) ....'47 '74 C.800 B.M. L.809 J.D. Sr. Asst. City Atty.
**Schuetze, Steven M.** ....'63 '89 C.911 B.A. L.990 J.D. [A Hagenbaugh&M.]
Schulman, George A., (AV) ....'46 '73 C.112 B.A. L.426 J.D. 130 N. Brand Blvd.
Schultz, H. Robert ....'54 '91 C.1128 B.A. L.426 J.D. 516 Burchett St.
Schwartz, Bob M. '51 '82 C.659 B.A. L.678 J.D.
(adm. in WA; not adm. in CA) Pres., Kennedy/Schwartz, Inc.
Scott, David L. ....'66 '92 C.154 B.A. L.880 J.D. 1000 N. Central
Scott, Ruben H. ....'48 '80 C.208 B.A. L.1068 J.D. 100 W. Broadway
Scott, Walter ....'42 '70 C.605 B.A. L.426 J.D. 411 N. Central Ave.
**Senuty, Peter J.** ....'50 '75 C&L.813 A.B., J.D. [Knapp,P.&C.]
Serian, Robert B. ....'55 '80 C.800 A.B. L.1049 J.D. 801 N. Brand Blvd.
Shafer, B. Kay ....'54 '84 C&L.846 B.A., J.D. 1308 Randall St.
Shapiro, Corey B. ....'69 '94 C.112 B.A. L.94 J.D. 1000 N. Central
**Sheedy, Christopher M.**, (BV) ....'54 '84 C.1042 B.A. L.809 J.D. [Calendo,P.S.&D.]
*PRACTICE AREAS: Civil Litigation; Insurance Defense.
Shore, Harold B. ....'37 '61 C&L.309 A.B., LL.B. 700 Brand Blvd.‡
**Shpall, Mark H.** ....'67 '94 C.112 B.A. L.800 J.D. [A O'Flaherty&B.]
Silk, Joseph ....'13 '36 C.113 B.A. L.800 J.D. 525 S. Central Ave.
**Silver, Holly A.** ....'54 '79 C.518 B.A. L.276 J.D. Sr. Coun., Nestle USA, Inc.
*RESPONSIBILITIES: Employment Law.
Silverton-Buckner, Robin ....'60 '87 C.800 B.A. L.1136 J.D. Dep. City Atty.
Simmons, Philip S., Law Offices of '52 '93
C.228 B.S.E. L.1148 J.D. 101 N. Brand Blvd., Ste 1830
**Simon, Michael S.** ....'60 '87 C.112 B.A. L.426 J.D. [A Baker,O.L.&D.]
**Simonian, Gary P.** ....'65 '95 C.605 B.A. L.809 J.D. [A Hagenbaugh&M.]
*PRACTICE AREAS: Intellectual Property; Insurance Coverage.
Simonson, Richard G. ....'48 '83 C.1120 B.S. L.809 J.D. 550 N. Brand Blvd.
**Simpson, David B.** ....'57 '82 C.112 B.A. L.1068 J.D. [Wolflick&S.]
*PRACTICE AREAS: Labor; Employment Law.
Simpson, Thomas L., (AV) ....'47 '74 C&L.770 B.A., J.D. 801 N. Brand Blvd.
**Skebba, Jamie B.** ....'60 '86 C.959 B.A. L.990 J.D. [Hagenbaugh&M.]
Smith, Forrest B., (AV) ....'50 '78 C.101 B.S. L.1065 J.D. [Clark&S.]
Smith, H. Allen ....'09 '34 C&L.800 A.B., LL.B. 420 N. Louise St.‡
Smith, Janna O. ....'61 '87 C&L.800 A.B., J.D. 1545 Glenmont Dr.
**Smith, Robert C.** '26 '52 C.791 B.S. L.793 LL.B.
(adm. in SD; not adm. in CA; See Pat. Sect.) [A Wagner&M.]
Smith, Robert S., (AV) '53 '79 C.766 B.A. L.1065 J.D.
501 W. Glenoaks Blvd., Ste 809
Snyder, Bruce D. ....'53 '80 C.112 A.B. L.426 J.D. 1238 E. Wilson Ave.‡
Sobol, Neal H. ....'50 '87 C.476 B.S. L.809 J.D. 520 E. Bway.
Sorkow, Alan, (BV) ....'50 '76 [Samuelsen,G.V.&S.]
**Sotomayor, Jess E.** '52 '82 C.36 B.S. L.813 J.D.
Assoc. Gen. Coun. & Asst. Secy., IHOP Corp.
*LANGUAGES: Spanish.
*RESPONSIBILITIES: Corporate Law.
Spicer, Mary Ann '39 '65
C.763 B.A. L.1068 LL.B. Sr. Assoc. Coun., Glendale Fed. Bk., FSB
Spivack, Thomas M. ....'53 '93 C.112 B.A. L.809 J.D. 124 S. Isabel St.
**Stack, Kevin J.**, (AV) ....'51 '76 C.112 B.A. L.426 J.D. [Knapp,P.&C.]

**Stafford, Michael N., (AV) '38 '72 C.1097 B.A. L.426 J.D.**
**104 North Belmont Third Floor, 91206**
**Telephone: 818-247-4303 Fax: 818-247-1451**
***PRACTICE AREAS: Real Estate; Corporate; Business Law; Probate; Estate Planning.**
**General Civil and Trial Practice in all State and Federal Courts, Real Estate, Corporate and Business Law, Probate and Estate Planning, Arbitration and Mediation.**
*See Professional Biographies, GLENDALE, CALIFORNIA*

Stein, Neil N. ....'53 '83 C.1111 B.A. L.1137 J.D. 516 Burchett St.
**Steinman, Peter E.** '48 '76
C.563 B.E.M.E. L.564 J.D. V.P.-Gen. Coun., Walt Disney Imagineering
Stern, Julie A. ....'59 '91 C.112 B.A. L.1049 J.D. 516 Burchett St.
**Stewart, William D., (A P.C.)**, (AV) ....'43 '68 C.112 A.B. L.809 J.D. [Hagenbaugh&M.]
Stillwell, Parks ....'18 '41 C.934 L.910 LL.B. Ret. Supr. Ct. J.
**Stokes, Charles H.** ....'42 '73 C.112 B.A. L.809 J.D. [R.W.McLain]
Stoll, Charles W. ....'31 '59 C.823 A.B. L.800 LL.B. Supr. Ct. J.
**Stoterau, H. Peter**, (AV) ....'38 '68 C.1077 B.S. L.1068 J.D. [Jobe&S.]
*PRACTICE AREAS: Business; Real Estate; Corporations; Government Business.
Stovitz, James E. '54 '79 C.1097 B.A. L.1148 J.D.
V.P. & Sr. Title Coun., North American Title Insurance Co.
Strayer, Joy D. ....'42 '79 C&L.508 B.A., J.D. 220 N. Glendale Ave.
Stringfellow, Dean M. ....'47 '74 C.112 B.A. L.767 J.D. 550 N. Brand Blvd.
Stroh, Duane C. ....'49 '77 C.1188 B.S. L.1137 J.D. 111 E. Broadway
Stroh, Herbert A., (BV) ....'58 '85 C.112 B.A. L.426 J.D. [Whitesell&S.]
Sturges, Clyde W., (BV) ....'26 '57 C.352 B.A. L.800 LL.B. 628 E. Colorado St.‡

**Styskal, Wiese & Melchione, (AV)**
**550 North Brand Boulevard, Suite 550, 91203**
**Telephone: 818-241-0103 Fax: 818-241-5733**
**Members of Firm: Joseph S. Melchione; William J. Adler; Bruce A. Pearson. Associate: Donna M. Whooley.**
**General Corporate, Commercial and Consumer, Insurance and Computer Law as it affects Credit Unions.**
*See Professional Biographies, GLENDALE, CALIFORNIA*

**Subar, Daphne B.** ....'65 '90 C.112 B.A. L.904 J.D. [Knapp,P.&C.]
Sugarman, Sandra ....'38 '77 C.536 B.Ed. L.1190 J.D. 205 E. Bdwy.
**Sullivan, Kirk N.** ....'57 '84 C.061 B.S. L.990 J.D. [A Hagenbaugh&M.]
*REPORTED CASES: Dworkin v. Hustler Magazine, 668 F. Supp. 1408 (C.D. Cal. 1987); Dworkin v. LFP, 839 P.2d 903 (Wyo. 1992); Spence v. Flynt, 816 P. 2d 771 (Wyo. 1991); Aguayo v. Tomco Carburetor Co., 853 F.2d 744 (9th Cir. 1988); Leidoldt v. LFP, 647 F.Supp. 1283 (D.C. Wyo. 1986).
*PRACTICE AREAS: Intellectual Property; Fidelity and Surety; Business Litigation; Insurance Coverage.
Summer, Mark B., (AV) ....'48 '74 C.1077 B.A. L.809 J.D. [Knights&S.]
Szakall, Thomas S. ....'45 '74 C.1097 B.A. L.1049 J.D. 700 N. Brand Blvd.
**Szumiak, Paul G.** ....'54 '83 C.475 B.A. L.809 J.D. [Hagenbaugh&M.]
**Tang, K. Stephen** ....'56 '81 C.112 A.B. L.426 J.D. [Knapp,P.&C.]
**Tary, John J., (A P.C.)** ....'38 '73 C.1097 B.S. L.426 J.D. [Hagenbaugh&M.]
Taylor, Ben F., (AV) ....'25 '62 C.112 B.A. L.426 LL.B. [Zonni,G.&T.]
Taylor, Charles R. ....'55 '90 C.800 B.S. L.1148 J.D. 101 N. Brand Blvd., Suite 600
Taylor, Norman F. ....'53 '87 C.36 L.1190 J.D. 426 W. Broadway
**Taylor, Steven H.** ....'62 '92 C.800 B.S. L.1065 J.D. [A Ott&H.]
*LANGUAGES: Spanish.
*PRACTICE AREAS: Litigation.
Taylor, Tracy A. ....'61 '88 C.1077 B.A. L.426 J.D. 701 N. Brand Blvd.
Tennen, Randy ....'49 '75 C.604 B.A. L.564 J.D. 1219 N. Columbus Ave.
**Tenner, Kristina Ann** ....'62 '88 C.347 B.A. L.1065 J.D. [Knapp,P.&C.]
Thelin, Howard J. ....'21 '50 C.112 A.B. L.800 LL.B. 632 Robin Glen Dr.‡
**Thomas, Maureen F.** ....'57 '82 C.112 B.A. L.464 J.D. [Thomas&P.]©
*PRACTICE AREAS: Construction; Civil Litigation; Personal Injury; Medical Malpractice; Insurance Defense.
Thomas, Michael ....'38 '65 C.112 B.A. L.1065 J.D. 535 N. Brand Blvd., 5th Fl. (Pat.)
**Thomas, Michael**, (AV) ....'41 '68 C.112 B.A. L.809 LL.B. [Thomas&P.]©
*PRACTICE AREAS: Civil Litigation; Personal Injury; Medical Malpractice; Legal Malpractice; Wrongful Termination.

**Thomas & Price, (AV)** BB
**535 North Brand Boulevard, 7th Floor, 91203**©
**Telephone: 213-387-4800; 818-500-4800 FAX: 818-500-4822**
**Members of Firm: Michael Thomas; Bonnie R. Louis; Craig R. Donahue; Maureen F. Thomas. Associates: John P. DeGomez; Timothy A. Hodge; Linda B. Hurevitz; Christian E. Sanne; Benjimin M. Brees; Janet L. Keuper; Kevin M. McCormick. Of Counsel: Lawrence E. Price.**
**Insurance Defense, Medical Accounting, Legal Malpractice, Automobile Law, Product Liability, Construction and Premise Liability Law, Oilfield Exploration and Production Accidents, Wrongful Termination, Sexual Discrimination, Intellectual Property Law.**
**Ventura, California Office: 1655 Mesa Verde Avenue, Suite 230. Telephone: 805-642-6255. Fax: 805-642-4580.**
*See Professional Biographies, GLENDALE, CALIFORNIA*

Thompson, Stephan G., (AV) ....'48 '75 C.112 B.A. L.1065 J.D. 116 N. Maryland Ave.
Thyberg, Gregory A. ....'56 '81 C.112 B.A. L.1067 J.D. 550 N. Brand Blvd.
**Tilem, David A.**, (AV) ....'55 '82 C.103 A.B. L.426 J.D. [Tilem W.&W.]
*LANGUAGES: Spanish.
*PRACTICE AREAS: Bankruptcy; Workouts; Bankruptcy Litigation.

**Tilem White & Weintraub LLP, (AV)**
**701 North Brand Boulevard Suite 440, 91203**
**Telephone: 818-507-6000 Fax: 818-507-6800**
**David A. Tilem; C. Casey White; Daniel J. Weintraub; Jeanne C. Wanlass.**
**Bankruptcy, Workouts, Related Litigation, Creditor Rights in Marital Dissolution Proceedings, Bankruptcy Appellate Practice.**
*See Professional Biographies, GLENDALE, CALIFORNIA*

Tom, James F. .................................. '50 '78 C.1097 B.A. L.809 J.D. [Knights&S.]
**Tomsic, Gerald A., (AV) '50 '76 C.659 B.S. L.426 J.D.**
**625 West Broadway, Suite D, 91204-1997**
**Telephone: 818-500-4888; Fax: 818-241-2842**
**Estate Planning, Wills and Trusts, Probate, Taxation, Business, Corporate and Partnership Law, Real Estate, Limited Liability Companies.**
***See Professional Biographies, GLENDALE, CALIFORNIA***
**Tonya, Michael A.** .................. '52 '92 C.502 B.A. L.930 J.D. [⊠ Hagenbaugh&M.]
Toscano, Oscar E. ......................... '51 '78 C.112 B.A. L.426 J.D. 625 W. Bway.
Trainer, Owen A. ................................ '50 '81 C.94 B.A. L.818 J.D. P.O. Box 5165
**Trangsrud, Cynthia A.** ........................ '54 '82 C.300 B.A. L.494 J.D. [Knapp,P.&C.]
Traverse, Stephen E. '49 '80
C.112 B.A. L.1065 J.D. Sr. Assoc. Coun., Glendale Fed. Bk., FSB
**Trytten, Steven E.**, (AV) ........................ '52 '78 C&L.339 B.S., J.D. [S.E.Trytten]
*PRACTICE AREAS: Advanced Estate Planning (40%); Estate Planning (30%); Probate and Trust Administration (10%); Taxation (20%).
**Trytten, Steven E., A Professional Law Corporation, (AV)**
**500 North Brand Boulevard, Suite 1030, 91203**
**Telephone: 818-500-9969 Fax: 818-500-9979**
**Steven E. Trytten (Certified Specialist, Taxation Law, Estate Planning, Trust and Probate Law, The State Bar of California Board of Legal Specialization).**
**Advanced Estate Planning, Trust, Probate and Taxation.**
***See Professional Biographies, GLENDALE, CALIFORNIA***
Tucker, Rodney Alan ...... '51 '79 C.1042 B.A. L.1137 J.D. 550 N. Brand Blvd., 17th Fl.
Tuffin, Dennis F. ................................'50 '77 C.321 B.A. L.262 J.D. 516 Burchett St.
**Tukia, Phillip T. S.** ........................ '66 '96 C.1077 B.S. L.426 J.D. [Knapp,P.&C.]
Turchin, Florette S., (BV) ................'43 '74 C.112 B.A. L.1148 J.D. 516 Burchett St.
Turchin, Raymond L. ...................... '45 '79 C.1097 B.A. L.1148 J.D. 516 Burchett St.
Twigg, Alfred T., (AV) .......................'13 '37 C&L.770 B.A., LL.B. 1820 Bara Rd.‡
Uemura, Kazuaki ............. '56 '83 C.668 B.A. L.1067 J.D. Gen. Coun., Bidamar Corp.
**Unger, Charles J.**, (BV) ...............'55 '81 C.597 B.A. L.339 J.D. [Flanagan,B.U.&M.]
*PRACTICE AREAS: Criminal Law; Personal Injury Law.
Urick, Willis E., Jr., (AV) .............. '16 '41 C.976 B.A. L.309 J.D. 1958 Calle Sirena
Uyekawa, David T. ...................'45 '77 C.1042 A.B. L.809 J.D. U.S. Small Bus. Admn.
**Vaage, Susan L.**, (AV) ............................ '53 '78 C.112 B.A. L.426 J.D. [Laskin&G.]
*LANGUAGES: Spanish.
*PRACTICE AREAS: Commercial Litigation; Bankruptcy; Insolvency; Creditors' Rights; Financial Institution Law.
Vail, Lee E. ...............................'54 '80 C.112 B.S. L.767 J.D. 541 W. Colorado St.
Vallette, Kent Leeds ...................'45 '72 C.112 B.A. L.1068 J.D. 216 S. Louise St.
**Van Houten, Kathryn E.** .................. '59 '89 C.112 B.A. L.426 J.D. [Irsfeld,I.&Y.]
*PRACTICE AREAS: Business Litigation; Family Law; Probate Law.
**Vargas, Wilhelm Isaiah** ................. '61 '95 C.1042 B.A. L.809 J.D. [Wolflick&S.]
*LANGUAGES: Spanish.
*PRACTICE AREAS: Employment Law; Labor Law.
**Vega, Bridgette** .............. '57 '83 C.605 A.B. L.813 J.D. Sr. Coun., Nestle USA, Inc.
*LANGUAGES: Spanish.
*RESPONSIBILITIES: Litigation.
Vialla, Robin S. .......................'65 '92 C.112 B.A. L.809 J.D. 500 N. Brand Blvd.
Victoria, Rodolfo ......................'22 '53 C.990 L.1065 J.D. 1600 N. Verdugo Rd.‡
Vidmar, Lisa A. ........................ '65 '91 C.112 B.A. L.426 J.D. [⊠ Zonni,G.&T.]
Vincent, Sandra Lee ...................................'50 '79 L.1148 J.D. [Mozingo&V.]
Virgilio, Joseph A. ....................'52 '82 C.554 B.S. L.1148 J.D. [Najarian&V.]
**Wagner, John E.**, (AV) '26 '51 C.350 B.S.G.E. L.352 J.D.
[Wagner&M.] (See Pat. Sect.)
**Wagner & Middlebrook, (AV)**
**3541 Ocean View Boulevard, 91208**
**Telephone: 818-957-3340 Fax: 818-957-8123**
**Members of Firm: John E. Wagner; Theresa W. Middlebrook;—Robert C. Smith (Not admitted in CA).**
**Patent, Trademark and Copyright Law. Unfair Competition, Trade Secrets, Computer Law and related causes (transactional, administrative, prosecution and litigation in all state and federal courts).**
***See Professional Biographies, GLENDALE, CALIFORNIA***
**Waldorf, James J., (P.C.)**, (AV) ............'38 '66 C&L.426 B.B.A., J.D. [Irsfeld,I.&Y.]
*PRACTICE AREAS: Real Estate Law; Construction Law; Litigation; Real Estate.
**Walker, Diane L.** ...................... '59 '85 C.1077 B.A. L.990 J.D. [Irsfeld,I.&Y.]
*PRACTICE AREAS: Business Litigation; Real Property Law; Probate Law.
Wallace, Allan W., (AV) .............................. '25 '51 C&L.800 J.D. [Wallace&W.]
Wallace and Wallace, (AV) ...............................................220 S. Kenwood St.
**Waller, Antoinette S.** ........................ '65 '91 C.112 B.A. L.426 J.D. [Knapp,P.&C.]
**Walsh, Luanne** ......................'46 '89 C.69 B.A. L.809 J.D. [⊠ Hagenbaugh&M.]
**Wanlass, Jeanne C.** ........................ '68 '93 C.813 B.A. L.1066 J.D. [Tilem W.&W.]
*LANGUAGES: French.
*PRACTICE AREAS: Bankruptcy Law.
**Wanski, Nancy G.** ..............................'50 '88 C.16 B.S. L.800 J.D. [O'Flaherty&B.]
Warner, Olive Magee, (AV) ........... '37 '77 C.068 B.A. L.426 J.D. 501 N. Central Ave.
Warriner, Rhett P. ..................................'64 '89 C.112 A.B. L.800 J.D. [Beam&H.]
Watkins, Douglas A. ................... '56 '91 C.763 B.S. L.1049 J.D. [⊠ Zonni,G.&T.]
**Watson, Alexander M.** ................ '64 '91 C.293 B.A. L.300 J.D. [⊠ O'Flaherty&B.]
Wax, Alan Jay ................................. '59 '86 C.112 B.A. L.1190 J.D. [Wax&W.]
Wax, Harold W., (AV) ..........................'25 '52 C&L.800 A.B., J.D. [Wax&W.]
Wax & Wax, (AV) ..................................................................411 N. Central Ave.
**Weber, Mara L.** ............................... '51 '81 C.800 B.S. L.1068 J.D. [Knapp,P.&C.]
Weiner, Roberta L. .......................... '49 '74 C.690 A.B. L.910 J.D. P.O. Box 29014
**Weintraub, Daniel J.** ..................... '60 '87 C.112 B.A. L.800 J.D. [Tilem W.&W.]
*PRACTICE AREAS: Bankruptcy Law; Foreclosure Law; Business Law; Collections.
**Weisberger, Mark D.** '55 '80 C.112 B.A. L.809 J.D.
V.P., Legal, Secy. & Gen. Coun., IHOP Corp.
*RESPONSIBILITIES: Corporate Law.
**Wesierski & Zurek, (AV)**
**800 North Brand Boulevard, Suite 250, 91203⊙**
**Telephone: 818-543-6100 Telecopier: 818-543-6101**
**Partner: Ronald Zurek.**
**General Civil Litigation, Insurance Bad Faith, Defense and Coverage, Appellate Practice, Insurance Defense, Products Liability, Professional Liability, Representation of Employers and Employees, Premises Liability, Real Property (Land Subsidence), Toxic Torts and Intellectual Property.**
**Irvine, California Office: Suite 1500, 5 Park Plaza. Telephone: 714-975-1000. Telecopier: 714-756-0517.**
***See Professional Biographies, GLENDALE, CALIFORNIA***
Weyl, John A., (AV) ...............'13 '40 C.112 L.800 J.D. 100 W. Broadway, Ste. 900‡
**Wheat, Penny L.** ............................ '47 '77 C.823 B.A. L.809 J.D. [Knapp,P.&C.]
Wheatley, Carroll A., Jr. ....................'58 '84 C.238 B.S. L.809 J.D. [Zonni,G.&T.]
Whelan, Allan C. ......................'41 '72 C.1042 B.A. L.809 J.D. 330 Arden Ave.
**White, C. Casey** ............................'42 '84 C.112 B.A. L.1049 J.D. [Tilem W.&W.]
*PRACTICE AREAS: Bankruptcy; Litigation; Bankruptcy Appellate Practice.
White, Norman J., (AV) ....................... '35 '63 C.112 B.A. L.1068 LL.B. [N.J.White]
White, Norman J., A Professional Law Corporation, (AV) ........... 1156 N. Brand Blvd.
Whitehead, Ann F. ............................. '55 '90 C.999 R.N. L.809 J.D. 1000 N. Central
Whitesell, Charles E., (AV) ........................ '36 '62 C&L.800 B.A., J.D. [Whitesell&S.]
Whitesell & Stroh, (AV) .............................................................. 144 N. Glendale Ave.
**Whooley, Donna M.** ......................'68 '95 C.112 B.A. L.426 J.D. [⊠ Styskal,W.&M.]
*PRACTICE AREAS: Corporate Law; Consumer Law; Credit Union Law.
Wick, Michael G. ............ '53 '80 C.112 B.A. L.809 J.D. V.P. & Coun., Fidelity Fed. Bk.
Wiedner, Burke M., (AV) .................. '35 '70 C.112 B.A. L.809 J.D. [Molfetta,R.&W.]
Wiemans, Albert G., (AV) .................... '41 '74 C.112 L.809 J.D. 630 E. Colorado St.
Wildman, Richard W. '36 '62
C.994 B.A. L.569 LL.B. Sr. Assoc. Coun., Glendale Fed. Bk., FSB
Williams, Jack, (A Prof. Corp.) '31 '70 C.563 B.B.A. L.426 J.D.
3429 Ocean View Blvd.
Wilson, Roy C., Jr. ................. '45 '80 C.1097 B.A. L.1148 J.D. 700 N. Brand Blvd.
**Winter, David L.**, (BV) ............... '54 '79 C.473 B.A. L.464 J.D. [Hagenbaugh&M.]
Wolf, Perry S. ............................'53 '93 C.112 B.A. L.426 J.D. 516 Burchett St.
**Wolflick, Gregory D.** ..........................'56 '83 C.37 B.S. L.809 J.D. [Wolflick&S.]
*PRACTICE AREAS: Labor; Employment Law.
**Wolflick & Simpson**
**130 North Brand Boulevard, 4th Floor, 91203**
**Telephone: 818-243-8300**
**Members of Firm: Gregory D. Wolflick; David B. Simpson; Wilhelm Isaiah Vargas.**
**Labor, Employment Law.**
***See Professional Biographies, GLENDALE, CALIFORNIA***
**Wong, Claire** ........................................... '56 '90 L.061 LL.B. [Knapp,P.&C.]
**Wong, Laurence Y.** ................. '56 '82 C.1042 B.A. L.1137 J.D. [⊠ Hemer,B.&C.]
*PRACTICE AREAS: Medical Malpractice Defense.
**Wood, Merle W., II** .......... '42 '71 C.352 B.A. L.309 J.D. Sr. Coun., Nestle USA, Inc.
Woodhall, Phyllis A. .......................'65 '91 C.112 B.A. L.809 J.D. 1111 N. Brand Blvd.
Woolls, Paul, (AV) .........................'54 '79 C.894 A.B. L.665 J.D. 500 N. Brand Blvd.
**Wright, Peter C.**, (BV) ................. '43 '73 C.347 A.B. L.1119 J.D. [⊠ Irsfeld,I.&Y.]
*PRACTICE AREAS: General Civil Litigation; Business; Tort; Real Property; Extraordinary Writs.
Yablon, Al ........................... '18 '71 L.1095 J.D. Coun., Lumeni Productions Inc.
Yanz, Gordon I., (P.C.), (BV) ...............'34 '62 C.1043 B.S. L.1068 LL.B. [Yanz&H.]
Yanz & Hertz, (BV) ........................................................................ 801 N. Brand Blvd.
**Yocca, Mark W.** ........................ '63 '88 C.112 B.A. L.426 J.D. [Benjamin,L.&B.]
*PRACTICE AREAS: Business Litigation; Entertainment Law; Insurance Coverage; Insurance Bad Faith.
**Zanglis, Constance G.** ................. '59 '85 C.684 B.A. L.1067 J.D. [Knapp,P.&C.]
**Ziehm, Eugene C.** '32 '62 C.107 B.S. L.273 J.D.
(adm. in MD; not adm. in CA) Sr. Coun., Nestle USA, Inc.
*RESPONSIBILITIES: Intellectual Property Law.
Zonni, Marco J., (AV) ............................ '27 '50 C.813 L.809 [⊠ Zonni,G.&T.]
Zonni, Ginocchio and Taylor, Professional Corporation, (AV)
516 Burchett St. (⊙Santa Ana, Ventura & San Bernardino)
Zubrin, Douglas B. ........................ '47 '73 C.37 B.S. L.1068 J.D. 320 Arden Ave.
**Zuckerman, Alan R.** ........................ '51 '77 C.800 B.A. L.426 J.D. [Hagenbaugh&M.]
Zuckerman, Michael J. .....................'57 '83 C.112 B.A. L.1065 J.D. 100 W. Broadway
**Zurek, Ronald**, (AV) ...........................'52 '77 C.112 A.B. L.426 J.D. [Wesierski&Z.]⊙

## GLENDORA, 47,828, *Los Angeles Co.*

Anderson, Karen vom Lehn, (BV) '43 '77
C.575 B.A. L.426 J.D. 157 N. Glendora, Suite 207
Beitler, Roger, Law Corporation, (AV) ...... '35 '67 C.101 A.B. L.273 J.D. P.O. Box 524
Bess, Michael J., (BV) ...'45 '75 C.1075 B.S. L.398 J.D. 158 N. Glendora Ave., Suite "R"
Butler, Jean Smith ..................... '25 '81 C.550 B.A. L.1137 J.D. 2619 Country Club Dr.
Clowdus, Kenneth W. ..................................... '36 '71 L.809 J.D. 814 W. Bagnall St.
**DeWeese, Wendy M.** .................. '65 '93 C.668 B.A. L.809 J.D. [Stettner,E.&M.]
*LANGUAGES: Dutch; German and French.
*PRACTICE AREAS: Family Law.
Douglas, Walter M., (BV) ...........'34 '73 C.878 B.A. L.398 J.D. 209 W. Foothill Blvd.
Driskell, Robert L. ...................... '49 '76 C.112 B.A. L.426 J.D. 158 N. Glendora Ave.
Dyl, Mark S. ............................'48 '82 C.668 B.A. L.1066 J.D. 1103 Mullaghboy Rd.
**Eisenberg, Donald S.**, (AV) '47 '76
C.1042 B.A. L.1068 J.D. [Stettner,E.&M.] (⊙Los Angeles)
Ferguson, Matthew R., (BV) .... '51 '77 C.1074 B.A.B.S. L.809 J.D. 120 W. Bennett Ave.
Graham, Douglas D., (BV) .........'41 '70 C.878 B.S. L.145 J.D. 2001 E. Financial Way
Keijonen, Robert D. ......................... '46 '76 C.475 B.A. L.809 J.D. P.O. Box 426
Liddle, George Lee, Jr. ............................ '53 '85 C.112 B.S. L.426 J.D. [Liddle&L.]
Liddle, Layne L. .......................................... '51 '80 C.763 B.A. L.1003 J.D. [Liddle&L.]
Liddle & Liddle, A Prof. Corp. ............................................................310 S. Vermont Ave.
Meeder, Theodore H., Jr., (BV) ..........................'28 '58 C.112 L.1065 J.D. P.O. Box 506
Meyer, Robert E. ..........................'55 '81 C.112 B.A. L.464 J.D. Treasure Chest Co.
Morrill, Rodney T. '27 '52 C&L.966 B.A., LL.B.
(adm. in WI; not adm. in CA) 956 E. Cypress Ave.‡
**Morris, Charles J., Jr.** .......................... '56 '89 C.497 B.A. L.800 J.D. [Stettner,E.&M.]
*PRACTICE AREAS: Litigation; Family Law.
Pico, Tristan R. ...................................'46 '75 C.101 B.A. L.800 J.D. 2001 E. Financial Way
**Renninger, John H.** '50 '80
C.1075 B.S. L.1068 J.D. V.P. & Gen. Coun., Portland Cement Co.
Robusto, Anthony R., (BV) ........... '51 '76 C.1075 B.S. L.990 J.D. 1135 E. Alosta Ave.
Rose, Scott L., (BV) ...........................'49 '76 C.800 B.A. L.398 J.D. 1135 E. Alosta Ave.
**Silberman, Harvey A.** ..................... '57 '92 C.918 B.A. L.800 J.D. [⊠ Stettner,E.&M.]
*PRACTICE AREAS: Family Law; Testamentary; Civil; Probate.
Stanfill, Alan ..........................................'54 '88 C&L.101 B.S., J.D. 2001 Financial Way
**Stettner, Pamela P.**, (BV) ............. '48 '77 C.800 B.A. L.809 J.D. [Stettner,E.&M.]
*PRACTICE AREAS: Family Law.
**Stettner, Eisenberg & Morris, (AV)**
**1433 East Alosta Avenue, 91740-3747**
**Telephone: 818-914-2791 Facsimile: 818-914-3946**
**Members of Firm: Pamela P. Stettner; Donald S. Eisenberg (Certified Specialist, Family Law, The State Bar of California Board of Legal Specialization); Charles J. Morris, Jr. Associates: Harvey A. Silberman; Wendy M. DeWeese.**
**Family Law, including Dissolutions, Prenuptials, Cohabitation Agreements, Spousal Support, Custody and Adoptions, International Custody Disputes.**
***See Professional Biographies, GLENDORA, CALIFORNIA***
Tscharner, R. L., (BV) ..................... '11 '35 C.668 B.A. L.800 J.D. 109 S. County Club Rd.‡
Watkins, John F., (AV) ............ '40 '69 C.1097 B.S. L.800 J.D. 2605 E. Foothill Blvd.

## GLEN ELLEN, —, *Sonoma Co.*

Brandt-Hawley, Susan L. ..........................'51 '77 C.763 A.B. L.1067 J.D. 13760 Arnold
Ellis, Craig S. ........................ '48 '82 C.112 B.A. L.1197 J.D. 3382 Warm Springs Rd.
Millspaugh, Lynda ..................................... '45 '71 C.563 B.A. L.569 J.D. 10601 Slattery

## GOLD RIVER, —, *Sacramento Co.*

**Asperger, Robert E.** ............ '58 '84 C.112 B.A. L.1067 J.D. [⊠ Bullivant,H.B.P.&H.]
*PRACTICE AREAS: Insurance Defense Litigation; Professional Liability.

CAA113P

CALIFORNIA—GOLD RIVER
MARTINDALE-HUBBELL LAW DIRECTORY 1997

Beck, Patricia E. '55 '83
C.1060 B.A. L.464 J.D. Gen. Coun., Weststar Communications, Inc.
Beyer, Gregory R. ........ '55 '91 C.1020 L.1026 J.D. [Beyer&P.]
Beyer & Pongratz, A Prof. Law Corp., The Law Offices of ........ 11344 Coloma Rd.
**Boeck, Tamara L.** ........ '67 '93 C.267 B.S. L.464 J.D. [Ⓐ Bullivant,H.B.P.&H.]
*PRACTICE AREAS: Coverage Litigation; Insurance Defense Litigation; Environmental Litigation; Product Liability.

**Bullivant, Houser, Bailey, Pendergrass & Hoffman, A Professional Corporation, (AVⓉ)**
**11335 Gold Express Drive, Suite 105, 95670⊙**
**Telephone: 916-852-9100 FAX: 916-852-5777**
**URL: http://www.bullivant.com**
**James G. Driscoll; M. Taylor Florence;—Robert E. Asperger; Tamara L. Boeck; Gail E. Gearin; David R. Lane; Kathleen Ann Lynch; Kevin S. Mapes. Of Counsel: Jane O'Donnell.**
**Insurance Coverage; Insurance Defense; General Litigation; Environmental and Related Areas of Litigation.**
**Representative Clients: Reliance Insurance Co.; The Hanover Insurance Co.; United States Fidelity & Guaranty.; Federated Insurance Co.; Dean's & Homer; Houston General Insurance Co.; Grocers Insurance Co.; Standard Insurance Co.**
**Portland, Oregon Office: 300 Pioneer Tower, 888 S.W. Fifth Avenue, 97204-2089. Telephone: 503-228-6351. Facsimile: 503-295-0915.**
**Seattle, Washington Office: 2400 Westlake Office Tower, 1601 Fifth Avenue, 98101-1618. Telephone: 206-292-8930. Facsimile: 206-386-5130. Cable Address: Sealaw.**
**Vancouver, Washington Office: 300 First Independence Place, 1220 Main Street. 98660-2962. Telephones: 360-693-2424; 360-225-1100. Facsimile: 206-695-8504.**

*See Professional Biographies, GOLD RIVER, CALIFORNIA*

Cawley, Elaine M. ........ '53 '89 C.653 B.S. L.464 J.D. 11471 Round House Ct.
Couper, George E., (BV) ........ '26 '54 C.112 A.B. L.1065 J.D. 11344 Coloma Rd.
Dawn, William E. '37 '63 C&L.174 B.S., J.D.
(adm. in CO; not adm. in CA) Exec. V.P. & Gen. Coun., Springs Inc.
Dawson, Fred N., (AV) ........ '42 '69 C.112 B.A. L.1068 J.D. 11211 Gold Country Blvd.
Donahue, Leo F., (BV) ........ '40 '84 C.1070 B.S. L.464 J.D. 11246 Gold Express Dr.
**Driscoll, James G.**, (AVⓉ) ........ '48 '77 C.178 B.A. L.1051 J.D. [Bullivant,H.B.P.&H.]
*PRACTICE AREAS: Insurance Coverage; Environmental Litigation; Insurance Defense Litigation; Commercial Litigation.
Driver, Philip F. ........ '20 '45 C.999 L.1065 J.D. 11424 Tunnel Hill Way‡
**Florence, M. Taylor** ........ '60 '86 C&L.878 B.A., J.D. [Bullivant,H.B.P.&H.]
*PRACTICE AREAS: Environmental, Insurance and Commercial Litigation.
**Gearin, Gail E.** ........ '47 '88 C.1056 B.S. L.1051 J.D. [Ⓐ Bullivant,H.B.P.&H.]
*PRACTICE AREAS: Environmental Coverage and Defense Litigation; Insurance Defense Litigation; Insurance Coverage.
Hanks, Michael L., (BV) ........ '50 '75 C.112 B.S. L.464 J.D. 11211 Gold Country Blvd.
Kingsbury, David Reid ........ '58 '86 C.1320 B.A. L.464 J.D. 11344 Coloma Rd.
**Lane, David R.** ........ '51 '78 C.112 A.B. L.464 J.D. [Ⓐ Bullivant,H.B.P.&H.]
*PRACTICE AREAS: Insurance Coverage; Insurance Litigation.
**Lynch, Kathleen Ann** ........ '65 '94 C.1060 B.S. L.464 J.D. [Ⓐ Bullivant,H.B.P.&H.]
*PRACTICE AREAS: Insurance Defense; Insurance Coverage; Coverage Litigation.
Lyons, William M., (BV) ........ '37 '68 L.464 J.D. 11230 Gold Express Dr.
**Mapes, Kevin S.** ........ '67 '94 C.678 B.A. L.1051 J.D. [Ⓐ Bullivant,H.B.P.&H.]
*PRACTICE AREAS: Insurance Coverage; Coverage Litigation; Environmental Litigation.
Myers, Beverly J. ........ '52 '89 C.896 B.A. L.464 J.D. 2066 Promontory Point Lane
Nelson, Steven A. ........ '50 '82 C.768 B.A. L.770 J.D. 11626 N Carson Way
**O'Donnell, Jane** ........ '55 '81 C.800 B.A. L.809 J.D. [Ⓒ Bullivant,H.B.P.&H.]
*PRACTICE AREAS: Litigation.
Ohara, Maureen C. ........ '57 '91 C.112 B.A. L.408 J.D. 11211 Gold Co. Blvd.
Opdyke, Mona E. ........ '60 '88 C.112 B.A. L.1067 J.D. 11344 Coloma Rd.
Pongratz, Stephen G ........ '58 '84 C.999 B.A. L.184 J.D. [Beyer&P.]
Reiter, Susan M. ........ '55 '82 C.112 B.S. L.464 J.D. 11211 Glod Country Blvd.
Rosen, Etan Emanuel ........ '58 '94 C.846 B.B.A. L.464 J.D. 11344 Coloma Rd.
Spittler, John W. ........ '49 '75 C.766 B.A. L.464 J.D. 11344 Coloma Rd., Ste., 505
Tennant, David H., (BV) ........ '42 '72 C.1060 A.B. L.464 J.D. 11211 Gold Country Blvd.
**Westerberg, Dennis N.**, (AV) ........ '44 '74 C.112 B.S. L.464 J.D. [D.N.Westerberg]

**Westerberg, Dennis N., Law Corporation, (AV)**
**Suite 525, 11344 Coloma Road, 95670-4462**
**Telephone: 916-638-1506 Fax: 916-638-7833**
**Dennis N. Westerberg.**
**General Negligence Law. Professional Liability, Products Liability and Aviation Law. Trial Practice.**

*See Professional Biographies, GOLD RIVER, CALIFORNIA*

## GOLD RUN, —, *Placer Co.*

Coho, Kenneth F. ........ '40 '74 C.264 B.A. L.284 J.D. P.O. Box 42

## GOLETA, —, *Santa Barbara Co.*

Beluris, Terese A. Mosher ........ '— '83 C.860 B.A. L.426 J.D. Santa Barbara Svgs.
Bowden, Phyllis B. ........ '37 '81 C&L.999 B.S.L., J.D. 654 Dara Rd.
Cavalletto, George A., (AV) '13 '36 C.112 A.B. L.1066 LL.B.
777 Glen Annie Cyn Rd.‡
Eckert, Charles V., III, (BV) ........ '35 '61 C.112 B.A. L.1066 LL.B. 160 N. Fairview Ave.
Gans, W. Carl ........ '49 '89 C.112 B.S.M.E. L.769 J.D. 601 Vereda Leyenda

**Grokenberger & Wilson, A Professional Corporation, (BV)**
**160 North Fairview Avenue Suite 4, 93117⊙**
**Telephone: 805-964-4761 FAX: 805-967-0186**
**James H. Smith.**
**Family Law, Real Estate, Creditor work in Bankruptcy Court, Landlord-Tenant, Shopping Center and Condominium Law. General Business and Civil Litigation, Personal Injury Law, Probate and Estate Planning.**
**Santa Barbara, California Office: La Rinconada Building. 1004 Santa Barbara Street. Telephone: 805-564-1230. Fax: 805-965-2685.**

*See Professional Biographies, GOLETA, CALIFORNIA*

Halperin, Michael L. ........ '52 '76 C.112 B.A. L.809 J.D. 6380 Hollister Ave.
Locke, Robert B. ........ '47 '76 C.112 B.A. L.1137 J.D. 5901 Encina Rd.
Lunsford, Michael R. ........ '45 '92 C.763 B.A. L.769 J.D. 387 B. Cannon Green Dr.
**McGory, Michael P.** ........ '49 '74 C.112 B.A. L.770 J.D. Delco Electronics Corp.
Murray, William G. ........ '31 '64 C.999 B.A.,M.A. L.426 LL.B. 75 Coromar Dr.
**O'Gorman, Barrett Patrick** ........ '64 '90 C.112 B.A. L.426 J.D. [O'Gorman&O.]
*PRACTICE AREAS: Business Law; Finance; Bankruptcy Law; Consumer Finance.
**O'Gorman, C. Brian**, (BV) ........ '41 '66 C.178 A.B. L.1066 LL.B. [O'Gorman&O.]
*PRACTICE AREAS: Business Law; Probate; Finance; Bankruptcy Law.

**O'Gorman & O'Gorman, (BV)**
**Suite B-2, 5901 Encina Road, 93117**
**Telephone: 805-967-1215 FAX: 805-683-2058**
**C. Brian O'Gorman; Barrett Patrick O'Gorman.**
**Business, Probate, Finance and Bankruptcy Law.**

*See Professional Biographies, GOLETA, CALIFORNIA*

Pasternack, Kenneth C. ........ '49 '74 C.103 A.B. L.37 J.D. 966 W. Campus Ln.
Schmitt, Robert G. ........ '44 '76 C.602 A.B. L.312 J.D. Science Applications Intl. Corp.
**Schubert, William C.** '47 '79 C.1031 B.S. L.1066 J.D.
Santa Barbara Research Ctr. (Pat.)

**Smith, James H.**, (BV) ........ '51 '78 C.1060 B.A. L.1188 J.D. [Ⓐ Grokenberger&W.]⊙
*REPORTED CASES: Otanez v. Blue Skies Mobile Home Park (1991) 1 Cal App 4th 1521, 3 Cal. Rptr 2nd 210.
*PRACTICE AREAS: Real Estate; Construction Defects; Civil Litigation.
Tyler, Richard A., (BV) ........ '34 '62 C&L.477 B.S.E.E., LL.B. 160 N. Fairview Ave.
Wallis, Jonny D. ........ '46 '80 C.112 B.A. L.809 J.D. 5701 Gato Ave.‡
Watson, S. Derrin ........ '54 '80 C.101 B.S. L.1068 J.D. 5631 Kent Pl.
Williams, Jerry J., (AV) ........ '31 '62 C.112 A.B. L.1068 J.D. 6647 El Colegio Rd., #B-137

## GRAEAGLE, 1,000, *Plumas Co.*

Heaslett, David J., (BV) ........ '43 '74 C.112 B.A. L.1049 J.D. 7597 Hwy. 89

## GRANADA HILLS, —, *Los Angeles Co.*

(Part of the incorporated City of Los Angeles)

Barazani, Frederic R. ........ '43 '71 C.1077 B.A. L.1049 J.D. 17068 Chatworth St.
Brown, Frank R., (BV) ........ '21 '56 C.623 L.809 11960 Woodley Ave.
Bursk, Bonnie Marie, (AV) ........ '53 '76 C.1077 B.A. L.809 J.D. [Savin&B.]
Coller, Joseph M. ........ '51 '78 C.705 B.A. L.1095 J.D. 10324 Balboa Blvd.
Fagin, Earl H. ........ '41 '71 C.623 B.A. L.426 J.D. 10727 White Oak Ave.
Fox, Craig A. ........ '47 '75 C.894 B.A. L.1049 J.D. [Galindo&F.]
Fuchs, Howard M. ........ '52 '80 C.415 B.A. L.1095 J.D. Dep. City Atty.
Galindo, Marcia ........ '40 '70 [Galindo&F.]
Galindo & Fox ........ 17068 Chatsworth St.
Go, William Robert ........ '49 '77 C.1077 B.A. L.398 J.D. 17428 Chatsworth St.
Grossman, Bernard S., (BV) ........ '26 '56 C.112 B.A. L.426 J.D. 10324 Balboa Blvd.
Grossman, Leslie K., (Mr.) ........ '46 '74 C.112 B.A. L.809 J.D. [Grossman&M.]
Grossman and Mahan ........ 10324 Balboa Blvd.
Harrell, Jonathan E. ........ '52 '92 C.1232 B.A. L.426 J.D. 15600 Devonshire St.
Hoang, Son Thai ........ '57 '86 C.112 B.S. L.426 J.D. 17727 Tuscan Dr.
Jensen, Tamila C. ........ '47 '73 C.112 A.B. L.1067 J.D. 10324 Balboa Blvd.
Koroshec, Frank A., Jr. ........ '49 '77 C.755 B.A. L.1095 J.D. 10324 Balboa Blvd.
Korper, Rene ........ '48 '84 C.112 B.A. L.809 J.D. 17939 Chatsworth St. Ste. 133
Libis, Paul H. ........ '52 '80 C.1077 B.A. L.365 J.D. 17164 Sesnon Blvd.
Mahan, Christopher L. ........ '48 '75 C.1077 B.A. L.1095 J.D. [Grossman&M.]
McArthur, Francis R. '32 '60 C.755 B.A. L.494 J.D.
(adm. in MN; not adm. in CA) 13154 Courbet Ln.‡
Moser, James L., (AV) ........ '35 '70 C&L.1095 B.A., J.D. [Moser&O.]
Moser & Ostling, A Law Corporation, (AV) ........ 12008 Woodley Ave.
Myers, Donald M. ........ '33 '69 C.112 B.A. L.800 J.D. 12284 Woodley Ave.‡
Oliphant, David J. ........ '35 '66 C.1077 B.A. L.426 J.D. 11701 Verada Ave.
Oria, Charlotte ........ '37 '73 17930 Tulsa Pl.‡
Ostling, Herbert F. ........ '31 '71 C.112 B.A. L.809 J.D. [Moser&O.]
Pollack, Sidney L. '08 '32 C&L.597 B.S.L.
(adm. in IL; not adm. in CA) 12451 Jacqueline Pl.
Price, Gerald L., (AV) ........ '38 '65 C.768 B.S. L.30 J.D. P.O. Box 33084 (Pat.)
Price, Isabel, (Mrs.) '42 '66 C.4 L.564 LL.B.
(adm. in IN; not adm. in CA) P.O. Box 33084
Price, Martin J. ........ '56 '90 C.112 B.A. L.426 J.D. 16839 Horace St.
Prockiw, Orest M. '35 '63 C&L.893 B.A., LL.B.
(adm. in VA; not adm. in CA) Promex Corp.
Richards, David L. ........ '52 '82 C.878 B.S. L.1095 J.D. 17037 Chatsworth Ave.
Richards, Linda J. ........ '55 '81 L.1095 J.D. 17037 Chatsworth Ave.
Rink, Lawrence J. ........ '31 '60 C.112 B.S. L.1065 J.D. 10324 Balboa Blvd.
Sacks, Leonard M., (AV) ........ '28 '56 C.823 B.A. L.569 LL.B. 17241 Westbury Dr.
Savin, George J., Jr. ........ '47 '73 C.1042 B.S. L.900 J.D. [Savin&B.]
Savin & Bursk, (AV) ........ 10663 Yarmouth Ave.
Shapiro, Jerry ........ '45 '74 L.1221 J.D. 11214 Balboa Blvd.
Smith, Jack R. ........ '29 '67 C.809 L.398 LL.B. 17715 Chatsworth St.
Stedman, Alfred B. ........ '36 '73 C&L.1095 B.A., J.D. 10324 Balboa Blvd.
Steiker, Andrew R. ........ '51 '84 C.112 B.A. L.426 J.D. 17422 Chatsworth St.
Striff, Harlan D. ........ '31 '75 C.800 B.Mech.E. L.1095 J.D. 12151 Gothic Ave.
Turner, Davidson V. ........ '21 '72 C.800 L.1114 LL.B. 17512 Tuscan Dr.
Von Welzig, Robin R. ........ '— '67 C&L.800 A.B., J.D. 12646 Jimeno Ave.
Weitkamp, Fredrick J., (AV) ........ '27 '53 C.605 A.B. L.800 LL.B. [Weitkamp&W.]
Weitkamp, John F., (AV) ........ '53 '78 C.154 B.A. L.426 J.D. [Weitkamp&W.]
Weitkamp & Weitkamp, (AV) ........ 10724 White Oak Ave.
Wolf, Milton G. ........ '46 '84 C.1033 B.A. L.1148 J.D. 12461 Jacqueline Pl.

## GRAND TERRACE, 10,946, *San Bernardino Co.*

Bird, John D. ........ '42 '88 C.1075 B.S. L.1137 J.D. 22737 Barton Rd.
Fine, Gerald M. '19 '47 C&L.494 B.S.L., LL.B.
(adm. in MN; not adm. in CA) 22387 Tanager‡
Sogomonian, Aram M. ........ '31 '81 C.112 L.1137 J.D. 22365 Barton Rd.

## GRANITE BAY, —, *Placer Co.*

Brooks, Kay Upchurch ........ '56 '82 C.575 B.A. L.846 J.D. 4839 Waterbury Way
Motroni, Adrian R. ........ '35 '61 C.813 B.A. L.1065 J.D. P.O. Box 2025‡
Van Tassell, Sharyn J., (BV) ........ '46 '73 C.999 L.464 J.D. [S.J.Van Tassell]
Van Tassell, Sharyn J., A Law Corporation, (BV) ........ P.O. Box 2609

## GRASS VALLEY, 9,048, *Nevada Co.*

Baker, Stephen C. ........ '54 '83 C.813 B.A. L.1026 J.D. 131 S. Auburn St.
Baldwin, Milton L. ........ '25 '54 C.112 L.767 LL.B. 17709 Friendly Valley Place‡
Bell, Joseph J., (BV) ........ '47 '80 C.549 B.A. L.1230 J.D. 350 Crown Point Circle
Bellows, Ann Armstrong ........ '33 '80 C.569 B.S. L.976 J.D. 21500 Armstrong Rd.
Biddle, Claude L., Jr. ........ '39 '70 L.464 J.D. City Atty.
Brazier, John R. ........ '40 '89 C.174 B.S. L.770 J.D. [Brazier&E.]
Brazier & Erdmann ........ 120 Richardson St.
Browne, P. Scott, (BV) ........ '51 '76 C.976 B.A. L.1065 J.D. 131 S. Auburn St.
Cape, John A. ........ '28 '68 C.172 B.S.C.E. L.464 J.D. 19890 Venus Ct.‡
Caylor, Gary M. ........ '36 '61 C.940 B.A. L.1065 J.D. 120 Richardson St.
**Compton, Charles A.**, (BV) ........ '45 '76 C.813 B.A. L.1065 J.D. [Shine,C.&N.]
*PRACTICE AREAS: Estate Planning/Probate; Business; Personal Injury; Real Estate.
**Curtis, James A.**, (BV) ........ '48 '76 C.112 B.A. L.1137 J.D. [Shine,C.&N.]
*PRACTICE AREAS: Local Government (Public Agency); Land Use; Environmental; Employment.
Daus, Thomas E. ........ '33 '60 C.197 A.B. L.477 J.D. 970 E. Main St.
Davis, Gary D., (BV) ........ '44 '78 C.112 A.B. L.1065 J.D. 226 Colfax Ave.
Diamond, Craig A., (BV) ........ '54 '79 C.112 B.A. L.1065 J.D. 131 S. Auburn St.
Erdmann, Robert C. ........ '39 '89 C.111 Ph.D. L.770 J.D. [Brazier&E.]

**Farrar, Charles R., Jr., Law Offices of, (AV) '46 '72 C.112 A.B. L.1066 J.D.**
**120 Richardson Street, Suite D, 95945**
**Telephone: 916-273-0800 Fax: 916-273-0777 Email: crflawgodl@aol.com**
**Email: cflawgld@oro.net**
**Business and Commercial Transactions and Agreements, General Civil Trial and Appellate Practice, Easements and Real Property Law, Land Use and Environmental Law (C.E.Q.A.), Computer Law, Administrative and Municipal Law and Mediation Law.**

*See Professional Biographies, GRASS VALLEY, CALIFORNIA*

CAA114P

Franchi, Peter A. ............................'17 '62 L.464 LL.B. 17264 Franchi Pl.‡
Gilbert, Martin ....................'33 '67 C.1246 B.A. L.809 LL.B. 10563 Brunswick Rd.
Gottschalk, Michael P., (CV) ..............'51 '78 C.763 B.A. L.1065 J.D. 104 Fiddick Ln.
Hackler, Kristin S., (BV) ...................'46 '81 C.112 B.A. L.284 J.D. 10563 Brunswick
**Hawkins, Richard M.**, (AV) ..............'49 '74 C.112 B.S. L.1065 J.D. [R.M.Hawkins]

**Hawkins, Richard M., A Professional Corporation, (AV)**
**Suite 2, 10563 Brunswick Road, 95945**
**Telephone: 916-272-6733 Fax: 916-272-7861**
**Email: rhawk53@aol.com**
**Richard M. Hawkins (Certified Specialist, Estate Planning, Trust and Probate Law, The State Bar of California Board of Legal Specialization).**
**General Civil Practice, Probate, Estate Administration, Estate Planning, Wills, Trusts, Taxation and Corporate Law.**
***See Professional Biographies, GRASS VALLEY, CALIFORNIA***

Hohns, Christopher C..........................'54 '85 C.999 L.809 J.D. 120 Richardson St.
Honer, James A., (BV) ........ '43 '70 C.112 B.A. L.1066 J.D. 17247 Round Valley Circle
Kalman, Victoria L. ...........................'45 '87 C.740 B.A. L.464 J.D. 10563 Brunswick Rd.
Kamikawa, Janice A.............................'64 '91 C.112 B.A. L.464 J.D. 970 E. Main St.
Keefer, James O. .................................'47 '74 C.112 A.B. L.464 J.D. 113 Presley Way
Kepler, Patricia E., (BV) ...........'28 '71 C.174 A.B. L.1026 J.D. 13854 Garden Bar Rd.
Kierney, Roberta C., (BV) ......................'41 '79 C.999 B.A. L.464 J.D. [Kierney&T.]
Kierney and Thomsen, A Ptnrshp. incl. A Prof. Corp, (BV) ................128 Glasson Way
McGuire, Susan Kay, (CV) .................'57 '91 C.101 L.1026 J.D. 120 Richardson St.
Merritt, John J. ......................................'36 '71 L.1095 J.D. 113 Presley Way
Moore, Gerald L. ......................'32 '60 C.701 B.S.E.E. L.273 J.D. 10190 Luna Dr.‡
Mullane, Frances Hirschmann '43 '79 L.1137 J.D.
Dir., Nevada Co. Legal Assistance, Inc.
**Nelder-Adams, Maralee**, (BV) .............'56 '81 C.112 A.B. L.464 J.D. [Shine,C.&N.]
*LANGUAGES: French.
*PRACTICE AREAS: Family Law.
O'Connell, Francis A., Jr. '14 '39 C&L.262 LL.B.
(adm. in NY; not adm. in CA) 11534 Shockley Rd.‡
Oehler, Philip H. ....................'39 '77 C.197 B.A. L.990 J.D. 16102 Joshuas Horn Rd.
Paduck, Paul, (AV) ........................'11 '38 C.112 A.B. L.1066 LL.B. 10411 Sky Cir.‡

**Roach, Terry A.**
**(See Nevada City)**

Schneider, Richard J. .........................'38 '70 C.768 B.S. L.981 LL.B. P.O. Box 437‡
Schwartz, Stanley E. ..................'23 '52 C.112 B.A. L.1065 J.D. 111 Broadview Ave.‡
**Shine, Raymond E.**, (BV) ..................'48 '73 C.112 B.A. L.1066 J.D. [Shine,C.&N.]
*PRACTICE AREAS: Civil Litigation; Real Estate; Business; Local Government; Land Use.

**Shine, Compton & Nelder-Adams, (BV)**
**131 South Auburn Street, 95945**
**Telephone: 916-272-2686 Fax: 916-272-5570**
**Raymond E. Shine; Charles A. Compton; Maralee Nelder-Adams (Certified Specialist, Family Law, The State Bar of California Board of Legal Specialization); James A. Curtis.**
**General Civil and Real Estate Litigation, Environmental, Land Use, Family Law, Estate Planning/Probate, Business Law, Employment, Government and Public Agency Law and Personal Injury.**
***See Professional Biographies, GRASS VALLEY, CALIFORNIA***

Tassone, Augustine C., (BV) ........................'40 '66 C&L.767 B.S., LL.B. 110 Bank St.
Thompson, J. F. ...................................'48 '78 C.112 B.A. L.464 J.D. 12012 Sutton Way
Thompson, Thomas C.....................'50 '77 C.966 M.B.A. L.770 J.D. 120 Richardson St.
Thomsen, B. Scott ..................................'64 '89 C.1254 B.S. L.464 J.D. [Kierney&T.]
Todd, Leo J. .........................................'23 '51 C.999 L.767 LL.B. 140 Lidster Ave.‡
Toff, Jeffrey R., (BV) ..................'51 '76 C.112 B.A. L.1137 J.D. 10563 Brunswick Rd.
Wilcox, Richard .........................'43 '75 C.768 B.A. L.1026 LL.B. 20661 Post Chaise Circle
Wilkerson, Jennifer L., (BV) ................'55 '83 C.150 B.S. L.597 J.D. 131 S. Auburn St.

## GREENBRAE, —, *Marin Co.*

Adamson, Frank L., (AV) ..................'22 '50 C.178 A.B. L.477 J.D. 40 Corte Toluca St.‡
Andrade, Leo R. ...........................'30 '58 C.800 B.A. L.1065 J.D. 43 Via Cheparro St.
Baxter, J. Shelton '46 '75 C.178 B.A. L.1065 J.D.
(adm. in IL; not adm. in CA) 147 Bon Air Center‡
Bellings, David B. ..............................'53 '81 C.1033 B.S. L.809 J.D. 3 Los Cerros Dr.
**Brekhus, Matthew D.** ....................'60 '85 C.112 B.A. L.464 J.D. [Ⓐ Brekhus,W.W.&H.]
**Brekhus, Peter B.**, (AV) ..............'39 '65 C.767 B.S. L.1355 J.D. [Brekhus,W.W.&H.]⊙

**Brekhus, Williams, Wester & Hall, (AV)**
**1000 Drakes Landing Road, 94904⊙**
**Telephone: 415-461-1000 Fax: 415-461-7356**
**Members of Firm: Peter B. Brekhus; Scott A. Williams; Barry F. Wester; Robert P. Hall, Jr. Associates: Matthew D. Brekhus; Linda J. Philipps; Paula M. Weaver; Stacey Ann Lucas.**
**Civil Litigation and Appellate Practice. Insurance, Construction, Landslide and Subsidence, Personal Injury, Inverse Condemnation and Eminent Domain, Municipal and Zoning Law.**
**San Francisco, California Office: 44 Montgomery Street, Suite 1000, 94104-4612. Telephone: 415-296-9962.**
***See Professional Biographies, GREENBRAE, CALIFORNIA***

Brown, Linda J., (AV) ............'46 '72 C.228 B.A. L.1065 J.D. 100 Drakes Landing Rd.
Cohen, Melvin ..........................................'15 '39 C&L.145 A.B., J.D. 1131 S. Eliseo Dr.
Critchlow, Richard K. .....................'39 '66 C.112 B.A. L.1065 LL.B. [Critchlow&D.]
Critchlow & Diskint ........................................................300 Drakes Landing Rd.
**Diller, Nicole A.** .................................'66 '91 C.477 B.G.S. L.813 J.D. [Mills]
*PRACTICE AREAS: Civil RICO; Trust Litigation; Fiduciary Law; Consumer Class Action; Unfair Competition.
Diskint, Robert .......................................................................'45 '70 [Critchlow&D.]
Donovan, Leo T. ...........................'30 '61 C&L.846 B.B.A., LL.B. 44 El Portal Dr.
Giles, Frederic P. ...............'36 '70 C.813 B.A. L.1066 J.D. 511 Sir Francis Drake Blvd.‡
Graber, Peter H. F. ........................'31 '62 C.112 B.A. L.1066 LL.B. 138 Altura Way
Greene, Barbara Z. ............................'55 '80 C.856 B.A. L.770 J.D. 23 Corte Morada
Greene, Kenneth C., (BV) ...... '55 '80 C.1036 B.A. L.770 J.D. [Richman,L.M.G.C.F.&P.]
**Hall, Robert P., Jr.** ......................'52 '81 C.112 B.S. L.765 J.D. [Brekhus,W.W.&H.]⊙
**Howard, Derek G.** ...........................................'58 '85 C.659 B.A. L.284 J.D. [Mills]
*LANGUAGES: German.
*PRACTICE AREAS: Unfair Competition; Unfair Trade; Business Fraud; Consumer Class Actions; Civil Litigation.
Jones, Karen L. ......................'62 '89 C.1169 B.A. L.1067 J.D. 300 Drakes Landing Rd.
**Kohn, Richard S.** '42 '68 C.882 B.A. L.94 J.D.
(adm. in DC; not adm. in CA) [Mills]
*PRACTICE AREAS: Appellate Practice; Constitutional Law; Civil Rights; Consumer Fraud.
**Levenson, Lloyd S.** .............................................'59 '86 C.309 A.B. L.93 J.D. [Mills]
*LANGUAGES: French.
*PRACTICE AREAS: Commercial Litigation; Consumer Class Actions; Securities Class Action.
Long, Bertram M. '14 '42 C&L.339 A.B., LL.B.
(adm. in IL; not adm. in CA) 9015 S. Eliseo‡
**Lucas, Stacey Ann** .................'57 '91 C.112 B.A. L.767 J.D. [Ⓐ Brekhus,W.W.&H.]
**Luchenitser, Alexander J.** ......................................'69 '95 C.309 A.B. L.813 J.D. [Mills]
*LANGUAGES: Russian.
**Mills, Robert W.** ..................................................'49 '74 C.112 B.A. L.284 J.D. [Mills]
*PRACTICE AREAS: Consumer Class Actions; Business Fraud; Fiduciary Law; Business Litigation.

**Mills Firm, The**
**300 Drakes Landing, Suite 155, 94904**
**Telephone: 415-464-4770 Fax: 415-464-4777**
**Email: millsfrm@microweb.com**
**Robert W. Mills; Derek G. Howard; Richard S. Kohn (Not admitted in CA); Gilmur R. Murray; Lloyd S. Levenson; Nicole A. Diller; Steven R. Rhoads; Alexander J. Luchenitser.**
**Class Actions in Partnerships, Trusts, Securities, Consumer Fraud, Mass Torts, and Environmental Cases. General Civil and Trial Practice in all courts.**
***See Professional Biographies, GREENBRAE, CALIFORNIA***

**Murray, Gilmur R.** ..........................................'54 '83 C.145 A.B. L.1066 J.D. [Mills]
*PRACTICE AREAS: Unfair Competition; Unfair Trade; Business Fraud; Consumer Class Actions; Contract Fraud.
**Philipps, Linda J.** ..................'49 '83 C.1169 A.B. L.1066 J.D. [Ⓐ Brekhus,W.W.&H.]
**Rhoads, Steven R.** ..................................'57 '82 C.112 B.A. L.284 J.D. [Mills]
*PRACTICE AREAS: Unfair Business Practices; Business Litigation; Business Torts; Consumer Class Actions; Civil Litigation.
Richman, Lawrence, Mann, Greene, Chizever, Friedman & Phillips, A Professional Corporation, (AV)
300 Drakes Landing Rd. (⊙Beverly Hills)
Sammis, Robert J. ...........................'46 '71 C.112 B.A. L.477 J.D. 5 Corte Gracitas
Waldman, Susan K. '54 '80 C.477 B.A. L.94 J.D.
(adm. in MA; not adm. in CA) 79 Corte Baristo‡
**Weaver, Paula M.** ..................'53 '80 C.112 A.B. L.767 J.D. [Ⓐ Brekhus,W.W.&H.]
**Wester, Barry F.** ...................'53 '82 C.770 B.A. L.1065 J.D. [Brekhus,W.W.&H.]⊙
Whetstone, Martha Z. ...................'52 '86 C.45 B.S.E. L.767 J.D. 15 Via Hermosa
White, Wayne H., (AV) ..................'37 '62 C.878 B.S. L.1065 J.D. 271 Via Barranca
**Williams, Scott A.**, (BV) ............'48 '77 C.147 B.A. L.464 J.D. [Brekhus,W.W.&H.]⊙
Zubowski Bell, Linda '59 '90 C.354 B.A. L.776 J.D.
(adm. in NJ; not adm. in CA) 300 Drakes Landing, Ste 155

## GREENFIELD, 7,464, *Monterey Co.*

Roy, Donald E. ..........................................'45 '80 C.454 B.A. L.1095 J.D. Drawer 6

## GREENVILLE, 1,537, *Plumas Co.*

Kearns, William G. ..................................'42 '73 C.602 B.A. L.800 J.D. 220 Main St.

## GRIDLEY, 4,631, *Butte Co.*

Baggett, Joseph W. ..................................'52 '84 C.502 B.A. L.767 J.D. 660 Ohio St.
Harris, John T., (BV) ...........................'41 '66 C.112 A.B. L.1066 J.D. [Harris&S.]
Harris & Sanford, (BV) ..........................................................................660 Ohio St.
Jones, G. Steven ........................................'49 '75 C.101 L.464 J.D. P.O. Box 756‡
McNelis, Steven R. .................................'46 '75 C.147 B.A. L.809 J.D. Jus. Ct. J.
Millington, Robert, (BV) ..................'21 '50 C&L.813 A.B., J.D. [Millington&M.]
Millington & Millington, (BV) ...............................................446 Kentucky St.
Sanford, Thomas G., (BV) ....................'45 '74 C.112 B.A. L.1067 J.D. [Harris&S.]

## GRIZZLY FLAT, 150, *El Dorado Co.*

Grimes, Stewart '47 '81 C&L.93 B.A., J.D.
(adm. in MA; not adm. in CA) P.O. Box 328‡

## GROVELAND, 2,050, *Tuolumne Co.*

Gaarde, Ralph E., (BV) '38 '67 C.112 B.S. L.1132
11833 Powderhouse Rd. (⊙Modesto)
Jeffrey, R. Asahel ..................................'46 '88 C.770 B.S. L.284 J.D. Sursum Corda
Patrick, Dean R. ..................'24 '72 C.768 A.B. L.1026 J.D. 19976 Ridgecrest Way

## GROVER BEACH, —, *San Luis Obispo Co.*

Clark, Clifford H., (BV) ..............................'27 '51 C.508 L.800 J.D. 230 N. 9th St.
Norman, Roy A. .....................................'50 '75 C&L.802 B.B.A., J.D. 200 S. 13th St.

**Stockwell, Harris, Widom & Woolverton, A Professional Corporation, (AV)**
**Suite 307, 200 South 13th Street, 93433⊙**
**Telephone: 805-473-0720 Fax: 805-473-0635**
**Michael L. Terry (Managing Attorney).**
**Workers Compensation Insurance and Employment Matters.**
**Los Angeles, California Office: 6222 Wilshire Boulevard, Sixth Floor, P.O. Box 48917. Telephone: 213-935-6669; 818-784-6222; 310-277-6669. Fax: 213-935-0198.**
**San Bernardino, California Office: Suite 303, 215 North "D" Street. Telephone: 909-381-5553. Fax: 909-384-9981.**
**Santa Ana, California Office: Suite 500, 2551 N. Tustin Avenue, P.O. Box 11979. Telephone: 714-479-1180. Fax: 714-479-1190.**
**Ventura, California Office: 2021 Sperry Avenue, Suite 46. Telephone: 805-654-8994; 213-617-7290. Fax: 805-654-1546.**
**San Diego, California Office: Suite 400, 402 West Broadway. Telephone: 619-235-6054. Fax: 619-231-0129.**
***See Professional Biographies, GROVER BEACH, CALIFORNIA***

**Terry, Michael L.** ..................'49 '81 C.1097 B.A. L.426 J.D. [Stockwell,H.W.&W.]

## GROVER CITY, 11,656, *San Luis Obispo Co.*

Bass, James M. ..............................'50 '76 C&L.800 B.A., J.D. Workers Comp. J.
Herreras, William A., (BV) .....................'41 '67 C&L.426 B.A., LL.B. [W.A.Herreras]
Herreras, William A., A Prof. Law Corp., (BV) ...............................................P.O. Box 387
Koenen, Nita H., (CV) ..............................'35 '80 C.352 B.A. L.1186 230 N. 9th St.
LeCover, Michael .............................'51 '76 C.800 B.S. L.426 J.D. Worker's Comp. J.

## GUADALUPE, 5,479, *Santa Barbara Co.*

Quandt, Richard S. '49 '79 C.112 B.A. L.61 J.D.
Pres. & Gen. Coun., Grower-Shipper Vegetable Assn.

## GUALALA, —, *Mendocino Co.*

Cline, E. Roderick, (AV) ....................'36 '65 C&L.813 B.S., LL.B. P.O. Box 532 (Pat.)
Harrington, James H. ..........................'32 '56 C&L.502 B.A., LL.B. P.O. Box 447
Lizarraga, Frank J., Jr., Law Offices of ....'58 '87 C.398 B.A. L.1137 J.D. P.O. Box 1152
Reynolds, Robert L. ...................................'26 '67 L.464 J.D. 45575 Pacific Woods Rd.

## GUSTINE, 3,931, *Merced Co.*

Sousa, Bruce B. ......................................'51 '76 C&L.770 B.A., J.D. 306 5th St.

## HACIENDA HEIGHTS, 35,969, *Los Angeles Co.*

Agnihotri, Varun ...............................'60 '90 C&L.061 B.A., J.D. 15454 E. Gale Ave.
Bragg, Lawrence C. ............................'32 '63 C&L.112 B.S., LL.B. [L.C.Bragg]
Bragg, Lawrence C., Prof. Law Corp. .............................................15454 E. Gale Ave.
Brearley, David B. .......................................'41 '70 C.1097 L.1065 J.D. City Atty.
Chao, Calvin E. ...............'35 '65 C.112 B.A. L.426 LL.B. 15333 Mockingbird Hill Dr.
Chaparro, Reynaldo ...................'20 '64 C.800 B.S. L.809 LL.B. Ret. Mun. Ct. J.‡
Davis, John W. ........................................'23 '56 C&L.809 J.D. 3130 El Sebo

CAA115P

CALIFORNIA—HACIENDA HEIGHTS MARTINDALE-HUBBELL LAW DIRECTORY 1997

DeNorch, Daniel J. '12 '55 L.809 LL.B. 17078 E. Colima Rd.‡
Elhai, Del Decker '31 '78 C.621 B.A. L.1137 J.D. [Elhai&M.]
Elhai & McIntosh 1201 S. Hacienda Blvd.
Fierro, Arturo N. '60 '89 C.169 B.A. L.309 J.D. 15454 E. Gale Ave.
Fitzsimons, J. David '31 '67 C.684 A.B. L.61 J.D. 2440 S. Hacienda Blvd.
Garrity, Melissa L. '58 '83 C.112 B.A. L.426 J.D. 2936 Sisal Pl.
McIntosh, Owen L. '51 '79 C.1075 B.A. L.398 J.D. [Elhai&M.]
Nielsen, Kenneth P. '46 '78 C.1042 B.A. L.1136 J.D. 2440 Hacienda Blvd.
Ovieda, James G. '54 '91 C.1049 B.A. L.940 J.D. 34025 Hacienda Blvd.
Pennington, Laurence M. '19 '64 L.809 LL.B. 15735 La Subida Dr., Apt 1
Sackett, Harry E., Jr., (AV) '06 '31 C&L.546 B.A., LL.B. 901 S. 6th Ave.‡
White, William H. '39 '65 C&L.878 B.S., J.D. 2849 Sierra Canyon Way

## HALF MOON BAY, 8,886, *San Mateo Co.*

Bredenbeck, Arthur H., (AV) '39 '64 C&L.813 A.B., J.D. 60 San Andreas Ave.‡
Cherniss, David A. '54 '79 C.112 B.A. L.61 J.D. 225 S. Cabrillo Hwy. (⊙Moreno Valley)
Ferenz, Walter S. '26 '55 C.112 A.B. L.1065 J.D. 225 Cabrillo Hwy., S.‡
Firestone, Marvin H., & Associates '39 '81 C.645 B.S. L.174 J.D. 225 S. Cabrillo Hwy. Ste. 105-D
Gananian, Jeffrey S. '59 '86 C.800 B.A. L.61 J.D. Gen. Coun., Alternative Systems, Inc. (Pat.)
Garrison, Gregg S. '56 '89 C.805 B.A. L.802 J.D. [Garrison]
Garrison Law Corporation, P.C. 691 Myrtle St.

**Jones, Bryan, (BV) '31 '57 C.674 A.B. L.813 LL.B.**
**Shoreline Station, 225 S. Cabrillo Highway, Suite 111C, P.O. Box 967, 94019-0967⊙**
**Telephone: 415-726-7578 Fax: 415-726-9068**
**(Certified Specialist, Estate Planning, Trust and Probate Law, The State Bar of California Board of Legal Specialization).**
**Practice Limited to Estate Planning, Trust and Probate Law and Related Litigation, Real Estate Transactions.**
**Palo Alto, California Office: Embarcadero Suites 2465 East Bayshore Road. Telephone: 415-856-2211. Fax: 415-726-9068.**

Kahan, Joel '42 '69 C.685 B.A. L.813 LL.B. P.O. Box 968
Koenig, Carol '57 '85 C.766 B.A. L.767 J.D. 725 Main St.
Roma, Patricia, (CV) '43 '72 C.966 B.A. L.284 J.D. 745 Mill St.
Schur, Robert E. '59 '85 C&L.174 B.A., J.D. 225 S. Cabrillo Hwy.
Sponsler, Margret A. G. '— '82 L.1026 LL.B. 700 Mill St.
Weistrop, Harry '18 '59 C&L.569 B.A., LL.B. 890 Main St.

## HANFORD, * 30,897, *Kings Co.*

Altimus, Richard D., (CV) '56 '82 C.1074 B.S. L.809 J.D. 422 N. Douty St.
Barnes, Steven D. '49 '80 C.267 B.S. L.1137 J.D. P.O. Box 448
Behrens, Robert K., (BV) '42 '72 C.267 B.S. L.1065 J.D. [Behrens,S.&R.]
Behrens, Snyder & Romaine, (BV) 522 N. Redington St.
Berrett, Ralph E. '27 '76 C.878 B.S. L.1137 J.D. 425 W. Seventh St.
Bissig, Louis F. '45 '71 C.267 B.S. L.1067 J.D. Supr. Ct. J.
Buckley, Timothy S. '45 '73 C.112 A.B. L.770 J.D. Ct. of Apps. Jus.
Bumsted, Edmund J. '16 '58 C.112 B.A. L.809 LL.B. P.O. Box 71 (Pat.)
Byrd, Thomas R. '35 '86 C.160 B.S. L.1137 J.D. 5613 N. 11th Ave.‡
Caietti, Robert A. '36 '74 L.1026 J.D. Dep. Dist. Atty.

**Calhoun, Ronald L., Law Office of, (BV) '52 '88 L.1189 J.D.**
**607 North Douty Street, P.O. Box 1071, 93232-1071**
**Telephone: 209-587-0486 Fax: 209-587-0492**
**Civil Litigation and Family Law.**

**Conway, Richard C.**, (BV) '53 '78 C.112 B.A. L.1137 J.D. [Kahn,S.&C.]
DeSantos, Thomas, (CV) '56 '81 C.813 B.A. L.800 J.D. [Farley&D.]⊙
Dilling, Jas. R., (AV) '15 '53 C.813 A.B. L.765 LL.B. 544 E. Grangeville Blvd.
Doan, Glenda K., (BV) '44 '75 C.950 B.A. L.1189 J.D. Jus. Ct. J.
**Dowd, Robert M.**, (AV) '46 '76 C.766 B.A. L.61 J.D. [Griswold,L.C.D.&G.]
*PRACTICE AREAS: Civil Litigation; Agricultural Cooperative Law.
**Edwards, Randy L.** '53 '82 C.172 B.A. L.464 J.D. [Griswold,L.C.D.&G.]
*PRACTICE AREAS: Criminal; Civil Litigation.
Fadenrecht, Anne C. '57 '86 C.112 B.A. L.464 J.D. 422 N. Douty St.
Fadenrecht, Daniel M., (BV) '20 '48 C.112 B.A. L.813 J.D. 422 N. Douty St.
Farley, Michael L., (BV) '50 '75 C.838 B.S. L.802 J.D. [Farley&D.]⊙
Farley & DeSantos, (BV) 104 E. 7th St. (⊙Visalia)
**Gin, Robert W.**, (BV) '48 '82 C.1074 B.S. L.464 J.D. [Griswold,L.C.D.&G.]
*REPORTED CASES: Tos v. Mayfair Packing Co., 160 Cal App. 3rd 67, 206 Cal Rptr. 459; Plaza Tulare v. Tradewell Stores, Inc., 207 Cal App. 3rd 522, 254 Cal Rptr. 792.
*PRACTICE AREAS: Environmental Law; Corporate and Administrative Law; Business Transactions; Probate and Trusts.
**Griswold, Craig** '45 '84 C.112 B.A. L.1026 J.D. [Griswold,L.C.D.&G.]
*LANGUAGES: French.
*PRACTICE AREAS: Water Law; Agricultural Cooperative Law; Business Law.
**Griswold, Lyman D.**, (AV) '14 '40 C.112 A.B. L.1066 LL.B. [Griswold,L.C.D.&G.] ‡

**Griswold, LaSalle, Cobb, Dowd & Gin, L.L.P., (AV) [B]**
**311 North Douty Street, 93230**
**Telephone: 209-584-6656 Facsimile: 209-582-3106**
**Lyman D. Griswold (Retired); Steven W. Cobb (1947-1993). Members of Firm: Michael E. LaSalle; Robert M. Dowd; Robert W. Gin; Randy L. Edwards; Craig Griswold. Associates: Jack G. Willis; Jim D. Lee; Jeffrey L. Levinson; A. David Medeiros. Of Counsel: Julienne L. Rynda.**
**General Civil, Criminal, Trial and Appellate Practice in all State, Federal and Military Courts. Administrative, Environmental Law, Agricultural, Bankruptcy, Corporation, Creditors Rights, Estate Planning, Family Law, Insurance, Land Use, Oil and Gas, Personal Injury, Probate, Real Estate, Taxation, Water Rights, Workers Compensation and Zoning Law.**
**Representative Clients: Badasci Land Leveling, Inc.; David A. Bush, Inc.; Calcot, Ltd.; Kings County Housing Authority; Kings County Water District; Silvas Oil Co.; Stone Land Co.; Western Waste Industries; World Wide Sires, Inc.**
***See Professional Biographies, HANFORD, CALIFORNIA***

**Hardcastle, V. Wayne**, (BV) '51 '77 C.1212 B.A. L.1049 J.D. [Maroot,H.&H.]⊙
*PRACTICE AREAS: Personal Injury Law; Civil Litigation; Criminal Defense Law; Family Law.
**Hatherley, Dale J.**, (CV) '50 '77 C.112 B.A. L.1049 J.D. [Maroot,H.&H.]
*PRACTICE AREAS: Family Law; Bankruptcy Law; Personal Injury Law.
Hazen, William A. '38 '86 C.911 B.A. L.1189 J.D. 707 N. Douty
Helart, Gayle L. '65 '91 C.1165 B.A. L.61 J.D. Dep. Dist. Atty.

**Helding, Neil A., (AV) '34 '60 C.267 A.B. L.1065 J.D.**
**623 West Grangeville Boulevard, P.O. Box 1190, 93232**
**Telephone: 209-584-6601 Fax: 209-584-6375**
**General Civil and Trial Practice in all Courts. Personal Injury, Family, Corporation, Real Property, Estate Planning, Probate, Water Rights, Creditors Rights and Bankruptcy Law.**
***See Professional Biographies, HANFORD, CALIFORNIA***

Jahn, James H. '46 '78 C.763 B.S. L.809 J.D. Dep. Dist. Atty.
Jennings, Charles W., (AV) '14 '50 C.35 A.B. L.1065 J.D. 117 N. Irwin St.‡
Jones, Ronald Paul '47 '85 C.1074 B.S. L.94 J.D. 219 N. Douty St.

**Kahn, Jan L.**, (BV) '44 '73 C.267 B.A. L.464 J.D. [Kahn,S.&C.]

**Kahn, Soares & Conway, (BV)**
**Old Phone Building, 219 North Douty Street, P.O. Box 1376, 93230⊙**
**Telephone: 209-584-3337 Fax: 209-584-3348**
**Members of Firm: Jan L. Kahn (Resident); George H. Soares (Resident, Sacramento Office); Richard C. Conway; Michael J. Noland; Dale A. Stern (Resident, Sacramento Office).**
**General Civil and Trial Practice in State and Federal Courts. Personal Injury, Agricultural, Water, Environmental, Business, Corporation, Administrative, Real Property, Municipal Law, Land Use, Labor and Employment, Estate Planning and Probate Law, Government Relations.**
**In addition to the partners listed below, the firm currently employs four associates in the Hanford office, and three associates in the Sacramento office. The firm also retains Jack C. Parnell, former Deputy Secretary, United States Department of Agriculture, as a government relations advisor, resident in Sacramento and Washington, D.C.**
**Representative Clients: Beacon Oil Co.; Overland Stock Yards, Inc.**
**Reference: Bank of America (Hanford Branch).**
**Sacramento, California Office: Suite 200, 1112 "I" Street. Telephone: 916-448-3826. Fax: 916-448-3850.**
***See Professional Biographies, HANFORD, CALIFORNIA***

**Kimble, MacMichael & Upton, A Professional Corporation**
**(See Fresno)**

Kirkland, Kathryn '43 '77 C.112 B.A. L.1049 J.D. Dep. Dist. Atty. III
**LaSalle, Michael E.**, (BV) '45 '71 C.267 B.S. L.1067 J.D. [Griswold,L.C.D.&G.]
*PRACTICE AREAS: Estate, Probate and Trust Planning; Business Transactions (Agriculture).
Lee, Jennifer A. '65 '92 C.267 B.S. L.464 J.D. 311 N. Douty St.
**Lee, Jim D.** '50 '92 C.267 B.A. L.999 J.D. [Griswold,L.C.D.&G.]
*LANGUAGES: French.
*PRACTICE AREAS: Business Law; Civil Litigation.
**Levinson, Jeffrey L.** '55 '93 C.112 B.A. L.1189 J.D. [Griswold,L.C.D.&G.]
*PRACTICE AREAS: Civil Litigation; Creditor's Rights; Business Law.
Markle, Deanna L. '67 '92 C.999 B.A. L.1065 J.D. 219 N. Douty St.
**Maroot, K. Phillip**, (BV) '36 '62 C.668 B.A. L.813 J.D. [Maroot,H.&H.]⊙
*PRACTICE AREAS: Estate Planning; Probate Law; Corporate and Business Law; Real Estate Law.

**Maroot, Hardcastle & Hatherley, (BV)**
**429 North Redington Street, P.O. Box 1759, 93232-1759⊙**
**Telephone: 209-584-0131 Fax: 209-584-7625**
**K. Phillip Maroot; V. Wayne Hardcastle; Dale J. Hatherley (Certified Specialist, Family Law, The State Bar of California Board of Legal Specialization). Associate: John M. Melikian.**
**General Civil, Criminal, Trial and Appellate Practice. Estate Planning, Probate, Corporation, Partnerships, Family, Creditors Rights, Personal Injury and Water Rights Law. Employment Litigation, Bankruptcy, Domestic Relations, Real Property Law.**
**Visalia, California Office: 1001 North Demaree. Telephone: 209-734-3540.**
***See Professional Biographies, HANFORD, CALIFORNIA***

McCartney, James J. '23 '50 C&L.724 LL.B. 938 Lakewood Dr.‡
McCormick, Mark D. '59 '84 C&L.861 B.A., J.D. 525 W. 3rd.
McInturff, Patrick S. '46 '76 [Behrens,S.&R.]
**Medeiros, A. David** '62 '88 C.1074 B.A. L.464 J.D. [Griswold,L.C.D.&G.]
*PRACTICE AREAS: Civil Litigation; Business Litigation; Insurance; Personal Injury.
Medeiros, Joan M. '55 '93 C.112 B.A. L.464 J.D. 1006 4th St. 10th Fl.
**Melikian, John M.** '61 '90 C.267 B.S. L.1067 J.D. [Maroot,H.&H.]
*PRACTICE AREAS: Civil Litigation; Family Law; Corporate Law.
Meyer, Laurence E., (CV) '58 '88 C.267 B.S. L.1189 J.D. 117 N. Irwin
Murphy, Trudy Voigt '68 '93 C.884 B.A. L.128 J.D. 219 N. Douty St.
**Noland, Michael J.**, (BV) '53 '78 C.169 B.A. L.1137 J.D. [Kahn,S.&C.]
Norcross, Joe L. '50 '75 C.1130 B.A. L.990 J.D. 1048 E. Hoover Way
O'Rourke, John G. '35 '64 C.602 B.S. L.1065 J.D. Mun. Ct. J.

**Robinson, Palmer & Logan**
**(See Bakersfield)**

Romaine, William A., (CV) '55 '86 C.05 B.A. L.464 J.D. [Behrens,S.&R.]
Rosson, Robt R. '10 '36 C.112 B.A. L.1066 LL.B. Ret. Supr. Ct. J.
**Rynda, Julienne L.**, (BV) '53 '79 C.1042 B.A. L.1067 J.D. [Griswold,L.C.D.&G.]
*PRACTICE AREAS: Family Law; Children; Wills; Probate; Contracts.
Schultz, Peter M. '49 '74 C.813 A.B. L.1065 J.D. Supr. Ct. J.
Sharp, Sidney J. W., Jr., (BV) '34 '62 C.267 A.B. L.813 J.D. 429 N. Redington St.
Snyder, Thomas R., (CV) '45 '82 C.267 B.A. L.1189 J.D. [Behrens,S.&R.]
Trapp, Robert, Jr. '44 '72 C.112 B.A. L.1049 J.D. Dep. Dist. Atty.
Vierra, Manuel N., (BV) '43 '72 C.267 B.A. L.1132 310 N. Irwin St.

**Wild, Carter & Tipton**
**(See Fresno)**

**Willis, Jack G.** '47 '90 C.813 B.A. L.1189 J.D. [Griswold,L.C.D.&G.]
*PRACTICE AREAS: Business Law; Civil Litigation.
Woodbury, Michael R. '49 '77 C.112 B.A. L.1137 J.D. 823 N. Douty

## HARBOR CITY, —, *Los Angeles Co.*

(Part of the incorporated City of Los Angeles)

Hanover, G. Norden '42 '79 C.705 B.S.I.E. L.426 J.D. Corp. Pat. Coun., Judco Mfg., Inc.
Maltun, Dana R. '51 '78 C.940 B.A. L.809 J.D. 25311 S. Normandie Ave.

## HAWAIIAN GARDENS, 13,639, *Los Angeles Co.*

Schorr, Lawrence, (BV) '26 '57 C.205 A.B. L.1009 J.D. 12144-H Carson St.
Siegel, Eugene M., (BV) '49 '79 C.415 B.A. L.1137 J.D. 12144-H Carson St.

## HAWTHORNE, 71,349, *Los Angeles Co.*

Adamson, Stephen Michael '46 '73 C.800 B.A. L.809 J.D. City Atty.
Barbieri, Patricia '57 '88 C.378 B.A. L.1137 J.D. Fed. Aviation Admn., Off. of Asst. Chief Coun.
Busch, Carl J. '49 '77 C.93 B.S. L.809 J.D. Div. Coun.; Military Aircraft Div., Northrop Grumman Corp.
Chavez, Donald J. '62 '90 C.560 B.B.A. L.809 LL.M. Coun., Northrop Grumman Corp.
Epstein, Margaret Lynn '50 '87 C.112 A.B. L.1068 J.D. Coun., Northrop Grumman Corp.
Everett, Carmen Zervigon '64 '90 C&L.724 B.A., J.D. (adm. in CT; not adm. in CA) Fed. Aviation Admin. (Western-Pacific)
Fine, Bonnie N., (AV) '49 '75 C.112 B.A. L.800 J.D. [Fine&W.]
Fine & Woliung, A Professional Corporation, (AV) 5155 Rosecrans Blvd., Ste. 210
Gehringer, Mickeal S. '52 '85 C.147 B.A. L.61 J.D. Northrop Corp.
Gordon, Mark S. '58 '85 C.139 B.A. L.1137 J.D. Dep. City Atty.
Grieves, Richard W. '37 '67 C.674 B.A. L.1066 LL.B. Sr. Corp. Coun., Northrop Corp.
Keel, A. B. '23 '54 C.112 B.S. L.800 LL.B. 13527 Hawthorne Blvd.‡
Konell, Suzan V. '57 '92 C.1042 B.S. L.809 J.D. Gen. Coun., Robt. F. Kennedy Med. Ctr.
Lukacovic, Perry '48 '79 C.1042 B.A. L.770 J.D. Pres., Western Silversmiths
Marapese, Kenneth, (BV) '31 '57 L.426 J.D. 4477 W. 118th St.
Miller, Mark F. '54 '80 C.950 B.A. L.678 J.D. (adm. in WA; not adm. in CA) Northrop Corp.

CAA116P

**Nathanson, Janet L., Law Offices of '28 '82 C.112 B.A. L.1179 J.D.**
**13731 South Rossburn Avenue, 90250-6461**
**Telephone: 310-643-6247 Fax: 310-643-7271**
***PRACTICE AREAS: Elder Law; Estate Planning; Wills; Trust Law; Government Law.**
**Elder Law, Public Benefits, Probate and Estate Planning.**
***See Professional Biographies, HAWTHORNE, CALIFORNIA***

Paepke, Gail C. ........ '51 '84 C.1097 B.A.S.W. L.809 J.D. Vista Bay Med. Grp.
Pope, Ralph K. ........ '51 '77 C.999 B.A. L.818 J.D. Sr. Coun., Northrop Grumman Corp.
Rasmussen, Robert G. ....... '39 '74 C.911 B.S.E.E. L.1136 J.D. 12841 S. Hawthorne Blvd.
Renetzky, Martin ........ '47 '73 C.800 B.A. L.809 J.D. 14120 Hawthorne Blvd.
Simon, Carol Bremer ........ '51 '81 C.1060 B.A. L.464 J.D. [Simon&S.]⊙
Simon, David E. ........ '43 '69 C.112 B.S. L.800 J.D. [Simon&S.]⊙
Simon & Simon, Ltd. ........ 4477 W. 118th St., Suite 101 (⊙Manahattan Beach)
Wiczynski, Marilyn Ann, (BV) ........ '42 '79 C.851 B.A. L.1179 J.D. Dep. City Atty.
Woliung, Martha J., (AV) ........ '54 '79 C.150 B.A. L.426 J.D. [Fine&W.]

## HAYWARD, 111,498, *Alameda Co.*

**Adkins, Armand P.** ........ '69 '95 C.112 B.A. L.1065 J.D. [A W.W.Haskell&Assoc.]
*PRACTICE AREAS: Insurance Defense; General Civil Litigation; Insurance Coverage Law.
Akana, Michael P. ........ '51 '78 C.312 B.A. L.1049 J.D. [Akana&Y.]
Akana & Yee ........ 22693 Hesperian Blvd.
Allan, Laura J. ........ '64 '89 C.1169 B.A. L.813 J.D. 225 W. Winton
Anderson, Ernest L. ........ '41 '70 L.93 J.D. 22673 Hesperian Blvd.
Appleby, Seymour R. ........ '24 '79 C.339 B.S. L.1197 J.D. 1290 "B" St.‡
Arriola, Joseph T., (BV) ........ '56 '80 C.112 B.A. L.1065 J.D. 1065 "A" St.

**Bailin, Richard H., (AV) '35 '61 C.477 B.B.A. L.309 LL.B.**
**21790 Hesperian Boulevard, 94541-7003**
**Telephone: 510-783-5300 Fax: 510-782-3082**
**Real Estate, Business, Corporate, Estate Planning and Probate Law.**
***See Professional Biographies, HAYWARD, CALIFORNIA***

Baker, Raymond N., (BV) ........ '26 '51 C.659 A.B. L.1065 J.D. 770 A St.
Bell, Jaynelle K. ........ '53 '91 C.112 A.B. L.1065 J.D. Dep. City Atty.
Bequette, Todd L. ........ '65 '91 C.464 B.A. L.276 J.D. [A García&S.]
Bernhardt, Paul R., (AV) ........ '30 '61 C.112 B.S. L.1066 LL.B. 350 Winton Ave.
Biasotti, David E., (BV) ........ '41 '66 C.740 B.A. L.1065 J.D. 350 Winton Ave.
Bonjour, Jules F., Jr., (AV) ........ '39 '66 C.597 B.S. L.1066 J.D. [Bonjour&T.]
Bonjour & Thorman, (AV) ........ 24301 Southland Drive
Briegleb, John P., (BV) ........ '22 '50 C.112 L.1065 J.D. 21565 Foothill Blvd.‡
Browner, Betty J., (BV) ........ '18 '69 C.1073 B.A. L.1065 J.D. [Browner,P.&S.]
Browner, Pulido & Sheehan, (AV) ........ 1290 "B" St.
Bruno, Harry R., Jr. ........ '49 '75 C.112 B.A. L.1065 J.D. 25199 Campus Dr.
Carballo, Tony E., (CV) ........ '54 '83 C.1073 B.S. L.770 J.D. 338 Jackson St.
Cardoza, Rafael Y., (BV) ........ '42 '78 C.112 A.B. L.1066 J.D. 1065 "A" St.
Castle, Linval B. ........ '20 '67 C.813 A.B. L.809 J.D. 22693 Hesperian Blvd. (Pat.)‡
Dalby, Robert A. ........ '58 '87 C.112 B.A. L.284 J.D. 24808 Mission Blvd.
Davis & Dorward, (AV) ........ 1065 "A" St.
di Bene, John S. '61 '88 C.17 B.A. L.276 J.D.
(adm. in DC; not adm. in CA) 1290 B St., Suite 218
Doctors, Samuel I. '36 '67 C.472 B.S. L.309 LL.B.
(adm. in MA; not adm. in CA) Calif. State Univ.-Hayward
Dorward, Michael S., (AV) ........ '48 '77 C&L.112 B.S., J.D. [Davis&D.]
Dorward, Stephanie Davis, (AV) ........ '47 '77 C.188 B.A. L.1066 J.D. [Davis&D.]
Dresnick, Paul, A Professional Corporation, (BV) '44 '70
C.813 A.B. L.1065 J.D. 225 W. Winton Ave.
Duggan, Daniel A., Jr., (AV) ........ '43 '73 C.768 B.A. L.767 J.D. [D.A.Duggan,Jr.]
Duggan, Daniel A., Jr., Prof. Corp., (AV) ........ 1325 "B" St.
Dunn, G.M. ........ '28 '61 C.740 A.B. L.1026 LL.B. V.P., Zerowatt Mfg. Corp.
Dutton, David C., Jr., (AV) ........ '17 '42 L.1065 J.D. Asst. Dist. Atty.
Dzubur, Eric G., Law Offices of, (BV) '51 '78 C.112 B.A. L.765 J.D.
21565 Foothill Blvd.
Dzubur, Karen S. ........ '57 '85 C.112 B.A. L.765 J.D. 21565 Foothill Blvd.
Edgar, Dallas S. ........ '21 '59 C.112 A.B. L.1065 J.D. Ret. Mun. Ct. J.
Eisenberg, Mark L., (BV) ........ '48 '85 C.1073 B.A. L.464 J.D. 1290 "B" St.
Engel, Maurice, (AV) ........ '27 '53 C.112 A.B. L.1066 LL.B. 22320 Foothill Blvd.
Faria, Manuel A. ........ '48 '88 C.1073 B.A. L.765 J.D. 109 Jackson St.

**Flynn, Kevin D., (BV) '50 '76 C.768 B.A. L.767 J.D.**
**Suite 209, 21573 Foothill Boulevard, 94541**
**Telephone: 510-886-1166**
**Family Law.**
***See Professional Biographies, HAYWARD, CALIFORNIA***

Foley, Paul L., (BV) ........ '34 '67 C.770 L.765 LL.B. 21790 Hesperian Blvd.
**Fraser, Keith S.**, (AV) ........ '36 '61 C.813 B.S. L.1065 LL.B. [Varni,F.H.&R.]⊙
*PRACTICE AREAS: Real Estate; Land Use; Probate.
French, Cecil P., Jr., (BV) ........ '45 '80 C.112 B.A. L.1026 J.D. 1065 "A" St.
**Fuerch, Stephen M.**, (BV) ........ '45 '75 C.147 B.S. L.464 J.D. [Rifkind&F.]
*PRACTICE AREAS: Construction Law; Government Tort Liability; Products Liability; Personal Injury; Real Property.
Furtado, Manuel L., (AV) ........ '25 '62 C.169 A.B. L.1066 LL.B. [Furtado,J.&S.]
Furtado, Robert A., (AV) ........ '51 '79 C.112 B.S. L.770 J.D. [Furtado,J.&S.]
Furtado, Jaspovice & Simons, (AV) ........ 22274 Main St.
Galiga, Michael L. '55 '91 C.612 B.S. L.378 J.D.
(adm. in KS; not adm. in CA) 22301 Foothill Blvd., Suite MO2Y
García, Jesse J., (AV) ........ '48 '74 C.112 A.B. L.767 J.D. [García&S.]
García & Schnayerson, (AV) ........ 225 W. Winton, Ste., 208
Goldman, Paul Z., (BV) ........ '43 '71 C.696 B.A. L.1066 J.D. 1290 B St.
Gonella, Robert J. '50 '77
C.112 A.B. L.1065 J.D. Sr. Atty. & Legal Servs. Mgr., Mervyn's
Gonick, Harry ........ '11 '46 L.284 J.D. 838 Hancock St.‡
Gonzales, Robert ........ '45 '71 C.768 B.S. L.1065 J.D. Alameda Co. Legal Aid Soc.
Goodman, Louis J., (BV) ........ '53 '80 C.696 B.A. L.1065 J.D. 1290 "B" St.
**Goodman, Mark Alan** ........ '50 '87 C.112 B.S. L.1153 J.D. [A W.W.Haskell&Assoc.]
*PRACTICE AREAS: Insurance Defense; Construction and Business Litigation; Insurance Fraud; Personal Injury; General Civil.
Gorelick-Levine, Jo Lynn, (BV) ........ '56 '83 C.112 B.A. L.1065 J.D. 164 W. Jackson St.
Goulart, Frank, (BV) ........ '49 '81 C.112 L.1197 J.D. 22248 Main St.
Grant, Gerald ........ '38 '65 C.112 B.A. L.1065 J.D. 1728 B St.
**Greathouse, Michael J.** ........ '56 '81 C.1074 B.A. L.990 J.D. [Rifkind&F.]
Guinee, John F., (AV) ........ '18 '50 C&L.767 B.S., LL.B. 1065 A St.

**Haley, Purchio, Sakai & Smith, (AV) BB**
**P.O. Box 450, 22320 Foothill Boulevard, Suite 620, 94543**
**Telephone: 510-538-6400 Oakland: 510-351-1932**
**Members of Firm: J. Kenneth Birchfield (1920-1978); John K. Smith; Robert Sakai; Cynthia K. Smith. Of Counsel: John J. Purchio; Donald A. Pearce (1898-1982); Marlin W. Haley (1910-1993).**
**General Civil and Trial Practice. Business, Corporation, Real Property, Construction, Land Use, Municipal and Probate Law.**

(This Listing Continued)

**Haley, Purchio, Sakai & Smith (Continued)**

**Representative Clients: City Center Commercial (Shopping Center); Oak Hills, Walnut Hills, Creekwood (Apartment Complexes); R. Zaballos & Sons (General Contractors); Hospital Associates; Wolf Investment Co.; Chicago Title Company of Alameda County; Sunnyside Nurseries, Inc.; Mission Valley Rock Co. (quarry); LaVista Quarry.**
***See Professional Biographies, HAYWARD, CALIFORNIA***

Hamel, Hubert O., (BV) ........ '18 '60 C.112 B.A. L.767 225 W. Winton Ave.
Hardin, Richard D., (BV) ........ '43 '71 C.147 L.169 J.D. 22693 Hesperian Blvd.
Harper, Rita I., (BV) ........ '— '81 C.763 B.A. L.767 J.D. 225 W. Winton Blvd.
Hashimoto, Roy ........ '51 '76 C.112 A.B. L.464 J.D. Mun. J.

**Haskell, William W., & Associates, (AV) '42 '71 C.813 A.B. L.1065 J.D.**
**22320 Foothill Boulevard Suite 330, 94541**
**Telephone: 510-785-7400 Fax: 510-783-1501**
***PRACTICE AREAS: Insurance Defense Law; Personal Injury Law; Public Entity Law; Construction Litigation; Insurance Coverage Law.**
**Associates: Mark Alan Goodman; G. Randy Kasten; Kenneth R. Van Vleck; Armand P. Adkins; Lyn Davaly Tadlock.**
**General Civil and Trial Practice in State and Federal Courts. General Civil Litigation including Insurance Defense, Personal Injury, Construction, Real Property, Landslide, Subsidence and Business Litigation.**
***See Professional Biographies, HAYWARD, CALIFORNIA***

Hernandez, Juan B. ........ '54 '82 C.112 B.A. L.1066 J.D. 31400 Meadowbrook Ave.
Hertz, Howard, (AV) ........ '42 '68 C.112 B.A. L.1066 J.D. 295 W. Winton Ave.
Hillis, David, (BV) ........ '49 '82 C.112 B.A. L.284 J.D. 24072 Myrtle St.
Hinkston, Ulanda Denise Rippy '64 '89 C.269 B.A. L.309 J.D.
(adm. in NC; not adm. in CA) 22723 Olive Pl.‡
Hodge, Richard A. ........ '38 '65 C.611 B.A. L.145 J.D. Supr. Ct. J.
Holihan, Clare A. ........ '67 '94 C.216 B.A. L.1065 J.D. 23320 Foothill Blvd.
Holmes, Marjorie Randolph '44 '78
C.679 B.A. L.284 J.D. V.P., Human Res. & Gen. Coun., Mervyn's
Homen, Mark A. ........ '56 '83 C.1073 B.A. L.770 J.D. 22698 Mission Blvd.
Hora, Peggy F. ........ '46 '78 C.1073 B.A. L.765 J.D. Mun. Ct. J.
Humphrey, Richard F., (BV) ........ '35 '71 C.766 B.A. L.767 J.D. 713 "A" St.
Jaquint, David J., (BV) ........ '48 '79 C.1073 B.A. L.1065 J.D. 1728 "B" St.
Jaspovice, Martin L., (AV) ........ '47 '73 C&L.1066 A.B., J.D. [Furtado,J.&S.]
Jewell, Colin H. ........ '55 '86 C.112 A.B. L.767 J.D. 713 A St.
Johnson, Richard B., (BV) ........ '38 '67 C.112 A.B. L.1066 LL.B. 21550 Foothill Blvd.
**Kasten, G. Randy**, (BV) ........ '55 '84 C.685 B.A. L.284 J.D. [A W.W.Haskell&Assoc.]
*PRACTICE AREAS: Insurance Defense Law; General Civil and Construction Litigation; Products Liability; Taxation; Real Property.
Keith, June M. ........ '64 '88 C.740 B.A. L.1065 J.D. 313 W. Winton Ave.
Kirk, James W., (CV⊙) '49 '78 C&L.629 B.S., J.D.
(adm. in OR; not adm. in CA) 240 Cherry Way‡
Kock, Arlene D. ........ '51 '78 C.766 B.A. L.765 J.D. [A.D.Kock]
Kock, Arlene D., Law Offices of, A Professional Law Corporation ... 24301 Southland Dr.
Kraetzer, John F. ........ '37 '63 C.309 A.B. L.813 J.D. Supr. Ct. J.
Kurtz, Robert K. ........ '48 '73 C.112 A.B. L.1065 J.D. Supm. Ct. J.
Kyle, James M., III, (BV) ........ '31 '63 C.502 A.B. L.1065 J.D. 225 W. Winton
Lampi, Bill H., (BV) ........ '40 '65 C.766 A.B. L.1065 LL.B. 1276 A St.
Lewman, Bonnie ........ '47 '79 C.999 L.765 J.D. Sup. Ct. J.
Littlefield, Christina B. ........ '53 '83 C.483 B.A. L.1067 J.D. 1290 "B" St.
Lyons, Robert W. ........ '44 '70 C.112 B.A. L.767 J.D. 295 W. Winton Ave.
Martins, Edward E., A Professional Corporation, (AV) '27 '53
C.112 B.S. L.767 LL.B. 22698 Mission Blvd.
McBride, James P., (BV) ........ '43 '66 C.112 L.765 J.D. 1065 "A" St.
McCardle, John R., (BV) ........ '42 '70 C.112 B.S. L.284 J.D. 1728 B St.
McDonald, Dennis D., (AV) ........ '44 '71 C.1073 B.A. L.765 J.D. 1325 "B" St.
McDonald, Robert W. ........ '21 '47 C&L.339 A.B., J.D. 27948 Pueblo Serena‡
McNulty, William T., Jr. ........ '38 '76 C.112 B.A. L.1066 J.D. 389 Gresel St.
Mefford, Harold D., (AV) ........ '16 '49 C.174 A.B. L.1066 LL.B. 30063 Palomares Rd.‡
Meltzer, Ross M. ........ '58 '85 C.1044 B.A. L.284 J.D. 164 W. Jackson
Mendell, Preston K. ........ '26 '76 C.767 B.S. L.1026 J.D. 27940 Pueblo Serena
Mockus, Joseph E. ........ '52 '86 C.112 B.A. L.1065 J.D. [A García&S.]
Mooney, Michael R. ........ '57 '91 C.941 B.A. L.464 J.D. 1290 B St.
**Moruza, Christine Kasun** ........ '51 '76 C.112 B.A. L.1065 J.D. [A Varni,F.H.&R.]⊙
*PRACTICE AREAS: Business Litigation.
Moss, Glen L. ........ '43 '69 C.112 B.S. L.1066 J.D. [Moss&M.]
Moss & Murphy ........ 22693 Hesperian Blvd.
Murphy, Ann ........ '45 '75 C.483 B.A. L.284 J.D. [Moss&M.]
Nakatsu, Penny ........ '49 '74 C.766 A.B. L.1065 J.D. Asst. City Atty.
Newman, Edw. F., (BV) ........ '24 '52 C.112 B.S. L.1066 LL.B. 22274 Main St.
Osofsky, Gene L., (BV) ........ '44 '70 C.112 A.B. L.1068 J.D. 24301 Southland Dr.
Pasquali, Rolando W., (BV) ........ '57 '82 C.800 B.A. L.770 J.D. 22274 Main St.
**Peck, Ronald G.**, (AV) ........ '51 '77 C.169 B.A. L.464 J.D. [Schenone&P.]
*PRACTICE AREAS: Commercial Litigation; Real Property; Construction Disputes; Collection; Business Disputes.
**Phillips, James J.**, (AV) ........ '54 '80 C.112 B.S. L.1065 J.D. [J.J.Phillips]⊙

**Phillips, James J., A Professional Corporation, (AV)**
**1331 B Street, Suite 4, 94541⊙**
**Telephone: 510-886-2120 Fax: 510-463-8656**
**James J. Phillips (Certified Specialist, Estate Planning, Trust and Probate Law, The State Bar of California Board of Legal Specialization).**
**Estate Planning, Trust and Probate Law.**
**Pleasanton, California Office: 4900 Hopyard Road, Suite 260, 94588. Telephone: 510-463-1980.**
***See Professional Biographies, HAYWARD, CALIFORNIA***

Picetti, Gary M. ........ '47 '72 C.309 A.B. L.767 J.D. Mun. Ct. J.
Pulido, Stephen M., (AV) ........ '53 '78 C.112 B.A. L.1065 J.D. [Browner,P.&S.]
**Purchio, John J.**, (AV) ........ '15 '46 C&L.262 B.S., LL.B. [Haley,P.S.&S.]
Reitz, Norman E. ........ '41 '69 C.813 B.S. L.1066 J.D. 22693 Hesperian Blvd. (Pat.)
**Rifkind, Richard D.**, (AV) ........ '37 '63 C.112 A.B. L.1066 LL.B. [Rifkind&F.]

**Rifkind & Fuerch, A Professional Corporation, (AV)**
**Suite 614, 24301 Southland Drive, 94545**
**Telephone: 510-785-3101 Fax: 510-785-6828**
**Richard D. Rifkind; Stephen M. Fuerch; Michael J. Greathouse.**
**General Civil and Trial Practice. Insurance, Insurance Defense, Real Estate, Transportation Law, Fire Insurance, Products Liability, Automobile, Professional Liability, Landslide and Subsidence, Construction, Business, Municipal and Education Law.**
**Representative Clients: Fireman's Fund American Insurance Co.; City of Fremont (Self-Insured); Briggs & Stratton Inc.; Colonial-Penn Insurance Co.; J.C. Penny Insurance Co.; Orion Group Insurance Co.; Royal Insurance Co.**
***See Professional Biographies, HAYWARD, CALIFORNIA***

Riley, Patrick Z. ........ '45 '71 C.770 B.A. L.1066 J.D. 30100 Mission Blvd.
Sabraw, Ronald M. ........ '50 '76 C.637 B.A. L.464 J.D. Supr. Ct. J.
**Sakai, Robert**, (AV) ........ '45 '74 C.112 B.S. L.1065 J.D. [Haley,P.S.&S.]
Saunders, Reginald P. ........ '50 '84 C.112 A.B. L.767 J.D. Mun. J.
Scanlon, John W., (BV) ........ '21 '49 C.740 B.S. L.767 LL.B. 382 St. Andrews St.

CAA117P

CALIFORNIA—HAYWARD MARTINDALE-HUBBELL LAW DIRECTORY 1997

**Schenone, Bart J.**, (AV) ....................'49 '74 C.813 B.A. L.477 J.D. [Schenone&P.]
*PRACTICE AREAS: Estate Planning; Trust; Probate; Real Property.

**Schenone & Peck, (AV)**
**1260 B Street, Suite 350, 94541**
**Telephone: 510-581-6611 Fax: 510-581-6174**
**Members of Firm: Bart J. Schenone (Certified Specialist, Probate, Estate Planning and Trust Law, The State Bar of California Board of Legal Specialization); Ronald G. Peck.**
**Civil and Trial Practice Law. Real Property, Construction, Land Use, Estate Planning, Probate, Trusts, Business, Corporation and Commercial Law.**
*See Professional Biographies, HAYWARD, CALIFORNIA*

Schnayerson, Philip A., (AV) ..................'40 '68 C.705 B.S. L.569 J.D. [García&S.]
Schoenfelder, Peg A. '52 '79
C.488 B.S. L.1035 J.D. Dir., Legal Servs. & Asst. Secy., Mervyn's
Servatius, Brian J., (AV) ..................'43 '69 C.770 B.S.C. L.1066 J.D. 1276 "A" St.
Sheehan, Constance Cae, (BV) ......................'42 '83 L.1153 J.D. [Browner,P.&S.]
Sills, Milton ..........................'10 '32 C&L.145 Ph.B., J.D. 22320 City Center Dr.‡
Silva, Diane L., (BV) .............'43 '76 C.1073 B.A. L.1066 J.D. 225 W. Winton Ave.
Simons, Rick, (AV) ......................'50 '76 C.112 A.B. L.1066 J.D. [Furtado,J.&S.]
**Smith, Cynthia K.**, (BV) ...................'57 '83 C.770 B.S. L.1065 J.D. [Haley,P.S.&S.]
**Smith, John K.**, (AV) ....................'26 '55 C.813 B.A. L.1065 LL.B. [Haley,P.S.&S.]
Snyder, W. James, (BV) .......................................'40 '69 L.878 J.D. 1728 B St.
Stern, Ralph D. ...............'43 '67 C.105 A.B. L.145 J.D. Gen. Coun., Schools Legal Coun.
Stone, Richard C., (AV) ...................'41 '67 C.112 B.A. L.1066 J.D. 24072 Myrtle St.
**Tadlock, Lyn Davaly** .................'— '93 C.999 L.284 J.D. [⊠ W.W.Haskell&Assoc.]
*PRACTICE AREAS: Insurance Defense; General Civil Litigation.
Tarkington, Bruce K., (BV) .........'41 '78 C.766 B.A. L.1197 J.D. 21565 Foothill Blvd.
Thorman, Michael P., (AV) ...........................'49 '74 C.197 A.B. L.813 J.D. [Bonjour&T.]
Thorpe, John M. ..................'32 '57 C.813 B.A. L.1066 J.D. 21790 Hesperian Blvd.
Tully, Griffeth E., (BV) .................'36 '68 C.800 B.S. L.1065 J.D. P.O. Box 3789
**Van Vleck, Kenneth R.** ........'65 '93 C.813 A.B. L.1065 J.D. [⊠ W.W.Haskell&Assoc.]
*PRACTICE AREAS: Insurance Defense; General Civil and Construction Management Litigation.
**Varni, Anthony B.**, (AV) ...............'39 '64 C&L.770 B.A., LL.B. [Varni,F.H.&R.]⊙
*PRACTICE AREAS: Real Estate; Land Use; Eminent Domain; Inverse Condemnation.

**Varni, Fraser, Hartwell & Rodgers, (AV)**
**22771 Main Street, P.O. Box 570, 94543-0570⊙**
**Telephone: 510-886-5000; 352-4500 Fax: 510-538-8797**
**Members of Firm: Anthony B. Varni; Keith S. Fraser; Elizabeth E. Trutner (Resident, Livermore Office) (Certified Specialist, Estate Planning, Trust and Probate Law, The State Bar of California Board of Legal Specialization); John S. Hartwell (1924-1993); Lionel A. Rodgers (1942-1989). Associate: Christine Kasun Moruza.**
**State and Federal Court Business Litigation, Real Estate Development and Land Use, Environmental and Eminent Domain, Estate Planning and Probate Practice.**
**Representative Clients: Ameron Pipe Products Group (Northern California Division); Kaufman & Broad of Northern California, Inc.; Castro Valley Sanitary District; Glad-A-Way Gardens, Inc.**
**Livermore, California Office: 2109 Fourth Street, P.O. Box 511, 94550-0511. Telephone: 510-447-1222. Fax: 510-443-7831.**
*See Professional Biographies, HAYWARD, CALIFORNIA*

Watkins, Paul B. ..........................'53 '82 C.604 B.A. L.767 J.D. [⊠ Akana&Y.]
White, Barbara M. .................'45 '81 C.763 A.B. L.284 J.D. 26250 Industrial Blvd.
Wies, Louis B., (BV) .................'28 '66 C.112 B.A. L.770 J.D. 21573 Foothill Blvd.
Wiles, Robert J. ...................................'26 '54 C.112 L.1026 LL.B. 22734 Main St.‡
Wright, Kathleen K. '49 '82 C.259 B.S. L.262 J.D.
(adm. in NY; not adm. in CA) Univ. of Calif.
Yee, Darryl M. ..........................'59 '87 C.839 B.Ed. L.284 J.D. [Akana&Y.]

## HEALDSBURG, 9,469, *Sonoma Co.*

Butler, Larry D. ...................................'41 '79 C.628 B.S. L.1227 J.D. P.O. Box 1344‡
Fitzpatrick, Timothy D., (BV) ........'52 '79 C.209 B.S. L.1227 J.D. 465 Healdsburg Ave.
Forest, Joseph A., (AV) ..................'32 '63 C.871 B.S. L.813 J.D. 330 Healdsburg Ave.
Furth, Frederick P., (AV) .........................'34 '59 C&L.477 B.A., LL.B. [Furth,F.&M.]⊙
Furth, Fahrner & Mason, (AV) ....................10300 Chalk Hill Rd. (⊙San Francisco)
Gladden, Mark L., (BV) ..............'50 '75 C.767 B.A. L.770 J.D. [Passalacqua,M.&G.]
Groff, Richard P. .....'55 '90 C.1078 B.A. L.1227 J.D. 4723 E. Soda Rock Lane, Suite 200
Haiken, Marvin B. ......................................'32 '55 C&L.178 A.B., J.D. 407 N. St.
Heth, Jacob A. .........................................'67 '94 C.112 B.A. [⊠ Passalacqua,M.&G.]
Hunter, William C., (AV) ...................'39 '70 C&L.893 B.S., J.D. 465 Healdsburg Ave.
Jonas, Gail E. ...........................................'40 '77 C.446 B.S. L.1065 J.D. 521 Brown St.
Jordan, Thomas N., Jr. '35 '59 C.494 B.A. L.208 LL.B.
(adm. in CO; not adm. in CA) Jordan Operating
Kamm, Thomas A. ...................'25 '57 C.911 B.S. L.215 LL.B. 11000 Chalk Hill Rd.
Kinkade, Joseph C. ..........................'48 '92 C.147 B.A. L.1227 J.D. 141 N. St.
Leonhaeuser, Janet C. ...................'54 '78 C.112 A.B. L.1065 J.D. 7505 Mill Creek Rd.
Lopez, Lourdes ........................'61 '87 C.1042 B.A. L.426 J.D. [Passalacqua,M.&G.]
Manning, John H. ............................'40 '69 C.884 B.A. L.1065 J.D. 141 North St.
Marmor, Robert E., (CV) ....................'49 '78 C.112 A.B. L.464 J.D. 141 North St.
Mazzoni, James R., Jr., (AV) ..........'32 '57 C&L.813 A.B., LL.B. [Passalacqua,M.&G.]
Miller, Mark S. ............................'47 '79 C.112 A.B. L.1065 J.D. P.O. Box 1803
Passalacqua, Emil R. ...................'31 '76 C.767 B.S. L.1026 LL.B. [Passalacqua&P.]
Passalacqua, Joseph Richard .............'62 '88 C.147 B.S. L.770 J.D. [Passalacqua&P.]
Passalacqua, Richard Joseph ...................'61 '86 C&L.770 B.S., J.D. [Passalacqua&P.]
Passalacqua, Thomas R., (BV) .....'39 '65 C.767 B.S. L.1065 LL.B. [Passalacqua,M.&G.]
Passalacqua, Mazzoni & Gladden, (AV) ....................................1201 Vine St.
Passalacqua & Passalacqua .............................................152 Piper St.
Phillips, William B., III .....................'47 '78 C.950 B.A. L.596 J.D. 58 W. North St.
Rizzo, Albert G., Jr., (CV) .........................'34 '66 L.765 LL.B. 817 Brown St.
Short, John E., (CV) ............................'40 '72 C.112 B.A. L.1067 J.D. [J.E.Short]
Short, John E., A Professional Corporation, (CV) ...........................141 North St.
Smith, Phillip J., (BV) ......................'40 '65 C.112 A.B. L.1066 LL.B. 141 North St.
Welty, Michael H., (CV) ......................'45 '72 C.112 A.B. L.1067 J.D. P.O. Box 488
Wood, Gary James ........................'54 '79 C.597 B.A. L.813 J.D. 2190 Madrone Ave.

## HELENDALE, —, *San Bernardino Co.*

Sheridan, H. Ford ........................................'29 '79 C.1077 L.1095 J.D. P.O. Box 1796‡

## HEMET, 36,094, *Riverside Co.*

Amschel, Edward T. .............................'44 '75 C.112 B.A. L.972 J.D. [Amschel]
Amschel, Peter ..........................................'45 '73 C.112 B.A. L.972 J.D. [Amschel]
Amschel Law Corp. .........................................................120 South Harvard St.
Bauman, William H. '16 '50 C&L.208 B.S., LL.B.
(adm. in CO; not adm. in CA) 1810 Flametree Way‡
**Bloom-Rudibaugh, Kathlyn J.** ........'51 '78 C.763 B.A. L.1137 J.D. [Bloom,R.&G.]⊙
*PRACTICE AREAS: Family Law; Real Estate.

**Bloom, Rudibaugh & Gunn, (CV)**
**805 East Florida Avenue, 92543⊙**
**Telephone: 909-652-1400 Fax: 909-652-3990**
**Members of Firm: Kathlyn J. Bloom-Rudibaugh; C. Scott Rudibaugh; Rebecca L. Gunn.**

(This Listing Continued)

**Bloom, Rudibaugh & Gunn (Continued)**
**General Civil and Trial Practice. Family, Estate Planning, Probate, Bankruptcy and Criminal Law.**
**Temecula, California Office: 43517 Ridge Park Drive, Suite 100. Telephone: 909-676-2112. Fax: 909-694-0418.**
*See Professional Biographies, HEMET, CALIFORNIA*

Bray, Leland H. ...........................'32 '69 C.766 L.426 LL.B. 43946 Citrus View
Brown, Kevin R. ...................'63 '89 C.426 B.A. L.1065 J.D. 41555 E. Florida Ave.
Cain, Vera A. ........................'26 '78 C.112 B.A. L.1137 J.D. 1600 E. Florida Ave.‡
Camper, Beverly M. ...............'37 '86 C.629 B.A. L.1198 J.D. 41555 E. Florida Ave.
**Carpenter, Thomas M., (P.C.)**, (BV) ....'33 '66 C&L.424 B.S., J.D. [Swan,C.W.&M.]⊙
*PRACTICE AREAS: Estate Planning Law; Probate Law.
Clark, Julie M. ......................'58 '91 C.112 B.A. L.464 J.D. 805 E. Florida Ave.
Cornish, Handley M. ..............................'23 '64 C.494 L.112 J.D. 1600 E. Florida
Cornish, Jane D. ......................'36 '76 C.1065 B.S. L.1137 J.D. 1600 E. Florida Ave.
Cox, James A., (BV) ...................'53 '78 C.112 B.A. L.990 J.D. 805 E. Florida Ave.
Cox, Thomas M., (AV) .................'20 '51 C.902 B.S. L.813 J.D. 805 E. Florida Ave.
Cripps, James O., (CV) ...............'35 '61 C.112 B.A. L.1065 LL.B. 1001 E. Morton Pl.
Daugherty, Lawrence M. ..............'48 '74 C&L.426 B.B.A., J.D. 3550 E. Florida Ave.
Davis, Robert A., Jr. ..........................'62 '92 C.1110 B.A. L.101 J.D. 550 E. Latham
Farnsworth, William K. .................'15 '38 C&L.800 A.B., LL.B. 44533 Olive Ave.‡
Gallagher, Loren V. ..........................'46 '83 C.493 B.A. L.426 J.D. P.O. Box 280
Gritten, Darrell P. .....................'44 '73 C&L.972 B.A., J.D. 3550 E. Florida Ave.
**Gunn, Rebecca L.**, (CV) ...............'51 '80 C.494 B.E.S. L.426 J.D. [Bloom,R.&G.]⊙
*PRACTICE AREAS: Estate Planning, Probate and Tax.
Harr, James J. ..........................'48 '80 C.990 B.A. L.61 J.D. 133 N. Buena Vista
Jeglin, Marvin H. ..................'48 '79 C.1110 B.A. L.1198 J.D. 805 E. Florida Avenue
Kellner & Ybarrondo, (BV) ..........................................................901 E. Morton Pl.
Knowles, Thomas P. ...............................'12 '35 L.262 LL.B. 987 Woodland St.
**McKenzie, Kevin A.** ....................'57 '84 C.1253 B.A. L.800 J.D. [Swan,C.W.&M.]⊙
*PRACTICE AREAS: Estate Planning; Probate and Conservatorships; Real Estate; General Civil Litigation; Aviation Law.
Mowery, Karl D. ......................'60 '93 C&L.1351 B.S.L., J.D. 1109 E. Florida Ave.
Nielsen, Sherrill A. ........................'58 '88 C.112 B.S.L. L.1137 J.D. 550 E. Latham
Nishino, Gilbert Y. ....................'49 '81 C.112 B.A. L.1137 J.D. 1401 E. Florida Ave.
Patterson, Colleen Sue ......................'62 '89 C.398 B.A. L.1137 J.D. [Kellner&Y.]
Powers, Jude Thaddeus A., (BV) ..........'35 '68 C.766 A.B. L.1065 J.D. 950 N. State St.
Robson, Wayne D. ......................'51 '76 C.112 B.S. L.1049 J.D. 26160 Soboba St.
**Rudibaugh, C. Scott**, (CV) ...............'50 '80 C.294 A.B. L.1137 J.D. [Bloom,R.&G.]⊙
*PRACTICE AREAS: Family Law; Bankruptcy.
**Swan, D. Richard, (P.C.)**, (AV) .........'34 '61 C&L.174 B.A., LL.B. [Swan,C.W.&M.]⊙
*PRACTICE AREAS: Commercial Law; Family Law.

**Swan, Carpenter, Wallis & McKenzie, (AV)**
**A Partnership including Professional Corporations**
**1600 East Florida Avenue, Suite 211, 92544⊙**
**Telephone: 909-658-7162 Facsimile No.: 909-658-2231**
**D. Richard Swan (P.C.) (Certified Specialist, Family Law, The State Bar of California Board of Legal Specialization); Thomas M. Carpenter (P.C.) (Certified Specialist, Probate, Estate Planning and Trust Law, The State Bar of California Board of Legal Specialization); Bruce M. Wallis (P.C.); Kevin A. McKenzie.**
**General Civil Trial Practice. Corporate, Estate Planning, Probate, Real Property, Family and Commercial Law.**
**Reference: Security Pacific National Bank.**
**Sun City, California Office: 26858 Cherry Hills Boulevard. Telephone: 909-672-1881. Facsimile: 909-672-3164.**
*See Professional Biographies, HEMET, CALIFORNIA*

Thompson, Winthrop E. ................'18 '49 C.112 B.A. L.426 LL.B. 2106 El Toro Cir.
Van Order, William R. ..............'59 '86 C.120 B.A. L.1148 J.D. 380 N. San Jacinto St.
**Wallis, Bruce M., (P.C.)**, (BV) .........'45 '75 C.112 B.A. L.464 J.D. [Swan,C.W.&M.]⊙
*PRACTICE AREAS: Real Property Law; Commercial Law; Banking Law; General Civil Litigation.

**Welebir & McCune, A Professional Law Corporation**
**(See Redlands)**

Wheeler, William M. '62 '89 C.763 B.A. L.37 J.D.
(adm. in ID; not adm. in CA) 627 E. Wright St.★
Wickham, Donald C., (BV) ..........'34 '59 C.763 A.B. L.1068 J.D. 133 N. Buena Vista
Ybarrondo, James T., (BV) ..........................'48 '73 C.1075 B.S. L.61 J.D. [Kellner&Y.]

## HERALD, —, *Sacramento Co.*

Ridgway, Maureen Abbott '58 '87 C.911 B.A. L.596 J.D.
(adm. in WA; not adm. in CA) Center for Participating in Democracy

## HERCULES, 16,829, *Contra Costa Co.*

Gilbert, Wil D. ..........................................'38 '88 C.999 A.A. L.1153 J.D. 192 Rosti Pl.‡

## HERMOSA BEACH, 18,219, *Los Angeles Co.*

Baker, Brad N. ..........................................'49 '75 C.112 B.A. L.1068 J.D. [Baker&B.]
Baker & Burton, A Prof. Corp. ...........................................................515 Pier Ave.
Barr, Nancy M. '55 '83 C.112 B.A. L.472 J.D.
(adm. in FL; not adm. in CA) 515 Pier Ave.
Burton, Kent ..............................................'50 '75 C.800 B.A. L.112 J.D. [Baker&B.]
Cox, Ralph Frederick, Jr. ...................'53 '88 C.1341 M.D. L.1049 J.D. 1212 24th St.
Devine, Robert A. ..............................'43 '79 C.1024 B.S. L.1136 J.D. 555 Pier Ave.
**Edgerton, Samuel Y., III** ...................................'56 '82 C.94 B.S. L.128 J.D. [Nash&E.]⊙
*PRACTICE AREAS: Securities Brokerage Defense; Bankruptcy; Real Estate and Commercial Litigation.
Frank, Dale S. .........................................'48 '86 C.999 L.940 J.D. 555 Pier Ave.
Frank, Lawrence R. ..............................'49 '81 C.1044 B.A. L.1048 J.D. 555 Pier Ave.
Goldenberg, David H. .........................'41 '77 C.679 B.S.E.E. L.426 J.D. 504 24th Pl.
**Harwood, Deanna R.** ..................'60 '94 C.1077 B.S. L.809 J.D. [⊠ M.W.Monroe]
*PRACTICE AREAS: Insurance Defense; Admiralty; Trademark; Corporate Litigation.
Hershner, John D., Jr. ......................'47 '75 C.859 B.A. L.208 J.D. 435 Bayview Dr.
Hodges, Jana Park, (BV) .........'46 '80 C.430 B.A. L.1137 J.D. 2200 Pacific Coast Hwy.
Hodges, Robert R., (AV) ..............'40 '70 C.800 L.1137 J.D. 2200 Pacific Coast Hwy.
Holbrook, Nancy J. ..........................'51 '80 C.112 A.B. L.426 J.D. 936 Hermosa Ave.

**James, Norman D., (AV) '43 '69 C&L.339 A.B., J.D.**
**49 Pier Avenue 2nd Floor, 90254**
**Telephone: 310-798-4131 Fax: 310-798-4136**
***REPORTED CASES: United States v. Salerno 902 F.2d 1429 (9th Circuit 1990); Firstmark Capital Corp. v. Hempel Financial Corp. 859 F.2d 92 (9th Circuit 1988); United States v. Noti 731 F.2d 610 (9th Circuit 1984).**
**Civil Trials and Appellate Practice in all State and Federal Courts, Business Litigation and Federal Criminal Law.**
*See Professional Biographies, HERMOSA BEACH, CALIFORNIA*

**Johnson, K. D.** .......................'52 '80 C.619 B.S. L.1067 J.D. [⊠ M.W.Monroe]
*PRACTICE AREAS: Admiralty/Maritime; Insurance Defense, Business and Real Estate Litigation.
Kane, Gerald H. B. ...................'40 '71 C.668 B.A. L.1068 J.D. 2130 Monterey Blvd.‡
Kole, Cynthia Wicktom ....................'61 '88 C.976 B.A. L.273 J.D. 501 Herondo St.
Konicek, Thomas K. ...........................'54 '83 C.813 A.B. L.426 J.D. 410 29th St.

Lawson, Carol C. .......................... '43 '78 C.813 B.A. L.809 J.D. 728 24th St.‡
Lee, Robert R. .......................... '34 '67 C.628 B.S. L.800 J.D. 121 Herondo St.
Lundy, Albro L., III .......................... '59 '86 C.112 B.A. L.426 J.D. [A Baker&B.]
Lytle, Craig M. .......................... '42 '79 C.1097 B.A. L.1179 J.D. 1409 Monterey Blvd.
**Maurer, David** .......................... '51 '83 C.112 B.A. L.426 J.D. [Nash&E.]⊙
*PRACTICE AREAS: Securities; Business; Commercial Litigation.

**Monroe, Matthew W., Law Offices of '48 '90 C.1228 B.S. L.1241 J.D.**
**2200 Pacific Coast Highway Suite 312, 90254-2757**
**Telephone: 310-318-3595 Fax: 310-318-1257**
***LANGUAGES: Japanese, Vietnamese and French.**
***PRACTICE AREAS: Insurance Defense; Admiralty Law; Business Law; Civil Litigation; Military Law.**
**Associates: Tom R. Shapiro; Deanna R. Harwood; Steven D. Smelser; Dara S. Niad; Daniel A. Schuch.**
**Of Counsel: Ralph M. Singer, Jr.; K. D. Johnson.**
**General Practice.**
*See Professional Biographies, HERMOSA BEACH, CALIFORNIA*

**Nash, Savery L., (AV)** .......................... '33 '60 C.112 B.A. L.1068 LL.B. [Nash&E.]⊙
*PRACTICE AREAS: General Business Practice; Corporate; Contract; Finance; Real Property.
**Nash, Shelley** .......................... '59 '86 C.112 B.A. L.1049 J.D. [Nash&E.]⊙

**Nash & Edgerton, (AV)** BB
**A Limited Liability Partnership**
**2615 Pacific Coast Highway, Suite 322, 90254⊙**
**Telephone: 310-937-2066 Fax: 310-937-2063**
**Savery L. Nash; Samuel Y. Edgerton, III; Shelley Nash; David Maurer; Damon Rubin.**
**Commercial and Securities Litigation, Broker-Dealer Defense. General Business Practice. Corporate, Contract, Finance, Real Property Law, New Ventures and Partnership Law.**
**Torrance, California Office: 3625 Del Amo Boulevard, suite 360. Telephone: 310-370-8272. Fax: 310-214-9677.**
*See Professional Biographies, HERMOSA BEACH, CALIFORNIA*

Newton, Leslie Ann .......................... '47 '78 L.1179 J.D. 53 Pier Ave., 2nd Fl.
**Niad, Dara S.** .......................... '70 '95 C.703 B.S. L.809 J.D. [M.W.Monroe]
*PRACTICE AREAS: Insurance Defense; Admiralty; Civil Litigation; Civil Rights Defense.
Polinger, Thomas M., (BV) .......................... '51 '77 C.768 B.A. L.426 J.D. 555 Pier Ave.
Pope, Jaquelynn C. .......................... '— '77 L.1230 LL.B. [A Worthington&W.]
Portnoy, Zamira E. .......................... '— '65 C.102 B.A. L.569 J.D. P.O. Box 683
Radin, Marc S. .......................... '55 '82 C.37 B.S. L.809 J.D. 1536 Silver St.
Roberts, Laurel L. .......................... '44 '84 C.112 M.A. L.1136 J.D. 239 Pier Ave.
Rodgers, John Q. .......................... '54 '86 C.112 B.A. L.800 J.D. 326 10th St.
**Rubin, Damon** .......................... '70 '96 C.426 B.S. L.823 J.D. [A Nash&E.]
*PRACTICE AREAS: Civil Litigation.

**St. Clair, Grace Greer '61 '91 C.800 B.A. L.809 J.D.**
**657 Third Street, Suite 3, 90254**
**Telephone: 310-374-5479 Fax: 310-372-8502**
***PRACTICE AREAS: Real Estate.**
**Real Estate, Estate Planning, Trusts, Wills, General Business.**

**Schapira, Leonard L., Law Office of '52 '90 C.813 A.B. L.426 J.D.**
**555 Pier Avenue, Suite 4, 90254**
**Telephone: 310-318-9050 Fax: 310-376-3531**
**Real Estate, Lender Liability, Debt Restructuring, Business, Consumer and Commercial Law.**
*See Professional Biographies, HERMOSA BEACH, CALIFORNIA*

Schindler, Gary .......................... '48 '82 C.1350 B.A. L.284 J.D. American Airlines, Inc.
**Schuch, Daniel A.** .......................... '55 '88 C&L.838 B.A., J.D. [M.W.Monroe]
*PRACTICE AREAS: Insurance Defense; Admiralty; Trademark/Copyright; Civil Litigation.
Seidensticker, Kirk W. .......................... '56 '83 C.800 B.S. L.990 J.D. 734 Strand (Upper)
**Shapiro, Tom R.** .......................... '62 '86 C.354 B.S. L.128 J.D. [M.W.Monroe]
*PRACTICE AREAS: Civil Litigation; Civil Rights Litigation; Business Litigation.
**Singer, Ralph M., Jr., (BV)** .......................... '30 '77 C&L.426 B.B.A., J.D. [M.W.Monroe]
*PRACTICE AREAS: Business Law; Insurance Defense Law; Real Property Law.
**Smelser, Steven D.** .......................... '69 '95 C.112 B.S. L.426 J.D. [A M.W.Monroe]
*PRACTICE AREAS: Insurance Defense; Admiralty; Corporate Litigation.
Spaustat, James H., (BV) .......................... '43 '78 C.321 A.B. L.809 J.D. 555 Pier Ave.
Sternfield, Bertram F. '12 '41 C&L.724 B.S., LL.B.
(adm. in NY; not adm. in CA) 3007 The Strand‡
Thomas, Richard F.G., (AV) ....'54 '79 C.1097 B.A. L.1049 J.D. 2200 Pacific Coast Hwy.
Warshaw, Mark D. .......................... '52 '79 C.112 B.A. L.1065 J.D. 2164 Circle Dr.
Worthington & Worthington, (AV) .......................... P.O. Box 166 (⊙San Francisco)

## HESPERIA, 50,418, *San Bernardino Co.*

Hughes, Clifford B. .......................... '27 '53 C&L.800 A.B., J.D. 10898 4th Ave.
Lewis, Anne E. .......................... '54 '79 C&L.1137 B.S.L., J.D. [Lewis&P.]
Lewis & Padgett .......................... 18275 Bear Valley Rd.
McConahay, Charles L., Jr. .......................... '47 '77 C.154 B.A. L.1137 J.D. 14968 Main St.
Padgett, Troy Allen .......................... '61 '90 C.763 B.A. L.1137 J.D. [Lewis&P.]
Pope, Steven J. .......................... '40 '78 C&L.1198 B.S.L., J.D. 14321 Main St.
Raupp, Robert L. .......................... '38 '80 C.36 B.A. L.1224 J.D. 14888 Main St.

## HIDDEN HILLS, 1,729, *Los Angeles Co.*

Gruber, Milton E. .......................... '27 '53 C&L.494 B.S.L., LL.B. 5305 Old Farm Rd.
Kaufman, Bernard R. .......................... '27 '56 C.560 B.B.A. L.1009 LL.B. 24701 Robert Gray Rd.
Licht, Michele Habibi .......................... '53 '79 C.112 B.A. L.426 J.D. 5440 Round Meadow Rd.
Satzberg, Michael J. '60 '85 C.645 B.S. L.1019 J.D.
(adm. in PA; not adm. in CA) 23726 Long Valley Rd.‡

## HIGHLAND, 34,439, *San Bernardino Co.*

Cooper, Susan Starbuck .......................... '54 '87 C.112 B.S. L.426 J.D. 27258 Main St.
Feigenson, Claire .......................... '26 '79 L.1137 J.D. 6234 Stanton Ave.
Herwig, Bruce S. .......................... '44 '72 C.641 B.A. L.1068 J.D. 2660 E. 29th St.
Luoma, Jack O. .......................... '21 '51 L.818 LL.B. 1559 N. Buckeye St.‡
Mussell, Stanley, (AV) .......................... '24 '50 C.668 B.A. L.800 J.D. 3605 E. 29th St.‡

## HILLSBOROUGH, 10,667, *San Mateo Co.*

Berryman, Robert P. .......................... '24 '54 C&L.813 A.B., LL.B. 1260 Kenilworth Rd.‡
Cramer, Richard A. .......................... '41 '77 C.766 B.A. L.1065 J.D. 945 Baileyana Rd.
Creed, Christopher D. .......................... '43 '68 C.367 B.A. L.309 J.D. 1769 Forest View Ave.‡
Etcheverry, Bernard, Jr., (AV) .......................... '21 '49 C.112 A.B. L.1066 J.D. 25 Conifer Lane‡
Ferron, Mary Ellen .......................... '54 '81 C.1044 B.A. L.1065 J.D. DRG Finl. Corp.
Giordano, Joseph A., (BV) .......................... '29 '57 C&L.813 A.B., J.D. 447 El Centro Rd.
Gordon, Alan C. .......................... '40 '83 C.112 B.A. Sr. V.P., Wells Fargo Bk., N.A.
Hedden, William H. .......................... '54 '79 C.813 B.A. L.1065 J.D. 10 Willow Ct.‡
Hufford, Chas T., Jr. .......................... '22 '48 C&L.339 A.B., LL.B. 748 Jacaranda Circle‡
Inglese, Joseph H. .......................... '25 '53 C.112 B.S. L.767 LL.B. 20 Tamarack Dr.‡
Kiley, Thomas D., (AV) .......................... '43 '70 C.645 B.S.Ch.E. L.276 J.D. 986 Baileyana (Pat.)
Krabbenschmidt, Henry .......................... '18 '41 C&L.846 B.B.A., LL.B. 463 El Arroyo Rd.
Larson, Bianca G. .......................... '42 '80 C.273 B.A. L.284 J.D. 50 Knollcrest Rd.‡
Lauricella, Felix, (AV) .......................... '12 '35 L.767 1035 Woodland Dr.‡
Roberts, John M., (AV) .......................... '23 '50 C.112 A.B. L.1066 LL.B. 2230 Oakdale Rd.‡
Rosenblatt, Jerrold H. .......................... '48 '73 C.112 B.A. L.477 J.D. Pres., French Transit, Ltd.
Schnacke, June Borina .......................... '20 '42 C&L.813 A.B., J.D. 45 Genevra Rd.‡
Shannon, James W. .......................... '38 '67 C.363 B.S. L.209 J.D. 418 El Arroyo Rd.
Solvin, Francis J. .......................... '22 '48 C&L.767 B.S., LL.B. 1014 San Raymond Rd.
Stephenson, Polly Clarke .......................... '54 '81 C.813 B.A. L.61 J.D. 815 Vista Rd.
Terranella, Mary Ellen .......................... '54 '81 C.1044 B.A. L.1065 J.D. DRG Finl. Corp.
Tileston, Fred M., Jr. .......................... '47 '76 C.813 B.S. L.94 J.D. 1060 Barroilhet Dr.
Weil, Norman I. .......................... '51 '76 C.112 A.B. L.1067 J.D. 975 Vista Rd.
Wexler, Louis .......................... '08 '32 C.851 B.A. L.608 J.D. 363 Darrell Rd.‡

## HOLLISTER, * 19,212, *San Benito Co.*

Borelli, Frank P., Jr., (BV) .......................... '35 '61 C&L.770 B.S., LL.B. [O'Brien&B.]
Brady, Edw. L. .......................... '20 '49 C&L.813 A.B., LL.B. Ret. Supr. Ct. J.
Breen, Thomas P. .......................... '35 '64 C&L.770 B.S., LL.B. Supr. Ct. J.
Brown, Marie T. .......................... '49 '87 C.767 B.S. L.1226 J.D. [O'Brien&B.]
Coughlin, John R., (AV) .......................... '22 '49 C.755 A.B. L.494 LL.B. 390 5th St.‡
Coughlin, Paxton & Pipal, A Law Corporation, (AV) .......................... 390 5th St.
Engelhardt, Stephen E. .......................... '44 '70 C.112 A.B. L.1065 J.D. P.O. Box 679
Hamilton, Karen J., (BV) .......................... '45 '76 C&L.398 B.A., J.D. 210 San Benito
Helm, Greta Louise .......................... '— '90 C.914 B.S. L.770 J.D. 390 5th St.
LaForge, Gregory M. .......................... '61 '89 C.767 B.A. L.284 J.D. Dep. Dist. Atty.

**Lindsey, Bruce**
**(See Salinas)**

**Lombardo, Anthony, & Associates**
**(See Salinas)**

Marshall, Patrick E. .......................... '47 '75 C.1073 B.A. L.770 J.D. 345 5th St.

**Noland, Hamerly, Etienne & Hoss, A Professional Corporation**
**(See Salinas)**

Nutt, Harold L. .......................... '58 '86 C.1 B.S. L.809 J.D. Dep. Dist. Atty.
O'Brien, John H., (AV) .......................... '30 '57 C&L.770 B.S., LL.B. [O'Brien&B.]
O'Brien & Borelli, (AV) .......................... 350 5th St.
Paxton, James M., (AV) .......................... '27 '53 C&L.813 A.B., LL.B. [Coughlin,P.&P.]
Pipal, David E., (BV) .......................... '47 '74 C.494 B.A. L.809 J.D. [Coughlin,P.&P.]
Pleyte, James R. .......................... '43 '68 C&L.966 B.S., J.D. 514 Monterey St.
Russo, Steven Benito .......................... '56 '82 C.813 A.B. L.770 J.D. Dep. Dist. Atty.
Sanders, Steven R. .......................... '55 '83 C.112 B.A. L.464 J.D. Co. Coun.
Shipley, H. Anne .......................... '54 '81 C.767 B.S. L.1065 J.D. 50 Janets Ct.‡
Tobias, Harry J. .......................... '53 '78 C.112 B.A. L.1067 J.D. 3905th St.

## HOLLYWOOD, —, *Los Angeles Co.*

(See Los Angeles)

## HOLTVILLE, 4,820, *Imperial Co.*

Pliscou, Lee N. .......................... '57 '83 C.976 B.A. L.1065 J.D. 135 W. 7th St.★

## HOMELAND, 1,187, *Riverside Co.*

Nazario, Esther Joan Cid .......................... '44 '79 C.222 B.A. L.1198 J.D. 31393 Allen Ave.

## HORNBROOK, —, *Siskiyou Co.*

Dodd, Peter J. .......................... '44 '72 C.685 B.A. L.1066 J.D. P.O. Box 380
Ernst, Richard, (AV) .......................... '12 '39 C.494 B.A. L.976 LL.B. P.O. Box 289‡

## HUGHSON, 3,259, *Stanislaus Co.*

James, Stewart W., (BV) .......................... '39 '64 C.112 A.B. L.1066 LL.B. 7108 Hughson Ave.
Wright, William D. .......................... '49 '78 C.112 B.A. L.1065 J.D. 7108 Hughson Ave.

## HUNTINGTON BEACH, 181,519, *Orange Co.*

Adams, Carol Y. .......................... '63 '90 C.1310 B.S.B.A. L.809 J.D. 5200 Warner Ave.
Alter, Spencer R., (BV) .......................... '25 '57 C.1097 L.1065 J.D. 15956 Mariner Dr.
Amsbary, William S. .......................... '27 '58 C.1043 A.B. L.1068 LL.B. 20422 Craimer Lane‡
Anderson, Larry C. .......................... '43 '74 C.1109 B.A. L.1137 J.D. 16168 Beach Blvd.

**Armstrong, Alan Leigh '45 '84 C.112 B.A. L.1137 J.D.**
**18652 Florida Street, Suite 225, 92648-6006**
**Telephone: 714-375-1147 Fax: 714-375-1149**
**Email: armstrng@deltanet.com URL: http://users.deltanet.com/armstrng/**
**Probate, Trust and Estate, Real Estate, Commercial Real Estate, Admiralty, Small Business Law.**
*See Professional Biographies, HUNTINGTON BEACH, CALIFORNIA*

Baker, Celia Y. .......................... '12 '48 C.107 L.273 8251 Manifesto Cir.‡
Barron, Joseph C. .......................... '31 '65 C&L.426 B.S., J.D. Dep. City Atty.
Bauer, Charles A. .......................... '13 '38 C&L.378 B.A., LL.B. 1737 Park St.‡
Bechtold, William M. .......................... '46 '72 C.276 B.S.B.A. L.273 J.D. 18032 Starmont Lane
Beech, Dennis W., The Law Offices of '40 '82
C.502 B.S. L.1137 J.D. 19900 Beach Blvd. (⊙Lancaster)
Belsito, Floyd G., (BV) .......................... '34 '82 C.1109 B.A. L.1137 J.D. 17111 Beach Blvd.
Bisson, Barry A. .......................... '34 '63 C.550 B.S. L.273 LL.B. 17111 Beach Blvd. (Pat.)
Blanchard, Lester L. .......................... '28 '53 C.112 L.809 LL.B. 5901 Warner
Blank, Joel H. .......................... '57 '83 C.1109 B.A. L.426 J.D. 16261 Gentry Lane‡
Bloom, Donald L. '29 '58 C&L.546 B.S., J.D.
(adm. in NE; not adm. in CA) 21762 Starfire Ln.‡
Bonfa, Don P., (BV) .......................... '25 '52 C.734 B.S. L.477 J.D. 18582 Beach Blvd.
Bruce, Larry B., (A P.L.C.), (BV) .......................... '47 '73 C.763 B.A. L.61 J.D. 419 Main St.
Campbell, Vicki J. .......................... '44 '81 L.1137 J.D. P.O. Box 25
Cane, Michael A. .......................... '54 '78 C.112 B.A. L.800 J.D. Atty., Tele-Lawyer, Inc.
Carlson, C. William, Jr., (AV) .......................... '30 '59 C.223 B.S. L.477 J.D. [C.W.Carlson,Jr.]
Carlson, C. William, Jr., Inc., A Prof. Corp., (AV) .......................... Suite 140, 2130 Main Street
Catania, Robert F. .......................... '46 '78 C.813 B.A. L.426 J.D. McDonnell Douglas Aerospace
Chapin, William L. .......................... '36 '80 C.494 B.E.E. L.1137 J.D. 8732 Squires Cir. (Pat.)
Chasle, Dama C. .......................... '54 '84 C.1042 B.A. L.1137 J.D. 16835 Algonquin St.
Coen, Alvin M., (BV) .......................... '37 '62 C.1044 B.A. L.1349 LL.B. 16152 Beach Blvd.
Colaw, Frank D. '54 '81 C.934 B.A. L.502 J.D.
Dir., Contracts & Financial Mgmt., McDonnell Douglas Space Systems Co.
Coleman, Lori Ann ... '61 '87 C.800 B.S. L.990 J.D. Gen. Coun., Out-Patient Surgery Ctr.
Crawfis, Robert P. .......................... '50 '75 C.112 A.B. L.950 J.D. 2120 Main St.
Cubete, Samuel, (BV) .......................... '48 '75 C.1042 B.A. L.1148 J.D. 8071 Slater Ave.
Cully, Michael R. .......................... '51 '80 C.107 M.B.A. L.809 J.D. [Cully&R.]
Cully & Ryan, A Professional Corporation .......................... 8072 Warner Ave.
D'Alessandro, Paul David .......................... '62 '88 C.112 B.A. L.426 J.D. Dep. City Atty.
Deight, Blanche .......................... '26 '72 C.331 B.A. L.1068 J.D. 8912 Baywood Dr.‡
Delaloza, Arthur, Jr. .......................... '43 '76 C.990 M.P.P.A. L.1137 J.D. Dep. City Atty.
Doeringer, Jeffrey W. .......................... '49 '76 C.207 B.A. L.1137 J.D. 18377 Beach Blvd.
Dow, Robert .......................... '27 '74 C.823 A.B. L.1137 J.D. 8071 Slater Ave.
Drake, Dana L. .......................... '45 '70 C&L.800 B.A., J.D. 20301 Bluffside Cir.
Dreim, Lisa .......................... '60 '86 C.188 B.S. L.1044 J.D. 5301 Bolsa Ave.

Droege, Calvin L. ......... '43 '80 C.800 B.S. L.1179 J.D. [Droege,C.L.]
Droege, Calvin L., (A Prof. Corp.) ......... 2130 Main St.
Duverney, Ulric N. ......... '54 '80 C.415 B.S. L.1137 J.D. 602 Ashland Dr.
Eckert, L. M. ......... '06 '28 C&L.910 B.A., J.D. 22171 Wood Island Ln.‡
Feldman, Julius W., (BV) ......... '22 '51 C.112 A.B. L.1066 LL.B. 3801 Seascape Dr.
Flood-Smith, Dorothy Ann ......... '47 '79 C.1042 B.A. L.1001 J.D. 19471 Salmon Lane
Foster, Cecil G., Jr. .... '45 '72 C&L.846 B.A., J.D. 5200 Warner Ave. (⊙Las Vegas, NV)
Funkhouser, William Morry ......... '49 '81 C.112 B.A. L.878 J.D. 602 Oceanhill Dr.
Garrott, Valerie S. ......... '37 '77 C.932 B.S. L.1137 J.D. 200 Main St., #104-206
Gearhart, Glenn L. ......... '45 '77 C.854 B.S.E.E. L.1137 J.D. Sungrowth Equities Corp.
Georges, James ......... '31 '69 C.102 B.A. L.809 J.D. Dep. City Atty.‡
Gooding, Sandra J. '57 '86 C.999 B.S. L.37 J.D.
(adm. in AR; not adm. in CA) 5191 Meadowlark Drive★
Gray, John S. ......... '43 '76 C.763 A.B. L.284 J.D. 18141 Beach
Grossman, Jonathan C. '55 '83 C.112 B.A. L.809 J.D.
(adm. in IL; not adm. in CA) Gen. Coun. & V.P., Security Environmental Systems, Inc.
Guerin, John J. ......... '26 '49 C.174 L.426 J.D. 1118A Pacific Coast Hwy.
Gummerman, William E. ......... '24 '54 C&L.145 A.B., J.D. 16152 Beach Blvd.
Gumpel, Charles S. ......... '37 '74 C.679 B.S.C.E. L.1148 J.D. 9601 Onset
**Hallsted, L. Eugene**, (BV) ......... '45 '71 C.1163 B.A. L.950 J.D. [▣G.L.Rogers]
Harman, Thomas G., (BV) ......... '41 '69 C.375 B.S. L.426 J.D. 2130 Main St.
Hastings, Joyce E. ......... '— '72 L.1137 LL.B. 20422 Beach Blvd.
Hochfelsen, Steven I. ......... '58 '87 C.312 B.A. L.1065 J.D. 7755 Center Ave.
Holland, Robert B., (AV) ......... '27 '52 C&L.629 B.S., LL.B. 16411 Ladona Cir.‡
**Hood, Thomas W.**, (BV) ......... '47 '74 C.1042 B.A. L.1049 J.D. [Hood,W.&R.]
*REPORTED CASES: Harbour Landing-Dolfann, Ltd. v. Stanley C. Anderson (1996) 48 Cal.App.4th 260.
*PRACTICE AREAS: Real Property; Commercial Transactional Matters; Title Insurance Defense; General Business Negotiations.

**Hood, Wetzler & Reed, (AV)**
**18141 Beach Boulevard, Suite 300, 92648**
**Telephone: 714-842-6837 Fax: 714-841-6216**
**Email: INFO@HWRLAW.COM**
**Members of Firm: Thomas W. Hood; Sandra S. Wetzler; James T. Reed, Jr.**
**Civil Practice and Appellate practice including Real Property, Financial Institutions, Banking, Mortgage Lending, Title Insurance, Insurance Defense and Coverage, Transactional Matters, Commercial Litigation, Creditors' Rights, Bankruptcy, General Corporate, Probate.**
*See Professional Biographies, HUNTINGTON BEACH, CALIFORNIA*

Hutton, Gail, (BV) ......... '36 '73 C.112 B.A. L.990 J.D. City Atty.
Igo, Louis D ......... '39 '68 C.503 B.S. L.862 J.D. 16884 Sims St.
Jacob, J. Michael ......... '53 '79 C.1042 B.A. L.809 J.D. 16052 Beach Blvd.
Jan, Janet ......... '56 '87 C.800 B.S. L.809 J.D. 17456 Beach Blvd.‡
Kagel, Joseph H. ......... '41 '74 C.472 B.S.E.E. L.426 J.D. 6202 Hamshire‡
Katzen, Susan A. ......... '53 '78 C.958 B.S. L.1137 J.D. 8362 Laura Circle
Kelley, Fred F. ......... '06 '30 L.426 J.D. 21412 Dockside Cir.
Kelsey, Seth J. ......... '49 '74 C.273 B.A. L.1049 J.D. 7755 Center Ave.
Koffroth, Willis A. ......... '21 '72 L.1136 LL.B. 5011 Argosy Ave.
Kozich, S. David ......... '54 '82 C.1042 B.S. L.398 J.D. 17011 Beach Blvd.
Lejnieks, John H. ......... '46 '73 C.1042 B.A. L.1065 J.D. 19900 Beach Blvd.
Lewis, William J. ......... '42 '86 C.1042 B.S. L.1001 J.D. 19641 Ditmar Lane
Lopez, Beatriz M. ......... '40 '90 L.1137 J.D. 16541 Gothard St.
Loreto, Paul D. ......... '44 '79 C.433 B.M.E. L.809 J.D. 7402 Coho Dr.
**Loyd, Ralph R.** ......... '52 '80 C.1042 B.A. L.1137 J.D. [▣G.L.Rogers]
*PRACTICE AREAS: ERISA; General Trial Practice.
Lucas, Glen D. ......... '21 '52 C.999 L.809 LL.B. 16222 Monterey Lane
Mallon, Lawrence G. ......... '46 '73 C.276 B.S. L.245 J.D. 9041 Adlia Cir
Marcarelli, Ralph G. ......... '24 '74 C.831 B.Sc. L.1137 J.D. 10091 Birchwood Dr.
Mc Aneny, Redmond "Pete", (BV) ......... '45 '76 18141 Beach Blvd.
McDonald, Daniel J. ......... '56 '88 C.1042 B.A. L.1137 J.D. 6392 Talegate Dr.
Meyers, Mark J., (AV) ......... '50 '76 C.112 B.A. L.1137 J.D. 4952 Warner Ave
Moon, Linda Sapiro ......... '48 '80 C.112 B.A. L.1137 J.D. 2134 Main St.
Moore, Carol J. ......... '56 '81 C.681 A.B. L.309 J.D. 15892 Wicklow Lane
Moore, Neal ......... '45 '71 C&L.800 A.B., J.D. [Moore,R.&E.]⊙
Moore, Robert L., Jr. ......... '41 '69 C.112 A.B. L.800 J.D. 18090 Beach Blvd.
Moore, Rutter & Evans, (AV) ......... 2100 Main St., Ste. 280 (⊙Long Beach)
Morello, Arthur P. ......... '30 '63 C.112 L.809 J.D. 19361 Brookhurst St.
Morey, Christopher J. ......... '63 '90 C.800 B.S. L.1049 J.D. 4952 Warner Ave.
Nahm, David S. ......... '18 '51 C.312 A.B. L.94 J.D. 21841 Harbor Breeze Ln.‡
Nappa, Joseph A. ......... '54 '82 C.1042 B.S.L. L.1137 J.D. 315 3rd St.
Needham, Laura ......... '66 '91 C.112 B.A. L.426 J.D. 711 Ocean Ave. #114
Osborn, Jeffrey T. ......... '56 '89 C.1042 B.A. L.1137 J.D. 16162 Beach Blvd. #301
Parenzan, Annie R. Dozier ......... '— '79 C.1042 B.A. L.1068 J.D. 19126 Magnolia St.
Patton, Gary W. ......... '44 '74 L.1137 LL.B. P.O. Box 3597
Peroutka, Dale J. ......... '39 '77 C&L.1137 B.S., J.D. 16162 Beach Blvd.
Pierce, Donald J. ......... '15 '53 C.528 B.A. L.802 LL.B. 15452 Shasta Ln.
Potts, Howard A. ......... '26 '51 C.767 L.765 LL.B. 17881 Quintana Ln.
Raichelson, Michael H. ......... '67 '94 C.112 B.A. L.990 J.D. 17011 Beach Blvd.
**Reed, James T., Jr.**, (AV) ......... '48 '78 C.838 B.S. L.836 J.D. [Hood,W.&R.]
*PRACTICE AREAS: Financial Litigation; Creditors' Rights; Real Estate and Commercial Litigation.
Reilly, Paul A., (BV) ......... '38 '71 C.1042 B.S. L.1137 J.D. 7777 Ctr. Ave.
Rieck, Charles H. ......... '28 '74 C.1137 B.S.L. J.D. 6531 Peggy Circle
**Rogers, George L**, (AV) ......... '43 '69 C.112 B.A. L.1068 J.D. [G.L.Rogers]
*PRACTICE AREAS: Probate Law; Estate Planning; Taxation Law.

**Rogers, George L., A Law Corporation, (AV)**
**Suite 103, 17111 Beach Boulevard, 92647-5999**
**Telephone: 714-847-6041 Fax: 714-842-2151**
**Email: glralaw@1change.com**
**George L Rogers;—L. Eugene Hallsted; Ralph R. Loyd.**
**General Civil, Trial and Appellate Practice in all State and Federal Courts. Probate, Estate Planning, Tax, Business, Real Property, Domestic Relations and ERISA Transactions.**
*See Professional Biographies, HUNTINGTON BEACH, CALIFORNIA*

Rohm, Jeffrey P. '53 '79 C.839 B.A. L.790 J.D.
(adm. in SC; not adm. in CA) Coun., McDonnell Douglas Aerospace
Rokes, Dale S. ......... '36 '79 [D.S.Rokes]
Rokes, Dale S., A Prof. Law Corp. ......... 18377 Beach Blvd.
Ryan, Timothy J. ......... '56 '81 C.93 B.A. L.809 J.D. [Cully&R.]
Sage, William B. ......... '38 '69 C.112 B.A. L.426 J.D. Dep. City Atty.
Sangster, Robert C., (AV) ......... '41 '69 C.800 A.B. L.990 J.D. Dep. City Atty.
Schultz, Montana R. ......... '34 '71 C.1042 B.A. L.809 J.D. 17111 Beach Blvd.
Shaffer, R. James, (AV) ......... '31 '64 C.911 B.A. L.809 J.D. 1711 Beach Blvd, Ste 103
Sher, Rosalie M. ......... '— '75 C.999 L.765 J.D. 200 Pacific Coast Hwy.
Shinn, James M. ......... '49 '78 C.1042 B.A. L.1137 J.D. 6892 Vista Del Sol Dr.
Silber, Richard J. ......... '38 '64 C.216 A.B. L.273 LL.B. 2134 Main St.
Skerik, Dale O. ......... '30 '69 C.429 B.A. L.1068 J.D. 5200 Warner Ave.
Slates, Roger ......... '64 '90 C.1042 B.S. L.1066 J.D. 822 13th St.
Smith, Robert L. ......... '23 '56 C.800 B.S. L.809 LL.B. 2130 Main St.
Smith, Stephen H., (BV) ......... '43 '74 C.800 B.S. L.809 J.D. 2124 Main St.
Spiekerman, L Michael ......... '— '91 C.398 B.A. L.1137 J.D. 18377 Beach Blvd.
Steponovich, Stephen A. ......... '52 '88 C&L.1137 B.S.L., J.D. 5942 EdingerAve.
Stevens, Edward ......... '16 '41 C.976 B.A. L.800 LL.B. 21341 Compass Lane
Sunseri, James M. ......... '45 '76 C.107 B.A. L.823 J.D. 18652 Florida St.
Swanson, Martin H., Jr. ......... '45 '73 L.1137 J.D. 9441 Leilani Dr.
Taylor, Ronald L. '43 '74 C.475 B.S.E.E. L.912 J.D.
Intell. Prop. Coun., McDonnell Douglas Aerospace (Pat.)
Thibault, Alice O. ......... '44 '88 C&L.1137 B.S., J.D. 16682 Kettler Ln.
Trott, James E. ......... '55 '83 C.1042 B.S. L.464 J.D. 18632 Beach Blvd.
Tsai, Huai-Ching Robert ......... '51 '86 C.061 B.S. L.1067 J.D. 9202 Ellsworth Drive
Urban, William L. ......... '48 '73 C.112 B.A. L.1065 J.D. 9582 Hamilton Ave.
Van Holt, Karl A. ......... '41 '73 C.1042 B.A. L.1137 J.D. 16052 Beach Blvd.
Vaughan, Earle R. ......... '12 '35 C.33 L.29 LL.B. 8565 Sierra Circle‡
Vlachos, Dino ......... '35 '71 C.1077 B.S. L.809 J.D. 16052 Beach Blvd.
**Wetzler, Sandra S.**, (AV) ......... '47 '82 C.477 B.A. L.464 J.D. [Hood,W.&R.]
*PRACTICE AREAS: Civil Litigation and Appellate Practice; Corporate; Financial Litigation; Real Property; Commercial Litigation.
Young, Nevins D. ......... '27 '53 C.668 A.B. L.976 J.D. P.O. Box 852
Zwick, Kenneth T. ......... '53 '82 C.813 A.B. L.1066 J.D. 5471 Argosy Dr.

## HUNTINGTON PARK, 56,065, *Los Angeles Co.*

Burns, Wm. W. ......... '08 '44 C&L.809 [Lewis,S.&B.]
Carico, David B. ......... '33 '72 C.945 B.A. L.1152 J.D. Anchor Glass Container Corp.
Dapeer, Kenneth B. ......... '50 '76 C.1077 B.S. L.1095 J.D. [Dapeer,R.&L.]⊙
Dapeer, Rosenblit & Litvak, LLP, (AV) ......... 2770 E. Slauson Pk. (⊙Beverly Hills)
Dib, Michael G., (AV) ......... '44 '70 C.477 A.B. L.1068 J.D. 17111 Beach Blvd.
Glasberg, Jeffrey S. ......... '51 '78 C.895 L.1137 LL.B. 3400 E. Florence Ave.
Hapgood, Mark Wayne ......... '52 '87 C.330 B.A. L.809 J.D. 3400 E. Florence Ave.
Lewis, Alexander ......... '07 '32 L.800 LL.B. [Lewis,S.&B.]
Lewis, Signer & Burns ......... 2755 E. Florence Ave.
Luna, Ana Maria ......... '59 '84 C.112 B.A. L.800 J.D. Mun. J.
Nunez, Wilo B. ......... '50 '80 C.112 B.A. L.1068 J.D. 2675 Olive St.
Peguero, Eugene, Jr. ......... '57 '83 C.112 B.A. L.426 J.D. 2810-A E. Gage Ave.
Renteria, Hector A. ......... '54 '84 C.1131 B.A. L.1065 J.D. 6728 Seville Ave.
Rosenblit, Steven H. ......... '51 '76 C.112 B.S. L.1095 J.D. [▣Dapeer,R.&L.]
Schooling, Russell F. ......... '31 '60 C.112 B.A. L.1068 J.D. Mun. Ct. J.
Shafer, Roger S. ......... '44 '71 C.112 B.A. L.426 J.D. 2755 E. Florence Ave.
Willson, Geo. A., (BV) ......... '10 '44 C.800 L.999 3400 Florence Ave.

## HYDESVILLE, —, *Humboldt Co.*

Shulman, Adley M. ......... '31 '58 C.112 B.A. L.1068 J.D. [Shulman,S.&S.]
Shulman, Corinne S., (Mrs.) ......... '31 '57 C.112 B.A. L.1068 J.D. [Shulman,S.&S.]
Shulman, Shulman & Siegel ......... P.O. Box 642 (⊙Beverly Hills & Encino)

## HYNES, —, *Los Angeles Co.*

(See Paramount)

## IDYLLWILD, —, *Riverside Co.*

Clark, Jack H., (BV) ......... '45 '75 C.112 B.A. L.426 J.D. P.O. Box 1855
Nugent, Edward A., (AV) ......... '23 '52 C.385 B.A. L.309 LL.B. 26031 Hemstreet Pl.‡
Steele, J. Kent ......... '39 '70 C.767 B.S. L.61 J.D. 54380 N. Circle Dr.

## IMPERIAL, 4,113, *Imperial Co.*

**Stutz, Gallagher, Artiano, Shinoff & Holtz, A Professional Corporation**
**(See San Diego)**

## IMPERIAL BEACH, 26,512, *San Diego Co.*

Caster, Gary D. ......... '42 '88 C.679 B.S. L.61 J.D. 662 Ocean Lane
Kanner, John M., Sr. ......... '33 '67 C.434 B.S. L.426 LL.B. 244-C Evergreen Ave.‡
McGrew, Douglas A., (BV) ......... '38 '66 C.112 B.A. L.1066 J.D. 934 Palm Ave.
Schucker, Robert V., (BV) ......... '29 '62 C.763 A.B. L.1066 J.D. 238 Palm Ave.

## INDEPENDENCE, * —, *Inyo Co.*

Ashworth, Philip T. ......... '63 '90 C.147 B.A. L.1137 J.D. 436 N. Edwards St.
Bruce, Paul N. ......... '48 '78 C.1042 B.S. L.1049 J.D. Co. Coun.
Chapman, Don L. ......... '31 '60 C.101 A.B. L.800 J.D. Supr. Ct. J.
Gibbons, LaJoie H., Jr. ......... '41 '67 C.951 B.A. L.813 LL.B. Dist. Atty.
Gilbert, Bruce M. ......... '51 '77 C.112 B.A. L.1068 J.D. Dep. Dist. Atty.IV
Jones, Alicia ......... '50 '77 C.112 A.B. L.809 J.D. Dep. Co. Coun.
Livermont, Kirk K. ......... '54 '88 C.426 B.S. L.398 J.D. 251 N. Edwards St.

## INDIAN WELLS, 2,647, *Riverside Co.*

Christian, Alvern D. '34 '59 C.485 B.S. L.966 LL.B.
(adm. in WI; not adm. in CA) 45-645 Club Dr.‡

**Davis, Russell L. '39 '62 C.339 L.209 J.D.**
**74900 Highway 111, 92210**
**Telephone: 619-341-1040 Fax: 619-341-8084**
**Federal and State Taxation, Tax Litigation and Tax Controversies, Estate Planning, Probate and Probate Litigation.**
*See Professional Biographies, INDIAN WELLS, CALIFORNIA*

Ellmaker, Lee A., (BV) ......... '12 '39 C.629 L.950 LL.B. 76740 Sandpiper Ln.
Elm, J. Tucker '44 '72 C.1044 B.A. L.107 J.D.
Adm. Law J., State Agricultural Labor Relations Bd.
Foster, James C., (AV) ......... '29 '57 C.477 A.B. L.912 J.D. 74940 US Hwy. 111
Friedman, Orlan S., (AV) ......... '22 '51 C.112 B.A. L.426 J.D. 76-319 Fairway Dr.‡
Gibbons, Austin R., (AV) ......... '37 '64 C.740 A.B. L.1066 LL.B. [Gibbons,L.&C.]⊙
Gibbons, Lees & Conley, (AV) ......... 74-900 Hwy. III, Suite 216 (⊙Walnut Creek)

**Gibbs, Joseph A., (AV) '51 '78 C.1049 B.A. L.1137 J.D.** ▣
**74-900 Highway 111, Suite 211, 92210**⊙
**Telephone: 619-779-1790 Fax: 619-779-1780**
***PRACTICE AREAS: Civil Litigation; Real Estate; Business; Commercial.**
**Associate: Gregory R. Oleson.**
**Civil Litigation, Real Estate, Business, Commercial, Corporate and Partnership Law.**
**Palm Springs California Office: 901 E. Tahquitz Canyon Way, Suite C-203. Telephone: 619-320-7111. Fax: 619-320-6392.**
*See Professional Biographies, INDIAN WELLS, CALIFORNIA*

Hanlin, William K., (BV) ......... '38 '85 C.01 L.011 LL.B. 45-025 Manitou Dr.
Harnik, Brian S., (BV) ......... '57 '81 C.1349 B.A. L.94 J.D. [Roemer&H.]

**Healey & Healey**
**(See Palm Desert)**

Jackson, Randall S. ......... '71 '96 C.679 B.A. L.1339 J.D. [Roemer&H.]

**Johnson, Ronald W., (AV) '39 '68 C.37 B.S. L.1065 J.D.**
**45-025 Manitou Drive at Highway 111, 92210**
**Telephone: 619-360-8675 Fax: 619-360-1211**
**(Certified Specialist, Family Law, The State Bar of California Board of Legal Specialization).**
(This Listing Continued)

**Johnson, Ronald W. (Continued)**
*LANGUAGES: Spanish.
***PRACTICE AREAS: Family Law; Divorce; Adoptions; Child Custody; Premarital Agreements. Family Law, Divorce, Child and Spousal Support, Child Custody Disputes, Premarital and Separation Agreements, Living Arrangement Agreements.**
*See Professional Biographies, INDIAN WELLS, CALIFORNIA*

Lake, Jeffrey M. '41 '67 C.629 B.S. L.1068 J.D. 44345 Michigan Ct.
Lax, Martin, The Law Office of '63 '88 C.1097 B.A. L.1019 J.D. 45-025 Manitou Dr.
Long, Keith H. '29 '59 C.112 L.426 J.D. 75-370 Desert Valley Lane
Marshall, Lyle A. '25 '54 C.563 B.B.A. L.564 J.D. (adm. in NY; not adm. in CA) 44165 Mohave Ct.‡
**Martin, Douglas**, (AV) '37 '63 C.813 A.B. L.426 LL.B. [D.Martin]©
*PRACTICE AREAS: Estate Planning; Probate; Real Estate; Corporate Law; Taxation Law.

**Martin, Douglas, A Law Corporation, (AV)**
**Wall Street West, 74-785 Highway 111, Suite 201, 92210**
**Telephone: 619-776-1377 Fax: 619-776-1380**
**Douglas Martin.**
**Estate Planning, Probate, Real Estate, Corporate, Taxation and Business Law.**
*See Professional Biographies, INDIAN WELLS, CALIFORNIA*

**Oleson, Gregory R.** '67 '93 C.239 B.A. L.436 J.D. [J.A.Gibbs]
*PRACTICE AREAS: Civil Litigation; Real Estate; Business Litigation.
Poole, William H. '27 '57 C.999 L.596 J.D. (adm. in OR; not adm. in CA) 78585 Vista Del Fuente‡
Roemer, Richard I., (AV) '26 '54 C.112 A.B. L.426 J.D. [Roemer&H.]
Roemer & Harnik, (AV) 45-025 Manitou Dr. at Hwy. 111
Schmelzer, Gerald R., (AV) '29 '63 C.350 B.S. L.1065 J.D. 44-940 Lakeside Dr.
Wiese, Alvin O., Jr. '29 '54 C.174 B.S. L.800 LL.B. 45451 Cielito Dr.
Zeigler, G. Richard '42 '68 C&L.793 B.A., J.D. (adm. in SD; not adm. in CA) Prudential-Bache Securities

## INDIO, 36,793, *Riverside Co.*

Alexander, Audrey L. '44 '92 C.679 B.S. L.800 J.D. 82-500 Highway 11
**Anderson, Gregory T.** '— '93 C.446 B.A. L.284 J.D. [T.T.Anderson]
*PRACTICE AREAS: Plaintiffs Civil Trial; Plaintiffs Medical Malpractice.
**Anderson, Thomas T.**, (AV) '28 '55 C.629 B.B.A. L.767 LL.B. [T.T.Anderson]
*PRACTICE AREAS: Personal Injury; Highway Safety; Consumer Fraud; Insurance Bad Faith.

**Anderson, Thomas T., P.C., (AV)**
**45-926 Oasis Street, 92201**
**Telephone: 619-347-3364 Fax: 619-347-5572**
**Thomas T. Anderson;—David M. Chapman; Samuel F. Trussell; Gregory T. Anderson.**
**Negligence Law, Highway Safety, Products Liability, Insurance Bad Faith, Legal Malpractice and Consumer Fraud.**
**Reference: City National Bank.**
*See Professional Biographies, INDIO, CALIFORNIA*

Baker, Josephine '20 '44 C&L.800 A.B., LL.B. 45881 Salton St.
Belden, William L. '53 '84 C.1077 B.A. L.1065 J.D. Dep. Pub. Def.
Best, Lawrence P. '57 '82 C.1109 B.A. L.1068 J.D. Dep. Dist. Atty.
Bozich, Darinco '58 '83 C.1060 B.S. L.990 J.D. Dep. Dist. Atty.
Brand, Barbara M., (BV) '59 '85 C.426 B.S. L.990 J.D. 82500 Hwy. 111
Brhel, Martin C., Jr. '47 '77 C.1042 B.A. L.1137 J.D. Dep. Dist. Atty.
Brown, Chandler G. '45 '69 C.999 L.37 J.D. 82-634 Highway 111
Cabrera, Peter R. '50 '78 C.1109 B.A. L.602 J.D. P.O. Box 543
Carney, Dianne B. '47 '77 C.800 B.A. L.809 J.D. Dep. Dist. Atty.
Carnick, M. Lawrence, (A P.C.), (BV) '27 '51 C.25 A.B. L.188 J.D. 45-902 Oasis St., The Law Cntr.
Carroll, John P. '21 '52 C&L.426 B.B.A., J.D. Ret. Sup. Ct. J.
**Chapman, David M.**, (AV) '50 '77 C.36 B.S. L.1095 J.D. [T.T.Anderson]
*PRACTICE AREAS: Personal Injury Law; Products Liability Law; Insurance Law.
Cohen, Candice H. '53 '79 C.1077 B.A. L.1095 J.D. Dep. Pub. Def.
Coleman, Cal H. '24 '49 C&L.221 J.D. 78365 Silver Sage Dr.‡
Cribbs, Graham Anderson '40 '75 C.763 B.A. L.1137 J.D. Sup. Ct. J.
Dahl, Martin A. '34 '77 C.800 B.A. L.1137 J.D. 81106 U.S. Hwy. 111, #4F-87‡
Daily, Joseph A., (BV) '45 '76 C.1190 LL.B. Dep. Dist. Atty.
De Armond, Forest N., Sr. '21 '57 C.999 L.809 LL.B. 83-909 Pacifica Surf‡
Deaztlan, Roberto '49 '78 C.763 B.A. L.1049 J.D. 82500 Hwy. 111
Dougherty, H. Morgan, III '41 '66 C.770 A.B. L.1065 LL.B. Supr. Ct. J.
Douglass, Thomas N., Jr. '47 '72 C.1042 B.A. L.1065 J.D. Mun. Ct. J.
Downing, David B. '41 '79 C.745 B.A. L.1137 J.D. Dep. Dist. Atty.
Dunn, Robert N. '49 '79 C.112 B.A. L.809 J.D. Dep. Dist. Atty.
Ebert, Robert L. '40 '77 C.878 B.S. L.1137 J.D. Pub. Def.
Eckhardt, Thomas K. '50 '82 C.911 B.A. L.464 J.D. Dep. Dist. Atty.
Erwood, Richard A. '47 '73 C.909 B.A. L.1065 J.D. Supvr. Dept. Dist. Atty.
Fry, Lawrence W. '46 '76 C.112 B.A. L.61 J.D. Consolidated Cts. J.
Fryer, Brian Michael '51 '86 C.492 B.E.S. L.45 J.D. Inland Cos. Legal Servs.
Gianguzi, Charles J., Jr., (BV) '52 '81 C.651 B.A. L.1225 J.D. Dep. Dist. Atty.
Hanks, William J. '18 '48 C.623 A.B. L.896 LL.B. P.O. Box 1262

**Head, Clark '45 '76 C.1060 B.A. L.45 J.D.**
**82-500 Highway 111, Suite 5, 92201**
**Telephone: 619-347-3173 Fax: 619-347-0046**
***PRACTICE AREAS: Criminal Defense; Felonies; Civil Litigation.**
**Criminal Defense, Felonies, Civil Litigation.**
*See Professional Biographies, INDIO, CALIFORNIA*

Hemmer, John K. '34 '84 C.1242 B.A. L.1226 J.D. 82500 Hwy.
Hurley, Robert F. '40 '71 C.93 A.B. L.276 J.D. Chief Trial Deputy

**Ives, Kirwan & Dibble, A Professional Corporation**
**(See Palm Springs)**

Jevne, Franz P., III, (AV©) '42 '67 C.309 B.A. L.494 J.D. (adm. in MN; not adm. in CA) Pres., Cortima Co.
Katz, H. Alan '46 '80 C.112 B.A. L.1137 J.D. 46209 Oasis St.

**Kinkle, Rodiger and Spriggs, Professional Corporation**
**(See Riverside)**

**Koosed, Charles J. '67 '94 C.112 B.A. L.809 J.D.**
**82-500 Highway 111, Suite 5, 92201**
**Telephone: 619-347-6579**
***PRACTICE AREAS: Juvenile Law; Juvenile Dependency; Criminal Defence; Felonies; DUI.**
**Juvenile Law, Juvenile Dependency, Criminal Defense, Felonies, Criminal Defense, DUI.**
*See Professional Biographies, INDIO, CALIFORNIA*

Landon, Rick A '53 '87 C.1042 B.A. L.1137 J.D. 79-671 Port Royal Ave.
La Rocca, Phillip '34 '67 C.999 L.809 LL.B. Mun. Ct. J.
McDonald, Mark R., (BV) '60 '90 C.228 B.A. L.464 J.D. Dist. Atty. Off.
McKay, Donald C. '51 '80 C.1079 B.A. L.1137 J.D. 82-451 Hway. 111
McNulty, Ulrich Roy, (BV) '61 '86 C.174 B.A. L.1049 J.D. Sr. Dep. Dist. Atty.
Meckler, Renee B. '65 '92 C.112 B.A. L.809 J.D. Dep. Dist. Atty.
Miller, Douglas P. '52 '78 C.101 B.S. L.990 J.D. Consol. Ct. J.
Miller, Rosalind '59 '85 C.112 B.S. L.770 J.D. Dep. Dist. Atty.
Nelson, Fred M. '22 '45 C.502 B.A. L.477 J.D. 80000 Ave. 48
Retamal, Sergio A. '36 '71 C&L.420 J.D. 82-500 Hwy. 111
Scott, Shelly K. Hunt, (BV) '63 '90 C.628 B.S. L.1049 J.D. Dep. Dist. Atty.
Shelton, George C., Jr. '30 '60 C.668 B.A. L.1065 LL.B. Mun. J.

**Shuford, Jerry, (BV) '36 '70 C.766 B.A. L.809 J.D.**
**Suite 111, 82500 Highway III, P.O. Box 10370, 92202**
**Telephone: 619-347-3635 Fax: 619-347-0046**
***PRACTICE AREAS: Criminal Defense; Writs and Appeals; Drunk Driving Defense.**
**Practice Limited to Major Felonies and Drunk Driving Defense. Criminal Writs and Appeals.**
**Reference: El Dorado Bank.**
*See Professional Biographies, INDIO, CALIFORNIA*

Silva, James '47 '81 C.1077 B.A. L.398 J.D. 82-636 Highway 111
Stafford, Charles E., Jr., (BV) '47 '76 C.112 B.A. L.61 J.D. Dep. Pub. Def.
Steding, Sue F., (AV) '49 '75 C.911 B.A. L.1049 J.D. Asst. Dist. Atty.
**Trussell, Samuel F.**, (CV) '47 '85 C.766 B.A. L.809 J.D. [T.T.Anderson]
*LANGUAGES: Spanish.
*PRACTICE AREAS: Personal Injury; Consumer Fraud; Products Liability Law; Insurance Law.
Tweedle, Toni, (BV) '54 '81 C.388 B.A. L.61 J.D. Dep. Pub. Def.

**Welebir & McCune, A Professional Law Corporation**
**(See Redlands)**

Werbel, Julie S. '53 '81 C.605 B.A. L.1066 J.D. Pub. Def.
White, Randall D. '52 '78 C.112 B.A. L.426 J.D. Presiding J.

## INGLEWOOD, 109,602, *Los Angeles Co.*

Agate, Carol '34 '74 C.103 A.B. L.184 J.D. Admin. Law J., Unemployment Ins. App. Bd.
Baker, Richard M. '45 '71 C.347 B.S.B.A. L.813 J.D. Sr. V.P. & Gen. Coun., Imperial Bk.
Ballas, Jack '45 '71 C.800 B.A. L.426 J.D. Chf. Asst. City Atty.
Barnard, Bettye '— '75 C.1177 B.S. L.809 J.D. 110 S. La Brea Ave.
Berger, Jeanne S. '33 '69 L.1148 J.D. Adm. Law J., Calif. Unemployment Ins. App. Bd.
Boone, Elton D., (AV) '19 '49 C.813 B.A. L.800 J.D. 407 S. La Brea Ave.‡
Broady, Earl C., Jr., (AV) '30 '63 C.800 L.809 LL.B. 401 E. Manchester Blvd. #101
Broderick, Dennis S. '50 '81 C.329 B.A. L.1136 J.D. 101 N. La Brea Ave.

**Brown, John Clark, Jr., (AV) '43 '71 C.813 B.A. L.1068 J.D.**
**407 East Florence Avenue, 90301**
**Telephone: 310-419-2214**
**Real Estate, Business and Bankruptcy Litigation and Trial Practice in all Courts.**
**Reference: Metrobank, 10900 Wilshire Blvd., L.A., Calif.**
*See Professional Biographies, INGLEWOOD, CALIFORNIA*

Bueno-Flores, Mary H. '48 '82 C.1042 B.A. L.1136 J.D. 315 W. Manchester Blvd.
Cannon, Therese A. '50 '85 C.112 B.A. L.426 J.D. Dean, Univ. of W. Los Angeles
Castlen, Julia E. '63 '88 C.112 B.A. L.1066 J.D. Assoc. Gen. Coun., McNall Sports and Entertainment
Cohan, Charles G. '41 '76 C.1097 B.A. L.990 J.D. 111 N. La Brea Ave.
Collins, Caprice L. '54 '79 C.112 B.A. L.309 J.D. 3330 W. Manchester Blvd.
Cox, Wanda L. '49 '89 C.36 B.A. L.940 J.D. 3500 W. Manchester
Crawford, John E. '52 '80 C.112 B.A. L.1148 J.D. 705 S. Inglewood Ave.
Daugherty, L. Valson '32 '77 C.999 B.Mus. L.1179 J.D. 10252 2nd Ave.
Elias, Richard H., (AV) '37 '66 C.112 B.A. L.800 J.D. Dep. Dist. Atty.
Ellis, Philip C. '46 '79 C.605 A.B. L.284 J.D. V.P. & Sr. Coun., Imperial Bk.
Felix, Nadine G. '40 '87 C.309 B.S. L.329 J.D. Dept. of Housing & Community Development
Felthouse, Jack C., (BV) '25 '52 C&L.800 A.B., J.D. 9009 La Cienega Blvd.
Fierstadt, Edward T. '33 '69 C.112 B.S. L.1136 J.D. 318 E. Hillcrest Blvd.
Fitzhugh, Margaret S. '52 '78 C.170 B.A. L.36 J.D. Coun., Watts Health Found., Inc.
Franciscus, Mortimer G. '25 '53 C.605 A.B. L.800 LL.B. 1 Regent St.‡
Fukai, Janice Y. '54 '79 C&L.800 M.S., J.D. Dep. Pub. Def.
Furth, Marlene '52 '83 C.1169 A.B. L.1218 J.D. 1 Regent St.
Graham, Alma H. '56 '83 C.94 B.S. L.112 J.D. V.P. & Gen. Coun., Watts Health Found., Inc.
Green, Karen T. '57 '81 C.976 A.B. L.813 J.D. Dep. Pub. Def.
Hairston, Billy H. '30 '71 C.922 B.A. L.809 J.D. 401 E. Manchester Blvd.
Haydel, Augustavia J. '57 '88 C.597 B.A. L.1119 J.D. Staff Atty., Watts Health Found., Inc.
Jaffe, Doris N. '38 '65 C.112 L.809 J.D. Admn. Law J., Unemploy. Ins. App. Bd.
Jefferson, Bernard S. '10 '34 C.112 A.B. L.309 J.D. Univ. of West Los Angeles
Johnson, Barbara R. '— '80 C.976 B.A. L.61 J.D. Asst. City Atty.
Johnson-Parker, Jonnie H. '52 '84 C.900 B.A. L.705 J.D. [J.H.Johnson-Parker]
Johnson-Parker, Jonnie H., Inc. 111 N. La Brea Ave.
Katz, Seth H. '51 '81 C.813 A.B. L.1066 J.D. 601 W. Ellis Ave.
Labat, Germain, Jr. '46 '82 C.525 B.A. L.809 J.D. 9920 La Cienega Blvd.
Lee, David J. '24 '52 C.800 L.809 LL.B. 3500 W. Manchester Blvd.
Levine, Henry '43 '76 C.563 B.M.E. L.1148 J.D. 9920 S. La Cienega Blvd.
McAlpin-Grant, Lola M. '41 '67 C.525 B.A. L.426 LL.B. 1608 Centinela Ave.
Meigs, John '47 '81 C.112 B.A. L.426 J.D. Mun. Ct. J.
Meyer, Charles F. '58 '84 C&L.36 B.A., J.D. Assoc. Coun., Imperial Bk.
Mizrahi, Edward M. '35 '61 C.112 A.B. L.1068 LL.B. 9920 La Cinega Blvd.
Moss, Wardell G. '29 '62 C.112 B.A. L.809 LL.B. Mun. Ct. J.
Ochuru, Eke '64 '92 L.061 LL.B. (adm. in NY; not adm. in CA) 622 Austin Ave.
Orum, Wilbur C., Jr. '20 '52 C.37 A.B. L.796 LL.B. (adm. in TX; not adm. in CA) 3500 W. Manchester Bldg.‡
**Perzik, James L.**, (AV) '29 '63 C&L.800 B.S., J.D. Gen. Coun., Calif. Sports, Inc.
*RESPONSIBILITIES: Sports Law; Taxation Law.
Peters, Ann Davis '46 '81 C.112 B.A. L.1068 J.D. 1300 N. La Brea Ave.
Polski, Perry M. '27 '69 C.494 B.S. L.999 J.D. Univ. of West Los Angeles Sch. of Law
Potts, Jas. L., (AV) '18 '44 C&L.813 A.B., J.D. 116 S. Oak St.
Rosten, Howard, (AV) '43 '69 C.112 B.S. L.1049 J.D. City Atty.
Smith, Malcolm George, (AV) '35 '63 C.112 A.B. L.309 LL.B. Gen. Coun., The Centinela Grp.
Starr, Philip J. '50 '75 C.94 B.S.,B.A. L.809 J.D. Pres. & CEO, Tritech Biogenics, Inc.
Steuart, Timothy G. '59 '84 C.112 B.A. L.426 J.D. 812 E. La Brea Dr.
Sullivan, Harold V., II '40 '67 C&L.800 A.B., J.D. 9920 S. La Cienega Blvd.
Sulman, Frances J. '42 '83 C.881 A.B. L.426 J.D. Dep. Dist. Atty.
Tobenkin, Michele Mercer '51 '82 C.112 B.S. L.1136 J.D. Prof. of Law, Univ. of West Los Angeles
Vassie, Kenneth '33 '62 L.426 J.D. Mun. Ct. J.
Webster, Allen J., Jr. '41 '71 110 S. La Brea Ave.
Williams, Beverly A. '45 '78 C.329 B.A. L.426 J.D. 8615 Crewshaw Bldg.
Wright, Jeannette J. '35 '74 C.863 B.A. L.1136 J.D. 11222 La Cienega Blvd.

CAA121P

CALIFORNIA—INGLEWOOD MARTINDALE-HUBBELL LAW DIRECTORY 1997

Zieff, Linda G. .................... '44 '79 L.1136 J.D. 4635 Century Blvd.

## INVERNESS, —, *Marin Co.*

Behr, Peter H., (AV) .................... '15 '40 C&L.976 A.B., LL.B. P.O. Box 750‡
Cameron, Sarah T. .................... '48 '74 C.66 B.A. L.813 J.D. 19 Cameron St.
Cherrigan, Alan K. .................... '52 '86 C.112 B.A. L.284 J.D. P.O. Box 34‡
Duke, George F. .................... '35 '61 C.860 B.A. L.309 J.D. P.O. Box 224
Elke, Thomas, (AV) .................... '29 '52 C&L.813 B.S., J.D. P.O. Box 888
Hansen, Borah R. .......... '24 '49 C&L.813 A.B., J.D. 12732 Sir Francis Drake Bldg.
Hertz, Richard S. .................... '47 '73 C.575 B.A. L.818 J.D. P.O. Box 584
Kroninger, Robt. H. .................... '23 '48 C.112 B.S. L.1066 J.D. P.O. Box 500‡
Linderman, Jay S., (AV) .................... '40 '65 C.696 B.A. L.1066 LL.B. P.O. Box 888
Wagner, George W. .................... '32 '63 C.112 B.S. L.809 LL.B. P.O. Box 795

## IONE, 6,516, *Amador Co.*

Wood, Daved F. .................... '30 '77 C.112 A.B. L.464 J.D. 313 W. Marlette‡

## IRVINE, 110,330, *Orange Co.*

Abbott, Sharon Stoner .................... '57 '82 C.645 B.S. L.245 J.D. Unicare Ins. Co.
Abrams, Donald L. '46 '73 C.276 B.S. L.273 J.D.
(adm. in DC; not adm. in CA) Gen. Coun., Three D- Depts., Inc.
**Adair, Lance A.** .................... '59 '85 C.112 B.S. L.1065 J.D. [Jackson,D.&P.]
*PRACTICE AREAS: Litigation.
**Adams, Michael R.** .................... '60 '85 C.112 B.A. L.763 J.D. [Suchman,G.&P.]⊙
*PRACTICE AREAS: Business Law; Corporate Law; Estate Planning and Trust Law; Probate Law.
Addy, Susan P. .................... '56 '89 C&L.1241 B.A., J.D. 2030 Main St.
**Adelson, Jeffrey M.** .................... '52 '77 C.1109 B.A. L.1137 J.D. [Laughlin,F.L.&M.]
*PRACTICE AREAS: Workers' Compensation Defense; Employment Law.
Agler, Timothy B. .................... '52 '82 C.860 B.S. L.273 J.D. 150 Amherst Aisle‡
Ahrens, Leslie C., (P.C.), (AV) .................... '44 '75 C.112 B.A. L.809 J.D. 2010 Main St.
Alami, Iwona Joanna .................... '58 '92 C.112 B.A. L.426 J.D. Two Venture Plaza
**Albrecht, Richard J.**, (AV) .................... '48 '73 C&L.494 B.S., J.D. [Albrecht&B.]
*PRACTICE AREAS: Estate and Gift Tax Law; Estate and Business Planning; Asset Protection Planning.

**Albrecht & Barney, (AV)**
**1 Park Plaza, Suite 300, 92614**
**Telephone: 714-263-1040 Fax: 714-263-1099**
**Richard J. Albrecht; Colleen Barney. Associate: Commie Stevens.**
**Estate and Gift Tax Law, Estate Planning, Trust and Estate Administration, Asset Protection Planning.**

***See Professional Biographies, IRVINE, CALIFORNIA***

**Aldrich, Mark E.**, (AV) .................... '53 '79 C.426 B.A. L.800 J.D. [Aldrich&B.]
*PRACTICE AREAS: Banking; Commercial Code, Articles 3 & 4; Corporate and Securities.

**Aldrich & Bonnefin, P.L.C., (AV)** [BR]
**18200 Von Karman Avenue, Suite 730, P.O. Box 19686, 92623**
**Telephone: 714-474-1944 Telecopier: 714-474-0617**
**Email: 103132.2601@compuserve.com**
**Mark E. Aldrich; Janet M. Bonnefin; Mark Alan Moore; David Bustamante;—Eric G. Baron; Keith R. Forrester; Anne M. McEachran; Kristen Welles Lanham; Robert K. Olsen.**
**Banking, Business and Financial Law.**
**Representative Clients: Bankers' Compliance Group; Bank Leumi Le Israel, B.M.; California Commerce Bank; California Korea Bank; Fallbrook National Bank; State Bank of India (California); Valley Independent Bank; Valliwide Bank.**
**References: S. Suresh Kumar, President, Brentwood Bank of California; Curtis Reis, President, Alliance Bank.**

***See Professional Biographies, IRVINE, CALIFORNIA***

**Alexander, Marc D.** .................... '51 '81 C.1169 B.A. L.1068 J.D. [Jackson,D.&P.]
*LANGUAGES: French.
*PRACTICE AREAS: Litigation.
**Alexander, Melissa C.** .................... '65 '92 C.112 B.A. L.800 J.D. [Malpass&G.]
*LANGUAGES: French.
*PRACTICE AREAS: Bankruptcy; Business Litigation.
**Alexander, Sheila Anne** .................... '47 '90 C.112 B.A. L.1226 J.D. [[A] Baker,S.&K.]
*PRACTICE AREAS: Medical Malpractice; Dental Malpractice.
**Allen, Alyssa J.** '66 '92 C.990 B.A. L.1065 J.D.
[[A] Faustman,C.D.&F.] (⊙San Francisco)
*PRACTICE AREAS: Employment Law; Labor Law; Business Litigation.
Allen, J. Wayne .................... '60 '84 C&L.69 B.B.A., J.D. 2030 Main St.
**Allen, Stephanie E.**, (BV) .................... '54 '80 C.112 B.A. L.61 J.D. [Allen,R.&M.]
*PRACTICE AREAS: Banking; Corporate; Mergers and Acquisitions.
Allen, William R. .......... '26 '52 C.840 B.S. L.802 LL.B. 19900 MacArthur Blvd., 8th Fl.

**Allen, Matkins, Leck, Gamble & Mallory LLP, (AV)** [BR]
**A Limited Liability Partnership including Professional Corporations**
**Fourth Floor, 18400 Von Karman, 92715⊙**
**Telephone: 714-553-1313 Telecopier: 714-553-8354**
**Partners: John C. Gamble (Resident); Thomas C. Foster (Resident); R. Michael Joyce (Resident); Lawrence D. Lewis (P.C.) (Resident); Monica E. Olson (Resident); Thomas E. Gibbs (Resident); Dwight L. Armstrong (Resident); Paul D. O'Connor (Resident); S. Lee Hancock (Resident); Richard E. Stinehart (Resident); Stephen R. Thames (Resident); Anne E. Klokow (Resident); David W. Wensley (Resident); Gary S. McKitterick (Resident); Patrick J. Grady (Resident); Robert M. Hamilton (Resident); Vincent M. Coscino. Resident Associates: Bradley N. Schweitzer; Alan J. Gordee; Pamela L. Andes; Catherine M. Page; Leslie Tucker Fischer; Ralph H. Winter; Michael S. Greger; A. Kristine Floyd; Stephen J. Kepler; Michael A. Alvarado; Mary Kay Ruck; Susan E. Graham; Christopher G. Lund; Sally S. Costanzo; Allison Fong Greenberg; Jeffrey Mannisto; Tracy L Silva.**
**General Civil, Trial and Appellate Practice in all State and Federal Courts. Real Property and Construction Law. Land Use and Environmental Law, including Administrative and Regulatory Practice. Corporations, Securities, Partnerships and Public Bond Financings. Federal, State and Local Taxation. Labor and Employment Law (Management) and Wrongful Termination. Bankruptcy, Creditors Rights, Receiverships and Restructuring. Estate Planning and Trusts.**
**Los Angeles, California Office: Seventh Floor, 515 South Figueroa Street, 90071. Telephone: 213-622-5555. Telecopier: 213-620-8816.**
**San Diego, California Office: 501 West Broadway, Suite 900, 92101. Telephone: 619-233-1155. Facsimile: 619-233-1158.**
**West Los Angeles, California Office: 1999 Avenue of the Stars, 90067. Telephone: 310-788-2400. Fax: 310-788-2410.**

***See Professional Biographies, IRVINE, CALIFORNIA***

**Allen, Ross & Mooney, (AV)**
**2603 Main Street, Suite 1000, 92614**
**Telephone: 714-955-3334 Fax: 714-955-3723**
**Members of Firm: Stephanie E. Allen; James L. Ross; W. Ernest Mooney.**
**Civil Litigation, Banking, Business, Real Estate.**

***See Professional Biographies, IRVINE, CALIFORNIA***

**Allison, Jeffrey S.** .................... '67 '94 C.112 B.A. L.464 J.D. [[A] Gauntlett&Assoc.]
**Alpert, Mark D.** .................... '63 '88 C.112 B.A. L.880 J.D. [Willis,K.&A.]
*PRACTICE AREAS: Business; Real Estate and Land Use Litigation; Environmental Litigation.
**Alpin, Maureen M.** .................... '65 '92 C.972 B.S. L.464 J.D. [[A] Maher,L.&G.]
*PRACTICE AREAS: Financial Institutions Law; Transactions; Business Litigation; Construction Litigation; Commercial Law.
**Alsnauer, William E., Jr.** .................... '57 '82 C.294 A.B. L.607 J.D. [Suchman,G.&P.]⊙
*PRACTICE AREAS: Bankruptcy (Creditor Representation); Litigation; Commercial Law; Collection Law; Landlord and Tenant Law.

**Altman, Nancy J.** .................... '59 '87 C.1042 B.A. L.990 J.D. [[A] Mower,K.N.C.&H.]
**Alvarado, Michael A.** .................... '65 '92 C.112 B.A. L.813 J.D. [[A] Allen,M.L.G.&M.]
*PRACTICE AREAS: Real Estate.

**Alvarado, Smith, Villa & Sanchez, A Professional Corporation**
**(See Newport Beach)**

**Amante, Jerome L.** .................... '48 '83 C.1068 B.A. L.809 J.D. [Amante]
*PRACTICE AREAS: Business; Real Estate; Construction Litigation; Civil Trial Advocacy; Trial Consultation.

**Amante Law Firm, The**
**19800 MacArthur Boulevard Suite 1450, 92715-2442**
**Telephone: 714-724-4510 Telecopier: 714-724-4504**
**Jerome L. Amante. Associates: Catherine Stark Shiel. Of Counsel: Heidi Knapp Leanders; Janice M. Patronite.**
**General Civil and Trial Practice in all California State and Federal Courts. Business, Real Estate, Construction, Employment, Homeowner Association, Banking, Mortgage Brokerage, Partnership and Commercial Law. Bankruptcy, Insolvency, Corporate and Partnership Reorganization and Debtor and Creditor Rights Law.**

***See Professional Biographies, IRVINE, CALIFORNIA***

**Amber, Gregg** .................... '56 '81 C.675 B.A. L.813 J.D. [Snell&W.]
*PRACTICE AREAS: Corporate; Securities.
**Amo, Douglas A.** .................... '57 '85 C.112 B.A. L.464 J.D. [[A] Pivo&H.]
**Andersen, Jon D.** .......... '62 '94 C.1077 A.A.A.S. L.1109 J.D. [[A] Berger,K.S.M.F.S.&G.]
**Anderson, Gregory J.** .................... '67 '92 C.1259 B.S. L.629 J.D. [[A] D.R.Kurtz]
*PRACTICE AREAS: Estate Planning, Probate and Trusts; Business and Corporate Law; Business Litigation; General Litigation.
Anderson, Stephen E. '57 '82
C.1169 B.A. L.1065 J.D. Assoc. Coun., Fidelity Natl. Title Ins. Co.
**Andes, Pamela L.** .................... '63 '88 C.800 B.S. L.426 J.D. [[A] Allen,M.L.G.&M.]
*PRACTICE AREAS: Real Estate and Environmental.
**Andrade, Richard B.**, (AV) .................... '51 '77 C.763 B.S. L.61 J.D. [Andrade&M.]
*PRACTICE AREAS: Construction Litigation; Maritime Law; Labor Law and Environmental Law.

**Andrade & Muzi, (AV)** [BR]
**Marine National Bank Building, 18401 Von Karman, Suite 350, 92715⊙**
**Telephone: 714-553-1951 Telecopier: 714-553-0655**
**Members of Firm: Richard B. Andrade; Andrew C. Muzi; Ronald G. Holbert; Abilio Tavares, Jr.; Samuel G. Broyles, Jr.; Frank A. Satalino. Of Counsel: Kurt Kupferman.**
**Civil Trial and Appellate Practice, Construction Law, Insurance and Surety Litigation, General, Commercial, Civil Litigation, Bankruptcy, Real Estate and Business Law.**
**Representative Clients: American International Cos.; American Home Assurance; Lloyds of London; VECO International; VECO Drilling, Inc.; Shell Oil Co.; Unocal.**
**San Diego, California Office: Tokia Bank Building, 3111 Camino Del Rio North, Suite 1100. Telephone: 619-291-2481.**

***See Professional Biographies, IRVINE, CALIFORNIA***

**Andre, Christopher S.** .................... '64 '95 C.1109 B.A. L.426 J.D. [[A] Ramsay&J.]
*PRACTICE AREAS: First and Third Party Insurance Defense; Insurance Coverage.
**Andrews, Camilla N.** .................... '58 '86 C.770 B.A. L.426 J.D. [Nichols&A.]
*LANGUAGES: French.
*PRACTICE AREAS: Commercial Litigation; Creditors' Rights; Contract Disputes; Financial Institution Litigation; Creditor Bankruptcy.
**Andrews, Denver R., Jr.** .................... '49 '82 C.1128 B.A. L.809 J.D. [[A] Neuland&N.]
*PRACTICE AREAS: Civil Litigation; Business; Construction; Community Associations; Personal Torts.
**Andronico, Paul A.** .................... '67 '95 C.112 B.A. L.1049 J.D. [[A] Gibson,D.&C.]
**Anielski, Jeffrey M.** .................... '56 '86 C.610 B.A. L.809 J.D. [Kirtland&P.]
Annis, Michael ...... '46 '74 C.1042 B.A. L.1148 J.D. V.P. & Gen. Coun., Red Robin Intl.
**Antosh, Louis T., Jr.** .................... '64 '95 C.990 B.S. L.94 J.D. [[A] Kring&B.]
*PRACTICE AREAS: Business Litigation; Corporate Transactional; Construction Law.
Applegate, Douglas L. .................... '53 '79 C&L.36 B.S., J.D. One Park Plaza
Aprahamian, Constance E. .................... '— '87 C.823 B.A. L.1137 J.D. 16 Sycamore Creek
**Arens, Russell R.** .................... '62 '88 C.940 B.A. L.464 J.D. [[A] Kring&B.]
*REPORTED CASES: Swann v. Oliver (1994) 22 CA 4th 1334.
*PRACTICE AREAS: Civil and Business Litigation.
**Arguelles, John A.** .................... '27 '55 C.112 A.B. L.1068 LL.B. [[C] Gibson,D.&C.]
*PRACTICE AREAS: Alternative Dispute Resolution.
**Armstrong, Dwight L.** .................... '52 '77 C.813 B.A. L.800 J.D. [Allen,M.L.G.&M.]
*PRACTICE AREAS: Labor and Employment Law (Management).
**Armstrong, Wm. David** '49 '84 C&L.1137 B.S.L., J.D.
Legal Coun., Kawasaki Motors Corp., U.S.A.
*RESPONSIBILITIES: Products Liability Law; Personal Injury.
**Arnold, Thomas D.** .................... '58 '92 C.112 B.S. L.426 J.D. [[A] Jackson,D.&P.]
*PRACTICE AREAS: Litigation.
**Arnold, Wayne C.**, (BVⓉ) .................... '53 '77 C.1042 B.A. L.500 J.D. [Bryan C.]
*PRACTICE AREAS: Commercial Litigation; Products Liability; Employment Litigation.

**Arter & Hadden, (AV)**
**Five Park Plaza, 10th Floor, Jamboree Center, 92714⊙**
**Telephone: 714-252-7500 Facsimile: 714-833-9604**
**Members of Firm: Jack W. Fleming; Bruce G. Holden; Curtiss L. Isler; Randolf W. Katz; Stephen H. LaCount; Joseph J. Nardulli; Michael P. Ridley; H. Neal Wells III (Certified Specialist, Estate Planning, Trust and Probate, The State Bar of California Board of Legal Specialization). Associates: Rodney W. Bell; Marie A. Cioth; James K. Dierking; Christine E. Howson; David K. Marion; Mark T. Palin; Joseph P. Quinby; Peter K. Rundle. Of Counsel: Henry G. Kohlmann.**
**General Civil and Trial Practice. Antitrust, Banking, Corporation, Corporate Financing, Creditors Rights, Estate Planning, Trust, Probate, Government Contract, International Business, Labor and Employment, Oil and Gas, Products Liability, Negligence, Admiralty, Maritime, Workers Compensation, Public Utility, General Real Estate, Finance, Securities and Taxation Law.**
**In Cleveland, Ohio: 1100 Huntington Building, 925 Euclid Avenue. Telephone: 216-696-1100. Fax: 216-696-2645.**
**In Columbus, Ohio: 21st Floor, One Columbus, 10 West Broad Street. Telephone: 614-221-3155. Fax: 614-221-0479.**
**In Washington, D.C.: 1801 K Street, N.W., Suite 400K. Telephone: 202-775-7100. FAx: 202-857-0172.**
**In Dallas, Texas: 1717 Main Street, Suite 4100. Telephone: 214-761-2100. Fax: 214-741-7139.**
**In Los Angeles, California: 700 South Flower Street, 30th Floor. Telephone: 213-629-9300. Fax: 213-617-9255.**
**In Austin, Texas: 100 Congress Avenue, Suite 1800. Telephone: 512-479-6403. Fax: 512-469-5505.**
**In San Antonio, Texas: 7710 Jones Maltsberger, Harte-Hanks Tower, Suite 540. Telephone: 210-805-8497. Fax: 210-805-8519.**
**In San Francisco, California: 201 California Street, 14th Floor, 94111. Telephone: 415-912-3600. Fax: 415-912-3636.**
**In San Diego, California: 402 West Broadway, Fourth Floor, 92101. Telephone: 619-238-0001. Fax: 619-238-8333.**
**In Woodland Hills, California: 5959 Topanga Canyon Boulevard, Suite 244, 91367. Telephone: 818-712-0036. Fax: 818-346-6502.**
**Revisers of the Ohio Law Digest for this Directory.**

***See Professional Biographies, IRVINE, CALIFORNIA***

Ashley, Fred T. .................... '50 '78 C.112 B.A. L.426 J.D. 2201 Dupont Dr.
**Ashman, Kristi J.** .... '60 '93 C.112 B.A. L.800 J.D. Corp. Coun., Burlington Air Express
Aughenbaugh, Richard A. '50 '76 C.347 B.A. L.880 J.D.
(adm. in PA; not adm. in CA) Dir., Tax Resch. & Planning, Allergan, Inc.
**Augustini, Jeff** .................... '69 '95 C.112 B.A. L.276 J.D. [[A] Gibson,D.&C.]
**Augustini, Rick** .................... '67 '92 C.112 B.A. L.426 J.D. [[A] Case,K.B.&W.]⊙
**Ault, Thomas H., (Inc.)**, (AV) '45 '72
C.763 B.A. L.1049 J.D. [Ault,D.J.&G.] (⊙San Diego)

**Ault, Deuprey, Jones and Gorman, (AV)**
**A Law Partnership including Professional Corporations**
**AT&T Tower, 8001 Irvine Center Drive, Suite 980, 92718-2921⊙**
**Telephone: 714-450-8345 Facsimile: 714-450-8353**
**Thomas H. Ault (Inc.); Joseph P. Price.**
**General Civil and Trial Practice in all State and Federal Courts. Appellate Practice, Family, Negligence, Insurance and Medical and Legal Malpractice Law.**
**San Diego, California Office: 402 West Broadway, 16th Floor. Telephone: 619-544-8300. Fax: 619-338-0017.**
**Vista, California Office: 202 West Vista Way. Telephone: 619-631-1800. Fax: 619-631-1915.**
*See Professional Biographies, IRVINE, CALIFORNIA*

Baca, Walter E. ....................... '36 '73 C.112 B.S. L.426 J.D. 1920 Main St.

**Bachman, Robert L., Law Offices of '49 '73 C.1109 B.A. L.1067 J.D.**
**The Atrium, 19100 Von Karman Avenue Suite 380, 92715**
**Telephone: 714-955-0221 Telecopier: 714-955-0324**
***REPORTED CASES: Valley Circle Estates v. VTN Corporation.**
**Construction Defect, Mechanics Lien, Construction Claims, Bankruptcy, Transactional Matters and Labor Law.**
**Representative Clients: The Austin Co.; Hensel Phelps; Savala Construction; Al Shankle Construction; Steve P. Rados; The Griffith Co.**
*See Professional Biographies, IRVINE, CALIFORNIA*

Bahan, Cornelius P., (AV) .................. '47 '72 C.112 A.B. L.800 J.D. [C.P.Bahan]⊙
Bahan, Cornelius P., Inc., (AV) .......................... 2030 Main St. (⊙Santa Ana)

**Bainbridge Group, A Law Corporation, (AV)**
**18301 Von Karman Avenue, Suite 410, 92612**
**Telephone: 714-442-6600 FAX: 714-442-6609**
**Michael E. Johnson; David W. Greenman; Randy McDonald; Samuel M. Hung (Not admitted in CA).**
**General Business, Corporate, Partnership and Real Estate, Finance, Mergers and Acquisitions, Strategic Alliances and Technology Licensing.**
*See Professional Biographies, IRVINE, CALIFORNIA*

**Baker, Silberberg & Keener, (AV)**
**Newport Gateway, Suite 850, 19900 MacArthur Boulevard, 92612⊙**
**Telephone: 714-955-0900 Fax: 714-955-0909**
**Marshall Silberberg; Steven R. Van Sicklen; Mark V. Franzen;—Tobin J. Trobough; Constance A. Endelicato; Mark N. Maizel; Robert C. Mc Bride; Robert A. Cardwell; Robert E. Hess; Ross E. Shanberg; Sheila Anne Alexander; Kimberly A. Maynard.**
**General Civil and Business Litigation. Appellate, Professional Malpractice, Insurance Coverage/Bad Faith, Toxic Torts, Personal Injury and Products Liability Law, Architectural & Engineering, Legal Ethics.**
**Santa Monica, California Office: Suite 300, 2850 Ocean Park Boulevard. Telephone: 310-399-0900. Fax: 310-399-1644.**
*See Professional Biographies, IRVINE, CALIFORNIA*

**Ball, Angela L.** ................. '64 '91 C.112 A.B. L.800 J.D. [Ⓐ Sedgwick,D.M.&A.]
Ballo, Brian P ........... '56 '87 C.477 B.A. L.61 J.D. 19900 MacArthur Blvd., Ste., 650
Balmuth, Robert L. ....................... '52 '77 C.112 B.A. L.1049 J.D. [Davis&B.]
**Banki, Shireen G.** ............. '67 '92 C.112 B.A. L.809 J.D. [Ⓐ Berger,K.S.M.F.S.&G.]
*PRACTICE AREAS: Business Litigation; Insurance Coverage.
**Barajas, Monica E.** ......................... '61 '87 C.112 B.A. L.1065 J.D. [Ⓒ Bryan C.]
*LANGUAGES: Spanish.
*PRACTICE AREAS: Business Immigration.
Baran, Robert J. ......... '41 '69 C.705 B.S. L.776 J.D. Sr. Pat. Atty., Allergan, Inc. (Pat.)
**Barbin, Debra L.** ....................... '66 '91 C.112 B.A. L.1065 J.D. [Ⓐ Corbett&S.]
**Baren, Daniel H.** ..................... '66 '95 C.597 B.S. L.800 J.D. [Ⓐ Gibson,D.&C.]
**Barinholtz, Alec M.** .................. '57 '88 C.1183 B.S. L.809 J.D. [Ⓒ Ross,D.&M.]
**Barmettler, Michael A.** ............ '69 '96 C.35 B.S.B.A. L.1049 J.D. [Ⓐ Gibson,D.&C.]
**Barnes, Robert Samuel**, (AV) ........... '22 '50 C&L.813 A.B., LL.B. [Barnes,C.F.&Z.]
*PRACTICE AREAS: Business Related Matters; Civil Litigation.

**Barnes, Crosby, FitzGerald & Zeman, LLP, (AV) BR**
**2030 Main Street, Suite 1050, 92614**
**Telephone: 714-852-1100 Fax: 714-852-1501**
**Members of Firm: Robert Samuel Barnes; William M. Crosby; Michael J. FitzGerald; Larry S. Zeman; Mark H. Cheung; Alka N. Patel. Of Counsel: Frederick J. Stemmler.**
**Construction, Labor, Tort and Commercial Law.**
*See Professional Biographies, IRVINE, CALIFORNIA*

**Barnett, Richard L.**, (AV) ................. '53 '79 C.768 B.S. L.990 J.D. [Barnett&R.]
*PRACTICE AREAS: Bankruptcy Law.

**Barnett & Rubin, A Professional Corporation, (AV) BR**
**2 Park Plaza, Suite 980, 92614**
**Telephone: 714-261-9700 Facsimile: 714-261-9799**
**Email: Lawyers@Pacbell.net**
**Richard L. Barnett; Jeffrey D. Rubin;—Kathryn B. Salmond.**
**Civil Litigation, Receiverships and Bankruptcy.**
*See Professional Biographies, IRVINE, CALIFORNIA*

**Barney, Colleen** ......................... '66 '93 C.136 B.S. L.477 J.D. [Albrecht&B.]
*PRACTICE AREAS: Estate and Gift Tax Law; Estate Planning; Tax Law; Trust and Estate Administration.
**Baron, Eric G.** ......................... '51 '87 C&L.276 B.S.F.S., J.D. [Ⓐ Aldrich&B.]
*LANGUAGES: German and Hebrew.
*PRACTICE AREAS: Commercial Transactions; Real Estate Transactions; Documentary and Standby Letters of Credit; Environmental Law; Litigation.
**Barritt, Douglas A.** ..................... '62 '90 C.1074 B.S. L.426 J.D. [Ⓐ Payne&F.]
*PRACTICE AREAS: Employment Law; Wrongful Termination; Employment Discrimination; Unfair Competition Law.
Barth, Robert D. ...................... '58 '84 C.1042 B.S. L.809 J.D. 2532 Dupont Dr.
**Bartyczak, Michael A.** '59 '86 C&L.930 B.S., J.D.
Asst. Gen. Coun., Burlington Air Express Inc.
Bartz, Alan, (BV) ............................ '46 '77 C.97 B.A. L.1137 J.D. [A.Bartz]
Bartz, Knuppel and Chun, P.C., (BV) ........................ 19100 Von Karman Ave.
**Batliner, Jennifer** ........................ '69 '95 C.112 B.A. L.1049 J.D. [Ⓐ Pivo&H.]
Bazyler, Michael J. ................... '52 '78 C.112 A.B. L.800 J.D. 4 Venture St.
**Beam, Gregory B.** ..................... '48 '82 C.763 B.A. L.1049 J.D. [Horwitz&B.]
*PRACTICE AREAS: Civil Litigation; Banking Law; Real Estate.
**Beaton, Julie R.** ............. '61 '94 C.397 B.A. L.809 J.D. [Ⓐ Berger,K.S.M.F.S.&G.]
Beauchamp, Robert B. .................. '55 '87 C.267 B.A. L.800 J.D. 18881 von Karman
**Becker, Edward G.** '65 '90 C.502 B.S. L.276 J.D.
(adm. in MO; not adm. in CA) [Ⓒ Bryan C.]
*PRACTICE AREAS: International Law; Government Contracts; Litigation.
**Becker, Michael A.** '52 '78 C.763 B.S. L.1137 J.D.
Legal Coun., Kawasaki Motors Corp., U.S.A.
*RESPONSIBILITIES: Corporate; Commercial.
**Behrendt, Lawrence B.** ............... '55 '81 C.112 A.B. L.276 J.D. [Boutwell,B.&E.]⊙
*PRACTICE AREAS: Banking and Finance; Environmental; Corporate.
**Bell, Rodney W.** ........................ '57 '86 C.1077 B.A. L.809 J.D. [Ⓐ Arter&H.]
*PRACTICE AREAS: Business Law; Securities; Commercial Law.
**Bellenghi, Julian B.** ........................ '48 '81 C.276 B.S. L.1162 J.D. [Collins&B.]
*LANGUAGES: Spanish and Italian.
*REPORTED CASES: Barnes v. Litton Systems, Inc., 28 Cal.App 4th. 681, 33 Cal.Rptr.2d 652 (1994).
Bellomo, Lawrence P. ...... '55 '80 C.1109 B.A. L.1137 J.D. 18400 Von Karman, Ste 500
Benice, Jeffrey S. ............................ '53 '78 C.1109 B.A. L.1068 J.D. [Benice]
Benice Group, The, A Professional Corporation ............... 19700 Fairchild, Ste. # 230
Benninghoff, Huang & Ramirez
100 Pacifica (⊙San Juan Capistrano & Tijuana, Mexico)
Beral, Harold, (AV) .... '39 '64 C.112 B.S. L.309 LL.B. Pres., Gold State Developers, Inc.
**Beral, Shara C.** .......................... '71 '96 C.112 A.B. L.145 J.D. [Ⓐ Snell&W.]
*PRACTICE AREAS: Litigation.

**Berger, Kahn, Shafton, Moss, Figler, Simon & Gladstone, (AV)**
**A Professional Corporation including a Professional Corporation**
**Suite 650, 2 Park Plaza, 92714⊙**
**Telephone: 714-474-1880 Telecopier: 714-474-7265**
**Carole J. Buckner; Stephan S. Cohn; Samuel M. Danskin; Steven H. Gentry; James F. Henshall, Jr.; Harri J. Keto; Howard F. Kline; Lance A. LaBelle; Melody S. Mosley; Patrick E. Naughton; Robert W. Nelms; Timothy A. Nicholson; Teresa Ransom Ponder; Eric N. Riezman; Carol Peskoe Schaner; Craig S. Simon; Sherman M. Spitz; Jeffrey M. Spurlock; Jeffrey A. Swedo; Sara Schwab Trask;—Jon D. Andersen; Shireen G. Banki; Julie R. Beaton; Laura Farrel Bucher; Anne Barden Cleeland; Keri Flynn Corfield; Renee C. D'Agostino; Margaret M. Drugan; Riva I. Edwards; Philip T. Emmons; David B. Ezra; Areta Kay Guthrey; Eric B. Johnson; Ann K. Johnston; Richard O. Knapp; Catherine K. La Tempa; Jeffrey B. Lehrman; Mark F. Marnell; Margaret R. Miglietta; Julia A. Mouser; Robert S. Robinson; Stephen A. Shapiro; Fred Timothy Winters; Hali E. Ziff.**
**Insurance and Environmental Law, Real Estate, Tax and Probate, Music and Entertainment Law and Intellectual Property, General Civil and Trial Practice in all State and Federal Courts.**
**Los Angeles, California Office: 4215 Glencoe Avenue (Marina L.C. Del Rey), 90292-5634. Telephone: 310-821-9000. Telecopier: 310-578-6178.**
**Novato, California Office: Suite 304, 1701 Novato Boulevard, 94947. Telephone: 415-899-1770. Telecopier: 415-899-1769.**
**San Diego, California Office: 402 W. Broadway, Suite 400, 92101. Telephone: 619-236-8602. Telecopier: 619-236-0812.**
**Bend, Oregon Office: P.O. Box 1407, 97709. Telephone: 541-388-1400. Telecopier: 541-388-4731.**
*See Professional Biographies, IRVINE, CALIFORNIA*

**Bernstein, Andrew P.**, (AV) ............ '55 '80 C.112 B.A. L.1068 J.D. [Morrison&F.]
*PRACTICE AREAS: Real Estate.
**Berry-Smith, Bridgette A.** '59 '83 C.112 B.A. L.813 J.D.
Corp. Coun., Taco Bell Corp.
*RESPONSIBILITIES: Litigation/Employment.
**Bhakta, Kushal S.** ................. '70 '96 C.112 B.A. L.1065 J.D. [Ⓐ Malcolm,C.&H.]
*PRACTICE AREAS: Bankruptcy; Creditor's Rights; Commercial Litigation.
**Bick, Alan N.** ........................ '61 '90 C.197 B.A. L.813 J.D. [Ⓐ Gibson,D.&C.]
*PRACTICE AREAS: Environmental; Intellectual Property.
Bick, Kimberly L. .................. '63 '90 C&L.813 B.S., J.D. 19900 MacArthur Blvd.
**Bickel, Arthur S.** ............ '43 '79 C.823 B.A. L.1206 J.D. Discovision Assocs. (Pat.)
*RESPONSIBILITIES: Patent Prosecution.
Bidwell, Jane ...................... '61 '87 C.860 B.A. L.273 J.D. 19800 MacArthur Blvd.
**Biesty, McCool & Garretty, A Professional Corporation**
(See Los Angeles)
**Bigi, Donna M.** ..................... '59 '93 C.112 B.A. L.800 J.D. [Ⓐ Gibson,D.&C.]
*PRACTICE AREAS: Labor and Employment; Litigation.
**Bilas, Sharyl P.** ........................ '67 '92 C.112 B.A. L.276 J.D. [Ⓐ Gibson,D.&C.]
*PRACTICE AREAS: Labor and Employment Law.
**Billyou, Jean De Forest** ............. '66 '95 C.914 B.A. L.228 J.D. [Ⓐ Gibson,D.&C.]
**Binam, Robert M.** .................. '68 '95 C.800 B.A. L.426 J.D. [Ⓐ Wesierski&Z.]
**Binderow, Lawrence H.** ............ '56 '82 C.966 B.A. L.365 J.D. [Ⓐ Friedman P.&S.]
*PRACTICE AREAS: Trademarks; Copyright and Domestic and International Licensing.
**Bjerregaard, Kevin P.** .................. '59 '87 C.966 B.A. L.494 J.D. [Ⓒ Bryan C.]
*PRACTICE AREAS: Litigation.
Bjerum, RaeAnn ...................... '41 '84 C.101 B.A. L.1137 J.D. 13621 Onkayha‡
Black, Robin J. ......................... '59 '92 C.112 B.A. L.1137 J.D. 2010 Main St.
**Black, Shelli J.** ..................................... '61 '86 C.112 B.A. L.426 J.D. [Pinto&D.]
**Blaine, Stephen E.** ................... '53 '80 C.1077 B.A. L.426 J.D. [Callahan&B.]
*PRACTICE AREAS: Corporate Law; Business and Transactional Law; Real Property; Intellectual Property Litigation; Entertainment Law.
Blair, Rod ..................................... '49 '77 C.112 B.A. L.809 J.D. [Vance&B.]
**Blake, Laura Lee** ..................... '62 '90 C&L.352 B.A., J.D. [Connor,C.B.&G.]
Bleiman, Wendy A. .................... '54 '85 C.112 A.B. L.1065 J.D. Fluor Daniel, Inc.
**Blinn, S. David**, (AV) .......... '45 '70 C.918 B.A. L.802 J.D. [Gibson,D.&C.] (⊙L.A.)
**Block, Carrie** ................... '68 '93 C.112 B.A. L.426 J.D. [Ⓐ Simon,M.M.Z.S.&D.]
*PRACTICE AREAS: Family Law.
**Block, Hal G.**, (AV) ..................... '53 '82 C.46 B.Arch. L.365 J.D. [Musick,P.&G.]
*PRACTICE AREAS: Construction and Design Defect Litigation; Insurance Coverage; Business and Commercial Litigation.
Bober, Alan M. ................................. '48 '91 L.1137 J.D. [Ⓐ Silberman&C.]
Bohorquez, Elizabeth .............. '65 '92 C.1052 B.S. L.1065 J.D. 5 Pk. Plz., Ste., 830
**Bois, Thomas J., II, (P.C.)** ........ '55 '82 C.745 A.B. L.734 J.D. [Ⓒ Sedgwick,D.M.&A.]
**Bolduc, Lynne** ........................................ '66 '95 L.572 J.D. [Horwitz&B.]
*PRACTICE AREAS: Securities Law and Business Transactions.
Bolinger, Robert F., Jr., (BV) ....... '46 '78 C.585 B.S. L.809 J.D. 7700 Irvine Center Dr.
**Bollard, William C.**, (AV) ............ '54 '82 C.101 B.A. L.990 J.D. [Chapman,F.&B.]
*LANGUAGES: Spanish.
*PRACTICE AREAS: Litigation.
**Bollella, Donald** '59 '89 C.453 B.S. L.94 J.D.
(adm. in NY; not adm. in CA; Pat.) Discovision Assocs.
*RESPONSIBILITIES: Patent Prosecution.
**Bolt, Eduardo Guerini** ................ '48 '77 C.1077 B.S. L.1221 J.D. [Musick,P.&G.]
*LANGUAGES: Spanish, Italian and Portuguese.
*PRACTICE AREAS: Corporate; Business; Real Estate Transactions.
**Bonnefin, Janet M.**, (BV) ............... '57 '82 C.1042 B.A. L.426 J.D. [Aldrich&B.]
*PRACTICE AREAS: Consumer Financial Services (100%).

**Booth, Richard P., Jr., (AV) '44 '74 C.800 B.S. L.426 J.D.**
**2030 Main Street, Suite 1600, 92714**
**Telephone: 714-752-2145 FAX: 714-622-0206**
***PRACTICE AREAS: Medical Malpractice; Personal Injury Law; Employment Law.**
**Medical Malpractice, Personal Injury Law, Employment Law.**
*See Professional Biographies, IRVINE, CALIFORNIA*

**Borchard, Michael D.**, (AV) .............. '61 '87 C.478 B.A. L.94 J.D. [Borchard&W.]
*PRACTICE AREAS: Civil Litigation; Securities Litigation; Real Estate Litigation; Appellate Practice.

**Borchard & Willoughby, A Professional Corporation, (AV) BR**
**18881 Von Karman Avenue, Suite 1400, 92612**
**Telephone: 714-644-6161 Fax: 714-263-1913**
**Michael D. Borchard; Michael L. Willoughby; Mark A. Rodriguez;—Stephanie A. Pittaluga.**
**Civil Litigation.**
*See Professional Biographies, IRVINE, CALIFORNIA*

Borresen, Rand A. ......................... '57 '88 C&L.1137 B.S.L., J.D. 111 Pacifica
**Bouslog, Lynn M.** .................. '53 '85 C.927 B.S.Ed. L.221 J.D. [Mower,K.N.C.&H.]
**Boutwell, Sherrie M.** .............. '57 '83 C.112 B.A. L.1068 J.D. [Boutwell,B.&E.]
*PRACTICE AREAS: Pension/ERISA; Employee Benefits; Executive Compensation.

**Boutwell, Behrendt & Ennor**
**1 Park Plaza, Suite 490, 92714⊙**
**Telephone: 714-251-2888 Fax: 714-251-2889**
**Members of Firm: Sherrie M. Boutwell; Lawrence B. Behrendt; Sara Langford Ennor.**
**Banking, Finance, Mortgage Banking, Pensions/ERISA, Tax Exempt Entities, Corporate and Municipal Finance Law.**

(This Listing Continued)

CAA123P

CALIFORNIA—IRVINE MARTINDALE-HUBBELL LAW DIRECTORY 1997

**Boutwell, Behrendt & Ennor (Continued)**

**Los Angeles, California Office: 333 South Grand Avenue, 37th Floor. Telephone: 213-346-0070. Fax: 213-346-0071.**
**San Francisco, California Office: 221 Sansome Street, Suite 3. Telephone: 415-274-8511. Fax: 415-274-8513.**

*See Professional Biographies, IRVINE, CALIFORNIA*

**Bouzaglou, Lydia R.** '62 '88 C.112 A.B. L.464 J.D. [🄰 Stevens,K.A.&H.]
*PRACTICE AREAS: Construction Defect.
**Boyd, Larry C.** '52 '77 C&L.813 A.B., J.D. [Gibson,D.&C.]
*PRACTICE AREAS: Intellectual Property and Business Litigation.
Boylan, James O., III '39 '79 C.906 B.S. L.1095 J.D. 19800 MacArthur Blvd.
**Bradley, Donald E.** '63 '89 C.1109 B.A. L.1067 J.D. [🄰 Crowell&M.]
Brady, Donna L. '61 '85 C.112 B.A. L.1066 J.D. 18101 Von Karman Ave.
Brady, M. Christine '55 '82 C.1042 B.A. L.426 J.D. 2010 Main St.
Brady, M. Christine '55 '82 C.1042 B.A. L.426 J.D. 2010 Main St.
**Brand, Dulcie D.** '55 '81 C.839 B.A. L.273 J.D. [Jones,D.R.&P.]

**Brandlin, John J., Jr., (AV) '44 '74 C.37 B.A. L.809 J.D.**
**Suite 730, 7700 Irvine Center Drive, 92718-2929**
**Telephone: 714-453-2100 Fax: 714-453-7393; E-Mail: JBrandlin@earthlink.net**
**Email: JBrandlin@aol.com**
***PRACTICE AREAS: Business Law; Computers and Software; Litigation; Estate Planning and Probate; Bankruptcy.**
**Business, Corporate, Civil Litigation, Computers and Software, Bankruptcy, Estate Planning and Probate Law.**

*See Professional Biographies, IRVINE, CALIFORNIA*

Brandon, Stephen D. '42 '67
C.112 A.B. L.1066 J.D. Asst. Gen. Coun., Avco Fin. Servs., Inc.
Branman, Kathryn H. K. '52 '82 C.130 B.A. L.1137 J.D.
Sr. V.P. & Assoc. Coun., Fidelity National Title Insurance Co.
**Braun, Jeffrey I.** '67 '92 C.112 B.A. L.464 J.D. [🄰 Sedgwick,D.M.&A.]
**Braun, Robert T.** '63 '90 C.158 B.S. L.823 J.D. Discovision Assocs. (Pat.)
*RESPONSIBILITIES: Patent Law; Patent Licensing; Patent Prosecution; Patent Contracts; Patent Portfolio Management.

**Breckenridge, Hugh, Law Offices of, (AV) '46 '75 C.813 B.A. L.990 J.D.**
**4199 Campus Drive, Suite 700, 92715**
**Telephone: 714-854-2520 FAX: 714-854-4897**
**Email: HUGHBRECK@PRODIGY.COM**
***PRACTICE AREAS: Contract Law; Corporate Law; Real Estate Law; Partnership Law; Civil Litigation.**
**Real Estate and Business Transactions and Litigation, Settlement, Arbitration and Mediation.**

*See Professional Biographies, IRVINE, CALIFORNIA*

**Bremer, Keith G.** '64 '91 C.763 B.S. L.1137 J.D. [Kring&B.]
*PRACTICE AREAS: Civil Litigation; Business Litigation; Construction.
**Brennan, J. Michael**, (AV) '39 '72 C.262 A.B. L.1066 J.D. [Gibson,D.&C.]
*LANGUAGES: French.
*PRACTICE AREAS: Securities Litigation; Proceedings Before the Securities and Exchange Commission; Class Actions and Derivative Suits; Corporate and Partnership Takeover, Control and Dissolution Matters.
**Brennan, Sterling A.** '59 '86 C&L.101 B.A., J.D. [Smith,B.&D.]
*PRACTICE AREAS: Business Litigation; Real Estate; Environmental; Land Use; Construction.
Bresee, Mark R. '62 '92 C.112 B.A. L.426 J.D. [🄰 Parham&Assoc.]
**Bressi, Jess R.**, (AV) '57 '83 C.1077 B.S. L.809 J.D. [Cox,C.&N.]
*PRACTICE AREAS: Bankruptcy Law; Real Estate, Construction and Commercial Litigation; Creditor Rights Law.
Brewer, Lance A. '59 '86 C.878 B.S. L.1137 J.D. 2201 Dupont Dr.
**Brewsaugh, Gary D.** '53 '78 C.976 B.A. L.1137 J.D. [Kayajanian&B.]
*PRACTICE AREAS: Civil Litigation; Family Law; Personal Injury; Business Law; Construction.
**Brodie, Michael A.** '44 '69 C&L.945 A.B., J.D. [🄰 Pivo&H.]
*PRACTICE AREAS: Medical Malpractice.
**Bronson, Peter C.**, (AV) '50 '74 C.112 A.B. L.1068 J.D. [Bryan C.] (⊙Santa Monica)
*PRACTICE AREAS: Bankruptcy; Commercial Litigation.
**Brooks, Michael R.** '66 '93 C.1042 B.S. L.800 J.D. [🄰 Malcolm,C.&H.]
*LANGUAGES: French.
*PRACTICE AREAS: Commercial Litigation; Bankruptcy.
**Brosnan, Tiffanny** '71 '96 C&L.112 B.A., J.D. [🄰 Snell&W.]
Brower, Todd Gordon '54 '80 C.674 A.B. L.813 J.D.
Prof. of Law, Western State Univ. School of Law
Brown, Craig T. '47 '80 C.813 A.B, L.1137 J.D. V.P., Wells Fargo Bk., N.A.
**Brown, Cynthia J.** '58 '88 C.267 B.S.M.S. L.1137 J.D. [🄰 Laughlin,F.L.&M.]
*PRACTICE AREAS: Workers' Compensation.
Brown, David Allen, (A Professional Corporation) '46 '74
C&L.1137 B.S., J.D. [Brown&S.]
**Brown, David F.** '55 '81 C.112 B.S. L.1068 J.D. [Corbett&S.]
**Brown, Edwin B.** '51 '79 C.101 B.S. L.426 J.D. [Genson,E.C.&W.]
**Brown, Ernest C.**, (AV) '53 '78 C.453 B.S.C.E. L.1066 J.D. [Brown,P.H.&V.]⊙
*PRACTICE AREAS: Construction; Public Works; Environmental; Mediation.
**Brown, Gregory G.** '62 '87 C.36 B.S. L.1049 J.D. [Kring&B.]⊙
*PRACTICE AREAS: Civil and Business Litigation; Corporate Law; Real Estate; Estate Planning.
**Brown, Jeffrey K.** '65 '92 C.976 B.A. L.1066 J.D. [🄰 Payne&F.]
*PRACTICE AREAS: Labor and Employment Law; Wrongful Termination Defense; Employment Litigation; Employment Discrimination; Wage and Hour Law.
Brown, Kimberly '— '81 C&L.1137 B.S., J.D. 100 Pacifica Ste. 200
Brown, Michael R. '55 '83 C&L.101 B.S., J.D. 4199 Campus Dr., Ste 700
**Brown, Richard L.**, (AV) '52 '79 C&L.101 B.S., J.D. [🄲 Chapman,F.&B.]
*PRACTICE AREAS: General Civil Practice; Corporate Law; Probate; Professional Liability Defense; Environmental Law.

**Brown, Pistone, Hurley & Van Vlear, A Professional Corporation, (AV) BR**
**Suite 900 AT&T Building, 8001 Irvine Center Drive, 92618-2921⊙**
**Telephone: 714-727-0559 Fax: 714-727-0656**
**Email: BPHVLAW@AOL.COM**
**Ernest C. Brown; Thomas A. Pistone; Gregory F. Hurley; John E. Van Vlear; Michael K. Wolder;— Francis T. Donohue, III; Robert C. Schneider (Resident, Phoenix, Arizona Office); Sheila I. Patterson; Michael R. Gandee; Julia E. Kress. Of Counsel: Robert G. Mahan; Stephen M. Wontrobski; Brian A. Runkel (Not admitted in CA).**
**Construction, Environmental and Technology Trial Practice, Public Works, Contractor Professional Licensing and Bonding, Mechanics Liens, Insurance Coverage, Malpractice, International Projects, Arbitration, Environmental Law, Air and Water Permits, Trial and Appellate Practice.**
**Phoenix, Arizona Office: 2999 North 44th Street, Suite 300. Telephone: 602-968-2427. Fax: 602-840-0794.**
**San Diego, California Office: 4350 La Jolla Village Drive, Suite 300. Telephone: 619-546-4368. Fax: 619-453-2839.**
**Sacramento, California Office: 980 Ninth Street, 16th Floor. Telephone: 916-449-9541. Fax: 916-446-7104.**

*See Professional Biographies, IRVINE, CALIFORNIA*

Brown & Streza 7700 Irvine Ctr. Dr. Ste 900
**Broyles, Samuel G., Jr.** '61 '87 C.549 B.S. L.770 J.D. [Andrade&M.]⊙
*PRACTICE AREAS: Business Litigation; Mobile Home Park Litigation; Construction Litigation; Real Estate Litigation; Certain Transactional Matters.

**Brubaker, Mark E.** '55 '87 C.1262 B.S. L.809 J.D. [Wesierski&Z.]
*PRACTICE AREAS: Environmental Law; Construction Defect Litigation; Contract Law; Insurance Defense Law.
Brutoco, Roberto G., (P.C.) '57 '82 C.770 B.S.C. L.1068 J.D. 5 Pk. Plz., Ste., 800

**Bryan Cave LLP, (AV)**
**A Partnership including a Professional Corporation**
**18881 Von Karman, Suite 1500, 92715-1500⊙**
**Telephone: (714) 223-7000 Facsimile: (714) 223-7100 For attorney e-mails use: First initial, last name, firm name, e.g., rsmith@bryancavellp.com**
**Partners: Wayne C. Arnold; Peter C. Bronson; Peter T. Fagan; Gary J. Highland; Wilbur D. Layman; James B. O'Neal; Angelo A. Paparelli (Certified Specialist, Immigration and Nationality Law, The State Bar of California Board of Legal Specialization); Jeffrey W. Shields; Steven H. Sunshine. Of Counsel: Monica E. Barajas; Robert E. Dye. Counsel: Kevin P. Bjerregaard; Ren R Hayhurst. Resident Associates: Edward G. Becker (Not admitted in CA); J. Ira Burkemper; Mary Lynn K. Coffee; Mynette M. Dufresne; Adam J. Gillman; James R. Rouse.**
**Administrative and General Civil Practice. Antitrust, Aviation, Banking, Computer, Corporate Financing, Corporation, Environmental, Estate Planning, Government Contracts, Immigrations, International, Labor, Probate, Products Liability, Real Estate, Securities, Taxation, Technology, Transportation, Trust and University Law; U.S. Visa Law and Practice. General Civil Trial and Appellate Practice.**
**St. Louis, Missouri Office: One Metropolitan Square, 211 North Broadway, Suite 3600, 63102-2750. Telephone: (314) 259-2000. Facsimile: (314) 259-2020.**
**Washington, D.C. Office: 700 Thirteenth Street, N.W., 20005-3960. Telephone: (202) 508-6000. Facsimile: (202) 508-6200.**
**New York, N.Y. Office: 245 Park Avenue, 10167-0034. Telephone: (212) 692-1800. Facsimile: (212) 692-1900.**
**Kansas City, Missouri Office: 3500 One Kansas City Place, 1200 Main Street, 64141-6914. Telephone: (816) 374-3200. Facsimile: (816) 374-3300.**
**Overland Park, Kansas Office: 7500 College Boulevard, Suite 1100, 66210-4035. Telephone: (913) 338-7700. Facsimile: (913) 338-7777.**
**Phoenix, Arizona Office: 2800 North Central Avenue, Twenty-First Floor, 85004-1098. Telephone: (602) 230-7000. Facsimile: (602) 266-5938.**
**Los Angeles, California Office: 777 South Figueroa Street, Suite 2700, 90017-5418. Telephone: (213) 243-4300. Facsimile: (213) 243-4343.**
**Santa Monica, California Office: 120 Broadway, Suite 500, 90401-2305. Telephone: (310) 576-2100. Facsimile: (310) 576-2200.**
**London SW1H 9BU England Office: 29 Queen Anne's Gate. Telephone: 171-896-1900. Facsimile: 171-896-1919.**
**Riyadh 11465 Saudi Arabia Office: In Cooperation with Kadasah Law Firm, P.O. Box 20883. Telephone: 966-1-474-0888. Facsimile: 966-1-476-2881.**
**Kuwait City, Kuwait Office: Mashora Advocates & Legal Consultants, Sheraton Towers, Second Floor, P.O. Box 5902 Safat, 13060. Telephone: 965-240-4470/240-600. Facsimile: 965-245-9000.**
**Dubai, U.A.E. Office: Al-Mahairi Legal Consultants - Bryan Cave LLP, Dubai, Holiday Centre, Commercial Tower, Suite 1103, P.O. Box 13677, UAE. Telephone: 971-4-314-123. Facsimile: 971-4-318-287.**
**Abu Dhabi, U.A.E. Office: Al-Mehairi Legal Consultants - Bryan Cave LLP, Abu Dhabi, Dhabi Tower, Suite 304, P.O. Box 47645. Telephone: 971-2-260-335. Facsimile: 971-2-260-332.**
**Hong Kong Office: Suite 2106, Lippo Tower, 21/F, Lippo Centre, 89 Queensway. Telephone: 852-2522-2821. Facsimile: 852-2522-3830.**
**Shanghai, People's Republic of China Associated Office: 100 Fu Xing Xi Lu, 3C, 200031. Telephone: 86-21-6466-3845. Facsimile: 86-21-6466-4280.**

*See Professional Biographies, IRVINE, CALIFORNIA*

**Bucher, Laura Farrel** '61 '87 C.1109 B.S. L.990 J.D. [🄰 Berger,K.S.M.F.S.&G.]
**Buckner, Carole J.**, (BV) '59 '84 C.112 B.A. L.1065 J.D. [Berger,K.S.M.F.S.&G.]
Buckovich, Mark E. '63 '89 C.239 B.A. L.904 J.D.
(adm. in PA; not adm. in CA) 7700 Irvine Center Dr., Suite 700
**Bujold, Lawrence R.** '56 '85 C.112 B.A. L.1049 J.D. [Horwitz&B.]
*REPORTED CASES: Rubin v. Green (1993) 4 Cal. 4th 1187.
*PRACTICE AREAS: Litigation; Real Estate; Banking; Intellectual Property.
**Bukaty, Raymond M.** '57 '83 C.813 B.A. L.800 J.D. Fluor Corp.
**Bukovskis, Layne M.** '64 '92 C.112 B.S. L.1049 J.D. [🄰 Kirtland&P.]
*PRACTICE AREAS: Medical Malpractice Defense.
Bumiller, James B. '60 '86 C.1111 B.A. L.1137 J.D. [Tieger&B.]
Bumiller, Jolynn L. '60 '87 C.549 B.A. L.1137 J.D. 5 Park Plaza
**Burakoff, William L.** '59 '87 C.951 B.A. L.477 J.D. Atty., AirTouch Comm.
**Burden, Alice O.** '56 '82 C.986 B.A. L.809 J.D. [🄰 Laughlin,F.L.&M.]
*PRACTICE AREAS: Workers' Compensation.
Burge, Harland L., (AV) '32 '75 C.174 B.S.M.E. L.426 J.D. [Burge,S.&D.]
Burge, Strid & Dickinson, (AV) 100 Pacifica
**Burke, Gerald R.** '50 '75 C.629 B.S. L.61 J.D. [Laughlin,F.L.&M.]
*PRACTICE AREAS: Workers' Compensation.
**Burkemper, J. Ira** '62 '94 C.860 B.A. L.1068 J.D. [🄰 Bryan C.]
*LANGUAGES: German and Italian.
*PRACTICE AREAS: Immigration.
Burkitt, Susan Kelly '64 '89 C.893 B.A. L.602 J.D. Fluor Corp.
Burnes, James T. '54 '79 C.112 B.S. L.767 J.D. 19900 Macarthur Blvd.
**Burnett, Craig V.** '58 '92 C.339 B.S. L.128 J.D.
(adm. in TX; not adm. in CA; Pat.) Discovision Assocs.
*RESPONSIBILITIES: Patent Licensing; Patent Contracts; Patent Prosecution.
**Burnett, Michael W., (P.C.)** '53 '80 C.112 B.A. L.464 J.D. [Case,K.B.&W.]
*PRACTICE AREAS: Real Estate.
Burns, Melina J. '66 '92 C.1169 B.A. L.1068 J.D. 38 Corp. Pk.
**Burrows, Lee E.** '66 '94 C.112 B.A. L.809 [🄰 Stevens,K.A.&H.]
Burrows, Peter, (AV) '19 '49 C.112 L.800 J.D. [🄲 Morgan&W.]
**Burton, James A.** '62 '90 C.911 B.A. L.464 J.D. [🄰 Mower,K.N.C.&H.]
**Busch, Joseph P., III**, (AV) '48 '76 C.154 B.A. L.1066 J.D. [Gibson,D.&C.]
*PRACTICE AREAS: ERISA Litigation; Accounting Liability Litigation; Securities Litigation.
**Busch, Timothy R.**, (AV) '54 '78 C.932 B.B.A. L.912 J.D. [Busch]
*PRACTICE AREAS: Estate; Tax; Business Law.

**Busch Firm, The, (AV)**
**2532 Dupont Drive, 92612⊙**
**Telephone: 714-474-7368 Fax: 714-474-7732**
**Email: trb@buschfirm.com URL: http://www.buschfirm.com**
**Timothy R. Busch; Rudolph J. Fuchs; David L. Keligian; George P. Mulcaire; Layne T. Rushforth (Resident, Las Vegas, Nevada Office); James J. Scheinkman; Clay Stevens; Douglas M. Stevens; Allen B. Walburn; Rick S. Weiner.**
**Estate Planning and Trusts, Probate, Federal, State and Local Tax Planning, Real Estate Transactional, Corporate Transactional and Reorganization, Partnerships, and Limited Liability Companies.**
**Las Vegas, Nevada Office: Hughes Center Executive Suites, 3753 Howard Hughes Parkway, Suite 200, 89109. Telephone: 702-892-3789. Fax: 702-892-3992.**

*See Professional Biographies, IRVINE, CALIFORNIA*

**Bustamante, David** '55 '80 C.940 B.A. L.426 J.D. [Aldrich&B.]
*PRACTICE AREAS: Litigation; Regulatory Compliance - Operations; Negotiable Instruments; Contracts; Writs and Attachments (20%).
Butz, Douglas M., (AV) '49 '74 C.763 B.S. L.800 J.D. [Butz,L.&D.]⊙
Butz, Lucas & Dunn, A Professional Corporation, (AV) 1 Park Plaza (⊙San Diego)
Buzzard, Erik D. '66 '92 C&L.112 B.S., J.D. 18400 Von Karman Ave.
**Bye, Roland E.**, (AV) '46 '72 C.309 A.B. L.1066 J.D. [Bye,H.&R.]
*REPORTED CASES: Stewart Development IV v. Superior Court (1980) 108 Cal.App.3rd 266 (leading case on expungement of lis pendens under C.C.P. §409.1).
*PRACTICE AREAS: Business Litigation; Real Estate Litigation.

**Bye, Hatcher & Robinson, (AV)**
**A Partnership including a Professional Corporation**
**Suite 1100, Five Park Plaza, 92714**
**Telephone: 714-553-2404 Telecopier: 714-660-7212**
**Roland E. Bye; Patrick G. Hatcher (P.C.); David A. Robinson; Michael S. Winsten; Jonathan S. Pink.**
**General Trial Practice in all State and Federal Courts emphasizing Business, Real Estate and Products Liability Litigation.**
*See Professional Biographies, IRVINE, CALIFORNIA*

Cabezas, Fabio R. ....'61 '87 C&L.800 A.B., J.D. [Cone,C.&K.]
**Call, Christopher E.**, (AV) ....'51 '76 C.800 B.A. L.1066 J.D. [McKenna&S.]
*PRACTICE AREAS: Securities; Real Estate.
**Callahan, Daniel J., (A Professional Corporation)**, (AV) '49 '80 C.927 B.A. L.1067 J.D. [Callahan&B.]
*PRACTICE AREAS: Complex Business Litigation; Insurance Coverage; Unfair Competition; Bad Faith; Banking.
**Callahan, Marc K.** ....'67 '91 C.112 B.A. L.1065 J.D. [Jones,D.R.&P.]
**Callahan, Robert E.**, (AV) ....'49 '75 C.112 B.A. L.770 J.D. [Paone,C.M.&W.]
*PRACTICE AREAS: Family Law; Business; Real Property; Litigation; Sports Law.

**Callahan & Blaine, A Professional Law Corporation, (AV)**
**Suite 800, 18500 Von Karman, 92612**
**Telephone: 714-553-1155 Fax: 714-553-0784**
**Email: info@callahan-law.com**
**Daniel J. Callahan (A Professional Corporation); Stephen E. Blaine;—Kathleen L. Dunham; Jim P. Mahacek; Michael J. Sachs; Andrew A. Smits; Gary S. Spitzer; Edward Susolik; Graig R. Woodburn. Of Counsel: Shelley M. Liberto; Walt D. Mahaffa.**
**General Civil and Trial Practice in all State and Federal Courts including Banking, Commercial, Construction, Environmental, Insurance Coverage and Bad Faith, Intellectual Property, Real Property, Corporate and Securities Litigation, Transactional Representation in Corporate, Real Estate and Commercial Law.**
*See Professional Biographies, IRVINE, CALIFORNIA*

Calwell, Richard L. '47 '78 C.838 B.S. L.1137 J.D. V.P. & Assoc. Coun., Fidelity Natl. Title Ins. Co.
Campbell, Patrick J. ....'65 '94 C.768 B.S. L.1137 J.D. 18401 Von Karman, Ste. 350
**Campbell, Warren B.** ....'49 '76 C.1097 B.A. L.990 J.D. [Robinson&C.]
*PRACTICE AREAS: General Commercial; Construction; Insurance and Real Estate Litigation.
**Cane, David E.** ....'61 '87 C.112 B.A. L.809 J.D. [Fiore,W.R.&P.]
Cannan, Daniel P. ....'56 '81 C.763 B.S. L.1065 J.D. Professional Pension Consultants
Capp, Jonathan Charles ....'64 '95 C.061 L.054 LL.B. 38 Corporate Pk., Ste. 200
**Cappucci, Debora A.** ....'71 '96 C.188 B.S. L.208 J.D. [Woldt&H.]

**Card, Benjamin F., (AV) '39 '71 C.112 B.A. L.1137 J.D.**
**19800 MacArthur Boulevard, Suite 370, 92715**
**Telephone: 714-851-6900 FAX: 714-955-1626**
**Civil Litigation and Arbitration.**
**Reference: Bank of America.**
*See Professional Biographies, IRVINE, CALIFORNIA*

**Cardwell, Robert A.**, (AV) ....'42 '71 C.454 B.A. L.800 J.D. [Baker,S.&K.]
**Carey, Diane P.** ....'57 '83 C.602 B.A. L.902 J.D. [Jackson,D.&P.]
*PRACTICE AREAS: Real Estate.
**Carlton, Christopher W.** '56 '83 C.228 A.B. L.188 J.D. [Faustman,C.D.&F.] (⊙Los Angeles)
*PRACTICE AREAS: Employment Law; Labor Law; Business Litigation.
Carlton, Daniel C., (BV) ....'50 '77 C.112 B.A. L.1137 J.D. 19100 Von Karman Ave.
**Carney, Terence P.** ....'57 '82 C.169 B.A. L.426 J.D. [Wesierski&Z.]
*PRACTICE AREAS: Land Subsidence Law; Auto Law; Premises Liability Law; Products Liability; Sexual Harassment.
**Carpenter, Scott R.** ....'62 '89 C.813 B.A. L.1068 J.D. [Palmieri,T.W.W.&W.]
*PRACTICE AREAS: Litigation.
Carr, Richard F., (AV) ....'21 '50 C.679 B.S.M.E. L.1119 LL.B. 1920 Main St. (Pat.)
**Carreon, Patrick A.** ....'58 '85 C.309 B.A. L.1068 J.D. [Mower,K.N.C.&H.]
**Carroll, David B.**, (AV) ....'42 '81 C.05 A.B. L.426 J.D. [Groh,C.S.&R.]
*PRACTICE AREAS: Business Litigation; Real Estate Litigation; Personal Tort/Contract Litigation.
Carroll, Patrick C. ....'50 '76 C.1109 B.A. L.990 J.D. 8001 Irvine Ctr. Dr.
**Carter, James P.** ....'63 '90 C&L.101 B.A., J.D. [Ramsay&J.]
*LANGUAGES: French.
*REPORTED CASES: Carty v. American States Insurance Co., 7 Cal. App. 4th 399 (1992); Zands v. Nelson, 797 F.Supp. 805 (S.D. Cal. 1992).
*PRACTICE AREAS: Insurance Coverage and Defense; Civil Litigation; Bad Faith.
Casaudoumecq, Paul E. ....'65 '90 C.112 B.A. L.1065 J.D. [Morgan&W.]

**Case, Knowlson, Burnett & Wright, (AV)**
**A Partnership including Professional Corporations**
**5 Park Plaza, Suite 800, 92614⊙**
**Telephone: 714-955-1050 Telecopier: 714-851-9112**
**Daniel A. Case (P.C.) (Resident, Los Angeles Office); Arthur R. Knowlson, Jr., (P.C.); Michael W. Burnett (P.C.); Barry A. Yoch; Rick A. Cigel (Resident, Los Angeles Office); Michael F. Wright (Resident, Los Angeles Office); Patrick W. Walsh (Resident, Los Angeles Office). Associates: Rick Augustini. Of Counsel: David M. Luber (Resident, Los Angeles Office); Edwin I. Lasman; Daniel G. Jordan.**
**General Civil Trial and Appellate Practice in all State and Federal Courts. Corporate, Real Estate, Real Estate Finance, Taxation, Estate Planning, Trusts and Probate Law.**
**Los Angeles, California Office: Suite 1700, 2121 Avenue Of The Stars. Telephone: 213-552-2766. Telecopier: 213-552-3229.**
*See Professional Biographies, IRVINE, CALIFORNIA*

Casey, David W. ....'44 '75 C.118 A.B. L.851 J.D. Western State Univ.
**Casserly, Brian W.**, (AV) ....'49 '76 C.112 B.A. L.1065 J.D. [Jackson,D.&P.]
*PRACTICE AREAS: Real Estate Law; Real Estate Finance Law; Corporate Law.
**Castaldi, Cathrine M.** ....'65 '91 C.1068 B.A. L.763 J.D. [Rus,M.W.&S.]
*PRACTICE AREAS: Corporate Bankruptcy; Complex Business Litigation.
**Cates, William L.** ....'59 '85 C.1109 B.A. L.1065 J.D. [Cates&H.]
*PRACTICE AREAS: Corporate Transactions; Probate; Estate Planning Law; Tax.

**Cates & Han**
**19800 MacArthur Boulevard, Suite 1450, 92612**
**Telephone: 714-757-4104 Facsimile: 714-757-4107**
**Email: cateshan@aol.com**
**James W. Han; William L. Cates.**
**Business Transactions, Estate Planning, Litigation and Arbitration involving Franchising, Distribution, Unfair Competition, Trade Secrets and Business Torts.**
*See Professional Biographies, IRVINE, CALIFORNIA*

Cavallini, Angela ....'58 '90 C.766 B.S. L.1049 J.D. Coun., Avco Fin. Servs., Inc.
**Cavanaugh, James R.**, (AV) ....'49 '74 C&L.602 A.B., J.D. [Paone,C.M.&W.]
*PRACTICE AREAS: Real Property Transactions; Land Use.
Caviola, James Calvin, Jr. ....'55 '88 C.1042 B.A. L.1137 J.D. 2600 Michelson Dr.
**Cerutti, Larry A.** ....'57 '87 C.605 A.B. L.169 J.D. [Snell&W.]
*PRACTICE AREAS: Securities; Corporate.
Chairez, Joseph L. ....'54 '81 C&L.112 B.A., J.D. [Cone,C.&K.]
**Chambers, Dan E.** ....'66 '91 C.352 B.A. L.803 J.D. [Perkins,Z.&D.]
*LANGUAGES: Spanish, Italian.
*PRACTICE AREAS: Business, Real Estate, Construction and Insurance Litigation.
Chapin, Linda A., (AV) ....'50 '75 C.813 B.A. L.1065 J.D. 2172 Dupont Dr.

**Chapman, William D.**, (AV) ....'54 '81 C.101 B.S. L.990 J.D. [Chapman,F.&B.]
*LANGUAGES: Spanish.
*PRACTICE AREAS: Litigation.

**Chapman, Fuller & Bollard, (AV)**
**2010 Main Street, Suite 400, 92714**
**Telephone: 714-752-1455 Telecopier: 714-752-1485**
**Members of Firm: William D. Chapman; H. Daniel Fuller; William C. Bollard. Associate: Robert J. Hadlock. Of Counsel: Richard L. Brown.**
**General Civil, Trial and Appellate Practice, State and Federal Courts, Business and Real Estate Law, Products Liability, Construction Defect, Personal Injury, Employment Law, Trade Secrets, Trademark and Unfair Competition Litigation.**
*See Professional Biographies, IRVINE, CALIFORNIA*

Chaum, Elyn ....'60 '87 C.112 B.A. L.790 J.D. P.O. Box 19591
Chaya, Stephen D. '53 '78 C&L.36 B.S., J.D. (adm. in AZ; not adm. in CA) V.P. & Asst. Gen. Coun., Fidelity Nat'l Title Ins. Co.
Chen, Belle M. ....'68 '95 C.846 B.A. L.1066 J.D. 19900 MacArthur Blvd. Ste. 700
Chen, Shun C. ....'— '91 C.112 B.S. L.809 J.D. 4521 Campus Dr.
**Cheung, Mark H.** ....'61 '89 C.1036 B.A. L.93 J.D. [Barnes,C.F.&Z.]
*PRACTICE AREAS: Real Estate; Construction; Business Litigation; Tort Litigation.

**Chevalier, Allen & Lichman, LLP**
**5 Park Plaza, Suite 1500, 92614⊙**
**Telephone: 714-474-6967 Fax: 714-474-9606**
**Gary Mikel Allen; Roger P. Freeman; Berne C. Hart (Resident); Barbara E. Lichman; Frederick C. Woodruff (Not admitted in CA).**
**Commercial Litigation, Aviation Law and Litigation, Environmental Law and Litigation.**
**Torrance, California Office: 23430 Hawthorne Boulevard, Skypark 3, Suite 200. Telephone: 310-378-0975. Fax: 310-791-1546.**
*See Professional Biographies, IRVINE, CALIFORNIA*

**Chi, Joseph H.** ....'66 '93 C.112 B.S.E.E. L.800 J.D. [Morrison&F.] (Pat.)
*LANGUAGES: Mandarin.
Ching, Ernest F., Jr. ....'48 '77 C.897 B.A. L.1095 J.D. [Ching&Assoc.]
Ching & Associates, A Law Corp. .... 19200 Von Karman Ave., Ste. 400

**Chiu, Vivien M. '57 '92 C.038 B.S. L.1188 J.D.**
**2603 South Main Street, Suite 800, 92714**
**Telephone: 714-833-8239**
***PRACTICE AREAS: Family Law; Immigration Law.**
**Family Law, Immigration Law.**
*See Professional Biographies, IRVINE, CALIFORNIA*

**Chow, Lily** ....'62 '88 C.112 B.A. L.1068 J.D. [Sedgwick,D.M.&A.]
*LANGUAGES: Cantonese.
**Christensen, Eric L.** '45 '79 C.112 B.A. L.426 J.D. Asst. Gen. Coun., MAI Systems Corp.
*RESPONSIBILITIES: Contract; Securities; Business Law; Real Estate; Mergers and Acquisitions.
**Christian, Edward P.** ....'65 '95 C.112 B.A. L.800 J.D. [Lobel&O.]
*PRACTICE AREAS: Insolvency Law; Reorganization; Workouts.
**Christie, William P.**, (AV) ....'41 '78 C.560 B.S.Ch.E. L.1137 J.D. [Christie,P.&H.]

**Christie, Parker & Hale, LLP, (AV)**
**Suite 1440, 5 Park Plaza, 92714⊙**
**Telephone: 714-476-0757 Los Angeles: 213-681-1800 Cable Address: "Patlaw" Telex: ITT 4995129 (CP&H PSD) Telecopier: 714-476-8640**
**Members of Firm: William P. Christie (Resident); Vincent G. Gioia. Associates: John W. Eldredge.**
**Patent, Trademark and Copyright Law. Unfair Competition, Trade Secrets, Computer Law, Biotechnology, Licensing, Antitrust and Complex Business Litigation.**
**References: Lloyds Bank California (Pasadena, Calif. Main Office); Wells Fargo Bank (Pasadena, California Main Offices).**
**Pasadena, California Office: Fifth Floor, Wells Fargo Bank Building, 350 West Colorado Boulevard. Telephone: 818-795-9900.**
*See Professional Biographies, IRVINE, CALIFORNIA*

Chun, Tom S. ....'62 '87 C.1109 B.A. L.1065 J.D. [A.Bartz]
**Chung, Kenneth W.** ....'67 '93 C.112 B.S. L.767 J.D. [Kring&B.]
*LANGUAGES: Korean.
*PRACTICE AREAS: Civil Litigation; Business Litigation; Corporate Law; Real Estate Law; Intellectual Property Law.
**Cicione, Douglas D.** ....'51 '78 C.732 B.A. L.813 J.D. [D.D.Cicione]

**Cicione, Douglas D., A Professional Corporation**
**Suite 300, 19762 MacArthur Boulevard, 92612-2478**
**Telephone: 714-253-3499; 310-379-8602 Fax: 714-474-9392**
**Douglas D. Cicione (Certified Specialist, Taxation Law, Estate Planning, Trust and Probate Law, The State Bar of California Board of Legal Specialization).**
**Federal and State Taxation. Estate Planning, Trust and Probate. Tax Collection, Audit and Litigation. Corporate, Partnership and Business Tax Planning.**
*See Professional Biographies, IRVINE, CALIFORNIA*

**Cimpoeru, Ligia G.** ....'69 '94 C.1163 B.A. L.809 J.D. [Woldt&H.]
*LANGUAGES: Romanian.
*PRACTICE AREAS: Employment.
**Cioth, Marie A.** ....'64 '91 C.1109 B.A. L.966 J.D. [Arter&H.]
*PRACTICE AREAS: Corporate.
**Cipriani, Linda M.**, (AV⊤) ....'54 '79 C.1044 B.A. L.588 J.D. [Crowell&M.]
*PRACTICE AREAS: Insurance Coverage; First and Third Party Insurance Defense; Toxic Tort Defense; Superfund.
**Cisneros, Arturo M.** ....'59 '85 C.112 B.A. L.1068 J.D. [Malcolm,C.&H.]⊙
*PRACTICE AREAS: Bankruptcy; Creditor and Trustee Representation.
**Claire, Guy K.**, (AV) ....'25 '58 C&L.800 A.B., LL.B. [Gibson,D.&C.]
**Clark, Karen H.**, (AV) ....'44 '78 C.813 B.A. L.477 J.D. [Gibson,D.&C.]
*PRACTICE AREAS: Real Property and Business Transactions; Real Property Finance and Workouts; Commercial Leasing.
**Clark, Ronald J.** '36 '63 C.128 B.E.E. L.276 J.D. (adm. in CT; not adm. in CA; Pat.) Sr. V.P., Discovison Assocs.
*RESPONSIBILITIES: Intellectual Property; Patent Litigation; Patent Licensing; Patent Prosecution; Patent Contracts.
**Claster, William D.**, (AV) ....'52 '76 C.813 B.A. L.1068 J.D. [Gibson,D.&C.]
*PRACTICE AREAS: Labor and Employment Law; Employment Discrimination; Wrongful Discharge and Privacy Litigation; Federal and State Wage and Hour Law; Non-Competition Agreements.
**Clayton, Kent M.** ....'61 '90 C.472 B.M. L.893 J.D. [Snell&W.]
*PRACTICE AREAS: Securities; Business; Finance Law; Multimedia; Computer Law.
**Cleeland, Anne Barden** ....'56 '81 C.112 B.A. L.990 J.D. [Berger,K.S.M.F.S.&G.]
Cloud, W. Dean '52 '85 C.264 B.A. L.809 J.D. V.P. & Assoc. Coun., Fidelity Natl. Title Ins. Co.
Cochran, Sandra ....'61 '95 C.1075 B.S. L.1137 J.D. 2 Pk. Plaza
**Cochran, Thia M.** ....'61 '87 C.112 B.A. L.990 J.D. [Katten M.&Z.]
*PRACTICE AREAS: Real Estate Law.
**Cochrane, John W.** ....'55 '81 C.112 A.B. L.1068 J.D. [Jackson,D.&P.]
*PRACTICE AREAS: Business Litigation.
Codron, Keith ....'54 '80 C.145 B.A. L.365 J.D. 19800 MacArthur Blvd.
**Coffee, Mary Lynn K.** ....'63 '89 C.859 B.S. L.846 J.D. [Bryan C.]
*PRACTICE AREAS: Real Estate; Endangered Species; Wetlands Protection.
**Coffee, William D.** ....'64 '89 C&L.846 B.B.A., J.D. [Songstad,R.&U.]
Cohen, Peter J. ....'58 '82 C.813 A.B. L.145 J.D. Cosmotronic Co. Corp.

CAA125P

Cohn, David M. .......... '46 '74 C.800 B.A. L.910 J.D. [Silberman&C.]
**Cohn, Stephan S.** .......... '59 '86 C.112 A.B. L.1049 J.D. [Berger,K.S.M.F.S.&G.]
**Colaner, Deborah E.** .......... '68 '93 C.473 B.A. L.800 J.D. [Crowell&M.]
**Cole, Brian E.** '52 '82 C.684 B.A. L.940 J.D.
V.P. & Sr. Coun., Burlington Air Express Inc.
**Cole, Ronald M.** .......... '47 '90 C.112 B.A. L.426 J.D. [Palmieri,T.W.W.&W.]
*PRACTICE AREAS: Business Litigation.
**Coleman, Joseph L.** .......... '59 '86 C.145 A.B. L.831 J.D. [Corey,C.D.&D.]
*PRACTICE AREAS: Real Estate Finance; Real Estate; Business Law; Public Finance.
Coleman, Wendy Patricia .......... '59 '94 C.790 B.A. L.575 J.D. Quality Mtge. Corp.
**Colgan, David L.**, (AV) .......... '49 '75 C.378 B.A. L.986 J.D. [Nossaman,G.K.&E.]
*PRACTICE AREAS: Real Property and Land Use Law.
Collett, Charles T. .......... '51 '77 C.112 B.A. L.800 J.D. 5 Park Plaza
Collins, Bruce S. .......... '48 '77 C.1042 B.S. L.1137 J.D. 4000 Barranca Pkwy.
**Collins, Desmond J.** .......... '67 '95 C.112 B.A. L.809 J.D. [Raitt&M.]
*PRACTICE AREAS: Real Estate Litigation; Business Litigation; Insurance Law.
**Collins, Michael J.**, (AV) .......... '50 '75 C.988 B.A. L.426 J.D. [Collins&B.]

**Collins & Bellenghi, (AV)**
**18401 Von Karman Avenue, Suite 220, 92612-1542**
**Telephone: 714-851-9311 Fax: 714-851-9333**
**Michael J. Collins; Julian B. Bellenghi. Associates: Deborah S. Robbins.**
**Labor and Employment Law, Banking and Financial Institution Law, Complex Litigation, Consumer Law, Contract Disputes, Business Torts and Professional Liability Law.**
***See Professional Biographies, IRVINE, CALIFORNIA***

**Combs, A. Bennett**, (BV) .......... '45 '76 C.1043 L.1190 LL.B. [A.B.Combs]
*PRACTICE AREAS: Insurance Defense; Products Liability; Church/Clergy; Premises; Automobile.

**Combs, A. Bennett, A Professional Corporation, (BV)**
**14988 Sand Canyon, Suite 1-8, 92618**
**Telephone: 714-786-0023 Fax: 714-786-3864**
**A. Bennett Combs.**
**Insurance Defense, Products Liability, Church and Clergy, Premises, Automobile.**
***See Professional Biographies, IRVINE, CALIFORNIA***

**Condas, John C.** .......... '61 '89 C.145 A.B. L.800 J.D. [Jackson,D.&P.]
*PRACTICE AREAS: Land Use and Environmental Law and Litigation; Real Estate and Financial Institutions Litigation.
Conde, H. Victor .......... '47 '74 C.112 A.B. L.1067 J.D. 28 Agostino
**Condino, Debra Dahl** .......... '57 '82 C&L.770 B.S., J.D. Baxter Healthcare Corp. (Pat.)
Cone, John A., Jr., (BV) .......... '55 '82 C.1075 B.S. L.426 J.D. [Cone,C.&K.]
Cone, Chairez & Kassel, (BV) .......... 2603 Main St. Ste 1000
Conley, Timothy J. '48 '73 C.112 A.B. L.1068 J.D.
V.P. & Gen. Coun., Mazda Motor of Amer., Inc.
**Connor, Edmond M.**, (AV) .......... '50 '75 C.276 B.A. L.813 J.D. [Connor,C.B.&G.]

**Connor, Culver, Blake & Griffin LLP, (AV)**
**2600 Michelson Drive, Suite 1450, 92612**
**Telephone: 714-622-2600 Fax: 714-622-2626**
**Edmond M. Connor; Marilyn Martin Culver; Laura Lee Blake; Craig L. Griffin;—Roma R. Hanlon; David J. Hasseltime.**
**Business Litigation, with Areas of Concentration in Land Use, Construction Defect, Real Estate, Financial Institutions, Securities, Bankruptcy, Employment Law, including Sexual Harassment and Discrimination.**
***See Professional Biographies, IRVINE, CALIFORNIA***

**Conti, Alexander L.** .......... '65 '91 C.597 B.A. L.1049 J.D. [Snell&W.]
*PRACTICE AREAS: Business and Product Liability Litigation.
**Cook, Joseph T.**, (AV) .......... '41 '72 C.871 B.S. L.273 J.D. [Speiser,K.M.&C.]
*REPORTED CASES: Finley v. U.S., 490 U.S. 545 (1989); Estrada v. U.S., 967 F.2d 1421 (9th Cir. 1992); Steering Committee, et al. v. U.S., 6 F.3d 572 (9th Cir. 1993).
*PRACTICE AREAS: Aviation Accidents; International Aviation Law; Personal Injury and Wrongful Death Litigation; Mass Disaster Litigation; Products Liability.
**Copple, Brian W.** .......... '60 '87 C.813 A.B. L.1068 J.D. [Gibson,D.&C.]
*LANGUAGES: German.
*PRACTICE AREAS: Corporate Law; Securities; Venture Capital; Contracts; Technology and Science.
**Corbett, Bruce R.**, (AV) .......... '44 '70 C.659 B.A. L.188 J.D. [Corbett&S.]

**Corbett & Steelman, A Professional Law Corporation, (AV)**
**Suite 200, 18200 Von Karman, 92612**
**Telephone: 714-553-9266 Telecopier: 714-553-8454**
**Bruce R. Corbett; Ken E. Steelman; Richard B. Specter; David F. Brown;—Mark M. Monachino; Debra L. Barbin; Anthony L. Lanza; Robert H. Feigenbaum.**
**General Practice including Trial and Appellate Litigation in all State and Federal Courts. Corporate, Banking, Franchise, Real Property, Insurance, Antitrust, Trade Secret, Bankruptcy and Insolvency Matters.**
***See Professional Biographies, IRVINE, CALIFORNIA***

**Corey, Croudace, Dietrich & Dragun**
**5 Park Plaza, Suite 1050, 92714**
**Telephone: 714-251-2777 Fax: 714-251-2779**
**Members: Virginia P. Croudace; Debra M. Dietrich; Anthony J. Dragun. Associates: Mark A. Nitikman; Joseph L. Coleman. Of Counsel: Christianne F. Kerns.**
**Real Estate, Finance, Land Use and Business.**
***See Professional Biographies, IRVINE, CALIFORNIA***

**Corfield, Keri Flynn** .......... '62 '89 C.112 B.A. L.1049 J.D. [Berger,K.S.M.F.S.&G.]
Corie, Joseph '16 '46 C.799 B.C.S. L.180
(adm. in DC; not adm. in CA) 19191 Edgehill Dr.‡
**Cornwell, Kimberly H.** .......... '61 '87 C.823 B.S. L.564 J.D. [Ramsay&J.]
*PRACTICE AREAS: Insurance Coverage and Defense.
Corrado, Victoria F., (BV) .......... '53 '83 C.763 B.A. L.904 J.D. 100 Pacifica Ste. 200
Corris, Steve G. .......... '45 '77 C.260 B.S.B.A. L.981 LL.B. 19100 Von Karman
**Coscino, Vincent M.** '60 '85 C.605 B.A. L.1049 J.D.
[Allen,M.L.G.&M.] (©Los Angeles)
*PRACTICE AREAS: Bankruptcy Law; Insolvency Law; Commercial Law.
**Costanzo, Sally S.** .......... '58 '94 C.1169 B.A. L.1068 J.D. [Allen,M.L.G.&M.]
*PRACTICE AREAS: Employment Law.
**Cotter, Paul R.** .......... '67 '95 C.112 B.A. L.464 J.D. [Kirtland&P.]
**Couch, Laura Pavloff** .......... '69 '96 C.112 B.A. L.464 J.D. [S.M.Trager]

**Cox, Castle & Nicholson, LLP, (AV)**
**A Limited Liability Partnership including Professional Corporations**
**19800 MacArthur Boulevard, Suite 600, 92715©**
**Telephone: 714-476-2111 Fax: 714-476-0256**
**Resident Partners: Arthur O. Spaulding, Jr.; Lora Lee Moore; P. Jerold Walsh; Mark P. McClanathan; John A. Kincannon; Jess R. Bressi; D. Scott Turner. Resident Associates: Stathi George Marcopulos; Camellia Kuo Schuk; Colin C. Swainston; Robert J. Sykes.**
**General Civil, Trial and Appellate Practice in all State and Federal Courts. Real Property and Construction Law. Land Use and Environmental Law. Public Bond Financing. International Law. Labor Relations Bankruptcy, Receiverships and Creditors Rights. Taxation, Trusts, Estate Planning and Probate Law.**
**Los Angeles, California Office: 28th Floor, Two Century Plaza, 2049 Century Park East. Telephone: 310-277-4222. Fax: 310-277-7889.**
***See Professional Biographies, IRVINE, CALIFORNIA***

**Coyle, Michele C.**, (AV©) .......... '51 '78 C.546 B.A. L.1170 J.D. [Gibson,D.&C.]
*PRACTICE AREAS: Environmental Law; Toxics; Product Liability; Labor and Employment.
**Crandall, James L.**, (AV) .......... '45 '71 C.768 B.A. L.426 J.D. [Genson,E.C.&W.]
**Crary, E. Avery**, (AV) .......... '39 '68 C.276 B.S.F.S. L.799 LL.B. [Meserve,M.&H.]
Crary, Gordon B. .......... '47 '75 C.1201 B.S. L.426 J.D. [Crary&W.]
Crary & Wilcox .......... 8200 Von Karman Ave.
**Crinella, M. Peter** .......... '64 '89 C.1049 B.A. L.800 J.D. [Rus,M.W.&S.]
*PRACTICE AREAS: Civil Litigation; Bankruptcy.
Crisp, Geoffrey .......... '56 '83 C.101 B.A. L.1049 J.D. 19100 Von Karman Ave., Ste., 400
**Cron, Lawrence M.** .......... '63 '90 C.112 B.A. L.464 J.D. [Horwitz&B.]
*PRACTICE AREAS: Business Litigation; Commercial Litigation; Bankruptcy; Creditors Rights.
**Cronin, Frank**, (AV) .......... '44 '71 C&L.93 A.B., J.D. [Snell&W.]
*PRACTICE AREAS: Labor and Employment Law.
**Crooke, Steven C.**, (BV) .......... '51 '77 C.112 B.A. L.770 J.D. [Sikora&P.]
*PRACTICE AREAS: Real Estate Transactions; Business Law; Litigation.
**Crookes, Harold R.** .......... '— '76 C.477 B.B.A. L.802 J.D. Sr. Coun., AirToucn Comm.
**Crosby, William M.**, (AV) .......... '45 '71 C.112 A.B. L.426 J.D. [Barnes,C.F.&Z.]
*PRACTICE AREAS: Employment Law; Civil Litigation.
**Croudace, Virginia P.** .......... '54 '85 C.67 B.A. L.800 J.D. [Corey,C.D.&D.]
Crowell, Alton I., Jr. .......... '36 '67 C.871 B.S. L.893 LL.B. Exec. V.P., Carpenter & Co.

**Crowell & Moring LLP, (AV)**
**2010 Main Street, Suite 1200, 92714-7217©**
**Telephone: 714-263-8400 Fax: 714-263-8414**
**Members of Firm: Donald E. Sovie; Randall L. Erickson; Michael D. Newman. Of Counsel: Linda M. Cipriani; Steven A. Fink; Steven P. Rice. Associates: Cecelia A. Tripi; Donald E. Bradley; Stuart Einbinder; Diane Smith Daruty; Deborah E. Colaner; John F. Walsh.**
**General Practice.**
**Washington, D.C. Office: 1001 Pennsylvania Avenue, N.W. Telephone: 202-624-2500. Fax: 202-628-5116.**
**London, England Office: 180 Fleet Street, EC4A 2HD. Telephone: 011-44-171-413-0011. Fax: 011-44-171-413-0333.**
***See Professional Biographies, IRVINE, CALIFORNIA***

**Cullen, Joseph J.** .......... '52 '81 C.426 B.A. L.809 J.D. [Mower,K.N.C.&H.]
*LANGUAGES: Swedish.
*PRACTICE AREAS: Construction Defect Litigation; Bad Faith Law; Insurance Coverage; Insurance Defense Law; Construction Accidents.
**Culver, Marilyn Martin** .......... '57 '83 C.112 B.A. L.1068 J.D. [Connor,C.B.&G.]
**Cummings, Linda E.** .......... '59 '87 C.1044 B.A. L.1137 J.D. [Genson,E.C.&W.]
Cunningham, Ernest D. '34 '60 C&L.178 B.A., LL.B.
(adm. in NY; not adm. in CA) 13711 Onkayha Circle
Curtis, Jennifer Tolson .......... '55 '81 C.813 A.B. L.178 J.D. Sr. Coun., Fluor Daniel, Inc.
**Curtis, Michelle A.** .......... '68 '92 C&L.37 B.A., J.D. [Katten M.&Z.]
*LANGUAGES: Spanish.
*PRACTICE AREAS: Litigation.
Curtis, William M., (AV) .......... '40 '66 C.918 B.A. L.228 LL.B. [Curtis&V.]
Curtis & Vaccaro, (AV) .......... 5 Pk. Plaza
Cutler, M. Richard .......... '57 '84 C.101 B.A. L.178 J.D. Two Venture Plaza
Daggett, Dean E., (AV) .......... '46 '72 C.475 B.S. L.477 J.D. One Park Plz.
**D'Agostino, Renee C.** .......... '63 '91 C.549 B.S. L.426 J.D. [Berger,K.S.M.F.S.&G.]
Dale, A. Ennis, (AV©) '43 '70 C.477 B.B.A. L.1119 J.D.
(adm. in AZ; not adm. in CA)
Sr. V.P. & Corp. Coun., Fidelity National Title Insurance Co.
**D'Alessandro, Anna M.** .......... '64 '96 C.112 B.A. L.1137 J.D. [Kring&B.]
*PRACTICE AREAS: Construction Defects.
Damiani, John F. .......... '60 '86 C.569 B.A. L.262 J.D. 18500 Von Karman Ave., Suite 600
**Dannemeyer, Bruce W.** .......... '57 '82 C.879 B.A. L.1066 J.D. [Palmieri,T.W.W.&W.]
*PRACTICE AREAS: Litigation.
**Danskin, Samuel M.** .......... '63 '88 C.112 B.A. L.1049 J.D. [Berger,K.S.M.F.S.&G.]

**D'Antony, Joseph S., & Associates, (AV) '39 '73 C.607 Phar. B. L.990 J.D.**
**100 Pacifica, Suite 200, 92718-3320©**
**Telephone: 714-727-7077 Fax: 714-727-1284**
***PRACTICE AREAS: Malpractice Law; Personal Injury Law; Dental Malpractice Law; Alternative Dispute Resolution; Insurance Defense.**
**Daniel W. Doyle. Associates: Kelly A. Fortin.**
**Insurance Defense, Personal Injury, Medical Malpractice Defense.**
**Los Angeles, California Office: 2049 Century Park East, Suite 880, 90067-3110. Telephone: 310-843-2800. Facsimile: 310-843-2820.**
***See Professional Biographies, IRVINE, CALIFORNIA***

**Dapp, Melody Williams** .......... '57 '91 C.112 B.A. L.426 J.D. [Katten M.&Z.]
**Darling, Ellen L.** .......... '64 '90 C.37 B.A. L.1049 J.D. [Snell&W.]
*PRACTICE AREAS: Product Liability Litigation; Commercial Litigation; Environmental Litigation.
**Daruty, Diane Smith** .......... '63 '93 C.339 B.S. L.1067 J.D. [Crowell&M.]
Davey, Gerard P. .......... '49 '74 C.339 B.S. L.326 J.D. [G.P.Davey]
Davey, Gerard P., A Professional Law Corporation .......... 8001 Irvine Cntr., Dr.
**Davidson, Ann D.** '52 '79 C.610 B.A. L.201 J.D.
(adm. in OH; not adm. in CA)
Assoc. Gen. Coun. & V.P., Aerospace, Parker-Hannifin Corp.
Davies, Lori K. .......... '62 '86 C.813 A.B. L.1097 J.D. 2603 Main St., Ste., 1300
Davis, Glenn E. .......... '49 '74 C.169 A.B. L.1066 J.D. Asst. Gen. Coun., Allergan, Inc.
Davis, Russell D. .......... '43 '76 L.1137 LL.B. 2010 Main St.
Davis, Wesley L., (AV) .......... '43 '73 C.1042 B.S.M.E. L.1152 J.D. [Davis&B.]
Davis & Balmuth, (AV) .......... 111 Pacifica St.
Day, Brian L. .......... '63 '89 C.426 B.A. L.1065 J.D. 1 Park Plaza
Dayton, Christopher A. .......... '61 '92 C.1049 B.A. L.61 J.D. 1920 Main St. (Pat.)
**Dean, Robert Everett** .......... '51 '76 C.112 B.A. L.494 J.D. [Gibson,D.&C.]
*PRACTICE AREAS: General Corporate Law; Securities Law; Banking.
**De Corso, Nicholas** '54 '80 C.645 B.A. L.8 J.D.
Reg. Coun., Coml. Equip. Fin., GE Capital Corp.
**DeFelice, Ronald J.**, (AV) .......... '43 '69 C.813 A.B. L.309 J.D. [Morrison&F.]
*PRACTICE AREAS: Real Estate; Environmental; Land Use.
**DeForge, Dale R.** '49 '95 C.912 B.S. L.1137 J.D.
Staff Atty., Natl. Telephone & Communications, Inc.
*RESPONSIBILITIES: State and Federal Regulatory Compliance; Corporate; Business.
**DeGasperin, Toni L.** .......... '55 '83 C.608 B.S. L.1049 J.D. [Jones&D.]
*PRACTICE AREAS: Government Contracts; Contracts.
**Deihl, Richard T.** .......... '51 '77 C.940 B.A. L.990 J.D. [Rosenbaum&D.]
*PRACTICE AREAS: General Business; Corporate Law; Real Estate; Corporate Finance.
Delgado, Charles X. .......... '46 '72 C.767 B.S. L.426 J.D. [Wood&D.]
DeMarco, Donna L. .......... '53 '86 L.1137 J.D. 5 Park Plaza
**DeMarco, James R.**, (AV) .......... '40 '66 C.93 B.S. L.276 LL.B. [Jackson,D.&P.]
*PRACTICE AREAS: Litigation.
Dempsey, Pamela A. .......... '47 '84 L.1137 J.D. [Parham&Assoc.]
**Derevan, Richard A.**, (AV) .......... '49 '74 C.112 B.A. L.1065 J.D. [Snell&W.]
*PRACTICE AREAS: Appellate Law.
De Silva, Michael R. .......... '43 '72 C.171 M.E. L.1065 J.D. 8 Autumn Oak
**Deverich, Jay W.** .......... '55 '86 C.101 B.S. L.1066 J.D. [Smith,B.&D.]
*LANGUAGES: Japanese.
*PRACTICE AREAS: Real Estate Transactional; Land Use.

**de Veyra Gonzalez, Ferdinand** ............ '58 '88 C&L.061 B.A., J.D. [🄰 C.G.Tuohey]
*LANGUAGES: Tagalog.
*PRACTICE AREAS: Toxic Torts; Environmental Law; International Law.
Devine, John M., (AV) ................... '56 '82 C.339 B.A. L.990 J.D. [Floratos,L.&D.]
**Devine, William R.** .................. '51 '81 C.1075 B.S. L.101 J.D. [🄲 Paone,C.M.&W.]
*PRACTICE AREAS: Real Estate Development; Land Use; Environmental; Natural Resources.
**Dickerson, Donald D.** ................ '56 '82 C.1075 B.A. L.800 J.D. [Smith,B.&D.]
*PRACTICE AREAS: Business Litigation; Real Estate; Land Use; Environmental; Construction.
Dickinson, Scott J. ................ '55 '87 C.1109 B.S. L.1137 J.D. [Burge,S.&D.]
**Dierking, James K.** ................ '61 '90 C.1109 B.A. L.1049 J.D. [🄰 Arter&H.]
*PRACTICE AREAS: Construction; Commercial Litigation; Complex Contract Disputes; International Business.
**Dietrich, Debra M.** ..................... '60 '86 C.112 B.A. L.1066 J.D. [Corey,C.D.&D.]
**Di Fronzo, Pascal W.** ................ '64 '89 C.112 B.A. L.1065 J.D. [🄰 Ross,D.&M.]
Dillard, Thomas S., (BV) .......... '48 '77 C.1109 B.A. L.1137 J.D. 100 Pacifica Ste. 200
Dimitruk, David B., (BV) .................. '51 '77 C.1109 B.A. L.1137 J.D. 5 Corp. Park
**DiPinto, Ilse Harle**, (AV) ............. '53 '77 C.1109 B.A. L.1068 J.D. [DiPinto&S.]
*PRACTICE AREAS: Toxic Tort Defense Law; Construction Litigation; Products Liability Law; General Civil Litigation.

**DiPinto & Shimokaji, P.C., (AV)**
**2192 Martin Street, Suite 260, 92715**
**Telephone: 714-223-0838 Fax: 714-223-0845**
**Ilse Harle DiPinto; Michael A. Shimokaji.**
**Toxic Tort Defense, Construction Litigation, Products Liability, General Civil Litigation, Negligence, Intellectual Property, General Business.**
***See Professional Biographies, IRVINE, CALIFORNIA***

**DiSante, Marie D.** ..................... '63 '88 C.840 B.S. L.802 J.D. [Faustman,C.D.&F.]
*PRACTICE AREAS: Employment Law; Labor Law.
Dobrott, James E., Jr. .......'53 '81 C.426 B.A. L.809 J.D. 19900 MacArthur Blvd., 8th Fl.
Dodds, Debra A. ........................'56 '82 C.147 B.A. L.1049 J.D. 17th Fl., 3 Park Plaza
**Donato, Brian J.** ......................... '40 '71 C.433 B.A. L.893 J.D. [Hyman,P.&M.]
Dondanville, Jeffrey W. '51 '83 C.1077 B.A. L.1137 J.D.
V.P. & Assoc. Coun., Fidelity Natl. Title Ins. Co.
**Donnellan, Joan C.** ...................... '52 '78 C.940 B.A. L.990 J.D. [🄰 Ramsay&J.]
*PRACTICE AREAS: Commercial Law; Employment Law; Banking Law; Insurance Law.
Donnelly, John M. ........................ '62 '87 C.188 B.A. L.910 J.D. 101 Pacifica
**Donohue, Francis T., III** ........... '54 '82 C.1122 B.S. L.1040 J.D. [🄰 Brown,P.H.&V.]
*PRACTICE AREAS: Environmental Law; Construction Law; General Litigation.
**Donovan, Brian J.**, (AV) .................. '45 '75 C.1070 B.S. L.426 J.D. [Jones&D.]
*PRACTICE AREAS: Government Contracts; Contracts.
Douglas, Priscilla H. ......................... '60 '85 C.112 B.S. L.1065 J.D. [Ybarra&D.]
Downes, Roger P. ........................ '40 '72 C.107 B.A. L.169 J.D. 3 Park Plz., 9th Fl.
**Doyle, Daniel W.** ............ '63 '89 C.1102 B.A. L.1049 J.D. [J.S.D'Antony&Assoc.]
*PRACTICE AREAS: Personal Injury; Medical Malpractice; Construction Defects; Criminal Matters.
**Doyle, Mark C.** ............................ '58 '83 C&L.426 B.A., J.D. [Tredway,L.&D.]
*PRACTICE AREAS: Corporate Law; Real Estate Law.
**Doyle, Todd E.** '61 '86 C.112 B.A. L.426 J.D.
Gen. Coun. & Corp. Secy., Family Restaurants, Inc.
*RESPONSIBILITIES: Real Estate; Corporate; Commercial Litigation.
**Dragun, Anthony J.** ..................... '57 '86 C.112 B.S. L.1066 J.D. [Songstad,R.&U.]
**Dragun, Anthony J.** ..................... '57 '86 C.112 B.S. L.1066 J.D. [Corey,C.D.&D.]
**Dressler, Donald G.** ..................... '45 '70 C.375 B.A. L.813 J.D. [Meuers,D.&K.]
*PRACTICE AREAS: Labor and Employment; Corporate Law.
**Driscoll, Steven M.** ........................ '56 '90 C&L.426 B.S., J.D. [Feder,G.&S.]
*PRACTICE AREAS: Estate Planning; Administrative; Probate.
**Drugan, Margaret M.** ........... '69 '94 C.94 B.A.B.S. L.809 J.D. [🄰 Berger,K.S.M.F.S.&G.]
**Dubia, Christian F., Jr.**, (AV) ................. '48 '78 C.871 B.S. L.990 J.D. [Pinto&D.]
**Duffy, Anthony C.**, (AV) .............. '47 '72 C.813 B.A. L.976 J.D. [Smith,S.D.P.&W.]
**Dufresne, Mynette M.** ..................... '65 '91 C.1002 B.A. L.426 J.D. [🄰 Bryan C.]
**Dukellis, Gregory John** ................ '64 '91 C.800 B.S. L.426 J.D. [🄰 Watt,T.&H.]
*PRACTICE AREAS: Construction Law; Commercial Litigation; Government Contracts; Surety Law.
**Duncan, Richard G., Jr.**, (AV) ........ '38 '67 C.813 A.B. L.1068 LL.B. [Gibson,D.&C.]
*PRACTICE AREAS: Business, Corporate, Real Estate and Land Use Litigation.

**Duncan, John A., A Professional Corporation**
**(See Orange)**

**Dundas, David G.**, (AV) .......... '42 '69 C.112 B.A. L.809 LL.B. [Simon,M.M.Z.S.&D.]
*PRACTICE AREAS: Estate Planning; Business Law.
**Dunham, Kathleen L.**, (BV) ........... '50 '81 C.112 B.A. L.1068 J.D. [🄰 Callahan&B.]
*LANGUAGES: Spanish.
*PRACTICE AREAS: Civil Litigation; Business Law; Insurance Coverage Litigation; Creditors Rights.
**Dunn-Rankin, Dean** ........................... '58 '85 C.312 B.A. L.800 J.D. [Hewitt&M.]
*PRACTICE AREAS: Real Estate Law.
**Dunning, Kim G.** ......................... '49 '77 C.813 B.A. L.802 J.D. [🄰 Ramsay&J.]
*PRACTICE AREAS: First Party Insurance; Appellate Practice.
**Durbin, Mary** ........................ '60 '94 C.999 A.A. L.1137 J.D. [🄰 Morrison&L.]
*LANGUAGES: Greek.
*PRACTICE AREAS: Real Estate Litigation; Business Litigation; Civil Litigation; Personal Injury.
Dwyer, K. Scott ........................... '53 '80 C.1044 B.A. L.575 J.D. 5 Pk Plaza
**Dye, Robert E.** ........................ '48 '73 C.940 B.A. L.800 J.D. [🄲 Bryan C.]
**Dzida, Steven J.**, (AV) ............... '50 '74 C&L.426 B.A., J.D. [Jackson,D.&P.]
*PRACTICE AREAS: Real Estate.

**Earley, Jack M., (AV) '48 '74 C.1042 B.A. L.426 J.D.** 🄱🄱
**19100 Von Karman Avenue, Suite 950, 92715**
**Telephone: 714-476-8900 Fax: 714-476-0900**
**(Certified Specialist, Criminal Law, The State Bar of California Board of Legal Specialization).**
***REPORTED CASES: People v. Broderick; People v. Strawn; People v. Lee.**
***PRACTICE AREAS: Criminal Defense; Environmental; White Collar; Civil Litigation.**
**Criminal Defense and Environmental White Collar Civil Litigation.**
***See Professional Biographies, IRVINE, CALIFORNIA***

**Ebert, James R.** ........................ '56 '82 C.770 B.S.C. L.426 J.D. [Kitagawa&E.]
**Ebiner, Lawrence P.** ..................... '53 '85 C.426 B.A. L.1068 J.D. [Morrison&F.]
*PRACTICE AREAS: Litigation; Alternative Dispute Resolution; Real Property; Insurance; Energy.
Eddison, Jonathan B., (AV) '52 '79
C.918 B.A. L.276 J.D. V.P. & Gen. Coun., Pinnacle Micro
**Edwards, Riva I.** ............ '64 '89 C.139 B.A. L.1049 J.D. [🄰 Berger,K.S.M.F.S.&G.]
*PRACTICE AREAS: Insurance Defense; Business Litigation.
Egly, Jane H., (BV) .......... '42 '73 C.575 B.A. L.912 J.D. 7700 Irvine Center Dr., #700
Ehrlich, Steven A. .......................... '50 '76 C.1077 B.A. L.1148 J.D. 5 Park Plaza
**Eichten, David R.** ........ '48 '73 C.494 B.A. L.1049 J.D. [Meserve,M.&H.] (⊙San Diego)
**Einbinder, Stuart** ..................... '64 '91 C.112 B.A. L.1065 J.D. [🄰 Crowell&M.]

**Eisenberg, Lawrence S., (AV) '54 '83 C.107 B.A. L.809 J.D.**
**8001 Irvine Center Drive, Suite 1500, 92718**
**Telephone: 714-753-1500 FAX: 714-753-1516**
**Civil Trial Practice, Negligence, Products and Premises Liability, Professional Malpractice and Business Litigation, Wills and Trusts.**
***See Professional Biographies, IRVINE, CALIFORNIA***

**Eldredge, John W.** ...... '49 '92 C.67 B.S. L.1049 J.D. [🄰 Christie,P.&H.] (See Pat. Sect.)
*PRACTICE AREAS: Patent; Trademark; Copyright; Unfair Competition.
Elekes, John S., (BV) ............. '38 '74 C.36 B.S. L.1137 J.D. 18881 Von Karman Ave.
Elkins, Suzanne ... '53 '79 C.684 B.A. L.1068 J.D. Spec. Coun., Off. of Thrift Supervision
**Ellison, Michael W.** ....................... '63 '89 C.187 B.A. L.477 J.D. [Smith,B.&D.]
*PRACTICE AREAS: Business Litigation; Environmental Litigation.
**Emmons, Philip T.** .................. '54 '86 C.112 B.S. L.464 J.D. [🄰 Berger,K.S.M.F.S.&G.]
*PRACTICE AREAS: Labor & Employment; Environmental; Insurance Defense; Medical Malpractice; Products Liability.
**Emmons, Steven L.** .................. '51 '78 C.112 B.A. L.1068 J.D. Sr. Coun., PepsiCo., Inc.
*RESPONSIBILITIES: Franchising/Licensing.
**Endelicato, Constance A.** .................. '61 '88 C&L.546 B.A., J.D. [🄰 Baker,S.&K.]
England, Linda F. ....................... '43 '82 C.326 B.A. L.1137 J.D. 15375 Barranca Pkwy.
**Ennor, Sara Langford** ............. '52 '81 C.999 B.A. L.1355 J.D. [Boutwell,B.&E.]⊙
*PRACTICE AREAS: Pension Plans; ERISA; Fiduciary Law.
**Enriquez, Sally P.** ....................... '59 '95 C.476 B.A. L.1068 J.D. [🄰 Morrison&F.]
**Epstein, David G.**, (AV) .......... '43 '78 C.178 B.A. L.1068 J.D. [Kasdan,S.M.E.&M.]
*LANGUAGES: Portuguese, Spanish and French.
*PRACTICE AREAS: Construction Defect Litigation; Civil Litigation.
Erickson, James E., (AV) ....... '32 '58 C.684 B.A. L.500 LL.B. 18101 Von Karman Ave.
**Erickson, Mark D.** ......................... '57 '82 C.112 B.A. L.1065 J.D. [🄰 Pinto&D.]
**Erickson, Randall L.** ..................... '43 '71 C.966 B.S. L.228 J.D. [Crowell&M.]
*PRACTICE AREAS: Construction Law; Commercial Banking Law; Antitrust Law.
**Erskine, John P.** .................. '51 '78 C.1109 B.A. L.990 J.D. [Nossaman,G.K.&E.]
*PRACTICE AREAS: Real Property Law; Land Use Law; Environmental Law.
**Esten, Lawrence D.** ... '61 '86 C.112 B.A. L.426 J.D. [Manning,M.&W.] (⊙Los Angeles)
**Ettinger, Marc** ....................... '57 '88 C.763 B.A. L.1137 J.D. [Parilla,M.&S.]
*PRACTICE AREAS: Condominium Law; Contract Law; Real Estate Property Law; Civil Litigation; Construction Law.
**Evans, David W.**, (AV) ......................... '39 '71 C.770 B.S. L.426 J.D. [Snell&W.]
*PRACTICE AREAS: Estate Planning, Probate and Trust Law; Guardianship and Conservatorship; Estate and Gift Taxation.
Evans, Jeanne M. ............................................ '24 '79 C&L.1225 B.S., J.D. 2 Macon
Eversmeyer, John H. ............. '28 '71 C.800 B.S. L.426 J.D. 2081 Business Center Dr.
**Exon, Charles S.** .......................... '49 '83 C.502 B.A. L.800 J.D. [Hewitt&M.]
*PRACTICE AREAS: Corporate Law; Securities Law; Business Law.
**Ezra, David B.** ............... '63 '91 C.1109 B.A. L.800 J.D. [🄰 Berger,K.S.M.F.S.&G.]
**Fabiano, Michael D.** .................. '64 '93 C.691 B.A. L.1065 J.D. [🄰 Jones,D.R.&P.]
**Fabricant, Deborah** ....................... '52 '80 C.66 A.B. L.569 J.D. [🄰 Feder,G.&S.]
*PRACTICE AREAS: Litigation.
**Fagan, Peter T.** ............................ '48 '73 C&L.602 B.B.A., J.D. [Bryan C.]
*PRACTICE AREAS: Government Contracts; Construction Law; Civil Litigation.
**Falk, Barry D.** ........................... '62 '88 C.553 B.S. L.426 J.D. [Jeffers,W.&S.]
*PRACTICE AREAS: Corporate and Securities Law.
**Farrell, Teresa Joanning** ............ '58 '86 C.112 B.A. L.1065 J.D. [🄲 Gibson,D.&C.]
*PRACTICE AREAS: Real Estate; Finance.
**Farrington, Lisa M.** ........................ '66 '93 C.1042 L.426 J.D. [🄰 Snell&W.]
*PRACTICE AREAS: Bankruptcy Law; Commercial Litigation.
**Farrow, Jeffrey D.** .................. '67 '95 C.763 B.A. L.809 J.D. [🄰 Kring&B.]
*PRACTICE AREAS: Construction Defect; Insurance Bad Faith; Personal Injury.
**Faustman, David F.** '52 '78 C.800 B.S. L.1068 J.D.
[Faustman,C.D.&F.] (⊙San Francisco and Sacramento)
*PRACTICE AREAS: Employment Law; Labor Law; Business Litigation.

**Faustman, Carlton, DiSante & Freudenberger LLP**
**2600 Michelson Drive Suite 800, 92612⊙**
**Telephone: 714-622-1661 Facsimile: 714-622-1669**
**Members of Firm: David F. Faustman; Christopher W. Carlton; Marie D. DiSante; Timothy M. Freudenberger. Associates: Laura L. Saadeh; Christopher M. Robertson; Alyssa J. Allen; Leigh A. White; Diane L. Schlesinger; Jason L. Hoffman; Ann H. Qushair. Of Counsel: Ronna S. Reed; Kristine P. Nesthus.**
**On behalf of Employers, Employment Discrimination, Wrongful Discharge, Sexual Harassment and ERISA Litigation. Union Organizing Campaigns, Unfair Labor Practice Proceedings, Collective Bargaining Negotiations, Grievance Arbitration and other Labor Management Relations Issues. Wage and Hour and Occupational Safety and Health Proceedings. Trade Secrets and Unfair Competition Litigation. Employee Handbooks and Advice on Personnel Issues.**
**Los Angeles, California Office: 700 South Flower Street. Eleventh Floor, 90017. Telephone: 213-892-6308. Fax: 213-892-2263.**
**Sacramento, California Office: 711 9th Street, Suite 100, 95814. Telephone: 916-443-0999. Fax: 916-443-5140.**
**San Francisco, California Office: 388 Market Street, Suite 400, 94111. Telephone: 415-296-3813. Fax: 415-296-3814.**
**San Diego, California Office: 8910 University Center Lane, Suite 500, 92122. Telephone: 619-678-8446. Fax: 619-678-8447.**
***See Professional Biographies, IRVINE, CALIFORNIA***

**Fay, Alison Smith** ......................... '53 '81 C.813 A.B. L.1065 J.D. [Feder,G.&S.]
*PRACTICE AREAS: Employee Benefits.
**Fears, Daniel F.** ......................... '55 '83 C.1075 B.S. L.1049 J.D. [Payne&F.]
*PRACTICE AREAS: Labor Law; Employment Law and Related Litigation; Wrongful Termination Law; Employment and Housing Discrimination Law; Civil Rights Law.
Fedalen, Charles H., Jr. '56 '82
C.112 B.A. L.800 J.D. V.P. & Mgr., Wells Fargo Bk., N.A.
**Feder, Jon C.**, (AV) ....................... '41 '66 C.112 B.S. L.1065 J.D. [Feder,G.&S.]
*PRACTICE AREAS: Estate Planning.

**Feder, Goodman & Schwartz, Incorporated, (AV)**
**2 Park Plaza, Suite 450, 92614**
**Telephone: 714-251-2800 Telecopier: 714-251-2801**
**Jon C. Feder (Certified Specialist, Taxation Law, The State Bar of California Board of Legal Specialization); Randolph M. Goodman; John W. Schwartz; David I. Lesser; Alison Smith Fay; Michelle A. Wakino; Steven M. Driscoll; Donna T. Tonkon; Deborah Fabricant.**
**General Business and Taxation Law including Profit-Sharing, Employee Stock Ownership Plans and Employee Benefits, Estate Planning, Corporations, Business Sales and Acquisitions, Health Care, Finance, Securities, Tax Audits and Disputes, Tax Exempt Organizations and Real Estate Transactions and Related Litigation.**
***See Professional Biographies, IRVINE, CALIFORNIA***

**Feeley, John E.** ....................... '59 '84 C.1030 B.S. L.809 J.D. [Sedgwick,D.M.&A.]
**Feigenbaum, Robert H.** .................. '69 '96 C.1044 B.A. L.1049 J.D. [🄰 Corbett&S.]
Felchlin, Peter W. ......................... '49 '78 C.112 B.A. L.809 J.D. 7755 Center Ave.
Feliciano, Melanie A. ......... '65 '90 C.802 B.B.A. L.276 J.D. 18400 Von Karman, Ste., 600
Feller, Harriet Burns '42 '74 C&L.184 B.A., J.D.
Gen. Coun. & Sr. V.P., Western Financial Svgs. Bk., F.S.B.
Fenelli, Rick J., (BV) ..................... '50 '76 C.629 B.A. L.1137 J.D. 111 Pacifica
Fernandez, David ............................ '— '83 C.178 B.A. L.276 J.D. [🄰 Ching&Assoc.]
**Fidone, Kelly Lee** ................ '63 '88 C.112 B.A. L.426 J.D. [🄰 Sedgwick,D.M.&A.]
Finger, Robert J. .......................... '49 '80 C.813 B.S. L.1068 J.D. 40 Wetstone
**Fink, Steven A.** ........................... '54 '80 C&L.861 B.A., J.D. [🄲 Crowell&M.]
*PRACTICE AREAS: Business Litigation; Construction Law; Labor Law.
**Finlayson, Jesse S.** ..................... '70 '95 C.36 B.A. L.1049 J.D. [🄰 Gibson,D.&C.]
**Fiore, Richard S.**, (AV) ................. '42 '68 C.605 A.B. L.1065 J.D. [Fiore,W.R.&P.]

**Fiore, Walker, Racobs & Powers, A Professional Law Corporation, (AV)**
**Koll Center Irvine, 18400 Von Karmen, Suite 600, 92612-1514⊙**
**Telephone: 714-955-0560 Fax: 714-955-2894**

(This Listing Continued)

**Fiore, Walker, Racobs & Powers, A Professional Law Corporation (Continued)**
Richard S. Fiore; Bradley D. Walker; Peter E. Racobs; Janet L. S. Powers; Stephen D. McNamara; David E. Cane;—Chester A. Puchalski; Mark Hopkins; James C. Harkins, IV; Tracy Ann Stevenson.
Community Association, Real Property, Civil Litigation, Construction and Business.
Reference: Commerce Bank (Newport Beach).
Riverside, California Office: 6670 Alessandro, Suite B. Telephone: 909-789-8100. Fax: 909-789-8105.
Palm Desert, California Office: 74-361 Highway III, Suite 1. Telephone: 619-776-6511. Fax: 619-776-6517.

*See Professional Biographies, IRVINE, CALIFORNIA*

**Fischer, Leslie Tucker** ........... '65 '90 C.813 A.B. L.1068 J.D. [Ⓐ Allen,M.L.G.&M.]
*PRACTICE AREAS: Corporate Securities; General Corporate.
**Fisher, Christopher M.** .................. '61 '89 C.446 B.S. L.284 J.D. [Ⓐ Wesierski&Z.]
*PRACTICE AREAS: Personal Injury Law; Insurance Defense Law.
**Fisher, Don,** (BV) .................. '52 '80 C.589 B.A. L.1066 J.D. [Palmieri,T.W.W.&W.]
*PRACTICE AREAS: Litigation.
Fisher, Lawrence N. ............ '44 '69 C&L.800 B.A., J.D. Gen. Coun., Tax, Fluor Corp.
**Fisher, Robert A., II** ............... '65 '91 C.147 B.A. L.990 J.D. [Ⓐ Stevens,K.A.&H.]
*PRACTICE AREAS: Construction Defect Law; General Liability-Torts; Professional Liability; Products Liability; Litigation Defense.
Fitzer, Joel M. ................................ '41 '65 C&L.966 B.S., LL.B. [Santochi,F.&G.]
**FitzGerald, Michael J.** ................ '51 '76 C.1109 B.A. L.767 J.D. [Barnes,C.F.&Z.]
*PRACTICE AREAS: Commercial; Business Litigation.
**Fitzgerald, Robert M.,** (AV⊕) '47 '75 C&L.945 B.A., J.D.
(adm. in VA; not adm. in CA) [Watt,T.&H.] (⊙Mc Lean, VA)
*PRACTICE AREAS: Public Construction Law; Private Construction Law; Zoning.
Fivehouse, Derence V. ............ '56 '81 C.174 B.A. L.45 J.D. 1920 Main St. Ste. 1200
**Fleming, Jack W.** ........................ '50 '75 C.477 B.S.I.E. L.188 J.D. [Arter&H.]
*PRACTICE AREAS: Construction Law;-Public Contract Law; Business Litigation.
Fleming, Sheldon J. ........................ '57 '83 C.1042 B.S. L.990 J.D. 2030 Main St.
Fletcher, Ann E. ............................ '57 '83 C.605 A.B. L.770 J.D. 5 Park Plaza‡
Floratos, William A., (AV) ................ '57 '83 C&L.990 B.A., J.D. [Floratos,L.&D.]
Floratos, Loll & Devine, A Professional Law Corporation, (AV)
18201 Von Karman Ave.
Flores, Paul E. '53 '82 C.112 B.A. L.800 J.D.
V.P. & Assoc. Coun., Fidelity Natl. Title Ins. Co.
**Floyd, A. Kristine** ................. '66 '91 C.800 B.A. L.228 J.D. [Ⓐ Allen,M.L.G.&M.]
*PRACTICE AREAS: Litigation.
**Flynn, Jane M.** ............................. '64 '93 C.1169 B.A. L.1065 J.D. [Ⓐ Payne&F.]
**Flynn, John J., III** ................... '52 '77 C.112 B.A. L.1066 J.D. [Nossaman,G.K.&E.]
*PRACTICE AREAS: Litigation.
Flynn, Matthew J., (BV) ..................... '37 '76 C.112 B.A. L.990 J.D. 18 Sumter Dr.
Foley, William P., II '44 '74 C.870 B.S. L.911 J.D.
(adm. in AZ; not adm. in CA) CEO & Pres., Fidelity Natl. Title Ins. Co.
Foliart, Mary E. ......................... '48 '75 C.1077 B.A. L.1095 J.D. P.O. Box 18917‡
Fong, Cheryl Y. ............................................ '61 '90 C.788 A.B. L.974 J.D. AT&T
**Ford, Daniel J., Jr.,** (BV) ................ '57 '82 C.112 B.S. L.1049 J.D. [Wesierski&Z.]
*PRACTICE AREAS: Civil Litigation Law; Auto Liability Law; Insurance Law; Bad Faith Law.
**Forrester, Keith R.** ...................... '61 '87 C.884 B.A. L.990 J.D. [Ⓐ Aldrich&B.]
*PRACTICE AREAS: Commercial Litigation; Writs and Attachments; Commercial Transactions; Loan Workouts; Bank Regulatory Compliance.
**Forsythe, Marc C.** ......................... '61 '90 C.549 B.S. L.464 J.D. [Ⓐ Frankel&T.]
**Fortin, Kelly A.** .............. '66 '92 C.1154 B.A. L.912 J.D. [Ⓐ J.S.D'Antony&Assoc.]
*PRACTICE AREAS: Civil Litigation; Professional Liability; Medical Malpractice.
Foster, Jacquelyn A. .............. '43 '80 C.1109 B.A. L.1137 J.D. 8001 Irvine Center Dr.

**Foster, Lachlan,** (AV) '31 '58 C.475 B.A. L.976 LL.B.
**Suite 1250, One Park Plaza, 92614**
Telephone: 714-263-1010 Telecopier: 714-263-1693
Corporate, Securities and Business Practice.

*See Professional Biographies, IRVINE, CALIFORNIA*

**Foster, Richard J.** ..................... '51 '81 C.1042 B.A. L.426 J.D. [Paone,C.M.&W.]
*PRACTICE AREAS: Business Law; Real Estate Litigation; Construction; Eminent Domain.
Foster, Robert A., II, (AV) ................ '47 '75 C.549 B.A. L.464 J.D. [R.A.Foster,II]
**Foster, Thomas C.** ..................... '48 '75 C&L.800 B.S., J.D. [Allen,M.L.G.&M.]
*PRACTICE AREAS: Tax; Partnerships; General Corporate.
Foster, Robert A., II, A Law Corporation, (AV) ........ 18101 Von Karman Ave., Ste. 1400
Francisco, Emilio N. ........................................ '48 '76 C&L.1137 B.S., J.D. 17771 Fitch
**Frankel, Benjamin W.** ........................ '42 '66 C&L.813 A.B., J.D. [Frankel&T.]

**Frankel & Tennant, Professional Corporation**
**17875 Von Karman, Suite 350, 92614-6257**
Telephone: 714-252-4700 Fax: 714-252-5597
Benjamin W. Frankel; Douglas G. Tennant:—Marc C. Forsythe.
Real Property, Banking, Creditors' Rights, Loan Workouts/Foreclosure/Bankruptcy and Litigation.

*See Professional Biographies, IRVINE, CALIFORNIA*

**Franklin, Blake T.** ......... '42 '66 C.197 A.B. L.309 J.D. [Gibson,D.&C.] (⊙N.Y., NY)
*LANGUAGES: Spanish.
*PRACTICE AREAS: International Transactions (project finance, etc.); Banking Law; Corporate Law.
**Franks, Roger M.** ......................... '68 '93 C.112 B.S. L.426 J.D. [Jackson,D.&P.]
*PRACTICE AREAS: Real Estate and Commercial Litigation; Land Use.
**Fransz, Helene Z.** ............................ '60 '85 C.93 B.A. L.276 J.D. [Jackson,D.&P.]
*PRACTICE AREAS: General Business and Real Estate.
**Franzen, Mark V.,** (AV) ................... '51 '77 C.112 B.A. L.990 J.D. [Baker,S.&K.]
**Frasca, Joanne M.** ......................... '53 '77 C.184 B.A. L.602 J.D. [Frasca&Assoc.]
*PRACTICE AREAS: Business Litigation.

**Frasca & Associates**
**5 Park Plaza, Suite 1500, 92614**
Telephone: 714-553-8193 Fax: 714-553-8195
Joanne M. Frasca.
General Commercial Litigation Practice in both State and Federal Courts.

*See Professional Biographies, IRVINE, CALIFORNIA*

**Freeman, Douglas K.,** (AV) '45 '70
C.813 A.B. L.1068 J.D. [Freeman,F.&S.] (⊙Los Angeles)
*PRACTICE AREAS: Tax Law; Estate Law; Business Planning Law.
**Freeman, Roger P.** ........................ '46 '71 C.684 A.B. L.1068 J.D. [Chevalier,A.&L.]

**Freeman, Freeman & Smiley, LLP, (AV)**
A Limited Liability Partnership including Law Corporations
**2010 Main Street, Suite 580, 92614⊙**
Telephone: 714-833-7966 Facsimile: 714-833-9584
Members of Firm: Douglas K. Freeman (Certified Specialist, Taxation Law, The State Bar of California Board of Legal Specialization); Fred J. Marcus; Jane Peebles. Of Counsel: Ernest J. Schag, Jr. (Certified Specialist, Taxation Law, The State Bar of California Board of Legal Specialization) (Resident); Richard E. Gilbert.
Estate and Gift Planning, Probate, Real Estate, Corporate, Business Succession Planning, Civil Trial and Appellate Litigation.
Los Angeles, California Office: Penthouse, Suite 1200, 3415 Sepulveda Boulevard. Telephone: 310-398-6227. Facsimile: 310-391-4042.
San Francisco, California Office: One Market, Steuart Tower, 16th Floor. Telephone: 415-974-1930.

*See Professional Biographies, IRVINE, CALIFORNIA*

**Freisleben, Alan J.,** (AV) ........... '52 '78 C.800 B.A. L.426 J.D. [Sedgwick,D.M.&A.]

**Freudenberger, Timothy M.** '62 '88
C.112 B.A. L.106 J.D. [Faustman,C.D.&F.] (⊙San Diego)
*REPORTED CASES: Lee v. Bank of America NT&SA, 27 Cal.App.4th 197, 32 Cal.Rptr.2d 388 (1994).
*PRACTICE AREAS: Employment Law; Labor Law.
**Friedman, Alan J.** ............................ '61 '87 C.112 B.A. L.1065 J.D. [Ⓐ Lobel&O.]
*PRACTICE AREAS: Bankruptcy Law; Reorganization.
**Friedman, Bryan M., (A Professional Corporation)** ........... '46 '70 [Friedman P.&S.]
*PRACTICE AREAS: Domestic and International Business Transactions; Licensing and Trademarks; Copyright.
**Friedman, Philip N.** ........................ '56 '83 C.112 B.A. L.1065 J.D. [Horwitz&B.]
*PRACTICE AREAS: Civil Litigation; Real Estate and Broker Law; Business Transactions.

**Friedman Peterson & Stroffe**
A Partnership including Law Corporations
**19800 MacArthur Boulevard, Suite 1100, 92612-2425**
Telephone: 714-955-1086 Facsimile: 714-833-9436
Bryan M. Friedman (A Professional Corporation); Robert A. Peterson (A Professional Corporation); James D. Stroffe;—Brian F. Segall; Lawrence H. Binderow.
General Business, Corporate, Real Property, Construction, Unfair Competition, Licensing and Trademark Law. Litigation.

*See Professional Biographies, IRVINE, CALIFORNIA*

**Friess, K. Erik** ..................... '65 '90 C.112 B.A. L.1065 J.D. [Ⓐ Nossaman,G.K.&E.]
*PRACTICE AREAS: Litigation.
**Fuchs, Rudolph J.** ........................... '57 '92 C.1042 B.S. L.809 J.D. [Ⓐ Busch]
*PRACTICE AREAS: Tax Law.
Fuhrman, Sandra L. '50 '78 C.161 B.B.A. L.1049 J.D.
Underwriting Coun., Fidelity Natl. Title Ins. Co.
**Fujimoto, Michelle M.** ........... '62 '86 C.990 B.A. L.800 J.D. [Palmieri,T.W.W.&W.]
*PRACTICE AREAS: Product Liability; Commercial Litigation.
Fuller, David J., (BV) .............. '48 '76 C.1042 B.A. L.1137 J.D. 100 Pacifica Ste. 200
**Fuller, H. Daniel,** (AV) ................ '55 '82 C.112 B.A. L.101 J.D. [Chapman,F.&B.]
*LANGUAGES: Spanish.
*PRACTICE AREAS: Litigation.
Fullmer, Jerri A. ........'59 '94 C.112 B.A. L.426 J.D. 18500 Von Karman Ave., Suite 600
Funsten, Melanie F. ................ '63 '89 C.112 B.A. L.1065 J.D. 2 Park Plz., Suite 800
Gable, Bill L., (AV) ...................... '49 '75 C.988 B.A. L.800 J.D. [Santochi,F.&G.]
Gable, Marsha A. ..................... '52 '92 C.351 B.A. L.1188 J.D. 18101 Von Karman
**Gaetje, Clay E.** ............... '70 '94 C.158 B.S. L.1097 J.D. Discovision Assocs. (Pat.)
*RESPONSIBILITIES: Patent Litigation; Patent Licensing; Patent Contracts; Patent Prosecution.
Gagnon, Ron F., (BV) ............. '41 '71 C.1042 B.A. L.809 J.D. 8001 Irvine Center Dr.

**Galardi, Lawrence J., (AV) '35 '59 C.776 B.A. L.1009 LL.B.** BB
**Wells Fargo Tower, 2030 Main Street Suite 1050, 92714**
Telephone: 714-852-1100 Telecopier: 714-252-7780
***PRACTICE AREAS: Construction Defect; Aviation Law; Business Disputes; Products Liability Law; Civil Trial Practice.**
General Civil Litigation, Construction Defect, Business Disputes, Aviation and Products Liability Law. Trial Practice in all State and Federal Courts.

*See Professional Biographies, IRVINE, CALIFORNIA*

**Galfin, Ted A.,** (BV) ................. '53 '80 C.112 B.A. L.284 J.D. [Suchman,G.&P.]⊙
*PRACTICE AREAS: Litigation; Bankruptcy (Creditor Representation); Commercial Law; Landlord and Tenant Law; Banking Law.
**Gallagher, Mary-Cay** ........... '48 '85 C.112 B.A. L.1137 J.D. [Ⓐ Laughlin,F.L.&M.]
**Galloway, Edward A.** ..................... '56 '82 C.846 B.A. L.802 J.D. [Jackson,D.&P.]
*LANGUAGES: Russian and German.
*PRACTICE AREAS: Litigation.
Galusha, Timothy S. ................................ '68 '93 C.112 B.A. L.1065 J.D. 2603 Main St.
**Gamble, John C.,** (AV) ................ '45 '71 C.813 B.A. L.426 J.D. [Allen,M.L.G.&M.]
*PRACTICE AREAS: Real Estate.
**Gandee, Michael R.** ..................... '62 '93 C.446 B.S. L.990 J.D. [Ⓐ Brown,P.H.&V.]
*PRACTICE AREAS: Construction Law; Public Works.
**Garber, Bradley N.** ........................ '58 '84 C.49 B.A. L.990 J.D. [Parilla,M.&S.]
*PRACTICE AREAS: General Business Litigation; Real Estate Property Litigation.
**Garcia, Manuel** ........................ '63 '91 C.1075 B.A. L.1137 J.D. [Ⓐ Laughlin,F.L.&M.]
*PRACTICE AREAS: Workers' Compensation.
Garfinkle, David D. ................... '44 '72 C.94 B.S.B.A. L.818 J.D. 2201 Dupont Dr.
Garrison, David A. ...................... '57 '83 C.679 B.A. L.879 J.D. Fluor Daniel, Inc.
**Gartside, Jeri L.** ......................... '60 '86 C.475 B.A. L.1187 J.D. [Ⓐ J.E.Mudd]
*PRACTICE AREAS: Tax Controversy; Bankruptcy.
**Gary, Bruce J.,** (AV) ............................. '54 '80 C&L.494 B.S., J.D. [Sikora&P.]
*PRACTICE AREAS: Business Law; Real Estate Transactions; Probate Law; Estate Planning Law.
**Garza, Oscar** .............................. '63 '90 C.267 B.S. L.37 J.D. [Ⓐ Gibson,D.&C.]
*PRACTICE AREAS: Debtor and Creditor's Rights; Bankruptcy Litigation.
**Gates, Peter J.** ................................ '48 '74 C.1109 B.A. L.426 J.D. [Genson,E.C.&W.]
**Gauntlett, David A.,** (AV) ........... '54 '80 C.112 B.A. L.1066 J.D. [Gauntlett&Assoc.]
*LANGUAGES: French.
*PRACTICE AREAS: Insurance Coverage; Intellectual Property; Antitrust; Business; Environmental.

**Gauntlett & Associates, (AV)** BB
**18400 Von Karman, Suite 300, 92612**
Telephone: 714-553-1010 Fax: 714-553-2050
Email: ugauntlett@aol.com
David A. Gauntlett;—David A. Stall; Leo E. Lundberg, Jr.; Michael Danton Richardson; William P. Warden; Stanley H. Shure; Elizabeth A. Gillis (Not admitted in CA); Mark H. Plager (Not admitted in CA); Jeffrey S. Allison. Of Counsel: Gary L. Hinman; Jose Zorrilla, Jr.
Policyholder Insurance-Coverage Representation, Patent, Trademark, Copyright, Trade Secret, Antitrust, Business, Environmental and Labor Litigation as well as Business and Estate Planning.

*See Professional Biographies, IRVINE, CALIFORNIA*

**Gausewitz, Richard L.,** (AV) '25 '50
C.966 B.S.E.E. L.813 LL.B. [Oppenheimer P.S.] (Pat.) (⊙Los Angeles)
**Gebara, Joseph C.** ...................................... '63 '90 C.800 B.S. L.101 J.D. [Ramsay&J.]
*PRACTICE AREAS: Insurance Coverage; Insurance Defense; Civil Litigation.
**Geiler, Dennis L.,** (AV) ........................... '42 '68 C&L.800 B.S., J.D. [D.L.Geiler]
*PRACTICE AREAS: Business Law; Estate Planning Law; Real Estate Law.

**Geiler, Dennis L., Inc., A P.C., (AV)**
**19900 Mac Arthur Boulevard, Suite 700, 92715**
Telephone: 714-660-1040 Fax: 714-660-0342
Dennis L. Geiler; Warren Worth.
Business and Estate Planning including Corporation, Partnerships and Real Estate Business and Civil Litigation.

*See Professional Biographies, IRVINE, CALIFORNIA*

**Genson, Even, Crandall & Wade, A Professional Corporation, (AV)**
**7700 Irvine Center Drive, #700, 92718⊙**
Telephone: 714-753-1000 FAX: 714-753-1039
James L. Crandall; Peter J. Gates; Edwin B. Brown; William F. Zulch; K. Robert Gonter, Jr.;—Maria M. Rullo; Michael J. McGuire; Linda E. Cummings; Matthew M. Proudfoot; Richard W. Miller; Michelle M. Williams; Rosemarie B. Heard; Richard A. Muench; Roberta A. Kraus; James A. Teel; Sarah Yoseloff; Alan P. Trafton; James Louis Wilson; Robert Hamparyan.
Trial practice in State and Federal Courts: Employment Practices Liability, Third Party Violent Crime/Premises Security, Product Liability, Warranty Litigation, Insurance Coverage, Insurance Bad Faith, Insurance Fraud, HMO/Managed Care Defense, Medical Malpractice, Directors and Officers Liability, Professional Malpractice, Construction Defect, Government Liability, Premises Liability,

(This Listing Continued)

**Genson, Even, Crandall & Wade, A Professional Corporation (Continued)**
**Transportation Liability, Vehicle Liability, Environmental Liability, Recreational Sports and Leisure Activities Liability, Appellate Practice, Business Litigation (Class Action, Fraud, Misrepresentation, Breach of Contract, etc.).**
**Woodland Hills, California Office: 21031 Ventura Boulevard, Suite 801. Telephone: 818-999-4811. FAX: 818-999-1782.**
**Rancho Cucamonga, California Office: 9483 Haven Avenue, Suite 102. Telephone: 909-390-4811. FAX: 909-390-1907.**
**San Diego, California Office: 9988 Hibert Street, Suite 300. Telephone: 619-635-6300. FAX: 619-635-6306.**
***See Professional Biographies, IRVINE, CALIFORNIA***

**Gentile, Susan E.** ... '59 '85 C.112 B.A. L.426 J.D. [Malpass&G.]
*PRACTICE AREAS: Banking Law; Bankruptcy Litigation.
**Gentry, Steven H.** ... '43 '76 C.674 B.S.E. L.426 J.D. [Berger,K.S.M.F.S.&G.]
**George, Robert K.** ... '49 '74 [George&S.]
*PRACTICE AREAS: Business; Business Acquisitions; Real Estate; Personal Injury Litigation; Employment Law.

**George & Shields, LLP, (AV)** BR
**30 Corporate Park, Suite 300, 92714-5133**
**Telephone: 714-263-1085 Fax: 714-263-0585**
**Members of Firm: Robert K. George; Timothy F. Shields; David W. Sparks.**
**General Civil and Trial Practice in State and Federal Courts. Business, Real Estate, Construction, Insurance, Surety, Contract, Personal Injury and Negligence Litigation. Corporate, Partnership, and Limited Liability Company Formation and Maintenance. Business, Finance and Real Estate Transactions, including Secured Transactions. Special Counsel on Legal Ethics and Conflicts of Interest including Attorney-Client Fee Agreements and Disputes.**
***See Professional Biographies, IRVINE, CALIFORNIA***

Germann, J. Gary, (BV) ... '46 '73 C.267 B.A. L.767 J.D. [Germann&W.]
Germann & Welputt, (AV) ... 19762 MacArthur Blvd.
**Gess, Albin H.**, (AV) ... '42 '72 C.215 B.E.E. L.904 J.D. [Price,G.&U.] (See Pat. Sect.)
*REPORTED CASES: In re VE Holding v. Johnson Cos. Appliance, 917 F.2d 1574 (CAFC 1990). The U.S. Court of Appeals for the Federal Circuit cited Mr. Gess's writings in support of its decision; California Irrigation Services, Inc. v. Bartron Corp. 9 USPQ 2d 1859 (C.D. Cal. 1988).
*PRACTICE AREAS: Patent; Trademark; Copyright.
**Ghan, Dennis W., (A Professional Corporation)**, (AV) '52 '77
C.112 B.A. L.1065 J.D. [Palmieri,T.W.W.&W.]
*PRACTICE AREAS: Real Estate Law.
**Giannamore, Mark J.** ... '59 '86 C.112 B.A. L.809 J.D. [🄰 Wesierski&Z.]
*PRACTICE AREAS: Insurance Defense; Products Liability; Medical Malpractice Defense.
**Giannone, Terrence J.** ... '47 '88 C.1042 B.A. L.426 J.D. [🄰 Mower,K.N.C.&H.]
*PRACTICE AREAS: Insurance Defense; Personal Injury; Product Liability; Construction Defects; Auto.
**Gibbs, Thomas E.** ... '55 '80 C.112 B.A. L.1068 J.D. [Allen,M.L.G.&M.]
*PRACTICE AREAS: Litigation.
Gibson, Jacqueline J. '62 '91 C.1111 B.A. L.260 J.D.
Asst. V.P. & Assoc. Coun., Fidelity Natl. Title Ins. Co.
Gibson, L. J. ... '— '81 C.846 B.A. L.61 J.D. RTC
**Gibson, Robert B.** ... '66 '92 C.1074 B.S. L.464 J.D. [🄰 Kring&B.]
*PRACTICE AREAS: Litigation.
**Gibson, Robert J.**, (AVⓉ) ... '46 '77 C.36 B.S. L.37 J.D. [Snell&W.]
*PRACTICE AREAS: Product Liability Litigation; Environmental Litigation.
**Gibson, Robert V.**, (AV) ... '21 '50 C.912 L.767 LL.B. [Gibson,H.&J.]

**Gibson, Dunn & Crutcher LLP, (AV)**
**4 Park Plaza, Suites 1400, 1500, 1700 and 1800, 92614-8557⊙**
**Telephone: 714-451-3800 Telecopier: 714-451-4220**
**Partners: Kenneth E. Ristau, Jr.; Richard G. Duncan, Jr.; Ralph C. Wintrode; Blake T. Franklin (Irvine, California and New York City Offices); John C. Wells; J. Michael Brennan; Wayne W. Smith (Los Angeles and Irvine Offices); Dennis A. Gladwell; S. David Blinn (Los Angeles and Irvine Offices); Gerard J. Kenny; Gordon A. Schaller; Robert W. Loewen; Robert Everett Dean; Thomas D. Magill; William D. Claster; Joseph P. Busch III; Larry C. Boyd; E. Michael Greaney (Irvine, California and New York, N.Y. Offices); Karen H. Clark; Mark W. Shurtleff; Walter L. Schindler; Michele C. Coyle; Jeffrey T. Thomas; Craig H. Millet; Robert E. Palmer; Brian W. Copple; Timothy J. Kay; Geniene B. Stillwell. Advisory Counsels: Thomas B. Pitcher; Frank L. Mallory; Guy K. Claire. Of Counsels: John A. Arguelles; W. Richard Smith, Jr. Special Counsel: Teresa Joanning Farrell. Associates: Marianne Shipp; Liisa Anselmi Stith; Gunnar Blaise Gooding; Oscar Garza; Alan N. Bick; Andrea E. Neuman; Clark D. Stith; J. Fred Neuman; Scott M. Knutson; Jeffrey H. Reeves; John M. Williams, III; Gregg P. Goldman; Peter M. Stone; Mark J. Payne; Trygve M. Thoresen; Maryn L. Miller; Michelle D. Lustig; Sharyl P. Bilas; David A. Segal; Leslie R. Olson; Donna M. Bigi; Thomas S. Jones; Torrey A. Olins; Cosmas N. Lykos; Adam E. Muchnick; Mark N. Mazda; Paul A. Andronico; Michael E. Sanders; Jeff Augustini; Daniel H. Baren; Jesse S. Finlayson; Michael A. Barmettler; Jean De Forest Billyou. Staff Attorneys: Melinda Dalton Waterman; Brian R. Kirchoff.**
**General Civil, Trial and Appellate Practice, State and Federal Courts. Antitrust Law, Specialized Criminal Defense. General Corporation, Securities, Administrative, Labor and Employment, Real Estate, Taxation, Estate Planning, Probate and Trust, International Business, Entertainment, Commercial, Insolvency, Bankruptcy and Reorganization, Natural Resources, Oil and Gas, Environmental Energy, Municipal and Public Utility Law.**
**Los Angeles, California Office: 333 South Grand Avenue. Telephone: 213-229-7000. Telex: 188171 GIBTRASK LSA (TRT), 674930 GIBTRASK LSA (WUT). Telecopier: 213-229-7520. Cable Address: GIBTRASK LOS ANGELES.**
***See Professional Biographies, IRVINE, CALIFORNIA***

**Gibson, Haglund & Johnson, (AV)** BR
**2010 Main Street, Suite 400, 92714**
**Telephone: 714-752-1100 Fax: 714-752-1144**
**Members of Firm: Robert V. Gibson; Bruce H. Haglund; Paul H. Johnson.**
**Business, Corporate and Securities. Franchising, Real Estate, Municipal Finance, Investment Management and Financial Services, Mergers and Acquisitions.**
***See Professional Biographies, IRVINE, CALIFORNIA***

Giebel, Rita D. '58 '96 C.1060 B.S. L.1339 J.D.
(adm. in CO; not adm. in CA) P.O. Box 6503‡
**Gilbert, Richard E.**, (AV) '46 '73
C.30 B.A. L.904 J.D. [🄲 Freeman,F.&S.] (⊙Los Angeles)
*PRACTICE AREAS: Estate Planning; Tax and Business Planning.
Gillies, Robert D. ... '48 '91 C.112 B.A. L.1065 J.D. 18101 von Karman Ave.
**Gillis, Elizabeth A.** '60 '88 C.309 B.A. L.818 J.D.
(adm. in MA; not adm. in CA) [🄰 Gauntlett&Assoc.]
*LANGUAGES: Italian.
**Gillman, Adam J.** ... '69 '93 C.112 B.A. L.1065 J.D. [🄰 Bryan C.]
**Gioia, Vincent G.** ... '35 '60 C.171 E.Met. L.273 J.D. [Christie,P.&H.] (See Pat. Sect.)
*PRACTICE AREAS: Patents; Trademarks; Copyrights; Licensing; Plant Variety Protection Litigation.
Giovanatto, Attillio J. ... '62 '90 C.36 B.A. L.1049 J.D. [🄰 Cone,C.&K.]
**Gladwell, Dennis A.**, (AV) ... '43 '70 C&L.878 B.S., J.D. [Gibson,D.&C.]
*PRACTICE AREAS: Employment Law; Labor Law.
**Glaser, Herbert A.** '56 '81 C.373 B.A. L.477 J.D.
(adm. in DC; not adm. in CA) Corp. V.P., Assoc. Gen. Coun., Edison Mission Energy
*LANGUAGES: French.
Glaser, Jeremy D. ... '60 '85 C.228 B.A. L.309 J.D. 18400 Von Karman
Glass, Susan J. '42 '80 C.563 B.S. L.426 J.D.
Asst. Gen. Coun. & Asst. Secy., Allergan, Inc.
Glasser, Robert E., (BV) ... '44 '70 C.112 B.A. L.1068 J.D. 19782 MacArthur Blvd.
**Glen-Grossman, Hilary B.** ... '60 '86 C.112 B.A. L.1065 J.D. [Samuels&S.]
*LANGUAGES: Spanish.
*PRACTICE AREAS: Real Estate Transactional.

Goddard, Sara W ... '48 '87 C.331 B.A. 4330 Barranca Pkwy.
**Goddard, William A., IV** ... '59 '87 C.112 B.A. L.1065 J.D. [Maher,L.&G.]
*PRACTICE AREAS: Federal Income Tax Law and California Income; Franchise and ad valorem Property Tax Law; Corporate; Partnership; Real Estate and International Tax Planning.
Goetz, Charles A. '30 '74 C.103 Sc.B. L.990 J.D.
Prof., Western State Univ. Coll. of Law
Goldberg, Kathleen ... '61 '87 C.112 B.A. L.1065 J.D. 6 Venture
Goldin, Marc S. ... '62 '88 C&L.608 B.S.B.A., J.D. [🄰 O'Kain&J.]
**Goldman, Gregg P.** ... '65 '91 C&L.36 B.S., J.D. [🄰 Gibson,D.&C.]
**Golem, Donna A.** ... '63 '96 C.112 B.A. L.426 J.D. [Malcolm,C.&H.]
*PRACTICE AREAS: Commercial and Business Litigation; Bankruptcy.
Gonsky, Marshall I. '36 '62 C&L.350 B.B.A., J.D.
(adm. in IL; not adm. in CA) Los Angeles Unified School Dist.
**Gonter, K. Robert, Jr.** ... '56 '82 C.678 B.A. L.809 J.D. [Genson,E.C.&W.]
**Gooding, Gunnar Blaise** ... '63 '89 C.112 B.A. L.800 J.D. [🄰 Gibson,D.&C.]
*PRACTICE AREAS: Employment Litigation; Labor.
**Goodman, Randolph M.**, (AV) ... '48 '74 C.264 B.A. L.705 J.D. [Feder,G.&S.]
**Goodspeed, John M.** ... '50 '79 C.20 B.A. L.990 J.D. [Kirtland&P.]
**Gordee, Alan J.** ... '61 '87 C.976 B.A. L.94 J.D. [🄰 Allen,M.L.G.&M.]
*PRACTICE AREAS: Litigation.
Gordon, Suzanne ... '— '79 L.1137 J.D. Mgr., Govt. Contract Admin., Fluor Daniel, Inc.‡
**Gossage, Charles R.** ... '67 '93 C.36 B.S. L.990 J.D. [🄰 Sedgwick,D.M.&A.]
**Grable, Roger A.**, (AV) ... '44 '71 C.101 B.A. L.1065 J.D. [🄲 Paone,C.M.&W.]
*PRACTICE AREAS: Land Use; Environmental; Public Law.
**Grabowski, Richard J.** ... '61 '86 C.1042 B.A. L.1068 J.D. [Jones,D.R.&P.]

**Grace, Brandon, Hollis and Ramirez, (AV)**
**7700 Irvine Center Drive, Suite 800, 92718⊙**
**Telephone: 714-753-2860 Fax: 714-753-2899**
**Manuel L. Ramirez.**
**General Civil and Trial Practice with an emphasis on providing a defense in the following areas: Medical Negligence, Hospital Liability, Personal Injury, Construction Defect, Product Liability, Real Estate and Creditor's Remedies.**
**San Diego, California Office: 1010 Second Avenue, Suite 1800, 92101. Telephone: 619-595-0800. Fax: 619-595-0328.**
***See Professional Biographies, IRVINE, CALIFORNIA***

**Grad, Roger A.** ... '58 '85 C.112 B.A. L.464 J.D. [Jackson,D.&P.]
*PRACTICE AREAS: Tax Planning and Litigation; Estate Planning; Corporate and Partnerships; Business Transactional.
**Grady, Patrick J.** ... '59 '84 C.1042 B.S. L.800 J.D. [Allen,M.L.G.&M.]
*PRACTICE AREAS: Labor (Management).
**Graham, Steven T.** ... '56 '82 C.112 B.A. L.990 J.D. [Snell&W.]
*PRACTICE AREAS: Commercial; Environmental; Construction; Litigation.
**Graham, Susan E.** ... '64 '89 C.112 B.A. L.426 J.D. [🄰 Allen,M.L.G.&M.]
*PRACTICE AREAS: Real Estate Transactional Practice.
Graif, Jay R. ... '65 '92 C.755 B.A. L.990 J.D. 108 Pacifica
**Grant, David C., (P.C.)**, (AV) ... '47 '72 C.165 A.B. L.426 J.D. [Grant&L.]
*PRACTICE AREAS: Litigation.

**Grant & Laubscher, (AV)**
**A Partnership including a Professional Corporation**
**2030 Main Street, Suite 1600, 92714**
**Telephone: 714-660-1600 Telecopier: 714-660-6060**
**David C. Grant (P.C.); Barry R. Laubscher; James R. Percival; Mark A. Schadrack; Denise L. McKinney; DeeAnn M. Taylor; Gordon G. May; Lea B. Williams.**
**General Civil Trial Practice, with Emphasis in Areas of Antitrust, Business, Real Estate and Securities Litigation.**
***See Professional Biographies, IRVINE, CALIFORNIA***

Graves, Arthur A., III ... '51 '78 C.911 B.A. L.990 J.D. [Pratter&G.]⊙
**Gravitt, Timothy A.** '57 '84 C.112 B.A. L.1065 J.D.
[Meserve,M.&H.] (⊙Los Angeles & San Diego)
**Gray, Donald S.** '45 '74 C.1097 B.A. L.1065 J.D.
V.P., Gen. Coun. & Secy., Toshiba America Info. Systems, Inc.
*RESPONSIBILITIES: Corporate (10%); Business (90%).
**Gray, Gordon E., III** ... '69 '94 C.339 B.A. L.426 J.D. [🄰 Price,G.&U.]
*PRACTICE AREAS: Intellectual Property.
**Greaney, E. Michael** ... '52 '77 C.426 B.A. L.800 J.D. [Gibson,D.&C.] (⊙N.Y., NY)
*PRACTICE AREAS: Corporate Securities; Mergers and Acquisitions; General Business Law.
**Greco, Thomas A.** ... '48 '77 C.1109 B.A. L.990 J.D. [Greco,M.&O.]
*PRACTICE AREAS: Business and Real Estate Transactions; Partnerships and Corporations; Federal and State Taxation; Civil Litigation; Bankruptcy.

**Greco, Mollis & O'Hara, A Professional Corporation, (AV)** BR
**18400 Von Karman, Suite 500, 92612-1514**
**Telephone: 714-263-0600 Fax: 714-263-1513**
**Thomas A. Greco; Ronald A. Mollis (Certified Specialist, Taxation Law, The State Bar of California Board of Legal Specialization); Kevin O'Hara; Charles A. Mollis.**
**Taxation, Federal (State and Local), Real Estate Law, Corporate, Business Law, Bankruptcy, Probate, Wills and Trusts, and Trials and Appeals.**
***See Professional Biographies, IRVINE, CALIFORNIA***

**Greely, Adam M.** ... '64 '91 C.668 B.A. L.426 J.D. [Suchman,G.&P.]⊙
*PRACTICE AREAS: Litigation; Bankruptcy (Creditor Representation); Commercial Law; Collection Law.
Green, Marlon J. ... '61 '89 C.800 B.S. L.809 J.D. 18400 Von Karman, Ste., 600
Green, Thomas W. ... '40 '74 L.1137 LL.B. 7700 Irvine Center Dr.
**Greenberg, Allison Fong** ... '64 '95 C.112 B.S.Ch.E. L.426 J.D. [🄰 Allen,M.L.G.&M.]
*PRACTICE AREAS: Real Estate; Environmental.
**Greene, Lance Gordon** ... '61 '93 C.36 B.S. L.494 J.D. [🄰 Pivo&H.]
*PRACTICE AREAS: Medical Malpractice.
**Greene, Michael J., (A Professional Corporation)**, (AV) '46 '72
C.813 A.B. L.309 J.D. [Palmieri,T.W.W.&W.]
*PRACTICE AREAS: Real Estate Law; Partnership Law.
**Greenfield, Arthur P.**, (AV) '36 '64 C.112 A.B. L.37 LL.B.
[Snell&W.] (⊙Phoenix, AZ)
*PRACTICE AREAS: Civil Litigation; Product Liability Litigation; Commercial Litigation.
**Greengard, Gerald L.** ... '61 '86 C.112 B.A. L.477 J.D. [Oswald&Y.]
*PRACTICE AREAS: Commercial Litigation.
**Greenman, David W.** ... '52 '81 C.172 B.S. L.339 J.D. [Bainbridge]
*PRACTICE AREAS: Real Estate; Real Estate Finance; Partnerships; General Corporate.
**Greger, Michael S.** ... '66 '91 C.1109 B.A. L.809 J.D. [🄰 Allen,M.L.G.&M.]
*PRACTICE AREAS: Litigation; Bankruptcy.
Gregory, Keith M., (AV) ... '59 '85 C.112 B.A. L.1049 J.D. [Toledano&W.]
**Grenner, William B.** ... '62 '89 C.112 B.A. L.276 J.D. [🄰 Morrison&F.]
**Gresham, Allen B., II** ... '64 '91 C.605 A.B. L.425 J.D. [🄰 Sedgwick,D.M.&A.]
Grey, Steven L. ... '57 '83 C.145 B.A. L.569 J.D. Gen. Coun., Kia Motors America, Inc.
**Griffen, Thomas B.** ... '63 '88 C&L.800 B.A., J.D. [Horwitz&B.]
**Griffin, Craig L.** ... '57 '89 C.1042 B.S. L.101 J.D. [Connor,C.B.&G.]
Grimaila, Debra L. ... '58 '86 C.1077 B.S. L.426 J.D. 18400 Von Karman, Ste. 600
Gritsch, Norman R. ... '61 '86 C.276 B.S.F.S. L.990 J.D. 4 Park Plaza
**Groh, Martin C.**, (AV) ... '50 '77 C.223 B.S.B.A. L.884 J.D. [Groh,C.S.&R.]
*PRACTICE AREAS: Business; Tax; Corporate Transactional Law; Executive Employment.

CALIFORNIA—IRVINE MARTINDALE-HUBBELL LAW DIRECTORY 1997

**Groh, Carroll, Stern & Robinson, A Professional Corporation, (AV)**
**2600 Michelson, Suite 270, 92715**
**Telephone: 714-752-7600 Fax: 714-752-7661**
**Martin C. Groh; David B. Carroll; W. Rod Stern; Gregory E. Robinson.**
**General Business Law, with an emphasis in: Corporate, Tax, Real Estate and Employment Transactions; Business, Real Estate and Personal Tort/Contract Litigation; Business and Personal Tax Planning and Appeals; Conservatorship and Probate Proceedings.**

*See Professional Biographies, IRVINE, CALIFORNIA*

Gromet, Stevan J., (BV) ... '54 '81 C.976 B.A. L.846 J.D. 2 Park Plaza
Gropen, Moss ... '57 '91 C.112 B.A. L.61 J.D. [Floratos,L.&D.]
Grosenbaugh, Downey A., (AV) '15 '41 C&L.352 B.A., J.D. 18500 Von Karman Ave., Suite 600
**Gross, Dimitri P.** ... '66 '94 C.112 B.A. L.464 J.D. [🄰 Hanley&P.]
*PRACTICE AREAS: Business Litigation.
Grossberg, James E. ... '56 '85 C&L.893 B.A., J.D. 5 Park Plaza
**Gruber, Karen A.** ... '51 '87 C.112 B.A. L.1049 J.D. [Ramsay&J.]
*REPORTED CASES: Zands v. Nelson, 779 F.Supp. 1254 (S.D. Cal. 1991); Zands v. Nelson, 797 F.Supp. 805 (S.D. Cal. 1992).
*PRACTICE AREAS: Environmental Insurance Litigation; Environmental Law; Environmental Liability Law; Insurance Coverage; Insurance Defense Law.
**Guirgis, Ralph A.** ... '65 '89 C.1109 B.A. L.464 J.D. [🄰 Sedgwick,D.M.&A.]

**Gullstrand, Gregory R., (AV) '53 '80 C.112 B.A. L.1067 J.D.**
**18022 Cowan Suite 203 D, 92714**
**Telephone: 714-474-8501 Fax: 714-474-9883**
**General Civil Trial Practice in all State and Federal Courts. Construction, and Business Litigation.**

*See Professional Biographies, IRVINE, CALIFORNIA*

**Gunther, Victoria L.** ... '62 '89 C.1077 B.A. L.426 J.D. [Ramsay&J.]
*PRACTICE AREAS: Insurance Coverage.
**Gurwitz, Renee Friend** ... '70 '94 C.1060 B.A. L.464 J.D. [Ramsay&J.]
*PRACTICE AREAS: Insurance Coverage; Insurance Defense.
**Guthrey, Areta Kay** ... '59 '85 C.990 B.A. L.464 J.D. [🄰 Berger,K.S.M.F.S.&G.]
Guy, Terry ... '55 '81 C&L.846 B.A., J.D. The Restaurant Enterprises Group, Inc.
Hachmeister, John H. ... '44 '84 C.1147 B.A. L.809 J.D. 18400 Von Karman, Ste., 600
**Hadlock, Robert J.** ... '61 '94 C.1109 B.A. L.1065 J.D. [🄰 Chapman,F.&B.]
*PRACTICE AREAS: Litigation.
**Haglund, Bruce H.**, (AV) ... '51 '80 C&L.878 B.A., J.D. [Gibson,H.&J.]
*LANGUAGES: Japanese.
*PRACTICE AREAS: Corporate Law; Securities.
**Hagopian, David G.** ... '63 '89 C.112 B.A. L.800 J.D. [Smith,B.&D.]
*PRACTICE AREAS: Business Litigation; Employment Law; Insurance Coverage; Construction.
Haguewood, Steven A. ... '52 '80 C.112 A.B. L.426 J.D. 2010 Main St.
**Hahn, Beth J.** ... '50 '91 C.147 B.A. L.464 J.D. Sr. Legal Coun., Family Restaurants, Inc.
*RESPONSIBILITIES: Employment Law; Litigation.
**Halbreich, Eva S.**, (AV) ... '48 '75 C.771 B.A. L.1066 J.D. [Pivo&H.]
*LANGUAGES: French, Hebrew and Polish.
**Hall, Donald R.**, (AV) ... '54 '80 C.112 B.A. L.1049 J.D. [Hall&B.]
Hall, Thomas F. ... '64 '89 C.1042 B.S. L.809 J.D. 401 E. Ocean Blvd.

**Hall & Bailey, (AV)** BR
**5 Park Plaza Suite 1440, 92714⊙**
**Telephone: 714-553-8663 Facsimile: 714-476-8640**
**Donald R. Hall; John L. Bailey (Resident, Riverside Office).**
**General Civil, Trial and Appellate Practice in all State and Federal Courts. Commercial, Business, Real Estate, Financial Institution and Title Insurance Litigation.**
**Riverside, California Office: 6761 Brockton Avenue, 92506. Telephone: 909-682-7334.**

Halle, Dana L. ... '63 '88 C.668 B.A. L.1065 J.D. 2603 Main St.
**Halle, William E.** ... '63 '90 C.1097 B.A. L.477 J.D. [🄰 Jones,D.R.&P.]
Hallett, R. F. ... '12 '41 L.588 LL.B. 18300 Von Karman Ave.
**Halliday, Gregory H.**, (AV) ... '52 '78 C.813 B.A. L.1065 J.D. [Sedgwick,D.M.&A.]
**Halstead, Sherman O., Jr.** ... '60 '85 C.893 B.A. L.813 J.D. [Maher,L.&G.]
**Haluck, William L.**, (AV) ... '52 '78 C&L.426 B.B.A., J.D. [Mower,K.N.C.&H.]
*PRACTICE AREAS: Civil Trial; Insurance Coverage; Construction Defect Litigation; Medical Malpractice Law; Government Law.
**Ham, Scott W.** ... '63 '89 C.645 B.A. L.990 J.D. [Woldt&H.]
**Hamilton, Robert M.** ... '59 '84 C.800 B.S. L.426 J.D. [Allen,M.L.G.&M.]
*PRACTICE AREAS: Business Organizations; Tax Planning.
**Hamparyan, Robert** ... '64 '96 C.800 B.A. L.1137 J.D. [🄰 Genson,E.C.&W.]
**Han, James W.** ... '54 '83 C.112 A.B. L.1065 J.D. [Cates&H.]
**Hanagami, Steven S.** ... '59 '93 C.112 B.S. L.273 J.D. [Kasdan,S.M.E.&M.]
*PRACTICE AREAS: Construction Defect; Business Litigation.
**Hancock, S. Lee**, (AV) ... '55 '79 C.804 B.S. L.802 J.D. [Allen,M.L.G.&M.]
*PRACTICE AREAS: Securities; Corporate.
**Hanley, William B., (P.C.)**, (AV) ... '46 '74 C.229 B.A. L.990 J.D. [Hanley&P.]
*REPORTED CASES: Dawes v. Superior Court, 111 Cal. App. 3d 82; State Farm v. Davis, 937 F. 2d 1415.
*PRACTICE AREAS: Trials.

**Hanley & Patch, (AV)** BR
**A Partnership including Professional Corporations**
**19900 MacArthur Boulevard, Suite 650, 92715-2445**
**Telephone: 714-253-0800 Fax: 714-253-0870**
**William B. Hanley (P.C.); Ryan Mark Patch (P.C.); Joshua M. Wolff;—Paul Kim; Johanna Y. Hsu; Dimitri P. Gross.**
**General Civil Litigation Practice in State and Federal Courts. Commercial, Business, Complex and High Technology Litigation, Toxic and Hazardous Substance, Real Estate, Environmental and Employment.**

*See Professional Biographies, IRVINE, CALIFORNIA*

**Hanlon, Roma R.** ... '64 '93 C.112 B.A. L.770 J.D. [🄰 Connor,C.B.&G.]
**Hanna, Mona Z.** ... '62 '87 C.1097 B.A. L.1065 J.D. [Pivo&H.]
*LANGUAGES: Arabic.
Hannemann, Glenn P. ... '52 '79 C.675 B.A. L.1067 J.D. 2603 Main St.
Hannen, George M. ... '48 '78 C.198 A.B. L.1065 J.D. [G.Hannen]
Hannen, George, & Company, A Prof. Corp. ... 4199 Campus Dr. Suite 720
Hapeman, H. Vaughn ... '48 '73 C.112 B.A. L.61 J.D. 2030 Main St., 13th Fl.
**Harkins, James C., IV** ... '63 '89 C.446 B.A. L.904 J.D. [🄰 Fiore,W.R.&P.]
**Harraka, Joseph G., Jr.** ... '60 '85 C.776 B.A. L.602 J.D. [Smith,B.&D.]
*PRACTICE AREAS: Commercial Litigation; Environmental; Bankruptcy; Securities Arbitration.
**Harris, Charles L.** ... '63 '90 C.800 B.A. L.900 J.D. [Stevens,K.A.&H.]
*PRACTICE AREAS: Construction Defect; Environmental; Coverage and Liability; Personal and Commercial Casualty.
Harris, T. Michael ... '— '83 C.999 B.A. L.1065 J.D. [🄲 Ching&Assoc.]
**Harrison, Howard F.**, (AV) ... '37 '63 C.112 A.B. L.1066 LL.B. [Nossaman,G.K.&E.]
*PRACTICE AREAS: Civil Litigation.
**Harshman, David J.** '50 '77 C.608 B.I.E. L.1049 J.D. Asst. Gen. Coun., Toshiba America Info. Systems, Inc. (Pat.)
**Hart, Berne C.** ... '40 '91 C&L.1137 B.S.L., J.D. [Chevalier,A.&L.]
*PRACTICE AREAS: Civil Practice.
Harty, John T. ... '42 '67 C&L.602 A.B., J.D. [Harty&H.]
Harty, Maureen A. ... '44 '79 C.741 B.A. L.1137 J.D. [Harty&H.]
Harty & Harty ... 14 Mountain View

**Hartzell, Andrew K.** ... '63 '90 C.659 B.A. L.813 J.D. [Hewitt&M.]
*PRACTICE AREAS: Natural Resources Law; Environmental Law; Land Use Law.
Harvey, James C. ... '61 '89 C.112 B.A. L.426 J.D. 65 Eagle Run
Hassan, Stanley ... '46 '79 L.1137 J.D. 2515 McCabe Way
**Hasseltime, David J.** ... '70 '96 C.112 B.A. L.1049 J.D. [🄰 Connor,C.B.&G.]
**Hatcher, Patrick G., (P.C.)**, (BV) ... '44 '73 C.1097 B.A. L.1068 J.D. [Bye,H.&R.]
*PRACTICE AREAS: Products Liability; Business Litigation.

**Hatter, Rodney R., and Associates '44 '70 C.309 A.B. L.178 J.D.**
**19800 MacArthur Boulevard, Suite 1450, 92715**
**Telephone: 714-724-4558 Fax: 714-724-4551**
**Associates: Eric J. Stoop; Patricia L. Stoop.**
**Franchise, Corporate, Business, Real Estate and Civil Litigation.**

*See Professional Biographies, IRVINE, CALIFORNIA*

**Hawkins, Michael L.** ... '54 '85 C.608 B.A. L.884 J.D. [Morrison&F.]
*PRACTICE AREAS: Securities; Corporate Finance; Business Practice.
**Hayhurst, Ren R** ... '62 '87 C&L.878 B.S., J.D. [🄲 Bryan C.]
*LANGUAGES: German.
**Hays, David Edward** ... '66 '92 C.1109 B.A. L.800 J.D. [🄰 Rus,M.W.&S.]
*REPORTED CASES: In re Continental Capital & Credit, Inc., 158 B.R. 828 (Bankr. C.D.Cal. 1993, J. Wilson); In re Turner, 186 B.R. 108 (9th Cir. BAP 1995); In re National Environmental Waste Corporation, 191 B.R. 832 (Bankr. C.D.Cal. 1996, J. Wilson).
*PRACTICE AREAS: Complex Litigation; Creditors Rights; Bankruptcy Law.
**Hayward, Robin L.** ... '67 '94 C.112 B.A. L.1065 J.D. [🄰 Musick,P.&G.]
**Heard, Rosemarie B.** ... '37 '81 C.988 B.A. L.1190 J.D. [🄰 Genson,E.C.&W.]
Hedemann, G. Christian ... '43 '71 C&L.174 B.A., J.D. Corp. Coun., Fluor Corp.
**Heimerl, Lori L.** ... '69 '94 C.800 B.S. L.464 J.D. [Pinto&D.]
*PRACTICE AREAS: Real Estate.
Henderman, Keith B. ... '45 '70 C.800 B.A. L.1068 J.D. 96 Lehigh Aisle

**Hendrickson, Ray, (AV) '37 '73 C.579 B.S. L.1137 J.D.** BR
**University Tower, Suite 700, 4199 Campus Drive, 92612**
**Telephone: 714-833-0101; 854-8800 Fax: 714-854-4897**
**Divorce, Custody, Family and Negligence Law. Personal Injury, Civil and Business Litigation and actions relating to Psychic Trauma.**
**References: Mitsui Manufacturers Bank, Newport Beach, California; Bank of California, Newport Beach, California; Home Fed, Irvine, California.**

*See Professional Biographies, IRVINE, CALIFORNIA*

Hendrix, Joseph A. ... '62 '87 C&L.426 B.A., J.D. 17th Fl., 3 Park Plaza
**Hennessey, Patrick A.** ... '52 '78 C.112 B.A. L.1049 J.D. [Palmieri,T.W.W.&W.]
*PRACTICE AREAS: Condemnation Law; Litigation.
Henry, Richard M. ... '53 '78 C.813 B.A. L.1065 J.D. 100 Pacifica #250
**Henshall, James F., Jr.** ... '62 '87 C&L.763 B.A., J.D. [🄰 Berger,K.S.M.F.S.&G.]
**Henshel, Annie Glass** ... '43 '77 C.112 B.A. L.809 J.D. [Pivo&H.]
**Hensley, William Michael**, (AV) ... '54 '79 C.800 B.A. L.1292 J.D. [🄰 Jackson,D.&P.]
*PRACTICE AREAS: Real Property; Commercial Banks; Commercial Bankruptcy; Construction Defect; Liens.
**Hereford, Darren L.** ... '67 '93 C.665 B.A. L.426 J.D. [🄰 Jackson,D.&P.]
*PRACTICE AREAS: Real Estate Development and Subdivisions Law; Nonprofit Corporate Law; Contract.
**Hersh, Wayne A.** ... '45 '76 C.800 B.A. L.464 J.D. [Hinchy,W.W.A.&H.] (⊙San Diego)
*PRACTICE AREAS: Labor and Employment; Construction Law.
**Hess, Robert E.** ... '68 '95 C.112 B.A. L.426 J.D. [🄰 Baker,S.&K.]
**Hewitt, Hugh**, (AV) ... '56 '83 C.309 A.B. L.477 J.D. [Hewitt&M.]
*PRACTICE AREAS: Natural Resources Law; Land Use Law; Environmental Law.

**Hewitt & McGuire, (AV)**
**19900 MacArthur Boulevard, Suite 1050, 92715**
**Telephone: 714-798-0500 FAX: 714-798-0511**
**Email: HMLAW@INTERNETMCI.COM**
**Members of Firm: Dean Dunn-Rankin; Charles S. Exon; Andrew K. Hartzell; Hugh Hewitt; Mark R. McGuire; Dennis D. O'Neil; Jay F. Palchikoff; Paul A. Rowe; William L. Twomey; John P. Yeager.**
**Corporate, Business, Securities Law, Real Estate, Land Use, Natural Resources, Environmental, Public Finance Law, Corporate Finance.**

*See Professional Biographies, IRVINE, CALIFORNIA*

**Hickey, David E.** ... '64 '89 C.112 B.A. L.1065 J.D. [🄰 Neuland&N.]
*PRACTICE AREAS: Community Association Law; Real Property/Civil Litigation; Business.
**Hickey, William P.**, (AV) ... '38 '67 C.112 B.S. L.1068 J.D. [🄲 Neuland&N.]
*PRACTICE AREAS: Community Association Law; Probate.
**Highland, Gary J.**, (BV) ... '55 '79 C.112 B.A. L.800 J.D. [Bryan C.]
Highman, David R., (AV) ... '47 '78 C.1109 B.A. L.809 J.D. 100 Pacifica Ste. 200
Hiller, Mark A., (BV) ... '53 '79 C.112 B.A. L.1049 J.D. 7700 Irvine Ctr. Dr.
Hillgren, Nancy C., (BV) ... '54 '79 C.800 A.B. L.426 J.D. 2030 Main St.

**Hinchy, Witte, Wood, Anderson & Hodges, A Law Corporation, (AV)**
**2030 Main Street, Suite 1300, 92614⊙**
**Telephone: 714-260-4710 FAX: 714-260-4711**
**Wayne A. Hersh; Jon G. Miller (Resident).**
**General Civil Litigation, General Commercial, including Corporations, Limited Liability Companies, Partnerships and Taxation; Real Estate, Estate Planning and Probate; Financial Institutions, Mortgage Banking, Collection, Bankruptcy, Family Law, Labor Relations and Employment Law and Related Litigation, Agricultural Labor Relations, Employee Stock Ownership Plans (ESOPs), ERISA, Pension and Profit Sharing, Employee Benefits Law and Litigation.**
**Reference: Scripps Bank.**
**Rancho Bernardo, California Office: 11440 West Bernardo Court, Suite 280. Telephone: 619-487-7948; 586-7696. FAX: 619-487-2177.**
**San Diego, California Office: 525 B Street, Suite 1500. Telephone: 619-239-1901. FAX: 619-696-0555.**
**Palm Desert, California Office: 74-010 El Paseo, Suite 200. Telephone: 619-779-8569. FAX: 619-568-6175.**

*See Professional Biographies, IRVINE, CALIFORNIA*

**Hinman, Gary L.**, (AV) ... '40 '66 C&L.339 J.D. [🄲 Gauntlett&Assoc.]
*PRACTICE AREAS: Business; Corporate; Partnerships; Real Estate; Franchise.
Hirsch, Steven H. ... '49 '81 C.608 B.S. L.1230 J.D. Coun., ORION Scientific Systems
**Hirson, David**, (AV) ... '47 '80 L.061 [Hirson W.P.&S.] (⊙Los Angeles)
*PRACTICE AREAS: Immigration Law; International Law.

**Hirson Wexler Perl & Stark, A Professional Corporation, (AV)** BR
**Jamboree Center, One Park Plaza, Suite 950, 92614⊙**
**Telephone: 714-251-8844 Fax: 714-251-1545**
**Email: immigration_law@msn.com URL: http://www.immig.com**
**David Hirson (Certified Specialist, Immigration and Nationality Law, The State Bar of California Board of Legal Specialization); Mitchell L. Wexler (Certified Specialist, Immigration and Nationality Law, The State Bar of California Board of Legal Specialization); Gary B. Perl (Resident, San Diego, California and Dallas, Texas Offices); Joanne Trifilo Stark (Resident, Phoenix, Arizona Office). Of Counsel: Lance Kaplan.**
**Immigration and International Law Firm.**
**Los Angeles, California Office: 6310 San Vicente Boulevard, Suite 415, 90048. Telephone: 213-936-0200. Fax: 213-936-4488. E-Mail: 73411.37@compuserve.com. Web-Site: http://www.immig.com.**
**San Diego, California Office: 4275 Executive Square, Suite 800, 92037. Telephone: 619-452-5700. Fax: 619-452-1911. E-Mail: hkps@immiglaw.com. Web-Site: http://www.immig.com.**
**Phoenix, Arizona Office: 3443 North Central Avenue, Suite 706, 85012. Telephone: 602-266-4700. Fax: 602-265-8108. E-Mail: 73344.21@compuserve.com. Web-Site: http://www.immig.com.**
**Dallas, Texas Office: Heritage Square Tower II, 7th Floor, 5001 L.B.J. Freeway, 75244. Telephone: 214-991-7400. Fax: 214-991-1501. E-Mail: hkps@immig-law.com. Web-Site: http://www.immig.com.**

*See Professional Biographies, IRVINE, CALIFORNIA*

Hobart, Jean A., (AV) ... '43 '78 C&L.1137 B.S.L., J.D. 38 Corporate Park

**Holbert, Ronald G.** ........................ '48 '79 C.763 B.A. L.61 J.D. [Andrade&M.]
*PRACTICE AREAS: Real Estate.
Holbrook, Patricia A., (AV) ...................'56 '82 C.1108 B.S. L.884 J.D. 108 Pacifica
**Holden, Bruce G.**, (AV) ........................'51 '81 C.477 B.S. L.990 J.D. [Arter&H.]
*PRACTICE AREAS: Finance; Corporate Law; Real Estate Law.
**Holett, Steven G.** ............... '65 '94 C.1109 B.A. L.1137 J.D. [Ⓐ Mower,K.N.C.&H.]
*PRACTICE AREAS: Insurance Defense; Insurance Coverage; Construction Law.
**Holland, Jimmy D.** '48 '75 C.420 B.S. L.880 J.D.
(adm. in AR; not adm. in CA) Exec. V.P. & Gen. Coun., Amer. Svgs. Bk., F.A.
Holmen, Robert R. '63 '89
C.813 B.S. L.1066 J.D. Assoc. Corp. Coun., National Educ. Corp.
**Holmes, Curtis C., II** ................................ '61 '87 C.112 B.A. L.426 J.D. [Ⓐ Kirtland&P.]
Holmes, Mark D. ..............................'60 '91 C.1060 B.A. L.846 J.D. 5 Park Plz., Ste. 1500
hOLTHOUSE, Philip J. ........................................... '— '93 [Sherry&H.]
Holzer, Peter '54 '80 C.1044 B.A. L.809 J.D.
V.P. & Assoc. Coun., Fidelity Natl. Title Ins. Co.
Holzwarth, William C., Law Offices of, (AV) '40 '70
C.768 A.B. L.990 J.D. 15707 Rockfield Blvd, Ste 305
Hopkins, C. Mark, (BV) ........'47 '78 C.802 B.B.A. L.990 J.D. 18401 Van Karman Ave.
**Hopkins, Mark** ...................... '47 '78 C.802 B.B.A. L.990 J.D. [Ⓐ Fiore,W.R.&P.]
Horan, Michael A., (AV) ............. '45 '74 C.1042 B.S. L.1137 J.D. 30 Corporate Park
**Hori, Susan K.**, (AV) ...................'55 '80 C.911 B.A. L.1066 J.D. [Paone,C.M.&W.]
*PRACTICE AREAS: Land Use and Environmental Law.
**Horwitz, Lawrence W.** .................... '59 '84 C.112 B.S. L.1066 J.D. [Horwitz&B.]
*PRACTICE AREAS: General Business; Civil Litigation.

**Horwitz & Beam**
**Two Venture Plaza, Suite 380, 92618**
Telephone: 714-453-0300; 310-842-8574 Fax: 714-453-9416
Email: HOROWITZBEAM@EARTHLINK.NET
Members of Firm: Lawrence W. Horwitz; Gregory B. Beam. Associates: Lawrence R. Bujold; Lawrence M. Cron; Lynne Bolduc; Philip N. Friedman; Thomas B. Griffen.
General Business Practice. Corporate, Securities Offerings, Partnerships, Business Acquisitions and Dispositions. General Civil Litigation Practice in State and Federal Courts, Real Estate, Mobilehome Park, Administrative and Bankruptcy Law.
*See Professional Biographies, IRVINE, CALIFORNIA*

**Houser, Eric D.** ...................... '62 '87 C.112 B.A. L.1049 J.D. [Malcolm,C.&H.]
*PRACTICE AREAS: Commercial and Business Litigation; Bankruptcy.
**Howson, Christine E.** ........................ '63 '88 C.436 B.A. L.464 J.D. [Ⓐ Arter&H.]
**Hsu, Johanna Y.** ...................................'— '93 C.112 B.A. L.426 J.D. [Ⓐ Hanley&P.]
*LANGUAGES: Taiwanese.
*PRACTICE AREAS: Employment Litigation; Complex Business Litigation.
Huang, Geoffrey Chi Ho '51 '81 C.112 B.S. L.940 J.D.
[Benninghoff,H.&R.] (⊙San Juan Capistrano)
**Huber, Paul R.** ...................... '56 '89 C.112 B.A. L.1137 J.D. [Ⓐ Rosenbaum&D.]
*PRACTICE AREAS: Business Litigation; General Business.
**Huckabone, Joan M.** ................'69 '94 C.112 B.A. L.1065 J.D. D. [Jackson,D.&P.]
*PRACTICE AREAS: Business Litigation.
Hudson, Blake A. ..............'62 '94 C.112 B.A. L.800 J.D. 38 Corporate Pk. Suite 200
**Hudson, Dale A.**, (AV) .........'53 '78 C.1169 B.A. L.1066 J.D. [Ⓒ Sedgwick,D.M.&A.]
Hulsy, William S. ...........................'42 '68 C.112 B.A. L.1065 J.D. 17682 Mitchell N.
**Humphrey, Janet E.** .................... '63 '90 C.043 B.A. L.990 J.D. [Songstad,R.&U.]
**Hung, Samuel M.** '60 '85 C.838 B.A. L.145 J.D.
(adm. in NY; not adm. in CA) [Bainbridge]
*LANGUAGES: Mandarin Chinese and French.
*PRACTICE AREAS: Corporate; Securities.
**Hunter, Ellen E.** ........................'57 '87 C.6 B.A. L.1137 J.D. [Mower,K.N.C.&H.]
*PRACTICE AREAS: Insurance Defense; Construction Defect.
**Hurley, Gregory F.** ........................'58 '86 C.112 B.S. L.174 J.D. [Brown,P.H.&V.]
*PRACTICE AREAS: Construction Litigation; Business Litigation; Construction Project Insurance Coverage; Disabled Access Litigation; Environmental Law.
**Hurst, Charles W.** ...........................'57 '83 C.918 B.A. L.228 J.D. [Snell&W.]
*PRACTICE AREAS: Real Estate Law; Commercial Finance.
Hutchins, Holly, (BV) ...................'47 '75 C.112 B.A. L.426 J.D. 30 Corporate Park

**Hyman, Phelps & McNamara**
**2603 Main Street, 92614⊙**
Telephone: 714-553-7400 Telecopier: 714-553-7433
Brian J. Donato.
Practice before all Courts, Government Agencies and International Regulatory Authorities involving Foods, Drugs, Cosmetics, Medical Devices, Pesticides, Controlled Substances and Consumer Products.
Washington, D.C. Office: 700 Thirteenth Street, N.W., Suite 1200, 20005. Telephone: 202-737-5600. Telecopier: 202-737-9329.
*See Professional Biographies, IRVINE, CALIFORNIA*

**Igarashi, John Y.** ........................... '69 '95 C.112 B.A. L.426 J.D. [Oswald&Y.]
*PRACTICE AREAS: Commercial Litigation.
**Ihrke, Robert C., (A Professional Corporation)**, (AV) '41 '66
C.679 B.A. L.813 LL.B. [Palmieri,T.W.W.&W.]
*PRACTICE AREAS: Corporate Law; Real Estate Law.

**Inouye, Warren S., (AV) '51 '79 C&L.101 B.A., J.D.**
**2212 Dupont Drive, Suite B, 92715**
Telephone: 714-757-0757 Fax: 714-757-0759
*LANGUAGES: Japanese.
*PRACTICE AREAS: Real Estate Development; Contracts; Business Law.
Real Estate Development, Contracts and Business Law.
*See Professional Biographies, IRVINE, CALIFORNIA*

**Isler, Curtiss L.**, (AVⓉ) ......'45 '75 C.473 B.A. L.608 J.D. [Arter&H.] (⊙Los Angeles)

**Ivanjack & Lambirth, (AV)**
A Partnership including Professional Corporations
**5 Park Plaza, Suite 800, 92614⊙**
Telephone: 714-475-4477 Telecopier: 714-475-4475
Email: ivanjack@AOL.com
Of Counsel: Robert F. Nichols, Jr.; Camilla N. Andrews.
General Civil Trial and Appellate Practice in all State and Federal Courts, Commercial, Banking and Financial Institutions, Real Estate, Secured Transactions, Equipment Leasing, Creditors' Rights and Bankruptcy, Transactional Documentation, Operational and Regulatory Compliance Advice, Business and Construction.
Representative Clients: Bank of America; The Bank of California; Great Western Bank; General Electric Capital Corp.
Los Angeles, California Office: 12301 Wilshire Boulevard, Suite 600. 90025-1000. Telephone: 310-820-7211. Telecopier: 310-820-0687.
*See Professional Biographies, IRVINE, CALIFORNIA*

**Ives, Kirwan & Dibble, A Professional Corporation, (AV)**
**101 Pacifica, Suite 250, 92718⊙**
Telephone: 714-450-8900 FAX: 714-450-8908
Roger Erik Marken; Steven S. Marken.
Major Insurance Company Clients: American Mutual Insurance Co.; Utica Mutual Insurance Co.
Los Angeles, California Office: The Biltmore Court, Fourth Floor, 520 South Grand Avenue. Telephone: 213-627-0113. FAX: 213-627-1545.
Ventura-Santa Barbara Office: 5210 Carpinteria Avenue, P.O. Box 360, Carpinteria, California. Telephone: 805-684-7641. FAX: 805-684-9649.

(This Listing Continued)

**Ives, Kirwan & Dibble, A Professional Corporation (Continued)**
San Bernardino-Riverside Office: 777 Tahquitz Way, Suite 23, Palm Springs, California. Telephone: 619-788-2611. FAX: 619-778-2612.
*See Professional Biographies, IRVINE, CALIFORNIA*

**Jackson, C. Bennett, Jr.**, (AV) .............'39 '69 C.813 A.B. L.800 J.D. [Kendrick&J.]
**Jackson, F. Scott**, (AV) ......................'45 '72 C.1070 B.S. L.208 J.D. [Jackson,D.&P.]
*PRACTICE AREAS: Real Estate.
**Jackson, Jon Mitchell** .................... '57 '86 C.37 B.S. L.1137 J.D. [Jackson&W.]⊙
*PRACTICE AREAS: Tort Law; Business Law.
Jackson, Robert J. .................................. '47 '72 C.740 B.A. L.800 J.D. 4199 Campus Dr.

**Jackson, DeMarco & Peckenpaugh, A Law Corporation, (AV) BB**
**4 Park Plaza, 16th Floor, P.O. Box 19704, 92714**
Telephone: 714-752-8585 Fax: 714-752-0597
Lance A. Adair; Marc D. Alexander; Thomas D. Arnold; Diane P. Carey; Brian W. Casserly; John W. Cochrane; John C. Condas; James R. DeMarco; Steven J. Dzida; Roger M. Franks; Helene Z. Fransz; Edward A. Galloway; Roger A. Grad; William Michael Hensley; Darren L. Hereford; Joan M. Huckabone; F. Scott Jackson; Andrew V. Leitch; Thomas D. Peckenpaugh; John Petrasich; Andrew C. Schutz; David C. Smith; Douglas P. Smith; Jay R. Steinman; Michael L. Tidus.
Business and Real Estate Transactions, Financing and Construction, Taxation, Estate Planning, Corporate, Subdivision Law, Condominiums and Planned Developments, General Litigation, Land Use, Employment, Partnership, and Construction Defect Litigation and Appellate Practice.
*See Professional Biographies, IRVINE, CALIFORNIA*

**Jackson & Wilson**
**Ventura Plaza, 2 Ventura, Suite 280, 92618⊙**
Telephone: 714-450-1103 Fax: 714-450-1105
URL: http://www.jacksonwilson.com
Jon Mitchell Jackson; Lisa M. Wilson.
Civil Settlement, Mediation, Trial and Appellate service at the State and Federal Court level. Wrongful Death, Serious Personal Injury, Business Litigation, Products Liability, Professional Malpractice, Maritime, Aviation, Negligence, Professional Practice Disputes and Resolutions, Commercial Collections, and Insurance Matters involving Bad Faith. Litigation, including Bench and Jury Trials, Appeals, Writs, Arbitrations, Depositions, Law and Motion and Petitions for Injunctive Relief.
San Jose, California Office: 1228 Lincoln Avenue, Suite 102, 95125.
*See Professional Biographies, IRVINE, CALIFORNIA*

**Jacobs, Diane E.** ........................ '59 '95 C.112 B.A. L.1137 J.D. [Ⓐ Wesierski&Z.]
Jacobs, Leigh Marshall ......................'60 '89 C.999 B.S. L.1137 J.D. [Cone,C.&K.]
**Janecek, Jon J.** ....................................'62 '88 C.112 B.S. L.1065 J.D. [Ⓐ Snell&W.]
*PRACTICE AREAS: Real Estate Law; Commercial Finance.
**Jasper, Catherine R.** ........................... '51 '81 C.112 B.A. L.1137 J.D. [Jasper&J.]
**Jasper, Stuart P.**, (AV) ..........................'47 '73 C&L.472 A.B., J.D. [Jasper&J.]

**Jasper & Jasper, A Professional Corporation, (AV)**
**19900 MacArthur Boulevard, Suite 1120, 92612**
Telephone: 714-756-1560 Fax: 714-756-2251
Stuart P. Jasper; Catherine R. Jasper.
General Civil Trial Practice in all State and Federal Courts. Business, Franchise and Employment Litigation, Restaurant Industry Litigation.
*See Professional Biographies, IRVINE, CALIFORNIA*

**Jeffers, Michael B.** ..........................'40 '64 C&L.911 B.A., LL.B. [Jeffers,W.&S.]
*PRACTICE AREAS: Corporate and Securities Law.

**Jeffers, Wilson & Shaff, LLP, (CV)**
**Tower 17, 18881 Von Karman Avenue Suite 1400, 92715**
Telephone: 714-660-7700 Facsimile: 714-660-7799
Members of Firm: Michael B. Jeffers; Christopher A. Wilson; Michael E. Shaff (Certified Specialist, Taxation Law, The State Bar of California Board of Legal Specialization); Barry D. Falk.
Corporate Law, Securities, Mergers and Acquisitions, and Taxation.
*See Professional Biographies, IRVINE, CALIFORNIA*

Jenkins, Gregory P. ......... '57 '83 C.197 A.B. L.477 J.D. V.P., Legal, The Geneva Cos.
Jennings, E. L., Jr. '24 '49 C&L.436 B.S., J.D.
(adm. in WI; not adm. in CA) 44 Wetstone‡

**Jennings & Haug, (AVⓉ) BB**
**1920 Main Street, Suite Eight-Thirty, 92714⊙**
Telephone: 714-250-7800 Fax: 714-250-4913
Email: jhlaw@syspac.com
Robert A. Scheffing. Associate: Paul D. Kramer (Resident).
General Practice in State and Federal Courts and before Administrative Agencies. Commercial, Bankruptcy, Creditors Rights, Construction, Corporate, Labor and Employment Law, Estate Planning, Fidelity and Surety, Insurance, Personal Injury. Trials and Appeals.
Phoenix, Arizona Office: 2800 North Central Avenue, Suite Eighteen Hundred. Telephone: 602-234-7800.
*See Professional Biographies, IRVINE, CALIFORNIA*

**Jensen, Jacqueline M.**, (AV) ................'38 '78 C.856 B.A. L.862 J.D. [J.M.Jensen]
Jensen, Jeffrey V. ..............................'59 '84 C.112 B.A. L.1066 J.D. 2212 Dupont Dr.
Jensen, VerLyn N., (AV) ....... '39 '64 C.112 B.A. L.1066 J.D. 18101 Von Karman Ave.

**Jensen, Jacqueline M., Inc., (AV) BB**
**18006 Sky Park Circle, Suite 109, 92614**
Telephone: 714-261-0100 Fax: 714-261-0176
Jacqueline M. Jensen (Board Certified, Probate, Estate Planning and Trust Law, California Board of Legal Specialization).
Estate Planning, Estate Tax, Trusts, Asset Protection, Probate, Business Law and Elder Care.
*See Professional Biographies, IRVINE, CALIFORNIA*

**Jodis, Kristina M.** ...................... '67 '92 C.602 B.A. L.477 J.D. [Ⓐ Morrison&F.]
**Joens, Timothy L.**, (AV) ............ '51 '79 C.800 B.A. L.426 J.D. [T.L.Joens&Assoc.]
*PRACTICE AREAS: Civil Litigation; Franchise Law; Personal Injury; Professional Liability Law.

**Joens, Timothy L., & Assoc., A Prof. Corp., (AV) BB**
**Jamboree Center, Five Park Plaza, Suite 1480, 92714**
Telephone: 714-553-1950 Fax: 714-553-8835
Timothy L. Joens.
Trial and Appellate Litigation for Civil Matters in all State and Federal Courts, including Business, Real Property, Contract, Will Contests, Collection, Personal Injury, Professional Malpractice, Corporate, Partnership, Franchise, Surety, Lien and Construction Matters.
Representative Clients: Century 21 of the Pacific, Inc.; Century 21 Region V, Inc.; Century 21 Real Estate Corp.
*See Professional Biographies, IRVINE, CALIFORNIA*

**Johnson, Doyle B.** .......................'66 '95 C.112 BSEE L.990 J.D. [Price,G.&U.]
**Johnson, Eric B.** .............. '56 '85 C.494 B.A. L.1035 J.D. [Ⓐ Berger,K.S.M.F.S.&G.]
**Johnson, Judy J.**, (AV) .......................'52 '77 C.813 B.A. L.800 J.D. [Ramsay&J.]
*PRACTICE AREAS: Insurance Coverage/Bad Faith Law; Professional Errors and Omissions Law; Insurance Defense Law.
**Johnson, Kenneth D.** ................'57 '85 C.608 B.A. L.930 J.D. [Ⓐ Paone,C.M.&W.]
*LANGUAGES: French, Spanish and Russian.
*PRACTICE AREAS: Redevelopment; Affordable Housing; Real Property; Environmental Law.
**Johnson, Michael E.** ....................... '60 '87 C.763 B.S. L.1068 J.D. [Bainbridge]
*PRACTICE AREAS: Mergers and Acquisitions; Strategic Alliances; Corporate Finance; Technology Licensing.
**Johnson, Paul H.** ....................... '42 '74 C.1042 B.A. L.1137 J.D. [Gibson,H.&J.]
*PRACTICE AREAS: Corporate Law; Estate Planning.

CALIFORNIA—IRVINE MARTINDALE-HUBBELL LAW DIRECTORY 1997

Johnson, Paul R. .................. '57 '84 C.976 B.A. L.1066 J.D. 18101 Von Karman Ave.
**Johnson, Scott M.** .................'— '87 C.907 B.A. L.276 J.D. Atty., AirTouch Comm.
**Johnston, Ann K.** .............. '64 '89 C.112 B.A. L.990 J.D. [Ⓐ Berger,K.S.M.F.S.&G.]
**Jones, Brian D.** ................... '67 '95 C.112 B.A. L.990 J.D. [Ⓐ Sedgwick,D.M.&A.]
**Jones, Peter Best**, (AV) .................... '43 '68 C.197 A.B. L.178 LL.B. [Jones&D.]
*PRACTICE AREAS: Government Contracts; Contracts.
Jones, Richard D. ............. '33 '59 C.940 A.B. L.800 LL.B. 2091 Business Center Dr.
**Jones, Thomas S.** ..................... '67 '93 C&L.945 B.A., J.D. [Ⓐ Gibson,D.&C.]
*PRACTICE AREAS: Litigation.

**Jones, Day, Reavis & Pogue, (AV)** BR
**2603 Main Street, Suite 900, 92714-6232⊙**
**Telephone: 714-851-3939 Telex: 194911 Lawyers LSA Telecopier: 714-553-7539**
**Members of Firm in Irvine: Thomas R. Malcolm; Dulcie D. Brand; Richard J. Grabowski. Associates: J. Scott Schoeffel; Mark D. Kemple; William E. Halle; Marc K. Callahan; Jeffrey B. Kirzner; Michelle M. Nuszkiewicz; Michael D. Fabiano; James L. Poth; Heather A. McConnell.**
**General Practice.**
**In Los Angeles, California: 555 West Fifth Street, Suite 4600. Telephone: 213-489-3939. Telex: 181439 UD. Telecopier: 213-243-2539.**
**In Atlanta, Georgia: 3500 One Peachtree Center, 303 Peachtree Street, N.E. Telephone: 404-521-3939. Cable Address: "Attorneys Atlanta". Telex: 54-2711. Telecopier: 404-581-8330.**
**In Brussels, Belgium: Avenue Louise 480, 7th Floor, B-1050 Brussels. Telephone: 32-2-645-14-11. Telecopier: 32-2-645-14-45.**
**In Chicago, Illinois: 77 West Wacker. Telephone: 312-782-3939. Telecopier: 312-782-8585.**
**In Cleveland, Ohio: North Point, 901 Lakeside Avenue. Telephone: 216-586-3939. Cable Address: "Attorneys Cleveland." Telex: 980389. Telecopier: 216-579-0212.**
**In Columbus, Ohio: 1900 Huntington Center. Telephone: 614-469-3939. Cable Address: "Attorneys Columbus." Telecopier: 614-461-4198.**
**In Dallas, Texas: 2300 Trammell Crow Center, 2001 Ross Avenue. Telephone: 214-220-3939. Cable Address: "Attorneys Dallas." Telex: 730852. Telecopier: 214-969-5100.**
**In Frankfurt, Germany: Triton Haus, Bockenheimer Landstrasse 42, 60323 Frankfurt am Main. Telephone: 49-69-9726-3939. Telecopier: 49-69-9726-3993.**
**In Geneva, Switzerland: 20, rue de Candolle. Telephone: 41-22-320-2339. Telecopier: 41-22-320-1232.**
**In Hong Kong: 29th Floor, Entertainment Building, 30 Queen's Road Central. Telephone: 852-2526-6895. Telecopier: 852-2868-5871.**
**In London, England: Bucklersbury House, 3 Queen Victoria Street. Telephone: 44-171-236-3939. Telecopier: 44-171-236-1113.**
**In New Delhi, India: Pathak & Associates, 13th Floor, Dr. Gopal Das Bhavan, 28 Barakhamba Road. Telephone: 91-11-373-8793. Telecopy: 91-11-335-3761.**
**In New York, New York: 599 Lexington Avenue. Telephone: 212-326-3939. Cable Address: "JONESDAY NEWYORK." Telex: 237013 JDRP UR. Telecopier: 212-755-7306.**
**In Paris, France: 62, rue du Faubourg Saint-Honore. Telephone: 33-1-44-71-3939. Telex: 290156 Surgoe. Telecopier: 33-1-49-24-0471.**
**In Pittsburgh, Pennsylvania: 500 Grant Street, 31st Floor. Telephone: 412-391-3939. Cable Address: "Attorneys Pittsburgh." Telecopier: 412-394-7959.**
**In Riyadh, Saudi Arabia: The International Law Firm, Sulaymaniyah Center, Tahlia Street, P.O. Box 22166. Telephone: (966-1) 462-8866. Telecopier: (966-1) 462-9001.**
**In Taipei, Taiwan: 8th Floor, 2 Tun Hwa South Road, Section 2. Telephone: (886-2) 704-6808. Telecopier: (886-2) 704-6791.**
**In Tokyo, Japan: Toranomon MT Building, 4th Floor, 10-3, Toranomon 3-Chome, Minato-ku, Tokyo 105, Japan. Telephone: 81-3-3433-3939. Telecopier: 81-3-5401-2725.**
**In Washington, D.C.: Metropolitan Square, 1450 G Street, N.W. Telephone: 202-879-3939. Cable Address: "Attorneys Washington." Telex: 89-2410 ATTORNEYS WASH. Telecopier: 202-737-2832.**

***See Professional Biographies, IRVINE, CALIFORNIA***

**Jones & Donovan, A Prof. Corp., Law Offices of, (AV)**
**Centerpointe 6, Suite 230, 19782 MacArthur Boulevard, 92715**
**Telephone: 714-833-8893 Telecopier: 714-833-7555**
**Peter Best Jones; Brian J. Donovan;—Toni L. DeGasperin.**
**Government Contracts and related Commercial Contracts, including Litigation before all Courts and Boards of Contract Appeals.**

***See Professional Biographies, IRVINE, CALIFORNIA***

**Jordan, Daniel G.** .................'54 '81 C.112 B.A. L.1066 J.D. [Ⓒ Case,K.B.&W.]⊙
**Joseph, Christy D.** ........................'60 '88 C.112 B.A. L.1065 J.D. [Snell&W.]
*PRACTICE AREAS: Employment Litigation; Commercial Litigation; Product Liability Litigation.
**Joseph, E. George** ................ '58 '83 C.188 A.B. L.1068 J.D. [Nossaman,G.K.&E.]
*PRACTICE AREAS: Litigation.
Joy, Jeffrey C., (AV) .......................'52 '78 C.378 B.S. L.900 J.D. [O'Kain&J.]
**Joyce, R. Michael**, (AV) ..............'51 '77 C.674 A.B. L.800 J.D. [Allen,M.L.G.&M.]
*PRACTICE AREAS: Real Estate.
Judge, James A. ..............................'52 '85 L.1137 J.D. 19900 MacArthur Blvd.
Jurkoic, Paul M., (AV) '46 '75
C.475 B.S.E.E. L.912 J.D. Coun., Coml. Equip. Fin., GE Capital Corp.
**Kadotani, Cheri A.**, (BV) ..............'59 '85 C.112 B.A. L.1137 J.D. [Tredway,L.&D.]
*REPORTED CASES: In re Marriage of Simpson, 92 Daily Journal D.A.R. 18002 (1992).
*PRACTICE AREAS: Family Law.
Kalfa, Leda L. ......................'58 '87 C.112 B.A. L.1148 J.D. 100 Pacifica Ste. 200
Kaminsky, Larry M. '52 '77 C.112 B.A. L.1095 J.D.
V.P. & Asst. Gen. Coun., Fidelity Natl. Title Ins. Co.
Kamman, James M. ..................... '45 '76 C.477 B.A. L.990 J.D. 1 Pk. Plz. Ste 300
Kane, M'Liss Jones ... '52 '80 C.112 B.A. L.809 J.D. Fidelity National Title Insurance Co.
**Kania, Edward J.** '57 '86
C.1168 B.A. L.426 J.D. Mng. Atty. & Reg. V.P., Mission Energy Co.
Kaniewski, John A. ...........................'57 '83 C&L.426 B.A., J.D. [Morgan&W.]
**Kanter, Charles H., (A Professional Corporation)**, (AV) '51 '76
C.112 B.A. L.1067 J.D. [Palmieri,T.W.W.&W.]
*PRACTICE AREAS: Litigation.
**Kaplan, Lance** ...................... '63 '88 C.061 B.A. L.61 J.D. [Ⓒ Hirson W.P.&S.]
*LANGUAGES: Afrikaans and Hebrew.
*PRACTICE AREAS: Immigration Law; International Law.
**Karger, Pamela Z.** ......................... '53 '86 C.347 B.S. L.796 J.D. [Ⓐ Lobel&O.]
*PRACTICE AREAS: Bankruptcy Law; Reorganization.
**Kasdan, Kenneth S.**, (AV).......... '51 '76 C.1138 B.A. L.107 J.D. [Kasdan,S.M.E.&M.]
*PRACTICE AREAS: Construction Defect Litigation; Business Litigation.

**Kasdan, Simonds, McIntyre, Epstein & Martin, (AV)** BR
**2600 Michelson Drive, Tenth Floor, 92715**
**Telephone: 714-851-9000 Fax: 714-833-9455**
**Members of Firm: Kenneth S. Kasdan; Vance C. Simonds, Jr.; R. Donald McIntyre; David G. Epstein; Ronald B. Martin; Andrew D. Weiss. Associate: Henry P. Schrenker; Steven S. Hanagami.**
**General Civil and Trial Practice, State and Federal Courts. Business, Real Property, Financial Institutions, Product Liability, Corporate, Creditors Rights, Property Tax Assessment Appeals, Public Law and Construction Law.**
**Reference: Commerce Bank.**

***See Professional Biographies, IRVINE, CALIFORNIA***

Katsell, Jerome H. .................. '41 '88 C.112 B.A. L.1049 J.D. 3355 Michelson Dr.

**Katten Muchin & Zavis, (AV)**
**A Partnership including Professional Corporations**
**Katten Muchin & Zavis Established in 1974**
**Two Park Plaza, Suite 800, 92714-5976⊙**
**Telephone: 714-263-3500 Telecopier: 714-263-3533**
**Member of Firm: Thomas S. Mahr; Frederick H. Kranz; Stuart M. Richter. Associates: Thia M. Cochran; Michelle A. Curtis; Melody Williams Dapp; Eoin L. Kreditor.**
**Creditor's Rights, Environmental, Intellectual Property, Labor and Employment Law, Litigation and Trial Practice, Real Estate.**

(This Listing Continued)

CAA132P

**Katten Muchin & Zavis (Continued)**

**Chicago, Illinois Office: 525 West Monroe Street, Suite 1600. Telephone: 312-902-5200. Telecopier: 312-902-1061. Telex: 298264 ATLAW UR.**
**Los Angeles, California Office: 1999 Avenue of the Stars, Suite 1400. Telephone: 310-788-4400. Telecopier: 310-788-4471.**
**New York, New York Office: 40 Broad Street, Suite 2000. Telephone: 212-612-9500. Telecopier: 212-425-0266.**
**Washington, D.C. Office: 1025 Thomas Jefferson Street, N.W., East Lobby, Suite 700. Telephone: 202-625-3500. Telecopier: 202-298-7570. Telex: 211195 KMZ UR.**

***See Professional Biographies, IRVINE, CALIFORNIA***

**Katz, Randolf W.** ............................ '53 '78 C.112 A.B. L.1068 J.D. [Arter&H.]
*PRACTICE AREAS: Corporate Law; Securities Law.
Kaufman, Jeffrey S. .............. '66 '91 C.112 B.A. L.426 J.D. 1920 Main St. Ste. 1200
Kay, David G. ................................'53 '77 C.112 B.A. L.426 J.D. Univ. of Calif.
**Kay, James G.** ..........................'50 '91 C.846 B.B.A. L.276 J.D. [Ⓐ Payne&F.]
*PRACTICE AREAS: Business Litigation; Construction Litigation; Insurance Coverage Litigation.
**Kay, Timothy J.** ........................ '53 '87 C.767 B.A. L.813 J.D. [Gibson,D.&C.]
*PRACTICE AREAS: Trusts and Estates; Estate and Gift Tax Controversies; Nonprofit and Charitable Organizations; Taxation; Guardianship and Conservatorship.
**Kayajanian, Jack J.**, (BV) .............. '50 '77 C.267 B.A. L.1137 J.D. [Kayajanian&B.]
*PRACTICE AREAS: Criminal Law; Personal Injury; Business Law.

**Kayajanian & Brewsaugh, (BV)**
**18500 Von Karman Avenue, Suite 430, 92715**
**Telephone: 714-955-2254 Facsimile: 714-833-1556**
**Members of Firm: Jack J. Kayajanian (Certified Specialist, Family Law, The State Bar of California Board of Legal Specialization); Gary D. Brewsaugh.**
**Personal Injury, Business Law, Civil Litigation, Family Law, Construction.**

***See Professional Biographies, IRVINE, CALIFORNIA***

**Kearl, Jane Grilliot** .........................'65 '91 C.607 B.A. L.608 J.D. [Kendrick&J.]
**Keenan, Robert J.** ...................... '65 '90 C.1109 B.A. L.800 J.D. [Ⓐ Morrison&F.]
**Kegel, Debra L.** '57 '82 C.1109 B.A. L.1068 J.D.
V.P. & Assoc. Gen. Coun., Amer. Svgs. Bk., F.A.
**Keligian, David L.** ........................................ '56 '80 C&L.800 B.S., J.D. [Busch]
*PRACTICE AREAS: Estate; Tax; Business Law.
Keller, Coby N. ............'49 '75 C.139 B.A. L.462 J.D. 19900 MacArthur Blvd., 8th Fl.

**Keller, Jennifer L., Law Offices of, (AV) '53 '78 C.112 A.B. L.1065 J.D.** BR
**19100 Von Karman Avenue, Suite 950, 92612**
**Telephone: 714-476-8700 Fax: 714-476-0900**
**Email: HVDE71A@PRODIGY.COM**
**(Certified Specialist, Criminal Law, The State Bar of California Board of Legal Specialization).**
***REPORTED CASES: United States v. Stites, 56 F.3d 1020 (1995); People v. Sellers (1988) 203 Cal. App. 3d 1042; Betsworth v. WCAB (1994) 26 Cal. App. 4th 586.**
***PRACTICE AREAS: Criminal Defense; Civil Litigation.**
**Criminal Defense and Related Civil Litigation.**

***See Professional Biographies, IRVINE, CALIFORNIA***

**Keller, Timothy G.** ................ '49 '84 C.112 B.A. L.1153 J.D. [Ⓐ Laughlin,F.L.&M.]
*PRACTICE AREAS: Longshoremen; Harbor Workers' Act; Workers' Compensation.
Kemp, Roland L. ................................... '19 '64 L.1026 LL.B. 2 Park Vista‡
**Kemple, Mark D.** .......................'62 '89 C.112 B.A. L.800 J.D. [Ⓐ Jones,D.R.&P.]
**Kendig, David E.** ......................... '66 '91 C&L.800 B.A., J.D. [Willis,K.&A.]
*SPECIAL AGENCIES: Regional Water Quality Control Board - Santa Ana Region; California Department of Toxic Substances Control; Orange County Health Services Agency, Environmental Health; U.S. Army Corp of Engineers; California Water Resources Control Board.
*PRACTICE AREAS: Environmental Litigation; Environmental Insurance; Lender/Trustee Environmental Liability; Real Estate Transactions; Wetlands Regulation.
**Kendrick, John J., Jr.**, (AV) ................'46 '74 C.112 B.A. L.464 J.D. [Kendrick&J.]

**Kendrick & Jackson, (AV)**
**19800 MacArthur Boulevard Suite 270, 92612**
**Telephone: 714-261-6440 Facsimile: 714-261-5758**
**John J. Kendrick, Jr.; C. Bennett Jackson, Jr.; Jane Grilliot Kearl.**
**Business and Civil Litigation including Real Property, Insurance Banking, Construction and Employment Disputes.**

***See Professional Biographies, IRVINE, CALIFORNIA***

**Kenny, Gerard J.**, (AV) ................. '43 '73 C.102 B.A. L.800 J.D. [Gibson,D.&C.]
*PRACTICE AREAS: Taxation (Corporate, Partnership and Personal Income Tax); Federal and State Tax Controversies; Employee Compensation Programs; Mergers, Acquisitions and Divestitures; Partnerships.
Kenyon, Kyle, Law Office, (CVⓉ) ......................... '24 '52 C&L.966 J.D. 9 Orion
**Kepler, Stephen J.** ............... '65 '91 C.112 B.A. L.1066 J.D. [Ⓐ Allen,M.L.G.&M.]
*PRACTICE AREAS: Litigation and Employment Law.
**Kerns, Christianne F.** '58 '85
C.1109 B.A. L.800 J.D. [Ⓒ Corey,C.D.&D.] (⊙Los Angeles)
*PRACTICE AREAS: Real Estate Finance; Real Estate Workouts; Commercial Law; Business Law.
**Kerr, Douglas B.** .........................'56 '83 C.112 B.A. L.464 J.D. [Meuers,D.&K.]
*PRACTICE AREAS: Labor and Employment Law; Perishable Commodities; Corporate Law; ERISA.
Kerrigan, David L. '41 '68
C.112 B.S. L.1068 J.D. Exec. V.P. & Gen. Coun., Crowell Industries
**Kessel, Alan Jules**, (AV) .............. '62 '87 C.861 B.A. L.569 J.D. [Paone,C.M.&W.]
*LANGUAGES: Spanish.
*PRACTICE AREAS: Business; Real Estate; Land Use; Environmental Litigation.
**Keto, Harri J.**, (BV) ........... '49 '76 C.112 B.A. L.1049 J.D. [Berger,K.S.M.F.S.&G.]
*LANGUAGES: Finnish.
**Kew, Joel P.**, (BV) ................ '56 '82 C.112 B.A. L.767 J.D. [Palmieri,T.W.W.&W.]
*PRACTICE AREAS: Litigation.
Keyworth, William A. '24 '52 C&L.748 B.S., LL.B.
(adm. in MN; not adm. in CA) 5200 Irvine Blvd.‡
**Khouri, Michael J.**, (AV) ........... '56 '81 C&L.426 B.A., J.D. [Ⓒ Sedgwick,D.M.&A.]
Kichler, Benita K. '54 '83 C.1252 B.S. L.365 J.D.
(adm. in IL; not adm. in CA) Trademark Atty., Allergan, Inc.

**Kiken, Dale A. '53 '81 C.174 B.A. L.990 J.D.**
**18400 Von Karman Avenue, Suite 500, 92715**
**Telephone: 714-476-0270 Fax: 714-476-2883**
***PRACTICE AREAS: Business Litigation.**
**Business Litigation.**

***See Professional Biographies, IRVINE, CALIFORNIA***

**Kim, Esther Y.** ................. '57 '83 C.112 B.A. L.1066 J.D. Baxter Healthcare Corp.
**Kim, Jennifer Anne** ............ '68 '94 C.103 A.B. L.309 J.D. [Ⓐ Palmieri,T.W.W.&W.]
*PRACTICE AREAS: Real Estate.
**Kim, Paul** .............................. '66 '91 C.688 B.S. L.276 J.D. [Ⓐ Hanley&P.]
*PRACTICE AREAS: Business Law; Intellectual Property; Employment Law.
**Kimel, Metiner G.** .......................... '58 '91 C.659 B.A. L.911 J.D. [Ⓐ Lobel&O.]
Kimes, Phillip R. .................... '43 '69 C.1042 B.A. L.1188 J.D. 4199 Campus Dr.
**Kincannon, John A.** ...............................'55 '80 C&L.45 B.S., J.D. [Cox,C.&N.]
*PRACTICE AREAS: Real Property Law; Partnerships Law; Public Finance.
**King, Marian A.** ......'43 '77 C.1181 L.464 J.D. Sr. Grp. Envir. Coun., Waste Mgmt., Inc.
**Kirchanski, Stefan J.** ..... '49 '92 C.1097 B.A. L.426 J.D. [Ⓐ Price,G.&U.] (See Pat. Sect.)
*PRACTICE AREAS: Patent; Trademark; Copyright.

**Kircher, C. William, Jr., (Professional Corporation)**, (AV) '46 '72
C&L.813 B.A., J.D. [C.W.Kircher,Jr.]
*PRACTICE AREAS: Business Litigation; Securities Litigation; Commercial Litigation.

**Kircher, C. William, Jr., A Prof. Corp., Law Offices of, (AV)**
**19800 MacArthur Boulevard, Suite 1450, 92612-2442**
**Telephone: 714-720-9752 Fax: 714-720-8752**
**C. William Kircher, Jr., (Professional Corporation).**
**Civil Business, Commercial and Securities Litigation in Federal and State Courts.**
**Reference: First Los Angeles Bank (Main Branch).**

*See Professional Biographies, IRVINE, CALIFORNIA*

**Kirchoff, Brian R.** ... '50 '79 C.766 B.A. L.464 J.D. [S Gibson,D.&C.]
*PRACTICE AREAS: Real Estate.

**Kirtland & Packard LLP, (AV)**
**18101 Von Karman Avenue, Nineteenth Floor, 92715-1041⊙**
**Telephone: 714-263-9700 Fax: 714-263-9090**
**Members of Firm: Mark P. Poliquin; John M. Goodspeed; Jeffrey M. Anielski. Resident Associates Irvine Office: Robert W. Skripko, Jr.; C. Christopher Mulder; Curtis C. Holmes II; Joseph Stephen McMillen; Timothy D. Otte; Layne M. Bukovskis; Paul R. Cotter; Ronald J. Thommarson. Resident Partners Los Angeles Office: Harold J. Hunter, Jr.; Jacques E. Soiret; Michael L. Kelly; Joseph E. Gregorich; Robert A. Muhlbach; Robert M. Churella; Scott M. Schutz; Steven M. Maslauski; John M. Caron; Terrence J. Schafer.**
**General Civil and Trial Practice in State and Federal Courts. Aviation, Employment and Labor Law, Environmental, Insurance, Medical Malpractice, Professional and Product Liability and Toxic Torts Law.**
**Los Angeles, California Office: 1900 Avenue of the Stars, Twenty-Fifth and Twenty-Sixth Floors. Telephone: 310-552-9700. Cable Address: "Kirtpack". Fax: 310-552-0957.**

*See Professional Biographies, IRVINE, CALIFORNIA*

**Kirzner, Jeffrey B.** ... '66 '91 C.112 B.A. L.1065 J.D. [A Jones,D.R.&P.]
**Kitagawa, Lisa M.**, (AV) ... '59 '82 C.800 B.S. L.426 J.D. [Kitagawa&E.]⊙
*LANGUAGES: Japanese.

**Kitagawa & Ebert, P.C., (AV)**
**Formerly known as Kitsuta & Ebert, P.C.**
**8001 Irvine Center Drive, Suite 850, 92718⊙**
**Telephone: 714-727-0290 Fax: 714-727-0607**
**Lisa M. Kitagawa; James R. Ebert.**
**General Business, Corporate, International, Business and Tax Litigation, Employment Law, Employment Litigation, Collection Litigation, Estate Planning, Probate, Real Estate, Sports, Entertainment, Licensing, Restructuring, Mergers and Acquisitions.**
**Atlanta, Georgia Office: 400 Colony Square, Suite 200. 1201 Peachtree Street, N.E. Telephone: 404-870-0290. Fax: 404-870-0079.**

*See Professional Biographies, IRVINE, CALIFORNIA*

**Klawunder, Nina D.** ... '66 '91 C.112 B.A. L.426 J.D. [A Kring&B.]
*LANGUAGES: Armenian.
*PRACTICE AREAS: Civil Litigation.
Klein, Daniel S. ... '64 '91 C.763 B.S. L.809 J.D. 19762 MacArthur Blvd.
**Klein, Howard J.**, (AV) ... '50 '76 C.453 B.S. L.228 J.D. [Klein&S.] (See Pat. Sect.)
*SPECIAL AGENCIES: Federal Election Commission.
*PRACTICE AREAS: Intellectual Property Law; Election Law.

**Klein & Szekeres, (AV)**
**4199 Campus Drive, Suite 700, 92715**
**Telephone: 714-854-5502 FAX: 714-854-4897**
**Email: hjklein@mail.calypso.com**
**Members of Firm: Howard J. Klein; Gabor L. Szekeres.**
**Patent, Trademark and Copyright Law. Unfair Competition Law. Election Law.**
**Reference: Sanwa Bank.**

*See Professional Biographies, IRVINE, CALIFORNIA*

**Kline, Howard F.** ... '51 '76 C&L.999 B.A., J.D. [Berger,K.S.M.F.S.&G.]
Klingler, Lidia A. '— '85
C.420 B.A. L.705 J.D. Legal Coun., Westcorp Financial Servs., Inc.
**Klokow, Anne E.** ... '54 '80 C.112 B.A. L.800 J.D. [Allen,M.L.G.&M.]
*PRACTICE AREAS: Real Estate.

**Klunder, Carl J., (AV) '45 '77 C.103 B.G.S. L.1068 J.D.**
**108 Pacifica, 3rd Floor, P.O. Box 19799, 92623-9799**
**Telephone: 714-753-1229 Fax: 714-753-1413**
***PRACTICE AREAS: Insurance Coverage; Casualty Insurance Law; Environmental Insurance Litigation; Bad Faith; Excess Insurance Law.**
**Insurance Coverage, Casualty Insurance Law, Environmental Insurance Litigation, Bad Faith; Excess Insurance Law, Insurance Agents, Errors and Omissions, Life Insurance Law.**

*See Professional Biographies, IRVINE, CALIFORNIA*

Knapp, Kenneth L., (AV) ... '21 '55 L.809 LL.B. [K.L.Knapp]
**Knapp, Richard O.** ... '64 '89 C.112 B.A. L.1049 J.D. [A Berger,K.S.M.F.S.&G.]
Knapp, Kenneth L., A Law Corporation, (AV) ... 2600 Michelson Dr.
**Knowlson, Arthur R., Jr., (P.C.)**, (AV) '48 '74 C.705 B.A. L.1049 J.D.
[Case,K.B.&W.]
*PRACTICE AREAS: Tax; Estate Planning; Trust; Probate.
Knuppel, Neil W., (BV) ... '52 '79 C.112 B.A. L.1137 J.D. [A.Bartz]
**Knutson, Scott M.** ... '60 '92 C.906 B.A. L.494 J.D. [A Gibson,D.&C.]
*PRACTICE AREAS: Tax Law.
Kocalis, Steven S. ... '41 '79 C.1012 B.A. L.1042 J.D. 1 Descanso
**Koehler, Philip J.** ... '51 '91 C.846 B.A. L.800 J.D. [A Morrison&F.]
**Koeller, Keith D.**, (AV) ... '56 '81 C.800 B.A. L.426 J.D. [Mower,K.N.C.&H.]
*PRACTICE AREAS: Insurance Coverage; Insurance Defense; Bad Faith Law; Construction Defect Litigation; Construction Accidents.
Kofford, Cree-L, (AV) '33 '62
C.878 B.S. L.800 J.D. 19800 MacArthur Blvd. (⊙Pasadena)
**Kohlmann, Henry G.** ... '39 '74 C.768 B.S.E.E. L.1065 J.D. [C Arter&H.]

**Kolczynski, Phillip J., (AV) '47 '77 C.436 B.A. L.930 J.D.** BR
**Lakeshore Towers, 18101 Von Karman Avenue, Suite 1800, 92715**
**Telephone: 714-833-8999 Fax: 714-833-7878**
**Email: Klawcorp@aol.com**
**Aviation, Products Liability, Insurance, Business Litigation.**

*See Professional Biographies, IRVINE, CALIFORNIA*

**Kompa, Mark A., (AV) '55 '80 C.800 A.B. L.823 J.D.** BR
**2603 Main Street, Suite 1170, 92714**
**Telephone: 714-250-9500 Facsimile: 714-250-9515**
***REPORTED CASES: In re Victor Dye Works, Inc., 48 B.R. 943 (Bkrptcy.E.D. Pa. 1985); In re Zerodec Megacorp, Inc., 54 B.R. 814 (Bkrptcy.E.D. Pa. 1985); In re Oxford Royal Mushroom Products, Inc., 59 B.R. 926 (Bkrptcy.E.D. Pa. 1986); In re McCombs Properties VIII, Ltd., 91 B.R. 907 (Bkrptcy. C.D. Cal. 1988).**
***PRACTICE AREAS: Landlord and Tenant Law; Civil Litigation.**
**Real Estate, Landlord-Tenant, Creditors' Rights and Bankruptcy, Commercial and Business Law and Appellate Practice.**

*See Professional Biographies, IRVINE, CALIFORNIA*

**Kondzella, Michael A.** '27 '55
C.339 A.B. L.705 J.D. [Oppenheimer P.S.] (Pat.) (⊙Los Angeles)

**Kopeny, William J.**, (AV) ... '50 '74 C.112 B.A. L.800 J.D. [Kopeny&P.]
*REPORTED CASES: Powell v. Superior Court (People), 232 Cal.App.3d 785, 283 Cal.Rptr. 777 (1991); In Re Robinson, 216 Cal.App.3d 1510, 265 Cal.Rptr. 574 (1990); People P.2d 905, 229 Cal.Rptr. 131 1986); Freedom Newspapper, Inc. v. Superior Court (Orange County), 186 Cal.App.3d 1102, 231 Cal.Rptr. 189 (1986); Koon v. U.S., - U.S.-, 116 S.Ct.2035, 135 L.Ed.2d 392 (1996).
*PRACTICE AREAS: Appellate Practice; White Collar Trials Trials.

**Kopeny & Powell, (AV)** BR
**8001 Irvine Center Drive, Suite 1170, 92618**
**Telephone: 714-453-2243 Facsimile: 714-453-1916**
**Email: KPATKP@AOL.COM**
**William J. Kopeny (Certified Specialist, Criminal Law, The State Bar of California Board of Legal Specialization); John W. Powell.**
**Writs and Appeals in all State and Federal Courts, Tax Controversies and Defense of White Collar Crimes, Business Litigation, Tax and Estate Planning.**

*See Professional Biographies, IRVINE, CALIFORNIA*

**Koprowski, Donald J.** '42 '67 C.602 B.S. L.966 J.D.
V.P., Gen. Coun. & Secy., Kawasaki Motors Corp., U.S.A. (Pat.)
**Kornievsky, George M.**, (AV) ... '53 '78 C.770 B.A. L.1065 J.D. [G.M.Kornievsky]
*LANGUAGES: German.
*REPORTED CASES: In Re: Marriage of McCann (1996) 41 Cal. App. 4th 978.
*PRACTICE AREAS: Dissolution of Marriage; Support and Visitation; Pre-Nuptial Agreements; Appeals.

**Kornievsky, George M., A Professional Corporation, (AV)** BR
**18881 Von Karman Avenue, Suite 1260, 92612-1578**
**Telephone: 714-724-0888 Fax: 714-752-7035**
**Email: gmkapc@quick.com**
**George M. Kornievsky (Certified Specialist, Family Law, The State Bar of California Board of Legal Specialization).**
**Practice limited to Family Law.**

*See Professional Biographies, IRVINE, CALIFORNIA*

Kott, Alison Mellor ... '56 '82 C.169 B.A. L.1137 J.D. Sr. Atty., F.D.I.C.
Kracht, Dominic ... '63 '89 C.999 B.S. L.259 J.D. 2532 Dupont Dr.
**Kraemer, Steven Joseph** ... '66 '92 C.112 B.A. L.800 J.D. [A Rus,M.W.&S.]
*PRACTICE AREAS: Complex Litigation; Creditors Rights Law; Bankruptcy Law.
Kraetzer, Priscilla C., (BV) ... '49 '74 C.112 B.A. L.426 J.D. [Tovstein&K.]
**Kramer, Kenneth S.** ... '57 '82 C.659 B.A. L.800 J.D. [Paone,C.M.&W.]
*PRACTICE AREAS: Real Property Transactions and Finance; Commercial Leasing.
**Kramer, Paul D.** ... '63 '90 C.112 B.A. L.426 J.D. [A Jennings&H.]
*PRACTICE AREAS: Commercial and Construction Litigation; Surety, Contract and Real Property Litigation.
Kramer, Stacy J. ... '66 '92 C.112 B.A L.1049 J.D. 7700 Irvine Center Dr., #700
Kramer, Valerie L. ... '56 '84 C.1075 B.A. L.950 J.D. 18401 Von Karman Ave.
**Kranz, Frederick H.**, (BV) ... '47 '72 C.426 B.A. L.1068 J.D. [Katten M.&Z.]
*PRACTICE AREAS: Commercial and High-Tech Litigation.
**Kraus, Roberta A.** ... '59 '85 C.1109 B.A. L.1137 J.D. [A Genson,E.C.&W.]
**Krause, Charles F.**, (AV⊙) '31 '61 C.879 B.A. L.705 J.D.
(adm. in NY; not adm. in CA) [Speiser,K.M.&C.]⊙
**Kreditor, Eoin L.** ... '65 '90 C&L.800 B.A., J.D. [A Katten M.&Z.]
*PRACTICE AREAS: Business Litigation; Real Estate Litigation.
Kremer, J. W. ... '49 '83 C.1044 B.A. L.1137 J.D. 15202 Nantes Cir.
**Kress, Julia E.** ... '66 '91 C.424 B.B.A. L.426 J.D. [A Brown,P.H.&V.]
*SPECIAL AGENCIES: California Air Resources Board, South Coast Air Quality Management District; Department of Toxic Substances Control; State Water Quality Control Board; Office of Health Hazard Assessment; Cal-OSHA and The U.S. Environmental Protection Agency.
*PRACTICE AREAS: Environmental and Business Litigation; Environmental Compliance.
**Kring, Kyle D.** ... '60 '86 C.112 B.A. L.426 J.D. [Kring&B.]
*PRACTICE AREAS: Civil and Business Litigation; Personal Injury Defense; Construction Defect; Insurance Fraud.

**Kring & Brown**
**38 Corporate Park, Suite 200, P.O. Box 19782, 92623-9782⊙**
**Telephone: 714-261-7895 Telecopier: 714-261-7545**
**Members of Firm: Kyle D. Kring; Gregory G. Brown; Stuart A. Smith; Nicole Whyte; Keith G. Bremer;—Louis T. Antosh, Jr.; Russell R. Arens; Kenneth W. Chung; Anna M. D'Alessandro; Jeffrey D. Farrow; Robert B. Gibson; Nina D. Klawunder; Jeffrey A. Lake; Benjamin T. Ladinig; Jeffrey R. Marquart; Michelle McWhorter (Resident, Irvine Office); Raymond Meyer, Jr.; Robert Mougin; Mary Ann Noiroux; Rina K. Rai; Laurie Rau; Brent Reden; Paul A. Rianda; Joseph A. Robertson; Dirk E. Silva; Craig J. Silver; Paul N. Stam; Kere K. Tickner; Tonia Tompkins; Jon H. Van De Grift.**
**General Civil and Commercial Trial Practice in all State and Federal Courts, Construction, General Business, Corporate, Real Estate, Estate Planning, Insurance, Immigration.**
**Riverside, California Office: 5225 Canyon Crest Drive, Building 100, Suite 166. Telephone: 909-684-0332. Fax: 909-684-4376.**
**San Diego, California Office: 225 Broadway, Suite 2100. Telephone: 619-236-0668. Fax: 619-236-0809.**

*See Professional Biographies, IRVINE, CALIFORNIA*

**Kruger, Gilbert N.**, (AV) ... '41 '67 C.102 B.S. L.1065 LL.B. [Snell&W.]
*PRACTICE AREAS: Corporate Law; Securities Law; Emerging Business Law; Technology Law.
Kukta, Stephen H. ... '65 '91 C.98 B.A. L.426 J.D. 2 Park Plaza
Kunath, John F., Jr. ... '44 '72 C&L.426 B.A., J.D. 7700 Irvine Ctr. Dr.
**Kupferman, Kurt**, (BV) ... '22 '86 C.570 B.S. L.1137 J.D. [C Andrade&M.]
*LANGUAGES: German.
*PRACTICE AREAS: Criminal Law; Family Law; Business Law.

**Kurtz, Donald R. '55 '80 C.897 B.A. L.629 J.D.**
**8001 Irvine Center Drive, Suite 1140, 92718**
**Telephone: 714-753-8122 Facsimile: 714-753-8120**
***PRACTICE AREAS: Trusts and Estates; Corporate Law; Taxation Law; Bankruptcy.**
**—Gregory J. Anderson.**
**Business Law, Corporate Law, Estate Planning, Taxation, Bankruptcy.**

*See Professional Biographies, IRVINE, CALIFORNIA*

**LaBelle, Lance A.** ... '55 '82 C.494 B.A. L.300 J.D. [Berger,K.S.M.F.S.&G.]
**Labriola, Ronald T.** ... '65 '93 C.674 B.S.E. L.426 J.D. [A Snell&W.]
*PRACTICE AREAS: Product Liability Litigation.
**LaCount, Stephen H.** ... '50 '77 C.94 B.A. L.564 J.D. [Arter&H.]
*PRACTICE AREAS: Commercial Transactions; Business Law; Computer and Technology; Proprietary Rights; Licensing.
**Ladinig, Benjamin T.** ... '70 '96 C.112 B.A. L.809 J.D. [A Kring&B.]
Lamb, Steven A. ... '58 '87 C.154 B.A. L.800 J.D. 19900 MacArthur Blvd.
Lambert, Howard R. ... '29 '73 C.472 B.S. L.1068 J.D. Sr. Pat. Atty., Allergan, Inc. (Pat.)
**Lane, Gregory S.** ... '62 '89 C.112 B.S. L.990 J.D. [A Smith,S.D.P.&W.]

**Lane, William G. '37 '69 C.112 B.A. L.284 J.D.**
**18400 Von Karman Avenue Suite 500, 92715**
**Telephone: 714-474-9961 Fax: 714-474-9973**
***PRACTICE AREAS: Patents; Trademark Litigation; Intellectual Property.**
**Intellectual Property Law.**

*See Professional Biographies, IRVINE, CALIFORNIA*

Langford, Karin H. Ota ... '64 '91 C.112 B.A. L.1065 J.D. 1920 Main St. Ste. 800
Langmuir-Logan, Garfield ... '54 '79 C.800 B.S. L.426 J.D. 2532 Dupont Dr.
**Lanham, Kristen Welles** ... '67 '92 C.112 B.A. L.1148 J.D. [A Aldrich&B.]
*LANGUAGES: Spanish.
*PRACTICE AREAS: Corporate Banking; Business Litigation.
**Lanphere, Michael A.** ... '59 '85 C.36 B.S. L.426 J.D. [Tredway,L.&D.]
*PRACTICE AREAS: Banking Law; Civil Litigation.

CAA133P

CALIFORNIA—IRVINE MARTINDALE-HUBBELL LAW DIRECTORY 1997

Lans, Douglas ... '37 '64 C.112 A.B. L.1068 J.D. Reliance Ins. Co.
**Lanza, Anthony L.** ... '64 '91 C.602 B.A. L.1065 J.D. [Ⓐ Corbett&S.]
Larsen, Joseph Y., Jr. '21 '52 C&L.878 B.S., J.D.
(adm. in UT; not adm. in CA) 4 Mann St.‡
Larson, Chris ... '53 '80 C.188 B.A. L.1137 J.D. F.D.I.C.
**La Scalla, Paul B.** ... '71 '96 C.763 B.B.A. L.426 J.D. [Ⓐ Palmieri,T.W.W.&W.]
*PRACTICE AREAS: Products Liability; Business Litigation; Eminent Domain.
Lasezkay, George M. ... '51 '86 C.1044 B.S. L.800 J.D. Sr. Atty., Allergan, Inc.
**Lasman, Edwin I.**, (AV) ... '55 '82 C.112 B.A. L.1068 J.D. [Ⓒ Case,K.B.&W.]⊙
*LANGUAGES: French.
*PRACTICE AREAS: Corporate Law; Real Estate; Civil Litigation.
**La Tempa, Catherine K.** ... '55 '92 C.763 B.A. L.426 J.D. [Ⓐ Berger,K.S.M.F.S.&G.]
Lau, Elise K. Y. '62 '93 C.312 B.B.A. L.1065 J.D.
(adm. in HI; not adm. in CA) 2532 Dupont Dr.
**Laubscher, Barry R.**, (AV) ... '46 '72 C.363 B.S. L.188 J.D. [Grant&L.]
*PRACTICE AREAS: Litigation; Antitrust.

**Laughlin, Falbo, Levy & Moresi LLP, (AV)**
**A Partnership including Professional Corporations**
**3 Park Plaza, Suite 1400, P.O. Box 17659, 92713⊙**
**Telephone: 714-251-0120 Fax: 714-251-0125**
**Email: lflm@lflm.com URL: http://lflm.com/**
**Gerald R. Burke; Jeffrey M. Adelson;—Priscilla W. LLoyd; Stephanie H. Proffitt; Alice O. Burden; Manuel Garcia; Cynthia J. Brown; Timothy G. Keller; Mary-Cay Gallagher; Davil R. Vasquez.**
**General Civil and Trial Practice. Workers' Compensation Defense (State and Federal), Labor Relations and Employment Discrimination.**
**San Francisco, California Office: Two Embarcadero Center, Fifth Floor. Telephone: 415-781-6676. Fax: 415-781-6823.**
**Sacramento, California Office: 106 K Street - Second Floor. Telephone: 916-441-6045. Fax: 916-441-7067.**
**Redding, California Office: 930 Executive Way, Second Floor. Telephone: 916-222-0268. Fax: 916-222-5705.**
**Pasadena, California Office: 200 South Los Robles, Suite 500. Telephone: 818-568-9700. Fax: 818-568-3905.**
**Walnut Creek, California Office: 100 Pringle Avenue, Suite 630. Telephone: 510-210-0210. Fax: 510-210-0105.**
**San Jose, California Office: 1570 The Alameda, Suite 100. Telephone: 408-286-8801. Fax: 408-286-1935.**

***See Professional Biographies, IRVINE, CALIFORNIA***

Lavin, James R. ... '52 '82 C.684 B.A. L.61 J.D. Sr. Coun., Insco Ins. Servs., Inc.
Law, R. Zebulon ... '63 '88 C.415 B.A. L.904 J.D. 2532 Dupont Dr.
**Layman, Wilbur D.**, (AV) ... '31 '60 C.860 A.B. L.1066 J.D. [Bryan C.]

**Layman, Jones & Dye**
**(See Bryan Cave LLP)**

Leanders, Christopher J. ... '54 '81 C.800 B.S. L.426 J.D. 5 Park Plaza
**Leanders, Heidi Knapp**, (BV) ... '55 '80 C.800 B.S. L.1068 J.D. [Ⓒ Amante]
*PRACTICE AREAS: Bankruptcy-Debtors; Creditors; Creditors Committees; Trustee Representation; Civil and Bankruptcy Litigation.
Leatherby, Russell E. '53 '79 C.169 B.A. L.464 J.D.
Pres., COO & Gen. Coun., Unicare Fin. Corp.
**Leckie, Bernard A.**, (AV) ... '32 '60 C&L.800 B.S., LL.B. [Meserve,M.&H.]
**Lee, Karen J.** ... '44 '81 C.494 B.A.B.S. L.426 J.D. [Ⓒ Morrison&F.]
*PRACTICE AREAS: Land Use and Entitlement Litigation; Business Litigation.
**Lee, Raymond A.**, (AV) ... '51 '81 C.472 B.A. L.260 J.D. [Maher,L.&G.]
*PRACTICE AREAS: Corporate Law; Corporate (Corporation) Financing Law; Business Acquisitions Law; Real Estate (Property) Law.
Leguizamon, Martha P. ... '51 '83 C.426 B.A. L.800 J.D. [Cone,C.&K.]
Lehr, John F., Jr., (AV) ... '52 '78 C.154 B.A. L.880 J.D. 19100 Von Karman Ave.
Lehrfeld, Richard E. ... '42 '72 C.1060 B.A. L.464 J.D. 30 Diamante
**Lehrman, Jeffrey B.** ... '63 '89 C.1044 B.S. L.94 J.D. [Ⓐ Berger,K.S.M.F.S.&G.]
**Leibel, Dennis R.** '44 '70 C.102 B.S. L.1009 J.D.
(adm. in NY; not adm. in CA) Sr. V.P., AST Resch., Inc.
**Leifer, Michael H.** ... '62 '88 C.112 B.A. L.426 J.D. [Palmieri,T.W.W.&W.]
*PRACTICE AREAS: Real Estate Litigation; Business Litigation; Condemnation; Public Agency.
**Leitch, Andrew V.** ... '64 '89 C.668 B.A. L.990 J.D. [Ⓐ Jackson,D.&P.]
*PRACTICE AREAS: Real Estate; Corporate; Business Transactions.
Leiter, Carl H. '39 '65 C&L.477 B.B.A., LL.B.
(adm. in MI; not adm. in CA) 5 White Birch‡
Leonhardt, Harry J. '56 '83
C.999 B.Sc. L.800 J.D. Asst. Gen. Coun., Europe, Allergan, Inc.
**Lespier, Manfredo E.** ... '58 '90 C.112 B.A. L.1137 J.D. [Morrison&L.]
*LANGUAGES: Spanish.
*PRACTICE AREAS: Commercial Litigation; Bankruptcy Law (Creditors); Personal Injury; Civil Litigation; Banking Litigation.
**Lesser, David I.** ... '53 '79 C.696 B.A. L.178 J.D. [Feder,G.&S.]
**Leverett, John M.** ... '59 '93 C.112 B.S. L.423 J.D. [Ⓐ Pinto&D.]
**Lewis, Lawrence D., (P.C.)**, (AV) ... '46 '72 C.112 A.B. L.1066 J.D. [Allen,M.L.G.&M.]
*PRACTICE AREAS: Litigation.
**Liberto, Shelley M.** ... '53 '87 C.112 B.A. L.464 J.D. [Ⓒ Callahan&B.]
*LANGUAGES: Arabic and French.
*PRACTICE AREAS: Business Litigation; Computers and Software; Insurance Coverage; Legal Malpractices; Real Estate.
**Lichman, Barbara E.** ... '46 '88 C.1036 B.A. L.800 J.D. [Chevalier,A.&L.]
*PRACTICE AREAS: Aviation and Airport Access Regulation; Commercial Litigation; Environmental.
Lindquist, Mary Lee, (BV) ... '51 '78 C&L.1049 B.A., J.D. 111 Pacifica
**Lipman, Paul J.** ... '61 '91 C.112 B.A. L.426 J.D. [Ⓐ Wesierski&Z.]
*PRACTICE AREAS: Premises Liability; General Civil Trials and Appeals; Business Litigation; Toxic Torts; Insurance Defense Law.
**Lippert, Timothy J.** ... '65 '92 C.112 B.A. L.990 J.D. [Ⓐ Pivo&H.]
*PRACTICE AREAS: Medical Malpractice.
**Lister, John R.** ... '56 '82 C.112 B.A. L.1066 J.D. [Palmieri,T.W.W.&W.]
*PRACTICE AREAS: Litigation.
**Lister, Sonia A.** ... '67 '92 C.112 B.A. L.1067 J.D. [Ⓐ Morrison&F.]
**Livingston, Daniel M.** ... '57 '82 C.813 A.B. L.101 J.D. [Payne&F.]
*PRACTICE AREAS: Business; Construction Litigation.
Lloyd, Gregory M. ... '50 '77 C.112 B.A. L.1137 J.D. 2062 Business Ctr. Dr.
**LLoyd, Priscilla W.** ... '48 '79 C&L.831 A.B., J.D. [Ⓐ Laughlin,F.L.&M.]
*PRACTICE AREAS: Subrogation.
**Lobel, William N.**, (AV) ... '43 '69 C&L.472 B.B.A., J.D. [Lobel&O.]
*PRACTICE AREAS: Bankruptcy Law; Insolvency Law; Reorganization.

**Lobel & Opera, Professional Corporation, (AV)** BR
**Suite 1100, 19800 MacArthur Boulevard, P.O. Box 19588, 92713**
**Telephone: 714-476-7400 Fax: 714-476-7444**
**William N. Lobel; Robert E. Opera; Alan J. Friedman; Pamela Z. Karger; Cheryl A. Skigin; Tavi Claire Stanley; Metiner G. Kimel; Edward P. Christian; Robert J. Mrofka; Hamid R. Rafatjoo.**
**Bankruptcy, Insolvency, Corporate Reorganization and Commercial Litigation Matters.**

***See Professional Biographies, IRVINE, CALIFORNIA***

**Loewen, Robert W.**, (AV) ... '48 '75 C.668 B.A. L.809 J.D. [Gibson,D.&C.]
*PRACTICE AREAS: Business Litigation; Toxic Tort Litigation; Trade Secrets; Land Use and Real Estate Litigation; Insurance Coverage.
Loewenstein, Carol R. ... '50 '79 C.112 B.A. L.464 J.D. 11 Ramada‡

**Logan, Francis D., Jr.** ... '63 '92 C.228 B.A. L.800 J.D. [Ⓐ Nossaman,G.K.&E.]
*PRACTICE AREAS: Litigation.
**Logan, Michael J.**, (AV) ... '42 '73 C.800 B.S.F. L.809 J.D. [Ramsay&J.]
*PRACTICE AREAS: Insurance Defense and Coverage.
Loll, Robert A., (AV) ... '58 '85 C.1109 B.A. L.990 J.D. [Floratos,L.&D.]
**Lomenzo, Cristy G.** ... '70 '95 C.1109 B.A. L.1065 J.D. [Ⓐ Snell&W.]
*PRACTICE AREAS: Corporate and Securities Law; Real Estate and Commercial Finance.
**Long, Gary P.** ... '48 '79 C.668 B.A. L.1068 J.D. [Morrison&F.]
*PRACTICE AREAS: Real Estate; Financial Transactions; Financial Restructurings and Workouts.
**Long, Michael G.** ... '62 '87 C.276 B.A. [Watt,T.&H.]
*PRACTICE AREAS: Construction Law; Government Contracts; Surety Law.
**Losness, Charles W.** ... '50 '91 C.763 B.S. L.1137 J.D. [Ⓐ Turner&R.]
*PRACTICE AREAS: Construction Litigation; Eminent Domain/Condemnation Litigation; Real Estate Litigation.
**Lowe, Cary D.** ... '48 '74 C&L.800 B.A., J.D. [Ⓒ Paone,C.M.&W.]
*PRACTICE AREAS: Land Use Regulation; Real Estate; Environmental; Corporate; Nonprofit Organizations.
Lowry, Tracey L. ... '61 '89 C.800 B.A. L.426 J.D. 2 Park Plaza
Lubin, Howard G. ... '43 '74 C.1077 B.A. L.809 J.D. [H.G.Lubin]
Lubin, Howard G., Law Office of, A Professional Corp. ... 18400 Von Karman
**Lucas, Eric S.** ... '62 '89 C.701 B.S. Ch.E. L.347 J.D. Discovision Assocs. (Pat.)
*RESPONSIBILITIES: Patent Licensing; Patent Litigation; Patent Contracts; Patent Prosecution.
**Luckadoo, Carl P.** ... '54 '89 C.575 B.A. L.494 J.D. [Ⓐ Morrison&L.]
*PRACTICE AREAS: Real Estate Law; Creditors Bankruptcy Law; Banking Litigation; Corporate Law.
**Lund, Christopher G.** ... '62 '92 C.800 B.S. L.426 J.D. [Ⓐ Allen,M.L.G.&M.]
*PRACTICE AREAS: Real Estate Transactions.
**Lundberg, Leo E., Jr.** ... '55 '86 C.1253 B.S. L.426 J.D. [Ⓐ Gauntlett&Assoc.]
Lurner, Jefferey B. ... '55 '88 L.061 B.Proc. Jamboree Ctr., 1 Park Plz.
**Lustig, Michelle D.** ... '66 '92 C.112 B.A. L.426 J.D. [Ⓐ Gibson,D.&C.]
*PRACTICE AREAS: Corporations.
Lutz, G. Scott ... '63 '89 C.269 B.A. L.790 J.D. 3333 Michelson Dr.
**Lykos, Cosmas N.** ... '68 '94 C.216 B.A. L.228 J.D. [Ⓐ Gibson,D.&C.]
*PRACTICE AREAS: Corporate Law.
**Lyman, Patricia A. Jones** '49 '80 C.454 B.S. L.1068 J.D.
Corp. V.P., Asst. Gen. Coun. & Asst. Secy., Mission Energy Co.
**Lynch, Michele L.** ... '68 '93 C.112 B.A. L.1065 J.D. [Ⓐ Ross,D.&M.]
Lynn, John H. ... '— '76 C.861 B.S.E.E. L.365 J.D. 1920 Main St. (Pat.)
Lyons, Warren R. ... '45 '72 C&L.813 A.B., J.D. Pres., Avco Fin. Servs., Inc.
**MacLean, Kurt A.**, (AV) '53 '82
C.1042 B.A. L.1068 J.D. [Oppenheimer P.S.] (Pat.) (⊙Los Angeles)
Macy, Wendy G. '67 '92 C&L.309 A.B., J.D.
(adm. in PA; not adm. in CA) 5 Park Plaza‡
**Madole, Juanita M.** ... '49 '74 C.861 B.S. L.326 J.D. [Speiser,K.M.&C.]
*PRACTICE AREAS: Aviation Accidents; International Aviation Law; Personal Injury and Wrongful Death Litigation; Mass Disaster Litigation; Products Liability.
**Magill, Thomas D.** ... '50 '76 C.216 B.A. L.228 J.D. [Gibson,D.&C.]
*PRACTICE AREAS: Mergers, Acquisitions and Divestitures; Securities; Corporate Law.
**Mahacek, Jim P.** ... '47 '77 C.793 B.A. L.990 J.D. [Ⓐ Callahan&B.]
*PRACTICE AREAS: Administrative Law; Price Control Regulation; Civil Litigation; Appellate Practice.
**Mahaffa, Walt D.** ... '54 '80 C.426 B.A. L.990 J.D. [Ⓒ Callahan&B.]⊙
*PRACTICE AREAS: Litigation; Business Law; Real Estate Law.
Mahaffey, Douglas L. ... '61 '86 C.1 B.B.A. L.990 J.D. 2010 Main St.
**Mahan, Robert G.** ... '39 '80 C.800 B.S. L.1137 J.D. [Ⓒ Brown,P.H.&V.]
**Maher, Cynthia R.** ... '58 '82 C.112 B.A. L.426 J.D. [Maher,L.&G.]
*PRACTICE AREAS: Environmental Law; Real Estate Litigation; Land Use; Construction Litigation; Labor Law.
**Maher, Michael K.**, (AV) ... '49 '75 C.201 B.A. L.426 J.D. [Maher,L.&G.]
*PRACTICE AREAS: Business Law; Civil Practice; Employment Law; Insurance; General Practice.

**Maher, Lee & Goddard, LLP, (AV)** BR
**18500 Von Karman Avenue, Suite 700, 92715**
**Telephone: 714-721-7555 Facsimile: 714-721-7444**
**Michael K. Maher; Raymond A. Lee; William A. Goddard, IV; Cynthia R. Maher; Sherman O. Halstead, Jr.; Maureen M. Alpin.**
**General Civil and Business Practice, Environmental Law, Employment Law, Insurance Coverage, Trial and Appellate Practice.**

***See Professional Biographies, IRVINE, CALIFORNIA***

Mahony, Richard Vincent ... '56 '85 C.1109 B.A. L.1137 J.D. 18201 Von Karman Ave.
**Mahr, Thomas S.** ... '54 '81 C&L.472 B.M., J.D. [Katten M.&Z.] (⊙L.A.)
*PRACTICE AREAS: Business, Entertainment and Commercial Litigation.

**Mailly, Guy E. '54 '83 C.145 A.B. L.846 J.D.**
**7700 Irvine Center Drive, 92618**
**Telephone: 714-753-1676**
**General Practice.**

***See Professional Biographies, IRVINE, CALIFORNIA***

**Maizel, Mark N.** ... '65 '91 C.112 B.S. L.464 J.D. [Ⓐ Baker,S.&K.]
**Malcolm, Thomas R.**, (AV) ... '39 '66 C.112 A.B. L.1065 LL.B. [Jones,D.R.&P.]
**Malcolm, William G., (A Professional Corporation)** '59 '87
C&L.770 B.S.C., J.D. [Malcolm,C.&H.]
*PRACTICE AREAS: Bankruptcy; Reorganization; Creditors Rights; Bankruptcy Court Litigation.

**Malcolm, Cisneros & Houser**
**A Partnership including a Professional Corporation**
**Jamboree Center, 5 Park Plaza, Suite 830, 92714⊙**
**Telephone: 714-252-9400 Telecopier: 714-252-1032**
**Members of Firm: William G. Malcolm (A Professional Corporation); Arturo M. Cisneros; Eric D. Houser. Associates: Shawn R. Miller; Michael R. Brooks; Yvonne Ramirez; Donna A. Golem; Zachary J. Zaharek; Kushal S. Bhakta.**
**Commercial and Business Litigation in the Bankruptcy, District and State Courts. Creditors' Rights and Trustee Representation.**
**San Bernardino, California Office: 290 North "D" Street, Suite 723. 92401. Telephone: 909-884-6882. Fax: 909-884-8189.**

***See Professional Biographies, IRVINE, CALIFORNIA***

**Maleki, Joseph A.** ... '69 '95 C.1042 B.S. L.1137 J.D. [Tredway,L.&D.]
*PRACTICE AREAS: Civil Litigation.
**Mall, William J., III** ... '65 '90 C.152 B.A. L.831 J.D. [Ⓐ Pivo&H.]
*PRACTICE AREAS: Medical Malpractice.
**Mallory, Frank L.**, (AV) ... '20 '48 C&L.813 A.B., LL.B. [Ⓒ Gibson,D.&C.]
Maloof, John J. ... '49 '74 C.154 B.A. L.61 J.D. Exec. V.P. & Coun., Kline Develop. Co.
**Malpass, T. Edward**, (BV) ... '53 '77 C&L.174 B.A., J.D. [Malpass&G.]
*PRACTICE AREAS: Bankruptcy; Business and Commercial Litigation.

**Malpass & Gentile, (BV)**
**19800 MacArthur Boulevard Suite 350, 92715**
**Telephone: 714-553-2000 Facsimile: 714-553-2080**
**Members of Firm: T. Edward Malpass (Certified Specialist, Personal and Small Business Bankruptcy Law, The State Bar of California Board of Legal Specialization); Susan E. Gentile; Melissa C. Alexander.**
**Bankruptcy, Corporate Reorganization, Commercial, Banking and Business Law. Business, Real Estate and Bankruptcy Litigation and Appeals.**

***See Professional Biographies, IRVINE, CALIFORNIA***

Manly, John C., IV ... '64 '90 C.800 B.A. L.990 J.D. [Ⓐ Morgan&W.]

Mann, John M. ....................'48 '79 C.1183 B.A. L.1066 J.D. Sr. Atty., Allergan, Inc.

**Manning, Marder & Wolfe, (AV)**
**Suite 1450, 19800 MacArthur Boulevard, 92715⊙**
**Telephone: 714-556-0552**
**Email: rfs@mmw.com URL: http://www.mmw.com**
**Members of Firm: Lawrence D. Esten. Associate: Brian T. Moss; John Revelli; G. Andrew Nagle.**
**Insurance Defense, Police Civil Liability, General Civil Litigation, Private Security Litigation, Corporate Law, Business Formation and Securities Offerings, Employment Litigation, Entertainment Law, Workers' Compensation Defense, Professional Liability (Medical Malpractice, Legal Malpractice, Construction Malpractice), Appellate Law, Health Law, Bad Faith, Insurance Coverage, Loss Prevention and Risk Management.**
**Los Angeles, California Office: 45th Floor at First Interstate Tower, 707 Wilshire Boulevard. Telephone: 213-624-6900. Fax: 213-624-6999.**
**San Diego, California Office: 964 Fifth Avenue, Suite 214. Telephone: 619-699-5933.**
***See Professional Biographies, IRVINE, CALIFORNIA***

**Mannisto, Jeffrey** .................'66 '96 C.846 B.B.A L.500 J.D. [Ⓐ Allen,M.L.G.&M.]
*PRACTICE AREAS: Taxation, Estate Planning and Business Organization.
Manuele, Robert L. '32 '54 C&L.107 J.D.
V.P. & Chf. Underwriting Coun., World Title Co.
**Marcopulos, Stathi George** ..............'61 '87 C.813 B.A. L.1068 J.D. [Ⓐ Cox,C.&N.]
*PRACTICE AREAS: Real Property Law; Leasing; Real Estate Finance Law.
**Marcus, Fred J.**, (AV) .................'51 '81 C.999 B.A. L.426 J.D. [Freeman,F.&S.]⊙
*PRACTICE AREAS: Transactional Business; Tax Exempt Organizations; Estate Planning Law.
**Marion, David K.** ..........................'65 '93 C.656 B.A. L.117 J.D. [Ⓐ Arter&H.]
*PRACTICE AREAS: Commercial Litigation.
**Marken, Roger Erik**, (AV) '44 '72 C.911 B.S. L.809 J.D.
[Ives,K.&D.] (⊙Los Angeles)
**Marken, Steven S.** ..............................'65 '91 C.36 B.S. L.809 J.D. [Ⓐ Ives,K.&D.]
**Marking, John R.** ......................'67 '94 C.112 B.A. L.990 J.D. [Ⓐ Stevens,K.A.&H.]
*PRACTICE AREAS: Construction Defect; Personal Injury.
**Marks, Jeffrey Scott** ..........................'69 '95 C.112 B.A. L.426 J.D. [Ⓐ Snell&W.]
*PRACTICE AREAS: Litigation.
Marlett, Orville L. ....................'17 '60 C.966 A.B. L.800 J.D. 17910 Skypark Circle‡
**Marnell, Mark F.** ..............'53 '81 C.770 B.A. L.1066 J.D. [Ⓐ Berger,K.S.M.F.S.&G.]
**Marquart, Jeffrey R.** ......................'61 '87 C.46 B.S.M.E. L.602 J.D. [Ⓐ Kring&B.]
*LANGUAGES: German.
*PRACTICE AREAS: Civil Litigation; Business Litigation; Personal Injury; Products Liability; Medical Malpractice.
Marsh, Lindell L., (AV) .................'40 '67 C.112 A.B. L.1065 LL.B. [Siemon,L.&M.]
Marshall, Douglas E., (BV) ......................................'36 '66 C.112 A.B. L.1065 J.D. F.D.I.C.
**Marshall, Ellen R.**, (AV) ....................'49 '75 C.976 A.B. L.309 J.D. [Morrison&F.]
*PRACTICE AREAS: Corporate Finance; Financial Services and Transactions; Employee Benefit Plans.
Martin, Michael G. ..............'56 '84 C.347 A.B. L.1218 J.D. 18301 Von Karman Ave.
Martin, Richard A. ..................'61 '87 C.112 B.A. L.426 J.D. 18400 Von Karman Ave.
**Martin, Ronald B.**, (BV) ............'52 '78 C.112 B.A. L.426 J.D. [Kasdan,S.M.E.&M.]
*PRACTICE AREAS: Construction Defect Litigation; Real Estate Law.

**Martinez, Ralph G. '53 '78 C.1232 B.A. L.61 J.D.**
**8001 Irvine Center Drive, #1550, 92618**
**Telephone: 714-450-0123 Fax: 714-753-8069**
***PRACTICE AREAS: Business Litigation; Real Estate Litigation; Personal Injury.**
**Business Litigation, Real Estate Litigation and Personal Injury.**
***See Professional Biographies, IRVINE, CALIFORNIA***

**Mastan, David F.** .........................'63 '91 C.112 B.A. L.426 J.D. [Ⓐ Wesierski&Z.]
*PRACTICE AREAS: Civil Litigation.
Mathena, Larry ..........................'57 '80 C.645 B.B.A. L.665 J.D. 2532 Dupont Dr.
Matlaf, Michael J. ..........................'43 '72 C.1077 B.A. L.61 J.D. 4199 Campus Dr.
**Mattson, Robert M., Jr.**, (AV) ..............'48 '75 C.813 A.B. L.597 J.D. [Morrison&F.]
*PRACTICE AREAS: Corporate Finance; Securities.

**Mauthe, Andrew K. '43 '82 C.112 A.B. L.800 J.D.**
**18500 Von Karman, Suite 700, 92612-0504**
**Telephone: 714-833-7035 Fax: 714-721-7444**
**Email: amauthe@aol.com**
**Bankruptcy and Creditors Rights, Insolvency and Reorganization.**
***See Professional Biographies, IRVINE, CALIFORNIA***

Maxwell, Clyde R., (AV) .............'21 '45 C&L.911 B.S., LL.B. 2041 Business Ctr. Dr.
**May, Gordon G.** ..........................'66 '93 C.990 B.A. L.426 J.D. [Ⓐ Grant&L.]
*PRACTICE AREAS: Litigation.
Mayberry, David P. ..............'55 '83 C.658 B.S. L.1137 J.D. 18500 Von Karman Ave.
**Maynard, Kimberly A.** ...................'71 '96 C.112 B.A. L.1188 J.D. [Ⓐ Baker,S.&K.]
Maynard, Philip C., (AV) '54 '80 C.1109 B.A. L.426 J.D.
V.P., Secy. & Gen. Coun., National Educ. Corp.
**Mazda, Mark N.** .........................'68 '95 C.101 B.A. L.178 J.D. [Ⓐ Gibson,D.&C.]
*LANGUAGES: Portuguese.
**Mc Bride, Robert C.** ......................'61 '91 C.549 B.A. L.940 J.D. [Ⓐ Baker,S.&K.]
McCabe, Joseph V. '59 '91
Asst. V.P. & Assoc. Coun., Fidelity National Title Insurance Co.
McCaffrey, Michael D., (AV) ..........'46 '74 C.112 B.S. L.208 J.D. 4 Park Plz., 16th Fl.
McCall, Patrick A., (BV) .............'58 '83 C.1042 B.S. L.1137 J.D. 8001 Irvine Ctr. Dr.
McCann, Dean M. ....................'27 '55 C.800 B.S. L.1065 LL.B. 2525 Dupont Drive
McCarrel, Daniel J. ....................'60 '88 C.373 B.A. L.904 J.D. Waste Mgmt., Inc.
**McClanathan, Mark P.**, (AV) ..............'52 '77 C.966 B.B.A. L.800 J.D. [Cox,C.&N.]
*PRACTICE AREAS: Real Property Law; Corporate Law; Taxation Law.
**McConnell, Heather A.** ..................'70 '96 C.112 B.A. L.426 J.D. [Ⓐ Jones,D.R.&P.]
McDonald, Laurence D. ..................'49 '76 C.1044 B.A. L.809 J.D. 2603 Main St.
**McDonald, Randy**, (AV) .......................'49 '76 C.112 B.A. L.228 J.D. [Bainbridge]
*PRACTICE AREAS: General Business; Corporate and Partnerships; Real Estate; Real Estate and Corporate Finance; Technology Licensing.
**McEachran, Anne M.** .....................'66 '93 C.1042 B.S. L.940 J.D. [Ⓐ Aldrich&B.]
**McGinley, Joseph B.** .....................'55 '82 C&L.800 A.B., J.D. [Ⓐ Meserve,M.&H.]
**McGlinn, Lynnda A.** .........................'67 '92 C.800 B.S. L.426 J.D. [Ⓐ Pinto&D.]
**McGuire, Mark R.** ...........................'64 '90 C.112 B.A. L.813 J.D. [Hewitt&M.]
*PRACTICE AREAS: Real Estate Law; Land Use Law; Environmental Law.
**McGuire, Michael J.** ................'59 '86 C.602 B.A. L.809 J.D. [Ⓐ Genson,E.C.&W.]
**McHolm, Steven A.**, (AV) ............'49 '75 C.112 B.A. L.426 J.D. [Paone,C.M.&W.]
*PRACTICE AREAS: Real Property Transactions and Finance; Commercial Leasing.
**McIntyre, Caroline** .........................'66 '92 C.881 B.A. L.602 J.D. [Ⓐ Smith,B.&D.]
*LANGUAGES: Spanish.
*PRACTICE AREAS: Business Litigation.
**McIntyre, R. Donald**, (AV) ........'49 '75 C.112 B.A. L.1068 J.D. [Kasdan,S.M.E.&M.]
*PRACTICE AREAS: Real Estate Law; Construction; Real Property Tax and Assessment Appeals.
**McKenna, Charles A., Jr.**, (AV) ..........'38 '74 C.436 A.B. L.893 J.D. [McKenna&S.]
*PRACTICE AREAS: Real Estate; Real Estate Finance.
McKenna, Dina M. ........'61 '89 C.1042 B.A. L.800 J.D. 2600 Michelson Dr., Ste., 1000

**McKenna & Stahl, (AV) BB**
**2603 Main Street, Suite 1010, 92614-6232**
**Telephone: 714-752-2800 Facsimile: 714-752-6723**
**Charles A. McKenna, Jr.; Harry S. Stahl. Of Counsel: Christopher E. Call.**

(This Listing Continued)

**McKenna & Stahl (Continued)**

**Corporations, Corporate Finance And Securities, Real Estate, Real Estate Finance, Land Use, Partnerships, Limited Liability Companies and Taxation.**
***See Professional Biographies, IRVINE, CALIFORNIA***

McKenney, Larry B. ..............................'60 '88 C.871 B.S. L.846 J.D. 2100 E. Main St.
**McKinney, Denise L.** ..............................'65 '90 C.1097 B.A. L.1066 J.D. [Grant&L.]
*PRACTICE AREAS: Litigation.
**McKitterick, Gary S.** ..................'58 '84 C.813 B.A. L.426 J.D. [Allen,M.L.G.&M.]
*PRACTICE AREAS: Real Estate.
McKnight, Kathleen A. .......................'52 '77 C.813 B.A. L.800 J.D. 19 Cedar Ridge
**McMillen, Joseph Stephen** ...............'68 '94 C.112 B.A. L.1049 J.D. [Ⓐ Kirtland&P.]
**McNamara, Stephen D.** .........................'54 '87 C.763 B.A. L.61 J.D. [Fiore,W.R.&P.]
**McNamara, Valerie L.** ..........................'60 '86 C.112 A.B. L.1065 J.D. [Ⓐ Payne&F.]
*PRACTICE AREAS: Employment Law; Labor Law.
**McSwain, Valerie** ..........................'— '95 C.911 B.A. L.112 J.D. [Ⓐ Stevens,K.A.&H.]
**McWhorter, Michelle** ...........................'65 '92 C.549 B.A. L.464 J.D. [Ⓐ Kring&B.]
*PRACTICE AREAS: Construction Defect Defense; Personal Injury Defense.
**Mears, Christopher B.**, (AV) ..................'51 '82 C.1109 B.A. L.1137 J.D. [C.B.Mears]

**Mears, Christopher B., A P.C., (AV) BB**
**Old Town Irvine, 14988 Sand Canyon Avenue, Suite 1-8, 92618**
**Telephone: 714-551-2250 Fax: 714-551-0887**
**Email: CMEARS1031@AOL.COM**
**Christopher B. Mears.**
**General Tort Litigation. Medical and Legal Malpractice, Insurance, Negligence, Civil Rights, Personal Injury, Government, Products Liability and Wrongful Termination.**
***See Professional Biographies, IRVINE, CALIFORNIA***

Meedon, Carol L. ...................'64 '90 C.147 B.A. L.770 J.D. 19900 MacArthur Blvd.
**Melious, Jean O.** ........................'57 '84 C.732 B.A. L.309 J.D. [Ⓒ Nossaman,G.K.&E.]
*PRACTICE AREAS: Land Use Law; Environmental Law.
Mellor, James R., Jr. .........................................'54 '82 C.800 B.S. L.426 J.D. [Toledano&W.]
**Mersel, H. Mark** ...................................'62 '87 C.659 B.S. L.1065 J.D. [Ⓐ Morrison&F.]
**Meserve, J. Robert**, (AV) ..............'16 '42 C.112 A.B. L.1065 J.D. [Ⓒ Meserve,M.&H.]

**Meserve, Mumper & Hughes, (AV) BB**
**A Partnership**
**2301 Dupont Drive, Suite 410, 92612⊙**
**Telephone: 714-474-8995 Telecopier: 714-975-1065**
**Email: mmhir@ix.netcom.com**
**Members of Firm: Edwin A. Meserve (1863-1955); Shirley E. Meserve (1889-1959); Hewlings Mumper (1889-1968); Clifford E. Hughes (1894-1981); Bernard A. Leckie; David R. Eichten; Timothy A. Gravitt; E. Avery Crary; Lisa A. Roquemore. Of Counsel: J. Robert Meserve; Gary V. Spencer. Associates: Joseph B. McGinley; Wendy C. Satuloff.**
**General Civil and Trial Practice in all State and Federal Courts. Banking, Corporate, Real Estate, Labor, Life Insurance, Probate, Estate Planning, Family Law and Bankruptcy.**
**Los Angeles, California Office: 555 South Flower Street, 18th Floor. Telephone: 213-620-0300. Telecopier: 213-625-1930.**
**San Diego, California Office: 701 "B" Street, Suite 1080. Telephone: 619-237-0500. Telecopier: 619-237-0073.**
***See Professional Biographies, IRVINE, CALIFORNIA***

**Meuers, Dressler & Keaton, LLP**
**17620 Fitch Street, 92614⊙**
**Telephone: 714-260-6665 Fax: 714-260-6666**
**Donald G. Dressler; Douglas B. Kerr.**
**Perishable Agricultural Commodities Act, Agricultural Law, Bankruptcy and Creditors' Rights, Commercial Law and Litigation, Employment Law.**
**Naples, Florida Office: 2590 Golden Gate Parkway, Suite 109. telephone: 941-649-6100. Fax: 941-649-5414.**
***See Professional Biographies, IRVINE, CALIFORNIA***

Michalske, Michael A. '40 '65 C.734 B.S. L.930 J.D.
V.P. & Gen. Coun., Beszt Life Assurance Co.
Miede, Debbie L. ...........................'55 '81 C.112 B.A. L.1065 J.D. 2601 Main St.
**Miglietta, Margaret R.** ........'58 '84 C.1365 B.A. L.426 J.D. [Ⓐ Berger,K.S.M.F.S.&G.]
**Miliband, Joel S.**, (AV) ..........................'52 '77 C.112 B.A. L.1049 J.D. [Rus,M.W.&S.]
*REPORTED CASES: Hydrotech Systems, Ltd. v. Oasis Water Park, 52 Cal 3d. 488 (1991).
*PRACTICE AREAS: Business Litigation; Commercial Litigation; Bankruptcy Litigation; Real Estate Law.
**Militzok, Steven**, (AV) ....................'52 '78 C.800 B.A. L.1049 J.D. [Parilla,M.&S.]
*PRACTICE AREAS: Real Estate Development Law; Partnership Law; Business Law.
**Miller, Darren B.** ......'56 '91 C.112 B.A. L.1097 J.D. Contract Atty., Discovision Assoc.
*RESPONSIBILITIES: Patent Contracts; General Contracts.
Miller, Jack J., (BV) ..............'32 '61 C&L.184 B.A., J.D. 2082 Michelson Dr., Ste. 100
**Miller, Jon G.** ........'64 '90 C.112 B.A. L.426 J.D. [Hinchy,W.W.A.&H.] (⊙San Diego)
*PRACTICE AREAS: Labor and Employment; Construction Law; Business Litigation.
**Miller, Maryn L.** ......................'66 '92 C.112 B.A. L.1066 J.D. [Ⓐ Gibson,D.&C.]
**Miller, Richard W.** ......................'64 '91 C.477 B.S. L.912 J.D. [Ⓐ Genson,E.C.&W.]
**Miller, Shawn R.** .......................'66 '93 C.112 M.A. L.809 J.D. [Ⓐ Malcolm,C.&H.]
*LANGUAGES: Italian and Spanish.
*PRACTICE AREAS: Bankruptcy; Creditors Rights; Commercial Litigation.
**Miller, Terry L.** '48 '79
C.1159 B.S. L.879 J.D. [Oppenheimer P.S.] (Pat.) (⊙Los Angeles)
**Millet, Craig H.** ...............................'54 '82 C.800 B.A. L.990 J.D. [Gibson,D.&C.]
*PRACTICE AREAS: Bankruptcy Litigation; Insolvency; Creditors' Rights; International Bankruptcy.
**Mills, Creighton D.**, (AV) ......................'55 '81 C.112 B.A. L.1068 J.D. [Snell&W.]
*PRACTICE AREAS: Real Estate Law; Commercial Finance.
**Moffatt, Michael J.** ........................'62 '95 C.1042 BSME L.990 J.D. [Price,G.&U.]
*PRACTICE AREAS: Patents; Litigation; Trademarks.
Moll, Kurt A. ..................'50 '84 C.745 B.A. L.426 J.D. 7700 Irvine Center Dr., #700
**Mollis, Charles A.** .................'59 '85 C.1042 B.A. L.1137 J.D. [Greco,M.&O.]
*REPORTED CASES: Nanfito vs. Superior Court (1991) 2 C.A. 4th 315; 2 C.R. 2nd 876.
*PRACTICE AREAS: General Civil Trial Practice; Insurance Law; Construction Law; Products Liability Law; Environmental Law.
**Mollis, Ronald A.**, (AV) ..................'55 '81 C.1042 B.S. L.1137 J.D. [Greco,M.&O.]
*PRACTICE AREAS: Tax Law; Business Law; Federal, State and Local Taxation Law; Estate Planning; Business and Real Estate Transaction.
Mona, Joseph M. .....................'54 '80 C.940 B.S. L.426 J.D. 8001 Irvine Center Dr.
**Monachino, Mark M.** ..............'63 '89 C.602 B.S.EE./B.A. L.426 J.D. [Ⓐ Corbett&S.]
**Mooney, W. Ernest**, (AV) .....................'53 '78 C.338 B.S. L.800 J.D. [Allen,R.&M.]
*PRACTICE AREAS: Litigation.
**Moore, Lora Lee** ...............................'52 '77 C.940 B.A. L.426 J.D. [Cox,C.&N.]
*PRACTICE AREAS: Construction Law; Civil Litigation.
**Moore, Mark Alan** .........................'52 '83 C.112 B.A. L.145 J.D. [Aldrich&B.]
*PRACTICE AREAS: Consumer Financial Services; Financial Institutions; Payment Systems; Computer Law.
Moore, Patrick K., (AV) ..................'52 '77 C.112 B.A. L.1065 J.D. 2301 Dupont Dr.
**Moore, Randolph T.** ..........................'55 '85 C.94 B.A. L.93 J.D. [Snell&W.]
*PRACTICE AREAS: Commercial Litigation; Product Liability Litigation.
**Moran, Stephen M.** '56 '91 C.154 B.A. L.426 J.D.
Sr. Atty., Toshiba America Info. Systems, Inc.
*RESPONSIBILITIES: Contracts; Labor and Employment; International Law; Products Liability; Corporate Law.

**Morasse, Steven R.** ........................ '58 '85 C.426 B.A. L.1049 J.D. [Raitt&M.]
*PRACTICE AREAS: Business Law; Real Estate Law; Insurance Law; Litigation.
Moravek, John '47 '75 C.1042 B.A. L.990 J.D.
Sr. V.P. & Gen. Coun., Century 21 Real Estate Corp.
Morgan, Amy E. .................... '64 '90 C&L.426 B.A., J.D. 19900 MacArthur Blvd.
Morgan, Wm. Marshall, (AV) .............. '22 '50 C.665 B.A. L.800 J.D. [Morgan&W.]⊙
Morgan & Wenzel, Professional Corporation, (AV) ........ 19900 Macarthur Blvd. (⊙L.A.)
Morrell, Rivers J., III, (BV) ............... '47 '73 C.112 B.A. L.284 J.D. [R.J.Morrell,III]
Morrell, Rivers J., III, A Prof. Corp., (BV) ................................ 7700 Irvine Ctr. Dr.
Morring, Oweni L ............... '54 '87 C.112 B.A. L.990 J.D. 17901 Von Karman Ave.
Morris, Aaron P. .............................. '56 '87 C.37 B.A. L.809 J.D. 5 Park Plz.
Morris, Ronald L. ......................... '56 '84 C.684 B.S. L.464 J.D. 2603 Main St.
**Morrison, Steven C.** .................. '53 '79 C.347 B.S. L.345 J.D. [Morrison&L.]
*PRACTICE AREAS: Banking Litigation; Real Estate Litigation; Personal Injury; Title Insurance Litigation; Commercial.

**Morrison & Foerster LLP, (AV)**
**Twelfth Floor, 19900 MacArthur Boulevard, 92715-2445⊙**
**Telephone: 714-251-7500 Facsimile: 714-251-0900**
**URL: http://www.mofo.com**
**Members of Firm: Andrew P. Bernstein; Ronald J. DeFelice; Lawrence P. Ebiner; Michael L. Hawkins; Gary P. Long; Ellen R. Marshall; Robert M. Mattson, Jr.; Robert A. Naeve; Jane M. Samson; Charles E. Schwenck; Carl R. Steen; Josephine Staton Tucker; Thomas J. Umberg; Dean J. Zipser. Of Counsel: Karen J. Lee; Paul M. Smith. Associates: Joseph H. Chi; Sally P. Enriquez; William B. Grenner; Kristina M. Jodis; Robert J. Keenan; Philip J. Koehler; Sonia A. Lister; H. Mark Mersel; C Keith Mosley; Jeremy T. Naftel; Ronald P. Oines; Carole E. Reagan; Jennifer A. Riel; Brian C. Sinclair; Tamara Powell Tate; William B. Tate, II; Peter D. Taylor.**
**Other offices located in: San Francisco, Los Angeles, New York, Washington, D.C., London, Brussels, Hong Kong, Tokyo, Sacramento, Palo Alto, Walnut Creek and Denver.**
***See Professional Biographies, IRVINE, CALIFORNIA***

**Morrison & Lespier**
**3333 Michelson Drive Suite 605, 92715-1685**
**Telephone: 714-474-7755**
**Email: 74014.2126@compuserve.com URL: http://www.cal_law.com**
**Members of Firm: Steven C. Morrison; Manfredo E. Lespier;—Carl P. Luckadoo; Mary Durbin.**
**Civil and Business Litigation, Banking Litigation, Real Estate Litigation, Bankruptcy Litigation (Creditors), Commercial Litigation, Personal Injury, Title Insurance Litigation.**
***See Professional Biographies, IRVINE, CALIFORNIA***

Morse, James S. ..................... '56 '81 C.352 B.A. L.94 J.D. 2010 Main St., Ste., 400
**Mosley, C Keith** ........................... '64 '93 C.36 B.S. L.178 J.D. [[A] Morrison&F.]
**Mosley, Melody S.** .............. '54 '84 C.1042 B.A. L.809 J.D. [Berger,K.S.M.F.S.&G.]
**Moss, Brian T.** .... '63 '91 C.763 B.A. L.1049 J.D. [[A] Manning,M.&W.] (⊙Los Angeles)
**Mouser, Julia A.** .............. '59 '85 C.999 B.A. L.809 J.D. [[A] Berger,K.S.M.F.S.&G.]
**Mower, Jon R.**, (AV) ............... '50 '76 C.813 B.A. L.1068 J.D. [Mower,K.N.C.&H.]
*PRACTICE AREAS: Insurance Defense; Medical Malpractice Law; Government Law; Bad Faith Law; Civil Trial.

**Mower, Koeller, Nebeker, Carlson & Haluck, (AV) [BR]**
**108 Pacifica, P.O. Box 19799, 92713-9799⊙**
**Telephone: 714-753-1229 Fax: 714-753-1413**
**Members of Firm: Jon R. Mower; Keith D. Koeller; William L. Haluck; Joseph J. Cullen; Patrick A. Carreon; Lynn M. Bouslog; Edward W. Schmitt; Ellen E. Hunter;—Nancy J. Altman; Mark D. Newcomb; Terrence J. Giannone; Ferdinand M. Trampe; James A. Burton; Eric W. Smith; Steven G. Holett.**
**General Liability, Construction Defect, Environmental Law, Medical Malpractice, Product Liability, Business Litigation, Governmental Tort Liability, Insurance and Insurance Bad Faith Law.**
**San Bernardino, California Office: 412 West Hospitality Lane, Suite 300, 92408. Telephone: 909-381-3334. Fax: 909-889-2007.**
**San Diego, California Office: 225 Broadway, 21st Floor. Telephone: 619-233-1600. Fax: 619-236-0527.**
**Yuma, Arizona Office: 212 South 2nd Avenue, P.O. Bin 11791. Telephone: 520-782-2531. Fax: 520-782-5319.**
***See Professional Biographies, IRVINE, CALIFORNIA***

**Mrofka, Robert J.** .................... '51 '86 C.679 B.S.Ch.E. L.145 J.D. [[A] Lobel&O.]
**Muchnick, Adam E.** .................. '69 '95 C.813 A.B. L.145 J.D. [[A] Gibson,D.&C.]
*LANGUAGES: Spanish.
*PRACTICE AREAS: Corporate Law; International Law.
**Mudd, Joseph E.**, (AV) ............................ '47 '72 C&L.508 B.A., J.D. [J.E.Mudd]
*PRACTICE AREAS: Taxation Law; IRS Representation; Business Transactions; Corporate Planning; Business Reorganization.

**Mudd, Joseph E., P.L.C., (AV) [BR]**
**8001 Irvine Center Drive, Suite 1170, 92618**
**Telephone: 714-453-1012 Fax: 714-453-1516**
**Joseph E. Mudd (Certified Specialist, Taxation Law, The State Bar of California Board of Legal Specialization);—Jeri L. Gartside; Dennis M. Sandoval.**
**Corporate and Business Transactions and Representation with emphasis in the area of Taxation and Tax Controversy.**
***See Professional Biographies, IRVINE, CALIFORNIA***

**Muench, Richard A.** ........... '66 '94 C.602 B.B.A. L.1137 J.D. [[A] Genson,E.C.&W.]
**Mulcaire, George P.** ................................ '56 '84 C.112 B.A. L.770 J.D. [Busch]
*PRACTICE AREAS: Real Estate; Business and Tax Law.
**Mulder, C. Christopher** .................. '57 '91 C.397 B.S. L.426 J.D. [[A] Kirtland&P.]
**Murphy, John C.**, (AV) ............ '54 '80 C.112 B.A. L.800 J.D. [Nossaman,G.K.&E.]
*PRACTICE AREAS: Litigation.
**Murphy, Michele D.** ........... '57 '88 C.112 B.A. L.426 J.D. [[A] Palmieri,T.W.W.&W.]
*PRACTICE AREAS: Litigation.
**Murphy, Thomas M.** ........................ '62 '87 C&L.112 B.A., J.D. [Sutton&M.]
*PRACTICE AREAS: Personal Injury Law; Insurance Defense.

**Musick, Peeler & Garrett LLP, (AV)**
**2603 Main Street, Suite 1025, 92614-6232⊙**
**Telephone: 714-852-5122 Facsimile: 714-852-5128**
**Members of Firm: Hal G. Block; Eduardo Guerini Bolt. Associate: Robin L. Hayward.**
**General Practice. Trial and Appellate Practice. Corporation, Securities and Antitrust Law. Healthcare, Hospital, College and University Law. Insurance, Excess, Reinsurance and Coverage. Labor, Real Estate, Land Use, Environmental, Eminent Domain, Oil and Gas and Mining Law. Taxation, Trust, Probate, Estate Planning, Bankruptcy and Pension and Profit Sharing.**
**Los Angeles, California Office: Suite 2000, One Wilshire Boulevard. Telephone: 213-629-7600. Facsimile: 213-624-1376.**
**San Diego, California Office: 1900 Home Savings Tower, 225 Broadway. Telephone: 619-231-2500. Facsimile: 619-231-1234.**
**San Francisco, California Office: Suite 1300, Steuart Street Tower, One Market Plaza. Telephone: 415-281-2000. Facsimile: 415-281-2010.**
**Sacramento, California Office: Wells Fargo Center, Suite 1280, 400 Capitol Mall. Telephone: 916-557-8300. Facsimile: 916-442-8629.**
**Fresno, California Office: 6041 North First Street. Telephone: 209-228-1000. Facsimile: 209-447-4670.**
***See Professional Biographies, IRVINE, CALIFORNIA***

**Muzi, Andrew C.** ...................... '61 '87 C.1044 B.S. L.1137 J.D. [Andrade&M.]
*PRACTICE AREAS: Construction Litigation; Environmental Law; Business Litigation.
**Naeve, Robert A.** ......................... '55 '82 C.800 B.M. L.813 J.D. [Morrison&F.]
*PRACTICE AREAS: Labor and Employment; Litigation; Alternative Dispute Resolution.
**Naftel, Jeremy T.** ...................... '71 '96 C.668 B.A. L.800 J.D. [[A] Morrison&F.]
Nagel, A. Patrick, (AV) ........... '20 '50 C.645 B.A. L.209 J.D. 18881 Von Karman Ave.
**Nagle, G. Andrew** '54 '83 C.1042 B.A. L.809 J.D.
[[A] Manning,M.&W.] (⊙Los Angeles)
**Nardulli, Joseph J.**, (AV) .................... '47 '74 C.112 B.A. L.1049 J.D. [Arter&H.]
Narodick, Margaret '51 '79
C.589 B.A. L.424 J.D. V.P. & Coun., Century 21 Real Estate Corp.
Nash, Paul S. ............................................ '49 '77 C.1075 B.S. L.36 J.D. 2603 Main St.
Nasser, Albert ........................................ '18 '54 C.800 B.A. L.813 LL.B. 16 Morena
**Natcher, Stephen D.** '40 '66 C.813 A.B. L.1065 J.D.
Sr. V.P., Gen. Coun. & Secy., Wyle Electronics
*RESPONSIBILITIES: General Business Practice.
**Naughton, Patrick E.**, (BV) ........ '50 '78 C.267 B.S. L.990 J.D. [Berger,K.S.M.F.S.&G.]
**Needham, Crystal S.** '59 '84 C.668 B.A. L.1066 J.D.
Sr. Proj. Atty., Mission Energy Co.
**Nelms, Robert W.** ............ '58 '84 C.893 B.A. L.990 J.D. [Berger,K.S.M.F.S.&G.]
Nelson, Farrell L. '39 '74 C.800 B.S.E.E. L.426 J.D.
Gen. Coun., Toshiba America Electronic Components, Inc.

**Nelson, Harold S., (AV) '49 '77 C&L.101 B.A., J.D.**
**8001 Irvine Center Drive, Suite 1500, 92718**
**Telephone: 714-753-1921 FAX: 714-753-1888**
**(Certified Specialist, Estate Planning, Trust and Probate Law, The State Bar of California Board of Legal Specialization).**
***LANGUAGES: Japanese.**
***PRACTICE AREAS: Estate, Probate and Trusts; Estate and Trust Litigation; Real Estate; Corporate; Business.**

**Nesthus, Kristine P.** '55 '85 C.966 B.A. L.378 J.D.
[[A] Faustman,C.D.&F.] (⊙San Diego)
*PRACTICE AREAS: Employment Law; Labor Law; Business Litigation.
**Neuland, Richard P.**, (AV) ............... '46 '75 C.1042 B.S. L.990 J.D. [Neuland&N.]
*PRACTICE AREAS: Homeowner Association; Condominium Law; Real Estate; Business; Personal Injury.

**Neuland & Nordberg, A Professional Law Corporation, (AV)**
**One Technology Drive Suite I-803, 92718**
**Telephone: 714-453-7200 Fax: 714-453-7212**
**Richard P. Neuland; Daniel A. Nordberg;—Denver R. Andrews, Jr.; David E. Hickey; Robert F. Wilson; Dean E. Smart. Of Counsel: William P. Hickey.**
**Homeowner Association and Condominium Law, Real Property, Civil Litigation, Construction Law, Business, Personal Injury, Probate.**
**Reference: Bank of America (Laguna Hills Branch).**
***See Professional Biographies, IRVINE, CALIFORNIA***

**Neuman, Andrea E.** .................... '65 '90 C.893 B.S. L.890 J.D. [[A] Gibson,D.&C.]
*PRACTICE AREAS: Trust/Probate Litigation and General Commercial Litigation.
**Neuman, J. Fred** ..................... '65 '90 C.375 B.S. L.893 J.D. [[A] Gibson,D.&C.]
*PRACTICE AREAS: Antitrust; Litigation.
**Newcomb, Mark D.** .............. '62 '88 C.112 B.A. L.1068 J.D. [[A] Mower,K.N.C.&H.]
**Newman, Michael D.** ........................ '52 '85 C.604 A.B. L.273 J.D. [Crowell&M.]
Newman, Stephen T. '47 '77 C.1042 B.S. L.1068 J.D.
Gen. Coun., Bristol Park Medical Group, Inc.
**Ng, Pohleng**, (BV) '61 '91 C.914 B.A. L.1066 J.D.
Sr. Atty., Toshiba America Info. Systems, Inc.
*LANGUAGES: Malaysian, Cantonese, Mandarin, Taiwanese, Indonesian.
*RESPONSIBILITIES: General Corporate; Corporate Formation; Corporate Dissolutions; Corporate Governance; Corporate Reorganization.
**Nichols, Robert F., Jr.**, (AV) .......... '27 '66 C.1258 B.A. L.426 LL.B. [Nichols&A.]
*PRACTICE AREAS: Commercial Banking Law; Business Law; Real Estate Law; Corporate Law; Creditor's Rights.

**Nichols & Andrews, A Professional Law Corporation, (AV) [BR]**
**5 Park Plaza, Suite 800, 92614-6501**
**Telephone: 714-475-4477 Fax: 714-475-4475**
**Robert F. Nichols, Jr.; Camilla N. Andrews.**
**General Civil and Trial Practice. Commercial Law, Banking, Business, Creditor Bankruptcy, Construction, Real Estate, Personal Injury.**
***See Professional Biographies, IRVINE, CALIFORNIA***

**Nicholson, Timothy A.** ......... '62 '79 C.1110 B.A. L.1137 J.D. [Berger,K.S.M.F.S.&G.]
Niermann, Herbert N. .................. '39 '80 C.999 B.A. L.1137 J.D. 38 Corporate Pk.‡
**Nitikman, Mark A.** .................. '58 '88 C.112 A.B. L.800 J.D. [[A] Corey,C.D.&D.]
**Nix, Benjamin A.** ........................ '61 '88 C.1109 B.S. L.1065 J.D. [Payne&F.]
*PRACTICE AREAS: Business Litigation; Civil Litigation; Trade Secrets; Unfair Competition.
Nixen, Michael G. ........................................ '51 '76 C.112 B.A. L.800 J.D. [M.G.Nixen]
Nixen, Michael G., A P.C. ............................................................ 4199 Campus Dr.
Noble, Donna M. ........................ '53 '79 C.878 B.S. L.1137 J.D. Fluor Daniel, Inc.
**Noiroux, Mary Ann** ........................ '59 '91 C&L.1137 B.S.L., J.D. [[A] Kring&B.]
*PRACTICE AREAS: Wrongful Termination; Construction Defect; Medical Malpractice; Business Litigation.
**Nordberg, Daniel A.**, (AV) ................. '52 '77 C.112 B.A. L.990 J.D. [Neuland&N.]
*PRACTICE AREAS: Homeowner Association; Condominium Law and Litigation; Construction Defect Litigation; Real Estate; Personal Injury.
Norouzi, David N. ................ '66 '89 C.800 B.S. L.1049 J.D. 1 Park Plaza, Ste., 1250

**Nossaman, Guthner, Knox & Elliott, LLP, (AV)**
**Suite 1800, 18101 Von Karman Avenue, 92715-1007⊙**
**Telephone: 714-833-7800 Telefacsimile: 714-833-7878**
**Members of Firm: Howard F. Harrison; Robert D. Thornton; Gregory W. Sanders; John J. Flynn III; Rensselaer J. Smith IV; John C. Murphy; John P. Erskine; E. George Joseph; Adam H. Relin; James M. Picozzi; David L. Colgan. Resident Associates: Sue S. Okuda; K. Erik Friess; Rick E. Rayl; Francis D. Logan, Jr. Of Counsel: Jean O. Melious.**
**General Civil Practice, including Real Estate, Corporations and Litigation in all State and Federal Courts. Transportation, Land Use, Environmental, Hazardous Waste, Solid Waste and Legislative Law.**
**Reference: Union Bank (Los Angeles Headquarters Office).**
**Los Angeles, California Office: Thirty-First Floor, Union Bank Square, 445 South Figueroa Street. Telephone: 213-612-7800.**
**San Francisco, California Office: Thirty-Fourth Floor, 50 California Street. Telephone: 415-398-3600.**
**Sacramento, California Office: Suite 1000, 915 L Street. Telephone: 916-442-8888.**
**Washington, D.C. Office: c/o French & Company, The Homer Building, Suite 370-S, 601 13th Street, N.W. Telephone. 202-783-7272.**
***See Professional Biographies, IRVINE, CALIFORNIA***

**Nowak, Yolita J. '60 '86 C.999 L.1137 J.D.**
**18400 Von Karman Avenue, Suite 500, 92715-1514**
**Telephone: 714-851-5948 Facsimile: 714-851-0936**
***PRACTICE AREAS: Securities Law.**
**Corporate, Business Transactions, Partnerships and Securities and Investments.**
***See Professional Biographies, IRVINE, CALIFORNIA***

**Nuszkiewicz, Michelle M.** .............. '66 '92 C&L.800 B.A., J.D. [[A] Jones,D.R.&P.]
O'Brien, Sharon K. ........................................................ '— '86 L.1137 J.D. P.O. Box 6009
**O'Connor, Deborah L.** ........... '65 '91 C.147 B.A. L.1065 J.D. [[A] Sedgwick,D.M.&A.]
**O'Connor, Edward F.** '44 '71
C.477 B.S. L.347 J.D. [Oppenheimer P.S.] (Pat.) (⊙Los Angeles)
*LANGUAGES: Spanish.
O'Connor, Lee P., (BV) .................... '53 '79 C.1109 B.A. L.426 J.D. [O'Connor&S.]

**O'Connor, Paul D.** ... '55 '80 C.1109 B.S. L.426 J.D. [Allen,M.L.G.&M.]
*PRACTICE AREAS: Business Organization and Tax Planning.
**O'Connor, Sean P.** ... '65 '91 C.112 B.A. L.1065 J.D. [Ⓐ Palmieri,T.W.W.&W.]
*PRACTICE AREAS: Litigation; Condemnation Law.
O'Connor, Timothy J. ... '65 '90 C.1075 B.S. L.426 J.D. 8001 Irvine Center Dr.
O'Connor & Schmeltzer, A Law Corporation, (BV) ... 8001 Irvine Ctr. Dr.
O'Dell, Sherilyn L. ... '64 '89 C.59 B.A. L.990 J.D. 2 Park Plaza
Ogrod, Gregory D. ... '50 '80 C.112 B.A. L.464 J.D. Western Digital Corp. (Pat.)
**O'Hara, Kevin** ... '58 '83 C.112 B.A. L.426 J.D. [Greco,M.&O.]
*PRACTICE AREAS: Tax; Estate Planning; Probate; Corporate; Business.
**O'Hare, William S., Jr.**, (AV) ... '52 '78 C.423 A.B. L.1065 J.D. [Snell&W.]
*PRACTICE AREAS: Commercial Litigation.
**Oines, Ronald P.** ... '63 '90 C.1109 B.A. L.36 J.D. [Ⓐ Morrison&F.]
Oja, Richard W. ... '34 '76 C.475 B.A. L.1137 J.D. 2 Rainbow Lake
O'Kain & Joy, A Law Corporation, (AV) ... 18400 Von Karman Suite 580
Okin, Stuart L. ... '61 '93 C.1077 B.A. L.1137 J.D. P.O. Box 52291
**Okuda, Sue S.** ... '54 '89 C.112 B.A. L.1066 J.D. [Ⓐ Nossaman,G.K.&E.]
*PRACTICE AREAS: Litigation.
**Olins, Torrey A.** ... '69 '93 C.659 B.A. L.813 J.D. [Ⓐ Gibson,D.&C.]
*PRACTICE AREAS: Employee Benefits.
**Olsen, Robert K.** ... '58 '83 C.112 B.A. L.1068 J.D. [Ⓐ Aldrich&B.]
*PRACTICE AREAS: Banking.
Olsen, Thomas J. ... '62 '89 C.546 B.S. L.823 J.D. [Sims&O.] (⊙Oakland)
Olson, David ... '63 '93 C.1075 B.S. L.800 J.D. 1920 Main St., Ste., 1000
**Olson, Leslie R.** ... '64 '93 C.170 B.A. L.1049 J.D. [Ⓐ Gibson,D.&C.]
*PRACTICE AREAS: Corporate Law.
**Olson, Mary Ellen** ... '55 '84 C.1042 B.A. L.990 J.D. Reg. V.P., Mission Energy Co.
**Olson, Monica E.**, (AV) ... '54 '80 C.112 B.A. L.1068 J.D. [Allen,M.L.G.&M.]
*PRACTICE AREAS: Real Estate.
Olson, Neil ... '46 '76 C.668 B.A. L.809 J.D. Pres. & CEO, Calif. Market Data Coop., Inc.
O'Mahoney, Denis A. ... '43 '77 C.1056 B.S. L.1179 J.D. 30 Corporate Pk.
**O'Neal, James B.** ... '44 '69 C.500 B.B.A. L.846 J.D. [Bryan C.]
**O'Neil, Dennis D.**, (AV) ... '38 '66 C.800 B.A. L.1065 J.D. [Hewitt&M.]
*PRACTICE AREAS: Real Estate Law; Land Use Law; Health Law.
O'Neill, James G. ... '36 '67 C.588 B.S.M.E. L.273 LL.B. Cue Paging Corp. (Pat.)
**Opera, Robert E.**, (AV) ... '56 '81 C.659 B.A. L.1068 J.D. [Lobel&O.]
*PRACTICE AREAS: Reorganization; Bankruptcy Law.

**Oppenheimer Poms Smith, (AV) BR**
**1920 Main Street, Suite 1050, 92714⊙**
**Telephone: 714-263-8250 FAX: 714-263-8260**
**Email: owdlaw.com**
**Richard L. Gausewitz; Kurt A. MacLean; Edward F. O'Connor; Terry L. Miller; Michael A. Kondzella.**
**Medical Device, Health Care, Business/Technology, Labor and Employment, Antitrust, professional Liability and Securities, Banking and Finance, Real Estate, Corporate Finance, Employee Benefits, International Corporate, Tax/Trust and Estate, Environmental Law and Toxic Torts, Insurance, Products Liability, Transportation, Dispute Resolution/Arbitration, European Community, International Tax.**
**Reference: City National Bank (Century Plaza Office, Century City).**
**Los Angeles, California Office: 2029 Century Park East, 38th Floor, 90067. Telephone: 310-788-5000. FAX: 310-277-1297.**
**San Jose, California Office: 333 West Santa Clara Street, Suite 1000, 95113. Telephone: 408-275-8790. FAX: 408-275-8793.**
**Oppenheimer Wolff & Donnelly:**
**Brussels, Belgium Office: Avenue Louise 250, Box 31, 1050. Telephone: 32-2-626-0500. FAX: 32-2-626-0510.**
**Chicago, Illinois Office: Two Prudential Plaza, 45th Floor, 180 North Stetson Avenue, 60601.**
**Minneapolis, Minnesota Office: 3400 Plaza VII, 45 South Seventh Street, 55401. Telephone: 612-344-9300. FAX: 612-344-9376.**
**New York, N.Y. Office: Citicorp Center, 153 East 53rd Street, 10022. Telephone: 212-826-5000. Telecopier: 212-486-0708.**
**Paris, France Office: 53 Avenue Montaigne, 75008. Telephone: (33/1) 44 95 03 50. FAX: (33/1) 44 95 03 40.**
**St. Paul, Minnesota Office: 1700 First Bank Building, 55101. Telephone: 612-223-2500. FAX: 612-223-2596.**
**Washington, D.C. Office: 1020 Nineteenth Street, N.W., Suite 400, 20036. Telephone: 202-293-6300. FAX: 202-293-6200.**
**Detroit, Michigan Office: Timberland Office Park, Suite 250, 5445 Corporate Drive, 48098. Telephone: 810-267-8500. FAX: 810-267-8559.**
**Affiliated Offices:**
**Goudsmit & Branbergen, J.J. Viottastraat, 46 Amsterdam 1071. Telephone: 31-20-662-30-31. FAX: 31-20-673-65-58.**
**Pisano, DeVito, Maiano & Catucci, Piazza Del Duomo, 20, Milan 20122. Telephone: 39-2-878281. FAX: 39-2-861275.**
**Pisano, DeVito, Maiano & Catucci, Via G. Borsi, 3, Rome 00197. Telephone: 39-6-8079087. FAX: 39-6-8078407.**

***See Professional Biographies, IRVINE, CALIFORNIA***

Orr, Mary L. B., (BV) ... '49 '76 C.112 B.A. L.990 J.D. 111 Pacifica K
**Oswald, Michael A.**, (AV) ... '49 '79 C.602 B.A. L.426 J.D. [Oswald&Y.]

**Oswald & Yap, A Professional Corporation, (AV)**
**19900 MacArthur Boulevard, Suite 700, 92715**
**Telephone: 714-756-6000 Telefax: 714-756-6020**
**Michael A. Oswald; Calvin C.S. Yap; Gerald L. Greengard; Jeffrey E. Thomas; Niall Sweetnam; Gary R. White; Tzong-Bing Tsai; John Y. Igarashi.**
**General Civil and Trial Practice, Banking, Real Estate, Equipment Leasing, Secured Transactions, Securities and Commodities Litigation, Bankruptcy and Immigration.**

***See Professional Biographies, IRVINE, CALIFORNIA***

**Otte, Timothy D.** ... '63 '94 C.921 B.A. L.94 J.D. [Ⓐ Kirtland&P.]
*PRACTICE AREAS: Professional Liability Defense.
**Owen, Erin A.** ... '66 '96 C.800 B.A. L.990 J.D. [Pinto&D.]
**Page, Catherine M.** ... '57 '90 C.061 B.Sc. L.851 J.D. [Ⓐ Allen,M.L.G.&M.]
*PRACTICE AREAS: Litigation.
**Palchikoff, Jay F.** ... '55 '82 C.112 B.A. L.1068 J.D. [Hewitt&M.]
*PRACTICE AREAS: Real Estate Law; Business Law.
**Palin, Cynthia Caruso** ... '59 '86 C&L.36 B.S., J.D. [Ramsay&J.]
*REPORTED CASES: Martinez v. State Workman's Compensation Insurance Fund of the State of Arizona.
*PRACTICE AREAS: Property and Commercial Insurance Coverage and Defense; Legal Malpractice Defense; Personal Injury Law.
**Palin, Mark T.**, (AV) ... '53 '85 C.1109 B.A. L.1065 J.D. [Ⓐ Arter&H.]
*PRACTICE AREAS: Business Law; Personal Injury Litigation.
**Palmer, Charles A.**, (BV) ... '49 '77 C.1042 B.A. L.990 J.D. [Ⓐ Pivo&H.]
*PRACTICE AREAS: Construction Accident; Construction Defect; Trucking Accident; Toxic Injuries; Product Liability.
**Palmer, Robert E.**, (AV) ... '56 '84 C.546 B.A. L.990 J.D. [Gibson,D.&C.]
*PRACTICE AREAS: Litigation, with a focus on Complex Business Litigation including Intellectual Property; Environmental Counseling and Litigation.

**Palmieri, Tyler, Wiener, Wilhelm & Waldron, LLP, (AV) BR**
**A Limited Liability Partnership including Professional Corporations**
**East Tower - Suite 1300, 2603 Main Street, P.O. Box 19712, 92614-6228**
**Telephone: 714-851-9400 Telecopier: 714-851-1554; 851-3844; 757-1225**
**Email: general@ptwww.com**
**Members of Firm: Angelo J. Palmieri (A Professional Corporation) (1926-1996); Robert F. Waldron (A Professional Corporation); Alan H. Wiener (A Professional Corporation); Robert C. Ihrke (A**

(This Listing Continued)

**Palmieri, Tyler, Wiener, Wilhelm & Waldron, LLP (Continued)**

**Professional Corporation); James E. Wilhelm (A Professional Corporation); Dennis G. Tyler (A Professional Corporation); Michael J. Greene (A Professional Corporation); Frank C. Rothrock (A Professional Corporation); Dennis W. Ghan (A Professional Corporation); David D. Parr (A Professional Corporation); Charles H. Kanter (A Professional Corporation); George J. Wall; L. Richard Rawls; Patrick A. Hennessey; Don Fisher; Gregory N. Weiler; Warren A. Williams; John R. Lister; Bruce W. Dannemeyer; Cynthia M. Wolcott; Joel P. Kew; Michelle M. Fujimoto; Gary C. Weisberg; Michael H. Leifer;—Norman J. Rodich; Michele D. Murphy; Scott R. Carpenter; Richard A. Salus; D. Susan Wiens; Ronald M. Cole; Cynthia B. Paulsen; Sean P. O'Connor; Susan T. Sakura; Jennifer Anne Kim; Matthew W. Paskerian; Paul B. La Scalla.**
**General Civil and Trial Practice in all State and Federal Courts. Condemnation, Corporation, Estate Planning, Probate, Product Liability Defense, Real Property, Securities, Tax and Trust Law.**

***See Professional Biographies, IRVINE, CALIFORNIA***

Palumbo, Diane O. ... '58 '85 C.884 B.A. L.990 J.D. [Richter,S.&P.]⊙
Pandullo, Nicholas J. '37 '77 C.895 B.A. L.831 J.D.
V.P. & Corp. Coun., Insco/Dico Grp.
Panuska, Tandi S. ... '67 '93 C.112 B.S. L.464 J.D. 18400 Von Karman
**Paone, Kathleen Carothers**, (AV) ... '55 '80 C.112 A.B. L.426 J.D. [Ⓒ Paone,C.M.&W.]
*PRACTICE AREAS: Business, Real Estate and Land Use Litigation.
**Paone, Tim**, (AV) ... '49 '76 C.112 B.A. L.800 J.D. [Paone,C.M.&W.]
*PRACTICE AREAS: Land Use and Environmental Law.

**Paone, Callahan, McHolm & Winton, (AV)**
**Eighth Floor, 19100 Von Karman Avenue, P.O. Box 19613, 92713-9613⊙**
**Telephone: 714-955-2900 Facsimile: 714-955-9009**
**Email: info@paone.com URL: http://www.paone.com**
**Members of Firm: Robert E. Callahan; Richard J. Foster; Susan K. Hori; Alan Jules Kessel; Kenneth S. Kramer; Steven A. McHolm; Tim Paone; John F. Simonis; Martin J. Stein; Daniel K. Winton. Associate: Kenneth D. Johnson. Of Counsel: James R. Cavanaugh; William R. Devine; Roger A. Grable; Cary D. Lowe; Kathleen Carothers Paone; Carla K. Ryhal (Resident, Westlake Village); John E. Tawa, Jr.**
**Real Property, Land Use, Environmental, Partnership, Business, Commercial and Public Law, Banking, Business, Real Property, Land Use, Redevelopment and Family Law Litigation. General Civil Trial and Appellate Practice, State and Federal Courts. Sports Law.**
**Westlake Village, California Office: 200 North Westlake Boulevard, Suite 100. Telephone: 805-371-5755. Fax: 805-446-1915.**

***See Professional Biographies, IRVINE, CALIFORNIA***

**Paparelli, Angelo A.**, (AV) ... '49 '76 C.477 B.A. L.912 J.D. [Bryan C.] (⊙L.A.)
**Pappas, Christopher P.** ... '60 '90 C.119 B.S. L.1194 J.D. [Watt,T.&H.]
*PRACTICE AREAS: Construction Contract Litigation; Commercial Litigation.
**Paradis, Jon Pierre**, (AV) ... '42 '68 C.1042 B.A. L.1068 J.D. [J.P.Paradis]
*PRACTICE AREAS: Contracts; Business Litigation; Real Estate; Real Estate Litigation.

**Paradis, Jon Pierre, Inc., A Law Corporation, (AV)**
**18002 Cowan, First Floor, 92614-6812**
**Telephone: 714-477-2400 Facsimile: 714-851-0108**
**Jon Pierre Paradis (Member of Consumer Attorneys of California with recognized experience as a Trial Lawyer).**
**Civil and Appellate Litigation in Business, Commercial, Landlord and Tenant and Real Estate Law.**

***See Professional Biographies, IRVINE, CALIFORNIA***

Parham, Jackson E. ... '44 '84 C.684 B.A. L.1137 J.R. [Parham&Assoc.]
Parham & Associates, Inc. ... 18662 MacArthur Blvd.
**Parilla, Paul H.**, (AV) ... '48 '73 C.123 B.A. L.436 J.D. [Parilla,M.&S.]
*PRACTICE AREAS: Real Estate Law; Business and Real Estate Trial Practice.

**Parilla, Militzok & Shedden, LLP, (AV)**
**Suite 1250, 1 Park Plaza, 92614-8509**
**Telephone: 714-263-1010 Telecopier: 714-263-1693**
**Members of Firm: Marc Ettinger; Bradley N. Garber; Steven Militzok; Paul H. Parilla; Rhea S. Shedden.**
**General Civil and Trial Practice in all California State and Federal Courts. Real Estate and Homeowner Association Law. Corporate, Business, Partnership and Commercial Law. and Creditor Rights Law.**

***See Professional Biographies, IRVINE, CALIFORNIA***

**Parker, Keith M.** ... '52 '83 C.112 B.S. L.597 J.D. [Smith,S.D.P.&W.]
Parker, Viveca D. ... '56 '89 C.128 B.A. L.800 J.D. 18101 Von Karman Ave., Suite 1800
**Parmes, Penelope**, (AV) ... '47 '82 C.208 L.765 J.D. [Snell&W.]
*PRACTICE AREAS: Bankruptcy Law; Creditors' Remedies Law.
**Parr, David D., (A Professional Corporation)**, (AV) '51 '78
C.228 A.B. L.276 J.D. [Palmieri,T.W.W.&W.]
*PRACTICE AREAS: Corporate Law; Real Estate Law; Tax Law.
Partington, Donald E. '52 '77 C.610 B.A. L.1095 J.D.
Sr. V.P. & Asst. Gen. Coun., Fidelity Natl. Title Ins. Co.
**Parvin, Curtis D.** ... '56 '84 C.112 B.A. L.990 J.D. [Sedgwick,D.M.&A.]
**Paskerian, Matthew W.** ... '66 '96 C.112 B.S. L.1049 J.D. [Palmieri,T.W.W.&W.]
*PRACTICE AREAS: Corporate; Business Law.
**Pasqualini, David A.** ... '48 '86 C.473 B.S. L.188 J.D. [Ⓒ Tredway,L.&D.]
*PRACTICE AREAS: Estate Planning; Probate; Business Law.
**Passon, Kenneth D.** ... '53 '78 C.112 B.A. L.426 J.D. [Suchman,G.&P.]⊙
*REPORTED CASES: Dodd v. Citizens Bank of California (1990) 222 Cal. App. 3d 1624; Symonds v. Mercury Savings and Loan Assn. (1990) 225 Cal. App. 3d 1458.
*PRACTICE AREAS: Title Insurance Law; Commercial Law; Litigation; Banking Law; Receivership Law.
**Patch, Ryan Mark, (P.C.)** ... '60 '87 C.1308 B.S. L.809 J.D. [Hanley&P.]
*PRACTICE AREAS: Civil Litigation; Real Estate Loan Transactions.
**Patel, Alka N.** ... '60 '94 C.1077 B.S. L.809 J.D. [Ⓒ Barnes,C.F.&Z.]
*PRACTICE AREAS: Business Litigation; Tax; Bankruptcy; Estate Planning; Probate.
**Patronite, Janice M.**, (BV) ... '51 '76 C.112 B.A. L.426 J.D. [Ⓒ Amante]
*PRACTICE AREAS: Corporate; Business; Real Estate Law; Civil Litigation; Appellate Practice.
**Patterson, Sheila I.** ... '54 '82 C.112 B.A. L.426 J.D. [Brown,P.H.&V.]
*PRACTICE AREAS: Civil and Environmental Litigation; Land Use.
**Paulsen, Cynthia B.** ... '65 '90 C.112 B.A. L.1049 J.D. [Ⓐ Palmieri,T.W.W.&W.]
*PRACTICE AREAS: Corporate Law; Real Estate Law.
Paulson, Edward (Ted) B. ... '63 '90 C.101 B.S. L.878 J.D. 2010 Main St., Ste. 400
**Payne, Daniel J.** ... '57 '88 C.112 B.A. L.1068 J.D. [Ⓐ Payne&F.]
*PRACTICE AREAS: Business; Land Use; Environmental; Construction Litigation.
**Payne, James L.** ... '51 '82 C.112 B.A. L.424 J.D. [Payne&F.]
*PRACTICE AREAS: Employment Law and Related Litigation; Wrongful Termination Law; Employment Discrimination Law; Civil Rights Law; Wage and Hour Law.
**Payne, Mark J.** ... '64 '92 C.890 B.S. L.945 J.D. [Ⓐ Gibson,D.&C.]
*PRACTICE AREAS: Labor and Employment.

**Payne & Fears, (AV)**
**4 Park Plaza, Suite 1100, 92714**
**Telephone: 714-851-1101 Fax: 714-851-1212**
**Members of Firm: James L. Payne; Daniel F. Fears; Daniel M. Livingston; Daniel L. Rasmussen; Scott S. Thomas; Karen O. Strauss; Benjamin A. Nix;—Valerie L. McNamara; Douglas A. Barritt; Thomas L. Vincent; Mark A. Sacks; James G. Kay; Daniel J. Payne; Eric C. Sohlgren; Jeffrey K. Brown; Jane M. Flynn.**

***See Professional Biographies, IRVINE, CALIFORNIA***

Peabody, Thomas M. ... '68 '95 C&L.426 B.A., J.D. 19900 Macarthur Blvd.
**Peckenpaugh, Thomas D.**, (AV) ... '39 '66 C.1042 B.A. L.1068 J.D. [Jackson,D.&P.]
*PRACTICE AREAS: Business and Real Estate.
**Peebles, Jane** ... '51 '84 C.563 B.A. L.569 J.D. [Freeman,F.&S.] (⊙Los Angeles)

Peelor, Sharon G. ....................... '47 '88 C.37 B.A. L.597 J.D. Irvine Valley College
Pelt, Kent D. '60 '92 C.112 B.A. L.1137 J.D.
Asst. V.P. & Assoc. Coun., Fidelity Natl. Title Ins. Co.
Penticuff, Mark T. ....................... '61 '87 C.990 B.A. L.94 J.D. 5461 Catawba Ln.
**Pepper, Jeanne E.** .................. '70 '95 C.112 B.A. L.990 J.D. [Ⓐ Stevens,K.A.&H.]
*PRACTICE AREAS: Construction Defect Litigation; Insurance Defense; General Liability Defense; Professional Malpractice.
**Percival, James R.**, (AV) .................... '55 '81 C.352 B.B.A. L.813 J.D. [Grant&L.]
*PRACTICE AREAS: Litigation.
**Perkal, Julie I.** '62 '87 C.112 B.A. L.426 J.D.
Sr. Atty., Toshiba America Info. Systems, Inc.
**Perkins, Kenneth L., Jr.** ................ '56 '84 C.112 B.A. L.800 J.D. [Perkins,Z.&D.]
*PRACTICE AREAS: Business, Real Estate, Construction and Insurance Litigation.

**Perkins, Zarian & Duncan, P.C.**
**2030 Main Street, Suite 660, 92614⊙**
**Telephone: 714-475-1700 Fax: 714-475-1800**
**Kenneth L. Perkins, Jr.; John N. Zarian; Adam D. Duncan, Jr. (Resident, Los Angeles Office); Dan E. Chambers.**
**Business Litigation including Securities, Real Estate, Construction, Insurance, Antitrust, Environmental and Commercial Disputes.**
**Los Angeles, California Office: 1801 Century Park East, Suite 1100. Telephone: 310-203-4646. Fax: 310-203-4647.**

*See Professional Biographies, IRVINE, CALIFORNIA*

Petersen, Karen A. ...................... '54 '82 C.813 A.B. L.629 J.D. 4199 Campus Dr.
Peterson, Dale R. ............... '48 '74 C.1167 B.S.B.A. L.813 J.D. 2600 Michelson Dr.
**Peterson, Kathleen O.** ..................... '60 '86 C.813 A.B. L.1068 J.D. [Ⓐ Woldt&H.]
*REPORTED CASES: Nurmi v. Peterson, 10 U.S.P.Q. 2d 1775 (C.D. Cal. 1989); Microsoft Corp. v. A-Tech., 855 F.Supp. 308 (C.D. Cal. 1994); Fennessy v. Southwest Airlines, 91 F.3d 1359 (9th Cir. 1996).

**Peterson, Mark D., Law Offices of '61 '86 C.813 A.B. L.112 J.D.**
**Newport Gateway Towers, 19800 MacArthur Boulevard, Suite 1450, 92612**
**Telephone: 714-757-4143 Facsimile: 714-757-4148**
**Email: mpeterson2@aol.com**
***LANGUAGES: Spanish.**
***REPORTED CASES: Daniel E. Dyer v. Northbrook Property & Casualty Insurance Company, 210 Cal.App. 3d 1540 (1989); Allstate Insurance Company v. Interbank Financial Services, 215 Cal. App. 3d 825 (1989); Roger Marsh v. Stanley K. Burrell, a/k/a M.C. Hammer, 805 F. Supp. 1493 (1992).**
**Business Litigation, Insurance Coverage.**

*See Professional Biographies, IRVINE, CALIFORNIA*

Peterson, Richard M., (AV) ........ '53 '79 C&L.1137 B.S.L., J.D. 2010 Main St., Ste 400
**Peterson, Robert A., (A Professional Corporation)** '47 '73
C.112 B.A. L.1065 J.D. [Friedman P.&S.]
*PRACTICE AREAS: State and Federal Court Litigation; General Business; Real Property Law.
**Petrasich, John**, (AV) ......................'45 '71 C&L.800 B.A., J.D. [Jackson,D.&P.]
*PRACTICE AREAS: Litigation.
Petrokofsky, Robert .................'54 '81 C.705 B.A. L.1066 J.D. [Ⓐ S.A.Silverman]
**Phifer, Scott C.** '58 '85 C&L.494 B.S., J.D.
(adm. in MN; not adm. in CA) Corp. Coun., Pfizer Inc.
Phillips, Celeste ................................'53 '81 C.112 A.B. L.1065 J.D. 5 Park Plaza
Phillips, Wendy G. ................'59 '90 C.763 B.A. L.61 J.D. 5500 Irvine Center Dr.
**Picker, Todd Andrew** ..............'62 '87 C.911 B.A. L.464 J.D. [Sedgwick,D.M.&A.]
**Picozzi, James M.** ..................... '59 '88 C&L.976 B.A., J.D. [Nossaman,G.K.&E.]
*PRACTICE AREAS: Litigation.
**Pierce, Ronald B.**, (AV) .........'54 '79 C.112 A.B. L.1068 J.D. [Ⓒ Sedgwick,D.M.&A.]
Piggott, George B., (AV) ..................'50 '76 C.813 A.B. L.1068 J.D. [G.B.Piggott]
Piggott, George B., A Professional Corporation, (AV) ............ Ste., 1100, 5 Park Plaza
Pike, Robert L., (AV) ....................'40 '72 C&L.426 B.A., J.D. 38 Corporate Park
**Pink, Jonathan S.** ...........................'61 '95 C.112 B.A. L.809 J.D. [Bye,H.&R.]
*LANGUAGES: Business.
*PRACTICE AREAS: Business Litigation.
Pinto, Patricia Manning '54 '81 C.1109 B.A. L.1137 J.D.
Asst. V.P. & Claims Coun., Fidelity Natl. Title Ins. Co.
**Pinto, Saul B.**, (AV) ........................ '54 '79 C.112 A.B. L.800 J.D. [Pinto&D.]

**Pinto & Dubia, LLP, (AV)**
**2 Park Plaza, Suite 300, 92614**
**Telephone: 714-955-1177 FAX: 714-833-2067**
**Members of Firm: Saul B. Pinto; Christian F. Dubia, Jr.; Michael R. Tenerelli; Kenneth A. Ryder; Mark K. Worcester; Mark D. Erickson; Shelli J. Black. Associates: Lynnda A. McGlinn; J. Scott Russo; John M. Leverett; Lori L. Heimerl; Erin A. Owen.**
**Commercial, Industrial and Residential Real Estate. Real Property Acquisition, Development, Leasing and Finance. Toxic Substances, Property Management, Common Interest Communities, Foreclosure Law and Lender Workouts. Partnership, Corporation and Limited Liability Company Law. General Business Transactions. General Civil and Trial Practice, Complex Litigation, Unfair Competition and Business Torts. Construction Defect and Brokerage Litigation. Bankruptcy and Debtor-Creditor Reorganization.**

*See Professional Biographies, IRVINE, CALIFORNIA*

**Pistone, Thomas A.**, (AV) ........... '49 '77 C.1042 B.A. L.1065 J.D. [Brown,P.H.&V.]
*PRACTICE AREAS: Construction Litigation; Real Estate and Title Litigation; Business Litigation; Computer Products Litigation; Environmental Litigation.
**Pitcher, Thomas B.**, (AV) ......... '38 '67 C.260 B.S.B.A. L.228 J.D. [Ⓒ Gibson,D.&C.]
*PRACTICE AREAS: Business Law; Corporate Law; Securities; Mergers, Acquisitions and Divestitures; Commercial Law.
**Pittaluga, Stephanie A.** ............... '69 '96 C.1109 B.A. L.1137 J.D. [Ⓐ Borchard&W.]
*LANGUAGES: French.
**Pivo, Kenneth R.** ........................ '53 '78 C.112 B.S. L.1065 J.D. [Pivo&H.]

**Pivo & Halbreich, (AV)**
**1920 Main Street, Suite 800, 92714**
**Telephone: 714-253-2000**
**Kenneth R. Pivo; Eva S. Halbreich; Douglas A. Amo; Richard O. Schwartz; Mona Z. Hanna. Associates: Charles A. Palmer; William J. Mall, III; Kathleen E. Wilcox; Timothy J. Lippert; Michael A. Brodie; Lance Gordon Greene; Annie Glass Henshel; Jennifer Batliner.**
**General Civil and Trial Practice in State and Federal Courts. Professional and Products Liability, Medical Malpractice, Insurance, Disability Law and Elder Law, Conservatorships, Environmental and Employment Law, Trade Secrets. Social Security and Medi-Cal Appeals, Hospital Privileges Matters and Professional Medical Boards.**
**Representative Clients: Physicians and Surgeons Underwriters Corp.; Fremont Indemnity; American Continental Insurance Co.; AKROS Medico Enterprises; Kaiser Foundation Healthplan, Inc.; Caronia Corp.; The Doctor's Co.; Harbor Regional Center; Developmental Disabilities Regional Center; South Central Los Angeles Regional Center.**

*See Professional Biographies, IRVINE, CALIFORNIA*

**Plager, Mark H.** '64 '90 C.390 B.S. L.1029 J.D.
(adm. in NJ; not adm. in CA; Pat.) [Ⓐ Gauntlett&Assoc.]
**Poliquin, Mark P.** ........................ '55 '80 C.800 B.S. L.426 J.D. [Kirtland&P.]

**Poms, Smith, Lande & Rose**
**(See Oppenheimer Poms Smith, Los Angeles)**

**Ponder, Teresa Ransom** .........'53 '87 C.790 B.S. L.1137 J.D. [Berger,K.S.M.F.S.&G.]
**Poth, James L.** ...........................'67 '94 C.112 B.A. L.1065 J.D. [Ⓐ Jones,D.R.&P.]

Potter, Andrew G., (BV) ........................'52 '78 C.112 B.S. L.426 J.D. 4 Venture
**Powell, John W.** .......................... '47 '74 C.426 B.A. L.1068 J.D. [Kopeny&P.]
*REPORTED CASES: In Re: Edgar M., 14 Cal.3d 727, 122 Cal. Rptr. 574, 537 Pal 406 (19750; Manier v. Anaheim Business Center Co., 161 Cal. App. 3d 503, 207 Cal. Rptr. 508 (1984).
*PRACTICE AREAS: Appellate Practice; Taxation; Litigation.
Powell, Linda ...................'62 '88 C.990 B.A. L.464 J.D. 18400 Von Karman Ave.
**Powers, Janet L. S.** ..................... '55 '85 C.112 B.A. L.809 J.D. [Fiore,W.R.&P.]
**Pozin, Robert M.** ........................'54 '80 C.976 B.A. L.309 J.D. [Ross,D.&M.]
**Pratt, Steven G.** ............................... '65 '93 C.112 L.61 J.D. [Sutton&M.]
*PRACTICE AREAS: Personal Injury Law; Insurance Defense.
Pratter, Michael S., (BV) .................. '41 '67 C.347 B.A. L.912 J.D. [Pratter&G.]⊙
Pratter & Graves, (BV) ........................................ 3 Park Plaza (⊙Malibu)
**Presiado, Leo J.** ...........................'68 '93 C&L.112 B.A., J.D. [Ⓐ Rus,M.W.&S.]
*PRACTICE AREAS: Corporate; Bankruptcy Law; Complex Business Litigation; Creditor's Rights.
Price, Christopher ...................... '67 '92 C.112 B.A. L.990 J.D. 10 Corporate Pk.
**Price, Donald R.**, (AV) ................. '40 '66 C.1042 B.S. L.1068 LL.B. [Sikora&P.]
*PRACTICE AREAS: Litigation; Business Law; Real Property Transactions.
**Price, Joseph P.** ............'58 '84 C.754 B.S. L.300 J.D. [Ault,D.J.&G.] (⊙San Diego)
**Price, Joseph W., Jr.**, (AV) '41 '68
C.884 B.M.E. L.276 J.D. [Price,G.&U.] (See Pat. Sect.)
*REPORTED CASES: Angres v. Dioptics Medical Products, Inc., 2 USPQ 2d 1041 (C.D. Cal 1986).
*PRACTICE AREAS: Patent; Trademark; Copyright.

**Price, Gess & Ubell, P.C., (AV)**
**2100 S.E. Main Street, Suite 250, 92714**
**Telephone: 714-261-8433 Telecopier: 714-261-9072**
**Email: pgu@ix.netcom.com**
**Joseph W. Price, Jr.; Albin H. Gess; Franklin D. Ubell; Stefan J. Kirchanski; Doyle B. Johnson; Michael J. Moffatt; Gordon E. Gray, III.**
**Patent, Trademark, Copyright, Trade Secret and Antitrust Causes and Related Litigation and Counseling.**

*See Professional Biographies, IRVINE, CALIFORNIA*

**Proffitt, Stephanie H.** ........... '47 '81 C.1042 B.A. L.1148 J.D. [Ⓐ Laughlin,F.L.&M.]
*PRACTICE AREAS: Workers' Compensation.
**Proudfoot, Matthew M.** ........... '57 '91 C.112 B.A. L.1049 J.D. [Ⓐ Genson,E.C.&W.]
**Puchalski, Chester A.** ................. '62 '88 C.273 B.A. L.276 J.D. [Ⓐ Fiore,W.R.&P.]
**Quinby, Joseph P.** ......................... '56 '82 C.605 A.B. L.770 J.D. [Ⓐ Arter&H.]
*PRACTICE AREAS: Real Property Litigation; Civil Practice.
Quinlivan, Patrick C., (AV) .............. '48 '73 C.1077 B.A. L.1068 J.D. [Morgan&W.]
**Qushair, Ann H.** .................. '69 '95 C.112 B.A. L.188 J.D. [Ⓐ Faustman,C.D.&F.]
*PRACTICE AREAS: Employment Law; Labor Law.
**Racobs, Peter E.** .......................'57 '83 C.112 B.A. L.1067 J.D. [Fiore,W.R.&P.]⊙
**Rafatjoo, Hamid R.** ......................... '70 '95 C.112 B.A. L.426 J.D. [Ⓐ Lobel&O.]
*LANGUAGES: Farsi and French.
*PRACTICE AREAS: Reorganization; Creditors' Rights; Litigation.
**Rai, Rina K.** ...................................'— '96 C.112 B.A. L.990 J.D. [Kring&B.]
**Raitt, G. Emmett, Jr.**, (AV) ................. '51 '75 C.668 B.A. L.800 J.D. [Raitt&M.]
*PRACTICE AREAS: Real Estate Litigation; Business Litigation; Insurance Litigation.

**Raitt & Morasse, A Professional Corporation, (AV)**
**17320 Redhill Avenue, Suite 370, 92614-5644**
**Telephone: 714-261-1700 Fax: 714-261-2073**
**G. Emmett Raitt, Jr.; Steven R. Morasse;—Desmond J. Collins.**
**General Civil Litigation and Appellate Practice in all Courts. Real Estate, Corporation, Insurance and Business Law.**

*See Professional Biographies, IRVINE, CALIFORNIA*

Rajcic, John ........................... '55 '80 C.112 B.A. L.990 J.D. [Ⓐ Parham&Assoc.]
**Ramirez, Manuel L.** ................... '55 '82 C.763 B.A. L.61 J.D. [Grace,B.H.&R.]⊙
**Ramirez, Yvonne** .......................'66 '92 C&L.846 B.A., J.D. [Ⓐ Malcolm,C.&H.]
*PRACTICE AREAS: Bankruptcy; Creditors Rights; Commercial Litigation.
**Ramsay, Janice A.**, (AV) ....................'42 '70 C.347 A.B. L.767 J.D. [Ramsay&J.]
*REPORTED CASES: State Farm Fire & Casualty Company v. Tan, 690 F.Supp 886 (D.C. Cal. 1988); 690 F.Supp 886; Prudential - LMI Commercial Insurance Co. v. Superior Court of San Diego County, 51 Cal. 3d 674 (1990); Carty v. American States, 7 Cal. App. 4th 399 (1992).
*PRACTICE AREAS: Insurance Coverage/Bad Faith Litigation; Property Claim Coverage Issues; Environmental Insurance; Litigation; Insurance Fraud.

**Ramsay & Johnson, A Law Corporation, (AV)**
**Suite 750, 19800 MacArthur Boulevard, 92715**
**Telephone: 714-476-5070 Fax: 714-851-8659**
**Janice A. Ramsay; Judy J. Johnson; Phillip E. Smith; Stephen E. Smith; Karen A. Gruber; James P. Carter; Cynthia Caruso Palin; Kimberly H. Cornwell; Victoria L. Gunther; Michael J. Logan; Renee Friend Gurwitz; Joseph C. Gebara; Todd E. Wendel; Kim G. Dunning; Christopher S. Andre; Joan C. Donnellan.**
**Insurance Law and Civil Litigation. Insurance Coverage and Bad Faith, Subrogation and Insurance Defense.**

*See Professional Biographies, IRVINE, CALIFORNIA*

**Randall, Timothy L.** ................... '51 '78 C.172 B.A. L.1049 J.D. [Songstad,R.&U.]
Ranger, Richard J., (AV) ................'37 '66 C.112 B.S. L.1068 LL.B. P.O. Box 6023
**Rasmussen, Daniel L.**, (AV) ................ '59 '85 C.101 B.S. L.1066 J.D. [Payne&F.]
*PRACTICE AREAS: Business Litigation.
**Rau, Laurie** ...........................'69 '96 C.800 B.A. L.1137 J.D. [Ⓐ Kring&B.]
*LANGUAGES: Spanish, Japanese and Korean.
*PRACTICE AREAS: Contracts; Construction Defects; Personal Injury; Elder Law; Corporate Law.
Ravin, Wendy E. .......................'— '94 C.112 B.A. L.426 J.D. 18400 Von Karmen
**Rawls, L. Richard**, (AV) ......... '52 '77 C.800 B.A. L.276 J.D. [Palmieri,T.W.W.&W.]
*PRACTICE AREAS: Litigation; Product Liability Defense.
Ray, Glenn R. ...........'54 '78 C.112 B.S. L.629 J.D. CEO, Celeritas Technologies, Ltd.
**Ray, John J., III** '59 '83 C.454 B.A. L.221 J.D.
(adm. in IA; not adm. in CA) V.P., Grp. Gen. Coun., Waste Management
**Rayl, Rick E.** ..................... '69 '94 C.112 B.A. L.1066 J.D. [Ⓐ Nossaman,G.K.&E.]
*PRACTICE AREAS: Litigation.
**Reagan, Carole E.** ...................... '67 '92 C.112 B.A. L.1066 J.D. [Ⓐ Morrison&F.]
Rebney, Bjorn Eric ........................ '66 '93 C.610 B.A. L.464 J.D. 108 Pacifica
**Reed, Ronna S.** '55 '84 C.112 B.A. L.800 J.D.
[Ⓒ Faustman,C.D.&F.] (⊙Sacramento, Santa Rosa)
*PRACTICE AREAS: Employment Law; Labor Law.
**Reeves, Jeffrey H.** .................... '66 '91 C.839 B.S. L.326 J.D. [Ⓐ Gibson,D.&C.]
*PRACTICE AREAS: Commercial Litigation; Bankruptcy Litigation.
**Relin, Adam H.** ..................... '62 '87 C.112 A.B. L.1068 J.D. [Nossaman,G.K.&E.]
*PRACTICE AREAS: Environmental Law.
**Revelli, John** ....... '67 '94 C.1097 B.A. L.61 J.D. [Ⓐ Manning,M.&W.] (⊙Los Angeles)
Reynolds, Anson D. ........................'36 '80 C.953 B.S. L.1137 J.D. 4 Venture St.
**Reynolds, Michael B.** ..................... '69 '94 C.1067 B.A. L.426 J.D. [Ⓐ Snell&W.]
*PRACTICE AREAS: Bankruptcy Law.
**Reynolds, Richard J.**, (BV) .................. '54 '79 C&L.426 B.A., J.D. [Turner&R.]
*PRACTICE AREAS: Bankruptcy Law; Business Litigation; Real Estate Litigation.

**Rhodes, Terry L., (AV) '40 '69 C.1042 B.S. L.1068 J.D.**
**19762 MacArthur Boulevard, Suite 100, 92715**
**Telephone: 714-752-2285**
**General Business, Real Estate and Estate and Tax Planning.**

*See Professional Biographies, IRVINE, CALIFORNIA*

**Rianda, Paul A.** ........................ '64 '94 C.1042 B.S. L.1065 J.D. [Ⓐ Kring&B.]
*PRACTICE AREAS: Civil Litigation; Business Litigation; Corporate.
**Rice, Steven P.** ........................ '56 '80 C.605 B.A. L.309 J.D. [Ⓒ Crowell&M.]
*PRACTICE AREAS: Commercial Litigation; Unfair Business Practices; Real Estate Litigation.
Rich, Lisa Lenack ........................ '53 '78 C.112 A.B. L.809 J.D. 7 Laurelglen
**Richardson, Michael Danton** ...... '59 '87 C.1055 B.A. L.420 J.D. [Ⓐ Gauntlett&Assoc.]
**Richter, Stuart M.** .............. '61 '86 C.893 B.S. L.990 J.D. [Katten M.&Z.] (⊙L.A.)
*PRACTICE AREAS: Litigation.
Richter, Senn & Palumbo ........ 18301 Von Karman Ave. (⊙San Francisco & San Diego)
**Ridley, Michael P.** ........................ '47 '72 C.813 A.B. L.976 J.D. [Arter&H.]
**Riel, Jennifer A.** ........................ '69 '95 C.1042 B.M. L.1066 J.D. [Ⓐ Morrison&F.]
**Riezman, Eric N.** .............. '54 '80 C.273 B.A. L.1137 J.D. [Berger,K.S.M.F.S.&G.]
Riggs, Charles E. '41 '76 C&L.1136 B.S., J.D.
V.P. & Underwriting Coun., Fidelity Natl. Title Ins. Co.
Riggs, Janet C. .............. '51 '84 C&L.878 B.S., J.D. Waste Management, Inc.-West
Ringstad, Todd C. .................. '54 '80 C.112 B.A. L.1068 J.D. 4 Park Pl., 16th Fl.
**Ristau, Kenneth E., Jr.**, (AV) ............ '39 '65 C.165 B.A. L.569 J.D. [Gibson,D.&C.]
*PRACTICE AREAS: Management Labor Law; N.L.R.B. Practice; Equal Employment and Labor Law; Wrongful Termination Litigation; General Litigation.
**Robbins, Deborah S.** .................. '61 '93 C.1257 B.A. L.900 J.D. [Ⓐ Collins&B.]
**Robertson, Christopher M.** ........ '62 '88 C.674 B.A. L.477 J.D. [Ⓐ Faustman,C.D.&F.]
*PRACTICE AREAS: Employment Law; Labor Law.
**Robertson, Joseph A.** .................... '65 '90 C&L.502 B.A., J.D. [Ⓐ Kring&B.]
**Robinson, David A.** ........................ '57 '82 C.112 A.B. L.1065 J.D. [Bye,H.&R.]
**Robinson, Gregory E.** .................. '56 '83 C.101 B.A. L.878 J.D. [Groh,C.S.&R.]
*LANGUAGES: Italian.
*PRACTICE AREAS: Corporate; Real Estate; Real Estate Finance; Commercial Law.

**Robinson, Jeffrey A., (AV) '56 '83 C.878 B.A. L.101 J.D. BR**
**2301 Dupont Drive, Suite 410, 92612**
**Telephone: 714-752-7007 Fax: 714-752-7023**
***REPORTED CASES: Golden Cheese Company of California v. Voss, 230 Cal. App. 3d 547 & 727 (1991).**
***PRACTICE AREAS: General Civil Litigation; Dispute Resolutions; Trials; Appellate and Administrative Proceedings.**
**Specializing in the representation of domestic and foreign businesses in all aspects of commercial and administrative litigation, including trial, appellate and administrative proceedings in both state and federal courts.**

***See Professional Biographies, IRVINE, CALIFORNIA***

Robinson, Kevin E. ........................ '51 '79 C.766 B.A. L.464 J.D. 2030 Main St.
**Robinson, Robert C.**, (AV) .............. '56 '80 C.999 B.S. L.1009 J.D. [Robinson&C.]
*PRACTICE AREAS: Employment Litigation; Business Litigation; General Commercial Law; Real Estate; Litigation.
**Robinson, Robert S.** .......... '62 '87 C.112 B.A. L.800 J.D. [Ⓐ Berger,K.S.M.F.S.&G.]

**Robinson & Campbell, (AV)**
**One Park Plaza, Suite 1250, 92714**
**Telephone: 714-263-8790 Fax: 714-263-1793**
**Robert C. Robinson; Warren B. Campbell.**
**Trials and Appeals in State and Federal Courts and Alternative Dispute Resolution involving Real Estate, Finance and Construction Litigation, Partnership, Corporate, Business and Employment Disputes. Commercial Fraud, Business Torts, Breach of Contract, Collection and Insurance, Sexual Harassment, Wrongful Termination, Civil Rights and Discrimination.**

***See Professional Biographies, IRVINE, CALIFORNIA***

**Rodich, Norman J.** ............ '61 '86 C.112 A.B. L.1067 J.D. [Ⓐ Palmieri,T.W.W.&W.]
*PRACTICE AREAS: Litigation.
**Rodman, Daniel S.** ........................ '66 '91 C.800 B.S. L.426 J.D. [Ⓐ Snell&W.]
*PRACTICE AREAS: Product Liability Litigation.
**Rodriguez, Mark A.**, (AV) .............. '59 '87 C.426 B.A. L.309 J.D. [Borchard&W.]
*PRACTICE AREAS: Civil Litigation; Securities Litigation; Real Estate Litigation; Appellate Practice.
Roe, Troy D., (AV) ............ '50 '76 C.1042 B.A. L.990 J.D. 14988 Sand Canyon Ave.
Rofoli, Robert L. ................ '46 '91 C.1042 B.A. L.1137 J.D. 7700 Irvine Center Dr.
Roman, H. Scott .................... '51 '84 C.446 B.A. L.809 J.D. 8001 Irvine Center Dr.
Root, Walter H., (BV) .................. '51 '78 C.846 B.A. L.802 J.D. 2201 DuPont Dr.
**Roquemore, Lisa A.** .................... '62 '89 C.763 B.A. L.61 J.D. [Meserve,M.&H.]
*PRACTICE AREAS: Bankruptcy; Commercial and Business Litigation.
**Rorty, Bruce V.** .................... '57 '86 C.1169 B.A. L.1049 J.D. [Wesierski&Z.]
*PRACTICE AREAS: Insurance Bad Faith; Employment Law; Civil Litigation; Medical Malpractice.
Rosandic, Anton M. ............................ '64 '90 C.112 B.A. L.800 J.D. [Ⓐ Benice]
**Rosenbaum, Keith A.** .................. '58 '82 C.1109 B.A. L.61 J.D. [Rosenbaum&D.]

**Rosenbaum & Deihl, A Professional Corporation**
**8001 Irvine Center Drive, Suite 1500, 92718**
**Telephone: 714-753-1990 Fax: 714-753-1888**
**Keith A. Rosenbaum; Richard T. Deihl;—Paul R. Huber.**
**General Business, Corporate Law, Tax Law, Business Litigation, Estate Planning, Mergers and Acquisitions, Real Estate Law.**

***See Professional Biographies, IRVINE, CALIFORNIA***

Ross, Gary B., (BV) ............................ '51 '78 C.800 B.S. L.1148 J.D. [G.B.Ross]
**Ross, James L.**, (AV) .................... '57 '82 C.112 A.B. L.800 J.D. [Allen,R.&M.]
*PRACTICE AREAS: Real Estate.

**Ross, Dixon & Masback, L.L.P.**
**5 Park Plaza, Suite 1200, 92614-8529⊙**
**Telephone: 714-622-2700 Fax: 714-622-2739**
**Resident Member: Robert M. Pozin;—Pascal W. Di Fronzo; Michele L. Lynch. Resident Of Counsel: Alec M. Barinholtz.**
**General Trial and Appellate Practice before State and Federal Courts, Insurance Coverage Litigation and Counseling, Directors and Officers Liability, Professional Liability, Corporate, First Amendment, Media and Intellectual Property Litigation.**
**Washington, D.C. Office: 601 Pennsylvania Avenue, N.W., North Building, 20004-2688. Telephone: 202-662-2000.**

***See Professional Biographies, IRVINE, CALIFORNIA***

Ross, Gary B., (A Law Corporation), (BV) .......... 8001 Irvine Center Drive, Suite 1500
Rothenberg, Allan, (AV) ........ '24 '50 C.563 B.C.E. L.1009 LL.B. 1920 Main St. (Pat.)
**Rothrock, Frank C., (A Professional Corporation)**, (AV) '47 '72
C.605 A.B. L.1066 J.D. [Palmieri,T.W.W.&W.]
*REPORTED CASES: San Diego Gas & Electric Co. v. Superior Court, 13 Cal.3d 893 (1996); San Diego Gas & Electric Co. v. Superior Court, 38 Cal. Rptr. 2d 811 (1995); Ministry of Health v. Shiley, 858 F.Supp. 1426 (C.D. Cal. 1994); Artiglio v. Superior Court, 22 Cal.App.4th 1388 (1994); McGhan Medical Corp. v. Superior Court, 11 Cal.App.4th 804 (1992).
*PRACTICE AREAS: Pharmaceutical and Medical Device Product Liability; General Product Litigation; Civil Writs and Appeals.
Rothrock, Judith A. '41 '85 C.112 B.A. L.426 J.D.
V.P. & Assoc. Coun., Fidelity Natl. Title Ins. Co.
**Rouse, James R.** ........................ '43 '89 C.871 B.S. L.273 J.D. [Ⓐ Bryan C.]
*PRACTICE AREAS: Products Liability; Business Litigation.
Rovere, Michael V. .................. '66 '91 C.119 B.S. L.188 J.D. 18400 Von Karman
**Rowe, Paul A.** ............................ '58 '85 C.585 B.A. L.494 J.D. [Hewitt&M.]
*PRACTICE AREAS: Corporate Law; Securities Law; Real Estate Law; Business Law.
**Roy, Gerda M.** ........................ '62 '87 C.112 B.A. L.1066 J.D. [Ⓐ Snell&W.]
*PRACTICE AREAS: Business Litigation; State and Federal Appeals.
Rozakis, Patricia J. .................... '57 '87 C.112 B.A. L.1137 J.D. [Ⓐ Morgan&W.]

**Rubin, Jeffrey D.**, (AV) .................. '52 '79 C.1109 B.A. L.1137 J.D. [Barnett&R.]
*PRACTICE AREAS: Civil Practice; Commercial Law; Real Estate; Receivership Law.
**Ruck, Mary Kay** .................. '65 '92 C.967 B.A. L.477 J.D. [Ⓐ Allen,M.L.G.&M.]
*PRACTICE AREAS: Employment Law.

**Rudolph Law Group, The, A Professional Corporation**
**(See Costa Mesa)**

**Rullo, Maria M.** .................. '47 '79 C&L.1137 B.S.L., J.D. [Ⓐ Genson,E.C.&W.]
**Rundle, Peter K.** ........................ '59 '85 C.112 B.A. L.1065 J.D. [Ⓐ Arter&H.]
*PRACTICE AREAS: Litigation; Real Estate; Title Insurance.
**Runkel, Brian A.** '61 '87 C.273 B.A. L.309 J.D.
(adm. in MD; not adm. in CA) [Ⓒ Brown,P.H.&V.]
*PRACTICE AREAS: Environmental Law.
**Rus, Ronald**, (AV) ...................... '50 '75 C.800 B.A. L.990 J.D. [Rus,M.W.&S.]
*REPORTED CASES: In re Fietz, 852 F.2d 455, (9th Cir. 1988); In re American Continental Corporation/ Lincoln Sav. & Loan Securities Litigation, 794 F.supp. 1424, (D.Ariz., 1992); In re County of Orange, 183 B.R. 594, (Bankr. C.D. Cal 1995); In re Walters, 136 B.R. 256, (Bkrptcy. C.D. Cal., 1992).
*PRACTICE AREAS: Complex Litigation; Creditors Rights; Bankruptcy Litigation.

**Rus, Miliband, Williams & Smith, (AV) BR**
**Suite 700, 2600 Michelson Drive, 92612**
**Telephone: 714-752-7100 Fax: 714-252-1514**
**Ronald Rus; Joel S. Miliband; J. Scott Williams; Randall A. Smith; Laurel Zaeske;—M. Peter Crinella; Jeffrey H. Sussman; Cathrine M. Castaldi; David Edward Hays; Steven Joseph Kraemer; Leo J. Presiado.**
**General Civil and Trial Practice. Complex Commercial Litigation, Bankruptcy, Insolvency, Corporate Reorganization and Creditors Rights.**

***See Professional Biographies, IRVINE, CALIFORNIA***

**Russo, J. Scott** .......................... '65 '91 C.112 B.S. L.426 J.D. [Ⓐ Pinto&D.]
Rutten, Susan M., (BV) ........... '57 '82 C.770 B.S. L.990 J.D. 2010 Main St., Ste., 400
Ryan, Judith M. .......................... '42 '70 C.800 B.A. L.426 J.D. 2030 Main St.
**Ryder, Kenneth A.** .......................... '57 '82 C.602 B.A. L.569 J.D. [Pinto&D.]
**Saadeh, Laura L.** ................ '57 '87 C.1077 B.A. L.426 J.D. [Ⓐ Faustman,C.D.&F.]
*PRACTICE AREAS: Employment Law; Labor Law.
**Sachs, Michael J.** .......................... '62 '87 C.910 A.B. L.94 J.D. [Ⓐ Callahan&B.]
*PRACTICE AREAS: Business Litigation; Insurance Coverage Litigation; Securities Litigation.
**Sacks, Mark A.** .......................... '64 '91 C.112 B.A. L.309 J.D. [Ⓐ Payne&F.]
*PRACTICE AREAS: Labor and Employment Law; Wrongful Termination; Employment Discrimination.
**Sakura, Susan T.** .............. '67 '93 C.813 B.A. L.273 J.D. [Ⓐ Palmieri,T.W.W.&W.]
*PRACTICE AREAS: Business Litigation.
**Salmond, Kathryn B.** .................. '63 '88 C.112 B.A. L.800 J.D. [Ⓐ Barnett&R.]
*PRACTICE AREAS: Commercial Litigation; Real Estate; Receivership; Bankruptcy Law.
Salot, Susan E. ...................... '42 '85 C.800 B.S. L.1137 J.D. 100 Pacifica Ste. 200
**Salus, Richard A.** ............ '64 '89 C.112 B.A. L.1065 J.D. [Ⓐ Palmieri,T.W.W.&W.]
*PRACTICE AREAS: Corporate Law; Environmental; Estate Planning Law; Estate Administration Law.
Salyer, Timothy J., (BV) ..... '49 '74 C.139 L.990 J.D. 18400 Von Karman Ave., Ste. 600
**Samson, Jane M.** ...................... '58 '85 C.741 B.Mus. L.602 J.D. [Morrison&F.]
*PRACTICE AREAS: Land Use; Environmental; Real Estate.
**Samuels, Herbert N.**, (AV) .......... '30 '55 C.563 B.B.A. L.1009 LL.B. [Samuels&S.]
*PRACTICE AREAS: Corporate and Business; Real Estate Development; Commercial Development Law; Land Use Entitlement Law; Joint Ventures and Financing.

**Samuels & Steel, LLP, (AV)**
**18881 Von Karman Avenue Suite 1400, 92612**
**Telephone: 714-224-0140 FAX: 714-224-0141**
**Email: SamSteel@aol.com**
**Herbert N. Samuels; William L. Steel; Hilary B. Glen-Grossman.**
**General Practice.**

***See Professional Biographies, IRVINE, CALIFORNIA***

**Sanders, Gregory W.** .............. '47 '77 C.1109 B.A. L.990 J.D. [Nossaman,G.K.&E.]
*PRACTICE AREAS: Land Use Law; Real Property Law; Legislative Law.
**Sanders, Michael E.** .............. '58 '96 C.45 B.S.B.A. L.813 J.D. [Ⓐ Gibson,D.&C.]
**Sanders, Nanette D.** .......................... '58 '85 C.1075 B.S. L.426 J.D. [Snell&W.]
*PRACTICE AREAS: Bankruptcy; Reorganization; Commercial Litigation.
**Sandor, Geraldine G.**, (AV) ...... '42 '75 C.112 B.A. L.1066 J.D. [Simon,M.M.Z.S.&D.]
*PRACTICE AREAS: Family Law.
**Sandoval, Dennis M.** .................... '58 '96 C.1109 B.A. L.1137 J.D. [Ⓐ J.E.Mudd]
*PRACTICE AREAS: Estate Planning; Tax Controversy; Probate Administration; Retirement Planning/ Pension Distributions; Charitable Planning/Planned Giving.
Santochi, Fitzer & Gable, (AV) .................................. 3355 Michelson Dr.
**Sartain, Julianne** ........................ '65 '90 C.112 A.B. L.1068 J.D. [Ⓐ Snell&W.]
*PRACTICE AREAS: Commercial Litigation.
Sartoris, Stephanie J. '51 '83 C.1042 B.A. L.61 J.D.
V.P. & Assoc. Coun., Fidelity Natl. Title Ins. Co.
**Satalino, Frank A.** ...................... '63 '89 C.1044 B.A. L.1065 J.D. [Andrade&M.]
*PRACTICE AREAS: Construction Claims; Mechanic's Liens; Public and Private Projects; Construction Defect Actions; Insurance Litigation.
**Satuloff, Wendy C.** .................. '66 '92 C.112 B.A. L.426 J.D. [Ⓐ Meserve,M.&H.]
*PRACTICE AREAS: Bankruptcy.
Saur, John K., (BV) .................. '41 '75 C.800 B.A. L.1137 J.D. 7700 Irvine Ctr. Dr.
**Schadrack, Mark A.** .......................... '59 '85 C.112 A.B. L.426 J.D. [Grant&L.]
*PRACTICE AREAS: Litigation.
Schafer, Timothy J. .......................... '62 '89 C.174 B.S. L.1049 J.D. [Schafer]⊙
Schafer Law Offices .................... 8001 Irvine Center Dr., Suite 1170 (⊙Denver)
**Schag, Ernest J., Jr.**, (AV) ............ '33 '60 C&L.800 A.B., LL.B. [Ⓒ Freeman,F.&S.]
*PRACTICE AREAS: Estate Planning; Charitable Tax Planning and Private Foundations.
**Schaller, Gordon A.**, (AV) .............. '49 '73 C.350 B.S. L.494 J.D. [Gibson,D.&C.]
*PRACTICE AREAS: Estate Planning, Trust and Probate Administration; Tax Exempt Organizations; Charitable Tax Planning.
**Schaner, Carol Peskoe** .......... '55 '82 C.188 B.S. L.1049 J.D. [Berger,K.S.M.F.S.&G.]
Schanz, William L., (AV) .............. '51 '77 C.112 B.S. L.464 J.D. 8001 Irvine Ctr. Dr.
**Schappals, Julia A.** ............ '— '77 C.823 B.A. L.990 J.D. Sr. Atty., AST Resch., Inc.
**Scheffing, Robert A.**, (AVⓉ) ............ '42 '67 C.602 A.B. L.37 J.D. [Jennings&H.]⊙
*PRACTICE AREAS: Surety; Construction; Product Liability; Personal Injury; Design Professional Liability.
**Scheinkman, James J.** ...................... '58 '83 C.1044 B.A. L.569 J.D. [Ⓐ Busch]
*PRACTICE AREAS: Corporate; Securities; Commercial; Real Estate Transactional and Finance; Creditors Rights.
Schiff, Cathy R., (AV) .................. '49 '80 C.994 B.A. L.800 J.D. 8 Corporate Park
**Schiffer, Michael C.** '55 '80 C.705 B.S. L.1048 J.D.
Asst. Gen. Coun., Baxter Healthcare Corp. (Pat.)
Schiffman, Mark E. ............ '49 '74 C.112 B.A. L.502 J.D. Fidelity Natl. Title Ins. Co.
**Schindler, Walter L.** .................. '51 '80 C.976 B.A. L.309 J.D. [Gibson,D.&C.]
*PRACTICE AREAS: Corporate Law; Securities Law.
Schiralli, Beth S. .......................... '60 '86 C&L.546 B.A., J.D. 2 Park Plaza
**Schlesinger, Diane L.** '63 '88
C.112 B.A. L.1066 J.D. [Ⓐ Faustman,C.D.&F.] (⊙Los Angeles)
*PRACTICE AREAS: Employment Law; Labor Law; Business Litigation.
Schmeltzer, Norman B., (BV) ............ '49 '78 C.1042 B.S. L.426 J.D. [O'Connor&S.]
Schmidhauser, Paul A. '54 '81
C.800 A.B. L.1068 J.D. 2600 Michelson Dr. 12th Fl. Zone 3
**Schmitt, Edward W.**, (BV) ........ '56 '81 C.112 B.A. L.1065 J.D. [Mower,K.N.C.&H.]

CALIFORNIA—IRVINE MARTINDALE-HUBBELL LAW DIRECTORY 1997

Schneider, Kathleen Villarruel .........'61 '87 C.426 B.A. L.800 J.D. 17877 Von Karman
**Schoeffel, J. Scott** ...........................'54 '80 C.112 B.A. L.1066 J.D. [A Jones,D.R.&P.]

**Schoellerman, Jack L., (AV) '46 '72 C.154 B.A. L.1049 J.D.** BR
**2030 Main Street, Suite 1600, 92614**
**Telephone: 714-660-7000 Fax: 714-660-6096**
**Corporate, Partnership, Taxation and Estate Planning Law.**

***See Professional Biographies, IRVINE, CALIFORNIA***

Schoenberger, James A., Jr. '48 '81 C.339 B.A. L.146 J.D.
(adm. in IL; not adm. in CA) F.D.I.C.
**Schrenker, Henry P.** ............ '56 '78 C.347 B.S. L.1137 J.D. [A Kasdan,S.M.E.&M.]
*PRACTICE AREAS: Construction Defects; Real Estate Litigation.
**Schubert, Victor J.** ................ '63 '88 C.971 B.S.M.E. L.802 J.D. Discovision Assocs.
*RESPONSIBILITIES: Patent Litigation; Patent Licensing; Patent Prosecution.
**Schuk, Camellia Kuo** ...................'66 '91 C.112 B.A. L.188 J.D. [A Cox,C.&N.]
*PRACTICE AREAS: Real Estate Law.

**Schumacher, Stephen J., (AV) '42 '68 C.800 A.B. L.1065 J.D.** BR
**18201 Von Karman, Suite 220, 92612-1005**
**Telephone: 714-752-9425 Telecopier: 714-752-8170**
**Business, Tax and Estate Planning Practice. Corporation, Real Property, Probate, Trusts, Wills, Securities and Federal and State Taxation Law.**
**Reference: Bank of America (Irvine Industrial Branch).**

***See Professional Biographies, IRVINE, CALIFORNIA***

**Schutz, Andrew C.** .......................'43 '70 C.112 A.B. L.1068 J.D. [Jackson,D.&P.]
*PRACTICE AREAS: Business; Real Estate.
**Schwab, Charlotte** ..............'43 '80 C.929 B.S. L.1066 J.D. Baxter Healthcare Corp.
Schwartz, Jerome W. .....................'21 '75 C.24 B.S. L.1148 J.D. 18 Southern Wood‡
**Schwartz, John W.** ..........................'49 '75 C&L.188 B.A., J.D. [Feder,G.&S.]
**Schwartz, Richard O.** ..........................'52 '79 C.94 B.A. L.569 J.D. [Pivo&H.]
Schwarz, Michael E. ....................'54 '79 C.976 B.A. L.145 J.D. The Ayco Corp.
**Schweitzer, Bradley N.** ..............'57 '87 C.112 B.A. L.426 J.D. [A Allen,M.L.G.&M.]
*PRACTICE AREAS: Real Estate.
**Schwenck, Charles E.** ........................'45 '72 C.112 A.B. L.1066 J.D. [Morrison&F.]
*PRACTICE AREAS: International Project Development; International Project Finance; Construction; Public Utility.
**Scott, Spencer** '51 '85 C.112 B.A. L.809 J.D.
Legal Coun., Kawasaki Motors Corp., U.S.A.
*RESPONSIBILITIES: Products Liability Law.
Scranton, Drasan R. '64 '92 C.112 B.A. L.1097 J.D.
(adm. in PA; not adm. in CA) Fed. Deposit Ins. Corp.

**Sedgwick, Detert, Moran & Arnold, (AV)**
**A Partnership including Professional Corporations**
**17th Floor, 3 Park Plaza, 92714☉**
**Telephone: 714-852-8200 Fax: 714-852-8282**
**Email: E-Mail@SDMA.com**
**Members of Firm: Gregory H. Halliday; Alan J. Freisleben; Curtis D. Parvin; John E. Feeley; Todd Andrew Picker; Lily Chow. Special Counsel: Dale A. Hudson; Ronald B. Pierce; Michael J. Khouri; Thomas J. Bois, II, (P.C.). Of Counsel: Irene E. Ziebarth. Associates: Richard Wm. Zevnik; Kelly Lee Fidone; Ralph A. Guirgis; Angela L. Ball; Allen B. Gresham, II; Deborah L. O'Connor; Alan B. Unterman; Jeffrey I. Braun; Jill A. Tracy; Charles R. Gossage; Brian D. Jones.**
**General Civil Litigation and Trial Practice. Aviation, Business, Construction, Directors and Officers Liability, Employment and Labor, Entertainment, Environmental, Fidelity and Surety, General Liability, Health Care, Pharmaceuticals, Insurance and Reinsurance, Intellectual Property, Products Liability, and Professional Malpractice.**
**San Francisco, California Office: 16th Floor, One Embarcadero Center. Telephone: 415-781-7900. Cable Address: "Sedma". Fax: 415-781-2635.**
**Los Angeles, California Office: 801 South Figueroa Street, 18th Floor. Telephone: 213-426-6900. Fax: 213-426-6921.**
**New York, New York Office: 41st Floor, 59 Maiden Lane. Telephone: 212-422-0202. Fax: 212-422-0925.**
**Chicago, Illinois Office: The Rookery Building, Seventh Floor, 209 South La Salle Street. Telephone: 312-641-9050. Fax: 312-641-9530.**
**London, England Office: Lloyds Avenue House, 6 Lloyds Avenue, EC3N 3AX. Telephone: 0171-929-1829. Fax: 0171-929-1808.**
**Zurich, Switzerland Office: Spluegenstrasse 3, CH-8002. Telephone: 011-411-201-1730. Fax: 011-411-201-4404.**

***See Professional Biographies, IRVINE, CALIFORNIA***

**Segal, David A.** ........................ '67 '93 C.453 S.B. L.262 J.D. [A Gibson,D.&C.]
*PRACTICE AREAS: Intellectual Property Litigation and Counseling; Business Litigation.
**Segall, Brian F.** ..........................................'46 '70 L.061 [A Friedman P.&S.]
*PRACTICE AREAS: Domestic and International Business Transactions; Licensing and Trademarks; Copyright.
Seguin, Gregory N., (AV) ............'33 '74 C.912 B.S. L.1137 J.D. 8001 Irvine Ctr. Dr.
Seidler, Nancy C. '57 '85 C.999 B.S. L.1137 J.D.
(adm. in MT; not adm. in CA) 151 W. Yale Loop‡
Sesler, Timothy W. ......... '63 '89 C.375 B.S. L.1068 J.D. Coun., Avco Fin. Servs., Inc.
Sevier, Charles B. .........................'21 '48 C.337 B.A. L.910 J.D. 4712 Royce Rd.‡
Shaeffer, George William, Jr. .................'49 '75 C.112 B.A. L.809 J.D. 2030 Main St.
**Shaff, Michael E., (CV)** .................. '54 '79 C.178 A.B. L.569 J.D. [Jeffers,W.&S.]
*PRACTICE AREAS: Taxation.
**Shanberg, Ross E.** ...........................'70 '95 C.112 B.S. L.61 J.D. [A Baker,S.&K.]
Shapiro, Daniel R. .........................'51 '90 C.112 M.S. L.1137 J.D. P.O. Box 4415
Shapiro, Gary M. ...............................'51 '77 C.1077 B.A. L.398 J.D. 14771 Athel
**Shapiro, Stephen A.** ........... '65 '91 C.112 B.A. L.1065 J.D. [A Berger,K.S.M.F.S.&G.]
**Shedden, Rhea S.** ............................'49 '82 C.188 A.B. L.800 J.D. [Parilla,M.&S.]
*PRACTICE AREAS: Construction Law; Real Estate Property Law; Shopping Center Law.
**Sheets, Philip A.** '35 '74 C.679 B.S. L.990 J.D.
Dir., Prod. Litig., Kawasaki Motors Corp., U.S.A.
*RESPONSIBILITIES: Products Liability Law (100%).
Sherlock, Robert L., (AV) ......... '43 '73 C.93 B.S. L.810 J.D. 18201 Von Karman Ave.
**Sherlock, Sean Michael** .................... '64 '92 C.474 B.S. L.426 J.D. [A Snell&W.]
*PRACTICE AREAS: Environmental Law.
Sherman, Robert M. ..........................'66 '91 C.684 B.S. L.1148 J.D. 11 Stonepine
Sherry, Kevin L. ............................'60 '92 C.1075 B.S. L.426 J.D. [Sherry&H.]
Sherry & Holthouse, LL.P. ...................................................610 Newport Center Dr.
**Shewmaker, John R.** '41 '80 C.390 B.S.E.E. L.128 J.D.
Sr. Corp. Coun., Pfizer Inc. (Pat.)
**Shiel, Catherine Stark** .........................'53 '79 C.813 A.B. L.36 J.D. [A Amante]
*PRACTICE AREAS: Civil Litigation; Legal Writing; Trial and Appellate Practice; Bankruptcy Law.
**Shields, Jeffrey W.** ............................'57 '83 C&L.101 B.A., J.D. [Bryan C.]
*LANGUAGES: Japanese.
*PRACTICE AREAS: International Litigation; Real Estate Litigation; Employment Litigation; Financial Transactions Litigation; Bankruptcy Litigation.
**Shields, Timothy F., (AV)** ..................'57 '85 C.908 B.A. L.990 J.D. [George&S.]
*PRACTICE AREAS: Business; Real Estate; General Civil Litigation; Construction Claims; Labor and Employment Law.
Shier, Robert C., Jr. '65 '91 C.1021 B.B.A. L.982 J.D.
(adm. in NY; not adm. in CA) The Ayco Corp.
**Shimokaji, Michael A.** ......................'54 '80 C.112 B.A. L.809 J.D. [DiPinto&S.]
*PRACTICE AREAS: Products Liability; Negligence; Intellectual Property; General Business.

**Shipp, Marianne** ........................ '52 '87 C.980 B.S. L.1049 J.D. [A Gibson,D.&C.]
*PRACTICE AREAS: Labor and Employment; ERISA Litigation.
**Shirley, R. Bryce** ................'51 '77 C&L.813 B.A., J.D. Mng. Coun., PepsiCo, Inc.
*RESPONSIBILITIES: Real Estate.
**Shure, Stanley H.** .....................'54 '84 C.605 B.A. L.426 J.D. [A Gauntlett&Assoc.]
*LANGUAGES: French.
**Shurtleff, Mark W.** ........................ '53 '78 C.813 B.A. L.800 J.D. [Gibson,D.&C.]
*PRACTICE AREAS: Securities; Intellectual Property; Software; General Corporate.
Siemon, Larsen & Marsh, (AV) ..... Suite 350 (☉Chicago IL, Boca Raton FL, Aspen CO)
Siepler, James E. ..............................'54 '81 C.436 B.A. L.809 J.D. 5 Park Plz.
**Sikora, Warren,** (AV) ......................'21 '53 C.145 B.A. L.1068 J.D. [Sikora&P.]☉
*PRACTICE AREAS: Estate Planning; Real Estate Law; Business Law.

**Sikora and Price, Incorporated, (AV)** BR
**10 Corporate Park Suite 300, 92606**
**Telephone: 714-261-2233 Telecopier: 714-261-6935**
**Warren Sikora (Certified Specialist, Taxation Law, The State Bar of California Board of Legal Specialization); Donald R. Price; Steven C. Crooke; Bruce J. Gary (Certified Specialist, Estate Planning, Trust and Probate Law, The State Bar of California Board of Legal Specialization).**
**Federal and State Taxation Law. Estate Planning, Probate, Business and Real Estate Transactions, Partnerships, Corporation Law. Trials and Appeals.**

***See Professional Biographies, IRVINE, CALIFORNIA***

**Silbar, Lisa Welch** ........................ '58 '85 C.575 B.S. L.880 J.D. [Smith,S.D.P.&W.]
**Silberberg, Marshall,** (AV) ................ '48 '73 C.800 B.A. L.464 J.D. [Baker,S.&K.]
*PRACTICE AREAS: Professional Liability; Personal Injury.
Silberman, Leonard J., (AV) ............ '47 '72 C.1077 B.S. L.1065 J.D. [Silberman&C.]
Silberman & Cohn, (AV) ........................................ 2603 Main Street, Suite 800
Silliman, Dean J. ...........'69 '95 C.1042 B.A. L.861 J.D. 18401 Von Karman, Ste. 350
Silva, Alban P., (BV) ............................'32 '60 C.426 B.A. L.1066 J.D. Five Park Plaza
**Silva, Tracy L** ........................'63 '96 C.946 B.A. L.802 J.D. [A Allen,M.L.G.&M.]
*PRACTICE AREAS: Litigation.
**Silver, Craig J.** ...................................... '67 '93 C.763 B.S. L.990 J.D. [A Kring&B.]
*PRACTICE AREAS: Business Litigation; Professional Liability; Construction Defect.
Silverman, Sherman A., (AV) .............'35 '62 C.112 B.A. L.1068 J.D. [S.A.Silverman]
Silverman, Sherman A., A Law Corp., (AV) ........................ 19800 MacArthur Blvd.
**Simon, Craig S.** .................. '53 '77 C.112 B.A. L.426 J.D. [Berger,K.S.M.F.S.&G.]
Simon, William G., (AV) .....................'13 '40 C.740 A.B. L.1066 J.D. 18021 Cowan

**Simon, McKinsey, Miller, Zommick, Sandor & Dundas, A Law Corporation, (AV)**
**Suite 670, 4199 Campus Drive, 92715☉**
**Telephone: 714-856-1916 Facsimile: 714-856-3834**
**Geraldine G. Sandor (Certified Specialist, Family Law, The State Bar of California Board of Legal Specialization); David G. Dundas;—Carrie Block.**
**General Civil and Civil Trial Practice. Corporation, Real Estate, Estate Planning, Trust, Taxation, Probate, Negligence, Family Law, Local Government Administrative Hearings and Appeals.**
**Long Beach, California Office: 2750 Bellflower Boulevard. Telephone: 213-421-9354. Facsimile: 213-420-6455.**

***See Professional Biographies, IRVINE, CALIFORNIA***

**Simonds, Vance C., Jr.,** (AV) ....... '47 '78 C.813 A.B. L.426 J.D. [Kasdan,S.M.E.&M.]
*PRACTICE AREAS: Medical Products Liability; Business Litigation.
**Simonis, John F.,** (AV) ................ '61 '86 C.436 B.S. L.477 J.D. [Paone,C.M.&W.]
*PRACTICE AREAS: Real Property Transactions and Finance; Commercial Leasing; Land Use.
Simonson, Kirstin H. ...............................'— '82 C.1042 B.A. L.426 J.D. 1 Park Plaza
Simpson, Peter, (BV) ..... '47 '76 C.1042 B.S. L.1137 J.D. 14988 Sand Canyon, Ste., 1-8
Simpson, Richard D., Jr. ..................'49 '77 L.1137 J.D. Fidelity Natl. Title Ins. Co.
Sims, James A., Jr. ................'57 '83 C.282 B.A. L.809 J.D. [Sims&O.] (☉Oakland)
Sims & Olsen .......................................... 19000 Macarthur Blvd. (☉Oakland, CA.)
**Sinclair, Brian C.** ........................'69 '95 C.112 B.A. L.1067 J.D. [A Morrison&F.]
**Singer, Jeffrey B.,** (AV) ...............'56 '81 C.966 B.A. L.1049 J.D. [Tredway,L.&D.]
*REPORTED CASES: Eisenbaum v. Western Energy Resources, Inc. (1990) 218 Cal. App. 3d 314; Wu v. Interstate Consolidated Industries (1991) 226 Cal. App. 3d 1511.
*PRACTICE AREAS: Civil Litigation.
Singer, Melanie Rabin, (BV) ...........................'52 '77 C.112 B.A. L.426 J.D. 3 Nova‡
**Singer, Rachelle** ........................ '64 '89 C&L.608 B.A., J.D. [A Smith,S.D.P.&W.]
Sizemore, Rachna S. .............'71 '95 C.112 B.A. L.1066 J.D. 19900 MacArthur Blvd.
**Skigin, Cheryl A.,** (BV) ..........................'51 '76 C.367 B.A. L.245 J.D. [Lobel&O.]
*PRACTICE AREAS: Bankruptcy.
Sklan, Mark L. .............................................'51 '77 C&L.930 B.A., J.D. 38 Corp. Pk.
**Skripko, Robert W., Jr.** ......................'65 '90 C.112 B.A. L.800 J.D. [A Kirtland&P.]
Slavin-Cosel, Judith A. .........................'51 '77 C.608 B.A. L.161 J.D. 14252 Culver Dr.
**Smart, Dean E.** ...........................'59 '87 C.1109 B.A. L.990 J.D. [A Neuland&N.]
*LANGUAGES: Spanish.
*PRACTICE AREAS: Construction Defect; Community Association; Personal Injury; Commercial.
**Smith, Cameron M., Jr.,** (AV) ........'45 '73 C.976 B.A. L.893 J.D. [Smith,S.D.P.&W.]
Smith, Christine Boersma ............. '49 '83 C&L.276 B.S., J.D. 4 Park Plaza, 16th Fl.
**Smith, David C.** ..............................'66 '95 C.112 B.A. L.990 J.D. [Jackson,D.&P.]
*PRACTICE AREAS: Litigation.
**Smith, Diane R.,** (AV) ..............................'46 '75 C.112 A.B. L.1066 J.D. [Snell&W.]
*PRACTICE AREAS: Environmental Law; High Technology, Engineering and Construction Contracts.
**Smith, Douglas P.** .............................'56 '81 C.800 B.A. L.426 J.D. [Jackson,D.&P.]
*PRACTICE AREAS: Commercial; Business; Probate; Environmental Litigation.
**Smith, Eric W.** ................'39 '78 C.112 B.S.M.E. L.37 J.D. [A Mower,K.N.C.&H.]
Smith, Herbert F. '38 '64 C.813 A.B. L.1065 J.D.
Dir., Sr. V.P., Corp. Secy. & Gen. Coun., Avco Fin. Servs., Inc.
Smith, Kristin ..........................'55 '95 C&L.1137 B.S.L., J.D. 100 Pacifica Ste. 200
**Smith, Paul M.** ..................................'52 '77 C.800 B.A. L.426 J.D. [A Morrison&F.]
*PRACTICE AREAS: Commercial Litigation.
**Smith, Philip E.** .............................. '56 '81 C&L.893 B.A., J.D. [Smith,B.&D.]
*PRACTICE AREAS: Civil Litigation; Environmental; Antitrust; Real Estate; Insurance.
**Smith, Phillip E.** ..............................'60 '85 C.1253 B.A. L.426 J.D. [Ramsay&J.]
*REPORTED CASES: Nationwide Mutual Insurance Co. v. Devlin, 11 Cal. App. 4th 81 (1992).
*PRACTICE AREAS: Insurance Coverage; Bad Faith Law; Environmental Insurance Litigation; Excess Insurance Law; Casualty Insurance Law.
**Smith, Randall A.** .........................'58 '84 C.605 B.A. L.1068 J.D. [Rus,M.W.&S.]
*PRACTICE AREAS: Complex Litigation; Business Litigation; Creditors Rights; Bankruptcy Litigation.
**Smith, Rensselaer J., IV** ............ '56 '81 C.112 B.A. L.1068 J.D. [Nossaman,G.K.&E.]
*PRACTICE AREAS: Real Property Law.
Smith, Richard A. '45 '70 C.575 B.A. L.893 J.D.
(adm. in OH; not adm. in CA) 17901 Von Karman
**Smith, Stephen E.** .............................'60 '85 C.1253 B.A. L.800 J.D. [Ramsay&J.]
*PRACTICE AREAS: Insurance Coverage; Bad Faith Law; Litigation.
**Smith, Stuart A.** ...............................'59 '86 C.112 B.A. L.426 J.D. [Kring&B.]
*PRACTICE AREAS: Civil and Business Litigation; Plaintiff Personal Injury; Subrogation.
**Smith, W. Richard, Jr.** ..................... '60 '86 C.893 B.S. L.245 J.D. [C Gibson,D.&C.]
*PRACTICE AREAS: Computers and Software; Intellectual Property.
**Smith, Wayne W.,** (AV) .......'42 '72 C.1042 B.A. L.1068 J.D. [Gibson,D.&C.] (☉L.A.)
*PRACTICE AREAS: Business and Securities Litigation; Entertainment Litigation.

**Smith, Brennan & Dickerson, A Professional Corporation**
**19900 MacArthur Boulevard Seventh Floor, 92612**
**Telephone: 714-442-1500 Facsimile: 714-442-1515**
**Philip E. Smith; Donald D. Dickerson; Sterling A. Brennan; Jay W. Deverich; Joseph G. Harraka, Jr.; Michael W. Ellison; David G. Hagopian; Caroline McIntyre.**

(This Listing Continued)

**Smith, Brennan & Dickerson, A Professional Corporation (Continued)**

**Business and Civil Litigation in all State and Federal Courts, including Real Estate, Environmental, Land Use, Banking, Employment, Insurance, Construction, Contract, Antitrust, and Securities Litigation; Real Estate Transactions and Land Use.**

*See Professional Biographies, IRVINE, CALIFORNIA*

**Smith, Silbar, Duffy, Parker & Woffinden, (AV)**
**19100 Von Karman Avenue Suite 400, 92715**
**Telephone: 714-263-8066 Fax: 714-263-8073**
**Members of Firm: Cameron M. Smith, Jr.; Lisa Welch Silbar; Anthony C. Duffy; Keith M. Parker; Arlen D. Woffinden;—Rachelle Singer; Gregory S. Lane.**
**Alternate Dispute Resolution; Business Law, Commercial Law, Complex and Multi District Litigation, Litigation Defense, Government Contracts, Real Estate, Probate, Property Taxation, Corporate, Domestic Relations, Federal Tax, Non-Profit and Charitable Organizations, Taxation, Trademarks and Wills.**

*See Professional Biographies, IRVINE, CALIFORNIA*

**Smits, Andrew A.** ........ '63 '90 C.112 B.A. L.426 J.D. [🄰 Callahan&B.]
*PRACTICE AREAS: Business Litigation; Bankruptcy.
**Smyth, Lorraine Kay** ........ '57 '82 C.1074 B.A. L.61 J.D. [Suchman,G.&P.]⊙
*PRACTICE AREAS: Litigation; Landslide and Subsidence Law; Construction Law; Commercial Law.

**Snell & Wilmer, L.L.P., (AV) BB**
**1920 Main Street, Suite 1200, 92614⊙**
**Telephone: 714-253-2700 FAX: 714-955-2507**
**Members of Firm: Robert J. Gibson (Resident); Arthur P. Greenfield; Creighton D. Mills (Resident); Steven T. Graham (Resident); Christy D. Joseph; William S. O'Hare, Jr. (Resident); Diane R. Smith (Resident); Gary A. Wolensky (Resident); Gilbert N. Kruger (Resident); Charles W. Hurst (Resident); David W. Evans (Resident); Richard A. Derevan; Randolph T. Moore; Nanette D. Sanders; Luke A. Torres (Resident); Gregg Amber; Penelope Parmes; Frank Cronin. Associates: Shara C. Beral; Tiffany Brosnan; Larry A. Cerutti; Kent M. Clayton; Alexander L. Conti; Ellen L. Darling; Lisa M. Farrington; Jon J. Janecek; Ronald T. Labriola; Cristy G. Lomenzo; Jeffrey Scott Marks; Michael B. Reynolds; Daniel S. Rodman; Gerda M. Roy; Julianne Sartain; Sean Michael Sherlock; Martin W. Taylor.**
**General Civil Practice. Trials and Appeals before State and Federal Courts. Bankruptcy and Insolvency, Commercial Litigation, Corporate and Securities, Franchising, Labor and Employment, Product Liability Litigation. Construction, Real Estate, Environmental and Natural Resources, Computer and High Technology, Health Care, Estate Planning.**
**Phoenix, Arizona Office: One Arizona Center, 85004-0001. Telephone: 602-382-6000. Fax: 602-382-6070.**
**Tucson, Arizona Office: Norwest Tower, Suite 1500, One South Church Avenue, 85701-1612. Telephone: 520-882-1200. Fax: 520-884-1294.**
**Salt Lake City, Utah Office: Broadway Centre, 111 East Broadway, Suite 900, 84111-1004. Telephone: 801-237-1900. Fax: 801-237-1950.**

*See Professional Biographies, IRVINE, CALIFORNIA*

Snyder, Elizabeth A. '51 '82 C.770 B.A. L.426 J.D.
V.P. & Assoc. Coun., Fidelity Natl. Title Ins. Co.
Snyder, Eufrona A. .... '48 '74 C.1042 B.A. L.809 J.D. V.P. & Sr. Coun., World Title Co.
Snyder, Kent G., (BV) ........ '36 '66 C.112 B.S. L.1068 LL.B. 2212 Dupont Dr.
Snyder, Stephen L. ........ '42 '75 C.755 B.A. L.809 J.D. 111 Pacifica
**Sohlgren, Eric C.** ........ '55 '92 C.939 B.A. L.426 J.D. [🄰 Payne&F.]
*PRACTICE AREAS: Employment Law; Wrongful Termination; Employment Discrimination; Employee Benefits.
Solomonian, Patrick ........ '64 '91 C.1076 A.A. L.1137 J.D. 2182 Dupont Dr.
Song, John Y. ........ '— '94 C.659 B.A. L.112 J.D. [Ching&Assoc.]
**Songstad, L. Allan, Jr., (AV)** ........ '46 '71 C.800 A.B. L.1065 J.D. [Songstad,R.&U.]

**Songstad, Randall & Ulich, (AV)**
**2201 Dupont Drive, Suite 420, 92612**
**Telephone: 714-757-1600 Fax: 714-757-1613**
**William D. Coffee; Janet E. Humphrey; Timothy L. Randall; L. Allan Songstad, Jr.; Andrew K. Ulich. Of Counsel: Anthony J. Dragun.**
**General Practice.**

Sonnenschein, J. Dorian, (AV) ........ '48 '73 C.273 B.A. L.477 J.D. 2030 Main St.
Souders, J. Scott ........ '50 '76 C.763 B.S. L.1137 J.D. 111 Pacifica
**Sovie, Donald E., (AV)** ........ '44 '70 C.988 B.A. L.767 J.D. [Crowell&M.]
*PRACTICE AREAS: Government Contract Law; International Business Law; Federal Practice; Commercial Law.
**Sparks, David W.** ........ '68 '93 C.1075 B.A. L.990 J.D. [George&S.]
*PRACTICE AREAS: Civil Litigation; Business Law; Corporate Law; Torts; Personal Injury.
**Spaulding, Arthur O., Jr.** ........ '48 '73 C.976 B.A. L.1068 J.D. [Cox,C.&N.]
*PRACTICE AREAS: Resort and Residential Development Law; Real Estate and Receivables Finance Law; Real Property Law.
Specter, Jill Ossenfort ........ '54 '81 C.602 B.A. L.734 J.D. 37 Bull Run‡
**Specter, Richard B., (AV)** ........ '52 '77 C.910 B.A. L.273 J.D. [Corbett&S.]
**Speiser, Stuart M., (AV⊙)** '23 '48 C.659 L.178 J.D.
(adm. in NY; not adm. in CA) [🄲 Speiser,K.M.&C.] (⊙N.Y., NY & Rosslyn, VA)

**Speiser, Krause, Madole & Cook, (AV)**
**One Park Plaza Suite 470, 92614-8520⊙**
**Telephone: 714-553-1421 Fax: 714-553-1346**
**Joseph T. Cook; Juanita M. Madole; John J. Veth; Gerard R. Lear (Resident, Rosslyn, Virginia Office); Kenneth P. Nolan (Resident, New York, N.Y. Office); James Teague Crouse (Resident, Rosslyn, Virginia Office); Frank H. Granito, III (Resident, New York, N.Y. Office). Of Counsel: Stuart M. Speiser (Not admitted in CA); Charles F. Krause (Not admitted in CA).**
**General Civil Trial and Appellate Practice in State and Federal Courts, Aviation, Negligence, Products Liability, Medical Malpractice, Commercial Law and Complex Tort Litigation.**
**New York, N.Y. Office: Speiser, Krause, Madole & Nolan, Two Grand Central Tower, 140 East 45th Street. Telephone: 212-661-0011. Fax: 212-953-6483.**
**Rosslyn, Virginia Office: Speiser, Krause, Madole & Lear, 1300 North Seventeenth Street, Suite 310. Telephone: 703-522-7500. Fax: 703-522-7905.**
**Dallas, Texas Office: Speiser, Krause & Madole, P.C., Three Lincoln Centre, 5430 LBJ Freeway - Suite 1575. Telephone: 972-404-1401. Fax: 972-404-9797.**

*See Professional Biographies, IRVINE, CALIFORNIA*

**Spencer, Gary V., (AV)** ........ '44 '70 C.800 B.A. L.1066 J.D. [🄲 Meserve,M.&H.]
*PRACTICE AREAS: Construction Law; Mediation; Trademark Licensing; General Business.
Spengler, E. Gordon ........ '56 '81 C.723 B.S. L.494 J.D. 7700 Irvine Center Dr., #700
**Spikes, Martha A.** '54 '83 C.1163 B.A. L.990 J.D.
Corp. Secy. & Sr. Proj. Atty., Mission Energy Co.
*LANGUAGES: Spanish.
**Spitz, Sherman M.** ........ '52 '78 C.112 B.A. L.809 J.D. [Berger,K.S.M.F.S.&G.]
**Spitzer, Gary S.** ........ '65 '91 C.800 B.A. L.426 J.D. [🄰 Callahan&B.]
*LANGUAGES: German.
*PRACTICE AREAS: Business Litigation.
Sprecher, Steven W. ........ '55 '87 C.871 B.S. L.1068 J.D. 4 Park Plaza
**Spurlock, Jeffrey M.** ........ '63 '89 C&L.990 B.S., J.D. [Berger,K.S.M.F.S.&G.]
Stafford, William V., (BV) ........ '46 '72 C.1042 B.A. L.1068 J.D. 59 Thicket
**Stahl, Harry S., (AV)** ........ '43 '73 C.321 B.S. L.30 J.D. [McKenna&S.]
*PRACTICE AREAS: Corporate Law; Securities Law.

**Staight, Lisa, Law Office of, (BV) '50 '77 C.861 B.A. L.990 J.D.**
**2172 Dupont Drive, Suite 17, 92715**
**Telephone: 714-851-2111 Fax: 714-851-0161**
**(Certified Specialist, Family Law, The State Bar of California Board of Legal Specialization).**
***LANGUAGES: Spanish.**
***PRACTICE AREAS: Family Law; Divorce; Paternity; Child Custody; Child and Spousal Support.**

(This Listing Continued)

**Staight, Lisa, Law Office of (Continued)**

**Certified Family Law Specialist.**

*See Professional Biographies, IRVINE, CALIFORNIA*

**Stall, David A., (AV)** ........ '44 '69 C.436 A.B. L.365 J.D. [🄰 Gauntlett&Assoc.]
**Stam, Paul N.** ........ '65 '91 C.112 B.A. L.1137 J.D. [🄰 Kring&B.]
*PRACTICE AREAS: Civil Litigation; Personal Injury Defense; Business Litigation.
**Stanley, Tavi Claire** ........ '66 '93 C.112 B.A. L.800 J.D. [🄰 Lobel&O.]
*PRACTICE AREAS: Bankruptcy Law; Reorganization.
**Staples, Michele A.** ........ '60 '89 C.555 B.S. L.1049 J.D. [S.M.Trager]
*SPECIAL AGENCIES: U.S. Fish and Wildlife Service; California State Water Resources Control Board; Regional Water Quality Control Boards; Local Agency Formation Commissions; County Boards of Supervisors.
*PRACTICE AREAS: Endangered Species; Transactional Environmental Law; Water Rights; Reclaimed Water Contracts.
Starrett, Thomas C., (AV) ........ '44 '70 C&L.800 A.B., J.D. 2600 Michelson Dr.
**Steel, William L., (AV)** ........ '57 '82 C.112 B.A. L.800 J.D. [Samuels&S.]
*PRACTICE AREAS: Business Law; Real Property Transactions; Financing Law.
**Steelman, Ken E., (AV)** ........ '45 '72 C.352 B.S. L.61 J.D. [Corbett&S.]
**Steen, Carl R.** ........ '58 '86 C.1044 B.A. L.904 J.D. [Morrison&F.]
*PRACTICE AREAS: International Project Development; International Project Finance.
Steffensen, D. David, Jr. ........ '54 '82 C.36 B.A. L.990 J.D. The Lusk Co.
**Stein, Martin J., (AV)** ........ '50 '75 C.800 B.A. L.809 J.D. [Paone,C.M.&W.]
*PRACTICE AREAS: Real Estate Development; Subdivisions.
Steinbach, Ronald D., (BV) ........ '43 '69 C.36 B.S. L.1068 J.D. 2212 Dupont Dr.
**Steinman, Jay R.** ........ '50 '77 C.1075 B.A. L.800 J.D. [Jackson,D.&P.]
*PRACTICE AREAS: Real Estate Acquisition; Development and Financing.
**Stemmler, Frederick J.** ........ '48 '73 C.112 B.A. L.800 J.D. [🄲 Barnes,C.F.&Z.]
*PRACTICE AREAS: Real Estate; Commercial Transactions.
**Steponovich, Michael J., Jr., (AV)** '46 '77
C.1042 B.S. L.1137 J.D. [Steponovich&Assoc.]
*REPORTED CASES: Will v. Engebretson & Company, Inc. (1989) 213 CA 3d 1033; Douglas v. Superior Court of Orange County (1989) 215 CA 3d 155; Kelly-Zurian v. Wohl Shoe Company (1994) 22 CA 4th 397; Saltarelli & Steponovich v. Douglas (1995) 40 CA 4th 1.
*PRACTICE AREAS: Banking; Business and Commercial Litigation; Real Estate Litigation; Tort Litigation.

**Steponovich & Associates, A Professional Law Corporation, (AV) BB**
**Koll Center Irvine - Transamerica Tower, 18201 Von Karman Avenue, Suite 650, 92612-1005**
**Telephone: 714-852-1073 Fax: 714-852-1276**
**Email: STEPOLAW@aol.com**
**Michael J. Steponovich, Jr.**
**Litigation Practice in Banking, Business, Commercial, Family Law, Financial, Real Estate and Tort Matters.**

*See Professional Biographies, IRVINE, CALIFORNIA*

Stepp, Thomas E., Jr. ........ '46 '77 C.1109 B.A. L.1065 J.D. 2010 Main St.
Sterling, Alan DeNeve ..... '55 '88 C&L.1137 B.S.L., J.D. V.P., Chrysler 1st Coml. Corp.
**Stern, W. Rod, (BV)** ........ '55 '83 C.112 A.B. L.1065 J.D. [Groh,C.S.&R.]
*PRACTICE AREAS: Business Law; Tax Law; Conservatorships; Probate.
**Stevens, Carl R.** ........ '53 '78 C.800 B.A. L.1188 J.D. [Stevens,K.A.&H.]⊙
*PRACTICE AREAS: Defense of Legal and Medical Malpractice; General Insurance Defense Law; Insurance Coverage; Bad Faith; Wrongful Termination.
**Stevens, Clay** ........ '69 '96 C.605 A.B. L.990 J.D. [🄰 Busch]
*PRACTICE AREAS: Estate; Tax; Business Planning.
**Stevens, Commie** ........ '70 '96 C.112 B.A. L.990 J.D. [🄰 Albrecht&B.]
*PRACTICE AREAS: Estate and Gift Tax Law; Estate Planning; Trust and Estate Administration.
**Stevens, Douglas M.** ........ '64 '89 C&L.800 B.S., J.D. [🄰 Busch]
*PRACTICE AREAS: Business and Tax; Real Estate.

**Stevens, Kramer, Averbuck & Harris, A Professional Corporation, (AV)**
**18400 Von Karman Avenue, Suite 615, 92612⊙**
**Telephone: 714-253-9553 Fax: 714-253-9643**
**Carl R. Stevens; Charles L. Harris;—Valerie McSwain (Resident Irvine Office); Lee E. Burrows (Resident); Lydia R. Bouzaglou; John R. Marking; Robert A. Fisher, II; Jeanne E. Pepper.**
**General Civil Litigation Defense in all State and Federal Courts. Commercial and Personal Lines, Construction Defect, Bad Faith, Insurance Coverage and Declaratory Relief, Medical Malpractice, Environmental Law, Legal Malpractice, Wrongful Termination, Governmental Entity Defense.**
**Los Angeles, California Office: 1990 S. Bundy Drive, Suite 340, 90025. Telephone: 310-442-8435. Fax: 310-442-8441.**

*See Professional Biographies, IRVINE, CALIFORNIA*

**Stevenson, Tracy Ann** ........ '60 '92 C.1042 B.S. L.1137 J.D. [🄰 Fiore,W.R.&P.]
*PRACTICE AREAS: Construction Defect; Business Litigation; Probate.
**Stillwell, Geniene B.** ........ '62 '88 C.839 B.B.A. L.846 J.D. [Gibson,D.&C.]
*PRACTICE AREAS: Labor and Employment Law; Trade Secrets.
**Stinehart, Richard E., (AV)** ........ '56 '82 C.112 B.A. L.800 J.D. [Allen,M.L.G.&M.]
*PRACTICE AREAS: Real Estate.
**Stith, Clark D.** ........ '61 '91 C.378 B.S.,B.A. L.276 J.D. [🄰 Gibson,D.&C.]
*LANGUAGES: German and French.
*PRACTICE AREAS: Litigation; Intellectual Property.
**Stith, Liisa Anselmi** ........ '63 '88 C.602 B.B.A. L.228 J.D. [🄰 Gibson,D.&C.]
*PRACTICE AREAS: General Corporate and Securities.
Stoll, Charley M. ........ '48 '75 C.800 B.S. L.1137 J.D. [C.M.Stoll]
Stoll, Charley M., A Prof. Corp. ........ 5 Park Plaza
**Stolzman, Barry A.** '66 '92 C.475 B.S. L.912 J.D.
(adm. in MI; not adm. in CA) Discovision Assocs.
*RESPONSIBILITIES: Patent Licensing; Patent Prosecution; Patent Litigation.
**Stone, Peter M.** ........ '67 '92 C.112 B.A. L.1066 J.D. [🄰 Gibson,D.&C.]
*PRACTICE AREAS: Real Estate and Securities Litigation.
**Stoop, Eric J.** ........ '66 '93 C.1239 B.A. L.950 J.D. [🄰 R.R.Hatter&Assoc.]
**Stoop, Patricia L.** ........ '69 '94 C.886 B.A. L.950 J.D. [🄰 R.R.Hatter&Assoc.]
Stowe, Terrance W. '49 '81 C.347 B.A. L.1137 J.D.
V.P. & Assoc. Coun., Fidelity Natl. Title Ins. Co.
Strader, Timothy L., (AV) ........ '38 '64 C.363 B.S. L.1068 J.D. 2532 Dupont Dr.
**Strauss, Karen O.** ........ '63 '88 C.112 B.A. L.1066 J.D. [Payne&F.]
*PRACTICE AREAS: Employment Law; Wrongful Termination; Employment Discrimination; Trade Secrets and Unfair Competition; Labor Law.
**Strauss, Marcelle Suzanne** ........ '60 '86 C.112 B.A. L.464 J.D. [Suchman,G.&P.]⊙
*PRACTICE AREAS: Litigation; Construction Law; Insurance Defense Law; Employment Law; Title Insurance Law.
Streza, Richard E., (A Professional Corporation) '56 '82
C.1165 B.A. L.990 J.D. [Brown&S.]
Strid, Lawrence A., (BV) ........ '52 '78 C.1109 B.A. L.1137 J.D. [Burge,S.&D.]
**Stroffe, James D.** ........ '51 '77 C.309 B.A. L.1049 J.D. [Friedman P.&S.]
*PRACTICE AREAS: Real Property Law; Construction Law; Litigation.
Strukelj, Mark S. ........ '56 '81 C&L.426 B.B.A., J.D. Sr. Coun., Fluor Daniel, Inc.
**Suchman, Stewart R., (AV)** ........ '42 '70 C.112 B.A. L.1065 J.D. [Suchman,G.&P.]⊙
*PRACTICE AREAS: Corporate Law; Commercial Law; Litigation; Banking Law; Construction Law.

**Suchman, Galfin & Passon, LLP, (AV) BB**
**18101 Von Karman Avenue, Suite 1400, 92612-1043⊙**
**Telephone: 714-752-2444 Facsimile: 714-833-8256**
**Email: sgplaw1@aol.com**

(This Listing Continued)

CAA141P

**Suchman, Galfin & Passon, LLP (Continued)**

**Members of Firm: Stewart R. Suchman; Ted A. Galfin; Kenneth D. Passon; Lorraine Kay Smyth; Michael R. Adams; William E. Alsnauer, Jr.; Marcelle Suzanne Strauss; Adam M. Greely.**
**General Civil and Trial Practice, Commercial Litigation. Financial Institutions including Banks and Savings & Loan Associations, Corporate, Business, Real Estate, Title Insurance, Bankruptcy (Creditor Representation), Equipment Leasing, Construction, Mobilehome Law, Probate, Estate Planning and Trust Law.**
**Santa Ana, California Office: 2122 North Broadway, Suite 100. Telephone: 714-752-2444.**

*See Professional Biographies, IRVINE, CALIFORNIA*

Sukrau, Janis ............................. '48 '74 C.800 B.A. L.61 J.D. 24 Executive Pk.
Sukut, Keri Foley ......................... '63 '89 C.154 B.A. L.426 J.D. 38 Corp. Pk.
**Sullivan, James J.** ... '57 '85 C.800 B.S. L.426 J.D. V.P. & Coun., Amer. Svgs. Bk., F.A.
*RESPONSIBILITIES: Corporate Law; Banking Law.
**Sunshine, Steven H.**, (AV) ..................... '51 '76 C.112 B.A. L.1068 J.D. [Bryan C.]
**Susolik, Edward** ......................... '62 '90 C&L.800 B.A., J.D. [A Callahan&B.]
*PRACTICE AREAS: Complex Business Litigation; Insurance Bad Faith; Insurance Coverage; Constitutional Law.
**Sussman, Jeffrey H.** ..................... '65 '91 C.1066 B.A. L.800 J.D. [A Rus,M.W.&S.]
*PRACTICE AREAS: Bankruptcy.
**Sutton, Michael S.**, (BV) .................. '55 '80 C.1109 B.A. L.426 J.D. [Sutton&M.]
*PRACTICE AREAS: Personal Injury Law; Insurance Defense.

**Sutton and Murphy, (BV)**
**7700 Irvine Center Drive, Suite 830, 92718**
**Telephone: 714-753-5057**
**Members of Firm: Michael S. Sutton; Thomas M. Murphy; Steven G. Pratt.**
**Insurance Defense, Plaintiffs' Personal Injury, Civil Litigation.**

*See Professional Biographies, IRVINE, CALIFORNIA*

**Swainston, Colin C.** ......................... '63 '90 C&L.101 B.S., J.D. [A Cox,C.&N.]
*LANGUAGES: Spanish.
*PRACTICE AREAS: Civil Litigation.
Swanson, Randy E. .................. '49 '83 C.112 B.A. L.1137 J.D. 2082 Michelson Dr.
**Swedo, Jeffrey A.** ............ '53 '77 C.879 B.S.B.A. L.188 J.D. [Berger,K.S.M.F.S.&G.]
**Sweetnam, Niall** ........................................ '59 '83 C&L.999 B.A. [Oswald&Y.]
*PRACTICE AREAS: Commercial Litigation.
Swift, Barbara L. '49 '80 C.112 B.A. L.1137 J.D.
Gen. Coun., Mobile Community Mgmt.
**Sykes, Robert J.** ..................... '59 '90 C.911 B.B.A. L.1068 J.D. [A Cox,C.&N.]
*PRACTICE AREAS: Shopping Center Development; Commercial Leasing; Construction Law; Partnership Agreements.
Szabo, Joseph E. ......................... '33 '65 C.012 B.S.E.E. L.273 J.D. 5 Park Plaza
**Szekeres, Gabor L.**, (AV) .. '44 '77 C.1044 Ph.D L.1137 J.D. [Klein&S.] (See Pat. Sect.)
*LANGUAGES: Hungarian, German and Spanish.
*PRACTICE AREAS: Intellectual Property Law.
Tarr, Nathan W., (BV) ....................... '28 '55 C.112 B.A. L.800 J.D. 1 Park Plz.
**Tate, Tamara Powell** ................ '65 '89 C.112 B.A. L.1066 J.D. [A Morrison&F.]
**Tate, William B., II** ..................... '65 '88 C.800 A.B. L.813 J.D. [A Morrison&F.]
**Tavares, Abilio, Jr.** ......................... '56 '82 C.94 B.A. L.982 J.D. [Andrade&M.]
*PRACTICE AREAS: Contract; Construction; Entertainment; Insurance; Intellectual Property and Tort Litigation.
**Tawa, John E., Jr.** .................. '62 '87 C.164 B.A. L.893 J.D. [C Paone,C.M.&W.]
*LANGUAGES: French.
*PRACTICE AREAS: Civil Litigation.
**Taylor, DeeAnn M.** ............................. '66 '92 C.1097 L.564 J.D. [A Grant&L.]
*PRACTICE AREAS: Litigation.
**Taylor, Duncan H., Jr.** ............ '60 '88 C.101 B.A. L.1065 J.D. Discovision Assocs.
*LANGUAGES: Spanish.
*RESPONSIBILITIES: Patent Contracts.
Taylor, Kurt ............................................. '64 '91 C&L.101 B.S., J.D. 2010 Main St.
**Taylor, Martin W.** ......................... '— '90 C.1109 B.A. L.464 J.D. [A Snell&W.]
*PRACTICE AREAS: Bankruptcy Law; Reorganization Law; Commercial Litigation.
**Taylor, Peter D.** ........................ '65 '95 C.112 B.A. L.1068 J.D. [A Morrison&F.]
*LANGUAGES: Japanese.
Taylor, Richard L. '54 '79 C.352 B.S. L.221 J.D.
(adm. in IA; not adm. in CA) Gen. Coun, Greystone Mortgage Corp.

**Taylor, Lawrence**
**(See Long Beach)**

**Teel, James A.** ..................... '61 '90 C.112 B.A. L.1137 J.D. [A Genson,E.C.&W.]
Teel, Kenn L. ................... '58 '86 C.112 B.A. L.809 J.D. 19800 MacArthur Blvd.
**Tenerelli, Michael R.**, (AV) ..................... '51 '77 C&L.426 B.B.A., J.D. [Pinto&D.]
**Tennant, Douglas G.** ......................... '56 '83 C.976 B.A. L.178 J.D. [Frankel&T.]
**Thames, Stephen R.** .................. '56 '82 C.112 B.A. L.1068 J.D. [Allen,M.L.G.&M.]
*PRACTICE AREAS: Litigation.
**Thomas, Jeffrey E.** ......................... '55 '83 C.1042 B.A. L.1137 J.D. [Oswald&Y.]
*PRACTICE AREAS: Commercial Litigation.
**Thomas, Jeffrey T.** .................... '57 '82 C.112 B.A. L.1049 J.D. [Gibson,D.&C.]
*PRACTICE AREAS: Business Litigation; Land Use Litigation; Antitrust; Intellectual Property Litigation; Real Estate Litigation.
**Thomas, Scott S.** .......................... '54 '82 C&L.101 B.A., J.D. [Payne&F.]
*PRACTICE AREAS: Business Litigation; Insurance Coverage.
**Thommarson, Ronald J.** .............. '67 '94 C.813 B.A. L.800 J.D. [A Kirtland&P.]
Thompson, David A., (AV) '56 '83 C.276 B.S.,B.A. L.1068 J.D.
19900 MacArthor Blvd.
Thompson, Jeri Tabback ..................... '54 '92 C&L.1137 B.S.L., J.D. 2 Parl Plaza
Thompson, William C. ..................... '54 '82 C.800 B.A. L.1066 J.D. 6 Dickens Ct.
**Thoresen, Trygve M.** ................. '64 '93 C.112 B.A. L.1065 J.D. [A Gibson,D.&C.]
*PRACTICE AREAS: Mergers, Acquisitions and Divestitures; Securities.
**Thornton, Robert D.** ................ '50 '76 C.112 A.B. L.767 J.D. [Nossaman,G.K.&E.]
*PRACTICE AREAS: Environmental Law; Land Use Law; Hazardous Waste Law; Endangered Species; Transportation Law.
**Throckmorton, A. Robert** '33 '61
C.101 A.B. L.800 J.D. [Throckmorton,B.O.&T.] (⊙Pasadena)

**Throckmorton, Beckstrom, Oakes & Tomassian LLP, (AV)**
**A Partnership**
**19800 MacArthur Boulevard, Suite 350, 92612⊙**
**Telephone: 714-955-2280 Fax: 714-467-8081**
**Members of Firm: A. Robert Throckmorton (Resident); Serge Tomassian (Resident).**
**Construction (claims and defects), Real Estate, Insurance, Business, Commercial and Medical Legal Law. General Civil Litigation, Defense of Religious Institutions. All aspects of Trial and Appellate Work.**
**Pasadena, California Office: Corporate Center Pasadena, 225 South Lake Avenue, Suite 500. Telephone: 818-568-2500; 213-681-2321. Fax: 818-405-0786.**

*See Professional Biographies, IRVINE, CALIFORNIA*

**Tidus, Michael L.** ......................... '61 '86 C.112 B.A. L.800 J.D. [Jackson,D.&P.]
*PRACTICE AREAS: Land Use Litigation; Eminent Domain.
**Tieder, John B., Jr.**, (AV⊕) '46 '71 C.367 A.B. L.30 J.D.
(adm. in VA; not adm. in CA) [Watt,T.&H.]⊙
Tieger, Marcy, (AV) ........................ '60 '87 C.1109 B.A. L.1137 J.D. [Tieger&B.]
Tieger & Bumiller, Law Offices of, (AV) ......................................2 Park Plaza
Toledano, James, (AV) ..................... '44 '72 C.112 A.B. L.1066 J.D. [Toledano&W.]
Toledano & Wald, (AV) ................................................ 18201 Von Karman Ave.
**Toman, Richard J.** '48 '77 C.373 B.A. L.365 J.D.
(adm. in IL; not adm. in CA) Sr. Atty., Digital Equip. Corp.
**Tomassian, Serge**, (AV) '56 '84
C.800 B.A. L.464 J.D. [Throckmorton,B.O.&T.] (⊙Pasadena)
*LANGUAGES: French.
**Tompkins, Tonia** ............................ '67 '95 C.566 B.A. L.940 J.D. [A Kring&B.]
*PRACTICE AREAS: Civil Litigation.
**Tonkon, Donna T.** ........................ '50 '76 C.66 B.A. L.904 J.D. [Feder,G.&S.]
*PRACTICE AREAS: Estate Planning; Trust Planning; Estate Administration; Probate.
Torgeson, Penelope H. ................. '44 '78 C.546 B.S. L.1137 J.D. 6 Waterway‡
**Torres, Luke A.** .......................... '57 '82 C.112 B.A. L.1067 J.D. [Snell&W.]
*PRACTICE AREAS: Product Liability Litigation.
Tovstein, Marc Steven, (BV) .............. '50 '76 C.102 B.A. L.1137 J.D. [Tovstein&K.]
Tovstein & Kraetzer, (BV) ................................................... 1920 Main St.
Trachtman, Marc A. ......................... '68 '93 C.112 A.B. L.61 J.D. 1920 Main St.
**Tracy, Jill A.** .................... '65 '93 C.881 B.A. L.1218 J.D. [A Sedgwick,D.M.&A.]
**Trafton, Alan P.** ................. '69 '94 C.1049 B.B.A. L.61 J.D. [A Genson,E.C.&W.]
**Trager, Susan M.**, (AV) ..................... '47 '73 C.174 B.S. L.284 J.D. [S.M.Trager]
*SPECIAL AGENCIES: California Water Resources Control Board; California Department of Toxic Substances Control; California Department of Fish and Game; Regional Water Quality Control Boards; County Boards of Supervisors.
*PRACTICE AREAS: Water Rights Law; Land Use; Municipal Law; Environmental Law; Eminent Domain.

**Trager, Susan M., A Prof. Corp., Law Offices of, (AV)**
**The Landmark Building, Suite 104, 2100 S. E. Main Street, 92614**
**Telephone: 714-752-8971 Telefax: 714-863-9804**
**Susan M. Trager;—Michele A. Staples; Laura Pavloff Couch.**
**Administrative Proceedings and Civil Litigation relating to Water Rights, Species and Habitat Protection, Natural Resources, Hazardous Materials, Municipal Law, Eminent Domain, Land Use Planning and Environmental Law.**
**Representative Client: San Luis Rey Municipal Water District.**
**Reference: Sanwa Bank, CA.**

*See Professional Biographies, IRVINE, CALIFORNIA*

Traino, Michael L. '66 '91 C.597 B.S.E.E. L.188 J.D.
(adm. in MN; not adm. in CA; Pat.) Discovision Assocs.
*RESPONSIBILITIES: Patent Licensing; Patent Litigation; Patent Prosecution.
**Trampe, Ferdinand M.** ........... '62 '89 C.662 B.A. L.1068 J.D. [A Mower,K.N.C.&H.]
*LANGUAGES: Tagalog.
**Trask, Sara Schwab** ............ '60 '86 C.112 B.A. L.464 J.D. [Berger,K.S.M.F.S.&G.]
**Tredway, Harold T.** ................. '19 '55 C.807 B.A. L.426 LL.B. [Tredway,L.&D.]⊙

**Tredway, Lumsdaine & Doyle, LLP, (AV)**
**Suite 1000 1920 Main Street, 92714⊙**
**Telephone: 714-756-0684 Telecopier: 714-756-0596**
**Members of Firm: Joseph A. Lumsdaine (Resident at Downey Office); Mark C. Doyle; Jeffrey B. Singer; Michele S. Ahrens (Resident at Downey Office); Cheri A. Kadotani; Michael A. Lanphere; Harold T. Tredway (Retired); Matthew L. Kinley (Resident at Downey Office); Lynn L. Walker (1951-1994); Gary Lieberman (Resident at Downey Office); Daniel R. Gold (Resident at Downey Office); Sharisse E. Molyneux (Resident at Downey Office); Joseph A. Maleki. Of Counsel: David A. Pasqualini.**
**General Civil Trial Practice, Business, Corporate, Securities, Financial Institutions, Real Estate, Personal Injury, Employment, Environmental Law, Taxation, Probate, Estate Planning, and Family Law.**
**Reference: Southern California Bank.**
**Downey, California Office: 10841 Paramount Boulevard. Telephone: 310-923-0971; 714-750-0141. Telecopier: 310-869-4607.**

*See Professional Biographies, IRVINE, CALIFORNIA*

Trimble, P. Joseph '30 '55 C.28 B.A. L.846 LL.B.
Sr. V.P., Law, Engg. & Construction Group, Fluor Corp.
**Tripi, Cecelia A.** ......................... '59 '85 C.800 B.A. L.426 J.D. [A Crowell&M.]
**Trobough, Tobin J.** ...................... '61 '89 C.112 B.A. L.426 J.D. [A Baker,S.&K.]
Trotter, Steven D. ........... '62 '88 C.112 B.A. L.990 J.D. 7700 Irving Center Dr., #700
**Tsai, Tzong-Bing** ....................... '67 '94 C.293 B.A. L.284 J.D. [Oswald&Y.]
*PRACTICE AREAS: Commercial Litigation.
**Tucker, Josephine Staton** ................ '61 '86 C.947 B.A. L.309 J.D. [Morrison&F.]
*PRACTICE AREAS: Labor and Employment.
Tucker, Thomas J. '39 '69 C.347 B.A. L.345 J.D.
(adm. in IN; not adm. in CA)
Group Labor & Employ. Coun., Waste Management Inc.- West
Tunney, Francis R., Jr. '47 '73 C.264 A.B. L.229 J.D.
Corp. V.P., Secy. & Gen. Coun., Allergan, Inc.
**Tuohey, Conrad G.**, (AV) ................. '33 '62 C.273 B.A. L.477 J.D. [C.G.Tuohey]
*PRACTICE AREAS: Toxic Torts; Environmental Law; International Law.

**Tuohey, Conrad G., A Professional Law Corporation, (AV)**
**8001 Irvine Center Drive, Suite 1000, 92718-2996**
**Telephone: 714-453-1255 Fax: 714-453-9566**
**Conrad G. Tuohey;—Ferdinand de Veyra Gonzalez.**
**Toxic/Environmental Law and International Trials and Appeals.**

*See Professional Biographies, IRVINE, CALIFORNIA*

Turner, Clark Savage ..................... '54 '88 C.1113 B.S. L.1294 J.D. 1514 Verano Pl.
**Turner, D. Scott** .............................. '52 '82 C.112 B.S. L.464 J.D. [Cox,C.&N.]
*PRACTICE AREAS: Real Property Law.
**Turner, Frederick E.**, (BV) ................. '53 '80 C.1042 B.S. L.426 J.D. [Turner&R.]
*REPORTED CASES: The City v. Hart, (1985) 175 Cal. App. 3d 92.
*PRACTICE AREAS: Commercial Litigation; Business Litigation; Real Estate Litigation; Insurance Litigation; Construction Litigation.
**Turner, Steven D.** .................... '67 '94 C.101 B.A. L.990 J.D. [A Wesierski&Z.]
*LANGUAGES: Spanish.
*PRACTICE AREAS: Insurance Defense; Bad Faith; Alternative Dispute Resolution.

**Turner and Reynolds, A Law Corporation, (BV)**
**18400 Von Karman Avenue, Suite 500, 92612-1584**
**Telephone: 714-474-6900 Fax: 714-474-6907**
**Frederick E. Turner; Richard J. Reynolds;—Charles W. Losness; Robert F. Zwierlein.**
**General Civil Trial Practice. Business, Construction, Securities, Commodities, Real Property, Bankruptcy, Banking, Insurance, Environmental, Eminent Domain and Personal Injury Litigation.**
**Representative Client: Webb Service Co.**

*See Professional Biographies, IRVINE, CALIFORNIA*

Turpit, William J. .................................. '53 '78 C.228 B.A. L.464 J.D. The Lusk Co.
**Twomey, William L.**, (AV) .................. '55 '81 C.112 B.A. L.1068 J.D. [Hewitt&M.]
*PRACTICE AREAS: Corporate Law; Securities Law; Business Law.
**Tyler, Dennis G., (A Professional Corporation)**, (AV) '43 '70
C.112 B.A. L.1067 J.D. [Palmieri,T.W.W.&W.]
*PRACTICE AREAS: Real Estate Law.
**Ubell, Franklin D.** ....... '49 '75 C.339 B.S.E.E. L.273 J.D. [Price,G.&U.] (See Pat. Sect.)
*REPORTED CASES: Adray v. Adrayhart, Inc. 68 F.3d 362 (9th cir. 1995).
*PRACTICE AREAS: Patent; Trademark; Copyright.

**Ulich, Andrew K.** ... '56 '81 C.112 B.A. L.800 J.D. [Songstad,R.&U.]
*REPORTED CASES: Sachs v. Exxon, 9 CA 4th 1491 (1992).
*PRACTICE AREAS: Commercial, Construction and Environmental trial and Appellate Litigation.
**Umberg, Thomas J.**, (AV) ... '55 '80 C.112 B.A. L.1065 J.D. [Morrison&F.]
*PRACTICE AREAS: Litigation; Land Use and Environmental Law; Regulatory Law; Legislative.
**Unterman, Alan B.** ... '65 '91 C.112 B.S. L.1068 J.D. [🄰 Sedgwick,D.M.&A.]
*LANGUAGES: Dutch.
Urland, Karl W., (AV) ... '47 '73 C.112 B.A. L.800 J.D. 19800 MacArthur Blvd.
Urquhart, James R., III ... '51 '77 C.112 B.A. L.464 J.D. 2061 Business Ctr. Dr.
Vaccaro, Christopher M. ... '59 '86 C.684 B.A. L.1148 J.D. [🄰 Curtis&V.]
Vaccaro, San E., (AV) ... '33 '60 C&L.262 A.B., J.D. [Curtis&V.]
Vance, Thomas L. ... '57 '83 C.112 B.A. L.1049 J.D. [Vance&B.]
Vance and Blair ... 19900 MacArthur Blvd.
Van Cleave, Jonathan E. ... '45 '79 C.112 B.A. L.1137 J.D. 5 Corporate Park
Van Dam, James S., (AV) ... '47 '73 C.112 B.A. L.800 J.D. [Van Dam&V.]
Van Dam, Linda J. ... '54 '80 C.112 B.A. L.809 J.D. [Van Dam&V.]
Van Dam & Van Dam, A Prof. Law Corp., (AV) ... 108 Pacifica
Vanderwilt, Lester E. '21 '56 C.350 B.S. L.7 LL.B.
(adm. in OH; not adm. in CA) Fluor Corp.
Van Dyke, Keith F. ... '59 '86 C.112 B.A. L.990 J.D. [🄰 G.Hannen]
**Van Riper, Marianne** ... '63 '88 C.112 B.A. L.990 J.D. [Woldt&H.]
**Van Sicklen, Steven R.** ... '46 '72 C.800 B.A. L.464 J.D. [Baker,S.&K.]
*PRACTICE AREAS: Professional Liability; Personal Injury.
Van Tatenhove, Lester ... '14 '40 C.323 B.A. L.309 LL.B. 17 Lakeview‡
**Van Vlear, John E.** ... '62 '87 C.112 B.A. L.990 J.D. [Brown,P.H.&V.]
*SPECIAL AGENCIES: Federal Environmental Protection Agency (EPA), Region IX; California Department of Toxic Substances Control (DTSC) and Regional Water Quality Control Boards (RWQCB).
*TRANSACTIONS: Brownfields Redevelopment of Kaiser Ventures California Speedway; Waste disposal Inc.; Superfund Site; Roche Estate Oil Production Site.
*PRACTICE AREAS: Environmental Law; Cost Recovery Litigation; Regulatory Compliance; Site Assessment and Remediation; Real estate.
Vasels, Nicholas C. ... '50 '79 C.112 B.S. L.426 J.D. 2010 Main St.
**Vasquez, David R.** ... '60 '89 C.112 B.A. L.1067 J.D. [🄰 Laughlin,F.L.&M.]
*PRACTICE AREAS: Subrogation Law; Insurance Defense Law; Liability Defense Law; Business Litigation.
**Vaughn, Steve C.** '52 '77 C.999 B.S. L.178 J.D.
Assoc. Gen. Coun. & Asst. Secy., Parker-Hannifin Corp.
Verano, Beverly J. ... '50 '81 C.763 B.S. L.1049 J.D. [Verano&V.]
Verano, Hugh T., Jr. ... '49 '81 C.668 B.A. L.1051 J.D. [Verano&V.]
Verano & Verano, A Professional Law Corp. ... 108 Pacifica
**Veth, John J.** ... '41 '87 C.569 B.S. L.1137 J.D. [Speiser,K.M.&C.]
*PRACTICE AREAS: Aviation Accidents; International Aviation Law; Personal Injury and Wrongful Death Litigation; Mass Disaster Litigation; Products Liability.
**Vincent, Thomas L.** ... '62 '90 C.112 B.A. L.813 J.D. [🄰 Payne&F.]
*LANGUAGES: Portuguese.
*PRACTICE AREAS: Business; Real Estate; Construction Litigation.
Voet, Martin A. '42 '70 C.112 B.S. L.273 J.D.
Assoc. Gen. Coun. & Asst. Secy., Allergan, Inc. (Pat.)

**Vollmer, Michael V.**
**(See Newport Beach)**

Vujovich, George ... '54 '82 C.1075 B.A. L.464 J.D. 2100 Main St.
**Wagner, Donald P.** ... '60 '87 C.112 B.A. L.1065 J.D. [Wagner&Assoc.]
Wagner, John J. ... '35 '66 C.36 B.S.M.E. L.1026 J.D. 17880 Sky ParkCircle
**Wagner, Megan L.** ... '62 '87 C.112 B.A. L.1066 J.D. [Wagner&Assoc.] (ⓢSanta Rosa)
*PRACTICE AREAS: Civil Litigation; Civil Appeals.
Wagner, Michael J. ... '48 '75 C.770 B.S. L.426 J.D. Fluor Daniel, Inc.
Wagner, Timothy S. ... '51 '79 C&L.36 B.S., J.D. Beauchamp Enterprizes

**Wagner & Associates**
**5 Park Plaza, Suite 1500, 92714**
**Telephone: 714-474-6964 Fax: 714-756-0517**
**Donald P. Wagner; Megan L. Wagner (Resident).**
**General Civil Litigation, Commercial Law, Securities Arbitration, Landlord/Tenant Law.**
*See Professional Biographies, IRVINE, CALIFORNIA*

Wahl, Timothy S. '45 '76
C.884 A.B. L.61 J.D. Gen. Coun. & Mng. Dir., Geneva Companies
**Wakino, Michelle A.** ... '60 '89 C.1109 B.A. L.426 J.D. [Feder,G.&S.]
**Walburn, Allen B.** ... '60 '95 C.763 B.S. L.1049 J.D. [🄰 Busch]
*PRACTICE AREAS: Estate, Tax and Business Planning.
Wald, David E., (AV) ... '48 '73 C.1042 B.A. L.61 J.D. [Toledano&W.]
**Waldron, Robert F., (A Professional Corporation)**, (AV) '27 '55
C.112 B.A. L.1068 J.D. [Palmieri,T.W.W.&W.]
*PRACTICE AREAS: Condemnation Law; Litigation.
**Walker, Bradley D.**, (AV) ... '55 '81 C.966 B.S. L.990 J.D. [Fiore,W.R.&P.]
Walker, Brian D. '61 '87 C.169 B.S. L.464 J.D.
Envir. Risk Mgr., C R C Environmental Risk Management, Inc.
Walker, Jennifer W. ... '66 '91 C.112 B.A. L.1049 J.D. 2301 Dupont Sr., Suite 410
Walker, Thomas P., (AV) ... '05 '29 C.112 L.800 LL.B. 19191 Harvard Ave.‡
**Wall, George J.**, (AV) ... '48 '74 C.893 B.A. L.472 J.D. [Palmieri,T.W.W.&W.]
*PRACTICE AREAS: Corporate Law; Real Estate Law.
**Walsh, John F.** ... '62 '96 C.019 B.A. L.426 J.D. [🄰 Crowell&M.]
**Walsh, P. Jerold**, (AV) ... '37 '77 C.260 B.S. L.326 J.D. [Cox,C.&N.]
*PRACTICE AREAS: Environmental Law; Hazardous and Toxic Substances Law; Real Property Law.
Walz, William R. '60 '88 C.105 B.A. L.1065 J.D.
V.P. & Assoc. Coun., Fidelity Natl. Title Ins. Co.
Wanlass, Gregory K. ... '53 '80 C&L.101 B.A., J.D. 15 Studebaker, Suite 201
Wanvig, John F. ... '52 '85 C&L.999 B.A., J.D. [J.F.Wanvig&Assoc.]
Wanvig, John F., & Associates ... 4199 Campus Dr.
**Warden, William P.**, (AVⓉ) ... '48 '74 C.859 B.A. L.623 J.D. [🄰 Gauntlett&Assoc.]
Wassner, Kenneth B. ... '40 '72 C.763 B.A. L.1049 J.D. FDIC
**Waterman, Melinda Dalton** ... '68 '95 C.800 B.A. L.990 J.D. [🅂 Gibson,D.&C.]
*PRACTICE AREAS: Estate Planning.

**Watt, Tieder & Hoffar, L.L.P., (AVⓉ) [BR]**
**3 Park Plaza, Suite 1530, 92714⊙**
**Telephone: 714-852-6700 Telecopier: 714-261-0771**
**Members of Firm: John B. Tieder, Jr. (Not admitted in CA); Robert M. Fitzgerald (Not admitted in CA); Michael G. Long; Christopher P. Pappas. Associate: Gregory John Dukellis.**
**Government Contracts, Construction, Surety, Environmental, Commercial Litigation, International Business, Toxic Waste and Real Estate Law.**
**McLean Virginia Office: 7929 Westpark Drive, Suite 400, Telephone: 703-749-1000. Telecopier: 703-893-8029.**
**Washington, D.C. Office: 601 Pennsylvania Avenue, N.W. Suite 900, Telephone: 202-462-4697.**
*See Professional Biographies, IRVINE, CALIFORNIA*

Weber, Charles E. ... '53 '78 C.347 B.A. L.1137 J.D. 19900 MacArthur Blvd., 8th Fl.

**Weidberg, Bertrand H., (AV) '40 '65 C.188 B.S. L.178 J.D.**
**33 Silver Crescent, 92612**
**Telephone: 714-854-5221 Fax: 714-854-5220**
**Email: bweid@aol.com**
***PRACTICE AREAS: Corporate; International; Intellectual Property; Commercial; Computer.**
**Corporate, International, Intellectual Property, Commercial, Computer.**

**Weiler, Gregory N.** ... '56 '81 C.1042 B.A. L.1065 J.D. [Palmieri,T.W.W.&W.]
*PRACTICE AREAS: Real Estate and Land Use.
Weiman, S. Wyle ... '57 '84 C.1097 B.A. L.426 Weiman Coml. Real Estate
Weinberg, Elaine J., (BV) ... '29 '74 C.112 L.990 J.D. 18201 Von Karman Ave.
Weinberg, Martin B., (AV) ... '25 '54 C.800 B.A. L.1068 LL.B. 18201 Von Karman Ave.
**Weiner, Rick S.** ... '62 '90 C.112 B.A. L.36 J.D. [Busch]
*PRACTICE AREAS: Real Estate Transactional and Finance; Corporate and Business Planning Law.
**Weisberg, Gary C.** ... '60 '87 C.112 B.A. L.1065 J.D. [Palmieri,T.W.W.&W.]
*PRACTICE AREAS: Litigation; Condemnation Law.
**Weiss, Andrew D.** ... '60 '85 C.112 B.A. L.1049 J.D. [Kasdan,S.M.E.&M.]
*PRACTICE AREAS: Construction Defect Litigation; Civil Litigation.
**Weiss, Barry A.** ... '56 '84 C&L.188 B.S., J.D. Asst. Gen. Coun., Entergy Power Grp.
Weiss, Ruth A. ... '58 '90 C.260 B.A. L.188 J.D. 12 Bayside
Welch, Stephen H. ... '51 '79 C.1109 B.A. L.990 J.D. 5 Park Plaza
Wellman, Scott W. ... '53 '78 C.112 B.A. L.800 J.D. [Wellman&Assoc.]
Wellman & Associates ... 4 Venture St.
**Wells, H. Neal, III**, (AV) ... '36 '62 C&L.813 A.B., J.D. [Arter&H.]
**Wells, John C.**, (AV) ... '41 '67 C.813 B.A. L.1066 J.D. [Gibson,D.&C.]
Welputt, Keith C., (AV) ... '39 '65 C.675 B.A. L.813 J.D. [Germann&W.]
**Wendel, Todd E.** ... '62 '92 C.101 B.S. L.878 J.D. [🄰 Ramsay&J.]
*PRACTICE AREAS: Insurance Coverage; Insurance Defense.
**Wensley, David W.** ... '58 '84 C.800 B.S. L.1065 J.D. [Allen,M.L.G.&M.]
*PRACTICE AREAS: Real Estate; Environmental Law.
**Wesierski, Christopher P.**, (AV) ... '53 '79 C.1042 B.A. L.1049 J.D. [Wesierski&Z.]
*PRACTICE AREAS: Wrongful Termination Law; Medical Malpractice Law; Insurance Coverage Law; Premises Liability Law; Auto Liability.

**Wesierski & Zurek, (AV) [BR]**
**Suite 1500, 5 Park Plaza, 92714⊙**
**Telephone: 714-975-1000 Telecopier: 714-756-0517**
**Partners: Christopher P. Wesierski; Ronald Zurek (Resident, Glendale Office); Daniel J. Ford, Jr.; Terence P. Carney; Thomas G. Wianecki; Stephen M. Ziemann; Mark E. Brubaker. Associates: Christopher M. Fisher; Mark J. Giannamore; Paul J. Lipman; David F. Mastan; Steven D. Turner; Robert M. Binam; Diane E. Jacobs; Bruce V. Rorty.**
**General Civil Litigation, Insurance Bad Faith, Defense and Coverage, Appellate Practice, Insurance Defense, Products Liability, Professional Liability, Representation of Employers and Employees, Premises Liability, Real Property (Land Subsidence), Toxic Torts and Intellectual Property.**
**Glendale, California Office: 800 North Brand Boulevard, Suite 250. Telephone: 818-543-6100. Telecopier: 818-543-6101.**
*See Professional Biographies, IRVINE, CALIFORNIA*

Wesley, Brian R. ... '60 '87 C&L.426 B.A., J.D. 7700 Irvine Center Dr., #700
**Wexler, Mitchell L.** ... '60 '85 C.1019 B.A. L.809 J.D. [Hirson W.P.&S.]
*PRACTICE AREAS: Immigration and Naturalization Law; Nationality Law.
Whaling, Thomas M. ... '33 '65 C.770 A.B. L.426 J.D. One Technology
White, Claire Elizabeth ... '61 '86 C&L.802 B.B.A., J.D. 5 Park Plaza
**White, David G.** '60 '89 C.475 B.S. L.213 J.D.
(adm. in MI; not adm. in CA) Discovision Assocs.
*RESPONSIBILITIES: Patent Law; Patent Prosecution; Patent Licensing; Patent Litigation.
**White, Gary R.** ... '52 '85 C.112 A.B. L.911 J.D. [Oswald&Y.]
*PRACTICE AREAS: Commercial Litigation.
White, James D. ... '43 '70 C.112 A.B. L.1068 J.D. 4 Park Plz., 16th Fl.
**White, Leigh A.** ... '67 '93 C.45 B.S.B.A. L.802 J.D. [🄰 Faustman,C.D.&F.]
*PRACTICE AREAS: Employment Law; Labor Law; Business Litigation.
Whitesides, James B. '49 '76
C.877 B.A. L.1335 J.D. Gen. Coun., National Purchasing Corp.
**Whyte, Nicole** ... '65 '91 C&L.061 B.A., LL.B [Kring&B.]
*LANGUAGES: Afrikaans, French, Latin.
*PRACTICE AREAS: Construction; Civil Litigation; Immigration.
**Wianecki, Thomas G.**, (BV) ... '51 '76 C.112 B.A. L.426 J.D. [Wesierski&Z.]
*PRACTICE AREAS: Personal Injury Law; Construction Defect Litigation; Dental Malpractice; Premises Liability.
**Wick, Randall G.** ... '53 '79 C&L.494 B.E.E., J.D. Gen. Coun., AST Resch., Inc.
Wiechert, David W., (AV) ... '55 '80 C&L.477 B.A., J.D. 2600 Michelson Dr., Ste., 1000
**Wiener, Alan H., (A Professional Corporation)**, (AV) '41 '67
C.918 B.A. L.813 LL.B. [Palmieri,T.W.W.&W.]
*PRACTICE AREAS: Corporate Law; Real Estate Law; Tax Law.
**Wiens, D. Susan** ... '50 '89 C.112 B.A. L.426 J.D. [🄰 Palmieri,T.W.W.&W.]
*PRACTICE AREAS: Litigation; Product Liability Defense.
Wilcox, Jean C. ... '51 '81 C.1097 B.A. L.426 J.D. [Crary&W.]
**Wilcox, Kathleen E.** ... '62 '90 C.112 B.A. L.61 J.D. [🄰 Pivo&H.]
Wilens, Jeffrey N. ... '61 '85 C.112 B.A. L.1066 J.D. 18101 Von Karman Ave.
**Wilhelm, James E., (A Professional Corporation)**, (AV) '40 '69
C.1042 A.B. L.1068 J.D. [Palmieri,T.W.W.&W.]
*PRACTICE AREAS: Estate Planning Law; Estate Administration Law.
Willey, Frank P., Jr. '53 '78 C.1031 B.S. L.982 J.D.
(adm. in AZ; not adm. in CA) Exec. V.P. & Gen. Coun., Fidelity Natl. Title Ins. Co.
Williams, Gerold G., (AV) ... '41 '66 C.112 A.B. L.1065 LL.B. [G.G.Williams]
Williams, J. Craig ... '57 '87 C.891 B.S. L.352 J.D. 18500 Von Karman
**Williams, J. Scott** ... '56 '83 C&L.101 B.A., J.D. [Rus,M.W.&S.]
*LANGUAGES: German.
*PRACTICE AREAS: Bankruptcy, Insolvency and Commercial Litigation.
**Williams, John M., III** ... '63 '91 C.112 B.A. L.276 J.D. [🄰 Gibson,D.&C.]
*PRACTICE AREAS: Securities; Mergers, Acquisitions and Divestitures.
**Williams, Lea B.** ... '68 '93 C.36 B.A. L.846 J.D. [🄰 Grant&L.]
*LANGUAGES: Spanish.
*PRACTICE AREAS: Litigation.
**Williams, Michelle M.** ... '65 '93 C.112 B.A. L.1049 J.D. [🄰 Genson,E.C.&W.]
**Williams, S. Linn** '46 '71 C&L.976 B.A. L.309 J.D.
(adm. in MA; not adm. in CA) Corp. Sr. V.P. & Gen. Coun., Mission Energy Co.
**Williams, Warren A.** ... '53 '78 C.976 B.A. L.800 J.D. [Palmieri,T.W.W.&W.]
*PRACTICE AREAS: Real Estate Law; Corporate Law.
Williams, Gerold G., Incorporated, (AV) ... Ste. 370, 19800 MacArthur Blvd.
Williamson, E. Joseph '45 '81 C.967 B.A. L.912 J.D.
(adm. in MI; not adm. in CA) Toyota Motor Sales, U.S.A.,Inc.
**Willis, Geoffrey K.** ... '61 '86 C.668 B.A. L.1065 J.D. [Willis,K.&A.]
*SPECIAL AGENCIES: California Department of Toxic Substances Control; California Department of Fish and Game; South Coast Air Quality Management District; Orange County Health Services Agency; U.S. Fish and Wildlife Service.
*REPORTED CASES: KOLA v. U.S., 882 F. 2d 361 (9th cir. 1989); City of Rancho Cucamonga, et al v. Mackzum, 286 Cal. Rept. 39 (1991).
*PRACTICE AREAS: Environmental Litigation; Air Quality; Hazardous Waste; Land Use; Municipal Litigation.

**Willis, Kendig & Alpert**
**5 Park Plaza Suite 800, 92714-8501**
**Telephone: 714-440-7000**

(This Listing Continued)

**CAA143P**

**Willis, Kendig & Alpert (Continued)**

**Members of Firm: Geoffrey K. Willis; David E. Kendig; Mark D. Alpert.**
**Civil Litigation and Administrative Proceedings relating to Hazardous Materials, Land Use Planning, Municipal Law, Air Quality, Wetlands and General Environmental Law, as well as related Real Estate Issues and Business Litigation.**

***See Professional Biographies, IRVINE, CALIFORNIA***

**Willoughby, Michael L.**, (AV) ........... '49 '81 C.800 B.S. L.1066 J.D. [Borchard&W.]
*PRACTICE AREAS: Civil Litigation; Securities Litigation; Real Estate Litigation; Appellate Practice.
**Wilson, Christopher A.** .................... '59 '87 C&L.101 B.A., J.D. [Jeffers,W.&S.]
*LANGUAGES: French.
*PRACTICE AREAS: Corporate and Securities Law; Mergers and Acquisitions.
**Wilson, Douglas A.** '46 '77 C.940 B.S. L.1137 J.D.
Sr. Legal Coun., Kawasaki Motors Corp., U.S.A.
*RESPONSIBILITIES: Products Liability Law.
Wilson, Gerald E. ..................... '49 '75 C&L.893 B.S., J.D. 5 Park Plz., Ste. 1130
Wilson, Gerald G., (BV) .............. '47 '75 C.679 B.S. L.990 J.D. 8001 Irvine Ctr. Dr.
**Wilson, James Louis** ............... '68 '93 C.112 B.A. L.810 J.D. [🄰 Genson,E.C.&W.]
**Wilson, Lisa M.** ........................ '60 '86 C.800 B.A. L.1137 J.D. [Jackson&W.]⊙
*PRACTICE AREAS: Tort Law; Business Law.
**Wilson, Robert F.**, (BV) ................. '51 '78 C.112 B.A. L.61 J.D. [🄰 Neuland&N.]
*PRACTICE AREAS: Personal Injury; Insurance Defense; Corporation; Business; Real Estate.
**Wilson, Steven N.** ................. '— '77 C.668 B.A. L.990 J.D. Atty., AirTouch Comm.
**Winsten, Michael S.** ........................... '58 '86 C.188 B.S. L.800 J.D. [Bye,H.&R.]
*PRACTICE AREAS: Business Litigation.
**Winter, Ralph H.** ................ '62 '91 C.770 B.S.C. L.602 J.D. [🄰 Allen,M.L.G.&M.]
*PRACTICE AREAS: Corporate; Tax.
**Winters, Fred Timothy** ...... '50 '79 C.1077 B.A. L.426 J.D. [🄰 Berger,K.S.M.F.S.&G.]
*PRACTICE AREAS: Landlord and Tenant Law; Bankruptcy; Creditors Rights; Real Property; Business Litigation.
**Winton, Daniel K.**, (AV) ............. '47 '73 C.112 B.A. L.1066 J.D. [Paone,C.M.&W.]
*PRACTICE AREAS: Business and Real Property Transactions; Real Property Finance; Strategic Alliances; Joint Ventures and Partnerships.
**Wintrode, Ralph C.**, (AV) .................. '42 '67 C&L.800 B.S., J.D. [Gibson,D.&C.]
*PRACTICE AREAS: Real Estate; Land Use; Corporate; Mergers and Acquisitions; Bankruptcy.
**Witkow, Stanley P.** '48 '73
C.112 B.A. L.1065 J.D. V.P., Legal/Corp., MAI Systems Corp.
*RESPONSIBILITIES: Corporate; Business; Intellectual Property; Employment.
Wittman, Randall R. ........................... '53 '78 C.800 B.S. L.1065 J.D. 6 Venture
**Woffinden, Arlen D.** .................... '50 '77 C&L.101 B.A., J.D. [Smith,S.D.P.&W.]
**Wolcott, Cynthia M.** ............. '54 '85 C.197 B.A. L.800 J.D. [Palmieri,T.W.W.&W.]
*PRACTICE AREAS: Corporate Law; Real Estate Law.
**Wolder, Michael K.** ........... '60 '90 C.1042 B.S.M.E. L.1137 J.D. [Brown,P.H.&V.]⊙
*PRACTICE AREAS: Private Development; Public Works; Construction Litigation; Engineering.
**Woldt, Wendy A.** ......................... '56 '81 C.800 B.A. L.1065 J.D. [Woldt&H.]
*REPORTED CASES: Foreman vs. Knapp Press (1985) 173 Cal.App.3d 200, 218 Cal.Rptr. 815.

**Woldt & Ham, A Professional Law Corporation**
**2151 Michelson Drive, Suite 136, 92612-1311**
**Telephone: 714-833-5000 Fax: 714-833-5300**
**Wendy A. Woldt; Scott W. Ham;—Kathleen O. Peterson; Marianne Van Riper; Ligia G. Cimpoeru; Debora A. Cappucci.**
**Representing Management in the Defense of Employment Litigation and Labor Disputes and the Development and Implementation of Employment Policies and Procedures.**

***See Professional Biographies, IRVINE, CALIFORNIA***

**Wolensky, Gary A.**, (AVⓉ) .................... '54 '78 C&L.884 B.A., J.D. [Snell&W.]
*PRACTICE AREAS: Product Liability Litigation.
**Wolff, Joshua M.** .......................... '59 '88 C.112 A.B. L.273 J.D. [Hanley&P.]
*LANGUAGES: German.
*REPORTED CASES: %italic; Denney v. Lawrence %roman; (1994) 22 Cal. App 4th 927 (libel).
Wong, Rollin Y. L. ..................... '59 '84 C.312 B.A. L.1065 J.D. 8 Corporate Park
**Wontrobski, Stephen M.** ............. '47 '76 C.93 B.S. L.326 J.D. [🄲 Brown,P.H.&V.]
*PRACTICE AREAS: Construction Law; Environmental Law; Engineering; Insurance Law.
Wood, Patrick J. ............................. '50 '78 C.112 B.A. L.809 J.D. [Wood&D.]
Wood & Delgado .................................................. 1 Park Plza., Ste. 1250
**Woodburn, Graig R.** .................. '60 '88 C.308 B.A. L.276 J.D. [🄰 Callahan&B.]
*PRACTICE AREAS: Securities Litigation; Intellectual Property Litigation; Business Litigation.
Woodmansee, Glen D., (BV) .............. '27 '66 C.112 B.A. L.809 J.D. P.O. Box 4440
**Woodruff, Frederick C.** '37 '63 C.165 A.B. L.823 LL.B.
(adm. in NY; not adm. in CA) [Chevalier,A.&L.]
*PRACTICE AREAS: Aviation law (50%); Environmental Law (25%); Administrative Law (25%).
**Worcester, Mark K.** ........................ '55 '80 C&L.800 B.A., J.D. [Pinto&D.]
**Worth, Warren** ........................ '— '89 C&L.1137 B.S.L., J.D. [D.L.Geiler]
*PRACTICE AREAS: Tort Law; Real Estate (Property) Law; Contract Law.

**Wu, Charles C.H., & Associates '61 '93 C.800 B.S.E.E. L.1137 J.D.**
**2603 S.E. Main Street, Suite 800, 92614-6232**
**Telephone: 714-251-0111 Fax: 714-251-1588**
**Email: CWU@ODONT.CON**
***PRACTICE AREAS: Business Litigation; Business Transactions; Intellectual Property.**
**Business Litigation, Business Transactions, Intellectual Property.**

***See Professional Biographies, IRVINE, CALIFORNIA***

**Yamaguchi, Howard S.** '60 '85 C&L.800 A.B., J.D.
Sr. Group Coun., Waste Mgmt., Inc.
**Yap, Calvin C.S.** .......................... '56 '82 C.339 B.S. L.597 J.D. [Oswald&Y.]
*LANGUAGES: Taiwanese.
Ybarra, Wayne A. ......................... '45 '82 C.112 B.S. L.178 J.D. [Ybarra&D.]
Ybarra and Douglas .................................................. 5 Park Plaza
**Yeager, John P.**, (AV) ..................... '58 '83 C.112 B.A. L.1068 J.D. [Hewitt&M.]
*PRACTICE AREAS: Real Estate Law; Land Use Law; Public Finance Law.
**Yoch, Barry A.** ........................ '53 '78 C.112 B.S. L.1068 J.D. [Case,K.B.&W.]
*PRACTICE AREAS: Estate Planning; Tax Law.
**Yoseloff, Sarah** ..................... '— '87 C.94 B.S. L.1137 J.D. [🄰 Genson,E.C.&W.]
Young, Leo J., (AV) '37 '70 C.884 B.S.E.E. L.426 J.D.
V.P., Intell. Prop. Rights, Western Digital Corp. (Pat.)
Young, Merne E. .................. '37 '67 C.846 B.S. L.767 LL.B. 18751 San Rufino Dr.
Young, Ronald L. ...'46 '75 C.813 B.A. L.273 J.D. Corp. Coun., Entrepreneur Media, Inc.
Young, Timothy J. .......... '52 '80 C.112 B.A. L.1065 J.D. Sr. Coun., Fluor Daniel, Inc.
**Zaeske, Laurel** ......................... '60 '88 C.174 B.S. L.800 J.D. [Rus,M.W.&S.]
*PRACTICE AREAS: Civil Litigation; Bankruptcy Litigation.
**Zaharek, Zachary J.** .................... '68 '95 C&L.770 B.S., J.D. [Malcolm,C.&H.]
*PRACTICE AREAS: Bankruptcy; Creditors Rights; Commercial Litigation.
Zanton, Shirley L. .......................... '56 '81 C.597 B.A. L.309 J.D. 18 Abeto‡
**Zarian, John N.** ...................... '62 '89 C.878 B.A. L.800 J.D. [Perkins,Z.&D.]
*LANGUAGES: Spanish and Italian.
*PRACTICE AREAS: Securities, General Business and Commercial Litigation.
Zaslav, Barry A. '39 '65
C.575 B.A. L.276 LL.B. V.P. & Coun., Century 21 Real Estate Corp.
Zeisler, Jack F. '21 '52 C.608 B.S. L.209 J.D.
(adm. in IL; not adm. in CA) New Directions Business & Financial Consulting
**Zeman, Larry S.**, (AV) .................. '50 '75 C.473 B.A. L.597 J.D. [Barnes,C.F.&Z.]
*PRACTICE AREAS: Real Estate; Construction; Business Litigation; Tort Litigation.
**Zevnik, Richard Wm.** ............ '53 '85 C.112 B.A. L.426 J.D. [🄰 Sedgwick,D.M.&A.]
**Ziebarth, Irene E.**, (BV) ......... '43 '85 C.1109 B.A. L.426 J.D. [🄲 Sedgwick,D.M.&A.]
**Ziemann, Stephen M.** .................... '59 '87 C.101 B.S. L.800 J.D. [Wesierski&Z.]
*LANGUAGES: Japanese.
*PRACTICE AREAS: Civil Litigation; Product Liability; Premises Liability; Wrongful Termination; Unlawful Detainer.
**Ziff, Hali E.** .................. '59 '86 C.112 B.A. L.426 J.D. [🄰 Berger,K.S.M.F.S.&G.]
**Zipser, Dean J.**, (AV) .................. '55 '80 C.112 B.A. L.813 J.D. [Morrison&F.]
*PRACTICE AREAS: Litigation; Real Estate; Construction; Intellectual Property.
**Zorrilla, Jose, Jr.**, (BV) ............ '48 '74 C.800 A.B. L.61 J.D. [🄲 Gauntlett&Assoc.]
*LANGUAGES: Spanish.
*PRACTICE AREAS: Contract Law; Corporations Law; Patent, Trademark and Copyright.
**Zulch, William F.** ..................... '55 '80 C.112 B.A. L.809 J.D. [Genson,E.C.&W.]
**Zurek, Ronald**, (AV) .................. '52 '77 C.112 A.B. L.426 J.D. [Wesierski&Z.]⊙
*PRACTICE AREAS: Wrongful Termination; Medical Malpractice; Insurance Coverage; Premises Liability; Automobile Liability.
**Zwierlein, Robert F.** .................... '63 '88 C.763 B.A. L.800 J.D. [🄰 Turner&R.]
*LANGUAGES: German.
*PRACTICE AREAS: Business Law; Commercial Law; Real Estate Litigation; Personal Injury.

## IRWINDALE, 1,050, *Los Angeles Co.*

Atkinson, Richard M., II ..................... '34 '63 C.112 L.426 LL.B. P.O. Box 2365
Brannon, G. Sims .................... '55 '80 C.893 B.A. L.813 J.D. 4900 Rivergrade Rd.
Cook, Donald T. ..... '46 '74 C.112 B.S. L.106 J.D. Sr. Coun., Home Svgs. of Amer., FSB
Coughlin, Thomas M. ................ '50 '77 C.813 A.B. L.276 J.D. 4900 Rivergrade Rd.
Engman, John R. '31 '56 C.112 B.S. L.1065 LL.B.
Sr. Coun., Home Svgs. of Amer., FSB
Fletcher, Bruce W. '41 '68 C.1095 B.A. L.398 B.A.
Sr. Coun., Home Svgs. of Amer., FSB
Friedman, Michael J. '63 '89 C.112 B.A. L.1065 J.D.
Assoc. Coun., HSA Servicing Corp.
Gelsinger, J. Roger '37 '63 C.605 B.A. L.569 LL.B.
Sr. Coun., Home Svgs. of Amer., FSB
Glassett, Tim S. '56 '81 C&L.878 B.S., J.D.
Sr. V.P. & Asst. Gen. Coun., H. F. Ahmanson & Co.
Greenfield, Julia Leah .............. '51 '76 C.1044 B.A. L.884 J.D. 4900 Rivergrade Rd.
Gregory, George G., (AV) '32 '57 C&L.309 B.A., LL.B.
Exec. V.P., Govt. Affs., H. F. Ahmanson & Co
Halm, Willard K. ................. '51 '78 C.112 B.A. L.1066 J.D. H.F. Ahmanson & Co.
Hartley, Donald V. '43 '71 C.112 B.A. L.398 J.D.
Sr. Coun., Home Svgs. of Amer., FSB
Hartley, George R. '49 '74 C.454 A.B. L.276 J.D.
Sr. Coun., Home Svgs. of Amer., FSB
Holaday, Keith ..................... '26 '61 C.800 B.A. L.809 LL.B. 4900 Rivergrade Rd.
Johnson, J. Warren ................. '28 '64 C.112 B.A. L.1066 J.D. 1001 Commerce Dr.
Kleiner, Madeleine Ann, (AV) '51 '76 C.188 B.S. L.976 J.D.
Exec. V.P., Gen. Coun., H.F. Ahmanson & Co.
Langenfeld-Minasian, Christine M. '49 '80
C.112 B.A. L.813 J.D. Sr. Coun., Home Svgs. of Amer., FSB
Lyons, Tracie Tabor ...'62 '86 C.112 B.A. L.1066 J.D. Coun., Home Svgs. of Amer., FSB
Marzell, Hal M. .......'55 '81 C.1075 B.S. L.809 J.D. Coun., Home Servicing of America
Moseley, Susan D. ................. '52 '86 C.813 B.A. L.1065 J.D. 4900 Rivergrade Rd.
Parnell, Covert E., III ................ '46 '73 C.88 A.B. L.309 J.D. 4900 Rivergrade Rd.
Perez, Alex T. '60 '89 C.112 B.A. L.1065 J.D.
Assoc. Coun., Home Svgs. of Amer., FSB
Pisapia, Ronn A. .......'51 '80 C.1077 B.A. L.1095 J.D. Sr. Coun., Home Svgs. of Amer.
Pogue, Brian V. W. .................. '54 '85 C.112 B.A. L.800 J.D. 1001 Commerce Dr.
Root, Sherwin F. '51 '75 C.276 B.S.B.A. L.309 J.D.
Sr. Coun., Home Svgs. of Amer., FSB
Sama, Lillian '63 '89 C.112 B.A. L.800 J.D.
Assoc. Coun., Home Savings of America, FSB
**Tansey, Roger K., Jr.** '55 '83
C.930 A.B. L.93 J.D. Assoc. Coun., Home Svgs. of Amer., F.A.
Tobias, Barry I. '64 '92 C.994 B.A. L.978 J.D.
(adm. in NJ; not adm. in CA) Assoc. Coun., Home Svgs. of Amer., FSB
Tomkins, Ann M. '62 '87 C.988 B.A. L.1068 J.D.
Sr. Coun., Home Svgs. of Amer., FSB
Tyre, John Dulken, (AV) ........... '53 '82 C.1097 B.S. L.1179 J.D. 5200 Irwindale Ave.
Wurtzel, Franklin R., (BV) '42 '68
C.112 B.A. L.1068 J.D. Sr. Coun., Home Svgs. of Amer., FSB
Yamasaki, Makoto '57 '83 C.674 A.B. L.1066 J.D.
Sr. Coun., Home Svgs. of Amer., FSB
Yuen, Chuie-Wei .......'61 '86 C.813 B.A. L.659 J.D. Coun., Home Svgs. of Amer., FSB
Zipperstein, Diane Flanagan '58 '83 C.659 B.A. L.1067 J.D.
Home Svgs. of Amer., FSB

## JACKSON, * 3,545, *Amador Co.*

Allen, John B. .......................... '50 '85 C.112 B.S. L.464 J.D. 135 Summit St., #2
Anderson, Stephen W. ...................... '46 '82 C.767 B.A. L.999 J.D. 610 Court St.
Chisholm, Michael H. ...................... '41 '71 C.112 B.A. L.464 J.D. 39 Summit St.
Dixon, Larry L. ............................................ '43 '79 L.1148 J.D. Co. Dist. Atty.
Hamburger, Lon D. ...................... '52 '86 C.267 B.S. L.464 J.D. Dep. Dist. Atty.
Jordan, Carolyn S. '36 '77 C.813 B.S. L.845 J.D.
(adm. in TX; not adm. in CA) Stockton Unified School Dist.
Lacey, Laurence A. .................. '38 '65 C.813 B.A. L.1065 J.D. 100 French Bar Rd.
McNett, Mary Ann ..................... '59 '84 C.112 A.B. L.1065 J.D. Dep. Co. Coun.
Page, Helen O. ............................. '46 '80 C.1060 B.A. L.464 J.D. 8 Court St.
Reynolds, Guy E. .................. '31 '63 C.597 B.S. in Che. L.734 LL.B. 34 Summit St.
Rodman, Kevin D. ........................... '52 '82 C.1060 B.A. L.464 J.D. 17 Main St.
Ryan, Martin H. ............................................. '21 '54 C.112 L.1065 J.D. Supr. Ct. J.
Seaton, Jeffrey D. ........................ '51 '90 C.1060 B.A. L.464 J.D. 435 Court St.
Sides, Jimmie L. ...................... '40 '74 C&L.1137 B.S.L., J.D. Sr. Dep. Dist. Atty.
Stomberg, Nannette ................. '62 '93 C.112 B.A. L.464 J.D. 100 French Bar Rd.
Tremelling, Dennis S. .............. '48 '78 C.1060 B.A. L.1065 J.D. 10330 Argonaut Dr.
Valen, Mark ................................. '46 '78 C.33 B.A. L.767 J.D. 108 Water St.

**Zalkind, Stephen R., (AV) '42 '68 C.112 A.B. L.329 J.D.**
**833 Vogan Toll Road, 95642**
**Telephone: 209-223-2244 Fax: 209-223-5458**
**General Civil, Real Estate, Municipal, Business, Family Law, Probate and Related Litigation.**

***See Professional Biographies, JACKSON, CALIFORNIA***

## JAMESTOWN, —, *Tuolumne Co.*

Rosasco, Richard J., (CV) ............. '33 '71 C.112 B.S. L.1132 J.D. 18281-C Main St.

## JAMUL, —, *San Diego Co.*

Weigand, Penny D. ......................... '47 '84 C.763 B.A. L.1137 J.D. P.O. Box 650
Zickel, Mark ...................... '52 '77 C.31 B.A. L.94 J.D. 14794 Wild Stallion Pl.

**JOSHUA TREE, 1,211, *San Bernardino Co.***

Bynum, Jerry E., (BV) ................... '47 '74 C.1110 B.A. L.1049 J.D. Pub. Def. Off.
Cave, James W., III ..................... '54 '92 C.1004 B.A. L.284 J.D. Dep. Dist. Atty.
McGuire, James C. ............................ '46 '72 C&L.800 B.A., J.D. Supr. Ct. J.
Root, Linda A., (BV) ...................... '39 '82 C&L.1137 B.S.L., J.D. Dep. Dist. Atty.
Sasnett, William B., Jr. ................... '39 '74 C.36 B.A. L.1049 J.D. P.O. Box 2042‡
Swift, Bert L. ........................................................ '40 '77 L.1137 LL.B. Mun. J.
Weir, Bill J., Jr. ................... '48 '81 C&L.1190 B.S.L., J.D. 62762- 29 Palms Hwy.

**JULIAN, —, *San Diego Co.***

Carey, David W. '42 '75 C.763 B.S. L.1137 J.D.
Dir., Environmental Mgmt., Univ. of California, San Diego
Enstrom, Elmer M., Jr. .......................................... '15 '57 C.999 890 Knob Hill Dr.‡
Grum, Robert M., (AV) ..................... '19 '52 C.174 B.S. L.809 LL.B. P.O. Box 687
McCarty, Donald L. ................. '28 '73 C.912 B.F.A. L.1137 J.D. P.O. Box 1558

**KEENE, —, *Kern Co.***

Chavez, Federico "Freddy" G. .............. '51 '80 C.112 B.A. L.1066 J.D. P.O. Box 30
Lynch, Thomas P. .......................................................... '— '92 P.O. Box 310
Macri-Ortiz, Barbara ..................... '49 '87 C.1169 United Farm Workers, AFL-CIO
Schneider, Chris A. .......................................................... '56 '86 P.O. Box 30

**KELSEYVILLE, —, *Lake Co.***

Harpham, Wilfred J. ..................... '25 '53 C.112 B.S. L.1065 LL.B. Ret. Jus. Ct. J.

**KENSINGTON, 5,823, *Contra Costa Co.***

Brock, Diane C. ........................................................ '47 '79 21 Kingston Rd.
Fineman, Elliott L. '49 '81 C.604 B.A. L.64 J.D.
(adm. in MD; not adm. in CA; Pat.) 68 Stratford Rd.
Griffin, Myron R. ................................. '20 '59 L.426 LL.B. 458 Coventry Rd.
Gross, Herbert ................................ '29 '58 C.999 L.426 LL.B. 267 Lake Dr.‡
Heskin, Allan D. ................. '38 '64 C.112 B.S. L.1066 LL.B. 317 Vassar Ave.
Hironaka, Bruce A. ........................ '55 '80 C.112 A.B. L.813 J.D. 26 Lenox Rd.
Lyon, Beverly M., (Ms.), (BV) .......... '44 '70 C.112 B.A. L.1066 J.D. 388 Colusa Ave.
Parker, Nancy L. ......................... '49 '84 C.112 B.A. L.284 J.D. 382 Colusa Ave.
Rose, Ovid ................................... '10 '38 C.569 B.A. L.309 LL.B. 8 Kenyon Ave.
Sayles, Elda G., (Mrs.) ................. '17 '56 C&L.912 B.A., LL.B. 222 Stanford Ave.‡
Schulak, Donald ........................ '32 '60 C.608 B.S. L.851 LL.B. 19 Kingston Rd.
Ward, Richard O. '46 '78 C.112 B.S. L.950 J.D.
(adm. in OR; not adm. in CA) 42 Kingston Rd.‡
Welden, David R. ......................... '54 '81 C.112 A.B. L.765 J.D. [Welden&W.]
Welden, Jacques R., (AV) .................... '27 '55 C.112 L.1065 J.D. [Welden&W.]
Welden & Welden, (AV) ..................................................... 264 Arlington Ave.
Wolf, Chester J. ....................... '20 '47 C.112 A.B. L.1066 LL.B. 60 Highland Blvd.‡

**KENTFIELD, —, *Marin Co.***

Begg, John R. ................ '59 '88 C.284 B.A. L.767 J.D. 925 Sir Francis Drake Blvd.
Clark, Kim R., (AV) ......................... '36 '65 C.674 A.B. L.1066 J.D. 307 Kent Ave.
Dinkelspiel, Richard C., (AV) ............... '13 '37 C.112 A.B. L.1066 J.D. P.O. Box 511
Donoghue, Robin Paige, (AV) ............ '52 '75 C.112 B.A. L.767 J.D. 16 Treetop Way
**Dudley, Susannah M.** ........................ '68 '96 C.112 B.A. L.146 J.D. [⊡J.L.Fallat]
*PRACTICE AREAS: Insurance Defense; Family Law.

**Fallat, John L., Law Offices of '55 '84 C.112 B.A. L.61 J.D.**
**Suite 100, 907 Sir Francis Drake Boulevard, 94904-1502⊙**
**Telephone: 415-457-3773 Fax: 415-457-2667**
**Associates: Steven D. Schroeder; Susannah M. Dudley.**
**General trial and civil practice including insurance and surety defense, administrative law, transportation, collections, bankruptcy, probate and consumer class actions.**
**San Francisco, California Office: One Sansome Street, Suite 2100. 94104. Telephone: 415-399-1180; Fax: 415-951-4660.**
**Pasadena, California Office: 225 South Lake Avenue, Suite 300, 91101. Telephone: 818-296-0155. Fax: 818-432-5401.**

*See Professional Biographies, KENTFIELD, CALIFORNIA*

Granger, Hubert R., Jr. '42 '68 C&L.378 B.A., J.D.
(adm. in KS; not adm. in CA) 138 Cypress Ave.‡
Greenberg, Frank R. ..................... '39 '64 C.197 A.B. L.178 LL.B. 121 Kent Ave.
Hillard, Lila Anderson ........................ '50 '76 C.813 B.A. L.273 J.D. 1 Spring Rd.‡
Horton, Corwin R. .......... '33 '63 C.628 B.S. L.273 LL.B. The Park, 25 Mann Dr. (Pat.)
McGuire, E. Warren ...................................... '24 '51 C&L.767 LL.B. 1 Rosebank Lane‡
Neumeier, Edward J. ........................ '24 '72 C.908 A.B. L.284 J.D. 85 Berens Dr.‡
Ribar, Peter A. ..................... '13 '39 C.174 B.A. L.273 LL.B. Admin. Law J., OHA
Richert, Richard J. ............................. '16 '41 L.284 LL.B. 216 Foster Avenue‡
**Schroeder, Steven D.** ....................... '56 '85 C.966 B.S. L.61 J.D. [⊡J.L.Fallat]
*PRACTICE AREAS: Surety Defense; Real Estate; Personal Injury; Business.
Silen, Harold, (AV) ....................... '31 '57 C.112 B.A. L.1065 J.D. 8 Buckeye Way
Smith, Daniel U. ..................... '43 '68 C.674 A.B. L.1066 J.D. 21 Rancheria Rd.
Smith, Peter A. .......................... '25 '51 C&L.767 B.S., LL.B. Ret. Supr. Ct. J.
Sorensen, Karen S. ................................................ '43 '77 929 Sir Francis Drake Blvd.
Sylla, John R. .............................. '59 '86 C.309 A.B. L.145 J.D. P.O. Box 864
Ward, Edmond C., (AV) ......................... '26 '55 C&L.767 B.S., J.D. 4 Orchard Way‡
Wilner, Joseph M. ......................................... '19 '45 L.767 LL.B. 310 Evergreen Dr.‡

**KENWOOD, —, *Sonoma Co.***

Bowden, Leslie J. ........................ '42 '72 C.766 B.A. L.284 J.D. 8771 Sonoma Hwy.
Holm, Phillip H., (AVⓣ) '31 '55 C&L.597 B.S.L., LL.B.
(adm. in IL; not adm. in CA) P.O. Box 634‡
Phillips, Sarah J. ........................... '50 '85 C.72 B.A. L.1218 J.D. P.O. Box 714

**KERMAN, 5,448, *Fresno Co.***

Henry, Jerry E., (BV) ..................... '41 '74 C.768 B.A. L.1189 J.D. [J.E.Henry]⊙
Henry, Jerry E., Inc., (BV) ................................................ 441 S. Madera Ave. (⊙Fresno)
Markeson, Thomas A. ..................................... '52 '87 L.1051 J.D. [⊡J.E.Henry]
O'Malley, David T., (BV) ............ '44 '71 C.907 B.A. L.208 J.D. 188 S. Madera Ave.

**KERNVILLE, 1,660, *Kern Co.***

**Hix, Phyllis M., (AV) '36 '63 C&L.800 B.S., J.D.**
**112 Buena Vista Drive, P.O. Bin DD, 93238⊙**
**Telephone: 619-376-3761 Fax: 619-376-3764**
**Insurance Defense and Coverage Litigation. General Civil Practice with emphasis on Litigation.**
**Phoenix, Arizona Office: 910 East Osborn. Telephone: 602-248-9222.**

**KING CITY, 7,634, *Monterey Co.***

Anderson, Peter D., (BV) ..................... '40 '68 C&L.494 B.A., J.D. [Anderson&B.]
Anderson & Bolles, Inc., (BV) ............................................................ 523 Broadway
Bolles, Donald S., (BV) .................. '36 '71 C.24 B.A. L.1049 J.D. [Anderson&B.]
Foley, Edward J., (BV) .......................... '28 '53 C.755 B.A. L.494 J.D. City Atty.
Hutton, John W., (AV) .............................................. '15 '45 L.284 LL.B. 523 Broadway‡
Jacobs, Craig H. ........................................ '60 '88 C.101 B.S. L.1067 J.D. 510 Broadway
Moody, Robert F. ............................................... '43 '71 C.112 A.B. L.1065 J.D. Mun. Ct. J.

**Noland, Hamerly, Etienne & Hoss, A Professional Corporation, (AV)**
**104 South Vanderhurst, Suite D, 93930⊙**
**Telephone: 408-386-1080 Fax: 408-386-1083**
**James D. Schwefel, Jr.**
**Business and Commercial Litigation. Construction Litigation. General Business, Corporation, Probate, Estate Planning, Real Property, Land Use, Administrative Law, Tax Law and Family Law.**
**Salinas, California Office: Civic Center Building, 333 Salinas Street. Telephones: 408-424-1414; 372-7525. Fax: 408-424-1975.**
**Monterey, California Office: Heritage Harbor, 99 Pacific Street, Building 200, Suite C, 93940. Telephone: 408-424-1414. Fax: 408-373-4797.**

*See Professional Biographies, KING CITY, CALIFORNIA*

**Schwefel, James D., Jr.**, (BV) ........ '36 '64 C.112 A.B. L.1066 J.D. [Noland,H.E.&H.]⊙
*PRACTICE AREAS: Real Estate Law; Agricultural Law; Business Law.
Scott, Russell D., (BV) ........................... '52 '78 C.112 B.A. L.1226 J.D. Mun. J.

**KINGSBURG, 7,205, *Fresno Co.***

Coduti, Leonard L. ......................................... '19 '50 L.1065 J.D. Ret. Jus. Ct. J.
Falk, E. LeRoy ............................... '42 '91 C.112 B.A. L.1148 J.D. 2504 Birch Ct.
Hauenstein, James F. ..................... '44 '72 C.800 B.A. L.1068 J.D. 1776 Simpson St.
Kriebel, Barry F. .... '50 '75 C.813 B.A. L.276 J.D. Pres., Sun-Diamond Growers of Calif.

**KNEELAND, —, *Humboldt Co.***

Kossow, Richard E. .......................... '35 '60 C&L.494 B.S.L., LL.B. Ret. Jus. Ct. J.
Moore, Charles V. .............................................. '18 '50 C.230 A.B. L.1065 J.D.‡

**LA CANADA FLINTRIDGE, 19,378, *Los Angeles Co.***

Anderson, T. Reid ................... '20 '49 C&L.174 B.S.Ch.E., LL.B. 809 Milmada Dr.‡
Arman, Harold ......................... '17 '46 L.1001 LL.B. 5042 Gould Ave.‡
Bachand, Louis J., (AV) .............. '36 '61 C.321 B.S. L.569 LL.B. P.O. Box 1508 (Pat.)
Borden, Thomas W., (BV) ..... '42 '72 C.1097 B.S. L.1148 J.D. 4529 Angeles Crest Hwy.
Brunette, Robert A. ............................. '43 '73 C.869 B.S. L.426 J.D. 4443 Chevy Chase Dr.
Byung-Cho Chang, Kenneth ..... '29 '63 C.231 B.A. L.770 LL.B. 5618 Bramblewood Rd.
Forssen, Richard E. ..................... '23 '55 C.990 L.809 LL.B. 5181 Princess Anne Rd.
Gearhart, Donald C., (AV) ............................ '24 '56 L.1001 J.D. 1732 Bonita Vista Dr.
Googooian, Charles L. ................. '47 '74 C.800 A.B. L.61 J.D. 2214 Los Amigos St.
Grifka, Wilfred '15 '38 C.563 B.S. L.732 LL.B.
(adm. in NY; not adm. in CA) 4377 Beulah Dr.‡
Hanin, Daniel ......... '48 '75 C.1077 B.S. L.426 J.D. 5040 Ocean View Blvd., La Canada
Johnson, Don I., (AV) ............ '28 '54 C.112 B.S. L.477 J.D. 4529 Angeles Crest Hwy.
Johnson, Edward D. ............... '50 '74 C.1109 B.A. L.426 J.D. 5040 Ocean View Blvd.
Johnson, Heber E. ............................ '18 '48 C.383 B.S.C. L.597 J.D. Int. Rev. Serv.
Lewis, Evan W. ............................ '13 '35 C.112 L.809 LL.B. 5074 Walmar Ave.
Longo, Samuel C. ................... '55 '80 C.112 B.A. L.464 J.D. 535 Meadow Grove St.
Maharg, John D., (AV) ................ '13 '39 C.112 A.B. L.800 J.D. 5040 Oakwood Ave.‡
Mitchell, Harry H. ................................... '17 '43 C&L.976 B.A., LL.B. P.O. Box 848
Orlik, Deborah K. ........................ '54 '86 C.112 A.B. L.1065 J.D. 2222 Foothill Blvd.
Reynolds, Meredith B. '54 '80
C.813 B.A. L.665 J.D. V.P., Unified Sch. Dist. Governing Bd.
Rhine, Bertrand, (AV) ........................ '05 '30 C.813 A.B. L.800 J.D. 835 Milmade Dr.
Rodli, Lauren Thor '55 '83 C.112 B.A. L.209 J.D.
(adm. in IL; not adm. in CA) 4834 Oakwood Ave., La Canada‡
Rosker, Benjamin H. .................. '29 '54 C&L.930 B.S., J.D. 1045 W. Inverness Dr.‡
Samuels, Nancy B. ................... '51 '83 C.342 B.A. L.1068 J.D. 840 Greenridge Dr.
Schifferman, Robert P. ................. '27 '52 C&L.813 A.B., J.D. 3836 Hampstead Rd.‡
Smith, Joy ........................... '60 '85 C.112 B.A. L.1049 J.D. 4210 Hampstead Rd.
Snyder, Robert I., Jr. ................. '41 '74 C.112 B.A. L.809 J.D. 430 Foothill Blvd
Stell, Jos., (AV) ..................... '16 '41 C.112 A.B. L.800 LL.B. P.O. Box 848‡
Stevenson, Robert W. ................... '16 '41 C.112 B.A. L.1066 J.D. P.O. Box 687‡
Swink, Jack W. ...................... '24 '50 C.684 L.809 LL.B. 191 Starlight Crest Dr.‡
Taliaferro, Lewis E. ........................ '26 '63 C.999 L.809 LL.B. 5571 Stardust Rd.
White-Redmond, Marilyn S. ............... '50 '78 C.1077 B.A. L.426 J.D. P.O. Box 1248
Winer, Jane B. .......................... '47 '78 C.771 B.A. L.178 J.D. P.O. Box 805
Wright, Alton L., II ................ '42 '66 C&L.420 B.A., J.D. 5229 Vista Lejana Lane

**LA CRESCENTA, —, *Los Angeles Co.***

Asch, Sunny Charla ..................... '— '82 C.800 B.S. L.1148 J.D. 2606 Foothill Blvd.
Baldwin, Bernardine M. ................. '— '70 C.1097 B.A. L.1095 J.D. P.O. Box 8573
Cross, Susan Lynn ....................... '54 '82 C.605 B.A. L.846 J.D. 2771 Pinelawn Dr.
Eick, William E. ....................... '48 '73 C.112 B.A. L.800 J.D. 2604 Foothill Blvd.
Gamboa, Glenn J. ...................... '46 '71 C.112 B.A. L.763 J.D. 3400 Fairesta St.★
Gershik, Larry .................................................. '48 '79 5504 Terrace Dr.
Klahs, Curtis L. ................. '19 '56 C.999 B.A. L.809 LL.B. 2947 Manhattan Ave.‡
Klahs, Richard W. .................. '19 '56 C.999 L.809 LL.B. 2930 Manhattan Ave.‡
Klein, Marian M.J. .................. '56 '81 C.800 A.B. L.809 J.D. 2701 Mayfield Ave.
Kragulac, Robert Paul .............. '43 '81 C.347 B.S. L.1136 J.D. 2970 Honolulu Ave.
McNally, Gerald, Jr. ................ '47 '84 C.475 L.1148 J.D. 3800 La Crescenta Ave.
Pogue, G. Michael ................... '45 '79 C.1077 B.A. L.809 J.D. 2523 Foothill Blvd.
Prosser, Linda J. .................. '42 '82 C.112 B.S. L.809 J.D. 57 Northwoods Ln.
Ruygrok, Ellynn ..................... '52 '83 C.112 B.A. L.426 J.D. 8 Mountain Oaks‡
Variel, Richard P. .............. '16 '49 C.113 A.B. L.809 LL.B. 4807 Rosemont Ave.
Vient, Timothy C. ..................... '49 '89 C.1097 B.A. L.809 J.D. P.O. Box 8691

**LAFAYETTE, 23,501, *Contra Costa Co.***

Alderman, Kate K. ......................... '42 '74 C.788 A.B. L.1066 J.D. 1 Hartwood Ct.
Anderson, Robert T., (AV) .... '17 '46 C.267 A.B. L.1066 LL.B. 3565 Silver Springs Rd.‡
**Belzer, Robert A.**, (AV) .................. '43 '69 C.112 B.A. L.1065 J.D. [Belzer,H.&M.]
*PRACTICE AREAS: Real Estate Law; Estate Planning; Probate.

**Belzer, Hulchiy & Murray, (AV)**
**3650 Mt. Diablo Boulevard Suite 130, 94549-3765**
**Telephone: 510-284-9600 Fax: 510-284-9630**
**Members of Firm: Robert A. Belzer; Nicholas P. Hulchiy; William J. Murray. Associates: Robert P. Rich.**
**Civil Trial and Appellate Practice, Business, Real Estate, Landslide and Subsidence, Real Estate Syndications, Construction, Personal Injury, Professional Negligence, Insurance, Estate Planning and Probate Law.**

*See Professional Biographies, LAFAYETTE, CALIFORNIA*

Bernstein, Bruce R. ................. '57 '82 C.347 A.B. L.770 J.D. 3736 Mt. Diablo Blvd.
Bohren, J. Keith ....................... '56 '83 C.112 B.S. L.1065 J.D. 953 Dewing Ave.
Bruzzone, Kathryn A. .............. '52 '83 C.112 B.A. L.770 M.B.A. 877 Broadmoor Ct.
Burns, Thomas P. ............. '30 '71 C.112 L.1153 J.D. 959 Mountain View Dr.‡
Camp, Thomas F. ................. '39 '68 C.976 A.B. L.1066 LL.B. 3700 Mt. Diablo Blvd.
Carniato, John J., (AV) .............. '37 '64 C&L.770 B.S., J.D. 3736 Mt. Diablo Blvd.
Channell, William R. ................... '22 '50 C.813 L.1065 J.D. 1250 Medfield Rd.‡

CAA145P

CALIFORNIA—LAFAYETTE MARTINDALE-HUBBELL LAW DIRECTORY 1997

Clark, Diddo ........................................'50 '78 C.112 B.A. L.276 J.D. 6 Blackthorn Rd.
**Claytor, James D.**, (AV) .................. '47 '72 C.154 B.A. L.813 J.D. [Foley M.&F.]⊙
*PRACTICE AREAS: Business Litigation including Employment; Real Estate; Environmental Law; Insurance Coverage.
Converse, John R. ........................... '46 '75 C.112 B.S. L.1066 J.D. 3732 Mt. Diablo Blvd.
Crawford, William G., (BV) '26 '71
C.376 B.S. L.1132 J.D. 1333 N. California Blvd. ite 200
**Curtis, William H.** .......................... '57 '89 C.112 B.A. L.1065 J.D. [▣ Foley M.&F.]
*REPORTED CASES: Diamond Heights HOA v. Nat. Am. Ins. Co., (1991), 227 Cal. App. 3d 563; Patricia H. v. Berkeley Unified School Dist. (1993) 830 F. Supp. 1288.
*PRACTICE AREAS: Business; Commercial; Real Estate; Personal Injury; Insurance Coverage.
Dahl, Gregory G. ........'54 '86 C.1169 B.A. L.1065 J.D. Ste. 300, 3736 Mt. Diablo Blvd.
Dodge, Fred C., (BV) ............................'11 '38 C.169 L.1065 J.D. P.O. Box 1428
Dorband, F. William .............. '45 '74 C.966 B.B.A. L.1065 J.D. 3182 Old Tunnel Rd.
Dumke, Richard A. ............... '38 '66 C.112 B.S. L.1065 J.D. 3901 Happy Valley Rd.
Elliot, Jane ..........................................'46 '77 C.381 L.1197 J.D. P.O. Box 1428
**Feeley, Glenn M.** .......................... '51 '81 C.1133 B.S. L.1019 J.D. [Lorenz A.C.&R.]
*PRACTICE AREAS: Real Estate.
**Foley, William R.**, (AV) ......................'42 '69 C&L.767 B.S., J.D. [Foley M.&F.]
*PRACTICE AREAS: Real Property; Business Law; Estate Planning; Probate and Trust Administration.

**Foley McIntosh & Foley, Professional Corporation, (AV)**
**Suite 250, 3675 Mt. Diablo Boulevard, 94549**
**Telephone: 510-284-3020 Fax: 510-284-3029**
**James D. Claytor; William R. Foley; David L. Frey, Jr.; Thomas J. McIntosh; Jay Richard Strauss;— William H. Curtis; Kenneth W. Pritikin.**
**General Civil and Trial Practice in all Courts. Corporate, Business, Real Property, Tax and Probate Law.**
**References: Mechanics Bank, Albany; Lamorinda National Bank, Lafayette.**
*See Professional Biographies, LAFAYETTE, CALIFORNIA*

**Frey, David L., Jr.**, (AV) .............. '45 '71 C.112 A.B. L.1067 J.D. [Foley M.&F.]⊙
*PRACTICE AREAS: Business Law and Transactions; Taxation; Estate Planning; Probate Administration.
Furness, Stephanie A. .........................'52 '77 C.112 L.765 J.D. 1029 Dolores Dr.
Haile, Raymond A. ........... '30 '58 C.813 A.B. L.309 LL.B. 3658 Mount Diablo Blvd.
**Hall, Robert R.** ......................... '21 '53 C.675 A.B. L.477 LL.B. [▣ Pedder,S.H.&W.]
*PRACTICE AREAS: Estate and Will Contests; General Civil Practice.
Hallmark, M. F., (AV) ...........'10 '35 C.169 B.A. L.1066 LL.B. 1230 Monticello Rd.‡
Hanks, Judith A. ............. '49 '75 C.813 B.A. L.1065 J.D. Kemper-Bedford Properties
Harmon, Richard D., (AV) ................ '47 '76 C.112 A.B. L.284 J.D. [Harmon&T.]⊙
Harmon & Tootell, (AV) ........ 3650 Mt. Diablo Boulevard, Suite 220 (⊙San Francisco)
Hartinger, Lawrence W. ......................'48 '77 C.740 B.A. L.765 J.D. P.O. Box 516
Henry, Robert J. ........ '22 '55 C&L.851 B.E., J.D. 3812 Happy Valley Rd.-Box C (Pat.)‡
**Hesseltine, W. G.**, (AV) ................ '43 '70 C.800 B.S. L.284 J.D. [Pedder,S.H.&W.]
*PRACTICE AREAS: Criminal Law; General Civil Trial Practice; Domestic Relations.
Higham, Frank C., Jr. ............. '35 '64 C.101 A.B. L.1066 J.D. 1418 Reliez Valley Rd.
Hobbs, William P. ..................... '24 '53 C&L.174 B.S., LL.B. 3730 Meadow Lane‡
Hogan, Mary Christine '49 '80
(adm. in CO; not adm. in CA) 1605 Reliez Valley Rd.‡
Holmes, Samuel L., (AV) ..........'18 '43 C&L.878 A.B., LL.B. 3917 Happy Valley Rd.
Honegger, Scott C. '50 '77 C.813 B.A. L.208 J.D.
(adm. in CO; not adm. in CA) 3308 Las Huertas Rd.
Howard, Keith L., (AV) ...............'53 '86 C&L.260 B.S., J.D. 3468 Mt. Diablo Blvd.
**Hulchiy, Nicholas P.**, (BV) ............. '49 '73 C.477 B.A. L.209 J.D. [Belzer,H.&M.]
*PRACTICE AREAS: Real Estate Transactions; Real Estate Law; Construction Law; Civil Litigation.
Hyland, Richard W. ........................'42 '77 C.112 B.A. L.284 J.D. 3237 Deer Hill Rd.
Jones, James J., Jr. ..............................'27 '53 C.767 L.1065 J.D. 127 Marsha Place
Kellman, Robert C., (BV) ........................'48 '80 C.216 3447 Mount Diablo Blvd.
Kleinman, Ira M., (BV) ......................'45 '70 C.966 B.S. L.1065 J.D. [Sweet&K.]
**Klimmek, Dennis M.** .................... '44 '74 C.990 B.S. L.426 J.D. [Lorenz A.C.&R.]
Kurteff, Arthur W. ..................'36 '65 C.913 B.S. L.1065 J.D. 150 Haslemere Ct.
Lake, Sara M., (AV) .........................'44 '74 C.788 B.A. L.767 J.D. 1137 Garden Ln.‡
**Lenz, Stewart W.** ....................'57 '87 C.112 B.S.M.E. L.188 J.D. [▣ Pedder,S.H.&W.]
*PRACTICE AREAS: General Practice; Estate Planning Law; Contested Trusts and Estates; Business Law.
Lester, Helen M. '35 '59 C.436 L.424 J.D.
(adm. in IL; not adm. in CA) 3161 Teigland Rd.‡
Lewis, Paul, Law Office of, (BV) '49 '77 C.608 B.A. L.1230 J.D.
3700 Mt. Diablo Blvd.
Lewis, Regina Marie .....................'54 '84 C.766 B.A. L.1230 J.D. 935 Moraga Rd.
Li, Paul M. ..............................'38 '64 C.999 A.B. L.229 LL.B. 3370 Springhill Rd.
Lindquist, Rodney J., Jr. ...............'29 '56 C.112 B.S. L.1066 LL.B. 668 Doreen Way
Lombardo, Salvatore V., (BV) '41 '69
C.740 B.S. L.1026 LL.B. 3433 Golden Gate Way, E.
Lopez, Stephen B. ........................... '56 '86 C.112 B.S. L.813 J.D. P.O. Box 875

**Lorenz Alhadeff Cannon & Rose, (AV)**
**Lafayette Terrace, 3697 Mount Diablo Boulevard, Suite 100, 94549⊙**
**Telephone: 510-283-1599 Facsimile: 510-283-5847**
**Dennis M. Klimmek; Glenn M. Feeley.**
**General Civil and Trial Practice in all State and Federal Courts, Administrative Law, Antitrust, Banking, Bankruptcy, Reorganization and Creditors Rights, Business, Construction, Corporations, Environmental, International Business and Litigation, Public Finance, Real Estate Litigation, Real Estate Transactions, Federal and State Securities and Trade Regulation, White Collar Crime, Estate Planning, Probate, Criminal.**
**San Diego, California Office: 550 West "C" Street, Nineteenth Floor, 92101-3540. Telephone: 619-231-8700. Facsimile: 619-231-8323.**
**Temecula, California Office: The Tower Plaza, 27555 Ynez Road, Suite 203, 92591-4677. Telephone: 909-699-9088. Facsimile: 909-699-9878.**
**Riverside, California Office: The Orleans Building, 3638 University Avenue, Suite 256, 92501. Telephone: 909-369-3281. Facsimile: 909-683-4307.**
*See Professional Biographies, LAFAYETTE, CALIFORNIA*

Lustig, Norman I. .................. '38 '69 C.260 B.A. L.1066 J.D. 1020 Aileen St., Ste. A
MacArthur, Wallace F. .....................'23 '73 C.112 A.B. L.809 J.D. 1238 Barrott Rd.
Mastrangelo, Edward M., (BV) ...... '52 '78 C.1044 B.A. L.1065 J.D. [E.M.Mastrangelo]
Mastrangelo, Edward M., A Prof. Corp., Law Offices of, (BV) ..... 3447 Mt. Diablo Blvd.
McDowell, Dana Leahy ...............'50 '76 C.813 B.A. L.770 J.D. 3470 Mt. Diablo Blvd.‡
**McIntosh, Thomas J.**, (AV) ............ '30 '66 C.147 B.A. L.1065 J.D. [Foley M.&F.]
*PRACTICE AREAS: Business Law and Transactions; Taxation; Estate Planning; Probate Administration.

**Michelsen, Diane G., (AV) '45 '80 C.112 B.A. L.284 J.D.**
**3190 Old Tunnel Road, 94549-4133**
**Telephone: 510-945-1880 Fax: 510-933-6807**
***PRACTICE AREAS: Adoptions; Surrogacy Law.**
**Agency Adoption, Private Adoption, Independent Adoption and Surrogate Parenting Law.**
*See Professional Biographies, LAFAYETTE, CALIFORNIA*

Miller, Bayard J. ...........................'51 '86 C.112 B.A. L.1065 J.D. [Miller&P.]
Miller & Partridge, (AV) .......................... 3708 Mount Diablo Boulevard, Suite 210
Murphey, Elwood ........................'09 '33 C.112 A.B. L.1066 LL.B. 3280 Hillview Ln.‡
**Murray, William J.** ................... '53 '79 C.768 B.S.B.A. L.770 J.D. [Belzer,H.&M.]
*PRACTICE AREAS: Business Litigation; Real Estate Litigation; Construction Law; Insurance Litigation.
Nicolaisen, Lee K. ...............................'49 '75 C.112 B.A. L.284 J.D. 3264 Park Ln.

Partridge, Robert G., (AV) ........................'24 '52 C.112 B.A. L.1065 J.D. [Miller&P.]
Pasto, John R. ...........................'47 '75 C.763 B.A. L.1049 J.D. 3470 Mt. Diablo Blvd.
Pedder, Robert J., (AV) ................'13 '36 C.999 L.1065 J.D. 3445 Golden Gate Way
**Pedder, Stanley**, (AV) .....................'35 '61 C.169 B.A. L.1066 J.D. [Pedder,S.H.&W.]
*PRACTICE AREAS: Personal Injury Law; General Civil Litigation; Estate and Will Contests.

**Pedder, Stover, Hesseltine & Walker, LLP, (AV)**
**3445 Golden Gate Way, P.O. Box 479, 94549-0479**
**Telephone: 510-283-6816 Fax: 510-283-3683**
**Members of Firm: Stanley Pedder; John A. Stover; W. G. Hesseltine; Timothy B. Walker;—Robert R. Hall; Stewart W. Lenz; Melinda R. Self.**
**Emphasis in Estate and Will Contests. General Civil, Trial and Criminal Practice. Real Property, Personal Injury, Business, Taxation, Domestic Relations, Estate Planning, Probate, Livestock, Appellate Law.**
*See Professional Biographies, LAFAYETTE, CALIFORNIA*

Powlan, Roy Y. .......................................... '27 '66 C.01 B.S. L.284 LL.B. 1 Chapel Dr.‡
Pray, Thorsten John ..................'54 '92 C.112 B.A. L.1067 J.D. 3736 Mt. Diablo Blvd.
Pray, Thorston John ........................'54 '92 C&L.112 B.A., J.D. 3736 Mt. Diablo Blvd.
**Pritikin, Kenneth W.** ....................... '56 '83 C.112 B.A. L.1065 J.D. [Foley M.&F.]⊙
*PRACTICE AREAS: Business Litigation including Real Estate; Environmental Law; Insurance Coverage.
Randall, Craig Z., (BV) ..........................'22 '53 C.112 L.1065 J.D. P.O. Box 1428
Ratcliffe, Allen T., Jr. ...............'47 '72 C.150 B.A. L.208 J.D. 3732 Mt. Diablo Blvd.
Reyes, Edw. O., (BV) ........................'21 '53 C.112 A.B. L.1065 LL.B. P.O. Box 1428
Rhoades, John S. '21 '49 C&L.276 A.B., LL.B.
(adm. in DC; not adm. in CA) 613 Huntington Dr.‡
**Rich, Robert P.** .............................. '57 '82 C.821 B.A. L.1065 J.D. [▣ Belzer,H.&M.]
*PRACTICE AREAS: Litigation; Mediation.
Roberts, Justin A., (AV) ...... '43 '70 C.112 A.B. L.1065 J.D. 1078 Carol Lane, Suite 203
Robinson, Ned, (AV) ................'27 '52 C.112 A.B. L.1066 LL.B. 100 Lafayette Circle
Rockwell, Richard, (AV) ...........'21 '52 C.112 A.B. L.1065 J.D. 1618 Silver Dell Rd.‡
Rosen, Rena C.B. ..............'51 '90 C.66 B.A. L.767 J.D. Ste. 300, 3736 Mt. Diablo Blvd.
Russell, V. Eric .......................'51 '77 C.169 B.A. L.464 J.D. 941 Reliez Station Rd.
Samuelsen, J. Roger ......'36 '65 C.112 A.B. L.1066 J.D. Exec. Dir., Ctr. for Living Skills
Sarkisian, Thomas A. ..........................'50 '77 C.112 B.A. L.767 J.D. 3264 Judith Ln.
Sasse-Wood, Joyce, (BV) .....................'43 '82 C.763 B.A. L.1153 J.D. 1020 Aileen St.
**Self, Melinda R.** ...............'59 '91 C.1245 B.S.B.A. L.1153 J.D. [▣ Pedder,S.H.&W.]
*PRACTICE AREAS: Domestic Relations.
Sherrer, Charles W. '22 '50 C.378 B.S. L.986 J.D.
(adm. in MO; not adm. in CA) 3933 Woodside Ct.‡
Skinner, John W., (AV) ......................'10 '36 C.813 B.A. L.309 LL.B. 797 Solana Dr.
Snyder, Leslie B., Jr. ......................'10 '40 C.112 B.S. L.199 LL.B. 824 Solana Dr.‡
**Stover, John A.**, (BV) ..................'24 '56 C&L.336 B.S., LL.B. [Pedder,S.H.&W.]
*PRACTICE AREAS: Wills Law; Trusts Law; Probate Law.
**Strauss, Jay Richard** .................... '44 '73 C.1349 B.A. L.284 J.D. [Foley M.&F.]⊙
*SPECIAL AGENCIES: City of Lafayette Traffic Commission, 1991-1993; Lafayette Planning Commission, 1993— ; President, Lafayette Chamber of Commerce, 1994.
*PRACTICE AREAS: Business and Real Estate Transactions; Civil Litigation.
Sweet, Rodney M., (BV) ......................'40 '69 C.966 B.S. L.1065 J.D. [Sweet&K.]
Sweet & Kleinman, (BV) ..........................................1020 Aileen St., Suite A
Thompson, Charlotte M. ........................'16 '55 C.999 L.765 LL.B. 1091 Via Roble‡
Titmus, Janice Crosetti, (BV) ..............'43 '81 C.112 B.A. L.1153 J.D. P.O. Box 1428
Titmus, Thomas J., (BV) ....................'27 '64 C.768 L.284 LL.B. P.O. Box 1428
Tobin, William C. ........................'45 '77 C.767 B.S. L.464 J.D. 585 Silverado Dr.
Tootell, Megan ................................'52 '78 C.112 A.B. L.284 J.D. [Harmon&T.]⊙
Vaccaro, Ann .......................'63 '90 C.770 B.A. L.1065 J.D. Stalwart Mgmt. Co.

**Vanoli, Gerald C., (BV) '35 '61 C.767 B.S. L.770 LL.B.**
**3445 Golden Gate Way, 94549-0479**
**Telephone: 510-283-6856 Fax: 510-283-3683**
**Business Law, Bankruptcy, Real Estate Law, Civil Litigation, Will Contests.**

Wagley, William M., (BV) ...... '43 '71 C.1197 B.S. L.1132 J.D. 3433 Golden Gate Way
**Walker, Timothy B.** .......................'55 '80 C.330 L.1065 J.D. [Pedder,S.H.&W.]
*PRACTICE AREAS: Real Property Law; Business Law; Conservatorships; General Civil Litigation.
Wasson, George W. ...........'23 '52 C.679 B.S. L.215 LL.B. 3123 Indian Way (Pat.)‡
Weintraub, Donald J. ......................'46 '72 C.112 A.B. L.1066 J.D. 716 Moraga Rd.
Whitten, Thomas J. .................'31 '60 C.112 B.S. L.765 LL.B. 850 Rosedale Ave.
Wilson, Diane ..........................'47 '77 C.30 B.A. L.1065 J.D. 1314 Reliez Valley Rd.‡
Woods, Glenn R. .............................'43 '70 C.1074 B.S. L.1066 J.D. 12 Diablo Cir.
Young, Robert L., (BV) ...........'43 '70 C.112 B.S. L.284 J.D. 3470 Mt. Diablo Blvd.

## LAGUNA BEACH, 23,170, *Orange Co.*

Adler, John A., (BV) ................'41 '69 C.112 B.A. L.990 J.D. 380 Glenneyre, Ste G.
Aitken, Joslyn, (BV) ....................'49 '79 C.605 B.A. L.1137 J.D. 301 Forest Ave.
Arnold, William B. ...........................'11 '37 C&L.339 B.S., J.D. 178 Emerald Bay
Baim, Joseph M. ...........................'30 '53 C.37 B.A. L.209 J.D. 112 Sa La Senda Dr.
Balacek, Robert V. .................................................'38 '83 1241 Temple Hills Dr.
Basile, Rudolph J. ..........................'27 '53 C.128 L.724 LL.B. 276 Fairview St.
**Bates, Owen J.** ................................'49 '95 C.734 B.A. L.999 J.D. [▣ Levin&G.]
*PRACTICE AREAS: Intellectual Property Law; Litigation.
Bayless, Mark E. ...........................'51 '79 C.1077 B.A. L.1137 J.D. [M.E.Bayless]
Bayless, Mark E., Inc. ......................................................... 301 Forest Ave.
Beckwith, Geo. L. ..........................'11 '39 C.113 A.B. L.800 LL.B. 998 Emerald Bay
**Bidart, Michael J., (P.C.)**, (BV) ........'50 '74 C.1075 B.S. L.990 J.D. [Shernoff,B.&D.]
*LANGUAGES: Basque.
*PRACTICE AREAS: Insurance Bad Faith.
Bishop, James W. ..........................'45 '79 C.1042 B.S. L.1137 J.D. [Bishop&W.]
Bishop & Warren ..................................................................P.O. Box 322
Blacketer, Belinda .................................'46 '85 L.1137 J.D. 303 Broadway

**Boyd, Eva-Marie, (BV) '41 '88 C.840 B.A. L.1137 J.D.**
**1160 Catalina, 92651-2952**
**Telephone: 714-494-0374 Fax: 714-497-3148**
***LANGUAGES: German.**
***PRACTICE AREAS: Civil Litigation; Trademarks; Landlord Tenant; Contracts; Copyrights.**
**Trademarks, Copyrights, Contracts, Business Law, Art Law.**
*See Professional Biographies, LAGUNA BEACH, CALIFORNIA*

Brady, Charles R., (BV) ............'23 '65 C.506 B.A. L.1001 LL.B. 219 Broadway St.‡
Brinkman, Paul F., Jr. '47 '76 C.112 B.A. L.809 J.D.
(adm. in TX; not adm. in CA) 2815 Park Pl.‡
Butterwick, Kirk D. ....................'49 '75 C.800 B.A. L.809 J.D. 31755 S. Coast Hwy.
Carlton, Harry R. ......................'21 '49 C.112 A.B. L.1066 LL.B. 2576 Monaco Dr.
Catz, Sarah L. ..........................'57 '80 C.273 B.A. L.770 J.D. 31022 Aliso Circle
Coffin, Baird B., (AV) ..............'12 '36 C.385 Ph.B. L.273 J.D. 380 Glenneyre, Ste G.
Colman-Schwimmer, Arlene, (AV) '40 '64
C.102 B.A. L.1009 J.D. [A.Colman-Schwimmer]⊙
Colman-Schwimmer, Arlene, A Professional Corporation, (AV)
1400 S. Coast Hwy. (⊙Beverly Hills)
Cooper, T. Hatfield .......................'47 '72 C.112 B.A. L.1065 J.D. 420 Linden St.

**Darras, Frank N.**, (AV) ..............'54 '87 C.1365 B.S. L.1137 J.D. [Shernoff,B.&D.]
*LANGUAGES: Greek.
*PRACTICE AREAS: Insurance Bad Faith.
**Davis, Paul W.** ...........................'53 '79 C.813 A.B. L.1066 J.D. [McClung&D.]
*PRACTICE AREAS: Business Law; Real Property Law; Estate Planning Law; Appeals.
**Davis, Thomas P.**, (AV) ..................'50 '75 C.800 B.A. L.228 J.D. [Nokes,D.&Q.]
*PRACTICE AREAS: Business Litigation; Real Estate Litigation; Civil Litigation; Family Law; Probate Litigation.
Denton, Kenneth G. ..................... '46 '88 C.1109 B.A. L.1137 J.D. 801 Glenmeyre
Dickerson, Joy Edna Margaret .....'27 '81 C.112 B.A. L.1137 J.D. Laguna Business Ctr.‡

**Drozd, Donald L., (AV) '49 '74 C.112 B.A. L.1068 J.D.**
**401 Glenneyre Street, Suite H, 92651-2401**
**Telephone: 714-497-2453 Fax: 714-376-2618**
**Email: DDROZD@aol.com**
**(Certified Specialist, Estate Planning, Trust and Probate Law, The State Bar of California Board of Legal Specialization).**
**Estate Planning, Probate, Trust, Real Property, Business and Elder Law.**
***See Professional Biographies, LAGUNA BEACH, CALIFORNIA***

Egly, Paul ...................................'21 '49 C.112 A.B. L.273 LL.B. 339 Dartmoor‡

**Finley, Warren, (AV) '32 '60 C.813 B.A. L.800 LL.B.**
**564 Vista Lane, 92651**
**Telephone: 714-494-8960 Facsimile: 714-497-8477**
**Email: WFinley@SurEmail.com URL: http://www.SurEmail.com/finley**
***PRACTICE AREAS: Corporate Law; Real Estate; Taxation; Wills; Trust.**
**Commercial, Corporate, Real Estate, Partnership, Taxation and Estate Planning, Probate, Wills and Trust.**
***See Professional Biographies, LAGUNA BEACH, CALIFORNIA***

Fishman, Steven B., (BV) ................ '47 '72 C.112 B.S. L.910 J.D. 361 Forest Ave.
Folmer, Richard J. ......................... '44 '75 C.846 B.B.A. L.61 J.D. 410 Broadway

**Fulton, A. Jane, Law Offices, (AV) '38 '66 C.766 A.B. L.464 J.D.**
**Suite C, 301 Forest Avenue, 92651**
**Telephone: 714-494-9411; 714-494-5844**
**General Practice. Concentrating in Family Law and Criminal Law. Writs and Appeals in all Courts.**
***See Professional Biographies, LAGUNA BEACH, CALIFORNIA***

**Gluck, Peter J.** '64 '93 C.67 A.B. L.1218 J.D.
(adm. in NY; not adm. in CA; Pat.) [Levin&G.]
*LANGUAGES: French.
*PRACTICE AREAS: Patent; Trademark Law; Copyright Law; Biotechnology.
Goldberg, Dorothy P. .........................'30 '53 C.367 B.S. L.446 LL.B. 224 Viejo
Gratz, Eugene C. .......................'41 '75 C.994 B.A. L.705 J.D. 1400 S. Coast Hwy.
**Gutierrez, Sergio A.** .........................'68 '96 C.112 B.A. L.426 J.D. [Levin&G.]
*LANGUAGES: Spanish.
*PRACTICE AREAS: Intellectual Property Law; Litigation.
Haight, Betty Anne ........................ '44 '70 C.490 L.190 J.D. 1278 Glenneyre, #94
Haight, Raymond L., III .................'50 '75 C.800 B.A. L.61 J.D. 1278 Glenneyre #94
Harris, Ronald C. ........................'46 '78 C.112 B.A. L.1137 J.D. 32325 Coast Hwy.
Hasselbach, Gerard .................'47 '76 C.1044 B.S. L.1065 J.D. 765 Bluebird Canyon Dr.
**Hawes, James E.**, (AV) ..........'34 '62 C.339 B.S.E.E. L.273 J.D. [Levin&G.] (Pat.)‡
*PRACTICE AREAS: Patent, Trademark and Copyright Law.
Hayes, Lynne ................................'42 '90 C&L.1137 B.S.L., J.D. 384 Forest Ave.
Hazelbaker, Ralph Brian ...........'51 '79 C.381 B.G.S. L.608 J.D. 32325 S. Coast Hwy
Herman, Richard P., (AV) .......................'45 '72 C.223 B.S. L.800 J.D. [R.P.Herman]
Herman, Richard P., P.L.C., (AV) ............................................. 301 Forest Ave.

**Isaza, John J. '64 '90 C.260 B.A. L.93 J.D.**
**2670 Victoria Drive, 2nd Floor, P.O. Box 744, 92652**
**Telephone: 714-376-5517 Fax: 714-376-8355**
**Email: jisaza@aol.com**
***LANGUAGES: Spanish, French and German.**
***PRACTICE AREAS: Business Law; Immigration; Real Estate Litigation; Construction; Civil Trial.**
**Business Law, Immigration, Real Estate Litigation, Construction and Civil Trial.**
**References: Wells Fargo Bank.**

Joel, Donald G. '32 '58 C&L.280 B.B.A., LL.B.
(adm. in GA; not adm. in CA) 310 San Nicholas Ct.‡
Kennelly, David L., Law Offices of, (BV) '47 '78
C.35 B.S. L.990 J.D. 384 Forest Ave, Ste 24A
Killian, Donald W., Jr., (AV) ..............'29 '55 C&L.800 B.S., LL.B. 1170 Marine Dr.
Kruse, M. Russell, Jr., (AV) ........ '48 '73 C.823 B.A. L.802 J.D. 31732 Mar Vista Ave.
Kuyper, Adrian, (AV) ..................................'28 '56 C.821 B.A. L.145 J.D. 385 Ledroit St.
**Levin, William E.**, (AV) ..........................'54 '79 C.1365 B.A. L.472 J.D. [Levin&G.]
*PRACTICE AREAS: Trademark; Trade Dress; Copyright and Related Litigation.

**Levin & Gluck, (AV)**
**384 Forest Avenue, Suite 13, 92651**
**Telephone: 714-497-7676 Facsimile: 714-497-7679**
**URL: http://www.lagunalaw.com**
**Members of Firm: William E. Levin; Peter J. Gluck (Not admitted in CA). Associates: Owen J. Bates; Sergio A. Gutierrez. Of Counsel: James E. Hawes.**
**Patent, Trademark, Copyright, Trade Dress and Unfair Competition Law and Related Litigation.**
***See Professional Biographies, LAGUNA BEACH, CALIFORNIA***

**Lewin, Robert S.**, (AV)......................... '42 '72 C.112 B.A. L.1068 J.D. [R.S.Lewin]
*LANGUAGES: Chinese.

**Lewin, Robert S., A Law Corporation, (AV)**
**105 Crescent Bay Drive, Suite F, 92651**
**Telephone: 714-497-8897 FAX: 714-497-1714**
**Robert S. Lewin.**
**Business Litigation State and Federal, Legal Malpractice, Real Estate, Collections and Appellate.**
***See Professional Biographies, LAGUNA BEACH, CALIFORNIA***

Liljestrom, Roger, (AV) .........................'23 '52 C&L.800 A.B., J.D. 158 Sunset Terr.‡
Lorenze, Alan T. ............................'28 '51 C.339 B.A. L.813 LL.B. P.O. Box 41

**Luppi, Robert W., (BV) '45 '71 C.112 B.A. L.426 J.D.**
**401 Glennerye, Suite A, 96251**
**Telephone: 714-494-8553**
***PRACTICE AREAS: Personal Injury Law.**
**Personal Injury.**
***See Professional Biographies, LAGUNA BEACH, CALIFORNIA***

Macdonald, Andrew B. ......................'49 '78 C.800 B.A. L.990 J.D. 361 Forest Ave.
Marsh, Keith F. ...............................'43 '74 C.972 B.A. L.1190 J.D. 330 Cajon Ter.
Masin, Richard M., (AV) .............'44 '78 C.282 B.A. L.1137 J.D. 1409 Glenneyre St.
Maycock, James E. ............................'40 '73 C.112 B.S. L.990 J.D. 410 Broadway
**McClung, Charles E., (A Professional Corporation)**, (AV) '27 '52
C&L.813 A.B., J.D. [McClung&D.]
*PRACTICE AREAS: Health Care Law; Real Property Law; Probate Law; Estate Planning Law.
**McClung, Charles E., Jr.**, (BV) ........'53 '79 C.813 A.B. L.1067 J.D. [McClung&D.]
*PRACTICE AREAS: Family Law; Eminent Domain Law; Civil Rights Law; Litigation.

**McClung & Davis, (AV)**
**A Partnership including a Professional Corporation**
**32392 Pacific Coast Highway, Suite 250, 92677**
**Telephone: 714-499-8424 Facsimile: 714-499-8423**
**Email: 76530.556@compuserve.com**
**Charles E. McClung (A Professional Corporation); Charles E. McClung, Jr.; Paul W. Davis.**
**General Civil Practice. Business, Family Law, Real Property, Environmental, Administrative, Eminent Domain and Redevelopment, Government Relations Law, Civil Rights, Health Care, Probate and Estate Planning Law.**
**Northern California Office: Pioneer Hotel, 2925 Woodside Road, Woodside, California. Telephone: 415-851-9700. Fax: 415-851-9701.**
***See Professional Biographies, LAGUNA BEACH, CALIFORNIA***

**McMahon, Peter C.**, (BV) ............... '49 '76 C.112 B.A. L.1137 J.D. [McMahon&M.]
*PRACTICE AREAS: Real Estate; Construction Litigation; Personal Injury Law; Construction Defects.
**McMahon, Robert V.**, (BV) .................. '60 '84 C.112 B.A. L.809 J.D. [McMahon&M.]
*PRACTICE AREAS: Personal Injury Law; Civil Trial; Criminal Law.

**McMahon & McMahon, (BV)**
**Suite E, 401 Glenneyre Street, 92651**
**Telephone: 714-494-9785 Fax: 714-494-5970**
**Members of Firm: Peter C. McMahon; Robert V. McMahon.**
**General Civil and Criminal Trial Practice. Real Estate, Construction, Mechanics Lien, Commercial Collections and Personal Injury Law. Construction Defect Litigation.**
***See Professional Biographies, LAGUNA BEACH, CALIFORNIA***

Mead, H. Lawson .......................................'41 '69 C&L.800 B.S., J.D. 442 Monterey Dr.
Miller, Elyse Caraco ..........................'60 '89 C&L.800 A.B., J.D. 515 Emerald Bay
Miller, Gene ..........................'51 '77 C.563 B.A. L.990 J.D. 260 Saint Anns Dr.
Myers, Darin L. ..........................'53 '79 C.1042 B.S. L.800 J.D. 39 Woodswallow Ln.
Myers, Ralph M., Jr., (AV) ............... '24 '53 C&L.800 B.S., J.D. 380 Glenneyre Ste G.
**Nokes, Laurence P.**, (AV) ...........................'54 '82 C.878 B.A. L.464 J.D. [Nokes,D.&Q.]
*LANGUAGES: Italian.
*REPORTED CASES: Marsh & McLennan v. Superior Court, 49 C 3d 1, 1989.
*PRACTICE AREAS: Insurance Coverage; Construction Litigation; Real Estate Litigation.

**Nokes, Davis & Quinn, A Professional Corporation, (AV)**
**450 Ocean Avenue, 92651**
**Telephone: 714-376-3055 FAX: 714-376-3070**
**Laurence P. Nokes; Thomas P. Davis; Thomas P. Quinn, Jr.**
**Insurance Coverage, Construction Litigation, Commercial Litigation, Real Estate Litigation, Civil Litigation, Family Law and Business Litigation.**
***See Professional Biographies, LAGUNA BEACH, CALIFORNIA***

Penney, James F., (AV) ........................'27 '54 C.605 B.A. L.800 LL.B. 818 Emerald Bay‡
Phillips, Kathryn H. '52 '86 C.802 B.F.A. L.862 J.D.
(adm. in OK; not adm. in CA) 82 Emerald Bay‡
Pressman, Paul B. ........................'30 '59 C.685 B.A. L.1068 J.D. 1472 Morningside Circle‡
**Quinn, Thomas P., Jr.** ..........................'62 '87 C.602 B.A. L.464 J.D. [Nokes,D.&Q.]
*PRACTICE AREAS: Construction Litigation; Insurance Litigation; Real Estate Litigation; Business Litigation.

**Reilly, Thomas A., (AV) '33 '63 C.767 B.S. L.1065 J.D.**
**1400 South Coast Highway, Penthouse Suite, 92651**
**Telephone: 714-494-8575**
**General Civil and Criminal Trial Practice.**
***See Professional Biographies, LAGUNA BEACH, CALIFORNIA***

Reisman, Richard S. '53 '78
C.1349 B.A. L.273 J.D. Publisher, Orange Co. Business Journal
Ringers, Thomas J. ...........................'44 '79 C.112 B.A. L.1137 J.D. 824 La Vista Dr.
Robinson, Michael W., (AV) ..................'47 '74 C.112 B.A. L.464 J.D. [Robinson&W.]
Robinson & Wisbaum, A Law Corp., (AV) ..............................361 Forest Ave., Ste. 203
Rossi, Charles J. ...........................'47 '87 C.1042 B.A. L.1137 J.D. 1409 Glenneyre St.

**Rourke, James G., (AV) '26 '54 C.112 A.B. L.1066 J.D.**
**633 Alta Vista, 92651-4040**
**Telephone: 714-497-9652 Facsimile: 714-494-5570**
***PRACTICE AREAS: Municipal Law; Business Law.**
**Municipal Law, Business Law.**
***See Professional Biographies, LAGUNA BEACH, CALIFORNIA***

Sagar, Michael C., (BV) ..........................'33 '62 C&L.800 B.A., LL.B. 1437 Glenneyre St.
**Shernoff, William M., (P.C.)**, (AV) '37 '62
C.472 B.B.A. L.966 J.D. [Shernoff,B.&D.] (Palm Desert)
*PRACTICE AREAS: Insurance Bad Faith.

**Shernoff, Bidart & Darras, (AV)**
**A Partnership including Professional Corporations**
**130 Cleo Street, 92651**
**Telephone: 714-494-6714 Fax: 714-497-0825**
**Members of Firm: William M. Shernoff (P.C.); Michael J. Bidart (P.C.); Frank N. Darras.**
**Practice Limited to Plaintiff's Insurance Bad Faith, Automobile Insurance, Fire Insurance, Commercial Liability Insurance, Homeowners Insurance, Accident and Health Insurance, Catastrophic Personal Injury, Wrongful Death, Wrongful Termination, Lender's Liability and Consumer Law Litigation.**
**Claremont, California Office: 600 South Indian Hill Boulevard. Telephone: 909-621-4935. Fax: 909-625-6915.**
**Palm Desert, California Office: 73-111 El Paseo, Suite 208. Telephone: 619-568-9944.**
***See Professional Biographies, LAGUNA BEACH, CALIFORNIA***

**Simons, Barry T., (BV) '46 '72 C.30 B.S. L.564 J.D.**
**Lawyers Court, 260 St. Ann's Drive, 92651**
**Telephone: 714-497-1729 FAX: 714-497-3971 Email: simmslaw@primenet.com**
**Email: simonslaw@aol.com**
**Criminal Defense in State and Federal Courts, DUI/DWI, Juvenile Law and Appeals.**
***See Professional Biographies, LAGUNA BEACH, CALIFORNIA***

Smith, Eric L. ........................ '40 '72 C.112 B.S. L.273 J.D. 660 Temple Hills Dr.‡
Smith, Gregory M. ..........................'40 '72 C.605 B.A. L.1066 J.D. 639 Pearl St.‡
Soelberg, Glenn B. ...................... '12 '40 C&L.494 A.B., LL.B. 54 Blue Lagoon‡
**Solomon, John W.**, (AV) ......................... '08 '33 C&L.813 A.B., J.D. [K.O.Solomon] ‡
**Solomon, Kenneth O.**, (AV) .....................'44 '75 C.800 B.A. L.809 J.D. [K.O.Solomon]

**Solomon, Kenneth O., (AV)**
**243 Broadway, 92651**
**Telephone: 714-494-7527 Fax: 714-497-9351**
**Sherrill B. Osborne (1873-1949); John W. Solomon (Inactive); Kenneth O. Solomon.**
**Probate, Estate Planning & Trusts.**
**Reference: Bank of America National Trust & Savings Assn., (Laguna Beach Branch Office).**

Stocker, William ........................... '42 '69 C.1077 B.A. L.426 J.D. P.O. Box 4980
Sullivan, Mitchell ..............................'51 '83 C.37 B.A. L.1137 J.D. P.O. Box 1044
Warren, Bruce G. ...............................'20 '49 C.966 Ph.B. L.813 J.D. 10 Blue Lagoon‡
Warren, Roseline A. .............................................'34 '82 L.1137 J.D. [Bishop&W.]
Wilcoxen, William M., (AV) ...'32 '60 C.293 B.A. L.1066 J.D. Ste A, 801 Glenneyre St.‡
Williams, Keith P., Jr. '58 '85 C.934 B.A. L.734 J.D.
(adm. in MO; not adm. in CA) Cornerstone Mktg. Inc.
Wilson, Jennifer Hanson ................... '61 '88 C&L.101 B.A., J.D. 3074 Nestall Rd.‡

CAA147P

Wisbaum, Keith D. ... '54 '84 C.37 B.S. L.464 J.D. [Robinson&W.]
Wright, Frank C. ... '42 '76 C.1109 B.A. L.800 J.D. 800 Glenneyre
Zimmerman, Bruce G. ... '47 '72 C.813 B.A. L.800 J.D. Pres., Commercial Devco, Inc.

**LAGUNA HILLS, 13,676, *Orange Co.***

Adair, A. Lee, (AV) ... '30 '62 C.1042 L.426 LL.B. 23046 Avenida de la Carlota
Adamson, Dean H., (AV) ... '— '52 C.30 L.809 LL.B. [Adamson&A.]
Adamson, Gregory J. ... '53 '78 C.112 B.A. L.1095 J.D. 23101 Moulton Pkwy.
Adamson, LaVilla S., (AV) ... '— '51 C.273 L.800 LL.B. [Adamson&A.]
Adamson & Adamson, (AV) ... 23101 Moulton Pkwy.
Allebest, Edward F. ... '47 '74 C.101 B.A. L.273 J.D. 27581 Lost Trail Dr.
Archbold, Judith Woodward '53 '78
C.112 B.A. L.426 J.D. V.P. & Gen. Coun., SysteMed, Inc.
**Beck, Gregory M.**, (AV) ... '52 '78 C.426 B.S. L.1065 J.D. [Beck&Assoc.]
*PRACTICE AREAS: Taxation Law; Estate Planning Law; Corporate Law.

**Beck & Associates, A Professional Corporation, (AV)**
**23041 Mill Creek Drive, 92653**
**Telephone: 714-855-9250 Fax: 714-380-1128**
**Gregory M. Beck, Certified Specialist, Taxation and Estate Planning, Probate and Trust Law, The State Bar of California Board of Legal Specialization.;—Stephen L. Christian.**
**Taxation, Real Estate Law, Corporate and Business Law, Estate Planning, Wills and Trusts.**

Behm, Paul B. '11 '52 C.112 B.S. L.966 LL.B.
(adm. in WI; not adm. in CA) 2353 Via Mariposa W.‡
Bender, Martin R. ... '45 '80 C.1213 B.S. L.1137 J.D. 23331 Mill Creek
Berman, Samuel '23 '52 C.208 B.S.B.A. L.936 LL.B.
(adm. in CO; not adm. in CA) 320 Avenida Carmel‡
Bernhardt, A. J. ... '17 '41 C.813 B.A. L.309 LL.B. 5163 Belmez‡
Bibro, Vickie Lynn ... '56 '90 C.879 B.M. L.1049 J.D. 23161 Millcreek Rd.
Binford, Howard M. ... '08 '32 C.628 L.809 LL.B. 3373 Punta Alta‡
Blek, Charles L., Jr., (BV) ... '45 '72 C.800 B.A. L.426 J.D. 25255 Cabot Rd., Ste. 101
Bohrer, Thomas H. ... '49 '80 C.112 B.A. L.1065 J.D. 25251 Paseo de Alicia
Bradley, George E., (AV) ... '06 '30 C.813 A.B. L.800 J.D. 274 Avenida Sevilla‡
Bragman, Melvin, (CVⓉ) '24 '53 C.477 A.B. L.213 LL.B.
(adm. in MI; not adm. in CA) 392 Avenida Castilla‡

**Brown, Dennis R. '47 '75 C.112 B.A. L.1049 J.D.**
**24012 Calle De La Plata Suite 450, 92653-7626**
**Telephone: 714-859-3277 Facsimile: 714-951-8468**
***PRACTICE AREAS: Taxation.**
**Tax Law.**

**Brucker, William J.** '64 '90 C.1062 B.E.E. L.930 J.D.
[Ⓐ Stetina B.&B.] (See Pat. Sect.)
Bruinsma, Dirk ... '47 '78 C.1265 B.S. L.1187 J.D. [Bruinsma&H.]
Bruinsma & Hewitt, Trial Lawyers ... 25431 Cabot Rd.
**Brunda, Bruce B.**, (AV) '51 '78
C.570 B.S.E.E. L.1218 J.D. [Stetina B.&B.] (See Pat. Sect.)
Bryan, William L., Jr. ... '52 '84 C.276 B.S.F.S. L.800 J.D. 24461 Ridge Rte. Dr.
Buchanan, Richard W. ... '42 '67 C.376 B.A. L.378 J.D. 23332 Mill Creek Rd.
Bucknum, Daniel R., (BV) ... '36 '66 C.101 B.S. L.1067 J.A. 25256 Cabot Rd.
**Buyan, Robert Dean**, (AV) '53 '85
C.1062 B.S. L.117 J.D. [Stetina B.&B.] (See Pat. Sect.)
**Cabodi, K. J.**, (BV) ... '53 '80 C.339 B.A. L.990 J.D. [Small,H.&C.]
*PRACTICE AREAS: Personal Injury; Construction Law; Insurance Defense.
Carey, Charles B. ... '43 '69 C.770 B.A. L.1068 J.D. [C.B.Carey]
Carey, Charles B., Law Offices of, A Prof. Corp. ... 24012 Calle De La Plata
Carreon, Daniel T. ... '50 '76 C.426 B.B.A. L.1137 J.D. 23421 S. Pointe Dr., Ste., 280
**Chase, James L.** ... '62 '89 C&L.1137 B.S.L., J.D. [Ⓐ Small,H.&C.]
**Christian, Stephen L.** ... '60 '84 C&L.69 B.B.A., J.D. [Ⓐ Beck&Assoc.]
*PRACTICE AREAS: Taxation Law; Estate Planning Law.
Conte, Richard L. ... '53 '79 C.1109 B.A. L.800 J.D. Community Psychiatric Ctrs.
Cooper, Clarence P. ... '10 '34 C&L.546 A.B., J.D. 24552 Paseo De Valencia‡
Cooper, Daniel J., (BV) ... '42 '77 C.1097 B.S. L.1137 J.D. [Cooper&W.]
Cooper & Wolowski, A Prtnrshp. incl. A Prof. Corp., (BV) ... 24012 Calle De La Plata
Cullins, Douglas D. ... '56 '82 C.260 B.A. L.809 J.D. [Cullins&G.]
Cullins & Grandy ... 23141 Verdugo Dr.
**Deily, John P.**, (AV) ... '53 '80 C.112 B.A. L.1065 J.D. [Reynolds&D.]
*PRACTICE AREAS: Probate, Estate Planning and Trust Law; Probate, Trust and Conservatorship Litigation; Trial Practice.
DeLancy, David P., Jr., (BV) ... '32 '72 L.1137 B.L. 25301 Cabot Rd.
De Liema, Max B., (AV) ... '46 '75 C.112 B.A. L.426 J.D. 25283 Cabot Rd.
Donahue, Mark F. ... '51 '79 C.951 B.A. L.659 J.D. 24791 Nellie Gail Rd.‡
Donovan, Stephen ... '52 '87 C&L.012 B.S., LL.B. [Donovan&E.]
Donovan & Eastham ... 23046 Avenida De La Carlota
Ellsworth, Ernie M., (BV) ... '46 '76 C.36 B.A. L.990 J.D. 24422 Ave. De La Carlota
Epstein, David M. ... '32 '63 C.36 B.Sc. L.809 J.D. [Epstein,D.M.]
Epstein, Deanna Swagel ... '40 '80 C.66 A.B. L.990 J.D. 23521 Paseo de Valencia
Epstein, David M., (P.C.) ... 23521 Paseo De Valencia
Farrar, Mark E., (BV) ... '50 '76 C.36 B.A. L.1137 J.D. 23421 S. Pointe Dr.
Fay, Arthur E. '10 '36 C&L.276 A.B., J.D.
(adm. in DC; not adm. in CA) 566-A Avenida Sevilla‡
Feagles, Shirley L. ... '65 '90 C.436 B.A. L.1049 J.D. 24752 Hidden Hills Rd.
Field, Martin '11 '37 C.102 L.724 LL.B.
(adm. in NY; not adm. in CA) 472 Calle Cadiz‡
Freedman, Bernard W. '34 '66 C.705 A.B. L.776 J.D.
(adm. in NJ; not adm. in CA) 24811 Hon Ave.‡
Frimond, Bernard J., (BV) ... '47 '79 C.260 B.A. L.1137 J.D. 23175 La Cadena Dr.
**Garred, Mark B.** ... '64 '90 C.1062 B.M.E. L.161 J.D. [Ⓐ Stetina B.&B.] (See Pat. Sect.)
Geiser, Lew C., (AV) ... '47 '72 C.769 B.A. L.1065 J.D. [Geiser&H.]
Geiser & Heneghan, (AV) ... 23521 Paseo De Valencia
Godbe, Douglas E. ... '51 '76 C.605 A.B. L.1049 J.D. 23521 Paseo De Valencia K
Goethals, Thomas M., (AV) ... '52 '77 C.770 B.A. L.426 J.D. [Pohlson,M.&G.]
Goldenberg, Jay S. ... '54 '88 C.37 B.S. L.809 J.D. 24517 Madeira
Grace, Marilyn H. ... '30 '71 C.112 B.S. L.426 J.D. Calif. Unemployment Ins. App. Bd.
Grandy, James L. ... '54 '86 C.1193 B.S. L.1148 J.D. [Cullins&G.]
Groves, Byron D., (CV) ... '42 '71 C.260 B.A. L.421 J.D. 23232 Peralta Dr.

**Gunderson, Linda, (AV) '50 '78 C.999 B.F.A. L.464 J.D.**
**Oakbrook Plaza, Suite 385, 24422 Avenida de la Carlota, 92653**
**Telephone: 714-837-1060 Telecopier: 714-837-4594**
**(Certified Specialist, Probate, Estate Planning and Trust Law, The State Bar of California Board of Legal Specialization).**
**Probate and Trust Law.**
***See Professional Biographies, LAGUNA HILLS, CALIFORNIA***

Heneghan, Martin J., (AV) ... '33 '59 C.1041 B.A. L.262 LL.B. [Geiser&H.]
**Henstridge, Robert M.** ... '49 '76 C.1109 B.A. L.1049 J.D. [Ⓐ Small,H.&C.]
*PRACTICE AREAS: Construction Defects; Insurance; Personal Injury; Products Liability; Business Law.
Hewitt, Michael Conrad ... '61 '90 C.1074 B.S. L.284 J.D. [Bruinsma&H.]
Hill, Sherman R. ... '05 '30 C.221 L.273 LL.B. 2203-A Via Mariposa, E.‡
Hinkle, James R. '23 '50 C.337 A.B. L.352 J.D.
(adm. in IA; not adm. in CA) 589C Avenida Majorca‡
Hook, L. Harmon '26 '79 C.145 M.S. L.1000 J.D.
(adm. in GA; not adm. in CA) 5127 Brazo
Jaco, Lyston G., Jr. ... '21 '51 C.838 B.S. L.477 J.D. 5399 Via Carrizo‡
Jamroz, Judith Hurst ... '42 '85 C.477 A.B. L.1137 J.D. 24012 Calle de la Plata
Jennings, C. Ross ... '30 '60 C.679 B.S. L.347 J.D. P.O. Box 2723‡

**Jensen, Jacqueline M., Inc.**
**(See Irvine)**

Johnson, Edgar C., Jr. ... '43 '89 C.870 B.S. L.1137 J.D. 23151 Moulton Pkway.
Keeler, Kathleen P., (CV) ... '52 '85 C.139 B.A. L.1137 J.D. [Keeler&K.]
Keeler, Marie B. '17 '44 C&L.107 B.A., J.D.
(adm. in NY; not adm. in CA) [Keeler&K.] ‡
Keeler & Keeler, (CV) ... 23521 Paseo De Valencia
Kessler, Ernest A. ... '16 '50 C.112 A.B. L.800 J.D. 3364 Punta Alta
**Kimball, Stephen C.** ... '63 '91 C.101 B.A. L.1049 J.D. [Ⓐ R.T.Matthews]
*LANGUAGES: French.
*PRACTICE AREAS: Civil Litigation; Probate Litigation; Trust Litigation; Probate Administration; Estate Planning.
Kingdon, Grover C., Jr. ... '12 '52 L.809 23301 Ridge Rd. Dr.‡
Kirbens, Samuel M. ... '18 '42 C&L.546 B.A., J.D. Ret. J.‡
Klein, Robert D. ... '32 '75 L.990 J.D. 27061 Lost Colt Dr.
Kreber, Ronald P. ... '37 '72 C.112 L.1136 LL.B. Mun. Ct. J.
Landau, Samuel '07 '32 C&L.309 A.B., J.D.
(adm. in MA; not adm. in CA) 5462 Paseo Del Lago, E.‡
Larson, William G. ... '41 '73 C.560 B.A. L.426 J.D. 26962 Willow Tree Ln.
Lauson, Robert J. ... '58 '94 C.339 B.S.M.E. L.809 J.D. 24221 Calle de la Louisa
Lemkin, Laurence R., (BV) ... '34 '69 C.186 L.284 J.D. 25112 Mawson Dr.

**Lent, James W. '36 '89 C.321 B.S. L.818 J.D.**
**24031 El Toro Road, Suite 130, 92653**
**Telephone: 714-829-8009 Fax: 714-829-8209**
***PRACTICE AREAS: Probate and Estate Planning; Business; Elder Law.**
**Corporate Law, Business Law, Estate Planning, Probate, Elder Law.**
***See Professional Biographies, LAGUNA HILLS, CALIFORNIA***

**Lents, Michelle M.** ... '66 '93 C.763 B.A. L.1049 J.D. [Ⓐ M.A.Reinglass]
*PRACTICE AREAS: Business, Civil and Employment Litigation; Employment Discrimination; Sexual Harassment both State and Federal Courts.
Leydorf, Fred L., (AV) ... '30 '59 C.477 B.B.A. L.1068 J.D. 3078-D Via Serena S.
Lichtman, Andrew ... '47 '76 C.112 A.B. L.659 J.D. 23046 Carlsta, 6th Fl.
Lightholder, Roger Ellis ... '43 '74 C.1109 A.B. L.990 J.D. 24422 Avenida De La Carlota
Llorente, Alex J. ... '59 '95 C.1111 B.A. L.1137 J.D. 23046 Avenida De La Carlota
Logan, Henry T., (CV) ... '18 '53 C.684 B.A. L.1001 B.L. 25401 Cabot Rd.
MacAuley, Dan J., (AV) ... '50 '76 C.940 B.A. L.800 J.D. 24031 El Toro Rd.
Marticorena, Lynda E. ... '54 '80 C.1109 B.A. L.1137 J.D. 25541 Rapid Falls

**Mathews, Stanton T., & Associates, The Law Offices of, (AV) '52 '81**
**C.101 B.A. L.1137 J.D.**
**24012 Calle de la Plata, Suite 320, 92653**
**Telephone: 714-586-2235**
***LANGUAGES: Spanish.**
***REPORTED CASES: Budd v. American Excess Ins. Co.**
***PRACTICE AREAS: Personal Injury; Trial Practice; Professional Negligence; Products Liability; Insurance Coverage.**
**Associates: Paul W. Ralph.**
**Civil Trial and Appellate Practice, Personal Injury, Insurance Bad Faith, Professional Negligence, Products Liability, Wrongful Death, Premise Liability, Trucking Liability.**
***See Professional Biographies, LAGUNA HILLS, CALIFORNIA***

Matos, Paula C., (AV) ... '43 '80 C.36 B.A. L.1137 J.D. 24031 El Toro Rd. (⊙Orange)

**Matthews, Robert T., Law Offices of '54 '82 C.928 B.A. L.1225 J.D.**
**23382 Mill Creek Drive Suite 120, 92653**
**Telephone: 714-470-1390 Fax: 714-470-1337**
**(Certified Specialist, Estate Planning, Trust and Probate Law, The State Bar of California Board of Legal Specialization).**
***PRACTICE AREAS: Probate Law; Probate and Trust Litigation; Civil Law; Trial Practice; Estate Planning.**
**Associate: Stephen C. Kimball.**
**Probate and Estate Planning, Probate and Trust Litigation and Trust Law.**
***See Professional Biographies, LAGUNA HILLS, CALIFORNIA***

McCloskey, Paul N., Jr., (AV) ... '27 '53 C&L.813 A.B., J.D. 32392 Pacific Coast Hwy.
McKenzie, Patrick R. ... '41 '66 C.436 B.A. L.190 J.D. 25431 Cabot Rd.

**Medwied, Susan R. '53 '77 C.1029 B.A. L.776 J.D.**
**23046 Avenida De la Carlota, Suite 600, 92653**
**Telephone: 714-588-5703 Facsimile: 714-588-5777**
***PRACTICE AREAS: Business Planning; Constructions Liens; Mechanics Liens; Construction Contracts.**
**Breach of Contract, Mechanics Lien, Stop Notice, Attachment, Claim and Delivery, Judgement Enforcement, Business Planning.**
***See Professional Biographies, LAGUNA HILLS, CALIFORNIA***

Metzger, Jeffrey C., (AV) ... '55 '80 C.169 B.A. L.770 J.D. 23041 Mill Creek Dr.
Mirkin, Theodore '22 '56 C.569 B.S. L.1009 LL.B.
(adm. in NY; not adm. in CA) 22738 Via Mariposa E.‡
Moorhead, Gary L., (AV) ... '50 '76 C.770 B.S. L.809 J.D. [Pohlson,M.&G.]
Mudge, Richard T. ... '31 '59 C.267 B.A. L.112 J.D. 23521 Paseo de Valencia
Muench, Richard A., (BV) ... '42 '67 C&L.602 A.B., LL.B. 25231 Paseo de Alica
Mullen, J. Robert ... '59 '88 C.154 B.A. L.426 J.D. 23151 Moulton Pkwy.
Murphy, Roger T., (BV) '45 '75
C.597 B.S. L.1137 J.D. [R.T.Murphy] (⊙South Lake Tahoe)
Murphy, Roger T., A Professional Law Corporation, (BV)
23046 Avenida De La Carlota (⊙South Lake Tahoe)
**Naber, Thomas C.** '41 '72 C&L.208 B.S., J.D.
(adm. in CO; not adm. in CA; See Pat. Sect.) [Ⓐ Stetina B.&B.]
Nathanson, Milton N. ... '10 '36 C&L.659 B.S., LL.B. 3514-B Bahia Blanca W.‡
Naughton, Michael J., (AV) ... '40 '65 C.424 A.B. L.209 LL.B. 25231 Paseo de Alicia
Nelson, Byron, (BV) ... '43 '70 C.112 B.A. L.426 J.D. [B.Nelson]
Nelson, Gilbert F., (AV) ... '05 '31 C.339 A.B. L.800 J.D. 2392 Via Mareposa St. W.‡
Nelson, Ralph D. '22 '48 C.543 B.A. L.546 J.D.
(adm. in NE; not adm. in CA) 2001C Via Mariposa W.‡
Nelson, Thomas J., III ... '36 '75 C.999 B.S.E.E. L.1137 J.D. 23010 Lake Forest Dr.
Nelson, Byron, Prof. Corp., (BV) ... 25231 Paseo De Alicia
**Newboles, Matthew A.** '65 '93 C.1074 B.S. L.770 J.D.
[Ⓐ Stetina B.&B.] (See Pat. Sect.)
Newhouse, Gerald W. ... '44 '74 L.426 J.D. Glendale Fed. Bk. Bldg.
Nickerson, LaVelle ... '07 '41 C.113 L.809 LL.B. 5419 Calle Carmenita‡
Norman, Lawrence ... '33 '57 C.107 B.S.B.A. L.94 LL.B. [L.Norman]
Norman, Lawrence, Inc. ... 24031 El Toro Rd.

Owens, Karen J. .....................'47 '78 C.8 B.A. L.930 J.D. 23521 Paseo de Valencia
Parsons, William A. .....................'13 '47 C.112 B.A. L.800 J.D. 95 Calle Aragon‡
Pohlson, Gary M., (AV) .....................'50 '75 C.770 B.A. L.1068 J.D. [Pohlson,M.&G.]
Pohlson, Moorhead & Goethals, (AV) ..................... 23151 Moulton Pky.
Porterfield, Brad D. ..........'61 '88 C.608 B.S. L.1137 J.D. 23046 Avenida de la Carlota
**Powers, Krista Lee** .....................'68 '93 C.112 B.A. L.1049 J.D. [⊠ Reynolds&D.]
*PRACTICE AREAS: Estate and Tax Planning; Trust Law; Probate Law; Trust and Conservatorship Litigation.
Pratt, Charles W. ..................... '34 '83 C.627 B.S. L.809 J.D. 26166 Bridlewood Dr.
Prentice, Geo. B. ..................... '19 '53 C.800 A.B. L.426 LL.B. 25511 Gallup Cir.
Pummer, Erwin L. ..................... '11 '56 L.1001 LL.B. 5217 Elvira St.
**Pyles, Bryan D.** ..................... '60 '88 C.1109 B.A. L.1137 J.D. [⊠ Small,H.&C.]
**Ralph, Paul W.** ..................... '62 '91 C.1109 B.A. L.809 J.D. [⊠ S.T.Mathews&Assoc.]
*PRACTICE AREAS: Personal Injury; Medical Malpractice; Construction Defects.
Ransford, Anthony H. .....................'40 '76 C.1077 B.A. L.1137 J.D. 25401 Cabot Rd.
Rash, Wayne A. ..................... '48 '79 C.976 B.A. L.813 J.D. 24012 Calle De La Plata

**Reinglass, Michelle A., (AV) '54 '79 C&L.1137 B.S.L., J.D. BB**
**Suite 170 23161 Millcreek Road, 92653**
**Telephone: 714-587-0460 FAX: 714-587-1004**
***LANGUAGES: Spanish and French.**
**Associate: Michelle M. Lents.**
**Business, Civil and Employment Litigation, Employment Discrimination, Sexual Harassment, Wrongful Termination.**
*See Professional Biographies, LAGUNA HILLS, CALIFORNIA*

**Reynolds, Sallie Tiernan**, (AV) ........'23 '53 C.813 A.B. L.1068 LL.B. [Reynolds&D.]
*PRACTICE AREAS: Estate and Tax Planning and Trust Law; Probate Law.

**Reynolds & Deily, (AV)**
**Taj Mahal, Suite 115, 23521 Paseo De Valencia, 92653-3138**
**Telephone: 714-454-8800 FAX: 714-454-9207**
**Members of Firm: Sallie Tiernan Reynolds (Certified Specialist, Probate, Estate Planning and Trust Law, The State Bar of California Board of Legal Specialization); John P. Deily. Associates: Krista Lee Powers.**
**Estate Planning, Probate and Civil Litigation.**
*See Professional Biographies, LAGUNA HILLS, CALIFORNIA*

Ribakoff, Solomon '08 '30 L.986 J.D.
(adm. in MO; not adm. in CA) 24055 Paseo Del Lago, #603
Richmond, Scott D., (AV) ..................... '38 '65 C.813 A.B. L.1065 J.D. [Richmond&R.]⊙
Richmond & Richmond, (AV) .....................23521 Paseo de Valencia (⊙Orange)
**Rimer, Darren S.** ..................... '69 '95 C.112 B.A. L.809 J.D. [⊠ Stetina B.&B.]
Roberts, Louis .....................'52 '79 C.911 B.S. L.1137 J.D. 23201 Mill Creek Dr.
**Ross, Lawrence S.**, (AV) ..................... '48 '75 C.145 B.S. L.1068 J.D. [L.S.Ross]
*PRACTICE AREAS: Family Law; Estate Planning; Probate.

**Ross, Lawrence S., A Law Corporation, (AV)**
**Oakbrook Plaza, 24422 Avenida De La Carlota, Suite 365, 92653**
**Telephone: 714-581-3360 Fax: 714-581-2649**
**Lawrence S. Ross (Certified Specialist, Family Law; Estate Planning, Trust and Probate Law, The State Bar of California Board of Legal Specialization).**
**Family Law, Probate, Estate Planning, Trust Law.**
*See Professional Biographies, LAGUNA HILLS, CALIFORNIA*

Rostkowski, Eugene F. ..........'47 '78 C.705 A.B. L.1137 J.D. 24012 Calle De La Plata
Sack, Bernard ..................... '22 '46 C.102 B.A. L.178 J.D. 3187 Via Buena Vista B‡
Scholte, Gordon D. ..........'60 '86 C.1239 B.A. L.1049 J.D. 24012 Calle De La Plata
Sennett, Sandra .....................'— '73 187-D Avenida Majorica‡
Sikora, Warren, (AV) ..................... '21 '53 C.145 B.A. L.1068 J.D. [Sikora&P.]⊙
Sikora and Price, Incorporated, (AV) .....................23521 Paseo de Valencia (⊙Santa Ana)
Sivolella, Cosmo G., (BV) ..................... '20 '66 C.999 25231 Paseo De Alicia
**Small, Walter S.**, (BV) ..................... '27 '74 C.684 B.A. L.809 J.D. [Small,H.&C.]
*PRACTICE AREAS: Insurance Defense.

**Small, Henstridge & Cabodi, (BV)**
**24422 Avenida de la Carlota, Suite 460, 92653**
**Telephone: 714-837-5534 Fax: 714-837-6160**
**Walter S. Small (1972-1992); Robert M. Henstridge; K. J. Cabodi. Associates: Bryan D. Pyles; James L. Chase.**
**Insurance Defense.**
*See Professional Biographies, LAGUNA HILLS, CALIFORNIA*

Springer, Mel ..................... '14 '62 C.623 B.A. L.1068 LL.B. 3161-D Alta Vista
**Stetina, Kit M., (Mr.)**, (AV) '52 '78 C.36 B.S. L.990 J.D.
[Stetina B.&B.] (See Pat. Sect.)
*REPORTED CASES: No Fear, Inc. v. Imagine Films, Inc., 38 U.S.P.Q.2d 1374; Big Ball Sports, Inc. v. No Fear, Inc., 38 U.S.P.Q. 2d 1383.
*PRACTICE AREAS: Patent, Trademark, Copyright, Unfair Competition; Antitrust; Commercial Litigation; Computer.

**Stetina Brunda & Buyan, A Professional Corporation, (AV) BB**
**Suite 401, 24221 Calle De La Louisa, 92653**
**Telephone: 714-855-1246 Telex: 704355 Facsimile: 714-855-6371**
**Email: 104052.1330@compuserve.com**
**Kit M. Stetina (Mr.); Bruce B. Brunda; Robert Dean Buyan;—Mark B. Garred; William J. Brucker; Matthew A. Newboles; Thomas C. Naber (Not admitted in CA); Darren S. Rimer.**
**Intellectual Property Law including Patent, Trademark, Copyright, Unfair Competition, Trade Secret, Licensing, Computer Law and Related Antitrust Law, Hands-On Computer Law.**
*See Professional Biographies, LAGUNA HILLS, CALIFORNIA*

Stevens, Bruce M. .....................'46 '90 C.871 B.S. L.1137 J.D. 23461 S. Pointe Dr.

**Stone, Edward H., P.C.**
**(See Newport Beach)**

Swank, Elizabeth K. .....................'47 '84 C.112 B.A. L.1137 J.D. 25401 Cabot Rd.
Sweyd, Bruce ..................... '46 '76 C.1077 B.A. L.1095 J.D. 25852 Cedarbluff Terr.
**Tepper, Nancy Boxley**, (AV) .....................'33 '58 C.681 B.A. L.309 LL.B. [N.B.Tepper]

**Tepper, Nancy Boxley, A Professional Corporation, (AV) BB**
**24031 El Toro Road, Suite 130, 92653**
**Telephone: 714-830-6660 Fax: 714-830-6123**
**Nancy Boxley Tepper.**
**Tax and Estate Planning, Trust Administration, Probate Administration, Trust and Probate Litigation, Estate Administration, Will Contests.**
*See Professional Biographies, LAGUNA HILLS, CALIFORNIA*

Tevis, Jeffrey B. ..................... '46 '75 C&L.446 B.A., J.D. 5140 Miembro

**Thomas, Melvin D. '39 '78 C.616 B.S. L.1137 J.D.**
**Eldorado Bank Building, 24012 Calle De La Plata, Suite 480, 92653-7625**
**Telephone: 714-458-6700 Fax: 714-458-1362**
***PRACTICE AREAS: Civil Practice (40%, 10); Taxation Law (20%, 15); Real Estate Law (10%, 15); Family Law (20%, 10); Corporate Law (10%, 5).**
**Civil Litigation, Real Estate, Corporate/ Business Counsel, Corporate Formation, Dissolutions, Franchise Law, Shareholder Disputes, Complex or Unusual Tax/ Business Matters, Family Law, Probate, Multi-State Tax Return Preparation, Tax Audit/ Appeal Representation, Forensic Accounting Issues, Investment/ Tax Fraud Issues, General Tax Compliance, Trusts and Estates.**
*See Professional Biographies, LAGUNA HILLS, CALIFORNIA*

Tibbitts, Kent F., (BV) ....... '49 '76 C.101 B.A. L.990 J.D. 2422 Avenida De La Carlota
Toups, Mary Pat ..................... '28 '74 C.112 B.A. L.990 J.D. 3467B Bahia Blanca W.
Traumueller, Gerard E. .......... '23 '63 C.178 A.B. L.1068 LL.B. 4026 Calle Sonora Este
Tucker, James B., (AV) ..................... '19 '50 C.188 B.A. L.813 LL.B. 2254 Via Puerta‡
Umann, Harry M. ..................... '12 '42 L.809 LL.B. 23010 Lake Forest Dr.
Vanderveen, Jeffrey T., (BV) '54 '83 C.112 B.A. L.990 J.D.
24422 Avenida De la Carlota
Van Ness, Robert Terry ........ '— '85 C.205 B.Ch.E. L.1137 J.D. 23011 Moulton Pkwy.
Von Helms, John E. .....................'53 '79 C.1109 B.A. L.990 J.D. 2395 W. Via Mariposa

**Walkon, Craig S., Law Offices of '62 '89 C.475 B.A. L.912 J.D.**
**23151 Moulton Parkway, 92653**
**Telephone: 714-699-0177 Fax: 714-699-6792**
***PRACTICE AREAS: Medical Malpractice; Personal Injury; Employment Litigation; Hospital Law; Premises Liability.**
**civil Litigation including Medical Malpractice and Personal Injury.**
*See Professional Biographies, LAGUNA HILLS, CALIFORNIA*

**Wall, Genevieve**, (BV) ..................... '50 '81 C.112 B.A. L.1137 J.D. [G.Wall]
*PRACTICE AREAS: Trust Law; Estate Planning Law; Probate Law; Wills Law.

**Wall, Genevieve, A Law Corporation, (BV)**
**23521 Paseo De Valencia, Suite 201-B, 92653**
**Telephone: 714-859-0861**
**Genevieve Wall.**
**Estate Planning, Wills and Trusts, Estate Litigation, Guardianships.**
*See Professional Biographies, LAGUNA HILLS, CALIFORNIA*

**Weissenberger, Harry G.**, (AV) '28 '52
C.277 B.E.E. L.245 J.D. [H.G.Weissenberger] (See Pat. Sect.)
*LANGUAGES: German, French.
*PRACTICE AREAS: Intellectual Property Law.

**Weissenberger, Harry G., Inc., Law Offices of, (AV)**
**Glendale Federal Building, Suite 309, 24221 Calle de la Louisa, 92653-7602**
**Telephone: 714-380-4046 Fax: 714-380-1179**
**Email: weisspat@aol.com**
**Harry G. Weissenberger.**
**Patent, Trademark, Copyright and Unfair Competition Law. Trials in Federal and State Courts.**
*See Professional Biographies, LAGUNA HILLS, CALIFORNIA*

White, John M. ..................... '45 '81 24012 Calle De La Plata
Wolfson, Ilse M. ..................... '24 '78 C.145 L.1095 J.D. 838 C Ronda Sevilla
Wolowski, Hal W., (BV) ..................... '46 '79 C.112 B.A. L.1137 J.D. [Cooper&W.]
Wood, Karen G. .....................'47 '80 C.36 B.A. L.1148 J.D. 30011 Ivy Glenn Dr.

## LAGUNA NIGUEL, 44,400, *Orange Co.*

Apke, Thomas M. ..................... '45 '69 C.645 B.S. L.436 J.D. 29156 Mira Vista
Asch, Harry M. ..................... '34 '60 C.629 B.S. L.497 LL.B. I.R.S.

**Ashworth & Moran, (AV) BB**
**28202 Cabot Road, Suite 300, 92677-1249⊙**
**Telephone: 714-365-5776 Fax: 714-365-5720**
**Bernard L. Moran; Eric K. Billings.**
**Corporation, Business and Real Estate Law, General Civil, Trial and Appellate Practice. State and Federal Courts, Estate Planning.**
**Newport Beach, California Office: 18 Corporate Plaza, Suite 114. Telephone: 714-720-1477. Fax: 714-720-1478.**
*See Professional Biographies, LAGUNA NIGUEL, CALIFORNIA*

Avila, Manuel J. ..................... '05 '42 C.113 B.A. L.800 LL.B. 30381 Benecia Ave.‡
Babcock, John A. ..................... '46 '72 C&L.800 B.S., J.D. 30131 Town Center Dr.

**Baillie, Charlene L. '54 '83 L.809 J.D.**
**27762 Forkes Road, Suite 1, 92677**
**Telephone: 714-348-2929 Fax: 714-348-2987**
**Workers Compensation Defense.**
*See Professional Biographies, LAGUNA NIGUEL, CALIFORNIA*

**Belz, David L., (AV) '50 '75 C.1109 B.A. L.990 J.D.**
**28202 Cabot Road #215, 92677**
**Telephone: 714-347-0447 Fax: 714-364-0606**
***PRACTICE AREAS: Personal Injury Law (100%).**
**civil, Personal Injury.**
*See Professional Biographies, LAGUNA NIGUEL, CALIFORNIA*

**Billings, Eric K.** ..................... '58 '85 C&L.1137 B.S., J.D. [Ashworth&M.]
*LANGUAGES: Norwegian.
*PRACTICE AREAS: Business Litigation; Construction; Collections; Personal Injury; Torts.
Biram, James R. ..................... '26 '51 C.976 B.E. L.273 J.D. P.O. Box 6359‡
Burrows, Robert D. '37 '74 C.1145 B.S. L.818 J.D.
(adm. in MA; not adm. in CA) P.O. Box 6943‡
**Calcagnie, Kevin F.**, (AV) ..........'55 '83 C.1109 B.A. L.1137 J.D. [Robinson,P.&C.]⊙
*PRACTICE AREAS: Products Liability Law; Civil Litigation; Personal Injury Law.
Calton, Roger W. .....................'50 '75 C&L.502 B.S., J.D. 30131 Town Ctr. Dr.
Carolan, William B. ..................... '59 '92 C.338 B.S. L.1137 J.D. 28241 Crown Valley Pkwy.
Clark, James W. '— '80 C.911 B.A. L.336 J.D.
(adm. in WA; not adm. in CA) I.R.S.
**Coglianese, Christopher J.** ..................... '61 '90 C.705 B.A. L.1049 J.D. [⊠ Grady]⊙
*PRACTICE AREAS: Plaintiff Construction Defects.
Coleman, Gerald C. ............ '33 '76 C.420 B.S.M.E. L.1137 J.D. 30531 Paseo DelValle
Corsini, Richard A. ..................... '31 '59 C&L.426 B.A., LL.B. 28421 El Sur
**Davis, Allan F.** .....................'54 '83 C&L.972 B.S., J.D. [⊠ Robinson,P.&C.]⊙
*PRACTICE AREAS: Products Liability Law; Personal Injury Law.
Day, Charles F., (BV) ..................... '19 '47 C&L.262 B.S., J.D. 31332 Pardella Lane
Delesk, Suzanne M. .....................'58 '83 C.1109 B.A. L.809 J.D. 28202 Cabot Rd.
**Dicks, Michael Drew** ..................... '63 '89 C.763 B.S. L.61 J.D. [Grady]⊙
*PRACTICE AREAS: Plaintiff Construction; Defect Litigation.
**Dunning, Steven J.**, (BV) ..................... '49 '81 C.813 B.A. L.426 J.D. [Higham,M.&D.]
*PRACTICE AREAS: Corporate Law; Securities; Mergers and Acquisitions; Business Law; Real Estate Law.
Eby, Rickey L. ..................... '54 '89 C.629 B.S. L.1137 J.D. 28202 Cabot Rd.
Ettinghoff, Tracy H. ..................... '53 '84 C.112 B.A. L.769 J.D. 30011 Ivy Glen
Faber, Arnold L. .....................'27 '67 C.112 A.B. L.809 J.D. 30922 Westgreen Dr.
Fleming, Clark M. '08 '34 C.60 L.378 LL.B.
(adm. in KS; not adm. in CA) 31262 W. Nine Dr.‡
Floyd, Gerald L. '27 '61 C.623 B.S. L.862 LL.B.
(adm. in OK; not adm. in CA) 28921 Curlew Lane‡
Frank, Mari J. ..................... '47 '85 C.966 B.S. L.1137 J.D. 28202 Cabot Rd.
Frazee, Walter M., III, (A P.C.), (BV) ... '55 '80 C.800 B.S. L.1137 J.D. 30012 Ivy Glenn
Fredrick, William C. .....................'25 '81 C.898 B.S. L.1137 J.D. 29586 Teracina
Friedman, Miles D. ..................... '52 '76 C.1044 B.A. L.910 J.D. I.R.S.
Gardner, William R. ..................... '15 '49 C.112 L.800 LL.B. 31542 Crystal Sands Dr.‡
Gary, George R. '38 '64 C.659 B.A. L.912 J.D.
(adm. in MI; not adm. in CA) 23971 Swallowtail‡

CALIFORNIA—LAGUNA NIGUEL MARTINDALE-HUBBELL LAW DIRECTORY 1997

**Goode, Michael, (BV) '50 '77 C.424 B.A. L.990 J.D.**
**30101 Town Center Drive, Suite 100, 92677**
**Telephone: 714-249-2260 Fax: 714-495-3867**
***PRACTICE AREAS: Civil Litigation; Franchises and Franchising.**
**General Civil and Trial Practice. Franchise and Corporation Law.**
**References: Monarch Bank; Bank of America (Laguna Beach Office).**
*See Professional Biographies, LAGUNA NIGUEL, CALIFORNIA*

**Grady, Thomas**, (AV) .......... '45 '76 C.763 B.A. L.1049 J.D. [Grady]⊙
*PRACTICE AREAS: Construction Defect Litigation; Insurance; Personal Injury; Wrongful Death.

**Grady Law Firm, A Professional Corporation, (AV)**
**28202 Cabot Road, Suite 300, 92677⊙**
**Telephone: 714-752-1222**
**Thomas Grady; Michael Drew Dicks; Christopher J. Coglianese; Darlene Rohr Kowalczyk.**
**Construction Defect and Land Subsidence Litigation, Personal Injury, General Business and Litigation Practices.**
**San Diego, California Office: Aventine, 8910 University Center Lane, Suite 500, 92122-1085. Telephone: 619-535-1222. Fax: 619-535-0222.**
*See Professional Biographies, LAGUNA NIGUEL, CALIFORNIA*

**Guinn, Susan Lee** .......... '65 '92 C.560 B.S.N. L.208 J.D. [Ⓐ Robinson,P.&C.]⊙
*PRACTICE AREAS: Products Liability Law; Personal Injury Law; Medical Malpractice Law; Civil Litigation; Toxic Torts.

Halpern, Ronald D. .......... '49 '74 C.674 B.A. L.861 J.D. 30011 Ivy Glenn
Hamilton, Richard D. .......... '23 '51 C&L.911 B.A., LL.B. Ret. Mun. Ct. J.
**Higham, Douglas F.**, (AV) .......... '51 '78 C&L.101 B.S., J.D. [Higham,M.&D.]
*PRACTICE AREAS: Business Law; Corporate Law; Securities; Partnership Law; Taxation Law.

**Higham, McConnell & Dunning, (AV)**
**28202 Cabot Road, Suite 450, 92677-1250**
**Telephone: 714-365-5515 FAX: 714-365-5522**
**Email: HMDTI@AOL.com**
**Douglas F. Higham; Scott E. McConnell; Steven J. Dunning.**
**Corporate, Public and Private Securities, Venture Capital, Tax, Partnership, Technology Transfer, Real Estate and General Business Law, as well as Leveraged Buyouts and other Mergers and Acquisitions.**
*See Professional Biographies, LAGUNA NIGUEL, CALIFORNIA*

Hosmer, David E. .......... '51 '83 C.827 B.A. L.1288 J.D. 29773-F Niguel Rd.
Houts, Marshall W. '19 '40 C&L.494 B.S.L., J.D.
(adm. in TN; not adm. in CA) 33631 Magellan Isle‡
Hoy, William T., (BV) .......... '52 '78 L.999 J.D. 28202 Cabot Rd.
Huber, Gerd B. .......... '37 '77 C.1050 B.A. L.1190 J.D. 29262 Tierre
Hull, Richard S. .......... '13 '36 C.415 B.A. L.178 J.D. 15 Parkman Rd.‡
Hummer, John L. .......... '21 '82 C.813 Ph.D. L.273 J.D. P.O. Box 6427 (Pat.)
Jack, Louis B. .......... '51 '76 C.696 B.A. L.276 J.D. IRS
**Kowalczyk, Darlene Rohr** .......... '62 '88 C.763 B.A. L.426 J.D. [Grady]⊙
Krogmeier, Kevin G. '51 '87 C.436 B.A. L.1340 J.D.
(adm. in IN; not adm. in CA) Dir., Human Res., Furon Co.
Kuhn, Steven R., (AV) .......... '48 '73 C.112 B.A. L.809 J.D. [S.R.Kuhn]
Kuhn, Steven R., Law Offices of, A Prof. Corp., (AV) .......... 28202 Cabot Rd.
Lacy, James V. .......... '52 '78 C.800 A.B. L.990 J.D. [Lacy&L.]
Lacy, Janice A. '57 '82 C.473 B.A. L.608 J.D.
(adm. in OH; not adm. in CA) [Lacy&L.]
Lacy and Lacy .......... 30100 Town Ctr. Dr. #0-269
Lamons, Thomas R. .......... '57 '83 C&L.972 B.S., J.D. Dist. Coun., I.R.S.
Lance, I. Glenn .......... '21 '59 C.1027 B.S. L.184 LL.B. 7 St. Raphael
Leifer, Deborah L. .......... '54 '85 C.112 B.A. L.1137 J.D. [Ⓐ S.R.Kuhn]
Lindley, Wendy S. .......... '49 '79 C.800 B.S. L.990 J.D. Mun. J.
Lynn, Richard B. .......... '26 '57 C&L.813 B.S., J.D. P.O. Box 65350
Marshall, Adrian P., (AV) .......... '29 '56 C.800 B.S. L.1068 J.D. 15 Baroness Ln‡

**May, Gil, (BV) '48 '80 C.112 B.A. L.1137 J.D.**
**30101 Town Center Drive, Suite 100, 92677**
**Telephone: 714-831-5972 Fax: 714-495-3867**
***PRACTICE AREAS: Driving While Intoxicated; Misdemeanors; Felonies.**
**Driving While Intoxicated, Misdemeanors and Felonies.**

Maynard, John H. .......... '17 '41 C.604 A.B. L.477 J.D. 33605 Moonsail Dr.
**McConnell, Scott E.**, (AV) .......... '52 '78 C.800 B.S. L.1068 J.D. [Higham,M.&D.]
*PRACTICE AREAS: Corporate Law; Securities; Mergers and Acquisitions; Technology Transfer; Business Law.
McNames, William P. .......... '49 '75 C.112 B.A. L.990 J.D. Resch. Atty., Supr. Ct.
Molnar, Marie Elena .......... '— '85 C&L.1137 B.S.L., J.D. 30011 Ivy Glenn Dr.
**Moran, Bernard L.**, (AV) .......... '49 '79 C.800 B.A. L.101 J.D. [Ashworth&M.]
*PRACTICE AREAS: Commercial Law; Business Transactions.
Morrison, Charles R. '45 '71 C&L.575 B.S.B.A., J.D.
(adm. in NC; not adm. in CA) Estate & Gift Tax, I.R.S.
Peacock, James F. .......... '16 '65 C&L.800 A.B., J.D. 24082 Paseo Del Campo‡
Peron, Rochelle L. .......... '63 '90 C.112 B.A. L.1065 J.D. 29461 Drydock Cove
Peters, Roger P. '05 '38 C.846 B.A. L.569 LL.B.
(adm. in NY; not adm. in CA) 31582 Flying Cloud Dr.‡
**Phillips, Gordon G., Jr.** .......... '53 '79 C.800 B.S. L.426 J.D. [Robinson,P.&C.]⊙
*PRACTICE AREAS: Products Liability Law; Civil Litigation; Personal Injury Law.
Platt, D. Alexander '61 '88 C.98 B.S. L.8 J.D.
(adm. in PA; not adm. in CA) 25102 Camino Del Mar‡
Renfro, Roger D. .......... '38 '90 C.1095 B.A. L.1240 J.D. 30452 Via Estoril
Rice, Susan Braun .......... '55 '80 C.608 B.S.C.I.S. L.309 J.D. 27 New Haven‡
**Robinson, Jeoffrey L.**, (AV) .......... '55 '81 C.169 B.A. L.809 J.D. [Ⓐ Robinson,P.&C.]⊙
*PRACTICE AREAS: Products Liability; Personal Injury; Civil Litigation.
**Robinson, Mark P., Jr.**, (AV) .......... '45 '72 C.813 B.A. L.426 J.D. [Robinson,P.&C.]⊙
*PRACTICE AREAS: Products Liability Law; Civil Litigation; Personal Injury Law.

**Robinson, Phillips & Calcagnie, A Professional Corporation, (AV)** ▣
**Incorporated 1986**
**28202 Cabot Road Suite 200, 92677⊙**
**Telephone: 714-347-8855 Fax: 714-347-8774**
**Email: rpc@robinson-pilaw.com**
**Mark P. Robinson, Jr.; Gordon G. Phillips, Jr.; Kevin F. Calcagnie;—Allan F. Davis; Susan Lee Guinn; Jeoffrey L. Robinson.**
**Automobile Product Liability Litigation, Toxic Tort, Corporate Fraud, Serious Injury and Death Cases.**
**San Diego, California Office: 110 Laurel Street. Telephone: 619-338-4060. Fax: 619-338-0423.**
*See Professional Biographies, LAGUNA NIGUEL, CALIFORNIA*

Rosen, Charles F. .......... '45 '77 C.1077 B.A. L.1137 J.D. I.R.S.
Rosenfield, J. David .......... '37 '64 C.112 B.A. L.426 [Rosenfield]
Rosenfield Law Firm .......... P.O. Box 7086
Schmidt, Karen P. Goss .......... '51 '83 C.398 B.S. L.1095 J.D. [Schmidt&S.]
Schmidt, Philip, (BV) .......... '51 '79 C.1169 B.A. L.398 J.D. [Schmidt&S.]
Schmidt & Schmidt, (BV) .......... Suite 182, 30131 Town Center Drive
Seymour, Lauren .......... '45 '82 C.112 B.A. L.800 J.D. 32 Blue Horizon
Shaw, William D. .......... '30 '59 C.112 B.S.B.A. L.1068 J.D. Referee, L.A. Co. Sup. Ct.
Smith, J. Anthony, (BV) .......... '38 '76 C.1042 B.A. L.398 J.D. 28202 Cabot Rd.
Stahl, Dennis J. .......... '52 '78 C&L.800 B.S., J.D. 30131 Town Ctr. Dr.
Steelman, Ronald .......... '27 '57 C.659 B.A. L.309 J.D. Comr. Mun. Ct.
Stetson, Tracy Elizabeth .......... '64 '89 C&L.623 B.B.A., J.D. I.R.S.

**Stevens, Gary D. '35 '75 C.112 B.S. L.990 J.D.**
**30011 Ivy Glenn Drive, Suite 109, 92677-5014**
**Telephone: 714-249-9295**
**(Certified Specialist, Family Law, The State Bar of California Board of Legal Specialization).**
**Family Law, Business Law, Personal Injury Law, Civil Litigation.**
*See Professional Biographies, LAGUNA NIGUEL, CALIFORNIA*

Tandler, Moe L. '18 '49 C.563 B.A. L.1009 LL.B.
(adm. in NY; not adm. in CA) 21 Pemberton Pl.‡
Taylor, Lynda B. Cheung '51 '82 C.766 B.A. L.552 J.D.
(adm. in MA; not adm. in CA) I.R.S.
Tjandrasuwita, Maria Cecilia Inawati .......... '64 '90 C.66 B.A. L.1068 J.D. 25 S. Peak
Tucker, Ronald S. .......... '38 '67 C.112 B.S. L.426 LL.B. 9 Cala Moreya St.
Urbano, Gino D. .......... '31 '65 C.800 B.S. L.426 LL.B. 31 S. Peak
Westen, Marion L. '27 '67 C.66 A.B. L.472 J.D.
(adm. in WI; not adm. in CA) I.R.A.
Wilder, Sherri Spradley '56 '87 C.575 B.S. L.574 J.D.
(adm. in NC; not adm. in CA) Sr. Atty., I.R.S.
Wilson, Jacquelyn D. .......... '46 '76 C.945 B.A. L.426 J.D. 28915 La Carreterra
Wojciechowski, Zbigniew M. .......... '25 '72 C.999 B.S. L.809 J.D. 31317 East Nine Dr.‡
Wolf, Brian D. .......... '59 '86 C&L.1137 B.S.L., J.D. 12 Shallop

## LA HABRA, 51,266, *Orange Co.*

Anderson, Robert J. .......... '56 '85 C.684 B.A. L.426 J.D. 800 S. Beach A
Beau, John F. .......... '25 '76 C.158 B.E.E. L.1137 J.D. P.O. Box 752‡
Beckman, Gene W. .......... '27 '58 C.502 A.B. L.809 LL.B. 374 E. Avocado Crest Rd.
Birkland, Jack A. '19 '46 C.285 L.161 LL.B.
(adm. in OH; not adm. in CA) Hartford Ins. Co.
Burgess, Brian K. .......... '46 '72 C.768 B.S. L.1065 J.D. 800 S. Beach Blvd.
Creeden, Lawrence E. .......... '53 '79 C.1109 B.A. L.1137 J.D. P.O. Box 832
**Down, Carl V.** .......... '51 '84 C.112 B.A. L.678 J.D. Sr. Coun., Chevron U.S.A. Products Co.

**Fancher, C. Larry, (AV) '42 '82 C.909 B.A. L.1137 J.D.** ▣
**440 East La Habra Boulevard, 90631**
**Telephone: 714-870-9972; 310-691-1300**
**(Certified Specialist, Family Law, The State Bar of California Board of Legal Specialization).**
***PRACTICE AREAS: Family Law.**
**Family Law and Related Litigation.**
*See Professional Biographies, LA HABRA, CALIFORNIA*

Fazio, William A., (BV) .......... '31 '66 C&L.426 B.B.A., J.D. [W.A.Fazio]
Fazio, William A., Inc., A Prof. Law Corp., (BV) .......... 440 East La Habra Boulevard
**Gentner, Brian H.** '49 '77 C.37 B.A. L.464 J.D.
Sr. Coun., Chevron U.S.A. Products Co.
Glandfield, Philip J. .......... '52 '78 C.1109 B.A. L.809 J.D. 1601 Elmsford Ave.
**Goldstein, Jonathan A.**, (BV) .......... '50 '75 C.823 B.A. L.1049 J.D. [Goldstein&W.]
*PRACTICE AREAS: Business Litigation; Bankruptcy.

**Goldstein & Ward, Inc., (BV)**
**440 East La Habra Boulevard, 90631**
**Telephone: 310-694-3821; 714-870-9972 Fax: 310-697-8477**
**Burton H. Ward; Jonathan A. Goldstein;—David T. Ward.**
**Business Litigation and Bankruptcy Law.**
*See Professional Biographies, LA HABRA, CALIFORNIA*

Hix, Billy Joe .......... '25 '73 C.897 B.A. L.809 J.D. 360 E. Pinehurst Ave.‡
Holland, Clinton W., (BV) .......... '47 '73 C.763 B.A. L.1065 J.D. [C.W.Holland]
Holland, Clinton W., Inc., A Prof. Law. Corp., (BV) .......... 440 East La Habra Boulevard
Kamell, Rafik Y. .......... '58 '90 C.1164 B.A. L.990 J.D. 800 S. Beach Blvd.
**Kent, Jeffrey D.** .......... '67 '92 C.112 B.A. L.1137 J.D. [Ⓐ M.R.McDonnell]
*PRACTICE AREAS: Criminal Law; Juvenile; Federal and State.
Keywan, Thomas G. .......... '47 '73 C.112 B.A. L.61 J.D. 1861 E. Brooksdale Ave.
Launders, Robert J., II, (BV) .......... '50 '75 C.839 B.A. L.1049 J.D. 440 E. La Habra Blvd.
Mahoney, William D., (BV) .......... '39 '72 C.999 L.1137 LL.B. 800 S. Beach Blvd.
**McDonnell, Michael R.**, (AV) .......... '42 '68 C&L.1049 B.A., J.D. [M.R.McDonnell]
*PRACTICE AREAS: Criminal; Juvenile; Federal and State.

**McDonnell, Michael R., Inc., A Professional Corporation, (AV)**
**440 East La Habra Boulevard, 90631**
**Telephone: 310-694-3827; 714-870-9972 Fax: 310-694-4280**
**Michael R. McDonnell;—Jeffrey D. Kent.**
**Criminal Trial Practice in State and Federal Courts, Juvenile Law.**
**Reference: Landmark Bank.**
*See Professional Biographies, LA HABRA, CALIFORNIA*

Miller, Jack M., (AV) .......... '25 '60 C.628 B.S. L.1001 J.D. P.O. Box 3531‡
Petersen, Edward H. .......... '35 '62 C.101 B.S. L.1066 J.D. 800 S. Beach Blvd.
Pusavat, Keith N. .......... '67 '91 910 E. Woodcrest Ave.
Rallis, Ronald D., Sr. .......... '56 '82 C.35 B.S. L.809 J.D. [Rallis&C.]
Rallis & Chinen .......... 800 S. Beach Blvd.
Spencer, Douglas Charles .......... '58 '86 C.101 B.S. L.878 J.D. Landmark Bk.
Stone, Christina M., (BV) .......... '54 '84 C.1075 B.S. L.426 J.D. [W.A.Fazio]
Taaffe, Edw. J. .......... '13 '49 C.813 A.B. L.767 LL.B. Std. Oil Co. of Calif.
Talbert, Robert S. .......... '18 '64 C.668 L.809 LL.B. Hartford Ins. Grp.
**Ward, Burton H.**, (BV) .......... '40 '70 C.763 B.S. L.426 J.D. [Goldstein&W.]
*PRACTICE AREAS: Business Litigation; Bankruptcy.
**Ward, David T.** .......... '62 '89 C.101 B.A. L.188 J.D. [Ⓐ Goldstein&W.]
*LANGUAGES: Spanish.
*PRACTICE AREAS: Business Litigation; Bankruptcy.

## LA HABRA HEIGHTS, 6,226, *Los Angeles Co.*

Barcal, John J. .......... '44 '69 C.209 B.S. L.813 J.D. 1301 East Rd.
Christian, Dana C. .......... '51 '83 L.1179 J.D. 2009 El Cajonita Dr.
Hyslop, Richard S. .......... '44 '71 C.1109 B.A. L.1068 J.D. 1147 Picaacho Dr.
Newbre, Richard N. .......... '34 '76 C.596 L.809 J.D. 255 Canada Sombre

## LA JOLLA, —, *San Diego Co.*

(Part of the City of San Diego)

Aguirre, Gary J., (AV) .......... '40 '66 C&L.112 B.A., LL.B. 8498 El Paseo Grande
Allen, James M., (AV) '45 '75
C.846 B.B.A. L.1137 J.D. Pres., Action Foreclosure Servs., Inc.
Allen, Janet W. .......... '42 '79 C.112 B.A. L.477 J.D. 2223 Avenida De La Playa
Allison, James N. .......... '43 '75 C.174 B.A. L.1026 LL.B. 4180 LaJolla Village Dr.
**Armstrong, Robert G.** .......... '47 '76 C.112 B.A. L.1049 J.D. [Armstrong,F.&Assoc.]
*PRACTICE AREAS: Estate Planning Law.

**Armstrong, Fisch and Associates, P.C., (BV)**
**4250 Executive Square Suite 900, 92037**
**Telephone: 1-800-846-1666 Fax: 619-453-1147**

(This Listing Continued)

CAA150P

**Armstrong, Fisch and Associates, P.C. (Continued)**
**Robert G. Armstrong; Sanford Fisch.**
**Estate Planning, Probate, Trust Planning and Taxation Law.**
***See Professional Biographies, LA JOLLA, CALIFORNIA***

Bailey, Judy R. ........ '44 '72 C&L.851 B.A., J.D. [J.R.Bailey]
Bailey, Judy R., A Professional Corporation ........ 7855 Ivanhoe Ave. Ste 220
Baker, Edward G. ........ '41 '66 C.112 B.S. L.767 LL.B. P.O. Box 2287
Banoff, Grace K. ........ '16 '54 C.66 A.B. L.569 J.D. 733 Kline‡
Barkett, Lisa Ann ........ '59 '85 C.800 B.S. L.990 J.D. 864 Prospect St.
**Basden, Mildred** '49 '89 C.846 B.S.N. L.1049 J.D.
[Gray C.W.&F.] (⊙San Diego/Golden Triangle)
*PRACTICE AREAS: Trusts Law; Estates Law.
Baugh, Clyde A., (AV) ........ '16 '53 C.623 L.61 LL.B. 6929 Fairway Rd.‡
Bayer, Michael B. ........ '65 '91 C.228 B.A. L.575 J.D. 240 Playa del Norte
Beardsley, Nancy T. ........ '48 '84 C.629 B.S. L.1049 J.D. 737 Pearl St.
Begley, Thomas J., (BV) ........ '30 '54 C&L.878 B.S., LL.B. 8060 La Jolla Shores Dr.
Bell, Lynn L., (AV) '51 '82 C.37 B.S. L.1049 J.D.
Sr. V.P. & Gen. Coun., Amer. Residential Mtge. Corp.
**Benassi, John M.**, (AV) ........ '48 '75 C.339 B.S. L.273 J.D. [Lyon&L.] (See Pat. Sect.)
*PRACTICE AREAS: Intellectual Property.
Bennett, William R. ........ '46 '73 C.62 B.A. L.665 J.D. 5610 Desert View Dr.
Berke, Chuck '33 '58 C.966 B.B.A. L.597 J.D.
(adm. in IL; not adm. in CA) 7721 Eads Ave.‡
**Berkman, Charles S.** ........ '68 '93 C&L.846 B.S., J.D. [Lyon&L.] (See Pat. Sect.)
*PRACTICE AREAS: Patent, Unfair Competition, Antitrust; Intellectual Property.
Berol, John A. ........ '48 '81 C.119 B.A. L.1049 J.D. 8521 Ave. de las Ondas‡
**Biggs, Suzanne L.** ........ '48 '78 C.668 B.A. L.800 J.D. [Lyon&L.] (See Pat. Sect.)
*LANGUAGES: (Reading) German, French.
*PRACTICE AREAS: Patent, Trademark, Copyright, Unfair Competition, Licensing; Intellectual Property.
**Bingham, Douglas A.** '52 '85 C.446 B.S. L.1137 J.D.
V.P., Gen. Coun. & Chf. Pat. Coun., The Scripps Resch. Instit. (Pat.)
**Blanchard, Robert W.** ........ '53 '80 C.208 B.S.B.A. L.1049 J.D. [Blanchard,K.&F.]
*PRACTICE AREAS: Financial Institutions Law; Securities Regulation Law; Corporate Law; Real Estate Law.

**Blanchard, Krasner & French, A Professional Corporation, (AV)**
**7724 Girard Avenue, 3rd Floor, 92037**
**Telephone: 619-551-2440 FAX: 619-551-2434**
**Email: bkfl@aol.com**
**Robert W. Blanchard; Mark A. Krasner; Alan W. French;—Brad Rodriguez Bohrer; Glenn T. Macaluso.**
**General Civil Trial Practice. General Corporate and Commercial Law, Tax Estate Planning, International Transactions, Securities, Regulation, Financial Institutions, Copyright, Trademark and Licensing and Bankruptcy.**
***See Professional Biographies, LA JOLLA, CALIFORNIA***

Boehmer, Raymond '53 '78 C&L.546 B.S., J.D.
(adm. in WI; not adm. in CA) P.O. Box 995‡
**Bohrer, Brad Rodriguez** ........ '68 '93 C.802 B.B.A. L.990 J.D. [Blanchard,K.&F.]
*PRACTICE AREAS: International Sales and Trade Law; General Business Litigation; Real Estate; Tax.
Borchardt, Kurt '12 '39 C&L.145 A.B., J.D.
(adm. in DC; not adm. in CA) 1001 Genter St.‡
Bottomley, Robert B., (AV) ........ '25 '53 C.976 B.A. L.893 LL.B. P.O. Box 1377‡
Boyl, Charleen Cirese ........ '45 '73 C.768 B.A. L.1049 J.D. 9575 Poole St.
Brewer, David A., (BV) ........ '50 '75 C.112 B.A. L.1049 J.D. [Moore,B.&B.]
Brody, David W., (BV) ........ '57 '83 C.1102 B.S. L.1049 J.D. [Sullivan,M.B.&B.]
Brotman, Harris F. ........ '45 '89 C.1077 B.A. L.809 J.D. 202 Coast Blvd. Ste. 111 (Pat.)
Brown, Jeffrey M. ........ '63 '88 C.882 B.S. L.61 J.D. [J.M.Brown]
**Brown, Wayne B.** ........ '63 '92 C.309 B.A. L.1066 J.D. [Lyon&L.]
*PRACTICE AREAS: Patent, Trademark, Trade Secret, Unfair Competition and Business Tort Counseling and; Litigation; Trademark Prosecution; Intellectual Property.
Brown, Jeffrey M., A P.L.C., Law Offices of ........ 4275 Executive Sq., Ste. 320

**Burgart, Michele M. '44 '71 C.555 B.A. L.838 J.D.**
**The Wall Street Building, 7855 Ivanhoe Avenue, Suite 320, 92037**
**Telephone: 619-456-1190 FAX: 619-456-1244**
***PRACTICE AREAS: Wills; Trust Law; Probate Law.**
**Estate Planning and Administration.**
***See Professional Biographies, LA JOLLA, CALIFORNIA***

Busch, Douglas Dale '— '72 C.674 A.B. L.1049 J.D.
Dir., Legal Servs. & Tech. Transfer, Salk Institute, The
Campbell, Cameron ........ '59 '86 C.174 B.A. L.1049 J.D. 1020 Prospect St.
Campbell, Leon E., (BV) ........ '29 '54 C.597 B.S. L.629 J.D. [L.E.Campbell]
Campbell, Leon E., A Professional Corporation, (BV) ........ 1020 Prospect St.
Carl, Ronald A. ........ '60 '87 C.112 B.A. L.1049 J.D. 4180 La Jolla Village Dr.

**Carmellino, Joseph S. '49 '83 C.102 B.A. L.1049 J.D.**
**4225 Executive Square Suite 260, 92037-1483**
**Telephone: 619-457-4240 Fax: 619-457-0303**
**General Civil and Trial Practice. Criminal Appeals.**

Carroll, Eileen P. ........ '49 '78 C.881 A.B. L.813 J.D. 2330 Avenida De La Playa‡
Carson, Elizabeth H. '28 '53 C.881 B.A. L.659 J.D.
(adm. in IA; not adm. in CA) 1703 Soledad Ave.‡
Cerv, Marleen J. ........ '48 '79 C&L.1137 B.S., J.D. Asst. Corp. Coun., ICL North America
Chachas, George G. ........ '62 '87 C.763 B.A. L.61 J.D. [Wenthur&C.]
Chapman, Lawrence M. '34 '60 C.597 B.A. L.976 LL.B.
(adm. in NE; not adm. in CA) Pres., The Today Cos., Inc.
Chapman, Robert L., (BV) ........ '27 '54 C.477 B.B.A. L.813 J.D. 5469 Caminito Rosa
**Charney, Jack G.**, (AV) .... '46 '72 C.880 B.A. L.813 J.D. [Luce,F.H.&S.] (⊙San Diego)
*PRACTICE AREAS: Estate Law; Personal Tax Planning Law; Probate Law; Trust Administration Law.
**Chen, Anthony C.** ........ '66 '93 C.061 B.Sc. L.309 J.D. [Lyon&L.]
*LANGUAGES: Mandarin, Chinese.
*PRACTICE AREAS: Patent, Trademark, Trade Secret, Technology Licensing; Biotechnology Patent Prosecution; Litigation; Opinion Analysis.
Cheverton, Paul M. ........ '57 '83 C.813 B.A. L.800 J.D. 4275 Executive Sq.
Chien, Benny ........ '44 '73 C.813 A.B. L.1049 J.D. 2615 Ellentown Rd.
**Circuit, Richard K.**, (AV) ........ '43 '70 C.101 B.A. L.878 J.D. [Circuit,M.K.&R.]
*PRACTICE AREAS: Corporate Law; Business Law; Intellectual Property Law.

**Circuit, McKellogg, Kinney & Ross LLP, (AV)**
**1205 Prospect Street Suite 400, 92037**
**Telephone: 619-459-0581 Fax: 619-459-0690**
**Members of Firm: Richard K. Circuit; R. Keith McKellogg; Richard R. Kinney, Jr.; Scott Hunter Ross; Darl R. Danford; Phillip C. Wing; Daniel Pearl; Sheri Lynne Perlman.**
**General Civil, Trial, Arbitration and Appellate Practice. Antitrust, Bankruptcy, Corporation and Business Law, Employment, Estate Planning, Probate, Pension and Profit Sharing, Real Property, Taxation, Trusts, Health Care, Insurance Defense, Copyright and Trademark Law.**
***See Professional Biographies, LA JOLLA, CALIFORNIA***

Clark, Rita S. ........ '47 '79 C&L.1137 B.S.L., J.D. 5757 Soledad Rd.
Clarkson, Dessau ........ '30 '57 C.668 A.B. L.1068 J.D. 7875 Bellakaren‡
Cochran, Martha '54 '88 C.197 B.A. L.776 J.D.
(adm. in NJ; not adm. in CA) 2605 Ellentown Rd.‡
**Cohan, Darvy Mack, (AV) '43 '73 C.869 B.S. L.61 J.D.**
**Suite 550, 1200 Prospect Street, 92037**
**Telephone: 619-459-4432 Fax: 619-454-3548**
***PRACTICE AREAS: Civil Litigation; Commercial Litigation; Business and Corporate Litigation.**
**Civil, Business Law, Bankruptcy Law, Commercial Litigation, Insurance Law and Corporate Law.**
**Reference: Scripps Bank, La Jolla, CA.**
***See Professional Biographies, LA JOLLA, CALIFORNIA***

**Cohan, William A.**, (AV) ........ '47 '76 C.813 A.B. L.911 J.D. [W.A.Cohan]
*LANGUAGES: German; French; Spanish.
*PRACTICE AREAS: Complex Litigation; Criminal Tax Litigation; White Collar Defense Law.

**Cohan, William A., P.C., (AV)**
**7746 Herschel Avenue, 92037-4403**
**Telephone: 619-551-0939 Fax: 619-551-0193**
**Email: wcohan@aol.com**
**William A. Cohan.**
**Complex Civil and Criminal Litigation.**
***See Professional Biographies, LA JOLLA, CALIFORNIA***

**Consalvi, Mary S.** ........ '58 '83 C.679 B.S. L.209 J.D. [Lyon&L.] (See Pat. Sect.)
*LANGUAGES: Italian and French.
*PRACTICE AREAS: Patent, Trademark, Unfair Competition; Intellectual Property.
**Cordray, Monique L.** '64 '89 C.923 B.S. L.260 J.D.
(adm. in FL; not adm. in CA; See Pat. Sect.) [Fish&R.]
*PRACTICE AREAS: Intellectual Property; International Trade Commission Practice.
Cornblath, Dana '53 '90 C.910 B.A. L.61 J.D.
(adm. in PA; not adm. in CA) 5705 Caminito Pulsera‡
Corwin, John J. '09 '33 C&L.188 A.B., J.D.
(adm. in NY; not adm. in CA) 5822 Caminito Cardelia‡
**Cranston, Theodore J.**, (AV) '39 '65 C&L.813 B.A., J.D.
[Gray C.W.&F.] (⊙San Diego/Golden Triangle)
*PRACTICE AREAS: Taxation Law; Real Estate Law; Trusts Law; Estates Law.
Culver, Robert W., (A P.C.) ........ '32 '61 C.813 A.B. L.1065 J.D. P.O. Box 126‡
**Danford, Darl R.**, (BV) ........ '58 '84 C.174 B.A. L.623 J.D. [Circuit,M.K.&R.]
*PRACTICE AREAS: Business Civil Litigation; Intellectual Property Litigation; Employment Law; Health Care Law.
Dattan, Howard S. ........ '20 '49 C.800 A.B. L.770 LL.B. 4225 Exec. Sq.
Davis, Shirleymae ........ '— '64 C.436 L.424 J.D. 7541 Eads Ave.
Dechant, Donald J. ........ '54 '79 C.800 B.S. L.1067 J.D. 3129 Bremerton Pl.
DeMaria, Christine ........ '68 '93 C.104 A.B. L.383 J.D. 7211 Romero Dr.
Dillahunty, Benjamin P., (BV) .... '25 '64 C.802 B.B.A. L.1049 LL.B. 5428 Chelsea Ave.
Dillemuth, Walter F. '29 '55 C.262 A.B. L.724 LL.B.
(adm. in NY; not adm. in CA) 5888 Soledad Mt. Rd.‡
Dodge, Scott H., (BV) '46 '73 C.477 B.B.A. L.912 J.D.
Sr. Coun., Great Amer. Bk., FSB
**Dommel, Julia M.** ........ '51 '91 C.1349 B.A. L.1137 J.D. [Shapiro&M.]
*PRACTICE AREAS: Bankruptcy-Creditors; Real Property Foreclosure; Unlawful Detainers.
Dorr, Roderick A., (AV) ........ '37 '75 C&L.623 B.S., J.D. [Moore,B.&B.]
**Duft, Bradford J.** ........ '54 '80 C.174 B.A. L.61 J.D. [Lyon&L.] (See Pat. Sect.)
*PRACTICE AREAS: Intellectual Property.
Dunn, Brian J., (BV) ........ '55 '82 C&L.1049 B.B.A., J.D. 7855 Ivanhoe Ave.
Durbin, Winfield T. '12 '37 C.951 A.B. L.309 LL.B.
(adm. in IL; not adm. in CA) 7755 Sierra Mar Dr.‡
Durham, Robert J., (AV) ........ '16 '40 C.502 A.B. L.309 J.D. 1538 Kearsarge Rd.‡
**Durham, Robert J., Jr.**, (AV) '41 '75
C.951 B.A. L.813 J.D. [Luce,F.H.&S.] (⊙San Diego)
*PRACTICE AREAS: Estate Planning; Tax Planning; Probate Law; Estate and Trust Administration.
**Edep, Monique M.** ........ '65 '91 C&L.426 [Shapiro&M.]
*PRACTICE AREAS: Bankruptcy; Creditor Bankruptcy; Real Property; Foreclosures; Unlawful Detainers.
Edwards, John C., (BV) ........ '47 '77 C.763 B.A. L.1049 J.D. 2223 Avenida De La Playa
Edwards, Stephen W. ........ '23 '49 C&L.339 B.S., J.D. 2510 Torrey Pines Rd#316‡
Eger, John M. '40 '70 C.885 B.A. L.365 J.D.
(adm. in IL; not adm. in CA) Worldwide Media Grp., Inc.
Eichen, James J. ........ '62 '87 C.190 B.A. L.1067 J.D. 836 Prospect St.
Eischen, James J., Jr. ........ '62 '87 C.190 B.A. L.1067 J.D. 836 Prospect St.
Eisenberg, Herbert '33 '57 C.415 B.A. L.1009 LL.B.
(adm. in NY; not adm. in CA) 8939 Caminito Fresca St.‡
Elkind, Arnold B. '16 '39 C&L.569 B.S., LL.B.
(adm. in NY; not adm. in CA) 1547 Caminito Solidago‡
Epstein, Alan I. ........ '37 '61 C&L.477 B.B.A., J.D. 7140 Caminito Estrada‡
**Estle, Mark D.** ........ '55 '81 C.839 B.A. L.69 J.D. [M.C.Tremblay]
*PRACTICE AREAS: Business Litigation; Real Estate; Creditor Rights Law; Business; Real Estate Litigation.
Ezrin, Alvin '40 '67 C&L.273 B.S., LL.B.
(adm. in DC; not adm. in CA) V.P., Law & Secy., National Health Labs., Inc.
**Fanshaw, Judith L.** '55 '85 C.763 A.B. L.1049 J.D.
Gen. Coun., The Copley Press, Inc.
*RESPONSIBILITIES: Litigation Management; Contract Negotiation; Employment Issues; Access to Information.
**Ferguson, William E.**, (AV) ........ '23 '50 C.668 B.A. L.1066 LL.B. [Ferguson,N.&W.]
*PRACTICE AREAS: Estate Planning; Trust Law; Probate.

**Ferguson, Newburn & Weston, A Professional Corporation, (AV)**
**Suite 260, 7777 Fay Avenue, 92037**
**Telephone: 619-454-4233 Facsimile: 619-454-3052**
**Keith M. Ferguson (1903-1965); John L. Newburn (Retired, 1989); William E. Ferguson; David Weston (Certified Specialist, Estate Planning, Trust and Probate Law, The State Bar of California Board of Legal Specialization).**
**Estate Planning, Trust and Probate Law.**
**References: Union Bank (La Jolla Office); Scripps Bank (La Jolla Office).**
***See Professional Biographies, LA JOLLA, CALIFORNIA***

Filicia, James J ........ '60 '88 C.1031 B.S. L.1137 J.D. 4225 Executive Sq.
**Fisch, Sanford**, (BV) ........ '55 '80 C.94 B.A. L.1049 J.D. [Armstrong,F.&Assoc.]
*PRACTICE AREAS: Estate Planning; Probate; Trust Planning; Taxation Law.

**Fish & Richardson P.C., (AV)**
**4225 Executive Square, Suite 1400, 92037⊙**
**Telephone: 619-678-5070 Fax: 619-678-5099**
**Email: info@fr.com URL: http://www.fr.com**
**John F. Land; John R. Wetherell, Jr. (Not admitted in CA); Scott C. Harris (Not admitted in CA);—Monique L. Cordray (Not admitted in CA); Stacy L. Taylor; June Marie Learn; Lisa A. Haile; Christopher S. Marchese; Donald L. Wenskay.**
**Intellectual Property Law: Trials, Transactions, Patents, Trademarks, Copyrights, Trade Secrets, Entertainment Law, Telecommunications Law, Drug and Medical Device and Antitrust Law.**
**Boston, Massachusetts Office: 225 Franklin Street. Telephone: 617-542-5070. Fax: 617-542-8906.**
**Washington, D.C. Office: 601 13th Street, N.W. Telephone: 202-783-5070. Fax: 202-783-2331.**
**Houston, Texas Office: One Riverway, Suite 1200. Telephone: 713-629-5070. Fax: 713-629-7811.**
**Menlo Park, California Office: 2200 Sand Hill Road, Suite 100. Telephone: 415-322-5070. Fax: 415-854-0875.**
**Minneapolis, Minnesota Office: Fish & Richardson P.C., P.A., 60 South Sixth Street, Suite 3300. Telephone: 612-335-5070. Fax: 612-288-9696.**

(This Listing Continued)

CAA151P

CALIFORNIA—LA JOLLA MARTINDALE-HUBBELL LAW DIRECTORY 1997

**Fish & Richardson P.C. (Continued)**

New York, N.Y. Office: 45 Rockefeller Plaza, Suite 2800. Telephone: 212-765-5070. Fax: 212-258-2291.
*See Professional Biographies, LA JOLLA, CALIFORNIA*

**Fisher, David A.**, (AV) ....'51 '77 C.112 B.A. L.1137 J.D. [Fisher T.] (⊙Cincinnati, OH)
*PRACTICE AREAS: Corporate; Securities; Real Estate; Taxation.

**Fisher Thurber LLP, (AV)** BB
**La Jolla Executive Tower, 4225 Executive Square Suite 1600, 92037-1483**
**Telephone: 619-535-9400 Fax: 619-535-1616**
**David A. Fisher. Of Counsel: Marshall Thurber;—Timothy J. Fitzpatrick; Nancy L. Mauriello.**
**Finance, Securities, Real Estate, Tax, Corporate Law, Franchise.**
*See Professional Biographies, LA JOLLA, CALIFORNIA*

**Fitting, Thomas** '53 '89 C.112 B.A. L.1137 J.D.
Assoc. Chf. Pat. Coun., The Scripps Resch. Instit. (Pat.)
**Fitzpatrick, Timothy J.**, (BV) ..............'50 '79 C.112 B.A. L.1137 J.D. [Ⓐ Fisher T.]
*PRACTICE AREAS: Securities; Corporate; Franchise.
**Fleck, Melitta**, (AV) '48 '79 C.525 B.A. L.1065 J.D.
[Gray C.W.&F.] (⊙San Diego/Golden Triangle)
*PRACTICE AREAS: Estate Planning; Estate and Gift Taxation; Trust Administration; Probate Law; Fiduciary Law.
Foley, Matthew O., III .........'61 '86 C.966 B.A. L.436 J.D. 4180 La Jolla Village Dr.★
Forbes, George T. '25 '50 C.502 B.S. L.900 LL.B.
(adm. in KS; not adm. in CA) P.O. Box 8349‡
Ford, Larry A. ........................'39 '66 C&L.608 B.S.B.A., J.D. 5478 Soledad Rd.‡
Fox, Wm. W. ...............................'28 '55 C.763 L.809 LL.B. 7825 Fay Ave.
Franklin, J. David, (BV) ............'37 '68 C.108 B.A. L.347 J.D. 1055 Torrey Pines Rd.
Frantz, Roger C. ......................'42 '69 C.800 B.S. L.1068 J.D. 6767 Avenida Andorra
Fraser, Peter, (BV) ..........................'41 '68 C.178 A.B. L.262 J.D. [Fraser&R.]
Fraser & Rossman, (BV) ............................................... 202 Coast Blvd.
**French, Alan W.** ........................'64 '89 C.169 B.S. L.94 J.D. [Blanchard,K.&F.]
*PRACTICE AREAS: Business Law; Banking Law; Real Estate Law.
Friedman, Gary E., (AV) '47 '74 C.910 A.B. L.1066 J.D.
V.P. & Gen. Coun., Agouron Pharmaceuticals, Inc.
Furtek, Edward C. '46 '91 C.112 B.A. L.128 J.D.
(adm. in MD; not adm. in CA) Univ. of San Diego
**Fuson, Harold W., Jr.**, (AV) '45 '76
C.293 B.A. L.161 J.D. V.P., Law, The Copley Press, Inc.
*RESPONSIBILITIES: Communications and Media (30%); Business Law (30%); Labor and Employment (30%); Libel, Slander and Defamation (10%).

**Galvin, Thomas J. '51 '78 C.475 B.A. L.213 J.D.**
**7825 Fay Avenue, Suite 200, 92037**
**Telephone: 619-456-3590 Fax: 619-456-1835**
**Email: tgalvin@ix.netcom.com**
***TRANSACTIONS: Taco Bell Corp. 1988 (Comprehensive Properties Audit); Marriott Corp. 1989 (Conversion of Big Boy Restaurants to Allies); The Price Company, 1991 (Formation of Price REIT); Price Costco, Inc., 1994-1995 (Sale of 85 shopping centers); Pepsico 1994-1996 (Counsel for California Pizza Kitchens).**
**Commercial Real Estate, Commercial Leasing for Retail Office and Industrial Property, Multi-State, Multi-Property Purchase and Sales Transactions. General Business Law.**
**Representative Clients: Price Costco, Inc.; Pepsico.**
**Reference: Bank of America.**
*See Professional Biographies, LA JOLLA, CALIFORNIA*

Ganus, Walter David '37 '61 C&L.477 A.B., LL.B.
(adm. in MI; not adm. in CA) 7629 Girard Ave.‡
Garrett, Lewis, (AV) .......................'20 '51 C.769 A.B. L.809 J.D. 849 Coast Blvd.
Garrie, Julie L. ...............................'59 '86 C.112 B.A. L.813 J.D. 2155 Via Sinalda
Gaskins, Roger A. ..................'40 '78 C.763 B.A. L.61 J.D. 8950 Villa La Jolla Dr.
Gavin, Wm. F. ...................................'22 '46 C.858 L.262 LL.B. 7661 Hillside Dr.‡
Gay, Michael H. .............'44 '74 C.112 B.S. L.1065 J.D. Fujitsu Systems of Amer., Inc.
Gilbert, Caroline G. ........................'66 '95 C.800 B.A. L.1049 J.D. [Ⓐ Sullivan,M.B.&B.]
**Gillick, Mary F.**, (BV) ....'50 '84 C.446 B.S. L.1049 J.D. [Luce,F.H.&S.] (⊙San Diego)
*PRACTICE AREAS: Trust and Estate Litigation.
Gillooly, Craig Lewis ...................'60 '85 C.184 B.A. L.800 J.D. 7529 Draper Ave.
Gilman, Earl R. '17 '41 C&L.477 A.B., J.D.
(adm. in MI; not adm. in CA) 5810 Caminito Empresa‡
Gilmore, Maurice Wilky '40 '73 C.174 B.S. L.184 J.D.
(adm. in CT; not adm. in CA) 4225 Executive Sq.
Gleason, Jan M. ........................'32 '79 C&L.1137 B.S.L., J.D. 6333 Castejon Dr.
Godinez, Cynthia J. '50 '77 C&L.378 B.A., J.D.
(adm. in KS; not adm. in CA) 1830 Caminito Monrovia‡
Goldberg, Russell M. .......'41 '87 C.843 B.A. L.1241 J.D. 4275 Executive Sq., Ste. 1020
Goldberger, Peter C. ...........'48 '75 C.112 B.A. L.1049 J.D. 920 Kline St. (⊙El Centro)
Goode, Thomas B. ..........................'53 '85 C.602 B.A. L.1137 J.D. 4225 Exec. Sq.
Gordon, James S., (BV) ..................'48 '77 C.855 B.A. L.1049 J.D. 3251 Holiday Ct.
Gordon, Laura P. ..........................'65 '91 C.823 B.A. L.184 J.D. 8444 Via Sonoma
Gorman, Patrick J. '67 '92 C.861 B.A. L.64 J.D.
(adm. in MD; not adm. in CA) 6986 La Jolla Blvd.‡
Gotfredson, Thomas L. '56 '81 C.597 B.A. L.208 J.D.
V.P., Transamerican Properties, Inc.
Goulian, Susan H., (BV) ..............'38 '82 C.518 B.A. L.1049 J.D. 4225 Executive Sq.

**Gray Cary Ware & Freidenrich, A Professional Corporation, (AV)** BB
**Suite 575, 1200 Prospect Street, 92037⊙**
**Telephone: 619-454-9101 Telecopier: 619-456-3075**
**Email: info@gcwf.com URL: http://www.gcwf.com**
**Theodore J. Cranston (Resident, San Diego/Golden Triangle Office); Melitta Fleck (Resident, San Diego/Golden Triangle Office); Ellen H. Whelan (Resident, San Diego/Golden Triangle Office); Karl Zobell (Resident, La Jolla Office);—Mildred Basden, Resident, San Diego/Golden Triangle Office).**
**Languages: Spanish, German, French, Italian and Swedish.**
**General Civil and Trial Practice in all State and Federal Courts and Administrative Agencies. Admiralty, Agribusiness, Antitrust, Aviation, Banking, Bankruptcy and Insolvency, Business, Commercial, Computer Law, Compensation and Benefits, Condemnation, Construction, Copyright and Trademark, Corporation, Corporate Securities, Customs, Eminent Domain, Employment Counseling and Litigation, Environmental, Estate Planning, Family Law, Fidelity and Surety, Government Contracts, Hospital and Health Care, Immigration and Naturalization, Insurance, Intellectual Property, International Business and Litigation, Publishing, Labor, Land Use, Libel, Licensing, Multimedia Negligence, News Media, Pension and Profit Sharing, Privacy, Private Foundation, Probate, Products Liability, Professional Malpractice, Railroad, Real Property, Federal and State Securities, Taxation, Telecommunications, Trade Regulation, Unfair Competition, Wills and Trusts.**
**Representative Clients: The Copley Press, Inc.; Home Capital Corp.; Dr. Seuss Foundation; Ernest W. Hahn, Inc.; Imperial Corporation of America; La Jolla Bank & Trust Co.; La Jolla Real Estate Brokers Association; Merrill, Lynch, Pierce, Fenner & Smith; Scripps Clinic and Research Foundation; Timkin-Sturgis Foundation.**
**San Diego, California Office: 401 "B" Street, Suite 1700. Telephone: 619-699-2700.**
**San Diego/Golden Triangle, California Office: 4365 Executive Drive, Suite 1600, 92121. Telephone: 619-677-1400. Fax: 619-677-1477.**
**Palo Alto, California Office: 400 Hamilton Avenue. Telephone: 415-328-6561.**
**El Centro, California Office: 1224 State Street, P.O. Box 2890. Telephone: 619-353-6140.**
*See Professional Biographies, LA JOLLA, CALIFORNIA*

Greenwald, Clarence J. '27 '52 C.347 A.B. L.1119 J.D.
(adm. in IN; not adm. in CA) 2172 Caminito Circulo Sur‡
Guetz, Burton W. ..................'51 '76 C&L.972 B.S., J.D. 4275 Executive Sq., Ste. 320
Guggenheim, David M. .................'46 '74 C.679 B.S. L.861 J.D. 8289 Sugarman Dr.
**Guise, Jeffrey William** ......'59 '93 C.352 B.S. L.763 J.D. [Ⓐ Lyon&L.] (See Pat. Sect.)
*PRACTICE AREAS: Patent, Trademark, Copyright; Intellectual Property.
**Haile, Lisa A.** ..................'60 '92 C.699 B.A. L.61 J.D. [Ⓐ Fish&R.] (See Pat. Sect.)
*PRACTICE AREAS: Intellectual Property; Patents.
Haines, Jay A. ............................................'62 '89 C.931 B.A. L.61 J.D. [J.A.Haines]
Haines, Jay A., A Professional Law Corporation ............................ 4275 Executive Sq.
**Hallman, Jonathan** ........................'59 '96 C.338 B.S. L.1068 J.D. [Ⓐ Lyon&L.]
*PRACTICE AREAS: Intellectual Property.
Hanzlik, Rayburn '38 '75 C.675 B.S. L.893 J.D.
Chmn. & Gen. Coun., Lanxide Sports Intl., Inc.
Harris, Ruth M. ......................'— '56 C.597 B.S. L.209 J.D. 5363 La Jolla Blvd.‡
**Harris, Scott C.** '57 '87 C&L.273 B.S.E.E., J.D.
(adm. in PA; not adm. in CA; See Pat. Sect.) [Fish&R.]
*PRACTICE AREAS: Intellectual Property; Patents.
Haskell, Roger L. ............'58 '90 C.105 B.A. L.999 J.D. 4275 Executive Sq., Ste. 320
Hauser, Heather Kristin .....................'69 '94 C.112 B.A. L.61 J.D. [Ⓐ J.M.Brown]
**Heber, Sheldon O.** ........'60 '93 C.563 Ph.D. L.1188 J.D. [Ⓐ Lyon&L.] (See Pat. Sect.)
*PRACTICE AREAS: Patent; Intellectual Property.
Hedgecock, Roger A. ...........................'46 '72 C.112 A.B. L.1065 J.D. 625 Wrelton Dr.
**Hellenkamp, Amy Stark** ... '66 '96 C.645 B.S. L.1049 J.D. [Ⓐ Lyon&L.] (See Pat. Sect.)
*PRACTICE AREAS: Patent; Intellectual Property.
Hemme, Jerry D., (BV) ......'54 '81 C.763 B.A. L.1049 J.D. 1025 Prospect St., Suite 300
Henry, Dan O., (BV) .......................'11 '79 C.357 A.B. L.564 J.D. 1020 Prospect St.
**Henry, Sara A.** .....................................'65 '91 C.174 B.A. L.1188 J.D. [Ⓐ T.A.Henry,Jr.]

**Henry, Thomas A., Jr., Law Offices of, (AV) '38 '63 C&L.174 B.A., LL.B.**
**Suite 315, 875 Prospect Street, P.O. Box 1168, 92038**
**Telephone: 619-454-1780 Fax: 619-454-1792**
**—Sara A. Henry.**
**Estate Planning, Probate, Trust Administration and Conservatorship Law.**
**Reference: Scripps Bank.**
*See Professional Biographies, LA JOLLA, CALIFORNIA*

Hertzel, David E., (AV) '54 '80 C.426 L.878 J.D.
V.P. & Sr. Coun., Amer. Residential Mtge. Corp.
Higgins, Patrick H. ..........................'59 '93 C.446 B.S. L.1338 J.D. 317 Kolmar Ave.
Hillhouse, Andrew F., Jr. .................'20 '47 C.453 B.S. L.273 LL.B. P.O. Box 12708
**Holmes, Emily** .... '56 '95 C.172 B.S. L.1049 J.D. Assoc. Coun., The Scripps Resch. Inst.
Holsenback, J. Daniel ..................'64 '89 C.678 B.A. L.1067 J.D. 4180 La Jolla Village Dr.
Holthus, Thomas J. '59 '84 C.36 B.S. L.61 J.D.
Pres. & Gen. Coun., American Custody Corp.
Hom, Cynthia L. '51 '76 C.1049 B.A. L.112 J.D.
Asst. Corp. Coun., ICL North America
Howell, Joseph A. .....................'61 '89 C.1110 B.A. L.1137 J.D. 7855 Ivanhoe Ave.
Irons, Peter H. '40 '79 C.33 B.A. L.309 J.D.
(adm. in MA; not adm. in CA) Univ. of Calif. at San Diego
Jay, D. Frederick, Jr., (AV) '46 '75 C.878 B.S. L.61 J.D.
Assoc. Gen. Coun., Agouron Pharmaceuticals, Inc.
Jensen, J. Kenneth ........... '31 '62 C.112 B.A. L.1068 LL.B. 4180 La Jolla Village Dr.
Joehnk, Susan R. ..................'41 '90 C.890 B.A. L.1137 J.D. 1117 Wall St., Ste. 3
Jones, Julie A. ...........'52 '85 C.656 B.A. L.1049 J.D. [Mulvaney,K.&B.] (⊙San Diego)
Joyce, Robert J. .............................'48 '76 C.454 B.A. L.208 J.D. P.O. Box 8247
Kahan, Lawrence, (AV) '34 '62 C.763 A.B. L.893 J.D.
[Mulvaney,K.&B.] (⊙San Diego)
Kahn, Laurence M. ......................'47 '77 C.659 B.A. L.477 J.D. 5519 Waverly Ave.
**Kao, Carol K.** ...........'63 '91 C.112 B.A. L.800 J.D. [Ⓐ Luce,F.H.&S.] (⊙San Diego)
*PRACTICE AREAS: Estate Planning; Probate; Trust Administration.
**Karlen, Peter H.**, (AV) .......................'49 '74 C.112 B.A. L.1065 J.D. [P.H.Karlen]

**Karlen, Peter H., A Professional Law Corporation, (AV)**
**1205 Prospect Street, Suite 400, 92037**
**Telephone: 619-454-9696 Fax: 619-454-9777**
**Peter H. Karlen.**
**Art, Publishing and Intellectual Property including Copyrights and Trademarks.**

Kavanagh, Pierce M., (BV) ...............'31 '59 C.262 L.564 LL.B. 7300 Vista Del Mar
Keller, Lawrence R. ..................'37 '78 C.1074 B.S. L.1136 J.D. 1916 Hypatia Way
Kent, Karlyn R. '64 '90 C.112 B.A. L.1049 J.D.
V.P. & Coun., American Custody Corp.
Kerman, Arline S., (Mrs.) '39 '68 C&L.64 LL.B.
(adm. in GA; not adm. in CA) 1304 La Jolla Rancho Rd.‡
Kilburn, E. Miles '63 '89 C.911 B.A. L.597 J.D.
V.P. & Treas., Amer. Residential Mtge. Corp.
**Kinney, Richard R., Jr.**, (AV) .........'43 '69 C.611 B.A. L.608 J.D. [Circuit,M.K.&R.]
*PRACTICE AREAS: Estate Planning Law; Probate Law; Trust Law; Taxation Law; Health Care Law.
Kirchheimer, Arthur E. ............'31 '54 C.1093 B.A. L.823 LL.B. 2876 Palamino Circle
**Kolegraff, William J.** ......................'59 '96 C.792 B.S.E.E. L.1049 J.D. [Ⓐ Lyon&L.]
*PRACTICE AREAS: Patent; Trademark; Intellectual Property.
**Korniczky, Stephen S.** '63 '88 C.667 B.S.M.E. L.107 J.D.
[Ⓒ Lyon&L.] (See Pat. Sect.)
*PRACTICE AREAS: Litigation; Patent; Trademark; Copyright; Unfair Competition.
**Krasner, Mark A.**, (AV) .............'54 '81 C.763 B.S. L.1049 J.D. [Blanchard,K.&F.]
*LANGUAGES: Spanish.
*PRACTICE AREAS: Real Property Law; Business Law; Taxation Law.
**Land, John F.** ..................'53 '78 C.111 B.S. L.800 J.D. [Fish&R.] (See Pat. Sect.)
*PRACTICE AREAS: Intellectual Property; Copyrights; Patents; Trademarks; Trade Secrets.
Larkin, H. Robert '24 '49 C&L.910 J.D.
(adm. in MO; not adm. in CA) 4225 Executive Sq.
**Laurenson, Robert C.** .........'53 '87 C.453 S.B. L.273 J.D. [Lyon&L.] (See Pat. Sect.)
*PRACTICE AREAS: Litigation; Patent, Trademark, Copyright; Intellectual Property.
**Lautanen, W. Alan**, (AV) ..............'53 '80 C.381 B.B.A. L.228 J.D. [Lautanen&S.]
*PRACTICE AREAS: State and Local Tax Controversies (50%, 16); Federal Tax Controversies (50%, 16).

**Lautanen & Stanley, A Professional Law Corporation, (AV)**
**4225 Executive Square, Suite 525, 92037**
**Telephone: 619-554-1091 FAX: 619-554-1093**
**Email: stanley0@counsel.com**
**W. Alan Lautanen; Kimberly S. Stanley.**
**Federal, State and Local Tax Law, Administrative Tax Appeals and Tax Litigation.**
*See Professional Biographies, LA JOLLA, CALIFORNIA*

**Learn, June Marie** ..........'37 '88 C.112 Ph.D. L.426 J.D. [Ⓐ Fish&R.] (See Pat. Sect.)
*PRACTICE AREAS: Intellectual Property; Patents.
Leaverton, David G. .....................'37 '66 C.763 A.B. L.1066 LL.B. 7730 Herschel
Lee, S. Tamara .......................'48 '78 C.446 B.A. L.61 J.D. Salk Institute, The
Leigh, Lawrence S., (BV) ......'44 '70 C.763 B.A. L.1049 J.D. 4180 La Jolla Village Dr.
Levin, Richard L. '46 '71 C.347 B.A. L.893 J.D.
(adm. in IN; not adm. in CA) Pres., Blue Book Publishers, Inc.

CAA152P

Lewis, Bernard L., (AV) ..... '31 '57 C.112 A.B. L.1068 J.D. 6305 El Camino Del Teatro
**Lewis, Donald G.**, (AV) '47 '80 C.112 B.S. L.809 J.D.
Assoc. Pat. Coun., The Scripps Resch. Instit. (Pat.)
**Lithgow, Timothy J.** ........ '62 '91 C.999 B.A. L.1066 J.D. [Lyon&L.] (See Pat. Sect.)
*PRACTICE AREAS: Patent Law; Trademark Law; Intellectual Property.
Livett, Richard K. ........................ '33 '66 C.112 B.S. L.1049 J.D. P.O. Box 1800
**Logan, April C.** '52 '85 C.58 B.S. L.862 J.D.
Assoc. Pat. Coun., The Scripps Resch. Instit. (Pat.)
Low, Cynthia Hom ............ '51 '76 C.763 B.A. L.1066 J.D. 11085 N. Torrey Pines Rd.
Lowrie, James S. ................................'09 '35 L.494 LL.B. 7256 Dunemere Dr.‡
Lubin, Carol J., (BV) ................... '— '80 C.477 B.A. L.1049 J.D. 1205 Prospect St.

**Luce, Forward, Hamilton & Scripps LLP, (AV)**
**A Partnership including Professional Corporations**
**La Jolla Golden Triangle, 4275 Executive Square, Suite 800, 92037⊙**
**Telephone: 619-535-2639 Fax: 619-453-2812**
**URL: http://www.luce.com**
**Members of Firm: Jack G. Charney; Robert J. Durham, Jr.; Frederick R. Vandeveer; Mary F. Gillick; Daniel N. Riesenberg. Associates: Carol K. Kao; Philip J. Sullivan.**
**General Civil Practice and Litigation in all State and Federal Courts. Antitrust, Banking, Bankruptcy, Business, Commercial, Copyright, Corporate Finance, Corporations, Energy and Resource, Environmental, Estate Planning, Family, Fidelity and Surety, First Amendment, Foreign Investment, Health Care Organizations, Immigration and Naturalization, Insurance and Reinsurance, Intellectual Property, International Financial Transactions, Labor, Land Use, Mergers and Acquisitions, Municipal Finance, Partnership, Patent, Pension and Profit-Sharing, Probate, Probate Litigation, Product Liability and Warranty, Professional Responsibility, Public Utility, Real Property, Securities, Taxation, Trademark, Trust and Venture Financing Law, Water Law.**
**San Diego, California Office: 600 West Broadway, Suite 2600, 92101. Telephone: 619-236-1414. Fax: 619-232-8311.**
**Los Angeles, California Office: 777 South Figueroa, Suite 3600, 90017. Telephone: 213-892-4992. Fax: 213-892-7731.**
**San Francisco, California Office: 100 Bush Street, 20th Floor, 94104. Telephone: 415-395-7900. Fax: 415-395-7949.**
**New York, N.Y. Office: Citicorp Center, 153 East 53rd Street, 26th Floor, 10022. Telephone: 212-754-1414. Fax: 212-644-9727.**
**Chicago, Illinois Office: 180 North La Salle Street, Suite 1125, 60601. Telephone: 312-641-0580. Fax: 312-641-0380.**
*See Professional Biographies, LA JOLLA, CALIFORNIA*

**Lyon & Lyon LLP, (AV)**
**A Limited Liability Partnership Including Professional Corporations**
**Suite 660, 4250 Executive Square, 92037⊙**
**Telephone: 619-552-8400 FAX: 619-552-0159**
**Email: lyon@lyonlyon.com URL: http://www.lyonlyon.com**
**Resident Partners: Douglas E. Olson (A Professional Corporation); John M. Benassi; Mary S. Consalvi; Robert C. Laurenson. Resident Associates: Richard Warburg; Wayne B. Brown; Jessica R. Wolff; Sheldon O. Heber; Jeffrey William Guise; Charles S. Berkman; Sheryl Rubinstein Silverstein; Anthony C. Chen; Clarke W. Neumann, Jr.; Vicki Gee Norton; Timothy J. Lithgow; Gary H. Silverstein; Amy Stark Hellenkamp; William J. Kolegraff; Jonathan Hallman; Howard N. Wisnia. Resident Of Counsel: Bradford J. Duft; Suzanne L. Biggs; F.T. Alexandra Mahaney; Stephen S. Korniczky.**
**Intellectual Property Law including Patent, Trademark, Copyright, Trade Regulation, Unfair Competition and Antitrust Law. Litigation.**
**Los Angeles, California Office: First Interstate World Center, 47th Floor, 633 West Fifth Street. Telephone: 213-489-1600.**
**Costa Mesa, California Office: Suite 1200, 3200 Park Center Drive. Telephone: 714-751-6606.**
**San Jose, California Office: Suite 1150, 303 Almaden Boulevard. Telephone: 408-993-1555.**
*See Professional Biographies, LA JOLLA, CALIFORNIA*

Mabile, Marc D. ......................... '62 '89 C.800 B.A. L.1137 J.D. 4275 Executive Sq.
**Macaluso, Glenn T.** .................. '— '96 C.569 B.A. L.1049 J.D. [Blanchard,K.&F.]
Mackey, Linda C. ................ '41 '81 C.623 B.A. L.1137 J.D. 4180 La Jolla Village Dr.
Macpherson, Catherine R. '52 '78 C.610 B.A. L.851 J.D.
(adm. in OH; not adm. in CA) Pres., CR Macpherson & Assoc., Inc.
**Mahaney, F.T. Alexandra** '59 '86 C.103 B.S. L.1068 J.D.
[Lyon&L.] (See Pat. Sect.)
*PRACTICE AREAS: Intellectual Property Litigation; Patent, Trademark, Copyright, Unfair Competition, Antitrust.
**Marchese, Christopher S.** .....'64 '92 C.383 B.A. L.273 J.D. [Fish&R.] (See Pat. Sect.)
*PRACTICE AREAS: Intellectual Property; Patents; Copyrights; Trademarks; Trade Secrets.
Martin, Linda M. .............................. '54 '88 C.8 B.A. L.851 J.D. 7855 Ivanhoe Ave.
**Maurer, Charles D., Jr.**, (AV) ............................'46 '73 C.579 B.A. L.36 J.D. [Maurer]
*PRACTICE AREAS: Malpractice; Personal Injury; Insurance; Construction Defect; Business Litigation.

**Maurer Law Firm, (AV)**
**7825 Fay Avenue, Suite 200, 92037**
**Telephone: 619-456-5570 Fax: 619-551-8919**
**Charles D. Maurer, Jr.**
**Trial Practice, Professional Liability, Personal Injury, Products Liability, Insurance Law, Business Law and Sports Law.**
*See Professional Biographies, LA JOLLA, CALIFORNIA*

**Mauriello, Nancy L.** ..........................'58 '94 C.112 B.A. L.1137 J.D. [Fisher T.]
*PRACTICE AREAS: Securities; Corporate; Real Estate.
Mayer, Anne Wright '47 '86 C&L.1241 B.S., J.D.
Dir., Human Res., La Jolla Institute for Allergy & Immunology
McClue, Sidney G., Jr., (BV①) '43 '68 C.37 B.S. L.767 J.D.
(adm. in AZ; not adm. in CA) Pres., The Professional Advsry. Res. (PAR) Grp., Inc.

**McCue, Stephen V., (AV) '56 '83 C.112 B.A. L.1049 J.D.**
**Suite 240, 4180 La Jolla Village Drive, 92037-1471**
**Telephone: 619-455-5015 Fax: 619-455-7924**
***LANGUAGES: Spanish and French.**
***REPORTED CASES: Carver v. Teitsworth (1991), 1 Cal. App. 4th 845, 2 Cal. Rptr. 2d 446.**
**General Civil and Trial Practice. Real Estate and Business Law.**
*See Professional Biographies, LA JOLLA, CALIFORNIA*

McEvoy, John E., (BV) .........................'30 '67 C.178 B.S. L.284 J.D. State Prob. Ref.
McGowan, James P., Jr., (BV) ........'37 '64 C.763 A.B. L.800 LL.B. 7911 Herschel Ave.
**McKellogg, R. Keith**, (AV) ..................'47 '73 C.1109 B.A. L.1049 J.D. [Circuit,M.K.&R.]
*PRACTICE AREAS: Civil Litigation; Real Estate Law; Bankruptcy Law; Corporate Law.
McPherson, Kathleen Z. ...................... '48 '80 C.1169 B.S. L.770 J.D. P.O. Box 851
Melville, Charles W., Jr. ................................'26 '81 L.1137 J.D. 6359 Via Cabrera
Merkin, Donald, (BV) .........'35 '74 C.608 B.A. L.1049 J.D. 1025 Prospect St., Suite 300
Miller, Edwin L., Jr., (AV) ........................'26 '58 C.197 B.A. L.1068 LL.B. Dist. Atty.‡
Miller, Stephen R. .............'50 '74 C&L.352 B.A., J.D. 4225 Executive Sq., Ste., 1600
Montgomery, Matthew .........................................'70 '96 1025 Prospect St., Suite 300
Moore, Bonnie L. ........................ '— '85 C.800 B.A. L.1068 J.D. 1200 Prospect St.
Moore, Erik S. ................................'67 '95 C.1042 B.S. L.1137 J.D. [Moore&M.]⊙
Moore, Peggy L. ............................'41 '80 C.645 B.S. L.1137 J.D. [Moore&M.]⊙
Moore, Randy ..................................'49 '75 C.112 B.A. L.623 J.D. [Moore,B.&B.]⊙
Moore, Brewer & Burbott, A Professional Corporation, (AV)
4180 La Jolla Village Dr. (⊙San Dimas, CA, Austin, TX)
Moore & Moore, A Prof. Corp, Law Offices of .......... 7848 Ivanhoe Ave. (⊙San Diego)
Morelli, Douglas A. ............................'49 '78 C.208 B.A. L.1049 J.D. 6399 Castejon Dr.
Mosley, Edmond '14 '39 C&L.145 B.A., J.D.
(adm. in IL; not adm. in CA) 6413 Caminito Aronimink‡

Mulvaney, Kahan & Barry, A Professional Corporation, (AV)
7911 Herschel (⊙San Diego, Los Angeles, Orange)
Murfey, George John, Law Offices of, (AV) '48 '73
C.1188 B.A. L.61 J.D. 4180 La Jolla Village Dr.
Myer, Elspeth H., Mrs. ..................'40 '80 C.028 B.A. L.61 J.D. 5758 Dolphin Place‡
Naugle, Page ....................'40 '78 C.228 B.A. L.1137 J.D. Pres., Retirement Benefits, Inc.
Nelson, William E., (AV) ... '26 '52 C.990 B.S. L.426 J.D. Chmn. of the Bd., Scripps Bk.
**Neumann, Clarke W., Jr.** ... '63 '93 C.645 B.S. L.426 J.D. [Lyon&L.] (See Pat. Sect.)
*PRACTICE AREAS: Intellectual Property.
Newberry, Paul, (BV) ...................................'28 '55 C&L.800 B.A., J.D. 7855 Ivanhoe
**Newburn, John L.**, (AV) ..................'28 '57 C&L.800 B.A., LL.B. [Ferguson,N.&W.]
**Newnham, M. Kathryn** ...................'63 '91 C.763 B.A. L.608 J.D. [Nugent&N.]⊙
*PRACTICE AREAS: Trusts and Estates.
**Newnham, Stephen L.**, (AV) ...............'34 '63 C.197 A.B. L.659 LL.B. [Nugent&N.]⊙
*PRACTICE AREAS: Trusts and Estates.
Nichting, Joseph J. ..........................'57 '81 C.190 B.S.B.A. L.352 J.D. 1299 Prospect St.
Nissenberg, David N., (AV) ............ '39 '64 C.103 A.B. L.472 LL.B. [Nissenberg&N.]
Nissenberg, Merel Grey, (BV) ............ '48 '74 C.112 A.B. L.472 J.D. [Nissenberg&N.]
Nissenberg & Nissenberg, (AV) ............................................... P.O. Box 2063
Norris, David B., (BV) ..........'60 '90 C.546 B.A. L.1049 J.D. 6713 Vista del Mar Ave.
**Norton, Vicki Gee** ..........................'60 '94 C.112 Ph.D. L.1068 J.D. [Lyon&L.]
*PRACTICE AREAS: Patent; Intellectual Property.
Novick, Walter E. ...................................'54 '79 C.802 A.B. L.1049 J.D. 7905 Lowry Terr.

**Nugent & Newnham, A Professional Corporation, (AV)**
**875 Prospect Street, Suite 305, 92037⊙**
**Telephone: 619-459-3821 Fax: 619-459-6358**
**Stephen L. Newnham (Certified Specialist, Estate Planning, Trust and Probate Law, The State Bar of California Board of Legal Specialization);—M. Kathryn Newnham.**
**General Civil Trial Practice. Negligence, Taxation, Corporation, Real Property, Trusts and Estates, Pension and Profit Sharing, Employee Benefits, Health Care Law, Employer-Employee Relations, and Appellate Law.**
**Representative Clients: Pacific Theatres Corp.; Anesthesia Service Medical Group, Inc.; Specialty Medical Clinic, Inc.; San Diego County Medical Society; Trevellyan Oldsmobile Co.**
**San Diego, California Office: Suite 2200, 1010 Second Avenue. Telephone: 619-236-1323. Fax: 619-238-0465.**
*See Professional Biographies, LA JOLLA, CALIFORNIA*

Odegaard, Douglas N., (BV①) '29 '58 C.494 B.A. L.1035 LL.B.
(adm. in MN; not adm. in CA) 8019 Paseo Del Ocaso
O'Donnell, J. Brian ........................................ '43 '69 C&L.1049 B.A., J.D. P.O. Box 341
Olmstead, Patrick J. ...............................'50 '75 C&L.436 B.A., J.D. 5666 La Jolla Blvd.
**Olson, Douglas E., (A Professional Corporation)**, (AV) '37 '65
C.966 B.S.Ch.E. L.273 LL.B. [Lyon&L.] (See Pat. Sect.)
*PRACTICE AREAS: Patent, Trademark, Unfair Competition; Intellectual Property.
Pabarcus, William N., (BV) .....................'47 '74 C.763 A.B. L.1049 J.D. P.O. Box 1147
Pantoni, Anthony F. ..............................'56 '81 C.645 B.S. L.477 J.D. 4225 Executive Sq.
**Pearl, Daniel** .......................................'65 '94 C.112 B.A. L.61 J.D. [Circuit,M.K.&R.]
*PRACTICE AREAS: General Civil Litigation; Real Estate; Business Litigation; Real Property Transactions.
Pecheles, Joseph D. ..............................'49 '89 C.575 B.S. L.763 J.D. 7825 Fay Ave.

**Pecora, Robert J., (BV) '54 '82 C.696 B.A. L.61 J.D.**
**Suite 550, 1200 Prospect Street, 92037**
**Telephone: 619-454-4014 Fax: 619-454-3548**
**Email: rjpecora@rplaw.alphapacnet.com**
**Personal Injury, Civil Litigation.**
**Reference: Wells Fargo Bank.**
*See Professional Biographies, LA JOLLA, CALIFORNIA*

**Pederson, Charles B.**, (AV) ............... '48 '77 C.112 B.A. L.1049 J.D. [Toothacre&P.]
**Perlman, Sheri Lynne** ........................'67 '96 C.763 B.S. L.999 J.D. [Circuit,M.K.&R.]
*PRACTICE AREAS: Estate Planning; Probate Law; Trust Law.
Peterson, Laurence E., (BV) ............ '34 '73 C.101 B.S. L.770 J.D. 4225 Executive Sq.
Pillsbury, Laurence L. .................'34 '65 C.309 A.B. L.1065 L.L.B. 7730 Herschel Ave.
Pirtle, Elmer B., Jr. ..............................'18 '55 C.112 B.S. L.464 LL.B. 1135 Skylark Dr.
Popov, Chris ..........................................'50 '79 C.1060 B.A. L.1137 J.D. 7746 Herschel Ave.
Potomac, L. Lawrence ........'49 '77 C.813 B.A. L.188 J.D. Pres., Financial Insight Corp.
Price, Sol, (AV) .......................................'16 '38 C&L.800 B.A., J.D. 7979 Ivanhoe Ave.
Ravin, William W., (AV) '47 '72 C.763 A.B. L.1068 J.D.
V.P. & Gen. Coun., Pixel, Inc.
Reed, John W., (AV) ...........................................'47 '72 C.813 B.A. L.1049 J.D. [J.W.Reed]
Reed, Paul Lewis, (BV) ...................'54 '79 C.813 B.A. L.1066 J.D. 533 Coast Blvd. S.
Reed, John W., Law Offices of, A Prof. Corp., (AV) ............7713 Fay Avenue, Suite D
**Riesenberg, Daniel N.**, (AV) '49 '79 C.103 A.B. L.276 J.D.
[Luce,F.H.&S.] (⊙La Jolla)
*PRACTICE AREAS: Employee Benefits; ERISA; Pension and Profit Sharing Plans; Employee Stock Ownership Plans; Deferred Compensation.
Ripley, Robert W., Jr. ...............................................'44 '72 First Affiliated Secs.
Ritner, George, (BV) .............................'28 '56 C.112 B.S. L.1068 J.D. [G.Ritner]
Ritner, George, P.C., (BV) ........................................................7769 Starlight
Robinson, John M. '17 '46 C&L.494 B.S., J.D.
(adm. in MN; not adm. in CA) 1310 Dellcrest Lane‡
Robinson, Robert .................'43 '72 C&L.976 B.A., LL.B. 4180 La Jolla Village Dr.
**Ross, Scott Hunter**, (AV) ..............'50 '79 C.988 B.A. L.1049 J.D. [Circuit,M.K.&R.]
*PRACTICE AREAS: Civil Litigation; Business Litigation; Employment Law; Family Law.
Rossman, Linda ............................................'47 '77 C.494 B.A. L.1137 J.D. [Fraser&R.]
Rushing, Cynthia G. ................'52 '78 C.813 B.A. L.1068 J.D. 5805 Beaumont Ave.‡
Russo, Joseph ...........................................'50 '76 C.426 B.A. L.1049 J.D. 4275 Executive Sq.

**Schorr, Steven '56 '83 C&L.309 A.B., J.D.**
**5398 La Jolla Mesa Drive, 92037-8038**
**Telephone: 619-454-2261 Fax: 619-459-7187**
***REPORTED CASES: People v. Ivans (1992), 2 Cal. App. 4th 1654, 4 Cal. Rptr. 2d 66; People v. Brown (1991) 234 Cal. App. 3d 918; 285 Cal. Rptr. 824; People v. McGee (1993) 15 Cal. App. 4th 107, 19 Cal. Rptr. 2d 12; People v. Maestas (1993) 20 Cal. App. 4th 1482.**
***PRACTICE AREAS: Appellate Litigation; Criminal Law.**
**Appellate Litigation, Criminal Appellate.**
*See Professional Biographies, LA JOLLA, CALIFORNIA*

Schrader, Phyllis G. '45 '86 C.228 B.A. L.326 J.D.
(adm. in TX; not adm. in CA) 6093 Abbotswood⊙
Schram, W. Neal, (BV) .............'48 '74 C.112 B.S. L.602 J.D. 2223 Ave. De La Playa
Shannahan, William P., (AV) ..............'34 '58 C.215 A.B. L.276 J.D. 1200 Prospect St.

**Shapiro & Miles**
**4180 La Jolla Village Drive, Suite 405, 92037⊙**
**Telephone: 619-546-9480 Fax: 619-546-9455**
**Associates: Monique M. Edep; Julia M. Dommel; Amy L. Shuss.**
**Bankruptcy, Evictions, Civil Litigation and Foreclosure.**
**Santa Ana, California Office: 5 Hutton Centre Drive, Suite 1050. Telephone: 714-432-9000. Fax: 714-432-8125; 432-1221.**
**Walnut Creek, California Office: 2033 North Main Street, Suite 550. Telephone: 510-933-3700. Fax: 510-933-3425; 933-3784.**

(This Listing Continued)

CALIFORNIA—LA JOLLA MARTINDALE-HUBBELL LAW DIRECTORY 1997

**Shapiro & Miles (Continued)**

**Las Vegas, Nevada Office: 2030 East Flamingo Road, Suite 145. Telephone: 702-369-5960. Fax: 702-369-4955.**

**Shuss, Amy L.** ........ '64 '91 C.112 B.A. L.800 J.D. [A Shapiro&M.]
*PRACTICE AREAS: Bankruptcy-Creditors; Real Property Foreclosure; Unlawful Detainers.
Siegan, Bernard H. '24 '50 C.119 L.145 J.D.
(adm. in IL; not adm. in CA) 6005 Camino de la Costa St.‡
**Silverstein, Gary H.** ........ '55 '96 C.165 A.B. L.1049 J.D. [A Lyon&L.] (See Pat. Sect.)
*PRACTICE AREAS: Intellectual Property.
**Silverstein, Sheryl Rubinstein** .............. '61 '93 C.112 A.B. L.800 J.D. [A Lyon&L.]
*LANGUAGES: French.
*PRACTICE AREAS: Patent; Unfair Competition; Antitrust; Intellectual Property.
Simpson, Robert P., (AV) ...... '18 '50 C.877 B.S. L.813 J.D. 7881 Caminito El Rosario‡
Smallwood, Tim E. ............. '36 '69 C.800 B.S. L.426 J.D. 986 Muerlands Vista Way
**Stanley, Kimberly S.**, (AV) ................ '56 '85 C.101 B.S. L.273 J.D. [Lautanen&S.]
*PRACTICE AREAS: Federal Tax Controversies (75%, 11); State Tax Controversies (25%, 4).
Statsky, William P. '43 '68 C&L.93 B.A., J.D.
(adm. in NY; not adm. in CA) 8268 Prestwick Dr.‡
Stone, Susan W. ...... '58 '85 C.813 B.A. L.763 J.D. CEO & Corp. Coun., Blue Tech Inc.
Stubblefield, Dennis A. ............ '50 '76 C.112 A.B. L.800 J.D. 4180 La Jolla Village Dr.
Sullivan, J. Stacey, (AV) ............ '26 '55 C.178 B.S. L.597 J.D. 430 Westbourne St.‡
**Sullivan, Philip J.** ........ '63 '88 C.776 B.S. L.884 J.D. [A Luce,F.H.&S.] (©San Diego)
*PRACTICE AREAS: Estate Planning.
Sullivan, McDonald, Bramley & Brody, A Professional Corporation, (AV)
9404 Genesee Avenue, Suite 320 (©San Diego, CA)
Tarpin, G. Mark .............................................. '55 '84 L.1137 J.D. 1020 Prospect St.
**Taylor, Stacy L.** ................ '59 '86 C.1074 B.S. L.61 J.D. [A Fish&R.] (See Pat. Sect.)
*PRACTICE AREAS: Intellectual Property; Litigation; Trademarks; Copyrights.
**Teaff, Robert F.**, (AV) .................... '43 '68 C.1150 B.A. L.93 J.D. [Thomas&T.]
*PRACTICE AREAS: Real Estate; Trusts and Estates; Contracts; Sports Law; Business Law.
**Thomas, John H.**, (AV) .................... '34 '64 C&L.893 B.A., LL.B. [Thomas&T.]
*PRACTICE AREAS: Negligence; Real Estate; Trusts and Estates; Collections; Family Law.

**Thomas & Teaff, (AV)**
**Suite 2212, 8950 Villa La Jolla Drive, 92037**
**Telephone: 619-457-2330; 457-2470 Telecopier: 619-452-9484**
**Members of Firm: John H. Thomas; Robert F. Teaff.**
**General Civil and Trial Practice. Estates, Business, Real Property, Negligence, Enforcement of Judgments, Family, Entertainment and Sports Law.**
**References: Union Bank (La Jolla Branch); First Interstate Bank (La Jolla Branch); City National Bank (La Jolla Branch).**
*See Professional Biographies, LA JOLLA, CALIFORNIA*

**Thurber, Marshall** ................................ '43 '70 C.867 A.B. L.1065 J.D. [C Fisher T.]
*PRACTICE AREAS: Business; Management Practices.
Todd, Marilyn Ressler ................ '40 '87 C.585 B.S. L.1137 J.D. 4225 Executive Sq.
**Toothacre, Rod M.**, (BV) ..................... '35 '61 C&L.352 B.S., J.D. [Toothacre&P.]
**Toothacre, Scott H.** ........................ '62 '90 C.763 B.A. L.1137 J.D. [Toothacre&P.]

**Toothacre & Pederson, (AV)**
**4225 Executive Square, Suite 260, 92037**
**Telephone: 619-457-4240 Telecopier: 619-457-0303**
**Rod M. Toothacre; Charles B. Pederson; Scott H. Toothacre.**
**General Civil and Trial Practice. Real Estate, Corporation, Business, Domestic Relations, Probate, Personal Injury, Wrongful Termination, and Dental Malpractice Law.**
*See Professional Biographies, LA JOLLA, CALIFORNIA*

Torres, Moby ................................ '71 '95 C.061 L.1026 J.D. 7825 Fay Ave.
Tremblay, Donald P., (BV) ...... '51 '78 C.184 B.S. L.1137 J.D. 4180 La Jolla Village Dr.
**Tremblay, Maurile C.**, (AV) ............ '44 '69 C.184 B.A. L.276 J.D. [M.C.Tremblay]
*REPORTED CASES: La Jolla Mesa Vista Improvement Association v. La Jolla Mesa Vista Homeowners Association, 220 Cal. App. 3d 1187 (1990).
*PRACTICE AREAS: Civil Litigation; Title Insurance Law; Real Estate Law.

**Tremblay, Maurile C., A Prof. Corp., Law Offices of, (AV)** [B]
**4180 La Jolla Village Drive, Suite 210, 92037**
**Telephone: 619-558-3030 FAX: 619-558-2502**
**Maurile C. Tremblay; Mark D. Estle.**
**General Civil, Trial and Appellate Practice. Title Insurance Defense, Business and Securities Litigation, Insurance, Real Estate, Commercial and Creditor Rights Law.**
*See Professional Biographies, LA JOLLA, CALIFORNIA*

Tschirn, Darryl J., (BV⊕) '40 '64 C&L.425 B.B.A., LL.B.
(adm. in LA; not adm. in CA) 7825 Fay Ave.
Turney, Thomas A., (CV) ............ '25 '68 C.766 A.B. L.61 J.D. 8713 Caminito Abrazo
Valenzuela, Humberto A. '41 '67 C&L.37 B.S., J.D.
(adm. in AZ; not adm. in CA) 4150 Regents Park Rd.‡
**Vandeveer, Frederick R.**, (AV) '51 '80
C.878 B.A. L.101 J.D. [Luce,F.H.&S.] (©San Diego)
*PRACTICE AREAS: Estate Planning; Estate Administration; Trust Administration; Charitable Giving; Charitable Trusts and Foundations.
Verbeck, Bruno J., (AV) ...... '13 '42 C.339 B.S. L.424 J.D. 6502 Avenida Manana (Pat.)‡
Vesco, Paul A., Jr. ................ '41 '68 C.1049 B.B.A. L.61 J.D. 6833 Avenioa Andorra
Vibbard, Mark .............................. '58 '95 L.284 J.D. 8555 Ruette Monte Carlo
Wagner, Michael J. ...................... '46 '78 C.112 B.S. L.1137 J.D. P.O. Box 2447

**Walt, Christopher J. '50 '79 C.813 B.A. L.1066 J.D.**
**2223 Avenida De La Playa, Suite 100, 92037**
**Telephone: 619-459-5940 Fax: 619-459-7210**
***PRACTICE AREAS: General Business Law; Real Estate; Corporate Law; Securities Law; Mergers and Acquisitions Law.**
**General Business Law, Real Estate Law, Corporate Law, Securities Law, Mergers and Acquisitions Law.**
*See Professional Biographies, LA JOLLA, CALIFORNIA*

**Warburg, Richard** ......... '57 '90 C.061 B.Sc. L.818 J.D. [A Lyon&L.] (See Pat. Sect.)
*PRACTICE AREAS: Patent, Trademark, Copyright; Intellectual Property.
**Wenskay, Donald L.** .......... '54 '88 C.477 B.S. L.912 J.D. [A Fish&R.] (See Pat. Sect.)
*PRACTICE AREAS: Patent; Trademark; Intellectual Property.
Wenthur, Cris John ........................ '57 '82 C.326 B.A. L.1137 J.D. [Wenthur&C.]
Wenthur & Chachas ............................................. 4180 La Jolla Village Dr.
**Weston, David**, (AV) ................ '48 '77 C.763 A.B. L.1065 J.D. [Ferguson,N.&W.]
*PRACTICE AREAS: Estate Planning; Trust Law; Probate.
**Wetherell, John R., Jr.** '48 '85 C.260 B.S.Chem. L.776 J.D.
(adm. in DC; not adm. in CA; See Pat. Sect.) [Fish&R.]
*PRACTICE AREAS: Intellectual Property; Patents; Trade Secrets; Unfair Trade Practices.
**Whelan, Ellen H.**, (AV) '56 '84 C.112 B.A. L.813 J.D.
[Gray C.W.&F.] (©San Diego/Golden Triangle)
*PRACTICE AREAS: Trusts Law; Estates Law.
Whitney, John H., (AV) ............ '27 '56 C.668 A.B. L.1066 LL.B. 7301 Rue Michael‡
Whittemore, Ridgway, (P.C.), (BV) ...... '42 '66 C.112 B.A. L.1066 LL.B. 7752 Fay Ave.
Wildman, Richard C., Jr., (CV) '44 '77
C.174 B.A. L.1137 J.D. 7817 Ivanhoe Ave., Ste. 300
Wiles, Gary H., (BV) ...................... '32 '62 C.112 L.1049 LL.B. 1205 Prospect St.‡

Wilhelm, William G. ........................ '52 '78 C.1049 B.A. L.61 J.D. P.O. Box 1885
Wilson, Bonnie J. ................................. '— '89 C.112 B.A. L.1137 J.D. 2235 Bahia Dr.‡
**Wing, Phillip C.** ........................ '57 '85 C.101 B.S. L.1049 J.D. [Circuit,M.K.&R.]
*LANGUAGES: Spanish.
*PRACTICE AREAS: Civil Litigation; Business Litigation; Employment Law; Insurance Law; Real Estate Law.
**Wisnia, Howard N.** ......... '69 '96 C&L.273 B.S.E.E., J.D. [A Lyon&L.] (See Pat. Sect.)
*PRACTICE AREAS: Intellectual Property.
Wolf, Daniel H. '49 '86 C.685 B.A. L.309 J.D.
(adm. in MA; not adm. in CA) Univ. of Calif.
**Wolff, Jessica R.** ........... '64 '92 C.104 A.B. L.1068 J.D. [A Lyon&L.] (See Pat. Sect.)
*PRACTICE AREAS: Patent, Trademark, Copyright, Unfair Competition, Trade Secret; Intellectual Property.
Wolk, I. Louis ........................ '07 '33 C.494 B.S. L.276 J.D. 939 Coast Blvd. (Pat.)‡
Yanke, Gian-Carlo M. '57 '83 C.763 B.A. L.61 J.D.
Legal Dept., Pacific Intercultural Exchange, Inc.
Zimmerman, James Michael '58 '88
C.112 B.A. L.1049 J.D. 1320 Columbia St. (©Los Angeles)
**Zobell, Karl**, (AV) ........................ '32 '59 C.178 A.B. L.813 J.D. [Gray C.W.&F.]
*PRACTICE AREAS: Real Estate Transactions; Land Use Law; Trusts Law; Estates Law.

## LAKE ARROWHEAD, 2,682, *San Bernardino Co.*

Ehmann, Carl G. ........... '53 '79 C.605 B.S. L.1137 J.D. 28200 Hwy. 189, Bldg. F-240
Keating, John F. ............................ '39 '65 C.800 B.S. L.1065 J.D. P.O. Box 606
Rhoads, Donald Perry, (BV) ................ '44 '72 C.112 B.A. L.426 J.D. [D.P.Rhoads]
Rhoads, Donald Perry, A Professional Corporation, (BV) ........... 675 Grass Valley Rd.
Shore, Stephen B., (BV) ........................ '43 '69 C&L.800 B.S., J.D. 28200 Hwy. 189

## LAKE ELSINORE, 18,285, *Riverside Co.*

Jenkins, Richard E. ................................................... '40 '76 [Jenkins&O.]
Jenkins & O'Neil ................................................ 22860 Vista Del Agua
Lounsbery, Virgil E. ............................ '27 '75 L.1137 31915 Mission Trail
Nelson, Nancy K. ................ '44 '75 C.112 B.A. L.1148 J.D. 31915 Mission Trail
Neumann, Richard E. .............. '42 '77 C.112 B.A. L.1137 J.D. 31915 Mission Trail
O'Neil-Jenkins, Merilou P. .............. '43 '79 C.1042 B.A. L.1137 J.D. [Jenkins&O.]

## LAKE FOREST, —, *Orange Co.*

Anderson, James F. ........................ '58 '83 C.1042 B.S. L.1066 J.D. [McFarlin&A.]
Aynes, Patricia C. ............ '51 '82 C.1042 B.A. L.1137 J.D. 21927 Yellowstone Lane
Ballard, Ronald M. ................ '58 '83 C.154 B.A. L.1068 J.D. 22942 El Toro Rd.
Bartlett, Michael J. ...................... '41 '74 C.800 B.A. L.990 J.D. 22942 El Toro Rd.
**Beall, Kelly A.** ................................ '64 '92 C.112 B.A. L.464 J.D. [A Roup,L.&J.]
Berends, E. Robert, Jr. ................ '53 '89 C.1077 B.S. L.1137 J.D. 25132 Carolwood
Breaux, Melvin D. ...................... '48 '78 C.999 B.S.L. L.1137 J.D. 23331 Gondor Dr.
Coombs, Richard H., Jr., (BV) '49 '76
C.1109 B.A. L.1137 J.D. Coun., Attys. Equity Natl. Corp.
Cornelius, Robert S. ................ '59 '86 C.1109 B.A. L.1137 J.D. 23561 El Toro Rd.
DePol, Bruce F. ........................ '56 '87 C.884 B.S. L.61 J.D. 23695 Birtcher Dr.
**Gyorkos, John W.**, (BV) .................... '43 '73 C&L.1137 B.S., J.D. [Gyorkos&F.]
*PRACTICE AREAS: Business and Tort Litigation.

**Gyorkos & Fenton, A Law Corporation, (BV)**
**Lake Forest Plaza, 23072 Lake Center Drive Suite 104, 92630**
**Telephone: 714-837-7750 Fax: 714-837-6242**
**Fred C. Fenton (1908-1987); John W. Gyorkos;—David L. Rukstalis; Clayton B. Huntington.**
**General Civil and Trial Practice. Insurance, Business, Corporate and Family Law. Environmental and Toxic Substance Law.**
*See Professional Biographies, LAKE FOREST, CALIFORNIA*

**Huntington, Clayton B.** ................ '66 '95 C.112 B.S. L.1137 J.D. [A Gyorkos&F.]
*PRACTICE AREAS: Labor Law; Tort Litigation; Business and Tax Litigation; Family Law; General Litigation.
Jacobs, R. M. "Mac", (BV) .................... '45 '71 C.112 A.B. L.426 J.D. [Jacobs&J.]
Jacobs, Robert H., (AV) ...................... '24 '51 C.112 B.S. L.800 J.D. [Jacobs&J.]
Jacobs & Jacobs, A Professional Law Corporation, (AV) ............ 22942 El Toro Road
Johnson, James D. ........................ '38 '87 C.37 B.S. L.1137 J.D. 23591 El Toro Rd.
**Johnson, Michael W.** ........................ '65 '90 C.740 B.S. L.1049 J.D. [Roup,L.&J.]
Lee, David J. .......................... '33 '72 C.426 A.B. L.809 J.D. 23072 Lake Ctr. Dr.
Lloyd, Edward W. ................ '52 '80 C.446 B.A. L.1137 J.D. 25982 McKenna Ct.
**Loomis-Therrien, Tary C.** ................ '61 '88 C.1109 B.A. L.1137 J.D. [Roup,L.&J.]
McFarlin, George W. ................ '43 '78 C.813 B.S. L.1137 J.D. [McFarlin&A.]
McFarlin & Anderson ............................................ 23101 Lake Center Dr.
Moshenko, Terry M., (BV) ...... '42 '67 C.1042 B.A. L.1068 J.D. [Moshenko,D.W.T.&P.]
Moshenko, DePol, Winchel, Travieso & Pickelsimer, A P.L.C., (BV) ... 23695 Birtcher Dr.
Preston, Barry L. ...................... '64 '92 C.112 B.A. L.1137 J.D. 23695 Birtcher Dr.
Recchia, Peter L. ................................ '— '77 C.800 B.A. L.809 J.D. P.O. Box 206
**Roup, Ronald D.** ........................ '48 '80 C.923 B.S.A.E. L.1137 J.D. [Roup,L.&J.]

**Roup, Loomis & Johnson LLP**
**Suite 310, 23101 Lake Center Drive, 92630-6819**
**Telephone: 714-472-2377**
**Ronald D. Roup; Tary C. Loomis-Therrien; Michael W. Johnson;—Kelly A. Beall.**
**Real Estate, Civil Litigation and Bankruptcy.**
*See Professional Biographies, LAKE FOREST, CALIFORNIA*

**Rukstalis, David L.** ................ '56 '95 C.1241 B.B.A. L.426 J.D. [A Gyorkos&F.]
*PRACTICE AREAS: Contracts; Business Law; Family Law; Environmental Law; Toxic Substances Law.
Smith, Mark A. ........................ '45 '72 C&L.1137 B.S., J.D. 22956 El Toro Rd.
Tudor, Gary A. .................. '35 '67 C.800 B.A. L.809 LL.B. 20864 Serrano Creek
Werlhof, Bruce A. .................. '22 '49 C.112 L.1065 LL.B. 24001 Muirlands Blvd.
Williams, Wayne K. .................. '44 '74 C.781 B.A. L.809 J.D. 25216 Grovewood
Winchell, Sterling Scott ................ '56 '90 C.49 B.S. L.1137 J.D. 23695 Birtcher Dr.
Wright, Mark A. .................. '55 '80 C&L.1240 B.S., J.D. 23101 Lake Center Dr.
Young, Richard E. .................. '47 '74 C.112 B.A. L.990 J.D. 23161 Lake Ctr. Dr.

## LAKE HUGHES, —, *Los Angeles Co.*

(Part of the incorporated City of Los Angeles)

Johnson, Robert L. ............................ '28 '71 L.809 J.D. Ste. 2, 18257 Devere Ct.‡
Tyler, Bruce H. .................. '29 '62 C.813 B.S. L.800 LL.B. 2520 Pine Canyon Rd.

## LAKE ISABELLA, —, *Kern Co.*

Borsari, J. Thomas .................. '43 '74 C.1333 B.S. L.809 J.D. 3700 Golden Spur
Dean, John T. .......................... '46 '75 C.940 B.A. L.1137 J.D. P.O. Box X

## LAKEPORT, * 4,390, *Lake Co.*

Alvord, Edward L. ........................ '50 '79 C.766 B.S. L.999 J.D. [Alvord&E.]
Alvord & Ewing .............................................................. 995 S. Main St.
Anderson, Donald A. .............. '52 '89 C.768 B.S. L.1227 J.D. 485 No. Main St.
Bridges, Robert L. .............. '51 '76 C.112 A.B. L.767 J.D. Sr. Dep. Co. Coun.

**Brigham & Gaustad**
(See Ukiah)

Bronson, Edward D., Jr., (AV) ...'26 '53 C.770 L.1065 J.D. 55 1st St.
Brookes, Steven J., (CV) ...'57 '82 C.1169 B.A. L.284 J.D. City Atty.
Bruchler, Bruce B., (AV) ...'20 '51 C&L.813 A.B., LL.B. [Crump,B.&L.]
Campbell, Joyce Ann ...'48 '79 L.1221 J.D. Dist. Atty. Off.
Clark, Stephen E., (AV) ...'43 '69 C.976 B.A. L.309 J.D. 149 N. Main St.
Collins, Bruce D. ...'49 '80 C.330 B.A. L.1049 J.D. Sr. Dep. Dist. Atty.
Crawford, Phil N., (BV) ...'24 '53 C.112 A.B. L.309 LL.B. 160 5th St.
Crone, Robert L., Jr. ...'44 '72 C.37 B.A. L.1067 J.D. Supr. Ct. J.
Crump, Fredric S., (AV) ...'15 '47 C.112 L.765 J.D. [Crump,B.&L.]
Crump, Bruchler & La Velle, (AV) ...1175 N. Main St.
Druckman, Rebecca Carol ...'60 '89 C.426 B.A. L.464 J.D. Dep. Dist. Atty.
Drummond, John A. ...'44 '70 C.112 B.A. L.426 J.D. Lake Co. Off. of Education
Ewing, T. Michael ...'48 '81 C.813 B.S. L.1067 J.D. [Alvord&E.]
Feeney, William L. ...'32 '75 C.585 B.A. L.464 J.D. 304 N. Main, S.E.
Gibson, George W. ...'54 '80 C&L.1137 B.S.L., J.D. 199 N. Main St.
Golden, John J. ...'25 '51 C.623 B.A. L.1066 J.D. Supr. Ct. J.
Hartford, Donald M., Jr., (CV) ...'51 '82 C.454 B.A. L.770 J.D. 175 Park St.
Hauptman, Mitchell Z. ...'49 '78 C.999 B.A. L.1230 J.D. 333 Armstrong St.
Herrick, David W. ...'48 '75 C.169 B.A. L.1065 J.D. 485 N. Main St.
Kranz, William C. ...'44 '69 C.285 B.A. L.1065 J.D. 160 5th St.
Krones, Susan ...'59 '84 C.112 B.A. L.1065 J.D. Dist. Atty.★
La Velle, Edward H., III ...'55 '83 C.1060 B.A. L.464 J.D. [Crump,B.&L.]
Lunas, Michael S. ...'58 '82 C&L.1137 B.S.L., J.D. 306 N. Main St.
Magnuson, Richard H., Jr. ...'59 '86 C.636 B.S. L.464 J.D. 485 N. Main St.
Major, Tibor E. ...'47 '74 C.911 B.A. L.1066 J.D. 160 5th St.
Mann, Authur H. ...'47 '74 C.1078 B.A. L.1049 J.D. Mun. Ct. J.
Munter, Gavan R. ...'61 '88 C.154 B.A. L.1137 J.D. [Ⓐ Alvord&E.]
Pinto, Robert H. ...'38 '66 C.1074 B.S. L.1065 J.D. P.O. Box 775

**Rawles, Hinkle, Carter, Behnke & Oglesby**
(See Ukiah)

Reeves, Cameron L. ...'41 '74 C.763 B.A. L.464 J.D. Co. Coun.
Shaw, Patricia ...'51 '87 C&L.1137 B.S., J.D. [Ⓐ Alvord&E.]
Underwood, Debra M. ...'56 '82 C.112 B.A. L.1067 J.D. Senior Law Project, Inc.
Wiley, Robert W., (BV) ...'33 '75 C&L.1190 B.S.L., LL.B. Pub. Def.
Windrem, Peter F., (BV) ...'45 '69 C.169 B.A. L.893 LL.B. 401 N. Main
Wright, Gesford P. ...'15 '40 C.112 B.A. L.1066 LL.B. 450 Lakeport Blvd.‡

## LAKE SAN MARCOS, —, *San Diego Co.*

Coleman, Ray J. ...'06 '30 C&L.813 A.B., J.D. 1629 La Verde Dr.‡
Davis, DeMar W. ...'17 '51 C.112 B.A. L.800 J.D. 1306 San Julian Ln.‡
Kelly, Dennis P. ...'43 '68 C.373 B.A. L.477 J.D. 11325 San Marino Dr.
McAllister, Ray E. ...'15 '39 C&L.800 A.B., LL.B. 1176 San Pablo Dr.
Peterson, Clinton L. ...'43 '76 C.1109 B.A. L.765 J.D. 1132 San Marino Dr.
Powell, William H. ...'07 '32 C&L.378 LL.B. 1423 La Loma Dr.‡
Richmond, Delmas R., (AV) ...'07 '32 C&L.629 B.S., J.D. 1215 San Julian Pl.‡

## LAKESIDE, 11,991, *San Diego Co.*

Goodman, B. Kenneth ...'11 '35 C.112 A.B. L.1066 J.D. 13143 Hahanna Rd.‡
Graus, A. David ...'49 '77 C.705 A.B. L.054 LL.B. Eyecare U.S.A. of Calif.
Keller, Philip A. ...'48 '77 C.813 B.A. L.1137 J.D. 8665 Winter Gardens Blvd.
Mc Lean, Raymond L. ...'46 '80 L.1137 J.D. 12308 Gay Rio Dr.
Sullivan, Mary M. ...'33 '71 C.741 A.B. L.1049 J.D. Legal Aid Soc.
Walton, Victor B. ...'26 '53 C.763 B.S. L.426 LL.B. 9742 Los Coches‡

## LAKEWOOD, 73,557, *Los Angeles Co.*

Aid, Kenneth, (BV) ...'35 '64 C.112 A.B. L.1066 J.D. 12628 Lemming St.
Ainbinder, Michael D., (BV) ...'47 '73 C.1042 B.A. L.809 J.D. 4010 Watson Plaza Dr.
Antolinez, Joseph Henry '67 '95 C.259 L.990
(adm. in FL; not adm. in CA) P.O. Box 280287
Biggerstaff, Ralph A. ...'22 '51 C.999 L.809 LL.B. 4432 Fairway Dr.‡
Chapman, William N. ...'45 '76 C.112 B.A. L.426 J.D. 4239 Knoxville Ave.
Cope, H. Brooks ...'33 '74 C.112 L.1001 LL.B. 5230 N. Clark Ave.
Deatherage, Marion, (BV) ...'57 '84 C.174 B.S. L.809 J.D. 4010 Watson Plz. Dr.

**Fitzpatrick, Josephine A., (AV) '42 '79 L.1137 J.D.**
**4909 Lakewood Boulevard, Suite 303, 90712**
**Telephone: 310-630-1616 FAX: 310-360-2026**
**(Certified Specialist, Family Law, The State Bar of California Board of Legal Specialization).**
**Family, Adoption and Probate Law.**
*See Professional Biographies, LAKEWOOD, CALIFORNIA*

Friedman, Alva M. ...'30 '83 L.1001 J.D. 4909 Lakewood Blvd.
Hansen, Steven W. ...'61 '86 C.101 B.S. L.990 J.D. 5913 Lorelei Ave.
Hernandez, Enrique A. ...'46 '77 C&L.1137 B.S.L., J.D. 12536 Walcroft St.
Jones, Clyde A. ...'13 '53 L.1001 LL.B. 5838 Pennswood Ave.
Lyons, Charles J., Jr. ...'29 '53 C&L.800 B.S., LL.B. 3752 Parkview Dr.‡
Mendlovitz, Sidney, (BV) ...'29 '66 C.800 L.1001 LL.B. 4010 Watson Plaza Dr.
Norton, A. Jay, (BV) ...'47 '75 C.1109 B.A. L.426 J.D. 4010 Watson Plaza Dr.
Reino, Donald J. ...'53 '80 C.112 B.A. L.1148 J.D. 4010 Watson Plaza Dr.
Roche, Kathleen M. ...'47 '88 C.398 B.S. L.426 J.D. 3650 E. South St.
Sederholm, Carl R. ...'28 '57 C.101 B.S. L.878 J.D. 3215 Warwood Rd.‡
Shahon, Leon J. ...'44 '69 C.112 B.A. L.426 J.D. 5529 Del Amo Blvd.
Sullivan, Ted, (BV) ...'21 '51 C&L.800 B.S., J.D. 5505 Carson St.
Swick, James E. ...'49 '74 C.1042 B.A. L.809 J.D. 5505 Carson St.
Todd, John Sanford, A Professional Corporation, (AV) '19 '49
C&L.800 B.A., J.D. 4909 Lakewood Blvd.

## LA MESA, 52,931, *San Diego Co.*

Anderson, Clayton M., (AV) ...'48 '76 [Anderson&K.]
Anderson & Kriger, (AV) ...8220 University Avenue, 2nd Fl.
Armento, Donald F. ...'56 '82 C.299 B.A. L.436 J.D. 8765 Fletcher Pkwy., 3rd Fl.
Bailey, Richard ...'39 '81 C.1290 B.A. L.464 J.D. 7777 Alvarado Rd.
Bard, Norman R., (BV) ...'41 '66 C.112 B.A. L.1068 LL.B. 9701 Sierra Vista Ave.
Beard, J. William ...'20 '50 C.642 L.809 J.D. 7546 El Paso St.‡

**Bender, Clarence, (BV) '32 '64 C&L.378 B.S., LL.B.**
**9001 Grossmont Boulevard, 91941-4031**
**Telephone: 619-463-5500 FAX: 619-463-0701**
**Email: kucal57@aol.com**
**General Civil Trial Practice in both State and Federal Courts. Aviation Law, business Law, Workers Compensation, Personal Injury, Probate, and Family Law.**
*See Professional Biographies, LA MESA, CALIFORNIA*

Blue, Henry W., Jr. ...'31 '53 C&L.502 A.B., J.D. 5480 Baltimore Dr.
Bott, Charles A. ...'51 '88 C.763 B.S. L.1049 J.D. 8220 University Ave., 2nd Fl.
Boyle, Martin L. ...'28 '53 C&L.477 A.B., LL.B. 4611 Hillview Dr.‡
Braun, William R. ...'40 '69 C.112 B.S. L.809 J.D. 7991 Anders Cir.
Burke, Thomas ...'15 '74 L.1137 LL.B. 4527 3rd St.‡
Carlos, Bertha J. ...'25 '67 C.112 B.A. L.1049 J.D. 7330 Mohawk St.
Chadderdon, Norris '05 '29 C&L.546 A.B., J.D.
(adm. in NE; not adm. in CA) 5740 Lake Murray Blvd.‡
Cozart, Bruce W., (BV) ...'58 '85 C.172 B.S. L.1049 J.D. 4700 Spring St.
Davies, William F. ...'27 '54 C.763 A.B. L.800 LL.B. 10430 Sierra Vista Lane‡
de la Flor, George L. ...'58 '83 C.145 B.A. L.464 J.D. 8355 LaMesa Blvd.
de Milliano, Maryanne, (BV) ...'43 '82 C.424 B.S.N. L.1137 J.D. 7777 Alvarado Rd.
Dobbin, James J. ...'33 '75 C.763 B.A. L.1049 J.D. 10946 Fury Lane
Easler, Ray C. ...'23 '78 C&L.1137 B.S.L., J.D. 9830 Lyncarol Dr.‡
Egan, David B. ...'52 '80 C.763 B.A. L.1137 J.D. 8282 University Ave.
Farmer, Penelope Anne ...'45 '89 C.763 A.B. L.1137 J.D. 7777 Alvarado Rd.
Fenton, Alan N., (BV) ...'40 '66 C.112 A.B. L.1066 J.D. 8338 Center Dr.
Finrow, Thomas M. ...'50 '81 C&L.1137 B.S.L., J.D. 8265 Commercial St.
**Fischbeck, William L., (AV)** ...'48 '76 C.352 B.S. L.1137 J.D. [Fischbeck&O.]
*PRACTICE AREAS: Real Estate; Land Use; Environmental Law; Litigation.

**Fischbeck & Oberndorfer, A Professional Corporation, (AV)**
**5464 Grossmont Center Drive, Third Floor, 91942**
**Telephone: 619-464-1200 Fax: 619-464-6471**
**Email: LaMesaLaw@aol.com**
**William L. Fischbeck; Ron H. Oberndorfer;—Virginia S. Johnson.**
**Land Use, Environmental, Real Property, Estate Planning, Corporate, Transactional Matters, Hearing of Arbitrations, Mediations and Settlement Conferences.**
**Representative Clients: Baja Life Communications; Bron Development Self Storage; California Building and Consulting, Inc.; Coast Graphics, Inc.; Digital Outpost, Inc.; DYK Prestressed Tanks, Inc.; Eco-Air Products, Inc.; Gibson Properties; Kaminari, Inc.; Sounds Write Productions, Inc.**

Fougeron, Charles E., (BV) ...'44 '73 C.763 B.A. L.61 J.D. 8330 Allison Ave.
Fox, Joseph, (BV) ...'48 '74 C.763 B.A. L.37 J.D. 8220 University Ave., 2nd Fl.
Giuseppini, Irene S. ...'62 '90 L.1188 J.D. [Anderson&K.]
Greenberg, Linda Wesson ...'51 '88 C.112 B.A. L.1188 J.D. 7863 La Mesa Blvd.
Griffith, Edward '53 '77 C.1262 A.B. L.969 J.D.
(adm. in GA; not adm. in CA) 5832 Clay Ave.★
Grisafi, James Charles ...'56 '81 C.763 B.S. L.61 J.D. 9340 Fuerte Dr.
Haddad, Roland J., (AV) ...'43 '70 C.426 B.A. L.1049 J.D. 8844 La Mesa Blvd.
Hambleton, Kaye E., (BV) ...'43 '80 C.579 B.S. L.1049 J.D. 7777 Alvarado Rd.
Harelson, Gilbert ...'19 '49 C.37 L.800 LL.B. 10055 Pandora Dr.‡
Has-Ellison, M.D., (BV) ...'34 '74 C.381 B.S. L.1137 J.D. 7800 Univ. Ave. (ⒸRamona)
Hirst, Frank L. ...'18 '42 C&L.426 A.B., LL.B. 9205 Lemon Ave.
Horwick, Daniel M., (BV) ...'45 '70 C.112 A.B. L.1049 J.D. 8844 La Mesa Blvd.
**Johnson, Virginia S.** ...'53 '90 C.805 B.A. L.861 J.D. [Ⓐ Fischbeck&O.]
*PRACTICE AREAS: General Litigation; Employment Law.
Kartvedt, Maynard O., (BV) ...'37 '70 C.871 B.S. L.494 J.D. 5020 Baltimore Dr., #314D
Knutson, LeRoy W., (AV) ...'29 '57 C&L.966 B.S., LL.B. [Knutson&M.]
Knutson & Meyer, A Professional Corporation, (AV) ...9001 Grossmont Blvd.
Kriger, Joel M., (BV) ...'48 '73 C.831 B.B.A. L.1049 J.D. [Anderson&K.]
Kruer, Jay C. '47 '89 C.973 B.S. L.1049 J.D.
(adm. in KY; not adm. in CA) V.P., San Diego Dental Grp.
Kuhfal, David P., (CV) ...'39 '74 C.134 L.1137 J.D. 9001 Grossmont Blvd.
Logan, Charles C., II '37 '70 C.688 B.S. L.128 J.D.
(adm. in RI; not adm. in CA; Pat.) 7851 University Ave.
Lyman, Wells B., (BV) ...'43 '72 C.608 B.S. L.61 J.D. 8453 La Mesa Blvd.
Mac Farlane, Robert D., (BV) '34 '60 C&L.800 B.A., LL.B.
8415 La Mesa Blvd., Ste. 4
Marco, Corey H., (BV) ...'42 '76 C.112 B.A. L.813 J.D. 10152 Grandview Dr.
Martindill, Michael J. ...'49 '83 C&L.1137 B.S.L., J.D. 7373 University Ave.
McGill, Larry D. ...'51 '88 C.636 B.A. L.1137 J.D. 8155 Binney Pl.
Meeker, Keith L., (BV) ...'49 '75 C.763 B.A. L.1188 J.D. 7777 Alvarado Rd.
Meyer, John S., (AV) ...'40 '66 C.529 A.B. L.665 LL.B. [Knutson&M.]
Miller, Charles B. ...'48 '77 C.763 B.S. L.1137 J.D. 4656 Glen St.
Miller, Stephen L. ...'44 '86 C.966 B.S. L.61 J.D. 9555 Grossmont Blvd.
Moore, Mark R., (BV) ...'51 '77 C.763 A.B. L.1137 J.D. [Moore&B.]
Moore and Bailey, (BV) ...7777 Alvarado Rd.
Mueller, Howard R. ...'17 '57 C.763 L.426 LL.B. 8787 Alpine Ave.‡
Mulder, Gerald S., (AV) ...'37 '64 C.763 B.S. L.1066 J.D. 8550 La Mesa Blvd.
**Oberndorfer, Ron H., (AV)** ...'53 '78 C.684 B.A. L.61 J.D. [Fischbeck&O.]
*PRACTICE AREAS: Business/Corporate Transactions; Estate Planning; Business Litigation; Real Estate Litigation; Corporate Entities.

**O'Connor, Patrick F., (AV) '47 '73 C.210 B.A. L.276 J.D.**
**Wells Fargo Bank Building, 5464 Grossmont Center Drive, Third Floor, 91942**
**Telephone: 619-463-4284 Facsimile: 619-464-6471**
***PRACTICE AREAS: Employment Law-Discrimination; Serious Personal Injury; Business Litigation.**
**Employment Law, Serious Personal Injury, Business Litigation.**
*See Professional Biographies, LA MESA, CALIFORNIA*

Olander, Alexander J. ...'47 '79 C.645 B.A. L.1049 J.D. 9470 Grossmont Blvd.
Olander, Shelley T. ...'52 '77 C&L.107 B.A., J.D. 4670 Nebo Dr.
Ornish, Marty Chapman ...'52 '90 C.1090 B.S., M.S.W. L.1137 J.D. 4705 Maxapan Dr.
Philo, DuWayne A. ...'25 '77 C.763 A.B. L.1137 J.D. 6031 Sinton Place‡
Rayon, Howard W. ...'48 '78 C.763 B.S. L.1137 J.D. 6830 Delaware Ave.
Richards, R. Neal ...'28 '66 C.101 B.Sc. L.273 J.D. 7569 El Paso St.‡
Schleicher, Edward M. ...'53 '84 C.999 L.1137 J.D. 5360 Marengo Ave.
Schmidt, Charles J. ...'53 '80 C.763 B.A. L.1137 J.D. 4670 Nebo Dr.
Shapiro, Lee S. '31 '67 C.645 B.A. L.502 J.D.
(adm. in MO; not adm. in CA) Univ. of Phoenix, San Diego
Simone, Mathew W. ...'57 '83 C.646 B.S. L.1188 J.D. 9019 Park Plaza Dr.
Skube, John C. ...'53 '83 C.763 B.A. L.61 J.D. P.O. Box 515
Sorbo, John, (AV) ...'21 '49 C&L.813 A.B., LL.B. 10505 Grandview Dr.
Thaeler, Kent H. ...'60 '92 C.112 L.537 J.D. [Anderson&K.]
Underhill, Casey A. '42 '67 C.309 B.A. L.178 J.D.
(adm. in MN; not adm. in CA) 5700 Baltimore Dr.‡
Vaughn, Pierre, (BV) ...'52 '78 C.597 B.A. L.1066 J.D. 4817 Palm Ave.
Walsh, Joan M. ...'53 '83 C.208 B.A. L.1049 J.D. 7777 Alvarado Rd.
White, Brian J. ...'63 '91 C.763 B.S. L.990 J.D. 4265 Francis Way
White, John G. ...'37 '70 C.112 A.B. L.1049 J.D. 9412 La Cuesta Dr.
Williams, Charles A., (BV) ...'40 '74 C&L.1049 B.A., J.D. 9340 Fuerte Dr.
Willis, Wilford D., (BV) ...'22 '59 C.763 A.B. L.1049 LL.B. 4546 Mayapan Dr.
Wingfield, Steven F. ...'53 '79 C.801 B.A. L.1049 J.D. 8241 La Mesa Blvd.
Wright, Edward M. ...'29 '58 C.112 B.A. L.1065 J.D. 5736 Jeanette Ave.

## LA MIRADA, 40,452, *Los Angeles Co.*

Comroe, George ...'17 '76 L.1137 15906-B Alta Vista Dr.
Gleason, Eugene A., III, (AV) ...'55 '80 C.426 B.A. L.809 J.D. 15901 E. Imperial Hwy.
Guayante, Mary F. ...'57 '91 C&L.1137 B.S., J.D. Roy A. Hoff, Inc.
Jenkins, James T. ...'21 '56 C&L.309 A.B., LL.B. 12627 Santa Gertrudes Ave.

CAA155P

Land, Larry E. ... '43 '78 C.801 B.S. L.990 J.D. 15232 Greenworth Dr.
Mackey, Jerry D. ... '51 '79 Biola Coll.
Oppedahl, Olaus J. ... '29 '58 C&L.221 B.S., LL.B. 15512 Lofthill‡
Perryman, Steven ... '42 '72 C.870 B.S. L.1066 J.D. Gannon Mfg. Co. Inc.
Roman, Robert ... '52 '80 C.1109 B.A. L.1137 J.D. 14222 Jalisco Rd.
Shyer, Herbert M. ... '20 '59 C.112 B.S. L.809 LL.D. 14229 E. Imperial Hwy.
Summers, Sunshine A. ... '14 '53 C.387 B.A. L.61 J.D. 14509 Valeda Dr.
Tomeo, Kathleen A., (BV) ... '42 '78 C.1109 B.A. L.1137 J.D. 15901 E. Imperial Hwy
Turner, Jon E. ... '44 '76 C.37 B.A. L.1137 LL.B. P.O. Box 279

## LANCASTER, 97,291, *Los Angeles Co.*

**Ambill, David Edward, (CV) '48 '81 C.112 B.A. L.1137 J.D.**
**936 West Avenue J-4, Suite 203, 93534-4246**
**Telephone: 805-945-8733 Fax: 805-723-0160**
**Email: daveambill@aol.com**
***PRACTICE AREAS: Real Property; Residential; Brokers and Agents; Commercial Leasing; Partnerships and Joint Ventures.**
**Real Estate.**
***See Professional Biographies, LANCASTER, CALIFORNIA***

Amorosa, John C. '47 '74 C&L.986 B.S., J.D.
(adm. in KS; not adm. in CA) 641 W. Ave. J‡
Amspoker, Ross W., (AV) ... '21 '50 C.112 A.B. L.1066 LL.B. Supr. Ct. Ref.
**Baird, Terence A.**, (BV) ... '50 '83 C.101 B.S. L.464 J.D. [Gillon,L.M.&B.]
*LANGUAGES: German.
*PRACTICE AREAS: Business Law; Real Estate Law; Construction Law; Municipal Law; Land Use Law.
Beacham, Donald W. ... '40 '70 C&L.800 B.S., J.D. 641 W. Ave. J
Beech, Dennis W. '40 '82
C.502 B.S. L.1137 J.D. 43770 15th St. W. (⊙Huntington Beach)
**Bianchi, David W.**, (AV) ... '50 '79 C.259 B.S. L.1095 J.D. [Cosgrove,M.S.W.&B.]
*PRACTICE AREAS: Family Law; Adoptions; Estate Planning Law; Probate Law.
Brakemeyer, Doane ... '17 '54 C.911 B.A. L.809 J.D. 44826 Cedar St.‡
Bruns, James R. ... '50 '75 L.1095 J.D. 44905 10th St., W.
Campbell, Inlow H., (AV) ... '40 '72 C&L.1095 B.A., LL.B. 647 W. Ave. L-14
Campbell, Lionel T., (AV) ... '10 '37 C&L.336 B.A., LL.B. 2055 E. Glentree St.‡
Cannon, Dennis A., (A L.C.) ... '34 '67 C.763 B.A. L.61 J.D. P.O. Box 2256
Clark, William A. ... '47 '77 C.426 B.A. L.1095 J.D. 44421 N. 10th St., W.
**Collins, David T.**, (BV) ... '56 '83 C.1077 B.A. L.336 J.D. [Cosgrove,M.S.W.&B.]
*PRACTICE AREAS: Worker's Compensation; Personal Injury.
**Cosgrove, Leonard A.**, (AV) '24 '52
C.763 A.B. L.426 J.D. U.S. Mag. [Cosgrove,M.S.W.&B.]
*PRACTICE AREAS: Probate Law; Estate Planning Law; Living Trusts.

**Cosgrove, Michelizzi, Schwabacher, Ward & Bianchi, A Professional Corporation, (AV) BR**
**767 West Lancaster Boulevard, 93534-3135**
**Telephone: 805-948-5021 Telecopier: 805-948-5395**
**Philip M. Schwabacher (1913-1993); Leonard A. Cosgrove; Frank G. Michelizzi; Thomas J. Ward; David W. Bianchi (Certified Specialist, Family Law, The State Bar of California Board of Legal Specialization); David T. Collins;—James Lillicrap; Kevin L. Von Tungeln.**
**General Civil and Trial Practice. Probate, Estate Planning, Commercial, Business Law, Personal Injury, Workers Compensation, Real Estate, Family Law and Adoptions.**
***See Professional Biographies, LANCASTER, CALIFORNIA***

Cunningham & Lansden, (BV)
44404 16th St. W., #109 (⊙Oxnard, Simi Valley, Victorville, Fresno, Modesto & Sacramento)
Curtin, Richard P., (BV) ... '53 '79 C.112 B.A. L.1049 J.D. 44323 Lowtree
Delaney, Patrick M., (BV) ... '51 '80 C.1077 B.A. L.426 J.D. [Walsh,D.&Y.]
Dragan, Dennis T., (BV) ... '41 '72 C.608 B.S. L.426 J.D. P.O. Box 2113
Eberhardt, Michael C., (AV) ... '47 '75 C.999 L.1095 J.D. 44421 10th St. W.
Falls, Dell L. ... '20 '53 C.112 A.B. L.1068 LL.B. 702 W. Ave. J
**Gillon, Robert**, (BV) ... '46 '79 C.112 B.A. L.1148 J.D. [Gillon,L.M.&B.]
*PRACTICE AREAS: Real Estate; Representing Creditors in Bankruptcy, Condemnation; General Civil Practice.

**Gillon, Lepore, Menefee & Baird, (BV)**
**43825 North 10th Street West, P.O. Box 4379, 93539**
**Telephone: 805-948-1618 Facsimile: 805-948-4989**
**Email: avlaw@qnet.com**
**Members of Firm: Robert Gillon; Robert T. Lepore; Terry R. Menefee; Terence A. Baird.**
**Personal Injury, General Civil and Trial Practice. Probate and Real Estate Law. Insurance, Corporation, Commercial and Estate Planning Law.**
**References: Antelope Valley Bank; First Interstate Bank; First Valley National Bank.**
***See Professional Biographies, LANCASTER, CALIFORNIA***

Grant, Ian R. ... '29 '61 C.1043 B.A. L.809 LL.B. Mun. Ct. J.
Hales, Lawrence C. ... '52 '95 C.30 B.S.B.A. L.904 J.D. 44421 Tenth St. W.
Heiserman, Glenda L. ... '45 '90 C.101 B.S. L.1065 J.D. 43983 15th St., W.
Jackson, Frank Y. ... '48 '73 C.549 B.A. L.464 J.D. Sup. Ct. J.
Johnson, Robert K. ... '49 '78 C.629 B.S. L.1137 J.D. 44421 10th St.W.
Koch, William A. ... '50 '78 C.112 B.A. L.1137 J.D. 44540-10th St. W.
Langford, Stanley R. ... '31 '63 L.981 LL.B. 44526 Stanridge St.‡
Larson, Max W. ... '28 '72 C.579 B.S. L.981 LL.B. 202 W. Pondera St.
**Lepore, Robert T.**, (BV) ... '51 '81 C.728 B.S. L.809 J.D. [Gillon,L.M.&B.]
*PRACTICE AREAS: Personal Injury.
Levin, Marvin, (BV) ... '28 '52 C.209 L.365 LL.B. 44421 N. 10th St. W.
**Lillicrap, James** ... '62 '90 C.882 B.A. L.940 J.D. [Ⓐ Cosgrove,M.S.W.&B.]
*PRACTICE AREAS: Family Law.
Martinez, Manuel R., Jr. ... '38 '70 C.1077 B.S. L.1049 J.D. Dep. Pub. Def. IV
**Menefee, Terry R.**, (BV) ... '43 '77 C.766 B.A. L.464 J.D. [Gillon,L.M.&B.]
*PRACTICE AREAS: Insurance Law; Real Property Litigation; Personal Injury; Product Liability; Defamation.
**Michelizzi, Frank G.**, (AV) ... '29 '54 C.999 L.209 LL.B. [Cosgrove,M.S.W.&B.]
*PRACTICE AREAS: Personal Injury Law; Hospital Law.
Naranjo, Richard E. ... '52 '91 C.550 B.S. L.809 J.D. Co. Dist. Atty.
Nichols, Clifford C. ... '54 '85 C.112 B.A. L.597 J.D. 44444 16th St. W
Peters-Weaver, Claudia Ann, (BV) ... '50 '84 C.763 B.S. L.398 J.D. 43770 15th St. W.
**Pollock, Cynthia R.** ... '61 '91 C.134 B.S. L.426 J.D. [Ⓐ M.E.Thompson]
*PRACTICE AREAS: Probate; Wills; Trust Law; Estate Planning; Elder Law.
Reed, Brian E., (BV) ... '55 '80 C.763 B.A. L.1049 J.D. 1039 W. Ave. J.
Reichman, Victor I. ... '44 '70 C.112 A.B. L.800 J.D. Supr. Ct. Comr.
Rishoff, Stephen L. ... '49 '74 C.1077 B.S. L.809 J.D. 825 W. Ave. J (⊙Woodland Hills)

**Rogers, Randolph A., (BV) '54 '78 C&L.260 B.A., J.D.**
**857 West Lancaster Boulevard, 93534**
**Telephone: 805-945-4404 Facsimile: 805-723-7089**
**Civil Litigation and Trial Practice with emphasis on Business Partnership, Real Estate, Construction, Consumer, Civil Rights, Wrongful Death and Insurance Law.**
***See Professional Biographies, LANCASTER, CALIFORNIA***

Seelicke, William H. ... '41 '67 C.165 A.B. L.1065 J.D. Mun. Ct. J.
Smith, Brenda C. '62 '90 C.330 B.A. L.990 J.D.
[Ⓐ Cunningham&L.] (⊙Oxnard & Simi Valley)
Spann, Richard E. ... '34 '74 C.178 A.B. L.426 J.D. Mun. Ct. J., Antelope Jud. Dist.
Tafarella, Santi, Jr. ... '33 '72 C.112 A.B. L.981 LL.B. 2531 W. Ave. K‡
**Thompson, Mark E.**, (AV) ... '47 '77 L.1095 J.D. [M.E.Thompson]
*PRACTICE AREAS: Probate; Wills; Trust Law; Estate Planning; Elder Law.

**Thompson, Mark E., A Professional Corporation, (AV) BR**
**857 West Lancaster Boulevard, 93534**
**Telephone: 805-945-5868 Fax: 805-723-7089**
**Mark E. Thompson (Certified Specialist, Probate, Estate Planning and Trust Law, The State Bar of California Board of Legal Specialization);—Cynthia R. Pollock.**
**Probate, Wills, Trusts, Estate Planning, Conservatorships, and Elder Law.**
**Reference: Antelope Valley Bank, Lancaster, California.**
***See Professional Biographies, LANCASTER, CALIFORNIA***

Van Arsdale, Leah C., (CV) ... '40 '75 C.112 B.A. L.426 J.D. 44903 N. 10th St., W.
**Von Tungeln, Kevin L.** ... '64 '91 C.556 B.S.E.E. L.560 J.D. [Ⓐ Cosgrove,M.S.W.&B.]
*PRACTICE AREAS: Business Law.
Walsh, William, IV, (AV) ... '40 '66 C&L.426 B.A., LL.B. [Walsh,D.&Y.]
Walsh, Delaney & Yep, (AV) ... 42306 10th St.,W.
**Ward, Thomas J.**, (AV) ... '42 '68 C.767 B.A. L.1068 J.D. [Cosgrove,M.S.W.&B.]
*PRACTICE AREAS: Municipal Law; Real Property Law; Business Law.
Weaver, Claudia A. ... '50 '84 C.763 B.S. L.398 J.D. 43770 N. 15th St., W.
Werner, L. Rob ... '46 '75 C.1077 B.A. L.809 J.D. 1672 West Ave. J
Yep, Brian C. ... '60 '86 C.800 B.A. L.1067 J.D. [Walsh,D.&Y.]

## LA PALMA, 15,392, *Orange Co.*

Andrews, Deborah B. ... '49 '82 C.1042 B.A. L.1148 J.D. Calif. Unemp. Ins. App. Bd.
Brandenburg, Jay W. ... '49 '80 C.339 B.S. Engr. L.809 J.D. 7651 El Lobo Circle
De Mont, William E. ... '43 '75 C.1137 B.S. L.999 J.D. 4991 Sharon Dr.
Roth, Gregory L., (AV) ... '42 '67 C.350 B.S. L.352 J.D. 6 Centerpointe Dr. (Pat.)
Smoot, C. Timothy ... '45 '76 C.309 B.A. L.347 J.D. 7002 Moody St.
Vaughn, Amy A. ... '56 '85 C.201 B.S.B.A. L.1049 J.D. 5600 Orangethorpe
Yee, Chester W. ... '22 '71 C.112 B.A. L.809 LL.B. 5221 Dumaine Dr.‡

## LA PUENTE, 36,955, *Los Angeles Co.*

Gershenovitz, Edward P. ... '34 '60 C&L.494 B.A., LL.B. 1114 N. Hacienda St.
Hicks, Dwight G. ... '28 '71 C.800 B.S. L.398 J.D. 402 Clintwood Ave.
Lopez-Hicks, Gloria Y. ... '41 '73 C.061 L.1137 LL.B. 2211 S. Hacienda Blvd.
Netzley, Willard P., (BV) ... '22 '50 L.800 J.D. 15825-A Main St.

## LA QUINTA, 11,215, *Riverside Co.*

Correa, Glenn E., (AV) ... '17 '46 C.911 B.A. L.800 LL.B. 78-191 Calle Norte‡
Dalbey, Wm. Blair, (AV) ... '23 '53 C.1043 A.A. L.426 J.D. 54-604 Inverness
Daniel, Joseph T. ... '31 '79 C.871 B.S. L.1137 J.D. P.O. Box 269
Etinger, Seth R. ... '19 '66 C.608 B.S. L.426 LL.B. 78720 Avenida La Fonda
Harrell, William C. '47 '90 C.1042 B.S. L.61 J.D.
(adm. in AZ; not adm. in CA) P.O. Box 86
Holland, Jay Putnam ... '41 '82 C.112 B.A. L.284 J.D. P.O. Box 946
Linehan, Randolph ... '49 '80 C.976 B.A. L.1065 J.D. 50028 Calle Oaxaca
Mulcahey, Thomas J. '36 '69 C.1044 B.S. L.1009 J.D.
(adm. in NY; not adm. in CA) 79-350 Desert Rock Ct.
Rose, Charles T., (AV) ... '35 '66 C.276 B.S. L.846 J.D. 55-611 Winged Foot
Sanoff, Stanford, (BV) ... '26 '65 C.569 L.809 LL.B. 55/604 Pinehurst St.
Williams, Robert O., Jr. '50 '76 C.347 A.B. L.862 J.D.
(adm. in IN; not adm. in CA) P.O. Box 1687‡

## LARKSPUR, 11,070, *Marin Co.*

Barker, Eileen Evans, (AV) ... '54 '78 C.347 B.A. L.276 J.D. 700 Larkspur Landing Circle
Bartley, Daniel Robert ... '48 '72 C.235 B.B.A. L.383 J.D. 101 Larkspur Landing Circle
Benz, William R., (AV) ... '31 '66 C.112 A.B. L.1065 J.D. 900 Larkspur Landing Cir.
Bergman, John G. ... '49 '92 C.740 B.A. L.1241 J.D. 36 Elm Ave.
**Bierer, Joel D.** ... '49 '81 C.1044 B.A. L.767 J.D. [Katz,B.&B.]
**Brady, Steven J.** ... '60 '84 C.597 B.A. L.426 J.D. [Katz,B.&B.]
Brown, Tracy M. ... '47 '82 C&L.472 B.A., J.D. 26 Loma Vista Ave.
**Brown, Tyler A.** ... '60 '85 C.602 B.A. L.1065 J.D. [Ⓐ Jackson,L.S.&K.]
**Casey, A. Michael**, (AV) ... '42 '67 C.112 A.B. L.1065 J.D. [Weinberg,H.&C.]
*PRACTICE AREAS: Insurance Defense; Litigation; Personal Injury.
Colthurst, Wallace G., (AV) ... '23 '51 C&L.767 B.S., LL.B. P.O. Box 33‡
Davis, Donald R. ... '47 '83 C.262 B.A. L.178 J.D. 2200 Larkspur Landing Circle
Dickman, Norbert J. ... '43 '73 C.1256 B.A. L.1065 J.D. 100 Larkspur Landing Circle
Downes, John J. ... '16 '41 C.767 B.A. L.309 LL.B. 339 W. Baltimore Ave.
Duca, Steven J. ... '57 '83 C.112 B.A. L.1065 J.D. P.O. Box 1127
Fawcett, Margaret G. ... '42 '81 C.483 B.A. L.767 J.D. 72 Cypress Pl.
Fischer, John P. '44 '76 C.746 B.A. L.1049 J.D.
Exec. Dir., National Employment Law Institute
**Greenberg, Myron S.**, (AV) ... '45 '71 C.112 B.S. L.1068 J.D. [M.S.Greenberg]

**Greenberg, Myron S., A Professional Corporation, (AV)**
**700 Larkspur Landing Circle, Suite 205, 94939**
**Telephone: 415-461-5844 Fax: 415-461-5873**
**Email: taxlaw700@aol.com**
**Myron S. Greenberg (Certified Specialist, Taxation Law, The State Bar of California Board of Legal Specialization).**
**Federal and State Taxation Law. Probate and Estate Planning.**
***See Professional Biographies, LARKSPUR, CALIFORNIA***

**Hearne, William T.** '69 '94 C.862 B.A. L.861 J.D.
(adm. in MN; not adm. in CA) N.L.R.B. [Ⓐ Jackson,L.S.&K.]
**Hoffman, Joseph** ... '54 '84 C.1155 B.S. L.767 J.D. [Weinberg,H.&C.]
*LANGUAGES: German, Spanish and Portuguese.
*PRACTICE AREAS: Insurance Defense; Products Liability; Medical Malpractice Defense; Litigation; Personal Injury.

**Jackson, Lewis, Schnitzler & Krupman, (AV)**
**700 Larkspur Landing Circle Suite 167, 94939-1754⊙**
**Telephone: 415-461-5899 Facsimile: 415-461-5898**
**Members of Firm: John V. Nordlund. Associates: Tyler A. Brown; William T. Hearne (Not admitted in CA).**
**Labor Relations, Employment Discrimination, Wrongful Discharge and Other Employment-Related Litigation, Employee Benefits and Pension Law, Wage and Hour, OSHA, Immigration Law, Public Sector and State Labor Relations Law, On Behalf of Management.**
**Other offices located in: Atlanta, Georgia; Boston, Massachusetts; Chicago, Illinois; Dallas, Texas; Greenville, South Carolina; Hartford, Connecticut; Los Angeles, California; Miami, Florida; Morristown, New Jersey; New York, New York; Orlando, Florida; Pittsburgh, Pennsylvania; San Francisco, California; Stamford, Connecticut; Washington, D.C.; White Plains, New York; Woodbury, New York.**
***See Professional Biographies, LARKSPUR, CALIFORNIA***

Johann, Susan K. ... '46 '77 C.219 B.A. L.1137 J.D. 10 Bayview
Johnson, Steger P., (AV) ... '50 '78 C.112 B.A. L.1065 J.D. [Ⓒ Joost&A.]⊙
Joost, William E., Jr., (AV) ... '49 '75 C.668 B.A. L.284 J.D. [Joost&A.]

Joost & Allman, (AV) .......... 600 E. Sir Francis Drake Blvd.
**Katz, Richard L.**, (AV) .......... '38 '69 C.260 B.S.B.A. L.284 J.D. [Katz,B.&B.]

**Katz, Bierer & Brady, A Professional Corporation, (AV)**
**101 Larkspur Landing Circle, Suite 223, 94939**
Telephone: 415-925-1600 FAX: 415-925-0940
Richard L. Katz (Member of Consumer Attorneys of California, with recognized experience in the fields of General Personal Injury and Professional Negligence); Joel D. Bierer; Steven J. Brady. Of Counsel: Alvin J. Schifrin.
General Civil Trial Practice. Negligence, Product Liability, Legal and Medical Malpractice, Business Litigation, Wrongful Termination, Insurance Bad Faith, and Will Contests.
*See Professional Biographies, LARKSPUR, CALIFORNIA*

Konigsberg, Fred S. '47 '74 C.994 B.A. L.1009 J.D.
101 Larkspur Landing Cir., Ste., 223
Laubenthal, Marilu '44 '82 C.62 B.A. L.1003 J.D.
(adm. in OH; not adm. in CA) 1800 Lincoln Village Cir.‡
Lefkowitz, Ronald W. '34 '68 C.693 B.S. L.564 J.D.
(adm. in NJ; not adm. in CA) 420 Madrone Ave.‡
Marker, Marc L. .......... '41 '71 C.112 B.A. L.800 J.D. 471B Magnolia Ave.
Matyi, Phyllis A. .......... '51 '84 C.201 B.S. L.1230 J.D. P.O. Box 426
Meredith, Craig S. .......... '53 '78 C&L.326 B.S., J.D. [Meredith,W.&N.]
Meredith, Weinstein & Numbers, (AV) .......... 115 Ward St.
Nachtrieb, Harold C., (AV) '29 '59 C.813 A.B. L.1066 LL.B.
900 Larkspur Landing Cir.
**Nordlund, John V.** .......... '48 '79 C.354 B.A. L.564 J.D. [Jackson,L.S.&K.]
Numbers, Charles H. .......... '58 '86 C.112 B.A. L.1065 J.D. [Meredith,W.&N.]
Plummer, Norman C. .......... '42 '74 C.267 L.284 900 Larkspur Landing Circle
Pritzker, Bruce E. .......... '49 '75 C.94 B.A. L.818 J.D. P.O. Box 6
**Ropers, Mark** .......... '38 '73 C.813 B.A. L.1065 J.D. [Weinberg,H.&C.]
*PRACTICE AREAS: Insurance Defense Law; Litigation.
**Schifrin, Alvin J.** .......... '40 '65 C.178 A.B. L.659 J.D. [Katz,B.&B.]
Shepherd, Kathryn Ballentine .......... '49 '78 60 E. Sir Francis Drake Blvd.
Smith, Robert J. .......... '23 '49 C&L.767 A.B., LL.B. 89 Darthmouth Dr.‡
Thorner, Tom, (BV) .......... '32 '56 C.145 B.A. L.813 J.D. P.O. Box 830
Torres, Julie A. .......... '50 '77 C.1097 B.A. L.1065 J.D. [Joost&A.]
Veith, Nancy A., Law Offices of '49 '79
C.282 B.A. L.767 J.D. 700 Larkspur Landing Circle
**Weinberg, Ivan**, (AV) .......... '43 '68 C.813 A.B. L.1068 J.D. [Weinberg,H.&C.]
*PRACTICE AREAS: Medical-Legal; Medical Malpractice; Personal Injury; Insurance Defense; Medical Board Actions Defense.

**Weinberg, Hoffman & Casey, (AV)**
A Partnership including a Professional Corporation
**900 Larkspur Landing Circle, Suite 155, 94939**
Telephone: 415-461-9666 Fax: 415-461-9681
Ivan Weinberg; Joseph Hoffman; A. Michael Casey. Of Counsel: Mark Ropers.
General Civil and Trial Practice. Insurance Defense, Plaintiff Trial Practice. Medical Legal Practice including Medical Malpractice.
*See Professional Biographies, LARKSPUR, CALIFORNIA*

Weinstein, Barron L., (AV) .......... '49 '75 C.112 B.A. L.1065 J.D. [Meredith,W.&N.]
West, Gertrude C. .......... '32 '76 C.178 L.1197 J.D. 119 Elm Ave.

## LA SELVA BEACH, 1,171, *Santa Cruz Co.*

Votaw, Dow .......... '20 '49 C.170 B.A. L.309 LL.B. 321 Camino Al Mar‡
Woolsey, Helene S. .......... '38 '80 C.112 B.A. L.770 J.D. 212 Altivo Ave.‡
Woolsey, William H., (BV) .......... '30 '61 C.813 A.B. L.1066 LL.B. 212 Altivo Ave.‡

## LA VERNE, 30,897, *Los Angeles Co.*

Ashbaugh, Ralph W., Jr. .......... '56 '80 C.1075 B.A. L.398 J.D. 2535 College Lane
Hawkins, Howard R. .......... '53 '81 C.112 B.A. L.398 J.D. 3839 Emerald Ave.
Held, Kenneth .......... '37 '69 C.94 A.B. L.262 J.D. Dean, Univ. of La Verne Coll. of Law
Mason, Arthur P. '19 '47 C.964 L.966 J.D.
(adm. in WI; not adm. in CA) 4095 Fruit St.‡
Prager, Irving '40 '69 C.454 B.A. L.276 J.D.
Asst. Dean & Prof. of Law, Univ. of La Verne

## LAWNDALE, 27,331, *Los Angeles Co.*

Balton, Monroe P. '41 '75 C.378 B.A. L.705 J.D.
(adm. in NJ; not adm. in CA) Fed. Aviation Admn., Off. of Chief Coun.
Campana, David E. .......... '53 '79 C.112 B.A. L.284 J.D. [Kusion&C.]
Kusion, Eugene L. .......... '54 '80 C.112 B.A. L.1049 J.D. [Kusion&C.]
Kusion & Campana .......... 4541 Artesia Blvd.
Wittry, Richard G. '34 '59 C&L.424 B.S., J.D.
(adm. in IL; not adm. in CA) F.A.A.

## LEBEC, —, *Kern Co.*

Dale, Karen L. .......... '52 '83 C.1236 B.A. L.1068 J.D. P.O. Box 907‡
**Mullins, Dennis** .......... '52 '78 C.112 B.A. L.477 J.D. Gen. Coun., Tejon Ranch Co
**Onyshko, Gary J.** .......... '60 '88 C.112 B.A. L.464 J.D. Assoc. Coun., Tejon Ranch Co.
*RESPONSIBILITIES: Commercial; Farm Leases; Environmental Compliance/Natural Resources; Landlord/Tenant; Labor Law.
Wallace, Vicky .......... '37 '66 C&L.347 B.S., J.D. P.O. Box 1262

## LEMON GROVE, 23,984, *San Diego Co.*

Barwick, Kenneth A., (AV) .......... '26 '55 C.112 A.B. L.1068 J.D. [Barwick,R.&S.]
Barwick, Rutherford & Scott, A Prof. Corp., (BV) .......... 3434 Grove St.
Clabby, Rick .......... '53 '79 C.675 B.A. L.61 J.D. 1650 Angelus Ave.
Cochran, Brian, (BV) .......... '56 '82 C.112 B.A. L.1137 J.D. 7850 Golden Ave.
Dorman, James V., (BV) .......... '36 '65 C.668 B.A. L.61 J.D. [Dorman&D.]
Dorman, Vroman J. .......... '08 '32 C.800 A.B. L.813 LL.B. 6781 Hibiscus‡
Dorman, Wallace D., (BV) .......... '17 '49 C&L.813 A.B., LL.B. [Dorman&D.]
Dorman and Dorman, (BV) .......... P.O. Box 517
Rutherford, Timothy C., (BV) .......... '53 '78 C&L.813 A.B., J.D. [Barwick,R.&S.]
Scott, Charles T., Jr. .......... '52 '77 C.112 B.A. L.1066 J.D. [Barwick,R.&S.]
Stewart, Victoria A. .......... '56 '82 C.197 B.A. L.477 J.D. [Barwick,R.&S.]

## LEMOORE, 13,622, *Kings Co.*

Atkinson, Lynn C., (Mr.) .......... '47 '73 C.990 B.S. L.1067 J.D. Supr. Ct. J.
Hoover, William D. '40 '70 C&L.378 B.S., J.D.
Assoc. Prof., Embry-Riddle Aeronautical Univ.‡
Johnson, Charles R., (BV) .......... '40 '72 C.906 L.1137 LL.B. P.O. Box 147

## LEUCADIA, —, *San Diego Co.*

Austin, James W., III .......... '45 '76 C&L.763 B.A., J.D. 810 Peubla St.
Sanders, Dennis E. .......... '43 '75 C.1075 B.S.M.E. L.1137 J.D. 570 Southbridge Ct.‡

## LINCOLN, 7,248, *Placer Co.*

Ewing, John W., (BV) .......... '43 '74 C.999 L.464 J.D. P.O. Box 333
Kendall, Earl D., Sr., (CV) .......... '38 '71 L.464 J.D. 510 F St.
Langle, Gerald D. .......... '39 '72 C.999 A.A. L.464 J.D. Admin. Law J.
Sorensen, Kurt .......... '40 '69 C.597 B.A. L.1065 J.D. 4150 Wilson Way

## LINDSAY, 8,338, *Tulare Co.*

Kiesz, ReDoy, (BV) .......... '34 '66 C.1163 B.A. L.1132 J.D. City Atty.

## LITTLE RIVER, 500, *Mendocino Co.*

Frankston, Jay '28 '52 C.569 B.A. L.1009 LL.B.
Prof. of Law, College of the Redwoods
Herbert, James K., (AV) .......... '38 '63 C.813 B.S. L.1066 LL.B. 17415 Ave.‡
Lamb, William P. .......... '38 '64 C.976 A.B. L.309 LL.B. Jud. J.‡
Raymond, Robert L., (AV) .......... '26 '51 C&L.813 A.B., LL.B. P.O. Box 628‡

## LITTLE ROCK, —, *Los Angeles Co.*

Harper, Albert L., Jr. .......... '23 '53 C.800 B.S. L.809 LL.B. 11246 Juniper Hills Rd.

## LIVE OAK, 4,320, *Sutter Co.*

Dankman, Roy .......... '32 '66 C.910 B.S. L.1068 LL.B. 6820 Madden Ave.

## LIVERMORE, 56,741, *Alameda Co.*

**Allen, Tracy C.** .......... '60 '85 C.494 B.A. L.893 J.D. Coun., KENETECH Windpower, Inc.
Bakken, Lawrence H. .......... '31 '69 C.494 B.C.E. L.770 J.D. 1888 Buena Vista
Bernal, Albert L., II, (BV) .......... '47 '78 C.426 B.A. L.398 J.D. 1536 Holmes St.
Blea, Jacob, III, (BV) .......... '52 '81 C.1073 B.A. L.1066 J.D. 1789 4th St
Buginas, Scott J. .......... '33 '79 C.473 B.A. L.1026 J.D. 1207 Gonzaga Ct.
Butnick, Roland .......... '35 '71 C&L.569 B.A., J.D. 1046 Murrieta Blvd.‡
**Culley, Patricia** .......... '— '78 C.1073 B.A. L.999 J.D. [Culley *.G.]

**Culley * Goodwin, (BV)**
**2162 Fifth Street, 94550**
Telephone: 510-443-0822
Patricia Culley; Robert E. Goodwin.
Business Law and Family Law.
*See Professional Biographies, LIVERMORE, CALIFORNIA*

Davis, Cherie Thompson .......... '56 '89 C.1073 B.A. L.770 J.D. 1524 Holmes St.
Estrada, Armand M., (BV) .......... '56 '82 C.1073 B.S. L.284 J.D. [Estrada&T.]
Estrada & Thomson, (BV) .......... 203 South "S" Street
Feinberg, Susan B. .......... '51 '82 C.628 B.S. L.273 J.D. 490 Lindbergh Ave.‡
**Fraser, Keith S.**, (AV) .......... '36 '61 C.813 B.S. L.1065 LL.B. [Varni,F.H.&R.]
*PRACTICE AREAS: Real Estate; Land Use; Probate.
Frye, Dexter A. .......... '49 '75 C.154 B.A. L.930 J.D. P.O. Box 2539‡
**Goodwin, Robert E.**, (BV) .......... '43 '67 C&L.767 B.S., J.D. [Culley *.G.]
*PRACTICE AREAS: Business Law; Real Estate Law; Civil Litigation.
Graham, Keith Forrest '52 '77 C&L.770 B.A., J.D.
Asst. Lab. Coun., Lawrence Livermore Nat. Lab.
Lateiner, Emanuel .......... '49 '76 C.112 B.A. L.284 J.D. Lawrence Livermore Natl. Lab.
Lowell, Jonathan Peter .......... '59 '85 C.112 B.S. L.1065 J.D. Asst. City Atty.
Malloy, Alexandria .......... '61 '88 C.1104 B.A. L.1066 J.D. 1247 Laguna St.‡
McGrail, James Vincent .......... '54 '89 C.767 B.S. L.1153 J.D. 2600 Kitty Hawk Rd.
**Moruza, Christine Kasun** .......... '51 '76 C.112 B.A. L.1065 J.D. [Varni,F.H.&R.]
*PRACTICE AREAS: Business Litigation.
Mullinix, Karen E. .......... '53 '78 C.147 B.A. L.1065 J.D. Asst. City Atty.
Nice, Charles Casey .......... '58 '89 C.1073 B.S. L.284 J.D. Sheriffs Dept.
O'Neill, Lawrence J., III '47 '77 C.608 B.S. L.851 J.D.
(adm. in OH; not adm. in CA) Univ. of Calif. Lawrence Livermore Natl. Laboratory
Rauhut, Kathryn A. '58 '83 C&L.031 B.A., LL.B.
Coun., Lawrence Livermore Natl. Lab.
Rien, Timothy B., (AV) .......... '53 '77 C.1079 B.A. L.1137 J.D. 197 S. "S" St.

**Rifkind & Fuerch, A Professional Corporation**
(See Hayward)

Robertson, Frederick A. '25 '54 C.659 B.S. L.838 LL.B.
(adm. in TN; not adm. in CA; Pat.) U.S. Atomic Energy Comm.
Sartorio, Henry P. '44 '78 C.453 B.S. L.273 J.D.
Pat. Atty., Lawrence Livermore Natl. Lab. (Pat.)
Struthers, William, (BV) .......... '21 '53 C.813 A.B. L.767 J.D. 1789 4th St.
Thomson, William D. .......... '56 '82 C.147 B.S. L.284 J.D. [Estrada&T.]
Tipton, Robert R., (P.C.) .......... '26 '63 C.112 B.S. L.1065 J.D. 249 El Caminito (Pat.)
**Trutner, Elizabeth E.** .......... '58 '89 C.112 B.A. L.765 J.D. [Varni,F.H.&R.]
*LANGUAGES: French.
**Varni, Anthony B.**, (AV) .......... '39 '64 C&L.770 B.A., LL.B. [Varni,F.H.&R.]
*PRACTICE AREAS: Real Estate; Land Use; Eminent Domain; Inverse Condemnation.

**Varni, Fraser, Hartwell & Rodgers, (AV)**
**2109 Fourth Street, P.O. Box 511, 94550-0511**
Telephone: 510-447-1222 Fax: 510-443-7831
Members of Firm: Anthony B. Varni; Keith S. Fraser; Elizabeth E. Trutner (Resident) (Certified Specialist, Estate Planning, Trust and Probate Law, The State Bar of California Board of Legal Specialization); John S. Hartwell (1924-1993); Lionel A. Rodgers (1942-1989). Associate: Christine Kasun Moruza.
Estate Planning, Trusts, Probate, Real Estate Development and Land Use, Business Transactions, Environmental and Eminent Domain, State and Federal Court Business Litigation.
Representative Clients: Ameron Pipe Products Group (Northern California Division); Kaufman & Broad of Northern California, Inc.; Castro Valley Sanitary District; Glad-A-Way Gardens, Inc.
Hayward, California Office: 22771 Main Street, P.O. Box 570, 94543. Telephone: 510-886-5000. Fax: 510-538-8797.
*See Professional Biographies, LIVERMORE, CALIFORNIA*

Wharton, James C. '36 '75 C.911 B.A. L.767 J.D.
Univ. of Calif. Lawrence Livermore Natl. Laboratory
Willner, Patricia C. .......... '42 '78 C.1073 B.A. L.1137 J.D. 2162 Fifth St.

## LOCKEFORD, —, *San Joaquin Co.*

Lipelt, Donald R. .......... '28 '65 C.112 B.A. L.1066 LL.B. P.O. Box 23

## LODI, 51,874, *San Joaquin Co.*

**Adams, Stewart C., Jr.**, (AV) .......... '37 '63 C.813 B.A. L.1066 LL.B. [Adams,H.&E.]
*PRACTICE AREAS: Estate Planning Law; Probate Law; Living Trust Law; Real Estate Law; Water Rights Law.

**Adams, Horstmann & Edwards, Professional Corporation, (AV)**
**25 North School Street, 95240**
Telephone: 209-333-1414; 478-5356 Fax: 209-333-0104
Stewart C. Adams, Jr.; Herbert E. Horstmann; Roy D. Edwards.
General Civil Practice, Agricultural Water Rights, Probate, Estate Planning, Corporate, Construction, Commercial and Real Estate, Bankruptcy, Personal Injury, and Criminal Law in all Courts.
Reference: Farmers & Merchants Bank of Central California, Lodi, Calif.
*See Professional Biographies, LODI, CALIFORNIA*

Anderson, Dan R. .......... '47 '73 C.768 B.S. L.464 J.D. Anderson Co.
Anderson, Robert L. .......... '49 '90 C.549 B.S. L.464 J.D. 1802 Lakeshore Dr.

CALIFORNIA—LODI MARTINDALE-HUBBELL LAW DIRECTORY 1997

**Brown, Suzanne B.** ............'70 '95 C.112 B.A. L.1067 J.D. [Ⓑ Driscoll&Assoc.]
*PRACTICE AREAS: Family Law; Education; Government.
Cottrell, Steven J., (BV) ..............'50 '76 C.169 B.A. L.464 J.D. 125 N. Pleasant St.
**DeMera, James V., III** ..............'54 '89 C.267 B.S. L.464 J.D. [Mullen,S.&N.]
*PRACTICE AREAS: General Law; Civil Law; Business Law; Litigation; Construction Law.
**Driscoll, Thomas J., Jr.**, (BV) ........'55 '80 C.154 B.A. L.1067 J.D. [Driscoll&Assoc.]
*PRACTICE AREAS: Business; Real Estate; Construction Litigation; Education; Government.

**Driscoll & Associates, (BV)**
**801 South Ham Lane, Suite H, 95242**
**Telephone: 209-334-1935 Fax: 209-334-0178**
**Thomas J. Driscoll, Jr.;—Suzanne B. Brown.**
**Civil Litigation and Transaction Practice in Business, Real Estate, Government, Estate Planning and Family Law.**
***See Professional Biographies, LODI, CALIFORNIA***

Dutton, Donald D. ..............................'44 '86 C.1077 B.A. 1420 Arundel Ct.
**Edwards, Roy D.**, (CV) ....................'40 '73 C.1060 B.A. L.464 J.D. [Adams,H.&E.]
*PRACTICE AREAS: Accident and Personal Injury; Bankruptcy, Criminal Law; Family Law.
Elliott, Robert K., (AV) ..............................'27 '53 C&L.813 B.A., LL.B. [Rinn&E.]
Gavin, James M., (CV) ..............'40 '73 C.147 B.S. L.464 J.D. 1010 Port Chelsea Cir.
Gibson, George K., (BV) '51 '77
C.147 B.A. L.990 J.D. V.P. & Gen. Coun., Anderson Homes, Inc.
Hahn, Steven R. .......................'66 '96 C.267 B.S. L.464 J.D. 717 Ribier Ave.
Harris, Michael K. ...................'44 '81 C.112 B.A. L.966 J.D. 9970 E. Harney Lane
Hays, Randall A., (BV) ..........................'43 '70 C.768 B.A. L.770 J.D. 221 W. Pine St.
**Horstmann, Herbert E.**, (BV) ........'38 '63 C.154 B.A. L.1066 LL.B. [Adams,H.&E.]
*PRACTICE AREAS: Business Law; Construction; Family Law; Corporate Law; Litigation.
**Jordan, Jennifer Davena**, (CV) ...........'54 '81 C.763 B.A. L.61 J.D. [Mullen,S.&N.]
*PRACTICE AREAS: Civil Practice; Insurance Defense; Construction Defects; Litigation.
**Marshall, David R.**, (CV) ..................'47 '72 C.1066 A.B. L.1065 J.D. [Marshall&M.]

**Marshall & Marshall, (CV)**
**404 West Pine Street, 95240**
**Telephone: 209-369-2751 Fax: 209-369-3687**
**Members of Firm: Lindsay P. Marshall (1916-1996); David R. Marshall.**
**General Civil Practice. Personal Injury, Family Law, Probate and Estate Planning, Real Estate and Commercial Law.**
**References: Farmers and Merchants Bank of Central California, Lodi, California; Bank of Stockton, Lodi, California.**

McNatt, Bobby W. ..........................................'45 '80 L.1137 J.D. Supr. Ct. J.
Mertz, Robert J., (AV) ..................'23 '47 C.436 L.770 LL.B. 25 North School St.‡
Michael, Joseph D., (BV) ........................'19 '49 C&L.770 B.S., LL.B. P.O. Box 1570
**Mullen, Robert H.**, (AV) ..............'14 '38 C.112 J.C. L.1065 J.D. [Ⓑ Mullen,S.&N.]
*PRACTICE AREAS: Estate Planning Law; Probate Law; Real Estate Law; Railroad Law.

**Mullen, Sullivan & Newton, (AV)**
**1111 West Tokay Street, P.O. Box 560, 95241-0560**
**Telephone: 209-334-5144 Fax: 209-333-1034**
**Members of Firm: Thomas J. Newton; Craig Rasmussen; Stephen C. Snider; James V. DeMera, III; Jennifer Davena Jordan. Of Counsel: Robert H. Mullen; Cornelius M. (Bud) Sullivan, Jr.**
**Civil Practice with emphasis in Business, Real Estate, Construction, Agriculture, Commercial, Bankruptcy, Education, Municipal/Government, Estate Planning and Probate, Torts and Family Law. Trials and Appeals in all State and Federal Courts.**
***See Professional Biographies, LODI, CALIFORNIA***

**Neumiller & Beardslee, A Professional Corporation**
(See Stockton)

**Newton, Thomas J.**, (AV) ..............'42 '73 C.1365 B.A. L.464 J.D. [Mullen,S.&N.]
*PRACTICE AREAS: Personal Injury Law; Litigation.
Paskett, Herbert A. ......................'25 '54 C.800 B.S. L.1065 LL.B. 1160 Lucas Rd.
**Rasmussen, Craig**, (BV) ..............'53 '78 C.112 A.B. L.464 J.D. [Mullen,S.&N.]
*PRACTICE AREAS: Real Estate Law; Business Litigation.
Renschler, Sharon ..............................................'43 '89 L.1132 J.D. 600 York St.
Rice, Henry J. '35 '69 C.972 B.S.E.E. L.208 J.D.
(adm. in CO; not adm. in CA) P.O. Box 3006‡
Rinn & Elliott, (AV) .................................................................P.O. Box 1827
Rishwain, Ben M. ..............................'42 '69 C.169 A.B. L.770 J.D. P.O. Box 1567
Rosá, Randall W. ..........................'54 '82 C.628 B.A. L.276 J.D. 35 S. School St.
Salo, James D. '45 '71 C.768 A.B. L.1065 J.D.
(adm. in NV; not adm. in CA) 320 Kristmont St.‡
Seibly, J. Thomas ...............................'37 '63 C.1163 B.A. L.800 LL.B. Mun. J.
**Snider, Stephen C.**, (BV) ..............'56 '81 C.169 B.A. L.464 J.D. [Mullen,S.&N.]
*PRACTICE AREAS: General Practice.
Sternfels, Robert B., (BV) ...................'46 '73 C.112 B.A. L.61 J.D. 1101 W. Tokay St.
**Sullivan, Cornelius M. (Bud), Jr.**, (BV) '33 '61
C.1001 A.B. L.1066 J.D. [Ⓑ Mullen,S.&N.]
*PRACTICE AREAS: Real Estate Development Law; Education Law; Public Law.
Warner, David P., (CV) ..................'49 '75 C.1060 B.A. L.1132 J.D. 215 W. Oak St.

## LOMA LINDA, 17,400, *San Bernardino Co.*

Gathings, Susan D. '57 '92
C.1163 B.A. L.1137 J.D. Assoc. Legal Coun., Loma Linda Univ.
James, Richard A. '28 '67 C.1163 B.A. L.800 J.D.
Gen. Legal Coun., Loma Linda Univ.
McAnally, Larry L. '38 '63 C.1365 A.B. L.245 LL.B.
(adm. in GA; not adm. in CA) 25865 Sunrise Way
Snider, Jennifer J. '60 '90 C.170 B.A. L.1035 J.D.
(adm. in ND; not adm. in CA) 25590 Prospect Ave. 26C★
Spreen, Robert H. '12 '37 C.24 A.B. L.178 LL.B.
(adm. in NY; not adm. in CA) P.O. Box 458‡

## LOMITA, 19,382, *Los Angeles Co.*

Barker, Ernest E. .........................................'26 '71 L.1152 LL.B. P.O. Box 966
Barry, Patricia J. .................'43 '74 C.1097 B.A. L.1068 J.D. 25835 Narbonne Ave.
Goodwin, Susan Busby ............'42 '75 C.940 B.A. L.1137 J.D. 25124 Narbonne Ave.
Grotz, Arline A. ...................................'— '81 C.436 B.A. L.1179 J.D. P.O. Box 978
Lahendro, A. Lewis '43 '68 C.885 B.A. L.896 J.D.
(adm. in VA; not adm. in CA) 2022 Via Nova★
Rivera, Eduardo M. ...................'43 '72 C.1097 B.A. L.1068 J.D. 1962 Lomita Blvd.
Splinter, Robert G. ...................'46 '77 C.1077 B.A. L.1136 J.D. 25124 Narbonne Ave.
York, Phillip G. ...................'46 '80 C.145 A.B. L.1136 J.D. 2018 Pacific Coast Hwy.

## LOMPOC, 37,649, *Santa Barbara Co.*

Brown, Curtiss E. ...........................'30 '80 C.623 B.B.A. L.1186 J.D. 4311 Rigel Ave.‡
Carney, Matthew J. '56 '89 C.545 B.S. L.546 J.D.
(adm. in NE; not adm. in CA) U.S. Bur. of Prisons, Dept. of Jus.
**Cox, Terrill F.**, (AV) .....................'31 '58 C.112 B.A. L.1068 J.D. [Grossman,C.&J.]
*PRACTICE AREAS: Probate; Estate Planning; Personal Injury; Criminal; Banking Law.
Dunlap, Gary J. .............................'41 '67 C.112 B.A. L.1068 LL.B. [G.Dunlap]
Dunlap, Gary, P.C. ..............................................................100 South H St.
Gamble, William K., (BV) '39 '69 L.765 J.D.
437 N. H St. (⊙Santa Maria, Solvang, Arroyo Grande, San Luis Obispo)
Gerbac, Joseph E. ....................'39 '66 C.112 A.B. L.1068 LL.B. 1017 E. Ocean Ave.

**Grossman, Cox & Johnson, (AV)**
**121 North H Street, P.O. Box 458, 93438**
**Telephone: 805-736-8555 FAX: 805-736-6647**
**Lawrence C. Grossman (1914-1983); Terrill F. Cox; Leslie E. Johnson, II.**
**General Practice. Probate, Estate Planning, Real Estate, Corporation, Banking, Business, Personal Injury, Family Law and Criminal Law.**
***See Professional Biographies, LOMPOC, CALIFORNIA***

Hall, James M., (CV) .........................'47 '82 C.139 B.A. L.1137 J.D. 118 N. "G" St.
Hirsch, David H. ..................................'50 '77 C.1131 B.A. L.823 J.D. City Atty.
Hourigan, Brian F. ..............................'38 '70 521 E. Ocean Ave. (⊙Santa Barbara)
Huseman, Eugene L. ................................................'32 '57 C.1074 L.1065 J.D. Mun. J.
Huseman, James C., (BV) ....................'42 '70 C.1074 B.S. L.61 J.D. 308 N. H St.
Jacoby, Richard K. '28 '57 C.732 B.A. L.508 J.D.
(adm. in MT; not adm. in CA) 303 W. Walnut Ave.‡
**Johnson, Leslie E., II** ...................'52 '81 C.309 A.B. L.770 J.D. [Grossman,C.&J.]
*PRACTICE AREAS: Probate; Estate Planning; Corporation; Business; Real Estate Law.
Leyva, Cynthia Cochran ..............'56 '87 C.802 B.A. L.862 J.D. 1521 Riverside Dr.‡
Martin, Rodger L. ................'49 '81 C.8 B.S.E.E. L.1186 J.D. 101 Civic Center Plaza
Martinez, Eugene J. ........................'44 '76 C.112 B.A. L.770 J.D. Dep. Dist. Atty.
Motter, Dorothy Denise '51 '92
C.1012 B.A. L.769 J.D. Dist. Attys. Off., Family Support Div.
Stockton, Wendy S. .........................'58 '83 C.112 B.A. L.1068 J.D. Dep. City Atty.
Ward, Charles G., (CV) .................'35 '74 C.139 B.A. L.1065 J.D. 515 E. Ocean Ave.
Weinstock, Rita Barbee ............'55 '82 C.424 B.A. L.1068 J.D. 689 St. Andrews Way
Weiser, Sidney L., (BV) ...............'46 '72 C.415 B.A. L.724 J.D. Sr. Dep. Dist. Atty.
Weldon, Thomas P., III ..................'61 '95 C.686 B.A. L.426 J.D. Dep. Dist. Atty.

## LONE PINE, 1,241, *Inyo Co.*

Corpora, L. Elizabeth ....................................'50 '82 C.112 B.A. L.1049 J.D. 138 Bush
Odell, Donald W., (AV) .......................'25 '52 C.605 A.B. L.426 J.D. P.O. Box 128

## LONG BEACH, 429,433, *Los Angeles Co.*

**Abbott, Mary Nielsen**, (BV) ......'51 '77 C.112 A.B. L.464 J.D. [Stolpman K.E.M.&K.]
*PRACTICE AREAS: Premises/Construction Accident Law; Products Liability Law.
Accetta, Therese Ann ..............'55 '83 C.768 B.A. L.809 J.D. 780 Atlantic Ave., 3rd Fl.

**Ackerman, James H., Law Offices of, (AV) '17 '49 C&L.800 B.A., J.D. BB**
**Suite 1440, One World Trade Center, 90831-1440**
**Telephone: 310-436-9911 Cable Address: "Jimack" Telecopier: 310-436-1897**
**Admiralty, General Maritime, Personal Injury and International Law. Trial Practice.**
**References: Farmers and Merchants Bank (Long Beach Main Office); Sumitomo Bank of California (Long Beach Main Office).**
***See Professional Biographies, LONG BEACH, CALIFORNIA***

Adam, Elaine M. .......................'59 '85 C.112 B.A. L.809 J.D. 100 Oceangate
**Adams, Sandra L.** .................................'— '89 C.800 B.S. L.426 J.D. [Ⓑ Kegel,T.&T.]
Agins, Richard H. ........'43 '70 C.112 B.S. L.426 J.D. Gen. Coun., Eldon Industries Inc.
Aitken, Robert E., (AV) ........'30 '58 C.912 B.S. L.477 J.D. 301 E. Ocean Blvd., 7th Fl.
Aleccia, James P. ......................'56 '89 C.1044 B.A. L.790 J.D. 400 Oceangate Ave.
Alesso, Richard A., (BV) .........................'39 '67 C.426 B.A. L.809 LL.B. Dep. City Atty.
Allan, Steven H., (AV) ...........'43 '69 C.1042 A.B. L.1068 J.D. Ofc. of the Pub. Def.
**Allen, Mark C., III** ..........................'49 '74 C.293 B.A. L.426 J.D. [Wise,W.T.&W.]
*PRACTICE AREAS: Contract Law; Insurance Law; Litigation; Probate Law.
Allmeroth, Marc D., (BV) ..................'55 '81 C.605 B.A. L.809 J.D. [Garner,Z.&A.]
Alpert, Charles S. .......'46 '71 C.912 B.A. L.477 J.D. Gen. Coun., Earth Tech. Corp., The
Alvarado, Judith T. .....................'60 '91 C.112 B.A. L.800 J.D. [Carroll,K.&T.]
**Amaro, Michael L.**, (AV) ..............'58 '83 C.1109 B.A. L.809 J.D. [Prindle,D.&A.]
*PRACTICE AREAS: Insurance Defense; Amusement Park Litigation; Product Liability.
**Amberg, Robert R.** '52 '79 C.801 B.S. L.1026 J.D.
V.P. & Gen. Coun., Retirement Housing Found.
*RESPONSIBILITIES: Labor (20%); Corporate (20%); Real Estate (20%); Litigation (20%); Business (20%).
**Ammirato, Vincent A.**, (AV) ......'42 '72 C.1042 B.A. L.1049 J.D. [Burns,A.P.M.&B.]⊙
*PRACTICE AREAS: Products Liability; Construction Accident; General Trial Work.
**Anderson, Gary M.** '49 '81
C.112 B.S.M.E. L.809 J.D. [Ⓑ Fulwider P.L.&U.] (See Pat. Sect.)
*PRACTICE AREAS: Patent, Trademark, Copyright and Unfair Competition Law; Litigation.
Anderson, John T., (BV) ..........................'49 '75 L.809 J.D. 1741 E. Wardlow Rd.
Anderson, William B. ......................'62 '95 C.112 B.S. L.990 J.D. 100 Oceangate
Andrew, Laurie E. ......................'52 '87 C.349 B.S. L.426 J.D. Dep. Dist. Atty.
Andrews, Bradford L. ......................'44 '82 C.1042 B.A. L.1148 J.D. Mun. Ct. J.
Apostle, James A. ..............'56 '84 C.1042 L.1137 J.D. 4047 Long Valley Blvd.‡
**Appelbaum, Richard A.** '40 '70 C.869 B.S. L.273 J.D.
(adm. in FL; not adm. in CA) [Ⓑ Keesal,Y.&L.]
**Armitage, Michael L.** .........................'61 '87 C&L.861 B.A., J.D. [Keesal,Y.&L.]
*LANGUAGES: Spanish and Portuguese.
Armstrong, Robert W., (AV) ............'52 '78 C.112 B.A. L.464 J.D. [Demler,A.&R.]⊙
Arndt, Christopher J. ..............'55 '81 C.597 B.A. L.426 J.D. 301 E. Ocean Blvd.
Arneal, Richard G. ..........................'62 '89 C.112 B.A. L.1137 J.D. [Wolfe&W.]
Ashby, F. Paul, Jr., (BV) '43 '77 C.1042 B.A. L.1137 J.D.
Mng. Atty., Legal Aid Found.
**Ashby, John C.** ..............................'61 '89 C&L.477 A.B., J.D. [Ⓑ Lillick&C.]
Aspiz, Ira M. ..........................'55 '81 C.1042 B.A. L.426 J.D. 555 E. Ocean Blvd.
**Atlee, Elizabeth E.** ......................'65 '93 C.976 B.A. L.800 J.D. [Ⓑ Keesal,Y.&L.]
*LANGUAGES: Spanish.
August, George R. ....................'18 '72 C.112 B.S. L.1001 J.D. 6055 Lido Lane
Austin, Jack F. .....................................'27 '53 C.813 L.809 LL.B. 800 South St.
Austin, Robert G. ..............................'22 '52 C&L.809 LL.B. 471 Kakkis Dr.‡
Avirom, Cheryl R. ....................'51 '76 C.940 A.B. L.976 J.D. 440 Redondo Ave.
Ayers, Christan L., (BV) .............'55 '83 C.112 B.A. L.1065 J.D. 401 E. Ocean Blvd.
Bak-Boychuk, I. Michael, (BV) .......'39 '71 C.645 B.S. L.831 J.D. 401 W. 4th St. (Pat.)
Baker, Richard M., (AV) .................'48 '84 C.1077 B.A. L.426 J.D. [Cantrell,G.&P.]

**Baker & Hostetler, (AV) BB**
**300 Oceangate, Suite 620, 90802-6807⊙**
**Telephone: 310-432-2827 FAX: 310-432-6698**
**Members of Firm in Long Beach, California: Sheldon A. Gebb (Managing Partner, Los Angeles and Long Beach, California and Houston, Texas Offices). Partners: Robert E. Coppola (Partner in Charge); David A. Kettel; George T. Mooradian; Christina L. Owen. Associates: Kenneth E. Johnson; George M. Jones; Steven Y. Otera; Robert M. White, Jr. Of Counsel: Herbert W. Kalmbach.**
**General Practice.**
**In Cleveland, Ohio: 3200 National City Center, 1900 East Ninth Street. Telephone: 216-621-0200.**
**In Columbus, Ohio: Capitol Square, Suite 2100, 65 East State Street. Telephone: 614-228-1541.**
**In Denver, Colorado: 303 East 17th Avenue, Suite 1100. Telephone: 303-861-0600.**
**In Houston, Texas: 1000 Louisiana, Suite 2000. Telephone: 713-236-0020.**
**In Los Angeles, California: 600 Wilshire Boulevard. Telephone: 213-624-2400.**
**In Orlando, Florida: SunBank Center, Suite 2300, 200 South Orange Avenue. Telephone: 407-649-4000.**

(This Listing Continued)

CAA158P

**Baker & Hostetler (Continued)**

**In Washington, D. C.: Washington Square, Suite 1100, 1050 Connecticut Avenue, N. W. Telephone: 202-861-1500.**
**In College Park, Maryland: 9658 Baltimore Boulevard, Suite 206. Telephone: 301-441-2781.**
**In Alexandria, Virginia: 437 North Lee Street. Telephone: 703-549-1294.**
**In San Francisco, California: One Sansome Street, Suite 2000. Telephone: 415-951-4705.**

*See Professional Biographies, LONG BEACH, CALIFORNIA*

Bardales, Oscar, II, (BV) .... '49 '75 C.112 B.A. L.809 J.D. 350 Redondo Ave.
Barker, Elizabeth A. .... '48 '77 C&L.1137 B.S., J.D. 3605 Long Beach Blvd.
Barnes, Earl A., (BV) .... '27 '55 C.813 B.A. L.1001 LL.B. [Barnes&B.]
Barnes, Kenneth Logan, Jr. .... '46 '81 C.800 A.B. L.426 J.D. 5500 Atherton St.
**Barnes, Tahereh K.** .... '66 '91 C.112 B.A. L.809 J.D. [Ⓐ Prindle,D.&A.]
*PRACTICE AREAS: Insurance Coverage Defense; Environmental; Workers Compensation.
Barnes, Trent L. .... '57 '89 [Barnes&B.]
Barnes & Barnes, (BV) .... 3633 E. Bway.
**Barnett, Kathleen E.** .... '57 '87 C.112 B.A. L.1049 J.D. [Ⓐ O'Flaherty&B.]
*PRACTICE AREAS: Litigation; Appellate Work.
Barnhill, Steven M. .... '61 '87 C&L.1049 B.B.A., J.D. [Barnhill&M.]
Barnhill & McKasson .... 301 E. Ocean Blvd.
Barrad, Catherine M. '53 '80
C&L.1137 B.S.L., J.D. 6200 E. Spring St. (ⓞMakawao, Hawaii)
Barrera, Victor T. .... '39 '65 C&L.800 A.B., LL.B. Supr. Ct. J.
Barrett, Nelda K. .... '41 '84 C.1077 B.A. L.426 J.D. Off. of Pub. Def.
**Barrow, Brian P.** .... '68 '95 C.1169 B.A. L.1148 J.D. [Ⓐ O'Flaherty&B.]
**Bartholomew, David M.** .... '59 '87 C.918 B.A. L.800 J.D. [Keesal,Y.&L.]
Bartos, John F., (AV) .... '31 '62 C.112 B.S. L.1068 LL.B. [Bartos&W.]
Bartos & Weber, A Prof. Corp., (AV) .... 4001 Atlantic Ave.
**Bass, Stephen Chace** .... '52 '87 C.1042 B.A. L.1068 J.D. [Ⓒ Fisher&P.]
*PRACTICE AREAS: Maritime Law; Insurance Law; Commercial Litigation.
Batsakis, Theodore J. .... '54 '82 C.112 B.A. L.1137 J.D. 3960 N. Studebaker Rd.
Batson, Ron, (BV) .... '39 '72 C.1042 B.A. L.809 J.D. 4801 E. Anaheim St.
**Bauer, Dona Fay** .... '53 '85 L.940 J.D. [Ⓐ Johnson,C.&R.]
*PRACTICE AREAS: Municipality Defense; Premises Liability; Uninsured Motorist Litigation.
Bayles, Calvin D., (AV) .... '48 '76 C&L.101 B.A., J.D. [Martin&S.]
Beason, Joseph D. .... '38 '75 C.1042 L.1001 J.D. 110 W. Ocean Blvd.
Beatty, Sean D. .... '64 '91 C.1077 B.A. L.464 J.D. 4500 E. Pacific Hwy., 4th Fl.
**Beazley, Elizabeth P.** .... '61 '88 C.112 B.A. L.1049 J.D. [Keesal,Y.&L.]
**Beck, Dwayne S.** .... '61 '92 C.684 B.A. L.1137 J.D. [Prindle,D.&A.]
*PRACTICE AREAS: Insurance Defense; Amusement Park Litigation.
**Beck, Ronald**, (AV) .... '53 '78 C.154 B.A. L.1049 J.D. [Perona,L.&B.]
Becker, Eric F. .... '61 '89 C.446 B.A. L.128 J.D. [Ⓐ R.Helton]
Beeks, Gary E., (BV) .... '50 '77 C.668 B.A. L.990 J.D. 1412 E. Wardlow Rd.
Beeks, Mary Swift .... '15 '41 L.809 1412 E. Wardlow Rd.‡
**Behar, Jeffrey S.**, (AV) .... '52 '78 C.112 B.A. L.426 J.D. [Ford,W.H.&B.]
*PRACTICE AREAS: Construction Defect Litigation; Products Liability; Premises Liability; Security Related Litigation; Civil Environmental Litigation.
Bell, Ida May Peterson .... '26 '77 C.878 B.S. L.1137 J.D. Legal Aid of Long Beach
**Bennett, Charles J.**, (AV) '30 '71 C.112 B.A. L.1068 LL.B.
[Bennett&K.] (ⓞSan Rafael)
*PRACTICE AREAS: Personal Injury Defense; Medical Malpractice; Business Litigation; Insurance Coverage; Professional Malpractice.

**Bennett & Kistner, (AV) BB**
**115 Pine Avenue, Suite 600, 90802-4446**
**Telephone: 310-435-6675 Fax: 310-437-8375**
**Charles J. Bennett; Wayne T. Kistner; Richard R. Bradbury. Associate: Charles H. Smith. Of Counsel: Christopher Johns (Also Member of Johns, Helmueller & Christensen, San Rafael, California).**
**General Civil Litigation at Trial and Appellate levels in both State and Federal Courts. Personal Injury Defense, Medical Malpractice, Insurance Defense, Business Litigation, Professional Malpractice, Governmental Entities.**
**Representative Clients: The Hertz Corp.; Mattel, Inc.; Di Salvo Trucking Co.; Long Beach Community Medical Center; Los Angeles County Metropolitan Transportation Authority; Long Beach Memorial Medical Center; Saddleback Memorial Medical Center; Utah Home Fire Insurance; P.C.H. Enterprise, Inc.**
**Reference: Ken Walker of Farmers & Merchants Bank, Long Beach, California.**

Benson, Maurice A., (BV) .... '40 '67 C.563 B.E.E. L.426 J.D. 6615 E. Pacific Coast Hwy.
Berberian, Linda J. .... '53 '88 C.696 B.A. L.426 J.D. 301 E. Ocean Blvd.
**Berger, Susan D.** .... '60 '85 C.112 B.A. L.809 J.D. [Ford,W.H.&B.]
*LANGUAGES: Italian, Spanish and French.
Bergkvist, Carl M., (BV) .... '38 '67 L.426 J.D. 100 Oceangate
**Biard, Michael W.** .... '68 '96 C.178 B.A. L.426 J.D. [Ⓐ Keesal,Y.&L.]
**Billings, Julie H.** .... '68 '93 C.112 B.A. L.61 J.D. [Ⓐ Fields I.&B.]
**Binning, Michael W.** .... '54 '79 C.112 B.A. L.1067 J.D. [Fields I.&B.]
Birenbaum, Herbert A. .... '37 '64 C.659 B.S. L.831 J.D. Atlantic Richfield Co. (Pat.)
Blair, Keith J. .... '48 '75 C.800 B.S. L.1049 J.D. 780 Atlantic Ave.
Blakey, Robert M., (AV) .... '30 '56 C.154 A.B. L.800 J.D. [R.M.Blakey]
Blakey, Robert M., A Professional Law Corporation, (AV) .... 2750 N. Bellflower Blvd.
Blaskey, Richard J., (BV) .... '47 '79 C&L.999 B.S.L., J.D. 555 E. Ocean Blvd.
Blaustein, Joseph B. .... '46 '78 C.680 B.A. L.809 J.D. 3246 Woodruff Ave.
Block, Samuel P., (AV) .... '10 '31 C.112 L.109 LL.B. 3505 Long Beach Blvd.‡
**Blumberg, John P.**, (AV) .... '49 '76 C.1042 B.A. L.1137 J.D. [Blumberg]
*PRACTICE AREAS: Legal and Medical Malpractice; Personal Injury; Business Litigation; Mediation.
**Blumberg, Myron**, (AV) .... '19 '54 C.494 B.B.A. L.800 J.D. [Blumberg]ⓞ
*PRACTICE AREAS: Municipal Law; Dispute Resolution and Mediation.

**Blumberg Law Corporation, (AV)**
**100 Oceangate Suite 1100, 90802ⓞ**
**Telephone: 310-437-0403 Fax: 310-432-0107**
**Myron Blumberg; John P. Blumberg; Ave Buchwald.**
**General Civil Trial and Appellate Practice. Professional Liability and Mediation.**
**Mammoth Lakes Office: 1196 Majestic Pines Drive. P.O. Box 368, Mammoth Lakes, California, 93546. Telephone: 619-934-2907. Fax: 619-934-5499.**

*See Professional Biographies, LONG BEACH, CALIFORNIA*

**Bogoch, Anne-Elenore E.** .... '64 '89 C.197 B.A. L.94 J.D. [Ⓐ M.J.Emling]
*LANGUAGES: French.
*PRACTICE AREAS: Intellectual Property; Copyright; Trademark; Entertainment Law.
**Borg, Donn** .... '28 '59 C.869 B.S. L.276 J.D. [Kirlin,C.&K.]
**Boskovich, Violet M.** .... '53 '84 C.1042 L.1179 J.D. [Churchill&B.]
*PRACTICE AREAS: Probate; Estate Planning; Trust Administration.
**Boss, Gregory A.** .... '61 '87 C&L.800 B.S., J.D. [Ⓐ Keesal,Y.&L.]
**Bothwell, Bruce E.**, (AV) .... '54 '80 C.112 B.A. L.1049 J.D. [Pray,P.W.&R.]
*PRACTICE AREAS: Litigation; Personal Injury Law; Family Law; Business Law; Real Estate Law.
**Botti, Christopher E.** .... '64 '90 C.1044 B.S. L.1148 J.D. [Ⓐ Kerry,G.&L.]
*PRACTICE AREAS: Personal Injury Insurance; Business Litigation and Transactions.
**Bourette Schuur, Pamela** .... '59 '85 C.800 B.S. L.940 J.D. [Ⓐ Vandenberg,N.C.N.&S.]
*PRACTICE AREAS: Probate Litigation; Estate Planning; Conservatorships; Construction Law; Tax Litigation.
Boyd, James R. .... '58 '92 C.464 B.A. L.1137 J.D. 110 W. Ocean

**Bradbury, Richard R.** .... '46 '73 C.684 B.A. L.61 J.D. [Bennett&K.]
*PRACTICE AREAS: Personal Injury Defense; Medical Malpractice; Insurance Defense.
Brady, James .... '47 '90 C.1097 B.S. L.1137 J.D. 4500 E. Pacific Coast Hwy., 4th Fl.
Brady, James C. .... '42 '89 C.112 B.A. L.809 — 110 Pine Ave., 11th Fl.
**Brahms, Sharon A.** .... '46 '89 C.999 R.N. L.809 J.D. [Ⓐ O'Flaherty&B.]
Brakewood, Robert E. .... '38 '91 C.679 B.S. L.426 J.D. 100 Oceangate

**Brandmeyer, Brian K., Law Offices of, (BV) '37 '63 C&L.426 B.A., J.D.**
**One World Trade Center, Suite 1600, 90831-1600**
**Telephone: 310-499-2131 Fax: 310-499-2132**
***PRACTICE AREAS: Family Law; Personal Injury.**
**Family Law, Personal Injury.**

*See Professional Biographies, LONG BEACH, CALIFORNIA*

**Brandon, Lisa E. '60 '87 C.1109 B.A. L.809 J.D.**
**200 Oceangate, Suite 1580, 90802**
**Telephone: 310-901-9800 FAX: 310-983-9383**
***PRACTICE AREAS: Family Law; Civil Litigation.**
**Family Practice emphasizing Dissolution, Marital Contracts, Custody Issues, Wills, Trusts and Related Civil Litigation.**

*See Professional Biographies, LONG BEACH, CALIFORNIA*

Braude, Evan Anderson .... '47 '73 C.112 B.A. L.426 J.D. 115 Pine Ave.
Brayton, Thomas J. .... '50 '92 C.1042 B.A. L.1001 J.D. 3930 CharlemagneAve.
**Bridgen, William J.** .... '64 '89 C.282 B.A. L.831 J.D. [Ⓐ Keesal,Y.&L.]
Bright, David S., (AV) .... '49 '74 C.112 B.A. L.1049 J.D. [White&B.]ⓞ
Brizendine, Richard A., (BV) .... '31 '70 L.990 J.D. Dep. City Pros.
Brodsky, Ronald D., (BV) .... '34 '64 C&L.174 J.D. Dep. City Pros.
Bronn, Clyde L., (AV) .... '21 '55 C.546 L.800 J.D. 4968 Atherton St.
Brough, Melinda A. .... '68 '94 L.990 McDonnell Douglas Fin. Corp.
Brover, Richard D., (CV) .... '52 '77 C.112 B.A. L.426 J.D. 350 Redondo Ave.
Brown, Phyllis C. .... '48 '76 C&L.1137 B.S., J.D. 4000 Long Beach Blvd.
**Brucculeri, Frank C.** .... '63 '88 C.951 B.A. L.861 J.D. [Tabrisky B.&S.]
*REPORTED CASES: Griffith v. Martech Int'l, Inc., 754 F. Supp. 166 (C.D. Cal. 1989).
*PRACTICE AREAS: Jones Act; Longshore; Personal Injury Defense; Maritime Insurance; Property Casualty Litigation and Coverage.

**Brummett, Franklin J., (AV) '34 '64 C.670 B.S.Gen.Eng. L.800 LL.B.**
**111 W. Ocean Boulevard, Suite 1300, P.O. Box 2210, 90802**
**Telephone: 310-437-2926 Fax: 310-590-7909**
**Civil Litigation and Business Matters.**

*See Professional Biographies, LONG BEACH, CALIFORNIA*

**Buchwald, Ave** .... '51 '76 C.112 B.S. L.107 J.D. [Blumberg]
*PRACTICE AREAS: Real Estate; Civil Litigation; Appeals.
Buck, Robert, (AV) .... '15 '46 C.560 A.B. L.800 LL.B. 300 Oceangate‡
Buckley, Theodore A. '43 '76 C.1042 B.A. L.426 J.D.
Legal Adviser, Long Beach Unified Sch. Dist.
Buentgen, Bernadette .... '58 '85 C.112 B.A. L.1049 J.D. 320 Golden Shore Dr.
Burford, William H. .... '— '76 C.832 B.A. L.1068 J.D. 301 E. Ocean Blvd.
Burgos, Rosemarie .... '60 '87 C.800 B.S. L.1049 J.D. 5855 E. Naples Plaza
Burke, Sean M., (AV) .... '53 '81 C&L.800 A.B., J.D. [Thielen&B.]
**Burnight, Gregory J.** .... '66 '91 C.112 B.A. L.800 J.D. [Ⓐ Vandenberg,N.C.N.&S.]
*PRACTICE AREAS: Business and Corporations; Personal Injury; Estate Planning; Family Law; Probate Litigation.

**Burns, Ammirato, Palumbo, Milam & Baronian, A Professional Law Corporation, (AV) BB**
**One World Trade Center, Suite 1200, 90831-1200ⓞ**
**Telephone: 310-436-8338; 714-952-1047 Fax: 310-432-6049**
**Vincent A. Ammirato;—Grace C. Mori; Michael P. Vicencia; Michael E. Wenzel.**
**General Civil and Trial Practice in all Courts. Insurance Defense, Products Liability, Toxic Torts, Construction Litigation, Medical Malpractice, Personal Injury, Tort, Subrogation and Wrongful Termination.**
**Pasadena, California Office: 65 North Raymond Avenue, 2nd Floor. Telephone: 818-796-5053; 213-258-8282. Fax: 818-792-3078.**

*See Professional Biographies, LONG BEACH, CALIFORNIA*

Buzas, John S. .... '57 '85 C.800 A.B. L.809 J.D. 801 Pacific Ave.
Caffray, Donald B., (AV) .... '28 '53 C.112 B.S. L.800 J.D. [D.B.Caffray]
Caffray, Donald B., A Prof. Corp., Law Offices of, (AV) .... 444 West Ocean Boulevard
Calescibetta, C.C. .... '32 '89 C.763 B.A. L.1001 J.D. Med. Dir., St. Marys Med. Ctr.
Calhoun, John R., (AV) .... '33 '58 C&L.352 B.A., J.D. City Atty.

**Calvillo, Stevan R., (BV) '47 '75 C.763 B.S. L.1137 J.D.**
**200 Oceangate, Suite 430, 90802**
**Telephone: 310-983-6624 Facsimile: 310-983-6628**
**Business, Real Estate Litigation and Shareholder Litigation.**

*See Professional Biographies, LONG BEACH, CALIFORNIA*

**Cameron, Timothy C.**, (AV) .... '43 '73 C.112 A.B. L.61 J.D. [Cameron,M.P.G.&S.]

**Cameron, Madden, Pearlson, Gale & Sellars, (AV) BB**
**One World Trade Center Suite 1600, 90831-1600**
**Telephone: 310-436-3888 Telecopier: 310-437-1967**
**Members of the Firm: Timothy C. Cameron; Charles M. Gale; Patrick T. Madden; Paul R. Pearlson; James D. Sellars. Associate: Lillian D. Salinger.**
**General Civil Trial and Appellate Practice, State and Federal Courts, Real Estate, Land Use, Environmental, Administrative, Corporate, Partnership, Taxation, Estate Planning, Trust and Employment Law.**

*See Professional Biographies, LONG BEACH, CALIFORNIA*

**Cammarano, Dennis A., (AV) '57 '83 C.1044 B.A. L.262 J.D.**
**Fidelity Federal Plaza, 555 East Ocean Boulevard, Suite 501, 90802-5003ⓞ**
**Telephone: 310-495-9501 Facsimile: 310-495-3674**
***PRACTICE AREAS: Admiralty Law; Insurance Law; Transportation Law; Inland Marine Insurance; Casualty Defense.**
**Associate: Karen L. Donald; Elene Daley. Of Counsel: Gregory B. Gershuni.**
**Maritime and General Transportation Law, Inland Marine, Casualty Defense, Subrogation, Insurance Coverage and Policy Defense, Products Liability, General Business Litigation.**
**Representative Clients: Great American Insurance Companies; Mitsui Marine Group; Reliance Insurance Companies; Tokio Marine and Fire Insurance Co.; Zurich-American Insurance Group.**
**New York, N.Y. Office: 133 West 72nd Street, 10023. Telephone: 212-942-5676. Facsimile: 212-942-5721.**

Cantrell, Green & Pekich, A Professional Corporation, (AV) .... 200 Pine Ave., Suite 600
Caplan, Morton L., (AV) .... '32 '73 C.431 B.S.M.E. L.809 J.D. 100 Oceangate
Cardona, Elena .... '58 '86 C.112 B.A. L.1066 J.D. 401 E. Ocean Blvd.
**Carlin, Gary R.**, (BV) .... '42 '70 C.112 A.B. L.1065 J.D. [G.R.Carlin]
Carlin, Nancy G. .... '54 '83 C.66 B.A. L.1067 J.D. [Carlin&C.]
Carlin & Ceccia .... 1850 Redondo Ave.

**Carlin, Gary R., A Professional Corporation, (BV)**
**Suite 918, 555 East Ocean Boulevard, 90802**
**Telephone: 310-432-8933 Fax: 310-435-1656**
**Gary R. Carlin.**
**Civil Trials and Appeals. Wrongful Termination, Personal Injury, Business Litigation and Family Law.**

(This Listing Continued)

CAA159P

**Carlin, Gary R., A Professional Corporation (Continued)**
Reference: Bank of America.
*See Professional Biographies, LONG BEACH, CALIFORNIA*

Carroll, John E., (BV) .......... '30 '57 C.800 B.A. L.426 LL.B. [Carroll&C.]
Carroll, John H., Jr. .......... '37 '62 C.940 B.A. L.1068 LL.B. 3855 Lakewood Blvd.
Carroll, Richard D. .......... '54 '84 C.197 B.A. L.990 J.D. [Carroll,K.&T.]
Carroll, Vincent K., (BV) .......... '59 '84 L.1137 J.D. [Carroll&C.]
Carroll & Carroll, (BV) .......... 333 West Broadway
Carroll, Kelly & Trotter .......... 100 Oceangate
Carvajal, Roxane M. .......... '54 '80 C.112 L.1065 J.D. Dep. Dist. Atty.
Casey, Kathleen L. .......... '49 '75 C.770 B.A. L.426 J.D. 4510 E. Pacific Coast Hwy.
**Casey, Sean M.** '62 '95 C.94 B.S.A.E. L.809 J.D.
[Fulwider P.L.&U.] (See Pat. Sect.)
*PRACTICE AREAS: Patent; Copyright; Trademark Prosecution; Intellectual Property Litigation.
Castner, Jeffery P. .......... '46 '78 C&L.1137 B.S.L., J.D. Mun. Ct. Comr.
**Catron, John A.** .......... '61 '88 C.101 B.A. L.893 J.D. Div. Coun., Douglas Aircraft Co.
*RESPONSIBILITIES: Commercial; Contracts; Corporate Finance.
Cavanaugh, James Early .......... '49 '93 C.112 B.A. L.284 J.D. [Demler,A.&R.]
**Cayer, John J.**, (AV) .......... '28 '55 C.999 A.B. L.426 J.D. [Cayer,K.&C.]
*PRACTICE AREAS: Banking; Corporation; Estate Planning; Probate; Equine and Securities Law.

**Cayer, Kilstofte & Craton, A Professional Law Corporation, (AV)**
**Suite 700, 444 West Ocean Boulevard, 90802**
**Telephone: 310-435-6008 Fax: 310-435-3704**
**Email: CKCCRC@AOL.COM**
**John J. Cayer; Stephen R. Kilstofte; Curt R. Craton;—Cortlen R. Hauge.**
**General Business and Civil Trial Practice before all Federal and State Courts. Banking and Bank Litigation, Business Litigation, Corporations, Corporate Securities, Federal and State Taxation, Estate Planning, Probate, Real Property Sales and Financing, Equine Law and Syndication, Family Law, Personal Injury and Workers Compensation Law.**
*See Professional Biographies, LONG BEACH, CALIFORNIA*

**Cebula, T. J.**, (AV) .......... '57 '83 C.1042 B.A. L.426 J.D. [Johnson,C.&R.]
*PRACTICE AREAS: General Civil Law; Litigation; Insurance Defense Law; Fraud and Suspicious Claims.
Ceccia, Richard M. .......... '55 '86 C.112 B.A. L.426 J.D. [Carlin&C.]
Cecil, Cameron W., (AV) .......... '15 '43 C.674 B.A. L.309 LL.B. 133 Roswell St.
Chang, Lawrence L. .......... '64 '94 C.112 B.A. L.426 J.D. 310 Golden Shore
Charvat, Frank C. .......... '02 '26 C&L.190 A.B., LL.B. 301 E. Ocean Blvd., 7th Fl.
Charvat, Richard F. .......... '38 '64 C.112 B.A. L.1065 LL.B. Supr. Ct. J.
**Chavez, Robert J.** .......... '61 '87 C&L.800 B.S., J.D. [Ford,W.H.&B.]
**Chavez, Ronald A.** .......... '54 '85 C.1169 B.A. L.1068 J.D. [O'Flaherty&B.]
*LANGUAGES: Spanish.
Chel, Frederik W., (BV) .......... '29 '55 C.990 B.A. L.1068 J.D. 1711 Harbor Ave.‡
Chemeleski, John E., (AV) .......... '48 '75 C.1043 L.809 J.D. Trial Ct. Comr., Supr. Ct.
**Cho, Teresa** .......... '64 '92 C.112 B.S. L.1068 J.D. [La Torraca&G.]
**Chonoles, Stephen J.** .......... '55 '92 C.33 B.A. L.809 J.D. [Danner&C.]
*LANGUAGES: Japanese.
*PRACTICE AREAS: Wrongful Termination; Business Litigation; Products Liability.
**Chrzanowski, Eugene L.** .......... '48 '73 C.321 B.A. L.276 J.D. [Littler,M.F.T.&M.]
**Churchill, Carol A.** .......... '53 '83 C.172 B.S. L.1136 J.D. [Churchill&B.]
*PRACTICE AREAS: Probate; Estate Planning; Trust Administration; Estate Taxation.

**Churchill & Boskovich**
**401 East Ocean Boulevard, Suite 507, 90802**
**Telephone: 310-437-1559 Telecopier: 310-495-4311**
**Members of Firm: Carol A. Churchill (Certified Specialist, Probate, Estate Planning and Trust Law, State Bar of California Board of Legal Specialization); Violet M. Boskovich.**
**Probate, Estate Planning and Trust Law.**
*See Professional Biographies, LONG BEACH, CALIFORNIA*

Cislo & Thomas, (AV) .......... 4201 N. Long Beach Blvd. (Pat.) (©Santa Monica)
**Clapp, Theodore A.** .......... '64 '91 C&L.426 B.S., J.D. [Ford,W.H.&B.]

**Claveran-Lopez, Laura E.** '— '82 C.112 B.A. L.800 J.D.
**2703 East Seventh Street, 90804**
**Telephone: 310-433-0004 Fax: 310-433-4640**
**Email: lawrac@aol.com**
***PRACTICE AREAS: Personal Injury; Immigration and Naturalization; Art Law.**
**Personal Injury, Immigration and Naturalization, Art Law.**
*See Professional Biographies, LONG BEACH, CALIFORNIA*

Clayton, Sterling S., (AV) .......... '27 '54 C&L.813 B.A., J.D. 354 Empire Landing‡
Clemmer, Stephen B. .......... '48 '89 C.1042 B.A. L.1148 J.D. 444 W. Ocean Blvd.

**Cockriel, Stephen E., (BV)** '48 '73 C.800 B.S. L.426 J.D.
**333 West Broadway, Suite 306, 90802-4440**
**Telephone: 310-901-1447 FAX: 310-437-3492**
**Estate Planning, Probate, Real Estate and Business Law.**
*See Professional Biographies, LONG BEACH, CALIFORNIA*

Coffman, David R., (BV) .......... '46 '82 C&L.1338 B.A., J.D. 3605 Long Beach Blvd.
**Cogswell, Forrest R.** .......... '46 '75 C.197 A.B. L.145 J.D. [Williams W.C.N.&R.]
*LANGUAGES: Spanish.
*REPORTED CASES: Amando Martinez v. Korean Shipping Corp., Ltd., et al., 903 F.2d 606 (9th Cir. 1990); Katherine E. Rumberg, et al. v. Weber Aircraft Corporation, et al., 424 F. Supp. 294 (1976); Eliud A. Torres v. Johnson Lines and NYK Lines, 1989 AMC 1009; United Kingdom Mutual Steamship Assurance Association (Bermuda) Limited v. Continental Maritime of San Francisco, Inc., Inc., 1993 AMC 542.
*PRACTICE AREAS: Maritime Law; Transportation and International Law; Commercial Transactions and Litigation; Personal Injury; Product Liability.
Cohen, Arthur D. .......... '47 '75 C.112 B.A. L.276 J.D. 3855 Lakewood Blvd.

**Cohen, Jerome S., Law Offices of '39 '71 C.821 B.A. L.659 LL.B.**
**301 East Ocean Boulevard Suite 540, 90802-4828**
**Telephone: 310-983-1160 Fax: 310-983-1870**
***LANGUAGES: French.**
***PRACTICE AREAS: Bankruptcy; Civil Litigation.**
**Bankruptcy, Business Reorganization, Commercial Collections, Judgment Enforcement, Insolvency, Creditors' Rights, Domestic and International Commercial Law.**
*See Professional Biographies, LONG BEACH, CALIFORNIA*

**Cohen, Jodi S.** .......... '64 '90 C.1109 B.A. L.464 J.D. [Keesal,Y.&L.]
*PRACTICE AREAS: Securities.
Cohen, Nellie .......... '10 '66 C.831 B.A. L.800 LL.B. 3702 Faust Ave.
**Cohen, Nelson L.** .......... '60 '91 C.800 B.S. L.1148 J.D. [Perona,L.&B.]
**Cole, Montgomery** .......... '55 '80 C.1042 B.A. L.426 J.D. [Madden,J.C.&J.]
*PRACTICE AREAS: Personal Injury Litigation; Civil and Commercial Litigation.
**Collier, William H., Jr.** .......... '52 '78 C.691 B.A. L.861 J.D. [Keesal,Y.&L.]
Collins, Wynn L. .......... '43 '80 C.1042 B.A. L.990 J.D. 249 E. Ocean Blvd.
Colton, Jerome G., (BV) .......... '25 '53 C.112 L.809 LL.B. 800 South St.
Coniglio, Terry J. .......... '51 '80 C.1042 B.S. L.1137 J.D. [Coniglio&U.]
Coniglio & Uthoff, A Professional Law Corporation .......... 110 W. Ocean Blvd.
Conway, Richard E., (AV) .......... '48 '73 C.1042 B.S. L.426 J.D. 3233 E. Bway.
**Copeland, Gregory E.** .......... '46 '89 C.1169 B.A. L.426 J.D. [Keesal,Y.&L.]

**Coppola, Robert E.**, (AV) .......... '39 '66 C.178 A.B. L.276 LL.B. [Baker&H.]
*PRACTICE AREAS: Admiralty; Litigation; Insurance.
Corriere, Joette J. .......... '— '92 C.36 B.A. L.1137 J.D. Consumer Legal Centers
Cowan, Arnold M. .......... '21 '49 C.112 B.A. L.800 J.D. 35 Vista del Golfo
**Cox, James M.** .......... '60 '84 C.1109 B.A. L.800 J.D. [Wise,W.T.&W.]
*PRACTICE AREAS: Insurance Law; Litigation.
Cox, William, (BV) .......... '41 '74 C.999 A.S. L.809 J.D. 1435 E. Ocean Blvd.
**Crandall, Elizabeth C.** .......... '70 '95 C.112 B.A. L.464 J.D. [Keesal,Y.&L.]
**Craton, Curt R.** .......... '54 '85 C.1167 B.S. L.426 J.D. [Cayer,K.&C.]
*PRACTICE AREAS: Banking; Corporation; Tax; Estate Planning; Real Property Law.

**Cree & Prineas, (BV)**
**4047 Long Beach Boulevard, P.O. Box 7646, 90807**
**Telephone: 310-424-0417 FAX: 310-595-1174**
**William H. Cree, Jr. (1926-1983); Zachary T. Prineas.**
**Oil and Gas, Business and Real Estate, Probate, Estate Planning and Trust Law.**

Crutchfield, John J. .......... '53 '78 C&L.800 B.S., J.D. 1820 Nipomo Ave.
Culver, Howard L. .......... '41 '68 C.197 A.B. L.813 LL.B. Envir. Coun., Targhee Inc.
**Curtis, Mark**, (AV) .......... '54 '80 C.112 B.A. L.990 J.D. [Vandenberg,N.C.N.&S.]
*PRACTICE AREAS: Family Law; Probate Law; Estate Planning; Personal Injury Law.
Dachman, Jerome M. .......... '26 '51 C.930 B.A. L.1003 J.D. 775 Raymond Ave.
**Dale, Gregory T.** .......... '49 '77 C.169 B.A. L.464 J.D. [Mullen&F.]
**Dalessi, William T.**, (AV) .......... '22 '48 C&L.800 J.D. [Riedman,D.&D.]
*PRACTICE AREAS: Estate Planning; Probate Law; Business Law; Real Estate Law.
**Daley, Elene** .......... '58 '96 C.1015 B.A. L.800 J.D. [D.A.Cammarano]
*PRACTICE AREAS: Admiralty and Maritime.
Dalsimer, Vincent S. .......... '21 '50 C.999 L.809 J.D. 6240 Napoli Ct.‡
Dalton, George E. .......... '28 '65 C.878 B.A. L.800 J.D. 100 Oceangate
Dalton, Matthew J. .......... '63 '90 C.112 B.A. L.426 J.D. Dep. City Pros.
**Dalton, Phillip S.** .......... '48 '75 C.112 B.A. L.1068 J.D. [Lillick&C.]
*PRACTICE AREAS: Maritime; Defense of Shipowner Interests in Personal Injury and Cargo Matters; Construction; Products Liability Defense.
Danner, John .......... '47 '76 C.309 B.A. L.1066 J.D. 100 Oceangate
**Danner, Michael J.**, (AV) .......... '52 '77 C.352 B.A. L.809 J.D. [Danner&C.]
*LANGUAGES: Spanish.
*PRACTICE AREAS: Products Liability; Premises Liability; Construction Litigation.

**Danner & Chonoles, L.L.P., (AV)**
**100 Oceangate, Suite 840, 90802**
**Telephone: 562-983-8980 Fax: 562-983-8986**
**Michael J. Danner; Stephen J. Chonoles. Associate: Janet E. Glenny.**
**General Civil Trial and Appellate Practice in State and Federal Courts. Products Liability, Premises Liability, Wrongful Termination, Business Litigation.**
*See Professional Biographies, LONG BEACH, CALIFORNIA*

Darrow, Geraldine .......... '44 '78 C.1042 L.809 J.D. [Darrow&M.]
Darrow, Stephen Hal .......... '55 '84 C.1042 B.S. L.1137 J.D. 3950 N. Long Beach Blvd.
Darrow & Merrill .......... 5150 E. Pacific Coast Highway, Suite 200
**Dato, Robert M.** .......... '58 '83 C.763 B.A. L.1049 J.D. [O'Flaherty&B.]
Davert, Douglass S. .......... '64 '92 C.139 B.A. L.426 J.D. [Davert&L.]
Davert & Loe .......... 320 Pine Ave.
**Davidson, Jock R., (Inc., A Prof. Law Corp.)**, (BV) '43 '71
C.112 B.S. L.1068 J.D. [A.B.Weiss&Assoc.]
*PRACTICE AREAS: Civil Litigation; Probate Law; Negligence Law; Family Law.
Davis, David B., (BV) .......... '46 '71 C.1097 B.A. L.426 J.D. 301 E. Ocean Blvd., Ste 540
Davis, Robert B. .......... '43 '68 C&L.802 B.S., LL.B. 223 1/2 Argonne Ave.
Dayton, Steven A. .......... '55 '92 C.1109 B.A. L.1137 J.D. 5199 E. Pacific Coast Hwy.
**Decker, R. Joseph** .......... '47 '78 C.1109 B.A. L.809 J.D. [Prindle,D.&A.]
*PRACTICE AREAS: Admiralty; Real Estate Transactions; Business Transactions; Personal Injury; Property Damage.
DeJong, Barbara DePaola .......... '48 '88 C.679 B.A. L.1137 J.D. Princ. Dep. City Atty.
Delaterre, Norman F. .......... '47 '77 C.1042 B.A. L.1179 J.D. Mission Ins. Co.

**deMartino, Valerie K. '54 '84 C.1097 B.A. L.1136 J.D.**
**100 Oceangate, 12th Floor, 90802**
**Telephone: 310-628-5577 Fax: 310-628-5578**
***PRACTICE AREAS: Business; Probate; Litigation.**
**Corporate, Business Transactions, Probate, Conservatorships and Estate Planning, Commercial Law, Business and Probate Litigation.**
*See Professional Biographies, LONG BEACH, CALIFORNIA*

Demler, Edison J., (AV) .......... '16 '42 C.112 A.B. L.1066 LL.B. [Demler,A.&R.]
**Demler, Eric C.**, (BV) .......... '54 '80 C.1042 B.A. L.426 J.D. [Kaiser&S.]
Demler, Everett E., (AV) .......... '25 '51 C.112 B.A. L.809 LL.B. 369 Panama Ave.‡
Demler, Armstrong & Rowland, (AV)
4500 E. Pacific Coast Hwy., 4th Fl. (©San Diego)
Dennis, Anna .......... '61 '90 C.043 B.A. L.902 J.D. 3780 Kilroy Airport Way
**Denton, Debra L.** .......... '54 '93 C.800 B.S. L.1137 J.D. [O'Flaherty&B.]
Depew, M. Cecilia Gaudier '61 '92 C.112 B.S. L.1068 J.D.
Gen. Coun., Calif. State Univ.
Desmond, Walter J. .......... '09 '33 C.309 A.B. L.813 J.D. 110 Pine Ave.
Devon, Marcia A. .......... '54 '80 C.475 B.S. L.767 J.D. 333 W. Bway. (Pat.)
Dewire, Mary H. .......... '— '74 L.1137 LL.B. 2856 Monogram Ave.
**Dieffenbach, Richard P.** .......... '55 '82 C.21 B.A. L.910 J.D. [Wise,W.T.&W.]
*PRACTICE AREAS: Insurance Law; Real Property; Litigation.
**Dik, Daniel K.** .......... '59 '91 C.1042 B.S. L.800 J.D. [O'Flaherty&B.]
*LANGUAGES: Spanish.
Dingman, E. Wallace .......... '46 '72 C.768 B.A. L.950 J.D. 115 Pine Ave.
**Dipolito, Frank X.** .......... '51 '88 C.1044 B.S. L.426 J.D. [Swain&D.]
*PRACTICE AREAS: Admiralty and Maritime; Insurance Defense Coverage.
Dixon, Elliott J. .......... '38 '74 C.1097 B.A. L.800 J.D. 333 W. Bway.
Do, Andrew H. .......... '63 '90 C.112 B.A. L.1065 J.D. 300 Oceangate
Dobberpuhl, William E. .......... '46 '75 C.112 B.A. L.990 J.D. 3820 Jotham Pl.

**Dodson, C. Richard '36 '67 C.36 B.A. L.1066 J.D.**
**4100 Long Beach Boulevard, Suite 200, 90807**
**Telephone: 310-595-8771 Fax: 310-595-0723**
***PRACTICE AREAS: Real Estate Law; Litigation; Corporations Law.**
**Computer Law, Business Litigation, Transactions, Real Estate, Civil Trial, Commercial Litigation.**

**Donahue, Lisa Kaye** .......... '66 '91 C.188 B.A. L.1068 J.D. [Keesal,Y.&L.]
**Donald, Karen L.** .......... '60 '93 C.651 B.A. L.809 J.D. [D.A.Cammarano]
Donsbach, Jan S. J. '40 '65 C.107 B.S. L.276 J.D.
(adm. in NY; not adm. in CA) Soc. Sec. Admin.
**Douglas, E. Scott** .......... '58 '83 C.770 B.S. L.1049 J.D. [Keesal,Y.&L.]
Douglas, Gregory A. .......... '49 '90 C.1077 B.S. L.1179 J.D. [Matsuk&O.]
Downing, Charles, (AV) .......... '32 '71 C.453 S.B. L.1152 J.D. P.O. Box 21152
Draffin, Michael C. '52 '77 C.893 B.A. L.309 J.D.
V.P., Taxes & Assoc. Gen. Coun., McDonnell Douglas Fin. Corp.
Duncan, John K., (AV) .......... '28 '56 C.642 L.426 LL.B. 6086 Lido Lane‡
Dunlap, Mollie Busterud .......... '59 '85 C.668 B.A. L.352 J.D. Calif. State Univ.
Dunn, G. William .......... '30 '66 C.608 B.S. in Ed. L.800 J.D. Mun. Ct. J.

**Dunn, Kristin E.D.** '67 '92 C.800 B.S. L.426 J.D. [Ⓐ Prindle,D.&A.]
*PRACTICE AREAS: Insurance Coverage; Environmental.
Dunnett, Carolyn M. S. '40 '80 C.1042 B.A. L.1137 J.D. 3713 Iroquois Ave.
Dunnum, Carroll M. '17 '45 C.809 B.S. L.426 LL.B. Ret. Supr. Ct. J.
**Dybens, Bruce A.**, (BV) '50 '76 C.112 B.A. L.426 J.D. [Riedman,D.&D.]
*PRACTICE AREAS: Litigation; Personal Injury Law; Real Estate Law; Family Law.
Dyer, Don, (BV) '40 '66 C.1042 B.A. L.1068 J.D. 22 Windjammer Ct.
Edgmon, Jerry R., (BV) '35 '66 C.768 A.B. L.800 LL.B. 3835 E. 7th St.
Edmondson, Robert B., (BV) '48 '76 C.112 B.A. L.990 J.D. 5808 E. Naples Plz.
Efros, M. Nicholas Daniel '48 '78
C.560 B.U.S. L.862 J.D. V.P. & Gen. Coun., Worthington Ford, Inc.
Egli, David T. '55 '80 C.605 B.A. L.464 J.D. 4266 Atlantic Blvd. (ⓄL.A.)
Eisenstat, Jared Parnell '59 '87 C.112 B.A. L.978 J.D. 4326 Atlantic Ave.
Eiser, Jay N. '47 '76 C.800 B.A. L.809 J.D. 2355 Pacific Ave.
**Elber, Dennis M.** '51 '76 C.112 B.A. L.1068 J.D. [Stolpman K.E.M.&K.]
*PRACTICE AREAS: Construction Accidents Law; Products Liability Law; Maritime Accidents Law.
**Emling, Michael J.**, (AV) '57 '85 C.1169 B.A. L.767 J.D. [Moore,R.&E.] (Pat.)
*PRACTICE AREAS: Copyright; Trademark; Estate Planning; Business Torts; Insurance Defense.

**Emling, Michael J., Law Office of, (AV) '57 '85 C.1169 B.A. L.767 J.D.**
**555 East Ocean Boulevard Suite 500, 90802**
**Telephone: 310-491-1400 Fax: 310-491-3400**
**Email: emling@aol.com**
**(Also Of Counsel to Moore, Rutter & Evans).**
***REPORTED CASES: In Re Circuit Breaker Litigation, Cite: 852 F. Supp. 883 (C.D. Cal. 1994).**
***PRACTICE AREAS: Intellectual Property Litigation.**
**—Philip H. Haymond; Anne-Elenore E. Bogoch. Of Counsel: Sandra M. Parker.**
**Patent, Trademark, Copyright and Business Litigation.**
*See Professional Biographies, LONG BEACH, CALIFORNIA*

**Ericson, Robert B.** '58 '84 C.813 B.A. L.1068 J.D. [Keesal,Y.&L.]
**Evans, Donna R.** '54 '83 C.174 B.S. L.1137 J.D. [Ⓐ O'Flaherty&B.]
*PRACTICE AREAS: Medical Malpractice.
**Evans, William D., (P.C.)**, (AV) '53 '78 C.645 B.A. L.990 J.D. [Moore,R.&E.]
*PRACTICE AREAS: Civil Trial Practice; Criminal Trial Practice.
Eyre, Michael J. '60 '88 C.112 B.A. L.1137 J.D. 444 W. Ocean Blvd., 9th Fl.
Eyres, Patricia Stearns '51 '77 C.813 B.A. L.426 J.D. 5630 E. El Parque
Ezzell, Donald G. '63 '90 C.112 B.A. L.1065 J.D. 6242 Paramont Blvd.
Farrell, Raymond R. '22 '52 C.112 A.B. L.976 LL.B. Long Bch. City College
**Faulkner, Brian R.** '53 '83 C.112 B.A. L.1049 J.D. [Ⓐ Lillick&C.]
*PRACTICE AREAS: Product Liability; Insurance; Admiralty; Construction Litigation.
**Feighner, Robert D.** '51 '76 C.446 B.A. L.800 J.D. [Keesal,Y.&L.]
Feinberg, Cheryl Lackman, (BV) '57 '86 C.112 B.A. L.1137 J.D.
3740 Long Beach Blvd.
Fentis, John, (BV) '49 '77 C.112 B.A. L.1148 J.D. Dep. City Pros.
**Ferguson, Anna M.** '68 '93 C.112 B.A. L.990 J.D. [Ⓐ Prindle,D.&A.]
*PRACTICE AREAS: Insurance Defense.
Ferrari, Gary J., (BV) '45 '71 C.112 B.A. L.426 J.D. Dep. City Atty.
**Ferrer, Geoffrey D.** '55 '82 C.623 B.A. L.178 J.D. [Hill,B.&N.] (ⓄN.Y., NY)
**Field, Mark E.** '53 '77 C.112 B.A. L.1066 J.D. [Ⓐ L.Silver&Assoc.]
*REPORTED CASES: Felt v. Atchison, Topeka & Santa Fe Railroad, 831 F.Supp. 780 (C.D. Cal. 1993), rev'd 60 F3d 1416 (9th Cir. 1995); Dockside, Ltd. v. Sea Technology, Ltd., 875 F.2d 762 (9th Cir. 1989); Excess & Cas. Reinsurance Assn. v. Insurance Comr. etc., 656 F.2d 497 (9th Cir. 1981).
*PRACTICE AREAS: Litigation; Business Litigation.
**Fields, Gary D.**, (AV) '51 '76 C.112 A.B. L.809 J.D. [Fields I.&B.]

**Fields Israel & Binning LLP, (AV)**
**115 Pine Avenue, Suite 300, 90802**
**Telephone: 310-432-5111 Fax: 310-432-6333**
**Gary D. Fields; Albert S. Israel; Michael W. Binning;—Julie H. Billings. Of Counsel: Charles E. Greenberg; Sharon P. Kee.**
**General Civil, Trial and Appellate Practice, State and Federal, U.S. Tax and U.S. Claims Courts, including Business, Corporate, Commercial, Bankruptcy, Labor, Real Estate Transactions and Land Use, Environmental, Construction, Health Care, Insurance, Personal Injury, Product Liability, Maritime and International Law.**
*See Professional Biographies, LONG BEACH, CALIFORNIA*

**Finnerty, Daniel J.** '65 '93 C.1027 B.S. L.1356 J.D. [Ⓐ Keesal,Y.&L.]
Finzi, David B. '59 '85 C.800 B.S. L.990 J.D. Calfin Properties
**Fisher, Gerald M.**, (AV) '44 '73 C.1042 B.A. L.1049 J.D. [Fisher&P.]
*PRACTICE AREAS: Complex Litigation in Admiralty; Aviation; Transportation Law; Insurance; Insurance "Bad Faith" Defense.
Fisher, R. Rust '41 '72 C.1042 B.S. L.1065 J.D. 333 W. Broadway
Fisher, Thos. R. '13 '38 L.502 LL.B. 2857 Monogram Ave.‡

**Fisher & Porter, A Law Corporation, (AV) BB**
**110 Pine Avenue, 11th Floor, P.O. Box 22686, 90801-5686**
**Telephone: 310-435-5626 Telex: 284549 FPKLAW UR Fax: 310-432-5399**
**Gerald M. Fisher; David S. Porter; Therese G. Groff; Michael W. Lodwick; George P. Hassapis. Of Counsel: Stephen C. Klausen; Stephen Chace Bass; Anthony P. Lombardo;—Vicki L. Hassman; Linda A. Mancini; Michael J. McLaughlin; Sandra L. Gryder; Kenneth F. Mattfeld.**
**Admiralty, Insurance and General Business Litigation, Transportation and Aviation Law, Environmental Law.**
*See Professional Biographies, LONG BEACH, CALIFORNIA*

**Fitzer, Richard L. '66 '91 C.112 B.A. L.209 J.D.**
**P.O. Box 50053, 90815**
**Telephone: 310-494-4185 Fax: 310-597-7712**
**Email: Rollwyr@aol.com**
***PRACTICE AREAS: Intellectual Property Law; Entertainment Law; Criminal Law.**
**Entertainment, representing Musicians, Criminal Appeals.**
**Representative Clients: Standing Hawthorn; Soul Scream; California Appellate Project, Standing Hawthron; Eracism.**
*See Professional Biographies, LONG BEACH, CALIFORNIA*

Flanagan, James A., (BV) '55 '81 C.1042 B.A. L.809 J.D. 444 W. Ocean Blvd., 9th Fl.
**Flatebo, James R.** '59 '92 C.763 B.A. L.1148 J.D. [Ⓐ A.B.Weiss&Assoc.]
*PRACTICE AREAS: Civil Litigation; Real Estate.

**Flynn, Delich & Wise, (AV) BB**
**One World Trade Center, Suite 1800, 90831-1800Ⓞ**
**Telephone: 310-435-2626 Fax: 310-437-7555**
**Erich P. Wise; Nicholas S. Politis;—Thomas C. Jorgensen; Sook H. Lee.**
**Admiralty, Maritime, International Transportation, Insurance Coverage, Intellectual Property and Civil Litigation.**
**Representative Clients: American Hawaii Cruises; Holland America Line; Through Transport Mutual Insurance Association, Ltd.; The Britannia Steam Ship Insurance Association Limited; The Steamship Mutual Underwriting Association (Bermuda) Ltd.; General Steamship Corp., Ltd.; Commodore Cruise Line, Ltd.; Interocean Steamship Corporation; Sea-Land Service, Inc.; Hatteras Yachts.**
**San Francisco, California Office: Suite 1750, 580 California Street. Telephone: 415-693-5566. Fax: 415-693-0410.**
*See Professional Biographies, LONG BEACH, CALIFORNIA*

**Forbes, Lauren Sara** '67 '92 C.112 B.A. L.426 J.D. [Ⓐ Keesal,Y.&L.]
**Ford, G. Richard**, (AV) '41 '66 C.668 B.A. L.813 LL.B. [Ford,W.H.&B.]
*PRACTICE AREAS: Insurance Bad Faith; Auto Negligence; Police Misconduct.

**Ford, Walker, Haggerty & Behar, Professional Law Corporation, (AV) BB**
**One World Trade Center, Twenty Seventh Floor, 90831**
**Telephone: 310-983-2500 Telecopier: 310-983-2555**
**G. Richard Ford; Timothy L. Walker; William C. Haggerty; Jeffrey S. Behar; Mark Steven Hennings; Donna Rogers Kirby; Tina Ivankovic Mangarpan; Susan D. Berger; Joseph A. Heath; Robert J. Chavez; J. Michael McClure;—Arthur W. Schultz; Jon T. Moseley; Maxine J. Lebowitz; Timothy P. McDonald; K. Michele Williams; Stephen Ward Moore; James D. Savage; Todd D. Pearl; Patrick J. Gibbs; James O. Miller; David Huchel; Robert Reisinger; Theodore A. Clapp; Stanley L. Scarlett; Scott A. Ritsema; Michael Guy Martin; Colleen A. Strong; Thomas L. Gourde; Patrick J. Stark; Shayne L. Wulterin; Charles D. Jarrell; Charles J. Schmitt; Kyle A. Ostergrad; Todd L. Kessler. Of Counsel: Theodore P. Shield, P.L.C.**
**Alternative dispute resolution, Appellate practice, Automobile negligence, Insurance defense, Bad faith, Casualty defense, Commercial litigation, Construction defect litigation, Dental Malpractice, Declaratory relief, Employment discrimination, Civil Environmental litigation, False arrest, Fire losses, Fraudulent and suspect claims, Homeowners liability, Insurance coverage, Legal malpractice, Malicious prosecution, Mass catastrophe, Municipality defense, Pollution and toxic torts, Premises liability, Product liability, Security related litigation, Sexual harassment claims, Wrongful termination.**
*See Professional Biographies, LONG BEACH, CALIFORNIA*

Forrester, Donald S., (BV) '43 '72 C.800 B.S. L.809 J.D. 333 W. Broadway Ste. 202
Fort, John L., (BV) '37 '63 C.420 B.S. L.724 J.D. 3633 E. B'way
**Fougner, Robert B.**, (AVⓣ) '52 '78 C.273 B.B.A. L.861 J.D. [Ⓒ Hill,B.&N.]
Francis, Alan '20 '72 C.05 B.C. L.1001 J.D. 329 Claremont Ave.‡
**Frankart, Mary E.** '56 '88 C&L.426 B.A., J.D. [Ⓐ Madden,J.C.&J.]
*PRACTICE AREAS: Healthcare; Civil and Commercial Litigation.
Franks, Dean K., Jr. '48 '80 C.939 B.A. L.1238 J.D.
U.S. Admin. Law J., Soc. Sec. Admn.
Frazier, Jessica K. '49 '82 C.763 B.A. L.1068 J.D. Chf., Litig., Calif. State Univ.
Frerks, Harold C. '18 '46 C.684 A.B. L.800 LL.B. 393 Los Altos Ave.
Fritz, Albert G., Jr. '40 '71 C.645 B.S. L.1001 J.D. 3605 Long Beach Blvd.
**Fron, Michele R.** '58 '88 C.112 B.A. L.1137 J.D. [Keesal,Y.&L.]
*LANGUAGES: Spanish.
Fujii, Raymond T. '57 '81 C.112 B.A. L.1065 J.D. One World Trade Ctr.
Fuller, Jack A. '52 '78 C.112 B.A. L.464 J.D. 111 W. Ocean Blvd., Ste 625

**Fulwider Patton Lee & Utecht, LLP, (AV)**
**200 Oceangate, Suite 1550, 90802-4351Ⓞ**
**Telephone: 310-432-0453 Fax: 310-435-6014 Email: fulwidr@primenet.com**
**Email: fulwiderlb@aol.com**
**Member of Firm: Vern Schooley (Resident). Associates: Gunther D. Hanke (Resident); Gary M. Anderson (Resident); Russell C. Pangborn (Resident); Derrick W. Reed (Resident); JoAnne M. Ybaben (Resident); Sean M. Casey (Resident). Of Counsel: Francis A. Utecht (Resident).**
**Patent, Trademark, Copyright and Unfair Competition Law. Litigation.**
**Los Angeles, California Office: 10877 Wilshire Boulevard, 10th Floor. Telephone: 310-824-5555. Internet: fulwidr@primenet.com; fulwidr@aol.com. FAX: 310-824-9696.**
*See Professional Biographies, LONG BEACH, CALIFORNIA*

Gabel, Glenda '38 '82 C.1042 B.A. L.426 J.D. 5150 E. Pacific Coast Hwy.
Gabriel, Samuel E. '33 '69 C.475 B.A. L.215 J.D. 801 Pacific Ave.
**Galante, Fred** '69 '95 C.1077 B.A. L.426 J.D. [Ⓐ L.Silver&Assoc.]
*LANGUAGES: Spanish.
**Gale, Charles M.** '55 '80 C.347 A.B. L.813 J.D. [Cameron,M.P.G.&S.]
*PRACTICE AREAS: Environmental Law; Real Estate.
**Garcia, Andrew**, (AV) '42 '77 C.1077 B.A. L.809 J.D. [Kerry,G.&L.]
*LANGUAGES: Spanish.
*PRACTICE AREAS: Civil Trial; Personal Injury Insurance; Construction; Business Litigation and Transactions.
Gardner, Harry J. '24 '51 C.869 L.472 J.D. Adm. Law J., U.S. Coast Guard
Garner, Dwight F., (BV) '25 '54 C.112 B.A. L.800 J.D. [Garner,Z.&A.]
Garner, William T. '33 '63 C.1042 L.1001 J.D. Mun. Ct. J.
Garner, Zahn & Allmeroth, (BV) 2539 E. 7th St.
**Garrett, Stacey Myers** '66 '91 C.1074 B.S. L.1065 J.D. [Ⓐ Keesal,Y.&L.]

**Gasper, Robert W., (BV) '55 '80 C.112 B.A. L.1049 J.D.**
**Shoreline Square Tower, Sheraton Plaza, 301 East Ocean Boulevard, Suite 540, 90802-4828**
**Telephone: 310-436-2294 Fax: 310-590-8999**
**General Family Law Practice. Dissolution of Marriage, Child Custody, Support and Divorce Law.**
**Reference: International City Bank, Long Beach, California.**
*See Professional Biographies, LONG BEACH, CALIFORNIA*

**Gauhan, Dennis P., (A Law Corporation)**, (AV) '45 '72
C.112 B.S. L.426 J.D. [Gauhan&K.]
*PRACTICE AREAS: Torts; Negligence; Premises Liability; Products Liability; Construction Accidents.

**Gauhan and King, (AV)**
**A Partnership of Professional Corporations**
**Suite 610, 100 Oceangate, 90802**
**Telephone: 310-437-6661 Fax: 310-495-1642**
**Dennis P. Gauhan (A Law Corporation); Thomas C. King (A Law Corporation).**
**Tort Litigation, Personal Injury Law and Insurance Matters.**
**Reference: Wells Fargo Bank.**
*See Professional Biographies, LONG BEACH, CALIFORNIA*

Gaylord, Ned L., (AV) '39 '65 C.112 B.A. L.809 LL.B. 3530 Atlantic Blvd.
**Gebb, Sheldon A.**, (AV) '35 '64
C.112 A.B. L.1066 LL.B. [Baker&H.] (ⓄL.A. & Houston, Texas)
*PRACTICE AREAS: Admiralty; Litigation; Insurance.
George, Barbara C. '35 '57 C.999 B.A. L.352 J.D. Calif. State Univ.
**George, Edward P., Jr.**, (AV) '32 '60 C.112 B.A. L.1068 LL.B. [E.P.George,Jr.]
*PRACTICE AREAS: Criminal; Personal Injury; Appellate.

**George, K. Doyle '50 '76 C.401 B.A. L.276 J.D.**
**One World Trade Center, Suite 1600, 90831-1600**
**Telephone: 310-436-3888 Fax: 310-437-1967**
**Real Estate, Business Planning and Organization, Business Transactions Matters, Alternate Dispute Resolution, General Civil Litigation.**
*See Professional Biographies, LONG BEACH, CALIFORNIA*

**George, Edward P., Jr., Inc., A Prof. Corp., (AV) BB**
**Suite 430, 5000 East Spring Street, 90815**
**Telephone: 310-497-2900 Facsimile: 310-497-2904**
**Edward P. George, Jr.; Timothy L. O'Reilly. Of Counsel: Albert C. S. Ramsey.**
**General Civil and Criminal Practice in all Courts. Trials and Appeals, Personal Injury.**
**Reference: Harbor Bank, Long Beach.**
*See Professional Biographies, LONG BEACH, CALIFORNIA*

**Gershuni, Gregory B.**, (AV) '54 '78
C.112 B.A. L.426 J.D. [Ⓒ D.A.Cammarano] (ⓄLos Angeles)
*PRACTICE AREAS: Civil Practice; Business Law; Real Estate Law; Personal Injury Law.
Gerson, Richard I. '49 '76 C.37 B.S. L.1001 J.D. 3835 E. 7th St.
**Gertler, Cheryl F.** '57 '82 C.112 B.A. L.1067 J.D. [Ⓒ Swain&D.]
*LANGUAGES: Japanese.
*PRACTICE AREAS: Corporate; Commercial; Real Estate; Immigration.
**Gibbons, James E.** '53 '87 C.766 B.A. L.94 J.D. [Ⓐ Haines&L.]
**Gibbs, Patrick J.** '64 '89 C.1253 B.A. L.990 J.D. [Ford,W.H.&B.]
**Gill, Geoffrey W.** '46 '75 C.1027 B.S. L.262 J.D. [Kirlin,C.&K.]

CAA161P

Gilligan, John J. ....................'54 '81 C.1044 B.S. L.1137 J.D. 4201 Long Beach Blvd.
**Glenny, Janet E.** .....................................'— '93 C.1077 B.A. L.809 J.D. [▣ Danner&C.]
*PRACTICE AREAS: Products Liability; Landlord-Tenant Litigation.
**Gless, Michael M.**, (AV) ........................'40 '66 C&L.800 B.S., LL.B. [Keesal,Y.&L.]
**Gmelich, Thomas P.** ......................'67 '93 C.112 B.A. L.426 J.D. [▣ Prindle,D.&A.]
*PRACTICE AREAS: Insurance Defense.
**Goettsch, Raymond H.** ..........................'47 '82 C.589 B.A. L.464 J.D. [La Torraca&G.]
*REPORTED CASES: David Kleis, Inc. v. Superior Court, 37 Cal.App. 4th 1035 (2d Dist., 1995); %italic; Safeco Insurance Company of America vs. Pemcon International, Inc., d.b.a. General Magnetics, %roman; 935 F2d 275 (9th Cir., 1991); %italic.
*PRACTICE AREAS: Personal Injury Law; Products Liability Law; Malpractice Law; Commercial Litigation; Bad Faith Law.
**Goetz, Andy J.** ..........................'61 '86 C.112 B.A. L.426 J.D. [▣ Prindle,D.&A.]
*PRACTICE AREAS: Environmental; Asbestos Personal Injury; Property Damage; Insurance Defense.
Goldstein, Barney, (AV) .................'41 '67 C.768 B.S. L.1068 J.D. 2290 Pacific Ave.
Gordon, David A. ................................'47 '78 C.1042 B.S. L.1137 J.D. Dep. City Pros.
Gordon, Norman W. .............................'26 '53 C.112 B.A. L.800 J.D. Supr. Ct. J.
Gorman, Edward G. ..........................'31 '63 C&L.724 B.A., LL.B. 1506 E. 4th St.‡
Gottlieb, Arthur J. ...................'29 '62 C.112 B.A. L.1001 LL.B. 215 Prospect Ave.‡
**Gourde, Thomas L.** ..........................'62 '90 C&L.878 B.A., J.D. [▣ Ford,W.H.&B.]
*LANGUAGES: French.
*PRACTICE AREAS: Litigation; Professional Malpractice Defense.
Graham, Larry G., (AV) .............................'39 '71 C.575 B.A. L.896 J.D. [Martin&S.]
**Graham, Susan** ...........................'63 '92 C.454 B.A. L.426 J.D. [▣ Perona,L.&B.]
Grayson, Martin L., (AV) ..........'44 '82 C.1222 B.A. L.861 J.D. One World Trade Ctr.
Green, Bjorn C. .........................'68 '93 C.769 B.A. L.990 J.D. [▣ Demler,A.&R.]
Green, Marilyn S., (AV) ........................'28 '52 C&L.813 B.A., LL.B. [Cantrell,G.&P.]
**Greenberg, Charles E.**, (AV) ..........'33 '60 C.197 B.A. L.800 LL.B. [▣ Fields I.&B.]

**Greenhill, Lorna C., (AV) '42 '78 C.1042 B.A. L.1068 J.D.**
**60 Elm Avenue, 90802**
**Telephone: 310-437-2973**
**General Civil Practice. Family, Real Estate, Personal Injury, Probate and Estate Planning Law.**
**Reference: Bank of America, Main Branch, Long Beach, California.**
*See Professional Biographies, LONG BEACH, CALIFORNIA*

Grew, Frank J., (AV) ................................................'20 '69 200 Pine Ave.
Griffin, Thos. D. ........................'19 '49 C.768 A.B. L.800 LL.B. 56 Rivo Alto Canal‡
Grisham, Donald E., (BV) ......................'27 '55 C&L.800 B.A., J.D. 555 E. Ocean Blvd.
Groff, Paul E. ...................'43 '73 C.1042 B.S. L.426 J.D. 3505 Long Beach Blvd.
**Groff, Therese G.**, (BV) ............................'59 '84 C&L.426 B.B.A., J.D. [Fisher&P.]
*PRACTICE AREAS: Transportation Law; Admiralty; Aviation; "Bad Faith" Insurance Defense; ICC and FMC Tariffs.
Gross, Donald W. ......................'42 '79 C.1042 B.S. L.1152 J.D. 3311 Julian Ave.
**Gryder, Sandra L.** ............................'59 '85 C&L.426 B.A., J.D. [▣ Fisher&P.]
Gyler, Emanuel, (BV) ....................'19 '49 C&L.494 B.S.L., J.D. 4201 Long Beach Blvd.
Hagee, Talmadge M. ......................'15 '40 C.623 L.192 LL.B. State Comr. on Aging
Hagemeyer, Michael A. ..........'61 '89 C&L.190 B.A., J.D. 5150 E. Pacific Coast Hwy.
**Haggerty, William C.**, (AV) ..................'49 '77 C.103 B.A. L.770 J.D. [Ford,W.H.&B.]
*PRACTICE AREAS: Dental Malpractice; Professional Liability; Products Liability; Premises Liability.
Haigh, Douglas M., (BV) .... '46 '77 C.454 B.A. L.588 J.D. Supr. Ct. Comr. [Sievers&H.]

**Haines & Lea, A Law Corporation, (AV)**
**100 West Broadway, #595, 90802⊙**
**Telephone: 310-437-0400 Fax: 310-437-0206**
**Gregg Vorwerck; Robert B. Ryder; James E. Gibbons.**
**General Civil and Trial Practice. Financial Institutions, Corporation, Labor Relations and Employment Law, Real Estate, Construction Law and Probate Law.**
**San Francisco, California Office: 235 Pine St., Suite 1300. Telephone: 415-981-1050. Fax: 415-989-3561.**
*See Professional Biographies, LONG BEACH, CALIFORNIA*

**Hake, William Murray**, (AV) .......... '51 '83 C.768 B.S. L.464 J.D. [▣ Prindle,D.&A.]⊙
*PRACTICE AREAS: Trials; Professional Liability; Complex and Multi-District Litigation; Asbestos Toxic Torts; Insurance Defense.
Hall, Richard G., (BV) ...........................'23 '49 C.800 A.B. L.426 LL.B. [Hall&K.]
Hall & Kent, (BV) ........................................................ 3230 Claremore Ave.
**Hamada, Paul I.** ............................'64 '92 C.112 B.A. L.426 J.D. [▣ Keesal,Y.&L.]
**Hanke, Gunther D.** '55 '86 C.800 B.S. L.809 J.D.
[▣ Fulwider P.L.&U.] (See Pat. Sect.)
*LANGUAGES: German.
*PRACTICE AREAS: Patent, Trademark, Copyright and Unfair Competition Law; Litigation.
Hankins, Scott H. '55 '80 C.605 A.B. L.813 J.D.
Sr. Coun., McDonnell Douglas Fin. Corp.
**Hannesson, John D.** '52 '75 C.675 L.426 J.D.
V.P., Gen. Coun. & Secy., BW/IP Intl., Inc.
*RESPONSIBILITIES: General Corporate Law; Securities Law; International Law.
**Hardy, Kelly M.** ...........................'62 '92 C.1109 B.A. L.1137 J.D. [▣ Kegel,T.&T.]
**Hardy, William D.** ..............................'66 '95 C.112 B.S. L.809 J.D. [▣ O'Flaherty&B.]
Harmon, Thomas M., (BV) .........'47 '74 C.800 B.A. L.61 J.D. 4017 Long Beach Blvd.
Harre, Gary L. ..........................'38 '77 C.339 B.S. L.1001 J.D. 2939 E. Anaheim St.
Harrington, Curtis L., Jr. .... '53 '83 C.10 B.S. L.326 J.D. 6300 State University Dr. (Pat.)
Hart, George A., Jr., (AV) .......'14 '38 C&L.800 A.B., LL.B. 301 E. Ocean Blvd. 7th Fl.

**Hartman, Eric S., (BV) '44 '70 C.940 B.A. L.1066 J.D.**
**Suite 245, 6615 East Pacific Coast Highway, 90803**
**Telephone: 310-598-9753 Fax: 310-430-4218**
**Business, Corporate, Real Estate, Wills, Trusts and Probate Law.**
**Reference: Harbor Bank (Marina Office).**
*See Professional Biographies, LONG BEACH, CALIFORNIA*

**Hassapis, George P.** ...............................'65 '90 C.145 A.B. L.1049 J.D. [Fisher&P.]
*LANGUAGES: Greek.
*REPORTED CASES: Tai Ping Ins. Co. v. Northwest Airlines, Inc., 94 F.3d 29 (3d. Cir. 1996).
*PRACTICE AREAS: Admiralty and Transportation Litigation; Construction Litigation; Insurance Litigation and Coverage Disputes; Environmental and Toxic Tort Litigation; "Bad Faith" Defense.
**Hassman, Vicki L.** ..........................'66 '93 C.174 B.S.B.A. L.245 J.D. [▣ Fisher&P.]
*PRACTICE AREAS: Commercial Litigation; Transportation Law; Insurance Coverage; Trials and Appeals.
**Hauge, Cortlen R.** .............................'45 '93 C.493 B.A. L.426 J.D. [Cayer,K.&C.]
*PRACTICE AREAS: Civil Litigation; Bankruptcy; Banking; General Business Law.
Haughton, William B. ....................'26 '52 C.668 B.A. L.813 J.D. 400 Golden Slove
**Haymond, Philip H.** ..................'57 '90 C.112 B.A. L.767 J.D. [▣ M.J.Emling] (Pat.)
*PRACTICE AREAS: Patent, Trademark and Copyright Law.
**Heath, Joseph A.** .................................'58 '86 C.112 B.A. L.809 J.D. [Ford,W.H.&B.]
**Heim, Kristen J.** ...........................'59 '87 C.112 B.A. L.990 J.D. [O'Flaherty&B.]
Heimburger, Ray A. ......................'10 '38 C.273 L.537 LL.B. 281 Argonne Ave.‡
Helton, Ralph G. .........................'48 '80 C.112 B.A. L.1137 J.D. [R.Helton]
Helton, Ralph, Associates ...................................... 301 East Ocean Boulevard Suite 1700
Helwick, Christine, (AV) '47 '73
C.813 B.A. L.1065 J.D. Interim Gen. Coun., Calif. State Univ.
Henderson, George S. ..................'48 '77 C&L.1049 B.A., J.D. 555 E. Ocean Blvd.
**Hendricks, Jonathan A.** ...................'66 '94 C.668 B.A. L.464 J.D. [▣ La Torraca&G.]

**Hennings, Mark Steven** ............................'53 '81 C.1109 B.A. L.426 J.D. [Ford,W.H.&B.]
*PRACTICE AREAS: Fraudulent and Suspect Claims; Automobile Negligence.
Hernandez, Mateo M. '33 '57 L.662 LL.B.
(adm. in NY; not adm. in CA) 2460 Pine Ave.
Hernandez, Matthew .........................................'33 '87 L.662 LL.B. 2501 Pacific Ave.
Heumann, H. David ........'49 '75 C&L.546 B.S.B.A., J.D. McDonnell Douglas Fin. Corp.
Hill, Forest D. ...........................'59 '85 C.112 B.A. L.426 J.D. 3646 Long Beach Blvd.

**Hill, Betts & Nash LLP, (AV⊙)**
**A Limited Liability Partnership including Professional Corporations**
**Arco Center, 200 Oceangate, Suite 400, 90802-4302⊙**
**Telephone: 310-437-4407 Rapifax: 310-437-6057**
**Members of Firm: Geoffrey D. Ferrer; Lynn E. Moyer (Resident). Counsel: Robert B. Fougner (Resident). Associates: Brian B.A. McAllister.**
**General Practice. Admiralty, Aviation, Banking, Corporate, Employee Benefits, Environmental, Estates, Insurance, International, Securities and Taxation Law.**
**Reference: First Interstate Bank of California.**
**New York, N.Y. Office: Suite 5215, One World Trade Center. Telephone: 212-839-7000. Telex: ITT 426284; 667170. Telecopier: 212-839-7105. Rapifax: 212-466-0514. Cable Address: "Hillbetts."**
**Washington, D.C. Office: 1615 New Hampshire Avenue, N.W. Telephone: 202-319-0800. Telex: ITT 440083. Fax: 202-319-0804.**
**Newark, New Jersey Office: One Gateway Center, Suite 1203. Telephone: 201-623-0800. Fax: 201-623-1188.**
*See Professional Biographies, LONG BEACH, CALIFORNIA*

**Hirose, Kathleen N.** ...........................'69 '95 C.112 B.A. L.426 J.D. [▣ Keesal,Y.&L.]
**Hirota, Ryan K., (A Prof. Law Corp.)** '52 '81
C.112 B.S. L.1137 J.D. [▣ A.B.Weiss&Assoc.]
*PRACTICE AREAS: Real Estate; Business Litigation.
Hitchens, Linda S. .......... '49 '82 C.205 B.S. L.426 J.D. 4205 E. Anaheim St. Apt. 303
Hitt, Harman M., (AV) ............'20 '49 C&L.477 B.A., J.D. 301 E. Ocean Blvd., 7th Fl.
**Holden, Craig E.** ........................ '70 '94 C.112 B.A. L.1065 J.D. [▣ Keesal,Y.&L.]
**Hollingworth, Lisa Ann** ............................'54 '85 C.1042 B.S. L.426 J.D. [Spaltro&L.]
*REPORTED CASES: Santa Monica Hospital Medical Center v. Superior Court (1988), 203 Cal. App. 3rd 1026.
*PRACTICE AREAS: Civil Rights; Insurance Defense; Premises Liability; Products Liability; Insurance Fraud Defense.
**Holmes, Reginald A.** '50 '78
C.260 B.S.E.E. L.276 J.D. Asst. Gen. Coun., Douglas Aircraft Co.
*LANGUAGES: Mandarin Chinese.
*RESPONSIBILITIES: Intellectual Property; Licensing; Export.
Horner, Linda P. ..........................'51 '78 C.169 B.A. L.1068 J.D. 1217 Umatilla Ave.
Houston, Patrick J. ......................'34 '77 C.546 B.S. L.1001 J.D. 280 Claremont Ave.‡
Hovden, Lisa Chorness, (BV) ............'54 '78 C.112 B.A. L.990 J.D. World Trade Ctr.
Hroma, Catherine L. ............................................'— '86 C.339 B.A. L.800 J.D. Dep. Dist. Atty.
**Huchel, David** ....................................'65 '90 C.1060 B.A. L.464 J.D. [Ford,W.H.&B.]
Humphries, L. Lee ........................'20 '49 C.350 B.S.E.E. L.878 J.D. 7821 Tibana St.
**Hurwitz, Andres C.** ..............................'65 '90 C.93 B.A. L.276 J.D. [La Torraca&G.]
*PRACTICE AREAS: Civil Practice; Accident and Personal Injury Law; Insurance Defense Law; Bad Faith Law; Product Liability Law.
Ibarra, Olivia T., (AV) ......................'51 '76 C.1042 B.A. L.800 J.D. 5318 E. Second St.
**Im, Tae J.** ..........................................'63 '88 C.367 B.A. L.112 J.D. [▣ Wise,W.T.&W.]
*PRACTICE AREAS: Insurance Coverage; Insurance Defense.
**Ingler, Michael A.** ............................ '46 '75 C.1077 B.A. L.1095 J.D. [Kegel,T.&T.]
**Isaac, Kathleen Mahon** ........................ '47 '77 C.502 B.A. L.276 J.D. [Lillick&C.]
*PRACTICE AREAS: Transportation Regulation; Maritime; Immigration; Corporate.
**Island, E. R.** '43 '72 C.254 B.A. L.309 J.D.
V.P. & Assoc. Gen. Coun., Douglas Aircraft Co.
**Israel, Albert S.**, (BV) ..........................'51 '76 C.112 A.B. L.426 J.D. [Fields I.&B.]
Jaeckel, Uwe L., (Mr.) '40 '75 C.302 B.S. L.64 J.D.
(adm. in MD; not adm. in CA) Pres., Uwe Jaeckel, Inc.
**Janes, Alissa B.** ...........................'62 '93 C.976 B.A. L.1068 J.D. [▣ Keesal,Y.&L.]
*LANGUAGES: Italian, French.
**Jarrell, Charles D.** ........................'67 '94 C.556 B.A. L.800 J.D. [▣ Ford,W.H.&B.]
Jenson, Mary Ann D. ............................................'30 '52 C&L.221 LL.B. P.O. Box 50139‡
Jimenez, David G. .............................'54 '81 C.1109 B.A. L.276 J.D. [Jimenez&S.]
Jimenez & Small ........................................................................100 Oceangate
**Johns, Christopher**, (BV) ...................'50 '79 C.112 B.A. L.1065 J.D. [▣ Bennett&K.]
*PRACTICE AREAS: Insurance Law; Bad Faith Litigation; Products Liability; Personal Injury; Construction Law.
Johnson, George R., (AV) ................'17 '40 C.112 B.A. L.1066 LL.B. 60 Elm Ave.
**Johnson, Kenneth E.** .............................'52 '79 C.732 B.S. L.1009 J.D. [▣ Baker&H.]
*PRACTICE AREAS: Admiralty; Customs and Trade Law.
**Johnson, Philip L.** ........................'39 '73 C.674 A.B. L.800 J.D. [▣ Lillick&C.]
*PRACTICE AREAS: Aviation; Products Liability; Insurance Defense.
Johnson, Preston W. ............................'12 '37 C.112 B.A. L.809 LL.B. P.O. Box 2210‡
**Johnson, R. Scott** .........................'52 '79 C.309 A.B. L.800 J.D. [Johnson,C.&R.]
*PRACTICE AREAS: Insurance Coverage; Bad Faith; Tort Litigation.
Johnson, Randy H. '54 '80
C.112 B.A. L.1068 J.D. Pres. & Corp. Coun., Harbor Chevrolet Corp.
Johnson, Robert R., (AV) ....'43 '68 C.112 B.A. L.800 J.D. [Johnson&J.] & [Madden,J.C.]

**Johnson, Cebula & Rygh, A Professional Corporation, (AV)**
**Fifth Floor, 115 Pine Avenue, 90802**
**Telephone: 310-437-0307 Fax: 310-495-1894**
**R. Scott Johnson; T. J. Cebula; John M. Rygh;—Dona Fay Bauer; David C. Williamson; Barbara M. McAndrews; Michael D. Lind; Tamar Poladian; David Brian Rosenberg; Theodore S. Okazaki; Connie A. McHugh.**
**Automobile Negligence, Insurance Defense, Bad Faith, Complex Litigation, Construction Defect Litigation, Fraudulent and Suspect Claims, Insurance Coverage, Municipality Defense, Premise Liability, Product Liability, Medical Malpractice, Wrongful Termination and Appellate Practice.**
*See Professional Biographies, LONG BEACH, CALIFORNIA*

Johnson & Johnson, (AV) ............................................................ 111 W. Ocean Blvd.
**Jones, George M.** ........................................'56 '92 C.312 B.A. L.767 J.D. [▣ Baker&H.]
*PRACTICE AREAS: Civil Litigation.
Jones, Michael B. ............................ '52 '79 C.1042 B.S. L.809 J.D. 4001 Atlantic Ave.
**Jones, Steven A.**, (BV) ..........................'53 '79 C.1042 B.S. L.990 J.D. [Madden,J.C.&J.]
*PRACTICE AREAS: Healthcare; Business Law; Real Estate.
Jones, W. Steven '47 '75 C.902 B.S. L.208 J.D.
(adm. in CO; not adm. in CA) Atlantic Richfield Co.
**Jorgensen, Thomas C.** .....................'63 '91 C.966 B.A. L.477 J.D. [▣ Flynn,D.&W.]
*PRACTICE AREAS: Admiralty and Maritime Law; International Transportation; Civil Litigation.
**Kaiser, Raymond T.**, (AV) ...............................'51 '76 C.800 B.A. L.426 J.D. [Kaiser&S.]

**Kaiser & Swindells, (AV)**
**Suite 900 Sumitomo Tower, 444 West Ocean Boulevard, 90802-4516**
**Telephone: 310-590-8471 Telecopier: 310-437-0903**
**Email: ks@kaiserlaw.com URL: http://www.crl.com/~kaiser/**
**Raymond T. Kaiser; Pamela A. Swindells. Associates: Wayne D. Louvier; Eric C. Demler.**
**Civil Trial Practice. Insurance Defense, Personal Injury, Products Liability, Construction, Common Carrier, Condominium and Homeowners Association Law, Insurance Fraud, Environmental, Trucking, Professional Negligence, Vertical Transportation, Business Torts and Litigation.**
*See Professional Biographies, LONG BEACH, CALIFORNIA*

**Kalmbach, Herbert W.** ... '21 '52 C&L.800 B.S., J.D. [Ⓒ Baker&H.]
Kamm, Warren ... '46 '75 C.112 B.A. L.464 J.D. 555 E. Ocean Blvd.
Kander, Roger A. ... '28 '61 C.1042 B.A. L.1001 LL.B. 4266 Atlantic Ave.
**Katrinak, R. Paul** ... '63 '93 C.446 B.S. L.1049 J.D. [Ⓐ Perona,L.&B.]
**Katzman, Bernard, (Inc.)**, (AV) '35 '64
C.112 B.A. L.1068 LL.B. [Stolpman K.E.M.&K.]
*LANGUAGES: Spanish.
*PRACTICE AREAS: Workers Compensation Law.
Kaup, Paul R. '23 '63 C.145 A.B. L.365 J.D.
(adm. in IL; not adm. in CA) 7124 Marina Pacifica Dr. N.‡
**Kee, Sharon P.** ... '50 '77 C.112 B.A. L.426 J.D. [Ⓒ Fields I.&B.]
*PRACTICE AREAS: Labor and Employment Law; Wage and Hour Law; Employment Contracts; Wrongful Termination; WARN Act.
Keeler, Frederic S., Jr. ... '39 '70 C.813 B.A. L.1065 J.D. 3855 Lakewood Blvd.
**Keesal, Samuel A., Jr.**, (AV) '39 '66
C.1042 B.S. L.800 LL.B. [Keesal,Y.&L.] (⊙San Francisco, CA)

**Keesal, Young & Logan, A Professional Corporation, (AV)**
**400 Oceangate, P.O. Box 1730, 90802-1730⊙**
**Telephone: 310-436-2000 Telex: KEESAL LGB 656460 Telecopier: 310-436-7416**
**Samuel A. Keesal, Jr.; J. Stephen Young; Robert H. Logan; Michael M. Gless; Peter R. Boutin (Resident, San Francisco Office); Scott T. Pratt; Terry Ross; John D. Giffin (Resident, San Francisco Office); William H. Collier, Jr.; Robert D. Feighner; Philip McLeod (Resident, San Francisco Office); Neal Scott Robb; Ben Suter (Resident, San Francisco Office); Stephen C. Clifford (Resident, San Francisco Office); E. Scott Douglas; Shannon L. McDougald (Resident, Seattle, Washington Office); William E. McDonnell, Jr. (Resident, San Francisco Office); Michael A. Thurman; Dawn M. Schock; Timothy N. Will; Albert E. Peacock, III (Resident, Anchorage, Alaska Office); Cameron Stout (Resident, San Francisco Office); John R. Loftus; David M. Bartholomew; Jeffrey D. Warren; Robert J. Stemler; Lisa M. Bertain (Resident, San Francisco Office); Janet M. Simmons; Robert J. Bocko (Resident, Seattle, Washington Office); Michele R. Fron; Robert A. S. Bleicher (Resident, San Francisco Office); Michael L. Armitage; Robert B. Ericson; Elizabeth P. Beazley; Paul J. Schumacher; Brian L. Zagon (Resident, San Francisco Office). Associates: Douglas R. Davis (Resident, Anchorage, Alaska Office); Elizabeth A. Kendrick; John A. Treptow (Resident, Anchorage, Alaska Office); Susan Wright Mason (Resident, Anchorage, Alaska Office); Jon W. Zinke (Resident, Hong Kong Office); Linda A. Loftus; Eric Swett (Resident, San Francisco Office); Gregory E. Copeland; Joseph A. Walsh, II; Michael C. Licosati; Jodi S. Cohen; Mark W. Nelson; Philip R. Lempriere (Resident, Seattle, Washington Office); Leslie M. Sullivan; Herbert H. Ray, Jr. (Resident, Anchorage, Alaska Office); E. Scott Palmer; Jill Elizabeth Olofson; Julie LeAnn Taylor (Resident, San Francisco Office); Lisa Kaye Donahue; Stacey Myers Garrett; Michael A. Sitzman (Resident, San Francisco Office); Gordon Craig Young (Resident, San Francisco Office); William J. Bridgen; Gregory A. Boss; Richard William Smirl; Paul I. Hamada; Elizabeth J. Lindh; Lauren Sara Forbes; Peter J. Morgan, III (Resident, San Francisco Office); Jeffrey Scott Simon; Kelly J. Moynihan (Resident, San Francisco Office); Alissa B. Janes; Elizabeth E. Atlee; Daniel J. Finnerty; Gabrielle L. Walker (Resident, San Francisco Office); Thaddeus I. Paul (Resident, Seattle, Washington Office); Craig E. Holden; Esther S. Kim (Resident, San Francisco Office); Kimberly Wong; John M. Whelan; Lauren N. Schwake; Teresa Solomon Mack; Christine Ann Miller; Elizabeth C. Crandall; David Shane Brun (Resident, San Francisco Office); Dena L. Murphy; Kathleen N. Hirose; Sarah Tong Sangmeister; Ted Fyke Angus, Jr. (Resident, San Francisco Office); Shannon S. Wagoner (Resident, San Francisco Office); Adym W. Rygmyr; Pamela J. Reeder; Michael W. Biard; Jilana L. Miller. Of Counsel: Michael H. Woodell (Resident, Anchorage, Alaska Office); Reese H. Taylor, Jr.; Richard A. Appelbaum (Not admitted in CA).**
**General Civil Trial, Appellate and Business Practice, Securities, Employment, Admiralty, Commodities, Professional Malpractice, Insurance, Real Estate, Employment, Real Estate, Corporate, Environmental, Franchise, Labor, Intellectual Property, Products Liability and Administrative Law.**
**Reference: Union Bank (Long Beach Main Office).**
**San Francisco, California Office: Four Embarcadero Center, Suite 1500. Telephone: 415-398-6000. Telecopier: 415-981-7729; 415-362-8535. Telex: KEESAL SF 656460.**
**Anchorage, Alaska Office: 1029 W. 3rd Avenue, Suite 650. Telephone: 907-279-9696. Telecopier: 907-279-4239. Telex: KEESAL LGB 656460.**
**Seattle, Washington Office: 1301 Fifth Avenue, Suite 2714. Telephone: 206-622-3790. Telecopier: 206-343-9529. Telex: KEESAL LGB 656460.**
**Hong Kong Office: 1603 The Centre Mark, 287 Queen's Road Central. Telephone: 852-285-41718. Telecopier: 852-254-16189.**

***See Professional Biographies, LONG BEACH, CALIFORNIA***

**Kegel, Robert A.**, (AV) '27 '53
C.112 B.S. L.800 LL.B. [Kegel,T.&T.] (⊙L.A. & San Diego)

**Kegel, Tobin & Truce, A Professional Corporation, (AV)**
**330 Golden Shore Drive, Suite 150, 90802⊙**
**Telephone: 310-437-1108 Facsimile: 310-435-3742**
**Email: comp-law@ktt.com**
**Robert A. Kegel (Certified Specialist, Workers Compensation Law, The State Bar of California Board of Legal Specialization); W. Joseph Truce (Certified Specialist, Workers Compensation Law, The State Bar of California Board of Legal Specialization); Michael A. Ingler;—D'Arcy T. Swartz; Sandra L. Adams; Kelly M. Hardy.**
**Workers Compensation, Longshore and Harborworkers, Public Employment, Retirement Law. Insurance Law, Third Party Subrogation.**
**Reference: Union Bank, Wilshire & Vermont, Los Angeles, California.**
**Los Angeles, California Office: 3580 Wilshire Boulevard, 10th Floor, P.O. Box 76907. Telephone: 213-380-3880. FAX: 213-383-8346.**
**Ventura, California Office: 5450 Ralston Street, Suite 204, P.O. Box 7779. Telephone: 805-644-2216. Facsimile: 805-644-8625.**
**Rancho Cucamonga, California Office: 10737 Laurel Street, #240, P.O. Box 3329. Telephone: 909-466-5555. Facsimile: 909-466-5562.**
**San Diego, California Office: 2535 Kettner Boulevard, Suite 2A1. Telephone: 619-696-0906.**
**Van Nuys, California Office: 14545 Friar Street, Suite 104. Telephone: 818-947-0300. Facsimile: 818-947-0303.**

***See Professional Biographies, LONG BEACH, CALIFORNIA***

Keiser, William H., (BV) ... '33 '64 C.668 A.B. L.1066 LL.B. Dep. City Atty.
Kelly, John C. ... '59 '86 C.112 B.A. L.809 J.D. [Carroll,K.&T.]
Kelner, Richard W., (BV) ... '31 '59 C.911 B.A. L.1068 J.D. 3505 Long Beach Blvd.
**Kendrick, Elizabeth A.** ... '59 '86 C.112 B.A. L.426 J.D. [Ⓐ Keesal,Y.&L.]
Kepka, Fredk. A. ... '17 '47 C&L.477 A.B., J.D. Mun. J.
**Kerry, William H.** ... '47 '77 C.1042 B.A. L.1136 J.D. [Kerry,G.&L.]
*PRACTICE AREAS: Aviation litigation and certificate actions; Personal Injury Insurance; Business Litigation and Transactions.

**Kerry, Garcia & Lewis, (AV)**
**320 Golden Shore Drive, Suite 480, 90802**
**Telephone: 310-436-1234 Fax: 310-495-2590**
**Andrew Garcia; William H. Kerry; Daniel G. Lewis;—Christopher E. Botti; Lee B. Madinger; Mark A. Sayed.**
**Civil Trial and Appellate Practice emphasizing Defense and Plaintiff Personal Injury, Premises Liability, Products Liability, Professional Negligence, Construction, Aviation, Insurance, Business Litigation and Transaction matters, Commercial, Corporate and Real Estate Transactions, Alternative Dispute Resolution.**
**Reference: First Interstate Bank (Market Place Branch).**

***See Professional Biographies, LONG BEACH, CALIFORNIA***

**Kessler, Todd L.** ... '66 '92 C.174 B.S. L.999 J.D. [Ⓐ Ford,W.H.&B.]
*PRACTICE AREAS: Construction Defect Defense; Automobile Defense.
**Kettel, David A.** ... '60 '86 C.112 B.A. L.861 J.D. [Baker&H.]
*PRACTICE AREAS: Admiralty; Oil and Gas; General Litigation.
Kight, Mason T., (BV) ... '31 '60 C.112 B.S. L.800 LL.B. 300 Oceangate
Kilpatrick, R. J., (AV) ... '21 '49 C.755 A.B. L.145 J.D. 5407 Heron Bay‡
**Kilstofte, Stephen R.** ... '51 '78 C.1042 B.A. L.809 J.D. [Cayer,K.&C.]
*PRACTICE AREAS: Business Litigation; Family; Personal Injury; Workers Compensation.
Kim, Richard S. ... '62 '89 C.1097 B.A. L.1065 J.D. Off. of Pub. Def.
Kim, Ryul ... '55 '84 C.112 B.A. L.1137 J.D. [R.Kim&Assoc.]⊙
**Kim, Susie E.** ... '67 '94 C.112 B.A. L.1067 J.D. [Ⓐ Madden,J.C.&J.]
*PRACTICE AREAS: Estate Planning; Probate; Civil Litigation.
Kim, Ryul, & Associates ... 444 W. Ocean Blvd. (⊙Seoul, Korea)
Kincaid, Mark L. ... '— '85 [Westrup,K.&K.]
King, Floyd H. ... '20 '54 C.112 L.1065 J.D. 2999 E. Ocean Blvd.
King, Michael W. ... '53 '85 C.814 B.S. L.629 J.D. 4500 E. Pacific Coast Hwy., 4th Fl.
**King, Thomas C., (A Law Corporation)**, (AV) '45 '72
C.1097 B.S. L.426 J.D. [Gauhan&K.]
*PRACTICE AREAS: Torts; Negligence; Premises Liability; Products Liability; Construction Accidents.

**Kinkle, Rodiger and Spriggs, Professional Corporation**
**(See Santa Ana)**

Kinsey, Eugene E. ... '49 '76 C.1042 B.A. L.990 J.D. 4201 Long Beach Blvd.
**Kirby, Donna Rogers** ... '49 '83 C.851 B.A. L.800 J.D. [Ford,W.H.&B.]
*PRACTICE AREAS: Insurance Coverage; Bad Faith Litigation.
Kirkpatrick, Robert R., (AV) ... '32 '58 C.112 B.S. L.1068 J.D. 444 W. Ocean Blvd.

**Kirlin, Campbell & Keating**
**301 East Ocean Boulevard, Suite 540, 90802-4804⊙**
**Telephone: 310-491-1267 Fax: 310-590-8999**
**Resident Partners: Donn Borg; Geoffrey W. Gill. Resident Of Counsel: Joseph R. McFaul.**
**General Practice. General Civil Trial and Appellate Practice. Admiralty and Maritime, International, Corporate, Administrative, Finance, Labor, Trusts and Estates, Tax, Insurance Coverage and Defense, Reinsurance, Personal Injury, Environmental, Oil Pollution and Coast Guard Proceedings, Bankruptcy and Real Estate Law**
**Other Offices Located in: New York, New York, Washington, D.C., Stamford, Connecticut and Caldwell, New Jersey.**

***See Professional Biographies, LONG BEACH, CALIFORNIA***

**Kistner, Wayne T.**, (AV) ... '53 '81 C.1042 B.A. L.809 J.D. [Bennett&K.]
*PRACTICE AREAS: Personal Injury Defense; Medical Malpractice; Business Litigation; Insurance Coverage; Professional Malpractice.
**Klausen, Stephen C.** ... '46 '73 C.112 B.A. L.1068 J.D. [Ⓒ Fisher&P.]
*PRACTICE AREAS: Defense of Complex Personal Injury; Products Liability; Property Damage; Construction; Environmental and Commercial Claims.
Klein, A. Joel '40 '67 C.46 B.S. L.424 J.D.
(adm. in IL; not adm. in CA) Pres., Sunrise Consulting Servs., Inc.
**Klein, Neil B.** ... '54 '79 C.061 B.Proc. [Walsh,D.L.&K.]
*LANGUAGES: Afrikaans.
Klick, Rhonda ... '57 '87 C.999 [Westrup,K.&K.]

**Klink, Richard W. W. '36 '73 C.1042 B.A. L.1001 J.D.**
**444 West Ocean Boulevard, 9th Floor, 90802-4526**
**Telephone: 310-432-7838 Fax: 310-432-7455**
**Criminal Defense, White Collar Crime, DUI Litigation.**

***See Professional Biographies, LONG BEACH, CALIFORNIA***

**Knight, Linda M.** ... '— '78 C.560 B.S. L.1001 J.D. Coun., Douglas Aircraft Co.
*RESPONSIBILITIES: Commercial Transactions; Product Liability.
Knight, William G. ... '47 '72 C&L.800 B.A., J.D. Asst. Gen. Coun., Calif. State Univ.
Knopf, Travor ... '67 '92 C.112 B.A. L.809 J.D. [Ⓐ Demler,A.&R.]
**Kolostian, Richard G., Jr** ... '67 '94 C.112 B.A. L.940 J.D. [Ⓐ O'Flaherty&B.]
Kravitz, Peter S. ... '69 '95 C.401 B.A. L.1292 J.D. 100 Oceangate
Krieger, Linda Guthmann ... '65 '90 C.339 B.A. L.112 J.D. [Krieger&Assoc.]
Krieger, Terrence B. ... '66 '92 C.112 B.A. L.94 J.D. [Krieger&Assoc.]
Krieger & Associates ... 115 Pine Ave., 5th Fl.
**Krissman, Joel**, (AV) ... '48 '73 C.112 B.A. L.1049 J.D. [Stolpman K.E.M.&K.]
*PRACTICE AREAS: Products Liability Law; Maritime Accidents Law; Premises/Construction Accidents.
Kulis, Merrillyn Erskine ... '47 '73 C&L.800 B.A., J.D. 3841 Jotham Pl.
Kurz, Michael J. ... '54 '83 C&L.426 B.S., J.D. [M.J.Kurz]
Kurz, Michael J., Law Office of ... 115 Pine Ave.
Lach, JoAnn ... '54 '79 C.112 B.A. L.1066 J.D. Dep. Dist. Atty.
Lackman, Lawrence H., (AV) ... '26 '58 L.1001 J.D. 3740 Long Beach Blvd.
**Lallande, M. Lawrence** ... '57 '84 C&L.990 B.S., J.D. [Perona,L.&B.]
*LANGUAGES: Spanish.
Lambert, Edgar Folk, III ... '42 '72 C.880 B.A. L.309 J.D. 300 Oceangate
**Lamhofer, Eric T.** ... '59 '84 C.112 B.A. L.464 J.D. [Spaltro&L.]
*PRACTICE AREAS: Insurance Defense; Automobile and Premises Liability; Commercial Trucking Accidents; Insurance Coverage; Product Liability.
Landes, Richard L., (BV) ... '39 '69 C.813 A.B. L.1065 J.D. Dep. City Atty.
Lane, Gary ... '46 '72 C.994 B.A. L.1049 J.D. Sr. Assoc. Coun., Memorial Health Servs.
Lane, John S. ... '25 '49 C.1365 B.A. L.902 J.D. Mun. Ct. J.
**Langer, Major A.**, (AV) ... '42 '66 C.1044 B.A. L.724 LL.B. [Perona,L.&B.]⊙
**Larkin, Blake W.** ... '55 '86 L.061 LL.B. [Williams W.C.N.&R.]
*PRACTICE AREAS: Maritime Law; Environmental Law; Transportation and International Law; Commercial Transactions and Litigation; Personal Injury.
Larson, Ralph E. '45 '72 C.911 B.A. L.546 J.D.
(adm. in NE; not adm. in CA) 5911 Walton St.‡
Lashlee, C. Timothy ... '51 '76 C.684 B.A. L.990 J.D. 4201 Long Beach Blvd.
**La Torraca, Henry B.**, (AV) ... '51 '76 C.1042 B.S. L.426 J.D. [La Torraca&G.]
*PRACTICE AREAS: Insurance Coverage; Third Party Defense; Business Litigation; Insurance Bad Faith Law; Insurance Law.

**La Torraca and Goettsch, (AV)**
**A Law Partnership**
**211 East Ocean Boulevard, Suite 400, P.O. Box 21978, 90801-4978**
**Telephone: 310-436-1887 Telecopier: 310-436-8489**
**Members of Firm: Henry B. La Torraca; Raymond H. Goettsch. Associates: Teresa Cho; Andres C. Hurwitz; Susan Koehler Sullivan; Eric R. Little; Nicola Migliaccio; Jonathan A. Hendricks; Scott K. Murch; David James Reinard.**
**General Civil Litigation including Insurance Coverage, Insurance Bad Faith, Insurance Defense, Insurance Fraud, Toxic Tort Law, Personal Injury, Products Liability, Malpractice, Commercial Litigation, Defamation, Unfair Competition, Real Property Litigation, Construction Defects Litigation, Complex Litigation and Civil Appeals. Trial Practice in all State and Federal Courts.**

***See Professional Biographies, LONG BEACH, CALIFORNIA***

Latting, Holcomb B. '21 '50 C&L.862 B.A., LL.B.
(adm. in OK; not adm. in CA) 3855 Lakewood Blvd.
Lear, Sherry Anne ... '65 '90 C.589 B.A. L.1068 J.D. 100 Oceangate
LeBeau, Jeffrey O ... '55 '86 C.112 B.A. L.426 J.D. 401 E. Ocean Blvd.
**Lebowitz, Maxine J.** ... '44 '82 C.999 B.S. L.809 J.D. [Ford,W.H.&B.]
Lee, Donna David ... '49 '89 C&L.1137 B.S.L., J.D. 4480 Myrtle Ave.
**Lee, Sook H.** ... '57 '92 C.061 B.A. L.809 J.D. [Ⓐ Flynn,D.&W.]
*LANGUAGES: Korean.
*PRACTICE AREAS: Admiralty and Maritime Law.
Lemieux, James Philip ... '68 '93 C.946 B.S. L.990 J.D. [Ⓐ Demler,A.&R.]
Lentzner, Jay R. ... '52 '77 C.605 B.A. L.800 J.D. 4500 E. Pacific Coast Hwy., 4th Fl.
LePore, Vincent J., III '53 '82 C.112 B.A. L.1049 J.D.
Gen. Coun. & Corp. Secy., Edgington Oil Co.
Lew, Cheryl J. ... '55 '83 C.112 B.S. L.1068 J.D. 3855 Lakewood Blvd.
**Lewis, Daniel G.** ... '58 '85 C.999 B.A. L.950 J.D. [Kerry,G.&L.]
*PRACTICE AREAS: Arbitration; Civil Trial; Personal Injury Insurance.
Lewis, Stephen G. ... '51 '77 C.112 A.B. L.426 J.D. 444 W. Ocean Blvd.

CAA163P

CALIFORNIA—LONG BEACH MARTINDALE-HUBBELL LAW DIRECTORY 1997

**Liberto, Charles J.** '40 '65 C.605 B.A. L.426 LL.B.
**4201 Long Beach Boulevard, Suite 327, P.O. Box 7737, 90807-0737**
Telephone: 310-424-7441 Fax: 310-424-2231
Practice limited to Estate Planning, Trust and Probate Law.
Reference: National Bank of Long Beach (Long Beach Main Office).
*See Professional Biographies, LONG BEACH, CALIFORNIA*

**Licosati, Michael C.** ........................'64 '89 C&L.763 B.A., J.D. [A Keesal,Y.&L.]
Liebson, Susan D. ........................'54 '78 C&L.800 B.A., J.D. Atlantic Richfield Co.

**Lillick & Charles LLP, (AV)**
**One World Trade Center, Suite 950, 90831-0950⊙**
Telephone: 310-499-7000 Cable Address: "Lillickchs LGB" Telex: 188652 LILLICKCHS LGB
FAX: 310-437-5957
Long Beach Partners: Phillip S. Dalton; Kathleen Mahon Isaac; William L. Robinson; Robert B. Yoshitomi. Of Counsel: Philip L. Johnson. Long Beach Associates: John C. Ashby; Brian R. Faulkner.
General Civil and Trial Practice. Aviation, Banking, Bankruptcy/Creditors' Rights, Commercial, Computer Law, Construction, Corporate, Environmental, Estate and Trust, Finance, Governmental Regulation, Independent Power, Insurance, International Business, Labor, Maritime, Products Liability, Project Finance, Real Estate, Tax, Toxic Tort, Trademark, Visa and Immigration.
San Francisco, California Office: Two Embarcadero Center, Suite 2600, 94111-3996. Telephone: 415-984-8200. Cable Address: "Lillickchs SF." Telex: 184983 LILLICKCHS SF. FAX: 415-984-8300.
Parsippany, New Jersey Office: 119 Cherry Hill Road, Second Floor, 07054-1114. Telephone: 201-334-8100. Telex: 178727 LILLICKCHS NJ. FAX: 201-334-9559.
*See Professional Biographies, LONG BEACH, CALIFORNIA*

**Lind, Michael D.** ..................'62 '88 C.1042 B.A. L.1065 J.D. [A Johnson,C.&R.]
*PRACTICE AREAS: General Civil Law; Insurance Coverage; Bad Faith; General Civil Appellate Practice; Insurance Defense.
**Lindh, Elizabeth J.** ........................'66 '92 C.37 B.A. L.1065 J.D. [A Keesal,Y.&L.]
Ling, Joe, (AV) ..............'29 '58 C.112 B.S. L.1068 J.D. 555 E. Ocean Blvd, Ste 500‡
Lipson, Steve ........................'58 '84 C.112 B.A. L.629 J.D. 2755 Vuelta Grande
Liptak, Charlotte S. ........................'53 '78 C.509 B.A. L.424 J.D. P.O. Box 21542
**Little, Eric R.** ........................'63 '93 C.464 B.A. L.767 J.D. [A La Torraca&G.]

**Littler, Mendelson, Fastiff, Tichy & Mathiason, A Professional Corporation, (AV)**
**401 E. Ocean Boulevard, Suite 204, 90802⊙**
Telephone: 310-437-2441 Facsimile: 310-435-0406
URL: http://www.littler.com
—Eugene L. Chrzanowski.
Offices located in: California — Bakersfield, Fresno, Los Angeles, Menlo Park, Oakland, Sacramento, San Diego, San Francisco, San Jose, Santa Maria, Santa Rosa and Stockton; Denver, Colorado; Washington, D.C.; Atlanta, Georgia; Baltimore, Maryland; Reno and Las Vegas, Nevada (a partnership with the Law Offices of Hicks & Walt); Morristown, New Jersey; New York, New York; and Dallas and Houston, Texas.
*See Professional Biographies, LONG BEACH, CALIFORNIA*

Lobdell, Robert C., (AV) ..................'26 '51 C&L.813 A.B., LL.B. 925 Hillside Dr.‡
**Lodwick, Michael W.**, (BV⊙) ..................'46 '81 C.420 B.A. L.425 J.D. [Fisher&P.]
*REPORTED CASES: Flota Mercante Grancolombiana, S.A. v. Florida Const. Equip. Inc., 798 F.2d 143 (5th Cir. 1986); Louis Dreyfus Corp. v. Plaquemines Port, Harbor & Terminal Dist., 21 S.R.R: 1072 (F.M.C. 1982); All Pacific Trading, Inc. v. M /V Hanjin Yosu, 7 F.3d 1427 (9th Cir. 1993); TRW, Inc. v. TWI Int'l Exhibition Logistics, 29 F.3d 634 (9th Cir. 1994) (opinion at 1994 U.S. App. LEXIS 16416); Tai Ping Ins. Co. v. Northwest Airlines, Inc. 94 F.3d 29 (2d Cir. 1996).
*PRACTICE AREAS: Marine, Inland Marine and Property Insurance Coverage and Defense; Hull and Cargo Subrogation and Hull Defense; Toxic Torts; Maritime Administrative Law; Civil Trials and Appeals.
Loe, David C. ..................................................'64 '90 [Davert&L.]
**Loftus, John R.** ........................'58 '87 C.745 B.A. L.1148 J.D. [Keesal,Y.&L.]
**Loftus, Linda A.** ........................'56 '88 C.112 B.A. L.426 J.D. [A Keesal,Y.&L.]
**Logan, Robert H.**, (AV) ........................'48 '73 C.813 A.B. L.800 J.D. [Keesal,Y.&L.]
Loggins, John F., (BV) ..................'41 '72 C.1097 B.A. L.426 J.D. 2530 Atlantic Ave.
**Lombardi, Christopher**, (BV) ..........'49 '80 C.1042 B.A. L.1137 J.D. [Lombardi&P.]

**Lombardi & Perry, LLP, (BV)**
**110 Pine Avenue, 12th Floor, 90802**
Telephone: 310-983-3616 Fax: 310-983-3618
Christopher Lombardi; Scott D. Perry.
Personal Injury including Insurance Defense.
Representative Clients: A-Best Products; Combustion Engineering Inc.; Stauffer Chemical; Connecticut Valley Claim Service Co., Inc.
*See Professional Biographies, LONG BEACH, CALIFORNIA*

**Lombardo, Anthony P.** ........................'61 '91 C&L.734 B.A., J.D. [B Fisher&P.]
*PRACTICE AREAS: Insurance Coverage; Cargo Claims; Business Litigation.

**Long, Jay B.** '53 '82 C.112 B.S. L.1067 J.D.
**Greater Los Angeles World Trade Center, One World Trade Center, Suite 800, 90831-0800⊙**
Telephone: 310-983-8146; Fax: 310-983-8199
Email: jayblong@ix.netcom.com
Environmental and Energy Law, including Regulatory and Legislative Matters; Insurance Coverage Law; Construction and Design Law; Sports, Sponsorship and Event Law; Advertising, Marketing and Distribution Law; Select Business, Real Estate, other Civil Litigation and Trial Practice in all State and Federal Courts; Alternate Dispute Resolution.
Monterey, California Office: 500 Camino El Estero, Suite 200, 93940. Telephone: 408-649-3877. Fax: 408-649-4705.
*See Professional Biographies, LONG BEACH, CALIFORNIA*

Lossing, Elizabeth A. ..................'— '89 C.990 B.S. L.1001 J.D. 1 World Trade Ctr.
Lough, Lyman W. ........................'12 '35 C.999 L.809 LL.B. 1154 Los Altos Ave.‡
**Louvier, Wayne D.** ........................'57 '83 C.112 B.A. L.1137 J.D. [A Kaiser&S.]
Ludmerer, Richard C. ..........'50 '77 C.95 A.B. L.276 J.D. Coun., Calif. State Univ.
Lund, Jeffrey ........................'49 '79 C.800 B.A. L.1001 J.D. 354 W. Ocean Blvd.
Lund, Robert H., (AV) ..................'26 '54 C.893 B.A. L.1001 LL.B. 354 W. Ocean St.
Lyman, Richard W., Jr. ........................'46 '72 C.112 A.B. L.426 J.D. Mun. J.
Lynn, Elizabeth A. ........................'53 '83 C.1042 B.A. L.1137 J.D. Pub. Def. Off.
Lyon, Jeffrey J. ........................'42 '73 C.436 A.B. L.426 J.D. 3852 Pacific Ave.
**Lyon, Stanley W.** '39 '72 C.763 B.S. L.1049 J.D.
Asst. Gen. Coun., Douglas Aircraft Co.
MacAllister, Linda S. ..................'52 '89 L.1001 J.D. Univ. Coun., Calif. State Univ.
**Machit, Monte H.** ........................'57 '89 C.1042 B.A. L.426 J.D. [Prindle,D.&A.]
*PRACTICE AREAS: Insurance Coverage Defense; Amusement Park Litigation.
**Mack, Teresa Solomon** ..................'63 '94 C.1077 B.S. L.800 J.D. [A Keesal,Y.&L.]
Madariaga, David ..................................................'64 '92 [A Davert&L.]
**Madden, Patrick T.**, (AV) ..........'44 '72 C.112 A.B. L.800 J.D. [Cameron,M.P.G.&S.]
**Madden, Philip M.**, (AV) ..........'37 '63 C.112 A.B. L.1066 LL.B. [Madden,J.C.&J.]
*PRACTICE AREAS: Business Law; Civil Litigation.

**Madden, Jones, Cole & Johnson, A Professional Corporation, (AV)**
**Suite 1300, 111 West Ocean Boulevard, 90802**
Telephone: 310-435-6565 Fax: 310-590-7909
Email: MJCJLAW@AOL.COM
Philip M. Madden; Steven A. Jones; Montgomery Cole; Robert R. Johnson;—John Vita; Mary E. Frankart; Susie E. Kim.
Civil Litigation, Business, Corporate, Healthcare, Construction, Personal Injury, Real Estate, Probate, Tax and Estate Planning Matters.

(This Listing Continued)

CAA164P

**Madden, Jones, Cole & Johnson, A Professional Corporation (Continued)**
Counsel for: Ameritone Paint Corp.; St. Mary Medical Center; St. Bernardine Medical Center; Farmers & Merchants Trust Co.; Wells Fargo Bank; Mack Truck, Inc.; Long Beach Public Transportation.
*See Professional Biographies, LONG BEACH, CALIFORNIA*

**Madinger, Lee B.** ........................'48 '90 C.902 B.A. L.1148 J.D. [A Kerry,G.&L.]
*PRACTICE AREAS: Personal Injury Insurance; Business Litigation and Transactions; Appellate Work.
**Magee, Scott R.** ........................'57 '85 C.1042 B.S. L.990 J.D. [Taubman,S.Y.&S.]
*PRACTICE AREAS: Business; Taxation; Estate Planning.
Mahood, Heather A. ..............'57 '82 C.112 B.A. L.1068 J.D. Princ. Dep. City Atty.
Mains, David D. ..................'59 '87 C.454 B.B.A. L.1137 J.D. 320 Golden Shore Dr.
Mais, Michael J., (BV) ..................'53 '79 C&L.1049 B.A., J.D. Dep. City Atty.
Makin, Cynthia C., (A Professional Corporation) '63 '88
C.1042 B.S. L.990 J.D. [Makin&M.]⊙
Makin & Masoner ........................401 E. Ocean Blvd., 6th Fl. (⊙Los Angeles)
**Malmgren, Robert T.** '39 '64 C&L.597 B.S.C.E., J.D.
(adm. in IL; not adm. in CA) Secy. & Gen. Coun., Taisei America Corp.
**Mancini, Linda A.** ........................'60 '90 C.687 B.A. L.990 J.D. [A Fisher&P.]
*PRACTICE AREAS: Insurance Defense; Commercial Litigation; Cargo Subrogation; Environmental and Toxic Tort Litigation.
**Mandel, Elaine** ........................'67 '92 C&L.112 B.A., B.A. [A Stolpman K.E.M.&K.]
*LANGUAGES: Spanish.
*PRACTICE AREAS: Construction Accidents Law; Products Liability Law.
**Mandel, Leonard H.**, (AV) ........'38 '67 C.813 B.S. L.800 J.D. [Stolpman K.E.M.&K.]
*LANGUAGES: Spanish.
*PRACTICE AREAS: Products Liability Law; Construction Accident Law.
**Mangarpan, Tina Ivankovic** ..............'59 '85 C.222 B.A. L.990 J.D. [Ford,W.H.&B.]
*PRACTICE AREAS: Premises Liability; Security Related Litigation; Product Liability; Construction Defect Litigation.
Marin, Paul J. ........................'23 '60 C.112 A.B. L.1068 Dep. Dist. Atty.
Martin, Clive Standlee, Jr., (BV) '38 '67
C.800 B.A. L.809 J.D. 310 Golden Shore St., 4th Fl.
**Martin, Michael Guy** ..................'59 '93 C.766 B.A. L.398 J.D. [A Ford,W.H.&B.]
Martin, Steven M., (AV) ........................'15 '49 C&L.426 B.B.A., J.D. [B Martin&S.]
Martin, Thomas ........................'53 '81 C.1042 B.A. L.1137 J.D. 301 E. Bixby Rd.
Martin, Thomas ........................'32 '71 C.911 B.A. L.426 J.D. 555 E. Ocean Blvd.‡
Martin and Stamp, A Professional Corporation, (AV) ..........110 Pine Ave. (⊙Anaheim)
Mason, Asa D. ........................'28 '63 C.800 B.S. L.809 J.D. 201 Covina Ave.
Matsuk, Leonard A., (AV) ..................'50 '77 C.1042 B.A. L.990 J.D. [Matsuk&O.]
Matsuk and Orr, (AV) ..................................................111 West Ocean Boulevard
**Mattfeld, Kenneth F.** ........................'54 '96 C.477 B.S. L.945 J.D. [Fisher&P.]
*PRACTICE AREAS: Marine; Environmental and Toxic Tort Litigation.
Mayer, Martin J. ........................'41 '66 C.331 B.A. L.724 J.D. 110 W. Ocean Blvd.
**McAllister, Brian B.A.** ........................'67 '93 C.299 B.A. L.1065 J.D. [A Hill,B.&N.]
*LANGUAGES: French.
**McAndrews, Barbara M.** ..............'62 '88 C.112 B.S. L.809 J.D. [A Johnson,C.&R.]
*PRACTICE AREAS: Insurance Coverage; Environmental Law; Transactional Law; Receiverships.
McBrearty, John ........................'50 '87 L.1137 J.D. 3454 E. Anaheim St.
McCabe, James N. ........................'44 '69 C.112 A.B. L.1066 J.D. Dep. City Atty.
**McClure, J. Michael** ..................'53 '86 C.586 B.A. L.1136 J.D. [Ford,W.H.&B.]
Mccoy, Roche S. ........................'59 '92 C.1042 B.S. L.809 J.D. 801 Pacific Ave.
McCulloch, Wendell H. '21 '49 C.273 A.B. L.976 J.D.
Dir., Intl. Business Programs, Calif. State Univ.
McDonald, Sean K. ........................'65 '91 C.800 B.A. L.990 J.D. Dep. Pub. Def.
**McDonald, Timothy P.** ..................'58 '86 C.1030 B.A. L.1049 J.D. [Ford,W.H.&B.]
**McFaul, Joseph R.** ........................'53 '83 C.869 B.S. L.678 J.D. [Kirlin,C.&K.]
McGuire, Michael T. ........................'36 '72 C&L.800 J.D. 1803 E. Ocean Blvd.
**McHugh, Connie A.** ..................'61 '92 C.1042 B.S. L.1137 J.D. [A Johnson,C.&R.]
*PRACTICE AREAS: Civil Law; Litigation; Insurance Defense.
McKasson, John K. ........................'62 '88 C.763 B.S. L.1049 J.D. [Barnhill&M.]
McKenna, Robert L., III ..................'67 '93 C.112 B.A. L.426 J.D. [Carroll,K.&T.]
McKnight, Cherre M. ..........'47 '89 C.1042 B.A. L.1001 J.D. 1025 Palo Verde Ave.‡
**McLaughlin, Michael J.** ........................'66 '92 C&L.426 B.B.A., J.D. [A Fisher&P.]
*PRACTICE AREAS: Maritime Personal Injury; Inland Marine; Transportation; Insurance Litigation.
McMillan, James T. '26 '56
C.800 B.E. L.1068 LL.B. Pres., McDonnell Douglas Fin. Corp. (Pat.)
McWilliams, Richard L., (Inc.), (AV) '24 '51
C.249 B.A. L.800 LL.B. 111 W. Ocean Blvd.
Menke, Bruce R. ..............'57 '84 C.809 B.S. L.800 J.D. 5199 E. Pacific Coast Hwy.
Mepham, Robert J., Jr. ........................'24 '54 C.744 L.426 LL.B. P.O. Box 14843
Merrill, Kenneth B. ........................'48 '79 C.36 B.S. L.809 J.D. [Darrow&M.]
Merryman, Robin K. ..................'55 '83 C.766 B.A. L.1065 J.D. 4320 Atlantic Ave.
Metcalfe, Chas. R. ........................'23 '55 C.999 L.809 6222 E. Conant St.
Meyer, Donald W., (AV) ..................'34 '64 C.347 B.A. L.1065 J.D. 649 Park Ave.‡
**Migliaccio, Nicola** ........................'63 '92 C.1042 B.A. L.464 J.D. [A La Torraca&G.]
**Miller, Arthur W.**, (AV) ..........'28 '53 C.976 B.A. L.569 J.D. [Simon,M.M.Z.S.&D.] ‡
**Miller, Christine Ann** ........................'65 '95 C&L.800 B.S., J.D. [A Keesal,Y.&L.]
Miller, Douglas C., (BV) ..................'43 '69 C.112 B.A. L.813 J.D. 60 Elm Ave.
**Miller, James O.** ........................'48 '91 C.112 B.A. L.809 J.D. [Ford,W.H.&B.]
**Miller, Jilana L.** ........................'70 '96 C.800 B.A. L.1049 J.D. [A Keesal,Y.&L.]
Miller, John D., (AV) ........................'27 '53 C&L.813 B.A., J.D. [J.D.Miller]
Miller, Randall B. ..................'37 '63 C.112 A.B. L.800 LL.B. 2810 Temple Ave.
Miller, John D., A Professional Corporation, (AV) ..............................3838 Cedar Ave.
Mills, Don Harper, (AV) ..................'27 '58 C.150 B.S. L.800 J.D. 700 E. Ocean Blvd.
Minsky, Larry ........................'50 '80 C.763 A.B. L.1238 J.D. 110 Pine Ave.
**Mirkovich, Joseph N.**, (AV) ..................'39 '70 C.112 B.S. L.767 J.D. [Russell&M.]
*PRACTICE AREAS: Maritime; International; Commercial; Business Litigation.
Mitchell, Gary R., (AV) ..................'39 '65 C.1042 A.B. L.1065 J.D. 333 W. Bway.
Mittelstadt, Louis R. ..................'43 '80 C.1075 B.A. L.398 J.D. [Mittelstadt&M.]
Mittelstadt and Moreno ..................................................3300 E. 59th
Moghaddam, B. Alexander '62 '89 C.966 B.S. L.846 J.D.
301 E. Ocean Blvd., Ste. 1200
**Mooradian, George T.**, (AV) ..................'54 '79 C&L.477 B.A., J.D. [Baker&H.]
*PRACTICE AREAS: Tax Law; Estate Planning Law.
**Moore, Neal** ........................'45 '71 C&L.800 A.B., J.D. [Moore,R.&E.]⊙
*PRACTICE AREAS: Public Entity Defense; Law Enforcement Defense; Insurance Defense.
**Moore, Stephen Ward** ..................'61 '89 C.800 B.A. L.426 J.D. [Ford,W.H.&B.]
*LANGUAGES: Spanish.

**Moore, Rutter & Evans, (AV) BB**
A Partnership including a Professional Corporation
**555 East Ocean Boulevard, Suite 500, 90802-5090⊙**
Telephone: 310-494-6667; 435-4499 Facsimile: 310-495-4229
Resident Partners: Neal Moore; Mark D. Rutter; William D. Evans (P.C.). Of Counsel: Michael J. Emling.
General Civil, Maritime and Trial Practice in all State and Federal Courts, Appellate Practice, Automobile Negligence, Business Torts, Casualty Defense, Commercial Litigation, Construction De

(This Listing Continued)

**Moore, Rutter & Evans (Continued)**

**fect Litigation, Environmental Torts, Estate Planning, Insurance Coverage, Inverse Condemnation, Law Enforcement Defense, Municipality Defense, Premises Liability, Products Liability and Wrongful Termination.**
**Huntington Beach, California Office: 2100 Main Street, Suite 280, 92648. Telephone: 714-374-3333.**

*See Professional Biographies, LONG BEACH, CALIFORNIA*

Moreno, Kathleen ........................................ '49 '83 [Mittelstadt&M.]
**Mori, Grace C.** .................. '68 '93 C.112 B.S. L.809 J.D. [[A] Burns,A.P.M.&B.]⊙
*PRACTICE AREAS: General Civil Litigation.
Morimoto, Mary Ann ....... '57 '82 C.813 B.A. L.569 J.D. 4060 Lakewood Blvd., 6th Fl.
Morris, Laurence D. ...................... '49 '90 C&L.862 B.S., J.D. 2290 Pacific Ave.
**Moseley, Jon T.** ......................... '58 '84 C.112 B.A. L.990 J.D. [Ford,W.H.&B.]
Moseley, William J., IV '57 '84 C.112 B.A. L.990 J.D.
One World Trade Center, 27th Fl.
Moses, Thomas J. ..... '59 '84 C.1042 B.A. L.464 J.D. 4500 E. Pacific Coast Hwy., 4th Fl.
Moss, Alfred G. .................. '39 '67 C.939 B.A. L.911 J.D. One World Trade Ctr.
**Moyer, Lynn E.** ............................ '53 '87 C&L.1137 B.S., J.D. [Hill,B.&N.]
Mulholland, Maryjane, (BV) ............ '41 '70 C.923 B.A. L.893 J.D. [M.Mulholland]⊙
Mulholland, Maryjane, P.C., (BV) ..................... 203 Quincy Ave. (⊙Summerland)

**Mullen & Filippi, (AV)**
**400 Oceangate Avenue, Suite 400, 90802⊙**
**Telephone: 310-491-0369**
**Member of Firm: Gregory T. Dale. Associate: Georgene K. Tibbetts.**
**Insurance Defense, Workers Compensation, Liability and Subrogation.**
**Other California Offices: San Francisco, San Jose, Sacramento, Fresno, Santa Rosa, Salinas, Stockton, Bakersfield, Redding, Woodland Hills and Oakland.**

*See Professional Biographies, SAN FRANCISCO, CALIFORNIA*

Mulloy, Eric E. '47 '72 C.309 A.B. L.477 J.D.
Assoc. Gen. Coun., McDonnell Douglas Aerospace-Military Transport Aircraft
Mulrooney, Celeste M. ................ '51 '77 C.37 B.A. L.1148 J.D. 1 World Trade Ctr.
**Murch, Scott K.** .................. '68 '94 C.112 B.A. L.1065 J.D. [[A] La Torraca&G.]
**Murphy, Dena L.** .................... '69 '95 C.1042 B.S. L.1049 J.D. [[A] Keesal,Y.&L.]
**Murray, James G.** ........................ '60 '85 C.112 B.A. L.426 J.D. [Prindle,D.&A.]
*PRACTICE AREAS: Insurance Defense; Environmental; Product Liability.
**Nakazawa, Alan**, (AV) ........... '51 '78 C.976 B.A. L.800 J.D. [Williams W.C.N.&R.]
*REPORTED CASES: North River Ins. Company v. Fed Sea/Fed Pac, 647 F.2d 985 (9th Cir. 1981); Mobil Sales & Supply Corporation v. Panamax Venus, 804 F.2d 541, 1987 AMC 305 (9th Cir. 1986); Carman Tool & Abrasives, Inc. v. Evergreen Lines, 871 F.2d 897 (9th Cir. 1989); Mori Seiki USA, Inc. v. M.V. Alligator Triumph, 990 F.2d 444 (9th Cir. 1993); North End Oil v. Norman Spirit, 1993 AMC 88 (C.D. Cal. 1992).
*PRACTICE AREAS: Maritime Law; Transportation and International Law; Commercial Transactions and Litigation; Immigration.
**Nanos, John M.** ............ '47 '72 C.347 A.B. L.597 J.D. Princ. Coun., BW/IP Intl., Inc.
*RESPONSIBILITIES: Corporate Law; International Law; Securities Law; Finance Law.
**Nelson, Keith A.**, (BV) ..................... '45 '75 L.1137 J.D. [Vandenberg,N.C.N.&S.]
*PRACTICE AREAS: Personal Injury Law; Negligence and Trials; Civil Trial Law.
**Nelson, Mark W.** .................. '65 '90 C.1060 B.A. L.1049 J.D. [[A] Keesal,Y.&L.]
*PRACTICE AREAS: Maritime Litigation; Securities Litigation; General Litigation.
**Nessel, Cheryl P.** .................... '55 '82 C.1077 B.A. L.809 J.D. [[A] O'Flaherty&B.]
**Newell, Frank R.**, (BV) ......... '50 '75 C.1042 B.A. L.800 J.D. [Vandenberg,N.C.N.&S.]
*PRACTICE AREAS: Probate; Real Estate Law; Business and Corporations; Estate Planning.
Newman, Linda Haley .... '48 '79 C.1042 B.A. L.426 J.D. 6475 E. Pacific Coast Highway
Nichols, Scott E., (BV) ............ '46 '75 C.800 B.A. L.990 J.D. City Atty. [Siegel&N.]
Nicholson, Gerald G. ............... '50 '78 C.1042 B.A. L.1137 J.D. 5375 E. Second St.
**Nick, Jack C.** ......................... '67 '92 C.769 B.A. L.426 J.D. [[A] Prindle,D.&A.]
*PRACTICE AREAS: Insurance Defense; Amusement Park Litigation; Product Liability.
**Nikas, Richard J.** .................. '68 '96 C&L.800 B.A., J.D. [[A] Williams W.C.N.&R.]
*LANGUAGES: Greek, Russian and Spanish.
*PRACTICE AREAS: Admiralty and Maritime Law; International Law; Litigation.
Nishkian, Michael A. .................. '44 '72 C.813 B.S. L.800 J.D. 3640 Atlantic Ave.
Nolte, Ronald A. ....................... '38 '64 C.675 B.A. L.597 J.D. 4245 Cedar Ave.
**Nursall, John G.** ........................... '53 '88 C.800 B.A. L.990 J.D. [Swain&D.]
*PRACTICE AREAS: Admiralty and Maritime; Labor and Employment.
Nutter, Melvin L., (BV) ................. '39 '65 C.668 B.A. L.1066 J.D. 200 Oceangate
Oakley, Susan C., (BV) ................ '46 '81 C.1042 B.A. L.1137 J.D. Dep. City Atty.

**O'Flaherty & Belgum, (AV)**
**100 Oceangate Suite 500, 90802-4312⊙**
**Telephone: 310-437-0090 Fax: 310-437-5550**
**Email: oandb&primenet.com URL: http://www.oandb-law/oandb**
**Resident Partners: Todd C. Theodora; John J. Weber; Lynn E. Ovando; Stephen L. Schumm; Kristen J. Heim. Resident Associates: Robert M. Dato; Donna R. Evans; Sharon A. Brahms; Johanna A. Schleuter; Cheryl P. Nessel; Ronald A. Chavez; Kathleen E. Barnett; Daniel K. Dik; Debra L. Denton; Richard G. Kolostian, Jr; William D. Hardy; Brian P. Barrow.**
**General Civil, Trial and Appellate Practice in State and Federal Courts. Medical and Dental Malpractice, Products Liability, General Insurance Law, Insurance Coverage, Wrongful Termination, Worker's Compensation, Business and Environmental Litigation.**
**Glendale, California Office: 1000 North Central, Suite 300, 91202-2957. Telephone: 818-242-9229. Fax: 818-242-9114.**
**Orange County, California Office: 222 South Harbor Boulevard, Suite 600, Anaheim, 92805-3701. Telephone: 714-533-3373. Fax: 714-533-2607.**
**Riverside, California Office: 3880 Lemon Street, Suite 450, 92501-3301. Telephone: 909-341-0049. Fax: 909-341-3919.**
**Ventura, California Office: 840 County Square Drive, Suite 200, 93003-5406. Telephone: 805-650-2600. Fax: 805-650-2658.**

*See Professional Biographies, LONG BEACH, CALIFORNIA*

**Okazaki, Theodore S.** ................ '62 '89 C.112 B.A. L.809 J.D. [[A] Johnson,C.&R.]
*LANGUAGES: Japanese.
*PRACTICE AREAS: Premises Liability; Tort Litigation; Government Entities; Insurance Defense.
Olifant, Scott B. .................... '58 '90 C.1222 B.B.A. L.809 J.D. 4480 Myrtle Ave.
**Olofson, Jill Elizabeth** ............ '65 '91 C.112 B.S./B.A. L.424 J.D. [[A] Keesal,Y.&L.]
Olsen, Terri L. ...................... '58 '91 C.1131 B.S. L.809 J.D. 330 Golden Shore Dr.
O'Melia, Brendan A. .................. '62 '94 C.1077 B.A. L.809 J.D. 400 Oceangate ave.
**O'Reilly, Timothy L.** ................ '64 '90 C.1042 B.A. L.1148 J.D. [[A] E.P.George,Jr.]
*PRACTICE AREAS: Criminal; Personal Injury; Appellate.
Orr, Robert M., (AV) ........................ '54 '79 C.112 B.A. L.990 J.D. [Matsuk&Q.]
Osaki, Kerry G., (BV) ............... '53 '78 C.769 B.A. L.426 J.D. [Wheatley O.&Assoc.]
**Ostergrad, Kyle A.** ........................ '70 '95 C.112 B.A. L.770 J.D. [Ford,W.H.&B.]
O'Sullivan, Dennis J. ............. '50 '77 C.346 B.S. L.1137 J.D. 3701 Long Beach Blvd.
**Otera, Steven Y.** ........................ '65 '91 C.112 B.A. L.426 J.D. [[A] Baker&H.]
*PRACTICE AREAS: Admiralty Personal Injury Defense; Insurance Coverage and Defense; General Business Litigation.
Ottenweller, Solan & Park, (AV) .................. 301 E. Ocean Blvd. (⊙San Francisco)
Otto, Douglas W., (AV) .............. '48 '78 C.813 B.A. L.145 J.D. 111 W. Ocean Blvd.
**Ovando, Lynn E.**, (BV) ................ '57 '83 C.740 B.A. L.1292 J.D. [O'Flaherty&B.]
**Owen, Christina L.**, (BV) .................. '46 '72 C.112 B.S. L.800 J.D. [Baker&H.]
*PRACTICE AREAS: Admiralty; Litigation; Insurance Coverage.
**Padley, Albert F., III** .................. '53 '78 C.602 B.A. L.426 J.D. [Wise,W.T.&W.]
*PRACTICE AREAS: Insurance Coverage; Insurance Defense.
**Palmer, E. Scott** ...................... '66 '91 C.112 B.S. L.800 J.D. [[A] Keesal,Y.&L.]
Palmer, Edward S. ................. '66 '91 C.112 B.S. L.800 J.D. 310 Golden Shore St.
Palmer, Gregory P. ........................ '58 '88 L.1137 J.D. 110 W. Ocean Blvd., 7th Fl.
**Pangborn, Russell C.** '66 '94
C.813 B.A. L.1065 J.D. [[A] Fulwider P.L.&U.] (See Pat. Sect.)⊙
*PRACTICE AREAS: Trademark; Copyright; Patent Litigation; Trade Secret.
Park, Arthur A., Jr., (AV) ..................................... '40 '66 [Ottenweller,S.&P.]⊙
Parker, Howard Craig .................. '48 '76 C.112 B.A. L.809 J.D. 2290 Pacific Ave.

**Parker, Larry H. '48 '73 C.1097 B.A. L.809 J.D.**
**3605 Long Beach Boulevard Suite 100, 90807**
**Telephone: 800-872-0000 Fax: 310-595-4908**
***PRACTICE AREAS: Personal Injury.**
**Environmental Law, Asbestos Toxic Torts, Chemical Exposure, Hazardous Materials and Substances, Management, Hazardous Waste, Toxic Injuries, Toxic Exposure, Construction Defects, Insurance Bad Faith, Personal Injury, Medical Malpractice, Maritime Accidents, Aviation Accidents, Automobile, Bus and Train Accidents.**

*See Professional Biographies, LONG BEACH, CALIFORNIA*

Parker, Robert B. ................... '— '93 C.800 M.S.E.E. L.1137 J.D. 329 LaJolla Ave.
**Parker, Sandra M.** ............ '— '92 C.800 M.S.E.E. L.1137 J.D. [[C] M.J.Emling] (Pat.)
*LANGUAGES: French and Russian.
*PRACTICE AREAS: Intellectual Property.
Parker, Sandra M. ........... '— '92 C.800 M.S.E.E. L.1137 J.D. 329 La Jolla Ave. (Pat.)
Parry, Alaine R. .......................... '58 '83 C.605 A.B. L.1065 J.D. 400 Oceangate
Patko, Yvette A. G. ........................ '69 '92 C.112 B.A. L.990 J.D. [[A] Makin&M.]
Patterson, Thomas G. ................ '44 '75 C.1042 B.S. L.809 J.D. 4266 Atlantic Ave.
Paulsin, Joanna L. ... '63 '88 C.1042 B.S. L.1137 J.D. 4500 E. Pacific Coast Hwy., 4th Fl.
**Pearce, Michael J.**, (AV) .............. '52 '79 C.051 B.A. L.228 J.D. [Wise,W.T.&W.]
*PRACTICE AREAS: Contract Law; Insurance Law; International Law; Litigation.
**Pearl, Todd D.** ............................ '64 '90 C.112 B.A. L.770 J.D. [Ford,W.H.&B.]
**Pearlson, Paul R.** ................ '55 '80 C.112 A.B. L.813 J.D. [Cameron,M.P.G.&S.]
*PRACTICE AREAS: Business Litigation.
Pekich, Donald M., (AV) .............. '35 '76 C.1042 B.A. L.1137 J.D. [Cantrell,G.&P.]
**Pepys, Mark B.**, (AV) .............. '37 '64 C.112 B.A. L.1066 LL.B. [[C] Prindle,D.&A.]
*PRACTICE AREAS: Products Liability; Professional Liability; Construction Defects.
Perella, Jack ............................ '44 '84 C.112 B.A. L.1227 J.D. 601 Pacific Ave.
**Perona, James T.**, (AV) .................. '35 '63 C&L.950 B.S., LL.B. [Perona,L.&B.]

**Perona, Langer & Beck, A Professional Corporation, (AV) [BR]**
**300 East San Antonio, 90807⊙**
**Telephone: 310-426-6155 Facsimile: 310-490-9823**
**James T. Perona; Major A. Langer; Ronald Beck; Wayne M. Robertshaw; John C. Thornton; M. Lawrence Lallande; Ellen R. Serbin;—Nelson L. Cohen; R. Paul Katrinak; Susan Graham; Edward T. Trumper; Richard L. Stuhlbarg; Rhonda Ann Visniski.**
**Personal Injury, Products Liability, Malpractice, Insurance (Bad Faith), Commercial Litigation and Trial Practice in all Courts and Administrative Agencies. Landslide and Subsidence Law. Construction Defect.**
**Los Angeles, California Office: 9255 Sunset Boulevard, Suite 920. Telephone: 800-435-7542.**

*See Professional Biographies, LONG BEACH, CALIFORNIA*

Perry, James David ............ '46 '87 C.684 B.A. L.1137 J.D. 3780 Kilroy Airport Way
**Perry, Scott D.** ....................... '62 '94 C.1109 B.A. L.1137 J.D. [Lombardi&P.]
Peters, Michael M. ................... '58 '85 C.426 B.B.A. L.1137 J.D. Dep. City Atty.
Petersen, Einar C., (AV) ............. '36 '61 C.813 A.B. L.1065 J.D. Sr. Dep. City Atty.
Petersen, Mark E., (BV) .................. '56 '82 C.1042 B.A. L.809 J.D. [[A] Martin&S.]
Petersen, Ronald E. .................. '42 '72 C.1097 B.A. L.809 J.D. 211 E. Ocean Blvd.
Peterson, John E., Jr., (BV) ............. '30 '65 C.112 A.B. L.426 LL.B. Dep. City Atty.
Peterson, Orlin C. ...................... '19 '49 C.112 B.A. L.800 J.D. 2727 E. 7th St.‡
Pheil, David B. ......................... '54 '80 C.763 B.A. L.1049 J.D. 301 E. Ocean Blvd.
Phillips, Herschel A. ................ '22 '50 C.112 A.B. L.309 LL.B. 6 Rivo Alto Canal‡
**Picking, Jay H.**, (BV) ...................... '54 '80 C.608 B.A. L.61 J.D. [Pray,P.W.&R.]
*PRACTICE AREAS: Litigation; Construction Law; Personal Injury Law; Family Law.
Pierce, James B. ..................................... '51 '74 C.1163 B.A. L.464 J.D. Supr. Ct. J.
Pierce, Robert G. ................ '49 '84 C.684 B.A. L.1137 J.D. 215 Long Beach Blvd.
Pike, Mark W. ....................... '59 '88 C.1042 B.S. L.1137 J.D. 301 E. Ocean Blvd.
Pillsbury, Wm. T. ......................... '19 '53 C.999 L.426 LL.B. 111 W. Ocean Blvd.
Platt, Lisa Slayton ........................ '57 '85 C.378 B.A. L.61 J.D. 320 Golden Shore
Pokras, Sheila, (Mrs.) ................................ '35 '70 C.831 B.S. L.990 J.D. Supr. Ct. J.
**Poladian, Tamar** .................. '64 '91 C.112 B.A. L.809 J.D. [[A] Johnson,C.&R.]
*LANGUAGES: Armenian.
*PRACTICE AREAS: General Civil Law; Litigation; Insurance Defense; Premises Liability.
Poland, Richard L, (BV) .................... '48 '73 C.228 A.B. L.846 J.D. 333 W. Bway.
**Politis, Nicholas S.** ........................ '54 '80 C.112 B.A. L.1068 J.D. [Flynn,D.&W.]
*PRACTICE AREAS: Admiralty and Maritime Law; International Transportation; Civil Litigation; Insurance Coverage.
Polsky, Alexander S., (AV) .......... '51 '77 C.912 B.S.E. L.1095 J.D. 5911 E. Spring St.
**Porter, David S.**, (AV) ........................ '55 '80 C.112 B.A. L.1068 J.D. [Fisher&P.]
*REPORTED CASES: Foss Launch & Tug Co. v. Char Ching Shipping U.S.A., Ltd., 808 F.2d 697 (9th Cir. 1987); Interpool Limited v. Char Yigh Marine (Panama) S.A., 890 F.2d 1453 (9th Cir. 1989); Alexander v. Circus Circus Enterprises, Inc., 972 F.2d 261 (9th Cir. 1992).
*PRACTICE AREAS: Trials and Appeals; Insurance Coverage and "Bad Faith" Defense; Marine P & I Coverage and Defense.
Porter, Robert L., (BV) ..................... '30 '65 C.112 B.A. L.800 LL.B. [R.L.Porter]
Porter, Steven R. '55 '81 C.813 B.A. L.477 J.D.
(adm. in AK; not adm. in CA) ARCO Transportation Co.
Porter, Theodore Carl ............. '54 '84 C.659 B.S. L.800 J.D. 3638 San Anseline Ave.
Porter, Robert L., A Professional Corporation, (BV) ............... 110 Pine Ave. 11th Fl.
Post, Barry J. .................... '52 '76 C.112 B.A. L.1049 J.D. 3780 Kilroy Airport Way
**Pratt, Scott T.**, (BV) .................... '50 '75 C.800 B.S. L.1068 J.D. [Keesal,Y.&L.]

**Pray, Price, Williams & Russell, (AV)**
**810 Fidelity Federal Plaza Building, 555 East Ocean Boulevard, 90802**
**Telephone: 310-436-1231 Facsimile: 310-435-6384**
**Members of Firm: Russell H. Pray (1892-1971); Wm. A. Williams; James B. Russell, Jr.; William C. Price; Jay H. Picking; Bruce E. Bothwell; David M. Price.**
**General Civil and Criminal Trial Practice. Corporation, Real Estate, Estate Planning, Trust, Taxation, Probate, Negligence and Family Law.**
**References: Bank of America National Trust & Savings Assn., Farmers & Merchants Bank (Long Beach Main Branches).**

*See Professional Biographies, LONG BEACH, CALIFORNIA*

Pretre, Andrea G. .......................... '40 '88 L.1137 J.D. 4047 Long Beach Blvd.
**Price, David M.** ......................... '58 '85 C.101 B.A. L.1067 J.D. [Pray,P.W.&R.]
*LANGUAGES: German.
*PRACTICE AREAS: Litigation; Commercial Law; Construction Law; Corporations Law; Family Law.
**Price, William C.**, (AV) ................ '47 '73 C.101 A.B. L.1068 J.D. [Pray,P.W.&R.]
*LANGUAGES: French and Tahitian.
*PRACTICE AREAS: Probate and Estate Planning Law; Family Law; Litigation; Construction Law; Personal Injury.
**Prindle, Kenneth B.**, (AV) ............ '53 '78 C.112 B.A. L.809 J.D. [Prindle,D.&A.]⊙
*PRACTICE AREAS: Environmental; Asbestos Personal Injury; Property Damage; Insurance Coverage Defense.

**Prindle, Decker & Amaro, (AV)**
**310 Golden Shore 4th Floor, P.O. Box 22711, 90801-5511⊙**
**Telephone: 310-436-3946 Fax: 310-495-0564**
**Email: LAWPDA1@aol.com**

(This Listing Continued)

CAA165P

**Prindle, Decker & Amaro (Continued)**
**Members of Firm: Kenneth B. Prindle; R. Joseph Decker; Michael L. Amaro; Andy J. Goetz; Mary Kirk Hillyard (Resident, San Francisco Office); Gary E. Yardumian; Monte H. Machit. Associates: Tahereh K. Barnes; Jack R. Reinholtz; Jack C. Nick; Kristin E.D. Dunn; James G. Murray; Anna M. Ferguson; Thomas A. Steig (Resident, San Francisco Office); Thomas P. Gmelich; Peter A. Pogue (Resident, San Francisco Office); Dwayne S. Beck; Darren B. Rosenberg; Amy E. Ahlers (Resident, San Francisco Office); Haleh Rahimzadeh. Of Counsel: William Murray Hake; Mark B. Pepys.**
**General Litigation Practice including Insurance Defense, Asbestos Personal Injury and Property Damage, Personal Injury, Products Liability, Recreation and Amusement Park Litigation, Environmental, Admiralty, Business Transaction, Real Estate Transaction, Superfund, Workers Compensation, Construction Litigation and Coverage.**
**San Francisco, California Office: 369 Pine Street, Suite 800. 94104. Telephone: 415-788-8354. Fax: 415-788-3625.**

*See Professional Biographies, LONG BEACH, CALIFORNIA*

**Prineas, Zachary T.**, (BV) ....'52 '75 C&L.800 A.B., J.D. [Cree&P.]
Pugsley, George L. ....'31 '67 C.112 B.A. L.426 J.D. Mun. Ct. Comr.
Pulley, Pamela Abney ....'65 '91 C.597 B.A. L.184 J.D. 401 E. Ocean Blvd., Suite 600
**Pynchon, Victoria** ....'52 '80 C.112 B.A. L.1067 J.D. [🄰 L.Silver&Assoc.]
*REPORTED CASES: Harris v. Smith, 157 Cal.App. 3d 100 (1984); Ziller Electronics Lab v. Superior Court, 206 Cal.App. 3d 1222 (1988); Geophysical Systems Corp. v. Seismograph Service Corp., 738 F.Supp. 348 (1990).
*PRACTICE AREAS: Litigation; Business Litigation.
Quiel, Cynthia A. ....'57 '83 C&L.1137 B.S., J.D. Wkrs. Comp. App. Bd. J.
Quinn, Jean Ann ....'59 '89 C.906 B.A. L.800 J.D. Atty., Calif. State Univ.
**Rahimzadeh, Haleh** ....'71 '96 C.569 B.A. L.800 J.D. [🄰 Prindle,D.&A.]
*LANGUAGES: Persian and French.
*PRACTICE AREAS: Litigation.
**Ramsey, Albert C. S.**, (AV) ....'12 '37 C.112 B.A. L.800 LL.B. [🄲 E.P.George,Jr.]
*PRACTICE AREAS: Criminal; Personal Injury; Appellate.
**Ramsey, Thomas A.**, (AV) ....'36 '65 C.605 A.B. L.800 LL.B. [T.A.Ramsey]
*PRACTICE AREAS: Business Law; Probate Law; Entertainment; Estate Planning Law; Real Estate.

**Ramsey, Thomas A., A P.C., (AV)**
**200 Oceangate, Suite 1550, 90802**
**Telephone: 310-436-7713 Fax: 310-436-7313**
**Thomas A. Ramsey.**
**Business, Healthcare, Entertainment, Real Estate and Estate Planning.**

Rasmussen, Judith A. ....'42 '85 C.1042 L.809 J.D. 111 W. Ocean Blvd.
**Rasmussen, Lynne** ....'53 '84 C.1042 B.A. L.426 J.D. [🄰 Stolpman K.E.M.&K.]
*PRACTICE AREAS: Appeals; Construction Accidents Law; Products Liability Law; Maritime Accidents Law.
Rasmussen, Norman, (AV) ....'32 '60 C.112 B.S. L.1001 LL.B. 11 Golden Shore
Reagan, Margaret L. ....'44 '87 C.1075 B.S. L.1137 J.D. 2530 Atlantic Ave.
Rebeck, Joseph P. ....'34 '61 C.645 B.S. L.1068 LL.B. Wkrs. Comp. Apps. Bd. J.
Recknagel, Robert R., (AV) ....'39 '65 C.766 A.B. L.1065 J.D. Dep. City Pros.
**Reed, Derrick W.** '69 '95
C.112 B.S.E.E. L.426 J.D. [🄰 Fulwider P.L.&U.] (See Pat. Sect.)
*PRACTICE AREAS: Patent Prosecution; Patent Litigation; Trademark Law; Unfair Competition Law; Intellectual Property Law.
**Reeder, Pamela J.** ....'71 '96 C.112 B.A. L.426 J.D. [🄰 Keesal,Y.&L.]
Reid, Edward C. ....'48 '74 C.1042 B.A. L.990 J.D. 5855 Naples Plaza
Reidder, William A. ....'41 '69 C.112 B.S. L.809 J.D. Sr. Dep. City Atty.
**Reinard, David James** ....'61 '91 C.426 B.A. L.809 J.D. [La Torraca&G.]
*PRACTICE AREAS: General Liability.
**Reinholtz, Jack R.** ....'62 '90 C.426 B.S. L.770 J.D. [🄰 Prindle,D.&A.]
*PRACTICE AREAS: Insurance Defense; Construction Litigation.
**Reisinger, Robert** ....'64 '91 C.763 B.S. L.61 J.D. [Ford,W.H.&B.]
Rhoads, Thomas J. ....'48 '76 C.800 M.B.A. L.1137 J.D. 5150 Pacific Coast
Rhodes, Daniel James ....'55 '90 C.101 B.A. L.990 J.D. 100 Oceangate
Rhorer, William G., Jr. ....'45 '76 C.800 B.S.B.A. L.61 J.D. 5330 El Prado
**Rice, Steven C.** ....'59 '83 C.309 A.B. L.1067 J.D. [Wise,W.T.&W.]
*PRACTICE AREAS: Insurance Law; Litigation.
Richardson, Bruce M. '42 '70 C.101 B.A. L.1066 J.D.
Dep. Gen. Coun., Calif. State Univ.
Richardson, Elizabeth L. ....'55 '80 C.112 B.S. L.1049 J.D. 333 W. Ocean Blvd., 11th Fl.
**Riedman, Fred L.**, (AV) ....'30 '57 C.684 A.B. L.800 J.D. [Riedman,D.&D.]
*PRACTICE AREAS: Real Estate Law.
Riedman, Fred M. ....'03 '31 C.684 A.B. L.800 LL.B. 200 Oceangate, Ste 330

**Riedman, Dalessi & Dybens, (AV)**
**200 Oceangate, Suite 440, 90802**
**Telephone: 310-436-5203; 435-5608 Fax: 310-437-8225**
**Members of Firm: William T. Dalessi; Fred L. Riedman; Bruce A. Dybens.**
**General Civil and Trial Practice in all Courts. Business and Corporate, Real Property, Estate Planning, Trust and Probate Law. Family Law. Personal Injury.**

*See Professional Biographies, LONG BEACH, CALIFORNIA*

Riley, Peter F. ....'43 '78 C.1097 B.S. L.426 J.D. 3885 Gundry Ave.
Risi, Domenico ....'40 '90 C.1042 B.A. L.1001 J.D. 333 W. Bway.
**Ritsema, Scott A.** ....'61 '88 C.112 B.A. L.1067 J.D. [🄰 Ford,W.H.&B.]
*PRACTICE AREAS: Civil Litigation.
**Robb, Neal Scott**, (BV) ....'57 '82 C.112 B.A. L.1065 J.D. [Keesal,Y.&L.]
Robbe, Fletcher A. ....'50 '75 C.1077 B.A. L.809 J.D. 147 Quincy Ave.
Robbins, Paul S., (BV) ....'41 '73 C.588 B.S. L.809 J.D. Dep. City Pros.
**Robertshaw, Wayne M.** ....'49 '74 C.940 B.A. L.426 J.D. [Perona,L.&B.]
**Robinson, William L.** ....'46 '79 C.871 B.S.E.E. L.1066 J.D. [Lillick&C.]
*PRACTICE AREAS: Aviation; Products Liability; Toxic Tort, Environmental and Commercial Litigation.
Roddy, Wilton J., Jr., (BV) ....'40 '74 L.1152 J.D. One World Trade Ctr., 8th Fl.

**Rodenborn, Michelle M., Law Offices of '48 '74 C&L.352 B.A., J.D.**
**One World Trade Center, Suite 1600, 90831-1600**
**Telephone: 562-436-5456 Fax: 562-437-1967**
**Email: customs@rodenborn.com URL: http://www.rodenborn.com**
***LANGUAGES: Russian, French and Spanish.**
**Customs, International Trade and Transportation Law. Trial and Appellate Practice in all State and Federal Courts. Practice before Federal Administrative Agencies. Export Licensing.**

*See Professional Biographies, LONG BEACH, CALIFORNIA*

Rodrick, Scott S. ....'59 '91 C.112 B.A. L.61 J.D. Advsr., U.S. Dept. of Labor
**Rohaidy, Maria M.** ....'63 '89 C.472 B.A. L.940 J.D. [🄰 Taubman,S.Y.&S.]
*LANGUAGES: Spanish.
*PRACTICE AREAS: Litigation.
Rose, Klein & Marias, (AV)
110 Pine Ave. (©L.A., Pomona, San Bernardino, Santa Ana, San Diego & Ventura)
Roseman, Steven, (BV) ....'25 '59 C.112 B.A. L.809 LL.B. 3939 Atlantic Ave.
Rosen, George M. ....'36 '61 C.339 B.S. L.597 J.D. 4060 Lakewood Blvd., 6th Fl.
**Rosenberg, Darren B.** ....'70 '95 C.103 A.B. L.809 J.D. [🄰 Prindle,D.&A.]
**Rosenberg, David Brian** ....'60 '86 C.1077 B.A. L.940 J.D. [🄰 Johnson,C.&R.]
*PRACTICE AREAS: Premises Liability; Tort Litigation.
**Rosenberger, Paul D.** ....'63 '89 C.112 B.A. L.809 J.D. [Strain&R.]
*PRACTICE AREAS: International, Federal and State Taxation Law; Probate and Estate Planning.
Ross, Barry A. ....'49 '73 C.112 B.A. L.426 J.D. Dep. City Atty.
Ross, James Michael ....'41 '76 C.37 B.S. L.813 J.D. 4801 E. Anaheim St.
Ross, Terry, (AV) ....'48 '73 C.813 A.B. L.800 J.D. [Keesal,Y.&L.]
Rothenberg, Marc S., (BV) ....'51 '76 C.705 B.A. L.990 J.D. 4326 Atlantic Ave.
Rothschild, Toby J., (BV) '44 '70
C.766 A.B. L.1068 J.D. Exec. Dir., Legal Aid Found. of Long Beach
Rouin, Carole C., (BV) ....'39 '83 C.629 B.A. L.464 J.D. 1 World Trade Ctr.
Rowland, Terry A., (AV) ....'51 '76 C.112 A.B. L.1068 J.D. [Demler,A.&R.]
Royer, Donald L. ....'23 '75 C.605 L.1221 J.D. 3855 Lakewood Blvd., MS 35-35‡
Rudolph, Richard B. ....'60 '92 C.1042 B.S. L.809 J.D. 110 W. Ocean Blvd.
**Russell, Carlton E.**, (AV) ....'28 '60 C.869 B.S. L.273 J.D. [Russell&M.]
*PRACTICE AREAS: Maritime; Environmental; Personal Injury.
**Russell, James B., Jr.**, (AV) ....'29 '59 C.1042 B.A. L.800 LL.B. [Pray,P.W.&R.]
*PRACTICE AREAS: Litigation Related to Negligence Law; Injury Accidents both Plaintiff and Defense; Family Law; Construction Law; Criminal Defense Law.
**Russell, Thomas A.** ....'53 '83 C.112 B.S. L.800 J.D. [Williams W.C.N.&R.]
*REPORTED CASES: Sea-Land Service, Inc. v. Murrey & Son's Co., 824 F.2d 740, 1988 AMC 1, 24 SRR 393 (9th Cir. 1987); Hong Kong Islands Line America S.A. v. Distribution Services Limited, 795 F.Supp. 983, 1992 AMC 82, 25 SRR 1601 (1991) aff'd 963 F.2d 378 (9th Cir. 1992); Key Bank of Maine v. M/V Asever, 1993 AMC 263 (C.D. Cal. 1992); Maryland National Bank v. The Vessel Madam Chapel, 46 F.3d 895, 1995 AMC 850, 27 SRR 279 (9th Cir, 1995); Dietrich v. Key Bank, N.A. 72 F.3d 1509, 1996 AMC 609, 27 SRR 448 (11th Cir, 1996), Logistics Management, Inc. v. Pyramid Tent Arena, 86 F.3d 908 1996 AMC 1826, 27 SRR 838 (9th Cir. 1996).
*PRACTICE AREAS: Maritime Law; Commercial Transactions and Litigation; Business; Regulatory; Immigration.

**Russell & Mirkovich, (AV)** BRI
**One World Trade Center, Suite 1450, 90831-1450**
**Telephone: 310-436-9911 FAX: 310-436-1897**
**Carlton E. Russell; Joseph N. Mirkovich.**
**General Civil, Trial and Appellate Practice in State and Federal Courts, Admiralty, Maritime, International, Environmental and Commercial Law, Personal Injury and Business Litigation.**

*See Professional Biographies, LONG BEACH, CALIFORNIA*

Ruszak, John A. ....'49 '74 C.426 B.A. L.770 J.D. 1118 E. Bixby Rd.
**Rutter, Mark D.**, (AV) ....'48 '73 C.112 B.A. L.426 J.D. [Moore,R.&E.]
*REPORTED CASES: Cooper v. Bray 21 Cal. 3d 841, 148 Cal. Rptr. 148, 1978; Tri-Chem, Inc. v. County of Los Angeles 60 Cal. App. 3d 306, 132 Cal. Rptr. 142, 1976; Garcia v. Joseph Vince Company 84 Cal. App. 3d 868, 148 Cal. Rptr. 743, 1978; Huizar v. Albex Corp. 156 Cal. App. 3d 534, 203 Cal. Rptr. 47, 1984; Cowing v. City of Torrance 60 Cal. App. 3d 757, 131 Cal. Rptr. 830, 1976.
*PRACTICE AREAS: Insurance Defense; Public Entity Defense; Products Liability; Premises Liability.
**Ryder, Robert B.** ....'56 '82 C.770 B.S.C. L.1049 J.D. [Haines&L.]
*PRACTICE AREAS: General Civil Tort Litigation; Trials; Appeals.
**Rygh, John M.** ....'53 '86 C.172 B.A. L.809 J.D. [Johnson,C.&R.]
*PRACTICE AREAS: Construction Defect; Insurance Defense; Employment Law; Governmental Entities.
**Rygmyr, Adym W.** ....'69 '96 C.678 B.A. L.800 J.D. [🄰 Keesal,Y.&L.]
St. John, Eric M. ....'50 '76 C.112 B.A. L.1137 J.D. 780 Atlantic Ave.
**Salinger, Lillian D.** ....'67 '92 C.112 B.A. L.1066 J.D. [🄰 Cameron,M.P.G.&S.]
Salisbury, David L. ....'50 '77 C.1042 B.A. L.800 J.D. Legal Aid Foundation

**Salmon, Samuel M., (AV) '31 '57 C.112 L.1065 J.D.**
**Suite 520, 200 Oceangate, Arco Center, 90802**
**Telephone: 310-437-0841 Fax: 310-432-3610**
**Trial Litigation Matters in State and Federal Courts and Arbitration Proceedings in Business, Contract, Fraud, Legal Malpractice and Bankruptcy Reorganization.**

*See Professional Biographies, LONG BEACH, CALIFORNIA*

Salmond, Andrew W. ....'63 '93 C.267 B.S. L.1148 J.D. [Carroll,K.&T.]
Samarin, Paul W. ....'56 '89 C.112 L.424 J.D. 1 World Trade Ctr.
Sanborn, Warren L. ....'28 '73 L.1136 J.D. 5199 E. Pacific Coast Hwy.
**Sandor, David L.**, (AV) ....'42 '68 C.976 B.A. L.1066 J.D. [Simon,M.M.Z.S.&D.]
*PRACTICE AREAS: Family Law.
**Sangmeister, Sarah Tong** ....'69 '94 C.597 B.S. L.990 J.D. [🄰 Keesal,Y.&L.]
San Jose, Jon A. ....'60 '91 C.1071 B.A. L.1068 J.D. 4326 Atlantic Ave.
**Savage, James D.** ....'63 '89 C.37 B.A. L.1049 J.D. [Ford,W.H.&B.]
Sawyer, Stephen D. ....'48 '75 C.1077 B.A. L.1049 J.D. 6700 E. Pacific Coast Hwy.
**Sayed, Mark A.** ....'57 '87 C.112 B.A. L.809 J.D. [🄰 Kerry,G.&L.]
*PRACTICE AREAS: Personal Injury Insurance; Real Estate Transactions; Federal Employer's Liability Act; Common Carrier Liability; Professional Malpractice.
**Scarlett, Stanley L.** ....'58 '87 C.766 B.A. L.1066 J.D. [🄰 Ford,W.H.&B.]
Schein, Cynthia Dersh ....'52 '77 C.112 B.A. L.809 J.D. 2750 N. Bellflower Blvd.
Schlackman, Marvin I. ....'46 '92 C.563 B.S. L.1136 J.D. 1 World Trade Ctr.
**Schleuter, Johanna A.** ....'41 '89 C.610 B.S. L.1137 J.D. [🄰 O'Flaherty&B.]
*PRACTICE AREAS: Wrongful Termination.
**Schmitt, Charles J.** ....'68 '94 C.112 B.A. L.809 J.D. [🄰 Ford,W.H.&B.]
Schmitt, Nancy ....'60 '87 C.1060 B.A. L.1067 J.D. P.O. Box 30302
Schmocker, John B. ....'51 '77 C.112 B.A. L.770 J.D. 4017 Long Beach Blvd.
**Schock, Dawn M.** ....'57 '85 C.585 B.A. L.464 J.D. [Keesal,Y.&L.]
**Schooley, Vern**, (AV) '37 '67
C.475 B.S.M.E. L.1049 J.D. [Fulwider P.L.&U.] (See Pat. Sect.)
*PRACTICE AREAS: Patent, Trademark, Copyright and Unfair Competition Law; Litigation.
Schorr, Gloria P. ....'26 '57 C.331 B.A. L.1009 J.D. 8045 Ring St.‡
Schreiber, Gary E. ....'60 '89 C.112 B.A. L.61 J.D. One World Trade Cntr., 11th Fl.
Schroeter, Mary J. ....'34 '83 C.813 B.A. L.1137 J.D. Dep. City Pros.
Schuchert, Joseph S. ....'59 '84 C.112 B.A. L.1049 J.D. 400 Oceangate
**Schultz, Arthur W.** ....'46 '77 C.112 L.426 J.D. [Ford,W.H.&B.]
**Schumacher, Paul J.**, (BV) ....'51 '84 C.770 B.S. L.426 J.D. [Keesal,Y.&L.]
**Schumm, Stephen L.**, (BV) ....'50 '83 C.1097 B.A. L.809 J.D. [O'Flaherty&B.]
Schuster, Jeremy G. ....'63 '89 C.1213 B.S. L.818 J.D. 3594 Armourdale Ave.
**Schwake, Lauren N.** ....'69 '94 C.659 B.A. L.426 J.D. [🄰 Keesal,Y.&L.]
Schweizer, William G. ....'47 '76 C.4 B.A. L.800 J.D. 100 Oceangate
Scully, Daniel J., (AV) ....'17 '42 C&L.585 LL.B. 3505 Long Beach Blvd.
**Sellars, James D.** ....'52 '78 C.1042 B.S. L.990 J.D. [Cameron,M.P.G.&S.]
*PRACTICE AREAS: Taxation; Estate Planning; Commercial Law; Corporate Law.
**Serbin, Ellen R.** ....'59 '87 C.1168 B.A. L.1049 J.D. [Perona,L.&B.]
Seymour, Marilyn J. ....'59 '85 C.1042 B.A. L.464 J.D. Dep. Dist. Atty.
Shafer, Harry T. ....'13 '38 C.976 B.A. L.178 LL.B. Ret. Supr. Ct. J.
Shafer, Phil J. ....'28 '55 C.112 A.B. L.309 LL.B. 908 Stevely Ave.‡
Shapiro, Anita Rae ....'41 '66 C.483 B.A. L.659 LL.B. Comr., Los Angeles Supr. Ct.
Sharzer, Elizabeth Gale ....'58 '85 C.477 B.A. L.1068 J.D. 316 Monrovia Ave.
Shaw, Carol A. ....'44 '89 C.112 B.S. L.809 J.D. 333 W. Ocean Blvd.
Shaw, Steven M. ....'49 '76 C.1097 B.A. L.1137 J.D. 1018 E. 3rd.
Sheldon, Charles D. ....'32 '61 C.951 B.A. L.893 LL.B. Supr. Ct. J.
Shelton, Howard W., (AV) ....'25 '50 C.813 A.B. L.880 LL.B. 4047 Long Beach Blvd.
Sheridan, E. W. ....'14 '44 C.352 A.B. L.1065 J.D. 200 Oceangate

**Shibley, William H., (BV) '46 '73 C.813 B.S. L.846 J.D.**
**555 East Ocean Boulevard, Suite 500, P.O. Box 1731, 90801-1731**
**Telephone: 213-437-6654 Telecopier: 310-491-5400**
**Email: shib@ix.netcom.com**
***LANGUAGES: German, Spanish, Portuguese and Arabic.**
**General Civil, Business Intellectual Property and Criminal Trial Practice with emphasis on Plaintiff Personal Injury, Criminal Defense, Maritime Injury, Longshore Compensation.**

*See Professional Biographies, LONG BEACH, CALIFORNIA*

Shick, Susan F. ....'47 '78 C.293 B.A. L.990 J.D. Dir., Community Develop.

**Shield, Theodore P., P.L.C.,** (AV) ........... '20 '49 C.112 L.800 LL.B. [Ford,W.H.&B.]
Shulman, Karen R. ........................ '49 '90 C.112 B.S. L.1137 J.D. 4106 E. 5th St.
Shupack, Bernard M. .......... '40 '77 C.563 B.S.M.E. L.809 J.D. 3628 N. Studebaker Rd.
Siegel, Samuel, (AV) ............ '20 '61 C.555 B.A. L.1001 J.D. Dep. City Atty. [Siegel&N.]
Siegel & Nichols, (AV) ................................ 3610 Long Beach Blvd., 2nd Fl.
Siemer, Robert E. ...... '45 '76 C.1032 B.S. L.809 J.D. Gen. Coun., Memorial Health Servs.
Sievers, Ronald, (BV) .............. '41 '67 C.426 B.B.A. L.1068 LL.B. [Sievers&H.]
Sievers & Haigh, (BV) ................................................ 110 Pine Ave.
**Silver, Donna** .................... '54 '79 C.112 A.B. L.800 J.D. [Stolpman K.E.M.&K.]
*PRACTICE AREAS: Appellate Practice.
**Silver, Edwin,** (AV) ............. '22 '50 C.112 L.800 LL.B. [Ⓐ Stolpman K.E.M.&K.]
*PRACTICE AREAS: Workers Compensation Law.

**Silver, Gregory S., (BV) '53 '82 C.1042 B.S. L.1137 J.D.**
**Suite 410, 200 Oceangate, P.O. Box 1967, 90801**
**Telephone: 310-491-1212 Fax: 310-590-8181**
***REPORTED CASES: In re the Marriage of Roberta J. & D. Michael Trainotti, 212 CAL App. 3d, 381, 1072.**
**General Civil and Criminal Trial Practice, Real Estate, Commercial, Workers Compensation, Personal Injury and Family Law.**
*See Professional Biographies, LONG BEACH, CALIFORNIA*

**Silver, Lawrence,** (AV) ........................... '44 '68 C&L.966 B.S., J.D. [L.Silver&Assoc.]
*REPORTED CASES: Summit Health v. Pinhas, 500 U.S. 322, 111 S.Ct. 1842, (1991) affirming; Pinhas v. Summit Health, Ltd., 894 F.2d 1024 (9th Cir. 1989); Pennsylvania v. New Jersey, 426 U.S. 660, 96 C.Ct. 2333, (1976); First National Monetary Corp. v. Commodity Futures Trading Commission, 677 F2d 522 (6th Cir. 1982), cert. denied sub nom., Monex International v. Commodity Futures Trading Commission 459 U.S. 1016; Aldens Inc. v. Packel, 524 F2d 38 (3d Cir. 1975), cert. denied, 425 U.S. 943 (1976).
*PRACTICE AREAS: Litigation; Business Litigation.

**Silver, Lawrence, & Associates, A Law Corporation, (AV)**
**111 West Ocean Boulevard Suite 1900, 90802-4649**
**Telephone: 310-901-4500 Facsimile: 310-901-4520**
**Email: lsilver@lsilver.com**
**Lawrence Silver;—Mark E. Field; Victoria Pynchon; Jeffrey M. Tanzer; Fred Galante.**
**General Civil and Trial Practice before all Federal and State Administrative Agencies and Courts. Business, Real Estate, Antitrust, Securities, Commodities, Labor, Corporate, Automotive Dealer Law, Physicians/Hospital Relations Law and Health Law, Computer and Internet Law.**
**Reference: The Bank of California (Los Angeles Branch).**
*See Professional Biographies, LONG BEACH, CALIFORNIA*

Silverman, Jerry, (AV) .................. '29 '55 C.112 B.S. L.1068 J.D. P.O. Box 21338‡
**Simmons, Janet M.** ..................... '62 '87 C.112 B.A. L.426 J.D. [Keesal,Y.&L.]
**Simon, Jeffrey Scott** ................... '64 '93 C.1049 B.B.A. L.93 J.D. [Ⓐ Keesal,Y.&L.]

**Simon, McKinsey, Miller, Zommick, Sandor & Dundas, A Law Corporation, (AV)**
**2750 Bellflower Boulevard, 90815⊙**
**Telephone: 310-421-9354 Facsimile: 310-420-6455**
**Harry J. Simon (1922-1977); Thomas W. McKinsey (1920-1990); Arthur W. Miller (Retired); Kenneth Zommick; David L. Sandor (Certified Specialist, Family Law, The State Bar of California Board of Legal Specialization); Geraldine G. Sandor (Certified Specialist, Family Law, The State Bar of California Board of Legal Specialization) (Resident, Irvine Office); David G. Dundas (Resident, Irvine Office);—Robert M. Stone; Carrie Block (Resident, Irvine Office).**
**General Civil and Civil Trial Practice. Corporation, Real Estate, Estate Planning, Trust, Taxation, Probate, Negligence, Family Law, Local Government Administrative Hearings and Appeals.**
**Irvine, California Office: Suite 670, 4199 Campus Drive. Telephone: 714-856-1916. Facsimile: 714-856-3834.**
*See Professional Biographies, LONG BEACH, CALIFORNIA*

Simonian, Kenneth C. .................. '49 '75 C.112 B.A. L.809 J.D. 3640 Atlantic Ave.
Simpson, Robert L. ......................... '21 '79 C.616 B.B.A. L.1137 J.D. [Ⓐ Thomas]
Simpson, Robert M. ..................... '38 '64 C.313 A.B. L.477 J.D. [Rose,K.&M.]
Sine, David M. ................... '45 '78 C.426 B.S. L.1136 J.D. 5199 E. Pacific Coast Hwy.
Singer, Morris ..................... '24 '55 C.112 B.S. L.767 LL.B. 3436 Val Verde Ave.‡
Slick, Janet M., (CV) ........................... '47 '73 C.1042 L.990 J.D. [Slick&S.]
Slick, Ronald J. ......................................... '42 '72 L.990 J.D. [Slick&S.]
Slick & Slick, (CV) .................................................. 780 Atlantic Ave., 3rd Fl.
Small, Carol S. .......................... '56 '82 C.696 B.A. L.276 J.D. 100 Oceangate
**Smirl, Richard William** ............... '67 '92 C.112 B.A. L.426 J.D. [Ⓐ Keesal,Y.&L.]
**Smith, Charles H.** ..................... '60 '85 C.1188 B.A. L.426 J.D. [Ⓐ Bennett&K.]
*PRACTICE AREAS: Civil Litigation; Business Litigation; Personal Injury Litigation.
Smith, Edward D. ................ '41 '82 C.225 B.A. L.1137 J.D. 6242 E. Beachcomber Dr.
Smith, James H. ........................... '35 '75 C.347 B.S. L.1136 J.D. 2400 E. 2nd St.
Smith, Jeffrey ........................... '65 '90 C&L.940 B.A., J.D. 301 E. Ocean Blvd.
Smith, Mark S. ..................... '58 '92 C.1131 B.A. L.1148 J.D. 444 W. Ocean Blvd.
**Smith, Stephen M.** ....................... '58 '83 C.800 A.B. L.426 J.D. [Wise,W.T.&W.]
*PRACTICE AREAS: Insurance Coverage.
Soden, Mary Ann ..................... '58 '90 C.112 B.A. L.800 J.D. 111 W. Ocean Blvd.
Solan, Kevin M., (AV) ............................................. '47 '73 [Ottenweller,S.&P.]⊙
Solomon, Phillip E. ............ '32 '79 C.112 B.S. L.1001 J.D. 925 E. San Antonio Dr.‡
Sowers, Donald G. ....................... '53 '86 C.999 A.S. L.809 J.D. [Takakjian&S.]⊙
**Spaltro, James P.,** (BV) .................. '50 '82 C.1248 B.A. L.1049 J.D. [Spaltro&L.]
*REPORTED CASES: Weinrot and Son, Inc. vs. Jackson, (1985) 40 Cal. 3d 327.
*TRANSACTIONS: Authored Resolution 9-5-85 to amend California Civil Code 49, Legislative Committee, Long Beach Bar Association.
*PRACTICE AREAS: Insurance Defense; Automobile and Premises Liability; Commercial Trucking Accidents; Insurance Coverage; Product Liability.

**Spaltro & Lamhofer, (BV)**
**3760 Kilroy Airport Way, Suite 260, 90806-2455**
**Telephone: 310-988-1027 Facsimile: 310-988-1163**
**James P. Spaltro; Eric T. Lamhofer; Lisa Ann Hollingworth.**
**Insurance Defense, Automobile and Premises Liability, Commercial Trucking Accidents, Insurance Coverage, Product Liability, Insurance Fraud Law, Construction Defect and Subrogation.**
*See Professional Biographies, LONG BEACH, CALIFORNIA*

**Stacker, Patrick C. '— '76 C.10 B.S.I.E. L.809 J.D.**
**One World Trade Center, Suite 1600, 90831-1600**
**Telephone: 310-436-7963 Fax: 310-437-1967**
**Real Estate, Corporate, Estate Planning and Dispute Resolution.**
*See Professional Biographies, LONG BEACH, CALIFORNIA*

Stamos, Gregory, (AV) ........................... '46 '72 [Rose,K.&M.] (⊙Los Angeles)
Stamp, Lloyd V., (AV) .................... '30 '55 C.999 L.1065 J.D. 110 Pine Ave.
Stanton, John R., Jr. ................................ '22 '49 L.800 LL.B. Ret. Supr.Ct. J.
**Stark, Patrick J.** ....................... '64 '89 C.958 B.S. L.990 J.D. [Ⓐ Ford,W.H.&B.]
Steffire, Greg P., (BV) ........................................ '44 '71 L.809 J.D. [G.P.Steffire]
Steffire, Greg P., A Law Corporation, (BV) ............ Suite 201, 4028 Long Beach Blvd.
**Stein, Kathy W.** ......................... '52 '87 C.112 B.A. L.1148 J.D. [Tabrisky B.&S.]
*REPORTED CASES: North End Oil, Ltd. v. M/V Ocean Confidence, 777 F.Supp. 12 (C.D. Ca. 19910); Trent v. Princess Cruises, Inc. 50 F.3d 16 (9th Cir. 1995).
*PRACTICE AREAS: Maritime Personal Injury; Passenger Cruise Ship Work; Charter Parties; Cargo Disputes; Commercial and General Business Litigation.
Steinberg, John D. ....... '59 '86 C.604 B.A. L.813 J.D. One World Trade Cntr., Ste., 1600
Steingisser, I. Robert ................... '51 '76 C.112 A.B. L.426 J.D. P.O. Box 4493
**Stemler, Robert J.** ........................ '62 '87 C&L.800 B.A., J.D. [Keesal,Y.&L.]
Stilman, Scott J. ........................ '59 '85 C.112 B.A. L.978 J.D. [Ⓐ Makin&M.]
**Stolpman, Thomas G., (Inc.),** (AV) '49 '76
C.112 B.A. L.800 J.D. [Stolpman K.E.M.&K.]⊙
*PRACTICE AREAS: Products Liability Law; Professional Negligence Law; Maritime Accidents Law.

**Stolpman • Krissman • Elber • Mandel & Katzman LLP, (AV)**
**A Partnership including Professional Corporations**
**Nineteenth Floor, 111 West Ocean Boulevard, 90802-4649⊙**
**Telephone: 310-435-8300 Telecopier: 310-435-8304**
**Members of Firm: Thomas G. Stolpman (Inc.); Leonard H. Mandel; Bernard Katzman (Inc.); Joel Krissman; Mary Nielsen Abbott; Donna Silver; Dennis M. Elber. Associates: Edwin Silver; Lynne Rasmussen; Elaine Mandel.**
**Tort Litigation, Trials, Appeals and Workers Compensation.**
**Los Angeles (Westwood) Office: Suite 1800, 10880 Wilshire Boulevard.**
*See Professional Biographies, LONG BEACH, CALIFORNIA*

**Stone, Robert M.** .............. '56 '82 C.112 B.A. L.1065 J.D. [Ⓐ Simon,M.M.Z.S.&D.]
*PRACTICE AREAS: Business Law.
**Stoner, John E.** ........... '58 '86 C.1142 B.B.A. L.802 J.D. Coun., Douglas Aircraft Co.
*RESPONSIBILITIES: General Corporate; Securities; Energy.
**Strain, John A.,** (AV) ........................ '48 '74 C.154 B.A. L.145 J.D. [Strain&R.]
*LANGUAGES: Spanish.
*PRACTICE AREAS: International, Federal and State Taxation Law; Estate Planning; Pension and Profit Sharing Law; Employee Benefit Law.

**Strain & Rosenberger, A Law Corporation, (AV)**
**Union Bank Building, 400 Oceangate, Suite 520, 90802-4356**
**Telephone: 310-436-2900 Fax: 310-436-5393**
**Email: 103504.312@compuserve.com**
**John A. Strain (Certified Specialist, Taxation Law, The State Bar of California Board of Legal Specialization); Paul D. Rosenberger.**
**International, Federal and State Taxation Law. Pension and Profit Sharing Law. Employee Benefit Law. Estate Planning.**
*See Professional Biographies, LONG BEACH, CALIFORNIA*

Straub, Betse C., (CV) ........................ '21 '60 C.999 L.809 1800 E. Ocean Blvd.
**Strong, Colleen A.** ..................... '67 '93 C.1060 B.S. L.464 J.D. [Ⓐ Ford,W.H.&B.]
*PRACTICE AREAS: Insurance; Personal Injury Defense; Municipality Defense.
Stuart, Jack ........... '37 '83 C.102 A.B. L.426 J.D. Coun., Rep. Cities & Police Agcys.
**Stuhlbarg, Richard L.** ................... '64 '95 C.95 A.B. L.426 J.D. [Ⓐ Perona,L.&B.]
*LANGUAGES: Japanese, Spanish and French.
Sudan, Ravi .................... '56 '90 C&L.061 B.S., LL.B. 4500 E. Pacific Coast Hwy.
**Sulentor, William J.,** (AV) ........... '46 '72 C&L.426 B.B.A., J.D. [Taubman,S.Y.&S.]
*PRACTICE AREAS: Business; Real Estate; Environmental; Oil and Gas.
**Sullivan, Leslie M.** ........................ '59 '86 C.112 B.S. L.426 J.D. [Ⓐ Keesal,Y.&L.]
**Sullivan, Susan Koehler** ............... '65 '91 C.911 B.A. L.112 J.D. [Ⓐ La Torraca&G.]
*PRACTICE AREAS: Bad Faith Law; Insurance Law.
**Swain, Michael L.** ......................... '58 '83 C.264 B.A. L.861 J.D. [Swain&D.]
*PRACTICE AREAS: Admiralty and Maritime; Transportation; General Liability; Business.

**Swain & Dipolito**
**555 East Ocean Boulevard Suite 400, 90802-5051**
**Telephone: 310-983-7833 Fax: 310-983-7835**
**Members of Firm: Michael L. Swain; Frank X. Dipolito; John G. Nursall. Of Counsel: Cheryl F. Gertler.**
**General Civil, Trial and Appellate Practice in all State and Federal Courts. Admiralty and Maritime, Transportation, Labor and Employment, General Liability and Insurance Law.**
*See Professional Biographies, LONG BEACH, CALIFORNIA*

**Swartz, D'Arcy T.** ..................... '61 '87 C.112 B.A. L.1049 J.D. [Ⓐ Kegel,T.&T.]
*PRACTICE AREAS: Workers Compensation Law; Personal Injury Law.
**Swindells, Pamela A.** .......................... '49 '88 C.684 B.A. L.1040 J.D. [Kaiser&S.]
Sword, C. Daniel ..................... '27 '74 C.893 B.A. L.1152 J.D. 512 Redondo Ave.
Szczepaniak, William E. ........... '52 '78 C.426 B.A. L.1049 J.D. 4085 Long Beach Blvd.
**Tabrisky, Joseph P.** ................... '60 '85 C.112 B.A. L.770 J.D. [Tabrisky B.&S.]
*REPORTED CASES: All Pacific Trading, Inc. v. M/V Hanjin Yosu, 7F.3d 1427, 1994 AMC 365 (9th Cir. 1993), cert. denied, U.S. 127 L.Ed.2d 693, 114 S.Ct. 1301 (1994); In re Korea Shipping Corp. Ltd., 1990 AMC 190 (C.D.Cal. 1989), 919 F.2d. 601, 1991 AMC 499 (9th Cir. 1990), cert. denied; Hanjin Container Lines v. Tokio Marine & Fire Insurance Co., Ltd., 499 U.S. 961, 113 L.Ed.2d 651, 111 S.Ct. 1586 (1991); Tokio Marine & Fire Insurance Co., Ltd. v. M/V Sammi Aurora, 903 F.2d 1244, 1990 AMC 2235 (9th Cir. 1990); In re M/V F.P. Clipper, SMA No. 3119 (1994).
*PRACTICE AREAS: Commercial Litigation and Transactions; International Business and Maritime Litigation; Environmental and Toxic Tort Claim; Insurance; Maritime Personal Injury.

**Tabrisky Brucculeri & Stein, LLP**
**301 East Ocean Boulevard Suite 270, 90802**
**Telephone: 310-901-4852 Fax: 310-901-4854**
**Email: marlaw@tbsllp.com URL: http://www.tbsllp.com**
**Joseph P. Tabrisky; Frank C. Brucculeri; Kathy W. Stein.**
**Commercial Litigation and Transactions, International Business, Aviation, Maritime, Insurance, Defense of Bad Faith, Personal Injury, Maritime Products Liability, Environmental cases and Appellate Practice in all Courts.**
*See Professional Biographies, LONG BEACH, CALIFORNIA*

Tadolini, Antoinette M. '51 '78 C.1165 B.A. L.208 J.D.
(adm. in AK; not adm. in CA) Sr. Coun., Atlantic Richfield Co.
Takakjian, Paul, (BV) '53 '79 C.112 B.A. L.426 J.D.
[Takakjian&S.] (⊙L.A., Oxnard, Orange & Encino)
Takakjian & Sowers, (BV)
Suite 800, World Trade Center (⊙Los Angeles, Oxnard, Orange, Pasadena & Encino)
**Talley, Stuart C.** ......................... '69 '95 C.112 B.A. L.990 J.D. [Taubman,S.Y.&S.]
*PRACTICE AREAS: Business; Litigation.
**Tanzer, Jeffrey M.** ................. '52 '84 C.1169 B.A. L.508 J.D. [Ⓐ L.Silver&Assoc.]
*PRACTICE AREAS: Business Litigation.

**Taubman, Simpson, Young & Sulentor, (AV)**
**249 East Ocean Boulevard, Suite 700, P.O. Box 22670, 90801-5670**
**Telephone: 310-436-9201 FAX: 310-590-9695**
**E. C. Denio (1864-1952); Geo. A. Hart (1881-1967); Geo. P. Taubman, Jr. (1897-1970); Matthew C. Simpson (1900-1988); Richard G. Wilson (1928-1993); Roger W. Young; William J. Sulentor; Peter M. Williams; Scott R. Magee; Maria M. Rohaidy; Stuart C. Talley.**
**General Civil and Criminal Trial Practice. Business, Taxation, Real Estate, Environmental, Oil and Gas, Eminent Domain, Estate Planning and Probate, Commercial.**
**Attorneys for: Bixby Land Co.; Renick Cadillac, Inc.; Oil Operators Inc.**
**Local Counsel: Crown Cork & Seal Co., Inc.**
*See Professional Biographies, LONG BEACH, CALIFORNIA*

**Taylor, Lawrence, (AV) '42 '70 C.112 B.A. L.1068 J.D.**
**3780 Kilroy Airport Way, Suite 200, 90806**
**Telephone: 310-594-6278; 714-752-1550 Facsimile: 310-598-4603**
**Email: letaylor@msn.com URL: http://law.net/sponsors/taylor/**
***PRACTICE AREAS: Drunk Driving Defense.**
**Criminal Defense practice limited to Drunk Driving Defense.**
*See Professional Biographies, LONG BEACH, CALIFORNIA*

**Taylor, Reese H., Jr.,** (AV⑦) .......... '28 '54 C.813 B.A. L.188 LL.B. [Ⓐ Keesal,Y.&L.]
*PRACTICE AREAS: Transportation; Railroads; Trucking.
**Theodora, Todd C.,** (AV) ............ '60 '85 C.1042 B.A. L.1049 J.D. [O'Flaherty&B.]
Thielen, Joseph E., (AV) ................... '49 '74 C.800 B.A. L.809 J.D. [Thielen&B.]

Thielen and Burke, A Professional Corporation, (AV) .................. 3233 E. Broadway
Thom, Susan M. ............ '54 '84 C.1042 B.S. L.1137 J.D. 6475 E. Pacific Coast Hwy.
Thomas, Allen L., (AV) ............................'55 '82 C.1042 B.A. L.990 J.D. [Thomas]
Thomas, Charles H. ..................... '42 '70 C.339 B.S. L.209 J.D. [Cislo&T.] (Pat.)
Thomas Law Firm, (AV) ..................................... 3780 Kilroy Airport Way
Thompson, Neal B., Jr., (AV) .......... '36 '72 C.112 B.A. L.426 J.D. 4001 Atlantic Ave.
**Thornton, John C.**, (AV) ..................'50 '78 C.1131 B.A. L.809 J.D. [Perona,L.&B.]
**Thurman, Michael A.** .......................'57 '85 C.813 A.B. L.629 J.D. [Keesal,Y.&L.]
**Tibbetts, Georgene K.** .....................'53 '80 C.426 B.A. L.1137 J.D. [Ⓐ Mullen&F.]
**Timmons, Duane H.**, (AV) ........... '45 '72 C.309 A.B. L.813 J.D. [Wise,W.T.&W.]⊙
*PRACTICE AREAS: Insurance Law; Litigation; Medical Malpractice; Personal Injury; Products Liability.
Trager, Thomas R. ............'45 '71 C.210 B.A. L.910 J.D. Sr. Coun., Calif. State Univ.
**Trainotti, D. Michael**, (AV) ........... '44 '74 C.1042 B.A. L.809 J.D. [D.M.Trainotti]

**Trainotti, D. Michael, A Professional Law Corporation, (AV)**
**Suite 410, 200 Oceangate, 90802**
**Telephone: 310-590-8621 Fax: 310-590-8181**
**D. Michael Trainotti.**
**General Tax Practice. Real Estate, Trust and Probate Law, Estate Planning, Corporation and Partnership Law. Real Estate Pass Through Entities.**
**Reference: Farmers & Merchants Bank; Harbor Bank.**
*See Professional Biographies, LONG BEACH, CALIFORNIA*

Trotter, Michael J. ...................................... '63 '88 C.276 B.A. L.800 J.D. [Carroll,K.&T.]
**Truce, W. Joseph**, (AV) .......... '43 '71 C.911 B.A. L.284 J.D. [Kegel,T.&T.] (⊙L.A.)
**Trumper, Edward T.** ............. '65 '92 C.1163 B.B.A. L.1049 J.D. [Ⓐ Perona,L.&B.]
Tshudy, Thomas P. '57 '83 C.645 B.A. L.1017 J.D.
(adm. in PA; not adm. in CA) 5301 Bolsa Ave.
Tubin, Bradley D. .........................'54 '78 C&L.1136 B.S.L., J.D. 4450 N. California Pl.
**Turner, James D.** ................ '50 '76 C.1131 B.A. L.809 J.D. [Ⓒ A.B.Weiss&Assoc.]
*PRACTICE AREAS: Civil Litigation; Insurance Coverage; Personal Injury Defense.
Unitan, Richard T. .................. '39 '75 C.1042 B.A. L.1137 J.D. 4237 Atlantic Ave.
**Utecht, Francis A.**, (AV) '23 '52
C.800 B.S.M.E. L.809 J.D. [Ⓒ Fulwider P.L.&U.] (See Pat. Sect.)
*PRACTICE AREAS: Patent; Trademark Law; Copyright Law; Unfair Competition Law; Litigation.
Uthoff, Stephen M. .....................................'65 '89 C&L.800 B.A., J.D. [Coniglio&U.]
**Valdes, Todd A.** ............... '63 '93 C.309 A.B. L.800 J.D. [Ⓐ Williams W.C.N.&R.]
*PRACTICE AREAS: Business Litigation; Commercial Litigation; Admiralty and Maritime Law.
Valentine, Wm. J. '16 '52 C.871 B.S. L.276 J.D.
(adm. in DC; not adm. in CA) 1036 E. 45th Way‡
Van Camp, Julie C. ........ '47 '80 C.518 A.B. L.276 J.D. Assoc. Prof., Calif. State Univ.

**Vandenberg, Newell, Curtis, Nelson & Schuur, A Professional Corporation, (AV)**
**Suite 400 Harbor Bank Building, 11 Golden Shore Drive, 90802**
**Telephone: 310-435-7471 Facsimile: 310-435-7405**
**Email: VNCNS@earthlink.net**
**Jack M. Vandenberg (1921-1986); Frank R. Newell; Mark Curtis; Keith A. Nelson; Pamela Bourette Schuur;—Gregory J. Burnight.**
**General Civil and Trial Practice. Corporation, Real Estate, Estate Planning, Trust and Probate Law. Tax Litigation. Trials and Appeals. Negligence and Family Law.**
**Representative Client: Economy Reconveyance Corp.**
*See Professional Biographies, LONG BEACH, CALIFORNIA*

Vander Lans, John A., (AV) .......................'30 '57 C.112 B.A. L.426 LL.B. City Pros.
**Vande Wydeven, Mathew J.** ..............'63 '88 C.112 B.A. L.426 J.D. [Wise,W.T.&W.]
*PRACTICE AREAS: Insurance Defense.
Vanley, Jerry T. ............................'53 '80 C.112 B.A. L.1049 J.D. 4458 Myrtle Ave.
**Vicencia, Michael P.** ...............'64 '90 C.1109 B.A. L.169 J.D. [Ⓐ Burns,A.P.M.&B.]⊙
*PRACTICE AREAS: Civil Defense.
Villalobos, Edward A., (BV) ............ '42 '73 C.1042 B.A. L.426 J.D. 3888 Cherry Ave.
Villeneuve, Michael S. .......... '52 '78 C.800 A.B. L.93 J.D. Coun., Dept. of Indus. Rel.
**Visniski, Rhonda Ann** .......................'66 '95 C.645 B.A. L.426 J.D. [Ⓐ Perona,L.&B.]
**Vita, John** ..........................................'53 '89 C.102 B.S. L.426 J.D. [Ⓐ Madden,J.C.&J.]
*PRACTICE AREAS: Civil Litigation; Commercial Litigation; Securities Litigation.
**Vorwerck, Gregg**, (AV) ...................... '48 '76 C.112 B.A. L.800 J.D. [Haines&L.]
*PRACTICE AREAS: Personal Injury Law; Municipality Defense; Premise Liability; Medical Malpractice; Dental Malpractice.
Vose, Donna M. .......................... '50 '79 C.1042 B.A. L.1137 J.D. 4444 Olive Ave.
Vyse, Thomas A., (BV) .................. '32 '63 C.674 A.B. L.1065 J.D. Dep. City Atty.
Wade, Michael E. .......................... '46 '77 C.1042 B.S. L.990 J.D. [Demler,A.&R.]
Waestman, Robert R., (AV) ................. '34 '61 C.813 L.426 LL.B. 4001 Atlantic Ave.
**Walker, Timothy L.**, (AV) ....................'47 '72 C.112 B.A. L.426 J.D. [Ford,W.H.&B.]
*PRACTICE AREAS: Construction Defects Litigation; Civil Environmental Litigation; Legal Malpractice; Bad Faith; Municipality Defense.
Wallace, Alexander W. .............'50 '77 C.605 B.A. L.809 J.D. 4047 Long Beach Blvd.
Wallace, Donald C., Jr., (AV) ...... '24 '51 C.871 B.S. L.813 J.D. 4047 Long Beach Blvd.
**Walsh, Joseph A., II** ................................'61 '89 C.1027 B.S. L.37 J.D. [Ⓐ Keesal,Y.&L.]
**Walsh, Thomas G.** ............. '67 '94 C.602 B.A. L.800 J.D. [Ⓐ Williams W.C.N.&R.]
*LANGUAGES: Mandarin and Spanish.
*PRACTICE AREAS: Admiralty and Maritime Law; International Law; Commercial Law; Litigation.

**Walsh, Donovan, Lindh & Keech, (AV)**
**301 East Ocean Boulevard, Suite 1200, 90802-4828⊙**
**Telephone: 310-901-4848 Telefax: 310-901-4850; Telex: 384-831**
**Neil B. Klein.**
**General Civil and Trial Practice. Admiralty, Commercial, Construction, Bankruptcy, Franchising, International Practice and Insurance Law.**
**San Francisco, California Office: Suite 2000, 595 Market Street. Telephone: 415-957-8700. Telefax: 415-543-9388. Telex: WU 384831 WADINH SFO; RCA 286833 WDL UR; ESL 62756007.**
**Los Angeles, California Office: Suite 2600, 445 South Figueroa Street. Telephone: 213-612-7757. Telefax: 213-612-7797. Telex: WU 401760 WADINH LSA ESL 62949341.**
*See Professional Biographies, LONG BEACH, CALIFORNIA*

Walz, John D. '42 '66 C&L.846 A.B., LL.B.
(adm. in TX; not adm. in CA) Sr. Litig. Coun., U.S. Small Bus. Admn.
Wandner, William J. '65 '93 C.156 B.A. L.273 J.D.
(adm. in MD; not adm. in CA) 1107 E. 3rd St., #6
Warner, Samuel W. '36 '60 C&L.846 B.A., LL.B.
(adm. in TX; not adm. in CA) Soc. Sec. Admn.
**Warren, Jeffrey D.** ..........................'56 '81 C.679 B.A. L.326 J.D. [Keesal,Y.&L.]
Warriner, Martha A. ........... '45 '77 C.802 B.A. L.426 J.D. 6475 E. Pacific Coast Hwy.
Wasserman, Benjamin P., (BV) ..... '38 '65 C&L.800 A.B., LL.B. 419 W. Broadway Apt.
Webb, Jas. C. ..................................................'— '40 C&L.809 320 Pine Ave.
Weber, Ferrell A. ....................................................................'45 '73 [Bartos&W.]
**Weber, John J.**, (BV) ............................'47 '72 C.426 B.A. L.800 J.D. [O'Flaherty&B.]
Weems, Eleanor O. ........................ '16 '57 C.555 B.A. L.1001 LL.B. 4501 E. Bway.
Weems, Thomas M., Jr. ...................'46 '74 C.602 B.A. L.426 J.D. 4501 E. Broadway
Weil, David G. ..................................'48 '75 C.112 B.A. L.809 J.D. 110 W. Ocean Blvd.
Weinberg, Laurence M., (AV) '10 '33
C&L.813 A.B., J.D. 210 East Ocean Blvd., Unit 916‡
Weinberg, Marion T. ...................................... '11 '35 L.1001 J.D. 210 E. Ocean Blvd.‡

**Weinberg, Robert A., (AV) '57 '83 C.112 B.A. L.990 J.D.**
**4335 Atlantic Avenue, 90807**
**Telephone: 310-424-1798 Fax: 310-424-0047**
***PRACTICE AREAS: Collections; Construction; General Business; Estate Planning.**
**Collections, Business and Construction Law. Estate Planning, Banks Receivables.**
*See Professional Biographies, LONG BEACH, CALIFORNIA*

**Weiss, Allan B., (A Prof. Corp.)**, (AV) '44 '69
C.813 A.B. L.800 J.D. [A.B.Weiss&Assoc.]
*PRACTICE AREAS: Civil Litigation; Real Estate; Corporate Law; International Law; Hazardous Waste.

**Weiss, Allan B., and Associates, (AV)**
**5000 E. Spring Street Suite 430, 90815-1270**
**Telephone: 310-421-6333 Telecopier: 310-421-6903**
**Allan B. Weiss (A Professional Law Corporation);—Jock R. Davidson, (Inc., A Professional Law Corporation); Ryan K. Hirota (A Professional Law Corporation); James R. Flatebo; Mira Susan Wolff. Of Counsel: James D. Turner.**
**General Civil and Trial Practice. Corporation, Real Estate, General Business, Probate, International, Hazardous Waste, Negligence, Employment, Insurance (coverage and defense), and Domestic Relations.**
**Reference: Wells Fargo Bank, Long Beach Main Branch; Bank of America, Belmont Shore and Bixby Knolls Branches; National Bank of Long Beach.**
*See Professional Biographies, LONG BEACH, CALIFORNIA*

**Welden, William B., (BV) '50 '77 C.350 B.S. L.221 J.D.**
**5150 East Pacific Coast Highway, 90804-3393**
**Telephone: 310-986-1201 Fax: 310-597-2174**
***PRACTICE AREAS: General Civil and Trial Practice; Insurance Bad Faith; Insurance Coverage; Arbitrator.**
**General Civil and Trial Practice in all Courts. Insurance Bad Faith, Insurance Coverage, Arbitrator.**
*See Professional Biographies, LONG BEACH, CALIFORNIA*

Wellen, Warren R. ........................... '61 '89 C.112 B.A. L.800 J.D. 100 Oceangate
Wellsand, Ingrid J. ................................................ '43 '81 L.809 J.D. 4229 Virginia Rd.
Weltman, Jordan S. .......... '53 '78 C.976 B.A. L.659 J.D. 4060 Lakewood Blvd., 6th Fl.
Wendorff, E. Susie ........................ '63 '93 C.112 B.S. L.800 J.D. [Ⓐ Demler,A.&R.]
Wenke, Robert A. ................................'26 '51 C&L.546 B.A., J.D. 4216 E. 2nd St.
**Wenzel, Michael E.** ................ '45 '75 C.755 B.A. L.990 J.D. [Burns,A.P.M.&B.]⊙
*PRACTICE AREAS: General Trial; Premises; Malpractice; Construction; Insurance Defense.
Westrup, R. Duane ................................'45 '74 C.990 B.A. L.426 J.D. [Westrup,K.&K.]
Westrup, Kincaid & Klick ..................................................... 444 W. Ocean Blvd.
Wheatley Osaki & Associates, (BV) ........... 3780 Kilroy Airport Way (⊙Fullerton, Ca.)
**Whelan, John M.** ........................'61 '94 C.477 B.A. L.800 J.D. [Ⓐ Keesal,Y.&L.]
Whitaker, Robert L. ............................'56 '89 C.37 B.A. L.809 J.D. 292 Ravena Rd.
White, Bruce H., (A P.C.), (AV) ................'33 '66 C.940 B.A. L.61 J.D. [White&B.]⊙
**White, Robert M., Jr.** ................ '53 '90 C.838 B.S.B.A. L.011 LL.B. [Ⓐ Baker&H.]
*PRACTICE AREAS: Admiralty; Marine Construction; Personal Injury Defense.
White, Wm. L., (BV) ............... '23 '56 C.800 B.S. L.1001 LL.B. Comr., Human Rel.
White and Bright, A Professional Corporation, (AV)
3780 Kilroy Airport Way, Suite 200 (⊙Escondido)
Whiteleather, Tania L. ............ '53 '89 C.1042 B.A. L.1137 J.D. 4427 Charlemagne Ave.
**Wiezorek, Anthony F.**, (AV) .............'41 '72 C.112 B.A. L.426 J.D. [Wise,W.T.&W.]
*PRACTICE AREAS: Insurance Law; Litigation.
**Will, Timothy N.** ..................................'59 '86 C.169 B.S. L.1049 J.D. [Keesal,Y.&L.]
Willens, D. Damon ....................'63 '88 C.154 B.A. L.426 J.D. 444 W. Ocean Blvd.
Willens, William N. ....................'26 '52 C.112 A.B. L.813 J.D. 401 E. Ocean Blvd.
**Williams, K. Michele** .................. '43 '87 C.1158 B.A. L.1148 J.D. [Ford,W.H.&B.]
Williams, Paul S. ............................................'47 '77 L.1001 J.D. 1150 E. San Antonio Dr.
**Williams, Peter M.**, (AV) .............'44 '70 C.813 B.A. L.800 J.D. [Taubman,S.Y.&S.]
*PRACTICE AREAS: Trial Practice.
**Williams, Reed M.**, (AV) .... '26 '54 C.1250 B.S. L.1065 LL.B. [Williams W.C.N.&R.]⊙
*REPORTED CASES: Orient Steam Navigation Co., Ltd. v. United States of America (Kearsarge-Oriana), 231 F.Supp. 469, 1964 AMC 2163 (S.D. Cal. 1964); Chervy v. Peninsular & Oriental Steam Navigation Co., Ltd. (Arcadia), 364 F.2d 908, 1966 AMC 226 (9th Cir. 1966); Waterman Steamship Corp. v. Gay Cottons (Chickasaw) 414 F.2d 724, 1969 AMC 1682 (9th Cir. 1969); Japan Line, Ltd. v. County of Los Angeles, 441 U.S. 434, 99 S.Ct. 1813, 16 L.Ed.2d 336, 1979 AMC 881 (1979); Lubick v. Travel Service, Inc., 573 F.Supp. 904 (D.V.I. 1983).
*PRACTICE AREAS: Maritime Law; Transportation and International Law; Commercial Transactions and Litigation; Personal Injury.
**Williams, Wm. A.**, (AV) ...................... '27 '54 C.800 L.809 J.D. [Pray,P.W.&R.]
*PRACTICE AREAS: Commercial Law; Litigation; Real Property Law; Construction Law; Cooperative Housing Law.

**Williams Woolley Cogswell Nakazawa & Russell, (AV) BB**
**111 West Ocean Boulevard, Suite 2000, 90802-4614⊙**
**Telephone: 310-495-6000 Telecopier: 310-435-1359; 310-435-6812 Telex: ITT: 4933872; WU: 984929**
**Email: wwlaw@msn.com**
**Members of Firm: Reed M. Williams; David E. R. Woolley; Forrest R. Cogswell; Alan Nakazawa; Blake W. Larkin; Thomas A. Russell. Associates: Todd A. Valdes; Thomas G. Walsh; Richard J. Nikas.**
**Commercial Transactions and Litigation, Maritime Law, Transportation and International Law, Environmental Law, Immigration Law, Personal Injury and Product Liability Litigation.**
**Rancho Santa Fe, California Office: P.O. Box 9120, 16236 San Dieguito Road, Building 3, Suite 3-15, 92067. Telephone: 619-497-0284. Fax: 619-759-9938.**
**Port Hueneme, California Office: 237 E. Hueneme Road, Suite A, 93041. Telephone: 805-488-8560. Fax: 805-488-7896.**
*See Professional Biographies, LONG BEACH, CALIFORNIA*

**Williamson, David C.** ......................'56 '82 C&L.546 B.A., J.D. [Ⓐ Johnson,C.&R.]
*PRACTICE AREAS: Entertainment Law.
Wilson, Edwin J., (AV) ................. '15 '55 C.153 A.B. L.1001 LL.B. 320 Pine Ave.‡
Wilson, Paul E. '46 '75 C.276 A.B. L.446 J.D.
(adm. in MD; not adm. in CA) Reg. Coun., U.S. Customs Serv.
Wilson, Walter J., (BV) .......................... '46 '75 C.1042 B.A. L.800 J.D. 333 W. Bway.
**Wise, Erich P.**, (AV) .......................'48 '74 C.309 A.B. L.145 J.D. [Flynn,D.&W.]
*PRACTICE AREAS: Admiralty and Maritime Law; International Transportation; Civil Litigation; Insurance Coverage.
**Wise, George E.**, (AV) ....................... '24 '49 C.393 L.145 J.D. [Wise,W.T.&W.]
*PRACTICE AREAS: General Civil Practice; Corporate; Real Property; Probate; Estate Planning.
**Wise, Susan E. Anderson**, (AV) ..........'48 '74 C.399 B.A. L.145 J.D. [Wise,W.T.&W.]
*PRACTICE AREAS: Civil Litigation; Employment Law; General Business Litigation; Insurance Coverage; Real Property Law.

**Wise, Wiezorek, Timmons & Wise, A Professional Corporation, (AV) BB**
**3700 Santa Fe Avenue, Suite 300, P.O. Box 2190, 90810⊙**
**Telephone: 310-834-5028 Fax: 310-834-8018**
**George E. Wise; Duane H. Timmons; Anthony F. Wiezorek; Susan E. Anderson Wise; Albert F. Padley, III; Michael J. Pearce; Mark C. Allen, III; Richard P. Dieffenbach; Steven C. Rice; Stephen M. Smith; Thomas J. Yocis; James M. Cox; Mathew J. Vande Wydeven; Tae J. Im.**
**General Civil and Trial Practice in State and Federal Courts. Corporation, International Business, Insurance, Real Property, Immigration, Estate Planning, Probate and Tax Law.**
**Redding, California Office: 443 Redcliff Drive, Suite 230. Telephone: 916-221-7632. Fax: 916-221-8832.**
*See Professional Biographies, LONG BEACH, CALIFORNIA*

Wolf, Virginia .................................... '39 '85 C.1042 L.1001 J.D. 1960 E. Jackson

CAA168P

Wolfe, Stuart B. ........................ '65 '91 C.112 B.A. L.464 J.D. [Wolfe&W.]
Wolfe & Wyman ........................ 1 World Trade Ctr., 11th Fl.
**Wolff, Mira Susan** .............. '66 '92 C.1042 B.A. L.809 J.D. [🄰 A.B.Weiss&Assoc.]
*PRACTICE AREAS: Business Litigation; Employment; Civil Litigation.
Wolter, Stevan B. .................'54 '87 C.112 B.A. L.1137 J.D. 3605 Long Beach Blvd.
Wong, James, Jr. .................. '56 '84 C.112 B.A. L.426 J.D. Atlantic Richfield Co.
**Wong, Kimberly** .................... '70 '94 C.1077 B.A. L.1065 J.D. [🄰 Keesal,Y.&L.]
Wood, James J., (AV) ..........................'28 '61 L.1001 LL.B. 3441 E. Broadway‡
Woodcock, Raymond L. '55 '83 C&L.178 B.A., J.D.
(adm. in NY; not adm. in CA) P.O. Box 21447‡
**Woolley, David E. R.** ............ '46 '73 C.015 B.A. L.1066 J.D. [Williams W.C.N.&R.]
*REPORTED CASES: Melwire Trading Co., Inc. v. M/C Cape Antibes, 811 F.2d 1271, 1987 AMC 1217 (9th Cir. 1986); Flexi-Van Leasing, Inc. v. M/V C.C. San Francisco, 808 F.2d 697 (9th Cir. 1987); and GF Company v. Pan Ocean Shipping Co., Ltd., 23 F.3d 1498 (9th Cir. 1994); All Pacific Trading, Inc. v. M/V Hanjin Yosu 7 F.3d 1427, 1994 AMC 365 (9th Cir. 1994); Slaven v. BP America, Inc., 973 F.2d 1468, 1993 AMC 9, 22 ELR 21500 (9th Cir. 1992).
*PRACTICE AREAS: Maritime Law; Environmental Law; Transportation and International Law; Commercial Transactions and Litigation; Personal Injury.
Wright, James L. ................................ '37 '72 C.976 L.1001 J.D. Mun. Ct. J.
Wu, Howard L. .................. '48 '73 C.33 B.A. L.1066 J.D. 3855 Lakewood Blvd.
Wulfsohn, Julius G., (BV) .......'25 '79 C&L.061 B.A., LL.B. 4201 N. Long Beach Blvd.
**Wulterin, Shayne L.** .............. '66 '91 C.1239 B.A. L.1148 J.D. [🄰 Ford,W.H.&B.]
*PRACTICE AREAS: Automobile Fraud; Automobile Liability; Construction Defect; Police Misconduct.
Wyman, Samuel A. ........................ '67 '92 C.112 B.A. L.464 J.D. [Wolfe&W.]
**Yardumian, Gary E.** .................. '61 '87 C.1074 B.S. L.809 J.D. [Prindle,D.&A.]
*PRACTICE AREAS: Construction Litigation; Coverage; Insurance Defense.
Yates, William R. .................. '29 '59 C.339 B.S. L.178 LL.B. 6208 Tobruk Ct.
**Ybaben, JoAnne M.** '66 '94 C.112 B.A. L.61 J.D.
[🄰 Fulwider P.L.&U.] (See Pat. Sect.)
*PRACTICE AREAS: Patents and Trademark Prosecution and Litigation.
Yim, Carrie Downey '65 '91 C.1145 B.S. L.128 J.D.
(adm. in GA; not adm. in CA) J. Advocate Gen.'s Corp. Atty.
**Yocis, Thomas J.**, (BV) ................'56 '81 C.1151 B.A. L.145 J.D. [Wise,W.T.&W.]
*PRACTICE AREAS: Contract Law; Corporate Law; Estate Planning; Probate Law; Tax Planning.
**Yoshitomi, Robert B.**, (AV) '44 '73
C.674 A.B. L.1066 J.D. [Lillick&C.] (©Parsippany, N.J.)
*PRACTICE AREAS: Trade and Transportation Regulation; Maritime; Immigration; Corporate.
**Young, J. Stephen**, (AV) ....................'48 '73 C.112 B.A. L.800 J.D. [Keesal,Y.&L.]
*PRACTICE AREAS: Securities and Commodity Futures Litigation; Securities and Commodity Futures Regulatory Work and Employment Litigation.
**Young, Mary Jane** ................'— '87 C.426 A.B. L.809 J.D. Atty., BW/IP Intl., Inc.
*RESPONSIBILITIES: Corporate Law; Securities Law.
**Young, Roger W.**, (AV) ..............'21 '49 C.602 A.B. L.309 J.D. [Taubman,S.Y.&S.]
*PRACTICE AREAS: Taxation; Estate Planning and Probate.
Zabel, Ronald C. ......................'45 '73 C.911 B.A. L.273 J.D. U.S. Coast Guard
Zager, Jennifer Lynn ....................'69 '93 C.861 B.A. L.1137 J.D. 100 Oceangate
Zahn, Victor S. ............................'17 '61 C.999 L.1001 LL.B. 711 Molino Ave.
Zaks, Richard, (AV) ............................................ '43 '77 P.O. Box 1700
Zeligs, David M. ........................'54 '82 C.112 B.A. L.464 J.D. 1 World Trade Ctr.
**Zommick, Kenneth**, (AV) ........'38 '65 C.112 B.A. L.1066 J.D. [Simon,M.M.Z.S.&D.]
*PRACTICE AREAS: Estate Planning; Personal Injury; Medical Malpractice.
**Zugsmith, George S., Jr.**, (AV) .........'39 '69 C.1254 B.S. L.1095 J.D. [G.S.Zugsmith]

**Zugsmith, George S., A Professional Law Corporation, (AV)**
**Suite 430, 5000 East Spring Street, 90815-1270**
**Telephone: 310-420-6164 Fax Number: By Request**
**George S. Zugsmith, Jr.**
**Family Law, Child Support, Spousal Support, Divorce, Custody and Visitation.**
**Reference: Farmers & Merchants Bank, Long Beach.**
***See Professional Biographies, LONG BEACH, CALIFORNIA***

## LOOMIS, 5,705, *Placer Co.*

Beckett, Belinda D. ........................ '52 '80 C.813 A.B. L.1065 J.D. 6105 Barton Rd.
Brentnall, Gerald J., Jr. ....................... '47 '78 C.768 B.S. L.464 J.D. 9190 Vista Ct.★
Dwyer, W. P., Jr., (AV) .............'11 '36 C&L.813 B.A., LL.B. 7935 Morningside Dr.‡
Isles, Ted W. ..................'28 '60 C.871 B.S. L.705 LL.B. 7525 Auburn-Folsom Rd.‡
Joehnck, Robert N. ....................'41 '67 C.112 A.B. L.1066 J.D. 4300 Hansen Rd.
Liebert, Martin ......................'30 '75 C.563 B.S. L.1152 J.D. 7410 Shelborne Dr.‡
Lyon, LeRoy E., Jr. ...................'20 '50 C&L.800 A.B., LL.B. 7230 Morningside Dr.‡
McCarthy, Wilson ............................'43 '69 L.878 J.D. 3625 Holly Hill Lane
Rodgers, Bobby D. ........................'39 '69 C.613 B.S. L.464 J.D. P.O. Box 1407‡
Vorpagel, Russell E. '27 '59 C.966 B.S. L.436 LL.B.
(adm. in WI; not adm. in CA) Legaprover, Inc.

## LOS ALAMITOS, 11,676, *Orange Co.*

Andrews, Karen M. ...................'54 '83 C.705 B.A. L.800 J.D. 2901 Coleridge Dr.
Barham, E. Thomas, Jr. ..................... '45 '82 C.800 B.S. L.426 J.D. [Barham&O.]
Barham & Ostrow ...............................................3349 Cerritos Ave.
Bloom, Joyce ...................'33 '82 C.102 B.A. L.1137 J.D. 3152 Inverness Dr.
Carson, Richard C. ................'48 '73 C&L.1137 B.S., J.D. 3502 Katella Ave.
Drukker, William R. .............. '46 '72 C.112 B.A. L.1066 J.D. Asst. Prof. of Crim. Jus.
Ensley, Gerry Lee .....................'42 '71 C.112 B.A. L.1065 J.D. 11771 Montecito
Fink, Theresa H. ..........................'56 '86 C&L.1137 B.S., J.D. 2962 Copa De Oro
Flax, David Allen ....................'38 '73 C.1042 A.B. L.809 J.D. 3532 Katella Ave.
Frambach, Willis A. ...................'24 '79 C.112 B.S. L.1152 J.D. 3662 Katella Ave.
Frazer, Ira '54 '80 C.659 B.S. L.477 J.D.
Gen. Coun. & Dir., Admin., Daihatsu Amer., Inc.
Golanty, Lorriee M. ......................'— '80 C.1042 A.B. L.1137 J.D. 5030 Katella Ave.
Greer, Elwin H. ..............'24 '72 C.112 B.A. L.1137 J.D. 11771 Marthe Ann Dr.‡
Lachina, Andrew C., (AV) ................'38 '65 C.688 B.M.E. L.800 J.D. 5212 Katella Ave.
Landreau, Linda A. .................'49 '78 C.112 B.A. L.426 J.D. 12551 Silver Fox Rd.
Maxwell, Georges A., (BV) .......'25 '64 C.999 L.809 J.D. 11362 Wallingsford Rd. (Pat.)‡
Meyrelles, Joseph A., III ..........................'54 '79 C.967 B.A. L.678 J.D. P.O. Box 1324
Miller, Robert O. ...........................'50 '81 C.1042 B.S. L.1137 J.D. 3502 Katella Ave.
Morrow, Margaret Eddy ..............'63 '89 C.147 B.A. L.770 J.D. 3221 Oak Grove Rd.
Nelms, Robert L. ....................... '39 '68 C.800 B.S. L.1068 J.D. 5030 Katella
Oftedal, Richard H. .................. '41 '64 C.273 B.A. L.800 LL.B. 11291 Davenport Rd.
Ogorzalek, John F. .................... '40 '76 C.971 B.S. L.1137 J.D. 4281 Katella Ave.
Ostrow, Shirley ............................. '41 '83 C.659 B.S. L.426 J.D. [Barham&O.]
Peachee, Russell L. ...................'16 '55 C.623 B.S. L.800 LL.B. 2732 St. Albans Dr.
Peters, Samuel A. ...............'34 '61 C.569 B.A. L.262 LL.B. 11471 Kensington Rd.‡
Pintek, Michael D. ........................'47 '75 C.37 B.S. L.1190 J.D. 3888 Cerritos Ave.
Posner, Gayle R., (BV) .................'36 '74 C.1036 B.A. L.990 J.D. 3281 Wendy Way
**Sabo, Kenneth B.**, (AV) ......................'38 '67 C.800 A.B. L.809 J.D. [K.B.Sabo]

**Sabo, Kenneth B., A Professional Corporation, (AV)**
**3551 Florista Avenue, Suite 1A, 90720**
**Telephone: 310-594-8787 Fax: 310-594-8780**
**Kenneth B. Sabo.**

(This Listing Continued)

**Sabo, Kenneth B., A Professional Corporation (Continued)**
**General Business, Corporate, Partnership, Insurance, Real Estate, Commercial Law and Related Litigation. Civil Trials and Appeals in all State and Federal Courts.**
***See Professional Biographies, LOS ALAMITOS, CALIFORNIA***

Shahinian, George C. ....................'28 '72 C.94 B.A. L.809 J.D. 4132 Katella Ave.
Shaw, John Robert ..........................'52 '86 C.112 B.A. L.1049 J.D. [Shaw&W.]
Shaw & Weitz ..................................................... 5030 Katella Ave.
Stephens, Garland G. .....................'21 '57 C.999 L.1001 LL.B. 3012 Brimhall Dr.
Sublett, Edward .................... '48 '82 Western Reg. Coun., GTE Directories Corp.
Wagner, James J. .......................'51 '80 C.1042 B.A. L.426 J.D. P.O. Box 1069
Weitz, Mark ......................................'49 '88 C.545 B.A. L.809 J.D. [Shaw&W.]

## LOS ALTOS, 26,303, *Santa Clara Co.*

Abbott, Douglas J., (BV) ...........'48 '72 C.112 B.A. L.1065 J.D. 4966 El Camino Real
**Acquesta, Mary**, (BV) ....................'58 '83 C.112 B.A. L.770 J.D. [Nelson,P.&L.]
*PRACTICE AREAS: Insurance Defense; Products Liability; Professional Malpractice; Personal Injury; Civil Litigation.
Alcala, Brett A. .................... '61 '86 C.768 B.S. L.770 J.D. 5150 El Camino Real
**Anderson, Jason H.** ....................'69 '94 C.1049 B.A. L.802 J.D. [🄰 Langley,L.K.&M.]
*PRACTICE AREAS: Civil Litigation; Business Litigation; Products Liability; Personal Injury; Wrongful Termination.
**Andrews, Joyce D.** ................'49 '85 C.1019 B.A. L.770 J.D. [🄰 Langley,L.K.&M.]
*LANGUAGES: French, Spanish and German.
*PRACTICE AREAS: Trials and Appeals; Defense of Personal Injury; Insurance Coverage; Litigation.
Antonioli, William, (BV) ............ '29 '54 C&L.770 A.B., LL.B. 4410 El Camino Real
Atherton, Michael, (A Professional Corporation), (BV) '32 '57
C.112 B.A. L.813 J.D. 300 3rd St.
Auger, Diana J. ..........................'16 '41 C.999 A.B. L.588 J.D. 38 Woods Lane‡
Beban, Alan, (AV) ..................'32 '64 C.112 B.S. L.813 LL.B. 1466 Clubview Terr.
Blaufarb, Gerard A. .............'28 '55 C&L.174 B.A., J.D. 433 Yerba Buena Ave. (Pat.)
Bradley, Michael J. ..................'39 '66 C&L.352 B.A., J.D. 877 Highlands Circle‡
Brock, Joe E. ..................................'61 '89 C.112 B.A. L.770 J.D. 5150 El Camino Real
Burdick, Lee ..........................'59 '89 C.502 B.A. L.180 J.D. Prima Legal Servs.
Callaway, William H. '47 '81 C.154 B.A. L.999 J.D.
V.P., Austgen Biojet Waste Water Systems, Inc.
Casas, Daniel L. .....................'59 '84 C.267 B.S. L.770 J.D. [Reynolds,R.P.C.&R.]
Coleman, Patricia A. ............................'30 '66 C.381 B.A. L.767 P.O. Box 606‡
Courture, Peter J., (AV) ................'54 '79 C.976 B.A. L.813 J.D. 993 Highland Cir.
Cowans, Daniel R., (AV) ...........'22 '51 C.112 A.B. L.1066 J.D. 5150 El Camino Real

**Denebeim, Robert L., (BV) '53 '80 C.112 B.A. L.765 J.D.**
**885 North San Antonio Road, Suite K, 94022-1305**
**Telephone: 415-941-7327 Facsimile: 415-941-7328**
***REPORTED CASES: Henslee v. DMV, 168CA3d 445; Marvin v. DMV, 191CA3d 171.**
***PRACTICE AREAS: Family Law; Civil Litigation; Business Law.**
**General Practice/Family Law.**
***See Professional Biographies, LOS ALTOS, CALIFORNIA***

Dornig, Joseph A., Jr. '39 '64 C.1200 B.S.B.A. L.93 LL.B.
(adm. in MA; not adm. in CA) 6 Cypress Ct.‡
Dozier, James H., (BV) ...................... '22 '72 C.896 B.S. L.770 J.D. [Dozier&D.]
Dozier, Joseph W., (CV) .....................'51 '81 C.330 B.A. L.1137 J.D. [Dozier&D.]
Dozier & Dozier, (BV) ........................................................ 180 2nd St.
Durham, Sheldon D., (CV) ...............'20 '52 C&L.813 A.B., LL.B. 387 Alicia Way
Endersby, Kelly B. ........................'61 '85 C.112 B.A. L.770 J.D. 250 Margarita Ct.
Erdelyi, Gabor ..........................'27 '81 C.061 M.A. L.999 J.D. 571 Panchita Way‡
Eustice, W. Gordon ............................'16 '48 C&L.813 A.B., J.D. Drawer 400‡
Evans, Marjorie W. .........................'21 '72 C.174 A.B. L.813 J.D. 101 First St.‡
Fenner, Randee G. ....................'54 '80 C.813 B.A. L.1067 J.D. 280 Vernal Ct.
Ferrari, Gerald B., (BV) ............................'24 '57 C&L.813 B.S., LL.B. [Ferrari&F.]
Ferrari, Maria A., (BV) ........................'58 '84 C.1051 B.A. L.770 J.D. [Ferrari&F.]
Ferrari & Ferrari, A Law Corp., (BV) ............................................ 300 Second St.
Fisher, Harold J. ...............................'10 '34 C&L.800 B.S., LL.B. 1568 Plateau St.‡
Fletcher, Robert L., (BV) ................'51 '81 C.197 B.A. L.94 J.D. 854A Jordan Ave.
Fry, Dennis G. .............................'48 '75 C.112 B.A. L.1065 J.D. 754 Filip Rd.
Gamel, Gary E., (BV) ..................'38 '74 C.768 B.S. L.1153 J.D. 4966 El Camino Real
Giles, Rita L., (AV) .......................'44 '77 C.696 A.B. L.813 J.D. 27800 Saddle Ct.‡
Gotlieb, Heidi B. '61 '89 C.112 B.A. L.813 J.D.
Corp. Coun., Amer. Restaurant Grp., Inc.
**Graves, Eric L.** .......................'69 '95 C.1109 B.A. L.464 J.D. [🄰 Langley,L.K.&M.]
Gross, Laddy H. ......................'15 '39 C.911 A.B. L.477 LL.B. 924 Riverside Dr.‡
Gruber, Stephen C. ....................'44 '72 C.813 B.A. L.950 J.D. 4966 El Camino Real
Handel, Richard T. '54 '83
C.112 A.B. L.1065 J.D. Corp. Coun., Amer. Restaurant Grp., Inc.
**Hawley, Melvin L.**, (AV) .......... '20 '52 C.976 B.A. L.813 LL.B. [Myers,H.M.M.&M.]
Herbert, Leon F. .............'22 '53 C.128 B.A. L.276 J.D. 610 Twelve Acres Dr. (Pat.)‡
Hickey, Barbara J. ..........................................'— '91 C.788 B.A. L.770 J.D. P.O. Box 45
Hines, Leelane E. ......................'37 '59 C&L.813 B.A., LL.B. 1048 Dartmouth Lane‡
Hoffman, William P., (AV) ...............'20 '52 C.112 B.S. L.813 J.D. 736 Panchita Way‡
Horsey, William F., Jr. '61 '88
C.169 B.A. L.767 J.D. 4984 El Camino Real (©Santa Rosa)
Howard, Susan W. ........................'41 '77 C.112 B.A. L.1095 J.D. 27827 Saddle Ct.
**James, Kim** ......................................'46 '82 C.1060 B.A. L.464 J.D. [Nelson,P.&L.]
*PRACTICE AREAS: Insurance Defense; Products Liability; Professional Malpractice; Personal Injury; Civil Litigation.
Janz, James R., (BV) '48 '79 C.679 B.S. L.145 J.D.
Chf. Real Estate Coun., Amer. Restaurant Grp., Inc.
Johnson, Clarence G., (AV) ...........................'15 '39 L.626 LL.B. P.O. Box 1117
Johnson, Margaret S., (BV) ....................... '44 '78 C.054 B.S. L.767 J.D. One First St.

**Kaye, Kenneth R., (AV) '43 '70 C.659 B.S. L.813 J.D.**
**Suite A, 220 State Street, 94022**
**Telephone: 415-949-1660 Fax: 415-949-5024**
***PRACTICE AREAS: Real Estate Law; Real Estate Transactions; Tax Deferred Exchanges; Estate Planning; Trusts and Probate.**
**Real Estate, Taxation, Tax Deferred Exchanges, Estate Planning, Trusts, Corporate and Business Law.**
***See Professional Biographies, LOS ALTOS, CALIFORNIA***

Kelley, Mary Katherine L. ...................'— '76 C.611 A.B. L.273 J.D. P.O. Box 422
Kelvie, Patrick J. '51 '76 C.112 A.B. L.309 J.D.
Gen. Coun. & Secy., Amer. Restaurant Grp., Inc.
**Konevich, Marian Malovos**, (AV) .........'49 '75 C.112 B.A. L.464 J.D. [Malovos&K.]
*PRACTICE AREAS: Probate; Estate Planning; Trust Law; Corporation.
**Konevich, Robert W.**, (AV) ...............'47 '82 C.112 B.A. L.770 J.D. [Malovos&K.]
*PRACTICE AREAS: Real Property; Business; Family Law.
Kramer, Linda C. .........................'42 '88 C.684 B.A. L.284 J.D. 280 Second St.

CALIFORNIA—LOS ALTOS MARTINDALE-HUBBELL LAW DIRECTORY 1997

**Kreger, Brian S.** .... '54 '82 C.112 B.A. L.770 J.D. [Langley,L.K.&M.] (⊙San Francisco)
*REPORTED CASES: Kohn v. Superior Court (1983, 1st Dist) 142 Cal. App. 3d 323; Mid-Century Insurance Co. v. Hartford Casualty Insurance Co., 26 Cal. App. 4th 1783; Worthington v. Rusconi, et al, 29 Cal App 4th 1488 (1994).
*PRACTICE AREAS: Trials and Appeals; Defense of Personal Injury; Wrongful Termination; Product Liability; Construction Defect Cases.
Kuhr, Harvey N. '12 '38 C.194 A.B. L.477 LL.B.
(adm. in NE; not adm. in CA) 1449 Arbor Ave.‡
Ladd, Donald M., Jr. .................. '23 '51 C.207 A.B. L.813 J.D. 1034 Golden Way‡
Lagorio, Anthony, (BV) ......................... '27 '55 C.740 L.767 LL.B. 300 3rd St.
**Lamberto, Peter N.**, (BV) '47 '74
C&L.767 B.A., J.D. [Langley,L.K.&M.] (⊙San Francisco)
*REPORTED CASES: Mid-Century Insurance Co. v. Hartford Casualty Insurance Co., 26 Cal. App. 4th 1783.
*PRACTICE AREAS: Civil Litigation; Defense of Toxic Torts; Personal Injury; Product Liability; Construction Law.
**Langley, Larry D.**, (AV) '42 '73
C.612 B.Arch.E. L.767 J.D. [Langley,L.K.&M.] (⊙San Francisco)
*REPORTED CASES: Magnolia Square HOA v. Safeco Insurance Company of America (1990) 221 CA 3d 1049; National Union v. Siliconix (1989) 729 Fed. Supp. 77; State Farm Mutual Automobile Insurance Co., Becker v., 52 Cal. App. 3d 282, 124 Cal. Rptr. 739 (1975).
*PRACTICE AREAS: Product Liability; Personal Injury; Construction; Environmental; Business and Employment Litigation.
**Langley, Lisa A.** ................. '70 '96 C.112 B.A. L.1202 J.D. [Langley,L.K.&M.]

**Langley, Lamberto, Kreger & Moher, (AV)**
**4984 El Camino Real, Second Floor, 94022-1433⊙**
**Telephone: 415-428-1100 Fax: 415-428-1102**
**Members of Firm: Larry D. Langley; Peter N. Lamberto; Brian S. Kreger; James P. Moher; Joyce D. Andrews. Associates: Bonnie L. Miller; Philip R. Soderquist; J. Penny Oliver; Kristi J. Spiering; Alan J. Zacharin; Elizabeth van der Toorren; Jason H. Anderson; Eric L. Graves; Lisa A. Langley.**
**Trial and Appellate Practice, Insurance Defense, Insurance Law and Coverage, Environmental and Toxic Tort Claims, Business Litigation, Personal Injury, Bad Faith, Products Liability, Professional Liability, Landslide/Subsidence Claims, Construction, Arson and Fraud Claims, Insurance Appraisals.**
**San Francisco, California Office: 465 California Street, Suite 1285, 94104. Telephone: 415-394-9900. Fax: 415-394-9997.**
**Santa Rosa, California Office: 404 Mendocino Avenue, Suite 200, 95401. Telephone: 707-577-0895. Fax: 707-526-5864.**
***See Professional Biographies, LOS ALTOS, CALIFORNIA***

**Leary, Patricia M.** ..................... '51 '80 C.061 B.A. L.765 J.D. [Nelson,P.&L.]
*PRACTICE AREAS: Insurance Defense; Products Liability; Professional Malpractice; Personal Injury; Civil Litigation.
**Lee, Mark S.**, (AV) ........................ '54 '79 C.990 B.A. L.770 J.D. [Nelson,P.&L.]
*PRACTICE AREAS: Insurance Defense; Products Liability; Professional Malpractice; Personal Injury; Civil Litigation.
Le Fevre, Eugene de D. '26 '52 C.222 A.B. L.188 J.D.
(adm. in NY; not adm. in CA) 1299 St. Joseph Ave.‡
Levine, Marcia D. '57 '88 C.770 B.S. L.356 J.D.
(adm. in MS; not adm. in CA) 729 Vista Grande Ave.
Lockhart, Robert D. .................. '65 '91 C.112 A.B. L.770 J.D. 339 S. Antonio Rd.
Loebner, Barbara M. ...................... '55 '85 C.999 B.A. L.770 J.D. 1644 Newcastle
Madden, James P., (BV) ..................... '49 '74 C.112 B.A. L.767 J.D. 300 3rd St.
**Malovos, Kenneth R.**, (AV) ........................ '08 '33 C&L.813 A.B., J.D. [Malovos&K.] ‡

**Malovos & Konevich, (AV)** BB
**Los Altos Plaza, 5150 El Camino Real, Suite A-22, 94022**
**Telephone: 415-988-9700 Facsimile: 415-988-9639**
**Marian Malovos Konevich (Certified Specialist, Probate, Estate Planning and Trust Law, The State Bar of California Board of Legal Specialization); Robert W. Konevich. Retired Founding Partner: Kenneth R. Malovos.**
**General Civil Practice. Real Property, Probate and Estate Planning, Corporation, Business and Family Law.**
***See Professional Biographies, LOS ALTOS, CALIFORNIA***

Massey, Donald L. ............................ '43 '70 C.767 B.A. L.770 J.D. 18 Los Altos Sq.
**McDonnell, John P.** ................ '50 '77 C.767 B.A. L.1066 J.D. [Myers,H.M.M.&M.]
*REPORTED CASES: Lettieri v. Equitable Life Assur. Soc. 627 F.2d 930 (9th Cir. 1980).
McGowen, Richd. M. .................. '29 '56 C.605 L.1065 J.D. 4410 El Camino Real
McLean, Robert J. ............................. '20 '48 C&L.178 B.A., J.D. 530 Patrick Way‡
Metzger, Christine L. ................. '65 '92 C.768 B.A. L.770 J.D. 5150 El Camino Real
Michaud, Frederick C., (AV) ...... '40 '66 C.813 A.B. L.1066 J.D. 27709 Via Cerro Gordo
Mickel, George E. '09 '33 C&L.546 A.B., J.D.
(adm. in NE; not adm. in CA) 580 Los Altos Ave.‡
**Miller, Bonnie L.** ................................ '50 '84 L.765 J.D. [Ⓐ Langley,L.K.&M.]
*PRACTICE AREAS: Construction; Personal Injury Litigation; Juvenile; Family Law.
**Moher, James P.** '54 '82 C.1169 B.A. L.1065 J.D.
[Langley,L.K.&M.] (⊙San Francisco)
*PRACTICE AREAS: Business Litigation; Commercial Litigation; Personal Injury Law; Construction Law; Insurance Coverage.
**Morley, Sam R.**, (AV) ................. '32 '60 C&L.813 A.B., LL.B. [Myers,H.M.M.&M.]
Morris, Richd. C. ................... '16 '52 C.911 B.S. L.813 LL.B. 24131 Summerhill Ave.
Muir, Brenda C. ................. '39 '64 C.966 B.A. L.813 LL.B. 175 S. San Antonio Rd.‡
**Myers, Alexander P.** ................ '62 '88 C.112 B.A. L.767 J.D. [Myers,H.M.M.&M.]
**Myers, Paul I., Jr.**, (AV) ............ '28 '51 C&L.813 A.B., LL.B. [Myers,H.M.M.&M.]
**Myers, Paul I. "Chico", III**, (AV) '50 '76 C.813 B.A. L.1197 J.D.
[Myers,H.M.M.&M.]
*REPORTED CASES: People v. Phillips (1985) 41 Cal. 3d 29.

**Myers, Hawley, Morley, Myers & McDonnell, (AV)**
**An Association of Attorneys**
**166 Main Street, P.O. Box 280, 94022**
**Telephone: 415-948-1600 Fax: 415-949-3581**
**Paul I. Myers, Jr. (1928-1991); Sam R. Morley; Paul I. "Chico" Myers, III; John P. McDonnell; Alexander P. Myers. Of Counsel: Melvin L. Hawley.**
**General Civil and Trial Practice. Taxation, Corporate, Family, Real Property, Business, Estate Planning, Trusts and Probate.**
**Reference: Wells Fargo Bank.**
***See Professional Biographies, LOS ALTOS, CALIFORNIA***

Nelson, Elaine T. ............. '44 '72 C.788 A.B. L.1066 J.D. 27261 Black Mountain Rd.
**Nelson, Thomas F.**, (AV) ................... '35 '63 C&L.767 B.S., LL.B. [Nelson,P.&L.]
*PRACTICE AREAS: Insurance Defense; Products Liability; Professional Malpractice; Personal Injury; Civil Litigation.

**Nelson, Perlov & Lee, A Professional Corporation, (AV)**
**339 South San Antonio Road, 94022**
**Telephone: 415-941-6161 Fax: 415-949-0695**
**Thomas F. Nelson; Florence T. Perlov (Retired); Mark S. Lee; Kim James; Patricia M. Leary; Mary Acquesta.**
**General Civil and Trial Practice. Insurance, Products Liability, Malpractice and Personal Injury Law.**
***See Professional Biographies, LOS ALTOS, CALIFORNIA***

Newlander, Roger A. .............. '26 '69 C.46 B.S.E.E. L.1026 J.D. 1504 Redwood Dr.
Nichols, E. L. ..................... '10 '37 C.878 L.273 LL.B. 391 South Gordon Way‡
Nyquist, Charles W. ............... '12 '37 C&L.494 B.B.A., LL.B. 327 Mariposa Ave.‡

**Oliver, J. Penny** ............................ '49 '87 C.506 B.A. L.770 J.D. [Ⓐ Langley,L.K.&M.]
*LANGUAGES: French.
*REPORTED CASES: Magnolia Square HOA v. Safeco Insurance Company of America (1990) 221 CA3d 1049.
*PRACTICE AREAS: Trials and Appeals; Defense of Personal Injury; Insurance Coverage.
Penland, Lee S., (AV) ............................ '12 '40 C&L.767 LL.B. 11970 Rhus Ridge Dr.
**Perlov, Florence T.**, (AV) ................ '— '74 C.813 B.A. L.770 J.D. [Nelson,P.&L.] ‡
Price, Harry I., (AV) ................ '52 '77 C.347 B.A. L.1119 J.D. [Reynolds,R.P.C.&R.]
Reynolds, James E., (AV) ........ '36 '67 C.679 B.S.E.E. L.770 J.D. [Reynolds,R.P.C.&R.]
Reynolds, Roux, Price, Casas & Riley, (AV) ........................ 5150 El Camino Real
Riley, Sheila M., (AV) ................... '59 '84 C&L.770 B.A., J.D. [Reynolds,R.P.C.&R.]
Riter, Bruce D. ........................ '49 '75 C.801 B.S.E.E. L.597 J.D. 101 First St. (Pat.)
Roux, Henry W., (BV) ................. '51 '76 C&L.770 B.S., J.D. [Reynolds,R.P.C.&R.]
Samuel, Mervin R. ........................................ '13 '37 C.999 L.1065 J.D. 471 Panchila Way
Shaevitz, Jerald P. ............... '44 '71 C.112 B.S. L.1068 J.D. 24175 Dawridge Dr.
Sines, John B., (BV) ...................... '47 '73 C.813 A.B. L.1065 J.D. 300 3rd St.
Smith, Margaret A. ................ '45 '86 C.273 B.A. L.770 J.D. 175 S. San Antinie Rd.
**Soderquist, Philip R.** ................. '54 '86 C.112 B.A. L.1065 J.D. [Ⓐ Langley,L.K.&M.]
*PRACTICE AREAS: Trials and Appeals; Complex Construction Litigation; Personal Injury.
**Spiering, Kristi J.** ........................ '63 '91 C.1051 B.A. L.150 J.D. [Ⓐ Langley,L.K.&M.]
*PRACTICE AREAS: Tort Litigation; Insurance Coverage; Insurance Defense.
Stapleton, James A. ......................... '32 '56 C&L.215 LL.B. 670 Panchita Way
Staskus, Kim David, (AV) ........ '53 '80 C.112 B.A. L.1137 J.D. 371 1st St. (⊙San Jose)
Stearns, Patricia H., (BV) .................... '47 '83 C.322 B.A. L.770 J.D. 474 Tyndall St.
Thede, David M. ........................ '52 '77 C.813 A.B. L.1066 J.D. 26540 Conejo Ct.
Umeda, Wesley T. .................... '47 '82 C.112 A.B. L.770 J.D. 5150 El Camino Real
VanAssenderp, John A. '10 '60 L.326 J.D.
(adm. in TX; not adm. in CA) 1460 Aura Way‡
Van Buren, Paul B. ............... '38 '64 C.793 B.A. L.813 J.D. 1206 Woodview Terrace
**van der Toorren, Elizabeth** .......... '66 '92 C.112 B.A. L.767 J.D. [Ⓐ Langley,L.K.&M.]
Vaughters, Cecilie A. '53 '79 C.610 B.B.A. L.276 J.D.
(adm. in DC; not adm. in CA) 1635 Candace Way‡
Vivian, Carlson ........................................................................ '51 '80 [Dozier&D.]
Voet, Leo C. '15 '42 C.973 B.S.C. L.1340 J.D.
(adm. in OH; not adm. in CA) 440 Juanita Way‡
Wait, William B. '19 '42 C&L.861 A.B., LL.B.
(adm. in LA; not adm. in CA) 12364 Prisolla Ln.
Wetenkamp, Jean High ........................................ '46 '76 C.347 B.S. L.770 J.D. Mun. J.
Wise, Ellen J. ........................ '53 '80 C.788 B.A. L.770 J.D. 24301 Elise St. (Pat.)
**Zacharin, Alan J.** '47 '90 C.112 B.S. L.464 J.D.
[Ⓐ Langley,L.K.&M.] (⊙San Francisco)
*PRACTICE AREAS: Civil Litigation.

## LOS ALTOS HILLS, 7,514, *Santa Clara Co.*

Barnett, George H. ................. '14 '39 C&L.930 B.A., LL.B. Superior Court J. (Ret.)
Block, Richard A. ............... '47 '72 C.659 B.S. L.976 J.D. 26790 Arastradero Rd.‡
Hawkins, Jack D. ................................ '21 '47 C&L.228 LL.B. 26464 Taaffe Rd.
Henley, Albert Thomas .............. '16 '41 C&L.813 A.B., LL.B. 26631 Taaff Rd.‡
Oberlin, John C. '14 '38 C.309 A.B. L.930 LL.B.
(adm. in OH; not adm. in CA; Pat.) 26140 Robb Rd.‡
Siegel, William M. ................... '21 '50 C&L.477 A.B., LL.B. 24905 La Loma Ct.‡
Silver, Mary Ellen F. '46 '72 C&L.930 B.A., J.D.
(adm. in OH; not adm. in CA) 24840 Prospect Ave.‡
Spector, David M. .... '60 '85 C.103 B.A. L.309 J.D. Pres., Legal Advantage Invests., Inc.
Wardenburg, Barbara J. '37 '80 C.813 B.A. L.184 J.D.
(adm. in CT; not adm. in CA) 12143 Hilltop Dr.‡
Wolff, Miriam E. ................... '18 '40 C&L.813 B.A., LL.B. 25623 Elena Rd.‡

## LOS ANGELES, * 3,485,398, *Los Angeles Co.*

A number of communities in the Los Angeles area have individual identities, and therefore, in addition to the lawyers listed in the following Bar Roster, other lawyers and firms appear under the names of those towns and sections, some of which are part of the incorporated City of Los Angeles, while others are either unincorporated or separately incorporated. See list of towns and cities shown under the heading of Los Angeles County in index appearing on the first page of California Lawyers.

Aalto, Laura A. ............................ '39 '76 C.174 B.A. L.569 J.D. Dep. Dist. Atty.
**Aardal, Dan C.** ...................... '47 '75 C&L.208 B.A., J.D. [Brown R.M.F.&S.]
*PRACTICE AREAS: Computer Law; Banking; Real Estate Finance.
**Aarestad, Joan E.** ...................... '53 '80 C.1075 B.S. L.800 J.D. [Meserve,M.&H.]
**Aaron, Jaculin** ............................ '58 '85 C.942 B.A. L.378 J.D. [Shearman&S.]
Aaron, Roy H., (AV) ............... '29 '57 C.112 B.A. L.800 LL.B. 234 S. Canyonview Dr.
**Aaronoff, Steven J.** ........ '64 '89 C.309 A.B. L.597 J.D. [Ⓐ Christensen,M.F.J.G.W.&S.]
*PRACTICE AREAS: Litigation.
Aaronson, Susan Alane ................. '50 '81 C.112 A.B. L.800 J.D. Dep. Pub. Def. IV

**Aaronson & Aaronson**
**(See Encino)**

Abarams, Michael S., Law Offices of, A Professioal Corp. .......... 1880 Century Park E.
**Abascal, Manuel A.** ..................... '65 '94 C.154 B.A. L.976 J.D. [Ⓐ Munger,T.&O.]
*LANGUAGES: Spanish.
Abbey, William S. ....................... '45 '71 C.112 B.A. L.1068 J.D. Dep. Atty. Gen.
Abbitt, Diane R., (AV) ......................... '43 '79 C.112 B.A. L.1095 J.D. [Abbitt&B.]
Abbitt & Bennett, (AV) ............................................. 12121 Wilshire Blvd.
**Abbott, Bruce A.** .................... '66 '92 C.668 B.A. L.976 J.D. [Ⓐ Munger,T.&O.]
Abbott, Louis Lee, (AV) ................ '24 '50 C.453 L.800 J.D. 1951 Bel Air Rd.‡
**Abbott, Mark Bruce** ................ '64 '89 C.276 B.S.F.S. L.1066 J.D. [Ⓐ Latham&W.]
**Abbott, Michael J.** ................ '44 '72 C.813 B.A. L.1068 J.D. [Jones,B.S.A.&F.]
*PRACTICE AREAS: Business Law; Securities Litigation.
**Abbott, Mitchell E.** .................... '50 '75 C.112 A.B. L.893 J.D. [Richards,W.&G.]
*PRACTICE AREAS: Environmental Litigation; Unfair Competition Law; Appeals.
**Abbott, Thomas M.** ........................ '54 '84 C.871 B.S. L.273 J.D. [McKenna&C.]
*PRACTICE AREAS: Government Contracts; Litigation; White Collar Criminal Defense; International Arbitration.
Abbott, Thomas P. ..................... '61 '87 C.740 B.A. L.990 J.D. 1200 Wilshire Blvd.
Abdulaziz, Sam K., (A Law Corporation), (AV) '39 '72
C.112 B.S. L.426 J.D. [Abdulaziz&G.]
Abdulaziz & Grossbart, (AV) ........ 6454 Coldwater Canyon Avenue (North Hollywood)
Abdullah, Mace ........................... '50 '90 C.1097 B.S. L.426 J.D. 3250 Wilshire Blvd.
**Abdur-Rahman, Aisha H.** '50 '86 C.188 B.S. L.569 J.D.
(adm. in OH; not adm. in CA) [Ⓐ Skadden,A.S.M.&F.]
**Abel, David B.** ........................ '57 '91 C.339 B.S. L.426 J.D. [Ⓐ Graham&J.] (Pat.)
*PRACTICE AREAS: Intellectual Property Law; Patent Law.
**Abele, George W.** ........................ '63 '90 C.893 B.A. L.1068 J.D. [Ⓐ Paul,H.J.&W.]
**Abeles, Jerrold E.** ................ '63 '88 C.112 B.A. L.800 J.D. [Ⓐ LeBoeuf,L.G.&M.]
*PRACTICE AREAS: Commercial Litigation; Business Torts.
Abell, Leslie B., (AV) ................. '51 '75 C.800 B.S. L.426 J.D. [Myman,A.F.G.&R.]
Abels, Ulma A. .................... '17 '46 C.767 B.S. L.1065 LL.B. 2115 S. Curson Ave.

CAA170P

**Abelson, Lawrence A.** .................... '67 '92 C.860 B.A. L.112 J.D. [Epport&R.]
*LANGUAGES: French.
*PRACTICE AREAS: Real Property; Bankruptcy; Commercial Litigation.
**Abelson, Leroy A.**, (BV) .................. '42 '73 C.906 B.S. L.426 J.D. [O'Neill,H.&A.]
*PRACTICE AREAS: Eminent Domain; Direct and Inverse Condemnation; Related Fields.
**Abelson, Michael Bruce** .................. '63 '87 C.605 B.A. L.569 J.D. [Latham&W.]
**Abend Bauman, Michelle** ........... '67 '93 C.154 B.A. L.800 J.D. [Mitchell,S.&K.]
*PRACTICE AREAS: Labor Law; Employment Law.
**Aberbook, Donald J.** ................... '58 '90 C.112 B.A. L.809 J.D. [Dale,B.&H.]
**Abernathy, Michele L.** ................... '70 '95 C.1075 B.S. L.990 J.D. [Gifford&D.]
*PRACTICE AREAS: Trusts; Wills; Real Estate Transactions; Conservatorships; Probate Administration.
Abernathy, R. Wayne ............... '52 '92 C.846 B.S. L.809 J.D. 5700 Wilshire Blvd.
**Abitanta, Susan E.** .................. '49 '83 C.421 B.A. L.802 J.D. [Quisenberry&B.]
*PRACTICE AREAS: Civil Litigation; Insurance Coverage.
Ableser, Gary D. ..................... '48 '73 C.112 B.A. L.1068 J.D. 5455 Wilshire Blvd.
**Ablon, Herman**, (AV) ......... '31 '61 C.563 B.B.A. L.800 LL.B. [Anderson,A.L.&G.]
*LANGUAGES: French.
*PRACTICE AREAS: Real Estate; Tax; Corporate.
Ablon, Paul S. ..................... '48 '74 C.112 B.A. L.1066 J.D. 16311 Ventura Blvd.
Abraham, Anslyene A. ...................... '47 '74 C&L.346 B.A., J.D. [Harris,B.&A.]
**Abraham, Susan** ................ '57 '86 C.347 B.S. L.1068 J.D. [Weinstock,M.R.S.&N.]
*PRACTICE AREAS: Estate Planning and Probate Law.
**Abrahams, Colin P.** ........... '52 '82 C&L.061 B.Sc., LL.B. [Ladas&P.] (See Pat. Sect.)
**Abrahams, Peter**, (AV) ...................... '45 '70 C.112 B.A. L.426 J.D. [Horvitz&L.]
Abram, Morris B., Jr. ...................... '49 '91 C.309 B.A. L.809 J.D. Dep. Dist. Atty.
**Abram, Steven** ...................... '54 '80 C.112 B.A. L.1068 J.D. [Brown,W.&C.]
*PRACTICE AREAS: Real Property Transactions; Commercial Leasing.
Abramoff, Robert W. ..................... '61 '88 C.94 B.A. L.800 J.D. [Kaslow,A.&A.]
**Abrams, Gregory S.** ..................... '54 '80 C.800 B.A. L.999 J.D. [Shawn,M.&N.]
*PRACTICE AREAS: Bankruptcy Law; Commercial Law.
**Abrams, Jeffrey I.** ..................... '67 '92 C.112 B.A. L.188 J.D. [Katten M.&Z.]
Abrams, Judith ............................ '39 '77 C.1365 B.A. L.1136 J.D. Mun. Ct. J.

**Abrams, Michael L., Law Offices of, (AV) '44 '69 C.1044 L.107 J.D.**
**12121 Wilshire Boulevard, Suite 900, 90025**
**Telephone: 310-268-1000 Fax: 310-207-1508**
**Civil Litigation in all State and Federal Courts with Special Emphasis on Family Law, Banking, Contracts and Real Property Law.**

Abrams, Michael S. ......................... '53 '81 C.659 B.A. L.597 J.D. [M.S.Abrams]
Abrams, Norman '33 '56 C&L.145 A.B., J.D.
(adm. in IL; not adm. in CA) Prof. of Law, Univ. of Calif.
Abrams, Paul L. ................ '58 '83 C.112 A.B. L.1066 J.D. Bet Tzedek Legal Servs.
Abrams, Ronald P. .............. '62 '89 C.446 B.S. L.1148 J.D. 221 N. Figueroa St. (Pat.)
**Abramson, Howard Andrew** ................. '63 '88 C.659 B.A. L.309 J.D. [Behr&A.]
*PRACTICE AREAS: Entertainment Law.
**Abramson, Joe R.** .................. '56 '82 C.112 B.A. L.426 J.D. [Glass,A.G.&C.]
*PRACTICE AREAS: Commercial Law; Construction Litigation; Real Estate Development.
Abramson, Michael A. ............... '51 '78 C.112 B.A. L.809 J.D. 4851 S. Alameda St.
Abreu, Elizabeth I. ................................ '52 '77 C.105 B.A. L.1065 J.D. I.R.S.
**Abrolat, Nancy L.** ....................... '65 '90 C.464 B.A. L.1065 J.D. [Abrolat&T.]

**Abrolat & Teren**
**5777 West Century Boulevard, Suite 1550, 90045**
**Telephone: 310-410-9111 Facsimile: 310-410-1687**
**Members of Firm: Nancy L. Abrolat; Pamela McKibbin Teren. Associate: Kevin P. Berg.**
**Employment Litigation, Representing Employees and Employers, Sexual Harassment, Discrimination, Wrongful Termination, Disability Discrimination, Whistle Blower Cases, Civil Rights Litigation.**
*See Professional Biographies, LOS ANGELES, CALIFORNIA*

**Abshez, Allan J.** ....................... '56 '84 C.112 A.B. L.1066 J.D. [Irell&M.]
**Abu-Assal, Nabil L.** ......... '62 '88 C.154 B.A. L.1068 J.D. [Christensen,M.F.J.G.W.&S.]
*LANGUAGES: Arabic and French.
*PRACTICE AREAS: Civil Litigation.
Acalin, David T. ..................... '58 '84 C.112 B.A. L.990 J.D. 4221 Wilshire Blvd.
Accinelli, Thomas F. ........................ '50 '79 C.112 B.A. L.588 J.D. P.O. Box 34817
Acevedo, Lucy ..................................... '51 '78 C.813 B.A. L.1065 J.D. N.L.R.B.
Aceves, William J. ........................ '64 '90 C.154 B.A. L.800 J.D. 6435 W. 87th Pl.
Acheson, Richard M., Jr. .................. '44 '72 C.36 C.P.A. L.426 J.D. Gen. Coun., BSI
Achor, Robert T. .. '32 '58 C.976 B.A. L.477 J.D. V.P., Secy. & Gen. Coun., Glaser Bros.
Ackel, Elena H. ........................................ '43 '72 C&L.800 B.A., J.D. Legal Aid
**Acker, Allison-Claire** ................ '61 '88 C.112 B.A. L.1068 J.D. [Kelley D.&W.]
*PRACTICE AREAS: Business Immigration.
**Acker, Stephen**, (AV) ................... '51 '75 C.112 B.A. L.1065 J.D. [Acker,K.&W.]
*LANGUAGES: Spanish.
*PRACTICE AREAS: Professional Liability; Products Liability.

**Acker, Kowalick & Whipple, A Professional Corporation, (AV)**
**World Trade Center Suite 900, 350 South Figueroa Street, 90071**
**Telephone: 213-687-3933 Fax: 213-626-3561**
**Stephen Acker; W. Frederick Kowalick; Anthony Henry Whipple; Brian F. Drazich;—D. Alton Kelly; Bernhard E. Bihr; Jerri L. Johnson; Catherine L. Rhodes; A. Gina Hogtanian; Tawnya L. Southern.**
**Civil Trial Practice in State and Federal Courts. Insurance Law. Products Liability, Personal Injury, Malpractice, Subrogation and Business Litigation.**
*See Professional Biographies, LOS ANGELES, CALIFORNIA*

**Ackerknecht, Richard E.** ................ '61 '87 C&L.800 B.S., J.D. [Mitchell,S.&K.]
*PRACTICE AREAS: Corporate Law; Commercial Law.
Ackerman, Lee B. ........................ '50 '76 C.112 B.A. L.426 J.D. [L.B.Ackerman]
**Ackerman, Michael S.** ...................... '57 '82 C&L.339 B.S., J.D. [Jones,K.&A.]
*PRACTICE AREAS: Real Estate; Secured Lending; Corporate.
**Ackerman, Peter B.** ......................... '54 '84 C.112 B.A. L.94 J.D. [O'Melveny&M.]
**Ackerman, Richard L.**, (AV) ............ '45 '72 C.112 B.S. L.1068 J.D. [Herzfeld&R.]
*PRACTICE AREAS: Product Liability; Insurance; Insurance Defense Law; Litigation.
Ackerman, Robert S. ......................... '46 '72 C.112 B.A. L.1068 J.D. [Corleto&A.]
Ackerman, Shelley M. ................... '58 '84 C&L.608 B.A., J.D. L. A. Co. Bar Assn.
**Ackerman, Steve W.** ..................... '59 '84 C.188 B.S. L.1019 J.D. [Baker&H.]
*PRACTICE AREAS: Intellectual Property.
Ackerman, Lee B., P.C. ................................................. 865 S. Figueroa St.
**Ackermann, Robert A.** ............. '64 '91 C.112 A.B. L.426 J.D. [Walker,W.T.&W.]
**Ackland, Thomas B.** .......................... '40 '71 C.197 A.B. L.930 J.D. [Barger&W.]
*PRACTICE AREAS: Aviation Law; Securities Litigation; Insurance Law.
Acosta, Annemarie ....................... '53 '86 C.740 B.A. L.809 J.D. Dep. Dist. Atty.
**Acosta, Maritoni** ................ '69 '95 C.112 B.A. L.426 J.D. [Weinstock,F.M.&K.]
*PRACTICE AREAS: General Civil Litigation; Family Law.
Acosta, Philip H. ...................................... '48 '74 C&L.426 B.A., J.D. [P.H.Acosta]
Acosta, Philip H., P.C. .............................................................. 333 S. Grand Ave.
**Acret, James**, (AV) ............... '30 '57 C.112 B.A. L.1068 LL.B. [Gibbs,G.L.&A.]
*PRACTICE AREAS: Construction Litigation; Construction Arbitration; Insurance Coverage of Construction Claims.
**Adair, K. Eric** ............................... '62 '90 C&L.101 B.A., J.D. [Zevnik H.G.&M.]
*LANGUAGES: Spanish.
*PRACTICE AREAS: Environmental Insurance Coverage; General Litigation.

**Adair, Sidney A., (AV) '28 '60 C.1155 B.S. L.800 J.D.**
**Suite 104, 444 North Larchmont Boulevard, 90004-3030**
**Telephone: 213-464-4875 Fax: 213-464-1817**
**Trust, Estate Planning, Probate and Taxation Law. Corporation, Real Property.**
**References: Union Bank of California, N.A. (Los Angeles Main Office) Wells Fargo Bank (Larchmont Branch).**
*See Professional Biographies, LOS ANGELES, CALIFORNIA*

Adam, Jane .......... '54 '78 C&L.502 B.A., J.D. Mng. Tax Coun., Atlantic Richfield Co.
**Adamek, Charles A.**, (AV) .................... '44 '69 C&L.477 A.B., J.D. [Lord,B.&B.]
*PRACTICE AREAS: Insurance Coverage Law; Professional Liability Law; Railroad Tort Defense Law.
**Adams, Carol J.** ................. '52 '85 C.1042 B.A. L.809 J.D. [Patterson,R.L.G.&J.]
**Adams, Carolyn** '56 '82 C.169 B.A. L.464 J.D.
Sr. Coun., Transamerica Financial Servs.
*RESPONSIBILITIES: Real Property; Creditors Remedies; Regulatory Matters.
Adams, Charles Curtis .............. '26 '59 C&L.597 B.S., LL.B. 2072 Roscomare Rd.‡
**Adams, Christine M.** ................ '68 '94 C.112 B.A. L.976 J.D. [O'Melveny&M.]
Adams, Margaret I. '47 '75
C.813 B.A. L.228 J.D. Sr. V.P. & Gen. Coun., MS Mgmt. Servs.
Adams, Randall E. ..................... '56 '82 C.267 B.s. L.1068 J.D. Mercury Gen. Corp.
Adams, Scot Earle .................. '55 '80 C.112 B.A. L.1148 J.D. Park Hill Productions
Adams, Victoria Lewis ................... '58 '84 C.770 B.A. L.1068 J.D. Dep. Dist. Atty.
Adams, William J. '29 '57 C&L.878 B.S., LL.B.
(adm. in UT; not adm. in CA) 3460 Wilshire Blvd.‡
**Adamson, Scott E.** ..................... '63 '88 C.1068 B.A. L.800 J.D. [Rodi,P.P.G.&C.]
Adamson, Susan C. ..................... '56 '83 C&L.813 A.B., J.D. 1888 Century Park E.
Addison, Bradley R. ....................... '48 '73 C&L.309 A.B., J.D. 2712 La Cuesta Dr.
**Addison, David C.** ........................ '57 '89 C&L.312 B.A., J.D. [Manning,M.&W.]
**Adel, Hilary** ................................. '67 '95 C.882 B.A. L.588 J.D. [Arnold&P.]
*PRACTICE AREAS: Litigation.
Adel, Nancy P., (BV) ............................................. '45 '75 C&L.107 [Adel&P.]
Adel & Pollack, A Professional Corporation, (BV) ........................... 10940 Wilshire
Adell, Hirsch, (AV) ....................... '31 '63 C.112 B.A. L.1068 LL.B. [Reich,A.C.&C.]
**Adelman, Fred** ................. '62 '87 C.1253 B.A. L.1049 J.D. [Verboon,W.H.&P.]
*PRACTICE AREAS: Complex Civil Litigation.
Adelman, Jeffrey S. .................... '66 '91 C.1066 B.A. L.1065 J.D. [Gurewitz&L.]
Adelman, Steven .................. '56 '81 C.1349 B.A. L.809 J.D. 12100 Wilshire Blvd.
**Adelson, Michael**, (AV) .......................... '41 '66 C.215 L.213 J.D. [Epstein,A.&R.]
*PRACTICE AREAS: Criminal Law.
Adelson, Thea J. Nesis .............. '62 '87 C.112 B.A. L.426 J.D. East West Capital

**Adelstein, Bruce '64 '92 C.112 B.A. L.145 J.D.**
**11661 San Vicente Boulevard, Suite 1015, 90049**
**Telephone: 310-979-3565 Fax: 310-826-8242**
**Email: adelstein@appellatelaw.com**
**Appellate Practice, Civil and Criminal in all State and Federal Courts.**
*See Professional Biographies, LOS ANGELES, CALIFORNIA*

**Adkins, Katherine E.** .............. '62 '91 C.546 B.A. L.426 J.D. [Walker,W.T.&W.]
**Adler, Alan S.** ............................ '67 '96 C.164 B.A. L.94 J.D. [Latham&W.]
**Adler, Anthony A., (A Professional Corporation)** '50 '79
C.154 B.A. L.800 J.D. [Mitchell,S.&K.]
*PRACTICE AREAS: Loan Workouts; Mergers and Acquisitions Law; Corporate Law.
**Adler, Douglas B.** ..................... '52 '78 C.188 A.B. L.93 J.D. [Skadden,A.S.M.&F.]
**Adler, Erwin E.** ........................ '41 '66 C.477 B.A. L.309 J.D. [Richards,W.&G.]
*PRACTICE AREAS: Trial Law; Appellate Litigation; Insurance Coverage.
Adler, Frederic R. ................. '22 '78 C&L.1136 B.S.L., J.D. 10501 Wilshire Blvd.‡
Adler, Irene Brooks .......................... '11 '32 C&L.1001 1239 N. Vista Street‡
Adler, Jack I. ............................... '47 '81 C.475 B.A. L.1179 J.D. 4700 Wilshire Blvd.
**Adler, James E.** ............................ '52 '77 C.112 B.A. L.426 J.D. [D.B.Bloom]
**Adler, James N., (P.C.)**, (AV) ............... '36 '61 C.674 B.S.E. L.477 J.D. [Irell&M.]
Adler, Jerome ................... '35 '64 C.112 B.S. L.1068 J.D. 12350 W. Olympic Blvd.
**Adler, Michael I.**, (AV) .............. '49 '77 C.112 B.A. L.1068 J.D. [Lichter,G.N.&A.]
*PRACTICE AREAS: Entertainment Law; Corporate Law.
**Adler, Phillip E., (A P.C.)**, (AV) ............ '42 '67 C.112 A.B. L.1066 J.D. [Loeb&L.]
*PRACTICE AREAS: Corporate Law; Intellectual Property.
Adler, Richard A. ............................................ '46 '72 C.112 A.B. L.426 J.D. Mun. Ct. J.
Adler, Robert C. ................. '58 '85 C.1239 B.A. L.990 J.D. 4676 Admiralty Way Ste. 300
**Adler, Robert L.**, (AV) ............................. '47 '74 C&L.309 A.B., J.D. [Munger,T.&O.]
Adler, Sara, (AV) ...................................... '42 '70 C.145 B.A. L.112 J.D. 1034 Selby Ave.
Adler, Scott Z., (P.C.) ........... '55 '80 C.112 A.B. L.1065 J.D. 828 Moraga Dr., 2nd Fl.
Adler, Susan Kahn ................ '41 '82 C.990 B.A. L.1136 J.D. 1875 Century Park E.
Admire, Leslie Quinlan ............................. '45 '82 C.312 B.A. L.1067 J.D. Mun. Ct.
**Adriano, Sarah B.** '60 '90 C.1294 B.A. L.1049 J.D.
(adm. in NY; not adm. in CA; See Pat. Sect.) [Merchant&G.]
Advani, Mukesh, (AV) '59 '81
C&L.061 B.Com., LL.B. 11500 Olympic Blvd. (San Francisco)
Advincula, Cenon S. ............. '37 '75 C.662 B.S.B.A. L.999 LL.B. 3460 Wilshire Blvd.
Adwar, Gary S. ........................... '63 '88 C.472 B.A. L.978 J.D. [Kaslow,A.&A.]
Africk, Allan V. ................... '33 '65 C.112 B.S. L.809 LL.B. 1901 Ave. of the Stars
**Agajanian, Cary J. C.**, (AV) ............. '41 '67 C&L.800 B.S., LL.B. [Agajanian&M.]
*REPORTED CASES: Hoffman v. Sports Car Club of America, et al. (1986) , 180 Cal. App. 3d 119, Cite as 225 Cal. Rptr. 359, Dummit & Agajanian, Cary Agajanian, Los Angeles, for amicus curiae K & K Ins. Co.; National and International Brotherhood of Street Racers Inc. v. Superior Court of Los Angeles County (1989), 215 Cal. App. 3d 943, 264 Cal. Rptr. 44, Agajanian and McFall, Cary Agajanian, Universal City for K & K Ins. Co.; Ford v. Gouin (1992), 3 Cal. 4th 339, 11 Cal. Rptr. 2d 30, 834 P2d 724, Agajanian, McFall & Tomlinson, Cary Agajanian, Universal City for amicus curiae K & K Ins. Co.
Agajanian, Tim M., (AV) ................. '61 '87 C.800 B.S. L.809 J.D. [Casterline&A.]

**Agajanian & McFall, (AV)**
**346 North Larchmont Boulevard, 90006-3012**
**Telephone: 213-993-0198**
**Members of Firm: Cary J. C. Agajanian; Scott B. McFall; Philip D. Weiss;—Christine M. Yocca; Abbie Crist; Paul L. Tetreault; Kenneth M. Von Helmolt.**
**Defense of Medical and Hospital Malpractice, Motor Sports Litigation, Governmental Litigation, Products Liability, General Insurance, Hospital, and Business Litigation.**
*See Professional Biographies, LOS ANGELES, CALIFORNIA*

**Agapay, Joe M., Jr.**, (AV) ................ '36 '62 C&L.800 A.B., LL.B. [Agapay,L.&H.]
*PRACTICE AREAS: Complex Civil Litigation; Construction.

**Agapay, Levyn & Halling, A Professional Corporation, (AV)**
**Fourth Floor, 10801 National Boulevard, 90064**
**Telephone: 310-470-1700 Fax: 310-470-2602**
**Joe M. Agapay, Jr.; Thomas S. Levyn; Chris W. Halling;—Glen R. Segal (Resident Member, Orange Office); Peter J. Krupinsky; Laurie J. Bergren; Tracey P. Hom; Richard D. Coats; Steven A. Sokol; Pamela J. Paluga. Of Counsel: Alan B. Grass; Glen Dresser; Nanci E. Murdock.**
**General Civil Practice. Real Estate, Construction, Corporation, Computer Law, Business, Banking, Unfair Competition, Taxation, Commercial Law and Related Litigation and Risk Management.**
**Orange, California Office: One City Boulevard West, Suite 835, 92668. Telephone: 714-634-1744. Fax: 714-634-0417.**
*See Professional Biographies, LOS ANGELES, CALIFORNIA*

Agawa, Thomas K. ........................ '60 '95 C.112 A.B. L.426 J.D. [Kramer&K.]

CAA171P

CALIFORNIA—LOS ANGELES MARTINDALE-HUBBELL LAW DIRECTORY 1997

Ageson, Martin, (BV) ..................... '53 '80 C.112 A.B. L.145 J.D. Dep. Atty. Gen.
**Aghabegian, Alan** ..................... '68 '95 C.1077 B.A. L.990 J.D. [Ⓐ Lynberg&W.]
*LANGUAGES: French, Armenian, Persian.
*PRACTICE AREAS: Insurance Defense.
Aghishian, Ara ........... '60 '87 C.999 A.A. L.1190 J.D. 6255 Sunset Blvd., Hollywood
Agliozzo, Joseph D. ..................... '63 '93 C.112 B.A. L.800 J.D. 1999 Ave. the Stars
**Agmon, Elizabeth S.** ..................... '61 '88 C.112 A.B. L.990 J.D. [Ⓐ Meyers,B.&M.]
*PRACTICE AREAS: Litigation; Professional Liability; Products Liability; General Liability; Insurance Coverage.

**Agnew & Brusavich**
**(See Torrance)**

**Agran, Michael C., (AV) '42 '67 C.112 B.S. L.309 J.D.**
**Suite 1225, 10960 Wilshire Boulevard, 90024**
**Telephone: 310-477-5544 FAX: 310-477-8768**
**(Certified Specialist, Taxation Law, The State Bar of California Board of Legal Specialization).**
**Federal and State Taxation, Business, Trusts and Estate Planning and Probate Law.**
***See Professional Biographies, LOS ANGELES, CALIFORNIA***

**Agrusa, Angela C.** ..................... '62 '87 C.112 B.A. L.426 J.D. [Baker&H.]
*PRACTICE AREAS: Litigation.
**Agtagma, Andrew M.** ..................... '70 '95 C.112 B.A. L.1066 J.D. [Ⓐ Foley L.W.&A.]
*PRACTICE AREAS: Litigation.
Aguilar, Evelyn ..................... '59 '87 C.112 B.A. L.1068 J.D. 725 S. Figueroa St.
Aguilar, Louis V. ..................... '38 '72 C.800 B.A. L.809 J.D. Asst. Co. Coun.
**Aguilera, Jacqueline M.** ..................... '66 '95 C.112 B.S. L.262 J.D. [Ⓐ Jones,D.R.&P.]
Aguiluz, Heroico M. ............. '37 '59 C&L.662 B.S.J., LL.B. 1240 S. Crenshaw Blvd.
Aguirre, Manuel ..................... '59 '90 C&L.061 4661 W. Pico Blvd.
Aguirre, Rodolfo '31 '79 C.112 B.S.M.E. L.1179 J.D.
Staff Coun., State Comp. Ins. Fund
**Aharonian, Taline A.** ..................... '69 '95 C.605 A.B. L.813 J.D. [Ⓐ Milbank,T.H.&M.]
*LANGUAGES: French, Spanish, Russian, Armenian, Farsi.
Ahart, Alan M. ..................... '49 '76 C.112 B.A. L.107 J.D. U.S. Bkrptcy. J.
Ahdoot, Bobby ..................... '68 '94 C.112 B.A. L.990 J.D. 725 S. Figueroa St., 19th Fl.
Ahearn, Thomas ..................... '56 '83 C.1083 B.A. L.809 J.D. Dep. Pub. Def.

**Aherne, Brian W., & Associates**
**(See Burbank)**

Ahn, Charles ..................... '56 '86 C.813 B.S.M.E. L.1066 J.D. [Ahn&L.]
Ahn & Lee ..................... 3435 Wilshire Blvd.
**Aidikoff, Philip M.** ..................... '48 '75 C.112 B.A. L.809 J.D. [Aidikoff&K.]
*PRACTICE AREAS: Securities Arbitration.

**Aidikoff & Kesluk**
**9255 Sunset Boulevard Suite 411, 90069**
**Telephone: 310-273-3180 Fax: 310-273-6137**
**Email: paidi@aol.com**
**Members of Firm: Philip M. Aidikoff; Brian S. Kesluk. Of Counsel: Robert A. Uhl.**
**Securities Arbitration and Civil Litigation, Plaintiff Personal Injury.**
***See Professional Biographies, LOS ANGELES, CALIFORNIA***

Aidlin, Joseph W., (AV) ..................... '10 '33 C.112 B.A. L.1066 J.D. 5143 Sunset Blvd.‡
Aiken, Lorn ..................... '45 '79 L.1221 J.D. 714 Ducommun St.
**Aiken, Michael J.** ..................... '55 '81 C&L.800 B.A., J.D. [Ⓐ Berger,K.S.M.F.S.&G.]
**Aikenhead, David S.**, (AV) ........... '46 '72 C.105 A.B. L.665 J.D. [Aikenhead,C.&S.]

**Aikenhead, Cipes & Supanich, (AV)**
**Equitable Plaza, 30th Floor, 3435 Wilshire Boulevard, 90010-2050**
**Telephone: 213-738-9700 Fax: 213-380-3308**
**Members of Firm: David S. Aikenhead; Andrew P. Cipes; Dennis M. Supanich.**
**General Business, including formation and counseling of corporations, partnerships and limited liability companies, mergers and acquisitions, estate and succession planning, probate, estate and trust administration, commercial lending, creditor bankruptcy representation, environmental law and real estate law.**
**Representative Clients: Los Angeles Convention & Visitors Bureau; United Aeronautical Corp.; USA Properties Fund, Inc.; American Feed & Farm Supply, Inc.; Bank United of Texas, FSB; Bloomfilm; Freedom Management Co.; AHT Architects, Inc.**
***See Professional Biographies, LOS ANGELES, CALIFORNIA***

**Ailin, June** ..................... '55 '83 C.446 B.A. L.846 J.D. [Ⓐ Kane,B.&B.]
*PRACTICE AREAS: Real Property Law; Eminent Domain Litigation.
**Aisenson, David J.** ..................... '24 '56 C.112 B.A. L.809 J.D. [Ⓒ Veatch,C.G.&N.] ‡
**Aitken, William M.** ..................... '50 '78 C.112 A.B. L.1068 J.D. [Ⓒ Berman,B.&B.]
**Aiwasian, Deborah Ann** ..................... '61 '86 C&L.800 B.A., J.D. [Ⓐ Gibson,D.&C.]
*PRACTICE AREAS: Litigation; Insurance.
**Ajalat, Charles R., (A Professional Corporation)**, (AV) '47 '72
C.309 B.A. L.1066 J.D. [Ajalat,P.&A.]
*SPECIAL AGENCIES: Assessment Appeals Boards; State Board of Equalization; Franchise Tax Board; City Tax Boards, Employment Development Department.
*PRACTICE AREAS: State and Local Tax Law.

**Ajalat, Polley & Ayoob, (AV)** ⊞
**A Partnership including Professional Corporations**
**Suite 200, 643 South Olive Street, 90014**
**Telephone: 213-622-7400 Fax: 213-622-4738**
**Members of Firm: Charles R. Ajalat (A Professional Corporation) (Certified Specialist, Taxation Law, The State Bar of California Board of Legal Specialization); Terry L. Polley (A Professional Corporation) (Certified Specialist, Taxation Law, The State Bar of California Board of Legal Specialization); Richard J. Ayoob.**
**State and Local Taxation Law: Real and Personal Property Taxes, Franchise and Income Taxes, Sales and Use Taxes, Gross Receipts Taxes.**
**Reference: Bank of America (Los Angeles Main Office).**
***See Professional Biographies, LOS ANGELES, CALIFORNIA***

Ajemian, David R. ..................... '61 '94 C.1097 B.S. L.809 J.D. 11766 Wilshire Blvd.
Akbar, Raymond ..................... '65 '92 C.1214 B.A. L.569 J.D. 777 S. Figueroa St.
**Akens, Susan E.** ..................... '62 '88 C.705 B.S. L.893 J.D. [Ⓒ O'Melveny&M.]
*PRACTICE AREAS: Entertainment Law.
Akhlaghi, Lily ..................... '66 '92 C.1253 B.S. L.309 J.D. 11377 W. Olympic Blvd.
**Akins, Kelly D.** ..................... '62 '88 C.859 B.A. L.846 J.D. [Ⓐ Lewis,D.B.&B.]
**Akiyama, Carol Lynn** ..................... '46 '71 C&L.800 B.A., J.D. [Ⓒ J.M.Donovan]
*LANGUAGES: Spanish.
*PRACTICE AREAS: Labor Law; Entertainment Law.
**Akre, M. Jan**, (AV) ..................... '47 '75 C.426 B.A. L.93 J.D. [Akre,B.&C.]
*PRACTICE AREAS: Banking Law; Financial Transactions; General Corporate.

**Akre, Bryan & Chang, (AV)**
**355 South Grand Avenue Suite 4100, 90071-3103**
**Telephone: 213-626-0100 Fax: 213-626-1428**
**M. Jan Akre; Geoffrey L. Bryan; WooJin (Eugene) Chang; Steven K. Hazen; Ronald J. Selgrath; Joseph F. Daniels. Of Counsel: Ronald H. Malin.**
**Banking and Financial Institutions, Corporate, Corporate Finance, Employment Law, Business Litigation, International Law, Intellectual Property and Real Estate.**
***See Professional Biographies, LOS ANGELES, CALIFORNIA***

Alarcon, Arthur L. ..................... '25 '52 C&L.800 A.B., LL.B. U.S. Sr. Cir. J.
Alazraki, Howard S. ..................... '63 '88 C.1044 B.S. L.800 J.D. 725 S. Figueroa St.

Albala, Allan, (AV) ..................... '35 '59 C.112 B.S. L.309 J.D. [Ⓒ Levine&Assoc.]
*PRACTICE AREAS: Real Estate; Shopping Center Leasing and Development; Business Law; Contract Law; Corporations and Partnerships.
**Albers, Wendy S.** ..................... '66 '93 C.770 B.A. L.426 J.D. [Ⓐ Perkins C.]
*PRACTICE AREAS: Litigation.
Alberstadt, Samuel L. '48 '87 C&L.273 B.S.C.E., J.D.
(adm. in IL; not adm. in CA; Pat.) 1000 Wilshire Blvd.
Alberstone, Dale S. ..................... '51 '76 C.1077 B.A. L.426 J.D. [Alberstone&E.]
**Alberstone, Daniel** ..................... '56 '82 C.112 B.A. L.809 J.D. [Alschuler G.&P.]
**Alberstone, Todd T.** ..................... '59 '85 C.112 A.B. L.1066 J.D. [Ⓐ Katten M.&Z.]
*PRACTICE AREAS: Intellectual Property; Entertainment Law; Business Litigation.
Alberstone & Evangelatos, (AV) ..................... 1801 Ave. of the Stars (Century City)
**Albert, Caroline M.** ..................... '66 '93 C.228 B.S. L.426 J.D. [Ⓐ Murchison&C.]
*PRACTICE AREAS: Civil Litigation.
Albert, Elaine H. '42 '68
C.112 B.A. L.1068 J.D. Jewish Federation Council of Greater L.A.
**Albert, Mark Anchor** ..................... '61 '88 C.112 A.B. L.1066 J.D. [Ⓐ Sidley&A.]
*LANGUAGES: French, Spanish, Portuguese, Italian.
*PRACTICE AREAS: Commercial and International Litigation.
**Albert, Richard M.** ..................... '53 '79 C&L.477 B.B.A., J.D. [Foley L.W.&A.]
*SPECIAL AGENCIES: National Labor Relations Board; National Mediation Board; Equal Employment Opportunity Commission and State Counterparts; Wage and Hour Division and State Counterparts.
*PRACTICE AREAS: Labor and Employment; Wrongful Termination; Employment Discrimination; Wage and Hour Law; Administrative Law.
Albertine, John M. .......... '45 '71 C&L.339 A.B., J.D. Dep. State Atty., Dept. of Trans.
Albertini, Eugene J., (BV) ..................... '30 '65 C.112 B.A. L.809 J.D. [Albertini&G.]
Albertini & Gill, (BV) ..................... 3350 Barham Boulevard
**Alberts, Ronald K.** ..................... '55 '81 C.112 B.A. L.1067 J.D. [Frye,A.&M.]
*LANGUAGES: French.
*PRACTICE AREAS: Bad Faith Litigation; Insurance Law; Life and Health Insurance Law; ERISA Litigation; Fidelity and Surety Law.
**Albin-Riley, Debra J.** ..................... '59 '83 C.112 B.A. L.800 J.D. [Fried,F.H.S.&J.]
*LANGUAGES: French.
*PRACTICE AREAS: Business Torts; Intellectual Property; Entertainment and Franchise Litigation.
**Albino, Frank** ..................... '45 '70 C.724 B.A. L.309 J.D. [Parker,M.C.O.&S.]
*TRANSACTIONS: $100 million sale of liquor manufacturing company; Structuring and documentation of partnership and financing for development and operation of major Atlantic City Hotel Casino; Structuring and documentation of partnership for mixed-use commercial development of Farmer's Market property in Los Angeles.
*PRACTICE AREAS: Health Law (Defense of Physicians in licensing-disciplinary proceedings; Mergers, Contracts and Structuring of Modern Health-care practices & delivery systems); Professional Corporations Practice; Real Estate; ERISA/Employee Benefits.
Albino, Robert C., (AV) ........... '39 '68 C.500 B.B.A. L.472 J.D. 420 Boyd St., 4th Fl
Albracht, James A. ..................... '40 '68 C.139 B.A. L.1068 J.D. Supr. Ct. J.
Albrecht, Bonnie K. ..................... '44 '92 C.966 B.S. L.1136 J.D. State Comp. Ins. Fund
Albrecht, Donald H., (AV) ..................... '28 '56 C.174 L.1065 J.D. Pres., Terramics Inc.
**Albrecht-Buehler, Christine G.** ..................... '69 '95 C.597 B.A. L.426 J.D. [Ⓐ D.Q.Dern]
*PRACTICE AREAS: Entertainment Law.
**Albright, Alan M.** ..................... '49 '76 C.112 B.A. L.1068 J.D. [Dewey B.]
*PRACTICE AREAS: Corporate.
Albright, Clifton W. ..................... '55 '81 C.1042 B.S. L.426 J.D. [Albright,Y.&S.]
**Albright, Katharine M.** ..................... '67 '94 C.951 B.A. L.276 J.D. [Ⓐ Latham&W.]
Albright, Yee & Schmit ..................... 333 S. Grand Ave.
**Albus, Paul D.** ..................... '67 '93 C.112 B.A. L.569 J.D. [Ⓐ Charlston,R.&W.]
*PRACTICE AREAS: Environmental Insurance Coverage Defense; General Litigation.
Alcala, Michael ..................... '59 '89 C.112 B.A. L.1068 J.D. Fed. Pub. Def. Off.
**Alcaraz, Sharyn G.** ..................... '67 '93 C.112 B.A. L.770 J.D. [Ⓐ Murchison&C.]
*REPORTED CASES: %italic; Han v. City of Pomona%roman; (1995) 37 Cal. App. 4th 552.
*PRACTICE AREAS: Law and Motion; Appellate.
**Alch, Thomas S.** ..................... '63 '88 C.112 B.A. L.426 J.D. [Ⓐ La Follette,J.D.F.&A.]

**Alcorn, John R., Law Offices of**
**(See Newport Beach)**

**Alcumbrac, Marta A.** ..................... '66 '96 C.36 B.S. L.809 J.D. [Ⓐ Bonne,B.M.O.&N.]
*PRACTICE AREAS: Medical Malpractice Defense.
Alden, John W. '34 '60 C&L.813 B.S., J.D.
Assoc. Gen. Coun., Occidental Petroleum Corp.
**Alden, John W. (Jack), Jr.** ..................... '65 '90 C.813 A.B. L.228 J.D. [Ⓐ Morrison&F.]
Alden, Richard F., (AV) ..................... '24 '49 C&L.800 B.A., J.D. 11340 W. Olympic Blvd.‡
**Alderman, Daniel S.** ..................... '61 '86 C.112 B.A. L.464 J.D. [Kinkle,R.&S.]
**Alderton, Scott W.** ..................... '59 '85 C.112 B.A. L.426 J.D. [Troop M.S.&P.]
*PRACTICE AREAS: General Corporate Law; Corporate Securities Law; Mergers and Acquisitions Law.
**Aldisert, Gregory J.** ..................... '59 '84 C.453 B.S. L.1066 J.D. [Kinsella,B.F.&T.]
*PRACTICE AREAS: Entertainment Law; Commercial Litigation.
**Aldover, Ernesto F.** ..................... '65 '91 C.112 B.A. L.770 J.D. [Ⓐ Knopfler&R.]
*PRACTICE AREAS: Construction Defect Litigation; Personal Injury; Insurance Coverage.
Alef, Daniel, (AV) ..................... '44 '70 C.112 B.S. L.1068 J.D. 11845 W. Olympic Blvd.‡
**Alexander, Allan L.**, (AV) ...... '40 '66 C.813 A.B. L.309 LL.B. [Armstrong H.J.T.&W.]
*PRACTICE AREAS: Real Estate; Corporate; Business Law.
**Alexander, Anthony E.** ..................... '45 '74 C.112 B.S. L.800 J.D. [Ⓒ Atkins&E.]
*PRACTICE AREAS: Civil Litigation; Criminal Litigation.
Alexander, Daniel J. ..................... '68 '94 C.329 B.A. L.1068 J.D. 3699 Wilshire Blvd.
**Alexander, J. Bernard, III** ..................... '60 '87 C.112 B.A. L.809 J.D. [Alexander&Y.]
*PRACTICE AREAS: Civil Litigation; Insurance Defense; Insurance Fraud; Municipality and Peace Officer Defense; Business.
Alexander, L. Wayne ..................... '51 '76 C.112 A.B. L.976 J.D. [Alexander,H.N.&R.]
**Alexander, Lisa C.** ..................... '58 '86 C.112 B.A. L.800 J.D. [Kessler&K.]
*PRACTICE AREAS: Estate Planning; Corporate Law; Real Estate Law; Partnership Law; Limited Liability Company Law.
**Alexander, Lorie M.** ..................... '66 '92 C.112 B.A. L.1065 J.D. [Ⓐ Morrison&F.]
**Alexander, Mary C.** ..................... '59 '88 C.112 B.A. L.809 J.D. [Alexander&Y.]
*LANGUAGES: Spanish.
*PRACTICE AREAS: Probate, Trusts, Wills, Estate; Real Estate Transactions; Family Law.
**Alexander, Sarira D.** ..................... '62 '94 C.112 kB.A. L.1065 J.D. [Ⓐ Lewis,D.B.&B.]
*LANGUAGES: Farsi and French.
*PRACTICE AREAS: Intellectual Property; International Law.
**Alexander, Stephen D.** ..................... '49 '76 C.429 B.A. L.494 J.D. [Fried,F.H.S.&J.]
Alexander, Halloran, Nau & Rose, (AV) ..................... 2029 Century Park E.

**Alexander & Yong**
**10940 Wilshire Boulevard, Suite 2200, 90024**
**Telephone: 310-824-5254 Fax: 310-208-3493**
**Members of Firm: J. Bernard Alexander, III; Jeffrey S. Yong; Mary C. Alexander. Associates: Arturo D. Sanchez.**
**Business Litigation, Insurance Defense, Real Property, Bankruptcy, Trust and Estate Planning, Taxation, Probate, Conservatorships, China Trade and Investments, Corporate Transactions.**
***See Professional Biographies, LOS ANGELES, CALIFORNIA***

**Alexson, Harriet B.** ..................... '50 '83 C.94 B.S. L.800 J.D. [Ⓒ Buchalter,N.F.&Y.]
*PRACTICE AREAS: Corporate and Commercial Matters; Real Estate Law; Healthcare Matters; Software Licensing.
**Alfonzo, Rafael E.** ..................... '72 '96 C.477 B.A. L.273 J.D. [Brown,W.&C.]
*LANGUAGES: Spanish.

CAA172P

**Alger, Timothy L.** .................... '55 '92 C.776 B.A. L.426 J.D. [Ⓐ Gibson,D.&C.]
*PRACTICE AREAS: Media and Entertainment Litigation; Business Litigation.
Alikhan, Arif .................... '68 '93 C.112 B.A. L.426 J.D. 1800 Ave. of the Stars

**Alkana, Eugene S.**
**(See Pasadena)**

**Alkov, Leonard A.** .................... '47 '77 Hughes Aircraft Co.
**Allan, Aaron P.** .................... '61 '89 C.1097 B.A. L.426 J.D. [Ⓐ Proskauer R.G.&M.]
**Allan, Wallace M.** .................... '54 '81 C.112 A.B. L.273 J.D. [O'Melveny&M.]
*PRACTICE AREAS: Automobile Manufacturers Dealers Disputes; General Commercial Litigation.

**Allard, William J. '36 '73 C.1258 B.A. L.426 J.D.**
**12304 Santa Monica Boulevard, 3rd Floor, 90025-2558**
**Telephone: 310-442-6688 Fax: 310-442-6691**
***PRACTICE AREAS: Surety and Fidelity Law; Probate Law; Construction Law; Insurance Law. Surety and Fidelity, Probate, Construction and Insurance Law.**

**Allderdice, Linda Auerbach**, (AV) .................... '49 '73 C.966 B.A. L.273 J.D. [Allderdice&D.]
*PRACTICE AREAS: Labor and Employment Law (Management) and Related Litigation; Intellectual Property Litigation.
**Allderdice, Michael B.**, (AV) .................... '48 '74 C.902 B.S. L.273 J.D. [Ⓐ King,W.E.&B.]
*PRACTICE AREAS: Business; Real Estate and Land Use; Housing; Economic Development; Redevelopment.

**Allderdice and Denman, (AV)**
**Wilshire Park Place Suite 820, 3700 Wilshire Boulevard, 90010-3085**
**Telephone: 213-383-9500 Facsimile: 213-383-9666**
**Email: allden@aol.com**
**Members of Firm: Linda Auerbach Allderdice; Alexandra Denman. Of Counsel: Floran L. Fink.**
**Labor and Employment Law (Management), Entertainment and Intellectual Property Law and Related Litigation.**

***See Professional Biographies, LOS ANGELES, CALIFORNIA***

**Allegra, Kelly Marie** .................... '67 '94 C&L.800 B.S., J.D. [Ⓐ Wolf,R.&S.]
*PRACTICE AREAS: Community Association Law; Real Estate.
**Alleguez, Tina M.** .................... '61 '88 C.112 B.A. L.990 J.D. [Ⓐ Manning,M.&W.]
*LANGUAGES: Spanish; French.
**Allemeier, Daniel R.** .................... '48 '78 C.870 B.S. L.464 J.D. Hughes Aircraft Co.
Allen, Barbara A. .................... '59 '85 C.788 B.A. L.976 J.D. 300 S. Grand Ave.
Allen, Brian D. '62 '90 C.1209 B.S. L.1194 J.D.
(adm. in NY; not adm. in CA) IBM Corp.
**Allen, David S.** .................... '55 '81 C.112 A.B. L.1067 J.D. [Jackson,L.S.&K.]
**Allen, Frederick L.**, (AV) .................... '39 '67 C.813 A.B. L.1065 LL.B. [Allen,M.L.G.&M.]
*PRACTICE AREAS: Real Estate.
Allen, Gizella L., (Mrs.) .................... '12 '35 C.112 B.A. L.800 LL.B. 548 So. Spring St.‡
**Allen, Jeffrey S.** .................... '48 '65 C.813 B.S. L.1066 J.D. [Ⓒ Orrick,H.&S.]
*PRACTICE AREAS: Real Estate Law.
Allen, John D. S., (BV) .................... '42 '72 C.112 B.A. L.1065 J.D. Dep. Dist. Atty.
**Allen, John J.** .................... '48 '76 C.1042 B.A. L.426 J.D. [Graham&J.]
*PRACTICE AREAS: Environmental Law.
**Allen, Laurie A.** .................... '60 '89 C.112 B.A. L.245 J.D. [Brobeck,P.&H.]
**Allen, Mark C., Jr., (Professional Corporation)**, (AV) '22 '50
C&L.800 A.B., LL.B. [Ⓒ Burke,W.&S.]
*PRACTICE AREAS: Municipal Law.
**Allen, Philip C.** .................... '53 '77 C.1097 B.A. L.1049 J.D. [McHale&C.]
*PRACTICE AREAS: Insurance Defense; Products Liability; Construction.
Allen, Robin E. .................... '64 '91 C.112 B.A. L.464 J.D. Dep. Dist. Atty.
Allen, Ronald V. '58 '88 C.880 B.A. L.1137 J.D.
(adm. in DC; not adm. in CA) Resch. Atty., Calif. Supr. Ct.
**Allen, Terrence R.** .................... '67 '93 C&L.800 B.A.B.S., J.D. [Ⓐ O'Melveny&M.]
**Allen, Todd B.** .................... '69 '95 C.112 B.A. L.1068 J.D. [Ⓐ Hawkins,S.L.&B.]
Allen, Warren D. .................... '21 '51 C.112 L.1065 J.D. Supr. Ct. J.

**Allen, Matkins, Leck, Gamble & Mallory LLP, (AV)** BR
**A Limited Liability Partnership including Professional Corporations**
**Seventh Floor, 515 South Figueroa Street, 90071**⊙
**Telephone: 213-622-5555 Telecopier: 213-620-8816**
**Partners: Frederick L. Allen; John C. Gamble (Resident, Irvine Office); Brian C. Leck; Richard C. Mallory; Michael L. Matkins; Marvin E. Garrett; Michael E. Gleason (P.C.) (Resident, San Diego Office); Thomas C. Foster (Resident, Irvine Office); Robert J. Cathcart; R. Michael Joyce (Resident, Irvine Office); Gerben Hoeksma (Resident, West Los Angeles Office); Thomas W. Henning; Patrick E. Breen; Lawrence D. Lewis (P.C.) (Resident, Irvine Office); George T. McDonnell; Michael F. Sfregola; David A. B. Burton (P.C.); Monica E. Olson (Resident, Irvine Office); Thomas E. Gibbs (Resident, Irvine Office); Vernon C. Gauntt (Resident, San Diego Office); Dwight L. Armstrong (Resident, Irvine Office); Paul D. O'Connor (Resident, Irvine Office); S. Lee Hancock (Resident, Irvine Office); David L. Osias (San Diego and Los Angeles Offices); William R. Harmsen; Debra Dison Hall; Anton N. Natsis (Resident, West Los Angeles Office); George J. Berger (Resident, San Diego Office); Michael C. Pruter (Resident, San Diego Office); Michael H. Cerrina; Richard E. Stinehart (Resident, Irvine Office); Stephen R. Thames (Resident, Irvine Office); John K. McKay; Dana I. Schiffman (Resident, San Diego Office); Anne E. Klokow (Resident, Irvine Office); Neil N. Gluck; David W. Wensley (Resident, Irvine Office); Gary S. McKitterick (Resident, Irvine Office); Patrick J. Grady (Resident, Irvine Office); Ray B. Gliner (Resident, San Diego Office); Anthony S. Bouza; Charles N. Kenworthy (Resident, West Los Angeles Office); Anthony J. Oliva; Robert M. Hamilton (Resident, Irvine Office); David R. Zaro; Janet A. Winnick; Robert R. Barnes (Resident, San Diego Office); Vincent M. Coscino; Jeffrey R. Patterson (Resident, San Diego Office); Mark R. Hartney; John M. Tipton (Resident, West Los Angeles Office). Associates: Cheryl S. Rivers (Resident West Los Angeles Office); Craig D. Swanson (Resident, San Diego Office); Bradley N. Schweitzer (Resident, Irvine Office); Gregory G. Gorman; Alan J. Gordee (Resident, Irvine Office); Pamela L. Andes (Resident, Irvine Office); Rebecca L. Gundzik; Adela Carrasco (Resident, West Los Angeles Office); Martha K. Guy (Resident, San Diego Office); George W. Kuney (Resident, San Diego Office); Daniel L. Goodkin; Catherine M. Page (Resident, Irvine Office); Scott P. Schomer; Kelli L. Fuller (Resident, San Diego Office); Leslie Tucker Fischer (Resident, Irvine Office); Michael J. Kiely; David Adam Swartz (Resident, West Los Angeles Office); Ralph H. Winter (Resident, Irvine Office); Michael S. Greger (Resident, Irvine Office); A. Kristine Floyd (Resident, Irvine Office); Robert A. Lurie (Resident, West Los Angeles Office); Susan G. Spira; Cynthia Ann Eder; Michael A. Alvarado (Resident, Irvine Office); Hadar Gonen Goldstein; Mary Kay Ruck (Resident, Irvine Office); Eric J. Shelby (Resident, West Los Angeles Office); Susan E. Graham (Resident, Irvine Office); Martin L. Togni (Resident, San Diego Office); David T. Hathaway; Christopher G. Lund (Resident, Irvine Office); Loraine L. Pedowitz (Resident, San Diego Office); Randy J. Myricks; John G. Piano; Mark J. Hattam (Resident, San Diego Office); Michael R. Farrell; Stephen J. Kepler (Resident, Irvine Office); Steve Wellington (Resident, San Diego Office); Sally S. Costanzo (Resident, Irvine Office); Ann Marie Maas (Resident, San Diego Office); Todd E. Whitman; Allison L. Malin (Resident, West Los Angeles Office); Reon Roski-Amendola (Resident, West Los Angeles Office); Allison Fong Greenberg (Resident, Irvine Office); Jeffrey Mannisto (Resident, Irvine Office); Pamela M. Everett; Jeffrey N. Strug; Kathryn D. Horning; Jordan Fishman (Resident, West Los Angeles Office); Tracy L Silva (Resident, Irvine Office); Francis N. Scollan; Darren A. Manibog; Veena D. Persaud. Of Counsel: John G. Davies (Resident, San Diego Office); Joe M. Davidson (Resident, San Diego Office); Michael J. Murphy.**
**General Civil, Trial and Appellate Practice in all State and Federal Courts. Real Property and Construction Law. Land Use and Environmental Law, including Administrative and Regulatory Practice. Corporations, Securities, Partnerships and Public Bond Financings. Federal, State and Local Taxation. Labor and Employment Law (Management) and Wrongful Termination. Bankruptcy, Creditors Rights, Receiverships and Restructuring. Estate Planning and Trusts.**
**Reference: Wells Fargo Bank (Los Angeles Main Office).**
**Irvine, California Office: Fourth Floor, 18400 Von Karman, 92715. Telephone: 714-553-1313. Telecopier: 714-553-8354.**
**San Diego, California Office: 501 West Broadway, Suite 900, 92101. Telephone: 619-233-1155. Facsimile: 619-233-1158.**
**West Los Angeles, California Office: 1999 Avenue of the Stars, Suite 1800, 90067. Telephone: 310-788-2400. Fax: 310-788-2410.**

***See Professional Biographies, LOS ANGELES, CALIFORNIA***

**Allen-Niesen, Keith A.** .................... '61 '89 C.112 B.A. L.1067 J.D. [Ⓐ Pillsbury M.&S.]

**Allen, Rhodes, Sobelsohn & Johnson, LLP, (AV)** BR
**10866 Wilshire Boulevard, Suite 200, 90024**⊙
**Telephone: 310-475-0875; 213-879-9660**
**Members of Firm: Bernard Sobelsohn (Certified Specialist, Workers Compensation Law, The State Bar of California Board of Legal Specialization); Michael E. Johnson (Resident, Santa Barbara Office). Of Counsel: David B. Allen; J. Richard Rhodes (Certified Specialist, Workers' Compensation Law, The State Bar of California Board of Legal Specialization).**
**Workers Compensation, Subrogation, Insurance Law. Employment Law and Appellate Practice.**
**Reference: Wells Fargo Bank.**
**Santa Barbara, California Office: 125 East De La Guerra, 2nd Floor. Telephone: 805-965-5236.**

***See Professional Biographies, LOS ANGELES, CALIFORNIA***

Allenby, Leslie L. .................... '59 '88 C.336 B.A. L.809 J.D. Off. of Pub. Def.
Allensworth, Michael R. .................... '43 '70 C.112 B.A. L.1049 J.D. Dep. Pub. Def.
Allis, Nicholas R., Law Offices of .... '42 '71 C.976 B.A. L.276 J.D. 11601 Wilshire Blvd.
**Allison, Barney A.** .................... '54 '79 C.31 B.A. L.800 J.D. [Nossaman,G.K.&E.]
*PRACTICE AREAS: Municipal Finance Law.
**Allison, Dean B.** .................... '48 '74 C.103 B.A. L.569 J.D. [Jones,D.R.&P.]
**Allison, Susan** .................... '53 '80 C.813 B.A. L.1065 J.D. [Jeffer,M.B.&M.]
*PRACTICE AREAS: Civil Litigation.
**Allman, Kim** .................... '64 '92 C.66 B.B.A. L.1049 J.D. [Buchalter,N.F.&Y.]
*PRACTICE AREAS: Financial Institutions Litigation; Business Litigation.
Allread, Laurie K. .................... '60 '92 C.1111 B.A. L.1148 J.D. 1055 W. 7th St.
Allred, Gloria R. .................... '41 '75 C.659 B.A. L.426 J.D. [Allred,M.&G.]
**Allred, Kevin S.** .................... '60 '86 C.339 B.A. L.1066 J.D. [Munger,T.&O.]
Allred, Maroko & Goldberg, (AV) .................... 6300 Wilshire Blvd.
Allshouse, Mark W. .................... '53 '81 C&L.477 A.B., J.D. 1835 S. Shenandoah St.
**Allyn, Russell L.** .................... '64 '89 C.112 B.A. L.1065 J.D. [Katz,H.S.&K.]
*REPORTED CASES: In re Kingsley, Jennison McNulty & Morse, Inc., Adm. Prac. File No. 3-7446; Securities and Exchange Commission, Initial Decision, Release No. 24, 1991 SEC LEXIS 2587, November 14, 1991.
*PRACTICE AREAS: Business Litigation.
**Almeter, Kevin** .................... '62 '88 C.112 B.A. L.1067 J.D. [Ⓐ Cummins&W.]
*PRACTICE AREAS: Insurance Defense; Litigation.
Almond, Honi M. '52 '78 C.112 B.A. L.426 J.D.
Sr. V.P., Bus. Affs., Vin Di Bona Productions
Almond, Paul S. .................... '43 '68 C.112 B.S. L.1068 J.D. V.P., New World Pictures
**Alonzo, Arlyn** .................... '62 '96 C.800 B.S.A.E. L.426 J.D. [Ⓐ Lyon&L.]
*LANGUAGES: Taiwanese, Mandarin, Tagalog.
*PRACTICE AREAS: Patents; Trademarks; Copyrights; Intellectual Property.
**Alper, Andrew K.**, (AV) .................... '53 '79 C.112 B.A. L.426 J.D. [Glass,A.G.&C.]⊙
*PRACTICE AREAS: Banking Law; Commercial Law; Insolvency; Equipment/Personal Property Leasing; Secured Transactions.
Alper, Marilyn Weiss '50 '82 C.800 A.B. L.1136 J.D.
Sr. Jud. Research Atty., Ct. of App.
Alperin, Anthony S. .................... '46 '72 C.112 A.B. L.1068 J.D. Asst. City Atty.
Alpern, Eugene D. .................... '30 '59 C.112 L.426 J.D. 3030 W. Temple St.
**Alpert, Peter H., (Professional Corporation)** '48 '74
C.112 B.A. L.1065 J.D. [Resch P.A.&B.]
*PRACTICE AREAS: Real Estate; Business Law.

**Alpert, Barr and Gross, A Professional Law Corporation**
**(See Encino)**

Alschuler, Natt D, (BV) .................... '— '83 C.112 B.A. L.426 J.D. [Alschuler,A.A.&A.]
Alschuler, Walter W. .................... '18 '60 C.112 L.809 LL.B. [Alschuler,A.A.&A.]
Alschuler, Alschuler, Alschuler & Alschuler, A Professional Corporation, (BV)
1271 W. 2nd St.

**Alschuler Grossman & Pines LLP, (AV)** BR
**2049 Century Park East, Thirty-Ninth Floor, 90067-3213**
**Telephone: 310-277-1226 Fax: 310-552-6077**
**Email: info@agplaw.com URL: http://www.agplaw.com**
**Members of Firm: Leon S. Alschuler (1910-1987); Daniel Alberstone; Bruce D. Andelson; Jeffrey C. Briggs; Michael J. Brill (P.C.); Michael L. Cypers; Melvyn B. Fliegel (P.C.); Andrew D. Friedman; Bruce A. Friedman (P.C.); Dale J. Goldsmith; Marshall B. Grossman (P.C.); Carole E. Handler; Gerald B. Kagan (P.C.); Frank Kaplan (P.C.); Karen Kaplowitz (P.C.); Dana N. Levitt (P.C.); Kenneth S. Meyers; Burt Pines (P.C.); Gwyn Quillen; Paul H. Rochmes; John A. Schwimmer; Michael A. Sherman; Sandra G. Slon; William S. Small (P.C.); Pierre Vogelenzang (P.C.); Bruce Warner (P.C.); Karen Africk Wolfen; Joan A. Wolff. Associates: M. Cris Armenta; Betty Bales; Julian Brew; Rebecca Edelson; Yael Feinreich; Grant E. Finkle; Donald P. Harris; Johnnie A. James; Caroline S. Lee; Jonathan A. Loeb; Dana Milmeister; Jeffrey H. Mintz; Michael A. Taitelman. Of Counsel: Stanley S. Arkin; Eric van Ginkel.**
**General Civil and Trial Practice in all State and Federal Courts. Corporation, Securities, Real Estate, Land Use, Entertainment Law, Taxation, Antitrust, Administrative, Financial Institutions, Insurance, Municipal, Probate and Professional Liability Defense.**

***See Professional Biographies, LOS ANGELES, CALIFORNIA***

Alshuler, Herbert E .................... '57 '83 C.1077 B.S.B.A. L.809 J.D. [Alschuler,A.A.&A.]
**Alsnauer, Mary Ann** .................... '60 '85 C.294 B.A. L.930 J.D. [Ⓐ Murchison&C.]
*PRACTICE AREAS: Trial Practice; Products Liability Law; Premises Liability; Inadequate Security; Business Litigation.
**Alt, Trevor L.** .................... '68 '94 C.1060 B.S. L.990 J.D. [Pick&B.]
*PRACTICE AREAS: Bankruptcy; Civil Litigation; Telemarketing Law.
Altagen, Robert S. .................... '46 '73 C.112 B.A. L.1065 J.D. 12301 Wilshire Blvd.
Altenburg, John J. .................... '31 '68 C.112 B.A. 973 Bluegrass Lane
Alter, Marlene L. .................... '47 '85 C.112 B.A. L.1026 J.D. 10401 Wilshire Blvd.
Altfeld, Jennifer K. '65 '91 C.31 B.A. L.145 J.D.
1800 Ave. of the Stars, Suite 900 (Century City)
Althaus, Thomas Edward .................... '53 '81 C.112 B.A. L.426 J.D. Pub. Def. Off.
Althouse, Dennis L. .................... '65 '91 C&L.546 B.S., J.D. 624 S. Grand Ave.
**Altman, Bryan C.** .................... '60 '86 C.112 A.B. L.178 J.D. [Ⓐ McCambridge,D.&M.]
Altman, Donald A. '31 '63 C.102 B.S. L.564 LL.B.
(adm. in NY; not adm. in CA) Admn. Law J., Dept. of H. & H. S.
Altman, Jeffrey A., (AV) .................... '47 '74 C.112 B.A. L.61 J.D. [Reifman&A.]
**Altman, Jonathan E.** .................... '— '94 C.178 B.A. L.276 J.D. [Ⓐ Munger,T.&O.]
**Altman, Louis H.**, (AVⓉ) .................... '53 '78 C&L.846 B.A., J.D. [Cummins&W.]
*PRACTICE AREAS: Commercial Litigation; Bankruptcy.
Altman, Robert T. .................... '39 '64 C.112 A.B. L.309 LL.B. Supr. Ct. J.

**Altman & Schoemaker**
**(See Encino)**

**Altmayer, Thomas L.** .................... '66 '91 C.112 B.A. L.800 J.D. [Ⓐ Burke,W.&S.]
*PRACTICE AREAS: Corporate and Municipal Litigation; Environmental Law.
Altschul, John A. .................... '36 '63 C.112 A.B. L.1068 LL.B. 1180 S. Beverly Dr.
**Altschuld, Bruce E.** .................... '54 '83 C.567 B.A. L.809 J.D. [Ⓐ Fierstein&S.]
*PRACTICE AREAS: Real Estate; Business Law; Litigation.
Altschuler, Douglas H. .................... '55 '84 C&L.37 B.A., J.D. 611 W. 6th St., 20th Fl.
Alumbaugh, Scott E. .................... '58 '89 C.1169 B.A. L.1067 J.D. 550 S. Hope St.
Alva, Susan .................... '52 '83 L.1137 J.D. Coalition for Humane Immigrant Rights of L. A.
Alvarado, Donald G. '54 '82 C.426 B.A. L.800 J.D.
V.P. & Gen. Coun., Smart & Final Stores Corp.

CAA173P

CALIFORNIA—LOS ANGELES MARTINDALE-HUBBELL LAW DIRECTORY 1997

**Alvarado, Raymond G.**, (AV) ........'36 '72 C.800 B.A. L.809 J.D. [Alvarado,S.V.&S.]
*PRACTICE AREAS: Secured Transaction Litigation; Business Litigation.
Alvarado, Robert V., Jr. ................'58 '83 C.800 B.A. L.426 J.D. [Wapnick&A.]

**Alvarado, Smith, Villa & Sanchez, A Professional Corporation, (AV)**
**611 West Sixth Street, Suite 2650, 90017⊙**
**Telephone: 213-229-2554 Facsimile: 213-617-8966**
**URL: http://www.Alvarado-Smith.com**
**Residents: Raymond G. Alvarado; Fernando Villa; Raúl F. Salinas; J. Michelle Hickey; Frances Q. Jett; Susan Bade Hull;—Steven M. Lawrence; Robert W. Brown, Jr.; Steven C. Yung.**
**Sophisticated Business Transactions and Complex Litigation.**
**Newport Beach, California Office, 4695 MacArthur Court, Suite 800. 92658. Telephone: 714-955-1433. Fax: 714-955-1704.**
*See Professional Biographies, LOS ANGELES, CALIFORNIA*

Alvarez, Edna R.S., (AV) .....'39 '67 C.766 A.B. L.911 J.D. 10850 Wilshire Blvd., 4th Fl.
**Alvarez, M. Michelle** ......................'— '95 C.104 B.A. L.813 J.D. [Ⓐ Latham&W.]
*LANGUAGES: Spanish.
**Alvarez, Paul** ..............................'58 '84 C.112 B.A. L.426 J.D. [Kearney,B.&C.]
*LANGUAGES: Spanish.
Amado, Ralph A. ....................................'42 '69 C.800 B.S. L.1095 J.D. Mun. Ct. Comr.
Amador, Alicia ......................'61 '89 C&L.846 B.S.W., J.D. Offc. of U.S. Atty.
**Amador, Eric A.** ..................'63 '89 C.112 A.B. L.1065 J.D. [Bronson,B.&M.]
**Amador, Richard S.** .....................'63 '88 C.112 B.A. L.1066 J.D. [Sanchez&A.]
*PRACTICE AREAS: Business Litigation; Employment; Trademark Protection; Unfair Business Practices.
**Amantea, Chris M.** ...................'55 '89 C.112 B.S. L.46 J.D. [McDermott,W.&E.]
**Amberg, John W.** ..............................'51 '80 C.674 A.B. L.477 J.D. [Bryan C.]
*PRACTICE AREAS: Business and Commercial Litigation; Products Liability Law; Professional Liability Law.

**Ambrose, Dean V., (AV) '38 '65 C&L.208 B.S., J.D.**
**1901 Avenue of the Stars Suite 1551, 90067**
**Telephone: 310-785-9700 Fax: 310-556-1266**
**Partnership, Real Estate, Corporate, Securities and General Business Law.**
*See Professional Biographies, LOS ANGELES, CALIFORNIA*

Ambrose, Dean V., (AV) '38 '65
C&L.208 B.S., J.D. 10960 Wilshire Blvd. (⊙Santa Monica)
Ambrose, S. Robert, (AV) ...................'36 '62 C&L.426 B.S., LL.B. Asst. Co. Coun.
**Amdursky, Eric E.** ...................'69 '95 C.112 B.A. L.426 J.D. [Ⓐ O'Melveny&M.]
*PRACTICE AREAS: Corporate Law.
Ament, Gerald .......................'46 '71 C.569 B.A. L.94 J.D. 2861 Woodwardia Dr.‡
**Amer, A. (John) F.** ..........................'67 '94 C.112 B.A. L.426 J.D. [Ⓐ Lim,R.&K.]
*PRACTICE AREAS: Civil Litigation.
**Amer, Cynthia Lynn** '64 '94 C.1077 B.A. L.426 J.D.
Corp. Coun., The Times Mirror Co.
Amerson, Andrew D. ...................'44 '70 C.477 B.A. L.1068 J.D. Dep. Atty. Gen.
Amico, Joseph ..............................'37 '65 C&L.426 B.S., LL.B. Dep. Dist. Atty.
**Amini, Farzad E.** ...............'66 '96 C.800 B.S.E.E. L.426 J.D. [Ⓐ Blakely,S.T.&Z.]
**Amiri, Michael A.** ..................'67 '94 C.112 B.A. L.1065 J.D. [Ⓐ Jones,B.S.A.&F.]
Amkraut, D. M. H. ...................................'— '93 C.1169 B.S. 900 Wilshire Blvd.
Ammeian, Benjamin V. ........ '47 '79 C.1097 B.A. L.1136 J.D. 1605 W. Olympic Blvd.
**Ammeter, April L.** ..................................'63 '88 C&L.352 B.A., J.D. [Kirkland&E.]
*PRACTICE AREAS: Litigation.
**Ammons, David W.** '69 '94 C.800 B.A. L.477 J.D.
(adm. in OH; not adm. in CA) [Ⓐ Baker&H.]
*PRACTICE AREAS: Litigation.
**Amsden, John L.** ...............................'61 '88 C.506 B.S. L.276 J.D. [Hennigan,M.&B.]
Amtmanis, Liza ...................'47 '79 C.112 B.A. L.767 J.D. 555 S. Flower St., 29th Fl.
**Anabtawi, Iman** .....................'63 '92 C.668 B.A. L.813 J.D. [Ⓐ O'Melveny&M.]

**Ananda & Krause**
**(See Westlake Village)**

**Anapol, Neil R.** ............................'62 '89 C.597 B.S. L.112 J.D. [Ⓐ Pollak,V.&F.]
**Anastasia, Damon C.** ......................'66 '92 C.112 B.A. L.93 J.D. [Ⓐ Andrews&K.]
*PRACTICE AREAS: General Civil Litigation; Insurance Litigation; Commercial Litigation.
Anav, Gil ..........................................'63 '90 C.1036 B.A. L.178 J.D. 550 S. Hope St.
**Ancel, Mark G.**, (AV) ...................'24 '51 C&L.813 B.A., LL.B. [Stephens,B.&L.]
*PRACTICE AREAS: State and Local Tax; Probate; Estate Tax Valuation.
Ancker, Deanne B. ..........................'64 '90 C.893 B.A. L.276 J.D. Dep. Dist. Atty.
Andelson, Arlen H., (AV) ...............'44 '69 C.112 A.B. L.800 J.D. 8485 Melrose Pl.
**Andelson, Bruce D.**, (AV) ..........'50 '74 C.103 A.B. L.813 J.D. [Alschuler G.&P.]
Andersen, David G. ...............................'65 '91 C.112 B.A. L.596 J.D. 555 W. 5th st.
**Andersen, Susan K.** ......................'65 '90 C.489 B.A. L.809 J.D. [Ⓐ Grace,S.C.&S.]
*PRACTICE AREAS: Products Liability Law.

**Andersen, Keleher & Spata**
**(See Manhattan Beach)**

Anderson, Alison G. '43 '69 C.681 B.A. L.1066 J.D.
(adm. in MD; not adm. in CA) Prof. of Law, Univ. of Calif.
**Anderson, Allan E.** .....................'61 '88 C.112 A.B. L.767 J.D. [Ropers,M.K.&B.]
*PRACTICE AREAS: Civil Litigation.
**Anderson, C. David**, (AV) .................'43 '67 C.976 B.A. L.145 J.D. [Tuttle&T.]
*PRACTICE AREAS: Tax; Executive Employment Benefits.
Anderson, Carol F. .........................'47 '87 C.1077 B.A. L.809 J.D. [Anderson&W.]
**Anderson, Charles E.** ............'30 '55 C.800 B.B.A. L.597 LL.B. [Ⓟ Pillsbury M.&S.]
**Anderson, Charles R.**, (AV) .........'27 '53 C&L.347 B.S., J.D. [Ⓟ Anderson,A.L.&G.]
*PRACTICE AREAS: Corporate; Tax; Business.
Anderson, Edor G., III .......'57 '83 C.605 A.B. L.1049 J.D. 801 S. Grand Ave., 11th Fl.
**Anderson, Gregory L.** ......................'60 '87 C.768 B.S. L.809 J.D. [Ⓐ Dwyer,D.B.&B.]
**Anderson, Jeffrey M.** '64 '91
C.165 B.A. L.1356 J.D. [Ⓐ McCutchen,D.B.&E.] (⊙San Francisco)
*PRACTICE AREAS: Health Care; General Corporate.
Anderson, John E., (AV) ..................'17 '51 C.112 B.S. L.426 J.D. [Ⓟ Kindel&A.]
**Anderson, Judith L.** ...................'47 '86 C.696 B.A. L.1065 J.D. [Ⓐ Stroock&S.&L.]
**Anderson, Kenneth W.**, (AV) ............'40 '66 C&L.309 B.A., LL.B. [Gibson,D.&C.]
*PRACTICE AREAS: Labor Law Matters; Wrongful Termination Litigation; Title VII and EEO Matters; Collective Bargaining; Labor Arbitration.
**Anderson, Leighton M.** ....................'53 '78 C.154 B.A. L.178 J.D. [Smaltz,A.&F.]
*REPORTED CASES: Rebel Oil Co., Inc. v. ARCO, 51 F.3d 1421 (9th Cir. 1995); Little Oil Co., Inc. v. ARCO, 852 F.2d 441 (9th Cir. 1988); Orloff v. Allman, 819 F.2d 904 (9th Cir. 1987); Dyke v. Gulf Oil Corp., 601 F.2d 557 (Em. Appl. 1979); Southern Nevada Shell Dealers Assoc. v. Shell Oil Co., 725 F. Supp. 1104 (D. Nov. 1989).
*PRACTICE AREAS: Complex Business Litigation; Antitrust; Environmental.
**Anderson, LeRoy** .........................'49 '74 C.543 B.S. L.546 J.D. [Frandzel&S.]
*PRACTICE AREAS: Business Litigation; Bankruptcy Litigation; Bankruptcy Reorganization; Creditors' Rights; Secured Leasing.
**Anderson, Leslie G.**, (AV) ..................'35 '65 C.339 B.S. L.1065 J.D. [Ibold&A.]
Anderson, Linda Diane ................'46 '80 C.1077 B.A. L.809 J.D. 835 Wilshire Blvd.
Anderson, Lisa A. ........................'69 '93 C.813 A.B. L.112 J.D. 725 S. Figueroa St.
**Anderson, Melody G.** .....................'65 '94 C&L.800 B.A., J.D. [Ⓐ Goldman&G.]
*PRACTICE AREAS: Bankruptcy Law; Commercial Litigation; Debtor-Creditor Law.

**Anderson, Michael T.** ........................'63 '89 C&L.309 B.A., J.D. [Troop M.S.&P.]
*PRACTICE AREAS: Business Litigation; Entertainment Litigation.
Anderson, Patricia E. ........................'51 '76 C.112 B.A. L.1068 J.D. [Mantalica&T.]
**Anderson, Percy** ...................'49 '75 C.112 B.A. L.1068 J.D. [Sonnenschein N.&R.]
*PRACTICE AREAS: Litigation.
Anderson, Peter C. ..........................'57 '83 C.800 B.S. L.426 J.D. [Roquemore,P.&M.]
**Anderson, Robert M.** ..............'51 '77 C.260 B.A. L.1065 J.D. [Ⓐ Wilson,E.M.E.&D.]
**Anderson, Roy L.**, (AV) ........'57 '82 C.340 B.A. L.273 J.D. [Lyon&L.] (See Pat. Sect.)
*PRACTICE AREAS: Litigation; Patent, Trademark, Unfair Competition, Antitrust; Intellectual Property.

**Anderson, Sandra Jones '— '80 C.112 B.A. L.1148 J.D.**
**Thirty Seventh Floor, 777 South Figueroa Street, 90017-5800**
**Telephone: 213-892-7478 Facsimile: 213-892-7481**
**Email: sanderson@greenheart.com**
***PRACTICE AREAS: Health Care; Elder Law; Probate; Nonprofit and Charitable Organizations. Probate, Trusts, and Estate Planning, Tax Exempt Organizations, Real Estate, Elder Law.**
*See Professional Biographies, LOS ANGELES, CALIFORNIA*

**Anderson, Steven M.** .............'64 '89 C.112 B.S. L.309 J.D. [Ⓐ Quinn E.U.&O.] (Pat.)
*PRACTICE AREAS: Intellectual Property.
Anderson, Terry J. '36 '64 C.378 B.S.M.E. L.900 J.D.
Sr. Corp. Coun., Northrop Grumman Corp. (Pat.)
Anderson, Trent G., Jr., (AV) .....'17 '46 C.112 A.B. L.800 LL.B. 126 S. Windsor Blvd.‡
**Anderson, Victoria Lynn** '— '95 C.813 B.S. L.178 J.D.
(adm. in CT; not adm. in CA) [Ⓐ Skadden,A.S.M.&F.]
*LANGUAGES: French.
**Anderson, William G.** ...........'47 '75 C.701 B.S.M.E. L.365 J.D. [Ⓟ Graham&J.] (Pat.)
*PRACTICE AREAS: Intellectual Property.
Anderson, William H., (AV) ...............'21 '61 L.981 LL.B. 6222 Wilshire Blvd. 6th Fl.

**Anderson, Ablon, Lewis & Gale, LLP, (AV) BB**
**Suite 2000 Equitable Plaza Building, 3435 Wilshire Boulevard, 90010⊙**
**Telephone: 213-388-3385 Telecopier: 213-388-8432**
**Members of Firm: Robert E. Lewis; Jerald E. Gale; Harris D. Bass. Associates: Farhad Kazemzadeh; Candace Connart Bleifer; Robert David Schwartz. Of Counsel: Charles R. Anderson (Retired); Herman Ablon (Retired).**
**Civil Trial Practice, State and Federal Courts. Business Law, Commercial, Corporation, Taxation, Securities, Trusts, Probate and Real Property Law.**
**Representative Clients: Maremont Corp.; Chansler & Lyon Co., Inc.**
**Reference: Bank of America (Wilshire Center Branch).**
**Thousand Oaks, California Office: 220-H Briarwood Building, 299 West Hillcrest Drive, 91360. Telephone: 805-373-5273. Fax: 805-495-1456.**
*See Professional Biographies, LOS ANGELES, CALIFORNIA*

**Anderson, McPharlin & Conners, (AV)**
**A Partnership including Professional Corporations**
**One Wilshire Building, Nineteenth Floor, 624 South Grand Avenue, 90017-3320⊙**
**Telephone: 213-688-0080; 714-669-1609 Telecopier: 213-622-7594**
**Newton E. Anderson (1897-1967); William J. Conners (1911-1986); Kenneth E. Lewis (1919-1990). Members of Firm: Michael C. Phillips (P.C.); Thomas J. Casamassima; David T. DiBiase; Eric A. Schneider; Gary J. Valeriano; Jesse S. Hernandez; Joel A. Osman; Paul F. Schimley; Michael S. Robinson; Mark E. Aronson; Ann Graupmann Zuckerman; Brian S. Mizell (Resident, Riverside Office); Jane Ellen Randolph; Carleton R. Burch; Lisa Marie Le Nay Coplen. Associates: G. Wayne Murphy (P.C.); John J. Immordino; Wayne B. Ducharme; Paula G. Tripp; Marci L. Bolter; Jeanette E. Jerles; Ernest J. Bartlett; Steven R. Yee; Arnold W. Holaday (Resident, Riverside Office); Michael S. Barrett; Stewart Dennis Reid (Resident, Riverside Office); Judy Hawthorne-Waters; Regina R. Wong. Of Counsel: Eldon V. McPharlin; Nelson P. Steitz.**
**General Civil and Trial Practice in all State and Federal Courts. Fidelity and Surety, Environmental Litigation (Hazardous Waste, Toxic Torts), Products Liability, Property Insurance, Title Insurance, Maritime, Fire Insurance, Commercial and General Liability Insurance Defense, Insurance Coverage, Bad Faith Litigation, Business Torts, Architects' and Engineers' Errors and Omissions, Construction Litigation, Commercial Litigation, Banking, Labor and Professional Malpractice Law.**
**Representative Clients: American Reinsurance Co.; Employers Reinsurance Corp.; Fireman's Fund Insurance Co.; Ohio Casualty Insurance Co.; Globe Indemnity Co.; Royal Indemnity Co.; U.S. Fire Insurance Co.; Maryland Casualty Co.; U.S. Fidelity & Guaranty Co.**
**Riverside, California Office: 3750 University Avenue, Suite 225. Telephone: 909-787-1900. Telecopier: 909-787-6749.**
*See Professional Biographies, LOS ANGELES, CALIFORNIA*

**Anderson & Salisbury**
**(See Pasadena)**

Anderson & Wood ................................................. 12121 Wilshire Blvd.
Andion, James L., Law Offices of '50 '77 C.475 B.A. L.477 J.D.
409 N. Soto (⊙Pasadena)
**André, Gary Paul** ..........................'50 '83 C.475 B.S. L.1095 J.D. [Clopton,P.&B.]
**Andrea, Janet** ......................'60 '86 C.800 B.A. L.1065 J.D. [Ⓐ Bronson,B.&M.]
*PRACTICE AREAS: Civil Litigation; Bad Faith Litigation.
**Andrea, Nicholas R.** ......................'68 '93 C.999 B.A. L.990 J.D. [Ⓐ Lynberg&W.]
*PRACTICE AREAS: Environmental Insurance Coverage; Toxic Tort.
**Andreani, Robert P.** ...............................'55 '80 C.813 B.A. L.800 J.D. [Arter&H.]
*LANGUAGES: Italian, French, Spanish.
*PRACTICE AREAS: Real Estate; Corporate and Commercial Law; Environmental Law.
**Andrew, Joanne M.**, (CV) ..........'49 '82 C.1109 B.A. L.1137 J.D. [Ⓐ Veatch,C.G.&N.]
Andrews, Alexandrea ................'— '93 C.280 A.B.J. L.174 J.D. 5757 Wilshire Blvd.
**Andrews, Camilla N.** .....................'58 '86 C.770 B.A. L.426 J.D. [Ⓟ Ivanjack&L.]
*LANGUAGES: French.
*PRACTICE AREAS: Commercial Litigation; Creditors' Rights; Contract Disputes; Financial Institution Litigation; Creditor Bankruptcy.
Andrews, Cecelia R. '48 '74 C.659 B.S. L.309 J.D.
Exec. V.P., Bus. Affs., Network T.V. Group, Paramount Pictures Corp.
**Andrews, Dawn R.** ......................'66 '92 C.446 B.S. L.112 J.D. [Ⓐ Freilich,K.F.&S.]
**Andrews, Douglas W.** ...........'58 '85 C&L.101 B.A., J.D. [Breidenbach,B.H.H.&H.]⊙
**Andrews, John E.** ...........................'50 '82 C.550 B.A. L.982 J.D. [Blecher&C.]
*PRACTICE AREAS: Antitrust; Intellectual Property; Entertainment Litigation.
**Andrews, Joseph M.**, (AV) ................'51 '78 C.112 B.A. L.1065 J.D. [Andrews&H.]
*REPORTED CASES: Employers Reinsurance Corp. v. Phoenix Insurance Co., 186 Cal. App. 3d 545, 230 Cal. Rptr. 792 (1986); Kane, Kane & Kritzer v. Altagen, 107 Cal. App. 3d 36, 165 Cal. Rptr. 534 (1980).
*PRACTICE AREAS: Civil Litigation.
**Andrews, Kathleen K.** ......................'60 '87 C.112 B.A. L.809 J.D. [Ⓐ Pollak,V.&F.]

**Andrews & Hensleigh, LLP, (AV)**
**700 South Flower Street 11th Floor, 90017**
**Telephone: 213-892-6364 Fax: 213-892-2265**
**Members of Firm: Joseph M. Andrews; Barbara J. Hensleigh. Associate: John J. Aumer.**
**General Civil Trial, Business Litigation, Commercial Litigation, Insurance Law and Tort.**
*See Professional Biographies, LOS ANGELES, CALIFORNIA*

**Andrews & Kurth L.L.P., (AV) BB**
**Suite 4200, 601 S. Figueroa Street, 90017⊙**
**Telephone: 213-896-3100 Telecopier: 213-896-3137**
**Members of Firm: Steven H. Haney; David J. Johnson, Jr.; William H. Lancaster; Carl B. Phelps; Shelly Rothschild; Ralph W. Tarr; Michael T. Williams. Of Counsel: Marta Thoerner Kurland; Diane C. Weil. Associates: Damon C. Anastasia; Graeme Lawrence Currie; Jon L. R. Dalberg; John L. House; Diana J. Hunt; Charles Gustaf Klink (Not admitted in CA); Gregg J. Loubier; David W. Meadows; Gabriela Mejia; Audra M. Mori; Rebecca O'Malley; Daniel F. Passage (Not admitted in CA); Steven L. Satz.**
**General Civil Practice, Antitrust, Asset Securitization, Bankruptcy and Business Reorganization, Biotechnology, Corporate and Securities, Energy Regulatory, Environmental, Natural Resources,**

(This Listing Continued)

**Andrews & Kurth L.L.P. (Continued)**

**Health and Safety, Finance, Intellectual Property, International, Labor and Employment, Litigation, Oil and Gas, Real Estate, Taxation, Utility. Trial of Civil Cases in all Courts.**
**Houston, Texas Office: Suite 4200, 600 Travis, 77002. Telephone: 713-220-4200. Telecopier: 713-220-4285. E-Mail: webmaster@andrews-kurth.com.**
**Washington, D.C. Office: Suite 200, 1701 Pennsylvania Avenue, N.W. Telephone: 202-662-2700. Telecopier: 213-896-3137.**
**Dallas, Texas Office: Suite 4400, 1601 Elm Street. Telephone: 214-979-4400. Telecopier: 214-979-4401.**
**The Woodlands, Texas Office: Suite 150, 2170 Buckthorne Place, 77380. Telephone: 713-220-4801. Telecopier: 713-364-9538. E-Mail: hightech@andrews-kurth.com.**
**New York, N.Y. Office: 425 Lexington Avenue. Telephone: 212-850-2800. Telecopier: 212-850-2929.**
**London, England Office: 2 Creed Court, 5-11 Ludgate Hill, EC4M 7AA. Telephone: 0171-236-3456. Telefax: 0171-236-4276.**

***See Professional Biographies, LOS ANGELES, CALIFORNIA***

Androlia, William L., (AV) '44 '73 C.112 B.S.E.E. L.426 J.D. 1880 Century Pk. E. (Pat.)
Andrues, Mary Carter .... '54 '88 C.378 B.S. L.800 J.D. U.S. Atty's Off.
**Andrus, Sarah K.** .... '69 '94 C.477 A.B. L.1068 J.D. [🄰 Fainsbert,M.&S.]
Angarella, Steven V. .... '60 '85 C.676 B.A. L.990 J.D. [Vastano&A.]
Angel, Frank P. .... '53 '84 C.061 L.1068 LL.M. 10951 W. Pico Blvd., 3rd Fl.
**Angel, Michael A.**, (AV) .... '47 '73 C.112 B.A. L.1049 J.D. [Angel&N.]
*PRACTICE AREAS: Civil Litigation; Corporate.
**Angel, Richard S.** .... '58 '83 C.112 B.S. L.800 J.D. [Buchalter,N.F.&Y.]
*PRACTICE AREAS: Real Estate Development; Acquisition; Sales & Leasing.
Angel, Robert M. .... '53 '78 C.112 A.B. L.1068 J.D. [Myman,A.F.G.&R.]

**Angel and Neistat, A Professional Corporation, (AV) BB**
**28th Floor 555 South Flower Street, 90017-2205**
**Telephone: 213-689-4500 Fax: 213-689-4651**
**Michael A. Angel; Douglas M. Neistat; Alan Holmberg; Steven L. Crane; Steven A. Schwaber; Alan J. Stomel; Gary R. Wallace; Daniel H. Reiss.**
**Civil Litigation in State and Federal Courts. Business, Real Property, Secured Transactions, Bankruptcy, Insolvency, Corporation and Banking Law.**

***See Professional Biographies, LOS ANGELES, CALIFORNIA***

Angelastro, Linette B. .... '65 '90 C.112 B.A. L.1292 J.D. Dist. Coun., I.R.S.
**Angelo, Christopher E.**, (AV) .... '49 '76 C.112 B.A. L.426 J.D. [Mazursky,S.&A.]
*REPORTED CASES: Trial and appellate counsel: Mora v. Baker Commodities (1989) 210 Cal.App. 3d 771, 258 Cal. Rptr. 699 (Also Basi; 8. 20. 1); Street v. Superior Court (1990) 224 Cal. App. 3d 1397, 274 Cal. Rptr. 595; Moore v. Regents of the University of California (1990) 51 Cal. 3d 120, 271 Cal. Rptr. 146; Lipton v. Lawyers Mutual, 56 Cal. Rptr. 2d 341.
*PRACTICE AREAS: Insurance Law; Commercial Bad Faith Law; Products Liability Law; Environmental Torts; Professional Liability Law.

**Anglea & Bannon, A Professional Corporation**
**(See Pasadena)**

**Anglin, John M.**, (AV) .... '47 '72 C&L.800 A.B., J.D. [Walker,W.T.&W.]
*PRACTICE AREAS: Real Estate; Corporate; Banking.
**Angvire, Leon S., (P.C.)**, (AV) .... '28 '55 C.112 B.S. L.1068 LL.B. [Hill,F.&B.]
*PRACTICE AREAS: Federal Taxation; State Taxation; Corporate Tax Planning; Closely Held Corporations; Probate Administration.
Anh, William Vu Tam .... '66 '93 C.112 B.A. L.426 J.D. 1880 Century Park East
**Aniel, Jan Harris** .... '53 '82 C.112 B.A. L.800 J.D. Sr. Coun., Bank of Amer.

**Anker & Hymes, A Law Corporation**
**(See Encino)**

**Annick, Nancy McAniff** .... '64 '91 C.276 B.A. L.1066 J.D. [🄰 Sheppard,M.R.&H.]
**Annis, Michael B.** .... '63 '92 C.629 B.S. L.276 J.D. [🄰 Graham&J.]
**Ansberry, Susan W.** .... '60 '85 C.770 B.A. L.1066 J.D. [🄰 Folger L.&K.]⊙
**Anschell, Jonathan H.** .... '68 '92 C&L.025 B.A., LL.B. [🄰 White O.C.&A.]
*PRACTICE AREAS: Civil Litigation; Media Law; Entertainment Law.
Anschultz, Andrew S. .... '61 '96 C.1042 B.A. L.940 J.D. 12400 Wilshire Blvd.
Ansell, Gerald, (AV) .... '33 '59 C.112 B.A. L.800 LL.B. 611 S. Shatto Pl.
**Ansis, Fredric W.**, (AV) .... '41 '69 C.105 B.A. L.262 J.D. [Hall D.K.F.&W.]
*PRACTICE AREAS: Entertainment Law; Intellectual Property Law; Advertising Law.
Anson, Jeffrey M. .... '47 '77 C.766 B.A. L.426 J.D. 3660 Wilshire Blvd.
Antablin, Drew R. .... '52 '77 C.112 B.A. L.426 J.D. [Cheong&D.]
Anthony, Bert V. .... '46 '73 C.112 B.A. L.1067 J.D. 3250 Wilshire Blvd.
**Anthony, Chow Siu Wo** '56 '91 C.038 B.A.S. L.472 J.D. (adm. in NY; not adm. in CA) [🄰 Arnberger,K.B.&C.]
*LANGUAGES: Cantonese, English and Mandarin.
*PRACTICE AREAS: Corporate and Commerical; Litigation; Real Estate and Mortgage Remedies.
**Anthony, Elizabeth Skorcz** .... '64 '92 C.951 B.A. L.1068 J.D. [🄰 Horvitz&L.]
Anthony, Pamela M. .... '47 '79 C.494 L.1148 J.D. 888 S. Figueroa St.
**Antin, Michael**, (AV) .... '38 '64 C.112 B.S. L.1066 J.D. [Antin&T.]
*PRACTICE AREAS: Taxation Law; Estate Planning Law; Corporate Planning Law; Probate Law.

**Antin & Taylor, (AV) BB**
**1875 Century Park East, Suite 700, 90067**
**Telephone: 310-788-2733 Fax: 310-788-0754**
**Email: mantin@ix.netcom.com**
**Members of Firm: Michael Antin (Certified Specialist, Taxation Law, The State Bar of California Board of Legal Specialization); Michael L. Taylor.**
**Taxation, Estate Planning, Pension and Profit Sharing and General Business Law.**

***See Professional Biographies, LOS ANGELES, CALIFORNIA***

**Antion, D. Stephen** .... '61 '86 C.112 A.B. L.1066 J.D. [O'Melveny&M.]
*PRACTICE AREAS: Corporate Law; Securities; Mergers, Acquisitions and Divestitures; Computers and Software.
**Antola, A. Victor**, (AV) .... '45 '70 C.112 A.B. L.477 J.D. [Latham&W.]
**Antoni, John D.** .... '67 '93 C.228 B.A. L.800 J.D. [🄰 Charlston,R.&W.]
**Aoyama, K. Tomoko** .... '64 '93 C.914 B.A. L.93 J.D. [🄰 Heller E.W.&M.]
*LANGUAGES: Japanese.
**Aparicio, Francisco Javier** .... '59 '87 C.800 A.B. L.1068 J.D. [🄰 Kelley D.&W.]
*PRACTICE AREAS: Project Finance; Real Estate; Political Law.
Apel, Richard T., (AV) .... '31 '59 C.112 A.B. L.1068 J.D. Co. Supr. Ct.
**Apfel, Gary** .... '52 '77 C.569 B.A. L.178 J.D. [Kaye,S.F.H.&H.]
*PRACTICE AREAS: Contract Law; Corporate Law; Private Placements; Project Finance; Public Offerings.
**Aponte, Lester F.** .... '64 '89 C.311 B.A. L.178 J.D. [🄰 Epstein B.&G.]
*PRACTICE AREAS: Labor and Employment Law; Litigation.
**Appel, Howard M.** .... '54 '92 C.112 B.S. L.1066 J.D. [🄰 Hughes H.&R.]
**Appel, Martin S.**, (AV) .... '33 '56 C&L.597 B.S., J.D. [Troop M.S.&P.]
**Appel, Sherry L.** .... '65 '93 C.112 B.S. L.1066 J.D. [🄰 Tuttle&T.]
Appell, Marc J. .... '65 '91 C.112 B.A. L.464 J.D. 1801 Century Park E.
Apperson, Ron '34 '63 C.668 B.A. L.1066 LL.B. Legal Advsr., Los Angeles Unified School Dist.
Apple, Irving D. .... '25 '56 8752 Holloway Dr.
**Applebaum, Amy L.** .... '44 '80 C.319 B.A. L.1068 J.D. [Sidley&A.]
*PRACTICE AREAS: Litigation; Insurance Coverage Disputes.
**Applebaum, Martha L.** .... '64 '90 C.881 B.A. L.262 J.D. [🄰 Graham&J.]
Applebaum, Mindy A. .... '64 '90 C.112 B.A. L.800 J.D. 2049 Century Park E.
Applegate, Susan L. .... '— '90 C.787 B.A. L.1065 J.D. Propaganda Films

**Applequist, Kimberly F.** .... '66 '95 C.878 B.A. L.800 J.D. [🄰 Foley L.W.&A.]
*PRACTICE AREAS: Health Care; Hospitals; Corporate Law.
Appleton, Byron Y. .... '31 '65 C.112 A.B. L.809 J.D. 3122 S. Bentley Ave.
**Appleton, Heather** .... '67 '92 C.112 B.A. L.426 J.D. [🄰 Appleton,P.&P.]
**Appleton, Mary Moss** .... '48 '94 C.1077 B.A. L.112 J.D. [🄰 Gansinger,H.B.&P.]
**Appleton, Peter M.**, (AV) .... '42 '67 C.112 A.B. L.1068 J.D. [Appleton,P.&P.]

**Appleton, Pasternak & Pasternak, A Law Corporation, (AV)**
**1925 Century Park East, Suite 2140, 90067-2722**
**Telephone: 310-553-1500 Facsimile: 310-553-1540**
**Peter M. Appleton; Cynthia F. Pasternak; David J. Pasternak;—Heather Appleton.**
**The Firm Practice includes Receiverships and Litigation in the areas of Complex Business, Employment, Environmental Law, Family Law, Personal Injury, Real Estate, Unfair Competition and Alternative Dispute Resolution.**

***See Professional Biographies, LOS ANGELES, CALIFORNIA***

Aprahamian, Mark H. .... '46 '79 C.1097 B.S. L.1136 J.D. 3250 Wilshire Blvd.
**April, Rand S.** .... '51 '76 C.597 B.A. L.178 J.D. [Skadden,A.S.M.&F.]
**Apt, Gloria Kurman** .... '54 '80 C.112 B.A. L.1148 J.D. [🄰 Fonda,G.H.&D.]
*LANGUAGES: Spanish and French.
*PRACTICE AREAS: Medical Malpractice Defense Law.
Aquavia, James '34 '63 C.191 B.A. L.910 J.D. Reg. Coun., Prudential Ins. Co. of Amer., The
Aragon, Ellen .... '55 '83 C.276 B.S.F.S. L.800 J.D. Dep. Dist. Atty.
**Aragon, Rebecca M.** .... '57 '87 C.976 B.A. L.276 J.D. [Parker,M.C.O.&S.]
*LANGUAGES: Spanish.
*SPECIAL AGENCIES: California Department of Fair Employment and Housing; Equal Employment Opportunity Commission.
*PRACTICE AREAS: Employment; Labor Law and Litigation; Management; Civil Litigation.
**Arai, Toshiyuki** .... '56 '85 C.061 B.A. L.188 LL.M. [Paul,H.J.&W.]
Arakawa, Gregory P. .... '63 '94 C.800 B.A. L.809 J.D. 624 S. Grand Ave.
**Araki, Kenneth T.** .... '63 '90 C.312 B.A. L.1066 J.D. [🄰 Paul,H.J.&W.]
Aran, Kenneth J., (AV) .... '40 '66 C.112 B.S. L.1068 J.D. [Aran&M.]
Aran & Miller, (AV) .... 11766 Wilshire Blvd.
Aranas, Pauline M. .... '54 '82 C.112 B.A. L.800 J.D. Assoc. Dir., USC Law Ctr.
**Aranoff, Mel, (P.C.)**, (AV) .... '50 '75 C.112 B.A. L.1068 J.D. [Horgan,R.B.&C.]
*LANGUAGES: Hebrew.
*PRACTICE AREAS: Complex Commercial Litigation; Bankruptcy; Creditors' Rights; Real Estate Receiverships; Loan Work-Outs.
Aranovich, Florencia R. .... '68 '94 C.112 B.A. L.276 J.D. 1925 Century Park East
**Arant, Gene W.**, (AV) '20 '50 C.628 B.S.E.E. L.800 J.D. [Arant,K.L.&R.] (See Pat. Sect.)
*PRACTICE AREAS: Counseling; Alternative Dispute Resolution; Licensing; Domestic and Foreign Patent and Trademark Prosecution.

**Arant, Kleinberg, Lerner & Ram, LLP, (AV)**
**Suite 1080, 2049 Century Park East (Century City), 90067-3112**
**Telephone: 310-557-1511 Telex: 5101012414 AKL LAX Cable Address: "PTCLAW" Facsimile: 310-557-1540**
**Members of Firm: Gene W. Arant; Marvin H. Kleinberg; Marshall A. Lerner; Michael J. Ram; Bradford E. Mattes; Michael R. Diliberto. Associate: Michael T. Smith.**
**Civil Trial and Appellate Practice in All State and Federal Courts Regarding Patents, Trademarks, Copyrights, Antitrust, Unfair Competition and Intellectual Property Law, Entertainment and Music Litigation and General Business Litigation. Transactional Matters For Corporate and Entertainment Law.**
**Reference: First Los Angeles Bank, Avenue of the Stars, Los Angeles, Calif.**

***See Professional Biographies, LOS ANGELES, CALIFORNIA***

**Arao, John**, (AV) .... '51 '81 C.309 A.B. L.976 J.D. [Loeb&L.]
*PRACTICE AREAS: Taxation.
**Arar, Roger M.** .... '55 '83 C.976 B.A. L.178 J.D. [Loeb&L.]
*LANGUAGES: French.
*PRACTICE AREAS: Entertainment Law.
**Arata, Elsa Ward** .... '68 '92 C&L.425 B.A., J.D. [🄰 Kaye,R.]
Aratani, Dana M. .... '59 '89 C.1097 B.S. L.940 J.D. Dep. Dist. Atty.
**Arato, Alexander G.** .... '63 '89 C.112 B.A. L.978 J.D. [🄰 Heller E.W.&M.]
**Arato, Cynthia S.** .... '64 '91 C.659 B.A. L.178 J.D. [🄰 Blanc W.J.&K.]
*REPORTED CASES: Abdul-Jabbar v. General Motors Corp., 75 F.3d 1391 (9th Cir. 1996).
*PRACTICE AREAS: Commercial Litigation; Proprietary Rights Litigation; Employment Law; Discrimination Law.
**Arbetter, Brian S.** .... '66 '92 C.910 B.S. L.145 J.D. [🄰 Mitchell,S.&K.]
*PRACTICE AREAS: Labor Law; Employment Law; Employment Discrimination Law.
**Arbisser, Aton** .... '56 '84 C.674 A.B. L.1066 J.D. [Kaye,S.F.H.&H.]
*PRACTICE AREAS: Administrative Law Litigation; Antitrust Law; False Advertising Litigation; Trademark Litigation; Unfair Competition Claims.
**Arbiter, Ross** .... '51 '77 C.112 A.B. L.800 J.D. [Solish,A.&G.]
*PRACTICE AREAS: Business Transactions; Medical Compliance; Real Estate; Tax.
**Arboles, Monika M.** .... '67 '94 C.112 B.A. L.800 J.D. [🄰 Breidenbach,B.H.H.&H.]
*LANGUAGES: Spanish.
**Arbuss, Steven B.** .... '59 '84 C.188 B.S. L.1068 J.D. [🄲 Pircher,N.&M.]
*PRACTICE AREAS: Real Estate Law; Entertainment; Multimedia.
**Archer, Steven D.**, (AV) .... '48 '75 C.112 B.A. L.426 J.D. [Robins,K.M.&C.]
*PRACTICE AREAS: Medical Malpractice; Product Liability Law; Professional Liability; Tort and Personal Injury; Workers Compensation.
Archer, William .... '56 '86 C&L.37 B.A., J.D. 555 W. 5th St.
Archuletta, Gilbert M. .... '39 '75 C.999 L.1152 J.D. 355 S. Grand Ave.
**Arciniega, Jorge**, (AV) .... '57 '83 C.112 B.A. L.309 J.D. [Graham&J.]
*LANGUAGES: Spanish.
*PRACTICE AREAS: International Law; Intellectual Property; Business.
Ardis, Stephen B. .... '62 '92 C.112 B.A. L.800 J.D. [🄰 Pollet&W.]
Ardura, Carol J. '34 '68 C.1042 L.809 LL.B. Div. Claims Mgr., Auto. Club of Southern Calif.
Arenberg, Stanley I. .... '33 '61 C&L.597 B.Sc., J.D. 11377 W. Olympic Blvd.
Arenella, Peter L. '47 '72 C.918 B.A. L.309 J.D. (adm. in MA; not adm. in CA) Prof. of Law, U.C.L.A. Law Sch.
**Arens, John J.** .... '67 '95 C&L.1049 B.A., J.D. [🄰 Booth,M.&S.]
**Arentz, Paul F.** .... '66 '93 C.37 B.A. L.1188 J.D. [🄰 Bonne,B.M.O.&N.]
*LANGUAGES: German.
Arfa, Fay .... '51 '81 C.112 B.A. L.809 J.D. 10850 Wilshire Blvd.
**Argue, Douglas W.**, (AV) .... '31 '56 C&L.846 B.A., LL.B. [Richards,W.&G.]
*PRACTICE AREAS: Federal Income and Estate Taxation; State Income; Sales, Employment and Property Taxation; Tax Planning; Administrative Practice.
**Argue, John C.**, (AV) .... '32 '57 C.605 A.B. L.800 LL.B. [Argue P.H.&M.]

**Argue Pearson Harbison & Myers, (AV)**
**A Partnership including a Professional Corporation**
**801 South Flower Street Suite 500, 90017-4699**
**Telephone: 213-622-3100 Telecopier: 213-622-7575**
**Members of Firm: Louis W. Myers (1943-1993); Don M. Pearson (A Professional Corporation); Stephen F. Harbison; William A. Jones; Jerry K. Staub; Douglas F. Galanter; Anthony M. Vienna; Philip J. Kaplan; Richard G. Rasmussen. Associates: Thomas Schalow; Patricia Venegas; Scott Chaplan; Andrea L. Esterson. Of Counsel: John C. Argue.**

(This Listing Continued)

CAA175P

**Argue Pearson Harbison & Myers (Continued)**

General Business and Civil Litigation Practice. Corporation, Securities, Real Estate and Partnership Law. Finance, Regulatory, International, Federal and State Taxation, Pension and Profit Sharing, Labor and Employment, Estate Planning, Trust and Probate Law, Insurance Coverage, Nonprofit Corporation.

*See Professional Biographies, LOS ANGELES, CALIFORNIA*

Argueta, Silvia R. ....................'63 '89 C.112 B.A. L.1065 J.D. 3435 Wilshire Blvd.
**Arias, Mickel M.** ....................'59 '84 C.1102 B.S. L.990 J.D. [Arias&O.]
*PRACTICE AREAS: Business Litigation; Entertainment Litigation; Personal Injury; Negligence; Sports Law.
**Arias, Richard M.** ....................'46 '73 C&L.426 B.S., J.D. [Murchison&C.]
*PRACTICE AREAS: General Insurance Defense Litigation.
Arias, Yolanda ....................'61 '87 C.800 B.A. L.1068 J.D. Legal Aid Found. of L.A.

**Arias & Ozzello, A Professional Corporation**
**11766 Wilshire Boulevard Suite 720, 90025-6538**
Telephone: 310-478-1212 Fax: 310-474-8884
Mickel M. Arias; Mark A. Ozzello.
Civil Litigation, Corporate, Business and Entertainment Litigation, Real Estate and Investment Fraud, Major Personal Injury, Product Liability, Negligence, Insurance Law and Class Action Litigation. Construction Defect, Wrongful Death, Harassment, Discrimination, Premises and Product Liability, Breach of Contract, Insurance Defense.

*See Professional Biographies, LOS ANGELES, CALIFORNIA*

**Arico, James S.** ....................'58 '87 C.800 B.S. L.426 J.D. [Clark&T.]
*PRACTICE AREAS: Real Estate; Real Estate Leasing; Sports Law; General Corporate.
Ariel, Frank Y. ....................'66 '92 C.112 B.A. L.1148 J.D. 1801 Century Park E.
**Ariey, Janine Y.** ....................'49 '80 C.112 B.A. L.1068 J.D. [A Riordan&M.]
*PRACTICE AREAS: Real Estate.
**Aristei, J. Clark, (AV)** ....................'48 '75 C.1042 B.A. L.1049 J.D. [Baum,H.A.G.&D.]
*REPORTED CASES: Penner v. Falk, 153 Cal. App. 3d 858, 200 Cal. Rptr. 661 (1984); Geffen v. County of Los Angeles, 197 Cal. App. 3d 188, 242 Cal. Rptr. 492 (1987).
*PRACTICE AREAS: Catastrophic Injury; School Bus Accidents; Wrongful Death; Products Liability; Railroad Accidents and Injuries.
**Arjomand, Mehran** ....................'69 '95 C&L.112 B.S., J.D. [A Troop M.S.&P.]
*PRACTICE AREAS: General Business Litigation.
**Arkin, Allison Sher** ....................'63 '92 C.918 B.A. L.262 J.D. [A McDermott,W.&E.]
Arkin, Edward D. ....................'43 '93 C.112 B.S. L.890 J.D. 16055 Ventura Blvd. (Encino)
Arkush, J. Robert, (AV) ....................'06 '32 C.112 A.B. L.813 J.D. 3580 Wilshire Blvd.
Arky, Lauren S. ....................'56 '81 C.1111 B.A. L.809 J.D. City Atty's. Off.
Arlen, Jennifer '59 '87 C.309 B.A. L.569 J.D.
(adm. in NY; not adm. in CA) Prof. of Law, Univ. of Calif.
**Arlow, Donna P.** ....................'56 '81 C.1042 B.A. L.1049 J.D. [Bronson,B.&M.]
*PRACTICE AREAS: Insurance Coverage Litigation.
Armagost, John W., (P.C.), (AV) ....................'30 '57 C&L.813 A.B., LL.B. [B Kindel&A.]
**Armbrister, Cyril E. "Ted", Jr., (AV)** '40 '68
C.668 B.A. L.809 [Long&L.] (⊙Santa Monica)
Armbruster, Mark S., (AV) ....................'49 '78 C.112 B.A. L.426 J.D. 828 Moraga Dr., 2nd Fl.
Armen, Christopher T. ....................'55 '82 C.112 B.A. L.809 J.D. 205 S. Broadway.
**Armenta, M. Cris** ....................'— '95 C.112 B.A. L.426 J.D. [A Alschuler G.&P.]
**Armitage, Angela J.** ....................'68 '94 C.112 B.A. L.426 J.D. [A Kern,S.&G.]
*PRACTICE AREAS: Employment Discrimination; Medical Malpractice; Products Liability.
**Armstrong, Arthur O., (AV)** '29 '59 C.763 B.S. L.1066 LL.B.
[B Armstrong H.J.T.&W.]
*PRACTICE AREAS: Corporate; Securities Law; Taxation.
Armstrong, David W. ....................'64 '92 C.112 B.A. L.800 J.D. 1200 Wilshire Blvd.
**Armstrong, James S., Jr., (AV)** ....................'43 '72 C.813 B.A. L.1066 J.D. [Armstrong&T.]
*REPORTED CASES: Lee v. Takao Building Development Co. Ltd. 175 Cal. App. 3d 565, 220 Cal. Rptr. 782 (1986).
*PRACTICE AREAS: Civil Trial; Commercial; Corporate; Insurance; Surety.
**Armstrong, Michael L.** ....................'61 '92 C&L.101 B.A., J.D. [A Brobeck,P.&H.]
*LANGUAGES: Cantonese Chinese and Mandarin Chinese.
*PRACTICE AREAS: Insolvency.
Armstrong, Orville A. ....................'29 '57 C.846 B.B.A. L.800 LL.B. Assoc. Jus., Ct. of App.
Armstrong, Robert W. ....................'23 '51 C.990 B.A. L.800 J.D. Supr. Ct. J.
Armstrong, Robert W. ....................'43 '73 C.1077 B.A. L.1095 J.D. 1150 S. Olive St.
**Armstrong, Roger L.** ....................'57 '95 C.112 B.A. L.424 J.D. [A Baker&H.]
*PRACTICE AREAS: Business Law; Entertainment Law.
Armstrong, Timothy B. ....................'60 '87 C.112 B.A. L.426 J.D. [Johnson,R.&W.]

**Armstrong Hirsch Jackoway Tyerman & Wertheimer, A Professional Corporation, (AV)**
**Suite 1800, 1888 Century Park East (Century City), 90067**
Telephone: 310-553-0305 Fax: 310-553-5036
Allan L. Alexander; Karl R. Austen; Joseph D'Onofrio; Alan J. Epstein; J. Gunnar Erickson; Andrew L. Galker; Robert S. Getman; George T. Hayum; Barry L. Hirsch; James R. Jackoway; Jonathan D. Kaufelt; Christianne F. Kerns; James C. Mandelbaum; Marcy S. Morris; Michele M. Mulrooney; Geoffry W. Oblath; Randy M. Schienberg; Scott A. Stein; Robert Stulberg; Barry W. Tyerman; Robert S. Wallerstein; Eric C. Weissler; Alan S. Wertheimer. Of Counsel: Ronald J. Bass; Geraldine S. Hemmerling; Arthur O. Armstrong.
Entertainment, Corporation, Taxation, Real Estate, Estate Planning and Securities Law.

*See Professional Biographies, LOS ANGELES, CALIFORNIA*

**Armstrong & Tabor, (AV)**
**1901 Avenue of the Stars, Suite 1050, 90067**
Telephone: 310-203-0005 Fax: 310-553-0851
Members of Firm: James S. Armstrong, Jr.; Stephen H. Tabor.
General Civil and Trial Practice in all State and Federal Courts. Commercial, Corporate, Insurance, Mergers and Acquisitions, Surety and Real Property Law, Insurance Brokers and Agencies.

*See Professional Biographies, LOS ANGELES, CALIFORNIA*

**Arnberger, Kim, Buxbaum & Choy, (AV)**
**515 South Flower Street, Suite 3500, 90071-2201⊙**
Telephone: (213) 426-6255; (213) 426-4355 Facsimile: (213) 426-6222
Members of the Firm: David S. Kim; H. Bennett Arnberger (San Francisco Office); David C. Buxbaum (Hong Kong Office); Kenneth Y. Choy (New York Office); Douglas L. Bryan. Of Counsel: Michael A. Brand; Robert W. Dziubla; Charles K. Kolstad; Roger S. Saxton (Not admitted in CA); Kazuko Itoh; Duck-Soon Chang; Deborah S. Chew; Christina Y. Chen; Li Zhuogen (Hong Kong Office); Constance M. Burke (Not admitted in CA); Michael J. Orlofsky (Not admitted in CA). Hong Kong Associates: Lee Kui Lam (Not Admitted in United States); Wong Sui Kwan (Not Admitted in United States); Pang Ka Kwong (Not Admitted in United States); Chow Siu Wo Anthony (Not admitted in CA); Fung Tik Lung (Not Admitted in United States); Fong Chun Kwong (Not Admitted in United States); Chan Shing Che Phileas (Not Admitted in United States); Wong Shun Foon (Not Admitted in United States); Wong Suk Har (Not Admitted in United States); Sze Wai Shan (Not Admitted in United States); Zhou Jian Hong (Not Admitted in United States). Associates: Lan Mingliang (Beijing Office); C. Sophia Ng (San Francisco Office); Ping Ye (San Francisco Office); Robert M. Shannon (Hong Kong Office); Hao Xiaodong (Beijing Office); Lin Jia (Beijing Office); Byambaa Bayarmaa (Mongolia Office); Huang Jiang-Xiong (Xiamen Office); Lin Yong (Shanghai Office); Wu Hongliang (Shanghai Office); Wang Xiaogang; Lin Chang (Guangzhou Office); Feng Ruiding (Guangzhou Office); Zhong Wenya (Shenzhen Office); Du Lei (Not Admitted United States); Steven P. Leavenworth (Beijing Office); Dashsambuu Odongua (Not Admitted in United States); Wang Xinhua (Not Admitted in United States); Wei Zheng (Not Admitted in United States); Wu Fanxiang (Not Admitted in United States); Li Zhiguang (Not Admitted in United States); Terence J. Denigan (Not admitted in CA); Lei Shanying (Not Admitted in United States); Hu Jie (Not Admitted in United States); Teng Li (Not Admitted in United States); Wu Hong Liang (Not Admitted in United States).
General Business, Corporate and Commercial Transaction and Civil Litigation Practice involving Foreign Trade and International Business Transactions, Intellectual Property and Technology Trans-

(This Listing Continued)

**Arnberger, Kim, Buxbaum & Choy (Continued)**

fers, Corporate Formation and other Start-Ups, Securities and Commodities, Mergers and Acquisitions, Real Estate and Construction, Regulatory and Insurance Matters, Products Liability and General Casualty, Employment Law and Immigration, Cross-border Financing and International Taxation, Natural Resources, and Environmental Law, Aircraft and Equipment Leasing, Admiralty and Maritime, and Complex Commercial Litigation and Arbitration.
Other Los Angeles, California Office: 3731 Wilshire Boulevard, Suite 910, West Tower, Los Angeles, California, 90010. Telephone: (213) 380-7780. Facsimile: (213) 380-5798.
New York Office: 100 Maiden Lane, 16th Floor, Suite 1600B, New York, New York, 10038. Telephone: (212) 504-6109. Fax: (212) 412-7016. E-Mail: akbc.ny@juno.com; Choylaw@earthlink.net.
San Francisco, California Office: 555 Montgomery Street, Suite 1405, San Francisco, California, 94111. Telephone: (415) 362-7601. Fax: (415) 753-4512. E-Mail: jurisprude@aol.com.
Hong Kong Office: 3201 Citibank Tower, 3 Garden Road, Central, Hong Kong. Telephone: (852) 2523-7001. Fax: (852) 2845-0947. E-Mail: AKBC@hk.super.net.
Beijing (Peking), People's Republic of China Office: China World Trade Centre, Suite 2518, No. 1 Jian Guo Men Wai Avenue, Beijing, P.R.C. Telephone: (86)(10) 6505-2288 Ext: 2523/2518. Fax: (86)(10) 6505-2538. E-Mail: akbcbjo@public.bta.net.cn.
Guangzhou (Canton), People's Republic of China Office: China Hotel Office Tower, Suite 512, Guangzhou, P.R.C. Telephone: (86)(20) 86663388 Ext: 2512. Fax: (86)(20) 8669-1217. Email:gzakbcgz@public1.guangzhou.gd.cn.
Xiamen, People's Republic of China Office: Foreign Trade Centre, Suite 519, No. 15 Hu Bing North Road, Xiamen City, P.R.C. Telephone: (86)(592) 506-3059. Facsimile: (86)(592) 511-1044 Ext: 519. E-Mail: akbcxmo@xpublic.fz.fj.cn.
Shenzhen, People's Republic of China Office: Shenzhen Development Center, Suite 2103, Renmin Nan Lu, Shenzhen, P.R.C. Telephone: (86)(755) 229-8009. Facsimile: (86)(755) 229-8011. E-Mail: szakbcsz@public.szptt.net.cn.
Shanghai, People's Republic of China Office: Room 1907, Astronaut Building, No. 525 Sichuan Bei Road, Shanghai 200085, P.R.C. Telephone: (86)(21) 6357-5676; (86)(21) 6357-5677. Fax: (86)(21) 6357-5679. E-Mail: akbcsho @public.sta.net.cn.
Ulaanbaatar, Mongolia Office: Mongolian Business Development Agency, Prime Minister Amar's Street, Ulaanbatar, Mongolia. Telephone: (976)(1) 31-3492. Facsimile: (976)(1) 32-5102. E-Mail: akbc@magicnet.mn.
Reviser of the People's Republic of China and Mongolia Law Digests for this Directory.

*See Professional Biographies, LOS ANGELES, CALIFORNIA*

**Arndt, Christina Bull** ....................'67 '94 C.518 B.A. L.1068 J.D. [A Luce,F.H.&S.]
*PRACTICE AREAS: Insurance; Reinsurance; Litigation.
**Arndt, Craig R., (P.C.)** ....................'37 '62 C&L.976 B.A., LL.B. [Arndt&V.]
*LANGUAGES: French.
*PRACTICE AREAS: Commercial Law; Corporate Law; International Law.
**Arndt, Kyle B.** ....................'67 '94 C.1169 B.A. L.1068 J.D. [A Riordan&M.]

**Arndt & Van Patten, (AV)**
A Law Partnership of Professional Corporations
**523 West Sixth Street Suite 310, 90014⊙**
Telephone: 213-622-7174 Fax: 213-622-8026
Members of Firm: Craig R. Arndt (P.C.); Anthony J. Van Patten (P.C.). Of Counsel: Robert H. Takeuchi (P.C.).
General Commercial and Corporate Law. International Law.
Reference: First Los Angeles Bank (Downtown Branch).
Bangkok, Thailand Office: Associated Lawyers & Consultants Ltd., 4th Floor, Panunee Building, 518/3 Ploenchit Road. Telephone: 662-252-0177; 251-9832. Fax: 662-251-2323. E-Mail: arndt@ksc.av.ac.th.
Yangon, Myanmar Affiliated Office: Maw Htoon & Partners Law Offices, 49/51 31st Street. Telephone: (951) 71919. Facsimile: (951) 34586.

*See Professional Biographies, LOS ANGELES, CALIFORNIA*

**Arnelle, Hastie, McGee, Willis & Greene, (AV)⊙**
**2049 Century Park East, Suite 800, 90067⊙**
Telephone: 310-552-3200 Fax: 310-552-3214
Members of Firm: Reginald D. Greene (Resident); William H. Hastie. Special Counsel: John A. Minor III (Resident). Associates: Robert Shayne Figgins (Resident); Michael V. Lee (Resident); Scott K. Liner (Resident); Brandon M. Tesser (Resident).
Civil Litigation. Bankruptcy. Business. The Civil Litigation Practice includes Commercial, Construction, Environmental, Toxic, Insurance, Intellectual Property, Labor and Employment, Products Liability and Professional Malpractice.
San Francisco, California Office: One Market, Steuart Street Tower, 9th Floor. 94105-1310. Telephone: 415-495-4747. Telecopier: 415-495-5123.

*See Professional Biographies, LOS ANGELES, CALIFORNIA*

**Arneson, Delynn Y.** ....................'63 '94 C.35 B.S. L.990 J.D. [B Sanchez&A.]
*LANGUAGES: German.
*PRACTICE AREAS: Trademark Protection; Entertainment.
Arney, Neil L. ....................'60 '86 C.792 B.S. L.352 J.D. 725 S. Figueroa St.
Arnhem, Erik M. ....................'36 '62 C.061 L.1008 J.D. 4250 Wilshire Blvd., 2nd Fl. (Pat.)
**Arnold, Brian G.** ....................'70 '96 C.668 B.A. L.426 J.D. [A Jones,B.S.A.&F.]
*PRACTICE AREAS: Business Law; Securities Litigation.
**Arnold, Bryan B.** ....................'65 '90 C.187 B.A. L.276 J.D. [Troop M.S.&P.]
*PRACTICE AREAS: Litigation and Government Contracts.
**Arnold, Carol G.** ....................'53 '87 C.893 B.A. L.809 J.D. [A Gray,Y.D.&R.]
*PRACTICE AREAS: Insurance Defense; Construction Defect; Premises Liability; Personal Injury Defense; Appellate.
**Arnold, Dennis B., (AV)** ....................'50 '76 C.1044 B.A. L.976 J.D. [Gibson,D.&C.]
*PRACTICE AREAS: Real Estate; Banking; Debt Restructure; Commercial Law and Secured Transactions; Bankruptcy/Reorganization.

**Arnold & Porter, (AV)**
**44th Floor, 777 Figueroa Street, 90017-2513⊙**
Telephone: 213-243-4000 Telecopy: 213-243-4199
Partners: Brian K. Condon; Lawrence A. Cox; Eric L. Dobberteen; David S. Eisen; Gregory C. Fant; James I. Ham; Matthew T. Heartney; Craig N. Hentschel; Polly Horn; Laurence J. Hutt; Theodore G. Johnsen; Maurice A. Leiter; Margaret M. Morrow; J. David Oswalt; John J. Quinn; Ellen Kelly Reisman (Not admitted in CA); Richard C. Smith; James F. Speyer; Mark J. Spooner; Julie M. Ward; Edward W. Zaelke. Of Counsel: Susan J. Eliot; Russel I. Kully. Associates: Hilary Adel; John D. Bandiera; Steven H. Bergman; Theodore J. Bro; Carey C. Chern; Martha Jeannette Clark; Sharon L. Douglass; Mark R. Drozdowski; William H. Forman; James D. Layden; Patricia A. Libby; John D. Lombardo; Tracy L. Merritt; Diane S. Ponce-Gomez; Kelley P. Potter; Michael H. Walizer; Mina S. Yang.
General Practice.
Washington, D.C. Office: Thurmond Arnold Building, 555 Twelfth Street, N.W., 20004-1202. Telephone 202-942-5000. Telecopy: 202-942-5999.
Denver, Colorado Office: 1700 Lincoln Street, 80203-4540. Telephone: 303-863-1000. Telecopy: 303-832-0428.
New York, N.Y. Office: 399 Park Avenue, 10022-4690. Telephone: 212-715-1000. Telecopy: 212-715-1399.
The United Kingdom Office: One, St. Paul's Churchyard, London, England, EC4M 8SH. Telephone: 011-44-171-236-3626. FAX: 011-44-171-236-3610.

*See Professional Biographies, LOS ANGELES, CALIFORNIA*

**Arnone, James L.** ....................'65 '90 C.112 B.A. L.309 J.D. [A Latham&W.]
Arnopole, David L. ....................'46 '73 C.259 B.A. L.809 J.D. 6500 Wilshire Blvd.
**Aron, Simon** ....................'54 '83 C.112 B.A. L.809 J.D. [Jeffer,M.B.&M.]
*PRACTICE AREAS: Bankruptcy; Creditors' Rights; Financial Restructurings.
**Aronoff, David** ....................'60 '86 C.112 B.A. L.1065 J.D. [A Leopold,P.&S.]
*PRACTICE AREAS: Entertainment; Civil Litigation; Copyright and Trademark; Libel and Slander; Unfair Competition.
**Aronoff, David L.** ....................'61 '91 C.800 B.A. L.809 J.A. [A Buchalter,N.F.&Y.]
*PRACTICE AREAS: Civil Litigation.

**Aronoff, Robert C.**, (AV) .................... '51 '76 C.112 B.A. L.208 J.D. [Aronoff&S.]
*PRACTICE AREAS: Commercial Litigation; Real Estate Litigation; Landlord and Tenant Law; Bankruptcy Law.

**Aronoff & Soukup, A Professional Law Corporation, (AV)**
**11726 San Vicente Boulevard, Suite 600, 90049**
**Telephone: 310-207-6700 Fax: 310-207-6714**
**John F. Soukup; Robert C. Aronoff (Certified Specialist, Personal and Small Business Bankruptcy Law, The State Bar of California Board of Legal Specialization);—Scott A. Schiff; Edward J. Candelaria, II (1965-1995); Adam S. Rossman.**
**Real Estate, Bankruptcy, Commercial Litigation, Transactions, and Landlord-Tenant Law.**
**Reference: First Interstate Bank.**

***See Professional Biographies, LOS ANGELES, CALIFORNIA***

**Aronson, Alan D.** .................... '62 '87 C.813 A.B. L.1068 J.D. [Rosenfeld&W.]
*PRACTICE AREAS: Corporate Law; Real Estate Law.

**Aronson, Brian** .................... '66 '91 C.30 B.A. L.276 J.D. [[A] Davis&F.]
*LANGUAGES: Afrikaans.
*PRACTICE AREAS: Real Estate Law; Environmental Law.

**Aronson, Mark E.** .................... '54 '79 C.1044 B.A. L.607 J.D. [Anderson,M.&C.]

**Aronson, Peter** .................... '67 '92 C.30 B.A. L.276 J.D. [[A] Paul,H.J.&W.]

**Aronson, Peter**, (AV) .................... '33 '60 C.339 B.A. L.800 LL.B. [Foley L.W.&A.]
*LANGUAGES: German.
*REPORTED CASES: Wilson v. Blue Cross, 271 Cal Rptr. 876 (1990).
*PRACTICE AREAS: Commercial Litigation; Administrative Law; Business Torts; Legal Law; Antitrust.

**Aronson, Robert M.** .................... '53 '78 C.112 B.A. L.426 J.D. [[B] Fulbright&J.]
*PRACTICE AREAS: Litigation; Bankruptcy; Real Estate.

**Aronson, Seth** .................... '55 '81 C.610 B.B.A. L.426 J.D. [O'Melveny&M.]
*PRACTICE AREAS: Securities Litigation; RICO; Professional Liability Defense; Advertising Liability; Unfair Competition.

**Aronzon, Paul S.**, (AV) .................... '54 '79 C.1077 B.A. L.809 J.D. [Milbank,T.H.&M.]

**Arouesty, Erica S.** .................... '57 '90 C.1168 B.A. L.426 J.D. [[A] Hewitt&P.]
*PRACTICE AREAS: Medical and Dental Malpractice Defense; Insurance Coverage Disputes; Professional Negligence Defense.

Aroustamian, Ara .................... '60 '86 C.112 B.A. L.990 J.D. 3171 Los Feliz Blvd.

Aroz, Raoul '52 '87 C.1042 B.A. L.426 J.D.
Chf. Admin. Offr. & House Coun., Catholic Charities of L.A., Inc.

**Arrache, Marissa R.** .................... '70 '96 C.112 B.A. L.770 J.D. [[A] Stevens,K.A.&H.]
*PRACTICE AREAS: Insurance Defense.

Arredondo, David .................... '50 '76 C.112 A.B. L.1068 J.D. [Arredondo&M.]

Arredondo & Mendoza .................... 5429 E. Beverly Blvd.

**Arriandiaga, Marta B.** .................... '53 '85 C.205 B.A. L.767 J.D. [Ropers,M.K.&B.]
*LANGUAGES: Spanish.
*PRACTICE AREAS: Insurance Coverage and Bad Faith Litigation.

**Arrington, Jeffrey L.** .................... '60 '89 C.878 B.S. L.426 J.D. [[A] Irell&M.]

Arrow, Allan H. .................... '26 '67 C.800 A.B. L.809 J.D. 2045 Selby Ave.‡

**Arrow, Paul S.** .................... '56 '88 C.112 B.A. L.809 J.D. [[A] Buchalter,N.F.&Y.]
*PRACTICE AREAS: Insolvency.

**Arroyo, Felipe J.** .................... '66 '93 C.112 B.A. L.976 J.D. [[A] O'Melveny&M.]

**Arshonsky, Richard I.** .................... '67 '91 C.210 B.M. L.426 J.D. [Marcus,W.S.&D.]
*PRACTICE AREAS: Real Property; Business Law.

**Artan, Michael H. '56 '81 C.112 B.A. L.1068 J.D.**
**445 South Figueroa Street Twenty-Seventh Floor, 90071**
**Telephone: 213-688-0370 Facsimile: 213-627-9201**
***LANGUAGES: Armenian.**
***PRACTICE AREAS: Criminal Defense; Civil Litigation.**
**Criminal Defense in all Federal and State Courts, including White Collar Crime, Civil and Licensing Defense.**

***See Professional Biographies, LOS ANGELES, CALIFORNIA***

**Arter & Hadden, (AV) [BR]**
**700 South Flower Street, 30th Floor, 90017-4101⊙**
**Telephone: 213-629-9300 Cable Address: "Oslaw" Facsimile: 213-617-9255**
**Members of Firm: Robert P. Andreani; Kathleen M. K. Brahn; James S. Bryan; Steven J. Coté; Jay M. Davis; William S. Davis; Eric D. Dean; David R. Decker; Richard D. De Luce; Edwin W. Duncan; James E. Durbin; Richard N. Ellner; Donald C. Erickson; Jack Goldman; Wayne S. Grajewski; John L. Hosack; Curtiss L. Isler; John E. James; Bart L. Kessel; Craig G. Kline; Michael S. Kogan; Julie Dean Larsen; Kenneth J. Murphy; Bruce H. Newman; Richard R. Pace; J. Douglas Post; Kay Rustand; Andrea Y. Slade; Stephen T. Swanson; John R. Tate; Jacqueline I. Valenzuela; Ronald Warner; Kim W. West; Michael C. Zellers. Retired Partners: Robert Henigson; Richard F. Outcault, Jr.; Reed A. Stout. Of Counsel: Michael L. Coates; Barbara R. Diamond; Judith A. Gilbert; Ronald M. Griffith; Steven T. Gubner. Associates: Julian Bach; Victor M. Bartholetti; Susan C. Bergemann; Linley Clare Bizik; Katessa M. Charles; Robert M. Forester; Adam Gubner; Holly A. Hayes; David M. Hershorin; Tammy L. Kahane; Kathryn L. Kempton; Wendy L. Linder; Brenda J. Logan; Mary Devereaux Mackey; Michelle McAloon; Maura B. O'Connor; John M. Orr; Jane H. Root; Alexander G. Rufus-Isaacs; Helen A. Sabo; Michael D. Schwarzmann; Robert G. Soper; Juliana Stamato; Karen M. Stuckey; Neil M. Sunkin; Daniel R. Villegas; David B. Zolkin.**
**General Civil and Trial Practice. Antitrust, Banking, Bankruptcy and Commercial Transactions, Corporation, Corporate Financing, Creditors Remedies, Environmental, Estate Planning, Trust, Probate, Government Contract, Intellectual Property, International Business, Labor and Employment, Oil and Gas, Products Liability, Negligence, Admiralty, Maritime, Workers Compensation, Public Utility, General Real Estate, Finance, Securities and Taxation Law.**
**Representative Clients: Chevron Corp.; American International Group; ADT, Inc.; PacTel Properties; The Bank of California, N.A.; Brunswick Corp.; Reliance Steel & Aluminum Co.; Scope Industries; National Railroad Passenger Car; Boral Industries, Inc.**
**In Cleveland, Ohio: 1100 Huntington Building, 925 Euclid Avenue. Telephone: 216-696-1100. Fax: 216-696-2645.**
**In Columbus, Ohio: 21st Floor, One Columbus, 10 West Broad Street. Fax: 614-221-0479. Telephone: 614-221-3155.**
**In Washington, D.C.: 1801 K Street, N.W., Suite 400K. Telephone: 202-775-7100. Fax: 202-857-0172.**
**In Dallas, Texas: 1717 Main Street, Suite 4100. Telephone: 214-761-2100. Fax: 214-741-7139.**
**In Irvine, California: Five Park Plaza, 10th Floor, Jamboree Center. Telephone: 714-252-7500. Fax: 714-833-9604.**
**In Austin, Texas: 100 Congress Avenue, Suite 1800. Telephone: 512-479-6403. Fax: 512-469-5505.**
**In San Antonio, Texas: 7710 Jones Maltsberger, Harte-Hanks Tower, Suite 540. Telephone: 210-805-8497. Fax: 210-805-8519.**
**In San Francisco, California: 201 California Street, 14th Floor, 94111. Telephone: 415-912-3600. Fax: 415-912-3636.**
**In San Diego, California: 402 West Broadway, Fourth Floor, 92101. Telephone: 619-238-0001. Fax: 619-238-8333.**
**In Woodland Hills, California: 5959 Topanga Canyon Boulevard, Suite 244, 91367. Telephone: 818-712-0036. Fax: 818-346-6502.**
**Revisers of the Ohio Law Digest for this Directory.**

***See Professional Biographies, LOS ANGELES, CALIFORNIA***

Arthur, Stacey L. .................... '52 '82 C.112 A.B. L.1067 J.D. Whittier Law Sch.

**Arthur, Thomas S.** .................... '49 '76 C.763 B.A. L.1049 J.D. [Frandzel&S.]

**Arturo, Peter J.**, (AV) .................... '40 '72 C.800 B.A. L.809 J.D. [[C] Gibson,D.&C.]
*PRACTICE AREAS: Medical Malpractice; Product Liability.

Artz, Jon Bryant .................... '43 '72 C.112 B.A. L.1068 J.D. 11755 Wilshire Blvd.

**Arvin, Anne E.** .................... '59 '95 C.1 B.A. L.990 J.D. [[B] Manning,M.&W.]

**Arya, John D.** .................... '66 '91 C.37 B.A. L.1068 J.D. [[C] McClintock,W.B.R.R.&M.]
*REPORTED CASES: Stell v. Jay Hayes Development Co., 11 Cal. App. 4th 1214, 15 Cal. Rptr. 2d 220, 1992.
*PRACTICE AREAS: Business Litigation; Franchise Litigation.

**Asakura, Hidetoshi** .................... '43 '80 C.061 B.A. L.911 LL.M. [Graham&J.]
*PRACTICE AREAS: International Business Law; Corporate Law; Real Estate (Property) Law; Mergers and Acquisitions.

**Asamura, Saskia Tsushima** .................... '57 '91 C.054 B.Sc. L.1068 J.D. [Richards,W.&G.]
*LANGUAGES: French.
*REPORTED CASES: Sinaloa Lake Owners Assoc. v. Stephenson, 805 F.Supp. 824 (C.D. Cal. 1992).
*PRACTICE AREAS: Litigation.

Asari, Yoichi J. .................... '43 '70 C.813 A.B. L.1065 J.D. Dep. Dist. Atty.

Asay, Jeffrey S. '46 '72 C.112 B.A. L.1068 J.D.
Asst. Gen. Solr., Union Pacific R.R. Co.

Asayama, Phyllis C. .................... '55 '79 C&L.800 A.B., J.D. Dep. Dist. Atty.

**Aschieris, Katherine F.** .................... '56 '80 C.1042 B.A. L.1065 J.D. [[B] Burke,W.&S.]
*PRACTICE AREAS: Municipal Prosecution; Municipal Law; Civil Litigation.

**Asel, Colette M.** .................... '67 '93 C.112 B.A. L.893 J.D. [[A] Crosby,H.R.&M.]
*LANGUAGES: German.

**Ashe, Brian T.** .................... '61 '89 C.93 B.A. L.273 J.D. [[A] Seyfarth,S.F.&G.]
*PRACTICE AREAS: Labor and Employment Law.

Ashen, Mark M. .................... '51 '84 C.112 B.A. L.809 J.D. Dep. Dist. Atty.

**Ashen, Robert M.**, (AV) '34 '58
C.679 B.S.M.E. L.309 J.D. [Ashen,G.&L.] (See Pat. Sect.)⊙

**Ashen, Golant & Lippman, (AV) [BR]**
**2029 Century Park East, Suite 2610, 90067⊙**
**Telephone: 310-203-0303 Fax: 310-203-8803**
**Members of Firm: Robert M. Ashen; Joseph H. Golant; Peter I. Lippman; Elizabeth L. Swanson.**
**Patent, Trademark and Copyright Law. Intellectual Property Litigation and Licensing. Unfair Competition, Trade-Secret, Computer and High-Technology Law.**
**Reference: City National Bank (Beverly Hills Office).**
**Beverly Hills, California Office: 1737 Franklin Canyon Drive, 90210. Telephone: 310-274-8060. Fax: 310-858-1922.**
**Chicago, Illinois Office: 70 West Madison Street, 1700, 60602. Telephone: 312-422-0729. Fax: 312-422-0730.**
**Montrose, California Office: 4385 Ocean View Boulevard. Telephone: 818-249-5961. Fax: 818-249-8384.**

***See Professional Biographies, LOS ANGELES, CALIFORNIA***

**Asher, Raymond L.**, (AV) .................... '45 '72 C.112 A.B. L.1068 J.D. [R.L.Asher]

**Asher, Raymond L., A Professional Corporation, (AV)**
**2040 Avenue of the Stars, Suite 400, 90067**
**Telephone: 310-277-4510 Fax: 310-277-7623**
**Email: ASHERLAW@Loop.com**
**Raymond L. Asher.**
**Civil Trial and Appellate Practice in State and Federal Courts. Real Estate, Taxation, Corporation, Partnership, Entertainment, Intellectual Property and Computer Law.**

***See Professional Biographies, LOS ANGELES, CALIFORNIA***

**Asherson, Neville** .................... '39 '75 C.061 B.S. L.1188 L.D. [Asherson&K.]
*PRACTICE AREAS: Immigration; Customs Law; International Law; Civil Litigation; Business Law.

**Asherson & Klein**
**9150 Wilshire Boulevard Suite 210, 90212**
**Telephone: 310-247-6070 Fax: 310-278-8454**
**Members of Firm: Neville Asherson. Associates: Anna Darbinyan (Not admitted in the United States).**
**Immigration, General Civil Practice, Litigation and Business Law.**

Ashkar, Albert J., II .................... '42 '70 C.426 B.B.A. L.809 J.D. 10960 Wilshire Blvd.

Ashland, Calvin K. .................... '33 '64 C.350 B.S. L.273 J.D. Chf. U.S. Bkrptcy. J.

**Ashley, Lane J.**, (AV) .................... '52 '76 C.339 B.A. L.1068 J.D. [Sedgwick,D.M.&A.]

Ashley, Odette L. .................... '59 '84 C.112 B.S. L.809 J.D. 1901 Ave. of the Stars, 20th Fl.

**Ashley, Stephen D.** .................... '47 '73 C.309 B.A. L.976 J.D. [Goldstein&A.]
*PRACTICE AREAS: Entertainment Law; Non Union Employment; Contract Law; Copyrights; Trademarks.

**Ashley-Farrand, Margalo**
**(See Pasadena)**

Ashouri, Pardis P. .................... '61 '92 C&L.1190 B.S.L., J.D. 1925 Century Park E.

**Ashton, Bruce L.**, (AV) .................... '45 '71 C.691 B.A. L.802 J.D. [Reish&L.]
*PRACTICE AREAS: Employee Benefits; ESOPs; Employee Relations.

**Ashworth, Christopher, Law Offices of, (AV) '42 '73 C.112 B.A. L.1065 J.D.**
**540 North Santa Cruz Avenue Suite 270, 95030⊙**
**Telephone: 408-867-1573 Fax: 408-867-4387**
***PRACTICE AREAS: Interstate Commercial Litigation; Commercial Constitutional Litigation.**
**Interstate Commerce, Public Utilities, Transportation and Complex Civil Litigation.**
**Los Gatos, California Office: 540 North Santa Cruz Avenue, Suite 270. Telephone: 408-867-1573. Fax: 408-867-4387.**

**Asiedu, Kwasi A.** .................... '55 '88 C&L.061 B.A., B.L. [Asiedu&L.]
*LANGUAGES: English.
*PRACTICE AREAS: Business Law; Civil Litigation; Employment Litigation; Real Estate.

**Asiedu & Lubega**
**1900 Avenue of the Stars, Suite 790, 90067-4308**
**Telephone: 310-551-0200 Facsimile: 310-563-5256**
**Kwasi A. Asiedu; Stephen K. Lubega.**
**Business Litigation, Employment Litigation, Wrongful Termination, Securities Litigation, Real Litigation, Family and Appeals.**

Asif, Lisa A. .................... '60 '89 C.426 B.A. L.809 J.D. [[A] Ivie,M.&W.]

Asimow, Michael .................... '39 '64 C.112 B.S. L.1065 J.D. Prof. of Law, UCLA Law School

Aspaturian, Nancy Lee .................... '58 '85 C.112 B.A. L.1065 J.D. Co. Pub. Def. Off.

Aspenson, Everett H. .................... '33 '57 C.747 L.966 LL.B. 8622 Olin St.

Asper, Maynard W., (BV) .................... '38 '65 C.800 B.A. L.809 LL.B. Asst. City Atty.

**Asperger, James R.**, (AV) .................... '53 '78 C.112 B.A. L.1068 J.D. [O'Melveny&M.]
*PRACTICE AREAS: Litigation; Securities Enforcement; White Collar Criminal Defense.

**Aspessi, Francis P.** .................... '56 '85 C.178 B.A. L.800 J.D. [[A] Radcliff,F.&D.]

**Aspinwall, Mark A.** '56 '81 C.800 L.878 J.D.
Asst. Gen. Coun., Litig. Dir., Teledyne, Inc.

**Aspinwall, Marla J.** .................... '59 '84 C.878 B.A. L.800 J.D. [Tuttle&T.]
*PRACTICE AREAS: Agricultural Cooperatives; Tax.

**Astor, Sanford**, (AV) .................... '37 '63 C.679 B.S.Ch.E. L.273 J.D. [Stall,A.&G.]
*SPECIAL AGENCIES: U.S. Patent and Trademark Office.
*PRACTICE AREAS: Civil Litigation; Corporate; Probate; Real Estate; Intellectual Property.

**Astor & Phillips, A Professional Law Corporation, (AV)**
**800 Wilshire Boulevard, Fifteenth Floor, 90017-2619⊙**
**Telephone: 213-680-9212 Facsimile: 213-891-2910**
**Email: astorphill@aol.com**
**George R. Phillips; Mark E. LaBounty; John Kelly Astor (Resident at Orange Office); Gary R. Phillips. Of Counsel: Z. Harry Astor (Resident at Orange Office);—Ronald N. Sarian; Gary Y. Tanaka; Lya Kingsland-Canada (Resident at Orange Office); Eric B. LaBounty.**
**Business, Real Estate, Corporate, Estate Planning, Probate, Taxation, Solid Waste Management/ Environmental Law. General Trial Practice in Business, Real Estate, Eminent Domain, Commercial and Trust Litigation, Governmental Affairs, Family Law.**
**Orange County Office: 333 City Boulevard West, 17th Floor. Orange, California. Telephone: 714-634-8050.**

***See Professional Biographies, LOS ANGELES, CALIFORNIA***

Athanasiou, Christina D. .................... '58 '85 C.1074 B.S. L.767 J.D. 3435 Wilshire Blvd.

**Atkins, Erin K.** .................... '65 '92 C.426 B.A. L.809 J.D. [[A] Manatt,P.&P.]
*PRACTICE AREAS: Litigation.

**Atkins, Nelson L.**, (AV) ... '39 '65 C.1097 B.A. L.426 LL.B. [Atkins&E.]
*PRACTICE AREAS: Personal Injury Defense Law; Employment Law; Construction Law; Business Litigation; Labor and Employment.
Atkins, Patricia S. ... '45 '89 C.172 L.809 J.D. 3580 Wilshire Blvd.

**Atkins & Evans, (AV)**
**5900 Wilshire Boulevard, Suite 2750, 90036**
**Telephone: 213-933-4100 Fax: 213-933-4157**
**Nelson L. Atkins; Irwin S. Evans. Associates: Karen Labat Wells; Syna N. Dennis; Herbert N. Wiggins; Darlene Diane Gartrell; Henry L. Heins, III. Of Counsel: Anthony E. Alexander; Lee R. Young, Jr.**
**General Casualty Litigation, Products Liability, Government Agencies, Tort Liability, Employment Litigation, Commercial Litigation and Criminal Defense, Taxation and Entertainment, Construction, Real Estate.**
**Representative Clients: County of Los Angeles; City of Inglewood; Kaiser Foundation; Los Angeles Unified School District; Ford Motor Co. Dupont.**
***See Professional Biographies, LOS ANGELES, CALIFORNIA***

**Atkinson, Karen L.** ... '68 '96 C.381 B.B.A. L.1049 J.D. [[A] Hennelly&G.]
*PRACTICE AREAS: Business Litigation; Products Liability.
**Atkinson, Mark W.** ... '49 '74 C.813 B.A. L.1068 J.D. [Paul,H.J.&W.]
**Atkinson, Paula G.** ... '64 '92 C.69 B.B.A. L.178 J.D. [[A] Loeb&L.]

**Atkinson, Andelson, Loya, Ruud & Romo, A Professional Corporation**
**(See Cerritos)**

Atkisson, B. E., (BV) ... '21 '53 C.763 L.1065 J.D. 320 N. Vermont Ave.
Atlas, Alan G. ... '49 '82 C&L.1029 B.S., J.D. [[A] Liebert,C.&F.]
**Atlee, Steven** ... '65 '90 C.976 B.A. L.800 J.D. [[A] Latham&W.]
**Attanasio, Edward T.** ... '— '85 C.188 B.S. L.813 J.D. [[A] Morgan,L.&B.]
Attaway, James H. ... '49 '79 C.1224 A.A. L.1221 J.D. 4700 Wilshire Blvd.
**Attenborough, Roland M.**, (AV) ... '38 '65 C.112 B.S. L.1065 LL.B. [Reish&L.]
*PRACTICE AREAS: ESOPs; Financing Law; Business and Corporate Law.
Attie, Maurice J. ... '40 '65 C.112 B.S. L.1068 J.D. 11500 W. Olympic Blvd.
**Attwood, Mark R.** ... '59 '86 C&L.878 B.S., J.D. [Jackson,L.S.&K.]
**Au, Alan** ... '67 '92 C.188 B.A. L.1066 J.D. [[A] Sidley&A.]
*PRACTICE AREAS: Environmental Law.
**Aubert, Garth W.** ... '67 '92 C.800 B.A. L.464 J.D. [[A] Mendes&M.]
Au Coin, Jeanne H. ... '57 '92 C.1077 L.1148 J.D. [[A] Swedelson&G.]
**Auden, Nichole M.** ... '70 '95 C.770 B.A. L.1067 J.D. [[A] Hennigan,M.&B.]
*PRACTICE AREAS: Complex Business Litigation.
**Audet, Gregg M.** ... '65 '92 C.321 B.A. L.477 J.D. [[A] Bannan,G.S.&F.]
*PRACTICE AREAS: Civil Litigation; Products Liability.
Audet, Louis A., (AV) ... '11 '38 C&L.809 LL.B. [Audet&O.] ‡
Audet & O'Reilly, (AV) ... 4221 Wilshire Blvd.
Auerbach, Arthur H. ... '63 '90 C.112 B.A. L.990 J.D. Dep. Atty. Gen.
**Auerbach, Lee L.** ... '55 '90 C.354 B.S. L.426 J.D. [[A] Sidley&A.]
*PRACTICE AREAS: Civil Litigation; Environmental Litigation; Tort and Insurance Coverage Litigation.
Auerbach, Philip I. ... '37 '64 C.112 B.S. L.1068 LL.B. 8531 Alcott St.
August, Jon L. ... '43 '71 C.475 B.A. L.912 J.D. 6363 Wilshire Blvd.
**August, Julie A.** ... '68 '93 C.112 B.A. L.767 J.D. [[A] Schaffer&L.]
*LANGUAGES: Spanish.
**August, Kenneth A.** ... '47 '93 C.813 B.A. L.178 J.D. [Ziffren,B.B.&F.]
*PRACTICE AREAS: Entertainment Transactions.
**August, Marshall J.** ... '57 '82 C.112 B.A. L.809 J.D. [Frandzel&S.]
**August, Richard Lee**, (AV) ... '49 '74 C.339 B.S. L.800 J.D. [Russ,A.&K.]
*PRACTICE AREAS: Real Estate Transactions; Business Transactions.
**Augustine, Joseph P.** ... '66 '93 C&L.823 B.S., J.D. [[A] Grace,S.C.&S.]
*LANGUAGES: Spanish.
*PRACTICE AREAS: Insurance Coverage; Environmental; Products Liability; Employment Law; Sexual Harassment.
Augustine, Mark E., (P.C.) ... '42 '74 C.172 B.S. L.800 J.D. 221 N. Figueroa St.
**Augustini, Alfred E.**, (AV) ... '42 '69 C.93 A.B. L.276 J.D. [Augustini,W.&D.]
**Augustini, Rick** ... '67 '92 C.112 B.A. L.426 J.D. [[A] Case,K.B.&W.]⊙

**Augustini, Wheeler & Dillman, LLP, (AV)**
**Pacific Center, Suite 300, 523 West Sixth Street, 90014**
**Telephone: 213-629-8888 Telecopier: 213-688-7600**
**Members of Firm: Alfred E. Augustini; David C. Wheeler; Kirk D. Dillman. Associates: John M. Bowers; Lawrence C. Jones. Of Counsel: Peter H. Strong.**
**General Civil Trial and Appellate Litigation in all State and Federal Courts and Arbitrations; with emphasis on Business Contract and Tort Litigation; including real estate and real property matters; hazardous waste, pollution and environmental matters; RTC matters, banking and lender liability; and corporate and partnership litigation.**
**Representative Clients: Toyota Motor Sales, U.S.A., Inc.; Home Savings and Loan Assn.; Watt Industries, Inc.; Trammell Crow Co.; U.S. Bank Note; Goldrich & Kest Industries; The Hewson Co.; The Larwin Co.; Tiger Real Estate Partners.**
***See Professional Biographies, LOS ANGELES, CALIFORNIA***

Aull, Roger J., (Law Corporation) ... '46 '72 C.347 A.B. L.1119 J.D. 1000 Wilshire Blvd.
**Aumer, John J.** ... '59 '87 C.112 B.A. L.1065 J.D. [[A] Andrews&H.]
*PRACTICE AREAS: Civil Litigation.
**Austen, Karl R.** ... '64 '89 C.31 B.A. L.309 J.D. [Armstrong H.J.T.&W.]
*LANGUAGES: French.
*PRACTICE AREAS: Entertainment.
**Austin, Joseph R.**, (AV) ... '39 '65 C.162 A.B. L.309 LL.B. [McCutchen,D.B.&E.]
*PRACTICE AREAS: Business Litigation.
Austin, Maureen T. ... '61 '86 C.477 B.A. L.276 J.D. Dep. Pub. Def.
Autrey, James K. ... '63 '89 C.112 B.A. L.1068 J.D. 12100 Wilshire Blvd.
**Avanzado, Melvin N.A.** ... '62 '88 C.112 B.S. L.602 J.D. [White O.C.&A.]
*LANGUAGES: Tagalog.
*PRACTICE AREAS: Civil Litigation; Entertainment; Sports Law.
Avazian, Arthur ... '42 '68 [Avazian&A.]
Avazian, Eric ... '42 '73 [Avazian&A.]
Avazian & Avazian ... 800 Wilshire Blvd.
**Avchen, Terry D.** ... '51 '77 C.112 B.A. L.1068 J.D. [Christensen,M.F.J.G.W.&S.]
*PRACTICE AREAS: Civil Litigation; Environmental Law.
Avedissian, Azita ... '62 '93 C.112 B.S. L.809 J.D. 11355 W. Olympic Blvd.
Avedissian, Lucy ... '50 '94 L.1190 J.D. [[A] Davis&W.]
**Aver, Raymond H.** ... '57 '83 C.112 B.A. L.1065 J.D. [Fainsbert,M.&S.]
*PRACTICE AREAS: Insolvency Law; Real Estate Law; Business Litigation.
**Averbach, Zane S., (A Professional Corporation)**, (AV) '51 '77
C.112 B.A. L.426 J.D. [Goldfarb,S.&A.]
*PRACTICE AREAS: Taxation Law; Real Estate Law; Estate Planning Law.
**Averbuck, Clayton C.**, (AV) ... '50 '79 C&L.898 B.A., J.D. [Stevens,K.A.&H.]
*PRACTICE AREAS: Defense of Legal and Medical Malpractice; Personal Casualty Liability; Commercial Casualty Liability; Public Entities.
**Avery, Robert Dean** ... '44 '71 C.597 B.A. L.178 J.D. [Jones,D.R.&P.]
**Avery, Wesley** ... '58 '91 C&L.112 B.A., J.D. [[A] Sulmeyer,K.B.&R.]
*PRACTICE AREAS: Bankruptcy.
**Avila, Felix** ... '68 '94 C.1075 B.A. L.1066 J.D. [[A] Mendes&M.]
**Avila, Jonathan D.** ... '56 '86 C.976 B.A. L.309 J.D. Litig. Coun., CBS Inc.
**Avila, Michael F.** ... '66 '92 C.112 B.A. L.800 J.D. [[A] Morris,P.&P.]

**Avitia, Javier R.** '61 '87 C.112 A.B. L.309 J.D.
Sr. Legal Coun., Univision Communication Grp.
*LANGUAGES: Spanish.
*RESPONSIBILITIES: Corporate Law; Entertainment Law; Intellectual Property.
Avner, Correy B. ... '52 '78 C.37 B.S. L.1049 J.D. 11835 W. Olympic Blvd.
**Avrith, Charles** ... '56 '80 C.1036 B.A. L.813 J.D. [Hughes H.&R.]
*PRACTICE AREAS: Litigation.
Avrutin, Roberta ... '— '78 C.112 B.A. L.284 J.D. 351 S. Fuller Ave.
**Axel, Douglas A.** ... '— '94 C.112 B.S. L.1065 J.D. [[A] Munger,T.&O.]
Axel, Robert B. ... '42 '67 C.1077 L.1068 J.D. Comr. Supr. Ct.
Axelrad, Bernard, (AV) ... '19 '48 C.563 B.B.A. L.309 J.D. 11941 Wilshire Blvd.‡
**Axelrad, David M.** ... '50 '77 C.813 B.A. L.1065 J.D. [Horvitz&L.]
**Axelrod, Charles D.**, (AV) ... '41 '67 C.165 B.A. L.228 J.D. [Stutman,T.&G.]
*PRACTICE AREAS: Bankruptcy; Insolvency; Corporate Reorganization; Commercial Litigation.
Axelrod, G. Carla '53 '80 C.112 B.A. L.426 J.D.
V.P. & Sr. Coun., Wells Fargo Bk., N.A.
Axelrod, Ronald B. ... '54 '84 C.680 B.A. L.1065 J.D. 2039 Century Park East
**Axelrood, Bryan J.** ... '54 '80 C.112 B.A. L.426 J.D. [[C] Ruben&M.]
*PRACTICE AREAS: Federal and California Taxation; Estate Planning; Corporate Formation; Dissolution; Mergers and Acquisitions.
Axtell, James H. ... '59 '85 C.112 B.A. L.1065 J.D. Deputy City Atty.
Ayala, Renee I ... '60 '95 C.424 B.S. L.1136 J.D. [Grayson,G.&M.]
**Ayazi, Armand F.** ... '60 '92 C.112 B.S. L.426 J.D. [[A] Lyon&L.]
*PRACTICE AREAS: Patent, Trademark, Copyright, Unfair Competition; Antitrust, Civil Litigation; Business Transaction; Intellectual Property.
**Ayers, Paul R.** ... '51 '91 C.112 B.A. L.1148 J.D. [[A] Irwin&R.]
*PRACTICE AREAS: Aviation; Products Liability; General Civil Practice; Trial Practice.
**Ayles, Richard P.** ... '51 '80 C.1044 B.A. L.472 J.D. [[C] Kopple&K.]
*PRACTICE AREAS: International Business Law; Business Law; Corporate Law; Real Property Law.
**Ayoob, Richard J.**, (AV) ... '53 '78 C.800 B.S. L.1065 J.D. [Ajalat,P.&A.]
*SPECIAL AGENCIES: State Board of Equalization; Franchise Tax Board; Assessment Appeals Boards; City Tax Board; Employment Development Department.
*PRACTICE AREAS: State and Local Tax Law.
**Azad, Susan S.** ... '62 '89 C.628 B.S. L.1068 J.D. [Latham&W.]
*PRACTICE AREAS: Civil Litigation.
**Azrael, Julia** ... '50 '82 C.813 B.A. L.262 J.D. [Belcher,H.&B.]
*LANGUAGES: Russian and French.
*PRACTICE AREAS: Civil Trials.
Baaden, Marianne ... '66 '92 C.112 B.A. L.426 J.D. 611 W. 6th
Babayi, Robert S. '59 '92 C.1222 B.S.E.E. L.472 J.D.
(adm. in FL; not adm. in CA; Pat.) 444 S. Flower St.
Babb, Steven C. ... '48 '73 C.668 B.A. L.800 J.D. Sr. Corp. Coun., Northrop Corp.
**Babbe, David B.** ... '55 '81 C.112 B.A. L.1068 J.D. [Morrison&F.]
*PRACTICE AREAS: Business Litigation.
**Babbitt, W. Thomas** '61 '93 C.112 B.S. L.464 J.D.
[[A] Blakely,S.T.&Z.] (See Pat. Sect.)
**Babok, Barry S.** ... '57 '87 C.477 B.A. L.146 J.D. [[A] Klein&M.]
**Baca, Elena R.** ... '67 '92 C.36 B.S. L.602 J.D. [[A] Paul,H.J.&W.]
Baca, Marie G. ... '55 '84 C.800 B.S. L.426 J.D. 1701 Clinton St.
**Bach, Julian** ... '64 '92 C.112 B.S. L.464 J.D. [[A] Arter&H.]
Bachmann, Peter H. '57 '82 C.732 B.A. L.94 J.D.
(adm. in MA; not adm. in CA) Exec. V.P., Bus. Affs., Imagine Films Entertainment, Inc.
Bachner, Monica ... '56 '81 C.309 B.A. L.178 J.D. Asst. U.S. Atty.
Bachrach, Donald B. ... '49 '74 C.37 B.S.B.A. L.209 J.D. [Iglow&B.]
**Backus, Stephen L.** ... '51 '80 C.165 B.A. L.990 J.D. [Bronson,B.&M.]
*PRACTICE AREAS: Civil Litigation; Construction and Real Estate Law and Professional Liability.
**Bacon, Barbara J.** ... '66 '92 C.763 B.S. L.309 J.D. [[A] McKenna&C.]
**Bacon, David L.**, (AV) ... '44 '69 C&L.309 A.B., J.D. [Thelen,M.J.&B.]
*PRACTICE AREAS: Management Labor Law; Civil Rights Litigation; Employee Benefit Plan Law; Insurance Law; Appeals.
**Bacon, Robert L.**, (AV) ... '28 '52 C.642 L.1065 J.D. [Bacon&M.]
*PRACTICE AREAS: Corporations; Tax; Transactions; Estate Planning; Real Estate.
**Bacon, Steven W., (P.C.)**, (AV) ... '48 '74 C.674 A.B. L.813 J.D. [Hill,F.&B.]

**Bacon & Mills, LLP, (AV)** [BR]
**800 Wilshire Boulevard, Suite 950, 90017**⊙
**Telephone: 213-486-6500 Fax: 213-486-6552**
**Robert Parker Mills; Robert L. Bacon; Theodore E. Bacon (Resident at West Covina Office); James W. Colfer; Carl Andrew Botterud; Adam J. Gerard; Howard S. Hou.**
**General Civil Trial and Appellate Practice in Federal and State Courts. Insurance Defense, Employment, Corporate, Federal and State Taxation Law, Environmental, Probate and Estate Planning.**
**West Covina, California Office: 100 North Barranca Street, 11th Floor. Telephone: 818-915-6555. Fax: 818-915-8855.**
***See Professional Biographies, LOS ANGELES, CALIFORNIA***

**Badal, Robert G.**, (AV) ... '47 '74 C.659 B.A. L.309 J.D. [Belin R.&B.]
Bader, Hans ... '69 '94 C.893 B.A. L.309 J.D. 445 S. Figueroa St., 31st Fl.
Bader, Jonathan David ... '58 '82 C.1349 B.A. L.276 J.D. Paramount Pictures Corp.
Bado, Peter James ... '59 '86 C.112 B.A. L.426 J.D. 777 S. Figueroa St., 10th Fl.
**Bae, I. Paul** ... '64 '91 C.112 B.A. L.464 J.D. [[A] Ropers,M.K.&B.]
*LANGUAGES: Korean.
*PRACTICE AREAS: Products and General Civil Litigation.
**Baer, James K.** ... '58 '83 C.112 B.A. L.426 J.D. [Katten M.&Z.]
*PRACTICE AREAS: Mergers and Acquisitions; Corporate Securities/Venture Capital.
Baer, John J., (AV) ... '— '57 C.061 L.981 LL.B. [J.J.Baer]
**Baer, Laura I.** ... '58 '88 C.800 B.A. L.1179 J.D. [[A] Murchison&C.]
*PRACTICE AREAS: General Insurance Defense Litigation.
Baer, Mark B. ... '65 '91 C.112 B.A. L.426 J.D. 1901 Ave. of the Stars, Ste. 390
Baer, John J., A Law Corporation, (AV) ... 1801 Ave. of the Stars
**Baerwitz, Herbert G.**, (AV) ... '20 '47 C.112 B.A. L.800 LL.B. [[C] Carlsmith B.W.C.&I.]
*PRACTICE AREAS: Intellectual Property; Entertainment Law; Copyrights; Business Law.
Baerwitz, Stephen ... '52 '78 C.112 B.A. L.1095 J.D. 10940 Wilshire Blvd., #1400
**Baev, Andrei A.** ... '65 '95 L.813 J.D. [[A] Mayer,B.&P.]
**Baev, Gail M.** ... '53 '81 C.388 B.A. L.424 J.D. [Lord,B.&B.]
*LANGUAGES: Spanish and French.
*PRACTICE AREAS: Insurance Coverage Litigation; Tort Litigation; Business Litigation.
Baggaley, James H., (BV) '34 '59
C.846 B.A. L.800 LL.B. Claims Atty., Auto. Club of Southern Calif.
**Baghdassarian, Alex R.** ... '63 '89 C.145 B.A. L.800 J.D. [[A] Whitman B.A.&M.]
*LANGUAGES: Armenian, French and Arabic.
**Bagnaschi, Christopher J.** ... '64 '91 C.1109 B.A. L.809 J.D. [[A] Knopfler&R.]
*PRACTICE AREAS: Construction Litigation; Insurance; Environmental; Products Liability; Business Litigation.
**Bagneris, Michele Beal** ... '59 '84 C.813 A.B. L.1066 J.D. [Richards,W.&G.]
*PRACTICE AREAS: Public Law.
**Bahar, Farhad** ... '62 '87 C.105 B.A. L.813 J.D. [[A] Pillsbury M.&S.]
**Bahar, Sarvenaz** ... '66 '94 C.659 B.A. L.976 J.D. [[A] Morrison&F.]
*LANGUAGES: French and Persian.
Bail, Alan C. ... '53 '79 C.1077 B.A. L.426 J.D. 3549 Maplewood Ave.
**Bailey, Barbara J.**, (AV) ... '42 '79 C.112 B.A. L.1148 J.D. [[C] Freeman,F.&S.]
*PRACTICE AREAS: Probate; Conservatorships; Probate and Trust Litigation.
**Bailey, Brett H.** ... '62 '91 C.878 B.A. L.276 J.D. [[A] Pillsbury M.&S.]

**Bailey, Bruce R., Law Offices of, (AV) '41 '66 C.112 B.A. L.1068 J.D.** BR
**1900 Avenue of the Stars, Suite 1630, 90067**
**Telephone: 310-286-9900 Telecopier: 310-286-9907**
**Email: brbailey@netcom.com URL: http://www.baileyfirm.com**
**(Certified Specialist, Taxation Law, The State Bar of California Board of Legal Specialization).**
**Associates: Gregory R. Schenz; John R. Denny; Richard Charles Herman. Of Counsel: Claudio O. Wolff; Steven U. Ross.**
**International Transactions, Taxation, Corporate Law, Real Estate, Promotion, Marketing and Advertising Law, Employee Benefits.**
**References: First Interstate Bank; Security Pacific National Bank.**

*See Professional Biographies, LOS ANGELES, CALIFORNIA*

**Bailey, Craig B.** ...... '52 '78 C.105 B.A. L.273 J.D. [Fulwider P.L.&U.] (See Pat. Sect.)
*PRACTICE AREAS: Patent, Trademark, Copyright and Unfair Competition Law; Litigation.
**Bailey, Jack S.** ........ '68 '93 C&L.276 B.S.F.S., J.D. [Ⓐ Littler,M.F.T.&M.]
**Bailey, Kathleen E.** ........ '58 '92 C&L.326 B.S., J.D. [Ⓐ Baker&H.]
*PRACTICE AREAS: Litigation; Insurance Coverage.
Bailey, Patricia S. ........ '65 '90 C.976 B.A. L.1068 J.D. Dep. Pub. Def.
**Bailey, Terry R.** ........ '60 '90 C.1077 B.A. L.1067 J.D. [Ⓐ Quisenberry&B.]
*REPORTED CASES: Fleming v. Gallegos 23 Cal.App.4th 68 (1994).
Baird, Alison Kaye ........ '61 '88 C.112 B.A. L.809 J.D. 3832 Wilshire Blvd.

**Baird, James R., Jr. '29 '54 C&L.813 A.B., J.D.**
**2791 La Castana Drive, 90046-1330**
**Telephone: 213-874-3442 Fax: 213-876-7699**
**Counsel for: Los Angeles Macintosh Group; Log Cabin Political Action Committee.**

**Baird, Lisa M.** ........ '— '95 C.112 B.A. L.426 J.D. [Ⓐ Crosby,H.R.&M.]
Baird, Lourdes G. ........ '35 '76 C.112 B.A. L.1068 J.D. U.S. Dist. J.
Baird, Rita J. ........ '45 '82 C.684 B.A. L.809 J.D. [Harris,B.&A.]
**Bajak, Curtis W.** ........ '57 '88 C&L.976 B.A., J.D. [Ⓐ Loeb&L.]
*LANGUAGES: German, Japanese and Swedish.
Bakaly, Charles G., Jr., (AV) ........ '27 '53 C.813 A.B. L.800 J.D. 400 S. Hope St.
**Baker, Annie Kun** ........ '47 '81 C.112 B.A.M.A. L.1068 J.D. [Carlsmith B.W.C.&I.]
*LANGUAGES: French, Italian, German and Russian.
*PRACTICE AREAS: Business Law; Corporate Law; Real Estate; International Law.
**Baker, Christopher R.** ........ '69 '96 C.790 B.S. L.893 J.D. [Ⓐ Rogers&W.]
Baker, Christopher R., (AV) '53 '80
C.1169 B.B.A. L.1148 J.D. 12400 Wilshire Blvd., 13th Fl.
Baker, Debra ........ '59 '85 C.297 B.A. L.494 J.D. 601 S. Figueroa
**Baker, Donald P.**, (AV) ........ '47 '73 C.684 B.A. L.1068 J.D. [Latham&W.]
Baker, Jerry L. ........ '33 '58 Calif. Dept. of Corps.
Baker, John, (AV) ........ '14 '40 C.112 L.800 J.D. 12400 Wilshire Blvd.
**Baker, Lisa M.** ........ '69 '95 C.800 B.A. L.809 J.D. [Ⓐ Lynberg&W.]
*PRACTICE AREAS: Business Litigation; Insurance Coverage.
**Baker, Louis R.**, (AV) ........ '15 '38 C.112 A.B. L.1066 J.D. [Ⓐ Stephens,B.&L.]
*PRACTICE AREAS: Corporate; Health Care; Probate.
Baker, Mia Ahrens ........ '40 '85 C.813 B.A. L.809 J.D. Spec. Asst. Dist. Atty.
Baker, Michael A. ........ '49 '75 C.800 A.B. L.809 J.D. 11443 Rose Ave.
Baker, Michael J. ........ '59 '84 C.209 B.S. L.990 J.D. 2029 Century Park E.
Baker, Pomphylia G. ........ '58 '86 C.800 B.S. L.325 J.D. P.O. Box 8574
Baker, Robert '49 '80 C.1077 B.S. L.1095 J.D.
(adm. in GA; not adm. in CA) 1145 S. Clark Dr.‡
Baker, Robert E. ........ '33 '72 C.668 B.A. L.813 LL.B. State of Calif. Real Estate

**Baker, Robert K., (AV) '40 '66 C&L.813 B.A., LL.B.**
**601 South Figueroa Street, 41st Floor, 90017-5758**
**Telephone: 213-612-0800 Facsimile: 213-689-7607**
***PRACTICE AREAS: Complex Litigation; Antitrust Law; Securities Litigation; Trade Secrets Law. General Civil Trial, Criminal Antitrust, Securities and Tax, Commercial Litigation, Trademark, Trade Secrets.**

*See Professional Biographies, LOS ANGELES, CALIFORNIA*

**Baker, Robert P.**, (AV) ........ '50 '75 C.93 A.B. L.309 J.D. [Baker&J.]
*PRACTICE AREAS: Business; Commercial; Real Estate Litigation.
Baker, Sandra L. ........ '62 '87 C.679 B.A. L.770 J.D. Resch. Atty., L.A. Supr. Ct.

**Baker, Scott L., (AV) '59 '85 C.608 B.S. L.930 J.D.**
**2029 Century Park East, Suite 2750, 90067**
**Telephone: 310-553-2253 Fax: 310-553-2254**
**Email: bake@earthlink.net**
**General Civil Practice including Business, Contract, Art and Entertainment, Insurance Defense and Accident Litigation.**

*See Professional Biographies, LOS ANGELES, CALIFORNIA*

**Baker, Shirley A.** ........ '52 '92 C.1109 B.A. L.1137 J.D. [Ⓐ Herzfeld&R.]
Baker, Valerie L. ........ '49 '75 C.112 B.A. L.1068 J.D. Supr. Ct. J.

**Baker & Hostetler, (AV)** BR
**600 Wilshire Boulevard, 90017-3212**⊙
**Telephone: 213-624-2400 FAX: 213-975-1740**
**Members of Firm in Los Angeles, California: Edward J. McCutchen (1857-1933); Harold A. Black (1895-1970); George Harnagel (1903-1962); G. William Shea (1911-1986); Sheldon A. Gebb (Managing Partner-Los Angeles, Long Beach, California and Houston, Texas Offices). Partners: Angela C. Agrusa; William P. Barry; Patrick J. Cain; Penny M. Costa; Richard A. Deeb; David A. Destino; Jack D. Fudge; Richard A. Goette; Byron Hayes, Jr.; Emil W. Herich; Dennis F. Hernandez; Bradley R. Hogin; Joseph B. Hudson, Jr.; Peter W. James; Michael M. Johnson; Anthony M. Keats; Lynn S. Loeb; Larry W. McFarland; John C. Mueller; Dean G. Rallis Jr.; Jill Sarnoff Riola; Thomas G. Roberts; Jack I. Samet; David C. Sampson; Bill E. Schroeder; Diane C. Stanfield; Teresa R. Tracy; Ralph Zarefsky. Associates: Steve W. Ackerman; David W. Ammons (Not admitted in CA); Roger L. Armstrong; Kathleen E. Bailey; David Caplan; Maria T. CeloCruz; Norman C. Davis; Andrew J. Durkovic; Keith A. Fink; Megan E. Gray; James E. Houpt (Not admitted in CA); Lisa F. Hinchliffe; Susan Horwitz (Not admitted in CA); Thomas Johnson; Jeffrey K. Joyner; Kirstin M. Larson; Marcia T. Law; Stephen Nakata; Peggy A. Propper; Gregg A. Rapoport; Marc I. Seltzer; Cranston J. Williams; Dennis L. Wilson. Of Counsel: Janet S. Hoffman; Glen A. Smith; John R. Sommer.**
**General Practice.**
**In Cleveland, Ohio: 3200 National City Center, 1900 East Ninth Street. Telephone: 216-621-0200.**
**In Columbus, Ohio: Capitol Square, Suite 2100, 65 East State Street. Telephone: 614-228-1541.**
**In Denver, Colorado: 303 East 17th Avenue, Suite 1100. Telephone: 303-861-0600.**
**In Houston, Texas: 1000 Louisiana, Suite 2000. Telephone: 713-236-0020.**
**In Long Beach, California: 300 Oceangate, Suite 620. Telephone: 310-432-2827.**
**In Orlando, Florida: SunBank Center, Suite 2300, 200 South Orange Avenue. Telephone: 407-649-4000.**
**In Washington, D. C.: Washington Square, Suite 1100, 1050 Connecticut Avenue, N. W. Telephone: 202-861-1500.**
**In College Park, Maryland: 9658 Baltimore Boulevard, Suite 206. Telephone: 301-441-2781.**
**In Alexandria, Virginia: 437 North Lee Street. Telephone: 703-549-1294.**
**In San Francisco, California: One Sansome Street, Suite 2000. Telephone: 415-951-4705.**

*See Professional Biographies, LOS ANGELES, CALIFORNIA*

**Baker and Jacobson, A Professional Corporation, (AV)** BR
**Suite 500, 11377 West Olympic Boulevard, 90064-1683**
**Telephone: 310-914-7990 Fax: 310-914-7913**
**Robert P. Baker; Lawrence M. Jacobson.**
**General Business and Commercial Litigation, including Complex Financial and Securities Fraud, Litigation under the Racketeer Influenced and Corrupt Organizations Act, Shareholders' Disputes, Wrongful Termination, Construction Matters, Bankruptcy Practice, Accountant's and Lawyer's Collections and Liability, and Real Estate Litigation of all types, including representation of Sellers, Purchasers, Developers, Lenders, Landlords, Contractors and Brokers.**

*See Professional Biographies, LOS ANGELES, CALIFORNIA*

**Baker, Manock & Jensen, A Professional Corporation**
**(See Fresno)**

**Baker, Silberberg & Keener**
**(See Santa Monica)**

Bakhshian, Varoujan ........ '60 '91 C.112 B.A. L.426 J.D. [Ⓐ Hagen H.&H.]
Bakker, Andrew M. ........ '43 '80 C.1246 B.S.C. L.1065 J.D. 3550 Wilshire Blvd.
**Bakley, Whitney E.** '64 '87 C.1278 B.A. L.276 J.D.
(adm. in FL; not adm. in CA) [Troop M.S.&P.]
Bakman, Larry M. ........ '53 '79 C.112 B.A. L.809 J.D. 12424 Wilshire Blvd., Bldg. 1430
**Baldocchi, Jennifer Stivers** ........ '68 '93 C.112 B.A. L.426 J.D. [Ⓐ Paul,H.J.&W.]
Baldonado, Arthur ........ '32 '61 C.112 B.A. L.276 J.D. Supr. Ct. J.
**Baldridge, Mary Ellen**, (AV) ........ '50 '76 C.972 B.A. L.178 J.D. [Coskey&B.]
*PRACTICE AREAS: Debtor/Creditor; Secured Transactions; Landlord and Tenant; Commercial Litigation and Documentation; Bankruptcy.
Baldwin, James W., (AV) ........ '23 '53 C.940 A.B. L.1068 J.D. 333 S. Grand Ave.
**Balekjian, Arpie** ........ '61 '89 C.605 B.A. L.426 J.D. [Ⓐ Quinn E.U.&O.]
**Bales, Betty** ........ '63 '91 C.112 B.A. L.569 J.D. [Ⓐ Alschuler G.&P.]
**Bales, Michael V.** ........ '55 '81 C.112 A.B. L.1067 J.D. [Greenberg G.F.C.&M.]
*PRACTICE AREAS: Corporate; Business; Entertainment.
**Balesh, James R.** ........ '67 '94 C.602 B.A. L.770 J.D. [C.A.Lloreda]
*PRACTICE AREAS: Civil Litigation; Personal Injury (Plaintiff and Defendant); Business Transactions.
**Balfus, Jonathan C.** ........ '63 '89 C&L.569 B.A., J.D. [Ⓐ Wilson,E.M.E.&D.]
**Balgenorth, Charles R.** '62 '92 C.912 B.S.E.E. L.477 J.D.
[Ⓐ Lyon&L.] (See Pat. Sect.)
*PRACTICE AREAS: Intellectual Property.
**Balian, Habib A.** ........ '70 '95 C&L.800 B.S., J.D. [Ⓐ Mitchell,S.&K.]
*PRACTICE AREAS: Litigation.
**Balisok, Russell S.**, (AV) ........ '46 '75 C.1097 L.809 J.D. [Houck&B.]
Balkin, Jeffrey G. ........ '43 '68 C&L.912 Ph.B., J.D. 1 Wilshire Bldg.
**Ball, Byron T.** ........ '64 '90 C.880 B.A. L.990 J.D. [Ⓐ Hill,F.&B.]
*PRACTICE AREAS: Civil Litigation.
**Ball, David N.** ........ '62 '88 C.112 B.A. L.426 [Biesty,M.&G.]
*PRACTICE AREAS: Insurance Defense Litigation; Construction Litigation; Real Estate; Family Law; Business Litigation.
Ball, James M. H. '51 '78 C.312 B.A. L.940 J.D.
C, University of Southern Calif. (Gen. Coun. Off)
**Ball, Joseph A.**, (AV) ........ '02 '27 C.190 A.B. L.800 J.D. [Carlsmith B.W.C.&I.]
*PRACTICE AREAS: Litigation.
Ball, Philip L. ........ '34 '59 C&L.339 B.S., LL.B. Gen. Coun., Caesars World, Inc.
Ball, Robert M. ........ '58 '88 C.1131 B.A. L.800 J.D. 555 S. Flower St., 23rd Fl.
**Ball, Robin D.** ........ '60 '86 C.145 B.A. L.309 J.D. [Ⓐ Chadbourne&P.]
Ball, Sally W. '55 '82 C.378 B.A. L.1338 J.D.
(adm. in PA; not adm. in CA) Plastic Mgmt. Co.
**Ballantyne, R. Curtis** ........ '46 '73 C.112 B.A. L.878 J.D. [Hill,F.&B.]
*LANGUAGES: French.
*PRACTICE AREAS: Public Utilities Commission Law.
Ballantyne, Robert B., (AV) '15 '43 C.112 A.B. L.309 J.D.
131161 Boca De Canon Lane‡
**Ballard, Laurel R.** ........ '55 '86 C.668 B.A. L.800 J.D. [Cox,C.&N.]
*PRACTICE AREAS: Real Estate and Business Litigation; Construction Litigation.
Ballard, Norma Crippen ........ '59 '86 C.668 B.A. L.809 J.D. Dept. of Jus.
**Ballard, Sean J.** ........ '67 '92 C.112 B.A. L.800 J.D. [Ⓐ Manning,L.B.&B.]
*PRACTICE AREAS: Business Litigation.
**Ballard, Shawna L.** ........ '65 '91 C.36 B.S. L.37 J.D. [Ⓐ Hennigan,M.&B.]
*PRACTICE AREAS: Commercial Law.
**Ballas, Stephen B.**, (AV) ........ '54 '79 C.112 B.A. L.800 J.D. [Williams&B.]⊙
*PRACTICE AREAS: Tax Law; Estate Planning Law; Probate.
**Ballesteros, Deanna L.** ........ '63 '92 C.66 A.B. L.128 J.D. [Ⓐ Burke,W.&S.]
*PRACTICE AREAS: Litigation.
**Ballmer, Bruce D.**, (AV) ........ '42 '74 C.112 A.B. L.309 J.D. [Kane,B.&B.]
*TRANSACTIONS: In San Diego: Horton Plaza Retail/Entertainment Center, Koll Center, America Plaza, Meridian, Santa Fe Depot Property, Emerald-Shapery Center, Lyceum Theaters, Gateway Center Industrial Parks. In Santa Clara: Great America Theme Park, Bella Vista Residential Development, Convention Center/Hotel/High Tech Trade Center Complex.
*PRACTICE AREAS: Redevelopment Law; Housing Law; Land Use Law.
Ballou, Robert B. ........ '29 '57 C.999 L.809 LL.B. 5757 W. Century Blvd.
**Ballsun, Kathryn A.**, (AV) ........ '46 '76 C.800 B.A. L.426 J.D. [Katten M.&Z.]
*PRACTICE AREAS: Estate Planning; Post Death Administration (Probate and Revocable Trust); Individual Tax Planning.
**Baluyot, Reuel M.** ........ '68 '95 C.662 B.A. L.809 J.D. [Ⓐ Freid&G.]
*LANGUAGES: Tagalog.
*PRACTICE AREAS: Family Law.
**Bamberger, David T.** ........ '54 '79 C.112 B.A. L.1067 J.D. [Selman B.]
**Bandiera, John D.** ........ '50 '94 C.012 B.A. L.813 J.D. [Ⓐ Arnold&P.]
*PRACTICE AREAS: Business Litigation.
Bandiera, Michael P., Jr. ...... '54 '81 C.107 B.A. L.809 J.D. 6320 Commodore Sloat Dr.
**Bandlow, Lincoln D.** ........ '66 '94 C.112 B.A. L.94 J.D. [Ⓐ Gibson,D.&C.]
*PRACTICE AREAS: Media and Intellectual Property Litigation.
Bane, George D. ........ '35 '70 C.112 B.A. L.809 J.D. 1180 S. Beverly Dr.
**Bank, Ira Eugene**, (AV) ........ '49 '76 C.36 B.S. L.1136 J.D. [I.E.Bank]
*REPORTED CASES: BIA, Matter of Amesquita, 16 I. & N. Dec. 318.
**Bank, Jonathan F.** ........ '43 '68 C.623 B.B.A. L.190 J.D. [Chadbourne&P.]

**Bank, Ira Eugene, A Law Corporation, (AV)**
**6300 Wilshire Boulevard, Suite 1010, 90048**
**Telephone: 213-653-4514 Facsimile: 213-651-5938**
**Email: 73032.342@Compuserve.com**
**Ira Eugene Bank (Certified Specialist, Immigration and Nationality Law, The State Bar of California Board of Legal Specialization).**
**Immigration and Nationality Law.**

**Banko, Nicholas** ........ '52 '84 C.112 B.A. L.426 J.D. [Selman B.]
**Bannan, C. Forrest**, (AV) ........ '46 '70 C&L.770 B.S.C., J.D. [Bannan,G.S.&F.]
*PRACTICE AREAS: Trial Practice; Antitrust; Employment Law; White Collar Criminal Defense; Commercial Litigation.

**Bannan, Green, Smith & Frank, (AV)**
**555 South Flower Street Forty Fourth Floor, 90071**
**Telephone: 213-362-1177 Fax: 213-362-1188**
**Email: BGSF.com**
**Members of Firm: C. Forrest Bannan; Ward D. Smith; Lesley C. Green; Ronald F. Frank. Associates: Gregg M. Audet; Gary J. Goodstein; Russell G. Petti; Kristina E. Weaver.**
**General Civil Trial and Appellate Practice in all State and Federal Courts, Product Liability, Environmental, Employment Law, Securities, Commercial Litigation, White Collar Criminal Defense including Antitrust.**

*See Professional Biographies, LOS ANGELES, CALIFORNIA*

Banner, Steven J. ........ '58 '82 C.112 B.A. L.800 J.D. 4700 Wilshire Blvd., 3rd Fl.
**Bant, Jill N.** ........ '68 '95 C.966 B.A. L.800 J.D. [Ⓐ Hawkins,S.L.&B.]
**Barabander, Michael** '53 '80 C.994 B.A. L.982 J.D.
(adm. in NJ; not adm. in CA) [Grotta,G.&H.]⊙
Barajas, Cecilia M. ........ '62 '89 C.112 B.A. L.893 J.D. 2133 Balsam Ave.
**Barajas, Dino** ........ '68 '93 C.112 B.A. L.309 J.D. [Ⓐ Milbank,T.H.&M.]

CAA179P

**Barak, Deborah** ... '57 '81 C.112 B.A. L.426 J.D. Asst. Gen. Coun., CBS Inc.
**Barak, Randee J.** ... '67 '93 C&L.112 B.A., J.D. [🄰 Sidley&A.]
*PRACTICE AREAS: General Civil, Health Care and Employment Litigation.
**Barak, Ronald S.**, (AV) ... '43 '69 C&L.800 B.S., J.D. [Manatt,P.&P.]
*PRACTICE AREAS: Real Estate; Leasing; Lease Audits; Finance.
**Baran, John M.** ... '55 '80 C&L.800 A.B., J.D. Asst. Gen. Coun., Ernst & Young LLP
Barasch, Stuart T. ... '51 '77 C.608 B.A. L.809 J.D. 767 N. Hill St.
**Barash, Martin R.** ... '68 '92 C.674 A.B. L.112 J.D. [Stutman,T.&G.]
*PRACTICE AREAS: Bankruptcy; Corporate Reorganization; Corporate Insolvency; Commercial Litigation.
**Baratta, James M.**, (AV) ... '47 '72 C.112 B.A. L.426 J.D. [Daniels,B.&F.]
*PRACTICE AREAS: Trial Law; Insurance.
**Baray, Enrique "Henry"** '51 '77 C.843 B.A. L.309 J.D.
Sr. V.P. & Gen. Coun., Univision Communication Grp.
*LANGUAGES: Spanish.
*RESPONSIBILITIES: Corporate Law; Media Law; International Law; Litigation.
Barbakow, Daniel R., (AV) ... '48 '73 C.1077 B.A. L.61 J.D. [Barbakow&L.]
Barbakow & Lerner, (AV) ... 11661 San Vicente Blvd.
**Barbanel, Alan H.** ... '55 '83 C.588 B.S. L.1049 J.D. [Quisenberry&B.]⊙
*REPORTED CASES: North Star Reinsurance Corporation v. Superior Court, 10 Cal. App. 4th 1815 (1992); General Star Indemnity Company v. Superior Court, 96 Daily Journal D.A.R. 9263 (1996).
**Barbanel, Debra Spangler** ... '57 '82 C.741 B.A. L.1049 J.D. [🄲 Pircher,N.&M.]
*PRACTICE AREAS: Real Estate Law; Finance.
**Barbarosh, Alison M.** ... '71 '96 C.112 B.A. L.426 J.D. [🄰 Graham&J.]
**Barbee, Michael P.** ... '61 '90 C.846 B.A. L.309 J.D. [🄰 Hughes H.&R.]
*LANGUAGES: German and Spanish.
**Barber, Bryan M.** ... '59 '85 C.473 B.A. L.893 J.D. [Zelle&L.]
*PRACTICE AREAS: Litigation; Insurance Coverage; Environmental Law; Product Liability.
**Barber, Jeremy W.** ... '66 '94 C.050 B.A. L.276 J.D. [🄰 Loeb&L.]
**Barber, John L.** ... '67 '92 C.934 B.A. L.426 J.D. [🄰 Gray,Y.D.&R.]
*PRACTICE AREAS: Business Law; Labor and Employment Law.
**Barber, Michele L.** ... '69 '95 C.112 B.A. L.800 J.D. [🄰 Paul,H.J.&W.]
**Barbosa, Henry S., (P.C.)**, (AV) ... '48 '74 C.112 B.A. L.1068 J.D. [Barbosa G.&B.]
*REPORTED CASES: Campbell v. City of Monrovia (1978) 84 Cal.App.3d 341; Doyle v. City of Chino (1981) 117 Cal.App.3d 673; Salvaty v. Falcon Cable TV (1985) 165 Cal.App.3d 798; Salazar v. City of Montebello (1987) 190 Cal.App.3d 953.
*PRACTICE AREAS: Municipal Law; Land Use and Zoning Law; Redevelopment Law; Environmental Law; CATV Law.

**Barbosa Garcia & Barnes, (AV)** 🄱🅁
**A Partnership including a Professional Corporation**
**Suite 390, 500 Citadel Drive, 90040**
**Telephone: 213-889-6600 FAX: 213-889-6605**
**Henry S. Barbosa (P.C.); Bonifacio Bonny Garcia; Douglas D. Barnes; Peter E. Langsfeld; Kenneth T. Fong; Jonathan B. Stone;—Augustin R. Jimenez; Rajeev M. Talwani; Erick L. Solares; Lorie A. Campos; Charisma T. Tan-Sanchez; Diana M. Carbajal; Sylvia J. Trujillo. Of Counsel: Norman Lieberman; John F. Lagle.**
**Education, Municipal, Administrative, Land Use, Real Estate, Corporate, Banking and Commercial, Employment, Environmental, Public Finance, Public Sector Labor. General Business and Commercial Litigation, State and Federal Civil and Appellate Litigation.**

***See Professional Biographies, LOS ANGELES, CALIFORNIA***

Barcena, Gustavo A. ... '51 '77 C.1060 B.A. L.1068 J.D. 6334 Whittier Blvd.
Barchiesi, Chester A. ... '31 '77 C.871 B.S. L.1095 J.D. Dept. of Trans.
**Barclay, Andrew W.**, (AV) ... '38 '65 C.112 B.A. L.1065 LL.B. [Clopton,P.&B.]
Barclay, James ... '41 '74 C.312 B.A. L.809 J.D. Gen. Atty., Union Pacific R.R. Co.
Bardach, Sheldon G., (AV) ... '37 '62 C.102 A.B. L.1068 J.D. 11755 Wilshire Blvd.
**Bardellini, Keith B.** ... '52 '77 C.112 B.A. L.1065 J.D. [Buchalter,N.F.&Y.]
*REPORTED CASES: Cole v. Fair Oaks Fire Protection District (1987) 43 Cal 3d 148.
*PRACTICE AREAS: Civil Litigation; Employment Litigation; Labor Law.
**Bardin, Richard A.**, (AV) '34 '65
C.112 B.S.E. L.800 J.D. [Fulwider P.L.&U.] (See Pat. Sect.)
*PRACTICE AREAS: Patent, Trademark, Copyright and Unfair Competition Law; Litigation.
Bardugo, Judy S. '41 '79 C.112 B.A. L.1068 J.D.
1800 Ave. of the Stars, Suite 900 (Century City)‡
**Baren, Charles H.** ... '62 '88 C.1097 B.A. L.426 J.D. [Wolf,R.&S.]
*PRACTICE AREAS: Community Associations Law; Civil Litigation.
Barens, Arthur H. ... '44 '69 C.112 B.A. L.800 J.D. [Barens,A.H.]
Barens, Arthur H., A P.C. ... 10209 Santa Monica Blvd.
**Barer, Daniel P.** ... '65 '90 C.112 B.A. L.1065 J.D. [🄰 Pollak,V.&F.]
Barfield, Barry B. ... '54 '84 C.767 B.A. L.426 J.D. Calif. Assn. of Realtors
**Barger, Glenn T.** ... '66 '91 C.112 B.A. L.990 J.D. [🄰 Chapman&G.]
*PRACTICE AREAS: General Negligence; Construction Litigation; Product Liability; Environmental Law; Professional Liability.
**Barger, Richards D.**, (AV) ... '28 '54 C.347 B.S. L.800 LL.B. [Barger&W.]
*PRACTICE AREAS: General Corporate Law; Insurance Law; Regulatory Law.

**Barger & Wolen, (AV)**
**515 South Flower Street, 34th Floor, 90071**⊙
**Telephone: 213-680-2800 Facsimile: 213-614-7399**
**Email: barwol@ix.netcom.com**
**Members of Firm: Richards D. Barger; Victor B. Levit (Resident, San Francisco Office); Kent Keller; Thomas B. Ackland; Robert Wood Hogeboom; Stephen C. Klein; S. Stuart Soldate; Royal Forest Oakes; Don R. Adkinson (Resident, Newport Beach Office); Dennis W. Harwood (Resident, Newport Beach Office); John M. Meindl (Resident, Newport Beach Office); John J. Richmond; Steven H. Weinstein; Gail E. Cohen; Sandra I. Weishart; John S. Pierce (Resident, San Francisco Office); Martin E. Rosen; Larry M. Golub; Edwin A. Oster (Resident, Newport Beach Office); J. Russell Stedman; Henry F. White, Jr. (Resident, New York Office); John C. Holmes; David C. Park; Robert J. McKennon; Richard G. De La Mora; John E. McPherson; Michael L. Rosenfield. Associates: David J. McMahon (Resident, San Francisco Office); Randall A. Doctor; Scott J. Therrien; Gregory B. Scarlett; Linda R. Caruso; Audrey M. Lyness; Gary A. Bresee (Resident, San Francisco Office); J. Ronald Ignatuk (Resident, Newport Beach Office); Heather Peters; Thomas R. Beer (Resident, San Francisco Office); John M. Le Blanc; J. Steven Bingman; Robert K. Renner (Resident, Newport Beach Office); Kimberly D. Griffin (Resident, San Francisco Office); Beverly A. Brand (Resident, San Francisco Office); Robert J. Cerny; Marina M. Maniatis; Gregory O. Eisenrich; Russell H. Birner; Michael J. Rothman; Pablo M. Zylberglait; Erin E. Martens; John P. Newell. Of Counsel: Alan R. Wolen; William A. Kurlander.**
**General Civil and Trial Practice in State and Federal Courts. Corporation, Securities, Real Estate, Real Estate Financing, Insurance, Banking, Probate, Trademark, Antitrust and Administrative Law. General Business, Legislative and Appellate Practice.**
**San Francisco, California Office: 47th Floor, 101 California Street, 94111. Telephone: 415-434-2800. FAX: 415-434-2533.**
**Newport Beach, California Office: 19800 MacArthur Boulevard, Suite 800, Irvine, California, 92715. Telephone: 714-757-2800. FAX: 714-752-6313.**
**Sacramento, California Office: 925 "L" Street, Suite 1100, 95814. Telephone: 916-448-2800. FAX: 916-442-5961.**
**New York, N.Y. Office: 100 Park Avenue, 23rd Floor, 10017. Telephone: 212-557-2800. FAX: 212-213-1199.**

***See Professional Biographies, LOS ANGELES, CALIFORNIA***

Barich, Richd. J., (AV) ... '23 '51 C&L.800 B.S., J.D. 2020 Ave. of the Stars
**Barker, Charles F.** ... '51 '76 C.800 A.B. L.1068 J.D. [Sheppard,M.R.&H.]
*PRACTICE AREAS: Labor and Employment Law.
**Barker, Jeffrey A.** ... '64 '93 L.1068 [🄰 Dewey B.]
Barker, Julie L. ... '68 '95 C.112 B.A. L.990 J.D. 1291 Stradella Rd.‡
**Barker, Linda Daves** ... '55 '83 C.800 B.S. L.426 J.D. [🄲 Heller E.W.&M.]
Barker, M. H., (AV) ... '17 '40 C&L.800 B.A., J.D. V.P., Arden Group, Inc.
**Barker, Norman B.**, (AV) ... '28 '54 C.112 B.S. L.1068 LL.B. [Gibson,D.&C.]
*PRACTICE AREAS: Federal, State and Local Taxation; International Taxation; Tax Controversies.
**Barker, Timothy S.**, (AV) ... '50 '76 C.112 B.S. L.1049 J.D. [🄰 Fragomen,D.&B.]
Barker, William G. '46 '72
C.112 B.A. L.426 J.D. Dir., Tax Planning, The Times Mirror Co.

**Barker & Romney, A Professional Corporation**
**(See Pasadena)**

Barlow, June Babiracki '54 '80
C&L.101 B.S., J.D. Assoc. Gen. Coun., Calif. Assn. of Realtors
**Barlow, Wayne E.**, (AV) ... '42 '68 C.112 B.A. L.800 J.D. [Barlow&K.]
*LANGUAGES: Spanish, Italian.
*PRACTICE AREAS: Management Labor Law; Employment Law; Discrimination Law.
**Barlow, William H.** '53 '86
C.101 B.S. L.426 J.D. Assoc. Gen. Coun., The Times Mirror Co.

**Barlow & Kobata, (AV)**
**2029 Century Park East, Suite 3230, 90067**
**Telephone: 310-277-7556 Fax: 310-277-2982**
**Members of Firm: Wayne E. Barlow; Mark T. Kobata. Associates: James E. Hall.**
**Management Labor, Employment, Personnel, Discrimination and Administrative Law. Litigation.**

***See Professional Biographies, LOS ANGELES, CALIFORNIA***

**Barmann, Bernard C., Jr.** ... '66 '90 C.154 B.A. L.178 J.D. [🄰 O'Melveny&M.]
**Barna, Susan L.** ... '65 '93 C.112 B.A. L.569 J.D. [🄰 Quinn E.U.&O.]
Barnard, Richard E. ... '34 '62 C.112 B.A. L.1068 J.D. 10880 Wilshire Blvd.
**Barnes, Angela** '69 '94 C.914 B.A. L.178 J.D.
(adm. in IL; not adm. in CA) [🄰 Christensen,M.F.J.G.W.&S.]
*PRACTICE AREAS: Corporate Law.
**Barnes, Brent E.** ... '53 '82 C.1042 B.S. L.426 J.D. [Dale,B.&H.]
*PRACTICE AREAS: Real Estate Law; Construction Defect Law; Banking Law; Product Liability Law; Insurance Coverage Law.
**Barnes, Christopher A.** ... '62 '87 C.659 B.A. L.893 J.D. [Howrey&S.]
*PRACTICE AREAS: Government Contract Law.
**Barnes, Craig S.** ... '56 '86 C.331 B.A. L.1068 J.D. [Sedgwick,D.M.&A.]
**Barnes, Douglas D.** ... '52 '79 C.668 B.A. L.1068 J.D. [Barbosa G.&B.]
*REPORTED CASES: Sounhein v. City of San Dimas, 11 Cal.App. 4th 1255.
*PRACTICE AREAS: Municipal Law; Personnel Law; Civil Rights Law; Tort Liability.
Barnes, James H. ... '48 '73 C.475 B.A. L.477 J.D. 15760 Ventura Blvd. (Encino)
**Barnes, Mary K.** ... '58 '83 C.800 A.B. L.1068 J.D. [Troop M.S.&P.]
*PRACTICE AREAS: General Business Litigation; Insurance Coverage Litigation; Entertainment Litigation.
Barnes, Minda F. ... '54 '80 C.1168 B.A. L.426 J.D. 1900 Ave. of Stars
**Barnes, Robert** ... '52 '85 C.051 B.A. L.1068 J.D. [Kaye,S.F.H.&H.]
*PRACTICE AREAS: Litigation; Entertainment.
**Barnes, Robert C.** ... '54 '83 C.103 A.B. L.659 J.D. [🅂 Fulbright&J.]
*PRACTICE AREAS: Real Estate.
**Barnes, Robert W.** ... '53 '80 C.1168 B.A. L.1068 J.D. [Greenberg G.F.C.&M.]
*PRACTICE AREAS: General Civil Litigation; Alternative Dispute Resolution; Labor Law; Employment Law.
**Barnes, Willie R.**, (AV) ... '31 '60 C.112 B.A. L.1068 LL.B. [Musick,P.&G.]
*PRACTICE AREAS: Corporate Law; Securities; Franchises and Franchising.
Barnes, McGhee & Pryce, (AV) ... 333 S. Grand Ave.
Barness, Ron Nathan ... '61 '86 C.112 B.A. L.426 J.D. 11440 San Vicente Blvd.
**Barnet, Irwin G.**, (AV) ... '38 '62 C.918 B.A. L.309 LL.B. [Sanders,B.G.S.&M.]
Barnett, Donald ... '37 '62 C.112 A.B. L.1068 J.D. 1801 Century Pk., E.
Barnett, Gary, (A Professional Corporation) '42 '67
C.112 B.S. L.1068 J.D. 3832 Wilshire Blvd.
**Barnett, James E.** ... '42 '66 C&L.802 B.B.A., LL.B. [🄲 Cox,C.&N.]
*PRACTICE AREAS: Taxation Law.
**Barnett, Lawrence R.** ... '56 '83 C.813 B.A. L.800 J.D. [Gipson H.&P.]

**Barnett, Leslie Ann '45 '92 C.347 B.A. L.426 J.D.**
**12400 Wilshire Boulevard, Suite 400, 90025**
**Telephone: 310-571-3680 Fax: 310-571-3682**
**Trusts and Estates, Probate, Wills, Guardianship and Conservatorship.**

Barnett, Paula Winner ... '— '90 C&L.178 A.B., J.D. 11111 Santa Monica Blvd.
Barnett, Philip ... '22 '52 C.472 B.A. L.809 LL.B. 2237 Sunset Blvd.
**Barnouw, Benjamin** ... '67 '93 C.846 B.A.,B.S. L.1066 J.D. [🄰 Richards,W.&G.]
*PRACTICE AREAS: Insurance Coverage; Business Litigation.
**Barnouw, Faye Chen** ... '68 '93 C.309 A.B. L.1066 J.D. [🄰 Parker,M.C.O.&S.]
*LANGUAGES: Mandarin Chinese, French, Portuguese.
*PRACTICE AREAS: Litigation; Bankruptcy Law; Commercial Law.
**Barns, Laura J.** ... '55 '80 C.112 A.B. L.809 J.D. [🄰 A.M.Klein]
*PRACTICE AREAS: Business Litigation; Antitrust; Lemon Law; Copyright and Trademark; Employment.

**Barnum, Jerome D.**
**(See Pasadena)**

Baron, Elizabeth A. ... '41 '77 L.1095 J.D. Supr. Ct. J.
Baron, Randall J. ... '64 '90 C.174 B.A. L.1049 J.D. Dep. Dist. Atty.
Baron, Stephen A. ... '45 '74 C.1077 B.A. L.1065 J.D. Dep. Dist. Atty.
**Baronsky, Kenneth J.** ... '62 '88 C&L.911 B.A., J.D. [Milbank,T.H.&M.]
**Barquist, Charles S.**, (AVⓉ) ... '53 '79 C.477 A.B. L.309 J.D. [Morrison&F.]
*PRACTICE AREAS: Intellectual Property Litigation; Product Liability; Business Litigation; Alternative Dispute Resolution.
Barr, Bruce W. ... '52 '85 C.893 B.A. L.1067 J.D. State Dept. of Transp.
**Barr, Colin E.** ... '66 '91 C.207 B.A. L.930 J.D. [🄰 Knopfler&R.]
*PRACTICE AREAS: Construction Defect Litigation; Suretyship.
**Barr, William B.** ... '39 '65 C&L.800 B.S.L., LL.B. [🄲 Oliver,V.S.M.&L.]
*PRACTICE AREAS: Eminent Domain; Inverse Condemnation; Civil Litigation.
**Barrall, James D. C.**, (AV) ... '50 '75 C.112 A.B. L.1068 J.D. [Latham&W.]
**Barrera, Patricio T.D.** ... '64 '90 C.805 B.B.A. L.846 J.D. [🄰 Hancock R.&B.]
*LANGUAGES: Spanish.
**Barrera, Teresa R.** ... '59 '87 C.309 A.B. L.1067 J.D. [Beck,D.D.B.&O.]
Barrero, Nestor ... '56 '84 C.112 B.A. L.1065 J.D. V.P. & Sr. Coun., Union Bk.
Barrero, Zinnia C. '60 '87 C.800 B.S. L.1065 J.D.
Assoc. Coun., Calif. Assn. of Realtors
Barreto-Morehouse, Margaret A. ... '49 '80 C.112 B.A. L.809 J.D. Dep. Dist. Atty.
Barrett, Bernard John, Jr. ... '53 '80 C.197 A.B. L.178 J.D. Legal Prof., Univ. of Calif.
**Barrett, David K.** ... '65 '90 C.813 B.A. L.1068 J.D. [🄰 Morrison&F.]
**Barrett, Edmont T.** ... '46 '77 C&L.426 B.A., J.D. [🄰 M.B.F.Biren&Assoc.]
*PRACTICE AREAS: Personal Injury.
Barrett, Eleanor Edie ... '45 '78 C.216 B.A. L.1148 J.D. Dep. Dist. Atty.
**Barrett, Ian R.** ... '56 '91 C.112 B.A. L.575 J.D. [🄰 Pillsbury M.&S.]
**Barrett, Jane H.**, (AV) ... '47 '72 C.1042 B.A. L.800 J.D. [Preston G.&E.]
**Barrett, John D., Jr.** ... '51 '76 C.426 B.A. L.809 J.D. [Parker S.]

**Barrett, Marilyn, (AV) '52 '78 C.378 B.S. L.1068 J.D.**
**1900 Avenue of the Stars Suite 1450, 90067**
**Telephone: 310-788-0028 Fax: 310-788-0215 E-Mail: mbarr@counsel.com**
**Email: mbarr@Counsel.com**
***PRACTICE AREAS: Business Law; State and Federal Tax Law.**
**Business Law. State and Federal Tax Law.**

***See Professional Biographies, LOS ANGELES, CALIFORNIA***

**Barrett, Michael S.** ....................'65 '94 C.546 B.S. L.190 J.D. [A] Anderson,M.&C.]
*PRACTICE AREAS: Surety Litigation.
Barrett, Newell ........................ '16 '47 C.112 B.A. L.1066 LL.B. Supr. Ct. J.
**Barrientos, Sandra Isabel** ................'63 '93 C&L.112 B.A., J.D. [Dale,B.&H.]
*LANGUAGES: Spanish and Italian.
Barrington, Betty G. ..........'40 '82 C.1097 B.A. L.800 J.D. 1933 Crenshaw Blvd.
**Barrios, Alfredo, Jr.** ......................'69 '94 C&L.309 A.B., J.D. [A] O'Melveny&M.]
Barrios, Gloria ..................'50 '80 C.112 B.A. L.770 J.D. Fair Employ. & Housing
**Barron, Eric A.** .......................'64 '90 C.309 B.A. L.477 J.D. [Troop M.S.&P.]
*PRACTICE AREAS: General Business Litigation.
**Barron, Jeffrey S.** ......................'49 '75 C.112 B.S. L.1068 J.D. [Morris,P.&P.]
**Barrow, Quinn M.** ......................'55 '80 C.569 A.B. L.94 J.D. [Richards,W.&G.]
*PRACTICE AREAS: Public Law; Litigation; Land Use Law.
**Barry, John S.** ...................'51 '77 C.112 B.A. L.426 J.D. Sr. Coun., Bank of Amer.
Barry, Kirk M. .................'55 '81 C.112 B.A. L.1066 J.D. 11669 Santa Monica Blvd.
**Barry, Robert S., Jr.** ......................'49 '76 C.112 B.A. L.1049 J.D. [Loeb&L.]
*PRACTICE AREAS: Corporate Law.
Barry, Stephen A. ..............'44 '77 C.800 B.S. L.426 J.D. 9800 S. Sepulveda Blvd.
Barry, Steven M., (AV) ..............'49 '75 C.119 B.F.A. L.398 J.D. 5750 Wilshire Blvd.
**Barry, William P.** ......................'48 '78 C.871 B.S. L.128 J.D. [Baker&H.]
*PRACTICE AREAS: Admiralty Law; Maritime Litigation; Environmental Litigation.
Barry & Duque ................................................ P.O. Box 251619
Barshop, Steven M. ......................'43 '71 C.112 B.A. L.809 J.D. Dep. Dist. Atty.
Barsook, Bruce A. .....................'51 '76 C.112 B.A. L.1068 J.D. [Liebert,C.&F.]
Barta, Robert M., (P.C.), (AV) ..............'57 '83 C.112 B.A. L.809 J.D. [Rosoff,S.&B.]
**Bartell, Steven R.** ..................'53 '88 C.845 B.A. L.1335 J.D. [A] Koletsky,M.&F.]
*LANGUAGES: Spanish, German.
*PRACTICE AREAS: Construction Defect Litigation; Litigation; Insurance; Business; Corporate.
**Bartenetti, Philip W.**, (AV) .....................'42 '72 C.767 B.S. L.1065 J.D. [Clark&T.]
*PRACTICE AREAS: General Business Litigation; Commercial Litigation; Insurance Litigation; Securities Litigation; Unfair Competition Litigation.
**Barth, Karen A.** ....................'66 '95 C.172 B.A. L.1067 J.D. [A] Baum,H.A.G.&D.]
*PRACTICE AREAS: Class Actions; Complex and Multi-District Litigation; Wrongful Death; Products Liability; Mass Disaster Litigation.
**Barth, Lawrence C.** .........................'54 '85 C.186 L.978 J.D. [Munger,T.&O.]
Barth, Marilyn L. ........................'34 '60 C.112 B.A. L.809 LL.B. [Goldflam&B.]
Barth, Stuart I. .........................'38 '62 C.494 B.A. L.37 LL.B. [Goldflam&B.]
**Bartholetti, Victor M.** ......................'62 '88 C&L.800 B.A., J.D. [A] Arter&H.]
Bartilson, Laurie Neiger ..................'55 '79 C&L.339 B.A., J.D. 6255 Sunset Blvd.
**Bartlett, Ernest J.** ..................'59 '91 C.1169 B.A. L.767 J.D. [A] Anderson,M.&C.]
*PRACTICE AREAS: Environmental, Surety and Probate Litigation; Bankruptcy.
**Bartlett, George M.** .....................'43 '73 C.813 A.B. L.61 J.D. [O'Melveny&M.]
*PRACTICE AREAS: Mutual Funds; Securities Regulation; Corporate Finance.
**Bartlett, Joseph P.** ...................'58 '85 C.112 A.B. L.1065 J.D. [Kinsella,B.F.&T.]
*PRACTICE AREAS: Corporate Financing Law; Securities Law; Corporate Law; Business Law.
**Bartnof, Howard M.** ..................'49 '75 C.1077 B.S. L.809 J.D. [C] J.M.Donovan]
*PRACTICE AREAS: Probate Law; Estate Planning; Trust Law.
**Barton, Alan J.**, (AV) ....................'38 '64 C.112 A.B. L.1066 LL.B. [Paul,H.J.&W.]
**Barton, Brenda S.** ...................'63 '92 C.112 B.A. L.145 J.D. [A] Mitchell,S.&K.]
*PRACTICE AREAS: General Civil; Bankruptcy Litigation.
Barton, David J. .......'56 '81 C.112 B.A. L.309 J.D. V.P. & Gen. Coun., Sizzler Intl., Inc.
Barton, Donald A. ..................'57 '82 C.800 B.S. L.1068 J.D. 2049 Century Park E.
Barton, Edmund C., (AV) ..............'40 '71 C.602 B.A. L.309 J.D. 6144 Burrows Dr.‡
Barton, Howard '27 '51 C.823 B.A. L.597 J.D.
Sr. V.P., Network TV Div., Paramount Pictures Corp.
**Barton, Robert M.**, (AV) ............'22 '45 C.378 A.B. L.477 J.D. [C] Barton,K.&O.]⊙
*PRACTICE AREAS: Business Law; Taxation; Estate Planning; Estate Administration.

**Barton, Klugman & Oetting, (AV)** [BB]
**A Partnership including Professional Corporations**
**37th Floor, 333 South Grand Avenue, 90071-1599**⊙
**Telephone: 213-621-4000 Telecopier: 213-625-1832**
**Counsel to Firm: Robert M. Barton†; Robert H. Klugman†; Richard F. Oetting†. Members of Firm: David F. Morgan†; William D. Herz†; Charles J. Schufreider†; Robert Louis Fisher†; Gilbert D. Jensen†; David J. Cartano†; Martin J. Spear; Tod V. Beebe†; Ronald R. St. John; Mark A. Newton†; Margot I. McLeay. Associates: Barbara W. G. Crowley; Reiko L. Furuta; Jaleen Nelson.**
**General Civil and Trial Practice. Taxation, Corporation, Banking, Probate and Trust Law. Antitrust, Corporate Securities, Real Property, Environmental, Oil and Gas, Labor and International Business Law. Professional Liability Defense, Insurance Coverage, Directors and Officers Defense and Coverage.**
**References: The Bank of California (Southern California Headquarters); Wells Fargo Bank, N.A. (Wells Fargo Center, Los Angeles).**
**Newport Beach Office: Suite 700, 4400 MacArthur Boulevard, P.O. Box 2350, 92660. Telephone: 714-752-7551. Telecopier: 714-752-0288.**
**†Denotes a lawyer whose Professional Corporation is a member of the partnership or is Counsel to the Firm**
***See Professional Biographies, LOS ANGELES, CALIFORNIA***

**Bartosh, Wendy A.** ............'61 '89 C.112 B.A. L.800 J.D. Broadcast Coun., CBS Inc.
**Barza, Harold A.**, (AV) .........................'52 '77 C.94 A.B. L.178 J.D. [Loeb&L.]
*LANGUAGES: French.
*PRACTICE AREAS: Litigation.
Baseman, Neal S. .......'52 '77 C.1044 B.A. L.94 J.D. Sr. V.P., Bus. Affs., Turner Pictures
**Basich, Anthony M.** ....................'56 '81 C.813 B.S. L.273 J.D. [Troop M.S.&P.]
*PRACTICE AREAS: General Business Litigation; Environmental Litigation; Wrongful Termination Litigation; Entertainment Litigation.
**Basile, Paul L., Jr.**, (AV) ......................'45 '72 C.605 A.B. L.1068 J.D. [Basile&L.]

**Basile & Lane, L.L.P., (AV)** [BB]
**11400 West Olympic Boulevard, 9th Floor, 90064-1565**
**Telephone: 310-478-2114 Fax: 310-478-0229**
**Members of Firm: Paul L. Basile, Jr. (Certified Specialist, Taxation Law, The State Bar of California Board of Legal Specialization); Jeff W. Lane.**
**Taxation, Estate Planning, Corporate and International Law.**
***See Professional Biographies, LOS ANGELES, CALIFORNIA***

**Basileo, Steven** .........................'64 '92 C.145 B.A. L.846 J.D. [A] O'Melveny&M.]
**Basini, Elisabeth A.** ..........'66 '91 C.1044 B.A. L.1068 J.D. [A] Greenberg G.F.C.&M.]
*PRACTICE AREAS: Litigation.
Basist, Wayne S. ....................'60 '87 C.1068 B.A. L.426 J.D. 1801 Ave. of the Stars
Baskett, John M, III ...........................................'47 '73 Principal Dep. Co. Coun.
Baskett, W. Paul ..................'59 '87 C.668 B.A. L.464 J.D. 2049 Century Park E.
**Bass, Adam Joel** ....................'65 '91 C&L.1049 B.A., J.D. [A] Buchalter,N.F.&Y.]
*LANGUAGES: Spanish.
*PRACTICE AREAS: Business Litigation; Real Property Litigation; Commercial Litigation; Loan Workouts.
**Bass, David M.** ..........................'58 '84 C.112 A.B. L.800 J.D. [Katten M.&Z.]
*PRACTICE AREAS: Litigation.
**Bass, Harris D.** ...................'52 '77 C.184 B.S. L.1068 J.D. [Anderson,A.L.&G.]
*PRACTICE AREAS: Corporate; Tax; Estate Planning; Real Estate; Trust and Probate Law.
**Bass, Jessica R.** ....................'69 '94 C.112 B.A. L.426 J.D. [A] Troop M.S.&P.]
*PRACTICE AREAS: Corporate.
**Bass, Lawrence**, (AV) ....................'50 '74 C.112 B.A. L.800 J.D. [Murphy,W.&B.]
*PRACTICE AREAS: Business Workouts; Bankruptcy Reorganizations; Creditors Remedies.

**Bass, Ronald J.** .....................'42 '68 C.813 A.B. L.309 J.D. [C] Armstrong H.J.T.&W.]
*PRACTICE AREAS: Entertainment.
**Bassett, Randall C.**, (AV) ......................'45 '70 C.112 B.A. L.309 J.D. [Latham&W.]
Bassett, Schuyler H. ....................'47 '75 C.112 B.A. L.809 J.D. 10460 Holman Ave.

**Bassin, Michael Robert, (AV) '48 '76 C.1077 B.A. L.426 J.D.**
**City National Bank Building, 16133 Ventura Boulevard Suite 1175 (Encino), 91436-2415**
**Telephone: 818-905-6096 Fax: 818-905-9145**
***REPORTED CASES: Elder v. Carlisle 1987, 2nd App. Dist. 193 Cal App. 3rd 1313; United Electric v. National Bonding 1983, 711 P.2d 131; Cornish v. Superior Court (Capital Bond & Insurance Co., real party interest) (1989) 209 Cal.App.3d 467.**
**General Business, Civil Litigation, Negligence and Insurance Law, Construction, Surety and Guaranty.**
***See Professional Biographies, LOS ANGELES, CALIFORNIA***

Bastiaanse, Gerard C. .............................'35 '64 C.94 B.S. L.893 LL.B. [Kindel&A.]
Bate, Bettina A. .........................'26 '64 C.112 L.809 J.D. Presiding Wkrs. Comp. J.
**Bate, David H.** .............................'57 '82 C.154 B.A. L.1068 J.D. [A] White&C.]
**Bateman, Mark R.** ....................'66 '91 C.800 B.S. L.1065 J.D. [A] Morrison&F.]
**Bates, Andre Y.** .............................'— '95 C.871 B.S. L.1068 J.D. [A] Morgan,L.&B.]
**Bates, Jeffrey R.** ....................'54 '83 C.970 B.A. L.276 J.D. [C] Foley L.W.&A.]
*SPECIAL AGENCIES: Provider Reimbursement Review Board.
*PRACTICE AREAS: Medicare and Medicaid; Health Care; Long Term Care.
**Bates, Terry B.** ....................'59 '84 C.112 B.A. L.1065 J.D. [Crosby,H.R.&M.]
*PRACTICE AREAS: Business Litigation; Insurance; Malpractice.
**Bath, Daniel G.** ...........................'57 '85 C.112 B.A. L.464 J.D. [Cummins&W.]
*PRACTICE AREAS: Bankruptcy; Commercial Litigation; Debtor-Creditor Disputes; Personal Injury Insurance Coverage and Litigation.
**Battaglia, David Alan** ...................'62 '87 C.276 B.A. L.1068 J.D. [Gibson,D.&C.]
**Battaglia, Philip M.**, (AV) ......................'35 '59 C&L.800 B.S.L., J.D. [Sidley&A.]
Battelstein, Nancy ....................'69 '96 C.860 B.A. L.990 J.D. Ernst & Young, LLP
**Battenfeld, John S.** ....................'59 '85 C.311 B.A. L.1068 J.D. [C] Morgan,L.&B.]
**Battle, W. Michael** ....................'64 '92 C&L.800 A.B., J.D. [A] Seyfarth,S.F.&G.]
*PRACTICE AREAS: Labor and Employment.

**Battle Fowler LLP, (AV Ⓣ)**
**A Limited Liability Partnership**
**1999 Avenue of the Stars, Suite 2700, 90067**⊙
**Telephone: 310-277-9090**
**Members of Firm: George Gordon Battle (1897-1949); Ludlow S. Fowler (1924-1961); Sanford C. Presant.**
**General and International Practice.**
**New York, N.Y. Office: Park Avenue Tower, 75 East 55th Street, 10022. Telephone: 212-856-7000.**
***See Professional Biographies, LOS ANGELES, CALIFORNIA***

**Battles, Charles S., Jr.**, (AV) ..........'34 '63 C.674 A.B. L.976 LL.B. [Gibson,D.&C.]
*PRACTICE AREAS: Alternative Dispute Resolution; Litigation; Constitutional; Securities.
Batzkovich, Chad B. .............................'56 '90 L.061 J.D. 3580 Wilshire Blvd.
**Bauer, Catherine Ellen** ..........'60 '85 C.112 B.A. L.800 J.D. Sr. Coun., Bank of Amer.
Bauer, Ginger G. ....................'54 '80 C.172 B.S. L.800 J.D. 333 S. Grand Ave.
Bauer, S. Harold ....................................'16 '41 C.145 L.146 J.D. P.O. Box 29034‡
Baum, Eric I ....................'54 '88 C.112 B.A. L.1065 J.D. 5757 Wilshire Blvd.
**Baum, Michael L.**, (AV) ..............'52 '85 C.112 B.A. L.1068 J.D. [Baum,H.A.G.&D.]
*PRACTICE AREAS: Aviation Accidents and Injuries; Complex and Multi-District Litigation; Products Liability; Mass Disaster Litigation; Wrongful Death.
Baum, Richard T. ....................'52 '78 C.112 A.B. L.809 J.D. 2040 Ave. of the Stars

**Baum, Hedlund, Aristei, Guilford & Downey, A Professional Corporation, (AV)** [BB]
**Suite 950, 12100 Wilshire Boulevard, 90025**⊙
**Telephone: 310-207-3233; 800-827-0087 Facsimile: 310-820-7444**
**Email: bhagd@bhagd.com URL: http://www.bhagd.com/attorneys/**
**Michael L. Baum; Paul J. Hedlund; J. Clark Aristei; Robert E. Guilford; William J. Downey III;—John A. Greaves; Cara L. Belle (Not admitted in CA); Robert F. Foss; Karen A. Barth; V. Neil Forn, II.**
**Languages: Spanish, German and French**
**Limited only to Plaintiff's Serious Personal Injury and Wrongful Death Accident Litigation nationwide and worldwide; including Aviation Accident Litigation, Airplane Accidents, Bus Accidents, Tractor-Trailer Accidents, Train Accidents, Public Transportation Accidents, General Tort, Mass Disaster Litigation, Multi-District Litigation and Product Liability including Drug Litigation.**
**Reference: Union Bank.**
**Washington, D.C. Office: 1250 24th Street, N.W., Suite 300. Telephone: 202-466-0513; 800-827-0097. Facsimile: 202-466-0527.**
***See Professional Biographies, LOS ANGELES, CALIFORNIA***

Bauman, Janet E. '66 '94 C.813 A.B. L.145 J.D.
1800 Ave. of the Stars, Suite 900 (Century City)

**Bauman, Joan S., (AV) '50 '77 C.1077 B.A. L.1095 J.D.**
**2029 Century Park East, Suite 2610, 90067**
**Telephone: 310-203-8267 Fax: 310-203-8644**
**Email: JoanBauman@aol.com**
**(Certified Specialist, Family Law, The State Bar of California Board of Legal Specialization).**
***REPORTED CASES: In Re Marriage of White, 1987, 192 CA3d 1022.**
**Family and Divorce Law, Premarital Agreements, Arbitration and Mediation.**
***See Professional Biographies, LOS ANGELES, CALIFORNIA***

**Bauman, Scott H.** ....................'64 '89 C.691 B.A. L.1066 J.D. [A] Mitchell,S.&K.]
*PRACTICE AREAS: Litigation; Copyright Law.
**Bauman, Stephen A.**, (AV) ............'35 '69 C.112 B.S. L.813 J.D. [Seyfarth,S.F.&G.]
*PRACTICE AREAS: Taxation Law; Estate Planning Law; Probate Law.
**Baumann, Merrill J., Jr.** ....................'59 '86 C.197 A.B. L.800 J.D. [C] Graham&J.]
*PRACTICE AREAS: Attorney Ethics; Corporate Law.
**Baumann, Michael E.** ....................'54 '79 C.674 A.B. L.945 J.D. [Kirkland&E.]
*PRACTICE AREAS: Litigation.
**Baumann, Richard G.**, (AV) ..........'38 '64 C&L.966 B.S., J.D. [Sulmeyer,K.B.&R.]
*PRACTICE AREAS: Commercial Law.
Baumeister, Madonna Shannon ...........'59 '86 C.741 B.A. L.1065 J.D. 400 S. Hope St.
Baumer, Charles B. ....................................'43 '69 C.112 B.A. L.546 J.D. [Schaffer&B.]
Baumer, Edward F. '13 '37 C&L.705 A.B., J.D.
(adm. in NJ; not adm. in CA) Chmn. of the Bd., E. F. Baumer & Co.
Baumgarten, Ronald N., (AV) ..............'42 '70 C&L.339 B.A., J.D. [R.N.Baumgarten]
Baumgarten, Ronald N., P.C., (AV) .................... 12304 Santa Monica Blvd., 3rd Fl.
Baumgold, Sharon .......'53 '77 C.112 B.A. L.1068 J.D. Sr. Writs Atty., Calif. Ct. of App.
**Baumoel, James L.** ....................'46 '73 C.473 B.S. L.477 J.D. [Jones,D.R.&P.]
**Baute, Mark D.** ....................'61 '86 C.911 B.A. L.1068 J.D. [Lamb&B.]
*PRACTICE AREAS: Complex Business Litigation; Labor; Employment; Real Estate; Antitrust.
**Bautista, Leopoldo A.** ....................'62 '90 C.813 B.A. L.1066 J.D. [A] J.V.Jordan]
*LANGUAGES: Spanish.
*PRACTICE AREAS: Business Litigation; Intellectual Property Law and Litigation; Franchise Law and Litigation; Trademarks; Premises Liability Defense.
**Bava, Gordon M., (P.C.)**, (AV) ........'48 '74 C.276 B.S.F.S. L.800 J.D. [Manatt,P.&P.]
*PRACTICE AREAS: Corporate Law; Securities Law; Financial Institutions Law; Mergers and Acquisitions.
Bavnick, Stewart '41 '79 C.330 B.A. L.809 J.D.
L.A. County Assessor, Prin. Prop. Assess. Spec. Atty.
Bax, John W. ....................................'42 '70 C.36 B.A. L.1066 J.D. Dep. Dist. Atty.

CAA181P

CALIFORNIA—LOS ANGELES MARTINDALE-HUBBELL LAW DIRECTORY 1997

**Baxter, Judith L.** ..........................'62 '87 C.800 B.A. L.608 J.D. [Ⓐ Epstein B.&G.]
*PRACTICE AREAS: Labor and Employment Law; Construction; Litigation.
**Baxter, Thomas W.** .......................... '54 '83 C.170 B.A. L.1065 J.D. [O'Melveny&M.]
*PRACTICE AREAS: Corporate Banking; Corporate Finance; Securities; Structured Finance.
Bay, James S. .......................... '34 '60 C.112 B.S. L.1066 LL.B. 11845 W. Olympic Blvd.
**Bayard, Michael J.** ..........................'53 '79 C.112 A.B. L.1065 J.D. [Sonnenschein N.&R.]
*PRACTICE AREAS: Construction Law; Alternative Dispute Resolution.
Bayer, Kenneth H. ..........................'56 '82 C.112 B.A. L.1148 J.D. 6922 Hollywood Blvd.
Bayer, Leon D., (AV) .......................... '53 '79 C.1077 B.A. L.1095 J.D. 201 N. Figueroa St.
**Bayer, Ronald M.**, (AV) .......................... '48 '72 C.112 A.B. L.1068 J.D. [Shearman&S.]
Bayman, Lindsey .......................... '63 '89 L.054 LL.B. 2506 Canyon Dr.
**Baymiller, Roger B.**, (AV) ..........................'41 '69 C.36 B.A. L.800 J.D. [Carlsmith B.W.C.&I.]
*PRACTICE AREAS: Corporate Finance; Securities; Corporate Formation; Commercial Real Estate Acquisitions; Commercial Real Estate Sales.
Bayne, Donald S., (BV) '49 '78
C.691 B.A. L.744 J.D. 12400 Wilshire Blvd. (©San Antonio, TX)
Baynes, James M. .......................... '46 '74 C.770 B.A. L.1065 J.D. [Hogan,B.&H.]
**Bazan, John Francis** .......................... '61 '94 C.1075 B.A. L.1068 J.D. [Ⓐ Mendes&M.]
Bazar, Darin N. .......................... '60 '85 C.1044 B.S. L.1068 J.D. 4215 Glencoe Ave.
**Bazar, Gerald M.**, (AV) ..........................'35 '59 C.112 B.A. L.1068 J.D. [King,W.E.&B.]
*PRACTICE AREAS: Business Law; Real Property.
**Bazis, Jeanette M.** .......................... '66 '93 C.831 B.B.A. L.494 J.D. [Ⓐ Gibson,D.&C.]
*PRACTICE AREAS: General Commercial Litigation; Intellectual Property Litigation.
Beadel, Robert H. .......................... '66 '92 C.197 B.A. L.990 J.D. 624 S. Grand Ave.
**Beal, Robert F.** ..........................'70 '95 C.93 B.A. L.1049 J.D. [Coleman&W.]
*PRACTICE AREAS: Civil Litigation; Torts; Insurance Defense; Products Liability.
**Beall, L. Anthony** ..........................'61 '87 C.112 B.A. L.426 J.D. [Ⓐ Heller E.W.&M.]
Beam, Elsworth M. .......................... '22 '50 C.668 A.B. L.800 J.D. Supr. Ct. J.

**Beam, Brobeck & West**
(See Santa Ana)

Beaman, Patricia A. .......................... '51 '81 C.800 B.A. L.426 J.D. Asst. U.S. Atty.
**Beanum, John O.** ..........................'69 '95 C&L.602 B.A., J.D. [Ⓐ Sheppard,M.R.&H.]
**Beard, Ronald S.**, (AV) .......................... '39 '65 C.207 B.A. L.976 LL.B. [Gibson,D.&C.]
*PRACTICE AREAS: Corporate Law; Mergers, Acquisitions and Divestitures; Securities.
Beasley, Sheryl M. .......................... '56 '85 C.605 A.B. L.1065 J.D. 3550 Wilshire Blvd.
Beason, Candace Joan .......................... '53 '80 C.112 B.A. L.809 J.D. Supr. Ct. J.
**Beattie, R. Bret** .......................... '60 '90 C.1253 B.S. L.990 J.D. [Ⓐ Schaffer&L.]
*PRACTICE AREAS: Products Liability; Complex Personal Injury; Chemical Exposure; Business Interruption; Property Damage.
**Beatty, Heather C.** ..........................'65 '92 C.112 B.A. L.426 J.D. [Ⓐ Burke,W.&S.]
*PRACTICE AREAS: Litigation; Employment Law; Labor Relations.
Beaubein, Andrea Kemp .......................... '56 '91 C.112 B.A. L.426 J.D. 11000 Wilshire Blvd.
Beaubien, Andrea K. .......................... '56 '91 C.112 B.A. L.426 J.D. N.L.R.B.
**Beaubien, James P.** ..........................'63 '91 C.674 A.B. L.1068 J.D. [Ⓐ Latham&W.]
**Beaudet, Teresa A.** .......................... '53 '80 C&L.426 B.A., J.D. [Mayer,B.&P.]
**Beaudry, Robert V.** ..........................'46 '74 C.112 B.A. L.809 J.D. [Ⓒ Kirtland&P.]
**Beawy, Adel F.** ..........................'67 '96 C.145 B.A. L.659 J.D. [Ⓐ Latham&W.]
Bechman, Carolyn .......................... '51 '83 C.339 B.A. L.37 J.D. Chief Coun., I.R.S.
**Beck, Devan D.** .......................... '60 '88 C&L.101 B.A., J.D. [Ⓐ Milbank,T.H.&M.]
**Beck, Douglas W.** ..........................'49 '75 C.674 A.B. L.1066 J.D. [Tuttle&T.]
*PRACTICE AREAS: Civil Litigation; Real Estate and Environmental Litigation.
**Beck, Kelley K.**, (AV) .......................... '55 '79 C.878 B.S. L.846 J.D. [Hawkins,S.L.&B.]
Beck, Leonard S. .......................... '29 '53 C.800 L.426 LL.B. 11737 Darlington Ave.
**Beck, Mark E.**, (AV) ..........................'50 '75 C.813 B.A. L.276 J.D. [Beck,D.D.B.&O.]
**Beck, Paul A.**, (AV) ..........................'50 '76 C.309 B.A. L.273 J.D. [McDermott,W.&E.]
*PRACTICE AREAS: Bankruptcy; Insolvency; Litigation.
**Beck, Paul J.** ..........................'59 '84 C.154 B.A. L.1066 J.D. [Ⓐ Knapp,M.J.&D.]
*PRACTICE AREAS: Construction Law; Government Contracts Law; Litigation; Public Entity Law.
Beck, Robert S., (AV) .......................... '39 '67 C.112 B.S. L.800 J.D. 1251 Norman Pl.‡
Beck, Thomas E. ..........................'46 '78 C.415 B.A. L.1136 J.D. 3435 Wilshire Blvd.

**Beck, De Corso, Daly, Barrera & Oh, A Professional Law Corporation, (AV)**
**601 West Fifth Street, 12th Floor, 90071-2025**
**Telephone: 213-688-1198 Fax: 213-489-7532**
**Email: beckdecorso@earthlink.net URL: http://www.earthlink.net/~beckdecorso**
**Mark E. Beck; Anthony A. De Corso; Bryan D. Daly; Teresa R. Barrera; Angela E. Oh;—Peter J. Diedrich; Joan M. Steinmann; Evan Scheffel. Of Counsel: Godfrey Isaac.**
**Civil and Criminal Litigation in State and Federal Courts and before Administrative Agencies.**
*See Professional Biographies, LOS ANGELES, CALIFORNIA*

**Becker, Arto C.**, (AV) ..........................'55 '81 C.178 A.B. L.262 J.D. [Hawkins,D.&W.]
**Becker, Bartley L.** .......................... '47 '76 C.112 A.B. L.426 J.D. [Lewis,D.B.&B.]
**Becker, David J.** .......................... '66 '94 C.112 B.A. L.1066 J.D. [Ⓐ McCambridge,D.&M.]
*LANGUAGES: French.
Becker, Diane Lynn, (AV) ..........................'50 '73 C.112 B.A. L.1068 J.D. 1801 Century Park E.
**Becker, Marc A.** .......................... '64 '88 C.025 B.S. L.1066 J.D. [Munger,T.&O.]
**Becker, Norman H.** ..........................'67 '92 C.112 A.B. L.1068 J.D. [Behr&A.]
*PRACTICE AREAS: Entertainment Law.
Becker, Richard G. ..........................'48 '75 C.1077 B.A. L.809 J.D. 6255 Sunset Blvd.
Becker, Todd B. .......................... '60 '87 C.112 B.A. L.990 J.D. 6380 Wilshire Blvd.
**Becker, William J., Jr.** .......................... '54 '88 C.549 B.A. L.1049 J.D. [Ⓐ Koletsky,M.&F.]
*REPORTED CASES: Kuperstein v. Superior Court, (1988) 204 Cal. App.3d 598; Allstate v. Interbank Financial Services (1989) 215 Cal. App.3d 825.
*PRACTICE AREAS: Construction Defect Defense; General Liability Defense.
Becket, Jody .......................... '55 '90 C.259 B.S. L.809 J.D. 1750 N. Harvard Blvd.
**Beckham, Robert P.**, (AV) ..........................'48 '73 C.112 B.A. L.767 J.D. [Horgan,R.B.&C.]
*PRACTICE AREAS: Commercial Litigation; Employee Relations.
**Beckhart, Leslie Kent** .......................... '61 '93 C.309 A.B. L.800 J.D. [Ⓐ Sidley&A.]
*PRACTICE AREAS: Taxation.
Beckler, Howard E., (AV) .......................... '31 '59 C&L.608 B.Sc., J.D. 6922 Hollywood Blvd.
**Beckman, Bruce A.**, (AV) .......................... '30 '59 C.112 B.A. L.1068 LL.B. [Beckman,D.S.&R.]
*PRACTICE AREAS: Life, Health and Disability Insurance Law; Appellate Practice; Constitutional Law; Environmental Law; Real Estate.

**Beckman, Davis, Smith & Ruddy LLP, (AV)**
**601 South Figueroa Street, Suite 2600, 90017-5704**
**Telephone: 213-624-4900 Facsimile: 213-624-5300**
**Members of Firm: Bruce A. Beckman; Richard T. Davis, Jr.; Jeffrey P. Smith; Catherine Hunt Ruddy. Of Counsel: Sidney W. Bishop; Cheryl A. De Bari. Associates: Laura L. Chapman; Brian F. Rowe.**
**General Civil Trial and Appellate Practice, Insurance, Employment and Discrimination, Products Liability, Environmental and Probate Law.**
*See Professional Biographies, LOS ANGELES, CALIFORNIA*

**Beckner, Nancy M.**, (AV®) ..........'44 '79 C.446 B.A. L.312 J.D. [Carlsmith B.W.C.&I.]
*PRACTICE AREAS: International Taxation; International Estate Planning; Corporate and Partnership Tax; Non-Profit Tax Law.
Becks, Harold G., (BV) ..........................'48 '74 C.813 B.A. L.659 J.D. [Wilson&B.]
Beckstrand, Peggy .......................... '49 '82 C.846 B.F.A. L.1179 J.D. Dep. Dist. Atty.
**Beckwith, Cynthia** .......................... '55 '92 C.019 B.A. L.990 J.D. [Ⓐ McKenna&C.]
Beckwith, Douglas C. .......................... '51 '82 C&L.546 B.A., J.D. 2359 Nicholas Canyon Rd.
Beckwith, Francis B., Jr. .......................... '30 '70 1647 S. Orange Dr.
Bednarski, Marilyn E. .......................... '58 '82 C.112 B.A. L.426 J.D. Fed. Pub. Def.

Bedrosian, John C. ..........................'34 '60 C.112 B.S. L.800 LL.B. 11620 Wilshire Blvd.‡
Beebe, James Warren, (A Law Corporation), (AV) '20 '50
C.813 A.B. L.800 LL.B. 4069 Cromwell Ave.
**Beebe, Tod V.**, (AV) .......................... '56 '81 C.800 B.A. L.1066 J.D. [Barton,K.&O.]
*PRACTICE AREAS: Trial Practice; Insurance Coverage; Securities; Banking; Entertainment.
Beechen, Paul D., (AV) .......................... '48 '74 C.112 A.B. L.1068 J.D. [P.D.Beechen]
Beechen, Paul D., Inc., (AV) .......................... 1900 Ave. of Stars

**Beehler & Pavitt**
(See Culver City)

**Beeman, Michael R.** .......................... '64 '89 C.154 B.A. L.178 J.D. [Ⓐ Dewey B.]
Beerman, David Mark ..........................'45 '72 C.1077 B.A. L.426 J.D. 7060 Hollywood Blvd.
**Beers, Everitt G.** ..........................'50 '80 C.17 B.A. L.1065 J.D. [Ⓒ Graham&J.]
*PRACTICE AREAS: Civil Litigation; Intellectual Property Law; Computers and Software; Copyrights; Online and Internet Law.
**Behar, Howard D.** .......................... '50 '82 C.178 B.S. L.813 J.D. [Proskauer R.G.&M.]
*PRACTICE AREAS: Entertainment Law.
**Behnia, Hatef** .......................... '53 '81 C.685 B.A. L.800 J.D. [Gibson,D.&C.]
**Behr, Joel, (A P.C.)**, (AV) .......................... '42 '68 C.800 B.S. L.145 J.D. [Behr&A.]
*PRACTICE AREAS: Entertainment Law.

**Behr and Abramson, (AV)**
**A Partnership including A Professional Corporation**
**2049 Century Park East, 26th Floor, 90067**
**Telephone: 310-556-9200 Telecopier: 310-556-9229**
**Joel Behr (A P.C.); Howard Andrew Abramson; Dennis N. Cline; Norman H. Becker; Adam David Kaller.**
**Entertainment and Technology Transactions.**
*See Professional Biographies, LOS ANGELES, CALIFORNIA*

**Behrendt, John T.** .......... '45 '71 C.815 B.A. L.494 J.D. [Gibson,D.&C.] (©N.Y., NY)
*PRACTICE AREAS: Litigation; Accountant's Liability.
**Behrens, Erica S.** ..........................'69 '95 C.112 B.A. L.1065 J.D. [Ⓐ Monteleone&M.]
*LANGUAGES: Spanish.
*PRACTICE AREAS: Construction Law; Business Litigation; Business Law; Corporate Law.
Behrle, F. Keenan ..........'42 '70 C.426 B.A. L.1068 J.D. 1999 Ave. of the Stars, 26th Fl.
Behrstock, Victor .......................... '12 '35 C.800 L.809 LL.B. 2741 Anchor Ave.‡
**Beightol, Claudia T.** .......................... '65 '92 C.112 B.A. L.426 J.D. [Ⓐ Kern,S.&G.]
*PRACTICE AREAS: Premises Liability; Products Liability; Medical Malpractice; Defamation; Wrongful Termination.
**Beilinson, Marc A.**, (BV) .......................... '58 '83 C.112 B.A. L.1067 J.D. [Pachulski,S.Z.&Y.]
Beker, Semion Alon ..........................'64 '89 C.112 B.A. L.1065 J.D. 8421 Lincoln Blvd.
Belanger, Debra A. ...... '61 '94 C.446 B.S.B.A. L.809 J.D. 515 S. Figueroa St., Ste. 1200
**Belcher, John A.** ..........................'56 '81 C.112 A.B. L.1066 J.D. [Hanna&M.]
*PRACTICE AREAS: Insurance Coverage; Litigation; Appellate Practice.
Belcher, Martha M. .......................... '58 '83 C.282 B.A. L.1065 J.D. 777 Figueroa St.
**Belcher, Michael J.**, (AV) ..........................'42 '70 C&L.426 B.A., J.D. [Wright,R.O.&T.]
*PRACTICE AREAS: Insurance Bad Faith; Insurance Coverage; Employment Law; Product Liability; Commercial Litigation.

**Belcher, Henzie & Biegenzahn, A Professional Corporation, (AV)** BB
**333 South Hope Street, Suite 3650, 90071-1479**
**Telephone: 213-624-8293 Telecopier: 213-895-6082**
**Frank B. Belcher (1891-1979); David Bernard (1931-1978); John S. Curtis; E. Lee Horton; William T. DelHagen; Julia Azrael;—Jeffrey L. Horwith; Georgette Renata Herget; David L. Bonar; Raymond E. Hane, III; James C. Hildebrand; Robert S. Cooper; Wun-ee Chelsea Chen; John Erin McOsker; Mary E. Gram. Of Counsel: George M. Henzie; Leo J. Biegenzahn; James M. Derr.**
**Aviation, Product Liability, General Civil Trial and Appellate Practice, Insurance Defense, Personal Injury.**
**Reference: Bank of America (Los Angeles Main Office).**
*See Professional Biographies, LOS ANGELES, CALIFORNIA*

Beld, Todd Daniel .......................... '60 '86 C.684 B.A. L.426 J.D. 1500 Quail St.
Belevetz, Timothy D. '67 '93 C.31 B.A. L.945 J.D.
(adm. in VA; not adm. in CA) U.S. Sec. & Exch. Comm.
**Belfield, Carol Laurene** ..........................'55 '81 C.112 A.B. L.1068 J.D. [Loeb&L.]
*LANGUAGES: French.
*PRACTICE AREAS: Litigation.
**Belfield, George M.** .......................... '54 '81 C.401 B.S. L.800 J.D. [Manatt,P.&P.]
*PRACTICE AREAS: Litigation.
**Belgrad, Christine H.** .......................... '64 '91 C.659 B.S. L.846 J.D. [Rutter,G.&H.]
*PRACTICE AREAS: Litigation.
**Belin, Daniel N.**, (AV) .......................... '38 '62 C.477 B.S. L.309 LL.B. [Belin R.&B.]

**Belin Rawlings & Badal, (AV)** BB
**11601 Wilshire Boulevard, Suite 2200, 90025-1758**
**Telephone: 310-575-5300 Fax: 310-445-0884**
**Members of Firm: Daniel N. Belin; Douglas M. Rawlings; Robert G. Badal; Paul N. Sorrell; Burton Falk. Associates: Stephanie Blackman; John A. Schlaff. Of Counsel: Martin S. Schwartz (Certified Specialist, Taxation Law, The State Bar of California Board of Legal Specialization); James Edward Doroshow.**
**General Commercial Litigation Practice in all State and Federal Courts. Arbitration, Mediation and Dispute Resolutions. Administrative Hearings and Appeals, International Litigation. Firm Specialties include: securities, antitrust, financial institutions, real estate and construction defect litigation.**
*See Professional Biographies, LOS ANGELES, CALIFORNIA*

Belinsky, Russell A. ..........................'60 '85 C.912 B.B.A. L.276 J.D. Chanin & Co.
**Belke, Becky J.** ..........................'67 '95 C.960 B.S. L.809 J.D. [Ⓐ Meserve,M.&H.]
*PRACTICE AREAS: Insurance Bad Faith Defense; Labor (Management Defense).
Bell, Anthony E. .......................... '63 '88 C.112 B.A. L.1066 J.D. 515 S. Flower St.
**Bell, Carolyn Pierce** .......................... '47 '91 C.112 B.S.N. L.809 J.D. [Ⓐ Quisenberry&B.]
*PRACTICE AREAS: Business Litigation; Insurance Coverage; Bankruptcy.
**Bell, Charles F.** ..........................'38 '65 C.112 A.B. L.1066 J.D. Sr. Reg. Coun., Unisys Corp.
**Bell, Craig H.** ..........................'53 '78 C.112 B.A. L.426 J.D. [Ⓐ Chapin,F.&W.]
*REPORTED CASES: Warner v. Fire Ins. Exch. (1991) 230 Cal. App.3d 1029; Beaty v. Truck Ins. Exch. (1992) 6 Cal. App 4th 1455.
*PRACTICE AREAS: Civil Appeals; Insurance Coverage; Bad Faith Litigation.
**Bell, David L.** ..........................'53 '90 C.623 B.S. L.809 J.D. [Ⓐ La Follette,J.D.F.&A.]
**Bell, Kimber K.** ..........................'— '93 C&L.990 B.A., J.D. [Ⓐ Hughes H.&R.]
Bell, Leslie F., (AV) '40 '65 C.339 B.S. L.37 J.D.
V.P., CFO & Gen. Coun., Salick Health Care, Inc.
**Bell, Marcella A.** .......................... '66 '94 C.426 B.A. L.1136 J.D. [Ⓐ S.L.Hartmann]
*LANGUAGES: Italian, Spanish.
*PRACTICE AREAS: Civil Rights.
**Bell, Michael F.**, (AV) ..........................'54 '79 C.840 B.A. L.813 J.D. [Galton&H.]
*PRACTICE AREAS: Civil Litigation.
Bell, Robert McKim .......................... '47 '73 C.813 B.A. L.426 LL.B. Dep. Atty. Gen.
**Bell, Theodore M., (AV) '41 '67 C.112 A.B. L.1066 J.D.**
**1901 Avenue of the Stars, 11th Floor, 90067**
**Telephone: 310-553-5572 Fax: 310-277-7947**
**Email: tedbell9@aol.com**
**Corporations, Partnerships, Taxation, International Investments and Taxation, Securities, Real Estate, Estate Planning.**
*See Professional Biographies, LOS ANGELES, CALIFORNIA*

Bellach, Francine A. .......................... '59 '85 C.1036 B.A. L.978 J.D. 1950 N. Tamarind Ave.

CAA182P

**Bellah, Jennifer** . . . . '56 '83 C.104 B.A. L.1066 J.D. [Gibson,D.&C.]
*LANGUAGES: French.
*PRACTICE AREAS: Corporations; Securities; General Corporate; International.
**Bellanca, Angela M.** . . . . '68 '94 C.602 B.B.A. L.112 J.D. [A] O'Melveny&M.]
**Belland, Stanton P.**, (AV) . . . . '31 '60 C.112 A.B. L.1068 LL.B. [S.P.Belland]
*PRACTICE AREAS: Closely Held Businesses; Corporate Reorganizations; International Corporate Law; Strategic Business Planning.

**Belland, Stanton P., P.C., (AV)**
**10 Universal City Plaza, Suite 2000, 91608-7806**
**Telephone: 818-754-3770 Telecopier: 818-754-3780**
**Stanton P. Belland.**
**General Corporate and Business Practice with emphasis on Closely Held Business Planning, Acquisitions and Finance and International Business Transactions.**
*See Professional Biographies, LOS ANGELES, CALIFORNIA*

**Beller, Richard D.** . . . . '69 '94 C.69 B.A. L.846 J.D. [A] O'Melveny&M.]
**Belleville, Philip F.**, (AV) . . . . '34 '61 C&L.477 B.A. in Econ., J.D. [Latham&W.]
Bellordre, Catherine Anne . . . . '67 '95 C.112 B.A. L.861 J.D. 12121 Wilshire Blvd.
Bellows, Joel J. . . . . '39 '65 C.145 B.A. L.365 J.D. [Bellows&B.]©
Bellows, Laurel G. . . . . '48 '74 C.659 B.A. L.424 J.D. [Bellows&B.]©
Bellows and Bellows, A Prof. Corp. . . . . 601 S. Figueroa St. (©Chicago, Ill.)
Belmont, C. Elizabeth . . . . '63 '89 C.801 B.A. L.424 J.D. 11355 W. Olympic Blvd.
Belshaw, Robert . . . . '48 '83 C.112 B.A. L.1136 J.D. 3550 Wilshire Blvd.
Belton, Rudy D. . . . . '46 '79 C.378 B.A. L.1148 J.D. 924 Westwood Blvd.
**Belusko, Vincent J.** . . . . '57 '81 C.910 B.S.C.E. L.273 J.D. [Graham&J.] (Pat.)
*PRACTICE AREAS: Intellectual Property Law; Litigation.
Bemel, Babette . . . . '52 '79 C.174 B.A. L.809 J.D. 801 S. Grand Ave., 18th Fl.
**Ben-Porat, Laura** . . . . '63 '88 C.112 B.A. L.426 J.D. [B] Gibson,D.&C.]
*PRACTICE AREAS: Entertainment; Intellectual Property.
**Ben-yehuda, Michelle** . . . . '64 '91 C.112 B.A. L.813 J.D. [Kinsella,B.F.&T.]
*LANGUAGES: Hebrew.
*PRACTICE AREAS: Litigation.
**Ben-Zvi, Daniel P.** . . . . '56 '81 C.705 B.A. L.978 J.D. [A] Schmeltzer,A.&S.]
**Ben-Zvi, Henry** . . . . '53 '82 C.342 B.A. L.1068 J.D. [Proskauer R.G.&M.]
*PRACTICE AREAS: Litigation.
**Benardo, Stephen M.** . . . . '62 '92 C.494 B.A. L.1068 J.D. [A] Knee&M.]
*LANGUAGES: Spanish.
*PRACTICE AREAS: Wrongful Termination Defense; Employment Discrimination; Sexual Harassment; Occupational Safety and Health; Occupational Injury.
**Benbassat, Kenneth R.**, (AV) . . . . '47 '72 C.112 B.A. L.309 J.D. [Loeb&L.]
*PRACTICE AREAS: Corporate; Securities; Commercial; International.
**Bence, David R.**
**(See Torrance)**
Bendel, Randy E. . . . . '61 '87 C.154 B.A. L.1068 J.D. [Murray&B.]
**Bendell, Adam S.** . . . . '61 '87 C.188 B.A. L.145 J.D. [A] Gibson,D.&C.]
*PRACTICE AREAS: Technology; Practice Systems.
**Bendell, Spencer E.** . . . . '— '95 C.188 B.A. L.309 J.D. [A] Irell&M.]
Bender, Carole L. . . . . '45 '86 C.966 B.A. L.426 J.D. 333 S. Hope St., 30th
**Bender, Charles W.**, (AV) . . . . '35 '65 C&L.309 A.B., LL.B. [O'Melveny&M.]
Bender, Christine W. . . . . '49 '76 C.914 B.A. L.309 J.D. Comr., Dept. of Corps.
**Bender, David P., Jr.** . . . . '56 '86 C.602 B.A. L.809 J.D. [Epstein B.&G.]
Bender, Earl O. . . . . '41 '73 C.154 B.A. L.800 J.D. [E.O.Bender]
**Bender, Ellen M.** . . . . '57 '84 C.602 B.A. L.1068 J.D. [B] Pachulski,S.Z.&Y.]
**Bender, Kenneth R.** . . . . '50 '75 C.154 B.A. L.309 J.D. [Brobeck,P.&H.]
*PRACTICE AREAS: Corporate Law; Business Law.
Bender, Marc Lee . . . . '56 '87 C.766 B.A. L.1065 J.D. Bet Tzedek Legal Servs.
Bender, Marie Meyer '54 '80 C.768 B.A. L.276 J.D.
Sr. V.P. & Assoc. Gen. Coun., Trust Company of the West
**Bender, Ron** . . . . '64 '89 C.659 B.S. L.813 J.D. [Levene,N.&B.]
*PRACTICE AREAS: Bankruptcy.
Bender, Earl O., A Professional Corporation . . . . 11755 Wilshire Blvd.
Bendix, Helen I. . . . . '52 '76 C.188 B.A. L.976 J.D. 601 S. Figueroa St.
**Bendy, Jacqueline** . . . . '66 '94 C.276 B.A. L.1066 J.D. [A] Hennigan,M.&B.]
Benedek, John Douglas . . . . '52 '78 C&L.597 B.A., J.D. 7985 Santa Monica Blvd.
Benes, Edward D. . . . . '39 '68 C.1060 B.A. L.1065 J.D. 9911 W. Pico Blvd.
Benezra, Gerald C., (AV) . . . . '33 '63 C.112 A.B. L.1068 LL.B. [Israel&B.]
Benezra, Marc L. . . . . '58 '85 C.112 B.A. L.1065 J.D. [B] Hammel&P.]
**Bengston, Dean** . . . . '68 '95 C.112 B.A. L.1067 J.D. [A] Daniels,B.&F.]
**Benjamin, Alan G.**, (AV) . . . . '53 '77 C.112 A.B. L.1068 J.D. [Orrick,H.&S.]
*PRACTICE AREAS: Banking and Finance.
Benjamin, Bruce D. . . . . '47 '72 C.112 B.A. L.1068 J.D. 1900 Ave. of the Stars
Benjamin, Donald E. . . . . '43 '68 C&L.800 B.S., J.D. 9200 Sunset Blvd.
**Benjamin, Julie R.** '68 '93
(adm. in IL; not adm. in CA) [A] Katten M.&Z.]
Benjamin, Linda Hope . . . . '64 '90 C&L.494 B.S., J.D. [Davis&B.]
**Benjamin, Lugosi & Benjamin, LLP**
**(See Glendale)**
**Benko, Istvan** . . . . '54 '80 C.112 B.A. L.1068 J.D. [Troy&G.]
*PRACTICE AREAS: Corporate Law; Securities Law; International Law.
Bennett, Alice J. . . . . '42 '79 C.999 B.S. L.1148 J.D. 3863 Glenfeliz Blvd.
**Bennett, Bruce**, (AV) . . . . '58 '82 C.103 Sc.B. L.309 J.D. [Hennigan,M.&B.]
*TRANSACTIONS: Counsel for the County of Orange chapter 9 debt adjustment case; Reorganization counsel for debtors in Federated Stores, Inc., chapter 11 reorganization; Storage Technology Corporation, chapter 11 reorganization; First Capital Holdings corporation, chapter 11 reorganization; Ticor, chapter 11 reorganization.
*PRACTICE AREAS: Bankruptcy; Insolvency; Corporate Reorganization; Commercial Litigation.
**Bennett, Carla J.** . . . . '46 '88 C.112 B.A. L.1068 J.D. [A] O'Melveny&M.]
*PRACTICE AREAS: Litigation; ERISA; Corporate.
**Bennett, Charles A.**, (AV) . . . . '42 '74 C.112 B.S. L.426 J.D. [Dennison,B.&P.]
*PRACTICE AREAS: Construction Defect Litigation; Products Liability; Earth Movement and Drainage Litigation; Property Insurance Coverage Issues; Property Damage Litigation.
Bennett, Eric D. . . . . '57 '84 C.112 B.A. L.1065 J.D. 12424 Wilshire Blvd.
Bennett, F. Ray . . . . '10 '35 C.113 A.B. L.1066 LL.B. Ret. J. of L.A. Supr. Ct.
**Bennett, Fred Gilbert**, (AV) . . . . '46 '74 C.878 B.A. L.1068 J.D. [Gibson,D.&C.]
*PRACTICE AREAS: International and Domestic Arbitration and Dispute Resolution; Technical, Construction and Commercial Litigation and Contract Drafting; Intellectual Property and Patent Litigation; Real Estate Litigation; Corporate and Partnership Dissolutions.
Bennett, Frederick R. . . . . '45 '71 C.112 A.B. L.1068 J.D. Asst. Co. Coun.
**Bennett, Joel I., (P.C.)** . . . . '55 '82 C.178 B.A. L.477 J.D. [Jeffer,M.B.&M.]
*PRACTICE AREAS: General Corporate; Securities.
Bennett, Lawrence A., (AV) . . . . '41 '76 C.767 B.S. L.464 J.D. [Bennett&R.]©
Bennett, Mary M. . . . . '49 '76 C.112 B.A. L.426 J.D. [Cheong&D.]
Bennett, Paula P. . . . . '61 '86 C.813 A.B. L.1066 J.D. 555 W. 5th St.
**Bennett, Robert E., Jr.**, (AV) . . . . '44 '70 C.575 B.A. L.228 J.D. [Greenberg G.F.C.&M.]
*PRACTICE AREAS: Probate, Estate Planning and Trust Law.
Bennett, Roberta, (AV) . . . . '42 '79 C.1077 B.A. L.1095 J.D. [Abbitt&B.]
**Bennett, Simone Margaret** . . . . '— '94 C.228 B.A. L.1068 J.D. [A] Buchalter,N.F.&Y.]
*PRACTICE AREAS: Commercial Litigation; Labor Litigation; Financial Institutions Litigation.
Bennett, Vincent F. . . . . '61 '91 C.1131 B.A. L.1068 J.D. 11766 Wilshire Blvd.
Bennett, William B. . . . . '55 '80 C.112 B.A. L.809 J.D. [Manulkin,G.&B.]
**Bennett, Joel R.**
**(See Pasadena)**
**Bennett & Kistner**
**(See Long Beach)**
**Bennett, Leon F.**
**(See Woodland Hills)**
Bennett & Rowland, (AV) . . . . 11255 Wilshire Blvd. (©San Francisco)
Bennion, Sydney B. '54 '80 C&L.101 B.A., J.D.
Sr. Dep. Gen. Coun., Metropolitan Water Dist. of Southern Calif.
Benoff, Stephan . . . . '42 '72 C.112 A.B. L.800 J.D. 119 N. Bundy Dr.
**Benoit, Luc P.**, (AV) . . . . '— '68 C.061 L.426 J.D. [Benoit] (Pat.)

**Benoit Law Corporation, (AV)**
**2551 Colorado Boulevard, 90041-1040**
**Telephone: 213-255-0000; 213-254-9307 Telecopier: 213-254-4538**
**Luc P. Benoit.**
*See Professional Biographies, LOS ANGELES, CALIFORNIA*

**Bensch, Jennifer A.** . . . . '66 '94 C.174 B.A. L.273 J.D. [A] Skadden,A.S.M.&F.]
**Benshoof, Ward L.**, (AV) . . . . '46 '73 C.429 B.A. L.569 J.D. [McClintock,W.B.R.R.&M.]
*REPORTED CASES: Cose v. Getty Oil Co., 4 F.3d 700 (9th Cir. 1993); Ascon Properties, Inc. v. Mobil Oil Co., 866 F 2d 1149 (9th Cir. 1989); Abujdeh v. Mobil, 841 F. 2d 310 (9th Cir. 1988); Davis v. Gulf Oil, 572 F. Supp. 1393 (D.C. Calif. 1983); People v. Mobil Oil Corp., 143 Cal. App.3d 261, 192 Cal. Rptr. 155 (1983).
*PRACTICE AREAS: Environmental/Superfund Litigation; Business Litigation; Petroleum Marketing; Trade Regulation; Unlawful Termination.
**Bensinger, Grayson & Ritt**
**(See Pasadena)**
**Benson, Patricia H., (A Professional Corporation)**, (AV) '49 '74
C.813 B.A. L.800 J.D. [Mitchell,S.&K.]
*PRACTICE AREAS: Securities Litigation; Intellectual Property Litigation; Employment Litigation.
Benson, Robert W. . . . . '42 '70 C.178 A.B. L.1066 J.D. Loyola Univ. Sch. of Law
**Benson, Ruth** . . . . '— '77 C.239 A.B. L.1068 J.D. [A] Littler,M.F.T.&M.]
Benson, Steven I. . . . . '63 '90 C.867 B.A. L.569 J.D. 725 S. Figueroa St.
**Bentler, Robin S.** . . . . '63 '90 C.112 B.A. L.809 J.D. [A] Kirtland&P.]
**Bentley, Alicia J.** . . . . '63 '88 C.8 B.A. L.608 J.D. [A] Gibson,D.&C.]
*PRACTICE AREAS: Litigation.
**Benton, Orr, Duval & Buckingham, A Professional Corporation**
**(See Ventura)**
Bentsi-Enchill, Kofi C. . . . . '62 '91 C.454 B.A. L.1068 J.D. [A] Ivie,M.&W.]
**Benudiz, P. Peter, (P.C.)** . . . . '61 '87 C.112 A.B. L.309 J.D. [Jeffer,M.B.&M.]
*PRACTICE AREAS: Hospitality Industry; Real Estate Workouts, Finance, Acquisitions/Sale.
**Benveniste, Nancy R.** . . . . '54 '84 C.1169 B.A. L.1065 J.D. [A] Walter,F.&R.]
*PRACTICE AREAS: Corporate Law; Commercial Transactions; Employment Law; Non-Profit Corporations Law.
**Berard, Douglas C.** . . . . '45 '79 C.152 B.A. L.809 J.D. [Berger,K.S.M.F.S.&G.]
Berardo, David J. . . . . '42 '68 C.668 B.A. L.1068 J.D. 1901 Ave. of the Stars
**Berberich, Joseph E.**, (AV) . . . . '37 '69 C.999 B.A. L.426 J.D. [Manning,L.B.&B.]
*PRACTICE AREAS: Automotive Dealer Law; Business Purchases and Sales; Association and Commercial Law.
**Berchild, John D., Jr.**, (AV) . . . . '42 '72 C.964 B.S. L.494 J.D. [Sheppard,M.R.&H.]
*PRACTICE AREAS: Commercial Secured Transactions; UCC Law; Bankruptcy Law; Debtor/Creditor Law; Finance Law.
Berchin, Jerome J. . . . . '26 '72 C.800 O.D. L.1148 J.D. 3034 Elvill Dr.‡
Berejian, Silva . . . . '59 '89 C&L.112 B.A., J.D. 801 S. Grand Ave., 11th Fl.
Berend, Robert E. . . . . '56 '88 C.112 B.A. L.809 J.D. Assoc. Coun., Calif. Assn. of Realtors
**Berenson, Mitchell** . . . . '65 '91 C&L.061 B.A., LL.B. [A] B.P.Wolfsdorf]
*PRACTICE AREAS: Immigration Law.
Beres, Linda S. . . . . '51 '88 C.161 B.S. L.800 J.D. Assoc. Prof., Loyola Law Sch.
Berg, Denise S. . . . . '55 '81 C.112 B.A. L.770 J.D. 3484 Ashwood Ave.
**Berg, Eric** . . . . '62 '88 C.1049 B.A. L.800 J.D. [A] Engstrom,L.&L.]
**Berg, Jeffrey P.**, (AV) . . . . '48 '74 C.1077 B.A. L.809 J.D. [Matthias&B.]
*PRACTICE AREAS: Corporate Finance; Mergers and Acquisitions; Asset Securitization; Municipal Finance; Securities.
**Berg, Kevin P.** . . . . '68 '96 C.800 B.A. L.990 J.D. [A] Abrolat&T.]
*PRACTICE AREAS: Employment Litigation; Sexual Harassment; Discrimination; Whistle-Blower Cases; Wrongful Termination.
Berg, Michael . . . . '32 '60 C.112 B.A. L.800 LL.B. Supr. Ct. J.
**Berg, Randy A.** . . . . '59 '87 C.112 B.A. L.426 J.D. [A] Schell&D.]
Berg, Richard . . . . '59 '89 C.112 B.A. L.1066 J.D. 1015 Gayley Ave.
**Berg, Richard G.**, (AV) . . . . '37 '71 C.679 B.S. L.809 J.D. [Tharp&B.]
*PRACTICE AREAS: General Commercial Litigation; Litigation of Will Contests and other Contested Fiduciary Proceedings; Real Estate Law; Construction Law; Environmental Law.
**Berg, Richard P.**, (AV) '45 '76 C.800 B.S.E.E. L.1049 J.D.
[Ladas&P.] (See Pat. Sect.)
Bergdahl, Lars H. . . . . '36 '88 C.446 B.S. L.1026 J.D. Legal Dept., Calif. Dept. of Trans.
Berge, Jonathan M. . . . . '45 '71 C.112 B.S. L.1068 J.D. 3450 Sawtelle St.‡
**Bergemann, Susan C.** . . . . '56 '82 C.352 B.A. L.904 J.D. [A] Arter&H.]
*PRACTICE AREAS: Civil Litigation; Products Liability; Insurance.
Bergen, Barbara Hart '38 '75 C.1019 B.A. L.1221 J.D.
Assoc. Western States Coun., Anti-Defamation League
Bergen, Richard C., (AV) . . . . '14 '39 C.597 B.S. L.309 LL.B. 400 S. Hope St.
Bergener, John E. . . . . '13 '36 C.145 L.999 J.D. 865 S. Figueroa St., 24th Fl.
**Berger, Cary J. A.** . . . . '63 '89 C.178 B.A. L.813 J.D. [Irell&M.]
*LANGUAGES: Italian.
**Berger, Donald I.** . . . . '57 '82 C.112 A.B. L.1068 J.D. [Morrison&F.]
*PRACTICE AREAS: Land Use; Environmental; Real Estate.
Berger, Jerold F. '41 '68 C.563 B.B.A. L.273 J.D.
(adm. in NY; not adm. in CA) Dep. Pub. Def.‡
**Berger, Laura B.** . . . . '69 '96 C.112 B.A. L.426 J.D. [A] O'Melveny&M.]
*LANGUAGES: Spanish.
Berger, Lawrence W. . . . . '54 '79 C.112 B.A. L.1068 J.D. 11611 San Vicente Blvd.
Berger, Louis H. . . . . '38 '64 C.1221 L.809 LL.B. 523 W. 6th St.
**Berger, Marcus J.** . . . . '47 '89 C.1183 L.809 J.D. [A] Howarth&S.]
*REPORTED CASES: Freeman v. Hale, 30 Cal. App. 4th 1388, 36 Cal. Rptr. 2d 418 (1994); Barrus v. Sylvania, 55 F.3d 468 (9th Cir. 1995).
**Berger, Matthew D.** . . . . '64 '92 C.188 B.A. L.1065 J.D. [A] Manatt,P.&P.]
*PRACTICE AREAS: Intellectual Property; High Technology/Electronic Commerce.
**Berger, Michael D.** . . . . '46 '85 C.339 B.A. L.101 J.D. [Matthias&B.]
*LANGUAGES: Chinese (Mandarin), Russian and French.
*PRACTICE AREAS: Securities Offerings; Commercial Litigation.
**Berger, Paul S.**, (AV) . . . . '36 '64 C.112 B.S. L.1068 J.D. [B] Berger,K.S.M.F.S.&G.]
**Berger, Richard S.**, (AV) . . . . '41 '67 C.813 B.S. L.1065 J.D. [Tuttle&T.]
*PRACTICE AREAS: Civil Litigation; Bankruptcy and Creditors' Rights; Appellate Practice.
**Berger, Sheldon P., (Professional Corporation)**, (AV) '49 '74
C&L.665 B.A., J.D. [Resch P.A.&B.]
*PRACTICE AREAS: Real Estate; Business Law.

CAA183P

**Berger, Kahn, Shafton, Moss, Figler, Simon & Gladstone, (AV)**
**A Professional Corporation including a Professional Corporation**
**4215 Glencoe Avenue (Marina Del Rey), 90292-5634⊙**
**Telephone: 310-821-9000 Telecopier: 310-578-6178**
**Email: lawyers@bergerkahn.com**
**William Berger (1903-1974); Douglas C. Berard; Carole J. Buckner (Resident, Irvine Office); Stephan S. Cohn (Resident, Irvine Office); Samuel M. Danskin (Resident, Irvine Office); Paul Figler; Steven H. Gentry (Resident, Irvine Office); Leon J. Gladstone; William J. Glazer; David A. Helfant; James F. Henshall, Jr. (Resident, Irvine Office); Harri J. Keto (Resident, Irvine Office); Howard F. Kline (Resident, Irvine Office); Lance A. LaBelle (Resident, Irvine Office); Alan H. Lazar; Robert W. Mehr (Resident, Novato Office); G. Arthur Meneses; Allen L. Michel; Melody S. Mosley (Resident, Irvine Office); Jon Roger Moss; Patrick E. Naughton (Resident, Irvine Office); Robert W. Nelms (Resident, Irvine Office); Timothy A. Nicholson (Resident, Irvine Office); Teresa Ransom Ponder (Resident, Irvine Office); Eric N. Riezman (Resident, Irvine Office); Carol Peskoe Schaner (Certified Specialist, Taxation Law, The State Bar of California Board of Legal Specialization) (Resident, Irvine Office); Anthony E. Shafton; Craig S. Simon (Resident, Irvine Office); Owen J. Sloane; Sherman M. Spitz (Resident, Irvine Office); Jeffrey M. Spurlock (Resident, Irvine Office); Jeffrey A. Swedo (Resident, Irvine Office); Arthur J. Swerdloff; Roberta S. Taylor (Resident, San Diego Office); Sara Schwab Trask (Resident, Irvine Office); Roger M. Vosburg (Resident, Novato Office); Bruce M. Warren;—Michael J. Aiken; Dale A. Amato (Resident, San Diego Office); Jon D. Andersen (Resident, Irvine Office); Shireen G. Banki (Resident, Irvine Office); Julie R. Beaton (Resident, Irvine Office); James K. Beriker; Laura Farrel Bucher (Resident, Irvine Office); Patricia J. Campbell; Anne Barden Cleeland (Resident, Irvine Office); Keri Flynn Corfield (Resident, Irvine Office); Renee C. D'Agostino (Resident, Irvine Office); Kimberly A. Donlon; Margaret M. Drugan (Resident, Irvine Office); Riva I. Edwards (Resident, Irvine Office); Philip T. Emmons (Resident, Irvine Office); David B. Ezra (Resident, Irvine Office); Lindsey S. Feldman; Gary Ganchrow; Daniel J. Goodstein; Areta Kay Guthrey (Resident, Irvine Office); Reid S. Honjiyo; Amy Hsieh; Eric B. Johnson (Resident, Irvine Office); Susanne Berry Johnson; Ann K. Johnston (Resident, Irvine Office); Richard O. Knapp (Resident, Irvine Office); Catherine K. La Tempa (Resident, Irvine Office); Jeffrey B. Lehrman (Resident, Irvine Office); Denise A. MacRae; Mark F. Marnell (Resident, Irvine Office); Carolyn A. Mathews; Kevin P. McNamara; Margaret R. Miglietta (Resident, Irvine Office); Julia A. Mouser (Resident, Irvine Office); Nancy N. Potter; Robert S. Robinson (Resident, Irvine Office); Stephen A. Shapiro (Resident, Irvine Office); Steven H. Silverman; Maxim Vaynerov; Fred Timothy Winters (Resident, Irvine Office); Hali E. Ziff (Resident, Irvine Office). Of Counsel: Paul S. Berger; Charles H. Kahn; James B. Krug; Kenji Machida (A Professional Corporation).**
**Insurance Law, Real Estate, Music and Entertainment Law; Tax, Probate, Intellectual Property, General Civil and Trial Practice in all State and Federal Courts.**
**Reference: Santa Monica Bank.**
**Irvine, California Office: Suite 650, 2 Park Plaza. Telephone: 714-474-1880. Telecopier: 714-474-7265.**
**Novato, California Office: Suite 304, 1701 Novato Boulevard. Telephone: 415-899-1770. Telecopier: 415-899-1769.**
**San Diego, California Office: 402 W. Broadway, Suite 400. Telephone: 619-236-8602. Telecopier: 619-236-0812.**
**Bend, Oregon Office: P.O. Box 1409, 97709. Telephone: 541-388-1400. Telecopier: 541-388-4731.**

***See Professional Biographies, LOS ANGELES, CALIFORNIA***

**Berger & Norton, A Law Corporation**
**(See Santa Monica)**

**Bergerson, John M.** ... '60 '86 C.800 B.A. L.809 J.D. [Roper&F.]
*PRACTICE AREAS: Accidents; Personal Injury; Construction Defect Litigation; Defamation; Intentional Torts.
**Berges, Ronald A.**, (AV) ... '45 '72 C.1042 B.A. L.426 J.D. [Williams,B.&S.]
*PRACTICE AREAS: Negligence; Products Liability; Probate; Insurance; Mediation.
**Bergfeld, Michael M.** ... '49 '88 C.1109 B.A. L.1065 J.D. [🄰 Cummins&W.]
*PRACTICE AREAS: Appellate Law; Litigation.
**Bergman, Alan M.**, (AV) ... '41 '65 C.705 A.B. L.776 LL.B. [Saltzburg,R.&B.]
*PRACTICE AREAS: Real Estate Law; Business Law; Partnership Law; Entertainment Law.
Bergman, Ben Z. ... '24 '80 C.563 B.C.E. L.1095 J.D. Univ. of Judaism‡
Bergman, G. Merle ... '20 '48 C.145 B.A. L.597 J.D. 446 N. Sweetzer Ave.‡
**Bergman, Gregory M.**, (AV) ... '47 '75 C.112 B.A. L.809 J.D. [Bergman&W.]
*PRACTICE AREAS: Business Litigation; Commercial Real Property; Commercial Litigation; Professional Liability Defense; Commercial Insurance.
Bergman, Paul B. ... '43 '69 C.112 A.B. L.1066 J.D. Univ. of Calif. Law Sch.

**Bergman, Robert D., (AV) '56 '83 C.112 B.A. L.809 J.D.**
**Eighth Floor, 10100 Santa Monica Boulevard, 90067-4012**
**Telephone: 310-557-1888 Fax: 310-557-9888**
**Business, Corporate, Real Estate, Estate Planning, Probate and Taxation Law.**
**Reference: Century Bank (West Los Angeles Branch).**

***See Professional Biographies, LOS ANGELES, CALIFORNIA***

**Bergman, Steven H.** ... '63 '95 C.112 B.S. L.1068 J.D. [🄰 Arnold&P.]
*PRACTICE AREAS: Litigation.

**Bergman & Wedner, Inc., (AV)** 🅱🅱
**Suite 900, 10880 Wilshire Boulevard, 90024**
**Telephone: 310-470-6110 Fax: Available on Request**
**Gregory M. Bergman; Gregory A. Wedner; Mark E. Fingerman; Alan Harvey Mittelman; Robert M. Mason III; Kristi Anne Sjoholm-Sierchio; Keith A. Robinson; John P. Dacey;—John V. Tamborelli; Blithe Ann Smith; Lisa S. Shukiar; Daphne M. Humphreys; Suzanne Z. Shbaro. Of Counsel: Lloyd A. Bergman (1923-1994); Jacob A. Wedner. Special Counsel: Richard V. Godino.**
**Business, Professional Liability, Real Estate, Land Use, Earth Movement, Banking, Securities, Taxation, Condominium, Insurance, Public Entity, Environmental, Computer Litigation, Toxic Tort, Product Liability, Entertainment, Construction, Fraud and Recession Action, Employment and White-Collar Criminal Law and Federal and State Litigation.**

***See Professional Biographies, LOS ANGELES, CALIFORNIA***

**Bergren, Laurie J.** ... '58 '85 C.350 B.A. L.221 J.D. [🄰 Agapay,L.&H.]
**Bergsten, Robert T.** ... '68 '93 C.94 B.A. L.990 J.D. [🄰 Koletsky,M.&F.]
*LANGUAGES: Spanish.
*PRACTICE AREAS: General Liability; Product Liability; Construction Defect; Insurance Coverage.
**Beriker, James K.** ... '65 '93 C.025 B.A. L.06 LL.B. [🄰 Berger,K.S.M.F.S.&G.]
*LANGUAGES: French.
Berk, Ellen R. ... '59 '84 C.112 B.A. L.1065 J.D. Dep. Dist. Atty.
Berk, Jerry S. ... '19 '42 C.999 L.146 LL.B. 3030 W. Temple St.‡
**Berk, Michael D.**, (AV) ... '43 '67 C.112 B.A. L.1068 J.D. [Rogers&W.]
*PRACTICE AREAS: Banking Litigation; Business Litigation; Business Insurance; Business Torts; Real Estate Litigation.
Berke, Jeff ... '54 '81 C.1042 B.S. L.1068 J.D. 11766 Wilshire Blvd.
Berke, Robert G. ... '67 '90 C.1044 B.A. L.809 J.D. 3250 Wilshire Blvd.
Berkey, Dennis A. '44 '73
C.766 B.A. L.421 J.D. V.P. & Corp. Coun., Nations Holding Grp.
**Berkin, Geoffrey A.** ... '51 '83 C.112 A.B. L.1068 J.D. [Manatt,P.&P.]
*PRACTICE AREAS: Intellectual Property Law; Computer and Multimedia Law; Entertainment Law.
Berkley, Stuart ... '56 '81 C.1044 B.A. L.1049 J.D. 3701 Wilshire Blvd.
**Berkman, Isidoro** ... '40 '64 C.209 B.S.C. L.597 J.D. [Nossaman,G.K.&E.]
*LANGUAGES: Spanish.
*PRACTICE AREAS: Taxation Law.
Berkman, Stephen I. ... '66 '92 C.112 B.S. L.1068 J.D. 1999 Ave. of the Stars
**Berkowitz, Barbara Lee** ... '61 '89 C.94 B.A. L.464 J.D. [🄰 Iverson,Y.P.&H.]
*PRACTICE AREAS: Entertainment Law; Defamation and Privacy Litigation; Civil Litigation and Appellate Practice.
**Berkowitz, Ellen** ... '57 '89 C.1036 B.A. L.426 J.D. [Manatt,P.&P.]
*PRACTICE AREAS: Administrative Law; Land Use; Government Practice.
Berkowitz, Elliot S., (P.C.), (AV) ... '48 '77 C.4 B.A. L.1190 J.D. [E.S.Berkowitz]
**Berkowitz, Eric D.** ... '58 '84 C.1169 B.A. L.767 J.D. [🄲 Fenigstein&K.]
*PRACTICE AREAS: Business; Litigation.

**Berkowitz, Harold D., (A P.C.)**, (AV) ... '18 '42 C.563 B.S. L.569 LL.B. [🄲 Loeb&L.]
*PRACTICE AREAS: Entertainment Law.
Berkowitz, Steven E. '57 '83 C.659 B.A. L.276 J.D.
(adm. in DC; not adm. in CA) Screen Actors Guild
Berkowitz, Elliot S., A Professional Corporation, (AV) ... 6500 Wilshire Blvd.
**Berle, Elihu M.**, (AV) ... '43 '70 C.102 B.A. L.178 J.D. [Chrystie&B.]
*PRACTICE AREAS: Business Law; Commercial Litigation; Business Litigation.
Berlie, Karen Margaret ... '46 '72 C.112 A.B. L.1068 J.D. Second Dist. Ct. of App.
**Berliner, Brian M.** ... '58 '91 C.588 B.S.E.E. L.426 J.D. [🄰 Graham&J.] (Pat.)
*PRACTICE AREAS: Intellectual Property Law.
**Berliner, Jill H.** ... '— '84 C.1169 B.A. L.800 J.D. [King,P.H.P.&B.]
*LANGUAGES: French and Spanish.
*PRACTICE AREAS: Music Law; General Entertainment Law.
Berliner, Norman S. ... '27 '56 C.112 B.S. L.809 LL.B. 330 S. Mission Rd.
**Berliner, Robert**, (AV) ... '35 '62 C.563 B.S. L.213 J.D. [Robbins,B.&C.] (See Pat. Sect.)
*PRACTICE AREAS: Patents Law; Copyright Law; Trademark Law; Federal Litigation; Licensing Law.
**Berliner, Roger A.**, (AVⓉ) ... '51 '83 C.197 B.A. L.464 J.D. [Brady&B.]⊙
*PRACTICE AREAS: Litigation; Appellate Advocacy; North American Energy Law and Trade; Federal and State Legislation.
**Berliner, Steven A.** ... '64 '91 C.918 B.A. L.112 J.D. [🄰 Wehner&P.]
**Berls, Bruce D.** ... '54 '80 C.154 B.A. L.1168 J.D. [🄲 Gansinger,H.B.&P.]
*PRACTICE AREAS: Civil Litigation; Insurance Coverage; Travel Law.
**Berman, Ada** ... '71 '96 C.112 B.A. L.426 J.D. [🄰 Stevens,K.A.&H.]
*LANGUAGES: Russian.
*PRACTICE AREAS: Personal Injury; Premises Liability; Construction Defects.
Berman, Alan S. ... '59 '85 C.1036 B.A. L.1068 J.D. 12424 Wilshire Blvd.
Berman, Bruce E. J. '55 '80
C.112 B.A. L.1066 J.D. V.P. & Gen. Coun., Charles Barone, Inc.
**Berman, Charles** ... '43 '78 C&L.999 B.S., LL.B. [Merchant&G.] (See Pat. Sect.)
Berman, Daniel A. ... '67 '92 C.1169 B.A. L.426 J.D. 624 S. Grand Ave.
Berman, David M. ... '43 '70 C.477 B.B.A. L.309 J.D. 9130 W. Sunset Blvd.
**Berman, Evan A.** ... '64 '90 C.911 B.A. L.990 J.D. [Berman,B.&B.]
**Berman, Jeffrey A.**, (AV) ... '46 '72 C.112 B.A. L.1068 J.D. [Proskauer R.G.&M.]
*PRACTICE AREAS: Labor and Employment Law.
Berman, Jerome A., (AV) ... '22 '53 C.800 B.A. L.809 LL.B. 3315 Glendale Ave.‡
**Berman, Joel J., (P.C.)**, (AV) ... '54 '79 C&L.309 A.B., J.D. [Jeffer,M.B.&M.]
*PRACTICE AREAS: Commercial; Real Estate; Corporate; Insolvency and Creditors' Rights.

**Berman, Kenneth R., (BV) '56 '82 C.112 B.A. L.426 J.D.**
**3315 Glendale Boulevard, Suite 1, 90039**
**Telephone: 213-660-8120 Fax: 213-669-1712**
***PRACTICE AREAS: Workers Compensation Law; Personal Injury Law.**
**Workers Compensation Applicants, Personal Injury Plaintiff.**

***See Professional Biographies, LOS ANGELES, CALIFORNIA***

**Berman, Laurence M.**, (AV) ... '55 '80 C.966 B.A. L.1068 J.D. [Berman,B.M.&R.]
*PRACTICE AREAS: Commercial Litigation; Intellectual Property Litigation; Real Estate Litigation; Insurance Litigation; Telecommunications Law.
**Berman, Martha A. H.** ... '54 '80 C.597 B.A. L.208 J.D. [🄰 Bonne,B.M.O.&N.]
Berman, Martin R. ... '61 '86 C.112 B.A. L.426 J.D. 1801 Century Park E., 9th Flr
Berman, Myles L., (AVⓉ) ... '54 '80 C.339 B.A. L.146 J.D. 9255 Sunset Blvd.
**Berman, Rachael H.** ... '68 '94 C.112 B.A. L.1065 J.D. [🄰 Buchalter,N.F.&Y.]
*PRACTICE AREAS: Bankruptcy.
**Berman, Rod S.** ... '55 '82 C.112 B.S. L.426 J.D. [Jeffer,M.B.&M.] (Pat.)
**Berman, Ronald S.**, (AV) ... '38 '72 C.112 B.S. L.426 J.D. [Berman,B.&B.]
**Berman, Stephanie J.** ... '68 '93 C.112 B.A. L.426 J.D. [Berman,B.&B.]

**Berman, Berman & Berman, (AV)**
**11900 West Olympic Boulevard, 6th Floor, 90064-1151⊙**
**Telephone: 310-447-9000 Fax: 310-447-9011**
**Email: rberman156@aol.com**
**Ronald S. Berman; Evan A. Berman; Myra L. Markey (Not admitted in CA; Resident, Chicago, Illinois Office); Stephanie J. Berman. Associates: Matthew S. Shorr; Mark Lowary; Charles G. Whitehead; Christopher C. McNatt, Jr. Of Counsel: Pamela A. Davis; Robert C. Fishman; William M. Aitken.**
**General Insurance Defense and Business Litigation. Professional Liability including Design Professionals, Real Estate Brokers, Appraisers, Lawyers, Insurance Brokers, Psychologists and Accountants. Product Liability, Employment Law, Insurance Coverage and Construction Defects. Monitoring Counsel, Litigation Management, Insurance Regulations and Consulting to the Insurance Industry.**
**Chicago, Illinois Office: Berman, Berman & Markey, 30 North LaSalle Street, Suite 1530, 60602. Telephone: 312-201-9191. Fax: 312-201-9195.**

***See Professional Biographies, LOS ANGELES, CALIFORNIA***

**Berman, Blanchard, Mausner & Resser, A Law Corporation, (AV)** 🅱🅱
**4727 Wilshire Boulevard, Suite 500, 90010**
**Telephone: 213-965-1200 Telecopier: 213-965-1919**
**Email: BBMR@ix.netcom.com**
**Laurence M. Berman; Lonnie C. Blanchard, III; Jeffrey N. Mausner; Bernard M. Resser;—Paul A. Hoffman; Eric Levinrad; Cary P. Ocon; Lisé Hamilton.**
**General Civil Trial and Appellate Practice in all State and Federal Courts and Administrative Agencies, with emphasis on Litigation in the following areas: Copyright, Trademark, Trade Secrets, Computer Law, Securities, Antitrust, Unfair Competition, Real Estate, Construction, Torts, Insurance, Employment, Probate and General Commercial Litigation.**

***See Professional Biographies, LOS ANGELES, CALIFORNIA***

Bermingham, Robert P. '44 '70 C.800 B.A. L.426 J.D.
Sr. V.P., Gen. Coun. & Secy., Westfield Corp., Inc.
Bernabo, Cathi L. ... '56 '91 C.846 B.S. L.800 J.D. 300 N. Los Angeles St.
**Bernacchi, Michael B.** ... '65 '92 C.112 B.A. L.426 J.D. [🄰 Galton&H.]
*PRACTICE AREAS: General Litigation.
**Bernacchi, Richard L., (P.C.)**, (AV) ... '38 '65 C.770 B.Sc. L.800 LL.B. [Irell&M.]
Bernal, Jesus G. ... '63 '90 C.926 B.A. L.813 J.D. 601 S. Figueroa St.
Bernardi, John P. ... '43 '69 C&L.112 A.B., J.D. Dep. Dist. Atty.
**Berner, William E., Jr.** '67 '93 C.150 B.S.M.E. L.800 J.D.
[🄰 McClintock,W.B.R.R.&M.]
*PRACTICE AREAS: Commercial Litigation; Environmental Litigation.
**Bernhard, Herbert A., (P.C.)**, (AV) '27 '58 C.570 B.S.E.E. L.477 J.D.
[Jeffer,M.B.&M.]
*PRACTICE AREAS: Business Litigation; Appeals.
Bernhard, Laurie ... '51 '77 C.112 B.A. L.426 J.D. 227 N. Seltair Ave.
**Bernhard, Lazare F.**, (AV) ... '08 '32 C&L.813 A.B., J.D. [🄲 Sanders,B.G.S.&M.]
Bernheim, Steven J. ... '61 '89 C.309 A.B. L.659 J.D. 333 S. Grand Ave.
**Bernholz, A. Blair** ... '64 '92 C.94 B.A. L.309 J.D. [🄰 B.Tarlow]
*PRACTICE AREAS: Criminal Law.

**Bernick, Kathy F.**
**(See Marina Del Rey)**

**Bernsley, Mark, A Prof. Corp., Law Offices of**
**(See Encino)**

Bernstein, Barry O., (AV) ... '40 '69 L.1095 LL.B. 1901 Ave. of the Stars
Bernstein, Florence ... '29 '65 C&L.800 B.S.L., J.D. Supr. Ct. J.
Bernstein, Irving A. ... '20 '51 C.112 B.S. L.426 J.D. 2768 Monte Mar Ter.‡
**Bernstein, Joel J.** ... '63 '89 C.178 A.B. L.659 J.D. [🄰 Reboul,M.H.M.&K.]
*LANGUAGES: Spanish.

**Bernstein, Joel M.** ....................'45 '71 C.477 B.A. L.145 J.D. [McDermott,W.&E.]
*PRACTICE AREAS: Corporate Law; Finance; Securities.
**Bernstein, Maria Victoria** ...............'67 '96 C.560 B.A. L.1066 J.D. [🄰 Cox,C.&N.]
*LANGUAGES: Spanish.
*PRACTICE AREAS: Real Property; Healthcare.
Bernstein, Marvin N. ..................'28 '78 C.112 B.A. L.809 J.D. 2566 Overland Ave.
Bernstein, Michael R. .........................'61 '85 C.112 B.S. L.1066 J.D. [Schiff&B.]
Bernstein, Robert M. ................'— '93 C.831 B.A. L.426 J.D. 15456 Ventura Blvd.
Bernstein, Sharon Yvonne '59 '83 C.477 B.A. L.831 J.D.
(adm. in PA; not adm. in CA) I.R.S.
Berris, Norman, (AV) .................'28 '54 C.800 L.809 J.D. 11661 San Vicente Blvd.
**Berry, Amy L. Kincaid** ................'63 '88 C.880 B.A. L.228 J.D. [Troop M.S.&P.]
*PRACTICE AREAS: Insurance Coverage and General Business Litigation.
**Berry, David W.** ......................'70 '95 C.112 B.A. L.1065 J.D. [🄰 Brobeck,P.&H.]
**Berry, Graham E.** ...........................'50 '81 C&L.061 LL.B. [Musick,P.&G.]
Berry, James G. ..............................'37 '69 L.1095 LL.B. Dep. Dist. Atty.‡
Berry, James H., Jr. ..................'52 '77 C.880 B.A. L.976 J.D. 2049 Century Park E.
Berry, Michael I. ......................'62 '89 C.112 B.A. L.1066 J.D. 300 S. Grand Ave.
**Berry, Patricia M.** ......................'53 '91 C.684 B.A. L.800 J.D. [🄰 Paul,H.J.&W.]
Berry, Richard G. ..........................'30 '55 C.112 A.B. L.1068 LL.B. Mun. Ct. J.
Berry, Sean R. .......................'59 '87 C.602 B.B.A. L.597 J.D. Asst. U.S. Atty.
**Berry, Stephen L.** ..........................'54 '81 C&L.101 B.S., J.D. [Paul,H.J.&W.]
**Bersch, Amy** .......................'69 '95 C.66 B.A. L.426 J.D. [🄰 Milbank,T.H.&M.]
**Bersch, Phyllis J.**, (AV) ............'54 '79 C.112 B.A. L.1068 J.D. [🄰 Quisenberry&B.]
*PRACTICE AREAS: Family Law; Business Litigation.
Bershon, Nicole C. '67 '92 C.674 B.A. L.112 J.D.
1800 Ave. of the Stars, Suite 900 (Century City)
Bertero, John B., III ...........'60 '86 C.813 B.A. L.1068 J.D. 515 S. Figueroa St., 8th Fl.
**Bertero, Karen E.** .....................'57 '81 C.112 A.B. L.1068 J.D. [Gibson,D.&C.]
*PRACTICE AREAS: General Corporate; Securities.
Bertonneau, Kevin L. ................'66 '93 C.112 B.A. L.426 J.D. 3699 Wilshire Blvd.
**Bertram, Manya M., (Mrs.)**, (AV) ...........................'— '63 L.809 J.D. [🄲 J.Fogg]
*LANGUAGES: Yiddish.
*PRACTICE AREAS: Wills; Trust Law; Trust Administration.
**Bertrando, Nancy A.** .............'57 '85 C.763 B.A. L.800 J.D. [Greenberg G.F.C.&M.]
*PRACTICE AREAS: Employment Law.
**Bertwell, Ellie Mask** ......................'57 '89 C.446 B.A. L.426 J.D. [🄰 Sidley&A.]
*PRACTICE AREAS: Environmental Law.

**Bertz, Michael A., (AV) '41 '67 C.112 B.S. L.1066 J.D.**
**Suite 2400, 1801 Century Park East, 90067**
**Telephone: 310-277-2811 Fax: 310-277-2914**
**Securities and Corporate Litigation.**
***See Professional Biographies, LOS ANGELES, CALIFORNIA***

**Bertzyk, Scott D.** .......................'59 '84 C.966 B.B.A. L.846 J.D. [Jones,D.R.&P.]
**Berwin, Victor R.** ..........................'68 '93 C.228 B.A. L.800 J.D. [🄰 Epport&R.]
Besnyl, Timothy .............'63 '89 C.112 B.A. L.426 J.D. Auto. Club of Southern Calif.
Besser, Andrew K. ...........................'58 '87 C.105 B.S. L.426 J.D. [Schmid&V.] ‡
Besser, Robert S., (BV) ..........'43 '70 C.188 B.A. L.569 J.D. 12011 San Vicente Blvd.
**Besser, Stephen N.** '36 '63 C.112 B.A. L.426 J.D.
[Christensen,M.F.J.G.W.&S.] (⊙San Francisco)
*PRACTICE AREAS: Governmental Relations.
**Bessolo, James P.** ..............'53 '78 C.800 B.A. L.426 J.D. Sr. Coun., Bank of Amer.
Beswick, Brenda A. .....................'63 '88 C&L.477 A.B., J.D. 12121 Wilshire Blvd.
Beswick, Robert H. ....................'49 '79 C.911 B.A. L.1095 J.D. [Beswick,K.&W.]
Beswick, Kiss & Weiss ........................................... 2029 Century Pk. E.
Beton, I. Robert ..........................'23 '57 C.800 B.S. L.426 2049 Century Pk. E.
**Beuerlein, Michele E.** .........................'66 '90 C.112 B.A. L.800 J.D. [🄰 Loeb&L.]
*LANGUAGES: German.
*PRACTICE AREAS: General Corporate Law; Franchising Law; Securities Law.
Beugelmans, Jacques ...........'51 '76 C.1169 A.B. L.284 J.D. 1901 Avenue of the Stars
**Beverlin, Wesley G.**, (AV) ..............'52 '77 C.800 B.A. L.426 J.D. [Knapp,M.J.&D.]
*SPECIAL AGENCIES: Interstate Commerce Commission; California Public Utilities Commission.
*REPORTED CASES: Blackburn Truck Lines Inc. v. Francis 723 F.2d 730; U.S. v. Montrose Chemical Corp., 827 F.Supp. 1453; County Sanitation Dist. v. Watson Land Co., 17 Cal.App. 4th 1268; 22 Cal Rptr. 2d 117.
*PRACTICE AREAS: Trials and Appeals; Public Entity Law; Eminent Domain Law; Transportation Law; Public Utility Law.
**Beverly, Robert G.**, (AV) ..................'25 '52 C.112 L.426 LL.B. [Richards,W.&G.]
Bewick, Joseph F. .......'49 '77 C.754 B.S. L.215 J.D. Admin. Law J., Wkrs. Comp. Bd.

**Bewley, Lassleben & Miller**
**(See Whittier)**

Bey, Jeffrey D. ........................'56 '84 C.112 B.A. L.426 J.D. 2900 W. Sunset Blvd.
**Beyer, Kent S.** .........................'50 '82 C.893 B.A. L.1068 J.D. [Katten M.&Z.]
*PRACTICE AREAS: Real Estate Law; Finance Law.
Beyer, Patricia A. ....'53 '83 C.763 B.A. L.1049 J.D. Assoc. Gen. Coun., ABM Indus. Inc.
**Biancamano, J. Keith** ...............'66 '91 C.188 B.A. L.112 J.D. [🄰 Pillsbury M.&S.]
**Bianchi, James S.**, (AV) ................'45 '70 C.112 B.S. L.1068 J.D. [Meyers,B.&M.]
*PRACTICE AREAS: Litigation; Product Liability; Professional Liability; Coverage.
**Biblin, Allan E., (A Professional Corporation)**, (AV) '38 '63
C.339 B.S. L.145 J.D. [Mitchell,S.&K.]
*PRACTICE AREAS: Taxation Law; Estate Planning Law; Business Planning Law.
Bickenbach, Paul H. .........................'48 '74 C.112 B.A. L.809 J.D. [Herstead&B.]

**Biddle, Jonathan W.**
**(See Beverly Hills)**

**Biderman, David T., A Prof. Corp.** .........'54 '81 C.1365 B.A. L.893 J.D. [Perkins C.]
*PRACTICE AREAS: Commercial Litigation; Bankruptcy Law.
Biderman, Joseph S. ..................'55 '81 C.893 B.A. L.1068 J.D. 725 S. Figueroa St.
**Biederman, Donald E.** '34 '59 C.188 B.A. L.309 J.D.
Exec. V.P., Bus. Affs. & Gen. Coun., Warner/Chappell Music
**Biederman, Robert W., (P.C.)**, (AVⓉ) '52 '78 C.771 B.A. L.424 J.D.
[Cantilo,M.&H.]⊙
*PRACTICE AREAS: Bankruptcy; Insurance Insolvency; Commercial Litigation.
Biegel, Stuart ..........................'45 '85 C.112 L.809 1041 Moore Hall, U.C.L.A.
**Biegenzahn, Leo J.**, (AV) .................'26 '54 C&L.813 A.B., J.D. [🄲 Belcher,H.&B.]

**Bienstock & Clark**
**(See Santa Monica)**

**Bierenbaum, Susan**, (AV) ..............'55 '81 C&L.705 B.A., J.D. [🄰 Fragomen,D.&B.]
*LANGUAGES: Spanish.
**Bierman, Ivy Kagan** ................'58 '85 C.228 B.A. L.597 J.D. [🄰 Kaye,S.F.H.&H.]
*PRACTICE AREAS: Entertainment; Employment and Labor.
**Bierman, Michael H.** ..........................'50 '76 C&L.309 B.A., J.D. [Tuttle&T.]
*PRACTICE AREAS: Professional Liability Litigation; False Claims Act Litigation; Trademark; Copyright.
**Bierstedt, Peter R.** ........................'43 '69 C&L.178 A.B., J.D. [🄲 J.M.Donovan]
*PRACTICE AREAS: Entertainment Industry Contracts.
Biesterfeld, Bryan D. ..................'64 '93 C.208 B.S.B.A. L.112 J.D. 1055 W. 7th St.

**Biesty, James T.** ..........................'40 '78 C.112 B.S. L.809 J.D. [Biesty,M.&G.]
*PRACTICE AREAS: Insurance Defense Law; Insurance Coverage; Bad Faith Law; Construction Law; Arbitration.

**Biesty, McCool & Garretty, A Professional Corporation**
**725 South Figueroa Street, Suite 2200, 90017**
**Telephone: 213-617-9193 Facsimile: 213-620-0746**
**James T. Biesty; Clinton T. McCool; Reetha Haynes-Garretty;—David N. Ball; Marina M. Morrison; Brett G. Hampton.**
**Insurance Defense. Legal, Real Estate, Insurance Agents and Brokers' Errors & Omissions. Construction Defect and Family Law. Governmental Tort Liability. General Civil Litigation, Alternate Dispute Resolution.**
***See Professional Biographies, LOS ANGELES, CALIFORNIA***

**Bigbee, Deborah A.** .......................'66 '92 C.46 B.S. L.1065 J.D. [🄰 Latham&W.]
**Bigelow, David N.** .........................'52 '95 C.940 B.A. L.1049 J.D. [Girardi&K.]
*PRACTICE AREAS: Personal Injury; Professional Liability; Toxic Torts.
Bigelow, M. Ross ..................................'24 '52 C&L.800 B.S., J.D. Supr. Ct. J.

**Bigelow, Moore & Tyre**
**(See Pasadena)**

**Bigley, Paul A.** ..........................'59 '85 C.112 B.A. L.426 J.D. [Gilbert,K.C.&J.]
*PRACTICE AREAS: Personal Injury Defense; Premises Liability; Construction Defect; Entertainment Law; Medical Malpractice.
Bigony, Bruce A. ...........'54 '82 C.597 B.A. L.1068 J.D. V.P. & Sr. Coun., Union Bk.
**Bihr, Bernhard E.** ....................'47 '74 C.1097 B.A. L.426 J.D. [🄰 Acker,K.&W.]
*PRACTICE AREAS: Construction Defect; Professional Liability; Insurance Defense.
Bilac, Eva .......................'56 '82 C&L.800 B.A., J.D. 3255 Wilshire Blvd. 12th Fl.
**Bilbeaux, Raymon B., III** ...........'59 '91 C.1077 B.A. L.800 J.D. [🄰 Bronson,B.&M.]
**Biles, Barbara** ..............'54 '80 C.112 B.A. L.1068 J.D. [McClintock,W.B.R.R.&M.]
*LANGUAGES: Spanish.
*PRACTICE AREAS: Real Estate Law; Environmental Law.
**Bilger, L. Victor, Jr.** ...............'45 '78 C.1167 B.S. L.426 J.D. [Wilson,E.M.E.&D.]
Bilgore, Paul S. '29 '55 C.976 B.A. L.178
(adm. in NY; not adm. in CA) 355 S. Windsor Blvd.‡
**Biller, Dimitrios P.** ..................'62 '89 C.112 B.A. L.426 J.D. [🄰 Pillsbury M.&S.]
**Billet, Jerome S., (A Professional Corporation)**, (AV) '35 '63
C.112 B.A. L.1068 J.D. [🄲 Billet&K.]
*PRACTICE AREAS: Civil Litigation.

**Billet & Kaplan, (AV)**
**A Partnership of Professional Corporations**
**Suite 1700, 1888 Century Park East, 90067-1721**
**Telephone: 310-551-1700 Fax: 310-277-7062**
**Member of Firm: Terry S. Kaplan (A Professional Corporation); Ronald J. Sokol (A Professional Corporation); Gregory A. Dawley (A Professional Corporation). Associates: Michael K. Dewberry; Paul N. Glasser; Jordan Trachtenberg; Roger C. Glienke; Todd M. Lander. Of Counsel: Jerome S. Billet (A Professional Corporation); Arthur L. Rolston (A Professional Law Corporation).**
**General Civil and Commercial Litigation, including Title Insurance Litigation, Financial Institution Litigation, Real Estate Litigation, Insolvency and related Litigation, Wrongful Termination Litigation, Fidelity and Blanket Bond Litigation.**
***See Professional Biographies, LOS ANGELES, CALIFORNIA***

**Billey, Cynthia J.** ..................'62 '91 C.112 B.A. L.1066 J.D. [🄰 Konowiecki&R.]
*PRACTICE AREAS: General Business; Health Care Law; Corporate.
Bin, Enrique P. ..........................'37 '71 C.061 B.A. L.809 J.D. 2700 W. 3rd St.
**Bin, Rachelle Marie** '63 '89 C.112 B.A. L.1068 J.D.
Sr. Legal Coun., Univision Communication Grp.
*LANGUAGES: Spanish and French.
*RESPONSIBILITIES: Media Law; Labor Law; Litigation.
Binder, David A. ................'34 '60 C.112 A.B. L.813 LL.B. Prof. of Law, U.C.L.A.
**Binder, Lisa** ...............................'67 '94 C&L.309 A.B., J.D. [🄰 Latham&W.]
*LANGUAGES: German, Latin, Greek, Spanish and Classical Arabic.
**Binder, Maureen F. Wolfe**, (AV) ..........'46 '76 C.770 B.A. L.426 J.D. [Larwill&W.]
*PRACTICE AREAS: Probate; Estate Planning; Real Property.
**Binder, Nancy R.** ...................'62 '90 C.112 B.A. L.809 J.D. [🄰 Saltzburg,R.&B.]
*PRACTICE AREAS: Bankruptcy; Receiverships; Business Law.
**Binford, Heidi M.** ................................'65 '93 C&L.800 B.S., J.D. [🄰 Dewey B.]
**Bing, Peter R.** ................'54 '79 C.597 B.A. L.800 J.D. [🄰 La Follette,J.D.F.&A.]
*PRACTICE AREAS: Product Liability; General Liability; Construction Defect.
**Bingham, John J., Jr., (A Professional Corporation)**, (AV) '46 '77
C.800 B.A. L.809 J.D. [Danning,G.D.&K.]
**Bingham, Melanie J.** ......................'65 '93 C.31 B.A. L.1068 J.D. [🄰 Danner&M.]
**Bingham, Patrick D.** ...............'56 '81 C.813 B.A. L.1068 J.D. [🄰 Meyers,B.&M.]
*PRACTICE AREAS: Product Liability; Insurance Related Issues.
Bingham, Patrick E. ....................'54 '89 C.37 B.A. L.1068 J.D. 4929 Wilshire Blvd.
**Bingman, J. Steven** ........................'60 '91 C.347 B.S. L.990 J.D. [🄰 Barger&W.]
Binns, James J., (AVⓉ) '39 '65 C.397 B.S. L.884 J.D.
355 S. Grand Ave. (⊙NY, SD Ca, LV NV, Bo MA, DC, Dal TX, SJ PR, Den CO, Phil PA)
Binstock, Sydney L. ...............'25 '80 C.665 B.S. L.1221 J.D. 12121 Wilshire Blvd.
Binstock, Yvonne ........................'36 '78 C.112 L.1221 J.D. 12121 Wilshire Blvd.
**Bird, Brian James** ...........................'49 '78 C.976 B.A. L.426 J.D. [Fried,B.&C.]
*PRACTICE AREAS: Business Litigation - General Civil and Trial Practice in all State and Federal Courts; Lender Liability; Insurance Coverage; Securities; Bankruptcy.
**Bird, Terry W.**, (AV) ...............'46 '70 C.813 B.A. L.1097 J.D. [Bird,M.B.W.&M.]

**Bird & Bird, A Law Corporation**
**(See Torrance)**

**Bird, Marella, Boxer, Wolpert & Matz, A Professional Corporation, (AV)**
**1875 Century Park East, 23rd Floor, 90067-2561**
**Telephone: 310-201-2100 Facsimile: 310-201-2110**
**Terry W. Bird; Joel E. Boxer; Vincent J. Marella; A. Howard Matz; Dorothy Wolpert; Jason D. Kogan; Mark T. Drooks; Ronald J. Nessim; Thomas R. Freeman; Gary S. Lincenberg;—Efrem M. Grail; Kristin L. Jameson; John Milton McCoy, III; Elizabeth A. Newman; Thomas V. Reichert; Ekwan E. Rhow. Of Counsel: Louise A. LaMothe (A Professional Corporation).**
**Civil and Criminal, Trial and Appellate Litigation.**
**Reference: Bank of California (Downtown Los Angeles Branch).**
***See Professional Biographies, LOS ANGELES, CALIFORNIA***

**Biren, Matthew B. F., & Associates, (AV) '48 '73 C.112 B.A. L.426 J.D.** BR
**815 Moraga Drive, 90049-1633**
**Telephone: 310-476-3031; 381-5609 FAX: 310-471-3165**
**Email: mbfba@primenet.com**
***PRACTICE AREAS: Products Liability; Personal Injury (with Complex Technological Issues); Professional Negligence; Neurolaw; Insurance Bad Faith.**
**—Marc J. Katzman; Debra J. Tauger; Edmont T. Barrett.**
**Practice Limited to Personal Injury, Products Liability, Neurolaw, Business Torts and Professional Negligence.**
**Reference: First Los Angeles Bank (Century City, Los Angeles, Branch).**
***See Professional Biographies, LOS ANGELES, CALIFORNIA***

**Birenbaum, Charles S.** '57 '83
C.604 B.A. L.276 J.D. [Thelen,M.J.&B.] (⊙San Francisco)
*PRACTICE AREAS: Labor Litigation.

CAA185P

**Birk, Jodi** '— '96 C.813 B.A. L.893 J.D.
(adm. in MD; not adm. in CA) [Skadden,A.S.M.&F.]
**Birke, Charles L.**, (AV) ... '37 '62 C.910 B.A. L.309 LL.B. [Sandler&R.]
**Birker, Craig C.** ... '54 '79 C.1077 B.A. L.426 J.D. [Sandler&R.]
Birmingham, William B. ... '37 '72 C.1077 B.A. L.477 J.D. [Standish&B.]
**Birnbaum, Mark** ... '66 '91 C.1349 B.A. L.112 J.D. [Perkins C.]
*PRACTICE AREAS: Real Estate Law.
**Birnberg, James R.**, (AV) ... '39 '66 C.668 B.A. L.1066 J.D. [Loeb&L.]
*PRACTICE AREAS: Trusts and Estates.
**Birner, Russell H.** ... '63 '91 C.1271 B.A. L.861 J.D. [Barger&W.]
**Birnholz, Richard M.** ... '65 '90 C.813 B.A. L.112 J.D. [Irell&M.]
**Birnie, Brian W.** ... '52 '79 C.605 B.A. L.1148 J.D. [La Follette,J.D.F.&A.]
*PRACTICE AREAS: Medical Malpractice Litigation.
**Bisceglia, Julie J.** ... '46 '85 C.813 B.A. L.1068 J.D. [Shapiro,R.&C.]
*LANGUAGES: French and Italian.
*PRACTICE AREAS: Commercial and Entertainment Litigation.
Bischel, Charlotte L. ... '69 '94 C.188 B.S. L.309 J.D. 601 S. Figueroa St.
Bise, Lester ... '20 '47 L.209 LL.B. 3030 W. Temple St.
**Bisetti, Richard L.**, (AV) ... '48 '75 C.800 B.A. L.1136 J.D. [Magaña,C.&M.]
*PRACTICE AREAS: Automobile Product Liability; Construction Accident; Premises Liability Law; Products Liability Law; Wrongful Death Law.
**Bisgaard, Christopher P., (P.C.)**, (AV) '47 '72 C.800 B.A. L.1068 J.D.
[Lewis,D.B.&B.]
**Bishin, William R.**, (AV) '39 '64 C.178 B.A. L.309 J.D.
[R.Edwards] (©Seattle, WA)
**Bishop, Anthony J.** ... '56 '81 C&L.800 A.B., J.D. [Sheppard,M.R.&H.]
**Bishop, J. Douglas** ... '61 '91 C.112 B.A. L.1065 J.D. [Pillsbury M.&S.]
**Bishop, Kendall R.**, (AV) ... '39 '65 C.813 A.B. L.1066 J.D. [O'Melveny&M.]
*PRACTICE AREAS: Corporate Law; Securities; Mergers, Acquisitions and Divestitures.
**Bishop, Leah Margaret**, (AV) ... '54 '80 C.1036 B.A. L.178 J.D. [O'Melveny&M.]
*PRACTICE AREAS: Estate Administration; Taxation; Estate Planning; Tax Exempt Organizations, Non-profit and Charitable Organizations.
**Bishop, Nadia M.** ... '69 '96 C.025 B.A. L.813 J.D. [Quinn E.U.&O.]
**Bishop, Sidney W.** ... '26 '50 C.686 B.S. L.936 J.D. [Beckman,D.S.&R.]
*PRACTICE AREAS: Disability Insurance; Insurance Regulation; Life and Health Insurance; Unfair Insurance Practices; Reinsurance.
Bishop-Thompson, Avis ... '61 '89 C.811 B.A. L.770 J.D. 5757 Wilshire Blvd., Ste., 560
**Bishton, Norris J., Jr.**, (AV) ... '36 '60 C&L.602 A.B., J.D. [Bishton G.]
*PRACTICE AREAS: Civil Trial; Appellate; Business; Bankruptcy; Corporate.

**Bishton • Gubernick, (AV)**
**2029 Century Park East, Suite 3150, 90067**
**Telephone: 310-556-1801 Fax: 310-556-1050**
**Members of Firm: Norris J. Bishton, Jr.; Jeffrey S. Gubernick.**
**Civil Trial and Appellate Practice in all State and Federal Courts. Real Estate, Business, Bankruptcy, Corporate, Construction Law and Insurance Coverage.**
***See Professional Biographies, LOS ANGELES, CALIFORNIA***

Bisno, Alice Cohen ... '49 '76 C.112 B.A. L.1068 J.D. Auto. Club of Southern Calif.

**Bisno & Samberg**
**(See Pasadena)**

Bisnow, James S. ... '50 '75 C.112 B.A. L.910 J.D. 880 W. 1st St.
Bissell, Henry M., III, (AV) ... '25 '58 C.494 B.E.E. L.705 LL.B. [H.Bissell] (Pat.)
Bissell, Henry M. (Chip), IV ... '65 '92 C.112 B.S. L.426 J.D. 6327 Riggs Pl.
Bissell, Olivia O. ... '55 '85 C.705 B.A. L.61 J.D. 4215 Glencoe Ave.
Bissell, Henry, Prof. Law Corp., (AV) ... 6820 La Tijera Blvd. (Pat.)
**Bisset, William T.** ... '47 '73 C.696 B.S. L.477 J.D. [Hughes H.&R.]
*PRACTICE AREAS: Litigation.
**Bissett, Brenda Adams** ... '57 '84 C.112 B.A. L.426 J.D. [Lord,B.&B.]
Bissonnette, Karen L ... '55 '87 C.813 B.A. L.112 J.D. Dep. Atty. Gen.
**Bistline, Gregory D.** ... '51 '76 C.1097 B.A. L.426 J.D. [Kearney,B.&C.]
**Bitting, William M., (P.C.)**, (AV) ... '39 '66 C.112 A.B. L.1068 J.D. [Hill,F.&B.]

**Bivona & Cohen**
**Two Century Plaza, 2049 Century Park East, 90067©**
**Telephone: 310-553-4114 Telex: 691681 Telecopier: (310) 553-2510**
**Laurence A. Dornstein; Marla M. Stewart; Laura Lyn Lipscomb.**
**General Defense, Appellate and Trial Practice. Product Liability, Malpractice, Property, Casualty and Surety Insurance Law. Toxic and Hazardous Waste Litigation.**
**New York, N.Y. Office: Wall Street Plaza. Telephone: 212-363-3100. Telex: 640179. Cable Address: "Insurlaw" Telecopier: (212) 363-9824.**
**Warren, New Jersey Office: 15 Mountain Boulevard. Telephone: 908-757-7800. Telecopier: 908-757-8039.**
***See Professional Biographies, LOS ANGELES, CALIFORNIA***

Bixby, Kelly W. ... '47 '72 C.112 B.A. L.1049 J.D. 1901 Ave. of the Stars
**Bizik, Linley Clare** ... '70 '95 C.37 B.S.B.A. L.1068 J.D. [Arter&H.]
Bizzini, Karen L. ... '59 '85 C.800 B.S. L.309 J.D. 601 S. Figueroa
Blachman, Rochel S. '52 '77
C.112 B.A. L.1066 J.D. Sr. V.P., Bus. Affs., Orion Pictures Corp.
Black, David H. ... '53 '79 C.994 B.A. L.1095 J.D. 914 S. Robertson Blvd., 2nd Fl.
**Black, Donna R.**, (AV) ... '47 '75 C.37 B.A. L.1068 J.D. [Manatt,P.&P.]
*PRACTICE AREAS: Environmental Law; Land Use; Administrative Law.
Black, Felicia Duque ... '27 '78 C.1097 B.A. L.809 J.D. I.R.S.
Black, Kathryn J. ... '47 '92 C.1097 B.A. L.426 J.D. 777 S. Figueroa St., 10th Fl.
Black, Kenneth A. ... '49 '74 C.1044 B.A. L.1068 J.D. Supr. Ct. J.
**Black, Randall W.** ... '60 '83 C.112 B.A. L.1066 J.D. [Cox,C.&N.]
*PRACTICE AREAS: Corporate Law; Real Property Law.
Black, Richard M. ... '23 '71 C.178 A.B. L.1136 J.D. P.O. Box 710
**Black, Robert H.**, (AV) ... '41 '81 C.605 B.A. L.809 J.D. [Black C.H.&L.]
*PRACTICE AREAS: Insurance Coverage; Coverage Litigation; Bad Faith Litigation; Insurance Defense; Appellate Practice.
**Black, Timothy A.** ... '64 '92 C.112 B.A. L.770 J.D. [Nordstrom,S.N.&J.]
*PRACTICE AREAS: Plaintiffs Litigation; Products Liability.

**Black Compean Hall & Lenneman, (AV)** BB
**One Wilshire, Suite 1000 624 South Grand Avenue, 90017**
**Telephone: 213-629-9500 FAX: 213-629-4868**
**Email: bchl@earthlink.net**
**Members of Firm: Robert H. Black; Michael D. Compean; Frederick G. Hall; Annette J. Lenneman. Associates: William J. Light; Vicente Valencia, Jr.; Margie Castillo; Lara Michelle Brya; Meredith A. Czapla.**
**Trial and Appellate Practice in all State and Federal Courts, Concentrating in the areas of Insurance Coverage, Coverage Litigation, Insurance Guarantee Association Practice, Reinsurance and Insurance Related Matters.**
**Reference: Sterling Bank.**
***See Professional Biographies, LOS ANGELES, CALIFORNIA***

**Blackburn, James S.** ... '69 '94 C.112 B.A. L.1066 J.D. [Blanc W.J.&K.]
*PRACTICE AREAS: Commercial Litigation; Proprietary Rights Litigation.
**Blacker, Richard A.**, (AV) ... '37 '72 C.188 B.Ch.E. L.1068 J.D. [Foley L.W.&A.]
*PRACTICE AREAS: Health Care; Hospitals; Nonprofit Corporations; Business Law.
**Blackman, Lee L.**, (AV) ... '50 '75 C&L.800 B.A., J.D. [McDermott,W.&E.]
*PRACTICE AREAS: Constitutional Law; Environmental; Litigation.
**Blackman, Stephanie** ... '61 '87 C.174 B.A. L.1068 J.D. [Belin R.&B.]
Blackshaw, Julie Fox, (AV) ... '53 '79 C.813 B.A. L.1065 J.D. Asst. U.S. Atty.
Blackstone, Mary Louise ... '41 '82 C.446 B.A. L.1148 J.D. Sr. Jud. Atty., Ct. of App.
Blackwell, Glenette ... '34 '61 C.800 B.A. L.809 LL.B. 4219 Don Alanis Pl.
Blackwell, William W. ... '51 '78 C.174 B.S. L.1137 J.D. 1901 Ave. of the Stars
**Blades, Steven D.** ... '54 '90 C.1074 B.A. L.809 J.D. [Manning,M.&W.]
**Blady, I. Benjamin** ... '66 '92 C.112 B.A. L.426 J.D. [Epstein B.&G.]
*PRACTICE AREAS: Labor and Employment Law; Litigation.
**Blagden, Kathryn** ... '71 '95 C.813 A.B. L.1067 J.D. [Jones,D.R.&P.]
Blaine, Cheryl L. ... '58 '89 C.112 B.A. L.809 J.D. [Simkin&B.]
Blais, Simone Marie-Louise ... '34 '85 C.684 B.A. L.1136 J.D. Worker's Comp. J.
Blaisch, Harold, (BV) ... '32 '66 C.112 B.S. L.809 LL.B. 1661 Ventura Blvd. (Encino)
**Blake, Guy S.** '67 '93 C.629 B.A., B.S. L.990 J.D.
Assoc. Dir., Legal & Bus. Affs., Warner/Chappell Music
**Blake, Lawrence J.**, (BV) ... '50 '76 C.1031 B.A. L.309 J.D. [Manatt,P.&P.]
*PRACTICE AREAS: Music.
Blake, Natalie ... '64 '89 C.112 A.B. L.1065 J.D. 11601 Wilshire Blvd.
**Blake, Samantha E.** ... '65 '93 C.911 B.A. L.426 J.D. [Kehr,C.T.&F.]
*LANGUAGES: French.
*PRACTICE AREAS: Real Estate; Corporate Litigation; Business Litigation; Civil Litigation.
Blake, Thomas A., (AV) ... '43 '72 C&L.767 B.S., J.D. 300 South Spring St.
**Blakeley, Scott E.** ... '— '89 C.990 B.S. L.809 J.D. [Blakeley&B.]

**Blakeley & Brinkman**
**333 South Grand Avenue, 37th Floor, 90071-1599**
**Telephone: 213-628-2190 Telecopier: 213-625-1832**
**Members of Firm: Scott E. Blakeley; Daren R. Brinkman.**
**Bankruptcy, Creditors Rights, Commercial Litigation, Business Litigation and Real Estate.**
***See Professional Biographies, LOS ANGELES, CALIFORNIA***

**Blakely, Elizabeth B.** ... '53 '78 C.605 A.B. L.800 J.D. [Rodi,P.P.G.&C.]
*PRACTICE AREAS: Corporate; Partnership and Real Estate Transactions; Tax Planning.

**Blakely, Sokoloff, Taylor & Zafman, (AV)**
**A Limited Liability Partnership**
**7th Floor, 12400 Wilshire Boulevard, 90025©**
**Telephone: 310-207-3800 Facsimile: 310-820-5988**
**Email: BSTZ_mail@bstz.com URL: http://www.bstz.com**
**Members of Firm: Roger W. Blakely, Jr.†; Stanley W. Sokoloff†; Edwin H. Taylor†; Norman Zafman†; Eric S. Hyman; Stephen D. Gross (1953-1995); George W Hoover II; Lori N. Boatright; Dennis G. Martin. Of Counsel: Stephen L. King; Ronald W. Reagin;—Thomas M. Coester; Michael W. Hicks; Eric Ho; W. Thomas Babbitt; Karen L. Feisthamel; Dinu Gruia; Anand Sethuraman; George G.C. Tseng; Farzad E. Amini.**
**Intellectual Property Law, including Patents, Trademarks, Copyrights, Related Prosecution and Litigation.**
**Sunnyvale, California Office: 1279 Oakmead Parkway. Telephone: 408-720-8598. Facsimile: 408-720-9397.**
**Costa Mesa, California Office: Suite 850, 611 Anton Boulevard. Telephone: 714-557-3800. Facsimile: 714-557-3347.**
**Lake Oswego, Oregon Office: Suite 101, 5285 SW Meadows Road. Telephone: 503-684-6200. Facsimile: 503-684-3245.**
**†Indicates A Law Corporation.**
***See Professional Biographies, LOS ANGELES, CALIFORNIA***

**Blakey, Daniel R.** ... '60 '89 C.951 B.A. L.1065 J.D. [Lane P.S.L.]
*PRACTICE AREAS: Toxic Tort Litigation; Products Liability; General Litigation.
**Blakey, Elizabeth E.** ... '61 '88 C.602 B.A. L.426 J.D. [Hecker&H.]
**Blalock, Steven W.**, (AV) ... '52 '77 C.684 B.A. L.426 J.D. [Blalock&G.]
*PRACTICE AREAS: Immigration and Nationality Law.

**Blalock & Gray, (AV)**
**11726 San Vicente Boulevard, Suite 650, 90049**
**Telephone: 310-447-5665 Fax: 310-820-7143**
**Email: B&G@BBS.la.com**
**Members of Firm: Humberto R. Gray; Steven W. Blalock (Certified Specialist, Immigration and Nationality Law the State Bar of California Board of Legal Specialization). Associate: Cristina E. Perez.**
**Practice Limited to Immigration and Nationality Law.**
***See Professional Biographies, LOS ANGELES, CALIFORNIA***

**Blamires, Bradley R.** ... '61 '90 C.101 B.S. L.169 J.D. [Wilson,E.M.E.&D.]
**Blanc, Ronald L., (P.C.)**, (AV) ... '37 '62 C.174 B.S. L.569 LL.B. [Blanc W.J.&K.]

**Blanc Williams Johnston & Kronstadt, (AV)**
**A Partnership including Professional Corporations**
**Suite 1700, 1900 Avenue of the Stars, 90067**
**Telephone: 310-552-2500 Telecopier: 310-552-1191**
**Members of Firm: Ronald L. Blanc (P.C.) (Certified Specialist, Taxation Law, The State Bar of California Board of Legal Specialization); Harley J. Williams (P.C.); Ronald L. Johnston (P.C.); John A. Kronstadt; James R. Farrand; Gary A. David; Allen R. Grogan; Richard T. McCoy III; Regina A. Stagg; John C. Rawls III; Sam C. Mandel;—Suzanne V. Wilson; Dawn Weekes Glenn; Cynthia S. Arato; Gio Hunt; James S. Blackburn. Of Counsel: Sol Rosenthal; Samuel J. Fox; Mona D. Miller.**
**Commercial, Computer and Technology, Proprietary Rights, including Copyright, Trademark, Trade Secret and Patent Law, Corporate and Securities, Entertainment, Federal and State Taxation, International Business and Taxation and Real Property Law and Employment Law. General Civil and Trial Practice in all State and Federal Courts.**
**Reference: First Los Angeles Bank (Main Office).**
***See Professional Biographies, LOS ANGELES, CALIFORNIA***

Blancarte, James E. ... '53 '79 C.668 B.A. L.1068 J.D. [J.E.Blancarte]
Blancarte, James E., A Professional Corporation, Law Offices of
1875 Century Park East, Suite 700
**Blanch, Joey L.** ... '72 '96 C.877 B.A. L.309 J.D. [Fried,F.H.S.&J.]
**Blanchard, Lonnie C., III**, (AV) ... '54 '80 C.347 B.S. L.1068 J.D. [Berman,B.M.&R.]
*PRACTICE AREAS: Commercial Litigation; Real Estate; Real Estate Litigation; Probate Litigation; Construction Litigation.
**Blanchard, Timothy P.** ... '60 '86 C.612 B.S. L.734 J.D. [McDermott,W.&E.]
*PRACTICE AREAS: Health Care; Medicare and Medicaid.
Blanco, Alicia Yoko ... '66 '91 C.426 B.A. L.809 J.D. Dep. Fed. Pub. Def.
**Bland, Charles N., Jr.** ... '54 '80 C.860 B.A. L.276 J.D. [Bronson,B.&M.]
*PRACTICE AREAS: Employment; Wrongful Termination; Commercial Litigation; Construction Litigation.
Blaney, Doyle O., (AV) ... '30 '59 C.112 B.A. L.1068 J.D. [Kahn,S.&B.]
Blank, Bess ... '59 '84 C.112 A.B. L.426 J.D. [Colton M.]
Blank, Douglas S. ... '57 '88 C.112 B.S. L.1137 J.D. 3600 Wilshire Blvd.
Blank, Julius N. ... '14 '39 C.113 B.A. L.800 LL.B. 103 W. 11th St.

**Blank, Martin H., Jr.**, (AV) '42 '66 C.112 A.B. L.1066 LL.B. BB
**11755 Wilshire Boulevard, Suite 1400, 90025-1520**
**Telephone: 310-477-5455 Fax: 310-444-9203**
**Email: marty@general.net**
**General Civil Practice. Corporation, Real Property, Business and Estate Planning Law.**
***See Professional Biographies, LOS ANGELES, CALIFORNIA***

**Blankenship, Marlena M.** ... '54 '89 C.112 B.A. L.426 J.D. [Tourtelot&B.]
**Blanton, Patricia L.** ... '58 '84 C.695 B.A. L.990 J.D. [Parker S.]
*PRACTICE AREAS: Insurance Defense Law; General Liability Law.
Blasberg, Teresa A., (AV) ... '56 '82 C.813 B.A. L.1068 J.D. 811 W. Seventh St.

**Blashek, Robert D., III** . . . '54 '80 C.103 A.B. L.178 J.D. [O'Melveny&M.]
*PRACTICE AREAS: Federal Income Tax; California State Income Tax.
Blasi, Gary L. . . . '45 '76 C.623 B.A. Actg. Prof., UCLA School of Law
Blatner, Margaret '— '80
C.768 B.A. L.770 J.D. Sr. V.P., Bus. Affs., New Line Cinema Corp.
Blatt, Jeffrey J., (BV) '56 '81
C.112 B.S. L.1051 J.D. 1800 Ave. of the Stars, Suite 900 (Pat.)

**Blau, Edward, Law Offices of, (AV) '22 '51 C.563 B.B.A. L.309 J.D.**
**10100 Santa Monica Boulevard Suite 250, 90067**
**Telephone: 310-556-8468; 310-556-0833 Fax: 310-282-0579; 203-0311**
**Entertainment Law.**

Blau, Louis C., (AV) . . . '15 '38 C.112 A.B. L.800 J.D. Pres., Adak Productions Inc.
**Blaufarb, Tamar** . . . '68 '94 C.112 B.A. L.1065 J.D. [Ⓐ Frye,A.&M.]
Blaustein, Alan S. . . . '53 '78 C.597 B.A. L.339 J.D. 8631 W. 3rd St.
Blavin, Sheree A. . . . '— '86 C.112 B.A. L.809 J.D. 601 W. 5th St., Suite 300
**Blaylock, Michael I.**, (AV) . . . '42 '67 C.605 A.B. L.800 J.D. [Hanna&M.]
*PRACTICE AREAS: Taxation; Estate Planning; General Practice.
Blaylock, Robert J. . . . '30 '59 C.112 B.A. L.1068 LL.B. Ct. Comr.
**Bleau, Thomas P.** . . . '65 '91 C.457 B.A. L.398 J.D. [Bleau,F.&G.]
*PRACTICE AREAS: Complex Litigation; Insurance Bad Faith; Medical Malpractice; Legal Malpractice; Business Litigation.

**Bleau, Fox & Goldberg, A Professional Law Corporation**
**3575 Cahuenga Boulevard, West, Suite 580, 90068**
**Telephone: 213-874-8613 Fax: 213-874-1234**
**Thomas P. Bleau; Martin R. Fox; Seth M. Goldberg.**
**Litigation in all State and Federal Courts. Complex Tort Liability, Intellectual Property, Contract and Real Estate Litigation, Unfair Competition, Trademark, Trade Dress and Copyright Matters, Royalty Reclamation, High Profile Civil Rights and Discrimination Claims, Personal Injury, Medical and Legal Malpractice and Insurance Bad Faith Claims.**
*See Professional Biographies, LOS ANGELES, CALIFORNIA*

**Blecher, Maxwell M.**, (AV) . . . '33 '55 C.209 B.A. L.800 LL.B. [Blecher&C.]
*PRACTICE AREAS: Antitrust; Complex Business Litigation; Intellectual Property; Professional Malpractice; Patent Infringement.

**Blecher & Collins, A Professional Corporation, (AV) ⊞**
**611 West Sixth Street, 20th Floor, 90017**
**Telephone: 213-622-4222 Telecopier: 213-622-1656**
**Maxwell M. Blecher; Harold R. Collins, Jr.; John E. Andrews; Florence F. Cameron; Ralph C. Hofer; William C. Hsu; James Robert Noblin; Donald R. Pepperman; Alicia G. Rosenberg.**
**Complex Business Litigation in Federal and State Courts. Antitrust, Intellectual Property, Professional Malpractice, Patent and Trademark Infringement, Contract and Fraud Litigation, Sports Law, Trials and Appeals.**
*See Professional Biographies, LOS ANGELES, CALIFORNIA*

**Blechner, Paul A.** . . . '66 '92 C.605 A.B. L.569 J.D. [Ⓐ Greenberg G.F.C.&M.]
*PRACTICE AREAS: Litigation.
**Bledsoe, Steven E.** . . . '61 '91 C.1042 B.A. L.101 J.D. [Ⓐ Kirkland&E.]
*PRACTICE AREAS: Litigation.
**Bleichner, Brad D.** . . . '53 '85 C.446 B.A. L.1136 J.D. [Selman B.]
**Bleifer, Candace Connart** . . . '60 '92 C.896 B.B.A. L.426 J.D. [Ⓐ Anderson,A.L.&G.]
*PRACTICE AREAS: Business Litigation.
**Bleifer, Scott D.** . . . '67 '92 C.112 B.A. L.426 J.D. [Dale,B.&H.]
**Blencowe, Paul S.**, (AV) . . . '53 '79 C.966 B.A. L.813 J.D. [Fulbright&J.]
*PRACTICE AREAS: Corporate Law; Mergers, Acquisitions and Divestitures; Securities.
**Blendell, Elizabeth A.** . . . '50 '80 C.518 B.A. L.93 J.D. [Latham&W.]
**Blessey, Raymond L.** . . . '47 '95 C.800 M.S. L.809 J.D. [Ⓐ Bonne,B.M.O.&N.]
**Blevit, Stephen D.** . . . '70 '95 C.209 B.S. L.800 J.D. [Ⓐ Latham&W.]
*PRACTICE AREAS: Finance; Real Estate.
Blewitt, J. Justin, Jr. . . . '45 '70 C.754 A.B. L.884 J.D. Sr. Coun., Calif. Fed. Bk.
**Bley, Kenneth B.**, (AV) . . . '39 '74 C.112 B.S. L.309 J.D. [Cox,C.&N.]
*PRACTICE AREAS: Appellate Litigation; Land Use Litigation; Land Use and Eminent Domain Law.
**Blinn, S. David**, (AV) . . . '45 '70 C.918 B.A. L.802 J.D. [Gibson,D.&C.] (©Irvine)
**Blint, Laura S.** . . . '71 '96 C.112 B.A. L.800 J.D. [Ⓐ Wolf,R.&S.]
*PRACTICE AREAS: Community Association Law.
Bliss, Ina N. . . . '— '92 C.800 B.A. L.1136 J.D. 395 Huntley Dr.
Blissert, Jane A. . . . '54 '82 C.605 B.A. L.426 J.D. Dep. Dist. Atty.
**Blitstien, Lori S.** . . . '49 '90 C.339 B.S. L.426 J.D. [Ⓐ Cotkin&C.]
*PRACTICE AREAS: Insurance Coverage and Bad Faith Litigation; General Civil Litigation; Professional Liability.
Bloch, Jonathan, (P.C.) '53 '79 C.112 B.A. L.1049 J.D.
Exec. V.P., Micor Ventures, Inc.
**Block, Alan P.** . . . '64 '89 C.188 B.S. L.112 J.D. [Oppenheimer P.S.] (Pat.)
*PRACTICE AREAS: Intellectual Property.
Block, Alan Robert . . . '46 '72 C.800 B.A. L.1049 J.D. [A.R.Block]
Block, Brian T. . . . '62 '88 C.659 B.A. L.978 J.D. 11669 Santa Monica Blvd.
Block, Joseph D., (AV) . . . '53 '78 C.813 B.A. L.426 J.D. 1901 Avenue of The Stars
**Block, Karl E.**, (AV) . . . '58 '83 C.367 B.A. L.800 J.D. [Robinson,D.B.&K.]
*LANGUAGES: French.
*REPORTED CASES: In re Commercial Consortium of California, 135 B.R. 120 (Bankr C.D. Cal. 1991);In re Hathaway Ranch Partnership, 127 B.R. 859 (Bankr C.D. Cal. 1990); In re Altabon Foods, Inc., 998 F. 2d 718 (9th Cir., 1993).
*PRACTICE AREAS: Bankruptcy Law; Insolvency Law; Creditors' Rights Law; Commercial Law.
**Block, Kenneth L.** . . . '53 '82 C.238 B.A. L.424 J.D. [Katten M.&Z.]
*PRACTICE AREAS: Banking.
**Block, Mark L.** . . . '59 '84 C.838 B.A. L.597 J.D. [Christensen,M.F.J.G.W.&S.]
*PRACTICE AREAS: Civil Litigation.
Block, Mitchell J. . . . '49 '77 C.994 B.A. L.300 J.D. Mun. Ct. Comr.
Block, Ralph L., (AV) . . . '43 '68 C.112 A.B. L.1068 J.D. [Graven P.B.B.&Q.]
Block, Robert N., (AV) . . . '50 '78 C.112 B.A. L.1068 J.D. U.S. Mag.
Block, Alan Robert, P.C. . . . 1901 Ave. of the Stars
**Blodgett, Mary** . . . '62 '88 C&L.352 B.A., J.D. [Kirkland&E.]
*PRACTICE AREAS: Litigation.
Blonder, David . . . '11 '35 C&L.800 A.B., LL.B. 727 W. 7th St.
Bloom, Alan '45 '75 C.145 B.A. L.30 J.D.
(adm. in MD; not adm. in CA) Maxicare Health Plans, Inc.
Bloom, Allan . . . '34 '62 C.475 B.A. L.912 J.D. [Bloom&R.]
**Bloom, David B.**, (AV) . . . '49 '73 C.800 B.A. L.426 J.D. [D.B.Bloom]
**Bloom, Dena L.** . . . '62 '87 C.112 B.A. L.1065 J.D. [Latham&W.]
Bloom, Irwin N. . . . '34 '62 C.494 B.S.L. L.809 LL.B. Dep. Dist. Atty.
**Bloom, Jerry R.** . . . '52 '81 C.273 B.A. L.472 J.D. [Morrison&F.]
*PRACTICE AREAS: Energy; Project Development.
**Bloom, Judith Ilene**, (AV) . . . '50 '75 C.112 B.A. L.426 J.D. [Clark&T.]
*PRACTICE AREAS: Banking; Bankruptcy; Creditors Rights; Collateral Recovery; Financial Institutions Law.
Bloom, Lisa . . . '61 '87 C.112 B.A. L.976 J.D. 6300 Wilshire Blvd.
Bloom, Richard H. . . . '53 '78 C.112 B.A. L.426 J.D. 11755 Wilshire Blvd.
**Bloom, Steven N.** . . . '53 '79 C.800 A.B. L.426 J.D. [Frandzel&S.]

**Bloom, David B., A Prof. Corp., Law Offices of, (AV) ⊞**
**3325 Wilshire Boulevard, Ninth Floor, 90010**
**Telephone: 213-938-5248; 384-4088 Telecopier: 213-385-2009**
(This Listing Continued)

**Bloom, David B., A Prof. Corp., Law Offices of (Continued)**
**David B. Bloom;—Stephen S. Monroe (A Professional Corporation); Raphael A. Rosemblat; James E. Adler; Bonni S. Mantovani; Roy A. Levun; Cherie S. Raidy; Jonathan Udell; Susan Carole Jay; Edward Idell; Sandra Kamenir; Steven Wayne Lazarus; Andrew Edward Briseno; Harold C. Klaskin; Shelley M. Gould; Peter O. Israel.**
**General Civil Practice, Litigation, Insurance, Personal Injury, Bankruptcy, Creditors Rights, Probate, Real Property, Banking and Entertainment Law.**
*See Professional Biographies, LOS ANGELES, CALIFORNIA*

**Bloom, Hergott, Cook, Diemer & Klein, LLP**
**(See Beverly Hills)**

Bloom & Ruttenberg, (AV) . . . 11111 Santa Monica Blvd.
**Bloomberg, Coe A., (A Professional Corporation)**, (AV) '43 '72
C.277 B.M.E. L.426 J.D. [Lyon&L.] (See Pat. Sect.)
*PRACTICE AREAS: Intellectual Property.
**Bloomberg, Vivian Rigdon**, (AV) . . . '54 '86 C.30 B.A. L.273 J.D. [Peterson&R.]
**Bloomfield, Tammy Cain** . . . '64 '91 C.1349 B.A. L.94 J.D. [Ⓐ Mitchell,S.&K.]
*PRACTICE AREAS: Litigation.
**Bloomgarden, Craig S.** . . . '58 '83 C.893 B.A. L.309 J.D. [Macklin T.]
*PRACTICE AREAS: Environmental Litigation; Insurance Coverage Litigation.
Bloomgarden, David . . . '40 '66 C.477 B.A. L.1068 LL.B. 419 N. Fairfax
**Blue, John A.**, (AV) . . . '43 '73 C.119 B.S. L.309 J.D. [Hughes H.&R.]
*PRACTICE AREAS: Business Torts; Accountants Liability; Securities Arbitration; Securities Litigation.
**Bluebond, Sheri A.** . . . '61 '85 C.112 B.A. L.1068 J.D. [Irell&M.]
**Bluestein, Elizabeth S.** . . . '68 '93 C.309 B.A. L.1066 J.D. [Ⓐ Sullivan&C.]
**Bluestone, Randall J.** . . . '68 '95 C.112 B.S. L.1068 J.D. [Ⓐ Hecker&H.]
Blum, Harry N. . . . '32 '57 C&L.477 B.B.A., LL.B. Pres., The Blum Grp., Inc.
**Blum, Ivon B.**, (AV) . . . '34 '61 C.112 A.B. L.1068 J.D. [Blum,P.&H.]
**Blum, L. Amy** . . . '61 '88 C.1169 B.A. L.770 J.D. [Ⓐ Crosby,H.R.&M.]
Blum, Warren I. . . . '51 '79 C.809 L.426 J.D. 7916 Melrose

**Blum, Propper & Hardacre, Incorporated, (AV)**
**Suite 905, 12100 Wilshire Boulevard, 90025**
**Telephone: 310-826-7900 Fax: 310-826-1480**
**Email: BPHINC@AOL.COM**
**Grant E. Propper; Ivon B. Blum; David W. Hardacre;—Edwin Grantley Hardacre.**
**Corporate, Business and Securities Law. Insurance, Negligence and Family Law. Probate, Trusts, Estate Planning and Copyright Law, Business Litigation.**
*See Professional Biographies, LOS ANGELES, CALIFORNIA*

Blumberg, Grace Ganz . . . '40 '72 C.174 B.A. L.107 J.D. Prof. of Law, Univ. of Calif.
**Blumberg, Robert S.** . . . '67 '92 C.112 B.S. L.569 J.D. [Ⓐ Littler,M.F.T.&M.]
Blume, David A. . . . '33 '57 C.813 L.966 LL.B. Robert Stevenson, Inc.
**Blumenfeld, Michael** . . . '48 '73 C.112 A.B. L.426 J.D. [Fierstein&S.]
*PRACTICE AREAS: Business and Commercial Litigation; Real Property Litigation; Federal and State Courts Employment Law; Securities Industry Litigation and Employment Disputes.
**Blumenfeld, Stan** . . . '62 '89 C.1044 B.A. L.1068 J.D. [Ⓒ O'Melveny&M.]
*PRACTICE AREAS: Litigation.
Blumenthal, Allen '58 '83 C.1349 B.A. L.1068 J.D.
Dep. Trial Coun., State Bar of Calif.
**Blumenthal, David A.**, (AV) '45 '74 C.945 B.S. L.273 J.D.
(adm. in VA; not adm. in CA; Pat.) [Foley L.W.&A.]
(©Washington, D.C. & Annapolis, MD.)
*PRACTICE AREAS: Intellectual Property.
Blumenthal, Ellen . . . '55 '85 C.112 B.S. L.809 J.D. Staff Atty., Bet Tzedek Legal Servs.
Blumenthal, Norman R. . . . '23 '63 C.112 B.A. L.1068 11030 San Monica Blvd.
Blumenthal, Richard L., (AVⓉ) '39 '64 C.477 B.B.S. L.178 LL.B.
(adm. in NY; not adm. in CA) [Ⓒ Wyman,I.B.&L.] (©N.Y., NY)
**Blumer, Kenneth R.**, (AV) . . . '42 '67 C.112 A.B. L.1068 J.D. [Troy&G.]
*PRACTICE AREAS: Real Estate Development; Finance; Lease Law.
Blumofe, Robt. F. . . . '09 '33 C&L.178 A.B., J.D. 1100 Alta Loma Rd.‡
**Blut, Monica A.** . . . '67 '92 C.112 B.A. L.301 J.D. [Ⓐ Stevens,K.A.&H.]
*LANGUAGES: Spanish.
Bluth, Edmund W. . . . '38 '66 C&L.800 A.B., J.D. Asst. Coun., Unocal Corp.
Blutinger, Jeffrey C. . . . '61 '88 C&L.1097 B.A., J.D. 777 Figueroa St.
**Bly, William F.** . . . '64 '93 C.205 B.S./B.A. L.273 J.D. [Ⓐ Troop M.S.&P.]
*PRACTICE AREAS: Insurance Coverage; Litigation; Environmental.
**Blye, Jeffrey D.** . . . '62 '87 C.112 B.A. L.1066 J.D. [Del,R.S.M.&D.]
*PRACTICE AREAS: Entertainment Law; Television Law; Motion Picture Law.
**Blythe, Robert E.** . . . '48 '81 C.1077 B.A. L.809 J.D. [Ⓐ Nordstrom,S.N.&J.]
Boadt, Eleanor P. . . . '06 '31 C.113 B.A. L.800 LL.B. 1516 Glendon Ave.‡
Boags, Charles D. . . . '29 '56 C.415 B.S. L.1009 LL.B. 4076 Tropico Way
**Boatright, Lori N.** . . . '59 '84 C.804 B.A. L.502 J.D. [Blakely,S.T.&Z.]
Bobb, Aviva K. . . . '46 '72 C.914 B.A. L.1066 J.D. Supr. Ct. J.

**Bobb, Merrick J., (AV) '46 '72 C.197 B.A. L.1066 J.D.**
**355 South Grand Avenue, 40th Floor, 90071-3101**
**Telephone: 213-683-8759 Fax: 213-683-0225**
***PRACTICE AREAS: Law Enforcement; Civil Litigation; Antitrust.**
**Police and Public Entity Lose Prevention and Risk Management, Business Litigation and Antitrust.**
*See Professional Biographies, LOS ANGELES, CALIFORNIA*

Bobrowsky, Samuel . . . '11 '34 C&L.262 LL.B. 930 Shenandoah St.‡
Bobys, Hugh M. . . . '41 '66 C.800 A.B. L.1068 LL.B. 444 N. Kenter Ave.
**Bocarsly, Lance S.** . . . '62 '88 C.112 B.A. L.1068 J.D. [Riordan&M.]
**Bocchieri, Breton August** . . . '55 '85 C.705 B.A. L.1218 J.D. [Bronson,B.&M.] (Pat.)
*PRACTICE AREAS: Intellectual Property Litigation emphasis on litigation involving complex technologies.
**Bochner, Dean A.** . . . '69 '94 C.813 B.A. L.477 J.D. [Ⓐ Tuttle&T.]
**Bockman, Craig R.** . . . '58 '82 C.112 B.A. L.426 J.D. [Jones,B.S.A.&F.]
*PRACTICE AREAS: Litigation; Real Estate; Appellate Practice.
Bodenstein, Janette S. . . . '62 '89 C.112 B.S. L.978 J.D. [Ⓐ Revere&W.]
**Bodkin, Henry G., Jr.**, (AV) . . . '21 '48 C&L.426 B.S., J.D. [Ⓒ Sullivan,W.&D.]
*PRACTICE AREAS: Business Litigation.
Bodner, Hal . . . '62 '87 C.705 B.A. L.1292 J.D. 7985 Santa Monica Blvd.
Bodow, Joel M. C. . . . '55 '82 C.1036 B.A. L.93 J.D. 10940 Wilshire Blvd.
**Boeck, William A.** . . . '60 '87 C&L.426 B.A., J.D. [Sedgwick,D.M.&A.]
Boeh, Richard E. '61 '89 C.900 B.A. L.796 J.D.
(adm. in NV; not adm. in CA) F.B.I.
**Boehmer, Richard A.**, (AV) . . . '51 '76 C.800 B.A. L.426 J.D. [O'Melveny&M.]
*PRACTICE AREAS: Corporate Finance; Mergers, Acquisitions and Divestitures; General Corporate Law.
**Boesch, Philip W., Jr., (Professional Corporation)**, (AV) '49 '74
C.103 A.B. L.228 J.D. [Kinsella,B.F.&T.]
*PRACTICE AREAS: Litigation; Communications Law.
**Boese, Randall** . . . '67 '95 C.112 B.A. L.809 J.D. [Ⓐ Howarth&S.]
**Boga, Terence R.** . . . '69 '94 C.674 A.B. L.309 J.D. [Ⓐ Richards,W.&G.]
*PRACTICE AREAS: Public Law.
Bogart, John H. . . . '55 '93 C.1169 B.A. L.813 J.D. 601 S. Figueroa St.
Bogda, Russell W., (AV) . . . '37 '64 C.112 B.S. L.309 LL.B. 555 S. Flower St.
**Bogdanoff, Lee R.**, (AV) . . . '60 '85 C.112 A.B. L.1066 J.D. [Stutman,T.&G.]
*PRACTICE AREAS: Bankruptcy; Insolvency; Corporate Reorganization; Commercial Litigation.

CAA187P

**Bogeaus, Geoffrey Forsythe** .......'41 '74 C.976 B.A. L.1068 J.D. [C Buchalter,N.F.&Y.]
*PRACTICE AREAS: Complex Civil Litigation.
**Bogen, Andrew E.**, (AV) ..............'41 '67 C.668 B.A. L.309 LL.B. [Gibson,D.&C.]
*PRACTICE AREAS: Corporate; Securities.
Boggs, James N. .... '42 '74 C.610 B.A. L.61 J.D. Off. of Dist. Coun., Dept. of Vets. Affs.
**Boggs, T. Hale** ..............................'61 '86 C.813 B.A. L.1068 J.D. [Manatt,P.&P.]
*PRACTICE AREAS: Banking Law; Corporate and Securities Law.
Bogigian, Janet G. ...............................'54 '79 C.589 B.S. L.94 J.D. Dep. City Atty.
Bogin, Bonnie I. '56 '82 C.681 A.B. L.1066 J.D.
V.P., Legal Affs. & Sr. Litig. Coun., Fox, Inc.
Bogna, Annette Roberts ... '62 '89 C.112 B.A. L.1065 J.D. Coun., Calif. Assn. of Realtors
**Bogucki, Raymond A.**, (AV) '22 '52
C.602 B.S. in M.E. L.494 LL.B. [Merchant&G.] (See Pat. Sect.)
Bogust, Henry J., (AV) .......................'26 '55 C.112 L.426 LL.B. [Chase,R.D.&B.]
**Bogy, Vernon C., III** '55 '83 C.800 B.S. L.426 J.D.
Sr. Corp. Coun., Farmers Grp., Inc.
*RESPONSIBILITIES: Property and Casualty Insurance; Real Estate; General Corporate Law; Litigation; Regulatory.
**Bohen, Mary Catherine M.** .............'60 '85 C.112 B.A. L.1065 J.D. [Musick,P.&G.]
*PRACTICE AREAS: Litigation; Insurance.

**Bohorquez, Claudia C., Law Offices of '65 '90 C.846 B.A. L.276 J.D.**
**445 South Figueroa Street, Suite 2400, 90071-1628**
**Telephone: 213-488-0545 Fax: 213-488-0344**
***LANGUAGES: Spanish; French.**
***PRACTICE AREAS: Commercial Law; Banking Law; Business Litigation; Bankruptcy; Corporate and Real Estate.**
**Commercial Law and Litigation. Bankruptcy, Banking, Corporate Law, Real Estate and International Law.**

***See Professional Biographies, LOS ANGELES, CALIFORNIA***

Boland, Paul .........................................'42 '69 C.426 B.A. L.800 J.D. Supr. Ct. J.
Bolden, Dwight M. ...........................'57 '85 C.800 B.A. L.309 J.D. [Bolden&M.]
Bolden & Martin ...............................................................3731 Wilshire Blvd.
**Boldra, Patricia E.** ..........................'45 '77 C.112 B.A. L.809 J.D. [Boldra&K.]
*PRACTICE AREAS: Estate Planning; Bankruptcy; Real Estate Law.

**Boldra & Klueger**
**15760 Ventura Boulevard, Suite 1900, 91436**
**Telephone: 818-716-7710 FAX: 818-716-0042**
**Members of Firm: Robert F. Klueger; Patricia E. Boldra.**
**Tax Litigation and Controversies, Tax Planning, Estate Tax Planning, Estate Planning.**

***See Professional Biographies, LOS ANGELES, CALIFORNIA***

**Boldt, C. Robert** ..........................'66 '95 C.112 B.A. L.602 J.D. [A Kirkland&E.]
*PRACTICE AREAS: Litigation.
**Boldt, Ronald M.** ..................'47 '77 C.112 A.B. L.1067 J.D. [Weinstein,B.R.H.&C.]
*PRACTICE AREAS: Tax; Business Law; Business Transactions.
**Bolender, Jeffrey S.** ........................'61 '95 C.1077 B.A. L.809 J.D. [A Selman B.]
*PRACTICE AREAS: Insurance Law; Personal Injury Litigation.
**Boles, Martin R.** .............................'58 '86 C.197 B.A. L.813 J.D. [Kirkland&E.]
*PRACTICE AREAS: Litigation.
**Bolger, Bruce S.** .................'54 '82 C.800 B.M. L.809 J.D. [A Sedgwick,D.M.&A.]
**Boling, Kristen C.** ...................'67 '92 C.309 A.B. L.880 J.D. [A Zevnik H.G.&M.]
*LANGUAGES: French.
**Bolkin, Bruce I.** ......................'63 '92 C.276 B.S. L.569 J.D. [A Kinsella,B.F.&T.]
*PRACTICE AREAS: Business Litigation; Entertainment Litigation.
**Bollinger, Bernard D., Jr.** .............'61 '87 C.800 B.A. L.426 J.D. [Buchalter,N.F.&Y.]
*PRACTICE AREAS: Bankruptcy.
**Bolson, Jeffrey T.** ...........................'57 '81 C.684 B.S. L.464 J.D. [Engstrom,L.&L.]
*PRACTICE AREAS: Insurance Policy Interpretation; Bad Faith Defense; Entertainment Insurance; Professional Liability; Excess Insurance.
**Bolstad, David C.** ........................'58 '91 C.1042 B.S. L.426 J.D. [A Mayer,B.&P.]
**Bolter, Marci L.** ....................'64 '89 C.1077 B.A. L.800 J.D. [A Anderson,M.&C.]
*PRACTICE AREAS: General Litigation; Personal Injury; Construction Defect; Product Liability; Toxic Torts.

**Bolton, Dunn & Yates**
**(See Santa Monica)**

**Boltz, Howard O., Jr.** ..........................'51 '76 C.112 A.B. L.309 J.D. [Bryan C.]
Bomes, Melissa J. ...................'67 '93 C.569 B.A. L.262 J.D. 10940 Wilshire Blve.
Bomes, Stephen D., (AV) ............ '48 '72 C.94 B.S. L.1065 J.D. 1000 Wilshire Blvd.
**Bonaparte, Ronald H.**, (AV) ...........'35 '59 C.668 A.B. L.813 J.D. [Bonaparte&M.]⊙
*PRACTICE AREAS: Immigration and Nationality Law.

**Bonaparte & Miyamoto, A Professional Law Corporation, (AV) BR**
**11911 San Vicente Boulevard, Suite 355, 90049⊙**
**Telephone: 310-471-3481 FAX: 310-471-1686**
**Email: 73344.441@Compuserve.com**
**Ronald H. Bonaparte (Certified Specialist, Immigration and Nationality Law, The State Bar of California Board of Legal Specialization); Lynn Miyamoto (Certified Specialist, Immigration and Nationality Law, The State Bar of California Board of Legal Specialization);—Thomas E. Cummings.**
**Practice limited to Immigration and Nationality Law.**
**Other Los Angeles Office: 919 South Grand Avenue, Suite 208E. Telephone: 213-688-8872. FAX: 213-688-8887.**
**Newport Beach, California Office: 5030 Campus Drive. Telephone: 714-955-2012. FAX: 714-833-1423.**

***See Professional Biographies, LOS ANGELES, CALIFORNIA***

**Bonar, David L.** .......................'57 '90 C.154 B.A. L.426 J.D. [A Belcher,H.&B.]
*PRACTICE AREAS: Aviation Products Liability Litigation.
Bonaventura, Thomas C., (AV) ...... '36 '64 C.426 B.B.A. L.1068 LL.B. Asst. City Atty.
**Bond, Lisa** .........................'69 '94 C&L.846 B.B.A., J.D. [A Richards,W.&G.]
*PRACTICE AREAS: Environmental Litigation; Oil and Gas Law.
Bond, Robert L. ..........................'44 '70 C.477 B.B.A. L.1065 J.D. 633 W. 5th St.
**Bonenfant, Mark A.** ..............'53 '78 C.1077 B.A. L.1049 J.D. [Buchalter,N.F.&Y.]
*PRACTICE AREAS: Corporate Securities Mergers and Acquisitions; General Corporate; Venture Capital; General Business.
**Bongini, Stephen** .......'69 '95 C.472 B.S.E.E. L.1068 J.D. [A Loeb&L.] (See Pat. Sect.)
*PRACTICE AREAS: Patent Law.
Bonifazio, Jack '45 '96 C.563 B.B.A. L.1190 J.D.
12512 Chandler Blvd. (Valley Village)
Bonino, John M. .....'48 '73 C.800 B.S. L.813 J.D. Sr. V.P., Wedbush, Noble, Cooke, Inc.
**Bonne, Bruce J.**, (AV) ..............'28 '57 C.57 B.A. L.1068 J.D. [C Bonne,B.M.O.&N.]

**Bonne, Bridges, Mueller, O'Keefe & Nichols, Professional Corporation, (AV) BR**
**3699 Wilshire Boulevard, 10th Floor, 90010-2719⊙**
**Telephone: 213-480-1900 Fax: 213-738-5888**
**Ried Bridges; Kenneth N. Mueller; David J. O'Keefe; James D. Nichols; George E. Peterson; Joel Bruce Douglas; Alexander B. T. Cobb; Peter R. Osinoff; Margaret Manton Holm (Resident in Santa Ana Office); Jeffrey C. Moffat; N. Denise Taylor; Patricia K. Ramsey (Resident in Santa Barbara Office); Theodore H. O'Leary; Michael D. Lubrani (Resident in Riverside Office); Christopher B. Marshall (Resident in Riverside Office); Thomas M. O'Neil; Mark B. Connely (Resident in San Luis Obispo Office); Peter G. Bertling (Resident in Santa Barbara Office); Thomas R. Bradford;—Louis W. Pappas; Yuk Kwong Law; Mary A. Seliger; Thomas G. Scully (Resident in Santa Ana Office); Janice B. Lee; Martha A. H. Berman; Carmen Vigil; Kathryn S. Pyke; Robert W. Bates (Resident in Riverside Office); Douglas C. Smith (Resident in Riverside Office); Henry Yekikian (Resident in Riverside Office); Donna Bruce Koch; Julianne M. DeMarco; John H. Dodd; Kippy L. Wroten**

(This Listing Continued)

**Bonne, Bridges, Mueller, O'Keefe & Nichols, Professional Corporation (Continued)**

**(Resident in Santa Ana Office); Sara E. Hersh; Heather J. Higson (Resident in Santa Ana Office); Barbara Springe Kilroy (Resident in Santa Barbara Office); Mary Lawrence Test; Gregory Reyna Bunch; George E. Nowotny, III (Resident in Santa Ana Office); Marie E. Colmey; Gregory D. Werre; Brian L. Hoffman; Alison J. Vitacolonna (Resident in Santa Ana Office); Kathleen M. Walker; Jennifer L. Sturges; Andrew S. Levey; Brian H. Clausen (Resident in Santa Barbara Office); Patricia M. Egan; Russell M. Mortyn; Robert A. Mosier (Resident in Santa Ana Office); Cynthia M. Herrera (Resident in Riverside Office); John A. Haughton; Melanie C. Butts; Paul F. Arentz; Jeannette Lynne Van Horst; Robert A. Madison; Barbara Kamenir Frankel; Raymond J. Mc Mahon; Mitzie L. Dobson; Diana L. Kreinman; Raymond L. Blessey; Jo Lynn Valoff (Resident in Santa Ana Office); Yoshiaki C. Kubota (Resident in Riverside Office); Kimberly Netta (Resident in Riverside Office); Holly H. McGregor (Resident in Riverside Office); Mark S. Salz; James A. Keens; Michael L. Bazzo (Resident in Riverside Office); Kevin A. Duffis; Marta A. Alcumbrac; Cynthia C. Miller; Melanie M. Frayer; Nana Nakano. Of Counsel: Bruce J. Bonne.**
**General Insurance Defense, Professional Malpractice, Products Liability Claims, Drug and Medical Device Claims, Environmental and Toxic Tort Claims, Insurance and Wrongful Termination, Professional Administrative Hearing Counsel.**
**Representative Clients: Southern California Physicians Insurance Exchange, Doctor's Co.; Cooperative of American Physicians; Norcal Mutual Insurance Co.**
**Santa Ana, California Office: 1750 East Fourth Street, Suite 450, P.O. Box 22018, 92702-2018. Telephone: 714-835-1157. Fax: 714-480-2585.**
**Santa Barbara, California Office: 801 Garden Street, Suite 300, 93101-5502. Telephone: 805-965-2992. Fax: 805-962-6509.**
**Riverside, California Office: 3403 Tenth Street, Suite 800, 92501-0749. Telephone: 909-788-1944. Fax: 909-683-7827.**
**San Luis Obispo, California Office: 1060 Palm Street, 93401-3221. Telephone: 805-541-8350. Fax: 805-541-6817.**

***See Professional Biographies, LOS ANGELES, CALIFORNIA***

**Bonner, Joel E., III** '54 '82 C.575 B.A. L.276 J.D.
Asst. Gen. Coun., Ernst & Young LLP
**Bonner, Robert C.**, (AV) '42 '66 C.446 B.A. L.276 J.D.
[Gibson,D.&C.] (⊙Wash., DC)
*PRACTICE AREAS: Business Crime Matters; Complex Civil Cases and Implementation of Corporate Compliance Programs.
Bonoff, Jennifer C. ...........................'69 '96 C.976 B.A. L.309 J.D. 555 S. Flower St.
**Boock, Corey A.** ............................'65 '90 C.913 B.A. L.112 J.D. [A O'Melveny&M.]
**Bookbinder, Barry L.** .......................'63 '90 C.112 B.A. L.426 J.D. [A Lynberg&W.]
*PRACTICE AREAS: Litigation.
**Bookman, Lloyd A.** ........................'54 '79 C.112 B.S. L.1068 J.D. [Hooper,L.&B.]
*PRACTICE AREAS: Healthcare Law; Hospital Law.
**Boone, Robert E., III** ..................................................'62 '87 C&L.880 J.D. [Bryan C.]
*PRACTICE AREAS: Product Liability; Employment and Commercial Litigation.
**Booth, Hillary Arrow** ..................'59 '86 C.1077 B.A. L.809 J.D. [Grossblatt&B.]
*PRACTICE AREAS: Litigation.
**Booth, Jason M.** ..........................'61 '89 C.112 B.A. L.809 J.D. [A Lynberg&W.]
Booth, Lawrence R., (AV) ...............'35 '60 C.999 L.800 LL.B. 12301 Wilshire Blvd.

**Booth, Mitchel & Strange, (AV) BR**
**30th Floor-Equitable Plaza, 3435 Wilshire Boulevard, 90010-2050⊙**
**Telephone: 213-738-0100 Fax: 213-380-3308**
**Members of Firm: Bates Booth (1903-1967); Norman R. Willian (1917-1968); Michael D. Kellogg (1949-1996); William F. Rummler; Michael T. Lowe (Resident, Costa Mesa Office); Joseph A. Burrow; Seth W. Whitaker; Walter B. Hill, Jr. (Resident, Costa Mesa Office); Robert H. Briggs (Resident, Costa Mesa Office); David R. Kipper; Marla Lamedman Kelley (Resident, Costa Mesa Office); Kevin K. Callahan; Robert F. Keehn; Paul R. Howell; Craig E. Guenther (Resident, Costa Mesa Office); David L. Hughes (Resident, Costa Mesa Office); Daniel M. Crowley; Steven M. Mitchel; Robert C. Niesley; James G. Stanley (Resident, Costa Mesa Office). Of Counsel: George C. Mitchel; Owen W. Strange. Associates: John J. Arens; Richard W. Davis; James A. Holl, III; Robert W. Huston; Thomas T. Johnson; Cory J. King; Michelle M. La Mar; Christopher C. Lewi; Clinton Davis Robison; Robert H. Shaffer, Jr. Resident Associates Costa Mesa Office: Elizabeth Currin Bonn; Stacie L. Brandt; David F. McPherson; Scott S. Mizen; Sean T. Osborn; Laila Morcos Santana. Resident Associates San Diego Office: Derek J. Emge; Robert F. Tyson, Jr.**
**General Civil and Commercial Trial Practice in all State and Federal Courts. Construction, Professional Liability, Environmental, Corporation, Real Property, Savings and Loan, Tax, Insurance, Surety, Estate Planning, Trust and Probate Law.**
**Representative Clients: Southern California Gas Co.; Southern Counties Title Insurance Co.**
**Costa Mesa, California Office: 3080 Bristol Street, Suite 550. Telephone: 714-641-0217. Fax: 714-957-0411.**
**San Diego, California Office: 550 West "C" Street. Suite 1560. Telephone: 619-238-7620. Fax: 619-238-7625.**

***See Professional Biographies, LOS ANGELES, CALIFORNIA***

Borchert, David A. ....................'59 '83 C.56 B.A. L.1068 J.D. 624 S. Grand Ave.
**Bordewieck, Douglas W.** ..............'54 '84 C.821 B.A. L.309 J.D. [Mitchell,S.&K.]
*PRACTICE AREAS: Civil Litigation; Trademark; Patent Law; Environmental Law; Bankruptcy Law.
**Bordo, Gregory M.** .....................'— '91 C.112 B.A. L.426 J.D. [A Freeman,F.&S.]
Bordon, Julius, (AV) ...........................'10 '34 C.112 B.A. L.1066 LL.B. [Bordon&B.]
Bordon & Bordon, (AV) ...........................................................3009 Patricia Ave.
**Boren, Jeffrey M.**, (AV) ......................'47 '73 C.800 B.S. L.426 J.D. [C Gipson H.&P.]
*PRACTICE AREAS: Real Estate Law; General Business Law.
Boren, Morton H., (AV) .................................'32 '58 C&L.912 LL.B. 205 S. Bway.
Boren, Roger W. ............. '41 '73 C.112 B.A. L.1068 J.D. Presiding Jus., Ct. of App.
Borenstein, Jacob B. .......................'51 '79 C.112 B.A. L.809 J.D. 2503 Beverly Blvd.
**Borenstein, Mark A.**, (AV) ......................'51 '76 C.107 B.A. L.273 J.D. [Tuttle&T.]
*PRACTICE AREAS: Civil and Probate Litigation; Professional Liability Litigation.
Borges, Antonio R. ....................'55 '82 C.800 B.S. L.809 J.D. 1625 W. Olympic Blvd.
Bork, Terry A. ....................................'57 '86 C.636 B.S. L.990 J.D. Dep. Dist. Atty.
**Borkowski, George M., (A Professional Corporation)** '62 '88
C.107 B.A. L.309 J.D. [Mitchell,S.&K.]
*LANGUAGES: Polish.
*PRACTICE AREAS: Intellectual Property; Antitrust and Securities Litigation.
Bormaster, Melody B. ...........................'47 '79 C.112 B.A. L.809 J.D. Dep. City Atty.
Bornstein, David J. .............................'50 '75 C.112 B.A. L.767 J.D. Atty. Gen. Off.
Borofsky, Gary M., (AV) .....................'44 '71 C.112 B.S. L.1068 J.D. [Borofsky&S.]
**Borofsky, Gary M.**, (AV) ......'44 '71 C.112 B.S. L.1068 J.D. [C Weinstock,M.R.S.&N.]
*PRACTICE AREAS: Corporate; Business; Tax; Estate Planning; Probate/Trusts.
Borofsky and Solarz, A Law Corporation, (AV) ..................... 1875 Century Park E.
Boronkay, Carl, (AV) '29 '55 C.112 A.B. L.1068 LL.B.
Gen. Mgr., Metropolitan Water Dist. of Southern Calif.
**Borow, Jennifer L.** .......................'64 '88 C.788 B.A. L.976 J.D. [C O'Melveny&M.]
*PRACTICE AREAS: Corporate Law; Corporate Acquisitions and Dispositions.
**Borow, Richard H., (P.C.)**, (AV) ............'35 '59 C.331 A.B. L.178 LL.B. [Irell&M.]
Borsook, Lana '— '69 C.112 A.B. L.1068 J.D.
Union Bank Sq., 445 S. Figueroa St., 24th Fl.
**Borthwick, Maribeth A.**, (AV) ..................'51 '76 C.800 B.A. L.1068 J.D. [Loeb&L.]
*PRACTICE AREAS: Real Estate Law; Banking Law; Workout Law.
Borthwick, Robert J. ...................'64 '92 C.813 A.B. L.477 J.D. 333 S. Grand Ave.
**Borthwick, Wm. Harold, (P.C.)**, (AV) ......'48 '74 C.112 A.B. L.1068 J.D. [Hill,F.&B.]
*PRACTICE AREAS: Commercial Real Estate Finance; Commercial Real Estate Foreclosures; Commercial Real Estate Sales; Commercial Real Estate Acquisitions; Estate Planning.
Bortman, David .........................'38 '66 C&L.477 B.A., J.D. 2049 Century Park E.

**Borton, Petrini & Conron, (AV)**
**707 Wilshire Boulevard, Suite 5100, 90017⊙**
**Telephone: 213-624-2869 Fax: 213-489-3930**
**Email: bpcla@bpclaw.com**
**Members of Firm: Robert N. Ridenour; Richard M. Macias; George J. Hernandez, Jr.; Steven G. Gatley; Rosemarie Suazo Lewis. Associates: Dennis D. Resh; Steven P. Owen; Guy Chirinian; Sharon P. McAleenan.**
**Commercial/Real Estate Litigation, Insurance Law, General Civil Trial and Appellate Practice in State and Federal Courts, Personal Injury and Casualty Defense Litigation, Insurance Bad Faith and Coverage, Labor and Employment, Toxic Torts, Real Estate, Land Use Planning, Zoning, Municipal, Professional Errors and Omissions, Healthcare Provider Malpractice Defense, Products Liability, Oil and Gas, Water, Natural Resources, Environmental, Public Entity, Administrative, Agricultural, Banking, Contracts, Corporations, Partnerships, Taxation, Creditor's Remedies, Bankruptcy, Probate, Estate Planning, Family Law.**
**Bakersfield, California Office: The Borton, Petrini & Conron Building, 1600 Truxtun Avenue, P.O. Box 2026. Telephone: 805-322-3051. Fax: 805-322-4628. Email: bpcbak@bpclaw.com.**
**San Luis Obispo, California Office: 1114 Marsh Street. Telephone: 805-541-4340. Fax: 805-541-4558. Email: bpcslo@bpclaw.com.**
**Visalia, California Office: 206 South Mooney Boulevard, P.O. Box 1028. Telephone: 209-627-5600. Fax: 209-627-4309. Email: bpcvis@bpclaw.com.**
**Fresno, California Office: T. W. Patterson Building, 2014 Tulare Street, Suite 830. Telephone: 209-268-0117. Fax: 209-237-7995. Email: bpcfrs@bpclaw.com.**
**Sacramento, California Office: 2233 Watt Avenue, Suite 290. Telephone: 916-484-3555. Fax: 916-484-3550. Email: bpcsac@bpclaw.com.**
**Santa Barbara, California Office: 211 East Victoria Street, Suite D. Telephone: 805-564-2404. Fax: 805-564-2176. Email: bpcsb@bpclaw.com**
**San Diego, California Office: John Burnham Building, 610 West Ash Street, 9th Floor. Telephone: 619-232-2424. Fax: 619-531-0794. Email: bpcsd@bpclaw.com.**
**Newport Beach, California Office: 4675 MacArthur Court, Suite 1150. Telephone: 714-752-2333. Fax: 714-752-2854. Email: bpcnb@bpclaw.com.**
**Modesto, California Office: The Turner Building, 900 "H" Street, Suite D. Telephone: 209-576-1701. Fax: 209-527-9753. Email: bpcmod@bpclaw.com.**
**San Francisco, California Office: 111 Pine Street, Suite 730. Telephone: 415-981-4415. Fax: 415-391-5538. Email: bpcsf@bpclaw.com.**
**Redding, California Office: 280 Hemsted Drive, Suite 100. Telephone: 916-222-1530. Fax: 916-222-4498. Email: bpcred@bpclaw.com.**
**San Bernardino, California Office: 290 North "D" Street, Suite 500. Telephone: 909-381-0527. Fax: 909-381-0658. Email: bpcsbdo@bpclaw.com.**
**San Jose, California Office: 2 North Second Street. Telephone: 408-298-3997. Fax: 408-298-3365. Email: bpcsj@bpclaw.com.**
**Ventura, California Office: 1000 Hill Road, Suite 310. Telephone: 805-650-9994. Fax: 805-650-7125. Email: bpcvta@bpclaw.com.**
**Santa Rosa, California Office: 50 Santa Rosa Avenue, Suite 300. Telephone: 707-527-9477. Fax: 707-527-9488. Email: bpcsr@bpclaw.com.**

*See Professional Biographies, LOS ANGELES, CALIFORNIA*

**Borys, Lawrence, (Professional Corporation)**, (AV) '50 '74 C.112 A.B. L.1068 J.D. [Wilson,K.&B.]
**Bos, Carole D.**, (AVⓉ) '49 '81 C.1265 B.A. L.1187 J.D. (adm. in MI; not adm. in CA) [🄲 Meyers,B.&M.] (⊙Grand Rapids, MI)
*PRACTICE AREAS: Environmental Insurance Defense Litigation; Insurance Coverage Litigation; Personal Injury.
Bosbyshell, Edw. C., Jr. ....... '17 '41 C&L.813 1637 N. Vine St.
Bosco, Blau, Ward & Nopar
2049 Century Park E., Suite 2400 (⊙San Jose, Santa Monica and New York, N.Y.)
**Boshnaick, Michael H.** ....... '65 '93 C.569 B.A. L.809 J.D. [🄰 Fragomen,D.&B.]
*LANGUAGES: Spanish, French.
**Bosl, Phillip L.**, (AV) ....... '45 '75 C.769 B.A. L.800 J.D. [Gibson,D.&C.]
*PRACTICE AREAS: Securities and Business Litigation; Arbitrations and Mediation.
**Bossen, William A.** ....... '61 '87 C.352 B.G.S. L.990 J.D. [Musick,P.&G.]
*PRACTICE AREAS: Litigation.
**Bosserman, Gordon E.**, (AV) ....... '48 '75 C.112 B.A. L.426 J.D. [🄲 Ginsburg,S.O.&R.]
**Bossetti, Lisa M.** ....... '72 '96 C&L.112 B.A., J.D. [🄰 O'Melveny&M.]
**Bost, Stephen A.** '55 '81 C.945 B.S. L.809 J.D. [Ives,K.&D.] (⊙San Bernardino-Riverside)
**Bost, Thomas G.**, (AV) ....... '42 '67 C.1 B.S. L.880 J.D. [Latham&W.]
**Boston, Derrick O.** ....... '64 '90 C&L.309 B.A., J.D. [Irell&M.]
*LANGUAGES: French.

**Bostwick, Gary L.**
**(See Santa Monica)**

Bothman, Sanford B. ....... '29 '60 C&L.1068 B.A., LL.B. Friedman Bag Co., Inc.
**Bothwell, Pamela G.** ....... '52 '85 C.66 B.A. L.174 J.D. [🄲 Tuttle&T.]
*LANGUAGES: French and Sanskrit.
*REPORTED CASES: Korea Exchange Bank vs. Yang, 200 Cal. App. 3d 1471 (1988).
*PRACTICE AREAS: Special Tax and Assessment Lien Foreclosures; Civil Trial; Real Estate.
**Bothwell, William W.** ....... '50 '80 C.910 A.B. L.174 J.D. [Orrick,H.&S.]
*PRACTICE AREAS: Public Finance Law.
**Botnick, Shoshana B.** ....... '61 '87 C.66 B.A. L.273 J.D. [🄰 Donovan L.N.&I.]
*LANGUAGES: Hebrew.
*PRACTICE AREAS: Corporate; Real Estate.
Botsford, Elizabeth ....... '65 '92 L.054 LL.B. 7th Fl., 515 S. Figueroa St.
**Botterud, Carl Andrew** ....... '56 '92 C.605 A.B. L.1148 J.D. [Bacon&M.]
*PRACTICE AREAS: Business Litigation; Employment Law; Insurance Defense.
**Bottger, William C., Jr.** ....... '41 '72 C.197 A.B. L.893 J.D. [Latham&W.]

**Bottum & Feliton, A Professional Corporation, (AV)** BR
**Suite 1500, South Tower, 3200 Wilshire Boulevard, 90010⊙**
**Telephone: 213-487-0402 Fax: 213-386-9803**
**Roswell Bottum (1936-1993); John R. Feliton, Jr.; Robert A. Wooten, Jr.; Steve Johnson; Mark A. Oertel; Alexander F. Giovanniello;—Kenneth C. Feldman; Jerry Garcia; Paul K. Schrieffer; Scott A. Hampton; Gregg S. Garfinkel; Brian E. Cooper; Julie A. Covell; Karl R. Loureiro; Sean T. Hamada; Gary F. Werner; Victor I. King; Andrea J. Lang; Linwood Warren, Jr.**
**Professional Malpractice Defense. General Civil, Trial and Appellate Practice. Fidelity and Surety. Insurance. Corporations.**
**San Diego, California Office: Suite 400 Emerald Plaza, 402 West Broadway. Telephone: 619-595-4857. Fax: 619-595-4863.**

*See Professional Biographies, LOS ANGELES, CALIFORNIA*

**Botz, Thomas** ....... '56 '83 C&L.05 B.Com., LL.B. [🄰 Jones,D.R.&P.]
**Boubelik, Jane E.** ....... '64 '91 C.112 B.A. L.464 J.D. [🄰 McDermott,W.&E.]
Boucher, Raymond P. ....... '57 '84 C.1262 B.S. L.990 J.D. 12400 Wilsjire Blvd., Ste. 1400
**Boudreau, Laura R.** ....... '65 '94 C.821 B.A. L.309 J.D. [🄰 Morrison&F.]
*LANGUAGES: Japanese.
Boudreaux, Albert, III ....... '34 '75 C.1097 B.A. L.1136 J.D. 4735 W. Washington Blvd.
**Boughton, Nancy L.** '61 '87 C.30 B.A. L.276 J.D. (adm. in MD; not adm. in CA) [🄲 Howrey&S.]
*PRACTICE AREAS: Government Contract Law; Export International Law; Litigation.
**Boukidis, Constance E.** ....... '58 '92 C.1169 B.A. L.94 J.D. [🄰 Stall,A.&G.]
Bourbin, Bryan M. ....... '65 '92 C.659 B.A., B.S. L.94 J.D. 1 Wilshire Blvd.
**Bourgault, Lynne S.** ....... '62 '95 C&L.112 B.A., J.D. [🄰 Folger L.&K.]⊙
Bourgeois, Denise L. ....... '62 '89 C.112 B.A. L.426 J.D. 3250 Wilshire Blvd.

**Bourke, Thomas K., (AV) '46 '72 C.602 A.B. L.569 J.D.**
**One Bunker Hill, 8th Floor, 601 West Fifth Street, 90071-2094**
**Telephone: 213-623-1092 Fax: 213-680-4060**

(This Listing Continued)

**Bourke, Thomas K. (Continued)**
***REPORTED CASES: Layman v. Combs, 994 F.2d 1344 (9th Cir.) cert. denied, 114 S.Ct. 303 (1993); McGonigle v. Combs, 968 F.2d 810, 814-15 (9th Cir.), cert. dismissed, 113 S.Ct. 399 (1992); Schultz v. Hembree, 975 F.2d 572 (9th Cir. 1992).**
**Civil Litigation with emphasis on Unfair Competition, Insurance, Sales, Secured Transactions, Collection of Judgements and Securities Litigation.**

*See Professional Biographies, LOS ANGELES, CALIFORNIA*

**Boutwell, Behrendt & Ennor**
**(See Irvine)**

**Bouza, Anthony S.** ....... '60 '85 C.31 B.A. L.145 J.D. [Allen,M.L.G.&M.]
*PRACTICE AREAS: Real Estate.
**Bovard, Kenneth C.** ....... '47 '73 C.112 B.A. L.1049 J.D. [Frandzel&S.] (⊙Irvine)
*PRACTICE AREAS: Banking; Financial Practice; Real Estate; Commercial Law.
**Bovasso, Louis J.**, (AV) ....... '35 '67 C.570 B.S.M.E. L.128 J.D. [Oppenheimer P.S.] (Pat.)
*PRACTICE AREAS: Intellectual Property.
Bovee, Philip S. ....... '52 '77 C&L.972 B.S., J.D. 11693 San Vicente Blvd.
**Bovitz, J. Scott**, (AV) ....... '55 '80 C.112 B.A. L.426 J.D. [Bovitz&S.] & [🄲 Dixon&D.]
*PRACTICE AREAS: Bankruptcy Chapter 11; Bankruptcy Law; Business Reorganization; Secured Transactions Law; Creditor Bankruptcy.
**Bovitz, J. Scott**, (AV) ....... '55 '80 C.112 B.A. L.426 J.D. [🄲 Dixon&J.]
*PRACTICE AREAS: Bankruptcy Chapter 11; Bankruptcy Law; Business Reorganization; Secured Transactions Law; Creditor Bankruptcy.

**Bovitz & Spitzer, (AV)**
**Wells Fargo Center, 333 South Grand Avenue, Suite 2000, 90071-1524**
**Telephone: 213-346-8300 FAX: 213-620-1811**
**Email: bovitz@mrinter.net**
**Members of the Firm: J. Scott Bovitz (Certified Specialist, Personal and Small Business Bankruptcy Law, The State Bar of California Board of Legal Specialization); Susan Michelle Spitzer.**
**Bankruptcy and Workouts, Uniform Commercial Code Matters, Related Litigation, Alternative Dispute Resolution and Mediation in Bankruptcy.**

*See Professional Biographies, LOS ANGELES, CALIFORNIA*

**Bowen, Scott W.** ....... '46 '73 C&L.813 A.B., J.D. [Folger L.&K.]⊙
*PRACTICE AREAS: Environmental Law; Administrative Law; Bankruptcy Law.
**Bower, Allan M.**, (AV) ....... '36 '69 C.350 B.S. L.472 J.D. [Lane P.S.L.]
*PRACTICE AREAS: Aviation Law; Product Liability Law; Medical Malpractice; Insurance; Toxic Torts.
**Bower, David E.** ....... '51 '82 C.1044 B.A. L.809 J.D. [🄲 Hornberger&C.]
*PRACTICE AREAS: Business Law; Litigation; Commercial Law; Construction Law.
**Bower, John E., Jr.** ....... '49 '77 C.1077 B.A. L.809 J.D. [🄰 Bragg,S.S.&K.]
*PRACTICE AREAS: Insurance Defense.
**Bower, Paul G.**, (AV) ....... '33 '64 C.691 B.A. L.813 LL.B. [🄲 Gibson,D.&C.]
**Bowers, John M.** ....... '56 '91 C.260 B.S. L.990 J.D. [🄰 Augustini,W.&D.]
*PRACTICE AREAS: Litigation.
Bowers, Kelly C. '58 '84 C.907 B.A. L.990 J.D. (adm. in WA; not adm. in CA) Asst. Reg. Admr., Securities & Exch. Comm.‡
Bowers, Peter J. ....... '64 '91 C.473 B.A. L.1068 J.D. 515 S. Figueroa St.
Bowers, Ronald E. ....... '40 '67 C.112 B.A. L.800 J.D. Off. of Dist. Atty.
Bowers, Stephen A. ....... '50 '91 C.347 B.F.A. L.990 J.D. 11845 W. Olympic Blvd.
Bowers, Terree Allan, (AV) ....... '54 '79 C&L.846 B.A., J.D. U.S. Atty.
**Bowie, Scott O.** ....... '60 '88 C.605 A.B. L.1068 J.D. [Latham&W.]
*LANGUAGES: French.
**Bowles, James A., (P.C.)**, (AV) ....... '54 '79 C.347 A.B. L.276 J.D. [Hill,F.&B.]
*LANGUAGES: Spanish.
*SPECIAL AGENCIES: National Labor Relations Board, Equal Employment Opportunity Commission, California Department of Fair Employment and Housing, California Occupational Safety and Health Appeals Board, California Agricultural Labor Relations Board.
*REPORTED CASES: Wholesale and Retail Food Distribution Local 63 v. Santa Fe Terminal Services, Inc., 836 F.Supp. 326 (C.D. Cal. 1993); Graefenhain v. Pabst Brewing Co., 870 F.2d 1198 (7th Cir., 1989); Cardinal Distributing Co. v. ALRB, 159 Cal.App. 3d 758 (1984); Southern California Pipe Trades Trust Funds v. Franchise Tax Board, 909 F.2d 1266 (9th Cir. 1990). USCP-Wesco v. NLRB, 827 F.2d 581 (9th Cir. 1987).
*PRACTICE AREAS: Labor and Employment Law.
Bowles, Timothy ....... '49 '77 C.112 B.A. L.1067 J.D. [Bowles&M.]
Bowles-Gray, Kelly ....... '54 '86 C.800 B.A. L.1148 J.D. 2029 Century Park E., Ste. 1200
Bowles & Moxon ....... 6255 Sunset Blvd.
**Bowling, Norman D.** ....... '60 '86 C.154 B.A. L.426 J.D. [Gibbs,G.L.&A.]
*PRACTICE AREAS: Commercial Law; Business Litigation; Construction Law.
Bowling, Traci Denise ....... '62 '88 C.112 B.A. L.464 J.D. S.E.C.
Bowman, Alana L. ....... '48 '83 C.801 B.A. L.910 J.D. Dep. City Atty.
**Bowman, John M.** ....... '59 '88 C.350 B.S. L.809 J.D. [🄰 Reznik&R.]
*PRACTICE AREAS: Zoning and Land Use; Environmental Administrative Law and Litigation.
**Bowman, Lori A.** ....... '55 '84 C.347 A.B. L.1119 J.D. [Orrick,H.&S.]
*PRACTICE AREAS: Labor and Employment Law.

**Bowman and Brooke**
**(See Torrance)**

**Bowne, Robert R.**
**(See Burbank)**

**Boxer, Joel E.**, (AV) ....... '44 '72 C.112 B.A. L.309 J.D. [Bird,M.B.W.&M.]
Boxer, Lester, (AV) ....... '35 '62 C.112 B.S. L.800 LL.B. 1875 Century Park E.

**Boxer, Sandor T., (AV) '39 '65 C.112 A.B. L.1068 LL.B.** BR
**Suite 900 2049 Century Park East, 90067-3111**
**Telephone: 310-282-8118 Fax: 310-282-8077**
**Email: tedb@themall.net**
**Commercial, Bankruptcy, Business Law, and Business Litigation.**

*See Professional Biographies, LOS ANGELES, CALIFORNIA*

Boyack, Dean C. ....... '15 '56 C.101 A.B. L.809 J.D. Prof. of Law, Southwestern Univ.
Boyajian, Berj ....... '38 '74 C.061 B.A. L.426 J.D. [Boyajian&Assoc.]
Boyajian & Associates, Law Offices of ....... 2020 Avenue of the Stars
**Boyce, David S.**, (AV) ....... '49 '78 C.188 A.B. L.260 J.D. [Jones,D.R.&P.]
Boyce, Leslie A. ....... '59 '93 C.976 B.A. L.893 J.D. 1999 Ave. of the Stars
**Boyce, William R.** ....... '43 '82 C.1077 B.A. L.809 J.D. [Dummit,F.&B.]
**Boyd, Bruce M.** ....... '47 '73 C.112 B.A. L.1066 J.D. [🄲 Coudert] (⊙San Jose & San Fran.)
*PRACTICE AREAS: Real Estate; International Business; Corporate.
**Boyd, Carol**, (AV) ....... '45 '81 C.1275 L.398 J.D. [Neumeyer&B.]
*PRACTICE AREAS: Appellate Practice; Insurance Coverage; Insurance Bad Faith.
**Boyd, Debra L.** ....... '50 '82 C.112 B.A. L.426 J.D. [🄰 O'Melveny&M.]
**Boyd, Earl E.**, (AV) ....... '41 '66 C.593 B.A. L.502 J.D. [Stilz&B.]
**Boydston, Brian** ....... '64 '91 C.112 B.A. L.426 J.D. [Pick&B.]
**Boyer, Bradley P.** ....... '70 '95 C.475 B.A. L.1049 J.D. [🄰 Ropers,M.K.&B.]
Boyers, Steven R. ....... '42 '70 C.705 B.A. L.145 J.D. Gen. Coun., Kirk-Mayer, Inc.

**Boyk, Carol S. '42 '78 C.685 B.A. L.426 J.D.**
**11340 West Olympic Boulevard, Suite 175, 90064-1613**
**Telephone: 310-479-3813 FAX: 310-477-7248**
**Civil Litigation, Appellate Practice, and Pretrial Preparation.**

**Boykin, Jeffery P. '61 '87 C.575 B.A. L.990 J.D.**
**4484 Wilshire Boulevard, Second Floor, 90010**
**Telephone: 213-857-7175 Fax: 213-857-7185**

(This Listing Continued)

CAA189P

CALIFORNIA—LOS ANGELES MARTINDALE-HUBBELL LAW DIRECTORY 1997

**Boykin, Jeffery P. (Continued)**

**General Civil Trial in all State and Federal Courts, Personal Injury, Plaintiff and Defense, Criminal Law, Family Law, Commercial Litigation including Collections.**

*See Professional Biographies, LOS ANGELES, CALIFORNIA*

Boykin, Samuel S. '67 '92 C.390 B.A. L.1068 J.D. 445 S. Figueroa St.
**Boyko, David R.** '62 '95 C.188 B.S.M.E. L.1068 J.D. [Ⓐ Fried,F.H.S.&J.]
**Boylan, Jean M.** '61 '86 C&L.426 B.S., J.D. [Gibbs,G.L.&A.]
*PRACTICE AREAS: Construction Law; Business Litigation; Public Contract Law.
Boyle, Brian J. '55 '80 C.838 B.A. L.426 J.D. 10780 Santa Monica Blvd.
Boyle, David '65 '91 C.112 B.A. L.861 J.D. Legal Affairs, Propaganda Films, Inc.
**Boyle, Emily R.** '56 '80 C.112 B.A. L.809 J.D. [Ⓒ Jackson,L.S.&K.]
Boyle, Jacque, (AV) '19 '49 L.800 J.D. 201 N. Figueroa St.
**Boyle, John D.** '57 '82 C.112 B.A. L.1065 J.D. [Bronson,B.&M.]
*PRACTICE AREAS: Insurance Bad Faith; Professional Liability; Civil Litigation.

**Boyle, Olson & Robinson**
(See Pasadena)

**Boysaw, Marsha A.** '61 '87 C.1142 B.A. L.846 J.D. [Katten M.&Z.]
*PRACTICE AREAS: Finance and Reorganization.
Bozajian, James R. '65 '90 C.112 B.A. L.800 J.D. Dep. Dist. Atty.
Bozanich, Peter Andre, (AV) '44 '72 C.1042 B.S. L.1068 J.D. Dep. Dist. Atty.

**Bozeman, Marc H. '45 '72 C.112 A.B. L.1066 J.D.**
**Suite 1600 One Century Plaza, 2029 Century Park East, 90067**
Telephone: 310-553-4876 Fax: 310-553-3316
Email: MHB@DC4.HHLAW.COM
(Counsel, Hogan & Hartson L.L.P., Washington, D.C.).
*PRACTICE AREAS: Food, Drug, Biologics, Medical Device and Cosmetic (FDA) Law.
Food, Drug, Biologics, Medical Device and Cosmetic (FDA) Law.

*See Professional Biographies, LOS ANGELES, CALIFORNIA*

**Bozof, Richard P.** '47 '77 C.197 B.A. L.1066 J.D. [Nossaman,G.K.&E.]
*PRACTICE AREAS: Environmental Law.
**Bozung, Linda J.** '44 '78 C.679 B.S. L.818 J.D. [Brobeck,P.&H.]
*PRACTICE AREAS: Land Use Law; Zoning, Entitlement and California Quality Act Law.
**Braaf, Estelle M.** '51 '88 C.102 B.A. L.800 J.D. [Ⓐ Cox,C.&N.]
*PRACTICE AREAS: Real Estate and Business Litigation.
**Bracker, Andrew J.** '63 '91 C.1169 B.A. L.309 J.D. [Demetriou,D.S.&M.]
*PRACTICE AREAS: Environmental Law; Civil Litigation.
**Brackins, Charles G.** '48 '73 C&L.260 B.A., J.D. [Ⓐ Sherwood&H.]
*PRACTICE AREAS: Real Estate Litigation; Business Litigation.
Bradford, Christopher T. '54 '89 C.112 B.A. L.809 J.D. [Scherer&B.]
Bradford, Peggie J. '65 '93 C.911 B.A. L.809 J.D. 1900 Ave. of the Stars
Bradford, Rufus '45 '77 C.605 A.B. L.800
(adm. in PA; not adm. in CA) 3704 Country Club Dr.
Bradford, Scott F. '48 '78 C.1077 B.A. L.1095 J.D. [Gittler,W.&B.]
**Bradford, Stephen L.** '58 '87 C.101 B.S. L.893 J.D. [Carlsmith B.W.C.&I.]
*LANGUAGES: Spanish.
*PRACTICE AREAS: Latin America Trade; Corporate Law.
**Bradford, Thomas R.** '50 '83
C.884 B.S. L.809 J.D. [Bonne,B.M.O.&N.] (ⓞSanta Barbara)
Bradisse, Anthony J., (AV) '20 '54 C.339 A.B. L.809 LL.B. 1540 Wilshire Blvd.
Bradkin, Brandon F.R. '— '92 C&L.309 A.B., J.D. 400 S. Hope St.
**Bradley, Barry A.**, (AV) '60 '86 C.763 B.S. L.426 J.D. [Manning,M.&W.]
*PRACTICE AREAS: Private Security Litigation; Premises Liability; Police Civil Liability; General Civil Liability.
**Bradley, Brent D.** '63 '96 C.112 B.A. L.426 J.D. [Ⓐ Christensen,M.F.J.G.W.&S.]
*PRACTICE AREAS: Corporate Law; Real Estate Law.
**Bradley, Lawrence D., Jr.**, (AV) '20 '51 C.869 B.S. L.813 J.D. [Pillsbury M.&S.]
Bradley, Nancy Evers '51 '76 C.1169 A.B. L.1065 J.D. 2184 Roscomare Ed.‡
**Bradley, Sheila M.** '70 '95 C.112 A.B. L.309 J.D. [Ⓐ Howarth&S.]
**Bradley, Tom** '17 '57 C.112 L.809 J.D. [Ⓒ Brobeck,P.&H.]
*PRACTICE AREAS: Corporate Law.
**Bradshaw, James T., Jr.**, (AV) '23 '49 C.990 L.800 LL.B. [Burke,W.&S.]
*PRACTICE AREAS: Corporate Law; Commercial Law; Trade Regulation Law.
**Bradshaw, Mark L.** '62 '88
C.352 B.B.A. L.846 J.D [Ⓒ O'Melveny&M.] (ⓞSan Francisco)
*PRACTICE AREAS: Bankruptcy Law.
Brady, Brendan P. '57 '82 C.770 B.A. L.1065 J.D. 777 S. Figuerda St., 10th Fl.
Brady, David S. '58 '86 C.101 B.S. L.862 J.D. Asst. Coun., Unocal Corp.
Brady, Donley L. '22 '54 C&L.602 LL.B. 300 S. Grand Ave.
**Brady, Jacqueline R.** '65 '92 C.602 B.A. L.1066 J.D. [Ⓐ Mayer,B.&P.]

**Brady & Berliner, (AVⓉ)**
**1875 Century Park East, Suite 700, 90067ⓞ**
Telephone: 310-282-6848 Telecopy: 310-282-6841
Roger A. Berliner.
Administrative Law, Commercial Litigation, Appellate Advocacy, Intergovernmental Affairs, Legislative Practice, Health Policy, International Trade, North American Energy Transactions, Oil and Gas Law and Public Utility Law.
References: Canadian Embassy; City of Vernon, California; Pacific Gas Transmission Co.; Polyisocyanurate Insulation Manufacturers Assn.; Watson Cogeneration Co.
Washington, D.C. Office: 1225 Nineteenth Street, N.W., Suite 800. Telephone: 202-955-6067. Telecopy: 202-822-0109.
Berkeley, California Office: 2560 Ninth Street, Suite 316. Telephone: 510-549-6926. Telecopy: 510-649-9793.
Sacramento, California Office: 1121 L Street, Suite 606. Telephone: 916-448-7819. Telecopy: 916-448-1140.

*See Professional Biographies, LOS ANGELES, CALIFORNIA*

Braff, Nelson M. '59 '83 C.102 B.A. L.245 J.D.
(adm. in NY; not adm. in CA) 10920 Wilshire Blvd.
**Braga, M. Thereza** '62 '85 C&L.061 J.D.
(adm. in Brazil; not adm. in CA) [Verboon,W.H.&P.]
*LANGUAGES: Portuguese, French, Italian and Spanish.
*PRACTICE AREAS: Construction Litigation.
**Brager, Dennis N.**, (AV) '53 '78 C.1040 B.B.A. L.569 J.D. [D.N.Brager]
Brager, Jeannine '50 '82 C.763 B.S. L.1136 J.D. 8420 Coreyell Pl.

**Brager, Dennis N., A Prof. Corp., Law Offices of, (AV)**
**2029 Century Park East, Suite 600, 90067**
Telephone: 310-277-1734 Fax: 310-277-6431
Dennis N. Brager (Certified Specialist, Tax Law, The State Bar of California Board of Legal Specialization).
Civil and Criminal Tax Litigation. Federal and State Tax Controversies.

*See Professional Biographies, LOS ANGELES, CALIFORNIA*

**Bragg, Robert A.**, (AV) '51 '81 C.767 B.A. L.765 J.D. [Bragg,S.S.&K.]ⓞ
*PRACTICE AREAS: Insurance Defense.

**Bragg, Short, Serota & Kuluva, (AV)**
**801 South Figueroa Street, Suite 2100, 90017-2575ⓞ**
Telephone: 213-612-5335 Fax: 213-612-5712

(This Listing Continued)

**Bragg, Short, Serota & Kuluva (Continued)**

Robert A. Bragg; Carol D. Kuluva. Associates: Louis E. Goldberg; Thomas J. McDermott; Andrew Mancini; Gail D. Rackliffe; John E. Bower, Jr.; Amelia M. Eng (Certified Specialist, Workers' Compensation Law, The State Bar of California Board of Legal Specialization); Zahava Aroesty Stroud.
Insurance Defense, Products Liability, Personal Injury, Directors and Officers, and Worker's Compensation.
Representative Client: Chubb Group of Insurance Companies.
San Francisco, California Office: Bragg & Dziesinski, Two Embarcadero Center, Suite 1400. Telephone: 415-954-1850. Fax: 415-434-2179.
Newport Beach, California Office: 4695 MacArthur Court, Suite 530. Telephone: 714-442-4800. Fax: 714-442-4816.

*See Professional Biographies, LOS ANGELES, CALIFORNIA*

**Bragin, Ronald A.**, (AV) '50 '75 C.112 A.B. L.800 J.D. [Golob,B.&S.]
*PRACTICE AREAS: Real Property Law; Business Litigation; Corporate Law; Probate Litigation.
Braginsky, Julius '29 '55 C.112 B.S. L.800 LL.B. 10980 Rose Ave.
**Brahn, Kathleen M. K.** '54 '82 C.959 B.F.A. L.767 J.D. [Arter&H.]
*PRACTICE AREAS: Business Litigation.
Brainard, Lauren R. '42 '71 C.112 B.A. L.1065 J.D.
Sr. Dep. Gen. Coun., Metropolitan Water Dist. of Southern Calif.
Brainard, Robert L. '49 '76 C.1097 B.S. L.976 J.D. [Roquemore,P.&M.]
Brakensiek, Warren N. '46 '72 C.605 A.B. L.1067 J.D. 600 W. 9th St.
**Braker, Jeffrey L.** '61 '88 C.178 A.B. L.477 J.D. [Ⓐ Seyfarth,S.F.&G.]
*PRACTICE AREAS: Corporate/Business Law; Real Estate Law.
**Bramhall, Samuel E.** '60 '89 C.446 B.A. L.893 J.D. [Troop M.S.&P.]
*PRACTICE AREAS: Litigation.
Bramson, David H. '51 '77 C.112 B.A. L.861 J.D. 12400 Wilshire Blvd.
**Branca, John G.**, (AV) '50 '75 C.605 A.B. L.1068 J.D. [Ziffren,B.B.&F.]
*PRACTICE AREAS: Entertainment Law.
Branch, Deborah K. '60 '86 C.103 A.B. L.309 J.D.
(adm. in NY; not adm. in CA) 10940 Wilshire Blvd.
**Branch, K. Christopher** '62 '88 C.800 A.B. L.426 J.D. [Phillips&B.]
*PRACTICE AREAS: Insurance Coverage; Bad Faith; Commercial Litigation.
Brand, Eric S. '63 '89 C.763 B.A. L.990 J.D. Dep. Pub. Def.
**Brand, Julia W.** '58 '85 C.112 B.A. L.800 J.D. [Ⓐ Katten M.&Z.]
*PRACTICE AREAS: Bankruptcy Litigation.
**Brand, Michael A.** '52 '77 C.347 A.B. L.309 J.D. [Ⓒ Arnberger,K.B.&C.]
*PRACTICE AREAS: Real Estate Law; International Transactions; Loan Workouts.
**Brand, Michael A.** '52 '77 C.347 A.B. L.309 J.D. [Brand F.D.F.&K.]
*PRACTICE AREAS: Real Estate Law; International Law.

**Brand Farrar Dziubla Freilich & Kolstad, LLP, (AV)** 🅱🅱
Counsellors at Law
**515 South Flower Street, Suite 3500, 90071-2201**
Telephone: 213-228-0288 Facsimile: 213-426-6222
Michael A. Brand; David W. Farrar; Robert W. Dziubla; Amy E. Freilich; Charles K. Kolstad; Margaret G. Graf. Of Counsel: H. Bennett Arnberger; David C. Buxbaum; Sherry L. Geyer; Manender M. Grewal (Not admitted in the United States); Julia Marie Shymansky; Yelena Yeruhim; Norman A. Chernin; Joan M. Marquardt.
General Corporate, International Tax, Finance, Real Estate, Public-Private Development, Land Use and Workouts.
Correspondent Offices: Hong Kong, Shanghai, Beijing, Guangzhou, Xiamen, Shenzhen, Ulaanbaatar, New York and San Francisco.

*See Professional Biographies, LOS ANGELES, CALIFORNIA*

**Brandler, Jonathan M., (P.C.)**, (AV) '46 '71 C.112 A.B. L.800 J.D. [Hill,F.&B.]
*SPECIAL AGENCIES: National Labor Relations Board; Department of Labor; Equal Employment Opportunity Commission; California Department of Fair Employment and Housing; California Labor Commissioner.
*PRACTICE AREAS: Labor Relations (Management); Employment Discrimination; Wrongful Discharge; Wage and Hour; Safety and Health.
Brandlin, J. J., (AV) '13 '38 C.339 A.B. L.800 LL.B. 15496 Milldale Dr.
**Brandmeyer, Kent T.** '63 '89 C&L.426 B.A., J.D. [Ⓐ La Follette,J.D.F.&A.]
*PRACTICE AREAS: Medical Malpractice.
**Brandon, Jack** '54 '84 C.1051 B.S. L.1068 J.D. [Gipson H.&P.]
*PRACTICE AREAS: Domestic and International Tax Law.
**Brandon-Brown, Elizabeth** '48 '91
C.260 B.S. L.128 J.D. [Ⓒ Sanchez&A.] (ⓞMarina Del Rey)
*PRACTICE AREAS: Securities; Corporate; Business Law.

**Brandon, Lisa E.**
(See Long Beach)

Brandt, Gina Francesca '50 '76 C.112 B.A. L.800 J.D. 325 N. Kenter Ave.
**Brandt, Kevin M.** '53 '80 C&L.276 A.B., J.D. [Buchalter,N.F.&Y.]
*PRACTICE AREAS: Real Estate Development; Real Estate Finance; Real Estate Restructuring; Bankruptcy.
**Brandt, Robert C.**, (AV) '49 '77 C.763 A.B. L.809 J.D. [R.C.Brandt]

**Brandt, Robert C., A Prof. Corp., Law Offices of, (AV)**
**Suite 1780 12100 Wilshire Boulevard, 90025-7117**
Telephone: 310-473-6101 Telecopier: 310-473-9511
Robert C. Brandt (Certified Specialist, Family Law, The State Bar of California Board of Legal Specialization).
Family Law, Child Custody, Business and Personal Injury Litigation.

Branion, John M., III '63 '96 C.228 A.B. L.112 J.D. 10940 Wilshire Blvd.
Bransky, Harlan L. '58 '84 C.112 B.A. L.426 J.D. [Ⓐ Gittler,W.&B.]
**Bransten, Peter M.** '57 '84 C.112 B.A. L.800 J.D. [McDermott,W.&E.]
**Brant, Lisa R.** '69 '94 C.112 B.A. L.1068 J.D. [Ⓐ O'Donnell,R.&S.]
*PRACTICE AREAS: Litigation.
Brant and Pettitt, (AV) Ste. 410, 626 Wilshire Blvd.
**Branton, Gary G.** '44 '92 C.823 MBA L.464 J.D. [Kirshman&H.]ⓞ
*PRACTICE AREAS: Personnel; Labor Relations (Management) Law.
Branton, Leo, Jr. '22 '49 3460 Wilshire Blvd.
Brassel, Richard T. '59 '86 C.602 B.A. L.128 J.D.
(adm. in NY; not adm. in CA) 535 Westmount Dr.
Brassell, Roselyn S. '30 '63 C.420 B.A. L.1068 J.D. 645 N. Wilcox Ave.
Bratman, Marc P. '48 '73 C.1077 B.S. L.1068 J.D. 2029 Century Park E.‡
Braudrick, Arthur C., Jr., (BV) '41 '72 C.112 A.B. L.1067 J.D. Off. of Pub. Def.
**Brauer, Jeffrey** '55 '84 C.860 B.A. L.569 J.D. [Ⓒ Katz,G.&F.]
Braun, Brent A. '— '88 C.1077 B.A. L.809 J.D. FBI
Braun, David A., (AV) '31 '55 C&L.178 A.B., LL.B. 1901 Ave. of the Stars
Braun, Donald N. '34 '62 C.930 B.B.A. L.1068 11901 Santa Monica Blvd.
Braun, Ernest A., (AV) '11 '40 C.061 L.145 J.D. Suite 1015, 1880 Century Park East
**Braun, Harland W.**, (AV) '42 '67 C.112 B.A. L.1068 J.D. [H.W.Braun]
*PRACTICE AREAS: Criminal Law.
Braun, Janet L. '60 '85 C&L.608 B.S.I.S.E., J.D. 400 S. Hope St.
**Braun, Lawrence M.** '54 '81 C.705 B.A. L.597 J.D. [Sheppard,M.R.&H.]
*PRACTICE AREAS: Corporate Law; Mergers and Acquisitions; Venture Capital.
Braun, Michael D. '68 '93 C.112 B.A. L.426 J.D. 10940 Wilshire Blvd.
**Braun, Robert E., (P.C.)** '57 '81 C.112 A.B. L.1068 J.D. [Jeffer,M.B.&M.]
*PRACTICE AREAS: Corporate; Securities; Banking.

CAA190P

**Braun, Harland W., Professional Corporation, (AV)**
**Suite 1800, Two Century Plaza Building, 2049 Century Park East, 90067**
**Telephone: 310-277-4777**
**Harland W. Braun.**
**Practice Limited to Criminal Law, State Bar Defense and Medical Board Defense.**
**Reference: Bank of America (Century City Office).**
*See Professional Biographies, LOS ANGELES, CALIFORNIA*

Braveman, Peter E. .......... '50 '77 C.674 B.A. L.878 J.D. V.P., Cedars-Sinai Med. Ctr.
**Braveman, Wayne S.**, (AV) .......... '53 '80 C.222 B.A. L.309 J.D. [Heller E.W.&M.]
*PRACTICE AREAS: Appellate and Complex Civil Litigation.

**Brawerman, Richard S., (AV) '16 '39 C&L.477 A.B., J.D.**
**1901 Avenue of the Stars, Suite 1100, 90067**
**Telephone: 310-556-4660 FAX: 310-556-8945**
**Federal and State Income, Gift and Estate Taxation and Tax Exempt Organizations.**

Bray, Debra L. .......... '55 '87 C.112 B.S. L.800 J.D. [Liebert,C.&F.]
Bray, Gregory A., (AV) .......... '58 '84 C.112 B.A. L.426 J.D. 2049 Century Park E.
**Bray, Jana W.** .......... '65 '91 C.518 B.A. L.893 J.D. [[A] Ross,S.&G.]
*PRACTICE AREAS: Estate, Trust and Conservatorship Litigation; Business Litigation.
**Bray, Karen M.** .......... '67 '93 C&L.112 B.A., J.D. [[A] Perkins C.]
*PRACTICE AREAS: Litigation.
**Braybrooke, Scott E.** .......... '61 '87 C.264 B.A. L.800 J.D. [[A] Gilbert,K.C.&J.]
*PRACTICE AREAS: Insurance Defense; Products Liability.
**Brazil, Anthony G.**, (AV) .......... '53 '78 C.800 B.S. L.426 J.D. [Morris,P.&P.]
**Brazil, Leonard**, (AV) .......... '57 '82 C.800 B.S. L.426 J.D. [Clark&T.]
*PRACTICE AREAS: General Business Litigation; Commercial Litigation; Products Liability Litigation; Unfair Competition Law; Trade Secrets Litigation.
Breckenridge, Emily .......... '65 '91 C.813 A.B. L.1068 J.D. 333 S. Grand Ave.
Breedy-Richardson, Wilberta .......... '49 '83 C.1136 B.S. L.809 J.D. City Atty's. Office
**Breen, John E.** .......... '62 '94 C.770 B.S. L.426 J.D. [[A] Hancock R.&B.]
**Breen, Patrick E.** .......... '53 '78 C.770 B.S.C. L.1066 J.D. [Allen,M.L.G.&M.]
*PRACTICE AREAS: Trials; Litigation; Land Use; Environmental; Bankruptcy.
Bregman, Jenn Swenson .......... '60 '89 C.208 B.M. L.1068 J.D. 3413 Moore St.
Bregman, Jerry L. .......... '62 '90 C.112 B.A. L.1068 J.D. 11845 W. Olympic Blvd.
**Breidenbach, Francis**, (AV) ..... '30 '57 C&L.585 Ph.B., J.D. [Breidenbach,B.H.H.&H.]
*PRACTICE AREAS: Business Litigation; Casualty Insurance; Insurance Defense Appeals; Probate Litigation.

**Breidenbach, Buckley, Huchting, Halm & Hamblet, A Law Corporation, (AV)**
**611 West Sixth Street, Thirteenth Floor, 90017-3100⊙**
**Telephone: 213-624-3431 Fax: 213-488-1493**
**Email: law@bbhhh.com**
**Francis Breidenbach; Howard L. Halm; Stephen H. Huchting; Gary A. Hamblet; Daniel J. Buckley; Randi S. Lewis; Douglas W. Andrews; Shari L. Rosenthal; Lance S. Gams; Eugene J. Egan;—Mark K. Kitabayashi; Randi J. Theodosopoulos; M. Kendall Caudry; Leon A. Victor;—Michele VanRiper; Monika M. Arboles; Mark W. Waterman; Brian W. Rhodes; Christina O. Nyhan; Kimberly A. Millington; Paul B. Hundley; Angela T. Edwards; Jason S.J. Kim; Mark E. Clouser; Ricki J. Shoss; Gregory M. Sinderbrand; Michael P. Bryant; Aide C. Ontiveros; Suzanne M. Henderson; Kenneth R. Pedroza; Jennifer L. Walsleben. Of Counsel: Donald A. Way. Retired: Howard D. Swainston (Retired).**
**Civil Trial and Appellate Practice. Environmental, Toxic Torts, Products Liability, Professional Liability, Property and Casualty Insurance Coverage and Litigation, Fire Subrogation, Decedent's Estate Litigation and Business, Construction Defect.**
**Representative Clients: Pacific Indemnity Co.; The Travelers Insurance Co.**
**Riverside, California Office: 3403 Tenth Street, Seventh Floor. Telephone: 909-686-7058.**
**Orange County Office: 1851 East First Street, Ninth Floor, Santa Ana, California. Telephone: 714-564-2515.**
*See Professional Biographies, LOS ANGELES, CALIFORNIA*

Breier, David H., (AV) .......... '37 '66 C&L.494 B.A., LL.B. [Sandler&B.]
Breier, Sheldon I. .......... '42 '73 C.112 L.809 J.D. 12021 Wilshire Blvd.
**Breitburg, David** .......... '56 '81 C.150 B.A. L.809 J.D. [[A] Tharpe&H.]
**Breitman, Craig R.**, (AV) .......... '55 '82 C.112 B.A. L.809 J.D. [Selman B.]
**Bremer, Laura C.** '67 '92 C.112 B.A. L.477 J.D.
[[A] O'Melveny&M.] (⊙San Francisco)
**Brennan, Lawrence P., Jr.** '64 '91
C.103 A.B. L.1068 J.D. [[A] McClintock,W.B.R.R.&M.]
*PRACTICE AREAS: Business Litigation; Real Estate; Environmental Litigation.
**Brennan, Maureen V.** .......... '71 '96 C.112 B.A. L.1068 J.D. [[A] Crosby,H.R.&M.]
**Brennan, Thomas P., (P.C.)**, (AV) ...... '41 '66 C.262 B.S. L.309 LL.B. [Paul,H.J.&W.]
**Brenner, Jonathan M.** .......... '66 '92 C.112 B.A. L.1065 J.D. [[A] Sidley&A.]
*PRACTICE AREAS: Litigation.
**Brenner, Lee S.** .......... '70 '95 C.966 B.S. L.1065 J.D. [[A] White O.C.&A.]
*PRACTICE AREAS: Litigation.
**Brenner, Steven G.**, (AV) .......... '49 '74 C.112 A.B. L.426 J.D. [Clopton,P.&B.]
*PRACTICE AREAS: Workers Compensation; Defense; Subrogation.
Breslin, Thomas P., II, (AV) .......... '32 '61 C.426 B.A. L.800 LL.B. 210 W. Temple St.‡
**Breslo, James A.** .......... '67 '92 C.112 B.S. L.597 J.D. [[A] Seyfarth,S.F.&G.]
*PRACTICE AREAS: Employment; Labor; Litigation.
Breslow, Karen '62 '88 C.188 B.A. L.178 J.D.
1800 Ave. of the Stars, Suite 900 (Century City)
**Bressan, Paul L.** .......... '47 '76 C.262 A.B. L.178 J.D. [Kelley D.&W.]
*REPORTED CASES: Lead counsel for company on appeal in Fortino, et al. v. Quasar Company, 950 F.2d 389 (7th Cir. 1991).
*PRACTICE AREAS: Employment Discrimination Law; Management Labor Relations; Wrongful Discharge.

**Bressler, Howard J., (AV) '41 '66 C.800 B.A. L.1065 J.D.**
**Suite 1245, 11845 West Olympic Boulevard, 90064**
**Telephone: 310-312-8141 FAX: 310-312-8014**
**General Corporate and Real Estate Law Practice.**

**Bretoi, Jeffrey S.** .......... '62 '88 C.999 L.1137 J.D. [[A] Williamson,R.&D.]
*PRACTICE AREAS: Insurance Defense; Governmental; Municipal; Business Litigation; Construction Defect.
Brettauer, Karin H. .......... '49 '76 C.1097 B.A. L.426 J.D. 845 Thayer Ave.
**Bretz, Robert H.**, (AV) .......... '43 '73 C&L.37 B.S., J.D. [R.H.Bretz]
*REPORTED CASES: Stahl v. Gibraltar Financial Corp., 967 F.2d 335 (9th Cir. 1992).

**Bretz, Robert H., A Professional Corporation, (AV)**
**520 Washington Boulevard, Suite 428, 90292**
**Telephone: 310-578-1957 FAX: 310-578-5443**
**Robert H. Bretz.**
**Corporate, Corporate Finance and Securities Law. Commercial Litigation.**
*See Professional Biographies, LOS ANGELES, CALIFORNIA*

Breuer, Teri L. .......... '66 '92 C.112 B.A. L.800 J.D. 444 S. Flower St.
**Breuner, Katrina L.** .......... '60 '90 C.112 B.S. L.1065 J.D. [[A] Manatt,P.&P.]
*PRACTICE AREAS: Healthcare; Long-Term Care.
**Brew, Alexandra J.** .......... '67 '92 C.276 A.B. L.569 J.D. [[A] Katten M.&Z.]
*PRACTICE AREAS: General Business Litigation; Conservatorships.
**Brew, Julian** .......... '66 '90 C.472 B.A. L.145 J.D. [[A] Alschuler G.&P.]
Brewer, Gail Lynn .......... '56 '88 C.525 B.S.N. L.809 J.D. 865 S. Figueroa St.
**Brewer, Michael A.** .......... '57 '85 C.1109 B.A. L.1148 J.D. [Hornberger&C.]
*PRACTICE AREAS: Products Liability; Personal Injury; Construction Defect; Premises Liability; Trial Practice.

Brewster, George L. .......... '36 '67 C.813 B.A. L.765 J.D. 12441 Mitchell Ave.
Brewster, Lee .......... '34 '72 C.1097 B.A. L.809 J.D. 8929 S. Sepulveda Blvd., Ste. 312
**Brian, Brad D.**, (AV) .......... '52 '77 C.112 B.A. L.309 J.D. [Munger,T.&O.]
**Briand, Pamela** .......... '— '96 C.549 B.A. L.569 J.D. [[A] Christensen,M.F.J.G.W.&S.]
*PRACTICE AREAS: Litigation.
Brice, Gary .......... '50 '83 C.1097 B.A. L.809 J.D. 4077 Camino Real
Brice, Vinson .......... '11 '57 C.208 L.809 2148 Manning Ave.‡
**Bricker, Andrea H.** .......... '52 '77 C.112 B.A. L.1068 J.D. [[A] Hughes H.&R.]
*PRACTICE AREAS: Corporate Law; Securities Law.
**Brickman, Boaz M.** .......... '66 '92 C.025 B.A.Sc. L.1068 J.D. [[A] Kirkland&E.]
*PRACTICE AREAS: Litigation; Intellectual Property Law.
Brickwood, Susan C. .......... '46 '80 C.821 B.A. L.800 J.D. 6500 Wilshire Blvd.
**Bridge, Catherine S.** .......... '69 '95 C.112 B.A. L.94 J.D. [[A] Latham&W.]
*LANGUAGES: Spanish.
**Bridges, Harold A.** .......... '55 '80 C&L.426 B.A., J.D. [Burke,W.&S.]
*PRACTICE AREAS: Litigation; Public Law; Business Law; Employment Litigation; Education Law.
**Bridges, Ried**, (AV) ... '27 '54 C&L.800 B.S., J.D. [Bonne,B.M.O.&N.] (⊙Santa Barbara)
Bridgman, Stan W. '21 '51 C&L.502 LL.B.
(adm. in MO; not adm. in CA) Johnson & Higgins
Bridwell, Kent M., (AV) .......... '47 '73 C.112 B.A. L.426 J.D. 3620 Jasmine Ave.
**Brigante, Brad J.** .......... '66 '96 C.1074 B.S. L.861 J.D. [[A] Jeffer,M.B.&M.]
*PRACTICE AREAS: Federal and State Taxation.
**Brigden, John F.** .......... '64 '91 C.679 B.S.E.E. L.276 J.D. [[A] Howrey&S.]
*PRACTICE AREAS: Commercial Litigation; Intellectual Property Litigation.
**Briggs, Jeffrey C.**, (AV) .......... '56 '81 C&L.494 B.A., J.D. [Alschuler G.&P.]
**Briggs, Jeffrey T.** .......... '67 '93 C.112 B.A. L.809 J.D. [[A] Selman B.]
Briggs, Richard O. .......... '47 '77 C&L.597 B.A., J.D. 879 W. 190th St., Suite 540

**Brigham, Constance G., Law Offices of '54 '79 C.773 B.A. L.1065 J.D.**
**600 Wilshire, 17th Floor, P.O. Box 861791, 90086**
**Telephone: 213-489-8950 Fax: 213-489-8951**
***PRACTICE AREAS: Banking; Civil Business Litigation; Bankruptcy; Collections; Business.**

**Bright, Gregory P.** .......... '63 '91 C.800 B.A. L.990 J.D. [[A] Gartner&Y.]
*PRACTICE AREAS: Labor and Employment Law.
**Bright, Patrick F.**, (AV) ...... '43 '69 C.276 B.S. L.273 J.D. [Bright&L.] (See Pat. Sect.)
*PRACTICE AREAS: Patent, Copyright, Trademark, Trade Secret and Antitrust including Litigation.

**Bright and Brown**
**(See Glendale)**

**Bright & Lorig, A Professional Corporation, (AV)** [BB]
**633 West Fifth Street, Suite 3330, 90071**
**Telephone: 213-627-7774 Telecopier: 213-627-8508**
**Frederick A. Lorig; Patrick F. Bright;—Lois A. Stone; Sidford Lewis Brown; Edward C. Schewe; Bruce R. Zisser.**
**Patents, Trademarks, Copyright, Antitrust and Unfair Competition Law. Trials.**
**Reference: Manufacturers Bank (Headquarters Office).**
*See Professional Biographies, LOS ANGELES, CALIFORNIA*

**Brill, Martin J.**, (AV) .......... '46 '72 C.112 B.A. L.1068 J.D. [Robinson,D.B.&K.]
*PRACTICE AREAS: Bankruptcy Law; Insolvency; Reorganization.
**Brill, Michael J., (P.C.)**, (AV) .......... '45 '74 C.156 B.A. L.1009 J.D. [Alschuler G.&P.]
Brill, Thomas R. .......... '60 '86 C.112 B.A. L.809 J.D. 633 W. 5th St.
Brin, Benjamin A. .......... '62 '89 C.597 B.A. L.94 J.D. 601 W. 5th St.‡
**Brindisi, Thomas J.** .......... '69 '95 C.119 B.S. L.64 J.D. [[A] Lyon&L.] (See Pat. Sect.)
*PRACTICE AREAS: Intellectual Property.
**Brindze, Paul L.**, (AV) .......... '45 '74 C.112 B.A. L.1068 J.D. [Ziffren,B.B.&F.]
*PRACTICE AREAS: Entertainment Law.
Bringas, Martha C. .......... '48 '96 C.112 B.A. L.178 J.D. 1901 Ave. of the Stars
**Brink, R. Scott** .......... '63 '88 C.310 B.A. L.546 J.D. [[A] Jeffer,M.B.&M.]
*PRACTICE AREAS: Labor and Employment Law.
**Brinkman, Daren R.** .......... '61 '88 C.101 B.A. L.1066 J.D. [Blakeley&B.]
*PRACTICE AREAS: Bankruptcy; Creditor's Rights.
**Brinsley, John H.**, (AV) .......... '33 '61 C&L.188 B.A., LL.B. [Paul,H.J.&W.]
**Brisbin, Scott T.** .......... '54 '81 C.112 B.A. L.276 J.D. [Kleinberg L.L.B.&C.]
*PRACTICE AREAS: Entertainment Law; Copyright Law.
Brisbois, Patricia Lea ...... '58 '93 C.990 B.S. L.426 J.D. Pro Se Staff Atty., U.S. Dist. Ct.
**Brisbois, Roy M., (P.C.)**, (AV) .......... '47 '72 C.112 B.A. L.1068 J.D. [Lewis,D.B.&B.]
Briscoe, Joseph Jackson, IV .......... '56 '83 C&L.990 B.A., J.D. [Gibeaut,M.&B.]
Briseno, A. Edward .......... '58 '83 C.112 B.A. L.464 J.D. 3325 Wilshire Blvd., 9th Fl.
**Briseno, Andrew Edward** .......... '58 '83 C.112 B.A. L.464 J.D. [[A] D.B.Bloom]
*LANGUAGES: Spanish.
**Briskin, Jeffrey F.** .......... '48 '78 C.800 B.A. L.1137 J.D. [Schell&D.]
*LANGUAGES: Spanish.
Briskin, Morton .......... '13 '36 C.800 L.809 146 N. Almont St.
Briskin, Robert A., (AV) .... '52 '77 C.477 B.A. L.912 J.D. 1875 Century Park E., 15th Fl.
**Brittenham, Harry M.**, (AV) .......... '41 '71 C.1070 B.S. L.1068 J.D. [Ziffren,B.B.&F.]
*PRACTICE AREAS: Entertainment Law.
Britton, Layne Leslie .......... '55 '81 C.426 B.A. L.1068 J.D. 3677 Boise Ave.
Brizzolara, Christopher .......... '58 '83 C.800 B.A. L.861 J.D. [[A] Williams&Assoc.]
**Bro, Theodore J.** .......... '69 '95 C.477 B.G.S. L.276 J.D. [[A] Arnold&P.]
*PRACTICE AREAS: Litigation.
**Broadhead, Tracey N.** .......... '67 '94 C.112 B.A. L.1065 J.D. [[A] Sedgwick,D.M.&A.]

**Brobeck, Phleger & Harrison LLP, (AV)** [BB]
**A Partnership including a Professional Corporation**
**550 South Hope Street, 90071-2604⊙**
**Telephone: 213-489-4060 Facsimile: 213-745-3345 Cable Address: "Brobeck" Telex: 181164 BPH LSA**
**Managing Partner: Thomas P. Burke. Resident Partners: Laurie A. Allen; Kenneth R. Bender; Linda J. Bozung; Edmond R. Davis (Certified Specialist, Taxation Law, The State Bar of California Board of Legal Specialization); Gregg A. Farley; William B. Fitzgerald; David M. Halbreich; Susan B. Hall; Jeffery D. Hermann; David M. Higgins; John Francis Hilson; Drew Jones; Albert R. Karel; George H. Link; Debra E. Pole; Todd B. Serota; V. Joseph Stubbs; William K. Swank; Jeffrey S. Turner; Daniel J. Tyukody; Kenneth L. Waggoner; Gerard J. Walsh; John J. Wasilczyk; Michael S. Whalen (Board Certified, Estate Planning, Trust and Probate Law, The State Bar of California Board of Legal Specialization); Michael T. Zarro. Of Counsel: Tom Bradley; Chris Steven Jacobsen; Earle Miller; John A. Payne, Jr.; Thomas H. Petrides. Resident Associates: Michael L. Armstrong; David W. Berry; Kara L. Bue; Richard L. Daniels; Paul M. Gleason; Marcia Z. Gordon; John Hameetman; Bruce W. Hepler (Not admitted in CA); Bernard C. Jasper; Jamie L. Johnson; Wayne E. Johnson; Brian W. Kasell; Patty H. Le; Howard L. Magee; Christopher J. Menjou; Cynthia M. Patton; Braden W. Penhoet; Howard M. Privette; Douglas C. Rawles; Steven J. Renshaw; Eddie Rodriguez; David L. Schrader; Konrad F. Schreier, III; Jody L. Spiegel; Raymond T. Sung; Edward D. Totino; David R. Venderbush; Daniel I. Villapando; Todd W. Walker; Perrie M. Weiner; Daniel Weisberg; Pamela J. Yates; Thomas B. Youth; Gregg Zucker. Contract Attorney: Gary D. Rothstein.**
**General Practice, including Business and Technology, Litigation, Real Estate Litigation, Insurance Coverage Litigation, Securities Litigation, Technology Litigation, Environmental Litigation, Product Liability Litigation, Labor and Employment Law, Financial Services and Insolvency (including Bankruptcy and Loan Workout), Real Estate, and Tax/Estate Planning.**
**San Francisco, California Office: Spear Street Tower, One Market. Telephone: 415-442-0900. Facsimile: 415-442-1010.**
**Palo Alto, California Office: Two Embarcadero Place, 2200 Geng Road. Telephone: 415-424-0160. Facsimile: 415-496-2885.**
**San Diego, California Office: 550 West C Street, Suite 1300. Telephone: 619-234-1966. Facsimile: 619-236-1403.**

(This Listing Continued)

# CALIFORNIA—LOS ANGELES        MARTINDALE-HUBBELL LAW DIRECTORY 1997

**Brobeck, Phleger & Harrison LLP** (Continued)
Orange County, California Office: 4675 MacArthur Court, Suite 1000, Newport Beach. Telephone: 714-752-7535. Facsimile: 714-752-7522.
Austin, Texas Office: Brobeck, Phleger & Harrison LLP, 301 Congress Avenue, Suite 1200. Telephone: 512-477-5495. Facsimile: 512-477-5813.
Denver, Colorado Office: Brobeck, Phleger & Harrison LLP, 1125 Seventeenth Street, 25th Floor. Telephone: 303-293-0760. Facsimile: 303-299-8819.
New York, N.Y. Office: Brobeck, Phleger & Harrison LLP, 1633 Broadway, 47th Floor. Telephone: 212-581-1600. Facsimile: 212-586-7878.
Brobeck Hale and Dorr International Office:
London, England Office: Veritas House, 125 Finsbury Pavement, London EC2A 1NQ. Telephone: 44 071 638 6688. Facsimile: 44 071 638 5888.

*See Professional Biographies, LOS ANGELES, CALIFORNIA*

Brock, Christopher M. ............ '63 '90 C.350 B.A. L.477 J.D. [🅐 Proskauer R.G.&M.]
*PRACTICE AREAS: Litigation; Intellectual Property.
Brock, John A. ........... '42 '69 C.813 B.A. L.1068 J.D. Dep. Pub. Def.
**Brock, Larry J.** ............... '65 '90 C.221 B.S. L.990 J.D. [Lewis,D.B.&B.]
Brockie, Pamela J. '50 '75 C.112 B.A. L.1068 J.D.
   Sr. V.P., Bus. Affs., Intl. Creative Mgmt., Inc.
**Brockmeyer, Neal H.**, (AV) ........... '38 '64 C.813 A.B. L.1066 J.D. [Heller E.W.&M.]
*PRACTICE AREAS: Corporate Finance; Mergers and Acquisitions; Securities Law; Corporate Law.
**Brod, Jonathan A.**, .............. '46 '71 C.679 B.A. L.188 J.D. [J.A.Brod]
**Brod, Jonathan A., Law Corporation**, (AV)
1801 Century Park East, 25th Floor, 90067
Telephone: 310-556-2282 Facsimile: 310-556-2024
Jonathan A. Brod.
Estate Planning, Probate, Wills and Trusts, Tax Planning and Litigation, Pensions, Corporate and General Business.

*See Professional Biographies, LOS ANGELES, CALIFORNIA*

Broder, Jamie ................. '49 '76 C.1036 A.B. L.569 J.D. [Paul,H.J.&W.]
**Broderick, Brett Michael** ............ '66 '93 C.1097 B.S. L.809 J.D. [🅐 Buchalter,N.F.&Y.]
*PRACTICE AREAS: Insolvency.
**Broderick, Camilla L.** ............... '52 '77 C.276 B.A. L.426 J.D. [🅐 J.A.Broderick,Jr.]
*PRACTICE AREAS: Estate Planning & Probate; Adoption Law; Corporate Law.
**Broderick, James A., Jr.**, (AV) '15 '44 C.276 A.B. L.426 LL.B.
Suite 1226 Wilshire Financial Tower, 3600 Wilshire Boulevard, 90010
Telephone: 213-384-1134 Fax: 213-385-0276
*PRACTICE AREAS: Probate and Estate Planning; Adoption Law; Corporate Law.
Associates: Camilla L. Broderick.
Probate and Estate Planning Law. Adoption Law. General Civil and Corporation Law.
Reference: Bank of America National Trust & Savings Assn. (Wilshire Center Branch, Los Angeles).
**Broderick, James H., Jr.** ............ '52 '81 C.309 A.B. L.94 J.D. [Graham&J.]
*PRACTICE AREAS: Litigation.
**Broderick, Roger J.**, (AV) '33 '61 C.112 A.B. L.1068 LL.B.
700 South Flower Street, Suite 500, 90017
Telephone: 213-626-8711
Insurance Defense.

*See Professional Biographies, LOS ANGELES, CALIFORNIA*

Brodka, Mark A. ............. '56 '82 C&L.426 B.A., J.D. 12100 Wilshire Blvd.
Brody, Arthur '25 '50 C.145 Ph.B. L.309 LL.B.
   Prof., Southwestern Univ. School of Law
**Brody, Harold M.** ............. '50 '75 C.659 A.B. L.597 J.D. [Proskauer R.G.&M.]
*PRACTICE AREAS: Alternative Dispute Resolution; Employment Discrimination Law; Equal Employment Law.
Brody, Howard P. ............. '43 '75 C.569 A.B. L.809 J.D. [Graven P.B.B.&Q.]
**Brody, Michael J.** ............. '59 '84 C&L.352 B.B.A., J.D. [Latham&W.]
**Brody, Stuart L.** ............. '46 '72 C.112 B.A. L.800 J.D. [🅐 Neumeyer&B.]
*REPORTED CASES: Prudential-LMI Commercial Insurance v. Superior Court (1990) 51 Cal.3d 674, 274 Cal.Rptr. 387; Chu v. Canadian Indemnity Company (1990) 224 Cal.App.3d 86, 274 Cal.Rptr. 20; Home Insurance Company v. Landmark Insurance Company (1988) 205 Cal.App.3d 1388, 253 Cal. Rptr. 277; Preston v. Goldman (1986) 42 Cal.3d 108, 227 Cal.Rptr. 817; Poland v. Martin (9th Cir. 1985) 761 F.2d 546.
*PRACTICE AREAS: Appellate Practice; Insurance Coverage; Insurance Bad Faith.
**Brody, William S.** ............. '62 '88 C.112 B.A. L.1049 J.D. [🅐 Buchalter,N.F.&Y.]
*PRACTICE AREAS: Insolvency.
Broemer, Glen .............. '60 '93 C.37 B.A. L.1065 J.D. 12400 Wilshire Blvd., 13th Fl.
**Broerman, Kevin K.** ............. '61 '93 C.36 B.S. L.1137 J.D. [🅐 Robinson,D.&W.]
*PRACTICE AREAS: Litigation; Insurance Law; Products Liability; Personal Injury; Tort Defense.
Broersma, Amy-Hannah ............. '54 '83 C.787 B.A. L.767 J.D. Dep. Dist. Atty.
Broersma, Dirk P. ............. '55 '95 C.1074 B.S. L.809 J.D. 1520 Wilshire Blvd., 6th Fl.
**Broffman, Edward C.** ............. '48 '75 C.112 A.B. L.426 J.D. [Fierstein&S.]
*PRACTICE AREAS: Business Law; Construction Defect Litigation; Real Property Litigation (Federal and State Courts) Law.
Broffman, Scott L. ............. '53 '84 C.112 B.S. L.809 J.D. 5455 Wilshire Blvd.
Broffman, Sidney ............. '14 '38 C.102 L.1009 LL.B. 611 Wilshire Blvd.‡
**Brogan, Kevin H.**, (AV) ............ '53 '79 C.112 B.S. L.1065 J.D. [Hill,F.&B.]
*REPORTED CASES: City of Vista v. Fiedler (1996 Cal. 4th; 96 Daily Journal D.A.R. 8977; Los Angeles Unified School Dist. v. Trump Wilshire Assoc. (1996) 42 Cal. App. 4th 1982; Pincus v. Pabst Brewing Co. (1990) 893 F2d 1544; S.C.R.T.D. v. Bolen (1992) 1 Cal. 4th 654.
*PRACTICE AREAS: Business and Real Estate Litigation; Eminent Domain; Inverse Condemnation.
**Broido, Erica M.** ............. '66 '92 C.112 B.A. L.770 J.D. [🅐 Pollak,V.&F.]
Broidy, Alan F., (BV) ......... '54 '79 C.112 B.A. L.1068 J.D. 1999 Ave. of the Stars, 27th Fl.
Broidy, Steven D. ............. '38 '63 C.112 A.B. L.1066 LL.B. City Natl. Bk.
**Broiles, Steven A.** ............. '40 '66 C.684 B.A. L.1066 J.D. [🅒 LeBoeuf,L.G.&M.]
*PRACTICE AREAS: Environmental.
Bromberg, Michael S. ............. '44 '69 C.563 B.A. L.1009 J.D. 2601 So. Figueroa St.
**Bromley, Alexander H.** ............. '66 '95 C.569 B.F.A. L.178 J.D. [🅐 McDermott,W.&E.]
**Bronowski, Clare** ............. '55 '83 C.309 B.A. L.1068 J.D. [Christensen,M.F.J.G.W.&S.]
*PRACTICE AREAS: Real Estate; Land Use; Environmental.
**Bronson, Eric E.** ............. '58 '83 C.475 B.A. L.477 J.D. [🅐 B.S.Lemon]
**Bronson, Glenn R.** ............. '61 '91 C.878 B.A. L.101 J.D. [🅐 Chadbourne&P.]
*LANGUAGES: Italian.
**Bronson, Mark** ............. '63 '89 C.112 B.A. L.813 J.D. [🅐 Paul,H.J.&W.]
**Bronson, Bronson & McKinnon LLP**, (AV) 🌐
A Partnership including Professional Corporations
444 South Flower Street, 24th Floor, 90071☉
Telephone: 213-627-2000 Fax: 213-627-2277
Resident Partners: Eric A. Amador; Donna P. Arlow; Stephen L. Backus; Charles N. Bland, Jr.; Breton August Bocchieri; John D. Boyle; Stephen T. Carpenter; William B. Creim; L. Morris Dennis (A Professional Corporation); Lucinda Dennis (A Professional Corporation); Elizabeth A. Erskine; Edwin W. Green; Claudia L. Greenspoon; Stuart I. Koenig; Ralph S. LaMontagne, Jr.; Richard C. Macias; Dani H. Rogers; Manuel Saldaña; David M. Walsh; Sheldon J. Warren. Of Counsel: David L. Horgan; Robert Weber, Jr. Resident Associates: Janet Andrea; Raymon B. Bilbeaux, III; Laurie K. Jones; Laurie S. Julien; Charles E. Koro; Kathleen R. O'Laughlin; Hayley L. Sneiderman; John F. Stephens; Nancy L. Tetreault; James B. Yobski.
General Civil, Trial and Appellate and General Business Practice. Commercial Law and Secured Transactions, Bankruptcy, Insolvency, Business Reorganization, Real Estate, Federal and State Litigation, Corporate Partnerships, Federal, State and Local Taxation, Financial Institutions, Estate Planning.
San Francisco, California Office: 505 Montgomery Street. Telephone: 415-986-4200.

(This Listing Continued)

CAA192P

**Bronson, Bronson & McKinnon LLP** (Continued)
San Jose, California Office: 10 Almaden Boulevard, Suite 600. Telephone: 408-293-0599.

*See Professional Biographies, LOS ANGELES, CALIFORNIA*

**Bronstein, John D.** ............. '56 '81 C.112 B.A. L.426 J.D. [Ramsey,B.&D.]
*PRACTICE AREAS: Tractor-Trailer; Automotive Dealers Litigation; Products Liability Litigation; Negligence.
**Bronstein, Marc A.** ............. '52 '77 C.1042 B.S.A. L.426 J.D. [🅐 Isen&G.]
Bronstein, Paul A. ............. '43 '68 C.112 B.S. L.1068 J.D. Dep. Dist. Atty.
**Bronston, Edythe L., Law Offices of**, (AV) '36 '80 C.1077 B.A. L.426 J.D. 🌐
11377 West Olympic Boulevard, Suite 900, 90064-1683
Telephone: 310-914-7972 Fax: 310-914-7973
Bankruptcy, Receivership, Creditors' Rights, Civil Litigation.

*See Professional Biographies, LOS ANGELES, CALIFORNIA*

**Brook, Bradley E.** ............ '60 '86 C.597 B.S. L.1065 J.D. [🅒 Pachulski,S.Z.&Y.]
Brook, Fiona A. ........... '70 '94 C&L.061 B.A., J.D. 11611 San Vicente Blvd.
Brook, Renée Turkell ............. '56 '83 C.112 B.A. L.1068 J.D. 400 S. Hope St.
**Brookey, Dawn S.** ............. '64 '93 C.112 B.A. L.426 J.D. [🅐 Pillsbury M.&S.]
**Brooklier, Anthony P.**, (AV) ............. '46 '72 C.426 B.A. L.1066 J.D. [Marks&B.]
**Brooks, Dana Carli** ............. '58 '86 C.800 A.B. L.426 J.D. [Rubinstein&P.]
*REPORTED CASES: Quackenbush California Insurance Commissioner v. Allstate Ins. Co. 116 S.Ct.1712 (1996); In re Mission Insurance Company (Imperial Casualty), 41 Cal. App. 4th 828 (1995); In re Executive Life (Ins. Co.), 32 Cal. App. 4th 344 (1995); Sunburst Bank N.A. v. Executive Life, 24 Cal. App. 4th 1156 (1994); Garamendi v. Mission Ins. Co., 15 Cal. App. 4th 1277 (1993).
*PRACTICE AREAS: Business and Commercial Litigation; Insurance; Reinsurance; Insurance Insolvency; Insurance Rate Regulation.
**Brooks, James C.** ............. '48 '79 C.911 B.S. L.276 J.D. [Lyon&L.] (See Pat. Sect.)
*PRACTICE AREAS: Patent, Trademark, Copyright, Unfair Competition, Trade Secret; Intellectual Property.
Brooks, Michael I. ............. '47 '79 L.054 LL.B. [M.I.Brooks]
**Brooks, Mylene J.** ............. '63 '94 C.1075 B.S. L.426 J.D. [🅐 Troop M.S.&P.]
*PRACTICE AREAS: Labor and Employment.
**Brooks, Preston W.** ............. '64 '91 C.309 A.B. L.976 J.D. [🅐 Cox,C.&N.]
*LANGUAGES: French.
*PRACTICE AREAS: Environmental Litigation and Regulatory Law.
**Brooks, Scott Ashford** ............. '64 '92 C.112 B.A. L.426 J.D. [🅐 Daniels,B.&F.]
**Brooks, Scott D.** ............. '63 '89 C.188 B.A. L.976 J.D. [Cox,C.&N.]
*PRACTICE AREAS: Real Property Law.
**Brooks, Seeley Ann** ............. '64 '91 C.309 A.B. L.178 J.D. [🅐 Gibson;D.&C.]
*PRACTICE AREAS: Real Estate.
Brooks, Michael I., P.C., Law Offices of ............. 3255 Wilshire Blvd.
Brookwell, Frederick J., (AV) ........... '54 '80 C.103 B.A. L.809 J.D. [Brookwell K.]
Brookwell Karic, A Law Corporation, (AV) ........... 300 S. Grand Ave., Ste. 1345
**Broom, Deborah** ............. '57 '87 C.1110 B.A. L.990 J.D. [Knopfler&B.]
*PRACTICE AREAS: Insurance Law; Environmental; Construction Law
**Brophy, Carol R.** ............. '— '91 C.813 A.B. L.809 J.D. [🅐 McKenna&C.]
*PRACTICE AREAS: Environmental; Litigation; Administrative Law.
**Brophy, Fiona A.** ............ '69 '96 C.276 B.S. L.1066 J.D. [🅐 Christensen,M.F.J.G.W.&S.]
*PRACTICE AREAS: Litigation.
Brophy, Pollyann L. '54 '84 C.37 B.A. L.426 J.D.
   Sr. Coun., Pacific Telesis Legal Group
Brosio, Robert L., (AV) ............ '36 '61 C&L.813 B.A., LL.B. Asst. U.S. Atty.
**Brostrom, Ellen R.** ............ '67 '95 C.93 B.A. L.1068 J.D. [🅐 Crosby,H.R.&M.]
**Brot, Ronald F.**
(See Woodland Hills)
Brott, Irving H. ........... '14 '42 C.137 L.365 LL.B. 321 N. Saltair Ave.‡
Brotz, Beth Y. ........... '— '90 C.1044 B.A. L.426 J.D. 400 S Hope St.
**Brotzen, Peter P.**, (AV) ............ '42 '72 C.1179 B.S. L.1136 J.D. [Dwyer,D.B.&B.]
*PRACTICE AREAS: Civil Trials; Aviation; Products Liability; Construction Law; Bad Faith.
Broudy, Leonard C. ........... '33 '69 C.112 L.1148 J.D. 2566 Overland Ave.
Brougham, David C. ........... '62 '88 C.1250 B.A. L.990 J.D. P.O. Box 17927
Brourman, Michael, (AV) ........... '46 '75 C.665 B.A. L.273 J.D. 2029 Century Park E.
Broussard, Thomas Rollins, (AV) ........... '43 '68 C.659 B.A. L.309 J.D. [Broussard&Assoc.]
Broussard & Associates, Ltd., A Professional Corporation, (AV)
   5757 Wilshire Boulevard, Suite 648
Brouwer, Richard T. ............. '64 '92 C.1077 B.A. L.809 J.D. 1888 Century Park East
**Brown, A. Steven**, (AV) ........... '51 '77 C.602 B.A. L.426 J.D. [Holley&G.]
**Brown, Arthur Wm., Jr.**, (AV) ........... '46 '75 C.597 B.A. L.800 J.D. [Sheppard,M.R.&H.]
*PRACTICE AREAS: Corporate and Securities Law; Acquisitions, Divestitures and Mergers; International Business Law.
**Brown, Avery R.** ............. '64 '89 C.659 B.S. L.1068 J.D. [🅒 O'Melveny&M.]
*LANGUAGES: French.
*PRACTICE AREAS: Mergers and Acquisition Transactions.
**Brown, Baird A.**, (AV) ........... '46 '73 C.597 B.A. L.813 J.D. [B.A.Brown]
Brown, Barbara ............. '43 '79 C.611 B.A. L.1068 J.D. First Interstate Bank
**Brown, Barry D.**, (AV) ............. '51 '77 C&L.767 B.A., J.D. [Gray,Y.D.&R.]
*REPORTED CASES: Gurkewitz v. Hobermon (1982) 137 Cal.App. 3d 328; Stoil v. Superior Court (1992) 9 Cal.App. 4th 1362; Bellows v. Aliquot (1994) 25 Cal.App. 4th 426.
Brown, Bradford S. ............. '51 '77 C.112 B.A. L.426 J.D. Dep. Dist. Atty.
Brown, Bruce I. ............. '— '86 C.174 B.A. L.940 J.D. 11611 San Vicente Blvd.
**Brown, Charles D.** ............. '45 '75 C&L.426 B.S.E.E., J.D. Hughes Aircraft Co. (Pat.)
Brown, Charles H, II ............. '51 '86 C.831 B.S. L.809 J.D. 3255 Wilshire Blvd., 12th Fl.
**Brown, Charles T.** ............. '59 '89 C.1097 B.A. L.101 J.D. [🅐 Callahan,M.&W.]
Brown, Chester L. ............. '40 '69 C.911 B.A. L.327 J.D. 9000 Sunset Blvd., 15th Fl.
**Brown, Daniel R.** ............. '68 '94 C.37 B.A. L.284 J.D. [🅐 Veatch,C.&N.]
**Brown, David S.** ............. '62 '88 C.273 B.A. L.107 J.D. [🅐 Kirtland&P.]
Brown, David W. T. ............. '61 '90 C.1056 B.S. L.596 J.D. American Intl. Grp.
**Brown, Deborah J.** ............. '63 '88 C.112 B.A. L.1068 J.D. [🅒 O'Melveny&M.]
*PRACTICE AREAS: Real Estate Law.
Brown, Dennis C., (A Professional Corporation), (AV) '39 '71
   C.112 A.B. L.1068 J.D. [Munger,T.&O.]
**Brown, Diana K.** ............. '63 '88 C.66 B.A. L.477 J.D. [Manatt,P.&P.]
*PRACTICE AREAS: Health'Law.
**Brown, Donald** ............. '56 '90 C.821 B.A. L.999 J.D. [🅐 Manatt,P.&P.]
*PRACTICE AREAS: Litigation.
Brown, Eileen A. ............. '51 '77 C.605 B.A. L.1068 J.D. Pres., Ages & Stages
**Brown, Elizabeth Coppage** ............. '63 '92 C.859 B.S. L.1067 J.D. [🅐 McKenna&C.]
**Brown, Ella L.** ............. '62 '89 C.95 A.B. L.893 J.D. [🅐 Orrick,H.&S.]
**Brown, Elliot N.** ............. '— '90 C&L.309 A.B., J.D. [Irell&M.]
Brown, Emma L. ............. '36 '76 C.1131 B.A. L.1068 J.D. Legal Aid Found. of L.A.
**Brown, Gary** '44 '72 C.112 B.S. L.1068 J.D.
1888 Century Park East, Suite 1550, 90067-1706
Telephone: 310-201-0007 Facsimile: 310-277-2293
Email: browngrp@postoffice.worldnet.att.net
*PRACTICE AREAS: Litigation (70%); Real Estate (25%).
General Practice.

*See Professional Biographies, LOS ANGELES, CALIFORNIA*

Brown, Gary E. ............. '48 '79 C.679 L.1095 J.D. 11611 San Vicente Blvd.

**Brown, Geoffrey C.** ....................'49 '79 C.112 A.B. L.1068 J.D. [Musick,P.&G.]
*PRACTICE AREAS: Litigation.
**Brown, George H.** ....................'57 '88 C.494 B.S. L.1068 J.D. [O'Melveny&M.]
**Brown, Gina M.** ....................'62 '88 C.976 B.A. L.309 J.D. [Ⓐ Peterson&R.]
**Brown, Howard B.**, (AV) ....................'22 '49 C.112 B.A. L.800 J.D. [Ⓒ Moss,L.&M.]
*REPORTED CASES: J.A. Jones Construction Co. v. Superior Court, 27 Cal.App.4th 1568 (1994); Sawyer Nurseries v. Galardi, 181 Cal.App.3d 663 (1986); Sukut Const. Co. v. Cabot, Cabot & Forbes Land Trust, 95 Cal.App.3d 527 (1979); Rodeffer Industries v. Chambers Estates, 263 Cal.App. 2d 116 (1968); Avalon Painting Co. v. Alert Lumber Co., 234 Cal.App.2d 178 (1965).
*PRACTICE AREAS: Construction Law; Title Insurance Law; General Trial Law; Civil Litigation.
**Brown, J. Kenneth**, (AV) ....................'35 '61 C.363 B.S.S. L.930 LL.B. [Brown,W.&C.]
*PRACTICE AREAS: Redevelopment; Municipal Law; Real Estate.
Brown, J. Russell, Jr. ....................'34 '71 C.112 B.S. L.1095 J.D. [J.R.Brown,Jr.]
Brown, Jack L. ....................'44 '75 C.112 A.B. L.800 J.D. Asst. City Atty.
**Brown, Jacqueline C.** ....................'67 '95 C.112 B.A. L.464 J.D. [Ⓐ Lord,B.&B.]
*PRACTICE AREAS: Civil Litigation.
Brown, James E. ....................'40 '74 C.112 B.A. L.1068 J.D. 4988 N. Figueroa St.
Brown, Jamie N. ....................'56 '87 C.941 B.A. L.678 J.D. 221 N. Figueroa St.
**Brown, Jeffrey N.** ....................'57 '82 C.112 B.A. L.426 J.D. [Morgan,L.&B.]
**Brown, Jill I.** ....................'65 '92 C.309 A.B. L.1068 J.D. [Ⓐ Heller E.W.&M.]
Brown, Kevin L. ....................'55 '90 C.302 B.A. L.112 J.D. Dep. Dist. Atty.
**Brown, Kyle D., (P.C.)**, (AV) ....................'40 '65 C&L.800 B.A., LL.B. [Hill,F.&B.]
*PRACTICE AREAS: Employment Law; Labor Law; Equal Opportunity Law (Management).
**Brown, L. Douglas**, (AV) ....................'43 '70 C&L.800 B.A., J.D. [Ⓒ Reinis&R.]
*TRANSACTIONS: Sale of Northrop Corporation Headquarters Building, 1989; Purchase of Ford Motor Company Pico Rivera Facility, 1982.
*PRACTICE AREAS: Business and Commercial Litigation; Insolvency Practice and Reorganizations; Real Estate; General Business and Corporate Law.
Brown, Lane R. ....................'56 '82 C.860 B.A. L.273 J.D. Dep. Co. Coun.
Brown, Leslie E. ....................'52 '77 C.112 B.A. L.1067 J.D. Asst. City Atty.
**Brown, Lester O.** ....................'52 '85 C.188 B.A. L.276 J.D. [Jones,D.R.&P.]
Brown, Lisa J. ....................'58 '92 C.1111 B.A. L.809 J.D. [Bolden&M.]
**Brown, Louis M.**, (AV) ....................'09 '33 C.800 A.B. L.309 J.D. [Ⓒ Sanders,B.G.S.&M.]
**Brown, Lowell C.** ....................'54 '83 C&L.878 B.A., J.D. [Foley L.W.&A.]
*LANGUAGES: Spanish.
*SPECIAL AGENCIES: Division of Health Standards and Quality; Health Care Financing Administration.
*REPORTED CASES: Scripps Memorial Hospital v. Superior Court, 87 Cal.App.4th 1720 (1995); Mir v. Charter Suburban Hospital, 27 Cal. App. 4th 1471 (1994); Bollengier v. Doctors Medical Center, 222 Cal.App. 3d 1115 (1990).
*PRACTICE AREAS: Health Care; Hospitals; Integrated Health Care Delivery; Medical Staff; Health Care Facility Licensing and Regulation.
**Brown, Marc E.** '52 '79
C.124 B.S.E.E. L.273 J.D. [Oppenheimer P.S.] (Pat.) (ⓞSan Jose, CA)
*PRACTICE AREAS: Intellectual Property; Computer Law; Litigation.
**Brown, Marc L.** ....................'51 '78 C.966 B.A. L.976 J.D. [Tuttle&T.]
*PRACTICE AREAS: Business Law; Securities.
**Brown, Marguerite L.** ....................'57 '83 C.1097 B.A. L.950 J.D. [Ⓒ Lord,B.&B.]
Brown, Maria Dante ....................'57 '86 C.1077 B.A. L.813 J.D. Dep. Atty. Gen.
**Brown, Mark K.**, (AV) ....................'54 '79 C.813 B.A. L.1066 J.D. [Kinsella,B.F.&T.]
*PRACTICE AREAS: Business Litigation; Real Estate; UCC; Bankruptcy Law.
**Brown, Michael K.**, (BV) ....................'56 '82 C.276 A.B. L.767 J.D. [Crosby,H.R.&M.]
*PRACTICE AREAS: Civil Litigation; Products Liability; Pharmaceuticals and Medical Device Litigation; Intellectual Property; Business Litigation.
**Brown, Naida L.** ....................'56 '85 C.560 B.A. L.1049 J.D. [Ⓐ Ginsburg,S.O.&R.]
Brown, Nancy ....................'35 '61 C.347 A.B. L.813 LL.B. Supm. Ct. J.
**Brown, Patrick S.** ....................'69 '95 C&L.112 B.A., J.D. [Ⓐ Sullivan&C.]
**Brown, Peter C.** ....................'61 '95 C.112 B.A. L.990 J.D. [Ⓐ Knopfler&R.]
*PRACTICE AREAS: Civil Litigation; Construction Defect; Real Property; Personal Injury.
Brown, Peter J. ....................'64 '90 C.1349 B.A. L.1019 J.D. [Ⓐ Liebert,C.&F.]
Brown, Philip Michael ....................'42 '68 C.112 B.A. L.1068 J.D. [Egerman&B.]
Brown, Phyllis E. ....................'57 '84 C&L.800 A.B., J.D. 4050 Buckingham Rd.
Brown, R. Donald, (Law Offices of) '38 '84 C.1109 B.A. L.678 J.D.
(adm. in WA; not adm. in CA) 419 N. Larchmont Blvd.
**Brown, Richard A.**, (AV) ....................'43 '72 C.1097 B.S. L.1068 J.D. [Manatt,P.&P.]
*PRACTICE AREAS: Insurance Regulation; Insurance Legislation; Insurance Transactions; Corporate-Level Insurance Litigation Reinsurance.
Brown, Richard D. ....................'48 '75 C.629 B.S. L.169 J.D. Coun., Blackfield Enterprises
**Brown, Richard M.** ....................'42 '68 C.112 B.A. L.1068 J.D. [Jeffer,M.B.&M.]
*PRACTICE AREAS: Sports and Broadcasting.
Brown, Robert K., Jr. ....................'60 '86 C.178 B.A. L.902 J.D. 555 W. 5th St.
**Brown, Robert W., Jr.** ....................'49 '77 C.1097 B.S. L.1068 J.D. [Ⓐ Alvarado,S.V.&S.]
*PRACTICE AREAS: Real Estate; Business; Banking.
Brown, Ronald L. ....................'54 '80 C.800 A.B. L.1068 J.D. Dep. Pub. Def.
Brown, Samuel H. ....................'41 '73 C.39 B.S. L.800 J.D. 3646 Homeland Dr.
**Brown, Scott M.** ....................'68 '95 C.951 B.A. L.800 J.D. [Ⓐ Milbank,T.H.&M.]
Brown, Sheldon H., (AV) ....................'29 '57 C.112 B.S. L.1068 LL.B. 11684 Ventura Blvd.
**Brown, Sidford Lewis** ....................'55 '82 C.112 B.A. L.800 J.D. [Ⓐ Bright&L.]
*PRACTICE AREAS: Intellectual Property Law; Antitrust; Litigation.
Brown, Stanley D. ....................'36 '60 C&L.477 B.A., J.D. 11805 Mayfield Ave.
**Brown, Terry L.** ....................'55 '91 C.112 B.A. L.426 J.D. [Ⓐ McKenna&C.]
*PRACTICE AREAS: Labor and Employment Law; Litigation.
**Brown, Thomas M.** ....................'57 '85 C&L.426 B.A., J.D. [Ⓒ Sheppard,M.R.&H.]
*PRACTICE AREAS: Criminal Law and Parallel Civil Proceedings; Internal Corporate Investigations; Criminal Trial Practice.
**Brown, Thomas P., IV**, (AV) ....................'46 '75 C.831 B.A. L.880 J.D. [Epstein B.&G.]

**Brown, V. Emile, Law Office of '59 '90 C.197 B.A. L.1068 J.D.**
**One Wilshire Building, 624 South Grand, 29th Floor, 90017**
Telephone: 213-426-6533 Fax: 213-426-6562
General Civil Trial, Consumer Protection, specializing in Lemon Law. Real Estate and Business Law.
*See Professional Biographies, LOS ANGELES, CALIFORNIA*

**Brown, Valerie A.** ....................'67 '91 C.112 B.A. L.426 J.D. [Ⓐ Jones,D.R.&P.]
Brown, Volney V., Jr. ....................'26 '52 C.112 L.800 J.D. Ret. Chf. U.S. Mag. J.
**Brown, W. Clark** ....................'54 '89 C.1307 B.A. L.1068 J.D. [Ⓐ Bucksbaum&S.]
*PRACTICE AREAS: Business Litigation; Intellectual Property; Unfair Competition; Securities Fraud.
Brown, William C. ....................'56 '89 C.1302 B.A. L.1068 J.D. 2121 Ave. of the Stars

**Brown, Baird A., A Professional Corporation, (AV)**
**1000 Wilshire Boulevard, Suite 620, 90017**
Telephone: 213-688-7795 Fax: 213-688-1080
Baird A. Brown.
Trial and Appellate Practice in State and Federal Courts. Business Law.
*See Professional Biographies, LOS ANGELES, CALIFORNIA*

Brown-Curtis, Vera ....................'43 '82 [Mallory&B.]
**Brown Fletcher, Lolita** ....................'62 '90 C.112 B.A. L.426 J.D. [Nelson&B.]
*PRACTICE AREAS: Employment; Labor; Insurance Defense; Real Estate Construction; Banking.
Brown, J. Russell, Jr., A Law Corporation ....................5455 Wilshire Boulevard, Suite 1600

**Brown, John Clark, Jr.**
(See Inglewood)

**Brown, Pistone, Hurley & Van Vlear, A Professional Corporation**
(See Irvine)

**Brown Raysman Millstein Felder & Steiner LLP, (AV)**
**1925 Century Park East, Eleventh Floor, 90067ⓞ**
Telephone: 310-789-2100 Fax: 310-789-2129
Email: brownraysman.com
Members of Firm: Dan C. Aardal (Resident); Henry J. Silberberg; Maureen McGuirl; Benzion J. Westreich (Resident). Associates: Timothy J. Martin; Ron Burnovski (Resident).
General Practice. Litigation, Arbitration, Computer, Corporate, Securities, Copyright, High Technology, Bankruptcy, Equipment Leasing, Tax, Patent, Trade Secrets, Insurance and Real Estate Law. Trial and Appellate Practice.
New York, New York Office: 120 West Forty-Fifth Street. Telephone: 212-944-1515. Fax: 212-840-2429.
Hartford, Connecticut Office: City Place I, 185 Asylum Street, 37th Floor. Telephone: 860-275-6400. Fax: 860-275-6410.
Newark, New Jersey Office: One Gateway Center. Telephone: 201-596-1480. Fax: 201-622-3317.
*See Professional Biographies, LOS ANGELES, CALIFORNIA*

**Brown, Winfield & Canzoneri, Incorporated, (AV) ⒷⒷ**
**Suite 1500 California Plaza, 300 South Grand Avenue, 90071-3125**
Telephone: 213-687-2100 Fax: 213-687-2149
J. Kenneth Brown; Thomas F. Winfield, III; Anthony Canzoneri; Vicki E. Land; James C. Camp; Steven Abram; Dennis S. Roy; Mark Steres; Katharine Araujo Miller; Christopher Norgaard; C. Geoffrey Mitchell; Scott H. Campbell; Joshua C. Gottheim; Donald Paul Ries; Muira K. Sethi; Seth I. Weissman; John H. Holloway; Rafael E. Alfonzo; Sonya L. Karpowich.
General Civil and Appellate Trial Practice in all State and Federal Courts. Municipal, Administrative, Corporation, Business, Banking, Real Property, Estate Planning, Trust, Probate and Tax Law.
Reference: Wells Fargo Bank.
*See Professional Biographies, LOS ANGELES, CALIFORNIA*

**Brown & Wood LLP, (AV)**
**10877 Wilshire Boulevard, 90024ⓞ**
Telephone: 310-443-0200 Telecopier: 310-208-5740
Partner: Paul C. Pringle.
General Practice.
New York, New York Office: One World Trade Center, 10048-0557.
Telephone: 212-839-5300.
Washington, D.C. Office: 815 Connecticut Avenue, N.W., Suite 701, 20006-4004.
Telephone: 202-973-0600.
San Francisco, California Office: 555 California Street, 94104-1715.
Telephone: 415-772-1200.
London, England Office: Blackwell House, Guildhall Yard.
Telephone: 011-44-171-778-1800.
Hong Kong Office: 2606 Asia Pacific Finance Tower, Citibank Plaza, 3 Garden Road, Central.
Telephone: 011-852-2509-7888.
Sao Paulo, Brazil Office: Rua da Consolacao, 247 - 5° Andar.
Telephone: 011-55-11-256-9785.
Beijing, China Office: 2315, China World Tower, 1 Jian Guo Men Wai Avenue.
Telephone: 011-8610-6505-5359; 011-8610-6505-1807.
*See Professional Biographies, LOS ANGELES, CALIFORNIA*

Browne, David M. ....................'55 '80 C.112 B.A. L.629 J.D. 12400 Wilshire Blvd.
Browne, John T. ....................'48 '74 C.112 A.B. L.770 J.D. Dep. Dist. Atty.
**Browne, Rochelle** ....................'38 '77 C.112 A.B. L.1068 J.D. [Richards,W.&G.]
*PRACTICE AREAS: Litigation; Public Law; Land Use Law.

**Browne & Woods LLP**
(See Beverly Hills)

**Browning, J. Taylor** ....................'71 '96 C.112 B.A. L.1066 J.D. [Ⓐ O'Melveny&M.]
**Browning, John R.**, (AV) ....................'39 '65 C.1042 B.A. L.1068 LL.B. [Musick,P.&G.]
*PRACTICE AREAS: Healthcare; Hospitals; Corporate Law; Finance.
**Browning, Nicholas, III** ....................'46 '75 C.508 B.S. L.809 J.D. [Herzfeld&R.]
*PRACTICE AREAS: Business and Litigation Law; Federal Practice.
**Brownstein, Adrianne J.** ....................'66 '90 C.260 B.A. L.893 J.D. [Ⓐ Jeffer,M.B.&M.]
*PRACTICE AREAS: Commercial and Business Litigation.
**Brownstein, Amy R.** ....................'70 '95 C.860 B.A. L.426 J.D. [Ⓐ Jones,D.R.&P.]
**Bruce, Megan M.** ....................'69 '94 C.276 B.S./B.A. L.1068 J.D. [Ⓐ Coudert]
**Brucker, Alex M.**, (AV) ....................'45 '74 C.763 B.S. L.1148 J.D. [A.M.Brucker]
*PRACTICE AREAS: Employee Benefits Law.

**Brucker, Alex M., A Law Corporation, (AV) ⒷⒷ**
**10880 Wilshire Boulevard, Suite 2210, 90024**
Telephone: 310-475-7540 Fax: 310-470-4806
URL: http://www.pensionlawyers.com
Alex M. Brucker;—Linda Russano Morra; Michael L. Cotter; Scott E. Hiltunen.
Taxation, ERISA, Employee Benefits, Qualified Pension and Profit Sharing Plans and Non-qualified Deferred Compensation Plans.
*See Professional Biographies, LOS ANGELES, CALIFORNIA*

**Bruder, Walter F., Jr.** ....................'33 '60 C.684 B.A. L.1068 LL.B. [Manning,L.B.&B.] ‡
**Brueggemann, James R.**, (AV) '46 '75
C.112 B.S. L.1068 J.D. [Sheppard,M.R.&H.] (Pat.)
*PRACTICE AREAS: Patents; Trademarks; Copyrights; Unfair Competition.
**Brugge, Robert D.** ....................'54 '80 C.426 B.A. L.809 J.D. [Spray,G.&B.]
**Bruguera, S. Paul** ....................'56 '81 C.154 B.A. L.426 J.D. [Ⓐ T.J.Feeley]
*PRACTICE AREAS: Eminent Domain; Environmental Law; Civil Rights; Public Law; General Litigation.
**Bruinsma, Tim C.**, (AV) ....................'47 '74 C.154 B.A. L.426 J.D. [Fulbright&J.]
*PRACTICE AREAS: Corporate Law; Mergers and Acquisitions; International Law.
**Brull, Richard P.** ....................'58 '87 C.264 B.A. L.273 J.D. [Brull&P.]
*PRACTICE AREAS: Entertainment; New Media; Intellectual Property; Litigation; Technology.

**Brull & Piccionelli**
**1901 Avenue of the Stars, Twentieth Floor, 90067**
Telephone: 310-553-3375 Facsimile: 310-553-4120
Richard P. Brull; Gregory A. Piccionelli.
Entertainment, New Media, Intellectual Property including Patent, Copyright, Trademark and Trade Secret Protection, Telecommunications, Technology Licensing and Protection, Biotechnology and Litigation Practice in State and Federal Courts.

Brumder, George A. ....................'37 '62 C.813 B.A. L.309 LL.B. 801 S. Figueroa St.
Brumer, Herbert S., (AV) ....................'26 '55 C.112 B.S. L.809 LL.B. 3600 Wilshire Blvd.
**Brunel, André J.** ....................'63 '90 C.276 B.A. L.846 J.D. [Ⓐ Irell&M.]
*LANGUAGES: German.

**Brunell, Norman E., (BV) '46 '73 C.971 B.S.E.E. L.818 J.D.**
**2049 Century Park East, Suite 1080, 90067-3112**
Telephone: 310-553-0100 Fax: 310-553-1452
Email: nbrunell@netcom.com
*PRACTICE AREAS: Patent and Trademark Law (Computer and Software).
Practice limited to Patent and Trademark Law, specializing in preparation of Domestic and International Patent and Trademark Applications, Novelty, Infringement and Validity Searches, Studies and Opinions and Domestic and International Licensing Business Negotiations.
Representative Clients: Litton Industries; California Institute of Technology; Jet Propulsion Laboratory (JPL); NASA; Northrop Corp.; Hughes Aircraft Corp.; Hewlett Packard Co.; Applied Materials, Inc.; Western Atlas Int'l., Inc.
*See Professional Biographies, LOS ANGELES, CALIFORNIA*

**Brunet, Craig W.** ....................'56 '83 C.426 B.S. L.464 J.D. [Ⓐ Robie&M.]
*PRACTICE AREAS: Insurance Coverage; Construction Defect.
**Brunette, Richard W., Jr.**, (AV) ....................'53 '78 C.966 B.A. L.228 J.D. [Sheppard,M.R.&H.]
*PRACTICE AREAS: Bankruptcy Law; Commercial Law; Creditors Rights Law.
Bruni, A. Victor ....................'54 '80 C.674 A.B. L.813 J.D. 333 S. Grand Ave.

CAA193P

**Bruno, Toni Rae**, (AV) .............. '44 '70 C.1097 B.A. L.800 J.D. [Dwyer,D.B.&B.]
*SPECIAL AGENCIES: Los Angeles County Superior Court Panel of Arbitrators and Mediators, 1974—
*REPORTED CASES: Eisen v. Carlisle & Jacquelin, et al. 417 U.S. 156; Mireles v. Waco 502 U.S. 9; Bermudez v. Municipal Court 1 Cal.4th 855; Secrest Machine Corp. v. Superior Court 33 Cal.3d 664; Purdy v. Pacific Auto Ins. Co. 157 Cal.App.3d 59.
*PRACTICE AREAS: Litigation; Appellate Practice; Construction Law; Contracts; Insurance.

Brunon, Bradley W., (AV) '42 '69 C.1042 B.A. L.1068 J.D. 12100 Wilshire Blvd., 15th Fl.
Brunson, Lyle E. ........................ '46 '83 C.1109 B.A. L.1137 J.D. 11340 Olympic
Brunsten, Donald J. ...................... '54 '79 C&L.813 A.B., J.D. 622 Midvale Ave.
**Brunsten, William S., (P.C.)** ............ '47 '74 C.112 B.A. L.1068 J.D. [Manatt,P.&P.]
*PRACTICE AREAS: Financial Services; Real Estate.

**Brunswick, Alan M.**, (AV) ............... '47 '72 C.260 B.A. L.276 J.D. [Manatt,P.&P.]
*PRACTICE AREAS: Labor and Employment; Motion Pictures and Television.

Brunwin, Christopher M. '62 '92 C.112 B.A. L.1066 J.D. 300 S. Grand Ave., Suite 3000
Brustin, Arnold B. '42 '67 C&L.966 B.S., J.D. (adm. in WI; not adm. in CA) 601 N. Saltair St.‡
**Brutocao, Scott A.** .............. '69 '94 C.602 B.A. L.1068 J.D. [A Sheppard,M.R.&H.]
**Brya, Lara Michelle** ................ '69 '95 C.770 B.S. L.800 J.D. [A Black C.H.&L.]
Bryan, Christopher ...................... '67 '93 C.800 B.S. L.893 J.D. 633 W. Fifth St.
**Bryan, Douglas L.** ............... '60 '91 C.1074 B.S. L.809 J.D. [Arnberger,K.B.&C.]
*PRACTICE AREAS: Tax Law; Corporate Law; Corporate Reorganizations; Constitutional Law; Insurance.

**Bryan, Geoffrey L.** ....................... '52 '80 C.119 B.S. L.813 J.D. [Akre,B.&C.]
*LANGUAGES: French.
*REPORTED CASES: Ziello v. Superior Court (First Fed'l Bank) (1995) 36 Cal. App. 4th 321, 42 Cal. Reptr. 2d 251.
*PRACTICE AREAS: Commercial Litigation; Appellate; Employment Law; Trade Secrets; Intellectual Property.

**Bryan, Greyson Lee** ................. '49 '76 C.813 B.A. L.309 J.D. [O'Melveny&M.]
*LANGUAGES: French and Japanese.
*PRACTICE AREAS: International Business Transactions; International Trade; General Corporate Law.

**Bryan, James S.**, (AV) ..................... '44 '72 C.309 A.B. L.659 J.D. [Arter&H.]
*PRACTICE AREAS: Labor and Employment Law; Civil Litigation.

**Bryan, Karen Smith** ..................... '50 '79 C.104 A.B. L.800 J.D. [Latham&W.]

**Bryan Cave LLP, (AV)**
**A Partnership including a Professional Corporation**
**777 South Figueroa Street Suite 2700, 90017-5418⊙**
**Telephone: (213) 243-4300 Facsimile: (213) 243-4343 For attorney e-mails use: First initial, last name, firm name, e.g., rsmith@bryancavellp.com**
**Partners: John W. Amberg; Gerald E. Boltz (Resident, Santa Monica, California Office); Howard O. Boltz, Jr.; Robert E. Boone III; Ronald W. Buckly (Resident, Santa Monica, California Office); William I. Chertok (Resident, Santa Monica, California Office); Bonita L. Churney (Resident, Santa Monica, California Office); Stephen J. Densmore (Resident, Santa Monica, California Office); Curt M. Dombek; David I. Gindler; Lawrence H. Heller (Certified Specialist, Taxation Law, The State Bar of California Board of Legal Specialization) (Resident, Santa Monica, California Office); Bruce L. Ishimatsu; Norman H. Lane (Resident, Santa Monica, California Office); Thomas S. Loo (Resident, Santa Monica, California Office); M. Sean McMillan (A Professional Corporation) (Resident, Santa Monica, California Office); Agatha M. Melamed; Frank E. Merideth, Jr. (Resident, Santa Monica, California Office); Grace N. Mitsuhata (Resident, Santa Monica, California Office); Jeffrey W. Morof; Angelo A. Paparelli; Jon A. Pfeiffer (Resident, Santa Monica, California Office); Catherine F. Ratcliffe (Resident, Santa Monica, California Office); Pamela M. Soderbeck (Resident, Santa Monica, California Office); Harry R. Stang; Lynn K. Thompson; Robert D. Vogel; Barrye L. Wall (Resident, Santa Monica, California Office). Of Counsel: Donald K. Garner (Resident, Santa Monica, California Office); Hugh T. Scogin, Jr. (Not admitted in CA; Resident, Santa Monica, California Office). Counsel: Katherine Fleming Ashton (Resident, Santa Monica, California Office); Elizabeth A. King (Resident, Santa Monica, California Office); Kenneth G. Petrulis (Resident, Santa Monica, California Office). Associates: Michelle D. Boydston (Resident, Santa Monica, California Office); Pamela C. Calvet; Christopher L. Dueringer (Resident, Santa Monica, California Office); Thomas N. Fitzgibbon (Resident, Santa Monica, California Office); Andrew H. Friedman; Claire M. Goldbloom (Resident, Santa Monica, California Office); Catherine L. Haight (Resident, Santa Monica, California Office); Leslie L. Hecht Helmer; Kevin A. Kyle (Resident, Santa Monica, California Office); Maureen M. Muranaka (Resident, Santa Monica, California Office); Richard C. Ochoa (Resident, Santa Monica, California Office); Julie E. Patterson; Tracey A. Quinn; Michael W. Souveroff; Michael D. Stein; Adam J. Thurston; Christine M. Torre; Robert E. Wynner (Resident, Santa Monica, California Office); Karen D. Yardley (Resident, Santa Monica, California Office); Lesley D. Young.**
**Administrative and General Civil Practice. Antitrust, Aviation, Banking, Computer, Corporate Financing, Corporation, Estate Planning, Government Contracts, International, Labor, Probate, Products Liability, Real Estate, Securities, Taxation, Technology, Transportation, Trust and University Law. General Civil Trial and Appellate Practice.**
**St. Louis, Missouri Office: One Metropolitan Square, 211 North Broadway, Suite 3600, 63102-2750. Telephone: (314) 259-2000. Facsimile: (314) 259-2020.**
**Washington, D.C. Office: 700 Thirteenth Street, N.W., 20005-3960. Telephone: (202) 508-6000. Facsimile: (202) 508-6200.**
**New York, N.Y. Office: 245 Park Avenue, 10167-0034. Telephone: (212) 692-1800. Facsimile: (212) 692-1900.**
**Kansas City, Missouri Office: 3500 One Kansas City Place, 1200 Main Street, 64141-6914. Telephone: (816) 374-3200. Facsimile: (816) 374-3300.**
**Overland Park, Kansas Office: 7500 College Boulevard, Suite 1100, 66210-4035. Telephone: (913) 338-7700. Facsimile: (913) 338-7777.**
**Phoenix, Arizona Office: 2800 North Central Avenue, Twenty-First Floor, 85004-1098. Telephone: (602) 230-7000. Facsimile: (602) 266-5938.**
**Santa Monica, California Office: 120 Broadway, Suite 500, 90401-2305. Telephone: (310) 576-2100. Facsimile: (310) 576-2200.**
**Irvine, California Office: 18881 Von Karman, Suite 1500, 92715-1500. Telephone: (714) 223-7000. Facsimile: (714) 223-7100.**
**London, SW1H 9BU England Office: 29 Queen Anne's Gate. Telephone: 171-896-1900. Facsimile: 171-896-1919.**
**Riyadh 11465 Saudi Arabia Office: In Cooperation with Kadasah Law Firm, P.O. Box 20883. Telephone: 966-1-474-0888. Facsimile: 966-1-476-2881.**
**Kuwait City, Kuwait Office: Mashora Advocates & Legal Consultants, Sheraton Towers, Second Floor, P.O. Box 5902 Safat, 13060. Telephone: 965-240-4470/240-6000. Facsimile: 965-245-9000.**
**Dubai, U.A.E. Office: Al-Mehairi Legal Consultants - Bryan Cave LLP, Dubai, Holiday Centre, Commercial Tower, Suite 1103, P.O. Box 13677, UAE. Telephone: 971-4-1-314-123. Facsimile: 971-4-318-287.**
**Abu Dhabi, U.A.E. Office: Al-Mehairi Legal Consultants - Bryan Cave LLP, Abu Dhabi, Dhabi Tower, Suite 304, P.O. Box 47645. Telephone: 971-2-260-335. Facsimile: 971-2-260-332.**
**Hong Kong Office: Suite 2106, Lippo Tower, 21/F, Lippo Centre, 89 Queensway. Telephone: 852-2522-2821. Facsimile: 852-2522-3830.**
**Shanghai, People's Republic of China Associated Office: 100 Fu Xing Xi Lu, 3C, 200031. Telephone: 86-21-6466-3845. Facsimile: 86-21-6466-4280.**

*See Professional Biographies, LOS ANGELES, CALIFORNIA*

**Bryant, Michael P.** ........... '67 '94 C.112 B.A. L.464 J.D. [A Breidenbach,B.H.H.&H.]
Bryant-Kambe, Madeleine .................. '50 '79 C&L.1136 B.S.L., J.D. 900 Wilshire
**Bubb, Brian D.** ........................... '62 '88 C.21 B.S. L.990 J.D. [Howarth&S.]
**Bubman, Michael E.** .................. '62 '89 C.112 B.A. L.426 J.D. [Horgan,R.B.&C.]
*PRACTICE AREAS: Business; Banking; Real Property Litigation.

**Buch, Robert E.**, (AV) ............... '46 '74 C.800 B.A. L.426 J.D. [Seyfarth,S.F.&G.]
*PRACTICE AREAS: Workers' Compensation.

Buchalter, Irwin R., (AV) ................... '10 '33 C.494 L.809 J.D. 601 S. Figueroa St.
**Buchalter, Stuart D.**, (AV) ...... '37 '63 C.112 B.A. L.309 LL.B. [C Buchalter,N.F.&Y.]
*PRACTICE AREAS: Banking; Corporate; Finance.

**Buchalter, Nemer, Fields & Younger, A Professional Corporation, (AV)**
**24th Floor, 601 South Figueroa Street, 90017⊙**
**Telephone: 213-891-0700 Fax: 213-896-0400**
**Email: buchalter@earthlink.net URL: http://www.buchalter.com**
**Murray M. Fields; Richard Jay Goldstein; Michael L. Wachtell; Robert C. Colton; Gary A. York; Arthur Chinski; Jay R. Ziegler; Michael J. Cereseto; Bernard E. Le Sage; Gregory Keever; Roger D. Loomis, Jr.; Philip J. Wolman (Certified Specialist, Taxation Law, The State Bar of California Board of Legal Specialization); Keith B. Bardellini; Mark A. Bonenfant; David S. Kyman; James H. Turken; Kevin M. Brandt; Jeffrey S. Wruble; Randye B. Soref; Pamela Kohlman Webster; Matthew W. Kavanaugh; Richard S. Angel; Bryan Mashian; Robert J. Davidson; Bernard D. Bollinger, Jr. Of Counsel: Ronald E. Gordon; Stuart D. Buchalter; Barry A. Smith; Geoffrey Forsythe Bogeaus; Scott O. Smith; Holly J. Fujie; Elizabeth S. Trussell; Harriet M. Welch; William Mark Levinson; Harriet B. Alexson; Barry F. Soosman;—Janis S. Penton; Jerry A. Hager; Jonathan D. Fink; Julie A. Goren; Glenn L. Savard; Paul S. Arrow; William S. Brody; Amy L. Rubinfeld; Dean Stackel; Abraham J. Colman; Monika L. McCarthy; Mary LePique Dickson; Shirley Sheau-Lih Lu; Robert A. Willner; Adam Joel Bass; David L. Aronoff; Kim Allman; William P. Fong; Helen Goldberger Palmer; Brett Michael Broderick; Robert Alexander Pilmer; Kirk H. Sharpe; Nicolas M. Kublicki; Vincent I.S. Hsieh (Not admitted in CA); Simone Margaret Bennett; Christina M. Carlson; Rachael H. Berman; Daniel Joseph Kolodziej; Elizabeth H. Murphy; Lance R. Dixon; Allan R. Mouw; Daniel C. Wong.**
**References: City National Bank; Wells Fargo Bank; Metrobank.**
**New York, New York Office: 15th Floor, 605 Third Avenue. Telephone: 212-490-8600. Fax: 212-490-6022.**
**San Francisco, California Office: 29th Floor, 333 Market Street. Telephone: 415-227-0900. Fax: 415-227-0770.**
**Newport Beach, California Office: Suite 1450, 620 Newport Center Drive. Telephone: 714-760-1121. Fax: 714-720-0182.**

*See Professional Biographies, LOS ANGELES, CALIFORNIA*

**Buchanan, Brian F.** ..................... '52 '79 C.154 B.A. L.174 J.D. [Buchanan&K.]
*PRACTICE AREAS: Civil Litigation.

Buchanan, George G. ...................... '21 '59 C.339 L.426 LL.B. Asst. City Atty.
**Buchanan, John D.** ................... '58 '85 C.1075 B.A. L.1065 J.D. [A Lord,B.&B.]
Buchanan, Laura L. .................. '65 '91 C.813 B.S.E.E. L.1066 J.D. Alesis Corp.
**Buchanan, Michele A.** ............. '63 '92 C.966 B.A. L.1136 J.D. [A B.P.Wolfsdorf]
*LANGUAGES: Mandarin Chinese.
*PRACTICE AREAS: Immigration and Naturalization.

**Buchanan & Kindem, (AV)**
**420 Boyd Street, Suite 400, 90013**
**Telephone: 213-625-2974 Fax: 213-625-2668**
**Members of Firm: Brian F. Buchanan; Peter R. Dion-Kindem. Of Counsel: Lawrence W. Chamblee. General Civil Trial and Appellate Practice in all State and Federal Courts and Administrative Agencies with emphasis on Litigation. General Business and Commercial Litigation, Securities, Unfair Competition, Real Estate, Construction, Copyright, Trademark, Trade Secrets, Intellectual Property, Computer Law, Tort Litigation, Insurance, Employment Litigation, Probate and Family Law.**

*See Professional Biographies, LOS ANGELES, CALIFORNIA*

Buchberg, Carl G. ................. '50 '78 C.1077 B.A. L.1095 J.D. 6300 Wilshire Blvd.
**Buchen, Katarzyna A.** '66 '95 C.518 B.A. L.178 J.D. (adm. in NY; not adm. in CA) [A Jones,D.R.&P.]
**Bucher, James B.** ...................... '65 '91 C.165 B.A. L.245 J.D. [A Shearman&S.]
**Buchignani, Antony E.** ............... '71 '96 C.740 B.A. L.1065 J.D. [A Troop M.S.&P.]
*PRACTICE AREAS: Litigation; Insurance Coverage.

**Buchman, Joseph P.** .................. '63 '90 C.112 B.A. L.426 J.D. [A Burke,W.&S.]
*PRACTICE AREAS: Bankruptcy/Litigation; Debtor/Creditor/Trustee; Creditors' Rights; Real Property Transactions; Litigation.

Buck, Thomas K., (AV) ................. '49 '76 C.813 B.A. L.1065 J.D. Asst. U.S. Atty.
**Buckley, Brian L.** ................... '54 '80 C.197 A.B. L.945 J.D. [Gansinger,H.B.&P.]
*REPORTED CASES: Securities and Exchange Commission v. American Principals Holding, Inc., 817 F.2d 1349 (9th cir, 1987).
*PRACTICE AREAS: Complex Commercial Litigation; Unfair Competition.

**Buckley, Daniel J.**, (AV) ......... '55 '80 C&L.602 B.A., J.D. [Breidenbach,B.H.H.&H.]
*PRACTICE AREAS: Environmental Law; Government Tort Liability; Insurance Agents and Brokers Errors and Omissions; Casualty Defense; Civil Litigation.

Buckley-Weber, Illece Hillary ............ '57 '87 C&L.208 B.A., J.D. [A Rosner,O.&N.]
Bucklin, Stephen L. .................... '56 '85 C&L.911 B.A., J.D. [A Countryman&M.]
**Buckner, Richard W.** ............... '54 '82 C.1209 B.S. L.800 J.D. [C O'Melveny&M.]
*PRACTICE AREAS: Insurance Litigation; Business Law.

**Bucksbaum, Deborah S.** .............. '54 '83 C.112 B.A. L.276 J.D. [Bucksbaum&S.]
*PRACTICE AREAS: Business Litigation; Real Estate Litigation; Intellectual Property Litigation.

**Bucksbaum & Sasaki, A Professional Corporation**
**1900 Avenue of the Stars, Suite 1800, 90067**
**Telephone: 310-286-3396**
**Deborah S. Bucksbaum; Judith M. Sasaki;—W. Clark Brown; Kathleen M. Wood.**
**General Business Litigation, including Real Estate, Business Fraud, Financial Institution, Intellectual Property and Unfair Competition Litigation.**

*See Professional Biographies, LOS ANGELES, CALIFORNIA*

**Budare, Justin E.** .................... '59 '84 C.477 A.B. L.1068 J.D. [Marcus,W.S.&D.]
**Budd, Paige E.** ................... '67 '93 C&L.945 B.A., J.D. [A Parker,M.C.O.&S.]
*REPORTED CASES: Bill-Rea v. National Fin. Serv., 860 F. Supp. 1181 (WD. TX. 1994).
*PRACTICE AREAS: Litigation; General Transactional/Contract (in area of Telecommunications).

Budde, Alan F. ........................ '47 '73 C.112 A.B. L.1065 J.D. Dep. Pub. Def.
Budman, Robert L. ............................ '44 '77 C.800 L.809 J.D. Dep. Dist. Atty.
**Bue, Kara L.** ......................... '64 '93 C.103 A.B. L.426 J.D. [A Brobeck,P.&H.]
**Buehler, George W.**, (AV) ................ '48 '74 C.605 B.A. L.800 J.D. [Howrey&S.]
*PRACTICE AREAS: Complex Commercial and Business Litigation; Directors and Officers Liability; White Collar Criminal Defense.

Bueno, Antonio G. ........................ '34 '60 C.112 A.B. L.1065 J.D. [Bueno&D.]
Bueno & Dresselhaus ...................................... 853 W. Washington Blvd.
Bufford, Samuel ...................... '43 '75 C.937 B.A. L.477 J.D. U.S. Bkrptcy. J.
Bufford, Takashi A. '52 '79 C.329 B.A. L.1068 J.D. (adm. in DC; not adm. in CA) 1942 Grace Ave.‡
**Bui, Marguerite L.** ...................... '66 '91 C.813 A.B. L.1066 J.D. [A Loeb&L.]
*LANGUAGES: French, Vietnamese.

**Bullock, Victor A.** .................. '68 '94 C.112 B.A. L.1065 [A Sedgwick,D.M.&A.]
**Bunch, Gregory Reyna** .......... '52 '90 C.112 B.S. L.1148 J.D. [A Bonne,B.M.O.&N.]
**Bunger, Brian C.** .................. '63 '89 C.112 B.A. L.1065 J.D. [A Folger L.&K.]⊙
Bunn, Gerrie Morgan .................. '50 '81 C.112 B.A. L.426 J.D. State Ct. of App.
**Bunnell, Susan E.** ................ '66 '94 C.112 B.A. L.1068 J.D. [A Neff&Assoc.]⊙
*LANGUAGES: Spanish.
*PRACTICE AREAS: Computers and Software; Licensing; International Law; Copyright; Intellectual Property.

**Burbach, Stephen D.** ........... '59 '94 C.1165 B.S.E.E. L.112 J.D. [A Darby&D.] (Pat.)
*PRACTICE AREAS: Patent Law; Trademark Law.

Burby, William E., Jr. ..................... '29 '58 C.800 B.S. L.1068 LL.B. Supr. Ct. J.
**Burch, Carleton R.** ................. '61 '87 C.170 B.A. L.1065 J.D. [Anderson,M.&C.]
*LANGUAGES: Japanese and Spanish.
*PRACTICE AREAS: Commercial Law; Business Litigation; Fidelity and Insurance Coverage Matters.

**Burch, Cynthia L.** ...................... '52 '79 C.378 B.A. L.900 J.D. [Munger,T.&O.]
*PRACTICE AREAS: Environmental.

Burch, David R. '50 '75 C&L.420 B.A., J.D. (adm. in LA; not adm. in CA) Asst. Dir., USC Law Ctr.
Burch, Dorothy N. .........'— '80 C.835 B.S. L.426 J.D. Sr. Jud. Atty., Calif. Ct. of App.

## PRACTICE PROFILES

## CALIFORNIA—LOS ANGELES

**Burch, Robert D.**, (AV) ..............'28 '54 C.112 B.S. L.1066 LL.B. [G Gibson,D.&C.]
*PRACTICE AREAS: Trusts and Estates; Tax Law.
**Burch, W. Jeffrey** ...............'64 '91 C.172 B.A. L.1065 J.D. [A Monteleone&M.]
*PRACTICE AREAS: General Business Litigation; Construction; Construction Defect.
Burchette, Anastasia ............'59 '82 C&L.800 B.S., J.D. 4050 Buckingham Rd.
**Burdett, Joseph W.**, (AV) ........'36 '66 C.98 B.S. L.813 J.D. [G Heller E.W.&M.]
*PRACTICE AREAS: Federal and State Income Taxation; Tax Controversies.
**Burdge, Richard J., Jr.**, (AV) ........'49 '79 C.976 B.S. L.1068 J.D. [Dewey B.]
*PRACTICE AREAS: Litigation.
Burdick, Mary S. ......'47 '73 C.608 B.A. L.893 J.D. Western Ctr. on Law & Poverty, Inc.
**Burdick-Bell, Christine** ...'54 '79 C.112 B.S. L.813 J.D. [G Christensen,M.F.J.G.W.&S.]
*PRACTICE AREAS: Corporate.
**Bures, Matthew Clark** .............'61 '89 C.112 B.S.A.L. L.188 J.D. [A Loeb&L.]
*PRACTICE AREAS: Litigation.
**Burg, David L.** ..........'57 '87 C.112 B.A. L.1066 J.D. [G Goldberg&S.] (⊙Walnut Creek)
*PRACTICE AREAS: Commercial Litigation; Entertainment Litigation; Real Estate Litigation.

**Burg, Leslie C. '28 '55 C.112 B.S. L.426 LL.B.**
**4929 Wilshire Boulevard, Suite 410, 90010**
Telephone: 213-653-8222 Fax: 213-937-0958
Worker's Compensation Plaintiff and Probate.

Burg, Louis ................'21 '57 C.563 B.B.A. L.1009 LL.B. 2316 Nottingham Ave.‡
Burg, Philip A. ........................'11 '47 L.809 LL.B. [Burg&F.]
Burg & Farnham .....................................6630 Whitley Ter.
Burg & Silverman, Law Corp. .............................3580 Wilshire Blvd.
Burger, Barry John ..........'42 '74 C.273 B.A. L.800 J.D. 4700 Wilshire Blvd.
Burger, David P. ...............'59 '85 C.813 B.A. L.770 J.D. 1200 Wilshire Blvd.
**Burger, Ernest P.**, (BV) ..........'47 '73 C.426 B.S. L.1068 J.D. [G Sonnenschein N.&R.]
*LANGUAGES: German.
*PRACTICE AREAS: Corporate Law; Real Estate Transactions; Acquisition Law; Leasing Law; Construction Law.
Burgess, Holly S. .............'55 '82 C.628 B.S. L.765 J.D. 16133 Ventura Blvd., 7th Fl.
**Burgess, James M.** ............'62 '90 C.154 B.A. L.800 J.D. [A Sheppard,M.R.&H.]
*PRACTICE AREAS: Commercial Litigation; Insurance Litigation; Banking Litigation.
**Burgin, Stephen M.** .............'43 '70 C.112 B.A. L.1068 J.D. [G Latham&W.]
*PRACTICE AREAS: Trusts and Estates.
Burgos, Edwin A. .............'65 '91 C.951 B.A. L.1066 J.D. 1000 Wilshire Blvd.
Burgos, Olivia A. ..............'68 '94 C.112 B.A. L.1068 J.D. [A Posner&R.]
**Burhenn, David W.** ..............'53 '82 C&L.477 A.B., J.D. [Sidley&A.]
*PRACTICE AREAS: Environmental Law.
Burik, Michael A. ......'61 '88 C.145 B.A. L.1068 J.D. Sr. Coun., The Capital Grp., Inc.
Burk, Robert M ...........'41 '67 C.112 B.S. L.1068 LL.B. 611 Woodruff Ave.
Burk, Walter E. ......'—' '81 C.791 B.A. L.1127 J.D. Calif. Assn. of Realtors
**Burkdall, Lisa M.** .............'60 '75 C.112 B.A. L.1065 J.D. [A Musick,P.&G.]
Burke, Barbara A. ............'43 '70 C.112 B.A. L.770 J.D. Wkrs. Comp. J.
Burke, Constance M. '44 '82 C.524 B.A. L.1009 J.D.
(adm. in NY; not adm. in CA) [G Arnberger,K.B.&C.]⊙
*PRACTICE AREAS: Trial and Appellate Litigation in all Courts.
**Burke, Dennis P.**, (AV) ...........'42 '68 C&L.426 B.A., J.D. [Burke,W.&S.]
*PRACTICE AREAS: Corporate Law; Real Estate Law; Bankruptcy Law.
Burke, Jean F ............'59 '87 C.1097 B.S. L.940 J.D. Dep. Pub. Def. II
Burke, Kathleen J. '51 '77 C.906 B.A. L.276 J.D.
Exec. V.P. & Dir., Human Res., Security Pacific Corp.
**Burke, Martin J.**, (AV) ..........'03 '27 C&L.426 Ph.B., LL.B. [Burke,W.&S.] ‡
*PRACTICE AREAS: Business Law; Reorganizations Law; Commercial Law.
**Burke, Martin L.**, (AV) ...........'36 '62 C&L.426 B.S., LL.B. [Burke,W.&S.]
*PRACTICE AREAS: Corporate Law; Aviation Law; Education Law.
**Burke, Mary Courtney** ..............'63 '92 C.813 B.A. L.276 J.D. [A Mitchell,S.&K.]
*PRACTICE AREAS: Employment Law; Labor Law.
**Burke, Matthew F.** ..............'66 '93 C.174 B.A. L.1065 J.D. [A Troop M.S.&P.]
*PRACTICE AREAS: General Corporate; Securities; Mergers and Acquisitions.
**Burke, Paul W.** .............'59 '88 C.426 B.A. L.809 J.D. [A Tharpe&H.]
Burke, Peter A. ..................'55 '83 C.918 B.A. L.1162 J.D. SEC
Burke, Robert B., (AV) ........'42 '72 C.112 B.A. L.1068 J.D. 277 S. Irving Blvd.
**Burke, Siobhan McBreen** ...........'58 '83 C.788 A.B. L.339 J.D. [Paul,H.J.&W.]
**Burke, Thomas P.**, (AV) ...........'38 '66 C.426 B.S. L.1068 J.D. [Brobeck,P.&H.]

**Burke, Williams & Sorensen,** (AV)
A Partnership including a Professional Corporation
**611 West Sixth Street, 25th Floor, 90017⊙**
Telephone: 213-236-0600 Telecopiers: 213-236-2760; 236-2800 Telex: 671-1271 Cable Address: 'BWSLA UW'
Email: bws@bwslaw.com URL: http://www.bwslaw.com
Members of Firm: Harry C. Williams (1912-1967); Royal M. Sorensen (1914-1983); James T. Bradshaw, Jr.; Martin L. Burke; Carl K. Newton; J. Robert Flandrick; Edward M. Fox (Certified Specialist, Taxation Law, The State Bar of California Board of Legal Specialization); Dennis P. Burke; Leland C. Dolley (Resident, Orange County Office); Neil F. Yeager; Brian A. Pierik (Resident, Ventura County Office); Charles M. Calderon; Jerry M. Patterson (Resident, Orange County Office); Harold A. Bridges; Cheryl J. Kane; Barry S. Glaser; B. Derek Straatsma; Don G. Kircher (Resident, Ventura County Office); Michele R. Vadon; Mary Redus Gayle (Resident, Ventura County Office); Rufus C. Young, Jr.; Timothy B. McOsker; Thomas C. Wood (Resident, Orange County Office); Thomas W. Allen (Resident, Orange County Office); Steven J. Dawson; Stephen R. Onstot; Mark D. Hensley; John J. Welsh. Associates: Carleton H. Morrison, Jr.; Joseph P. Buchman; Gregory T. Dion; William A. Vallejos; Thomas L. Altmayer; Billy D. Dunsmore; Gregory G. Diaz (Resident, Orange County Office); Kenneth D. Rozell; Deanna L. Ballesteros; Elizabeth M. Calciano; Carol R. Victor; Heather C. Beatty; Elizabeth R. Feffer; Craig S. Gunther; Thomas P. Carter; Susan Geier Mejia; Robert F. Messinger; Anna Park Kang; Joseph M. Montes; Maj-Le R. Tate; Christopher R. Cheleden; Timothy L. Davis; Bryan Cameron LeRoy (Resident, Orange County Office); Nedy A. Williams. Of Counsel: Mark C. Allen, Jr., (Professional Corporation); Katherine F. Aschieris. Retired Partner: Martin J. Burke (Retired).
General Civil and Trial Practice in all State and Federal Courts. Securities, Corporate, Taxation, Insurance and Commercial Law. Municipal and Public Agency Representation. Local Government Financing, Taxation and Assessments. Community Redevelopment, Eminent Domain, Environmental and Land Use Law. Employee Benefit Plans, Probate and Estate Planning. Health Care, Medical Research, College and University and Non-Profit Organization Law, Employment and Personnel Law. Tort, Workers Compensation and Insurance Defense.
Orange County Office: 3200 Park Center Drive, Suite 750, Costa Mesa, California. Telephone: 714-545-5559.
Ventura County Office: 2310 Ponderosa Drive, Suite 1, Camarillo, California. Telephone: 805-987-3468.

See Professional Biographies, LOS ANGELES, CALIFORNIA

Burkenroad, David C. ..............'— '83 C.112 B.A. L.1068 J.D. [Roquemore,P.&M.]
Burkett, Robert L. ....................'45 '72 2828 Dumfries Rd.
**Burkholder, John A.** ..............'49 '78 C.976 B.A. L.30 J.D. [G McKenna&C.]
*PRACTICE AREAS: Administrative Law; Civil Practice; Contract Law; Government Contract Law; Litigation.
Burkholder, Paul C. ..'55 '82 C&L.966 B.A., J.D. Sr. Coun., Northrop Grumman Corp.
**Burkley, Walter R., III** ............'66 '96 C.197 A.B. L.880 J.D. [A O'Melveny&M.]

**Burkley, Greenberg, Fields & Whitcombe, L.L.P.**
(See Torrance)

**Burkow, Steven H.** ............'55 '78 C.668 A.B. L.1068 J.D. [Ziffren,B.B.&F.]
*PRACTICE AREAS: Entertainment Law.

**Burks, Sylvia K.** ...............'56 '84 C.999 B.A. L.846 J.D. [A Coudert]
*LANGUAGES: German.
*PRACTICE AREAS: Corporate; International Transaction.
**Burleigh, Paul H.** ..........'56 '83 C.1077 B.A. L.990 J.D. [A Wright,R.O.&T.]
*PRACTICE AREAS: Products Liability Law; Toxic Torts; Insurance Defense Law; Personal Injury Law; Wrongful Death Litigation.
Burman, David B. ..........'58 '83 C.174 B.S. L.426 J.D. 1801 Century Park E.
Burman, Jennifer M. ...............'64 '89 C.770 B.A. L.602 J.D. 515 S. Flower St.
Burner, Susan L., (P.C.) ......'50 '76 C.112 B.A. L.1068 J.D. 12301 Wilshire Blvd. Ste. 600
Burnett, Marvin A., (AV) .............'12 '35 C.813 B.A. L.309 J.D. 4201 Wilshire Blvd.
**Burney, Carol B.** ............'62 '87 C.696 B.A. L.426 J.D. [A Meserve,M.&R.]
Burnison, Chantal S. .......................'56 '81 P.O. Box 66910
**Burnovski, Ron** ...............'69 '94 C.1349 B.A. L.112 J.D. [A Brown R.M.F.&S.]
*PRACTICE AREAS: Litigation; Insurance Defense; Bad Faith; Product Liability.
**Burns, Cara R.** ..................'63 '88 C.1036 B.A. L.94 J.D. [Manatt,P.&P.]
*PRACTICE AREAS: Entertainment; Intellectual Property.
**Burns, Donald E.**, (AV) ..........'38 '65 C.276 A.B. L.976 LL.B. [Burns&G.]
*PRACTICE AREAS: Financial Institutions; Public Finance; Real Estate.
Burns, Frank J., (AV) ................'27 '54 C.112 B.A. L.800 J.D. 532 N. McCadden Pl.‡
**Burns, Hugh R.** ..............'62 '90 C.101 B.A. L.809 J.D. [A La Follette,J.D.F.&A.]
*LANGUAGES: Spanish.
*PRACTICE AREAS: General Liability; Medical Malpractice.
**Burns, Marvin G.**, (Professional Corporation), (AV) '30 '55
C.37 B.A. L.309 J.D. [G Resch P.A.&B.]
*PRACTICE AREAS: Land Use Law; Entertainment Litigation; Business Litigation; Real Estate Litigation.
**Burns, Melissa L.** ............'66 '92 C.788 B.A. L.112 J.D. [A McCambridge,D.&M.]
Burns, Rita ............'46 '92 L.1136 J.D. 1800 Ave. of the Stars, Suite 900 (Century City)
**Burns, Shannon H.** ............'52 '86 C.112 B.A. L.1148 J.D. [A P.L.Stanton]
*PRACTICE AREAS: Estate Planning; Fiduciary Litigation.

**Burns, Ammirato, Palumbo, Milam & Baronian, A Professional Law Corporation**
(See Pasadena)

**Burns & Goldstone, P.C.,** (AV)
**1900 Avenue of the Stars, Suite 2700, 90067-4301**
Telephone: 310-553-1900 Telecopier: 310-553-4207
Donald E. Burns; Hilary F. Goldstone.
General Business, Commercial and Corporate Law. Financial Institutions Law, Public Finance, International Business Transactions, Real Estate, Business and Civil Litigation. Administrative, Trade Association. Fiduciary Law and Public Pension Fund Law.
Reference: Union Bank.

See Professional Biographies, LOS ANGELES, CALIFORNIA

**Burraston, Kenneth N.** ...............'63 '95 C.101 B.A. L.273 J.D. [A Graham&J.]
Burrill, Janice H. ..........'57 '82 C&L.426 B.S., J.D. V.P. & Mgr., Wells Fargo Bk.
**Burrow, Joseph A.** ...............'37 '73 C.112 B.A. L.426 J.D. [Booth,M.&S.]
**Burrows, Christopher A.** ..........'58 '83 C.668 B.A. L.426 J.D. [Whitman B.A.&M.]
*PRACTICE AREAS: Labor and Employment Law.
**Burrus, Eugene A.** ......'64 '91 C.623 B.S.A.E. L.893 J.D. [G McClintock,W.B.R.R.&M.]
*PRACTICE AREAS: Commercial and Business Litigation; Franchise Litigation; Antitrust; Environmental Litigation.
Burrus, Karen L. ....................'65 '93 C.112 B.A. L.1066 J.D. 555 W. 5th st
**Burry, Kenneth L.** ............'66 '93 C.477 B.A. L.30 J.D. [A Troop M.S.&P.]
*PRACTICE AREAS: Entertainment and Business Litigation.
Burstein, Laurie E. ...............'61 '91 C.112 B.A. L.426 J.D. Paramount Pictures Corp.
Burstein, Mark ...............'48 '73 C&L.966 B.A., J.D. P.O. Box 34324
Burstein, Richard D. ........'48 '73 C.112 A.B. L.1066 J.D. 11355 W. Olympic Blvd.
**Burt, Chris** ..................'70 '95 C&L.145 A.B., J.D. [A Latham&W.]
**Burt, Jeffrey C.** ...............'59 '86 C.112 B.A. L.770 J.D. [Wilson,K.&B.]
*REPORTED CASES: Montrose Chemical vs. Superior Court (1993) 6 Cal 4th 287; Montrose Chemical vs. Admiral Insurance (1995) 10 Cal 4th 645.
*PRACTICE AREAS: Insurance Coverage Litigation.
**Burten, Barry L.** ...............'48 '74 C.165 B.A. L.309 J.D. [Jeffer,M.B.&M.]
*PRACTICE AREAS: Corporate; Securities; Bankruptcy.
Burton, Andrew M. ..............'68 '93 C.659 B.S. L.178 J.D. 444 S. Flower St.
**Burton, David A. B., (P.C.)** ............'55 '81 C.31 B.A. L.813 J.D. [Allen,M.L.G.&M.]
*PRACTICE AREAS: Real Estate.
Burton, David E. .................'34 '58 C&L.508 B.A., J.D. [D.E.Burton]
Burton, Elaine Minow ............'32 '82 C.597 B.S. L.426 J.D. 3221 Barry Ave.
Burton, Frank R. ......'50 '89 C.112 B.A. L.1136 J.D. State Comp. Ins. Fund, Staff Coun.
Burton, Grant T. .............'58 '91 L.1136 J.D. Dep. Gen. Coun., Metro. Water Dist.
Burton, Lura L. .............'61 '86 C.923 B.S., J.D. Broadcast Coun., CBS Inc.
**Burton, P. Scott** ..........'66 '94 C.112 B.A. L.1068 J.D. [A McCutchen,D.&E.]
*PRACTICE AREAS: Environmental Law.
Burton, Stephen L. ..........'55 '84 C.112 B.A. L.1148 J.D. 16530 Ventura Blvd. (Encino)
Burton, David E., A Professional Corporation ................11661 San Vincente Blvd.

**Burton & Norris**
(See Pasadena)

**Busch, Carole A.** ..............'64 '91 C.339 B.S. L.910 J.D. [A Tharpe&H.]
*PRACTICE AREAS: Civil Litigation; Insurance Defense; Construction Defects.
**Busch, Jolie L.** '62 '88 C.94 B.A. L.978 J.D.
(adm. in NY; not adm. in CA) [G Schifino&L.]
*PRACTICE AREAS: Securities Litigation; General Civil Litigation.
**Bush, D. Michael**, (BV) ..........'56 '81 C.560 B.A. L.809 J.D. [A Veatch,C.G.&N.]
*PRACTICE AREAS: Insurance Defense; Automobile Claims.
Bush, Joanna R. ............'56 '92 C.1241 B.A. L.398 J.D. 801 S. Grand Ave., 11th Fl.
**Bush, Lawrence A.** ............'31 '60 C.112 B.S. L.1068 J.D. [Harrington,F.D.&C.]
*PRACTICE AREAS: Products Liability Law; Personal Injury Defense Law.
Bushling, Bryant E. ...........'54 '82 C.1042 B.A. L.464 J.D. Dep. Dist. Atty.
**Bushnell, David H.** ............'54 '91 C.976 B.A. L.112 J.D. [A Chapin,F.&W.]

**Bustamante, Andrés Z. '55 '90 C.112 B.A. L.1238 J.D.**
**811 West 7th Street 11th Floor, 90017**
Telephone: 213-891-9009 Fax: 213-627-1655
*LANGUAGES: Spanish.
Criminal Law and Deportation Defense including Juvenile and Adult cases in State and Federal Court as well as Immigration Consequences of a Criminal Conviction both Pre and Post Conviction.

See Professional Biographies, LOS ANGELES, CALIFORNIA

Busterud, Gretchen A. .........'55 '80 C.112 B.A. L.1065 J.D. Coun., Teledyne, Inc.
**Butcher, John F.** .................'49 '83 C.319 B.A. L.365 J.D. [Iwasaki&S.]
*PRACTICE AREAS: Real Estate; General Practice; Family Law.
Buter, Irwin, (AV) ..............'31 '57 C.112 L.426 LL.B. [Spector,B.H.&B.]
Butler, Felicita Therese ..........'50 '82 C.112 B.A. L.426 J.D. [A J.G.Butler]
Butler, James G., (AV) ..............'20 '48 C.749 A.B. L.276 J.D. [J.G.Butler]
**Butler, James R., Jr.**, (AV) .............'46 '69 C.112 B.A. L.1066 J.D. [Jeffer,M.B.&M.]
*PRACTICE AREAS: Hospitality Industry; Real Estate Workouts; Banking and Corporate Finance.
**Butler, Jeffry** ...............'61 '95 C.112 B.A. L.1066 J.D. [Sonnenschein N.&R.]
*PRACTICE AREAS: Litigation; Insurance.
Butler, Joel M. ..........'44 '73 C.1019 B.A. L.1068 J.D. 2049 Century Pk. E.
**Butler, Joseph F.** .........'50 '75 C.112 B.A. L.1049 J.D. [Stephens,B.&L.]
*PRACTICE AREAS: Business Litigation; Employment Litigation; Environmental Litigation; Insurance Litigation.

**Butler, Laurie J., (P.C.)**, (AV) ............'49 '78 C.347 B.A. L.426 J.D. [Tourtelot&B.]
*LANGUAGES: French and Spanish.
*PRACTICE AREAS: State and Federal Court Business Litigation; Defamation; Unfair Competition; Real Estate; Corporate.
Butler, L'Tanya ..............................'66 '92 C.112 B.A. L.976 J.D. 555 W. 5th St.
**Butler, M. Chadwick** ...........'50 '84 C.685 B.A. L.1066 J.D. Sr.Coun., Bank of Amer.
Butler, Marilyn E. ..........................'58 '82 C.112 B.A. L.426 J.D. Dep. Fed. Pub. Def.
Butler, Thomas Sean .............'55 '85 C.477 B.A. L.213 J.D. 11835 W. Olympic Blvd.

**Butler, Douglas**
**(See Torrance)**

Butler, James G., A Professional Corporation, (AV) ...................533 S. Rimpau Blvd.
Buttita, Sandra Lynn ....................'44 '78 C.1131 B.A. L.1068 J.D. Dep. Dist. Atty.
**Butts, Melanie C.** ..................'67 '93 C.112 B.A. L.809 J.D. [A] Bonne,B.M.O.&N.]
*PRACTICE AREAS: Medical Malpractice.
Buzard, Glenn S., (BV) .............................................'49 '74 [Spector,B.H.&B.]
Bycel, Benjamin ........... '42 '75 C.768 B.A. L.1067 J.D. Exce. Dir., City Ethic Comm.
Byer, Timothy G. ..........................'58 '94 C.112 B.A. L.426 J.D. 1990 S. Bundy Dr.
Byers, Torrie M. '— '85 C.425 B.B.A. L.861 J.D.
Claims Coun., Commonwealth Land Title Ins. Co.
**Byrd, Christine W. S.**, (AV) ......................'51 '76 C.813 B.A. L.893 J.D. [Irell&M.]
**Byrne, Jerome C.**, (AV) ..............'25 '52 C.1121 A.B. L.309 J.D. [B] Gibson,D.&C.]
*PRACTICE AREAS: Labor; Employment; Employee Benefits Law.
Byrne, John M. ...........................'65 '92 C.112 B.A. L.602 J.D. 444 S. Flower St.
Byrne, John P. ..............'62 '88 C&L.477 B.A., J.D. 777 S. Figueroa St., 10th Fl.
Byrne, Mark A., (AV) ...... '59 '84 C.1068 B.A. L.602 J.D. Crim. Div., Off. of U.S. Atty.
**Byrne, Mary Lou** .......................'58 '88 C.990 B.S. L.800 J.D. [Nossaman,G.K.&E.]
*PRACTICE AREAS: Litigation.
**Byrne, Michael A.**, (AV) ..................'41 '69 C.966 B.A. L.424 J.D. [McKay,B.&G.]
*PRACTICE AREAS: Civil Trial; Insurance Defense; Personal Injury.
Byrne, Richard P. ...............'33 '59 C.112 A.B. L.800 LL.B. 116 N. Las Palmas Ave.
Byrne, William M., Jr. ...............................'30 '56 C&L.800 B.S., LL.B. U.S. Dist. J.
**Byrnes, David A.** ...............................'— '93 C.112 B.A. L.1068 J.D. [A] Loeb&L.]
*PRACTICE AREAS: Music; Motion Picture; Television; General Entertainment.
**Byrnes, Denise Renee** ..................'68 '96 C.112 B.A. L.809 J.D. [A] Iverson,Y.P.&H.]
*LANGUAGES: German.
*PRACTICE AREAS: Civil Litigation; Appellate Practice.
**Byrnes, Logan B.** ..............................'65 '92 C.800 B.A. L.940 J.D. [A] Dale,B.&H.]
Byrnes, William F. '31 '65
C.112 A.B. L.1066 LL.B. Admin. Law J., Off. of Admin. Hearings
Byron, Harvey E., (AV) ......................'28 '58 C.999 L.809 LL.B. 14401 Sylvan St.
Byun, Chai B. ..........................'36 '76 C.111 E.E. L.809 J.D. 3600 Wilshire Blvd.
Cabanday, Orlando F. ...............'67 '93 C.800 B.S. L.1067 J.D. 10940 Wilshire Blvd.
Cabell, Walter B. .........................'48 '73 C.668 B.A. L.966 J.D. 4311 Wilshire Blvd.
**Cabral, Carlos C.** ..............................'64 '92 C.112 B.A. L.1068 J.D. [A] Spray,G.&B.]
*LANGUAGES: Spanish.
Cabral, Michael Joseph ...................'59 '86 C.147 B.A. L.809 J.D. Off. of Dist. Atty.
**Cadarette, John R., Jr.** ................'58 '83 C.477 B.B.A. L.602 J.D. [Pillsbury M.&S.]
Cadish, Robert D. ...............................'46 '74 C.112 B.A. L.770 J.D. 633 W. 5th St.
Caditz, Allan M., (AV) ...................'29 '53 C&L.145 B.A., J.D. 10460 Le Conte Ave.‡

**Cadwalader, Wickersham & Taft, (AV)**
**660 South Figueroa Street, 90017**⊙
**Telephone: 213-955-4600 Telecopier: 213-955-4666**
**Email: postmaster@cadwalader.com URL: http://www.cadwalader.com**
**Members of Firm: Richard C. Field; Joseph M. Malinowski; John E. McDermott; Roger W. Rosendahl; Michael A. Santoro. Counsel: Robert E. Campbell; Philip G. Grant.**
**General Practice.**
**New York, N.Y. Office: 100 Maiden Lane, 10038. Telephone: 212-504-6000. Cable Address: "LABELLUM". Telex: 12-9146/667465. Telecopier: 212-504-6666.**
**Washington, D.C. Office: 1333 New Hampshire Avenue, N.W., 20036. Telephone: 202-862-2200. TWX: 710-822-1934. Cable Address: "LABELLUM WASHINGTON". Telecopier: 202-862-2400.**
**Charlotte, North Carolina Office: Suite 1510, 201 South College Street. Telephone: 704-348-5100. Fax: 704-348-5200.**
***See Professional Biographies, LOS ANGELES, CALIFORNIA***

Cady, Kathleen M. ........................'62 '89 C.112 B.A. L.809 J.D. Dist. Atty. Off.
**Caffee, Karen A.** ...............'58 '90 C.170 B.A. L.276 J.D. [B] McCutchen,D.B.&E.]
*LANGUAGES: French.
*PRACTICE AREAS: Environmental and Transactional; Environmental and Compliance.
**Cafferata, Reynolds T.** ..................'66 '92 C.273 B.A. L.809 J.D. [A] Riordan&M.]
*PRACTICE AREAS: Estate Planning; Planned Charitable Giving; Probate Litigation.
Cahan, Jerry R. .........................................'37 '72 C.1097 B.S. L.426 J.D. 633 W. 5th
**Cahill, James S.** ....................'51 '76 C.112 B.A. L.426 J.D. [B] Rossbacher&Assoc.]
*PRACTICE AREAS: Complex Commercial, Class Action and Labor Litigation; Business Transactions.
**Cahill, John D.**, (AV) ......................'29 '54 C.116 L.107 LL.B. [Rodi,P.P.G.&C.]
*PRACTICE AREAS: Real and Personal Property Tax Litigation; Sales and Use Tax Litigation; Probate Litigation.
**Cahill, John G.** .......................'63 '89 C.30 B.A. L.36 J.D. [A] Mendes&M.]
Cahill, Michael Edward '51 '78 C.03 B.A. L.029 LL.B.
Mng. Dir. & Gen. Coun., Trust Company of the West
Cahill, Randall C. ...............................'57 '85 C.502 B.S. L.734 J.D. U.S. Dept. of Jus.
Cahill, Robert V. '31 '57 C&L.276 B.S., LL.B.
(adm. in DC; not adm. in CA) Exec. V.P. & Gen. Coun., Chartwell Partnership Grp.
**Cahn, Joseph M.**, (AV) ...........'31 '73 C.453 B.S. L.426 J.D. [Greenberg G.F.C.&M.]
*PRACTICE AREAS: Litigation; Real Estate; Technology.
Caiafa, Douglas ......................................'57 '83 C.93 B.A. L.990 J.D. [Caiafa]
Caiafa Professional Law Corporation ...............................11845 W. Olympic Blvd.
**Cain, Patrick J.** ...............................'57 '82 C.426 B.A. L.1068 J.D. [Baker&H.]
*PRACTICE AREAS: Employment Litigation; Wrongful Termination; Unfair Competition; Workplace Violence.
**Caine, Andrew W.**, (AV) ...............'58 '83 C.597 B.A. L.1068 J.D. [Pachulski,S.Z.&Y.]
*REPORTED CASES: In re Madison Associates, 183 B.R. 206 (Bankr. C.D. California 1995); Gregorian v. National Convenience Stores, Inc., 174 Cal. App. 3d 944 (1985).
*TRANSACTIONS: Represented Official Creditors Committee of Madison Associates, FKA Pannell Kerr Foster; Merisel, Inc. and Advanced Research Laboratories in defense of various preference actions; Paine Webber Partnerships in guarantee litigation; Holiday Inns, Inc. in contract litigation.
**Cairl, Jack G., Jr.** ..........................'55 '82 C.976 B.A. L.1068 J.D. [Kinsella,B.F.&T.]

**Cairns, J. T., & Associates, (AV) '52 '77 C.188 A.B. L.1065 J.D.** [BB]
**200 N. Larchmont Boulevard, 90004**
**Telephone: 213-962-5588 Telecopier: 213-463-4412**
**Associates: Deann Hampton.**
**Business, Real Estate and Commercial Law, Civil Trial and Transactions. Bankruptcy, Aviation Law, Travel Law, Probate and Estate Planning.**
***See Professional Biographies, LOS ANGELES, CALIFORNIA***

**Cairns, James R.** .......................'59 '88 C.1049 B.A. L.1068 J.D. [A] White&C.]

**Cairns, Doyle, Lans, Nicholas & Soni**
**(See Pasadena)**

**Calaba, Frank V.** ...............................'45 '72 C.112 B.S. L.426 J.D. [B] Troy&G.]
*PRACTICE AREAS: Corporate Law; Taxation Law; Trusts and Estates Law.
Calabrese, Gina M. ...........'65 '91 C.178 B.A. L.262 J.D. 777 S. Figueroa St., 10th Fl.
**Calabrese, Joseph A.** ..........................'56 '81 C.93 A.B. L.188 J.D. [O'Melveny&M.]
*PRACTICE AREAS: Entertainment Law; Media Law; Finance.
**Calciano, Elizabeth M.** ......................'66 '92 C.95 A.B. L.1065 J.D. [A] Burke,W.&S.]
*PRACTICE AREAS: Public Law; Land Use; Environmental Law; Litigation.
**Caldera, Eva Orlebeke** ...................'63 '89 C&L.309 A.B., J.D. [A] Munger,T.&O.]
*LANGUAGES: French.
**Calderon, Charles M.** ....................'50 '75 C.1097 B.A. L.1067 J.D. [Burke,W.&S.]
*PRACTICE AREAS: Municipal Law.
Calderon, Dennis A. .................'66 '95 C.1075 B.S. L.809 J.D. 601 S. Figueroa St.
**Caldwell, Christopher G.**, (AV) ..............'57 '82 C.378 B.A. L.309 J.D. [Hedges&C.]

**Calendo, Puckett, Sheedy & DiCorrado**
**(See Glendale)**

**Calfas, John A.**, (AV) ..........................'26 '57 C.112 B.S. L.1068 LL.B. [J.A.Calfas]
**Calfas, Scott J.** .............................'65 '91 C.112 B.A. L.477 J.D. [A] Gibson,D.&C.]

**Calfas, John A., A Professional Corporation, (AV)** [BB]
**11601 Wilshire Boulevard Suite 1920, 90025**
**Telephone: 310-477-1920 FAX: 310-477-7132**
**John A. Calfas.**
**Corporation, Securities, Taxation, Estate Planning, Trust and Probate Law.**
***See Professional Biographies, LOS ANGELES, CALIFORNIA***

**Calfo, Alexander G.** ........................'64 '91 C.436 B.A. L.190 J.D. [A] Yukevich&S.]
*REPORTED CASES: Rinauro v.Honda Motor Co. (1995) 31 Cal. App. 4th 506, 37 Cal. Rptr. 2d 181.
*PRACTICE AREAS: Products Liability; Civil Litigation.
**Calhoun, Gordon J.** .........................'53 '78 C.367 B.A. L.813 J.D. [Lewis,D.B.&B.]
Calhoun, Jon Robert ...................'45 '73 C.813 B.A. L.1068 J.D. [A] Dumas&Assoc.]
**Caliman, Meredith L.** ..................'60 '87 C.674 A.B. L.1068 J.D. [Hamburg,H.E.&M.]
*PRACTICE AREAS: Civil Litigation.
**Calkins, Colleen Daphne, (P.C.)** .......'55 '78 C.112 B.A. L.800 J.D. [Reinstein,P.&C.]
*PRACTICE AREAS: Employee Benefits Law; Business Law; Corporate Law; Estate Planning and Probate Law; Health Care Law.
**Calkins, George D., II**, (AV) ...............'46 '73 C.112 B.A. L.426 J.D. [Cox,C.&N.]
*PRACTICE AREAS: Real Estate and Construction Litigation; Bankruptcy Law; Insurance Law.
**Calkins, Mary Craig** ....................'50 '81 C.112 B.A. L.426 J.D. [Troop M.S.&P.]
*PRACTICE AREAS: Insurance Coverage Litigation; General Business Litigation; Entertainment Litigation; Employment Litigation.
Calkins, Victoria L. .......................'65 '91 C.911 B.A. L.945 J.D. 355 S. Grand Ave.
**Call, Gregory D.** ..........................'58 '85 C.813 A.B. L.1066 J.D. [Folger L.&K.]⊙
**Call, Gregory L.** ........................'— '94 C&L.101 B.A., J.D. [A] Milbank,T.H.&M.]
**Call, John R.** ...........................'46 '93 C.37 B.A. L.813 J.D. [A] Quinn E.U.&O.]
*LANGUAGES: Castilian Spanish.
**Call, Merlin W.**, (AV) ..............................'31 '53 C&L.813 A.B., J.D. [Tuttle&T.]
*PRACTICE AREAS: Trust and Probate Administration; Engineering; Business.
Callahan, John P. ...............................................'18 '59 L.426 LL.B. 6607 W. 87th Pl.
**Callahan, Kevin K.** .........................'59 '84 C.103 B.A. L.1068 J.D. [Booth,M.&S.]
Callahan, Matilda Radalj .............'32 '84 C.112 B.A. L.1148 J.D. 1923 Camden Ave.
Callahan, Timothy J. .....................'42 '71 C.426 B.A. L.809 J.D. 8703 Truxton Ave.

**Callahan, McCune & Willis, (AV)**
**Suite 1200, 11755 Wilshire Boulevard, 90025**⊙
**Telephone: 310-312-1860 Fax: 310-477-3481**
**Members of Firm: John J. Tasker; Steven A. Simons; John A. Nojima; Allison L. Jones; Charles T. Brown; Pamela S. Cooke; Jeremy L. Tissot. Associate: Michael C. Rogers.**
**Civil, Trial and Appellate Practice. Insurance Defense, Personal Injury, Products and Professional Liability, Property Damage, Construction Law, Litigation, Employment Discrimination, Business Litigation and Medical Malpractice.**
**Tustin, California Office: 111 Fashion Lane, 92680. Telephone: 714-730-5700. Fax: 714-730-1642.**
**San Diego, California Office: 402 West Broadway, Suite 800, 92101. Telephone: 619-232-5700. Fax: 619-232-2206.**
***See Professional Biographies, LOS ANGELES, CALIFORNIA***

**Callanan, Charles F.** ....................'42 '68 C.262 B.A. L.128 J.D. [Sullivan,W.&D.]
*PRACTICE AREAS: Corporations Law; Real Estate Law; Commercial Law.
Callanan, Geo. T. ........................'24 '50 C&L.800 B.S., LL.B. 1301 N. Western Ave.‡
Calle, Nancy S. ............................'62 '90 C.800 B.S. L.990 J.D. 3435 Wilshire Blvd.
Callender, William L. ... '33 '60 C.267 A.B. L.800 J.D. Pres. & CEO, Calif. Fed. Bk. FSB
Callion, Luther ....................................'30 '68 C.1097 B.A. L.809 LL.B. Supr. Ct. Comr.
**Callobre, Anthony R.** ........................'60 '85 C.103 A.B. L.94 J.D. [A] Kelley D.&W.]
*PRACTICE AREAS: Commercial Finance; Loan Restructurings and Workouts.
**Calvelli, Gina M.** ..........................'56 '91 C.231 B.A. L.813 J.D. [A] Riordan&M.]
**Calver, Tracey A.** .......................'62 '96 C.1109 B.A. L.1049 J.D. [A] McKenna&C.]
*PRACTICE AREAS: Government Contracts; Civil Litigation.
**Calvet, Pamela C.** ...........................'58 '83 C&L.800 B.S., J.D. [A] Bryan C.]
*PRACTICE AREAS: Labor and Employment Law.

**Calvillo, Stevan R.**
**(See Long Beach)**

**Camacho, Elizabeth A.** ......................'67 '94 C.604 B.A. L.1066 J.D. [A] Irell&M.]
Camacho, Mike, Jr. ..........................'61 '88 C.1032 B.A. L.1137 J.D. Dep. Dist. Atty.
**Camara, Mario** ............................'48 '73 C.112 B.A. L.1068 J.D. [Cox,C.&N.]
*PRACTICE AREAS: Real Property Law; Construction Law.
**Camel, David J.** ........................'57 '83 C.112 B.A. L.309 J.D. [Weinstein,B.R.H.&C.]
*PRACTICE AREAS: Tax.
**Cameron, Florence F.** .....................'58 '87 C&L.178 B.A., J.D. [Blecher&C.]
*PRACTICE AREAS: Antitrust; Business Litigation; Intellectual Property; Business Torts.
**Cameron, Stephanie Yost** ..............'60 '94 C.112 B.A. L.809 J.D. [A] Gibson,D.&C.]
*PRACTICE AREAS: Entertainment and the Arts; Intellectual Property.

**Cameron, Madden, Pearlson, Gale & Sellars**
**(See Long Beach)**

Camerota, Frank P. .............'39 '80 C.223 B.S.M.E. L.809 J.D. 1850 N. Whitley Ave.
Camhi, Ronald R. ........'66 '91 C.112 B.A. L.809 J.D. 11400 W. Olympic Blvd., 9th Fl.
Caminker, Evan H. ..............'61 '87 C.112 B.A. L.976 J.D. Prof. of Law, Univ. of Calif.
**Cammarano, Terri Wagner** .........'63 '88 C.1176 B.S. L.616 J.D. [A] Foley L.W.&A.]
*SPECIAL AGENCIES: Franchise Tax Board, State Board of Equalization, California Public Utilities Commission, Federal Energy Regulatory Commission.
*PRACTICE AREAS: Health Care; Business Law; Tax Planning; Tax Controversies; Tax Exempt Organizations.
Camp, Alida D. ... '55 '81 C.1044 B.A. L.178 J.D. Concorde-New Horizons Picture Corp.
**Camp, James C.** ..........................'51 '76 C.228 A.B. L.245 J.D. [Brown,W.&C.]
*PRACTICE AREAS: Real Property; Commercial Law; Finance; Corporate.
**Camp, Warren D.** ..............................'64 '91 C.025 B.A. L.031 J.D. [A] Trope&T.]
*PRACTICE AREAS: Family Law.
Campbell, Alice C. '21 '44 C.927 L.339 J.D.
Corp. Secy. & Chf. Fin. Offr., Robt. Campbell Co.
**Campbell, Bruce L.** ........................'67 '93 C.674 A.B. L.309 J.D. [A] O'Melveny&M.]
**Campbell, Cannon Quigley** ..........'67 '93 C.813 B.A. L.309 J.D. [A] O'Melveny&M.]
**Campbell, Charles R., Jr.** ..........'57 '82 C.112 B.A. L.800 J.D. [Sonnenschein N.&R.]
*PRACTICE AREAS: Real Property; Corporate; Workouts; Environmental.
Campbell, Denis W., (AV) ....................'40 '75 C.1042 B.A. L.809 J.D. P.O. Box 990
Campbell, Frank P. ...........................'31 '62 C.229 L.426 J.D. 4700 Wilshire Blvd.
**Campbell, Gwyneth A.** .......................'64 '89 C.69 B.A. L.846 J.D. [A] Paul,H.J.&W.]

Campbell, Kevin D., Law Offices of ... '55 '83 C.608 B.A. L.809 J.D. 5455 Wilshire Blvd.
Campbell, Mark R. ... '— '92 C.1259 B.S. L.800 J.D. [Roquemore,P.&M.]
Campbell, P. David ... '54 '80 C.273 B.S. L.30 J.D. Asst. Dist. Atty.
**Campbell, Patricia J.** ... '57 '91 C.1097 B.A. L.800 J.D. [Ⓐ Berger,K.S.M.F.S.&G.]
Campbell, Renee L. ... '56 '82 C.398 B.A. L.1068 J.D. 221 N. Figueroa St.
Campbell, Robert Cleaver ... '46 '74 C.675 B.A. L.426 J.D. 12304 Santa Monica Blvd.
**Campbell, Robert E.** ... '52 '77 C.105 B.A. L.880 J.D. [Ⓒ Cadwalader,W.&T.]
**Campbell, Robert G.** ... '56 '82 C.112 B.A. L.800 J.D. [Thelen,M.J.&B.]
*PRACTICE AREAS: Business and Construction Litigation; Representation of Professional Athletes.
**Campbell, Robin C.** ... '51 '76 C.112 B.A. L.178 J.D. [Walker,W.T.&W.]
*PRACTICE AREAS: Litigation; General Business Practice.
**Campbell, Scott H.** ... '61 '87 C.112 B.A. L.1068 J.D. [Brown,W.&C.]
*PRACTICE AREAS: Business Litigation; Municipal Litigation.
Campbell, Sean Robbie Gibson ... '65 '89 C.878 B.A. L.846 J.D. 221 N. Figueroa St.
**Campbell, Thomas N.** ... '54 '89 C.800 B.A. L.796 J.D. [Ⓐ Hanna&M.]
*LANGUAGES: French.
*PRACTICE AREAS: General Practice; Civil Trial.
**Campbell, William B.**, (AV) ... '36 '63 C.350 B.S. L.813 LL.B. [Orrick,H.&S.]
**Campo, Joseph C.** ... '65 '90 C.262 B.A. L.569 J.D. [Ⓐ Lewis,D.B.&B.]
Campos, Guillermo ... '61 '92 C.112 B.A. L.1066 J.D. 555 S. Flower St.
**Campos, Lorie A.** ... '67 '93 C.112 B.S. L.813 J.D. [Ⓐ Barbosa G.&B.]
*PRACTICE AREAS: Education Law; Litigation.
Campos, Raymond Q. ... '40 '74 C.1077 B.A. L.426 J.D. 2966 Wilshire Blvd.
Camras, Barbara J. ... '38 '87 C.477 B.A. L.1136 J.D. State Comp. Ins. Fund
Camras, Michael J. ... '38 '63 C.477 B.B.A. L.1066 J.D. [M.J.Camras]
Camras, Michael J., Inc. ... 11500 W. Olympic Blvd.
**Canady, Karen S.** ... '— '96 C.637 B.S. L.911 J.D. [Ⓐ Merchant&G.]
**Canby, William Nathan** ... '57 '96 C&L.976 B.A., J.D. [Ⓐ Heller E.W.&M.]
**Candelaria, William A.** ... '70 '96 C.813 A.B. L.309 J.D. [Ⓐ O'Melveny&M.]
Candland, Richard W. '13 '39 C&L.878 J.D.
(adm. in UT; not adm. in CA) 12121 Wilshire Blvd.
**Cane, Joseph C., Jr.** ... '68 '94 C.188 L.426 J.D. [Ⓐ Robins,K.M.&C.]
*PRACTICE AREAS: General Civil Practice; Litigation; Medical Malpractice; Product Liability Law.
**Cane, Paul W., Jr.** ... '54 '81 C.197 A.B. L.1066 J.D. [Paul,H.J.&W.]
Canepa, Nanette C. ... '66 '91 C.691 B.A. L.1068 J.D. 333 S. Grand Ave.
**Canfield, Ann Therese** ... '57 '82 C&L.426 B.A., J.D. [Ibold&A.]
**Cannizzaro, Frank** ... '— '92 C.112 B.A. L.809 J.D. [Ⓐ Gilbert,K.C.&J.]
*PRACTICE AREAS: Workers' Compensation.
**Cannon, Anthon S., Jr.**, (AV) ... '38 '67 C.878 B.S. L.309 J.D. [Pillsbury M.&S.]
Cannon, Tristan C. ... '52 '80 C.878 B.A. L.1049 J.D. 1925 Century Park E.
Cantella, Kathleen M. ... '44 '83 L.1190 J.D. 2263 S. Harvard Blvd.
**Canter, David H.**, (AV) '37 '65 C.679 B.S. L.800 J.D.
[Harrington,F.D.&C.] (⊙Orange)
*PRACTICE AREAS: Products Liability Law; Toxic Torts Law; Medical Malpractice Law.
Canter, Ronald M. ... '54 '79 C.608 B.A. L.1095 J.D. 3580 Wilshire Blvd.

**Cantilo, Maisel & Hubbard, L.L.P., (AV Ⓣ)**
**A Partnership of Professional Corporations**
**11500 West Olympic Boulevard Fourth Floor, 90064⊙**
**Telephone: 310-478-7586 Fax: 310-312-2464**
**Members of Firm: Robert W. Biederman (P.C.); Christopher M. Maisel (P.C.): Of Counsel: Jeffrey H. Karlin (P.C.).**
**Bankruptcy, General Corporate, Health Care Law, Insolvencies, Insurance, Litigation, Mergers and Acquisitions, Real Estate, Workouts and Reorganizations.**
**Austin, Texas Office: 111 Congress Avenue, Suite 1700. Telephone: 512-478-6000. Fax: 512-404-6550.**
**Dallas, Texas Office: 1717 Main Street, Suite 3200, 75201. Telephone: 214-740-4600. Fax: 214-740-4646.**
***See Professional Biographies, LOS ANGELES, CALIFORNIA***

**Cantor, Linda F.** ... '56 '88 C&L.477 A.B., J.D. [Pachulski,S.Z.&Y.]
**Cantor, Lynn D.** '66 '95 C.262 B.A. L.178 J.D.
(adm. in TN; not adm. in CA) [Ⓐ Graham&J.]
Cantore, Jami L. ... '67 '93 C.112 B.A. L.990 J.D. [Ⓐ Casterline&A.]
Cantore, Robert A. ... '48 '75 C.415 B.A. L.724 J.D. [Gilbert&S.]
Cantú, Patricia Ann ... '52 '78 C.560 B.A. L.309 J.D. V.P. & Sr. Coun., Sanwa Bk. Calif.
**Canzoneri, Anthony**, (AV) ... '46 '72 C.1109 B.A. L.1068 J.D. [Brown,W.&C.]
*PRACTICE AREAS: Real Estate; Governmental Law; Finance; Real Estate Development; Environmental.
Capalbo, Thomas E. ... '48 '89 C.433 B.S. L.1137 J.D. 6825 E. Washington Blvd.
Capata, Julian Eli ... '41 '72 C.1077 B.A. L.426 J.D. 3600 Wilshire Blvd.
**Capella, Richard A.** ... '57 '87 C.766 B.A. L.1095 J.D. [Knopfler&R.]
*PRACTICE AREAS: Insurance Law; Construction Surety and Bonds; Business Litigation; Construction Defect Litigation.
Capiro, Rafael M. ... '53 '79 C.112 B.A. L.426 J.D. [Capiro&Assoc.]
Capiro and Associates ... 11650 N. Riverside #8
**Caplan, David** ... '69 '95 C.951 B.A. L.588 J.D. [Ⓐ Baker&H.]
*PRACTICE AREAS: Intellectual Property.
**Caplan, George T.**, (AV) ... '42 '69 C.112 A.B. L.178 LL.B. [Dewey B.]
*PRACTICE AREAS: Litigation.
Caplan, Richard H., (A Law Corp.) '44 '70
C.966 B.S. L.1068 J.D. 12400 Wilshire Blvd. Ste. 400
**Caplan, Sara L.** ... '55 '83 C&L.912 B.A., J.D. [Ⓒ Christensen,M.F.J.G.W.&S.]
*PRACTICE AREAS: Criminal Defense; Business Litigation; Commercial Litigation; Civil Litigation; Appeals.
**Capobianco, Anthony** ... '65 '92 C.36 B.S. L.1065 J.D. [Ⓐ Sonnenschein N.&R.]
*PRACTICE AREAS: Litigation.
**Capoccia, Rachel M.** ... '61 '96 C.1213 B.S. L.800 J.D. [Ⓐ Munger,T.&O.]
**Capozzola, Damian D.** ... '71 '96 C.112 B.A. L.893 J.D. [Ⓐ Kirkland&E.]
*PRACTICE AREAS: Litigation.
**Cappadona, Louis A.**, (AV) ... '39 '65 C.749 B.S. L.744 J.D. [Gray,Y.D.&R.]
*SPECIAL AGENCIES: Federal: National Labor Relations Board; U.S. Department of Labor; Equal Employment Opportunity Commission. California: Department of Fair Employment and Housing; Division of Labor Standards Enforcement; Employment Development Department.
*REPORTED CASES: Auchmoody v. 911 Emergency Services, Inc., 214 Cal App. 3d 1510; Automated Business Systems v. N.L.R.B., 497 F 2d 262, CA 6; Guidance and Control Systems v. N.L.R.B., 217 N.L.R.B., No. 34, 538 F2 336 (enforcement denied) CA9.
*PRACTICE AREAS: Labor and Employment Law.
Cappai, Ronald E. ... '41 '66 C.770 B.S. L.1065 J.D. Supr. Ct. J.
**Capps, William F., (P.C.)** ... '47 '73 C.940 B.A. L.1066 J.D. [Jeffer,M.B.&M.]
*PRACTICE AREAS: Corporate; Securities; Real Estate.
**Cappy, Rod J.** ... '63 '88 C.259 B.S. L.245 J.D. [Ⓐ Grace,S.C.&S.]
*PRACTICE AREAS: Product Liability Law; Insurance Defense Law; Appellate Law.
**Capriotti, Roger P.** ... '70 '96 C.893 B.A. L.309 J.D. [Ⓐ Gibson,D.&C.]
*LANGUAGES: Italian.
**Caps, Thomas L.**, (AV) ... '26 '55 C.112 B.S. L.1068 J.D. [Ⓒ Riordan&M.]
Capuano, Patrick J. ... '63 '89 C.367 B.A. L.893 J.D. 1801 Century Park E., 9th Flr.
**Caputo, Philip D.** ... '69 '96 C.970 B.A. L.1338 J.D. [Ⓐ A.R.Hamrick,III]
**Caragozian, John S.** ... '53 '79 C.112 A.B. L.309 J.D. [Stegman&C.]
*PRACTICE AREAS: Business Litigation; Real Estate Litigation; Business Torts; Arbitration.
Caras, Norma G. ... '— '73 L.1148 LL.B. IBM Corp.
Caras, William G. ... '58 '83 C.800 B.S. L.813 J.D. 1801 Ave. of Stars

**Carbajal, Diana M.** ... '63 '95 C.1109 B.A. L.426 J.D. [Ⓐ Barbosa G.&B.]
*PRACTICE AREAS: Litigation; Criminal.
Carberry, Vincent E. ... '54 '82 C.342 B.A. L.809 J.D. Dep. Dist. Atty.
**Carbone, Joseph A.** ... '24 '62 C.676 B.S. L.800 LL.B. [Ⓒ Riordan&M.]
Carbone, Steven S. ... '60 '92 C.112 B.A. L.1190 J.D. 801 S. Grand Ave.
**Card, David M.**, (AV) ... '45 '73 C.813 A.B. L.800 J.D. Sr. Coun., Bank of Amer.
**Carden, Douglas L.** ... '51 '77 C.145 B.A. L.770 J.D. [Shapiro,R.&C.]
*PRACTICE AREAS: Business Litigation and Franchising Law.
Cardenas, Raymond ... '31 '61 C.112 B.A. L.1068 LL.B. Supr. Ct. J.
**Cardenas Conn, Gloria** ... '64 '91 C.112 B.A. L.1065 J.D. [Ⓐ Serritella&P.]
*PRACTICE AREAS: Civil and Business Litigation; Public Entity Defense.
Cardiner, Scott A. ... '52 '77 C.696 B.A. L.1068 J.D. 8490 W. Sunset Blvd.
**Cardwell, Robert L.** ... '59 '85 C.968 B.A. L.990 J.D. [Ⓐ Tharpe&H.]
**Carero, William M.** ... '55 '82 C&L.426 B.A., J.D. [Stockwell,H.W.&W.]
**Carey, Stevens A.**, (AV) ... '51 '78 C.112 B.A. L.1066 J.D. [Pircher,N.&M.]
*PRACTICE AREAS: Real Estate Law.

**Carico, Christopher D.**
**(See Manhattan Beach)**

**Caris, Gary Owen**, (AV) ... '55 '79 C.1077 B.A. L.1068 J.D. [Frandzel&S.]
**Carl, Kenneth J.** ... '60 '85 C.145 A.B. L.309 J.D. [Ⓐ Hooper,L.&B.]
*PRACTICE AREAS: Corporate Law; Healthcare.
Carleton, David P. ... '49 '75 C.112 A.B. L.426 J.D. Head Dep. Alternate Pub. Def.
**Carleton, Douglas C.** ... '63 '94 C.893 B.A. L.800 J.D. [Ⓐ Riordan&M.]
**Carlin, Marnie S.** ... '64 '91 C.112 B.A. L.426 J.D. [Ⓐ Tuttle&T.]
Carlin, Robert Michael ... '55 '86 C.112 B.A. L.1068 J.D. 6145 Lindenhurst Ave.
**Carlisle, R. Jeff** ... '51 '77 C.112 B.A. L.800 J.D. [Lynberg&W.]
Carloni, August G. ... '27 '56 C.381 B.A. L.1003 J.D. 5455 Wilshire Blvd.
Carlow, Jack ... '20 '42 C.800 L.426 LL.B. 1311 Roscomare Rd.‡
**Carlsen, Nicki Marie Varyu** '61 '90
C.339 B.S. L.800 J.D. [Ⓐ McClintock,W.B.R.R.&M.]
*PRACTICE AREAS: Business Litigation; Environmental Litigation; Land Use Litigation.

**Carlsmith Ball Wichman Case & Ichiki, (AV) BB**
**A Partnership including Law Corporations**
**555 South Flower Street, 25th Floor, 90071⊙**
**Telephone: 213-955-1200 Cable Address: CWCMI LOSANGELESCALIFORNIA Fax: 213-623-0032; 213-624-7183**
**Members of Firm: Annie Kun Baker; Joseph A. Ball; Roger B. Baymiller; Nancy M. Beckner; Stephen L. Bradford; Albert H. Ebright; Terrence A. Everett; Jonathan R. Hodes; Robert F. Kull; John R. McDonough; Randolph G. Muhlestein; Joseph D. Mullender, Jr.; David S. Olson; James M. Polish; Jonathan L. Smoller; Allan Edward Tebbetts; Donald C. Williams; Duane H. Zobrist. Resident Associates: Peter N. Greenfeld; Ann Luotto Wolf. Resident Of Counsel: Herbert G. Baerwitz; Dagmar V. Halamka; Tom K. Houston; Robert R. Thornton.**
**Admiralty & Maritime, Administrative, Banking & Finance, Corporate, Environmental, Foreign Investment Interests, Hotel, Resort & Entertainment, Immigration, International, Labor & Employment, Litigation and Dispute Resolution, Public Utilities, Real Property and Land Use, Tax, Trusts, and Comparative Planning.**
**Honolulu, Hawaii Office: Suite 2200, Pacific Tower, 1001 Bishop Street. P.O. Box 656. Telephone: 808-523-2500.**
**Kapolei, Hawaii Office: Kapolei Building, Suite 318, 1001 Kamokila Boulevard. Telephone: 808-523-2500.**
**Wailuku, Maui Hawaii Office: One Main Plaza, Suite 400, 2200 Main Street, P.O. Box 1086. Telephone: 808-242-4535.**
**Kailua-Kona, Hawaii Office: Second Floor, Bank of Hawaii Annex Building, P.O. Box 1720. Telephone: 808-329-6464.**
**Hilo, Hawaii Office: 121 Waianuenue Avenue, P.O. Box 686. Telephone: 808-935-6644.**
**Agana, Guam Office: 4th Floor, Bank of Hawaii Building, P.O. Box BF. Telephone: 671-472-6813.**
**Saipan, Commonwealth of the Northern Mariana Islands Office: Carlsmith Building, Capitol Hill, P.O. Box 5241. Telephone: (011) 670-322-3455.**
**Washington, D.C. Office: 700 14th Street, N.W., 9th Floor. Telephone: 202-508-1025.**
**Mexico City, Mexico Office: Monte Pelvoux 111, Piso 1, Col. Lomas de Chapultepec 11000, Mexico, D.F. Telephone: (011-52-5) 520-8514. Fax: (011-52-5) 540-1545.**
**Mexico, D.F. Office of Carlsmith Ball Garcia Cacho y Asociados, S.C. (Authorized to practice Mexican Law): Monte Pelvoux 111, Piso 1, Col. Lomas de Chapultepec, 11000 Mexico, D.F. Telephone: (011-52-5) 520-8514. Fax: (011-52-5) 540-1545.**
**Revisers of the Hawaii Law Digest for this Directory.**
***See Professional Biographies, LOS ANGELES, CALIFORNIA***

**Carlson, Chris A.** ... '55 '82 C.813 B.A. L.1065 J.D. [Manatt,P.&P.]
*PRACTICE AREAS: Real Estate Law; Public Finance.
**Carlson, Christina M.** ... '63 '94 C.112 B.A. L.426 J.D. [Ⓐ Buchalter,N.F.&Y.]
*PRACTICE AREAS: Bankruptcy Litigation.
**Carlson, Edwin A.** ... '63 '96 C.012 B.S. L.1068 J.D. [Ⓐ McKenna&C.]
*PRACTICE AREAS: Environmental.
Carlson, Eric Matthew ... '60 '89 C.494 B.A. L.1066 J.D. Bet Tzedek Legal Servs.
**Carlson, Grant A.** ... '64 '91 C.112 B.A. L.426 J.D. [Ⓐ Gelfand&G.]
*PRACTICE AREAS: Civil Litigation.
**Carlson, Mark C.** ... '68 '93 C.1253 B.A. L.809 J.D. [Ⓐ Morris,P.&P.]
*PRACTICE AREAS: Real Estate Law; Insurance Law; Commercial Law.
Carlson, Robert C., (A Professional Corporation), (AV) '18 '41
C&L.16 A.B., J.D. 3926 Wilshire Blvd.
**Carlson, Robert E.**, (AV) ... '30 '59 C.629 B.S. L.1065 LL.B. [Paul,H.J.&W.]
**Carlson, Robert R.** ... '70 '95 C.112 A.B. L.309 J.D. [Ⓐ Paul,H.J.&W.]
**Carlton, Christopher W.** '56 '83 C.228 A.B. L.188 J.D.
[Faustman,C.D.&F.] (⊙Irvine)
*PRACTICE AREAS: Employment Law; Labor Law; Business Litigation.
Carlton, John L. ... '51 '79 C.112 A.B. L.1068 J.D. Asst. U.S. Attorney
**Carlton, R. David** ... '49 '74 C&L.902 B.A., J.D. [Howrey&S.]
*PRACTICE AREAS: Government Contract Law.
**Carluccio, Charles G., III** ... '62 '86 C.262 B.S. L.1188 J.D. [Mendes&M.]
Carman, Nancy W. '64 '91
C.800 B.A. L.823 J.D. Asst. Gen. Atty., Union Pacific R.R. Co.
**Carner, Gretchen S.** ... '61 '87 C.112 A.B. L.767 J.D. [Long&L.]
Carnevale, Steven J. ... '47 '73 C.1097 B.A. L.426 J.D. Principal Dep. Co. Coun.
**Caron, Sean M.** ... '67 '95 C.112 B.A. L.800 J.D. [Ⓐ O'Melveny&M.]
**Caron, John M.** ... '63 '87 C.347 B.S. L.809 J.D. [Kirtland&P.]
Carp, Mitchell A ... '56 '88 C.1077 B.S. L.940 J.D. Auto. Club of Southern Calif.
**Carpenter, John C.** ... '48 '76 C&L.767 B.A., J.D. [Ⓒ Thorpe&T.]
*PRACTICE AREAS: Business; Corporate; Entertainment; Real Estate Law.
Carpenter, Martin L. ... '48 '76 C.112 B.A. L.809 J.D. [Carpenter&R.]
Carpenter, Robert D. ... '28 '75 C.112 B.S. L.809 J.D. 727 W. 7th St.
**Carpenter, Thomas T.** ... '48 '81 C.871 B.S. L.284 J.D. [Bronson,B.&M.]
*PRACTICE AREAS: Aviation; Transportation; Product Liability; Civil Litigation.
Carpenter & Rothans ... 11601 Wilshire blvd.
**Carr, Christine L.** ... '66 '95 C.112 B.A. L.800 J.D. [Ⓐ O'Melveny&M.]
*PRACTICE AREAS: Corporate Law.
**Carr, James P.**, (AV) ... '50 '76 C&L.602 B.A., J.D. [J.P.Carr]
Carr, Larry Brannon ... '41 '86 C.1222 B.A. L.1153 J.D. 4700 Wilshire Blvd.
**Carr, Linda B.** ... '50 '88 C.741 B.A. L.809 J.D. [Ⓐ Hancock R.&B.]
**Carr, Willard Z., Jr.**, (AV) ... '27 '51 C.679 B.S. L.1119 LL.B. [Ⓒ Gibson,D.&C.]
*PRACTICE AREAS: Labor Arbitration; Employment Law including Wrongful Termination; Negotiations; Strikes; Drug and Alcohol Testing.

CAA197P

**Carr, James P., A Professional Corporation, (AV)**
**11755 Wilshire Boulevard, Suite 1170, 90025**
**Telephone: 310-444-7179 Fax: 310-473-0708**
**James P. Carr.**
**Trial Practice in all State and Federal Courts. Product Liability, Governmental Liability, Negligence, Professional Malpractice.**
***See Professional Biographies, LOS ANGELES, CALIFORNIA***

**Carrasco, Adela** ................ '63 '89 C.813 B.A. L.1066 J.D. [▣ Allen,M.L.G.&M.]
*LANGUAGES: Spanish.
*PRACTICE AREAS: Commercial Litigation.
**Carraway, James D.** ................ '59 '89 C.312 B.A. L.990 J.D. [▣ Murchison&C.]
*PRACTICE AREAS: Products Liability Law.
**Carrey, Neil**, (AV) ................ '42 '68 C.659 B.S. L.813 J.D. [De Castro,W.&C.]
*PRACTICE AREAS: Business Law; Qualified Retirement Plans Law; Retirement Benefits Law; Taxation Law and Health Care Law.
**Carrick, Roger Lane** ................ '51 '80 C.309 A.B. L.1066 J.D. [Preston G.&E.]
**Carrick, Timothy J.**, (AV) '55 '85 C.475 B.A. L.809 J.D.
[Dale,B.&H.] (⊙Walnut Creek)
*PRACTICE AREAS: Business Law; Land Subsidence Law; Products Liability Law.
Carrier, George B., III '51 '76
C.911 B.A. L.813 J.D. V.P. & Sr. Coun., Wells Fargo Bk., N.A.
**Carroll, Douglas G.** ................ '44 '81 C.1077 B.A. L.426 J.D. [▣ Sullivan]
*LANGUAGES: German and Russian.
*PRACTICE AREAS: Business Litigation.
**Carroll, Elizabeth A.** ................ '64 '92 C.112 B.A. L.1066 J.D. [▣ Howrey&S.]
*PRACTICE AREAS: Commercial Litigation.
Carroll, Irene S. ................ '48 '72 C.185 A.B. L.893 J.D. I.R.S.
**Carroll, James J., III**, (AV) ................ '46 '74 C.813 A.B. L.1065 J.D. [Sheppard,M.R.&H.]
*PRACTICE AREAS: Business Litigation; Estate Planning Law.
**Carroll, Laura J.** ................ '51 '85 C.473 B.A. L.1068 J.D. [Tuttle&T.]
*PRACTICE AREAS: Environmental Law; Business; Real Estate; Toxic Tort Litigation.
Carroll, Margaret C. ................ '— '89 C.66 B.A. L.569 J.D. 333 S. Grand Ave.
**Carroll, Michael J.** ................ '63 '90 C&L.477 B.A., J.D. [Latham&W.]
**Carroll, Michelle M.** ................ '68 '93 C.154 B.A. L.1066 J.D. [▣ Latham&W.]
Carroll, Ronald H., (AV) ................ '36 '66 C.605 A.B. L.809 LL.B. Head Dep. Dist. Atty.
Carroll, Roscoe C., (AV) ................ '10 '51 C.411 A.B. L.809 LL.B. 1101 S. Gramercy Dr.‡
**Carroll, Rosemary** ................ '55 '81 C.228 B.A. L.813 J.D. [Codikow&C.]⊙
*LANGUAGES: Spanish and Russian.
Carroll, Stephen C. ................ '59 '91 C.1322 B.F.A. L.809 J.D. 11766 Wilshire Blvd.
**Carron, Eugene J.** ................ '46 '72 C&L.724 B.S., J.D. [Orrick,H.&S.]
*PRACTICE AREAS: Public Finance Law.
**Carron, Paul A.** ................ '60 '86 C.602 B.B.A. L.477 J.D. [▣ Hewitt&P.]
*PRACTICE AREAS: Civil Litigation in States and Federal Courts.
**Carson, John**, (AV) ................ '42 '68 C.770 B.S. L.310 J.D. [Robbins,B.&C.] (See Pat. Sect.)
*PRACTICE AREAS: Patent Law; Trademark Law; Copyright Law; Trade Secret Law; Unfair Competition Law.
**Carson, Maryanne** ................ '60 '86 C.696 B.A. L.569 J.D. [▣ Stroock&S.&L.]
*LANGUAGES: French.
**Carson, Nicole** ................ '69 '95 C.477 B.A. L.1065 J.D. [▣ McKenna&C.]
*PRACTICE AREAS: Litigation; Government Contracts; Criminal Defense; Constitutional Law.
**Carstens, Rand Dunn** ................ '59 '86 C.1262 B.A. L.809 J.D. [▣ Kern&W.]
**Cartano, David J.** ................ '49 '76 C.911 B.A. L.188 J.D. [Barton,K.&O.]
*PRACTICE AREAS: Taxation; Corporate Law.
**Cartelli, Michael A.** ................ '54 '79 C&L.426 B.A., J.D. [▣ Lynberg&W.]
*PRACTICE AREAS: Insurance Litigation; Injury Litigation.
**Carter, Bret R.** ................ '59 '87 C.350 B.S. L.990 J.D. [▣ Hart&W.]
*REPORTED CASES: Clavell vs. North Coast 232 Cal. App. 3d 328 (1991).
*PRACTICE AREAS: Civil Litigation; Insurance Litigation; Real Estate Litigation; Business Litigation; Corporate Litigation.
**Carter, Geraldine C.** ................ '53 '83 C.184 B.A. L.426 J.D. [G.C.Carter]
*LANGUAGES: Spanish.
*PRACTICE AREAS: Real Estate; Business and Corporate; Financial Institutions; Environmental.
**Carter, Grace A.** ................ '55 '81 C.112 B.A. L.1066 J.D. [Paul,H.J.&W.]
Carter, Karen B. ................ '60 '86 C.112 B.A. L.1136 J.D. 3255 Wilshire Blvd. 12th Fl.
**Carter, Kevin B.** ................ '— '94 C&L.112 B.A., J.D. [▣ O'Melveny&M.]
**Carter, Richard D.** ................ '60 '86 C.763 B.A. L.464 J.D. [Chapin,F.&W.]
**Carter, Susan K.**, (AV) ................ '41 '78 C.112 B.A. L.1095 J.D. [Wasser,R.&C.]
**Carter, Thomas P.** ................ '63 '93 C&L.426 B.A., J.D. [▣ Burke,W.&S.]
*PRACTICE AREAS: General Civil Litigation.
Carter, Vereline F. ................ '31 '76 C.217 B.A. L.1095 J.D. 4050 Buckingham Rd.

**Carter, Geraldine C., Law Offices of**
**2029 Century Park East, Suite 600, 90067-3012**
**Telephone: 310-551-1714 Telecopier: 310-556-7975**
**Geraldine C. Carter. Of Counsel: Kirtley M. Thiesmeyer.**
**Business, Corporate, Real Property, with Emphasis in the Areas of Secured and Unsecured Financing, Leasing, Acquisitions, Property Management, Hazardous Materials Compliance and Remediation and International Trade.**
***See Professional Biographies, LOS ANGELES, CALIFORNIA***

**Cartwright, Brian G.** ................ '47 '80 C.976 B.S. L.309 J.D. [Latham&W.]
**Cartwright, David W.** ................ '56 '81 C.945 A.B. L.339 J.D. [O'Melveny&M.]
*LANGUAGES: French.
*PRACTICE AREAS: Real Estate; Government Contracts.
**Cartwright, Robert C.** ................ '60 '89 C.112 B.A. L.426 J.D. [▣ Crawford&R.]
*PRACTICE AREAS: Business Litigation; Environmental Litigation; Construction Litigation; Employment Litigation.
**Caruso, Joanne E.** ................ '60 '86 C&L.93 B.A., J.D. [Howrey&S.]
*PRACTICE AREAS: Antitrust Law; Complex Litigation; Litigation.
**Caruso, Linda R.** ................ '64 '89 C.321 B.A. L.273 J.D. [▣ Barger&W.]
Caruso, Rick J. ................ '59 '83 C.800 B.S. L.990 J.D. Pres., Caruso Affiliated Holdings
Caruso, Vito ................ '57 '90 C.1069 B.A. L.426 J.D. Dep. Alternate Pub. Def.
**Carver, Richard**, (AV) ................ '33 '58 C&L.813 A.B., J.D. [▣ Latham&W.]
**Cary, N. Dwight** ................ '48 '75 C.668 B.A. L.813 J.D. [Murphy,W.&B.]⊙
*PRACTICE AREAS: Secured Financing; Commercial Lending; Creditors Remedies; Real Estate Finance.
**Casamassima, Thomas J.**, (AV) ... '41 '68 C.1077 B.A. L.1068 LL.B. [Anderson,M.&C.]
*PRACTICE AREAS: Trial Practice; Environmental Litigation; Insurance Coverage; Construction Law; Surety Law.
**Case, Daniel A., (P.C.)**, (AV) ................ '51 '76 C.453 B.S. L.1066 [Case,K.B.&W.]
*PRACTICE AREAS: Corporate; Real Estate.
Case, John A., Jr. ................ '62 '86 C.178 A.B. L.813 J.D. 1875 Century Park E.

**Case, Knowlson, Burnett & Wright, (AV)**
**A Partnership including Professional Corporations**
**Suite 1700, 2121 Avenue of the Stars, 90067⊙**
**Telephone: 310-552-2766 Telecopier: 310-552-3229**
**Daniel A. Case (P.C.); Rick A. Cigel; Michael F. Wright; Patrick W. Walsh; Rick Augustini. Of Counsel: David M. Luber; Edwin I. Lasman; Daniel G. Jordan.**
**General Civil Trial and Appellate Practice in all State and Federal Courts. Corporate, Real Estate, Real Estate Finance, Taxation, Estate Planning, Trusts and Probate Law.**
**Irvine, California Office: 5 Park Plaza, Suite 800. Telephone: 714-955-1050. Telecopier: 714-851-9112.**
***See Professional Biographies, LOS ANGELES, CALIFORNIA***

**Casey, Edward J.** ................ '60 '85 C.1019 B.A. L.145 J.D. [McClintock,W.B.R.R.&M.]
*PRACTICE AREAS: Hazardous Waste; Environmental Litigation; CEQA Litigation.
**Casey, Elizabeth A.** ................ '62 '88 C.154 B.A. L.273 J.D. [Troop M.S.&P.]
*PRACTICE AREAS: General Commercial Litigation; Entertainment Litigation.
Casey, Marylynne B. ................ '55 '83 C.1109 B.A. L.1137 J.D. P.O. Box 45045
**Cashdan, Russ Alan** ................ '63 '90 C.1044 B.A. L.800 J.D. [▣ Kaye,S.F.H.&H.]
*PRACTICE AREAS: Corporate (Finance, Mergers and Acquisitions General); Entertainment.

**Cashion, David C.**
**(See Pasadena)**

Caskey, Marshall A., (AV) ................ '43 '75 C.378 B.S.J. L.502 J.D. 6255 Sunset Blvd.
Cass, Paul D. ................ '48 '81 C.685 B.A. L.976 J.D. [Stettin&C.]
Cassady, Ralph, (P.C.), (AV) ................ '32 '62 C.813 A.B. L.1068 LL.B. 1000 Wilshire Blvd.
**Cassel, Joel A., (P.C.)** ................ '40 '66 C.103 B.A. L.569 LL.B. [Jeffer,M.B.&M.]
*PRACTICE AREAS: Real Estate; General Business; Secured Financing Transactions.
Casselman, Gary S., (AV) ................ '49 '78 C.477 B.A. L.809 J.D. 11340 W. Olympic Blvd.
Cassidy, Daniel C. ................ '37 '69 C.800 B.S. L.426 J.D. [Liebert,C.&F.]
Cassidy, Seán M. ................ '57 '86 C.112 B.A. L.1068 J.D. 2029 Century Park E.
Cassman, Alan H., (AV) ................ '22 '49 C&L.659 B.A., LL.B. 8929 S. Sepulveda Blvd.
**Castanares, Anthony**, (AV) ................ '43 '71 C.112 B.A. L.569 J.D. [▣ Hennigan,M.&B.]
*LANGUAGES: Spanish.
*PRACTICE AREAS: Complex Business Litigation.
Casteel, Kimler G. ................ '39 '66 C.112 B.S. L.1068 J.D. 777 S. Figueroa St., 10th Fl.
Castellanos, Anita L. '39 '64
C&L.800 B.S.L., LL.B. Claims Atty., Auto. Club of Southern Calif.
Castellanos, Richard H. ................ '65 '90 C.112 B.A. L.1066 J.D. Los Angeles AIDS Project
**Castellon, Ruben A.** '63 '91 C.740 B.S.B.A. L.1068 J.D.
[▣ Radcliff,F.&D.] (⊙San Fran.)
*LANGUAGES: Spanish.
Casterline, David L., (AV) ................ '42 '67 C.63 B.S. L.1119 J.D. [Casterline&A.]
Casterline & Agajanian, LLP, (AV) ................ Ste. 1000, 550 S. Hope St.
**Castillo, Angel F.** ................ '64 '89 C&L.813 A.B., J.D. [▣ Levy,S.&L.]
*PRACTICE AREAS: Commercial Finance; Secured Transactions.
Castillo, Jose M. ................ '34 '65 C.112 B.A. L.809 J.D. 444 S. Flower St.
**Castillo, Margie** ................ '57 '94 C.723 B.S. L.310 J.D. [▣ Black C.H.&L.]
*LANGUAGES: Spanish.
*PRACTICE AREAS: Insurance Coverage; Coverage Litigation; Bad Faith Litigation; Appellate Practice.
Castillo, Martin G. ................ '31 '62 C&L.425 B.S., LL.B. 5408 E. Beverly Blvd.
Castillo, Pedro V. ................ '65 '92 C.813 B.A. L.37 J.D. Dep. Fed. Pub. Def.
Castle, Christian L. '50 '88 C.112 B.A. L.1068 J.D.
V.P., Bus. & Leg. Affs., A & M Records, Inc.
**Castle, Mary C.**, (AV) ................ '50 '77 C.309 A.B. L.273 J.D. [Folger L.&K.]⊙
**Castner, Laura D.** ................ '66 '92 C.705 B.A. L.178 J.D. [▣ Morrison&F.]
*LANGUAGES: French.
**Castorina, Bryan T.** ................ '66 '92 C.112 B.A. L.1066 J.D. [▣ McDermott,W.&E.]
**Castricone, Andrew D.** ................ '63 '91 C.1044 B.S. L.464 J.D. [▣ Ropers,M.K.&B.]
*PRACTICE AREAS: Litigation.
**Castrilli, Anthony, Jr.** ................ '66 '91 C.145 B.A. L.659 J.D. [▣ Dewey B.]
Castro, Emma ................ '52 '78 C.112 B.A. L.1068 J.D. P.O. Box 32157
**Castro, Eric C.** ................ '53 '79 C.976 B.A. L.800 J.D. [Lewis,D.B.&B.]
**Castro, Leonard E.**, (AV) ................ '34 '63 C.112 A.B. L.1068 J.D. [Musick,P.&G.]
*PRACTICE AREAS: Corporate Law; Securities.
**Castruccio, Eugenia L.** ................ '70 '96 C.321 B.A. L.145 J.D. [▣ Jones,D.R.&P.]
**Castruccio, Louis M., (P.C.)**, (AV) ................ '38 '65 C.770 A.B. L.800 LL.B. [Irell&M.]
**Catalino, Cynthia F.** ................ '66 '93 C.881 B.A. L.990 J.D. [▣ Manatt,P.&P.]
*PRACTICE AREAS: Trusts and Estates.
**Cate, Jan H.** ................ '64 '89 C.112 B.A. L.94 J.D. [▣ Pillsbury M.&S.]
**Cates, Richard B.** '63 '93 C.174 B.S. L.1065 J.D.
[▣ Fulwider P.L.&U.] (See Pat. Sect.)
*PRACTICE AREAS: Patent; Trademark; Copyright; Litigation.
Cates, Richard E. ................ '49 '77 C.112 B.A. L.1148 J.D. Sr. Atty., Calif. Ct. of App.

**Cates & Han**
**(See Irvine)**

**Cathcart, Daniel C., (Professional Corporation)**, (AV) '32 '57
C&L.800 LL.B. [▣ Magaña,C.&M.]
*PRACTICE AREAS: Airplane Crash Litigation; Aviation Law; Personal Injury Law; Products Liability Law; Wrongful Death Law.
**Cathcart, David A.**, (AV) ................ '40 '68 C.813 A.B. L.309 LL.B. [Gibson,D.&C.]
*PRACTICE AREAS: Labor and Employment Law; Litigation; Alternative Dispute Resolution; Administrative Law.
**Cathcart, Patrick A.**, (AV) ................ '45 '75 C.813 A.B. L.1065 J.D. [Hancock R.&B.]
**Cathcart, Peter T., (Professional Corporation)** '55 '80
C.800 B.S. L.426 J.D. [Magaña,C.&M.]
*PRACTICE AREAS: Airplane Crash Litigation; Aviation Law; Bad Faith Law; Personal Injury Law; Products Liability Law.
**Cathcart, Robert J.**, (AV) ................ '45 '72 C.813 A.B. L.911 J.D. [Allen,M.L.G.&M.]
*PRACTICE AREAS: Litigation; Construction Law.
**Cathey, William L.**, (AV) ................ '47 '77 C.575 B.S. L.477 J.D. [Munger,T.&O.]
**Catlow, James T.**, (AV) ................ '48 '74 C.112 B.A. L.1049 J.D. [▣ Williamson,R.&D.]
*PRACTICE AREAS: Insurance Coverage; Bad Faith; Complex Litigation; Construction Defect; Professional Malpractice.
**Caudle, Sheila R.** ................ '50 '87 C.549 B.A. L.128 J.D. [▣ Gibson,D.&C.]
*PRACTICE AREAS: Litigation; General Practice.
**Caudry, M. Kendall** ................ '64 '89 C&L.426 B.B.A., J.D. [▣ Breidenbach,B.H.H.&H.]
Cavalluzzi, Maria ................ '63 '87 C.426 B.A. L.809 J.D. Dep. Pub. Def.
**Cavanagh, John E.** ................ '18 '49 C.629 A.B. L.273 J.D. [McKenna&C.]
Cavanaugh, Gerald A., Jr. '44 '76
C.573 B.B.A. L.602 J.D. 1745 Camino Palmero St., Apt. 214
Cavanaugh, Thomas G. ................ '62 '90 C.178 B.A. L.1068 J.D. Fox, Inc.
Cavna, Arthur D. ................ '39 '88 C.284 B.A. L.999 J.D. Dept. of Industrial Relations
Cawile, Lourdes C. ................ '60 '87 C.112 B.A. L.1137 J.D. Dep. Pub. Def.

**Cayer, Kilstofte & Craton**
**(See Long Beach)**

Cayo, Felix B. ................ '32 '63 C.309 B.A. L.976 LL.B. 10793 Ashton Ave.
**Cazier, Edward C., Jr.**, (AV) ................ '24 '52 C.112 A.B. L.800 LL.B. [▣ Morgan,L.&B.]
**Cazzulino, Claude** ................ '54 '85 C.103 B.A. L.588 J.D. [Schwartz,S.D.&S.]
*PRACTICE AREAS: ERISA; Employee Benefit Law; Labor and Employment Law.
Cebeci, Rabia A. ................ '64 '89 C.112 B.A. L.426 J.D. Secs. Exch. Comm.
**Ceccon, Robert C.** ................ '60 '84 C.178 B.A. L.1068 J.D. [Richards,W.&G.]
*PRACTICE AREAS: Insurance Coverage; Litigation.
**Ceder, Christine E.** ................ '68 '94 C.763 B.S. L.990 J.D. [▣ Goldfarb,S.&A.]
*PRACTICE AREAS: Estate Planning; Transactional.
Cederberg, Jon C., (AV) ................ '52 '77 C&L.477 B.A., J.D. One Wilshire Blvd.
Ceely, Frederick ................ '48 '91 C.994 B.A. L.990 J.D. 5757 W. Century Blvd.
**Ceglar, Frank J., Jr.** '46 '74 C.8 B.S.A. L.7 J.D.
Asst. V.P. & Assoc. Gen. Coun., Farmers Grp., Inc.
*RESPONSIBILITIES: Property and Casualty Insurance.

CAA198P

**Celebrezze, Bruce D.**, (AV) '54 '79
C.602 A.B. L.477 J.D. [Celebrezze&W.] (⊙San Fran.)

**Celebrezze & Wesley, A Professional Corporation, (AV)**
**444 South Flower Street, Suite 2300, 90071⊙**
**Telephone: 213-243-1277 Facsimile: 213-243-1286**
**Email: 7345748@mcimail.com**
**Bruce D. Celebrezze; Nancy M. Wesley; Katherine Cranston Potter; Graziella Walsh Coggan; Howard S. Vallens; Jeffrey A. Meyers. Of Counsel: Scott Conley; Steven X. Schwenk.**
**Insurance Coverage, Insurance Litigation and Business Litigation.**
**San Francisco, California Office: 655 Montgomery Street, 17th Floor, 94111. Telephone: 415-288-3900. Facsimile: 415-288-3919. Email: 7365740@mcimail.com.**
**San Luis Obispo, California Office: 763 B Foothill Boulevard, Suite 146, 93405. Telephone: 805-927-9700. Facsimile: 805-927-9701. Email: 7305744@mcimail.com.**
***See Professional Biographies, LOS ANGELES, CALIFORNIA***

Celli, Thomas M. ... '37 '72 C.37 B.S. L.809 J.D. 3055 Wilshire Blvd.
**CeloCruz, Maria T.** ... '46 '93 C.788 A.B. L.94 J.D. [Ⓐ Baker&H.]
*PRACTICE AREAS: Labor and Employment Law.
**Center, Brian** ... '67 '93 C.378 B.A. L.112 J.D. [Ⓐ Christensen,M.F.J.G.W.&S.]
*PRACTICE AREAS: Business Litigation.
**Ceperley, Tim G.** ... '50 '84 C.216 B.A. L.426 J.D. [Rodi,P.P.G.&C.]
*PRACTICE AREAS: Civil Litigation; Products Liability Construction and Insurance Law.
Cephas, Dana ... '57 '93 C.184 B.S. L.145 J.D. 300 S. Grand Ave., Suite 3000
**Ceran, Allan E.** ... '54 '80 C.94 B.A. L.1068 J.D. [Rogers&W.]
Cercos, Theodore R. ... '59 '87 C.112 B.A. L.1067 J.D. [Lincoln,G.&C.]⊙
**Cereseto, Michael J.** ... '48 '73 C.112 B.A. L.1068 J.D. [Buchalter,N.F.&Y.]
*PRACTICE AREAS: Real Estate Litigation.
**Cermak, John F., Jr.** ... '56 '82 C.94 B.A. L.30 J.D. [Rodi,P.P.G.&C.]
*LANGUAGES: German.
*REPORTED CASES: Long Beach Unified School District v. Dorothy B. Goodwin, 32 F. 3d 1364 (9th Cir. 1994); AISI v. EPA, 886 F.2d 390 (D.C. Cir. 1989); Center for Auto Safety v. Thomas, 847 F. 2d 843 (D.C. CIr. 1988); Phillips Petroleum Co. v. EPA, 803 F.2d 545 (10th Cir. 1986); B.R. MacKay & Sons v. EPA, 633 F. Supp. 1290 (D. Utah 1986).
*PRACTICE AREAS: Environmental; Health and Safety; Civil Litigation.
Cermak, Thomas A. '43 '82
C.800 L.1137 J.D. Claims Atty., Auto. Club of Southern Calif.
**Cerny, Robert J.** ... '66 '92 C&L.93 B.A., J.D. [Ⓐ Barger&W.]
Cerra, Sharla '54 '81 C&L.502 B.A., J.D.
(adm. in MO; not adm. in CA) U.S. Atty.'s Off.
**Cerrina, Michael H.** ... '57 '82 C.800 B.S. L.426 J.D. [Allen,M.L.G.&M.]
*PRACTICE AREAS: Real Estate.
Cerutti, Romeo ... '62 '92 L.061 633 W. 5th St.
Cha, Jason S. ... '58 '85 C.145 B.A. L.665 J.D. 695 S. Vermont AVe.
**Cha, John S.** ... '61 '87 C.597 B.A. L.910 J.D. [Rodi,P.P.G.&C.]
*LANGUAGES: Korean.
*PRACTICE AREAS: Commercial Litigation; Insurance Law; Environmental Law; Professional Malpractice; Construction Law.

**Chadbourne & Parke LLP, (AV)** [BR]
**601 South Figueroa Street, 90017⊙**
**Telephone: 213-892-1000 Facsimile: 213-622-9865**
**Partners: Richard J. Ney; Jonathan F. Bank; Harvey I. Saferstein; Peter R. Chaffetz; Jay R. Henneberry; Linda Dakin-Grimm; Kenneth J. Langan. Resident Counsel: William J. Kelley, III. Resident Associates: Robin D. Ball; Glenn R. Bronson; Peter M. DelVecchio (Not admitted in CA); Anahid Gharakhanian; Armen K. Hovannisian; Kevin D. Hughes (Not admitted in CA); George Lasko; Marvin D. Mohn; Ann K. Penners; Mary Louise Serafine.**
**General Practice.**
**New York, N.Y. Office: 30 Rockefeller Plaza, 10112. Telephone: 212-408-5100. Facsimile: 212-541-5369.**
**Washington, D.C. Office: 1101 Vermont Avenue, N.W., 20005. Telephone: 202-289-3000. Facsimile: 202-289-3002.**
**London, England Office: 86 Jermyn Street, SW1 6JD. Telephone: 44-171-925-7400. Facsimile: 44-171-839-3393.**
**Moscow, Russia Office: 38 Kosmodamianskaya Naberezhnaya, 113035. Telephone: 7095-974-2424. Facsimile: 7095-974-2425. International satellite lines via U.S.: Telephone: 212-408-1190. Facsimile: 212-408-1199.**
**Hong Kong Office: Suite 3704, Peregrine Tower, Lippo Centre, 89 Queensway. Telephone: 852-2842-5400. Facsimile: 852-2521-7527.**
***See Professional Biographies, LOS ANGELES, CALIFORNIA***

Chaffetz, Nancy G. '53 '79 C&L.145 B.A., J.D.
(adm. in NY; not adm. in CA) 10473 Lindebrook Dr.‡
**Chaffetz, Peter R.**, (AV) ... '52 '79 C.309 A.B. L.145 J.D. [Chadbourne&P.]
Chahin, Sonia Elizabeth ... '63 '88 C.800 B.A. L.1049 J.D. 900 Wilshire Blvd.
**Chahine, Steve S.** ... '71 '96 C.309 A.B. L.1068 J.D. [Ⓐ Loeb&L.]
**Chais, Wrenn E.** ... '62 '89 C.840 B.B.A. L.990 J.D. [Ⓐ Stroock&S.&L.]
*PRACTICE AREAS: Business Litigation; White Collar Crime; Bankruptcy Litigation; Accountant Liability.
Chait, Robert J. ... '40 '66 C.659 B.S. L.569 LL.B. 1st V.P., Security Pacific Natl. Bk.
**Chakravorty, Pinaki** ... '69 '96 C.309 A.B. L.976 J.D. [Ⓐ O'Melveny&M.]
*LANGUAGES: French, Bengali, Hindi.

**Chaleff & English**
**(See Santa Monica)**

Chalfant, James C., (AV) ... '52 '79 C.668 B.A. L.1066 J.D. 444 S. Flower St., 11th Fl.
**Chamberlain, Harry W. R., II**, (AV) ... '57 '80 C.763 B.A. L.1065 J.D. [Musick,P.&G.]
*PRACTICE AREAS: Litigation; Insurance; Appellate Law.
**Chamberlin, Kirk C.** ... '62 '87 C.347 B.A. L.352 J.D. [Charlston,R.&W.]
**Chamberlin, Michael S.** ... '66 '94 C.112 B.A. L.1068 J.D. [Ⓐ Morrison&F.]
Chambers, Jon Charles ... '39 '70 C.608 B.A. L.1119 J.D. Dep. Co. Pub. Def.
**Chamblee, Lawrence W.** ... '42 '73 C&L.446 A.B., J.D. [Ⓒ Buchanan&K.]
*LANGUAGES: French.
*PRACTICE AREAS: Civil Litigation.
**Champ, Michael W.** ... '53 '80 C.1073 B.A. L.990 J.D. [Spray,G.&B.]
**Champion, Daniel E.** ... '58 '83 C.1265 B.S. L.477 J.D. [Ⓒ Graham&J.]
*PRACTICE AREAS: Litigation; Commercial Collection Law; Commercial; Enforcement of Judgements; Prejudgement Remedies.
**Chan, Antonia M.** ... '67 '83 C.112 B.A. L.426 J.D. [Ⓐ Lynberg&W.]
*LANGUAGES: Cantonese.
Chan, David R. ... '48 '73 C.112 B.A. L.1068 J.D. Dir., Kenneth Leventhal & Co.
**Chan, Lorita M.** ... '67 '93 C.112 B.A. L.426 J.D. [Ⓐ Nelson&B.]
*LANGUAGES: Cantonese, Spanish.
*PRACTICE AREAS: Construction Defect Litigation; Employment Litigation; Insurance Defense.
Chan, Mary M. ... '54 '83 C.668 B.A. L.800 J.D. V.P., Edward Properties
**Chan, Paul S.** ... '70 '95 C&L.309 A.B., J.D. [Ⓐ Quinn E.U.&O.]
**Chan, Sandra J.**, (AV) ... '56 '79 C.112 A.B. L.1067 J.D. [Perkins C.]
*LANGUAGES: Mandarin.
*PRACTICE AREAS: Estate Planning; Probate Law; Decedents Trust Administration.
**Chan, Thomas T.** ... '50 '79 C.965 B.A. L.966 J.D. [Chan]
*LANGUAGES: Chinese.
*REPORTED CASES: Z-Nix v. Microsoft.
*PRACTICE AREAS: Patent, Trademark and Copyrights; Computer Law; International Law.

**Chan Law Group, A Professional Law Corporation**
**911 Wilshire Boulevard, Suite 2288, P.O. Box 79159, 90017-3451**
**Telephone: 213-624-6560 Fax: 213-622-1154**
**Email: chanlaw@counsel.com URL: http://CHANLAW.COM**
**Thomas T. Chan; Ronald M. St. Marie; Ruby P. Shimomura.**
**Patent, Trademark, Copyright, Unfair Competition, Trade Secret, Licensing, Computer, Commercial, Acquisition and Merger, Corporation, International, China Trade and Customs, Export Control, Antitrust, Civil Litigation in all Courts.**
***See Professional Biographies, LOS ANGELES, CALIFORNIA***

Chandler, Catherine J. '60 '89 C.276 B.S. L.93 J.D.
(adm. in MA; not adm. in CA) P.O. Box 17576
Chandler, Susan Kay ... '47 '79 C.1042 B.A. L.1066 J.D. 801 S. Figueroa St.
**Chandra, Subodh** ... '67 '95 C.813 A.B. L.976 J.D. [Ⓐ Christensen,M.F.J.G.W.&S.]
*LANGUAGES: Hindi.
*PRACTICE AREAS: General Litigation; Entertainment Litigation; Governmental Law; Defense Litigation.
Chang, Alan ... '67 '93 C.569 B.A. L.94 J.D. 221 N. Figueroa St.
**Chang, Christine M.** ... '70 '96 C.1097 B.A. L.310 J.D. [Ⓐ Lim,R.&K.]
*PRACTICE AREAS: Civil Litigation.
Chang, Dennis W. ... '56 '88 C.1097 B.A. L.1065 J.D. [Chang&L.]
Chang, Howard F. '60 '89 C&L.309 A.B., J.D.
(adm. in NY; not adm. in CA) Assoc. Prof. of Law, Univ. of Southern Calif.
**Chang, J. June** ... '67 '92 C.104 B.A. L.831 J.D. [Ⓐ Tharpe&H.]
*PRACTICE AREAS: Insurance Defense.
Chang, Julian C. L. ... '61 '87 C.636 B.S. L.1049 J.D. 221 N. Figueroa St.
**Chang, Karen McLaurin** ... '61 '90 C.112 B.A. L.800 J.D. [Demetriou,D.S.&M.]
*PRACTICE AREAS: Environmental Law; Civil Litigation.
Chang, Lena C. ... '64 '91 C.188 A.B. L.1065 J.D. [Ⓐ Milberg W.B.H.&L.]
**Chang, Pei-Wen** ... '56 '91 C.061 B.A. L.426 J.D. [Ⓐ Graham&J.]
*LANGUAGES: Mandarin.
*PRACTICE AREAS: Admiralty and Maritime Law; Products Liability; Labor and Employment.
Chang, Te Jung ... '63 '90 C.112 B.A. L.284 J.D. 12121 Wilshire Blvd.
**Chang, Timothy P.** ... '65 '92 C.112 B.S. L.464 J.D. [Ⓐ Harrington,F.D.&C.]
*LANGUAGES: Japanese.
*PRACTICE AREAS: Coverage Litigation; Construction Defect; General Liability.
**Chang, Wendy Wen Yun** ... '70 '95 C.112 B.A. L.426 J.D. [Ⓐ Selman B.]
*LANGUAGES: Mandarin (conversational; verbal).
*PRACTICE AREAS: Insurance Coverage; Construction Defect; Coverage Litigation.
**Chang, Wonkoo** ... '64 '90 C&L.112 B.A., J.D. [Ⓐ Hillsinger&C.]
*LANGUAGES: Korean.
**Chang, WooJin (Eugene)** '59 '88 C.453 B.S. L.1066 J.D.
[Akre,B.&C.] (⊙Seoul, Korea)
*LANGUAGES: Korean and Japanese.
*PRACTICE AREAS: International Law; High Technology.
Chang and Lim ... 3325 Wilshire Blvd., 9th Fl.
**Chantland, James M.** ... '55 '80 C.800 B.A. L.426 J.D. [Morris,P.&P.]
Chapel, J. Alicia ... '47 '92 C.112 B.A. L.1066 J.D. 400 S. Hope St.

**Chapin, Fleming & Winet, (AV)**
**Suite 401, 12121 Wilshire Boulevard, 90025⊙**
**Telephone: 310-826-0133 Fax: 310-207-4236**
**Craig H. Bell; David H. Bushnell; Richard D. Carter; George Chuang; Robert Ehrenreich (Resident); Howard L. Hoffenberg; Dana Marie Lawson; Jeffrey J. Leist; Tonya L. Morgan; David A. Myers; Brenda J. Pannell; Thomas V. Perea; Spencer C. Skeen; Howard Smith; Grace I. Wang. Of Counsel: Arthur D. Rutledge; Jeffrey C. Stodel; Irwin Waldman (A P.C.).**
**Insurance Bad Faith and Coverage Practice in Liability, Disability, Life, Property, Health, Accident, Marine, Malpractice, Surety, Aviation, Self-Insurance Law, General Business, Corporate and Real Estate Litigation.**
**San Diego, California Office: Library, 501 West Broadway, 15th Floor. Telephone: 619-232-4261. Telefax: 619-323-4840.**
**Vista, California Office: 410 South Melrose Drive, Suite 101. Telephone: 619-758-4261. Telefax: 619-758-6420.**
**Palm Springs, California Office: 225 North El Cielo Road, Suite 470. Telephone: 619-416-1400. Telefax: 619-416-1405.**
***See Professional Biographies, LOS ANGELES, CALIFORNIA***

**Chapkis, Richard A.** ... '65 '91 C.103 B.A. L.1066 J.D. [Ⓐ Troop M.S.&P.]
*PRACTICE AREAS: Insurance Coverage Litigation; General Business Litigation.
**Chaplan, Scott** ... '64 '91 C.990 B.S. L.800 J.D. [Ⓐ Argue P.H.&M.]
*PRACTICE AREAS: Civil Litigation; Business Transactions.
**Chapman, Arthur J.** ... '51 '77 C.112 B.A. L.426 J.D. [Chapman&G.]
*PRACTICE AREAS: Business and Commercial Litigation; Products Liability; Negligence; Coverage; Professional Malpractice.
**Chapman, Bruce G.** ... '60 '87 C.215 B.Mech. L.273 J.D. [Ⓐ Lyon&L.] (See Pat. Sect.)
*PRACTICE AREAS: Intellectual Property.
**Chapman, K. Leigh** ... '64 '89 C.228 A.B. L.178 J.D. [Ⓒ O'Melveny&M.]
*PRACTICE AREAS: Labor and Employment Law.
**Chapman, Laura L.** ... '64 '93 C.788 A.B. L.800 J.D. [Ⓐ Beckman,D.S.&R.]
*PRACTICE AREAS: Insurance Litigation; Employment Litigation; Commercial Litigation.
**Chapman, Lloyd K.** ... '60 '86 C.112 B.A. L.1067 J.D. [Ⓐ Friedlander&W.]
*PRACTICE AREAS: Business and Commercial Litigation; Real Estate Litigation.
**Chapman, Robert S.** ... '51 '76 C.112 A.B. L.1067 J.D. [Greenberg G.F.C.&M.]
*PRACTICE AREAS: Entertainment Litigation; Defamation; General Business Litigation.
Chapman, Rosalyn M. ... '43 '69 C.477 B.A. L.1066 J.D. U.S. Mag.
**Chapman, Shawn Snider** ... '62 '88 C.112 B.A. L.809 J.D. [Ⓐ J.L.Cochran,Jr.]
*PRACTICE AREAS: Criminal Defense; Personal Injury.
Chapman, Stacy ... '66 '91 C.934 B.A. L.426 J.D. Staff Atty., Inner City Law Ctr.
Chapman, Stuart Alan ... '41 '68 C.112 B.A. L.800 J.D. Dep. Pub. Def.
Chapman, Timothy Jon '60 '88
C.1075 B.A. L.1148 J.D. 4215 Glencoe Ave. (Marina Del Rey)

**Chapman & Glucksman, A Professional Corporation, (AV)** [BR]
**11900 West Olympic Boulevard, Suite 800, 90064-0704**
**Telephone: 310-207-7722 Facsimile: 310-207-6550**
**Richard H. Glucksman; Arthur J. Chapman; Randall J. Dean; Wendy M. Housman; James C. Earle; Craig A. Roeb;—Thomas L. Halliwell; Dominic J. Fote; Christopher R. Kent; Andrew B. Cohn; Jeffrey A. Cohen; Glenn T. Barger; Christine L. Vanderbilt; Gregory Sabo; Rita Mongoven Miller; Todd M. Mobley; D. Scott Dodd; Jon A. Turigliatto; Karen S. Danto. Of Counsel: Thomas J. Pabst.**
**General Civil Practice in all State and Federal Trial and Appellate Courts. Commercial and Business Litigation and General Insurance Practice, including Products Liability, Professional Liability, Coverage, Construction Litigation, Complex and Multi-District Litigation, Commercial, Wrongful Termination, Corporation, Director and Officer Liability, Association Liability, Toxic and Hazardous Substance, Real Estate and Estate Planning, Excess and Surplus Insurance.**
**Reference: First Professional Bank, Santa Monica.**
***See Professional Biographies, LOS ANGELES, CALIFORNIA***

**Charles, Katessa M.** ... '63 '90 C.112 B.A. L.276 J.D. [Ⓐ Arter&H.]
*PRACTICE AREAS: Business and Employment Litigation.
**Charlston, Jeffrey A.** ... '50 '75 C.668 B.A. L.1068 J.D. [Charlston,R.&W.]

**Charlston, Revich & Williams LLP, (AV)**
**1840 Century Park East Third Floor, 90067-2104**
**Telephone: 310-551-7000 Telecopier: 310-203-9321**
**Partners of the Firm: Jeffrey A. Charlston; Ira Revich; Richard D. Williams; Howard N. Wollitz; Timothy J. Harris; Eugene C. Moscovitch; Stephen P. Soskin; Robert W. Keaster; Richard C. Giller; Robert D. Hoffman; Kirk C. Chamberlin. Associates: Paul D. Albus; John D. Antoni; David A.**

(This Listing Continued)

CAA199P

**Charlston, Revich & Williams LLP (Continued)**

**Eisenberg; Vanci Y. Fuller; Susan L. Germaise; Lisa M. Hatton; Margret J. Kim; David S. Levy; Shervin Mirhashemi; Robert P. Mitrovich; Elizabeth A. Moussouros; Robert A. Rosen; Guy M. Roy; Stephanie H. Scherby; Randolph C. Simpson; Wayne C. Smith; Bruce T. Smyth; Michael K. Staub; Patricia I. Taue; Christopher R. Wagner; Chad B. Wootton.**
**General Civil Trial and Appellate Practice before all State and Federal Courts. Insurance Coverage Litigation, Environmental, Toxic Torts and Hazardous Waste Law. Professional Liability, Officer and Director Liability, and Products Liability Coverage and Defense Litigation, Securities and Real Estate Litigation. Tax, Estate Planning and Trusts, and Business Law. Receivership Representation and Workouts and Wrongful Discharge Defense. Employment Law, Criminal Defense, White-Collar Fraud and Intellectual Property.**

*See Professional Biographies, LOS ANGELES, CALIFORNIA*

Charnay, John B. ........'49 '77 C.659 B.A. L.809 J.D. Natural History Museum of L.A.
Charnley, Richard L. B., (BV) .......'48 '76 C.112 B.A. L.990 J.D. 10880 Wilshire Blvd.
Chasalow, Irwin, (AV) ..........'32 '64 C.112 A.B. L.809 LL.B. 1900 Ave. of the Stars
Chasalow, Michael A. ............'62 '87 C.112 B.A. L.1066 J.D. 1900 Ave. of the Stars
Chasan, Mark S. ...................'57 '85 C&L.1137 B.S., J.D. 12424 Wilshire Blvd.
**Chase, Charles H.**, (AV) .....................'21 '49 C&L.546 B.S., J.D. [Smiland&K.]
*PRACTICE AREAS: Corporate Law; Tax Law; Estates; Trusts.
Chase, Rodney A. ............'39 '65 C.112 B.S. L.426 LL.B. 11911 San Vicente Blvd.
Chase, Stephen M. ...................'46 '71 C.112 B.A. L.426 J.D. State Dept. of Transp.
Chase, Rotchford, Drukker & Bogust, (AV) ............700 South Flower Street, Suite 500
Chasworth, Susan D. .................'58 '83 C.1044 B.A. L.800 J.D. Dist. Atty.'s. Off.
Chatfield, David Blake ...........'51 '79 C.800 B.A. L.1095 J.D. 2121 Ave. of the Stars
Chatman, Lynette G. ..........'50 '89 C.569 B.A. L.1068 J.D. Dep. Atty., Dept. of Trans.
Chaum, Elliot .........'28 '55 C.339 B.S. L.846 J.D. Gen. Coun., Motown Record Corp.
Chávez, Rosemary Elaine ..................'60 '88 C&L.1137 B.S.L., J.D. Dep. City Atty.
Chavez, Victor E., (AV) .............................'30 '60 C&L.426 B.S., J.D. Supr. Court J.
Chavez, Victoria Marie ...........................'53 '79 C.767 B.A. L.426 J.D. Supr. Ct. J.
Chayo, Leslie E. ...............'50 '75 C.1077 B.S. L.426 J.D. 1901 Ave. of the Stars
Cheeseman, Henry R. ............'46 '73 C.436 B.B.A. L.1068 J.D. 4929 Wilshire Blvd.
Cheleden, Algerdas N., Jr. ............'36 '63 C.611 B.A. L.1068 LL.B. 3435 Wilshire Blvd.
**Cheleden, Christopher R.** ............'68 '95 C.659 A.B. L.1067 J.D. [Burke,W.&S.]
*PRACTICE AREAS: Municipal Law; Environmental Law.
Cheleden, Robert A. ...............................'62 '91 C.112 B.A. L.809 J.D. Dep. Dist. Atty.
Chemerinski, Eliel .........'63 '89 C.260 B.S. L.861 J.D. 1901 Ave. of the Stars, 20th Fl.
**Chen, Alexander J.** ..............................'57 '82 C.112 B.A. L.1065 J.D. [Schaffer&L.]
**Chen, Christopher D.** ....................'65 '90 C.119 B.S. L.276 J.D. [Mayer,B.&P.]
**Chen, Connie C.** ...................................'71 '96 C.674 A.B. L.309 J.D. [Latham&W.]
*LANGUAGES: Madanrin and Taiwanese.
**Chen, David Y.** ..................'69 '94 C.228 A.B. L.813 J.D. [Skadden,A.S.M.&F.]
Chen, Denny D. .........................'54 '81 C.112 B.S. L.1066 J.D. 1200 Wilshire Blvd.
**Chen, Frank W.** ..................................'63 '88 C.813 A.B. L.1068 J.D. [Ku,F.L.&C.]
*LANGUAGES: Chinese (Mandarin and Taiwanese).
*PRACTICE AREAS: Civil Trial; Litigation; Real Estate Law; Business Law.
Chen, Jacques C. ..................................'59 '84 L.1137 J.D. 1999 Ave. of the Stars
**Chen, Jenny Chyi Ching** ..................'71 '96 C.813 B.A. L.569 J.D. [Klein&M.]
*LANGUAGES: Spanish, French, Mandarin.
**Chen, Kemble** .............................'70 '94 C.112 B.S. L.426 J.D. [Koletsky,M.&F.]
*LANGUAGES: Mandarin Chinese.
*PRACTICE AREAS: General Liability; Construction Defect; Immigration; Contracts; Criminal.
**Chen, Kurt Michael** ..................'54 '79 C.800 B.A. L.809 J.D. [Quinn E.U.&O.]
**Chen, Wun-ee Chelsea** ..................'64 '92 C.309 B.A. L.426 J.D. [Belcher,H.&B.]
*LANGUAGES: Taiwanese; Mandarin.
*REPORTED CASES: Continental Airlines, Inc. v. Intra Brokers, Inc., 24 F.3d 1099 (9th Cir. 1994).
*PRACTICE AREAS: Civil (General Civil) Practice; Appellate Practice; Aviation Law; Products Liability Defense; Business Law.
**Chen, Ying** .....................'63 '95 C.061 B.S. L.596 J.D. [Loeb&L.] (See Pat. Sect.)
*LANGUAGES: Chinese.
**Chenen, Arthur R.**, (AV) .........'46 '71 C.112 B.A. L.1068 J.D. [Ginsburg,S.O.&R.]
*PRACTICE AREAS: Health Law; Litigation; Contract Law; Administrative Law.
**Cheng, Brian I-An** ......................'70 '96 C.112 B.A. L.309 J.D. [Fried,F.H.S.&J.]
*LANGUAGES: Mandarin Chinese.
Cheng, Jennifer Y. ...................'60 '85 C.668 B.A. L.1067 J.D. 2601 S. Figueroa St.
Cheng, Ronald L. .........................'64 '88 C.976 B.A. L.178 J.D. 400 S. Hope St.
**Cheng, Rowland I.** ........................'68 '95 C.94 B.A. L.309 J.D. [Latham&W.]
*LANGUAGES: Mandarin Chinese.
Chenier, Maurice L. .............................'66 '93 C.767 B.A. L.770 J.D. [Wilson&B.]
Cheong, Wilkie ..................................'50 '76 C.112 B.A. L.426 J.D. [Cheong&D.]
Cheong & Denove, (AV) .......................................10100 Santa Monica Blvd.
Cher, David E. '57 '82 C.145 B.A. L.309 J.D.
Assoc. Reg. Coun., Prudential Ins. Co. of Amer., The
**Cherin, Alex H.** .................................'70 '96 C.477 B.A. L.426 J.D. [Lynberg&W.]
*LANGUAGES: Japanese.
*PRACTICE AREAS: Government Entity Litigation.
Cherin, Marvin S. ................................'47 '74 C.1077 B.A. L.809 J.D. [Cherin&Y.]
Cherin & Yelsky ..................................................12100 Wilshire Blvd.
**Chern, Carey C.** ..............................'66 '93 C.309 A.B. L.813 J.D. [Arnold&P.]
**Chernek, David M.** .....................'63 '90 C.112 B.A. L.93 J.D. [Heller E.W.&M.]
**Cherney, Nancy A.** .....................'52 '77 C.112 B.A. L.284 J.D. [Dixon&J.]
*PRACTICE AREAS: Corporate; Municipal Finance.
**Chernin, Norman A.** ................'46 '71 C.112 B.A. L.426 J.D. [Brand F.D.F.&K.]
*REPORTED CASES: People v. Orr (1972) 26 Cal. App.3d 849, 103 Cal. Rptr. 266.
*PRACTICE AREAS: Real Estate; Land Use.
**Chernof, Alpa Patel** .......................'66 '91 C.472 B.A. L.276 J.D. [Paul,H.J.&W.]
**Chernof, Kenneth L.** ....................'67 '91 C.309 A.B. L.276 J.D. [Heller E.W.&M.]
Chernove, Sheldon B., (AV) ..........'49 '75 C.1077 B.A. L.426 J.D. 700 S. Flower St.
Chernow, Eli .........................................'39 '65 C.112 B.S. L.809 LL.B. Supr. Ct. J.
Cheroske, John J. ..................................'35 '65 C&L.800 B.S., J.D. Supr. Ct. J.
Cherry, Richard ..................'48 '79 C.1077 B.S. L.1136 J.D. 1605 W. Olympic Blvd.
Chesebro, Marvin M., (AV) ............'13 '38 C.112 A.B. L.800 LL.B. [M.M.Chesebro]
Chesebro, Marvin M., A Professional Corporation, (AV) ..............1545 Wilshire Blvd.
Chester, Gerald E. '47 '88
C.477 A.B. L.426 J.D. Assoc. Coun., Auto. Club of Southern Calif.
**Chester, Jeffrey A.** ................................'55 '81 C.645 B.A. L.659 J.D. [Graham&J.]
*PRACTICE AREAS: Corporate Financing Law; Securities.
**Chester, Theodore A., Jr.** ......................'56 '82 C.813 B.A. L.426 J.D. [Smiland&K.]
*REPORTED CASES: Sumner Peck Ranch v. Bureau of Reclamation, 823 F. Supp. 715 (E.D. Cal. 1993); In re Westhaven Trust, Interior Sol. Op. M-36965 (1989).
*PRACTICE AREAS: Water Resources; Corporate Law; Tax Law; Estates; Trusts.
**Chester, Yvonne E.** ............................'58 '82 C.112 B.S. L.1066 J.D. [Troy&G.]
*PRACTICE AREAS: Corporate Law; Securities Law.
**Chevalier, Alisa M.** ...........................'67 '93 C.481 B.A. L.426 J.D. [Troop M.S.&P.]
*PRACTICE AREAS: Labor and Employment; Litigation.
Chevalier, Paul E. '39 '67 C&L.178 B.A., LL.B.
(adm. in IL; not adm. in CA) 2405 Glendower Ave.
**Chiappetta, Michael R.** .................'70 '96 C.165 B.A. L.800 J.D. [Troop M.S.&P.]
*PRACTICE AREAS: General Litigation.
Chiarello, Kevin R. ..................'60 '85 C.740 B.A. L.770 J.D. 1200 Wilshire Blvd.

**Chiasson, Stephen J.** .........................'58 '88 C.1134 B.S. L.1049 J.D. [Kinkle,R.&S.]
**Chiate, Kenneth R.**, (AV) ............'41 '67 C.154 B.A. L.178 LL.B. [Pillsbury M.&S.]
Chidsey, William R., Jr. .....................'39 '72 C.1042 B.S. L.800 J.D. Municipal Ct. J.
**Chieffo, Vincent H.**, (AV) ....................'45 '71 C.299 A.B. L.178 J.D. [Gipson H.&P.]
Chiella, Karen A ..........................'55 '80 C.112 B.A. L.1065 J.D. 7912 Beland Ave.
**Chierichella, John W.** '47 '73
C.188 A.B. L.178 J.D. [Fried,F.H.S.&J.] (©Washington DC)
*PRACTICE AREAS: Government Contracts; Litigation.
**Child, Bradford T.** ......................'54 '80 C.169 B.A. L.464 J.D. [Millard,P.H.&C.]
*PRACTICE AREAS: Insurance Defense; Civil Litigation.
**Child, John L.**, (AV) ...................'35 '63 C&L.336 B.A., LL.B. [Greenberg G.F.C.&M.]
*PRACTICE AREAS: Real Estate Transactions.
**Childers, Bradley P.** ..................'64 '89 C.112 B.A. L.990 J.D. [Millard,P.H.&C.]
*PRACTICE AREAS: Insurance Defense; Civil Litigation.
Childers, D. Bradley ....'64 '89 C.154 B.A. L.800 J.D. Coun., Occidental Petroleum Corp.
**Childers, John N.** ..........................'69 '95 C&L.112 B.A., J.D. [Thelen,M.J.&B.]
*LANGUAGES: French.
*PRACTICE AREAS: Business, Construction, Litigation and Insurance.
**Childress, Tyrone R.** ......................'63 '88 C.276 B.S. L.893 J.D. [Troop M.S.&P.]
*LANGUAGES: German.
*PRACTICE AREAS: Insurance Coverage Litigation; General Business Litigation; International Law.
Childs, Deborah L. .......................................'56 '85 C&L.426 B.A., J.D. Co. Coun.
**Childs, J. Mark** ........................'66 '92 C.112 B.A. L.1066 J.D. [Pillsbury M.&S.]
**Childs, James F., Jr.**, (AV) .............'40 '65 C.800 B.S. L.309 J.D. [Jones,D.R.&P.]
Childs, William F. ............'34 '83 C.472 B.S.M.E. L.426 J.D. 11355 W. Olympic Blvd.
Chilleri, Gino A. .............'56 '82 C.767 B.S. L.1065 J.D. V.P. & Sr. Coun., Union Bk.
**Chilton, Elizabeth G.**, (AV) .................'58 '83 C.112 B.A. L.1068 J.D. [Christa&J.]
*PRACTICE AREAS: Business Litigation; Real Estate Litigation; Land Use Litigation; Appellate Work.

**Chimicles, Jacobsen & Tikellis**
**First Interstate World Center, 633 West Fifth Street, Suite 3300, 90071**©
**Telephone: 213-623-8100 Telecopier: 213-623-9100**
**Resident Attorneys: Patrick J. Grannan; Trudy D. Johnson Opperman; Tina Bailer Nieves; Robin Bronzaft Howald; Marc A. Seligman.**
**Securities, Antitrust, Consumer, Environmental and Commercial Litigation.**
**Haverford, Pennsylvania Office: One Haverford Centre, 19041-0100. Telephone: 215-642-8500. Telecopier: 215-649-3633.**
**Wilmington, Delaware Office: One Rodney Square, 19801. Telephone: 302-656-2500. Telecopier: 302-656-9053.**

*See Professional Biographies, HAVERFORD, PENNSYLVANIA*

**Chin, Archie** ..........................'58 '89 C.112 B.A. L.940 J.D. [Prestholt,K.F.&V.]
*PRACTICE AREAS: Insurance Defense; Products Liability.
Chin, Benjamin M. ...........................'61 '87 C.174 B.S. L.446 J.D. 333 S. Hope St.
**Chin, Kena B.** ...............................'67 '95 C.112 B.A. L.770 J.D. [Daniels,B.&F.]
Ching, Anthony C. ......................'47 '75 C.768 B.A. L.659 J.D. 801 S. Figueroa St.
**Chinski, Arthur**, (AV) .................'45 '71 C.112 A.B. L.1067 J.D. [Buchalter,N.F.&Y.]
*PRACTICE AREAS: Labor and Employment Law (Management); Employment Litigation; Collective Bargaining/Union Organizing; Workplace Safety and Health; Employee Benefits.

**Chinski, Tobi J., Law Offices of, (AV) '47 '80 C.339 B.A. L.1136 J.D.**
**1801 Century Park East, Suite 2500, 90067**
**Telephone: 310-286-6767 Fax: 310-286-1633**
**Estate Planning, Probate and Trust Law, Charitable Tax Planning.**

*See Professional Biographies, LOS ANGELES, CALIFORNIA*

**Chirinian, Guy** ...............................'66 '92 C.112 B.A. L.809 J.D. [Borton,P.&C.]
*PRACTICE AREAS: Personal Injury; Automobile Accidents.
Chirlin, Judith C. ...........................................'47 '74 C.273 B.A. L.800 J.D. Supr. Ct. J.
**Chism, Edna M.** ...............................'60 '87 C.70 B.A. L.569 J.D. [Konowiecki&R.]
*PRACTICE AREAS: General Business; Corporate; Securities Law.
Chittenden, Russell W. ................................'53 '83 C&L.800 B.A., J.D. Off. of U.S. Atty.
Chiu, Agnes Sau-Chun ..............'64 '92 C.112 B.A. L.1068 J.D. 1200 Wilshire Blvd.
Chiu, Colin K. W. ...........................'42 '70 C.112 A.B. L.1065 J.D. Asst. City Atty.
**Chmura, Jennifer A.** ............................'67 '92 C.145 B.A. L.310 J.D. [Zelle&L.]
*PRACTICE AREAS: Environmental Litigation; Environmental Insurance Coverage; Civil Litigation.
Cho, Daniel D. ...........................'56 '82 C.1097 B.A. L.809 J.D. 3807 Wilshire Blvd.
**Cho, JoAn H.** .............................'71 '96 C.112 B.A. L.1066 J.D. [Graham&J.]
Cho, Johnna C. ......................'64 '90 C.914 B.A. L.1068 J.D. 801 S. Figueroa St.
**Choate, Joseph**, (AV) ...................................'00 '27 C&L.800 B.A., LL.B. [Choate&C.]
*PRACTICE AREAS: International.
**Choate, Joseph, Jr.**, (AV) .....................'41 '66 C.668 B.A. L.800 J.D. [Choate&C.]
*PRACTICE AREAS: International; Agricultural.

**Choate and Choate, (AV)**
**523 West Sixth Street, Suite 541, 90014**
**Telephone: 213-623-8136; 623-2297 Telecopier: 213-623-6429**
**Members of Firm: Joseph Choate; Joseph Choate, Jr.; Robert P. Lewis, Jr.; Bradley L. Cornell.**
**General Trial Practice. International, Agricultural and Probate Law.**

*See Professional Biographies, LOS ANGELES, CALIFORNIA*

**Chock, Patricia N.** ..........................'52 '87 C.112 B.A. L.800 J.D. [King,W.E.&B.]
*PRACTICE AREAS: Business; Real Estate; Estate Planning.
**Chodorow, Hilton I.**, (AV) .........'35 '63 C&L.846 B.B.A., LL.B. [De Castro,W.&C.]
*PRACTICE AREAS: Taxation Law; Business Law; Real Property Law.
**Chodos, David M.**, (AV) ......................'36 '67 C.112 B.A. L.426 LL.B. [Simke C.]
*PRACTICE AREAS: Business Litigation; White Collar Crime; Fiduciary Malpractice; Administrative Law; Contract Litigation.

**Chodos, Deborah, (AV) '53 '78 C.112 B.A. L.800 J.D.**
**12400 Wilshire Boulevard, Suite 400, 90025-1023**
**Telephone: 310-207-0569 Fax: 310-207-5313**
**General Business Litigation, Real Estate and Construction Litigation, Insurance Bad Faith and Personal Injury Litigation.**

*See Professional Biographies, LOS ANGELES, CALIFORNIA*

Chodos, Hillel, (AV) ............'33 '62 C.145 A.B. L.1068 LL.B. 1559 S. Sepulveda Blvd.
Chodos, Jonathan P. ..............'56 '83 C.112 B.A. L.284 J.D. 1559 S. Sepulveda Blvd.
**Choi, Albert B.** .....................................'67 '92 C.846 B.A. L.178 J.D. [Dewey B.]
Choi, John H. ...................................................'64 '90 C&L.112 B.S., J.D. I.R.S.
**Choi, William C.** ..............................'59 '85 C.768 B.S. L.800 J.D. [Rodríguez,H.&C.]
*LANGUAGES: Korean.
**Choi, Yun Y.** ...........................'67 '92 C.309 B.A. L.1066 J.D. [Proskauer R.G.&M.]
*LANGUAGES: Korean.
Chooljian, Jacqueline .........................'61 '86 C.112 B.A. L.800 J.D. Asst. U.S. Atty.
Choper, Laura B. .................................'59 '91 C.112 B.A. L.770 J.D. 1055 W. 7th St.
**Chopra, Apalla U.** ......................'66 '92 C.112 B.A. L.1065 J.D. [O'Melveny&M.]
Chotiner, Kenneth Lee ...........................'37 '70 C.112 B.A. L.426 J.D. Mun. Ct. J.
**Chotiner, Lori** ..........................'71 '96 C.1077 B.A. L.426 J.D. [Daniels,B.&F.]
**Choudhry, Nargis** .....................'— '90 C.605 B.A. L.112 J.D. [Sonnenschein N.&R.]
*PRACTICE AREAS: Real Estate.
**Christ, Roxanne E.** .....................'60 '85 C.112 B.A. L.426 J.D. [Paul,H.J.&W.]
**Christa, Laura Kassner**, (AV) ..............'55 '81 C.1036 B.A. L.659 J.D. [Christa&J.]
*PRACTICE AREAS: Litigation.

CAA200P

**Christa & Jackson, (AV)**
**Suite 1100 1901 Avenue of the Stars, 90067-6002**
**Telephone: 310-282-8040 Fax: 310-282-8421**
**Email: lchrista@christalaw.com URL: http://www.Christalaw.com**
**Members of Firm: Laura Kassner-Christa; Laurence D. Jackson; Ann Loeb. Associates: Carol K. Samek. Of Counsel: Elizabeth G. Chilton.**
**Business Litigation Practice on behalf of Domestic and International Clients, in Courts and other Adjudicative Tribunals on Matters Involving General Contract, Securities, Intellectual Property, Real Property and Construction, Travel and Tourism, Business Torts and Related Business Disputes.**
*See Professional Biographies, LOS ANGELES, CALIFORNIA*

**Christensen, David E.** ....'69 '96 C.188 B.A. L.1068 J.D. [Ⓐ Latham&W.]
*LANGUAGES: Italian.
**Christensen, Julius G.** ....'65 '95 C.112 B.A. L.309 J.D. [Ⓐ Sullivan&C.]
Christensen, Kim ....'71 '95 C.37 B.A. L.309 J.D. 633 W. 5th St.
**Christensen, Terry N.**, (AV) '41 '66 C.813 A.B. L.800 J.D. [Christensen,M.F.J.G.W.&S.]
*PRACTICE AREAS: Corporate; Entertainment; Civil Litigation.

**Christensen, Jay D., and Associates**
**(See Pasadena)**

**Christensen, Miller, Fink, Jacobs, Glaser, Weil and Shapiro, LLP, (AV)**
**2121 Avenue of the Stars Eighteenth Floor, 90067**⊙
**Telephone: 310-553-3000 Fax: 310-556-2920**
**Members of Firm: Terry N. Christensen; Barry E. Fink; Gary N. Jacobs; Louis R. Miller, III; Patricia Glaser; Robert L. Shapiro; Peter M. Weil; James S. Schreier; Janet S. McCloud; Terry D. Avchen; J. Jay Rakow; Roger H. Howard; Eric N. Landau; Sean Riley; Mark G. Krum; Clare Bronowski; Brett J. Cohen; Stephen N. Besser; Peter C. Sheridan; Carolyn Comparet Jordan; Ronald E. Guttman; David A. Giannotti; Nabil L. Abu-Assal; Mark L. Block; Jeffrey C. Soza. Of Counsel: Stephen D. Silbert (A Professional Corporation); Christine Burdick-Bell; Alisa J. Freundlich; Karen L. Filipi; Sara L. Caplan; Kenneth G. McKenna. Associates: Gerard R. Kilroy; Alisa M. Morgenthaler; Mark K. Li; Kevin J. Leichter; Steven J. Aaronoff; Anthony J. Sarkis; Cynthia M. Takács; Risa B. Winograd; Peter E. Garrell; Christopher R. O'Brien; David J. Nachman; Eric P. Early; Kimberlee A. Konjoyan; Talin V. Yacoubian; Robert James Shilliday III; Paul R. Rosenbaum; Seong Hwan Kim; Brian Center; Nicolas Morgan; Lisa D. Singer; Soroush Richard Shehabi; Gary J. Gorham; Mitchell M. Chupack; Angela Barnes (Not admitted in CA); Amy Lew Powell; Robert J. Muller (Not admitted in CA); Richard D. Roll; Joie Marie Gallo; David N. Lake; Jane McClure; Xianchun J. Vendler; Michael A. Minden; Joshua D. Helderman; Subodh Chandra; Tonie M. Franzese-Damron; Brent D. Bradley; Pamela Briand; Fiona A. Brophy; Robert J. Comer; Julie Giacopuzzi; Deborah R. Goldberg; Adrienne W. Goldstone; John E. Hoffman; Jon M. Konheim; Donald E. Leonhardt; D. Michael Oberbeck; Eric Michael Sherman; Michael W. Whitaker; Norman Y. Wong.**
**General Civil and Trial Practice in all State and Federal Courts. Corporation, Securities, Banking, Real Estate and General Business Law. International and Entertainment Law. Taxation, Estate Planning, Trust, Probate, Insurance, Environmental Law, Energy Law, Constitutional and Civil Rights, Employment, Copyright and Trademark, Toxic Tort, Government Relations, Regulatory and Administrative Law.**
**San Francisco, California Office: 650 California Street, Suite 2200. 94108. Telephone: 415-288-1377. Fax: 415-362-1021.**
*See Professional Biographies, LOS ANGELES, CALIFORNIA*

Christian, Cynthia J. ....'64 '91 C.112 B.A. L.1068 J.D. 400 S. Hope St.
Christian, Lisa A. ....'61 '87 C.788 B.A. L.813 J.D. Asst. U.S. Atty.
**Christian, William R.**, (AV) ....'50 '74 C.1109 B.A. L.1065 J.D. [Rodi,P.P.G.&C.]
*PRACTICE AREAS: Closely Held Business and Individual Tax and Business Planning; Estate Planning; Real Estate; Tax Law.
**Christianson, Greg A.** ....'66 '95 C.674 B.A. L.813 J.D. [Ⓐ McCutchen,D.B.&E.]
*PRACTICE AREAS: Environmental.

**Christie, Parker & Hale, LLP**
**(See Pasadena)**

**Christl, Frank C.**, (AV) ....'22 '52 C.800 A.B. L.809 LL.B. [Tuttle&T.]
*PRACTICE AREAS: Civil Litigation; Bankruptcy and Creditors' Rights.
**Christofferson, Carla J.** ....'67 '92 C.585 B.A. L.976 J.D. [Ⓐ O'Melveny&M.]
**Christopher, Daniel G.** ....'64 '89 C.884 B.E.E. L.178 J.D. [Irell&M.]
**Christopher, John S.** ....'46 '83 C.174 B.S.E.E. L.770 J.D. [Ⓐ Lewis,D.B.&B.] (Pat.)
Christopher, Thomas P. ....'— '94 C.1077 B.A. L.809 J.D. [Roquemore,P.&M.]
**Christopher, Warren**, (AV) ....'25 '49 C.800 B.S. L.813 LL.B. [O'Melveny&M.]
**Christovich, Jeffrey J.**, (BV Ⓣ) ....'59 '85 C.902 B.A. L.861 J.D. [Ⓐ Tressler,S.M.&P.]
Christy, Jeannette ....'39 '69 C.112 A.B. L.809 LL.B. Ref., Supr. Ct.
**Chrystie, Stephen**, (AV) ....'36 '63 C.112 B.A. L.309 LL.B. [Chrystie&B.]
*PRACTICE AREAS: Financial Institutions Law; Entertainment Law; Bankruptcy Law.

**Chrystie & Berle, A Prof. Corp., Law Offices, (AV)**
**Suite 2200, 1925 Century Park East, 90067**
**Telephone: 310-788-7700 Fax: 310-201-0436**
**Stephen Chrystie; Elihu M. Berle; Sherilyn L. Williams (1958-1994). Of Counsel: Arthur L. Stashower.**
**General Civil, Trial and Appellate Practice in all State and Federal Courts. Bankruptcy and Insolvency Law, Entertainment, Commercial, Corporate, Banking, Financial Transactions, Real Estate.**
*See Professional Biographies, LOS ANGELES, CALIFORNIA*

**Chu, Mary H.** ....'65 '91 C.112 B.A. L.1068 J.D. [Ⓐ Hennigan,M.&B.]
*LANGUAGES: Mandarin Chinese.
*PRACTICE AREAS: Litigation; Bankruptcy.
**Chu, Morgan**, (AV) ....'50 '76 C.112 A.B. L.309 J.D. [Irell&M.]
Chu, Thomas S. '64 '92 C.112 B.A. L.1049 J.D. (adm. in PA; not adm. in CA) 523 W. 6th St.
**Chuang, Diana K.** ....'72 '96 C.813 B.A. L.228 J.D. [Ⓐ Orrick,H.&S.]
**Chuang, George**, (AV) ....'60 '85 C.112 B.A. L.1049 J.D. [Chapin,F.&W.]
**Chuck, Catherine Endo** ....'56 '85 C.112 B.A. L.426 J.D. [McBirney&C.]
*PRACTICE AREAS: Corporate; Non Profit Organizations; Probate and Estate Planning.
**Chuck, Evan Y.** '68 '93 C.367 B.A. L.273 J.D. (adm. in VA; not adm. in CA) [Ⓐ Jeffer,M.B.&M.]
*LANGUAGES: Chinese, French.
*PRACTICE AREAS: Corporate Securities; International Business; International Trade; Representation before U.S. Government and Agencies.
Chudacoff, Gregory S. ....'56 '81 C.112 B.A. L.990 J.D. 12100 Wilshire Blvd.
Chudnow, David ....'49 '75 C.966 B.A. L.1068 J.D. 1801 Century Park E., 24th Fl.
Chulay, Cornell '55 '81 C&L.112 B.A., J.D. V.P., Gen. Coun. & Bus. Affs., Group W Productions
Chuman, Frank F. ....'17 '45 C.112 B.A. L.446 J.D. 201 N. Figueroa St., 7th Fl.
**Chung, D. James** ....'63 '95 C.477 B.S.C.E. L.800 J.D. [Ⓐ Mitchell,S.&K.]
*LANGUAGES: Korean.
**Chung, Jay J.** ....'67 '95 C.112 B.A. L.426 J.D. [Ⓐ Dale,B.&H.]
*LANGUAGES: Korean.
*PRACTICE AREAS: Personal Injury Defense; Construction Litigation; Commercial Contracts.
**Chung, John J.** ....'60 '85 C.910 B.A. L.309 J.D. [Katten M.&Z.]
*PRACTICE AREAS: Commercial Litigation.
Chung, Lisa M. ....'66 '92 C.881 B.A. L.861 J.D. Dep. Dist. Atty.
**Chung, Timothy J.** ....'63 '94 C.154 B.A. L.426 J.D. [Ⓐ Oliver,V.S.M.&L.]
*PRACTICE AREAS: Municipal Law.
Chung, Tong Soo "T.S." ....'55 '84 C.309 B.A. L.1068 J.D. 1055 W. 7thSt.
Chung, Yungeun T ....'60 '87 C.112 A.B. L.1068 J.D. Dep. Atty. Gen.
**Chupack, Mitchell M.** ....'62 '92 C.112 A.B. L.1066 J.D. [Ⓐ Christensen,M.F.J.G.W.&S.]
*LANGUAGES: Spanish.
*PRACTICE AREAS: Real Estate Law.

Churchill, Randall J. ....'59 '90 C.932 B.B.A. L.347 J.D. Bowne of Los Angeles
**Churella, Robert M.** ....'49 '77 C.453 B.S. L.800 J.D. [Kirtland&P.]
Chusid, Lawrence A. '24 '76 C.415 B.S. L.1148 J.D. 11500 W. Olympic Bldg., Rm. 335
Chyten, Kenneth E. ....'52 '79 C.112 B.A. L.1066 J.D. [Levin,S.C.&S.]
Ciafone, Frank C., Jr. ....'43 '68 C.676 B.A. L.724 J.D. 1056 S. Ogden Dr.
**Ciasulli, Anthony** ....'57 '82 C.311 B.A. L.1068 J.D. [Morgan,L.&B.]
**Ciasulli, Joseph, (A Professional Corporation)** '52 '78 C.659 B.S. L.178 J.D. [Mitchell,S.&K.]
*PRACTICE AREAS: Corporate Law; Securities Law; Motion Picture Financing Law.
**Ciccone, James J.** ....'63 '89 C.860 B.S. L.273 J.D. [Troop M.S.&P.]
*PRACTICE AREAS: Insurance Coverage Litigation; Business Litigation.
**Ciccone, Karen Palladino** ....'64 '89 C.112 B.A. L.426 J.D. [Troop M.S.&P.]
*PRACTICE AREAS: Insurance Coverage; Environmental Compliance and Litigation.
Cicone, Vincent P. ....'41 '88 C.112 B.A. L.999 J.D. 4700 Wilshire Blvd.
**Cigel, Rick A.** ....'56 '82 C.963 B.S. L.597 J.D. [Case,K.B.&W.]
*PRACTICE AREAS: Tax; Estate Planning; Trust; Probate.
Cincore, Lydia V. ....'— '91 C.425 B.S. L.329 J.D. 4216 Enoro Dr.
**Ciolino, Barbara** ....'59 '89 C.454 B.A. L.93 J.D. [Ⓐ Quisenberry&B.]
*PRACTICE AREAS: General Business Litigation.
**Cione, Anthony L.** ....'63 '92 C.945 B.B.A. L.800 J.D. [Ⓐ Selman B.]
**Cipes, Andrew P.**, (AV) ....'50 '76 C.112 B.A. L.426 J.D. [Aikenhead,C.&S.]
Ciriello, Nicholas G. ....'38 '64 C.976 B.A. L.309 LL.B. 418 So. Lucerne Blvd.‡
Cischke, Steven M. ....'56 '86 C&L.477 B.A., J.D. [Mink&M.]
Cissna, Robert L. ....'40 '80 C.911 B.A. L.809 J.D. 1617 3/4 N. Micheltorena
**Citron, Brad D.** ....'56 '85 C.259 B.S. L.1137 J.D. [Ⓐ La Follette,J.D.F.&A.]
*PRACTICE AREAS: General Liability.
**Citron, Richard K.**, (AV) ....'45 '70 C.112 B.S. L.1068 J.D. [Citron&D.]

**Citron & Deutsch, A Law Corporation, (AV)**
**Suite 970, Westwood Place, 10866 Wilshire Boulevard, 90024**
**Telephone: 310-475-0321 Fax: 310-475-1368**
**URL: http://www.candlaw.globalcenter.net**
**Richard K. Citron; David R. Deutsch.**
**Entrepreneurial Business Law, General Business Law including formation, purchase and sale of businesses, and Wills and Trusts, Estate Planning, Real Estate Transactions and Employment Law.**
*See Professional Biographies, LOS ANGELES, CALIFORNIA*

**Citron, Joel F., Law Offices of**
**(See Santa Monica)**

**Civale, Kevin M.** ....'59 '85 C.93 B.A. L.262 J.D. [Hawkins,D.&W.]
**Clair, John J., Jr.**, (AV) ....'46 '73 C.103 A.B. L.659 J.D. [Latham&W.]
Clairday, John C. '51 '86 C.800 B.A. L.426 J.D. Dep. Gen. Coun., Metropolitan Water Dist. of Southern Calif.
**Claman, Stephen**, (AV) ....'32 '60 C.112 A.B. L.1068 LL.B. [Greenberg G.F.C.&M.]
*PRACTICE AREAS: Real Estate; Corporate; Business.
**Clampitt, Russell W.** ....'56 '86 C.597 B.S. L.426 J.D. [Ruben&M.]
*PRACTICE AREAS: Business Litigation; Professional Liability; Appellate Advocacy.
**Clapp, Peter W.** ....'46 '82 C.178 B.A. L.1065 J.D. [Ⓑ Skadden,A.S.M.&F.]
**Clare, Andrew S., (A P.C.)**, (AV) ....'45 '72 C.112 B.A. L.1066 J.D. [Loeb&L.]
*PRACTICE AREAS: Insolvency Law; Workout Law.
Clare, Daniel A. ....'63 '91 C.950 B.S. L.809 J.D. 1900 Ave. of the Stars
Clare, Marilyn ....'46 '73 C.112 A.B. L.1066 J.D. 2417 Nottingham Ave.
**Clark, Alan B.**, (AV) ....'46 '75 C.16 B.S. L.893 J.D. [Latham&W.]
**Clark, Alfred M., III** ....'54 '81 C.813 A.B. L.426 J.D. [Hill,F.&B.]
*PRACTICE AREAS: Real Estate Finance Law; General Real Estate Law; Creditors' Rights.
Clark, Amy M. ....'68 '94 C.813 B.A. L.94 J.D. 10940 Wilshire Blvd.
Clark, Bob, Jr. '49 '83 C.893 B.S. L.145 J.D. (adm. in IL; not adm. in CA) 3580 Wilshire Blvd.
Clark, Bruce E., (AV) ....'22 '49 C.605 A.B. L.800 J.D. 6525 Sherbourne Dr.
Clark, David, (AV) ....'41 '70 C.112 B.A. L.1066 J.D. [Chase,R.D.&B.]
**Clark, Donald P.**, (AV) ....'35 '60 C.813 A.B. L.800 LL.B. [Clark&T.]
*PRACTICE AREAS: General Corporate; Corporate Securities and Finance; Mergers and Acquisitions; Venture Capital.
Clark, Edith Lee Anne ....'42 '77 C.112 B.A. L.426 J.D. Dep. City Atty.
Clark, Efrem A. ....'59 '87 C.604 B.A. L.800 J.D. 4050 Buckingham Rd.

**Clark, Elford H. '48 '89 C.260 B.A. L.1137 J.D.**
**1910 West Sunset Boulevard, Suite 200, 90026**
**Telephone: 213-484-1925 Fax: 213-484-4471**
**Email: mopar_49@ix.netcom.com**
***PRACTICE AREAS: Probate; Estate Planning; Religious Nonprofit Corporation Law; Personal Injury.**
**Probate and Estate Planning, Conservatorship, Bus Transactions, Corporations, Non-Profit Organizations.**
*See Professional Biographies, LOS ANGELES, CALIFORNIA*

**Clark, Ernest M., Jr.**, (AV) ....'19 '49 C.813 A.B. L.426 LL.B. [Smiland&K.] ‡
**Clark, Frank W., Jr.**, (AV) ....'17 '46 C.113 B.S. L.1065 J.D. [Parker,M.C.O.&S.]
**Clark, Frederick A.**, (AV) ....'42 '68 C.813 B.A. L.800 J.D. [Stephens,B.&L.]
*PRACTICE AREAS: Antitrust and Trade Litigation; Business Litigation; Copyright and Trademark Litigation.
**Clark, Gary A.**, (AV) ....'48 '75 C.1042 B.S.E. L.1068 J.D. [Sheppard,M.R.&H.] (Pat.)
*PRACTICE AREAS: Patents; Trademarks; Copyrights; Unfair Competition; Litigation.
Clark, James Bryce ....'57 '91 C&L.494 B.S., J.D. 777 S. Figueroa St., 10th Fl.
**Clark, James P.**, (AV) ....'48 '74 C.276 A.B. L.569 J.D. [Gibson,D.&C.]
*PRACTICE AREAS: Entertainment and Intellectual Property Litigation; Antitrust and Trade Regulation; White Collar Criminal; Complex Civil Litigation and Unfair Competition; Business Torts.
Clark, Jeffrey A., (BV) ....'51 '76 C.112 A.B. L.809 J.D. [Clark&K.]
**Clark, John A.** ....'61 '86 C.112 B.A. L.1066 J.D. Sr. Coun., Bank of Amer.
**Clark, John B.**, (AV) '36 '62 C&L.813 B.S., LL.B. [Thelen,M.J.&B.] (⊙San Francisco)
*PRACTICE AREAS: Construction Litigation.
Clark, Karen A. ....'63 '90 C.93 B.A. L.800 J.D. 11766 Wilshire Blvd.,
Clark, Kenneth J. ....'50 '83 C.354 B.S. L.426 J.D. Dir., W. Los Angeles V.A. Med. Ctr.
**Clark, Lisa A.** ....'62 '88 C.154 B.A. L.1049 J.D. [Ⓐ Sedgwick,D.M.&A.]
**Clark, Martha Jeannette** ....'56 '84 C.813 B.A. L.1065 J.D. [Ⓐ Arnold&P.]
**Clark, R. Bradbury**, (AV) ....'24 '52 C&L.309 A.B., LL.B. [Ⓑ O'Melveny&M.]
*PRACTICE AREAS: Corporations; Nonprofit Corporations; Limited Liability Companies; Limited Liability Partnerships; Project Finance.
**Clark, Randall L.** ....'69 '94 C.990 B.S. L.228 J.D. [Ⓐ Morrison&F.]
*LANGUAGES: Spanish and German.
Clark, Ray G. ....'31 '73 C.329 B.S.E.E. L.809 J.D. 4050 Buckingham Rd.
Clark, Richard ....'39 '63 C&L.477 A.B., J.D. 600 Wilshire Blvd.
**Clark, Richard A.** ....'41 '67 C.112 A.B. L.1065 LL.B. [Parker,M.C.O.&S.]
*PRACTICE AREAS: Civil Litigation; Securities Litigation; Directors and Officers Liability Defense.
Clark, Sheila J. ....'43 '77 C.112 L.1148 J.D. 600 Wilshire Blvd.
**Clark, Stephen P.** ....'68 '95 C.896 B.A. L.1065 J.D. [Ⓐ Greenberg G.F.C.&M.]
*PRACTICE AREAS: Litigation.
**Clark, Taylor L.** ....'65 '94 C.17 B.B.A. L.990 J.D. [Ⓐ Wright,R.O.&T.]
*LANGUAGES: French.
*PRACTICE AREAS: Business Litigation; Intellectual Property/Antitrust; Employment Law.

CAA201P

**Clark, James Dexter**
**(See Pasadena)**

Clark & Kramer, A Professional Corporation, (BV) .........2999 Overland Ave., Ste. 204

**Clark & Trevithick, A Professional Corporation, (AV)** BR
**800 Wilshire Boulevard, 12th Floor, 90017⊙**
**Telephone: 213-629-5700 Telecopier: 213-624-9441**
**Donald P. Clark; Alexander C. McGilvray, Jr.; Philip W. Bartenetti; Kevin P. Fiore; Dolores Cordell; Vincent Tricarico; John A. Lapinski; Leonard Brazil; Dean I. Friedman (Certified Specialist, Taxation Law, The State Bar of California Board of Legal Specialization); Robert F. DeMeter (Certified Specialist, Taxation Law, The State Bar of California Board of Legal Specialization); Michael K. Wofford; Leslie R. Horowitz; Brent A. Reinke; Arturo Santana Jr.; Kerry T. Ryan; James S. Arico. Of Counsel: John A. Tucker, Jr.; Judith Ilene Bloom.**
**General Business Practice and Litigation Practice in all State and Federal Courts and Arbitration Tribunals. General Corporate, Corporate Securities and Finance, Mergers and Acquisitions, Venture Capital, Federal, State and Local Taxation, Estate Planning, Trusts and Probate, Partnerships, Real Estate, Real Estate Leasing, Real Estate Finance and Land Use, Pension and Profit Sharing, Antitrust and Trade Regulation Litigation, General Business and Commercial Litigation, Banking, Credit Law, Bankruptcy, Creditors Rights, Collateral Recovery and Financial Institutions Law, Employer-Employee Litigation, Insurance Defense and Personal Injury Litigation, Products Liability Litigation, Real Estate Litigation, Securities Litigation, Unfair Competition and Trade Secrets Litigation; Sports Law.**
**References: Wells Fargo Bank (Los Angeles Main Office); National Bank of California.**
**San Francisco, California Office: 456 Montgomery Street, 20th Floor. Telephone: 415-288-6520. Fax: 415-398-2820.**

***See Professional Biographies, LOS ANGELES, CALIFORNIA***

**Clarke, Deborah J.** ......................'63 '89 C&L.623 B.A., J.D. [Ⓐ Gibson,D.&C.]
*PRACTICE AREAS: Labor and Employment Law.
Clarke, Michael F. ....................'50 '80 C.884 B.A. L.1136 J.D. 999 N. Doheny Dr.
Clarkson, Robert L. ........'56 '81 C.902 B.A. L.990 J.D. 1999 Ave. of the Stars, 27th Fl.

**Clarkson & Gore**
**(See Torrance)**

**Clary, Donald M.** ..................'53 '79 C.112 B.A. L.426 J.D. [Ⓐ Whitman B.A.&M.]
Clary, Everett B., (AV) ......................'21 '49 C&L.813 B.A., LL.B. 400 S. Hope St.
**Clary, Susan** ....................................'49 '78 C.691 B.A. L.846 J.D. [J.P.Tierney]
*PRACTICE AREAS: Entertainment Litigation; Commercial Litigation.
Clasen, Robert L. ...................................'51 '77 C.1042 B.A. L.1068 J.D. [Silva,C.&R.]
**Classen, R. Derek** ................. '67 '92 C.112 B.A. L.1049 J.D. [Ⓐ Federman,G.&G.]
Clausen, Kenneth H., (AV) .......................'16 '50 L.809 LL.B. 624 S. Grand Ave.
Claypool, Brian E. ..........................'61 '88 C.645 B.A. L.884 J.D. 777 S. Figueroa St.
**Clayton, Robert B.** ..........................'62 '88 C.367 B.A. L.477 J.D. [Ⓐ Trope&T.]
*PRACTICE AREAS: Family Law; Civil Litigation.
Clayton, William J. .....................'24 '62 C.1042 B.S. L.800 J.D. P.O. Box 17520‡
Clearwaters, Lon R., (AV) ..........................'41 '67 C.112 B.A. L.800 J.D. [Miller&C.]
Cleary, Loretta .....................'54 '83 C.112 B.A. L.426 J.D. Asst. Dist. Atty.

**Cleary, Richard D. '52 '81 C&L.276 B.S.F.S., J.D.**
**601 West Fifth Street, 8th Floor, 90071-2094**
**Telephone: 213-627-0464 Telecopier: 213-627-1964**
**Civil Trials and Appeals in all Courts. Business Litigation, Trust and Estate Litigation.**

***See Professional Biographies, LOS ANGELES, CALIFORNIA***

Cleary, Richard M. ..................'50 '85 C.436 B.A. L.426 J.D. 1801 Century Park E.
**Cleary, Thomas M.** ..................'63 '89 C.602 B.S.Ch.E. L.1066 J.D. [Riordan&M.]

**Cleary, William J., Jr., (BV) '42 '67 C.728 A.B. L.884 J.D.**
**1853 1/2 North Canyon Drive, 90028**
**Telephone: 213-465-3633 Fax: 310-202-6068**
***REPORTED CASES: Hernandez v. Temple (1982) 142 Cal. App. 3d 286; Woods v. Young (1991) 53 Cal. 3d 315; U.S. v. Chaidez (1990) 916 F.2d 563; Wilcox v. Ford (1988) 206 Cal. App. 3d 1170.**
**Appeals in Federal and State Courts. General Civil Trial Practice.**

Cleaves, Robert N., (BV) ................'30 '61 C&L.800 B.S.L., J.D. 1224 Roberto Lane
Clebowicz, Francine E. ...................................'60 '85 C.94 B.A. P.O. Box 17927
Clem, Carol A. .........................'55 '80 C.354 B.S. L.1068 J.D. Dep. Pub. Def.
Clemens, Kathleen L., (AV) .............. '46 '74 C.525 B.A. L.426 J.D. [Glassman&C.]
Clemens, Keith M. ......................'42 '73 C.112 B.A. L.1068 J.D. Comr., Supr. Ct.
Clemens, Patricia A. ...................'50 '74 C.800 B.A. L.426 J.D. Asst. City Atty.‡
Clement, Daniel G. ..........................'48 '74 C.813 B.A. L.659 J.D. 633 W. 5th St.

**Clements, Richard R., A Professional Corporation**
**(See Los Angeles)**

Clemons, James E. ......................'38 '79 C.1097 M.A. L.426 J.D. [Stearns&C.]
**Clemons, William T., III** ..................'41 '84 C.800 B.A. L.426 J.D. [Engstrom,L.&L.]
*LANGUAGES: Spanish.
*PRACTICE AREAS: Aviation; Products Liability; Professional Liability; Governmental Agency Defense; General Trials.
Cleveland, Catherine A. ....................'58 '90 C.112 B.A. L.1066 J.D. 555 W. 5th St.
Clevenger, William C. ..................'43 '72 C.150 B.A. L.607 J.D. 9044 Melrose Ave.
Clinco, Peter L., (BV) ..........................'52 '78 C.800 A.B. L.426 J.D. [Clinco,F.&D.]
Clinco, Fisher & Diamond, (AV) ..................................1801 Century Park E., 26th Fl.
**Cline, Dennis N.** ..................................'54 '87 C.112 B.A. L.1066 J.D. [Behr&A.]
*LANGUAGES: Spanish.
*PRACTICE AREAS: Entertainment Law.
Cline, Kelly Kevin '56 '87 C.800 A.B. L.285 J.D.
V.P., Twentieth Century Fox Film Corp.
**Clinnin, John A.** ...............................'59 '91 C.1049 B.A. L.1148 J.D. [Clinnin&C.]
*PRACTICE AREAS: Insurance Defense; Consumer Litigation Defense; Products Liability; Civil Trial Litigation.
**Clinnin, Mark G.** ...............................'55 '88 C.770 B.A. L.809 J.D. [Clinnin&C.]
*PRACTICE AREAS: Insurance Defense; Consumer Litigation Defense; Products Liability; Civil Trial Litigation.
**Clinnin, Robert G., (A Professional Corporation)**, (AV) '23 '54
C.424 L.426 LL.B. [Clinnin&C.]
*PRACTICE AREAS: Insurance Defense; Products Liability; Civil Trial Litigation.

**Clinnin & Clinnin, (AV)**
**A Partnership including a Professional Corporation**
**Suite 2875, 333 South Grand Avenue, 90071**
**Telephone: 213-895-4343 FAX: 213-895-4423**
**Members of Firm: Robert G. Clinnin (A Professional Corporation); Mark G. Clinnin; John A. Clinnin.**
**General Civil, Trial and Appellate Practice in All State and Federal Courts. Products Liability and Negligence Law. Administrative, Insurance, Corporate and Real Property Law.**
**Representative Clients: Chrysler Corp.; Alfa Romeo Distributors of North America; Cagiva North American, Inc.; Weber Trucking and Distribution; Van Pool Services, Inc.; Truesdail Laboratories, Inc.; Steve P. Rados Construction; Dana Corp.; Chumo Construction; Gallager Bassett Services.**

***See Professional Biographies, LOS ANGELES, CALIFORNIA***

Clinton, DeWitt W. ...............................'36 '62 C&L.426 B.S., LL.B. Co. Coun.
**Clolery, Denise M.** '— '83 C.112 B.A. L.309 J.D.
[O'Melveny&M.] (⊙New York, N.Y.)
*LANGUAGES: Spanish and German.
*PRACTICE AREAS: Entertainment Transactional; Entertainment and Media Finance; Telecommunications; Complex Media Acquisitions; Interactive Multimedia.

**Clopton, Penny & Brenner, A P.C., (AV)**
**1055 West Seventh Street, Suite 3000, 90017-2570**
**Telephone: 213-629-6680 Fax: 213-629-6668**
**Email: steveb@cpandb.com**
**Theodore A. Penny (Certified Specialist, Workers Compensation Law, The State Bar of California Board of Legal Specialization); Steven G. Brenner; Ronald R. Kollitz (Certified Specialist, Workers Compensation Law, The State Bar of California Board of Legal Specialization);—Louise G. Morse (Certified Specialist, Workers Compensation Law, California Board of Legal Specialization); Marlene C. Tassone; Gary Paul André; Jay A. Siegel; Gary A. Kanter; Elliott Kushner; Andrew W. Barclay (Certified Specialist, Workers Compensation Law, The State Bar of California Board of Legal Specialization); R. Randolph Reck; Penny R. Hand; Gilbert Katen; James C. Spoeri; Dennis N. Roman.**
**Workers Compensation Defense and Subrogation.**

***See Professional Biographies, LOS ANGELES, CALIFORNIA***

**Close, M. Douglas** '50 '75 C.112 A.B. L.1068 J.D.
Assoc. Gen. Coun., Farmers Grp., Inc. & V.P. & Gen. Coun., Farmers New World Life
*RESPONSIBILITIES: General Counsel, Life Cos.; Litigation; Legislative and Regulatory.
**Close, Richard H.**, (AV) ..................'45 '69 C.659 B.S. L.94 J.D. [Shapiro,R.&C.]
**Cloud, Scott B.** ..........................'63 '89 C&L.990 B.A., J.D. [Ⓐ Hornberger&C.]
*PRACTICE AREAS: Products Liability; Premises Liability; Commercial Disputes; Construction Defect.
Clough, William J. ..........................'51 '91 C.767 B.A. L.1065 J.D. P.O. Box 65768
**Clouser, Mark E.** .............'63 '92 C.945 B.A. L.809 J.D. [Ⓐ Breidenbach,B.H.H.&H.]
*PRACTICE AREAS: Civil Litigation; Business Transactions.
**Clouser, Michael A.** .................'63 '89 C.945 B.S. L.472 J.D. [Ⓐ Gansinger,H.B.&P.]
*LANGUAGES: Spanish.
*PRACTICE AREAS: Business Litigation; Civil Litigation.
Clover, Suzette ..........................'54 '79 C.800 B.A. L.1068 J.D. U.S. Atty's. Off.
Clymer, Steven David ........'58 '83 C&L.188 B.A., J.D. Asst. U.S. Atty., Dept. of Justice
Clyne, Dana P. ..........................'56 '88 C.990 B.S. L.1136 J.D. 880 W. 1st St.
Coady, James M. ........'57 '82 C.112 B.A. L.809 J.D. Dep. Pub. Def., L.A. Co. Pub. Def.
Coady, Paul J. ..........................'53 '78 C.197 B.A. L.309 J.D. [Kindel&A.]
Coane, Suzanne M. ..........................'51 '82 C.112 B.A. L.1068 J.D. F.A.A.
**Coates, Michael L.** ..........................'60 '87 C.800 B.S. L.464 J.D. [Ⓒ Arter&H.]
Coats, Benjamin F., Jr. ..................'60 '88 C.112 B.A. L.1153 J.D. 4700 Wilshire Blvd.
**Coats, Richard D.** ..........................'54 '84 C.112 B.A. L.464 J.D. [Ⓐ Agapay,L.&H.]
*PRACTICE AREAS: Commercial Leasing Transactions.
**Cobb, Alexander B. T.**, (AV) ........'46 '72 C.861 B.A. L.1065 J.D. [Bonne,B.M.O.&N.]
Cobb, John F. ..........................'20 '47 C&L.800 A.B., LL.B. 2601 S. Figueroa St.
**Cobb, Kristi L.** ..........................'68 '96 C.228 A.B. L.1068 J.D. [Ⓐ Riordan&M.]
*LANGUAGES: Japanese.
*PRACTICE AREAS: Labor and Employment Litigation.
**Cobb, Regina Liudzius** ............'59 '85 C.112 B.A. L.1068 J.D. [Demetriou,D.S.&M.]
*PRACTICE AREAS: Complex Litigation; General Civil Litigation; Environmental Law.
**Coben, Jerome L.**, (AV) ............'44 '69 C.103 A.B. L.569 J.D. [Skadden,A.S.M.&F.]
Coble, Paul R. ..........................'47 '87 C.768 B.A. L.426 J.D. Capt., Pol. Dept.
Cochran, Bruce W. ..........................'53 '79 C.698 B.A. L.502 J.D. [Cochran&P.]
**Cochran, James S.** ..........................'55 '87 C.918 B.A. L.846 J.D. [Ⓐ Dewey B.]
*LANGUAGES: Spanish and Portuguese.
*PRACTICE AREAS: Entertainment.
**Cochran, Joan E.** ..........................'59 '87 C&L.117 B.A., J.D. [Mendes&M.]
**Cochran, Johnnie L., Jr.**, (AV) ......'37 '62 C.112 B.S. L.426 LL.B. [J.L.Cochran,Jr.]⊙
*PRACTICE AREAS: Personal Injury; Entertainment; Sports Law; Professional Liability; Business Litigation.
**Cochran, Steve** ..........................'57 '82 C.1169 B.A.B.A. L.1066 J.D. [Katten M.&Z.]
*PRACTICE AREAS: Federal and State Criminal Litigation.
**Cochran-Bond, Walter**, (AV) ....'48 '74 C.821 B.A. L.1068 J.D. [Ⓒ Proskauer R.G.&M.]
*PRACTICE AREAS: Labor; Employment Discrimination.

**Cochran, Johnnie L., Jr., A Prof. Corp., Law Offices of, (AV)**
**4929 Wilshire Boulevard, Suite 1010, 90010⊙**
**Telephone: 213-931-6200 Fax: 213-931-9521**
**Johnnie L. Cochran, Jr.; Carl E. Douglas; Ralph L. Lotkin;—Eddie J. Harris; Eric G. Ferrer; Cameron A. Stewart; Shawn Snider Chapman; Brian T. Dunn. Of Counsel: Donald K. Wilson, Jr.; Dion-Cherie Raymond.**
**Personal Injury, Entertainment, Sports Law, Civil Litigation, Employment, Criminal and Civil Rights Law, Mass Tort Litigation.**
**Representative Clients: Automobile Club of Southern California; Atlantic Richfield Co.; Council of Black Administrators; Federal Depository Insurance Corp.; Food 4 Less (ABC, Alpha Beta, The Boys, Viva, et al.); Fred S. Moltrie Accountancy Corp.; James M. Montgomery Consulting Engineers, Inc.; Los Angeles County Transporation Commission (LACTC); PRWT; Resolution Trust Corp. (RTC).**
**Washington, D.C. Office: 201 Massachusetts Avenue, N.E. Capitol Hill West Building, 20002. Telephone: 202-547-9225.**

***See Professional Biographies, LOS ANGELES, CALIFORNIA***

Cochran & Pirtle ..................................................1875 Century Park, E.

**Cockriel, Stephen E.**
**(See Long Beach)**

Codd, Norman L. ..................'44 '79 C.1068 B.S.E. L.809 J.D. 7561 Clinton Ave.
**Codding, Richard J.** .........'44 '70 C.277 B.E.E. L.309 J.D. [Loeb&L.] (See Pat. Sect.)
*PRACTICE AREAS: Patent; Trademark; Copyright; Litigation.
**Coddon, Eve Mary** .................... '61 '86 C.112 B.A. L.1049 J.D. [Paul,H.J.&W.]
**Codikow, David** ..................................'60 '87 L.426 J.D. [Codikow&C.]

**Codikow & Carroll, P.C.**
**9113 Sunset Boulevard, 90069-3106⊙**
**Telephone: 310-271-0241 Fax: 310-271-0775**
**David Codikow; Rosemary Carroll;—Janine S. Natter; Kelly Ann Coleman.**
**Entertainment and Corporate Law.**
**New York, New York Office: 40 West 57th Street, Suite 2104. Telephone: 212-489-6300. Fax: 212-489-3230.**

Codrington-Lee, Carol .........'59 '87 C&L.426 B.A., J.D. 1925 Century Pk. E., 10th Fl.
Cody, Marnie Christine ............ '64 '90 C.800 B.A. L.426 J.D. 4640 Admiralty Way
Coen, Ronald S. ..........................'48 '73 C.1077 B.A. L.61 J.D. Supr. Ct. J.
**Coester, Thomas M.** '67 '94 C&L.352 B.S.E.E., J.D.
[Ⓐ Blakely,S.T.&Z.] (See Pat. Sect.)
**Coffee, James R.**, (AVⓉ) '34 '59 C.840 B.S. L.846 J.D.
(adm. in TX; not adm. in CA) Dep. Gen. Coun., Atlantic Richfield Co.
**Coffeen, Debra Burchard** ................'63 '90 C.112 B.A. L.426 J.D. [Ⓐ Holley&G.]
*PRACTICE AREAS: Environmental; Property Tax.
**Coffin, Adrienne M.** ................'54 '82 C.741 B.A. L.602 J.D. [Ⓒ Jeffer,M.B.&M.]
*PRACTICE AREAS: Insolvency; Creditors Rights, including Cross-Border Insolvencies with Japan and other Countries; Real Estate; Banking; Finance.
Coffino, Michael J., (AV) ...........'48 '79 C.563 B.S. L.1066 J.D. 1875 Century Pk. E.
Coffman, Edward M., (AV) ...........'37 '67 C.208 B.S. L.146 J.D. 4700 Wilshire Blvd.
**Cogan, Efrat M.** ..........................'62 '87 C.112 B.A. L.800 J.D. [Ⓐ Russ,A.&K.]
*LANGUAGES: Hebrew and French.
*REPORTED CASES: Cawdrey v. Redondo Beach.
*PRACTICE AREAS: Land-Use; Civil Rights; Commercial Litigation.
**Cogan, Ram F.** ..........................'61 '87 C.112 B.A. L.1068 J.D. [Hawkins,S.L.&B.]
Cogen, Pearl G. ..........................'— '67 C.102 B.A. L.809 J.D. 444 Comstock Ave.
**Coggan, Graziella Walsh** '58 '83 C.767 B.A. L.1065 J.D.
[Celebrezze&W.] (⊙San Fran.)

Coggan, Roger '50 '75 C.659 B.A. L.800 J.D.
Legal Servs. Dir., Gay & Lesbian Comm. Serv. Ctr.
Coghlan, Michael R., (BV) ....'39 '67 C.668 A.B. L.1065 J.D. Dep. Pub. Def.
Cohan, Edward M., (AV) ....'41 '72 C.436 B.S. L.800 J.D. [Cohan&C.]
Cohan, John A. ....'47 '72 C.112 B.A. L.426 J.D. 2049 Century Park E.
Cohan, John R., (P.C.), (AV) '31 '56
C.37 B.S. L.813 LL.B. 1800 Ave. of the Stars, Suite 900
**Cohan, Peter E.** ....'71 '95 L.813 [Dewey B.]
Cohan and Cohen, (AV) ....12301 Wilshire Boulevard
**Cohanne, Polin** ....'50 '75 C.645 B.A. L.884 J.D. [Langberg,C.&D.]
*PRACTICE AREAS: Entertainment.
Cohen, Alan G., (A Professional Corporation) '44 '75
C.912 B.S. L.426 J.D. [Rosner,O.&N.]
**Cohen, Alan Jay** ....'51 '78 C.156 B.A. L.365 J.D. [Katz,H.S.&K.]
*LANGUAGES: French.
*PRACTICE AREAS: Business Litigation; Prejudgment Remedies; Debtor/Creditor Relations; Personal Property Leasing.
Cohen, Albert M. ....'52 '77 C.178 B.A. L.94 J.D. 15456 Ventura Blvd.
**Cohen, Arthur D.** ....'27 '54 C.112 B.A. L.800 LL.B. [Quan,C.K.Y.S.&H.]
*PRACTICE AREAS: Commercial Litigation; Business Law.
**Cohen, Bradford S.**, (AV) ....'53 '79 C.588 B.A. L.1019 J.D. [Cohen P.&F.]
**Cohen, Brett J.** ....'58 '85 C.188 B.S. L.1068 J.D. [Christensen,M.F.J.G.W.&S.]
*PRACTICE AREAS: Real Estate; Land Use; Environmental.
**Cohen, Bruce M.** ....'54 '78 C.112 A.B. L.1068 J.D. [Cohen&L.]
*PRACTICE AREAS: Architects and Engineers Representation; Construction Law; Environmental Law; Entertainment Law; General Business Litigation.
Cohen, Carole H. ....'42 '81 C.119 B.S. L.809 J.D. 11601 Wilshire Blvd.
**Cohen, Cynthia M.**, (AV) ....'45 '71 C.188 A.B. L.569 J.D. [Morgan,L.&B.]
**Cohen, David B.** ....'60 '86 C&L.659 B.A., J.D. [Rogers&W.]
Cohen, David J. ....'63 '88 C.1044 B.A. L.1068 J.D. 5959 W. Century Blvd.
**Cohen, David M.** ....'66 '92 C.659 B.S. L.112 J.D. [Liner,Y.&S.]
*PRACTICE AREAS: Business Civil Litigation.
Cohen, Dennis A. '46 '75
C.36 B.A. L.1068 J.D. Center for Enforcement of Family Support
Cohen, Donald H. ....'38 '69 C.112 B.A. L.426 J.D. 12021 Wilshire Blvd.
Cohen, Eddie E. ....'58 '85 C.763 B.A. L.1097 J.D. 2040 Davies Way
Cohen, Elizabeth Rosenfeld ....'57 '82 C.112 B.A. L.464 J.D. 3424 Wilshire Blvd.
Cohen, Evan Seth ....'60 '85 C.112 B.A. L.464 J.D. [Cohen&C.]
**Cohen, Frederic D.**, (AV) ....'48 '73 C.1167 B.S. L.800 J.D. [Horvitz&L.]
*LANGUAGES: German.
**Cohen, Gail E.** ....'53 '79 C.156 B.A. L.1292 J.D. [Barger&W.]
*PRACTICE AREAS: Litigation; Insurance Law.
**Cohen, Gary J.**, (AV) ....'49 '75 C.112 B.A. L.1068 J.D. [Freid&G.]
*PRACTICE AREAS: Family Law; Civil Appeals.
**Cohen, Gary J.**, (AV) ....'46 '75 C.667 B.S. L.1066 J.D. [Sidley&A.]
*PRACTICE AREAS: Business Transactions and Corporation Law.
Cohen, Harold J. '13 '35 C&L.309 S.B., LL.B.
(adm. in IL; not adm. in CA) 11937 Gorham Ave., Apt. 6‡
**Cohen, Howard W.** ....'55 '85 C.112 B.A. L.477 J.D. [Foley L.W.&A.]
*PRACTICE AREAS: Commercial Litigation; Business Torts; Health Care Litigation; Insurance Coverage and Bad Faith Litigation.
Cohen, Isabel R. ....'39 '69 C.823 B.A. L.569 LL.B. Supr. Ct. J.
**Cohen, Jamey** ....'56 '90 C.813 A.B. L.309 J.D. [Ziffren,B.B.&F.]
*PRACTICE AREAS: Entertainment Law.
**Cohen, Jeffrey A.** ....'65 '90 C.36 B.S. L.990 J.D. [Chapman&G.]
*PRACTICE AREAS: General Negligence; Professional Liability; Commercial and Business Litigation; Construction Litigation; Wood Destroying Organism Litigation.
**Cohen, Jeffrey H.** ....'63 '88 C.659 B.S. L.1068 J.D. [Skadden,A.S.M.&F.]
**Cohen, Jeryll S.** ....'59 '86 C.112 B.A. L.426 J.D. [Ross,S.&G.]
*PRACTICE AREAS: Estate Planning; Probate and Trust Administration.
**Cohen, Jordan S.** ....'66 '91 C.112 B.A. L.880 J.D. [White&C.]
Cohen, Laura R. ....'58 '83 C.112 B.A. L.1066 J.D. Dept. Chf. of Staff to Assemblyman
**Cohen, Lawrence S.** '39 '66 C.588 B.S.M.E. L.94 J.D.
[Freilich,H.&R.] (See Pat. Sect.)
*PRACTICE AREAS: Patent, Trademark and Copyright Law; Unfair Competition Law; Litigation; Licensing Law; Technology Transfer.
**Cohen, Leslie A.** ....'56 '80 C.112 B.A. L.1068 J.D. [Robinson,D.B.&K.]
*REPORTED CASES: In re Oak Creek Energy Farms, Ltd., Debtor. Energy Enterprises, Inc., Plaintiff, v. Oak Creek Energy Systems, Inc., Dean Beckett, Steve Cummings, Oak Creek Energy Farms, Ltd., Defendant, No. 187-00644-A-11 Chapter 11, Adv. No.; In re Skyler Ridge, Debtor, No. LA 87-13216-SB Chapter 11, United States Bankruptcy Court for the Central District of California, 80 Bankr. 500; 1987 Bankr. Lexis 1935; Bankr. L. Rep. (CCH) P72,167; 16 Bankr. Ct. Dec. (CRR) 1122, November 2, 1987, December 15, 1987.
*PRACTICE AREAS: Bankruptcy.
**Cohen, Marc H.** ....'63 '93 C.932 B.S.E.E. L.930 J.D. [Pretty,S.&P.]
*PRACTICE AREAS: Patents; Trademarks; Copyrights; Unfair Competition; Litigation.
**Cohen, Marc S.**, (AV) ....'50 '74 C.188 B.A. L.569 J.D. [Greenberg G.F.C.&M.]
*PRACTICE AREAS: Corporate Reorganization; Bankruptcy.
Cohen, Martin ....'31 '61 C.112 B.A. L.1068 LL.B. [Cohen&C.]
Cohen, Michael A., (AV) '58 '84 C.154 B.A. L.597 J.D.
(adm. in IL; not adm. in CA) Princ., Cohen Financial
**Cohen, Michael C.** ....'55 '80 C.453 B.S. L.1066 J.D. [De Castro,W.&C.]
*PRACTICE AREAS: Tax Litigation.
**Cohen, Michael C.** ....'47 '72 C.112 B.A. L.426 J.D. [Donovan L.N.&I.]
**Cohen, Mitchell I.** ....'60 '88 C.112 B.A. L.464 J.D. [Tharpe&H.]
**Cohen, Mitchell Steven** ....'58 '88 C.605 A.B. L.178 J.D. [Gibson,D.&C.]
*PRACTICE AREAS: Corporate Law; Mergers, Acquisitions and Divestitures.
**Cohen, Nancy J.** ....'67 '93 C.813 B.A. L.1068 J.D. [Irell&M.]
*LANGUAGES: Spanish.
**Cohen, Nancy Sher** ....'51 '78 C.846 B.A. L.426 J.D. [Heller E.W.&M.]
*PRACTICE AREAS: Products Liability and Insurance Coverage Litigation.
Cohen, Norman R., (AV) ....'37 '61 C&L.659 B.S., LL.B. [Cohan&C.]

**Cohen, Paul F., (AV) '38 '64 C.659 B.A. L.569 LL.B.**
**4929 Wilshire, Suite 410, 90010**
**Telephone: 213-937-7105 Fax: 213-965-9907**
**Email: paulfred@aol.com**
**Business law, Complex and Multi-District Litigation and Probate Law.**
*See Professional Biographies, LOS ANGELES, CALIFORNIA*

Cohen, Peter R. ....'31 '58 C.882 B.A. L.309 LL.B. 1708 Westridge Rd.‡
Cohen, Robert L., (AV) ....'39 '71 C.999 L.1095 J.D. Dep. Dist. Atty.
Cohen, Robert M. ....'47 '73 C.112 B.A. L.1068 J.D. 1901 Ave. of the Stars, 18th Fl.

**Cohen, Robert M., (AV) '40 '65 C&L.94 B.A., LL.B.**
**2049 Century Park East, Suite 2790, 90067**
**Telephone: 310-277-1127 Fax: 310-277-6722**
**Family Law and Sports Law.**
*See Professional Biographies, LOS ANGELES, CALIFORNIA*

**Cohen, Ronald C.** ....'62 '87 C.668 B.A. L.145 J.D. [Sidley&A.]
*PRACTICE AREAS: Litigation.
**Cohen, Ronald S.** ....'70 '95 C.112 B.A. L.597 J.D. [Sheppard,M.R.&H.]
*PRACTICE AREAS: Business Litigation.
**Cohen, Ronan** ....'— '93 C.112 B.A. L.94 J.D. [Konowiecki&R.]
*PRACTICE AREAS: General Business; Health Care.
**Cohen, Sharon L.** ....'63 '88 C.112 B.A. L.426 J.D. [Skadden,A.S.M.&F.]
**Cohen, Sheri E.** ....'62 '95 C.763 A.B. L.426 J.D. [Mitchell,S.&K.]
*PRACTICE AREAS: Federal Taxation; Employment Taxation; Tax Exempt Organizations.
Cohen, Steven L. ....'60 '91 C.763 B.A. L.398 J.D. [Derdiger&C.]
**Cohen, Steven M.** ....'59 '85 C.112 B.A. L.904 J.D. [Wehner&P.]
*PRACTICE AREAS: Business Litigation.
Cohen, Sy R. ....'30 '63 C.563 B.B.A. L.426 LL.B. 11835 W. Olympic Bl.
**Cohen, Theodore A.** ....'65 '90 C.112 B.A. L.1067 J.D. [Levy,S.&L.]
*PRACTICE AREAS: Commercial Litigation; Bankruptcy.
Cohen, Warren H. '44 '69 C.976 B.A. L.309 LL.B.
(adm. in AZ; not adm. in CA) Prof., Whittier College Sch. of Law‡

**Cohen, Alexander & Clayton, A Professional Corporation**
**(See Thousand Oaks)**

Cohen and Cohen ....740 N. La Brea Ave.
**Cohen-Cutler, Olivia J.** '53 '78 C.783 B.A. L.93 J.D.
(adm. in MA; not adm. in CA) V.P., Labor Rels., Capital Cities/ABC, Inc.

**Cohen, Hilary Huebsch, A Prof. Corp., Law Offices of**
**(See Torrance)**

**Cohen, Jerome S., Law Offices of**
**(See Long Beach)**

**Cohen & Lord, A Professional Corporation**
**Suite 200, 4720 Lincoln Boulevard (Marina Del Rey), 90292**
**Telephone: 310-821-1163 Facsimile: 310-821-7828**
**Bruce M. Cohen; Scott R. Lord;—Ari J. Lauer; Cynthia R. Hodes; Jeffrey L. Linden. Of Counsel: Doug Gummerman.**
*See Professional Biographies, LOS ANGELES, CALIFORNIA*

Cohen-Milch, Janis ....'47 '74 C.112 B.A. L.329 J.D. P.O. Box 26-B99

**Cohen Primiani & Foster, A Professional Corporation, (AV)**
**2029 Century Park East, Suite 480, 90067**
**Telephone: 310-277-3963 Fax: 310-277-4351**
**Marc S. Primiani; Bradford S. Cohen; Michael D. Foster; Bernard Oster; Samuel Israel; Jeffrey Forer.**
**Federal, State, Local and International Taxation. Entertainment Tax, Tax Litigation and Controversies, Corporate, Real Estate and Partnership Law. Estate Planning, Probate, Trust and General Business Law.**
**Reference: Western Bank (Los Angeles, Calif.).**
*See Professional Biographies, LOS ANGELES, CALIFORNIA*

**Cohn, Andrew B.** ....'64 '90 C.94 B.A. L.426 J.D. [Chapman&G.]
*LANGUAGES: French.
*PRACTICE AREAS: General Negligence; Construction Litigation; Coverage.
**Cohn, Eileen M.** ....'53 '87 C.705 B.A. L.426 J.D. [Langberg,C.&D.]
*PRACTICE AREAS: General Business Litigation; Complex Business Litigation; Entertainment and the Arts; Government Regulations.
**Cohn, Hillel T.** ....'49 '74 C.860 B.A. L.309 J.D. [Graham&J.]
*PRACTICE AREAS: Securities; International Investment.
**Cohn, Jonathon E.** ....'60 '88 C.668 B.A. L.1068 J.D. [Foley L.W.&A.]
*PRACTICE AREAS: Commercial Litigation; Health Care; Bankruptcy; Workers Compensation.
Cohn, Martin '59 '85 C.228 A.B. L.178 J.D.
(adm. in NY; not adm. in CA) 161 4th Anita Dr.‡
**Cohn, Ronald R.**, (AV) ....'48 '74 C.112 B.A. L.464 J.D. [Glass,A.G.&C.]
*PRACTICE AREAS: Creditors Rights; Commercial Law; Insolvency; Equipment/Personal Property Leasing; Secured Transactions.
Cohn, Sheldon J. '56 '82 C.112 B.A. L.426 J.D.
V.P. & Gen. Coun., Home Budget Loans

**Cohn, Terri E., Law Office, (AV) '61 '86 C.684 B.A. L.464 J.D.**
**1801 Century Park East, 23rd Floor, 90067**
**Telephone: 310-553-8333 Fax: 310-553-8337**
***LANGUAGES: French, German and Russian.**
***PRACTICE AREAS: Business Law; Transactions (Domestic and International); Telecommunications; Corporate Law; Business Litigation.**
**Business Transactions, Domestic and International; Telecommunications; Corporate Law; Business Litigation.**
*See Professional Biographies, LOS ANGELES, CALIFORNIA*

Cohon, Bennett B. ....'37 '70 C.608 B.S.Ed. L.426 J.D. [Cohon&G.]
Cohon & Gardner, P.C. ....2049 Century Pk. E.
**Cohoon, James B.** ....'53 '80 C.906 B.S. L.1049 J.D. [Kearney,B.&C.]
Coker, Thomas D. '55 '85 C.801 B.S. L.365 J.D.
(adm. in IL; not adm. in CA) Asst. U.S. Atty.
**Colantuono, Michael G.** ....'61 '89 C.309 B.A. L.1068 J.D. [Richards,W.&G.]
*PRACTICE AREAS: Public and Municipal Law; Land Use Law.
**Colbert, James W., III**, (AV) ....'45 '70 C.976 B.A. L.309 J.D. [O'Melveny&M.]
**Colclough, Robert T., III** ....'68 '95 C.93 B.A. L.940 J.D. [Hillsinger&C.]
**Cole, Araceli K.** ....'60 '90 C.426 B.S. L.1066 J.D. [Sheppard,M.R.&H.]
*LANGUAGES: Spanish.
**Cole, Curtis A.**, (AV) ....'46 '72 C.112 A.B. L.1068 J.D. [Thelen,M.J.&B.]
*PRACTICE AREAS: Torts; Insurance; Health Care Law.
Cole, Dana M. ....'54 '79 C.112 A.B. L.1065 J.D. [Cole&L.]
Cole, Debra A. ....'62 '88 C.112 B.A. L.426 J.D. Dep. Pub. Def.
Cole, Diana L. ....'46 '76 C.678 B.A. L.809 J.D. 3960 Wilshire Blvd.
Cole, Gerald M. ....'46 '72 C.112 A.B. L.1068 J.D. Fed. Labor Rel. Auth.
**Cole, Leslie M. B.** ....'59 '88 C.1036 B.A. L.765 J.D. [Koletsky,M.&F.]
*LANGUAGES: French, German, Spanish.
*PRACTICE AREAS: Construction Defect Litigation; General Liability Litigation; Insurance Fraud Litigation.
**Cole, Stephen T.** ....'53 '80 C.506 B.A. L.569 J.D. [Fulbright&J.]
*PRACTICE AREAS: Municipal Finance; Finance.
**Cole, William L., (A Professional Corporation)**, (AV) '52 '77
C.112 A.B. L.813 J.D. [Mitchell,S.&K.]
*PRACTICE AREAS: Labor Law; Employment Litigation; Employee Benefits Law.
Cole & Loeterman ....1875 Century Pk. E., 8th Fl.
Colella, Benedetto ....'59 '89 C.472 B.S. L.940 J.D. Dep. Dist. Atty.
**Coleman, Catherine H.** ....'53 '79 C.813 A.B. L.309 J.D. [Kinsella,B.F.&T.]
*LANGUAGES: French and German.
**Coleman, Christine E.** ....'— '89 C&L.813 A.B., J.D. [O'Melveny&M.]
*PRACTICE AREAS: Entertainment Law.
**Coleman, Craig J.** ....'71 '96 C.93 B.A. L.276 J.D. [O'Melveny&M.]
Coleman, Edward S., (BV) ....'29 '53 C.112 B.A. L.800 J.D. [E.S.Coleman]
Coleman, George W., (AV) ....'25 '56 C.893 B.C.E. L.765 J.D. 10100 Santa Monica Blvd.
**Coleman, Howard D.** ....'45 '70 C.112 A.B. L.1066 J.D. [Nossaman,G.K.&E.]
*PRACTICE AREAS: Natural Resources Law; Real Property Law.
**Coleman, John M.**, (AV) ....'52 '78 C.276 B.A. L.398 J.D. [Coleman&W.]
*PRACTICE AREAS: Civil Litigation; Torts; Insurance Defense; Products Liability.

CAA203P

**Coleman, Kelly Ann** .... '64 '89 C.477 A.B. L.1067 J.D. [Ⓐ Codikow&C.]
*PRACTICE AREAS: Commercial Litigation; Entertainment; Real Estate.
**Coleman, Patricia M.** .... '46 '82 C.112 B.A. L.426 J.D. [Grace,S.C.&S.]
*PRACTICE AREAS: Insurance Defense Law; Product Liability Law; Construction Defect Law.
**Coleman, Richard M.**, (AV) .... '35 '60 C.276 A.B. L.309 J.D. [Coleman&R.]
**Coleman, Roland L., Jr.** .... '49 '74 C.800 B.A. L.421 J.D. [Wilson,E.M.E.&D.]
*PRACTICE AREAS: Product Liability; Government Tort Liability; Employment Law; Civil Rights Litigation; Construction Law.
Coleman, Thomas F. .... '48 '73 C.912 B.A. L.426 J.D. P.O. Box 65756
**Coleman, Thomas Henry**, (AV) .... '40 '66 C.813 B.A. L.1068 J.D. [Troy&G.]
*PRACTICE AREAS: Bankruptcy; Securities Litigation.
Coleman, Edward S., A Prof. Law Corp., (BV)
1516 S. Bundy Dr. (⊙Las Vegas, Nevada)

**Coleman & Richards, A Professional Corporation, (AV)**
**Suite 810, 1801 Avenue of the Stars (Century City), 90067**
**Telephone: 310-277-2700**
**Richard M. Coleman; Laurie J. Richards.**
**General Civil and Criminal Trial and Appellate Practice in all State and Federal Courts, Mediation and Arbitration.**

***See Professional Biographies, LOS ANGELES, CALIFORNIA***

**Coleman & Wright, (AV)**
**333 South Grand Avenue, Suite 3950, 90071**
**Telephone: 213-624-4292 Telecopier: 213-624-1354**
**Members of Firm: John M. Coleman; Patricia E. Wright; Kenneth K. Tanji, Jr.; Tracy Kawano; Charles K. Collins; Matthew J. Luce; Robert F. Beal; Robert Montes, Jr. Of Counsel: John J. Quinn (Not admitted in CA).**
**Civil Litigation. Torts and Insurance Defense. Products Liability.**

***See Professional Biographies, LOS ANGELES, CALIFORNIA***

**Coletti, Michael A.** .... '62 '88 C.454 B.A. L.990 J.D. [Ⓐ Tuverson&H.]
**Colfer, James W.** .... '62 '88 C.112 B.A. L.1066 J.D. [Bacon&M.]
*PRACTICE AREAS: Business; Insurance Defense; Employment Law.
Coli, Robert J. .... '53 '78 C&L.770 B.S., J.D. First Interstate Bank (⊙Las Vegas, NV)
**Colladay, Sharli** .... '66 '95 C.800 B.S. L.1065 J.D. [Ⓐ Sheppard,M.R.&H.]
Collari, Richard L., Jr. .... '66 '91 C.197 B.A. L.93 J.D. 1055 W. 7th St.
Collias, Philip J. '62 '87 C.165 B.A. L.188 J.D.
Assoc. Corp. Coun., Kaufman and Broad Home Corp.
**Colliau, Michael T.** .... '55 '85 C.628 B.S. L.878 J.D. [Morris,P.&P.]
Collie, Frank S. .... '64 '91 C.112 B.A. L.770 J.D. 1900 Ave. of the Stars
**Collier, Alan H.** .... '64 '90 C.1 B.A. L.990 J.D. [Ⓐ Mendes&M.]
**Collier, Charles A., Jr.**, (AV) .... '30 '55 C&L.309 A.B., LL.B. [Ⓒ Irell&M.]
Collier, Mark S. .... '52 '81 C.426 B.A. L.809 J.D. Dist. Atty's. Off.
Collingsworth, Terrence P. '56 '82 C.161 B.A. L.228 J.D.
(adm. in WA; not adm. in CA) Assoc. Prof., Loyola Law School
Collins, Andrea J. .... '59 '90 C.37 B.S. L.990 J.D. 1200 Wilshire Blvd, 6th Fl.
Collins, Audrey B. .... '45 '77 C.329 B.A. L.1068 J.D. Dist. J.
**Collins, C. Guerry** .... '44 '84 C.976 B.A. L.800 J.D. [Lord,B.&B.]
Collins, Candice J. .... '49 '85 C.763 B.A. L.426 J.D. 2029 Century Park E.
**Collins, Cathleen** .... '47 '84 C.706 B.A. L.569 J.D. [Kinsella,B.F.&T.]
**Collins, Charles K.** .... '51 '81 C.1042 B.A. L.426 J.D. [Ⓐ Coleman&W.]
*PRACTICE AREAS: Personal Injury Law; Business Litigation.
**Collins, Daniel P.** .... '63 '89 C.309 A.B. L.813 J.D. [Ⓐ Munger,T.&O.]
**Collins, Harold R., Jr.**, (AV) .... '38 '65 C.763 A.B. L.1065 J.D. [Blecher&C.]
*PRACTICE AREAS: Antitrust; Business Litigation; Intellectual Property; Professional Malpractice; Patent Infringement.
Collins, Horace C. '50 '78 C&L.309 A.B., J.D.
(adm. in NY; not adm. in CA) 2049 Century Pk. E.
**Collins, Kathleen M.** .... '62 '89 C.30 B.A. L.426 J.D. [Marcus,W.S.&D.]
*PRACTICE AREAS: Real Estate Title; Business Law.
**Collins, Kevin** .... '63 '93 C.1168 B.A. L.426 J.D. [Ⓐ Kamine,S.&U.]
**Collins, Michael D.** .... '55 '89 C.1077 B.A. L.426 J.D. [Ⓐ Ford]
**Collins, Michael K.**, (AV) .... '43 '70 C&L.910 A.B., J.D. [Greenberg G.F.C.&M.]
*PRACTICE AREAS: Civil Appeals; Business; Real Estate and Attorney Malpractice Litigation.
Collins, Mildred L. .... '38 '84 C.840 L.1001 J.D. [Liebert,C.&F.]
Collins, Patricia L. .... '53 '79 C.107 B.A. L.276 J.D. Supr. Ct. J.
**Collins, Timothy R., Jr.** .... '68 '95 C.813 B.A. L.976 J.D. [Ⓐ Mitchell,S.&K.]
*PRACTICE AREAS: Motion Picture and Television Law.

**Collins, Collins, Muir & Traver**
**(See Pasadena)**

**Collins, Robillard & Katz**
**(See Torrance)**

**Collinson, Lisa D.** .... '66 '95 C.112 B.A. L.809 J.D. [Ⓐ Hillsinger&C.]
**Collodel, Douglas J.** .... '59 '84 C.602 A.B. L.464 J.D. [Morris,P.&P.]
**Collyer, Glen B.** .... '58 '87 C&L.101 B.S., J.D. [Latham&W.]
**Colman, Abraham J.** .... '64 '89 C.1138 B.B.A. L.262 J.D. [Ⓐ Buchalter,N.F.&Y.]
*PRACTICE AREAS: Business Litigation; Creditor's Rights.
**Colman, Arlene A.**, (AV) .... '42 '81 C.766 B.A. L.1049 J.D. [Gray,Y.D.&R.]
*PRACTICE AREAS: Labor and Employment Law; Discrimination Law; Insurance Law; Appellate Practice.
Colman, Jonathan H., (AV) .... '52 '80 C.112 B.A. L.809 J.D. 12121 Wilshire Blvd.
**Colmey, Marie E.** .... '63 '89 C.628 B.S. L.950 J.D. [Ⓐ Bonne,B.M.O.&N.]
**Cologne, Knox M., III** '43 '68 C.763 A.B. L.813 J.D.
Sr. V.P. & Assoc. Gen. Coun., Bank of Amer.
Colón-Latta, Gisela .... '66 '90 C.677 B.A. L.809 J.D. 601 S. Figueroa St.
**Colorado, Gabriel** .... '57 '85 C.800 B.A. L.1068 J.D. Sr. Coun., Bank of Amer.
Colton, Edward A. '43 '81
C.1097 B.S. L.809 J.D. V.P. & Gen. Coun., Alpha Therapeutic Corp.
Colton, Lee F., (BV) .... '36 '62 C.112 B.S. L.1068 LL.B. [Colton M.]
**Colton, Robert C.**, (AV) .... '43 '69 C.174 B.A. L.1068 J.D. [Buchalter,N.F.&Y.]
*PRACTICE AREAS: Banking; Corporate; Finance.
Colton Mann Partnership, (AV) .... 1801 Century Park E., 19th Fl.
Colwell, Misty L. .... '63 '90 C.1075 B.A. L.1049 J.D. 555 S. Flower St., 25th Fl.
**Combs, Christopher W.** .... '62 '90 C.309 A.B. L.813 J.D. [Ⓐ Wynne S.I.]
*LANGUAGES: French and German.
*PRACTICE AREAS: Bankruptcy.
**Comer, Robert J.** .... '63 '96 C.1077 B.A. L.426 J.D. [Ⓐ Christensen,M.F.J.G.W.&S.]
*PRACTICE AREAS: Real Estate Law; Land Use Law; Environmental Law.
Comparet, Thomas M., (AV) .... '33 '62 C&L.477 B.A., LL.B. 4929 Wilshire Blvd.
**Compean, Michael D.** .... '52 '86 C.112 B.A. L.1068 J.D. [Black C.H.&L.]
*REPORTED CASES: Pruyn vs. Agricultural Ins. Co. (1995), Cal. App. 4th [42 Cal. Rptr. 2d 2985] ; Stonewall Ins. Co. vs. City of P.V. Estates (1992) 29 Cal.App.4th 98 (9 Cal.2d 663).
*PRACTICE AREAS: Insurance Coverage; Coverage Litigation; Bad Faith Litigation; Insurer Insolvency; Reinsurance.
Comsky, David, (AV) .... '28 '53 C.112 A.B. L.1068 J.D. 11377 W. Olympic Blvd.

**Comstock & Sharpe, Inc.**
**(See Culver City)**

Conant, Ardis M. .... '47 '83 C.813 B.A. L.767 J.D. [Wilson&B.]

**Concoff, Gary O.**, (AV) .... '36 '62 C.112 B.S. L.309 LL.B. [Troy&G.]
*PRACTICE AREAS: Entertainment Law; Motion Picture and Television Law; Finance Law; Intellectual Property Law.
**Condon, Brian K.** .... '63 '88 C.112 B.A. L.1065 J.D. [Arnold&P.]
*PRACTICE AREAS: Litigation.

**Condon & Forsyth, (AV)**
**1900 Avenue of the Stars, 90067⊙**
**Telephone: 310-557-2030 Telecopier: 310-557-1299**
**Resident Partners: Frank A. Silane; Roderick D. Margo; Stephen R. Ginger; Jennifer J. Johnston.**
**Resident Associates: William T. MacCary; Kevin R. Sutherland; Erin L. Nordby.**
**Civil and Commercial Litigation, Transactional and Regulatory, Aviation, Business, Employment, Products Liability, Administrative and Insurance Law.**
**New York, N.Y. Office: 1251 Avenue of the Americas. Telephone: 212-921-5100. Telex: 426978. Telecopier: 212-575-3638**
**Washington, D.C. Office: 1016 Sixteenth Street, N.W. Telephone: 202-289-0500. Telecopier: 202-289-4524.**

***See Professional Biographies, LOS ANGELES, CALIFORNIA***

**Conkle & Olesten**
**(See Santa Monica)**

**Conley, Mark A.** .... '51 '78 C.659 B.A. L.178 J.D. [McDermott,W.&E.]
Conley, Pamela A. '66 '93
C.112 B.S. L.446 J.D. Assoc. Gen. Coun., Directors Guild of Amer.
**Conley, Scott**, (AV) '23 '49 C&L.976 B.A., LL.B.
[Ⓒ Celebrezze&W.] (⊙San Francisco)
**Conn, Bernice** .... '53 '92 C.112 B.A. L.426 J.D. [Ⓐ Robins,K.M.&C.]
*PRACTICE AREAS: General Civil Practice; Litigation; Medical Malpractice; Product Liability Law; Tort and Personal Injury.
**Conn, Lawrence C.** .... '59 '85 C.674 B.A. L.813 J.D. [Foley L.W.&A.]
*PRACTICE AREAS: Health Care; Hospitals; Integrated Health Care Delivery Systems; Long Term Care; Business Law.
**Conn, Richard S.** .... '49 '75 C.178 B.A. L.1068 J.D. [Musick,P.&G.]
*PRACTICE AREAS: Litigation.
**Connell, Michael J.**, (AV) .... '38 '65 C&L.309 A.B., LL.B. [Morrison&F.]
*PRACTICE AREAS: Corporate Finance; Securities.
**Connelly, Blair G.** .... '69 '94 C&L.276 A.B., J.D. [Ⓐ Latham&W.]
Conner, Bren C. .... '62 '88 C.112 A.B. L.1065 J.D. 550 S. Hope St.
**Conner, Christopher B.** .... '62 '90 C.668 B.A. L.1066 J.D. [Ⓐ Folger L.&K.]⊙
**Conner, Jeffrey B.** '57 '89 C.112 B.A. L.309 J.D.
(adm. in PA; not adm. in CA) [Ⓐ Gibson,D.&C.]
*PRACTICE AREAS: Corporations; Securities.
Conner, Lindsay .... '56 '80 C.112 B.A. L.309 J.D. 10960 Wilshire Blvd.
**Connolly, John G.**, (AV) .... '59 '84 C.1036 B.A. L.1068 J.D. [Zimmermann,K.&C.]
*PRACTICE AREAS: Business Litigation; Real Estate; Labor Litigation.
**Connolly, Patrick A., III** .... '67 '94 C.273 B.A. L.1148 J.D. [Ⓐ Koletsky,M.&F.]
*PRACTICE AREAS: Construction Defect Insurance; Defense.
Connolly, Patrick E. .... '64 '92 C&L.1049 B.A., J.D. Dep. Dist. Atty.
Connolly, Paul A. .... '35 '78 C.734 A.B. L.809 J.D. 3219 Ettrick St.‡
**Connon, Nicholas P.** .... '64 '90 C.347 B.S. L.178 J.D. [Ⓐ Proskauer R.G.&M.]
*PRACTICE AREAS: Employment Litigation; Employment Counseling; Labor.
Connor, Gerald W. .... '50 '74 C.757 B.A. L.276 J.D. 3225 Club Dr.
Connor, Jacqueline A. .... '51 '76 C&L.800 A.B., J.D. Supr. Ct. J.
**Connor, Jan Allen**, (AV) .... '32 '66 C.1043 B.S. L.809 LL.B. [McHale&C.]
*PRACTICE AREAS: Insurance Defense; Products Liability; Construction.
Connor, Patrick T. .... '55 '79 [De Carlo,C.&S.]
Conroy, Roberta A. '54 '80
C.112 A.B. L.426 J.D. Asst. Gen. Coun., The Capital Grp., Inc.
Consolver, Carol A. .... '49 '76 C.188 A.B. L.800 J.D. 633 W. 5th St.
**Contarino, Alfred V.** .... '35 '65 C.94 B.S. L.1065 J.D. [Cotchett&P.]
Conti, Laura G. .... '60 '86 C.112 B.A. L.1136 J.D. [Ⓒ Thompson,M.&F.]
**Contopulos, Stephen G.**, (BV) .... '46 '72 C.1097 B.A. L.426 J.D. [Sidley&A.]
Contreras, Priscilla .... '50 '78 C.174 B.S. L.112 J.D. Gen. Atty., Union Pacific R.R. Co.
**Convy, Catherine** .... '57 '95 C.705 B.A. L.990 J.D. [Ⓐ Manning,M.&W.]
**Conway, Catherine A.**, (AV) .... '53 '78 C.679 B.A. L.1119 J.D. [Manatt,P.&P.]
*PRACTICE AREAS: Labor and Employment Law; Litigation.
**Conway, John C.** .... '56 '95 C.793 B.S. L.800 J.D. [Ⓐ Gibson,D.&C.]
**Conway, Kathryn M.** .... '62 '90 C.788 B.A. L.276 J.D. [Ⓐ Howrey&S.]
*PRACTICE AREAS: Commercial Litigation.

**Conway, Jack K.**
**(See San Marino)**

**Cook, Arthur B., II, (P.C.)** .... '48 '75 C.813 B.A. L.800 J.D. [Hill,F.&B.]
*REPORTED CASES: Surfside Colony, Ltd. v. California Coastal Commission, (1991) 226 Cal. App 3d 1260, 277 Cal. Rptr. 371.
**Cook, Bethany A.** .... '62 '93 C.446 B.A. L.724 J.D. [Ⓐ Musick,P.&G.]
*PRACTICE AREAS: Employment Law.
**Cook, Danna L., (A Professional Corporation)** '59 '85
C.605 B.A. L.976 J.D. [Mitchell,S.&K.]
*LANGUAGES: Spanish.
*PRACTICE AREAS: Music Law; General Entertainment Law; Entertainment Litigation.
Cook, Donald C. .... '43 '76 C.1042 B.A. L.1148 J.D. 800 S. Figueroa St.
Cook, Edward M., III .... '39 '66 C.769 B.A. L.1065 J.D. Dep. Pub. Def.
**Cook, Paul C.** .... '66 '94 C.1077 B.A. L.1188 J.D. [Ⓐ Ford]
**Cook, Philip E.** .... '55 '90 C.999 B.A. L.1068 J.D. [Ⓐ Jones,D.R.&P.]
Cook, Virginia .... '24 '57 C.846 B.A. L.800 J.D. 8616 La Tijera Blvd.
**Cooke, Michelle A.** .... '67 '93 C&L.893 B.A., J.D. [Ⓐ Small L.&K.]
*PRACTICE AREAS: Trademark; Litigation.
**Cooke, Pamela S.** .... '61 '86 C.1019 B.A. L.809 J.D. [Ⓐ Callahan,M.&W.]
**Cooke, Ronald J.** .... '47 '72 C.112 A.B. L.884 J.D. [Littler,M.F.T.&M.]
**Cookerly, Jacqueline A.** .... '66 '93 C.112 B.A. L.1068 J.D. [Ⓐ Riordan&M.]
**Cooley, Paul S.** .... '64 '90 C&L.426 B.A., J.D. [Ⓐ Tisdale&N.]
*PRACTICE AREAS: Business; Securities; Intellectual Property; Construction; Unfair Competition.
Cooley, Stephen L. .... '47 '73 C.1097 B.A. L.800 J.D. Head Dep. Dist. Atty.
**Cooley, Susan J.**, (AV) .... '52 '80 C.112 B.A. L.809 J.D. [Oldman&C.]
*REPORTED CASES: In re Estate of DiPinto, 188 Cal. App. 3d. 625 231 Cal Rptr. 612, 1986.
*PRACTICE AREAS: Probate; Conservatorship; Guardianship Administration; Trust Administration; Trust Litigation.
**Coomber, Skip R., III** .... '61 '90 C.112 B.A. L.426 J.D. [Coomber]⊙
*PRACTICE AREAS: Business Law.

**Coomber Law Firm**
**601 South Figueroa Street, 41st Floor, 90017-5704⊙**
**Telephone: 213-622-2200 Fax: 213-243-0000**
**Email: scoomber@aol.com**
**Skip R. Coomber, III.**
**Business Transactions and Business Litigation.**
**Rancho Santa Fe, California Office: 16909 Via de Santa Fe, Suite 200. P.O. Box 7299, 92067-7299. Telephone: 619-759-3939. Facsimile: 619-759-3930.**

***See Professional Biographies, LOS ANGELES, CALIFORNIA***

**Coombs, Chad Chase** .... '59 '91 C.1073 B.S. L.800 J.D. [Ⓐ Fulbright&J.]
*PRACTICE AREAS: Bankruptcy.

**Cooney, William N.** ................. '42 '72 C.679 B.S.E.E. L.966 J.D. [O'Melveny&M.]
*PRACTICE AREAS: Real Estate.
**Coons, Ann McCallister** '45 '72 C.880 B.A. L.1119 J.D.
Assoc. Gen. Coun. & Asst. Secy., The Times Mirror Co.
**Coons, Michael H.** ......................... '62 '89 C&L.101 B.S., J.D. [Johnson,P.C.&S.]
*LANGUAGES: Spanish.
*PRACTICE AREAS: Business Law; Estate Planning; Probate Law; Real Estate; Personal Injury.
**Cooper, Bertrand M.**, (AV) ........... '42 '70 C.976 B.A. L.597 J.D. [O'Melveny&M.]
*PRACTICE AREAS: Antitrust; Litigation; Lender Liability; Commercial Disputes.
**Cooper, Brian E.** ......................... '65 '90 C.112 B.A. L.426 J.D. [Bottum&F.]
Cooper, Candace D. ........................................ '48 '74 C&L.800 B.A., J.D. Supr. Ct. J.
**Cooper, Christopher K.** ................ '60 '86 C.112 A.B. L.426 J.D. [Sullivan,W.&D.]
*PRACTICE AREAS: Real Estate Transactions; Real Estate Acquisitions; Sales; Financing; Workouts.
**Cooper, Clayton E.**, (AV) .............. '43 '70 C.112 B.A. L.426 J.D. [Gilbert,K.C.&J.]
*PRACTICE AREAS: Insurance Defense; Construction Defect.
Cooper, Florence Marie ...................................... '40 '75 L.1148 J.D. Supr. Ct. J.
Cooper, Gary, (A Prof. Law Corp.), (AV) '34 '62
C.602 B.Ph. L.426 LL.B. 1801 Century Park, E.
**Cooper, Jay L.**, (AV) ........................................ '29 '51 C&L.209 J.D. [Manatt,P.&P.]
*PRACTICE AREAS: Entertainment Law (Movie, Film, Television); Intellectual Property Law; Multimedia Law.
Cooper, Jean A. ........................ '63 '88 C.188 B.A. L.309 J.D. 1000 Wilshire Blvd.
**Cooper, Jill F.** ................... '65 '91 C.674 B.A. L.1097 J.D. [McCutchen,D.B.&E.]
**Cooper, Leon M.**, (AV) ................. '24 '49 C.112 A.B. L.309 J.D. [Lewis,D.B.&B.]
*PRACTICE AREAS: Corporate Law; Corporate Securities; Public Offerings; Private Placements; Mergers and Acquisitions.
**Cooper, M. Scott**, (AV) ....................... '50 '79 C.112 A.B. L.1068 J.D. [Sidley&A.]
*PRACTICE AREAS: Real Estate; Finance.
**Cooper, Marlene S.** '53 '78
C.112 B.A. L.1068 J.D. Sr. Coun., Pacific Telesis Legal Group
Cooper, Martin A. ......................... '41 '76 C.667 B.S. L.1136 J.D. 8833 Sunset Blvd.
Cooper, Natasha S. ........................ '61 '86 C.1042 B.A. L.809 J.D. Dep. Dist. Atty.
**Cooper, Robert E.**, (AV) ............... '39 '65 C.597 A.B. L.976 LL.B. [Gibson,D.&C.]
*PRACTICE AREAS: Antitrust; Business Tort Litigation.
**Cooper, Robert S.** ....................... '60 '92 C.112 B.A. L.426 J.D. [Belcher,H.&B.]
*LANGUAGES: Spanish.
*PRACTICE AREAS: Civil Trials; Appellate Practice; Aviation Law; Products Liability; Toxic Tort Law.
**Cooper, Scott P.** ......................... '55 '81 C.602 B.A. L.276 J.D. [Proskauer R.G.&M.]
*PRACTICE AREAS: Litigation.
Cooper, Stephen L. ................... '40 '67 C.800 B.S. L.1095 J.D. 2049 Century Park E.
**Cooper, Steven M.** .................. '64 '89 C.112 B.A. L.1065 J.D. [O'Melveny&M.]
*PRACTICE AREAS: Toxic Tort Litigation; Employment Discrimination.
**Cooper, Victor G.** ... '56 '94 C.1077 B.S.E.E. L.426 J.D. [Merchant&G.] (See Pat. Sect.)
*PRACTICE AREAS: Patent Law; Copyright Law; Trademark Law.
Cooper, William P., III ............. '45 '76 C.112 A.B. L.809 J.D. 414 N. Beachwood Dr.
**Cooper & Hemar**
**(See Santa Monica)**
Cooperman, Barnet M. ........................ '22 '49 C.112 A.B. L.1066 J.D. Supr. Ct. J.
**Cooperman, Bruce E.**, (AV) ................. '52 '77 C.112 B.A. L.1068 J.D. [Trope&T.]
*PRACTICE AREAS: Family Law.
**Cope, Stephen L.** ......................... '63 '94 C.674 B.A. L.112 J.D. [Lord,B.&B.]
*PRACTICE AREAS: General Litigation; Insurance Bad Faith; Insurance Coverage.
**Copeland, Erin M.** ........................... '61 '87 C.93 B.A. L.273 J.D. [Levine&Assoc.]
*PRACTICE AREAS: Litigation; Real Estate; Gaming Law; Licensing and Regulation; Indian Law.

**Copeland, Trent B. '62 '88 C.197 B.A. L.273 J.D.**
**1999 Avenue of the Stars, Suite 2800, 90067**
**Telephone: 310-789-1050 Fax: 310-286-7285**
**Criminal Law, Business and Civil Litigation.**

Copeland, Yolanda ................ '47 '82 C.1097 B.A. L.1221 J.D. 3350 Wilshire Blvd.
Copes, Wilson B., (AV) ................. '22 '51 C.112 B.S. L.426 LL.B. [Kopesky&W.]
**Coplen, Lisa Marie Le Nay** ............. '63 '89 C.800 B.S. L.426 J.D. [Anderson,M.&C.]
Coplen, R. Bruce ........................... '52 '77 C.546 B.S. L.1065 J.D. Dep. City Atty.
**Coppenrath, Walter G., Jr., (P.C.)** '46 '78 C.770 B.A. L.1068 J.D.
[Mahoney,C.J.&P.]
*PRACTICE AREAS: Business; Real Estate; Maritime; Insurance; Construction Litigation.
**Corash, Michèle B.**, (AV) ... '45 '71 C.518 B.A. L.569 J.D. [Morrison&F.] (San Fran.)
*LANGUAGES: French.
*PRACTICE AREAS: Land Use; Environmental; Health and Safety.
Corbeill, Gregory G. ......................... '62 '87 C.429 B.A. L.145 J.D. 400 S. Hope St.
**Corbett, Kevin A.** ......................... '69 '95 C.659 B.A. L.861 J.D. [Hooper,L.&B.]
*PRACTICE AREAS: Health Care Law; Corporation Law.
Corbett, Kevin A. '54 '80 C.188 A.B. L.94 J.D.
V.P. & Dir., Coldwell Banker Real Estate Grp., Inc.
**Corbin, Robert L.**, (AV) ...................... '45 '72 C.165 B.A. L.262 J.D. [R.L.Corbin]

**Corbin, Robert L., P.C., Law Offices of, (AV)**
**601 West Fifth Street, 12th Floor, 90071**
**Telephone: 213-612-0001 Facsimile: 213-612-0061**
**Robert L. Corbin;—Michael W. Fitzgerald. Of Counsel: Kevin F. Ruf.**
**Criminal and Civil Litigation in State and Federal Courts and before Administrative Agencies.**
*See Professional Biographies, LOS ANGELES, CALIFORNIA*

**Corcoran, T. Stephen** .................. '63 '93 C.112 B.A. L.1137 J.D. [Dale,B.&H.]
Corda, Sharon C. ............................ '52 '77 C.1036 B.A. L.145 J.D. 633 W. 5th St.
**Cordell, Dolores** ................................ '47 '77 C.112 B.A. L.800 J.D. [Clark&T.]
*PRACTICE AREAS: General Business Litigation; Commercial Litigation; Collections Litigation; Employer-Employee Litigation; Unfair Competition.
**Cordelli, B. Gerard** ..................... '57 '83 C.273 B.B.A. L.1068 J.D. [Long&L.]
*PRACTICE AREAS: Insurance Coverage; Products Liability; Commercial Litigation; Intellectual Property; ERISA.
**Cordero, C. Darryl** ..................... '56 '83 C.846 B.A. L.309 J.D. [Foley L.W.&A.]
*PRACTICE AREAS: Insurance Coverage and Bad Faith; Antitrust; Federal Litigation; Commercial Litigation.
**Cordero, Mario** ........................................ '52 '80 C.1042 L.770 J.D. [Ochoa&S.]
*LANGUAGES: Spanish.
*PRACTICE AREAS: Workers Compensation.
**Cordrey, David M.** ............................ '64 '88 C.112 B.A. L.426 J.D. [Lavely&S.]
*PRACTICE AREAS: Entertainment Litigation; Business Litigation.
**Coren, Arthur A.** .......................... '55 '79 C&L.831 B.A., J.D. [Horgan,R.B.&C.]
*PRACTICE AREAS: Banking; Corporate and Corporate Securities.
Corey, Edward E. .......................... '61 '86 C.800 B.A. L.464 J.D. [E.E.Corey]
Corey, Edward E., A P.C., Law Offices of
3580 Wilshire Boulevard 17th Floor (San Francisco)
**Corinblit, Jack, A Law Corporation**, (AV) ... '23 '51 C.912 L.145 J.D. [Corinblit&S.]
*REPORTED CASES: Beacon Theatres, Inc. v. Westover, 359 U.S. 500 (1959); In re Equity Funding Corp. of America Securities Litigation, 438 F.Supp. 1303 (C.D. Cal. 1977).
*PRACTICE AREAS: Complex Civil Litigation; Antitrust; Securities.

**Corinblit & Seltzer, A Professional Corporation, (AV)**
**Suite 820 Wilshire Park Place, 3700 Wilshire Boulevard, 90010-3085**
**Telephone: 213-380-4200 Telecopier: 213-385-7503; 385-4560**
**Email: mseltzer@AOL.com**

(This Listing Continued)

**Corinblit & Seltzer, A Professional Corporation (Continued)**
**Marc M. Seltzer; Christina A. Snyder. Of Counsel: Jack Corinblit, A Law Corporation; Earl P. Willens;—Gretchen M. Nelson; George A. Shohet; Moses Garcia.**
**General Civil and Trial Practice in all State and Federal Courts. Antitrust, Securities and Corporation Law.**
*See Professional Biographies, LOS ANGELES, CALIFORNIA*

Cork, Gregory M. ........................... '65 '93 C&L.893 B.A., J.D. 777 S. Figueroa
Corless, Thomas C. .......................... '55 '81 C&L.101 B.A., J.D. 611 W. 6th St.
Corleto, Richard A., (AV) ..................... '46 '71 C.112 B.S. L.1068 J.D. [Corleto&A.]
Corleto & Ackerman, (AV) ................................................. 15760 Ventura Boulevard
**Corman, Craig A.** ..................... '59 '84 C.813 B.A. L.477 J.D. [O'Melveny&M.]
*LANGUAGES: French.
**Corman, Karen Leili** ............... '62 '88 C.112 B.A. L.309 J.D. [Skadden,A.S.M.&F.]
**Corman, Marc H.** ......................... '57 '82 C.800 B.A. L.1068 J.D. [Jones,K.&A.]
*PRACTICE AREAS: Real Estate Transactions and Litigation; Secured Lending; Bankruptcy.
Corn, John M. '30 '55 C.62 A.B. L.262 J.D.
(adm. in DC; not adm. in CA) Korean Community Servs.
Cornelius, Alexandre Ian ...................... '66 '95 C.36 B.S. L.990 J.D. [Costell&J.]
**Cornell, Bradley L.** ......................... '63 '92 C.668 B.A. L.426 J.D. [Choate&C.]
*PRACTICE AREAS: International; Agricultural.
**Cornell, W. Glenn** ........................... '46 '73 C.264 A.B. L.813 J.D. [Thelen,M.J.&B.]
*PRACTICE AREAS: Torts; Insurance Law.
Cornwell, Donald L. ................... '52 '78 C.280 B.B.A. L.893 J.D. 12100 Wilshire Blvd.
Corpening, Robert B. .......... '19 '48 C.575 B.S. L.309 LL.B. 7770 Hollywood Blvd.‡
Corral L., Dalila ........................... '58 '85 C.800 B.S. L.1066 J.D. Dep. Co. Coun.
**Correnti, John G.** ................ '63 '96 C.112 B.A. L.1148 J.D. [Seyfarth,S.F.&G.]
*PRACTICE AREAS: Government Contract Law.
**Corrigan, Brian T.** .................. '61 '89 C.426 B.S. L.809 J.D. [Kaye,S.F.H.&H.]
*PRACTICE AREAS: Bankruptcy; Corporate Reorganization; Debt Restructure; Workouts.
Cortez, Elizabeth M. ..................... '51 '87 C.112 B.A. L.426 J.D. Sr. Dep. Co. Coun.
Cortez, Jesse, Jr. ............................. '34 '68 C.999 A.A. L.809 LL.B. Dep. Dist. Atty.
**Cortson, Michael D.** ..................... '51 '85 C.932 B.S. L.1179 J.D. [Spray,G.&B.]
**Corwin, David M.** ..................... '— '88 C.178 B.A. L.276 J.D. [King,P.H.P.&B.]
*PRACTICE AREAS: Litigation.
Cory, Larry D. ............................... '41 '70 C.770 B.S.C. L.1049 J.D. Asst. Co. Coun.
**Coscino, Vincent M.** ...... '60 '85 C.605 B.A. L.1049 J.D. [Allen,M.L.G.&M.] (Irvine)
*PRACTICE AREAS: Bankruptcy Law; Insolvency Law; Commercial Law.
Cosel, Stephen R. ......................... '49 '76 C.112 B.S. L.61 J.D. 1822 Colby Ave.
**Cosgrove, Philip R.**, (AV) ............... '54 '80 C.705 B.A. L.426 J.D. [Grace,S.C.&S.]
*PRACTICE AREAS: Product Liability Law; Insurance Coverage Law and Bad Faith Law (including Environmental); Insurance Defense Law; Professional Liability Law; Appellate Law.
**Coskey, Hal L.**, (AV) ................................. '30 '54 C&L.813 B.A., J.D. [Coskey&B.]
*PRACTICE AREAS: Bankruptcy; Insolvency; Debtor Creditor; Secured Transaction; Landlord and Tenant.

**Coskey & Baldridge, (AV)**
**16th Floor, 1801 Century Park East, 90067-2317**
**Telephone: 310-277-7001 Telecopier: 310-277-9704**
**Members of Firm: Tobias Coskey (1896-1974); Hal L. Coskey; Mary Ellen Baldridge.**
**Negotiation, Documentation and Litigation of Commercial Transactions including Lending, Sales, Real Estate, Landlord Tenant, Bankruptcy, Insolvency and Debtor-Creditor Matters.**
*See Professional Biographies, LOS ANGELES, CALIFORNIA*

Coskran, William G. ........................ '34 '60 C&L.426 B.S., J.D. Prof., Loyola Law Sch.
**Cossack, Roger L.**, (AV) ................ '39 '67 C.112 B.A. L.1068 J.D. [Michaelson&L.]
Cossey, Woodrow R. ................. '44 '69 C.112 B.A. L.846 J.D. 10960 Wilshire Blvd.
**Cossi, Lidia A.** ............... '58 '83 C.93 B.A. L.990 J.D. Staff Coun., Hughes Aircraft Co.
**Cossman, Jill A.** .................... '46 '83 C.183 B.A. L.800 J.D. [Greenberg G.F.C.&M.]
*PRACTICE AREAS: Corporate; Business.
**Cost, John J., (P.C.)**, (AV) .................. '34 '64 C.431 B.A. L.309 LL.B. [Irell&M.]
**Costa, Christine** ................................ '64 '91 C.980 B.A. L.273 J.D. [Cox,C.&N.]
Costa, Joseph P. ........................ '61 '87 C.112 B.A. L.273 J.D. 814 S. Westgate Ave.
**Costa, Penny M.** ................................. '51 '83 C.166 B.A. L.1068 J.D. [Baker&H.]
*PRACTICE AREAS: Litigation.
**Costales, Dianne M.** .......... '67 '92 C.112 B.A. L.800 J.D. [Selman B.] (San Diego)
**Costales, Marco D.** ............................. '62 '89 C.813 A.B. L.1066 J.D. [Loeb&L.]
**Costanza, Jean M.** ................................. '48 '81 L.800 J.D. [LeBoeuf,L.G.&M.]
*PRACTICE AREAS: Municipal; Corporate.
**Costanzo, Vito A.** .................... '62 '87 C.112 B.A. L.426 J.D. [Whitman B.A.&M.]
Costell, Jeff L. ................................... '55 '80 C.823 B.A. L.276 J.D. [Costell&J.]
Costell & Joelson, LLP, (AV) ............................................ 1999 Ave. of the Stars, 15 Fl.
**Costello, Dawn M.** .................... '59 '89 C.101 B.S. L.809 J.D. [Veatch,C.G.&N.]
*LANGUAGES: American Sign.

**Costello, Edward J., Jr., (AV) '39 '64 C.262 B.A. L.569 J.D.**
**2950 Mandeville Canyon Road, 90049-1010**
**Telephone: 310-471-7330 Fax: 310-471-7330**
**Email: ARB-OR-MED@AOL.COM**
***PRACTICE AREAS: Alternative Dispute Resolution; Arbitration Law; Mediation Law.**
**Practice limited to service as dispute resolution neutral and consultant on dispute resolution.**

**Costello, Francis W.**, (AV) ........... '46 '74 C&L.178 B.A., J.D. [Whitman B.A.&M.]
*PRACTICE AREAS: Business Law; Corporate Law; International Law; Pacific Rim Trade.
Costello, Gerald A. ...... '44 '75 C.813 B.A. L.659 J.D. Dep. Atty., Dept. of Transportation
Costello, Jan Clifford ................. '50 '77 C&L.976 B.A., J.D. Prof., Loyola Law Sch.
**Costello, Karen M.** ....................... '56 '84 C.966 B.A. L.424 J.D. [Gabriel,H.&P.]
*PRACTICE AREAS: Insurance Coverage; Professional Liability; Directors and Officers Liability; Fiduciary Liability; Bad Faith Litigation.
**Costello, Kenneth R.** ................................ '53 '78 C.426 B.A. L.770 J.D. [Loeb&L.]
*PRACTICE AREAS: Franchise Law; Trademark; Corporate Law; Intellectual Property Law.
**Costello, T. Brent** '52 '78 C.976 B.A. L.276 J.D.
(adm. in NY; not adm. in CA) [Kaye,S.F.H.&H.]
*PRACTICE AREAS: Corporate Finance.
**Cotchett, Joseph W.**, (AV) .......... '39 '65 C.1074 B.S. L.1065 LL.B. [Cotchett&P.]

**Cotchett & Pitre, (AV)**
**Suite 1100, 12100 Wilshire Boulevard, 90025**
**Telephone: 310-826-4211**
**Email: CandPLegal@aol.com**
**Joseph W. Cotchett; Frank M. Pitre; Alfred V. Contarino.**
**Practice limited to Tort Law, Environmental, Products Liability, Securities, Antitrust and Commercial Litigation. General Trial and Appellate Practice.**
**Reference: Peninsula Bank of Commerce, Millbrae.**
**Burlingame, California Office: San Francisco Airport Office Center, Suite 200, 840 Malcolm Road. Telephone: 415-697-6000.**
**Affiliated Office: Friedlander & Friedlander, P.C., 2018 Clarendon Boulevard, Arlington, Virginia 22201. Telephone: 703-525-6750.**
*See Professional Biographies, LOS ANGELES, CALIFORNIA*

**Coté, Steven J.** ..................................... '57 '83 C.776 B.S. L.1049 J.D. [Arter&H.]
**Cotkin, Raphael**, (AV) ....................... '39 '65 C.112 B.A. L.800 J.D. [Cotkin&C.]
*PRACTICE AREAS: Insurance Coverage Law; Toxic Substances Litigation; Professional Liability Litigation and Coverage.

**Cotkin & Collins, A Professional Corporation, (AV)**
**1055 West Seventh Street, Suite 1900, 90017-2503**
Telephone: 213-688-9350 FAX: 213-688-9351
Email: cotkinla@sprynet.com
Raphael Cotkin; James P. Collins, Jr. (Resident, Santa Ana Office); Steven L. Paine; William D. Naeve (Resident, Santa Ana Office); Terry C. Leuin; Roger W. Simpson; Joan M. Dolinsky; Robert G. Wilson; David A. Winkle (Resident, Santa Ana Office); Philip S. Gutierrez (Resident, Santa Ana Office); Karen C. Freitas (Certified Specialist, Family Law, The State Bar of California Board of Legal Specialization); Brian R. Hill (Resident, Santa Ana Office);—Lori S. Blitstien; Carrie F. Smith; Gregory A. Sargenti (Resident, Santa Ana Office); Terry L. Kesinger (Resident, Santa Ana Office); Bradley W. Jacks; Scott P. Ward; Ellen M. Tipping (Resident, Santa Ana Office).
General Civil and Appellate Practice. Insurance Coverage, Regulatory and Administrative Law and Litigation, Professional and Product Liability Defense, Family Law, Health Law
References: American City Bank (Downtown Branch); Security Pacific Bank (7th and Grand Branch); Bank of America.
Santa Ana, California Office: 200 West Santa Ana Boulevard, Suite 800. Telephone: 714-835-2330. FAX: 714-835-2209.
*See Professional Biographies, LOS ANGELES, CALIFORNIA*

Cotler, Valerie K. . . . '62 '91 C.918 B.A. L.705 J.D. 500 S. Grand Ave.
Cotora, Craig, (P.C.) . . . '51 '76 C.813 A.B. L.1068 J.D. [C.Cotora]
Cotora, Craig, Inc., A Professional Law Corporation
10940 Wilshire Boulevard, Suite 1600 (Newport Beach)
Cotrel, Sally A. . . . '63 '89 C.112 B.A. L.1068 J.D. 221 N. Figueroa St.
Cott, Phillip M. . . . '51 '85 C.112 B.A. L.1136 J.D. Dep. Dist. Atty.
**Cotten, Robert M.** . . . '48 '74 C.112 A.B. L.309 J.D. Intl. Coun., Hughes Aircraft Co.
Cotter, George Edward '18 '46 C.918 A.B. L.188 LL.B.
(adm. in CT; not adm. in CA) 1033 Chantilly Rd.
Cotter, James J. . . . '38 '63 C&L.276 A.B., J.D. Int. Rev. Serv.
**Cotter, Michael L.** . . . '49 '75 C.426 B.A. L.809 J.D. [A.M.Brucker]
*PRACTICE AREAS: Employee Benefits Law.
**Cotton, Huey P.** . . . '56 '82 C.31 B.A. L.831 J.D. [Cozen&O.]
*PRACTICE AREAS: Products Liability Law; Insurance Coverage; Uniform Commercial Code.
**Cotton, John W., (AV)** . . . '47 '72 C.770 B.A. L.1065 J.D. [LeBoeuf,L.G.&M.]
*PRACTICE AREAS: Litigation; Securities Regulation.
Cotton, Karen K. . . . '56 '92 C.267 B.A. L.809 J.D. 11111 Santa Monica Blvd.

**Coudert Brothers, (AV)**
**1055 West Seventh Street, Twentieth Floor, 90017**
Telephone: 213-688-9088 Telecopier: 213-689-4467
URL: http://www.coudert.com
Members of Firm: Richard J. Garzilli (Resident); David Huebner; Robert R. Jesuele; Ralph C. Navarro; Seth A. Ribner; Richard G. Wallace (Resident). Of Counsel: Bruce M. Boyd. Resident Associates: Megan M. Bruce; Sylvia K. Burks; Lillian Hou; J. Monica Kim; Stephen G. Mason; John Robert Renner; Glenn W. Trost; William M. Walker.
General Practice.
New York, N.Y. 10036-7703: 1114 Avenue of the Americas.
Washington, D.C. 20006: 1627 I Street, N.W.
San Francisco, California 94111: 4 Embarcadero Center, Suite 3300.
San Jose, California 95113: Suite 1250, Ten Almaden Boulevard.
Denver, Colorado 80202: 1999 Broadway, Suite 2235.
Paris 75008, France: Coudert Frères, 52 Avenue des Champs-Elysees.
London, EC4M 7JP, England: 20 Old Bailey.
Brussels B-1050, Belgium: Tour Louise - Box 8, 149 Avenue Louise.
Berlin 10707, Germany: Kurfürstendamm 52.
Beijing, People's Republic of China 100020: 2708-09 Jing Guang Centre, Hu Jia Lou, Chao Yang Qu.
Hong Kong: Nine Queen's Road Central, 25th Floor.
Singapore 049319: Tung Centre, #21-00, 20 Collyer Quay.
Sydney N.S.W. 2000, Australia: Suite 2202, Colonial Centre, 52 Martin Place.
Tokyo 107, Japan: 1355 West Tower, Aoyama Twin Towers, 1-1-1 Minami-Aoyama, Minato-ku.
Moscow 109004, Russia: Ul. Nikoloyamskaya 54 (formerly Ulyanovskaya).
St. Petersburg 191011, Russia: U1. Italianskaya 5, Office 56/57.
Bangkok 10500, Thailand: Bubhajit Building, 20 North Sathorn Road, 10th Floor.
Ho Chi Minh City, Vietnam: c/o Saigon Business Centre, 58 Dong Khoi Street, Suite 3B, District 1.
Hanoi, Vietnam: 38 Bui Thi Xuan Street, Hai Ba Trung District.
Revisers of the France Law Digest for this Directory.
*See Professional Biographies, LOS ANGELES, CALIFORNIA*

**Coulson, Dawn M.** . . . '60 '90 C.846 B.A.,B.B.A. L.208 J.D. [Leland,P.S.F.M.&M.]
*LANGUAGES: Japanese and Spanish.
*PRACTICE AREAS: Banking; Business; Employment; Bankruptcy Litigation.
Countryman, Byron E., (AV) . . . '48 '75 C.800 B.A. L.809 J.D. [Countryman&M.]
Countryman & McDaniel, (AV) . . . 5933 W. Century Blvd.
Courteau, Diana L. . . . '57 '84 C&L.800 B.A., J.D. 12400 Wilshire Blvd.
Courtney, Colleen M. . . . '— '88 C.1077 B.A. L.398 J.D. 2121 Ave. of the Stars
**Courtney, John K.** . . . '62 '88 C&L.426 B.A., J.D. [Girardi&K.]
*PRACTICE AREAS: Professional Liability; Toxic Torts.
Courtney, Ralph A., III . . . '47 '72 C.112 B.A. L.1065 J.D. Dep. Pub. Def. IV
**Cousineau, Maria Louise** . . . '59 '85 C.112 B.A. L.809 J.D. [Robie&M.]
*REPORTED CASES: In Re Couch (Taxel v. Equity General) 80 B.R. 512 (1987); Orr v. Byers (1988) 198 Cal. App 3d 666.
*PRACTICE AREAS: Insurance Bad Faith; Insurance Agency Malpractice; Professional Malpractice.
**Cousins, Nathanael M.** . . . '70 '95 C.813 B.A. L.1065 J.D. [Greenberg G.F.C.&M.]
*PRACTICE AREAS: Litigation.
Couwenberg, Patrick . . . '49 '76 C.1075 B.S. L.398 J.D. Off. of Dist. Atty.
**Covarrubias, Marita T.** . . . '63 '91 C.112 B.A. L.426 J.D. [Loeb&L.]
**Covell, Julie A.** . . . '65 '91 C.1042 B.A. L.426 J.D. [Bottum&F.]
**Coven, Roger B.** . . . '47 '79 C.860 B.A. L.818 J.D. [Whitman B.A.&M.]
**Coventon, Kevin E.** . . . '63 '92 C.990 B.S. L.705 J.D. [Manning,M.&W.]
**Covert, Kasey A.** . . . '64 '91 C.147 B.A. L.1049 J.D. [Murchison&C.]
*LANGUAGES: Spanish.
*PRACTICE AREAS: Securities; Employment Litigation.
Covey, Margaret Lee, (AV) . . . '50 '77 C.605 B.A. L.904 J.D. [Schmid&V.]

**Covington & Crowe**
(See Ontario)

**Covitt, Reginam (Ginger)** . . . '52 '81 C.454 B.A. L.1068 J.D. [O'Melveny&M.]
*PRACTICE AREAS: Trusts and Estate.

**Cowan, David J., (BV) '63 '88 C.178 B.A. L.1065 J.D.**
**The Wiltern Theatre Tower, 3780 Wilshire Boulevard, Suite 910, 90010**
Telephone: 213-386-7957 FAX: 213-386-7958
*REPORTED CASES: Daniels v. Centennial Group, 16 Cal. App. 4th 467 (1993); Ocean Services Corp. v. Ventura Port District, 15 Cal. App. 4th 1762 (1993); Kim v. Sumitomo Bank, 17 Cal. App. 4th 974 (1993).
Business Litigation including Real Estate, Banking, Contracts, Bankruptcy, Insurance, Partnerships, Corporate and Securities Matters.
*See Professional Biographies, LOS ANGELES, CALIFORNIA*

**Cowan, Eugene G.** . . . '55 '81 C.112 B.A. L.1066 J.D. [Riordan&M.]
*LANGUAGES: Spanish.
Cowan, Henry N., (AV) . . . '12 '36 C.112 B.A. L.1066 J.D. 2049 Century Park, E.‡
**Cowan, James R.** . . . '64 '92 C.309 A.B. L.1065 J.D. [White&C.]
**Cowan, Jeffrey W.** . . . '64 '92 C.188 B.A. L.112 J.D. [Kendig&R.]
*PRACTICE AREAS: Business Litigation.
**Cowan, Melissa M.** . . . '70 '94 C.1042 B.S. L.1068 J.D. [Galton&H.]
*PRACTICE AREAS: General Civil Practice; Probate.

Cowell, Michael A. . . . '40 '70 C.014 B.A. L.1068 LL.B. Supr. Ct. J.
Cowen, Donald W. . . . '35 '60 C.156 A.B. L.976 LL.B. Prof. of Law, Loyola Law Sch.
**Cowles, Shawn E.** . . . '67 '93 C.990 B.A. L.893 J.D. [Hawkins,S.L.&B.]
Cowley, Charles F., III . . . '59 '93 C.800 B.S. L.809 J.D. [Dumas&Assoc.]
**Cowley, Deborah A.** . . . '63 '89 C.573 B.A. L.1148 J.D. [La Follette,J.D.F.&A.]
*PRACTICE AREAS: Medical Malpractice.
**Cox, David S.** . . . '68 '95 C.674 B.A. L.1068 J.D. [Zevnik H.G.&M.]
**Cox, Donald J., Jr.** . . . '63 '92 C.705 B.S.E.E. L.464 J.D. [Small L.&K.] (See Pat. Sect.)
*PRACTICE AREAS: Patent, Copyright and Trademark; Computer Law.
**Cox, George M., (AV)** . . . '24 '51 C.112 A.B. L.800 J.D. [Cox,C.&N.] ‡
**Cox, Joseph P.** . . . '48 '77 C.112 B.A. L.1049 J.D. [Stein S.S.&O.]
*PRACTICE AREAS: Customs Law; International Trade Law; Export Law.
**Cox, Lawrence A., (AV)** . . . '52 '77 C.112 A.B. L.1066 J.D. [Arnold&P.]
*REPORTED CASES: Keating v. National Union, 754 F. Supp. 1431 (C.D.Cal. 1990); Smith v. Montoro, 648 F. 2d 602 (9th Cir. 1981).
*PRACTICE AREAS: Litigation; Litigation of Securities; Health Care; Insurance; Legal Malpractice.
Cox, Richard A. . . . '42 '78 C.800 B.A. L.426 J.D. 5143 Sunset Blvd.
**Cox, Vincent, (AV)** . . . '52 '76 C.999 B.A. L.107 J.D. [Leopold,P.&S.]
*PRACTICE AREAS: Entertainment; Civil Litigation; Copyright and Trademark; Libel and Slander; Unfair Competition.

**Cox, Castle & Nicholson, LLP, (AV)**
**A Limited Liability Partnership including Professional Corporations**
**28th Floor, Two Century Plaza, 2049 Century Park East, 90067**
Telephone: 310-277-4222 Fax: 310-277-7889
George M. Cox (Retired); Richard N. Castle (1932-1992). Resident Partners: Phillip R. Nicholson (A Professional Corporation); Lawrence Teplin; Ronald I. Silverman (A Professional Corporation); Mario Camara; George D. Calkins, II; John H. Kuhl; Arthur O. Spaulding, Jr. (Irvine Office); Jeffrey Lapota; David A. Leipziger; John S. Miller, Jr.; Kenneth B. Bley; Ira J. Waldman; John F. Nicholson; Charles E. Noneman; William Kamer; Marlene D. Goodfried; Barry P. Jablon; Jeffrey D. Masters; Robert D. Infelise; Tamar C. Stein; Douglas P. Snyder; Gary A. Glick; Lora Lee Moore (Irvine Office); Lewis G. Feldman; P. Jerold Walsh (Irvine Office); Mark P. McClanathan (Irvine Office); John A. Kincannon (Irvine Office); Stanley W. Lamport; Randall W. Black; Perry D. Mocciaro; Jess R. Bressi (Irvine Office); Gregory J. Karns; D. Scott Turner (Irvine Office); Samuel H. Gruenbaum; Sandra C. Stewart; Mathew A. Wyman; Randy P. Orlik; Kenneth Williams; Laurel R. Ballard; Amy H. Wells; Scott D. Brooks; Gary P. Downs; Valerie L. Flores. Resident Of Counsel: James E. Barnett; Edward C. Dygert. Resident Associates: Maria Victoria Bernstein; Estelle M. Braaf; Preston W. Brooks; Christine Costa; Kevin J. Crabtree; Susan S. Davis; Sherry M. DuPont; Scott L. Grossfeld; Robert M. Haight, Jr.; John A. Henning, Jr.; Herbert Jay Klein; Mark T. Lammas; Mark Moore; Carlisle G. Packard; Scott Price; Edward F. Quigley, III; Anne-Marie Reader; David S. Rosenberg; John D. Rosenfeld; Stephanie Ann Schroeder; Cynthia K. Simons; Sharon L. Tamiya; Paul J. Titcher; Daniel J. Villalpando; Lisa A. Weinberg; Adam B. Weissburg.
General Civil, Trial and Appellate Practice in all State and Federal Courts. Real Property and Construction Law. Land Use and Environmental Law. Public Bond Financing. International Law. Labor Relations. Receiverships and Creditors Rights. Taxation, Trusts, Estate Planning and Probate Law.
Reference: Bank of America National Trust & Savings Assn. (Beverly Hills Main Branch, Beverly Hills).
Irvine, California Office: 19800 MacArthur Boulevard, Suite 600. Telephone: 714-476-2111. Fax: 714-476-0256.
*See Professional Biographies, LOS ANGELES, CALIFORNIA*

Coyle, Marshall A. . . . '56 '89 C.999 B.A. L.940 J.D. 5757 W. Century Blvd.
**Coyne, Joseph F., Jr.** . . . '55 '80 C.602 B.B.A. L.813 J.D. [Sheppard,M.R.&H.]
*PRACTICE AREAS: Government Contracts Law; Antitrust Law; Commercial Litigation.
**Coyoca, Lucia E., (A Professional Corporation)** '61 '86
C.112 B.A. L.1067 J.D. [Mitchell,S.&K.]
*PRACTICE AREAS: Business Litigation; Insurance Coverage; Entertainment Litigation.
**Cozart, Bert C.** . . . '65 '92 C.575 B.S. L.1068 J.D. [Troop M.S.&P.]
*PRACTICE AREAS: Insurance Coverage Litigation; Business Litigation.

**Cozen and O'Connor, A Professional Corporation, (AV)**
**777 Tower, 777 South Figueroa Street Suite 2850, 90017**
Telephone: 213-892-7900 800-563-1027 Fax: 213-892-7999
Firm Members in Los Angeles: Huey P. Cotton; Mark S. Roth;—Jennifer L. Larson; Colbern C. Stuart.
Property Insurance Law; Subrogation and Recovery; Casualty Defense; Insurance Coverage; Arson and Fraud Defense; Environmental and Toxic Tort; Primary/Excess and Re-Insurance Claims and Defense; Professional Liability Defense; Architects and Engineers Errors and Omissions; Agent and Brokers Errors and Omissions Defense; Employment Law; Directors and Officers Errors and Omissions Defense; Business and Commercial Litigation; Securities Litigation; RICO; Trade Secrets and Restrictive Covenants; Copyright Infringement; Construction Litigation; Lender Liability; White Collar Criminal Defense; Environmental; Medicare Fraud and Taxation; Corporate; Real Estate; Taxation; Labor and Employee Relations; Securities; Bankruptcy; Health Care.
Representative Clients: Available upon request.
Philadelphia, Pennsylvania Office: 1900 Market Street, 19103. Telephones: 215-665-2000; 800-523-2900; Fax: 215-665-2013.
Charlotte, North Carolina Office: One First Union Plaza, 301 South College Street, Suite 2100, 28202. Telephones: 704-376-3400; 800-762-3575. Fax: 704-334-3351.
Columbia, South Carolina Office: The Palmetto Center, 1426 Main Street, 29201. Telephones: 803-799-3900; 800-338-1117. Fax: 803-254-7233.
Dallas, Texas Office: Suite 4100, NationsBank Plaza, 901 Main Street, 75202. Telephones: 214-761-6700; 800-448-1207. Fax: 214-761-6788.
New York, N.Y. Office: 45 Broadway Atrium, 16th Floor, 10006. Telephones: 212-509-9400; 800-437-9400. Fax: 212-509-9492.
San Diego, California Office: Suite 1610, 501 West Broadway, 92101. Telephones: 619-234-1700; 800-782-3366. Fax: 619-234-7831.
Seattle, Washington Office: Suite 5200, Washington Mutual Tower, 1201 Third Avenue, 98101. Telephones: 206-340-1000; 800-423-1950. Fax: 206-621-8783.
Westmont, New Jersey Office: 316 Haddon Avenue, 08108. Telephones: 609-854-4900; 800-523-2900. Fax: 609-854-1782.
Atlanta, Georgia Office: Suite 2200, One Peachtree Center, 303 Peachtree Street, N.E., 30308. Telephones: 404-572-2000; 800-890-1393. Fax: 404-572-2199.
*See Professional Biographies, LOS ANGELES, CALIFORNIA*

**Crabb, Kelly Charles** . . . '46 '85 C.101 B.A. L.178 J.D. [Dewey B.]
*PRACTICE AREAS: Entertainment and Media; Japan Trade.
**Crabtree, Kevin J.** . . . '69 '95 C.605 A.B. L.990 J.D. [Cox,C.&N.]
**Craft, Jeffrey F.** . . . '54 '81 C.477 B.S. L.912 J.D. [Pretty,S.&P.] (See Pat. Sect.)
*PRACTICE AREAS: Patents; Trademarks; Copyrights; Unfair Competition; Litigation.
Crahan, Marcus E., Jr., (Law Corporation), (AV) '29 '57
C.154 B.A. L.1068 LL.B. [Crahan,J.&V.H.]
Crahan, Javelera & Ver Halen, (AV) . . . 1000 Wilshire Blvd.
**Craig, Jerome H., (AV)** . . . '42 '67 C&L.800 B.S., J.D. [Morrison&F.]
*PRACTICE AREAS: Business Litigation; Alternative Dispute Resolution.
Craig, John W., III . . . '59 '86 C.1105 B.A. L.802 J.D. 4201 Via Marisol
**Craig, Joyce I.** . . . '— '84 C.112 A.B. L.1068 J.D. [Kirsch&M.]
**Craigie, Alex W.** . . . '66 '93 C.112 B.A. L.426 J.D. [Grace,S.C.&S.]
*PRACTICE AREAS: Product Liability; Construction Defect Litigation; Insurance Coverage; Insurance Bad Faith.

**Craigo, Richard W., (AV) '34 '67 C.45 B.A. L.800 J.D.**
**10580 Wilshire Boulevard, Suite 3 S.E., 90024**
Telephone: 310-470-9647 Fax: 310-470-9687
(Certified Specialist, Taxation Law, The State Bar of California Board of Legal Specialization).
Equine/Horse Law, Taxation Law including Federal and State Income Tax Planning and Dispute Resolution and handling State Sales and Use Tax Disputes, General Business.
*See Professional Biographies, LOS ANGELES, CALIFORNIA*

Crain, Christopher M. . . . '61 '86 C.112 A.B. L.426 J.D. 400 S. Hope St.

Crain, Michael I., (BV) .............. '45 '73 C.800 B.S. L.426 J.D. 12121 Wilshire Blvd.
**Cramer, John**, (AV) ........................'39 '66 C.813 B.S. L.1066 J.D. [Ezer&W.]
Cramer, Robert ...............................'46 '73 C.112 B.S. L.426 J.D. Asst. City Atty.
**Cramin, Chet A.** ........................'62 '86 C.112 B.A. L.464 J.D. [Sherwood&H.]
*PRACTICE AREAS: Real Estate Litigation; Business Litigation.
Crane, Jonathan B. ............................'53 '77 C.477 B.A. L.800 J.D. [Dumas&Assoc.]
Crane, Michael C., (BV) .......... '40 '67 C.112 B.S. L.426 LL.B. 2331 W. Allview Ter.
Crane, Norma .................................'31 '78 Dept. of Fair Employ. & Housing

**Crane, Paul N., (AV) '37 '63 C.112 B.S. L.309 J.D.**
**Suite 900, Two Century Plaza, 2049 Century Park East, 90067-3111**
**Telephone: 310-282-8118 FAX: 310-282-8077**
**Real Estate Law. General Business Practice.**
*See Professional Biographies, LOS ANGELES, CALIFORNIA*

**Crane, Steven L.** ........................... '52 '81 C.1169 B.A. L.1068 J.D. [Angel&N.]
*PRACTICE AREAS: Civil Litigation; Bankruptcy.
**Crane, Steven M.** ............................ '56 '80 C&L.174 B.A., J.D. [Morris,P.&P.]
**Cranston, David E.** ......................'59 '86 C.763 B.A. L.1067 J.D. [Pircher,N.&M.]
*PRACTICE AREAS: Environmental Law and Litigation; Insurance Coverage.
Cranston, Kim Christopher '51 '79 C.1169 B.A. L.1065 J.D.
Chief of Staff, to Lt. Gov.‡
**Crawford, Christa L.** '69 '94 C.154 B.A. L.309 J.D.
(adm. in KY; not adm. in CA) [Heller E.W.&M.]
Crawford, Crystal D. .............'65 '93 C.197 A.B. L.569 J.D. 11355 W. Olympic Blvd.
**Crawford, David, III** ..................'55 '85 C.549 B.A. L.990 J.D. [Prestholt,K.F.&V.]
*PRACTICE AREAS: Insurance Defense Law; Plaintiff Personal Injury Law; General Practice Law.
**Crawford, Thomas W.**, (AV) ...........'57 '82 C.112 B.A. L.1068 J.D. [Crawford&R.]
*PRACTICE AREAS: Business Litigation; Environmental Litigation; Real Estate Litigation; Construction Litigation.

**Crawford & Bangs**
**(See West Covina)**

**Crawford & Reimann LLP, (AV)**
**15th Floor, 11755 Wilshire Boulevard, 90025**
**Telephone: 310-478-7442 Fax: 310-575-4575**
**Members of Firm: Thomas W. Crawford; David W. Reimann. Associate: Robert C. Cartwright; Glenn D. Hamovitz.**
**Civil Litigation in all Courts, including Business, Construction, Environmental, Real Estate and Insurance Litigation.**
**Reference: Santa Monica Bank, Brentwood Office.**
*See Professional Biographies, LOS ANGELES, CALIFORNIA*

Cray, Richard C. .........'56 '84 C.1169 B.A. L.1068 J.D. Assoc. Coun., EMI Music Inc.
**Creim, William B.** ......................'54 '79 C.112 B.A. L.800 J.D. [Bronson,B.&M.]
*PRACTICE AREAS: Commercial Law and Secured Transactions; Creditors' Rights, Bankruptcy and Antitrust.
**Creutz, Mary G.**, (AV) ............................'31 '55 C.525 L.426 LL.B. [Creutz&C.]

**Creutz and Creutz, (AV)**
**206 Brentwood Square Building, 11661 San Vicente Boulevard, 90049**
**Telephone: 310-826-3545; 213-879-0339**
**Gregory M. Creutz (1892-1966); Mary G. Creutz. Associate: Regine Derrendinger.**
**Estate Planning, Probate, Wills and Trusts. Real Estate Law.**
**Reference: Union Bank, Brentwood Branch.**
*See Professional Biographies, LOS ANGELES, CALIFORNIA*

Creyaufmiller, Timothy P. .........'58 '86 C.607 B.A. L.245 J.D. 4422 E. Olympic Blvd.
**Cribbs, Daniel A.** ........................'69 '94 C.112 B.A. L.1148 J.D. [Magaña,C.&M.]
*PRACTICE AREAS: Personal Injury Law; Aviation Law; Products Liability; Wrongful Death.
Crickard, Jack A. ...................................'20 '49 C.112 B.S. L.800 J.D. Supr. Ct. J.
Crigger, Raymond F. ..................'23 '54 C&L.597 B.S.L., J.D. 2135 Roscomare Rd.‡
Criley, Suzanne .................. '60 '86 C.112 B.A. L.1068 J.D. 10351 Santa Monica Blvd.
Crispi, Jos. E. ......................'17 '57 C.061 L.1068 J.D. 490-498 San Vicente Blvd.
Crispo, Lawrence W. ................................'34 '61 C&L.426 B.S., J.D. Supr. Ct. J.
**Crist, Abbie** ....................................'58 '85 C.112 B.A. L.426 J.D. [Agajanian&M.]
Crist, Jane Katz, (BV) ...............'37 '78 C.518 B.A. L.426 J.D. 12100 Wilshire Blvd.
**Criswell, Leslie E.** ............................'50 '80 C.112 B.A. L.809 J.D. [Hornberger&C.]
*PRACTICE AREAS: Insurance Defense Law; Trial Practice; Products Liability Law; Premises Liability Law; Employment Discrimination.
**Crochetiere, David P.** ........................................'58 '84 C.154 L.477 J.D. [Lamb&B.]
*PRACTICE AREAS: Business Litigation; Copyright, Trademark and Unfair Competition; Real Estate; Appellate; Entertainment Law.
Crockett, K. David ...................'61 '91 C.705 B.A. L.1049 J.D. 633 W. 5th St. (Pat.)
**Crockett, Karen B.** ................................'56 '84 C&L.101 B.S., J.D. Price Waterhouse
**Crockett, Robert D.**, (AV) ........................ '54 '82 C&L.101 B.S., J.D. [Latham&W.]
**Crockwell, Craig D.**, (AV) ............... '43 '69 C.813 B.A. L.1068 J.D. [Katten M.&Z.]
*PRACTICE AREAS: Real Estate Law.
**Croke, Thomas B., IV** .................. '65 '91 C.112 B.A. L.800 J.D. [Hooper,L.&B.]
*PRACTICE AREAS: Commercial Litigation; Products Liability.
Croker, Joan M. ............................'59 '84 C.012 B.A. L.990 J.D. Dep. Pub. Def. IV
**Croll, Alan D.**, (AV) .................. '39 '65 C.309 A.B. L.477 LL.B. [Katten M.&Z.]
*PRACTICE AREAS: Litigation.
**Cronenwalt, Nancy** ..........................'58 '88 C.1077 B.A. L.426 J.D. [Trope&T.]
Cronin, Ann Reid '51 '76 C.734 B.A. L.309 J.D.
(adm. in IL; not adm. in CA) Nat. Labor Rel. Bd.
**Croninger, Marsha S.** ................'47 '77 C.184 B.A. L.464 J.D. [McDermott,W.&E.]
**Cronthall, André J.** .....................'58 '84 C&L.800 B.S., J.D. [Sheppard,M.R.&H.]
*PRACTICE AREAS: Insurance Law; Product Liability Law; Business Litigation.
**Crook, George D.**, (AV) ..................'42 '74 C.1258 B.A. L.426 J.D. [Kehr,C.T.&F.]
*LANGUAGES: Spanish.
*PRACTICE AREAS: Real Estate; Business Litigation.
**Crooke, Elizabeth Lane** ...............'52 '79 C.112 B.A. L.426 J.D. [Engstrom,L.&L.]
*PRACTICE AREAS: Insurance Policy Interpretation; Bad Faith Defense; Environmental Coverage; Construction Litigation; Aviation and Governmental Agency Defense.
**Crosby, Magara Lee** ...................'53 '82 C.112 B.A. L.1068 J.D. [Morgan,L.&B.]
Crosby, Tami S. ......................'60 '87 C.139 B.A. L.1137 J.D. 801 S. Grand 18th Fl.

**Crosby, Heafey, Roach & May, Professional Corporation, (AV)**
**700 South Flower Street, Suite 2200, 90017⊙**
**Telephone: 213-896-8000 FAX: 213-896-8080**
**URL: http://www.chrm.com**
**Terry B. Bates (Resident); Michael K. Brown (Resident); James D. DeRoche (Resident); Lorenzo E. Gasparetti; Roy Ai-Ji Goto (Resident); M. Reed Hunter (Resident); William Paul Kannow (Resident); James C. Martin (Resident); Anna Segobia Masters (Resident); Marilyn A. Moberg (Resident); Kurt C. Peterson (Resident); Richard Salcido (Resident); Linda Margolies Salem (Resident); Robert S. Schulman (Resident); Philip L. Siracuse (Resident);—Colette M. Asel; Lisa M. Baird; L. Amy Blum; Maureen V. Brennan; Ellen R. Brostrom; Amy E. Deutsch; Mallory J. Garner; Scott C. Glovsky; Ginger F. Heyman; Peter J. Kennedy; Janet H. Kwuon; Stacey L. Meltzer; Theodore F. Monroe; Garet D. O'Keefe; Eric S. Oto; Laura G. Peraino; Douglas H. Riegelhuth; Thomas P. Seltz; Benjamin G. Shatz; Richard K. Shuter; Kenneth N. Smersfelt; Matthew A. Smith; Tamara C. Smith; Barry J. Thompson. Of Counsel: Lauren T. Diehl; Kristin Hubbard; Nancy A. Newhouse-Porter.**
**General Civil Practice and Litigation in all State and Federal Courts. Litigation: Product Liability; Pharmaceutical and Medical Device; Insurance Coverage and Claims; Business Litigation; Labor and Employment; Intellectual Property; Environmental/Toxic Tort; Property, Land Use and Condemnation; Construction; Professional Liability; Antitrust; Appellate; Bankruptcy and Creditors' Rights;**

(This Listing Continued)

**Crosby, Heafey, Roach & May, Professional Corporation (Continued)**
**Media and First Amendment Rights; Health Care. Business: Real Estate; General Corporate and Partnership; Commercial Transactions; Mergers and Acquisitions, Trust and Estate Planning; Tax; Finance and Banking; Securities.**
**Representative Clients: Dean Witter Reynold, Inc.; Syntex Laboratories, Inc.; Union Pacific Railroad Co.; Westinghouse Electric Corp.**
**Oakland, California Office: 1999 Harrison Street. Telephone: 510-763-2000. FAX: 510-273-8832.**
**San Francisco, California Office: One Market Plaza, Spear Street Tower, Suite 1800. Telephone: 415-543-8700. FAX: 415-391-8269.**
**Santa Rosa, California Office: 1330 N. Dutton. Telephone: 707-523-2433. FAX: 707-546-1360.**
*See Professional Biographies, LOS ANGELES, CALIFORNIA*

**Crose, John A., Jr.** ......................'59 '84 C.112 B.A. L.1068 J.D. [O'Melveny&M.]
*PRACTICE AREAS: Litigation; Intellectual Property; Mass Torts; Insurance Coverage; Commercial Contracts.
Croskey, H. Walter ..........................................'33 '59 C&L.800 B.S., LL.B. Assoc. Jus.
Cross, James E., (AV) ........................'21 '49 C.352 B.S.C. L.800 LL.B. 400 S. Hope St.
**Cross, Michael A.** ...................................'55 '80 C.112 B.A. L.309 J.D. [Dempsey&J.]
*PRACTICE AREAS: Corporate Law; Corporate Securities; Public Offerings; Private Placements; Mergers and Acquisitions.
**Crossman, John K.** '62 '87 C.860 B.S. L.94 J.D.
(adm. in CT; not adm. in CA) [Zevnik H.G.&M.]⊙
Crost, Paul E., (AV) ................................'43 '67 C.112 B.A. L.1066 J.D. [Reich,A.C.&C.]⊙
**Crotta, Carol A.** .........................'56 '95 C.976 B.A. L.112 J.D. [Zevnik H.G.&M.]
*LANGUAGES: Italian.
*PRACTICE AREAS: Environmental Insurance; General Litigation.
**Crouch, Charles L., III** .......................'52 '78 C.154 B.A. L.426 J.D. [Lord,B.&B.]
*PRACTICE AREAS: Corporate Law; Insurance Regulatory Law.
**Crouchley, John S.** ...........................'58 '84 C.190 B.A. L.426 J.D. [Talcott,L.V.&S.]
*PRACTICE AREAS: Criminal Defense Law; Civil Litigation; Appellate Law.
Crouse, Jacqueline S. '55 '80 C.645 B.S. L.665 J.D.
Sr. V.P. & Sr. Tax Coun., First Interstate Bancorp
**Croutch, Barbara L.** .....................'61 '90 C.525 B.S. L.426 J.D. [Pillsbury M.&S.]
**Crow, Carl Timothy** ........................'60 '88 C.906 B.A. L.878 J.D. [Gibson,D.&C.]
*PRACTICE AREAS: Federal Income; Taxation.
**Crowder, Douglas A.** ............................'53 '77 C.162 B.A. L.352 J.D. [D.A.Crowder]
*PRACTICE AREAS: Bankruptcy; Debtor and Creditor; Litigation; Business Law; Family Law.

**Crowder, Douglas A., Law Offices of, A Professional Corporation**
**World Trade Center, 350 South Figueroa Street Suite 190, 90071**
**Telephone: 213-621-2115 Fax: 213-621-2900**
**Email: DOUG@CROWDER7.COM URL: http://www.crowder7.com**
**Douglas A. Crowder.**
**Bankruptcy, Family Law.**
*See Professional Biographies, LOS ANGELES, CALIFORNIA*

**Crowe & Day**
**(See Santa Monica)**
**Crowell, Douglas G.** .............. '62 '95 C.112 B.S. L.602 J.D. [Greenberg G.F.C.&M.]
**Crowell & Moring LLP**
**(See Irvine)**

Crowley, Arthur J., (AV) ...........................................'25 '48 C&L.800 J.D. [A.J.Crowley]
**Crowley, Barbara W. G.** ........................ '24 '74 C.145 B.A. L.426 J.D. [Barton,K.&O.]
*PRACTICE AREAS: Probate; Estate Planning; Nonprofit and Charitable Organizations.
**Crowley, Carolyn Wagner** ...........'65 '90 C.112 B.A. L.770 J.D. [Gilbert,K.C.&J.]
**Crowley, Daniel M.** ..............................'60 '87 C.770 B.S. L.1049 J.D. [Booth,M.&S.]
**Crowley, James B.**, (AV) ...........................'30 '54 L.426 LL.B. [Gilbert,K.C.&J.]
**Crowley, Michael J.** ...............................'67 '93 C.309 A.B. L.228 J.D. [Pillsbury M.&S.]
Crowley, Arthur J., P.C., (AV) ................................................... 9200 Sunset Blvd.
Crump, Gerald F. ..........................'35 '60 C.112 A.B. L.1066 LL.B. Chf. Asst. Co. Coun.
**Crumpacker, David W., Jr.**, (AV) ..............'55 '81 C.174 B.A. L.273 J.D. [Fried,B.&C.]
*PRACTICE AREAS: Real Estate - Leasing and Lease Enforcement; Acquisitions and Dispositions of Real Property; Construction Law; Loan Workout and Debt Restructuring; Real Estate Lending.
**Crumpacker, Diane J.** ..........'55 '82 C.112 A.B. L.1068 J.D. [Greenberg G.F.C.&M.]
*PRACTICE AREAS: Labor Law; Employment Law; Employment Litigation.
**Crumpacker, John W.** ..........'57 '83 C.174 B.A. L.1051 J.D. [McCambridge,D.&M.]

**Cruz, Leonard G. '59 '86 C.112 B.A. L.1068 J.D.**
**12100 Wilshire Boulevard 15th Floor, 90025-7115**
**Telephone: 310-826-9315 Telecopier: 310-207-3230**
**Email: Lawoff_LeonardCruz@MSN.Com**
**Business Litigation Practice. Probate, Unlawful Detainer and Real Estate.**
*See Professional Biographies, LOS ANGELES, CALIFORNIA*

Cruz, Mariano D. '31 '80 L.662 LL.B.
(adm. in NY; not adm. in CA) 137 N. Wetherly Dr.‡
**Cruz, Mercedes** ..........................'59 '85 C.1042 B.A. L.1066 J.D. [Lewis,D.B.&B.]
*PRACTICE AREAS: Litigation; Product Liability; Intellectual Property; Labor Law.
Csathy, Peter D. ..........................'63 '90 C.494 B.A. L.309 J.D. 11150 Olympic Blvd.
Csathy, Peter Denis '63 '90 C.494 B.A. L.309 J.D.
Dir., Bus. & Legal Affairs, New Line Cinema Corp.
**Csato, Peter**, (AV) ..................................'51 '79 C.112 B.A. L.426 J.D. [Frandzel&S.]
**Cuddy, Christine S.**, (AV) ..........'50 '74 C.681 B.A. L.813 J.D. [Kleinberg L.L.B.&C.]
*LANGUAGES: Spanish.
*PRACTICE AREAS: Entertainment Law; Copyright Law.
Cuen, Robert M. ...................'61 '88 C.112 B.A. L.426 J.D. 6033 W. Century Blvd.
**Cuesta Aragon, Angeli** ........................'60 '95 C&L.112 B.A., J.D. [Ruben&M.]
*PRACTICE AREAS: Business Litigation; Professional Liability; Appellate Advocacy.
**Cuff, Terence F.**, (AV) ........................'49 '77 C.1169 A.B. L.800 J.D. [Loeb&L.]
*PRACTICE AREAS: Taxation.
Cukier, Linda ............'58 '84 C.771 B.A. L.426 J.D. 11377 W. Olympic Blvd., 2nd Fl.

**Cukier, Linda '58 '84 C.771 B.A. L.426 J.D.**
**Second Floor 11377 West Olympic Boulevard, 90064-1683**
**Telephone: 310-312-3229 Fax: 310-268-7972**
**(Also of Counsel, Deutsch & Rubin).**
***LANGUAGES: French.**
**Family and Domestic Relations.**
*See Professional Biographies, LOS ANGELES, CALIFORNIA*

Culbert, Mary B. ... '54 '85 C.966 B.S. L.426 J.D. Western Law Ctr. for Disability Rights
Cullen, William C. ..................................'52 '80 C.679 B.S. L.1095 J.D. U.S. Atty. Off.
Culliton, Daniel J., (AV) .............'16 '46 C.321 A.B. L.94 LL.B. 1541 N. Ogden Dr.‡
Culp, Sara Anne ................'59 '87 C.788 A.B. L.262 J.D. 777 S. Figueroa St., 10th Fl.
**Culver, Charlene Rudio** .............'43 '88 C.602 B.A. L.284 J.D. [Ropers,M.K.&B.]
*PRACTICE AREAS: Environmental Coverage Litigation; Business Litigation; Probate and Trust Litigation.
Culverwell, Kathleen E. ...................'63 '91 C.112 B.A. L.809 J.D. 444 S. Flower St.
**Cummings, Charles D.**, (AV) ..............'49 '74 C&L.426 B.A., J.D. [Sullivan,W.&D.]
*PRACTICE AREAS: Real Estate Law; Business Litigation; Real Estate Transactions.
Cummings, Emma M. '06 '42 C.103 L.818 J.D.
(adm. in MA; not adm. in CA) 12121 Wilshire Blvd.‡

**Cummings, M. Neil '51 '77 C.112 B.S. L.1065 J.D.**
**1800 Avenue of the Stars, Suite 1000, 90067-4212**
**Telephone: 310-277-7550 FAX: 310-277-7553**

(This Listing Continued)

CAA207P

**Cummings, M. Neil (Continued)**
**Corporate, Licensing, Banking. Business Litigation in State and Federal Courts.**
***See Professional Biographies, LOS ANGELES, CALIFORNIA***

**Cummings, Thomas E.** .... '27 '57 C.768 L.770 LL.B. [Ⓐ Bonaparte&M.]
*LANGUAGES: Spanish and Italian.
*PRACTICE AREAS: Immigration and Nationality Law.
**Cummins, Joseph H.**, (AV) .... '16 '40 C.210 A.B. L.597 J.D. [Ⓒ Cummins&W.]
*PRACTICE AREAS: Malpractice; Negligence; Products Liability; Arbitration and Mediation; Transportation Law.

**Cummins & White, LLP, (AV)**
**Limited Liability Partnership, including Professional Corporations**
**865 South Figueroa Street, 24th Floor, 90017⊙**
**Telephone: 213-614-1000 Telecopier: 213-614-0500**
**Email: cwllp@netcom.com URL: http://www.cwnb@cwoc.usa.com**
**Members of Firm: James D. Otto (Professional Corporation); Larry M. Arnold (Professional Corporation) (Resident, Newport Beach Office); Francis X. Sarcone; Marshall W. Vorkink; Robert E. Perkins; Gene A. Weisberg; David B. Shapiro; James R. Wakefield (Resident, Newport Beach Office); Clyde E. Hirschfeld; Daniel G. Bath; David Lee Carollo (Resident, Newport Beach Office); Robert W. Bollar (Resident, Newport Beach Office); Karen L. Taillon (Resident, Newport Beach Office); Michael T. Fox; Annabelle Moore Harris (Resident, Newport Beach Office); Sherry L. Pantages; Louis H. Altman; Blenda Eyvazzadeh; John E. Peer. Of Counsel: Thomas W. Burton (Resident, Newport Beach Office); Joseph H. Cummins; Marshall T. Hunt (Resident, Newport Beach Office); Jay F. Stocker (Resident, Newport Beach Office); Alan K. Stazer; William Bruce Voss (Resident, Newport Beach Office); James O. White, Jr. Associates: David M. Smithson; Lawrence E. Johnson (Resident, Newport Beach Office); Kevin Almeter; Michael M. Bergfeld; Henry Shyn; Laura N. MacPherson (Resident, Newport Beach Office); Bradley V. Black (Resident, Newport Beach Office); J. Thomas Gilbert; Esther P. Holm; Patti L. Whitfield (Resident, Newport Beach Office); Jeffrey Daniel Mansukhani (Resident, Newport Beach Office); Randy A. Moss; Susan M. Oglesby (Resident, Newport Beach Office); Michael A. McLain; Heather Skinner Nevis (Resident, Newport Beach Office); Rondi Jan Walsh; Patricia M. Michelena; Chinye Uwechue-Akpati; Monica J. Walker; Sabrina Kong; Joette Marea Gonzalez; Ian C. Ullman; D. Todd Parrish; Roger G. Honey; Lisa Emily Eisma.**
**Administrative, Appellate, Banking, Bankruptcy, Business Litigation, Business Transactions, Condemnation and Land Use, Construction, Construction Defect, Entertainment, Environmental, Estates and Trusts, Healthcare, Insurance, Intellectual Property, International Law, Maritime, Personal Injury, Products Liability, Professional Liability, Railroad and Transportation, Real Estate, Regulatory Law and Securities.**
**Orange County Office: 2424 S.E. Bristol Street, Suite 300, P.O. Box 2513, Newport Beach. Telephone: 714-852-1800. Telecopier: 714-852-8510.**
**Affiliated Taipei, Taiwan Office: Chang & Associates, No. 12 Jen-Ai Road, Section 21, Seventh Floor, Taipei, Taiwan, Republic of China. Telephone: (02) 341-4602. Fax: (02) 321-6388.**
***See Professional Biographies, LOS ANGELES, CALIFORNIA***

Cuneo, J. Nicholas, (AV) .... '53 '79 C.813 B.A. L.1068 J.D. 9200 Sunset Blvd.
**Cuneo, Steven R., Jr.** .... '69 '94 C.112 B.A. L.1068 J.D. [Ⓐ Gibbs,G.L.&A.]
*PRACTICE AREAS: Construction Law; Insurance Law; Business Litigation.
Cunningham, Alan T. '42 '71 C.994 B.A. L.724 J.D.
V.P. & Dep. Gen. Coun., Transamerica Occidental Life Ins. Co.
**Cunningham, David S., III** .... '55 '81 C.800 B.A. L.569 J.D. [Ⓐ Jackson&L.]
*LANGUAGES: Spanish.
*PRACTICE AREAS: Eminent Domain; Inverse Condemnation; Construction; Real Estate Litigation Redevelopment Law.
Cunningham, Gerald P. .... '59 '84 C.1044 B.A. L.262 J.D. 5670 Wilshire Blvd.
**Cunningham, Linda N.** .... '53 '87 C.549 A.B. L.1065 J.D. [Ⓐ Nossaman,G.K.&E.]
*PRACTICE AREAS: Real Property Law; Corporations Law.
**Cunningham, Mark G.** .... '59 '85 C.426 B.B.A. L.823 J.D. [McKay,B.&G.]
*PRACTICE AREAS: Civil Trial; Insurance Defense; Personal Injury.
Curcio, Rick V. .... '52 '79 C.112 B.A. L.1068 J.D. Sr. Jud. Atty., Ct. of App.‡
**Curfman, Shirley E.** .... '48 '79 C.1232 B.A. L.1068 J.D. [LeBoeuf,L.G.&M.]
*PRACTICE AREAS: Corporate; Real Estate; Bankruptcy.
Curl, Ann H. .... '23 '76 C.331 B.A. L.1095 J.D. Dept. Health & Human Servs.
Curlee, Brett B. .... '63 '90 C.37 B.A. L.800 J.D. 445 S. Figueroa St.
Curls, G. Michael .... '40 '73 C.1097 B.A. L.809 J.D. 4340 Leimert Blvd.
Curran, Jeanne Knox .... '35 '85 C.112 M.A. L.1068 J.D. [Notkoff&C.]
**Curran, Raymond L.**, (AV) .... '22 '53 C.112 B.S. L.477 LL.B. [Ⓒ Gibson,D.&C.]
**Curran, Stephen J.** .... '63 '91 C.763 B.A. L.276 J.D. [Ⓐ Sonnenschein N.&R.]
*PRACTICE AREAS: Litigation.
**Currey, Brian S.** .... '56 '81 C.112 B.A. L.893 J.D. [O'Melveny&M.]
*PRACTICE AREAS: Business Litigation; Environmental Litigation.
**Currie, Graeme Lawrence** .... '59 '85 C.882 B.A. L.902 J.D. [Ⓐ Andrews&K.]
*PRACTICE AREAS: Contract Law; Real Estate Law; Patent, Trademark and Copyright Law; Bankruptcy Law.
**Currie, Matthew T.** .... '63 '91 C.112 B.A. L.426 J.D. [Ⓐ Meserve,M.&H.]
Currier, Marjorie Hamano .... '51 '86 C.112 B.A. L.426 J.D. Dep. City Atty.
Curry, Barbara A. .... '62 '87 C.116 B.A. L.597 J.D. U.S. Attys. Off.
Curry, Daniel A. .... '37 '61 C&L.426 B.S., LL.B. Supr. Ct. J.
**Curry, James E.** .... '58 '84 C.813 B.A. L.145 J.D. [White O.C.&A.]
*PRACTICE AREAS: Civil Litigation.
Curry, Mary Judith .... '48 '89 C.623 B.S. L.1136 J.D. Dep. Pub. Def.
**Curtin, Colleen E.** .... '70 '95 C.165 B.A. L.1049 J.D. [Ⓐ Shapiro,H.&M.]
*LANGUAGES: Spanish.
*PRACTICE AREAS: Medical Malpractice; Legal Malpractice; Products Liability; Personal Injury.
Curtis, Charles Emeride .... '49 '77 C.154 B.A. L.1068 J.D. First Interstate Bank
Curtis, James B. .... '57 '83 C.234 B.A. L.800 J.D. Sr. Atty., Calif. Fed. Bk.
**Curtis, John E., Jr.**, (AV) .... '45 '70 C.855 B.A. L.893 J.D. [McDermott,W.&E.]
*PRACTICE AREAS: ESOPS Law; ERISA.
**Curtis, John S.**, (AV) .... '45 '72 C.684 B.A. L.1065 J.D. [Belcher,H.&B.]
*PRACTICE AREAS: General Negligence Trials & Appeals; Insurance Defense Law; Products Liability Law (Defective Products); Casualty Insurance Law; Federal Practice.
**Curtis, Jonathan C.** .... '59 '86 C.112 B.A. L.426 J.D. [Ⓒ Paul,H.J.&W.]
**Curtis, Linda L.** .... '60 '88 C.674 A.B. L.813 J.D. [Ⓐ Gibson,D.&C.]
*PRACTICE AREAS: Corporate Finance; Mergers and Acquisitions.
Curtis, Shirley A. .... '47 '85 C.1097 B.A. L.809 J.D. 865 S. Figueroa St. #3100
**Curtiss, Thomas, Jr.**, (AV) .... '41 '71 C.976 B.A. L.309 J.D. [McKenna&C.]
*PRACTICE AREAS: Trusts and Estates; Conservatorships and Guardianships; Estate Planning.
Cushman, Barry J. .... '60 '86 C.36 B.A. L.893 J.D. 300 S. Grand Ave.
**Cushnir, Andrew** .... '63 '93 C.112 B.A. L.1065 J.D. [Ⓐ Manatt,P.&P.]
*PRACTICE AREAS: Financial Services.
Cusick, James E., (AV) .... '22 '54 C.112 B.S. L.809 LL.B. 4411 Los Feliz Blvd.
Custer, Barbara Ann '45 '77 C.856 A.B. L.809 J.D.
V.P., Bus. & Legal Affs., Orion Pictures Corp.
**Custer, Eric J.** .... '68 '93 C.375 B.A. L.846 J.D. [Ⓐ Latham&W.]
Cutler, Felice R., (AV) .... '37 '61 C.102 B.A. L.976 LL.B. [Cutler&C.]
Cutler, Gordon B. .... '35 '58 C&L.912 B.A., J.D. [Maupin,C.T.&W.]
Cutler, Richard B., (AV) .... '31 '59 C.878 B.S. L.976 LL.B. [Cutler&C.]
Cutler & Cutler, (AV) .... 10601 Wilshire Blvd., 19th Fl.
**Cutrow, Allan B., (A Professional Corporation)**, (AV) '46 '72
C.112 B.A. L.1068 J.D. [Mitchell,S.&K.]
*PRACTICE AREAS: Estate Planning; Estate and Trust Administration and Litigation.
Cuttler, Michele K. .... '66 '92 C.112 B.A. L.770 J.D. [Ⓐ Garfield,T.E.&T.]
Cvitan, Alexander B. .... '52 '78 [Reich,A.C.&C.]
**Cypers, Michael L.** .... '56 '81 C.112 A.B. L.1066 J.D. [Alschuler G.&P.]

**Czapla, Meredith A.** .... '70 '96 C.477 B.A. L.494 J.D. [Ⓐ Black C.H.&L.]
*PRACTICE AREAS: Insurance Coverage; Bad Faith Litigation.
**Czepiel, Lori Anne** .... '63 '87 C.597 B.A. L.94 J.D. [Ⓒ Skadden,A.S.M.&F.]
**Daar, David**, (AV) .... '31 '56 C.1060 A.B. L.426 J.D. [Daar&N.]
**Daar, Jeffery J.** .... '57 '82 C.154 B.A. L.1067 J.D. [Ⓐ Daar&N.]

**Daar & Newman, Professional Corporation, (AV)** [BR]
**Suite 2500, 865 South Figueroa Street, 90017-2567**
**Telephone: 213-892-0999 FAX: 213-892-1066**
**David Daar; Michael R. Newman; Jeffery J. Daar; Marsha McLean-Utley; Michael J. White. Of Counsel: Rodney W. Loeb; William F. White, Jr.; Samuel T. Rees.**
**Insurance, Insurance Coverage, Corporation, Business, Aviation, Antitrust and Securities Law. Litigation and Appellate Practice.**
**Representative Clients: Allianz Insurance Co.; American Income Life Insurance Co.; American Life and Casualty Insurance Co.; Balboa Insurance Co.; California Casualty Insurance Co.; National Benefit Life Insurance Co.; Capital Life Insurance Co.; Charter National Life; Columbian Mutual Life; Connecticut Mutual Life Insurance Co.**
***See Professional Biographies, LOS ANGELES, CALIFORNIA***

**Dacey, John P.** .... '57 '88 C.1269 B.A. L.809 J.D. [Bergman&W.]
*PRACTICE AREAS: Environmental Liability; Commercial Real Property; Business Litigation; Civil Fraud; Construction Liability.
Dadaian, Shaghig I. .... '60 '87 C.112 B.A. L.426 J.D. 5757 Wilshire Blvd
Dahl, Robert H., (AV) .... '32 '59 C&L.426 B.B.A., J.D. [Wadsworth,F.&D.]
Dahle, David S. .... '50 '78 C.800 A.B. L.809 J.D. Dist. Atty.
Daigh, Gary E. .... '52 '77 C.800 B.S. L.426 J.D. Supr. J.
**Dailey, Joseph P.**, (AV⊙) '44 '70 C&L.276 A.B., J.D.
(adm. in NY; not adm. in CA) [Whitman B.A.&M.]
*PRACTICE AREAS: Litigation.
**Dailey, Steven M.** .... '65 '93 C.174 B.S. L.426 J.D. [Ⓐ Schaffer&L.]
*PRACTICE AREAS: Products Liability; Environmental Litigation; Business Litigation.
**Dakin-Grimm, Linda** .... '60 '85 C.976 B.A. L.309 J.D. [Ⓐ Chadbourne&P.]
**Dal Soglio, Robin D.** .... '64 '91 C.1077 B.S. L.800 J.D. [Ⓐ Latham&W.]
*PRACTICE AREAS: Employment Litigation.
**Dalberg, Jon L. R.** .... '55 '87 C.061 B.A. L.976 LL.M. [Ⓐ Andrews&K.]
*PRACTICE AREAS: Bankruptcy Law.
**Dale, George D.**, (BV) .... '59 '85 C.112 B.A. L.809 J.D. [Dale,B.&H.] (⊙Walnut Creek)
*LANGUAGES: Spanish.
*REPORTED CASES: Braude vs. City of Los Angeles, 226 Cal. App. 3d, 83 276 Cal. Rptr. 256 (1990).
*PRACTICE AREAS: Construction Defect/Injury Litigation; Insurance Coverage; Real Estate and Commercial Litigation; Creditor's Rights/Bankruptcy; Corporation Representation.
Dale, Louise D., (AV) .... '32 '60 C.112 B.A. L.1068 J.D. 2029 Century Park E.

**Dale, Braden & Hinchcliffe, A Professional Law Corporation, (AV)**
**3415 South Sepulveda Boulevard, Suite 900, 90034⊙**
**Telephone: 310-398-5517 Fax: 310-398-5317**
**George D. Dale; Timothy J. Carrick; Everett S. Hinchcliffe; Donald J. Aberbook; Roger O. Scouton; Susan R. Scouton; John F. Ramey; Henry J. Weinblatt; Logan B. Byrnes; Jack A. Marsh; Jill A. Spitz; Callie C. O'Hara; Ted L. Travis; Jay J. Chung; Tom A. Kerr; Joan Thompson Lind; Sandra Isabel Barrientos; Scott D. Bleifer; Willie Wang; Brent E. Barnes (Resident); Joanne K. Leighton; T. Stephen Corcoran.**
**Construction, Insurance Defense and Business Litigation, Real Estate Litigation, Corporate Representation, Creditor's Rights/Bankruptcy.**
**Representative Clients: AXA Marine & Aviation; Bain Hogg; Calvert Insurance Co.; Excess Insurance Co.; Generali; Global Special Risks; Hogg Insurance Brokers; Investors Insurance Group; Jardine Insurance Brokers International; Lloyds of London Claims Office; London Special Risks; Maness Industries; McCoy Construction Co.; Reliance National Insurance Co.; Sirius (UK) Insurance; Sukut Construction Co.; Transamerica Insurance Group; Willis Corroon Inc.; Yorkshire Insurance Co., Ltd.**
**Walnut Creek, California Office: 500 Ygnacio Valley Road, Suite 490. Telephone: 510-934-9011. Fax: 510-934-8983.**
**San Diego, California Office: 550 West "C" Street, Suite 620. Telephone: 619-702-5588. Fax: 619-702-9199.**
**Ventura, California Office: 121 North Fir Street, Suite H. Telephone: 805-643-4140. Fax: 805-643-1802.**

**Daley, Todd A.** .... '67 '93 C.112 B.A. L.1065 J.D. [Ⓐ Hawkins,S.L.&B.]
**Dalmore, Jean A.** .... '62 '94 C.112 B.S. L.800 J.D. [Ⓐ Murchison&C.]
*PRACTICE AREAS: Products Liability; Construction; General Civil Litigation; Toxic Tort; Insurance Coverage.
Dalrymple, Ronald D. .... '42 '81 C.640 B.S. L.1148 J.D. Dist. Coun., I.R.S.
**Dalton, Barbara E.** .... '— '95 C.112 B.A. L.426 J.D. [Ⓐ S.L.Hartmann]
*PRACTICE AREAS: Civil Rights.
Dalton, Douglas, (AV) .... '29 '56 C.112 B.A. L.800 LL.B. 555 S. Flower St., 25th Fl.
**Daly, Bryan D.** .... '59 '85 C.1269 B.A. L.1292 J.D. [Beck,D.D.B.&O.]
**Daly, Diane M.** .... '61 '90 C.1077 B.A. L.426 J.D. [Ⓐ Fonda,G.H.&D.]
**Daly, John A.**, (AV) .... '31 '57 C.770 B.S. L.800 LL.B. [Dwyer,D.B.&B.]
Dam, Lawrence W., (AV) .... '46 '72 C.911 B.A. L.477 J.D. Pres., UNIVISA, Inc.
D'Amato, George G. '25 '52 C&L.262 B.B.S., LL.B.
(adm. in NY; not adm. in CA) 221 N. Figueroa St. (⊙N.Y., N.Y.)
**D'Amato, John P.** .... '63 '89 C.276 B.A. L.93 J.D. [Quinn E.U.&O.]
*PRACTICE AREAS: General Commercial Litigation; Securities; Antitrust Law; Unfair Competition; Employment.
Dana, Saml. M. .... '21 '49 C.112 A.B. L.1066 LL.B. 8787 Shoreham Dr.‡
Dane, Karen Daniels .... '60 '89 C.1228 B.A. L.575 J.D. 400 S. Hope St.
**Dane, Ted** .... '64 '89 C.309 A.B. L.813 J.D. [Munger,T.&O.]
Daneman, Cara R. .... '57 '82 C.940 B.A. L.1068 J.D. [Ⓐ Spector,B.H.&B.]
Daneshrad, Joseph .... '55 '90 C.800 B.S. L.426 J.D. 12400 Wilshire Blvd.
**Danforth, Tanya K.** '45 '85 C.1097 B.S. L.1148 J.D.
(adm. in HI; not adm. in CA) [Ⓐ Marks&M.]
D'Angelo, James S., (AV) .... '19 '55 C.800 L.1001 LL.B. 2601 So. Figueroa St.‡
**D'Angelo, Vincent P.** .... '53 '80 C.262 B.S. L.426 J.D. [Wilson,E.M.E.&D.]
Dangl, John R., Jr. .... '57 '83 C.103 A.B. L.800 J.D. 700 S. Flower St.
Daniel, Eleanor .... '— '90 C.659 B.A.,B.S. L.809 J.D. Dep. Dist. Atty.
Daniel, H. D. .... '59 '87 C&L.112 B.A., J.D. 900 Wilshire Blvd.
**Daniel, Jonathan L.** '51 '77
C.112 B.A. L.1068 J.D. Sr. Coun., Pacific Telesis Legal Group
Daniel, Judith Palotay .... '42 '88 C.1211 B.S. L.1136 J.D. 3435 Wilshire Blvd., 18th Fl.
**Daniels, Christopher M.** .... '59 '88 C.966 B.B.A. L.846 J.D. [Ⓐ Ginsburg,S.O.&R.]
Daniels, Joan T. .... '38 '87 L.1136 J.D. 2126 Glendon Ave.
**Daniels, John P., (Inc.)**, (AV) .... '37 '64 C.197 A.B. L.800 J.D. [Daniels,B.&F.]
*PRACTICE AREAS: Trial Law; Products Liability; Insurance.
**Daniels, Joseph F.** .... '70 '96 C.112 A.B. L.800 J.D. [Akre,B.&C.]
**Daniels, Paula A.** .... '55 '81 C.800 B.A. L.809 J.D. [Kudo&D.]
*REPORTED CASES: Danielson v. ITT Industrial Credit Co. (1988) 199 Cal. App. 3d 645, 245 Cal. Rptr. 126.
*PRACTICE AREAS: Products Liability; Medical, Dental, Legal, Accountant and Realtor Malpractice; Construction Accidents.
**Daniels, Richard L.** .... '61 '89 C.475 B.A. L.809 J.D. [Ⓐ Brobeck,P.&H.]
*PRACTICE AREAS: Litigation; Products Liability.
**Daniels, Robert D.** .... '52 '79 C.1044 B.A. L.1068 J.D. [Manning,L.B.&B.]
*PRACTICE AREAS: Automotive Dealer Law; Civil Trial; Bankruptcy; Commercial Law.

**Daniels, Baratta & Fine, (AV)** BR
A Partnership including a Professional Corporation
**1801 Century Park East, 9th Floor, 90067**⊙
Telephone: 310-556-7900 Telecopier: 310-556-2807
Members of Firm: John P. Daniels (Inc.); James M. Baratta; Paul R. Fine; Nathan B. Hoffman; Mary Hulett; Michael B. Geibel; James I. Montgomery, Jr.; Lance D. Orloff; Mark R. Israel. Associates: Ilene Wendy Kurtzman; Janet Sacks; Michael N. Schonbuch; Scott M. Leavitt; Michelle R. Press; Scott Ashford Brooks; Craig A. Laidig; Robin A. Webb; Craig S. Momita; Spencer A. Schneider; Angelo A. Du Plantier, III; Leslie E. Wright, III.; Erin B. Hallissy; Kena B. Chin; Dean Bengston; Peter Anders Nyquist; Jeannie Masse; Lori Chotiner; Maureen M. Michail. Of Counsel: Timothy J. Hughes; Drew T. Hanker; Mark A. Vega.
General Civil Trial and Appellate Practice in all State and Federal Courts. Insurance, Products Liability, Tort, Wrongful Termination and Employment Discrimination, Business, Entertainment, Real Estate and Construction Law, Environmental and Toxic Torts.
Bakersfield, California Office: 5201 California Avenue, Suite 400. Telephone: 805-335-7788. Telecopier: 805-324-3660.

*See Professional Biographies, LOS ANGELES, CALIFORNIA*

Danielson, George E., (AV) ..........'15 '41 C&L.546 B.A., J.D. Assoc. Ct. of App. Jus.
Danielson, Joan Lewis ......'52 '87 C.36 B.S. L.1188 J.D. 221 N. Figueroa St., Ste., 1200
**Danker, Ashleigh A.** ..................'63 '88 C.228 B.A. L.800 J.D. [Weiss,S.S.D.&S.]
*PRACTICE AREAS: Bankruptcy Law.
**Danner, Robert C.** ......................... '53 '78 C.800 A.B. L.426 J.D. [Danner&M.]

**Danner & Chonoles, L.L.P.**
(See Long Beach)

**Danner & Martyn, LLP, (AV)**
**Watt Plaza-Suite 1070, 1925 Century Park East, 90067-2799**
Telephone: 310-789-3800 Telecopier: 310-789-3814
Robert C. Danner; Daniel E. Martyn, Jr.; David S. Poole;—Melanie J. Bingham; Adryane R. Omens.
General Commercial Practice, Bankruptcy, Reorganization and Workouts, Commercial Transactions, Corporations and Business Law , Creditors' Rights, Environmental, Financial Services and Commercial Lending, Litigation and Appellate Practice, Mergers and Acquisitions, Real Estate, White Collar Crime, Zoning, Land Use and Condemnation Law.

*See Professional Biographies, LOS ANGELES, CALIFORNIA*

**Dannhausen, John W.** ........................'49 '80 C.608 B.A. L.607 J.D. [Parker S.]
**Danning, Curtis B., (A Professional Corporation)**, (AV) '20 '53
C.112 A.B. L.1068 LL.B. [Ⓒ Danning,G.D.&K.]

**Danning, Gill, Diamond & Kollitz, LLP, (AV)** BR
A Limited Liability Partnership Composed of Professional Corporations
**2029 Century Park East, Suite 1900, 90067-3005**
Telephone: 310-277-0077 Fax: 310-277-5735
Email: dgdk@dgdk.com
Members of Firm: David A. Gill (A Professional Corporation); Richard K. Diamond (A Professional Corporation); Howard Kollitz (A Professional Corporation); John J. Bingham, Jr., (A Professional Corporation); Steven E. Smith (A Professional Corporation); Eric P. Israel (A Professional Corporation); David M. Poitras (A Professional Corporation); George E. Schulman (A Professional Corporation). Associates: Robert A. Hessling; Kevin L. Hing; Barry Lurie; Kathy Bazoian Phelps; Daniel H. Gill; Glenn C. Kelble; Sarah E. Petty; Elan R. Schwartz. Of Counsel: Curtis B. Danning (A Professional Corporation); James J. Joseph (A Professional Corporation).
Bankruptcy, Business Reorganization, Insolvency, Corporate Dissolutions, Partnership Dissolutions, Commercial Law, Bankruptcy Trusteeships, Federal Receiverships and State Receiverships.

*See Professional Biographies, LOS ANGELES, CALIFORNIA*

Dansby, Shelia R. '58 '84 C.326 B.A. L.325 J.D.
(adm. in TX; not adm. in CA) I.R.S.
**Dant, Mary F.** ..........................'60 '89 C.112 B.A. L.178 J.D. [Ⓐ Horvitz&L.]
**Danto, Karen S.** ........................'67 '94 C.112 B.A. L.990 J.D. [Ⓐ Chapman&G.]
*PRACTICE AREAS: Insurance Defense; General Negligence; Auto Liability; Professional Liability; Construct Defect.
Dantzer, M. Kathleen '45 '78 C.734 B.S. L.128 J.D.
Sr. Assoc. Coun., National Med. Enterprises, Inc.
**Dantzler, Amy** ......................'64 '90 C.668 B.A. L.426 J.D. [Ⓐ Quisenberry&B.]
Dapeer, Philip D. ...........................'47 '72 C.112 A.B. L.1068 J.D. [Dapeer&H.]
Dapeer & Hirsch, A Law Corporation, Law Offices of ..............5670 Wilshire Blvd.

**Dapeer, Rosenblit & Litvak, LLP**
(See Beverly Hills)

**Dapper, David P.** .........................'53 '78 C.112 A.B. L.800 J.D. [Wickwire G.]
*PRACTICE AREAS: Construction; Public Agency; Fidelity and Surety Law.
Dapser, Wayne R. .....................'49 '80 C.339 B.A. L.809 J.D. 3530 Wilshire Blvd.
Darakjian, Hagop A. ....................'50 '78 C.1097 B.A. L.1190 J.D. 6255 Sunset Blvd.
**Darby, G. Harrison** '42 '67 C.529 B.A. L.1009 LL.B.
(adm. in NY; not adm. in CA) [Jackson,L.S.&K.]
**Darby, Robert E.**, (AV) .................. '47 '76 C.705 A.B. L.1066 J.D. [Fulbright&J.]
*PRACTICE AREAS: Business Law; Bankruptcy; Creditors Rights.

**Darby & Darby, Professional Corporation, (AV)**
**707 Wilshire Boulevard Thirty Second Floor, 90017**⊙
Telephone: 213-243-8000 Telecopier: 213-243-8050
Byard G. Nilsson; Harold E. Wurst; Robert A. Green;—Clarke A. Wixon; Stephen D. Burbach; John E. Wurst (Not admitted in CA); Lance M. Kreisman. Of Counsel: William P. Green (Law Corporation).
Intellectual Property and Technology, including Patent, Trademark, Copyright, Computer, Trade Secrets, Unfair Competition, Licensing and Related Antitrust Law.
New York, New York Office: 805 Third Avenue. Telephone: 212-527-7700. Telecopier: 212-753-6237. Telex: 236687.

*See Professional Biographies, LOS ANGELES, CALIFORNIA*

**D'Arcangelo, S. Ellen** ........... '60 '91 C.1111 B.A. L.990 J.D. [Ⓐ Sheppard,M.R.&H.]

**Darling, Hall & Rae, (AV)** BR
**777 South Figueroa, 37th Floor, 90017**
Telephone: 213-627-8104 Fax: 213-627-7795
Email: 71555.1466@Compuserve.com
Members of Firm: Hugh W. Darling (1901-1986); Edward S. Shattuck (1901-1965); George Gaylord Gute (1922-1981); Donald Keith Hall (1918-1984); Matthew S. Rae, Jr.; Richard L. Stack; Edwin Freston. Of Counsel: John L. Flowers.
Trust, Estate Planning, Probate, Corporation, Business and Real Property. Civil and Trial Practice in all State and Federal Courts.
Reference: City National Bank (Pershing Square Office, Los Angeles, California).

*See Professional Biographies, LOS ANGELES, CALIFORNIA*

**Darrow, Christopher**, (AV) '45 '76
C.851 B.S.M.E. L.1148 J.D. [Oppenheimer P.S.] (Pat.)
*PRACTICE AREAS: Intellectual Property.

**Dart, Geraldine Mele, Law Offices of '47 '74 C.1099 B.A. L.94 J.D.**
**611 West Sixth Street, Suite 2500, 90071-3102**
Telephone: 213-489-2456 Fax: 213-489-2457
General Civil Practice, Plaintiff's Employment including Wrongful Discharge, Sexual Harassment, Sex, Race, Age, National Origin, Disability, Discrimination, Federal, State and County Employment, Plaintiff's Personal Injury including Vehicular, Premises Liability and Business Litigation.

*See Professional Biographies, LOS ANGELES, CALIFORNIA*

Dash, Ralph B., (AV) ......................'51 '76 C.930 B.A. L.426 J.D. Admin. Law J.

**Dasovich, Caroline L.** ................. '59 '88 C.931 B.A. L.61 J.D. [Ⓐ Koletsky,M.&F.]
*LANGUAGES: Spanish.
*PRACTICE AREAS: Insurance Defense Litigation; Construction Defect Litigation; General Liability Defense Litigation; Premises Liability.
Dassoff, Nancy L. ........................... '52 '78 C.1168 B.A. L.426 J.D. [Salerno&D.]
**Dasteel, Jeffrey H.** .................'53 '83 C.112 B.A. L.426 J.D. [Skadden,A.S.M.&F.]
**Dastin, Barry L.** .......................'54 '79 C.976 A.B. L.309 J.D. [Kaye,S.F.H.&H.]
*PRACTICE AREAS: Corporate Law; Securities Law; Mergers and Acquisitions; Banking and Financing.
Daswick, Michael ............ '57 '83 C.178 B.A. L.770 J.D. V.P., Calif. Pow-R-Ped Inc.
**Datomi, Christopher A.** ..................'55 '87 C.800 B.A. L.426 J.D. [Ⓐ Tuverson&H.]
Datomi, Jan M. ...............................'60 '91 C.1077 L.809 J.D. Off. of Pub. Def.
Dau, Ralph W., (AV) ........................'38 '66 C&L.846 B.A., LL.B. 400 S. Hope St.
**Daucher, Donald A.**, (AV) ................'45 '72 C.696 B.S. L.228 J.D. [Paul,H.J.&W.]
**Dauer, Risa C.** ........................ '68 '93 C.477 B.A. L.1009 J.D. [Ⓐ Koletsky,M.&F.]
*PRACTICE AREAS: Construction Defect; General Liability; Insurance Coverage.
DaVanzo, Frank J., (BV) .......... '46 '72 C.112 A.B. L.1068 J.D. Princ. Dep. Co. Coun.
Dave, Danelle K. ...................... '64 '90 C.914 B.A. L.426 J.D. 11718 Barrington Ct.
Dave, Jamiel G. ......................... '49 '76 C.1077 B.S. L.426 J.D. 633 W. 5th St.
**Dave, Michael G.** ......................'39 '65 C.112 B.S. L.1068 J.D. [Marcus,W.S.&D.]
*PRACTICE AREAS: Corporate Partnership; Real Property; Construction Law; Business Law.
Davenport, Patricia A. .... '39 '67 C&L.326 B.A., LL.B. Adm. Law J., State Personnel Bd.
Davenport, Robert R. '50 '80 C.478 B.A. L.724 J.D.
(adm. in NY; not adm. in CA) 564 Midvale
Daves, Ira A., III ......................... '58 '91 C.813 B.A. L.309 J.D. 400 S. Hope St.
**David, Darlene R.** .................... '61 '86 C.800 B.A. L.990 J.D. [Ⓐ Sherwood&H.]
*PRACTICE AREAS: Real Estate Litigation; Business Litigation.
**David, Deborah A.**, (AV) ................. '50 '75 C.773 B.A. L.1068 J.D. [Lebovits&D.]
*LANGUAGES: French.
*REPORTED CASES: Rose v. Volkswagen - verdict - judgment - $3.5 Million; Leal v. Golden - Verdict/Judgment - $14.9 Million; Goodstein v. Superior Court.
*PRACTICE AREAS: Products Liability; Professional Negligence; Aviation Law; Insurance Bad Faith; Personal Injury.
**David, Gary A.** ....................... '50 '77 C.112 B.A. L.1068 J.D. [Blanc W.J.&K.]
*PRACTICE AREAS: Mergers and Acquisitions; Proprietary Rights; Real Estate; Computer Law.
**David, Henry S.** ............................ '54 '79 C.111 B.S. L.569 J.D. [Graham&J.]
*PRACTICE AREAS: Litigation; Collection Law.
**Davidoff, Brian L.**, (AV) ............. '56 '82 C.061 B.Proc. L.472 LL.M. [Rutter,G.&H.]

**Davidoff & Davidoff**
(See Beverly Hills)

**Davids, Ronn S.** ..........................'65 '95 C.860 B.A. L.178 J.D. [Ⓐ Riordan&M.]
*LANGUAGES: Hebrew.
**Davidson, Ben M.** ....'68 '95 C.867 B.S.E.E. L.273 J.D. [Ⓐ Merchant&G.] (See Pat. Sect.)
*LANGUAGES: French and Japanese.
*PRACTICE AREAS: Litigation; Patent Prosecution.
Davidson, Cary, (AV) ..........................'54 '78 C.154 B.A. L.145 J.D. [Reed&D.]⊙
**Davidson, Jeffrey H.**, (AV) ............... '52 '77 C&L.309 B.A., J.D. [Stutman,T.&G.]
*SPECIAL AGENCIES: Bankruptcy Court and Office of U.S. Trustee.
*TRANSACTIONS: Attorney for Debtor in Possession in Chapter 11 Reorganization of Barry's Jewelers, Inc.; Attorney for Debtor in Possession in Chapter 11 Reorganization of Lamont's Apparel, Inc.; Attorney for Debtor in Possession in Chapter 11 Reorganization of Castle Entertainment, Inc.; Attorney for Executive Life Insurance Co. in Chapter 11 Reorganization of Continental Airlines, Inc.; Attorney for Executive Life Insurance Co. in Restructuring of LVI Group, Inc.
*PRACTICE AREAS: Business Bankruptcy; Insolvency; Corporate Reorganization.
**Davidson, Jeffrey S.** ...................... '47 '73 C.894 A.B. L.1119 J.D. [Kirkland&E.]
*PRACTICE AREAS: Litigation.
**Davidson, M. Katharine** .......... '52 '84 C.800 B.A. L.426 J.D. [Weinstein,B.R.H.&C.]
*PRACTICE AREAS: Tax.
**Davidson, Peter A.**, (AV) .............'52 '77 C.112 B.A. L.1068 J.D. [Saltzburg,R.&B.]
*PRACTICE AREAS: Receivership Law; Bankruptcy Law; Debtor Creditor Law.
**Davidson, Robert J.** ......................'58 '85 C&L.800 B.S., J.D. [Buchalter,N.F.&Y.]
*PRACTICE AREAS: Banking; Corporate; Finance.
Davies, John G. ............................'29 '61 C.477 B.A. L.1068 LL.B. U.S. Dist. J.
Davies, John Griffith, Jr. .............. '64 '91 C.103 B.A. L.800 J.D. 355 S. Grand Ave.
**Davies, M. Randel** .................'51 '76 C.112 B.A. L.800 J.D. [Nebenzahl K.D.&L.]
*PRACTICE AREAS: Real Property Law; Finance Law; Business Litigation.
**Davies, Veronica** ....................'69 '94 C.112 B.A. L.426 J.D. [Ⓐ Milbank,T.H.&M.]
**Davine, Jeffrey D.** .................. '60 '85 C.112 B.S. L.1068 J.D. [Ⓐ Mitchell,S.&K.]
*PRACTICE AREAS: Taxation; Tax Controversy and Litigation; Exempt Organizations-Nonprofit.
**Davis, Albert F.** '— '95 C.339 B.S.C.E. L.966 J.D.
(adm. in WI; not adm. in CA) [Ⓐ Merchant&G.]
*PRACTICE AREAS: Patent; Trademark; Entertainment; Copyright.
**Davis, Annette E.** ........................'64 '90 C&L.846 B.A., J.D. [Ⓐ Gaims,W.W.&E.]
**Davis, Barbra L.** ........................... '45 '85 C.112 B.A. L.1068 J.D. [Paul,H.J.&W.]
**Davis, Bret J.** .................................'55 '83 C.477 A.B. L.178 J.D. [Davis&D.]
*LANGUAGES: French, Japanese.
*PRACTICE AREAS: Bankruptcy; Business Reorganization; Insolvency; Asset Protection; Commercial Litigation.
**Davis, C. Stephen**, (AV) ................'55 '80 C.112 B.A. L.426 J.D. [Stephens,B.&L.]
*SPECIAL AGENCIES: California State Board of Equalization, Local Assessment Appeals Boards.
*PRACTICE AREAS: State and Local Tax; Commercial Litigation.
**Davis, Calvin E.**, (AV) ......................... '55 '81 C.112 B.A. L.426 J.D. [Davis&F.]
*PRACTICE AREAS: Trial Practice in State and Federal Courts; Business Litigation; Real Estate Litigation; Entertainment Litigation.
**Davis, Christopher L.** ..................'66 '92 C.813 B.A. L.1068 J.D. [Ⓐ Orrick,H.&S.]
Davis, Colette T. ............................'60 '89 C.1097 B.A. L.809 J.D. 400 S. Hope St.
Davis, Craig C. '19 '53 C.277 B.S. L.309 LL.B.
(adm. in DC; not adm. in CA) 10501 Wilshire Blvd.‡
**Davis, Deborah** ....................... '57 '85 C.446 B.S. L.1009 J.D. [Ⓐ R.L.Zukerman]
*PRACTICE AREAS: Family Law; Commercial Litigation; Real Estate.
**Davis, Deborah Neufeld** ...................... '57 '85 C.446 B.S. L.1009 J.D. [Davis&D.]
*PRACTICE AREAS: Commercial Litigation; Bankruptcy; Family Law.
Davis, Donald G., (AV) ..................'49 '70 C.1075 B.S. L.800 J.D. 300 S. Grand Ave.
**Davis, Edmond R.**, (AVⓉ) .................'28 '53 C.990 L.1065 J.D. [Brobeck,P.&H.]
*PRACTICE AREAS: Trusts and Estates Law; Planning and Litigation.
Davis, Eric K. ...................... '57 '86 C.1109 B.M. L.770 J.D. 2049 Century Park E.
**Davis, Eva Herbst** ........................'65 '90 C.228 A.B. L.309 J.D. [Ⓐ Latham&W.]
*PRACTICE AREAS: Corporate; Securities; Corporate Finance; Mergers and Acquisitions.
**Davis, George M.** ...................... '57 '83 C&L.472 B.S., J.D. [Ⓐ Nelson,G.F.&L.]
*PRACTICE AREAS: Motion Pictures Law (100%).
**Davis, Gleam O.** ... '56 '81 C.800 A.B. L.309 J.D. Sr. Coun., Pacific Telesis Legal Group
Davis, Herbert, (P.C.), (BV) '36 '60 C.102 B.Acct. L.569 LL.B.
601 W. 5th St., Suite 800
Davis, J. Alan ................................. '61 '88 C.802 B.A. L.846 J.D. [Davis&B.]
Davis, James H., (AV) ............. '30 '55 C.112 A.B. L.813 LL.B. 2960 Wilshire Blvd.
Davis, Jamie C. ..................'61 '88 C.112 B.A. L.309 J.D. 11845 W. Olympic Blvd.
Davis, Jane Clay ..........................'— '80 C.421 B.A. L.940 J.D. 444 S. Flower St.
**Davis, Jay M.** .................................'46 '72 C.999 B.S. L.1049 J.D. [Arter&H.]
Davis, John R. ........................... '47 '73 C.112 B.A. L.426 J.D. Dep. Dist. Atty.
Davis, Joseph A. .............................'52 '77 C.800 B.S. L.426 J.D. [Davis&W.]
Davis, Julia M. ............................. '50 '83 C.945 B.A. L.276 J.D. [D.A.Lapin]

Davis, Karl L., Jr., (AV) ............'30 '56 C.813 B.A. L.1068 LL.B. 515 S. Flower St.‡
Davis, Kelley R. ..........................'— '68 C.602 B.A. L.273 LL.B. [Johnson,R.&W.]
**Davis, Kevin Matthew** ....................'58 '89 C.36 B.S. L.990 J.D. [Ⓐ Knopfler&R.]
*PRACTICE AREAS: Construction Litigation; Business Litigation; Products Liability Law.
**Davis, Laurie E.** ...............................'57 '82 C.477 B.A. L.800 J.D. [Demetriou,D.S.&M.]
*PRACTICE AREAS: General Business Corporate Law/Transactions; Securities Law/Transactions.
**Davis, Leah D.** ...............................'55 '92 C.1097 B.A. L.1049 J.D. [Ⓐ Gilbert,K.C.&J.]
*PRACTICE AREAS: Workers Compensation.
Davis, LeRoy R. ..................'38 '63 C.112 B.A. L.1068 LL.B. 1925 Century Park E.
Davis, Margaret L. ..................'58 '85 C.276 B.A. L.809 J.D. 617 S. Irving Blvd.
**Davis, Mary Laura** ..........................'38 '78 C.331 B.A. L.245 J.D. [Gibson,D.&C.]
*PRACTICE AREAS: Litigation including Medical Malpractice; Products Liability; Personal Injury; Antitrust.
Davis, Maynard D. ..................'28 '55 C.1016 L.809 LL.B. 11111 W. Olympic Blvd.
**Davis, Norman C.** ..............'42 '93 C.1109 M.B.A. L.1137 J.D. [Ⓐ Baker&H.]
*PRACTICE AREAS: Healthcare Law; Business Law.
**Davis, Pamela A.** ..........................'60 '83 C.999 D.E.C. L.012 J.D. [Ⓑ Berman,B.&B.]
*LANGUAGES: French and Spanish.
*SPECIAL AGENCIES: Member, Penal Code 987 Panel, Burbank Municipal Court; Director, Westside Village Civic Association; Member, Los Angeles City Attorney's Task Force on Economic Recovery.
Davis, Paul M. ..............'37 '70 C.1114 B.S. L.1190 LL.B. 4731 Angeles Vista Blvd.
**Davis, Philip, (A Professional Corporation)**, (AV) '45 '71
C.112 A.B. L.800 J.D. [Mitchell,S.&K.]
*PRACTICE AREAS: Entertainment Law.
**Davis, Phillip A.** ..................'58 '83 C.813 B.A. L.1065 J.D. [Sheppard,M.R.&H.]
*PRACTICE AREAS: Securities, Business, Commercial and Real Estate Litigation.
Davis, Richard B. ......................'53 '79 C.30 B.A. L.800 J.D. First Interstate Bank
Davis, Richard D. ...............'61 '91 C.330 B.A. L.990 J.D. 11111 W. Olympic Blvd.
**Davis, Richard F., (P.C.)** ...............'45 '71 C.112 A.B. L.1068 J.D. [Katten M.&Z.]
*PRACTICE AREAS: Real Estate and International Law.
Davis, Richard J., Jr. ..........................'43 '71 C.112 A.B. L.1068 J.D. [Pappy&D.]
**Davis, Richard S.** ..................................'— '94 C.659 L.800 J.D. [Ⓐ Latham&W.]
**Davis, Richard T., Jr.**, (AV) ...........'45 '71 C&L.846 B.A., J.D. [Beckman,D.S.&R.]
*PRACTICE AREAS: Professional Liability Defense and Insurance Coverage; Life, Health and Disability Insurance Law; Products Liability; Real Estate and Commercial Litigation.
**Davis, Richard W.** ...........................'67 '92 C.112 B.A. L.990 J.D. [Ⓐ Booth,M.&S.]
Davis, Roger H., (AV) ..............'23 '52 C.112 A.B. L.1066 LL.B. 251 N. Layton Dr.‡

**Davis, Roxanne A., Law Offices of '61 '87 C.569 B.A. L.800 J.D.**
**1801 Avenue of the Stars, Suite 934, 90067**
**Telephone: 310-551-1222 Fax: 310-551-1333**
***LANGUAGES: Italian.**
**Associate: Frank Hakim.**
**Labor and Employment**
***See Professional Biographies, LOS ANGELES, CALIFORNIA***

**Davis, Shedrick O., III** '62 '87
C.112 A.B. L.1068 J.D. Litig. Atty., The Chase Manhattan Bk., N.A.
Davis, Stephanie M. ......'60 '87 C&L.426 B.A., J.D. U.S. Securities & Exchange Comm.
Davis, Stephanie R. ..............'58 '90 C.1077 B.A. L.999 J.D. 11601 Wilshire Blvd.
**Davis, Steven D.** ..........................'50 '79 C.112 B.A. L.809 J.D. [Fonda,G.H.&D.]
**Davis, Steven S.** ..........................'52 '77 C.197 B.A. L.1068 J.D. [Gaims,W.W.&E.]
**Davis, Susan S.** ..........................'52 '86 C.426 B.A. L.809 J.D. [Ⓐ Cox,C.&N.]
*PRACTICE AREAS: Bankruptcy; Loan Workouts; Real Estate Litigation.
**Davis, Thomas R.** ..........................'69 '95 C.103 B.A. L.569 J.D. [Ⓐ Morrison&F.]
*LANGUAGES: Spanish.
**Davis, Timothy L.** ..........................'70 '96 C.740 B.A. L.469 J.D. [Ⓐ Burke,W.&S.]
*PRACTICE AREAS: General Civil Litigation.
**Davis, Tracy T.** ..........................'63 '89 C.112 B.A. L.809 J.D. [Ⓐ Fonda,G.H.&D.]
*LANGUAGES: French and Spanish.
**Davis, William S.** ..........................'49 '74 C.684 B.A. L.1068 J.D. [Arter&H.]
Davis & Benjamin ..................................................... 2049 Century Park East

**Davis & Davis, L.L.P.**
**1875 Century Park East, Suite 700, 90067**
**Telephone: 310-229-1200 Fax: 310-229-1205**
**Members of Firm: Bret J. Davis; Deborah Neufeld Davis.**
**Bankruptcy, Business Reorganization, Insolvency, Family Law, Commercial Litigation.**
***See Professional Biographies, LOS ANGELES, CALIFORNIA***

**Davis & Fox, (AV)**
**1901 Avenue of the Stars, Suite 400, 90067**
**Telephone: 310-286-2915 Fax: 310-286-2916**
**Members of Firm: Calvin E. Davis; Steven A. Fox. Associates: Brian Aronson; Amy L. Freisleben; Susan R. Peck. Of Counsel: Herbert D. Meyers.**
**General Civil Litigation including Business, Real Estate and Entertainment Litigation, Insurance Coverage Disputes, Real Estate Transactions, Business Transactions and Environmental Law.**
***See Professional Biographies, LOS ANGELES, CALIFORNIA***

Davis & Winston ..........................................................9911 W. Pico Blvd.

**Davis Wright Tremaine LLP, (AV)**
**A Partnership including Professional Corporations**
**Suite 600, 1000 Wilshire Boulevard, 90017**⊙
**Telephone: 213-633-6800 FAX: 213-633-6899**
**URL: http://www.dwt.com**
**Resident Partners: Richard D. Ellingsen; Zhi-Ying James Fang; Andrew R. Hall; Charles Pereyra-Suarez; Kelli L. Sager; Robert A. Steinberg; Henry J. Tashman; Michael John Tichon. Resident Associates: Karen Nancy Frederiksen; Mary H. Haas; Carole A. Klove; Elizabeth Staggs-Wilson; Todd D. Thibodo; Steven J. Westman; Susan E. Wogoman. Of Counsel: Marc E. Jacobowitz; James R. Lahana.**
**Healthcare, Corporate, Tax, Securities, International, Media and Communications, Litigation.**
**Anchorage, Alaska Office: Suite 1450, 550 W. Seventh Avenue. 99501. Telephone: 907-257-5300. FAX: 907-257-5399.**
**Bellevue, Washington Office: 1800 Bellevue Place, 10500 NE 8th Street. 98004. Telephone: 206-646-6100. FAX: 206-646-6199.**
**Boise, Idaho Office: Suite 911, 999 Main Street, 83702-9010. Telephone: 208-338-8200. FAX: 208-338-8299.**
**Honolulu, Hawaii Office: 1360 Pauahi Tower, 1001 Bishop Street, 96813. Telephone: 808-538-3360. FAX: 808-526-0101.**
**Portland, Oregon Office: 2300 First Interstate Tower, 1300 SW Fifth Avenue. 97201. Telephone: 503-241-2300. FAX: 503-778-5299.**
**Richland, Washington Office: Suite 3A, 601 Williams Boulevard, 99352. Telephone: 509-946-5369. FAX: 509-946-4211.**
**San Francisco, California Office: One Embarcadero Center, Suite 600, 94111. Telephone: 415-276-6500. FAX: 415-276-6599.**
**Seattle, Washington Office: 2600 Century Square, 1501 Fourth Avenue. 98101. Telephone: 206-622-3150. FAX: 206-628-7040.**
**Washington, D.C. Office: Suite 700, 1155 Connecticut Avenue, N.W., 20036. Telephone: 202-508-6600. FAX: 202-508-6699.**
**Shanghai, China Office: Suite 1008/1009 Jin Jiang Hotel, 59 Mao Ming Road (S), 200020. Telephones: 011-8621-6472-3344; 011-8621-6415-3002. FAX: 011-8621-6415-3003.**
***See Professional Biographies, LOS ANGELES, CALIFORNIA***

**Davisson, Michael R.** ................'53 '78 C.112 A.B. L.1065 J.D. [Sedgwick,D.M.&A.]
**Davisson, William C., III** ................'70 '95 C.112 A.B. L.569 J.D. [Ⓐ Latham&W.]

**Davitt, Vincent J.** ..................'61 '87 C.770 B.S. L.276 J.D. [Ⓐ LeBoeuf,L.G.&M.]
*PRACTICE AREAS: Business Litigation; Insurance.
Daw, Alison E. ..........................'61 '88 C.112 B.A. L.276 J.D. 444 S. Flower St.
**Dawley, Gregory A., (A Professional Corporation)** '54 '85
C.1074 B.A. L.1148 J.D. [Billet&K.]
Dawson, Howard ..........................'53 '79 C.112 B.A. L.809 J.D. 425 Shatto Pl.
**Dawson, Jeanne R.** ..........................'47 '84 C.1042 B.A. L.426 J.D. [Ⓐ Paul,H.J.&W.]
Dawson, Mitchell J., (AV) ..................'47 '72 C.112 B.A. L.426 J.D. [M.J.Dawson]
Dawson, Richard A. ..................'37 '64 C&L.426 B.B.A., LL.B. Asst. City Atty.
**Dawson, Robert M.**, (AV) ..................'54 '78 C.770 B.A. L.1068 J.D. [Fulbright&J.]
*LANGUAGES: French.
*PRACTICE AREAS: Business Law; Business Litigation.
Dawson, Robert W. ..................'34 '65 C.575 A.B. L.800 J.D. Dep. Dist. Atty.
**Dawson, Steven J.** ..................'59 '87 C.813 A.B. L.1065 J.D. [Burke,W.&S.]
*LANGUAGES: French.
*PRACTICE AREAS: Business Litigation; Real Estate/Commercial Law; Labor Law; Trials and Appeals; Commercial Litigation.
Dawson, Mitchell J., A Professional Law Corporation, (AV)
2040 Avenue of the Stars, Suite 400
**Day, Graham L. W.** ..................'71 '96 C.734 B.A. L.659 J.D. [Ⓐ Irell&M.]
**Dayen, Michael** ..................'61 '91 C.494 B.A. L.1068 J.D. [Ⓐ Milbank,T.H.&M.]
**Dayton, Lee W.** ..................'51 '82 C.101 B.A. L.1137 J.D. [Ramsey,B.&D.]
*LANGUAGES: Spanish.
*PRACTICE AREAS: Municipality; Products Liability; General Negligence.
Dayvault, Jay J. '61 '92 C.612 B.S. L.990 J.D.
Staff Coun., Legal Div., Dept. of Soc. Serv.
Dea, Hong S. ..................'49 '73 C.112 B.S. L.800 J.D. Asst. U.S. Atty.
**Deacon, Linda Van Winkle** ..................'48 '74 C.939 A.B. L.145 J.D. [Morgan,L.&B.]
**Dean, Eric D.** ..................'48 '73 C.112 B.A. L.1068 J.D. [Arter&H.]
**Dean, Lauren A.** ..................'68 '94 C.112 B.A. L.37 J.D. [Ⓐ Goldstein,K.&P.]
*PRACTICE AREAS: Labor and Employment; Civil Litigation.
**Dean, Randall J.** ..................'57 '83 C.112 B.A. L.426 J.D. [Chapman&G.]
*PRACTICE AREAS: Products Liability; Professional Liability Law; Commercial Law; Business Litigation; Environmental Law.

**Dear & Kelley**
**(See Pasadena)**

Dearden-Trepanier, Lisa ..................'68 '91 C.101 B.A. L.188 J.D. 333 S. Hope St.
**Dearing, Henry H.**, (BV) ..................'48 '74 C.309 A.B. L.94 J.D. [Gifford&D.]
*PRACTICE AREAS: Wills; Trusts; Probate Administration; Litigation.
Deason, Susan Bryant ..................'46 '80 C.112 B.A. L.809 J.D. Supr. Ct. J.

**Deason, Edward J.**
**(See Torrance)**

**De Bari, Cheryl A.** ..................'59 '84 C.216 B.A. L.767 J.D. [Ⓑ Beckman,D.S.&R.]
*PRACTICE AREAS: Insurance Law; ERISA; Subrogation; Products Liability.
Debbaudt, Marc ..................'55 '83 C.112 B.A. L.426 J.D. Dep. Dist. Atty. III
De Biase, Nicholas R. ..................'63 '89 C.390 A.B. L.659 J.D. 2121 Ave. of the Stars
**DeBlase, Patrick** ..................'67 '93 C.112 B.A. L.1148 J.D. [Ⓐ Nordstrom,S.N.&J.]
*PRACTICE AREAS: Civil Litigation; Plaintiff Personal Injury.
**de Bodo, Richard** ..................'56 '87 C&L.309 B.A., J.D. [Irell&M.]
DeBose, Debra Jenkins ..................'— '74 C.988 L.1068 J.D. [DeBose&D.]
DeBose, James R. ..................'50 '74 C.1109 B.A. L.1068 J.D. [DeBose&D.]
DeBose & DeBose ..................................................911 Wilshire Blvd.
deBrauwere, John E. ..................'29 '75 C.1097 B.A. L.1190 LL.B. 4765 Eagle Rock Blvd.
deBrier, Donald P. '40 '67 C.674 B.A. L.659 J.D.
(adm. in NY; not adm. in CA)
Exec. V.P., Gen. Coun. & Secy., Occidental Petroleum Corp.
**De Bryn, R. Joseph**, (AV) ..................'48 '74 C&L.770 B.S., J.D. [Musick,P.&G.]
*PRACTICE AREAS: Litigation; Insurance.
De Carlo, John T. ..................'50 '76 C.884 B.S. L.1095 J.D. [De Carlo,C.&S.]
De Carlo, Connor & Selvo, A Professional Corporation ..................500 S. Virgil Ave.
**DeCarolis, Patrick, Jr.**, (AV) ..................'53 '78 C.1042 B.A. L.1148 J.D. [P.DeCarolis,Jr.]

**DeCarolis, Patrick, Jr., A Professional Law Corporation, (AV)**
**2029 Century Park East, Suite 2860, 90067**
**Telephone: 310-552-3312 Telecopier: 310-552-0441**
**Patrick DeCarolis, Jr. (Certified Specialist, Family Law, The State Bar of California Board of Legal Specialization).**
**Practice Limited to Family Law.**
***See Professional Biographies, LOS ANGELES, CALIFORNIA***

**De Castro, David M.** ..................'64 '91 C.112 B.S. L.426 J.D. [Ⓐ Selvin&W.&W.]
*PRACTICE AREAS: Civil Litigation.
**de Castro, Hugo D.**, (AV) ..................'35 '61 C.112 B.S. L.1068 J.D. [De Castro,W.&C.]
*PRACTICE AREAS: Business Law; Real Property Law; Taxation Law.
**De Castro, Luis C.**, (AV) '38 '65
C.112 B.S. L.1068 J.D. [Ⓑ Goodson&W.] (⊙Santa Monica)
*LANGUAGES: Spanish.
*PRACTICE AREAS: Tax Controversy and Litigation; Complex Business Litigation.

**De Castro, West & Chodorow, Inc., (AV)**
**Eighteenth Floor, 10960 Wilshire Boulevard, 90024-3804**
**Telephone: 310-478-2541 Telecopier: 310-473-0123**
**Email: dwandc@aol.com**
**Hugo D. de Castro; Hilton I. Chodorow; Jerome A. Rabow; Neil Carrey; Bruce S. Glickfeld; Buddy Epstein; James A. Ginsburg; Menasche M. Nass; David T. Stowell; David C. Ruth; Jonathan I. Reich; Scott M. Mendler; Richard S. Zeilenga; Michael C. Cohen; Henry A. Reitzenstein; Richard D. Furman; James D. Vaughn; Neal B. Jannol.**
**General Civil and Business Practice, including Federal, State, Local, and International Taxation, Corporations, Partnerships, Real Estate, Pension Planning and ERISA, Health Care Law, Estate Planning, Trusts and Probates, Civil and Criminal Tax Litigation, Business Trial and Appellate Litigation in State and Federal Courts, including Litigation in Connection with Environmental, Land Use and Toxic Tort Matters, Estate and Trust Disputes, and General Business Litigation.**
***See Professional Biographies, LOS ANGELES, CALIFORNIA***

Decio, Jamee '53 '80 C&L.602 B.A., J.D.
(adm. in IN; not adm. in CA) 1033 Hilgard Ave.‡
Decker, Antoinette ..................'46 '77 C.502 B.S. L.1136 J.D. Dep. Dist. Atty.‡
Decker, David J. ..................'68 '93 C.216 B.A. L.426 J.D. 801 S. Figueroa St.
**Decker, David R.**, (AV) ..................'42 '67 C.401 B.A. L.893 LL.B. [Arter&H.]
*PRACTICE AREAS: Corporate Law; Securities Regulation Law; Mergers and Acquisitions Law.
Decker, Norman E. '30 '56 C&L.966 B.S., LL.B.
(adm. in WI; not adm. in CA) Scudder, Stevens & Clark, Inc.
**Decker, Richard J.** ..................'59 '84 C.867 B.A. L.94 J.D. [Ⓑ Ginsburg,S.O.&R.]
**De Corso, Anthony A.** ..................'53 '83 C.679 B.A. L.426 J.D. [Beck,D.D.B.&O.]
**de Costa, Karl J.** ..................'71 '96 C.170 B.A. L.1068 J.D. [Ⓐ Mitchell,S.&K.]
*PRACTICE AREAS: Trusts and Estates; Probate; Civil Litigation.
**Decyk, Julian B.** ..................'50 '84 C.31 B.A. L.309 J.D. [Ⓑ Paul,H.J.&W.]
**Dederer, James W.** '46 '73 C.112 B.A. L.1065 J.D.
Exec. V.P., Gen. Coun. & Corp. Secy., Transamerica Occidental Life Ins. Co.

**Dee, John J.**, (AV) .................... '41 '70 C.770 B.A. L.1026 J.D. [Sullivan,W.&D.]
*PRACTICE AREAS: Eminent Domain Law; Zoning Law; Land Use Regulation Law; Real Estate Litigation.
**Deeb, Richard A.** ........................................ '63 '87 C&L.426 B.A., J.D. [Baker&H.]
*PRACTICE AREAS: Litigation and Product Liability.
**Deeley, Kathleen T.** .......................... '54 '87 C.800 B.A. L.1068 J.D. [Ⓐ Selman B.]
*REPORTED CASES: Austin v. Allstate Insurance Co. (1993) 16 Cal.App.4th 1812.
*PRACTICE AREAS: Environmental Law; Insurance Coverage.
**Deems, Douglas H.** .................. '62 '87 C.605 A.B. L.1065 J.D. [Ⓐ Pillsbury M.&S.]
Deems, Joseph E., (BV) ......................... '48 '75 C.426 B.A. L.809 J.D. [Deems&C.]
Deems & Carpenter, (BV) ................................................ 10880 Wilshire Blvd.
**Deere, Elizabeth A.** ..................... '57 '92 C.188 B.S. L.1068 J.D. [Ⓐ Morrison&F.]
Dees, Russell L. .......................... '55 '90 C.810 B.A. L.1066 J.D. 555 W. 5th St.
**Deetjan, Jose M.** ...................................... '37 '79 C.999 L.810 [Ⓐ Milbank,T.H.&M.]
Deetz, Tonya S. ................................ '62 '88 C.608 B.S. L.426 J.D. Dep. Pub. Def.
**DeFelice, Diane C.** ................................ '62 '90 C.112 B.A. L.990 J.D. [W.D.Ross]
*PRACTICE AREAS: Business; Civil Trial; Real Estate.
**De Feo, Robert M.** ................................ '65 '90 C.597 B.A. L.990 J.D. [Ⓒ J.K.Pierson]
*LANGUAGES: Finnish and Russian.
*PRACTICE AREAS: Civil Litigation.
Deffense, Clare '54 '84 C.112 A.B. L.1066 J.D.
1800 Ave. of the Stars, Suite 900 (Century City)
DeFrantz, Anita L. '52 '77 C.183 B.A. L.659 J.D.
(adm. in PA; not adm. in CA) 2141 W. Adams Blvd.‡
DeFurio, Frank A. ........................ '46 '71 C.686 B.A. L.208 J.D. Shuwa Investments Corp.
Degnan, James G., (AV) ....................... '29 '53 C&L.477 A.B., J.D. One Wilshire Blvd.‡
**de Gravelles, Patrick P.** .... '65 '95 C.276 B.S.F.S. L.1068 J.D. [Ⓐ Greenberg G.F.C.&M.]
*PRACTICE AREAS: Litigation.
**de Gyarfas, Victor** ........................................ '61 '94 C.1167 B.S. L.809 J.D. [Ⓐ Graham&J.]
*PRACTICE AREAS: Intellectual Property.
de Haaff, Stuart M. .......................................... '46 '72 C.112 B.A. L.1068 601 S. Figueroa St.
**De Haas, Louis H.**, (AV) ...... '41 '67 C.800 B.A. L.1065 LL.B. [La Follette,J.D.F.&A.]
*REPORTED CASES: Atienza v. Tamb MD., 194 Ca 3rd 388; Bolanos v. Khalatian MD., 91 Daily Journal D.A.R. 8439; The L.A. Free Press Juc. v. The City of Los Angeles 9 Ca 3rd 448; Willie Leonard v. City of Los Angeles 31 Ca 3rd 473; The City of Los Angeles v. Superior Court of the State of California 176 Ca 3rd 856.
*PRACTICE AREAS: Medical Malpractice Litigation; Wrongful Termination Litigation.
Deihl, Penelope M. ................................ '67 '93 C.36 B.A. L.37 J.D. 1055 W. 7th St.
Deitch, Philip ............................ '32 '59 C.112 B.A. L.800 LL.B. 4929 Wilshire Blvd.
Deitch, Russell ................................ '63 '88 C.112 B.A. L.1067 J.D. Fed. Trade Comm.
**Deixler, Bert H.**, (AV) ............ '52 '76 C.273 B.A. L.178 J.D. [McCambridge,D.&M.]
**de Jong, Hendrik** ........................................ '46 '69 C&L.145 A.B., J.D. [Latham&W.]
De Jute, David A. .......... '62 '91 C.602 B.S. L.309 J.D. 1901 Ave. Of The Stars, 7th Fl.
**Del, Ernest**, (AV) .................................... '52 '76 C.112 A.B. L.813 J.D. [Del,R.S.M.&D.]
*PRACTICE AREAS: Entertainment Law; Television Law; Motion Picture Law.
**de la Cruz, Alfred M.** .............. '61 '90 C.112 B.S. L.1066 J.D. [Ⓐ Manning,M.&W.]
Delahoussaye-Turner, Audre .......... '57 '88 C.800 B.S. L.1136 J.D. 3775 Jasmine Ave.
**De La Mora, Richard G.** .......................... '58 '85 C.112 B.A. L.800 J.D. [Barger&W.]
*PRACTICE AREAS: General Corporate Law; Insurance Regulation Law; Reinsurance; Administrative Law.
**Delancey, Leah E.** .................................... '63 '90 C.112 B.A. L.800 J.D. [Ⓐ Manatt,P.&P.]
*PRACTICE AREAS: Tax; Estate and Trust.
**Delaney, Daniel P.** .................................. '65 '92 C.813 A.B. L.112 J.D. [Ⓐ Paul,H.J.&W.]
Delaney, Michael J. ........ '46 '73 C&L.276 B.S., J.D. Co. Dist. Atty., Envir. Crimes Div.
**Delaney, Thomas A.** ............... '67 '92 C&L.426 B.A., J.D. [Ⓐ Sedgwick,D.M.&A.]
**De La Peña, Patricia M.** .............................. '64 '91 C&L.112 B.A., J.D. [Ⓐ Long&L.]
de la Poterie, Marceline A. ......................'— '66 C.053 L.809 LL.B. 1501 Viewsite Terr.
De La Riva, Jesús ............ '61 '90 C.800 B.S. L.1068 J.D. One Stop Immigration
de la Sota, Richard .............................. '44 '70 C.112 A.B. L.800 J.D. Dep. Dist. Atty.
**De Laurentis, Dina M.** .................. '67 '93 C.436 B.A. L.809 J.D. [Ⓐ Lynberg&W.]
*LANGUAGES: French.
Delavigne, John A. ........................................ '33 '70 C.800 B.S. L.809 J.D. Co. Dist. Atty.
Delbick, Judi A. .............................. '64 '89 C.112 B.A. L.800 J.D. 1925 Century Park E.
**Del Duca, Patrick** .......................... '57 '83 C&L.309 B.A., J.D. [Kelley D.&W.]
*LANGUAGES: French, Italian and Spanish.
*PRACTICE AREAS: Environmental and International Law; Project Finance.
**Delello, Richard J.** '54 '83 C.188 B.S. L.776 J.D.
(adm. in NJ; not adm. in CA) [Grotta,G.&H.]⊙
**DeLeo, Alfred F.** .................................... '52 '78 C.276 B.S.L. L.273 J.D. [Pircher,N.&M.]
*LANGUAGES: French and German.
*PRACTICE AREAS: Tax Law.
**Delevie, Harold J.**, (AV) ........................ '31 '57 C.112 A.B. L.1068 J.D. [H.J.Delevie]
*PRACTICE AREAS: Business Law; Business Transactions; Real Property Law; Estate Planning.

**Delevie, Harold J., Incorporated, (AV)**
**1875 Century Park East, Fifteenth Floor, 90067-2516**
**Telephone: 310-277-7490; Direct Dial: 310-282-9475 Fax: 310-277-8923**
**Harold J. Delevie.**
**Business Law, Business Transactions, Real Property Law, Estate Planning.**
***See Professional Biographies, LOS ANGELES, CALIFORNIA***

**Delfino, Rebecca** .............................. '68 '93 C.112 B.A. L.1067 J.D. [Ⓐ Quinn E.U.&O.]
Delgadillo, Lydia N. ...................... '52 '80 C.1042 B.A. L.426 J.D. 210 W. Temple St.
Delgadillo, Rockard J. .......................... '60 '86 C.309 A.B. L.178 J.D. 400 S. Hope St.
**Delgado, Andree D.** ................. '66 '91 C.575 B.A. L.1068 J.D. [Ⓐ Morrison&F.]
**Delgado, Marcus** .......................... '70 '93 C.94 B.A. L.1068 J.D. [Ⓐ Graham&J.]
*PRACTICE AREAS: Corporate Transactional.
Delgado-Krebs, Rosemarie ........ '62 '89 C.1109 B.A. L.1068 J.D. 10900 Wilshire Blvd.
**Del Greco, Peter F.** ...................... '55 '93 C.1349 B.A. L.1068 J.D. [Ⓐ Gipson H.&P.]
*PRACTICE AREAS: Litigation.
**Del Guercio, James P.**, (AV) .... '33 '58 C.112 A.B. L.426 LL.B. [Ⓒ Demetriou,D.S.&M.]
*PRACTICE AREAS: Banking Transactions; Compliance; Business Law.
**Del Guercio, Richard A.**, (AV) ...... '28 '52 C.112 A.B. L.426 LL.B. [Ⓒ Demetriou,D.S.&M.]
*PRACTICE AREAS: Eminent Domain; Civil Litigation.
**Del Guercio, Ronald J.**, (AV) ...... '31 '60 C&L.800 A.B., LL.B. [Ⓒ Demetriou,D.S.&M.]
*PRACTICE AREAS: Business Law.
**Del Guercio, Stephen A.** .............. '61 '86 C&L.800 B.A., J.D. [Demetriou,D.S.&M.]
*PRACTICE AREAS: Health Care; Business Law.
**DelHagen, William T.**, (AV) .......... '44 '75 C.453 B.S.A.E. L.426 J.D. [Belcher,H.&B.]
*PRACTICE AREAS: Airplane Crash Litigation; Products Liability Law; Litigation Defense Law; Accident and Personal Injury Law; Business Law.
**De Lisle, Desiree** ................................ '69 '95 C.602 B.A. L.802 J.D. [Ⓐ Zelle&L.]
*PRACTICE AREAS: Insurance Coverage; Environmental.
Dell, George M., (AV) '25 '53 C.870 B.S. L.800 J.D.
Ste. 1015, 11661 San Vicente Blvd.
**Dellafiora, Mary Jane** .................. '62 '87 C.893 B.A. L.990 J.D. [Ⓐ Murchison&C.]
*PRACTICE AREAS: Law and Motion Law; Appellate Practice; Insurance Coverage and Bad Faith Litigation.
**DellAngelo, Robert L.** .................. '61 '92 C.178 B.A. L.1068 J.D. [Ⓐ Munger,T.&O.]
**Dellaverson, John J.**, (AV) .................... '46 '78 C.665 B.S. L.262 J.D. [Loeb&L.]
*LANGUAGES: Italian.
*PRACTICE AREAS: Labor Law; Entertainment Law.

**Delling, Anthony R.**, (AV) ........................ '53 '78 C&L.813 B.A., J.D. [Pillsbury M.&S.]
**Delmendo, Fernando L.** ...................... '— '93 C.112 B.A. L.767 J.D. [Ⓐ Reish&L.]
*PRACTICE AREAS: Employee Benefits Law.
**Delmendo, Wendi J.** ...................... '64 '92 C.112 B.S. L.911 J.D. [Ⓐ Sheppard,M.R.&H.]
*PRACTICE AREAS: Labor and Employment Law.
**de Lorimier, Paul A.** .......................... '54 '83 C.1097 B.A. L.809 J.D. [McKay,B.&G.]
*PRACTICE AREAS: Civil Trial; Insurance Defense; Products Liability; Construction Law.
deLorrell, Walter J., Jr. ...................... '41 '76 C.1097 B.A. L.1095 J.D. 9130 Bellanca Blvd.
**Del Propost, John J.** ...................... '62 '89 C.970 B.A. L.990 J.D. [Ⓐ Marks&M.]

**Del, Rubel, Shaw, Mason & Derin, A Law Corporation, (AV)**
**2029 Century Park East, Suite 3910, 90067-3025**
**Telephone: 310-772-2000 Telecopier: 310-772-2777**
**Ernest Del; Michael A. Rubel; Nina L. Shaw; Greg David Derin; Jean E. Tanaka; Jeffrey D. Blye; Jeffrey S. Finkelstein; Jonathan D. Moonves;—Jay Aaron Goldberg.**
**Entertainment, Television, Motion Picture, Theatre, Corporation, Partnership, Taxation, Real Property Law, Litigation in State and Federal Courts and Arbitration.**
***See Professional Biographies, LOS ANGELES, CALIFORNIA***

**Del Tondo, Douglas J.** ........................ '58 '81 C.262 B.A. L.809 J.D. [Del Tondo&S.]
*LANGUAGES: Italian and Spanish.
*PRACTICE AREAS: Civil Trial; Complex Litigation; Insurance Defense; Insurance Coverage.

**Del Tondo & Sheehan, (AV)**
**11355 West Olympic Boulevard, Suite 500, 90064**
**Telephone: 310-312-0027 Fax: 310-477-5021**
**Members of Firm: Joseph J. Sheehan; Douglas J. Del Tondo.**
**Complex Litigation, Civil Trials, Insurance Defense, Insurance Coverage, Entertainment Litigation.**
***See Professional Biographies, LOS ANGELES, CALIFORNIA***

**De Luce, Richard D.**, (AV) ...................... '28 '55 C.112 A.B. L.813 J.D. [Arter&H.]
Del Valle, Sonia H. .........'59 '86 C.846 B.A. L.1068 J.D. 12100 Wilshire Blvd., 15th Fl.
**DelVecchio, Peter M.** '57 '88 C.1073 B.A. L.976 J.D.
(adm. in MA; not adm. in CA) [Ⓐ Chadbourne&P.]
DeMarco, John M. ...................... '58 '86 C.800 A.B. L.990 J.D. 801 S. Grand Ave.
**DeMarco, Julianne M.** ............ '56 '87 C.575 B.A. L.809 J.D. [Ⓐ Bonne,B.M.O.&N.]

**De Marco, Frank, Jr.**
**(See South Pasadena)**

**DeMarrais, Jennifer A.** .................. '69 '95 C.951 B.A. L.276 J.D. [Ⓐ Shapiro,R.&C.]
**DeMeire, Jana L.** ........................ '58 '85 C.881 B.A. L.893 J.D. [Ⓐ Epstein B.&G.]
*PRACTICE AREAS: Labor and Employment Law; Education Law; Litigation.
Demerjian, David E. ...................... '54 '83 C.1109 B.A. L.1137 J.D. Dep. Dist. Atty.
**Demet, James D.** ...................... '62 '87 C.880 B.A. L.472 J.D. [Hennelly&G.]
*PRACTICE AREAS: Business Litigation; Products Liability.
**DeMeter, Robert F.**, (AV) ...................... '48 '75 C.608 B.A. L.904 J.D. [Clark&T.]
*PRACTICE AREAS: Taxation Law; Business Law; Estate Planning Law.
**Demetriou, Andrew J.** ...................... '54 '79 C.112 A.B. L.1066 J.D. [Jones,D.R.&P.]

**Demetriou, Del Guercio, Springer & Moyer, LLP, (AV)** 🄱🄱
**801 South Grand Avenue, 10th Floor, 90017**
**Telephone: 213-624-8407 Telecopy: 213-624-0174**
**Email: ddsm@juno.com URL: http://www.ddsm.com**
**Members of Firm: Chris G. Demetriou (1915-1989); Jeffrey Z. B. Springer; Craig A. Moyer; Angela Shanahan; Stephen A. Del Guercio; Michael A. Francis; Regina Liudzius Cobb; Laurie E. Davis; Gregory D. Trimarche; Karen McLaurin Chang; Leslie M. Smario; Andrew J. Bracker; Kimberly E. Lewand; Jennifer T. Taggart; Robert P. Silverstein. Of Counsel: Ronald J. Del Guercio; Richard A. Del Guercio; James P. Del Guercio.**
**General Civil Practice and Litigation in all State and Federal Courts. Environmental, Eminent Domain, Energy, Oil and Gas, Business Law and Taxation, Securities Law, Commercial Law, Administrative, Health Care, Estate Planning, Trust and Probate, International Business and Real Estate Law.**
**Reference: Bank of America, L.A. Main Office, Los Angeles, Calif.**
***See Professional Biographies, LOS ANGELES, CALIFORNIA***

**De Meules, James H.**, (AV) ............ '45 '71 C.939 A.B. L.178 J.D. [O'Melveny&M.]
*PRACTICE AREAS: Banking; Financial Transactions; Project Finance; Corporate Law.
Demko, Adelle M. '46 '73 C.028 B.A. L.228 J.D.
(adm. in NY; not adm. in CA) V.P., Wedbush Morgan Securities, Inc.
**Demoff, Marvin A., (A Professional Corporation)** '42 '69
C.112 B.A. L.426 J.D. [Ⓒ Mitchell,S.&K.]
*PRACTICE AREAS: Sports Law.
**Dempsey, Michael D.**, (AV) ............ '43 '69 C.1077 B.A. L.1068 J.D. [Dempsey&J.]
*PRACTICE AREAS: Business Litigation; Securities Fraud; Directors and Officers Liability; Accountant's Liability.

**Dempsey & Johnson, P.C., (AV)**
**1925 Century Park East, Suite 2350, 90067-2724**
**Telephone: 310-551-2300 Facsimile: 310-556-2021**
**Michael D. Dempsey; Stephen C. Johnson;—Robert D. Donaldson; Heather M. Noelte. Of Counsel: Michael A. Cross.**
**General Civil and Trial Practice in all State and Federal Courts, Real Estate, Corporation, Corporate Securities and Probate.**
***See Professional Biographies, LOS ANGELES, CALIFORNIA***

Dempster, Katie A., (BV) ............ '55 '82 C.800 B.S.B.A. L.426 J.D. [Tanenbaum&D.]
**DeMuro, Paul R.**, (AV) ...... '54 '79 C.446 B.A. L.910 J.D. [Latham&W.] (⊙San Fran.)
*PRACTICE AREAS: Healthcare Law; Business Law; Administrative Law.
**Demyanek, Walter, Jr.** ...................... '60 '90 C.35 B.S. L.809 J.D. [Ⓐ Parker S.]
**Denenny, Yvonne D.** .................. '69 '94 C.914 B.A. L.1068 J.D. [Ⓐ Morrison&F.]
**Denham, Reid L.** ...................... '54 '87 C.101 B.S. L.990 J.D. [Ⓐ Neumeyer&B.]
*PRACTICE AREAS: Appellate Practice; Insurance Coverage; Insurance Bad Faith.
Denham, Robert E., (AV) ...... '45 '72 C.846 B.A. L.309 J.D. 355 S. Grand Ave., 35th Fl.
**Denham, S. Mark** .................. '67 '95 C.999 B.S. L.893 J.D. [Ⓐ Paul,H.J.&W.]
**Denigan, Terence J.** '66 '96 C.112 B.A. L.284 J.D.
(adm. in WA; not adm. in CA) [Ⓐ Arnberger,K.B.&C.]
*LANGUAGES: English, Spanish and Turkish.
*PRACTICE AREAS: International Corporate Law (Foreign Investment); Civil Litigation; Criminal Defense.
**Denise, Mary A.** ...................... '61 '89 C.273 B.A. L.260 J.D. [Ⓐ Howrey&S.]
*PRACTICE AREAS: Government Contracts Law.
**Denison, Colleen McGrath** ........ '60 '90 C.112 B.A. L.426 J.D. [Ⓐ Fragomen,D.&B.]
*LANGUAGES: Spanish.
**Denison, James W.** ...................... '60 '91 C.112 B.A. L.800 J.D. [Ⓐ Stroock&S.&L.]
*PRACTICE AREAS: Litigation.
**Denison, Michael C.**, (AV) .............. '47 '74 C.112 A.B. L.426 J.D. [Kinsella,B.F.&T.]
*PRACTICE AREAS: Civil Litigation; Directors and Officers Liability Insurance Law.
**Deniston, Martin K.** .............. '56 '82 C.112 B.A. L.990 J.D. [Wilson,E.M.E.&D.]
*LANGUAGES: Spanish.
Denius, Wofford '52 '77 C.846 B.B.A. L.802 J.D.
(adm. in TX; not adm. in CA) 2812 Angelo Dr.‡
**Denlinger, Michael C.** .................. '56 '87 C.1259 B.A. L.809 J.D. [Ⓐ Hornberger&C.]
**Denman, Alexandra** .................. '47 '73 C.881 B.A. L.273 J.D. [Allderdice&D.]
*PRACTICE AREAS: Entertainment Law; Intellectual Property.

**Denney & Oths**
**(See Glendale)**

**Dennis, B. Maria** ...................... '66 '92 C.976 B.A. L.276 J.D. [Ⓐ Jones,D.R.&P.]

CAA211P

CALIFORNIA—LOS ANGELES MARTINDALE-HUBBELL LAW DIRECTORY 1997

**Dennis, Dean E.** .................................'58 '83 C.674 A.B. L.800 J.D. [Hill,F.&B.]
*SPECIAL AGENCIES: Planning and Zoning Commissions, Coastal Commission.
*REPORTED CASES: Southern California Rapid Transit Dist. v. Bolen (1992) 1 Cal. 4th 654; City of Manhattan Beach v. Superior Court (1996) 13 Cal. 4th 232; City of Vista v. Fielder, California Supreme Court No. S046856 (decision pending); Los Angeles Unified School District v. Trump Wilshire Associates (1996) 42 Cal. App. 4th 1682; Kalmanovitz v. Bitting (1996) 43 Cal. App. 4th 311.
*PRACTICE AREAS: Appeals; Land Use Law; Zoning Law; Eminent Domain Law.
**Dennis, L. Morris, (A Professional Corporation),** (AV) '39 '65
C.813 B.A. L.1068 J.D. [Bronson,B.&M.]
*PRACTICE AREAS: Taxation; Estate Planning; Bankruptcy; Corporations and Partnerships.
**Dennis, Lucinda, (A Professional Corporation),** (AV) '41 '66
C.174 B.A. L.1068 J.D. [Bronson,B.&M.]
*PRACTICE AREAS: Creditors Rights; Bankruptcy; Business Reorganization; Commercial Law; Secured Transactions.
**Dennis, Patrick W.** .......................'52 '82 C.112 B.S. L.1068 J.D. [Gibson,D.&C.]
*SPECIAL AGENCIES: California Department of Toxic Substances Control, Regional Water Quality Control Boards; United States Environmental Protection Agency; South Coast Air Quality Management District.
*PRACTICE AREAS: Environmental Litigation; Environmental Due Diligence; Environmental Compliance.
**Dennis, Polly Towill** ...........................'59 '85 C.184 B.A. L.276 J.D. [Sheppard,M.R.&H.]
*PRACTICE AREAS: Litigation; Government Contracts Law.
**Dennis, Syna N.** ..............................'62 '88 C.112 B.A. L.1066 J.D. [Ⓐ Atkins&E.]
*PRACTICE AREAS: Civil Litigation.
**Dennison, Bruce B.,** (AV) ..............'47 '72 C.112 B.S. L.1068 J.D. [Dennison,B.&P.]
*PRACTICE AREAS: Insurance and Tort Defense; Products Liability; Wrongful Termination and Discrimination; Sexual Harassment; Insurance Coverage and Bad Faith Law.

**Dennison, Bennett & Press, LLP, (AV)**
**Warner Center, 21031 Ventura Boulevard, 12th Floor (Woodland Hills), 91364**
**Telephone: 818-716-7200 Fax: 818-347-5284**
**Email: DbANDPLAW@aol.com**
**Members of Firm: Bruce B. Dennison; Charles A. Bennett; Stephen M. Press; James H. Goudge; Thomas A. Stewart; Lisa G. Rosenwasser. Associates: Michael Kaplan; Leonard P. Janner; Sheila E. Schaefer; Robert Scott Silver; Deborah A. Lieber; Timothy McWilliams; Phillip M. Hayes; Michael Tudzin.**
**General Civil, Trial and Appellate Practice in all State and Federal Courts. Insurance and Tort Defense, Business Litigation, Products Liability, Earth Movement, Construction Defects, Wrongful Termination and Discrimination, Sexual Harassment, and Insurance Coverage and Bad Faith Law.**
*See Professional Biographies, LOS ANGELES, CALIFORNIA*

Denniston, Karol K. .......................'59 '85 C.181 B.S. L.923 J.D. 601 S. Figueroa St.
Denny, George V., III, (AV) ............'30 '59 C&L.813 B.A., LL.B. 11130 Cashmere St.
**Denny, John R.** .................................'57 '94 C.112 B.A. L.426 J.D. [Ⓐ B.R.Bailey]
*PRACTICE AREAS: Litigation.
**Denny, Leslie Anne** ...................'63 '88 C&L.623 B.B.A., J.D. [Ⓐ Robinson,D.&W.]
*PRACTICE AREAS: General Civil Trial and Appellate Practice in all State and Federal Courts; Insurance; Products Liability; Negligence and Professional Liability; Common Carrier.
Denove, John F., (AV) ..........................'51 '76 C.112 B.A. L.426 J.D. [Cheong&D.]
**Denson-Low, Wanda K.** '56 '83 C.688 B.S. L.1009 J.D.
(adm. in CT; not adm. in CA) Hughes Aircraft Co.
**Dent, John R.** ...................................'63 '90 C.112 B.A. L.145 J.D. [Ⓐ Tuttle&T.]
Dent, Lloyd A. '38 '76 C.1044 B.A. L.426 J.D.
4804 Laurel Canyon Blvd., Valley Village
Denton, Gregory J. ..............................'53 '78 C.112 B.A. L.61 J.D. Dep. Dist. Atty.
**Denzer, Paul P.** ..............................'54 '81 C.698 B.S.B.A. L.1068 J.D. [Ⓒ Freeman,F.&S.]
**DePasquale, David L.** ....................'57 '86 C.112 B.A. L.1049 J.D. [DePasquale&P.]⊙
*PRACTICE AREAS: Corporate; Real Estate; Business Litigation; Bankruptcy; Creditors' Rights.
DePasquale, Paul R. ..........................'45 '71 C.112 A.B. L.1066 J.D. 523 W. 6th St.

**DePasquale & Paulson**
**World Trade Center, 350 South Figueroa Street, Suite 900, 90071**⊙
**Telephone: 213-895-0685 Fax: 213-895-0686**
**Members of Firm: David L. DePasquale.**
**General Civil Practice. Corporate, Taxation, Real Estate, Estate Planning, Business Litigation, Bankruptcy, Creditors' Rights and General Business Law.**
**Santa Ana, California Office: 4 Hutton Center Drive, Suite 200. Telephone: 714-755-3055. Fax: 714-755-1570.**
*See Professional Biographies, LOS ANGELES, CALIFORNIA*

**De Petris, Celeste V.** .........................'66 '93 C.161 B.A. L.809 J.D. [Ⓐ Lane P.S.L.]
**Depew, Brian D.** ...........................'48 '79 C.1077 B.A. L.809 J.D. [Engstrom,L.&L.]
*PRACTICE AREAS: Medical Professional Liability; Chiropractic Professional Liability; Products Liability; General Trials.
Depietro, Susan C. ...........................'49 '92.C.1068 B.S. L.426 J.D. 6305 Yucca St.
DePould, Diane Elizabeth ......'48 '75 C.273 B.A. L.904 J.D. 1650 Veteran Ave., No. 308
**Derby, Loyd P.,** (AV) ........................'39 '67 C.112 A.B. L.1066 J.D. [Morgan,L.&B.]
Derdiger, Ira G. ....................................'60 '86 C.36 B.S. L.209 J.D. [Derdiger&C.]
Derdiger & Cohen ..................................................................... 2049 Century Park E.
**de Recat, Craig J.** ..........................'53 '82 C.112 B.A. L.426 J.D. [Graham&J.]
*PRACTICE AREAS: Environmental Law; Real Property; Toxic Torts.
**Derewetzky, Marc J.** ....................'56 '87 C.1349 B.A. L.1065 J.D. [Hancock R.&B.]
Derian, Steven K. ...................'52 '83 C.112 A.B. L.1065 J.D. Univ. of Calif. Law Sch.
Derian, Susan Morton ............'54 '83 C.914 B.A. L.1065 J.D. 333 S. Hope St., 48th Fl.
**Derin, Greg David,** (AV) ...................'54 '79 C.112 B.A. L.1066 J.D. [Del,R.S.M.&D.]
*PRACTICE AREAS: Civil Litigation; Appellate Litigation; Commercial Law; Intellectual Property Litigation.
Derkum, Sharon F., (BV) ....................'42 '82 C&L.1137 B.S., J.D. Dep. Atty. Gen.
**Dern, Dixon Q.,** (AV) ............................'29 '54 C&L.813 A.B., J.D. [D.Q.Dern]
*LANGUAGES: German.
*PRACTICE AREAS: Entertainment Law; Copyright Law; Communications Law.
**Dern, Warren D.** ...........................'64 '91 C.112 B.A. L.809 J.D. [Ⓐ Nelson,G.F.&L.]
*LANGUAGES: Spanish.
*PRACTICE AREAS: Entertainment Law; Copyright Law; Communication Law.

**Dern, Dixon Q., P.C., (AV)**
**Suite 400, 1901 Avenue of the Stars, 90067**
**Telephone: 310-557-2244 Fax: 310-557-2224**
**Dixon Q. Dern;—Christine G. Albrecht-Buehler.**
**Entertainment, Copyright and Communication Law.**
*See Professional Biographies, LOS ANGELES, CALIFORNIA*

**DeRoche, James D.,** (BV) ..............'48 '76 C.770 B.A. L.169 J.D. [Crosby,H.R.&M.]
**Derr, James M.,** (BVⓉ) '45 '80 C.1077 B.A. L.809 J.D.
[Ⓒ Belcher,H.&B.] (⊙Charlotte Amalie, St. Thomas, Virgin Islands)
*PRACTICE AREAS: Business Law; Aviation Law; Airplane Crash Litigation; Civil Practice; Insurance Defense Law.
**Derrendinger, Regine** .......................'45 '92 C.061 L.809 J.D. [Ⓐ Creutz&C.]
*LANGUAGES: French and Spanish.
Derry, Carol D. ......................'58 '89 C.112 B.A. L.1137 J.D. 865 S. Figueroa St.
Derwin, Nancy ........................'65 '90 C.112 B.A. L.426 J.D. 1801 Century Park E.
**Desai, Asim K.** .............................'68 '94 C.112 B.A. L.809 J.D. [Ⓐ Selman B.]
*PRACTICE AREAS: Insurance Coverage.
DeSantis, Richard A., (BV) .........'31 '59 C.705 A.B. L.976 J.D. 1900 Ave. of the Stars
Desmond, Bridget G. ..................'49 '75 C&L.426 B.A., J.D. 3255 Wilshire Blvd.
**Desmond, David F.** ...............'64 '93 C.999 B.A. L.112 J.D. [Ⓐ Rossbacher&Assoc.]
*LANGUAGES: French.
**Desmond, Marjorie Turk** ..................'67 '92 C.813 B.A. L.426 J.D. [Ⓐ Graham&J.]
*LANGUAGES: German.
*PRACTICE AREAS: Maritime Law; Transportation and International Law; Commercial Transactions and Litigation.
**Desmond, Robert** ........................'57 '93 C.1070 B.S.E.E. L.426 J.D. [Ⓐ Graham&J.]
**Desoer, Michele M.** ..........................'60 '85 C.112 B.S. L.1066 J.D. [Katten M.&Z.]
*LANGUAGES: French.
*PRACTICE AREAS: Litigation; Entertainment; Employment.
Desser, Franklin M. ................'13 '46 C.569 B.S. L.724 LL.B. 930 Linda Flora Dr.
**De Stefano, Louis Robert** ................'47 '76 C.724 B.S. L.800 J.D. [Lewis,D.B.&B.]
**Destian, Tony** ...................................'59 '89 C.454 B.A. L.809 J.D. [Parsons&D.]
*PRACTICE AREAS: General Insurance Litigation; Complex Coverage; Writs and Appeals.
**Destino, David A.** ...............................'44 '70 C.184 B.S. L.94 J.D. [Baker&H.]
*PRACTICE AREAS: Litigation; Antitrust.
**Destouet, Maurice P.** ..........................'48 '78 C.813 B.A. L.800 J.D. [Ⓐ S.L.Hartmann]
Destouet, Maurice Peter ..............'48 '78 C.813 B.A. L.800 J.D. 12424 Wilshire Blvd.
**De Toro, Anthony D.** ......................'59 '84 C.569 B.A. L.767 J.D. [Ⓒ Fenigstein&K.]
*PRACTICE AREAS: Business Litigation; Securities Arbitration and Litigation.
**Detre, Peter A.** ..............................'58 '96 C.012 B.Sc. L.976 J.D. [Ⓐ Munger,T.&O.]
*LANGUAGES: Hungarian, French.
*PRACTICE AREAS: Litigation.
**Detrick, Lisa Ann** ..............................'— '83 C.575 B.A. L.880 J.D. [Ⓐ Morgan,L.&B.]
**Dettelbach, Alan M.** ..............................'61 '88 C.665 B.S. L.426 J.D. [Troy&G.]
*PRACTICE AREAS: Environmental Law; Securities and Real Estate Litigation.
**Dettmann, Steven J.** ..........................'67 '95 C.112 B.A. L.426 J.D. [Ⓐ Morrison&F.]
**Deukmejian, George,** (AV) ..................'28 '52 C.1021 B.A. L.724 J.D. [Sidley&A.]
*PRACTICE AREAS: Business Transactions; Governmental Consultation.
**Deutsch, Amy E.** ......................'70 '96 C.910 B.A. L.1068 J.D. [Ⓐ Crosby,H.R.&M.]
**Deutsch, David R.** .................................'49 '78 C.994 B.A. L.1068 J.D. [Citron&D.]
**Deutsch, Joel David, (P.C.)** ..............'53 '82 C.154 B.A. L.813 J.D. [Jeffer,M.B.&M.]
*PRACTICE AREAS: Land Use; Eminent Domain; Business; Real Estate; Commercial Litigation.
Deutsch, Phyllis Z. .....................'18 '39 C.597 B.S. L.596 J.D. 816 Masselin Ave.‡
Deutsch, Robert ..............................'49 '85 L.1190 LL.B. 201 N. Figueroa St., 7th Fl.
**Deutsch, Shirley D.** ....................'52 '77 C.112 B.A. L.813 J.D. [Littler,M.F.T.&M.]
*LANGUAGES: French.

**Deutsch & Rubin, (AV)** ⒷⒷ
**Second Floor, West Tower, 11377 West Olympic Boulevard, 90064-1683**
**Telephone: 310-312-3222 FAX: 310-312-3205**
**Members of Firm: Miles J. Rubin (A Professional Corporation); Wendy A. Herzog; Lauri A. Kritt. Of Counsel: Linda Cukier.**
**Family, Domestic Relations, Matrimonial and Divorce Law.**
*See Professional Biographies, LOS ANGELES, CALIFORNIA*

**De Vaney, Kathleen D.** ....................'63 '91 C.112 B.A. L.426 J.D. [Ⓐ Manatt,P.&P.]
*PRACTICE AREAS: Business Litigation; Bankruptcy Law.
**Devereaux, Peter W.** ..........................'54 '85 C.886 B.S. L.976 J.D. [Latham&W.]
*PRACTICE AREAS: Professional Liability, Securities, Financial Institutions and other Business Litigation.
**Devereux, Robin J.** ........................'64 '94 C.674 B.A. L.990 J.D. [Ⓐ Ropers,M.K.&B.]
*PRACTICE AREAS: Insurance Defense; Malpractice.
Devey, Mark R. ...............................'57 '89 C&L.101 B.A., J.D. 3255 Wilshire Blvd.
Devich, Robert R. '26 '65
C.670 B.A. L.809 LL.B. Assoc. Jus., Ct. of App., 2nd Dist., Div. 1
Devin, Marilyn ..................................................................'— '83 L.1148 J.D. I.R.S.
**Devirian, Donald B.,** (AV) ....................'45 '71 C.684 B.A. L.1068 J.D. [Devirian&S.]
*PRACTICE AREAS: General Trial Law; Civil Litigation; Construction Law.

**Devirian & Shinmoto, A Professional Corporation, (AV)**
**Wellesley Plaza, Suite 215, 12304 Santa Monica Boulevard, 90025**
**Telephone: 310-571-1600 Fax: 310-571-1609**
**Donald B. Devirian; Lynn A. Shinmoto;—Armenak Kavcioglu.**
**General Practice.**
*See Professional Biographies, LOS ANGELES, CALIFORNIA*

De Vita, E. Michele .......................'54 '82 C.184 B.A. L.809 J.D. 3109 Waverly Dr.
Devitre, Mark P. '65 '91 C.112 B.A. L.809 J.D.
Dir., Bus. & Legal Affs., Multimedia Motion Pictures, Inc.
Devitt, Dennis M. ..........................'42 '73 C.770 B.A. L.426 J.D. Dep. Co. Coun.
Devlin, Mary '54 '89 C.800 B.S. L.426 J.D.
TV Credits Admr., Writers Guild of America West, Inc.
DeVorkin, Alexander D. '49 '79
C.112 B.A. L.426 J.D. Dep. Atty. IV, Legal Div., Dept. of Trans.‡
Devorris, Guy E. '51 '77 C.1155 B.S.B.A. L.1202 J.D.
(adm. in MA; not adm. in CA) Associated Financial Corp.
**Devroom, Marney E.** '48 '77
C.012 B.Sc. L.101 J.D. Asst. Gen. Coun., Envir., Teledyne, Inc.
Dew, Scott C. ..........................'58 '85 C.475 B.A. L.477 J.D. 1801 Ave. of the Stars
**Dewar, Stephen M.** '57 '81 C&L.061 BPROC
(adm. in SAfric; not adm. in CA) [Ⓐ B.P.Wolfsdorf]
*PRACTICE AREAS: Immigration Law.
**Dewberry, Michael K.** ........................'52 '90 C.309 A.B. L.800 J.D. [Ⓐ Billet&K.]
*PRACTICE AREAS: Litigation.
Dewees, Rebecca S. ...........................'62 '87 C.112 B.A. L.1066 J.D. Asst. U.S. Atty.
**Dewell, John C.** ....................'62 '88 C.112 B.A. L.800 J.D. [Harrington,F.D.&C.]
Dewell, Louise .............................'50 '81 C.813 A.B. L.426 J.D. 2029 Century Pk. E.
**Dewey, Sandra A.** ......'61 '87 C.1060 B.S. L.1067 J.D. Coun., Turner Bdcstg., Sys., Inc.

**Dewey Ballantine, (AV)**
**333 South Hope Street, 90071-1406**⊙
**Telephone: 213-626-3399 Fax: 213-625-0562**
**Resident Partners: Alan M. Albright; Richard J. Burdge, Jr.; George T. Caplan; Kelly Charles Crabb; Lee Smalley Edmon; Robert W. Fischer, Jr.; David S. McLeod; Robert M. Smith; Kathy TeStrake Wales; Alan Wayte; Jeffrey R. Witham; Robert Woll; Donald F. Woods, Jr. Counsel: Scotta E. McFarland. Of Counsel: John K. Van De Kamp. Resident Associates: Jeffrey A. Barker; Michael R. Beeman; Heidi M. Binford; Anthony Castrilli, Jr.; Albert B. Choi; James S. Cochran; Peter E. Cohan; John P. Flynn; Eric P. Geismar; Jon M. Greenbaum; Chihoe Hahn; David A. Hamburger; Maren H. Hendricks; Allen W. Hubsch, Jr.; Howard M. Levkowitz; Brian D. McAllister; Harry A Olivar Jr.; Peter G. Phan; Kurt A. Ressler; Patrick S. Schoenburg; Lisa Dearden Trepanier; Matthew M. Walsh; Andrew E. Zobler.**
**General Practice.**
**Other offices: New York, New York; Washington, D.C.; London, England; Hong Kong; Budapest, Hungary; Prague, Czech Republic; and Warsaw, Poland.**
*See Professional Biographies, LOS ANGELES, CALIFORNIA*

DeWinne, Werner K. ......................'33 '70 C.999 L.809 J.D. 1605 W. Olympic Blvd.
DeWitt, Caroline L. ......................'67 '94 C.659 B.A. L.30 J.D. 601 S. Figueroa St.
**DeWitt, Nicholas,** (AV) ........................'50 '79 C.347 B.S. L.426 J.D. [Paul,H.J.&W.]
**DeWitt, Robert A., (P.C.),** (AV) .........'31 '63 C.112 B.A. L.813 LL.B. [Paul,H.J.&W.]
**De Witt, Susan J.** ..............................'61 '87 C.112 B.S. L.276 J.D. [Ⓐ White&C.]
Dey, Sally C. ..........................'62 '95 C.112 B.A. L.809 J.D. 12424 Wilshire Blvd., Ste. 900
**DeYoung, Laurie** ..............................'66 '91 C.569 B.A. L.990 J.D. [Ⓐ Fonda,G.H.&D.]

CAA212P

**Dhillon, Janet L.** .................'62 '92 C.605 B.A. L.1068 J.D. [A Skadden,A.S.M.&F.]
**Dial, William K.**, (AV) ...............'40 '68 C.976 A.B. L.1066 J.D. [Pillsbury M.&S.]
**Diamant, Lawrence A.**, (AV) .......'42 '67 C&L.1068 B.A., LL.B. [Robinson,D.B.&K.]
*PRACTICE AREAS: Bankruptcy Law; Insolvency; Reorganization.
**Diamond, Alan J.** .......................'50 '74 C.569 B.F.A. L.273 J.D. [M.A.Lotman]
Diamond, Andrew W. .......................'48 '73 C.1077 L.1095 J.D. Dep. Dist. Atty.
**Diamond, Barbara R.** .......................'29 '75 C.70 B.A. L.705 J.D. [Arter&H.]
**Diamond, Charles P.**, (AV) ............'47 '73 C.112 B.A. L.569 J.D. [O'Melveny&M.]
*PRACTICE AREAS: Litigation; Entertainment Litigation.
Diamond, Donna G. .......................'54 '86 C.183 B.A. L.276 J.D. 633 W. 5th St.
Diamond, Eric J. .......................'61 '87 C.893 B.A. L.1068 J.D. [Clinco,F.&D.]
Diamond, Jacqueline ...............'60 '87 C.112 B.A. L.426 J.D. 11859 Wilshire Blvd.
Diamond, Larry .......................'48 '74 C.112 B.A. L.1068 J.D. Dep. Dist. Atty.
**Diamond, Richard K., (A Professional Corporation)**, (AV) '50 '76
C.112 A.B. L.1068 J.D. [Danning,G.D.&K.]
Diamond, Richard S., (AV) '35 '62
C.112 B.S. L.1068 LL.B. 3620 Mandeville Canyon Rd.
**Diamond, Scott R.**, (AV) '52 '80 C.1029 B.S. L.809 J.D.
[Dummit,F.&B.] (©San Diego)
**Diamond, Stanley J.**, (AV) ...............'27 '53 C.112 A.B. L.800 J.D. [Diamond&W.]
*PRACTICE AREAS: Entertainment Law; Music Recording Law; Motion Picture Law; Television Law.

**Diamond & Wilson, (AV)**
**Suite 300, 12304 Santa Monica Boulevard, 90025**
**Telephone: 310-820-7808 Fax: 310-826-9658**
**Members of Firm: Stanley J. Diamond; James J. Wilson.**
**Entertainment, Music, Motion Picture, Television, Copyright and Intellectual Property Law.**
**Reference: City National Bank, Beverly Hills.**
***See Professional Biographies, LOS ANGELES, CALIFORNIA***

**Diaz, Charles R.** .......................'53 '81 C.1168 B.A. L.800 J.D. [Ives,K.&D.]
**Diaz, Dennis S.** .......................'52 '80 C.112 B.A. L.1068 J.D. [Musick,P.&G.]
*PRACTICE AREAS: Healthcare; Hospitals; Corporate Law.
Diaz, Humberto .......................'57 '92 C.46 B.S. L.1068 J.D. Dep. Fed. Pub. Def.
**Diaz, Kristina M.** .......................'64 '90 C.154 B.A. L.1066 J.D. [A Troop M.S.&P.]
*PRACTICE AREAS: General Business Litigation; Securities Litigation.
**Diaz, Manuel J.** .......................'63 '92 C&L.112 B.A., J.D. [A Stringfellow&Assoc.]
*LANGUAGES: Spanish.
Diaz, Mario E., (A Professional Corporation) '52 '77
C.800 B.S. L.770 J.D. 6255 Sunset Blvd.
**DiBiase, David T.**, (AV) ...............'48 '73 C.800 B.A. L.1068 J.D. [Anderson,M.&C.]
*PRACTICE AREAS: Surety and Fidelity Bond Law; Legal Professional Liability Defense; Title Insurance Law; Real Estate (Property) Law; Bad Faith Litigation.
**DiBiase, Michael J.** .......................'53 '79 C.112 B.A. L.1068 J.D. [Hill,F.&B.]
*PRACTICE AREAS: Securities Law; Corporate Finance Law; Mergers & Acquisitions Law; Corporate Governance Law; Partnership Law.
Dicker, Barry R. .......................'42 '69 C.112 A.B. L.1068 J.D. 1326 N. Wetherly Dr.
Dickerman, Robert S. ........'19 '49 C.112 B.S. L.426 J.D. 2121 Ave. of the Stars, 6th Fl.
Dickerman, William .......................'51 '77 C.112 B.A. L.800 J.D. 2049 Century Park E.
Dickerson, Charles E., III .......................'52 '80 C.329 B.S. L.904 J.D. 1717 Virginia Rd.
**Dickerson, Jaffe D.** .......................'50 '77 C.321 B.A. L.93 J.D. [Littler,M.F.T.&M.]
Dickerson, Kenneth R. .....'35 '60 C&L.466 B.A., LL.B. Sr. V.P., External Affs., ARCO
**Dickerson, Robert W.** ..........'50 '79 C.112 B.S. L.809 J.D. [Lyon&L.] (See Pat. Sect.)
*PRACTICE AREAS: Intellectual Property.
Dickey, Todd R. '64 '93 C.112 B.A. L.800 J.D.
Univ. Coun., University of Southern Calif.
**Dicks, Mark Jeffry** .......................'56 '86 C.502 B.A. L.1068 J.D. [A Hooper,L.&B.]
*LANGUAGES: French.
*PRACTICE AREAS: Health Care; Business Law.
**Dickson, B. Alan**, (AV) .......................'43 '69 C.976 B.A. L.309 J.D. [Epstein B.&G.]
**Dickson, Gary L.** .......................'49 '78 C&L.629 B.S., J.D. [Latham&W.]
Dickson, Janet H. .......................'58 '91 C.112 B.A. L.1068 J.D. 555 W. 5th St.
**Dickson, Mary LePique** ...........'60 '91 C.346 B.S. L.809 J.D. [A Buchalter,N.F.&Y.]
*PRACTICE AREAS: Real Estate Development; Real Estate Finance.

**Dickson, Carlson & Campillo**
**(See Santa Monica)**

**Didak, Mark F.**, (AV) .......................'57 '82 C.685 B.A. L.800 J.D. [Didak&J.]
*PRACTICE AREAS: Insurance Coverage and Defense; Bad Faith; Legal Malpractice; Statutory Corporations; Civil Appeals.

**Didak & Jack, (AV)** [BB]
**11755 Wilshire Boulevard, 15th Floor, 90025**
**Telephone: 310-473-7173 Fax: 310-312-1077**
**Members of Firm: Mark F. Didak; Travis R. Jack.**
**Insurance Coverage/Bad Faith; Legal Malpractice; Torts/Contract Litigation; Statutory Corporations; Fidelity Insurance; Real Estate. Civil Appeals.**
***See Professional Biographies, LOS ANGELES, CALIFORNIA***

**Diederichs, Brenda L.** .......................'57 '90 C.1074 B.A. L.426 J.D. [Richards,W.&G.]
*PRACTICE AREAS: Labor Law; Employment.
**Diedrich, Peter J.** .......................'55 '81 C.112 B.A. L.276 J.D. [A Beck,D.D.B.&O.]
*PRACTICE AREAS: Business and Commercial Litigation; Real Estate Litigation; Construction Litigation.
**Diehl, Katia T.** .......................'67 '93 C.112 B.A. L.1065 J.D. [A Manatt,P.&P.]
*PRACTICE AREAS: Family Law; Litigation.
**Diehl, Lauren T.**, (BV) .......................'55 '83 C.976 B.A. L.276 J.D. [Crosby,H.R.&M.]
Dierberger, Wesley A. '10 '38 C.911 B.B.A. L.273 J.D.
(adm. in DC; not adm. in CA) Int. Rev. Serv.
**Digby, Matthew E.** .......................'51 '79 C.602 B.A. L.178 J.D. [Marks&M.]
*LANGUAGES: Japanese.
Di Giuseppe, James .......................'28 '56 C.877 B.S. L.1068 LL.B. Mun. Ct. J.
**Di Lando, Michael A.**, (AV)........'59 '85 C.1077 B.A. L.426 J.D. [Robinson,D.&W.]©
*PRACTICE AREAS: Professional Errors and Omissions; Product Liability.
**Diliberto, Michael R.** .......................'58 '87 C&L.472 B.M., J.D. [Arant,K.L.&R.]
*LANGUAGES: Spanish.
*PRACTICE AREAS: Intellectual Property Litigation; Intellectual Property Law; Copyright Law; Trademark Law; Entertainment Law.
**Dilkes, C. Edward** .......................'42 '71 C.605 A.B. L.800 J.D. [Richards,W.&G.]
*REPORTED CASES: HFH v. Superior Court (Vons) 15 Cal 3rd 508 (1975); Regus v. Baldwin Park 70 Cal App. 3d 968 (1977).
*PRACTICE AREAS: Eminent Domain; Municipal Law; Environmental Law; Litigation.
Dill, David G. '40 '68 C.610 B.B.A. L.608 J.D.
(adm. in OH; not adm. in CA) Sr. V.P., Karsten Realty Advisors
**Dillingham, Blase P.** .......................'46 '76 C.813 B.A. L.800 J.D. [Pillsbury M.&S.]
**Dillman, Kirk D.**, (AV) ...............'56 '83 C.685 B.A. L.1068 J.D. [Augustini,W.&D.]
**Dillman, Lori Huff** .......................'58 '83 C.608 B.S. L.309 J.D. [Sidley&A.]
*PRACTICE AREAS: Business Litigation; Products Liability; Reinsurance.
**Dillon, Marian J.** '62 '88
C.352 B.B.A. L.846 J.D. [O'Melveny&M.] (©New York, N.Y.)
*PRACTICE AREAS: Corporate Law.
**Dilts, Gregory A.** .......................'64 '93 C.1128 B.S. L.990 J.D. [A Kearney,B.&C.]
DiMaria, Mark E., (AV) ...............'54 '79 C&L.800 A.B., J.D. 1900 Ave. of the Stars
**DiMeglio, David J.** .......................'62 '87 C.112 B.A. L.813 J.D. [Jones,D.R.&P.]

**D'Incognito, Myrna L.** ...............'55 '90 C.1075 B.A. L.809 J.D. [A Ginsburg,S.O.&R.]
**Dinerman, Kristina H.** .......................'69 '94 C&L.426 B.A., J.D. [A Paul,H.J.&W.]
**Ding, Boise A.** .......................'67 '94 C.103 A.B. L.309 J.D. [A Mayer,B.&P.]
**DiNicola, Ronald A., (A Professional Corporation)** '56 '82
C.309 A.B. L.276 J.D. [Mitchell,S.&K.]
*PRACTICE AREAS: Litigation; Entertainment Law.
**Dinielli, David C.** .......................'68 '95 C.309 A.B. L.477 J.D. [A Munger,T.&O.]
**Dinino, Karen R.** .......................'64 '89 C.112 B.A. L.800 J.D. [A Stroock&S.&L.]
*PRACTICE AREAS: Employment Litigation; Business Litigation; Real Estate Litigation.
**Dinneen, Edith N.** .......................'48 '74 C.788 A.B. L.93 J.D. [Lane P.S.L.]
*PRACTICE AREAS: Employment Law, Litigation and Communications Law.
Dinsmore, Scott D. .......................'63 '90 Century Park East, 15th Fl.
**Dintzer, Jeffrey David** .......................'62 '88 C.112 B.A. L.94 J.D. [A Gibson,D.&C.]
*PRACTICE AREAS: Environmental Litigation; Environmental Due Diligence; Business Litigation.
**Dion, Gregory T.** .......................'63 '90 C.112 B.A. L.426 J.D. [A Burke,W.&S.]
*PRACTICE AREAS: Civil Litigation; Employment Law; Environmental Law; Land Use Law.
**Dion, Raymond C.** .......................'55 '88 C.1077 B.A. L.426 J.D. [A A.R.Hamrick,III]
*PRACTICE AREAS: Insurance Coverage; Insurance Defense; Civil Litigation; Bad Faith Litigation; Wrongful Termination and Employment Litigation.
**Dion-Kindem, Peter R.**, (AV) ...............'55 '80 C.747 B.A. L.1068 J.D. [Buchanan&K.]
*REPORTED CASES: Epstein v. MCA Inc., 50 F.3d 644 (9th. Cir. 1995); California Air Resources Board v. Hart, 21 Cal.App.4th 289 (1993); McCann v. Welden, 153 Cal.App.3d 814 (1984); Stevens v. Rifkin, 608 F.Supp. 710 (N.D.Cal. 1984).
*PRACTICE AREAS: Securities Litigation; Commercial Litigation; Insurance; Partnership Disputes; Corporate Law.
**Di Saia, Steven D.** .......................'66 '92 C.112 B.A. L.1065 J.D. [A Sedgwick,D.M.&A.]
Disse, Werner .......................'59 '89 C.813 B.A. L.569 LL.M. 1801 Ave. of the Stars
**Dito, John A.**, (AV) .......................'35 '62 C.813 B.A. L.309 LL.B. [Sinnott,D.M.&P.]
*PRACTICE AREAS: Insurance Coverage; General Litigation; Trial Practice.
Divens, Jon A. .......................'55 '89 C&L.1097 B.A., J.D. 8961 W. Sunset Blvd.
**Dix, Simon** ...............'50 '86 C.050 M.A. L.856 J.D. [Forward&D.] (©Bologna, Italy)
*LANGUAGES: Italian and French.
*PRACTICE AREAS: International Business; Business; Entertainment.
**Dixon, Lance R.** .......................'70 '94 C&L.061 B.A., LL.B. [A Buchalter,N.F.&Y.]
*PRACTICE AREAS: Business Law; Commerical Litigation; International Transactions and Litigation.
Dixon, Howell, Westmoreland & Newman, (AV) .......................924 Westwood Blvd.

**Dixon & Jessup, Ltd., L.L.P.**
**Suite 2000, Wells Fargo Center, 333 South Grand Avenue, 90071-1524©**
**Telephone: 213-346-8310 Fax: 213-620-1811**
**Clifton R. Jessup, Jr. (Not admitted in CA). Of Counsel: J. Scott Bovitz (Certified Specialist, Personal and Small Business Bankruptcy Law, The State Bar of California Board of Legal Specialization); Susan Michelle Spitzer; Nancy A. Cherney, Senior Vice President, General Counsel and Corporate Secretary.**
**Bankruptcy, Banking, Securities, Corporate, Commercial Finance, International, Real Estate, Insurance Regulation, Legislation, Litigation, and Employment.**
**Omaha, Nebraska Office: One First National Center, Sixteenth & Dodge Streets, Suite 1800, 68102. Telephone: 402-345-3900. Fax: 402-345-0965 or 402-345-3341.**
**Washington, D.C. Office: 1850 M Street, N.W., Suite 450, 20036. Telephone: 202-452-1034. Fax: 202-452-1822.**
**Dallas, Texas Office: Suite 5500, Fountain Place, 1445 Ross Avenue, 75202-2733. Telephone: 214-754-0155. Fax: 214-754-0704.**
**Kuwait City Office: Al-Hilali Street, Murgab, Al-Burrak Building 2, P.O. Box 22833 SAFAT, 13089. Telephone: 011-965-241-5617. Fax: 011-965-240-7030.**
***See Professional Biographies, LOS ANGELES, CALIFORNIA***

**Dizenfeld, Bruce E.** .......................'53 '78 C.800 B.A. L.1068 J.D. [Ginsburg,S.O.&R.]
*PRACTICE AREAS: Healthcare; Business Organization; Intellectual Property; Licensing.
Djeu, Deborah Daphne .........'62 '88 C.477 B.A. L.209 J.D. U.S. Secs. & Exch. Comm.
Dlug, Sam .......................'42 '67 C.112 B.S. L.1068 LL.B. 6357 Colgate St.
**Doan, R. Stephen**, (AV) ...............'49 '74 C.112 B.A. L.1068 J.D. [Morrison&F.]
*PRACTICE AREAS: Business; Real Estate; Tax; Estate Planning; Probate.
**Dobberteen, Eric L.**, (AV) ...............'48 '73 C.932 B.A. L.945 J.D. [Arnold&P.]
*PRACTICE AREAS: White Collar Criminal Defense Law; Complex Civil Litigation.
Dobberteen, Kenyon F., (BV) ...........'45 '71 C.112 B.A. L.1068 J.D. [Dobberteen&L.]
Dobberteen & Luna, (BV) .......................3540 Wilshire Blvd.
Dobbs, Ann, (AV) '37 '84 C.999 L.809 J.D.
Asst. Dean, Southwestern Univ. School of Law
Doble, Arthur V. .......................'32 '58 C.912 B.S. L.213 LL.B. [Shaffer,D.P.&G.]
Dobrin, Jon-Marc, (AV) .......................'52 '77 C.112 B.A. L.426 J.D. [J.Dobrin]©
Dobrin, Jon-Marc, A Prof. Corp., (AV) .......................12400 Wilshire Blvd.
**Dobson, Mitzie L.** .......................'63 '94 C.378 B.S.J. L.426 J.D. [A Bonne,B.M.O.&N.]
**Dobson, Thomas W.**, (AV) .......................'42 '67 C.426 B.A. L.800 J.D. [Latham&W.]
Dockweiler, Frederick C., (AV) ...............'09 '35 C.813 A.B. L.276 J.D. [Dockweiler&D.]
Dockweiler & Dockweiler, (AV) .......................2650 West Temple Street
**Doctor, Randall A.** .......................'62 '87 C.112 B.A. L.1065 J.D. [A Barger&W.]
*PRACTICE AREAS: General Corporate Law; Insurance Regulatory Law.
**Doctors, Jerome P.** .......................'63 '89 C.112 B.A. L.809 J.D. [A Lynberg&W.]
*REPORTED CASES: Sargoy v. Resolution Trust Corporation, et al. 10 Cal. Rptr. 2d 889 (Cal. App. 2 Dist. 1992).
*PRACTICE AREAS: Probate Law; Civil Litigation.
**Dodd, D. Scott** .......................'67 '94 C.112 B.A. L.800 J.D. [A Chapman&G.]
*PRACTICE AREAS: Construction Defect; Personal Injury; Premises Liability; Insurance Coverage.
**Dodd, John H.** .......................'61 '88 C.112 B.A. L.809 J.D. [A Bonne,B.M.O.&N.]
Dodd, Yvonne Jensen .......................'— '85 C.813 B.A. L.426 J.D. Dep. Dist. Atty.
**Dodds, Douglas A.** .......................'50 '76 C.112 A.B. L.1067 J.D. [Morgan,L.&B.]
Doddy, Robert V., (AV) .......................'42 '68 C.940 B.A. L.1068 J.D. Dep. Pub. Def.
Dodell, Herbert .......................'39 '64 C.665 B.A. L.1009 J.D. [H.Dodell]
Dods, Laurie Bierman .....'66 '92 C.112 B.A. L.426 J.D. Legal Div., State Dept. of Trans.
Doheny, William H., Jr. .......................'47 '75 C.813 B.A. L.426 J.D. Doheny Asset Mgmt.‡
Doherty, Frank W., (AV) ...........'15 '40 C.770 B.S. L.426 LL.B. 811 Wilshire Blvd.‡
**Doherty, John J.**, (BV) .......................'46 '76 C.800 L.426 J.D. [Williamson,R.&D.]
*PRACTICE AREAS: Insurance Defense; Bad Faith; Professional Malpractice; Products Liability; Business Litigation.
**Doherty, Mary Katherine** .......'58 '89 C.112 B.A. L.426 J.D. [A La Follette,J.D.F.&A.]
*PRACTICE AREAS: Medical Malpractice.
**Doherty, Moira** .......................'63 '90 C.156 B.A. L.30 J.D. [Katz,H.S.&K.]
*PRACTICE AREAS: Civil Litigation; Bankruptcy; Debtor/Creditor Relations; Business Law.
**Doherty, Penelope D.** .......................'67 '93 C.36 B.A. L.37 J.D. [A Morris,P.&P.]
Dohi, Gregory A. .......................'65 '91 C.309 L.1066 Dep. Dist. Atty.
Dohr, Heidi L. .......................'66 '92 C.800 B.A. L.990 J.D. [A Casterline&A.]
Dohrmann, Barbara H. ........'37 '63 C&L.800 B.S., LL.B. Gen. Coun., Charles Dunn Co.
**Dohrmann, Robert M.**, (AV) ...........'35 '63 C.770 B.S. L.800 LL.B. [Schwartz,S.D.&S.]
*PRACTICE AREAS: Labor and Employment Law; Employee Benefits Litigation; Public Sector Employment Relations; Collective Bargaining Law.
**Doi, Steven S.** ...........'62 '87 C.668 B.A. L.1068 J.D. [Graham&J.] (©Tokyo, Japan)
*PRACTICE AREAS: International Business Law.
**Dolan, Peter Brown**, (AV) ...............'39 '67 C.871 B.S. L.800 J.D. [Morgan,L.&B.]
Dolan, Robert T. .......................'57 '83 C.93 B.A. L.990 J.D. [Gaglione&D.]
**Doland, Michael C.**, (AV) .......................'51 '77 C&L.276 B.A., J.D. [Doland&G.]
*LANGUAGES: Italian, French, Spanish.

CAA213P

**Doland & Gould, (AV)**
**10866 Wilshire Boulevard, Suite 300, 90024**
**Telephone: 310-478-1000 FAX: 310-446-1363**
**Email: EUROLEX@AOL.COM**
**Michael C. Doland; Howard N. Gould.**
**Domestic and International Business and Real Estate Transactions and Litigation, Insurance and Bankruptcy Law.**
***See Professional Biographies, LOS ANGELES, CALIFORNIA***

Dolezel, Janine M. ....... '46 '72 C.770 B.A. L.813 J.D. Chief Coun., U.S. Dept. of H.U.D.
**Dolginer, Charles I.**, (AV) .................. '37 '65 C.112 B.A. L.174 J.D. [Stone,D.&W.]
*PRACTICE AREAS: Personal Injury; Malpractice; Products Liability; Aviation; Civil Trial.

**Dolin, Norman M., (AV) '32 '60 C.112 B.A. L.426 J.D.**
**Suite 2200, 1925 Century Park East (Century City), 90067-2723**
**Telephone: 310-552-9338 Fax: 310-552-1922**
**(Certified Specialist, Family Law, The State Bar of California Board of Legal Specialization).**
***PRACTICE AREAS: Family Law.**
**Associates: Lynn Langley; Ani M. Garikian.**
**Family Law.**
***See Professional Biographies, LOS ANGELES, CALIFORNIA***

**Dolinsky, Joan M.** .......................... '49 '76 C.483 B.A. L.884 J.D. [Cotkin&C.]
*LANGUAGES: French.
*PRACTICE AREAS: Insurance Coverage; Insurance Bad Faith Litigation; Complex Business Litigation; Legal Malpractice Defense; Employment Practices Litigation.
**Dollbaum, Margaret R.** .................. '50 '80 C.112 B.A. L.1068 J.D. [Folger L.&K.]⊙
Dolle, Carol L. ............................'— '78 C.800 B.S. L.809 J.D. Princ. Dep. Co. Coun.
**Dolle, Hodge L., Jr.**, (AV) ...................... '34 '62 C&L.800 B.S., J.D. [Dolle&D.]
*PRACTICE AREAS: Condemnation Law; Inverse Condemnation Law; Zoning and Land Use Law.

**Dolle and Dolle, A Professional Corporation, (AV)**
**11766 Wilshire Boulevard, Suite 1450, 90025**
**Telephone: 310-478-7516 Fax: 310-478-2780**
**Hodge L. Dolle, Jr.;—Lawrence H. Thompson; Thomas M. Garcin. Of Counsel: Hodge L. Dolle (1908-1989).**
**Condemnation, Inverse Condemnation, Zoning and Land Use.**
***See Professional Biographies, LOS ANGELES, CALIFORNIA***

Dollinger, Jeffrey A. ........................ '63 '90 C.112 B.A. L.94 J.D. 601 S. Figueroa
**Dollinger, Thomas W.** ............. '50 '79 C.1062 B.A. L.1009 J.D. [Proskauer R.G.&M.]
*PRACTICE AREAS: Corporate.
**Dolman, Maurice H., (P.C.)**, (AV) .......... '13 '54 C.112 B.S. L.426 J.D. [Dolman&S.]
*PRACTICE AREAS: Tax Law; Probate Law; Trust Law; Estate Planning.

**Dolman & Samuels, (AV)**
**A Partnership of Professional Corporations**
**Suite 2300, 1900 Avenue of the Stars, 90067**
**Telephone: 310-201-0777 Telecopier: 310-556-1346**
**Maurice H. Dolman (P.C.) (Certified Specialist, Taxation Law, The State Bar of California Board of Legal Specialization); S. Zachary Samuels (P.C.).**
**Corporation, Real Property, Estate Planning, Probate, State and Federal Tax Law. Administrative, Commercial Law.**
**Reference: 1st Business Bank, Los Angeles.**
***See Professional Biographies, LOS ANGELES, CALIFORNIA***

**Dombek, Curt M.** .................................... '58 '83 C&L.309 A.B., J.D. [Bryan C.]
*LANGUAGES: German.
*PRACTICE AREAS: Litigation; International Arbitration; International Trade Regulation; Aviation and Space Law.
Domingo, Socrates G. .................... '56 '88 C&L.061 B.A., B.L. 3701 Wilshire Blvd.
**Dominguez, Juan Carlos** ...... '63 '89 C.800 B.A.B.S. L.112 J.D. [[A] McDermott,W.&E.]
*LANGUAGES: Spanish.
Dominguez, Juan J. .......... '57 '87 C.1042 B.A. L.1065 J.D. 3250 Wilshire Blvd., Pthse.
Don, Jeffrey J. ...................................... '53 '78 C.112 B.A. L.800 J.D. 727 W. 7th St.

**Donahoe, Karen Phillips, Law Offices of, (AV) '55 '80 C.112 B.A. L.1065 J.D.**
**12100 Wilshire Boulevard 16th Floor, 90025**
**Telephone: 310-442-1488 Fax: 310-442-1490**
***PRACTICE AREAS: Family Law; Divorce Law; Custody Law; Pre-Nuptial Agreements.**
**General Civil Litigation in all State and Federal Courts.**
***See Professional Biographies, LOS ANGELES, CALIFORNIA***

**Donahue, Michael D.**, (AV) ................ '44 '69 C.602 B.A. L.174 J.D. [Donahue&M.]
*SPECIAL AGENCIES: United States Securities Exchange Commission; State Securities Administrators; New York Stock Exchange; American Stock Exchange; National Association of Securities Dealers, Inc.
*PRACTICE AREAS: Securities; General Business and Corporate; Investment Banking and Venture Capital; Securities Litigation and Arbitration.
**Donahue, Thomas E.** ............................ '61 '91 C.627 B.A. L.809 J.D. [[A] Fonda,G.H.&D.]

**Donahue & Mesereau, (AV)**
**A Partnership including a Professional Corporation**
**1900 Avenue of the Stars Suite 2700, 90067**
**Telephone: 310-277-1441 Telecopier: 310-277-2888**
**Email: SECORPLAW@AWOL.com**
**Michael D. Donahue; Thomas A. Mesereau, Jr. (Professional Corporation); Dave Lenny; Asher M. Leids; Susan H. Tregub.**
**General and International Business and Corporate Matters. Securities Transactions and Regulations. Investment Banking, Venture Capital, Mergers and Acquisitions, Franchising. Securities Litigation and Arbitration. Business Litigation in State and Federal Courts. Criminal Defense (State and Federal).**
***See Professional Biographies, LOS ANGELES, CALIFORNIA***

**Donaldson, Robert D.** ..................... '44 '73 C.976 B.A. L.880 J.D. [[A] Dempsey&J.]
*PRACTICE AREAS: Business Litigation; Securities Fraud; Directors and Officers Liability; Accountant's Liability.
Donegan, John C., (BV) .............. '50 '77 C.766 B.A. L.464 J.D. Prob. Atty., Supr. Ct.
**Donfeld, Jeffrey E., (A Professional Corporation)**, (AV) '43 '69
C.112 B.A. L.1066 J.D. [Donfeld,K.&R.]
*PRACTICE AREAS: Real Estate Acquisitions; Leasing; Workouts; Land Use; Partnership Formations.

**Donfeld, Kelley & Rollman, (AV)**
**A Partnership including a Professional Corporation**
**Suite 1245, 11845 West Olympic Boulevard, 90064**
**Telephone: 310-312-8080 Telecopier: 310-312-8014**
**Jeffrey E. Donfeld (A Professional Corporation); Paul M. Kelley; Fredric A. Rollman;—Amy Semmel.**
**Real Estate, Acquisitions, Leasing, Work-outs and Land Use, Partnership Formations, Corporations, Unfair Competition and Trade Regulation, General Business and Business Litigation, Construction and Construction Defect Defense, Employer/Employee Dispute Resolution, Family Law. General Civil Trial and Appellate Practice.**
**Reference: Marathon National Bank.**
***See Professional Biographies, LOS ANGELES, CALIFORNIA***

Dong, Braden V. ........................ '64 '91 C.685 B.A. L.112 J.D. 12400 Wilshire Blvd.
**Dongell, Richard A.** ..................... '61 '87 C.645 B.A. L.831 J.D. [Radcliff,F.&D.]
**Doniger, Thomas**, (AV) ....................... '45 '77 C.112 B.A. L.800 J.D. [Doniger&F.]
*PRACTICE AREAS: Business Litigation; Entertainment Litigation; Civil Appeals.

**Doniger & Fetter, (AV)**
**606 South Olive Street, Suite 530, 90014**
**Telephone: 213-488-7733 Facsimile: 213-488-7734**

(This Listing Continued)

**Doniger & Fetter (Continued)**
**Members of Firm: Thomas Doniger; Henry David Fetter.**
**General Civil Trial and Appellate Practice, Entertainment and General Business Litigation.**
***See Professional Biographies, LOS ANGELES, CALIFORNIA***

Donin, Dean M.; (BV) ........................ '45 '74 C.112 B.S. L.809 J.D. P.O. Box 34400
**Donlan, James F.** ............................ '52 '78 C.674 A.B. L.309 J.D. [[C] Sidley&A.]
*LANGUAGES: French and Italian.
*PRACTICE AREAS: Business Transactions; Real Estate Law.
**Donlon, Kimberly A.** ........... '61 '93 C.800 B.A. L.809 J.D. [[A] Berger,K.S.M.F.S.&G.]
**Donnelly, Brian J.** ........................ '37 '66 C.980 B.A. L.30 J.D. [[C] Paul,H.J.&W.]
Donnelly, John A. ................... '37 '67 C&L.426 A.B., J.D. Sr. Coun., Calif. Fed. Bk.

**Donnelly, Clark, Chase & Smiland**
**(See Smiland & Khachigian)**

**Donnenfeld, Bernard, (A Professional Corporation)**, (AV) '26 '50
C&L.569 B.A., J.D. [[C] Mitchell,S.&K.]
*PRACTICE AREAS: Entertainment Law; Intellectual Property and Copyright Law.
**D'Onofrio, Joseph** .................. '56 '82 C.674 A.B. L.659 J.D. [Armstrong H.J.T.&W.]
*PRACTICE AREAS: Real Estate.
Donoghue, Laurence B. ..................... '41 '72 C.112 B.S. L.284 J.D. Dep. Dist. Atty.

**Donovan, James M., Law Offices of, (AV) '43 '69 C.128 B.A. L.472 J.D.**
**515 South Figueroa Street, Suite 1000, 90071-3327**
**Telephone: 213-629-4861 Telecopier: 213-689-8784**
**Email: tdolaw@aol.com**
**Associates: Mark D. Maisonneuve; Michael J. Glenn. Of Counsel: Louis LaRose (1914-1986); Robert L. Fairman; Egon Dumler (Not admitted in CA); Richard S. Missan (Not admitted in CA); Peter R. Bierstedt; Martin Habdank (Not admitted in the United States); Graham L. Sterling, III; Carol Lynn Akiyama; Stephen M. Losh; Richard J. Kellum; John S. Preston; Walt D. Mahaffa; Babak Sotoodeh; Richard D. Saba (Not admitted in CA); Howard M. Bartnof.**
**General Commercial Practice. Business, International Business, Corporate, Securities, Real Estate, Labor, Agricultural, Estate Planning, Trust, Probate, Tax, State and Federal Criminal Trials, Entertainment, Advertising, Publishing and Family Law, Life Insurance, Commercial Casualty Insurance and Business Litigation.**
**Reference: Bank of California, Los Angeles Main Office.**
***See Professional Biographies, LOS ANGELES, CALIFORNIA***

**Donovan, John A.** ........................ '42 '67 C.309 A.B. L.262 J.D. [Skadden,A.S.M.&F.]
Donovan, Philip J. ..................... '18 '51 C.426 B.S. L.800 J.D. 3255 Wilshire Blvs.
Donovan, Thomas B. ............ '35 '63 C.112 A.B. L.1066 LL.B. U.S. Bankruptcy J.

**Donovan Leisure Newton & Irvine, (AV)**
**Suite 4100, 333 South Grand Avenue, 90071⊙**
**Telephone: 213-253-4000 Cable Address: "Donlard, L.A." Telecopier: 213-617-2368; 213-617-3246**
**Members of Firm: Michael C. Cohen; James B. Hicks; Kathy A. Jorrie; Howard B. Soloway. Resident Associates: Shoshana B. Botnick; Christie Gaumer; Mithra Sheybani. Resident Counsel: Norman A. Jenkins, III (Not admitted in CA).**
**General Practice.**
**New York, New York Office: 30 Rockefeller Plaza. Telephone: 212-632-3000. Cable Address: "Donlard, N.Y." Telecopiers: 212-632-3315; 212-632-3321; 212-632-3322.**
**Paris, France Office: 130, rue du Faubourg Saint-Honoré, 75008 Paris. Telephone: 011-33-01-53-93-77-00. Telecopier: 011-33-01-42-56-08-06.**
**Palm Beach, Florida Office: 450 Royal Palm Way, Suite 450, 33480. Telephone: 561-833-1040. Telecopier: 561-835-8511.**
***See Professional Biographies, LOS ANGELES, CALIFORNIA***

**Donovan & Sapienza, Law Offices of**
**(See Santa Monica)**

**Donoyan, Maral** ................................. '65 '90 C.112 B.A. L.1097 J.D. [[A] Ford&H.]
Dooley, Jas. R. .............................. '20 '50 C.73 B.S. L.365 J.D. U.S. Bkrptcy. J.
**Dorais, Claude J.**, (AV) ...................... '49 '74 C.112 A.B. L.1067 J.D. [Dorais&W.]

**Dorais & Wheat, A Professional Law Corporation, (AV)**
**11726 San Vicente Boulevard, Suite 550, 90049**
**Telephone: 310-826-4400 FAX: 310-820-7397**
**Claude J. Dorais; Sheldon R. Emmer; Lawrence O. Graeber, III; Maureen A. Grattan; Eric Anthony Joe; Marilyn A. Monahan; James F. Wheat (1938-1985).**
**Insurance Corporate, Business and Regulatory Law. Employee Benefit Law. Litigation. Uniform Commercial Code Transactions.**
***See Professional Biographies, LOS ANGELES, CALIFORNIA***

**Doran, A. J. Connick** ......................... '21 '72 C.674 A.B. L.800 J.D. [[C] Stone,D.&W.]
**Doran, Carolyn Wade** ........... '56 '82 C.605 B.A. L.1148 J.D. [[A] Patterson,R.L.G.&J.]
**Doran, Kenneth M.** ........................ '55 '81 C.813 A.B. L.800 J.D. [Gibson,D.&C.]
*PRACTICE AREAS: Securities; Mergers, Acquisitions and Divestitures; Business Law; Corporate Law; Real Estate.
**Doran, Thomas A.** ........................ '39 '68 C.112 B.S. L.426 J.D. [Knapp,M.J.&D.]
*PRACTICE AREAS: Public Entity Law; Business Litigation; Workers Compensation Law; Construction Law.
**Doren, Richard J.** ......................... '60 '86 C.112 B.A. L.1049 J.D. [Gibson,D.&C.]
*PRACTICE AREAS: Litigation; Insurance.
**Dorian, Charissa** ............................ '64 '89 C.1077 B.A. L.809 J.D. [[A] Lord,B.&B.]
Dorland, William A. ................... '41 '66 C&L.813 B.A., LL.B. 633 W. 5th St.
Dorn, Albert A. .......................... '16 '38 L.588 LL.B. 5710 W. Manchester Ave.
Dorne, Robert ...................... '45 '71 C.112 B.A. L.1068 J.D. 1015 Gayley Ave.
Dornstein, Judith C., (BV) ............ '40 '72 C&L.569 B.A., J.D. 1888 Century Park E.
**Dornstein, Laurence A.** .................. '39 '64 C.188 B.S. L.569 LL.B. [Bivona&C.]⊙
**Doroshow, James Edward** ................. '53 '79 C.910 B.A. L.813 J.D. [[C] Belin R.&B.]
*PRACTICE AREAS: Litigation; Business; Construction Defect; Real Estate; Financial Institutions.
Dorris, Michael P. '57 '92 C.1042 B.S. L.796 J.D.
(adm. in TX; not adm. in CA) Spec. Agent, F.B.I.
**Dorrough, Stephen B.** ..................... '67 '94 C.101 B.A. L.878 J.D. [[A] Gibson,D.&C.]
*LANGUAGES: Cantonese, Mandarin.
*PRACTICE AREAS: Corporate Law; Securities.
**Dorse, Kevin A.** ............................ '61 '88 C.103 A.B. L.472 J.D. [[A] Jones,D.R.&P.]
Dorsey, Earl A. ............... '52 '88 C.1106 B.A. L.809 J.D. Thomas Sports Mgmt., Inc.
Dorsey, Paul R. .............. '25 '61 C.800 B.F.S. L.809 LL.B. 5827 E. Beverly Blvd.
**Dorsey, Steven Lee** ..................... '48 '73 C&L.813 A.B., J.D. [Richards,W.&G.]
*PRACTICE AREAS: Public Law; Government Contracts Law.
Doss, Wayne D., (AV) ................. '50 '76 C.112 B.A. L.426 J.D. Dep. Dist. Atty. IV
**Dossick, Harrison J.** ..................... '60 '87 C.477 B.G.S. L.94 J.D. [Troop M.S.&P.]
*PRACTICE AREAS: Entertainment Litigation; Business Litigation.
**Dotson, Jerald B.** ............................ '67 '94 C.277 B.S. L.1068 J.D. [[A] Irell&M.]
**Doty, Andrew K.** ......................... '62 '88 C.597 B.A. L.1068 J.D. [[A] Iverson,Y.P.&H.]
*PRACTICE AREAS: Employment Law; Civil Litigation.
Doty, G. Richard, (AV) ................. '28 '53 C&L.813 B.A., LL.B. 600 Wilshire Blvd.
**Doty, Martha Schreiber** '62 '89 C.112 B.A. L.1068 J.D.
[[A] McClintock,W.B.R.R.&M.]
*PRACTICE AREAS: Civil Appellate Practice; Business Litigation; Employment Law; Petroleum Marketing/Franchise Litigation.
Doty, Rod ........................ '50 '81 C&L.800 B.A., J.D. V.P. & Coun., Sanwa Bk. Calif.
**Dougherty, E. Paul, Jr.** '56 '81 C.276 B.S.B.A. L.884 J.D.
(adm. in NJ; not adm. in CA) [Wilson,E.M.E.&D.]
Dougherty, Michael H., (AV) ......... '34 '66 C.339 B.S. L.800 J.D. Chief Asst. City Atty.

CAA214P

Dougherty, Michelle J. '62 '87 C.473 Ph.B. L.880 J.D. 7700 Emerson Ave.
**Douglas, Carl E.**, (AV) '55 '81 C.597 B.A. L.1066 J.D. [J.L.Cochran,Jr.]
*PRACTICE AREAS: Civil Rights Litigation; Personal Injury; Business Litigation; Entertainment Litigation; Criminal Defense.
Douglas, Harry E., IV '62 '88 C.145 B.A. L.1066 J.D. 5900 Wilshire Blvd.
**Douglas, J. Andrew** '68 '93 C.112 B.A. L.800 J.D. [Long&L.]
**Douglas, Joel Bruce**, (AV) '48 '73 C.1077 B.A. L.426 J.D. [Bonne,B.M.O.&N.]
Douglas, John E. '54 '91 L.800 J.D. Pub. Def.

**Douglas, Keith W., Law Offices of, (AV) '42 '69 C.112 B.A. L.61 J.D.**
**12424 Wilshire Boulevard, Suite 900, 90025-1043**
**Telephone: 310-207-2727 Fax: 310-442-6400**
**Real Property Litigation, including Condemnation, Inverse Condemnation, Land Use, and related Environmental and Civil Rights Litigation.**
***See Professional Biographies, LOS ANGELES, CALIFORNIA***

Douglas, Marion Elizabeth '38 '73 C.112 B.A. L.809 J.D. Dep. Co. Coun.
**Douglas, Michael L.**, (AV) '52 '78 C.112 B.A. L.426 J.D. [Ibold&A.]
**Douglass, Sharon L.** '64 '90 C.154 B.A. L.426 J.D. [Arnold&P.]
*PRACTICE AREAS: Business Litigation.
Doumani, Edward M. '36 '60 C&L.800 B.S.L., LL.B. 2600 Aberdeen Way
Doumani, Peter J. '46 '72 C.112 B.S. L.426 J.D. P.O. Box 35558
Dowds, Norman R. '20 '44 C&L.800 B.A., LL.B. Supr. Ct. J.
Dowell, Mary L. '52 '77 C.112 B.A. L.1067 J.D. [Liebert,C.&F.]
Dowell, Michael A. '57 '83 C.679 B.S.Ph. L.1119 J.D. [Miller&H.]
**Dowling, Alan G.** '51 '76 C.477 B.A. L.800 J.D. [Shapiro,R.&C.]
*LANGUAGES: French.
*PRACTICE AREAS: Litigation; Entertainment Law.
**Dowling, Thomas J.**, (AV) '40 '72 C.426 B.A. L.800 J.D. [Kinkle,R.&S.]
Downer, Carol A. '33 '91 L.1148 J.D. One Wilshire Blvd.
**Downer, Michael J.** '55 '82
C.112 B.A. L.809 J.D. Asst. Gen. Coun., Capital Grp. Cos., Inc.
*RESPONSIBILITIES: Securities.
Downey, Julie P., (BV) '37 '77 C.112 B.A. L.426 LL.B. Asst. City Atty.
Downey, Peter Michael '61 '89 C.589 B.A. L.61 J.D. 12400 Wilshire Blvd.
**Downey, William J., III**, (AV) '47 '88 C.588 B.S. L.818 J.D. [Baum,H.A.G.&D.]
*PRACTICE AREAS: Catastrophic Injury; Products Liability - Drugs and Medical Devices; Products Liability; Construction Accidents; Mass Disaster Litigation.
**Downs, Gary P.** '62 '88 C.210 B.A. L.1065 J.D. [Cox,C.&N.]
*PRACTICE AREAS: Public Finance.
**Doyen, Michael R.** '55 '84 C.112 B.A. L.309 J.D. [Munger,T.&O.]
**Doyle, Brooks S., Jr.** '43 '68 C.125 B.A. L.896 J.D.
(adm. in NC; not adm. in CA) Coun., Hughes Aircraft Co.
**Doyle, Colleen P.** '53 '85 C.112 A.B. L.426 J.D. [McCutchen,D.B.&E.]
*PRACTICE AREAS: Environmental Law.
Doyle, D. Barton '50 '78 C.103 B.A. L.665 J.D. 550 S. Hope St.
Doyle, Julie M. '68 '94 C.976 B.A. L.309 J.D. 2049
**Doyle, Laura O.** '60 '93 C.1042 B.S. L.800 J.D. [McKenna&C.]
*PRACTICE AREAS: Government Contracts.
Doyle, Patricia K. '46 '80 C.959 B.S. L.809 J.D. Dep. Dist. Atty.
Doyle, Suzan Gail '60 '86
C.636 B.S. L.1067 J.D. Assoc. Coun., Auto. Club of Southern Calif.
Drachlis, Bernard P. '40 '69 C.112 B.S. L.1148 J.D. 5012 Eagle Rock Blvd. (Pat.)
**Dragna, James J.** '53 '79 C.112 B.A. L.426 J.D. [McCutchen,D.B.&E.]
*PRACTICE AREAS: Environmental Law.
**Dragonette, John A.** '67 '93 C.112 B.A. L.426 J.D. [Stephens,B.&L.]
*PRACTICE AREAS: Medical Malpractice.
**Drake, Donna** '65 '93 C.1042 B.S. L.426 J.D. [Howrey&S.]
*PRACTICE AREAS: Government Contracts; General Litigation.
Drake, William A. '18 '57 C.800 L.809 Supr. Ct. J.
**Draper, Jack Alden, II**, (BV) '50 '75 C.605 B.A. L.800 J.D. [J.A.Draper]
*LANGUAGES: German, Indonesian, Spanish and Cantonese.
*PRACTICE AREAS: Environmental; Natural Resources; Employment Law; Real Estate; International Law.
**Draper, Robert S.**, (AV) '42 '68 C.112 A.B. L.1066 J.D. [O'Melveny&M.]
*PRACTICE AREAS: Antitrust; Civil Trials; Accounting Law; Intellectual Property Litigation.

**Draper, Jack A., Law Offices of, (BV)**
**2121 Avenue of the Stars, Suite 1750, 90067**
**Telephone: 805-322-7272 FAX: 805-322-9359**
**Jack Alden Draper II.**
**Environmental, Natural Resources, Employment, Real Estate and International Law, Trials in all Courts.**
**Bakersfield, California Office: 901 Tower Way, Suite 301. Telephone: 805-322-7272. FAX: 805-322-9359.**
***See Professional Biographies, LOS ANGELES, CALIFORNIA***

**Drapkin, Larry C., (A Professional Corporation)**, (AV) '56 '81
C.112 B.A. L.1066 J.D. [Mitchell,S.&K.]
*PRACTICE AREAS: Labor Law; Employment Litigation.

**Drapkin, Steven, Law Offices of, (AV) '50 '76 C.112 B.A. L.1068 J.D.**
**11377 West Olympic Boulevard, Suite 900, 90064-1683**
**Telephone: 310-914-7909 Fax: 310-914-7959**
***REPORTED CASES: (Partial Listing) Foley v. Interactive Data, 47 Cal.3d 654 (1988); Newman v. Emerson Radio, 48 Cal.3d 973 (1989); Moore v. Conliffe, 7 Cal.4th 634 (1994); Jennings v. Marralle, 8 Cal.4th 121 (1994); Gantt v. Sentry Insurance Co. 1 Cal.4th 1083 (1992).**
**Lee W. Rierson.**
**All aspects of Labor and Employment Law. Exclusively representing Management including Arbitration, Litigation and Appellate Practice.**
***See Professional Biographies, LOS ANGELES, CALIFORNIA***

Drasin, Lawrence, (AV) '34 '57 C.102 B.A. L.178 J.D. 1849 Sawtelle Blvd.
Dray, Janet A. W. '56 '87 C.112 B.A. L.426 J.D. 555 S. Flower St.
**Drazich, Brian F.** '42 '80 C.1032 B.S. L.966 J.D. [Acker,K.&W.]
Drell, Michael, (A Prof. Corp.) '— '81 2049 Century Park, E.
**Dresie, Lee A.** '57 '82 C.311 B.A. L.1068 J.D. [Greenberg G.F.C.&M.]
*PRACTICE AREAS: Litigation.
Dresselhaus, Carl D. '27 '60 C.112 A.B. L.1065 J.D. [Bueno&D.]
Dressler, Thomas W., (BV) '55 '79 C.611 B.A. L.597 J.D. [Dressler,R.&E.]
Dressler, Rein & Evans, (BV) 1800 Century Park East
Dressner, Tracy J. '60 '90 C.112 B.A. L.800 J.D. Jud. Clk., U.S. Dist. J.
**Dreuth, Sybille** '65 '93 C.112 B.A. L.1068 J.D. [Pillsbury M.&S.]
**Drew, Mark K.** '62 '95 C.112 B.A. L.426 J.D. [Pick&B.]
*PRACTICE AREAS: Insurance Coverage; Complex Securities Litigation; Criminal Law; ERISA and Tort Litigation.
**Drewry, Anthony B.**, (AV) '47 '72 C.813 B.A. L.1068 J.D. [Richards,W.&G.]
*PRACTICE AREAS: General Litigation.
**Drewry, Philip M.** '65 '94 C.893 B.A. L.990 J.D. [Morris,P.&P.]
**Dreyer, Scott Monro** '64 '89 C.112 A.B. L.1066 J.D. [Gibson,D.&C.]
*PRACTICE AREAS: Environmental; Insurance.
Dreyfuss, Gilbert, (AV) '26 '54 C.800 B.S. L.426 J.D. 311 S. Spring St.‡
Dreyfuss, Karen E. '61 '86 C.668 B.A. L.112 J.D. Dep. Pub. Def.
Dribin, Eileen Wilansky '45 '74 C.446 B.A. L.174 J.D. 325 S. Saltair Ave.
Dribin, Leland G. '44 '68 C&L.273 B.A., J.D. 325 S. Saltair Ave.
Drinkwater, John H., Jr. '52 '79 C&L.339 B.M., J.D. 2121 Ave. of the Stars
Driscoll, Christopher L. '68 '93 C.154 B.A. L.426 J.D. 445 S. Figueroa St., 27th Fl.
**Driscoll, William P.** '51 '78 C.800 B.S. L.809 J.D. [Hornberger&C.] (Pasadena)
*PRACTICE AREAS: Eminent Domain; Municipal Law; Government; Real Estate.
Drobny, Pablo J. '45 '74 C.367 B.A. L.309 J.D. Sr. Jud. Atty., Ct. of App.
**Drooks, Mark T.**, (AV) '57 '82 C.188 B.A. L.309 J.D. [Bird,M.B.W.&M.]
Drooyan, Richard E., (AV) '50 '75 C.154 B.A. L.309 J.D. U.S. Attys. Off.
**Drooz, Deborah** '56 '86 [Langberg,C.&D.]
*REPORTED CASES: Dangerfield v. Star 7 F. 3d 856 (1993).
*PRACTICE AREAS: Intellectual Property; Libel, Slander and Defamation; Litigation; Appellate Practice; Entertainment and the Arts.
Drown, Daniel D. '43 '77 C.1019 B.A. L.809 J.D. 365 S. Cochran Ave.
**Drozdowski, Mark R.** '62 '93 C.273 B.A. L.1068 J.D. [Arnold&P.]
**Drucker, Barry A.** '63 '89 C.273 B.A. L.990 J.D. [Newkirk,N.&R.]
*PRACTICE AREAS: Personal Injury Law.
Drucker, Bruce I. '54 '79 C&L.107 B.S., J.D.
(adm. in NY; not adm. in CA) Chf. Fin. Offr., The PDC Group, Ltd.
**Drucker, I. Morley, (A Professional Corporation)**, (AV) '31 '59
C.453 B.Sc. L.809 J.D. [Fulwider P.L.&U.] (See Pat. Sect.)
*REPORTED CASES: Oromeccanica, Inc. v. Ottmar Botzenhardt GmbH & Co. KG, 226 USPQ 996 (USDC, D.C. Calif. 1985); MWS Wire Industries, Inc. v. California Fine Wire Industries, Inc., 230 USPQ 873 (Ct of Appeals, 9th Cir. 1986); Cento Group S.p.A. v. OroAmerica, Inc., 822 F. Supp 1058 (USDC, SDNY, 1993).
*PRACTICE AREAS: Patent Law; Trademark Law; Copyright Law; Unfair Competition Law.
**Drucker, Jon E.** '55 '88 C.112 B.A. L.1068 J.D. [Troop M.S.&P.]
*PRACTICE AREAS: General Business Litigation; Insolvency and Creditors' Rights Law.
Drucker, Michael S. '50 '77 C.112 B.S. L.1065 J.D. 5455 Wilshire Blvd. (Oak Park)
Drucker, Peri J. '59 '86 C.94 B.S. L.800 J.D. 12424 Wilshire Blvd.
Drulias, Dean W. '47 '77 C.112 B.A. L.426 J.D. 11755 Wilshire Blvd.
Drumm, Lawrence E., (AV) '08 '32 C&L.800 B.A., LL.B. 296 Bronwood Ave.‡
**Drummy, James P.** '48 '73 C.112 A.B. L.1066 J.D. [Poindexter&D.]
*PRACTICE AREAS: Real Estate; Commercial Transactions; Corporate.
**Drummy, Kathleen L. Houston** '51 '77 C.112 B.A. L.1068 J.D. [McDermott,W.&E.]
*PRACTICE AREAS: Health Care; Hospitals; Medicare and Medicaid.
Drushall, Stephen D. '42 '67 C.112 B.A. L.1068 J.D. 427 S. Fuller Ave.
**Dryfoos, Glenn A.** '61 '87 C.674 A.B. L.569 J.D. [Greenberg G.F.C.&M.]
*PRACTICE AREAS: Bankruptcy; Corporate Reorganization; Business.
Duarte, Michael J. '55 '83 C&L.426 B.A., J.D. Off. of Dist. Atty.
**Dub, Daria A.** '65 '90 C.665 B.A. L.990 J.D. [Weinhart&R.]
*PRACTICE AREAS: Bankruptcy; Secured Creditor's Rights.
Duberstein, Ronnie '— '90 C.188 B.S. L.309 J.D. Dep. Pub. Def.
**Dubin, Cindy Zimmerman** '62 '88 C.112 B.A. L.145 J.D. [Troop M.S.&P.]
*PRACTICE AREAS: Corporate Law; Franchise Law.
Dubin, Leonard R., (AV) '37 '62 C&L.966 B.S., J.D. [L.R.Dubin]
**Dubin, Stephen L.** '63 '92 C.477 B.A. L.424 J.D. [Monteleone&M.]
*PRACTICE AREAS: Business Litigation; Construction Law; Business Law; Corporate Law.
Dubin, Leonard R., A Professional Corporation, (AV) 12121 Wilshire Blvd.
**Dubinsky, Jamie L.** '58 '87 C.112 B.A. L.1068 J.D.
Sr. Corp..Coun., Farmers Grp., Inc.
*RESPONSIBILITIES: Agency Litigation; Employment Litigation; Counselling in Labor and Agency.

**Dubrow, Dennis R., (AV) '39 '65 C&L.477 A.B., LL.B.**
**Suite 2000, 1925 Century Park East, 90067**
**Telephone: 310-277-2236 FAX: 310-556-5653**
**(Certified Specialist, Family Law, The State Bar of California Board of Legal Specialization). Practice Limited to Family Law.**
***See Professional Biographies, LOS ANGELES, CALIFORNIA***

**Dubrow, Eli B.**, (AV) '35 '61 C.112 B.S. L.1066 LL.B. [Harrington,F.D.&C.]
*PRACTICE AREAS: Real Estate Law; Probate and Trusts Law; Estate Planning Law; Business Law.
**Ducharme, Wayne B.** '43 '86 C.1077 B.S.B.A. L.1065 J.D. [Anderson,M.&C.]
*PRACTICE AREAS: Construction; Real Estate; Business Litigation; Surety Law.
**Duchene, Kate W.** '63 '90 C.813 B.A. L.569 J.D. [O'Melveny&M.]
**Duchesneau, Peter R.** '63 '93 C.690 B.A. L.809 J.D. [Graham&J.] (Pat.)
Duckler, Geordie '59 '87 C.628 B.S. L.596 J.D. 3172 S. Barrington Ave.
Dudley, David M. '54 '85 C.605 B.A. L.309 J.D. 1999 Ave. of the Stars
**Duea, Bradford David** '68 '96 C.112 B.A. L.1049 J.D. [O'Melveny&M.]
**Duesberg, Nancy J.** '67 '94 C.1077 B.S. L.990 J.D. [Koletsky,M.&F.]
*PRACTICE AREAS: Construction Defect.
Duff, James T. '43 '69 C&L.273 B.B.A., J.D. 1 Wilshire Blvd.
**Duff, Suzanne F.** '37 '81 C.999 L.809 J.D. [O'Melveny&M.]
*PRACTICE AREAS: Business Litigation.
Duffey, Michael M., (AV) '43 '71 C.112 A.B. L.1068 J.D. Dep. Pub. Def.
**Duffis, Kevin A.** '53 '96 C.800 B.A. L.426 J.D. [Bonne,B.M.O.&N.]
*LANGUAGES: Spanish.
*PRACTICE AREAS: Medical Malpractice; General Civil Litigation.
**Duffy, John J.**, (AV) '51 '80 C.602 B.A. L.809 J.D. [Gray,Y.D.&R.]
*PRACTICE AREAS: Insurance Law; Bad Faith; Medical Malpractice; Appellate Practice; Employment Law.
**Duffy, John J.**, (AV) '39 '73 C.999 B.A. L.569 J.D. [Pillsbury M.&S.]
**Duffy, Julie G.** '65 '90 C.276 A.B. L.94 J.D. [Pillsbury M.&S.]
**Duffy, Patrick J., III (P.C.)**, (AV) '44 '70 C&L.426 B.A., J.D. [Monteleone&M.]
*PRACTICE AREAS: Contract Litigation; Construction Litigation; Business Litigation; Contract Formation and Negotiation; Real Estate Transactions and Litigation.
**Duffy, Robert E.** '46 '71 C.999 B.A. L.326 J.D. [Troop M.S.&P.]
*PRACTICE AREAS: Real Estate Law; Real Estate Finance Law.
Duffy-Lewis, Maureen '— '77 C.800 B.A. L.426 J.D. Mun. J.
Duggan, Danl. L. '13 '41 C.113 L.800 J.D. 12751 Evanston St.‡
Dukelow, Gayle L., (Mr.) '47 '72 C.112 B.A. L.1066 J.D. Ct. of App., Sr. Jud. Atty.
Dukeminier, Jesse '25 '52 C.309 A.B. L.976 LL.B.
(adm. in NY; not adm. in CA) Prof. of Law, Univ. of Calif.
**Dulberg, Jeffrey W.** '70 '95 C.821 B.A. L.112 J.D. [Robinson,D.B.&K.]
*PRACTICE AREAS: Bankruptcy.
Dulgarian, George H. '46 '73
C.112 B.S. L.426 J.D. V.P., Standard Nickel-Chromium Plating Co.
**Dull, David A.** '49 '82 C&L.976 B.A., J.D. [Irell&M.]
**Dumas, Beth F.** '64 '90 C.112 B.A. L.1065 J.D. [Langberg,C.&D.]
*PRACTICE AREAS: Litigation; Libel, Slander and Defamation; Intellectual Property; Wrongful Termination.
Dumas, James A., Jr., (AV) '50 '77 C.112 B.A. L.1066 J.D. [Dumas&Assoc.]
Dumas & Associates, (AV) 445 S. Figueroa St., 24th Fl.
**Dumler, Egon** '29 '56 C.563 B.S. L.564 LL.B.
(adm. in NY; not adm. in CA) [J.M.Donovan]
*PRACTICE AREAS: Entertainment Law; Motion Picture Law; Theater Law; Television Law; Advertising Law.
**Dummit, Craig S.**, (AV) '46 '72 C.1042 B.S. L.800 J.D. [Dummit,F.&B.]

**Dummit, Faber & Briegleb, (AV)**
**11755 Wilshire Boulevard, 15th Floor, 90025**
**Telephone: 310-479-0944 Fax: 310-312-3836**

(This Listing Continued)

CALIFORNIA—LOS ANGELES
MARTINDALE-HUBBELL LAW DIRECTORY 1997

**Dummit, Faber & Briegleb (Continued)**

**Members of Firm: Craig S. Dummit; Christopher J. Faber; B. John Briegleb (Resident, Sacramento Office); Scott R. Diamond; Ann L. Holiday; William R. Boyce; Bruce S. Bailey (Resident, San Diego Office). Associates: John E. Tiedt; Lawrence A. Greenfield; Scott D. Buchholz (Resident, San Diego Office); Douglas H. Swope (Resident, San Diego Office); Randall R. McKinnon (Sacramento and Las Vegas, Nevada Office); Ronald W. Aitken (Resident, Sacramento Office); Paul A. Buckley (Resident, San Diego Office); Janet E. Trapp; Steven E. Kushner; Susan J. Veis; B. Elizabeth Gast; Jeffry A. Miller (Resident, San Diego Office); Michael A. Scherago; K. Sue Hummel; Lane E. Webb (Resident, San Diego Office); Cynthia L. Pertile; Steven J. Bechtold. Of Counsel: Richard C. DuPar.**
**Civil Litigation in all State and Federal Courts. Professional Malpractice, Products Liability, Negligence, Insurance Defense, Hospital, Business, Entertainment, Sports and Labor Law.**
**Sacramento, California Office: 1661 Garden Highway, 95833. Telephone: 916-929-9600. Fax: 916-927-5368.**
**San Diego, California Office: 750 B Street, Suite 1900, 92101. Telephone: 619-231-7738. Fax: 619-231-0886.**
**Las Vegas, Nevada Office: 808 South Seventh Street, 89101. Telephone: 702-471-0090. Fax: 702-386-8626.**

***See Professional Biographies, LOS ANGELES, CALIFORNIA***

Dunaway, Jack .... '14 '54 6255 Sunset Blvd.
**Duncan, Adam D., Jr.** .... '64 '90 C.878 B.A. L.809 J.D. [Perkins,Z.&D.]
*PRACTICE AREAS: Real Estate, Environmental, Securities and Commercial Litigation.
Duncan, Benjamin R. .... '51 '81 C.347 B.A. L.809 J.D. I.R.S.
**Duncan, Edwin W.**, (AV) .... '45 '70 C.112 A.B. L.1065 J.D. [Arter&H.]
*REPORTED CASES: Western Electric Company v. LaHoma Smith, 99 Cal. App.3d 629 (1979); Pacific Telephone and Telegraph Company v. Workers' Compensation Appeals Board and Thomas Blackburn 112 Cal. App.3d 241 (1980); Chevron U.S.A. vs. Bragg Crane & Rigging, 180 Cal. App.3d 639 (1986); Bartram vs. FDIC, 235 Cal. App. 3d 1749 (1991); Twenty-Nine Pals Band Mission Indians v. Pete Wilson, 925 F.Supp.1470 (C.D.CA 1996).
*PRACTICE AREAS: Commercial; Tort; Product Liability Litigation.
Duncan, Frank P. .... '28 '55 C.112 A.B. L.1065 J.D. 880 W. 1st St.
**Duncan, Helen L.** .... '52 '81 C.347 B.A. L.809 J.D. [LeBoeuf,L.G.&M.]
*PRACTICE AREAS: Litigation; Tax.
**Duncan, Mal**, (BV) '47 '72
C.112 B.A. L.800 J.D. [Tipler] (☉Andalusia, AL; Atlanta, GA)
**Dundas, Derek D.** .... '69 '96 C.112 B.A. L.276 J.D. [Ⓐ Latham&W.]
**Dung, Joseph W.** .... '64 '95 C.145 B.A. L.800 J.D. [Ⓐ Stroock&S.&L.]
**Dunham, Scott H.**, (AV) .... '50 '75 C.906 B.A. L.911 J.D. [O'Melveny&M.]
*PRACTICE AREAS: Labor and Employment Law.
Dunkel-Bradley, Dorothy A. '49 '89 C.527 B.A. L.940 J.D.
(adm. in PA; not adm. in CA) U.S. Dept. of Jus.
Dunlap, Richd. H. .... '21 '49 C.112 A.B. L.1066 LL.B. 444 N. LaBrea Ave.
**Dunlap, Thomas Paine**, (AV) .... '49 '74 C.112 B.A. L.1068 J.D. [Ⓐ Trope&T.]
*LANGUAGES: Spanish and Arabic.
*REPORTED CASES: In Re Marriage of Templeton, 14 CA 4th, 607 1993; In Re Marriage of Dick, 15 CA 4th 144, 1993; In Re Marriage of Quay, 18 CA 4th 961, 1993; Estevez v. Superior Court, 22 CA 4th 423. 1994; In Re Marriage of Gigliotti (1995) 33 CA App. 4th 518.
*PRACTICE AREAS: Family Law; Family and Civil Appeals; Business Litigation.
**Dunlavey, Dean C.**, (AV) .... '25 '55 C.309 B.S. L.1066 LL.B. [Ⓒ Gibson,D.&C.]
*PRACTICE AREAS: Litigation.
**Dunn, Brian T.** .... '68 '95 C.112 B.A. L.477 J.D. [Ⓐ J.L.Cochran,Jr.]
*PRACTICE AREAS: Personal Injury; Police Misconduct; Civil Rights Litigation.
**Dunn, Franklin T.** .... '66 '92 C.800 B.S. L.426 J.D. [Ⓐ Lord,B.&B.]
**Dunn, Gala E.** .... '53 '89 C.1097 B.S. L.426 J.D. [Ⓐ Parker S.]
*PRACTICE AREAS: Litigation.
Dunn, Geoffrey R. .... '69 '95 C.188 B.A. L.1068 J.D. 1999 Ave. of the Stars
**Dunn, James F.** .... '60 '95 C.870 B.S. L.1068 J.D. [Ⓐ Proskauer R.G.&M.]
*PRACTICE AREAS: Litigation; Labor.
**Dunn, Lisa Bondy** .... '68 '93 C.112 B.A. L.426 J.D. [Ⓐ Knopfler&R.]
*PRACTICE AREAS: Construction Law; Insurance Law; Personal Injury Defense.
**Dunn, Loryn D.** .... '68 '96 C.309 B.A. L.813 J.D. [Ⓐ O'Melveny&M.]
*LANGUAGES: Japanese.
**Dunn, Pamela E.** .... '49 '85 C.1111 B.A. L.809 J.D. [Robie&M.]
*REPORTED CASES: Waller v. Truck Insurance Exchange 1995 11 Cal. 4th; Kasparian v. County of Los Angeles 1995 386 App. 4th 242; State Farm v. Superior Court 1994 45 Cal. App. 4th 1093; Winans v. State Farm Fire and Casualty Co., 968 F 2d 884 (9th Cir. 1992); Almon v. State Farm Fire and Casualty Co., 724 F. Supp. 765 (S.D. Cal. 1989).
*PRACTICE AREAS: Appellate Law.
Dunne, Lisa J. .... '65 '90 C.112 B.A. L.1068 J.D. 700 S. Flower St.
**Dunnett, Cynthia M.** .... '57 '85 C.112 B.A. L.1065 J.D. [Riordan&M.]
Dunsay, Richard C. .... '40 '64 C.36 B.S. L.209 J.D. 6404 Wilshire Blvd.‡
**Dunsmore, Billy D.** .... '50 '79 C.623 B.S. L.208 J.D. [Ⓐ Burke,W.&S.]
*PRACTICE AREAS: Labor Law; Employment Law; Personnel Law.
**DuPar, Richard C.**, (AV) .... '33 '60 C&L.800 B.S., J.D. [Ⓒ Dummit,F.&B.]
*PRACTICE AREAS: Personal Injury Law; Insurance Law; Civil Trial; Products Liability Law; Medical Malpractice Law.
**Du Plantier, Angelo A., III** .... '66 '92 C.112 B.A. L.464 J.D. [Ⓐ Daniels,B.&F.]
**Duplantis, Stephen S.** .... '67 '92 C.420 B.G.S. L.990 J.D. [Ⓒ Huang&M.]
*PRACTICE AREAS: Litigation; Tort Law; Appellate Practice.
**Dupont, Norman A.** .... '53 '79 C.813 B.A. L.276 J.D. [Shapiro,H.&M.]
**DuPont, Sherry M.** .... '62 '90 C.112 B.A. L.800 J.D. [Ⓐ Cox,C.&N.]
*PRACTICE AREAS: Real Estate and Business Litigation; Lender Liability; Receiverships.
**Dupuis, Thomas I.** .... '69 '94 C.597 B.S.Ed. L.800 J.D. [Ⓐ Tuttle&T.]
Duque, Thomas E. .... '57 '89 C.770 B.S. L.809 J.D. [Barry&D.]
**Duraiswamy, Vijayalakshmi D., (Ms.)** '— '83
C.061 M.S. L.1066 J.D. Pat. Coun., Hughes Aircraft Co. (Pat.)
*LANGUAGES: English, Tamil.
Duran, John J. .... '59 '87 C.1042 B.S. L.1137 J.D. [Duran,L.&R.]
Duran, Percy .... '43 '74 Comr. of Pub. Works
**Duran, Robert N.** .... '56 '87 C.1109 B.A. L.770 J.D. [Ⓐ Riordan&M.]
*PRACTICE AREAS: International Business and Tax Planning; Corporation; Limited Liability Company; Partnership Taxation.
Duran, Loquvam & Robertson .... 9000 W. Sunset Blvd., West Hollywood (☉Anaheim)
Durante, Felix L. .... '19 '54 C.999 L.809 LL.B. 758 Colorado Blvd.
**Durbin, James E.**, (AV) .... '44 '73 C.1070 B.S. L.426 J.D. [Arter&H.]
Durchfort, David E. .... '56 '83 C.1077 B.A. L.1068 J.D. [Kosnett&D.]
Durfee, Karen M. .... '42 '85 [Sandler,R.&M.]
**Durko, Marsha E.** .... '55 '80 C.112 B.S. L.1068 J.D. [Ⓐ Jones,D.R.&P.]
**Durkovic, Andrew J.** .... '60 '93 C.112 B.A. L.426 J.D. [Ⓐ Baker&H.]
*LANGUAGES: Spanish.
**DuRocher, Jeffrey L.**, (AV) .... '45 '71 C.597 B.S. L.178 J.D. [Riordan&M.]

**DuRoss, Daniel V., Law Offices of**
**(See Manhattan Beach)**

Dushkes, Larry S., (BV) .... '57 '82 C.813 A.B. L.1068 J.D. 16830 Ventura Blvd.
**Dusseault, Christopher D.** .... '69 '95 C.976 B.A. L.228 J.D. [Ⓐ Gibson,D.&C.]
*PRACTICE AREAS: Litigation; Antitrust and Trade Regulation.
Dutton, Rosanne B. '42 '76 C.788 B.A. L.705 J.D.
Dir., USC Patent & Copyright Admn., Univ. of Southern Calif.
Duuglas, Darlene .... '46 '77 C.112 B.A. L.1068 J.D. Dep. Dist. Atty.
Duvernay, Marc S. .... '61 '88 C.112 B.A. L.329 J.D. 5757 W. Century Blvd.
**Dveirin, Brant H.** .... '61 '87 C.112 B.A. L.1065 J.D. [Ⓐ Loeb&L.]

**Dworsky, Marc T. G.** .... '61 '89 C.035 B.A. L.029 LL.B. [Munger,T.&O.]
*LANGUAGES: Hebrew and Afrikaans.
**Dwyer, John P.** .... '51 '81 C.210 B.S. L.1066 J.D. [Katz&Assoc.]
*PRACTICE AREAS: Environmental Law; Appellate Practice.
**Dwyer, Michael G.** .... '61 '86 C.893 B.A. L.724 J.D. [Ⓐ Jeffer,M.B.&M.]
*LANGUAGES: Spanish.
*PRACTICE AREAS: Labor and Employment.
**Dwyer, Ronald A.**, (AV) .... '29 '58 C&L.426 B.A., LL.B. [Dwyer,D.B.&B.]

**Dwyer, Daly, Brotzen & Bruno, LLP, (AV)**
**550 South Hope Street, Suite 1900, 90071**
**Telephone: 213-627-9300**
**Email: DB2LAW@ix.netcom.com**
**Partners: Ronald A. Dwyer; John A. Daly; Peter P. Brotzen; Toni Rae Bruno. Associates: Douglas W. Schroeder (Resident); Gregory L. Anderson; Patricia M. Muñoz; Diane A. Singleton; Gregory J. Salute.**
**General Civil Litigation and Appellate Practice in all State and Federal Courts, Business Litigation, Aviation, Product Liability, Premises Liability, Construction, Bad Faith, Labor and Employment Law, Professional Negligence, Legal Malpractice, Accountant Malpractice.**

***See Professional Biographies, LOS ANGELES, CALIFORNIA***

**Dyal, Sylvia Anne** .... '58 '89 C.112 B.A. L.1065 J.D. [Ⓐ Wilson,K.&B.]
Dyal-Chand, Rashmi .... '— '95 C.293 B.A. L.588 J.D. [Ⓐ Hall&Assoc.]
Dyas, Cherisse C. .... '54 '86 C.174 B.A. L.767 J.D. 6222 Wilshire Blvd.
Dybens, Mary T. .... '56 '85 C.1042 B.S. L.1137 J.D. 4700 Wilshire Blvd.

**Dye, Carolyn A. '49 '76 C.421 B.A. L.383 J.D.**
**445 South Figueroa Street Twenty Fourth Floor, 90071-1628**
**Telephone: 213-489-2620 Facsimile: 213-489-2019**
**Business and Corporate Securities Practice; Corporate Bankruptcy and Dissolution Matters.**

**Dye, Gary G.** .... '57 '86 C.877 B.S. L.1049 J.D. [Harrington,F.D.&C.]
**Dye, Paul T.**, (AV) .... '51 '78 C.188 A.B. L.477 J.D. [Saltzburg,R.&B.]
*REPORTED CASES: Steinberg v. Amplica, 42 Cal 3d 1198 (1986); California Digital v. Union Bank, 705 F.Supp 489 (CD Cal 1989).
*PRACTICE AREAS: Litigation; Business Law; Financial Institutions Law; Entertainment Law.
**Dye, Robert A.** .... '60 '86 C.1073 B.S. L.464 J.D. [Epstein B.&G.]
*PRACTICE AREAS: Labor and Employment Law; Litigation.
**Dyer, Hollis O.**, (AV) .... '33 '64 L.809 LL.B. [Ⓐ Veatch,C.G.&N.]
*LANGUAGES: Spanish.
*PRACTICE AREAS: Medical Malpractice Law (25%, 15); Products Liability Law (25%, 25); General Liability Law (Auto, Premises, etc.) (50%, 75).
**Dygert, Edward C.**, (AV) .... '46 '73 C.1109 B.A. L.1049 J.D. [Ⓒ Cox,C.&N.]
*REPORTED CASES: %italic; City of Oakland v. Oakland Raiders %roman; (1985), 174 Cal.App.3d 414.
*PRACTICE AREAS: Land Use Law; Eminent Domain Law; Environmental Law.
Dyler, Pattie .... '49 '92 L.809 J.D. [Frisenda,Q.&N.]
Dymally, Hazel M. .... '35 '79 C.1097 B.A. L.1136 J.D. 1843 S. Bedford St.
**Dzida, Joseph S., Jr.**, (BV) .... '55 '79 C&L.426 B.A., J.D. [Sullivan,W.&D.]
*PRACTICE AREAS: Business Law; Real Estate Litigation.
Dziuba, Catherine .... '51 '79 C.112 B.A. L.426 J.D. Sr. Dep. Co. Coun.
**Dziubla, Robert W.**, (AVⓉ) .... '52 '80 C&L.597 B.A., J.D. [Ⓒ Arnberger,K.B.&C.]
*LANGUAGES: English and Japanese.
*PRACTICE AREAS: International Transactions; Finance; Trade; Technology; Transfers.
**Dziubla, Robert W.**, (AV) .... '52 '80 C&L.597 B.A., J.D. [Brand F.D.F.&K.]
*LANGUAGES: Japanese.
*PRACTICE AREAS: Finance; Real Estate; International Trade.
Eamer, Richard K. '28 '60 C&L.800 B.S., LL.B.
Chmn. of the Bd., National Med. Enterprises, Inc.
**Earl, Joyce E.** .... '48 '88 C.112 B.A. L.464 J.D. [Ⓐ Ochoa&S.]
*PRACTICE AREAS: Education, Labor and Employment Law.
**Earle, James C.** .... '52 '86 C.1116 B.A. L.284 J.D. [Chapman&G.]
*PRACTICE AREAS: Construction Litigation; Products Liability; Coverage; Business Litigation; Trial.
Earles, Carl A. .... '22 '52 C.944 A.B. L.809 LL.B. 1111 E. Vernon Ave.‡
**Early, Eric P.** .... '58 '93 C.569 B.F.A. L.809 J.D. [Ⓐ Christensen,M.F.J.G.W.&S.]
*PRACTICE AREAS: Commercial; Entertainment; Litigation.
**Early, John D.** .... '68 '93 C.602 B.A. L.1068 J.D. [Ⓐ White&C.]
Early, Maslach & Price, (AV) .... 4700 Wilshire Boulevard
Easterwood, Larry J. '47 '78 C.1077 B.A. L.1068 J.D.
1605 W. Olympic Blvd., Suite 900
Eastman, Donald N. .... '40 '66 C.112 B.A. L.1068 LL.B. Head Dep. Dist. Atty.
**Eastman, Richard A.**, (AV) '37 '66 C&L.309 B.A., LL.B.
[Whitman B.A.&M.] (☉New York, N.Y., Tokyo, Japan)
*LANGUAGES: Japanese.
**Easton, Harold, (P.C.)**, (AV) .... '13 '37 C.112 A.B. L.1066 J.D. [Easton&S.]
**Easton, Mark C.** .... '63 '93 C.821 B.A. L.309 J.D. [Ⓐ O'Melveny&M.]
**Easton, Rosa Kwon** .... '64 '94 C.788 B.A. L.93 J.D. [Ⓐ Konowiecki&R.]
*LANGUAGES: Korean and Japanese.
*PRACTICE AREAS: Business Litigation; Employment Litigation.

**Easton & Schiff, (AV)**
**A Partnership of Professional Corporations**
**Suite 2610 One Century Plaza, 2029 Century Park East, 90067**
**Telephone: 310-557-2436 FAX: 310-785-0027**
**Members of Firm: Harold Easton (P.C.); Michael J. Schiff (P.C.).**
**General Civil and Trial Practice in all State and Federal Courts. Corporation, Tax, Business, Real Property, Trust and Probate Law. Estate Planning. Arbitration and Mediation.**
**References: Bank of America National Trust & Savings Assn. (Los Angeles Main Office); City National Bank (Century Towers Office).**

***See Professional Biographies, LOS ANGELES, CALIFORNIA***

**Eatman, Louis P.**, (AV) .... '48 '74 C.276 B.S.F.S. L.813 J.D. [Mayer,B.&P.]
Eaton, Claudia D. .... '60 '88 C.329 B.A. L.426 J.D. Dir., Legal Affs., KCET
**Eaton, Daniel E.** .... '63 '89 C.276 B.S.F.S. L.309 J.D. [Ⓐ Proskauer R.G.&M.]
*PRACTICE AREAS: Commercial Litigation; Business; Political Law.

**Ebbert, Richard P., (AV) '38 '66 C.112 B.S. L.1068 LL.B.**
**2418 Wild Oak Drive, 90068**
**Telephone: 213-939-9091 Fax: 213-856-0412**
**Trust, Estate, Business and Real Estate Law.**

**Ebershoff, David A.**, (AV) .... '39 '66 C.228 B.A. L.477 J.D. [Fulbright&J.]
*PRACTICE AREAS: Corporate Law; Securities; Utilities; Healthcare.
Ebner, Ruth .... '47 '81 C.339 B.A. L.809 J.D. Dep. City Atty.
**Ebright, Albert H.**, (AV) .... '33 '59 C.112 A.B. L.426 LL.B. [Carlsmith B.W.C.&I.]
*PRACTICE AREAS: Commercial Litigation; Commercial Law; Corporate Litigation.
**Ebright, James N.** '27 '52
C&L.608 B.Sc., J.D. Sr. V.P. & Gen. Coun., Ashland Tech. Corp.
Ebright, Mitchell A. '43 '72 C.1042 B.S. L.1068 J.D.
V.P., Gen. Coun. & Secy., Baker Commodities, Inc.
**Eck, F. Thomas, IV** .... '64 '89 C&L.800 B.A., J.D. Coun., Bank of Amer.
**Eckardt, Richard W.**, (AV) .... '38 '67 C.608 B.A. L.800 J.D. [Eckardt&K.]
*PRACTICE AREAS: Business Litigation; Real Property Title Litigation; Transactions; Estate Planning and Probate.

**Eckardt & Khoury, (AV)**
**333 South Grand Avenue Suite 3700, 90071**
**Telephone: 213-626-5061 Cable Address: "Richeck" Fax: 213-626-3629 ABA/Net: ABA 18857**
**Email: REckardt95@aol.com**

(This Listing Continued)

**Eckardt & Khoury (Continued)**
**Richard W. Eckardt; Robert P. Khoury.**
**General Civil and Trial Practice in all State and Federal Courts. Banking, Corporation, Construction, Insurance, Real Property, Estate Planning, Trust, Probate, Corporate Financing and International Business Law.**
*See Professional Biographies, LOS ANGELES, CALIFORNIA*

Economos, Gregory G. ...............'62 '92 C.228 B.S.E. L.30 J.D. 10877 Wilshire Blvd.
**Eddy, Edward D., III** ...........................'51 '83 C.976 B.S. L.477 J.D. [Sidley&A.]
*LANGUAGES: French.
*PRACTICE AREAS: Banking Law; Corporate Law.
**Edel, Scott** ...............'59 '87 C.105 B.S. L.800 J.D. [Kleinberg L.L.B.&C.]
*PRACTICE AREAS: Entertainment Law.
Edelman, Edmund D., (AV) ......'30 '58 C.112 B.A. L.1068 LL.B. Co. Bd. of Supervisors
Edelman, Emily Shappell, (AV) ..............'38 '76 C.66 A.B. L.1148 J.D. [Schenck&E.]
**Edelman, Jerry**, (AV) ..............'29 '57 C.112 B.S. L.1068 J.D. [▣ King,W.E.&B.]
*PRACTICE AREAS: Real Estate; Business Litigation.
**Edelman, Scott A.** ...................'59 '84 C.813 B.A. L.1066 J.D. [Gibson,D.&C.]
*PRACTICE AREAS: Litigation; Entertainment and the Arts; Intellectual Property; Trade Secrets; Labor and Employment.
Edelman, Susan Scheiber ..................'63 '87 C&L.813 A.B., J.D. 333 S. Grand Ave.
**Edelson, Rebecca** ..................'61 '90 C.659 B.A. L.1068 J.D. [▣ Alschuler G.&P.]
Edelstein, Gerald F., (AV) ..............'39 '65 C.882 B.A. L.188 LL.B. [Edelstein,L.&S.]
**Edelstein, Mark**, (AV) ..............'45 '69 C.107 B.A. L.705 J.D. [Gordon,E.K.G.F.&G.]
*PRACTICE AREAS: Workers Compensation Law; Social Security Law.
Edelstein, Laird & Sobel, P.C., (AV) ....................................9255 Sunset Blvd
Edelstone, Gary H., (AV) ...............'48 '76 C.112 B.A. L.426 J.D. [Surpin,M.&E.]
Eden, Joy D. ..............................'61 '94 C.890 B.A. L.1049 J.D. 601 S. Figueroa
**Eder, Cynthia Ann** ..............'62 '92 C.1040 B.A. L.800 J.D. [▣ Allen,M.L.G.&M.]
*PRACTICE AREAS: Real Estate.
**Edic, William S.** ...........................'63 '88 C.112 B.A. L.464 J.D. [▣ Kirtland&P.]
**Edlund, Lee A.** ...........................'68 '94 C.112 A.B. L.1066 J.D. [▣ Fierstein&S.]
*PRACTICE AREAS: Real Estate Finance; Insolvency; Workout.
**Edmon, Lee Smalley** ...............................'55 '81 C.92 B.A. L.339 J.D. [Dewey B.]
*PRACTICE AREAS: Litigation.
**Edmunds, Eric F., Jr.**, (AV) ..........'53 '78 C.674 A.B. L.1068 J.D. [Saltzburg,R.&B.]
*PRACTICE AREAS: Litigation; Real Estate Law; Business Law.
Edmunds, John M. ..........................'51 '84 C.101 B.S. L.809 J.D. 333 S. Grand Ave.
**Edmundson, D. Barclay** ...............'47 '79 C.800 A.B. L.1068 J.D. [Munger,T.&O.]
**Edson, Eldon S.** ...................................'66 '93 C.112 B.A. L.990 J.D. [▣ Selman B.]
*PRACTICE AREAS: Personal Injury.
**Edwards, Angela T.** ..............'70 '95 C.800 B.S. L.112 J.D. [▣ Breidenbach,B.H.H.&H.]
*PRACTICE AREAS: Environmental; Torts; Insurance; Construction Litigation.
**Edwards, Anne K.** ...........................'51 '83 C.446 B.A. L.1137 J.D. [▣ Fulbright&J.]
*PRACTICE AREAS: Creditors Rights; Litigation.
**Edwards, Anthony C.** ...........................'56 '82 C.813 B.A. L.426 J.D. [▣ R.Edwards]
**Edwards, Barry G.** .....................'60 '86 C.347 B.S. L.426 J.D. [Hamburg,H.E.&M.]
*PRACTICE AREAS: Taxation Law; Real Estate Law; General Business Law.
Edwards, Barry R. ...........................'47 '72 C.800 B.A. L.809 J.D. [Spiegelman&E.]
**Edwards, Brian L.** ..........................'63 '89 C&L.846 B.J., J.D. [Greenberg G.F.C.&M.]
**Edwards, Bryant B.** .................................'54 '81 C.101 B.A. L.145 J.D. [Latham&W.]
Edwards, Charles W., II .................'53 '87 C.1042 B.A. L.809 J.D. 3255 Wilshire Blvd.
**Edwards, Douglas W.** .........'49 '74 C.112 B.A. L.1068 J.D. Broadcast Coun., CBS Inc.
Edwards, Drew E. ...................'59 '88 C.813 A.B. L.1066 J.D. Dep. Fed. Pub. Def.
Edwards, Jerome, (AV) ..................'12 '34 C&L.569 B.S., J.D. 10701 Wilshire Blvd.‡
**Edwards, Linda Harrison** ..................'66 '93 C.859 B.A. L.846 J.D. [▣ Latham&W.]
*LANGUAGES: Spanish.
*PRACTICE AREAS: Corporate.
Edwards, Maridee Farnquist '54 '88
C.1201 B.A. L.809 J.D. Dep. Trial Coun., Calif. State Bar Assn.
**Edwards, Rick**, (AV) ...............................'47 '72 C.813 A.B. L.800 J.D. [R.Edwards]
**Edwards, Valerie C.** ..............................'67 '95 C.813 B.A. L.112 J.D. [▣ Sullivan&C.]
**Edwards, Weston A.** ...........'65 '92 C.101 B.A. L.846 J.D. [▣ Sonnenschein N.&R.]
*PRACTICE AREAS: Litigation; Construction Law.

**Edwards, Edwards & Ashton, A Professional Corporation**
**(See Glendale)**

**Edwards, Rick, Inc., (AV) ▣**
**20th Floor, 1925 Century Park East, 90067**
**Telephone: 310-277-6464 Telecopier: 310-286-9501**
**Rick Edwards;—Anthony C. Edwards; Ken Yuwiler. Of Counsel: William R. Bishin.**
**Litigation.**
**Reference: Union Bank, 445 South Figueroa Street, Los Angeles, California 90071.**
*See Professional Biographies, LOS ANGELES, CALIFORNIA*

**Edwards, Thomas H.**
**(See Pasadena)**

**Effron, Gary L.** ..........................'42 '68 C.112 B.S. L.1065 J.D. [Lewis,D.B.&B.]
Egan, Eleanor M., (BV) ..............'39 '74 C.289 B.A. L.800 J.D. 4095 Overland Ave.
**Egan, Eugene J.** ...................'62 '87 C.112 B.A. L.426 J.D. [Breidenbach,B.H.H.&H.]
*LANGUAGES: French.
Egan, Michael J. ...........................'61 '90 C.911 B.A. L.1067 J.D. 515 S. Flower St.
**Egan, Patricia M.** ..................'59 '92 C.426 B.A. L.285 J.D. [▣ Bonne,B.M.O.&N.]
Egerman, William M., (AV) ..............'42 '66 C.112 B.A. L.1068 J.D. [Egerman&B.]
Egerman & Brown, LL.P., (AV) ....................................5750 Wilshire Boulevard
Egers, Mitchell W., (AV) ............................'34 '59 C.112 B.A. L.800 J.D. [Hanson&E.]

**Egger & Hallett, Professional Law Corporation**
**(See San Bernardino)**

Eggert, Kurt '59 '84 C.691 B.A. L.1066 J.D.
Supervising Atty., Bet Tzedek Legal Servs.
Eglash, Louis R. ...........................'22 '46 C.999 L.426 LL.B. 5631 Park Oak Pl.
Egli, David T. .........'55 '80 C.605 B.A. L.464 J.D. 10940 Wilshire Blvd. (©Long Bch.)
**Ehling, Dennis M. P.** ...................'68 '93 C.674 A.B. L.602 J.D. [▣ Musick,P.&G.]
*PRACTICE AREAS: Litigation - Insurance Defense/Professional Malpractice; Insurance Coverage; Breach of Contract Defense.
**Ehrenberg, Howard M.**, (AV) .........'61 '86 C.112 B.A. L.800 J.D. [Sulmeyer,K.B.&R.]
*PRACTICE AREAS: Bankruptcy.
**Ehrenpreis, Ralph**, (AV) ..........................'42 '67 C.477 A.B. L.813 LL.B. [R.Ehrenpreis]

**Ehrenpreis, Ralph, A Professional Law Corporation, (AV) ▣**
**Suite 450, 1801 Century Park East, 90067**
**Telephone: 310-553-6600 Telefax: 310-553-2616 Cable Address: "Immlaw"**
**Ralph Ehrenpreis;—Bernard J. Lurie.**
**Immigration and Nationality Law.**
**References: City National Bank (Beverly Hills Office, Beverly Hills, California); Great American Bank (Century City Office, Los Angeles, California).**
*See Professional Biographies, LOS ANGELES, CALIFORNIA*

**Ehrenreich, Robert** ...............'60 '86 C.37 B.S. L.464 J.D. [▣ Chapin,F.&W.]
**Ehrgott, Catherine A.** ....................'62 '88 C.800 B.S. L.426 J.D. [▣ Jones,D.R.&P.]
Ehrlich, Anat ...........................................'63 '89 C.188 B.A. L.94 J.D. U.S.E.E.O.C.
Ehrlich, Barbara J. ...........................'61 '87 C.260 B.S. L.426 J.D. Staff Atty., KCET
Ehrlich, Gail A. ....................'57 '84 C.860 B.A. L.273 J.D. 1150 N. San Fernando Rd.
Ehrlich, Jerome L. ....................'10 '34 C&L.800 A.B., J.D. 2324 S. Bev. Glen Blvd.‡
**Ehrlich, Kenneth A.** ...........................'65 '90 C.112 B.A. L.770 J.D. [Reznik&R.]
*LANGUAGES: French.
*SPECIAL AGENCIES: Federal Deposit Insurance Corporation (FDIC).
*PRACTICE AREAS: Environmental and Land Use Litigation.

**Ehrmann, Frances, (AV) '34 '63 C.112 B.A. L.1068 J.D.**
**Suite 1800, 2049 Century Park East, 90067**
**Telephone: 310-553-2049 Fax: 310-553-8820**
***PRACTICE AREAS: Property Damage Subrogation; Property and Liability Insurance Coverage; Trial and Appellate Practice.**
**Property Insurance and Liability Insurance Coverage, Subrogation, Civil Trial and Appellate Practice.**
*See Professional Biographies, LOS ANGELES, CALIFORNIA*

**Ehrmann, Herbert Z., (AV) '32 '55 C.112 B.A. L.1068 LL.B.**
**1875 Century Park East, 15th Floor, 90067**
**Telephone: 310-553-5500 Fax: 310-553-8613**
**Civil Litigation, Insurance Coverage, Property and Business Insurance Appraisals, Property and Casualty Insurance Law. Property Damage and Subrogation.**
*See Professional Biographies, LOS ANGELES, CALIFORNIA*

Eicher, Tamara J. ...........................'67 '93 C.839 B.A. L.990 J.D. 520 S. Grand Ave.
**Eichler, Peter M.**, (BV) .........'36 '61 C.918 A.B. L.178 J.D. [▣ Troop M.S.&P.] (Pat.)
*LANGUAGES: Spanish.
*PRACTICE AREAS: International Business Transactions; International Trademarks; World-wide Licensing and Merchandising.
Eick, Charles F. ...........................'54 '78 C.861 B.A. L.846 J.D. U.S. Mag. J.
Eid, Richard N. .....................'63 '89 C.184 B.S. L.30 J.D. 11355 W. Olympic Blvd.
Eiler, James O. ...........................'61 '87 C.549 B.S. L.1137 J.D. [▣ Chase,R.D.&B.]
**Eilert, Anita M.** ...............'58 '87 C.763 B.A. L.1137 J.D. [▣ Kaye,R.] (©San Diego)
Einboden, Ronald J. ..........'37 '69 C.1077 B.S. L.1095 J.D. 281 S. Figueroa St., 2nd Fl.
Einhorn, Bruce J. ..........................'54 '80 C.178 A.B. L.569 J.D. U.S. Immig. Ct. J.

**Einhorn, Irving M., Law Offices of, (AV) '41 '72 C.831 B.S. L.879 J.D.**
**11900 Olympic Boulevard, Suite 510, 90064-1151**
**Telephone: 310-207-8994 Telecopier: 310-442-7663**
**Email: irveinhorn@earthlink.net**
***PRACTICE AREAS: Securities Arbitration; Securities Regulation; Securities Fraud; Regulatory Investigations; Self Regulatory Agency Investigations.**
**Securities Law.**
*See Professional Biographies, LOS ANGELES, CALIFORNIA*

Einstein, Gary ...........................'52 '76 C.112 B.A. L.1049 J.D. [Einstein&S.]
**Einstein, Gordon H.** .........'69 '95 C.1036 B.A. L.800 J.D. [▣ Weinstock,M.R.S.&N.]
*LANGUAGES: German.
*PRACTICE AREAS: General Practice; Business Law; Corporate Law.
Einstein & Spiegel .........................................................5243 E. Beverly Blvd.
**Eisen, David S.** .......................................'56 '81 C.112 B.A. L.800 J.D. [Arnold&P.]
*PRACTICE AREAS: Law Firm and Other Partnership Disputes; Complex Business Litigation; Legal Malpractice Litigation Defense; Employment Law.
**Eisen, Deborah H.** ...........................'55 '83 C.112 B.A. L.188 J.D. [Weinstein&E.]
**Eisen, Jeffrey K.** ...............................'67 '91 C.659 B.S. L.569 J.D. [▣ Mitchell,S.&K.]
*PRACTICE AREAS: Estate Planning and Probate.
**Eisenbaum, Michael S.** ....................'64 '90 C.172 B.A. L.990 J.D. [▣ Gray,Y.D.&R.]
*PRACTICE AREAS: Insurance Defense; Public Entity; Civil Litigation.
**Eisenberg, David A.** ...............'61 '91 C.112 B.A. L.1066 J.D. [▣ Charlston,R.&W.]
*PRACTICE AREAS: Litigation; Insurance Coverage.
Eisenberg, Gary P. ..............'— '78 C.476 B.B.A. L.809 J.D. 7131 W. Manchester Ave.
**Eisenberg, Jon B.** ...........................'53 '79 C.112 B.A. L.1065 J.D. [▣ Horvitz&L.]
**Eisenberg, Joseph A., (P.C.)**, (AV) ....'46 '72 C.112 B.A. L.1066 J.D. [Jeffer,M.B.&M.]
*PRACTICE AREAS: Insolvency.
**Eisenberg, Lucy T.**, (AV) ...............'41 '75 C.681 A.B. L.1068 J.D. [Munger,T.&O.]
Eisenberg, Michael M. .........'47 '79 C.1077 B.S. L.1136 J.D. 10474 Santa Monica Blvd.
Eisenberg, Sheldon ......'57 '81 C.112 A.B. L.1066 J.D. 1800 Ave. of the Stars, Suite 900
**Eisenberg, Theodore M.**, (AV©) '49 '75 C.188 B.A. L.276 J.D.
(adm. in NJ; not adm. in CA) [Grotta,G.&H.]©
**Eisenrich, Gregory O.** ...................'66 '92 C.112 A.B. L.1066 J.D. [▣ Barger&W.]
**Eisfelder, Robert W.**, (AV) ..............'47 '72 C.112 B.A. L.1065 J.D. [R.W.Eisfelder]
*PRACTICE AREAS: Commercial Litigation; Insurance Law; Bad Faith Litigation; Family Law.

**Eisfelder, Robert W., P.C., Law Offices of, (AV) ▣**
**Suite 400, 11726 San Vicente Boulevard, 90049-5047**
**Telephone: 310-820-4500**
**Robert W. Eisfelder.**
**General Civil and Trial Practice in all State and Federal Courts. Commercial, Insurance, Bad Faith, Personal Injury, Accident and Health Insurance and Family Litigation.**
*See Professional Biographies, LOS ANGELES, CALIFORNIA*

**Eisma, Lisa Emily** ..........................'69 '95 C.112 B.A. L.1067 J.D. [▣ Cummins&W.]
*PRACTICE AREAS: Insurance Defense Litigation; Subrogation.
Eisner, Eric ...........................'48 '73 C&L.178 B.A., J.D. 9130 Sunset Blvd.
Eisner, Paul D. ......................'51 '76 C.112 B.A. L.426 J.D. 11050 LaGrange Ave.
Eisner, Richard J. ...................'51 '82 C.1077 B.A. L.809 J.D. 520 S. Lafayette Park Pl.
Eisner, Robert A. '42 '67 C.563 B.S. L.724 LL.B.
(adm. in NY; not adm. in CA) Asst. V.P., Legal Comp. Dept., Jefferies & Co., Inc.
**Eisner, Sheri F.** ...........................'66 '92 C.112 A.B. L.800 J.D. [▣ Pillsbury M.&S.]
**Eisner, Steven G.** ..................'70 '95 C.112 B.A. L.1068 J.D. [▣ O'Melveny&M.]
*PRACTICE AREAS: Corporate.
**Ejikeme, Ada E.** ...........................'64 '95 C.325 B.A. L.178 J.D. [▣ Milbank,T.H.&M.]
**Elconin, Teresa F.** ...................'65 '92 C.1077 B.S. L.426 J.D. [▣ Sheppard,M.R.&H.]
*PRACTICE AREAS: Employment Law; Labor Relations; Public Law.

**Elden, David A. '42 '70 C.763 B.S. L.1049 J.D.**
**1975 Century Park East, Suite 2200, 90067**
**Telephone: 310-788-7775 Fax: 310-843-9933**
**Criminal Law, Federal and State Appellate.**
*See Professional Biographies, LOS ANGELES, CALIFORNIA*

**Elder, Brad M.** ......'67 '94 C.1109 B.A. L.1137 J.D. [▣ Harrington,F.D.&C.] (©Orange)
*PRACTICE AREAS: Civil Defense Litigation.
**Elder, Charles E.** ...........................'70 '96 C.813 B.A. L.145 J.D. [▣ Irell&M.]
Eldridge, Rose P. ..................................................'— '15 450 N. Rossmore St.‡
**Elerding, Gene R.** ...........................'49 '75 C.800 B.A. L.602 J.D. [Manatt,P.&P.]
*PRACTICE AREAS: Financial Services.
Elias, Emilie H. ...........................'46 '71 C.112 A.B. L.800 J.D. Comr., Supr. Ct.
Elias, Theodore J., (AV) ...........................'07 '31 C&L.813 B.A., LL.B. 6208 Warner Dr.
**Eliasberg, Michael J.**, (AV) ...............'45 '71 C.112 A.B. L.309 J.D. [▣ Gibson,D.&C.]
*PRACTICE AREAS: Entertainment.

**Eliaser, James R., The Law Offices of, (AV) '47 '72 C.763 B.A. L.426 J.D.**
**12100 Wilshire Boulevard, Suite 1600, 90025**
**Telephone: 310-820-7971 Fax: 310-820-7071**
***PRACTICE AREAS: Family Law.**
(This Listing Continued)

**Eliaser, James R., The Law Offices of (Continued)**
Family Law.
*See Professional Biographies, LOS ANGELES, CALIFORNIA*

**Elie, Steven J.** ............'62 '87 C.1044 B.A. L.1065 J.D. [Musick,P.&G.]
*PRACTICE AREAS: Litigation; Insurance.
**Eliot, Susan J.** ............'57 '81 C&L.800 B.A., J.D. [Arnold&P.]
*PRACTICE AREAS: Civil Litigation; Financial Institutions.
**Elkin, Craig S.** ............'51 '77 C.112 B.A. L.1148 J.D. [Firestein&F.]
*PRACTICE AREAS: Subrogation; Insurance; Civil Litigation.
**Elkind, Michael S.**, (AV) '48 '74 C.112 B.S. L.309 J.D. [Robbins,B.&C.] (See Pat. Sect.)
*PRACTICE AREAS: Patent Law; Trademark Law; Copyright Law; Trade Secret Law; Unfair Competition Law.
Elkins, Herschel T., (AV) ............'29 '56 C.112 B.A. L.1068 J.D. Sr. Asst. Atty. Gen.
**Elkins, Keith D.** ............'62 '87 C.112 B.A. L.1065 J.D. [Jeffer,M.B.&M.]
*PRACTICE AREAS: Real Estate.
Elkins, Randolph H. ............'46 '75 C.659 B.A. L.93 J.D. 444 S. Flower St.
**Elkins, Steven J.** ............'58 '93 C.597 B.M. L.178 J.D. [Proskauer R.G.&M.]
Eller, Robert M., (AV) ............'40 '66 C.472 B.A. L.800 J.D. 660 S. Figueroa St.
Ellicott, Vernon L. ............'54 '94 C.635 B.A. L.809 J.D. [R.G.Reinjohn]
**Ellingsen, Richard D.**, (AV) ............'54 '79 C.911 B.A. L.228 J.D. [Davis W.T.]

**Elliot, Lamb, Leibl & Snyder**
(See Encino)

Elliott, Charles M. W. ............'28 '72 C.112 B.S. L.1136 J.D. Dep. Alternate Pub. Def.
**Elliott, J. Jean** ............'32 '72 L.1095 J.D. 1707 Micheltorena St.
**Elliott, James F.**, (AV) ............'53 '80 C&L.37 B.A., J.D. [Irell&M.]
Elliott, Jay Jeffrey ............'57 '82 C.813 B.A. L.1068 J.D. [Thomas&E.]
**Elliott, Mark E.** ............'66 '92 C.112 B.A. L.1065 J.D. [Parker,M.C.O.&S.]
Elliott, William M. ... '34 '62 C&L.502 B.A., J.D. Sr. V.P. & Gen. Coun., Northrop Corp.
**Ellis, Bradley H.** ............'57 '83 C&L.339 B.A., J.D. [Sidley&A.]
**Ellis, Dennis S.** ............'67 '95 C.1109 B.B.A. L.329 J.D. [Paul,H.J.&W.]

**Ellis, George H., Law Offices of, (AV) '38 '66 C.813 A.B. L.1065 J.D.**
**811 West 7th Street, Suite 1220, 90017**
Telephone: 213-622-9001 Fax: 213-622-5949
General Civil and Trial Practice in all State Courts. Insurance Litigation, Products Liability, Personal Injury, Malpractice and Criminal Law. Appellate Practice.
Reference: First Interstate Bank.
*See Professional Biographies, LOS ANGELES, CALIFORNIA*

**Ellis, James H.** ............'63 '95 C.309 A.B. L.112 J.D. [Munger,T.&O.]
**Ellis, Jeffrey B.** ............'53 '78 C.659 B.A. L.426 J.D. [Gaims,W.W.&E.]
Ellis, Malcolm G. ............'38 '70 C.472 L.1127 LL.B. 6320 Commodore Sloat Dr.
**Ellis, Patricia A.** ............'59 '87 C.1032 B.A. L.809 J.D. [Meserve,M.&H.]
**Ellis, Steven A.** ............'64 '94 C.309 A.B. L.112 J.D. [Sidley&A.]
*PRACTICE AREAS: Litigation.
**Ellis, William D.** ............'57 '82 C.605 A.B. L.477 J.D. [Morgan,L.&B.]

**Ellis, Ronald D.**
(See Torrance)

Ellison, Laura Conway ............'62 '88 C.1097 B.A. L.426 J.D. Dep. Dist. Atty.
**Ellison, Roger**, (AV) ............'37 '65 C&L.494 B.S.L., LL.B. [Manatt,P.&P.]
*PRACTICE AREAS: Private Placements; Secured Financing; Securitization; Real Estate.
**Ellman, Dennis B.** ............'51 '77 C.94 B.A. L.569 J.D. [Greenberg G.F.C.&M.]
*PRACTICE AREAS: Real Estate.
**Ellner, Richard N.**, (AV) ............'29 '54 C&L.309 A.B., LL.B. [Arter&H.]
**Ellrod, Anthony J.**, (BV) ............'61 '88 C.1111 B.A. L.990 J.D. [Manning,M.&W.]
*PRACTICE AREAS: Insurance Fraud; Complex Business; Securities Litigation; Insurance Coverage; Recreational and Sports Litigation.
**Ellsworth, David G.**, (AV) ............'41 '66 C&L.800 B.S., LL.B. [Morgan,L.&B.]
Elperin, William, (AV) '47 '72 C.1077 B.A. L.1068 J.D. 10390 Santa Monica Blvd., 4th Fl.
**El-Saden, Dhiya**, (AV) ............'52 '77 C.112 B.A. L.1068 J.D. [Gibson,D.&C.]
*PRACTICE AREAS: Corporate Finance; Mergers and Acquisitions; Real Estate Investment Trusts; Investment Companies; Financial Institutions.
**Elson, David**, (AV) ............'45 '71 C.605 B.A. L.813 J.D. [Manatt,P.&P.]
*PRACTICE AREAS: Litigation; White Collar Criminal Defense.
**Elson, Hilari Hanamaikai** ............'69 '93 C.112 A.B. L.309 J.D. [Troop M.S.&P.]
*PRACTICE AREAS: Litigation; Environmental; Insurance Coverage.
Elson, John, (A Professional Corporation) '49 '80 C.388 L.809 J.D. 141 S. Windsor Blvd.
**Elstein, Matthew C.** ............'70 '94 C.112 B.A. L.273 J.D. [Luce,F.H.&S.]
*PRACTICE AREAS: Insurance; Reinsurance; Business Litigation.
**Elwell, Christopher L.** ............'66 '96 C.276 B.S.F.S. L.813 J.D. [Latham&W.]
*LANGUAGES: French.
**Elwood, Katherine M.** ............'62 '88 C.813 A.B. L.309 J.D. [Jones,D.R.&P.]
**Emanuel, Eric**, (AV) ............'52 '81 C.723 B.A. L.1068 J.D. [Quinn E.U.&O.]
*REPORTED CASES: Zimmerman v. Stotter, 160 Cal. App. 3d 1067 (1984); Youngblood v. Wilcox, 207 Cal. App. 3d 1368 (1989); Chamberlain v. Cocola Associates, 958 F.2d 282 (9th Cir. 1992); Downey Community Hosp. v. Wilson, 977 F.2d 470 (9th Cir. 1992).
*PRACTICE AREAS: Employment; Construction; ERISA.
**Emanuel, William J.**, (AV) ............'38 '63 C.436 A.B. L.276 J.D. [Morgan,L.&B.]
Embree, Melvyn C. ............'54 '80 C&L.309 B.A., J.D. 3530 Wilshire Blvd., Ste., 1600
Embry, Garcelle M. Jones ............'56 '84 C.112 B.A. L.426 J.D. Dep. City Atty.
**Emer, William H.**, (AV) ............'46 '72 C.112 B.A. L.1068 J.D. [Riordan&M.]
*SPECIAL AGENCIES: National Labor Relations Board, Office of Federal Contract Compliance Program, Equal Employment Opportunity Commission, Department of Labor.
*PRACTICE AREAS: Traditional Labor Law; Employment Discrimination; Employment Law; Wrongful Termination.
**Emery, Scott R.** ............'70 '95 C.112 B.A. L.309 J.D. [Quinn E.U.&O.]
**Emge, Derek J.** ............'67 '92 C.154 B.A. L.1049 J.D. [Booth,M.&S.]
**Emhoff, Douglas C.** ............'64 '90 C.1077 B.A. L.800 J.D. [Pillsbury M.&S.]
*PRACTICE AREAS: Litigation.
Emi, Gregory M. ............'62 '88 C.112 B.A. L.800 J.D. One Wilshire Blvd.
**Emmer, Sheldon R.** ............'52 '81 C.154 B.A. L.1095 J.D. [Dorais&W.]
*PRACTICE AREAS: Employment Benefits.
Emmick, Michael W. ............'52 '80 C.112 B.A. L.1068 J.D. U.S. Atty's Off.
Emquies, Moise ............'62 '91 C.800 B.A. L.809 J.D. 1801 Century Park E.
Emrick, Shannon T. ............'63 '89 C.112 B.A. L.770 J.D. 1416 S. Armacost Ave.
**Emry, Cynthia Jane** ............'64 '92 C.112 B.A. L.990 J.D. [Engstrom,L.&L.]
**Enders, Robert J.** ............'46 '75 C.966 B.B.A. L.1068 J.D. [Foley L.W.&A.]
*SPECIAL AGENCIES: Federal Trade Commission.
*PRACTICE AREAS: Antitrust and Trade Regulation; Business Torts; Unfair Competition; Advertising and Marketing.
Enders, Robert J., Jr. ............'55 '82 C.112 A.B. L.426 J.D. 4215 Glencoe Ave.
**Endicott, John L.**, (AV) ............'27 '54 C.705 B.A. L.976 LL.B. [Gibson,D.&C.]
Endman, James ............'42 '69 C.112 B.S. L.809 J.D. Comr., Supr. Ct.
**Enerle, Stephen D.** ............'53 '82 C.1077 B.A. L.398 J.D. [Veatch,C.G.&N.]
*PRACTICE AREAS: Insurance Defense; General Litigation.

**Eng, Amelia M.** ............'— '78 C.1097 B.A. L.809 J.D. [Bragg,S.S.&K.]
*PRACTICE AREAS: Workers Compensation Law.
Eng, David S. ............'52 '80 C.112 B.A. L.767 J.D. Dep. Dist. Atty.
Eng, Edward J. ............'24 '62 C.284 B.A. L.809 J.D. 2321 N. Commonwealth Ave.‡
Eng, Gordon K. ............'59 '83 C.994 B.A. L.262 J.D. 555 W. 5th St.
**Eng, Leslie J.**, (AV) ............'57 '86 C.112 B.A. L.426 J.D. [Liebman&R.]
Eng, Peter M. ............'58 '86 C.112 B.A. L.770 J.D. Sr. Litigator, State Bar of Calif.
Engel, Donald S., (AV) ............'29 '59 C.563 B.S. L.569 LL.B. [Engel&E.]
Engel, Judith Edelman ............'41 '70 C&L.569 B.A., J.D. [Engel&E.]
Engel, Lisa R. ............'56 '82 C.1349 B.A. L.273 J.D. 12233 W. Olympic Blvd.‡
Engel & Engel, A Professional Corporation, (AV) ............9200 Sunset Boulevard
**Engelskirchen, Adam G.** ............'68 '94 C.154 B.A. L.800 J.D. [Sidley&A.]
*LANGUAGES: French, Spanish.
*PRACTICE AREAS: Real Estate.
**Enger, William K.** ............'63 '89 C.112 A.B. L.1068 J.D. [Hancock R.&B.]
England, Timothy N. ............'60 '89 C.1049 B.A. L.276 J.D. 550 S. Hope St.
**English, Jerone J.** ............'52 '81 C.1060 B.S. L.464 J.D. [Pillsbury M.&S.]
**English, Stephen R.** ............'46 '75 C.112 A.B. L.309 J.D. [Morgan,L.&B.]
**Engstrom, Paul W.**, (AV) ............'41 '66 C.597 B.A. L.209 J.D. [Engstrom,L.&L.]
*PRACTICE AREAS: Insurance Policy Interpretation; Bad Faith Defense; Environmental Coverage; Construction Litigation; Aviation.

**Engstrom, Lipscomb & Lack, A Professional Corporation, (AV)**
**16th Floor, 10100 Santa Monica Boulevard, 90067**
Telephone: 310-552-3800 Telecopier: 310-552-9434
URL: http://www.elllaw.com
Paul W. Engstrom; Lee G. Lipscomb; Walter J. Lack; Jerry A. Ramsey; Steven C. Shuman; Elizabeth Lane Crooke; Brian D. Depew; Jeffrey T. Bolson; Alan B. Nishimura; Gary A. Praglin; William T. Clemons III; Matthew J. Saunders; Robert J. Wolfe;—Daniel G. Whalen; Brian J. Heffernan; Eric Berg; Karen-Denise Lee; Adam D. Miller; Jill L. Feinberg; Dawn M. Flores-Oster; Paul A. Traina; Cynthia Jane Emry; Brian J. Leinbach; Joy L. Robertson; Jill P. McDonell; Laura M. Watkins; Mark Evans Millard; Stuart R. Fraenkel; Tracy Michelle Tuso; David M. Robinson; Karen L. Hindin; Troy H. Slome; Daniel J. Padova.
General Civil and Trial Practice in all State and Federal Courts. Aviation, Corporation, Domestic and International Insurance, Maritime, Professional Liability, Products Liability and Real Property Law.
Reference: Comerica Bank.
*See Professional Biographies, LOS ANGELES, CALIFORNIA*

**Ennis, Kevin G.** ............'60 '86 C.154 B.A. L.426 J.D. [Richards,W.&G.]
*PRACTICE AREAS: Public Law; Water Law.
Enns, Jean A. ............'33 '83 C.011 B.S. L.1136 J.D. 1925 Century Park, E.
Enomoto, Michael A., Jr. ............'69 '94 C.309 B.A. L.1066 J.D. 801 S. Figueroa St.
Enright, Paul M. ............'43 '74 C.1077 B.A. L.809 J.D. Dep. Pub. Def.
**Ensbury, Linda K.** '58 '83 C.112 B.A. L.1068 J.D. V.P. & Gen. Coun., ING Real Estate Investors, Inc.
*RESPONSIBILITIES: Real Estate (30%); Creditors Rights (30%); Real Estate Finance (30%); Land Use (10%).
Enslow, Ray B. ............'46 '82 C.1275 B.A. L.809 J.D. 1738 Canyon Dr.
**Enzminger, David P.** ............'63 '88 C.684 B.A. L.36 J.D. [O'Melveny&M.]
*LANGUAGES: German.
*PRACTICE AREAS: Litigation.
**Eoff, Joanna M.** ............'68 '95 C.112 B.A. L.1068 J.D. [Galton&H.]
*PRACTICE AREAS: Civil Litigation.
**Epport, Victor M., (A Law Corporation)**, (AV) '29 '53 C.112 B.A. L.1068 J.D. [Epport&R.]

**Epport & Richman, (AV)**
A California General Partnership
**Suite 1450, 10100 Santa Monica Boulevard, 90067**
Telephone: 310-785-0885 Telecopier: 310-785-0787
Members of Firm: Steven N. Richman; Mark Robbins; Beth Ann R. Young. Associates: Steven C. Huskey; Laura E. McSwiggin; Wendy K. Shapnick; Victor R. Berwin; Amir Yariv; Scott H. Noskin; Philip H. R. Nevinny; Michael D. Shore; Francis Curtis Hung, Jr.; Renu Mago Setaro; Lawrence A. Abelson; Paul A. Fuhrman. Of Counsel: Victor M. Epport (A Law Corporation); Linda A. Netzer.
General Civil and Trial Practice in all State and Federal Courts. Banking, Secured Transactions, Corporation, Real Property, Commercial and Bankruptcy Law.
Reference: First Regional Bank (Century City Office).
*See Professional Biographies, LOS ANGELES, CALIFORNIA*

**Epstein, Alan J.** ............'60 '87 C.966 B.B.A. L.1068 J.D. [Armstrong H.J.T.&W.]
*PRACTICE AREAS: Taxation; Business Law.
Epstein, Bob J. ............'58 '90 C.112 B.A. L.809 J.D. [J.R.Brown,Jr.]
**Epstein, Buddy**, (AV) ............'48 '74 C.112 B.A. L.1068 J.D. [De Castro,W.&C.]
*PRACTICE AREAS: Real Estate Law; Taxation Law; Business Law.
Epstein, David B., (AV) ............'45 '69 C.112 B.S. L.1068 J.D. [Garfield,T.E.&T.]
Epstein, David J. ............'39 '65 C.112 B.S. L.1068 LL.B. 1801 Century Pk., E.
Epstein, Eric M. ............'46 '72 C.1036 B.A. L.94 J.D. [Epstein&R.]
Epstein, Hymen L., (BV) ............'27 '76 C.112 B.S. L.1148 J.D. 3700 Wilshire Blvd.
**Epstein, James M.**, (AV) ............'40 '67 C.813 B.A. L.1068 J.D. [Epstein,A.&R.]
*PRACTICE AREAS: Criminal Law.
**Epstein, Marc, (P.C.)**, (AV) ............'49 '74 C.112 B.S. L.1068 J.D. [Gaims,W.W.&E.]
**Epstein, Mark H.** ............'59 '85 C.112 B.A. L.1066 J.D. [Munger,T.&O.]
**Epstein, Paul C.** ............'56 '86 C.112 L.809 J.D. [Sullivan,W.&D.]
*PRACTICE AREAS: Civil Litigation; Real Estate Litigation; Eminent Domain Law.
**Epstein, Scott M.** ............'62 '90 C.112 B.A. L.813 J.D. [Irell&M.]

**Epstein, Adelson & Rubin, (AV)**
**East Tower, 11835 West Olympic Boulevard, Suite 1235, 90064**
Telephone: 310-473-6447 Fax: 310-473-3097
Members of Firm: James M. Epstein (Certified Specialist, Criminal Law, The State Bar of California Board of Legal Specialization); Michael Adelson; Alan Rubin.
Practice Limited to Criminal Law.
Reference: City National Bank.
*See Professional Biographies, LOS ANGELES, CALIFORNIA*

**Epstein Becker & Green, (AV)**
**Suite 500, 1875 Century Park, East, 90067**
Telephone: 310-556-8861 Facsimile: 310-553-2165
Members of the Firm: David P. Bender, Jr.; Thomas P. Brown IV; B. Alan Dickson; Robert A. Dye; Cynthia E. Gitt; James A. Goodman; David Jacobs; Mark A. Kadzielski; John P. Krave; Angel Manzano, Jr.; Alan E. Walcher. Senior Attorneys: Abbie P. Maliniak; Alyce Ann Rubinfeld;—Lester F. Aponte; Judith L. Baxter; I. Benjamin Blady; Jana L. DeMeire; Gregory S. Glazer; Pamela G. Gross; Daniel J. Hammond; Elona Kogan; Patricia Y. Miller; Margaret B. Reynolds; Ralph M. Semien.
General Practice. Corporation, Securities, Commercial Law and Bankruptcy. Health Care and Hospital Law. Management Labor Relations and Employee Benefits Law. Equal Employment Opportunity and Affirmative Action Law and Practice. Taxation, Insurance, Government Procurement, Municipal Finance, Real Estate, Political Activities, Legislation and Election Law. Arbitration, Administrative Proceedings, State and Federal Civil and Appellate Practice.
San Francisco, California Office: Two Embarcadero Center, Suite 1650. Telephone: 415-398-3500.
New York, N.Y. Office: Epstein Becker & Green, P.C., 250 Park Avenue. Telephone: 212-351-4500.
Washington, D.C. Office: Epstein Becker & Green, P.C., 1227 25th Street, N.W., Suite 700. Telephone: 202-861-0900.
Dallas, Texas Office: Epstein Becker & Green, P.C., Park Central VII, 12750 Merit Drive, Suite 1320. Telephone: 972-490-3143.
Stamford, Connecticut Office: Epstein Becker & Green, P.C., Suite 603, Six Landmark Square. Telephone: 203-348-3737.

(This Listing Continued)

**Epstein Becker & Green (Continued)**

**Newark, New Jersey Office: Epstein Becker & Green, P.C., Seventh Floor, The Legal Center, One Riverfront Plaza. Telephone: 201-642-1900.**
**Miami, Florida Office: Suite 100, 2400 South Dixie Highway. Telephone: 305-856-1100.**
**Boston, Massachusetts Office: Epstein Becker & Green, P.C., 75 State Street. Telephone: 617-342-4000.**
**Alexandria, Virginia Office: Epstein Becker & Green, P.C., Suite 301, 510 King Street. Telephone: 703-684-1204.**

*See Professional Biographies, LOS ANGELES, CALIFORNIA*

Epstein & Reed, A Professional Corporation ........................ 2049 Century Park E.
**Erasmus, Gavin M.** ..................'58 '86 C&L.061 B.Com., B.L. [O'Neill,H.&A.]
*PRACTICE AREAS: Eminent Domain; Just Compensation; Direct Takings and Inverse Condemnation; Compensation for Expropriation (Nationally, Comparatively and Internationally); Related Fields.
**Erb, Jason R.** ............................'71 '95 C.112 B.S. L.228 J.D. [Ⓐ Pillsbury M.&S.]
Erbsen, Philip ............................................... '10 '33 L.1001 LL.B. Supr. Ct. Comr.
**Erbstoesser, Eugene R.**, (AV) '48 '74
C.800 B.A. L.1065 J.D. Assoc. Gen. Coun., Ernst & Young LLP
Erdman, Jeffrey W. ........................'63 '95 C.911 B.A. L.809 J.D. [Ⓐ Anderson&W.]
Erenberg, Douglas D. ..................'51 '76 C.813 B.A. L.990 J.D. 8747 Beverly Blvd.‡
Ericksen, Lisa Strenger ..............'52 '87 C.37 B.A. L.1148 J.D. 3530 Wilshire Blvd.

**Ericksen, Arbuthnot, Kilduff, Day & Lindstrom, Inc., (AV)**
**835 Wilshire Boulevard, Suite 500, 90017-2603**⊙
**Telephone: 213-489-4411 Fax: 213-489-4332**
**Thomas J. McDonnell; Mark L. Kiefer; Deborah S. Tropp; Bud Spencer.**
**General Civil, Trial and Appellate Practice in all State and Federal Courts. Corporate, Probate and Insurance Law.**
**Oakland, California Office: 530 Water Street, Port Building, Suite 720. Telephone: 510-832-7770. Fax: 510-832-0102.**
**San Francisco, California Office: 260 California Street, Suite 1100. Telephone: 415-362-7126. Fax: 415-362-6401.**
**Sacramento, California Office: 100 Howe Avenue, Suite 240N. Telephone: 916-483-5181. Fax: 916-483-7558.**
**Fresno, California Office: 2440 West Shaw Avenue, Suite 101. Telephone: 209-449-2600. Fax: 209-449-2603.**
**San Jose, California Office: 152 North Third Street, Suite 700. Telephone: 408-286-0880. Fax: 408-286-0337.**
**Walnut Creek, California Office: 2700 Ygnacio Valley Road, Suite 280. Telephone: 510-947-1702. Fax: 510-947-4921.**
**Riverside, California Office: 1770 Iowa Avenue, Suite 210. Telephone: 909-682-3246. Fax: 909-682-4013.**

*See Professional Biographies, LOS ANGELES, CALIFORNIA*

**Erickson, Donald C.**, (AV) ........................ '50 '76 C.112 B.A. L.800 J.D. [Arter&H.]
**Erickson, Eric J.** ..............................'53 '82 C.112 B.A. L.61 J.D. [Ⓐ Gray,Y.D.&R.]
*PRACTICE AREAS: Construction Defects Litigation; Product Liability Litigation; Business Litigation; Personal Injury Litigation.
**Erickson, J. Gunnar** ..................'46 '75 C.813 B.A. L.976 J.D. [Armstrong H.J.T.&W.]
*PRACTICE AREAS: Entertainment.
**Erickson, Lauren** ..........................'59 '94 C.112 B.A. L.1068 J.D. [Ⓐ Musick,P.&G.]
Erickson, Lloyd E. ............... '30 '58 C.112 B.A. L.1066 J.D. Asst. Coun., Unocal Corp.
Erickson, Marjorie Lakin ................ '43 '80 C.33 B.A. L.426 J.D. Asst. U.S. Trustee
**Erickson, Neil C.** ..........................'55 '83 C.813 B.A. L.1065 J.D. [Jeffer,M.B.&M.]
*PRACTICE AREAS: General Business Litigation; Real Estate; Banking and Securities Litigation.
Erickson, Ralph E., (AV) ................ '28 '56 C.188 B.S. L.309 J.D. 555 W. 5th St.‡
Erickson, Ralph Hull ..... '31 '58 C.399 B.S. L.477 J.D. Admin. Law J., Soc. Sec. Admin.
Erickson Harris, Cherie ............... '46 '75 C.339 B.A. L.800 J.D. 1901 Ave. of the Stars
**Erigero, Stephen J.** ...................'59 '85 C.426 B.A. L.1065 J.D. [Ropers,M.K.&B.]
*PRACTICE AREAS: Insurance Coverage; Construction and General Civil Litigation; Bad Faith Litigation.
Erlich, Henry P. .........................'11 '34 C&L.800 B.A., J.D. 3634 Shannon Rd.‡
Erlich, Kenneth P. ................................................'49 '77 Off. of Pub. Def.
**Erlinger, Michael J.** ...................'69 '94 C.276 B.A. L.1068 J.D. [Ⓐ Pillsbury M.&S.]
Ernst, David D. ......................'61 '90 C.339 B.S. L.37 J.D. 3699 Wilshire Blvd.
Ernster, John H. ...................'47 '74 C.112 A.B. L.426 J.D. 500 Citadel Dr., 2nd Fl.
Errante, Diane M. ...................... '58 '84 C.37 B.S. L.1065 J.D. 621 Sunset Blvd.
**Erskine, Andrew** ..................................'50 '81 C&L.800 A.B., J.D. [Manatt,P.&P.]
*PRACTICE AREAS: Commercial Transactions; Secured Lending and Loan Workouts; Financial Institutions; Mortgage Banking.
**Erskine, Elizabeth A.** ..........................'56 '86 C.588 B.S. L.93 J.D. [Bronson,B.&M.]
*PRACTICE AREAS: Business Litigation; Banking Litigation; Professional Liability Litigation.
**Ersoff, Victoria L.** .......................'66 '92 C.36 B.S. L.1148 J.D. [Ⓐ Koletsky,M.&F.]
*PRACTICE AREAS: Construction Defect Defense; General Liability Defense; Toxic Tort Defense.

**Ervin, Cohen & Jessup LLP**
**(See Beverly Hills)**

**Erwin, Philippe O.** .............'66 '92 C.696 B.S. L.93 J.D. [Ⓐ Loeb&L.] (See Pat. Sect.)
**Esbenshade, Richard D., (A Professional Corporation)**, (AV) '29 '58
C.813 A.B. L.309 LL.B. [Munger,T.&O.]
**Escalante, Kristin Sherratt** ...............'63 '94 C&L.800 B.A., J.D. [Ⓐ Munger,T.&O.]
Eschenasy, Aveeram E. '66 '92 C.309 A.B. L.178 J.D.
(adm. in NY; not adm. in CA) 116 N. Robertson Blvd.
Eschenasy, Avy '66 '92 C.309 A.B. L.178 J.D.
V.P., Bus. & Legal Affairs, New Line Cinema Corp.
Escobar, Ana Maria ........................ '61 '88 C.813 B.A. L.1049 J.D. [Ⓐ Morgan&W.]
Escobedo, Mildred ....................'62 '90 C.112 B.A. L.940 J.D. 1541 Wilshire Blvd.
Escutia, Martha M. ........................ '57 '85 C.800 B.S. L.276 J.D. United Way, Inc.
**Eshaghian, George M.** ..........'66 '91 C.1077 B.S. L.1068 J.D. [Ⓐ Skadden,A.S.M.&F.]
Eskanos, David M. ........................'62 '90 C.112 B.A. L.284 J.D. 10650 Kinnard Ave.
**Eskenazi, Bonnie E.** .................'60 '85 C.893 B.A. L.813 J.D. [Greenberg G.F.C.&M.]
*PRACTICE AREAS: Litigation.
**Eskenazi, Phillip J.** ................'66 '92 C.112 B.S. L.1065 J.D. [Ⓐ Sheppard,M.R.&H.]
**Eskilson, James R.** ..................'59 '85 C.1077 B.A. L.1065 J.D. [Sanders,B.G.S.&M.]
**Eskridge, Gayle L.** ..................'59 '88 C.502 B.A. L.537 J.D. [Ⓐ Hornberger&C.]
**Esmail, Aaftab P.** ...........................'62 '86 C.112 B.A. L.309 J.D. [Riordan&M.]
**Esner, Stuart B.** ..........................'57 '82 C.112 B.A. L.426 J.D. [Esner H.&C.]⊙
*PRACTICE AREAS: Appellate Law.

**Esner Higa & Chang**
**523 West Sixth Street, 90014**⊙
**Telephone: 213-630-1990 Fax: 213-630-1999**
**Stuart B. Esner; Billie Ann U. Higa.**
**Appellate Practice.**
**San Francisco, California Office: 625 Market St., 10th Floor. Telephone: 415-882-4056. Fax: 415-495-4566.**

*See Professional Biographies, LOS ANGELES, CALIFORNIA*

Espo, Caryn S. ..........................'51 '76 C.112 B.A. L.1068 J.D. [Ⓐ Williams&Assoc.]
**Esquibias, Bridgett** ...................'66 '95 C.112 B.A. L.1049 J.D. [Ⓐ Gray,Y.D.&R.]
*PRACTICE AREAS: Labor and Employment Law; Litigation.
**Essex, Susan R.** ..........................................'— '90 C.684 B.A. L.276 J.D. [Ⓐ Morgan,L.&B.]
**Essner, Lee B.** ..........................'66 '91 C.112 B.A. L.800 J.D. [Ⓐ Skadden,A.S.M.&F.]
**Esten, Lawrence D.** .......... '61 '86 C.112 B.A. L.426 J.D. [Manning,M.&W.] (⊙Irvine)
**Esterkin, Richard W.**, (AV) ..........'51 '76 C.154 B.A. L.1068 J.D. [Ⓒ Morgan,L.&B.]
**Esters, Cory D.** ...........................'68 '94 C.112 B.A. L.426 J.D. [Ⓐ Mendes&M.]
**Esterson, Andrea L.** ....................'63 '92 C.800 B.S. L.426 J.D. [Ⓐ Argue P.H.&M.]
Estes, Mark ..................................'56 '83 C.339 B.A. L.1049 J.D. [Frisenda,Q.&N.]
**Estrada, Michael** ......................'56 '87 C.112 B.A. L.1066 J.D. [Richards,W.&G.]
*LANGUAGES: Spanish.
*PRACTICE AREAS: Municipal; Redevelopment; Solid Waste; Affordable Housing.
Estradas, Anthony R. ........................'44 '80 C.112 B.A. L.800 J.D. P.O. Box 49339
Estrich, Susan ........'52 '80 C.914 B.A. L.309 J.D. Prof. of Law, Univ. of Southern Calif.
**Estuar, Paul J.** ..............................'— '93 C.178 A.B. L.426 J.D. [Ⓒ J.Y.Lauchengco,Jr.]
*LANGUAGES: Tagalog.
Etezadi, David ................... '60 '86 C.112 B.A. L.1068 J.D. Legal Aid Found. of L.A.
**Ettinger, David S.** ..........................'56 '80 C.264 B.A. L.426 J.D. [Horvitz&L.]
**Ettinger, Warren**, (AV) ............'29 '56 C&L.800 B.S., LL.B. [Ⓒ Skadden,A.S.M.&F.]
**Etzioni, Michael R.** ...............................'67 '94 C&L.477 B.A., J.D. [Ⓐ Latham&W.]
**Eugenio, Lawrence A.** ...................'69 '95 C.724 B.A. L.112 J.D. [Ⓐ Lewis,D.B.&B.]
Eule, Julian N. '49 '74 C.1350 B.A. L.188 J.D.
(adm. in NY; not adm. in CA) Prof., UCLA Sch. of Law
**Eum, David** ..................................'61 '93 C.112 B.A. L.101 J.D. [Ⓐ Wehner&P.]
*LANGUAGES: Korean.
Evangelatos, Andrew, (AV) ............'25 '54 C.1246 B.A. L.809 LL.B. [Alberstone&E.]
**Evans, April McGandy** ..................'— '86 C.906 B.A. L.1068 J.D. [Ⓒ Gibson,D.&C.]
*PRACTICE AREAS: Banking; Corporations.
Evans, David G. ..........................................'46 '77 C&L.1137 B.S.L., J.D. Dep. Dist. Atty.
**Evans, David L.** ...............................'65 '91 C.170 B.A. L.426 J.D. [Ⓐ A.R.Hamrick,III]
*LANGUAGES: German.
*PRACTICE AREAS: Litigation; Insurance Defense; Bad Faith Litigation; Entertainment Litigation.
**Evans, Gareth T.** ..............................'61 '88 C.112 B.A. L.569 J.D. [Ⓐ Gibson,D.&C.]
*PRACTICE AREAS: Securities Litigation; General Business Litigation; Insurance Coverage and Bad Faith Litigation; Professional Liability.
Evans, Gregory B. ........................ '48 '74 C.846 B.S. L.744 J.D. [Nishiyama,M.L.E.&S.]
**Evans, Gregory Lawrence** ................'60 '90 C.800 B.S. L.602 J.D. [Preston G.&E.]
*LANGUAGES: Spanish.
*PRACTICE AREAS: Civil Litigation.
**Evans, H. Alix** ..........................'58 '87 C.893 B.A. L.880 J.D. [Ⓐ Sedgwick,D.M.&A.]
**Evans, Irwin S.**, (AV) ................................ '38 '66 C.1097 B.A. L.426 J.D. [Atkins&E.]
*PRACTICE AREAS: Product Liability Law; Personal Injury Law; Commercial Law.
Evans, J. Gregg, (AV) ..................'17 '51 C.800 B.S. L.809 J.D. 434 N. Larchmont Blvd.
**Evans, James R., Jr.** ............................'59 '85 C.800 B.S. L.1066 J.D. [Hill,F.&B.]
*LANGUAGES: Spanish.
*PRACTICE AREAS: Surety Law and Litigation; Business Litigation; Plaintiff's Tort Litigation (Insurance Bad Faith, Personal Injury, Medical Malpractice).
**Evans, Jeffrey A.** ..............................'61 '89 C.1074 B.S. L.767 J.D. [Ⓐ Long&L.]
Evans, John R. ........................'45 '71 C&L.309 A.B., J.D. Sr. Atty., Calif. Ct. of App.
**Evans, John W.** ................................'55 '81 C.112 B.A. L.809 J.D. [Ⓐ Liebman&R.]
Evans, Jonathan W. ......................'49 '75 C.112 A.B. L.809 J.D. [J.W.Evans&Assoc.]
Evans, Mark H. ......................'59 '85 C.112 B.A. L.800 J.D. 430 S. Fuller Ave.
Evans, Mark L. ...........................'51 '86 C.1042 B.S. L.426 J.D. Dep. Dist. Atty.
**Evans, Michael G.** ............................'54 '80 C.112 B.A. L.426 J.D. [Gascou,G.&T.]
*REPORTED CASES: Escrow Agents Fidelity Corp. v. Superior Court, (1992) 4 Cal. 4th 491.
*PRACTICE AREAS: Fidelity; Commercial Litigation; Real Estate Litigation; Legislation; Creditor Rights.
Evans, Patrick J. ..............................'55 '83 C.112 B.A. L.1068 J.D. [Dressler,R.&E.]
Evans, Jonathan W. & Associates ................................................ 201 N. Figueroa St.
**Everett, Pamela M.** '62 '96 C.549 B.A. L.1049 J.D.
[Ⓐ Allen,M.L.G.&M.] (⊙San Diego)
*PRACTICE AREAS: Real Estate; Bankruptcy.
**Everett, Terrence A.** ...................'53 '78 C.112 A.B. L.426 J.D. [Carlsmith B.W.C.&I.]
*PRACTICE AREAS: Corporate Law; Corporate Organization; Hotel and Resort Development; International Financial Real Estate.
Evers, Reid A. '51 '76 C.94 A.B. L.800 J.D.
2nd V.P. & Asst. Gen. Coun., Transamerica Occidental Life Ins. Co.
Ewell, Christine Cleveland ................ '61 '86 C.839 B.A. L.309 J.D. Asst. U.S. Atty.
**Ewen, Philip** ......................................'61 '87 C.36 B.S. L.800 J.D. [Musick,P.&G.]
*PRACTICE AREAS: Labor and Employment.
Ewing, Deborah E. ...................'57 '82 C.1109 B.A. L.809 J.D. 6310 San Vicente Blvd.
**Extavour, N. Kemba** ...................'70 '96 C.813 B.A. L.1066 J.D. [Ⓐ McKenna&C.]
*PRACTICE AREAS: Litigation; Government Contracts.
**Eyrich, John F.** ..................................'67 '94 C.766 B.S. L.770 J.D. [Ⓐ Ross,S.&G.]
**Eyvazzadeh, Blenda** ......................'60 '85 C.112 B.A. L.426 J.D. [Cummins&W.]
*PRACTICE AREAS: Personal Injury.
**Ezer, Mitchel J.**, (AV) ...............................'35 '60 C.597 B.S. L.976 J.D. [Ezer&W.]
*PRACTICE AREAS: Real Estate; Foreclosures; Partnership; Business and Probate Litigation.

**Ezer, Sment & Williamson**
**(See Michael R. Sment, Ventura and Los Angeles)**

**Ezer & Williamson, LLP, (AV)**
**(Formerly Rich & Ezer)**
**1888 Century Park East, Suite 1550 (Century City), 90067-1706**
**Telephone: 310-277-7747 Telecopier: 310-277-2576**
**Mitchel J. Ezer; Richard E. Williamson. Of Counsel: John Cramer. Associates: Frederick D. Hale.**
**General Civil, Trial and Appellate Practice in all State and Federal Courts. Real Estate, Corporate, Partnership Law, Business, Construction, Foreclosures, Probate, Creditors Rights.**

*See Professional Biographies, LOS ANGELES, CALIFORNIA*

Fabe, Jacqueline M. ........................ '48 '74 C.788 B.A. L.800 J.D. 4700 Wilshire Blvd.
**Faber, Cameron H.** ..........................'55 '81 C.112 B.A. L.426 J.D. [Parker,M.C.O.&S.]
*PRACTICE AREAS: Commercial Litigation.
**Faber, Christopher J.**, (AV) ...............'54 '81 C.269 B.A. L.990 J.D. [Dummit,F.&B.]
**Faber, Diane L.** ...............................'62 '87 C.976 B.A. L.309 J.D. [Manatt,P.&P.]
*PRACTICE AREAS: Entertainment Industry; Intellectual Property; Business Litigation.
Faber, Stuart J. ........................'33 '61 C.966 B.S. L.426 LL.B. 3255 Wilshire Blvd.
Fabrick, Douglas C. ......................'63 '91 C.112 B.A. L.426 J.D. 2121 Ave. of the Stars
**Fabrick, Howard D.**, (AV) ............'38 '63 C&L.813 B.A., J.D. [Proskauer R.G.&M.]
*PRACTICE AREAS: Labor; Entertainment Law.
**Fabrikant, Robert**, (AV) ..........................'43 '68 C.659 B.A. L.276 J.D. [Sidley&A.]
*PRACTICE AREAS: Health Care; Antitrust; White Collar Criminal; Complex Commercial Litigation.
Fabrizi, Larry David, (Mr.) ..........................'53 '82 C.645 L.809 J.D. 3701 W. 6th
**Facer, Mark S.** ...........................................'54 '83 C&L.101 B.S., J.D. [Mendes&M.]
**Fadel, Alfred** ..............................'41 '68 C.800 B.S. L.1095 J.D. [Gibbs,G.L.&A.]
*PRACTICE AREAS: Construction Law; Design; Real Estate.
**Fagan, Christopher B.** ........................'52 '79 C.668 B.A. L.767 J.D. [Goldman&K.]
*PRACTICE AREAS: Probate; Trusts; Wills.
Fagan, James W. ..........................................'39 '72 C.800 B.A. L.602 J.D. Dep. Dist. Atty.
Fagan, Seymour, (AV) .....................'28 '55 C.112 B.S. L.1068 LL.B. [Ⓒ Tyre K.K.&G.]
Fagelbaum, Jerold ........................'48 '73 C.823 B.A. L.276 J.D. [Fagelbaum&H.]
Fagelbaum & Heller, LLP .................................................. 2029 Century Pk. E.
Fager, Christopher B. '48 '73 C.165 B.A. L.94 J.D.
(adm. in MA; not adm. in CA) 7250 Franklin Ave.‡
Fagiani, Gabriel F. .......................'65 '91 C.800 B.A. L.809 J.D. 1880 Century Pk. E.
**Fagin, Norman A.** ......................'51 '79 C.1077 B.S. L.1095 J.D. [Ⓐ Saltzburg,R.&B.]
*PRACTICE AREAS: Estate Planning; Wills; Trusts; Probate.
**Fagin, Vernon A.** ........................'49 '82 C.112 B.A. L.228 J.D. [Ⓐ Wilson,E.M.E.&D.]

**Fahey, William F.**, (AV) ..................'51 '76 C.800 B.S. L.1068 J.D. [Smaltz,A.&F.]
*PRACTICE AREAS: White Collar Crime; Securities; Environmental; Complex Business Litigation.
Faierman, Stacy Lyn ..........................'66 '91 C.112 B.A. L.276 J.D. 515 S. Figueroa St.

**Fain, Harry M.**
**(See Beverly Hills)**

**Fainsbert, Stephen B., (A P.C.)**, (AV) '36 '66 C.659 B.S. L.1068 J.D. [Fainsbert,M.&S.]
*PRACTICE AREAS: Real Estate; Real Estate-Commercial Law; Real Estate Finance; Title Insurance Law.

**Fainsbert, Mase & Snyder, (AV)**
**A Partnership including Professional Corporations**
**Suite 1100, 11835 West Olympic Boulevard, 90064**
**Telephone: 310-473-6400 Telecopier: 310-473-8702**
**Members of Firm: Stephen B. Fainsbert (A P.C.); John A. Mase (A P.C.) (Certified Specialist, Taxation Law, The State Bar of California Board of Legal Specialization); Lawrence A. Snyder (A P.C.) (Certified Specialist, Taxation Law, The State Bar of California Board of Legal Specialization); Raymond H. Aver. Associates: Colin J. Tanner; Sarah K. Andrus.**
**Real Property, Federal and State Taxation, Business, Corporate, Partnership, Estate Planning, Probate and Entertainment Law. General Civil and Trial Practice in State and Federal Courts, Creditors Rights.**
***See Professional Biographies, LOS ANGELES, CALIFORNIA***

**Fairbank, Robert Harold**, (AV) ..........'48 '77 C.813 A.B. L.569 J.D. [Fairbank&V.]
*PRACTICE AREAS: Complex Business Litigation; Securities; Consumer Class Actions; Competitive Business Torts; Director and Officer Liability.

**Fairbank & Vincent, (AV)**
**11755 Wilshire Boulevard, Suite 800, 90025**
**Telephone: 310-996-5520 Fax: 310-996-5530**
**Email: fairvin@earthlink.net**
**Members of Firm: Robert Harold Fairbank; Dirk L. Vincent.**
**General Civil Trial and Appellate Practice in all Courts.**
***See Professional Biographies, LOS ANGELES, CALIFORNIA***

Fairbanks, Phyllis Kelly '30 '58 C.112 A.B. L.1068 LL.B. Sr. Atty., Off. of State Controller
**Fairclough, Michael J.**, (AV) ....................'44 '72 C&L.878 J.D. [O'Melveny&M.]
*LANGUAGES: French.
*PRACTICE AREAS: Investment Companies; Investment Advisors; Mergers and Acquisitions; Partnerships; Securities.
**Fairley, Alan H.** .........................'— '95 C.112 B.A. L.1068 J.D. [Ⓐ Rogers&W.]
**Fairman, Robert L.**, (AV) '35 '63 C&L.800 A.B., LL.B. [Norton&F.] & [Ⓒ J.M.Donovan]
*PRACTICE AREAS: Insurance Bad Faith; Life Insurance; Health Insurance; Disability Insurance; ERISA.

**Fairshter & Associates**
**(See Pasadena)**

Falco, James A ..................................'55 '87 C.674 B.A. L.940 J.D. Dep. Dist. Atty.
Falcone, A. V. ...................................'06 '31 C.112 L.1251 LL.B. 727 W. 7th St.
**Falcone, Angelo C.**, (AV) ......................'51 '78 C.112 B.A. L.809 J.D. [Riordan&M.]
*PRACTICE AREAS: International Business; Tax Law.
Falcone, Dewey L. ...................................'31 '56 C.770 B.S. L.800 LL.B. Supr. Ct.J.
**Falk, Burton**, (AV) ...........................'57 '81 C.339 B.A. L.477 J.D. [Belin R.&B.]
*PRACTICE AREAS: Business; Entertainment Litigation; Family Law.
**Falk, Ethan J.**, (AV) ............................'54 '79 C.1044 B.A. L.477 J.D. [Falk&S.]
*PRACTICE AREAS: Corporate.

**Falk & Sharp, A Professional Corporation, (AV)**
**660 South Figueroa Street, Suite 1600, 90017-3452**
**Telephone: 213-622-6868 FAX: 213-622-4486**
**Ethan J. Falk; Keith A. Sharp.**
**General Corporate and Labor.**
***See Professional Biographies, LOS ANGELES, CALIFORNIA***

**Fall, Mark Scott** .............................'61 '92 C.112 B.A. L.1068 J.D. [Ⓐ Lord,B.&B.]
*PRACTICE AREAS: Civil Litigation.
**Falzetta, Frank** ......................'61 '86 C.197 B.A. L.477 J.D. [Sheppard,M.R.&H.]
*PRACTICE AREAS: Litigation.
Fang, Kenneth T. H. ......................'57 '85 C.112 B.A. L.1065 J.D. Dep. Pub. Def.
**Fang, Zhi-Ying James** ..........'50 '84 L.911 LL.M. [Davis W.T.] (⊙Shanghai, China)
*LANGUAGES: Mandarin Chinese and Shanghai Dialect.
**Fannan, Richard** ................'47 '77 C.112 B.A. L.1066 J.D. [Leland,P.S.F.M.&M.]
*PRACTICE AREAS: Business Litigation.
**Fant, Gregory C.** ..........................'51 '76 C.112 B.A. L.1068 J.D. [Arnold&P.]
*PRACTICE AREAS: Corporation Law; Business Law; Banking Law; Real Estate Law.
**Farach, Horacio A.** .....'55 '89 C.790 B.S. L.796 J.D. [Ⓐ Robbins,B.&C.] (See Pat. Sect.)
*LANGUAGES: Spanish.
*PRACTICE AREAS: Patent Law (Biotechnology); Trademark Law; Copyright Law; Federal Litigation.
Farber, Mark A. ......................'51 '76 C.477 B.A. L.912 J.D. Exec. Dir., AFTRA-L.A.
Farber, Mia Darbonne ................'62 '87 C.1168 B.A. L.426 J.D. 3255 Wilshire Blvd.
**Farber, Michael B.** ......'47 '87 C.111 B.S. L.809 J.D. [Ⓐ Merchant&G.] (See Pat. Sect.)
*PRACTICE AREAS: Patents; Trademarks.
**Fargo, Raymond J.** ..............................'38 '75 C.1097 B.A. L.809 [Roper&F.]
*PRACTICE AREAS: Accidents; Personal Injury; Malpractice Defense; Uninsured Motorist; Products Liability Law.
**Farhat, Vince L.** ..........................'66 '96 C.30 B.A. L.426 J.D. [Ⓐ Jones,D.R.&P.]
**Faris, Cheryl J.** ........ '47 '83 C.455 B.A. L.426 J.D. Atty., Pacific Telesis Legal Group
**Faris, Sharon L.** ......................'62 '93 C.112 B.A. L.426 J.D. [Ⓐ Jones,D.R.&P.]
**Farjami, Farshad** ..........................'64 '96 C.112 B.S. L.426 J.D. [Ⓐ Lyon&L.]
*LANGUAGES: Persian.
*PRACTICE AREAS: Patents; Trademarks; Copyrights; Intellectual Property.
Farkas, Richard D. ......................'54 '79 C.174 B.S. L.1068 J.D. 820 Moraga Dr.
**Farley, Gregg A.** ......................'58 '84 C.112 A.B. L.1068 J.D. [Brobeck,P.&H.]
Farley, Lisa G. ...............................'58 '90 C.1232 L.809 J.D. [Farley&M.]
Farley & Mihell ................................................ 12100 Wilshire Blvd.
Farmer, John R. ......................'54 '81 C.1109 B.A. L.990 J.D. 3530 Wilshire Blvd.
Farmer, Kevin P. ..............'58 '84 C.716 B.S. L.724 J.D. 777 S. Figueroa St., 10th Fl.
**Farmer, Robert L., (A Professional Corporation)**, (AV) '22 '49 C.112 B.S. L.800 LL.B. [Farmer&R.]
*PRACTICE AREAS: Taxation; Estate Planning; Transactional Law.

**Farmer & Ridley, (AV)**
**A Partnership including Professional Corporations**
**Suite 2300, 444 South Flower Street, 90071**
**Telephone: 213-626-0291 Fax: 213-687-9807**
**Robert L. Farmer (A Professional Corporation); Terry R. Finucane (A Professional Corporation); Allan J. Graf; Perry E. Maguire (A Professional Corporation); John G. Powers (A Professional Corporation); Robert W. Ridley (A Professional Corporation); Robert L. Weaver (A Professional Corporation).**
**Federal and State Taxation, Corporation, Real Property and Land Use. Estate Planning, Probate and Trust Law, Securities, Pension and Profit Sharing. General Civil and Trial Practice in all State and Federal Courts and Administrative Agencies.**
***See Professional Biographies, LOS ANGELES, CALIFORNIA***

Farnham, Charlotte ......................................'18 '53 L.1001 LL.B. [Burg&F.]

**Farrah, Sasha E.** '62 '89 C.30 B.A. L.276 J.D. (adm. in PA; not adm. in CA) [Ⓐ Small L.&K.]
*LANGUAGES: Spanish.
*PRACTICE AREAS: Trademark; Copyright; Unfair Trade; Litigation.
**Farrand, James R.** .......................'45 '72 C.668 B.A. L.1066 J.D. [Blanc W.J.&K.]
*PRACTICE AREAS: Securities and Corporate Law; Mergers and Acquisitions; Partnerships; Business Law; Patent Law.
**Farrand, Laura K.** ..........................'48 '76 C.966 B.A. L.276 J.D. [Ⓐ Goodson&W.]
*PRACTICE AREAS: Tax; Estate Planning; Business Transaction.
**Farrar, David W.**, (AV) ......................'42 '73 C&L.893 B.A., J.D. [Brand F.D.F.&K.]
*SPECIAL AGENCIES: Special Counsel to U.S. District Court in Keith v Volpe with respect to administration of the $500 million Century Freeway Housing Program, 1990—.
*PRACTICE AREAS: Real Estate Development and Finance; Public-Private Development; Real Estate Asset Management; Public Agency Representations; Affordable Housing.
**Farrar, Stanley F.**, (AV) ......................'43 '68 C.112 B.S. L.1066 J.D. [Sullivan&C.]
**Farrell, Edmund G., III** ..................'55 '83 C.112 B.S. L.770 J.D. [Murchison&C.]
*REPORTED CASES: Danner v. Himmelfarb (1988) 858 F.2d 515; St. Mary Med. Center v. Cristiano (1989) 724 F.Supp 732; O'Dell v. Freightliner (1992) 10 CA 4th 645; Mitchell v. Scott Wetzel (1991) 227 CA 3d 1474; Semsch v. Henry Mayo Newhall Mem. Hospital (1985) 171 CA 3d 162.
*PRACTICE AREAS: Appellate Practice; Professional Malpractice Defense.
Farrell, Edward C., (AV) ....................'30 '55 C&L.800 A.B., LL.B. Chf. Asst. City Atty.
**Farrell, Ellen L.** ............................'64 '94 C.691 B.A. L.426 J.D. [Ⓐ Gibson,D.&C.]
Farrell, James J. ......................'68 '93 C.188 B.A. L.1068 J.D. 2121 Ave. of the Stars
**Farrell, John M.** ....................'68 '95 C&L.976 B.A., J.D. [Ⓐ O'Melveny&M.]
*PRACTICE AREAS: Entertainment Law.
Farrell, Michael J. ..................'38 '66 C.112 B.A. L.426 J.D. U.S. Trustee in Bkrptcy.
**Farrell, Michael R.** .........................'67 '94 C.976 B.A. L.800 J.D. [Ⓐ Allen,M.L.G.&M.]
*PRACTICE AREAS: Litigation.
**Farrell, Patrick J.** ..........................'69 '96 C&L.112 B.A., J.D. [Ⓐ Fenigstein&K.]
*PRACTICE AREAS: Business Litigation; General Corporate.
Farrell, Thomas G. '31 '71 C.645 B.A. L.809 J.D. Spec. Coun., U.S.A.F. Space & Missile Systems Ctr.
**Farrer, William C., (P.C.)**, (AV) ..............'22 '50 C.112 A.B. L.228 J.D. [Hill,F.&B.] ‡
Farrow, Kenneth R. ..................'63 '93 C.1168 B.A. L.1148 J.D. 12100 Wilshire Blvd.
**Farruggia, Samuel A.**, (AV) ......................'45 '73 C.339 B.A. L.209 J.D. [Firestein&F.]
*PRACTICE AREAS: Subrogation; Premium and Deductible Collections; Insurance.
**Fasi, Gioia M.** ..............................'63 '94 C.94 B.A. L.770 J.D. [Ⓐ Iverson,Y.P.&H.]
*LANGUAGES: Italian.
*PRACTICE AREAS: Civil Litigation.
**Fasiska, Barbara C.** ....................................'44 '81 C&L.665 B.S., J.D. [Schaffer&L.]
**Fasso, Jill** ..........................................'69 '95 C.705 B.A. L.990 J.D. [Feldman&S.]
*PRACTICE AREAS: Labor Law; Environmental Law; General Civil Practice.
Fasteau, Theodore ..............................'38 '70 C.1043 B.S. L.809 J.D. Dep. Pub. Def.
**Fatemi, Kayhan M.** ............................'64 '93 C.112 B.A. L.990 J.D. [Ⓐ Wickwire G.]
**Faucher, Joseph C.** ............................'62 '88 C.352 B.A. L.1067 J.D. [Reish&L.]
*PRACTICE AREAS: Business Litigation; Employee Benefits Litigation; Employment Law.
Faust, Kevin J. ..............................'64 '94 C.112 B.S. L.426 J.D. 1200 Wilshire Blvd.

**Faustman, Carlton, DiSante & Freudenberger LLP**
**700 South Flower Street, Eleventh Floor, 90017⊙**
**Telephone: 213-892-6308**
**Members of Firm: Christopher W. Carlton. Associate: Diane L. Schlesinger.**
**On behalf of Employers, Employment Discrimination, Wrongful Discharge, Sexual Harassment and ERISA Litigation. Union Organizing Campaigns, Unfair Labor Practice Proceedings, Collective Bargaining Negotiations, Grievance Arbitration and other Labor Proceedings. Trade Secrets and Unfair Competition Litigation. Employee Handbooks and Advice on Personnel Issues.**
**Irvine, California Office: 2600 Michelson Drive, Suite 800, 92612. Telephone: 714-622-1661. Fax: 714-622-1669.**
**Sacramento, California Office: 711 9th Street, Suite 100, 95814. Telephone: 916-443-0999. Fax: 916-442-5140.**
**San Francisco, California Office: 388 Market Street, Suite 400, 94111. Telephone: 415-296-3813. Fax: 415-296-3814.**
**San Diego, California Office: 8910 University Center Lane, Suite 500, 92122. Telephone: 619-678-8446. Fax: 619-678-8447.**
***See Professional Biographies, LOS ANGELES, CALIFORNIA***

**Fauvre, John** '45 '70 C.668 B.A. L.309 J.D. (adm. in GA; not adm. in CA) Sr. Coun. & Team Leader, Bank of Amer.
Favish, Bruce I. ...........................'54 '82 C.910 B.A. L.665 J.D. 1901 Ave. of the Stars
**Favre, Francois R.** ............................'43 '72 C.061 B.A. L.1114 J.D. [Ⓒ Hillsinger&C.]
Fay, Marion C., (AV) .........'44 '74 C.914 B.A. L.800 J.D. 777 S. Figueroa St., 38th Fl.
Fay-Bustillos, Theresa ..........................'53 '81 C.112 B.A. L.1068 J.D. M.A.L.D.E.F.
Fayollat, James E. ..........................'42 '75 C.910 A.B. L.426 J.D. 8251 Hollywood Blvd.
**Feder, Frank E., (A P.C.)**, (AV) '28 '55 C.976 B.A. L.309 LL.B. [Loeb&L.] (⊙New York, NY)
*PRACTICE AREAS: Real Estate Law; Banking Law.
**Feder, James J.**, (AV) ..............................'43 '75 C.112 B.A. L.800 J.D. [Feder&M.]
*LANGUAGES: German.
*REPORTED CASES: In re THC Financial Corp., 659 F.2d 951 (9th Cir. 1981) Cert. den. 456 U.S. 977 (1982); Falcon Capital Corporation Shareholders v. Osborne, 679 F.2d 784 (9th Cir. 1982); In re Manoa Finance Co., 853 F.2d 687 (9th Cir. 1988).
*TRANSACTIONS: Examiner, First Capital Holdings Corp., First Capital Life Insurance Group, Inc. and Fidelity Bankers Life Insurance Group Inc., 1991; Examiner, The Wickes Companies, 1982; California Target Enterprises, 1993. Lead Counsel for Chapter X reorganization of THC Financial Corp., 1976 and the Chapter 11 reorganization of American Continental Corp., 1989; Castle Entertainment/Malibu Grand Prix Chapter 11 acquisition, 1984.
*PRACTICE AREAS: Insolvency Law; Commercial Litigation; Appeals.
Feder, Julia M. ..........................'54 '95 C.112 B.A. L.426 J.D. 3255 Wilshire Blvd.
**Feder, Philip N.**, (AV) ..........................'54 '79 C.813 A.B. L.178 J.D. [Paul,H.J.&W.]

**Feder & Mills, A Professional Corporation, (AV)**
**1901 Avenue of the Stars, Seventh Floor, 90067**
**Telephone: 310-201-2075 Facsimile: 310-284-6020; 310-284-6018**
**James J. Feder; John W. Mills, III.**
**Corporate Reorganization, Bankruptcy, Insolvency, Debtor-Creditor Relations, Business and Commercial Law, Arbitration and Mediation.**
***See Professional Biographies, LOS ANGELES, CALIFORNIA***

**Federman, Robert J.**, (AV) ................'31 '57 C&L.930 B.A., J.D. [Federman,G.&G.]
*PRACTICE AREAS: Complex Litigation; Insurance; Reinsurance; Excess Surplus Lines; Insurance Coverage Law.

**Federman, Gridley & Gradwohl, A Professional Law Corporation, (AV)**
**Suite 1060, One Century Plaza, 2029 Century Park East (Century City), 90067⊙**
**Telephone: 310-552-9181 FAX: 310-552-3121**
**Robert J. Federman; Bruce C. Gridley; Alan J. Gradwohl; Temple K. Harvey; Marc R. Ward;—Robert Nation; R. Derek Classen; Debra Hartman Warfel; Robert B. Klepa; Stuart E. Supowit.**
**Civil Trial and Appellate Practice in all California State and Federal Courts, Insurance and Reinsurance, Excess and Surplus Lines Law, and General Civil Litigation.**
**Reference: First Los Angeles Bank (Century City).**
**San Luis Obispo (Central Coast), California Office: 992 Monterey Street #D, 93401. Telephone: 805-542-9002. Fax: 805-544-5837.**
***See Professional Biographies, LOS ANGELES, CALIFORNIA***

**Feeley, Michael Scott** ........................'61 '88 C.197 A.B. L.309 J.D. [Latham&W.]
*LANGUAGES: Italian and Spanish.

**Feeley, Thomas J.**, (AV) ....................... '37 '69 C.426 B.S. L.809 J.D. [T.J.Feeley]
*PRACTICE AREAS: Civil Trial; Municipal Law.

**Feeley, Thomas J., P.C., Law Offices of, (AV)**
**700 South Flower Street, Fourth Floor, 90017**
**Telephone: 213-236-9670 Facsimile: 213-627-2561**
**Thomas J. Feeley;—S. Paul Bruguera.**
**General Civil and Municipal Law.**
*See Professional Biographies, LOS ANGELES, CALIFORNIA*

**Feemster, Karrin** ................. '62 '89 C.1077 B.A. L.1148 J.D. [▣ Saltzburg,R.&B.]
*PRACTICE AREAS: Business Litigation; Bankruptcy Law; Receiverships; Debtor Creditor Law; Business Litigation.
Feenberg, G. Ronald, (AV) '45 '71 C.1068 A.B. L.1049 J.D.
801 S. Grand Ave. 18th Fl.
**Feess, Gary A.**, (AV) ...................'48 '74 C.608 B.A. L.1068 J.D. [Quinn E.U.&O.]
*REPORTED CASES: U.S. v. Schaflander, 743 F.2d 714 (9th Cir. 1984); U.S. v. Michaels, 796 F.2d 1112 (9th Cir. 1986); U.S. v. Stafford, 831 F.2d 1479 (9th Cir. 1987); U.S. v. Flewitt, 874 F.2d 669 (9th Cir. 1989); U.S. ex rel. Madden, et al. v. General Dynamics Corp., 4 F.3d 827 (9th Cir. 1993).
*PRACTICE AREAS: White Collar Crime; Appellate Litigation; Government Contracts and Regulations; Employment; General Trial Practice.
**Feffer, Elizabeth R.** ........................'68 '93 C.112 B.A. L.800 J.D. [▣ Burke,W.&S.]
*PRACTICE AREAS: Municipal Litigation.
Feffer, Irving S. ........................................'31 '58 C&L.800 B.S., J.D. Supr. Ct. J.
Feffer, Kerry C. .............................'53 '81 C.112 B.A. L.426 J.D. Sec. & Exchange Comm.
**Feffer, Suzanne R.** .......................'60 '85 C.112 B.A. L.1148 J.D. [▣ Schaffer&L.]
Fegen, Paul F. ......................'34 '61 C.112 B.S. L.800 LL.B. 1999 Ave. of the Stars
**Feher, Vincent B.** .............. '67 '91 C.112 B.A. L.309 J.D. Broadcast Coun., CBS Inc.
**Fehrman, David L.** ................ '52 '77 C.880 B.E.E. L.910 J.D. [Graham&J.] (Pat.)
*PRACTICE AREAS: Intellectual Property Law; Patent Law.
Fein, Alan ................................ '41 '80 C.563 B.A. L.1137 J.D. 8946 Kramerwood Pl.
**Fein, Ronald L.**, (AV) ................... '43 '70 C.112 A.B. L.1049 J.D. [Stutman,T.&G.]
*PRACTICE AREAS: General Corporate; Corporate Securities; Corporate Reorganization.
**Fein, Steven A.** ...'56 '81 C.667 B.A. L.982 J.D. Sr. Coun., Heller Real Estate Fin. Servs.
Feinberg, Gregory L. ........................'63 '89 C.112 B.A. L.1065 J.D. 1800 Century Pk. E.
**Feinberg, Irwin** .....................'54 '79 C.112 B.A. L.1067 J.D. [Weinstock,F.M.&K.]
**Feinberg, Jill L.** ...................... '63 '89 C.112 B.A. L.767 J.D. [▣ Engstrom,L.&L.]
**Feinberg, Margo A.** ..................'56 '81 C.112 B.A. L.1065 J.D. [Schwartz,S.D.&S.]
*PRACTICE AREAS: Labor and Employment Law; Public Employment Relations Law; Sexual Harassment; Education Law; Employment Discrimination Law.
**Feinberg, Michael R.** ...................'52 '79 C.800 B.A. L.426 J.D. [Schwartz,S.D.&S.]
*REPORTED CASES: Paramount Unified School Dist. v. Teachers Ass'n. of Paramount, Cal.App.4th, 32 Cal.Rptr.2d 311 (1994); Combs v. Rockwell International Corp., 927F.2d 486 (9th Cir. 1991); Wiman v. Vallejo City Unified School Dist., 221 Cal.App.3d 1486, 271 Cal.Rptr. 142 (1990); Dixon v. Bd. of Trustees of Saugus Union School Dist., 216 Cal.App.3d 1269, 265 Cal.Rptr. 511 (1989); California Teachers Ass'n. v. Cory, 155 Cal.App.3d 484, 202 Cal.Rptr. 611 (1984).
*PRACTICE AREAS: Labor and Employment Law; Employment Discrimination; Sexual Harassment; Wage and Hour Law; Education Law.
**Feinerman, Deborah S.**, (AV) ......... '55 '80 C.112 B.A. L.426 J.D. [▣ Gibson,D.&C.]
*PRACTICE AREAS: Entertainment and the Arts; Bankruptcy.
**Feinfield, Kenneth A.**, (AV) .............'44 '75 C.112 B.A. L.398 J.D. [Stephens,B.&L.]
*PRACTICE AREAS: Estate Planning; Trust and Probate.
**Feingold, Kenneth A.**, (AV) ............... '49 '75 C.1169 B.A. L.767 J.D. [Feingold&S.]
*PRACTICE AREAS: Civil Trial; Real Property Litigation and Transactions; Property Management Law; Construction Law; Alternative Dispute Resolution.

**Feingold & Spiegel, (AV)**
**Suite 175 Commerce Plaza, 11340 West Olympic Boulevard, 90064**
**Telephone: 310-477-7007 Fax: 310-477-7248**
**Members of Firm: Kenneth A. Feingold; Ronald L. Spiegel.**
**General Civil Trial Practice. Real Property, Property Management, Construction Law, Corporate Law, Alternative Dispute Resolution and Commercial Law.**
*See Professional Biographies, LOS ANGELES, CALIFORNIA*

**Feinreich, Yael** ......................'70 '95 C.112 B.A. L.1068 J.D. [▣ Alschuler G.&P.]
Feinstein, Janice Lynn ............. '52 '76 C.668 B.A. L.1068 J.D. 3372 Cabrillo Blvd.‡
**Feinstein, Marc F.** ..................... '62 '91 C.976 B.A. L.309 J.D. [▣ O'Melveny&M.]
Feinstein, N. Mitchell, (AV) ......'44 '68 C.446 B.A. L.800 J.D. 11111 W. Olympic Blvd.
**Feinstein, Robert W.** ................. '50 '76 C.696 B.A. L.910 J.D. [Littler,M.F.T.&M.]
**Feinstein, William L.** ................ '57 '81 C.154 B.A. L.1068 J.D. [▣ Reinstein,P.&C.]
*PRACTICE AREAS: Taxation Law; Probate; Estate Planning.
Feinswog, Kenneth A. ................. '57 '82 C.855 B.A. L.472 J.D. 10880 Wilshire Blvd.
**Feis, William J.**, (AV) ...................................... '31 '67 C&L.309 A.B., LL.B. [Troy&G.]
*PRACTICE AREAS: Corporate Law; Securities Law.
**Feisthamel, Karen L.** '65 '90 C.103 B.Sc. L.276 J.D.
[▣ Blakely,S.T.&Z.] (See Pat. Sect.)
**Feit, Dorette S.** ................................'54 '79 C.446 B.A. L.1066 J.D. [Irell&M.]
**Felder, B. Otis** ........................... '67 '94 C.477 A.B. L.1355 J.D. [▣ Hancock R.&B.]

**Feldhake, Robert J., Law Offices of**
**(See Costa Mesa)**

**Feldman, Andrew**, (AV) '43 '69 C&L.107 B.A., J.D.
(adm. in NY; not adm. in CA) [▣ Meyers,B.&M.] (Buffalo, NY & New York, NY)
*PRACTICE AREAS: Insurance; Professional Malpractice; Medical Malpractice; Environmental; Toxic Tort.
**Feldman, Carla J.** ..............................'59 '85 C.112 B.A. L.1049 J.D. [Feldman&S.]
*PRACTICE AREAS: Environmental Law; Employment Law; Toxic Torts; Products Liability Law.
Feldman, Edward G. ......................'42 '67 C.112 B.S. L.1068 LL.B. Dep. Dist. Atty.
**Feldman, Kenneth C.** ...................'62 '87 C.1077 B.S. L.426 J.D. [▣ Bottum&F.]
Feldman, Lee S. ................ '49 '75 C.1042 B.A. L.426 J.D. 500 S. Virgil Ave., 4th Fl.
**Feldman, Lewis G.** .........................'56 '82 C.1169 B.A. L.1067 J.D. [Cox,C.&N.]
*PRACTICE AREAS: Public Financing Law; Land Use Law; Real Property Law.
**Feldman, Lindsey S.** ...........'52 '77 C.823 B.S. L.1068 J.D. [▣ Berger,K.S.M.F.S.&G.]
**Feldman, Marc S.**, (BV) ....................'58 '83 C.260 B.S. L.809 J.D. [Koletsky,M.&F.]
*PRACTICE AREAS: Construction Defect Defense Litigation; General Liability Defense Litigation; Toxic Tort Defense Litigation; Product Liability Defense Litigation.
**Feldman, Mark A.** ........................ '65 '91 C.112 B.A. L.800 J.D. [▣ Poindexter&D.]
*PRACTICE AREAS: Construction Law; Surety Law; Real Estate; Probate Litigation.
Feldman, Michael H., (AV) .............'58 '82 C.197 A.B. L.477 J.D. 7230 Franklin Ave.

**Feldman, Phillip, Law Offices of '32 '67 C.1097 B.S. L.800 J.D.**
**15250 Ventura Boulevard, Suite 604 (Sherman Oaks), 91403-3287**
**Telephone: 310-LEG-MALP Fax: 818-986-1757**
***LANGUAGES: French.**
**Professional Liability: Legal Malpractice. Professional Liability: Expert Witness Legal Malpractice. Professional Responsibility: Legal Ethics and Discipline Defense Expert.**

Feldman, Raymond ......................... '56 '80 C&L.446 B.A., J.D. 3921 Wilshire Blvd.
**Feldman, Stacie L.** ..................... '71 '96 C.112 B.A. L.94 J.D. [▣ Mitchell,S.&K.]
*PRACTICE AREAS: Civil Litigation.
**Feldman, Steven L.** ..........................'49 '74 C.112 B.A. L.426 J.D. [Goldfarb,S.&A.]
*PRACTICE AREAS: Real Estate Law; Construction Law; Business Litigation; Environmental Law; Administrative Law.

**Feldman & Feldman, A Professional Corporation**
**(See Woodland Hills)**

**Feldman & Shaffery**
**611 West Sixth Street, 26th Floor, 90017**
**Telephone: 213-955-5400 Facsimile: 213-489-3677**
**Members of Firm: Carla J. Feldman; John Shaffery;—Jill Fasso.**
**Labor and Employment, Environmental, Toxic Torts, General Liability, Products Liability, Aviation and General Civil Litigation in all State and Federal Courts.**
*See Professional Biographies, LOS ANGELES, CALIFORNIA*

Feldsted, John F. ..................................... '55 '81 C.188 B.S. L.426 J.D. One Wilshire Blvd.
**Feldstein, Alan H.** .........'55 '84 C.112 B.A. L.809 J.D. [▣ Hall D.K.F.&W.] (N.Y.C.)
**Feldstein, Hydee R.** ............................ '58 '82 C.821 B.A. L.178 J.D. [Paul,H.J.&W.]
**Feliciano, Sahily H.** ............................ '61 '95 C.36 B.A. L.809 J.D. [▣ Gibson,D.&C.]
*LANGUAGES: Spanish.
**Feliton, John R., Jr.**, (AV) ..........................'48 '73 C.823 A.B. L.426 J.D. [Bottum&F.]
*PRACTICE AREAS: Professional Liability; Civil Law; Trial Practice; Appellate Practice; Insurance Law.
Felixson, Robert J. ............................ '20 '43 C&L.930 B.A., J.D. 10787 Wilshire Blvd.‡
Felker, Lonnie A., (AV) ................................ '47 '75 C.1077 B.A. L.809 J.D. Dep. Dist. Atty.
**Felker, Patti C.** ............................................. '58 '83 C.867 B.A. L.1066 J.D. [Nelson,G.F.&L.]
*PRACTICE AREAS: Entertainment Law.
Fella, Diane Lynn .................. '47 '89 C.1097 B.A. L.940 J.D. 1559 S. Sepulveda Blvd.
Fellman, Teri W. ........................ '55 '86 C.112 B.A. L.990 J.D. 4700 Wilshire Blvd.
Felman, Edward L. ................... '51 '77 C.112 B.A. L.309 J.D. 1801 Ave. of the Stars
**Felsen, Barry**, (AV) ......................... '50 '76 C.112 B.A. L.1068 J.D. [Goldman&K.]
*PRACTICE AREAS: Entertainment.

**Felsenthal, David B.**
**(See Santa Monica)**

Felt, Deborah Perfetti ........'54 '79 C&L.426 B.A., J.D. Sr. Atty., Atlantic Richfield Co.
**Felton, Richard I.**, (AV) ...........'51 '76 C.112 B.A. L.284 J.D. [Gordon,E.K.G.F.&G.]
*LANGUAGES: Spanish.
*PRACTICE AREAS: Workers Compensation Law; Social Security Law.
Fenelon, Carol .............................'57 '84 C.976 B.A. L.1065 J.D. 9113 Sunset Blvd.
**Feng, Paul Y.** '60 '90 C.966 B.S.M.E. L.494 J.D.
[▣ Fulwider P.L.&U.] (See Pat. Sect.)
*LANGUAGES: Chinese (Mandarin).
*PRACTICE AREAS: Patent Prosecution; Intellectual Property; Trademark Law.
**Fenigstein, S. Jack**, (AV) .................'47 '75 C.696 B.A. L.477 J.D. [Fenigstein&K.]
*PRACTICE AREAS: Corporate; Real Estate; Business; Health Care and Commercial Law; Estate Planning.

**Fenigstein & Kaufman, A Professional Corporation, (AV)**
**(Formerly Chasalow, Fenigstein & Kaufman, Established 1979)**
**Suite 2300, 1900 Avenue of the Stars (Century City), 90067-4314**
**Telephone: 310-201-0777 Telecopier: 310-556-1346**
**S. Jack Fenigstein; Ron S. Kaufman; David F. Tilles; Karl S. Thurmond;—Stephanie G. Pearl; Henry Lien; Patrick J. Farrell. Of Counsel: Lynne Drohlich Kaufman; Harold J. Tomin; Eric D. Berkowitz; Anthony D. De Toro.**
**Business Litigation. Corporate, Real Estate, Business, and Commercial Law. Health Care Law. Tax and Estate Planning.**
*See Professional Biographies, LOS ANGELES, CALIFORNIA*

Fennelly, Jane C., (AV) .......................'42 '74 C.188 A.B. L.426 J.D. 444 S. Flower St.
**Fenning, Alan M.** ................. '50 '75 C.154 B.A. L.1066 J.D. [▣ Milbank,T.H.&M.]
Fenning, Lisa Hill ......................... '52 '75 C.914 B.A. L.976 J.D. U.S. Bkrptcy. J.
**Fenno, Edward T.** ......................... '66 '94 C.674 B.A. L.800 J.D. [▣ Musick,P.&G.]
Fensten, Julian B. .........................'31 '57 C.112 B.A. L.1068 LL.B. 950 S. Grand Ave.
Fenster, Leo, (BV) ................................ '22 '51 C.112 L.809 LL.B. 961 Bluegrass Way
**Fenster, Marc A.** .............................. '69 '95 C.112 B.S. L.1068 J.D. [▣ Irell&M.]
Fenton, Ben P. .................................. '09 '32 C&L.800 A.B., J.D. 833 S. Spring St.
**Fenton, Linda** ......................'60 '87 C.112 B.A. L.1148 J.D. [▣ Weinstock,F.M.&K.]
*PRACTICE AREAS: General Civil Litigation; Construction Defect; Personal Injury.
**Fenton, Mitchell L.** .................... '56 '84 C.763 B.A. L.1049 J.D. [▣ Tuverson&H.]
**Feo, Edwin F.** ...............................'52 '77 C.112 B.A. L.1068 J.D. [Milbank,T.H.&M.]
**Ferber, Brian J.** ............................... '65 '91 C.763 B.A. L.284 J.D. [▣ Tharpe&H.]
*PRACTICE AREAS: Insurance Defense; Wrongful Termination; Premises Liability.
Ferber, Robert A. ................................ '52 '79 C.264 B.A. L.176 J.D. Asst. City Atty.
**Ferch, Richard A.** ............................'50 '82 C.1109 B.A. L.426 J.D. [▣ Tharpe&H.]
**Ferenczy, Ilene Hirsch** ...................... '56 '92 C.112 A.B. L.1139 J.D. [▣ Reish&L.]
*PRACTICE AREAS: Pension/Employee Benefits.

**Ferguson, Franklin L., Jr. '68 '94 C.659 B.A. L.569 J.D.**
**4929 Wilshire Boulevard, Suite 930, 90010**
**Telephone: 213-936-4375 Fax: 213-930-0338**
**Email: FLFERGUSONJR@IGC.ORG**
**Civil Rights, Labor (Plaintiffs - Employment Discrimination), Police Misconduct, Criminal Defense.**
*See Professional Biographies, LOS ANGELES, CALIFORNIA*

Ferguson, Linda T. ........................ '48 '73 C.112 B.A. L.1068 J.D. 1283 So. La Brea
Feringa, Andrew O. ......................'39 '69 C.1042 B.A. L.1049 J.D. 3845 Crestway Dr.
Ferkich, Roy S. ................................................ '29 '54 C.999 L.809 LL.B. Mun. Ct. J.
**Ferlauto, Thomas M.** ..................... '66 '91 C&L.846 B.S., J.D. [▣ Fierstein&S.]
*PRACTICE AREAS: State and Federal Courts Litigation.
Ferleger, Daniel S. '59 '85
C.1044 B.A. L.800 J.D. Coun., Twentieth Century Fox Film Corp.
Fern, Joseph J. ....................................... '45 '72 C&L.665 B.A., J.D. 4700 Wilshire Blvd.
**Fern, Martin D.**, (AV) ....................... '43 '67 C.563 B.A. L.569 J.D. [Loeb&L.]
*PRACTICE AREAS: Corporate Law; Franchising Law; Intellectual Property Law.
Fernandez, Antonio M., (AV) ........'28 '56 C.871 B.S. L.276 J.D. 2933 Motor Ave. (Pat.)
Fernandez, Lazaro E. ................ '62 '88 C.1109 B.A. L.112 J.D. 445 S. Figueroa, Ste. 2600
**Fernandez, Louise Ann** ..................'53 '79 C.813 B.A. L.273 J.D. [Jeffer,M.B.&M.]
*PRACTICE AREAS: Labor and Employment; Litigation.
**Fernandez, Marta M.** .................. '60 '85 C.426 B.A. L.800 J.D. [▣ Jeffer,M.B.&M.]
*LANGUAGES: Spanish.
*PRACTICE AREAS: Labor and Employment; Health and Hospital.
Fernandez, Santiago '54 '80
C.112 B.A. L.1065 J.D. Gen. Coun., Los Angeles Dodgers, Inc.
Fernandez-McEvoy, Josefina '60 '90
C&L.831 B.A., J.D. 1999 Ave. of the Stars, Suite 1400
**Fernhoff, Michael D.**, (AV) ..........'53 '78 C.966 B.B.A. L.1068 J.D. [Kaye,S.F.H.&H.]
*PRACTICE AREAS: Corporate, Partnership, Individual and International Taxation; Mergers and Acquisitions; Corporate Law; International Business Law; Partnership Law.
Ferrari, Charles D. ........................ '58 '87 C.1077 B.A. L.1067 J.D. 221 N. Figueroa St.
**Ferreira, Marco P.** .............'63 '90 C.1077 B.A. L.426 J.D. [▣ Sedgwick,D.M.&A.]
*LANGUAGES: Portuguese, Spanish and French.
**Ferrer, Eric G.** ............................'56 '82 C.1350 B.A. L.1068 J.D. [▣ J.L.Cochran,Jr.]
*PRACTICE AREAS: Personal Injury; Police Misconduct; Civil Rights Litigation.
**Ferrer, Feliciano M. (Bud)** ............... '62 '88 C.477 B.S. L.800 J.D. [▣ Frye,A.&M.]
Ferrier, Debra J. ...........'54 '87 C.1097 B.S. L.809 J.D. Sr. Coun., Calif. Assn. of Realtors
**Ferris, Brian W.** '48 '78
C.555 B.A. L.339 J.D. Asst. Gen. Coun. & Asst. Secy., CalMat Co.
**Ferro, Catherine L.** ........................ '61 '87 C.1077 B.A. L.426 J.D. [Lynberg&W.]
**Ferro, James L.** ............................ '57 '83 C.1077 B.S. L.426 J.D. [Gibbs,G.L.&A.]
*PRACTICE AREAS: Construction Law; Fidelity and Surety Law; Business Litigation.
Ferry, Joseph P., (AV) ......................'57 '83 C.473 B.A. L.1049 J.D. [Thompson,M.&F.]

CAA221P

CALIFORNIA—LOS ANGELES MARTINDALE-HUBBELL LAW DIRECTORY 1997

Fertig, Ralph D.H. ................'30 '80 C.145 B.A. L.1068 J.D. Admin. Law J., EEOC
**Fesler, Donald C.**, (AV) ..........'48 '73 C.112 B.S. L.1068 J.D. [La Follette,J.D.F.&A.]
*PRACTICE AREAS: Medical Malpractice; General Litigation.
Fesler, Roberta M. ..................'49 '74 C&L.112 B.A., J.D. Asst. Co. Coun.
**Fetter, Henry David**, (AV) ..........'49 '77 C&L.309 A.B., J.D. [Doniger&F.]
*PRACTICE AREAS: Business Litigation; Entertainment Litigation; Copyright Law.
**Feuer, Joel A.** ......................'54 '81 C.668 B.A. L.1066 J.D. [Gibson,D.&C.]
*PRACTICE AREAS: Securities Litigation; Business Litigation; Real Property Litigation; Professional Liability.
Feuer, Michael N. ...................'58 '83 C&L.309 B.A., J.D. 145 S. Fairfax Ave.
Feuerstein, Herman .................'28 '61 C.112 L.1065 J.D. P.O. Box 351284
Fichman, Glen S. ..............'52 '79 C.112 B.A. L.1068 J.D. Coun., Univ. of Calif.
Fick, John S. ......................'37 '70 C.174 L.765 J.D. 555 W. 5th St.
**Ficksman, David L.** ..................'44 '70 C.860 A.B. L.569 J.D. [Loeb&L.]
*PRACTICE AREAS: Corporate Law.
Fidler, Larry .........................'47 '74 C.1077 B.A. L.426 J.D. Supr. J.
**Fidone, Gary P.**, (AV) ............'46 '74 C.1074 B.S. L.426 J.D. [Prestholt,K.F.&V.]⊙
*PRACTICE AREAS: Insurance Defense Litigation; Complex Commercial Trial Practice.
**Field, Bradley O.** ..................'66 '93 C.112 B.A. L.426 J.D. [A A.R.Hamrick,III]
*PRACTICE AREAS: Insurance Coverage; Insurance Defense; Bad Faith Litigation; Entertainment Litigation.
**Field, Joanne S.** ..................'68 '95 C.860 B.A. L.893 J.D. [A Gibson,D.&C.]
**Field, Marc D.** .....................'67 '95 C.860 B.A. L.893 J.D. [A Jones,D.R.&P.]
**Field, Morton R.**, (AV) ..............'23 '49 C.339 B.A. L.209 LL.B. [B Loeb&L.]
**Field, Richard C.**, (AV) ............'40 '66 C.112 B.A. L.309 J.D. [Cadwalader,W.&T.]
**Field, Susan J.**, (AV) ...............'54 '79 C.1044 B.A. L.724 J.D. [Musick,P.&G.]
*PRACTICE AREAS: Litigation; Insurance.
**Fields, Bertram**, (AV) ..........'29 '53 C.112 B.A. L.309 LL.B. [Greenberg G.F.C.&M.]
*PRACTICE AREAS: Communications; Entertainment; Commercial Transactions and Litigation.
Fields, Brian Jay .....'62 '88 C.800 B.A. L.426 J.D. Litig. Coun., Alpha Therapeutic Corp.
**Fields, Henry M.**, (AV) ...............'46 '73 C.309 B.A. L.976 J.D. [Morrison&F.]
*LANGUAGES: French.
*PRACTICE AREAS: International Banking and Investment; Financial Services; Corporate Finance.
Fields, Jerome K. ......................'26 '53 C.112 B.S. L.800 LL.B. Supr. Ct. J.
**Fields, Kenneth S.** ....................'62 '89 C.112 B.A. L.426 J.D. [B Tisdale&N.]
*PRACTICE AREAS: Real Property; Environmental Law; Insurance Law; Real Estate Finance; Corporate.
Fields, Lori A. ..............'59 '89 C.112 B.A. L.426 J.D. 10850 Wilshire Blvd., 6th Fl.
**Fields, Murray M.**, (AV) ...............'09 '35 C.228 L.569 LL.B. [Buchalter,N.F.&Y.]
*PRACTICE AREAS: Construction; General Business; Legal Malpractice; Real Property.
**Fields, Patrick J.** .....................'56 '82 C.112 A.B. L.309 J.D. [B Graham&J.]
*PRACTICE AREAS: International Business Law; Banking Law.
Fields, Peter A. ...........................'35 '62 C&L.800 B.A., LL.B. Guild Mgmt.
**Fields, Stacey B.** .......................'60 '87 C.800 B.S. L.990 J.D. [Winn&F.]
Fields, Toy R., III ..............'63 '88 C.800 B.S. L.1066 J.D. 1801 Ave. of the Stars

**Fields, Michael S.**
(See Beverly Hills)

**Fierberg, Ira M., Law Office of**
(See Manhattan Beach)

Fierro, Gerard A. ...............'63 '88 C.645 B.S. L.800 J.D. 3250 Wilshire Blvd.

**Fierstein & Sturman, Law Corporation, (AV)**
**1875 Century Park East, Fifteenth Floor, 90067**
**Telephone: 310-553-5500 Fax: 310-552-3228**
**Herbert D. Sturman (Certified Specialist, Taxation Law, The State Bar of California Board of Legal Specialization); Harvey Fierstein (1923-1984); Michael Blumenfeld; Edward C. Broffman; William T. King; Richard M. Johnson, Jr.;—Tasha Dian Levinson; Bruce E. Altschuld; Leslie E. Wallis; Lee A. Edlund; Thomas M. Ferlauto; Allan S. Williams. Of Counsel: Marvin Jubas.**
**General Civil and Appellate Practice in all State and Federal Courts. Corporate, Tax Planning, Commercial Transactions, Litigation, Wrongful Termination, Securities (NYSE, NASD and SEC), Construction Defect, Environmental, Real Estate, Insolvency, Workout, Estate Planning, Probate and Entertainment Law.**
*See Professional Biographies, LOS ANGELES, CALIFORNIA*

Fieselman, Lawrence R., (BV) ........'46 '78 C.375 B.A. L.809 J.D. [Roquemore,P.&M.]
**Fife, Lorin M.** '53 '83 C.871 B.S. L.800 J.D.
Sr. V.P. & Gen. Coun., Regul. Affs., SunAmerica Inc.
*LANGUAGES: Hebrew and German.
*RESPONSIBILITIES: General Corporate Practice.
**Figgins, Robert Shayne** ............'66 '92 C&L.990 B.S., J.D. [A Arnelle,H.M.W.&G.]
Figgins, Shayne .......................'66 '92 C&L.990 B.A., J.D. 21031 Ventura Blvd.
**Figler, Paul**, (BV) ...................'41 '71 C.112 L.809 J.D. [Berger,K.S.M.F.S.&G.]
Figueroa, Rafael S. ..................'65 '92 C.813 B.A. L.1068 J.D. Occidental College‡
**Fikre, Ted** .............................'67 '94 C.674 A.B. L.813 J.D. [A Latham&W.]
**Fileti, Thomas R.** .....................'56 '81 C.188 A.B. L.659 J.D. [Morrison&F.]
*PRACTICE AREAS: Real Estate.
**Filipi, Karen L.** ...........'58 '86 C.36 B.S. L.1148 J.D. [B Christensen,M.F.J.G.W.&S.]
*PRACTICE AREAS: Criminal Defense; Civil Litigation.
Finch, George W., (AV) ........'38 '67 C&L.910 B.S.M.E., J.D. 725 S. Figueroa St. (Pat.)
**Finch, Kevin L.** .........................'63 '92 C.112 B.S. L.1068 J.D. [A Irell&M.]
**Finch, Roxanne P.** ....................'62 '87 C.112 B.A. L.800 J.D. [Rubenstein&F.]
*PRACTICE AREAS: Civil Litigation; Real Estate Litigation; Personal Injury Litigation; Business Litigation; Insurance Defense.
Finck, Robert S. ......................'26 '51 C.112 B.S. L.800 LL.B. 610 Hanley Way
Findlater, John W. ...................'13 '40 C&L.800 B.S., LL.B. 201 Chadbourne Ave.
Findley, Roger W. ...................'35 '61 C.210 A.B. L.477 J.D. Loyola Law School
**Fine, Arthur, (A Professional Corporation)**, (AV) '42 '68
C.112 A.B. L.1066 J.D. [Mitchell,S.&K.]
*PRACTICE AREAS: Litigation; Environmental Law; Administrative Law.
Fine, Edward S. ...............'57 '91 C.112 B.A. L.1136 J.D. 1875 Century Park E.
**Fine, Jerry**, (AV) ....................'23 '51 C.112 B.A. L.426 J.D. [Sanders,B.G.S.&M.]
Fine, Mickey L. ..............'59 '86 C.800 B.S. L.1148 J.D. 5757 Wilshire Blvd.
**Fine, Paul R.**, (AV) ....................'47 '72 C.112 B.A. L.426 J.D. [Daniels,B.&F.]
*PRACTICE AREAS: Trial Law; Insurance; Business; Real Estate and Construction.
**Fine, Richard I.**, (AV) ...............'40 '64 C.966 B.S. L.145 J.D. [R.I.Fine&Assoc.]
**Fine, Robert M., Jr.** '50 '75 C.942 B.B.A. L.326 J.D.
(adm. in TX; not adm. in CA) Atlantic Richfield Co.
Fine, Ronald A. .............'45 '71 C.112 B.A. L.426 J.D. 11845 W. Olympic Blvd.

**Fine, Richard I., & Associates, A Prof. Corp., Law Offices of, (AV)**
**Suite 1000, 10100 Santa Monica Boulevard (Century City), 90067-4090**
**Telephone: 310-277-5833 Rapifax: 310-277-1543**
**Richard I. Fine;—Sunny S. Huo; Genalin Y. Sulat.**
**Complex Litigation, Class Action, Taxpayer, Government Misuse of Funds and Unique Cases. General Civil and Trial Practice in all State and Federal Courts. Corporation, Antitrust, International, Trade Regulation, Government, Business Law.**
*See Professional Biographies, LOS ANGELES, CALIFORNIA*

Finell, Marvin, (AV) ...................'24 '50 C&L.309 A.B., LL.B. 9255 Doheny‡
Fineman, Thomas J., (AV) .............'45 '71 C.112 A.B. L.800 J.D. [Myman,A.F.G.&R.]
Finer, David A. ..........................'47 '79 C.1077 B.S. L.1136 J.D. [Lebe&F.]
**Finer, Dustin K.** .......................'69 '95 C.112 B.A. L.464 J.D. [A Katten M.&Z.]

**Finer, Kim & Stearns**
(See Torrance)

**Finestone, William**, (AV) .................'43 '69 C.112 B.S. L.1068 J.D. [Walter,F.&R.]
*PRACTICE AREAS: Taxation Law; Estate Planning Law.
Finfer, Stephen J. ................'62 '88 C.1036 B.A. L.978 J.D. 6464 W. Sunset Blvd.
**Fingerman, Mark E.** ..........................'54 '81 C.112 B.A. L.61 J.D. [Bergman&W.]
*LANGUAGES: French.
*PRACTICE AREAS: Earth Movement; Toxic Torts; Construction Liability; Insurance Fraud; Personal Injury Defense.
Fink, Albert J., (AV) '33 '61 C.112 B.A. L.1066 LL.B.
1800 Ave. of the Stars, Suite 900 (Century City)
**Fink, Amy J.** ...........................'68 '93 C.1049 B.A. L.1065 J.D. [A Troop M.S.&P.]
*LANGUAGES: French and German.
*PRACTICE AREAS: Insurance Coverage.
Fink, Baret C. ..................'42 '66 C.800 B.S. L.1068 LL.B. 1840 Century Park East
**Fink, Barry E.**, (AV) ......'38 '63 C.209 B.S.C. L.145 J.D. [Christensen,M.F.J.G.W.&S.]
*PRACTICE AREAS: Corporation; Taxation; Tax Litigation; Corporate; Business Law.
Fink, Barry M. ...................'49 '80 C.1077 B.A. L.1221 J.D. 6404 Wilshire Blvd.
**Fink, David E.** ..........................'66 '93 C.112 B.A. L.1065 J.D. [A White O.C.&A.]
*PRACTICE AREAS: Business; Entertainment Litigation.
**Fink, Dean M.** '68 '93 C.37 B.A. L.178 J.D.
(adm. in AZ; not adm. in CA) [A Kirkland&E.]
*PRACTICE AREAS: Litigation; Construction Law; Government Contract Law; Public Contract Law.
**Fink, Deborah L.** .......................'69 '94 C.788 B.A. L.800 J.D. [A Katten M.&Z.]
**Fink, Floran L.** ...........................'49 '75 C.771 B.A. L.273 J.D. [B Allderdice&D.]
*PRACTICE AREAS: Labor; Employment Law; Business Litigation; Intellectual Property Litigation.
**Fink, Henry Einar** .....................'59 '87 C.112 B.A. L.1065 J.D. [A Mayer,B.&P.]
**Fink, Jonathan D.** .................'58 '83 C.659 B.A. L.94 J.D. [A Buchalter,N.F.&Y.]
*PRACTICE AREAS: Bank and Financial; Commercial; Real Estate; Appeals and Employment Litigation.
**Fink, Keith A.** ..............................'62 '90 C.112 B.A. L.809 J.D. [Baker&H.]
*REPORTED CASES: %italic; Brooks v. Cook %roman; 938 F.2d 1038 (9th Cir. 1991); %italic; Romberg v. Nichols %roman.
*PRACTICE AREAS: Labor Law; Civil Rights; Business Litigation; Appellate Law; Personal Injury Defense.
Fink, Robert S., (A Prof. Corp.) .....'47 '75 C.1077 B.A. L.1148 J.D. 6404 Wilshire Blvd.
**Finkel, Alan H.** ......................'55 '80 C.145 A.B. L.1068 J.D. [A Proskauer R.G.&M.]
Finkel, Edwin L. ........................'29 '56 C&L.659 B.S., LL.B. 2195 Stradella Rd.
**Finkel, Evan** ....................'56 '81 C.1044 B.S. L.1065 J.D. [Loeb&L.] (See Pat. Sect.)
*PRACTICE AREAS: Trademark; Patent; Copyright; Trade Secret and Unfair Competition; Computer and Multimedia Law.
Finkelberg, Ellen S. .......................'47 '77 C.112 B.A. L.426 J.D. [Finkelberg&F.]
Finkelberg, Louis I. .......................'51 '77 C.112 B.A. L.1095 J.D. [Finkelberg&F.]
Finkelberg & Finkelberg, A Professional Corporation .......................205 S. Bway.
Finkelstein, Don B., (AV) '29 '62 C.659 B.S.M.E. L.800 J.D.
5670 Wilshire Blvd. (Pat.)
**Finkelstein, Henry D.** ............'55 '81 C.165 A.B. L.910 J.D. [Greenberg G.F.C.&M.]
*PRACTICE AREAS: Real Estate.
**Finkelstein, Jeffrey S.** ..................'57 '87 C.112 B.A. L.1066 J.D. [Del,R.S.M.&D.]
*PRACTICE AREAS: Entertainment Law; Television Law; Motion Picture Law.
Finkelstein, Robert A. ...............'47 '72 C.112 B.A. L.276 J.D. 1999 Ave. of the Stars
Finkle, David G., (AV) ..............'41 '68 C.1077 A.B. L.426 J.D. 6500 Wilshire Blvd.
**Finkle, Grant E.** ....................'68 '94 C&L.112 B.A., J.D. [A Alschuler G.&P.]
**Finn, Brian J.** ...................'58 '89 C.549 B.A. L.1065 J.D. [Prestholt,K.F.&V.]⊙
*PRACTICE AREAS: Civil Defense Litigation; Products Liability; Bad Faith.
**Finn, Jeffrey A.** ......................'63 '96 C.339 B.S.E.E. L.800 J.D. [A Pretty,S.&P.]
*PRACTICE AREAS: Intellectual Property; Patent Litigation and Prosecution; Trademark Litigation and Prosecution.
**Finnegan, Michael J.** ..................'62 '88 C&L.426 B.B.A., J.D. [Pillsbury M.&S.]
**Finnerty, Robert W.** ......................'55 '85 C.112 B.A. L.990 J.D. [Girardi&K.]
*PRACTICE AREAS: Civil Litigation; Toxic Torts; General Negligence; Legal Negligence.
**Finney, Tal Clifton** .................'64 '91 C.1097 B.A. L.426 J.D. [B Radcliff,F.&D.]
**Finney, William P.** ..................'47 '80 C.959 B.A. L.966 J.D. [Harrington,F.D.&C.]
*PRACTICE AREAS: Toxic Torts Law; Personal Injury Defense Law; Construction Defects Law.
Finston, Steven L. ...............'47 '74 C.112 B.S. L.1065 J.D. 124 N. Crescent Heights
**Finucane, Terry R., (A Professional Corporation)** '46 '73
C.112 B.A. L.1065 J.D. [Farmer&R.]
*PRACTICE AREAS: Corporate; Business; Tax; Employee Benefit Law.
**Fiore, Kevin P.**, (AV) .....................'42 '70 C&L.426 B.B.A., J.D. [Clark&T.]
*PRACTICE AREAS: Real Estate; Real Estate Leasing; Real Estate Finance; Land Use.
**Firestein, Martin L.**, (AV) ..............'49 '78 C.1077 B.A. L.1095 J.D. [Firestein&F.]
*PRACTICE AREAS: Subrogation; Insurance; Business Litigation.
**Firestein, Michael A.** ................'58 '83 C.103 A.B. L.597 J.D. [McCambridge,D.&M.]

**Firestein & Farruggia, (AV)**
**Suite 550, 5900 Sepulveda Boulevard (Van Nuys), 91411**
**Telephone: 818-785-1999 Fax: 818-785-8347**
**Members of Firm: Samuel A. Farruggia; Martin L. Firestein. Of Counsel: Craig S. Elkin; Toni Lewis; John S. Levitt.**
**Subrogation, Premium and Deductible Collections, Insurance, Civil Litigation and Business Litigation.**
*See Professional Biographies, LOS ANGELES, CALIFORNIA*

**Firestone, Lauren R.** .................'59 '88 C.72 B.S. L.705 J.D. [A Fried,F.H.S.&J.]
**First, Alyssa** .........................'63 '90 C.477 A.B. L.262 J.D. [A Pillsbury M.&S.]
Fisch, Carol .........................'58 '84 C.1044 B.A. L.809 J.D. Dep. Dist. Atty.
Fisch, Paul H. .............................'27 '70 C.280 B.B.A. L.1148 J.D. N.L.R.B.
Fischbach, Bernard J. ...........'45 '70 C.112 B.A. L.1065 J.D. 1925 Century Park E.
Fischbach, Gregory E. ...........'42 '67 C.766 B.S. L.1065 J.D. 1925 Century Park E.
Fischel, Elaine B. ..............'21 '53 C.112 B.A. L.800 LL.B. 4727 Wilshire Blvd.
Fischer, Bernard D., (AV) ................'32 '58 C.112 B.S. L.1068 J.D. [B.D.Fischer] ‡
**Fischer, Dale S.**, (AV) ................'51 '80 C.258 B.A. L.309 J.D. [B Heller E.W.&M.]
*REPORTED CASES: Mirkin v. Wasserman, 5 Cal. 4th 1082 (1993); Texas Commerce Bank v. Garamendi, 11 Cal. App. 4th 460 (1992).
*PRACTICE AREAS: Civil Practice; Complex Litigation; Probate and Trust Litigation; ERISA Litigation; Employment Litigation.
**Fischer, David B.** .......................'53 '94 C.178 B.A. L.1068 J.D. [A Jones,D.R.&P.]
**Fischer, Debra L.** .................'64 '89 C.112 A.B. L.1066 J.D. [McCutchen,D.B.&E.]
*PRACTICE AREAS: Employment and General Commercial Litigation.
Fischer, James M. ..........................'47 '73 L.426 J.D. 1200 Wilshire Blvd.
Fischer, John David .......'50 '77 C.112 B.A. L.426 J.D. 2121 Ave. of the Stars, 22nd Fl.
**Fischer, L. Bruce** .......................'57 '82 C.112 B.A. L.800 J.D. [Mayer,B.&P.]
Fischer, Richard A. .................'45 '71 C.112 B.S. L.809 J.D. 10866 Wilshire Blvd.
**Fischer, Robert W., Jr.**, (AV) ...............'48 '73 C.605 B.A. L.1068 J.D. [Dewey B.]
*PRACTICE AREAS: Litigation.
**Fischer, Samuel N.**, (AV) ..............'56 '82 C.103 B.A. L.1068 J.D. [Ziffren,B.B.&F.]
*PRACTICE AREAS: Entertainment Law.
Fischer, Bernard D., Inc., A Professional Corporation .................1957 Holmby Ave.
Fischmann, B. Wallace ..............'23 '51 C.112 B.A. L.800 LL.B. 655 Bonhill Rd.
Fisenne, Mary Ellen ......'59 '86 C.1019 B.A. L.978 J.D. 5757 Wilshire Blvd., Suite 600
Fish, Robert D. ...........................'53 '90 C.659 B.A. L.61 J.D. 633 W. 5th St. (Pat.)

CAA222P

Fishback, James A. '52 '77 C.477 B.S.E. L.976 J.D.
Div. Coun., National Med. Homecare
**Fishburn, C. Randolph** ........................'56 '81 C.800 A.B. L.1065 J.D. [White&C.]
Fishelman, Bruce C. ........................'49 '75 C.771 A.B. L.800 J.D. [Stanbury,F.&L.]
Fisher, Barry A. ........................'43 '68 C.112 A.B. L.1068 J.D. [Fleishman,F.&M.]
Fisher, Craig A. '49 '75 C.150 B.B.A. L.945 J.D.
Employee Benefits Coun., Occidental Petroleum Corporation
**Fisher, Damon R.** ........................'69 '95 C.112 B.A. L.426 J.D. [⊠ Perkins C.]
*PRACTICE AREAS: General Litigation.
**Fisher, Girard**, (AV) ........................'45 '73 C.112 A.B. L.1049 J.D. [Pollak,V.&F.]
Fisher, Howard S., (AV) ........................'51 '76 C.800 B.S. L.809 J.D. [Clinco,F.&D.]

**Fisher, James Q. '43 '68 C&L.800 A.B., J.D.**
**1801 Century Park East, Suite 2400, 90067-2326**
**Telephone: 310-556-3300 Facsimile: 310-556-2424**
**(Certified Specialist, Estate Planning, Trust and Probate Law, The State Bar of California Board of Legal Specialization).**
**Estate Planning (Wills and Trusts), Tax Planning, Business Transactions, Real Estate, Corporations and Partnerships.**
***See Professional Biographies, LOS ANGELES, CALIFORNIA***

**Fisher, Jeffrey M.** ........................'66 '91 C.597 B.A. L.339 J.D. [⊠ Sidley&A.]
*PRACTICE AREAS: Litigation.
Fisher, Leanne J. ........................'61 '88 C.959 B.S. L.426 J.D. 333 S. Grand Ave.
**Fisher, Raymond C.**, (AV) ........................'39 '67 C.112 B.A. L.813 LL.B. [Heller E.W.&M.]
*PRACTICE AREAS: Antitrust; Financial Institutions; Securities Litigation; Intellectual Property.
**Fisher, Richard N.**, (AV) ........................'43 '70 C.684 B.A. L.1066 J.D. [O'Melveny&M.]
*PRACTICE AREAS: Labor and Employment.
**Fisher, Robert Louis**, (AV) ........................'44 '72 C.112 A.B. L.1068 J.D. [Barton,K.&O.]
*PRACTICE AREAS: General Civil Practice; Trial Practice; Real Property Litigation; Commercial Litigation.
**Fisher, Ruth E.** ........................'55 '80 C.773 B.A. L.1068 J.D. [Munger,T.&O.]

**Fisher, Scott D. '60 '87 C.37 B.S.B.A. L.36 J.D.**
**12424 Wilshire Boulevard, Suite 900, 90025-1043**
**Telephone: 310-442-7171 Fax: 310-442-6400**
***LANGUAGES: Spanish.**
**Real Estate and Business Litigation, Insurance Defense, Employment Law, Discrimination/Civil Rights and Personal Injury Law, Conservatorships, Probate Litigation.**
***See Professional Biographies, LOS ANGELES, CALIFORNIA***

Fisher, Tia Graves ........................'58 '85 C.112 B.A. L.966 J.D. Dep. Dist. Atty.
**Fisher, Tina** ........................'60 '91 C.804 B.S. L.575 J.D. [⊠ Lewis,D.B.&B.]

**Fisher & Phillips**
**(See Newport Beach)**

**Fisher & Porter**
**(See Long Beach)**

Fishler, Matthew R. ........................'68 '93 C.918 B.A. L.1068 J.D. 12011 San Vicente Blvd.
**Fishman, Howard A.** ........................'66 '92 C.37 B.F.A. L.800 J.D. [⊠ Troop M.S.&P.]
*PRACTICE AREAS: Entertainment Finance.
**Fishman, Joel L.** ........................'47 '77 C.112 A.B. L.800 J.D. [Katz,G.&F.]
*PRACTICE AREAS: Business Law; Real Estate Law.
**Fishman, Jordan** ........................'68 '96 C.659 B.S. L.1065 J.D. [⊠ Allen,M.L.G.&M.]
*PRACTICE AREAS: Real Estate.
**Fishman, Karen S.** ........................'59 '84 C.188 A.B. L.273 J.D. [K.S.Fishman]
*REPORTED CASES: United Technologies Corp. v. United States, 830 F.2d 1121 (Fed. Cir. 1987); Nuclear Research Corp. v. United States, 814 F.2d 647 (Fed. Cir. 1987); Rogers v. Overseas Ed. Ass'n, 814 F.2d 1549 (Fed. Cir. 1987); Dominquez v. Department of Air Force, 803 F.2d 680 (Fed. Cir. 1986); Smith v. United States Postal Service, 789 F.2d 1540 (Fed. Cir. 1986).
Fishman, Mark D. ........................'42 '69 C&L.608 B.S., J.D. 1293 So. Beverly Glen Blvd.
Fishman, Richard L. ........................'38 '63 C.659 B.S. L.93 J.D. Princ. Tax Coun., Unocal Corp.
**Fishman, Robert C.** ........................'54 '79 C.881 A.B. L.94 J.D. [⊠ Berman,B.&B.]
*REPORTED CASES: Dumas v. Research Testing Labs, Inc. (In re EPI Products USA, Inc.), 162 B.R. 1 (Bankr. C.D. Cal. 1993).
**Fishman, Stacey K.** ........................'67 '92 C.112 B.A. L.1068 J.D. [⊠ Katten M.&Z.]
*PRACTICE AREAS: Real Estate.

**Fishman, Karen S., A Law Corporation**
**1901 Avenue of the Stars, 7th Floor, 90067**
**Telephone: 310-277-9350 Fax: 310-277-9032**
**Karen S. Fishman.**
**Complex Business Litigation.**
***See Professional Biographies, LOS ANGELES, CALIFORNIA***

Fisk, David P. '49 '84
C.605 B.A. L.1190 J.D. Assoc. Coun., Auto. Club of Southern Calif.
Fiszer, Michael C. ........................'61 '88 C.112 B.A. L.426 J.D. 1900 Avenue of The Stars

**Fitch, Even, Tabin & Flannery**
**(See San Diego)**

**Fitzer, Richard L.**
**(See Long Beach)**

**Fitzgerald, Barbara A.** ........................'60 '90 C.112 B.S. L.800 J.D. [⊠ Seyfarth,S.F.&G.]
*PRACTICE AREAS: Employment Litigation.
**Fitzgerald, Donald J.** '45 '73 C.575 A.B. L.228 J.D.
[Manatt,P.&P.] (©Washington, DC)
*PRACTICE AREAS: Taxation.
**Fitzgerald, Elizabeth T.** ........................'63 '92 C.112 B.A. L.426 J.D. [⊠ Millard,P.H.&C.]
*LANGUAGES: French, German.
*PRACTICE AREAS: Insurance Defense; Civil Litigation.
**Fitzgerald, G. Edward**, (AV) ........................'28 '53 C.112 A.B. L.813 LL.B. [⊠ Gibson,D.&C.]
**Fitzgerald, James E.** ........................'54 '80 C.276 B.S.B.A. L.262 J.D. [Luce,F.H.&S.]
*PRACTICE AREAS: Insurance and Reinsurance; Professional Liability; Business Litigation.
**Fitzgerald, John K.** '50 '93 C.209 B.S. L.1148 J.D.
[⊠ Fulwider P.L.&U.] (See Pat. Sect.)
*PRACTICE AREAS: Patent; Trademark; Copyright.
FitzGerald, Joseph T. ........................'64 '92 C.588 B.S.E.E. L.180 J.D. 801 S. Figueroa St. (Pat.)
**Fitzgerald, Kevin K.** ........................'56 '81 C.25 B.A. L.228 J.D. [Jones,B.S.A.&F.]
*PRACTICE AREAS: Litigation; Broker-Dealer Regulation; Class Actions.
**Fitzgerald, Michael W.** ........................'59 '87 C.309 A.B. L.1066 J.D. [⊠ R.L.Corbin]
*REPORTED CASES: United States v. Alvarez-Sanchez, 975 F. 2d 461 (9th Cir. 1991); United States v. Mejia, 953 F.2d 461 (9th Cir. 1991); Doganiere v. United States, 914 F. 2d 165 (9th Cir. 1990); United States v. Affinito, 873 F. 2d 1261 (9th Cir. 1989); United States v. Pace, 709 F Supp. 948 (C.D. Cal. 1989), affirmed, 893 F. 2d 1103 (9th Cir. 1990).
Fitzgerald, Patrick R. ........................'59 '88 C.309 A.B. L.1068 J.D. 355 S. Grand Ave., 35th Fl.
**Fitzgerald, Teresa M.** ........................'65 '91 C.221 B.A. L.352 J.D. Corp. Coun., Farmers Grp., Inc.
*RESPONSIBILITIES: Labor/Employment and Agency.
**Fitzgerald, William B.**, (AV) ........................'36 '61 C.976 B.A. L.309 J.D. [Brobeck,P.&H.]
*LANGUAGES: French, Italian.
*PRACTICE AREAS: Litigation; Products Liability Litigation; General Commercial Litigation.
**Fitzgibbons, Dana** ........................'62 '89 C.923 B.S. L.426 J.D. [⊠ McKenna&C.]
*PRACTICE AREAS: Government Contracts Law.
Fitzgibbons, John Carl ........................'42 '67 C&L.608 B.A., J.D. 500 Citadel Dr.

**Fitzhugh, Nancy E.** ........................'55 '80 C.951 B.A. L.1019 J.D. [Wright,R.O.&T.]
*PRACTICE AREAS: Commercial; Commercial Litigation; General Civil; Pharmaceutical/Device; Workers Compensation.
**Fitzhugh, Timothy B.**, (AV) ........................'53 '78 C.112 B.A. L.809 J.D. [⊠ Herzfeld&R.]
Fitzpatrick, Brian F. ........................'64 '93 C.101 B.S. L.1066 J.D. 300 S. Grand Ave., Suite 3000
Fitzpatrick, Donald K. ........................'34 '65 C.870 B.S. L.800 J.D. 725 S. Figueroa St., 19th Fl
Fitzpatrick, T. Robert ........................'35 '61 C.426 B.S. L.800 LL.B. 626 Wilshire Blvd.
FitzRandolph, John A. ........................'35 '65 L.800 J.D. Dean, Whittier Law Sch.
Fitzwater, Robert L. ........................'48 '75 C.112 B.A. L.800 J.D. 3330 S. Sepulveda Blvd.
**Flachs, Robert J.** ........................'71 '96 C.112 B.A. L.309 J.D. [⊠ Irell&M.]
**Fladell, Matthew** ........................'55 '82 C.043 B.A. L.05 LL.B. [⊠ Wolf,R.&S.]
*PRACTICE AREAS: Entertainment Law; Business Law.
**Flagel, Mark A.** ........................'58 '83 C.112 B.A. L.1066 J.D. [Latham&W.]
*PRACTICE AREAS: Intellectual Property; Litigation.
Flagg, Cynthia Platt ........................'48 '82 C.112 B.A. L.426 J.D. 860 S. Los Angeles St.
**Flahavan, William F.**, (AV) ........................'46 '72 C.740 B.A. L.1067 J.D. [Gray,Y.D.&R.]
*PRACTICE AREAS: Insurance Litigation; Professional Malpractice; Personal Injury.
**Flaherty, Michael P.** '45 '72 C.94 B.A. L.128 J.D.
(adm. in DC; not adm. in CA) [⊠ O'Donnell,R.&S.]
*LANGUAGES: German.
*PRACTICE AREAS: Litigation; Financial Institutions; Government Contracts; Regulatory Agency Law.
Flaig, Joseph L. ........................'13 '58 C.494 A.B. L.810 LL.B. 355 S. Grand Ave.
**Flaig, Robert B.**, (AV) ........................'41 '67 C&L.800 A.B., J.D. [Sheppard,M.R.&H.]
*PRACTICE AREAS: Construction Law; Construction and Commercial Litigation.
Flanagan, Sharon E. ........................'47 '78 C.112 B.A. L.1068 J.D. Sr. Atty., Ct. of App.
**Flanagan, Tara A.** ........................'58 '87 C.298 B.A. L.990 J.D. [⊠ McKenna&C.]
Flanagan, William J. ........................'45 '74 C.999 B.A. L.472 J.D. Bet Tzedek Legal Servs.

**Flanagan, Booth, Unger & Moses**
**(See Glendale)**

Flanderka, Peter C. ........................'56 '89 C.1077 B.A. L.426 J.D. 3255 Wilshire Blvd.
Flannery, Sandra J. ........................'59 '85 C.112 B.A. L.1049 J.D. 210 W. Temple
Flannes, Martin A. ........................'52 '77 C.813 A.B. L.1068 J.D. 300 S. Grand Ave.
Flattery, Michael P., (A Prof. Law Corp.), (BV) '52 '78
C.112 B.A. L.809 J.D. 8752 Holloway Dr.
Flattery, Thomas L., (AV) ........................'22 '55 C.870 B.S. L.1068 J.D. 333 S. Grand Ave. (Pat.)
**Flattum, Susan P.** ........................'68 '93 C.800 B.S. L.276 J.D. [⊠ Latham&W.]
Flaum, Joseph D., (AV) ........................'11 '36 C.910 C.L.734 J.D. 818 N. Doheny Dr.‡
Fleischli, Steven E. ........................'68 '94 C.174 B.A. L.1068 J.D. 444 S. Flower St.
Fleischman, William O., (BV) ........................'45 '71 C.112 B.A. L.1068 J.D. 1900 Ave. of the Stars
Fleishman, Stanley ........................'20 '44 C.102 L.178 LL.B. [Fleishman,F.&M.]
Fleishman, Stephen M., (P.C.) ........................'37 '65 C.112 B.S. L.426 LL.B. 1901 Ave. of the Stars
Fleishman, Fisher & Moest ........................ 2049 Century Pk. E.
**Fleming, David W.**, (AV) '34 '60 C.57 B.A. L.1068 J.D.
[⊠ Latham&W.] (©Univ. City)
Fleming, Frederick J. ........................'46 '71 C.112 L.809 J.D. 3701 Wilshire Blvd.
**Fleming, G. Thomas, III** ........................'51 '76 C.800 B.A. L.1065 J.D. [Jones,B.S.A.&F.]
*PRACTICE AREAS: Litigation; Arbitration; Real Estate; Regulatory Matters.
Fleming, J. Patrick, Jr. ........................'52 '77 C.112 B.A. L.276 J.D. 2029 Century Park E.
Fletcher, Freddie ........................'55 '88 C.309 A.B. L.1068 J.D. 323 S. La Fayette Pk.
Fletcher, Julie A. '61 '86 C.375 B.A. L.900 J.D.
(adm. in KS; not adm. in CA) Sr. Acct. Exec., LEXIS-NEXIS
**Fletcher, Kathryn Paige** ........................'66 '92 C.911 B.A., J.D. [⊠ Quisenberry&B.]
**Fletcher, Michael Gerard** ........................'51 '76 C.813 A.B. L.800 J.D. [Frandzel&S.]
*PRACTICE AREAS: Commercial Litigation; Bankruptcy; Bankruptcy Litigation; Real Estate; Workout Negotiations and Documentation.
Fletcher, Michael W. ........................'52 '80 C.1081 B.S. L.836 J.D. 116 N. Robertson Blvd.
Flette, Norman N. '44 '71 C&L.112 B.A., J.D.
Dep. Gen. Coun., Metropolitan Water Dist. of Southern Calif.
**Flewelling, Mark T.** ........................'55 '80 C.605 A.B. L.800 J.D. [Walker,W.T.&W.]
*PRACTICE AREAS: Banking; Litigation.
**Flick, Robert T.** ........................'53 '78 C.589 B.S. L.813 J.D. [Katten M.&Z.]
*LANGUAGES: French.
*PRACTICE AREAS: Real Estate Law.
**Flick, Wayne S.** ........................'63 '90 C.188 B.S. L.94 J.D. [⊠ Latham&W.]
*PRACTICE AREAS: Employment Law.
**Fliegel, Melvyn B., (P.C.)**, (AV) ........................'36 '62 C.112 A.B. L.309 J.D. [Alschuler G.&P.]
Fligsten, Monte C. ........................'41 '66 C.112 B.S. L.1068 J.D. Dep. Dist. Atty.
Flint, Mitchell L., (BV) ........................'23 '57 C.112 B.S. L.1068 LL.B. 6255 Sunset Blvd.
Flockhart, Monica M. ........................'62 '87 C.112 B.A. L.809 J.D. 4484 Wilshire Blvd.
**Flores, Delia** ........................'55 '81 C.309 A.B. L.1068 J.D. [⊠ R.D.Walker]
*PRACTICE AREAS: Employment Discrimination; Negligence; Product Liability; Medical-Legal Law; Unfair Competition.
**Flores, Mark K.** ........................'64 '93 C.800 B.S. L.426 J.D. [⊠ McNicholas&M.]
**Flores, Valerie L.** ........................'60 '88 C.112 B.A. L.990 J.D. [Cox,C.&N.]
*PRACTICE AREAS: Real Estate and Business Litigation.
**Flores-Oster, Dawn M.** ........................'58 '91 C.112 B.A. L.809 J.D. [⊠ Engstrom,L.&L.]
*LANGUAGES: French, Spanish.
*PRACTICE AREAS: Civil Litigation Defense; Civil Litigation Plaintiff.
**Flory, Mark W.** ........................'54 '80 C.112 B.A. L.1068 J.D. [Harrington,F.D.&C.]
*REPORTED CASES: D'Hondt v. Regents of the University of California (1984) 153 Cal. App. 3d 723. Williams v. Transport Indemnity Co. (1984) 157 Cal. App. 3d 953. Mann v. Cracchiolo (1985) 38 Cal. 3d 18. Insurance Company of the State of Pennsylvania v. Associated International Insurance Co. 922 F. 2d 516 (9th Cir. 1990). Span v. Associated International Insurance Co. (1991) 227 Cal. App. 3d 463.
*PRACTICE AREAS: Insurance Coverage Law; Commercial Litigation; Appellate Practice.
Floum, Richard H., (AV) ........................'31 '59 C.645 B.A. L.659 LL.B. [R.H.Floum]
Floum, Richard H., Inc., (AV) ........................ 1801 Century Park East
**Flowers, John L.**, (AV) ....'41 '66 C&L.800 B.S.L., J.D. [⊠ Darling,H.&R.] (©Pasadena)
*REPORTED CASES: Springs Industries, Inc. v. Kris Knit, Inc. (9th Circuit 1989) 880 F.2d 1129.
*PRACTICE AREAS: Civil Litigation; Trust Planning; Business Planning; Estate Planning; Trust and Estate Litigation.
**Floyd, Daniel S.** ........................'60 '86 C.112 B.A. L.1066 J.D. [Gibson,D.&C.]
*PRACTICE AREAS: Litigation.
**Flugge, Valerie V.** ........................'59 '83 C.793 B.A. L.800 J.D. [Slaff,M.&R.]
*PRACTICE AREAS: General Business Litigation; Entertainment; Copyright and Trademark.
Flusty, Ned ........................'33 '59 C.112 B.A. L.1068 LL.B. Asst. City Atty.
Flynn, Elizabeth Meinicke ........................'63 '90 C&L.945 B.A., J.D. 300 S. Grand Ave.
Flynn, Harry C., (AV) ........................'20 '51 C&L.426 A.B., J.D. 2728 S. LaCienega Blvd.
**Flynn, Jeanne Morales** ........................'69 '95 C.813 B.A. L.602 J.D. [⊠ O'Melveny&M.]
Flynn, John E. ........................'40 '67 C.478 B.A. L.178 LL.B. The Flying Tiger Line, Inc.
**Flynn, John P.** ........................'62 '88 C&L.477 B.A., J.D. [⊠ Dewey B.]
Flynn, Paul G. ........................'39 '69 C.276 A.B. L.767 J.D. Supr. Ct. J.
Flynn, Taylor ........................'64 '92 C.197 B.A. L.178 J.D. Amer. Civil Liberties Union
Fogel, Illyssa I. ........................'49 '83 C.549 B.A. L.809 J.D. 1901 Ave. of the Stars

**Fogel, Feldman, Ostrov, Ringler & Klevens, A Law Corporation**
**(See Santa Monica)**

**Fogelman, James P.** ........................'67 '92 C.659 B.S. L.1067 J.D. [⊠ Gibson,D.&C.]
**Fogelson, Noah T.** ........................'70 '95 C.813 B.A. L.1066 J.D. [⊠ Howrey&S.]
Fogelson, Steven M. ........................'53 '90 C.112 B.A. L.800 J.D. [⊠ Engel&E.]

CAA223P

**Fogg, Janice '48 '89 C.112 B.A. L.1068 J.D.**
**10880 Wilshire Boulevard, Suite 2200, 90024**
**Telephone: 310-446-9773 Fax: 310-470-6735**
**Email: JEFogg@AOL.com**
**(Certified Specialist, Estate Planning, Trust and Probate Law The State Bar of California Board of Legal Specialization).**
***PRACTICE AREAS: Probate; Trust Law; Estate Planning; Wills.**
**Of Counsel: Manya M. Bertram (Mrs.).**
**Probate, Estate Planning, Estates, Gift Taxation, Conservatorship, Trusts and Wills.**
*See Professional Biographies, LOS ANGELES, CALIFORNIA*

**Fohrman, Burton H.**, (AV) ....'39 '64 C.800 A.B. L.1068 J.D. [White&C.]
**Foker, Eric B.** .... '66 '95 C.16 B.A. L.276 J.D. [Ⓐ Pillsbury M.&S.]
Foland-Priver, Laura ....'58 '84 C.347 B.A. L.1148 J.D. Dep. Dist. Atty.
**Foley, John A.**, (BV) ....'53 '82 C.1077 B.A. L.809 J.D. [Ⓐ Wasser,R.&C.]
**Foley, Martin J.** .... '46 '75 C&L.800 B.A., J.D. [Sonnenschein N.&R.]
*PRACTICE AREAS: Aviation and Aerospace Litigation; Technology Law; Intellectual Property.

**Foley Lardner Weissburg & Aronson, (AV) BR**
**35th Floor, One Century Plaza, 2029 Century Park East (Century City), 90067-3021⊙**
**Telephone: 310-277-2223 Facsimile: 310-557-8475**
**Robert A. Klein; Peter Aronson; Carl Weissburg; Richard A. Blacker; Mark S. Windisch; J. Mark Waxman; Carl H. Hitchner (Resident at San Francisco Office); Robert D. Sevell; Richard F. Seiden; Gregory W. McClune (Resident at San Francisco Office); George L. Root, Jr. (Resident at San Diego Office); James R. Kalyvas; Michael G. McCarty (Resident, San Diego Office); Richard M. Albert; Ralph B. Kostant; Laurence R. Arnold (Resident at San Francisco Office); Anita D. Lee; Samuel F. Hoffman (Resident at San Diego Office); Samuel H. Weissbard (Not admitted in CA); Thomas L. Driscoll (Resident, San Francisco Office); Jonathan M. Lindeke (Resident at San Francisco Office); C. Darryl Cordero; Denise R. Rodriguez; Stephen W. Parrish (Resident at San Francisco Office); R. Michael Scarano, Jr. (Resident at San Diego Office); David A. Blumenthal (Not admitted in CA; Resident also at Foley & Lardner, Washington, D.C. & Annapolis, Maryland Offices); Lowell C. Brown; Gregory V. Moser (Resident at San Diego Office); Robert E. Goldstein; Tami S. Smason; Lawrence C. Conn; Mark T. Schieble (Resident at San Francisco Office); Robert C. Leventhal; Larry L. Marshall (Resident at San Diego Office); Clare Richardson; Carol Isackson (Resident at San Diego Office); Dorothy J. Stephens (Resident at Sacramento Office); Paul Gustav Neumann (Resident at San Francisco Office); Charles B. Oppenheim; James N. Godes; Ingeborg E. Penner (Resident at San Francisco Office); Robyn A. Meinhardt. Of Counsel: Judith E. Solomon (Resident at San Diego Office); Robert J. Enders; Mark E. Reagan (Resident at San Francisco Office); Frederick Martin, Jr. (Resident at San Diego Office); Mary K. Norvell (Resident at San Diego Office); Jeffrey R. Bates; Adam B. Schiff;—Shirley J. Paine; Howard W. Cohen; Jonathon E. Cohn; Steven J. Simerlein (Resident at San Diego Office); Amy B. Hafey; Diane Ung; Christopher E. Love; Terri Wagner Cammarano; Leila Nourani; Karen R. Weinstein; Lorna D. Hennington; Braulio Montesino; Shana T. Torem; David A. Renas (Resident at San Diego Office); Ioana Petrou (Resident at San Francisco Office); T. Joshua Ritz; Sharon M. Kopman; Kimberly F. Applequist; Lynn R. Goodfellow (Resident, San Diego Office); James D. Nguyen; Andrew M. Agtagma; John H. Douglas (Resident, San Francisco Office); Margaret M. McCahill (Resident, San Diego Office); David T. Morris (Resident, San Francisco Office); Nathan D. Schmidt (Resident, Sacrament Office); Paula C. Ohliger (Resident, San Francisco Office); Michael J. Sieradzki (Resident, San Francisco, Office); Lisa Goodwin Michael; René Bowser (Resident, San Francisco Office); Jeffrey M. Pomerance; Charles R. Zubrzycki; Lisa A. Palombo; Daron L. Tooch; Julie Christine Ashby (Resident at San Diego Office); Monica Gonzalez Brisbane (Resident at Sacramento Office); Robert J. Wenbourne, Resident at Sacramento Office).**
**Health Care; Hospitals; Medicare and Medicaid; Litigation; Labor and Employment; Business, Corporate and Commercial Law; Administrative and Legislative Practice before all State and Federal Agencies; Finance; Real Estate; Employee Benefits; Municipal Law.**
**Sacramento, California Office: Suite 1050, 770 L Street. Telephone: 916-443-8005. Facsimile: 916-443-2240.**
**San Diego, California Office: 402 West Broadway, 23rd. Floor. Telephone: 619-234-6655. Facsimile: 619-234-3510.**
**San Francisco, California Office: One Maritime Plaza, 6th Floor. Telephone: 415-434-4484. Facsimile: 415-434-4507.**
*See Professional Biographies, LOS ANGELES, CALIFORNIA*

**Folger, Peter M.**, (AV) ....'45 '73 C.813 A.B. L.767 J.D. [Folger L.&K.]⊙

**Folger Levin & Kahn LLP, (AV)**
**28th Floor, 1900 Avenue of the Stars, 90067⊙**
**Telephone: 310-556-3700 FAX: 310-556-3770**
**John P. Levin; Peter M. Folger; Michael A. Kahn; Donald E. Kelley, Jr.; Thomas P. Laffey; Scott W. Bowen; Samuel R. Miller; Mary C. Castle; Richard Keenan; Roger B. Mead; Douglas W. Sullivan; Teressa K. Lippert; Margaret R. Dollbaum; James Goldberg; Lisa McCabe van Krieken; Gregory D. Call; Janice B. Lawrence; Susan W. Ansberry; Thomas F. Koegel; Katharine Livingston; Adam Sachs; Wesley D. Hurst; J. Daniel Sharp; Margaret E. Murray. Associates: Charles R. Perry; Brian C. Bunger; Christopher B. Conner; M. Kay Martin; Julie M. Kennedy; Roland Valayre; Frieda A. Taylor; Kenneth R. Hillier; Theresa I. McFarland; Michael F. Kelleher; Raquel L. Wilkening; G. Jiyun Lee; Theresa A. Nagle; Karen J. Petrulakis; Jennifer L. Wright; Kelvin T. Wyles; Robert A. McFarlane; Beatrice B. Nguyen; Ernst A. Halperin; Jessica M. Karner; Kimberly A. Simpson; Nancy E. Yaffe; Lynne S. Bourgault; Stuart J. Mackey; Maxwell S. Peltz; Angela C. Miller.**
**General Practice.**
**San Francisco, California Office: Embarcadero Center West, 23rd Floor, 275 Battery Street. Telephone: 415-986-2800. FAX: 415-986-2827.**
*See Professional Biographies, LOS ANGELES, CALIFORNIA*

**Folino, Domenic**, (AV) ....'38 '64 C&L.823 B.A., LL.B. [Roper&F.]
*PRACTICE AREAS: Construction Insurance; Insurance Subrogation; Trial Practice; Environmental Law; Environmental Insurance Litigation.
Folinsky, Barry M. ....'46 '72 C.1077 B.A. L.426 J.D. 3600 Wilshire Blvd.
Folke, Duane R. ....'57 '83 C.990 B.A. L.213 J.D. 629 N. Alta Vista Blvd.
Follett, David B. ....'46 '73 C.112 B.A. L.61 J.D. 633 W. 5th St.
**Fond, Richard A.**, (AV) ....'48 '72 C&L.800 A.B., J.D. [Ⓐ Simke C.]
*PRACTICE AREAS: Business Litigation; Creditors' Rights and Remedies; Provisional Remedies.
**Fonda, Peter M.**, (AV) ....'47 '73 C.475 B.A. L.1068 J.D. [Fonda,G.H.&D.]

**Fonda, Garrard, Hilberman & Davis, A Professional Corporation, (AV) BR**
**1888 Century Park East, 21st Floor, 90067**
**Telephone: 310-553-1121 FAX: 310-553-4232**
**Donald A. Garrard; Peter M. Fonda; Joe W. Hilberman; Steven D. Davis; Patrick W. Mayer;—Gloria Kurman Apt; Diane M. Daly; Tracy T. Davis; Laurie DeYoung; Thomas E. Donahue; Frederick James; David M. Samuels.**
**General Civil, Trial and Appellate Practice. Insurance Defense, Property and Casualty Insurance, Medical Malpractice Defense, Personal Injury and Products Liability Law. Insurance Coverage (Primary, Excess and Reinsurance) and Bad Faith, Insurance Fraud.**
**Representative Clients: Utica Mutual Insurance Co.; Truck Ins. Exchange; Twentieth Century Ins.; Allstate Ins. Co.; Regents of California; State Farm Ins. Co.**
**Reference: Sanwa Bank of California (Los Angeles Headquarters Corporate Office).**
*See Professional Biographies, LOS ANGELES, CALIFORNIA*

Fong, Evelyn Jane ....'65 '90 C.112 B.A. L.813 J.D. 801 S. Figueroa St.
**Fong, H. G. Robert**, (AV) ....'46 '72 C.112 B.S. L.426 J.D. [Ku,F.L.&C.]
*PRACTICE AREAS: Civil Trial; Litigation; Intellectual Property Law.
**Fong, Kenneth T.** ....'61 '89 C.1097 B.S. L.426 J.D. [Barbosa G.&B.]
*PRACTICE AREAS: Redevelopment Law; Corporate Law; Real Estate Law.
Fong, Thomas Y. K. ....'49 '77 C&L.101 B.S., J.D. U.S. Immig. J.
**Fong, William P.** ....'65 '92 C.178 B.A. L.800 J.D. [Ⓐ Buchalter,N.F.&Y.]
*PRACTICE AREAS: Bankruptcy.
Fonte, Raquel M. '70 '96 C.30 B.A. L.128 J.D.
(adm. in MD; not adm. in CA) CARECEN
**Fontenot, Lisa A.** ....'68 '94 C.276 B.S.F.S. L.893 J.D. [Ⓐ Sidley&A.]
*LANGUAGES: French.
*PRACTICE AREAS: Corporate.

**Foos, Nicole M.** ....'59 '85 C.112 B.A. L.94 J.D. [Ⓐ Manning,M.&W.]
Foote, Emmerline ....'55 '87 C.976 B.A. L.329 J.D. Dep. Dist Atty.
**Forbes, Amy R.** ....'59 '84 C.674 B.S.E. L.800 J.D. [Gibson,D.&C.]
*PRACTICE AREAS: Real Estate; Land Use Planning.
**Forbes, Charles F.**, (AV) ....'29 '56 C&L.800 B.S., J.D. [Musick,P.&G.]
*PRACTICE AREAS: Healthcare; Hospitals; Corporate Law.
Forbes, Lawrence A. ....'45 '76 C.800 B.S. L.1095 J.D. 670 S. La Fayette Park Pl.
**Force, Joshua S.** ....'66 '91 C.311 B.A. L.309 J.D. [Ⓐ Lane P.S.L.]
*PRACTICE AREAS: Admiralty and Maritime Law; Insurance Law.
Ford, Bryan B. ....'58 '86 C.309 A.B. L.813 J.D. 5757 Wilshire Blvd., Ste. 560
**Ford, Donald H.**, (AV) ....'06 '32 C.628 B.S. L.477 J.D. [Overton,L.&P.]
*PRACTICE AREAS: Oil and Gas; Corporate Law; Farm and Ranch Law.
**Ford, F. Joseph, Jr.**, (BV) ....'50 '77 C.627 B.S. L.990 J.D. [Ⓐ Pierry&M.]
*PRACTICE AREAS: Admiralty/Maritime; Personal Injury; Products Liability (Plaintiff).
Ford, H. Jay, III ....'60 '85 C&L.878 B.U.S., J.D. [Tyre K.K.&G.]
Ford, Michael D. ....'42 '70 C.112 B.A. L.1068 J.D. Principal Dep. Co. Coun.
**Ford, Robert W.** ....'56 '80 C.800 B.A. L.990 J.D. [Ⓐ Pierry&M.]
*LANGUAGES: Spanish.
*PRACTICE AREAS: Admiralty/Maritime; Personal Injury; Products Liability (Plaintiff); Workmans Compensation.
**Ford, William H., III**, (AV) ....'44 '71 C.770 B.A. L.426 J.D. [Ford]
*PRACTICE AREAS: Insurance Coverage; Civil Litigation; Insurance Bad Faith.

**Ford & Harrison, (AV) BR**
**333 South Grand Avenue Suite 3680, 90071⊙**
**Telephone: 213-680-3410 FAX: 213-680-4161**
**Members of Firm: Michael L. Lowry; Glen H. Mertens. Associates: Maral Donoyan; Kari Haugen.**
**Labor Relations, Equal Employment, Wage and Hour, Airline Labor Law, OSHA, Environmental Law, Commercial Litigation, Employee Benefits and Immigration Law.**
**Representative Clients: Coca-Cola Enterprises; Columbia/HCA Healthcare Corp.; Delta Air Lines, Inc.; Federal Express Corp.; Kellogg Co.; Knight Publishing Co.; Landmark Communications, Inc.; LIN Television Corp.; Nestle USA, Inc.; Regional Airline Assn.**
**Atlanta, Georgia Office: 600 Peachtree at the Circle Building, 1275 Peachtree Street, N.E., 30309. Telephone: 404-888-3800. Fax: 404-888-3863.**
**Miami, Florida Office: Alley and Alley/Ford & Harrison. 516 Ingraham Building, 25 S.E. 2nd Avenue, 33131. Telephone: 305-379-3811. Fax: 305-358-5933.**
**Tampa, Florida Office: Alley and Alley/Ford & Harrison. 205 Brush Street, P.O. Box 1427, 33601. Telephone: 813-229-6481. Fax: 813-223-7029.**
**Washington, D.C. Office: 1920 N Street, N.W., Suite 200, 20036. Telephone: 202-463-6633. Fax: 202-466-5705.**
*See Professional Biographies, LOS ANGELES, CALIFORNIA*

**Ford Law Firm, The, (AV)**
**12400 Wilshire Boulevard, Suite 540, 90025**
**Telephone: 310-826-2648 Facsimile: 310-826-2658**
**William H. Ford, III. Associates: Claudia J. Serviss; George H. Kim; Michael D. Collins; Paul C. Cook.**
**Business Litigation, Trials and Appeals, Insurance Bad Faith Litigation.**
*See Professional Biographies, LOS ANGELES, CALIFORNIA*

**Ford, Walker, Haggerty & Behar**
**(See Long Beach)**

**Forer, Jeffrey** ....'55 '83 C.112 B.A. L.809 J.D. [Cohen P.&F.]
**Forester, Robert M.** ....'69 '95 C.861 B.A. L.800 J.D. [Ⓐ Arter&H.]
*PRACTICE AREAS: Business Litigation.
**Forgey, Darrell A.**, (AV) ....'47 '73 C.1077 B.A. L.426 J.D. [Hillsinger&C.]
**Forgey, Donald G.**, (AV) ....'50 '79 C.1077 B.A. L.809 J.D. [Hillsinger&C.]
**Forgie, Peter S.** ....'49 '75 C.800 B.A. L.990 J.D. [Sands N.F.L.&L.]
**Forgnone, Robert**, (AV) ....'36 '70 C.1042 L.426 J.D. [Gibson,D.&C.]
*PRACTICE AREAS: General Litigation; Business Law; Products Liability; Aviation Law; Equine Law.
Fork, Allan C. ....'38 '66 C&L.37 B.S., J.D. Dep. Dist. Atty.
Forkus, Kris J. ....'68 '94 C.1109 B.A. L.809 J.D. [Ⓐ Liebert,C.&F.]
Formaker, Marilyn W. ....'29 '87 C.800 A.B. L.1068 J.D. Sr. Jud. Atty. to Ct. of App.
**Formaker, Susan L.** ....'58 '87 C.112 A.B. L.1068 J.D. Sr. Coun., Bank of Amer.
**Forman, Cindy F.** ....'57 '85 C.66 B.A. L.276 J.D. [Ⓒ Shapiro,H.&M.]
**Forman, Dan** ....'64 '91 C.347 B.A. L.276 J.D. [Ⓐ Manatt,P.&P.]
*PRACTICE AREAS: General Business Litigation.
**Forman, Judith R., (P.C.)**, (AV) ....'42 '75 C.659 B.A. L.884 J.D. [Manatt,P.&P.]
*PRACTICE AREAS: Family Law.
**Forman, Richard S.** ....'60 '87 C.659 B.A. L.569 J.D. [Stroock&S.&L.]
*PRACTICE AREAS: Securities; Corporate; Mergers and Acquisitions.
**Forman, William H.** ....'65 '90 C.674 A.B. L.309 J.D. [Ⓐ Arnold&P.]
*PRACTICE AREAS: Litigation.
**Forn, V. Neil, II** ....'57 '96 C.809 M.A. L.990 J.D. [Ⓐ Baum,H.A.G.&D.]
*PRACTICE AREAS: Personal Injury; Wrongful Death; Mass Disaster Litigation; Complex and Multi-District Litigation.
Fornias, Vincent I. ....'56 '89 C.112 B.A. L.1190 J.D. 5140 York Blvd.
Forrest, Ernestine ....'48 '74 C.112 A.B. L.1066 J.D. P.O. Box 19221A
**Forry, John I.**, (AV) ....'45 '70 C.31 A.B. L.309 J.D. [Rogers&W.]
*PRACTICE AREAS: International Taxation; Foreign Investment in the United States; Project Finance.
**Forsley, Alan W.** ....'61 '95 C.112 B.S. L.1049 J.D. [Ⓐ Manning,L.B.&B.]
*PRACTICE AREAS: Civil Litigation; Bankruptcy.
Fortier-Duguay, Thierry ....'62 '88 C.112 B.A. L.426 J.D. 333 S. Grand Ave.
Fortman, Brian E. ....'66 '91 C.37 B.A. L.178 J.D. 9255 Sunset Blvd.
Fortner, Raymond G., Jr. ....'44 '68 C.112 L.800 J.D. Sr. Asst. Co. Coun.
**Forward, Robert H., Jr.**, (AV) ....'45 '70 C.813 B.A. L.309 J.D. [Forward&D.]
*LANGUAGES: French, Italian and Spanish.
*PRACTICE AREAS: Real Estate; Land Use; International Business; Entertainment.

**Forward & Dix, (AV)**
**2049 Century Park East, Suite 880, 90067⊙**
**Telephone: 310-785-9770 Fax: 310-785-9775**
**Robert H. Forward, Jr.; Simon Dix.**
**International and United States Business Law, Real Estate and Land Use Law, Entertainment Law.**
**Bologna, Italy Office: Studio Legale de Capoa-Guiducci & Associati. Via Albertazzi, 22, 40137. Telephone: (39-51) 346 062/348835. Telecopier: (39-51) 344 125.**
*See Professional Biographies, LOS ANGELES, CALIFORNIA*

**Foss, Robert F.** ....'52 '94 L.999 J.D. [Ⓐ Baum,H.A.G.&D.]
*PRACTICE AREAS: Wrongful Death; Personal Injury; Mass Disaster Litigation; Aviation Accidents and Injuries; Products Liability.

**Foss & Roberts**
**(See Pasadena)**

Foster, Charles E. '35 '64 C.165 B.A. L.37 LL.B.
Assoc. Gen. Coun., Occidental Petroleum Corp.
**Foster, Christopher G.** ....'56 '85 C.813 B.S. L.1065 J.D. [Smiland&K.]
*REPORTED CASES: Setliff v. E.I. DuPont de Nemours, 32 Cal. App. 4th 1525 (1995); Teitel v. First Los Angeles Bank, 231 Cal. App. 3d 1593 (1991).
*PRACTICE AREAS: Air Pollution; Water Resources; Commercial Litigation.
Foster, Eric C. ....'62 '87 C.569 B.S. L.1009 J.D. 1315 Angelus Ave.
Foster, Glenn B. '58 '89 C.971 B.S. L.128 J.D.
(adm. in NY; not adm. in CA; Pat.) 444 S. Flower St., Ste. 2000
Foster, James O. ....'38 '74 C&L.800 B.S.L., J.D. 4929 Wilshire Blvd.
Foster, Lisa Ann ....'57 '85 C.813 B.A. L.309 J.D. Exec. Dir., Calif. Common Cause

**Foster, M. Joan**, (AVⓉ) '39 '76 C.228 B.A. L.776 J.D.
(adm. in NJ; not adm. in CA) [Grotta,G.&H.]⊙
**Foster, Michael C.**, (AV) .... '55 '82 C.1077 B.S. L.426 J.D. [Konowiecki&R.]
*PRACTICE AREAS: Health Care Law; Mergers and Acquisitions; Corporate; Partnership; Securities Law.
**Foster, Michael D.** .... '55 '81 C&L.912 B.S., J.D. [Cohen P.&F.]
**Foster, Sharon E.** .... '61 '88 C.112 B.A. L.426 J.D. [Gibbs,G.L.&A.]
*PRACTICE AREAS: General Business Litigation; Commercial Law.
**Fote, Dominic J.** .... '61 '87 C.188 B.A. L.990 J.D. [🄰 Chapman&G.]
*PRACTICE AREAS: Insurance Coverage; General Negligence; Products Liability; Construction Litigation; Professional Liability.
**Four, Michael D.** .... '56 '81 C.112 A.B. L.426 J.D. [Schwartz,S.D.&S.]
*PRACTICE AREAS: Labor and Employment Law; Campaign Finance Law.
**Fournie, Thomas A.** .... '39 '70 C.339 B.S.E.E. L.208 J.D. [🄲 Goldstein,K.&P.] (Pat.)
*LANGUAGES: French and Spanish.
*PRACTICE AREAS: Litigation; Real Estate Law; Business and Tort Litigation.
Foust, Richard T., (BV) .... '38 '80 C.768 B.A. L.1136 J.D. 11340 W. Olympic Blvd.
Fowkes, Richard O. '46 '74 C.569 B.A. L.273 J.D.
(adm. in NY; not adm. in CA) Sr. V.P., Paramount Pictures Corp.
**Fowler, James M.** .... '57 '92 C&L.1136 B.S., J.D. [🄰 Meyers,B.&M.]
*PRACTICE AREAS: Product Liability; Insurance Related Issues.
Fowler, Janine R. .... '60 '87 C.112 B.A. L.990 J.D. Dep. Atty., State Dept. of Transp.
Fowler, Randall D., (AV) '48 '74
C.1074 B.A. L.1068 J.D. 2121 Ave. of the Stars (ⓒSan Marino)
Fowles, Julian .... '46 '72 C.569 A.B. L.309 J.D. 6253 Hollymont Dr.
**Fox, Angelee** .... '68 '96 C.805 B.B.A. L.800 J.D. [🄰 Latham&W.]
**Fox, Dana A.** .... '60 '85 C.1097 B.A. L.464 J.D. [Lynberg&W.]
**Fox, David M.** .... '60 '86 C.112 B.A. L.1137 J.D. [Kehr,C.T.&F.]
*PRACTICE AREAS: Entertainment Law; Real Estate; Business Law.
**Fox, Deborah J.** .... '58 '83 C.477 B.A. L.1049 J.D. [Freilich,K.F.&S.]
*REPORTED CASES: Santa Fe Realty Corp. v. City of Westminster (C.D. Cal. 1995) 906 F.Supp. 1341; Eldorado Drive v. City of Mesquite (D. Nev. 1994) 863 F.Supp. 1252.
**Fox, Edward M.**, (AV) .... '33 '57 C&L.602 A.B., J.D. [Burke,W.&S.]
*PRACTICE AREAS: Taxation Law; Corporate and Business Law; Estate Planning Law; Probate Law.
Fox, Edward M. .... '55 '86 C.339 B.A. L.809 J.D. [Klass,H.&R.]
Fox, Frank O. .... '60 '85 C.1077 B.S. L.426 J.D. [Firm of Fox&F.]
**Fox, Gerard P.** .... '60 '85 C.692 B.S. L.276 J.D. [Fox&S.]
*PRACTICE AREAS: Litigation; Intellectual Property; Infringement.
Fox, Henry A., (AV) .... '16 '46 C.610 A.B. L.800 LL.B. [Firm of Fox&F.]
Fox, James E. .... '54 '79 C.112 A.B. L.1065 J.D. [Fox&F.]
Fox, Jamie Beth .... '54 '80 C.831 B.A. L.61 J.D. 10866 Wilshire Blvd.
Fox, Janet S. .... '50 '76 C.1029 B.S. L.1095 J.D. Dep. Dist. Atty.
**Fox, Martin R.** .... '63 '91 L.398 J.D. [Bleau,F.&G.]
*PRACTICE AREAS: Business Litigation; Insurance Bad Faith; Contracts; Employment Law; Personal Injury.
**Fox, Michael A.** .... '64 '91 C.612 B.S. L.776 J.D. [🄰 Morris,P.&P.]
Fox, Michael K. .... '42 '71 C.112 B.A. L.1065 J.D. 200 N. Main
**Fox, Michael L.** .... '69 '94 C.659 B.S. L.990 J.D. [🄰 McKay,B.&G.]
**Fox, Michael T.** .... '47 '74 C.112 A.B. L.1049 J.D. [Cummins&W.]
*PRACTICE AREAS: Personal Injury; Premises Liability.
Fox, Robert M., (AV) .... '25 '52 C.659 B.S. L.809 J.D. [Fox&F.]
**Fox, Ronda** .... '59 '87 C.112 B.A. L.1067 J.D. [Fox&F.]
*PRACTICE AREAS: Business; Real Estate Litigation.
**Fox, Samuel J.** .... '44 '70 C.188 B.A. L.569 J.D. [🄲 Blanc W.J.&K.]
*PRACTICE AREAS: Entertainment; Music Publishing; International Copyright; Television Production; Syndication Licensing.
Fox, Stephen M. .... '49 '78 C.602 B.B.A. L.1136 J.D. Sr. Atty., Ct. of App.
**Fox, Steven A.** .... '54 '85 C.1109 B.A. L.588 J.D. [Davis&F.]
*LANGUAGES: Hebrew.
*PRACTICE AREAS: Business Litigation; Insurance Coverage Disputes; Real Estate Litigation; Professional Liability.
Fox, Warren S. .... '42 '70 C.1077 L.1095 J.D. 10100 Santa Monica Blvd.
Fox & Fox, (AV) .... 15233 Ventura Blvd.
Fox and Fox, The Law Firm of, (AV) .... 4201 Wilshire Blvd.

**Fox & Frumkin**
**11377 West Olympic Boulevard, Suite 1000, 90064**
**Telephone: 310-235-2414 Fax: 310-235-2479**
**Members of Firm: Ronda Fox; Arthur S. Frumkin.**
**General Civil Practice in State and Federal Courts. Trials and Appeals. Business, Construction and Real Estate Litigation.**

***See Professional Biographies, LOS ANGELES, CALIFORNIA***

Fox, Richard P., and Max Gest, A Professional Law Corporation .... 9911 W. Pico Blvd.

**Fox & Spillane, P.C.**
**10866 Wilshire Boulevard, Suite 900, 90024**
**Telephone: 310-441-5202 Fax: 310-441-5207**
**Gerard P. Fox; Jay M. Spillane;—Cynthia A. Vroom.**
**General Civil Litigation including Entertainment, Intellectual Property, Real Estate, Sports, Partnership and Product Liability Litigation.**

***See Professional Biographies, LOS ANGELES, CALIFORNIA***

**Foxx, Richard A.**, (AV) .... '18 '50 C.112 B.A. L.800 LL.B. [Harrington,F.D.&C.] ‡
Foy, Allan B. .... '29 '61 C.446 B.A. L.273 LL.B. Pres., Farr Co.
**Frackman, Russell J., (A Professional Corporation)**, (AV) '46 '71
C.597 B.A. L.178 J.D. [Mitchell,S.&K.]
*PRACTICE AREAS: Intellectual Property Litigation; Entertainment Litigation.
**Fraenkel, Stuart R.** .... '63 '94 C.1333 B.S. L.809 J.D. [🄰 Engstrom,L.&L.]
**Fragner, Matthew C.** .... '54 '78 C.976 B.A. L.1066 J.D. [Sonnenschein N.&R.]
*LANGUAGES: German.
*PRACTICE AREAS: Real Estate; Corporate.

**Fragomen, Del Rey & Bernsen, P.C., (AV)**
**11400 West Olympic Boulevard, Suite 1050, 90064⊙**
**Telephone: 310-473-8700 Facsimile: 310-473-5383**
**URL: http://www.fragomen.com**
**Peter H. Loewy; Cynthia J. Lange;—Timothy S. Barker; Susan Bierenbaum; Michael H. Boshnaick; Colleen McGrath Denison; Michael K. Molitz.**
**U.S. and Foreign Immigration and Nationality Law.**
**New York, New York Office: 515 Madison Avenue. Telephone: 212-688-8555. Facsimile: 212-319-5236; 212-758-7215.**
**Washington, D.C. Office: 1212 New York Avenue, N.W., Suite 850. Telephone: 202-223-5515. Facsimile: 202-371-2898.**
**Coral Gables, Florida Office: 890 South Dixie Highway. Telephone: 305-666-4655. Facsimile: 305-666-4467.**
**San Francisco, California Office: 88 Kearny Street, Suite 1300. Telephone: 415-986-1446. Facsimile: 415-986-7964.**
**Palo Alto, California Office: 525 University Avenue, Suite 1450. Telephone: 415-323-7557. Facsimile: 415-323-5030.**
**Chicago, Illinois Office: 300 South Wacker Drive, Suite 2900. Telephone: 312-263-6101. Facsimile: 312-431-0517.**
**Stamford, Connecticut Office: Fragomen Del Rey & Bernsen, 1177 High Ridge Road. Telephone: 203-321-1278. Facsimile: 203-321-1279.**
**Short Hills, New Jersey Office: Fragomen, Del Rey & Bernsen, 51 John F. Kennedy Parkway. Telephone: 201-564-5222. FAX: 201-564-5230.**

***See Professional Biographies, LOS ANGELES, CALIFORNIA***

Fraley, Franklin R., Jr. .... '64 '91 C.347 A.B. L.911 J.D. 801 S. Figueroa St.
**Framson, Jay E.** .... '58 '92 C.103 B.A. L.426 J.D. [🄰 Sedgwick,D.M.&A.]
Franceschi, Ernest J., Jr. .... '57 '84 C.800 B.S. L.809 J.D. 445 S. Figueroa St.
Francis, Caryn A. Y. .... '64 '89 C.586 B.A. L.846 J.D. 48th Fl., 333 S. Hope St.
Francis, Edna E. J. .... '45 '75 C.329 B.A. L.426 J.D. [E.E.J.Francis]
**Francis, Merrill R.**, (AV) .... '32 '60 C.668 B.A. L.813 J.D. [Sheppard,M.R.&H.]
*PRACTICE AREAS: Insolvency Law; Bankruptcy Law; Creditors Rights Law; Secured Transactions.
**Francis, Michael A.** .... '56 '87 C.801 B.S. L.809 J.D. [Demetriou,D.S.&M.]
*PRACTICE AREAS: Environmental Law; Business Law.

**Francis, Arthur W., Jr., A Prof. Corp., Law Offices of**
**(See Redondo Beach)**

Francis, Edna E. J., A Professional Corporation .... P.O. Box 65556
**Franck, Richard L.** .... '26 '53 C.940 L.426 J.D. [🄲 Parker,M.C.O.&S.]
*PRACTICE AREAS: Condemnation; Inverse Condemnation; Real Estate Valuation Litigation.
**Francken, Karla A.** .... '67 '94 C.966 B.S. L.436 J.D. [🄰 McCutchen,D.B.&E.]
*PRACTICE AREAS: Healthcare; Corporate/Business.
**Francone, Carol A.** .... '48 '77 C.37 B.A. L.1066 J.D. Sr. Coun., Bank of Amer.
**Frandsen, Russell Mackay**, (AV) .... '49 '76 C.101 B.A. L.228 J.D. [Radcliff,F.&D.]
*LANGUAGES: German.

**Frandzel & Share, A Law Corporation, (AV)**
**6500 Wilshire Boulevard 17th Floor, 90048-4920⊙**
**Telephone: 213-852-1000 Telecopier: 213-651-2577**
**Robert D. Frandzel (1942-1996); Richard Hudson Share; Thomas M. Robins, III; John A. Graham; Ronald L. Gruzen; Michael Gerard Fletcher; Steven N. Bloom; Peter Csato; Gary Owen Caris; David K. Golding; Stephen H. Marcus; Lisa A. Ogawa; Howard S Fredman; Stephen M. Skacevic; Thomas S. Arthur; Lesley Anne Hawes; Marshall J. August; LeRoy Anderson; Kenneth C. Bovard; Patricia Yamamoto Trendacosta; Craig A. Welin; Julia E. Sylva;—Henry G. Weinstein; Robb Michael Strom; Shirley D. Ramirez; Bruce D. Poltrock; Suzanne Kahn Wynne; Judy Man-Ling Lam; Robert Gonzalez; Joon W. Song; Amy Jessica Frankel.**
**Banking, Commercial Creditors Rights and Bankruptcy Law. General Civil, Trial Practice and Real Estate Law.**
**References: Cathay Bank; Community Bank; Kawasaki Motor Corp. USA; Phoenix Leasing; Sanwa Bank; Tokai Credit Corp.**
**San Francisco, California Office: 100 Pine Street, 26th Floor. Telephone: 415-788-7400. Telecopier: 415-291-9153.**

***See Professional Biographies, LOS ANGELES, CALIFORNIA***

Frank, David E. .... '34 '75 C.1077 B.A. L.426 J.D. 1801 Ave. of the Stars
**Frank, Debra Susan** .... '49 '77 C.94 B.A. L.809 J.D. [D.S.Frank]
**Frank, Douglas B.** .... '62 '89 C.597 B.A. L.426 J.D. [🄰 Mayer,B.&P.]
**Frank, John B.** .... '56 '85 C.918 B.A. L.477 J.D. [Munger,T.&O.]
**Frank, Leslie E.** .... '— '92 C.119 B.A. L.1067 J.D. [🄰 King,P.H.P.&B.]
Frank, Leslie J., (AV) .... '46 '72 C.763 B.A. L.426 J.D. [Frank,G.&S.]
Frank, Ralph R. .... '19 '53 C.178 L.809 LL.B. 2566 Overland Ave.
**Frank, Ronald F.**, (BV) .... '57 '82 C.105 B.A. L.893 J.D. [Bannan,G.S.&F.]
*PRACTICE AREAS: Product Liability; Asbestos Defense; Mass Toxic Torts; General Trial Practice.
Frank, Sidney C. .... '15 '38 C.563 B.B.A. L.569 LL.B. 357 S. Burnside Ave.

**Frank, Debra S., A Professional Law Corporation**
**Two Century Plaza, Suite 1800, 2049 Century Park East, 90067-3120**
**Telephone: 310-277-5121 Fax: 310-277-5932**
**Debra Susan Frank.**
**Family Law, Divorce Mediation, Civil, Personal Injury and Criminal Litigation.**

***See Professional Biographies, LOS ANGELES, CALIFORNIA***

Frank, Greenberg & Simone, (AV) .... 3530 Wilshire Blvd.
**Frankel, Amy Jessica** .... '69 '94 C.112 B.A. L.1065 J.D. [🄰 Frandzel&S.]
*PRACTICE AREAS: Commercial Litigation; Civil Litigation.
**Frankel, Barbara Kamenir** .... '50 '93 C.112 B.S. L.809 J.D. [🄰 Bonne,B.M.O.&N.]
**Frankel, Jeffrey H.** .... '65 '91 C.188 B.S. L.1068 J.D. [🄰 Mitchell,S.&K.]
*PRACTICE AREAS: Entertainment Law; Entertainment Industry Transactions; Copyright Law.
**Frankenheimer, John T., (A P.C.)**, (AV) .... '46 '73 C.154 B.A. L.1068 J.D. [Loeb&L.]
*PRACTICE AREAS: Entertainment Industry Law.
Frankley, Lawrence R., (AV) .... '28 '53 C&L.800 A.B., J.D. 2751 Forrester Dr.‡
Franklin, Benjamin C. .... '41 '69 Princ. Dep. Co. Coun.
Franklin, Carl M., (AV) '11 '65 C.911 A.B. L.893 J.D.
V.P., Emeritus & Prof. of Law, Univ. of Southern Calif.
Franklin, Cassandra S. .... '56 '85 C.37 B.A. L.228 J.D. 405 Hilgard Ave.
**Franklin, Christine C.** .... '49 '80 C.93 B.A. L.1068 J.D. [Thelen,M.J.&B.]
*PRACTICE AREAS: Commercial Litigation; Insurance.
**Franklin, Jill A.** .... '59 '87 C.605 A.B. L.426 J.D. [Schaffer&L.]
Franklin, Lair C. .... '49 '79 C.1097 B.A. L.1068 J.D. 3550 Wilshire Blvd.
Franklin, Sidney, Jr. .... '38 '65 C.112 A.B. L.1065 LL.B. 3600 Wilshire Blvd.
**Franklin, Terrence M.** .... '63 '89 C.597 B.S. L.309 J.D. [Ross,S.&G.]
*PRACTICE AREAS: Estate, Trust and Conservatorship Litigation; Appellate Practice; Business Litigation.
**Franks, Dennis B.** .... '57 '83 C.813 A.B. L.800 J.D. [🄲 Manatt,P.&P.]
*PRACTICE AREAS: Antitrust and Trade Regulation Law; Business Litigation; Financial Institution Litigation.

**Franscell, Strickland, Roberts & Lawrence, A Professional Corporation**
**(See Pasadena)**

**Franzen, Corinne A.** .... '66 '94 C.112 B.A. L.494 J.D. [🄰 Gibson,D.&C.]
*PRACTICE AREAS: Labor and Employment.
**Franzen, Edwin H., (P.C.)**, (AV) .... '27 '55 C.339 B.S. L.426 LL.B. [🄲 Hill,F.&B.]
**Franzese-Damron, Tonie M.** '65 '96
C.477 A.B. L.213 J.D. [🄰 Christensen,M.F.J.G.W.&S.]
*PRACTICE AREAS: Litigation.
**Fraser, Bruce W.** .... '57 '81 C.178 A.B. L.309 J.D. [Paul,H.J.&W.]
Fraser, E. L., (AV) .... '18 '48 C.602 B.S. L.800 LL.B. [Wadsworth,F.&D.]
**Fraser, E. Scott** .... '59 '84 C.813 A.B. L.426 J.D. [🄰 Nelson&N.]
*PRACTICE AREAS: Litigation; Business; Personal Injury; Employment.
Fraser, G. Howden, (AV) .... '47 '73 C.605 A.B. L.569 J.D. 444 S. Flower St.
**Fraser, James D.** .... '49 '75 C.112 B.A. L.1068 J.D. [Lewis,D.B.&B.]
Fraser, Linda D. .... '49 '87 C.1097 B.A. L.1068 J.D. 865 S. Figaroa St. #3100
Fraser, Robert B. .... '38 '70 C.871 B.S. L.1068 J.D. 801 S. Grand Ave.
Fraser, Shelley A. .... '53 '89 C.668 B.A. L.800 J.D. 3580 Wilshire Blvd.
Fratianne, Nicholas J. .... '57 '83 C.1077 B.S. L.809 J.D. Dep. City Atty.
Fratianne, Robert J. .... '67 '93 C.1077 B.A. L.809 J.D. Off. of City Atty.
**Frauman, David C. L.** .... '46 '76 C.178 B.A. L.705 J.D. [Milbank,T.H.&M.]
Frawley, Michael T. .... '56 '82 C.800 B.A. L.809 J.D. 2049 Century Pk. E.
**Frayer, Melanie M.** .... '71 '96 C&L.426 B.A., J.D. [🄰 Bonne,B.M.O.&N.]
*LANGUAGES: French.
Frazier, Kevin P. .... '64 '91 C.911 B.A. L.893 J.D. 10990 Wilshire Blvd.
Frazier, Rawls H. .... '20 '49 C&L.896 B.S., J.D. Adm. Law J., Soc. Sec. Admin.
**Frazier-Thomas, Avis** '54 '81 C.789 B.A. L.790 J.D.
Corp. Coun., The Times Mirror Co.
Fred, Alex Denny, (AV) .... '14 '41 C.1068 B.A. L.800 LL.B. P.O. Box 241589
Frederick, Barry R. .... '34 '74 C.1097 B.A. L.426 J.D. 1021 S. Union Ave.
**Frederickson, David H.**, (AV) .... '39 '69 C.766 B.A. L.1066 J.D. [Frederickson&Y.]
*PRACTICE AREAS: Business Litigation; Real Estate Litigation; Commercial Litigation; Civil Litigation; Partnership Disputes.

CAA225P

**Frederickson & Young, (AV)** BB
**Suite 481, 5757 Wilshire Boulevard, 90036-3664**
Telephone: 213-964-7373 Fax: 213-964-7377
Email: FNYMAN@AOL.com
Members of Firm: David H. Frederickson; Robert E. Young. Associates: Brian M. Plessala.
Business Litigation, Administrative, Real Property, Construction, Commercial and General Transactional Law. General Civil and Trial Practice in State and Federal Courts.
Representative Clients: Information International, Inc.; Nordoff Investments, Inc.; International Broadcasting, Inc.; Patrick Media Group; Palm Plaza Development; Cobe Laboratories, Inc.; Amusements International; Oxford Group of Companies.
*See Professional Biographies, LOS ANGELES, CALIFORNIA*

**Frederiksen, Karen Nancy** ............ '60 '88 C.1077 B.A. L.1068 J.D. [A Davis W.T.]
*PRACTICE AREAS: Media Law; Constitutional Law; Business Litigation.
**Fredman, Howard S**, (AV) ..................'44 '70 C.674 A.B. L.178 J.D. [Frandzel&S.]
*PRACTICE AREAS: Antitrust; Civil Appeals; Lender Liability; Business Torts; Business Litigation.
Fredricksen, David Scott '61 '89 C.112 B.A. L.398 J.D.
1000 S. Westgate Ave., Apt. 313

**Freeburg, Judy & Nettels**
(See Pasadena)

Freed, Evan Phillip ........................ '46 '79 C.1097 B.A. L.1136 J.D. Dep. City Atty.
Freed, Joanne ..........................'54 '79 C.103 A.B. L.659 J.D. 627 N. Cherokee St.‡
**Freedenthal, Michele** ...................'63 '90 C.659 B.S. L.846 J.D. [A Paul,H.J.&W.]
Freedland, Sumner '19 '41 L.818 LL.B.
(adm. in MA; not adm. in CA) 2400 S. Beverly Dr.‡
Freedman, Bryan Joel ........................ '64 '91 C.112 B.A. L.464 J.D. [Nelson&F.]
**Freedman, Daniel M.** '53 '79 C.881 A.B. L.94 J.D.
(adm. in NY; not adm. in CA) [C O'Melveny&M.]
*PRACTICE AREAS: Securities; Corporate Finance; Mergers and Acquisitions.
**Freedman, Dara L.** ...................... '66 '92 C.691 B.A. L.245 J.D. [A Gibson,D.&C.]
*LANGUAGES: Spanish.
*PRACTICE AREAS: Taxation.
**Freedman, David G.** ..................'52 '78 C.112 B.A. L.426 J.D. [C Jackson,L.S.&K.]
Freedman, Jack E. ...................'40 '67 C.107 B.S. L.1068 LL.B. 407 Denslow Ave.
Freedman, James J. ..................... '54 '85 C.112 B.F.A. L.426 J.D. 400 S. Hope St.
**Freedman, Jeffrey C.**, (AV) ...........'44 '69 C.605 B.A. L.1068 J.D. [Rexon,F.K.&H.]
*PRACTICE AREAS: Labor and Employment Litigation; Public and Private Sectors.
Freedman, Jerry L. .......... '52 '76 C.1044 B.S. L.809 J.D. 15821 Ventura Blvd. (Encino)
**Freedman, Leora D.** .................'59 '87 C.918 B.A. L.1068 J.D. [C Shapiro,H.&M.]
*LANGUAGES: French.
**Freedman, Margo E.** ........................'66 '92 C&L.477 B.B.A., J.D. [A Paul,H.J.&W.]
**Freedman, Neil H.**, (AV) ................... '45 '71 C.112 B.A. L.426 J.D. [Silver&F.]
*PRACTICE AREAS: Business Litigation; General Civil Litigation; Family Law.
**Freedman, Robert M.** .......................... '49 '89 C&L.999 B.S., J.D. [A Tharpe&H.]
*LANGUAGES: French.
**Freedman, Scott Alan** ........................'61 '87 C.276 B.A. L.990 J.D. [Hornberger&C.]
*PRACTICE AREAS: Civil Litigation; Employment Law; Products Liability; Premises Liability; Negligence.
**Freedman, Susan M.** .......................'59 '91 C.525 B.A. L.426 J.D. [A Weinhart&R.]
*PRACTICE AREAS: Business Litigation.
**Freedman, William H.** .............'57 '82 C.910 B.S. L.245 J.D. [McCutchen,D.B.&E.]
**Freeling, Kenneth A.** .................... '57 '82 C&L.276 B.A., J.D. [Kaye,S.F.H.&H.]
**Freeman, Barry V.**, (AV) ..................'38 '63 C.112 A.B. L.1068 J.D. [Morgan,L.&B.]
**Freeman, Douglas K.**, (AV) '45 '70 C.813 A.B. L.1068 J.D.
[Freeman,F.&S.] (©Irvine)
*PRACTICE AREAS: Tax; Estate Planning; Exempt Organizations.
**Freeman, Joseph M.** .......................'64 '93 C.309 A.B. L.1066 J.D. [A Irell&M.]
**Freeman, Karin E.** .......................'70 '96 C.112 B.A. L.800 J.D. [A Wolf,R.&S.]
*PRACTICE AREAS: Real Estate; Bankruptcy; Community Association.
Freeman, Malik Dantala .............. '53 '90 C&L.911 B.A., J.D. 3255 Wilshire Blvd.
**Freeman, Richard D.**, (AV) ............ '44 '70 C.112 B.A. L.426 J.D. [Freeman,F.&S.]
*PRACTICE AREAS: Estate Planning; Business Succession Planning.
Freeman, Robert L., Jr. .......................'63 '89 C.426 B.A. L.276 J.D. 221 N. Figueroa St.
Freeman, Russell A., (AV) ................. '32 '57 C.31 B.A. L.982 LL.B. 400 S. Hope St.
**Freeman, Steven A.** ...........................'46 '70 C&L.800 B.S., J.D. [Neumeyer&B.]
*PRACTICE AREAS: Appellate Practice; Insurance Coverage; Insurance Bad Faith.
**Freeman, Thomas R.** ....................'60 '87 C.699 B.A. L.597 J.D. [Bird,M.B.W.&M.]
**Freeman, William B.** .................'63 '88 C.477 B.A. L.1065 J.D. [A Pillsbury M.&S.]

**Freeman, Freeman & Smiley, LLP, (AV)**
A Limited Liability Partnership including Law Corporations
**Penthouse, Suite 1200, 3415 Sepulveda Boulevard, 90034-6060**©
Telephone: 310-398-6227 Facsimile: 310-391-4042
Douglas K. Freeman (Certified Specialist, Taxation Law, The State Bar of California Board of Legal Specialization); Richard D. Freeman; Bruce M. Smiley; Glenn T. Sherman; Fred J. Marcus; Laurence L. Hummer; Bruce L. Gelb; Jane Peebles; Richard E. Gilbert. Associates: Stephen F. Weltman; Warren O. Hodges, Jr.; Kyle M. Robertson; Martin P. Hochman; Paul J. Goldman; Gregory M. Bordo. Of Counsel: Paul P. Denzer; Michael R. Magasin; Barbara J. Bailey (Certified Specialist, Probate, Estate Planning and Trust Law, The State Bar of California Board of Legal Specialization); Steven M. Kraus; Arthur Mazirow; Steven L. Ziven; Ernest J. Schag, Jr. (Resident, Irvine Office); Lynda S. Moerschbaecher.
Estate and Gift Planning, Probate, Real Estate, Corporate, Business Succession Planning, Trial and Appellate Litigation.
Reference: Union Bank (Beverly Hills, California).
Irvine, California Office: 2010 Main Street, Suite 580. Telephone: 714-833-7966. Facsimile: 714-833-9584.
San Francisco, California Office: One Market, Steuart Tower, 16th Floor. Telephone: 415-974-1930.
*See Professional Biographies, LOS ANGELES, CALIFORNIA*

Freese, Paul L., (AV) ........................'29 '58 C.276 B.S. L.813 J.D. [C Kindel&A.]
Frego, James P. ......................'63 '90 C.477 B.A. L.1068 J.D. 3255 Wilshire Blvd., 12th Fl.
**Freiberg, Thomas A., Jr.**, (AV) ..........'37 '65 C.976 B.A. L.800 LL.B. [Fulbright&J.]
*PRACTICE AREAS: Eminent Domain; Land Use.
**Freid, Manley**, (AV) ...............................'37 '62 C.831 B.S. L.1068 J.D. [Freid&G.]
*PRACTICE AREAS: Family Law.

**Freid and Goldsman, A Professional Law Corporation, (AV)** BB
**2029 Century Park East, Suite 860, 90067**
Telephone: 310-552-2700 Telecopier: 310-552-2770
Manley Freid (Certified Specialist, Family Law, The State Bar of California Board of Legal Specialization); Melvin S. Goldsman (Certified Specialist, Family Law, The State Bar of California Board of Legal Specialization); Gary J. Cohen; Marci R. Levine; Joanne D. Ratinoff; Heather Rickett Graham; Lori A. Loo;—Janet Kaplan; Reuel M. Baluyot.
General Civil and Trial Practice. Family Law.
*See Professional Biographies, LOS ANGELES, CALIFORNIA*

**Freier, Elliot G.** ........................... '61 '86 C.893 B.A. L.976 J.D. [Irell&M.]
**Freilich, Amy E.** ......................'62 '87 C.145 A.B. L.309 J.D. [Brand F.D.F.&K.]
*PRACTICE AREAS: Real Estate Law; Land Use Law; Environmental Quality Act Compliance; Public-Private Development.
**Freilich, Arthur**, (AV) '35 '62
C.688 B.E.E. L.273 LL.B. [Freilich,H.&R.] (See Pat. Sect.)
*PRACTICE AREAS: Patent Law; Trademark Law; Licensing Law; Litigation; Technology Business Startups.

**Freilich, Hornbaker & Rosen, P.C., (AV)** BB
**Suite 1434, 10960 Wilshire Boulevard, 90024**
Telephone: 310-477-0578 Telex: 298725 Patl Ur Telecopy: 310-473-9277
Arthur Freilich; Robert D. Hornbaker; Leon D. Rosen; Timothy T. Tyson; Lawrence S. Cohen; Lee Jay Mandell.
Patent, Trademark, Copyright, Unfair Competition and Antitrust Law. Trials in State and Federal Courts.
Reference: Bank of America (Wilshire-Westwood Branch).
*See Professional Biographies, LOS ANGELES, CALIFORNIA*

**Freilich, Kaufman, Fox & Sohagi**
**Wilshire Landmark, Suite 1230, 11755 Wilshire Boulevard, 90025-1518**©
Telephone: Telephone: 310-444-7805 Facsimile: 310-477-7663
Members of Firm: Benjamin Kaufman; Deborah J. Fox; Margaret Moore Sohagi. Associate: Dawn R. Andrews. Of Counsel: Terry P. Kaufmann Macias.
Land Use, Zoning, Environmental, Municipal Finance, State and Local Government Law, Civil Litigation.
Kansas City, Missouri Office: Freilich, Leitner & Carlisle, 1000 Plaza West, 4600 Madison. Telephone: 816-561-4414. Facsimile: 816-561-7931.
*See Professional Biographies, LOS ANGELES, CALIFORNIA*

**Freimann, Vicki L.** .........................'46 '81 C.112 B.A. L.1137 J.D. [Leland,P.S.F.M.&M.]
*PRACTICE AREAS: Banking; Business Litigation; Creditors' Remedies.
**Freisleben, Amy L.** ......................... '59 '85 C.112 B.A. L.809 J.D. [A Davis&F.]
*PRACTICE AREAS: Business Litigation.
Freistat, Lana L. ........................'51 '77 C.112 B.A. L.1068 J.D. 142 S. Windsor Ave.
Freitas, Alfred M. ......................'37 '78 C.1077 B.A. L.809 J.D. 3345 Wilshire Blvd.
**Freitas, Karen C.**, (BV) ..................... '56 '82 C.312 B.B.A. L.426 J.D. [Cotkin&C.]
*PRACTICE AREAS: Family Law.
**Freitas, Robert E.** ...............................'52 '77 C.629 B.S. L.1065 J.D. [Orrick,H.&S.]
*PRACTICE AREAS: Litigation; Antitrust Law; Insurance Coverage.
**Fresch, Elaine K.** .......................... '60 '85 C.112 A.B. L.1049 J.D. [Selman B.]

**Freshman, Marantz, Orlanski, Cooper & Klein, A Law Corporation**
(See Beverly Hills)

**Freston, Edwin**, (AV) ...........................'37 '63 C&L.800 B.A., J.D. [Darling,H.&R.]
*REPORTED CASES: Cal. 1976. Archibald v. Cinerama Hotels, 126 Cal.Rptr. 811, 15 Cal.3d 853, 544 P.2d 947 Cal. 1965; Powell v. California Dept. of Employment, 45 Cal.Rptr. 136, 403 P.2d 392, 63 Cal.2d 103; Cal.App. 2 Dist. 1993; A Local and Regional Monitor v. City of Los Angeles, 16 Cal.Rptr.2d 358, 12 Cal.App.4th 1773; Cal.App. 2 Dist. 1993.
*PRACTICE AREAS: Probate; Trust; Real Property Litigation; Real Property Transactions.
Freund, Jonathan D. ..................'66 '91 C.112 B.A. L.426 J.D. 1999 Ave. of the Stars
**Freundlich, Alisa J.** ........'60 '85 C.112 B.A. L.426 J.D. [C Christensen,M.F.J.G.W.&S.]
*PRACTICE AREAS: Real Estate Finance; Real Estate Development.
**Frey, Cynthia M.** ........................... '62 '90 C.112 B.A. L.273 J.D. [A Lord,B.&B.]
**Frey, J. Patrick** ...........................'68 '94 C.188 B.A. L.846 J.D. [A Shearman&S.]
**Frey, Richard J.** ................................'69 '94 C.112 B.A. L.990 J.D. [A Loeb&L.]
**Frey, Sandford L.** .....................'55 '82 C.1077 B.A. L.1136 J.D. [Robinson,D.B.&K.]
**Frick, Richard J.** ..........................'47 '72 C.112 B.A. L.145 J.D. [C Jones,D.R.&P.]
**Fricks, John W.** ............................ '64 '90 C.1074 B.S. L.94 J.D. [A Gibson,D.&C.]
*PRACTICE AREAS: Litigation; Commercial Real Estate.
**Fridkis, Cliff, (P.C.)**, (AV) .....................'47 '74 C.645 B.A. L.273 J.D. [Wintroub&F.]
*REPORTED CASES: Crawford vs. Board of Education (1980) 113 Cal. App. 3d 633; Paul vs. State Farm Fire & Casualty Co. (1987) 193 Cal. App. 3d 223.
*PRACTICE AREAS: Civil Litigation.
Fridkis, Judy Gray ........................'50 '75 C.112 B.A. L.1068 J.D. Dep. Dist. Atty.
Fridlington, John J. '52 '77
C.707 B.A. L.602 J.D. Assoc. Gen. Coun., Calif. Assn. of Realtors
**Fried, Jack**, (AV) ................................'49 '74 C.112 A.B. L.1068 J.D. [Fried,B.&C.]
*PRACTICE AREAS: Financial Institutions Law - General Corporate and Regulatory Representation; Mergers and Acquisitions; Bank Applications and Organizations; Corporate Securities.

**Fried, Bird & Crumpacker, A Professional Corporation, (AV)** BB
**10100 Santa Monica Boulevard, Suite 300, 90067-6031**
Telephone: 310-551-7400 Facsimile: 310-556-4487
Jack Fried; Brian James Bird; David W. Crumpacker, Jr.; Nikki Wolontis; David M. Schachter;—David K. Johnson.
Banking, Corporate, Securities, Real Estate, General Civil Litigation and Trial Practice in all State and Federal Courts, Insurance, Bankruptcy and Creditors Rights.
*See Professional Biographies, LOS ANGELES, CALIFORNIA*

**Fried, Frank, Harris, Shriver & Jacobson, (AV)**
A Partnership including Professional Corporations
**350 South Grand Avenue, Thirty-Second Floor, 90071**©
Telephone: 213-473-2000 Telecopier: 213-473-2222
Email: postmaster@ffhsj.com
Resident Partners: Debra J. Albin-Riley; Stephen D. Alexander; John W. Chierichella; Barbara A. Reeves; David K. Robbins; Edward S. Rosenthal; Louis D. Victorino. Resident Associates: Joey L. Blanch; David R. Boyko; Brian I-An Cheng; Lauren R. Firestone; Don A. Hernandez; Jody Rene Katz; Ray La Soya; Maribel S. Medina (Not admitted in CA); Darrel C. Menthe; Malena R. Neal; William A. Molinski; Karen B. Seto; Stacy J. Weinstein.
General Practice.
New York, New York Office: One New York Plaza. Telephone: 212-859-8000. Cable Address: "Steric New York." W.U. Int. Telex: 620223. W.U. Int. Telex: 662119. W.U. Domestic: 128173. Telecopier: 212-859-4000 (Dex) 6200).
Washington, D.C. Office: Suite 800, 1001 Pennsylvania Avenue, N.W. Telephone: 202-639-7000.
London, England Office: 4 Chiswell Street, London EC1Y 4UP. Telephone: 011-44-171-972-9600. Fax: 011-44-171-972-9602.
Paris, France Office: 7, Rue Royale, 75008. Telephone: (+331) 40 17 04 04. Fax (+331) 40 17 08 30.
*See Professional Biographies, LOS ANGELES, CALIFORNIA*

Friedberg, Jerome H. ...................... '60 '86 C.112 B.A. L.1066 J.D. Off. of U.S. Atty.
Friedberg, Michael ...................'48 '80 C.112 B.A. L.809 J.D. [Nishiyama,M.L.E.&S.]
**Friederichs, Teresa J.** ..................................... '59 '92 L.1136 J.D. [A Robie&M.]
*PRACTICE AREAS: Civil Litigation.
Friedland, Patricia A. .............. '60 '88 C.165 B.A. L.800 J.D. 2035 Linda Flora Dr.
**Friedlander, Martin S.**, (AV) ................ '38 '63 C.563 B.B.A. L.597 J.D. [Herzfeld&R.]
*PRACTICE AREAS: Business; Partnership; Real Estate; Construction and Mechanics Lien Law; Litigation.
**Friedlander, Michael I.** .................'48 '79 C&L.061 B.A., LL.B. [Friedlander&W.]
*PRACTICE AREAS: International Business and Licensing Transactions; General Corporate; Business; Commercial Transactions; Business Immigration Matters.

**Friedlander & Werlin LLP**
**11611 San Vicente Boulevard, Suite 615, 90049**
Telephone: 310-820-4778 Fax: 310-820-6588
Members of Firm: Michael I. Friedlander; Leslie M. Werlin. Associates: Lloyd K. Chapman; Tracy L. Sneed; Valerie M. Rierdan; Peter K. Zweighaft. Of Counsel: Jeanine Jacobs Goldberg.
Civil Litigation, Business and Commercial Litigation and Transactions, Immigration, Tax, International Business.
*See Professional Biographies, LOS ANGELES, CALIFORNIA*

Friedler, Edith .........................'42 '80 L.426 J.D. Prof. of Law, Loyola Law School
Friedman, Aaron R. ...................'59 '87 C.1077 B.A. L.426 J.D. City Atty. Office
**Friedman, Alan E.**, (AV) ............................ '46 '71 C.31 B.A. L.813 J.D. [Tuttle&T.]
*PRACTICE AREAS: Civil Business Litigation.
**Friedman, Alan V., (A Professional Corporation)**, (AV) '38 '63
C.659 A.B. L.903 LL.B. [Munger,T.&O.]

Friedman, Andrew ... '47 '72 C.112 B.A. L.1068 J.D. Comr., Police Pemit Review Panel
**Friedman, Andrew D.** ... '58 '83 C.896 B.A. L.273 J.D. [Alschuler G.&P.]
**Friedman, Andrew H.** ... '63 '90 C.880 B.A. L.188 J.D. [🄰 Bryan C.]
*PRACTICE AREAS: Labor and Employment Law; Litigation.
Friedman, Barry L., (AV) ... '45 '71 C.659 B.S. L.310 J.D. 10960 Wilshire Blvd.
**Friedman, Bruce** ... '60 '92 C.94 B.S.B.A. L.800 J.D. [🄰 Loeb&L.]
**Friedman, Bruce A., (P.C.)** ... '50 '76 C.154 B.A. L.273 J.D. [Alschuler G.&P.]
**Friedman, Daniel J.** ... '59 '85 C.293 B.A. L.1068 J.D. [🄰 Loeb&L.]
Friedman, David B. ... '57 '89 C.112 B.A. L.1068 J.D. Catellus Dev. Corp.
**Friedman, Dean I.**, (AV) ... '50 '76 C.800 A.B. L.809 J.D. [Clark&T.]
*PRACTICE AREAS: Federal, State and Local Taxation; Estate Planning; Trusts and Probate.
Friedman, Douglas ... '56 '82 C.112 B.A. L.990 J.D. 3250 Wilshire Blvd.
**Friedman, Gavin** ... '67 '95 C.012 B.B.S. L.1066 J.D. [🄰 Morrison&F.]
Friedman, Gerald ... '11 '40 C.112 A.B. L.809 LL.B. State. Dept. of Indus. Relations
Friedman, Gerald D. '49 '74 C.659 B.A. L.1068 J.D.
Sr. V.P., Bus. & Legal Affs., Fox Television Stations, Inc.
**Friedman, Gerald Lloyd**, (AV) ... '38 '63 C.165 A.B. L.188 J.D. [🄲 Wolf,R.&S.]
*PRACTICE AREAS: Matrimonial Law; Business Law.
Friedman, Gilbert H. ... '52 '84 C.1097 B.A. L.426 J.D. Bet Tzedek Legal Servs.
**Friedman, Gillian E.** ... '67 '93 C.112 B.A. L.809 J.D. [Horgan,R.B.&C.]
*PRACTICE AREAS: Business Law; Commercial Litigation; Bankruptcy.
**Friedman, Harold, (A Professional Corporation)**, (AV) '24 '52
C.309 A.B. L.976 J.D. [Mitchell,S.&K.]
*PRACTICE AREAS: Corporate Law; Motion Picture Television Law; Real Estate Law; Banking Law; International Law.
**Friedman, Harvey R.**, (AV) ... '38 '64 C.309 B.A. L.477 J.D. [Greenberg G.F.C.&M.]
*PRACTICE AREAS: Business Litigation; Real Estate Litigation.
Friedman, Henry, (BV) ... '34 '57 C.112 L.1065 J.D. [H.Friedman]
Friedman, Howard A. '49 '74
C.1077 B.A. L.809 J.D. Asst. Gen. Coun., L.A. Unified Sch. Dist.‡
**Friedman, Howard I., (A P.C.)**, (AV) ... '28 '52 C.623 B.A. L.976 LL.B. [🄲 Loeb&L.]
*PRACTICE AREAS: Litigation; Arbitration; Mediation.
**Friedman, J. Bennett** ... '62 '88 C.339 B.A. L.426 J.D. [🄰 Levinson,M.J.&P.]
*LANGUAGES: French.
*PRACTICE AREAS: Bankruptcy; Business Litigation.
**Friedman, James D.** ... '53 '79 C.659 B.S. L.1068 J.D. [Loeb&L.]
*PRACTICE AREAS: Real Estate Law.
Friedman, Jerald ... '44 '70 C.112 A.B. L.1068 J.D. [Kornwasser&F.]
**Friedman, Jonathan L.** ... '63 '88 C.659 B.S.E. L.813 J.D. [🄰 Skadden,A.S.M.&F.]
Friedman, Jud J. '56 '83 C.976 B.A. L.309 J.D.
(adm. in NY; not adm. in CA) 8159 Hollywood Blvd., Hollywood
Friedman, Leonard M. ... '53 '78 C.112 B.A. L.809 J.D. 6404 Wilshire Blvd.
Friedman, Linda J. ... '66 '92 C&L.597 B.S., J.D. 10940 Wilshire Blvd.
Friedman, Louis P. ... '10 '33 C&L.339 B.A., LL.B. 411 Gretna Green Way
Friedman, Mark J. ... '57 '87 C.112 B.A. L.800 J.D., Sr. Atty., Atlantic Richfield Co.

**Friedman, Michael N. '59 '85 C.112 B.A. L.800 J.D.**
**1901 Avenue of the Stars, Suite 1901, 90067-6020**
**Telephone: 310-552-3336 Fax: 310-552-1850**
***PRACTICE AREAS: Toxic Exposure Tort Law; ERISA; Land Use Law; Appellate Law; Family Law.**
**Toxic Torts and Long-Term Disability Claims for Chemical Injuries.**
***See Professional Biographies, LOS ANGELES, CALIFORNIA***

Friedman, Nathaniel J. ... '36 '62 C.800 A.B. L.809 LL.B. [N.J.Friedman]
**Friedman, Randel P.** ... '68 '94 C.197 B.A. L.472 J.D. [🄰 Manning,M.&W.]
Friedman, Richard A. ... '56 '81 C.966 B.A. L.178 J.D. 801 S. Figueroa St., 18th Fl.
**Friedman, Richard S.**, (AV) ... '44 '68 C&L.339 B.A., J.D. [Hughes H.&R.]
*PRACTICE AREAS: Real Estate Law.

**Friedman, Robert P., (AV) '52 '78 C.112 B.A. L.276 J.D.**
**827 Moraga Drive (Bel Air), 90049**
**Telephone: 310-471-3413 Facsimile: 310-472-7014**
**(Also Of Counsel to Peter J. McNulty).**
**Real Estate, Corporate and Business Law and Civil Litigation.**
***See Professional Biographies, LOS ANGELES, CALIFORNIA***

**Friedman, Sharon G.** ... '65 '93 C.112 B.S. L.426 J.D. [🄰 Koletsky,M.&F.]
*PRACTICE AREAS: Construction Defect Defense; General Liability Defense.
**Friedman, Stacey R.** ... '70 '94 C.1077 B.A. L.1148 J.D. [🄰 Koletsky,M.&F.]
*PRACTICE AREAS: Construction Defect Defense Litigation; General Liability Defense Litigation.
**Friedman, Steven M.** ... '63 '88 C.112 B.A. L.1065 J.D. [🄰 Heller E.W.&M.]
Friedman, Henry, A P.C., (BV) ... 11611 San Vicente Blvd.

**Friedman, Michael, Law Offices of**
**(See Torrance)**

Friedman, Nathaniel J., P.C. ... 1875 Century Park E.
Friedmann, Ellen Taratoot ... '50 '83 C.597 B.A. L.426 J.D. Dep. City Atty.
Friedrich, Penny L. ... '52 '91 C.1042 B.A. L.809 J.D. 523 W. 6th St.
**Friedrichs, John E.** ... '68 '94 C.861 B.A. L.1066 J.D. [🄰 Sidley&A.]
*LANGUAGES: French and Spanish.
**Friel, Alan L.** ... '66 '92 C.1059 B.S. L.588 J.D. [🄰 Kaye,S.F.H.&H.]
*PRACTICE AREAS: Commercial and Entertainment Litigation and Transactions.
**Frieman, Joshua R.** ... '70 '95 C.112 A.B. L.309 J.D. [🄰 Latham&W.]
Friend, Gerald L. ... '51 '81 C.1040 B.A. L.809 J.D. 3250 Wilshire Blvd.
Friend, Zachary S. ... '33 '65 C.112 B.A. L.809 J.D. 1925 Century Pk. E.
Frierson, Susan Lee ... '44 '76 C.112 B.A. L.426 J.D. Dep. Atty. Gen.
Fries, Judith Anne ... '51 '76 C.112 A.B. L.1066 J.D. Princ. Dep. Co. Coun.
**Frim, Gerald S.** ... '58 '84 C&L.659 B.A., J.D. [🄰 Nebenzahl K.D.&L.]
*LANGUAGES: Hebrew.
*PRACTICE AREAS: Business Law; Real Estate Litigation; Health Care.
**Frimmer, Paul N., (P.C.)**, (AV) ... '45 '70 C.994 B.A. L.262 J.D. [Irell&M.]
Frisch, Brian T. ... '65 '90 C.367 B.A. L.1068 J.D. 5750 Wilshire Blvd.
Frisch, Randi Gail ... '56 '81 C.112 B.A. L.426 J.D. 1875 Century Pk. E.
**Frischling, Gary N.** ... '62 '87 C.112 B.S. L.1068 J.D. [Irell&M.]
Frisenda, Frank, Jr., (A Professional Corporation), (BV) '50 '79
C.563 B.Ch.E. L.809 J.D. [Frisenda,Q.&N.] (Pat.)
Frisenda, Quinton & Nicholson, (BV)
11755 Wilshire Boulevard 10th Floor (Pat.) (©N.Y., N.Y.)
**Frishman, David M.** ... '62 '87 C.338 B.S. L.809 J.D. [🄰 Schaffer&L.]
Frith, Sara A. ... '60 '88 C.051 B.A. L.054 1999 Ave. of the Stars, Suite 1400
**Fritz, Arthur A.** ... '46 '72 C.112 B.A. L.1065 J.D. Sr. Coun., Bank of Amer.
Froehlich, Kent B. ... '36 '63 C.112 B.S. L.800 LL.B. 651 N. Wilcox Ave.
Froeling, Lori J. ... '58 '85 C.352 B.A. L.145 J.D. 300 S. Grand Ave., 29th Fl.
Frohreich, Pamela J. G. ... '47 '77 C.112 B.A. L.426 J.D. Dep. Dist. Atty.
**Fromholz, Ann Haley** ... '68 '94 C.197 B.A. L.800 J.D. [🄰 Morgan,L.&B.]
Fromholz, Haley J., (AV) ... '38 '67 C.569 A.B. L.228 LL.B. 555 W. 5th St.
Frommer, Roger ... '26 '67 C.763 B.A. L.426 J.D. 2500 Wilshire Blvd.
**Frost, F. Daniel**, (AV) ... '22 '48 C.112 L.37 J.D. [🄲 Gibson,D.&C.]
**Frost, Jeffrey D.** ... '64 '89 C.112 B.A. L.861 J.D. [🄰 Pillsbury M.&S.]
**Frost, Jess B.** ... '67 '96 C.112 B.A. L.426 J.D. [🄰 O'Melveny&M.]

Frost, Otis L., Jr. ... '17 '47 C.880 B.A. L.1066 LL.B. 2740 Monte Mar Ter.‡
Frotiner, Elizabeth J. ... '53 '79 C.37 B.A. L.809 J.D. P.O. Box 24476
Fruin, Richard L., Jr., (AV) ... '39 '66 C.659 B.A. L.1066 J.D. 700 S. Flower St.
**Frumes, Howard M.**, (AV) ... '49 '74 C.154 B.A. L.309 J.D. [Manatt,P.&P.]
*PRACTICE AREAS: Entertainment Law; International Law; Dispute Resolution.
**Frumkin, Arthur S.** ... '58 '85 C.112 B.A. L.1065 J.D. [Fox&F.]
*PRACTICE AREAS: Business; Construction; Real Estate Litigation.
Fry, Laurence F. ... '56 '94 C&L.061 Asst. Coun., Unocal Corp.
Fry, Thomas W. ... '57 '83 C.605 A.B. L.426 J.D. 4375 York Blvd.‡
**Frye, John N.**, (AV) ... '44 '70 C.112 B.A. L.309 J.D. [Frye,A.&M.]
*PRACTICE AREAS: Litigation; General Commercial; Business Disputes; Insurance Law; Property and Casualty Insurance.

**Frye, Alberts & Malchow, (AV)**
**1901 Avenue of the Stars, Suite 390, 90067©**
**Telephone: 310-553-7733 FAX: 310-553-7730**
**John N. Frye; Ronald K. Alberts; E. Lynn Malchow (Resident at San Francisco Office). Associates: Jeffrey A. Katz; Feliciano M. (Bud) Ferrer; Eugenie A. Gifford; Tamar Blaufarb. Of Counsel: Gary A. Schlessinger; Samuel M. Zaif.**
**Civil Litigation in all State and Federal Trial and Appellate Courts, including General Commercial and Business, Property, Casualty, Life, Health, Fidelity and Surety Insurance, Bad Faith, ERISA, Employment, Construction, Franchise and Unfair Trade Practices.**
**San Francisco, California Office: 225 Bush Street, 16th Floor. Telephone: 415-439-8315. Facsimile: 415-439-8317.**
***See Professional Biographies, LOS ANGELES, CALIFORNIA***

**Frye & Hsieh LLP**
**A Partnership including A Professional Corporation**
**626 Wilshire Boulevard, Suite 800, 90017©**
**Telephone: 310-820-5545**
**Stewart Hsieh.**
**General Civil and Trial Practice in all Courts. Corporation, Business, State, Federal and International Taxation, Estate Planning, Real Estate, Securities, Administrative, Professional Liability, Negligence Law and Government Finance.**
**Malibu, California Office: 23955 Pacific Coast Highway, Suite A201. Telephone: 310-456-0800. Fax: 310-456-0808.**

**Fuad, Peter H.** ... '49 '77 C.629 B.A. L.426 J.D. Sr. Coun., Bank of Amer.
Fuchs, David, (BV) ... '24 '49 C.569 L.1009 LL.B. 4317 Melbourne Ave.
Fuchs, John R., (P.C.) ... '46 '78 C.178 B.S. L.800 J.D. [Fuchs&M.]
Fuchs, Sandor C. ... '43 '76 1467 Echo Park Ave.
Fuchs & Marshall ... 12100 Wilshire Blvd.
**Fudacz, Frederic A.** ... '47 '72 C.813 B.A. L.309 J.D. [Nossaman,G.K.&E.]
*PRACTICE AREAS: Litigation.
**Fudge, Jack D.**, (AV) ... '34 '64 C.768 A.B. L.1065 LL.B. [Baker&H.]
*PRACTICE AREAS: Litigation.
Fuentes, Ernesto V. '47 '74 C.426 B.S. L.705 J.D.
(adm. in DC; not adm. in CA) Inspector Gen., So. Calif. Rapid Transit Dist.
**Fugate, Andrea A.** ... '70 '95 C.477 B.A. L.809 J.D. [🄰 Trope&T.]
*LANGUAGES: German.
*PRACTICE AREAS: Family Law; Civil Litigation.
**Fuhrman, Paul A.** ... '69 '95 C.112 B.A. L.426 J.D. [🄰 Epport&R.]
*PRACTICE AREAS: Real Property; Bankruptcy; Commercial Litigation.
Fuhrman, Robynne R. ... '52 '78 C.112 A.B. L.800 J.D. 2267 Talmadge St.
**Fujie, Holly J.** ... '55 '78 C.112 B.A. L.1066 J.D. [🄲 Buchalter,N.F.&Y.]
*PRACTICE AREAS: Civil Litigation; Insurance Coverage Law; Reinsurance Coverage.
**Fujii, John M.** ... '66 '94 C.112 B.S. L.1066 J.D. [🄰 Jeffer,M.B.&M.]
*PRACTICE AREAS: Environmental Law; General Business Litigation.
**Fujii, Rodney A.** ... '48 '75 C.426 B.A. L.30 J.D. [Graham&J.]
*PRACTICE AREAS: Employee Benefit Law; Executive Compensation.
**Fujikawa, Ronald K., (Professional Corporation)**, (AV) '48 '73
C&L.813 A.B., J.D. [Kinsella,B.F.&T.]
Fujioka, Fred J. ... '51 '77 C.800 B.A. L.1066 J.D. 3435 Wilshire Blvd.
Fujisaki, Hiroshi ... '36 '63 C.112 A.B. L.1068 LL.B. Supr. Ct. J.
**Fujita, Sharon M.** ... '61 '94 C.800 B.S. L.1065 J.D. [🄰 Pretty,S.&P.]
*PRACTICE AREAS: Patents; Trademarks; Copyrights; Unfair Competition; Litigation.
**Fujitani, Jay Masa** ... '59 '87 C.112 B.A. L.1066 J.D. [Munger,T.&O.]
**Fukano, Russ M.** ... '57 '84 C.1042 B.S. L.800 J.D. [Troy&G.]
*PRACTICE AREAS: Securities Litigation; Business Litigation; Real Estate Litigation.
**Fukui, Alexander H.** ... '64 '91 C.112 B.S. L.1066 J.D. [🄰 LeBoeuf,L.G.&M.]
*LANGUAGES: Japanese.
*PRACTICE AREAS: Corporate Law.

**Fulbright & Jaworski L.L.P., (AV)**
**865 South Figueroa Street 29th Floor, 90017-2571©**
**Telephone: 213-892-9200 Fax: 213-680-4518**
**Email: info@fulbright.com URL: http://www.fulbright.com**
**Members of Firm: Paul S. Blencowe; Tim C. Bruinsma; Stephen T. Cole; Robert E. Darby; Robert M. Dawson; David A. Ebershoff; Thomas A. Freiberg, Jr.; Timothy R. Greenleaf; Harry L. Hathaway; Donald L. Hunt; Richard L. Kornblith; Colin Lennard; Richard R. Mainland; Peter H. Mason; Jesse D. Miller; John A. O'Malley; Michael G. Smooke; Douglas W. Stern. Of Counsel: Fred G. Yanney. Associates: Chad Chase Coombs; Judith A. Holiber; Larissa A.J. Kehoe; Lisa R. Klein; Frederick S. Kuhlman; Joshua D. Lichtman; J. Kelly Moffat; Hardy Kay Murphy; Todd M. Sorrell; Jarlon Tsang; Kimberly R. Wells; Beth Mezoff Wilson. Staff Attorneys: Robert M. Aronson; Robert C. Barnes; Anne K. Edwards; James M. Gilbert; Ana M. Inguanzo; Paul E. Liguori.**
**General Civil Practice. Trial and Appellate Practice, Antitrust and Trade Regulation, Administrative Law, Banking, Bankruptcy, Reorganization and Creditors' Rights, Corporate and Securities, International, Labor and Employment, Probate, Public Utilities, Public Finance, Real Estate, Taxation.**
**Houston, Texas Office: 1301 McKinney, Suite 5100, 77010. Telephone: 713-651-5151. Fax: 713-651-5246.**
**Washington, D.C. Office: Market Square, 801 Pennsylvania Avenue, N.W., 20004. Telephone: 202-662-0200. Fax: 202-662-4643.**
**Austin, Texas Office: 600 Congress Avenue, Suite 2400, 78701. Telephone: 512-474-5201. Fax: 512-320-4598.**
**San Antonio, Texas Office: 300 Convent Street, Suite 2200, 78205. Telephone: 210-224-5575. Fax: 210-270-7205.**
**Dallas, Texas Office: 2200 Ross Avenue, Suite 2800, 75201. Telephone: 214-855-8000. Fax: 214-855-8200.**
**New York, New York Office: 666 Fifth Avenue, 31st Floor, 10103. Telephone: 212-318-3000. Fax: 212-752-5958**
**London, England Office: 2 St. James's Place, SW1A 1NP. Telephone: 011-44171-629-1207. Fax: 011-44171-493-8259.**
**Hong Kong Office: The Hong Kong Club Building, Nineteenth Floor, 3A Chater Road, Central. Telephone: 011-852-2523-3200. Fax 011-852-2523-3255.**
***See Professional Biographies, LOS ANGELES, CALIFORNIA***

Fulginiti, Mary E. ... '64 '89 C.93 B.A. L.276 J.D. 2121 Ave. of the Stars
Fuller, Irving ... '35 '61 C.309 B.A. L.477 LL.B. 8727 W. 3rd St.‡
**Fuller, Michael R.** ... '68 '94 C.502 B.S.B.A. L.809 J.D. [Thorne]
*PRACTICE AREAS: Entertainment Law.
Fuller, Timothy ... '56 '81 C.112 B.A. L.990 J.D. 3712 Somerset Dr.
**Fuller, Vanci Y.** ... '69 '94 C.684 B.A. L.990 J.D. [🄰 Charlston,R.&W.]
*PRACTICE AREAS: Civil Litigation; Environmental Insurance Coverage Litigation.

**Fuller & Fuller**
**(See Woodland Hills)**

**Fulwider Patton Lee & Utecht, LLP, (AV)** BR
**10877 Wilshire Boulevard, 10th Floor, 90024**⊙
**Telephone: 310-824-5555 FAX: 310-824-9696 Email: fulwidr@primenet.com**
**Email: fulwidr@aol.com**
**Members of Firm: Robert W. Fulwider (1903-1979); John M. Lee (1921-1978); Warren L. Patton (1912-1985); Richard A. Bardin; Gilbert G. Kovelman; Vern Schooley (Long Beach Resident Partner); James W. Paul; Craig B. Bailey; John S. Nagy; Stephen J. Strauss; Thomas H. Majcher; Thomas A. Runk. Associates: David G. Parkhurst; Paul M. Stull; Gunther D. Hanke (Long Beach Resident Associate); Gary M. Anderson (Long Beach Resident Associate); Ronald E. Perez; Robert L. Kovelman; Pamela G. Maher; John V. Hanley; Paul T. LaVoie; John K. Fitzgerald; James Juo (Not admitted in CA); Russell C. Pangborn (Long Beach Resident Associate); Richard B. Cates; Derrick W. Reed (Long Beach Resident Associate); Paul Y. Feng; JoAnne M. Ybaben (Long Beach Resident Associate); Sean M. Casey (Long Beach Resident Associate); Muriel C. Haritchabalet. Of Counsel: Francis A. Utecht (Resident, Of Counsel, Long Beach Office); I. Morley Drucker (A Professional Corporation); Howard N. Sommers.**
**Patent, Trademark, Copyright and Unfair Competition Law. Litigation.**
**Long Beach, California Office: 200 Oceangate, Suite 1550. Telephone: 310-432-0453. Fax: 310-435-6014. Internet: fulwidrlb@aol.com.**

***See Professional Biographies, LOS ANGELES, CALIFORNIA***

**Funderburk, William W., Jr.** .......... '61 '91 C.976 B.A. L.276 J.D. [[A] Radcliff,F.&D.]
**Fung, Jill Chiang** .......................'71 '96 C.788 B.A. L.426 J.D. [[A] Mendes&M.]
*LANGUAGES: Mandarin, Shanghainese, Taiwanese.
Fung, Kathleen Marie ..............'61 '87 C.112 B.A. L.1067 J.D. 11755 Wilshire Blvd.
Fung, Rodney G. .................................... '49 '78 L.767 J.D. F.B.I.
Fung, Ronald G. ......................... '53 '78 C.112 B.S. L.813 J.D. P.O. Box 71007
**Funk, John C.** ......................... '44 '72 C.800 A.B. L.309 J.D. [Paul,H.J.&W.]
Funk, Randy J. ......................... '55 '91 C.966 B.A. L.911 J.D. 400 S. Hope St.
**Funk, Roger L.** ..................'40 '83 C.333 A.B. L.1068 J.D. [Greenberg G.F.C.&M.]
*PRACTICE AREAS: Litigation.

**Funsten & Franzen**
**(See Beverly Hills)**

Furen, Herman M. ..................... '32 '71 C.878 B.S.Ch.E. L.426 J.D. Dep. Pub. Def.
**Furlong, Randall Collins** ...................'58 '96 C.691 B.A. L.276 J.D. [[A] Loeb&L.]
*LANGUAGES: German, Chinese, French, Italian.
Furlotti, Alexander ..............'48 '73 C.112 B.A. L.1068 J.D. CEO, Quorum Properties
**Furman, Danielle F.** ............ '68 '95 C.112 B.A. L.990 J.D. [[A] Sands N.F.L.&L.]
Furman, Leila Saidenberg '60 '86
C.103 B.A. L.976 J.D. V.P. & Tax Coun., First Interstate Bancorp
**Furman, Richard D.** ................ '66 '91 C.659 B.S. L.1068 J.D. [De Castro,W.&C.]
*PRACTICE AREAS: Tax Law; Business Law.
**Furman, Roger** ............................ '55 '82 C.976 B.A. L.1065 J.D. [Furman U.]
*PRACTICE AREAS: Antitrust Litigation.
Furman, Stanley A. ..................... '12 '38 C.569 B.S. L.309 J.D. 2401 Century Hill‡

**Furman Usher, Inc.**
**1901 Avenue of the Stars, Seventh Floor, 90067**
**Telephone: 310-201-0075 Facsimile: 310-201-0313**
**Principal Shareholders: Roger Furman; Richard S. Usher.**
**Domestic and International Corporate Matters, Commercial Litigation.**

**Furness, Donald G.** ................ '61 '92 C.75 B.A. L.800 J.D. [[A] Harrington,F.D.&C.]
*LANGUAGES: German; French.
*PRACTICE AREAS: Banking; Business Litigation.
**Furst, George A.** ...............................'46 '72 C.112 B.A. L.309 J.D. [Hughes H.&R.]
*PRACTICE AREAS: Real Estate.

**Furstman, Scott S.**
**(See Santa Monica)**

**Furth, Helmut F.** ......................... '30 '56 C&L.309 A.B., LL.B. [Shapiro,R.&C.]
*LANGUAGES: German.
*PRACTICE AREAS: Litigation.
**Furuta, Reiko L.** ...................... '66 '93 C.112 B.A. L.1065 J.D. [[A] Barton,K.&O.]
*PRACTICE AREAS: Business Litigation; Probate Administration; Estate Planning.
Fuson, Todd A. ..................'64 '91 C.1097 B.A. L.426 J.D. Research Atty., Supr. Ct.

**Fuss, Marshall R., (AV) '49 '74 C.112 A.B. L.188 J.D.**
**2029 Century Park East, Suite 2550, 90067**
**Telephone: 310-277-0378 FAX: 310-277-0521**
**Advising Clients in the Organization, Operation and Financing of Businesses. Computer and Internet Law.**

**Futami, Norman A.** ...................... '60 '84 C.976 B.A. L.309 J.D. [Paul,H.J.&W.]
**Futch, Jennifer L.** ..................... '69 '94 C.420 B.A. L.990 J.D. [[A] Gartner&Y.]
*PRACTICE AREAS: Labor and Employment Law.
Futerman, Kimberly M. .....'62 '86 C.112 B.A. L.1067 J.D. 700 S. Flower St., Suite 2200
**Futter, Cynthia** ............................ '59 '84 C&L.800 B.A., J.D. [Manatt,P.&P.]
*PRACTICE AREAS: Corporate Recovery/Insolvency; Financial Services.
Futterman, Michelle Lynne ........... '70 '95 C.112 B.A. L.426 J.D. 5750 Wilshire Blvd.
**Fybel, Richard D.**, (AV) .................. '46 '72 C.112 A.B. L.1068 J.D. [Morrison&F.]
*PRACTICE AREAS: Business Litigation; Alternative Dispute Resolution.
**Gabai, Joseph** ............................ '52 '76 C.645 B.A. L.659 J.D. [Morrison&F.]
*PRACTICE AREAS: Financial Services.
Gable, Ashley G. '66 '93 C.309 A.B. L.276 J.D.
1800 Ave. of the Stars, Suite 900 (Century City)
**Gabor, David R.** .................'64 '89 C.881 B.A. L.1068 J.D. [[A] McDermott,W.&E.]
*LANGUAGES: Hungarian.
**Gabriel, Allan**, (AV) ..................'47 '75 C.994 B.A. L.1292 J.D. [Gabriel,H.&P.]
*REPORTED CASES: Clamp Manufacturing Co. v. Enco Manufacturing Co., 870 F.2d 512 (9th Cir. 1989); American Credit Indemnity v. Sacks, 213 Cal.App.3d 622 (1989); Abba Rubber Co., Inc. v. Seaquist, 235 Cal.App.3d 1 (1991); Berg v. Leason, 32 F.3d 422 (9th Cir. 1995); Taylor Made Golf Company, Inc., v. Trend Precision Golf, Inc., 903 F.Supp. 1506 (M.D. Fla. 1995).
Gabriel, James ........................ '55 '86 C.112 B.A. L.426 J.D. 4929 Wilshire Blvd.
Gabriel, John F. ...................... '38 '63 C&L.262 A.B., LL.B. 1334 S. Central Ave.
**Gabriel, Larry W.** .................. '48 '74 C.801 B.A. L.209 J.D. [Pachulski,S.Z.&Y.]
*REPORTED CASES: In re County of Orange, Orange County Employers Assn., et al. v. County of Orange, 1995 WL 95157 (Bankr. C.D. Cal); Quackenbush as Insurance Commissioner, Etc., Plaintiff and Respondent, v. Aurora, et al., Defendants and Respondents, Commercial National Bank in Shreveport, et al., Defendants and Appellants (32 Cal. App. 4th 344, 38 Cal Rptr. 2d 453); Commercial National Bank in Shreveport, et al., v. Garamendi, 14 Cal. App. 4th 393, 17 Cal. Rptr. 2d 884 (1993); Texas Commerce Bank v. Garamendi, 11 Cal. App. 4th 460, 491, 14 Cal. Rptr. 854, 874 (1992); Federal Deposit Insurance Corporation v. Imperial Bank, 859 F.2d p.101 (9th Cir. 1988).

**Gabriel, Herman & Peretz, (AV)**
**1800 Century Park East, 5th Floor, 90067-1508**
**Telephone: 310-286-1300 Fax: 310-286-1331**
**Members of Firm: Allan Gabriel; Dean B. Herman; Avi S. Peretz; Peter Schwartz; Albert J. Tumpson; John H. Odendahl. Associates: Lynda M. Riley; Lindsay S. Johnson; Karen M. Costello; Deborah Schmidt; Leonard R. Schwigen; Matthew J. Hafey.**
**Business and Commercial Litigation, Insurance Coverage and Defense, Professional Liability, Business Transactions, Real Estate, Finance and General Business Law.**

***See Professional Biographies, LOS ANGELES, CALIFORNIA***

**Gabrielson, Jan C.**, (AV) ................'44 '70 C.112 A.B. L.1068 J.D. [J.C.Gabrielson]
*LANGUAGES: French, Spanish and Italian.

**Gabrielson, Jan C., A Law Corporation, (AV)**
**1875 Century Park East, Suite 2150, 90067-2710**
**Telephone: 310-785-9731**

(This Listing Continued)

**Gabrielson, Jan C., A Law Corporation (Continued)**
**Jan C. Gabrielson (Certified Specialist, Family Law, The State Bar of California Board of Legal Specialization).**
**Practice Limited to Family Law.**

***See Professional Biographies, LOS ANGELES, CALIFORNIA***

**Gach Ray, Linda**, (BV) ....................'54 '79 C.112 B.A. L.1068 J.D. [Owens&G.]
Gackle, G. Steven .................... '55 '92 C.502 B.A. L.426 J.D. 1900 Ave. of the Stars
**Gackle, Gerhard S.** ....................'55 '92 C.986 B.A. L.426 J.D. [[A] Murchison&C.]
*LANGUAGES: German.
**Gadbois, Barbara R.** .................. '60 '85 C.597 B.A. L.1068 J.D. [Gibbs,G.L.&A.]
*PRACTICE AREAS: Construction Law; Public Contracts; Business Litigation.
Gaffney, Edward M., Jr. '41 '75 C.1256 B.A. L.128 J.D.
(adm. in DC; not adm. in CA) Loyola Law School
**Gagliardi, Jeffrey A.** ..................'65 '91 C.446 B.S. L.1065 J.D. [[A] Radcliff,F.&D.]
Gaglione, Claudia L. ........................ '58 '82 C.724 B.S. L.800 J.D. [Gaglione&D.]
Gaglione & Dolan, A Prof. Corp. ...........................11377 W. Olympic Blvd., 5th Fl.
Gahagan, Marian .......... '62 '88 C.990 B.A. L.426 J.D. 354 S. Cochran Ave., Apt. 107
Gail, Lawrence R. '46 '75
C.112 B.A. L.767 J.D. Chf. Trial Coun., Industrial Indemnity Co.
**Gailen, Scott R.** ................................'54 '80 C.1077 B.A. L.1095 J.D. [S.Gailen]
*LANGUAGES: Spanish.

**Gailen, Scott, Inc., A Prof. Law Corp.**
**Suite 830, 21700 Oxnard Street, (Woodland Hills), 91367-3666**
**Telephone: 818-715-7070 Fax: 818-715-7076**
**Scott R. Gailen.**
**Criminal Defense, Family Law, Insurance Defense, Civil Litigation, Personal Injury, Bankruptcy, Debt Consolidation, Entertainment Litigation.**

***See Professional Biographies, LOS ANGELES, CALIFORNIA***

**Gaims, John**, (AV) .........................'34 '68 C.112 B.A. L.800 J.D. [Gaims,W.W.&E.]

**Gaims, Weil, West & Epstein, LLP, (AV)**
**A Partnership including a Professional Corporation**
**1875 Century Park East, Twelfth Floor, 90067**
**Telephone: 310-553-6666 Fax: 310-277-2133 Answer Back: Wild West Telex: 910678746**
**Members of Firm: John Gaims; Barry G. West; Alan Jay Weil; Marc Epstein (P.C.); Steven S. Davis; Jeffrey B. Ellis; Amy L. Rice; Corey E. Klein. Associates: Peter L. Steinman; Scott A. Schneider; Annette E. Davis; Sylvia M. Virsik; Jessica D. Lazarus.**
**General Civil Trial and Appellate Practice in all State and Federal Courts and Government Agencies. Business Litigation, Insurance Coverage, Professional Liability, Antitrust, White Collar Criminal Defense, and International Law.**

***See Professional Biographies, LOS ANGELES, CALIFORNIA***

Gaines, Cheryl Newman ....................'62 '87 C&L.426 B.A., B.A. Dep. Dist. Atty.
**Gaines, Fred N.** ...........................'59 '86 C.112 B.A. L.1066 J.D. [Reznik&R.]
*SPECIAL AGENCIES: Los Angeles County Metropolitan Transit Authority (MTA).
*REPORTED CASES: Jama Construction Co. v. City of Los Angeles, 938 F.2d 1045 (9th Cir. 1991); Save Our Residential Environment v. City of West Hollywood, 9 Cal App. 4th 1745, 12 Cal. Rptr. 2d 308 (1992).
*PRACTICE AREAS: Zoning and Land Use; Environmental Law; Administrative Law and Related Litigation.
**Gaines, Frederic N.**, (AV) ............'40 '66 C.319 B.A. L.1068 LL.B. [Mayer,G.&G.]
*PRACTICE AREAS: Entertainment Law; Television Law; Motion Picture Law; Publishing Law; Intellectual Property Law.
Gaines, Howard R., (AV) '53 '79
C.112 B.A. L.1065 J.D. 11755 Wilshire Blvd. (⊙Phoenix, Arizona)
**Galanter, Douglas F.** ...................'55 '80 C.1044 B.S. L.800 J.D. [Argue P.H.&M.]
*PRACTICE AREAS: Civil Litigation; Business Litigation.
**Galanty, Caroline Canning**, (AV) '56 '85 C.604 B.A. L.1067 J.D.
Coun., Bank of Amer.
**Galaz, Raul Carl** ..........................'62 '88 C.112 B.A. L.813 J.D. [[A] Loeb&L.]
*PRACTICE AREAS: Entertainment Industry Transactions; Copyright.
Galbreath, Roxanna J., (BV) ......................'41 '79 L.1148 J.D. 6118 W. 77th St.
Galceran, Rafael H., Jr. ....................................'21 '49 C&L.800 B.A., LL.B. Ret. Supr, Ct. J.
Gale, Barry Lee ..........................'47 '88 C.1077 B.A. L.1136 J.D. Dep. Dist. Atty.
**Gale, Jerald E.**, (AV) ...............'54 '81 C.112 B.A. L.1065 J.D. [Anderson,A.L.&G.]
*PRACTICE AREAS: Litigation; Business; Commercial; Real Property; Escrow and Title Litigation.
Gale, Lawrence E. .......................'42 '69 C.800 B.S. L.1065 J.D. 9911 W. Pico Blvd.
Gale, Mary Ellen ...............'40 '72 C.681 A.B. L.976 J.D. Prof., Whittier Law School
Gale, Rhonda '53 '79 C.112 B.A. L.426 J.D.
V.P., Bus. Affs. Dept., Orion Pictures Corp.
Gale, Shari Kim ............'52 '79 C.813 B.A. L.608 J.D. Staff Coun., Unified Sch. Dist.
**Galen, Albert J.**, (AV) .................................'28 '52 C&L.508 B.A., J.D. [Holley&G.] ‡
**Galer, Scott D.** .......................... '66 '92 C.112 B.A. L.309 J.D. [[A] Troop M.S.&P.]
*PRACTICE AREAS: Corporate Law; Securities Law.
**Galinsky, Marsha D.** ......................'58 '84 C.309 B.A. L.800 J.D. [Sheppard,M.R.&H.]
*PRACTICE AREAS: Bankruptcy, Workouts and Commercial Litigation.
**Galker, Andrew L.** ...............'65 '92 C.976 B.A. L.813 J.D. [[A] Armstrong H.J.T.&W.]
*PRACTICE AREAS: Entertainment.
**Gall, John U.**, (AV) .............................'28 '54 C.502 B.S. L.1068 LL.B. [Gall&G.]

**Gall & Gall, (AV)**
**37th Floor, 333 South Grand Avenue, 90071-1599**
**Telephone: 213-628-7269**
**Members of Firm: Herbert Gall (1900-1984); John U. Gall.**
**Corporation, Real Estate, Trust and Probate Law. Commercial Law and Collections. General Civil and Trial Practice in all State and Federal Courts.**
**Reference: Union Bank.**

***See Professional Biographies, LOS ANGELES, CALIFORNIA***

Gallagher, Dennis M. ......................'37 '68 C.112 A.B. L.1068 J.D. Dep. Pub. Def.
Gallagher, Helen L. ..............................'17 '56 C.208 B.S. L.426 LL.B. 314 W. 1st St.‡
**Gallagher, James J.**, (AV) ..................'39 '66 C.602 B.B.A. L.276 LL.B. [McKenna&C.]
Gallagher, John V. ........ '31 '62 C&L.426 B.A., LL.B. Prof. of Law, Southwestern Univ.
Gallagher, Owen L. ...........................'46 '74 C.1077 B.A. L.1095 J.D. Sr. Dep. Co. Coun.
**Gallagher, Sean J.** .....................'63 '89 C.94 B.S. L.472 J.D. [[A] Seyfarth,S.F.&G.]
*PRACTICE AREAS: Workers Compensation; Labor and Employment.
Gallagher, Sharon M. .....................'43 '83 C.112 B.A. L.426 J.D. P.O. Box 48897
**Gallarello, Donna M.** ............'65 '91 C.569 B.A. L.1009 J.D. [[A] Nossaman,G.K.&E.]
*PRACTICE AREAS: Bankruptcy.
**Galleberg, Paul A.** .............................'60 '86 C.477 A.B. L.309 J.D. [Latham&W.]
*PRACTICE AREAS: Communications Law; Corporate Law.
**Gallegos, Hector G.** .................'62 '94 C.426 B.S.E.E. L.1068 J.D. [[A] Morrison&F.]
*LANGUAGES: Spanish.
**Gallenson, Mavis S.**, (AV) ........ '51 '79 C&L.878 B.S., J.D. [Ladas&P.] (See Pat. Sect.)
**Gallo, Joie Marie** ........'62 '95 C.569 B.F.A. L.426 J.D. [[A] Christensen,M.F.J.G.W.&S.]
*PRACTICE AREAS: Civil Litigation.
**Gallo, Jon J.**, (AV) ..............'42 '68 C.605 B.A. L.1068 J.D. [Greenberg G.F.C.&M.]
*PRACTICE AREAS: Estate Planning.

**Gallo, James A.**
**(See Pasadena)**

Gallon, Stanley J. ......................... '16 '54 C.112 L.809 LL.B. 3032 Fernwood Ave.‡

CAA228P

Gallop, Wayne E., (AV) ... '31 '59 C.622 B.S. L.623 LL.B. [Noble&C.]
**Galloway, James C., Jr. (A Professional Corporation)** '42 '70
C.800 B.S. L.809 J.D. [Veatch,C.G.&N.]
*REPORTED CASES: Hector v. Cedars-Sinai Medical Center, 180 Cal.App.3d 493, 225 Cal.Rptr. 595, Prod. Liab. Rep. (CCH)P. 11,014 (Cal.App.2 Dist., Apr 29, 1986) (NO.CIV. B012677); Jones v. McCollister, 159 Cal.App.2d 708, 324 P.2d 639 (Cal.App., Apr 28, 1958) (NO. CIV. 17718).
*PRACTICE AREAS: Dental and Medical Malpractice; Construction Defects; Products Liability; Vehicle and Government Tort Liability Defense Law.
Galt, Bonnie Chambless ... '— '87 C.112 B.S. L.878 J.D. Cedars-Sinai Med. Ctr.
**Galt, Douglas H.** ... '56 '81 C.813 B.A. L.1068 J.D. [Ⓐ Long&L.]
**Galton, Stephen H.**, (AV) ... '37 '70 C&L.800 B.A., J.D. [Galton&H.]
*PRACTICE AREAS: Civil Litigation.

**Galton & Helm, (AV) BB**
**500 South Grand Avenue, Suite 1200, 90071⊙**
**Telephone: 213-629-8800 Telecopier: 213-629-0037**
**Members of Firm: Stephen H. Galton; Hugh H. Helm; Michael F. Bell; Daniel W. Maguire (Resident at Palm Desert); David A. Lingenbrink. Associates: Chris D. Olsen; Melissa M. Cowan; Edith Sanchez Shea; Joanna M. Eoff; Michael B. Bernacchi; Mark A. Riekhof (Resident, Glendale Office).**
**Civil Litigation Practice in State and Federal Courts. Insurance Defense. (Life, Accident and Health, Bad Faith Defense, Professional Negligence, Reinsurance Law and ERISA).**
**Palm Desert, California Office: 73-290 El Paseo, Suite 377. Telephone: 619-776-5600. Fax: 619-776-5602.**

***See Professional Biographies, LOS ANGELES, CALIFORNIA***

**Galvez-Lantion, Mae R., The Law Offices of '55 '79 C&L.662 A.B., LL.B.**
**3250 Wilshire Boulevard, Suite 1110, 90010**
**Telephone: 213-385-4040 Fax: 213-385-0444**
**Email: gllaw@worldnetaccess.com**
***LANGUAGES: Filipino.**
***PRACTICE AREAS: Business Law; Civil Litigation; Estate Planning and Trusts; Personal Injury. General Civil Litigation and Appellate Practice in all State and Federal Courts. Business, Corporate, Commercial, Personal Injury, Estate Planning and Trusts.**

***See Professional Biographies, LOS ANGELES, CALIFORNIA***

Gam, Gary A. ... '53 '80 C.112 B.A. L.426 J.D. [Shaffer,D.P.&G.]
**Gambill, M. Art** ... '67 '96 C.976 B.A. L.1068 J.D. [Ⓐ Heller E.W.&M.]
Gamble, Carol E. '46 '79 C.477 B.A. L.284 J.D.
Resch. Atty., Continuing Educ. of the Bar
**Gamboa, Mark F.** ... '62 '93 C.1097 B.A. L.800 J.D. [Ⓐ Lynberg&W.]
*PRACTICE AREAS: Environmental Coverage; Toxic Tort.
**Gamboa, René I., IV** ... '63 '88 C&L.767 B.A., J.D. [Ⓐ Zelle&L.]
*LANGUAGES: Spanish.
*PRACTICE AREAS: Insurance Defense; Civil Litigation.
Games, Alene M. ... '54 '90 C.1042 B.S. L.426 J.D. Dep. Atty. Gen.
**Gamliel, Eyal** ... '70 '96 C.112 B.A. L.800 J.D. [Ⓐ Latham&W.]
*LANGUAGES: Hebrew and Spanish.
**Gams, Lance S.** ... '61 '86 C.339 B.A. L.800 J.D. [Breidenbach,B.H.H.&H.]
Ganahl, Mary Catherine ... '50 '80 C.770 B.A. L.426 J.D. Dep. Dist. Atty.
**Ganchrow, Gary** ... '68 '93 C.978 B.A. L.262 J.D. [Ⓐ Berger,K.S.M.F.S.&G.]
**Gandara, Kathy M.** ... '60 '95 C.999 A.S. L.398 J.D. [Ⓐ Lynberg&W.]
*PRACTICE AREAS: Civil Litigation.

**Gang, Tyre, Ramer & Brown, Inc.**
**(See Beverly Hills)**

Gann, Gregg ... '48 '80 C.1097 B.A. L.426 J.D. Pres.
Gannon, Richard H. ... '40 '71 C.1056 B.S. L.629 J.D. Dist. Coun., I.R.A.
**Gans, Bernard R.**, (AV) '48 '73 C.112 B.S.M.E. L.1068 J.D.
[Oppenheimer P.S.] (Pat.)
**Gans, Gary E.** ... '53 '79 C.918 B.A. L.1066 J.D. [Richards,W.&G.]
*PRACTICE AREAS: Business Litigation; Entertainment Litigation; Intellectual Property Litigation.
**Gansinger, James M.**, (AV) ... '45 '70 C.105 B.A. L.813 J.D. [Gansinger,H.B.&P.]
*PRACTICE AREAS: Complex Commercial Litigation; Construction; Securities; Trade Regulation.

**Gansinger, Hinshaw, Buckley & Padilla, LLP, (AV)**
**300 South Grand Avenue Suite 3850, 90071**
**Telephone: 213-229-2500 FAX: 213-625-0755**
**Members of Firm: James M. Gansinger; David C. Hinshaw; Brian L. Buckley; Jose L. Padilla, Jr. Associates: T.A. Taurino; Michael A. Clouser; Mary Moss Appleton. Of Counsel: Bruce D. Berls.**
**General Civil Litigation. Construction, Securities, Insurance Coverage, Unfair Competition and Receivership.**

***See Professional Biographies, LOS ANGELES, CALIFORNIA***

**Gantz, David F.** ... '53 '80 C.1109 B.A. L.1066 J.D. [Jeffer,M.B.&M.]
*PRACTICE AREAS: General Real Estate; Real Estate Leasing; Construction Development; Acquisition and Financing.

**Gantz, Emmett J., Law Office of**
**(See Beverly Hills)**

**Ganz, Philip J., Jr.**, (AV) ... '48 '73 C.475 B.A. L.477 J.D. [Ganz&G.]
*REPORTED CASES: Hyatt v. Northrop Corporation, 80 F3d 1425 (9th Cir. 1996).
*PRACTICE AREAS: Civil Trials; Employment Law; Business Litigation.

**Ganz & Gorsline, A Law Partnership, (AV)**
**11620 Wilshire Boulevard, Suite 340, 90025-1769**
**Telephone: 310-235-1700 Fax: 310-235-1707**
**Email: Info@GanzGorsLaw.com URL: http://www.GanzGorsLaw.com**
**Philip J. Ganz, Jr.; Laurie Susan Gorsline.**
**Employment Law, Civil Trial, Business Litigation.**

***See Professional Biographies, LOS ANGELES, CALIFORNIA***

Garau, Olga H. ... '60 '86 C.112 B.A. L.1068 J.D. Dep. City Atty.
**Garb, Andrew S., (A P.C.)**, (AV) ... '42 '68 C.112 A.B. L.309 LL.B. [Loeb&L.]
*PRACTICE AREAS: Trusts and Estates Law and Related Litigation.
Garber, Adolfo B. ... '57 '85 C.800 B.A. L.1068 J.D. 3580 Wilshire Blvd.
Garber, Albert C., (AV) ... '20 '48 C.569 B.A. L.800 J.D. [Garber&G.]
Garber, Leonard N., (BV) ... '46 '71 C.112 B.A. L.1068 J.D. [Garber&G.]
Garber & Garber, (AV) ... 3550 Wilshire Blvd.
Garcetti, Gil, (AV) ... '41 '68 C.800 B.S. L.1068 J.D. Dist. Atty.
**Garcia, Alarice M.** ... '67 '93 C.112 B.A. L.1038 J.D. [Ⓐ Serritella&P.]
*PRACTICE AREAS: Government Defense Litigation; Appellate Law.
Garcia, Alex ... '37 '67 5410 E. Beverly Blvd.
**Garcia, Alfred M.** ... '65 '89 C.260 B.S.B.A. L.309 J.D. [Ⓐ Jeffer,M.B.&M.]
*LANGUAGES: Spanish.
*PRACTICE AREAS: Federal, State, Local and International Taxation.
**Garcia, Bonifacio Bonny** ... '56 '81 C.426 B.A. L.309 J.D. [Barbosa G.&B.]
*PRACTICE AREAS: Negotiations; Commercial; Corporate; Real Estate; General Business.
Garcia, Daniel P., (AV) ... '47 '74 C.426 B.B.A. L.1068 J.D. 355 S. Grand Ave., 35th Fl.
**Garcia, David R.** ... '54 '80 C.309 B.A. L.276 J.D. [Ⓒ O'Melveny&M.]
*PRACTICE AREAS: Securities Litigation; SEC Enforcement; Antitrust Counseling and Litigation.
Garcia, Enedina F. ... '56 '87 C.940 B.A. L.426 J.D. Dep. Pub. Def.
**Garcia, Gilbert A.** ... '64 '92 C.1109 B.A. L.1240 J.D. [Ⓐ Veatch,C.G.&N.]
*PRACTICE AREAS: General Casualty Defense Law; Workers Compensation Defense Law.
**Garcia, J. Luis** ... '59 '86 C.800 B.A. L.426 J.D. [Parker S.]
*LANGUAGES: Spanish.

**Garcia, Jerry** ... '56 '87 C.1042 B.A. L.1067 J.D. [Ⓐ Bottum&F.]
*LANGUAGES: Spanish.
Garcia, Luis A. ... '61 '90 C.112 B.A. L.1068 J.D. 6500 Wilshire Blvd.
Garcia, Luis H. ... '24 '66 C.1043 L.809 LL.B. 311 S. Spring St.
Garcia, Manuel, Jr. ... '61 '88 C.1075 B.S. L.464 J.D. Off. of Dist. Atty.
Garcia, Marilyn L. ... '51 '77 C.813 B.A. L.976 J.D. 221 N. Figueroa St., 10th Fl.
Garcia, Michael ... '57 '89 C.605 A.B. L.426 J.D. Dep. U.S. Pub. Def.
**Garcia, Moses** ... '66 '94 C.972 B.S. L.602 J.D. [Ⓐ Corinblit&S.]
*LANGUAGES: French, Spanish.
*PRACTICE AREAS: Complex Civil Litigation.
Garcia, Norma Iris ... '57 '84 C.674 B.A. L.1068 J.D. 333 S. Grand Ave.
Garcia, Robert ... '52 '78 C&L.813 B.A., J.D. NAACP Legal Def. & Educ. Fund, Inc.
Garcia, Stephen M. ... '60 '85 C&L.426 B.A., J.D. 3700 Wilshire Blvd.
Garcia, Teresa M. ... '62 '88 C.556 B.S. L.276 J.D. 2029 Century Park E.
**Garcia-Barron, Gerard L.** ... '65 '92 C.112 B.A. L.1148 J.D. [Ⓐ Parker S.]
*LANGUAGES: Spanish.
*PRACTICE AREAS: Civil Litigation.
Garcin, Robert W., (AV) '28 '59
C.1043 B.A. L.800 LL.B. V.P. & Gen. Coun., Pacific Greystone Corp.
Garcin, Thomas E., (AV) ... '25 '53 C.800 L.426 LL.B. 3699 Wilshire Blvd.
**Garcin, Thomas M.** ... '62 '88 C.800 B.S. L.426 J.D. [Ⓐ Dolle&D.]
*PRACTICE AREAS: Condemnation Law; Inverse Condemnation Law; Zoning and Land Use Law.
Gardiner, Patrick J. ... '39 '71 C.800 A.B. L.809 J.D. Principle Dep.Co. Coun.
Gardner, Bruce E. '53 '81 C.112 B.A. L.823 J.D.
(adm. in IL; not adm. in CA) I.R.S.
Gardner, Cathy A. ... '51 '83 C.1097 B.A. L.1238 J.D. Off. of Pub. Def.
**Gardner, Christopher W.** ... '47 '72 C.797 B.A. L.259 J.D. [Ⓐ Patterson,R.L.G.&J.]
Gardner, Dana F. ... '66 '91 C.112 B.A. L.976 J.D. 444 S. Flower St.
**Gardner, Daniel L.** ... '48 '74 C.112 B.A. L.1065 J.D. [Grace,S.C.&S.]
*PRACTICE AREAS: Insurance Defense Law (Casualty and First Party); Product Liability Law; Insurance Coverage and Bad Faith Law; Professional Liability Law.
Gardner, Peter J., A Prof. Corp., (AV) '45 '77
C.823 B.A. L.809 J.D. 12424 Wilshire Blvd.
Gardner, Steven H. ... '51 '76 C.763 A.B. L.426 J.D. [Cohon&G.]
Gardner, William D. '43 '78 C&L.607 B.A., J.D.
(adm. in NY; not adm. in CA) West Publishing Corp.
**Garelick, Andrew D.** ... '69 '94 C.163 B.S. L.1065 J.D. [Ⓐ Orrick,H.&S.]
Garelick, Nancy O. ... '69 '94 C.112 B.A. L.1065 J.D. 777 S. Figueroa St., 10th Fl.
Garell, Karin Mason ... '64 '89 C.112 B.A. L.1066 J.D. 601 S. Figueroa St.
Garey, Howard B. ... '30 '76 C.563 B.B.A. L.1136 J.D. 2219 S. Bentley Ave.‡
**Garey, Michael J.** ... '56 '81 C.1042 B.A. L.809 J.D. [Ibold&A.]
Garfield, Alice J. ... '52 '81 C.273 B.A. L.61 J.D. NLRB
Garfield, Elizabeth Jo ... '52 '77 C.813 B.A. L.477 J.D. 3780 Wilshire Blvd.
Garfield, Franklin R., (AV) ... '46 '71 C.112 A.B. L.1066 J.D. [Garfield,T.E.&T.]
Garfield, Harold T. ... '14 '38 L.588 LL.B. Legal Dept., Vet. Admn.
Garfield, Tepper, Epstein & Turner, P.C., (AV) ... 1925 Century Pk. E.
**Garfinkel, Gregg S.** ... '65 '91 C.1077 B.A. L.464 B.A. [Ⓐ Bottum&F.]
Garfinkel, Irwin H. ... '30 '59 C.112 B.S. L.809 LL.B. Supr. Ct. Comr.
**Garfinkel, Michael B.** ... '66 '91 C.477 B.A. L.1068 J.D. [Ⓐ Rintala,S.J.&R.]
Garfinkle, Steven E. ... '52 '88 C.1097 B.S. L.1190 J.D. 4700 Wilshire Blvd.
**Gargaro, William J., Jr.**, (AV) ... '39 '65 C&L.276 A.B., LL.B. [W.J.Gargaro,Jr.]
*PRACTICE AREAS: Medical Malpractice Law; Personal Injury Law.

**Gargaro, William J., Jr., A Professional Corporation, (AV) BB**
**Suite 1800, 2049 Century Park East, 90067**
**Telephone: 310-552-0633 Fax: 310-552-9760**
**William J. Gargaro, Jr.**
**Medical Malpractice Law. Federal and State Trial and Appellate Practice.**
**Reference: Wells Fargo Bank.**

***See Professional Biographies, LOS ANGELES, CALIFORNIA***

**Garikian, Ani M.** ... '65 '89 C.112 B.A. L.426 J.D. [Ⓐ N.M.Dolin]
*LANGUAGES: Armenian.
*PRACTICE AREAS: Family Law.
**Garland, David W.** '58 '85 C.945 B.A. L.273 J.D.
(adm. in NJ; not adm. in CA) [Grotta,G.&H.]⊙
Garland, James E. ... '30 '72 C.999 L.809 J.D. Sr. Dep. Co. Coun.
Garland, Norman M. '39 '65 C&L.597 B.S., J.D.
(adm. in DC; not adm. in CA) Prof., Southwestern Univ. School of Law
**Garland, Seth D.** ... '70 '95 C.659 B.A. L.112 J.D. [Ⓐ Robinson,D.B.&K.]
*PRACTICE AREAS: Bankruptcy.
Garlock, Edward Sanfern '50 '77 C.813 A.B. L.597 J.D.
Grp. Gen. Coun., Corp. Servs. & Comm. Banking, First Interstate Bank
Garmus, Mark A. ... '54 '80 C.112 B.A. L.1068 J.D. 500 Citadel Dr., 2nd Fl.
**Garner, Lisa K.** ... '— '91 C.112 B.A. L.426 J.D. [Ⓐ Wilson,K.&B.]
**Garner, Mallory J.** ... '63 '89 C&L.273 B.A., J.D. [Ⓐ Crosby,H.R.&M.]
**Garner, R. Lee, III** ... '67 '92 C.862 B.S. L.800 J.D. [Ⓐ Milbank,T.H.&M.]
**Garnett, Mary J.** ... '62 '87 C.426 B.A. L.1065 J.D. [Ⓐ Jones,D.R.&P.]
**Garnett, Robert H.** ... '66 '92 C&L.846 B.B.A., J.D. [Ⓐ Lewis,D.B.&B.]
Garnett, Terrence D. ... '61 '90 C.174 B.A. L.1068 J.D. 777 S. Fugueroa St.
Garr, Donna L. ... '60 '86 C.112 B.A. L.1066 J.D. Sanwa Bk. Calif.
**Garrard, Donald A.**, (AV) ... '44 '70 C.112 A.B. L.426 J.D. [Fonda,G.H.&D.]
**Garrell, Peter E.** ... '66 '91 C.156 B.A. L.1029 J.D. [Ⓐ Christensen,M.F.J.G.W.&S.]
*PRACTICE AREAS: Civil Litigation; Liability Defense.
**Garrett, Anne Elizabeth** ... '66 '94 C.813 B.A. L.1068 J.D. [Ⓐ O'Melveny&M.]
*PRACTICE AREAS: Labor and Employment.
**Garrett, Katherine E.** ... '63 '94 C.112 B.A. L.1066 J.D. [Ⓐ O'Melveny&M.]
Garrett, Mark ... '55 '81 C.930 B.A. L.1068 J.D. 1929 Beloit Ave. #10
**Garrett, Marvin E.**, (AV) ... '41 '70 C.597 B.S.I.E. L.800 J.D. [Allen,M.L.G.&M.]
*PRACTICE AREAS: Litigation.
Garrett, Mitchel O. ... '53 '78 C.31 B.A. L.188 J.D. 13018 San Vicente Blvd.‡
Garrett, Mitchell A. ... '57 '84 C.112 A.B. L.1190 J.D. 12555 W. Jefferson Blvd.
Garrett, Terry P. ... '44 '88 C.1042 B.A. L.1137 J.D. 3255 Wilshire Blvd.

**Garrett & Tully, A Professional Corporation**
**(See Pasadena)**

**Garrick, John M.** ... '56 '83 C.112 B.A. L.878 J.D. [Iverson,Y.P.&H.]
*PRACTICE AREAS: Civil Litigation and Appellate Practice; Products Liability; Unitary Tax and Tax Litigation; Antitrust; Libel and Defamation.
Garrie, Leon J. ... '17 '39 C&L.209 LL.B. 1948 Mount Olympus Dr.
Garrison, Michael W. '45 '82 C.612 B.S. L.862 J.D.
(adm. in OK; not adm. in CA) Asst. Gen. Coun., Occidental Petro. Corp.
Garrott, Clifton H. ... '38 '63 C.880 B.A. L.208 J.D. Dep. Dist. Atty.
Garrott, Joan W. ... '40 '77 C.1042 B.A. L.990 J.D. Pub. Def.
Garrotto, Greg W. ... '53 '79 C.112 B.A. L.809 J.D. 3580 Wilshire Blvd., 10th Fl
**Garscia, Mark**, (AV) ... '55 '85 C.494 B.S. L.564 J.D. [Pretty,S.&P.] (See Pat. Sect.)
*PRACTICE AREAS: Patents; Trademarks; Copyrights; Unfair Competition; Litigation.
**Gartenberg, Edward** ... '49 '75 C&L.178 B.A., J.D. [Gartenberg J.G.&S.]
*PRACTICE AREAS: Civil Litigation; Securities Law.

CAA229P

**Gartenberg Jaffe Gelfand & Stein, LLP, (AV)**
**11755 Wilshire Boulevard, Suite 1230, 90025-1518**
**Telephone: 310-479-0044 Fax: 310-477-7663**
**Edward Gartenberg; Sheldon M. Jaffe; Edward S. Gelfand; Craig J. Stein. Associate: Torgny R. Nilsson.**
**Securities, Corporate and Litigation in State and Federal Courts.**
***See Professional Biographies, LOS ANGELES, CALIFORNIA***

**Gartner, Harold H., III, (A Professional Corporation)**, (BV) '48 '72 C.274 L.426 J.D. [Patterson,R.L.G.&J.] (⊙Ventura)
**Gartner, Lawrence J.**, (AV) .......... '45 '71 C.112 B.A. L.309 J.D. [Gartner&Y.]
*PRACTICE AREAS: Labor and Employment Law.

**Gartner & Young, A Professional Corporation, (AV)** BR
**1925 Century Park East, Suite 2050, 90067-2709**
**Telephone: 310-556-3576 Fax: 310-556-8459**
**Naomi Young; Lawrence J. Gartner;—Christopher Adams Thorn; Kimberly M. Talley; Jennifer L. Futch; Jill Henson; Angela J. Reddock; Gregory P. Bright.**
**Labor Relations, Management, Public and Private Sectors.**
***See Professional Biographies, LOS ANGELES, CALIFORNIA***

**Gartrell, Darlene Diane** .......... '62 '93 C.549 B.A. L.36 J.D. [Ⓐ Atkins&E.]
*PRACTICE AREAS: Civil Litigation; Insurance Defense; Governmental Defense; Employment Law.
**Gartside, Frederick W.** .......... '62 '87 C.605 B.A. L.800 J.D. [Jeffer,M.B.&M.]
*PRACTICE AREAS: Corporate.
**Garvey, George M.** .......... '54 '79 C.976 B.A. L.309 J.D. [Munger,T.&O.]
Garvin, Pamela A. '57 '85 C.800 B.A. L.809 J.D. 1801 Century Park E., 24th Fl. (⊙Westlake Village)
**Gary, Donald J., Jr.** .......... '56 '92 C.64 B.S. L.809 J.D. [D.J.Gary,Jr.]
Gary, E. Jean .......... '47 '82 C.801 B.S.Ed. L.1136 J.D. 1149 S. Hill St.

**Gary, Donald J., Jr., P.C.**
**445 South Figueroa Street Twenty-Sixth Floor, 90017⊙**
**Telephone: 213-439-5385**
**Harry M. Halstead (1918-1995); Donald J. Gary, Jr.**
**Federal and State Taxation, Probate and Estate Planning, General Business, Corporation, Partnerships, Limited Liability Company.**
**Riverside, California Office: 3700 Sixth Street at Main, Second Floor. P.O. Box 664. 92502-0664. Telephone: 909-786-0100. Facsimile: 909-683-8458.**
***See Professional Biographies, LOS ANGELES, CALIFORNIA***

**Garzilli, Richard J.**, (AV) .......... '47 '73 C.976 B.A. L.569 J.D. [Coudert]
*LANGUAGES: Spanish, Italian and French.
**Gascou, René J., Jr.** .......... '45 '72 C.800 B.A. L.276 J.D. [Gascou,G.&T.]
*LANGUAGES: German.
*PRACTICE AREAS: Fidelity Law; Suretyship Law; Construction Law; Trials.

**Gascou, Gemmill & Thornton, (AV)**
**15th Floor 10866 Wilshire Boulevard, 90024**
**Telephone: 310-470-4226 Fax: 310-470-1360**
**Email: ggt@leonardo.net**
**René J. Gascou, Jr.; William P. Gemmill; Bruce M. Thornton; Michael G. Evans; Ronald W. Hopkins. Associates: Carlos V. Yguico; Carolyn Taylor McQueen; John M. Hamilton; Mona H. Young; Deborah J. Wilson.**
**General Civil, Trial and Appellate Practice in all State and Federal Courts. Fidelity and Surety, Insurance, Corporate, Probate and Escrow Law.**
***See Professional Biographies, LOS ANGELES, CALIFORNIA***

**Gasparetti, Lorenzo E.** .......... '62 '88 C.112 B.A. L.1066 J.D. [Crosby,H.R.&M.]
*PRACTICE AREAS: Business Litigation; Product Liability; Legal Malpractice; Insurance.
**Gassman, Catherine A.** .......... '56 '82 C&L.174 B.A., J.D. 555 S. Flower St.
**Gast, B. Elizabeth** .......... '63 '92 C.1164 B.A. L.990 J.D. [Ⓐ Dummit,F.&B.]
*PRACTICE AREAS: Civil Litigation.
Gast, Nancy S. .......... '50 '78 C.112 A.B. L.426 J.D. Dep. Pub. Def.
**Gasteier, Philip A.** .......... '52 '77 C.608 B.A. L.659 J.D. [Robinson,D.B.&K.]
*REPORTED CASES: In re Qintex Entertainment, Inc., 950 F.2nd 1492 (9th Cir. 1991); in re Mercon Industries, Inc., 37 B.R. 549 (Bankr. E.D. Pa., 1984).
*PRACTICE AREAS: Bankruptcy Law; Insolvency; Reorganization.
Gastler, Debra A. .......... '53 '81 C.788 A.B. L.569 J.D. V.P., Taxes, The Times Mirror Co.
Gastley, Harry L. .......... '43 '69 C&L.446 B.A., J.D. U.S. Immig. J., Dept. of Jus.

**Gaston, Robert A., (AV) '30 '58 C.16 A.B. L.893 J.D.**
**11755 Wilshire Boulevard, 15th Floor, 90025-1506**
**Telephone: 310-477-9744 Fax: 310-479-7612**
**Certified Specialist, Family Law, The State Bar of California Board of Legal Specialization.**
**Family, Domestic Relations, Matrimonial and Divorce Law.**
***See Professional Biographies, LOS ANGELES, CALIFORNIA***

**Gaswirth, Mitchell M.** .......... '57 '82 C.112 B.A. L.1066 J.D. [Proskauer R.G.&M.]
*PRACTICE AREAS: Taxation.
**Gatarz, Craig S.** '62 '87 C.93 B.A. L.893 J.D. (adm. in NJ; not adm. in CA) [Ⓐ Jones,D.R.&P.]
Gates, Donald N. .......... '26 '54 C.112 L.1065 J.D. Ret. Ct. of Appeal J.‡
**Gates, George Henry, III** '57 '89 C.608 B.S.C.I.S. L.1035 J.D. [Merchant&G.] (See Pat. Sect.)
**Gates, Marlyn M.** .......... '69 '94 C&L.990 B.A., J.D. [Ⓐ Mendes&M.]
**Gatley, Steven G.** .......... '65 '91 C.112 B.A. L.426 J.D. [Borton,P.&C.]
**Gatti, John M.** .......... '63 '88 C&L.800 B.S., J.D. [White O.C.&A.]
*PRACTICE AREAS: Civil Litigation; Entertainment Litigation; Entertainment Law.
**Gatti, Marina** .......... '61 '92 C.112 A.B. L.893 J.D. [Ⓐ Parker,M.C.O.&S.]
*LANGUAGES: Italian.
*PRACTICE AREAS: Labor and Employment Law; Litigation.

**Gauhan and King**
**(See Long Beach)**

**Gaumer, Christie** .......... '62 '90 C&L.846 B.B.A., J.D. [Ⓐ Donovan L.N.&I.]
*PRACTICE AREAS: Commercial Litigation; Business Litigation; Trademark and Copyright Law.
**Gausewitz, Richard L.**, (AV) '25 '50 C.966 B.S.E.E. L.813 LL.B. [Oppenheimer P.S.] (⊙Irvine)
**Gaut, Kevin, (A Professional Corporation)** '57 '85 C&L.309 B.A., J.D. [Mitchell,S.&K.]
*PRACTICE AREAS: Litigation; Business Torts; Securities Regulation.
**Gauthier, Andrea M.** .......... '65 '92 C&L.309 A.B., J.D. [Ⓐ Horvitz&L.]
Gauthier, Edward P. .......... '47 '73 C.1077 B.A. L.1068 J.D. 200 N. Main St.
Gauthier, Joseph T. .......... '67 '94 C.228 A.B. L.1068 J.D. [Egerman&B.]
**Gawne, Cathryn S.** .......... '57 '82 C.813 A.B. L.1068 J.D. [Shapiro,R.&C.]
*PRACTICE AREAS: Corporate Law; Securities Law.
Gaxiola, Henry R. .......... '60 '88 C.1097 B.S. L.800 J.D. 6500 Wilshire Blvd.
Gay, Matthew T. '46 '73 C.976 B.A. L.569 J.D. (adm. in NY; not adm. in CA) Asst. Gen. Coun., Occidental Petro. Corp.
**Gaynor, Eric A.** .......... '66 '93 C.112 B.A. L.800 J.D. [Ⓐ Latham&W.]
*PRACTICE AREAS: Corporate.

**Gaynor, Gilbert** .......... '52 '82 L.1148 J.D. [Ⓒ Langberg,C.&D.]
*REPORTED CASES: Feminist Women's Health Center v. Philibosian, 157 Cal.App.3d 1076 (1984), stay denied, 469 U.S. 1303 (mem.opn. of Rehnquist, J.), cert. denied, 470 U.S. 1052 (1984); Pines v. Tomson, 160 Cal.App.3d. 370 (1984); Martin v. International Olympic Committee, 740 F.2d 670 (9th Cir. 1984); Alamo Foundation v. Donovan, 471 U.S. 290 (1985); Gay Rights Coalition v. Georgetown University, 536 A.2d.1 (D.C.App. 1987).
*PRACTICE AREAS: Appellate Practice; Civil Litigation.
**Geary, John J., Jr.**, (AV) .......... '42 '74 C.208 B.A. L.809 J.D. [Lane P.S.L.]
*PRACTICE AREAS: Litigation; Toxic Torts; Products Liability; Personal Injury; Construction Defects.
**Geary, Stephen W.** .......... '66 '94 C.813 A.B. L.1066 J.D. [Ⓐ Sidley&A.]
*LANGUAGES: German.
*PRACTICE AREAS: Litigation.
**Gebb, Sheldon A.**, (AV) '35 '64 C.112 A.B. L.1066 LL.B. [Baker&H.] (⊙Long Bch. & Houston, Texas)
*PRACTICE AREAS: Admiralty; Litigation; Insurance.
Gedanke, Barbara .......... '41 '79 C.1097 B.A. L.1238 J.D. 12240 Venice Blvd.
Gedo, Nicholas M. .......... '60 '87 C.605 B.A. L.1065 J.D. 624 S. Grand Ave.
**Gee, Dolly M.** .......... '59 '84 C.112 B.A. L.1068 J.D. [Schwartz,S.D.&S.]
*PRACTICE AREAS: Labor and Employment Law; Public Employment Relations Law; Education Law.
Geer, LouAnn S. .......... '54 '79 C.94 B.A. L.1068 J.D. Prof. of Law, Univ. of Calif.
Geerdes, Cynthea E .......... '61 '87 C.114 B.A. L.569 J.D. 7200 Hughes Ter.
Geernaert, Bruce R. .......... '28 '53 C.112 L.1065 J.D. Supr. Ct. J.
Geffen, Harold D. .......... '07 '30 C&L.809 LL.B. 4973 Noeline Ave.‡
Geffen, Laura I. .......... '50 '80 C.1044 B.A. L.809 J.D. Jud. Atty., Ct. of App.
Geffner, Patricia J. .......... '43 '85 C.102 B.A. L.800 J.D. Dept. of Veterans Affairs-Staff Atty.
Geffner, Randi R. .......... '60 '84 C.112 B.A. L.809 J.D. [Geffner&G.]
Geffner, Steve .......... '58 '87 C.259 B.S. L.809 J.D. [Geffner&G.]
Geffner & Geffner .......... 12301 Wilshire Blvd.
Geher, Thomas M. .......... '62 '87 C.208 B.A. L.990 J.D. 1875 Century Pk. E.
**Gehring, Thomas G.** .......... '54 '79 C.112 B.A. L.990 J.D. [Solish,A.&G.]
**Geibel, Michael B.** .......... '50 '81 C.112 B.A. L.426 J.D. [Daniels,B.&F.]
*PRACTICE AREAS: Trial and Appellate Law; Insurance.
**Geibelson, Michael** .......... '70 '95 C.112 B.A. L.426 J.D. [Ⓐ Robins,K.M.&C.]
*PRACTICE AREAS: Medical Malpractice; Product Liability Law; Mass Tort.
**Geiger, Roy S.**, (AV) .......... '50 '79 C.112 B.A. L.1066 J.D. [Irell&M.]
Geisendorfer, Henry A., III .......... '31 '66 C.477 B.B.A. L.800 J.D. Dep. Pub. Def.
**Geisler, Frederick V.** .......... '52 '76 C.813 B.A. L.1065 J.D. [Ⓒ Sheppard,M.R.&H.]
**Geismar, Eric P.** .......... '61 '94 L.800 [Ⓐ Dewey B.]
Geist, Debra Velez .......... '62 '89 C.424 B.A. L.1068 J.D. 10100 Santa Monica Blvd.
Geisz, James W. .......... '53 '78 C&L.309 B.A., J.D. 12100 Wilshire Blvd.
**Gelb, Andrew S.** .......... '56 '81 C.267 B.S. L.1068 J.D. [Ⓐ Wolf,R.&S.]
*PRACTICE AREAS: Intellectual Property Law; Employment Law; Litigation; Business Law.
**Gelb, Bruce L.** .......... '51 '78 C.665 B.A. L.831 J.D. [Freeman,F.&S.]
*PRACTICE AREAS: Real Estate; Business; Civil Litigation.
**Gelber, Robert T.**, (AV) .......... '35 '61 C.111 B.S. L.309 LL.B. [Gibson,D.&C.]
*LANGUAGES: French.
*PRACTICE AREAS: International and Domestic Arbitration; Negotiation; Corporate and Business Transactions; International Law (Business Transactions).
**Gelblum, Peter B., (A Professional Corporation)** '52 '82 C.918 B.A. L.809 J.D. [Mitchell,S.&K.]
*PRACTICE AREAS: Litigation; Business Torts; Alternative Dispute Resolution; Estate and Trust Litigation.
Gelfan, Gregory '50 '77 C.112 A.B. L.809 J.D. Sr. V.P., Bus. Affs., Paramount Pictures Corp.
**Gelfand, Edward S.** .......... '48 '76 C.1016 B.S. L.1095 J.D. [Gartenberg J.G.&S.]
*PRACTICE AREAS: Public and Private Securities Offerings; Securities Arbitration; Broker-Dealer; Investment Adviser Regulation; NASD Arbitration.
**Gelfand, Martin N.**, (AV) .......... '41 '65 C.339 L.209 LL.B. [Irell&M.]
**Gelfand, Marvin, (A Professional Corporation)**, (AV) '48 '72 C.1077 B.A. L.800 J.D. [Gelfand&G.]
*PRACTICE AREAS: Corporate and Business Law and Litigation.

**Gelfand & Glaser, (AV)**
**A Partnership including a Professional Corporation**
**Suite 1000, 11111 Santa Monica Boulevard, 90025-3333**
**Telephone: 310-477-7446 Facsimile: 310-473-0906**
**Marvin Gelfand (A Professional Corporation); Steven H. Glaser. Associates: Jennifer B. Goosenberg; Grant A. Carlson; Robert D. Sencer.**
**Reference: City National Bank, Sunset/Doheny Branch (L.A.).**
***See Professional Biographies, LOS ANGELES, CALIFORNIA***

Geller, Jonathan .......... '66 '92 C.112 B.A. L.426 J.D. Off. of Co. Coun.
Geller, Paul Edward .......... '39 '76 C.145 B.A. L.800 J.D. 12100 Wilshire Blvd.

**Gelles, Peter A., (AV) '44 '70 C&L.051 B.A., J.D.**
**1801 Century Park East 16th Floor, 90067**
**Telephone: 310-201-7900 Facsimile: 310-201-4746**
***PRACTICE AREAS: U.S. and International Real Estate and Business Transactions.**
**Real Estate, Business and International Law.**
***See Professional Biographies, LOS ANGELES, CALIFORNIA***

Gelles, Richard Marc .......... '61 '87 C.823 B.S. L.809 J.D. 3575 Cahuenga Blvd. W.
Gelletich, Joseph F. '30 '61 C&L.280 B.B.A., LL.B. (adm. in GA; not adm. in CA) Dep. Ex. Dir. L.A. Housing Auth.
Gelman, Marc S. .......... '58 '83 C.994 B.A. L.978 J.D. 8417 Beverly Blvd.
Gelman, Pamela J. .......... '44 '82 C.112 B.A. L.1148 J.D. Dep. Dist. Atty.
Geminder, Lynne .......... '48 '79 C.112 B.A. L.426 J.D. State Bar of Calif.
**Gemmill, William P.** .......... '48 '76 C.112 B.A. L.178 J.D. [Gascou,G.&T.]
*LANGUAGES: French and Japanese.
*PRACTICE AREAS: Trials and Appeals; Insurance Coverage; Defense; Suretyship Law; Fidelity Law.
**Gemoets, Travis M.** .......... '69 '94 C.112 B.A. L.1065 J.D. [Ⓐ Sheppard,M.R.&H.]
*LANGUAGES: French.
Gendler, Michael S. '53 '80 C.112 A.B. L.1068 J.D. 1800 Ave. of the Stars, Suite 900 (Century City)
Genelin, Alan M. .......... '36 '64 C.112 B.A. L.1068 J.D. Head Dep. Dist. Atty.
**Genga, John M.** .......... '62 '86 C.813 B.A. L.477 J.D. [Troop M.S.&P.]
*PRACTICE AREAS: Copyright Litigation; General Entertainment Litigation; General Business Litigation.
Gentile, Joseph F., A Professional Corporation, (AV) '34 '67 C.768 B.A. L.398 J.D. P.O. Box 491117
Gentile, Marion, (AV) .......... '— '77 C.1057 B.A. L.1136 J.D. Dept. of Indus. Rel.
Gentile, Maury D., (AV) .......... '26 '53 C.112 L.426 LL.B. 924 Westwood Blvd.
**Gentile, Tina L.** .......... '57 '88 C.768 B.A. L.1068 J.D. [Ⓐ Kern,S.&G.]
*PRACTICE AREAS: Premises Liability; Products Liability; General Negligence; Defamation; Contract.
**Gentin, Jennifer L.** .......... '62 '90 C.103 B.A. L.978 J.D. [Ⓐ Troy&G.]
*PRACTICE AREAS: Business, Entertainment and Real Estate Litigation.
Gentino, Robert E. .......... '54 '80 C.184 B.A. L.188 J.D. 6922 Hollywood Blvd.
Gentry, Kathleen M. .......... '50 '77 C.112 B.A. L.809 J.D. Dep. Dist. Atty.
**Genz, Wendy K.** .......... '57 '89 C.101 B.A. L.421 J.D. [Rexon,F.K.&H.]
*LANGUAGES: Spanish.
*PRACTICE AREAS: Labor and Employment Litigation; Administrative Proceedings.

CAA230P

**Genzmer, George V., III**, (AV) ..........'43 '72 C.629 B.A. L.809 J.D. [Murchison&C.]
*PRACTICE AREAS: Errors and Omissions Defense; Directors and Officers Defense; Excess and Reinsurance Liability; Lawyers Professional Liability Defense; Insurance Agents & Real Estate Professional Liability Defense.
George, James, (AV) ..........'27 '54 L.1068 [George&B.]
George, Kristine A. ..........'66 '91 C.473 B.S. L.1340 J.D. 5750 Wilshire Blvd., Ste., 655
George & Buch, A Law Corporation, (AV) .......... 930 S. La Brea Ave.
**George, Edward P., Jr., Inc., A Prof. Corp.**
**(See Long Beach)**
**Georgelos, Demetra V.** ..........'67 '92 C.976 B.A. L.112 J.D. [🄰 Murphy,W.&B.]
**Geragos, Mark J.** ..........'57 '83 C.311 B.A. L.426 J.D. [Geragos&G.]
*PRACTICE AREAS: Criminal Law.
**Geragos, Matthew J.** .......... '58 '91 C.800 B.S. L.809 J.D. [Geragos&G.]
*PRACTICE AREAS: Civil Litigation; Criminal Law; Transactional Law.
**Geragos, Paul J.**, (AV) ..........'27 '57 C.112 B.A. L.800 LL.B. [Geragos&G.]
*PRACTICE AREAS: Criminal Law; Civil Litigation.

**Geragos & Geragos, (AV) BR**
**201 N. Figueroa Street 5th Floor, 90012-2628**
**Telephone: 213-250-5055 Fax: 213-250-2828**
**Paul J. Geragos; Mark J. Geragos; Matthew J. Geragos. Of Counsel: Susan P. Strick.**
**Criminal Defense and Civil Litigation.**
***See Professional Biographies, LOS ANGELES, CALIFORNIA***

**Gerard, Adam J.** ..........'63 '93 C.1109 B.A. L.990 J.D. [Bacon&M.]
*PRACTICE AREAS: Business and Civil Litigation; Insurance Defense.
Gerard, Melissa K. ..........'63 '89 C.112 B.A. L.800 J.D. 515 S. Figueroa St.
**Gerardi, Michael M.** ..........'59 '88 C.453 S.B.Ch.E. L.280 J.D. [🄰 Jeffer,M.B.&M.] (Pat.)
*PRACTICE AREAS: Patent Law.
Gerber, Ludwig H. ..........'11 '33 C&L.724 LL.B. 1567 Bluejay Way
**Gerber, Peggy A.** .......... '41 '81 C.446 B.S. L.426 J.D. [Gibbs,G.L.&A.]
*PRACTICE AREAS: Construction; Litigation; Real Estate.
**Gerchick, Randy G.** .......... '— '94 C.605 B.A. L.1068 J.D. [🄰 Hughes H.&R.]
*PRACTICE AREAS: Business Litigation; Insurance Litigation; Products Liability Litigation; Real Property Litigation.
**Gerdes, Ted F.** ..........'52 '81 C.1044 B.A. L.61 J.D. [🄲 Kirsch&M.]
*PRACTICE AREAS: Entertainment Law; Intellectual Property Law; Media Counselling Law; Litigation.
Gerdts, Marlene, Law Offices of '46 '80
C.112 B.A. L.767 J.D. 1901 Ave. of the Stars, 20th Fl.
Gerecht, Donald Leon .......... '45 '72 C.112 B.A. L.426 J.D. Dep. Dist. Atty.
**Geri, Joseph** .......... '59 '93 C.112 B.S. L.809 J.D. [🄰 Kirtland&P.]
*PRACTICE AREAS: Construction; Business Litigation.
**Geringer, Aylene M.** ..........'50 '84 C.112 B.A. L.809 J.D. [Rodarte&G.]
*PRACTICE AREAS: Toxic Tort/Environmental Litigation; Products Liability; Medical Device Litigation.
**Gerisch, Alfred W., Jr.** ..........'48 '73 C.800 B.S. L.426 J.D. [La Follette,J.D.F.&A.]
*PRACTICE AREAS: General Litigation.
Germain, Daniel L. ..........'64 '89 C.112 B.A. L.426 J.D. 1925 Century Park E.
**Germain, Michael D.** ..........'65 '91 C.763 B.A. L.990 J.D. [Maguire&O.]
*PRACTICE AREAS: Construction Law; Surety Law; Business Litigation.
**Germaise, Susan L.** .......... '67 '93 C.861 B.A. L.734 J.D. [🄰 Charlston,R.&W.]
**German, Judith Fournier** .......... '— '93 C.112 B.A. L.426 J.D. [Karpman&Assoc.]
Gerner, Michael G. ..........'49 '75 C.1109 B.A. L.1148 J.D. State Bar of Calif.
Gerry, Richard W. .......... '47 '73 C.197 B.A. L.309 J.D. 746 S. Los Angeles St.‡
Gersbacher, Jane .... '41 '64 C.861 A.B. L.339 LL.B. U.S. Immig. & Naturalization Serv.
**Gersh, David L.**, (AV) ..........'42 '67 C.112 B.S. L.309 J.D. [Paul,H.J.&W.]
*PRACTICE AREAS: Corporate Law; Securities Law; Acquisitions, Divestitures and Mergers Law.
Gershan, Howard ..........'30 '62 C.112 B.S. L.426 LL.B. 205 S. Bway.

**Gershman, Stephen A. '50 '76 C.645 B.A. L.990 J.D.**
**1901 Avenue of the Stars Suite 1800, 90067**
**Telephone: 310-553-5465 Fax: 310-553-5430**
***PRACTICE AREAS: Family Law (90%); Personal Injury (10%).**
**Family Law, Civil Litigation.**
***See Professional Biographies, LOS ANGELES, CALIFORNIA***

**Gershon, Deborah S.** ..........'55 '80 C.112 B.A. L.800 J.D. Sr. Coun., Bank of Amer.
**Gershon, Harry L.**, (AV) .......... '22 '49 C.112 A.B. L.800 LL.B. [Richards,W.&G.]
*PRACTICE AREAS: Antitrust Law; Intellectual Property Law; Business Litigation; Land Use; Environmental Litigation.
Gershuni, Gregory B., (AV) '54 '78
C.112 B.A. L.426 J.D. 10850 Wilshire Blvd. (©Long Beach)
Gerson, Morton M., (A Prof. Law Corp.), (AV) '34 '59
C.112 B.A. L.800 LL.B. 1875 Century Pk., E.
Gerst, Robert J., (AV) .......... '35 '60 C&L.800 B.A., LL.B. 2029 Century Park East
**Gertler, Gary B.** ..........'59 '86 C.112 B.S. L.800 J.D. [McDermott,W.&E.]
*PRACTICE AREAS: Health Care; Hospitals; Mergers, Acquisitions and Divestitures.
Gertler, Robin Tolmas ..........'61 '87 C.112 B.A. L.426 J.D. Atty. Gens. Off.
Gertz, Bette .......... '— '62 C.112 B.A. L.1068 LL.B. 750 N. Genesee Ave.
Gertz, Howard .......... '51 '78 C.494 B.A. L.426 J.D. 6320 Commodore Sloat Dr.
Gertz, Ronald H. ..........'47 '77 C.1077 B.A. L.1095 J.D. Clearing House Ltd.
**Gervin, Edward J.** ..........'68 '95 C.602 B.A. L.426 J.D. [🄰 Goldstein,K.&P.]
*PRACTICE AREAS: Labor and Employment; Civil Litigation.
**Gesner, Cynthia Farrelly** ..........'62 '89 C.860 B.A. L.94 J.D. [🄰 Lichter,G.N.&A.]
*LANGUAGES: French.
*PRACTICE AREAS: Entertainment Law.
Gessler, Charles A., (AV) .......... '33 '62 C.260 B.A. L.800 LL.B. Co. Pub. Def.
**Gest, Howard D.** .......... '52 '77 C.112 A.B. L.1065 J.D. [Sidley&A.]
*PRACTICE AREAS: Environmental Law.
Gest, Max ..........'45 '70 C.1097 B.A. L.426 J.D. [Fox,R.P.&M.G.]
Gesvi-Sharif, & Associates ..........1019 N. Avalon Blvd.
**Getman, Robert S.** ..........'56 '81 C.1044 B.A. L.188 J.D. [Armstrong H.J.T.&W.]
*PRACTICE AREAS: Entertainment; Intellectual Property.
**Getto, Ernest J.**, (AV) ..........'44 '70 C.188 B.A. L.880 J.D. [Latham&W.]
**Getzoff, Laurence D.** ..........'57 '82 C.813 A.B. L.273 J.D. [Hooper,L.&B.]
*SPECIAL AGENCIES: Medical Board of California; Provider Reimbursement Review Board; California Department of Health Services - Office of Administrative Appeals.
*REPORTED CASES: Mir vs. Little Company of Mary Hospital; Silverman vs. St. Rose Hospital.
*PRACTICE AREAS: Health Care Law (General); Medical Staff Relations Law; Reimbursement Law.
**Geyer, Bruce C.** .......... '62 '91 C.665 B.S. L.800 J.D. [🄰 Riordan&M.]
*PRACTICE AREAS: Real Estate.
**Geyer, Sherry L.** .......... '48 '88 C.112 B.A. L.426 J.D. [🄲 Brand F.D.F.&K.]
*PRACTICE AREAS: Real Estate; General Corporate.
Geyser, Lewis P. .......... '36 '61 C.309 B.A. L.178 LL.B. 5757 Wilshire Blvd.‡
**Gharakhanian, Anahid** ..........'66 '92 C.112 B.A. L.309 J.D. [🄰 Chadbourne&P.]
*LANGUAGES: Armenian, Farsi.
**Ghazarians, Ann M.** ..........'60 '85 C.112 B.A. L.809 J.D. [Hornberger&C.]
*REPORTED CASES: A-Mark Finance v. Pacific Indemnity Corp. (1995) 34 Cal. App. 4th 1179.
*PRACTICE AREAS: General Liability; Civil Litigation; Bad Faith; Insurance Coverage; Broker-Agent Liability.
Ghose, Rabindra Nath ...... '25 '79 C.911 M.S. L.339 LL.B. 8167 Mulholland Terr. (Pat.)
**Giacopuzzi, Julie** ..........'71 '96 C.112 B.A. L.800 J.D. [🄰 Christensen,M.F.J.G.W.&S.]
*PRACTICE AREAS: Litigation.
**Giali, Dale J.** .......... '65 '90 C.112 B.A. L.1049 J.D. [🄰 Howrey&S.]
Giannini, Peter E. .......... '21 '45 C.112 B.S. L.1066 LL.D. Ret. Supr. Ct. J.
**Giannotti, David A.**, (AV) '47 '72 C.354 B.A. L.245 J.D.
[Christensen,M.F.J.G.W.&S.]
*PRACTICE AREAS: Environmental Law.
Gibbon, Denise Hargleroad ..........'47 '88 C.770 B.A. L.767 J.D. 2049 Century Park E.
Gibbon, Elizabeth Johanna '39 '86 C.174 B.S. L.692 J.D.
(adm. in MD; not adm. in CA) 700 S. Flower St.
Gibbons, John J. ..........'26 '52 C.906 B.A. L.911 LL.B. 2035 N. Edgemont St.
Gibbons, Sheila M. .......... '31 '77 C.994 B.A. L.724 J.D. V.P. & Secy., Northrop Corp.
Gibbs, Geoffrey Taylor ..........'61 '89 C.309 A.B. L.1066 J.D. 10940 Wilshire Blvd.
**Gibbs, Kenneth C.**, (AV) .......... '49 '74 C.112 A.B. L.1068 J.D. [Gibbs,G.L.&A.]
*PRACTICE AREAS: Construction Law; Business Litigation; Public Contract Law.
Gibbs, Robert W., (AV) .......... '29 '53 C.112 A.B. L.309 LL.B. [R.W.Gibbs]
**Gibbs, Travis C.** ..........'56 '86 C.260 B.S.B.A. L.846 J.D. [O'Melveny&M.]
*PRACTICE AREAS: Federal Taxation; Municipal Finance.

**Gibbs, Giden, Locher & Acret, (AV)**
**One Century Plaza, 34th Floor, 2029 Century Park East, 90067**
**Telephone: 310-552-3400 Facsimile: 310-552-0805**
**Kenneth C. Gibbs; Joseph M. Giden; William D. Locher; Glenn E. Turner, III; Gerald A. Griffin; Anya Stanley; James D. Lipschultz; Jeriel C. Smith; Theodore L. Senet; James L. Ferro; Norman D. Bowling; Barbara R. Gadbois; Jean M. Boylan; Peter F. Lindborg; Peggy A. Gerber; Mary A. Salamone; Richard J. Wittbrodt; Robert E. Kent; Sharon E. Foster;—Steven R. Cuneo, Jr.; Michael I. Giden; Barbara L. Hamilton; John F. Heuer; Matthew P. Kanny; Larry T. Lasnik; Leon F. Mead, II; Dana M. Rudnick; Gary Edward Scalabrini; Jill R. Schecter. Of Counsel: James Acret; Alfred Fadel; Ronald S. Sofen; John H. Stephens; Barry C. Vaughan.**
**Construction, Public Contract, Fidelity and Surety, Title Insurance, Commercial, Business Litigation, Real Property, Commercial Leasing and Labor and Employment Law.**
***See Professional Biographies, LOS ANGELES, CALIFORNIA***

Gibbs, Robert W., A Prof. Corp., Law Offices of, (AV) ..... 8th Fl., 1875 Century Park E.
Gibeaut, Gary R., (AV) .......... '51 '76 C.800 B.A. L.809 J.D. [Gibeaut,M.&B.]
Gibeaut, Greg W., (AV) .......... '54 '78 C.800 B.A. L.809 J.D. [Gibeaut,M.&B.]
Gibeaut, Mahan & Briscoe, (AV) .......... 6701 Center Dr. W., Ste. 611
**Gibson, Bradley N.** ..........'70 '96 C.112 B.S. L.426 J.D. [🄰 Tuverson&H.]
**Gibson, Colin J.** ..........'59 '91 C.30 B.S. L.426 J.D. [🄰 Wright,R.O.&T.]
*PRACTICE AREAS: Negligence; Products Liability; Business/Contracts.
Gibson, Dorithea W. .......... '34 '73 C.802 B.B.A. L.426 J.D. 11459 Woodbine St.
**Gibson, Elizabeth Barrowman** ..........'64 '88 C.339 B.A. L.477 J.D. [Jeffer,M.B.&M.]
*PRACTICE AREAS: Business Litigation; Intellectual Property.
**Gibson, John S.** .......... '60 '86 C.309 A.B. L.477 J.D. [Paul,H.J.&W.]
Gibson, Joy .......... '34 '69 C.642 L.809 J.D. 5317 N. Figueroa St.
Gibson, Paul R. .......... '50 '85 C.112 B.A. L.1065 J.D. 308 N. Mansfield
Gibson, Paula Lauren .......... '56 '81 C.112 B.A. L.809 J.D. Dep. Atty. Gen.
**Gibson, Richard H.**, (AV) .......... '58 '83 C.1169 B.A. L.770 J.D. [R.H.Gibson]
*PRACTICE AREAS: Banking; Bankruptcy; Real Estate; Corporate Law; Civil Litigation.
**Gibson, Stanley M.** .......... '66 '92 C.112 B.A. L.228 J.D. [🄰 Jeffer,M.B.&M.]
*PRACTICE AREAS: Litigation.

**Gibson, Dunn & Crutcher LLP, (AV) BR**
**333 South Grand Avenue, 90071-3197⊙**
**Telephone: 213-229-7000 Telex: 188171 GIBTRASK LSA (TRT), 674930 GIBTRASK LSA (WUT)**
**Telecopier: 213-229-7520; 213-229-7268 Cable Address: GIBTRASK LOS ANGELES**
**Jas. A. Gibson (1852-1922); W. E. Dunn (1861-1925); Albert Crutcher (1860-1931). Partners: Norman B. Barker; Robert S. Warren; Ronald E. Gother; Stephen E. Tallent (Los Angeles and Washington, D.C. Offices); Robert E. Cooper; Ronald S. Beard; John H. Sharer; Wesley G. Howell, Jr. (New York City and Los Angeles, California Offices); John F. Olson (Washington, D.C. Office); Andrew E. Bogen; Robert K. Montgomery (Century City and Los Angeles Offices); Theodore B. Olson (Washington, D.C. Office); John J. Swenson; John T. Behrendt (Los Angeles and New York City Offices); Charles K. Marquis (New York City and Los Angeles Offices); William J. Kilberg (Washington, D.C. Office); Charles S. Battles, Jr.; Robert T. Gelber; Kenneth E. Ristau, Jr. (Irvine Office); Bruce L. Gitelson (San Francisco and Palo Alto Offices); Dean Stern; Jack H. Halgren; Roy J. Schmidt, Jr. (Century City Office); Richard G. Duncan, Jr. (Irvine Office); John A. Ruskey; Fred F. Gregory; Kenneth W. Anderson; Stephen M. Blitz (Denver, Colorado Office); Ralph C. Wintrode (Irvine Office); Dwight L. Nye (Dallas, Texas Office); James G. Phillipp; Blake T. Franklin (New York City and Irvine Offices); David A. Cathcart; Robert C. Bonner (Washington, D.C. and Los Angeles, California Offices); Steven Alan Meiers; Arthur L. Sherwood; John C. Wells (Irvine Office); James R. Martin; Richard A. Strong; Richard D. Hall; William Stinehart, Jr. (Century City Office); R. Randall Huff; Lawrence Calof (San Francisco Office); John Edd Stepp, Jr.; Robert Forgnone; Charles C. Ivie; Bruce D. Meyer; Meldon E. Levine (Los Angeles and Washington, D.C. Offices); C. Ransom Samuelson II; J. Anthony Sinclitico, III (San Diego Office); Peter J. Wallison (Washington, D.C. Office); J. Michael Brennan (Irvine Office); Don Parris (Century City Office); Joseph H. Price (Washington, D.C. Office); Marc R. Isaacson; Michael D. Ryan; James C. Opel; Martin Carl Washton; Cantwell Faulkner Muckenfuss III (Washington, D.C. Office); Scott August Kruse; Wayne W. Smith (Los Angeles and Irvine Offices); Peter L. Baumbusch (Washington, D.C. Office); Richard Paul Levy; Robert D. Sack (New York City Office); Dennis A. Gladwell (Irvine Office); S. David Blinn (Los Angeles and Irvine Offices); Ronald S. Orr; Jonathan M. Landers (San Francisco Office); Irwin F. Sentilles, III (Dallas, Texas Office); Aulana L. Peters (Los Angeles and Washington, D.C. Offices); Fred Gilbert Bennett; Gerard J. Kenny (Irvine Office); James P. Clark (Century City Office); John A. Herfort (New York City Office); Lawrence J. Hohlt (New York City Office); Jerry J. Strochlic (New York City Office); Bennett L. Silverman; Kirk A. Patrick; Thomas E. Holliday; Peter F. Ziegler; Stephen C. Johnson (Dallas, Texas Office); Christopher H. Buckley, Jr. (Washington, D.C. Office); Gordon A. Schaller (Irvine Office); David R. Johnson (Washington, D.C. Office); Donald Harrison (Washington, D.C. Office); David G. Palmer (Denver, Colorado Office); Pamela A. Ray (Denver, Colorado Office); Gaynell C. Methvin (Dallas, Texas Office); Richard Michael Russo (Denver, Colorado Office); Phillip L. Bosl; Wayne A. Schrader (Washington, D.C. Office); William F. Highberger; Rex S. Heinke; Robert W. Loewen (Irvine Office); Anthony Bonanno (London, England Office); Peter H. Turza (Washington, D.C. Office); Jonathan L. Sulds (New York City Office); Charles F. Feldman (New York City Office); Conor D. Reilly (New York City Office); Dennis B. Arnold; Steven R. Finley (New York City Office); John J. A. Hossenlopp (New York City Office); Martin B. McNamara (Dallas, Texas Office); Michael L. Denger (Washington, D.C. Office); F. Joseph Warin (Washington, D.C. Office); Charles M. Schwartz (Dallas, Texas Office); Lawrence J. Ulman; Jane Lindsey Wingfield; Robert Everett Dean (Irvine Office); Thomas D. Magill (Irvine Office); George B. Curtis (Denver, Colorado Office); William D. Claster (Irvine Office); Joseph P. Busch III (Irvine Office); Pamela Lynn Hemminger; Donald E. Sloan (San Francisco Office); Daniel Q. Callister (Washington, D.C. Office); Fred L. Pillon (San Francisco Office); Denis R. Salmon (Palo Alto Office); Scott Blake Harris (Washington, D.C. Office); Larry C. Boyd (Irvine Office); E. Michael Greaney (Irvine, California and New York, N.Y. Offices); Nancy P. McClelland; Mary Laura Davis (Century City Office); H. Richard Dallas (New York City Office); John D. Fognani (Denver, Colorado Office); Howard B. Adler (Washington, D.C. Office); Karen H. Clark (Irvine Office); Dhiya El-Saden; Dean J. Kitchens; Jeffrey Reid Hudson; Charles A. Larson (Century City Office); Mark W. Shurtleff (Irvine Office); Christopher J. Martin (San Francisco and Palo Alto Offices); Lesley Sara Wolf; Peter Sullivan; Shari Leinwand (Century City Office); Gary L. Justice; Jonathan K. Layne; Scott A. Fink (San Francisco Office); William D. Connell (San Francisco Office); Gail Ellen Lees; Marjorie Ehrich Lewis; Timothy L. Dickinson (Washington, D.C. Office); David West; Russell C. Hansen (Century City Office); Walter L. Schindler (Irvine Office); William Edward Wegner (Los Angeles and Century City Offices); Meryl L. Young (San Diego Office); Larry L. Simms (Washington, D.C. Office); John H. Sturc (Washington, D.C. Office); Jonathan C. Dickey (Palo Alto Office); Scott R. Hoyt (Dallas, Texas Office); Rhonda S. Wagner (San Diego Office); Elizabeth A. Grimes; Paul D. Inman (Dallas, Texas Office); Mitchell A. Karlan (New York City Office); Thomas C. McGraw (Dallas, Texas Office); Michael A. Barrett (Washington, D.C. Office); Hatef Behnia; Joel A. Feuer; Kenneth M. Doran (Los Angeles and Century City Offices); J. Nicholson Thomas; Michael A. Monahan; Michele C. Coyle (Irvine Office); Susan Erburu Reardon; Karen E. Bertero; Robert C. Eager (Washington, D.C. Office); Ray T. Khirallah (Dallas, Texas Office); Robert L. Weigel (New York City Office); Mark E. Weber; Todd H. Baker (San Francisco Office); Stephen L. Tolles; Cheryl D. Justice; Jeffrey T. Thomas (Irvine Office); Steven Eugene Sletten; Baruch A. Fellner (Washington, D.C. Office); Patrick W. Dennis; Craig H. Millet (Irvine Office); Robert Bruce Vernon (New York City Office); Michael A. Rosenthal (Dallas, Texas Office); Mitri J. Najjar (London, England Office); Jennifer Bellah; Joel S. Sanders (San Francisco Office); Phillip Howard Rudolph (Washington, D.C. Office); Rory Michael Hernandez; Arthur David Pasternak (Washington, D.C.**

(This Listing Continued)

**Gibson, Dunn & Crutcher LLP (Continued)**

Office); Paul R. Harter (London, England Office); Terence P. Ross (Washington, D.C. Office); Kathryn Anne Coleman (San Francisco Office); John C. Millian (Washington, D.C. Office); Brian D. Kilb; Robert B. Krakow (Dallas, Texas Office); Thomas Satrom; M. Byron Wilder (Dallas, Texas Office); Robert E. Palmer (Irvine Office); Steven P. Buffone (New York City Office); Mark S. Pécheck; Daniel G. Swanson; Gregory J. Kerwin (Denver, Colorado Office); Scott A. Edelman (Los Angeles and Century City Offices); David B. Pendarvis (San Diego Office); David B. Rosenauer (New York City Office); Raymond B. Ludwiszewski (Washington, D.C. Office); Amy R. Forbes; David I. Schiller (Dallas, Texas Office); John R. Crews (Dallas, Texas Office); Kenneth R. Lamb (San Francisco Office); Joerg H. Esdorn (New York City Office); Daniel S. Floyd; William R. Lindsay; Clay A. Halvorsen (Century City Office); Robert Francis Serio (New York City Office); Kimmarie Sinatra (New York City Office); Steven A. Ruben; Thomas R. Denison (Denver, Colorado Office); Paul S. Issler; Kay Ellen Kochenderfer; Joseph M. Salamunovich; Richard J. Doren; Jesse Sharf; Sean P. Griffiths (New York City Office); Julia A. Dahlberg (Washington, D.C. Office); Patricia S. Radez (San Francisco Office); Timothy J. Hatch; Bradford P. Weirick; James P. Ricciardi (New York City Office); David Alan Battaglia; Theodore J. Boutrous, Jr. (Washington, D.C. Office); Brian W. Copple (Irvine Office); James Edward Bass (Hong Kong Office); Kevin S. Rosen; Hsiao-chiung Li (Hong Kong Office); Janet Popofsky Vance (New York City Office); Steven Mark Schultz; Judith A. Lee (Washington, D.C. Office); A. James Isbester (San Francisco Office); Bernard Grinspan (Paris, France Office); Jeffrey M. Trinklein (Dallas, Texas Office); Ronald O. Mueller (Washington, D.C. Office); Timothy J. Kay (Irvine Office); Douglas R. Cox (Washington, D.C. Office); Geniene B. Stillwell (Irvine Office); Chad S. Hummel; Steven R. Shoemate (New York City Office); Gregory Toll Davidson (San Francisco Office); John Novak (New York City Office); Kimberly S. McGovern (San Francisco Office); Susan M. Marcella; Thomas G. Hungar (Washington, D.C. Office); Wendy M. Singer (London, England and Paris, France Offices) (European Partner). Advisory Counsels: Sherman Seymour Welpton, Jr.; Julian O. von Kalinowski; F. Daniel Frost; Sharp Whitmore (San Diego Office); Francis M. Wheat; Arthur W. Schmutz; William F. Spalding; James R. Hutter; Robert D. Burch (Century City Office); John L. Endicott; John J. Hanson; Jerome C. Byrne; George W. Bermant (Denver, Colorado Office); Willard Z. Carr, Jr.; G. Edward Fitzgerald; Russell L. Johnson; Thomas B. Pitcher (Irvine Office); George H. Whitney; Frank L. Mallory (Irvine Office); John T. Pigott (Century City Office); Raymond L. Curran; Dean C. Dunlavey; Roy D. Miller; Guy K. Claire (Irvine Office); Herbert Kraus; Irwin F. Woodland; James M. Murphy; Paul G. Bower; Charles R. Collins (San Francisco Office); Leo G. Ziffren (Century City Office); Bruce A. Toor; Lester Ziffren (Century City Office); Michael E. Alpert (San Diego Office). Of Counsels: John A. Arguelles (Irvine Office); Peter J. Arturo; Kevin W. Barrett (New York City Office); Paul Blankenstein (Washington, D.C. Office); Susan B. Burr (Palo Alto Office); Sheila R. Caudle; Ellen J. Curnes (Dallas, Texas Office); Michael J. Eliasberg (Century City Office); Deborah S. Feinerman (Century City Office); Cynthia Leap Goldman (Denver, Colorado Office); Mark A. Grannis (Washington, D.C. Office); Xuhua Huang (New York City and Hong Kong Offices); Joanne Franzel (New York City Office); David W. Jackson (Jeddah, Saudi Arabia Office); Gary M. Joye; Sungyong Kang; David H. Kennedy (Washington, D.C. Office); Richard G. Lyon (Dallas, Texas Office); Robert A. McConnell (Washington, D.C. Office); Robert E. Mellor (San Francisco Office); John A. Mintz (Washington, D.C. Office); Nathan I. Nahm (New York City Office); John O'Halloran (Century City Office); Gonzalo Pardo de Zela (New York City Office); Malcolm R. Pfunder (Washington, D.C. Office); Thomas M. Piccone (Denver, Colorado Office); Therese D. Pritchard (Washington, D.C. Office); Amy G. Rudnick (Washington, D.C. Office); W. Richard Smith, Jr. (Irvine Office); Lawrence W. Treece (Denver, Colorado Office); Stephanie Tsacoumis (Washington, D.C. Office); William M. Wiltshire (Washington, D.C. Office). Special Counsels: Deborah E. Miller (New York City Office); Josiah O. Hatch III (Denver, Colorado Office); David Andrew Cheit (San Francisco Office); Derry Dean Sparlin Jr. (Washington, D.C. Office); Teresa Joanning Farrell (Irvine Office); April McGandy Evans; Marilyn G. McDowell; Brent M. Cohen (San Francisco Office); David C. Mahaffey (Washington, D.C. Office); I. Richard Levy (Dallas, Texas Office); Laura Ben-Porat (Century City Office); Thomas D. Boyle (Dallas, Texas Office); Stephen H. Willard (Washington, D.C. Office); Steven James Johnson (San Francisco Office); Kevin R. Nowicki (San Diego Office); John Masao Iino; Gary M. Roberts. Associates: Deborah Ann Aiwasian; Adam S. Bendell; Marianne Shipp (Irvine Office); Markus U. Diethelm (New York City Office); D. Eric Remensperger; Gregory L. Surman; Michael J. Keliher (Dallas, Texas Office); Alicia J. Bentley; Lawrence M. Isenberg; Mitchell Steven Cohen; Liisa Anselmi Stith (Irvine Office); Riaz A. Karamali (Palo Alto Office); Jeffrey David Dintzer; Carl Timothy Crow; Gregory J. Conklin (San Francisco Office); Peter C. D'Apice (Dallas, Texas Office); Leonard H. Hersh (New York City Office); Duncan T. O'Brien (New York City Office); Deborah J. Clarke; Vivienne Angela Vella; Margaret B. Graham (Denver, Colorado Office); Lawrence S. Achorn (San Francisco Office); Gunnar Blaise Gooding (Irvine Office); Cynthia L. Salmen; Scott Monro Dreyer; Adam H. Offenhartz (New York City Office); Gareth T. Evans; Jeffrey F. Webb; Rodney J. Stone; Desmond Cussen (San Francisco Office); Mark Snyderman (Washington, D.C. Office); Christopher J. Bellini (Washington, D.C. Office); David W. Mayo (New York City Office); Lawrence Byrne (New York City Office); Janet M. Weiss (New York City Office); Walter J. Scott, Jr. (Dallas, Texas Office); Margaret C. McCulla (Washington, D.C. Office); Diana Gale Richard (Washington, D.C. Office); Linda L. Curtis; Seeley Ann Brooks; J. Mark Dunbar (San Diego Office); Meredith C. Braxton (New York City Office); Stanton P. Eigenbrodt (Dallas, Texas Office); Oscar Garza (Irvine Office); Alan N. Bick (Irvine Office); John W. Fricks; Jeffrey T. Gilleran (Washington, D.C. Office); Kim A. Thompson (San Francisco Office); Cheryl Wright Olsen; Michael F. Flanagan (Washington, D.C. Office); Andrea E. Neuman (Irvine Office); John Andrew Yu-Cheng Chang; Clark D. Stith (Irvine Office); Eugene Scalia (Washington, D.C. Office); Robert E. Malchman (New York City Office); Henry A. Thompson (Jeddah, Riyadh and Washington, D.C. Offices); Christopher L. Thorne (Denver, Colorado Office); J. Fred Neuman (Irvine Office); Jerry S. Fowler, Jr. (Washington, D.C. Office); M. Sean Royall (Washington, D.C. Office); Ralph H. Blakeney (Dallas, Texas Office); Eben Paul Perison (Century City Office); Peter J. Beshar (New York City Office); Richard D. Gluck (San Diego Office); Jeffrey B. Conner (Not admitted in CA); Noël C. Lohr; Frédérique Sauvage (Not admitted in CA; Not admitted in United States); Scott M. Knutson (Irvine Office); Karl G. Nelson (Dallas, Texas Office); William A. MacArthur; Jeffrey H. Reeves (Irvine Office); William J. Gallagher (New York City Office); Marshall R. King (New York City Office); Scott J. Calfas; Jodi M. Newberry; J. Mitchell Dolloff (New York City Office); Mark R. Dunn (Dallas, Texas Office); Kristine D. Ristaino; Michael S. Udovic; Robert H. Wright; Laura A. Zwicker; John M. Williams, III (Irvine Office); Gregg P. Goldman (Irvine Office); David A. Levine (Washington, D.C. Office); Steven K. Talley (Denver, Colorado Office); Holly B. Windham (Dallas, Texas Office); Audrey S. Trundle (New York City Office); W. James Biederman (Washington, D.C. Office); Antoinette D. Paglia; Shahin Rezai (Washington, D.C. Office); Peter M. Stone (Irvine Office); Tracey Nelson Tiedman (Denver, Colorado Office); Mark J. Payne (Irvine Office); Charles F. Kester; Tanya S. McVeigh; Brian L. Duffy (Denver, Colorado Office); Rebecca A. Womeldorf (Washington, D.C. Office); James C. Dougherty (Washington, D.C. Office); Mark A. Perry (Washington, D.C. Office); Michele L. Sheldon (New York City Office); Leeanna Izuel; Preeta D. Bansal (New York City Office); Dara L. Freedman; Alan R. Struble (Dallas, Texas Office); James P. Fogelman; Cori L. MacDonneil; Craig V. Richardson (Denver, Colorado Office); Timothy L. Alger; Stella S. Leung (Hong Kong and Dallas, Texas Offices); Michael P. De Simone (New York City Office); Trygve M. Thoresen (Irvine Office); Richard B. Levy; Ignacio M. Foncillas (New York City Office); Maryn L. Miller (Irvine Office); Leslie Ellen Moore (New York City Office); Patricia E. Foley (Denver, Colorado Office); Jody L. Johnson; Michelle D. Lustig (Irvine Office); William L. Menard (Washington, D.C. Office); Elise D. Charbonnet (New York City Office); Maya R. Crone (Washington, D.C. Office); Sharyl P. Bilas (Irvine Office); Michael A. Levy (San Francisco Office); Chris D. Biondi (New York City Office); Brian E. Casey (Denver, Colorado Office); Lawrence J. La Sala (New York City Office); Matthew Ben Hinerfeld (San Francisco Office); David A. Segal (Irvine Office); Alan Lawhead (San Diego Office); Boyd M. Johnson III (New York City Office); Peter P. Murphy (Washington, D.C. Office); Steven N. Gofman; H. Mark Lyon (Palo Alto Office); Paul J. Collins (Palo Alto Office); Linda Greif (New York City Office); Timothy D. Blanton (Palo Alto Office); Daniel W. Nelson (Washington, D.C. Office); Leslie Y. Kim; Debra Alligood White; Jeffrey A. Fiarman (Washington, D.C. Office); Monique Michal Drake (Denver, Colorado Office); T. Michael Crimmins (Denver, Colorado Office); Timothy J. Hart; Leslie R. Olson (Irvine Office); Peter E. Seley (Washington, D.C. Office); Lisa A. Sleboda (New York City Office); Lindsey F. Buss (Washington, D.C. Office); Lisa M. Landmeier (Washington, D.C. Office); D. Jarrett Arp (Washington, D.C. Office); Lincoln D. Bandlow; Jeffrey D. Goldstein; Kathleen M. Vanderziel; Jon G. Shepherd (Dallas, Texas Office); Jason C. Murray (Los Angeles and Century City Offices); Donna M. Bigi (Irvine Office); Jonathan K. Tycko (Washington, D.C. Office); Kimberly Ann Udovic; Thomas S. Jones (Irvine Office); Stephanie Yost Cameron; Jonathan L. Israel (New York City Office); O. Rey Rodriguez (Dallas, Texas Office); Jeanette M. Bazis (Century City Office); Jessica Bolger Lee (Denver, Colorado Office); Deborah A. Hulse (Washington, D.C. Office); Torrey A. Olins (Irvine Office); Georgiana G. Rodiger; Stephen B. Dorrough; Catherine Herrin Gorecki (Washington, D.C. Office); Paul B. Lackey (Dallas, Texas Office); Charles R. Bogle (New York City Office); Stacy V. Brown (New York City Office); Corinne A. Franzen; Thomas G. Mackey; Frederick A. Walters (New York City Office); Rebecca Sanhueza (San Francisco Office); Cosmas N. Lykos (Irvine Office); Shelley R. Meacham; William M. Rustum (Century City Office); Mary Sikra Thomas; Michelle M. Brissette (Denver, Colorado Office); Laura C. Roche (Palo Alto Office); Mary K. Porter (Denver, Colorado Office); Brian Jaywoo Kim; David N. King; Lila E. Rogers; Hilary Joy Hatch; Michael L. Reed (Century City Office); Lara M. Krieger (New York City Office); Albert R. Morales (New York City Office); Theodore A. Russell; Todd M. Noonan (San Francisco

(This Listing Continued)



**Gibson, Dunn & Crutcher LLP (Continued)**

Office); Tracey M. Whitney; Christopher D. Dusseault; Jeffrey E. Oraker (Denver, Colorado Office); Simone Procas (New York City Office); Christina L. Rooke (San Francisco Office); Alex E. Sadler (Washington, D.C. Office); Adam E. Muchnick (Irvine Office); Ellen L. Farrell; Sue J. Nam (New York City Office); Pauline H. Yoo (New York City Office); C. Glen Morris (Dallas, Texas Office); Sabrina Y. T. Fang (Hong Kong Office); Sean E. Andrussier (Washington, D.C. Office); Helgard C. Walker (Washington, D.C. Office); Hillary S. Zilz (New York City Office); Brette S. Simon; Sahily H. Feliciano; Robert R. Stark, Jr. (Denver, Colorado Office); Andrew H. Caudal (Dallas, Texas Office); Kelby D. Hagar (Dallas, Texas Office); John C. Conway; Arun Jha; Mark N. Mazda (Irvine Office); Natalie Kay Sidles (Dallas, Texas Office); Paul A. Andronico (Irvine Office); James P. Maniscalco; Michael E. Sanders (Irvine Office); Todd D. Kantorczyk (Washington, D.C. Office); Connie J. Rand (San Diego Office); Dylan K. Remley (New York City Office); Lisa A. Alfaro (New York City Office); Rachael A. Simonoff; Douglas C. Freeman (New York City Office); Sean C. Carr (Washington, D.C. Office); Jeff Augustini (Irvine Office); Wendy A. Lutzker; Jennifer R. Poe (Dallas, Texas Office); Tiffany Doon Silva; Walker J. Wallace III (New York City Office); Daniel H. Baren (Irvine Office); Todd S. Cohen (New York City Office); Michele J. Herschkowitz (New York City Office); Laurie McLaughlin (New York City Office); Stacy S. Shibao (Washington, D.C. Office); Samuel G. Liversidge; Timothy S. Lykowski; Stewart L. McDowell (New York City Office); Hassan A. Zavareei (Washington, D.C. Office); Julie R. Zebrak (Washington, D.C. Office); Richard F. Romero; Joanne S. Field; Michael Pierovich; Kevin F. Mabrey; Holli H. Payne (San Diego Office); Sachin D. Adarkar (San Francisco Office); Jay P. Srinivasan; Thomas R. Greenberg; Robert H. Pritchard, Jr. (New York City Office); Daniel N. Shallman; Karin L. Wolff (New York City Office); Gavin A. Beske (San Francisco Office); Jeffrey L. Mengoli (San Diego Office); S. Elizabeth Foster (New York City Office); Michael D. Newton; Phillip F. Smith, Jr. (Denver, Colorado Office); Jesse S. Finlayson (Irvine Office); Allison C. Goodman (Washington, D.C. Office); Raymond Ku (Washington, D.C. Office); Linda Richichi Stahl (Dallas, Texas Office); Michael A. Barmettler (Irvine Office); Kate Jeffery Stoia (San Francisco Office); Jill M. Dennis (Washington, D.C. Office); Colleen R. McMillin (Dallas, Texas Office); Seth M. M. Stodder; Inna Idelchik (New York City Office); Roger P. Capriotti; Daisy C. Wu; Daniel T. Perini (Denver, Colorado Office); Jean De Forest Billyou (Irvine Office); Jonathan M. Fingeret (Denver, Colorado Office); Abdul Aziz I. Al-Ajlan (Riyadh, Saudi Arabia Office); Abdullah A. Al Habardi (Riyadh, Saudi Arabia Office). Staff Attorneys: William H. Boyles (Dallas, Texas Office); Margaret Ann Garner (Washington, D.C. Office); Sally Novak Janin (Washington, D.C. Office); Brian R. Kirchoff (Irvine Office); Sharon W. Koplan (Dallas, Texas Office); Christine Naylor; Linda Noonan (Washington, D.C. Office); Irene M. Ramirez (Dallas, Texas Office); Roberto Redondo (New York City Office); Randy Rhodes; Kenneth A. Schagrin (Washington, D.C. Office); Anna C. Silva (San Francisco Office); Sydney M. Smith (Washington, D.C. Office); Mark Oneal Suttle; Kathleen G. Vagt (Washington, D.C. Office); Melinda Dalton Waterman (Irvine Office).

General Civil, Trial and Appellate Practice, State and Federal Courts. Antitrust Law. Specialized Criminal Defense. General Corporation, Securities, Administrative, Labor and Employment, Taxation, Estate Planning, Probate and Trust, International Business, Entertainment, Commercial, Insolvency, Bankruptcy and Reorganization, Natural Resources, Oil and Gas, Environmental Energy, Municipal and Public Utility Law.

Century City, Los Angeles, California Office: 2029 Century Park East, Suite 4000. Telephone: 310-552-8500. Telecopier: 310-551-8741. Cable Address: GIBTRASKCC LOS ANGELES.

Irvine, California Office: 4 Park Plaza, Suites 1400, 1500, 1700 and 1800. Telephone: 714-451-3800. Telecopier: 714-451-4220.

San Diego, California Office: 750 B Street, Suite 3300. Telephone: 619-544-8000. Telecopier: 619-544-8190; 619-544-8191.

San Francisco, California Office: One Montgomery Street, 26th Floor and 31st Floor. Telephone: 415-393-8200. Telecopier: 415-986-5309.

Palo Alto, California Office: 525 University Avenue, Suite 220. Telephone: 415-463-7300. Telecopier: 415-463-7333.

Denver, Colorado Office: 1801 California Street, Suite 4100. Telephone: 303-298-5700. Telecopier: 303-296-5310.

Washington, D.C. Office: 1050 Connecticut Avenue, N.W. Telephone: 202-955-8500. Telex: 197659 GIBTRASK WSH (TRT), 892501 GIBTRASK WSH (WUT). Telecopier: 202-467-0539. Cable Address: GIBTRASK WASHINGTON DC.

New York, New York Office: 200 Park Avenue. Telephone: 212-351-4000. Telecopier: 212-351-4035. Cable Address: GIBTRASK NEWYORK.

Dallas, Texas Office: 1717 Main Street, Suite 5400. Telephone: 214-698-3100. Telecopier: 214-698-3400.

Paris, France Office: 104 Avenue Raymond Poincare, 75116. Telephone: 011-33-1-45-01-93-83. Telecopier: 011-33-1-45-00-69-59. Cable Address: GIBTRAK PARIS.

London, England Office: 30/35 Pall Mall, SW1Y 5LP. Telephone: 011-44-171-925-0440. Telex: 27731 GIBTRK G; 916176 GIBTRK G. Telecopier: 011-44-171-925-2465. Cable Address: GIBTRASK LONDON W1.

Affiliated Jeddah, Saudi Arabia Office: Law Office of Abdulaziz Fahad, Sixth Floor, Haji Hussein Alireza Building, Bab Makkah, Post Office Box 16206, Jeddah, 21464. Telephone: 011-966-2-644-2663. Telecopier: 011-966-2-643-5401.

Affiliated Riyadh, Saudi Arabia Office: Law Office of Abdulaziz Fahad, Jarir Plaza, 4th Floor, Olaya Street, Post Office Box 15870, Riyadh, 11454. Telephone: 011-966-1-464-8081. Telex: 406176 LAWS SJ. Telecopier: 011-966-1-462-4968.

Hong Kong Office: 10th Floor, Two Pacific Place, 88 Queensway. Telephone: 011-852-2526-6816. Telex: 65665 GIBTK HX. Telecopier: 011-852-2845-9144.

*See Professional Biographies, LOS ANGELES, CALIFORNIA*

**Gibson, Richard H., Law Offices of, (AV)** [BR]
**Wells Fargo Center, 333 South Grand Avenue, Suite 1860, 90071**
Telephone: 213-617-1185 Facsimile: 213-617-1902
Richard H. Gibson.
Bankruptcy, Real Estate, Business Law and Civil Litigation.

*See Professional Biographies, LOS ANGELES, CALIFORNIA*

**Gibson and Rivera**
(See Pasadena)

Gichtin, Karen L. .................... '63 '92 C.1097 B.S. L.426 J.D. 777 S. Figueroa St.
**Giddens, Brent Matthew** .......... '62 '88 C.178 B.A. L.800 J.D. [Sonnenschein N.&R.]
*PRACTICE AREAS: Labor/Employment for Management Law.
**Giden, Joseph M.**, (AV) ............. '33 '59 C.197 A.B. L.309 LL.B. [Gibbs,G.L.&A.]
*PRACTICE AREAS: Title Insurance Law; Fidelity and Surety Law; Construction Law.
**Giden, Michael I.** .................. '62 '93 C.311 B.A. L.1184 J.D. [Ⓐ Gibbs,G.L.&A.]
*PRACTICE AREAS: Construction Law; Title Insurance.
Giedzinski, Steven P. .................... '63 '93 C.112 B.A. L.800 J.D. Dep. Dist. Atty.
**Giesler, Gary H.** ........................ '41 '67 C.112 B.A. L.800 J.D. [Knapp,M.J.&D.]
*PRACTICE AREAS: Real Property Law; Business Law; Litigation.
**Gifford, Eugenie A.** ...................... '68 '93 C.31 B.A. L.112 J.D. [Ⓐ Frye,A.&M.]
*PRACTICE AREAS: Insurance Bad Faith; Insurance Coverage; Insurance Defense.
**Gifford, G. Grant**, (AV) .................. '45 '71 C.605 A.B. L.1068 J.D. [Gifford&D.]
*PRACTICE AREAS: Trusts; Private Foundations; Real Estate Transactions; Wills; Probate Administration.
**Gifford, L. Andrew**, (AV) ................. '46 '72 C.473 B.S. L.477 J.D. [Riordan&M.]
Gifford, Margaret Rawls ........ '58 '85 C.605 A.B. L.809 J.D. 500 S. Virgil Ave., 4th Fl.

**Gifford & Dearing, (AV)**
**Suite 1222, 700 South Flower Street, 90017**
Telephone: 213-626-4481 Fax: 213-627-3719
Members of Firm: G. Grant Gifford; Henry H. Dearing. Associate: Michele L. Abernathy.
General Civil and Trial Practice in all State Courts. Corporation, Estate Planning, Trust and Probate Law.
Reference: Bank of America, Los Angeles, California (Head Office, Trust Dept.).

*See Professional Biographies, LOS ANGELES, CALIFORNIA*

Gilbert, Allen L. ............... '53 '78 C.112 B.A. L.800 J.D. Metropolitan Theatres Corp.
**Gilbert, J. Thomas** ....................... '63 '87 C&L.69 B.F.A., J.D. [Ⓐ Cummins&W.]
*PRACTICE AREAS: Insurance Coverage and Litigation; Products Liability; Medical Malpractice; Commercial Litigation.
**Gilbert, James M.** ..................... '64 '90 C.1097 B.A. L.809 J.D. [Ⓢ Fulbright&J.]
*PRACTICE AREAS: Real Estate Litigation; Business Litigation; Banks and Banking; Litigation.

**Gilbert, Judith A.** .......... '46 '71 C.112 B.A. L.309 J.D. [Arter&H.]
*PRACTICE AREAS: Finance and Insolvency; Entertainment Finance; Insolvency; Copyright; Entertainment.
Gilbert, Julie A. '55 '81 C.112 B.A. L.1067 J.D.
V.P. & Gen. Coun., European Invest. Mgmt. Serv. Inc.
Gilbert, M. Glenn .......... '49 '75 C.800 B.S. L.1068 J.D. 801 S. Grand Ave.
Gilbert, Mark E. .......... '50 '77 C.1077 B.S. L.1137 J.D. Dep. Pub. Def.
Gilbert, Marlene F. '40 '79
C.012 B.A. L.1136 J.D. Sr. Coun., Auto. Club of Southern Calif.
Gilbert, Norman J. .......... '31 '55 C.912 B.S. L.477 J.D. Asst. Co. Coun.
Gilbert, Paul A. .......... '43 '79 C.800 A.B. L.1221 J.D. Smith, Barney & Co.
**Gilbert, Richard E.**, (AV) .......... '46 '73 C.30 B.A. L.904 J.D. [Freeman,F.&S.] (ⓞIrvine)
*PRACTICE AREAS: Estate Planning; Tax and Related Business Planning.
Gilbert, Robert W. .......... '20 '44 C.112 A.B. L.1066 LL.B. [Gilbert&S.]

**Gilbert, Kelly, Crowley & Jennett, (AV)**
**1200 Wilshire Boulevard, 90017ⓞ**
**Telephone: 213-580-7000 Fax: 213-580-7100**
**Members of Firm: W. I. Gilbert (1876-1940); W. I. Gilbert, Jr. (1906-1972); John D. St. Pierre (1930-1981); Thomas J. Viola; Robert W. Rau; Michael J. Maloney; Patrick A. Mesisca, Jr.; Clayton E. Cooper; Stephen M. Moloney; Arthur J. McKeon III; John J. Russo; Jon H. Tisdale; Peter J. Godfrey; Paul A. Bigley; Eugene J. Landau; Rodney L. Terrazone; Randall W. Kaler; Peter R. Nelson; James J. Perkins; Mary-Claire Mira. Of Counsel: Roger E. Kelly; James B. Crowley; William D. Jennett; Clifford H. Woosley; Lisa A. Satter. Associates: Scott E. Braybrooke; Frank Cannizzaro; Carolyn Wagner Crowley; Leah D. Davis; Owen E. Girard; Vanessa H. Hubert; Thomas Joseph Jennett; Cheryl Hannah Karz; Francine B. Kelly; Catherine Lukehart; Scott L. MacDonald; Ronald MaWhinney; Maureen O'Grady Nix; R. Timothy O'Connor; Gregory J. Pedrick; Derek A. Simpson; Rebecca J. Smith; Terry Lynn Smith.**
**General Civil and Trial Practice in all State and Federal Courts. Appellate Practice. Corporation and Insurance Law.**
**Orange County Office: Suite 310 Nexus Financial Center, 721 South Parker Street, Orange, California. Telephone: 714-541-5000. Fax: 714-541-0670.**
**Riverside County Office: 3801 University Avenue, Suite 700, Riverside, California. Telephone: 909-276-4000. Fax: 909-276-4100.**
**San Diego, California Office: 501 West Broadway, Suite 1260 Koll Center. Telephone: 619-687-3000. Fax: 619-687-3100.**
*See Professional Biographies, LOS ANGELES, CALIFORNIA*

**Gilbert-Lurie, Clifford W.** .......... '54 '79 C.112 A.B. L.1066 J.D. [Ziffren,B.B.&F.]
*PRACTICE AREAS: Entertainment Law.
Gilbert & Sackman, A Law Corp. .......... 6100 Wilshire Blvd.
**Gilbertson, John T.** .......... '62 '93 C.475 B.A. L.896 J.D. [Musick,P.&G.]
*PRACTICE AREAS: Healthcare; General Corporate.
**Gilchrest, Robert M.** .......... '61 '87 C.1307 B.A. L.597 J.D. [Jones,D.R.&P.]

**Gilchrist & Rutter, Professional Corporation, (AV)**
**355 South Grand Avenue, Suite 4100, 90071ⓞ**
**Telephone: 213-617-8000 Facsimile: 213-346-7973**
**Thomas E. Stindt.**
**Real Estate, Business, Corporate, Partnerships, Commercial, Taxation and Environmental Law, Civil, Business, Intellectual Property and Securities Litigation in State and Federal Courts, Debtor/Creditor Rights, Commercial Law and Corporate Reorganization, and Estate Planning.**
**Santa Monica, California Office: 1299 Ocean Avenue, Suite 900. Telephone: 310-393-4000. Facsimile: 310-394-4700.**
*See Professional Biographies, LOS ANGELES, CALIFORNIA*

Gilder, Mark H. .......... '47 '76 C.1077 B.S. L.809 LL.B. 5455 WilshireBlvd.
Giles, Margaret S. .......... '58 '92 C.197 B.A. L.426 J.D. 725 S. Figueroa St.
Gilfillan, Gail S. .......... '60 '93 C.112 B.S. L.990 J.D. [Fuchs&M.]
**Gilford, Andrew M.** .......... '63 '89 C&L.112 B.A., J.D. [McClintock,W.B.R.R.&M.]
*PRACTICE AREAS: Civil Appellate Practice; Environmental Litigation; Commercial and General Business Litigation.
**Gilhuly, Peter M.** .......... '61 '90 C.918 B.A. L.309 J.D. [Latham&W.]
*LANGUAGES: Nepali.
*TRANSACTIONS: Chapter 11 Debtor Representations: Wherehouse Entertainment, Inc.; Acme Holdings, Inc. (Prepackaged Bankruptcy); Cherokee, Inc.; First Executive Corporation.
*PRACTICE AREAS: Bankruptcy (80%); Corporate (20%).
**Gill, Daniel H.** .......... '63 '91 C.113 B.A. L.112 J.D. [Danning,G.D.&K.]
**Gill, David A., (A Professional Corporation)**, (AV) '36 '62
C.112 B.A. L.813 J.D. [Danning,G.D.&K.]
**Gill, Lawrence B.** .......... '66 '95 [Milbank,T.H.&M.]
**Gill, Michael J.**, (AV) .......... '44 '70 C.684 A.B. L.426 J.D. [Seaver&G.]
*PRACTICE AREAS: Probate and Trust Administration; Conservatorships; Probate, Trust and Elder Abuse Litigation; Estate Planning.
Gill, Michael Min-Taek .......... '51 '81 C.061 B.S. L.809 J.D. 3250 Wilshire Blvd.
**Gill, Thomas R.** .......... '55 '88 C.1077 B.A. L.426 J.D. [Manning,M.&W.]

**Gill and Baldwin**
**(See Glendale)**

Gillam, Anne C. .......... '59 '87 C.112 L.809 Pub. Def. Off.

**Gillam, Carol L., Law Offices of**
**(See Torrance)**

**Giller, Richard C.** .......... '58 '85 C.321 B.A. L.809 J.D. [Charlston,R.&W.]
**Giller, Ronald K.** .......... '63 '89 C.112 B.A. L.1068 J.D. [Paul,H.J.&W.]
**Gillespie, Margaret H.** .......... '65 '90 C.813 B.A. L.1068 J.D. [Orrick,H.&S.]
**Gillespie, William T.** .......... '59 '88 C.112 B.A. L.426 J.D. [Pillsbury M.&S.]
**Gillett, Mark T.** .......... '62 '90 C.999 B.A. L.309 J.D. [Morrison&F.]
Gillig, Susan Cordell .......... '46 '79 C.061 B.A. L.800 J.D. U.C.L.A. Sch. of Law
Gilliland, Jean E. .......... '61 '87 C.605 A.B. L.802 J.D. Asst. U.S. Atty.
Gillott, Eloise F. .......... '53 '83 C.1046 B.A. L.990 J.D. Dep. Dist. Atty.
Gilman, Christopher M. .......... '50 '75 C.112 B.S. L.1068 J.D. 2720 Midvale
Gilman, Hugh M. .......... '20 '78 C.102 B.A. L.1136 J.D. 3558 Barry Ave.‡
Gilmer, Michele D. .......... '58 '86 C.276 B.A. L.284 J.D. Dep. Dist. Atty.
**Gilmore, Danielle L.** .......... '67 '94 C.597 B.S. L.273 J.D. [Troop M.S.&P.]
*PRACTICE AREAS: Litigation; Insurance Coverage.
Gilmore, David J. .......... '53 '78 C.112 B.A. L.426 J.D. 633 W. 5th St.
**Gilmore, Scott L.**, (AV) .......... '53 '78 C&L.800 B.S., J.D. [Hill,F.&B.]
*PRACTICE AREAS: Business Litigation; Real Estate Litigation; Construction Litigation.
Gilson, James R. '51 '78 C.918 B.A. L.910 J.D.
V.P., Los Angeles Co. Museum of Natural History
Gilson, Stanley W. .......... '48 '80 C.1077 B.A. L.809 J.D. Legal Div., Dept. of Transp.
**Gindler, Burton J.**, (AV) .......... '27 '51 C&L.494 B.S.L., J.D. [Morrison&F.]
*PRACTICE AREAS: Environmental Law; Water Resources; Water Quality Law; Service Duplication Under California Public Utility Code; Privatization of Municipal Utilities.
**Gindler, David I.** .......... '59 '85 C.668 B.A. L.1068 J.D. [Bryan C.]
**Ginger, Stephen R.** .......... '56 '82 C.1131 B.A. L.809 J.D. [Condon&F.]
Gingold, Lawrence H. .......... '40 '71 C.112 B.S. L.809 J.D. 522 S. Greta Green Way‡
Ginnow, Amy J. .......... '51 '85 C.483 B.A. L.61 J.D. 3580 Wilshire Blvd.
Ginoza, Donn .......... '52 '79 C.604 A.B. L.665 J.D. Legal Aid Found. of L.A.
Ginsberg, David M. '51 '80 C&L.800 B.A., J.D.
Dir., Bus. Affs., Metrolight Studios, Inc.
**Ginsberg, Larry A.**, (AV) .......... '59 '86 C.966 B.A. L.990 J.D. [Harris G.]
*PRACTICE AREAS: Family Law.

**Ginsberg, Lawrence A., (A Professional Corporation)** '52 '80
C.1036 B.A. L.94 J.D. [Mitchell,S.&K.]
*PRACTICE AREAS: Labor Law; Employment Law; Litigation; Discrimination Law; Litigation.
**Ginsburg, James A.**, (AV) .......... '43 '69 C&L.494 B.S.B., J.D. [De Castro,W.&C.]
*PRACTICE AREAS: Real Estate Law; Business Law.
Ginsburg, Reuben .......... '65 '89 C.197 A.B. L.477 J.D. 11835 W. Olympic Blvd.
**Ginsburg, William H.**, (AV) .......... '43 '67 C.112 B.A. L.800 J.D. [Ginsburg,S.O.&R.]

**Ginsburg, Stephan, Oringher & Richman, P.C., (AV)**
**10100 Santa Monica Boulevard Eighth Floor, 90067-4012ⓞ**
**Telephone: 310-557-2009 Fax: 310-551-0283**
**William H. Ginsburg; George J. Stephan; Harvey T. Oringher; David S. Richman; Michael C. Thornhill;—Naida L. Brown; Christopher M. Daniels; Myrna L. D'Incognito; Linda Hatcher; Nancy B. Hersman; David J. Masutani; Gerald J. Miller; Dean J. Smith; Peter Weinberger. Of Counsel: Gordon E. Bosserman; Arthur R. Chenen; Richard J. Decker; Bruce E. Dizenfeld; Terrence M. King.**
**General Civil Practice, General Business Litigation, Health Care Law, Corporate and Business Transactions, Professional Liability Defense, Employment Litigation, Coverage Litigation, Intellectual Property Litigation, White Collar Criminal Defense, Real Estate Litigation, Product Liability, Securities Fraud and RICO Defense, Consumer Credit Litigation, Copyright, Trademark, Antitrust and Unfair Competition Law.**
**Costa Mesa, California Office: 535 Anton Boulevard, Suite 800, 92626-1902. Telephone: 714-241-0420. Fax: 714-241-0622.**
*See Professional Biographies, LOS ANGELES, CALIFORNIA*

Ginzburg, Daniel S. .......... '67 '93 C.1036 B.A. L.809 J.D. 1900 Ave. of the Stars
**Giovannetti, Robert J.**, (AV) .......... '46 '72 C.867 B.A. L.178 J.D. [Jackson,L.S.&K.]
**Giovanniello, Alexander F.** .......... '59 '86 C.1044 B.S. L.1049 J.D. [Bottum&F.]ⓞ
*LANGUAGES: Italian.
*PRACTICE AREAS: Professional Malpractice Law; Civil Law; Trial Practice; Insurance Law; Corporate Law.
**Gipson, Robert E. (Reg)**, (AV) .......... '46 '73 C.309 A.B. L.976 J.D. [Gipson H.&P.]
*PRACTICE AREAS: General Business; General Counsel for Private Companies; Tax Law; Real Estate Law.

**Gipson Hoffman & Pancione, A Professional Corporation, (AV)**
**Suite 1100, 1901 Avenue of the Stars, 90067-6002ⓞ**
**Telephone: 310-556-4660 Telex: 910-490-2531 GHST LAW; Fax: 310-556-8945, 310-556-4301**
**Email: mail@ghplaw.com**
**Markus W. Barmettler (Resident, Zurich, Switzerland Office); Lawrence R. Barnett; Jack Brandon; Vincent H. Chieffo; Peter F. Del Greco; Robert E. (Reg) Gipson; John R. McHale; Mara Morner-Ritt; Peter R. Pancione; Ann L. Parsons; Ellen J. Shadur; Kenneth I. Sidle; Mary K. Solberg; Corey J. Spivey; Robert H. Steinberg. Of Counsel: Jeffrey M. Boren; G. Raymond F. Gross; Julia L. Ross; Norman D. Sloan.**
**Business, Entertainment and Tax Litigation. Corporate and Banking. Corporate and Securities Matters. Domestic and International Taxation. General Business. Motion Picture Financing and Securities Transactions. Motion Picture, Television and Music Production, Distribution and Talent Representation. Real Estate and Real Estate Securities.**
**Zurich, Switzerland Office: Zeppelinstrasse 28, CH-8057. Telephone: 011-411-364-2600. Telefax: 011-411-364-2713.**
*See Professional Biographies, LOS ANGELES, CALIFORNIA*

Girard, Julia M. .......... '57 '84 C.426 B.A. L.1068 J.D. Times Mirror Sq.
**Girard, Owen E.** .......... '65 '95 C.546 B.A. L.190 J.D. [Gilbert,K.C.&J.]
*PRACTICE AREAS: Insurance Defense.
**Girard, Robert D.**, (AV) .......... '46 '71 C.112 A.B. L.976 LL.B. [Musick,P.&G.]
*PRACTICE AREAS: Healthcare; Hospitals; Corporate Law.
**Girardi, John A.**, (AV) .......... '47 '72 C.602 B.A. L.426 J.D. [Girardi&K.]
*PRACTICE AREAS: Civil Trials; Professional Negligence; Government Entity Negligence; Product Liability; Toxic Tort Litigation.
**Girardi, Thomas V.**, (AV) .......... '39 '65 C&L.426 B.S., LL.B. [Girardi&K.]
*PRACTICE AREAS: Professional Liability; Toxic Torts; Business Litigation; Entertainment Law Litigation.

**Girardi and Keese, (AV)**
**1126 Wilshire Boulevard, 90017-1904ⓞ**
**Telephone: 213-977-0211 FAX: 213-481-1554**
**Members of Firm: Thomas V. Girardi; Robert M. Keese; John A. Girardi; James B. Kropff; Robert W. Finnerty; James G. O'Callahan; V. Andre Rekte (Resident, San Bernardino Office); John K. Courtney; Amy Fisch Solomon; Thomas C. Morgan; David N. Bigelow; Carrie J. Rognlien.**
**General Civil and Trial Practice in all State and Federal Courts. Business Litigation, Entertainment Law, Professional Negligence, Environmental Law, Toxic Torts, Personal Injury, Products Liability, Appellate Practice.**
**References: Wells Fargo Bank (Los Angeles Head Office); Bank of Industry.**
**San Bernardino, California Office: 596 North Arrowhead. Telephone: 714-381-1551. FAX: 714-381-2566.**
*See Professional Biographies, LOS ANGELES, CALIFORNIA*

Gire, Richard O. .......... '48 '91 C.763 B.S. L.426 J.D. V.P., Legal & Bus. Affs., A.C.I.
**Giss, Deborah** .......... '63 '90 C.1077 B.A. L.208 J.D. [Katten M.&Z.]
*PRACTICE AREAS: Corporate Insurance; Healthcare.
Giss, Harvey, (AV) .......... '39 '65 C.112 B.A. L.1068 LL.B. Sr. Prosecutor, Dist. Atty. Off.

**Gitlin-Petlak, Laura, (BV) '57 '84 C.118 B.A. L.424 J.D.**
**9314 West Pico Boulevard, Suite 222, 90035**
**Telephone: 310-277-4272 FAX: 310-277-3837**
**(Certified Specialist, Family Law, The State Bar of California Board of Legal Specialization).**
***LANGUAGES: French.**
***PRACTICE AREAS: Family Law; Marital Law; Adoption Law; Domestic Relations Law; Children's Law.**
**Family Law, Divorce, Custody, Paternity, QDRO's, Adoption Law, Children's Law, Division of Assets and Debts.**

**Gitman, David, (Professional Corporation)** '52 '77
C.339 B.A. L.424 J.D. [Resch P.A.&B.]
*PRACTICE AREAS: Taxation; Business Law.
**Gitt, Cynthia E.**, (AV) .......... '46 '71 C.938 B.A. L.273 J.D. [Epstein B.&G.]
**Gitterman, Judith B.** .......... '57 '84 C.659 B.A. L.188 J.D. [Solish,A.&G.]
*REPORTED CASES: Cislaw v. 7-Eleven, 4 Cal. App. 4th 1284; Martin v. The Southland Corporation, Bus. Franchise Guide (CCH) ¶11,019 (Cal.App. 1996).
*PRACTICE AREAS: Franchise Law; Business Litigation; Appellate Law.
Gittler, Gregg J., (AV) .......... '48 '73 C&L.813 A.B., J.D. [Gittler,W.&B.]
Gittler, Wexler & Bradford, (AV) .......... 11620 Wilshire Boulevard, Suite 800
**Giunta, Joseph J.** .......... '48 '77 C.813 B.S. L.904 J.D. [Skadden,A.S.M.&F.]
**Giunta, Linda M.** .......... '65 '90 C.874 B.A. L.245 J.D. [Troop M.S.&P.]
*PRACTICE AREAS: Corporate; Securities; Mergers and Acquisitions.
Givens, C. Eugene, (AV) .......... '33 '65 C.197 A.B. L.597 J.D. 624 S. Grand Ave.
Givner, Bruce, (AV) .......... '50 '76 C.112 B.A. L.178 J.D. 12100 Wilshire Blvd.
Givner, Kathleen Graham .......... '55 '87 C.208 B.A. L.800 J.D. 12100 Wilshire Blvd.
**Givner, Ronald P.** .......... '45 '71 C.112 B.A. L.1068 J.D. [Jeffer,M.B.&M.]
*PRACTICE AREAS: Federal and State Securities; General Corporate; Mergers and Acquisitions.
**Glabach, G. Frank** .......... '55 '81 C.373 B.A. L.912 J.D. [Liner,Y.&S.]
*PRACTICE AREAS: Taxation Law; Business Law; Securities Law; Corporate Law; Partnership Law.
Glad, Edward N., (AV) .......... '19 '49 C.627 L.477 J.D. [Glad&F.]
Glad & Ferguson, (AV) .......... 606 S. Olive St. (ⓞSan Fran.)
Gladson, Marcie .......... '66 '92 C.112 B.A. L.1067 J.D. Bet Tzedek Legal Servs.
**Gladstone, Brian J.** .......... '63 '93 C.569 B.F.A., L.276 J.D. [Hawkins,S.L.&B.]
**Gladstone, Leon J.** .......... '51 '76 C.112 A.B. L.1065 J.D. [Berger,K.S.M.F.S.&G.]

CAA233P

CALIFORNIA—LOS ANGELES
MARTINDALE-HUBBELL LAW DIRECTORY 1997

**Glaser, Barry S.**, (AV) ... '47 '76 C.1077 B.A. L.809 J.D. [Burke,W.&S.]
*PRACTICE AREAS: Bankruptcy; Corporate Reorganization; Creditors Rights; Real Estate and Title Insurance Litigation.
Glaser, Harvey A., (AV) ... '28 '63 C.800 B.S. L.809 LL.B. 2566 Overland Ave.
Glaser, Jerome J., (AV) ... '35 '61 C.112 A.B. L.800 LL.B. 3313 Patricia St.
Glaser, John Stephen, (AV) ... '42 '79 C.800 B.A. L.426 J.D. [Manulkin,G.&B.]
**Glaser, Patricia**, (AV) ... '47 '73 C.30 B.A. L.1292 J.D. [Christensen,M.F.J.G.W.&S.]
*PRACTICE AREAS: Civil Litigation; Entertainment.
**Glaser, Steven H.** ... '58 '85 C.112 B.A. L.800 J.D. [Gelfand&G.]
*PRACTICE AREAS: Business Litigation.
Glass, Paul F., (AV) ... '54 '79 C.1077 B.A. L.1095 J.D. [West,P.&G.]
**Glass, Steven R.**, (AV) ... '50 '75 C.112 B.A. L.809 J.D. [Glass,A.G.&C.]⊙
*PRACTICE AREAS: Creditors Rights; Commercial Law; Insolvency; Equipment/Personal Property Leasing; Secured Transactions.

**Glass, Alper, Goldberg & Cohn, A Law Corporation, (AV)**
**856 South Robertson Boulevard, 90035-1601⊙**
**Telephone: 818-715-7000 Telecopier: 818-715-7025**
**Ronald R. Cohn; Marshall F. Goldberg; Andrew K. Alper; Steven R. Glass;—Joe R. Abramson.**
**Business, Commercial and Insolvency Litigation representing creditors, Banking, Creditors Rights, Equipment and Personal Property Leasing, Secured Transactions and Real Estate Law.**
**Representative Clients: Chase Commercial Corp.; General Electric Capital Corp.; McDonnell Douglas Finance Corp.**
**Woodland Hills, California Office: 21700 Oxnard Street, Suite 430.**

*See Professional Biographies, LOS ANGELES, CALIFORNIA*

**Glasser, Paul N.** ... '58 '86 C.112 B.A. L.629 J.D. [🄰 Billet&K.]
*PRACTICE AREAS: Civil Litigation.
**Glassman, Frederick J., (P.C.)**, (AV) '39 '66 C.352 B.A. L.1068 LL.B. [Mayer,G.&G.]
*PRACTICE AREAS: Family Law; Mediation; Divorce Litigation.
**Glassman, Jeffrey L.**, (AV) ... '47 '72 C.112 B.A. L.426 J.D. [Riordan&M.]
**Glassman, Jerold E.**, (AVⓉ) ... '35 '66 C.705 B.S. L.776 LL.B. [Grotta,G.&H.]⊙
Glassman, Joel T. ... '53 '79 C.112 B.A. L.426 J.D. [🄰 H.L.Thomas]
Glassman, Michael S., (AV) ... '48 '73 C.112 B.A. L.426 J.D. [Glassman&C.] ‡
**Glassman, Paul R.**, (AV) ... '52 '77 C.659 B.A. L.813 J.D. [P.R.Glassman]
*PRACTICE AREAS: Bankruptcy Law; Insolvency Law; Commercial Law.
Glassman, Stephen ... '42 '79 C.1093 B.S. L.426 J.D. P.O. Box 451278
Glassman and Clemens, A Professional Corporation, (AV) 3200 Wilshire Blvd., 14th Fl. S. Twr.

**Glassman, Paul R., P.C., (AV)**
**11400 West Olympic Boulevard, 2nd Floor, 90064**
**Telephone: 310-312-9505 Fax: 310-312-9507**
**Paul R. Glassman.**
**Business and Real Estate Bankruptcies, Corporate Reorganizations, Workouts, Debtor-Creditor Matters and Related Litigation.**

*See Professional Biographies, LOS ANGELES, CALIFORNIA*

**Glatt, Herman L.**, (AV) ... '29 '53 C.112 B.A. L.309 LL.B. [Stutman,T.&G.]
*PRACTICE AREAS: Bankruptcy; Insolvency; Corporate Reorganization; Commercial Litigation.
**Glave, Corey W.** ... '65 '93 C.1074 B.A. L.809 J.D. [🄰 Kramer&G.]
*PRACTICE AREAS: Labor-Employment; Public Employment; Administration Law; Litigation; Employment Discrimination Law.
Glaviano, Phillip G ... '63 '87 C.1042 B.S. L.426 J.D. Dep. Dist. Atty.
Glazer, Albert A. ... '34 '71 C.112 A.B. L.1148 J.D. 4922 Rangview Ave.
**Glazer, Gregory S.** ... '68 '94 C.112 B.A. L.800 J.D. [🄰 Epstein B.&G.]
*PRACTICE AREAS: Labor and Employment Law; Litigation.
**Glazer, Michael**, (AV) ... '40 '67 C.813 B.S. L.1068 J.D. [Paul,H.J.&W.]
**Glazer, William J.** ... '50 '75 C.112 B.A. L.426 J.D. [Berger,K.S.M.F.S.&G.]
**Glazier, Kenneth M.**, (AV) ... '48 '73 C.309 B.A. L.976 J.D. [Ross,S.&G.]
*PRACTICE AREAS: Business Litigation; Estate, Trust and Conservatorship Litigation.
**Gleason, Paul M.** ... '61 '91 C.1042 B.A. L.426 J.D. [🄰 Brobeck,P.&H.]
Gleckman, Roger J. ... '41 '69 C.454 B.A. L.1068 J.D. 3435 Wilshire Blvd.
Gleeman, Marsha ... '50 '77 C.800 A.B. L.426 J.D. 10940 Wilshire Blvd.
**Gleiberman, Melissa R.** ... '68 '94 C.659 B.A. L.813 J.D. [🄰 Irell&M.]
*LANGUAGES: French.
Gleitman, Steven L. ... '48 '78 C.112 B.S. L.809 J.D. 1925 Century Park E.
**Glenn, Dawn Weekes** ... '65 '92 C.112 B.A. L.1068 J.D. [🄰 Blanc W.J.&K.]
*PRACTICE AREAS: Entertainment; Corporate; Employment Law.
**Glenn, Michael J.** ... '54 '79 C&L.800 B.S., J.D. [🄰 J.M.Donovan]
Glenn, Wendy G., (AV) ... '54 '79 C.1168 B.A. L.426 J.D. [W.G.Glenn]
Glenn, Wendy G., A Professional Corporation, (AV) ... 1900 Ave. of the Stars, Ste. 2700
Glick, Adam D. ... '67 '94 C.197 B.A. L.800 J.D. 12424 Wilshire Blvd.
Glick, Alex '05 '27 C.912 L.213 LL.B. (adm. in MI; not adm. in CA) 7054 Hawthorn Ave. (Hollywood)‡
**Glick, Earl A.**, (AV) ... '30 '53 C.339 B.S. L.597 J.D. [Orrick,H.&S.]
*PRACTICE AREAS: Secured Transactions; Asset-based Lending; Workouts; Creditor Representation in Bankruptcy Proceedings.
**Glick, Gary A.** ... '54 '79 C.696 B.A. L.426 J.D. [Cox,C.&N.]
*PRACTICE AREAS: Shopping Center Development; Commercial Leasing.
Glick, Marshall A., (A Professional Corporation) '42 '69 C.769 B.A. L.1068 J.D. 10780 Santa Monica Blvd.
Glick, Stephen ... '47 '74 C.1077 B.A. L.809 J.D. 3580 Wilshire Blvd.
**Glicker, Brian I.** ... '58 '92 C.999 B.A. L.1065 J.D. [🄰 Knopfler&R.]
*LANGUAGES: Hebrew.
*PRACTICE AREAS: Construction Defect Litigation; Personal Injury Litigation; Environmental Litigation; Business Litigation; Employment and Labor Litigation.
**Glickfeld, Bruce S.**, (AV) ... '48 '72 C.112 B.A. L.1068 J.D. [De Castro,W.&C.]
*PRACTICE AREAS: Taxation Law; Real Estate Law; Business Law.
**Glickman, Gary S.** ... '59 '84 C&L.472 B.B.A., J.D. [🄰 Skadden,A.S.M.&F.]
Glickman, Harold B. ... '31 '58 C.1043 B.S. L.809 LL.B. 3435 Wilshire Blvd.
Glickman, Laura L. ... '46 '71 C.112 A.B. L.1068 J.D. Admin. Hearing Offr.
**Glienke, Roger C.** ... '50 '82 C.999 B.A. L.209 J.D. [🄰 Billet&K.]
*REPORTED CASES: Facilities Systems Engineering Corp. v. United States, 25 Cl.Ct. 76 1 (1992); Wilson v. Commissioner of Internal Revenue, 57 T.C.M. (CCH 576 T.C. Memo. 1989-266; Graff v. Commissioner, 52 T.C.M. 9cch0 1025, T.C. Memo. 1986-550; Rowles v. Commissioner, 51 TC.M. (CCH) 27, T.C. MEMO. 1985-266; Gabaldon v. Commissioner, 47 T.C.M. (CCH) 1218, T.C. Memo 1984-107.
Glikbarg, Allan S. ... '19 '55 C&L.813 A.B., J.D. [A.S.Glikbarg]
Glikbarg, A. S., A Professional Corporation ... 1100 Glenon Ave.
Glouberman, Robert ... '68 '93 C.813 A.B. L.1068 J.D. 633 W. 5th St.
**Glouberman, Steven J.** ... '— '95 C.112 B.A. L.426 J.D. [🄰 Morgan,L.&B.]
Glovin, Irving ... '24 '50 C&L.800 A.B., J.D. 400 N. Skyewiay Rd.
**Glovinsky, Jason L.** ... '63 '89 C.112 A.B. L.1068 J.D. [🄰 Golob,B.&S.]
*PRACTICE AREAS: Real Estate Law; Business Litigation.
**Glovsky, Scott C.** ... '67 '94 C.112 B.A. L.188 J.D. [🄰 Crosby,H.R.&M.]
*PRACTICE AREAS: Commercial Litigation; Insurance Litigation; European Community Law.
Glubok, David ... '52 '78 C.966 B.A. L.1068 J.D. 1801 Century Pk. E.
**Gluck, David T.** ... '65 '94 C.1060 B.S. L.1068 J.D. [🄰 Peterson&R.]
Gluck, Howard B. ... '52 '79 C.112 B.A. L.809 J.D. Dep. City Atty.
**Gluck, Jonathan** ... '65 '93 C.999 B.A. L.800 J.D. [🄰 Riordan&M.]
*LANGUAGES: Spanish, Hebrew, German.
*PRACTICE AREAS: Litigation.

**Gluck, Neil N.** ... '58 '83 C.454 B.B.A. L.813 J.D. [Allen,M.L.G.&M.]
*PRACTICE AREAS: Real Estate.
**Gluck, Scott** ... '70 '96 C.112 B.A. L.178 J.D. [🄰 Latham&W.]
**Glucksman, Richard H.**, (AV) ... '52 '77 C.112 B.A. L.426 J.D. [Chapman&G.]
*PRACTICE AREAS: Professional Malpractice; Construction Law; Business Litigation; Taxes and Hazardous Substance Litigation; Director and Officer Liability Litigation.
**Glucoft, Frida Popik, (A Professional Corporation)**, (AV) '53 '79 C.800 B.A. L.1068 J.D. [Mitchell,S.&K.]
*PRACTICE AREAS: Immigration and Nationality Law; Employment Law,
**Glushon, Robert L.**, (AV) ... '53 '80 C.112 B.A. L.426 J.D. [Richman,L.K.&G.]
*PRACTICE AREAS: Real Estate; Real Property; Land Use; Governmental; Business Law.
**Glusker, Philip**, (AV) ... '24 '51 C.112 B.A. L.976 LL.B. [Greenberg G.F.C.&M.]
*PRACTICE AREAS: Real Estate; ADR; Transaction; Litigation.
**Glynn, Gregory C.** ... '40 '67 C.321 B.S. L.976 LL.B. [Overton,L.&P.]
*PRACTICE AREAS: Securities Litigation; Commodities; Business Litigation.
**Go, I-Fan Ching** ... '70 '95 C.813 B.A. L.1068 J.D. [🄰 McCutchen,D.B.&E.]
*LANGUAGES: Chinese.
*PRACTICE AREAS: Health Care Transactions.
Goalwin, John A. ... '49 '76 C.112 B.A. L.1190 J.D. 2029 Century Park E.
Gochis, Djinna M. '54 '80 C.262 B.A. L.724 J.D. Sr. Trial Coun., State Bar of California
**Gochman, Mark A.** ... '60 '86 C.112 B.A. L.1068 J.D. [Greenberg G.F.C.&M.]
*PRACTICE AREAS: Entertainment; Intellectual Property.
**Gocke, Gregory H.** ... '46 '74 C.800 B.S. L.426 J.D. [Inglis,L.&G.]
*PRACTICE AREAS: Insurance Defense.
Godbold, Wilford D., Jr., (AV) '38 '67 C.813 A.B. L.1068 J.D. Pres. & CEO, Zero Corp.
Goddard, Joan M. ... '55 '83 C.763 B.A. L.770 J.D. 550 S. Hope St.
**Godes, James N.** ... '62 '87 C.169 B.A. L.800 J.D. [Foley L.W.&A.]
*SPECIAL AGENCIES: California State Dept. of Health Services, California Dept. of Social Services, California Medical Review, Inc.; U.S. Health Care Financing Administration; Dept. of Fair Employment and Housing; Equal Employment Opportunity Commission.
*PRACTICE AREAS: Labor and Employment Law; Litigation; Long Term Care; Health Care; Bioethics.
**Godfrey, Peter J.** ... '53 '80 C.999 B.A. L.800 J.D. [Gilbert,K.C.&J.]
**Godino, Richard V.**, (AV) ... '29 '60 C.813 A.B. L.767 J.D. [🄲 Bergman&W.]
*PRACTICE AREAS: Commercial Real Property; Public School Law; Public Entity Law.
Godoy, Ralph ... '66 '91 C.770 B.S. L.1049 J.D. 3699 Wilshire Blvd.
**Godshall, Brad R.** ... '57 '82 C.372 B.A. L.659 J.D. [Pachulski,S.Z.&Y.]
*REPORTED CASES: In re Outlook Century Ltd., 127 B.R. 65.
Goebel, Heidi L. '68 '94 C.150 B.A. L.851 J.D. (adm. in OH; not adm. in CA) Trial Atty., U.S. Immig. & Nat. Serv.
**Goette, Richard A.** ... '48 '75 C.732 B.A. L.809 J.D. [Baker&H.]
*PRACTICE AREAS: Litigation.
**Goetz, Richard B.** ... '60 '84 C.197 A.B. L.145 J.D. [O'Melveny&M.]
*PRACTICE AREAS: Insurance Coverage; Environmental Law.
**Goff, Gregory W.** ... '52 '78 C.112 B.A. L.426 J.D. [O'Melveny&M.]
*PRACTICE AREAS: Partnership and Real Estate Taxation, including Real Estate Investment Trusts.
Goff, Lionel E., Jr. ... '34 '64 C.339 A.B. L.813 J.D. 7060 Hollywood Blvd.
Goffin, George M., (AV) ... '29 '57 C&L.426 B.B.A., J.D. 12650 Riverside Dr.
**Gofman, Steven N.** ... '62 '92 C.910 B.S.B.A. L.188 J.D. [🄰 Gibson,D.&C.]
*PRACTICE AREAS: Corporate Law; Securities.
**Gohlke, Robin L.** ... '66 '91 C.69 B.A. L.893 J.D. [🄰 O'Melveny&M.]
*LANGUAGES: German.
*PRACTICE AREAS: Real Estate.
Goichman, Jane C. L. ... '44 '70 C.112 B.A. L.1066 J.D. 633 W. 5th St.
Goines, Edward T. ... '65 '93 C.813 B.A. L.1066 J.D. 600 Wilshire Blvd.
**Golant, Joseph H.**, (AV) '41 '66 C.399 B.S.M.E. L.145 J.D. [Ashen,G.&L.] (See Pat. Sect.)⊙
**Golay, Frank H., Jr.** ... '48 '78 C&L.188 B.A., J.D. [Sullivan&C.]
**Golbert, Albert S.**, (AV) ... '32 '57 C.800 B.S. L.208 LL.B. [Golbert L.]
*LANGUAGES: French, German and Italian.
*PRACTICE AREAS: International Business; Taxation; Trade; General Business.
**Golbert, Miriam J.**, (AV) ... '41 '79 C.477 B.A. L.1068 J.D. [🄲 Loeb&L.]

**Golbert Lee LLP, (AV)**
**601 West Fifth Street 8th Floor, 90071-2094**
**Telephone: 213-891-9641 Telecopier: 213-623-6130**
**Albert S. Golbert (Certified Specialist, Taxation Law, The State Bar of California Board of Legal Specialization); San San Lee. Of Counsel: Catherine Delarbre Parker.**
**General Corporate and Commercial Practice, including International Transactions and Disputes, International Trade, Investment and Taxation, Real Estate Transactions and Litigation, Technology Transfers.**

*See Professional Biographies, LOS ANGELES, CALIFORNIA*

Gold, Alan L. ... '65 '91 C.882 B.A. L.659 J.D. 801 S. Grand Ave.
Gold, Ann C. ... '49 '73 C.783 B.A. L.424 J.D. 11995 Darlington Ave.‡
Gold, Arnold H. ... '32 '55 C&L.813 A.B., J.D. Supr. Ct. J.
Gold, Barry I. ... '48 '73 C.800 B.A. L.61 J.D. [Shaffer,G.&R.]
**Gold, Bernard D.**, (AV) ... '30 '55 C.188 B.S. L.309 J.D. [Proskauer R.G.&M.]
*PRACTICE AREAS: Labor and Employment Law.
**Gold, Darren J.** ... '70 '95 C.112 B.A. L.477 J.D. [🄰 Irell&M.]
**Gold, Devon A.** ... '70 '96 C.112 B.A. L.477 J.D. [🄰 Munger,T.&O.]
**Gold, Geoffrey M.** ... '64 '89 C.696 B.A. L.1066 J.D. [Rutter,G.&H.]
*PRACTICE AREAS: Business Litigation; Real Estate Law.
**Gold, Judith**, (AV) ... '38 '74 L.1148 J.D. [Lynberg&W.]
**Gold, Kate Schneider** ... '66 '91 C.112 B.A. L.1066 J.D. [🄰 Tuttle&T.]
**Gold, Lessing E., (A Professional Corporation)**, (AV) '32 '57 C.597 B.S. L.800 J.D. [🄲 Mitchell,S.&K.]
*PRACTICE AREAS: General Corporate Law; Corporate Acquisitions; Representation of International Companies.
Gold, Lois Ellen ... '— '77 C.914 B.A. L.1148 J.D. Coun., Unocal Corp.
**Gold, Michael A.** ... '49 '79 C.184 B.A. L.809 J.D. [Jeffer,M.B.&M.]
*LANGUAGES: French.
*PRACTICE AREAS: Complex Business, Partnership, Real Estate and Bankruptcy Litigation.
Gold, Mitchell M., (AV) ... '31 '59 C.112 B.A. L.1068 LL.B. 10960 Wilshire Blvd.
**Gold, Seth** ... '66 '92 C.188 B.A. L.94 J.D. [🄰 Manatt,P.&P.]
*PRACTICE AREAS: General Business Litigation.
**Gold, Sharon R.** ... '66 '90 C.339 B.S. L.178 J.D. [🄰 Troy&G.]
*LANGUAGES: German.
**Gold, Stephanie H.** ... '68 '93 C.976 B.A. L.1066 J.D. [🄰 Greenberg G.F.C.&M.]
*PRACTICE AREAS: Litigation.
Gold, Victor J. ... '50 '75 C.112 B.A. L.1068 J.D. Loyola Law School
**Goldberg, A. Scott** ... '59 '85 C.1077 B.A. L.990 J.D. [Selman B.]
**Goldberg, Ada** '54 '81 C.112 B.A. L.1065 J.D. V.P., Bus. & Legal Affs., MTM Entertainment Inc.
Goldberg, Arthur L. ... '41 '71 C.112 B.A. L.705 J.D. 1467 Echo Park Ave.
**Goldberg, Deborah R.** ... '68 '96 C.103 B.A. L.112 J.D. [🄰 Christensen,M.F.J.G.W.&S.]
*LANGUAGES: German.
*PRACTICE AREAS: Litigation.
**Goldberg, Eric D.** ... '65 '92 C.188 B.S. L.309 J.D. [Stutman,T.&G.]
*PRACTICE AREAS: Bankruptcy; Insolvency; Corporate Reorganization.
**Goldberg, Garth** ... '57 '83 C.112 B.A. L.1067 J.D. [Wilson,K.&B.]

CAA234P

**Goldberg, Ilene M.** '63 '89 C.1349 B.A. L.1068 J.D.
Dir., Legal & Bus. Affs., Warner/Chappell Music
**Goldberg, James** .......................'53 '83 C.976 B.A. L.145 J.D. [Folger L.&K.]⊙
**Goldberg, Jay Aaron** ................'49 '75 C.178 B.A. L.309 J.D. [🄰 Del,R.S.M.&D.]
*PRACTICE AREAS: Entertainment Law; Television Law; Motion Picture Law.
**Goldberg, Jeanine Jacobs** ..........'39 '63 C.659 B.S. L.309 LL.B. [🄲 Friedlander&W.]
*PRACTICE AREAS: Tax; Tax Controversy; Estate Planning; Corporate; ERISA.
Goldberg, Lawrence A. ................. '49 '75 C.1077 B.A. L.809 J.D. [L.A.Goldberg]
**Goldberg, Louis E.** ..................... '36 '74 C.36 B.A. L.1152 J.D. [🄰 Bragg,S.S.&K.]
Goldberg, Marci R. ..................... '67 '93 C.112 B.A. L.309 J.D. 300 S. Grand Ave.
**Goldberg, Marshall F.**, (AV) ..........'54 '79 C.112 B.A. L.426 J.D. [Glass,A.G.&C.]⊙
*PRACTICE AREAS: Creditors Rights; Commercial Law; Insolvency; Equipment/Personal Property Leasing; Secured Transactions.
Goldberg, Nathan, (AV) ................. '46 '74 C.1160 A.B. L.426 J.D. [Allred,M.&G.]
**Goldberg, Perry M.** ....................... '69 '93 C.659 B.S. L.309 J.D. [🄰 Irell&M.]
Goldberg, Robert S., (AV) .........'38 '64 C.112 B.S. L.1068 LL.B. 10866 Wilshire Blvd.
**Goldberg, Seth M.** .......................'64 '92 C.112 B.A. L.398 J.D. [Bleau,F.&G.]
**Goldberg, Seymour S.**, (AV) ........... '30 '57 C.112 B.A. L.1068 J.D. [🄲 Hinojosa&K.]
*PRACTICE AREAS: Real Estate Law.
**Goldberg, Steven M.** ..................... '54 '78 C.309 A.B. L.569 J.D. [Goldberg&S.]
*PRACTICE AREAS: Commercial Litigation; Entertainment Litigation; Real Estate Litigation.
Goldberg, Theodore A. .............'34 '61 C.112 B.S. L.1068 LL.B. 6380 Wilshire Blvd.
Goldberg-Ambrose, Carole E. ...... '47 '72 C.788 B.A. L.813 J.D. Prof. of Law, U.C.L.A.
Goldberg, Lawrence A., A Prof. Law Corp. ................ 1800 Century Park E., 5th Fl.

**Goldberg & Scott**
**1901 Avenue of the Stars, Suite 1100, 90067**
**Telephone: 310-277-6790 Fax: 310-556-8945**
**Members of Firm: Steven M. Goldberg; Jeff E. Scott; Michele R. Van Gelderen. Of Counsel: David L. Burg.**
**Commercial, Entertainment and Real Estate Litigation.**
***See Professional Biographies, LOS ANGELES, CALIFORNIA***

**Goldbloom, Claire M.** ...... '66 '92 C.966 B.A. L.800 J.D. [🄰 Bryan C.] (⊙Santa Monica)
*LANGUAGES: French.
*PRACTICE AREAS: Corporate; Securities.
**Goldblum, Martin T.**, (AV) ................'40 '63 C.563 B.A. L.569 LL.B. [Troy&G.]
*PRACTICE AREAS: Taxation Law.
**Golden, Diane A.** ..........................'56 '83 C.860 B.A. L.569 J.D. [🄲 Katz,G.&F.]
*PRACTICE AREAS: Entertainment Law; Motion Pictures and Television; Multimedia Law.
Golden, Harry G. ..........................'43 '70 C.112 B.S. L.426 J.D. 3611 Motor Avenue
Golden, Jonathan K., (AV) ........'45 '71 C.112 A.B. L.1068 J.D. 1900 Ave. of the Stars

**Golden, Renée Wayne, (AV) '— '77 C.178 L.1095 J.D.**
**8983 Norma Place (West Hollywood), 90069**
**Telephone: 310-550-8232 FAX: 310-276-7736**
**Intellectual Property, Entertainment, Motion Picture, Television, Publishing, Theatre, Graphic Arts and Estate Planning Law.**

**Golden, Eugene**
**(See Beverly Hills)**

Goldenhersh, Lawrence E. '55 '81 C.228 A.B. L.893 J.D.
1800 Ave. of the Stars, Suite 900 (Century City)
**Goldfarb, Dale B.** ....................'50 '75 C.112 A.B. L.426 J.D. [Harrington,F.D.&C.]
*PRACTICE AREAS: Business and Commercial Litigation; Insurance Coverage; Employment Law; Appellate Practice.
Goldfarb, Jack Maurice, (AV) ....................'48 '73 C.112 B.S. 10866 Wilshire Blvd.
**Goldfarb, Samuel**, (AV) ....................'21 '56 C.112 L.426 J.D. [Goldfarb,S.&A.] ‡
*PRACTICE AREAS: Taxation Law; Corporate Law; Business Litigation.

**Goldfarb, Sturman & Averbach, (AV)**
**A Partnership including Professional Corporations**
**15760 Ventura Boulevard, 19th Floor, 91436**
**Telephone: 213-872-2204; 818-990-4414**
**Members of Firm: Samuel Goldfarb (Retired); J. Howard Sturman (1931-1991); Martin L. Sturman (A Professional Corporation); Zane S. Averbach (A Professional Corporation); Martin B. Snyder; Mark J. Phillips (Certified Specialist, Estate Planning, Trust and Probate Law, The State Bar of California Board of Legal Specialization); Steven L. Feldman; Cynthia Lu Rubin. Associates: Les J. Wolin; Christine E. Ceder. Of Counsel: William L. Winslow.**
**General Practice. Business, Real Estate, Estate Planning, Probate, Taxation Law, Civil Litigation.**
***See Professional Biographies, LOS ANGELES, CALIFORNIA***

**Goldflam, Hal D.** ...........................'70 '95 C.112 B.A. L.809 J.D. [🄰 Morris,P.&P.]
Goldflam, Sheldon L. ......................'29 '59 C&L.339 B.S., LL.B. [Goldflam&B.]
Goldflam, Stanley Z. ............ '37 '61 C&L.705 B.A., LL.B. 520 S. Lafayette Park Pl.
Goldflam & Barth ................................................1644 Wilshire Blvd.
Goldfried, Robert M. ......................... '44 '74 C.339 A.B. L.94 J.D. 333 S. Hope St.
**Goldich, Stanley E.** .................... '55 '80 C.855 B.A. L.813 J.D. [Pachulski,S.Z.&Y.]
*REPORTED CASES: In re Reed, 89 B.R. 100; In re Westworld Community Healthcare, Inc. 95 B.R. 730; In re Reed 940 F.2d 1317.
*TRANSACTIONS: Represented New West Federal Savings and Loan in Hollywood Roosevelt Hotel chapter 11 and sale; Truck Insurance Exchange in Maxicare chapter 11; Official Committee of Creditors Holding Unsecured Membership Claims in American Adventure, Inc. chapter 11; Commonwealth Equity Trust.
Goldie, Ron R. ..........................'51 '75 C&L.800 B.A., J.D. 2121 Ave of the Stars
Goldin, Leon, (AV) ......................'27 '64 C.112 A.B. L.809 LL.B. P.O. Box 481127
Goldin, Martha ........................................ '28 '64 C.112 B.A. L.1068 LL.B. Supr. Ct. J.
**Golding, David K.** ........................'37 '64 C.112 B.A. L.1066 J.D. [Frandzel&S.]
**Golding, Jonathan F.** ............'62 '90 C.112 B.A. L.426 J.D. [🄰 Sonnenschein N.&R.]
*PRACTICE AREAS: Litigation; Creditor's Rights.
**Goldman, Allan B.**, (AV) ..................... '37 '64 C&L.309 A.B., J.D. [Katten M.&Z.]
*PRACTICE AREAS: Litigation; Mass Torts; Class Actions; Insurance Coverage; Real Estate.
Goldman, Barry I., (AV) ..................... '38 '65 C.112 B.A. L.1065 J.D. [Rose,K.&M.]
**Goldman, Benjamin E.** ......................'40 '68 C.569 B.S. L.262 J.D. [Graham&J.]
*PRACTICE AREAS: Employment Law; Labor Law.
**Goldman, David B.** ..................... '65 '92 C.165 B.A. L.477 J.D. [🄰 O'Melveny&M.]
Goldman, David R. .....................'47 '74 C.976 B.A. L.813 J.D. Executive Car Leasing
Goldman, Deborah J. .........................'49 '80 C.112 A.B. L.94 J.D. 725 S. Figueroa
**Goldman, Donald A.**, (AV) .........'47 '72 C.112 B.A. L.1068 J.D. [McDermott,W.&E.]
*PRACTICE AREAS: Administrative Law; Health Care; Regulatory.
Goldman, Gene E., (BV) ..........'37 '64 C&L.800 A.B., J.D. 555 S. Flower St., 25th Fl.
Goldman, Hyman, (AV) ..........'10 '35 C.112 A.B. L.1066 J.D. 2049 Century Park, E.
**Goldman, Jack**, (AV) ......................... '40 '66 C.390 B.A. L.1068 J.D. [Arter&H.]
*PRACTICE AREAS: Corporate and Securities; Trade Regulations; Mergers and Acquisitions; Asset Based Lending; Health Law.
**Goldman, James L.** ...................... '48 '73 C.112 B.A. L.1068 J.D. [Pircher,N.&M.]
*PRACTICE AREAS: Commercial Litigation.
**Goldman, Jeffrey D.** ..................... '66 '91 C.112 B.A. L.1065 J.D. [🄰 Mitchell,S.&K.]
*PRACTICE AREAS: Antitrust; Intellectual Property Litigation.
**Goldman, Joel A.**, (AV) ..................'42 '67 C.293 B.A. L.800 J.D. [Stephens,B.&L.]
*PRACTICE AREAS: Complex Civil Litigation.
Goldman, Joseph ...............'24 '52 C.415 B.S. L.1009 LL.B. 524 S. Alandele Ave.‡
**Goldman, Kenneth A.**, (AV) ......'42 '68 C.674 A.B. L.1066 J.D. [Sanders,B.G.S.&M.]
**Goldman, Kenneth L.**, (AV) ............ '45 '69 C.112 B.A. L.1068 J.D. [K.L.Goldman]
*PRACTICE AREAS: Probate, Wills and Trusts; Probate Litigation; General Business.
Goldman, Lawrence M. .................'61 '86 C.112 B.A. L.1066 J.D. 400 S. Hope St.
**Goldman, Leonard A.**, (AV) ............. '30 '56 C&L.813 B.A., J.D. [Goldman&G.]
*REPORTED CASES: C.A.Cal. 1974. In re Kanter, 505 F.2d 228; C.A.Cal. 1973. Biggins v. Southwest Bank, 490 F. 2d 1304, 13 UCC Rep.Serv. 928; C.A.9 1973. Veeck v. Commodity Enterprises, Inc. 487 F.2d. 423; C.A.Cal. 1971. Parker v. Williams Const. Co., 443 F.2d 597; C.A.Cal. 1966. A. & E. Plastik Pak Co. v. Bowie, 358 F.2d 148.
*PRACTICE AREAS: Bankruptcy Law; Civil Litigation Law; Debtor-Creditor Law; Real Estate Finance Law.
Goldman, Louis L., (AV) ..............'12 '38 C&L.800 B.A., LL.B. 1801 Century Pk. E.
**Goldman, Lynda B.** ........................... '60 '85 C.112 A.B. L.426 J.D. [Lavely&S.]
*REPORTED CASES: Prieto v. State Farm Fire & Casualty Company, Cal.App. 3d 1188, 275 Cal.Rptr 362 (1990).
*PRACTICE AREAS: Entertainment Litigation; Defamation; Business Litigation.
**Goldman, Mark A.**, (AV) ..............'41 '68 C.112 B.A. L.1068 J.D. [Goldman&K.]
*REPORTED CASES: Marvin v. Marvin, 122 Cal. App. 3d 871, 176 Cal. Rptr. 555 (1981); Marvin v. Marvin, 18C 3d 660, 134 Cal. Rptr. 815 (1976).
*PRACTICE AREAS: Real Estate; Contracts; General Business.

**Goldman, Martin F. '44 '70 C.1077 B.S. L.426 J.D.**
**10880 Wilshire Boulevard, Suite 2240, 90024-4123**
**Telephone: 310-470-8487 FAX: 310-474-0653**
***PRACTICE AREAS: Creditor's Rights; Collection; Bankruptcy.**
**Commercial, Collection and Litigation.**
***See Professional Biographies, LOS ANGELES, CALIFORNIA***

Goldman, Norman .................'59 '85 C.33 B.A. L.426 J.D. 7060 Hollywood Blvd.
**Goldman, Paul J.** ..........................'64 '90 C.1042 B.S. L.800 J.D. [🄰 Freeman,F.&S.]
**Goldman, Richard D.**, (AV) ............'53 '78 C.112 B.A. L.800 J.D. [Goldman&K.]
*PRACTICE AREAS: Entertainment; Real Estate; General Business.
Goldman, Stanley A. ...........'49 '75 C.112 A.B. L.426 J.D. Loyola Univ. Sch. of Law

**Goldman & Gordon, L.L.P., (AV) BB**
**Suite 1920, 1801 Century Park East, 90067**
**Telephone: 310-277-7171 FAX: 310-277-1547**
**Members of Firm: A. S. Goldman (1895-1966); Leonard A. Goldman; Robert P. Gordon. Associate: Melody G. Anderson.**
**General Civil and Trial Practice in all State and Federal Courts. Commercial, Real Estate, Probate, Corporate, Bankruptcy, Consumer, Fidelity and Surety, Insolvency, Insurance and Subrogation Law.**
**References: Bank of America, Fourth and Spring Branch, Los Angeles; Bank of America, Wilshire-San Vincente Branch, Beverly Hills.**
***See Professional Biographies, LOS ANGELES, CALIFORNIA***

**Goldman & Kagon, Law Corporation, (AV) BB**
**1801 Century Park East, Suite 2222, 90067**
**Telephone: 310-552-1707 Telecopier: 310-552-7938**
**Mark A. Goldman; Barry Felsen; Richard D. Goldman; Charles D. Meyer; Christopher B. Fagan; Terry Mc Niff (Certified Specialist, Family Law, The State Bar of California Board of Specialization); Jared Laskin; Marco F. Weiss; Edmund S. Schaffer. Counsel: A. David Kagon.**
**Corporate, Entertainment, Family Law, Probate, Wills and Trusts, Real Estate, Civil Litigation and General Civil Practice.**
***See Professional Biographies, LOS ANGELES, CALIFORNIA***

**Goldman, Kenneth L., Professional Corporation, (AV) BB**
**1801 Century Park East, Suite 2222, 90067**
**Telephone: 310-552-1720 Fax: 312-552-7938**
**Kenneth L. Goldman.**
**Probate, Wills and Trusts, Probate Litigation and General Business Law.**
***See Professional Biographies, LOS ANGELES, CALIFORNIA***

Goldring, Charles ......................... '07 '36 C.112 A.B. L.809 9044 Melrose Ave.

**Goldring, Irwin D., (AV) '31 '57 C.112 B.S. L.1068 J.D.**
**Suite 2000, 1875 Century Park East, 90067**
**Telephone: 310-201-0304 FAX: 310-277-7994**
**(Certified Specialist, Taxation Law and Estate Planning, Trust and Probate Law, The State Bar of California Board of Legal Specialization).**
***PRACTICE AREAS: Estate Planning; Trust and Probate Law; Taxation Law.**
**Taxation, Estate Planning, Trust and Probate Law.**
**Reference: Western Bank.**
***See Professional Biographies, LOS ANGELES, CALIFORNIA***

Goldsby, Matthew W. ...............'60 '89 C.112 B.A. L.809 J.D. 10940 Wilshire Blvd.
**Goldschein, Robert D.** ................ '54 '80 C.112 B.A. L.1068 J.D. [Katten M.&Z.]
*PRACTICE AREAS: Commercial Finance; Trade Finance; Reorganization and Insolvency.
**Goldsman, Melvin S.**, (AV) .................. '47 '75 C.112 B.A. L.809 J.D. [Freid&G.]
*PRACTICE AREAS: Family Law.
**Goldsmith, Anthony E.** ...................'60 '86 C.112 B.A. L.800 J.D. [🄰 Weinhart&R.]
*PRACTICE AREAS: Business Law; Real Property Law.
**Goldsmith, Dale J.** ...............................'60 '85 C.976 B.A. L.145 J.D. [Alschuler G.&P.]
**Goldsmith, Gordon A.** ........................'55 '80 C.339 B.A. L.1068 J.D. [Tuttle&T.]
*PRACTICE AREAS: Commercial Litigation; Environmental Litigation; Professional Liability Litigation.
Goldsmith, Mark E. ...........................'60 '87 C.966 B.A. L.1065 J.D. 1925 Century Park E.
Goldsmith, Patricia .... '53 '85 C.685 B.A. L.596 J.D. Sr. Atty., Legal Aid Found. of L.A.
**Goldsmith, William I., (A Professional Corporation)**, (AV) '53 '78
C.112 B.A. L.1095 J.D. [Goldsmith&B.]
*PRACTICE AREAS: Commercial Litigation; Major Personal Injury Litigation; Real Estate; Collection.

**Goldsmith & Burns, (AV)**
**A Partnership including a Professional Corporation**
**18425 Burbank Boulevard, Suite 708 (Tarzana), 91356-2800**
**Telephone: 818-708-2585 Telecopier: 818-996-4537**
**William I. Goldsmith (A Professional Corporation); Jack D. Hull. Associates: Nancy Sandberg Ramirez; David M. Gonor.**
**Retail and Commercial Collection, Insurance Defense, Coverage, Subrogation, Personal Injury, Professional Malpractice, Negligence, Construction Defect Litigation, Probate, Estate Planning, Wills and Trusts, Conservatorship, Elder Law, Business Litigation and Commercial Litigation.**
***See Professional Biographies, LOS ANGELES, CALIFORNIA***

Goldstein, Aileen N. .......................'41 '81 C.112 B.A. L.809 J.D. [A.N.Goldstein]
**Goldstein, Arnie E.** ..............................'65 '96 C.36 B.A. L.809 J.D. [Prestholt,K.F.&V.]
**Goldstein, Charles H.**, (AV) ...........'39 '64 C.930 B.A. L.273 J.D. [Goldstein,K.&P.]
*PRACTICE AREAS: Labor and Employment; Civil Litigation.
**Goldstein, David A.** ............ '57 '85 C&L.1136 B.S.L., J.D. [🄰 Gordon,E.K.G.F.&G.]
*PRACTICE AREAS: Workers Compensation Law; Social Security Law.
Goldstein, David M. '51 '76
V.P. & Assoc. Gen. Coun., Transamerica Occidental Life Ins. Co.
**Goldstein, Don W.**, (AV) ...............'41 '66 C.112 A.B. L.1066 LL.B. [Stall,A.&G.]
*PRACTICE AREAS: Civil Litigation; Family Law; Insurance Defense.
**Goldstein, Donna Fields**, (AV) ..........'47 '72 C.70 B.A. L.1292 J.D. [Manatt,P.&P.]
*PRACTICE AREAS: Employment Law; Labor Law Litigation; Unfair Competition; Consumeration; General Business Litigation.
Goldstein, Douglas J. ..........'56 '82 C.994 B.A. L.61 J.D. 210 W. Temple St., 19th Fl.
Goldstein, Gary W. ..............'50 '78 C.112 B.A. L.284 J.D. 864 S. Robertson Blvd.
**Goldstein, Irwin L., (A Professional Corporation)**, (AV) '39 '64
C.912 B.A. L.800 LL.B. [Gordon,E.K.G.F.&G.]
*PRACTICE AREAS: Workers Compensation Law; Social Security Law.

CAA235P

CALIFORNIA—LOS ANGELES
MARTINDALE-HUBBELL LAW DIRECTORY 1997

**Goldstein, Jeffrey D.** .................... '68 '93 C.112 B.A. L.178 J.D. [Ⓐ Gibson,D.&C.]
*PRACTICE AREAS: Corporations.
Goldstein, Jerry J. .................... '43 '74 C.112 B.S. L.767 J.D. 1245 McClellan Dr.
**Goldstein, Mark A.** .................... '64 '94 C.178 B.A. L.809 J.D. [Ⓐ Harrington,F.D.&C.]
*PRACTICE AREAS: Insurance Coverage; Reinsurance Litigation; Insurance Bad Faith Litigation; Civil Defense Litigation; Trademark and Copyright.
**Goldstein, Marlo Ann** .................... '67 '94 C.659 B.S. L.893 J.D. [Ⓐ Sidley&A.]
*PRACTICE AREAS: Real Estate.
Goldstein, Marsh M. .................... '38 '63 C.401 B.A. L.229 LL.B. Dep. Dist. Atty.‡
**Goldstein, Marvin M.**, (AVⓉ) '44 '69 C.188 B.S. L.94 J.D.
(adm. in NJ; not adm. in CA) [Grotta,G.&H.]⊙
**Goldstein, Michael H.** .................... '59 '84 C.264 B.A. L.309 J.D. [Stutman,T.&G.]
*PRACTICE AREAS: Bankruptcy; Insolvency; Corporate Reorganization; Commercial Litigation.
**Goldstein, Michael R.** .................... '66 '91 C.668 B.A. L.800 J.D. [Ⓐ Musick,P.&G.]
**Goldstein, Neal M.**, (AV) .................... '52 '78 C.309 A.B. L.1065 J.D. [Goldstein&A.]
*PRACTICE AREAS: Civil Litigation; Entertainment Law; Contract Law; Real and Personal Property Law; Copyright Law.
Goldstein, Ned S. '55 '81
C.1044 B.S. L.1068 J.D. Sr. V.P. & Gen. Coun., Ticketmaster Corp.
**Goldstein, Richard Jay**, (AV) ..... '41 '66 C.813 B.A. L.1068 LL.B. [Buchalter,N.F.&Y.]
*PRACTICE AREAS: Financial Law; Personal Property; Secured Transactions; Workouts.
Goldstein, Robert D. '47 '77 C&L.309 B.A., J.D.
(adm. in MA; not adm. in CA) Prof., Univ. of Calif., Los Angeles, School of Law
**Goldstein, Robert E.** .................... '47 '73 C.184 B.A. L.818 J.D. [Foley L.W.&A.]
*PRACTICE AREAS: Employee Benefits; Tax Exempt Organizations; Taxation.
**Goldstein, Roy D.** .................... '55 '80 C.1044 B.A. L.426 J.D. [Ⓐ Herzfeld&R.]
Goldstein, Sherwin .................... '31 '59 C.112 A.B. L.1068 LL.B. 1801 Ave. of the Stars
**Goldstein, Stephen R.**, (AV) .................... '44 '69 C.112 B.S. L.188 J.D. [Jeffer,M.B.&M.]
*PRACTICE AREAS: Corporate, Real Estate and International Taxation; Taxation of Entertainers and Entertainment Companies.
Goldstein, Aileen N., P.C. .................... 3350 Barham Blvd.

**Goldstein & Ashley, (AV)**
**10990 Wilshire Boulevard, Suite 940, 90024**
**Telephone: 310-575-6100 Fax: 310-575-6101**
**Neal M. Goldstein; Stephen D. Ashley.**
***See Professional Biographies, LOS ANGELES, CALIFORNIA***

**Goldstein, Kennedy & Petito, (AV) 🅱🅱**
**Suite 1018, 1880 Century Park East (Century City), 90067**
**Telephone: 310-553-4746; 213-879-1401 Fax: 310-282-8070**
**Charles H. Goldstein; Gregory G. Kennedy; Deborah Hanna Petito;—Lauren A. Dean; Edward J. Gervin; Frank A. Magnanimo. Of Counsel: Thomas A. Fournie.**
**Labor and Public Employment Relations Law and Equal Opportunity Law. General Civil, Trial and Appellate Practice in all State and Federal Courts.**
***See Professional Biographies, LOS ANGELES, CALIFORNIA***

**Goldstone, Adrienne W.** '53 '87 C.145 B.A. L.1068 J.D.
[Ⓐ Christensen,M.F.J.G.W.&S.]
*PRACTICE AREAS: Corporations Law; Securities Law.
**Goldstone, Hilary F.**, (AV) .................... '47 '72 C.66 B.A. L.813 J.D. [Burns&G.]
*PRACTICE AREAS: Business; Civil Litigation; International; Real Estate; Commercial.
Goldstone, Raymond H. '42 '71
C.112 B.A.,M.A. L.1068 J.D. Dean of Students, Univ. of Calif.
**Goldwasser, Charles A.** .................... '50 '74 C.264 A.B. L.1068 J.D. [Kramer&G.]
*PRACTICE AREAS: Public Employment Law; Administration Law; Employment Discrimination Law.
Goldwater, Deena '48 '78 C.112 B.A. L.426 J.D.
V.P. & Corp. Real Estate Coun., The Decurion Corp.
**Goldzweig, Mark Jay** .................... '— '94 C.1169 B.A. L.426 J.D. [Ⓐ Perkins C.]
**Goller, Karlene Worthington** '61 '86
C.478 A.B. L.818 J.D. Assoc. Gen. Coun., L.A. Times

**Gollub & Golsan**
**(See Culver City)**

**Golob, Dennis E.** .................... '42 '68 C.112 B.S. L.800 J.D. [Golob,B.&S.]
*PRACTICE AREAS: Business and Contracts Law; Real Property Law; Commercial Transactions Law; Corporate and Business, Commercial and Real Property, Construction and related Litigation.

**Golob, Bragin & Sassoe, P.C., (AV)**
**Suite 1400, 11755 Wilshire Boulevard, 90025-1520**
**Telephone: 310-477-1050 Fax: 310-477-0988**
**Dennis E. Golob; Ronald A. Bragin; Albert L. Sassoe, Jr.;—Jason L. Glovinsky.**
**Business, Real Property, Corporate, Commercial Transactions, Federal and State Securities, Secured Lending, Mergers, Acquisitions, Taxation, Estate Planning, Insolvency, Health Care, Environmental, Franchise and Associated Litigation with these areas of law as well as Entertainment and Probate Litigation.**
***See Professional Biographies, LOS ANGELES, CALIFORNIA***

**Golub, Larry M.** .................... '57 '83 C.112 B.A. L.1065 J.D. [Barger&W.]
*PRACTICE AREAS: Insurance Coverage Law; Employment Law; Construction Law.
**Gomez, Angel, III** .................... '— '77 C.112 A.B. L.309 J.D. [Katten M.&Z.]
*PRACTICE AREAS: Employment and Labor Law; ERISA.
Gomez, Glynda B. .................... '64 '89 C.773 A.B. L.813 J.D. Dep. Atty. Gen.
**Gomez, John H.** .................... '65 '93 C.1049 B.B.A. L.976 J.D. [Ⓐ Latham&W.]
*LANGUAGES: Spanish.
**Gonen Goldstein, Hadar** .................... '67 '92 C.112 B.A. L.800 J.D. [Ⓐ Allen,M.L.G.&M.]
*PRACTICE AREAS: Real Estate Transactions.
**Gonor, David M.** .................... '67 '94 C.112 B.A. L.990 J.D. [Ⓐ Goldsmith&B.]
*PRACTICE AREAS: Commercial Collections; Retail Collections; Creditors Rights; Mechanics Liens; Business Litigation.
Gonzales, Dennis M. .................... '47 '74 C.1077 B.A. L.809 LL.B. Dep. Co. Coun.
**Gonzales, Leonor C.** .................... '57 '88 C.1131 B.A. L.1049 J.D. [Ⓐ Parker S.]
*PRACTICE AREAS: General Civil; Family Law; Government Benefits.
**Gonzales, Timothy A.** .................... '59 '84 C.911 B.A. L.477 J.D. [Hawkins,S.L.&B.]
Gonzales, Vincent M. ......'57 '87 C.311 B.A. L.800 J.D. Sr. Atty., Atlantic Richfield Co.
**Gonzalez, Christopher** .................... '68 '94 C.112 B.A. L.1148 J.D. [Ⓐ Ochoa&S.]
*LANGUAGES: Spanish.
*PRACTICE AREAS: Civil Litigation; Education.
**Gonzalez, Daniel J.** .................... '50 '77 C.276 B.S. L.813 J.D. [Horvitz&L.]
**Gonzalez, Edward E.** .................... '54 '80 C.674 A.B. L.178 J.D. [Skadden,A.S.M.&F.]
**Gonzalez, Esther** .................... '66 '93 C.112 B.A. L.426 J.D. [Ⓐ Harrington,F.D.&C.]
*LANGUAGES: Spanish.
**Gonzalez, Humberto** .................... '52 '80 C.112 B.S. L.1049 J.D. [Kegel,T.&T.]
**Gonzalez, Joette Marea** .................... '60 '94 C.112 B.S. L.464 J.D. [Ⓐ Cummins&W.]
*PRACTICE AREAS: Complex Insurance Coverage Litigation; Business Litigation; Insurance Defense.
Gonzalez, Mario F. .................... '51 '77 C.112 B.A. L.1068 J.D. [Lenard&G.]
**Gonzalez, Michael D.** .................... '58 '84 C.1077 B.A. L.809 J.D. [Kern,S.&G.]
*PRACTICE AREAS: Medical Malpractice.
**Gonzalez, Nancy B.** .................... '66 '93 C.112 B.A. L.1068 J.D. [Ⓐ Inglis,L.&G.]
*LANGUAGES: Spanish.
*PRACTICE AREAS: Insurance Defense.
**Gonzalez, Robert** .................... '65 '94 C.800 B.S. L.809 J.D. [Ⓐ Frandzel&S.]
*LANGUAGES: Spanish.
*PRACTICE AREAS: Creditor's Rights; Bankruptcy.
Gonzalez, Rosendo .................... '61 '87 C&L.326 B.A., J.D. 445 S. Figueroa St.

Gonzalez Funes, Elva Y. .................... '56 '87 C.1097 B.S. L.426 J.D. 3250 Wilshire Blvd.
González-Sfeir, Javier J. .................... '58 '83 C&L.309 A.B., J.D. 633 W. 5th St.
Good, Gregory S. .................... '45 '77 C.426 B.S. L.809 J.D. 10223 Autumn Leaf Circle
**Good, Michael D.** .................... '65 '95 C.659 B.A. L.990 J.D. [Ⓐ Jeffer,M.B.&M.]
*PRACTICE AREAS: Insolvency; Creditors Rights.

**Good, Ned, The Law Offices of**
**(See Pasadena)**

**Goodchild, André S.** .................... '46 '82 C.906 B.S. L.1148 J.D. [Ⓐ Veatch,C.G.&N.]
*PRACTICE AREAS: Vehicle Liability; Premises Liability; General Casualty Defense Law.
Gooden, Lisa Maree Campbell .................... '66 '91 C.994 B.A. L.569 J.D. 400 S. Hope St.
**Goodfried, Marlene D.**, (AV) .................... '54 '79 C.112 B.A. L.1068 J.D. [Cox,C.&N.]
*PRACTICE AREAS: Real Property Law; Commercial Leasing Law.
**Goodkin, Daniel L.** .................... '61 '87 C.112 B.A. L.426 J.D. [Ⓐ Allen,M.L.G.&M.]
*PRACTICE AREAS: General Real Estate Litigation; Construction Litigation; Real Estate Finance Litigation; Landlord Tenant Litigation; Bankruptcy.
**Goodkin, Olivia** .................... '56 '81 C.112 B.A. L.800 J.D. [Rutter,G.&H.]
*PRACTICE AREAS: Business Litigation; Employment Law.
**Goodkind, James P.** .................... '56 '87 C.597 B.S.S. L.1065 J.D. [Ⓐ Loeb&L.]
**Goodkind, Maryann Link** .................... '62 '87 C&L.800 B.S., J.D. [Ⓒ Musick,P.&G.]
*PRACTICE AREAS: Public Finance Law; Municipal Law.
**Goodman, Carlos K.** .................... '62 '89 C.103 B.A. L.1068 J.D. [Lichter,G.N.&A.]
*PRACTICE AREAS: Entertainment Law.
Goodman, Daniel S. .................... '62 '86 C&L.813 A.B., J.D. U.S. Atty. Off.

**Goodman, Earle Gary, (AV) '43 '69 C.112 B.A. L.1068 J.D. 🅱🅱**
**2934 1/2 Beverly Glenn Circle Suite 395, 90077**
**Telephone: 310-470-9033 Fax: 310-470-3494**
**Email: 23852@MSN.com**
**General Business Transactions, Real Property Sales and Lease Transactions, Construction and Development, Business Transactions and LLC, Corporation and Partnership Formation and Operation.**
**Reference: Bank of America, Westwood Village Office.**
***See Professional Biographies, LOS ANGELES, CALIFORNIA***

**Goodman, Eileen H.** '51 '90
C.623 B.A. L.809 J.D. Coun., Cushman & Wakefield of Calif., Inc.
**Goodman, James A.** .................... '53 '79 C.629 B.S. L.426 J.D. [Epstein B.&G.]
**Goodman, Katherine E.** .................... '63 '86 C.309 A.B. L.145 J.D. [Katten M.&Z.]
*PRACTICE AREAS: Entertainment Law.
**Goodman, Marc P.** .................... '65 '90 C.112 B.A. L.800 J.D. [Ⓐ Manatt,P.&P.]
*PRACTICE AREAS: Litigation.
Goodman, Max A., (AV) .................... '24 '48 L.426 J.D. Prof., Southwestern Univ. Sch. of Law
Goodman, Rebecca R. .................... '66 '96 C.178 B.A. L.809 J.D. 12100 Wilshire Blvd., 15th Fl.
**Goodman, Stanley L.** '53 '78 C.178 B.A. L.569 J.D.
(adm. in NJ; not adm. in CA) [Grotta,G.&H.]⊙
Goodman-Delahunty, Jane ... '52 '83 C.061 B.A. L.678 J.D. Admin. Law J., U.S. E.E.O.C.
**Goodnow, Jennifer E.** .................... '60 '87 C.183 B.A. L.94 J.D. Labor & Litig. Coun., CBS Inc.
**Goodrich, Brenton F.**, (AV) .................... '42 '68 C.918 A.B. L.813 J.D. [Parker,M.C.O.&S.]
*PRACTICE AREAS: Construction; Civil Litigation.
Goodson, Carol Boas .................... '47 '71 C.112 B.A. L.1137 J.D. Mun. Ct. J.
Goodson, Jonathan M. .................... '45 '71 C.813 B.A. L.976 LL.B. Mark Goodson Productions
**Goodson, Marvin**, (AV) .................... '18 '51 C.112 B.A. L.426 J.D. [Goodson&W.]
*PRACTICE AREAS: Tax; Estate Planning; Business Transaction Structuring; Corporate Transactions.

**Goodson and Wachtel, A Professional Corporation, (AV)**
**10940 Wilshire Boulevard, Suite 1400, 90024-3941**
**Telephone: 310-208-8282 Facsimile: 310-208-8582**
**Marvin Goodson (Certified Specialist, Taxation Law, The State Bar of California Board of Legal Specialization); Edward W. Wachtel; David W. Riley;—Laura K. Farrand. Of Counsel: Luis C. De Castro; Lance Jon Kimmel.**
**Federal Income, Estate, Gift and International Taxation Law. Estate Planning, Business Transactions, Corporations, Partnerships, Non-Profits, ESOPs, ERISA, Real Estate, Securities, Trusts, Probate and Wills.**
***See Professional Biographies, LOS ANGELES, CALIFORNIA***

**Goodstein, Daniel J.** .................... '53 '81 C.1077 B.A. L.398 J.D. [Ⓐ Berger,K.S.M.F.S.&G.]
**Goodstein, Gary J.** .................... '66 '93 C.766 B.A. L.426 J.D. [Ⓐ Bannan,G.S.&F.]
*PRACTICE AREAS: Business Litigation; Professional Liability; Insurance Coverage.
Goodstein, Maurice Mac, (AV) '09 '35
C.112 B.A. L.999 LL.B. 1880 Century Park E., 12th Fl.
Goodwin, Eugene S., (AV) .................... '15 '41 C.112 B.A. L.800 LL.B. 9911 W. Pico Blvd.
**Goon, Robert H.**, (AV) .................... '40 '66 C.112 B.A. L.1068 J.D. [Jeffer,M.B.&M.]
*PRACTICE AREAS: Corporate Mergers and Acquisitions; Financing and Securities Transactions.
**Goosenberg, Jennifer B.** .................... '65 '89 C.1036 B.A. L.1068 J.D. [Ⓐ Gelfand&G.]
*PRACTICE AREAS: Civil Litigation.

**Gorbis & Liberty**
**(See Beverly Hills)**

**Gordinier, Todd E.** .................... '53 '78 C.309 B.A. L.1066 J.D. [Orrick,H.&S.]
*PRACTICE AREAS: Complex Litigation.
Gordon, Albert L. .................... '15 '67 L.1095 LL.B. 734 N. Spaulding Ave.
Gordon, Christopher J. .................... '64 '94 L.061 LL.B. 333 S. Grand Ave.
**Gordon, David E.**, (AV) .................... '49 '72 C.308 A.B. L.309 J.D. [O'Melveny&M.]
*PRACTICE AREAS: Employee Benefits; Executive Compensation.
Gordon, Donald R. .................... '45 '78 C.763 B.A. L.818 J.D. 4215 Glencoe Ave.
**Gordon, Donald R.**, (AV) .................... '54 '79 C.390 A.B. L.145 J.D. [Leopold,P.&S.]
*PRACTICE AREAS: Entertainment; Civil Litigation; Copyright and Trademark; Libel and Slander; Unfair Competition.
**Gordon, Eric B.** .................... '61 '90 C.103 A.B. L.1068 J.D. [McDermott,W.&E.]
*PRACTICE AREAS: Health Care.
Gordon, Errol J. .................... '41 '70 C.999 A.A. L.809 LL.B. 1200 Wilshire Blvd.
Gordon, Gail .................... '41 '75 C.05 B.Ed. L.800 J.D. 725 S. Figueroa St., 11th Fl.
**Gordon, Gerald N.** .................... '34 '58 C&L.930 B.A., LL.B. [Sheppard,M.R.&H.]
*PRACTICE AREAS: Government Contract Law; Business Litigation; Construction Litigation.
**Gordon, Ilona** .................... '— '95 C.112 B.A. L.809 J.D. [Ⓐ Hillsinger&C.]
Gordon, James A., Jr. .................... '23 '61 C.285 L.809 LL.B. 4300 Sutro Ave.‡
Gordon, Jana L. .................... '63 '89 C.766 B.A. L.767 J.D. 3580 Wilshire Blvd., 10th Fl.
Gordon, Janice M., (AV) .................... '44 '77 C.112 B.A. L.1148 J.D. 3255 Wilshire Blvd.
**Gordon, Jeffrey S.**, (AV) .................... '42 '77 C.284 B.A. L.1067 J.D. [Kaye,S.F.H.&H.]
*PRACTICE AREAS: Complex Civil Litigation; Securities Law; Contract Law; Entertainment Law; Environmental Law.
Gordon, John S. .................... '58 '84 C.846 B.A. L.813 J.D. Asst. U.S. Atty.
**Gordon, Jonathan M.** .................... '52 '78 C.154 B.A. L.597 J.D. [McClintock,W.B.R.R.&M.]
*REPORTED CASES: Savers Federal Savings & Loan Assoc. v. Home Federal Savings & Loan Assoc., 721 F. Supp. 940 (W.D. Tenn. 1989); Resolution Trust Corporation v. State of California, 1944 WL 172267 (C.D.CAL.).
*PRACTICE AREAS: Business Litigation and Dispute Resolution; Mediation/Arbitration; Intellectual Property; Entertainment Disputes; Employment Law/Confidential Investigations.
**Gordon, Judith A.** .................... '54 '79 C.103 A.B. L.893 J.D. [Ⓐ Seyfarth,S.F.&G.]
*PRACTICE AREAS: Pension and Employee Benefits Law.
**Gordon, Judith E.** .................... '69 '93 C&L.112 B.A., J.D. [Ⓐ Horvitz&L.]
Gordon, Kenneth G. .................... '45 '71 C.569 B.A. L.1009 J.D. [Laski&G.]
**Gordon, L. Gail** .................... '41 '75 C.05 B.Ed. L.800 J.D. [Pillsbury M.&S.]

# PRACTICE PROFILES
## CALIFORNIA—LOS ANGELES

Gordon, Louis S. .................................................. '29 '60 Principal Dep. Co. Coun.
Gordon, Marc '64 '91 C.197 A.B. L.1068 J.D.
    1800 Ave. of the Stars, Suite 900 (Century City)
**Gordon, Marcia Z.** .................... '54 '82 C.66 B.A. L.1009 J.D. [Ⓐ Brobeck,P.&H.]
   \*PRACTICE AREAS: Real Estate Law.
Gordon, Mark A. .................... '66 '91 C.974 B.A. L.1066 J.D. 601 S. Figueroa
Gordon, Meryl .................... '64 '92 C.831 B.A. L.477 J.D. 1000 Wilshire Blvd.
Gordon, Michael A. .................... '40 '66 C.112 B.S. L.800 11812 San Vicente Blvd.
Gordon, Nathan W. '26 '61 C.978 A.B. L.564 LL.B.
    (adm. in DC; not adm. in CA) U.S. Dept. of Justice, Immigration Judge
Gordon, Peter D. .................... '48 '77 C.1169 B.A. L.426 J.D. 8052 Melrose Ave.
**Gordon, Robert P.**, (AV) .................... '35 '60 C.112 B.S. L.800 J.D. [Goldman&G.]
   \*REPORTED CASES: Plotsky v. Friedman, in re Jack Friedman, BAP-CAL, 1991 126 BR 63; In Re Daylin, Inc., 9th Circuit, 1979, 596 F2d 853; Ruiz v. Ruiz, 6CA 3d 58, 85 CR 674; Lujan v. Gordan, 70 CA 3d 260, 138 CR 389; Associates Capital Services v. Security Pacific National Bank, 91 CA 3d 819, 154 CR 392.
   \*PRACTICE AREAS: Bankruptcy Law; Civil Litigation Law; Debtor-Creditor Law; Collections Law; Post-Judgement Law.
**Gordon, Roger L.**, (AV) .................... '47 '72 C.112 B.A. L.426 J.D. [Gordon,E.K.G.F.&G.]
   \*PRACTICE AREAS: Personal Injury Law; Products Liability Law; Insurance Bad Faith Law.
**Gordon, Ronald E.**, (AV) .................... '32 '61 C.911 B.A. L.1066 LL.B. [Buchalter,N.F.&Y.]
   \*PRACTICE AREAS: Insolvency.
Gordon, Sam .................... '24 '52 C&L.800 B.A., LL.B. 19-117 Criminal Cts. Bldg.
Gordon, Seymour N. .................... '29 '57 C.339 B.S. L.209 J.D. 10724 Wilshire Blvd.
Gordon, Stuart J., (BV) .................... '30 '56 C.685 B.A. L.145 J.D. 1223 N. Bundy Dr.‡
**Gordon, Edelstein, Krepack, Grant, Felton & Goldstein**, (AV) 📧
   A Partnership including a Professional Corporation
   **Suite 1800, 3580 Wilshire Boulevard, 90010**
   Telephone: 213-739-7000 Fax: 213-386-1671
   Roger L. Gordon; Mark Edelstein (Certified Specialist, Workers Compensation Law, The State Bar of California Board of Legal Specialization); Howard D. Krepack; Sherry E. Grant (Certified Specialist, Workers Compensation Law, The State Bar of California Board of Legal Specialization); Richard I. Felton (Certified Specialist, Workers Compensation Law, The State Bar of California Board of Legal Specialization); Irwin L. Goldstein (A Professional Corporation); Steven J. Kleifield. Associates: Joshua M. Merliss; David A. Goldstein; Eugenia L. Steele.
   Personal Injury, Workers Compensation, Social Security, Products Liability and Insurance Bad Faith Law, Toxic Tort, Premises Liability, Construction, Wrongful Termination, Sexual Harassment, Professional Negligence.
   *See Professional Biographies, LOS ANGELES, CALIFORNIA*
Goren, Bruce G. .................... '54 '79 C.112 B.A. L.1065 J.D. 10850 Wilshire Blvd.
**Goren, Julie A.** .................... '53 '87 C.112 A.B. L.426 J.D. [Ⓐ Buchalter,N.F.&Y.]
   \*PRACTICE AREAS: Insolvency.
Goren, Leora I. .................... '63 '89 C.112 B.A. L.1065 J.D. [Ⓐ Garfield,T.E.&T.]
**Gorham, Gary J.** .................... '64 '94 L.823 J.D. [Ⓐ Christensen,M.F.J.G.W.&S.]
   \*PRACTICE AREAS: Litigation.
Gorman, Edward I. .................... '21 '45 C.112 A.B. L.800 J.D. Supr. Ct. J.
**Gorman, Gregory G.** .................... '62 '87 C&L.597 B.S., J.D. [Ⓐ Allen,M.L.G.&M.]
   \*PRACTICE AREAS: Litigation; Real Estate Law; Attorney Malpractice; Unfair Trade Practices; Trade Secrets Law.
**Gorman, Joseph G., Jr.**, (AV) .................... '39 '67 C.112 A.B. L.1068 J.D. [Sheppard,M.R.&H.]
   \*PRACTICE AREAS: Estate Planning Law; Taxation Law.
Gorman, Karen .................... '55 '79 C.768 B.S. L.1137 J.D. Dep. Trial Coun., State Bar of Calif.
Gorman, Robert M. .................... '69 '94 C.597 B.A. L.813 J.D. 2121 Ave. of the Stars
**Gorowitz, Francie R.** .................... '55 '81 C.1044 B.A. L.982 J.D. [Ladas&P.] (See Pat. Sect.)
**Gorry, Timothy J.** .................... '63 '89 C.112 B.A. L.1065 J.D. [Gorry&M.]
   \*PRACTICE AREAS: Business; Entertainment; Commercial Litigation.
**Gorry & Meyer L.L.P.**
   **2029 Century Park East Suite 480, 90067**
   Telephone: 310-277-5967 Facsimile: 310-277-1470
   URL: http://www.gorrymeyer.com
   Timothy J. Gorry; David C. Meyer. Associate: Bryan Wilson Jardine; Frank Sandelmann.
   Business Litigation, Commercial, Corporate, Real Estate and Entertainment.
   *See Professional Biographies, LOS ANGELES, CALIFORNIA*
Gorsline, Laurie Susan .................... '59 '86 C.112 B.A. L.426 J.D. [Ganz&G.]
   \*REPORTED CASES: Hyatt v. Northrop Corporation, 80 F3d 1425 (9th Cir. 1996).
   \*PRACTICE AREAS: Employment; Civil Litigation.
Gortler, Hugh P. .................... '60 '91 C.401 B.S.M.E. L.978 J.D. 2029 Century Park E.
Gorvetzian, Kenneth R. '60 '87
   C.1077 B.A. L.809 J.D. Sr. Coun., Capital Grp. Cos., Inc.
**Gosch, Gerald E.** .................... '53 '83 C&L.546 B.A., J.D. [McClintock,W.B.R.R.&M.]
   \*PRACTICE AREAS: Construction and Surety Law; Federal Government - Contract Law.
Gosney, Christine H. .................... '51 '83 C.112 B.A. L.1137 J.D. [Ⓐ Lynberg&W.]
**Goss, Kent E.** .................... '61 '87 C.605 B.A. L.1065 J.D. [Pillsbury M.&S.]
Gotha, Frederick
   (See Pasadena)
**Gother, Ronald E.**, (AV) .................... '32 '56 C&L.879 B.A., LL.B. [Gibson,D.&C.]
   \*PRACTICE AREAS: Estate and Personal Planning.
**Goto, Roy Ai-Ji** .................... '46 '77 C.597 B.A. L.910 J.D. [Crosby,H.R.&M.]
   \*PRACTICE AREAS: Insurance; Environmental Law; Medical Devices.
Gottesman, Donald S. .................... '53 '78 C.112 B.A. L.1065 J.D. [Kulik&G.]
Gottesman, Mark A. .................... '40 '66 C.800 B.S. L.1065 LL.B. [Gottesman&P.]
Gottesman & Polito .................... 1880 Century Park E.
Gottfried, Abraham, (AV) '08 '30
   C.112 A.B. L.1065 J.D. 2160 Century Park, E., Apt. 1206‡
**Gottfried, Michael I.** .................... '55 '88 C.1044 B.A. L.1009 J.D. [McDermott,W.&E.]
   \*PRACTICE AREAS: Bankruptcy; Debtor and Creditor.
**Gottheim, Joshua C.** .................... '63 '89 C.976 B.A. L.1066 J.D. [Brown,W.&C.]
   \*PRACTICE AREAS: Real Estate; Land Use; Local Government Law.
Gottlieb, Gerald H., (AV) .................... '18 '51 C&L.800 A.B., J.D. 10933 Wellworth Ave.
Gottlieb, Jason A., (AV) .................... '32 '59 C&L.94 A.B., LL.B. [Rose,K.&M.]
Gottlieb, Judah .................... '34 '60 C.978 B.A. L.564 LL.B. 130 No. Fuller Ave.
Gottlieb, Judith Kaplan '57 '82 C.339 B.A. L.477 J.D.
   (adm. in IL; not adm. in CA) 2765 Casiano Rd.‡
**Gottlieb, Laurence L.** .................... '68 '93 C.94 B.S. L.978 J.D. [Troop M.S.&P.]
   \*PRACTICE AREAS: Litigation.
Gottlieb, Sandra L. .................... '54 '78 C.35 B.A. L.1148 J.D. [Swedelson&G.]
**Gottschall, Kurt L.** .................... '70 '95 C.154 B.A. L.1065 J.D. [Ⓐ Sheppard,M.R.&H.]
   \*PRACTICE AREAS: Litigation.
Gottshall-Sayed, Linda .................... '58 '90 C.999 L.809 J.D. 4700 Wilshire Blvd.
**Goudge, James H.** .................... '45 '80 C.1077 B.A. L.426 J.D. [Dennison,B.&P.]
   \*PRACTICE AREAS: Insurance and Tort Defense; Business Litigation; Products Liability; Wrongful Termination and Discrimination; Sexual Harassment.
Goul, Barbara Y. .................... '58 '83 C&L.426 B.A., J.D. Dep. Co. Coun.
**Gould, Carl M.**, (AV) ............. '— '43 C.025 L.426 J.D. [Hill,F.&B.] ‡
**Gould, Charles P.**, (AV) .................... '09 '32 C.145 Ph.B. L.800 LL.B. [Spray,G.&D.]
**Gould, David**, (AV) .................... '40 '66 C.112 A.B. L.1066 LL.B. [McDermott,W.&E.]
   \*PRACTICE AREAS: Bankruptcy.
Gould, Ernest S., (AV) .................... '38 '65 C.112 B.A. L.309 J.D. P.O. Box 27851
**Gould, Howard N.**, (AV) .................... '51 '77 C.178 A.B. L.276 J.D. [Doland&G.]

Gould, Jay B. .................... '55 '83 C.911 B.A. L.128 J.D. Bank of Amer.
Gould, Julian S. .................... '24 '50 C.800 B.A. L.809 J.D. 1741 Ivar Ave., (Hollywood)
Gould, Laizer D. .................... '53 '80 C.1077 B.A. L.1095 J.D. 6255 W. Sunset Blvd.
**Gould, Laurence K., Jr.**, (AV) .................... '46 '72 C.976 B.A. L.813 J.D. [Ⓒ Sheppard,M.R.&H.]
   \*PRACTICE AREAS: Administrative, Probate and Estate Planning.
Gould, Morton H. .................... '24 '51 C.569 B.S. L.178 LL.B. 6255 Sunset Blvd.
**Gould, Shelley M.** .................... '52 '76 C.112 B.A. L.809 J.D. [Ⓐ D.B.Bloom]
**Gould, William D.**, (AV) .................... '38 '64 C.426 B.A. L.1068 J.D. [Troy&G.]
   \*PRACTICE AREAS: Corporate Law; Securities Law.
**Gould-Saltman, Dianna J.**, (AV) .................... '58 '85 C.112 B.A. L.809 J.D. [Gould-Saltman]
**Gould-Saltman, Richard F.**, (AV) .................... '54 '78 C.608 B.A. L.800 J.D. [Gould-Saltman]
**Gould-Saltman Law Offices, LLP**, (AV)
   **4727 Wilshire Boulevard, Suite 500, 90010**
   Telephone: 213-939-8400 Fax: 213-939-8405
   Email: dgsaltman@aol.com
   Dianna J. Gould-Saltman (Certified Specialist, Family Law, The State Bar of California Board of Legal Specialization); Richard F. Gould-Saltman (Certified Specialist, Family Law, The State Bar of California Board of Legal Specialization).
   Family Law, Domestic Partnerships, Mediation and Litigation.
   *See Professional Biographies, LOS ANGELES, CALIFORNIA*
Goulet, Camille A. '63 '86 C.112 A.B. L.464 J.D.
   Assoc. Gen. Coun., Los Angeles Comm. Coll. Dist.
Goupillaud, Rene T. '49 '74 C&L.623 B.A., J.D.
   (adm. in OK; not adm. in CA) Dir., Atlantic Richfield Co.
**Gourley, Steven**, (AV) '49 '73 C.112 B.A. L.1066 J.D.
   **11355 West Olympic Boulevard Suite 100, 90064**
   Telephone: 310-478-1524 Fax: 310-312-4224
   \*LANGUAGES: Spanish.
   \*PRACTICE AREAS: Securities Law; Real Estate Lending Law; Mortgage Lending Law.
   Business Litigation Securities and Mortgage Lending Law.
   *See Professional Biographies, LOS ANGELES, CALIFORNIA*
Gower, Richard S. .................... '47 '73 C.589 B.S. L.426 J.D. [Inglis,L.&G.]
   \*PRACTICE AREAS: Insurance Defense.
**Gowey, Eric A.** .................... '67 '94 C.112 B.A. L.770 J.D. [Ⓐ McNicholas&M.]
Grab, Frederick .................... '46 '77 C.667 B.S. L.800 J.D. Dep. Atty. Gen.
**Graboff, Deborah L.** .................... '57 '83 C.112 B.A. L.426 J.D. [Ⓐ R.L.Zukerman]
   \*PRACTICE AREAS: Family Law; Civil Litigation.
**Graboff, Marc J.** .................... '56 '83 C.112 B.A. L.426 J.D. [Troop M.S.&P.]
   \*PRACTICE AREAS: Entertainment Law.
**Grace, David W.** .................... '54 '82 C.1209 B.S. L.893 J.D. [Loeb&L.] (See Pat. Sect.)
   \*PRACTICE AREAS: Trademark; Copyright; Intellectual Property Litigation.
**Grace, Eugene R.**, (AV) .................... '29 '62 C.1043 B.S. L.809 J.D. [Grace,S.C.&S.]
   \*PRACTICE AREAS: Product Liability Law; Insurance Coverage Law (including Environmental); Insurance Defense Law; Professional Liability Law; Appellate Law.
Grace, Jo-Ann W. .................... '46 '70 C.800 A.B. L.846 J.D. Pres., Metropolitan News Co.
**Grace, Michael K.** .................... '59 '86 C.475 B.A. L.477 J.D. [Greenberg G.F.C.&M.]
   \*PRACTICE AREAS: Intellectual Property; Business.
Grace, Roger M. R. .................... '45 '70 C.800 A.B. L.846 J.D. Coun., Metropolitan News Co.
**Grace, Skocypec, Cosgrove & Schirm, A Professional Corporation**, (AV)
   **444 South Flower Street, Suite 1100, 90071**☉
   Telephone: 213-487-6660 Fax: 213-487-4896
   Eugene R. Grace; Ronald J. Skocypec; Philip R. Cosgrove; Barry R. Schirm; Susan Tandy Olson; Ralph J. Scalzo; Daniel L. Gardner; Donald D. Wilson; Derek S. Whitefield; Patricia M. Coleman. Of Counsel: Greg W. Marsh;—Rod J. Cappy; Thomas H. Hutchinson; Jeffrey A. Lewiston; Dommond E. Lonnie; David Keith Schultz; Lisa M. Kralik; Scott W. McEwen (Resident, San Diego Office); Randy L. Rezen; Terence M. Kelly; Carl E. Lovell, III; Robin James; Alex W. Craigie; Kurt A. Schlichter; Susan K. Andersen; Joseph P. Augustine; Ilya A. Kostenboym.
   General Civil Practice in all California and Federal Trial and Appellate Courts. Product Liability, Insurance 'Bad Faith', Insurance Coverage, Toxic Tort, Environmental, Labor Relations and Professional Malpractice Law.
   Reference: City National Bank, 606 South Olive Street, Los Angeles, California 90014.
   San Diego, California Office: First National Bank Building, 401 West A Street, Suite 1815. Telephone: 619-234-6660. Telecopier: 619-234-2721.
   *See Professional Biographies, LOS ANGELES, CALIFORNIA*
**Grad, Richard J.** .................... '57 '83 C.112 A.B. L.588 J.D. [Sidley&A.]
   \*PRACTICE AREAS: Business Litigation.
Graddis, Richard D. '45 '71 C.477 A.B. L.309 J.D.
   (adm. in MA; not adm. in CA) 8794 Lookout Mt. Ave.‡
**Gradstein, Donna Luskin** .................... '56 '80 C.352 B.A. L.64 J.D. [Gradstein,L.&V.]
**Gradstein, Henry D.**, (AV) .................... '56 '74 C.1111 B.A. L.800 J.D. [Gradstein,L.&V.]
**Gradstein, Luskin & Van Dalsem**, (AV)
   **12100 Wilshire Boulevard, Suite 350, 90025**
   Telephone: 310-571-1700 Fax: 310-571-1717
   Henry D. Gradstein; Donna Luskin Gradstein; Bruce E. Van Dalsem; Joel M. Kozberg; R. David Smith.
   Civil, Trial and Appellate Practice, in all State and Federal Courts, Specializing in Entertainment and Business Litigation.
   *See Professional Biographies, LOS ANGELES, CALIFORNIA*
**Gradwohl, Alan J.**, (AV) .................... '33 '77 C.112 B.S. L.1148 J.D. [Federman,G.&G.]
   \*PRACTICE AREAS: Complex Civil Litigation; Insurance Coverage.
**Grady, Deena Fraley** .................... '63 '91 C.800 B.S. L.1148 J.D. [Grady&G.]
   \*PRACTICE AREAS: Insurance Bad Faith; Real Estate; Corporate; Fire Insurance; Wrongful Termination.
Grady, Erik Matthew '52 '85 C.1042 B.A. L.284 J.D.
   Dir., MCEG Sterling Entertainment
Grady, Janet M. .................... '53 '79 C.477 B.A. L.273 J.D. 777 S. Figueroa St.
**Grady, Scott L.** .................... '63 '91 C.1044 B.A. L.564 J.D. [Grady&G.]
   \*PRACTICE AREAS: Insurance Bad Faith; Fire Insurance; Homeowners Insurance; Wrongful Termination; Corporate Law.
Grady, Stafford R., (AV) '21 '45 C&L.273 A.B., LL.B.
   V.P., Emeritus, Sanwa Bk. Calif.
**Grady & Grady**
   **654 North Sepulveda Boulevard Suite Twelve, 90049**
   Telephone: 310-476-5773 Fax: 310-471-1055
   Members of Firm: Deena Fraley Grady; Scott L. Grady.
   Corporate Law, Business and Transactional Law, Employment Law, Wrongful Discharge/Discrimination, Real Property Litigation, including Land Use, Property Insurance, Fire Insurance, Homeowners Insurance, Inverse Condemnation, Insurance Bad Faith, Earth Movement and Flood Damage. Trial and Appellate Practice in all State and Federal Courts.
   *See Professional Biographies, LOS ANGELES, CALIFORNIA*
Graeber, Lawrence O., III .................... '44 '82 C.197 A.B. L.426 J.D. [Dorais&W.]
**Graf, Allan J.** .................... '46 '73 C.367 B.A. L.178 J.D. [Farmer&R.]
   \*LANGUAGES: French and Spanish.
   \*PRACTICE AREAS: Litigation.
**Graf, Margaret G.** .................... '43 '74 C.350 B.S. L.188 J.D. [Brand F.D.F.&K.]
   \*PRACTICE AREAS: Corporate Law; Finance; Securities.
Graf, Mark A. .................... '54 '79 C.201 B.S. L.339 J.D. [Ⓒ Sedgwick,D.M.&A.]
Graf, Ruth E. .................... '55 '81 C.112 B.A. L.966 J.D. [Allred,M.&K.]
Graff, Gil .................... '52 '76 C.1016 B.A. L.1068 J.D. 9628 Lockford St.

CAA237P

**Graff, Noah** '65 '92 C.311 B.A. L.188 J.D.
(adm. in NY; not adm. in CA) [[A] Hughes H.&R.]
**Graff, Victoria A.** ... '70 '96 C.112 B.A. L.976 J.D. [[A] O'Melveny&M.]
*LANGUAGES: Spanish.
Graham, Alice M. ... '50 '78 C.112 B.A. L.426 J.D. 5777 W. Century Blvd. Ste. 1255
**Graham, Anthony G.** ... '59 '90 C.945 A.B. L.309 J.D. [[A] Mayer,B.&P.]
*LANGUAGES: French, Spanish and German.
Graham, Bret ... '63 '88 C.976 B.A. L.659 J.D. 555 S. Flower St., 18th Fl.
**Graham, Bruce J.** ... '54 '83 C.154 B.A. L.1068 J.D. [[A] Pircher,N.&M.]
*PRACTICE AREAS: Public Finance Law.

**Graham, Bruce N., (AV) '50 '79 C.608 B.A. L.851 J.D.**
**21241 Ventura Boulevard, Suite 283, 91364**
**Telephone: 818-347-9146 Fax: 818-347-9147**
**Email: bgraha00@Counsel.com**
**General Civil and Trial Practice with emphasis on Property and Casualty, Insurance Coverage, Bad Faith, Fraud, Subrogation, Health Insurance, Life and Disability Insurance, Surety and Construction Bonds.**

***See Professional Biographies, LOS ANGELES, CALIFORNIA***

**Graham, Curtis A.**, (AV) ... '53 '79 C.112 B.A. L.659 J.D. [Rutter,G.&H.]
*PRACTICE AREAS: Business Litigation; Real Estate Law; Business Planning.
Graham, David M. ... '60 '91 C.1042 B.A. L.809 J.D. 2029 Century Park East
Graham, Gordon J. ... '51 '82 C.766 B.A. L.1137 J.D. 1741 N. Ivar
**Graham, Heather Rickett** ... '65 '92 C.112 B.A. L.426 J.D. [Freid&G.]
*PRACTICE AREAS: Family Law.
**Graham, J. Susan** ... '62 '87 C.112 B.A. L.1068 J.D. [Pollak,V.&F.]
**Graham, John A.**, (AV) ... '50 '76 C.645 B.A. L.1049 J.D. [Frandzel&S.]
*PRACTICE AREAS: Bankruptcy Chapter 11; Bankruptcy Litigation; Bankruptcy Reorganization; Commercial Law; Uniform Commercial Code.
**Graham, Joseph M., Jr.** ... '68 '92 C.1105 B.A. L.145 J.D. [[A] Kirkland&E.]
*PRACTICE AREAS: Litigation.
Graham, Kenneth E., Jr. ... '35 '63 C&L.477 B.A., J.D. Prof. of Law, U.C.L.A.‡
**Graham, Kent V.**, (AV) ... '43 '70 C.112 B.A. L.426 J.D. [O'Melveny&M.]
*PRACTICE AREAS: Family Business Law; Corporate Law; Venture Capital; Start-Ups; Mergers, Acquisitions and Divestitures.
Graham, Richard ... '53 '80 1925 Century Park E.
**Graham, Robert L.**, (AV) ... '40 '72 C.170 B.A. L.426 J.D. [McKay,B.&G.]
*PRACTICE AREAS: Civil Trial; Products Liability.
**Graham, Stanley P.** ... '43 '70 C.37 B.A. L.1068 J.D. [[C] Williams&B.]
*PRACTICE AREAS: Tax Law; Estate Planning Law.
Graham, Stephen S. '38 '64 C&L.309 A.B., LL.B.
(adm. in IL; not adm. in CA) 9000 Sunset Blvd.‡
Graham Dunitz, Jody ... '55 '81 C.112 B.A. L.1067 J.D. 11355 W. Olympic Blvd.

**Graham & James LLP, (AV) [BB]**
**14th Floor, 801 South Figueroa Street, 90017⊙**
**Telephone: 213-624-2500 Telex: 4720414 GRJAUI Telecopier: 213-623-4581**
**Email: dmiyamoto@gj.com URL: http://www.gj.com**
**John J. Allen; Jorge Arciniega; Hidetoshi Asakura; Vincent J. Belusko; James H. Broderick, Jr.; Jeffrey A. Chester; Hillel T. Cohn; Henry S. David; Craig J. de Recat; Steven S. Doi; David L. Fehrman; Rodney A. Fujii; Benjamin E. Goldman; Randolph H. Gustafson; Yasuhiro Hagihara (Not admitted in CA); David L. Henty; John C. Holberton; J. Eric Isken; William J. James; Cheryl Lee Johnson; Wolfgang M. Kau; Joon Yong Kim; Stan H. Koyanagi; Ken M. Kurosu; Michael R. Lindsay; Thomas T. Liu; David A. Livdahl; Joseph T. Lynyak, III; Thomas J. Masenga; Stuart L. Merkadeau; David T. Miyamoto; John T. Nagai; Stephen T. Owens; Denis H. Oyakawa; Charles Paturick; Steven G. Polard; Pamela K. Prickett; Don A. Proudfoot, Jr.; Edwin B. Reeser, III; James C. Roberts; William J. Robinson; Minda R. Schechter; Brian E. Schield; Allan A. Shenoi; Wayne M. Smith; Brian A. Sullivan; Derrick K. Takeuchi; Martin J. Trupiano; Les J. Weinstein; Barry Leigh Weissman. Special Counsel: William G. Anderson; Everitt G. Beers; Larry W. Mitchell. Senior Counsel: Daniel E. Champion; Patrick J. Fields. Of Counsel: David A. Hayden; Richard P. Manson; William W. Wells; Eric E. Younger. Counsel: Merrill J. Baumann, Jr. Associates: David B. Abel; Michael B. Annis; Martha L. Applebaum; Alison M. Barbarosh; Brian M. Berliner; Kenneth N. Burraston; Lynn D. Cantor (Not admitted in CA); Pei-Wen Chang; JoAn H. Cho; Marcus Delgado; Victor de Gyarfas; Marjorie Turk Desmond; Robert Desmond; Peter R. Duchesneau; Shivbir S. Grewal; Jennifer R. Hasbrouck; Gerard A. Hekker; Jonathan E. Johnson III; Allen Choo Kim; Hyunu Lee; Jeanne M. Malitz; David J. Meyer; Rie Miyake; Hisako Muramatsu; Martin M. Noonen; David K. Ritenour; Bin Xue Sang; Thomas P. Schmidt; Eric Shih; Nao S. Shimato; Kristi Miki Springer; Milo M. Stevanovich; Jennifer M. Tsao; Brian Van Vleck; Kimberly G. Winer; Rami S. Yanni.**
**General Practice including Civil Litigation in State and Federal Courts, Corporation, Banking and Financial Services, Commercial, International Business, Tax, Labor, Real Estate, Environmental, Intellectual Property, Bankruptcy, Creditors' Rights, Immigration, ERISA and Employee Benefits.**
**Other offices located in: San Francisco, Orange County, Palo Alto, Sacramento and Fresno, California; Seattle, Washington; Washington, D.C.; New York, New York; Milan, Italy; Beijing, China; Tokyo, Japan; London, England; Dusseldorf, Germany.**
**Associated Offices: Deacons Graham & James, Hong Kong, Sydney, Melbourne, Brisbane, Perth and Canberra, Australia.**
**Affiliated Offices: Deacons Graham & James, Hanoi and Ho Chi Minh City, Vietnam; Taipei, Taiwan and Bangkok, Thailand; In association with Dewi Soeharto & Rekan, Jakarta, Indonesia; Graham & James in affiliation with Taylor Joynson Garrett, London, England, Bucharest, Romania and Brussels, Belgium; Mishare M. Al-Ghazali & Partners, Safat, Kuwait; Law Firm of Salah Al-Hejailan, Jeddah and Riyadh, Saudi Arabia.**

***See Professional Biographies, LOS ANGELES, CALIFORNIA***

**Grail, Efrem M.** ... '59 '86 C.597 B.A. L.178 J.D. [[A] Bird,M.B.W.&M.]
*LANGUAGES: Spanish.
*PRACTICE AREAS: Criminal Law; General Commercial Law; Securities Law; First Amendment Practice.
Graiwer, Manuel P. ... '43 '70 C.112 B.A. L.1069 J.D. 3600 Wilshire Blvd.
**Grajewski, Wayne S.** ... '51 '76 C.813 A.B. L.1066 J.D. [Arter&H.]
**Gralla, Donald A.**, (AV) ... '33 '59 C.112 B.S. L.1068 J.D. [[A] King,W.E.&B.]
*PRACTICE AREAS: Civil Litigation; Real Estate; Business Transactions.
**Gralnek, Donald D.** ... '45 '71 C.813 B.A. L.1066 J.D. [Jones,D.R.&P.]
**Gralnek, Gaelle H.** ... '65 '89 C&L.36 B.S., J.D. Sr. Coun., Ernst & Young LLP
**Gram, Mary E.** ... '56 '93 C.623 B.F.A. L.809 J.D. [[A] Belcher,H.&B.]
*PRACTICE AREAS: Civil Trial; Appellate Practice; Products Liability.
Granados, Raul R. ... '46 '74 C.1097 B.A. L.426 J.D. 5429 E. Beverly Blvd.
Granbo, Roger H., Jr. ... '55 '83 C.1042 B.A. L.1179 J.D. Sr. Dep. Co. Coun.
Grancell, Norin T., (AV) ... '42 '68 C.112 B.S. L.800 J.D. [Grancell,G.&M.]
Grancell, Grancell & Marshall, A Professional Corp., (AV) ... 6701 Center Dr. W., 12th Fl
Granet, Nicholas ... '11 '40 L.596 LL.B. 205 S. Broadway
**Graniez, John A.** ... '48 '79 C.262 B.A. L.426 J.D. [[C] Quisenberry&B.]
*PRACTICE AREAS: Insurance Coverage Litigation.
**Graniez, Laurie B.** ... '59 '88 C&L.800 B.A., J.D. [[A] Morrison&F.]
**Grannan, Patrick J.** ... '58 '84 C.311 B.A. L.564 J.D. [Chimicles,J.&T.]
Grannis, John F. ... '52 '79 C.105 B.A. L.464 J.D. 611 W. 6th St., 16th Fl.
Granof, Gerald H., (AV) ... '27 '51 C&L.966 B.B.A., J.D. [Tyre K.K.&G.]
**Grant, Adam D. H.** ... '64 '91 C.112 B.A. L.809 J.D. [[A] Negele&Assoc.]
*PRACTICE AREAS: Commercial Construction Law; Residential Construction Law; Insurance Law; Products Liability; Interstate Commerce.
**Grant, Ann E.** ... '62 '91 C.101 B.A. L.1049 J.D. [[A] Howrey&S.]
*PRACTICE AREAS: Complex Litigation; White Collar Criminal Defense.
**Grant, Charles M.** ... '61 '88 C.143 B.A. L.245 J.D. [[A] Shearman&S.]
Grant, Edward I. ... '37 '63 C.112 B.A. L.426 J.D. 1543 W. Olympic Blvd.
**Grant, Hugh Jeffrey** ... '65 '91 C.800 B.S. L.426 J.D. [[A] Murchison&C.]
*PRACTICE AREAS: Product Liability; General Commercial Litigation.
**Grant, James T.** ... '65 '91 C.813 B.A. L.477 J.D. [[A] McDermott,W.&E.]

**Grant, Jay H.**, (AV) ... '35 '59 C&L.494 B.S.L., J.D. [Isen&G.]
**Grant, Jay R.** ... '67 '93 C.309 A.B. L.1066 J.D. [[A] Manatt,P.&P.]
*PRACTICE AREAS: Labor and Employment Law.
Grant, John G. ... '19 '48 C.813 A.B. L.800 LL.B. 266 N. Ashdale Ave.‡
**Grant, Philip G.** ... '41 '83 C.112 B.A. L.846 J.D. [[C] Cadwalader,W.&T.]
**Grant, Richard S.** ... '60 '86 C&L.966 B.A., J.D. [[A] Wolf,R.&S.]
**Grant, Sherry E.**, (AV) ... '48 '74 C.94 B.A. L.426 J.D. [Gordon,E.K.G.F.&G.]
*PRACTICE AREAS: Workers Compensation Law; Social Security Law; Third Party Litigation.
Grant, Stephen B. ... '— '62 6363 Wilshire Blvd.
**Grantham, Robert A.** ... '52 '81 C.112 B.A. L.208 J.D. [Murchison&C.]
*PRACTICE AREAS: Business and Corporate Law; Products Liability; Environmental; International; Appeals.
Graskamp, Edward D. '54 '79 C.898 B.A. L.300 J.D.
(adm. in MN; not adm. in CA) McKinsey & Co., Inc.
**Grasmick, T.J. (Mick)** ... '48 '76 C.546 B.S. L.477 J.D. [Pillsbury M.&S.]
**Grass, Alan B.**, (BV) ... '42 '68 C.477 B.A. L.309 J.D. [[C] Agapay,L.&H.]
**Grassgreen, Debra** ... '66 '92 C&L.260 B.S.B.A., J.D. [[A] Pachulski,S.Z.&Y.]
*PRACTICE AREAS: Bankruptcy.

**Grassini, Wrinkle & Gallagher, A Law Corporation**
**(See Woodland Hills)**

**Gratch, Joshua A.** ... '67 '93 C.112 B.A. L.1068 J.D. [[A] Quisenberry&B.]
**Grattan, Maureen A.** ... '50 '81 C.112 A.B. L.1065 J.D. [Dorais&W.]

**Graubart, Jeffrey L., (AV) '40 '65 C.339 B.S. L.597 J.D.**
**2029 Century Park East, Suite 2700, 90067-3041**
**Telephone: 310-788-2650 Fax: 310-788-2657**
***REPORTED CASES: Los Angeles News Service vs. Tullo, 973 F.2d 791 (9th Cir. 1992).**
**Entertainment Law, International Law, Corporate and Business Law, Civil Litigation, Copyright Infringement, Trademark Infringement, Motion Pictures, Music, Music Publishing, Multimedia, Publishing and Theater Law.**

***See Professional Biographies, LOS ANGELES, CALIFORNIA***

**Graupmann Zuckerman, Ann** ... '57 '86 C.297 B.A. L.426 J.D. [Anderson,M.&C.]
*PRACTICE AREAS: Civil and Environmental Litigation; Insurance Coverage; Employment Law.
**Grausam, Jeffrey L.**, (AV) ... '43 '69 C.918 B.A. L.145 J.D. [Morgan,L.&B.]
Graven, Lawrence S., (AV) ... '29 '60 C&L.800 B.S., LL.B. [Graven P.B.B.&Q.]
Graven Perry Block Brody & Qualls, A Professional Corporation, (AV)
523 West Sixth St.
**Graves, Anna M.** ... '59 '85 C.188 A.B. L.893 J.D. [[C] Paul,H.J.&W.]
Graves, Jeffrey R. ... '54 '80 C.1097 B.A. L.426 J.D. Dep. Pub. Co. Def.
**Graves, Philip J.** ... '61 '91 C.911 B.A. L.178 J.D. [[A] Irell&M.]
**Graves, Timothy R.** ... '60 '85 C&L.575 B.S., J.D. [Lewis,D.B.&B.]
**Gravitt, Timothy A.** '57 '84
C.112 B.A. L.1065 J.D. [Meserve,M.&H.] (⊙San Diego & Irvine)
Gravlin, E. William ... '42 '71 C.112 B.A. L.426 J.D. Dep. Dist. Atty.
**Gray, Gary S.**, (AV) ... '46 '75 C.1077 B.S. L.426 J.D. [Gray,Y.D.&R.]
*PRACTICE AREAS: Insurance Law; Environmental Law; Construction Law; Business Law.
**Gray, Humberto R.** ... '62 '88 C.940 B.A. L.1148 J.D. [Blalock&G.]
*PRACTICE AREAS: Immigration and Nationality Law.
Gray, Ione Young ... '47 '73 C.691 B.A. L.178 J.D. 2040 Ave. of the Stars
**Gray, Jeremy J. F.** ... '61 '90 C.182 B.A. L.426 J.D. [[A] Katten M.&Z.]
**Gray, Megan E.** ... '69 '95 C&L.846 B.A., J.D. [[A] Baker&H.]
*LANGUAGES: Russian.
*PRACTICE AREAS: Intellectual Property; Litigation.
**Gray, Pamela C.**, (AV) ... '44 '76 C.914 B.A. L.426 J.D. [O'Melveny&M.] (⊙Newport)
*PRACTICE AREAS: Income Tax; International Income Tax; Estate and Gift Taxation.
**Gray, Roger H.** ... '60 '85 C.800 A.B. L.128 J.D. [Margolis&M.]
*PRACTICE AREAS: General Practice; Litigation; Appeals (15%, 2).
Gray, Thomas A. ... '44 '72 C.705 A.B. L.1049 J.D. Dep. Dist. Atty.
Gray, Timothy ... '67 '94 C.112 B.A. L.276 J.D. 300 S. Grand Ave.
**Gray, Tracy Birnkrant** ... '66 '91 C.103 B.A. L.1068 J.D. [[A] Pillsbury M.&S.]

**Gray & Hirrel**
**(See Pasadena)**

**Gray, York, Duffy & Rattet, (AV) [BB]**
**15760 Ventura Boulevard, 16th Floor (Encino), 91436**
**Telephone: 818-907-4000; 310-553-0445 FAX: 818-783-4551**
**Members of Firm: Gary S. Gray; James R. York; John J. Duffy; Gary S. Rattet; Arlene A. Colman; Louis A. Cappadona; Barry D. Brown; William F. Flahavan; Jeffrey S. Stern. Associates: Amalia L. Taylor; Kenneth A. Hearn; Gabriel H. Wainfeld; John L. Barber; Miloslav Khadilkar; Michael S. Eisenbaum; Frank J. Ozello, Jr.; Eric J. Erickson; Bridgett Esquibias; Carol G. Arnold; David G. Marcus.**
**General Civil Trial and Appellate Practice in all State and Federal Courts. Insurance, Malpractice, Products Liability, Construction, Wrongful Termination, Public Liability and Business Law.**
**Reference: Marathon National Bank, Los Angeles, California.**

***See Professional Biographies, LOS ANGELES, CALIFORNIA***

Grayman, Peter M. ... '47 '88 L.061 [[A] Gittler,W.&B.]
Graysen, WilliamT. ... '52 '79 C.112 B.A. L.1136 J.D. 2049 Century Pk. E.
**Grayson, Jim G.** ... '48 '74 C&L.36 B.S., J.D. [[C] Morrison&F.]
*PRACTICE AREAS: Real Estate; Public Finance.
Grayson, Mark ... '56 '81 C.1077 L.809 J.D. [Grayson,G.&M.]
Grayson, Saul, (AV) ... '27 '53 C.112 B.A. L.1068 LL.B. [Grayson,G.&M.]
Grayson, Stephen P. ... '51 '76 C.112 B.A. L.1067 J.D. 10850 Wilshire Blvd.
Grayson, Grayson & Mansell, A Professional Corporation, (AV) ... 10880 Wilshire Blvd.
**Greaves, John A.** ... '48 '92 C.502 B.A. L.221 J.D. [[A] Baum,H.A.G.&D.]
*PRACTICE AREAS: Airplane Crash litigation; Aviation Accidents and Injuries; Aviation Products Liability; Helicopter Crash Litigation; Complex and Multi-District Litigation.
**Grecky, Maria E.** ... '67 '92 C.659 B.S. L.800 J.D. [[A] Proskauer R.G.&M.]
**Green, Christopher R.** ... '65 '90 C&L.494 B.A., J.D. [[A] Lewis,D.B.&B.]
**Green, Edwin W.**, (AV) ... '35 '60 C&L.800 B.S., LL.B. [Bronson,B.&M.]
*PRACTICE AREAS: Jury Trials.
**Green, Elizabeth C.** ... '53 '78 C.976 A.B. L.145 J.D. [[C] Preston G.&E.]
**Green, Gary H., II** ... '69 '94 C.902 B.A. L.309 J.D. [[A] Thelen,M.J.&B.]
*PRACTICE AREAS: Labor and Employment Law; Litigation; Federal Litigation.
Green, Harold B. ... '23 '74 C.930 L.1136 J.D. 3550 Wilshire Blvd., 7th Fl.
**Green, Ian M.** ... '63 '89 C.112 B.A. L.1065 J.D. [[A] Hill,F.&B.]
*PRACTICE AREAS: Business Litigation.
Green, Jerry H. ... '51 '76 C.112 B.A. L.800 J.D. 2029 Century Pk., E.
Green, Joan Whiteside, (BV) ... '44 '79 C.1097 B.A. L.1148 J.D. 3580 Wilshire Blvd.
**Green, Lesley C.** ... '47 '83 L.800 J.D. [Bannan,G.S.&F.]
*PRACTICE AREAS: Employment Law; First Party Insurance Bad Faith; ERISA Litigation.
Green, Michael B. ... '45 '72 C.102 B.A. L.569 J.D. Asst. Gen. Coun., Sizzler Intl., Inc.
Green, Richard ... '36 '88 C.823 A.B. L.976 J.D. U.C.L.A.
**Green, Robert A.**, (AV) ... '49 '75 C.112 B.S. L.1068 J.D. [Darby&D.] (Pat.)
*PRACTICE AREAS: Patent Law; Trademark Law; Copyright Law.
Green, Scott M. '56 '80 C.597 B.A. L.94 J.D.
(adm. in IL; not adm. in CA) V.P. & Assoc. Reg. Coun., Chicago Title Ins. Co.
Green, Stella M. ... '62 '87 C&L.800 B.A., J.D. ITC Entertainment Grp.
**Green, Steven M.** ... '61 '85 C.145 A.B. L.629 J.D. [[A] Kegel,T.&T.]

**Green, Susan H.** ...'56 '81 C.597 B.A. L.1068 J.D. [Ring&G.]
*PRACTICE AREAS: Business; Commercial; Corporate Litigation.
Green, Terry A. ...'47 '72 C&L.800 A.B., J.D. Supr. Ct. J.
Green, Tracy ...'60 '88 C.36 B.A. L.37 J.D. 3580 Wilshire Blvd.
**Green, William P., (Law Corporation),** (AV) '20 '47
C.337 B.A. L.597 J.D. [Ⓒ Darby&D.] (Pat.)
Greenbaum, Felice G. ...'58 '82 C&L.978 B.A., J.D. 9333 Duxbury Rd.
**Greenbaum, Jon M.** ...'68 '93 C.112 B.A. L.1068 J.D. [Ⓐ Dewey B.]
**Greenbaum, Michael S.** '55 '82 C&L.061 B.A., LL.B.
(adm. in SAfric; not adm. in CA) [Ⓐ B.P.Wolfsdorf]
*PRACTICE AREAS: Immigration Law.
**Greenbaum, Richard W.** ...'54 '80 C.150 B.B.A. L.990 J.D. [Herzfeld&R.]
*PRACTICE AREAS: Litigation; Product Liability; Insurance Defense Law.
**Greenberg, Amy E.** ...'68 '94 C.477 B.A. L.426 J.D. [Ⓐ Riordan&M.]
*PRACTICE AREAS: Labor and Employment.
**Greenberg, Arthur N.,** (AV) '27 '53 C.112 A.B. L.1068 LL.B.
[Greenberg G.F.C.&M.]
*PRACTICE AREAS: Litigation; Alternative Dispute Resolution; Business Litigation; Corporate and Business.
Greenberg, Bert D. ...'41 '67 C.331 B.A. L.1009 J.D. 3530 Wilshire Blvd.
**Greenberg, Blaine Eric** ...'58 '82 C.881 A.B. L.813 J.D. [Troop M.S.&P.]
*PRACTICE AREAS: Environmental/Toxic Tort Litigation; Commercial Litigation; Family Law Litigation.
Greenberg, Bruce A. ...'54 '78 C.800 B.S. L.809 J.D. 1200 Wilshire Blvd.
Greenberg, David, (AV) ...'38 '65 C.112 B.S. L.1068 LL.B. [Greenberg&P.]
**Greenberg, Gordon A.** ...'54 '80 C.339 B.A. L.146 J.D. [Sheppard,M.R.&H.]
*PRACTICE AREAS: Antitrust Law; Criminal Law; Business Crimes; Trial Practice.
Greenberg, Harold ...'39 '65 C.645 B.A. L.831 LL.B. 2263 S. Harvard Blvd.
**Greenberg, Jeffrey B.** ...'71 '96 C.800 B.A. L.597 J.D. [Ⓐ Latham&W.]
**Greenberg, Karen L.** '58 '87 C.112 B.A. L.809 J.D.
Asst. V.P. & Coun., CB Coml. Real Estate Grp., Inc.
*RESPONSIBILITIES: Litigation; Transactional.
Greenberg, Linda B. ...'45 '77 C.563 B.S. L.426 J.D. Dep. Dist. Atty.
Greenberg, Mark Howard '53 '78
C&L.309 B.A., J.D. Western Ctr. on Law & Poverty, Inc.
Greenberg, Mark S. ...'48 '79 C.1077 B.S. L.767 J.D. 1801 Avenue of the Stars
**Greenberg, Maxwell E.,** (AV) ...'22 '50 C.112 A.B. L.309 LL.B. [Ⓒ Jeffer,M.B.&M.]
*PRACTICE AREAS: Estate Planning and Probate; Corporate; Real Estate Transactions.
Greenberg, Mead I. ...'45 '70 C.154 B.A. L.276 J.D. 333 S. Grand Ave., 37th Fl.
**Greenberg, Paul R., Inc.,** (AV) ...'42 '69 C.112 A.B. L.178 LL.B. [P.R.Greenburg]
*PRACTICE AREAS: Corporate Law.
Greenberg, Stanley I., (AV) ...'41 '66 C&L.502 A.B., J.D. 11845 W. Olympic Blvd.
**Greenberg, Thomas R.** ...'58 '96 C.72 B.A. L.30 J.D. [Ⓐ Gibson,D.&C.]

**Greenberg Glusker Fields Claman & Machtinger LLP, (AV)**
**21th Floor, 1900 Avenue of the Stars (Century City), 90067**
**Telephone: 310-553-3610 Fax: 310-553-0687**
**Members of Firm: Arthur N. Greenberg; Philip Glusker; Sidney J. Machtinger; Stephen Claman; Bertram Fields; Harvey R. Friedman; Bernard Shearer; Jon J. Gallo; Paula J. Peters; Michael K. Collins; John L. Child; C. Bruce Levine; Michael A. Greene; Joseph M. Cahn; Garrett L. Hanken; Norman H. Levine; William A. Halama; James E. Hornstein; Robert S. Chapman; Robert F. Marshall; Robert E. Bennett, Jr.; Marc S. Cohen; Charles N. Shephard; Dennis B. Ellman; Gary L. Kaplan; Robert W. Barnes; Lawrence Y. Iser; E. Barry Haldeman; Mark Stankevich; Martin H. Webster; Michael V. Bales; Henry D. Finkelstein; Diane J. Crumpacker; Jean Morris; Elizabeth Watson; Jill A. Cossman; Peter J. Niemiec; Roger L. Funk; Richard A. Kale; Debby R. Zurzolo; Arnold D. Kahn (Certified Specialist, Probate, Estate Planning and Trust Law, The State Bar of California Board of Legal Specialization); Mark A. Gochman; Eve H. Wagner; Gerald L. Sauer; Nancy A. Bertrando; Bonnie E. Eskenazi; Glenn A. Dryfoos; Richard E. Posell; Jeffrey Spitz; Steven J. Lurie; Brian L. Edwards; Stanley W. Levy; Michael K. Grace. Associates: Lee A. Dresie; Nancy C. Hsieh; Nanette Lynn Klein; David R. Mersten; Patricia A. Millett; Elisabeth A. Basini; Jeffrey A. Krieger; Carla M. Roberts; Edward N. Sabin; Michael W. Scholtz; Joan E. Smiles; Mark S. Weinstock; Kevin L. James; Sheri E. Porath; Stephanie H. Gold; Matthew M. Johnson; Wendy M. Mesnick; Stephen S. Smith; Marc M. Stern; Curtis P. Holdsworth; Karen E. Pointer; Paul A. Blechner; Stephen P. Clark; Nathanael M. Cousins; Patrick P. de Gravelles; Kristen L. Jacobsmeyer; Barry D. Kellman; Kelly L. Sather; Bradley Small; Douglas G. Crowell; Gregory J. Sater.**
**General Civil, Trial and Appellate Practice; Alternative Dispute Resolution; Real Estate; Corporate and Business; Securities; Entertainment; Communications and Publishing; Intellectual Property; International, Federal and State Taxation; Estate Planning and Probate; Labor and Employee Relations; Bankruptcy; Corporate Reorganizations and Financial Institutions; Environmental.**
**Reference: Wells Fargo Bank, 1801 Century Park East, Los Angeles, CA 90067.**
***See Professional Biographies, LOS ANGELES, CALIFORNIA***

Greenberg & Panish, A Prof. Corp., (AV) ...3832 Wilshire Blvd.

**Greenberg, Paul R., Inc., (AV)**
**1875 Century Park East Seventh Floor, 90067**
**Telephone: 310-277-6109 Facsimile: 310-277-6115**
**Email: Paulgreenb@aol.com**
**Paul R. Greenberg, Inc.**
**General Corporate Representation, both Domestic and Foreign, with emphasis on Network Marketing Law.**

**Greene, David A.** ...'63 '89 C.990 B.A. L.809 J.D. [Ⓐ Saltzburg,R.&B.]
*PRACTICE AREAS: Bankruptcy Law; Debtor Creditor Law; Litigation.

**Greene, Gary S., (AV) '49 '75 C.112 B.A. L.426 J.D.**
**157 South Fairfax Avenue Second Floor, 90036-2106**
**Telephone: 213-525-1800 Fax: 213-525-1300**
**Business, Real Property, Personal Injury, Probate and Creditors Rights Law. General Civil and Trial Practice in State and Federal Courts.**
**Counsel for: K-G Properties.**
***See Professional Biographies, LOS ANGELES, CALIFORNIA***

Greene, Gerald ...'43 '75 C.994 B.A. L.1009 J.D. 1901 Ave. of the Stars
Greene, James C., (AV) ...'15 '40 C&L.976 B.A., LL.B. 400 S. Hope St.
**Greene, Marvin, (A P.C.),** (AV) ...'24 '51 C.813 B.A. L.767 J.D. [Ⓒ Loeb&L.]
*PRACTICE AREAS: Corporate Law; Securities Law; Arbitration.
Greene, Michael ...'45 '71 C.112 B.A. L.800 J.D. 1900 Ave. of the Stars
**Greene, Michael A.,** (AV) ...'45 '71 C.112 A.B. L.800 J.D. [Greenberg G.F.C.&M.]
*PRACTICE AREAS: Litigation.
**Greene, Reginald D.,** (AV) ...'51 '78 C.277 B.E.E.S. L.477 J.D. [Arnelle,H.M.W.&G.]
*PRACTICE AREAS: Litigation; Products Liability; Intellectual Property; Construction; Structural Defects.
**Greene, Richard J.,** (AV) ...'47 '75 C.1077 B.S. L.809 J.D. [Welter&G.]
*PRACTICE AREAS: Business Law; Corporate; Real Estate Law.
Greene, Robert L. ...'59 '85 C.800 A.B. L.276 J.D. 960 Dexter St.
Greene, Susanne L. ...'46 '78 C.1077 B.A. L.1095 J.D. 9000 Sunset Blvd.
Greene, Thomas J. ...'38 '64 C.602 B.A. L.477 LL.B. 7319 Ogelsby Ave.‡
**Greene, Warren G.,** (AV) ...'49 '74 C.813 A.B. L.800 J.D. [Rutter,G.&H.]
*PRACTICE AREAS: Business Litigation.
**Greene, William N.,** (AV) ...'18 '41 C&L.623 LL.B. [Ⓒ Hanna&M.]
*PRACTICE AREAS: Taxation; Real Estate; Probate; Estate Planning; Trusts.

**Greene, Broillet, Taylor, Wheeler, & Panish**
**(See Santa Monica)**

Greene-Frieden, Charlotte ...'38 '79 C.112 B.A. L.1238 LL.D. 5300 E. Beverly Blvd.

**Greenfeld, J. Steven** ...'52 '77 C.385 A.B. L.1065 J.D. [Rodgers&G.]
*PRACTICE AREAS: General Civil Trial Practice; Appellate Practice.
**Greenfeld, Peter N.** ...'63 '91 C.881 B.A. L.426 J.D. [Ⓐ Carlsmith B.W.C.&I.]
*PRACTICE AREAS: Business Litigation; Environmental Law.
Greenfield, Albert N. ...'18 '55 C.446 B.S. L.426 LL.B. 2795 McConnell Dr.‡
**Greenfield, Larry S.,** (AV) ...'50 '75 C.188 A.B. L.569 J.D. [McCambridge,D.&M.]
**Greenfield, Lawrence A.** ...'57 '85 C.1077 B.A. L.809 J.D. [Ⓐ Dummit,F.&B.]
Greenfield, Leslie H. '34 '65
C.472 B.B.A. L.809 J.D. Admin. Law J., Off. of Admin. Hearings
Greenfield, Mark S., (AV) '50 '74 C.112 B.A. L.1066 J.D.
1801 Century Park E., 16th Fl.
**Greenfield, Robert A.,** (AV) ...'41 '67 C.112 B.S. L.309 LL.B. [Stutman,T.&G.]
*PRACTICE AREAS: Bankruptcy; Insolvency; Corporate Reorganization; Commercial Litigation.
**Greenfield, Scott I.** ...'68 '93 C.112 B.A. L.426 J.D. [Ⓐ Jeffer,M.B.&M.]
*PRACTICE AREAS: General Business; Real Estate Litigation.
**Greenleaf, Christopher J.** ...'64 '94 C.112 B.A. L.800 J.D. [Lewis,D.B.&B.]
**Greenleaf, Timothy R.** ...'56 '81 C.112 A.B. L.426 J.D. [Fulbright&J.]
*PRACTICE AREAS: Taxation; Mergers and Acquisitions.
**Greenslade, Joseph L.** ...'63 '89 C.112 B.A. L.426 J.D. [Ⓐ Walter,F.&R.]
*PRACTICE AREAS: Litigation.
Greenspan, Eric R. ...'50 '75 C.228 B.A. L.904 J.D. [Myman,A.F.G.&R.]
Greenspan, Jonathan H. ...'47 '75 C.112 B.A. L.426 J.D. 2049 Century Pk., E.
**Greenspoon, Claudia L.** ...'57 '83 C.112 B.A. L.809 J.D. [Bronson,B.&M.]
*LANGUAGES: Hebrew.
*PRACTICE AREAS: Commercial and Business Litigation; Real Estate Brokerage Defense.
Greenstein, Robert S. ...'55 '81 C.188 L.809 J.D. 2049 Century Pk. E.
Greenwald, Alvin G. ...'20 '46 C.112 B.A. L.800 J.D. [Greenwald,A.G.&R.G.]
Greenwald, Carol A. ...'46 '84 C.1042 B.A. L.1137 J.D. Dep. Atty. Gen.
Greenwald, James C. ...'56 '81 C.228 A.B. L.770 J.D. 886 Hilgard Ave.
**Greenwald, Nicole A.** ...'68 '94 C.978 B.A. L.426 J.D. [Ⓐ Pollak,V.&F.]
Greenwald, Randy ...'— '74 [Greenwald,A.G.&R.G.]
Greenwald, Alvin G., & Randy Greenwald, A P.C. ...6010 Wilshire Blvd.

**Greenwald, Hoffman & Meyer**
**(See Glendale)**

**Greenwalt, Karen K.** ...'45 '93 C.605 B.A. L.426 J.D. [Ⓐ Paul,H.J.&W.]
Greer, Denise H. ...'54 '88 C.1044 B.S.N. L.809 J.D. [Schmid&V.] ‡
**Greer, Douglas A.** ...'49 '87 C.112 B.A. L.426 J.D. [Ⓐ Robins,K.M.&C.]
*PRACTICE AREAS: Insurance Coverage Law; Bad Faith Litigation; Business Litigation.
Greer, Robert W. ...'45 '73 C&L.1049 B.A., J.D. 11845 W. Olympic Blvd.
**Grefe, Andrea Jane,** (AV) ...'48 '78 C.597 B.A. L.1065 J.D. [Manatt,P.&P.]
*PRACTICE AREAS: Entertainment Law.
Gregg, Gene E., (AV) ...'19 '50 C.112 A.B. L.174 J.D. 1 Wilshire Blvd.‡
**Gregora, Peter J.,** (AV) ...'46 '71 C.684 B.A. L.976 J.D. [Irell&M.]
**Gregorich, Joseph E.** ...'38 '72 C.1024 B.A. L.426 J.D. [Kirtland&P.]
**Gregory, Edward G.** ...'49 '87 C.816 B.E. L.426 J.D. [Ⓒ O'Melveny&M.]
*PRACTICE AREAS: Labor and Employment Law.
**Gregory, Fred F.,** (AV) ...'41 '66 C.112 B.A. L.1066 LL.B. [Gibson,D.&C.]
*PRACTICE AREAS: Litigation; Insurance Coverage Disputes; Commercial Contract Disputes; Appellate Practice.
Gregory, Jacob G. ...'40 '69 C.768 B.A. L.1068 J.D. 934 Benton Way‡
Gregory, Nicholas A. ...'49 '74 C.800 B.A. L.1049 J.D. Princ. Dep. Co. Coun.
Gregory, Walter E. ...'29 '54 C.112 B.A. L.1068 J.D. 1875 Century Park E.
Greiff, Murray ...'42 '72 C.36 B.S. L.809 J.D. 11400 W. Olympic Blvd.
**Greiner, Paul H.** ...'58 '85 C.1109 B.A. L.426 J.D. [Heller E.W.&M.]
*PRACTICE AREAS: General Corporate; Securities and Venture Capital Transactions; Mergers and Acquisitions; Export Regulation and Corporate Investigations.

**Greines, Martin, Stein & Richland**
**(See Beverly Hills)**

**Greissinger, G. Karl** ...'66 '94 C.112 B.A. L.426 J.D. [Ⓐ Troop M.S.&P.]
*PRACTICE AREAS: Corporate; Securities.
Greitzer, Nathan ...'16 '54 C.112 B.Ed. L.800 J.D. 611 S. Catalina St.
**Gresenz, Kurt G.** ...'64 '89 C.228 B.A. L.846 J.D. [Ⓐ Hawkins,S.L.&B.]
**Greta, Richard** ...'56 '91 C.426 B.S.M.E. L.1068 J.D. [Ⓐ Mayer,B.&P.]
**Grewal, Shivbir S.** ...'59 '90 C&L.061 B.A., LL.B. [Ⓐ Graham&J.]
*LANGUAGES: Hindi and Punjabi.
*PRACTICE AREAS: Corporate Law.
**Grguric, Sherry** ...'64 '92 C.294 B.A. L.1148 J.D. [Ⓐ McHale&C.]
Gribow, Dale S., (AV) ...'43 '70 C.800 B.A. L.426 J.D. [D.S.Gribow]⊙
Gribow, Dale S., A Professional Corporation, (AV)
1925 Century Pk. E. Ste. 2250 (⊙Palm Desert)
**Gridley, Bruce C.,** (AV) ...'47 '73 C.966 B.A. L.800 J.D. [Federman,G.&G.]
**Griecci, John A.** ...'60 '94 C.339 B.S. L.188 J.D. [Ⓐ Pretty,S.&P.]
*PRACTICE AREAS: Patents; Trademarks; Copyrights; Unfair Competition; Litigation.
Grieco, Mary L. ...'61 '88 C.112 B.A. L.426 J.D. 1925 Century Pk., E.
Grienauer, John V. ...'49 '77 C.800 B.A. L.426 J.D. 107 S. Serrano Ave.
**Grieve, Timothy P.** ...'64 '96 C.813 B.A. L.276 J.D. [Ⓐ Munger,T.&O.]
*PRACTICE AREAS: Litigation.
**Griffen, Lorie S.** ...'62 '88 C.170 B.S.C. L.800 J.D. [Ⓐ Mayer,B.&P.]
*LANGUAGES: Spanish and Portuguese.
**Griffey, Linda Boyd** ...'49 '80 C.352 B.S. L.228 J.D. [O'Melveny&M.]
*PRACTICE AREAS: ERISA; Employee Benefits; Executive Compensation.
**Griffin, Fred B.** ...'46 '75 C.112 B.A. L.800 J.D. [Loeb&L.]
*PRACTICE AREAS: Employment Law.
**Griffin, Gerald A.** ...'47 '77 C.112 A.B. L.990 J.D. [Gibbs,G.L.&A.]
*PRACTICE AREAS: Business Litigation; Labor Law; Employment Law; Commercial Law.
Griffin, Kenneth G., (AV) ...'40 '65 C&L.813 B.A., LL.B. 333 S. Grand Ave., 37th Fl.
Griffin, Philip C. ...'31 '59 C&L.112 B.A., LL.B. Dep. Atty. Gen.

**Griffin, Richard T., (AV) '31 '58 C.426 B.S. L.1068 J.D.**
**Bradbury Building, Suite 225, 304 South Broadway, 90013**
**Telephone: 213-628-5595 Fax: 213-628-8470**
**Immigration and Nationality. Trial and Appellate Practice in all State and Federal Courts.**
***See Professional Biographies, LOS ANGELES, CALIFORNIA***

**Griffin, Sarah Heck** ...'54 '84 C.800 B.A. L.174 J.D. [Jones,D.R.&P.]
**Griffin, Thomas J.** ...'58 '89 C.676 B.A. L.1137 J.D. [Nelson G.]
*PRACTICE AREAS: Insurance Fraud Defense; Personal Injury.
**Griffis, Linda L.** ...'49 '81 C.37 B.A. L.426 J.D. [Ⓐ Rossbacher&Assoc.]
*LANGUAGES: French.
*PRACTICE AREAS: Federal Habeas Corpus; Complex Business Litigation.
**Griffith, Ronald M.** ...'46 '73 C.860 B.A. L.659 J.D. [Ⓒ Arter&H.]
*PRACTICE AREAS: Real Estate; Banks and Banking.
**Griggs, Johnny D.** ...'57 '83 C.1051 B.S. L.976 J.D. [Sidley&A.]
*PRACTICE AREAS: Business Litigation.
Grignon, Margaret Morrow ...'50 '77 C.112 B.A. L.426 J.D. Assoc. Jus., Ct. of App.
**Grigsby, Daniel M.** ...'54 '81 C.112 B.A. L.1148 J.D. [Nossaman,G.K.&E.]
*PRACTICE AREAS: Sports Law; Entertainment Law; General Business Law.
Grilli, Diana F. ...'45 '85 C.112 B.A. L.809 J.D. 4215 Glencoe Ave. (Marina Del Rey)
**Grime, Richard W.** ...'64 '91 L.051 [Ⓐ Morrison&F.]

**Grimes, Elizabeth A.** ....................'54 '80 C.846 B.A. L.813 J.D. [Gibson,D.&C.]
*LANGUAGES: Spanish.
*PRACTICE AREAS: Litigation; Franchises and Franchising; Administrative Law.
Grimm, Dale L., (AV) ....................'31 '64 C.999 L.809 J.D. [Medearis&G.]
Grimm, Richard N. ....'46 '73 C.169 B.A. L.809 J.D. 671 S. Westmoreland Ave.
Grimm, Trevor A., (AV) ....'38 '63 C.813 A.B. L.800 LL.B. [Kaplanis&G.]

**Grimwade, Richard L. '45 '71 C.399 B.A. L.966 J.D.**
**333 South Grand Avenue Suite 3700, 90071-1599⊙**
**Telephone: 213-346-9370 Fax: 213-625-1832**
**Civil Litigation including Wrongful Termination, Business, Related Litigation, Professional Liability, Real Estate and Insurance Bad Faith.**
**Newport Beach Office: 4400 MacArthur Boulevard, 7th Floor. Telephone: 714-752-7551. Fax: 714-752-0288.**

***See Professional Biographies, LOS ANGELES, CALIFORNIA***

Grinfeld, Michael J. ....'50 '75 C.94 B.A. L.1202 J.D. 4700 Wilshire Blvd.
Grinnalds, Robin A. ....'55 '85 C.184 B.S. L.809 J.D. 11766 Wilshire Blvd.
Grinstead, Amy R ....'59 '87 C.112 B.A. L.800 J.D. Dep. City Atty.
Griott, Michael A. '48 '73
C.800 A.B. L.426 J.D. Claims Atty., Auto. Club of Southern Calif.
**Grivakes, Christopher** ....'61 '87 C.478 B.A. L.1065 J.D. [Ives,K.&D.]
**Grizel, Jon S.** ....'62 '88 C.112 B.A. L.800 J.D. [Ⓐ Katten M.&Z.]
*PRACTICE AREAS: Real Estate - Transactional.
**Grizzi, Michael** ....'64 '96 C.597 B.S. L.112 J.D. [Ⓐ Irell&M.]
Grob, Rudy R. ....'62 '90 C.112 B.A. L.809 J.D. 6701 Ctr. Dr. W., 12th Fl.
Grobe, Charles S., Law Offices of, (AV) '35 '62
C.112 B.S. L.813 J.D. 501 N. Cliffwood Ave.
**Grode, Matthew L.** ....'62 '86 C.1044 B.S. L.990 J.D. [Ⓐ Wolf,R.&S.]
*PRACTICE AREAS: Real Estate; Construction Litigation; Civil Litigation; Products Liability Law.
**Grode, Susan A.**, (AV) ....'— '77 C.188 B.F.A. L.800 J.D. [Ⓒ Kaye,S.F.H.&H.]
*PRACTICE AREAS: Entertainment Law; Intellectual Property Law; Multimedia Law; Publishing Law; Licensing.
**Grodin, Jay H.**, (AV) ....'44 '70 C.800 B.S. L.1066 J.D. [White&C.]
Grodon, Monte S. ....'31 '72 C.475 B.A. L.1095 J.D. 10311 Clusterberry Ct.
Grodsky, Ben ....'10 '34 C&L.145 Ph.B., J.D. 1137 Point View St.‡
Grodsky, Michael E. ....'41 '68 C.112 A.B. L.1065 J.D. State Prob. Ref.
**Groeneveld, Greg R** ....'63 '93 C.802 B.B.A. L.178 J.D. [Ⓐ Luce,F.H.&S.]
*PRACTICE AREAS: Insurance; Reinsurance; Labor.
**Grogan, Allen R.** ....'53 '79 C.604 A.B. L.800 J.D. [Blanc W.J.&K.]
*PRACTICE AREAS: Computer and Technology; Proprietary Rights; Licensing; Commercial Transactions.
Grogan, Robert A. ....'48 '78 C.1042 B.S. L.1148 J.D. Tr. Div., United Calif. Bk.
**Grogan, Virginia Sollenberger** ....'51 '79 C.605 B.A. L.800 J.D. [Latham&W.]
Grogman, Bruce I. ....'52 '79 C&L.339 B.S., J.D. 16633 Ventura Blvd. (Encino)
Groh, Rupert J., Jr. '33 '60
C.694 B.A. L.436 J.D. U.S. Mag., U.S. D.C., Central Dist. of Calif.
**Groman, Arthur, (A Professional Corporation)**, (AV) '14 '39
C.800 A.B. L.976 J.D. [Mitchell,S.&K.]
*PRACTICE AREAS: Litigation.

**Gronemeier & Barker**
**(See Pasadena)**

Gronemeyer, Lyman S. '36 '61 C.112 B.A. L.1068 LL.B.
Dep. Gen. Coun. & Exec. V.P., Legal Affs., Twentieth Century Fox Film Corp.
Gronich, Daphne '56 '82 C.061 B.A. L.1019 J.D.
V.P., Bus. & Legal Affairs, Fox Television Stations, Inc.
Grosbard, Alan Z. ....'53 '76 C&L.260 B.A., J.D. 1888 Century Park E
Grosberg, Lawrence S. ....'41 '68 C.1077 B.A. L.800 J.D. 1900 Ave. of the Stars
Groskopf, Aubrey W. '31 '58 C&L.996 B.S., LL.B.
(adm. in WI; not adm. in CA) 10560 Wilshire Blvd.‡
**Gross, Allen J., (A Professional Corporation)**, (AV) '48 '74
C.608 B.S. L.276 J.D. [Mitchell,S.&K.]
*PRACTICE AREAS: Labor Law; Employment Law.
**Gross, Andrew W.** ....'61 '90 C.112 A.B. L.1068 J.D. [Irell&M.]
Gross, Brad H. ....'58 '84 C.112 B.A. L.800 J.D. 1015 Gayley Ave., 3rd Fl.
**Gross, Byron J.** ....'48 '77 C.976 B.A. L.1066 J.D. [Hooper,L.&B.]
*PRACTICE AREAS: Health Care Law.
**Gross, Clark D.** ....'52 '87 C.112 L.1148 J.D. [Robbins,B.&C.] (See Pat. Sect.)
*PRACTICE AREAS: Patent, Trademark and Copyright Litigation.
**Gross, Diane Arkow** ....'68 '94 C.228 B.A. L.800 J.D. [Ⓐ Richards,W.&G.]
*PRACTICE AREAS: Litigation; Labor and Employment.
**Gross, G. Raymond F.** ....'56 '81 C.103 A.B. L.178 J.D. [Ⓒ Gipson H.&P.]
*TRANSACTIONS: Acquisition of Ed Sullivan Show library for Sofa Entertainment. Negotiation of Prime Time Entertainment Network License Agreement with Warner Bros.
*PRACTICE AREAS: Entertainment Law; Motion Picture and Television Financing Law.
Gross, Gary P. ....'69 '94 C.112 B.A. L.276 J.D. 801 S. Grand Ave.
**Gross, Howard** ....'62 '95 C.112 B.A. L.426 J.D. [Kinkle,R.&S.]
**Gross, Irving M.**, (AV) ....'47 '72 C.112 B.A. L.1066 J.D. [Robinson,D.B.&K.]
*REPORTED CASES: First Pacific Bancorp., Inc. v. Bro, 847 F.2d 542 (9th Cir. 1988); In re Rossi, 86 B.R. 220 (9th Cir. BAP, 1988); In re Qintex Entertainment, Inc., 950 F.2d 1492 (9th Cir. 1991); Bergman v. Rifkind & Sterling, Inc., 227 Cal. App. 3d 1380 (1991); In re Qintex Entertainment, Inc., 8 F. 3d 1353 (9th Cir. 1993.
*PRACTICE AREAS: Bankruptcy Law; Insolvency; Commercial Litigation; Employment Litigation.
Gross, Kenneth I. ....'59 '85 C.21 B.A. L.809 J.D. 900 Wilshire Blvd.
Gross, Marc D. ....'56 '81 C.112 B.A. L.800 J.D. [Gross,G.&S.]
Gross, Marvin, (AV) ....'28 '55 C.112 B.A. L.1068 J.D. [Gross,G.&S.]
Gross, Murray B. ....'47 '74 C.112 B.A. L.426 J.D. Supr. Ct. Comr.
**Gross, Owen P.** ....'66 '95 C&L.800 A.B., J.D. [Ⓐ Orrick,H.&S.]
**Gross, Pamela G.** ....'45 '92 C.477 B.A. L.1068 J.D. [Ⓐ Epstein B.&G.]
*PRACTICE AREAS: Health Law.
Gross, Ron S. ....'69 '95 C.112 B.A. L.426 J.D. 777 S. Figueroa St., 10th Fl.
**Gross, Ronen** ....'69 '95 C.112 B.A. L.426 J.D. [Ⓐ Morrison&F.]
*LANGUAGES: Hebrew.
Gross, Gross & Simon, P.C., (AV) .... 10880 Wilshire Blvd.
Grossan, Melissa F. ....'53 '79 C.112 B.A. L.809 J.D. 1875 Central Pk. E.
Grossbart, Kenneth S., (A Law Corporation) '53 '79
C.800 B.S. L.1136 J.D. [Abdulaziz&G.]

**Grossblatt, Fred J. '53 '78 C.112 B.A. L.809 J.D.**
**1900 Avenue of the Stars Seventeenth Floor, 90067-4403**
**Telephone: 310-552-2002 Facsimile: 310-552-2324 E-Mail: fredjg@primenet.com**
**Commercial, Collection, Creditors Rights and Business Litigation.**

***See Professional Biographies, LOS ANGELES, CALIFORNIA***

**Grossblatt, Jennifer B.** ....'60 '87 C.112 B.S. L.809 J.D. [Grossblatt&B.]

**Grossblatt & Booth**
**2029 Century Park East, Suite 1700, 90067**
**Telephone: 310-556-9766 Fax: 310-556-9765**
**Members of Firm: Jennifer B. Grossblatt; Hillary Arrow Booth.**

(This Listing Continued)

**Grossblatt & Booth (Continued)**

**Business Litigation in all State and Federal Courts, involving Unfair Competition, Trade Secrets, Labor, Real Property and Contractual Disputes.**

**Grossenbacher, Gary M.** ....'62 '88 C&L.846 B.A., J.D. [Ⓐ Leopold,P.&S.]
*PRACTICE AREAS: Civil Litigation; Entertainment Law; Media Law; Copyrights and Idea Submissions; Contract Disputes.
Grossfeld, Claudia Zusman '59 '83 C.112 B.A. L.800 J.D.
U.S. Sec. & Exchange Comm.
**Grossfeld, Scott L.** ....'66 '91 C.477 B.A. L.800 J.D. [Ⓐ Cox,C.&N.]
*PRACTICE AREAS: Commercial Leasing; Retail Development.
Grosslight, Peter L. ....'46 '72 C&L.1068 B.A., J.D. The William Morris Agcy.
**Grossman, Allan I.**, (AV) ....'45 '70 C.102 B.S. L.309 J.D. [Ⓒ O'Melveny&M.]
*PRACTICE AREAS: Employee Benefits; ERISA; Employee Stock Ownership Trusts; Pension and Profit Sharing Plans.
**Grossman, Anthony C.** ....'66 '94 C.856 B.A. L.809 J.D. [Ⓐ Herzfeld&R.]
**Grossman, Brian M.** ....'68 '93 C.659 B.A. L.112 J.D. [Ⓐ Jeffer,M.B.&M.]
*PRACTICE AREAS: Commercial Litigation.
**Grossman, Craig A.** ....'69 '94 C.813 B.A. L.309 J.D. [Ⓐ Irell&M.]
Grossman, Felix T., (AV) ....'34 '60 C.951 B.A. L.178 LL.B. 523 W. Sixth St.

**Grossman, Harvey M., (AV) '29 '56 C.112 A.B. L.1068 LL.B.**
**P.O. Box 36E19, 90036-1419**
**Telephone: 213-957-1236**
**Civil Appellate Practice in all State and Federal Courts.**
**Reference: City National Bank (Fairfax Office, Los Angeles, California).**

***See Professional Biographies, LOS ANGELES, CALIFORNIA***

**Grossman, Keith D.** ....'62 '87 C.860 B.A. L.569 J.D. [Ⓐ Morgan,L.&B.]
**Grossman, Kurtiss Lee** ....'56 '92 C.612 B.A. L.623 J.D. [Ⓐ Loeb&L.]
*PRACTICE AREAS: Litigation; Insurance Coverage; Municipal Code Prosecution.
**Grossman, Marshall B., (P.C.)**, (AV) '39 '65
C.112 B.S.L. L.800 LL.B. [Alschuler G.&P.]
**Grossman, N. Matthew** ....'34 '59 C.309 A.B. L.178 LL.B. [Parker,M.C.O.&S.]
*TRANSACTIONS: Attorney for: Western Gear Corporation sale to Bucyrus-Erie Company; Bayly, Martin & Fay sale to Bass Brothers; BWIP International, Inc. purchase of United Centrifugal Pumps.
*PRACTICE AREAS: Estates and Trust; Business Law; Mergers and Acquisitions; Tax.
**Grossman, Paul**, (AV) ....'39 '65 C.31 A.B. L.976 LL.B. [Paul,H.J.&W.]
**Grossman, Peter**, (AV) ....'47 '74 C.309 B.A. L.1066 J.D. [Lichter,G.N.&A.]
*PRACTICE AREAS: Entertainment Law.
Grossman, Richard A. ....'39 '70 C.912 L.215 J.D. 2029 Century Pk. E.
**Grossman, Rick L.**, (AV) ....'55 '79 C.112 B.A. L.809 J.D. [Manatt,P.&P.]
*PRACTICE AREAS: Health; Taxation; Nonprofit/Tax Exempt Organizations.
Grossman, Robert J. ....'27 '54 C.112 A.B. L.1068 J.D. Admin. Law J., Soc. Sec. Admn.

**Grossman, Robert Jay, (AV) '49 '78 C.966 B.B.A. L.1068 J.D.**
**1801 Century Park East, 24th Floor, 90067**
**Telephone: 310-282-8330 Fax: 310-282-8454**
**Email: RJG_LAW@CompuServe.com**
***PRACTICE AREAS: Real Estate; Tax; Corporate Law.**
**Real Estate, Corporate, Finance, Tax, Contract and Transactional Law, Formation of Developmental Entities.**

***See Professional Biographies, LOS ANGELES, CALIFORNIA***

**Grossman, Grant & Cramer**
**(See Santa Monica)**

Grosz, David ....'48 '76 C.453 S.B. L.1068 J.D. [Fleishman,F.&M.]
**Grosz, Philip J.** ....'52 '77 C.966 B.A. L.976 J.D. [Loeb&L.]
*PRACTICE AREAS: Entertainment Law.
**Grosz-Salomon, Penny** ....'55 '80 C.112 B.A. L.426 J.D. [Reznik&R.]
*PRACTICE AREAS: Environmental Insurance Coverage; Real Estate Litigation.
**Grotta, Harold E.**, (AV⊤) '11 '34 C&L.893 B.S., J.D.
(adm. in NJ; not adm. in CA) [Grotta,G.&H.]⊙

**Grotta, Glassman & Hoffman, A Professional Corporation, (AV⊤)**
**Two Century Plaza, 2049 Century Park East, Suite 1800, 90067⊙**
**Telephone: 310-556-8786**
**Harold E. Grotta (Not admitted in CA); Jerold E. Glassman; Harold L. Hoffman (Not admitted in CA); Marvin M. Goldstein (Not admitted in CA); Stephen A. Ploscowe (Not admitted in CA); Desmond Massey (Not admitted in CA); Theodore M. Eisenberg (Not admitted in CA); Joseph J. Malcolm (Not admitted in CA); M. Joan Foster (Not admitted in CA); Richard J. Delello (Not admitted in CA); Michael Barabander (Not admitted in CA); Stanley L. Goodman (Not admitted in CA); Jed L. Marcus (Not admitted in CA); Ilene Lainer (Not admitted in CA); Jedd Mendelson (Not admitted in CA); David W. Garland (Not admitted in CA). Of Counsel: Kenneth J. McCulloch (Not admitted in CA). Practice Limited exclusively to the representation of management in all facets of labor and employment law: Employment Discrimination, Wrongful Discharge, ERISA and other employment related litigation, in state and federal courts and before federal and state administrative agencies nationwide; Union Organizing Campaigns; Negotiations; Arbitrations; Wage and Hour; OSHA; Immigration; Public Sector Labor Relations; Affirmative Actions Plans; Employee Benefits and Pension Law.**
**Roseland, New Jersey Office: 75 Livingston Avenue, 07068. Telephone: 201-992-4800. Telecopier: 201-992-9125.**
**New York, N.Y. Office: 125 West 55th Street, 10019. Telephone: 212-315-3510. Telecopier: 212-315-3992.**

***See Professional Biographies, LOS ANGELES, CALIFORNIA***

**Grotts, Charles L.** ....'48 '74 C.910 B.A. L.339 J.D. [Mahoney,C.J.&P.]
*PRACTICE AREAS: Business; Real Estate; Probate Litigation.
Grove, Ann W. ....'66 '93 C.165 B.A. L.880 J.D. 427 1/2 N. Hayworth‡
Grove, David S. ....'63 '88 C.375 B.A. L.37 J.D. [Lincoln,G.&C.]⊙
**Groveman, Barry C.** ....'53 '78 C.966 B.A. L.809 J.D. [Proskauer R.G.&M.]
*PRACTICE AREAS: Environmental Law.
Grover, Melvin B. ....'21 '55 C.769 L.809 Supr. Ct. J.
Grover, Susan S. ....'54 '82 C.1051 B.A. L.904 J.D. 725 S. Figueroa St.
**Growdon, Karen R.**, (AV) ....'48 '78 C.880 B.A. L.426 J.D. [Ⓒ O'Melveny&M.]
*PRACTICE AREAS: Civil Litigation; Environmental Insurance Coverage Litigation.
Grubbs, James L., (AV) ....'17 '46 C&L.813 B.A., J.D. 1620 Mandeville Canyon Rd.‡
**Grube, E. Jeffrey** ....'64 '93 C.112 B.A. L.800 J.D. [Ⓐ Paul,H.J.&W.]
**Gruber, Richard J.** ....'55 '82 C.1036 B.A. L.1068 J.D. [Pachulski,S.Z.&Y.]
Gruber, Susan W. ....'58 '82 C.800 B.A. L.809 J.D. Dep. Dist. Atty.
Gruen, Paul D. ....'51 '79 [Sandler,R.&M.]
**Gruenbaum, Samuel H.**, (AV) ....'52 '78 C.1077 B.S. L.426 J.D. [Cox,C.&N.]
*PRACTICE AREAS: Corporate Law; Securities Law.
**Gruenberg, David M.** ....'64 '91 C.112 B.A. L.767 J.D. [Ⓐ Seyfarth,S.F.&G.]
*PRACTICE AREAS: Workers' Compensation Defense; Labor.
Grueskin, Ronald J., (AV) ....'34 '62 C.597 B.A. L.1068 LL.B. [Hinden&G.]
**Gruettner, Allison B.** ....'68 '93 C.112 A.B. L.426 J.D. [Ⓐ Manatt,P.&P.]
*PRACTICE AREAS: Litigation.
**Gruia, Dinu** ....'62 '95 C.061 B.S.E.E. L.818 J.D. [Ⓐ Blakely,S.T.&Z.]
**Grumer, Carl** ....'50 '75 C.112 B.A. L.1068 J.D. [Manatt,P.&P.]
*PRACTICE AREAS: Business Litigation.
**Grunebach, Georgann Shelby** '55 '87 C.665 B.S. L.229 J.D.
Hughes Aircraft Co. (Pat.)
Gruner, Richard S. '53 '79
C.111 B.S. L.800 J.D. Prof. of Law, Whittier Coll. School of Law

**Grunfeld, Aaron A.**, (AV) . . . . . . . . . . . . '46 '72 C.112 A.B. L.178 J.D. [🄲 Resch P.A.&B.]
*PRACTICE AREAS: Corporate and Partnership Law; Securities Regulation.
**Grunfeld, Daniel** . . . . . . . . . . . . . . . . . . . . '59 '87 C.223 B.S. L.188 J.D. [McDermott,W.&E.]
*PRACTICE AREAS: Environmental Law; Franchises and Franchising; Litigation.

**Grunfeld, Desiderio, Lebowitz & Silverman LLP, (BV)**
**A Partnership**
**Suite 5555, 707 Wilshire Boulevard, 90017⊙**
**Telephone: 213-624-1970 Telecopy: 213-624-1678**
**Resident Partner: Barry E. Powell.**
**Customs and International Trade Law, Trade Regulations and Administrative Law. Trials and Appeals.**
**New York, N.Y. Office: 33rd Floor, 245 Park Avenue. Telephone: 212-557-4000. Fax: 212-557-4415.**
**Washington, D.C. Office: Suite 680, 1500 K Street N.W. Telephone: 202-783-6881. Telecopy: 202-783-0405.**
**Boston, Massachusetts Office: Grunfeld, Desiderio, Lebowitz, Silverman & Wright, Old City Hall, 45 School Street, 2nd Floor. Telephone: 617-742-8550. Telecopy: 617-523-9429.**
**Atlanta, Georgia Office: Suite 4860, One Atlantic Center, 1201 West Peachtree Street, N.E. Telephone: 404-874-3882. Telecopy: 408-874-6895.**
**Houston, Texas Office: 1100 Louisiana, Suite 1275. Telephone: 713-650-6590. Fax: 713-650-6591.**
***See Professional Biographies, LOS ANGELES, CALIFORNIA***

**Grunweig, Jonathan H.** . . . . . . . . . . '63 '89 C.188 B.A. L.309 J.D. [🄰 Skadden,A.S.M.&F.]
**Grupp, Anne R.** '40 '66 C.112 B.A. L.1065 LL.B.
Asst. Gen. Coun. & V.P., Litig., Turner Bdcstg. Sys., Inc.
**Gruppie, Guy R.** . . . . . . . . . . . . . . . . . . . . . '62 '91 C.800 B.A. L.426 J.D. [🄰 Murchison&C.]
*PRACTICE AREAS: Products Liability; Construction; Accident; Construction Defect.

**Grush, Julius S., (BV) '37 '65 C.112 B.S. L.809 LL.B.**
**2121 Avenue of the Stars, 22nd Floor, 90067**
**Telephone: 310-785-1111 Fax: 310-785-0720**
**Email: juglaws1@aol.com**
***PRACTICE AREAS: Construction/Mechanic's Lien Litigation; Personal Injury Litigation; Business Litigation.**
**General Practice.**
***See Professional Biographies, LOS ANGELES, CALIFORNIA***

Grush, Michael J. . . . . . . . . . . . . . . . . . . . '56 '81 C.112 A.B. L.1049 J.D. 3701 Wilshire Blvd.
**Grushkin, Mark J.**, (AV) . . . . . . . . . . . . . . '53 '78 C.1097 B.S. L.809 J.D. [Musick,P.&G.]
*PRACTICE AREAS: Employee Benefits.
**Gruskin, Mark S.** . . . . . . . . . . . . . . . . . . . . . . '58 '85 C.112 B.A. L.990 J.D. [🄰 Selman B.]
*PRACTICE AREAS: Personal Injury; Construction Defect/Property Damage; Real Property.
**Gruzen, Ronald L.**, (AV) . . . . . . . . . . . . . . . . '48 '73 C.112 B.A. L.770 J.D. [Frandzel&S.]
*PRACTICE AREAS: Business Litigation; Lender Liability Defense; Debt Collection; Creditors' Rights.
**Gubernick, Jeffrey S.** . . . . . . . . . . . . . . . . . . . '58 '84 C.401 B.A. L.564 J.D. [Bishton G.]
*PRACTICE AREAS: Civil Trial; Appellate; Business; Bankruptcy; Corporate.
**Gubner, Adam** . . . . . . . . . . . . . . . . . . . . . . . '68 '93 C.112 B.A. L.464 J.D. [🄰 Arter&H.]
*PRACTICE AREAS: Bankruptcy; Corporate Reorganization; Creditors Rights.
**Gubner, Steven T.** . . . . . . . . . . . . . . . . . . . . . . '66 '91 C.112 B.A. L.464 J.D. [🄲 Arter&H.]
*PRACTICE AREAS: Commercial Bankruptcy Law; Appellate Law; Real Estate Litigation; Asset Based Financing; Commercial Collection Actions.
Gudis, Alexander . . . . . . . . . . . . . . . . . . '57 '91 C.1097 B.S. L.1148 J.D. 3932 Wilshire Blvd.
Gueli, John . . . . . . . . . . . . . . . . . . . . '65 '93 C.1044 B.A. L.188 J.D. 15760 Ventura Blvd.
Guerin, Jane . . . . . . . . . . . . '56 '81 C.1365 B.A. L.208 J.D. 1999 Ave. of the Stars 15th Fl.
**Guerra, Rodrigo A., Jr.** . . . . . . . . . . '56 '83 C.813 B.A. L.1068 J.D. [Skadden,A.S.M.&F.]
**Guevara, Delia** . . . . . . . . . . . . . . . . . . . . . '64 '90 C.112 B.A. L.1097 J.D. [🄰 Paul,H.J.&W.]
**Guggenheim, Alfred Kim** . . . . . . . . . . . . . '46 '72 C.668 A.B. L.309 J.D. [Nelson,G.F.&L.]
*LANGUAGES: German.
*PRACTICE AREAS: Entertainment Law.
**Guibord, Barbara B.**, (AVⓉ) '51 '77 C.183 B.A. L.262 J.D.
(adm. in NY; not adm. in CA) [Zevnik H.G.&M.]⊙
*LANGUAGES: French.
*PRACTICE AREAS: Environmental Law; Insurance Coverage.
**Guilford, Robert E.**, (AV) . . . . . . . . . '33 '59 C.966 B.B.A. L.309 J.D. [Baum,H.A.G.&D.]
*REPORTED CASES: Curry v. Continental Airlines, 513 F.2d 691 (9th Cir. 1975); Baker v. Kipnis, 547 F.2d 1174 (9th Cir. 1976); Pratali v. Gates, 4 Cal. App. 4th 632, 5 Cal. Rptr. 2d 733 (1992); Datner v. Mann Theatres Corp., 145 Call, App. 3d 768, 193 Cal. Rptr. 676 (1983); The People exrel, Department of Public Works v. Salem Dev. Co., 216 Cal,App. 2d 652, 31 Cal Rptr. 193 (1963).
*PRACTICE AREAS: Airplane Crash Litigation; Aviation Accidents and Injuries; Aviation Products Liability; Aviation Torts; Helicopter Crash Litigation.
**Guillén, Elizabeth** . . . . . . . . . . . . . . . . . . '53 '88 C.1201 B.A. L.208 J.D. [🄰 S.L.Hartmann]
*PRACTICE AREAS: Civil Rights; Civil Rights Monitoring; Immigration; Education.
Guinan, June G. . . . . . . . . . . . . . . . . . . . . . . . '59 '84 C.112 B.A. L.1068 J.D. Dep. Pub. Def.
**Guise, Steven L., (A Professional Corporation)** '46 '71
C.477 A.B. L.880 J.D. [Munger,T.&O.]
Guizot, Damon, (AV) . . . . . . . . . . . . . . . . . . . . '50 '76 C.800 B.S. L.426 J.D. [Guizot&M.]
Guizot & Mouser, (AV) . . . . . . . . . . . . . . . . . . . . . . . . . . . . . . . . . 12400 Wilshire Blvd.
Gumbiner, Marshall, (BV) '18 '43
C.112 A.B. L.800 LL.B. 1030 N. Fairfax Ave., West Hollywood
Gummere, Koreen L. . . . . . . . . . . . . . . . . . . '56 '88 C.1193 B.S. L.208 J.D. 550 S. Hope St.
**Gummerman, Doug** . . . . . . . . . '51 '82 C.112 B.A. L.1065 J.D. [🄲 Cohen&L.] (⊙Torrance)
*PRACTICE AREAS: Corporate Law; Taxation.
**Gumpert, Joy K.** . . . . . . . . . . . . . . . . . . . . '68 '95 C.823 B.S. L.904 J.D. [🄰 Troop M.S.&P.]
*PRACTICE AREAS: Litigation.
**Gumport, Leonard L.**, (AV) . . . . . . . . . . . '50 '78 C.976 B.A. L.178 J.D. [Gumport,R.&M.]
*PRACTICE AREAS: Business and Bankruptcy Litigation; Receiverships.

**Gumport, Reitman & Montgomery, (AV)**
**550 South Hope Street, Suite 825, 90071-2627**
**Telephone: 213-452-4900 Fax: 213-623-3302**
**Members of Firm: Leonard L. Gumport; John P. Reitman; Susan I. Montgomery.**
**Commercial Litigation, Bankruptcy, Mediation, Receiverships, Real Estate and General Corporate.**
***See Professional Biographies, LOS ANGELES, CALIFORNIA***

Gunadi, Cindy T. '64 '90 C.112 B.A. L.1067 J.D.
Amer. Federation of State, Co. & Mun. Employees
Gunderson, Elmer M. '29 '56 C.494 L.190 LL.B.
(adm. in NE; not adm. in CA) Prof., Southwestern University School of Law
**Gunderson, Erik** . . . . . . . . . . . . . . . . . '70 '94 C.112 B.A. L.426 J.D. [🄰 Harrington,F.D.&C.]
*PRACTICE AREAS: Personal Injury Litigation; Business Litigation.
**Gundzik, Aaron C.** . . . . . . . . . . . . . . . . '62 '87 C.174 B.S. L.800 J.D. [🄰 LeBoeuf,L.G.&M.]
*PRACTICE AREAS: Litigation; Products Liability; Environmental Law; Insurance Coverage.
**Gundzik, Rebecca L.** . . . . . . . . . . . . . . . '63 '88 C.112 B.A. L.800 J.D. [🄰 Allen,M.L.G.&M.]
*PRACTICE AREAS: Litigation.
Gunn, Frenee M. . . . . . . . . . . . . . . . . . . . . '48 '76 C.766 B.A. L.1065 J.D. 3300 Overland Ave.
Gunn, John C. . . . . . . . . . . . . . . . . . . . . . . . . . . '24 '55 C.112 B.A. L.809 LL.B. Mun. Ct. J.
**Gunn, Patrick P.** . . . . . . . . . . . . . . . . . . . . . '68 '94 C.174 B.A. L.94 J.D. [🄰 Lewis,D.B.&B.]
*LANGUAGES: Russian and Slovak.
*PRACTICE AREAS: Litigation; International Business Law.
**Gunner, Arlen Ross** . . . . . . . . . . . . . . . . . . . . '49 '74 C.665 B.A. L.724 J.D. [🄲 Knopfler&R.]
*PRACTICE AREAS: Real Estate Development Law; Real Estate and Corporate Finance Law; Tax Exempt Bond Financing Law; Joint Venture and Partnership Law; Commercial and Business Law.
Gunning, Richard W. . . . . . . . . '47 '72 C.597 B.A. L.893 J.D. 3255 Wilshire Blvd. 12th Fl.
**Gunny, Deborah L.** . . . . . . . . . . . . . . . '56 '81 C.112 A.B. L.1067 J.D. [Sanders,B.G.S.&M.]
**Gunther, Craig S.** . . . . . . . . . . . . . . . . . '59 '93 C.112 B.S.E.E. L.426 J.D. [🄰 Burke,W.&S.]
*PRACTICE AREAS: Corporate Law; General Civil Litigation; Environmental Law; Communications.

Guren, Aliza Karney . . . . . . . . . . . . . . . . . . '54 '80 C.681 A.B. L.309 J.D. 12720 Hanover St.
Gurewitz, David . . . . . . . . . . . . . . . . . . . . . . . '49 '77 C.494 B.S. L.1068 J.D. [Gurewitz&L.]
Gurewitz & Lieb . . . . . . . . . . . . . . . . . . . . . . . . . . . . . . . . . . . . . . 10780 Santa Monica Blvd.
**Gurfein, Peter J.**, (AV) . . . . . . . . . . . . '48 '76 C.569 B.A. L.273 J.D. [Sonnenschein N.&R.]
*PRACTICE AREAS: Bankruptcy.
**Gurnee, Steven H.**, (AV) . . . . . . . . . . . . . '49 '75 C.112 B.A. L.1065 J.D. [🄲 Hillsinger&C.]
**Gussner, J. Walter** . . . . . . . . . . . . . . . . . . . . . . . '52 '79 C.112 B.A. L.426 J.D. [🄰 J.G.Hayes]
Gustafson, Charles R. . . . . . . . . . . . . . . . '38 '68 C.118 B.A. L.494 J.D. Calif. Teachers Assn.
Gustafson, James D. . . . . . . . . . . . . '61 '86 C.112 B.A. L.1065 J.D. 1055 W. 7th St., 20th Fl.
Gustafson, Randall D., (BV) . . . . . . . . . . . . '59 '84 C.37 B.A. L.1049 J.D. [Lincoln,G.&C.]⊙
**Gustafson, Randolph H.** . . . . . . . . . . . . . . . . . . . . '54 '81 C.880 B.A. L.145 J.D. [Graham&J.]
*LANGUAGES: Russian.
*PRACTICE AREAS: Real Property Law; Construction Law.
**Gustafsson, Ann Birgitta** . . . . . . . . . '51 '90 C.112 B.A. L.767 J.D. [🄰 Patterson,R.L.G.&J.]
*LANGUAGES: Swedish.

**Gustin, Jay Jordan, and Associates, (AV) '24 '74 C&L.1095 B.A., J.D.**
**Suite 1240 1901 Avenue of the Stars (Century City), 90067**
**Telephone: 310-552-2403; 271-1147 FAX: 310-553-9259**
***PRACTICE AREAS: Creditor's Rights; Bankruptcy; Sales Representative Affairs; Shopping Center Leasing; Business.**
**Of Counsel: David A. Schechet. Associates: Michael Libraty.**
**Commercial Practice. Bankruptcy, Insolvency, Debtor-Creditor Relationship, Corporations, Real Estate, UCC.**
**Reference: Bank of America, Century City Branch.**
***See Professional Biographies, LOS ANGELES, CALIFORNIA***

Gustlin, Philip R., (AV) . . . . . . . . . . . . . '34 '64 C.112 B.S. L.800 J.D. 11755 Wilshire Blvd.
**Gutcho, Lawrence B.** . . . . . . . . . . . . . . . . . . . . . . . '57 '82 C.976 B.A. L.309 J.D. [Loeb&L.]
*PRACTICE AREAS: Insolvency; Workout; Creditors Rights.
Gutenplan, Michael Alan . . . . . . . . . . . . '54 '79 C.112 B.A. L.809 J.D. 10866 Wilshire Blvd.
Guterman, Barry L., (AV) . . . . . . . . . . . '50 '75 C.763 B.A. L.767 J.D. 1925 Century Park E.
**Guterman, Mark B.** . . . . . . . . . . . : '62 '88 C.763 B.A. L.990 J.D. [🄰 La Follette,J.D.F.&A.]
*PRACTICE AREAS: Medical Malpractice.
Guterson, Eliot B. . . . . . . . . . . . . . . . . . . . '58 '85 C.1077 B.A. L.398 J.D. 12021 Wilshire Blvd.
**Guth, Theodore E.**, (AV) . . . . . . . . . . . . . . . . . . . . '54 '78 C.602 B.S. L.976 J.D. [Irell&M.]
Guthman, David H., (AV) . . . . . . . . . . . . . . . '42 '70 C.1042 A.B. L.273 J.D. Co. Dist. Atty.
**Guthner, William E., Jr.**, (AV) . . . . . . '32 '56 C.597 B.S. L.477 J.D. [Nossaman,G.K.&E.]
*PRACTICE AREAS: Corporations Law; Securities Law.
**Guthrie, Jeffrey** . . . . . . . . . . . . . '58 '85 C.679 B.S. L.800 J.D. Sr. Coun., Home Box Office
Gutierrez, Francisco H. . . . . . . . . . . . . . . . . . . . . '53 '80 C.976 B.A. L.800 J.D. [Gutierrez&G.]
**Gutiérrez, Jocelyn M.** . . . . . . . . . . . . . . . . '69 '95 C.309 A.B. L.1066 J.D. [🄰 Jones,D.R.&P.]
Gutierrez, Oscar H. . . . . . . . . . . . . . . . . . . . . . . '49 '76 C.426 B.S. L.800 J.D. [Gutierrez&G.]
**Gutierrez, Robert S.** . . . . . . . . . . . . . . . . . '62 '89 C.309 B.A. L.813 J.D. [🄰 Leopold,P.&S.]
*PRACTICE AREAS: Entertainment; Civil Litigation; Copyright and Trademark; Libel and Slander; Unfair Competition.
Gutierrez & Associates, (AV) . . . . . . . . . . . . . . . . . . . . . 333 S. Grand Ave. (⊙San Francisco)
Gutierrez & Gutierrez . . . . . . . . . . . . . . . . . . . . . . . . . . . . . . . . . . . . . . . . 2966 Wilshire Blvd.
Gutman, Paul . . . . . . . . . . . . . . . . . . . . . . . . . . . . . '31 '58 C&L.569 B.A., J.D. Supr. Ct. J.
**Gutterridge, Larry G.** . . . . . . . . . . . . . . . . . . . . . . '45 '71 C&L.339 B.S., J.D. [Sidley&A.]
*PRACTICE AREAS: Environmental Law; Health and Safety Law.
**Guttman, Ronald E.**, (AVⓉ) '43 '70
C.260 B.A.E. L.1009 J.D. [Christensen,M.F.J.G.W.&S.]
*PRACTICE AREAS: Litigation; Entertainment; Media; Employment.
Guy, Amy Mason . . . . . . . . . . . . . . . . . . . . . . '58 '88 C.1042 B.A. L.940 J.D. Dep. Pub. Def. II
Guy, John . . . . . . . . . . . . . . . . . . . . . . . . . . . . . '47 '74 C&L.800 B.S., J.D. 624 S. Grand Ave.
Guyer, Paul M. . . . . . . . . . . . . . . . . . . . . . . . . . . . . . '23 '68 L.809 LL.B. 4477 Hollywood Blvd.
**Guzik, Samuel S.** . . . . . . . . . . . . . . . . . . . . . '52 '79 C.188 B.S. L.813 J.D. [Guzik&Assoc.]

**Guzik & Associates**
**1800 Century Park East Fifth Floor, 90067**
**Telephone: 310-788-8600 Telecopier: 310-788-2835**
**Samuel S. Guzik.**
**Business, Corporate, Securities, Transactional, Corporate Litigation.**
***See Professional Biographies, LOS ANGELES, CALIFORNIA***

Guzin, Lawrence N., (AV) . . . . . . . . . . . . . '46 '73 C&L.112 A.B., J.D. 4525 Wilshire Blvd.
Guzman, Hector M. . . . . . . . . . . . . . . . . . . . . . '61 '89 C.478 B.A. L.596 J.D. Dep. Dist. Atty.
Guzman, Jorge . . . . . . . . . . . . . . . . . . . . . . . . . '61 '88 C.976 B.A. L.813 J.D. Dep. Pub. Def.
Guzman, Lisa . . . . . . . . . . . . . . . . . . . . . '63 '89 C.112 B.A. L.1066 J.D. ARCO Products Co.
**Gweon, Henry** . . . . . . . . . . . . . . . . . . . . . . . . . . . . . . . . . . . . . . . . . . . . . . '64 '91 [Hong&C.]
*LANGUAGES: English and Korean.
*PRACTICE AREAS: Business Litigation; Corporate Law; Commercial Law; Banking; Finance.
Haag, John Randolph . . . . . . . . . . . . . . . . '57 '82 C.112 B.S. L.1065 J.D. 725 S. Figueroa St.
Haakh, Gilbert E., (AV) . . . . . . . . . . . . . . . . . . '23 '52 C.112 A.B. L.309 LL.B. [🄲 Kindel&A.]
**Haas, Mary H.** . . . . . . . . . . . . . . . . . . . . . . . . . '65 '90 C.477 B.A. L.128 J.D. [🄰 Davis W.T.]
*PRACTICE AREAS: General Litigation; Real Estate Litigation.
Haase, Robert C., Jr., (AV) . . . . . . . . . . . . . . '31 '56 C&L.426 B.B.A., J.D. 601 S. Figueroa
**Haber, Jeffrey S.** . . . . . . . . . . . . . . . . . . . . . . . . '62 '87 C&L.976 B.A., J.D. [🄲 Latham&W.]
Haber, Steven J. . . . . . . . . . . . . . . . . . . . . '48 '77 C.112 B.S. L.809 J.D. 12301 Wilshire Blvd.
Haber, William . . . . . . . . . . . . . . . . . '38 '68 C.1097 B.S.M.E. L.809 J.D. 1180 S. Beverly Dr.
Haberbush, David R. . . . . . . . . . . . . . . . . '— '82 C.940 B.A. L.1148 J.D. [Roquemore,P.&M.]
Haberfeld, Sharon Burton . . . . . . . . . . . . . . . . '40 '72 C.112 B.A. L.309 J.D. [Haberfeld&H.]
Haberfeld, Stephen E. . . . . . . . . . . . . . . . . . . . '44 '71 C.112 A.B. L.309 J.D. [Haberfeld&H.]
Haberfeld & Haberfeld . . . . . . . . . . . . . . . . . . . . . . . . . . . . . . . . . . . . . . 8224 Blackburn Ave.
**Haberfelde, Ann** . . . . . . . . . . . . . . . . . . . . . . '55 '93 C.112 B.A. L.1065 J.D. [🄰 Morrison&F.]
**Habtu, Haimanot** . . . . . . . . . . . . . . . . . . . '65 '96 C.061 B.B.A. L.809 J.D. [🄰 Kirkland&E.]
*LANGUAGES: Amharic.
**Hachmeister, Lydia E.** . . . . . . . . . . . . . . . . . . '49 '84 C.612 B.S. L.809 J.D. [Neumeyer&B.]
*PRACTICE AREAS: Appellate Practice; Insurance Coverage; Insurance Bad Faith.
**Hackbert, Andrew J.** . . . . . . . . . . . . . . . . . '69 '94 C.309 B.A. L.1066 J.D. [🄰 Katten M.&Z.]
*PRACTICE AREAS: Corporate Litigation.
Haddad, Henry G. . . . . . . . . . . . . . . . . . . . . . . '57 '81 C.426 B.A. L.61 J.D. 3600 Wilshire Blvd.
**Haden, Patrick C.**, (AV) . . . . . . . . . . . . . . . . . '53 '83 C.800 B.A. L.426 J.D. [🄲 Riordan&M.]
**Hadlen, David A.** . . . . . . . . . . . . . . . . . . . . . . . . . '47 '72 C&L.426 B.A., J.D. [🄰 Pollak,V.&F.]
**Hadley, Lawrence M.** . . . . . . . . . . . . . . . '61 '91 C.1027 B.S. L.273 J.D. [🄰 O'Melveny&M.]
**Hadnot, Evan F.** . . . . . . . . . . . . . . . . . . . . . . . . '44 '89 C.502 B.S. L.1137 J.D. [🄰 Ochoa&S.]
*LANGUAGES: Spanish.
*PRACTICE AREAS: Workers' Compensation; Personal Injury; Bankruptcy; Family Law.

**Haefliger, William W.**
**(See Pasadena)**

**Haeusler, Rita M.** . . . . . . . . . . . . . . . . . . . . . . . '58 '83 C.112 B.A. L.1068 J.D. [Hughes H.&R.]
*PRACTICE AREAS: Intellectual Property and Entertainment Litigation; Representation of Receivers.
Hafenstein, Lance A. . . . . . . . . . . . . . . . . . . . . . '65 '91 C.112 B.A. L.1065 J.D. Dep. Dist. Atty.
**Hafey, Amy B.** . . . . . . . . . . . . . . . . . . . . . . . . . . '67 '93 C.66 B.A. L.800 J.D. [🄰 Foley L.W.&A.]
*PRACTICE AREAS: Health Care; Hospitals; Medicare and Medicaid; Administrative Law.
**Hafey, Matthew J.** . . . . . . . . . . . . . . . . . . . . . . '64 '93 C.178 A.B. L.426 J.D. [🄰 Gabriel,H.&P.]
**Haffner, Nancy G.** . . . . . . . . . '48 '75 C.910 B.A. L.208 J.D. Pres., The Haffner Group, Inc.
**Hagemeister, C. Steve** . . . . . . . . . . . . . . '68 '96 C.1109 B.A. L.1049 J.D. [🄰 Jones,D.R.&P.]

**Hagen, Catherine Burcham**, (AV) '43 '78
C.605 B.A. L.426 J.D. [O'Melveny&M.] (⊙Newport Beach)
*PRACTICE AREAS: Labor and Employment; Sexual Harassment and Disability Discrimination.
Hagen, David S., (AV) .................. '55 '83 C.112 B.A. L.426 J.D. [Hagen H.&H.]
Hagen, Earle, (AV) .................. '25 '63 C.112 B.S. L.809 LL.B. [Hagen H.&H.]
Hagen, Jeffrey J .................. '60 '89 C.112 B.S. L.426 J.D. [Hagen H.&H.]
Hagen Hagen & Hagen, (AV) .................. 17525 Ventura Blvd. (Encino)

**Hagenbaugh & Murphy**
(See Glendale)

Hagendorf, Wayne A. .................. '65 '90 C.264 B.A. L.800 J.D. 1901 Ave. of the Stars
**Hager, Jerry A.** .................. '57 '82 C.1077 B.A. L.990 J.D. [Ⓐ Buchalter,N.F.&Y.]
*PRACTICE AREAS: Real Estate Litigation; Bankruptcy; Real Estate Transactions.
**Hager, John V.**, (AV) ...... '49 '74 C&L.800 A.B., J.D. [Kinkle,R.&S.] (⊙Santa Barbara)
**Hagerott, Edward C., Jr.** .................. '65 '90 C&L.800 B.A., J.D. [Ⓐ Munger,T.&O.]
Hagerup, Eric '36 '62 C&L.966 B.S., LL.B.
(adm. in WI; not adm. in CA) V.P., Manufacturers Hanover Tr. Co.
Haggard, Mark L. '— '88 C.629 B.A. L.1065 J.D.
(adm. in OR; not adm. in CA) Sec. & Exch. Comm.
Haggerty, John F., (AV) .................. '33 '62 C&L.426 B.S., LL.B. Asst. City Atty.
**Hagihara, Yasuhiro** '37 '71 L.061 LL.B.
(adm. in DC; not adm. in CA) [Graham&J.] (⊙Wash., DC)
*PRACTICE AREAS: International Trade Law; Corporate Law.
**Hagle, Jennifer C.** .................. '61 '87 C.112 B.A. L.1065 J.D. [Sidley&A.]
*LANGUAGES: French.
*PRACTICE AREAS: Bankruptcy Law.
Hagle, Robert L. .................. '60 '87 C.740 B.S. L.1065 J.D. V.P. & Sr. Coun., Union Bk.
**Hahm, Jeannette** .................. '68 '92 C.112 B.A. L.1068 J.D. [Ⓐ Mitchell,S.&K.]
*LANGUAGES: Korean.
*PRACTICE AREAS: Estate Planning; Wills; Trusts; Probate Law; Conservatorship.
**Hahn, Chihoe** .................. '64 '92 C.976 B.A. L.569 J.D. [Ⓐ Dewey B.]
*PRACTICE AREAS: Corporate.
**Hahn, Elliott J.**, (AV) .................. '49 '74 C&L.659 B.A., J.D. [Sonnenschein N.&R.]
*LANGUAGES: Japanese and Spanish.
*PRACTICE AREAS: International Corporate; Real Estate; Banking.
**Hahn, Shenne J.** .................. '68 '94 C.112 B.A. L.800 J.D. [Wilson,K.&B.]

**Hahn & Hahn**
(See Pasadena)

Haig, Jerome J. .................. '62 '87 Off. of Co. Pub. Def.
**Haight, Robert M., Jr.** .................. '63 '88 C.770 B.S. L.1067 J.D. [Ⓐ Cox,C.&N.]
*PRACTICE AREAS: Public Finance.

**Haight, Brown & Bonesteel**
(See Santa Monica)

Haile, Lawrence B., (AV) .................. '38 '61 C&L.846 B.A., LL.B. [Haile&S.]
Haile & Simon, (AV) .................. 12304 Santa Monica Blvd.
**Haines, Steven M.** .................. '68 '93 C.93 B.A. L.1068 J.D. [Ⓐ Morrison&F.]
**Hairapetian, Armen** .................. '61 '86 C.112 B.A. L.800 J.D. [Lewis,D.B.&B.]
*PRACTICE AREAS: Product Liability and Reinsurance Litigation.
**Haith, Scott C.** .................. '46 '76 C.1042 B.S. L.1137 J.D. [Ⓒ Knopfler&R.]
*PRACTICE AREAS: General Civil and Trial Practice; Insurance Law; Products Liability; Insurance Bad Faith.
**Hakim, Afshin** .................. '71 '96 C.112 B.A. L.426 J.D. [Ⓐ O'Melveny&M.]
*LANGUAGES: Farsi.
**Hakim, Frank** .................. '68 '94 C.112 B.S. L.940 J.D. [Ⓐ R.A.Davis]
*LANGUAGES: Farsi.
Hakim, George .................. '50 '87 C.061 B.S. L.398 J.D. 1543 W. Olympic Blvd.
**Hakman, Deborah R.** .................. '61 '88 C.112 B.A. L.426 J.D. [Richards,W.&G.]
*LANGUAGES: Hebrew.
*PRACTICE AREAS: Public Law.
**Halama, William A.**, (AV) ......... '40 '67 C.293 B.A. L.145 J.D. [Greenberg G.F.C.&M.]
*PRACTICE AREAS: Real Estate; Real Estate Litigation.
**Halamka, Dagmar V.** .................. '42 '73 C.554 L.426 J.D. [Ⓒ Carlsmith B.W.C.&I.]
Halbe, Shailendra N. .................. '69 '94 C.228 A.B. L.1068 J.D. 445 S. Figueroa St.
**Halberstadter, David** .................. '57 '82 C.188 B.A. L.276 J.D. [Troop M.S.&P.]
*PRACTICE AREAS: Entertainment Litigation; Intellectual Property/Unfair Competition Law; General Commercial Litigation.
**Halbreich, David M.** .................. '58 '83 C.1044 B.A. L.273 J.D. [Brobeck,P.&H.]
*PRACTICE AREAS: Insurance Coverage Law; Antitrust Law; General Commercial Litigation.
**Haldeman, E. Barry**, (AV) ...... '44 '70 C.112 A.B. L.1068 J.D. [Greenberg G.F.C.&M.]
*PRACTICE AREAS: Entertainment.
Hale, Bruce M. .................. '50 '77 C.112 B.A. L.1068 J.D. Sr. Dep. Co. Coun.
**Hale, Frederick D.** .................. '60 '95 C.147 B.S. L.464 J.D. [Ⓐ Ezer&W.]
*PRACTICE AREAS: Construction; Real Estate; Business.
**Hale, G. Robert, (P.C.)** .................. '36 '64 C.999 L.1065 LL.B. [Monteleone&M.]
*PRACTICE AREAS: Construction Litigation; Government Contracts; Appellate Practice.
**Hale, M. Kevin** .................. '62 '89 C.475 B.A. L.1356 J.D. [Ⓐ Hawkins,D.&W.]
*PRACTICE AREAS: Municipal Finance; Corporate Securities.
Hale, Robert J. .................. '— '90 C.362 B.F.A. L.426 Dep. Dist. Atty.
**Haleblian, Lisa S.** .................. '70 '95 C.1077 B.S. L.800 J.D. [Ⓐ Thelen,M.J.&B.]
*LANGUAGES: Armenian.
*PRACTICE AREAS: Business Litigation; Insurance; Employment.
**Halfhide, Roger G.**, (AV) .................. '54 '80 C.112 B.A. L.464 J.D. [Weinstein,B.R.H.&C.]
*PRACTICE AREAS: Tax; Pensions; Estate Planning.
**Halgren, Jack H.**, (AV) .................. '40 '66 C.918 B.A. L.813 J.D. [Gibson,D.&C.]
*PRACTICE AREAS: Labor Law; Employment Law; Civil Rights; Housing Discrimination.
**Halkett, Alan N.**, (AV) .................. '31 '62 C.112 B.S. L.1068 LL.B. [Ⓒ Latham&W.]
**Halkett, Kent A.** .................. '56 '82 C.112 B.S. L.880 J.D. [Sidley&A.]
*PRACTICE AREAS: Commercial and International Litigation.
**Hall, Andrew R.** .................. '56 '86 C.659 B.A. L.1068 J.D. [Davis W.T.]
*LANGUAGES: French.
*PRACTICE AREAS: Litigation.
Hall, Carlyle W., Jr., (AV) .................. '42 '70 C.976 B.A. L.309 LL.B. [Hall&Assoc.]
**Hall, Debra Dison** .................. '52 '81 C.111 B.S. L.800 J.D. [Allen,M.L.G.&M.]
*PRACTICE AREAS: Corporate.
Hall, Eugene .................. '20 '53 C&L.912 B.A., LL.B. 4715 Presidio Dr.
**Hall, Frederick G.** .................. '62 '87 C.800 B.S. L.809 J.D. [Black C.H.&L.]
*REPORTED CASES: R.J. Reynolds Co. v. Cal. Ins. Guarantee Assn. (1991) 235 Cal.App.3d 595 (1 Cal.Rept.2d.405); Cal. Ins. Guarantee Assn. v. Argonaut Ins. Co. (1991) 227 Cal.App.3d 624 (278 Cal.Rptr. 23); Abraugh v. Gillespie (1988) 203 Cal.App.3d 462 (250 Cal.Rptr. 21); Isaacson v. Cal. Ins. Guarantee Association (1988) 44 Cal.3d.775 (244 Cal.Rptr. 655,750 P.2d.297).
*PRACTICE AREAS: Appellate Practice; Insurance Coverage; Coverage Litigation; Insurance Guarantee Association Practice.
**Hall, James E.** .................. '54 '80 C.1169 B.A. L.61 J.D. [Ⓐ Barlow&K.]
*PRACTICE AREAS: Management Labor Law; Employment Law; Discrimination Law.
Hall, John Joseph, (AV) .................. '26 '53 C.309 A.B. L.800 J.D. 1631 Beverly Blvd. (Pat.)
Hall, Joseph E. .................. '22 '50 C.437 A.B. L.273 LL.B. 205 S. Bway., Top Fl.
Hall, Keith E. .................. '44 '79 C.959 B.S. L.1190 J.D. 3700 Wilshire Blvd.
Hall, Kevin P. .................. '58 '85 C.855 B.A. L.178 J.D. 601 S. Figueroa St.
**Hall, Lynn E.** .................. '46 '72 C.813 B.A. L.976 J.D. [Ⓒ Kamine,S.&U.]

**Hall, Richard D.**, (AV) .................. '42 '70 C.431 B.A. L.309 J.D. [Gibson,D.&C.]
*PRACTICE AREAS: Professional Liability; Legal Ethics and Professional Responsibility; Litigation; Insurance; Antitrust.
Hall, Robert E. .................. '45 '73 C.112 A.B. L.426 J.D. Dep. Pub. Def.
**Hall, Robert M.** '42 '68 C.813 A.B. L.800 J.D.
Staff V.P., Asst. Gen. Coun. & Secy., Hughes Aircraft Co.
*RESPONSIBILITIES: Corporate Law; Business Law; Finance Law; Securities.
**Hall, Susan B.**, (AV) .................. '51 '83 C.763 B.A. L.1049 J.D. [Brobeck,P.&H.]
*PRACTICE AREAS: Bankruptcy and Loan Workout Law.
Hall, William H. .................. '19 '45 C.267 L.813 P.O. Box 48378
Hall & Associates, (AV) .................. 10951 W. Pico Blvd., 3rd Fl.

**Hall Dickler Kent Friedman & Wood LLP, (AV)**
**A Partnership including Professional Corporations**
**2029 Century Park East Suite 3760, 90067⊙**
**Telephone: 310-203-8410 Telecopier: 310-203-8559**
**Members of Firm: Fredric W. Ansis (Resident); Douglas J. Wood (Not admitted in CA); Christopher P. O'Connell. Associates: Alan H. Feldstein; Sally Koenig (Resident).**
**General Corporate, Securities, Taxation, International, Real Estate, Estate Planning, Probate, Copyright, Advertising, Marketing, Unfair Competition, Radio, Television (CATV), Entertainment, Trade Regulation, Literary Property, Computer Law, Matrimonial and Federal and State Litigation.**
**New York, N.Y. Office: 27th Floor, 909 Third Avenue. Telephone: 212-339-5400. Telecopier: 212-935-3121. Telex: 239857 GONY UR. Cable Address: "Halcasro".**
**White Plains, New York Office: 11 Martine Avenue. Telephone: 914-428-3232.**
**Bucharest, Romania Office: Hall, Dickler (Romania), SRL. World Trade Center, Boulevard Expozitiei, Nr. 2, Suite 225, 78334 Bucharest, Romania. Telephone: (+401) 222-8888. Fax: (+401) 223-4444.**
**Revisers of the Romania Digest for this Directory**
*See Professional Biographies, LOS ANGELES, CALIFORNIA*

Hallam, Jeffrey C. '66 '92 C.770 B.S. L.597 J.D.
1800 Ave. of the Stars, Suite 900 (Century City)
**Hallberg, Kathleen**, (AV) .................. '51 '76 C.112 B.A. L.1065 J.D. [Ziffren,B.B.&F.]
*PRACTICE AREAS: Entertainment Law.
**Hallem, Timi Anyon**, (AV) .................. '46 '72 C.788 A.B. L.1068 J.D. [Tuttle&T.]
*PRACTICE AREAS: Real Estate; Land Use; Secured Financing; Corporate Law.
Haller, Nina J. .................. '65 '92 C.1036 B.A. L.1065 J.D. 11377 W. Olympic Blvd.
**Hallinan, Kathleen M.** .................. '67 '93 C.813 A.B. L.178 J.D. [Ⓐ Troop M.S.&P.]
*PRACTICE AREAS: Intellectual Property Litigation; General Business Litigation.
**Halling, Chris W.**, (BV) .................. '53 '79 C.112 B.A. L.800 J.D. [Agapay,L.&H.]
*PRACTICE AREAS: Business Litigation; Corporations; Computer Law; Intellectual Property; Real Estate.
**Hallissy, Erin B.** .................. '69 '95 C.767 B.A. L.464 J.D. [Ⓐ Daniels,B.&F.]
**Halliwell, Thomas L.** .................. '54 '86 C.684 B.S. L.426 J.D. [Ⓐ Chapman&G.]
*PRACTICE AREAS: Construction Litigation; Products Liability; Professional Liability.
**Halloran, Finola G.** .................. '69 '95 C.112 B.A. L.990 J.D. [Ⓐ Manning,M.&W.]
Halloran, Mark E. .................. '53 '78 C.112 A.B. L.1065 J.D. [Alexander,H.N.&R.]
Hallowitz, Carol J. .................. '52 '77 C.604 A.B. L.94 J.D. Dep. Pub. Def.
**Halm, David** .................. '69 '95 C.112 B.A. L.426 J.D. [Ⓐ Valensi,R.&M.]
*PRACTICE AREAS: Litigation.
**Halm, Howard L.**, (AV) ......... '42 '69 C.112 B.A. L.1049 J.D. [Breidenbach,B.H.H.&H.]
*PRACTICE AREAS: Environmental Insurance Defense; Governmental Tort Liability; Municipal Defense; Products Liability Defense.
Halper, Samuel W., (AV) .................. '28 '56 C.112 B.A. L.1068 LL.B. 1880 Century Pk. E.
**Halper, Stephen I.** .................. '52 '77 C.910 B.A. L.494 J.D. [Ⓒ Levinson,M.J.&P.]
**Halperin, Ernst A.** .................. '64 '94 C.813 B.S. L.846 J.D. [Ⓐ Folger L.&K.]⊙
Halperin, Ivan W. .................. '46 '72 C.800 B.S. L.1065 J.D. [I.W.Halperin]
**Halperin, Lawrence N.** .................. '50 '76 C.309 A.B. L.477 J.D. [Lewis,D.B.&B.]
Halperin, Ivan W., Law Offices of .................. 12100 Wilshire Blvd.
Halpern, Eleanor S. .................. '30 '81 L.1148 J.D. 15510 Aqua Verde Dr.‡
Halpern, Irving L., (AV) .................. '31 '56 C&L.477 A.B., J.D. 221 N. Figueroa St.
**Halpern, Jason P.**, (AV) .................. '44 '71 C.102 B.A. L.851 J.D. [J.P.Halpern]
*LANGUAGES: French.
Halpern, Mindy S. .................. '60 '92 C.94 B.A. L.426 J.D. 660 S. Figueroa St., Suite 1500
Halpern, Paul .................. '61 '90 C.685 B.A. L.813 J.D. 1801 Ave. of the Stars
**Halpern, Sheldon A.** .................. '45 '70 C&L.659 B.A., J.D. [Pircher,N.&M.]
*PRACTICE AREAS: Real Estate Law.

**Halpern, Jason Paul, A Professional Corporation, (AV)**
**10880 Wilshire Boulevard Suite 1800, 90024-4174**
**Telephone: 310-478-2722 Facsimile: 310-470-7003**
**Jason P. Halpern.**
**Personal Injury, Wrongful Death, Wrongful Termination, Employee Discrimination and Harassment, Medical and Professional Malpractice, Business Litigation and Transactional Law Domestically and Internationally including Contract Preparation and Negotiation, including Severance Packages.**
*See Professional Biographies, LOS ANGELES, CALIFORNIA*

**Halstead, Baker & Olson**
(See Baker, Olson, LeCroy & Danielian, A Law Corporation, Glendale)

Haltom, Catherine E. ......... '67 '92 C.112 B.A. L.1068 J.D. 1901 Ave. Of The Stars, 7th Fl.
Halverson, Jerry F., (AV) .................. '29 '54 C&L.800 A.B., J.D. L.A. Unified Sch. Dist.
**Halvorsen, Clay A.** .................. '59 '85 C.1077 B.A. L.800 J.D. [Gibson,D.&C.]
*PRACTICE AREAS: Corporate Law; Securities; Mergers, Acquisitions and Divestitures; Partnerships; Franchises and Franchising.
**Ham, James I.** .................. '56 '81 C.800 A.B. L.1068 J.D. [Arnold&P.]
*REPORTED CASES: Hartbrodt v. Burke (1996) 42 Cal.App.4th 168, 49 Cal. Rptr. 2d 562.
*PRACTICE AREAS: Commercial Litigation; Products Litigation; Employment Law; Legal Ethics.
Hamada, Muneyuki Victor .................. '52 '80 C.800 B.A. L.426 J.D. 3550 Wilshire Blvd.
**Hamada, Sean T.** .................. '66 '93 C.112 B.A. L.802 J.D. [Ⓐ Bottum&F.]
**Hamblet, Gary A.**, (AV) ......... '53 '79 C.813 B.A. L.1292 J.D. [Breidenbach,B.H.H.&H.]
*PRACTICE AREAS: Business Litigation; Civil Rights Defense; Insurance Bad Faith; Subrogation; Professional Malpractice.
**Hambleton, Debby R.** .................. '59 '84 C.549 B.A. L.990 J.D. [Rexon,F.K.&H.]
*PRACTICE AREAS: Labor and Employment Litigation.
Hambly, Michael R. .................. '59 '85 C.882 B.A. L.309 J.D. 2121 Ave. of the Stars
**Hamburg, Sidney A.** .................. '52 '77 C.112 L.1095 J.D. [Hamburg,H.E.&M.]
*PRACTICE AREAS: Real Estate Law; General Business Law; State and Federal Court Receiver.

**Hamburg, Hanover, Edwards & Martin**
**2029 Century Park East Suite 1640, 90067-3086**
**Telephone: 310-552-9292 Fax: 310-552-9291**
**Email: HHEMLaw@Aol.com**
**Members of Firm: Sidney A. Hamburg; John D. Hanover; Barry G. Edwards; Gregg A. Martin; Meredith L. Caliman.**
**General Civil Practice in all State and Federal Courts. General Real Estate, Corporate, Employment, Business, Construction, Entertainment, Taxation, Immigration, Environmental, Zoning, Insurance and Insurance Defense, Administrative, Tradenames and Trademarks Infringement, and Copyright Enforcement.**
*See Professional Biographies, LOS ANGELES, CALIFORNIA*

**Hamburger, David A.** .................. '70 '95 L.800 [Ⓐ Dewey B.]
Hamburger, Edmund A., (AV) .................. '27 '53 C.667 B.E.E. L.262 J.D. [E.A.Hamburger]
Hamburger, Edmund A., A Professional Corporation, (AV) .................. 10540 Wilshire Blvd.
**Hameetman, John** .................. '— '94 C.674 A.B. L.309 J.D. [Ⓐ Brobeck,P.&H.]
*PRACTICE AREAS: Securities; Corporate.
Hamel, Charles .................. '26 '57 C.999 L.809 12304 Santa Monica Blvd.

CAA242P

**Hamer, Spencer** '69 '96 C.477 B.A. L.800 J.D. [Ⓐ Musick,P.&G.]
*LANGUAGES: Spanish.
**Hamersmith, Harold E.** '55 '79 C.339 A.B. L.477 J.D. [Sheppard,M.R.&H.]
*PRACTICE AREAS: Business Litigation; Construction Law; Public Contract Law.
**Hamilton, Barbara L.** '60 '92 C.112 B.A. L.1068 J.D. [Ⓐ Gibbs,G.L.&A.]
*PRACTICE AREAS: Title Insurance; Real Property; Construction Law.
**Hamilton, James A.**, (AV) '44 '70 C.696 B.A. L.846 J.D. [Riordan&M.]
**Hamilton, John M.** '62 '91 C.821 B.A. L.800 J.D. [Ⓐ Gascou,G.&T.]
*PRACTICE AREAS: Commercial Litigation; Bankruptcy.
**Hamilton, Lisé** '59 '93 C.705 B.A. L.976 J.D. [Ⓐ Berman,B.M.&R.]
*PRACTICE AREAS: Commercial Litigation; Intellectual Property Litigation; Corporate; Entertainment.
**Hamilton, Melissa** '66 '92 C.16 B.A. L.178 J.D. [Ⓐ Williams&B.]
*PRACTICE AREAS: Estate Planning.
**Hamilton, Paul R.**, (AV) '34 '66 C.800 B.S. L.809 LL.B. [Jeffer,M.B.&M.]
*REPORTED CASES: Orange Productions Credit Association vs. Frontline Ventures Ltd., 801 F.2d 1581 (1986); Long Beach Equities vs. County of Ventura, 231 Cal.App.3d 1016 (1991); Southwest Diversified Inc. vs. City of Brisbane, 229 Cal.App.3d 1548 (1991); Westlake North Homeowners Association vs. City of Thousand Oaks, 915 F.2d 1301 (9th Circuit 1990); Lacher vs. Superior Court, 230 Cal.App.3d 1038 (1991).
*PRACTICE AREAS: Land Use Law and Entitlement Litigation; Real Estate Litigation; Construction Defect Litigation; Appellate Matters.
Hamilton, Sandra B. '46 '77 C.331 B.A. L.809 J.D. 12735 San Vicente Blvd.

**Hamilton & Cumare**
**(See Pasadena)**

Hamilton-Klein, Lisa '59 '84 C.597 B.A. L.1068 J.D. 1801 Century Pk. E., 7th Fl.
Hamlin, Richard, (AV) '45 '71 C.112 A.B. L.426 J.D. 4640 Admiralty Way
Hammel & Peterson, A Professional Corporation
1901 Ave. of the Stars, 18th Fl. (⊙Sacramento & Walnut Creek)
Hammer, Peter '64 '93 C.285 B.S. L.477 J.D. 400 S. Hope St.
Hammers, Stephen '65 '92 C.112 B.A. L.91 J.D. 10100 Santa Monica Blvd.
**Hammill, Jeffrey** '66 '92 C.605 A.B. L.1148 J.D. [Ibold&A.]
Hammock, Randolph M. '58 '84 C.763 B.A. L.1049 J.D. [Hammock&H.]
Hammock & Hedges 1545 Wilshire Blvd., Eight Fl.
**Hammond, Daniel J.** '58 '89 C&L.494 B.S., J.D. [Ⓐ Epstein B.&G.]
*PRACTICE AREAS: Labor and Employment Law; Education Law; Litigation.
**Hammond, John** '55 '92 C.1154 B.A. L.426 J.D. [Ⓐ La Follette,J.D.F.&A.]
*PRACTICE AREAS: Medical Malpractice.
Hammond, Lisa Rae Brooks '66 '92 C.674 A.B. L.813 J.D. 11355 W. Olympic Blvd.

**Hammond, Zuetel & Cahill**
**(See Pasadena)**

**Hamovitz, Glenn D.** '63 '88 C.112 B.A. L.426 J.D. [Ⓐ Crawford&R.]
*REPORTED CASES: Fundamental Investment Etc. Realty Fund v. Gradow (1994) 28 Cal. App. 4th 966, 33 Cal. Rptr. 2d 812 (review den.).
*PRACTICE AREAS: Real Estate Litigation; Business Litigation; Construction Litigation.
Hampar, Armen '18 '52 C&L.813 A.B., LL.B. 880 W. First St.
**Hampton, Brett G.** '63 '89 C.112 B.A. L.990 J.D. [Ⓐ Biesty,M.&G.]
**Hampton, Carolyn A.** '66 '91 C.112 B.A. L.426 J.D. [Ⓐ Katten M.&Z.]
*LANGUAGES: French, German.
*PRACTICE AREAS: Civil Litigation.
**Hampton, Deann** '66 '94 C.112 B.A. L.426 J.D. [Ⓐ J.T.Cairns&Assoc.]
*PRACTICE AREAS: Real Estate; Civil Trial.
**Hampton, Scott A.** '64 '91 C.112 B.A. L.426 J.D. [Ⓐ Bottum&F.]
**Hamre, Mareta C.** '63 '90 C.309 B.A. L.1066 J.D. [Stutman,T.&G.]
*PRACTICE AREAS: Bankruptcy; Insolvency; Corporate Reorganization; Commercial Litigation.
**Hamrick, A. Raymond, III** '53 '80 C.763 A.B. L.770 J.D. [A.R.Hamrick,III]
*PRACTICE AREAS: Insurance Coverage; Insurance Defense; Civil Litigation; Bad Faith Litigation; Business Law.
**Hamrick, Robert S., (Professional Corporation)**, (AV) '46 '73
C.475 B.A. L.767 J.D. [Schell&D.]

**Hamrick, A. Raymond, III, A Law Corporation**
**Suite 2055, 10 Universal City Plaza (Universal City), 91608**
**Telephone: 818-763-5292 Fax: 818-763-2308**
**A. Raymond Hamrick, III;—David L. Evans; Bradley O. Field; Raymond C. Dion; David A. Tabb; Jill Anne Hillman; Philip D. Caputo.**
**Insurance Coverage, including Casualty, Property, Construction Defect and Environmental Claims , Insurance Defense, Bad Faith Litigation, Alternative Dispute Resolution, Civil Litigation, Construction Defect Litigation, Business Litigation, General Liability Litigation, Business Law.**
***See Professional Biographies, LOS ANGELES, CALIFORNIA***

Hamwi, Joseph F., (AV) '28 '59 C.112 B.S. L.426 J.D. 480 Tuallitan Rd.‡
Hamwi, Susan L. '64 '89 C.112 B.A. L.426 J.D. 865 S Figueroa St., #3100
**Han, Andrew** '68 '93 C.178 B.A. L.145 J.D. [Ⓐ Latham&W.]
*PRACTICE AREAS: Corporate.
Han, David T. '62 '89 C.178 B.A. L.228 J.D. 333 S. Hope St., 48th Fl.
**Hanagami, William K.**, (AV) '56 '85 C.112 B.A. L.426 J.D. [King&W.]
Hanan, Catherine B. '54 '77 C.112 B.S. L.1068 J.D. [C.B.Hanan]
Hanan, Catherine B., A Prof. Corp. 2049 Century Park E.
Hance, Bryan S. '62 '91 C.112 B.A. L.990 J.D.
Dir., Christian Conciliation Serv. of L. A.
**Hancock, Heller-Ann C.** '59 '84 C.446 B.S. L.990 J.D. [Lynberg&W.]

**Hancock Rothert & Bunshoft LLP, (AV)**
**17th Floor, 515 South Figueroa Street, 90071-3334⊙**
**Telephone: 213-623-7777 Telecopy: 213-623-5405**
**Members of Firm: Patrick A. Cathcart; Patricia Shuler Schimbor; Earl J. Imhoff, Jr.; Deborah Pitts; Vito C. Peraino; Yvette D. Roland; Marc J. Derewetzky; Robert V. Richter. Senior Counsel: Albert I. Moon, Jr. Associates: Linda B. Carr; William K. Enger; Mark A. Robbins; Jennifer A. Vane; Patricio T.D. Barrera; Vipal J. Patel; Dominique R. Shelton; R. Christopher Rhody; Laura A. Pace; Melissa M. Harnett; Frank A. Yokoyama; Jennifer D. McKee; John E. Breen; Daniel W. Nugent; B. Otis Felder; Peter T. Imhof; Steven C. Uribe; Christopher J. Keene.**
**General Civil and Trial Practice in all State and Federal Courts. Corporation, Business, Insurance, Admiralty, Probate, Tax and International Law.**
**San Francisco, California Office: 10th Floor, Four Embarcadero Center, 94111-4168. Telephone: 415-981-5550. Telex: 470369. Telecopy: 415-955-2599.**
**Tahoe City, California Office: Lighthouse Center, 850 North Lake Boulevard, Suite 15, P.O. Box 7199, 96145-7199. Telephone: 916-583-7767. Telecopy: 916-581-3215.**
**London Office: Forum House, 15/18 Lime Street, Sixth Floor, London EC3M 7AP, England. Telephone: 071-220-7567. Telecopy: 071-220-7609.**
**Associated Office: Staiger, Schwald & Sauter. Genferstrasse 24, 8002 Zurich, Switzerland. Telephone: 01-282-8686. Telecopy: 01-282-8787. Telex: 813-273-GND.**
***See Professional Biographies, LOS ANGELES, CALIFORNIA***

Hand, Alice '47 '78 C.112 B.A. L.809 J.D. Dep. City Atty.
**Hand, Penny R.** '41 '92 C.800 B.A. L.1136 J.D. [Clopton,P.&B.]
Handel, Jonathan L. '60 '90 C&L.309 A.B., J.D. P.O. Box 691781
**Handel, Sheri R.** '68 '95 C.112 B.A. L.426 J.D. [Ⓐ Firm of R.M.Moneymaker]
*PRACTICE AREAS: Bankruptcy.
**Handelman, David Y.**, (AV) '38 '63 C.659 A.B. L.309 LL.B. [Ⓒ Troy&G.]
*PRACTICE AREAS: Corporate Law; Entertainment Law.
Handle, Jonathan '60 '90 C&L.309 B.A., J.D. 2049 Century Park E., 26th Fl.
**Handler, Adam M.**, (AV) '59 '84 C.976 B.S. L.813 J.D. [Sidley&A.]
*PRACTICE AREAS: Taxation Law.
**Handler, Carole E.** '— '75 C&L.659 A.B., J.D. [Alschuler G.&P.]

**Handler & Schrage**
**(See Santa Monica)**

**Handy, Nelson J.** '— '90 C.1077 B.S. L.426 J.D. [Ⓐ Reish&L.]
*PRACTICE AREAS: Estate Planning; Taxation; Business Law.
**Handzlik, Jan Lawrence**, (AV) '45 '71 C.800 B.A. L.1068 J.D. [Kirkland&E.]
*PRACTICE AREAS: Litigation; White Collar Criminal Defense.
**Hane, Raymond E., III** '60 '90 C.112 B.A. L.809 J.D. [Ⓐ Belcher,H.&B.]
*LANGUAGES: Spanish.
*PRACTICE AREAS: General Civil Trials and Appellate Practice; Aviation Law; Products Liability Law.
**Haney, Steven H.** '57 '85 C.1060 B.A. L.1067 J.D. [Andrews&K.]
*PRACTICE AREAS: Civil Litigation; White Collar Criminal Defense; Contract Law; Real Estate Law.
**Hanken, Garrett L.**, (AV) '48 '73 C.684 A.B. L.813 J.D. [Greenberg G.F.C.&M.]
*PRACTICE AREAS: General Civil Trial and Appellate Practice.
**Hanker, Drew T.** '57 '83 C.105 B.A. L.800 J.D. [Ⓒ Daniels,B.&F.]
*LANGUAGES: French.
*PRACTICE AREAS: Trial Law; Hotel and Innkeeper Law; Products Liability; Wrongful Termination; Employment Discrimination.
Hankin, David Lee '61 '87 C.112 B.A. L.880 J.D. 1925 Century Pk. E.

**Hankin, Marc B., (AV) '50 '80 C.766 B.A. L.426 J.D.**
**11355 West Olympic Boulevard Suite 100, 90064-1614**
**Telephone: 310-996-2699 FAX: 310-996-2695**
**Email: Marc_B_Hankin@postoffice.worldnet.att.net**
***LANGUAGES: French.**
**Conservatorships, Elder Law, Estate Planning and Probate with an emphasis on Probate, Trust and Elder Abuse Litigation.**
***See Professional Biographies, LOS ANGELES, CALIFORNIA***

**Hankin, Marc E.** '61 '94 C.94 B.A. L.659 J.D. [Ⓐ Pretty,S.&P.] (See Pat. Sect.)
*PRACTICE AREAS: Patent Litigation and Prosecution; Trademark Litigation and Registration; Copyright Litigation and Registration; Trade Secrets Litigation.
**Hanley, John V.** '62 '92 C.112 B.S.M.E. L.767 J.D.
[Ⓐ Fulwider P.L.&U.] (See Pat. Sect.)
*PRACTICE AREAS: Patent; Trademark; Copyright; Unfair Competition; Litigation.
Hanley, Scott R. '52 '87 C.339 B.A. L.464 J.D. U.S. Dept. of Jus.
Hanley, Thomas F., III, (AV) '51 '79
C.426 B.B.A. L.809 J.D. 4215 Glencoe Ave. (Marina Del Rey)
Hanlon, Dolores M. '50 '83 C.94 A.B. L.1067 J.D. Dep. Dist. Atty.
Hanlon, Mary Kathleen '60 '85 C&L.477 B.A., J.D. Dep. Dist. Atty.
**Hanna, Denise E.** '61 '87 C.145 A.B. L.813 J.D. [Ⓒ Konowiecki&R.]
*PRACTICE AREAS: Corporate; Mergers and Acquisitions; General Business; Health Care.
Hanna, J. Terence '55 '80 C.763 A.B. L.1065 J.D.
V.P., Develop. & Opers., Kaufman & Broad Home Corp.
Hanna, Zaher N. '30 '75 L.061 LL.B. 350 S. Figueroa St.

**Hanna and Morton, (AV)** [BR]
**A Partnership including Professional Corporations**
**Seventeenth Floor, Wilshire-Grand Building, 600 Wilshire Boulevard, 90017**
**Telephone: 213-628-7131 Facsimile: 213-623-3379**
**Members of Firm: Byron C. Hanna (1887-1951); Harold C. Morton (1895-1978); John H. Blake (1916-1971); Edward S. Renwick (A Professional Corporation); James P. Lower; Robert M. Newell, Jr.; James P. Modisette; Michael I. Blaylock (Certified Specialist, Taxation Law, The State Bar of California Board of Legal Specialization); David A. Ossentjuk; Judith A. Lower; John A. Belcher. Of Counsel: William N. Greene; Milo V. Olson; David A. Thomas. Associates: Thomas N. Campbell; Robert J. Roche; Michael P. Wippler; Daniel Y. Zohar.**
**Trial and General Business Practice. Civil Trial and Appellate Practice. General Business and Corporate Law. Legal and Tax Aspects of Asset Management. Private Foundations and other Charitable and Non-Profit Organizations. Antitrust. Securities. Insurance. Taxation, Employment Law. Real Property. Probate. Trust and Estate Planning Law. Agricultural Law. Natural Resources Law including Energy, Oil and Gas, Environmental, Hazardous Waste, Air Resources and Water Law.**
***See Professional Biographies, LOS ANGELES, CALIFORNIA***

**Hannan, Susan F.** '49 '81 C.705 B.A. L.426 J.D. [Ⓐ Sedgwick,D.M.&A.]
**Hanneman, Brian G.** '65 '93 C.1333 B.S. L.809 J.D. [Ⓐ Morris,P.&P.]
**Hanni, Clint M.** '63 '92 C.1335 B.A. L.178 J.D. [Ⓐ O'Melveny&M.]
Hannifin, Bret '59 '84 C.813 B.A. L.1068 J.D.
V.P. & Assoc. Div. Coun., Chicago Title Ins. Co.
Hannig, Jack F. '28 '60 C.800 A.B. L.1068 LL.B. P.O. Box 83743
Hannon, Michael B. '36 '66 C.1097 L.809 J.D. [Hannon,P.&L.]
Hannon, Park and Lennon 3550 Wilshire Blvd.
**Hanover, John D.** '61 '86 C.860 B.A. L.880 J.D. [Hamburg,H.E.&M.]
*LANGUAGES: French and Hebrew.
*REPORTED CASES: T&R Painting Construction, Inc. v. St. Paul Fire & Marine Insurance Co., (2nd Dist., Div. 2 1994) 23 Cal. App. 4th 738.
*PRACTICE AREAS: Complex Business Litigation; Real Estate Litigation; Construction Litigation; Insurance Litigation; Employment Litigation.
**Hanrahan, Thomas P.** '50 '75 C.262 B.A. L.178 J.D. [Sidley&A.]
*PRACTICE AREAS: Business Litigation.
**Hansell, Dean** '52 '77 C.207 B.A. L.597 J.D. [LeBoeuf,L.G.&M.]
*PRACTICE AREAS: Litigation; Insurance; Environmental.
**Hansen, Dennis B., (P.C.)** '44 '72 C.101 B.S. L.1068 J.D. [Overton,L.&P.]
*PRACTICE AREAS: Business Law; Probate; Trusts and Estates; Estate Planning.
Hansen, Joan '51 '86 C.174 B.A. L.800 J.D. V.P., Twentieth Century Fox Film Corp.
**Hansen, Mark T.** '59 '84 C.770 B.S. L.1065 J.D. [Sonnenschein N.&R.]
*PRACTICE AREAS: Litigation.
Hansen, Raymond L. '33 '62 C.112 A.B. L.1066 LL.B.
Chf. Coun., Calif. Teachers Assn.
**Hansen, Russell C.** '55 '80 C.674 A.B. L.813 J.D. [Gibson,D.&C.]
*PRACTICE AREAS: Corporate Law; Securities; Mergers, Acquisitions and Divestitures; Finance; Business Law.
**Hansen, Scott R.** '63 '93 C.112 B.S. L.347 J.D. [Oppenheimer P.S.] (Pat.)
**Hansen, Shannon M.** '65 '94 C.119 B.S.Ch.E. L.813 J.D. [Ⓐ Kirkland&E.]
*PRACTICE AREAS: Litigation; Intellectual Property.

**Hansen, Jacobson, Teller & Hoberman**
**(See Beverly Hills)**

Hanson, Earl L., (AV) '33 '61 C.112 B.A. L.800 LL.B. [Hanson&E.]
**Hanson, John J.**, (AV) '22 '52 C.208 A.B. L.309 LL.B. [Ⓒ Gibson,D.&C.]
*PRACTICE AREAS: Antitrust and Trade Regulation.
Hanson, Joseph D. '30 '60 C.112 B.A. L.178 LL.B. City Atty.
Hanson, Paul T. '42 '72 C.767 B.A. L.1065 J.D. Dep. Co. Coun.
Hanson & Egers, (AV) 205 S. Bway.
**Hanzlick, Claudia H.** '63 '90 C.235 B.A. L.608 J.D. [Ⓐ Lynberg&W.]
*LANGUAGES: Spanish.
**Harber, Stephen M.** '59 '85 C.800 B.S. L.464 J.D. [Lynberg&W.]
**Harbin, John A.** '56 '92 C.767 B.A. L.426 J.D. [Tax C.]
Harbinger, Richard '23 '70 C.112 B.A. L.602 J.D. Dep. Dist. Atty.
**Harbison, Stephen F.**, (AV) '43 '69 C&L.813 A.B., LL.B. [Argue P.H.&M.]
*PRACTICE AREAS: Civil Litigation.
**Hardacre, David W.** '40 '69 C.139 B.A. L.426 J.D. [Blum,P.&H.]
**Hardacre, Edwin Grantley** '62 '93 C.139 B.A. L.1148 J.D. [Ⓐ Blum,P.&H.]
Harder, Patrick D. '60 '86 C.426 B.A. L.1068 J.D. 12424 Wilshire Blvd.

CAA243P

**Hardgrove, Kenneth M.**, (AV) .......... '51 '79 C.1046 B.A. L.990 J.D. [Sherwood&H.]
*PRACTICE AREAS: Real Estate Litigation; Business Litigation; Negotiation and Drafting of Real Property Leases.

**Hardie, Les Glenn**
(See Santa Monica)

**Harding, Richard C.**
(See Pasadena)

Hardwick, Gary C. .............................. '60 '85 C.477 B.A. L.912 J.D. Dept. of Jus.

**Hardy, John D., Jr.**, (AV) '43 '72
C&L.893 B.M.E., J.D. [O'Melveny&M.] (ⓞSan Francisco)
*PRACTICE AREAS: Corporate Law; Securities; Securitization; Mergers and Acquisitions.

Hardy, Karen A. ..................................'48 '79 L.1136 J.D. 1925 Century Park E.

**Hardy, Maria Snyder** ............... '60 '93 C.800 B.A. L.426 J.D. [Ⓐ O'Melveny&M.]

Hardy, William J. .......................... '32 '71 C.112 A.B. L.809 J.D. Alt. Def. Coun.

**Hargraves, Charles N.** ................. '64 '89 C.164 B.A. L.990 J.D. [Ⓐ Wilson,K.&B.]

**Haritchabalet, Muriel C.** '68 '94
C.764 B.A. L.990 J.D. [Ⓐ Fulwider P.L.&U.] (See Pat. Sect.)
*LANGUAGES: French and Spanish.
*PRACTICE AREAS: Trademarks.

**Hariton, Nicholas T.** ................. '56 '84 C.112 B.A. L.800 J.D. [Ⓢ Resch P.A.&B.]
*LANGUAGES: Swedish; Danish.
*PRACTICE AREAS: Business Law; Banking; Admiralty Law.

Harkavy, Dennis G. ............... '30 '55 C.659 B.S. L.1009 J.D. 2263 S. Harvard Blvd.

**Harlow, Yale M. '38 '66 C.1077 B.A. L.1065 J.D.**
**777 South Figuerora Street, Suite 3700, 90017**
**Telephone: 213-236-3860 Fax: 213-236-3861**
**Email: AW357@LAFN.ORG**
**Bankruptcy, Commercial Litigation and Collections.**
***See Professional Biographies, LOS ANGELES, CALIFORNIA***

Harman, Mark E. ............. '56 '86 C.362 B.A. L.1137 J.D. State Dept. of Corporations

Harmer, David J. .............................. '62 '88 C&L.101 B.A., J.D. 400 S. Hope St.

**Harmon, William J.** '42 '73 C.950 B.A. L.1065 J.D.
Sr. Corp. Coun., Farmers Grp., Inc.
*RESPONSIBILITIES: Labor and Agency; Corporate; Intellectual Property.

Harms, Dulany R. ........................'54 '86 C.502 B.S.C.E. L.426 J.D. 611 W. 6th St.

**Harmsen, William R.**, (AV) ......... '46 '72 C.154 B.A. L.1065 J.D. [Allen,M.L.G.&M.]
*PRACTICE AREAS: Litigation.

Harn, Joy M. Fernbach ............'67 '92 C.684 B.A. L.464 J.D. 611 W. 6th St. (ⓞBrea)

Harn, William Davis .................'— '93 C.112 B.S. L.464 J.D. 333 S. Hope St., 48th Fl.

Harnett, Daniel J. .................'30 '53 C.585 B.S. L.436 J.D. 763 S. Burlingame Ave.

**Harnett, Melissa M.** .......................'66 '93 C.112 B.A. L.800 J.D. [Ⓐ Hancock R.&B.]
*LANGUAGES: German.

**Harney, David M.** ........................................ '24 '49 C.426 L.800 J.D. [Harney]
*PRACTICE AREAS: Civil Trial; Product Liability Law; Medical Malpractice Law; Aviation Law.

**Harney, David T.** ................................ '54 '89 C.1169 B.A. L.1136 J.D. [Harney]
*PRACTICE AREAS: Civil Trial; Products Liability Law; Medical Malpractice Law; Aviation Law; Professional Liability Law.

**Harney, Julie A.** ................................ '61 '88 C.112 B.A. L.1136 J.D. [Harney]
*PRACTICE AREAS: Civil Trial; Products Liability Law; Medical Malpractice Law.

**Harney Law Offices, A Legal Corporation, (AV)** ⒷⒷ
**Suite 1300 Figueroa Plaza, 201 North Figueroa Street, 90012-2636**
**Telephone: 213-482-0881 Fax: 213-250-4042**
**David M. Harney; David T. Harney; Julie A. Harney; Andrew J. Nocas; Vincent McGowan; Thomas A. Schultz.**
**Negligence and Complex Personal Injury Law. Trials and Appeals. Medical Legal, Products Liability, Railroad and Aviation Law.**
**Reference: Bank of America.**
***See Professional Biographies, LOS ANGELES, CALIFORNIA***

**Harnsberger, Thomas L.**, (AV) ............'49 '74 C.112 B.A. L.477 J.D. [Riordan&M.]

Haroonian, Alexander .....'55 '84 C.112 B.A. L.809 J.D. 5455 Wilshire Blvd., Bldg. 1110

Harper, Lynne L. ..................'30 '81 C.112 B.S. L.1238 J.D. 1011 S. Hudson Ave.‡

**Harr, Kevin M.** ...................................'— '90 C&L.846 B.B.A., J.D. [Ⓐ O'Melveny&M.]

Harrel, Linda Cohen .....................'53 '78 C.1077 B.A. L.426 J.D. Dept. of Transp.

**Harriman, J. D., II**, (AV) '57 '84 C.608 B.S.E. L.800 J.D.
[Hecker&H.] (See Pat. Sect.)
*PRACTICE AREAS: Patent and Trademark; Intellectual Property; Computer Law; Unfair Competition.

Harriman, John H. ...................'20 '49 C.197 A.B. L.813 J.D. 245 S. Plymouth Blvd.‡

**Harriman, Jordon E.** ..............'57 '84 C.608 B.A. L.800 J.D. [Ⓢ Sedgwick,D.M.&A.]

Harrington, Chris ...........................'66 '93 C.154 B.A. L.1049 J.D. 3200 Wilshire Blvd.

**Harrington, Christopher J.** ............... '66 '93 C.154 B.A. L.1049 J.D. [Ⓐ Selman B.]
*PRACTICE AREAS: Insurance Coverage; Insurance Coverage Litigation.

**Harrington, Greg** ...................................'53 '80 C.112 B.A. L.800 J.D. [Orrick,H.&S.]
*PRACTICE AREAS: Public Finance Law.

Harrington, Lee K. ..................................'46 '75 C.112 B.A. L.800 J.D. 555 W. 5th St.

**Harrington, Scott D.** ..........................'56 '84 C.184 B.A. L.228 J.D. [Manatt,P.&P.]
*PRACTICE AREAS: Music.

**Harrington, Foxx, Dubrow & Canter, (AV)**
**Thirtieth Floor, 611 West Sixth, 90017ⓞ**
**Telephone: 213-489-3222 Facsimile: 213-623-7929**
**Members of Firm: Richard Hunt Sampson (1901-1952); Lowell L. Dryden (1909-1967); Robert S. Harrington (1913-1983); Brian L. Goller (1954-1992); Richard A. Foxx (Retired); Eli B. Dubrow; David H. Canter; Lowell M. Ramseyer; Lawrence A. Bush; Dale B. Goldfarb; Craig F. Sears; Martin C. Kristal; Edward R. Leonard; Mark A. Juhas; Mark W. Flory; William P. Finney; Thomas E. Lotz (Resident, San Diego Office); Thomas O. Russell, III; Henry A. Wirta, Jr.; Michael F. Cressey (Resident, San Diego Office); Nancy J. Mindel; Gary G. Dye; Beth Isaacs Golub (Resident, San Diego Office); John C. Dewell. Associates: Alan M Schnitzer; Marguerite Coyne Hill; Peter A. Schneider (Resident, Orange Office); Jeffrey S. Doggett (Resident San Diego Office); Mark S. Salzberg (Resident, San Francisco Office); Pamela Harrington Munro; Edward W. Lukas, Jr.; K. Erin Lennemann; Elizabeth J. Miller; Angela Lui Walsh; David R. Catalino (Resident, San Diego Office); Stephen L. Smith (Resident, San Diego Office); Mark W. Eisenberg (Resident, Orange Office); Brad M. Elder; Michael W. Jacobs (Resident, San Diego Office); Kimberlee S. Stubbs (Resident, San Diego Office); Erik Gunderson; Donald G. Furness; Kelly A. Ward; Esther Gonzalez; Mark W. Norman; Ann Michael; Timothy P. Chang; Kirk J. Retz; Daniel E. Kenney; Mark A. Goldstein; J. Jason Hill (Resident, San Diego Office).**
**General Civil and Trial Practice in all State and Federal Courts and before Federal and State Administrative Agencies. Real Estate, Corporation, Business, Estate Planning, Trust, Probate, Medical, Products Liability, Health and Insurance Law.**
**Representative Clients: Farmers Insurance Group; Pet, Inc.; Royal Insurance Co.; Transport Indemnity Co.; Underwriters at Lloyd's, London.**
**Reference: Security Pacific National Bank (Los Angeles Main Office, Sixth and Spring Streets).**
**Orange, California Office: Suite 1020, 1100 Town and Country Road. Telephone: 714-973-4595. Facsimile: 714-973-7923.**
**San Diego, California Office: Suite 1150, 401 West A Street. Telephone: 619-233-5553. Fax: 619-233-0005.**
**San Francisco, California Office: 444 Market Street, Suite 3050. Telephone: 415-288-6600. Facsimile: 415-288-6618.**
***See Professional Biographies, LOS ANGELES, CALIFORNIA***

Harris, Charles E. ........................'49 '74 C.267 B.S. L.1049 J.D. [Mommaerts&R.]

Harris, David A. ..........................'62 '87 C.112 B.A. L.1068 J.D. 55 S. Flower St.

**Harris, David M.** .......................'64 '89 C.112 B.A. L.800 J.D. [Ⓐ Sinnott,D.M.&P.]
*PRACTICE AREAS: Business Litigation; Trial Practice; Insurance Coverage Litigation; Real Property Law; Corporate Law.

Harris, David Paul ...........................'66 '92 C.112 B.A. L.813 J.D. Dep. Atty. Gen.

**Harris, Dean M.** ........................ '49 '76 C.347 A.B. L.477 J.D. Atlantic Richfield Co.

**Harris, Donald P.** ...................... '64 '94 C.1077 B.S. L.426 J.D. [Ⓐ Alschuler G.&P.]

**Harris, Eddie J.** ........................ '39 '75 C.14 B.A. L.1068 J.D. [Ⓐ J.L.Cochran,Jr.]
*PRACTICE AREAS: Personal Injury Law; Criminal Law; Business Litigation.

Harris, H. Elizabeth .........................'— '73 C.1023 B.A. L.800 J.D. [Harris,B.&A.]

**Harris, James M.** ........................ '51 '76 C.103 A.B. L.145 J.D. [Sidley&A.]
*PRACTICE AREAS: Appellate and Civil Litigation.

Harris, Jeffrey B. .......................................'57 '82 C.228 A.B. L.464 J.D. [J.B.Harris]

**Harris, Jennifer** ........................... '64 '89 C.112 B.A. L.426 J.D. [Ⓢ Thorpe&T.]
*LANGUAGES: French, Spanish and Japanese.
*PRACTICE AREAS: Probate Law; Trusts and Estates; Corporate Law; Real Estate.

Harris, John D. ...................................... '34 '60 C.112 A.B. L.1066 J.D. Mun. Ct. J.

Harris, John F., (AV) ......................................'41 '66 C&L.426 LL.B. [J.F.Harris]

**Harris, John Joseph** ..................'52 '80 C.112 B.A. L.1065 J.D. [Richards,W.&G.]
*PRACTICE AREAS: Environmental Law; Oil and Gas Law; Business Litigation.

Harris, John W. ........................'50 '75 C.112 A.B. L.1068 J.D. 911 Wilshire Blvd.

Harris, Jonathan A. .......................'62 '90 C&L.813 A.B., J.D. 725 S. Figueroa ST.

Harris, Jonathan D. '61 '86 C.112 B.A. L.1066 J.D.
Sr. Dir., Bus. Affs., Turner Pictures Worldwide

Harris, Joseph ...............................................'11 '35 9508 Monte Mar Dr.

Harris, Joseph B., (BV) ............'31 '60 C.011 B.A. L.800 LL.B. 2301 N. Catalina St.

Harris, Lara Drino ...........................'67 '93 C.112 B.A. L.1148 J.D. City Atty. Off.

**Harris, Michael**, (AV) ......................'35 '60 C.813 B.A. L.1068 J.D. [Rogers&H.]
*PRACTICE AREAS: Civil Practice; Real Property; Entertainment; Corporation; Probate.

**Harris, Michael D.**, (AV) ........ '46 '73 C.679 B.S. L.904 J.D. [Oppenheimer P.S.] (Pat.)
*PRACTICE AREAS: Intellectual Property.

Harris, Michael Richard ............'36 '81 C.813 B.A. L.1068 J.D. 12424 Wilshire Blvd.

**Harris, Michael S.** ......................... '46 '77 C.112 B.A. L.426 J.D. [Kirshman&H.]ⓞ
*PRACTICE AREAS: Corporate; Securities Law; Business Law; Civil Litigation; Estate Planning.

Harris, Mitchel J. .............................. '43 '67 C.107 B.A. L.1009 LL.B. Dep. Dist. Atty.

**Harris, Monica Y.** ........................'66 '92 C.674 A.B. L.309 J.D. [Ⓐ Kinsella,B.F.&T.]
*PRACTICE AREAS: Intellectual Property; Legal Malpractice.

**Harris, Nathan H.** ........................ '44 '72 C.763 B.A. L.1065 J.D. [Ⓐ Sulmeyer,K.B.&R.]
*PRACTICE AREAS: Commercial Law.

**Harris, Peter F.** .........................'50 '81 C.980 B.S. L.7 J.D. [Lewis,D.B.&B.]

**Harris, Philecia L.** ....................'62 '94 C.1070 B.S. L.608 J.D. [Ⓐ Seyfarth,S.F.&G.]

Harris, Philip H., (AV) '20 '47 C.813 A.B. L.309 LL.B.
5959 W. Century Blvd., Ste. 100

**Harris, Rand F.**, (AV) ............................ '45 '70 C.112 A.B. L.1065 J.D. [R.F.Harris]
*PRACTICE AREAS: Family Law; Criminal Law; Workers Compensation Defense; Personal Injury.

Harris, Randall G. ............................'48 '78 C.1060 B.A. L.1065 J.D. Dep. Dist. Atty.

**Harris, Richard G.** ............................'55 '81 C.1169 B.A. L.770 J.D. [Tuverson&H.]
*PRACTICE AREAS: Insurance Defense Law; Defense of Medical Malpractice; business Torts Litigation.

Harris, Richard S. .......'12 '34 C&L.800 A.B., LL.B. 1999 Ave. of the Stars, Suite 1400‡

Harris, Rita H. ..........................................'48 '72 C.112 A.B. L.1065 J.D. Dep. Pub. Def.

**Harris, Robin D.** ................................'59 '87 C.338 B.S. L.339 J.D. [Richards,W.&G.]
*PRACTICE AREAS: Public Law; Public Finance.

Harris, Sandra J. ..........'58 '88 C.1077 B.A. L.800 J.D. Securities and Exchange Comm.

**Harris, Sara T.** ........................................'52 '86 L.1190 J.D. [Ⓐ Saltzburg,R.&B.]
*PRACTICE AREAS: Litigation; Real Estate Law; Bankruptcy Law; Receivership Law.

**Harris, Steven I.**, (AV) .......... '40 '67 C.112 B.A. L.1068 LL.B. [Stockwell,H.W.&W.]

**Harris, Susan L.** '57 '81 C.112 A.B. L.800 J.D.
Sr. V.P., Gen. Coun., Corp. Affs., & Secy., SunAmerica Inc.
*RESPONSIBILITIES: General Corporate Practice.

**Harris, Suzanne**, (AV) ....................... '40 '77 C.1131 B.A. L.1068 J.D. [Harris G.]
*PRACTICE AREAS: Family Law.

**Harris, Timothy J.** ......................'53 '78 C.911 B.A. L.1068 J.D. [Charlston,R.&W.]

Harris, Timothy S. ......................'49 '74 C&L.188 B.A., J.D. 11500 W. Olympic Blvd.

Harris, William E. ...................'46 '77 C.1042 B.A. L.990 J.D. 11755 Wilshire Blvd.

Harris, Baird & Abraham ............................................... 880 W. First St.

**Harris • Ginsberg, LLP, (AV)**
**11755 Wilshire Boulevard, Suite 1650, 90025**
**Telephone: 310-444-6333 Fax: 310-444-6330**
**Members of Firm: Suzanne Harris (Certified Specialist, Family Law, The State Bar of California Board of Legal Specialization); Larry A. Ginsberg.**
**Specializing in all aspects of Dissolution of Marriage, Custody and Visitation, Paternity Issues, Adoption and Pre-Nuptial and Post-Nuptial Agreements.**
***See Professional Biographies, LOS ANGELES, CALIFORNIA***

Harris, Jeffrey B., A Professional Corporation ........333 South Grand Avenue, Suite 3400

Harris, John F., P.C., (AV) .............................................. P.O. Box 83789

**Harris, Rand F., A Prof. Corp., Law Offices of, (AV)**
**Riverside Law Building, 12650 Riverside Drive, Suite 205, 91607-3492**
**Telephone: 818-755-4848 Facsimile: 818-760-2583**
**Rand F. Harris.**
**Family Law, Criminal Law, Personal Injury, Workers Compensation Defense, Business and Real Estate.**
***See Professional Biographies, LOS ANGELES, CALIFORNIA***

Harrison, Gary S. .......................'55 '89 C.1036 B.A. L.1066 J.D. [Harrison&R.]

Harrison, Gordon J. .................'48 '75 C.112 B.A. L.1049 J.D. 10866 Wilshire Blvd.

Harrison, Hugh R. ..............'48 '74 C.112 A.B. L.1068 J.D. Legal Aid Found. of L.A.

**Harrison, Jeff A.** ..............................'65 '90 C.1042 B.S. L.800 J.D. [Ⓐ Karns&K.]
*PRACTICE AREAS: Administrative Law; Corporate Law; Business Law; Litigation; Trust Probate.

Harrison, Michael S. ...............'61 '89 C.112 B.A. L.990 J.D. 611 W. 6th St., 16th Fl.

Harrison, Robert ........................'57 '84 C.112 B.A. L.426 J.D. 6300 Wilshire Blvd.

**Harrison, Robert G.** ...............'59 '85 C.169 B.A. L.1065 J.D. [Ⓐ Wright,R.O.&T.]
*PRACTICE AREAS: Insurance Defense Litigation and Appeals; Public Entity Liability Law; Aviation Law.

**Harrison, Steven M.** .............................'44 '70 C.112 B.A. L.800 J.D. [Ⓐ Reinis&R.]
*TRANSACTIONS: Real Estate, Partnership, Corporate, Limited Liability, Business Purchase and Sales, and License Agreements.
*PRACTICE AREAS: Real Estate; Business Litigation; Trade Secret; Unfair Competition Litigation; Securities Litigation.

**Harrison, Stewart S.** ................'59 '92 C.893 B.A. L.1068 J.D. [Ⓐ Pillsbury M.&S.]

Harrison & Rodriguez ........................................................4727 Wilshire Blvd.

Harriton, Norman, (AV) ............'25 '71 C.112 B.A. L.809 J.D. 1870 N. Vermont Ave.

Hart, Albert M. ...........................'19 '47 C.112 A.B. L.813 LL.B. 972 Norman Pl.‡

Hart, Anthony W. ....................'41 '84 C&L.1190 B.S.L., J.D. 1901 Ave. of the Stars

**Hart, Charles R., Jr.**, (AV) ................ '39 '65 C.112 B.S. L.1065 LL.B. [Hart&W.]
*PRACTICE AREAS: Corporate Law; Business Law; Real Estate Law; Estate Planning; Tax Law.

**Hart, Douglas R.** ........................'58 '84 C.506 B.S. L.546 J.D. [Sheppard,M.R.&H.]
*PRACTICE AREAS: Employment Law.

Hart, Harris Spencer ..........................'64 '91 C.112 B.A. L.800 J.D. Jud. Law Clk.

Hart, Heidi Susan ..........................'61 '86 C.112 B.A. L.426 J.D. [Ⓐ Herrig&V.]

**Hart, Howard F.** .........................'47 '73 C.188 A.B. L.309 J.D. [Ⓢ Hughes H.&R.]
*PRACTICE AREAS: Real Estate Law; Corporate Law; Securities Law; Administrative Law.

Hart, James P., Jr. ....'65 '91 C.112 B.A. L.426 J.D. 505 Shatto Pl.
**Hart, Jana L.** ....'55 '84 C.1078 B.A. L.1148 J.D. [Hart&H.]
*PRACTICE AREAS: Franchising Mediation; Corporation Formation; Corporate Organization; Business.
Hart, Janet K. ....'51 '77 C.420 B.A. L.800 J.D. 10880 Wilshire Blvd.
Hart, Jennifer L. ....'65 '95 C.914 B.A. L.569 J.D. 333 S. Hope St.
**Hart, John K.** ....'50 '75 C.105 B.A. L.665 J.D. Sr. Coun., Bank of Amer.
**Hart, Larry C.**, (AV) ....'42 '74 C.172 B.S. L.426 J.D. [Musick,P.&G.]
*PRACTICE AREAS: Litigation.
**Hart, Maurice A.**, (AV) ....'27 '63 C&L.800 B.S., J.D. [Hart&H.]
*PRACTICE AREAS: Franchising; Mergers and Acquisitions; Receivable Financing; Corporate Formation; Corporate Governance.
Hart, Ross R. ....'51 '76 C.112 B.A. L.426 J.D. 3055 Wilshire Blvd., 7th Fl.‡
**Hart, Stephanie J.** ....'59 '87 C.112 B.A. L.990 J.D. [▣ Rexon,F.K.&H.]
*PRACTICE AREAS: Litigation; Labor and Employment Law; Employee Benefits; Family Law.
**Hart, Timothy J.** ....'64 '93 C.1057 B.A. L.1049 J.D. [▣ Gibson,D.&C.]
*PRACTICE AREAS: Securities; Mergers and Acquisitions.
**Hart, William S.**, (AV) ....'42 '72 C.453 S.B. L.426 J.D. [▣ Hillsinger&C.]
Hart-Franklin, Cassandra D. ....'63 '90 C.668 B.A. L.309 J.D. Wells Fargo Bk., N.A.

**Hart & Hart, (AV)**
**1925 Century Park East, Suite 2000, 90067**
**Telephone: 310-277-2236 Telecopier: 310-556-5653**
**Maurice A. Hart; Jana L. Hart.**
**General Business, Corporate and Partnership, Mergers and Acquisitions, Finance, Franchising, Real Property and Timeshare Law.**
**Reference: Union Bank, Century City Branch.**

Hart-Nibbrig, Harold C. ....'38 '72 C.112 B.A. L.1068 J.D. [Tyre K.K.&G.]

**Hart & Watters, A Professional Law Corporation, (AV)**
**12400 Wilshire Boulevard, Suite 450, 90025-1061**
**Telephone: 310-826-5202 FAX: 310-442-0181**
**Charles R. Hart, Jr.; Thomas L. Watters; Keith A. Lovendosky;—Bret R. Carter.**
**Civil Litigation Trial and Appellate Practice in all State and Federal Courts. Negligence, Business, Corporate, Insurance and Real Estate Law and Litigation. Probate, Trust and Estate Planning.**
**Reference: Santa Monica Bank.**
*See Professional Biographies, LOS ANGELES, CALIFORNIA*

Harten, Marvin A. ....'31 '67 C.667 B.M.E. L.426 LL.B. 578 Crestline Dr.
Harter, Gene G. ....'41 '72 C.813 B.A. L.1066 J.D. 445 S. Figueroa St.
Harter, Robert J., Jr. '44 '70 C.813 A.B. L.800 J.D.
Sr. V.P., Gen. Coun. & Secy., Tiger Intl., Inc.
**Hartgens, Amber N.** ....'67 '95 C.178 B.A. L.1066 J.D. [▣ White&C.]
**Hartigan, John F.** ....'50 '75 C.339 B.S. L.276 J.D. [Morgan,L.&B.]
**Hartigan, Mary K.** ....'62 '91 C.276 B.S. L.602 J.D. [▣ Jones,D.R.&P.]
Hartley, Judy L. ....'57 '83 C.1109 B.A. L.809 J.D. Calif. Dept. of Corps.
Hartman, Daniel M. ....'63 '89 C.645 B.A. L.276 J.D. 400 S. Hope St.
**Hartman, Roger C.**, (AV) ....'42 '69 C.112 B.A. L.1065 J.D. [Hartman&Assoc.]
**Hartman, Tricia J.** ....'64 '93 C.112 B.A. L.309 J.D. [▣ Quinn E.U.&O.]

**Hartman and Associates, (AV)**
**12401 Wilshire Boulevard, Second Floor, 90025-1015**
**Telephone: 310-207-9100 Fax: 310-207-5101**
**Roger C. Hartman. Associates: Douglas J. Workman.**
**Business, Real Property, Commercial, Corporate, Securities, Housing and Urban Development, Partnership and Limited Liability Company Law.**
*See Professional Biographies, LOS ANGELES, CALIFORNIA*

**Hartmann, Ronald A.** ....'58 '84 C.16 B.S. L.846 J.D. [Verboon,W.H.&P.]
*PRACTICE AREAS: Construction Defects Litigation; Real Estate Litigation; Insurance Litigation.

**Hartmann, Sharon Lybeck, Law Offices of '39 '79 C.112 A.B. L.1066 J.D.**
**5757 Wilshire Boulevard, Suite 560, 90036**
**Telephone: 213-965-5600 Facsimile: 213-965-5613**
**Email: Lybeck@aol.com**
***PRACTICE AREAS: Civil Rights Monitoring of Consent Decrees; Civil Rights Litigation; Bankruptcy Litigation; Civil Litigation.**
**Elizabeth Guillén; Lisa Ann Hollingworth; Susan M. Woolley. Associates: Marcella A. Bell; Barbara E. Dalton; Maurice P. Destouet; Mona Hathout; Leigh M. Leonard; William M. Litt; Doreena Wong.**
**Boutique practice in the monitoring of Civil Rights Consent Decrees and Injunctions; Civil Rights Litigation.**
*See Professional Biographies, LOS ANGELES, CALIFORNIA*

**Hartney, Mark R.** ....'62 '88 C.112 B.A. L.1067 J.D. [Allen,M.L.G.&M.]
*PRACTICE AREAS: Litigation; Environmental; Land Use.
Hartsfield, Arnett L., Jr., (AV) ....'18 '56 C&L.800 B.A., LL.B. 8745 S. Harvard Blvd.
**Hartston, Amos E.** ....'71 '96 C.112 B.A. L.276 J.D. [▣ Latham&W.]
Hartwick, Ronald S., (AV) ....'43 '68 C&L.976 B.S., J.D. 550 S. Hope‡
**Hartz, Jay N.**, (AV) ....'48 '73 C.228 B.A. L.145 J.D. [Hooper,L.&B.]
*SPECIAL AGENCIES: Medical Board of California; California State Department of Health Services.
*PRACTICE AREAS: Commercial Litigation; Health and Hospital Law; Bioethics Law.
**Hartzler, Mark B.** ....'63 '94 C.37 B.A. L.846 J.D. [▣ Zevnik H.G.&M.]
*LANGUAGES: Arabic.
*PRACTICE AREAS: Insurance Coverage; General Civil Litigation.
**Harvey, Marian A.** ....'59 '90 C.112 B.A. L.1049 J.D. [▣ Latham&W.]
*PRACTICE AREAS: Environmental; Land Use.
Harvey, Mark Richard ....'61 '91 C.1097 B.A. L.426 J.D. 1411 N. Hayworth Ave.
**Harvey, Temple K.** ....'51 '79 C.347 B.A. L.990 J.D. [Federman,G.&G.]
**Harvill, Saheli Datta** ....'65 '90 C.112 B.S. L.178 J.D. [▣ Morrison&F.]
Harwin, Gay L. ....'53 '78 C.1168 B.A. L.426 J.D. 10940 Wilshire Blvd.
Harwin, Michael B. ....'47 '72 C.705 B.A. L.569 J.D. Supr. Ct. J.
**Hasbrouck, Jennifer R.** ....'70 '96 C.602 B.A. L.1068 J.D. [▣ Graham&J.]
Hasencamp, Laurie F. '58 '85 C.668 B.A. L.800 J.D.
Dir., Legal Research, Legal Research Network, Inc.
Haskins, Ann ....'48 '74 C.112 B.A. L.1068 J.D. Chief Dep., City Coun.
**Hassan, James M.** ....'48 '73 C.800 B.S. L.1065 J.D. [Musick,P.&G.]
*PRACTICE AREAS: Taxation; Estate Planning; Trusts and Estates; Non-Profit and Charitable Organizations.
**Hassenberg, Barry** ....'52 '76 C.1077 B.A. L.809 J.D. [McKay,B.&G.]
*PRACTICE AREAS: Civil Trial; Insurance Defense; Products Liability.
Hassett, Charlotte ....'49 '89 C.576 B.S. L.809 J.D. 10850 Wilshire Blvd., 8th Fl.
Hasson, Aron P. ....'52 '80 C.112 B.A. L.1095 J.D. 10850 Wilshire Blvd.
**Hastie, William H.**, (AV) '47 '73 C.31 A.B. L.1066 J.D.
[Arnelle,H.M.W.&G.] (©San Francisco, Calif.)
*PRACTICE AREAS: Commercial Litigation; Employment Law; Business.
**Hasting, Carl D.** ....'57 '82 C.173 B.S. L.990 J.D. V.P. & Corp. Coun., Coalinga Corp.
*RESPONSIBILITIES: In House Legal; Tax Research; Tax Compliance; Family Estate Planning.
Hastings, J. Gary ....'43 '72 C.800 B.S. L.809 J.D. Jus., Ct. of App.
Hastings, John T. ....'15 '40 C.113 B.A. L.1066 LL.B. 527 Burlingame Av.‡
Hastings, Stephen Ross ....'40 '74 C.1097 B.S. L.809 J.D. 3125 Hollyridge Dr.‡
**Hata, Harumi** ....'60 '86 C&L.426 B.A., J.D. [LeBoeuf,L.G.&M.]
*PRACTICE AREAS: Corporate; International; Real Estate.
Hatamiya, Julie Y. ....'52 '88 C.800 B.M. L.1137 J.D. 33rd Fl., 611 W. 6th St.
**Hatch, Hilary Joy** ....'69 '94 C.112 B.A. L.426 J.D. [▣ Gibson,D.&C.]
*PRACTICE AREAS: Corporate Law; Securities.

**Hatch, R. Noel**, (AV) ....'32 '60 C.112 A.B. L.813 LL.B. [▣ Iverson,Y.P.&H.]
*PRACTICE AREAS: Civil Litigation and Appellate Practice; Wrongful Termination and Employment Discrimination; Labor; Real Property.
**Hatch, Timothy J.** ....'55 '83 C&L.966 B.B.A., J.D. [Gibson,D.&C.]
*PRACTICE AREAS: Government Contracts; Litigation; White Collar Crime; Computers and Software.
**Hatcher, Linda** ....'62 '94 C.531 B.S. L.426 J.D. [▣ Ginsburg,S.O.&R.]
**Hathaway, David T.** ....'67 '93 C.112 B.A. L.426 J.D. [▣ Allen,M.L.G.&M.]
*PRACTICE AREAS: Litigation.
**Hathaway, Harry L.**, (AV) ....'37 '63 C.112 B.S. L.800 J.D. [Fulbright&J.]
*PRACTICE AREAS: Corporate Law; Trusts and Estates.
Hathaway, Jeffrey D. ....'54 '80 C.800 B.A. L.426 J.D. [Mommaerts&R.]
Hathaway, Karen L. ....'50 '77 C.312 B.A. L.1136 J.D. Pres., LAACO Ltd.
**Hatherley, John E., (A Professional Corporation)** '44 '74
C.112 A.B. L.1067 J.D. [Mitchell,S.&K.]
*PRACTICE AREAS: Real Estate Law; Business Law.
**Hathout, Mona** ....'— '93 C.112 B.A. L.426 J.D. [▣ S.L.Hartmann]
*PRACTICE AREAS: Civil Rights; Corporate Law.
**Hattenbach, Benjamin** ....'70 '96 C.1167 B.S. L.1066 J.D. [▣ Irell&M.]
**Hattler, Eric Reed** ....'65 '93 C.31 B.A. L.145 J.D. [▣ Riordan&M.]
**Hatton, Lisa M.** ....'68 '93 C.112 B.A. L.800 J.D. [▣ Charlston,R.&W.]
*PRACTICE AREAS: Litigation; Environmental Insurance Coverage.
**Hauge, David F.** ....'43 '74 C.763 A.B. L.862 J.D. [Lord,B.&B.]
**Haugen, Kari** ....'59 '88 C.939 B.A. L.178 J.D. [▣ Ford&H.]
**Haughton, John A.** ....'63 '93 C.112 B.A. L.1148 J.D. [▣ Bonne,B.M.O.&N.]
Haughton, Thomas H. ....'38 '70 C.800 L.1148 LL.B. 2965 Waverly Dr.
Hauk, A. Andrew ....'12 '38 C.686 A.B. L.128 LL.B. U.S. Sr. Dist. J.
**Haupt, Renee A.** ....'70 '95 C&L.800 B.S., J.D. [▣ Mendes&M.]
Hauptman, H. Ronald ....'32 '61 C&L.705 A.B., LL.B. Supr. Ct. Comr.
**Hausladen, Erin M.** ....'69 '96 C&L.112 B.A., J.D. [▣ Hughes H.&R.]
**Hausmann, Edwin D.**, (AV) ....'41 '72 C.597 B.S. L.1066 J.D. [Hausmann&S.]
*REPORTED CASES: G.E. Hetrick & Assoc. v. Summit Const. 11 Cal App. 4th 318, 13 Cal Rptr. 2nd 803 (1992); U.S. v. Hughes Tool Co. 415 F. Supp. 637 (C.D. Cal, 1976).

**Hausmann & Shrenger, LLP, (AV)**
**333 South Grand Avenue, Thirty-Third Floor, 90071-1504**
**Telephone: 213-625-8886 Facsimile: 213-625-1388**
**Edwin D. Hausmann; Justin J. Shrenger.**
**General Civil Litigation in State and Federal Courts with emphasis on Real Estate, Commercial Law and International Law emphasizing Greater China.**
*See Professional Biographies, LOS ANGELES, CALIFORNIA*

**Havel, Richard W.**, (AV) ....'46 '72 C.602 B.A. L.1068 J.D. [Sidley&A.]
*PRACTICE AREAS: Corporate Reorganization Law; Bankruptcy Law.
**Haven, Peter T.** ....'65 '94 C.813 A.B. L.1068 J.D. [▣ Musick,P.&G.]
**Havens, Sylvia** ....'62 '88 C.705 B.A. L.809 J.D. [▣ Schell&D.]
**Haviland, Peter L.** ....'— '89 C.309 A.B. L.813 J.D. [▣ Kaye,S.F.H.&H.]
*LANGUAGES: Portuguese, Spanish.
*PRACTICE AREAS: Civil and Criminal Trials; CERCLA/Superfund; Copyright and Trademark; Insurance Recovery; Entertainment (Record, Film, TV).
Havkin, Stella Anne ....'61 '88 C.035 B.A. L.1065 J.D. 2049 Century Pk. E., Ste. 1100
Hawekotte, Robert S., Jr. ....'54 '84 C.870 B.S. L.930 J.D. 11835 W. Olympic Blvd.
**Hawes, Lesley Anne** ....'59 '84 C&L.800 A.B., J.D. [Frandzel&S.]
*PRACTICE AREAS: Creditors' Rights in Insolvency Proceedings and Workouts; Secured Transactions; Bankruptcy.
**Hawk, Dennis J.** ....'59 '87 C.1074 B.S. L.276 J.D. [Stein P.&H.]
*PRACTICE AREAS: Entertainment (50%); Corporate (30%); Medical (10%); Real Estate (10%).
Hawkes, Diane E. ....'63 '90 C.659 B.S. L.1068 J.D. Asst. U.S. Atty.
**Hawkins, Roger E.**, (AV) ....'40 '70 C.1097 B.S. L.1068 J.D. [Hawkins,S.L.&B.]
**Hawkins, Steven W.** ....'66 '94 C.813 A.B. L.112 J.D. [▣ Munger,T.&O.]

**Hawkins, Delafield & Wood, (AV)**
**First Interstate World Center, 633 West Fifth Street Suite 3550, 90071©**
**Telephone: 213-236-9050 Fax: 213-236-9060**
**Members of Firm: Arto C. Becker; Kevin M. Civale. Associates: M. Kevin Hale; Kenneth E. James.**
**Municipal Law, Municipal Finance, Redevelopment, Real Estate, Civil and Business Litigation, Corporate, Finance and Eminent Domain Law.**
**New York, N.Y. Office: 67 Wall Street. Telephone: 212-820-9300. Cable Address: "Hawkdel, New York". Telecopier: 212-514-8425.**
**Hartford, Connecticut Office: City Place. Telephone: 203-275-6260.**
**Newark, New Jersey Office: One Gateway Center. Telephone: 201-642-8584.**
**Washington, D.C. Office: 1015 15th Street, N.W., Suite 930. Telephone: 202-682-1480.**
*See Professional Biographies, LOS ANGELES, CALIFORNIA*

**Hawkins, Schnabel, Lindahl & Beck, (AV) BB**
**660 South Figueroa Street, Suite 1500, 90017**
**Telephone: 213-488-3900 Telecopier: 213-486-9883**
**Email: 102175.3573@compuserve.com**
**Members of Firm: Roger E. Hawkins; Laurence H. Schnabel; George M. Lindahl; Kelley K. Beck; Jon P. Kardassakis; William E. Keitel; Rena Denton Stone; Timothy A. Gonzales; R. Timothy Stone; Richard C. Weston; Ram F. Cogan; Randy M. McElvain;—Kurt G. Gresenz; David C. Moore; Wendy Anne Scholl; Robert J. Prata; Todd A. Daley; Laura E. Hogan; Todd B. Allen; Julie A. Mote; Jill N. Bant; Brian J. Gladstone; Shawn E. Cowles.**
**General Civil and Trial Practice in all State and Federal Courts. Products Liability, Professional Liability, Business Litigation, Environmental Law, Insurance Law and Bad Faith Litigation, Maritime Law and Employment Discharge Litigation.**
*See Professional Biographies, LOS ANGELES, CALIFORNIA*

Haworth, Greason P. ....'45 '79 C.1042 B.A. L.1137 J.D. [Hogan,B.&H.]
Haworth, Stephen A. ....'35 '66 C.112 B.S. L.800 J.D. 1875 Century Pk.
**Hawthorne, Andrew W.** ....'63 '89 C.605 A.B. L.426 J.D. [▣ Monteleone&M.]
*PRACTICE AREAS: Construction Law; Business Litigation.
**Hawthorne-Waters, Judy** ....'68 '95 C.112 B.A. L.426 J.D. [▣ Anderson,M.&C.]
Hayase, Helen M. ....'58 '82 C.813 B.A. L.1068 J.D. Law Clk. to Ct. of App. J.
**Hayashi, Kim A.** ....'56 '81 C&L.800 A.B., J.D. [▣ Hollins&R.]©
**Hayden, David A.** ....'38 '64 C.112 A.B. L.1066 LL.B. [▣ Graham&J.]
*LANGUAGES: Japanese, Chinese and German.
*PRACTICE AREAS: International Business Law.
Hayden, Frances J. ....'56 '86 C.907 B.A. L.1068 J.D. 1532 N. Hayworth Ave.
Hayden, John R. ....'43 '75 C.1126 B.A. L.809 J.D. Sr. Corp. Coun.
Hayden, Richard F. C. ....'17 '45 C.112 A.B. L.1066 LL.B. Supr. Ct. J.
**Hayden, Robert C.** ....'53 '78 C.813 B.S. L.1066 J.D. [▣ Konowiecki&R.]
*PRACTICE AREAS: Labor and Employment Law; Employment Litigation; General Business Litigation.
**Hayes, Byron, Jr.**, (AV) ....'34 '60 C.668 B.A. L.309 LL.B. [Baker&H.]
*PRACTICE AREAS: Business Transactions; Real Estate Law; Financial Institutions Law.
**Hayes, Daniel B.** ....'67 '92 C.472 B.B.A. L.800 J.D. [▣ Manatt,P.&P.]
*PRACTICE AREAS: Music.
**Hayes, Frederick Brevard** ....'61 '93 C.880 B.S. L.1148 J.D. [▣ Iverson,Y.P.&H.]
*PRACTICE AREAS: Civil Litigation.
Hayes, Gail H. ....'53 '87 C.339 B.F.A. L.1066 J.D. Sr. Atty., AT&T
**Hayes, Holly A.** ....'52 '89 C.483 B.A. L.426 J.D. [▣ Arter&H.]
**Hayes, Jacqueline Jourdain** '67 '94 C&L.309 B.A., J.D.
(adm. in NY; not adm. in CA) [▣ Troop M.S.&P.]
*PRACTICE AREAS: Corporate; Financial Services; Intellectual Property.
Hayes, James A., (BV) ....'21 '53 C.112 L.1065 J.D. 707 Wilshire Blvd.
**Hayes, Jeanine L.** ....'68 '96 C.696 B.S. L.426 J.D. [▣ Pretty,S.&P.]

Hayes, John Gardner, (AV) ....................'41 '68 C.112 B.A. L.1068 J.D. [J.G.Hayes]
Hayes, M. Jonathan, (AV) ............'49 '79 C.285 B.A. L.426 J.D. 12100 Wilshire Blvd.
**Hayes, Melinda L.** ............... '60 '86 C.494 B.S.B. L.1068 J.D. [McCutchen,D.B.&E.]
*PRACTICE AREAS: Healthcare.
**Hayes, Phillip M.** .................... '57 '91 C.602 B.A. L.809 J.D. [A Dennison,B.&P.]
Hayes, Richard A. '46 '74 C.645 B.A. L.569 J.D.
Sr. V.P. & Dir., Taxes, First Interstate Bancorp
Hayes, Russell E. .............'48 '73 C.154 B.A. L.893 J.D. Dir., Legal Affs., Hydril Co.
Hayes, Steven L. ........................'47 '79 C.45 B.A. L.767 LL.B. 1015 Oneonta Dr.
Hayes, William K. ...................'48 '73 C.1097 B.S. L.1068 J.D. 5225 Wilshire Blvd.

**Hayes, John Gardner, A Professional Corporation, (AV)**
**Suite 600, 11400 West Olympic Boulevard, 90064**
**Telephone: 310-478-4711 Fax: 310-575-4171**
**John Gardner Hayes;—J. Walter Gussner.**
**Civil Trials, Insurance Defense, Personal Injury Litigation, Product Liability, Medical and Professional Malpractice, Bad Faith and Casualty Insurance Law, Employment Law, Discrimination.**
***See Professional Biographies, LOS ANGELES, CALIFORNIA***

**Hayman, Russell** ..........................'58 '83 C.228 B.A. L.976 J.D. [Latham&W.]
**Haymer, Robert D.** ...................... '56 '87 C.112 B.A. L.426 J.D. [O'Melveny&M.]
*PRACTICE AREAS: Corporate Law; Securities; Partnerships; Joint Ventures; Mergers and Acquisitions.
Haymes, Catherine Anne '58 '84
C.112 B.A. L.1068 J.D. Pres., Advantage Legal Search & Consulting
Haynes, Marcelita V. ................................. '51 '77 C.1097 B.A. L.1068 J.D. NLRB
**Haynes-Garretty, Reetha** ...............'54 '86 C.1097 B.A. L.1190 J.D. [Biesty,M.&G.]
*PRACTICE AREAS: Insurance Defense Litigation; Construction Litigation; Business Litigation; Family Law.
Hays, Robert P. ........................... '42 '74 C.112 B.A. L.426 J.D. 1455 Wildwood Dr.
Haythorn, Joseph D. '47 '76 C.210 B.A. L.678 J.D.
(adm. in WA; not adm. in CA) Prof. & Libr., Whittier Law Sch.
**Hayum, George T.**, (AV) .........'45 '73 C.674 A.B. L.976 J.D. [Armstrong H.J.T.&W.]
*LANGUAGES: French.
*PRACTICE AREAS: Entertainment.
**Hayutin, David L.**, (AV) ................. '30 '58 C&L.800 A.B., J.D. [Pillsbury M.&S.]
**Hayutin, Marc I.**, (AV)......................... '44 '69 C.813 B.A. L.309 J.D. [Sidley&A.]
*LANGUAGES: French.
*PRACTICE AREAS: Commercial Real Estate Financial and Acquisitions; Partnerships; Corporate Mergers and Acquisitions; Computer; Telecommunications Technology.
**Hayworth, L. Keven** ................'67 '92 C.846 B.A. L.900 J.D. [A Pillsbury M.&S.]
**Hazarabedian, Arthur J.** ............'62 '88 C.112 B.A. L.426 J.D. [A Oliver,V.S.M.&L.]
*PRACTICE AREAS: Eminent Domain; Inverse Condemnation; Land Use; Appeals.
**Hazard, Susan J.**, (AV) ..................'53 '78 C.112 B.A. L.1068 J.D. [Musick,P.&G.]
*PRACTICE AREAS: Estate Planning; Trust and Estate Administration.
**Hazen, Steven K.**, (AV) ...................'49 '76 C.990 B.A. L.145 J.D. [Akre,B.&C.]
*PRACTICE AREAS: Corporate; International Business.
**Hazzard, Yakub** ........................'64 '90 C.813 B.A. L.1068 J.D. [A Mitchell,S.&K.]
*PRACTICE AREAS: Intellectual Property; Litigation; Sports Law.
Healey, Richard B. .....................'48 '72 C.112 A.B. L.1068 J.D. Dep. Dist. Atty.
**Healy, Brett** ...........................'70 '95 C.188 B.A. L.800 J.D. [A Orrick,H.&S.]
Healy, Gerard A. ..........................'48 '85 C.4 B.S. L.1029 J.D. First Interstate Bank
**Heaney, Mark O.**, (AV) ........................'46 '72 C.228 A.B. L.659 J.D. [A B.Tarlow]
*PRACTICE AREAS: Criminal Law.
**Heard, Viddell L., Jr.** .................. '68 '94 C.112 B.A. L.1068 J.D. [A Kirkland&E.]
*PRACTICE AREAS: Litigation.
**Hearn, Kenneth A.** ....................'52 '79 C.112 B.A. L.1095 J.D. [A Gray,Y.D.&R.]
*PRACTICE AREAS: Insurance Law; Environmental Law; Appellate Practice.
Hearne, Victoria E. '52 '78 C.846 B.A. L.796 LL.B.
(adm. in TX; not adm. in CA) 7519 Mulholland Dr.‡
Heartfield, Alison A. ...................'68 '93 C.668 B.A. L.1068 J.D. 444 S. Flower St.
**Heartney, Matthew T.** ......................'53 '79 C.604 B.A. L.976 J.D. [Arnold&P.]
*PRACTICE AREAS: Litigation; Antitrust.
Heath, John W., Jr. ......................'35 '69 C.800 B.A. L.809 LL.B. 3668 Olympiad Dr.
**Heather, Fred D.** .......................'43 '78 C.105 A.B. L.1019 J.D. [Troop M.S.&P.]
*PRACTICE AREAS: White Collar Criminal Defense; Complex Civil Litigation; Civil False Claims Act Defense.
Heaton, Thomas H., III '37 '66 C.472 B.A. L.818 LL.B.
(adm. in MA; not adm. in CA) 1728 S. La Cienega Blvd.
Heberton, Pamela M. ........................'58 '84 C.165 A.B. L.1119 J.D. U.S. Atty's Off.
**Hecht, Mervyn L.** ..........................'38 '64 C.112 B.A. L.309 J.D. [B Hecht&R.]
*LANGUAGES: French.
Hecht, Richard W., (AV) ................... '30 '61 C.112 L.809 J.D. Ret. Dist. Att. Off.‡

**Hecht, Steven '48 '75 C.605 B.A. L.1068 J.D.**
**1901 Avenue of the Stars Suite 1600, 90067-6017**
**Telephone: 310-286-3044 Fax: 310-286-2644**
***PRACTICE AREAS: International Business; Limited Liability Companies; Corporate Organization; Business Formation; Closely Held Corporations.**
**Business Law, Corporations, Limited Liability Companies, Partnerships, Finance, Investment, Mergers and Acquisitions and International Business Transactions.**
***See Professional Biographies, LOS ANGELES, CALIFORNIA***

**Hecht Helmer, Leslie L.** ......................'63 '90 C.813 B.A. L.1068 J.D. [A Bryan C.]
*PRACTICE AREAS: Labor and Employment Law.

**Hecht & Riskin, (AV)**
**1925 Century Park East Suite 2000, 90067**
**Telephone: 310-277-2236 Facsimile: 310-556-5653**
**Ira D. Riskin. Of Counsel: Mervyn L. Hecht.**
**General Civil and Trial Practice in all State and Federal Courts. Real Property, Corporation, Securities, Franchise, Estate Planning, Trust and Probate Law. International and Taxation Law.**
***See Professional Biographies, LOS ANGELES, CALIFORNIA***

**Heck, Christopher J.** ..................... '68 '94 C.178 A.B. L.228 J.D. [A Kirkland&E.]
*PRACTICE AREAS: Litigation.
**Hecker, Gary A.**, (AV) '55 '81 C.690 B.S.M.E. L.1049 J.D.
[Hecker&H.] (See Pat. Sect.)
*PRACTICE AREAS: Patent, Trademark and Copyright; Intellectual Property; Computer Law; Unfair Competition.

**Hecker & Harriman, (AV)**
**2029 Century Park East, 16th Floor, 90067**
**Telephone: 310-286-0377 Facsimile: 310-286-0488; 310-785-0016 Telex: 6503743401**
**Gary A. Hecker; J. D. Harriman II. Associates: Frank M. Weyer; Elizabeth E. Blakey; Carole A. Quinn; Ross D. Snyder; Randall J. Bluestone.**
**Intellectual Property Law including Patent, Trademark, Copyright, Computer Law, Unfair Competition, and Trade Secret. Technology Licensing and Litigation in Federal and State Courts and the International Trade Commission.**
***See Professional Biographies, LOS ANGELES, CALIFORNIA***

**Hedges, George R.**, (AV) ....................'52 '78 C.659 B.A. L.800 J.D. [Hedges&C.]
Hedges, James K. ..............................'59 '85 C.813 B.A. L.1066 J.D. [Hammock&H.]

**Hedges & Caldwell, A Professional Corporation, (AV) BB**
**606 South Olive Street, Suite 500, 90014**
**Telephone: 213-629-9040 Telecopier: 213-629-9022**
(This Listing Continued)

**Hedges & Caldwell, A Professional Corporation (Continued)**
**Christopher G. Caldwell; George R. Hedges; H. Jay Kallman; Michael R. Leslie; Joan Mack; Sherryl Elise Michaelson; Mary Newcombe; David Pettit. Of Counsel: Ralph H. Nutter; Jan B. Norman. General Civil and Criminal Trial and Appellate Practice in all State and Federal Courts and Administrative Agencies.**
***See Professional Biographies, LOS ANGELES, CALIFORNIA***

**Hedgpeth, Tiffany R.** '69 '94
C.112 B.S. L.1068 J.D. [A McCutchen,D.B.&E.] (☉San Francisco)
*PRACTICE AREAS: Environmental Counseling and Litigation.
**Hedlund, Karen J.** ......................'48 '74 C.681 A.B. L.276 J.D. [B Nossaman,G.K.&E.]
*PRACTICE AREAS: Project Finance Law; Municipal Finance Law; Transportation Law.
**Hedlund, Paul J.**, (AV) ....'46 '73 C.477 B.S.M.E. L.1068 J.D. [Baum,H.A.G.&D.] (Pat.)
*REPORTED CASES: Sigala v. Anaheim City School District, 15 Cal. App. 4th 661, 19 Cal. Rptr. 2d 38 (1993); Curry v. Continental Airlines, 513 F.2d 691 (9th Cir. 1975).
*PRACTICE AREAS: Airplane Crash Litigation; Aviation Accidents and Injuries; Mass Disaster Litigation; Railroad Accidents and Injuries; School Bus Accidents.
Heedwohl, Paula .......................................'54 '82 C.800 B.A. L.809 J.D. 505 Shatto Pl.
Heeger, Phillip L., Law Offices of '53 '82
C.112 A.B. L.809 J.D. 16830 Ventura Blvd. (Encino)

**Heenan Blaikie**
**(See Beverly Hills)**

**Heeseman, Rex**, (AV) ...................... '42 '68 C.154 B.A. L.813 J.D. [Luce,F.H.&S.]
*PRACTICE AREAS: Commercial Torts; Insurance Coverage Law.
**Heffernan, Brian J.** ..................... '61 '87 C.426 B.A. L.464 J.D. [A Engstrom,L.&L.]
**Heffernan, Joseph P., (A P.C.)**, (AV) ............'36 '68 C&L.724 B.A., LL.B. [Loeb&L.]
*PRACTICE AREAS: Real Estate Law; Finance.
Heflin, Robert P., (AV) ............'44 '70 C.768 B.A. L.1066 J.D. Head Dep. Dist. Atty.
**Hegedus, Joseph K.** ......................... '50 '75 C.188 B.S. L.831 J.D. [Lewis,D.B.&B.]
Hehmann, Denise Ann ..... '56 '82 C.112 B.A. L.426 J.D. 3550 Wilshire Blvd., Ste. 1250
**Heib, Malcolm G.**, (AV) ..................'34 '70 C.1046 B.A. L.809 J.D. [B Schlothauer,C.&M.]
*PRACTICE AREAS: Trial Practice (100); Civil Practice (300); Insurance Defense; Personal Injury; Construction Defect Cases.
**Heide, H. Elliott** ...........'61 '89 C.846 B.S. L.426 J.D. [A McClintock,W.B.R.R.&M.]
*SPECIAL AGENCIES: California and United States EPA, California Water Boards, California Air Board and local Air Districts.
*PRACTICE AREAS: Environmental and Corporate Compliance; Environmental Litigation.
**Heidelberg, Evelyn F.** ...................'51 '91 C.205 B.A. L.464 J.D. [A McKenna&C.]
*PRACTICE AREAS: Environmental; Litigation.
**Heileson, Marvin D.** ......................'41 '66 C.336 B.A. L.309 J.D. [Morrison&F.]
*PRACTICE AREAS: Banking and Financial Transactions; Loan Workouts; Bankruptcy and Insolvency; Creditors' Rights.
Heilman, Karen L. ...............................'55 '83 C.668 B.A. L.800 J.D. 725 S. Figueroa St.
Heimberg, Steven A. ....................'53 '84 C.838 B.S. L.1068 J.D. 2049 Century Park E.
**Heine, D. William, Jr.** ..............'53 '83 C.1044 B.A. L.1066 J.D. [Schwartz,S.D.&S.]
*PRACTICE AREAS: Labor and Employment Law; Employment Discrimination Law; Campaign Finance Law; Employee Drug Testing.
**Heinke, Rex S.**, (AV) .......................'50 '75 C.061 B.A. L.178 J.D. [Gibson,D.&C.]
*PRACTICE AREAS: Media Law; Constitutional Law; Appellate Practice; Copyrights/Trademarks; Entertainment and the Arts.
**Heins, Henry L., III** ........................'65 '94 C.511 B.A. L.1136 J.D. [A Atkins&E.]
**Heintz, Jeffrey A.** ...........................'60 '85 C.607 B.S. L.608 J.D. [Munger,T.&O.]
*PRACTICE AREAS: Real Estate.
Heinz, Jessica F. .............................'53 '78 C.800 B.A. L.1068 J.D. Asst. City Atty.
**Heinz, Judith A.** ......................... '— '95 C.1188 B.A. L.426 J.D. [A O'Melveny&M.]
*PRACTICE AREAS: Civil Litigation.
**Heisz, Kenneth L.**, (BV) .................. '57 '89 C.379 B.A. L.426 J.D. [Valensi,R.&M.]
*PRACTICE AREAS: Litigation; Business Litigation; Real Estate Litigation; Unfair Competition; Landlord/Tenant.

**Heiting & Irwin**
**(See Riverside)**

**Heitner, Howard M.** ......................'55 '82 C.105 B.A. L.145 J.D. [O'Melveny&M.]
*PRACTICE AREAS: Real Estate; Purchases and Sales; Finance; Low Income Housing Tax Credits; Historic Preservation.
**Heitz, Kenneth R.**, (AV) ..........................'47 '72 C.112 B.A. L.309 J.D. [Irell&M.]
**Hekker, Gerard A.** '60 '92 C.197 B.A. L.767 J.D.
[A Graham&J.] (☉Jakarta, Indonesia)
*LANGUAGES: Mandarin Chinese.
*PRACTICE AREAS: Immigration.
Held, David .........'46 '73 C.994 B.A. L.1009 J.D. Exec. V.P., Paramount Pictures Corp.
**Helderman, Joshua D.** '70 '95 C.228 B.S.B.A. L.597 J.D.
[A Christensen,M.F.J.G.W.&S.]
*PRACTICE AREAS: Litigation.
**Helfant, David A.** ................'55 '80 C.1044 B.A. L.809 J.D. [Berger,K.S.M.F.S.&G.]
**Helfen, Spencer J.** .........................'61 '88 C.112 B.A. L.1066 J.D. [Murphy,W.&B.]
*PRACTICE AREAS: Workouts; Bankruptcy Reorganization; Creditors Remedies.
**Helfferich, Krista** ...................'67 '96 C.569 B.F.A. L.426 J.D. [A O'Melveny&M.]
Helfing, Laurie ...........................................'53 '81 C.112 A.B. L.1095 J.D. Dist. Atty.
**Helfing, Robert F.** ..................'54 '79 C.112 B.A. L.809 J.D. [Sedgwick,D.M.&A.]
Helfrick, William F. ...........................'45 '70 C.347 B.S. L.284 J.D. Vet. Admin.
Helgeson, Richard M., (AV) ...............'43 '70 C.965 B.B.A. L.436 J.D. Asst. City Atty.
**Heller, Dona L.** ...............................'47 '74 C.104 A.B. L.659 J.D. [Saphier&H.]
*LANGUAGES: Spanish and French.
*PRACTICE AREAS: Health Care Law.
Heller, Elizabeth A. ..........................'— '80 C.112 B.A. L.426 J.D. Dep. Pub. Def.
**Heller, J. Dean**, (AV) ......................'44 '69 C.228 B.A. L.976 LL.B. [Morgan,L.&B.]
Heller, Philip ...............................'52 '79 C.309 B.A. L.94 J.D. [Fagelbaum&H.]
**Heller, Steven C.** ........................'59 '95 C.112 B.A. L.1068 J.D. [Howrey&S.]
**Heller, Steven P.** ......................'67 '95 C.112 B.A. L.1066 J.D. [A Parker,M.C.O.&S.]
**Heller, Thomas G.** ......................'67 '92 C.477 A.B. L.1068 J.D. [A Kirkland&E.]
*PRACTICE AREAS: Litigation.

**Heller & Edwards**
**(See Beverly Hills)**

**Heller Ehrman White & McAuliffe, (AV)**
**A Partnership including Professional Corporations**
**601 S. Figueroa Street, 90017-5758☉**
**Telephone: 213-689-0200 Facsimile: 213-614-1868**
**URL: http://www.hewm.com**
**Members of Firm: Wayne S. Braveman††; Neal H. Brockmeyer††; Nancy Sher Cohen††; Raymond C. Fisher††; Paul H. Greiner††; Robert B. Hubbell††; Joan K. Irion††; Jeffery W. Johnson††; Gary W. Maeder††; Stephen E. Newton††; Ronald C. Peterson††; Jon L. Rewinski††; Deborah Crandall Saxe; A. Timothy Scott††; Carlos Solis††; G. Thomas Stromberg, Jr.††; Steven R. Tekosky††; Stephen A. Tuggy††; Steven O. Weise††. Special Counsel: Linda Daves Barker; Dale S. Fischer; Carol A. Pfaffmann; Daniel K. Slaughter. Of Counsel: Joseph W. Burdett; James H. Kindel, Jr.; Gavin Miller. Associates: K. Tomoko Aoyama; Alexander G. Arato; L. Anthony Beall; Jill I. Brown; William Nathan Canby; David M. Chernek; Kenneth L. Chernof; Christa L. Crawford (Not admitted in CA); Steven M. Friedman; M. Art Gambill; Seth D. Hilton; Roger W. Janeway; Heather A. Mactavish; Patricia A. McBride; Robert Oliver; Ann I. Park; Paul W. Poareo; Rhonda M. Reaves; Thomas E. Reiber; Jeffrey A. Richmond; Reynold L. Siemens; Edward J. Slizewski; Deanna M. Wilcox. General Practice.**
(This Listing Continued)

**Heller Ehrman White & McAuliffe (Continued)**

**San Francisco, California Office: 333 Bush Street. Telephone: 415-772-6000. Facsimile: 415-772-6268. Cable Address "Helpow". Telex: 340-895; 184-996.**
**Palo Alto, California Office: 525 University Avenue, Suite 1100. Telephone: 415-324-7000. Facsimile: 415-324-0638.**
**Seattle, Washington Office: 6100 Columbia Center, 701 Fifth Avenue. Telephone: 206-447-0900. Facsimile: 206-447-0849.**
**Portland, Oregon Office: 200 S.W. Market Street, Suite 1750. Telephone: 503-227-7400. Facsimile: 503-241-0950.**
**Anchorage, Alaska Office: 1900 Bank of America Center, 550 West 7th Avenue. Telephone: 907-277-1900. Facsimile: 907-277-1920.**
**Tacoma, Washington Office: 1400 First Interstate Plaza, 1201 Pacific Avenue. Telephone: 206-572-6666. Facsimile: 206-572-6743.**
**Washington, D.C. Office: 815 Connecticut Ave., N.W., Suite 200. Telephone: 202-785-4747. Facsimile: 202-785-8877.**
**Hong Kong Office: 1902A, 19/F, Peregrine Tower, Lippo Centre, 89 Queensway, Hong Kong. Telephone: (011) 852-2526-6381. Facsimile: (011) 852-2810-6242.**
**Singapore Office: 50 Raffles Place, 17-04 Shell Tower. Telephone: (011) 65 538-1756. Facsimile: (011) 65 538-1537.**
**††Lawyer who is a stockholder and an employee of a professional corporation which is a member of the firm**

***See Professional Biographies, LOS ANGELES, CALIFORNIA***

**Hellow, John R.**, (AV) '56 '82 C.1154 B.A. L.734 J.D. [Hooper,L.&B.]
*SPECIAL AGENCIES: Provider Reimbursement Review Board; Health Care Financing Administration; California Department of Health Services, Office of Administrative Appeals.
*PRACTICE AREAS: Healthcare Government Payment Disputes; Administrative Litigation; Government Contract Disputes; Federal Block Grant Funding.
**Helm, Catherine H.** '59 '83 C&L.309 A.B., J.D. [Irell&M.]
**Helm, Hugh H.**, (AV) '41 '70 C&L.800 B.S., J.D. [Galton&H.]
*PRACTICE AREAS: Civil Litigation.
**Helm, Mark B.** '56 '84 C&L.309 A.B., J.D. [Munger,T.&O.]
Helman, Joseph S. '48 '74 C.1077 B.A. L.809 J.D. [Klass,H.&R.]

**Helms, Hanrahan & Myers**
**(See Arcadia)**

**Helton, Sabina A.** '64 '91 C.112 B.A. L.1065 J.D. [Ⓐ Pillsbury M.&S.]
**Helwig, Stephen J.** '67 '95 C.477 A.B. L.309 J.D. [Ⓐ Skadden,A.S.M.&F.]
**Helyar, L. Rachel Lerman** '60 '95 C.976 B.A. L.1066 J.D.
(adm. in ID; not adm. in CA) [Ⓐ Horvitz&L.]

**Hemar, Rousso & Garwacki**
**(See Encino)**

**Hemer, Barkus & Clark**
**(See Glendale)**

**Heming, Martin M.** '42 '72 C.705 A.B. L.94 J.D. [Reish&L.]
*PRACTICE AREAS: Employee Benefits Law; ESOPs.
**Hemmerling, Geraldine S.**, (AV) '28 '53
C.112 B.S. L.1066 J.D. [Ⓒ Armstrong H.J.T.&W.]
*PRACTICE AREAS: Probate and Estate Planning.
**Hemminger, Pamela Lynn**, (AV) '49 '76 C.668 B.A. L.990 J.D. [Gibson,D.&C.]
*PRACTICE AREAS: Labor and Employment Law; Occupational Safety and Health; Litigation; ERISA.
Henderson, Alexander T. '59 '88 C.112 A.B. L.1068 J.D. Dep. Pub. Def.
Henderson, Andrew R. '57 '90 C.770 B.S.C. L.575 J.D. [Ⓐ Hall&Assoc.]
**Henderson, Kevin L.** '62 '90 C.999 B.B.A. L.809 J.D. [Ⓐ Veatch,C.G.&N.]
*PRACTICE AREAS: General Casualty; Construction Defects; Products Liability Defense Law.
Henderson, Mark C., (BV) '51 '79 C.763 B.A. L.464 J.D. 333 S. Hope St., 30th Fl.
Henderson, Randall S. '47 '77 C.871 B.S. L.896 J.D. 555 S. Flower St.
Henderson, Richard C. '56 '82
C.940 B.A. L.1148 J.D. Ste. 410, 626 Wilshire Blvd. (⊙Fresno)
**Henderson, Suzanne M.** '68 '93 C.770 B.S. L.1066 J.D. [Ⓐ Breidenbach,B.H.H.&H.]
*PRACTICE AREAS: Environmental Litigation; Environmental Compliance.
Henderson, Vanessa I. '52 '83 C.112 B.A. L.1136 J.D. 6222 Wilshire Blvd.

**Henderson, Wohlgemuth & Bohl, A Professional Corporation**
**(See Ventura)**

Hendlish, Martin A. '64 '91 C.800 B.S. L.1148 J.D. 10940 Wilshire Blvd.
**Hendricks, Maren H.** '67 '92 L.1068 [Ⓐ Dewey B.]
Hendricks, Mark C. '61 '89 C.800 B.S. L.101 J.D. 725 S. Figueroa St.
**Hendricks, Robert Jon** '— '95 C.112 A.B. L.1066 J.D. [Ⓐ Morgan,L.&B.]
Hendricks, Terence R. '63 '90
C.1049 B.B.A. L.426 J.D. Assoc. Coun., Auto. Club of Southern Calif.
**Hendrickson, D. John** '55 '81 C.813 B.A. L.990 J.D. [Russ,A.&K.]
*PRACTICE AREAS: Commercial Law; Communications; Entertainment; Product Licensing; General Business.
**Hengesbach, Scott** '63 '90 C.684 B.A. L.464 J.D. [Ⓐ Murchison&C.]
*PRACTICE AREAS: Product Liability; Medical Device Litigation; Insurance Defense-General.
**Henick, Richard D.** '66 '91 C.112 B.A. L.831 J.D. [Ⓐ Lim,R.&K.]
*PRACTICE AREAS: Real Estate; General Corporate; Bankruptcy.
**Henig, Assaf J.** '68 '94 C.674 A.B. L.1068 J.D. [Ⓐ Latham&W.]
**Henigson, Robert**, (AV) '25 '56 C.111 B.S. L.309 LL.B. [Arter&H.]
Henke, Raymond L., (AV) '53 '79 C.312 B.A. L.767 J.D. 836 N. Hilldale Ave.
**Henneberry, Jay R.** '55 '83 C.860 B.A. L.569 J.D. [Chadbourne&P.]
**Hennelly, John J., Jr.**, (AV) '43 '70 C&L.734 A.B., J.D. [Hennelly&G.]
*PRACTICE AREAS: Litigation; Products Liability.
**Hennelly, Victoria J.** '57 '83 C&L.800 B.A., J.D. [Ⓐ Hennelly&G.]
*PRACTICE AREAS: Litigation.

**Hennelly & Grossfeld, (AV)**
**17383 West Sunset Boulevard, Suite 420, 90272⊙**
**Telephone: 310-573-7800 Fax: 310-573-7806**
**Email: 104066.3016@compuserve.com**
**John J. Hennelly, Jr.; Kenneth B. Grossfeld (Resident, Sacramento, California Office); Susan J. Williams; James D. Demet. Associates: Brian M. Englund (Resident, Sacramento, California Office); Victoria J. Hennelly; Michael G. King; Karen L. Atkinson.**
**General Civil Trial Practice in all State and Federal Courts and Administrative Agencies, Antitrust, Aviation, Bankruptcy, Business, Commercial, Corporate, Employment Counselling and Litigation, Environmental, Insurance, Intellectual Property, Negligence, Personal Injury, Product Liability, Professional Malpractice, Real Estate, Trade Regulation, Trade Secrets, Unfair Competition.**
**Sacramento, California Office: 3600 American River Drive, Suite 205, 95864. Telephone: 916-488-1000.**

***See Professional Biographies, LOS ANGELES, CALIFORNIA***

**Hennigan, Brian J.** '52 '76 C&L.597 B.A., J.D. [Irell&M.]
**Hennigan, J. Michael**, (AV) '43 '70 C&L.37 B.A., J.D. [Hennigan,M.&B.]
*PRACTICE AREAS: Antitrust; Commercial; Complex Litigation; Litigation; Insurance Coverage.

**Hennigan, Mercer & Bennett, (AV) BR**
**601 South Figueroa Street, Suite 3300, 90017**
**Telephone: 213-694-1200 Fax: 213-694-1234**
**Email: Silverm@hmb.com**
**J. Michael Hennigan; James W. Mercer; Bruce Bennett; John L. Amsden; C. Dana Hobart; Jeanne E. Irving; Pamala J. King; Laura Lindgren; Bruce R. MacLeod; Elizabeth D. Mann; Robert L. Palmer; Lauren A. Smith; Peter J. Most; Lee W. Potts. Associates: Nichole M. Auden; Jacqueline Bendy; Mary H. Chu; A. Ann Hered; Gregory K. Jones; Ellen M. Keane; Linda A. Kontos; Jennifer Sulla; Michael Swartz; Shawna L. Ballard; Claudia Schweikert; David H. Martin. Of Counsel: Anthony Castanares.**

(This Listing Continued)

**Hennigan, Mercer & Bennett (Continued)**

**Commercial and Complex Litigation; Corporate Reorganization, Insolvency, and Bankruptcy Law and Related Litigation; Antitrust Litigation; and Securities Litigation.**

***See Professional Biographies, LOS ANGELES, CALIFORNIA***

**Henning, John A., Jr.** '62 '92 C.823 B.S. L.1066 J.D. [Ⓐ Cox,C.&N.]
*PRACTICE AREAS: Land Use Law.
Henning, John L. '38 '66 C.112 B.S. L.1065 J.D. Supr. Ct. J.
Henning, Sonja L. '69 '95 C.813 B.A. L.228 J.D. 1925 Century Park East
Henning, Stephen J. '63 '89 C&L.546 B.S., J.D. 624 S. Grand Ave.
**Henning, Thomas W.** '49 '76 C.112 B.A. L.276 J.D. [Allen,M.L.G.&M.]
*PRACTICE AREAS: Tax, Joint Ventures and Business Organizations.
**Henninger, David P.** '50 '83 C.105 B.A. L.273 J.D. [Hooper,L.&B.]
*PRACTICE AREAS: Health Care Law.
**Hennington, Lorna D.** '65 '94 C.112 B.A. L.800 J.D. [Ⓐ Foley L.W.&A.]
*PRACTICE AREAS: Health Care; Hospitals; Medicare and Medicaid; Administrative Law.
**Henri, David C.** '43 '72 C.1046 B.S. L.862 J.D. [Ⓒ Quinn E.U.&O.]
*PRACTICE AREAS: Employment; General Commercial Litigation.
Henrichs, John '56 '89 C.1147 B.B.A. L.616 J.D. [Ⓐ Gutierrez&Assoc.]
**Henricks, James A.** '56 '84 C&L.37 B.S., J.D. [Oppenheimer P.S.] (Pat.)
*PRACTICE AREAS: Intellectual Property.
Henry, Anna '46 '91 C.665 Ph.D. L.1137 J.D. Assoc. Gen. Coun., ABM Indus. Inc.
Henry, Donald W., (Inc.)
**Henry, H. David** '62 '87 C&L.800 B.A., J.D. [Ⓐ Yukevich&S.]
*PRACTICE AREAS: Products Liability; Business Litigation.
Henry, Karl H. '36 '70 C.254 L.809 J.D. 2814 Martin Luther King Blvd.
Henry, Robert S. '48 '73 C.112 A.B. L.309 J.D. Dep. Atty. Gen.
**Henshaw, Georgeanne** '55 '80 C.228 B.A. L.477 J.D. [Seyfarth,S.F.&G.]
*PRACTICE AREAS: Labor Law; Employment Law.
**Hensleigh, Barbara J.** '55 '85 C.1142 B.A. L.846 J.D. [Andrews&H.]
*PRACTICE AREAS: Litigation; Commercial.
Hensley, Katherine L., (AV) '37 '78 C.668 B.A. L.800 J.D. 400 S. Hope St.
**Hensley, Kelly L.** '63 '88 C.112 B.A. L.426 J.D. [Ⓐ Sheppard,M.R.&H.]
**Hensley, Mark D.** '60 '89 C.112 A.B. L.426 J.D. [Burke,W.&S.]
*PRACTICE AREAS: Public Law; Municipal and Business Litigation; Public and Private Employment Law.
**Henson, Jill** '72 '96 C.556 B.B.A. L.990 J.D. [Ⓐ Gartner&Y.]
*PRACTICE AREAS: Labor and Employment Law.
Hentell, Marc A. '42 '78 C.800 B.S.B.A. L.999 J.D. 210 W. Temple St.
**Hentschel, Craig N.**, (AV) '50 '75 C.112 A.B. L.426 J.D. [Arnold&P.]
**Hentschel, Naomi A.** '54 '84 C.112 B.A. L.1066 J.D. [Ⓐ Reboul,M.H.M.&K.]
**Henty, David L.** '54 '83 C.02 B.Sc. L.05 LL.B. [Graham&J.] (Pat.)
*PRACTICE AREAS: Intellectual Property Law; Patent Law.
**Henzie, George M.**, (AV) '20 '49 C&L.813 B.A., J.D. [Ⓒ Belcher,H.&B.]
**Hepler, Bruce W.** '68 '94 C.197 B.A. L.1294 J.D.
(adm. in ME; not adm. in CA) [Ⓐ Brobeck,P.&H.]
*PRACTICE AREAS: Financial Services.
Heppel, Alan B. '51 '81 C.309 A.B. L.813 J.D.
V.P. & Leg. Coun., Paramount Pictures Corp.
**Herald, Alice A.** '50 '76 C.800 B.S. L.1065 J.D. Asst. Gen. Coun., Bank of Amer.

**Herbert, Daniel B., & Associates '63 '90 C.234 B.A. L.940 J.D.**
**Twenty Fifth Floor 1801 Century Park East (Century City), 90067**
**Telephone: 310-843-0210 Facsimile: 310-201-0143**
**General Civil and Trial Practice, State and Federal Courts. Business, Real Estate, Securities and Entertainment Litigation. Bankruptcy, Reorganization and Commercial Litigation Law. Probate and Conservatorship Estates.**

***See Professional Biographies, LOS ANGELES, CALIFORNIA***

Herbert, Dodell, A Law Corp. 3415 S. Sepulveda Blvd.
**Hered, A. Ann** '70 '94 C.697 B.A. L.188 J.D. [Ⓐ Hennigan,M.&B.]
*PRACTICE AREAS: Intellectual Property; Litigation.
**Herget, Georgette Renata** '49 '80 C.1044 B.A. L.1148 J.D. [Ⓐ Belcher,H.&B.]
*PRACTICE AREAS: Insurance Defense Law; Aviation Law; General Civil Practice; Accident and Personal Injury Law; Insurance Coverage Law.
**Herich, Emil W.** '57 '84 C.112 B.A. L.1068 J.D. [Baker&H.]
*PRACTICE AREAS: Litigation.
**Herman, Dean B.**, (AV) '52 '77 C.1109 B.A. L.426 J.D. [Gabriel,H.&P.]
*REPORTED CASES: Taub v. First State, 44 Cal.App.4th 811 (1995); Concha v. London, 62 F.3d 1493 (9th Cir. 1995); Trulis v. Barton, 67 F.3d779 (9th Cir. 1995); Trulis v. Burton, 67 F.3d 779 (9th Cir. 1995).
**Herman, Joseph E.**, (AV) '42 '66 C&L.309 A.B., LL.B. [Morgan,L.&B.]
**Herman, Michael G.**, (AV) '53 '80 C.813 A.B. L.767 J.D. [Warren&H.]
*PRACTICE AREAS: Real Property Law; General Corporate Practice; Commercial.
**Herman, Richard Charles** '63 '95 C.174 B.A. L.426 J.D. [Ⓐ B.R.Bailey]
Herman, Stuart P., (AV) '42 '68 C.112 B.A. L.1066 J.D. [Herman&W.]
Herman & Wallach, Professional Corporation, (AV) 1875 Century Pk., E.
**Hermann, Jeffery D.** '52 '77 C&L.312 B.S.M.E., J.D. [Brobeck,P.&H.]
*PRACTICE AREAS: Bankruptcy Law; Commercial Insolvency Law; Loan Workouts.
**Hermann, Karen L.** '67 '95 C.1075 B.S. L.112 J.D. [Ⓐ Pillsbury M.&S.]
Hermosillo, Teresa J. '49 '75 C.988 B.A. L.602 J.D. 333 S. Grand Ave.
**Hernand, David M.** '66 '92 C.112 B.A. L.276 J.D. [Ⓐ Latham&W.]
**Hernand, Stephanie Kaufman** '66 '92 C.659 B.A.,B.S.E. L.276 J.D. [Ⓐ Irell&M.]
Hernandez, Antonia '48 '74 C.112 B.A. L.1068 J.D. Pres. & Gen. Coun., M.A.L.D.E.F.
Hernandez, Bernice '54 '80 C.800 B.A. L.1068 J.D. Dep. Pub. Def.
**Hernandez, Dennis F.** '53 '81 C.426 B.A. L.276 J.D. [Baker&H.]
*LANGUAGES: Spanish.
*PRACTICE AREAS: First Amendment Law and Litigation; Intellectual Property.
**Hernandez, Don A.** '61 '86 C.309 A.B. L.813 J.D. [Ⓐ Fried,F.H.S.&J.]
**Hernandez, Evangelina P. Fierro** '66 '93 C.813 B.A. L.36 J.D. [Ⓐ Parker S.]
*LANGUAGES: Spanish.
**Hernandez, George J., Jr.** '55 '83 C.1077 B.A. L.1051 J.D. [Borton,P.&C.]
*LANGUAGES: Spanish, Italian, French and American Sign Language.
*PRACTICE AREAS: Civil Litigation; Construction Litigation; Public Entity Defense; Wrongful Termination.
**Hernandez, Jesse S.** '51 '80 C.112 B.A. L.426 J.D. [Anderson,M.&C.]
**Hernandez, Rory Michael** '54 '83 C.1097 B.A. L.809 J.D. [Gibson,D.&C.]
Herold, Henry L. '24 '72 C.112 A.B. L.1136 J.D. 1233 Amherst Ave.‡
Heron, Robert A. '42 '73 C.426 B.B.A. L.809 J.D. Supervising Dep. Atty. Gen.
Heron, Robert D. '37 '65 C.800 A.B. L.1068 LL.B. 10941 Sproul Ave.‡
**Herr, Richard C.** '31 '68 C.800 B.A. L.809 LL.B. Asst. Gen. Coun., Bank of Amer.
Herriford, David V. '58 '82 C&L.813 A.B., J.D. 880 W. 1st St.
Herrig & Vogt, (AVⓉ)
100 Wilshire Boulevard, #950 (⊙Kennewick, WA, Rancho Cordova, CA, Redmond, WA)
Herring, Paul J. '— '90 C.966 B.A. L.494 J.D. 221 N. Figueroa St.
**Herron, David L.** '59 '90 C.37 B.S.B.A. L.911 J.D. [Ⓐ O'Melveny&M.]
*LANGUAGES: Japanese.
**Herron, Vincent H.** '— '94 C.112 B.A. L.800 J.D. [Ⓐ Latham&W.]

CAA247P

**Herscher, Daniel M., (AV) '27 '55 C.112 B.S. L.800 J.D.**
**10100 Santa Monica Boulevard, Suite 250, 90067**
**Telephone: 310-556-0833 Fax: 310-788-2814**
**(Also Of Counsel, David A. Lapin, A Professional Corporation).**
***LANGUAGES: Spanish.**
***REPORTED CASES: First Western Bank and Trust Company, a California Corporation, v. Bookasta, 73 Cal.Rptr, 657, 267 Cal.App.2d 910, 5 UCC Rep.Serv. 1181; Feary v. Aaron Burglar Alarm, Inc., 108 Cal.Rptr. 242, 32 Cal.App. 3d 553, 12 UCC Rep. Serv. 881; Acosta v. County of Los Angeles, 363, P.2d 473, 14 Cal.Rptr. 433, 56 Cal.2d 208, 88 A.L.R.2d 1417; Peskin v. Herron, 26 CalRptr. 821, 210 Cal.App.2d 482.**
**Real Estate and Business Law.**

***See Professional Biographies, LOS ANGELES, CALIFORNIA***

Herscovitz, Martin L. .... '53 '78 C.112 A.B. L.809 J.D. Dep. Dist. Atty.
Hersh, Kathy L. .... '50 '88 C.112 B.A. L.809 J.D. 633 W. 5th St.
**Hersh, Leonard W.** .... '60 '86 C.477 A.B. L.145 J.D. [Ⓐ Skadden,A.S.M.&F.]
**Hersh, Sara E.** .... '53 '89 C.860 B.S. L.61 J.D. [Ⓐ Bonne,B.M.O.&N.]
**Hershenson, Joseph B.** .... '61 '89 C.309 B.A. L.813 J.D. [Troop M.S.&P.]
*LANGUAGES: French, Italian and German.
*PRACTICE AREAS: Corporate Law; Securities Law.
**Hershorin, David M.** .... '64 '90 C.800 B.S. L.1148 J.D. [Ⓐ Arter&H.]
*PRACTICE AREAS: Commercial Litigation; Real Estate Litigation.
Herskovitz, David .... '55 '80 C.112 B.A. L.1148 J.D. 11377 W. Olympic Blvd.
Herskovitz, Mark H. .... '61 '88 C.112 B.A. L.978 J.D. 3530 Wilshire Blvd.
**Hersman, Nancy B.** .... '54 '86 C.112 B.A. L.426 J.D. [Ⓐ Ginsburg,S.O.&R.]
Herstead, John W. .... '49 '81 C.546 B.S. L.990 J.D. [Herstead&B.]
Herstead & Bickenbach .... 2000 Riverside Dr., 3rd Fl.
**Hertan, Gaye E.** .... '61 '87 C.112 B.A. L.800 J.D. [Ⓐ Seyfarth,S.F.&G.]
*PRACTICE AREAS: Labor and Employment Law.
Hertz, John F. .... '49 '82 C.33 B.A. L.597 J.D. 236 S. Coronado St.
**Hertzberg, Robert M.** .... '54 '79 C.684 B.A. L.1065 J.D. [Ⓒ Reznik&R.]
**Hervatin, Lydia A.** .... '58 '92 C.209 B.A. L.426 J.D. [Ⓐ Mendes&M.]
**Herz, William D.** .... '43 '69 C.475 B.A. L.477 J.D. [Barton,K.&O.]
*PRACTICE AREAS: Real Estate; Corporate Law; Probate; Estate Planning.
Herzberg, Judith K. ... '47 '81 C.1109 B.A. L.1137 J.D. Sr. Coun., Calif. Assn. of Realtors

**Herzfeld & Rubin, (AV)**
**1925 Century Park East, 90067⊙**
**Telephone: 310-553-0451 Telefax: 310-553-0648**
**Resident Partners: Richard L. Ackerman; Martin S. Friedlander; Seymour Kagan; Nicholas Browning, III; Craig L. Winterman; Michael A. Zuk; Richard W. Greenbaum. Resident Associates: Gary S. Yates; Roy D. Goldstein; Timothy B. Fitzhugh; Alan I. Kaplan; Mary A. Kiker; Steven I. Smith; Matthew H. Kagan; Napoleon G. Tercero, III; Suhasini S. Sawkar; Anthony C. Grossman; Shirley A. Baker.**
**General Practice. Corporation, Antitrust, Administrative, International, Products and Professional Liability, Insurance, Trademark, Copyright and Unfair Competition, Probate, Real Estate, Taxation, Business and Commercial Law. Trials and Appeals.**
**Orange County, California Office: Herzfeld & Rubin, 625 The City Drive, Fourth Floor, Orange. Telephone: 714-750-0901. Telefax: 714-750-4708.**
**Affiliated Offices:**
**New York, N.Y.: Herzfeld & Rubin, P.C., 40 Wall Street. Telephone: 212-344-5500. Telefax: 212-344-3333.**
**Miami, Florida: Herzfeld & Rubin, 801 Brickell Avenue, Suite 1501. Telephone: 305-381-7999. Telefax: 305-381-8203.**
**Ft. Lauderdale, Florida: Herzfeld & Rubin, Gulf Atlantic Center, 1901 West Cypress Creek Road, Suite 400. Telephone: 954-772-3599. Telefax: 954-772-2469.**
**Orlando, Florida: DeCiccio, Herzfeld & Rubin, 20 North Orange Avenue, Suite 807. Telephone: 407-841-6391. Telefax: 407-648-0494.**
**Tampa, Florida: Barr, Murman, Tonelli, Herzfeld & Rubin, Enterprise Plaza, Suite 901, 201 East Kennedy Boulevard. Telephone: 813-223-3951. Telefax: 813-229-2254.**
**Jacksonville, Florida: Bullock, Childs, Pendley, Reed, Herzfeld & Rubin, 233 East Bay Street, Suite 711. Telephone: 904-354-0286. Telefax: 904-354-2778.**
**Newark, New Jersey: Chase Kurshan Suhr Herzfeld & Rubin, The Legal Center, Suite 500, One Riverfront Plaza. Telephone: 201-596-9484. Telefax: 201-596-0762.**
**Howell, New Jersey: Chase Kurshan Suhr Herzfeld & Rubin, 405 Candlewood Commons, Building 4. Telephone: 908-901-2929. Telefax: 908-901-9438.**
**Bucharest, Romania: Herzfeld & Rubin (Romania) S.R.L., 62 Stada Dionisie Lupu, Sector 1. Telephone: 40-1-22.333.58. Telefax: 40-1-22.333.77.**
**Düsseldorf, Germany: Couvenstrasse 2, 40211. Telephone: (49) 211 36 35 35. Telefax: (49) 211 36 35 37.**

***See Professional Biographies, LOS ANGELES, CALIFORNIA***

Herzhaft, Marilyn Jacobs .... '33 '75 C.112 B.A. L.426 J.D. 1243 Daniels Dr.
Herzog, Gary Drew .... '64 '89 C.112 B.A. L.94 J.D. 1632 N. Formosa Ave.
Herzog, Richard C. .... '49 '79 Dist. Atty. Off.
**Herzog, Wendy A.**, (AV) .... '50 '83 C.339 B.A. L.1065 J.D. [Deutsch&R.]
*PRACTICE AREAS: Family Law; Domestic Relations Law; Matrimonial Law; Divorce Law.
Hess, Donald J. .... '52 '87 C&L.061 B.Sc., LL.B. 725 S. Figueroa St.
**Hess, Mark H.**, (AV) .... '56 '80 C.1138 B.B.A. L.178 J.D. [Jeffer,M.B.&M.]
*PRACTICE AREAS: Pensions; Employee Benefits; Taxation; Exempt Organizations; Estate Planning.
Hess, Philip J. .... '50 '76 C&L.145 A.B., J.D. 155 S. Hudson Ave.
Hess, Robert L. .... '48 '76 C.668 B.A. L.800 J.D. Mun. Ct. J.
**Hess, Robert P.**, (AV) .... '42 '67 C.401 B.A. L.813 J.D. [R.P.Hess]
**Hess, William R.** .... '54 '81 C.1036 B.A. L.978 J.D. [Ⓐ Mihaly,S.&M.]

**Hess, Robert P., P.C., (AV)**
**445 South Figueroa Street Suite 3040, 90071**
**Telephone: 213-312-9495 Fax: 213-312-9499**
**Robert P. Hess.**
**Tax and Estate Planning. Business Planning.**

***See Professional Biographies, LOS ANGELES, CALIFORNIA***

**Hesse, Paul D.** .... '58 '83 C.549 B.S. L.770 J.D. [Musick,P.&G.]
*PRACTICE AREAS: Litigation; Insurance.
**Hessenius, Richard S., (A Professional Corporation)**, (AV) '51 '77 C.668 B.A. L.800 J.D. [Mitchell,S.&K.]
*PRACTICE AREAS: Real Estate Litigation; Insurance Litigation; Municipal Administrative Law.
**Hessling, Robert A.** .... '55 '80 C.546 B.A. L.37 J.D. [Ⓐ Danning,G.D.&K.]
*REPORTED CASES: In re Rivers, 55 B.R. 699 (Banks, C.D. Cal. 1984); Taxel v. Electronic Sports Research, 111 B.R. 892 (Bank v. S.D. Cal. 1990).
Hester, John W. '47 '74 C.299 B.A. L.1009 J.D. (adm. in NY; not adm. in CA) Exec. V.P., Gen. Coun. & Secy., Orion Pictures Corp.
Hetson, Jack .... '35 '74 C.102 B.A. L.426 J.D. 1021 S. Union Ave.
**Hettrick, Clyde M., III** .... '61 '87 [Troop M.S.&P.]
*PRACTICE AREAS: Insurance Coverage; Business Litigation.
Heuer, Henry T. .... '41 '76 C.105 B.S. L.800 J.D. 2029 Century Park E.
**Heuer, John F.** .... '65 '93 C.105 B.A.P.S. L.810 J.D. [Ⓐ Gibbs,G.L.&A.]
*PRACTICE AREAS: Commercial; Construction; Business Litigation.
**Heumann, Michael** .... '49 '75 C.674 B.A. L.1066 J.D. [Nossaman,G.K.&E.]
*PRACTICE AREAS: Litigation.
**Hevener, James J.** .... '64 '90 C.945 B.A. L.911 J.D. [Ⓐ McClintock,W.B.R.R.&M.]
*PRACTICE AREAS: Commercial and General Business Litigation; Employment Litigation; Environmental Litigation.
**Hewitt, Joan E.** .... '56 '83 C.385 B.A. L.990 J.D. [Ⓐ Veatch,C.G.&N.]
*PRACTICE AREAS: Appellate Practice.

**Hewitt, Stephen L., (A Professional Corporation)**, (AV) '53 '82 C.112 B.A. L.61 J.D. [Hewitt&P.]
*PRACTICE AREAS: Insurance Defense; Architects and Engineers; Medical Malpractice; Dental Malpractice; Professional Malpractice.

**Hewitt & Prout, (AV)**
**A Partnership including a Professional Corporation**
**4605 Lankershim Boulevard, Suite 540 (North Hollywood), 91602⊙**
**Telephone: 818-509-0311 Fax: 818-509-0402**
**Members of Firm: Stephen L. Hewitt (A Professional Corporation); R. Mac Prout (Resident, Sacramento Office). Associates: Erica S. Arouesty; Laura L. Horton; Daniel A. Rozansky; Keith M. Staub; Samuel M. Huestis; John C. Notti; Jerry R. Sparks; Paul A. Carron; Anthony V. Seferian.**
**Professional Malpractice, Medical, Dental, Real Estate, Architectural, Engineering, Legal and Accounting, Motor Sports Litigation, Products Liability, Negligence, Insurance Defense Coverage, Hospital, Business and Environmental Law.**
**Sacramento, California Office: 980 Ninth Street, Suite 1750, 95814. Telephone: 916-443-4849. Fax: 916-325-2322.**

***See Professional Biographies, LOS ANGELES, CALIFORNIA***

Heyck, Theodore D. .... '41 '80 C.103 A.B. L.564 J.D. Dep. City Atty.
Heydon, Kathleen M. '58 '85 C.800 B.A. L.426 J.D. Asst. Gen. Coun., Caesars World, Inc.
Heyert, Martin D. .... '34 '59 C.165 A.B. L.569 LL.B. 515 S. Flower St.
Heyler, David B., Jr., (AV) .... '26 '52 C&L.813 B.A., J.D. 2049 Century Park E.
**Heyman, Ginger F.** .... '67 '92 C.477 B.A. L.424 J.D. [Ⓐ Crosby,H.R.&M.]
Heyman, Roger P. .... '45 '70 C.390 B.A. L.309 J.D. 11835 W. Olympic Blvd.
**Hibner, Don T., Jr.**, (AV) .... '34 '63 C&L.813 B.A., J.D. [Sheppard,M.R.&H.]
*PRACTICE AREAS: Antitrust and Trade Regulation Law; Product Distribution Law; Domestic and International Competition Law.
**Hickey, J. Michelle** .... '63 '89 C.112 B.A. L.1066 J.D. [Alvarado,S.V.&S.]
*PRACTICE AREAS: Environmental Law; Litigation.
Hickey, James R. .... '51 '77 C.940 B.A. L.1065 J.D. Dep. Dist. Atty.
Hickman, Carol .... '48 '86 L.1179 J.D. 3660 Wilshire Blvd.
**Hicks, Jack B., III** .... '60 '86 C.800 B.A. L.426 J.D. [O'Melveny&M.]
*PRACTICE AREAS: Real Estate.
**Hicks, James B.** .... '59 '82 C.976 B.A. L.309 J.D. [Donovan L.N.&I.]
*PRACTICE AREAS: Commercial Litigation; Intellectual Property; Labor; Securities Litigation; Unfair Competition.
**Hicks, L. Westcott, Jr.** .... '45 '70 C.597 B.A. L.339 J.D. [MacArthur,U.H.&M.]
*PRACTICE AREAS: State, Local, Federal and International Tax Planning; Tax Compliance; Tax Controversies; Estate Planning.
**Hicks, Michael W.** '62 '88 C.838 B.A. L.665 J.D. [Ⓐ Blakely,S.T.&Z.] (⊙Sunnyvale, CA)
**Hicks, Pamela S.** .... '64 '94 C.1077 B.S. L.990 [Ⓐ Manning,M.&W.]
Hicks, Rick .... '44 '74 C.336 B.A. L.1065 J.D. 1900 Ave. of the Stars
Hidalgo, Manuel .... '29 '60 C.475 B.A. L.912 LL.B. 5220 E. Beverly Blvd.
Hidalgo, Rolando .... '61 '86 C.976 B.A. L.477 J.D. 5220 E. Beverly Blvd.
Hiddleson, Christopher .... '60 '88 C.30 B.A. L.990 J.D. Dep. Atty., Dept. of Transp.
Hidley, Ondrea D. .... '64 '89 C.684 B.A. L.426 J.D. 445 S. Figueroa St.
**Hieber, Darrel J.** .... '53 '81 C.112 B.A. L.1068 J.D. [Skadden,A.S.M.&F.]
**Hieronymus, Edward W.**, (AV) .... '43 '68 C.388 A.B. L.228 J.D. [Ⓒ O'Melveny&M.]
*PRACTICE AREAS: Real Property; Natural Resources; Water Law; Environmental Law.
**Higa, Billie Ann U.** .... '57 '81 C.1097 B.S. L.809 J.D. [Esner H.&C.]⊙
*PRACTICE AREAS: Appellate Law.
Higa, Robert J. .... '37 '67 C.112 B.A. L.1068 LL.B. Supr. Ct. J.
**Higgins, Anne Yeager** .... '59 '84 C.112 B.A. L.426 J.D. [Musick,P.&G.]
*PRACTICE AREAS: Litigation; Insurance.
**Higgins, Barbara A.** '57 '84 C.454 B.S. L.809 J.D. Asst. V.P. & Coun., CB Coml. Real Estate Grp. Inc.
*RESPONSIBILITIES: Litigation.
**Higgins, David M.**, (AV) .... '44 '69 C.112 A.B. L.1068 J.D. [Brobeck,P.&H.]
**Higgins, John J.** '34 '58 C.1021 A.B. L.262 LL.B. Sr. V.P. & Gen. Coun., Hughes Aircraft Co.
**Higgins, Karen Nielsen** .... '57 '90 C.1232 B.A. L.426 J.D. [Ⓐ Loeb&L.]
Higgins, Ronald J. .... '44 '82 C.974 B.A. L.1152 J.D. 3660 Wilshire Blvd.
**Higgins, Warren J.** .... '69 '95 C.112 B.A. L.1065 J.D. [Ⓐ Tharpe&H.]
*PRACTICE AREAS: Employment Litigation; Products Liability; Bad Faith Litigation; Construction Defect Litigation.
**Higham, Terry Lees** .... '— '90 C.878 B.A. L.464 J.D. [Ⓐ Wilson,E.M.E.&D.]
*LANGUAGES: Spanish, German.
**Highberger, William F.** .... '50 '76 C.674 A.B. L.178 J.D. [Gibson,D.&C.]
*LANGUAGES: French.
*SPECIAL AGENCIES: National Labor Relations Board; Equal Employment Opportunity Commission; Calif. Dept. of Fair Employment & Housing; Calif. Division of Occupational Safety & Health.
*PRACTICE AREAS: Labor and Employment; Employee Benefits; Trade Secrets; Occupational Safety and Health; Alternative Dispute Resolution.
**Hight, B. Boyd**, (AV) .... '39 '67 C.228 B.A. L.976 LL.B. [O'Melveny&M.]
*PRACTICE AREAS: Tort Litigation; Commercial Litigation; Securities Litigation.

**Hightower, George W. '39 '83 C.800 B.S.E.E. L.1136 J.D.**
**2040 Avenue of the Stars, Suite 400, 90056**
**Telephone: 310-556-1407 Fax: 310-670-6731**
***LANGUAGES: German.**
**Probate, Wills and Trusts including Related Real Estate Matters.**

***See Professional Biographies, LOS ANGELES, CALIFORNIA***

Higuchi, Edward James .... '54 '80 C.112 B.S. L.464 J.D. [Higuchi&H.]
Higuchi, Peter T. '56 '82 C.378 B.A. L.900 J.D. (adm. in KS; not adm. in CA) Touche Ross & Co.
Higuchi, Wiley H. .... '20 '46 C.113 L.209 LL.B. [Higuchi&H.]
Higuchi & Higuchi .... 3435 Wilshire Blvd.
**Hilario, Carlos** .... '63 '90 C.1097 B.A. L.1136 J.D. [Ⓐ Ochoa&S.]
*LANGUAGES: Pilipino and Spanish.
*PRACTICE AREAS: Workers Compensation; Civil Litigation.
**Hilberman, Joe W.**, (AV) .... '48 '73 C.112 A.B. L.1068 J.D. [Fonda,G.H.&D.]

**Hilbert, John S. '58 '85 C&L.420 B.A., J.D.**
**11755 Wilshire Boulevard, 15th Floor, 90025**
**Telephone: 310-479-0944 Fax: 310-312-3836**
**Email: 103061.1712@Compuserve.com**
**Probate and General Civil Litigation.**

***See Professional Biographies, LOS ANGELES, CALIFORNIA***

**Hildebrand, James C.** .... '55 '90 C.112 B.A. L.809 J.D. [Ⓐ Belcher,H.&B.]
*PRACTICE AREAS: Civil Trials; Appellate Practice; Aviation Law; Products Liability; Insurance Defense.
Hilderley, Susan H. .... '64 '89 C.659 B.A. L.309 J.D. Geffen Records

**Hill, C. Dickinson, (AV) '44 '76 C.816 B.E. L.1095 J.D.**
**12400 Wilshire Boulevard, Suite 700, 90025-1026**
**Telephone: 310-207-1115 Fax: 310-820-5988**
**Business Law. Business, Commercial and Intellectual Property Transactions. State and Federal Tax. Mergers, Acquisitions and Divestitures.**

***See Professional Biographies, LOS ANGELES, CALIFORNIA***

Hill, Christina L. .... '51 '80 C.273 B.A. L.809 J.D. State Bar of Calif.

**CAA248P**

Hill, Christopher M. ........ '60 '90 C&L.112 B.A., J.D. 4215 Glencoe Ave.
**Hill, Deirdre Hughes** ........ '60 '87 C.112 B.A. L.426 J.D. [Saltzburg,R.&B.]
*PRACTICE AREAS: Litigation; Business Law; Commercial Law.
**Hill, Dennis D.**, (AV) ........ '41 '67 C.112 B.A. L.1068 J.D. [Troop M.S.&P.]
*PRACTICE AREAS: Financial Institutions Law; Mortgage Banking Law; Real Estate Law.
**Hill, Frederick W.**, (AV) ........ '37 '65 C.932 B.A. L.1065 J.D. [Overton,L.&P.]
*PRACTICE AREAS: Banking Law; General Corporate Law; International Business Law; Mexico Trade; Japan Trade.
Hill, Irving ........ '15 '39 C.546 B.A. L.309 LL.B. U.S. Sr. Dist. J.
Hill, Jay S. ........ '55 '81 C.608 B.S. L.990 J.D. 10 Universal City Plaza, 28th Fl.
**Hill, Jeffrey W.** ........ '55 '80 C.674 A.B. L.800 J.D. [Pillsbury M.&S.]
**Hill, Jerry M.**, (AV) ........ '42 '67 C.375 B.A. L.502 J.D. [Seyfarth,S.F.&G.]
*PRACTICE AREAS: Litigation; Gaming.
**Hill, Marguerite Coyne** ........ '60 '85 C.801 B.S. L.426 J.D. [Harrington,F.D.&C.]
Hill, Melissa ........ '50 '76 C.112 B.A. L.767 J.D. Dist. Ct. of App.
**Hill, Thomas E.** ........ '53 '81 C.112 B.A. L.426 J.D. [Thelen,M.J.&B.]
*PRACTICE AREAS: Labor and Employment.
**Hill, Trenton J.** ........ '63 '89 C.668 B.A. L.800 J.D. [Jones,B.S.A.&F.]
*PRACTICE AREAS: Business; Real Estate.

**Hill, Farrer & Burrill LLP, (AV)**
**A Limited Liability Partnership including Professional Corporations**
**35th Floor, Union Bank Square, 445 South Figueroa Street, 90071**
**Telephone: 213-620-0460 Fax: 213-624-4840**
**William M. Farrer (1894-1971); Alfred J. Hill (1881-1953); Stanley S. Burrill (1902-1957). Members of Firm: Leon S. Angvire (P.C.); Stanley E. Tobin (P.C.); Jack R. White (P.C.); Kyle D. Brown (P.C.); William M. Bitting (P.C.); Stuart H. Young, Jr., (P.C.); Steven W. Bacon (P.C.); Wm. Harold Borthwick (P.C.); Arthur B. Cook, II, (P.C.); James G. Johnson (P.C.); George Koide (P.C.); Jonathan M. Brandler (P.C.); Scott L. Gilmore; Kevin H. Brogan; James A. Bowles (P.C.); Neil D. Martin; Michael J. DiBiase; Alfred M. Clark, III; Daniel J. McCarthy; Ronald W. Novotny (P.C.); David E. Parry; Benjamin B. Salvaty; Dean E. Dennis; Thomas F. Reed; Suzanne J. Holland; William A. White; R. Curtis Ballantyne; James R. Evans, Jr.; G. Cresswell Templeton III; Curtis A. Westfall; Jennifer Cook Lewis; Michael S. Turner; Michelle A. Meghrouni; Jennifer L. Pancake; Barry Van Sickle. Of Counsel: Edwin H. Franzen (P.C.); Darlene Fischer Phillips (P.C.). Retired: Carl M. Gould; Vincent C. Page; William C. Farrer (P.C.). Associates: Ian M. Green; Byron T. Ball; Dean A. Reeves; Paul M. Porter; Leslie G. Van Zyl; Arnold D. Woo; Karen S. Seigel; Stacey A. Sullivan.**
**General Civil and Trial Practice in all State and Federal Courts. Corporation, Securities, Antitrust, Real Estate (Finance Development and Environmental), Eminent Domain, Taxation, Bankruptcy and Creditors Rights, Labor Relations and Employment Law, Probate, Trust, Oil and Gas, Insurance, Government Contract and Administrative Law.**
*See Professional Biographies, LOS ANGELES, CALIFORNIA*

**Hill, John, & Associates**
**(See Torrance)**

**Hill-Yonis, Jeannette M.** ........ '— '96 C.800 B.A./B.S. L.569 J.D. [Latham&W.]
**Hillen, Jens H.** ........ '66 '94 C.112 B.S.M.E. L.800 J.D. [Latham&W.]
Hiller, Laurie B. ........ '61 '91 C.813 B.A. L.1068 J.D. 1900 Ave. of the Stars
**Hilliard, Terri Eileen** ........ '60 '89 C.112 B.A. L.426 J.D. [Knopfler&R.]
*REPORTED CASES: Howard v. Superior Court (1992) 2 Cal.App. 4th 745.
*PRACTICE AREAS: Business/Commercial Litigation; Construction Litigation; Securities Litigation; Insurance Coverage.
**Hillier, Kenneth R.** ........ '64 '92 C.112 B.A. L.477 J.D. [Folger L.&K.]⊙
Hillman, Brenda G ........ '55 '87 C.1136 L.940 J.D. [Spector,B.H.&B.]
**Hillman, Jill Anne** ........ '60 '93 C.1222 B.B.A. L.1158 J.D. [A.R.Hamrick,III]
Hillman, Stephen J. ........ '50 '75 C.112 B.A. L.911 J.D. U.S. Mag.J.
Hillmer, Siegfried O. ........ '25 '66 L.981 LL.B. Asst. City Atty.
**Hillsberg, Sanford J.**, (AV) ........ '48 '73 C.659 B.A. L.309 J.D. [Troy&G.]
*PRACTICE AREAS: Corporate Law; Securities Law.
**Hillsinger, George R.**, (AV) ........ '26 '52 C.642 L.809 LL.B. [Hillsinger&C.] (⊙Orange)

**Hillsinger and Costanzo, Professional Corporation, (AV)**
**12th Floor, 3055 Wilshire Boulevard, 90010-1161⊙**
**Mailing Address: P.O. Box 60858 Terminal Annex, 90060-0858**
**Telephone: 213-388-9441 Cable Address: "Hilcolaw" Los Angeles, CA. Telecopier: 213-388-1592**
**John J. Costanzo (1924-1985); George R. Hillsinger; Darrell A. Forgey; Carol A. Salmacia (Resident, Orange Office); Jean Stone; Thomas C. Hurrell; Robert S. Ruffalo; Donald G. Forgey; Michael C. Kellar; Linda Star; Gregory G. Lynch; Seana B. Thomas (Resident, Santa Barbara Office);—Lisa Martinelli; Michael J. Elsberry (Resident, Orange Office); Wonkoo Chang; Lisa M. Agrusa (Resident, Orange Office); Tyrone I. Toczauer; Lisa D. Collinson; Laura M. Booth (Resident, Orange Office); Robert T. Colclough, III; Valerie D. Rojas; Ada Rud Pentz; Ilona Gordon. Of Counsel: William S. Hart; Edward A. DeBuys (Resident, Orange Office); Francois R. Favre; Steven H. Gurnee; Wallace C. Reed; Roxanna Huddleston.**
**General Civil and Appellate Trial Practice in all State and Federal Courts. Insurance, Corporation, Products Liability and Malpractice Law.**
**Orange, California Office: 701 South Parker Street, Suite 6000. Telephone: 714-542-6241. Telecopier: 714-667-6806.**
**Santa Barbara, California Office: 220 East Figueroa Street. Telephone: 805-966-3986. Telecopier: 805-965-3798.**
**Rancho Cucamonga, California Office: 10737 Laurel Street, Suite 110 - Main Floor. Telephone: 909-483-6200. Telecopier: 909-483-6277.**
*See Professional Biographies, LOS ANGELES, CALIFORNIA*

**Hillyer, Kevin Pauley** ........ '65 '92 C.1165 B.S. L.990 J.D. [Tuverson&H.]
*LANGUAGES: Spanish.
**Hilson, John Francis** ........ '52 '77 C.94 B.A. L.174 J.D. [Brobeck,P.&H.]
**Hilton, Seth D.** ........ '68 '96 C.309 A.B. L.1067 J.D. [Heller E.W.&M.]
Hilton, Susan McHenry ........ '— '83 C.436 L.809 J.D. 201 North Figueroa
**Hiltunen, Scott E.** ........ '59 '93 C.477 B.A. L.800 J.D. [A.M.Brucker]
*PRACTICE AREAS: Employee Benefits Law.
**Himmelrich, Sue L.** ........ '53 '83 C.681 B.A. L.178 J.D. [Sonnenschein N.&R.]
*PRACTICE AREAS: Litigation.

**Himrod, Robert M., (AV) '18 '47 C.668 B.A. L.426 LL.B.**
**1055 Wilshire Boulevard, Suite 1890, 90017**
**Telephone: 213-250-5722 Fax: 213-250-1894**
**Email: trhimrod@aol.com**
***PRACTICE AREAS: Estate Planning; Probate and Trusts; Estate Tax; Real Estate.**
**Associates: Thomas E. Himrod.**
**Probate, Estate Planning, State and Federal Tax, Non-Profit Organizations, Charitable Trusts and Foundations, Corporation and Real Property Law. General Civil Practice.**
**Representative Clients: La Mirada Water Co.; Precision Coil Spring Co., Inc.**
*See Professional Biographies, LOS ANGELES, CALIFORNIA*

**Himrod, Thomas E.**, (AV) ........ '50 '76 C.668 B.A. L.276 J.D. [R.M.Himrod]
*PRACTICE AREAS: Charitable Trusts and Foundations; Non-Profit Organizations; Estate Planning; Probate.
**Hinchcliffe, Everett S.**, (AV) '45 '74
C.1097 B.S.E.E. L.426 J.D. [Dale,B.&H.] (⊙Walnut Creek)
*REPORTED CASES: Buchan v. U.S. Cycling Federation (1991) 227 C.A. 3d. 134; Farmers Ins. Exchange v. Schepler (1981) 115 C.A. 3d 200.
**Hinchliffe, Lisa F.** ........ '60 '87 C.914 B.A. L.800 J.D. [Baker&H.]
*LANGUAGES: Spanish.
*PRACTICE AREAS: Employment Litigation; Business Law; Constitutional Law.
Hinden, Barry H. ........ '43 '74 C.1077 B.A. L.809 J.D. [Hinden&G.]
Hinden, David R., (AV) ........ '46 '71 C.188 B.S. L.976 J.D. 2250 S. Beverly Dr.
Hinden & Grueskin, A Prof. Law Corp., (AV) ........ 4661 W. Pico Blvd.
**Hindin, Karen L.** ........ '69 '94 C.112 B.A. L.770 J.D. [Engstrom,L.&L.]
Hindin, Robert M. ........ '48 '75 C.37 B.A. L.1137 J.D. 11755 Wilshire Blvd.
**Hinds, James Andrew, Jr.** ........ '51 '76 C.197 A.B. L.309 J.D. [Shapiro,H.&M.]
**Hinerfeld, Robert E.**, (AV) ........ '34 '60 C&L.309 A.B., LL.B. [Manatt,P.&P.]
*PRACTICE AREAS: Litigation and Professional Responsibility.
**Hing, Kevin L.** ........ '62 '88 C.112 B.A. L.800 J.D. [Danning,G.D.&K.]
**Hinojosa, Lynard C.**, (AV) ........ '42 '68 C.976 B.A. L.1068 J.D. [Hinojosa&K.]
*PRACTICE AREAS: Probate Law and Litigation.

**Hinojosa & Khougaz, (AV)**
**Suite 1000, 11111 Santa Monica Boulevard, 90025-3344**
**Telephone: 310-473-7000 Facsimile: 310-473-0906**
**Lynard C. Hinojosa; Gregory J. Khougaz. Associates: Susan Jabkowski. Of Counsel: Seymour S. Goldberg.**
**Probate Litigation, Estate Administration and Planning, General Business and Corporate Law. Business and Real Estate Litigation.**
*See Professional Biographies, LOS ANGELES, CALIFORNIA*

**Hinshaw, David C.**, (AV) ........ '50 '77 C.502 B.A. L.309 J.D. [Gansinger,H.B.&P.]
*PRACTICE AREAS: Civil Litigation; Insurance Coverage; Securities.

**Hinton, Robert F., The Law Offices of '55 '81 C.674 A.B. L.309 J.D.**
**One Century Plaza, Suite 2600, 2029 Century Park East, 90067-2081**
**Telephone: 310-552-3670 Telecopier: 310-201-4776**
**Business Litigation, Entertainment Litigation, Attorney Malpractice, Medical Malpractice, Professional Negligence Litigation, Real Estate Litigation, Insurance Law and Construction Litigation.**
*See Professional Biographies, LOS ANGELES, CALIFORNIA*

**Hinz, William A.** ........ '49 '81 C.3 B.A. L.1137 J.D. [Ibold&A.]
**Hirano, Ronald M.** ........ '43 '83 C.112 A.B. L.426 J.D. [Quan,C.K.Y.S.&H.]
*PRACTICE AREAS: Business Law; Commercial Litigation; Employment Law.
Hirose, Paul O. ........ '62 '91 C.112 B.A. L.276 J.D. 777 S. Figueroa St.
**Hirsch, Barry L.**, (AV) ........ '33 '58 C.112 L.800 LL.B. [Armstrong H.J.T.&W.]
*PRACTICE AREAS: Entertainment.
Hirsch, Ephraim J., (AV) ........ '30 '58 C.112 A.B. L.1068 LL.B. 2049 Century Park East
Hirsch, Howard E. ........ '42 '73 C.112 L.1136 J.D. 8130 Gould Ave.

**Hirsch, Joel G. '51 '76 C.112 A.B. L.1066 J.D.**
**10100 Santa Monica Boulevard Suite 300, 90067**
**Telephone: 310-552-6080 Telecopier: 310-552-7917**
**General Business, Real Estate and Corporate Law.**
*See Professional Biographies, LOS ANGELES, CALIFORNIA*

Hirsch, Perry L. ........ '48 '72 C.112 A.B. L.309 J.D. [Dapeer&H.]
Hirsch, Richard M. ........ '58 '85 C.1077 B.A. L.426 J.D. Dist. Atty's. Off.

**Hirschberg, Gert K., (AV) '26 '51 C.800 B.A. L.809 J.D.**
**10390 Wilshire Boulevard, Suite 1610, 90024-6431**
**Telephone: 310-276-5302 Fax: 310-276-4878**
***PRACTICE AREAS: Civil Trial; Products Liability Law; Medical Malpractice Law; Professional Malpractice.**
**State Bar Disciplinary Defense of Attorneys.**
*See Professional Biographies, LOS ANGELES, CALIFORNIA*

Hirschberg, Gert K., (AV) ........ '26 '51 C.800 B.A. L.809 J.D. 10390 Wilshire Blvd.
**Hirschberger, Ted L.** ........ '50 '87 C.415 B.S. L.800 J.D. [Stockwell,H.W.&W.]
**Hirschfeld, Clyde E.** ........ '52 '81 C.1109 B.A. L.1068 J.D. [Cummins&W.]
*PRACTICE AREAS: Litigation; Environmental Law; Insurance Coverage and Bad Faith; Utility Ratemaking.

**Hirschmann, Ralph F., Law Offices of '53 '78 C.674 B.A. L.976 J.D.**
**777 South Figueroa Street, Suite 3612, 90017**
**Telephone: 213-891-1700 Telecopy: 213-891-1556**
***PRACTICE AREAS: Business Litigation; Criminal Law.**
**Associates: Jeffrey P. Siegel; Sharon A. Ligorsky.**
**Business Litigation. Criminal Law.**
*See Professional Biographies, LOS ANGELES, CALIFORNIA*

Hirschmann, Ross A. ........ '63 '89 C.112 B.A. L.1065 J.D. Legal Coun., Calif. Med. Assn.
Hirschtick, Steven R. '46 '71 C&L.339 B.S., J.D.
Gen. Coun. & Sr. V.P., Rad/Net Mgmnt., Inc.
Hirshfield, Thomas ........ '52 '78 C.112 B.A. L.1136 J.D 12223 W. Olympic Blvd.
**Hirson, David**, (AV) ........ '47 '80 L.061 [Hirson W.P.&S.] (⊙Irvine)
*PRACTICE AREAS: Immigration Law; International Law.

**Hirson Wexler Perl & Stark, A Professional Corporation, (AV)**
**6310 San Vicente Boulevard, Suite 415, 90048⊙**
**Telephone: 213-936-0200 Fax: 213-936-4488**
**Email: 73411.37@compuserve.com URL: http://www.immig.com**
**David Hirson (Certified Specialist, Immigration and Nationality Law, The State Bar of California Board of Legal Specialization).**
**Immigration and International Law Firm.**
**Irvine, California Office: Jamboree Center, One Park Plaza, Suite 950. Telephone: 714-251-8844. Fax: 714-251-1545. E-Mail: immigration_law@msn.com. Web-Site: http://www.immig.com.**
**San Diego, California Office: 4275 Executive Square, Suite 800, 92037. Telephone: 619-452-5700. Fax: 619-452-1911. E-Mail: hkps@immiglaw.com. Web-Site: http://www.immig.com.**
**Phoenix, Arizona Office: 3443 North Central Avenue, Suite 706, 85012. Telephone: 602-266-4700. Fax: 602-265-8108. E-Mail: 73344.21@compuserve.com. Web-Site: http://www.immig.com.**
**Dallas, Texas Office: Heritage Square Tower II, 7th Floor, 5001 L.B.J. Freeway, 75244. Telephone: 214-991-7400. Fax: 214-991-1501. E-Mail: hkps@immig-law.com. Web-Site: http://www.immig.com**
*See Professional Biographies, LOS ANGELES, CALIFORNIA*

**Hittelman, Paul M., (AV) '38 '63 C.112 B.A. L.309 LL.B.**
**1925 Century Park East, Suite 2200, 90067**
**Telephone: 310-788-7730 Fax: 310-203-8195**
**Litigation Practice including Business, Real Property, Intellectual Property, Medical-Legal Matters.**
*See Professional Biographies, LOS ANGELES, CALIFORNIA*

**Hiura, Stephen K.** ........ '62 '90 C.1097 B.S. L.809 J.D. [La Follette,J.D.F.&A.]
*PRACTICE AREAS: General Liability; Medical Malpractice.
**Ho, Edward C.** ........ '68 '95 C.112 A.B. L.802 J.D. [Margolis&M.]
**Ho, Eric** ........ '68 '94 C.112 B.S. L.800 J.D. [Blakely,S.T.&Z.] (See Pat. Sect.)
**Hoag, Hallack W.**, (AV) ........ '05 '32 C.347 A.B. L.976 LL.B. [Hoag&O.]⊙
*PRACTICE AREAS: Probate; Trust Law; Tax.

**Hoag & Overholt, (AV)**
**Suite 1902 Wilshire Financial Tower, 3600 Wilshire Boulevard, 90010⊙**
**Telephone: 213-386-7848 Fax: 213-386-0194**
**Members of Firm: E. Llewellyn Overholt (1897-1978); Hallack W. Hoag; David G. Overholt. Associates: Carl L. McGinnis.**
**Probate and Trust Law. Federal and State Taxation. Corporation. General Civil Practice.**
**Reference: Bank of America (Harvard & Wilshire Branch).**
**Newport Beach, California Office: 5030 Campus Drive. Telephone: 714-955-2260.**
*See Professional Biographies, LOS ANGELES, CALIFORNIA*

**Hobart, C. Dana** ........ '60 '86 C&L.800 B.A., J.D. [Hennigan,M.&B.]
**Hobbs, Franklin D., III**, (AV) ........ '52 '77 C.154 B.A. L.1068 J.D. [Rutter,G.&H.]
*PRACTICE AREAS: Business Litigation; Real Estate Law.
Hobbs, Lynne M. ........ '65 '92 C.811 B.A. L.178 J.D. 550 S. Hope St.
Hobbs, William C. ........ '39 '64 C.426 B.A. L.800 J.D. 1441 W. Olympic Blvd.
**Hobel, Michael S.** ........ '54 '81 C.309 B.A. L.107 J.D. [O'Melveny&M.]

CAA249P

CALIFORNIA—LOS ANGELES MARTINDALE-HUBBELL LAW DIRECTORY 1997

Hoberman, Michael A. ....................'50 '76 C.1167 B.S. L.800 J.D. [Spector,B.H.&B.]
**Hobson, Paula A.** ....................'— '94 L.800 J.D. [A Sheppard,M.R.&H.]
**Hochhausler, John M.** ....................'64 '89 C.112 A.B. L.1067 J.D. [A Lord,B.&B.]
*PRACTICE AREAS: Construction Litigation; Business Litigation.
**Hochman, Harry D.** ....................'58 '87 C.477 A.B. L.1068 J.D. [B Pachulski,S.Z.&Y.]
*REPORTED CASES: Kelly v. Gordon (In re Gordon) 988 F.2d 1000 (9th Cir. 1993); Greyhound Real Estate Finance Co. v. Official Unsecured Creditors' Committee (In re Northview Corp.) 130 B.R. 543 (9th Cir. BAP 1991).
**Hochman, Martin P.** ....................'62 '93 C.65 B.A. L.426 J.D. [A Freeman,F.&S.]
**Hochman, Salkin and DeRoy, A Professional Corporation**
(See Beverly Hills)
**Hodes, Cynthia R.** ....................'51 '84 C.851 B.A. L.276 J.D. [Cohen&L.]
*PRACTICE AREAS: Business; Wrongful Termination; Unfair Competition; Securities Litigation.
**Hodes, Jonathan R.** ....................'45 '71 C.188 A.B. L.705 J.D. [Carlsmith B.W.C.&I.]
*PRACTICE AREAS: Maritime Finance; Corporate Law; Contracts; Commercial Law; Corporate Finance.
**Hodge, Stephen T.** ....................'63 '92 C&L.101 B.S., J.D. [A Wehner&P.]
**Hodge, Richard E., Inc.**
(See Santa Monica)
**Hodges, Robert W.** ....................'63 '88 C&L.800 B.A., J.D. [A Rintala,S.J.&R.]
**Hodges, Warren O., Jr.** ....................'63 '90 C.976 B.A. L.800 J.D. [A Freeman,F.&S.]
**Hodgkins, J. Scott** ....................'60 '92 C&L.800 B.S., J.D. [A Latham&W.]
*PRACTICE AREAS: Corporate; Securities.
Hodgman, William W. ....................'52 '78 C.112 B.A. L.1065 J.D. Dep. Dist. Atty.
Hodgson, Cheryl L. ....................'51 '76 C.418 B.A. L.208 J.D. 2118 Wilshire Blvd.
**Hodson, Kendra S. Meinert** ....................'67 '93 C.915 B.A. L.809 J.D. [A Meserve,M.&H.]
**Hoecherl, Heather** '— '96
C.429 B.A. L.813 J.D. [A McCutchen,D.B.&E.] (⊙San Francisco)
*PRACTICE AREAS: Environmental.
**Hoeksma, Gerben,** (AV) ....................'47 '72 C&L.800 B.A., J.D. [Allen,M.L.G.&M.]
*PRACTICE AREAS: Real Estate.
Hoelting, Cheryl A. ....................'62 '92 C&L.546 B.A., J.D. 3954 Farmouth Dr.
Hofberg, Adam E. ....................'53 '80 C.112 B.A. L.1068 J.D. V.P. & Sr. Coun., Union Bk.
Hofeld, Frederick R. '07 '33 C.137 L.365 LL.B.
(adm. in IL; not adm. in CA) 5873 S. Orlando Ave.‡
**Hofer, Ralph C.** ....................'53 '79 C.112 B.A. L.800 J.D. [Blecher&C.]
*LANGUAGES: German and Spanish.
*PRACTICE AREAS: Antitrust; Business Litigation; Intellectual Property.
**Hoff, Amy A.** ....................'64 '90 C.112 B.A. L.800 J.D. [A Morrison&F.]
**Hoff, Kenneth M. H.** ....................'58 '83 C.112 A.B. L.1067 J.D. [Matthias&B.]
*PRACTICE AREAS: Corporate Law; Securities Law.
Hoff, Michael R. ....................'40 '72 L.981 LL.B. Supr. Ct. J.
Hoff, Robin J. ....................'45 '89 C.139 B.A. L.1001 J.D. Dept. of Transp.
**Hoffenberg, Howard L.** ....................'59 '85 C.339 B.S. L.209 J.D. [Chapin,F.&W.] (Pat.)
**Hoffman, Aggie R., (AV) '46 '76 C.8 B.A. L.1095 J.D.** BB
**6300 Wilshire Boulevard, Suite 1560, 90048**
**Telephone: 213-655-0123 Fax: 213-655-3345**
**(Certified Specialist, Immigration and Nationality Law, The State Bar of California Board of Legal Specialization).**
***LANGUAGES: Spanish, Russian, Hungarian and Hebrew.**
***PRACTICE AREAS: Immigration and Nationality Law.**
**Immigration and Nationality Law, with emphasis on Business Related Immigration of Professionals, Executives, Extraordinary Aliens and U.S. National Interest Cases.**
*See Professional Biographies, LOS ANGELES, CALIFORNIA*
**Hoffman, Brian L.** ....................'63 '90 C.112 B.S. L.809 J.D. [A Bonne,B.M.O.&N.]
**Hoffman, Carla M.** ....................'65 '91 C.112 B.S. L.426 J.D. [A Morris,P.&P.]
Hoffman, Daniel E. ....................'54 '82 C.1077 B.A. L.426 J.D. 6500 Wilshire Blvd.
Hoffman, David ....................'60 '89 C.112 B.A. L.809 J.D. 1801 Avenue of the Stars
Hoffman, Edward A. ....................'37 '64 C.112 A.B. L.800 J.D. 3656 Westwood Blvd.
**Hoffman, Edward A., Law Offices of '65 '93 C.178 B.A. L.800 J.D.**
**11620 Wilshire Boulevard, Suite 340, 90025**
**Telephone: 310-575-3540 Fax: 310-575-6107**
**Email: eah@hoffmanlaw.com URL: http://www.hoffmanlaw.com**
***PRACTICE AREAS: Litigation; Appellate Practice.**
**General Civil Litigation, Business Litigation and Appellate Practice in all State and Federal Courts.**
*See Professional Biographies, LOS ANGELES, CALIFORNIA*
**Hoffman, Eric J.** ....................'69 '96 C.112 B.A. L.800 J.D. [A Paul,H.J.&W.]
**Hoffman, Harold L.,** (AV⊕) '40 '66 C.30 B.S. L.705 LL.B.
(adm. in NJ; not adm. in CA) [Grotta,G.&H.]⊙
**Hoffman, Janet S.** ....................'55 '83 C.104 A.B. L.477 J.D. [B Baker&H.]
*LANGUAGES: French and Spanish.
*PRACTICE AREAS: Business.
Hoffman, Jeffrey S. ....................'50 '76 [Hoffman&R.]
**Hoffman, John E.,** (AV) '47 '72 C&L.800 B.S.E.E., J.D.
[A Christensen,M.F.J.G.W.&S.]
Hoffman, Marilyn L. ....................'35 '76 C.1077 B.A. L.1095 J.D. 110 N. Grand Ave.
Hoffman, Mark S. ....................'57 '83 C&L.426 B.A., J.D. [Labowe,L.&H.]
Hoffman, Michael R. ....................'58 '93 C.112 B.A. L.769 J.D. 3055 Wilshire Blvd.
**Hoffman, Nancy Ruth, (AV) '41 '77 C.597 B.A. L.800 J.D.**
**10880 Wilshire Boulevard, Suite 2200, 90024**
**Telephone: 310-441-0664 Fax: 310-441-1153**
**(Certified Specialist, Family Law, The State Bar of California Board of Legal Specialization).**
**Practice Limited to Family Law.**
*See Professional Biographies, LOS ANGELES, CALIFORNIA*
**Hoffman, Nathan B.,** (AV) ....................'53 '79 C.800 B.A. L.426 J.D. [Daniels,B.&F.]
*PRACTICE AREAS: Trial Law; Insurance; Construction; Business.
Hoffman, Nathan V. ....................'60 '87 C.30 B.S. L.426 J.D. 750 S. Spaulding Ave.
**Hoffman, Norman J.,** (AV) ....................'40 '66 C.1122 B.B.A. L.823 LL.B. [N.J.Hoffman]
**Hoffman, Paul A.** ....................'60 '88 C&L.101 B.A., J.D. [A Berman,B.M.&R.]
*LANGUAGES: Spanish.
*REPORTED CASES: Tuchman v. Aetna, 44 Cal. App. 4th 1607 (1996); LMV Leasing, Inc. v. Conlin, 805 P.2d 189 (Vt. App. 1991).
*PRACTICE AREAS: Appellate Law; Commercial Litigation; Probate Litigation; Landlord/Tenant; Real Estate Litigation.
**Hoffman, Paul Gordon,** (AV) ....................'50 '76 C.112 B.S. L.1068 J.D. [Hoffman,S.&W.]
*PRACTICE AREAS: Taxation Law; Estate Planning Law.
**Hoffman, Paul S.** ....................'59 '85 C.801 B.S. L.809 J.D. [Manatt,P.&P.]
*PRACTICE AREAS: Bankruptcy and Creditor-Debtor Rights; Commercial; Real Estate Workouts.
Hoffman, Peter M., (AV) ....................'49 '75 C.222 A.B. L.976 J.D. CineVisions
**Hoffman, Robert D.** ....................'60 '86 C.164 B.A. L.93 J.D. [Charlston,R.&W.]
Hoffman, Ronald N. ....................'51 '76 C.1077 B.A. L.1095 J.D. 6300 Wilshire Blvd.
**Hoffman, Susan L.** ....................'48 '79 C.112 B.A. L.976 J.D. [McCutchen,D.B.&E.]
*PRACTICE AREAS: General Business Litigation; Securities Litigation; Health Care Related Litigation.
Hoffman, Thomas A., (AV) ....................'31 '63 C.755 B.A. L.276 J.D. [Early,M.&P.]
**Hoffman, Norman J., Inc., A Professional Corporation, (AV)**
**Penthouse Suite A, 16133 Ventura Boulevard, 91436**
**Telephone: 818-986-8080 Fax: 818-379-4017**
(This Listing Continued)

**Hoffman, Norman J., Inc., A Professional Corporation (Continued)**
**Norman J. Hoffman (Certified Specialist, Taxation Law, The State Bar of California Board of Legal Specialization).**
**Automobile Law, Tax Law, Estate Planning, Wills, Trusts, Real Estate and Probate.**
*See Professional Biographies, LOS ANGELES, CALIFORNIA*
Hoffman & Robin ....................1950 Sawtelle Blvd.
**Hoffman, Sabban & Watenmaker, A Professional Corporation, (AV)**
**10880 Wilshire Boulevard, Suite 2200, 90024**
**Telephone: 310-470-6010 Fax: 310-470-6735**
**Paul Gordon Hoffman; Nina Madden Sabban; Alan S. Watenmaker (Certified Specialist, Estate Planning, Trust and Probate Law, The State Bar of California Board of Legal Specialization); Jonathan C. Lurie;—Mary K. Ramsden (Certified Specialist, Estate Planning, Trust and Probate Law, The State Bar of California Board of Legal Specialization); Loretta Siciliano; Linda J. Retz; Henry J. Moravec, III. Of Counsel: Kenneth S. Wolf (Certified Specialist, Estate Planning, Trust and Probate Law, The State Bar of California Board of Legal Specialization).**
**Estate Planning, Trust and Estate Administration, Taxation.**
*See Professional Biographies, LOS ANGELES, CALIFORNIA*
**Hoffmann, James W. E. '51 '80 C.172 B.A. L.1095 J.D.**
**Suite 225, 15821 Ventura Boulevard, 91436-2938⊙**
**Telephone: 818-905-6924 Telecopier: 818-907-6709**
**Associates: Tracy A. Naegele. Of Counsel: Howard M. Fields.**
**Professional Malpractice, Bad Faith, Insurance Coverage, Product Liability, Insurance Defense, General Civil Litigation.**
**Denver, Colorado Office: 1700 Broadway, Suite 910. Telephone: 303-831-7610. Fax: 303-831-7650.**
*See Professional Biographies, LOS ANGELES, CALIFORNIA*
**Hoffmeier Zamora, Nancy** ....................'60 '88 C.309 A.B. L.1068 J.D. [Zamora&H.]
*PRACTICE AREAS: Bankruptcy; Real Estate; Land Use; Litigation.
**Hogaboom, Kathleen M.** ....................'51 '80 C.112 B.A. L.1068 J.D. [Pircher,N.&M.]
*PRACTICE AREAS: Real Estate Law; Real Estate Finance; Corporate.
**Hogan, Brian J.** '57 '82 C.602 B.A. L.145 J.D.
(adm. in IL; not adm. in CA) [A McBreen,M.&K.]
**Hogan, Laura E.** ....................'67 '93 C.112 B.A. L.1065 J.D. [A Hawkins,S.L.&B.]
**Hogan, Mary Ellen** ....................'55 '80 C.597 B.A. L.1119 J.D. [McDermott,W.&E.]
*PRACTICE AREAS: Environmental Law; Aviation and Aerospace; Toxic Torts.
Hogan, Maurice R., Jr. ....................'24 '52 C.800 L.809 LL.B. Supr. Ct. J.
**Hogan, Maurya** ....................'54 '87 C.112 B.A. L.1066 J.D. [A Kamine,S.&U.]
Hogan, Paul M. '30 '61 C.299 B.A. L.1065 LL.B.
Admin. Law J., Off. of Hearing & App.
Hogan, Timothy A. ....................'49 '75 C&L.426 B.A., J.D. Asst. City Atty.
Hogan, Timothy J., (AV) ....................'47 '73 C.740 B.A. L.767 J.D. [Hogan,B.&H.]
Hogan, Baynes & Haworth, (AV) ....................3600 Wilshire Blvd.
**Hogeboom, Robert Wood** ....................'47 '74 C.813 B.A. L.61 J.D. [Barger&W.]
*PRACTICE AREAS: Insurance Law; Corporate Law; Administrative Law.
Hogg, John L. ....................'45 '72 C&L.16 B.S., J.D. 3550 Wilshire Blvd.
**Hogin, Bradley R.** ....................'58 '89 C.112 A.B. L.904 J.D. [Baker&H.]
*PRACTICE AREAS: Environmental and Natural Resources Law; Litigation.
**Hogoboom, William P.,** (AV) ....................'18 '49 C.605 A.B. L.800 J.D. Coun., Univ. of So. Calif.
**Hogtanian, A. Gina** ....................'65 '94 C.112 B.A. L.940 J.D. [A Acker,K.&W.]
*LANGUAGES: Armenian, Russian and French.
**Hogue, Amy D.** ....................'52 '79 C&L.228 A.B., J.D. [Pillsbury M.&S.]
**Hohl, Doren E.** ....................'55 '84 C.264 A.B. L.426 J.D. Corp. Coun., Farmers Grp., Inc.
*RESPONSIBILITIES: Life Insurance; Corporate Matters.
Hoiby, Randall C. '43 '70 C.800 B.A. L.1095 J.D.
V.P. & Assoc. Gen. Coun., Transamerica Occidental Life Ins. Co.
**Hokanson, Charles W.** ....................'64 '92 C.813 A.B. L.1065 J.D. [A Sonnenschein N.&R.]
**Hokanson, Jon E.,** (AV) ....................'48 '80 C.20 B.A. L.273 J.D. [Small L.&K.] (See Pat. Sect.)
*PRACTICE AREAS: Patent, Trademark and Copyright.
Hokinson, Thomas C., (AV) ....................'41 '66 C.679 B.S. L.1068 J.D. Sr. Asst. City Atty.
**Holberton, John C.,** (AV) ....................'46 '72 C&L.813 B.A., J.D. [Graham&J.]
*PRACTICE AREAS: Taxation Law.
**Holbrook, Brian M.** ....................'63 '89 C.893 B.A. L.813 J.D. [A Meserve,M.&H.]
*PRACTICE AREAS: Wrongful Termination; Employment Discrimination; Personal Policy Counseling; Wage and Hour.
**Holbrook, William F.** ....................'39 '85 C.95 B.A. L.426 J.D. [B Thelen,M.J.&B.]
*PRACTICE AREAS: Business and Insurance Litigation.
**Holchin, James W.** ....................'64 '92 C.112 B.A. L.426 J.D. [A Inglis,L.&G.]
*PRACTICE AREAS: Insurance Defense.
**Holcomb, John W.** ....................'63 '93 C.453 S.B. L.309 J.D. [A Irell&M.]
Holcomb, William W. ....................'48 '80 C.197 B.A. L.978 J.D. [Tyre K.K.&G.]
**Holdsworth, Curtis P.** ....................'67 '94 C.112 B.A. L.800 J.D. [A Greenberg G.F.C.&M.]
*PRACTICE AREAS: Litigation.
Holen, Marvin L., (AV) ....................'29 '59 C.112 B.A. L.1068 J.D. [Van Petten&H.]
Holguin, Claudia Roberta ....................'52 '83 C.813 B.A. L.276 J.D. 3660 Amesbury Rd.
Holguin, Henry A. ....................'51 '76 C.800 B.S. L.1067 J.D. [Miller&H.]
Holguin, Steven R. ....................'53 '84 C.1042 B.A. L.1068 J.D. 3780 Wilshire Blvd.
**Holiber, Judith A.** ....................'68 '95 C.881 B.A. L.276 J.D. [A Fulbright&J.]
*PRACTICE AREAS: Litigation.
**Holiday, Ann L.,** (AV) ....................'58 '84 C.112 B.A. L.990 J.D. [Dummit,F.&B.]
**Holl, James A., III** ....................'70 '95 C.112 B.A. L.990 J.D. [A Booth,M.&S.]
Holl, Philip K. '49 '75 C.705 B.A. L.1292 J.D.
(adm. in NJ; not adm. in CA) V.P. & Assoc. Gen. Coun., Trust Company of the West
Holland, Greg ....................'49 '77 C.339 B.S. L.1068 J.D. Dep. Co. Coun.
**Holland, Robert A.** ....................'68 '94 C.112 B.A. L.1066 J.D. [A Sidley&A.]
*PRACTICE AREAS: Civil and Appellate Litigation.
**Holland, Suzanne J.** ....................'46 '81 C.665 B.A. L.426 J.D. [Hill,F.&B.]
**Hollander, David A.** ....................'61 '85 C.659 B.S. L.813 J.D. [B O'Melveny&M.]
*PRACTICE AREAS: Bankruptcy; Banking and Finance.
**Holley & Galen, (AV)** BB
**800 South Figueroa, Suite 1100, 90017**
**Telephone: 213-629-1880 Fax: 213-895-0363**
**Members of Firm: Clyde E. Holley (1891-1980); Albert J. Galen (Retired); W. Michael Johnson (Certified Specialist, Taxation Law, California Board of Legal Specialization); A. Steven Brown. Associates: Debra Burchard Coffeen; Charles A. Jordan.**
**Taxation (Federal and State), Business, Estate Planning, Probate, Antitrust, Corporate, Real Property and Commercial Law. Trial and Appellate Practice.**
*See Professional Biographies, LOS ANGELES, CALIFORNIA*
**Holliday, Susan J.** '46 '74 C.966 B.A. L.1068 J.D.
Sr. V.P. & Dep. Gen. Coun., CBS Inc.
**Holliday, Thomas E.,** (AV) ....................'48 '74 C.813 B.A. L.800 J.D. [Gibson,D.&C.]
*PRACTICE AREAS: White Collar Criminal Defense.
**Hollinger, Chris** ....................'64 '90 C.197 B.A. L.145 J.D. [B O'Melveny&M.]
*PRACTICE AREAS: Railway Labor Act Litigation.
**Hollingworth, Lisa Ann** ....................'54 '85 C.1042 B.S. L.426 J.D. [S.L.Hartmann]
*REPORTED CASES: Santa Monica Hospital Medical Center v. Superior Court (1988), 203 Cal. App. 3rd 1026.
*PRACTICE AREAS: Civil Rights; Insurance Defense; Premises Liability; Products Liability; Insurance Fraud Defense.

CAA250P

**Hollins, Byron S.**, (AV) ............... '50 '84 C.502 B.S. L.1221 J.D. [Hollins&R.]⊙
*PRACTICE AREAS: Legal Malpractice; Legal Malpractice Defense; Coverage Defense; Insurance Defense; Medical Malpractice.

**Hollins & Rice, A Professional Corporation, (AV)**
**1925 Century Park East, Suite 920, 90067⊙**
**Telephone: 310-553-3510**
**Byron S. Hollins; Andrea Lynn Rice;—Kim A. Hayashi; Adam L. Johnson.**
**Professional Liability, Medical Malpractice, Legal Malpractice, Insurance Coverage and Bad Faith, Personal Injury, Products Liability and Toxic Tort Law. General Civil, Trial and Appellate Practice in all State and Federal Courts.**
**Representative Clients: Safeco Insurance Cos.; Utica Mutual Insurance Cos.; Lawyers Mutual Insurance Cos.; Texas Lawyers Insurance Exchange; Minnesota Lawyers Mutual Insurance Co.; Media Professional Insurance Co.; First State Insurance Co.; The Kemper Group; State Farm Fire & Casualty Co.**
**Reference: Union Bank.**
**San Diego, California Office: 402 West Broadway, Fourth Floor. Telephone: 619-232-0222.**
*See Professional Biographies, LOS ANGELES, CALIFORNIA*

Hollombe, Jos. B. ........................ '10 '36 6120 Barrows Dr.
**Hollomon, Michael P., Jr.** ............... '62 '89 L.1136 J.D. [A Liebman&R.]
Hollos, Cynthia ............... '55 '85 C.112 B.A. L.1068 J.D. Off. of Pub. Def.
Holloway, George ............ '46 '82 C.1097 B.A. L.1136 J.D. 2916 W. Florence Ave.
**Holloway, John H.** ............... '66 '95 C.945 B.A. L.861 J.D. [Brown,W.&C.]
**Holm, Esther P.** ............... '54 '89 C.112 B.A. L.770 J.D. [A Cummins&W.]
*PRACTICE AREAS: Insurance Coverage; Insurance Bad Faith; Personal Injury; Insurance Broker Malpractice.
Holm, Thomas W. ............... '64 '94 C.118 B.A. L.494 J.D. 555 W. 5th St.
**Holman, Brian L.** ............... '55 '80 C.800 B.S. L.309 J.D. [White&C.]
**Holman, R. Craig** ............... '54 '89 C.878 B.A. L.101 J.D. [A McKenna&C.]
*LANGUAGES: Portuguese.
*PRACTICE AREAS: Government Contracts Law; Litigation; Commercial Contracts; Construction.
**Holman, Randy B.** ............... '55 '82 C.101 B.A. L.1066 J.D. [C Hughes H.&R.]
**Holmberg, Alan** ............... '49 '75 C.604 A.B. L.800 J.D. [Angel&N.]
*PRACTICE AREAS: Civil Litigation; Bankruptcy.
**Holmberg, Brian D.** ............... '42 '74 C.800 B.S. L.61 J.D. [Prestholt,K.F.&V.]
*PRACTICE AREAS: Civil Trial Litigation; Insurance Casualty Defense.
Holmberg, Julie Tatsugi ........... '58 '84 C.112 B.A. L.800 J.D. 1999 Ave. of The Stars
Holmen, Gary L., (BV) ............ '44 '76 C.1070 B.S. L.208 J.D. 4700 Wilshire Blvd.
**Holmes, Catherine DeBono** ........... '53 '77 C.112 B.A. L.1066 J.D. [Jeffer,M.B.&M.]
*PRACTICE AREAS: Corporate, Partnership and Securities; Mortgage Banking.
Holmes, Gary ............... '54 '90 C&L.893 B.A., J.D. 2121 Ave. of the Stars
Holmes, H. Thomas ............... '39 '69 C.623 B.A. L.276 J.D. Dep. Dist. Atty.
**Holmes, James J. S.** ............... '61 '86 C&L.36 B.S., J.D. [C Sedgwick,D.M.&A.]
*LANGUAGES: French.
**Holmes, John C.** ............... '59 '85 C.112 B.A. L.800 J.D. [Barger&W.]
*PRACTICE AREAS: Insurance Coverage Law; Insurance Insolvency Law; Business Litigation.
**Holmes, Keith T.** ............... '— '77 C.597 B.A. L.659 J.D. [King,P.H.P.&B.]
*PRACTICE AREAS: Real Estate Law; Business Law; Banking.
**Holmes, Peter L.** ............ '64 '94 C.608 B.S.E.E. L.809 J.D. [Oppenheimer P.S.] (Pat.)
*PRACTICE AREAS: Intellectual Property.
**Holo, Robert E.** '66 '93 C.1169 B.A. L.112 J.D.
(adm. in NY; not adm. in CA) [A Munger,T.&O.]
**Holo, Sanford**, (AV) ............... '39 '64 C.477 B.A. L.309 J.D. [C Thorpe&T.]
*PRACTICE AREAS: Individual & Business Tax Planning & Business Transactions.
Holroyd, Ira W. ............ '29 '58 C.112 A.B. L.1068 J.D. Legal Div., Dept. of Transp.
**Holscher, Mark C.** ............... '62 '88 C.112 B.S. L.1066 J.D. [C O'Melveny&M.]
Holston, Dixon M. ............... '39 '65 C&L.800 B.S., J.D. Sr. Dep. Co. Coun.
Holt, Patricia Hurst '37 '64 C&L.813 A.B., J.D.
Directing Atty., Los Angeles County Bar Assn.
Holtdorf, Kristi A. ............... '— '89 C.350 B.S. L.426 J.D. [Wilson&B.]
Holtz, Craig A. ............... '58 '86 C.1077 B.A. L.940 J.D. [Hogan,B.&H.]
**Holtz, Michael D.** ............... '64 '90 C.477 A.B. L.569 J.D. [A Thelen,M.J.&B.]
*PRACTICE AREAS: Litigation.
Holtzman, Howard L. ............... '33 '58 1204 Beverwil Dr.
**Holtzman, Robert A., (A P.C.)**, (AV) ...... '29 '55 C.112 A.B. L.800 LL.B. [C Loeb&L.]
*PRACTICE AREAS: Litigation; Arbitration; Mediation.
Holtzman, Seymour R. ............... '12 '50 C.145 L.809 J.D. 947 Tiverton Ave.‡
**Holweger, Marie Polizzi** ............... '54 '80 C&L.426 B.S., J.D. [Millard,P.H.&C.]
*PRACTICE AREAS: Insurance Defense; Civil Litigation.
Holz, Stephen D. ............... '53 '78 C.1077 B.A. L.1065 J.D. 1 Wilshire Blvd.
**Holzer, Stephen T.** ............... '48 '74 C&L.976 B.A., J.D. [Parker,M.C.O.&S.]
*PRACTICE AREAS: Environmental Law; Hazardous Materials Management.
Holzhaus, Dominic T. ........... '58 '87 C.061 B.S. L.178 J.D. 355 S. Grand Ave. 35th Fl.
**Holzman, Ruth N.** ............... '52 '77 C.112 A.B. L.1066 J.D. [Sanders,B.G.S.&M.]
Hom, Howard, (AV) ............... '51 '76 C.112 B.A. L.426 J.D. 3731 Wilshire Blvd.
Hom, Mon Bill, (A Professional Law Corporation) '48 '73
C.112 B.A. L.426 J.D. 3550 Wilshire Blvd.
**Hom, Tracey P.** ............... '56 '90 C.800 B.S. L.426 J.D. [A Agapay,L.&H.]
Homer, Gregg ............... '54 '79 C.342 B.A. L.426 J.D. [G.Homer]
Homer, Gregg, P.C. ............... 2980 Beverly Glen Circle
**Homsy, Joseph G.** '45 '78 C.659 B.A. L.1202 J.D.
(adm. in NY; not adm. in CA) [Zevnik H.G.&M.]⊙
*PRACTICE AREAS: Environmental Law.
Honea, Sterling ............... '47 '72 C.1259 B.A. L.1049 J.D. Princ. Dep. Co. Coun.
**Honey, Roger G.** ............... '64 '94 C.763 B.A. L.800 J.D. [A Cummins&W.]
*PRACTICE AREAS: Insurance Coverage; Construction Defect.
Hong, H. David ............... '59 '84 C.299 B.A. L.569 J.D. 800 West Sixth Street
**Hong, Nowland C.**, (AV) ............... '34 '61 C.668 B.A. L.800 J.D. [Parker,M.C.O.&S.]
*PRACTICE AREAS: Business Litigation; Insurance Coverage Litigation; Representation of and Litigation against Public Entities.
**Hong, Ryan S.** ............... '68 '94 C.112 B.S.B.A. L.178 J.D. [A Riordan&M.]
*PRACTICE AREAS: Corporate.
**Hong, Sebong**, (AV) ............... '49 '78 C.30 B.A. L.904 J.D. [Hong&C.]
*LANGUAGES: Korean.
*PRACTICE AREAS: Corporate and Commercial Transactions; Banking and Finance; Real Estate Transactions.
Hong, Simon Song-Jin ............... '60 '90 C.112 B.A. L.276 J.D. 800 W. 6th St.

**Hong & Chang, (AV)**
**Suite 1010, 800 West Sixth Street, 90017⊙**
**Telephone: 213-629-5611 Telecopier: 213-629-1170**
**Sebong Hong; Richard W. Swartz; Rick D. Navarrette; Henry Gweon.**
**Commercial, Banking, Corporate, Real Property, Business Trials and Litigation, Bankruptcy.**
**Seoul, Korea Associated Office: Kim & Chang, Seyang Building, 223, Naeja-Dong, Chongro-Ku, Seoul, Korea. Telephone:(+82 2) 737-4455. Telecopier: (+82 2) 737-9091-3. E-Mail: lawkim@soback.kornet.nm.kr; Web Site Address: http://www.kimchang.com**
*See Professional Biographies, LOS ANGELES, CALIFORNIA*

Honig, Barbara ............... '49 '74 C.112 B.A. L.809 J.D. [Silbiger&H.]
Honig, Eric ............... '54 '81 C.94 B.S. L.861 J.D. 1901 Ave. of the Stars
**Honig, Keith C.** ........... '60 '90 C.800 B.S. L.464 J.D. Assoc. Coun., SunAmerica Inc.
*RESPONSIBILITIES: General Corporate Practice.
**Honig, Kelly Bennett** ............... '62 '90 C.112 B.A. L.464 J.D. [A Sands N.F.L.&L.]
Honig, Melvyn '38 '68 C.1097 B.S. L.809 LL.B.
1901 Ave. of the Stars, 20th Fl (Century City)
**Honjiyo, Reid S.** ............... '62 '87 C.112 A.B. L.1068 J.D. [A Berger,K.S.M.F.S.&G.]
**Honn, Richard A.**, (AV) ............... '52 '79 C.112 B.A. L.426 J.D. [Honn&S.]
*PRACTICE AREAS: Litigation; Business Law; Real Property; Insurance Law.

**Honn & Secof, (AV)** BB
**510 West Sixth Street, Suite 910, 90014-1310**
**Telephone: 213-629-3900 Telecopier: 213-624-5362**
**Richard A. Honn; Howard S. Secof. Associates: Wayne T. Kasai.**
**General Civil and Trial Practice. Business, Commercial and Insolvency Law and Banking, Corporate, Probate and Real Estate Law, Entertainment Law, Tort and Insurance Law.**
**Reference: Wells Fargo Bank.**
*See Professional Biographies, LOS ANGELES, CALIFORNIA*

Honold, Kristin ............ '49 '75 C.800 B.A. L.426 J.D. Sr. Staff Coun., Northrop Corp.
Honold, Ted C. ............... '52 '77 C.210 A.B. L.608 J.D. 1000 Wilshire Blvd.
**Honus, Kimberly L.** ............... '— '95 C.37 B.A. L.990 J.D. [A Howarth&S.]
*PRACTICE AREAS: Litigation; Products Liability.
Hood, Marcus M. ............... '27 '56 C.1097 L.1001 LL.B. 3600 Wilshire Blvd.‡
**Hood, Wetzler & Reed**
**(See Huntington Beach)**
**Hook, Lynne Marie** ............... '69 '93 C.112 B.A. L.602 J.D. [A Jeffer,M.B.&M.]
*PRACTICE AREAS: Labor and Employment Law.
**Hooper, Mark A.** ............... '65 '94 C.101 B.S. L.990 J.D. [A Lynberg&W.]
*PRACTICE AREAS: Insurance Defense; Bad Faith Litigation.
**Hooper, Patric**, (AV) ............... '48 '73 C.112 A.B. L.1049 J.D. [Hooper,L.&B.]
*PRACTICE AREAS: Healthcare Law; Hospital Law.

**Hooper, Lundy & Bookman, Inc., (AV)** BB
**Watt Plaza, Suite 1600, 1875 Century Park East, 90067-2517**
**Telephone: 310-551-8111 Telecopier: 310-551-8181**
**Robert W. Lundy, Jr.; Patric Hooper; Lloyd A. Bookman; W. Bradley Tully; John R. Hellow; Angela A. Mickelson; Laurence D. Getzoff; Jay N. Hartz; Byron J. Gross; David P. Henninger; Todd E. Swanson;—Gina Reese; Jonathan P. Neustadter; Kenneth J. Carl; Julia Schollenberger; Thomas B. Croke IV; Michele Melden; Mark Jeffry Dicks; Salvatore A. Zoida; Kevin A. Corbett; Betty J. Levine; William A. Larkin.**
**Healthcare and Hospital Law (General Business Matters, Joint Ventures, Managed Care, Health Care Financing, Third-Party Payment Programs, Medical Staff, Licensing and Certification Issues, Administrative Law and Regulatory Litigation).**
**Representative Clients: Tenet Healthcare Corp.; Kaiser Foundation Health Plan; City of Hope National Medical Center; County of Los Angeles; Physicians and Surgeons Laboratories, Inc.; Queen of Angels/Hollywood Presbyterian Medical Center; Beach Cities Health District; Kauai Medical Group; Vista Health Plans.**
**Reference: City National Bank.**
*See Professional Biographies, LOS ANGELES, CALIFORNIA*

**Hoover, George W, II** '46 '86 C.112 B.S. L.426 J.D.
[Blakely,S.T.&Z.] (See Pat. Sect.)
**Hope, Inez D.** ............... '52 '92 C.453 S.B.S.M. L.112 J.D. [A Munger,T.&O.]
**Hope, John E.** ............... '54 '81 C.911 B.A. L.1049 J.D. [Inglis,L.&G.]
*PRACTICE AREAS: Business Litigation.
Hope, Tamia L. ............... '46 '72 C.483 B.A. L.1065 J.D. Dep. Dist. Atty.
Hopkins, Dana ............... '42 '68 C.605 B.A. L.309 LL.B. P.O. Box 26871
**Hopkins, Ronald W.** ............... '54 '81 C.813 A.B. L.1068 J.D. [Gascou,G.&T.]
*LANGUAGES: French, Italian, Spanish and German.
*PRACTICE AREAS: Fidelity; Suretyship; Construction Law.
**Hopkins, Stacy M.** ............... '58 '94 C.1077 B.S. L.990 J.D. [A Paul,H.J.&W.]
Hopkins-Luder, John M. ............... '53 '88 C.1097 B.A. L.940 J.D. Dep. Dist. Atty.
**Horacek, Joseph, III, (P.C.)**, (AV) ... '41 '67 C.112 B.A. L.1068 LL.B. [C Manatt,P.&P.]
*PRACTICE AREAS: Entertainment; Motion Picture and Television.
**Horan, Brian R.** ............... '50 '79 C.112 B.A. L.809 J.D. [Stockwell,H.W.&W.]
Hording, Kyle ........... '43 '85 C.684 B.A. L.398 J.D. Coun., ML Settlement Servs., Inc.
Horenstein, Suzanne M. ............... '61 '87 C.154 B.A. L.188 J.D. 1373 Brinkley Ave
**Horgan, David L.** ............... '56 '81 C&L.800 B.A., J.D. [C Bronson,B.&M.]
*LANGUAGES: Japanese.
*PRACTICE AREAS: International Law; Corporate and Business; Financial Institutions; Bankruptcy.
**Horgan, Gary M.** ............... '47 '74 C.770 B.A. L.1068 J.D. [Horgan,R.B.&C.]
*PRACTICE AREAS: Administrative; Banking; Finance; Secured Transactions; Corporate.
Horgan, Paul C. ............... '44 '71 C.112 B.A. L.426 J.D. 800 Wilshire Blvd.

**Horgan, Rosen, Beckham & Coren, (AV)**
**A Partnership including Professional Corporations**
**21700 Oxnard Street, Suite 1400 (Woodland Hills), 91365-4335**
**Telephone: 818-340-6100; 310-552-2010; 619-295-3160 Fax: 818-340-6190**
**Members of Firm: S. Alan Rosen (A Professional Corporation); Robert P. Beckham; Arthur A. Coren; Gary M. Horgan; Alan M. Mirman; Mel Aranoff (P.C.); Michael E. Bubman; Gillian E. Friedman.**
**Administrative, Banking, Bankruptcy, Civil and Commercial Litigation in all State and Federal Courts. Corporate, Corporate Securities and Finance. Creditors' Rights, Labor, Real Estate and Secured Transactions.**
*See Professional Biographies, LOS ANGELES, CALIFORNIA*

**Horii, Dwayne M.** ............... '60 '86 C.112 B.S. L.477 J.D. [Rodríguez,H.&C.]
Horikawa, Harvey M. ............... '48 '73 C.1042 B.A. L.1068 J.D. 3250 Wilshire Blvd.
**Horn, Gerson S., (AV) '39 '67 C.1097 B.A. L.112 J.D.**
**11835 West Olympic Boulevard, Suite 1235, 90064**
**Telephone: 310-231-3419 Fax: 310-231-3422**
**(Certified Specialist, Criminal Law, The State Bar of California Board of Legal Specialization).**
***REPORTED CASES: Avital v. Superior Ct. 1114 Cal App. 3rd 297; IN RE: Letters Rogatory From the Tokyo District Prosecutor's Office 16 Fed. 3 1016; Tomlin v. Myers 30 Fed.3rd 1235; U.S. v. Isgrow 974 Fed.2d 1091; U.S. v. $277,000 and One 1986 Dodge Ram Charger 69 Fed.3d 1491.**
***PRACTICE AREAS: Criminal Law.**
**Federal and State Criminal Law.**
*See Professional Biographies, LOS ANGELES, CALIFORNIA*

Horn, Gregory C. ............... '48 '75 C&L.1136 B.S.L., J.D. 16501 Ventura Blvd.
Horn, H. Chester, Jr. ............... '47 '72 C.112 B.A. L.1068 J.D. Dep. Atty. Gen.
Horn, Martin R., (AV) ........... '28 '55 C.112 B.S. L.1068 J.D. 1880 Century Pk. E. (Pat.)
**Horn, Polly**, (AV) ............... '35 '78 C.880 A.B. L.800 J.D. [Arnold&P.]
*PRACTICE AREAS: Commercial Litigation; Legal Malpractice.
Horn, Robert H. ............... '58 '88 C.112 A.B. L.1065 J.D. [A Tyre K.K.&G.]
Horn, Robert J. ............... '54 '79 C.813 A.B. L.1066 J.D. 444 S. Flower St.
**Hornbaker, Robert D.**, (AV) '26 '49
C.350 B.S.E.E. L.352 J.D. [Freilich,H.&R.] (See Pat. Sect.)
*PRACTICE AREAS: Litigation; Patent Law; Trademark Law; Unfair Competition Law.
**Hornberger, Nicholas W.**, (AV) ............... '46 '72 C.112 B.S. L.767 J.D. [Hornberger&C.]
*PRACTICE AREAS: Insurance Bad Faith; Eminent Domain; Environmental; Employment Termination; Products Liability.

**Hornberger & Criswell, (AV)** BB
**444 South Flower, 31st Floor, 90071**
**Telephone: 213-488-1655 Facsimile: 213-488-1255**
**Email: kbranch0@counsel.com**
**Members of Firm: Nicholas W. Hornberger; Leslie E. Criswell; Ann M. Ghazarians; Michael A. Brewer; Scott Alan Freedman. Associates: Marlin E. Howes; Christopher T. Olsen; Scott B. Cloud; James M. Slominski; Michael C. Denlinger; Gayle L. Eskridge. Of Counsel: David E. Bower; William P. Driscoll.**

(This Listing Continued)

CAA251P

**Hornberger & Criswell (Continued)**

**General Civil Trial, Litigation and Appellate Practice in State and Federal Courts, Negligence, Products Liability, Labor and Employment, Insurance Coverage and Bad Faith, Construction Defect, Premises Liability, Commercial, and Environmental Law, Inverse Condemnation, Eminent Domain.**

*See Professional Biographies, LOS ANGELES, CALIFORNIA*

**Horning, Kathryn D.** '59 '96
C.112 B.A. L.1049 J.D. [▣ Allen,M.L.G.&M.] (⊙San Diego)
*PRACTICE AREAS: Litigation; Bankruptcy.
**Hornstein, James E.**, (AV) ....... '50 '75 C.575 B.A. L.976 J.D. [Greenberg G.F.C.&M.]
*PRACTICE AREAS: Entertainment Litigation; Labor Litigation; Intellectual Property Litigation; General Business Litigation.
**Horoupian, Grace** .......... '69 '95 C.1077 B.A. L.426 J.D. [▣ Selman B.]
*PRACTICE AREAS: Insurance Coverage; Litigation.
**Horoupian, Mark S.** .......... '69 '94 C.112 L.426 J.D. [▣ Sulmeyer,K.B.&R.]
**Horowitz, Edward J.**, (AV) .......... '42 '67 C.112 A.B. L.309 J.D. [E.J.Horowitz]
Horowitz, Harold W. .......... '23 '50 C.112 A.B. L.309 LL.B. Univ. of Calif. Law Sch.
**Horowitz, Leslie R.**, (AV) .......... '54 '81 C.605 A.B. L.809 J.D. [Clark&T.]
*PRACTICE AREAS: Banking; Credit Law; Bankruptcy; Creditors Rights; Collateral Recovery.

**Horowitz, Edward J., A Professional Corporation, (AV) ▣**
**Suite 1015, 11661 San Vicente Boulevard, 90049**
**Telephone: 310-826-6619 Fax: 310-826-8242**
**Email: Horowitz@appellatelaw.com**
**Edward J. Horowitz (Certified Specialist, Appellate Law, The State Bar of California Board of Legal Specialization).**
**Appellate Practice, Civil and Criminal.**
**Reference: Union Bank (Brentwood Branch).**

*See Professional Biographies, LOS ANGELES, CALIFORNIA*

Horrigan, Philip K. .......... '20 '53 C.112 A.B. L.309 LL.B. 1100 Glendon St.
**Horrow, Avigal** .......... '65 '92 C.446 B.S. L.61 J.D. [Prestholt,K.F.&V.]
*PRACTICE AREAS: Insurance Defense; Civil Litigation.
Horstman, Gregory C. .......... '55 '89 C.492 B.A. L.1035 J.D. 1200 Wilshire Blvd.
**Horton, E. Lee**, (AV) .......... '44 '73 C.112 B.A. L.809 J.D. [Belcher,H.&B.]
*PRACTICE AREAS: Airplane Crash Litigation; Aviation Law; Products Liability Law; Labor Law; Business Law.
**Horton, Elizabeth** .......... '59 '95 C.945 B.A. L.1068 J.D. [▣ Skadden,A.S.M.&F.]
Horton, Jack K. .......... '16 '41 C.813 A.B. L.999 LL.B. 315 S. Windsor St.‡
**Horton, Laura L.** .......... '57 '92 C.36 B.S. L.990 J.D. [▣ Hewitt&P.]
*PRACTICE AREAS: Professional Malpractice; Sport and Leisure Liability; Insurance Coverage; General Civil.
**Horton, Michel Yves** .......... '51 '84 C.1090 B.S. L.945 J.D. [Zevnik H.G.&M.]⊙
*PRACTICE AREAS: Insurance Coverage; Commercial Litigation.
Horton-Billard, Theodore P., Jr., (BV) '55 '84
C.940 B.A. L.1148 J.D. 4700 Wilshire Blvd., 3rd Floor
**Horvitz, Ellis J.**, (A P.C.), (AV) .......... '28 '51 C.145 A.B. L.813 J.D. [Horvitz&L.]

**Horvitz & Levy, (AV) ▣**
**A Partnership including Professional Corporations**
**18th Floor, 15760 Ventura Boulevard (Encino), 91436**
**Telephone: 818-995-0800; 213-872-0802 FAX: 818-995-3157**
**Ellis J. Horvitz (A P.C.); Barry R. Levy (A P.C.); Peter Abrahams (Certified Specialist, Appellate Law, The State Bar of California Board of Legal Specialization); David M. Axelrad (Certified Specialist, Appellate Law, The State Bar of California Board of Legal Specialization); Frederic D. Cohen; S. Thomas Todd; David S. Ettinger; Daniel J. Gonzalez; Mitchell C. Tilner; Christina J. Imre; Lisa Perrochet; Stephen E. Norris; Sandra J. Smith; John A. Taylor, Jr.;—Mary F. Dant; Ari R. Kleiman; Lisa R. Jaskol; Julie L. Woods; Holly R. Paul; H. Thomas Watson; Andrea M. Gauthier; Elizabeth Skorcz Anthony; Christine A. Pagac; Judith E. Gordon; Patricia Lofton; L. Rachel Lerman Helyar (Not admitted in CA). Of Counsel: Jon B. Eisenberg.**
**All Civil Appeals and Related Appellate Practice, including Trial Consultations, with Emphasis in the Areas of Business Law, Commercial Law, Contracts, Health Care, Hospitals, Insurance and Insurance Defense (including Coverage and Bad Faith), Legal Ethics and Professional Responsibility, Legal and Medical Malpractice, Negligence, Personal Injury, Products Liability, Professional Liability, and Torts.**
**Reference: Bank of California (Los Angeles, California Office).**

*See Professional Biographies, LOS ANGELES, CALIFORNIA*

**Horwich, Willard D., (AV) '29 '59 C.112 B.S. L.1068 J.D.**
**1875 Century Park East, Suite 2150, 90067**
**Telephone: 310-556-3378 FAX: 310-286-0865**
**Federal and State Taxation. Probate Law and Bankruptcy Tax Litigation.**

*See Professional Biographies, LOS ANGELES, CALIFORNIA*

**Horwith, Jeffrey L.** .......... '56 '83 C&L.800 B.S., J.D. [▣ Belcher,H.&B.]
*PRACTICE AREAS: Litigation; Products Liability Law; Insurance Defense Law; Motor Vehicle Litigation; Aviation Law.
Horwitz, David M. .......... '43 '68 C.112 B.A. L.1068 J.D. Mun. Ct. J.
**Horwitz, Howard L.**, (AV) .......... '57 '82 C.112 B.A. L.1065 J.D. [Oberstein,K.&H.]
**Horwitz, John H.** .......... '47 '88 C.112 B.A. L.426 J.D. [Schaffer&L.]
*PRACTICE AREAS: Insurance Coverage; Bad Faith.
Horwitz, Merle H. .......... '29 '55 C.800 B.A. L.1065 LL.B. 1059 S. Hayworth‡
Horwitz, Roger D. .......... '41 '73 C.1036 A.B. L.309 J.D. [R.D.Horwitz]
**Horwitz, Susan** '51 '82 C.1078 B.A. L.1065 J.D.
(adm. in FL; not adm. in CA) [▣ Baker&H.]
*PRACTICE AREAS: Intellectual Property; Litigation.
Horwitz, Wendi A. .......... '63 '88 C.347 B.S. L.1065 J.D. Dep. Atty. Gen.
Horwitz, Roger D., A Professional Corporation .......... 1500 N. Kings Rd.
**Hosack, John L.**, (AV) .......... '44 '69 C.911 L.767 J.D. [Arter&H.]

**Hoskins, Philip J. '38 '65 C&L.112 B.A., LL.B.**
**10940 Wilshire Boulevard, Suite 1400, 90024**
**Telephone: 310-209-8080 Fax: 310-208-8582**
**Email: philip_hoskins@msn.com URL: http://ntnet.com/pjhbase.htm**
**Civil Trial and Appellate Practice in State and Federal Courts, Family Law, Probate and Estate Planning.**

*See Professional Biographies, LOS ANGELES, CALIFORNIA*

**Hosp, Gilbert & Associates, A Law Corporation**
**(See Pasadena)**

Hotchkis, Preston B., (AV) '29 '57
C.112 B.S. L.1066 LL.B. Chmn. of the Bd., Bixby Ranch Co.
Hotchkiss, S. David, (BV) .......... '51 '77 C.1042 B.A. L.809 J.D. Dep. City Atty.
**Hou, Howard S.** .......... '66 '92 C.184 B.S. L.1067 J.D. [Bacon&M.]
*LANGUAGES: Mandarin Chinese.
*PRACTICE AREAS: Taxation; Estate Planning; Corporate.
**Hou, Lillian** .......... '62 '91 L.228 J.D. [▣ Coudert]
Houchen, Nancy L. .......... '— '81 C.597 B.S. L.146 J.D. 6399 Wilshire Blvd.

**Houck & Balisok, (AV)**
**1925 Century Park East, Suite 2000, 90067-2721**
**Telephone: 310-277-2236 Telecopier: 310-556-5653**
**Members of Firm: Alden F. Houck (1917-1988); Russell S. Balisok.**
**Civil Litigation including Business, Elder Abuse, Nursing Home Malpractice.**

*See Professional Biographies, LOS ANGELES, CALIFORNIA*

Hough, Steven H., (AV) .......... '38 '66 C.147 B.S.B.A. L.1065 LL.B. Head Dep. Pub. Def.

**Houlé, Gregory** .......... '48 '74 C.112 B.A. L.1066 J.D. [Houlé&S.]
*PRACTICE AREAS: Public Entity Defense; Insurance Defense; Personal Injury Litigation.
**Houlé, Richard** .......... '53 '92 C.112 B.A. L.809 J.D. [▣ Houlé&S.]

**Houlé & Sedin**
**800 Wilshire Boulevard, Suite 1450, 90017**
**Telephone: 213-624-4779 Fax: 213-624-5843**
**Members of Firm: Gregory Houlé; Tammy L. Sedin. Associates: Richard Houlé.**
**Public Entity Defense, Insurance Defense and Personal Injury Litigation.**

*See Professional Biographies, LOS ANGELES, CALIFORNIA*

**Houpt, James E.** '51 '92 C.147 B.A. L.309 J.D.
(adm. in VA; not adm. in CA) [▣ Baker&H.]
*PRACTICE AREAS: General Litigation; First Amendment; Freedom of Information.
**House, John L.** .......... '50 '84 C.845 B.A. L.846 J.D. [▣ Andrews&K.]
*LANGUAGES: French and Spanish.
*PRACTICE AREAS: Energy; Oil and Gas; Real Estate; Corporate.
House, Korey J. .......... '64 '90 C.112 B.A. L.1068 J.D. Dep. Fed. Pub. Def.
House, Lawrence P. .......... '56 '88 C.846 B.S. L.1137 J.D. 11859 Wilshire Blvd.
Housman, Ronald S. .......... '59 '85 C.112 B.A. L.809 J.D. 3530 Wilshire Blvd.
**Housman, Wendy M.** .......... '58 '85 C.112 B.A. L.990 J.D. [Chapman&G.]
*PRACTICE AREAS: Products Liability Law; Coverage; Commercial and Business Litigation; Labor Law; Construction Litigation.
Houston, Steve L. .......... '43 '70 C.802 B.A. L.426 J.D. Principal Dep. Co. Coun.
**Houston, Tom K.** .......... '45 '72 C.674 A.B. L.813 J.D. [▣ Carlsmith B.W.C.&I.]
*PRACTICE AREAS: Environmental; Administrative Law; Occupational Safety and Health; Municipal Law.
**Hovannisian, Armen K.** .......... '62 '87 C.112 B.A. L.1068 J.D. [▣ Chadbourne&P.]
Hovannisian, Raffi K. .......... '59 '85 C.112 A.B. L.276 J.D. 2029 Century Pk., E.
**Howald, Michael** .......... '56 '82 C&L.813 B.A., J.D. [Kinsella,B.F.&T.]
**Howald, Robin Bronzaft** .......... '60 '83 C.66 B.A. L.813 J.D. [▣ Chimicles,J.&T.]
*PRACTICE AREAS: Litigation.
**Howard, C. Stephen**, (AV) .......... '40 '69 C&L.976 B.A., LL.B. [Milbank,T.H.&M.]
Howard, Cecil W., Jr. .......... '61 '89 C.112 B.A. L.329 J.D. 3560 Hughes Way, #211
Howard, Edward P. .......... '63 '90 C.273 B.A. L.426 J.D. [▣ Hall&Assoc.]
Howard, Michael '47 '82 C.1097 B.A. L.1068 J.D.
Coun., Intl. Brotherhood of Elec. Wkrs., Local 18
**Howard, Nancy E.**, (AV) .......... '51 '77 C&L.813 B.A., J.D. [Tuttle&T.]
*PRACTICE AREAS: Partnership Taxation; Probate and Estate Planning.
**Howard, Roger H.**, (AV) .......... '44 '72 C&L.112 B.A., J.D. [Christensen,M.F.J.G.W.&S.]
*PRACTICE AREAS: Real Estate; Business Law.
Howard, Steven D. .......... '49 '75 C.112 B.A. L.809 J.D. 11661 San Vicente Blvd.
**Howarth, Don**, (AV) .......... '46 '72 C&L.309 B.A., J.D. [Howarth&S.]
*PRACTICE AREAS: Trial Practice; Antitrust Law; Products Liability Law.

**Howarth & Smith, (AV) ▣**
**Suite 2900, 700 South Flower Street, 90017**
**Telephone: 213-955-9400 Fax: 213-622-0791**
**Members of Firm: Don Howarth; Suzelle M. Smith; David K. Ringwood; Kenneth S. Tune; Brian D. Bubb;—Marcus J. Berger; Patricia Lee-Gulley; Thomas F. Vandenburg; Gregory S. Tamkin; Katy Jacobs; Sheila M. Bradley; Julia S. Swanson; Kimberly L. Honus; Randall Boese.**
**General Civil Practice. Litigation in all Courts.**

*See Professional Biographies, LOS ANGELES, CALIFORNIA*

**Howe, Lori A.** .......... '65 '90 C.1349 B.S. L.990 J.D. [▣ Trope&T.]
**Howell, Todd R.**, (AV) .......... '48 '73 C.112 B.A. L.61 J.D. [Tharpe&H.] (⊙Santa Maria)
*PRACTICE AREAS: General Casualty Defense; Coverage; Wrongful Termination; Contract Litigation; Sexual Harassment.
**Howell, Wesley G., Jr.**, (AV) '37 '66
C.878 B.S.E.E. L.178 LL.B. [Gibson,D.&C.] (⊙N.Y., NY)
**Howells, Dana D.** .......... '58 '82 C.846 B.A. L.1068 J.D. Sr. Coun., Capital Grp. Cos., Inc.
*RESPONSIBILITIES: Labor and Employment.
**Howes, Marlin E.** .......... '58 '88 C.1109 B.A. L.1049 J.D. [▣ Hornberger&C.]
*PRACTICE AREAS: Insurance Fraud; Environmental Law; Toxic Tort Law; Products Liability; Premises Liability.
Howitt, Ann .......... '58 '93 C.75 B.A. L.809 J.D. 1888 Century Park E.

**Howrey & Simon, (AV)**
**Suite 1400, 550 South Hope Street, 90071-2604⊙**
**Telephone: 213-892-1800 Fax: 213-892-2300**
**Members of Firm: Christopher A. Barnes; George W. Buehler; R. David Carlton; Joanne E. Caruso; David G. Meyer; Glenn E. Monroe (Not admitted in CA); Thomas J. Nolan; Richard S. Odom; Charles H. Samel; Elizabeth M. Weaver. Of Counsel: Nancy L. Boughton (Not admitted in CA). Resident Associates: John F. Brigden; Elizabeth A. Carroll; Kathryn M. Conway; Mary A. Denise; Donna Drake; Noah T. Fogelson; Dale J. Giali; Ann E. Grant; Steven C. Heller; Robert B. Humphreys; Bennet G. Kelley; Brian Sung Yun Kim; Joanne Lichtman; Christopher A. Mathews; Catherine Moore; Cheryl O'Connor Murphy; Georgia P. Saviola; John S. Schuster; Philip C. Tencer; Peter S. Veregge; Andrew E. Zirkelbach.**
**General and Trial Practice including Antitrust, Commercial Litigation, Corporate and Transactional, Environmental, Government Contracts, Insurance Coverage, Intellectual Property, International Trade, Products Liability, Securities Litigation, Supreme Court and Appellate and White Collar Criminal Defense.**
**Washington, D.C. Office: 1299 Pennsylvania Avenue, N.W., 20004-2402. Telephone: 202-783-0800. Fax: 202-383-6610.**
**Menlo Park, California Office: 301 Ravenswood Avenue, 94025. Telephone: 415-463-8100. Fax: 415-463-8400.**

*See Professional Biographies, LOS ANGELES, CALIFORNIA*

**Hoye, Brian M.** .......... '63 '88 C.112 A.B. L.800 J.D. [▣ Kaye,S.F.H.&H.]
*PRACTICE AREAS: Corporate Finance; Mergers and Acquisitions.
**Hoye, Maria P.** .......... '66 '91 C.1071 B.S. L.1068 J.D. [▣ Latham&W.]
*LANGUAGES: Spanish.
*PRACTICE AREAS: Environmental.
**Hsiao, Peter** .......... '60 '85 C.878 B.S. L.1066 J.D. [▣ McCutchen,D.B.&E.]
*REPORTED CASES: Gerritsen v. Consulado General De Mexico, 989 F. 2d 340 (9th Cir. Cal.) Mar. 30, 1993) (NO. 82-55226); Animal Lovers Volunteer Ass'n. Inc. v. Cheney, 795 F. Supp. 994 (C.D. Cal., Apr. 07, 1992) (No. CV 86-4992-RJK); Animal Lovers Volunteer Ass'n. Inc. v. Cheney, 795. Supp. 991 (C.D. Cal., Feb. 10, 1992); (NO. CV 86-4992-RJK); U.S. v. Montrose Chemical Corp. of California, 788 F. Supp. 1485, 35 ERC 1089, 22 Envtl. L. Rep. 21,333 (C.D. Cal., Mar. 31, 1992) (NO. CV 90-3122 AAH).
*PRACTICE AREAS: Environmental Litigation; NEPA/CEQA/Land-Use Planning.
**Hsieh, Amy** .......... '69 '94 C.112 B.A. L.767 J.D. [▣ Berger,K.S.M.F.S.&G.]
Hsieh, Louis T. .......... '64 '90 C.813 B.S. L.1066 J.D. 633 W. 5th St.
**Hsieh, Nancy C.**, (AV) .......... '62 '86 C.976 B.A. L.1066 J.D. [▣ Greenberg G.F.C.&M.]
*PRACTICE AREAS: Bankruptcy.
Hsieh, Richard W. .......... '48 '75 C.112 B.A. L.809 J.D. [R.W.Hsieh]
**Hsieh, Stewart** .......... '53 '88 C.1097 B.S. L.809 J.D. [Frye&H.]⊙
*PRACTICE AREAS: Business Transactions; Estate Planning; Probate; Corporations.
**Hsieh, Vincent I.S.** '64 '93 C.94 L.061 LL.B.
(adm. in NY; not adm. in CA) [▣ Buchalter,N.F.&Y.]
*LANGUAGES: Mandarin Chinese.
*PRACTICE AREAS: International Transactions; Corporate Practice.
Hsieh, Richard W., P.C. .......... 777 S. Figueroa St., 38th Fl.
**Hsu, Lillie** .......... '64 '92 C.309 A.B. L.813 J.D. [▣ Kaye,S.F.H.&H.]
**Hsu, Richard C.** .......... '67 '94 C.111 B.S. L.178 J.D. [▣ Lyon&L.]
*PRACTICE AREAS: Intellectual Property.
**Hsu, Victor** .......... '61 '87 C.674 A.B. L.976 J.D. [▣ Orrick,H.&S.]

**Hsu, William C.** ........................... '55 '83 C.112 B.A. L.1068 J.D. [Blecher&C.]
*PRACTICE AREAS: Antitrust; Intellectual Property.
Huang, Gail C. ..............'53 '92 C.112 B.A. L.1068 J.D. 777 S. Figueroa St., 10th Fl.
**Huang, Jade H.J.** ............. '69 '92 C.800 B.A. L.1066 J.D. Legal Coun., Guess ?, Inc.
*RESPONSIBILITIES: Intellectual Property.
Huang, Mark S. .......................'64 '90 C.367 B.A. L.800 J.D. 101 N. Brand Blvd.
**Huang, Patrick K.**, (AV) ..................'48 '75 C.112 B.A. L.1136 J.D. [Huang&M.]
*LANGUAGES: Cantonese Chinese.
*PRACTICE AREAS: Commercial Litigation; Arbitration; Mediation and Dispute Resolution in State and Federal Court; AAA and International Chamber of Commerce, Court of Arbitration, Paris, France; Commercial Transactions.
**Huang, Wendy W.** ....................'66 '93 C.188 B.A. L.94 J.D. [[A] Knapp,M.J.&D.]
*LANGUAGES: Mandarin Chinese and French.
*PRACTICE AREAS: Business Litigation; Public Agency Law.

**Huang & Mitchell, A Professional Law Corporation, (AV)**
**3250 Wilshire Boulevard Suite 1600, 90010**
**Telephone: 213-251-8199 Fax: 213-251-8188**
**Patrick K. Huang; Judith M. Mitchell. Of Counsel: Stephen S. Duplantis.**
**Languages: English, Cantonese Chinese, and German.**
**Commercial and Business Arbitration, Litigation, Mediation and Transactions; General Corporate Practice and International Arbitration.**
**References: Union Bank, Beverly Hills; First Interstate Bank, Catalina Branch.**
***See Professional Biographies, LOS ANGELES, CALIFORNIA***

Huard, David Leo ...........................'50 '76 C.770 B.A. L.276 J.D. 633 W. 5th St.
**Hubbard, Kristin** ......................'55 '83 C.813 B.A. L.800 [[C] Crosby,H.R.&M.]
Hubbard, Otis L. ............................'40 '69 C&L.861 B.A., J.D. Dep. Dist. Atty.
Hubbell, Richard C. ..........................'31 '59 C.112 A.B. L.1068 LL.B. Supr.Ct. J.
**Hubbell, Robert B.** ..........................'56 '81 C&L.426 B.A., J.D. [Heller E.W.&M.]
*PRACTICE AREAS: Professional Liability and Insurance Coverage Litigation.
Hubbs, Donald H. .......... '18 '57 C.36 B.A. L.809 J.D. Pres., Conrad N. Hilton Found.
Hubel, Gordon K. '48 '73 C.477 B.A. L.966 J.D.
Contract Admr., Southern Calif. Conference of Carpenters
**Huben, Brian D.** ..............................'62 '88 C&L.426 B.A., J.D. [[A] Robie&M.]
*PRACTICE AREAS: Commercial Litigation; Creditor Rights in Bankruptcy; Business Litigation; Banking.
**Huber, Birgit A.** .................... '62 '90 C.990 B.A. L.112 J.D. [[A] Sedgwick,D.M.&A.]
*LANGUAGES: German.
Huber, Terrance P. .......................................'43 '74 C&L.284 B.A., J.D. [T.P.Huber]
Huber, Terrance P., A Professional Corporation ............................9911 W. Pico Blvd.
**Hubert, Vanessa H.** ......................'59 '87 C.112 B.A. L.809 J.D. [[A] Gilbert,K.C.&J.]
**Hubsch, Allen W., Jr.** ..............................'64 '89 C.228 B.A. L.309 J.D. [[A] Dewey B.]
**Huchting, Stephen H.** .......... '48 '73 C&L.426 B.A., J.D. [Breidenbach,B.H.H.&H.]⊙
*PRACTICE AREAS: Arson and Insurance Fraud; First Party Property Insurance; Insurance Fraud; Property Insurance Coverage; Property Subrogation.
**Huddleston, Roxanna** ..................'56 '81 C&L.802 B.A.S., J.D. [[A] Hillsinger&C.]
*PRACTICE AREAS: Motions; Appeals.
Hudson, Dirk L. ...............................'37 '68 C.766 B.A. L.1066 J.D. Dep. Dist. Atty.
Hudson, Elbert T., (BV) ............ '20 '53 C.112 A.B. L.426 LL.B. 6500 Wilshire Blvd.
**Hudson, Jeffrey Reid** ........................'52 '78 C.154 B.A. L.309 J.D. [Gibson,D.&C.]
*PRACTICE AREAS: Finance; Banks and Banking; Mergers, Acquisitions and Divestitures; Debtor and Creditor.
**Hudson, Joseph B., Jr.** ...........................'39 '76 C.813 A.B. L.569 J.D. [Baker&H.]
*PRACTICE AREAS: Business.
Hudson, Paul C. '48 '74 C.112 B.A. L.1066 J.D.
Pres. & CEO, Broadway Fed. Svgs. & Loan Assn.
Hudson, Tighe F. ................................................... '49 '74 Sr. Dep. Co. Coun.
**Huebner, David** ............................'60 '89 C.674 A.B. L.976 J.D. [Coudert]
*LANGUAGES: Japanese and German.
Huebner, Harlan P., (AV) ............ '27 '58 C.800 B.S. L.809 J.D. [Huebner&R.] (Pat.)
**Huebner, Ted R.** ........................................ '50 '75 C.494 B.S. L.1068 J.D. [[A] Knee&M.]
*PRACTICE AREAS: Labor and Employment; Wrongful Termination; Employment Litigation; Employment Discrimination.
Huebner & Rosa, (AV) ................................................900 Wilshire Blvd. (Pat.)
**Hueckel, Donna L.** ............................'50 '81 C.668 B.A. L.800 J.D. [Sheppard,M.R.&H.]
Huerta, John E. .....'43 '70 C.1097 A.B. L.1066 J.D. Western Ctr. on Law & Poverty, Inc.
**Huestis, Carolyn M.** ......................'49 '75 C.112 B.A. L.426 J.D. [Pillsbury M.S.S.]
**Huestis, Samuel M.** .......................'54 '84 C&L.1137 B.S.L., J.D. [[A] Hewitt&P.]
Huey, Vanessa A. ...................'67 '93 C.112 B.A. L.339 J.D. 777 S. Figueroa St., 10th Fl.
**Huff, David M.** ..................................'67 '92 C.112 B.A. L.426 J.D. [Maguire&O.]
*PRACTICE AREAS: Construction Law; Business Litigation; Technology Litigation.
**Huff, R. Randall**, (AV) .......................'40 '70 C.101 B.A. L.228 J.D. [Gibson,D.&C.]
*PRACTICE AREAS: Litigation; Employment Law (Wrongful Discharge); Health Care; Fraud and Deceit; Unfair Competition.
**Hufstedler, Seth M.**, (AV) ............ '22 '50 C.800 B.A. L.813 LL.B. [[C] Morrison&F.]
*PRACTICE AREAS: Trial and Appellate Practice.
**Hufstedler, Shirley M.**, (AV) ........ '25 '50 C.560 B.B.A. L.813 LL.B. [[C] Morrison&F.]
*PRACTICE AREAS: Appellate Practice.
**Hugener, Janice Rourke** ........... '59 '86 C&L.426 B.A., J.D. [[A] Sedgwick,D.M.&A.]
Hughes, Irene Vera ...................................... '46 '77 L.1136 J.D. Pub. Def. Off.
**Hughes, James C.** ......................'54 '83 C.724 B.A. L.426 J.D. [Whitman B.A.&M.]
*PRACTICE AREAS: Real Estate; Commercial Real Estate Development; Shopping Center Development; Residential Real Estate Development; Land Use.
Hughes, Justin ....................'60 '87 C.604 B.A. L.309 J.D. 11355 W. Olympic Blvd.
**Hughes, Kevin D.** '68 '93 C.477 B.A. L.178 J.D.
(adm. in MD; not adm. in CA) [[A] Chadbourne&P.]
Hughes, Michael S. ..............'64 '89 C.976 B.A. L.309 J.D. 11355 W. Olympic Blvd.

**Hughes, Sharon Coverly, (AV) '51 '86 C.1097 B.A. L.1148 J.D.**
**12100 Wilshire Boulevard, Suite 945, 90025**
**Telephone: 310-442-7622 FAX: 310-442-9923**
**Business, Commercial and Bankruptcy Law.**
***See Professional Biographies, LOS ANGELES, CALIFORNIA***

**Hughes, Timothy J.** ..................'51 '78 C.426 B.A. L.1065 J.D. [[C] Daniels,B.&F.]
*LANGUAGES: Spanish.
*PRACTICE AREAS: Real Estate; Business Law.
Hughes, Wendy Marshall ....... '57 '86 C.801 B.A. L.1068 J.D. 11355 W. Olympic Blvd.

**Hughes Hubbard & Reed LLP, (AV)** [BB]
**350 South Grand Avenue, Suite 3600, 90071-3442⊙**
**Telephone: 213-613-2800 Telecopier: 213-613-2950**
**Resident Partners: Charles Avrith; William T. Bisset; John A. Blue; Richard S. Friedman; George A. Furst; Rita M. Haeusler; Richard J. Kaplan; Peter M. Langenberg; Theodore H. Latty; Charles D. Schoor; Daniel H. Slate; Mark R. Moskowitz; John R. Zebrowski. Special Counsel: Andrea H. Bricker; Randy B. Holman. Of Counsel: Howard F. Hart. Resident Associates: Howard M. Appel; Michael P. Barbee; Kimber K. Bell; Randy G. Gerchick; Noah Graff (Not admitted in CA); Erin M. Hausladen; Lois C. Jacobs Moonitz; David J. Shladovsky.**
**General Practice.**
**New York, New York Office: One Battery Park Plaza, 10004. Telephone: 212-837-6000. Telex: 427120. Telecopier: 212-422-4726.**
**Miami, Florida Office: 201 South Biscayne Boulevard, Suite 2500, 33131-4332. Telephone: 305-358-1666. Fax: 305-371-8759. Telex: 518785.**
**Paris, France Office: 47, Avenue Georges Mandel, 75116. Telephone: 33 (0)1 44 05 80 00. Telecopier: 33 (0)1 45 53 15 04.**

(This Listing Continued)

**Hughes Hubbard & Reed LLP (Continued)**
**Washington, D.C. Office: 1300 I Street, N.W., Suite 900 West, 20005. Telephone: 202-408-3600. Telex: 89-2674. Telecopier: 202-408-3636.**
***See Professional Biographies, LOS ANGELES, CALIFORNIA***

Hugstad, Vicki J. ......................'53 '85 C.494 B.A. L.976 J.D. Arthur Andersen & Co.
Huguenin, Edward R. ...................'68 '94 C.689 B.A. L.990 J.D. 444 S. Flower St.
**Hulett, Mary** ...............................'42 '77 C.813 B.A. L.273 J.D. [Daniels,B.&F.]
*PRACTICE AREAS: Trial and Appellate Law; Products Liability; Business; Wrongful Termination; Employment Discrimination.
**Hull, Christine A.** ..............................'68 '95 C.855 B.A. L.809 J.D. [[A] Morris,P.&P.]
Hull, Diane L. ..........................'58 '83 C&L.900 B.A., J.D. 11661 San Vicente Blvd.
**Hull, Jack D.** .......................................'51 '80 C.112 B.A. L.1095 J.D. [Goldsmith&B.]
*PRACTICE AREAS: Insurance Defense; Insurance Coverage; Professional Malpractice; Arbitration; Construction Defects.
**Hull, Robert Joe**, (AV) ......................'44 '69 C&L.846 B.A., J.D. [Sheppard,M.R.&H.]
*PRACTICE AREAS: Taxation Law; Partnership Law; Corporate Law.
**Hull, Susan Bade** .....................'63 '91 C.154 B.A. L.426 J.D. [Alvarado,S.V.&S.]
*PRACTICE AREAS: Environmental Law; Land Use Law.
Hullinger, Danny D. ...............'36 '77 C.267 B.A. L.1026 J.D. State Comp. Ins. Fund
Hulse, Sharon K. ....................'57 '90 C.1097 B.A. L.426 J.D. 2999 Overland Ave.
Hum, Craig William .......................'58 '86 C.1109 B.A. L.813 J.D. Dep. Dist. Atty.
**Humiston, Carol Ann** .........................'54 '84 C.1075 B.S. L.426 J.D. [Morris,P.&P.]
**Humiston, David M.**, (AV) ........'54 '79 C.112 B.A. L.1065 J.D. [Sedgwick,D.M.&A.]
**Hummel, Chad S.** ..............................'63 '88 C.309 B.A. L.145 J.D. [Gibson,D.&C.]
*PRACTICE AREAS: White Collar Crime; Litigation; Antitrust and Trade Regulation.
**Hummer, Laurence L.** ...................'51 '80 C.813 B.A. L.1068 J.D. [Freeman,F.&S.]
*PRACTICE AREAS: Civil; Business; Real Estate Litigation.
**Hummer, Maria D., (P.C.)**, (AV) ........'44 '76 C.773 B.A. L.1068 J.D. [Manatt,P.&P.]
*PRACTICE AREAS: Land Use; Administrative Law.
Humphrey, Theodore J. '69 '94 C.276 B.A. L.893 J.D.
(adm. in VA; not adm. in CA) Pinetree Entertainment, Inc.
**Humphreys, Daphne M.** ...........................'— '94 C.025 B.A. L.809 J.D. [[A] Bergman&W.]
*PRACTICE AREAS: Complex Litigation.
**Humphreys, Robert B.** ........................'68 '93 C.174 B.A. L.276 J.D. [[A] Howrey&S.]
*PRACTICE AREAS: White Collar Criminal Defense; Complex Civil Litigation.
**Humphries, Robin J.** .......'56 '84 C.112 B.A. L.800 J.D. [Weiss&H.] (⊙Newport Beach)
*PRACTICE AREAS: Corporate Law; Health Care Law.
**Hundley, Paul B.** ....................'61 '94 C.766 B.A. L.112 J.D. [[A] Breidenbach,B.H.H.&H.]
**Hung, Francis Curtis, Jr.** ...................'62 '91 C.800 B.S. L.1067 J.D. [[A] Epport&R.]
*PRACTICE AREAS: Creditors Rights Law; Bankruptcy; Commercial Litigation.
Hung, Maan-Huei (Ms.), Law Offices of ..........'47 '78 L.061 LL.B. 1055 Wilshire Blvd.
**Hungate, Richard**, (AV) ..................'09 '38 C.911 A.B. L.813 LL.B. [[C] Leopold,P.&S.]
*PRACTICE AREAS: Entertainment; Civil Litigation; Copyright and Trademark; Libel and Slander; Unfair Competition.
Hungerford, Rex S., Jr. ....................'48 '74 C.976 B.A. L.1068 J.D. 221 N. Figueroa St.
**Hunnius, Patrick O.** ..............................'69 '94 C&L.846 B.A., J.D. [[A] Irell&M.]
**Hunt, Derek W.** ..........................................'43 '72 C&L.188 A.B., J.D. [Troy&G.]
*PRACTICE AREAS: Securities Litigation; Business Litigation; Real Estate Litigation.
**Hunt, Diana J.** .........................'62 '93 C.112 B.A. L.426 J.D. [[A] Andrews&K.]
*PRACTICE AREAS: Litigation; Bankruptcy.
**Hunt, Donald L.** .......................................'49 '74 C.378 B.A. L.145 J.D. [Fulbright&J.]
*PRACTICE AREAS: Banks and Banking; Public Finance; Corporate Law.
**Hunt, Gio** .................................'66 '90 C.112 B.A. L.309 J.D. [[A] Blanc W.J.&K.]
*LANGUAGES: Spanish.
*PRACTICE AREAS: Corporate; Taxation; Proprietary Rights Law; Computers.
**Hunt, James W.** ...........................................'44 '76 C.1021 B.A. L.776 J.D. [Mendes&M.]
Hunt, Richard G. ....................'52 '79 C.763 B.S. L.426 J.D. 9200 Sunset Blvd., 3rd Fl.
Hunt, Steven D. .......................................'65 '92 C.147 B.A. L.423 J.D. [[A] R.G.Reinjohn]

**Hunt, Ortmann, Blasco, Palffy & Rossell, Inc.**
**(See Pasadena)**

**Hunter, Andrew R.** ....................... '61 '86 C.112 B.A. L.767 J.D. [[C] Jeffer,M.B.&M.]
*PRACTICE AREAS: Business; Construction and Real Estate Litigation.
Hunter, Anne L. .............................................'47 '88 C.813 B.A. L.809 J.D. Dep. Atty. Gen.
**Hunter, Craig C.** ..............................'46 '76 C.675 B.A. L.464 J.D. [[A] Zelle&L.]
*PRACTICE AREAS: Litigation; Securities; Insurance Coverage Litigation.
**Hunter, Edward O.**, (AV) .......... '47 '74 C.878 B.A. L.273 J.D. [[C] LeBoeuf,L.G.&M.]
*PRACTICE AREAS: Litigation; Product Liability.
**Hunter, Harold J., Jr.**, (AV) ..................... '33 '61 C&L.813 B.A., J.D. [Kirtland&P.]
**Hunter, James K. T.** ..................'51 '76 C.1275 B.A. L.309 J.D. [[C] Pachulski,S.Z.&Y.]
Hunter, Jesse W., Jr. ..............................'26 '69 C.302 B.S. L.809 J.D. 5326 Inadale Ave.‡
**Hunter, Larry D.**, (AV⊙) ................'50 '75 C.352 B.S. L.477 J.D. Hughes Aircraft Co.
**Hunter, M. Reed** ..............................'32 '61 C.101 B.S. L.878 J.D. [Crosby,H.R.&M.]
*PRACTICE AREAS: Appellate Expert in Land Use and Condemnation Law.
Hunter, Norma B. ....................................'35 '63 C&L.1097 B.A., B.A. 4700 Wilshire Blvd.
Huntington, John M. ..........................'31 '58 C.1032 B.A. L.813 J.D. Sr. Asst. Atty. Gen.
Huntoon, Martin T. ....................................'32 '66 C.112 L.1114 LL.B. 523 W. 6th St.
**Huo, Sunny S.** .....................'70 '95 C.112 B.A. L.1067 J.D. [[A] R.I.Fine&Assoc.]
*LANGUAGES: Mandarin Chinese.
*PRACTICE AREAS: Litigation; Antitrust; Government; Business; Class Actions.
**Hupe, Robert M.** ..............................'64 '89 C.112 B.S. L.893 J.D. [[A] Lane P.S.L.]
*PRACTICE AREAS: General Litigation; Toxic Torts; Products Liability.
Hupp, Harry L. ........................................'29 '56 C&L.813 A.B., LL.B. U.S. Dist. J.
**Hurewitz, Phalen G.**, (AV) ...............'36 '62 C.197 A.B. L.813 LL.B. [Manatt,P.&P.]
*PRACTICE AREAS: Entertainment Law.

**Hurey, Michael '62 '88 C.1075 B.S. L.426 J.D.**
**11679 Montana Avenue, Suite 10, 90049**
**Telephone: 310-471-3273 Fax: 310-471-5898**
**Intellectual Property Law, Patent, Trademark, Copyright and related Litigation.**
***See Professional Biographies, LOS ANGELES, CALIFORNIA***

Hurley, Andrew L. .......................'68 '93 C.112 B.A. L.1068 J.D. 444 S. Flower St.
Hurney, John W. .......................'66 '92 C.550 B.A. L.990 J.D. 801 S. Grand Ave.
**Huron, Jeffrey G.** ..........................'— '88 C.436 B.A. L.464 J.D. [Huron,Z.&K.]
*PRACTICE AREAS: Business; Real Estate; Lender Liability; Commercial Litigation.

**Huron, Zieve & Kierstead LLP**
**1901 Avenue of the Stars Eighteenth Floor, 90067⊙**
**Telephone: 310-284-3400 Fax: 310-772-0037**
**Members of Firm: Les Zieve; Jeffrey G. Huron.**
**Real Estate, Representation of Financial Institutions, Bankruptcy, Insurance Bad Faith Litigation, Business Litigation and Commercial Litigaton in State and Federal Courts.**
**Portland, Oregon Office: 1001 S.W. Fifth Avenue, Suite 1100, 97204. Telephone: 503-294-7075.**
***See Professional Biographies, LOS ANGELES, CALIFORNIA***

**Hurrell, Thomas C.** ......'60 '85 C.112 B.A. L.930 J.D. [Hillsinger&C.] (⊙Santa Barbara)
Hursh, Randal W. .........................'52 '81 C.136 B.F.A. L.1148 J.D. 2330 W. Third St.
Hurst, Jeffrey S. ..........................................'— '88 C&L.112 B.A., J.D. 725 S. Figueroa St.
Hurst, Walter E. ..................'30 '53 C.563 B.B.A. L.569 LL.B. 6253 Hollywood Blvd.
**Hurst, Wesley D.** ..............................'59 '87 C.112 B.A. L.284 J.D. [Folger L.&K.]⊙
Hurt, Arthur C., Jr., (AV) .............................'09 '33 C&L.813 A.B. 5867 W. 6th St.

CAA253P

**Hurwitz, David I.** '63 '88 C.659 B.A. L.145 J.D.
(adm. in IL; not adm. in CA) [🄲 O'Melveny&M.]
*PRACTICE AREAS: Commercial Trial and Appellate Practice; Class Action Litigation.
**Hurwitz, Mark D.** ........................'67 '90 C.112 B.S. L.1068 J.D. [🄱 Levy,S.&L.]
*PRACTICE AREAS: Business and Commercial Litigation.
Huryn, Marianna O. ..................... '63 '88 C.178 A.B. L.188 J.D. 333 S. Grand Ave.
**Husar, Linda S.** ........................ '55 '80 C.94 B.S. L.426 J.D. [Thelen,M.J.&B.]
*PRACTICE AREAS: Labor and Employment Law.
**Husdon, Ronald D.** .................. '53 '85 C&L.05 B.Comm., LL.B. [Kelley D.&W.]
*PRACTICE AREAS: Commercial Law; Joint Ventures; Mergers and Acquisitions.
**Huskey, Steven C.** .................. '64 '89 C.178 B.A. L.800 J.D. [🄱 Epport&R.]
*PRACTICE AREAS: Real Property and Banking Transactions; Bankruptcy; Litigation.
**Huskins, Louis A., (P.C.),** (AV) ................'43 '68 C.855 B.A. L.145 J.D. [Irell&M.]
Huss, William W. ..............................'32 '65 C&L.800 B.S., J.D. Ret. Supr. Ct. J.
**Hussey, John D.,** (AV) ...........'35 '61 C.668 B.A. L.1066 LL.B. [Sheppard,M.R.&H.]
*PRACTICE AREAS: Corporate Law; Securities Regulation Law; Venture Capital Law.
**Huston, J. Randolph** ...................'41 '67 C.276 A.B. L.800 J.D. [Walker,W.T.&W.]
*PRACTICE AREAS: Litigation; General Business Practice.
**Huston, Robert W.** .....................'68 '93 C.602 B.B.A. L.1049 J.D. [🄱 Booth,M.&S.]
Hutchinson, Daniel P. ........................ '48 '75 C.36 B.A. L.37 J.D. Univ. of Calif.
Hutchinson, David E. ........................................... '61 '90 Panorama Films
**Hutchinson, G. Calvin** .................'38 '88 C.119 B.S. L.1137 J.D. [🄱 Schaffer&L.]
Hutchinson, Gov ........ '57 '83 C.674 A.B. L.659 J.D. Sr. Coun., Calif. Assn. of Realtors
Hutchinson, Richard L. ........................'53 '80 C.976 B.A. L.800 J.D. University Park
**Hutchinson, Thomas H.** ................'54 '86 C.1131 B.A. L.426 J.D. [🄱 Grace,S.C.&S.]
*PRACTICE AREAS: Insurance Defense Law; Product Liability Law.
Huth, Patsy D. ................... '38 '83 C&L.999 B.A., J.D. Frank D. Lanterman Reg. Ctr.
Hutson, Robert ..........................................'19 '62 L.809 LL.B. 5020 Parklgen Ave.
**Hutt, Laurence J.,** (AV) ....................'50 '75 C.659 B.A. L.813 J.D. [Arnold&P.]
*PRACTICE AREAS: Real Estate and Banking Litigation; Sports Litigation; Commercial Litigation.
Huttenbrauck, Gail Eleanor ..................'44 '78 C.1102 B.A. L.809 J.D. Dep. Dist. Atty.
**Hutter, James R.,** (AV) ..................... '24 '51 C.112 B.S. L.813 J.D. [🄲 Gibson,D.&C.]
Hutton, Andrew D. ...........................'65 '91 C.378 B.A., B.S. L.494 J.D. 633 W. 5th St.
**Hwang, Catherine C.** ............................ '— '95 C.112 B.A. L.178 J.D. [🄱 Kirkland&E.]
*PRACTICE AREAS: Litigation; Intellectual Property.
**Hwang, Lee D.** .........................................'69 '93 C.197 A.B. L.309 J.D. [🄱 Latham&W.]
Hyatt, Clifford C. '58 '89 C.262 B.A. L.273 J.D.
(adm. in NY; not adm. in CA) S.E.C.
**Hyde, Daniel V.,** (AV) ...........................'47 '74 C.629 B.A. L.1065 J.D. [Knapp,M.J.&D.]
*LANGUAGES: German.
*PRACTICE AREAS: Trials and Appeals; Construction Law; Environmental Law; Public Entity Law.
Hydinger, David J. ........... '51 '90 C.848 B.A. L.809 J.D. Corp. Coun., Mission Ins. Co.
Hyer, Paul F. ....................................'35 '72 C.472 B.A. L.1095 J.D. 3921 Wilshire Blvd.

**Hyman, Andrew W., (AV) '53 '78 C.112 B.A. L.426 J.D.**
**15821 Ventura Boulevard, Suite 225 (Encino), 91436-2915**
**Telephone: 818-907-5200 Fax: 818-380-3387**
***PRACTICE AREAS: Business Law; Business Litigation; Commercial Law; Corporate Law; Creditors Rights.**
**Business Transactional Law including Business and General Civil Litigation Practice in all Courts.**

Hyman, Ansley Q. ....................................... '32 '64 C.112 B.A. L.809 J.D. 601 W. 5th St.
**Hyman, Eric S.** ..... '48 '79 C.800 B.S.E.E. L.1137 J.D. [Blakely,S.T.&Z.] (See Pat. Sect.)
**Hyman, Milton B., (P.C.),** (AV) ......................'41 '67 C.112 B.A. L.309 J.D. [Irell&M.]
**Hyman, Ursula H.** .......................................'51 '83 C.342 B.A. L.800 J.D. [Latham&W.]
*PRACTICE AREAS: Public Finance; FEMA; Public Entity/District Workouts.
**Hymanson, Marsha** .......................'46 '89 C&L.800 B.A., J.D. [🄱 Munger,T.&O.]
Hyun, Karen S. '62 '92 C.966 B.A. L.494 J.D.
(adm. in PA; not adm. in CA) Ogilvy & Mather
**Iaffaldano, Frank W.** .................'64 '89 C&L.597 B.A., J.D. [🄱 Sheppard,M.R.&H.]
*PRACTICE AREAS: Real Estate Law; Secured Transactions.
**Iancu, Andrei** ..........................'68 '96 C.112 B.S.A.E. L.1068 J.D. [🄱 Lyon&L.]
*LANGUAGES: Romanian.
*PRACTICE AREAS: Patents; Trademarks; Copyrights; Intellectual Property.
Iannucci, Salvatore J., Jr. ...................'27 '52 C.569 B.A. L.309 J.D. 255 Woodruff Ave.
Ibañez, Tania M. ..................'63 '89 C.1036 B.A. L.1068 J.D. 1900 Ave. of the Stars
**Ibekwe, Edebeatu C.** ..........................................'54 '83 C.473 A.B. L.1068 J.D. [Irell&M.]
Ibisi, Eric O. ............................'61 '86 C.1158 B.A. L.990 J.D. 3500 S. Figueroa St.
**Ibold, Charles R., Jr.,** (AV) ..........................................'35 '65 C.973 L.426 LL.B. [Ibold&A.]
**Ibold, James M.** ..................................... '64 '92 C.1109 B.A. L.276 J.D. [Ibold&A.]

**Ibold & Anderson, A Professional Corporation, (AV)**
**Paramount Plaza, 16th Floor, 3580 Wilshire Boulevard, 90010**
**Telephone: 213-380-7330 Fax: 213-380-5788**
**Charles R. Ibold, Jr.; Leslie G. Anderson; Michael I. Douglas; Marla Kelly; Michael J. Garey; Aurora Vasquez; Ann Therese Canfield; James M. Ibold; Robert E. Robinson; Jeffrey Hammill; William A. Hinz; Darryl N. Purks. Of Counsel: E. Bruce Thompson.**
**General Civil, Criminal and Trial Practice in all State and Federal Courts. Insurance, Workers Compensation, Corporation, Commercial, Real Property, Personal Injury, Family, Trust and Probate Law.**
**Reference: National Bank of California.**
***See Professional Biographies, LOS ANGELES, CALIFORNIA***

**Ichiho, Akemi** ...................'— '73 C.1097 B.A. L.426 J.D. Sr. Coun., Bank of Amer.
Ickowicz, Terry A., (AV) ..............'55 '80 C.800 B.S. L.1095 J.D. 2049 Century Park, E.
**Ickowitz, Allan H.** ........................ '51 '75 C&L.178 B.A., J.D. [Nossaman,G.K.&E.]
*PRACTICE AREAS: Debt Workout and Bankruptcy; Business Litigation; Real Estate Litigation.
**Idell, Edward** ........................................'55 '81 C.1350 B.A. L.472 J.D. [🄱 D.B.Bloom]
*LANGUAGES: Hebrew.
Ideman, James M. ................................ '31 '64 C.152 A.B. L.800 J.D. U.S. Dist. J.
Iglow, Lawrence I. ................................'46 '74 C.339 B.S. L.1049 J.D. [Iglow&B.]
Iglow, Robert A. ..................................'49 '74 C.112 B.A. L.1049 J.D. [Iglow&B.]
Iglow & Bachrach ..................................................... 1515 N. Crescent Heights Blvd.
**Ignatin, Gary R.** ...............................'68 '93 C.674 B.S.E. L.659 J.D. [🄱 Latham&W.]
**Iino, John Masao** ............................'62 '87 C.668 B.A. L.800 J.D. [🄲 Gibson,D.&C.]
*LANGUAGES: Japanese.
*PRACTICE AREAS: International Business; Corporate Law; Corporate Finance.
**Ikari, Ken** .......................................'64 '90 C.112 B.A. L.309 J.D. [🄱 Sullivan&C.]
**Ikuta, Sandra Segal** ..........................'54 '91 C.112 B.A. L.1068 J.D. [O'Melveny&M.]
*PRACTICE AREAS: Real Estate Law; Natural Resources and Environmental Law.
**Iler, Anthony T.** .......................................'60 '86 C.154 B.A. L.1066 J.D. [Irell&M.]
Illouz, Yael ................................................'64 '90 L.061 J.D. 2029 Century Pk. E.
**Im, Yongjin** ....... '66 '92 C.309 B.A. L.145 J.D. [🄱 O'Melveny&M.] (⊙New York, N.Y.)
*PRACTICE AREAS: General Corporate.
Imahara, Kathryn K. '61 '89 C&L.800 A.B., J.D.
Asian Pacific Amer. Legal Ctr. of Southern Calif.

**Imerman, Stanley C., (AV) '39 '66 C&L.813 B.A., LL.B.**
**1901 Avenue of the Stars, Suite 1100, 90067**
**Telephone: 310-553-5572 Fax: 310-277-7947**
***PRACTICE AREAS: General Civil Practice; Business; Commercial Litigation; Business Transactions.**

(This Listing Continued)

**Imerman, Stanley C. (Continued)**
**Corporations, Partnerships, Real Estate, Estate Planning, Probate and Business and Civil Litigation in all Federal and State Courts.**
***See Professional Biographies, LOS ANGELES, CALIFORNIA***

Imfeld, Michael D. ................. '50 '77 C.608 B.A. L.1065 J.D. 18425 Burbank Blvd
**Imhof, Peter T.** .................. '69 '95 C.674 B.A. L.1068 J.D. [🄱 Hancock R.&B.]
*LANGUAGES: German, French.
**Imhoff, Earl J., Jr.,** (AV) ...............'50 '79 C.602 B.A. L.966 J.D. [Hancock R.&B.]
Imhoff, Ronald Bruce ........... '49 '87 C.813 B.A. L.1068 J.D. 12350 W. Olympic Blvd.
**Immel, Melissa A.** ...................'63 '88 C.112 B.A. L.426 J.D. [🄱 Iverson,Y.P.&H.]
*PRACTICE AREAS: Products Liability; Employment Law; Civil Litigation; Appellate Practice.
**Immerman, William J.,** (AV) ..............'37 '64 C.966 B.S. L.813 J.D. [🄲 Kenoff&M.]
*PRACTICE AREAS: Entertainment Law.
**Immordino, John J.** ................ '52 '80 C.1077 B.A. L.809 J.D. [🄱 Anderson,M.&C.]
*PRACTICE AREAS: Surety; Construction Litigation; Commercial Litigation; Real Estate Litigation; Insurance Defense.
**Impastato, David J.** '63 '92 C.112 B.A. L.178 J.D.
(adm. in NY; not adm. in CA) [🄱 Milbank,T.H.&M.]
*LANGUAGES: Japanese.
**Imre, Christina J.,** (AV) ....................'50 '80 C.525 B.A. L.426 J.D. [Horvitz&L.]
Imrich, Ian J. ..............................'64 '90 C.112 B.A. L.950 J.D. 10850 Wilshire Blvd.
**Inamine, Brian S.** ........................ '56 '85 C.312 B.A. L.800 J.D. [🄱 Wright,R.O.&T.]
*PRACTICE AREAS: Insurance Coverage Law; Products Liability Law.
**Infelise, Robert D.** ......................'55 '80 C.112 A.B. L.1066 J.D. [Cox,C.&N.]
*REPORTED CASES: Resolution Trust Corp. v. Rossmoor Corp., 34 Cal. App. 4th 93 (1995).
*PRACTICE AREAS: Environmental Law; Civil Litigation.
Inferrera, John M. .......................................'50 '75 C.1036 B.A. L.426 J.D. [Royce&I.]
**Ingalls, Melissa D.** ...................... '68 '94 C.659 B.A. L.209 J.D. [🄱 Kirkland&E.]
*PRACTICE AREAS: Litigation.

**Ingber, Jeffrey C., (AV) '44 '70 C.401 B.A. L.976 LL.B.**
**1801 Century Park East, Suite 2400, 90067**
**Telephone: 310-552-1047**
***PRACTICE AREAS: Entertainment Law.**
**Entertainment Law.**
***See Professional Biographies, LOS ANGELES, CALIFORNIA***

Ingber, Joe, (AV) ........................... '30 '61 C.1043 B.A. L.1068 J.D. 205 S. Bway.
Ingber, Kenneth ............................... '69 '95 C.390 A.B. L.472 J.D. [Herman&W.]
**Ingham, Samuel D., III**
**(See Beverly Hills)**
**Inglin, Sonja A.** ........................ '54 '79 C.112 B.A. L.1066 J.D. [🄱 Rodi,P.P.G.&C.]
**Inglis, Michael K.,** (AV) ................'40 '67 C.112 A.B. L.1068 LL.B. [Inglis,L.&G.]
*PRACTICE AREAS: Mergers and Acquisitions Law; Corporate Law.

**Inglis, Ledbetter & Gower, (AV) BB**
**500 South Grand Avenue, 18th Floor, 90071-2612**
**Telephone: 213-627-6800 Facsimile: 213-622-2857**
**Members of Firm: Michael K. Inglis; Steven K. Ledbetter; Richard S. Gower; Richard G. Ritchie; Gregory H. Gocke; John E. Hope. Associates: Timothy E. Kearns; James W. Holchin; Nancy B. Gonzalez.**
**General Business and Commercial Law, Civil Trial and Appellate Practice, Insurance Defense, Probate and Estate Planning, Tax Law.**
**Representative Clients: Barnes-Dyer; Brehm Communications, Inc.; Inter-Insurance Exchange of the Automobile Club of Southern California; Presto Food Products, Inc.; Prudential Property and Casualty Insurance Co.; Safariland Ltd., Inc.; Cecil Saydah Co.**
***See Professional Biographies, LOS ANGELES, CALIFORNIA***

Ingram, Mark A. ..............'55 '80 C.940 B.A. L.990 J.D. Assoc. Coun., Coast Fed. Bk.
**Ingram, Thomas A., Jr.** ............'54 '88 C.999 B.A. L.990 J.D. [🄱 Negele&Assoc.]
*REPORTED CASES: Charter Point Homeowners Association v. Superior Court (1992) 6 Cal. App. 4th 1167.
*PRACTICE AREAS: Commercial Construction Litigation; Complex Multi-party Litigation; Land Subsidence; Insurance Litigation; Construction Law.
**Inguanzo, Ana M.** ................... '63 '89 C.800 B.A. L.1068 J.D. [🅂 Fulbright&J.]
*PRACTICE AREAS: Litigation.
Injejikian, Avo G. ....................'61 '87 C.112 B.A. L.1066 J.D. State Comp. Ins. Fund
Injeyan, Maral ............................'58 '87 C.112 B.A. L.809 J.D. 3600 Wilshire Blvd.
**Inlow, Laura S.** ................................. '62 '87 C&L.893 B.A., J.D. [Lewis,D.B.&B.]
**Inman, Steinberg, Nye & Stone, APC**
**(See Beverly Hills)**
**Innabi, Abdalla J.** ......................'67 '94 C.112 B.A. L.1252 J.D. [🄱 Yukevich&S.]
*LANGUAGES: Arabic.
Inoue, K. Anne ................................'61 '88 C.112 B.A. L.426 J.D. [Mink&M.]
**Inouye, Lawrence G.,** (AV) ...................'55 '81 C.800 B.S. L.770 J.D. [Shiotani&I.]
*PRACTICE AREAS: Corporate Law; Real Estate; Taxation; Estate Planning.
**Insel, Steven J.** ............................'54 '79 C.188 B.S. L.659 J.D. [Jeffer,M.B.&M.]
*PRACTICE AREAS: Broker-Dealer; Investment Adviser; Corporate Securities.
**Inskeep, James W.** ..................'61 '90 C.339 B.S. L.30 J.D. [Oppenheimer P.S.] (Pat.)
*PRACTICE AREAS: Intellectual Property; Medical Devices.
International Law et al
402 W. Bdwy., Ste. 1850 (⊙Los Angeles, Ca., London, England)
**Iorillo, Mario A.,** (AV) ................'39 '65 C.188 B.A. L.309 LL.B. [🄱 Tuverson&H.]
*PRACTICE AREAS: Insurance Defense; Bad Faith Defense; Personal Injury Defense; Automobile Liability; Automobile Law.
Irby, Gwendolyn L. '54 '80 C&L.800 B.A., J.D.
V.P., Legal Affs., Motown Record Corp.
**Iredale, Nancy L., (P.C.),** (AV) ........ '47 '73 C.276 B.S.F.S. L.976 J.D. [Paul,H.J.&W.]
**Irell, Lawrence E.,** (AV) .................. '12 '35 C.112 B.A. L.800 LL.B. [🄲 Irell&M.]

**Irell & Manella LLP, (AV) BB**
**A Law Partnership including Professional Corporations**
**Suite 900, 1800 Avenue of the Stars (Century City), 90067-4276⊙**
**Telephone: 310-277-1010 Cable Address: "Irella LSA" Telecopier: 310-203-7199**
**URL: http://www.irell.com**
**Members of Firm: Eugene M. Berger (1892-1944); Allan J. Abshez; James N. Adler (P.C.); Scott D. Baskin (P.C.) (Resident at Newport Beach); Cary J. A. Berger (Downtown Los Angeles Office); Richard L. Bernacchi (P.C.); Sheri A. Bluebond (Downtown Los Angeles Office); Richard H. Borow (P.C.); Derrick O. Boston; Christine W. S. Byrd; Frank A. Caput (Resident at Newport Beach); Louis M. Castruccio (P.C.); Daniel G. Christopher; Morgan Chu; Richard de Bodo; David A. Dull; James F. Elliott; Michael G. Ermer (Resident at Newport Beach); Dorette S. Feit; John C. Fossum (P.C.) (Resident at Newport Beach); Elliot G. Freier; Paul N. Frimmer (P.C.); Gary N. Frischling; Roy S. Geiger (Downtown Los Angeles Office); Martin N. Gelfand; Andra Barmash Greene (Resident at Newport Beach); Peter J. Gregora; Andrew W. Gross; Theodore E. Guth; Kenneth R. Heitz; Catherine H. Helm; Brian J. Hennigan (Downtown Los Angeles Office); Louis A. Huskins (P.C.); Milton B. Hyman (P.C.); Edebeatu C. Ibekwe (Downtown Los Angeles Office); Anthony T. Iler (Downtown Los Angeles Office); Thomas W. Johnson, Jr. (Resident at Newport Beach); Sandra Gerson Kanengiser; Edmund M. Kaufman (P.C.) (Downtown Los Angeles Office); Kyle S. Kawakami (Resident at Newport Beach); J. Christopher Kennedy (Downtown Los Angeles Office); Bruce D. Kuyper; Henry Lesser (Downtown Los Angeles Office); Joan L. Lesser (P.C.); Ronald M. Loeb (P.C.); Steven A. Marenberg; C. Kevin McGeehan; Richard J. McNeil (Resident at Newport Beach); Ashok W. Mukhey; Layn R. Phillips (Resident at Newport Beach); Anthony W. Pierotti (Resident at Newport Beach); S. Thomas Pollack; Joel Rabinovitz (P.C.); Susan Sakai; Lois J. Scali; Alvin G. Segel; Marvin S. Shapiro (P.C.); Richard M. Sherman, Jr.,(P.C.) (Resident at Newport Beach); Henry Shields, Jr., (P.C.); David Siegel;**

(This Listing Continued)

**Irell & Manella LLP (Continued)**

**Steven P. Sim; Steven L. Sloca; Gregory R. Smith; Howard J. Steinberg (Downtown Los Angeles Office); Jonathan H. Steinberg; Robert Steinberg; Steven E. Thomas; Ronald B. Tischler (P.C.); Bruce A. Wessel; Alexander F. Wiles; Richard C. Wirthlin (Downtown Los Angeles Office); Werner F. Wolfen (P.C.); Rob C. Zeitinger; Edward Zeldow. Of Counsel: Charles A. Collier, Jr.; John J. Cost (P.C.) (Downtown Los Angeles Office); Lawrence E. Irell; Thomas A. Kirschbaum; Arthur Manella (P.C.); David Nimmer; Alvaro Pascotto; Steven H. Shiffrin; Robert W. Stedman (P.C.) (Resident at Newport Beach); Lawrence M. Stone (P.C.) (Certified Specialist, Taxation Law, The State Bar of California Board of Legal Specialization); William D. Warren (Not admitted in CA). Associates: Jeffrey L. Arrington; Spencer E. Bendell; Richard M. Birnholz; Elliot N. Brown; André J. Brunel; Elizabeth A. Camacho; Nancy J. Cohen; Leigh Taylor Combs (Resident at Newport Beach); Graham L. W. Day; Jerald B. Dotson; Charles E. Elder; Scott M. Epstein; Marc A. Fenster; Kevin L. Finch; Robert J. Flachs; Joseph M. Freeman; Melissa R. Gleiberman; Darren J. Gold; Perry M. Goldberg; Philip J. Graves; Michael Grizzi (Downtown Los Angeles Office); Craig A. Grossman; Benjamin Hattenbach; Stephanie Kaufman Hernand; John W. Holcomb (Downtown Los Angeles Office); Steven W. Hopkins (Resident at Newport Beach); Patrick O. Hunnius; Peter M. Juzwiak (Downtown Los Angeles Office); Jonathan S. Kagan; Gregory B. Klein; Michael Krakovsky; Brian D. Ledahl; Richard Ung-Jin Lee (Downtown Los Angeles Office); Daniel P. Lefler; Francine J. Lipman (Resident at Newport Beach); Joseph M. Lipner; Wen Liu; Michael S. Lowe; Samuel Kai Lu; Marc S. Maister (Resident at Newport Beach); Benjamin R. Martin; Jennifer E. Meier; Roman Melnik; Philip H. Miller; Harry A. Mittleman; Joanna Moore; David Z. Moss; Maurine M. Murtagh; John M. Nakashima (Resident at Newport Beach); Ben D. Orlanski (Downtown Los Angeles Office); Elizabeth K. Penfil (Resident at Newport Beach); David J. Richter; Flavio Rose; David J. Rosmann; Kathryn Schaefer; David A. Schwarz; Alan D. Sege; Laura A. Seigle; Jeffrey N. Shapiro; Gail J. Standish; Ethan G. Stone; Douglas K. Sugimoto; Mary-Christine (M.C.) Sungaila (Resident at Newport Beach); Sana Swe; Craig Varnen; Eric A. Webber (Downtown Los Angeles Office); Toni Weinstein; Jessica Weisel; Ian C. Wiener; Wendy A. Wolf; Christopher F. Wong; Juliette Youngblood.**

**General Civil Practice and Litigation in all State and Federal Courts and Arbitration Tribunals, Administrative, Antitrust, Aviation, Computer, Corporate, Corporate Securities and Finance, Mergers and Acquisitions, Election and Redistricting, Entertainment, Estate Planning, Trusts and Probate, Federal, State and Local Taxation, First Amendment and Media, International Business and Taxation, Insolvency, Bankruptcy, Reorganization and Creditors Rights, Insurance, Labor Relations, Wrongful Termination and Discrimination, Pension and Profit Sharing, Real Estate, Real Estate Finance, Banking and Secured Transactions Law. Patent, Trademark and Copyright Law. Intellectual Property and Trade Secrets. High Technology Litigation, including Intellectual Property, Trade Secrets and Unfair Competition Litigation. Selected Criminal Defense.**

**Downtown Los Angeles Office: Suite 3300, 333 South Hope Street, 90071-3042. Telephone: 213-620-1555. Telecopier: 213-229-0515.**

**Newport Beach, California Office: Suite 500, 840 Newport Center Drive, 92660-6324. Telephone: 714-760-0991. Telecopier: 714-760-5200.**

*See Professional Biographies, LOS ANGELES, CALIFORNIA*

**Irey, James W.** ....................'64 '91 C.1094 B.S. L.1065 J.D. [Ⓐ White O.C.&A.]
*PRACTICE AREAS: General Commercial Litigation.

Irey, Stephanie S. ..............'65 '90 C.684 B.A. L.1065 J.D. 777 Figueroa St., 44th Fl.

**Iriarte-Abdo, Maria** ..............'60 '90 C.111 B.A. L.426 J.D. [Ⓐ Nordstrom,S.N.&J.]
*LANGUAGES: Spanish.
*PRACTICE AREAS: Plaintiffs Personal Injury.

**Irion, Joan K.**, (AV) ....................'53 '79 C.112 B.A. L.1067 J.D. [Heller E.W.&M.]
*PRACTICE AREAS: State and Local Taxation; Federal and State Tax Controversy.

Irmas, Sydney M., (AV) ..............'25 '55 C.112 B.S. L.800 J.D. 595 S. Mapleton Dr.‡

**Irons, John H., Jr.** ..............'61 '87 C.112 B.A. L.1068 J.D. [Ⓐ Pircher,N.&M.]
*PRACTICE AREAS: Real Estate Law and Finance.

**Irsfeld, Irsfeld & Younger LLP**
(See Glendale)

Irvin, Christopher J. ..........................'53 '78 C.112 B.A. L.61 J.D. [McLean&I.]

**Irvin, Diane A.** ....................'64 '90 C.112 B.A. L.990 J.D. [Ⓐ Jones,B.S.A.&F.]

Irvin, Robert G., (AV) ..............'21 '48 C.112 A.B. L.800 LL.B. 1612 W. Pico Blvd.

**Irvin, William B.**, (AV) ....................'18 '49 C.112 B.A. L.813 J.D. [McLaughlin&I.]

**Irvine, Douglas R.** ....................'60 '85 C.668 B.A. L.770 J.D. [Lewis,D.B.&B.]

**Irvine, Mark R.** ....................'63 '88 C.112 B.A. L.464 J.D. [Ⓐ Mendes&M.]

**Irving, Jeanne E.** ....................'53 '78 C.93 B.A. L.309 J.D. [Hennigan,M.&B.]
*PRACTICE AREAS: Securities Litigation; Complex Litigation; Accountants' Liability Litigation.

**Irving, Michael W. '59 '92 C.112 B.A. L.426 J.D.**
**1801 Century Park East, Suite 2500, 90067**
**Telephone: 310-284-3420 Fax: 310-277-1278**
***PRACTICE AREAS: Copyright Law (35%); Appellate Practice (30%); Guardianship Law (20%); Collections (15%).**
**Business Litigation, Appellate Law, Contracts, Collections, Enforcement of Judgements.**

*See Professional Biographies, LOS ANGELES, CALIFORNIA*

Irving, Paul D. ..........................'57 '82 C.30 B.S. L.1148 J.D. 810 S. Spring St.‡

**Irving, Paul H.** ....................'52 '80 C.569 B.F.A. L.426 J.D. [Manatt,P.&P.]
*PRACTICE AREAS: Banking; Corporate Finance; Entertainment and Media.

Irwin, Helen ..........................'— '84 C.129 B.S. L.978 J.D. 11740 Montana Ave.

**Irwin, James A.**, (AV) ....................'33 '63 C.112 A.B. L.1066 LL.B. [Irwin&R.]
*PRACTICE AREAS: Aviation; Products Liability; General Civil Practice; Trial Practice.

**Irwin, Michael J.** ....................'46 '78 C.846 B.A. L.809 J.D. [Roper&F.]
*PRACTICE AREAS: Products Liability Law; Tort Law; Legal Malpractice Law; Subrogation Law; Real Estate Errors and Omissions.

**Irwin, Philip D.**, (AV) ....................'33 '58 C.972 B.A. L.813 LL.B. [O'Melveny&M.]

**Irwin & Reily, (AV)**
**Suite 2040, 911 Wilshire Boulevard, 90017**
**Telephone: 213-624-3671 Fax: 213-688-7489**
**James A. Irwin; David H. Reily; Janine K. Jeffery. Associates: Paul R. Ayers.**
**Aviation, Products Liability, General Civil and Trial Practice.**

*See Professional Biographies, LOS ANGELES, CALIFORNIA*

**Irwin, Sandra McMahan**
(See Pasadena)

**Isaac, Godfrey**, (AV) ....................'25 '52 C.800 L.426 J.D. [Beck,D.D.B.&O.]
*PRACTICE AREAS: Trial Practice; Medical Law; White Collar Law; Criminal Defense Law; Wrongful Termination/Employment at Will.

**Isaacman, Kaufman & Painter**
(See Beverly Hills)

Isaacs, Bruce Alan, (AV) ..............'56 '81 C.668 B.A. L.426 J.D. [Wyman,I.B.&L.]

Isaacs, Jeffrey B. ..........................'60 '85 C.165 A.B. L.800 J.D. Asst. U.S. Atty.

Isaacson, Lon B. ..........................'49 '75 C.399 B.A. L.112 J.D. 2500 Wilshire Blvd.

**Isaacson, Marc R.**, (AV) ....................'45 '72 C&L.145 B.A., J.D. [Gibson,D.&C.]
*PRACTICE AREAS: Estate Planning; Trust and Estate Administration; Charitable Organizations.

Isaacson, Richard I. '64 '90 C.188 B.S. L.659 J.D.
(adm. in NY; not adm. in CA) V.P. & Gen. Mgr., Loud Records

**Isen, John M.** ..........................'48 '73 C.112 B.A. L.37 J.D. [Isen&G.]

**Isen, Julian C.**, (AV) ....................'17 '42 C.113 B.A. L.800 J.D. [Ⓒ Isen&G.]

**Isen and Grant, Incorporated, (AV)**
**10517 Santa Monica Boulevard, 90025**
**Telephone: 213-879-0303; 310-474-6504 Fax: 310-474-7234**
**Jay H. Grant (Certified Specialist, Taxation Law, The State Bar of California Board of Legal Specialization); John M. Isen;—Marc A. Bronstein. Of Counsel: Julian C. Isen.**
**Family Planning, Tax, Trust and Probate Law, Corporation, Real Property, Business.**

**Isenberg, Daniel** ..............'45 '70 C.1077 B.A. L.1065 J.D. Sr. Coun., Bank of Amer.

**Isenberg, Lawrence M.** ..............'58 '88 C.1044 B.A. L.809 J.D. [Ⓐ Gibson,D.&C.]

**Iser, Lawrence Y.** ..............'55 '80 C.477 B.A. L.1065 J.D. [Greenberg G.F.C.&M.]
*PRACTICE AREAS: Entertainment Litigation; Intellectual Property Law and Litigation; Real Estate Litigation; Business Litigation.

Ishikawa, Richard M. ..........................'49 '80 C.768 B.S. L.426 J.D. 555 W. 5th St.

**Ishimatsu, Bruce L.** ....................'52 '79 C.668 B.A. L.276 J.D. [Bryan C.]
*PRACTICE AREAS: Antitrust Law; Dealer and Distributor Termination; Litigation; International.

**Isken, J. Eric** ....................'52 '77 C.112 B.A. L.1065 J.D. [Graham&J.]
*PRACTICE AREAS: Litigation.

Iskyan, Tami A. ..............'59 '89 C.605 B.A. L.464 J.D. 11859 Wilshire Blvd.

**Isler, Curtiss L.**, (AVⓉ) ..............'45 '75 C.473 B.A. L.608 J.D. [Arter&H.] (ⓒIrvine)

Ison, Timothy M. ..............'60 '85 C.477 A.B. L.597 J.D. 601 S. Figueroa St.

**Israel, Eric P., (A Professional Corporation)** '59 '87
C.112 B.A. L.809 J.D. [Danning,G.D.&K.]

**Israel, Mark R.** ..............'62 '86 C.645 B.A. L.1068 J.D. [Daniels,B.&F.]⊙
*PRACTICE AREAS: Trial and Appellate Law; Insurance.

Israel, Mervyn R., (AV) ..............'35 '62 C.112 B.A. L.1065 J.D. [Israel&B.]

**Israel, Peter O.**, (AV) ..............'43 '72 C.112 B.A. L.426 J.D. [Ⓐ D.B.Bloom]

**Israel, Samuel** ..............'57 '82 C.1044 B.S. L.1068 J.D. [Cohen P.&F.]

Israel & Benezra, (AV) ..........................1545 Wilshire Blvd.

**Issacs, Asher D.** ..............'68 '95 C.165 B.A. L.1068 J.D. [Ⓐ McCutchen,D.B.&E.]
*PRACTICE AREAS: Business Litigation.

**Issagholian, Rita H.** ..............'63 '92 C.1077 B.A. L.809 J.D. [Ⓐ Selman B.]
*LANGUAGES: French, Armenian, Farsi, Spanish, Italian.
*PRACTICE AREAS: Insurance Coverage; Insurance Litigation; Insurance Bad Faith; Intellectual Property Litigation.

**Issler, Paul S.** ..............'60 '86 C.1077 B.S. L.800 J.D. [Gibson,D.&C.]
*PRACTICE AREAS: Corporate and Partnership Taxation; Tax aspects of Corporate and Partnership Formations; Mergers, Acquisitions, Dispositions; Reorganizations and Financings; Real Estate Investment Trusts.

Itatani, Elizabeth S. '— '79
C.800 A.B. L.426 J.D. Claims Atty., Auto. Club of Southern Calif.

**Itkin, Robbin L.**, (AV) ..............'59 '84 C.112 B.A. L.800 J.D. [Wynne S.I.]

Ito, Lance Allan ..............'50 '75 C.112 B.A. L.1066 J.D. Supr. Ct. J.

Ito, Patricia Masuye ..............'53 '81 C.112 A.B. L.1068 J.D. 11611 San Vicente Blvd.

**Ito, Ronald W.** ..............'60 '86 C.112 A.B. L.1065 J.D. [Ⓐ Wilson,K.&B.]

**Iungerich, Russell**, (AV) ..............'42 '69 C.154 B.A. L.1066 J.D. [R.Iungerich]
*PRACTICE AREAS: Administrative Law; Appellate Practice; Civil Trial; White Collar Criminal Defense; International Extradition.

**Iungerich, Russell, A Professional Law Corporation, (AV)**
**3580 Wilshire Boulevard, Suite 1920, 90010**
**Telephone: 213-382-8600 Fax: 213-382-5057**
**Email: riplc@ix.netcom.com**
**Russell Iungerich; Paul Spackman.**
**Appellate Practice. Civil and Criminal Trial Practice in all State and Federal Courts. Administrative, Constitutional and Criminal Law. International Practice.**

*See Professional Biographies, LOS ANGELES, CALIFORNIA*

**Ivanjack, Larry G., (P.C.)**, (AV) ..........'49 '75 C.112 B.A. L.1068 J.D. [Ivanjack&L.]
*REPORTED CASES: Bank of America National Trust and Savings Association v. Sanati, 11 Cal.App.4th 1079 (1992).

**Ivanjack & Lambirth, (AV) BR**
**A Partnership including Professional Corporations**
**12301 Wilshire Boulevard, Suite 600, 90025-1000⊙**
**Telephone: 310-820-7211 Telecopier: 310-820-0687**
**Email: ivanjack@AOL.com**
**Larry G. Ivanjack (P.C.); Timothy A. Lambirth (P.C.); Thomas E. Shuck (P.C.); Kathryn B. Milstead;—Joseph H. Lowther; Elise A. Ross; Gary Tokumori; Mary G. Lee. Of Counsel: Robert F. Nichols, Jr.; Camilla N. Andrews.**
**General Civil Trial and Appellate Practice in all State and Federal Courts, Commercial, Banking and Financial Institutions, Real Estate, Secured Transactions, Equipment Leasing, Creditors' Rights and Bankruptcy, Transactional Documentation, Operational and Regulatory Compliance Advice, Business and Construction.**
**Representative Clients: Bank of America; Citibank N.A.; Union Bank of California, N.A.; Sanwa Bank California; Great Western Bank; Imperial Bank; First Republic Thrift and Loan; General Electric Capital Corp.; Fleet Credit Corp.; Western Bank.**
**Irvine, California Office: 5 Park Plaza, Suite 800. 92614. Telephone: 714-475-4477. Telecopier: 714-475-4475.**

*See Professional Biographies, LOS ANGELES, CALIFORNIA*

**Ivener, Mark A.**, (AV) ....................'42 '68 C.339 B.A. L.1068 J.D. [M.A.Ivener]

**Ivener, Mark A., A Law Corporation, (AV) BR**
**11601 Wilshire Boulevard, Suite 1430, 90025**
**Telephone: 310-477-3000 Fax: 310-477-2652**
**Email: mark@ivener.com URL: http://www.ilw.com/ivener**
**Mark A. Ivener.**
**Practice Limited to Immigration and Nationality Law including Entertainment Related Matters.**
**Canadian Associate Office: 1300-808 Nelson Street, Vancouver, British Columbia V6Z 2H2. Telephone: 604-688-0558. FAX: 604-685-8972.**
**Japanese Associate Office: 13th Floor Urbannet Otemachi Building, 2-2-2 Otemachi, Chiyoda-Ku, Tokyo 100, Japan. Telephone: 813-3231-8888. Fax: 813-3231-8881.**

*See Professional Biographies, LOS ANGELES, CALIFORNIA*

**Iverson, Yoakum, Papiano & Hatch, (AV) BR**
**One Wilshire Building, 27th Floor 624 South Grand Avenue, 90017**
**Telephone: 213-624-7444 Telecopier: 213 629-4563**
**Paul E. Iverson (1907-1975); Frank B. Yoakum, Jr. (1906-1991). Members of Firm: Neil Papiano; Dennis A. Page; Patrick M. Mc Adam; Arnold D. Larson; John M. Garrick. Associates: Douglas C. Pease; Andrew K. Doty; Melissa A. Immel; Mary P. Lightfoot; Barbara Lee Berkowitz; Mark Pearson; Frederick Brevard Hayes; Gioia M. Fasi; Denise Renee Byrnes. Of Counsel: R. Noel Hatch.**
**General Civil Trial and Appellate Practice in State and Federal Courts including Corporation and Securities Law. Antitrust, Administrative, Insurance and Product Liability Law, Labor, Real Property, Entertainment, Commercial Tax and Municipal Law. Estate Planning, Probate and Trust Law, Wrongful Termination, Employment Discrimination and Construction Litigation.**
**Representative Clients: Lockheed Corp.; International Paper; Bridgestone/Firestone, Inc.**
**Reference: Security Pacific National Bank (Los Angeles Head Office).**

*See Professional Biographies, LOS ANGELES, CALIFORNIA*

**Ives, Kirwan & Dibble, A Professional Corporation, (AV)**
**The Biltmore Court, Fourth Floor, 520 South Grand Avenue, 90071⊙**
**Telephone: 213-627-0113 FAX: 213-627-1545**
**Eugene S. Ives (1903-1972); Darwin L. Dibble (1923-1990); Martin J. Kirwan (Retired from Firm); Thomas P. Minehan (Resident, Ventura-Santa Barbara Office); James M. McFaul (Resident, Ventura-Santa Barbara Office); Stephen A. Bost; Jerry E. McLinn (Resident, Ventura-Santa Barbara Office); Roger Erik Marken; Charles R. Diaz; Steven B. Kotulak; Neil D. Joseph; Joseph M. Walsh, Jr.; Keith M. Shishido; Christopher Grivakes; Steven S. Marken (Resident, Orange County Office); Jasmin A. Velarde.**
**Major Insurance Company Clients: American Mutual Insurance Co.; Utica Mutual Insurance Co.**
**Ventura-Santa Barbara Office: 5210 Carpinteria Avenue, P.O. Box 360, Carpinteria, California. Telephone: 805-684-7641. FAX: 805-684-9649.**
**Orange-San Diego County Office: 101 Pacifica, Suite 250, Irvine, California. Telephone: 714-450-8900. FAX: 714-450-8908.**
**San Bernardino-Riverside Office: 777 Tahquitz Way, Suite 23, Palm Springs, California. Telephone: 619-778-2611. FAX: 619-778-2612.**

*See Professional Biographies, LOS ANGELES, CALIFORNIA*

**Ivey, Robert L.**, (AV) ..........'41 '67 C.198 B.A. L.893 LL.B. [Whitman B.A.&M.]
*PRACTICE AREAS: Construction Litigation; Business Litigation.
**Ivey, Thomas J.** ..........'67 '93 C.112 B.A. L.1066 J.D. [A Skadden,A.S.M.&F.]
**Ivie, Charles C.**, (AV) ..........'47 '71 C.880 B.A. L.145 J.D. [Gibson,D.&C.]
Ivie, Rickey ..........'51 '77 C&L.112 B.A., J.D. [Ivie,M.&W.]
Ivie, McNeill & Wyatt, A Professional Law Corporation
201 North Figueroa Street, Suite 810
Iwanaga, S. Maya ..........'64 '90 C.112 B.A. L.1065 J.D. 333 S. Grand Ave.
**Iwanaga, Yuji** ..........'41 '84 L.1066 LL.M. [Pillsbury M.&S.]
**Iwasaki, Bruce Gen** ..........'51 '77 C.112 B.A. L.1068 J.D. [A O'Melveny&M.]
**Iwasaki, Robert Y.**, (AV) ..........'22 '52 C.930 B.A. L.365 J.D. [Iwasaki&S.]
*LANGUAGES: Japanese.
*PRACTICE AREAS: General Practice; International Business.

**Iwasaki & Sheffield, A Professional Association, (AV)**
**Not a Partnership**
**Fourth Floor, 420 Boyd Street, 90013**
**Telephone: 213-626-6462 Telecopier: 213-626-8203**
**Robert Y. Iwasaki; Chaney M. Sheffield; Koichi M. Yanagizawa; John F. Butcher.**
**International, Corporate, Immigration Business and Real Estate Law. Personal Injury, Probate, Estate Planning and Entertainment Law. General Civil and Trial Practice in all State and Federal Courts.**
**Reference: Kyowa Bank of California.**
*See Professional Biographies, LOS ANGELES, CALIFORNIA*

**Izenstark, Susan R.** ..........'52 '79 C.112 B.A. L.61 J.D. [A Oldman&C.]
*PRACTICE AREAS: Probate and Trust; Litigation; Conservatorships; Guardianships.
**Izuel, Leeanna** ..........'67 '91 C.112 B.A. L.1068 J.D. [A Gibson,D.&C.]
*PRACTICE AREAS: Securities; Mergers, Acquisitions and Divestitures.
**Jabkowski, Susan**, (BV) ..........'50 '75 C.112 B.A. L.809 J.D. [A Hinojosa&K.]
*PRACTICE AREAS: Probate; Conservatorship; Guardianship.
**Jablon, Barry P.**, (AV) ..........'40 '78 C.178 B.A. L.1066 J.D. [Cox,C.&N.]
*REPORTED CASES: %italic; Laborers Clean-Up Contract Administration Trust Fund v. Uriarte Clean-Up Service, Inc. %roman; , 736 F.2d 516, 9th Cir., 1984; %italic; Mattel, Inc. v. Hyatt %roman.
*PRACTICE AREAS: Real Property Law; Civil Litigation.
Jaburian, Shant ..........'66 '96 C.1077 B.S. L.1190 J.D. 3530 Wilshire Blvd.
Jacinto, Ruben A. ..........'37 '70 C.1097 B.A. L.809 5221 E. Beverly Blvd.
**Jack, J. Michael** ..........'— '86 C.1077 B.S. L.276 J.D. [A Morgan,L.&B.]
**Jack, Travis R.** ..........'52 '79 C.112 A.B. L.1065 J.D. [Didak&J.]
*PRACTICE AREAS: Insurance Coverage and Defense; Bad Faith; Real Estate; Suretyship.
**Jackoway, James R.** ..........'52 '78 C.610 B.A. L.976 J.D. [Armstrong H.J.T.&W.]
*PRACTICE AREAS: Entertainment.
Jackoway, Robin ..........'52 '80 C.610 B.S.C. L.184 J.D. Coun., Premium Collection Serv.
**Jacks, Bradley W.** ..........'58 '83 C.575 B.A. L.494 J.D. [A Cotkin&C.]
*PRACTICE AREAS: Professional Liability; Personal Injury; Insurance Coverage Litigation; Commercial Litigation.
**Jackson, Bryan C.** ..........'55 '87 C&L.101 B.A., J.D. [A Sonnenschein N.&R.]
*LANGUAGES: Portuguese.
*PRACTICE AREAS: Construction Litigation; Construction Contracts; Real Estate Litigation.
**Jackson, Christina E.** ..........'69 '94 C.1021 B.A. L.472 J.D. [A O'Neill,H.&A.]
*REPORTED CASES: People v. Ricciardi, 23 Cal.2d 390 (1943); People v. Superior Court, 145 Cal.App.2d 683 (1956); People v. Faus, 48 Cal.2d 672 (1957); Redevelopment Agency v. Gilmore, 38 Cal.3d 790 (1985); Gasser v. United States, 14 Cl.Ct. 476 (1988).
*PRACTICE AREAS: Eminent Domain; Direct and Inverse Condemnation; Land Use; Assessment Tax and Appeals; General Civil and Trial Practice.
**Jackson, G. Michael** ..........'56 '85 C.549 B.S. L.61 J.D. [A R.P.Slates]
*LANGUAGES: Spanish.
*PRACTICE AREAS: Bankruptcy; Business Litigation; Creditors Rights; Commercial Transfers; Commercial Litigation.
**Jackson, Gabrielle M.** ..........'61 '93 C.767 B.S. L.112 J.D. [A Robie&M.]
*PRACTICE AREAS: Civil Litigation.
Jackson, James M. '43 '68 C&L.546 B.A., J.D.
V.P. & Dep. Gen. Coun., Transamerica Occidental Life Ins. Co.
Jackson, Janet Crawford ..........'57 '83 C.800 B.A. L.629 J.D. Dep. City Atty.
**Jackson, Laurence D.**, (AV) ..........'55 '78 C.352 B.S. L.145 J.D. [Christa&J.]
*PRACTICE AREAS: Litigation.
Jackson, Martin T. ..........'46 '77 C.112 B.A. L.1148 J.D. 611 Wilshire Blvd.
Jackson, Murray ..........'28 '53 C.102 L.569 LL.B. 3700 Wilshire Blvd.
Jackson, Richard A. ..........'51 '76 C.339 B.S. L.597 J.D. 633 W. 5th St.
**Jackson, Samuel G., Jr.**, (AV) ..........'44 '70 C.31 B.A. L.178 J.D. [Jackson&L.]
*PRACTICE AREAS: Employment Law; Discrimination; Sexual Harassment; Products Liability; Environmental Law.
**Jackson, Shauna D.** ..........'— '91 C&L.813 A.B., J.D. [A Katten M.&Z.]
**Jackson, Theodore Warren** '52 '77
C.188 B.A. L.309 J.D. Sr. Corp. Coun., Hughes Aircraft Co.
Jackson, Virgil W., Jr. ..........'37 '71 C.1097 B.S. L.809 J.D. 3580 Wilshire Blvd.
**Jackson, William Howard** ..........'64 '90 C&L.813 B.A., J.D. [A Pircher,N.&M.]
*PRACTICE AREAS: Real Estate Law; Sports; Entertainment; Multimedia.

**Jackson & Lewis, (AV)**
**11400 West Olympic Boulevard, Suite 600, 90064**
**Telephone: 310-473-3100 Fax: 310-473-1720**
**Members of Firm: Samuel G. Jackson, Jr.; James W. Lewis; JoAnn Ellen Victor; Julie Yeh. Of Counsel: David S. Cunningham, III.**
**General Civil Litigation in State and Federal Courts, Trials and Appeals, Employment (wrongful termination, discrimination and harassment based on sex, ethnicity, age and disability), Environmental Law, including hazardous wastes and property damage claims, Professional Liability and Toxic Torts, Litigation including multi party "mega litigation," Personal Injury, Products Liability, Eminent Domain and Inverse Condemnation, Real Property Litigation.**
*See Professional Biographies, LOS ANGELES, CALIFORNIA*

**Jackson, Lewis, Schnitzler & Krupman, (AV)**
**1888 Century Park East Suite 1600, 90067⊙**
**Telephone: 310-203-0200 Facsimile: 310-203-0391**
**Members of Firm: David S. Allen (Resident); Mark R. Attwood; G. Harrison Darby (Not admitted in CA); Robert J. Giovannetti; Lawrence H. Stone. Of Counsel: Emily R. Boyle; David G. Freedman. Associates: Elizabeth Platte Johnson; Frank M. Liberatore; Anne-Marie P. Piibe; Marisa S. Ratinoff; Andrew L. Weiss; C. Craig Woo.**
**Labor Relations, Employment Discrimination, Wrongful Discharge and Other Employment-Related Litigation, Employee Benefits and Pension Law, Wage and Hour, OSHA, Immigration Law, Public Sector and State Labor Relations Law On Behalf of Management.**
**Other offices located in: Atlanta, Georgia; Boston, Massachusetts; Chicago, Illinois; Dallas, Texas; Greenville, South Carolina; Hartford, Connecticut; Larkspur, California; Miami, Florida; Morristown, New Jersey; New York, New York; Orlando, Florida; Pittsburgh, Pennsylvania; San Francisco, California; Stamford, Connecticut; Washington, D.C.; White Plains, New York; Woodbury, New York.**
*See Professional Biographies, LOS ANGELES, CALIFORNIA*

Jackson & Wallace, (AV) ..........2040 Ave. of the Stars (⊙San Francisco)
Jacob, Warren C. ..........'56 '83 C.963 B.S. L.800 J.D. [Jacob&P.]
Jacob & Pardo ..........1545 Wilshire Blvd., Ste. 800
**Jacobberger, Jeffrey M.** ..........'64 '89 C.276 A.B. L.1066 J.D. [Troop M.S.&P.]
*PRACTICE AREAS: Government Contracts; Insurance Coverage.
Jacobovitz, Victor ..........'47 '75 C.1077 B.A. L.809 J.D. 6255 Sunset Blvd.
**Jacobowitz, Marc E.** ..........'58 '82 C.1044 B.S. L.1068 J.D. [C Davis W.T.]
Jacobs, Andrew ..........'53 '78 C.112 B.A. L.426 J.D. 3530 Wilshire Blvd.
Jacobs, Carl P. ..........'50 '75 C.978 B.A. L.464 J.D. 6255 Sunset Blvd.
**Jacobs, Christina M.** ..........'50 '78 C.112 B.A. L.425 J.D. [C Ross,S.&G.]
*PRACTICE AREAS: Estate, Trust and Conservatorship Litigation; Business Litigation.
**Jacobs, David** ..........'— '77 C.112 B.A. L.569 J.D. [Epstein B.&G.]
**Jacobs, Gary N.**, (AV) ..........'45 '70 C.1036 B.A. L.976 LL.B. [Christensen,M.F.J.G.W.&S.]
*PRACTICE AREAS: Corporate; Securities; General Business Law.
**Jacobs, Gary S.**, (AV) ..........'35 '61 C.112 B.S. L.1068 J.D. [Levinson,M.J.&P.]
*PRACTICE AREAS: Family Law.
**Jacobs, Howard L.** ..........'66 '90 C.259 B.S. L.945 J.D. [A Sands N.F.L.&L.]
Jacobs, James David ..........'41 '72 C.1097 B.A. L.426 J.D. Dep. Dist. Atty.
Jacobs, John D ..........'61 '88 C.352 B.B.A. L.1068 J.D. Fed. Trade Comm.
**Jacobs, Katy** ..........'65 '94 C.330 B.A. L.769 J.D. [A Howarth&S.]
*PRACTICE AREAS: Trial Practice; Complex and Multi District Litigation; Products Liability; Federal Indian Law; Tribal Law.
Jacobs, Lawrence '11 '48 C.025 B.Com. L.209 J.D.
(adm. in IL; not adm. in CA) 617 1/2 N. Plymouth Blvd.‡
**Jacobs, Lisa** ..........'65 '90 C.477 B.A. L.425 J.D. [Kinkle,R.&S.]
**Jacobs, Marc Paul** ..........'48 '73 C.1077 B.S. L.800 J.D. [King,W.E.&B.]
**Jacobs, Micah R.** ..........'64 '94 C.112 B.A. L.1066 J.D. [A McCutchen,D.B.&E.]
*PRACTICE AREAS: General and Commercial Litigation.
Jacobs, Mitchell A. ..........'55 '81 C.1044 B.A. L.61 J.D. 815 Moraga Dr.
Jacobs, Paul A. ..........'41 '67 C.112 B.A. L.426 J.D. 5020 Sunset Blvd.
Jacobs, Randall Brian ..........'51 '78 C.335 B.A. L.1136 J.D. 522 S. Sepulveda Blvd.
Jacobs, Rex W., (AV) ..........'48 '73 C.112 B.A. L.904 J.D. [J.S.Matthew] (⊙Pasadena)
Jacobs, Robert N. ..........'55 '81 C.602 B.A. L.705 J.D. 12240 Venice Blvd.
**Jacobs, Robin L** ..........'69 '95 C.896 B.A. L.990 J.D. [A Ropers,M.K.&B.]
*PRACTICE AREAS: Litigation.
**Jacobs, Scott H.**, (AV) ..........'48 '78 C.1019 B.A. L.809 J.D. [Katz,H.S.&K.]
*REPORTED CASES: Datatronic Systems Corp. v. Speron, Inc. 176 Cal. App. 3d 1168 (1986).
*PRACTICE AREAS: Business Litigation; Bankruptcy; Debtor/Creditor Relations; Labor Law.
**Jacobs, Scott P.** ..........'60 '88 C.494 B.A. L.309 J.D. [A Shearman&S.]
**Jacobsen, Chris Steven** ..........'57 '81 C.426 B.A. L.1068 J.D. [C Brobeck,P.&H.]
*PRACTICE AREAS: General Corporate Law; Financial Services Law.
**Jacobsmeyer, Kristen L.** ..........'69 '95 C.112 B.A. L.1068 J.D. [A Greenberg G.F.C.&M.]
*PRACTICE AREAS: Litigation.
**Jacobson, Alan D.**, (AV) ..........'40 '65 C.188 A.B. L.976 LL.B. [Shapiro,R.&C.]
*PRACTICE AREAS: Corporate Law; Mergers and Acquisitions.
**Jacobson, David D.** ..........'55 '87 C.493 B.A. L.45 J.D. [A Seyfarth,S.F.&G.]
*PRACTICE AREAS: Litigation.
Jacobson, Eric '50 '78 C.331 A.B, L.564 J.D.
(adm. in NY; not adm. in CA) Sr. Gen. Atty., Capital Cities/ABC, Inc.
Jacobson, Eric S. ..........'52 '77 C.33 B.A. L.800 J.D. 3580 Wilshire Blvd.
Jacobson, Jerry A. ..........'66 '92 C.1077 B.S. L.1148 J.D. 10866 Wilshire Blvd.
**Jacobson, Lawrence M.** '56 '81
C.112 A.B. L.1068 J.D. [Baker&J.] & [C Glickfeld,F.&J.]
*PRACTICE AREAS: Bankruptcy Law; Commercial Litigation; Business Litigation; Creditors' Rights.
Jacobson, Robert D. ..........'61 '88 C.112 B.A. L.809 J.D. Ste. 600, 5757 Wilshire Blvd.
Jacobson, Ronald (Jake) '48 '73
C.800 B.A. L.1068 J.D. V.P., Bus. Affs., Paramount Pictures Corp.
Jacobson, Ruthe G. ..........'16 '39 C.339 L.209 J.D. 3580 Wilshire Blvd.
**Jacoby, Keith A.** ..........'65 '90 C.188 B.A. L.1068 J.D. [A Littler,M.F.T.&M.]
**Jacoby, Rachel S.** ..........'69 '93 C.999 B.S. L.978 J.D. [R.L.Zukerman]
Jacoves, Ira ..........'31 '62 C.112 B.S. L.426 LL.B. 545 Ave. 26, W. Los Angeles
Jaeger, Karl W. ..........'36 '67 C.900 A.B. L.809 J.D. Mun. Ct.J.
Jaenicke, Carol G. ..........'47 '73 C&L.569 B.A., J.D. 2566 Overland Ave.
**Jaenicke, J. Larson**, (AV) ..........'47 '72 C.797 B.A. L.569 J.D. [Rintala,S.J.&R.]
**Jaffe, Eve** ..........'63 '89 C.766 B.A. L.800 J.D. [Wynne S.I.]
Jaffe, F. Filmore, (AV) ..........'18 '45 C.809 L.1001 J.D. Supr. Ct. Ref.
Jaffe, Gail ..........'— '88 C.112 B.A. L.1065 J.D. Dep. Pub. Def.
**Jaffe, Howard M.**, **(P.C.)** ..........'36 '61 C&L.659 B.S., LL.B. [Mahoney,C.J.&P.]
*PRACTICE AREAS: Business, Professional and Employment Litigation; Business Transactions and Entities; Probate.
**Jaffe, Robert D.** ..........'64 '92 C.112 B.A. L.426 J.D. [A Pircher,N.&M.]
*PRACTICE AREAS: Real Estate Law; Entertainment; Sports; Multimedia.
**Jaffe, Saul** ..........'64 '91 C.846 B.A. L.464 J.D. [Richards,W.&G.]
**Jaffe, Sheldon M.**, (AV) ..........'34 '62 C.976 B.A. L.309 LL.B. [Gartenberg J.G.&S.]
Jagiello, Robert J. ..........'38 '65 C.339 L.426 LL.B. 1800 Ave. of the Stars
Jahn, Jerome J. ..........'36 '63 C.734 B.S. L.276 J.D. Exec. V.P., SFE Technologies
**Jahss, Neil Scot** ..........'67 '92 C.893 B.A. L.309 J.D. [A O'Melveny&M.]
Jalbuena, Arnel B. ..........'61 '91 C&L.9999 B.S., LL.B. 3250 Wilshire Blvd.
James, Becky S. ..........'65 '90 C&L.813 A.B., J.D. 400 S. Hope St.
James, Dana '54 '86 C.614 B.A. L.616 J.D.
(adm. in OK; not adm. in CA) U.S. Dept. of Jus.
James, Francis J. ..........'64 '91 C.602 B.A. L.1068 J.D. Off. of the Fed. Pub. Def.
**James, Frederick** ..........'55 '88 C.1131 B.A. L.809 J.D. [A Fonda,G.H.&D.]
**James, J. Chris** ..........'65 '94 C.679 B.S.M.E. L.846 J.D. [A Pretty,S.&P.]
*PRACTICE AREAS: Patents; Trademarks; Copyrights; Unfair Competition; Litigation.
**James, John E.** ..........'51 '76 C.1109 B.A. L.426 J.D. [Arter&H.]
*PRACTICE AREAS: Taxation Law; Partnership Law.
**James, Johnnie A.** ..........'63 '89 C.112 B.A. L.569 J.D. [A Alschuler G.&P.]
**James, Kenneth E.** ..........'67 '94 C.813 A.B. L.61 J.D. [A Hawkins,D.&W.]
*LANGUAGES: Spanish.
*PRACTICE AREAS: Public Finance.
**James, Kevin L.** ..........'63 '88 C.623 B.A. L.326 J.D. [A Greenberg G.F.C.&M.]
*PRACTICE AREAS: Litigation; Entertainment Litigation; Communications Litigation.
James, Michael A. '53 '79 C.893 B.A. L.976 J.D.
(adm. in NY; not adm. in CA) 8157 Mulholland Ter.‡
**James, Peter W.**, (AV) ..........'41 '68 C.813 B.A. L.976 LL.B. [Baker&H.]
*PRACTICE AREAS: Business Litigation; School Equal Protection Litigation.
**James, Robin** ..........'49 '90 C.112 B.A. L.426 J.D. [A Grace,S.C.&S.]
*PRACTICE AREAS: Insurance Coverage; Insurance Bad Faith; General Litigation.
**James, William J.**, (AV) ..........'44 '75 C.605 B.A. L.1065 J.D. [Graham&J.]
*PRACTICE AREAS: Litigation; Taxation Law.

**James, Norman D.**
**(See Hermosa Beach)**

Jameson, John B. ..........'56 '82 C.112 B.S. L.800 J.D. Pres., The Jameson Grp.
**Jameson, John M.** ..........'58 '85 C.188 B.A. L.1068 J.D. [Latham&W.]
**Jameson, Kristin L.** ..........'55 '80 C.763 B.A. L.800 J.D. [A Bird,M.B.W.&M.]
Jameson, William S. ..........'63 '90 C.112 B.A. L.426 J.D. 400 S. Hope St.
**Jan, Gloria Ching-hua** ..........'65 '93 C.103 Sc.B. L.976 J.D. [A Proskauer R.G.&M.]
**Janet, David M.** ..........'66 '93 C.945 B.A. L.228 J.D. [A Riordan&M.]
*PRACTICE AREAS: Corporate Transactional; Securities.
**Janeway, Roger W.** ..........'60 '95 C.976 B.A. L.1068 J.D. [A Heller E.W.&M.]
**Janger, Bruce** ..........'50 '77 C.813 A.B. L.1068 J.D. [McHale&C.]
*PRACTICE AREAS: Insurance Defense; Products Liability; Construction.
**Janisch, Richard A.** ..........'60 '88 C.426 B.A. L.809 J.D. [A Sedgwick,D.M.&A.]
**Janner, Leonard P.** ..........'61 '89 C.112 B.A. L.426 J.D. [A Dennison,B.&P.]

**Jannol, Henry N.** .......... '50 '75 C.112 A.B. L.809 J.D. [H.N.Jannol]
*PRACTICE AREAS: Commercial Litigation; Real Estate; Probate Litigation; Commercial Formation.
**Jannol, Martin B., (A Prof. Corp.)** .... '55 '80 C.668 B.A. L.809 J.D. [Woollacott J.&W.]
*PRACTICE AREAS: General Business and Real Estate Transactions; Corporate Law; Franchising; Real Property Law.
**Jannol, Neal B.** .......... '70 '95 C.112 B.A. L.1066 J.D. [[A] De Castro,W.&C.]
*LANGUAGES: Hebrew.
*PRACTICE AREAS: Tax Planning; Estates and Trusts.

**Jannol, Henry N., A Professional Corporation**
**1875 Century Park East, Suite 1400, 90067**
**Telephone: 310-552-7500 Telecopier: 310-552-7552**
**Email: hnj@la.saic.com**
**Henry N. Jannol.**
**Business Litigation and Real Estate Litigation.**

***See Professional Biographies, LOS ANGELES, CALIFORNIA***

Janofsky, Jack D. .......... '43 '69 C.112 B.A. L.1068 J.D. 315 W. 9th St.
**Janov, Jack A.**, (AV) .......... '54 '82 C.1077 B.A. L.426 J.D. [Wilson,E.M.E.&D.]
Jans, Ronald F. .......... '34 '64 C&L.800 LL.B. 2601 S. Figueroa St.
**Jansen, Lynn A.** .......... '66 '94 C.112 B.A. L.309 J.D. [[A] O'Melveny&M.]
Janson, Saul C. .......... '62 '90 C.659 B.A. L.112 J.D. 1900 Avenue Of The Stars
**Janson, Thomas C., Jr.** .......... '56 '82 C.453 B.S. L.472 J.D. [Skadden,A.S.M.&F.]
**Janssen, Kathryn R.**, (BV⊕) .......... '53 '81 C.813 B.A. L.1051 J.D. [Lane P.S.L.]
*PRACTICE AREAS: Products Liability Law; Employment Law; Toxic Tort Law.
**Janssen, Laurence F.**, (AV⊕) .......... '43 '67 C&L.629 B.S., J.D. [Lane P.S.L.]
*PRACTICE AREAS: Litigation; Toxic Torts; Products Liability.
Janzen, Thomas M. .......... '52 '82 C.629 B.A. L.464 J.D. 1900 Ave. of the Stars
**Jaques, Douglas A.** .......... '58 '84 C.813 B.A. L.1068 J.D. [McDermott,W.&E.]
*PRACTICE AREAS: Nonprofit and Charitable Organizations; Health Care; Taxation.
Jaquith, Peter C. '36 '65 C.197 A.B. L.494 LL.B.
(adm. in NY; not adm. in CA) 1801 Ave. of the Stars‡
Jaramillo, Philippe Francois .......... '63 '90 C&L.990 B.A., J.D. 11845 W. Olympic Blvd.
Jarboe, Hilmer U. .......... '46 '90 C.701 B.S.M.E. L.61 J.D. 611 W. 6th St.
**Jardine, Alisa** .......... '71 '96 C.112 B.A. L.1068 J.D. [[A] Orrick,H.&S.]
**Jardine, Bryan Wilson** .......... '62 '90 C.276 B.S. L.1068 J.D. [[A] Gorry&M.]
*LANGUAGES: Spanish.
*PRACTICE AREAS: Commercial; Real Estate; Insurance Bad Faith; Entertainment; Construction Litigation.
Jardine, Neal J. .......... '38 '85 L.1136 J.D. 3530 Wilshire Blvd.
Jarrin, Alfredo Xavier .......... '62 '87 C&L.800 B.S., J.D. Asst. U.S. Atty.
**Jaskol, Lisa R.** .......... '59 '88 C.104 A.B. L.976 J.D. [[A] Horvitz&L.]
**Jason, Robert M.**, (AV) .......... '56 '81 C&L.309 A.B., J.D. [Troop M.S.&P.]
*LANGUAGES: French.
*PRACTICE AREAS: Tax Law; Business Planning; Compensation Planning.
Jason, Samuel J. .......... '51 '79 C.150 B.A. L.05 LL.B. 9911 W. Pico Blvd.
**Jasper, Bernard C.** .......... '59 '85 C.793 B.S. L.800 J.D. [[A] Brobeck,P.&H.]
*PRACTICE AREAS: Business Law; Commercial Litigation.
Jasper, Patricia Marie .......... '48 '75 C.881 B.A. L.128 J.D. Campus Coun., Univ. of Calif.
**Jauffret, Jerome M.F.J.** .......... '54 '92 L.426 J.D. [[A] Mayer,B.&P.]
*LANGUAGES: French.
**Jauregui, Jesse M.** .......... '56 '87 C.976 B.A. L.426 J.D. [Ochoa&S.] (⊙Sacramento)
*LANGUAGES: Spanish.
*REPORTED CASES: Gonzalez v. Sup. Ct. 39 Cal Rptr 2d 896 (1995).
*PRACTICE AREAS: Civil Litigation; Construction Law.
Javelera, Lambert M. .......... '31 '59 C.800 B.S. L.426 J.D. [Crahan,J.&V.H.]
**Javier, Carolyn S.** .......... '68 '93 C.1365 B.A. L.426 J.D. [[A] Mitchell,S.&K.]
*LANGUAGES: Spanish, French.
*PRACTICE AREAS: Music Law; Music Publishing; Entertainment Law.
**Jay, Susan Carole** .......... '49 '85 C.763 B.A. L.1049 J.D. [[A] D.B.Bloom]
*LANGUAGES: Spanish.
Jaynes, Peter M. .......... '51 '80 C.800 B.A. L.1190 J.D. 865 S. Figeroa St. #3100
Jean, Lorri L. '57 '82 C.36 B.S. L.276 J.D.
Exec. Dir., L.A. Gay & Lesbian Community Servs. Ctr.
Jefchak, Karen G. .......... '52 '89 C.347 B.A. L.426 J.D. P.O. Box 17927
**Jeffer, Bruce P., (P.C.)**, (AV) .......... '42 '67 C.112 B.A. L.309 J.D. [Jeffer,M.B.&M.]
*LANGUAGES: Spanish.
*PRACTICE AREAS: Corporate; General Business; Syndication; Securities.

**Jeffer, Mangels, Butler & Marmaro LLP, (AV)**
**A Limited Liability Partnership including Professional Corporations**
**2121 Avenue of the Stars, Tenth Floor, 90067⊙**
**Telephone: 310-203-8080 FAX: 310-203-0567 Internet Address: attorney's 3 initials@jmbm.com (unless otherwise indicated)**
**URL: http://www.jmbm.com**
**Members of Firm: Bruce P. Jeffer (P.C.); Robert E. Mangels (P.C.); James R. Butler, Jr. (P.C.); Marc Marmaro (P.C.); Susan Allison; Simon Aron; Joel I. Bennett (P.C.); P. Peter Benudiz (P.C.); Joel J. Berman (P.C.); Rod S. Berman; Herbert A. Bernhard (P.C.); Robert E. Braun (P.C.); Patricia S. Brody (San Francisco Office); Richard M. Brown; Barry L. Burten; William F. Capps (P.C.); Joel A. Cassel (P.C.); Joel David Deutsch (P.C.); Randall G. Dick (San Francisco Office); Joseph A. Eisenberg (P.C.); Keith D. Elkins; Neil C. Erickson; Louise Ann Fernandez; Marta M. Fernandez; Nicholas S. Freud (San Francisco Office); David F. Gantz; Frederick W. Gartside; Elizabeth Barrowman Gibson; Michael A. Gold; Stephen R. Goldstein; Robert H. Goon; Paul R. Hamilton; Mark H. Hess; Catherine DeBono Holmes; Steven J. Insel; Patrick W. Jordan (San Francisco Office); Scott M. Kalt; Burton A. Mitchell (P.C.) (Certified Specialist, Taxation Law, The State Bar of California Board of Legal Specialization); Allen S. Resnick; Jeffrey L. Reuben (P.C.); Julia J. Rider (P.C.); Jeffrey K. Riffer; Richard A. Rogan (San Francisco Office); Mark M. Rosenthal; Robin M. Schachter (P.C.); Gary C. Sheppard (San Francisco Office); Michael S. Sherman (P.C.); Jeffrey W. Shopoff (San Francisco Office); Mark R. Sieke (P.C.); William S. Solari III (San Francisco Office); Jeffrey E. Steiner (P.C.); Jeffrey E. Sultan (P.C.); Paul L. Warner (San Francisco Office); William M. Weintraub (P.C.); Barry M. Weisz; Dennis J. White (San Francisco Office); Herbert N. Wolfe (P.C.). Of Counsel: Neil O. Andrus (San Francisco Office); Adrienne M. Coffin; Ronald P. Givner; Maxwell E. Greenberg; Andrew R. Hunter; David R. Kalifon; Timothy Lappen; Jennifer L. Long; Jeffrey I. Margolis (San Francisco Office); John E. Mason; Myron Meyers (P.C.); Fred Selan; David P. Waite (P.C.). Associates: Brad J. Brigante; R. Scott Brink; Adrianne J. Brownstein; Gregory S. Cavallo (San Francisco Office); Evan Y. Chuck (Not admitted in CA); Michael G. Dwyer; John M. Fujii; Alfred M. Garcia; Michael M. Gerardi; Stanley M. Gibson; Michael D. Good; Scott I. Greenfield; Brian M. Grossman; Lynne Marie Hook; Susan C. V. Jones; Victoria S. Kaufman; Steven M. Korbin; John G. Littell; Kenneth W. Muller (San Francisco Office); Mike D. Neue; Bradford K. Newman (San Francisco Office); Steven Plotkin; Linda A. Sampson; Dan P. Sedor; Maria Sendra; Robert Steinberg; Elizabeth A. Stone; Kathryn Ellen Suarez; Lazarus N. Sun; Alex O. Tamin; Elaine M. Taubenfeld; Deborah J. Tibbetts; Rebecca L. Torrey; Steven M. Weiss; James P. Williams; Isaac H. Winer (San Francisco Office); Stephen N. Yang (San Francisco Office).**
**General Civil Practice and Litigation in all State and Federal Courts. Corporate, Tax, Real Estate, Entertainment, Labor and Employment, Insolvency and Creditors' Rights, Antitrust, Environmental, Administrative, Corporate, Securities, Financial Institutions (including Banking, Savings and Loans), Fidelity and Surety, Insurance, Syndications, International, Oil and Gas, Apparel Industry, Health Care, Estate Planning, Probate/Trusts, Employee Benefits, Land Use, Hospitality Industry, Trademark, Intellectual Property, Patent, Copyright, Music and Music Publishing, Advertising, Sports, Technology. Member of INTERLAW, an international association of independent law firms in major world centers.**
**San Francisco, California Office: One Sansome Street, Twelfth Floor. Telephone: 415-398-8080. FAX: 415-398-5584. Internet Address: attorney's initials @jmbm.com.**

***See Professional Biographies, LOS ANGELES, CALIFORNIA***

**Jeffery, Janine K.**, (AV) .......... '59 '83 C.112 B.A. L.800 J.D. [Irwin&R.]
*PRACTICE AREAS: Aviation; Products Liability; General Civil Practice; Trial Practice.

**Jeffrey, Sheri** .......... '60 '85 C&L.426 B.S., J.D. [[C] Kaye,S.F.H.&H.]
*PRACTICE AREAS: Entertainment; Tax.
**Jeffries, D. Wayne**, (AV) .......... '45 '73 C.112 B.S. L.1065 J.D. [[A] Stroock&S.&L.]
Jeffries, Dan F. .......... '58 '83 C.112 B.A. L.1068 J.D. Dep. City Atty.
Jelenko, Martin M. .......... '45 '72 C.178 A.B. L.569 J.D. Mng. Dir., B T Capital Corp.
**Jelensky, Heather C.** .......... '71 '95 C.112 B.A. L.990 J.D. [[A] Lynberg&W.]
*PRACTICE AREAS: Insurance Coverage and Defense; General Defense; Litigation; Products Liability.
**Jenal, James Paul** .......... '54 '95 C&L.426 B.S., J.D. [[A] O'Melveny&M.]
*PRACTICE AREAS: Litigation.
Jenkins, Alfred .......... '36 '76 C.1097 B.A. L.426 J.D. 1480 Stearns Dr.‡
**Jenkins, Gayle I.** .......... '68 '93 C.139 B.A. L.1065 J.D. [[A] Thelen,M.J.&B.]
*PRACTICE AREAS: Insurance Litigation (Life, Health & Disability); Business Litigation.
**Jenkins, John D.** .......... '67 '92 C&L.800 B.A., J.D. [[A] Troop M.S.&P.]
*PRACTICE AREAS: Corporate.
Jenkins, Joseph S. .......... '56 '81 C.112 B.S. L.1066 J.D. 837 Traction Ave.
Jenkins, Mary L. .......... '51 '92 C.1131 B.A. L.426 J.D. 350 S. Grand Ave.‡
**Jenkins, Merrill E.** .......... '25 '69 C&L.813 B.A., J.D. [Stroock&S.&L.] ‡
**Jenkins, Michael** .......... '53 '78 C.311 B.A. L.228 J.D. [Richards,W.&G.]
*PRACTICE AREAS: Public Law; Land Use Law; Litigation.
Jenkins, Myron L. .......... '39 '71 C.17 B.B.A. L.1068 J.D. Dep. Dist. Atty.
**Jenkins, Nicholas G.** .......... '69 '94 C.911 B.A. L.276 J.D. [[A] O'Melveny&M.]
**Jenkins, Norman A., III** '50 '78 C.951 B.A. L.569 J.D.
(adm. in NY; not adm. in CA) [Donovan L.N.&I.]
**Jenness, Evan A.** .......... '62 '88 C.1036 B.A. L.178 J.D. [[A] B.Tarlow]
*PRACTICE AREAS: Criminal Law.
Jenness, Mark J. .......... '60 '86 C.112 A.B. L.800 J.D. 555 W. 5th St.
**Jennett, Thomas Joseph** .......... '59 '91 C.112 B.A. L.809 J.D. [[A] Gilbert,K.C.&J.]
**Jennett, William D.**, (AV) .......... '30 '59 C.112 L.426 LL.B. [[C] Gilbert,K.C.&J.]
Jensen, David L. .......... '45 '72 C&L.878 B.A., J.D. 10880 Wilshire Blvd.
**Jensen, Gilbert D.** .......... '46 '74 C.112 B.S. L.1066 J.D. [Barton,K.&O.]
*PRACTICE AREAS: International Law; Insurance Coverage; Securities; General Civil Practice; Trial Practice.
Jensen, Robert T. .......... '22 '50 C&L.597 B.S., J.D. 10610 Ashton Ave.‡
Jenson, Linda .......... '45 '72 C.878 B.A. L.1068 J.D. [Liebert,C.&F.]
Jenson, Linda .......... '46 '72 C.878 B.A. L.1068 J.D. 6033 W. Century Blvd.
**Jerles, Jeanette E.** .......... '64 '90 C.112 B.A. L.990 J.D. [[A] Anderson,M.&C.]
**Jessup, Clifton R., Jr.** '55 '79 C.999 B.A. L.477 J.D.
(adm. in NE; not adm. in CA) [Dixon&J.] (⊙Dallas, TX)
*PRACTICE AREAS: Bankruptcy Law; Creditors Rights Law; Corporate Reorganization.
**Jesuele, Robert R.** .......... '60 '86 C&L.426 B.B.A., J.D. [Coudert]
**Jeter, Kevin D.** .......... '59 '95 C.112 M.S. L.1067 J.D. [[A] Musick,P.&G.]
*PRACTICE AREAS: Litigation; Insurance; Environmental.
**Jett, Frances Q.** .......... '68 '95 C.112 B.A. L.1049 J.D. [Alvarado,S.V.&S.]
*PRACTICE AREAS: Business Litigation.
Jew, Kenneth A. .......... '65 '90 C.112 B.A. L.1065 J.D. 3255 Wilshire Blvd.
Jeys, Roy A. .......... '49 '77 C.112 B.A. L.309 J.D. [Wilson&B.]
**Jha, Arun** .......... '70 '95 C.188 A.B. L.800 J.D. [[A] Gibson,D.&C.]
**Jie, Hu** .......... '68 '93 [Arnberger,K.B.&C.]
*LANGUAGES: Chinese and English.
*PRACTICE AREAS: Economic Law; International Economic Law; Company Law.
**Jih, Victor** .......... '73 '96 C.813 B.A. L.309 J.D. [[A] O'Melveny&M.]
*LANGUAGES: Chinese (Mandarin).
**Jimbo, Thomas M.** .......... '57 '82 C.112 B.A. L.426 J.D. [Richards,W.&G.]
*PRACTICE AREAS: Litigation; Insurance Coverage Law.
**Jimenez, Alejandro** .... '61 '88 C.112 B.A. L.309 J.D. Atty., Pacific Telesis Legal Group
**Jimenez, Augustin R.** .......... '53 '80 C.1042 B.A. L.911 J.D. [[A] Barbosa G.&B.]
*REPORTED CASES: Supreme Court of the State of Washington: Seattle v. Williams, 101 Wn2d 445, 680 P2d 1051 (1984); Court of Appeals of the State of Washington: Seattle v. Gordon, 39 Wash. App. 437, 693 P2d 741 (1985); Seattle v. Tolliver, 31 Wash. App. 299, 641 P2d 719 (1982).
*PRACTICE AREAS: Municipal Law; Employment and Personnel Law; Litigation; Air Quality Law.
Jimenez, James M. .......... '53 '80 C.696 B.A. L.276 J.D. 12100 Wilshire Blvd., 15th Fl.
Jitner, Walter .......... '31 '72 C.776 B.S. L.426 J.D. 9073 Nemo St.
**Joannes, John A.**, (AV) .......... '34 '65 C.605 A.B. L.800 J.D. [J.A.Joannes]

**Joannes, John A., A Professional Corporation, (AV)** [BR]
**11911 San Vicente Boulevard Suite 375, 90049**
**Telephone: 310-440-4240 Facsimile: 310-471-2862**
**Email: jjoannespc@aol.com URL: http://www.primenet.com/~joannes/**
**John A. Joannes (Certified Specialist, Immigration and Nationality Law, The State Bar of California Board of Legal Specialization). Of Counsel: Stephen L. Teller.**
**Practice limited to Immigration and Nationality Law.**

***See Professional Biographies, LOS ANGELES, CALIFORNIA***

**Joe, Eric Anthony** .......... '54 '82 C.1169 B.A. L.426 J.D. [Dorais&W.]
**Joffe, Steven J.** .......... '57 '83 C.494 B.A. L.1137 J.D. [La Follette,J.D.F.&A.]
*PRACTICE AREAS: Bad Faith; General Liability.
John, Frederick E. .......... '46 '71 C.276 A.B. L.575 J.D. 555 W. 5th St.
**Johnsen, Theodore G.**, (AV) .......... '43 '69 C.112 B.A. L.1068 J.D. [Arnold&P.]
*PRACTICE AREAS: Corporate; Securities.

**Johnsen, Manfredi & Thorpe, A Professional Corporation**
**(See Perkins Coie)**

**Johnson, Adam L.** .......... '67 '93 C.668 B.A. L.909 J.D. [[A] Hollins&R.]⊙
*LANGUAGES: German.
Johnson, Andrea L. '56 '82 C.329 B.A. L.309 J.D.
(adm. in DC; not adm. in CA) Prof., Calif. Western Sch. of Law
Johnson, Arnold Melvin .......... '39 '72 C&L.329 B.S., J.D. 1200 Wilshire Blvd.
Johnson, B. Elliot .......... '43 '75 C.112 B.A. L.398 J.D. 16633 Ventura Blvd. (Encino)

**Johnson, Barbara E. '55 '80 C.112 B.A. L.426 J.D.**
**12650 Riverside Drive (North Hollywood), 91607**
**Telephone: 818-755-4848 FAX: 818-760-2583**
**General Civil Trial and Appellate Practice. Corporate, Real Property, Construction, Estate Planning, Trust and Probate Law, Personal Injury.**

Johnson, Barbara Jean .......... '32 '71 C&L.800 B.S., J.D. Supr. Ct. J.
**Johnson, Channing D.** .......... '51 '78 C.813 B.A. L.309 J.D. [Kaye,S.F.H.&H.]
Johnson, Cheryl Barnes .......... '— '76 624 S. Grand Ave
**Johnson, Cheryl Lee** .......... '50 '75 C.66 B.A. L.178 J.D. [Graham&J.]
*PRACTICE AREAS: Litigation; Antitrust; RICO; Banking Law.
**Johnson, Christine M.** '64 '91 C.112 B.S.E.E. L.1066 J.D.
Assoc. Coun., Bank of Amer.
**Johnson, Claire D.**, (AV) .......... '31 '58 C&L.546 B.S., J.D. [Parker,M.C.O.&S.]
*SPECIAL AGENCIES: California Department of Insurance.
*REPORTED CASES: Canadian Commercial Bank v. Findley, 229 Cal. App. 3d 1139; Shapiro v. United California Bank, 133 CA 3d 256.
*PRACTICE AREAS: Commercial Litigation; Class Action Defense; Securities Litigation; Directors and Officers Liability Defense.
**Johnson, Daren T.**, (AV) '28 '53 C.112 B.A. L.1068 J.D.
[La Follette,J.D.F.&A.] (⊙San Fran. & Santa Ana)
*PRACTICE AREAS: Bad Faith and General Liability Litigation; Insurance Law; Tort Law; Corporate Law.
Johnson, Darrell Lee .......... '29 '54 C.494 B.S. L.748 LL.B. 3580 Wilshire Blvd.

**Johnson, David J., Jr.** ... '56 '85 C&L.893 B.A., J.D. [Andrews&K.]
*PRACTICE AREAS: Corporate Law; Securities.
**Johnson, David K.** ... '60 '86 C.112 B.A. L.1049 J.D. [Ⓐ Fried,B.&C.]
*PRACTICE AREAS: Business Litigation - General Civil and Trial Practice in all State and Federal Courts; Lender Liability; Insurance Coverage; Securities; Bankruptcy.
Johnson, David M. ... '64 '88 C.763 B.A. L.273 J.D. 801 S. Grand Ave.
**Johnson, David Wayne, Jr.** ... '65 '93 C.228 A.B. L.896 J.D. [Ⓐ Rubinstein&P.]
*PRACTICE AREAS: Litigation.
Johnson, Earl, Jr. ... '33 '60 C.597 B.A. L.145 J.D. Assoc. Jus., Ct. of App.
**Johnson, Elizabeth Platte** ... '58 '83 C&L.790 B.A., J.D. [Jackson,L.S.&K.]
Johnson, Ernest E., (P.C.), (AV) ... '27 '54 C.579 B.S. L.477 J.D. 187 S. Beachwood Dr.
Johnson, Harvey G., (AV) ... '42 '74 C.877 B.S. L.276 J.D. [Johnson,R.&W.]
Johnson, Howard G. ... '39 '79 C.106 B.A. L.1198 J.D. 1406 S. Union Ave.
**Johnson, Hugh**, (AV) ... '40 '67 C.112 A.B. L.800 J.D. [Johnson&J.]
**Johnson, James C.** '52 '78 C&L.659 B.A., J.D.
Corp. V.P., Secy. & Asst. Gen. Coun., Northrop Grumman Corp.
*SPECIAL AGENCIES: Staff Attorney, SEC, Washington, D.C., 1977-1978.
*TRANSACTIONS: Purchase of Grumman Corporation $1.2 B. Vought Aircraft Company Acquisition $76 M. Various Credit Agreements totaling some $5 M.
*RESPONSIBILITIES: Corporate Law; Securities.
**Johnson, James G., (P.C.)**, (AV) ... '49 '74 C.112 A.B. L.61 J.D. [Hill,F.&B.]
*SPECIAL AGENCIES: National Labor Relations Board; EEOC; Department of Fair Employment and Housing; Division of Labor Standards Enforcement; U.S. Department of Labor.
*PRACTICE AREAS: Labor Management Law; Employer-Employee Relations; Employee Drug Testing; Employment Discrimination Law; Wrongful Discharge Law.
**Johnson, Jamie L.** ... '61 '87 C.112 B.A. L.1066 J.D. [Ⓐ Brobeck,P.&H.]
**Johnson, Jane Luecke** ... '42 '80 C.525 B.A. L.426 J.D. [Johnson&J.]
**Johnson, Jeffery W.** ... '62 '88 C.108 B.A. L.1119 J.D. [Heller E.W.&M.]
**Johnson, Jerri L.** ... '63 '89 C.228 B.S. L.990 J.D. [Ⓐ Acker,K.&W.]
*PRACTICE AREAS: Personal Injury Defense; Products Liability; Medical Malpractice; Professional Malpractice.
**Johnson, Jody L.** ... '66 '92 C.612 B.S. L.1066 J.D. [Ⓐ Gibson,D.&C.]
**Johnson, Jonathan E.**, (AV) ... '36 '64 C.188 B.S. L.273 J.D. [Johnson,P.C.&S.]
*PRACTICE AREAS: Family Law; Litigation; Estate Planning; Probate.
**Johnson, Jonathan E., III** ... '66 '93 C&L.101 B.A., J.D. [Ⓐ Graham&J.]
**Johnson, Julia R.** ... '— '93 C.112 B.A. L.569 J.D. [Ⓐ Pillsbury M.&S.]
**Johnson, Kathleen C.** ... '49 '82 C.112 B.A. L.1068 J.D. [Morgan,L.&B.]
**Johnson, Kenneth E.** ... '55 '83 C.309 B.A. L.178 J.D. [Ⓒ O'Melveny&M.]
*PRACTICE AREAS: Labor and Employment; Employee Benefits Litigation.
**Johnson, Kenneth W.** ... '65 '91 C.309 A.B. L.1066 J.D. [Ⓐ Robinson,D.&W.]
*PRACTICE AREAS: Civil Litigation; Legal Malpractice.
Johnson, Linda C. ... '59 '86 C.1239 B.A. L.1068 J.D. [Ⓐ Pollet&W.]
Johnson, Linda C. ... '52 '77 C.205 B.A. L.800 J.D. Dep. Atty. Gen.
**Johnson, Lindsay S.** ... '61 '86 C.112 B.A. L.1065 J.D. [Ⓐ Gabriel,H.&P.]
Johnson, Marion J. ... '33 '72 L.809 J.D. Mun. J.
Johnson, Mark D. ... '61 '88 C.800 B.S. L.426 J.D. 333 S. Hope St., 48th Fl.
**Johnson, Mark D.** ... '— '88 [Ⓐ Sheppard,M.R.&H.]
*PRACTICE AREAS: Environmental Law, Litigation.
Johnson, Mark T. ... '53 '79 C.813 A.B. L.770 J.D. Legal Aid Found. of L.A.
**Johnson, Matthew M.** ... '68 '93 C.705 B.A. L.569 J.D. [Ⓐ Greenberg G.F.C.&M.]
*PRACTICE AREAS: Transactional Entertainment.
Johnson, Michael C. ... '57 '85 C.112 B.A. L.128 J.D. U.S. Attys. Off.
**Johnson, Michael M.** ... '51 '76 C.112 B.A. L.1065 J.D. [Baker&H.]
*PRACTICE AREAS: Employment Law; Litigation.
Johnson, Morris T. ... '17 '49 C.671 A.B. L.309 LL.B. 2301 10th Ave.‡
Johnson, Neville L. ... '49 '75 C.112 B.A. L.809 J.D. 12121 Wilshire Blvd.
Johnson, Raymond L. ... '22 '64 C&L.329 B.S., LL.B. 3756 Santa Rosalia Dr.

**Johnson, Raymond Paul, The Law Offices of, (AV) '47 '83 C.569 M.S.Eng. L.945 J.D.**
**Suite 1150, 10990 Wilshire Boulevard (Westwood), 90024**
**Telephone: 310-246-9300 Fax: 310-312-1551**
**Aviation Law, Products Liability, Contract Actions, Technology-Related Litigation, Wrongful Termination, Entertainment Industry Disputes, Civil Trial Practice.**

*See Professional Biographies, LOS ANGELES, CALIFORNIA*

**Johnson, Richard M., Jr.** ... '— '87 C.911 B.A. L.770 J.D. [Fierstein&S.]
*PRACTICE AREAS: Real Estate Finance; Insolvency; Workout.
**Johnson, Robert K., (A Professional Corporation)**, (AV) '39 '65
C.309 A.B. L.813 J.D. [Munger,T.&O.]
Johnson, Robert M. ... '48 '77 C&L.426 B.A., J.D. 2578 S. Sepulveda Blvd.
**Johnson, Robert M.** ... '57 '84 C.299 B.A. L.893 J.D. [Ⓒ LeBoeuf,L.G.&M.]
*PRACTICE AREAS: Real Estate.
**Johnson, Robyn K.** ... '66 '91 C.339 B.A. L.276 J.D. [Ⓐ Russ,A.&K.]
*PRACTICE AREAS: Commercial Litigation; Real Estate Litigation; Intellectual Property Litigation; Unfair Competition Litigation.
**Johnson, Russell L.**, (AV) ... '33 '59 C.309 A.B. L.813 LL.B. [Ⓒ Gibson,D.&C.]
*PRACTICE AREAS: Real Estate; Financing and Leasing.
Johnson, Sherrill L. ... '50 '78 C.112 A.B. L.1068 J.D. First Interstate Bank
Johnson, Stephanie Emelle ... '65 '93 C.112 B.A. L.809 J.D. 2029 Century Park E.
**Johnson, Stephen C.** ... '61 '89 C.426 B.A. L.800 J.D. [Dempsey&J.]
*PRACTICE AREAS: Business Litigation; Securities Fraud; Officers and Directors Liability; Accountant's Liability; Employers Discrimination Defense.
**Johnson, Stephen D.** '57 '82 C.502 B.B.A. L.845 J.D.
(adm. in TX; not adm. in CA) Assoc. Gen. Coun., Farmers Grp., Inc.
*RESPONSIBILITIES: Claims Litigation; Claims Counseling.
**Johnson, Steve**, (AV) ... '55 '82 C.546 B.A. L.426 J.D. [Bottum&F.]
*PRACTICE AREAS: Professional Malpractice Law; Civil Law; Trial Practice; Appellate Practice; Fidelity and Surety Law.
**Johnson, Susanne Berry** ... '64 '89 C.861 B.A. L.990 J.D. [Ⓐ Berger,K.S.M.F.S.&G.]
**Johnson, Thomas** ... '— '92 C.317 B.A. L.284 J.D. [Ⓐ Baker&H.]
*PRACTICE AREAS: Bankruptcy Law.
Johnson, Thomas T. ... '23 '49 C&L.421 B.M.E., LL.B. Supr. Ct. J.
**Johnson, Thomas T.** ... '61 '92 C.1097 B.A. L.426 J.D. [Ⓐ Booth,M.&S.]
**Johnson, Virginia A.** ... '44 '84 C.1193 B.A. L.1067 J.D. [Ⓐ Sandler&R.]
**Johnson, W. Michael**, (AV) ... '42 '68 C.112 A.B. L.1068 J.D. [Holley&G.]
*PRACTICE AREAS: Taxation.
**Johnson, Wayne E.** ... '67 '92 C.188 B.A. L.659 J.D. [Ⓐ Brobeck,P.&H.]
Johnson, William D. ... '54 '81 C.101 B.A. L.178 J.D. [Johnson&Assoc.]
Johnson & Associates ... 350 S. Figueroa St.
Johnson, Bjornlie & Merritt ... 5455 Wilshire Blvd.

**Johnson, Cebula & Rygh**
**(See Long Beach)**

**Johnson & Johnson, A P.C., (AV)**
**11835 West Olympic Boulevard, Suite 1235, 90064**
**Telephone: 310-268-1606 FAX: 310-268-7999**
**Hugh Johnson; Jane Luecke Johnson.**
**General Business Practice, Real Estate, Civil Trial and Appellate Practice in all State and Federal Courts.**

**Johnson, Poulson, Coons & Slater, (AV)** BR
**10880 Wilshire Boulevard, Suite 1800, 90024**
**Telephone: 310-475-0611 Telecopier: 310-475-0143**

(This Listing Continued)

CAA258P

**Johnson, Poulson, Coons & Slater (Continued)**

**Members of Firm: Jonathan E. Johnson (Certified Specialist, Family Law, The State Bar of California Board of Legal Specialization); Lynn O. Poulson (Mr.); Michael H. Coons. Of Counsel: Martin R. Slater.**
**Corporation, Real Property, General Business. Family Law, Estate Planning, Probate, Civil Trial Practice in all State and Federal Courts.**

*See Professional Biographies, LOS ANGELES, CALIFORNIA*

Johnson, Rifenbark & Wylie, (AV) ... 3700 Wilshire Blvd.
**Johnston, Carol A.** ... '54 '79 C.478 B.A. L.145 J.D. [Ⓒ O'Melveny&M.]
*PRACTICE AREAS: Trusts and Estates.
**Johnston, James O., Jr.** ... '68 '93 C.813 B.A. L.800 J.D./M.A. [Ⓐ Stutman,T.&G.]
*PRACTICE AREAS: Bankruptcy; Insolvency; Corporate Reorganization.
**Johnston, Jennifer J.** ... '58 '86 C.1074 B.S. L.426 J.D. [Condon&F.]
**Johnston, Ronald L., (P.C.)**, (AV) ... '48 '73 C.1109 B.A. L.800 J.D. [Blanc W.J.&K.]
*REPORTED CASES: Abdul-Jabbar v. General Motors Corp., 75 F.3d 1391 (9th Cir. 1996); Balzer-Wolf Assoc., Inc. v. Parlex Corp., 753 F.2d 771 (9th Cir. 1985).
*PRACTICE AREAS: Commercial Litigation; Proprietary Rights; Antitrust; Computer Law.
**Johnstone, Kathryn I.** ... '57 '86 C.897 B.S.B.A. L.309 J.D. [Morrison&F.]
*PRACTICE AREAS: Business-Financial Transactions.
Jonas, Anderson L. ... '50 '79 C.800 B.S. L.426 J.D. 1925 Century Park E.
Jones, Abigail A. ... '52 '78 C.681 B.A. L.309 J.D. 400 S. Hope St.
Jones, Albert W. ... '25 '52 C&L.145 Ph.B., J.D. 3460 Wilshire Blvd.
**Jones, Allison L.** ... '66 '92 C.112 B.A. L.1065 J.D. [Ⓐ Callahan,M.&W.]
*PRACTICE AREAS: Civil Litigation.
Jones, Ann I. ... '55 '84 C.103 B.A. L.1066 J.D. 611 W. 6th St., 20th Fl.
Jones, Audrey B. ... '13 '58 C.838 B.S. L.809 J.D. 2716 S. Western Ave.
**Jones, Beth Finley** ... '58 '84 C.914 B.A. L.309 J.D. Litig. & Bdcst. Coun., CBS Inc.
**Jones, Carla N.** ... '68 '95 C.674 A.B. L.976 J.D. [Ⓐ Munger,T.&O.]
Jones, Charles E. ... '31 '66 C.1016 B.A. L.426 J.D. Supr. Ct. J.
**Jones, Christopher E.** ... '69 '94 C.276 B.S.B.A. L.1068 J.D. [Robinson,D.B.&K.]
*PRACTICE AREAS: Bankruptcy.
**Jones, David L.** ... '57 '83 C.426 B.A. L.990 J.D. [Selman B.]
*PRACTICE AREAS: Insurance Coverage; Insurance Bad Faith; Personal Injury; Product Liability.
**Jones, Donald H.**, (AV) ... '47 '72 C.800 B.S. L.1068 J.D. [Jones,K.&A.]
*PRACTICE AREAS: Real Estate; Corporate; Taxation; Estate Planning.
Jones, Donna Weisz ... '51 '75 C.112 B.A. L.426 J.D. Dep. City Atty.
**Jones, Drew**, (AV) ... '53 '78 C.112 A.B. L.1066 J.D. [Brobeck,P.&H.]
*PRACTICE AREAS: Business Law; Real Property Law; Finance Law; Development Law.
Jones, Elsa H. ... '53 '78 C.145 A.B. L.800 J.D. 624 S. Grand Ave., 27th Fl
Jones, Eric L. ... '48 '75 C.309 A.B. L.1068 J.D. 4929 Wilshire Blvd.
**Jones, Evan M.** ... '59 '84 C.228 B.A. L.1066 J.D. [O'Melveny&M.]
*PRACTICE AREAS: Bankruptcy.
Jones, G. Bradford ... '55 '81 C.309 A.B.A.M. L.813 J.D. 11150 Santa Monica Blvd.
**Jones, Gregory K.** ... '70 '95 C.112 B.A. L.1068 J.D. [Ⓐ Hennigan,M.&B.]
*PRACTICE AREAS: Bankruptcy Law; Commercial Law.
**Jones, James G.**, (AV) ... '43 '69 C.605 A.B. L.1065 J.D. [Knapp,M.J.&D.]
*PRACTICE AREAS: Business Law; Real Property Law; Business Civil Litigation; Transactional Tax Law.
Jones, Jewell ... '39 '74 C.112 B.A. L.809 J.D. Comr., Co. Supr. Ct.
**Jones, Jordan T.** ... '66 '93 C.674 B.S.E. L.1068 J.D. [Ⓐ Wilson,E.M.E.&D.]
Jones, Joseph M. ... '33 '59 C&L.813 A.B., J.D. 1800 Fairburn Ave.‡
**Jones, Laurie K.** ... '64 '95 C.958 B.A. L.809 J.D. [Ⓐ Bronson,B.&M.]
*PRACTICE AREAS: Bankruptcy; Creditors' Rights; Commercial Litigation.
**Jones, Lawrence C.** ... '53 '92 C.685 B.A. L.800 J.D. [Augustini,W.&D.]
Jones, Leo Paul ... '55 '81 C.424 B.A. L.426 J.D. Pres., The La Grange Grp.
**Jones, Lester L.** ... '50 '86 C.965 B.A. L.464 J.D. [Littler,M.F.T.&M.]
Jones, Lindley H. '43 '71 C&L.879 B.A., J.D.
(adm. in IL; not adm. in CA) V.P., Calif. Fed. Bk. FSB
Jones, Marc A. ... '65 '95 C.112 B.A. L.1068 J.D. 633 W. 5th St., Suite 1900
**Jones, Mark** ... '60 '88 C.112 B.A. L.426 J.D. [Ruben&M.]
*PRACTICE AREAS: Business Litigation; Professional Liability; Appellate Advocacy.
Jones, Mary S. ... '54 '79 C.426 B.S. L.61 J.D. Sr. Coun., Northrop Corp.
Jones, Milton Van ... '45 '75 C.112 B.A. L.800 J.D. [Wardlaw&J.]
**Jones, Patricia K** ... '69 '95 C.112 B.A. L.477 J.D. [Ⓐ Milbank,T.H.&M.]
*PRACTICE AREAS: Litigation.
Jones, Philip F. ... '20 '49 C&L.800 A.B., LL.B. Supr. Ct. J.
**Jones, Richard M.**, (AV) ... '49 '76 C.691 B.A. L.846 J.D. [O'Melveny&M.]
*PRACTICE AREAS: Government Finance; Government Infrastructure Projects.
**Jones, Rosalyn Evelyn** ... '61 '87 C&L.309 A.B., J.D. [Manatt,P.&P.]
*PRACTICE AREAS: Music.
**Jones, Royce K.** ... '55 '82 C&L.800 A.B., J.D. [Kane,B.&B.]
*SPECIAL AGENCIES: Counsel for Community Redevelopment Agency of the City of Los Angeles, San Diego Redevelopment Agency, Los Angeles County Community Development Commission, San Diego Redevelopment Agency, Lynwood Redevelopment Agency, Federal Deposit Insurance Corporation and Resolution Trust Corporation.
*REPORTED CASES: Centenial Estates v. Griffin Homes (Real Estate litigation); San Diego Redevelopment Agency v. San Diego Gas & Electric (Eminent Domain litigation); Lynwood Redevelopment Agency v. Lucky Stores (Eminent Domain litigation); Bank of America National Trust v. Nu-Med La Mirada (Judicial Foreclosure/Receivorship Action); J.E. Roberts Company, Inc. v. DeVere A. Anderson (Receivorship - Surety Bond Litigation).
*TRANSACTIONS: Broadway Spring Street Plaza, Chinatown Mall, San Diego College of Retail, Price Club, Chinese Mission (San Diego), Gateway Center East Industrial Park, Gateway Medical Center, Southcrest Plaza, Lynwood Plaza, KV Mart Stores, Mercado Housing Project, Kilgore Manor, Villa Malaga Housing Project, Habitat for Humanities, Brush Research Development, Central Imperial Redevelopment Plan Amendments, East Rancho Dominguez Plan Amendment.
*PRACTICE AREAS: Redevelopment; Municipal; Land Use; Eminent Domain; Affordable Housing Law.
**Jones, Scott L.** ... '57 '88 C.336 B.Arch. L.128 J.D. [Ⓐ Sonnenschein N.&R.]
*PRACTICE AREAS: Government Contracts; Construction; Litigation.
Jones, Stephen D. ... '65 '92 C.205 B.A. L.1148 J.D. Corp. Coun.

**Jones, Stephen L., Law Offices of '42 '76 C.846 B.A. L.477 J.D.**
**445 South Figueroa, Suite 2600, 90071**
**Telephone: 213-612-7701 Fax: 213-612-7702**
**Email: shibumi@loop.com**
***SPECIAL AGENCIES: Local Agencies: Planning Commissions, Zoning Administration, City Council, Mediation Dispute Resolution (1992).**
***REPORTED CASES: City of West Hollywood v. Beverly Towers, Inc. 52Cal 3rd 1184, 1991; V.D. Registry, Inc. v. State of California 34Cal App 4th 107, 1995;Korean American Legal Foundation v. City of Los Angeles 23Cal App 4th 376, 1994; Baker v. City of Santa Monica 181Cal App 3rd 972, 1986.**
***PRACTICE AREAS: Real Estate and Land Use Litigation; General Civil Litigation; Business Litigation; Commercial Litigation; Appellate Practice.**
**Real Estate and Land Use Litigation, General Civil Litigation, Business Litigation, Commercial Litigation and Appellate Practice.**

*See Professional Biographies, LOS ANGELES, CALIFORNIA*

**Jones, Susan C. V.** ... '63 '90 C.477 B.A. L.309 J.D. [Ⓐ Jeffer,M.B.&M.]
*PRACTICE AREAS: General Litigation.
**Jones, Suzanne Cate** ... '60 '91 C.800 A.B. L.426 J.D. [Ⓐ Sonnenschein N.&R.]
*PRACTICE AREAS: Litigation.
**Jones, Suzanne R.** ... '62 '88 C.112 B.S. L.426 J.D. [Pretty,S.&P.]
*PRACTICE AREAS: Patents; Trademarks; Copyrights; Unfair Competition; Litigation.
**Jones, William A.** ... '45 '74 C.674 A.B. L.273 J.D. [Argue P.H.&M.]
*PRACTICE AREAS: Business Transactions.

**Jones, Bell, Simpson, Abbott & Fleming, (AV)**
**601 South Figueroa Street, Twenty-Seventh Floor, 90017-5759**
**Telephone: 213-485-1555 Telecopier: 213-689-1004**
**Email: jonesbel@ix.netcom.com**
**Members of Firm: Maurice Jones, Jr. (1902-1987); Eugene W. Bell (1926-1996); C. Edward Simpson; Michael J. Abbott; G. Thomas Fleming III; Kevin K. Fitzgerald; Craig R. Bockman; Fredrick A. Rafeedie; Trenton J. Hill. Of Counsel: Richard F. Miller (Certified Specialist, Estate Planning, Trust and Probate Law, The State Bar of California Board of Legal Specialization). Associates: Diane A. Irvin; Michael A. Amiri; Alan S. Petlak; Brian G. Arnold.**
**General Civil, Trial and Appellate Practice in all State and Federal Courts. Antitrust, Arbitration, Franchise, Probate, Real Estate and Securities Law.**
**Reference: Sanwa Bank California, Los Angeles Main Office.**

***See Professional Biographies, LOS ANGELES, CALIFORNIA***

**Jones, Day, Reavis & Pogue, (AV)** BR
**555 West Fifth Street Suite 4600, 90013-1025**⊙
**Telephone: 213-489-3939 Telex: 181439 UD Telecopier: 213-243-2539**
**Members of Firm in Los Angeles: Bertram R. Zweig; James F. Childs, Jr. (Certified Specialist, Taxation Law, The State Bar of California Board of Legal Specialization); Ronald S. Rizzo; William G. Wilson; Ross E. Stromberg; Gerald W. Palmer; Victor G. Savikas; Gerry D. Osterland (Not admitted in CA); Elwood Lui; Robert Dean Avery; Donald D. Gralnek; James L. Baumoel; Frederick L. McKnight; Dean B. Allison; Norman A. Pedersen; David S. Boyce (Certified Specialist, Taxation Law, The State Bar of California Board of Legal Specialization); Andrew J. Demetriou; Thomas R. Mueller; Thomas M. McMahon; Eric V. Rowen; Louis L. Touton; Daniel J. McLoon; Scott D. Bertzyk; Sarah Heck Griffin; Jeffrey A. LeVee; Lester O. Brown; Kevin G. McBride (Not admitted in CA); David J. DiMeglio; Daniel D. McMillan. Of Counsel: Richard H. Koppes; David C. Zucker; Richard J. Frick; Patricia A. Van Dyke. Senior Attorney: Douglas F. Landrum; Lynn Leversen Kambe. Associates: Marsha E. Durko; Peter G. McAllen; Thomas Botz; Mary J. Garnett; Craig S. Gatarz (Not admitted in CA); Robert M. Gilchrest; Kevin A. Dorse; Catherine A. Ehrgott; Katherine M. Elwood; Kevin R. Lussier; Jeffrey A. Miller; Kenneth A. Remson; Bruce J. Shih; Philip E. Cook; Jane M. Nowotny; Ricky L. Shackelford; Valerie A. Brown; Mary K. Hartigan; Mark M. Kassabian; Stanley C. Morris; Maria K. Nelson; Gary W. Nugent; Wendy L. Thomas; Eugene Y. T. Won; B. Maria Dennis; Miwon Yi; Sharon L. Faris; Jeffrey S. Koenig; Susanne L. Meline; Elizabeth G. Moreno; Sophia Friedman Roslin; Alonzo B. Wickers, IV; Jinshu Zhang; David B. Fischer; Erin E. Nolan; Kirstin D. Poirier-Whitley; Karen R. Thorland; Jacqueline M. Aguilera; Kathryn Blagden; Amy R. Brownstein; Katarzyna A. Buchen (Not admitted in CA); Marc D. Field; Jocelyn M. Gutiérrez; C. Megan Laurance; Vick K. Mansourian; Ashley S.H. Sim; Susanne E. Stamey; Allan Z. Litovsky; Eugenia L. Castruccio; Vince L. Farhat; C. Steve Hagemeister; Gregory S.G. Klatt; Tristan B.L. Siegel.**
**General Practice.**
**In Irvine, California: 2603 Main Street, Suite 900. Telephone: 714-851-3939. Telex: 194911 Lawyers LSA. Telecopier: 714-553-7539.**
**In Atlanta, Georgia: 3500 One Peachtree Center, 303 Peachtree Street, N.E. Telephone: 404-521-3939. Cable Address: "Attorneys Atlanta". Telex: 54-2711. Telecopier: 404-581-8330.**
**In Brussels, Belgium: Avenue Louise 480, 7th Floor, B-1050 Brussels. Telephone: 32-2-645-14-11. Telecopier: 32-2-645-14-45.**
**In Chicago, Illinois: 77 West Wacker. Telephone: 312-782-3939. Telecopier: 312-782-8585.**
**In Cleveland, Ohio: North Point, 901 Lakeside Avenue. Telephone: 216-586-3939. Cable Address: "Attorneys Cleveland." Telex: 980389. Telecopier: 216-579-0212.**
**In Columbus, Ohio: 1900 Huntington Center. Telephone: 614-469-3939. Cable Address: "Attorneys Columbus." Telecopier: 614-461-4198.**
**In Dallas, Texas: 2300 Trammell Crow Center, 2001 Ross Avenue. Telephone: 214-220-3939. Cable Address: "Attorneys Dallas." Telex: 730852. Telecopier: 214-969-5100.**
**In Frankfurt, Germany: Triton Haus, Bockenheimer Landstrasse 42, 60323 Frankfurt am Main. Telephone: 49-69-9726-3939. Telecopier: 49-69-9726-3993.**
**In Geneva, Switzerland: 20, rue de Candolle. Telephone: 41-22-320-2339. Telecopier: 41-22-320-1232.**
**In Hong Kong: 29th Floor, Entertainment Building, 30 Queen's Road Central. Telephone: 852-2526-6895. Telecopier: 852-2868-5871.**
**In London England: Bucklersbury House, 3 Queen Victoria Street. Telephone: 44-171-236-3939. Telecopier: 44-171-236-1113.**
**In New Delhi, India: Pathak & Associates, 13th Floor, Dr. Gopal Das Bhaven, 28 Barakhamba Road. Telephone: 91-11-373-8793. Telecopier: 91-11-335-3761.**
**In New York, New York: 599 Lexington Avenue. Telephone: 212-326-3939. Cable Address: "JONESDAY NEWYORK." Telex: 237013 JDRP UR. Telecopier: 212-755-7306.**
**In Paris, France: 62, rue du Faubourg Saint-Honore. Telephone: 33-1-44-71-3939. Telex: 290156 Surgoe. Telecopier: 33-1-49-24-0471.**
**In Pittsburgh, Pennsylvania: 500 Grant Street, 31st Floor. Telephone: 412-391-3939. Cable Address: "Attorneys Pittsburgh". Telecopier: 412-394-7959.**
**In Riyadh, Saudi Arabia: The International Law Firm, Sulaymaniyah Center, Tahlia Street, P.O. Box 22166. Telephone: (966-1) 462-8866. Telecopier: (966-1) 462-9001.**
**In Taipei, Taiwan: 8th Floor, 2 Tun Hwa South Road, Section 2. Telephone: (886-2) 704-6808. Telecopier: (886-2) 704-6791.**
**In Tokyo, Japan: Toranomon MT Building, 4th Floor, 10-3, Toranomon 3-Chome, Minato-ku, Tokyo 105, Japan. Telephone: 81-3-3433-3939. Telecopier: 81-3-5401-2725.**
**In Washington, D.C.: Metropolitan Square, 1450 G Street, N.W. Telephone: 202-879-3939. Cable Address: "Attorneys Washington." Telex: 89-2410 ATTORNEYS WASH. Telecopier: 202-737-2832.**

***See Professional Biographies, LOS ANGELES, CALIFORNIA***

Jones Hirsch Connors & Bull LLP
1925 Century Park E. (⊙N.Y. & White Plains, NY, Newark, NJ & Stamford, CT)

**Jones, Kaufman & Ackerman LLP, (AV)** BR
**10960 Wilshire Boulevard, Suite 1225, 90024**
**Telephone: 310-477-8575 Fax: 310-477-8768**
**Donald H. Jones; Paul W. Kaufman; Michael S. Ackerman; Marc H. Corman; Ellen Roth Nagler.**
**Real Estate, Corporation, Finance, Secured Creditor Litigation, Estate Planning and Federal and State Taxation.**

***See Professional Biographies, LOS ANGELES, CALIFORNIA***

**Jones, Mahoney, Brayton & Soll**
**(See Claremont)**

Jonker, Peter E. '48 '79
C.800 B.S. L.1137 J.D. Dir., Governmental Affs., So. Calif. Gas Co.
**Joo, Anna Y.** ........................'69 '96 C.118 B.A. L.309 J.D. [Ⓐ Quinn E.U.&O.]
**Jordan, Carolyn Comparet** '62 '86 C.112 B.A. L.1068 J.D.
[Christensen,M.F.J.G.W.&S.]
*PRACTICE AREAS: Real Estate; Corporate Law.
**Jordan, Charles A.** ...................... '45 '77 C.1074 B.S. L.1137 J.D. [Ⓐ Holley&G.]
*PRACTICE AREAS: Business Law (Transactional and Litigation); Real Estate Litigation Law.
**Jordan, Daniel G.** ...................'54 '81 C.112 B.A. L.1066 J.D. [Ⓒ Case,K.B.&W.]⊙
**Jordan, Edward M.** ..................... '66 '95 C.112 b.S.M.E. L.426 J.D. [Ⓐ Lyon&L.]
*PRACTICE AREAS: Patent; Trademark; Copyright; Unfair Competition; Antitrust.

**Jordan, James V. '49 '75 C.112 B.A. L.1068 J.D.**
**12100 Wilshire Boulevard 15th Floor, 90025**
**Telephone: 310-826-2255 FAX: 310-207-3230**
**Email: JORDAN@SJAW.COM**
***REPORTED CASES: Cislaw v. 7-Eleven (1992) 4 Cal. App. 4th 1284; CIM v. United States, 641 F 2d 1441 (9th Cir. 1980); The Southland Corporation v. Emerald Oil, 789 F 2d 1441 (9th Cir. 1986).**
***PRACTICE AREAS: Securities; Franchise; Intellectual Property; Business; Commercial.**
**Associate: Leopoldo A. Bautista.**
**Franchise, Intellectual Property, Labor, Insurance, Business, Real Estate, Corporate, Tort, Administrative Law and Litigation and Appellate Practice in all State and Federal Courts before Municipal Administrative and Regulatory Boards, Agencies and Elected Councils, Banking and Finance.**

***See Professional Biographies, LOS ANGELES, CALIFORNIA***

**Jordan, Martha Barnhart** ............... '54 '83 C.645 B.S. L.1066 J.D. [Latham&W.]
Jordan, Susan Fox ...................... '59 '86 C.1042 B.A. L.426 J.D. [Schmid&V.] ‡
**Jordon, Leslie M.** ......................... '65 '90 C.103 B.A. L.597 J.D. [Ⓐ Trope&T.]
*LANGUAGES: French.

**Jorgensen, Darcy D.** ........................'62 '94 C.188 B.A. L.809 J.D. [Ⓐ Selman B.]
*PRACTICE AREAS: Insurance Defense.
**Jorgensen, Eric Todd** ............... '65 '94 C.112 B.A. L.1065 J.D. [Ⓐ Luce,F.H.&S.]
*PRACTICE AREAS: Insurance; Reinsurance; Litigation.
**Jorrie, Kathy A.** ....................'59 '85 C.112 B.A. L.1065 J.D. [Donovan L.N.&I.]
Jorstad, Kristofer ........................ '47 '75 C.37 B.A. L.1066 J.D. Dep. Atty. Gen.
Joseph, Alan A. ..............................'44 '69 C&L.37 B.S., J.D. 1680 Vine St.
Joseph, Howard L. ..........................'46 '71 C.685 B.A. L.309 J.D. [Joseph&J.]
**Joseph, James J., (A Professional Corporation)**, (AV) '47 '72
C.685 B.A. L.1066 J.D. [Ⓒ Danning,G.D.&K.]
Joseph, Michael D. ..........................'52 '78 C.112 B.A. L.1065 J.D. [Joseph&J.]
**Joseph, Neil D.** ..............................'57 '85 C.043 B.A. L.809 J.D. [Ives,K.&D.]
Joseph, Richard N. ..............'50 '86 C.1097 B.A. L.940 J.D. 116 N. Robertson Blvd.
Joseph & Joseph ........................................ 1875 Century Park East
Josephs, Steven H. ...................... '53 '79 C.112 B.S. L.426 J.D. 868 Moraga Dr.
Josephson, Barry S. ........................ '49 '73 C.112 B.A. L.477 J.D. [Ⓐ Segal&K.]

**Jossen, Sanford, (BV) '51 '82 C.415 B.A. L.1049 J.D.**
**Eighth Floor 1840 Century Park East, 90067-2101**
**Telephone: 310-201-0755; 201-0910 Telecopier: 310-553-2033**
***PRACTICE AREAS: Personal Injury; Business Litigation; Real Estate; Insurance Law.**
**Business Litigation of all types including: Corporate Dissolution, Entertainment (all Media), International Freight, Real Estate, Bad Faith Insurance, Personal Injury including Motor Vehicle, Slips, Trips and Falls, Medical Malpractice, Dental Malpractice. Also extensive Arbitration/Mediation experience.**

***See Professional Biographies, LOS ANGELES, CALIFORNIA***

**Joy, Thomas J.** ..........................'51 '76 C.426 B.B.A. L.809 J.D. [Ⓐ Ochoa&S.]
*PRACTICE AREAS: Immigration Law; Litigation.
**Joyce, Catherine** ..........................'58 '94 C.118 B.A. L.273 J.D. [Ⓐ Lyon&L.]
*PRACTICE AREAS: Patent; Trademark.
Joyce, J. Patrick .................'48 '77 C.1075 B.A. L.990 J.D. Sr. Dep. County Coun.
**Joye, Gary M.** ...................... '56 '82 C.502 B.A. L.1068 J.D. [Ⓒ Gibson,D.&C.]
*PRACTICE AREAS: Litigation.
**Joyner, Jeffrey K.** ...........................'69 '95 C.273 B.A. L.810 J.D. [Ⓐ Baker&H.]
*PRACTICE AREAS: Litigation; Intellectual Property.
Juarez, Angel N. ..................... '64 '91 C.605 A.B. L.112 J.D. Dep. Fed. Pub. Def.
**Juarez, George A.**, (AV) ......... '49 '77 C.112 B.A. L.1066 J.D. [Ⓒ Pachulski,S.Z.&Y.]
**Jubas, Marvin**, (AV) ................'29 '55 C.112 B.S. L.1068 J.D. [Ⓒ Fierstein&S.]
*PRACTICE AREAS: Trademark; Licensing; Copyright; Unfair Competition; Antitrust.
**Jubelt, Mark L.** ......................... '62 '87 C.1074 B.A. L.1067 J.D. [Selman B.]
Judd, Emilie D. .................'69 '74 C.112 B.A. L.1049 J.D. 1900 Ave. of the Stars
Judge, Michael P., (AV) ..........................'44 '69 C.112 B.A. L.1068 J.D. Pub. Def.
**Judson, Gerald R** .....................'44 '81 C.112 B.A. L.809 J.D. [Lewis,D.B.&B.]
**Juhas, Mark A.** .................. '54 '79 C.170 B.S. L.678 J.D. [Harrington,F.D.&C.]
*PRACTICE AREAS: Product Liability Law; Personal Injury Defense Law.
**Juhn, Sharon I.** ........................'64 '91 C.112 B.A. L.1068 J.D. [Rutter,G.&H.]
*LANGUAGES: Korean and Spanish.
*PRACTICE AREAS: Labor; Employment; General Litigation.
**Julien, Laurie S.** ................. '62 '88 C.112 B.A. L.1065 J.D. [Ⓐ Bronson,B.&M.]
*PRACTICE AREAS: Insurance Coverage and Bad Faith; Civil Litigation; Appellate.
**Jun, Joyce S.** ..............................'63 '89 C.112 B.A. L.1068 J.D. [Loeb&L.]
*LANGUAGES: Korean and Japanese.
*PRACTICE AREAS: Entertainment Law; International Transactions.
**Jun, Richard C.** '70 '96 C.309 A.B. L.178 J.D.
(adm. in NY; not adm. in CA) [Ⓐ Rogers&W.]
**Juo, James** '67 '93 C.158 B.S.E.E. L.273 J.D.
(adm. in VA; not adm. in CA; See Pat. Sect.) [Ⓐ Fulwider P.L.&U.]
*PRACTICE AREAS: Intellectual Property.
Jurecka, James R., (AV) ............'35 '66 C.691 B.A. L.273 J.D. 2029 Century Park E.
**Jurich, Lance N.** ............................ '62 '87 C.36 B.S. L.94 J.D. [Ⓐ Loeb&L.]
*PRACTICE AREAS: Insolvency and Workout.
**Justice, Cheryl D.** ...................... '45 '82 C.112 B.A. L.309 J.D. [Gibson,D.&C.]
*PRACTICE AREAS: Complex Commercial and Business Litigation; Defense of Federal Securities Class Actions; Professional Malpractice Actions; SEC Investigations.
**Justice, Gary L.**, (AV) ................. '54 '79 C.150 B.S. L.228 J.D. [Gibson,D.&C.]
*PRACTICE AREAS: Insurance "Bad Faith" and Coverage Litigation; Environmental Litigation; Products Liability and Toxic Torts; Commercial Litigation; Common Carrier Liability Law.
**Justman, Jennifer** ................. '60 '86 C.813 B.A. L.1068 J.D. [Ⓒ Katz,G.&F.]
*PRACTICE AREAS: Entertainment Law; Motion Pictures and Television; Multimedia Law.
**Justo, Justo M.** ............................'58 '92 C&L.061 B.S., LL.B. [Ⓐ Kern&W.]
**Juzwiak, Peter M.** ........................'61 '91 C.1111 B.A. L.800 J.D. [Ⓐ Irell&M.]
Kaas, Lisa K. ............................'64 '90 C.880 B.A. L.861 J.D. Dep. Dist. Atty.
**Kaasik, Raimo H.** .................. '63 '89 C&L.846 B.B.A., J.D. [Ⓐ Lewis,D.B.&B.]
**Kabat, Jules L.** .........................'49 '74 C.112 A.B. L.1068 J.D. [Russ,A.&K.]
*PRACTICE AREAS: Land Use Law; Real Property Law; Environmental Law; Complex Real Property and Business Litigation.
**Kabateck, Brian S.** ................. '61 '90 C.800 B.A. L.426 J.D. [Ⓐ Quisenberry&B.]
Kabert-Gerson, Marlene ...........'55 '81 C.112 B.A. L.809 J.D. 1605 W. Olympic Blvd.
**Kachel, Linda L.** ...................... '54 '88 C.597 B.S. L.800 J.D. [Ⓐ Katz&Assoc.]
Kaddo, James A. ..........................'34 '64 C.112 B.A. L.800 LL.B. Mun. Ct. J.
**Kadison, Stuart L.**, (AV) ...............'23 '48 C.446 A.B. L.813 LL.B. [Ⓒ Sidley&A.]
*PRACTICE AREAS: General Litigation.
**Kadlec, Robert W.** ........................'63 '88 C.575 B.S. L.569 J.D. [Ⓐ Sidley&A.]
*PRACTICE AREAS: Corporate Law.
**Kadue, David D.** .................. '52 '78 C.976 B.A. L.494 J.D. [Seyfarth,S.F.&G.]
*PRACTICE AREAS: Labor and Employment Law; Civil Litigation.
**Kadzielski, Mark A.** ...................'47 '76 C.363 A.B. L.659 J.D. [Epstein B.&G.]
*PRACTICE AREAS: Health and Hospital Law; Medical Staff Law.
**Kaften, Timothy W.** ........................ '59 '90 C.112 B.A. L.809 J.D. [Lovich&P.]
**Kagan, Gerald B., (P.C.)**, (AV) ........'43 '67 C.454 A.B. L.273 J.D. [Alschuler G.&P.]
**Kagan, Jonathan S.** ...................... '68 '93 C.659 B.S. L.1068 J.D. [Ⓐ Irell&M.]
**Kagan, Matthew H.** '62 '89
C.139 B.S. L.770 J.D. [Ⓐ Herzfeld&R.] (⊙Newport Beach, CA.)
**Kagan, Seymour** ....................... '30 '56 C.102 B.A. L.1009 J.D. [Herzfeld&R.]
*PRACTICE AREAS: Business; Environmental; Toxic Torts; Insurance Law; Litigation.
Kagel, David L. ...........................'38 '66 C.472 A.B. L.1009 LL.B. [D.L.Kagel]
Kagel, David L., Prof. Law Corp. ........................ 1801 Century Park, E., 25th Fl.
**Kagon, A. David**, (AV) .................. '18 '47 C&L.178 B.A., LL.B. [Ⓒ Goldman&K.]
*REPORTED CASES: Marvin v. Marvin, 122 Cal. App. 3d 871, 176 Cal. Rptr. 555 (1981); Marvin v. Marvin, 18 C.3d 660 (1976), 134 Cal. Rptr. 815; Watkins v. Watkins, 143 Cal. App. 3d 651, 192 Cal. Rptr. 54 (1983); Bergen v. Wood, 14 Cal. App. 4th 854, 18 Cal. Rptr. 2d 75 (1993).
*PRACTICE AREAS: Mediation and Arbitration; Family Law; Business Law; Real Property Law.
**Kahane, Tammy L.** ...................... '64 '89 C.112 B.A. L.426 J.D. [Ⓐ Arter&H.]
*PRACTICE AREAS: Commercial Litigation; Real Estate Litigation; Banking Law.
Kahanowicz, Alex ................ '22 '50 C.625 B.A. L.800 J.D. 214 N. Ridgewood Pl.
**Kahn, Arnold D.**, (AV) ........'39 '65 C.112 A.B. L.1068 LL.B. [Greenberg G.F.C.&M.]
*PRACTICE AREAS: Estate Planning; Probate and Trust Law.
**Kahn, Beth A.** ............................'61 '88 C.605 A.B. L.36 J.D. [Ⓐ Morris,P.&P.]
Kahn, Carole S. ....................... '54 '79 C&L.608 B.A., J.D. 4700 Wilshire Blvd.
**Kahn, Charles H.**, (AV) ...... '36 '61 C.188 B.A. L.597 J.D. [Ⓒ Berger,K.S.M.F.S.&G.]

CAA259P

Kahn, David L. .................... '42 '67 C.659 B.S. L.309 LL.B. 535 N. Hayworth Ave.
**Kahn, David O.** .......................... '60 '94 C.1077 B.S. L.309 J.D. [A Latham&W.]
*LANGUAGES: French.
Kahn, Lisa ..................................... '57 '84 C.800 B.S. L.809 J.D. Dep. Dist. Atty.
**Kahn, Lisa Hannah** ...................... '68 '93 C.763 B.A. L.1049 J.D. [A Selman B.]
**Kahn, Michael A., (AV)** ................. '49 '73 C.112 B.A. L.813 J.D. [Folger L.&K.]©
**Kahn, Ruth D.** ............................... '60 '85 C.174 B.S. L.930 J.D. [Lane P.S.L.]
*PRACTICE AREAS: Civil Litigation, Toxic Torts, Products Liability.
**Kahn, Susan Mapel** ..................... '48 '83 C.174 B.A. L.426 J.D. [A Sullivan,W.&D.]
Kahn, Stern & Blaney, (AV) ...................................5959 W. Century Blvd.
Kahng, Son Young ..................... '64 '92 C.103 A.B. L.1068 J.D. 1 Wilshire Blvd.
**Kaiman, Barry G., (P.C.)** ................ '49 '75 C.705 B.A. L.546 J.D. [Lewis,D.B.&B.]
Kairys, Cynthia M. ..................... '64 '90 C.426 B.A. L.809 J.D. 320 W. Temple St.
**Kaiser, Hayward J., (A Professional Corporation),** (AV) '50 '75
C.112 B.A. L.1068 J.D. [Mitchell,S.&K.]
*PRACTICE AREAS: Insurance Law; Contractual Litigation; Unfair Competition Law; Antitrust Litigation; Products Liability Law.
Kaiserman, Kenneth H. ................ '63 '89 C.112 B.A. L.800 J.D. 2788 Monte Mar Ter.

**Kajan Mather and Barish, A Professional Corporation**
**(See Beverly Hills)**

Kakita, Edward Y. ............................ '40 '66 C.800 B.S. L.1065 J.D. Supr. Ct. J.

**Kale, Michael A., (AV) '52 '78 C.763 B.A. L.990 J.D.**
**Suite 1225, 10960 Wilshire Boulevard, 90024-3715**
**Telephone: 310-473-3133 FAX: 310-477-6778**
***PRACTICE AREAS: Real Estate; Business Litigation.**
**Insurance Defense as related to Real Estate and Business Litigation, Construction Defect, Title Insurance Defense in all State and Federal Courts. Banking, Financial Institutions and Business Litigation.**
***See Professional Biographies, LOS ANGELES, CALIFORNIA***

**Kale, Richard A.** ................... '55 '80 C.112 A.B. L.976 J.D. [Greenberg G.F.C.&M.]
*PRACTICE AREAS: Real Estate Law.
**Kaler, Randall W.** ..................... '52 '82 C.506 B.S. L.990 J.D. [Gilbert,K.C.&J.]
Kalfayan, Lawrence J. ................... '55 '81 C.605 A.B. L.1065 J.D. 550 S. Hope St.
Kaliardos, Christine ........................ '— '89 C&L.477 B.S., J.D. 801 S. Grand Ave.
**Kalifon, David R.** ..................... '46 '88 C.705 B.A. L.1068 J.D. [© Jeffer,M.B.&M.]
*PRACTICE AREAS: Health; Professional Licensing; Contracts; Privileges; Peer Review.
Kalin, Neil D. ............ '60 '85 C.339 B.S. L.1068 J.D. Sr. Coun., Calif. Assn. of Realtors
Kalinski, George ................................ '35 '59 C&L.912 A.B., LL.B. Supr. Ct. Comr.

**Kalisch, Cotugno & Rust**
**(See Beverly Hills)**

**Kaliser, Laura B.** ......................... '66 '92 C.477 B.S. L.1148 J.D. [A Lewis,D.B.&B.]
Kallan, Roberta S. ........... '— '74 C.112 A.B. L.1065 J.D. 10866 Wilshire Blvd. Penthse

**Kallay, Thomas, Law Offices of, (AV) '37 '63 C.112 A.B. L.1068 J.D.** BB
**445 South Figueroa Street 27th Floor, 90071-1603**
**Telephone: 213-612-7717 Facsimile: 213-426-2181**
***LANGUAGES: German and Hungarian.**
***REPORTED CASES: Scofield v. Critical Air Medicine, Inc. (1996) 45 Cal. App. 4th 990; Photias v. Doertler (1996) 45 Cal. App. 4th 1014; Nguyen v. Los Angeles County Harbor/UCLA Medical Center (1995) 40 Cal. App. 4th 1433; International Engine Parts v. Fedderson (1995) 9 Cal.4th 606; Schultz v. Harney (1994) 27 Cal.App.4th 1611.**
***PRACTICE AREAS: Appellate Practice; Civil Trial.**
**Appellate Practice in State and Federal Courts.**
***See Professional Biographies, LOS ANGELES, CALIFORNIA***

**Kallberg, Candace E. Ahrens** .............. '53 '83 C.763 B.S. L.426 J.D. [A Schell&D.]
Kallberg, Delmer C. .............. '14 '54 C.494 B.A. L.487 LL.B. 12046 National Blvd.‡
Kallen, Norman H. ............... '42 '67 C.339 B.A. L.146 J.D. 1901 Avenue of the Stars
**Kaller, Adam David** ......................... '66 '91 C.800 B.S. L.1148 J.D. [Behr&A.]
*PRACTICE AREAS: Entertainment Law.
**Kallick, Ivan L., (AV)** .............. '55 '81 C.112 B.S. L.767 J.D. [McDermott,W.&E.]
*PRACTICE AREAS: Bankruptcy; Debtor and Creditor; Hotels.
Kalliomaa, Jill Freeman '61 '89 C&L.37 B.A., J.D.
Corp. Coun., Alpha Therapeutic Corp.
**Kallman, H. Jay** ..................................... '52 '91 C.012 B.A. L.813 J.D. [Hedges&C.]
**Kalmansohn, Mark E.** ................. '53 '77 C.112 B.A. L.1068 J.D. [McPherson&K.]
Kalnit, Arthur B. ............ '34 '59 C.367 B.A. L.178 LL.B. 11150 Santa Monica Blvd.
**Kaloyanides, David J.P.** ................. '64 '92 C.112 B.A. L.426 J.D. [A Quinn E.U.&O.]
**Kalpakian, Stephen M.** ................ '60 '90 C.940 B.S. L.426 J.D. [A Williams,B.&S.]
**Kalt, Scott M.** ............................... '63 '88 C&L.477 B.A., J.D. [Jeffer,M.B.&M.]
*PRACTICE AREAS: Real Estate; Acquisitions and Dispositions; Finance; Leasing.
Kalunian, Robert E. ........................... '48 '73 C.1097 B.A. L.809 J.D. Co. Pub. Def.
Kalustian, Richard P. ..................... '36 '64 C.800 B.S.M.E. L.426 LL.B. Supr. Ct. J.
**Kalyvas, James R.** ........................ '56 '81 C.1154 B.A. L.477 J.D. [Foley L.W.&A.]
*PRACTICE AREAS: Commercial Litigation; Information Systems; Health Care; Hospitals; Real Estate.
**Kam, Randall K. L.** .......................... '61 '91 C.800 B.S. L.809 J.D. [A Koletsky,M.&F.]
*PRACTICE AREAS: General Liability Defense Litigation.
**Kamanski, James B.** .......................... '67 '94 C.763 B.A. L.464 J.D. [A Selman B.]
*PRACTICE AREAS: Litigation.
**Kambe, Lynn Leversen** ................ '46 '81 C.770 B.A. L.426 J.D. [A Jones,D.R.&P.]
Kame, Margaret M. ................. '51 '87 C.768 B.S.H.S. L.809 J.D. 2960 Wilshire Blvd.
Kamei, Duane O. ........................ '54 '87 C.911 B.S. L.93 J.D. 1000 Wilshire Blvd.
Kamenir, Edward ........................... '22 '78 C.339 B.S. L.1136 J.D. 1224 Casiano Rd.
**Kamenir, Sandra** .............................. '49 '76 C.112 B.A. L.1095 J.D. [A D.B.Bloom]
**Kamenir-Reznik, Janice M., (AV)** ......... '52 '82 C.112 B.A. L.1068 J.D. [Reznik&R.]
*LANGUAGES: Hebrew.
*SPECIAL AGENCIES: Federal Deposit Insurance Corporation (FDIC); Los Angeles County Metropolitan Transit Authority (MTA).
*REPORTED CASES: Haskel vs. Superior Court, 33 Cal. App. 4th 963, Mod. 34 Cal. App. 4th 199e, rev. den. (June 29, 1995).
*PRACTICE AREAS: Environmental Law; Regulatory Compliance; Administrative Law; Hazardous Waste, State and Federal Superfund.
**Kamer, William, (AV)** ........................ '51 '78 C.881 A.B. L.94 J.D. [Cox,C.&N.]
*PRACTICE AREAS: Real Property Law.
**Kamine, Bernard S., (AV)** ................. '43 '69 C.208 B.A. L.309 J.D. [Kamine,S.&U.]
*PRACTICE AREAS: Construction.
Kamine, Marcia Haber ..................... '46 '78 C.112 B.S. L.809 J.D. Dep. City Atty.

**Kamine, Steiner & Ungerer, (AV)**
**Suite 250 World Trade Center, 350 S. Figueroa Street, 90071**
**Telephone: 213-972-0119**
**Bernard S. Kamine; Phyllis Ungerer. Associates: Maurya Hogan; Kevin Collins. Of Counsel: Matt Steiner; Lynn E. Hall.**
**Construction Industry Litigation, Business Litigation.**
***See Professional Biographies, LOS ANGELES, CALIFORNIA***

Kamins, Richard J., (AV) ....................... '25 '51 C&L.800 LL.B. [© Tyre K.K.&G.]
**Kaminsky, Michael J.** ................... '58 '86 C.228 B.A. L.94 J.D. [Stephens,B.&L.]
*PRACTICE AREAS: Real Estate; Community Association Law.
Kamm, Paul P. ................... '33 '63 C.1043 B.A. L.809 LL.B. 7200 W. 88th Pl.
**Kamm, Solomon M., (AV)** '38 '63 C.339 B.S. L.569 J.D.
V.P., Gen. Coun. & Secy., Capital Grp. Cos., Inc.
*RESPONSIBILITIES: Estate Planning; Estate Administration.
Kamon, Ralph .................. '23 '54 C.724 B.B.A. L.1009 LL.B. 11355 W. Olympic Blvd.
Kamornick, Phillip S. .................. '45 '74 C.112 B.A. L.1148 J.D. 344 N. Martel Ave.
Kamraczewski, Kevin P. .................. '56 '82 C.145 A.B. L.339 J.D. 601 S. Figueroa

**Kananack, Murgatroyd, Baum & Hedlund, A Professional Corporation**
**(See Baum, Hedlund, Aristei, Guilford & Downey)**

**Kanazawa, Sidney K.** ................... '52 '78 C.312 B.Ed. L.800 J.D. [Pillsbury M.&S.]
Kandel, Stanley T. ....................... '45 '70 C.1068 B.A. L.800 J.D. 2414 GuthrieDr.
**Kane, Brad S.** ................................ '65 '90 C.112 B.A. L.1065 J.D. [A Weisman&R.]
*PRACTICE AREAS: Business Litigation; Appellate Practice.
Kane, Harry N. ............................ '60 '89 C.112 B.A. L.1148 J.D. 4700 Wilshire Blvd.
**Kane, Kevin P.** .............................. '46 '71 C.676 B.A. L.309 J.D. [Kane&O.]
*PRACTICE AREAS: Business Litigation; Antitrust Law; Unfair Competition Law; Labor Law; Insurance Law.
**Kane, Margaret McDonald** .................. '44 '80 C.800 A.B. L.809 J.D. [Silver&F.]
*PRACTICE AREAS: Business Law; Corporate Law; Real Property Law.
**Kane, Mark** .................................. '56 '94 C.994 B.A. L.809 J.D. [A Robinson,D.&W.]
*PRACTICE AREAS: Litigation.
**Kane, Mark C., (AV)** ......................... '31 '61 C&L.426 LL.B. [Kane,W.&P.]
*PRACTICE AREAS: Insurance Defense; Civil Litigation.
**Kane, Murray O., (AV)** ...................... '46 '71 C.112 A.B. L.1068 J.D. [Kane,B.&B.]
*TRANSACTIONS: Fox Hills Mall, Culver City; Santa Monica Place, Santa Monica; Museum of Contemporary Art, Los Angeles; Watts Shopping Center, Los Angeles; Los Angeles Central Library restoration and expansion.
*PRACTICE AREAS: Redevelopment Law; Public Finance Law; Affordable Housing Law.
Kane, Paula, (AV) ...................... '49 '80 C.800 B.S. L.809 J.D. 1801 Century Park E.

**Kane, Ballmer & Berkman, A Law Corporation, (AV)**
**515 South Figueroa Street Suite 1850, 90071**
**Telephone: 213-617-0480 Telecopier: 213-625-0931**
**Murray O. Kane; Bruce D. Ballmer; Glenn F. Wasserman; R. Bruce Tepper, Jr.; Joseph W. Pannone; Royce K. Jones; Stephanie R. Scher;—June Ailin; Marc J. Manason; Michael J. Karger; Sonia J. Ransom.**
**Housing and Urban Development, Redevelopment, Municipal, Land Use, Real Estate, Eminent Domain, Environmental, Hazardous Waste and Local and State Government Law. Litigation in all Courts.**
**Special Counsel for Redevelopment: Cities of Glendale, Hawthorne, Lynwood, Moreno Valley, Redondo Beach, San Diego, Santa Ana, Santa Clara, Santa Monica, Vernon.**
***See Professional Biographies, LOS ANGELES, CALIFORNIA***

**Kane & O'Brien, A Professional Law Corporation**
**11766 Wilshire Boulevard, Suite 1580, 90025**
**Telephone: 310-575-1199 Fax: 310-575-1979**
**Kevin P. Kane; Mark A. O'Brien.**
**Civil Litigation and Trial Practice.**
***See Professional Biographies, LOS ANGELES, CALIFORNIA***

Kane-Ritsch, Julie '59 '84 C.208 B.A. L.209 J.D.
Asst. V.P., Bus. & Leg. Affs., Hanna-Barbera Productions, Inc.

**Kane, Wright & Paulos, (AV)**
**6055 Washington Boulevard, Suite 1000, 90040**
**Telephone: 213-728-8606 Fax: 213-728-8607**
**Mark C. Kane; Adam A. Wright; Nicholas Paulos.**
**General Civil and Trial Practice in all State and Federal Courts. Casualty, Property, Surety, Fire and Marine Insurance.**
**Representative Clients: Farmers Home Group; Deans & Homer; Western General Agency; Michigan Millers Insurance Co.; Liberty Mutual Insurance Co.; Vulcan Materials Co.; Ralphs Grocery Co.**

**Kanengiser, Sandra Gerson** ................... '55 '84 C.112 B.A. L.800 J.D. [Irell&M.]
**Kaneshiro, Wynn Cross** ........... '67 '92 C.061 B.A. L.1068 J.D. [A Sedgwick,D.M.&A.]
*LANGUAGES: Tagalog.
**Kang, Anna Park** ........................ '69 '94 C.112 B.A. L.1065 J.D. [A Burke,W.&S.]
*PRACTICE AREAS: Municipal Law; Bankruptcy Law.
**Kang, Jonathan Y.** ............ '61 '93 C.112 B.S. L.426 J.D. [A Loeb&L.] (See Pat. Sect.)
*LANGUAGES: Korean.
*PRACTICE AREAS: Patent; Trademark; Copyright.
**Kang, Sungyong** ............................ '48 '86 C.784 B.A. L.276 J.D. [© Gibson,D.&C.]
*LANGUAGES: Korean.
*PRACTICE AREAS: General Corporate.
Kanin, Paul R., (AV) ............... '51 '76 C.112 B.A. L.1148 J.D. 1801 Ave. of the Stars
**Kanjo, Christopher A.** ..................... '60 '87 C.112 B.A. L.800 J.D. [Wilson,K.&B.]
Kanne, Frank J., Jr., (AV) ............. '16 '41 C.112 A.B. L.1066 LL.B. 818 Devon Ave.‡
**Kannow, William Paul** ................. '51 '76 C&L.426 B.A., J.D. [Crosby,H.R.&M.]
*PRACTICE AREAS: Product Liability; Professional Negligence; Commercial Litigation.
**Kanny, Matthew P.** ........................ '64 '93 C.477 B.S. L.426 J.D. [A Gibbs,G.L.&A.]
*PRACTICE AREAS: Construction Litigation; Employment Law.
Kanode, Delno G. '30 '63
C.112 B.A. L.1068 LL.B. Sr. Real Estate Coun., Sizzler Intl., Inc.
**Kanoff, Mary Ellen** ......................... '56 '84 C.112 A.B. L.1066 J.D. [Latham&W.]
**Kanofsky, Gordon R.** ................ '55 '80 C.910 A.B. L.228 J.D. [© Sanders,B.G.S.&M.]
*PRACTICE AREAS: Corporate Law; Commercial Law; Securities Law; Intellectual Property Law.
Kanowsky, Carl J. ................ '54 '83 C.154 B.A. L.426 J.D. 2029 Century Park E.
Kanter, Deborah L. ........................ '63 '92 C.914 B.A. L.813 J.D. 400 S. Hope St.
**Kanter, Gary A.** ........................... '47 '72 C.37 B.A. L.426 J.D. [Clopton,P.&B.]
**Kanter, Sandra M.** ..................... '56 '81 C.1036 B.A. L.309 J.D. [Nossaman,G.K.&E.]
*PRACTICE AREAS: Real Property Law.
Kantor, Joel M. ........................ '46 '72 C.768 B.A. L.1067 J.D. 1990 S. Bundy Dr.
**Kao, Charles J.** ......................... '68 '94 C.112 B.A. L.188 J.D. [A Walker,W.T.&W.]
*LANGUAGES: Mandarin Chinese.
**Kao, Shane Y.** ............................ '70 '95 C.112 B.S. L.276 J.D. [A Morrison&F.]
Kapel, James R. ........................... '47 '72 C&L.608 A.B., J.D. Asst. City Atty.
Kapetan, Eugene V., (AV) ........... '28 '55 C.112 B.S. L.1068 LL.B. 3700 Wilshire Blvd.
**Kaplan, Alan I., (AV)** .................... '50 '79 C.188 B.A. L.426 J.D. [A Herzfeld&R.]
Kaplan, Benjamin L., (AV) ....... '14 '40 C.339 B.A. L.146 LL.B. 2222 Ave. of the Stars‡
Kaplan, David '44 '70 C.339 B.S. L.209 J.D.
(adm. in IL; not adm. in CA) 10551 Lindbrook Dr.‡
**Kaplan, David P.** ............................ '63 '88 C.674 A.B. L.1066 J.D. [A Katten M.&Z.]
*PRACTICE AREAS: Litigation.
**Kaplan, Frank, (P.C.)** ................... '46 '72 C.150 B.A. L.477 J.D. [Alschuler G.&P.]
**Kaplan, Gary L.** ..................... '49 '76 C.605 A.B. L.309 J.D. [Greenberg G.F.C.&M.]
*PRACTICE AREAS: Taxation; General Business.
**Kaplan, Gary R.** ........................... '58 '83 C.776 B.A. L.809 J.D. [A Sylvester&O.]
*PRACTICE AREAS: Governmental Tort Liability; Contracts; Bad Faith; Medical Malpractice; Legal Malpractice.
**Kaplan, Janet** .................................. '53 '94 C.188 B.S. L.426 J.D. [A Freid&G.]
*PRACTICE AREAS: Family Law.
Kaplan, Jay A., (AV) ...................... '51 '79 C.112 B.A. L.1148 J.D. [Kaplan]
Kaplan, Jeffrey A. .................... '47 '72 C.800 B.S. L.1066 J.D. 924 Westwood Blvd.
Kaplan, Jeffrey S. ......................... '67 '93 C.112 B.A. L.426 J.D. [A Gaglione&D.]
**Kaplan, Jonathon** ..................... '65 '90 C.1365 B.A. L.228 J.D. [A Lewis,D.B.&B.]

**Kaplan, Louis M.** ... '60 '87 C.112 B.S. L.426 J.D. [Troop M.S.&P.]
*PRACTICE AREAS: Real Estate Law.
**Kaplan, Mark Vincent**, (AV) ... '47 '73 C.339 B.A. L.809 J.D. [Trope&T.]
*LANGUAGES: Italian.
*PRACTICE AREAS: Family Law.
Kaplan, Marla J. ... '63 '92 C.112 B.A. L.809 J.D. 515 S. Flower St.
**Kaplan, Martin D.** ... '30 '79 C.800 Phar. D. L.1136 J.D. [Ⓒ Lynberg&W.]
Kaplan, Martin J. ... '51 '76 C.494 B.A. L.1068 J.D. Embassy TV
**Kaplan, Matthew I.** ... '67 '93 C.477 B.A. L.494 J.D. [Ⓐ Sonnenschein N.&R.]
*PRACTICE AREAS: Insurance Law; Construction Law; Commercial Litigation.
**Kaplan, Michael** ... '60 '86 C.112 B.A. L.1067 J.D. [Ⓐ Dennison,B.&P.]
Kaplan, Norman J. ... '28 '61 L.809 LL.B. P.O. Box 6458
Kaplan, Peter R. ... '51 '78 C.112 A.B. L.426 J.D. 11601 Wilshire Blvd.
**Kaplan, Philip J.** ... '54 '84 C.902 B.A. L.861 J.D. [Argue P.H.&M.]
*LANGUAGES: Spanish.
*PRACTICE AREAS: Civil Litigation; Entertainment Law.

**Kaplan, Raymond S., (AV) '40 '65 C.659 B.S. L.976 LL.B.**
**1901 Avenue of the Stars, Suite 1551, 90067**
**Telephone: 310-785-9700 Facsimile: 310-556-1266**
**(Also of Counsel to Richman, Lawrence, Mann, Greene, Chizever, Friedman & Phillips, Beverly Hills).**
***PRACTICE AREAS: Real Estate; Business.**
**Business and Real Estate Law.**

Kaplan, Richard B., (AV) ... '43 '68 C.685 A.B. L.976 LL.B. [R.B.Kaplan]
**Kaplan, Richard J.**, (AV) ... '48 '73 C.112 B.A. L.1068 J.D. [Hughes H.&R.]
*PRACTICE AREAS: Federal and State Taxation.
**Kaplan, Robert O.** ... '41 '66 C.197 A.B. L.1066 J.D. [Ⓒ Kenoff&M.]
*PRACTICE AREAS: Entertainment Law.
Kaplan, Ronald P., (AV) ... '48 '74 C.188 B.A. L.309 J.D. 2029 Century Pk., E.
Kaplan, Sherman Ian, (AV) ... '56 '80 C.112 B.A. L.809 J.D. [Kaplan,K.&R.]
**Kaplan, Stephen L.** ... '60 '86 C.154 B.A. L.426 J.D. [MacArthur,U.H.&M.]
**Kaplan, Steven J.** ... '53 '78 C.112 B.A. L.1066 J.D. [Krakow&K.]
*SPECIAL AGENCIES: Pacific Southwest Region, American Jewish Congress (Past President); Los Angeles Jewish Community Relations Committee.
*REPORTED CASES: Litton v. N.L.R.B., 501-U.S.-190, 111 S. Ct. 2215, 115 L.Ed.2d 177 (1991) (Brief only); Screen Extras Guild, Inc. v. Superior Court, 51 Cal.3d 1017 (1990); Graphic Communications Union v. GCLU-Employer Retirement Benefit Plan, 917 F.2d 1184 (9th Cir 1990); Foley v. Interactive Data Corporation, 47 Cal.3d 654 (1988); Carpenters Southern California Administrative Corp. v. El Capitan Development Co., 53 Cal.3d 1041 (1991) (Amicus Curiae).
*PRACTICE AREAS: Labor and Employment; Employee Benefits.
**Kaplan, Terry S., (A Professional Corporation)**, (AV) '44 '71 C.112 B.A. L.800 J.D. [Billet&K.]
*PRACTICE AREAS: Litigation.
Kaplan, Victor E., (AV) ... '14 '38 C.112 A.B. L.800 LL.B. [Ⓒ Kaplan]
**Kaplan, William M., (A Professional Corporation)** '24 '52 C.823 B.A. L.976 LL.B. [Ⓒ Mitchell,S.&K.]
*PRACTICE AREAS: Music Publishing Law; Motion Picture Music Law; Copyright Law.
Kaplan, Wm. ... '10 '34 C.112 B.A. L.1066 Wkms. Comp. App. Bd.
Kaplan, Klein & Rogen, (AV) ... 3600 Wilshire Blvd.
Kaplan Law Corporation, (AV) ... 5909 W. 3rd St.
Kaplan, Richard B., A Professional Corporation, (AV) ... 1015 Gayley Ave., #513
Kaplanis, Peter J., (AV) ... '35 '62 C&L.800 A.B., LL.B. [Kaplanis&G.]
Kaplanis & Grimm, (AV) ... 621 S. Westmoreland Ave.
**Kaplowitz, Karen, (P.C.)**, (AV) ... '46 '72 C.66 B.A. L.145 J.D. [Alschuler G.&P.]
**Kapor, Jeffrey H.**, (AV) ... '53 '78 C.112 B.A. L.809 J.D. [Katz,H.S.&K.]
*PRACTICE AREAS: Mergers and Acquisitions; Corporate Business Law; Commercial Law; Debtor/ Creditor Relations; Financial and Business Planning.
Kapp, Howard A. ... '53 '79 C.112 B.A. L.426 J.D. 6300 Wilshire Blvd.
Kappel, Karl G. ... '22 '49 C.800 L.809 LL.B. 12424 Wilshire Blvd.
**Kappler, Douglas D.**, (AV) ... '42 '71 C.1239 B.A. L.1066 J.D. [Robinson,D.B.&K.]
*REPORTED CASES: In re Tepper Industries, 74 B.R. 713 (9th Cir. BAP 1987) affirmed 840 F.2d 22; In re Matthews, 724 F.2d 798 (9th Dir. 1984).
*PRACTICE AREAS: Insolvency; Bankruptcy Law.
**Karabian, Walter J.**, (AV) ... '38 '64 C&L.800 B.A., J.D. [Karns&K.]
*PRACTICE AREAS: Administrative Law; Taxation; Education Law; Corporate Law; Business Law.
**Karaczynski, John A.** ... '53 '78 C&L.188 B.A., J.D. [Rogers&W.]
*PRACTICE AREAS: Antitrust; Complex Commercial Litigation; Media and First Amendment.
Karaffa, Jeanne M. ... '48 '92 C.1097 B.A. L.426 J.D. 1411 N. Hayworth Ave.
**Karapetian, Nick P.** ... '68 '94 C.1077 B.A. L.425 J.D. [Ⓐ Zevnik H.G.&M.]
*PRACTICE AREAS: Commercial Litigation; Environmental.
**Karasik, Eve H.** ... '62 '91 C.112 B.A. L.800 J.D. [Stutman,T.&G.]
*PRACTICE AREAS: Bankruptcy; Insolvency; Corporate Reorganization; Commercial Litigation.
**Karasik, Gregory N.** ... '59 '84 C.112 B.A. L.813 J.D. [Knee&M.]
*LANGUAGES: Spanish.
*PRACTICE AREAS: Wrongful Termination Defense; Sexual Harassment; Employment Discrimination; Management Labor Relations; Wage and Hour Law.
**Karasik, Louis A.** ... '56 '81 C.112 B.A. L.813 J.D. [McClintock,W.B.R.R.&M.]
*LANGUAGES: Spanish.
*SPECIAL AGENCIES: Cal-OSHA Appeals Board.
*REPORTED CASES: Ohandjanian v. Mobil Oil Corp., 1984 Bus. Franchise Rep. (CCH) §8249 (C.D. Cal. 1984).
*PRACTICE AREAS: Labor & Employment; Litigation and Trial; Alternative Dispute Resolution; Business Litigation; Environmental Litigation.
**Kardassakis, Jon P.** ... '54 '79 C.112 B.S. L.1067 J.D. [Hawkins,S.L.&B.]
**Karel, Albert R.** ... '42 '71 C&L.966 B.B.A., J.D. [Brobeck,P.&H.]
*PRACTICE AREAS: Insolvency of Banks Law; Financial Institutions Law.
**Karelis, Kim** ... '53 '94 C.493 B.A. L.809 J.D. [Ⓐ Selman B.]
*PRACTICE AREAS: Insurance Coverage.
**Karger, Michael J.** ... '48 '75 C.1349 B.A. L.107 J.D. [Ⓐ Kane,B.&B.]
*PRACTICE AREAS: Municipal Law.
**Kari, W. Douglas** ... '55 '85 C.112 A.B. L.1065 J.D. [Orrick,H.&S.]
*PRACTICE AREAS: Litigation and Entertainment Law.
Karic, Steven S. ... '54 '82 C.1169 B.A. L.861 J.D. [Brookwell K.]
**Karkanen, Janet L.** ... '63 '92 C.172 B.A. L.1065 J.D. [Ⓐ Woollacott J.&W.]
*PRACTICE AREAS: Business Litigation; Intellectual Property Law.
Karlan, Mark S. ... '— '84 C&L.309 A.B., J.D. State Prob. Ref.
Karlin, Amy M. ... '65 '90 C.112 B.S. L.426 J.D. Dep. Fed. Pub. Def.
**Karlin, Jeffrey H., (P.C.)**, (AV) ... '55 '80 C.1044 B.S. L.1065 J.D. [Ⓒ Cantilo,M.&H.]⊙
*PRACTICE AREAS: Business Transactions; Tax; Securities; Partnership; Insurance.
Karlin, Laurence M. ... '37 '63 C.112 B.S. L.1068 LL.B. 3301 Colby Ave.‡
Karlin, Louis W. ... '63 '88 C.178 A.B. L.1068 J.D. Off. of Atty. Gen.
**Karlin, Michael J. A.** ... '52 '80 C.050 B.A. [Morgan,L.&B.]
**Karlin, Peter A.** ... '57 '84 C.1077 B.A. L.61 J.D. [Ⓐ Liebman&R.]
Karlin, Samuel A. ... '07 '29 C&L.415 Ph.B., J.D. 10906 Bellagio Rd.
**Karner, Jessica M.** ... '67 '95 C.112 B.A. L.1066 J.D. [Ⓐ Folger L.&K.]⊙

**Karno, Schwartz, Friedman, Shafron & Warren**
**(See Encino)**

Karnos, Jean Pierre ... '41 '72 C.112 B.A. L.426 J.D. 1139 W. 6th St.
**Karns, Gregory J.** ... '56 '83 C.1169 B.A. L.426 J.D. [Cox,C.&N.]
*PRACTICE AREAS: Real Property Law.
**Karns, John**, (AV) ... '38 '64 C&L.800 B.S., J.D. [Karns&K.]
*PRACTICE AREAS: Administrative Law; Corporate Law; Business Law; Litigation; Real Property.

**Karns & Karabian, (AV)** BR
**Suite 530 Omni Centre, 900 Wilshire Boulevard, 90017**
**Telephone: 213-680-9522 FAX: 213-627-3602**
**Members of Firm: John Karns; Walter J. Karabian. Associates: Jeff C. Marderosian; David E. Kenney; Jeff A. Harrison.**
**General Civil Practice including Administrative, Corporate/Business, Education, Public and Private Sector, Labor and Employment Law, Litigation, Taxation, Real Property, Trusts and Probate Law. Government and International Business.**
***See Professional Biographies, LOS ANGELES, CALIFORNIA***

Karp, David C. ... '57 '83 C.338 B.S. L.426 J.D. 15760 Ventura Blvd.,16th Fl. (Encino)
Karp, Ivan M. ... '43 '70 C.012 B.A. L.184 J.D. 601 W. 5th St.
**Karp, Jonathan A.**, (AV) ... '51 '76 C.112 B.S. L.477 J.D. [Reish&L.]
*PRACTICE AREAS: Business Law; Estate Planning; Tax.
**Karp, Leslie R.** '63 '88 C.966 B.B.A. L.146 J.D. (adm. in IL; not adm. in CA) [Katten M.&Z.]
*PRACTICE AREAS: Tax and Estate Planning.
Karp, Steven M. ... '51 '76 C.563 B.A. L.1065 J.D. 3550 Wilshire Blvd., 17th Fl.
Karp, William H. '12 '34 C&L.494 B.A., J.D. (adm. in MN; not adm. in CA) 2257 Linnington Ave.‡
Karpel, Jeffrey E. ... '42 '68 C&L.1095 B.A., J.D. 1901 Ave. of the Stars
**Karpel, Philip**, (AV) ... '49 '77 C.1077 B.A. L.426 J.D. [Olincy&K.]
*PRACTICE AREAS: Tax Law; Estate Planning; Probate and Trust.
Karpf, Merrill H. ... '40 '67 C.1077 B.A. L.1068 2121 Ave. of the Stars
**Karpman, Diane L.**, (AV) ... '48 '75 C.112 B.A. L.1137 J.D. [Karpman&Assoc.]

**Karpman & Associates, (AV)**
**12100 Wilshire Boulevard, Suite 1600, 90025**
**Telephone: 310-447-6110**
**Diane L. Karpman. Associate: Judith Fournier German. Of Counsel: Daniel L. Rothman.**
**Attorney Professional Responsibility and Competence, Attorney Discipline and Legal Ethics, Admissions and Reinstatements, Conflict of Interest and Fiduciary Obligations of Lawyers.**
***See Professional Biographies, LOS ANGELES, CALIFORNIA***

**Karpowich, Sonya L.** ... '69 '95 C.800 B.S. L.809 J.D. [Brown,W.&C.]
*PRACTICE AREAS: Real Estate Transactions.
**Karr, Jeffrey S.** ... '71 '96 C.597 B.A. L.1065 J.D. [Ⓐ Tuttle&T.]
**Karsai, Liza Ilona** ... '66 '93 C.112 B.A. L.990 J.D. [Ⓐ Kaye,S.F.H.&H.]
*PRACTICE AREAS: Litigation.
Karsh, Bruce A. ... '55 '81 C.228 A.B. L.893 J.D. 10877 Wilshire Blvd., 12th Fl.
Karsh, Martha L. ... '56 '81 C&L.893 B.A., J.D. U.C.L.A. Student Legal Servs.
Karson, Emile ... '21 '60 L.976 S.J.D. 4331 Kingswell Ave.
Karst, Kenneth L. ... '29 '54 C.112 A.B. L.309 LL.B. Prof. of Law, Univ. of Calif.
**Karz, Cheryl Hannah** ... '69 '95 C.112 B.A. L.426 J.D. [Ⓐ Gilbert,K.C.&J.]
**Kasai, Wayne T.** ... '55 '89 C.800 B.S. L.1067 J.D. [Ⓐ Honn&S.]
*PRACTICE AREAS: Litigation; Business Law; Real Property; Probate; Trusts.
Kascle, Esther ... '29 '64 C.1043 B.S. L.800 J.D. 3481 La Sombra Dr.
**Kasdan, Sheldon David** ... '67 '92 C.112 B.A. L.426 J.D. [Ⓐ Littler,M.F.T.&M.]
**Kase, Beth A.** ... '51 '83 C.860 B.A. L.800 J.D. [Saphier&H.]
*LANGUAGES: Spanish.
*PRACTICE AREAS: Health Care Law.
**Kasell, Brian W.** ... '52 '89 C.563 B.S. L.809 J.D. [Ⓐ Brobeck,P.&H.] (Pat.)
*PRACTICE AREAS: Intellectual Property Litigation; Trademark and Patent Prosecution; Licensing.
**Kashani, Mir Saied** ... '65 '89 C&L.309 B.A.Ec., J.D. [Ⓐ Shearman&S.]
**Kashar, Gary A.** ... '67 '93 C&L.846 B.B.A., J.D. [Ⓐ Latham&W.]
*PRACTICE AREAS: Corporate.
Kashfian, Maurice ... '64 '87 C.112 B.A. L.800 J.D. 1875 Century Park E.
Kashian, James ... '47 '72 C.813 A.B. L.1068 J.D. Principal Dep. Co. Coun.
Kaskel, Helaine R. '62 '89 C.378 B.A.B.S. L.800 J.D. Pres., Benchmark Deposition Reporters
Kaslow, Harmon M. ... '62 '88 C.112 B.S. L.800 J.D. [Kramer&K.]
Kaslow, Abramoff & Adwar ... 1875 Century Park East, Suite 700
**Kaspar, Roland R., (Professional Corporation)**, (AV) '28 '61 C.546 B.S. L.1068 LL.D. [Schell&D.]
**Kasper, Dennis R.** ... '48 '74 C&L.61 B.A., J.D. [Lewis,D.B.&B.]
Kass, Deborah ... '54 '80 C.112 B.A. L.1049 J.D. Dist. Atty. Off.
**Kass, Dennis B.**, (BV) ... '62 '88 C.112 B.A. L.426 J.D. [Manning,M.&W.]
*PRACTICE AREAS: Insurance Fraud Litigation; Civil Litigation; Insurance Coverage Analysis; Bad Faith; Legal Malpractice.
Kass, Donald J. ... '54 '82 C.112 B.A. L.284 J.D. Dep. City Atty.
**Kass, Roberta E.** ... '55 '82 C.107 B.A. L.273 J.D. Atlantic Richfield Co.
*RESPONSIBILITIES: Bankruptcy Law; Commercial Law; Litigation.

**Kass, Gail D.**
**(See Beverly Hills)**

**Kassabian, Mark M.** ... '65 '91 C.197 A.B. L.1066 J.D. [Ⓐ Jones,D.R.&P.]
**Kasschau, Patricia L.** ... '46 '79 C&L.800 B.A., J.D. Staff Coun., Hughes Aircraft Co.
*RESPONSIBILITIES: Employment Law; Litigation; Labor Law; Arbitrations.
**Kassoy, Arnold D.**, (AV) ... '43 '69 C.112 B.S. L.1068 J.D. [Ⓒ Manatt,P.&P.]
*PRACTICE AREAS: Entertainment; Taxation; Estate Planning.
Kastner, Adam B. ... '65 '90 C.154 B.A. L.976 J.D. 9255 Sunset Blvd.
Katayama, Imogene M. N. ... '48 '85 C.605 B.A. L.990 J.D. Deputy Dist. Atty.
**Katel, Kenneth G.** ... '53 '79 C.339 B.A. L.1049 J.D. [Wright,R.O.&T.]
*PRACTICE AREAS: Litigation.
**Kateman, Jeffrey L.** ... '66 '93 C&L.178 A.B., J.D. [Ⓐ Latham&W.]
**Katen, Gilbert** ... '44 '70 C.112 B.S. L.1068 J.D. [Clopton,P.&B.]
*LANGUAGES: Spanish, English.
**Kater, Susie J.** ... '46 '86 C.446 B.S. L.464 J.D. [Ⓐ Neumeyer&B.]
*PRACTICE AREAS: Appellate Practice; Insurance Coverage; Insurance Bad Faith.
Kates, Lawrence ... '39 '65 C.80 B.S.E.E. L.426 LL.B. 1617 Pontius Ave., 3rd Ave.
**Kato, Dean M.** ... '65 '92 C.178 B.A. L.1066 J.D. [Ⓐ Latham&W.]
*LANGUAGES: Japanese.
Katofsky, Jeff ... '63 '88 C.112 B.A. L.1066 J.D. 2215 Colby Ave.
**Katovich, Kathleen D.** '48 '76 C.339 B.S. L.209 J.D. Sr. Corp. Coun., Farmers Grp., Inc.
*RESPONSIBILITIES: Employment; Agency; Labor Relations; Bankruptcy.
**Katris-Michael, Christina** ... '69 '93 C.597 B.A. L.990 J.D. [Ⓐ Long&L.]
Katsky, Ronald L., (AV) ... '38 '65 C.674 A.B. L.1068 J.D. [Katsky&L.]
Katsky & Lyon, (AV) ... 9200 Sunset Blvd., 3rd Fl.

**Katten Muchin & Zavis, (AV)**
**A Partnership including Professional Corporations**
**Katten Muchin & Zavis Established in 1974**
**1999 Avenue of the Stars, Suite 1400, 90067-6042**⊙
**Telephone: 310-788-4400 Telecopier: 310-788-4471**
**Members of Firm: James K. Baer; Kathryn A. Ballsun; David M. Bass; Kent S. Beyer; Kenneth L. Block; Marsha A. Boysaw; John J. Chung; Steve Cochran; Craig D. Crockwell; Alan D. Croll; Richard F. Davis (P.C.); Michele M. Desoer; Robert T. Flick; Allan B. Goldman; Robert D. Goldschein; Angel Gomez, III; Katherine E. Goodman; Leslie R. Karp (Not admitted in CA); Valerie E. Kincaid; Howard P. King (June 19, 1945-December 25, 1993); Thomas J. Leanse; Thomas S. Mahr; Zia F. Modabber; Stephen F. Moeller; Daniel M. Pelliccioni (P.C.); Stuart M. Richter; Charles M. Stern; Gail Migdal Title; Joel R. Weiner. Associates: Jeffrey I. Abrams; Todd T. Alberstone; Julie R. Benjamin (Not admitted in CA); Julia W. Brand; Alexandra J. Brew; Dustin K. Finer; Deborah L. Fink; Stacey K. Fishman; Deborah Giss; Jeremy J. F. Gray; Jon S. Grizel; Andrew J. Hackbert; Carolyn A. Hampton;**

(This Listing Continued)

**Katten Muchin & Zavis (Continued)**

**Shauna D. Jackson; David P. Kaplan; Stacey D. McKee Knight; Stacey R. Konkoff; George Mastras, Jr.; Sherylle Mills; Randee Schuster Motzkin; Nayssan L. Parandeh; James B. Pickell; Janette M. Redd; Jamie Rudman; Paul Schiada; E. Randol Schoenberg; Immanuel I. Spira; Mary Taten; Cheryl L. Van Steenwyk; Raymond Wu; Juan E. Zuniga.**
**Antitrust and Trade Regulation, Aviation, Banking and Commercial Finance, Bankruptcy and Reorganization, Commodities, Futures and Derivatives, Constitutional Law, Corporate, Corporate Insurance, Creditor's Rights, Customs, Employee Benefits and Executive Compensation, Entertainment, Environmental, Equipment and Facility Leasing, Estate Planning and Probate, Financial Services, Golf Course, Resort and Hotel Acquisition and Development, Governmental Affairs, Health Care, Insurance and Reinsurance, Intellectual Property, International Trade, International Business Transactions and Global Capital Markets, Investment Adviser and Investment Company Regulation, Joint Ventures, Labor and Employment Law, Litigation and Trial Practice, Mergers and Acquisitions, Municipal Law, Municipal Finance and Public Authority Financing Law, Partnerships, Product Liability, Product Manufacturing and Marketing, Professional Malpractice, Project Development and Finance, Real Estate, Real Estate Finance, Real Estate Taxation, Retail Leasing and Shopping Center Development, Securities, Securitization and Structured Finance, Sports, Stadium Financing, Syndications, Taxation-Federal and International, Technology and Computer Law, Thrift Institutions, Variable Insurance Products, Venture Capital, White Collar Civil and Criminal Litigation.**
**Chicago, Illinois Office: 525 West Monroe Street, Suite 1600. Telephone: 312-902-5200. Telecopier: 312-902-1061. Telex: 298264 ATLAW UR.**
**Irvine, California Office: Two Park Plaza, Suite 800. Telephone: 714-263-3500. Telecopier: 714-263-3533.**
**New York, New York Office: 40 Broad Street, Suite 2000. Telephone: 212-612-9500. Telecopier: 212-425-0266.**
**Washington, D.C. Office: 1025 Thomas Jefferson Street, N.W., East Lobby, Suite 700. Telephone: 202-625-3500. Telecopier: 202-298-7570. Telex: 211195 KMZ UR.**

*See Professional Biographies, LOS ANGELES, CALIFORNIA*

Katz, Allen M., (AV) .... '48 '72 C.1036 B.A. L.813 J.D. 355 S. Grand Ave.
**Katz, Andrew E., (A Professional Corporation)**, (AV) '47 '72 C.112 B.S. L.1068 J.D. [Mitchell,S.&K.]
*PRACTICE AREAS: Financial Institutions Law; Securities Offerings; Business Law.
Katz, Arthur J. .... '28 '52 C.824 B.A. L.178 LL.B. 818 N. Doheny Dr., W. Hollywood
**Katz, Arthur M.**, (AV) .... '34 '60 C.569 B.A. L.976 LL.B. [Ⓒ Saltzburg,R.&B.]
*PRACTICE AREAS: Business and Commercial Transactions; International.
**Katz, David A.**, (AV) .... '52 '82 C.112 B.A. L.1066 J.D. [Katz&Assoc.]
*LANGUAGES: Spanish.
*REPORTED CASES: U.S. v. Sterner, 23 F.3d 250 (9th Cir. 1994); U.S. v. Mett, 65 F.3d 1531 (9th Cir. 1995); U.S. v. U.S. District Court, 717 F.2d 478; U.S. v. McCollum, 802 F.2d 344; U.S. v. Fields, 783 F.2d 1382.
*PRACTICE AREAS: White Collar Criminal Defense Law; Health Claims Law; Commodities and Securities Fraud Defense Law; Banking and Savings and Loan Fraud Law.
**Katz, David J.** .... '63 '90 C.1077 B.S. L.426 J.D. [Ⓐ Mitchell,S.&K.]
*PRACTICE AREAS: Corporate; Securities; International Securities; Real Estate.
Katz, George L. .... '23 '57 C&L.800 B.A., J.D. 756 S. Broadway
Katz, Gloria J. .... '39 '83 C.112 B.A. L.426 J.D. Dep. Dist. Atty.
Katz, Howard J. .... '52 '79 C.1097 B.A. L.1148 J.D. 2429 Nottingham Ave.
**Katz, Ira Benjamin**, (AV) .... '— '78 C.112 B.A. L.1066 J.D. [I.B.Katz]
Katz, Jack .... '26 '52 C.209 L.365 LL.B. 11755 Wilshire Blvd.
**Katz, Jared M.** .... '67 '95 C.674 A.B. L.426 J.D. [Ⓐ LeBoeuf,L.G.&M.]
**Katz, Jason L.** '47 '73 C.1183 B.A. L.209 J.D. Sr. V.P. & Gen. Coun., Farmers Grp., Inc.
**Katz, Jeffrey A.** .... '62 '88 C.978 B.A. L.1065 J.D. [Ⓐ Frye,A.&M.]
**Katz, Jerry A.** .... '58 '83 C.112 B.S. L.1065 J.D. [Pircher,N.&M.]
*PRACTICE AREAS: Real Estate Law; Sports and Entertainment.
**Katz, Jody Rene** .... '71 '96 C.112 B.A. L.800 J.D. [Ⓐ Fried,F.H.S.&J.]
Katz, Leon, (AV) .... '23 '48 C&L.966 B.A., J.D. [Tyre K.K.&G.]
Katz, Leona Shapiro .... '44 '90 C.112 B.A. L.1136 J.D. 5750 Wilshire Blvd.
**Katz, Marc S.** .... '57 '81 C.112 B.A. L.1068 J.D. [Morris,P.&P.]
**Katz, Mark F., (Professional Corporation)**, (AV) '47 '72 C.674 A.B. L.477 J.D. [Kinsella,B.F.&T.]
*LANGUAGES: French, German and Mandarin Chinese.
Katz, Mark S. .... '52 '76 C.1077 B.A. L.1095 J.D. 6255 W. Sunset Blvd.
**Katz, Martin D.** .... '59 '83 C.597 B.A. L.477 J.D. [Troop M.S.&P.]
*PRACTICE AREAS: Insurance Coverage Litigation; General Business Litigation; Products Liability Defense.
Katz, Marvin S., (A Professional Law Corporation) '34 '63 C&L.800 B.A., LL.B. 1511 Thayer Ave.
**Katz, Maurice H.**, (AV) .... '37 '62 C.178 A.B. L.309 J.D. [M.H.Katz]
**Katz, Michael** .... '64 '93 C.309 A.B. L.569 J.D. [Ⓐ Morrison&F.]

**Katz, Michelle, (AV) '41 '78 C.188 B.A. L.1121 J.D.**
**1925 Century Park East, Suite 2000, 90067-2721**
**Telephone: 310-277-2236 Facsimile: 310-277-7065; 310-556-5653**
**Certified Specialist, Family Law, The State Bar of California Board of Legal Specialization.**
***PRACTICE AREAS: Family Law Mediation.**
**Family Law Mediation.**

*See Professional Biographies, LOS ANGELES, CALIFORNIA*

**Katz, Paul R.** .... '50 '75 C.112 A.B. L.1068 J.D. [Ⓒ Troop M.S.&P.]
*PRACTICE AREAS: Computer Law; Multimedia; Electronic Commerce; Telecommunications.
Katz, Robert F., (AV) .... '41 '67 C.112 A.B. L.1068 LL.B. Supvr., Dep. Atty. Gen.
Katz, Ronald S., (AV) .... '36 '64 C.861 B.S. L.208 J.D. 5750 Wilshire Blvd.
Katz, Shalom Zev .... '49 '80 C.112 B.A. L.809 J.D. [Thomas&E.]
**Katz, Steven**, (AV) .... '49 '74 C.299 A.B. L.309 J.D. [Katz,G.&F.]
*PRACTICE AREAS: Entertainment Law; Motion Pictures and Television.
**Katz, Steven B.** .... '62 '88 C&L.800 A.B., J.D. [Ⓐ Seyfarth,S.F.&G.]
*PRACTICE AREAS: Commercial; Real Estate; Employee Benefits; Employment Litigation.
Katz, Steven Ian .... '63 '89 C.112 B.A. L.1068 J.D. Dep. Dist. Atty.
Katz, William, (AV) .... '10 '32 L.809 2970 Queensberry Dr.

**Katz & Associates, (AV)**
**Eighteenth Floor, 2049 Century Park East (Century City), 90067**
**Telephone: 310-203-0701; 281-7380 Fax: 310-203-0312**
**David A. Katz; John P. Dwyer. Associates: Linda L. Kachel.**
**White Collar Criminal Defense and Appellate Practice in all State and Federal Courts; Health Claims Defense; Bankruptcy Fraud Defense; Environmental Law. Rights of Financial Institutions and Investors.**

*See Professional Biographies, LOS ANGELES, CALIFORNIA*

**Katz, Golden & Fishman, LLP, (AV)**
**10850 Wilshire Boulevard Suite 600, 90024**
**Telephone: 310-470-7777 Facsimile: 310-470-7481**
**Partners: Joel L. Fishman; Diane A. Golden; Steven Katz; Mary E. Sullivan. Of Counsel: Charles D. Silverberg (A Professional Corporation); Paul L. Migdal; Patricia A. McVerry; Jennifer Justman; Jeffrey Brauer.**

*See Professional Biographies, LOS ANGELES, CALIFORNIA*

**Katz, Hoyt, Seigel & Kapor LLP, (AV) BR**
**A Partnership including a Professional Corporation**
**Suite 820, 11111 Santa Monica Boulevard, 90025-3342**
**Telephone: 310-473-1300 Telecopier: 310-473-7138**
**Members of Firm: Charles J. Katz (1905-1983); Louis C. Hoyt (1905-1994); Benjamin S. Seigel (P.C.); Jeffrey H. Kapor; Scott H. Jacobs; Alan Jay Cohen; William Schoenholz; Jack R. Lenack; Russell L. Allyn; Douglas M. Lipstone; Moira Doherty; Marla Milner.**

(This Listing Continued)

**Katz, Hoyt, Seigel & Kapor LLP (Continued)**

**Commercial, Bankruptcy, Business, Real Estate, Trademark, Copyright, Unfair Competition, Probate, General Civil, Trial and Appellate Practice in all State and Federal Courts.**

*See Professional Biographies, LOS ANGELES, CALIFORNIA*

**Katz, Ira Benjamin, A Prof. Corp., Law Offices of, (AV)**
**1901 Avenue of the Stars, 20th Floor, 90067**
**Telephone: 310-282-8580 Fax: 310-282-8149**
**Ira Benjamin Katz.**
**Bankruptcy, Business, Commercial, Real Estate and Civil Litigation.**

*See Professional Biographies, LOS ANGELES, CALIFORNIA*

**Katz, Maurice H., A Professional Law Corporation, (AV)**
**Suite 612, 1880 Century Park East (Century City), 90067**
**Telephone: 310-553-8800 Fax: 310-553-8704**
**Maurice H. Katz.**
**General Civil and Trial Practice in all State and Federal Courts. Corporation, Real Property, Estate Planning.**

Katzan, Stephan Z. .... '31 '57 C.685 B.A. L.145 J.D. 1521 S. Oakhurst Dr.
**Katzenstein, Andrew M.**, (AV) .... '57 '82 C&L.477 B.A., J.D. [Manatt,P.&P.]
*PRACTICE AREAS: Health Law; Estates and Trusts.
**Katzman, Marc J.** .... '53 '92 C.112 B.A. L.398 J.D. [Ⓐ M.B.F.Biren&Assoc.]
Katzman, Richard A. .... '53 '76 C.1222 B.A. L.472 J.D. Sr. Dep. Co. Coun.
**Kau, Wolfgang M.** .... '50 '81 C&L.061 [Graham&J.] (ⓄDusseldorf, Germany)
*LANGUAGES: German.
*PRACTICE AREAS: International Business Law; Corporate Law; Entertainment-Media Law; EU Law.
**Kaufelt, Jonathan D.**, (AV) .... '52 '76 C.659 B.A. L.276 J.D. [Armstrong H.J.T.&W.]
*PRACTICE AREAS: Business Law; Entertainment; Taxation.
**Kaufer, Alvin S.**, (AV) .... '32 '60 C.918 B.A. L.477 J.D. [Nossaman,G.K.&E.]
*PRACTICE AREAS: Litigation.
**Kaufer, Julie M.** .... '64 '91 C.860 B.S. L.426 J.D. [Ⓐ Troop M.S.&P.]
*PRACTICE AREAS: General Corporate Law.
Kaufer, Robin F. .... '60 '86 C.911 B.A. L.1068 J.D. I.R.S.
Kauffman, Andrew C. .... '50 '75 C.800 B.A. L.1068 J.D. Los Angeles Mun. Ct.
Kauffman, D. Stephen .... '49 '76 C&L.629 B.S., J.D. Gen. Acctg. Off.

**Kaufman, Barry B., Law Offices of, (AV) '58 '83 C.112 B.A. L.800 J.D.**
**2121 Avenue of the Stars, Suite 1700, 90067**
**Telephone: 310-557-0404 Telecopier: 310-557-1010**
**Labor and Employment Law. General Civil Practice.**

*See Professional Biographies, LOS ANGELES, CALIFORNIA*

**Kaufman, Benjamin** .... '55 '84 C.188 B.S. L.800 J.D. [Freilich,K.F.&S.]
*REPORTED CASES: Ehrlich v. City of Culver City (1996); Hensler v. City of Glendale (1994) 8 Cal 4th 1, Cert. denied (1995) 115 5 Ct. 1176; Rogers v. Superior Court (City of Burbank) (1993) 19 Cal.App.4th 469; 3570 East Foothill Blvd. v. City of Pasadena (C.D. Calif., 1995) 912 F.Supp. 1257; Tensor Group, Ltd. v. City of Glendale (1993) 14 Cal.App.4th 154.
Kaufman, Bruce .... '56 '83 C.1077 B.A. L.809 J.D. 12121 Wilshire Blvd.
Kaufman, C. Bernard .... '27 '54 C&L.112 B.A., LL.B. Supr. Ct. J.
**Kaufman, Charles S.** .... '54 '94 C.112 B.A. L.1068 J.D. [Ⓐ Morrison&F.]
Kaufman, Clarice D. .... '12 '40 C.551 L.997 10501 Wilshire Blvd.‡
**Kaufman, Edmund M., (P.C.)**, (AV) .... '30 '60 C.112 B.S. L.178 LL.B. [Irell&M.]
Kaufman, George A. .... '55 '81 C.107 B.S. L.800 J.D. 1888 Centruy Park E.
Kaufman, Jerry .... '56 '81 C.1349 B.A. L.800 J.D. 3250 Wilshire Blvd.
Kaufman, Lynn J. .... '66 '91 C.575 B.A. L.893 J.D. 11755 Wilshire Blvd.
**Kaufman, Lynne Drohlich** .... '49 '74 C.112 A.B. L.1066 J.D. [Ⓒ Fenigstein&K.]
*PRACTICE AREAS: Health Care and Hospital Law.
Kaufman, Marjorie Hope .... '— '88 C.477 A.B. L.1066 J.D. 121 S. Hope St.
Kaufman, Melvin I. .... '26 '59 L.800 LL.B. 12100 Wilshire Blvd.
Kaufman, Michael J. .... '53 '80 C.1077 B.A. L.809 J.D. Corp. Coun., Joyce Intl., Inc.
**Kaufman, Paul W.** .... '57 '81 C.800 A.B. L.1066 J.D. [Jones,K.&A.]
*PRACTICE AREAS: Real Estate; Taxation; Corporate.
Kaufman, Peter L. .... '64 '89 C.1365 B.A. L.94 J.D. 1875 Century Pk. E., Century City
Kaufman, Philip S. .... '49 '74 C.112 B.A. L.426 J.D. 205 S. Broadway
**Kaufman, Ron S.**, (AV) .... '49 '74 C.112 B.A. L.1066 J.D. [Fenigstein&K.]
*PRACTICE AREAS: Business; Health Care; Employment and Real Estate Litigation.
**Kaufman, Stephen J.** .... '62 '87 C.112 B.A. L.1065 J.D. [Smith&K.]
*PRACTICE AREAS: Business Litigation; Campaign Finance; Election Law; Insurance Coverage; Insurance Defense.
**Kaufman, Thomas R.** .... '70 '95 C.339 B.A. L.112 J.D. [Ⓐ Seyfarth,S.F.&G.]
*LANGUAGES: Spanish and Japanese.
*PRACTICE AREAS: Litigation; Employment and Labor.
**Kaufman, Victoria S.** .... '64 '89 C.104 B.A. L.309 J.D. [Ⓐ Jeffer,M.B.&M.]
*PRACTICE AREAS: Bankruptcy; Corporate Insolvency.
**Kaufman, Warren W.**, (AV) .... '37 '64 C.112 A.B. L.1066 J.D. [W.W.Kaufman]
*SPECIAL AGENCIES: Armed Services Board of Contract Appeals.
*PRACTICE AREAS: Government Contract Law; Insurance Law; Product Liability Defense; Commercial Litigation; Construction Litigation.

**Kaufman, Warren W., Inc., (AV)**
**12650 Riverside Drive, 91607**
**Telephone: 818-755-4848 Fax: 818-508-0181**
**Warren W. Kaufman.**
**Government Contracts, Insurance, Product Liability Defense, Commercial Litigation, Construction.**

*See Professional Biographies, LOS ANGELES, CALIFORNIA*

**Kaufman & Young, A Professional Corporation**
**(See Beverly Hills)**

Kaufmann, Daniel .... '18 '46 C.112 A.B. L.800 LL.B. Supr. Ct. J.
Kaufmann, Ernest T. .... '36 '59 C&L.966 B.S., LL.B. 2049 Century Park E.
Kaufmann, Kenneth K., Jr. .... '30 '57 C.112 B.A. L.800 J.D. 633 W. 5th St.
**Kaufmann, Steven H.** .... '49 '74 C.112 B.A. L.426 J.D. [Richards,W.&G.]
*PRACTICE AREAS: State and Municipal Land Use and CEQA Litigation; Writs and Appellate Practice; Administrative Law; Coastal Law.
**Kaufmann Macias, Terry P.** .... '52 '88 C.112 B.A. L.426 J.D. [Freilich,K.F.&S.]
Kaus, Otto M., (AV) .... '20 '49 C.113 B.A. L.426 LL.B. 555 W. 5th St.

**Kavaller, Miles L., A Professional Law Corporation**
**(See Beverly Hills)**

Kavanau, Earl W. .... '32 '59 C.112 B.S. L.1068 J.D. 1157 S. Beverly Dr.
Kavanau, Richard A. .... '25 '53 C.112 A.B. L.426 LL.B. 10430 Wilshire Blvd.
**Kavanaugh, Matthew W.** .... '57 '83 C.112 B.A. L.1068 J.D. [Buchalter,N.F.&Y.]
*LANGUAGES: French.
*PRACTICE AREAS: Commercial Finance; Workouts; Problem Loan Restructuring; Equipment Leasing; Unsecured Lending.
**Kavanaugh, Michael T.** .... '47 '71 C&L.436 B.B.A., J.D. [McKenna&C.]
*PRACTICE AREAS: Government Contracts Law.
**Kavcioglu, Armenak** .... '69 '94 C.112 B.A. L.800 J.D. [Ⓐ Devirian&S.]
*LANGUAGES: Armenian, Turkish.
*PRACTICE AREAS: Civil Litigation; Construction Law; Bankruptcy.
Kawachi, Cynthia Y. .... '57 '83 C.112 B.A. L.1065 J.D. Dep. Dist. Atty.
Kawahara, Glenn N., (AV) .... '51 '77 C.800 B.A. L.809 J.D. 523 W. 6th St.
Kawahara, Ken K. .... '34 '66 C.312 B.A. L.1065 J.D. 1055 Wilshire Blvd.

CAA262P

Kawahara, Robert M. ................. '55 '80 C.112 B.A. L.767 J.D. 1055 Wilshire Blvd.
Kawahara, Russell K. ................... '57 '82 C.813 A.B. L.145 J.D. 777 S. Figueroa St.
**Kawakami, Thomas T.** ................. '60 '86 C.112 B.A. L.1049 J.D. [Musick,P.&G.]
*PRACTICE AREAS: Taxation; Business Law; Trusts and Estates.
Kawana, Teiji R. ....... '61 '88 C.918 B.A. L.426 J.D. Gen. Coun. & V.P., JSL Foods, Inc.
**Kawano, Tracy** .............................. '64 '91 C.112 B.A. L.426 J.D. [Coleman&W.]
*PRACTICE AREAS: Civil Litigation; Torts; Insurance Defense; Products Liability.
Kawasaki, Nobuo ............. '38 '64 C.628 B.S. L.629 LL.B. U.S. Sec. & Exch. Comm.
Kay, Catherine A. ............... '56 '80 C.112 B.A. L.800 J.D. 11355 W. Olympic Blvd.
**Kay, Richard K.** ................ '65 '92 C.112 B.A. L.800 J.D. [A La Follette,J.D.F.&A.]
*PRACTICE AREAS: Medical Malpractice.
**Kayaian, Richard T.**, (AV) ................. '39 '65 C&L.800 B.S., LL.B. [R.T.Kayaian]

**Kayaian, Richard T., A Professional Corporation, (AV)**
**444 South Flower, Suite 2030, 90071-2955**
**Telephone: 213-627-1450 FAX: 213-627-9858**
**Richard T. Kayaian.**
**General Business, Corporation and Probate Law, Litigation.**
**Reference: Sanwa Bank (Los Angeles Main Office).**
***See Professional Biographies, LOS ANGELES, CALIFORNIA***

Kayajanian, Patricia A. ...................... '41 '75 C.999 L.1136 J.D. 4700 Wilshire Blvd.
**Kaye, Barbara A.** ..................... '50 '82 C.1044 B.A. L.990 J.D. [C Pircher,N.&M.]
*PRACTICE AREAS: Real Estate; Business Law; Secured Creditors Rights; Mediation.
**Kaye, Barry D.** .......................... '68 '95 C&L.978 B.A., J.D. [A Russ,A.&K.]
*PRACTICE AREAS: Intellectual Property Litigation; Securities Litigation; Commercial Litigation; Bankruptcy.
Kaye, Claudia '— '86 C.881 B.A. L.262 J.D.
(adm. in NY; not adm. in CA) 1809 Brockton Ave.‡
**Kaye, Debbie** ................................ '58 '85 C.881 B.A. L.990 J.D. [Kegel,T.&T.]
**Kaye, Douglas M.** ........................ '61 '88 C.494 B.A. L.809 J.D. [C Zide&O.]
*PRACTICE AREAS: Commercial Collection; Retail Collection; Insolvency.
**Kaye, Jeffrey A.** ........................... '66 '91 C.978 B.A. L.659 J.D. [A Kopple&K.]
*LANGUAGES: Hebrew.
**Kaye, Lawrence W.**, (AV) ..... '55 '79 C.1033 B.A. L.1049 J.D. [Kaye,R.] (⊙San Diego)
*REPORTED CASES: Saroza v. Royal Caribbean Corp., 1992 A.M.C. 428 (C.D. Cal. 1991); aff'd 996 F.2d 1227 (9th Cir. 1993); Vander Lind v. The Atchison, Topeka and Santa Fe Railway System, 146 Cal.App. 3D 358, 194 Cal. Rptr. 209; Osborn v. Princess Tours, 1996 AMC 1481, 1995 AMC 2119 (S.D. Tex. 1995); Berman v. Royal Cruise Line, 1995 AMC 1926 (CA 1995).
Kaye, Leonard M. .................... '17 '46 C.569 B.A. L.1009 LL.B. 5001 Finley Ave.

**Kaye, Rose & Partners, (AV)**
**A Law Partnership**
**1801 Century Park East, #1250, 90067-2302⊙**
**Telephone: 310-277-1200 Fax: 310-277-1220 Telex: 371-7740**
**Email: krpla@aol.com**
**Lawrence W. Kaye; Bradley M. Rose (Resident); Anthony J. Passante, Jr. Associates: Anita M. Eilert; Elsa Ward Arata (Resident); Marva Jo Wyatt (Resident).**
**Maritime Law, Insurance Defense, General Civil Litigation, Customs and Trade Law, Entertainment, Medical Malpractice, Pollution, Legislative Affairs and Product Liability. Civil Trial and Appellate Practice in State and Federal Courts. Admiralty, Maritime, Marine Oil Spill, Construction, Insurance, Surety, Corporate, Product Liability and Business Litigation.**
**San Diego, California Office: 1230 Columbia Street, Suite 1000. Telephone: 619-232-6555. Fax: 619-232-6577.**
**San Francisco, California Office: 55 Francisco Street, Suite 610. Telephone: 414-433-6555. Fax: 415-433-6577.**
**Miami, Florida Office: One Biscayne Tower, 2 South Biscayne Boulevard, Suite 3750. Telephone: 305-358-6555. Fax: 305-374-9077.**
***See Professional Biographies, LOS ANGELES, CALIFORNIA***

**Kaye, Scholer, Fierman, Hays & Handler, LLP, (AV)** BR
**A New York Limited Liability Partnership**
**1999 Avenue of the Stars, Suite 1600, 90067-6048⊙**
**Telephone: 310-788-1000 Facsimile: 310-788-1200**
**Members of Firm: Gary Apfel; Aton Arbisser; Robert Barnes; T. Brent Costello (Not admitted in CA); Barry L. Dastin; Michael D. Fernhoff; Kenneth A. Freeling; Jeffrey S. Gordon; Channing D. Johnson; Barry H. Lawrence; Ronald L. Leibow; Hushmand Sohaili; William E. Thomson, Jr. Special Counsel: Cruz Reynoso. Counsel: Susan A. Grode; Peter L. Haviland; Sheri Jeffrey; Anthony R. Salandra; M. Kenneth Suddleson. Associates: Ivy Kagan Bierman; Russ Alan Cashdan; Brian T. Corrigan; Alan L. Friel; Brian M. Hoye; Lillie Hsu; Liza Ilona Karsai; Ronald E. Levinson; Gina LiMandri; Mitchell J. Steinberger; Bonnie Stylides; Rhonda Renee Trotter; Kym R. Wulfe; John A. Zecca.**
**New York, N.Y.: 425 Park Avenue, 10022-3598. Telephone: 212-836-8000. Telex: 234860 KAY UR. Facsimile: 212-836-8689.**
**Washington, D.C.: McPherson Building, 901 Fifteenth Street, N.W., Suite 1100, 20005-2327. Telephone: 202-682-3500. Facsimile: 202-682-3580.**
**Hong Kong: 9 Queen Road Centre, 18th Floor. Telephone: 852-28458989. Facsimile: 852-28453682; 2389.**
***See Professional Biographies, LOS ANGELES, CALIFORNIA***

Kays, Douglas B. ......................... '54 '80 C.950 B.S. L.809 J.D. 2239 Colby St.
Kayyem, Robert E. ................. '38 '64 C&L.1068 B.A., LL.B. 300 Comstock Ave.
**Kazan, Wayne** ................... '68 '95 C.174 B.S.B.A. L.800 J.D. [A Mitchell,S.&K.]
*PRACTICE AREAS: Music and Entertainment Law.
**Kazemzadeh, Farhad** ............. '42 '70 C.976 B.A. L.880 J.D. [A Anderson,A.L.&G.]
*LANGUAGES: Persian, Russian.
*PRACTICE AREAS: Real Estate; Title Insurance; Litigation.
Kean, Joseph A., (AV) ............. '15 '41 C&L.352 A.B., J.D. 234 S. Muirfield Rd.‡

**Kean, Lewis B., (AV) '17 '42 C.112 A.B. L.1066 LL.B.**
**Suite 808, 3440 Wilshire Boulevard, 90010**
**Telephone: 213-388-9341 Fax: 213-388-9344**
**Civil and Trial Practice. Corporation, Securities, Antitrust Law and Bankruptcy.**
**Reference: Bank of America, Main Office and Wilshire-Mariposa Office.**
***See Professional Biographies, LOS ANGELES, CALIFORNIA***

**Keane, Ellen M.** ...................... '68 '93 C&L.426 B.A., J.D. [A Hennigan,M.&B.]
**Keane, James L.** ....................... '47 '72 C.112 B.A. L.1068 J.D. [C Simke C.]
*PRACTICE AREAS: Business and Commercial; Appellate Practice.
**Keane, Shannon M.** ................... '68 '94 C.741 B.A. L.436 J.D. [A Rubinstein&P.]
*PRACTICE AREAS: Commercial Litigation.
**Kearney, Thomas A.** ..................... '52 '79 C.112 B.A. L.426 J.D. [Kearney,B.&C.]
Kearney, Thomas J. ......................... '59 '90 C.728 B.A. L.464 J.D. [Kopesky&W.]

**Kearney, Bistline & Cohoon, A Law Corporation**
**Suite 3265, 300 S. Grand, 90074**
**Telephone: 213-617-9209 Fax: 213-617-9325**
**James B. Cohoon; Gregory D. Bistline; Thomas A. Kearney; Larry J. Kent; Paul Alvarez; Ted H. Luymes; Gregory A. Dilts.**
**General Practice.**
***See Professional Biographies, LOS ANGELES, CALIFORNIA***

**Kearney, Gary W.**
**(See Pasadena)**

**Kearns, Timothy E.** ...................... '61 '89 C.1060 B.A. L.426 J.D. [A Inglis,L.&G.]
*PRACTICE AREAS: Insurance Defense.
**Keaster, Robert W.** .................. '59 '84 C.1077 B.A. L.990 J.D. [Charlston,R.&W.]
Keaton, Juliana J. ................... '64 '90 C.813 B.A. L.1065 J.D. 515 S. Figueroa St.
**Keats, Anthony M.** .......... '55 '86 C.103 B.A. L.767 J.D. [Baker&H.] (⊙San Francisco)
*PRACTICE AREAS: Intellectual Property.
**Keefer, Elizabeth J.** '48 '77 C.66 B.A. L.273 J.D.
(adm. in DC; not adm. in CA) Gen. Coun., Teledyne, Inc.
**Keehn, Robert F.** .............................. '59 '84 C.112 B.A. L.800 J.D. [Booth,M.&S.]
Keelan, Terrence P., (AV) '56 '81 C.602 B.A. L.190 J.D.
1888 Century Park E., 21st Fl.
**Keeler, Robert B.** ............................ '42 '73 C.101 B.A. L.1066 J.D. [A Reznik&R.]
*LANGUAGES: German.
*SPECIAL AGENCIES: California Public Utility Commission.
*PRACTICE AREAS: Public Utility Law; Energy Law; Administrative.
Keeley, Michael F. ............. '53 '80 C.602 B.A. L.477 J.D. COO, Off. of the Mayor
**Keenan, Kevin** ................................ '58 '85 C.112 B.S. L.1065 J.D. [C Manatt,P.&P.]
*PRACTICE AREAS: Health Law; Corporate Law; Corporate Securities.
**Keenan, Marcie A.** .......................... '69 '95 C.112 B.A. L.426 J.D. [A Selman B.]
**Keenan, Richard**, (AV) ................. '52 '77 C.602 B.B.A. L.976 J.D. [Folger L.&K.]⊙
**Keene, Christopher J.** ................... '70 '96 C.112 B.A. L.880 J.D. [A Hancock R.&B.]
Keene, William B., (AV) ............... '25 '53 C.112 B.A. L.1068 LL.B. [C Morgan&W.]
**Keener, Cynthia L.** ..................... '58 '88 C.476 B.B.E. L.245 J.D. [A Morris,P.&P.]
**Keens, James A.** ...................... '53 '95 C.112 B.A. L.61 LL.D. [A Bonne,B.M.O.&N.]
*PRACTICE AREAS: Medical Malpractice.
**Keese, Robert M.**, (AV) ................................ '43 '70 C&L.426 J.D. [Girardi&K.]⊙
*PRACTICE AREAS: Professional Liability; Toxic Torts.
**Keever, Gregory** ....................... '49 '74 C.575 A.B. L.893 J.D. [Buchalter,N.F.&Y.]
**Kegel, Robert A.**, (AV) '27 '53
C.112 B.S. L.800 LL.B. [Kegel,T.&T.] (⊙San Diego & Long Beach)

**Kegel, Tobin & Truce, A Professional Corporation, (AV)**
**3580 Wilshire Boulevard, 10th Floor, P.O. Box 76907, 90076-0907⊙**
**Telephone: 213-380-3880 Fax: 213-383-8346**
**Email: comp-law@ktt.com**
**Robert A. Kegel (Certified Specialist, Workers Compensation Law, The State Bar of California Board of Legal Specialization); John J. Tobin (Certified Specialist, Workers Compensation Law, The State Bar of California Board of Legal Specialization); Robert R. Wills (Certified Specialist, Workers Compensation Law, The State Bar of California Board of Legal Specialization) (Resident at Van Nuys); W. Joseph Truce (Certified Specialist, Workers Compensation Law, The State Bar of California Board of Legal Specialization); E. Charles Maki (Certified Specialist, Workers Compensation Law, The State Bar of California Board of Legal Specialization) (Resident at Ventura); Michael A. Ingler (Resident at Long Beach); Nancy J. Hankinson (Resident at Ventura); Jon E. von Leden; Theodore C. Hanf (Certified Specialist, Workers Compensation Law, The State Bar of California Board of Legal Specialization) (Resident at Van Nuys); Joseph D. Kieffer; Preeti G. Shah; Humberto Gonzalez; Timothy D. Sanford-Wachtel (Rancho Cucamonga and San Diego Offices); Debbie Kaye;—Paul M. Ryan, Jr.; Steven M. Green; D'Arcy T. Swartz (Resident at Long Beach); Sandra L. Adams (Resident at Long Beach); Daniel A. Dobrin (Resident at Rancho Cucamonga); Jeffrey E. Weiss; Kelly M. Hardy (Resident at Long Beach); Anju Khurana.**
**Workers Compensation, Longshore and Harborworkers', Public Employment, Retirement Law. Insurance Law, Third Party Subrogation.**
**Reference: American West Bank, Encino.**
**Ventura, California Office: 5450 Ralston Street, Suite 204, P.O. Box 7779. Telephone: 805-644-2216. Facsimile: 805-644-8625.**
**Rancho Cucamonga, California Office: 10737 Laurel Street, #240, P.O. Box 3329. Telephone: 909-466-5555. Facsimile: 909-466-5562.**
**San Diego, California Office: 2535 Kettner Boulevard, Suite 2A1. Telephone: 619-696-0906.**
**Long Beach, California Office: 330 Golden Shore Drive, Suite 150. Telephone: 310-437-1108. Facsimile: 310-437-3742.**
**Van Nuys, California Office: 14545 Friar Street, Suite 104. Telephone: 818-947-0300. Facsimile: 818-947-0303.**
***See Professional Biographies, LOS ANGELES, CALIFORNIA***

**Kehoe, Larissa A.J.** .................... '70 '95 C.976 B.A. L.1049 J.D. [A Fulbright&J.]
*PRACTICE AREAS: Litigation.
Kehr, Ellen Birnbaum ..................... '47 '72 C.112 B.A. L.800 J.D. Dep. Atty. Gen.
**Kehr, Robert L.**, (AV) ..................... '44 '70 C.188 B.A. L.178 J.D. [Kehr,C.T.&F.]

**Kehr, Crook, Tovmassian & Fox, A Professional Corporation, (AV)**
**11755 Wilshire Boulevard, Suite 1400, 90025**
**Telephone: 310-479-4994 Fax: 310-479-4855**
**Email: KCTFox@aol.com**
**Robert L. Kehr; George D. Crook; David M. Fox; Henry Tovmassian; Samantha E. Blake.**
**General Business, Corporate and Partnership Law, Real Estate Law, Condominium Law, Entertainment Law, Professional Liability and Ethics and General Civil Litigation and Appeals.**
***See Professional Biographies, LOS ANGELES, CALIFORNIA***

Keifer, Brian P. ................... '59 '89 C.1077 B.S. L.426 J.D. 11835 W. Olympic Blvd.
Keir, James M. ......................... '35 '61 C.112 B.A. L.1068 J.D. 10850 Wilshire Blvd.
Keiser, John ................................ '51 '74 C.800 L.425 J.D. 1010 Wilshire Blvd.
**Keisner, David A.** ........................... '56 '80 L.061 LL.B. [A Stringfellow&Assoc.]
Keitel, David Charles ................... '58 '85 C.112 B.A. L.426 J.D. 633 W. 5th St.
**Keitel, William E.** ......................... '54 '81 C.273 B.A. L.846 J.D. [Hawkins,S.L.&B.]
Keiter, Mitchell ................................ '67 '91 C.813 A.B. L.1068 J.D. Dep. Atty. Gen.
Keith, Susan R. ........................... '60 '86 C.518 B.A. L.245 J.D. 555 S. Flower St.
**Keitt, John K., Jr.** '54 '79 C.197 A.B. L.790 J.D.
(adm. in NY; not adm. in CA) [Rogers&W.] (⊙N.Y., NY)
Kekich, Barbara ........................ '48 '78 C.521 B.A. L.809 J.D. 1430 Holmby Ave.
Kelberg, Brian R. ......................... '50 '77 C.112 A.B. L.809 J.D. Dep. Dist. Atty.
**Kelble, Glenn C.** ....................... '66 '92 C.112 B.A. L.1068 J.D. [A Danning,G.D.&K.]
*PRACTICE AREAS: Bankruptcy; Litigation.
Kelcy, Michael C., (AV) ....................... '45 '76 C.821 B.A. L.659 J.D. 633 W. 5th St.
Keleti, S. Martin ............................ '63 '89 C.112 A.B. L.1065 J.D. [A Cohen&C.]
Kelhoffer, Alan C. ....................... '63 '89 C.276 B.A. L.809 J.D. 1200 Wilshire Blvd.
**Kellar, Michael C.** '52 '78
C.1253 B.A. L.1068 J.D. [Hillsinger&C.] (⊙Rancho Cucamonga)
Kelleher, J.D. .............................. '38 '76 C.1097 B.S. L.1095 J.D. 2020 Hillhurst Ave.
**Kelleher, Kathleen A.** ............... '64 '90 C.945 B.A. L.273 J.D. [A Manning,M.&W.]
**Kelleher, Michael F.** ................... '61 '93 C.878 B.A. L.1066 J.D. [A Folger L.&K.]⊙
Kelleher, Robert J. ......................... '13 '39 C.951 A.B. L.309 LL.B. U.S. Sr. Dist. J.
**Keller, Allison M.** ........................ '— '90 C.674 B.A. L.1068 J.D. [A O'Melveny&M.]
Keller, Barbara L. '46 '78
C.597 B.A. L.424 J.D. Assoc. Prof. of Bus. Law, Calif. State Univ.
**Keller, Kent**, (AV) .................................. '43 '69 C.804 B.A. L.910 J.D. [Barger&W.]
*PRACTICE AREAS: Litigation; Insurance Law; Insurance Regulation.
**Keller, Sarah D.** ................................. '— '92 L.145 J.D. [A Sheppard,M.R.&H.]
*PRACTICE AREAS: Business; Corporate; Securities.
Keller, William D. ......................... '34 '61 C&L.112 B.S., LL.B. U.S. Dist. J.

**Keller, Price & Moorhead**
**(See Redondo Beach)**

**Kellett, Thomas E.**, (AV) ................ '26 '52 C&L.494 B.A., J.D. [C Meserve,M.&H.]
**Kelley, Bennet G.** ..................................... '63 '90 C.30 B.S. L.276 J.D. [A Howrey&S.]
*PRACTICE AREAS: Complex Litigation; Insurance Coverage.
**Kelley, Donald E., Jr.**, (AV) ............. '48 '73 C.976 B.A. L.813 J.D. [Folger L.&K.]⊙
**Kelley, Michael C.** .............................. '54 '79 C.800 A.B. L.976 J.D. [Sidley&A.]
*PRACTICE AREAS: General Litigation; Antitrust; Securities Litigation.

**Kelley, Pamela Smith** ....................'67 '92 C.112 B.A. L.976 J.D. [⊠ Riordan&M.]
*PRACTICE AREAS: Litigation.
**Kelley, Paul M.** ....................'52 '79 C.855 B.A. L.464 J.D. [Donfeld,K.&R.]
*PRACTICE AREAS: Business Litigation; Unfair Competition and Trade Regulation; Real Property Litigation; Construction Defect Defense; Employer/Employee Dispute Resolution.
**Kelley, Peter C.** ....................'59 '86 C.976 B.A. L.1068 J.D. [O'Melveny&M.]
*LANGUAGES: French.
*PRACTICE AREAS: Partnerships; Real Estate Transactions; Limited Liability Companies.
Kelley, Robert Lane ....................'50 '84 C.112 B.A. L.990 J.D. [J.S.Matthew]
**Kelley, William J., III** ....................'57 '85 C.112 B.A. L.813 J.D. [⊠ Chadbourne&P.]

**Kelley Drye & Warren LLP, (AV)**
A Partnership including Professional Associations
**515 South Flower Street, 90071⊙**
Telephone: 213-689-1300 Fax: (213) 688-8150
Email: info@kelleydrye.com URL: http://www.kelleydrye.com
Paul L. Bressan; Patrick Del Duca; Ronald D. Husdon; William H. Kiekhofer, III; Theresa A. Kristovich; Michael Lublinski; Jun Mori; Kenneth A. O'Brien, Jr.; James D. Prendergast; Theodore J. Roper; Marshall C. Stoddard, Jr.; Shigeru Watanabe;—Allison-Claire Acker; Francisco Javier Aparicio; Anthony R. Callobre; Don S. Lemmer; Christina Lycoyannis (Not admitted in CA); Akiko Nakatani; Cynthia S. Papsdorf; Shari L. Prussin (Not admitted in CA); Katherine M. Windler; Rebecca J. Winthrop; Julia Zalba.
General Practice.
New York, N.Y. Office: 101 Park Avenue. Telephone: 212-808-7800. Telex: 12369. Fax: (212) 808-7897.
Stamford, Connecticut Office: Two Stamford Plaza, 281 Tresser Boulevard. Telephone: 203-324-1400. Fax: (203) 327-2669; (203) 964-3188.
Washington, D.C. Office: 1200 19th Street, N.W., Suite 500. Telephone: 202-955-9600. Fax: (202) 955-9792.
Miami, Florida Office: 201 South Biscayne Boulevard, 2400 Miami Center. Telephone: 305-372-2400. Fax: (305) 372-2490.
Parsippany, New Jersey Office: 5 Sylvan Way. Telephone: 201-539-0099. Fax: (201) 539-3167.
Chicago, Illinois Office: 303 West Madison Street, Suite 1400. Telephone: 312-346-6350. Fax: (312) 346-8982.
Brussels, Belgium Office: 106 Avenue Louise, 1050. Telephone: (011) (32) (2) 646-1110. Fax: (011) (32) (2) 640-0589.
Hong Kong Office: 509-10 Peregrine Tower, Lippo Centre, 89 Queensway. Telephone: (011) (85) (2) 2869-0821. Fax: (011) (85) (2) 2869-0049.
New Delhi, India Affiliated Office: Swarup & Co., J.K. Building, 6th Floor, Vipps Centre, 2 Masjid Moth, Greater Kailash II, 110 048. Telephone: (011) (91) (11) 646-6314. Fax: (011) (91) (11) 642-8939.
*See Professional Biographies, LOS ANGELES, CALIFORNIA*

**Kellman, Barry D.** ....................'53 '95 C.112 B.A. L.1068 J.D. [⊠ Greenberg G.F.C.&M.]
*PRACTICE AREAS: Litigation.
**Kellum, Richard J.** ....................'53 '79 C.800 B.A. L.426 J.D. [⊠ Norton&F.]
*PRACTICE AREAS: Insurance Bad Faith; Insurance Coverage; Appellate Practice.
Kelly, Brian J. ....................'66 '91 C.659 B.S. L.1068 J.D. 7th Fl. 515 S. Figueroa St.
**Kelly, Christopher W.** ....................'63 '92 C.1097 B.A. L.426 J.D. [⊠ White&C.]
**Kelly, D. Alton** ....................'51 '91 C.1201 B.A. L.809 J.D. [⊠ Acker,K.&W.]
*PRACTICE AREAS: Business Litigation; Civil Litigation; Construction Defects; Insurance Coverage.
**Kelly, Deidre M.** .................... '66 '89 C.800 B.A. L.426 J.D. [⊠ Paul,H.J.&W.]
Kelly, Faith A. ....................'56 '82 C.801 B.A. L.910 J.D. 725 S. Figueroa St.
**Kelly, Francine B.** ....................'58 '87 C.446 B.A. L.426 J.D. [⊠ Gilbert,K.C.&J.]
**Kelly, Genevieve M.** ....................'67 '93 C.103 A.B. L.276 J.D. [⊠ McDermott,W.&E.]
*LANGUAGES: French.
Kelly, Joel P. ....................'54 '80 C.94 A.B. L.276 J.D. 444 S. Flower St.
Kelly, Kevin M. '61 '91 C.813 B.A. L.1068 J.D.
1800 Ave. of the Stars, Suite 900 (Century City)
**Kelly, Marla**, (BV) ....................'46 '82 C.1097 B.S. L.1190 J.D. [Ibold&A.]
**Kelly, Michael L.**, (AV) ....................'53 '78 C.988 B.A. L.336 J.D. [Kirtland&P.]
**Kelly, Pamela Brown** ....................'59 '86 C.893 B.A. L.1068 J.D. [Latham&W.]
**Kelly, Patrick M.**, (AV) ....................'43 '70 C.668 B.A. L.426 J.D. [Wilson,E.M.E.&D.]
Kelly, Peter C. ....................'59 '85 C.309 A.B. L.1068 J.D. Coun., The Capital Grp., Inc.
**Kelly, Peter D.**, (AV) .................... '48 '77 C.1109 B.A. L.809 J.D. [Kelly&L.]
*PRACTICE AREAS: Administrative Law; Real Estate; Land Use.
Kelly, Robert A. ....................'65 '90 C.813 B.A. L.976 J.D. 333 S. Grand Ave.
**Kelly, Robert E., Jr.**, (AV) ....................'41 '73 C.734 B.S. L.569 J.D. [La Follette,J.D.F.&A.]
*PRACTICE AREAS: Products Liability; Environmental Law.
**Kelly, Roger E.**, (AV) ....................'16 '39 C&L.426 A.B., LL.B. [⊠ Gilbert,K.C.&J.]
**Kelly, Tara K.** ....................'68 '95 C.860 B.A. L.800 J.D. [⊠ Paul,H.J.&W.]
**Kelly, Terence M.** ....................'44 '79 C.112 B.A. L.1148 J.D. [⊠ Grace,S.C.&S.]
*PRACTICE AREAS: Medical Malpractice; Product Liability; Construction; Environmental; Insurance Defense Law.
**Kelly, Terry O.** .................... '45 '70 C.276 B.A. L.569 J.D. [Rogers&W.]
*PRACTICE AREAS: Business Litigation; Environmental; Intellectual Property.

**Kelly, Bauersfeld, Lowry & Kelley**
(See Woodland Hills)

**Kelly & Lytton, (AV)**
**1900 Avenue of the Stars Suite 1450, 90067**
Telephone: 310-277-5333 Facsimile: 310-277-5953
Members of Firm: Peter D. Kelly; Sheldon H. Lytton; Marshall G. Mintz; Bruce P. Vann; James D. Robinson. Of Counsel: Marilyn Barrett; Michael I. Sidley.
Administrative, Real Estate, Transactional, Entertainment, Business Law, Election Law, Family Law and Civil Litigation.
*See Professional Biographies, LOS ANGELES, CALIFORNIA*

Kelman, Joel B. ....................'40 '69 C.1077 B.A. L.398 J.D. 1741 N. Ivar Ave.
Kelner, Howard M. ....................'35 '70 C.112 B.A. L.398 J.D. Dep. Dist. Atty.
**Kelsberg, William G.** ....................'62 '89 C.05 B.A. L.1148 J.D. [⊠ Knopfler&R.]
*PRACTICE AREAS: Construction Defect Litigation; Personal Injury Defense.
Kelsey, David B. ....................'45 '75 C.112 B.A. L.426 J.D. Asst. Co. Coun.
Kelton, Lisa ....................'64 '91 C.112 B.A. L.1136 J.D. 2764 Krim Dr.‡
Kemalyan, Richard S. ....................'50 '76 C.112 B.A. L.426 J.D. [Chase,R.D.&B.]
Kemper, Bernard F. ....................'25 '67 C.912 L.809 LL.B. Mun. J.
Kemper, Carolyn V. ....................'61 '92 C.1213 B.S. L.940 J.D. Dependency Ct. Legal Servs.
Kemper, Elizabeth D. '54 '79 C.197 A.B. L.893 J.D.
Dir., Student Legal Servs. & Law Prof., Univ. of Calif.
**Kemper, Kevin M.** ....................'66 '94 C.112 B.A. L.1049 J.D. [⊠ Reznik&R.]
*SPECIAL AGENCIES: Los Angeles County Metroplitans Transit Authority (MTA).
*PRACTICE AREAS: Land Use; Zoning; Environmental; Administrative.
Kemper, Kurt C. '46 '73 C.918 B.A. L.880 J.D.
(adm. in DC; not adm. in CA) V.P. & Assoc. Tax Coun., Security Pacific Natl. Bk.
**Kempinsky, Louis E.**, (AV) ....................'55 '79 C.691 B.A. L.178 J.D. [Tuttle&T.]
*PRACTICE AREAS: Civil Litigation; Bankruptcy and Creditors' Rights; Environmental Litigation.
Kempler, Roger .................... '56 '87 C.1168 B.A. L.426 J.D. Auto. Club of Southern Calif.
**Kempton, Kathryn L.** .................... '69 '94 C.325 B.A. L.352 J.D. [⊠ Arter&H.]
*LANGUAGES: Spanish.
**Kendall, Richard B.**, (AV) ....................'52 '79 C.918 B.A. L.800 J.D. [Shearman&S.]
Kender, Randall F. ....................'61 '85 C.201 B.A. L.161 J.D. V.P. & Sr. Litig. Coun., Fox, Inc.
**Kendig, Dennis A.**, (AV) ....................'46 '74 C.210 B.A. L.976 J.D. [Kendig&R.]
*PRACTICE AREAS: Business Litigation; Securities Litigation; Franchise Litigation.
Kendig, Ellsworth H., Jr., (AV) .... '22 '50 C.477 B.A. L.912 LL.B. Liberty Mut. Ins. Co.
**Kendig, Holly E.**, (AV) .................... '47 '75 C.210 B.A. L.976 J.D. [O'Melveny&M.]

**Kendig & Ross, (AV)**
**1875 Century Park East, Suite 2150, 90067**
Telephone: 310-556-8100 Fax: 310-556-8140
Members of Firm: Dennis A. Kendig; Bradley D. Ross. Associate: Jeffrey W. Cowan.
Business Litigation and Employment/Labor Law.
*See Professional Biographies, LOS ANGELES, CALIFORNIA*

Kendis, Harold J. ....................'11 '34 C&L.190 Ph.B., J.D. 5866 Spring Oak Dr.‡
**Kendrick, Elwood S.**, (AV) ....................'12 '37 C.579 B.S. L.339 J.D. [E.S.Kendrick] (Pat.)

**Kendrick, Elwood S., Inc., (AV)**
**29th Floor, 555 South Flower Street, 90071-2498**
Telephone: 213-622-6030 Fax: 213-688-7564
Elwood S. Kendrick.
Complex Business Litigation. Class Actions.
*See Professional Biographies, LOS ANGELES, CALIFORNIA*

Keneipp, David M. '54 '80 C.802 B.F.A. L.705 J.D.
V.P., Bus. & Legal Affs., Fox Television Stations, Inc.
Kenmore, Christine F. '59 '84
C.66 B.A. L.94 J.D. V.P. & Sr. Coun., Wells Fargo Bk., N.A.
**Kenna, Timothy W., (Professional Corporation)**, (AV) '49 '75
C.112 B.A. L.767 J.D. [Wilson,K.&B.]
Kenneally, Dori D. ....................'60 '85 C.1077 B.A. L.800 J.D. 3443 Mandeville Canyon Rd.
**Kennedy, Alyssa Tara** ....................'71 '96 C.188 B.A. L.309 J.D. [⊠ Troop M.S.&P.]
*LANGUAGES: French, Spanish.
*PRACTICE AREAS: Corporate; Taxation.

**Kennedy, Brian J., (AV) '25 '52 C&L.426 A.B., J.D.**
**Suite 1226, 3600 Wilshire Boulevard, 90010**
Telephone: 213-385-0037 Fax: 213-385-0276
Real Property, Administrative, Corporation, Tax, Probate and Family Law. General Civil and Trial Practice in all State Courts.
Reference: Bank of America (Wilshire Harvard Branch, Los Angeles).

Kennedy, Donald C. ....................'64 '91 C.546 B.A. L.61 J.D. MCA Music Publishing
**Kennedy, Gregory G.** ....................'53 '78 C.112 B.A. L.426 J.D. [Goldstein,K.&P.]
*PRACTICE AREAS: Labor and Employment; Civil Litigation.
**Kennedy, J. Christopher** ....................'50 '76 C.309 B.A. L.893 J.D. [Irell&M.]
Kennedy, John M. ....................'64 '91 C.165 B.A. L.477 J.D. 11601 Wilshire Blvd.
**Kennedy, Julie M.** ....................'65 '91 C&L.813 B.A., J.D. [⊠ Folger L.&K.]⊙
Kennedy, Katharine B. ....................'12 '38 C&L.800 B.A., LL.B. 727 Burlingame Ave.‡
**Kennedy, Peter J.** ....................'67 '93 C.112 B.A. L.1068 J.D. [⊠ Crosby,H.R.&M.]
Kennedy, Sean K. ....................'64 '89 C&L.426 B.A., J.D. Fed. Pub. Def.
**Kennedy, Tracey A.** ....................'65 '90 C&L.846 B.A., J.D. [⊠ Sheppard,M.R.&H.]
Kennedy, Wm. John, (AV) ....'33 '57 C.674 B.S.E. L.309 LL.B. 777 S. Figueroa, 34th Fl.
**Kenney, Daniel E.** ....................'67 '94 C.1168 B.A. L.809 J.D. [⊠ Harrington,F.D.&C.]
*PRACTICE AREAS: Products Liability; General Liability; Medical Malpractice; Civil Rights.
**Kenney, David E.** ....................'53 '84 C.800 B.A. L.990 J.D. [⊠ Karns&K.]
*PRACTICE AREAS: Administrative Law; Taxation; Litigation; Government Law; Education Law.
Kenney, Mary Whitney ....................'50 '76 C.788 B.A. L.800 J.D. First Interstate Bank
Kennick, Michael Todd .................... '61 '87 C.1042 B.A. L.1148 J.D. [Hogan,B.&H.]
Kenninger, Steven C. ....................'52 '77 C.679 B.S. L.813 J.D. Pres., Koar Grp., Inc.
**Kennon, Randall H.** ....................'47 '73 C.976 B.A. L.1068 J.D. Sr. Coun., Bank of Amer.
**Kenny, Marc E.** .................... '69 '95 C.105 B.A. L.94 J.D. [⊠ Paul,H.J.&W.]
**Kenoff, Jay S.**, (AV) .................... '46 '70 C.112 A.B. L.309 J.D. [Kenoff&M.]
*PRACTICE AREAS: Entertainment; Real Estate; Business.

**Kenoff & Machtinger, (AV)**
**1999 Avenue of the Stars, Suite 1250, 90067**
Telephone: 310-552-0808 Fax: 310-277-0653
Jay S. Kenoff; Leonard S. Machtinger. Associate: Thomas S. Rubin; Courtney F. Lee. Of Counsel: William J. Immerman; Robert O. Kaplan; Lawrence E. May.
Entertainment (motion pictures, television and music), Civil Litigation (business and entertainment), Real Estate, Corporate, Banking, Tax.
*See Professional Biographies, LOS ANGELES, CALIFORNIA*

**Kent, Christopher R.** ....................'54 '88 C.1077 B.A. L.426 J.D. [⊠ Chapman&G.]
*PRACTICE AREAS: General Negligence; Products Liability Law; Environmental Law; Toxic and Hazardous Substance Litigation.
**Kent, Evan M.**, (BV⊙) ....................'55 '80 C.813 B.S. L.145 J.D. [Russ,A.&K.]
*PRACTICE AREAS: Trademark Law; Copyright Law; Patent Law; Trade Secrets; Unfair Competition.
**Kent, Jeffrey A.** ....................'52 '76 C.112 B.S. L.426 J.D. [Poindexter&D.]
*PRACTICE AREAS: Construction Litigation; Commercial Litigation.
**Kent, Larry J.** ....................'61 '86 C.112 B.A. L.426 J.D. [Kearney,B.&C.]
Kent, Norman '34 '62
C.112 A.B. L.800 LL.B. Claims Atty., Auto. Club of Southern Calif.
Kent, Rahel Eden ....................'62 '89 C.1077 B.A. L.940 J.D. 2700 E. Cahuenga Blvd.
**Kent, Robert E.** ....................'62 '89 C.103 A.B. L.426 J.D. [Gibbs,G.L.&A.]
*PRACTICE AREAS: Business Litigation; Employment Law; Labor Law.
**Kent, Ronald D.**, (AV) ....................'56 '81 C.112 B.A. L.1066 J.D. [Sonnenschein N.&R.]
*PRACTICE AREAS: Insurance Law; General and Environmental Litigation.
**Kenworthy, Charles N.** ....................'57 '85 C.112 B.A. L.1049 J.D. [Allen,M.L.G.&M.]
*PRACTICE AREAS: Business Litigation and Entertainment Law.
Kenyon, David V. ....................'30 '58 C.112 B.A. L.800 J.D. Sr. U.S. Dist. J.
Keosian, Armand ....................'34 '72 C.112 B.A. L.426 J.D. [Keosian&K.]
Keosian, Christopher ....................'63 '88 C.112 B.A. L.809 J.D. [Keosian&K.]
Keosian, Gregory ....................'61 '87 C.112 B.A. L.1136 J.D. [Keosian&K.]
Keosian & Keosian .................... 1801 Ave. of the Stars
**Kepner, Raymond R.** ....................'52 '77 C.346 B.A. L.477 J.D. [Morgan,L.&B.]
**Ker, Frank G.**, (AV) ....................'43 '67 C&L.813 A.B., LL.B. 555 S. Flower St.
Kerans, Susan A. ....................'59 '88 C.112 B.S. L.800 J.D. 725 S. Figueroa
Kerekes, Michael S. ....................'62 '87 C.112 A.B. L.309 J.D. 2029 Century Pk. E.
**Kerfes, Kathryn** ....................'46 '81 C.112 B.A. L.1148 J.D. [Sulmeyer,K.B.&R.]
*PRACTICE AREAS: Bankruptcy.
Kerlin, Karla D. ....................'64 '90 C.665 B.S. L.809 J.D. Dep. Dist. Atty.
Kerman, Thea J. ....................'49 '75 C.188 B.S. L.569 J.D. 720 Huntley Dr.
**Kern, Lee Ann** ....................'63 '91 C.1109 B.A. L.809 J.D. [⊠ Murchison&C.]
*PRACTICE AREAS: Insurance Defense-Litigation.
**Kern, René J., Jr.**, (AV) ....................'47 '81 C.173 B.S. L.1137 J.D. [Kern,S.&G.]
*PRACTICE AREAS: Product Liability; Premises Liability; Medical and Dental Malpractice; Employment Discrimination; General Negligence.
**Kern, Robert M.**, (AV) ....................'40 '71 C.1042 L.426 J.D. [Kern&W.]

**Kern, Streeter & Gonzalez, (AV) ⊞**
**601 West 5th Street, Suite 1100, 90071**
Telephone: 213-629-8100 Facsimile: 213-627-8765
Members of Firm: René J. Kern, Jr.; John W. Streeter; Michael D. Gonzalez. Associates: Tina L. Gentile; Claudia T. Beightol; Angela J. Armitage; Christina L. Young.
Product Liability, Medical and Dental Malpractice, Construction Defect, Premises Liability, Defamation, Employment Law, Insurance Law, and Brokerage Negligence, General Civil Trial and Appellate Practice in all State and Federal Courts.
*See Professional Biographies, LOS ANGELES, CALIFORNIA*

**Kern & Wooley, (AV)**
**Suite 1150, 10900 Wilshire Boulevard, 90024⊙**
**Telephone: 310-824-1777 Fax: 310-824-0892**
**Robert M. Kern; M. Eugene Wooley; William V. O'Connor; George Steven McCall (Resident, Irving, Texas Office); Douglas J. Pahl; John W. Shaw; Michael J. Terhar; Robert L. Greer (Resident, Mesa, Arizona Office); G. Don Swaim (Resident, Irving, Texas Office);—Peter T. Kirchen; Jonathan S. Morse; Stephen G. Good (Resident, Irving, Texas Office); Rand Dunn Carstens; John H. Ishikawa (Resident, Mesa, Arizona Office); Anthony G. Marriott; Justo M. Justo; John M. Schutza (Resident, Irving, Texas Office); Ellen Greer.**
**Aviation and Casualty Insurance Law. Products Liability Law; Business Litigation.**
**Irving, Texas Office: Suite 1700 The Central Tower at Williams Square, 5215 North O'Connor Road. Telephone: 214-869-3311. Fax: 214-869-2433.**
**Mesa, Arizona Office: Suite 10550 Financial Plaza, 1201 South Alma School Road; Telephone: 602-834-8811. Fax: 602-834-3433.**
*See Professional Biographies, LOS ANGELES, CALIFORNIA*

**Kerner, Karen D.** ............... '62 '89 C.1077 B.A. L.1066 J.D. [Ⓐ Rossbacher&Assoc.]
**Kerns, Christianne F.** '58 '85 C.1109 B.A. L.800 J.D.
[Armstrong H.J.T.&W.] (⊙Irvine)
*PRACTICE AREAS: Real Estate Finance; General Business; Finance.
**Keroes, Amy N.** ......................... '68 '93 C.597 B.A. L.1068 J.D. [Ⓐ Latham&W.]
**Kerr, Lance N., Law Offices of '48 '77 C.112 B.A. L.426 J.D.**
**8833 Sunset Boulevard, Suite 200, 90069**
**Telephone: 310-659-2929 Fax: 310-289-5240**
**Civil Litigation, Corporate and Business, Real Estate, Commercial.**
*See Professional Biographies, LOS ANGELES, CALIFORNIA*

**Kerr, Lisa M.** ............................ '61 '95 C.623 L.1066 J.D. [Ⓐ Smaltz,A.&F.]
*PRACTICE AREAS: Complex Business Litigation.
**Kerr, Michael F., (AV⊙)** ............... '53 '82 C.93 A.B. L.145 J.D. [Mayer,B.&P.]
Kerr, Robert Alexander ................... '40 '88 C.1077 B.S. L.398 J.D. 4015 Clayton Ave.
**Kerr, Tom A.** ............................ '46 '93 C.629 B.A. L.1068 J.D. [Ⓐ Dale,B.&H.]
Kerrigan, Thomas S. ......................... '39 '65 C.112 L.426 J.D. Off. of U.S. Atty.
Kerry, Jack T. ............................... '41 '72 C.154 B.A. L.1067 J.D. Dep. Atty. Gen.
**Kerry, Garcia & Lewis**
**(See Long Beach)**
**Kershaw, James J., III** ............... '67 '93 C.197 B.A. L.813 J.D. [Ⓐ Lichter,G.N.&A.]
*PRACTICE AREAS: Entertainment; Copyright.
**Kertell, Charles A.** ........................ '70 '95 C&L.188 B.S., J.D. [Ⓐ Lyon&L.]
*PRACTICE AREAS: Patent, Trademark, Copyright, Antitrust and Unfair Competition; Intellectual Property.
**Kesluk, Brian S.** ......................... '56 '84 C.645 B.A. L.809 J.D. [Aidikoff&K.]
*PRACTICE AREAS: Civil Litigation; Business Litigation; Plaintiff Personal Injury.
**Kesner, Matthew P.** ........................ '60 '85 C.763 B.S. L.1049 J.D. [Lane P.S.L.]
*PRACTICE AREAS: Insurance Coverage; Aviation Law; Product Liability Law.
**Kessel, Bart L.** ............................ '60 '86 C.880 B.S. L.1067 J.D. [Arter&H.]
Kessel, Elizabeth M. ................. '50 '85 C.1062 B.A. L.276 J.D. 3435 Wilshire Blvd.
Kesselman, Stanley W. W. ...... '44 '68 C&L.705 B.A., J.D. 6500 Wilshire Blvd., 17th Fl.
**Kessler, Fredric W.** ................... '52 '79 C.918 B.A. L.1065 J.D. [Nossaman,G.K.&E.]
*PRACTICE AREAS: Real Property Law.
**Kessler, Joan B.** ........................ '45 '87 C.477 A.B. L.426 J.D. [Kessler&K.]
*PRACTICE AREAS: Commercial Litigation; Bankruptcy Law; Business Litigation.
**Kessler, Remy** ......................... '60 '86 C.112 A.B. L.426 J.D. [Thelen,M.J.&B.]
*PRACTICE AREAS: Labor and Employment; Litigation; Municipal Law; Commercial.
**Kessler, Warren J., (AV)** ................ '45 '73 C.188 A.B. L.477 J.D. [Kessler&K.]
*PRACTICE AREAS: Taxation Law; Corporate Law; Real Estate Law; Partnership Law; Estate Planning.
**Kessler & Kessler, A Law Corporation, (AV)**
**2029 Century Park East, Suite 1520, 90067**
**Telephone: 310-552-9800 Fax: 310-552-0442**
**Email: skiplaw@ix.netcom.com**
**Warren J. Kessler; Joan B. Kessler; Lisa C. Alexander.**
**Taxation, Corporate, Real Estate, Commercial Litigation, Bankruptcy and General Business Litigation, Estate Planning.**
*See Professional Biographies, LOS ANGELES, CALIFORNIA*

**Kestenbaum, Paul T. '57 '84 C.1044 B.S. L.472 J.D.**
**2029 Century Park East Suite 480, 90067**
**Telephone: 310-277-9402 Facsimile: 310-277-4351**
**Email: ptk@westworld.com**
**Federal and State Tax Planning for Individuals and Business Entities. Estate Planning, General Business, Corporate and Real Estate Transactions.**
*See Professional Biographies, LOS ANGELES, CALIFORNIA*

**Kester, Charles F.** ................... '65 '92 C&L.893 B.A., J.D. [Ⓐ Gibson,D.&C.]
*PRACTICE AREAS: Litigation.
Kester, Kimberly L. ......................... '— '92 C.112 B.A. L.1068 J.D. 333 S. Grand Ave.
**Keto, Harri J., (BV)** ............ '49 '76 C.112 B.A. L.1049 J.D. [Berger,K.S.M.F.S.&G.]
*LANGUAGES: Finnish.
**Kettles, Gregg W.** ....................... '66 '94 C.902 B.A. L.976 J.D. [Ⓐ Munger,T.&O.]
Keup, Erwin J., (AV) ...... '30 '58 C&L.436 B.S., J.D. [Ⓐ Noble&C.] (⊙Newport Beach)
**Keutzer, Karin L.** ..................... '62 '88 C.629 B.A. L.276 J.D. [Ⓐ McKenna&C.]
**Kevane, Timothy D.** .................... '65 '91 C.276 B.S. L.426 J.D. [Ⓐ Thorpe&T.]
*LANGUAGES: Spanish, French.
*PRACTICE AREAS: Business Litigation.
**Keville, Terri Donna** .................... '51 '92 C.659 B.A. L.800 J.D. [Ⓐ Manatt,P.&P.]
*PRACTICE AREAS: Healthcare Law; Litigation.
Keyfauver, Mary Ann ........................................ '42 '86 L.1137 J.D. Dep. Dist. Atty.
**Keys, Brian S.** .......................... '69 '94 C.112 B.A. L.813 J.D. [Ⓐ Manatt,P.&P.]
*PRACTICE AREAS: Corporate Law; Securities Law.
Keys, William R. .................................. '29 '65 C.607 L.809 134 N. Vanness Ave.
**Khachigian, Kenneth L.** ................ '44 '70 C.112 B.A. L.178 J.D. [Smiland&K.]⊙
*PRACTICE AREAS: Public Law.
**Khadilkar, Miloslav** .................... '64 '91 C.112 B.A. L.990 J.D. [Ⓐ Gray,Y.D.&R.]
*LANGUAGES: Czech.
*PRACTICE AREAS: Insurance Defense; Premises Liability; Public Entity.
**Khajetoorians, Asteghik** ........... '65 '93 C.273 B.S. L.1148 J.D. [Ⓐ Parker,M.C.O.&S.]
*PRACTICE AREAS: Environmental.
Khalaf, Lucianne ......................... '62 '90 C.174 B.A. L.1068 J.D. Dep. Dist. Atty.
**Kharasch, Ira D.** ...................... '55 '83 C.339 B.A. L.1068 J.D. [Pachulski,S.Z.&Y.]
**Kheel, Alan J., (AV)** ..................... '57 '82 C.800 B.A. L.426 J.D. [Reznik&R.]
*SPECIAL AGENCIES: Federal Deposit Insurance Corporation (FDIC).
*PRACTICE AREAS: Real Estate Transactions; Subdivision Compliance and Environmental Matters.
**Khonsari, Arezou** ............ '67 '95 C.773 B.A. L.1148 J.D. [Ⓐ La Follette,J.D.F.&A.]
*LANGUAGES: Persian, French.
*PRACTICE AREAS: Medical Malpractice; General Liability.
**Khougaz, Gregory J.** ..................... '56 '83 C.112 B.A. L.426 J.D. [Hinojosa&K.]
*PRACTICE AREAS: Commercial Litigation; Real Estate Litigation; Probate Litigation; Labor Litigation.
**Khoury, John A. '43 '86 C.1109 B.A. L.809 J.D.**
**10880 Wilshire Boulevard, Suite 1050, 90024**
**Telephone: 310-475-3772 Fax: 310-470-8590**
***LANGUAGES: French and Arabic.**
**Aviation and International Law, Litigation and Entertainment Law.**
*See Professional Biographies, LOS ANGELES, CALIFORNIA*

Khoury, Louis J. ........................ '48 '73 C.112 B.A. L.1068 J.D. 1801 Century Park E.
**Khoury, Robert P., (BV)** .................. '47 '74 C.112 A.B. L.1065 J.D. [Eckardt&K.]
*LANGUAGES: German.
*PRACTICE AREAS: Banking; Civil Litigation.
**Khurana, Anju** ............................ '67 '92 C.119 B.A. L.809 J.D. [Ⓐ Kegel,T.&T.]
*LANGUAGES: Hindi, French.
**Kiaie, Bita M. '64 '89 C.800 B.A. L.809 J.D.**
**10877 Wilshire Boulevard, Suite 1401, 90024-4341**
**Telephone: 310-443-3229 Fax: 310-443-3233**
**Medical Malpractice, Personal Injury.**
*See Professional Biographies, LOS ANGELES, CALIFORNIA*

Kiang, William K. T. ............. '47 '89 C.629 B.S. L.1148 J.D. 634 S. Mansfield Ave.
**Kibre, Joseph, (AV)** .................... '46 '75 C.112 B.A. L.1068 J.D. [Oberstein,K.&H.]
**Kichaven, Jeffrey G.** .................. '56 '80 C.112 A.B. L.309 J.D. [Richman,L.K.&G.]
*PRACTICE AREAS: Mediation; Arbitration; Alternative Dispute Resolution.
**Kiddé, Thomas S., (AV)** ................ '50 '74 C.813 B.A. L.1065 J.D. [Small L.&K.]
*PRACTICE AREAS: Intellectual Property Litigation; Unfair Competition and Commercial Litigation; Trademark; Arbitration.
**Kidman, Scott B.** ......................... '59 '85 C.112 B.A. L.426 J.D. [Quinn E.U.&O.]
*PRACTICE AREAS: Employment; General Commercial Litigation.
Kidney, David A. ........................ '15 '41 C.276 A.B. L.262 J.D. 237 S. Plymouth Blvd.
**Kiefer, Mark L.** ..................... '59 '84 C.112 B.A. L.770 J.D. [Ericksen,A.K.D.&L.]
*PRACTICE AREAS: Insurance Litigation.
**Kieffer, George David, (AV)** ............ '47 '73 C.112 B.A. L.1068 J.D. [Manatt,P.&P.]
*PRACTICE AREAS: Government; Administrative; Regulatory; Legislative.
**Kieffer, Joseph D.** .......................... '49 '77 C.112 B.A. L.30 J.D. [Kegel,T.&T.]
Kiehne, Julie M. ........................ '64 '89 C.112 B.A. L.94 J.D. 221 N. Figueroa St.
**Kiekhofer, William H., III, (AV)** .......... '52 '80 C.966 B.A. L.800 J.D. [Kelley D.&W.]
*PRACTICE AREAS: Bankruptcy Law; Loan Workouts.
**Kiely, Michael J.** ................ '64 '89 C.276 B.S. L.1068 J.D. [Ⓐ Allen,M.L.G.&M.]
*PRACTICE AREAS: Real Estate Transactions.
Kightlinger, Jeffrey '59 '85
C.112 B.A L.770 J.D. Metropolitan Water Dist. of Southern Calif.
**Kightlinger, Kelly A.** .................. '64 '90 C.112 B.A. L.426 J.D. [Ⓐ Pillsbury M.&S.]
**Kiguchi, Mark** ........................... '22 '58 C&L.800 B.S.L., J.D. [Ⓒ Musick,P.&G.]
*LANGUAGES: Japanese.
**Kiker, Mary A.** .......................... '48 '76 C.805 B.A. L.846 J.D. [Herzfeld&R.]
*LANGUAGES: French.
**Kilb, Brian D.** ........................... '57 '83 C.188 B.S. L.309 J.D. [Gibson,D.&C.]
*PRACTICE AREAS: Banking; Commercial Law; Workouts and Financial Reorganizations.
**Kilbride, Wendy K.** ..................... '— '94 C.1077 B.A. L.276 J.D. [Ⓐ Morgan,L.&B.]
**Kiley, Anne Campbell** .......................... '64 '90 C&L.477 B.A., J.D. [Trope&T.]
*PRACTICE AREAS: Family Law.
**Kilkowski, James M.** ................... '47 '82 C.309 A.B. L.1066 J.D. [Williams&K.]
*REPORTED CASES: Abeytas v. Superior Court (1993) 17 Cal. App. 4th 1037.
**Killough, David E.** .... '55 '83 C.586 B.A. L.809 J.D. [O'Melveny&M.] (⊙San Francisco)
*PRACTICE AREAS: Environmental Law; Patent Litigation.
**Kilourie, Kathleen** ...................... '66 '94 C&L.800 B.S., J.D. [Ⓐ Latham&W.]
**Kilroy, Gerard R.** ............ '55 '80 C.112 B.A. L.426 J.D. [Ⓐ Christensen,M.F.J.G.W.&S.]
*PRACTICE AREAS: Civil Litigation.
**Kim, Alice J.** '71 '96 C.309 B.A. L.178 J.D.
(adm. in NY; not adm. in CA) [Ⓐ O'Melveny&M.]
*LANGUAGES: French, Korean.
**Kim, Allen Choo** ......................... '64 '91 C.112 B.A. L.276 J.D. [Ⓐ Graham&J.]
*LANGUAGES: Korean.
**Kim, Angela G.** ...................... '69 '95 C.112 B.A. L.61 J.D. [Ⓐ Nordstrom,S.N.&J.]
*PRACTICE AREAS: Plaintiff's Personal Injury; Asbestos Litigation.
**Kim, B. Tilden** ......................... '63 '89 C.112 B.S. L.1067 J.D. [Richards,W.&G.]
*LANGUAGES: Korean.
*PRACTICE AREAS: Litigation; Insurance Coverage.
**Kim, Brian Jaywoo** ...................... '68 '94 C.976 B.A. L.1066 J.D. [Ⓐ Gibson,D.&C.]
*LANGUAGES: Korean.
**Kim, Brian Sung Yun** ...................... '66 '96 C.813 B.S. L.309 J.D. [Ⓐ Howrey&S.]
*LANGUAGES: Korean.
*PRACTICE AREAS: Intellectual Property.
Kim, Cedina M. ....... '63 '90 C.309 A.B. L.93 J.D. U.S. Dept. of Health & Human Servs.
**Kim, Christine** ......................... '66 '94 C.518 B.A. L.94 J.D. [Ⓐ Poindexter&D.]
*PRACTICE AREAS: Commercial Litigation; Insurance Defense; Probate Litigation.
**Kim, Christopher, (AV)** .................. '52 '78 C.112 B.A. L.1068 J.D. [Lim,R.&K.]
*PRACTICE AREAS: Civil and Business Litigation.
Kim, Chul-Ho (Charles) ...................... '50 '80 C.061 B.A. L.178 J.D. [Kim&Assoc.]
**Kim, Claire H.** ....................... '65 '92 C.112 B.A. L.1051 J.D. [Ⓐ C.Shusterman]
*LANGUAGES: Korean.
*PRACTICE AREAS: Immigration and Naturalization Law.
**Kim, David S.** ........................ '61 '90 C.927 B.B.A. L.809 J.D. [Arnberger,K.B.&C.]
*LANGUAGES: English and Korean.
*PRACTICE AREAS: Litigation; Real Estate; Construction; Arbitration.
**Kim, Diann H.** ............................. '58 '85 C.309 B.A. L.477 J.D. [Tuttle&T.]
*PRACTICE AREAS: Civil Litigation; Antitrust and Unfair Business Practices Litigation; Civil Trial.
Kim, Erica M. ........................... '— '92 C.188 B.A. L.1068 J.D. [McVey&K.]⊙
**Kim, George H.** .................................. '66 '92 C.112 B.A. L.800 J.D. [Ⓐ Ford]
**Kim, Harry H.W.** ................... '64 '92 C.309 A.B. L.569 J.D. [Ⓐ Mitchell,S.&K.]
*PRACTICE AREAS: Corporate; Securities.
Kim, J. Eva ................................................. '64 '93 L.1067 333 S. Hope St.
**Kim, J. Monica** ........................... '— '91 C.112 B.A. L.1066 J.D. [Ⓐ Coudert]
*LANGUAGES: Korean.
**Kim, Jason S.J.** ............... '67 '92 C.112 B.A. L.1068 J.D. [Ⓐ Breidenbach,B.H.H.&H.]
*LANGUAGES: Korean.
*PRACTICE AREAS: Litigation.
**Kim, Jonathan J.** ................. '70 '95 C.228 A.B. L.309 J.D. [Ⓐ O'Melveny&M.]
*PRACTICE AREAS: Bankruptcy.
**Kim, Jong Han** ........................ '63 '89 C&L.276 B.S.F.S., J.D. [Ⓐ Paul,H.J.&W.]
**Kim, Joon-Soo** ............... '67 '93 C.112 B.A. L.426 J.D. [Ⓐ McClintock,W.B.R.R.&M.]
*PRACTICE AREAS: Environmental Compliance and Litigation.
**Kim, Joon Yong** ............................ '54 '83 C.800 A.B. L.276 J.D. [Graham&J.]
*LANGUAGES: Korean and Japanese.
*PRACTICE AREAS: International Business Law; Corporate Law.
Kim, Joseph D. '58 '86 C&L.976 B.A., J.D.
(adm. in NY; not adm. in CA) A & M Records, Inc.
**Kim, Joseph K.** ..................... '59 '86 C.112 B.A. L.309 J.D. [O'Melveny&M.]
*LANGUAGES: Korean.
*PRACTICE AREAS: Banking; Finance; Mergers, Acquisitions and Divestitures; Corporate Law.
**Kim, Leslie Y.** ..................... '64 '93 C.112 B.A. L.276 J.D. [Ⓐ Gibson,D.&C.]
*PRACTICE AREAS: Corporate Law; Securities.
**Kim, Linda J.** ............................ '70 '95 C.976 B.A. L.309 J.D. [Ⓐ Quinn E.U.&O.]
Kim, Linda M. ........................ '63 '88 C.966 B.S. L.477 J.D. 725 S. Figueroa St.
Kim, Lisa L. .............................. '64 '90 C.112 B.A. L.1065 J.D. [Egerman&B.]
**Kim, Margret J.** ................ '61 '89 C.800 B.A. L.809 J.D. [Ⓐ Charlston,R.&W.]
*LANGUAGES: Korean.
*PRACTICE AREAS: Environmental Insurance Law.
Kim, Michelle Yu .................. '61 '88 C.112 B.S. L.767 J.D. Legal Aid Found. of L.A.

CAA265P

CALIFORNIA—LOS ANGELES MARTINDALE-HUBBELL LAW DIRECTORY 1997

**Kim, Monica Y.** ........'70 '95 C.112 B.A. L.1065 J.D. [Levene,N.&B.]
*PRACTICE AREAS: Bankruptcy.
**Kim, Monica Yung-Min** ........'69 '95 C.112 B.A. L.976 J.D. [Latham&W.]
**Kim, Namyon** ........'67 '92 C.378 B.A. L.178 J.D. [Sonnenschein N.&R.]
*LANGUAGES: Korean.
*PRACTICE AREAS: General Litigation.
**Kim, Pio S.** ........'64 '91 C.112 B.A. L.1068 J.D. [Lim,R.&K.]
*LANGUAGES: Korean.
*PRACTICE AREAS: Civil Litigation.
Kim, Raymond B. ........'67 '92 C.112 B.A. L.800 J.D. [Marks&B.]
Kim, Richard Song-Uk ........'56 '88 C.910 B.S.B.A. L.1065 J.D. 3435 Wilshire Blvd.
**Kim, Seong Hwan** ........'68 '93 C&L.112 B.S., J.D. [Christensen,M.F.J.G.W.&S.]
*LANGUAGES: Korean.
*PRACTICE AREAS: Business Litigation.
**Kim, Stuart Y.** ........'65 '93 C.668 B.A. L.1068 J.D. [O'Melveny&M.]
**Kim, Sung Hui** ........'68 '93 C.245 B.A. L.309 J.D. [Riordan&M.]
*LANGUAGES: German and Korean.
*PRACTICE AREAS: General Corporate; Securities.
Kim, Tony K. ........'60 '87 C.112 B.A. L.1067 J.D. 3435 Wilshire Blvd.
Kim, Walter Y. ........'60 '88 C.112 B.A. L.1068 J.D. 624 S. Grand Ave.
Kim, Y. Maggie ........'67 '94 C.788 A.B. L.659 J.D. 444 S. Flower St.
**Kim, Y. Peter** ........'47 '78 C.061 B.A. L.831 J.D. [Morgan,L.&B.]
**Kim, Young J.** ........'68 '94 C.911 B.S./B.A. L.178 J.D. [Troy&G.]
*LANGUAGES: Korean.
*PRACTICE AREAS: Corporate; Mergers and Acquisitions; Securities.
Kim & Associates ........624 S. Grand Ave.
**Kimball, George** ........'52 '78 C.112 A.B. L.477 J.D. [Kimball&W.]
*LANGUAGES: French.
*PRACTICE AREAS: Computer Software, Systems and Services; International Business; Real Property; General Business.
**Kimball, R. Bartus** '45 '71 C.154 B.A. L.813 J.D.
Sr. Coun., Pacific Telesis Legal Group
**Kimball, Spencer L.** '18 '50 C.37 B.S. L.966 J.D.
(adm. in UT; not adm. in CA) [Manatt,P.&P.]
*PRACTICE AREAS: Insurance.

**Kimball, Tirey & St. John**
(See Newport Beach)

**Kimball & Weiner LLP, (AV)**
**555 South Flower Street, Suite 4540, 90071**
**Telephone: 213-538-3800 Fax: 213-538-3810**
**George Kimball; Matthew F. Maccoby; Jeffrey M. Weiner.**
**General Corporate and Commercial Practice, including Computer Software, Systems and Services, Real Estate Transactions, Corporate Finance and Securities, Mergers and Acquisitions and International Transactions.**
***See Professional Biographies, LOS ANGELES, CALIFORNIA***

Kimbell, Daniel R. ........'60 '88 C.112 B.S. L.426 J.D. 10877 Wilshire Blvd. (Pat.)
**Kimberlin, Diane L.** ........'52 '76 C.112 B.A. L.1068 J.D. [Littler,M.F.T.&M.]
Kimmel, James R. ........'54 '79 C.1042 B.A. L.800 J.D. Dep. Dist. Atty.

**Kimmel, Lance Jon, (AV) '54 '79 C.264 A.B. L.569 J.D.**
**Suite 1400, 10940 Wilshire Boulevard, 90024**
**Telephone: 310-208-0775 Telecopier: 310-208-8582**
**(Also Of Counsel to Goodson and Wachtel, A Professional Corporation).**
**Corporate, Securities, Business Transactions, Mergers and Acquisitions and Finance Law.**
**Reference: Bank of America.**
***See Professional Biographies, LOS ANGELES, CALIFORNIA***

Kimmell, Adam ....'51 '80 C.178 B.A. L.1066 J.D. 201 N. Figueroa St. (⊙Portland, OR)
**Kinaga, Patricia** ........'53 '86 C.112 B.A. L.276 J.D. [Seyfarth,S.F.&G.]
*PRACTICE AREAS: Public Sector; Employment Discrimination; Wrongful Termination; Discipline.
Kincaid, Nancy C. '38 '75
C.608 B.A. L.426 J.D. Claims Atty., Auto. Club of Southern Calif.
**Kincaid, Valerie E.** ........'61 '86 C.112 B.A. L.1068 J.D. [Katten M.&Z.]
*PRACTICE AREAS: Civil Litigation; Entertainment Litigation.
**Kindel, James H., Jr.**, (AV) ........'13 '41 C.112 A.B. L.426 LL.B. [Heller E.W.&M.]
*PRACTICE AREAS: Taxation; Trusts; Estate Planning.
Kindel & Anderson L.L.P., (AV)
Twenty-Ninth Floor, 555 South Flower Street (⊙Irvine, Woodland Hills & San Francisco)
**Kindred, Alan M.** ........'52 '86 C&L.061 B.A., LL.B. [Shaub&W.]
*LANGUAGES: German.
*PRACTICE AREAS: Transportation Litigation; Commercial and International Litigation; Bankruptcy Litigation.
King, Allen R. ........'52 '80 C.112 B.A. L.1065 J.D. 1101 Crenshaw Blvd.
King, Barry P., (AV) ........'47 '72 C.800 A.B. L.426 J.D. 1888 Century Park, E.
**King, Coby A.** ........'60 '92 C.112 B.A. L.276 J.D. [Manatt,P.&P.]
*PRACTICE AREAS: Election and Political Reform Law; Governmental and Administrative Law.
**King, Cory J.** ........'67 '95 C.101 B.A. L.1049 J.D. [Booth,M.&S.]
*LANGUAGES: Korean.
**King, David N.** ........'67 '94 C&L.800 A.B., J.D. [Gibson,D.&C.]
*PRACTICE AREAS: Labor and Employment.
**King, Donald L.**, (AV) ........'30 '57 C.112 A.B. L.1066 LL.B. [King,W.E.&B.]
*PRACTICE AREAS: Estate Planning; Gift Estate Tax; Real Estate Tax; Health Care; Pension and Employee Benefits.
King, George H. ........'51 '74 C.112 B.A. L.800 J.D. U.S. Dist. J.
**King, Gregory H.** ........'66 '93 C&L.101 B.A., J.D. [Luce,F.H.&S.]
*PRACTICE AREAS: Insurance Coverage; Business Litigation; Construction.
**King, Howard E.**, (AV) ........'— '77 C.112 B.A. L.1068 J.D. [King,P.H.P.&B.]
*PRACTICE AREAS: Real Estate; Finance; Business; Entertainment.
King, Kimberly Nilsen '61 '88 C.1075 B.A. L.800 J.D.
Corp. Secy. & Assoc. Coun., Kaufman & Broad Home Corp.
King, Leslie E. ........'— '92 C&L.800 B.A., J.D. 7907 Yorktown Ave.
King, Marcia ........'17 '61 L.809 LL.B. 800 W. 1st St.
King, Marian Beechen ........'— '72 C.112 B.A. L.1095 J.D. 809 Gretna Green Way
King, Melvin ........'33 '60 C.67 A.B. L.309 LL.B. 633 W. 5th St.
**King, Michael G.** ........'63 '89 C.93 B.A. L.1066 J.D. [Hennelly&G.]
*PRACTICE AREAS: Business Litigation; Products Liability.
**King, Michael P.**, (AV) ........'43 '69 C.112 B.A. L.426 J.D. [King&W.]
**King, Pamala J.** ........'56 '86 C.112 B.A. L.800 J.D. [Hennigan,M.&B.]
King, Peter N. ........'58 '88 C.911 B.A. L.950 J.D. Dep. City Atty.
**King, Sandra R.** ........'55 '80 C.1044 B.A. L.273 J.D. [Manatt,P.&P.]
*PRACTICE AREAS: Employment Law and Litigation.
King, Scottow A. "Scott" ....'57 '83 C.976 B.A. L.569 J.D. Coun., Occidental Petro. Corp.
**King, Stephen L.**, (AV) '31 '62
C.350 B.S.E.E. L.569 J.D. [Blakely,S.T.&Z.] (See Pat. Sect.)
**King, Terrence M.** ........'54 '83 C.1131 B.A. L.426 J.D. [Ginsburg,S.O.&R.]
**King, Victor I.** ........'64 '91 C.145 B.A. L.477 J.D. [Bottum&F.]
**King, William T.**, (AV) ........'33 '58 C.675 B.A. L.309 J.D. [Fierstein&S.]
*PRACTICE AREAS: Estate Planning; Family Law; Business Law.
King-Lautanen, Michelle R. '61 '88 C.381 B.A. L.1049 J.D.
V.P., TV Bus. Affs., Twentieth Century Fox Film Corp.

**King, Purtich, Holmes, Paterno & Berliner, LLP, (AV)**
**2121 Avenue of the Stars, Twenty Second Floor, 90067**
**Telephone: 310-282-8989 Facsimile: 310-282-8903**
**Howard E. King; Richard R. Purtich; Keith T. Holmes; Peter T. Paterno; Jill H. Berliner. Of Counsel: David M. Corwin;—Gregory A. Thomson; Tracy E. Loomis; Lisa E. Socransky; Leslie E. Frank.**
**Real Estate, Financial Institutions, Insolvency, Music, Media and Intellectual Property Law, General Corporate and Corporate Finance Matters, Insurance Bad Faith Litigation and Business Litigation in State and Federal Courts.**
***See Professional Biographies, LOS ANGELES, CALIFORNIA***

**King, Stephen Scott, A Professional Corporation**
(See Santa Monica)

**King, Weiser, Edelman & Bazar, A Law Corporation, (AV)**
**Suite 900, Two Century Plaza, 2049 Century Park East, 90067**
**Telephone: 310-553-1600 Panafax: 310-556-5687**
**Donald L. King; Herbert M. Weiser; Gerald M. Bazar; Marc Paul Jacobs. Of Counsel: Jerry Edelman; Herbert L. Weinberg;—Michael B. Allderdice; Patricia N. Chock; Donald A. Gralla; Christine S. Upton.**
**General Civil, Trial and Appellate Practice in all State and Federal Courts. Corporation and General Business Law. Corporate Financing, State and Federal Taxation, Health Care, Pension and Employee Benefit, Estate Planning, Trust and Probate Law, Limited Liability Companies, Real Property, Construction and Redevelopment Law. Public/Private Partnerships.**
**References: First Los Angeles Bank (Century City Office); Sanwa Bank of California.**
***See Professional Biographies, LOS ANGELES, CALIFORNIA***

**King & Williams, A Law Corporation, (AV)**
**10100 Santa Monica Boulevard, Eighth Floor, 90067-4012**
**Telephone: 310-553-1101 Telecopier: 310-277-4069**
**Michael P. King; Ralph O. Williams III; William K. Hanagami.**
**Civil Trial, Alternative Dispute Resolution and Appellate Practice. Business Litigation, Professional Liability, Real Property, Products Liability, Personal Injury and Insurance Law.**
***See Professional Biographies, LOS ANGELES, CALIFORNIA***

Kinjo, Richard I. ........'52 '82 C.800 B.A. L.426 J.D. 3550 Wilshire Blvd.
Kinkle, George P., Jr., (AV) ........'23 '52 C&L.800 B.E., LL.B. 621 Sunset Blvd.

**Kinkle, Rodiger and Spriggs, Professional Corporation, (AV)**
**600 North Grand Avenue, 90012⊙**
**Telephone: 213-629-1261 Fax: 213-629-8382**
**William B. Rodiger (Managing Attorney at Santa Ana Office); Everett L. Spriggs (Managing Attorney at Riverside Office); John V. Hager (Managing Attorney at Santa Barbara Office); Thomas J. Dowling (Managing Attorney); Guillermo W. Schnaider; Daniel S. Alderman; Stephen J. Chiasson; Emily E. Kordyban; James A. Stathas; Lisa Jacobs; Howard Gross.**
**General Trial Practice. Negligence, Malpractice, Products Liability, Construction and Insurance Law.**
**Santa Ana, California Office: 837 North Ross Street. Telephone: 714-835-9011. Fax: 714-667-7806.**
**Riverside, California Office: 3333 14th Street. Telephone: 909-683-2410; 800-235-2039. Fax: 909-683-7759.**
**San Diego, California Office: Suite 900 Driver Insurance Center, 1620 Fifth Avenue, P.O. Box 127900. Telephone: 619-233-4566. Fax: 619-233-8554.**
**Santa Barbara, California Office: 125 East De La Guerra Street. Telephone: 805-966-4700. Fax: 805-966-4120.**
***See Professional Biographies, LOS ANGELES, CALIFORNIA***

**Kinn, Jay T.** ........'62 '90 C.747 B.A. L.494 J.D. [Sheppard,M.R.&H.]
*PRACTICE AREAS: Real Estate Law (Finance, Leasing and Development).
**Kinnaird, Dennis E., (A Professional Corporation)**, (AV) '36 '65
C.763 B.A. L.1066 LL.B. [Munger,T.&O.]

**Kinnan, Richard P., (AV) '60 '86 C.611 B.A. L.426 J.D.**
**12424 Wilshire Boulevard, Ninth Floor, 90025-1043**
**Telephone: 310-820-5570 Facsimile: 310-820-6800**
**Civil Trial and Appellate Practice, Business and Casualty Law.**
***See Professional Biographies, LOS ANGELES, CALIFORNIA***

Kinnett, Gary E., (Inc.), (AV) '34 '63 C.605 A.B. L.1066 LL.B.
611 W. 6th St., 33rd Fl.
**Kinney, James H.**, (AV) ........'37 '66 C.1042 B.S. L.1068 LL.B. [O'Melveny&M.]
*PRACTICE AREAS: Real Estate.
Kinnon, Kelly ........'59 '87 C.112 B.S. L.800 J.D. Reg. Coun., Cornerstone Real Estate
Kinoshita, Dennis K. ........'38 '72 C.112 L.809 J.D. 4700 Wilshire Blvd.
**Kinsella, Dale F., (Professional Corporation)**, (AV) '48 '74
C&L.112 B.A., J.D. [Kinsella,B.F.&T.]

**Kinsella, Boesch, Fujikawa & Towle, (AV)**
**A Partnership including Professional Corporations**
**1901 Avenue of the Stars, Seventh Floor, 90067**
**Telephone: 310-201-2000 Fax: 310-284-6018**
**Members of Firm: Dale F. Kinsella (Professional Corporation)†; Philip W. Boesch, Jr., (Professional Corporation)†; Ronald K. Fujikawa (Professional Corporation)†; Edmund J. Towle, III, (Professional Corporation)†; Michael C. Denison; Mark F. Katz (Professional Corporation)†; Mark K. Brown; Michael J. Kump; Michael Howald; Jack G. Cairl, Jr.; David Andrew Pash; Cathleen Collins; Charles G. Smith; Gregory J. Aldisert; Joseph P. Bartlett. Associates: Alan R. Kossoff; Michelle Ben-yehuda; Bruce I. Bolkin; Helene E. Pretsky; Suzanne M. Madison; Jill Rosenthal; David P. Shebby; George T. Kliavkoff; Monica Y. Harris; Joshua A. Meyer. Of Counsel: Leonard M Tavera; Catherine H. Coleman.**
**General Civil Litigation, Corporation, Securities, Creditors Rights, Communication and Media, Real Estate, Finance, Commercial, Secured Transactions and Entertainment Law.**
**†Denotes a lawyer who is the sole employee of A Professional Corporation which is a member of the firm**
***See Professional Biographies, LOS ANGELES, CALIFORNIA***

Kinsler, David A. ........'24 '55 C.861 B.S. L.184 J.D. 11788 Bellagio Rd.‡
Kinsman, Terence J. ........'49 '78 C&L.178 A.B., J.D. 219 S. Barrington Ave.
**Kipper, David R.** ....'52 '82 C.112 B.A. L.1049 J.D. [Booth,M.&S.] (⊙Costa Mesa, CA)
**Kirbach, Rosemary Mahar** ........'— '90 C.645 B.S. L.178 J.D. [Paul,H.J.&W.]
**Kirby, Matthew T.**, (AV) '47 '74
C.321 A.B. L.767 J.D. [O'Melveny&M.] (⊙New York, N.Y.)
*PRACTICE AREAS: Banking and Creditor's Rights.
**Kirchen, Peter T.** ........'45 '76 C.426 B.S. L.1148 J.D. [Kern&W.]

**Kircher, C. William, Jr., A. Prof. Corp., Law Offices of**
(See Irvine)

**Kirios, Linda A.** ........'— '81 C.461 B.A. L.1068 J.D. [Pachulski,S.Z.&Y.]
*PRACTICE AREAS: Real Property Law.
**Kirk, Brandon L.** ........'68 '94 C.112 B.A. L.1067 J.D. [Rutter,G.&H.]
*PRACTICE AREAS: Litigation.
Kirk, Lawrence I., (AV) ........'39 '64 C.112 B.S. L.1068 J.D. [Grancell,G.&M.]
**Kirkbride, Rick S.** ........'54 '83 C.800 B.A. L.426 J.D. [Paul,H.J.&W.]
**Kirke, John C.** ........'68 '94 C&L.112 B.A., J.D. [Troop M.S.&P.]
*PRACTICE AREAS: Insurance Coverage; Litigation.
**Kirkland, J. Eric** ........'64 '90 C.1064 B.S. L.990 J.D. [J.K.Pierson]
*PRACTICE AREAS: Products Liability Law.

**Kirkland & Ellis, (AV)**
**A Partnership including Professional Corporations**
**300 South Grand Avenue, Suite 3000, 90071⊙**
**Telephone: 213-680-8400 Facsimile: 213-626-0010**
**Members of Firm: April L. Ammeter; Michael E. Baumann; Mary Blodgett; Martin R. Boles; Jeffrey S. Davidson; Jan Lawrence Handzlik; Eric C. Liebeler; Alexander F. MacKinnon; Tony L. Richard**

(This Listing Continued)

**Kirkland & Ellis (Continued)**

**son; Philip C. Swain; John A. Zackrison. Associates: Steven E. Bledsoe; C. Robert Boldt; Boaz M. Brickman; Damian D. Capozzola; Dean M. Fink (Not admitted in CA); Joseph M. Graham Jr.; Haimanot Habtu; Shannon M. Hansen; Viddell L. Heard Jr.; Christopher J. Heck; Thomas G. Heller; Catherine C. Hwang; Melissa D. Ingalls; Anna Kogan; Eric R. Lamison; Kevin P. Latek; Sally S. Liu; Michael S. McCauley; M. Scott McCoy (Not admitted in CA); Sydne Squire Michel; Charles Isaac Newton; Andrew E. Paris; Ephraim Starr; Suzanne E. Tracy.**
**General Practice.**
**Washington, D.C. Office: 655 Fifteenth Street, N.W. Telephone: 202-879-5000. Facsimile: (202)-879-5200.**
**Chicago, Illinois Office: 200 East Randolph Drive. Telephone: 312-861-2000. Telex: 25-4361.**
**New York, New York Office: Citicorp Center, 153 East 53rd Street. Telephone: 212-446-4800. Facsimile: (212)-446-4900.**
**London England Office: 199 Bishopsgate, London EC2M 3TY England. Telephone: 171 814 6682. Facsimile: 171 814 6622.**
***See Professional Biographies, LOS ANGELES, CALIFORNIA***

**Kirkpatrick, Cheryl A.** .................. '64 '90 C.426 B.A. L.809 J.D. [⊠ Knopfler&R.]
*PRACTICE AREAS: Personal Injury; Construction Defect.
**Kirsch, Jonathan L.**, (AV) ......................'49 '76 C.1169 B.A. L.426 J.D. [Kirsch&M.]
*PRACTICE AREAS: Copyrights; Trademarks; Publishing; Intellectual Property; Entertainment Law.

**Kirsch & Mitchell, (AV)**
**2029 Century Park East, Suite 2750, 90067**
**Telephone: 310-785-1200 Facsimile: 310-286-9573**
**Members of Firm: Jonathan L. Kirsch; Dennis Mitchell. Associates: Joyce I. Craig; Lawrence J. Zerner. Of Counsel: Ted F. Gerdes.**
**General Civil Practice. Civil Litigation, Copyright, Trademark and Intellectual Property, Real Estate, Corporation, Publishing. Administrative Law, Insurance Defense.**
***See Professional Biographies, LOS ANGELES, CALIFORNIA***

Kirschbaum, Lloyd ...................... '59 '84 C.446 B.A. L.809 J.D. 6477 W. 77th St.
**Kirschbaum, Thomas A.**, (AV) .............. '52 '77 C.31 B.A. L.1068 J.D. [⊠ Irell&M.]
Kirschenbaum, Robert S. '49 '74 C.696 B.A. L.1068 J.D.
Sr. Corp. Tax Coun., Alpha Therapeutic Corp.
Kirschner, Richard H., (P.C.), (AV) '44 '69 C.112 B.A. L.1068 J.D.
10850 Wilshire Blvd.‡
Kirschner, Steven J. ............ '57 '90 C.597 B.S. L.339 J.D. 444 S. Flower St., Ste. 2000
Kirshbaum, Marc D. ................ '68 '93 C.800 A.B. L.145 J.D. 2121 Ave. of the Stars
**Kirshman, Norman H.**, (AV) ........... '30 '58 C.178 B.S. L.188 J.D. [Kirshman&H.]⊙

**Kirshman & Harris, A Professional Corporation, (AV)**
**11500 West Olympic Boulevard, Suite 605, 90064⊙**
**Telephone: 310-312-4544 Telecopier: 310-312-4539**
**Norman H. Kirshman; Michael S. Harris; William E. Cooper (Not admitted in CA); Gary G. Branton.**
**General Civil and Trial Practice in all State and Federal Courts. Employment Relations Law Representing Management. Corporation and Corporate Securities Law.**
**Las Vegas, Nevada Office: Kirshman, Harris & Cooper, A Professional Corporation, 411 E. Bonneville Avenue, Suite 300. Telephone: 702-384-3877. Telecopier: 702-384-7057.**
***See Professional Biographies, LOS ANGELES, CALIFORNIA***

Kirste, Robert L. ..................... '28 '62 C.112 A.B. L.809 J.D. 3435 Wilshire Blvd.

**Kirtland & Packard LLP, (AV)**
**1900 Avenue of the Stars, Twenty-Fifth and Twenty-Sixth Floors, 90067⊙**
**Telephone: 310-552-9700 Fax: 310-552-0957**
**Members of Firm: Harold J. Hunter, Jr.; Jacques E. Soiret; Michael L. Kelly; Joseph E. Gregorich; Robert A. Muhlbach; Mark P. Poliquin (Resident Partner, Irvine Office); Robert M. Churella; Scott M. Schutz; John M. Goodspeed (Resident Partner, Irvine Office); Steven M. Maslauski; John M. Caron; Jeffrey M. Anielski (Resident Partner, Irvine Office); Terrence J. Schafer. Of Counsel: Robert C. Packard; Robert V. Beaudry. Associates: James T. La Chance; Gillian N. Pluma; Robert W. Skripko, Jr. (Resident, Irvine Office); William S. Edic; Michelle M. Moyer; Robin S. Bentler; Alice C. Longoria; David S. Brown; C. Christopher Mulder (Resident, Irvine Office); J. Conrad Schroeder; Curtis C. Holmes II (Resident, Irvine Office); Joseph Stephen McMillen (Resident, Irvine Office); Joseph Geri; Timothy D. Otte (Resident, Irvine Office); Layne M. Bukovskis (Resident, Irvine Office); Paul R. Cotter (Resident, Irvine Office); Ronald J. Thommarson (Resident, Irvine Office).**
**Architects and Engineers, ADR, Aviation and Aerospace, Business and Tax Planning and Litigation, Construction, Employment and Labor Law, Environmental and Toxic Tort, Estate Planning, Food Service and Hospitality, General Liability and Casualty, Health Care Providers Liability, Insurance, Mediation, Professional Liability, Product Liability, Real Estate, Risk Management and Loss Prevention and SIU.**
**Orange County Office: 18101 Von Karman Avenue, Nineteenth Floor, Irvine, California. Telephone: 714-263-9700. Fax: 714-263-9090.**
***See Professional Biographies, LOS ANGELES, CALIFORNIA***

**Kirwan, Betty-Jane**, (AV) ................. '47 '72 C.112 A.B. L.1066 J.D. [Latham&W.]
**Kirwan, Martin J.**, (AV) ................... '21 '52 C.545 L.426 LL.B. [Ives,K.&D.] ‡
**Kirwan, Ralph D.**, (AV) ................ '42 '69 C.112 A.B. L.767 J.D. [Pillsbury M.&S.]
Kiser, Lawrence L. '44 '69 C.335 B.A. L.336 J.D.
(adm. in ID; not adm. in CA) S.E.C.
Kiss, Benjamin ........... '60 '85 C.112 B.A. L.940 J.D. 2121 Ave. of the Stars, 22nd Fl.
Kissane, H. Franklin ..................... '27 '74 C.604 B.A. L.426 J.D. State Bar of Calif.
Kissee-Sandoval, Catherine J. '61 '91 C.976 B.A. L.813 J.D.
355 S. Grand Ave. 35th Fl.
Kita, George I. .......................... '64 '91 C.1097 B.A. L.1065 J.D. 1331 Sunset Blvd.
**Kitabayashi, Mark K.** ........... '60 '86 C.112 B.A. L.800 J.D. [Breidenbach,B.H.H.&H.]
**Kitano, Judith T.** ............................ '61 '88 C.112 B.A. L.813 J.D. [Munger,T.&O.]
**Kitchen, David S.** ..................... '65 '91 C.197 A.B. L.426 J.D. [⊠ O'Melveny&M.]
*LANGUAGES: French.
**Kitchens, Dean J.**, (AV) ................. '52 '78 C.112 A.B. L.1068 J.D. [Gibson,D.&C.]
*PRACTICE AREAS: Business, Commercial and Insurance Litigation.
**Kittleson, John W.** .......................... '65 '92 C.112 B.A. L.426 J.D. [⊠ Loeb&L.]
**Kittrell, B. Bruce** ......................... '40 '67 C.1042 B.S. L.1065 J.D. [B.B.Kittrell]

**Kittrell, B. Bruce, Law Offices of, P.C.**
**The Airport Center, 5959 West Century Boulevard, Suite 100, 90045**
**Telephone: 213-776-5679 Fax: 310-645-2218**
**B. Bruce Kittrell.**
**Civil Trial, Business, Corporate, Real Estate, Family, Personal Injury, Probate, Estate, Commercial Litigation.**
**Representative Clients: Tetraflour, Inc.; Centaur, Inc., KTS Services, Inc.; Intensity, Inc.; Master Design.**

Kivinski, Margaret A. '64 '94
C.112 B.S.Ch.E. L.1137 J.D. 10100 Santa Monica Blvd. (Pat.)
Klar, Deborah A., (AV) .............. '51 '79 C.659 B.A. L.564 J.D. 1801 Century Pk., E.
Klar, Jonathan M. ................................ '48 '74 C.112 A.B. L.1068 J.D. [Segal&K.]
Klaristenfeld, David M. .................. '63 '90 C.061 B.S. L.1068 J.D. 333 S. Hope St.
**Klaskin, Harold C.** ............................. '63 '92 C&L.1136 B.S., J.D. [⊠ D.B.Bloom]
**Klass, Barbara J.** ......................... '47 '87 C.112 B.A. L.426 J.D. [⊠ Lord,B.&B.]
Klass, Helman & Ross ........................................................ 11766 Wilshire Blvd.
**Klatsky, David L.** ......................... '62 '90 C.103 B.A. L.1068 J.D. [McDermott,W.&E.]
*LANGUAGES: Italian and French.
**Klatt, Gregory S.G.** ........................ '67 '96 C.767 B.A. L.1066 J.D. [⊠ Jones,D.R.&P.]

**Klausner, Gary E.**, (AV) ............... '49 '74 C&L.446 B.A., J.D. [Robinson,D.B.&K.]
*REPORTED CASES: In re Southeast Company, 868 F.2d 335 (9th Cir. 1989); In re Rubin, 769 F.2d 611 (9th Cir. 1986); In re Softalk Pub. Co., Inc., 856 F.2d 1328 (9th Cir. 1988); In re Victory Construction Co., 37 B.R. 222 (9th Dir. BAP 1984).
*PRACTICE AREAS: Bankruptcy Law; Insolvency; Reorganization.

**Klausner, Manuel S., (AV) '39 '63 C.112 A.B. L.569 LL.B.**
**One Bunker Hill, Eighth Floor, 601 West Fifth Street, 90071**
**Telephone: 213-680-9940 Fax: 213-680-4060**
**Email: mklaus@aol.com**
***REPORTED CASES: Crawford v. Honig, 37 F.3d 485 (9th Cir. 1994); Choice-in-Education League v Los Angeles Unified School Dist., 17 Cal. App. 4th 415 (1993); Amp Inc. v. Lantrans, Inc., 19 U.S.P.Q. 2d 1929 (C.D. Cal. 1991); Plasticolor Molded Products v. Ford Motor Co, 713 F. Supp. 1329 (C.D. Cal. 1989); Hernandez v. Six Flags Magic Mountain, Inc, 688 F. Supp 560 (C.D. Cal. 1988).**
***PRACTICE AREAS: Complex Litigation; Class Actions; Intellectual Property Law; Securities and Constitutional Litigation.**
**General Civil Trial and Appellate Practice in all State and Federal Courts. Business Litigation, Complex Litigation, Constitutional Litigation, Intellectual Property, Securities and Class Actions.**
***See Professional Biographies, LOS ANGELES, CALIFORNIA***

Klausner, R. Gary ............................ '41 '69 C.602 B.A. L.426 J.D. Supr. Ct. J.
Klavens, Kent J. '49 '78 C.659 B.S. L.809 J.D.
V.P., Legal & Bus. Affs., Famous Music Corp.
**Klawon, Lynette** ........................... '62 '88 C.1168 B.A. L.188 J.D. [⊠ Selman B.]
Klebanow, Anatole '50 '78 C.800 B.A. L.809 J.D.
Sr. Coun., Twentieth Century Fox Film Corp.
**Klee, Kenneth N.**, (AV) ................. '49 '75 C.813 B.A. L.309 J.D. [Stutman,T.&G.]
*REPORTED CASES: In re Standard Brands Paint Co., 154 B.R. 563 Bankr. C.D. Cal. 1993; In re Texaco Inc., 92 B.R. 38; In re Western Real Estate Fund, Inc., 75 B.R. 580, 17 Collier Bankr. Cas. 2d 577.
*TRANSACTIONS: Represented Pennzoil Co. in Texaco Chapter 11; Griffin Resorts, Inc. Noteholders' Committee in Resorts International, Inc. Chapter 11; Charter Medical Secured Bondholders' Group out-of-Court Restructuring; Bally's Inc. Junior Bondholders' Group out-of-Court Restructuring; Orion Pictures Bondholders' Group out-of-Court Restructuring.
*PRACTICE AREAS: Bankruptcy; Insolvency; Corporate Reorganization; Commercial Litigation; Expert Witness.
**Kleeger, Kenneth S.**, (BV) ......... '54 '82 C.1097 B.S. L.809 J.D. [Prestholt,K.F.&V.]⊙
*PRACTICE AREAS: Products Liability; Premises Liability; Governmental Torts; Business Torts; Trials.
**Kleiderman, Karen L.** ................. '62 '87 C.112 B.A. L.273 J.D. [⊠ Paul,H.J.&W.]
**Kleifield, Steven J.**, (AV) .......... '53 '80 C.910 A.B. L.273 J.D. [Gordon,E.K.G.F.&G.]
*PRACTICE AREAS: Major Personal Injury Litigation; Insurance Bad Faith; Products Liability; Professional Negligence; Government Liability.
**Kleiman, Ari R.** ......................... '58 '91 C.061 B.A. L.800 J.D. [⊠ Horvitz&L.]
*LANGUAGES: Hebrew.

**Kleiman, Mark Allen**
**(See Santa Monica)**

**Klein, Alan M., (AV) '47 '80 C.851 B.B.A. L.1148 J.D.**
**5757 West Century Boulevard Suite 880, 90045-6407**
**Telephone: 310-649-3141 Telecopier: 310-649-4349**
***PRACTICE AREAS: General Business Litigation; Real Estate Litigation; Construction Litigation; Transportation (Air and Ocean Cargo); Trademark Litigation.**
**Associates: Laura J. Barns.**
**Business Litigation in State and Federal Courts. Unfair Competition, Trademark and Copyright Litigation, Business Torts, Real Property, Equine, Employment, Transportation and Insurance Law.**
***See Professional Biographies, LOS ANGELES, CALIFORNIA***

Klein, Alan R., (AV) ......................... '50 '76 C.112 B.A. L.1095 J.D. [Kaplan,K.&R.]
Klein, Arnold Lewis ................. '42 '72 C.107 B.A. L.284 J.D. 2049 Century Pk., E.
Klein, Brett C. ........................................ '49 '72 C.188 B.A. L.659 J.D. Mun. J.
Klein, Clifford L. ............................ '51 '75 C.112 B.A. L.1066 J.D. Dep. Dist. Atty.
Klein, Conrad Lee ............ '28 '52 C&L.569 B.S., J.D. 1800 Century Park E., 15th Fl.
**Klein, Corey E.** ........................ '60 '87 C.112 B.S. L.1068 J.D. [Gaims,W.W.&E.]
Klein, Earl '25 '57 C.978 B.A. L.426 J.D.
Admin. Law J., Calif. Unemploy. Ins. App. Bd.
**Klein, Elise D.** ............................ '59 '83 C.668 B.A. L.1065 J.D. [Lewis,D.B.&B.]
**Klein, Eric A.**, (AV) ............................ '59 '86 C.674 A.B. L.94 J.D. [Klein&M.]
Klein, Gary H. ....................... '54 '79 C.1044 B.A. L.800 J.D. 4215 Glencoe Ave.
**Klein, Gregory B.** ........................ '71 '96 C.659 B.A., B.S. L.1068 J.D. [⊠ Irell&M.]
**Klein, Henry**, (AV) ........ '49 '75 C.1044 B.A. L.1049 J.D. [Ladas&P.] (See Pat. Sect.)
**Klein, Herbert Jay** ........................ '45 '70 C.112 B.A. L.1068 J.D. [⊠ Cox,C.&N.]
*PRACTICE AREAS: Labor Relations Law; Employee Benefits Law.
Klein, Herbert M. ................ '31 '62 C.112 B.A. L.809 LL.B. 4219 Don Alanis Place

**Klein, Howard S., (AV) '37 '63 C.112 B.A. L.1068 J.D.**
**11845 West Olympic Boulevard, Suite 1075, 90064**
**Telephone: 310-312-8182**
**(Certified Specialist, Estate Planning, Trust and Probate Law, The State Bar of California Board of Legal Specialization).**
***PRACTICE AREAS: Contested Trusts and Estates (40%); Conservatorships (20%); Family Law (20%); Estate Planning (20%).**
**Contested Trusts and Estates, Conservatorships, Estate Planning and Family Law.**
***See Professional Biographies, LOS ANGELES, CALIFORNIA***

**Klein, Jacqueline Redin** ................. '66 '92 C.112 B.A. L.1065 J.D. [⊠ Lord,B.&B.]
Klein, James William, (AV) ........ '47 '72 C.112 A.B. L.1066 J.D. 12400 Wilshire Blvd.
Klein, Joan Dempsey ........................ '24 '55 L.1068 LL.B. Pres. Jus., Ct. of App.
**Klein, Kenneth D.** .......................... '47 '73 C.477 B.A. L.178 J.D. [Riordan&M.]
**Klein, Lisa R.** ......................... '67 '92 C.112 B.A. L.1068 J.D. [⊠ Fulbright&J.]
*PRACTICE AREAS: Litigation.
**Klein, Michael F.** ....................... '68 '93 C.684 B.A. L.464 J.D. [⊠ Musick,P.&G.]
Klein, Michael S., (AV) ......................... '52 '76 C.347 A.B. L.976 J.D. [Klein&W.]
**Klein, Nanette Lynn** ......... '63 '89 C.1110 B.A. L.1065 J.D. [⊠ Greenberg G.F.C.&M.]
*PRACTICE AREAS: Entertainment Law.
**Klein, Nicholas F.** ................. '61 '86 C.112 B.A. L.1066 J.D. [⊠ Stroock&S.&L.]
*PRACTICE AREAS: Real Estate Law.
Klein, Paul J. ............................ '23 '52 C&L.966 B.A., J.D. 11438 Thurston Cir.
Klein, Raymond M., (A Prof. Law Corp.), (AV) '38 '62
C.951 A.B. L.309 J.D. 908 Kenfield Ave.
**Klein, Robert A.**, (AV) ..................... '33 '59 C&L.477 B.A., J.D. [Foley L.W.&A.]
*PRACTICE AREAS: Health Care; Hospitals; Medicare and Medicaid; Administrative Law.
**Klein, Robert G.** .......................... '51 '87 C.80 B.S. L.1136 J.D. [⊠ Schreiber&S.]
Klein, Robert M. ..................... '57 '84 C.37 B.A. L.809 J.D. 11611 San Vicente St.
**Klein, Sandra R.** ...................... '60 '92 C.459 B.A. L.426 J.D. [⊠ O'Melveny&M.]
**Klein, Scott P.** .............................. '62 '88 C.165 B.A. L.813 J.D. [Latham&W.]
**Klein, Stephen C.** ........................... '51 '75 C.112 B.A. L.809 J.D. [Barger&W.]
*PRACTICE AREAS: Litigation; Insurance Coverage; Reinsurance.
Klein, William A. '31 '58 C&L.309 A.B., LL.B.
(adm. in DC; not adm. in CA) Prof. of Law, U.C.L.A.

**Klein & Martin, (AV)**
**2029 Century Park East, Suite 2550, 90067**
**Telephone: 310-201-2581 Fax: 310-201-0108**
**Eric A. Klein; Clara Ruyan Martin. Associates: Barry S. Babok; Jenny Chyi Ching Chen; Samuel R. Spira.**

(This Listing Continued)

CAA267P

# Klein & Martin (Continued)

Corporate, Securities, Intellectual Property, Computer Law, Start-Up Companies and Venture Capital, Mergers and Acquisitions, Private Placements, Healthcare Transactions, Financing, Commercial and International Transactions.

See Professional Biographies, LOS ANGELES, CALIFORNIA

## Klein & Rosenbaum
(See Glendale)

Klein & Weisz, (AV) .................................................. 12424 Wilshire Blvd.
Kleinberg, Joel W. H., (AV) ............ '43 '68 C&L.976 B.A., J.D. [J.W.H.Kleinberg]
Kleinberg, Kenneth ........ '42 '68 C.112 B.A. L.1068 J.D. [Kleinberg L.L.B.&C.]
  *PRACTICE AREAS: Entertainment Law; Copyright Law.
Kleinberg, Marvin H., (AV) '27 '54
                    C.112 B.A. L.1066 J.D. [Arant,K.L.&R.] (See Pat. Sect.)
  *PRACTICE AREAS: Domestic and International Patent Prosecution; Intellectual Property; Patents; Trademarks; Intellectual Property Litigation.

## Kleinberg, Joel W. H., A Professional Corporation, (AV)
Suite 2420, One Wilshire Boulevard, 90017-3325
Telephone: 213-624-1990 Fax: 213-488-9890
Joel W. H. Kleinberg (Member of California Trial Lawyers Association, with recognized experience in the fields of Professional Negligence, Product Liability and General Personal Injury).
Plaintiffs Trial Practice. Professional Malpractice, Legal Malpractice, Medical Malpractice, Products Liability and Personal Injury Law. Tort Law. Contingent Fee Business Litigation.

See Professional Biographies, LOS ANGELES, CALIFORNIA

## Kleinberg Lopez Lange Brisbin & Cuddy, (AV)
2049 Century Park East, Suite 3180, 90067⊙
Telephone: 310-286-9696 Fax: 310-277-7145
Kenneth Kleinberg; Peter M. Lopez (Resident, Sherman Oaks Office); Robert M. Lange; Scott T. Brisbin (Resident, Sherman Oaks Office); Christine S. Cuddy; Scott Edel. Associates: Darren J. Lewis (Resident, Sherman Oaks Office); Mark L. Kovinsky (Resident, Sherman Oaks Office).
Entertainment Industry Transactions including Motion Picture, Television, Music, Amusement/Leisure Parks and Attractions. Intellectual Property Matters.
Sherman Oaks, California Office: 15250 Ventura Boulevard, Penthouse 1220, 91403-3201. Telephone: 818-995-5500. Fax: 818-995-5511.

See Professional Biographies, LOS ANGELES, CALIFORNIA

Kleinman, Gerald D., (A P.C.), (AV) ....... '33 '59 C.197 A.B. L.309 LL.B. [Ⓖ Loeb&L.]
  *PRACTICE AREAS: Real Estate Law.
Klekner, Michael L. ..................... '44 '78 C.112 A.B. L.809 J.D. Dep. City Atty.
Klem, Abigail ................... '68 '96 C.347 B.A. L.1065 J.D. [Ⓐ Troop M.S.&P.]
  *LANGUAGES: French.
  *PRACTICE AREAS: Entertainment.
Klepa, Robert B. .................... '64 '89 C.112 B.A. L.426 J.D. [Ⓐ Federman,G.&G.]
  *PRACTICE AREAS: Construction Defect; Business Litigation.
Klepetar, Ronald J., (AV) ........ '46 '71 C.339 B.A. L.209 J.D. [Rexon,F.K.&H.]
  *PRACTICE AREAS: Labor Negotiation; Arbitration; Labor Litigation; National Labor Relations Board Proceedings.
Kliavkoff, George T. .................. '67 '93 C.94 B.S. L.893 J.D. [Ⓐ Kinsella,B.F.&T.]
  *PRACTICE AREAS: Litigation.
Klibanow, Linda S. ................ '50 '77 C.681 B.A. L.976 J.D. [Parker,M.C.O.&S.]
  *SPECIAL AGENCIES: National Labor Relations Board; U.S. Equal Opportunity Commission; California Department of Fair Employment and Housing; U.S. Department of Labor; U.S. Department of Justice.
  *REPORTED CASES: Sahara-Tahoe Corporation v. NLRB, 648 F.2d 553, 9th Cir. (1980); Universal Paper Goods Company v. NLRB, 638 F2d. 1159, 9th Cir. (1979); NLRB v. Solar Turbines, Inc., 302 NLRB No. 3, (1991); Arbitration of Heinz Pet Products, 90-2 ARB ¶8468.
  *PRACTICE AREAS: Labor and Employment Law.
Klima Liner, Katherine E. ............. '64 '89 C&L.339 B.A., J.D. [Ⓐ Morris,P.&P.]
Klinck, Jonathan B. ................... '57 '85 C&L.893 B.A., J.D. [Ⓖ Reinstein,P.&C.]
  *PRACTICE AREAS: Business Litigation; Trademark and Copyright Law; Arbitration.
Kline, Alan S. '61 '88 C.273 B.A. L.776 J.D.
                            (adm. in PA; not adm. in CA) I.R.S.
Kline, Craig G. ........................ '51 '79 C.659 A.B. L.1065 J.D. [Arter&H.]
  *PRACTICE AREAS: Direct Insurance and Reinsurance; Environmental Law.
Kline, Jeremy B. ............ '61 '85 C.112 B.A. L.800 J.D. [Weinstock,F.M.&K.]
  *PRACTICE AREAS: General Civil Litigation; Family Law.
Kline, Judith M. .................. '66 '91 C.602 B.A. L.309 J.D. [Ⓐ Paul,H.J.&W.]
Kling, Frederick J. ............ '24 '51 C&L.659 A.B., LL.B. 3749 Shannon Rd.‡
Klinger, Leslie S., (AV) .......... '46 '71 C.112 A.B. L.1066 J.D. [Ⓐ Kopple&K.]
Klinghoffer, Jack H. '43 '70 C.563 B.B.A. L.1009 J.D.
                            (adm. in NY; not adm. in CA) I.R.S.
Klink, Charles Gustaf '65 '93 C.668 B.A. L.893 J.D.
                            (adm. in NY; not adm. in CA) [Ⓐ Andrews&K.]
  *LANGUAGES: Spanish.
  *PRACTICE AREAS: Asset Securitization; Corporate Securities; Bankruptcy and Reorganization.
Klotz, Adam M. ................ '67 '93 C.178 B.A. L.893 J.D. 300 S. Grand Ave.
Klotz, Dena L. ................. '68 '94 C.112 B.A. L.990 J.D. [Ⓐ S.D.Zimring]
  *PRACTICE AREAS: Estate Planning; Probate and Trust; Real Estate Law; Business; Elder Law.
Klove, Carole A. .............. '58 '86 C.228 B.S.N. L.809 J.D. [Ⓐ Davis W.T.]
Klowden, Michael L., (AV) ....... '45 '71 C.145 A.B. L.309 J.D. 801 S. Grand Ave.
Klueger, Robert F. ............... '45 '74 C.659 B.A. L.262 J.D. [Boldra&K.]
  *REPORTED CASES: Brockamp v. United States, 859 F. Supp. 1283 (1994) 67 F.3d 260 (9th Cir., 1995).
  *PRACTICE AREAS: Tax Litigation and Controversies; Tax Planning; Estate Tax Planning.
Klugman, Robert H., (AV) ......... '26 '50 C.976 B.A. L.597 J.D. [Barton,K.&O.]
  *PRACTICE AREAS: Business Law; Taxation; Real Estate; Environmental Law; Construction Law.
Klugman, Steven M. .................... '47 '73 C.112 B.A. L.597 J.D. [S.M.Klugman]
Klugman, Steven Mark, Law Offices of .................... 2049 Century Pk. E.
Klum, Charles A. ................ '48 '73 C.112 B.A. L.763 J.D. Dep. Pub. Def.
Klyman, Robert A. ................ '64 '89 C&L.477 B.A., J.D. [Latham&W.]
Kmieciak, Steven J. ........... '53 '79 C.602 B.A. L.446 J.D. [Seyfarth,S.F.&G.]
  *PRACTICE AREAS: Construction Law; Government Contracts Law.
Knapp, Stephen R. ............... '41 '68 C&L.188 B.A., J.D. [Wilson,E.M.E.&D.]
  *REPORTED CASES: Merchants Home Delivery Service, Inc. vs. Reliance Group Holdings Inc., et al.
  *PRACTICE AREAS: Business Law; Corporate Law; Commercial Law; Real Estate Law; Securities Law.

## Knapp, Marsh, Jones & Doran, (AV)
Suite 1400, Manulife Plaza, 515 South Figueroa Street, 90071-3329
Telephone: 213-627-8471 Telecopier: 213-627-7897
Members of Firm: B. Richard Marsh; Thomas A. Doran; James G. Jones; Daniel V. Hyde; Gary H. Giesler; Wesley G. Beverlin; Patricia M. Schnegg; Janette Sarmiento Knowlton. Associates: Eileen M. Whalen; Paul J. Beck; Alexander Shipman; Scott M. Olken; Mario A. Pichardo; Wendy W. Huang.
General Civil Practice in State and Federal Courts. Trial and Appellate Practice. Corporation, Estate Planning and Probate. Real Estate, Eminent Domain, Construction, Environmental, Public Entity, Transportation and Administrative Law. Public Entity, Securities, Taxation and Computer Law.

See Professional Biographies, LOS ANGELES, CALIFORNIA

## Knapp, Petersen & Clarke, A Professional Corporation
(See Glendale)

Knauss, Robert B. .................. '53 '81 C.309 A.B. L.477 J.D. [Munger,T.&O.]
Knecht, Peter, (BV) ............. '36 '64 C.800 A.B. L.809 LL.B. 9000 Sunset Blvd.
Knee, Howard M., (AV) ......... '47 '73 C.112 B.A. L.1068 J.D. [Knee&M.]
  *PRACTICE AREAS: Employment Litigation; Employment Discrimination; Labor Strikes; Collective Bargaining; Sexual Harassment.

## Knee & Mason, (AV)
A Partnership
Suite 2050, 2049 Century Park East, 90067
Telephone: 310-551-0909 Fax: 310-552-9818
Email: kmfirm@aol.com
Members of Firm: Howard M. Knee; Belle C. Mason; Gregory N. Karasik; Melanie C. Ross; Lora Silverman; Stephen M. Benardo; Lisa G. Sherman. Of Counsel: Ted R. Huebner; Heather A. Lindquist.
Employment Discrimination, Sexual Harassment and Wrongful Termination Defense, Management Labor Relations, Public Employment Relations, Wage and Hour Law, Employment Contracts, Occupational Safety and Health, Employee Benefits, State and Federal Litigation and Appellate Practice.

See Professional Biographies, LOS ANGELES, CALIFORNIA

Knickmeyer, Karl H., Jr., (AV) ...... '47 '77 C.112 B.A. L.61 J.D. 12100 Wilshire Blvd.
Knierim, K. Phillip ............... '45 '74 C.911 B.A. L.178 J.D. 279 Camino Del Sol‡
Knight, Jay Adams ............ '45 '72 C.154 B.A. L.1065 J.D. [Ⓖ Loeb&L.]
  *PRACTICE AREAS: Employee Benefit Plans.
Knight, Stacey D. McKee ......... '70 '95 C.684 B.A. L.464 J.D. [Ⓐ Katten M.&Z.]
  *PRACTICE AREAS: Labor and Employment Law.
Knight, Thelma Harris ............ '46 '87 C.112 B.S. L.464 J.D. Dep. Dist. Atty.
Knipstein, Julie E. ............ '65 '90 C.347 B.A. L.339 J.D. [Ⓐ Orrick,H.&S.]
  *PRACTICE AREAS: Public Finance Law.

## Knobbe, Martens, Olson & Bear, LLP
(See Newport Beach)

Knoblow, Carol J. ..................... '65 '90 C.25 B.A. L.990 J.D. [Ⓐ Meyers,B.&M.]
  *PRACTICE AREAS: Litigation; Professional Liability; Products Liability; General Liability; Insurance Coverage.
Knokey, David J. ............. '45 '75 C.800 B.S. L.1136 J.D. Dep. City Atty.
Knopf, Shirley Fuld .............. — '80 Prob. Atty., Supr. Ct.
Knopfler, George, (AV) .......... '55 '80 C.183 B.A. L.770 J.D. [Knopfler&R.]
  *PRACTICE AREAS: Insurance Law; Construction Law.

## Knopfler & Robertson, A Professional Law Corporation, (AV)
Suite 500, 21650 Oxnard Street (Woodland Hills), 91367
Telephone: 818-227-0770; 213-624-1111 Telefax: 818-227-0777
George Knopfler; Alexander Robertson, IV; Deborah Broom; Richard A. Capella; Edward D. Vaisbort; Jonathan S. Vick. Of Counsel: James H. Patton, Jr.; Arlen Ross Gunner; Scott C. Haith;— Kevin Matthew Davis; Richard P. Riley; Christina S. Robertson; Janice M. Michaels; William G. Kelsberg; Ernesto F. Aldover; Jeanine M. St. Pierre-Kumar; Terri Eileen Hilliard; James M. Pazos; Lisa Bondy Dunn; Brian I. Glicker; Colin E. Barr; Cynthia Coulter Mulvihill; Christopher J. Bagnaschi; Cheryl A. Kirkpatrick; Peter C. Brown.
General Civil Litigation in all State and Federal Courts with Special Emphasis on Construction, Insurance, Corporate, Real Estate and Business Law.

See Professional Biographies, LOS ANGELES, CALIFORNIA

Knott, Steven E. ................. '61 '90 C.112 A.B. L.1067 J.D. [Ⓐ Zevnik H.G.&M.]
  *PRACTICE AREAS: Environmental Law; Insurance Coverage.
Knowles, Robert ................. '— '88 C.1042 B.A. L.426 J.D. Dep. Dist. Atty.‡
Knowles, Steven, (AV) ........... '52 '77 C.800 B.A. L.309 J.D. [Trope&T.]
  *PRACTICE AREAS: Family Law; Civil Litigation.
Knowlton, Hugh E. ............. '43 '68 C&L.352 B.S., J.D. 1901 Ave. of the Stars, 7th Fl.
Knowlton, John S. ................. '57 '89 C.112 B.A. L.809 J.D. [Ⓐ Selman B.]
Knox, Franklin L., Jr., (AV) ........ '07 '33 C.112 A.B. L.813 J.D. 2650 W. Temple St.
Knox, William O. ................ '58 '85 C.184 B.A. L.1068 J.D. [Ⓐ Troy&G.]
  *PRACTICE AREAS: Securities Litigation; Business Litigation; Intellectual Property Litigation.
Knudsen, Kit L. .................. '63 '91 C.112 B.A. L.1065 J.D. 700 S. Flower St.
Knupfer, Nancy ..................... '— '90 C.33 B.A. L.809 J.D. [Ⓐ Dumas&Assoc.]
Ko, Daniel ..................... '— '95 C.111 B.S. L.813 J.D. [Ⓐ Skadden,A.S.M.&F.]
Kobata, Mark T. ................. '50 '77 C.112 B.A. L.809 J.D. [Barlow&K.]
  *PRACTICE AREAS: Management Labor Law; Employment Law; Discrimination Law.
Kobayashi, Naomi H. ........... '68 '94 C.178 B.A. L.976 J.D. [Ⓐ Latham&W.]
Kobrin, Janet A. ................ '42 '85 C.1036 B.A. L.1068 J.D. [Ⓐ Small L.&K.]
  *PRACTICE AREAS: Intellectual Property; Unfair Competition; Trade Secrets; Commercial Litigation.
Koch, Albin C., (AV) .......... '33 '60 C.976 B.A. L.309 J.D. 3900 W. Alameda
Koch, Donna Bruce .......... '49 '87 C.1097 B.S. L.398 J.D. [Ⓐ Bonne,B.M.O.&N.]
Koch-Weser, Kathleen R. '48 '80 C.540 B.A. L.1068 J.D.
                                                          U.C.L.A. Student Legal Servs.
Kochenderfer, Kay Ellen ........ '55 '86 C.112 B.A. L.800 J.D. [Ⓖ Gibson,D.&C.]
  *PRACTICE AREAS: Litigation; Class Actions.
Kocontes, Lonnie L. ................. '57 '93 C.546 B.A. L.846 J.D. [Ⓐ O'Melveny&M.]
Koda, H. Henry '43 '70 C&L.061 B.S., LL.B.
                    (adm. in NY; not adm. in CA; Pat.) 1880 Century Pk. E.
Koeblitz, Robert M. ............... '63 '92 C.999 B.S. L.1137 J.D. 444 S. Flower St.
Koeffler, Deborah P., (A Professional Corporation), (AV) '48 '75
                    C.966 B.A. L.1068 J.D. [Mitchell,S.&K.]
  *PRACTICE AREAS: Labor Law; Employment Litigation; Public Entity Labor Relations Law; Health Care Law.
Koegel, Thomas F. ................. '61 '86 C.602 B.A. L.1066 J.D. [Folger L.&K.]⊙
Koelzer, George J., (AV) ........... '38 '64 C&L.705 A.B., J.D. [Lane P.S.L.]
  *PRACTICE AREAS: Admiralty; Insurance; Federal Trial and Appellate Practice.
Koen, Elizabeth A. ............... '50 '75 C.668 B.A. L.426 J.D. 145 S. Hudson Ave.
Koenig, Jeffrey S. ............... '55 '93 C.112 B.A. L.800 J.D. [Ⓐ Jones,D.R.&P.]
Koenig, Joseph P. ............... '61 '90 C.112 B.A. L.809 J.D. 4215 Glencoe Ave.
Koenig, Robert A. ............... '62 '86 C&L.813 A.B., J.D. [Latham&W.]
Koenig, Sally ............... '61 '92 C.94 B.A. L.810 J.D. [Ⓐ Hall D.K.F.&W.]
  *PRACTICE AREAS: Entertainment Law; Licensing; Advertising Law.
Koenig, Stuart I. ............... '56 '82 C.112 B.A. L.426 J.D. [Bronson,B.&M.]
  *PRACTICE AREAS: Federal and State Litigation; Bankruptcy Litigation and Commercial Law.
Koepcke, William W. ........... '50 '85 C.1169 B.A. L.426 J.D. Dep. City Atty.

## Koepke, Scott P., Law Office of '59 '85 C.477 B.G.S. L.800 J.D.
One Bunker Hill, 8th Floor, 601 West Fifth Street, 90071-2094
Telephone: 213-623-7820 Fax: 213-680-4060
General Business and Unfair Competition Litigation in all State and Federal Courts. Employment, Construction and Real Property Litigation, Dispute Resolution, and Trials.

See Professional Biographies, LOS ANGELES, CALIFORNIA

Koffman, Linda S. ................. '63 '89 C.112 A.B. L.1065 J.D. [Ⓐ Orrick,H.&S.]
Kogan, Anna ................ '71 '94 C.813 B.A. L.597 J.D. [Ⓐ Kirkland&E.]
  *LANGUAGES: Russian.
  *PRACTICE AREAS: Litigation; Intellectual Property Law.
Kogan, Elona ................. '69 '94 C.66 B.A. L.809 J.D. [Ⓐ Epstein B.&G.]
  *PRACTICE AREAS: Health Law.
Kogan, Jason D., (AV) ............ '44 '69 C.645 A.B. L.273 J.D. [Bird,M.B.W.&M.]
Kogan, Michael L. ............ '44 '71 C.112 B.A. L.705 J.D. 1401 Calumet Ave.
Kogan, Michael S. ............... '55 '85 C.208 B.A. L.809 J.D. [Arter&H.]
Koh, Hyong S. ............... '59 '89 C.309 B.A. L.1067 J.D. [McDermott,W.&E.]
  *LANGUAGES: Korean.
Kohler, Jessie A. ............. '70 '95 C.112 B.A. L.800 J.D. [Ⓐ Sonnenschein N.&R.]
Kohler, Kenneth E. ............. '53 '81 C.112 B.S. L.976 J.D. [Mayer,B.&P.]

**Kohlweck, Carl E.**, (AV) ........... '46 '79 C.112 B.A. L.1136 J.D. [Parker,M.C.O.&S.]
*PRACTICE AREAS: Complex Commercial Litigation including Construction; Real Property; Trade Secrets, Unfair Business Practices and RICO; Computer Technology Licensing and Real Estate Transactions; Class Action Litigation.
Kohn, Barry D. ................................ '43 '69 C.112 L.800 J.D. Mun. Ct. Comr.
Kohn, Elaine N. ........................ '45 '76 C.112 B.A. L.1137 J.D. 8033 Sunset Blvd.
**Kohn, James A., (A Professional Corporation)**, (AV) '36 '62
C&L.309 A.B., LL.B. [Nebenzahl K.D.&L.]
*PRACTICE AREAS: Real Estate Law; Business Litigation; Environmental Law; Corporation Law.
Kohn, Sandra E. ..................... '41 '67 C.112 B.A. L.1068 J.D. 418 S. McCadden Pl.
Kohorn, Jay M. ............... '47 '74 C.112 B.A. L.1068 J.D. Asst. Dir., Calif. App. Proj.

**Kohrs, Fiske & Steur**
(See Santa Monica)

**Koide, George, (P.C.)** ........................ '45 '77 C.112 A.B. L.809 J.D. [Hill,F.&B.]
*PRACTICE AREAS: Estate Planning Law; Business Planning Law; Taxation Law.
Kolb, Hart B. ........................ '17 '55 C.404 B.A. L.426 LL.B. 620 Tuallitan Rd.
Kolb, Klaus J. ........................ '58 '84 C.475 B.A. L.309 J.D. 11755 Wilshire Blvd.
**Kolber, Richard A.** ..................... '61 '86 C.1044 B.A. L.464 J.D. [[C] Tisdale&N.]
*PRACTICE AREAS: Business, Corporate and Entertainment Litigation.
**Koletsky, Roy A.** ......................... '57 '82 C.605 B.A. L.809 J.D. [Koletsky,M.&F.]
*PRACTICE AREAS: Insurance Defense Litigation; Real Estate Litigation; Business Litigation.

**Koletsky, Mancini & Feldman, (BV)**
**Central Plaza, Eighth Floor, 3460 Wilshire Boulevard, 90010-2228**
**Telephone: 213-427-2350 Fax: 213-427-2366**
**Members of Firm: Marc S. Feldman; Roy A. Koletsky; Stephen C. Mancini; Caroline L. Dasovich; Andrew M. Morrow III. Associates: Steven R. Bartell; William J. Becker, Jr.; Robert T. Bergsten; Kemble Chen; Leslie M. B. Cole; Patrick A. Connolly, III; Risa C. Dauer; Nancy J. Duesberg; Victoria L. Ersoff; Sharon G. Friedman; Stacey R. Friedman; Randall K. L. Kam; Christian F. LaMond; Kim A. Neistadt; Peter Keith Pritchard; Ira L. Siskind; Brian P. Smith; Jeffery E. Stockley; Thomas N. Thrasher, Jr.; Timothy N. Thompson; John C. Volz; Eric P. Weiss; L. Scott Wertlieb.**
**Insurance Defense, General Civil Litigation.**
*See Professional Biographies, LOS ANGELES, CALIFORNIA*

Kolhoff, Terry W. .................. '38 '65 C.426 B.B.A. L.1068 LL.B. Dep. Co. Coun.‡
Kolkey, Daniel M. ...................... '52 '77 C.813 B.A. L.309 J.D. 333 S. Grand Ave.
**Kolkey, Peggy** ......................... '51 '90 C.1077 B.A. L.426 J.D. [[A] Lynberg&W.]
*PRACTICE AREAS: Insurance Defense Law.
**Kollar, Linda Randlett** ..................... '44 '86 C.773 B.A. L.990 J.D. [Weinhart&R.]
*PRACTICE AREAS: Administrative Law; Commercial Litigation.

**Kollender & Sargoy**
(See Santa Monica)

Koller, James E. ........................ '51 '77 C.1042 B.A. L.1136 J.D. Dep. Dist. Atty.
Kolliner, Max G., (AV) ................ '11 '35 C.813 B.A. L.309 J.D. 10526 Edgeley Pl.‡
**Kollitz, Howard, (A Professional Corporation)**, (AV) '48 '74
C.112 A.B. L.1068 J.D. [Danning,G.D.&K.]
**Kollitz, Ronald R.**, (AV) .................. '50 '74 C.112 B.A. L.1068 J.D. [Clopton,P.&B.]
*PRACTICE AREAS: Workers Compensation; Defense; Subrogation.
Kolod, Leonard, (AV) ................ '33 '61 C.112 B.A. L.1068 J.D. 11944 Foxboro Dr.‡

**Kolod & Wager**
(See Encino)

**Kolodziej, Daniel Joseph** .......... '69 '94 C.477 B.A. L.112 J.D. [[A] Buchalter,N.F.&Y.]
Koloff, Kevin ...... '56 '80 C.197 B.A. L.178 J.D. V.P., Bus. Affs., Nelson Entertainment
**Kolstad, Charles K.** ................ '53 '80 C.884 B.S. L.602 J.D. [[C] Arnberger,K.B.&C.]
*PRACTICE AREAS: International Taxation; Business Transactions; Mergers and Acquisitions; Aircraft and Equipment Leasings.
**Kolstad, Charles K.** ..................... '53 '80 C.884 B.S. L.602 J.D. [Brand F.D.F.&K.]
*PRACTICE AREAS: Taxation; International Trade and Finance.
Koltai, Mikael ...................... '50 '78 C.112 B.A. L.1137 J.D. 10866 Wilshire Blvd.

**Kolter, Raymond Kirk '62 '91 C.1050 B.A. L.990 J.D.**
**Suite 900, Gateway Los Angeles, 12424 Wilshire Boulevard, 90025-1043**
**Telephone: 310-826-6077 Fax: 310-442-6400**
**(Also Of Counsel to John K. Pierson).**
**Of Counsel: John K. Pierson.**
**Civil and Business Litigation, including Family, Divorce, Domestic Relations, Plaintiffs Personal Injury, Products Liability, Premises Liability and Bankruptcy Practice. General Civil and Trial Practice in all Courts.**
*See Professional Biographies, LOS ANGELES, CALIFORNIA*

Kolts, Jas. G. ............................... '24 '52 C.629 B.B.A. L.800 LL.B. Supr. Ct. J.

**Kolts and Nawa**
(See Pasadena)

**Koltun, Gregory B.** ......................... '62 '87 C.154 B.A. L.145 J.D. [Morrison&F.]
*PRACTICE AREAS: Litigation.
**Komorsky, Jason B.** ............. '64 '91 C.112 B.A. L.1065 J.D. [[A] Zevnik H.G.&M.]
*PRACTICE AREAS: Environmental; Securities; Insurance Coverage; Antitrust; General Business.
Kompaniez, Peter K., (A P.C.), (AV) '44 '70
C.976 B.A. L.1066 J.D. Pres., PDI Realty Enterprises
**Kondoleon, Nicholas L.** ............ '66 '91 C.608 B.S. L.569 J.D. [[A] Milbank,T.H.&M.]
**Kondon, Hayley J.** ..................... '69 '94 C.178 B.A. L.426 J.D. [[A] O'Melveny&M.]
**Kondzella, Michael A.** ...... '27 '55 C.339 A.B. L.705 J.D. [Oppenheimer P.S.] (⊙Irvine)
*PRACTICE AREAS: Intellectual Property.
Konell, Cheryl R. ................... '61 '90 C.112 A.B. L.999 J.D. 3600 Wilshire Blvd.
**Kong, Sabrina** ..................... '68 '93 C.800 B.S. L.809 J.D. [[A] Cummins&W.]
*PRACTICE AREAS: Corporate; Securities; Litigation.
**Konheim, Jon M.** ..... '70 '96 C.659 B.A.B.S. L.426 J.D. [[A] Christensen,M.F.J.G.W.&S.]
*PRACTICE AREAS: Real Estate Law; Corporate Law.
**Konishi, Lauri S.** ........................ '64 '92 C.800 B.A. L.94 J.D. [Troop M.S.&P.]
*PRACTICE AREAS: Insurance Coverage Litigation; General Litigation.
**Konjoyan, Kimberlee A.** ..... '65 '91 C.800 B.S. L.426 J.D. [Christensen,M.F.J.G.W.&S.]
*LANGUAGES: Spanish.
*PRACTICE AREAS: Litigation.
**Konkoff, Stacey R.** ..................... '67 '92 C.112 B.A. L.426 J.D. [[A] Katten M.&Z.]
**Konowiecki, Joseph S.**, (AV) ......... '53 '78 C.112 B.A. L.1065 J.D. [Konowiecki&R.]
*PRACTICE AREAS: Health Care Law; Mergers and Acquisitions; Corporate; Partnership and Securities; General Business.

**Konowiecki & Rank, (AV) BB**
**A Partnership including a Professional Corporation**
**First Interstate World Center, 633 West 5th Street, Suite 3500, 90071-2007**
**Telephone: 213-229-0990 Telefax: 213-229-0992**
**Peter C. Rank; Joseph S. Konowiecki; Michael C. Foster; Jon N. Manzanares; Kevin B. Kroeker; Peter Roan; Peter R. Mason; Denise E. Hanna. Associates: Cynthia J. Billey; Edna M. Chism; Ronan Cohen; Rosa Kwon Easton; Robert C. Hayden; Phillip R. Maltin; Scott J. Moore; John A. Mueller; Leslie Overfelt; Catherine M. Polisoto; Harold C. Pope.**
**Health Care Law. Mergers and Acquisitions. Corporate, Securities, Real Estate and Environmental Law. General Business and Civil Litigation.**
**Representative Clients: PacifiCare Health Systems, Inc.; UniHealth America; Columbia General Life Insurance Co.; Santa Clarita Health Care Assoc.; College Health Enterprises; Granada Hills Community Hospital; Redlands Community Hospital; Bay Shores Medical Group.**
**Reference: Bank of America.**
*See Professional Biographies, LOS ANGELES, CALIFORNIA*

**Konrad, William K.** ................ '52 '77 C&L.339 B.S., J.D. [Loeb&L.] (See Pat. Sect.)
*PRACTICE AREAS: Trademark; Patent; Copyright.
**Kontos, Linda A.** ..................... '69 '94 C.339 B.A. L.273 J.D. [[A] Hennigan,M.&B.]
*PRACTICE AREAS: Commercial Litigation.
**Kooistra, Melissa S.** ...................... '60 '86 C.112 B.A. L.990 J.D. [Rubinstein&P.]
*REPORTED CASES: Quackenbush California Insurance Commissioner v. Allstate Ins. Co. 116 S.Ct. 1712 (1996); In re Mission Insurance Company v. (Imperial Casualty) 41 Cal. App. 4th 828 (1995); Sunburst Bank, N.A. v. Executive Life, 24 Cal. App. 4th 1156 (1994); Prudential Ins. Co. v. Garamendi, 3 Cal. 4th 1118 (1992); California Automobile Assigned Risk Plan v. Garamendi, 232 Cal. App. 3d 904 (1991).
*PRACTICE AREAS: Litigation; Insurance Insolvency; Reinsurance.
**Koomer, Michael D.**, (AV) ........ '42 '69 C.112 A.B. L.800 J.D. [Zimmermann,K.&C.]
*PRACTICE AREAS: Employment Law; Business Litigation.
Koorenny, Mark K. ................. '65 '90 C.1163 B.B.A. L.426 J.D. 444 S. Flower St.
**Kooyman, Elizabeth A.** .................. '59 '84 C&L.221 B.A., J.D. [Meyers,B.&M.]
*PRACTICE AREAS: Litigation; Professional Liability; Products Liability; Coverage; Construction.
Kopelson, Arnold '35 '60 C.569 B.S. L.564 J.D.
Co-Chmn. of the Bd. & CEO, Arnold Kopelson Productions
**Kopenhefer, Richard W.** ..................... '54 '78 C.228 B.A. L.150 J.D. [Loeb&L.]
*PRACTICE AREAS: Labor Law.
Kopesky, William J. ........................ '48 '83 C.728 A.B. L.94 J.D. [Kopesky&W.]
Kopesky & Welke, (AV) ............................................... 611 W. 6th St.
Kopko, Maureen C. '50 '81 C.588 L.128 J.D.
(adm. in PA; not adm. in CA) I.R.S.
Koplof, Norman G. ........................ '44 '69 C.112 B.A. L.800 J.D. Dep. Pub. Def.
**Kopman, Sharon M.** ................... '68 '93 C.659 B.A. L.426 J.D. [[A] Foley L.W.&A.]
*LANGUAGES: Spanish.
*PRACTICE AREAS: Labor and Employment; Litigation; Personal Injury.
Koppekin, Stephen M. '44 '70 C.1046 B.A. L.705 J.D.
(adm. in NJ; not adm. in CA) Sr. V.P., Indus. Rel., Paramount Pictures Corp.
**Koppes, Richard H.** ..................... '46 '71 C.426 B.A. L.1068 J.D. [[C] Jones,D.R.&P.]
**Kopple, Robert C., (P.C.)**, (AV) .............. '44 '68 C&L.209 B.A., J.D. [Kopple&K.]

**Kopple & Klinger, (AV) BB**
**A Law Partnership including a Professional Corporation**
**2029 Century Park East, Suite 1040, 90067**
**Telephone: 310-553-1444 Facsimile: 310-553-7335**
**Members of Firm: Robert C. Kopple (P.C.); Leslie S. Klinger. Of Counsel: Richard P. Ayles. Associates: Douglas W. Schwartz; Jeffrey A. Kaye; Richard A. Marshall.**
**Federal and State Taxation, Estate Planning, Trust and Probate Law, Employee Benefits, Business Law.**
*See Professional Biographies, LOS ANGELES, CALIFORNIA*

Koral, Richard I. ........................ '53 '79 C.112 B.A. L.1048 LL.B. 935 S. Wall St.
Korbatov, Igor ......................... '63 '88 C.800 B.S. L.1066 J.D. [Korbatov,R.&R.]
Korbatov, Rose & Rubinstein ............................................ 1875 Century Park E.
**Korbin, Steven M.** .................. '66 '95 C.112 B.A. L.426 J.D. [[A] Jeffer,M.B.&M.]
*PRACTICE AREAS: Real Estate.
Korchak, Cheryl D. ............... '56 '80 C.1109 B.A. L.1137 J.D. 1714 S. Canfield Ave.
Kordic, Bruce D. ................. '50 '76 C.645 B.A. L.851 J.D. 5959 W. Century Blvd.
Korduner, David J. ....... '61 '92 C.1169 B.A. L.1068 J.D. Directors Guild of Amer., Inc.

**Korduner, Debra L., Law Offices of, (AV) '55 '82 C.112 B.A. L.426 J.D.**
**1801 Century Park East, 24th Floor, 90067-2326**
**Telephone: 310-277-3685 Fax: 310-277-5471**
***PRACTICE AREAS: Commercial Litigation; Civil Trial; Real Estate; Business Law.**
**Business and Real Estate Litigation.**
*See Professional Biographies, LOS ANGELES, CALIFORNIA*

**Kordyban, Emily E.** ..................... '65 '89 C.215 B.M.E. L.990 J.D. [Kinkle,R.&S.]
Koris, Gerald A. ............ '27 '51 C.696 A.B. L.966 LL.B. 2717 Bottlebrush Dr. (Pat.)
Korman, David C. ............................. '12 '36 C.999 L.146 LL.B. 9127 Cresta Dr.
Korman, Sharon M. ................. '68 '93 C.659 B.A. L.426 J.D. 12121 Wilshire Blvd.
Korn, Peter J. ..................................... '59 '90 C.112 B.A. L.273 J.D. Dep. Dist. Atty.
Kornberg, Howard Craig, (BV) ...... '53 '79 C.112 B.A. L.809 J.D. 10880 Wilshire Blvd.
**Kornblith, Richard L.** ..................... '47 '77 C.910 B.A. L.659 J.D. [Fulbright&J.]
*PRACTICE AREAS: Taxation; Finance; Municipal Finance.
**Kornfeld, Alan J.** ....................... '55 '87 C.112 B.A. L.1068 J.D. [Pachulski,S.Z.&Y.]
*LANGUAGES: Hebrew.
**Kornfeld, Linda D.** ..................... '65 '91 C.112 B.A. L.273 J.D. [[A] Troop M.S.&P.]
*PRACTICE AREAS: Insurance Coverage Litigation; General Litigation.
Kornwasser, Joseph ........................ '47 '72 C.112 B.S. L.1068 J.D. [Kornwasser&F.]
Kornwasser & Friedman ............................................................ 145 S. Fairfax Ave.
**Koro, Charles E.** ......................... '51 '92 C.454 B.A. L.809 J.D. [[A] Bronson,B.&M.]
Korsen, James G. ..................... '51 '76 C&L.800 B.A., J.D. [[C] Myman,A.F.G.&R.]
**Korshak, Stuart R.**, (AV) ......... '47 '76 C.976 B.A. L.1067 J.D. [Korshak,K.K.&S.]
*PRACTICE AREAS: Labor and Employment; Equal Opportunity Law; Civil Litigation.

**Korshak, Kracoff, Kong & Sugano, (AV)**
**11111 Santa Monica Boulevard Suite 910, 90025⊙**
**Telephone: 310-996-2340 Fax: 310-996-2334**
**Stuart R. Korshak; Richard J. Kracoff; Clement J. Kong (Resident, Sacramento Office); Takashi ("T.R.") Sugano (Resident, Sacramento Office); Anne Six Knight (Not admitted in CA; Resident, Chicago, Illinois Office); Michael W. Schoenleber; Lauren E. Zax. Of Counsel: Mamoru Sakuma (Resident, Sacramento Office); Ray W. Frederick (Not admitted in CA; Resident, Chicago, Illinois Office).**
**Labor and Employment Relations, Public Employment Relations, Equal Opportunity Law and Civil Litigation.**
**Representative Clients: Borenstein Associates Builders Co.; CalFarm Insurance Co.; Fairmont Hotels of San Francisco, Chicago, San Jose, New Orleans and Dallas; Marina Hotels; Resolution Trust Corp.; Southern Wine & Spirits of Nevada; Southern Wine & Spirits of America, Inc.; Zenith Insurance Co.**
**Sacramento, California Office: 25th & "J" Streets Building, 2430 "J" Street. Telephone: 916-441-6255. Fax: 916-448-8435.**
**Chicago, Illinois Office: 70 West Madison Street, Suite 525. Telephone: 312-346-2700. Fax: 312-346-2710.**
*See Professional Biographies, LOS ANGELES, CALIFORNIA*

Kort, Jordan R. '51 '89 C.800 B.S. L.426 J.D.
Exec. V.P. & Corp. Coun., Imperial Toy Corp.
Kortum, Frank D. ................................... '54 '83 L.1066 J.D. Asst. U.S. Atty.
Kosco, Keith J. ......................... '52 '79 C.478 A.B. L.309 J.D. 801 S. Grand Ave.
Koskoff, Richard B. ................. '46 '72 C.112 B.A. L.1067 J.D. 12301 Wilshire Blvd.
**Koslov, John**, (AV) ......................... '33 '72 C.800 B.A. L.809 J.D. [Koslov&M.]
*REPORTED CASES: Marsk v. Tilley Steel, 26 C3d. 486; Pacific Estates v. Sup. Ct. 13 CA 4th, 561; So. Calif. White Trucks v. Terezinski 190 CA3d 1393; Knox v. Streatfield, 79 CA3d 565.
*PRACTICE AREAS: Insurance Law; Products Liability Law; Real Estate Law; Construction Law; Personal Injury.

**Koslov & Medlen, (AV) BB**
**30141 Agoura Road, Suite 200, 91301-4334**
**Telephone: 818-597-9996 FAX: 818-597-8848**
**Members of Firm: John Koslov; William P. Medlen. Associate: Sabrina Simmons-Brill.**
**Insurance, Real Estate and Construction Law, Personal Injury, Products Liability, Insurance Brokerage. Trials.**
*See Professional Biographies, LOS ANGELES, CALIFORNIA*

Kosnett, James Victor ...................... '51 '76 C.976 B.A. L.1068 J.D. [Kosnett&D.]

CALIFORNIA—LOS ANGELES MARTINDALE-HUBBELL LAW DIRECTORY 1997

Kosnett & Durchfort ... 11601 Wilshire Blvd.
**Kossoff, Alan R.** ... '65 '90 C.228 B.A. L.1068 J.D. [Kinsella,B.F.&T.]
*PRACTICE AREAS: Litigation.
**Kostant, Ralph B.**, (AV) ... '51 '78 C.813 A.B. L.36 J.D. [Foley L.W.&A.]
*PRACTICE AREAS: Real Estate Development; Real Estate Finance; Real Estate Workouts; Real Estate Leasing; Secured Finance.
**Kostenboym, Ilya A.** ... '68 '94 C.112 B.A. L.990 J.D. [🄰 Grace,S.C.&S.]
*PRACTICE AREAS: Insurance Defense Law; Construction Defects Litigation; Personal Injury Defense Law.

**Kotarski, Kenneth A. '57 '81 C.1044 B.S. L.809 J.D.**
**Suite 755, 11150 Santa Monica Boulevard, 90025-3397**
**Telephone: 310-575-8685 Telecopier: 310-473-4645**
**General Civil Litigation, Practice in all State and Federal Courts with emphasis in Business, Commercial, Real Estate, Defamation and Insurance Law, Arbitration.**

**Kotlarski, Ann** ... '60 '85 C.597 B.A. L.767 J.D. [Quinn E.U.&O.]
*PRACTICE AREAS: Employment.
Kotlowitz, Steven '57 '83
C.112 B.A. L.990 J.D. Sr. V.P., Admn., Intl. Creative Mgmt., Inc.
**Kotto, Natasha A.** ... '65 '92 C.911 B.A. L.276 J.D. [🄰 McCambridge,D.&M.]
**Kotulak, Steven B.** ... '59 '85 C.554 B.S. L.809 J.D. [Ives,K.&D.] (⊙Palm Springs, Ca.)
Kough, Ann ... '52 '78 C.941 B.A. L.1068 J.D. Mun. J.
**Kouri, Dennett F.** ... '38 '63 C&L.800 B.S., LL.B. [Meserve,M.&H.]
**Kouri, Dennett F., Jr.** ... '68 '95 C.112 B.A. L.809 J.D. [🄰 Meserve,M.&H.]
*LANGUAGES: Spanish.
*PRACTICE AREAS: Civil Litigation.
Koury, Joel C. ... '60 '89 C.112 B.A. L.426 J.D. Dep. Pub. Def.
Koutsos, John C. ... '47 '77 C.178 A.B. L.1292 J.D. 1999 Ave. of the Stars
**Kouyoumdjian, Natalie A.** ... '69 '94 C.800 B.A. L.809 J.D. [🄰 Robie&M.]
*LANGUAGES: Armenian.
*PRACTICE AREAS: Civil Litigation.
**Kovacic, Gary A.**, (AV) ... '51 '76 C.112 B.A. L.809 J.D. [Sullivan,W.&D.]
*PRACTICE AREAS: Eminent Domain Law; Zoning Law; Land Use Regulation Law; Environmental Law.
Kove, Joseph F. ... '40 '69 C.112 B.S. L.809 LL.B. 11030 Santa Monica Blvd.
**Kovelman, Gilbert G.**, (AV) '36 '60
C.186 B.E.E. L.273 J.D. [Fulwider P.L.&U.] (See Pat. Sect.)
*PRACTICE AREAS: Patent, Trademark, Copyright and Unfair Competition Law; Litigation.
**Kovelman, Paul H.** ... '60 '92 C.1077 B.S.E.E. L.809 J.D. [🄰 Loeb&L.] (See Pat. Sect.)
*PRACTICE AREAS: Patent.
**Kovelman, Robert L.** '63 '91
C.112 B.A. L.809 J.D. [🄰 Fulwider P.L.&U.] (See Pat. Sect.)
*PRACTICE AREAS: Patent, Trademark, Copyright and Unfair Competition Law; Litigation.
**Kovinsky, Mark L.** ... '65 '90 C.477 B.A. L.1068 J.D. [🄰 Kleinberg L.L.B.&C.]
*PRACTICE AREAS: Entertainment Transactions.
**Kowal, James D.** ... '35 '60 C.763 A.B. L.813 J.D. [Smaltz,A.&F.]
**Kowalick, W. Frederick** ... '48 '73 C.1077 B.A. L.1068 J.D. [Acker,K.&W.]
*PRACTICE AREAS: Insurance Coverage Law and Litigation.
**Koyanagi, Stan H.** ... '60 '85 C.800 B.S. L.813 J.D. [Graham&J.]
*PRACTICE AREAS: Real Estate; Secured Transactions; Corporate Law; International Business Law.
**Kozberg, Joel M.**, (AV) ... '52 '79 C.112 A.B. L.800 J.D. [🄱 Gradstein,L.&V.]
**Kozuch, Carolyn J.** ... '59 '85 C.103 A.B. L.800 J.D. [🄰 Trope&T.]
*PRACTICE AREAS: Family Law.
**Kracoff, Richard J.** ... '59 '84 C.197 A.B. L.813 J.D. [Korshak,K.K.&S.]
*PRACTICE AREAS: Labor and Employment; Public Employment; Equal Opportunity Law; Civil Litigation.
**Kracov, Gideon** ... '71 '95 C.112 B.A. L.1066 J.D. [🄰 McClintock,W.B.R.R.&M.]
*PRACTICE AREAS: Environmental Litigation; Toxic Tort Litigation; Employment Litigation.
Kraemer, Glen E. ... '62 '87 C.154 B.A. L.1068 J.D. 444 S. Flower St.
Kraemer, Samuel H. ... '60 '85 C.112 B.A. L.800 J.D. 11611 San Vicente Blvd.
Krafchak, Stephanie L. ... '56 '83 C.1044 B.A. L.61 J.D. 2049 Century Park E.

**Krafft, M. Sue, Law Offices of**
**(See Covina)**

Kraft, Richard E. ... '56 '81 C.1036 B.A. L.800 J.D. Dep. City Atty.
Krag, Thomas R. ... '58 '88 C.1097 B.A. L.809 J.D. Dep. Dist. Atty.
Kraines, Lawrence J. ... '48 '73 C.112 B.A. L.429 J.D. Asst. U.S. Trustee
**Krakovsky, Michael** ... '69 '95 C.477 B.S.E.E. L.178 J.D. [🄰 Irell&M.]
**Krakow, Marvin E.**, (AV) ... '48 '74 C&L.976 B.A., J.D. [Krakow&K.]
*REPORTED CASES: Loder v. City of Glendale, 216 Cal. App. 777 (1989); Montecini v. I.N.S., 915 F.2d 518 (9th Cir. 1990); Funk v. Sperry Corp., 842 F.2d 1129 (9th Cir. 1990); Khalsa v. Weinberger, 787 F.2d 1288 (9th Cir. 1985); Knight v. Hallsthammar, 29 Cal. 3d 46 (1981) (amicus).
*PRACTICE AREAS: Wrongful Termination; Employment Discrimination; Civil and Constitutional Rights; Privacy and Free Expression; Government Misconduct.

**Krakow & Kaplan, (AV)**
**1801 Century Park East, Suite 1520, 90067-2302**
**Telephone: 310-229-0900 Fax: 310-229-0912**
**Marvin E. Krakow; Steven J. Kaplan.**
**Civil Trials and Appeals. Wrongful Termination, Civil and Constitutional Rights, Sexual Harassment, Privacy and Free Expression, Government and Business Misconduct, Insurance Bad Faith, ERISA, Union Representation.**
***See Professional Biographies, LOS ANGELES, CALIFORNIA***

**Krakowsky, Steven P.** ... '55 '80 C.112 B.A. L.809 J.D. [🄱 S.M.Mason]
*PRACTICE AREAS: Trials and Appeals.
**Kralik, Lisa M.** ... '65 '90 C&L.190 B.A., J.D. [🄰 Grace,S.C.&S.]
*PRACTICE AREAS: Appellate Law; Insurance Coverage Law; Insurance Bad Faith.
Kramar, Steven D. ... '47 '72 C.800 B.A. L.426 J.D. 845 N. Fairfax Ave.
Kramer, David M., (AV) ... '49 '79 C.1350 B.A. L.809 J.D. 12121 Wilshire Blvd.
Kramer, Eugene ... '31 '58 C.339 B.S. L.209 J.D. Asst. U.S. Atty.
Kramer, Eugene L. ... '29 '58 C.563 B.A. L.569 LL.B. 1875 Century Park E.
Kramer, Ian L. ... '56 '92 C.051 B.A. L.178 J.D. 606 S. Olive St.
**Kramer, Jeffrey S.**, (AV) ... '54 '80 C.768 B.S. L.809 J.D. [Stevens,K.A.&H.]
*REPORTED CASES: Debbie Reynolds v. Superior Court (1994) 25 CA 4th 222, 30 C.R. 2nd 514.
*PRACTICE AREAS: Defense of General Liability; Construction Defect; Intellectual Property; Public Carrier; Entertainment.
**Kramer, Jeffrey W.**, (AV) ... '51 '76 C.347 A.B. L.813 J.D. [Troy&G.]
*PRACTICE AREAS: Securities Litigation; Business and Financial Institutions Litigation; Real Estate Litigation; Employment Litigation.
Kramer, Katherine ... '58 '85 C.260 B.A. L.259 J.D. [Clark&K.]
**Kramer, Michael A.** ... '53 '78 C.800 B.A. L.809 J.D. [Veatch,C.G.&N.]
*REPORTED CASES: Mitchell v. Superior Court 37 Cal. 3rd, Page 591.
*PRACTICE AREAS: Product Liability; Vehicle Liability; Government Tort Liability; General Casualty Defense Law.
**Kramer, Ora D.** ... '62 '88 C.112 B.S. L.426 J.D. [🄰 Quisenberry&B.]
Kramer, Philip A., (AV) ... '59 '84 C.608 B.A. L.128 J.D. [Kramer&K.]
**Kramer, R. Brian** ... '55 '80 C.800 B.A. L.426 [Voorhies&K.]
*PRACTICE AREAS: Civil Trial; Insurance; Product Liability; Medical Malpractice; Negligence Law.
Kramer, Seth Daniel, (AV) ... '55 '80 C.846 B.J. L.809 J.D. 12100 Wilshire
**Kramer, Stephen W.**, (AV) ... '48 '76 C.800 A.B. L.1068 J.D. [Kramer&G.]
*PRACTICE AREAS: Estates Law; Trusts Law; General Business Law; Fine Arts Law.
**Kramer, Steven O.** ... '47 '73 C.174 B.A. L.146 J.D. [Pillsbury M.&S.]

**Kramer, William K.**, (AV) ... '34 '64 C.1258 B.A. L.426 J.D. [Richards,W.&G.]
*PRACTICE AREAS: Municipal Finance.
Kramer, William M. ... '20 '79 C.930 B.A. L.1136 J.D. 2049 Century Park E.

**Kramer & Goldwasser, (AV)**
**5670 Wilshire Boulevard Suite 2420, 90036**
**Telephone: 213-964-7100 FACSIMILE: 213-964-7107**
**Stephen W. Kramer; Charles A. Goldwasser; Jeffrey M. Pugh; Corey W. Glave.**
**General Business and Real Estate Transactions, Estate Planning and Probate, Entertainment and Visual Arts Law.**
***See Professional Biographies, LOS ANGELES, CALIFORNIA***

Kramer & Kaslow, (AV) ... 2029 Century Park E.

**Kramer & Kramer**
**(See Santa Monica)**

**Kramsky, Elliott N., Law Offices of**
**(See Woodland Hills)**

Krane, Jonathan D. ... '52 '77 C.999 B.A. L.976 J.D. Management Co. Entertainment Grp.
Kranitz, Ephraim P., P.C., (AV) ... '31 '59 C.112 B.S. L.1068 J.D. 4929 Wilshire Blvd.
**Krantz, David S.**, (AV) ... '48 '78 C.112 B.A. L.809 J.D. [Ostrove,K.&O.]
*PRACTICE AREAS: Business Litigation; Business Transactions; Real Estate Litigation; Real Estate Transactions; Corporate Law.
**Kranwinkle, C. Douglas**, (AV) '40 '66
C.597 B.A. L.477 J.D. [O'Melveny&M.] (⊙New York, NY.)
*PRACTICE AREAS: Securities; Mergers and Acquisitions; Complex Business Transactions.
**Krashin, Jeffrey B.** ... '50 '77 C.910 A.B. L.930 J.D. [Thompson&W.]
*PRACTICE AREAS: Government Contracts; Construction Law; Business Litigation.
Krasney, Robert L. ... '51 '79 C.608 B.A. L.1049 J.D. 3580 Wilshire Blvd.
Krattli, John F. ... '52 '78 C.112 B.A. L.1068 J.D. Asst. Co. Coun.
Kraus, David P. ... '57 '81 C.112 B.A. L.813 J.D. 333 S. Grand Ave.
**Kraus, Herbert**, (AV) ... '30 '55 C&L.813 A.B., LL.B. [🄱 Gibson,D.&C.]
*PRACTICE AREAS: Corporate Law; Securities Law.
Kraus, Sean Christopher ... '64 '89 C.367 B.A. L.245 J.D. 1801 Century Pk. E., 9th Fl.
**Kraus, Steven M.** ... '59 '84 C.112 B.A. L.1066 J.D. [🄱 Freeman,F.&S.]
*LANGUAGES: French.
*PRACTICE AREAS: Real Estate Sales and Acquisitions; Development; Leasing and Financing.
**Krause, Jeffrey C.**, (AV) ... '56 '80 C.112 B.S. L.1068 J.D. [Stutman,T.&G.]
*REPORTED CASES: In re Felburg, 39 Bankr. 591 (Bankr. C.D. Cal. 1984); Pistole V. Mellor (In re Mellor), 734 F. 2d 1396 (19th Cir. 1984); In re Safren, 65 Bankr. 566 (Bankr. C.D. Cal. 1986); Black & White Cattle Co. V. Shamrock Farms Co. (In re Black & White Cattle Co.), 30 Bankr. 508 (Bankr. 9th Cir. 1983), Rev'd. 746 F. 2d 1484 (9th Cir. 1984); Black & White Cattle Co. V. Granada Services, Inc. (In re Black & White Cattle Co.), 783 F. 2d 1454 (9th Cir. 1986).
*PRACTICE AREAS: Bankruptcy; Insolvency; Corporate Reorganization; Commercial Litigation.
Kraut, Nate G. ... '59 '83 C.1077 B.A. L.1065 J.D. Research Atty., Supm. Ct. Jus.
**Krave, John P.** ... '52 '80 C&L.426 B.A., J.D. [Epstein B.&G.]
*PRACTICE AREAS: Corporate Health Care.
Kravetz, Bryan ... '43 '68 C.112 A.B. L.178 J.D. [B.Kravetz]
Kravetz, Bryan, A P.C. ... 1801 Ave. of the Stars
Kravit, Stephen M. ... '39 '62 C.331 A.B. L.178 LL.B. Kings Rd. Entertainment Inc.
**Kravitz, Jeffrey S.** ... '50 '75 C.112 B.A. L.426 J.D. [Lord,B.&B.]
*PRACTICE AREAS: Professional Malpractice; Railroad Law; Business Litigation.
Kraybill, Nancy C. ... '54 '86 C.674 B.A. L.1068 J.D. 606 S. Olive St.
Krebs, Kathryn Lee '59 '84 C.259 B.S. L.192 J.D.
V.P., Sr. Lit. Coun., PaineWebber, Inc.
Kreeger, Margaret Ryan ... '53 '79 C.112 B.A. L.767 J.D. Sr. Atty., ARCO
Kregal, Irving W. ... '34 '66 C.911 B.S. L.426 LL.B. 11845 W. Olympic Blvd.
**Kreger, Wayne S.** ... '66 '91 C.94 B.A. L.990 J.D. [Kreger&S.]
*LANGUAGES: Spanish.

**Kreger & Stein**
**A Partnership**
**3518 Cahuenga Boulevard West, Suite 213, 90068**
**Telephone: 213-876-8118 Fax: 213-876-5612**
**Members of Firm: Wayne S. Kreger; Mitchell Reed Stein.**
**General Civil Litigation in all State and Federal Courts, Entertainment, Intellectual Property, Insurance Coverage and Bad Faith, Real Estate, Business, Commercial Litigation, Personal Injury.**
***See Professional Biographies, LOS ANGELES, CALIFORNIA***

Kreindler, Charles L. ... '61 '85 C.1044 B.A. L.94 J.D. Asst. U.S. Atty.
**Kreinman, Diana L.** ... '67 '94 C.112 B.A. L.464 J.D. [🄰 Bonne,B.M.O.&N.]
**Kreis, John P.**, (AV) ... '48 '73 C&L.602 B.A., J.D. [🄱 Orrick,H.&S.]
*PRACTICE AREAS: Bankruptcy and Corporate Reorganization Litigation; Debt Restructure; Workouts.
Kreisel, June E. ... '57 '85 C.1044 B.S. L.809 J.D. 4215 Glencoe Ave.
Kreisler, Richard M. ... '49 '74 C.112 B.A. L.1068 J.D. [Liebert,C.&F.]
**Kreisman, Lance M.** '64 '94 C.112 B.S.E.E. L.1148 J.D.
[🄰 Darby&D.] (See Pat. Sect.)
*PRACTICE AREAS: Patent Prosecution; Patent Litigation; Trademark.
**Kreisman, Norman J.** ... '48 '92 C.36 B.S. L.426 J.D. [Tax C.]
*LANGUAGES: Dutch, Punjabi.
*PRACTICE AREAS: Bankruptcy Law; Taxation Law.
Kreitenberg, Ernie B. ... '62 '92 C.112 B.A. L.1137 J.D. 10583 Eastborne Ave.
Kreitenberg, Mitchell H. ... '58 '83 C.112 B.A. L.426 J.D. 4055 Wilshire Blvd.
**Krekorian, Paul M.** ... '60 '84 C.800 A.B. L.1066 J.D. [🄰 Leopold,P.&S.]
*PRACTICE AREAS: Entertainment; Employment; Civil Litigation; Copyright and Trademark; Libel and Slander.
**Kreller, Thomas R.** ... '64 '92 C.357 B.S. L.1068 J.D. [🄰 Stutman,T.&G.]
*PRACTICE AREAS: Bankruptcy; Insolvency; Corporate Reorganization; Commercial Litigation.

**Krentzman, Donald A. '50 '75 C.112 B.A. L.208 J.D.**
**2049 Century Park East, Suite 1200, 90067-9777**
**Telephone: 310-277-6520**
**Estate Planning, Corporate Planning, Tax Planning, Tax Controversies, Limited Partnerships.**
***See Professional Biographies, LOS ANGELES, CALIFORNIA***

**Krepack, Howard D.**, (AV) ... '48 '74 C.112 A.B. L.1068 J.D. [Gordon,E.K.G.F.&G.]
*PRACTICE AREAS: Personal Injury Law; Products Liability Law; Insurance Bad Faith Law; Professional Negligence.
**Kreps, Allyn O.**, (AV) ... '30 '59 C.309 B.A. L.813 LL.B. [Troy&G.]
*PRACTICE AREAS: Complex Commercial; Corporate; Antitrust Litigation.
**Kreps, Theodore V.** ... '57 '89 C.30 B.A. L.809 J.D. [🄱 Lund]
*PRACTICE AREAS: Business; Commercial; General Civil Litigation.
**Kretzmer, Michael J.** ... '52 '83 C.112 A.B. L.426 J.D. [🄱 Pircher,N.&M.]
*PRACTICE AREAS: Real Estate; Litigation; Family Law.
Kricun, Newton, (AV) ... '40 '70 C.1097 B.A. L.809 J.D. 1670 Corinth Ave.
**Krieg, Barbara A.** ... '58 '95 C.602 B.A. L.1068 J.D. [🄰 Riordan&M.]
*PRACTICE AREAS: Litigation.
Krieger, Eliot F. ... '60 '92 C.112 B.A. L.309 J.D. 555 W. 5th St.
**Krieger, Jeffrey A.** ... '64 '91 C.821 B.A. L.1067 J.D. [🄰 Greenberg G.F.C.&M.]
*PRACTICE AREAS: Corporate Reorganization; Bankruptcy; Creditors Rights.
Krieger, Lisa R. ... '— '90 C.994 B.A. L.1148 J.D. 9314 W. Pico Blvd.
Krieger, Michael M. ... '41 '83 C.111 B.S. L.1068 J.D. [🄱 Rosner,O.&N.]
**Krieger, Spencer A.** ... '65 '94 C.112 B.A. L.464 J.D. [🄰 Sedgwick,D.M.&A.]
*LANGUAGES: Spanish, French and Portuguese.

CAA270P

Krikorian, Rosanne Joy '50 '76
C.112 A.B. L.1068 J.D. Assoc. Dir. of Law Libr., Whittier Law Sch.
**Krim, Lisa E.** ... '69 '95 C.813 A.B. L.112 J.D. [A] O'Melveny&M.]
Krimmel, Herbert T. ... '49 '75 C&L.800 B.S., J.D. Southwestern Univ. Sch. of Law
Krinsky, Miriam A. ... '59 '84 C.112 B.A. L.1068 J.D. U.S. Attys. Off.
**Krischer, Gordon E.**, (AV) ... '46 '72 C.339 B.S. L.309 J.D. [O'Melveny&M.]
*PRACTICE AREAS: Trial Practice; Labor and Employment Law; Toxic Torts; Civil Litigation.
**Krischer, Jason** ... '70 '96 C.339 B.S. L.809 J.D. [A] Mitchell,S.&K.]
*PRACTICE AREAS: Civil Litigation.
**Krischer, Joel E.** ... '51 '75 C.339 B.A. L.477 J.D. [Latham&W.]
**Krishel, Daniel L.** ... '63 '90 C.1077 L.426 J.D. [A] Stein P.&H.]
*PRACTICE AREAS: Business Litigation (100%).
Krislov, Maureen D., (BV) ... '52 '82 C.823 B.S. L.398 J.D. [Krislov&N.] (©Sacramento)
Krislov & Neuman, (BV) ... 2029 Century Park E.
**Kristal, Elliot B.**, (BV) ... '53 '77 C.112 B.A. L.1068 J.D. [B] Manatt,P.&P.]
*PRACTICE AREAS: Health Law; Estates and Trusts.
**Kristal, Martin C.**, (AV) ... '53 '77 C.112 B.A. L.1068 J.D. [Harrington,F.D.&C.]
*PRACTICE AREAS: Real Estate Law; Probate and Trusts Law; Estate Planning Law; General Business Law.
Kristovich, Marlene ... '— '78 C.800 B.S. L.426 J.D. Mun. J.
**Kristovich, Stephen M.** ... '53 '78 C.813 A.B. L.1066 J.D. [Munger,T.&O.]
**Kristovich, Theresa A.**, (AV) ... '— '75 C.813 B.A. L.1066 J.D. [Kelley D.&W.]
*PRACTICE AREAS: Business Litigation; Employment Disputes; Professional Negligence; White Collar Fraud.
Kristovich, Thomas B. ... '47 '73 C.800 B.S. L.426 J.D. 3200 Wilshire Blvd.
Kritt, Evi E. ... '52 '85 C&L.1137 B.S., J.D. Assoc. Gen. Coun., ABM Indus. Inc.
**Kritt, Lauri A.** ... '63 '90 C.154 B.A. L.770 J.D. [Deutsch&R.]
*PRACTICE AREAS: Family Law.
**Kroeker, Kevin B.**, (AV) ... '59 '86 C.623 B.A. L.1067 J.D. [Konowiecki&R.]
*PRACTICE AREAS: Health Care Law; General Business; Administrative.
**Kroft, Stephen A.**, (AV) ... '44 '69 C.112 B.A. L.813 LL.B. [McDermott,W.&E.]
*PRACTICE AREAS: Complex Business Litigation; Intellectual Property Litigation and Counseling; Entertainment Litigation and Counseling; Legal Malpractice Defense.
Krohn, Charles H. ... '51 '77 C.112 A.B. L.1049 J.D. 511 N. LaCienega Blvd.
**Krolikowski, Charles S.** ... '70 '96 C.112 B.S. L.800 J.D. [A] Mendes&M.]
Kroll, Gerald R., (AV) ... '37 '69 C.112 L.426 J.D. [Kroll,G.R.]
**Kroll, Howard A.** ... '56 '81 C.154 B.A. L.800 J.D. [Preston G.&E.]
Kroll, Gerald R., A P.C., (AV) ... 15760 Ventura Blvd. (Encino)

**Kroll & Tract, (AV)**
**6500 Wilshire Boulevard, 90048©**
**Telephone: 213-857-5080 Telecopier: 213-857-5090**
**Resident Associate: David Kam Ng.**
**General Insurance and Reinsurance Practice, Casualty, Professional Liability, Products Liability, Surety, Aviation, Marine and Life Insurance, Admiralty, Insurance Regulatory, Corporate and Securities Law, Trials and Appeals.**
**New York, N.Y. Office: 520 Madison Avenue. Telephone: 212-921-9100. Telex: WU 668838 KROLAWNY; WU 645461 KROLAWNY. Telecopier: 212-869-3657.**
**San Francisco, California Office: 120 Montgomery Street, Suite 340. Telephone: 415-989-2494. Fax: 415-989-2496.**
**Houston, Texas Office: 700 Louisiana Street. Telephone: 713-228-3100. Telex: 3710883. Telecopier: 713-228-2219.**
**Miami, Florida Office: 201 South Biscayne Boulevard. Telephone: 305-577-4848. Telex: 808094. Telecopier: 305-577-3417.**
**Mineola, New York Office: Suite 330, 120 Mineola Boulevard, Box 10. Telephone: 516-747-7333. Telecopier: 516-747-3540.**
**London, England Office: Asia House, 31/33 Lime Street, EC3M 7HR. Telephone: 621-1142. Telex: 8955700 KROLAW LDN. Telecopier: 283-6391.**
**Paris, France Office: 32, Rue la Boétie, 75008. Telephone: 4563.18.10. Telex: 643752 F. Telecopier: 45633494.**
**Boston, Massachusetts Office: 60 State Street, Suite 2080. Telephone: 617-742-3530. Telecopier: 617-227-0201.**
**Newark, New Jersey Office: One Gateway Center, 17th Floor. Telephone: 201-622-3955. Telecopier: 201-622-1112.**
**White Plains, New York Office: 11 Martine Avenue. Telephone: 914-946-0773. Telecopier: 914-946-2216.**
*See Professional Biographies, NEW YORK, NEW YORK*

**Kronemyer, David E.** ... '53 '76 C.112 A.B. L.800 J.D. [B] Rosen&Assoc.]
*PRACTICE AREAS: Entertainment Law; Corporate Law; Business Law.
Kronenberg, John R. ... '23 '59 C.623 L.425 LL.B. U.S. Mag. J.
**Kronstadt, John A.** ... '51 '77 C.188 B.A. L.976 J.D. [Blanc W.J.&K.]
*PRACTICE AREAS: Commercial Litigation; Environmental Law; Antitrust and Trade Regulation.
**Kropff, James B.** ... '54 '80 C.763 A.B. L.426 J.D. [Girardi&K.]
*PRACTICE AREAS: Appellate Practice.
Krotman, Howard E. ... '63 '88 C.112 B.A. L.978 J.D. 4215 Glencoe Ave.
Krown, Kenneth J. ... '59 '84 C.112 B.A. L.990 J.D. First Interstate Bank
Krueger, Cynthia A. ... '65 '94 C.494 B.A. L.112 J.D. 801 S. Figueroa St.
**Krug, James B.** ... '53 '78 C.112 B.A. L.426 J.D. [B] Berger,K.S.M.F.S.&G.]
**Krug, Kenneth** ... '58 '82 C.228 A.B. L.145 J.D. [B] Proskauer R.G.&M.]
*PRACTICE AREAS: Real Estate; Corporate.
**Kruger, Elizabeth J.** ... '65 '93 C.597 B.S. L.978 J.D. [A] Proskauer R.G.&M.]
**Kruger, Jodi L.** ... '68 '93 C&L.188 B.A., J.D. [A] Littler,M.F.T.&M.]
**Kruis, Elizabeth E.** ... '66 '93 C.112 B.A. L.426 J.D. [A] Perkins C.]
*PRACTICE AREAS: Litigation; Employment Law.
**Krum, Mark G.** ... '56 '83 C.937 B.A. L.597 J.D. [Christensen,M.F.J.G.W.&S.]
*PRACTICE AREAS: Civil Litigation; Securities Litigation; Corporate Governance.
Krumrey, Marilyn S. ... '68 '95 C&L.347 B.A., J.D. 2355 S. Bentley Ave
**Krupinsky, Peter J.** ... '54 '79 C.971 B.S. L.426 J.D. [A] Agapay,L.&H.]
**Kruppe, Michael A.** ... '59 '86 C.880 B.A. L.365 J.D. [Roper&F.]
*PRACTICE AREAS: Appellate Practice; Automobile Negligence; Construction Defect Litigation; Construction Accidents; Civil Rights Actions.
**Kruse, Scott August**, (AV) ... '47 '72 C.674 A.B. L.309 J.D. [Gibson,D.&C.]
*PRACTICE AREAS: Labor and Employment Law; Civil Rights; Occupational Safety and Health; Employee Benefits; Transportation.
Kruth, Joseph L. ... '47 '77 C.665 B.S. L.1068 J.D. 949 S Hope St.
Krystal, Sidney D., (AV) ... '07 '36 C.113 B.A. L.309 LL.B. 16460 Sloan Dr.‡
**Ku, Edward Y.** ... '42 '73 C.061 B.A. L.910 J.D. [B] Ku,F.L.&C.]
*LANGUAGES: Chinese (Mandarin).
*PRACTICE AREAS: International Law; Corporate; Business; Real Estate; Banking.

**Ku, Fong, Larsen & Chen, LLP, (AV)** [BB]
**523 West Sixth Street, Suite 528, 90014**
**Telephone: 213-488-1400 Telecopier: 213-236-9235**
**Members of Firm: H. G. Robert Fong; Paul A. Larsen; Frank W. Chen. Of Counsel: Edward Y. Ku. Associates: Jack S. Yeh; Victor S. Sze.**
**Corporate, Business, Real Estate, International, Insurance, Copyright, Trademark, Unfair Competition and Business Litigation Law. General Civil and Trial Practice in all State and Federal Courts.**
*See Professional Biographies, LOS ANGELES, CALIFORNIA*

Kubani, Thomas L. ... '31 '62 C.1229 B.S.M.E. L.273 LL.B. [A] Chase,R.D.&B.]
Kubec, Edward M. ... '63 '91 C.896 B.S. L.262 J.D. 9255 Sunset Blvd.
**Kubec, Kristin M.** ... '66 '91 C.112 B.A. L.464 J.D. [A] Wilson,K.&B.]
**Kubelun, Walter H.** ... '63 '91 C.1077 B.S. L.1049 J.D. [A] La Follette,J.D.F.&A.]
*PRACTICE AREAS: Medical Malpractice Litigation; Insurance Defense.

**Kuber, Douglas A.** ... '60 '87 C.1097 B.A. L.1065 J.D. [Quinn E.U.&O.]
*REPORTED CASES: Macaulay v. Norlander, 12 Cal. App. 4th 1 (1992).
*PRACTICE AREAS: General Commercial Litigation; Securities; Real Property Litigation.
Kubik, Frederick J. ... '40 '72 C.112 B.A. L.426 J.D. Dep. Dist. Atty.
**Kublicki, Nicolas M.** ... '66 '93 C.112 B.A. L.990 J.D. [A] Buchalter,N.F.&Y.]
*PRACTICE AREAS: Real Estate Finance; Environmental Law.
**Kuckelman, David J.** ... '50 '76 C.375 B.S. L.378 J.D. [Seyfarth,S.F.&G.]
*PRACTICE AREAS: Government Contract Law; International Contract Law; Corporate Law.
**Kudo, Richard K.** ... '51 '78 C.112 B.A. L.1065 J.D. [Kudo&D.]
*PRACTICE AREAS: Commercial Collections in Federal and State Courts; Real Estate; Business; Transactional Law; Personal Injury Litigation.

**Kudo & Daniels, LLP**
**12400 Wilshire Boulevard, Suite 400, 90025-1023**
**Telephone: 310-442-7900 Facsimile: 310-442-7999**
**Richard K. Kudo; Paula A. Daniels.**
**Real Estate, Business and Personal Injury Litigation; Commercial Collections in Federal and State Courts, Product Liability; Legal, Accountancy, Medical, Dental and Realtor Malpractice. Business, Corporate, Securities and Transactional Law. Arbitration and Mediation Services.**
*See Professional Biographies, LOS ANGELES, CALIFORNIA*

**Kuechle, John M., (A Professional Corporation)**, (AV) '51 '77
C.605 A.B. L.309 J.D. [Mitchell,S.&K.]
*PRACTICE AREAS: Real Estate Law; Corporate Law; Commercial Law.
**Kuelbs, John T.** '42 '73 C.723 B.S. L.190 J.D.
V.P. & Assoc. Gen. Coun., Hughes Aircraft Co.
Kuhl, Carolyn B. ... '52 '77 C.674 A.B. L.228 J.D. 355 S. Grand Ave., 35th Fl.
**Kuhl, John H.**, (AV) ... '49 '74 C.112 B.S. L.1067 J.D. [Cox,C.&N.]
*PRACTICE AREAS: Real Property Law; Real Estate Acquisitions and Finance.
**Kuhlman, Frederick S.** ... '53 '92 C.589 B.A. L.426 J.D. [A] Fulbright&J.]
*PRACTICE AREAS: Public Finance.
Kuhn, Ernest ... '25 '56 C.800 B.S. L.426 LL.B. 3326 Ocean Dr. (©Beverly Hills)
Kuhn, Robert E. ... '43 '76 C.1042 B.S. L.809 J.D. 3255 Wilshire Blvd. 12th Fl.
**Kula, Donald J.** ... '63 '89 C.339 B.A. L.477 J.D. [Riordan&M.]
Kulik, Glen L. ... '53 '78 C.112 B.A. L.426 J.D. [Kulik&G.]
Kulik & Gottesman ... 1880 Century Pk. E., Ste. 800
**Kull, Robert F.** ... '48 '76 C.112 A.B. L.1065 J.D. [Carlsmith B.W.C.&I.]
**Kully, Russel I.**, (AV) ... '32 '60 C.659 B.S. L.813 LL.B. [B] Arnold&P.]
*PRACTICE AREAS: Corporation Law; Non-Profit Law; Health Care Law.
**Kuluva, Carol D.** ... '55 '79 C.1077 B.A. L.1095 J.D. [Bragg,S.S.&K.]
*PRACTICE AREAS: Professional Liability Defense; Directors and Officers Errors and Omissions Law; Product Liability; Personal Injury Defense.
Kumagai, Duane ... '59 '86 C.881 A.B. L.569 J.D. 2029 Century Park E.
**Kumar, Aneeta** ... '66 '92 C.605 A.B. L.1067 J.D. [A] Troop M.S.&P.]
*PRACTICE AREAS: Insurance Coverage and General Litigation.
Kumar, Sanjay T. ... '65 '90 C.424 B.B.A. L.990 J.D. Dep. Atty. Gen.
Kumetz, Barbara A. ... '50 '89 C.1077 B.A. L.809 J.D. 3580 Wilshire Blvd.
Kumetz, Fred J., (AV) ... '48 '74 C.1077 L.809 J.D. 3580 Wilshire Blvd.
Kummer, Janis Gorby ... '51 '76 C.112 B.S. L.800 J.D. 225 S. Anita Ave.
**Kump, Michael J.** ... '52 '81 C.293 B.A. L.477 J.D. [Kinsella,B.F.&T.]
**Kumpis, Philip Bruno** ... '53 '89 C.871 B.S.E.E. L.1184 J.D. [A] McKenna&C.]
**Kunert, Gregory M.** ... '54 '80 C.605 A.B. L.800 J.D. [Richards,W.&G.]
*PRACTICE AREAS: Civil Litigation and Trials; Civil Rights Litigation; Land Use Litigation.
**Kunowski, Herbert P.** ... '58 '90 C.112 B.A. L.990 J.D. [A] Wilson,E.M.E.&D.]
Kunsberg, Sandra P. ... '48 '74 C.1036 B.A. L.178 J.D. 150 S. Bentley Ave.‡
**Kunstler, Peter M.** ... '48 '84 C.800 M.S. L.1097 J.D. [Ruben&M.]
*PRACTICE AREAS: Civil Litigation.
**Kupetz, Arnold L.**, (AV) ... '33 '56 C&L.208 B.S., J.D. [Sulmeyer,K.B.&R.]
*PRACTICE AREAS: Bankruptcy; Federal and State Court Receiverships.
**Kupetz, David S.** ... '61 '86 C.112 B.S. L.1065 J.D. [Sulmeyer,K.B.&R.]
*PRACTICE AREAS: Bankruptcy.
**Kupfer, Coralie** ... '48 '74 C.800 B.A. L.770 J.D. [Rodi,P.P.G.&C.]
*PRACTICE AREAS: Environmental Law; Air Quality Regulation; Transportation; Health and Safety.
Kupferman, Ellis H. '56 '83 C.415 B.S. L.1029 J.D.
(adm. in CT; not adm. in CA) F.B.I.
**Kupferstein, Phyllis**, (AV) ... '58 '82 C.112 B.A. L.426 J.D. [Quinn E.U.&O.]
*REPORTED CASES: Simon Oil Co., Ltd. v. Norman, 789 F.2d 780 (9th Cir. 1986); Mitsui Manufacturers Bank v. Texas Commerce Bank, 159 Cal. App. 3d 1051 (1984).
*PRACTICE AREAS: Employment; Health Care; ERISA; General Commercial Litigation; General Trial Practice.
**Kupietzky, Moshe J.**, (AV) ... '44 '69 C.563 B.B.A. L.309 LL.B. [Sidley&A.]
*LANGUAGES: Hebrew.
*PRACTICE AREAS: Corporate Law; Mergers and Acquisitions; Banking Law.
**Kurahashi, Eileen** ... '43 '75 C.483 B.A. L.800 J.D. [Quan,C.K.Y.S.&H.]
*PRACTICE AREAS: Commercial Litigation; Employment Law; Family Law.
**Kuriyama, John M.** ... '65 '92 C.312 B.B.A. L.813 J.D. [A] Latham&W.]
*LANGUAGES: Japanese.
Kuriyama, Lester C. ... '54 '83 C.1042 B.A. L.426 J.D. Dep. Dist. Atty.
**Kurland, Marta Thoerner** ... '58 '83 C.426 B.B.A. L.1066 J.D. [B] Andrews&K.]
*PRACTICE AREAS: Real Estate Law; Real Estate Finance Law; Business Law.
**Kurlander, William A.**, (AV) ... '26 '50 C.112 B.A. L.426 LL.B. [B] Barger&W.]
*PRACTICE AREAS: Litigation, Insurance Coverage.
**Kurosu, Ken M.** ... '58 '83 C.813 A.B. L.911 J.D. [Graham&J.] (©Tokyo, Japan)
*LANGUAGES: Japanese.
*PRACTICE AREAS: International Business Law.
Kurshner, Richard A. '49 '74 C.1044 B.A. L.273 J.D.
Sr. Atty., Bus. Affs., Paramount Pictures Corp.
**Kurtz, Barry**, (AV) ... '48 '73 C.112 B.A. L.809 J.D. [B] Shapiro,R.&C.]
*PRACTICE AREAS: Franchise Law; Business Law.
**Kurtz, Carol E.** ... '47 '92 C.112 B.A. L.809 J.D. [A] Proskauer R.G.&M.]
*PRACTICE AREAS: Environmental Law.
Kurtz, Gary A. ... '59 '84 C.260 B.A. L.880 J.D. [Sherman&K.]
Kurtz, Robin S. ... '53 '80 C.881 B.A. L.1040 J.D. [A] Gurewitz&L.]
Kurtz, Steven D. '60 '87 C.477 B.S. L.145 J.D.
(adm. in IL; not adm. in CA) 711 Wilcox Ave.‡
Kurtzman, Alvin M., (AV) ... '24 '61 C.112 B.S. L.426 J.D. [Kurtzman&S.]
**Kurtzman, Eric S.** ... '70 '96 C.112 B.A. L.1068 J.D. [A] Murphy,W.&B.]
**Kurtzman, Ilene Wendy** ... '58 '85 C.112 B.A. L.800 J.D. [A] Daniels,B.&F.]
Kurtzman & Sarfaty, A Law Corporation, (AV) ... 1880 Century Park E. (Century City)
**Kushman, Moshe J.** ... '56 '87 C.112 B.A. L.426 J.D. [B] Skadden,A.S.M.&F.]
**Kushner, Elliott**, (BV) ... '50 '75 C.112 B.A. L.426 J.D. [Clopton,P.&B.]
Kushner, James A. ... '45 '70 C.472 B.B.A. L.446 J.D. Southwestern Univ. Sch. of Law
Kushner, Michael F. ... '50 '77 C.1077 B.S.E. L.1095 J.D. [M.F.Kushner]
Kushner, Robert G. ... '66 '91 C.112 B.A. L.94 J.D. 1901 Ave. of the Stars
**Kushner, Steven E.** ... '49 '77 C.1049 B.A. L.61 J.D. [A] Dummit,F.&B.]
Kushner, Michael F., A Professional Corporation ... 1901 Ave. of the Stars, Ste. 1242

**Kussman, Russell S., (A Professional Corporation)**, (AV) '49 '81
C.94 B.A. L.1066 J.D. [Kussman&W.]
*PRACTICE AREAS: Medical Malpractice; Products Liability Law; Professional Liability; Personal Injury.

**Kussman & Whitehill, (AV)**
**A Partnership including a Professional Corporation**
**Suite 1470, 10866 Wilshire Boulevard, 90024**
**Telephone: 310-474-4411 Fax: 310-474-6530**
**Russell S. Kussman (A Professional Corporation); Michael H. Whitehill;—Steven G. Mehta.**
**Medical Malpractice, Insurance Bad Faith, Personal Injury, Products Liability and Professional Liability.**

*See Professional Biographies, LOS ANGELES, CALIFORNIA*

Kutler, Sara S. '57 '83 C.112 B.A. L.1066 J.D.
Gen. Coun., Quarterdeck Investment Partners, Inc.
**Kuyper, Bruce D.** .......................... '63 '89 C.112 B.S.E.E. L.1068 J.D. [Irell&M.]
**Kveton, Kyle** .......................... '59 '83 C.1044 B.A. L.800 J.D. [Robie&M.]
*PRACTICE AREAS: Business Litigation; Directors and Officers Errors and Omissions.
**Kwak, Erick** .......................... '70 '95 C.93 B.A. L.276 J.D. [Ⓐ Proskauer R.G.&M.]
*PRACTICE AREAS: Corporate.
Kwan, Hiram W., (A Prof. Law Corp.) ..... '24 '53 C&L.800 B.S., J.D. 808 N. Springs St.
Kwan, Leo W. .......................... '36 '65 C.112 A.B. L.1068 LL.B. 808 N. Spring St., 6th Fl.
Kwan, Ruth .......................... '56 '81 C.800 B.A. L.1065 J.D. Mun. J.
Kwan, Wellington Y., (AV) .......................... '22 '57 C.886 L.809 J.D. 3731 Wilshire Blvd.
Kwan, William C. .......................... '52 '89 C.763 B.S. L.809 J.D. Ernst & Young
Kwan-Gett, Mei Lin .......................... '67 '93 C.309 A.B. L.976 J.D. A.C.L.U.
**Kwasigroch, Lois M.** .......................... '— '87 C.766 B.A. L.426 J.D. [Lyon&L.] (See Pat. Sect.)
*PRACTICE AREAS: Intellectual Property.
**Kwasniewski, Gary K.** .......................... '51 '86 C.158 B.S. L.1340 J.D. [Ⓒ Sedgwick,D.M.&A.]
Kwok, Gino M. .......................... '63 '88 C.112 B.S. L.800 J.D. Summer Pro League
Kwong, Owen Lee .......................... '— '73 C.878 B.S. L.1068 J.D. Supr. Ct. J.
**Kwuon, Janet H.** .......................... '64 '89 C.112 B.A. L.464 J.D. [Ⓐ Crosby,H.R.&M.]
Kyle, David, (AV) .......................... '36 '73 C&L.1095 B.A., LL.B. 700 S. Flower St.
**Kyle, Deanne B.** .......................... '67 '93 C.280 B.B.A. L.846 J.D. [Ⓐ Munger,T.&O.]
*PRACTICE AREAS: Tax; Trusts and Estates.
Kyle, Gary W. .......................... '44 '70 C.1060 B.S. L.145 J.D. 633 W. 5th St.
**Kyman, David S.** .......................... '54 '79 C.112 B.A. L.809 J.D. [Buchalter,N.F.&Y.]
*PRACTICE AREAS: Banking; Corporate; Finance.
Kyman, Roberta H. .......................... '42 '79 L.1136 J.D. 12304 Santa Monica Blvd.
Kyriacou, Gig .......................... '59 '84 C.800 A.B. L.1066 J.D. [Plotkin,M.&K.]
La, Carolyn Y. .......................... '67 '92 C.112 B.A. L.1068 J.D. Asian Pacific Amer. Legal Ctr.
**LaBounty, Eric B.** .......................... '63 '94 C.147 B.A. L.1137 J.D. [Ⓐ Astor&P.]
**LaBounty, Mark E.** .......................... '53 '79 C.1042 B.S. L.426 J.D. [Astor&P.]
*PRACTICE AREAS: Estate Planning; Probate; Real Estate Law; Corporate Law.
Labovitch, Gerald .......................... '42 '73 C.1077 B.S. L.1136 J.D. 12400 Wilshire Blvd.
Labovitz, Laurence B. .......................... '46 '76 C.1077 B.A. L.809 J.D. 3055 Wilshire Blvd.
Labowe, Richard W. .......................... '57 '82 C.112 B.A. L.426 J.D. [Labowe,L.&H.]
Labowe, Ronald B., (AV) .......................... '30 '53 C.112 B.A. L.1068 LL.B. [Labowe,L.&H.]
Labowe, Labowe & Hoffman, (AV) .......................... 1631 Beverly Blvd., 2nd Fl.
**La Chance, James T.** .......................... '57 '82 C.1042 B.A. L.426 J.D. [Ⓐ Kirtland&P.]
*LANGUAGES: French.
Lachs, Stephen M. .......................... '39 '64 C.112 B.A. L.1068 LL.B. Supr. Ct. J.
**Lack, Walter J.**, (AV) .......................... '48 '73 C&L.426 B.A., J.D. [Engstrom,L.&L.]
*LANGUAGES: French.
*PRACTICE AREAS: Complex Business Litigation; Insurance Policy Interpretation; Bad Faith; Environmental Coverage; Professional Liability.
Lackner, Michael .......................... '53 '82 C.112 A.B. L.145 J.D. Dist. Coun., I.R.S.
**Laco, John A.** .......................... '64 '92 C.602 B.S.E.E. L.426 J.D. [Ⓐ O'Melveny&M.]
La Croix, Strohe D. .......................... '65 '91 C.112 B.A. L.800 J.D. [Casterline&A.]

**Ladas & Parry, (AV)**
**5670 Wilshire Boulevard, 90036⊙**
**Telephone: 213-934-2300 Telex: 240423 Cable Address: "Lawlan LSA" Telecopier: 213-934-0202**
**URL: http://www.ladas.com**
**Members of Firm: Richard P. Berg; Henry Klein; Colin P. Abrahams; Mavis S. Gallenson; Francie R. Gorowitz. Associates: Iris Smith-Hess; Richard J. Paciulan (Not admitted in CA); John Palmer. Of Counsel: Ira M. Siegel; Kam C. Louie.**
**Patent, Trademark, Copyright, Unfair Competition, Licensing, Entertainment and Litigation.**
**New York, New York Office: 26 West 61st Street. Telephone: 212-708-1800. Telex: 233288. Telecopy: 212-246-8959. Cable Address: "Lawlan New York".**
**Chicago, Illinois Office: 224 South Michigan Avenue. Telephone: 312-427-1300. Telex: 203649. Telecopy: 312-427-6663; 312-427-6668. Cable Address: "Lawlan Chicago".**
**London, England Office: High Holborn House, 52-54 High Holborn, WC1V 6RR. Telephone: 44-71-242-5566. Telex: 262433 MONREF G. Telecopy: 44-71-405-1908 (Groups 2 & 3). Cable Address: "Lawlan London W.C.1".**
**Munich, Germany Office: Altheimer Eck 2, D-80331 Munich. Telephone: (089) 269077. Fax: (089) 269040. Cable Address: "Lawlan Munich".**

*See Professional Biographies, LOS ANGELES, CALIFORNIA*

Ladenberger, Don A., (AV) .... '14 '38 C.933 B.A. L.352 J.D. 777 S. Figueroa St., 37th Fl.
Ladner, John .......................... '46 '73 C.112 A.B. L.426 J.D. L.A. Co. Mun. Ct. Comr.‡
Lafaille, David .......................... '40 '67 C.112 A.B. L.1068 LL.B. 1900 Ave. of the Stars
**Laffey, Thomas P.**, (AV) .......................... '48 '73 C.602 B.B.A. L.813 J.D. [Folger L.&K.]⊙

**La Follette, Johnson, De Haas, Fesler & Ames, A Professional Corporation, (AV)**
**865 South Figueroa Street, Suite 3100, 90017-5443⊙**
**Telephone: 213-426-3600 Fax: 213-426-3650**
**John T. La Follette (1922-1990); Daren T. Johnson; Louis H. De Haas; Donald C. Fesler; Dennis K. Ames (Manager/Shareholder, Santa Ana Office); Alfred W. Gerisch, Jr.; Brian W. Birnie; Peter J. Zomber; Robert E. Kelly, Jr.; G. Kelley Reid, Jr. (Resident, San Francisco Office); Dennis J. Sinclitico; Christopher C. Cannon (Resident, Santa Ana Office); Dorothy B. Reyes; Steven R. Odell (Santa Ana and Riverside Offices); Christopher L. Thomas (Santa Ana and Riverside Offices); Robert K. Warford (Resident, Riverside Office); John L. Supple (Resident, San Francisco Office); Vincent D. Lapointe; Steven J. Joffe; Mark M. Stewart; Bradley J. McGirr (Resident, Santa Ana Office); Sydney La Branche Merritt; Mark S. Rader (Resident, Riverside Office); Michael R. Packer (Resident, Santa Ana Office);—Peter R. Bing; Larry P. Nathenson; Donald R. Beck (Resident, Santa Ana Office); David J. Ozeran; Mark B. Guterman; Terry A. Woodward (Resident, Santa Ana Office); Stephen C. Dreher (Resident, Santa Ana Office); Tatiana M. Schultz (Resident, San Francisco Office); Peter E. Theophilos (Resident, San Francisco Office); Deborah A. Cowley; Kent T. Brandmeyer; Garry O. Moses; Jeffery R. Erickson (Resident, Riverside Office); Michael J. O'Connor; Elizabeth Anne Scherer (Resident, Santa Ana Office); Hugh R. Burns; Stephen K. Hiura; James G. Wold; Eileen S. Lemmon (Resident, Riverside, Office); David M. Wright; Larry E. White (Resident, Riverside Office); Michelle McCoy Wolfe; William T. Gray (Resident, Santa Ana Office); Daniel D. Sorenson (Resident, Riverside Office); Joanne Rosendin (Resident, San Francisco Office); Henry P. Canvel (Resident, San Francisco Office); Jay B. Lake; Erin L. Muellenberg (Resident, Riverside Office); Phyllis M. Winston (Resident, Riverside Office); John Calfee Mulvana (Resident, Santa Ana Office); David L. Bell; Brian T. Chu (Resident, Santa Ana Office); John Hammond; David Peim; Daniel V. Kohls (Resident, San Francisco Office); Joel E. D. Odou; Henry M. Su; Richard K. Kay; Annette A. Pelton; Brad D. Citron; Caren R. Weakley; Kevin J. Price; Arezou Khonsari; John Beall (Resident, Santa Ana Office); Walter H. Kubelun; Thomas S. Alch; E. Christine Vartanian (Resident, Santa Ana Office); Kristi A. Schifrin (Resident, San Francisco Office); Mary Katherine Doherty.**
**Civil Litigation, Employment Law, Medical Malpractice, Professional Liability, Insurance Defense Coverage and Bad Faith, Construction Law and Product Liability.**
**A list of References will be furnished upon request.**
**San Francisco, California Office: 50 California Street, Suite 3350. Telephone: 415-433-7610. Telecopier: 415-392-7541.**

(This Listing Continued)

**La Follette, Johnson, De Haas, Fesler & Ames, A Professional Corporation (Continued)**
**Santa Ana, California Office: 2677 North Main Street, Suite 901. Telephone: 714-558-7008. Telecopier: 714-972-0379.**
**Riverside, California Office: 3403 Tenth Street, Suite 820. Telephone: 714-275-9192. Fax: 714-275-9249.**

*See Professional Biographies, LOS ANGELES, CALIFORNIA*

**Lafond, Gerard A., Jr.** .......................... '54 '86 C.112 B.A. L.809 J.D. [Ⓐ Pollak,V.&F.]
Lager, Marvin M. .......................... '54 '79 C.994 B.A. L.178 J.D. Mun. J.

**Lagerlof, Senecal, Bradley & Swift, LLP**
**(See Pasadena)**

Lagin, Eric L. .......................... '53 '78 C.112 B.A. L.36 J.D. 116 N. Robertson Blvd.
**Lagle, John F.**, (AV) .......................... '38 '67 C.112 B.S. L.1068 J.D. [Ⓒ Barbosa G.&B.]
*PRACTICE AREAS: Real Property Law; Corporations Law; Finance Law; Securities Law.
Lagomarcino, John P., Jr. '36 '62 C.31 A.B. L.145 J.D.
(adm. in AZ; not adm. in CA) V.P., Amer. High Speed Rail Corp.
**La Guardia, Maryanne**, (AV) .......................... '43 '75 C.768 B.A. L.800 J.D. [Trope&T.]
*PRACTICE AREAS: Family Law.
**Lahammer, Douglas E.** .......................... '63 '90 C&L.494 B.A., J.D. [Ⓐ Paul,H.J.&W.]
**Lahana, James R.** .......................... '51 '76 C.112 B.A. L.1066 J.D. [Ⓒ Davis W.T.]
*PRACTICE AREAS: Health Care; Medical Staff Law.
**Laidig, Craig A.** .......................... '55 '92 C.112 B.A. L.426 J.D. [Ⓐ Daniels,B.&F.]
Laidman, Daniel H. .......................... '32 '72 C.112 B.S. L.426 J.D. 8425 W. 3rd St.
**Laifman, Jay S.** .......................... '63 '88 C.1169 B.A. L.1065 J.D. [Ⓐ Pircher,N.&M.]
**Lainer, Ilene** '58 '84 C.910 B.A. L.1019 J.D.
(adm. in NJ; not adm. in CA) [Grotta,G.&H.]⊙
Laird, Peter F. .......................... '44 '70 C.608 B.A. L.276 J.D. [Edelstein,L.&S.]
Laites, Sandra L. .......................... '49 '75 C.66 B.A. L.93 J.D. 1010 Wilshire Blvd.
**Lake, David N.** .......................... '69 '95 C.1036 B.A. L.767 J.D. [Ⓐ Christensen,M.F.J.G.W.&S.]
*PRACTICE AREAS: Litigation.
**Lake, Jay B.** .......................... '60 '88 C.112 B.S. L.426 J.D. [Ⓐ La Follette,J.D.F.&A.]
*PRACTICE AREAS: Medical Malpractice Defense.
**Lake, Timothy D.** .......................... '49 '74 C.800 B.A. L.809 J.D. [Tharpe&H.]
*PRACTICE AREAS: Construction Accident Litigation; Complex Fire Litigation.
**Lallas, Tom, (P.C.)**, (AV) .......................... '51 '75 C&L.813 B.A., J.D. [Levy,S.&L.]
*PRACTICE AREAS: Commercial, Bankruptcy and Real Estate Litigation and Transactions.
**Lam, Cynthia C.** .......................... '61 '88 C.112 B.A. L.990 J.D. [Ⓐ Stall,A.&G.]
**Lam, James F.** .......................... '69 '95 C.188 B.S.I.L.R. L.800 J.D. [Ⓐ Sheppard,M.R.&H.]
*PRACTICE AREAS: Labor and Employment Law; General Business Litigation.
**Lam, Judy Man-Ling** .......................... '65 '94 C.605 A.B. L.425 J.D. [Ⓐ Frandzel&S.]
*LANGUAGES: Chinese.
*PRACTICE AREAS: Litigation; Transactional; Banking Law; Commercial Law; Bankruptcy.
**La Mar, Michelle M.** .......................... '65 '92 C.112 B.A. L.426 J.D. [Ⓐ Booth,M.&S.]
Lamb, Brian J. .......................... '59 '84 C.37 B.A. L.1066 J.D. 355 S. Grand Ave.
**Lamb, David A.** .......................... '53 '79 C.770 B.S.C. L.1068 J.D. [Milbank,T.H.&M.]
**Lamb, Kevin J.** .......................... '60 '86 C&L.477 B.A., J.D. [Lamb&B.]
*PRACTICE AREAS: Real Property Law; Oil and Gas; Work-Outs; Reorganizations.

**Lamb & Baute**
**601 South Figueroa Street, Suite 4100, 90017**
**Telephone: 213-630-5000 Fax: 213-683-1225**
**Mark D. Baute; David P. Crochetiere; Kevin J. Lamb; Karl J. Lott; Dale M. Struman.**
**General Practice.**

*See Professional Biographies, LOS ANGELES, CALIFORNIA*

**Lambe, Deborah C.** .......................... '60 '95 C.112 A.B. L.1066 J.D. [Ⓐ Latham&W.]
Lambeck, Debra Tilson '58 '84 C.475 B.A. L.426 J.D.
V.P. & Gen. Coun., Daniel, Mann, Johnson & Mendenhall
Lambert, Mark A. .......................... '61 '86 C.112 A.B. L.1065 J.D. Dep. City Atty.
Lambert, Marnie C. .......................... '67 '93 C.473 B.A. L.990 J.D. 333 S. Grand Ave.
Lambert, Susan H. .......................... '50 '76 C.668 B.A. L.1065 J.D. 7th Fl., 515 S. Figueroa St.
**Lambert, Thomas P., (A Professional Corporation)**, (AV) '46 '71
C.426 B.A. L.1068 J.D. [Mitchell,S.&K.]
*PRACTICE AREAS: Securities Litigation; Intellectual Property Litigation; Antitrust Litigation.
**Lambillotte, Diane M.** .......................... '55 '93 C.1075 B.A. L.426 J.D. [Ⓐ Riordan&M.]
Lambirth, Dena J. Hayden .......................... '58 '87 C.112 B.S. L.426 J.D. [Schmid&V.] ‡
**Lambirth, Timothy A., (P.C.)**, (AV) .......................... '53 '78 C.112 B.A. L.1148 J.D. [Ivanjack&L.]
Lambrecht, Nancy S. .......................... '52 '92 C.966 B.A. L.809 J.D. 4215 Glencoe Ave.
**Lambros, John M.** .......................... '68 '95 C.597 B.A. L.846 J.D. [Ⓐ O'Melveny&M.]
*LANGUAGES: Greek.
*PRACTICE AREAS: Litigation.
**Lamison, Eric R.** .......................... '70 '95 C.475 B.S. L.477 J.D. [Ⓐ Kirkland&E.]
*PRACTICE AREAS: Litigation.
**Lamken, Mark L.**, (AV) .......................... '33 '61 C.112 A.B. L.1068 LL.B. [Richards,W.&G.]
*PRACTICE AREAS: Real Estate Development and Finance; Common Interest Developments.
**Lammas, Mark T.** .......................... '66 '92 C.112 B.A. L.1066 J.D. [Ⓐ Cox,C.&N.]
**LaMond, Christian F.** .......................... '66 '94 C.884 B.A. L.1148 J.D. [Ⓐ Koletsky,M.&F.]
*PRACTICE AREAS: Construction Defect Defense Litigation.
**LaMontagne, Ralph S., Jr.** .......................... '54 '79 C.112 B.A. L.809 J.D. [Bronson,B.&M.]
*PRACTICE AREAS: Insurance Coverage; Civil Appellate Law.
**LaMothe, Louise A., (A Professional Corporation)**, (AV) '46 '72
C&L.813 B.A., J.D. [Ⓒ Bird,M.B.W.&M.]
LaMothe, Rachel M. .......................... '63 '90 C.112 B.A. L.1068 J.D. 633 W. 5th St.
Lampkin, David P. .......................... '45 '71 C&L.188 B.A., J.D. 2410 Crest View Dr.
**Lamport, Stanley W.** .......................... '57 '82 C.800 A.B. L.597 J.D. [Cox,C.&N.]
*REPORTED CASES: %italic; Thompson v. Allert%roman; , 233 C.A. 3d 1462 (1991).
*PRACTICE AREAS: Civil Litigation; Land Use Law; Legal Ethics; Insurance Law.
**Lancaster, William H.** .......................... '51 '86 C.446 B.A. L.893 J.D. [Andrews&K.]
*PRACTICE AREAS: Business Litigation.
**Lance, Nicole D.** .......................... '66 '93 C.112 B.A. L.1067 J.D. [Robinson,D.B.&K.]
*PRACTICE AREAS: Bankruptcy.
Lancer, Phillip C. .......................... '40 '67 C.1033 B.S.B.A. L.477 J.D. 139 N. Mansfield Ave.
**Land, Vicki E.**, (AV) .......................... '40 '76 C.326 B.A. L.846 J.D. [Brown,W.&C.]
*PRACTICE AREAS: Litigation.
**Landau, Eric N.** .......................... '57 '82 C&L.910 B.A., J.D. [Christensen,M.F.J.G.W.&S.]
*PRACTICE AREAS: Civil Litigation; Securities Litigation; Corporate Governance.
**Landau, Eugene J.**, (AV) .......................... '14 '37 L.1001 LL.B. [Gilbert,K.C.&J.]
*PRACTICE AREAS: Estate Planning and Probate.
**Landau, Jennifer** .......................... '65 '91 C.31 B.A. L.145 J.D. [Ⓐ Sidley&A.]
*PRACTICE AREAS: Litigation.
**Landau, Lewis R.** .......................... '63 '89 C.1044 B.A. L.426 J.D. [McDermott,W.&E.]
Landau, Paul H. .......................... '40 '88 C.1097 B.A. L.1136 J.D. 5967 W. 3rd St.
**Landau, Rodger M.** .......................... '63 '90 C.311 B.A. L.145 J.D. [McDermott,W.&E.]
Landau, Ronald Barry .......................... '57 '82 C.705 B.A. L.228 J.D. Tax Coun., ARCO
Landau, Stephen R., (A Prof. Law Corp.) '39 '65
C&L.800 B.S., J.D. 1875 Century Park E.
**Lande, David** .......................... '67 '94 C&L.659 B.A., J.D. [Ⓐ Ziffren,B.B.&F.]
*PRACTICE AREAS: Entertainment Law.

**Lande, Gary E.**, (AV) .......... '34 '66 C.793 B.S. L.904 J.D. [Oppenheimer P.S.] (Pat.)
*PRACTICE AREAS: Intellectual Property.
Lande, Steven A., (AV) ......... '37 '64 C.112 B.S. L.1068 LL.B. 1888 Century Park E.‡
**Lander, Todd M.** .......... '68 '94 C.05 B.A. L.940 J.D. [Ⓐ Billet&K.]
Landes, Stanley J. .......... '49 '79 C.102 B.A. L.809 J.D. 8955 Beverly Blvd.
**Landesman, Laura**, (AV) .......... '59 '82 C.112 B.A. L.1068 J.D. [Ⓐ Wasser,R.&C.]
**Landfair, Stanley W.** .......... '54 '78 C.108 B.A. L.276 J.D. [McKenna&C.]
*PRACTICE AREAS: Environmental Law.
Landin, Dennis J. .......... '55 '80 C.605 B.A. L.1068 J.D. Chf. Dep. Fed. Pub. Def.
**Landis, Kipp A.** .......... '66 '95 C&L.990 B.A., J.D. [Ⓐ Mendes&M.]
Landis, William .......... '26 '57 C.347 B.B.S. L.800 J.D. 1901 Ave. of the Stars‡
**Landrum, Douglas F.**, (AV) ......... '49 '74 C.260 B.S.B.A. L.1065 J.D. [Jones,D.R.&P.]
**Landry, Edward A.**, (AV) .......... '39 '65 C.420 B.A. L.1068 J.D. [Musick,P.&G.]
*PRACTICE AREAS: Trusts and Estates; Non-Profit and Charitable Organizations.
**Landsberg, Barry S.** .......... '55 '80 C.446 B.A. L.245 J.D. [Manatt,P.&P.]
*PRACTICE AREAS: Health Care; Business Litigation.
**Landsberg, Perry L.**, (AV) .......... '56 '82 C.112 B.A. L.1065 J.D. [Sidley&A.]
*PRACTICE AREAS: Bankruptcy Law.
Lane, Franklin K., III .......... '24 '49 C&L.893 B.A., LL.B. 12304 Santa Monica Blvd.
**Lane, Jeff W.** .......... '50 '76 C.563 B.A. L.569 J.D. [Basile&L.]
*PRACTICE AREAS: Taxation Law; Estate Planning; Business Law.
**Lane, Mary D.** .......... '50 '76 C.66 B.A. L.1068 J.D. [Loeb&L.]
*PRACTICE AREAS: Insolvency and Workouts; Entertainment; Real Estate.
Lane, Mitchel Jay ..... '48 '75 C.107 B.A. L.1068 J.D. Gen. Coun., Dr. Ludington Toy Co.
Lane, Robert Gerhart, (AV) '31 '60 C&L.800 A.B., LL.B.
Gen. Coun., University of Southern California
**Lane, Robert T.** .... '59 '85 C&L.800 B.S., J.D. Sr. Coun., Transamerica Financial Servs.

**Lane Powell Spears Lubersky LLP, (AV)** BR
**A Partnership including Professional Corporations**
**333 South Hope Street, Suite 2400, 90071**⊙
**Telephone: 213-680-1010 FAX: 213-680-1784**
**Members of Firm: Allan M. Bower; Edith N. Dinneen; John J. Geary, Jr.; Kathryn R. Janssen; Laurence F. Janssen; Ruth D. Kahn; Matthew P. Kesner; George J. Koelzer; Lawrence P. Riff; Russell W. Roten; Carolyn J. Shields; Simon D. Wright; Robert J. Zapf (Not admitted in CA). Associates: Daniel R. Blakey; Celeste V. De Petris; Joshua S. Force; Robert M. Hupe; Kenneth W. Lord (Not admitted in CA); Jo-Ann Horn Maynard; Michael M. Murata; Constance E. Norton; Jay E. Smith; Lisa Stevens; Cynthia T. Soldwedel; Thomas H. Van Horn (Not admitted in CA); Philip Young.**
**Admiralty, Alternative Dispute Resolution, Antitrust, Appellate Practice, Aviation, Banking and Financial Institutions, Bankruptcy and Reorganizations, Construction, Employment Law, Corporate Finance, Emerging Companies, Employee Benefits, Environmental, Forest Products and Natural Resources, Hospital and Healthcare, Immigration, Insurance, Intellectual Property and Computer Law, International Transactions, Litigation, Public Finance, Real Estate and Land Use, Retailing, Securities, Taxation, Toxic Torts, Transportation, Trusts and Estates, White Collar Criminal Law.**
**Other Offices at: Seattle, Washington; Portland, Oregon; Anchorage, Alaska; San Francisco, California; Olympia and Mount Vernon, Washington; Fairbanks, Alaska; London, England.**

***See Professional Biographies, LOS ANGELES, CALIFORNIA***

**Lang, Andrea J.** .......... '62 '95 C.1077 B.A. L.1148 J.D. [Ⓐ Bottum&F.]
**Lang, Dudley M.**, (AV) .......... '36 '63 C.112 A.B. L.1068 J.D. [Stephens,B.&L.]
*PRACTICE AREAS: Taxation Law.

**Lang, Turley, Nevers & Palazzo, A Professional Law Corporation**
**(See Westlake Village)**

**Langan, Kenneth J.** '55 '81
C.276 B.S.F.S. L.178 J.D. [Chadbourne&P.] (⊙London, England)
*LANGUAGES: Spanish.
**Langberg, Barry B., (A Professional Corporation)**, (AV) '42 '71
C&L.767 J.D. [Langberg,C.&D.]
*REPORTED CASES: Carol Burnett vs. National Enquirer, 144 Cal. App. 3d 991, 193 Cal. Rptr. 206 (1983).
*PRACTICE AREAS: Entertainment and the Arts; Litigation; Libel, Slander and Defamation.
**Langberg, Mitchell J.** .......... '68 '94 C.464 B.S. L.800 J.D. [Langberg,C.&D.]

**Langberg, Cohn & Drooz, (AV)** BR
**A Partnership including a Professional Corporation**
**12100 Wilshire Boulevard Suite 1650, 90025**
**Telephone: 310-979-3200 Telecopier: 310-979-3220**
**Barry B. Langberg (A Professional Corporation); Eileen M. Cohn; Deborah Drooz; Beth F. Dumas; Mitchell J. Langberg; Mary L. Muir; Brian A. Murphy. Of Counsel: Peter C. Richards (A Professional Corporation); Gilbert Gaynor; Polin Cohanne; Milton Segal.**
**Libel and Slander, Entertainment Litigation, Intellectual Property Litigation, General Business Litigation, Real Estate Litigation.**

***See Professional Biographies, LOS ANGELES, CALIFORNIA***

**Lange, Cynthia J.**, (AV) .......... '59 '86 C.101 B.A. L.809 J.D. [Fragomen,D.&B.]
*LANGUAGES: German and Spanish.
Lange, Ellen E. .......... '64 '91 C.112 B.A. L.800 J.D. 633 W. 5th St.
**Lange, Joseph J. M.** .......... '61 '87 C.112 B.A. L.426 J.D. [Ⓒ Lebovits&D.]
*REPORTED CASES: Villa Pacific Building Company v. Superior Court, 223 Cal. App. 328 (1991).
*PRACTICE AREAS: Products Liability; Professional Negligence; Aviation Law; Insurance Bad Faith; Personal Injury.
**Lange, Robert M.** .......... '53 '80 C.912 B.S. L.477 J.D. [Kleinberg L.L.B.&C.]
*PRACTICE AREAS: Entertainment Law; Copyright Law.
**Langenberg, Peter M.** .......... '45 '77 C.674 A.B. L.1065 J.D. [Hughes H.&R.]
*LANGUAGES: Japanese.
*PRACTICE AREAS: International; Intellectual Property; General Commercial; Corporate.
**Langer, Greg R.** .......... '56 '81 C&L.276 B.S.B.A., J.D. [Ⓐ Troop M.S.&P.]
*PRACTICE AREAS: Real Estate.
**Langer, Major A.**, (AV) .......... '42 '66 C.1044 B.A. L.724 LL.B. [Perona,L.&B.]⊙
Langfus, Howard D. .......... '43 '78 C.112 B.S. L.1095 J.D. 6922 Hollywood Blvd.
Langfus, Stanley A. .......... '45 '71 C.112 A.B. L.169 J.D. 6922 Hollywood Blvd.
**Langley, Lynn** .......... '51 '86 C.112 B.A. L.800 J.D. [Ⓐ N.M.Dolin]
*PRACTICE AREAS: Family Law.
**Langlois, Joseph A.** .......... '58 '88 C.112 B.A. L.101 J.D. [Ⓐ Nachshin&W.]
*LANGUAGES: Spanish.
Langlois, Joseph T. .......... '56 '90 C.668 B.A. L.145 J.D. 726 Claymont Dr.
**Langs, Michael** .......... '40 '68 C.800 B.A. L.61 J.D. [Loeb&L.]
*PRACTICE AREAS: Structured Finance; Land Use; Workout and Development Law.
**Langsfeld, Peter E.** .......... '47 '88 C.1097 B.S. L.809 J.D. [Barbosa G.&B.]
*LANGUAGES: Hungarian and Spanish.
*PRACTICE AREAS: Municipal Tort Defense Law; Eminent Domain Law; Criminal Law.
**Langslet, Julie A.** .......... '54 '86 C&L.800 B.S., J.D. [Ⓐ Rossbacher&Assoc.]
*PRACTICE AREAS: Appellate; Business Litigation; Federal Habeas Corpus.
Langston, Cassandra Green '48 '92
C.800 B.A. L.426 J.D. Asst. Coun., Co. Metro. Transp. Auth.
**Lanphere, Darci A.** .......... '68 '93 C.103 A.B. L.1066 J.D. [Ⓐ Latham&W.]
Lansford, Steven D. .......... '55 '80 C.800 B.A. L.809 J.D. 1999 Ave. of the Stars
Lanter, Marvin S. .......... '51 '76 C.102 B.A. L.284 J.D. 1925 Century Park E.
**Lantry, Daniel B.** .......... '65 '91 C.112 B.S. L.1066 J.D. [Ⓐ McDermott,W.&E.]
**Lantry, Kevin T.** .......... '58 '91 C.636 B.A. L.1066 J.D. [Ⓐ Sidley&A.]
*PRACTICE AREAS: Bankruptcy Law.
**Lanyard, Eric M.** .......... '71 '96 C.1036 B.A. L.309 J.D. [Ⓐ Latham&W.]
LaPallo, Francis J. .......... '48 '77 C.705 B.S. L.273 J.D. 11355 W. Olympic Blvd.
Lapesarde, Kyle-Marie .......... '51 '83 C.800 B.A. L.1068 J.D. 6535 Wilshire Blvd.
Lapidus, Michael H. .......... '49 '73 C.112 A.B. L.1066 J.D. [M.H.Lapidus]
Lapidus, Michael H., Inc. .......... 10960 Wilshire Blvd.
Lapin, David A., (AV) .......... '52 '76 C.154 B.A. L.178 J.D. [D.A.Lapin]
Lapin, Herbert R. .......... '37 '65 C.36 L.809 LL.B. Dep. Dist. Atty.
Lapin, Ian S., (AV) .......... '39 '70 C.800 B.A. L.809 J.D. 12400 Wilshire Blvd.
Lapin, Jeffrey C. ..... '56 '83 C.112 B.A. L.426 J.D. Pres. & COO, Starwood Lodging Tr.
Lapin, David A., P.C., (AV) .......... 10100 Santa Monica Blvd.
**Lapinski, John A.**, (AV) .......... '47 '76 C.645 B.S. L.1136 J.D. [Clark&T.]
*PRACTICE AREAS: Banking; Credit Law; Bankruptcy; Creditors Rights; Collateral Recovery.
LaPlace, Anne Marie '64 '94
C.755 B.A. L.800 J.D. 15456 Ventura Blvd. 5th Fl. (Sherman Oaks)
**Lapointe, Vincent D.** .......... '53 '82 C.1154 B.A. L.809 J.D. [La Follette,J.D.F.&A.]
*PRACTICE AREAS: General Liability; Public Entities; Medical Malpractice.
**LaPorte, Lawrence R.** .......... '61 '87 C&L.494 B.S.M.E., J.D. [Lyon&L.]
*PRACTICE AREAS: Complex and Technical Litigation including Patent, Trademark, Copyright; Unfair Competition; Intellectual Property.
LaPorte, Richard G. '44 '71 C.602 B.A. L.228 J.D.
Sr. V.P. & Asst. Chf. Coun., Wells Fargo Bk., N.A.
**Lapota, Jeffrey**, (AV) .......... '46 '75 C.112 B.S. L.309 J.D. [Cox,C.&N.]
*PRACTICE AREAS: Estate Planning Law; Probate Law; Tax Law.

**Lapp, Stuart W., (AV) '30 '57 C.800 A.B. L.1066 LL.B.**
**700 South Flower Street, Suite 1100, 90017**
**Telephone: 213-627-7760 Fax: 213-627-3750**
**General Civil and Trial Practice. Corporation, Insurance, Probate, Trusts, Life Insurance, Mortgage and Real Estate Law.**
**Reference: Security Pacific National Bank (Wilshire Grand Office).**

***See Professional Biographies, LOS ANGELES, CALIFORNIA***

**Lappen, Chester I., (A Professional Corporation)**, (AV) '19 '43
C.112 B.A. L.309 LL.B. [Mitchell,S.&K.]
*PRACTICE AREAS: Corporate Law; Real Estate Law.
**Lappen, Jeremy A.** .......... '70 '96 C.112 B.A. L.800 J.D. [Ⓐ Mitchell,S.&K.]
*PRACTICE AREAS: Corporate.
Lappen, Miyuki M. .......... '42 '77 C.112 B.A. L.767 J.D. State Bar of Calif.
**Lappen, Timothy**, (AV) .......... '47 '75 C.112 A.B. L.1068 J.D. [Ⓒ Jeffer,M.B.&M.]
*PRACTICE AREAS: General Business; Real Estate; Corporate.
**La Prade, Jennie L.** .......... '53 '78 C.112 A.B. L.800 J.D. [Pillsbury M.&S.]
Lardiere, Eric G. .......... '54 '83 C.112 B.A. L.1068 J.D. 2049 Century Park E.
**Larin, Michael J.** .......... '50 '77 C.823 B.A. L.809 J.D. [Lynberg&W.]
**Larkin, Christopher C.** .......... '55 '81 C.813 B.A. L.178 J.D. [Small L.&K.]
*LANGUAGES: German.
*PRACTICE AREAS: Trademark; Copyright; Litigation.
**Larkin, Joan Kupersmith** .......... '53 '77 C.569 B.A. L.669 J.D. [Small L.&K.]
*PRACTICE AREAS: Trademark, Copyright and Unfair Competition.
**Larkin, William A.** .......... '64 '91 C.197 B.A. L.112 J.D. [Ⓐ Hooper,L.&B.]
*LANGUAGES: French.
**Larmore, Thomas R.**, (AV) .......... '44 '69 C.112 B.S. L.1068 J.D. [Pillsbury M.&S.]
Larner, Andrew S. .......... '64 '90 C.918 B.A. L.178 J.D. 400 S Hope St.
**Larsen, Julie Dean** .......... '59 '84 C&L.546 B.A., J.D. [Arter&H.]
**Larsen, Melodie K.** .......... '51 '83 C.1097 B.A. L.1066 J.D. [Rintala,S.J.&R.]
**Larsen, Paul A.** .......... '63 '88 C.112 A.B. L.1068 J.D. [Ku,F.L.&C.]
*PRACTICE AREAS: Litigation; Intellectual Property; Business Law.
**Larson, Arnold D.**, (AV) .......... '51 '77 C.112 B.A. L.809 J.D. [Iverson,Y.P.&H.]
*PRACTICE AREAS: Civil Litigation and Appellate Practice; Products Liability; Wrongful Termination and Employment Discrimination; Libel and Defamation; General Business and Commercial Litigation.
**Larson, Charles A.** .......... '52 '78 C.813 A.B. L.976 J.D. [Gibson,D.&C.]
*PRACTICE AREAS: Tax Law; Probate and Estate Planning.
**Larson, Douglas N.**, (AV) '52 '77 C.688 B.S.C.E. L.502 J.D.
[Oppenheimer P.S.] (Pat.)
*PRACTICE AREAS: Patent Law.
**Larson, Jennifer L.** .......... '70 '95 C.112 B.A. L.1065 J.D. [Ⓐ Cozen&O.]
**Larson, John B.** .......... '54 '83 C.490 B.S. L.809 J.D. [Roper&F.]
*PRACTICE AREAS: Environmental Insurance Litigation; Government Law; Construction Defect Litigation; Public Entity Law; Subrogation Law.
**Larson, Kirstin M.** .......... '70 '95 C.112 B.A. L.809 J.D. [Ⓐ Baker&H.]
*PRACTICE AREAS: General Litigation.
Larson, Marcia J. ........ '61 '86 C.1074 B.A. L.800 J.D. 1925 Century Park, E., 22nd Fl.
Larson, Sandra Twiss .......... '54 '83 C.112 B.A. L.809 J.D. State Bar of Calif.

**Larwill & Wolfe, (AV)**
**1631 West Beverly Boulevard, 90026**
**Telephone: 213-481-7377**
**Members of Firm: George R. Larwill (1895-1967); Charles W. Wolfe; Maureen F. Wolfe Binder.**
**General Civil and Trial Practice in all State and Federal Courts. Corporation, Business, Real Property, Estate Planning and Taxation, Trust and Probate Law.**

Lasarow, William J. .......... '22 '51 C.260 B.A. L.813 LL.B. U.S. Bkrptcy. J.
**Lasater, Richard W., II**, (AV) .......... '48 '74 C.813 B.A. L.1065 J.D. [Stephens,B.&L.]
*PRACTICE AREAS: Real Estate; Corporate and Corporate Securities; Probate; Estate Planning.
**Lascheid, Elizabeth M.** .......... '55 '91 C&L.426 B.A., J.D. [Ⓐ Wickwire G.]
*PRACTICE AREAS: Commercial; Corporate; Construction Law; Litigation.

**Lascher & Lascher, A Professional Corporation**
**(See Ventura)**

Lash, David A. ........ '55 '80 C.112 B.A. L.1068 J.D. Exec. Dir., Bet Tzedek Legal Servs.
Lasher, Allan .......... '35 '61 C.112 A.B. L.1068 LL.B. Mun. J.
Lashley, Lenore '34 '81 C.112 M.S.W. L.1065 J.D.
State Bar of Calif., Off. of Trial Coun.
Lasker, Edward, (AV) .......... '12 '55 C.976 A.B. L.1068 LL.B. 444 S. Flower St.
Laski, Mortimer L. .......... '40 '70 C.563 B.B.A. L.1009 J.D. [Laski&G.]
Laski & Gordon .......... 2049 Century Park E.
Laskin, Herbert .......... '35 '63 C.112 B.S. L.1068 LL.B. [H.Laskin]
**Laskin, Jared** .......... '62 '87 C.910 B.A. L.1068 J.D. [Ⓐ Goldman&K.]
*REPORTED CASES: Bergen v. Wood, 14 Cal. App. 4th 854, 18 Cal. Rptr. 2d 75 (1993).
*PRACTICE AREAS: Civil Litigation; Palimony Defense; General Business.

**Laskin & Graham**
**(See Glendale)**

Laskin, Herbert, A Law Corporation .......... 3145 Coolidge Ave.
**Lasko, George** .......... '68 '93 C.112 B.A. L.309 J.D. [Ⓐ Chadbourne&P.]
**Lasky, Aric H.** .......... '67 '94 C.112 B.A. L.800 J.D. [Ⓐ Paul,H.J.&W.]
Lasky, Gilbert P. .......... '31 '79 C.112 B.A. L.1136 J.D. 1432 Camden Ave.
**Lasky, Paul H.** .......... '40 '87 C.453 Sc.B. L.1136 J.D. [Ⓐ Tharpe&H.]
*PRACTICE AREAS: Construction Law; Toxic Tort; Product Liability; Professional Liability.
**Lasman, Edwin I.**, (AV) .......... '55 '82 C.112 B.A. L.1068 J.D. [Ⓒ Case,K.B.&W.]⊙
*LANGUAGES: French.
*PRACTICE AREAS: Corporate Law; Real Estate; Civil Litigation.
**Lasnik, Larry T.** .......... '47 '74 C.112 B.A. L.1068 J.D. [Ⓐ Gibbs,G.L.&A.]
*PRACTICE AREAS: Construction Litigation; Business Litigation; Insurance Defense.
**La Soya, Ray** .......... '64 '92 C.940 B.A. L.976 J.D. [Ⓐ Fried,F.H.S.&J.]
**Latek, Kevin P.** .......... '70 '96 C.276 B.S.B.A. L.893 J.D. [Ⓐ Kirkland&E.]
*PRACTICE AREAS: Litigation.
**Latham, J. Al, Jr.** .......... '51 '76 C.976 B.A. L.880 J.D. [Paul,H.J.&W.]

CAA273P

CALIFORNIA—LOS ANGELES

MARTINDALE-HUBBELL LAW DIRECTORY 1997

**Latham, Robert A., III** . . . . . . . . . . . . '53 '82 C.228 A.B. L.734 J.D. [Ⓐ Wilson,E.M.E.&D.]

**Latham & Watkins, (AV)** BR
**633 West Fifth Street, Suite 4000, 90071**⊙
**Telephone: 213-485-1234 Telecopier: 213-891-8763 TWX: 910-321-3733 Cable Address: "Lathwat"**
**URL: http://www.lw.com**

Members of Firm: Paul R. Watkins (1899-1973); Dana Latham (1898-1974); Ira M. Price, II (1919-1968); Philip F. Belleville; Irving Salem (New York City Office); William R. Nicholas; John P. McLoughlin; Alan I. Rothenberg; Francis K. Decker, Jr. (New York City Office); David H. Vena; Donald P. Newell (San Diego Office); Joseph A. Wheelock Jr. (Costa Mesa Office); Kenneth Conboy (New York City Office); J. Thomas Rosch (San Francisco Office); Kenneth M. Poovey (San Francisco Office); John J. Kirby, Jr. (New York City Office); Takashi Matsumoto (Tokyo, Japan Office); Robert E. Currie (Costa Mesa Office); Michael J. Shockro; John R. Light; James G. Hunter, Jr. (Chicago, Illinois Office); John P. Lynch (Chicago, Illinois Office); Thomas W. Dobson; Bruce R. Lederman; Thomas G. Bost; Selvyn Seidel (New York City Office); Alan W. Pettis (Costa Mesa Office); George Vradenburg III; Joseph I. Bentley (Costa Mesa Office); Fredric J. Zepp (San Francisco Office); Gary Olson; George A. Rice (Chicago, Illinois Office); Thomas L. Patten (Washington, D.C. Office); Randall C. Bassett; A. Victor Antola; James W. Daniels (Costa Mesa Office); Ernest J. Getto; Philip E. Coviello (New York City Office); Hendrik de Jong; Roger M. Zaitzeff (New York City Office); Barry A. Sanders; Morris A. Thurston (Costa Mesa Office); Peter H. Benzian (San Diego Office); David V. Lee; Michael S. Lurey; McGee Grigsby (Washington, D.C. Office); Robert J. Rosenberg (New York City Office); Paul H. Dawes (San Francisco Office); Christopher L. Kaufman (San Francisco Office); Hugh Steven Wilson (San Diego Office); Eric L. Bernthal (Washington, D.C. Office); William C. Kelly, Jr. (Washington, D.C. Office); William C. Bottger, Jr.; Laurence H. Levine (Chicago, Illinois Office); John F. Walker, Jr.; Robert A. Long; William J. Gibbons (Chicago, Illinois Office); Gary M. Epstein (Washington, D.C. Office); Roger H. Kimmel (New York City Office); Job Taylor, III (New York City Office); Jeffrey T. Pero (Costa Mesa Office); Betty-Jane Kirwan; William J. Meeske; John J. Clair, Jr.; Stephen S. Bowen (Chicago, Illinois Office); Erica H. Steinberger (New York City Office); Robert A. Greenspon (New York City Office); Gene A. Lucero; Richard L. Chadakoff (New York City Office); Bruce A. Tester (Costa Mesa Office); Barbara A. Caulfield (San Francisco Office); Donald P. Baker; James A. Cherney (Chicago, Illinois Office); Paul I. Meyer (San Diego Office); Robert M. Sussman (Washington, D.C. Office); James V. Kearney (New York City Office); Geoffrey K. Hurley (New York City Office); Thomas L. Pfister; Alan B. Clark; Dale K. Neal; Donald L. Schwartz (Chicago Office); David L. Mulliken (San Diego Office); Robert K. Break (Costa Mesa Office); Joel E. Krischer; James D. C. Barrall; Ronald W. Hanson (Chicago, Illinois Office); Leonard A. Zax (Washington, D.C. Office); John J. Lyons; John J. Huber (Washington, D.C. Office); W. Harrison Wellford (Washington, D.C. Office); Walter P. Loughlin (New York City Office); Miles N. Ruthberg; Jon D. Anderson (Costa Mesa Office); John B. Sherrell; Carl E. Witschy (Chicago, Illinois Office); Robert M. Dell (San Francisco Office); Mary B. Ruhl; Patrick T. Seaver (Costa Mesa Office); Thomas G. Gallatin, Jr. (New York City Office); Victoria E. Marmorstein; Peter A. Wald (San Francisco Office); Gary L. Dickson; Scott N. Wolfe (San Diego Office); Gregory P. Lindstrom (Costa Mesa Office); Joseph J. Wheeler (San Diego Office); Maureen E. Mahoney (Washington, D.C. Office); David J. Hayes (Washington, D.C. Office); Bruce P. Howard (Costa Mesa Office); Michael Chertoff (Newark, New Jersey, New York City and Washington, D.C. Offices); Jon D. Demorest (San Diego Office); Virginia Sollenberger Grogan; Kelley Michael Gale (San Diego Office); Karen Smith Bryan; Deanne P. George (San Diego Office); Edward Sonnenschein, Jr.; Milton A. Miller; Martin N. Flics (New York City Office); Paul R. DeMuro; Robert A. Waterman (San Francisco Office); Shelley B. O'Neill (New York City Office); Terrence J. Connolly (New York City Office); James F. Rogers (Washington, D.C. Office); George J. Mihlsten; Peter L. Winik (Washington, D.C. Office); Russell F. Sauer, Jr.; Steven Della Rocca (New York City Office); Jed W. Brickner (New York City Office); Elizabeth A. Blendell; Kevin A. Russell (Chicago, Illinois Office); Marc W. Rappel; Mary K. Westbrook (Costa Mesa Office); Mark S. Pulliam (San Diego Office); Robert A. Wyman, Jr.; Roger S. Goldman (Washington, D.C. Office); Bruce E. Rosenblum (Washington, D.C. Office); Brian G. Cartwright; Charles Stephen Treat (San Francisco Office); Marc D. Bassewitz (Chicago, Illinois Office); Kevin M. Murphy (Chicago, Illinois Office); Bryant B. Edwards; Christopher W. Garrett (San Diego Office); Everett C. Johnson, Jr. (Washington, D.C. Office); Paul D. Tosetti; William K. Rawson (Washington, D.C. Office); Mark W. Smith (San Francisco Office); David R. Hazelton (Washington, D.C. Office); G. Andrew Lundberg; Mark E. Newell (Washington, D.C. Office); John D. Shyer (New York City Office); Joshua Stein (New York City Office); John C. Hart (New York City Office); Edward J. Shapiro (Washington, D.C. Office); Samuel A. Fishman (New York City Office); Tomoaki Ikenaga (New York City Office); David C. Boatwright (San Diego Office); Mark A. Harris (Chicago, Illinois Office); Mark A. Stegemoeller (Chicago, Illinois Office); Robert P. Dahlquist (San Diego Office); Robert D. Crockett; David J. McLean; Thomas C. Sadler; Richard A. Levy (Chicago, Illinois Office); James E. Brandt (New York City Office); Sharon Y. Bowen (New York City Office); John L. Sachs (Washington, D.C. Office); Jerry R. Peters (San Francisco Office); Kenneth A. Wolfson (Costa Mesa Office); Pamela S. Palmer; Karl S. Lytz (San Francisco Office); William H. Voge (New York City Office); Nancy Scheurwater Hunter (Chicago, Illinois Office); Ursula H. Hyman; Martha Barnhart Jordan; Thomas A. Edwards (San Diego Office); David Booth Rogers; John D. Watson, Jr. (Washington, D.C. Office); Richard A. Conn, Jr. (Washington, D.C. Office); David S. Foster (Chicago, Illinois Office); Bennett J. Murphy; Eric A. Stern (Washington, D.C. Office); Lori E. Simon (Chicago, Illinois Office); Nancy L. Schimmel (Chicago, Illinois Office); J. Douglas Bacon (Chicago, Illinois Office); Cary K. Hyden (Costa Mesa Office); Peter W. Devereaux; Mark A. Flagel; Bruce P. Shepherd (San Diego Office); Edith R. Perez; David W. Barby (Costa Mesa Office); Juli Wilson Marshall (Chicago, Illinois Office); Robert G. Goldman (Chicago, Illinois Office); Michael J. Brody; Mary Ellen Kanoff; Peter F. Kerman (San Francisco Office); Kirk A. Davenport (New York City Office); Lucinda Starrett; Scott R. Haber (San Francisco Office); Kristine L. Wilkes (San Diego Office); Joel H. Mack (San Diego Office); Raymond Yung Lin (New York City Office); Robert J. Gunther, Jr. (New York City Office); Geoffrey S. Berman (New York City Office); Joseph D. Sullivan (Washington, D.C. Office); Richard S. Zbur; Douglas A. Freedman (Chicago, Illinois Office); John M. Jameson; John M. Newell; Linda S. Schurman (Chicago, Illinois Office); Glenda Sanders (Costa Mesa Office); Peter J. Wilson (Costa Mesa Office); Laurence J. Stein (Chicago, Illinois Office); Joseph Blum (London, England Office); Patricia Timko Sinclair; Kirk A. Wilkinson; Allen D. Haynie (San Diego Office); Reba W. Thomas; Kevin C. Blauch (New York City Office); David A. Hahn (San Diego Office); Richard L. Wirthlin (Moscow, Russia Office); Linda M. Inscoe (San Francisco Office); James F. Ritter (Washington, D.C. Office); David A. Gordon (New York City Office); Robert A. Koenig; Pamela Brown Kelly; Dennis B. Nordstrom (London, England Office); Paul A. Galleberg; Kevin Charles Boyle (Washington, D.C. Office); Glen B. Collyer; Richard W. Raushenbush (San Francisco Office); William J. Cernius (Costa Mesa Office); David K. Rathgeber (Chicago, Illinois Office); John H. Kenney (San Francisco Office); David T. I. Vong (Hong Kong Office); Andrew D. Singer (San Diego Office); Michael Bruce Abelson; Julia A. Hatcher (Washington, D.C. Office); Joseph A. Bevash (Hong Kong Office); Samuel R. Weiner (San Francisco Office); Dena L. Bloom; Cynthia H. Cwik (San Diego Office); Philip J. Perzek (Chicago, Illinois Office); Carolyne R. Hathaway (Washington, D.C. Office); Cary R. Perlman (Chicago, Illinois Office); Michael Scott Feeley; John P. Janka (Washington, D.C. Office); Steven M. Bauer (San Francisco Office); Linda Schilling (Costa Mesa Office); Brian C. Krisberg (New York City Office); Michael K. Hertz (New York City Office); Joseph B. Farrell (Costa Mesa Office); R. Ronald Hopkinson (New York City Office); Scott O. Bowie; David L. Shapiro (Chicago, Illinois Office); Tracy K. Edmonson (San Francisco Office); David S. Raab (Washington, D.C. Office); Anthony J. Richmond; Mark S. Mester (Chicago, Illinois Office); Michael G. Romey; Jeffrey R. Holmstead (Washington, D.C. Office); Scott P. Klein; Sosi Biricik Klijian (San Diego Office); Timothy B. Hardwicke (Chicago, Illinois Office); Robert A. Klyman; Ian B. Blumenstein (New York City Office); Barry J. Shotts (San Diego Office); Susan S. Azad; A. Brent Truitt (New York City Office); Timothy P. Crudo (San Francisco Office); Gay L. Bronson (New York City Office); Michael J. Carroll; Hyun Park (Hong Kong Office); Mary Rose Alexander (Chicago, Illinois Office); J. Drew Page (San Diego Office); Robert M. Howard (San Diego Office); Susan Paulsrud Welch; Nicholas W. Allard (Washington, D.C. Office); James I. Hisiger (New York City Office); Russell Hayman; David Miles (London, England Office); Mark D. Gerstein (Chicago Office). Of Counsel: John S. Welch; Clinton R. Stevenson; H. Randall Stoke; Richard Carver; John R. Stahr (Costa Mesa Office); Alan N. Halkett; Robert B. Wessling; Philip L. Reynolds; Warren B. Elterman (New York City Office); David A. York (San Francisco Office); Frederick M. Danziger (New York City Office); Beth R. Neckman (New York City Office); Patrick W. Duval (New York City Office); Regina M. Schlatter (Costa Mesa Office); Jeffrey S. Haber; Michael P. Vandenbergh (Washington, D.C. Office); Andrea L. Mersel (Costa Mesa Office); John P. Coffey (New York City Office); Austin H. Peck, Jr.; Scott R. Smith (New York City Office); Gerald J. Lewis (San Diego Office); Mark S. Fowler (Washington, D.C. Office); Stephen M. Burgin; David E. Novitski; David W. Fleming; Thomas B. Trimble (Washington, D.C. Office); Gordon Simonds (San Francisco Office); David M. Leive (Washington, D.C. Office); Desiree Icaza Kellogg (San Diego Office); Jean M. Donnelly (Costa Mesa Office); Yanlei Wu (Washington, D.C. Office); Hervé Gouraige (Newark, New Jersey and New York City Offices); Richard B. Ulmer Jr. (San Francisco Office); Daniel K. Settelmayer; Dean G. Dunlavey (Costa Mesa Office); James O. Copley (New York City Office); Gregory K. Miller (San Francisco Office); Jonathan S. Berck (London Office); Kenneth R. Whiting, Jr. (San Francisco Office); Bruce J. Prager (New York City Office); Bernard C. Byrnes (New York City Office); Lev S. Simkin (Moscow, Russia Office); Louise Zeitzew (New York City Office); Christopher R. Plaut (New York City Office); Jiyeon Lee Lim (New York City Office). Associates: Christopher D. Lueking (Chicago, Illinois Office); Carlos Alvarez (New York City Office); Adele K.

(This Listing Continued)

**Latham & Watkins (Continued)**

Cardoza (Costa Mesa Office); Elissa Ganbarg Benudis (New York City Office); Gail A. Matthews (New York City Office); Jeffrey T. Wald (New York City Office); Mark D. Beckett (New York City Office); Marc J. Veilleux (New York City Office); Katherine A. Lauer (San Diego Office); Marla S. Becker (New York City Office); J. Wesley Skow (San Francisco Office); Gregory A. Ezring (New York City Office); Kimberly M. McCormick (San Diego Office); Amos M. Levy (Not admitted in CA); Jeffrey G. Moran (Chicago, Illinois Office); John T. Brennan (New York City Office); Patrick J. Carty (New York City Office); Jeffrey M. Goodman (New York City Office); Elisabeth L. Goot (New York City Office); Dean T. Janis (San Diego Office); David C. Meckler (Costa Mesa Office); Jennifer C. Archie (Washington, D.C. Office); Mark I. Michigan (New York City Office); E. William Cattan, Jr. (New York City Office); Kenneth M. Fitzgerald (San Diego Office); Dorn G. Bishop (San Diego Office); Kim Natalie Alicia Boras (New York City Office); L. Susan McGinnis; Marian A. Harvey; Steven Atlee; James L. Arnone; Jeff D. Wesselkamper (San Francisco Office); Marcus A. McDaniel; Daniel T. Lennon (Washington, D.C. Office); Anya Goldin (Moscow, Russia Office); Eva Herbst Davis; David C. Flattum (Costa Mesa Office); Gregory N. Pimstone; Steven J. Levine (San Diego Office); Wayne S. Flick; Maureen Smith (New York City Office); Peter M. Gilhuly; Cynthia A. Rotell; Mark Bruce Abbott; Peter Huston (San Francisco Office); Andrew Marc Paley; Gregory M. Pettigrew; Ann K. O'Brien; Donna J. Williams (San Diego Office); William J. Caldarelli (San Diego Office); Jon L. Praed (Washington, D.C. Office); David F. Randell (Chicago, Illinois Office); James H. Barker, III (Washington, D.C. Office); Curtis P. Lu (Washington, D.C. Office); Jennifer Upham Saunders; Teresa D. Baer (Washington, D.C. Office); Jeffrey H. Koppele (New York City Office); David L. Schwartz (Washington, D.C. Office); S. H. Spencer Compton (New York City Office); David A. Barrett (Washington, D.C. Office); John R. Tinkham (Chicago, Illinois Office); Rebecca D. Roberts (Not admitted in CA); Scott R. McCaw (New York City Office); Regina L. Scinta (New York City Office); Andrew D. Richman (New York City Office); James S. Blank (New York City Office); Corinne M. Plummer (London, England Office); Howard A. Matalon (Newark, New Jersey Office); Kathryn Shaw Collins (Chicago, Illinois Office); Joseph M. Kronsnoble (Chicago, Illinois Office); Diana L. Day (San Diego Office); R. Brian Timmons (Costa Mesa Office); Ora T. Fruehauf (San Francisco Office); David Judson Barrett (San Diego Office); Ellen L. Marks (Chicago, Illinois Office); Scott C. Herlihy (Washington, D.C. Office); Robin D. Dal Soglio; Scott B. Garner (Costa Mesa Office); James P. Beaubien; Philip J. Perry (Washington, D.C. Office); Richard M. Trobman (New York City Office); Lisa A. Von Eschen; James R. Barrett (Washington, D.C. Office); Michael W. Sturrock; Kimberly L. Wilkinson (San Francisco Office); Robin M. Hulshizer (Chicago Office); Amy G. Nefouse (San Diego Office); Deborah A. Bigbee; Bruce D. Gellman (San Francisco Office); Paul J. Hunt (Washington, D.C. Office); Anthony I. Fenwick (San Francisco Office); Maria P. Hoye; Kathleen M. O'Prey Truman; Vivian Clara Strache (Washington, D.C. Office); Christopher J. Peters (Chicago, Illinois Office); Melissa A. Roper (New York City Office); Gwyn Goodson Timms (San Diego Office); Charles W. Cox, II (Costa Mesa Office); David T. Kraska (San Francisco Office); Marci L. Smith; Annette L. Hayes (Washington, D.C. Office); Scott C. Lewis; Whitney E. Peterson (San Diego Office); Charles K. Ruck (Costa Mesa Office); Julian Y. Kim (Washington, D.C. Office); Michael J. Guzman (Washington, D.C. Office); Kimberly Arouh (San Diego Office); Kenneth A. Schuhmacher (London, England Office); Paul N. Singarella (Costa Mesa Office); Maureen A. Riley (New York City Office); Greg S. Slater (Washington, D.C. Office); Maureen C. Shay (New York City Office); Peter J. Falconer (Chicago, Illinois Office); Dennis M. Walsh (New York City Office); Christopher Harrison (London, England Office); Tracy M. Preston (San Francisco Office); Stephen K. Phillips (San Francisco Office); James W. Baker (San Diego Office); J. Scott Hodgkins; David A. Nelson (Chicago, Illinois Office); Michael S. Wroblewski (Washington, D.C. Office); Hugh L. Burns (New York City Office); David M. Hernand; Michael A. Bell (Washington, D.C. Office); Dean M. Kato; Craig M. Garner (San Diego Office); Minh N. Vu (Washington, D.C. Office); Eric A. Gaynor; Andrew Han; Amy N. Keroes; Teri L. Witteman; Linda Harrison Edwards; Simon J. Dickens (Chicago, Illinois Office); Marc D. Jaffe (New York City Office); Daniel J. Ross (New York City Office); Peter M. Labonski (New York City Office); Michèle O. Penzer (New York City Office); Robert F. Kennedy (New York City Office); Kenneth D. Crews (Chicago, Illinois Office); Gary R. Ignatin; Jeffrey L. Kateman; Joseph A. Sullivan (Chicago, Illinois Office); Anat Hakim (New York City Office); Michelle M. Carroll; Eric J. Custer; Brian H. Levey; Stuart L. Leviton; Susan M. Marsch; Parris J. Sanz; John B. Duer (New York City Office); C. Chad Johnson (New York City Office); Lee D. Hwang; Darci A. Lanphere; Andrea S. Matiauda (Costa Mesa Office); Daniel A. Thomson (Costa Mesa Office); Pilar S. Parducci; Bruce R. Ledesma (San Francisco Office); Mary E. Britton (Washington, D.C. Office); Steven D. McKenney; David L. Kuiper (Costa Mesa Office); Kenneth G. Schuler (Chicago, Illinois Office); Daniel Scott Schecter; Susan P. Flattum; Daniel W. Burke (Costa Mesa Office); Michael J. Malecek (San Francisco Office); William C. Tayler (San Diego Office); Laura Gabriel (San Francisco Office); Sylvia A. Stein (Chicago, Illinois Office); John H. Gomez; William A. Voxman (Washington, D.C. Office); Naomi H. Kobayashi; Jerianne E. Mancini (New York City Office); Anton Leof (San Francisco Office); Randall D. Roth (New York City Office); Michael A. Bond (New York City Office); David N. Fong (New York City Office); Gary A. Kashar; Michael D. Smith (Chicago, Illinois Office); Deidre L. Schneider (San Diego Office); Jill H. Silfen; Alice S. Fisher (Washington, D.C. Office); Neil Cummings (New York City Office); Julia E. Parry (San Diego Office); Dawn D. Schiller (Chicago, Illinois Office); Marsha Y. Reeves (Washington, D.C. Office); Richard S. Davis; Ted Fikre; Francis Y. Park; Eric A. Richardson (New York City Office); Steven H. Schulman (Washington, D.C. Office); Claudia M. O'Brien (Washington, D.C. Office); Ian H. Fisher (Chicago, Illinois Office); Gregory O. Lunt; Daniel L. Martens; Christine LeGrand Lehman (San Francisco Office); James R. Dutro (San Francisco Office); Carolyn R. Worsley (New York City Office); Assaf J. Henig; Robert S. Michitarian (San Francisco Office); Matthew W. Walch (Chicago, Illinois Office); Jens H. Hillen; Kathleen Kilourie; Michael G. Mishik; Mary C. Tesh; Dominic K.L. Yoong; Tad J. Freese (San Francisco Office); Sony Ben-Moshe (San Diego Office); Michelle Duncan Bergman (New York City Office); JoAnn Laurentino (New York City Office); Denise R. Ben-Attar (New York City Office); Carole Ferguson Johnson (New York City Office); Rose Greenberg (New York City Office); Theodore K. Smith (Moscow, Russia Office); Roland S. Young (New York City Office); Christian B. McGrath (Chicago, Illinois Office); Lynne S. Hoffenberg (Chicago, Illinois Office); Andrew B. Munro; Laura I. Bushnell (Costa Mesa Office); R. Scott Shean (Costa Mesa Office); Malu S. Mercado (San Francisco Office); Donald A. Fishman (Washington, D.C. Office); Oswald B. Cousins, II (San Francisco Office); Hyen-ae Jane Sung (San Francisco Office); Lauren E. Passmore (New York City Office); Ian A. Gerard (New York City Office); Miriam T. Jona (Chicago, Illinois Office); Michael R. Etzioni; Vincent H. Herron; Blair G. Connelly; Mark A. Finkelstein (Costa Mesa Office); Debra N. Michelson (New York City Office); Mary A. Donovan (Costa Mesa Office); Lino J. Lauro (Chicago, Illinois Office); Wayne G. Nitti; David O. Kahn; Carol M. Mauch; John G. Holland (Washington, D.C. Office); Kyle W. Hoffman (San Diego Office); David Pitman (Costa Mesa Office); Kevin T. Kerns (Chicago, Illinois Office); Robert E. Burwell (San Diego Office); Sandra A. Muhlenbeck (Chicago, Illinois Office); Patrick Gibbs (Chicago, Illinois Office); Lane H. Blumenfeld (Washington, D.C. Office); Jacklyn Kay Bartlett (New York City Office); Scott R. Raber (New York City Office); David S. Dantzic (Washington, D.C. Office); Will B. Fitton (San Francisco Office); Elena C. Norman (New York City Office); Matthew D. Moren (New York City Office); Katharine M. Albright; Richard D. Strulson; John W. Creighton, III (Washington, D.C. Office); Craig D. Solar (New York City Office); Joseph M. Yaffe (Costa Mesa Office); Jared W. Johnson (Washington, D.C. Office); Scott B. Cooper (Costa Mesa Office); David L. London (Washington, D.C. Office); Eva Izsak-Niimura (New York City Office); Don Robert Spellmann (New York City Office); Grace Won; Jeffrey A. Brandon (New York City Office); Robert Braumuller (Washington, D.C. Office); Monica Yung-Min Kim; Leslie A. Pereira; David A. Kass (Washington, D.C. Office); Katherine M. Rollins (Washington, D.C. Office); Michele T. Blay (Chicago, Illinois Office); Sarah M. Ekdahl (Chicago, Illinois Office); Audrey Lee; Jacques Youssefmir; Ronit D. Earley (Costa Mesa Office); Mark W. Seneca (Costa Mesa Office); Bradley E. Kotler (Chicago, Illinois Office); Lenora Smith (Chicago, Illinois Office); Daniel P. Dillon (San Diego Office); Barbara L. Cammarata (San Diego Office); John C. Marchese (Washington, D.C. Office); Lynley A. Ogilvie (Washington, D.C. Office); Thomas R. Pappas (New York City Office); J. Erik Sandstedt (New York City Office); Shane M. Spradlin (New York City Office); Virginia C. Edwards (San Francisco Office); Rowland I. Cheng; Michael J. Lawrence; Jacklyn J. Park; Sally Shekou; Stephen F. Case (San Diego Office); Diana L. Strauss (San Diego Office); Fred B. Jacobsen (Chicago, Illinois Office); Clifford Mentrup (Chicago, Illinois Office); Peter J. Millones, Jr. (New York City Office); Mark D. Spoto (Washington, D.C. Office); Susan Finch Moore (Washington, D.C. Office); David E. Ross (Washington, D.C. Office); Patrick J. Devine (Washington, D.C. Office); Daniel S. Duane (New York City Office); Daniel McCray (New York City Office); Jennifer R. Fonner (San Francisco Office); Deborah C. Lambe; Holly M. Holt (San Diego Office); M. Michelle Alvarez; William C. Davisson, III; Robert M. O'Shea; Hoyt Sze; David M. Taub; Vivian W. Yang; Stefanie B. Isser (New York City Office); Chris Burt; Jamie L. Wine (Costa Mesa Office); Martin A. Sabarsky; Stephen R. Tetro, II (Chicago, Illinois Office); John D. Whipple (San Francisco Office); Karen E. Humphreys (San Francisco Office); Sangyeup Lee (New York City Office); Donna Herzing (New York City Office); Stephen D. Blevit; Joshua R. Frieman; Michael D. Lewis; Kelly J. Sosnow; Cheryl Miller Coe (Washington, D.C. Office); Eric Whitaker (San Francisco Office); Catherine S. Bridge; John M. Kuriyama; Ellen C. Waggoner; Sarah K. Freeman (San Diego Office); Thomas M. Reiter (Moscow Office); David E. Christensen; Stephen J. Newman; Susan E. McNeil (Washington, D.C. Office); James R. Hanna (Washington, D.C. Office); Martha Ann Mazzone (Washington, D.C. Office); Carter H. Strickland, Jr. (New York City Office); Maria E. Platsis (Washington, D.C. Office); Stephanie Switzer Brule (San Francisco Office); Christopher L. Elwell; T. Edward Smith; Steven J. Olson; Lauren G. Krasnow (New York City Office); Bradd L. Williamson

(This Listing Continued)

CAA274P

**Latham & Watkins (Continued)**

**(New York City Office); Marilyn M. Singleton (San Francisco Office); Mara I. Kapelovitz (San Francisco Office); Sanjay Bhandari (San Francisco Office); Maurine J. Neiberg (Chicago, Illinois Office); Eric A. Rosand (Washington, D.C. Office); Chunlin Leonhard (Chicago Office); Alan S. Adler; Randy R. Merritt; Brian E. Cromer (San Diego Office); Louis G. Alonso (San Diego Office); Meera Joshi Cattafesta (New York City Office); Stephanie H. Knutson (Costa Mesa Office); Gregory M. Saylin (Costa Mesa Office); Heidi E. Klein (Washington, D.C. Office); Monique Valbuena Pertchik (Washington, D.C. Office); Diana S. Doyle (Chicago Office); Matthew Fradin (Chicago Office); Katharine P. Moir (Chicago Office); Guy Giberson (New York City Office); Jena Kirsch (San Diego Office); Jill M. Houlahan (San Diego Office); Brett Rosenblatt (San Diego Office); David A. Becker (Washington, D.C. Office); Chris Carr (Washington, D.C. Office); Nandan M. Joshi (Washington, D.C. Office); Joseph M. Boyle (Washington, D.C. Office); Alyssa R. Harvey (Washington, D.C. Office); Paul M. Winters (Washington, D.C. Office); Arthur S. Landerholm (Washington, D.C. Office); Elizabeth T. Carlson (Washington, D.C. Office); Jocelyn M. Seitzman (Washington, D.C. Office); Meredith A. Berlin (Chicago Office); Katharine A. Wolanyk (Chicago Office); Adel F. Bebawy; Connie C. Chen; Scott Gluck; Eric M. Lanyard; Jason T. Miller; Jonn R. Beeson (Costa Mesa Office); Julie Vigil King (Costa Mesa Office); Stephen J. Venuto (Costa Mesa Office); Eric L. Czech (New York City Office); M. Christopher Hall (New York City Office); Perry J. Hindin (New York City Office); Anna C. Lincoln (New York City Office); Michael S. Winderman (New York City Office); Kevin C. May (Chicago Office); Steven J. Novatney (Chicago Office); Micaela H. Martín (San Francisco Office); Karen A. Merkle (New York City Office); Judy D. Stratton (New York City Office); Derek D. Dundas; Angelee Fox; Jeffrey B. Greenberg; Daniel W. S. Lawrence; Susan E. Leckrone; Deborah T. Lee; Lisa S. Prange; Nadia A. Shabaik; Mary J. Yoo; Jeannette M. Hill-Yonis; Stacey Sternberg; Amos E. Hartston; Loren M. Montgomery; Eyal Gamliel; Julie Vaughan (London, England Office); Dru Greenhalgh (San Diego Office); Melinda A. Pfeiffer (San Francisco Office); Scott K. Milsten (San Francisco Office); Dana N. Linker (San Francisco Office); Randall K. H. Ching (San Francisco Office); Clay Shevlin (Costa Mesa Office); Catherine Lamb (San Francisco Office); David B. Allen (Costa Mesa Office); Sharadchandra A. Samy (New York City Office); Matthew J. Rossman (New York City Office); Alexander S. Pesic (San Francisco Office); David A. Levitt (New York City Office); Lisa K. Eastwood (New York City Office); Theresa J. McPherson (San Francisco Office); Kenneth R. Morris (San Francisco Office); Dmitri A. Kounitsa (Moscow, Russian Office); Ivan A. Smolin (Moscow, Russia Office); Lisa Binder.**
**General Practice.**
**Costa Mesa, California Office: Suite 2000, 650 Town Center Drive. Telephone: 714-540-1235.**
**San Diego, California Office: Suite 2100, 701 B Street. Telephone: 619-236-1234.**
**San Francisco, California Office: 505 Montgomery Street, Suite 1990. Telephone: 415-391-0600.**
**Washington, D.C. Office: Suite 1300, 1001 Pennsylvania Avenue, N.W. Telephone: 202-637-2200.**
**Chicago, Illinois Office: Suite 5800 Sears Tower. Telephone: 312-876-7700.**
**Newark, New Jersey Office: One Newark Center. Telephone: 201-639-1234. Fax: 201-639-7298.**
**New York, N.Y. Office: Suite 1000, 885 Third Avenue. Telephone: 212-906-1200.**
**London, England Office: One Angel Court, EC2R 7HJ. Telephone: +-44-171-374 4444. Telecopier: +-44-171-374 4460.**
**Moscow, Russia Office: Suite C200, 113/1 Leninsky Prospeckt, 117198. Telephone: +-7 503 956-5555. Fax: +-7 503 956-5556.**
**Hong Kong Office: 11th Floor Central Building, Number One Pedder Street, Central Hong Kong. Telephone: 011-852-2841-7779. Fax: 011-852-2841-7749.**
**Tokyo, Japan Office: Infini Akasaka, 8-7-15 Akasaka, Minato-Ku, Tokyo 107, Japan. Telephone: 011 81 3 3423-3970. Fax: 011 81 3 3423-3971.**

***See Professional Biographies, LOS ANGELES, CALIFORNIA***

Lathers, Mary E. .......................... '63 '88 C.190 B.A. L.770 J.D. 555 W. 5th St.
Latin, Michael A. .......................... '59 '86 C.112 B.A. L.426 J.D. Dep. Dist. Atty.
Latiner, Forrest .....'31 '56 C.112 B.A. L.1068 LL.B. 6922 Hollywood Blvd. (Hollywood)
Latiolait, Anthony F. .................. '59 '87 C.1077 B.A. L.1148 J.D. [Ⓐ Morgan&W.]

**La Torraca and Goettsch**
**(See Long Beach)**

Lattaker, Pearl .......................... '46 '77 C.864 B.S. L.1068 J.D. Dep. Atty. Gen.

**Latter, Daniel S. '56 '81 C.339 B.A. L.273 J.D.**
**2029 Century Park East Suite 480, 90067**
**Telephone: 310-277-1358 Fax: 310-277-4351**
***LANGUAGES: French.**
**General Business Law and Transactions, Trademarks and Real Estate Law.**

***See Professional Biographies, LOS ANGELES, CALIFORNIA***

**Latty, Theodore H.** ..................... '54 '73 C.860 B.S. L.262 J.D. [Hughes H.&R.]
*PRACTICE AREAS: Corporate Law; Securities Law; Sports Law.
Lau, Peter W. .......................... '40 '75 C.1109 B.A. L.1095 J.D. 767 N. Hill St.
**Lau, Ying-Kit** ......... '53 '86 C.966 B.S. L.178 J.D. [Ⓐ Robbins,B.&C.] (See Pat. Sect.)
*LANGUAGES: Chinese (Mandarin and Cantonese).
*PRACTICE AREAS: International Technology Transfers Law; Pharmaceutical and Chemical Technology Law; Business Planning Law; Litigation in the Peoples' Republic of China.
**Laucella, Patricia L.** ................ '62 '93 C.569 B.S. L.309 J.D. [Ⓐ Lichter,G.N.&A.]
*PRACTICE AREAS: Entertainment Law.

**Lauchengco, José Y., Jr., (AV) '36 '72 C.662 A.B. L.426 J.D. BR**
**3545 Wilshire Boulevard, Suite 247, 90010**
**Telephone: 213-380-9897**
***LANGUAGES: Pilipino and Spanish.**
**Of Counsel: Paul J. Estuar.**
**Personal Injury and Criminal Practice. Trials in State and Federal Courts.**

***See Professional Biographies, LOS ANGELES, CALIFORNIA***

**Lauderdale, Helen J.** .................. '60 '85 C.118 B.A. L.597 J.D. [Thelen,M.J.&B.]
*PRACTICE AREAS: Litigation; Construction Law.
**Lauer, Ari J.** .......................... '65 '89 C.112 A.B. L.426 J.D. [Cohen&L.]
*PRACTICE AREAS: Construction; Real Estate; Unfair Competition; Wrongful Termination; Securities and Commodities Litigation.
Laufer, Theodore L. ................ '60 '88 C.054 M.Sc. L.1065 J.D. 8391 Beverly Blvd.
**Laughlin, Gary M.** ..................... '52 '78 C.823 B.A. L.184 J.D. [Pircher,N.&M.]
*PRACTICE AREAS: Real Estate Law.
**Laughlin, LouCinda** ..................... '54 '83 C&L.378 B.S., J.D. [Ⓐ Lord,B.&B.]
Laukenmann, Christopher B. ............ '62 '89 C&L.228 B.A., J.D. 515 S. Figueroa St.
**Launder, Pamela D.** ................. '67 '96 C.154 B.A. L.426 J.D. [Ⓐ McKenna&C.]
*PRACTICE AREAS: Government Contracts.
Launer, Lawrence B. ...................... '43 '69 C.154 B.A. L.426 J.D. Asst. Co. Coun.
**Laurance, C. Megan** ................. '69 '95 C.800 B.A. L.276 J.D. [Ⓐ Jones,D.R.&P.]
Laurents, Renee ....................... '39 '80 C.890 B.A. L.1148 J.D. Dep. City Atty.
Laurie, John David ........... '62 '87 C.800 B.A. L.990 J.D. 6326 Commodose Sloat Dr.
Laursen, Lisa K. .................. '64 '91 C&L.846 B.B.A., J.D. 1888 Century Park E.
Lautemann, John E. ............ '46 '73 C.763 B.S. L.1049 J.D. 11726 San Vincente Blvd.
Lautman, Kenneth Z., (BV) ..................... '30 '65 L.809 LL.B. 4311 Wilshire Blvd.
**Lauzon, Peter A.** ..................... '58 '91 C.112 B.A. L.990 J.D. [Ⓐ Mannis&P.]
*PRACTICE AREAS: Family Law.
LaValley, Melvin, (AV) ............................. '13 '65 L.426 LL.B. 205 S. Bway.
**Lavely, John H., Jr.**, (AV) .................. '43 '70 C.976 B.A. L.659 LL.B. [Lavely&S.]
*SPECIAL AGENCIES: California Labor Commissioner.
*REPORTED CASES: Richard Pryor, et al v. David McCoy Franklin, California Department of Industrial Relations, Division of Labor Standards Enforcement, Labor Commissioner, Case No. TAC 17 MP114; Bo Derek v. Karen Callan, California Department of Industrial Relations, Division of Labor Standards Enforcement, Labor Commissioner, Case No. TAC 18-80 SFMP 82-80; Selleck vs. Globe International, Inc., 166 Cal.App.3d 1123, 212 Cal.Rptr. 1123 (1985) (Rev. Denied); LaCienega Music Co. v. ZZ Top, 53 F. 3d 950 (9th Cir 1995), cert denied 116 S. Ct. 331 (1995); Gould v. Maryland Sound Industries, Inc., (1995) 31 Cal.App. 4th 1137, 37 Cal.Rptr. 2d 718 (Rev. denied).
*PRACTICE AREAS: Entertainment Litigation; Business Litigation; Right of Publicity and Privacy Law; Libel Law; Copyright Law.

**Lavely & Singer, Professional Corporation, (AV)**
**2049 Century Park East, Suite 2400, 90067**
**Telephone: 310-556-3501 Telecopier: 310-556-3615 Telex: 4995300 BURX LSA**
**John H. Lavely, Jr.; Martin D. Singer; Michael J. Plonsker; Brian G. Wolf; Lynda B. Goldman; Theresa J. Macellaro; David M. Cordrey; Max J. Sprecher; Eugene P. Sands.**
**Business Litigation, Contracts, Business Torts, Intellectual Property, Libel, Entertainment.**

***See Professional Biographies, LOS ANGELES, CALIFORNIA***

Laven, Bernard B. .................................. '05 '28 C&L.800 LL.M. [Laven&L.]
Laven, Peter J. ...................................................... '48 '74 [Laven&L.]
Laven & Laven ............................................1557 S. Beverly Glen Blvd.
Laverty, Roger M., III '47 '72
C&L.813 B.A., J.D. Pres. & CEO, Smart & Final Stores Corp.
Lavin, Laurence M. '40 '68 C.728 B.S. L.884 J.D.
(adm. in PA; not adm. in CA) Dir., Nat. Health Law Prog.
**Laviña, Salvador P.** ........................ '62 '88 C.112 B.A. L.178 J.D. [Ⓐ Trope&T.]
*PRACTICE AREAS: Real Estate; Commercial Litigation; Business Law.
Lavine, Joan C. ...................... '44 '71 C.800 A.B. L.1066 J.D. 123 N. Hobart Blvd.
**LaVoie, Paul T.** ........ '65 '94 C&L.101 B.A., J.D. [Ⓐ Fulwider P.L.&U.] (See Pat. Sect.)
*PRACTICE AREAS: Patent; Trademark.
**Law, Marcia T.** ............................ '63 '89 C.112 B.A. L.1067 J.D. [Ⓐ Baker&H.]
*PRACTICE AREAS: Litigation; Employment.
**Law, Yuk Kwong** ................ '58 '85 C.882 B.A. L.262 J.D. [Ⓐ Bonne,B.M.O.&N.]
*LANGUAGES: Chinese.
**Lawler, Jean M.**, (AV) .................. '54 '79 C&L.426 B.B.A., J.D. [Murchison&C.]
*REPORTED CASES: Michael Mitchell v. Scott Wetzel Services, 1991; Cristiano v. Hartford et al, 724 F Supp 732, 1989 (represented Arrow Coach).
*PRACTICE AREAS: Insurance Litigation; Insurance Coverage; Property Insurance; Casualty Insurance; Directors and Officers Liability.
**Lawler, Michael B.**, (AV) ............. '42 '72 C.426 B.B.A. L.809 J.D. [Murchison&C.]
*PRACTICE AREAS: General Insurance Defense Litigation; Construction and Land Subsidence Law; Premises and Automobile Liability; Employment Law; Wrongful Termination.

**Lawler, Bonham & Walsh**
**(See Oxnard)**

Lawlor, Karen L. ............................ '49 '91 C.549 L.464 J.D. 550 S. Hope St.
Lawrence, Amy .................. '57 '84 C.102 B.A. L.1068 J.D. 2049 Century Park E.
**Lawrence, Barry H.**, (AV) ............. '42 '67 C.112 B.S. L.1068 J.D. [Kaye,S.F.H.&H.]
*PRACTICE AREAS: Business Law; Real Estate; Securities; Real Estate Development and Finance.
**Lawrence, Daniel W. S.** ............. '68 '96 C.770 B.S.E.E. L.597 J.D. [Ⓐ Latham&W.]
**Lawrence, Frank R.** .............. '61 '89 C.1169 B.A. L.1065 J.D. [Ⓐ Levine&Assoc.]
*PRACTICE AREAS: Civil Litigation; Appellate Litigation; Administrative Law; Indian Law; Gaming Law.
**Lawrence, Janice B.** ................. '42 '83 C.66 B.A. L.1066 J.D. [Ⓐ Folger L.&K.]⊙
Lawrence, Lary ......... '49 '74 C.112 A.B. L.1066 J.D. Prof. of Law, Loyola Law School
Lawrence, Mary Frances ........... '47 '74 C.112 B.A. L.1066 J.D. Sr. Atty., Ct. of App.
**Lawrence, Michael J.** ................. '70 '95 C.112 B.A. L.276 J.D. [Ⓐ Latham&W.]
**Lawrence, Paul F.** .............. '67 '91 C.112 B.A. L.309 J.D. [Ⓐ McDermott,W.&E.]
Lawrence, Rick Leslie ......... '55 '79 C.154 B.A. L.178 J.D. 725 S. Figueroa, Ste. 3600
Lawrence, Robert L. ............. '46 '74 C.112 A.B. L.1066 J.D. 2029 Century Pk., E.
**Lawrence, Steven M.** ............. '57 '90 C.1097 B.A. L.112 J.D. [Ⓐ Alvarado,S.V.&S.]
*PRACTICE AREAS: Bankruptcy; Creditor Rights; Commercial Litigation.

**Lawrence & Harding, A Professional Corporation**
**(See Santa Monica)**

**Lawson, Dana Marie** .................. '70 '96 C.112 B.A. L.426 J.D. [Ⓐ Chapin,F.&W.]
*PRACTICE AREAS: Insurance Defense.
Lawson, Jeanne M. .................. '53 '79 C.112 B.A. L.990 J.D. 1875 Century Pk. E.
**Lawson, Linda M.** ....................... '52 '77 C.813 B.A. L.800 J.D. [Meserve,M.&H.]
Lawson, Louis W. ............................... '20 '49 C.112 L.800 LL.B. [L.W.Lawson]
**Lawson, Michael A.** ............... '53 '78 C.426 B.A. L.309 J.D. [Skadden,A.S.M.&F.]
**Lawson, Scott G.** ....................... '62 '94 C.112 B.A. L.878 J.D. [Ⓐ Orrick,H.&S.]
**Lawson, Thomas N.**, (AV) ........ '52 '77 C&L.546 B.S., J.D. [Ⓒ Weinstein,B.R.H.&C.]
*PRACTICE AREAS: Tax.
Lawson, Louis W., Inc. ............................................ 12424 Wilshire Blvd.
**Lax, Gerald B.** '50 '76 C.1077 B.A. L.809 J.D.
Sr. Coun., Transamerica Financial Servs.
Lax, Kathleen T. ..................... '45 '80 C.378 B.A. L.1068 J.D. U.S. Bkrptcy. J.
Lax, Paul A. ...................... '50 '80 C.37 B.A. L.1068 J.D. 1925 Century Park E.
**Lax, Stephen A.**, (AV) ................. '51 '79 C.1044 B.A. L.426 J.D. [Schaffer&L.]
**Layden, James D.** ..................... '62 '88 C.165 B.A. L.602 J.D. [Ⓐ Arnold&P.]
*PRACTICE AREAS: Commercial Litigation.
**Layne, Jonathan K.** .................... '53 '79 C.945 B.A. L.245 J.D. [Gibson,D.&C.]
*PRACTICE AREAS: Corporate Law; Securities; Finance; Mergers, Acquisitions and Divestitures; Business Law.
Layne, Michele ......................... '59 '85 C.112 B.A. L.800 J.D. 725 Figueroa St.
**Layton, Robert L.** ..................... '48 '74 C.112 B.A. L.1067 J.D. [McKenna&C.]
*PRACTICE AREAS: Health Care; Civil Litigation; Business Law.
**Lazar, Alan H.**, (AV) .......... '41 '70 C.112 A.B. L.1068 J.D. [Berger,K.S.M.F.S.&G.]
Lazar, Alyse M. '53 '79 C.659 B.S. L.734 J.D.
Asst. Chf. Trial Coun., State Bar of Calif.
**Lazar, John I.** ......................... '62 '92 C.860 B.A. L.477 J.D. [Ⓐ Manatt,P.&P.]
Lazar, Rubin M., (AV) ................. '28 '52 C.112 L.426 J.D. 12121 Wilshire Blvd.‡
Lazaro, Avelino Bill ............................ '28 '83 L.066 LL.B. 3434 W. 6th St.
Lazarus, Edward M. ............ '37 '63 C.16 B.A. L.1068 LL.B. 11400 W. Olympic Blvd.
**Lazarus, Jessica D.** ................. '70 '95 C.112 B.S. L.1068 J.D. [Ⓐ Gaims,W.W.&E.]
Lazarus, Ralph E., (AV) ............ '11 '36 C.813 B.A. L.800 LL.B. 2160 Century Pk. E.
**Lazarus, Steven Wayne** ............... '60 '88 C.1097 B.A. L.990 J.D. [Ⓐ D.B.Bloom]
Lazo, Ignacio J. ............... '55 '82 C.813 A.B. L.1066 J.D. 11377 W. Olympic Blvd.
**Le, Patty H.** ........................... '71 '96 C.112 B.A. L.309 J.D. [Ⓐ Brobeck,P.&H.]
**Leach, Timothy P.** '49 '76 C.112 B.A. L.770 J.D.
Assoc. Gen. Coun., Farmers Grp., Inc.
*RESPONSIBILITIES: Commercial Insurance and Reinsurance.
Leaf, Jacqueline R. .................. '46 '80 C.605 B.A. L.809 J.D. 4988 N. Figueroa St.
Leahy, Jean A. ....... '59 '84 C.103 B.A. L.966 J.D. Sr. Coun., Northrop Grumman Corp.
Leahy, Michael V. '47 '72 C.684 B.A. L.800 J.D.
Sr. Corp. Coun., Intl., Northrop Grumman Corp.
Leal, Dolores Y. ........................................ '58 '87 L.1137 J.D. [Allred,M.&G.]
**Leanse, Thomas J.**, (AV) .............. '54 '78 C.763 B.A. L.1049 J.D. [Katten M.&Z.]
*PRACTICE AREAS: Real Estate; Bankruptcy; Commercial and Business Litigation.
**Lear, Elizabeth D.** ....................... '58 '86 C.112 B.S. L.1066 J.D. [Ⓒ Zelle&L.]
*PRACTICE AREAS: Litigation.
**Leary, Thomas J.** ..................... '63 '88 C.112 B.A. L.1068 J.D. [O'Melveny&M.]
*PRACTICE AREAS: Corporate Law; Securities Matters.
Leatherwood, Felix E. ................ '53 '81 C.112 B.A. L.178 J.D. 1040 Masselin Ave.
**Leatherwood, Valerie L.** .............. '63 '91 C.64 B.A. L.426 J.D. [Ⓐ Lewis,D.B.&B.]
**Leaver, George E.**, (AV) ........... '29 '59 C&L.426 B.S., LL.B. [Manning,L.B.&B.] ‡
Leavitt, Laura Ann '49 '82 C.569 B.F.A. L.893 J.D.
(adm. in VA; not adm. in CA) N.L.R.B.
Leavitt, Richard B., (AV) ................ '35 '61 C.197 A.B. L.813 LL.B. Brentwood Ctr.

CAA275P

CALIFORNIA—LOS ANGELES

MARTINDALE-HUBBELL LAW DIRECTORY 1997

**Leavitt, Scott M.** .......................... '63 '91 C.112 B.A. L.426 J.D. [A Daniels,B.&F.]
Lebe, Melvin S., (AV) .......................... '35 '61 C.112 B.S. L.1068 LL.B. [Lebe&F.]
Lebe & Finer, (AV) .......................... 1800 Century Park E.
Le Bel, Christine Y. .......................... '68 '94 C.788 B.A. L.1194 J.D. 624 S. Grand Ave.
Lebenzon, Farrel F. .......................... '45 '87 C.112 L.809 J.D. Dep. Dist. Atty.
**LeBlanc, Jean B., II** .......................... '57 '87 C.1077 B.A. L.1068 J.D. [Murphy,W.&B.]
*PRACTICE AREAS: Creditors Remedies; Commercial Lending; Secured Financing; Business Workouts.
**Le Blanc, John M.** .......................... '59 '91 C.1042 B.A. L.809 J.D. [A Barger&W.]
LeBlanc, Yvon J.R.J. .......................... '40 '90 C.014 B.A. L.809 J.D. 4700 Wilshire Blvd.

**LeBoeuf, Lamb, Greene & MacRae, L.L.P., (AV)**
**A Limited Liability Partnership including Professional Corporations**
**Formerly LeBoeuf, Lamb, Leiby & MacRae**
**725 South Figueroa Street, Suite 3600, 90017-5436⊙**
**Telephone: 213-955-7300 Facsimile: 213-955-7399 Telex: 678982**
**Partners: Jean M. Costanza; John W. Cotton; Shirley E. Curfman; Helen L. Duncan; Dean Hansell; Harumi Hata; Richard R. Terzian; Lisalee Anne Wells. Associates: Jerrold E. Abeles; Vincent J. Davitt; Alexander H. Fukui; Aaron C. Gundzik; Jared M. Katz; R. Diane McKain; Stephen P. Pfahler; Kristin Pelletier; Allyson S. Taketa. Of Counsel: Steven A. Broiles; Edward O. Hunter; Robert M. Johnson; Charles F. Timms, Jr.**
**General Practice including Corporate Finance, Defense of Government Fraud Investigations, Energy, Environmental, Insolvency, Insurance, Public Utilities, Public Finance, Real Estate, Securities Litigation, Taxation, Trade Associations.**
**Eastern United States:**
**New York, N.Y. Office: 125 West 55th Street. Telephone: 212-424-8000. Facsimile: 212-424-8500. Telex: 156363 or 423416.**
**Washington, D.C. Office: 1875 Connecticut Avenue, N.W. Telephone: 202-986-8000. Facsimile: 202-986-8102. Telex: 440274.**
**Albany, New York Office: One Commerce Plaza, Suite 2020, 99 Washington Avenue. Telephone: 518-465-1500. Facsimile: 518-465-1585.**
**Boston, Massachusetts Office: 260 Franklin Street. Telephone: 617-439-9500. Facsimile: 617-439-0341; 439-0342.**
**Harrisburg, Pennsylvania Office: 200 North Third Street, Suite 300, P.O. Box 12105. Telephone: 717-232-8199. Facsimile: 717-232-8720.**
**Pittsburgh, Pennsylvania Office: 601 Grant Street. Telephone: 412-594-2300. Facsimile: 412-594-5237.**
**Hartford, Connecticut Office: Goodwin Square, 225 Asylum Street, 13th Floor. Telephone: 860-293-3500. Facsimile: 860-293-3555.**
**Newark, New Jersey Office: The Legal Center, One Riverfront Plaza. Telephone: 201-643-8000. Facsimile: 201-643-6111.**
**Western United States:**
**Salt Lake City, Utah Office: 1000 Kearns Building, 136 South Main Street. Telephone: 801-320-6700. Facsimile: 801-359-8256.**
**San Francisco, California Office: One Embarcadero Center, Suite 400. Telephone: 415-951-1100. Facsimile: 415-951-1180; 951-1881. Telex: 470167.**
**Denver, Colorado Office: 633 17th Street, Suite 2800. Telephone: 303-291-2600. Facsimile: 303-297-0422.**
**Portland, Oregon Office: KOIN Center, Suite 1600, 222 S.W. Columbia. Telephone: 503-294-3095. Fax: 503-294-3895.**
**Southern United States:**
**Jacksonville, Florida Office: 50 N. Laura Street, Suite 2800. Telephone: 904-354-8000. Facsimile: 904-353-1673.**
**European Offices:**
**Brussels, Belgium Office: Avenue des Arts, 19H, 1000 Brussels, Belgium. Telephone: 001-32-2-227-0900. Facsimile: 011-32-2-227-0909.**
**London, England Office: One Mincining Lane, 6th Floor, London EC3R 7AA England. Telephone: 011-44-171-459-5000. Facsimile: 011-44-171-459-5099.**
**Moscow, Russian Federation Office: Nikitsky Pereulok, 5 (formerly Ulitsa Belinskogo) 103009, Moscow, Russian Federation. Telephone: 011-7-503-956-3935. Facsimile: 011-7-503-956-3936.**
**Almaty, Kazakhstan Office: Ulitsa Zheltoksana, 83 480091 Almaty, Republic of Kazakhstan. Telephone: 011-7-3272-50-7575. Facsimile: 011-7-3272-50-7576.**
***See Professional Biographies, LOS ANGELES, CALIFORNIA***

LeBouef, John F. .......................... '39 '74 C.1044 B.S. L.990 J.D. P.O. Box 69618
**Lebovits, Moses**, (AV) .......................... '51 '75 C.112 B.A. L.1068 J.D. [Lebovits&D.]
*REPORTED CASES: Flood v. Wyeth, 183 Cal. App. 3d 1272, 228 Cal. Rptr. 700 (1986); Touri v. Walker - Verdict/Judgment - $7.5 Million; Rose v. Volkswagen - Verdict/Judgment - $3.5 Million ; Charlesworth v. USA, 840 F. Supp. 1484 (D. Utah 1994) - Verdict/Judgment - $1,128,000; Salazar v. Foroughe - Verdict/Judgment - $2.2 Million.
*PRACTICE AREAS: Product Liability; Professional Negligence; Aviation Law; Insurance Bad Faith; Personal Injury.

**Lebovits & David, A Professional Corporation, (AV) BB**
**Suite 3100, Two Century Plaza, 2049 Century Park East, 90067**
**Telephone: 310-277-0200 Fax: 310-552-1028**
**Moses Lebovits; Deborah A. David. Of Counsel: Joseph J. M. Lange.**
**Product Liability, Professional Negligence, Aviation Law, Insurance Bad Faith, Personal Injury and Business Litigation.**
**Reference: Imperial Bank (Main Office - Beverly Hills).**
***See Professional Biographies, LOS ANGELES, CALIFORNIA***

Lebovitz, Michael S. .......................... '59 '84 C.1042 B.A. L.426 J.D. 400 S. Hope St.

**Lebow, Carol A., (AV) '50 '75 C.112 B.A. L.880 J.D.**
**1999 Avenue of the Stars, 27th Floor, 90067**
**Telephone: 310-286-1999 Facsimile: 310-551-0027**
**Corporate, Real Estate, Partnership and Transactional Business Law. Federal, State, Local and International Taxation. Tax Litigation and Controversies.**
***See Professional Biographies, LOS ANGELES, CALIFORNIA***

Lebowitz, Donna S. .......................... '61 '88 C.112 B.A. L.398 J.D. Dep. Dist. Atty.
**Leck, Brian C.**, (AV) .......................... '45 '71 C.813 B.A. L.1068 J.D. [Allen,M.L.G.&M.]
*PRACTICE AREAS: Corporate.
**Leckrone, Susan E.** .......................... '69 '96 C.813 B.A. L.347 J.D. [A Latham&W.]
**LeCrone, John P.** .......................... '57 '84 C.800 B.S. L.809 J.D. [Manatt,P.&P.]
*PRACTICE AREAS: Labor/Employment Law; Litigation.
**Ledahl, Brian D.** .......................... '71 '96 C&L.178 B.A., J.D. [A Irell&M.]
**Ledakis, James M.** .......................... '58 '87 C.508 B.A. L.61 J.D. [A Parker S.] (⊙San Diego)
**Ledbetter, Steven K.** .......................... '47 '75 C.800 B.S. L.809 J.D. [Inglis,L.&G.]
*PRACTICE AREAS: Tax Law; Corporate Law.
Lederer, Les E. .......................... '46 '71 C.112 B.S. L.426 J.D. [L.E.Lederer]
Lederer, Les E, A Professional Law Corporation .......................... 1990 Westwood Blvd.
**Lederman, Bruce R.**, (AV) .......................... '42 '68 C.659 B.S. L.309 LL.B. [Latham&W.]
Lee, Albert .......................... '60 '88 C.112 B.A. L.1065 J.D. [Ahn&L.]
**Lee, Anita D.** .......................... '57 '82 C.813 A.B. L.1068 J.D. [Foley L.W.&A.]
*SPECIAL AGENCIES: Provider Reimbursement Review Board.
*PRACTICE AREAS: Health Care; Hospitals; Medicare and Medicaid; Administrative Law.
**Lee, Ann S.** .......................... '67 '92 C.112 B.A. L.188 J.D. [A Mitchell,S.&K.]
*PRACTICE AREAS: Litigation.
**Lee, Audrey** .......................... '70 '95 C.112 B.A. L.145 J.D. [A Latham&W.]
*LANGUAGES: Mandarin Chinese.
*PRACTICE AREAS: Corporate; Securities; Intellectual Property.
Lee, Benjamin T. .......... '65 '93 C&L.464 B.S., J.D. 4215 Glencoe Ave. (Marina Del Rey)
Lee, Bill L. .......... '49 '75 C.976 B.A. L.178 J.D. NAACP Legal Def. & Educ. Fund, Inc.
**Lee, Bub-Joo S.** .......................... '64 '92 C.309 A.B. L.188 J.D. [A Sheppard,M.R.&H.]
*LANGUAGES: Portuguese, Korean, Spanish (Reading).
*PRACTICE AREAS: Litigation.
**Lee, Caroline S.** .......................... '68 '92 C.976 B.A. L.1066 J.D. [A Alschuler G.&P.]
Lee, Corinne .......................... '— '80 Legal Div., Dept. of Transp.

**Lee, Courtney F.** .......................... '68 '96 C.65 B.A. L.1068 J.D. [A Kenoff&M.]
*PRACTICE AREAS: Entertainment Transactions.
Lee, Craig M. .......................... '55 '81 C.112 B.A. L.426 J.D. 4751 Wilshire Blvd.
**Lee, Daniel H.** .......................... '68 '94 C.112 B.A. L.1068 J.D. [A Musick,P.&G.]
*LANGUAGES: Korean.
*PRACTICE AREAS: Taxation; Business Law.
Lee, Daniel S. .......................... '65 '92 C.112 B.S. L.1065 J.D. 550 S. Hope St.
**Lee, Daniel W.** .......................... '54 '85 C.475 B.A. L.767 J.D. [A Whitman B.A.&M.]
*LANGUAGES: Korean.
**Lee, David K.** .......... '63 '92 C.112 B.A. L.464 J.D. [A Radcliff,F.&D.] (⊙San Fran.)
*LANGUAGES: Korean.
**Lee, David V.**, (AV) .......................... '43 '71 C.579 B.S. L.494 J.D. [Latham&W.]
Lee, Debbie Ling .......................... '63 '89 C.976 B.A. L.426 J.D. 601 S. Figueroa
**Lee, Deborah T.** .......................... '69 '96 C.659 B.S. L.1068 J.D. [A Latham&W.]
*LANGUAGES: Chinese.
Lee, Donna A. .......................... '60 '89 C.112 B.A. L.1049 J.D. Paramount Pictures Corp.
Lee, Edward M., Jr. .......................... '39 '66 C.770 B.S.C. L.800 J.D. 606 N. Larchmont
**Lee, Edward W.** .......................... '50 '87 C.112 B.A. L.809 J.D. [Oliver,V.S.M.&L.]
*PRACTICE AREAS: Municipal; Land Use and Real Estate Development Services; General Redevelopment Counsel Services; Real Estate.
**Lee, Ellen Ma** .......................... '48 '75 C.605 B.A. L.426 J.D. [A C.Shusterman]
*LANGUAGES: Chinese.
*PRACTICE AREAS: Immigration and Naturalization Law.
**Lee, G. Jiyun** .......................... '67 '92 C.112 B.A. L.309 J.D. [A Folger L.&K.]
*LANGUAGES: Korean and Japanese.
Lee, Gilbert W. .......................... '27 '61 C.112 B.A. L.800 J.D. Dep. City Atty.
**Lee, Henry M.** .......................... '66 '91 C.605 B.A. L.1068 J.D. [A Lim,R.&K.]
*PRACTICE AREAS: Civil Litigation.
**Lee, Hyunu** .......................... '68 '96 C.976 B.A. L.1068 J.D. [A Graham&J.]
*PRACTICE AREAS: Litigation.
**Lee, James C.** .......................... '70 '95 C.976 B.A. L.309 J.D. [A O'Melveny&M.]
*PRACTICE AREAS: Corporate Law.
Lee, Jang W. .......................... '45 '84 C.061 B.A. L.426 J.D. 3250 Wilshire Blvd.
**Lee, Janice B.** .......................... '46 '85 C.36 B.S. L.426 J.D. [A Bonne,B.M.O.&N.]
Lee, Jeffrey M. .......................... '45 '70 C.112 B.A. L.426 J.D. 10920 Wilshire Blvd.
Lee, Jin Sin .......................... '33 '64 C&L.800 A.B., J.D. 403 W. College St.
**Lee, Joseph D.** .......................... '57 '83 C.112 B.A. L.1066 J.D. [Munger,T.&O.]
Lee, Judy .......................... '65 '91 C.914 B.A. L.893 J.D. [Bolden&M.]
**Lee, Karen-Denise** .......................... '61 '87 C.1181 B.S. L.950 J.D. [A Engstrom,L.&L.]
Lee, Karen K. .......................... '63 '89 C.312 B.A. L.831 J.D. 1875 Century Pk. East
Lee, Katherine K. .......... '66 '94 C.800 B.S. L.809 J.D. Atty., Alpha Therapeutic Corp.
Lee, Linda Sue .......................... '49 '90 C.112 B.A. L.426 J.D. 1051 S. Beacon Ave.
**Lee, Mark S.** .......................... '54 '80 C&L.339 B.A., J.D. [Manatt,P.&P.]
*LANGUAGES: Japanese.
*PRACTICE AREAS: Intellectual Property; Litigation; International.
Lee, Martin T. .......................... '61 '87 C.112 B.A. L.1065 J.D. 601 S. Figueroa
Lee, Martin V. .......................... '55 '83 C.800 B.S. L.1068 J.D. Famco Investments
**Lee, Mary G.** .......................... '66 '94 C.128 B.A. L.904 J.D. [A Ivanjack&L.]
*PRACTICE AREAS: Bankruptcy; Commercial Litigation; Business Litigation; Real Estate.
Lee, Mary M. .......................... '55 '83 C.1168 B.A. L.1066 J.D. Legal Aid Found. of L.A.
Lee, Mavis K. .......................... '— '94 C.453 B.S. L.813 J.D. Asst. U.S. Atty.
**Lee, Michael V.** .......................... '69 '94 C&L.112 B.A., J.D. [A Arnelle,H.M.W.&G.]
*LANGUAGES: Vietnamese.
*PRACTICE AREAS: Products Liability Litigation; Commercial Law; Warranty Litigation.
Lee, Nicole D. .......................... '67 '92 C.112 B.A. L.990 J.D. 12100 Wilshire Blvd.
**Lee, Paul Y.** .......................... '53 '80 C.910 A.B. L.659 J.D. [Lewis,D.B.&B.]
**Lee, Pauline Ng** .......................... '64 '89 C.228 B.S. L.800 J.D. [A Sonnenschein N.&R.]
*PRACTICE AREAS: Bankruptcy; Commercial and Lending Litigation.
Lee, Peter V. '58 '93 C.112 A.B. L.800 J.D.
Dir., HMO Consumer Protec. Proj., Ctr. for Health Care Rights
**Lee, Philip Nelson** .......................... '45 '73 C.800 A.B. L.309 J.D. [Preston G.&E.]
*PRACTICE AREAS: Municipal Finance; Corporate Law.
Lee, R. Marilyn .... '48 '77 C.112 B.A. L.464 J.D. V.P., Human Res., Los Angeles Times
Lee, Randall R. .......................... '61 '91 C.976 B.A. L.1066 J.D. Asst. US Atty
**Lee, Richard Ung-Jin** .......................... '64 '90 C.976 B.A. L.178 J.D. [A Irell&M.]
**Lee, San San** .......................... '63 '88 C.154 B.A. L.1068 J.D. [Golbert L.]
*LANGUAGES: Mandarin, Japanese.
*PRACTICE AREAS: Real Estate and Corporate.
Lee, Steven J. .......................... '55 '88 C.101 B.A. L.426 J.D. [Roquemore,P.&M.]
**Lee, Tin Kin** .......................... '61 '87 C.800 B.S. L.178 J.D. [Manatt,P.&P.]
*PRACTICE AREAS: Healthcare; Finance; Corporate; Real Estate.
**Lee-Gulley, Patricia** .......................... '53 '89 C.800 B.A. L.1137 J.D. [A Howarth&S.]
*PRACTICE AREAS: Civil Litigation Law.
Leeb, Larry J. .......................... '49 '75 C.112 B.A. L.809 J.D. Calif. Custom Shapes
Leeds, Julie Ann .......................... '57 '88 C.800 B.S. L.1049 J.D. Pub. Def.
Leemon, Gary R. .......................... '49 '79 L.1136 J.D. 2639 E. 1st St.
Leen, Mark .......................... '60 '90 C.95 B.A. L.878 J.D. Dep. Pub. Def. II
Lees, Alan B. .......................... '26 '75 C.432 Ph.D. L.1114 J.D. 12301 Wilshire Blvd.
**Lees, Gail Ellen**, (AV) .......................... '50 '79 C.597 B.S. L.1068 J.D. [Gibson,D.&C.]
*PRACTICE AREAS: Advertising and Consumer Fraud Litigation; Securities Class Action and Derivative Litigation; Corporate Control; Entertainment Litigation.
Lees, Mindy J. .......................... '64 '90 C.1077 B.A. L.800 J.D. 333 S. Grand Ave.
Leewong, James D. .......................... '49 '74 C.800 B.S. L.426 J.D. [Nishiyama,M.L.E.&S.]
Lefcoe, George '38 '63 C.197 A.B. L.976 LL.B.
(adm. in FL; not adm. in CA) Prof., Univ. of Southern Calif. Law Ctr.
Lefevre, Suzanne M. .......................... '50 '74 C.112 B.A. L.426 J.D. 4700 Wilshire Blvd.
Leff, Holly Arden .......................... '62 '90 C.112 B.S. L.426 J.D. 1888 Century Park E.
**Leff, Randall S.**, (AV) .......................... '51 '77 C.605 B.A. L.1065 J.D. [Nebenzahl K.D.&L.]
*PRACTICE AREAS: Health Care; Business Litigation; Employment Law.
Lefkowitz, Richard A. ..... '57 '93 C.1077 B.A. L.1136 J.D. 18425 Burbank Blvd., Tarzana
**Lefler, Daniel P.** .......................... '65 '90 C.112 B.A. L.145 J.D. [A Irell&M.]
Legaspi, Leonard S. .......................... '32 '78 L.061 LL.B. 4643 W. Beverly Blvd.
Leggon, L. Marie .......................... '68 '93 C.813 B.A. L.178 J.D. 550 S. Hope St.
**Leh, Marc B.** .......................... '59 '86 C.174 B.A. L.800 J.D. [Morrison&F.]
*PRACTICE AREAS: Real Estate; Finance; Corporate Law; Mergers and Acquisitions.
Leher, Richard I., (AV) .......... '44 '70 C.605 A.B. L.1066 J.D. 11377 W. Olympic Blvd.
Lehman, Howard N., (AV) .......................... '32 '57 C.800 B.S. L.1068 J.D. [Rose,K.&M.]
Lehman, M. Lewis .......................... '01 '24 L.809 J.D. 5959 W. Century Blvd., Ste. 100
Lehman, Mary D. .......................... '39 '85 C.645 B.S. L.1068 J.D. [A Gittler,W.&B.]
Lehmann, J. Michael .......................... '65 '92 C.112 B.A. L.1068 J.D. 2049 Century Pk. E.
Lehmann, Kenneth H. '57 '83 C.994 B.A. L.262 J.D.
Gen. Coun., Longwood Mgmt. Corp.
Lehrer, David A. .......... '48 '73 C.112 B.A. L.1068 J.D. Dir., Anti-Defamation League
Lehrer, Keith M. '58 '84 C.1169 B.A. L.809 J.D.
(adm. in HI; not adm. in CA) 2238 Stradella Rd.‡
Lehrer-Graiwer, Jonathan .......................... '46 '71 C.112 B.A. L.1066 J.D. 4727 Wilshire Blvd.
**Lehrhoff, Steven J.** .......................... '68 '95 C.597 B.A. L.800 J.D. [A Sheppard,M.R.&H.]
*PRACTICE AREAS: Corporate; Securities.
**Leib, Alton**, (AV) .......................... '32 '59 C.112 B.A. L.1068 J.D. [A.Leib]

CAA276P

**Leib, Alton, (AV)**
**1801 Century Park East, Suite 2500, 90067-2326**
**Telephone: 310-286-0880 Fax: 310-286-1633**
**Alton Leib.**
**Languages: Italian and French.**
**Business Litigation.**
**Representative Clients: Western Dye House, Inc.; Cal-Pacific Dying & Finishing; Ideal Textile Co., Inc.**
*See Professional Biographies, LOS ANGELES, CALIFORNIA*

**Leibow, Ronald L.**, (AV) ....... '39 '66 C.1077 A.B. L.1068 J.D. [Kaye,S.F.H.&H.]
*PRACTICE AREAS: Insolvency; Bankruptcy; Corporate Reorganization; Debt Restructure; Workouts.
**Leichenger, Sheryl W.** ....... '64 '92 C.1077 B.S. L.426 J.D. [[A] Selman B.]
*PRACTICE AREAS: Insurance Coverage.

**Leichenger, David B.**
**(See Beverly Hills)**

**Leichnitz, Leonard P.** ....... '63 '91 C.605 B.A. L.1068 J.D. [[A] Munger,T.&O.]
*PRACTICE AREAS: Real Estate.
**Leichter, Kevin J.** ....... '61 '91 C.787 B.A. L.94 J.D. [[A] Christensen,M.F.J.G.W.&S.]
*PRACTICE AREAS: Civil Litigation; Entertainment Litigation; Bankruptcy Law.
Leidner, Joel D. ....... '39 '72 C&L.800 A.B., J.D. [Leidner&L.]
Leidner, Suzanne C. ....... '42 '79 C.112 B.A. L.1238 J.D. [Leidner&L.]
Leidner & Leidner, A Professional Corporation ....... 4622 Hollywood Blvd.
**Leids, Asher M.** ....... '61 '88 C.1044 B.A. L.276 J.D. [Donahue&M.]
*PRACTICE AREAS: Securities; Corporate Finance; Investment Banking and Venture Capital; Mergers and Acquisitions; Franchise Offerings.
Leight, Michelle S. ....... '54 '89 C.1042 B.S. L.1049 J.D. 444 S. Flower St.
**Leighton, Joanne K.** ....... '65 '93 C.754 B.A. L.831 J.D. [[A] Dale,B.&H.]
*PRACTICE AREAS: Civil Litigation.
Leighton, Steven L. ....... '39 '67 C.477 B.S.E. L.1068 LL.B. 3530 Wilshire Blvd.
**Leinbach, Brian J.** ....... '66 '92 C.174 B.A. L.990 J.D. [[A] Engstrom,L.&L.]
**Leinwand, Shari**, (AV) ....... '51 '76 C.112 A.B. L.800 J.D. [Gibson,D.&C.]
*PRACTICE AREAS: Estate Planning; Tax; Trusts and Estates; Probate; Charitable Organizations and Planning.
**Leipziger, David A.**, (AV) ....... '37 '68 C.309 A.B. L.1066 J.D. [Cox,C.&N.]
*PRACTICE AREAS: Bankruptcy Law; Creditors Rights Law; Real Property Law; Commercial Law.
Leis, Colin ....... '61 '89 C.309 A.B. L.800 J.D. 400 S. Hope St.
**Leiserowitz, Bruce H.** ....... '57 '84 C.813 A.B. L.1066 J.D. [[A] Silver&F.]
*LANGUAGES: French.
*PRACTICE AREAS: Commercial Litigation; Insurance Litigation; Surety Litigation.
**Leist, Jeffrey J.** ....... '56 '81 C.112 B.A. L.800 J.D. [[A] Chapin,F.&W.]
**Leiter, Maurice A.** ....... '58 '82 C.309 A.B. L.276 J.D. [Arnold&P.]
*PRACTICE AREAS: Civil Litigation; Products Liability; White Collar Criminal Defense.
**Leitereg, Elizabeth E.** ....... '54 '89 C.705 B.A. L.770 J.D. Hughes Aircraft Co.
Leland, N. Stanley, (AV) ....... '11 '34 C&L.800 A.B., J.D. 10100 Santa Monica Blvd.

**Leland, Parachini, Steinberg, Flinn, Matzger & Melnick, L.L.P., (AV)**
**500 South Grand Avenue, Suite 1100, 90071⊙**
**Telephone: 213-623-7505 Fax: 213-623-7595**
**Resident Partners: Richard Fannan; Vicki L. Freimann; Kenneth Miller. Resident Associates: Dawn M. Coulson; Thomas A. Vidano. Of Counsel: C. Timothy O'Malley.**
**General Civil and Trial Practice in all State and Federal Courts. Corporation, Business, Banking, Bankruptcy, Employment, Tax, Estate Planning, Probate, Trust, Family and Real Estate Law.**
**San Francisco, California Office: 27th Floor, 333 Market Street. Telephone: 415-957-1800. Fax: 415-974-1520.**
*See Professional Biographies, LOS ANGELES, CALIFORNIA*

**Lemann, Monte M., II** ....... '61 '88 C&L.309 B.A., J.D. [[A] Manatt,P.&P.]
*PRACTICE AREAS: General Corporate; Corporate Finance.
**Lemke, Elaine M.** ....... '58 '87 C.221 B.A. L.597 J.D. [McClintock,W.B.R.R.&M.]
*PRACTICE AREAS: Business Litigation; Environmental Litigation.
**Lemkin, Jeffrey W.** ....... '45 '72 C.95 A.B. L.94 J.D. [McDermott,W.&E.]
*PRACTICE AREAS: Business Law; Corporate Law; Health Care.
Lemle, Robert L. ....... '63 '90 C&L.260 B.S., J.D. 1888 Century Park E.
Lemlech, Bernard ....... '24 '59 C.112 B.S. L.1068 J.D. Kenneth Leventhal & Co.
**Lemmer, Don S.** ....... '51 '81 C.78 B.A. L.280 J.D. [[A] Kelley D.&W.]
**Lemoine, France D.** ....... '64 '89 C&L.014 LL.B. [[A] Russ,A.&K.]
*LANGUAGES: French.
*PRACTICE AREAS: Trademark; Copyright.

**Lemon, Boyd S., (AV) '40 '66 C&L.800 A.B., J.D.**
**12304 Santa Monica Boulevard, Suite 221, 90025⊙**
**Telephone: 310-979-4848 Fax: 310-979-4840**
***PRACTICE AREAS: Litigation; Business Litigation; Legal Malpractice; Ethics; Real Estate Litigation.**
**Associates: C. Kelly McCourt; Eric E. Bronson.**
**Expert Witness in Legal Malpractice Matters. General Civil and Trial Practice.**
**Paso Robles, California Office: 1111 Riverside Avenue, Suite 504, 93446. Telephone: 805-239-4184. Facsimile: 805-239-1049.**
*See Professional Biographies, LOS ANGELES, CALIFORNIA*

**Lenack, Jack R.** ....... '56 '85 C.112 B.A. L.809 J.D. [Katz,H.S.&K.]
*PRACTICE AREAS: Corporate Law; Real Estate Law; Commercial Law.
Lenahan, Dennis J. ....... '44 '72 C&L.800 B.S., J.D. Karsten Realty Advisors
Lenard, Allen D., (AV) ....... '42 '69 C.966 B.B.A. L.1068 J.D. [Lenard&G.]
Lenard & Gonzalez, A Ptnrshp. Including A Prof. Corp., (AV)
2121 Ave. of the Stars, 22nd Fl.
Lending, Patricia M. ....... '51 '85 C.339 B.A. L.809 J.D. 4215 Glencoe Ave.
Lenhart, Daniel A. B. ....... '43 '79 C.1042 B.S. L.1137 J.D. Off of Dist. Atty.
Lenke, Sharon L. ....... '44 '80 C.1077 B.S. L.809 J.D. 4151 Melrose Ave.
**Lenkov, Jeffrey M.** ....... '65 '91 C.012 B.A. L.589 J.D. [[A] Wilson,E.M.E.&D.]
*LANGUAGES: French.
*PRACTICE AREAS: Entertainment Law; Civil Litigation; Real Estate Law.
**Lennard, Colin**, (AV) ....... '42 '68 C.112 L.426 J.D. [Fulbright&J.]
*PRACTICE AREAS: Land Use; Environmental Law.
**Lenneman, Annette J.**, (AV) ....... '59 '86 C.710 B.A. L.894 J.D. [Black C.H.&L.]
*PRACTICE AREAS: Coverage Litigation; Bad Faith Litigation; Insurer Insolvency; Insurance Guarantee Association Practice; Insurance Defense.
**Lennemann, K. Erin** ....... '64 '91 C.1042 B.A. L.426 J.D. [[A] Harrington,F.D.&C.]
Lennon, Gerald E. ....... '36 '83 C.1077 B.A. L.1095 J.D. [Hannon,P.&L.]
**Lennon, Margaret E.**, (AV) ....... '59 '86 C.66 A.B. L.477 J.D. [Valensi,R.&M.]
*PRACTICE AREAS: Tax Law; Estate Planning Law.
**Lennox, Malissia R.** ....... '68 '94 C.36 B.A. L.813 J.D. [[A] Tuttle&T.]
**Lenny, Dave** ....... '50 '75 C.339 B.A. L.178 J.D. [Donahue&M.]
*SPECIAL AGENCIES: United States Department of Agriculture.
*REPORTED CASES: National Union Fire Insurance Company of Pittsburgh v. Stites Professional Law Corporation (Cal. App. 2nd Dist. 1991) 235 Cal. App. 3d 1718 1 Cal. Rptr. 2d 570.
*PRACTICE AREAS: Securities Arbitration and Litigation; Insurance Litigation; Bankruptcy Litigation; Real Estate Litigation; Attorney Malpractice Litigation.
Lentz, Jennifer Beth '58 '89 C.112 B.A. L.990 J.D.
Dep. Dist. Atty., Hardcore Gang Div.
Lentz, Robert H. ....... '24 '57 C.667 B.E.E. L.426 LL.B. 2877 Nicada Dr. (Pat.)‡
Lenzi, Stephen E. '47 '74 C.1060 B.A. L.464 J.D.
Dir., Pub. Affs., Auto. Club of Southern Calif.

**Leo, Thomas Glen** ....... '53 '78 C.453 S.B. L.800 J.D. [Troop M.S.&P.]
*PRACTICE AREAS: Secured Transactions; Entertainment Finance.
Leon, David M. ....... '56 '81 C.597 B.S. L.1068 J.D. 11766 Wilshire Blvd.
**Leon, Marvin, (A Professional Corporation)**, (AV) '29 '53
C.339 B.S. L.597 J.D. [Mitchell,S.&K.]
*PRACTICE AREAS: Real Estate Property Law; Real Estate Development Law; Real Estate Syndications Law.
**Leonard, Arthur A.** ....... '52 '81 C.112 B.A. L.861 J.D. [Sands N.F.L.&L.]
**Leonard, Christopher B., (A Professional Corporation)** '62 '88
C.477 B.A. L.1068 J.D. [Mitchell,S.&K.]
*PRACTICE AREAS: Litigation.
**Leonard, Edward R.**, (AV) '53 '78
C.763 B.A. L.1049 J.D. [Harrington,F.D.&C.] (⊙Orange)
*PRACTICE AREAS: Personal Injury Defense Law; Product Liability Law; Professional Negligence Law; Construction Defects Law.

**Leonard, James M., (AV) '46 '71 C.112 B.A. L.1068 J.D.**
**Suite 645, 11845 West Olympic Boulevard, 90064**
**Telephone: 310-312-8660 Fax: 310-312-8024**
**General Business Practice and Entertainment Law.**
*See Professional Biographies, LOS ANGELES, CALIFORNIA*

**Leonard, Leigh M.** ....... '59 '90 C.188 B.S. L.1068 J.D. [[A] S.L.Hartmann]
*PRACTICE AREAS: Civil Rights; Employee Benefits.
**Leonard, Michelle M.** ....... '67 '94 C.93 B.A. L.426 J.D. [[A] O'Melveny&M.]
Leonard, Robert T. ....... '63 '92 C.800 B.S. L.810 J.D. [[B] M.D.Pastor]

**Leonard, Dicker & Schreiber**
**(See Beverly Hills)**

**Leone, Lawrence E., (AV) '51 '77 C.112 B.A. L.426 J.D.**
**12100 Wilshire Boulevard Fifteenth Floor, 90025**
**Telephone: 310-207-1231 Fax: 310-207-5800**
**(Certified Specialist, Family Law, The State Bar of California Board of Legal Specialization).**
**Family Law.**
*See Professional Biographies, LOS ANGELES, CALIFORNIA*

**Leonhardt, Donald E.** ....... '68 '96 C.112 B.A. L.1065 J.D. [[A] Christensen,M.F.J.G.W.&S.]
*PRACTICE AREAS: Litigation.
Leoni, Andrew F., (AV) ....... '18 '46 C&L.767 LL.B. [Slate&L.]
Leonian, Leon, (BV) ....... '28 '56 C&L.800 B.A., J.D. 11620 Wilshire
**Leopold, A. Fredric**, (AV) ....... '19 '48 C.197 A.B. L.178 J.D. [Leopold,P.&S.]
*PRACTICE AREAS: Copyright; Trademark; Entertainment; Insurance; Errors and Omissions.

**Leopold, Petrich & Smith, A Professional Corporation, (AV) [BB]**
**(Formerly Youngman, Hungate & Leopold)**
**Suite 3110, 2049 Century Park East (Century City), 90067**
**Telephone: 310-277-3333 Telecopier: 310-277-7444**
**Gordon E. Youngman (1903-1983); A. Fredric Leopold; Louis P. Petrich; Joel McCabe Smith; Edward A. Ruttenberg; Vincent Cox; Donald R. Gordon; Walter R. Sadler; Daniel M. Mayeda. Of Counsel: Richard Hungate;—Paul M. Krekorian; David Aronoff; Gary M. Grossenbacher; Robert S. Gutierrez.**
**General Civil and Trial and Appellate Practice in all State and Federal Courts. Motion Picture, Television, Copyright, Trademark, Libel and Slander and Unfair Competition Law.**
*See Professional Biographies, LOS ANGELES, CALIFORNIA*

Lepak, Brian P. ....... '62 '87 C&L.966 B.A., J.D. 103 N. Robertson Blvd.
Lepape, Harry L. ....... '30 '56 C&L.813 B.S., LL.B. 633 W. 5th St.
**Leparulo, Peter V.** ....... '58 '85 C.165 B.A. L.1068 J.D. [Pillsbury M.&S.]
Leppek, Harry V., (BV) ....... '15 '41 C&L.426 B.B.A. 920 S. Ford Blvd.
**Lerman, Cary B.**, (AV) ....... '48 '72 C.339 B.S. L.1068 J.D. [Munger,T.&O.]
Lerman, Glenn E. ....... '64 '89 C.112 B.A. L.1066 J.D. 1900 Ave. of the Stars
Lerner, Marc, (AV) ....... '46 '71 C&L.800 B.S., J.D. [Barbakow&L.]
**Lerner, Marshall A.**, (AV) '41 '66
C.570 B.S.E.E. L.273 J.D. [Arant,K.L.&R.] (See Pat. Sect.)
*PRACTICE AREAS: Intellectual Property Litigation; Patent and Trademark Prosecution; Advertising Injury; Trade Secrets.
**Lerner, Neil S.** ....... '59 '86 C.831 B.A. L.273 J.D. [Sands N.F.L.&L.]
**Lerner, Perry A.**, (AV) '43 '69
C.154 B.A. L.309 J.D. [O'Melveny&M.] (⊙New York, NY.)
Lerner, Richard S. ....... '49 '74 C.1077 B.A. L.1049 J.D. 1801 Century Pk. E.
**Le Sage, Bernard E.**, (AV) ....... '49 '74 C.602 B.A. L.426 J.D. [Buchalter,N.F.&Y.]
*PRACTICE AREAS: Business and Financial Institution Litigation.
LeSage, Joan M. ....... '49 '82 C.741 B.A. L.1068 J.D. 633 W. 5th St.
**Lesansky, Stuart K.** ....... '52 '79 C.1044 B.A. L.1009 J.D. [Lesansky&Assoc.]
*PRACTICE AREAS: Unfair Competition; Securities Litigation; Aviation; Aerospace Law; Litigation.

**Lesansky & Associates**
**1875 Century Park East, Suite 700, 90067**
**Telephone: 310-226-2400 Fax: 310-226-2401**
**Email: lesans@ibm.net**
**Stuart K. Lesansky. Associates: Steven L. Weinberg; Christine M. Macfarlane.**
**Unfair Competition, Securities Litigation, Aviation and Aerospace Law and Litigation, Construction Defect Litigation, Intellectual Property, Professional Liability, Insurance Coverage, Probate Litigation, Directors and Officers, Errors and Omissions Litigation and General Commercial Law.**
*See Professional Biographies, LOS ANGELES, CALIFORNIA*

Lesel, Dov S. ....... '47 '73 C.112 B.A. L.1008 J.D. Asst. City Atty.
Leserman, Paul ....... '31 '81 C.976 B.A. L.1148 J.D. 3700 Wilshire Blvd.
Leslie, Jody R. ....... '54 '80 C.1111 B.A. L.800 J.D. 1999 Ave. of the Stars
**Leslie, Michael R.** ....... '57 '86 C.197 B.A. L.813 J.D. [Hedges&C.]
*LANGUAGES: Spanish.
**Lesmez, Arthur G.** ....... '59 '85 C.823 B.A. L.61 J.D. [[A] Liebman&R.]
Lesser, Gershon M. ....... '33 '77 C.112 B.A. L.1136 J.D. 8230 Beverly Blvd.‡
**Lesser, Henry**, (AV) ....... '47 '77 C.050 B.A. L.309 LL.M. [Irell&M.]
**Lesser, Joan L., (P.C.)**, (AV) ....... '47 '73 C.1036 B.A. L.800 J.D. [Irell&M.]
**Lesser, Peter J.** ....... '57 '84 C.604 B.A. L.893 J.D. [P.J.Lesser] & [[B] Wickens&L.]
**Lesser, Trudi J.** ....... '59 '85 C.1044 B.A. L.800 J.D. [[A] Nebenzahl K.D.&L.]
*PRACTICE AREAS: Business Law; Corporate Law; Real property Law; Business Litigation; Real Estate Litigation.

**Lesser, Peter J., Law Offices of**
**1801 Century Park East, Suite 2500, 90067**
**Telephone: 310-552-0599 Fax: 310-552-0596**
**Email: PETELESSER@AOL.COM**
**Peter J. Lesser. Of Counsel: Steven M. Rich.**
**Civil Litigation; Business Counseling and Litigation; Entertainment Transactions and Litigation; Probate and Estate Litigation; Criminal Defense.**
*See Professional Biographies, LOS ANGELES, CALIFORNIA*

**Lessley, Rebecca Hairston** ....... '58 '91 C.69 B.B.A. L.426 J.D. [[A] Thorpe&T.]
*PRACTICE AREAS: Construction; Business Litigation.
Lessner, Ronald D. ....... '47 '73 C.1077 B.A. L.800 J.D. 4221 Wilshire Blvd. Ste. 395
**Lester, David M.** ....... '60 '85 C.188 B.S. L.1068 J.D. [Musick,P.&G.]
*PRACTICE AREAS: Labor and Employment.
Letteau, Robert M. ....... '42 '68 C.813 B.A. L.1065 J.D. Supr. Ct. J.
**Letter, Gordon A.** ....... '52 '79 C.112 B.A. L.1065 J.D. [Littler,M.F.T.&M.]

CALIFORNIA—LOS ANGELES MARTINDALE-HUBBELL LAW DIRECTORY 1997

Lettieri, Joan T. ........................'56 '83 C.800 B.A. L.426 J.D. 2160 Century Park E.
Letts, J. Spencer ........................'34 '60 C.976 B.A. L.309 LL.B. U.S. Dist. J.
Letwin, Leon ........................'29 '52 C.145 Ph.B. L.966 LL.B. Prof. of Law, U.C.L.A.
**Leuin, Terry C.** ........................'46 '82 C.112 B.A. L.426 J.D. [Cotkin&C.]
*PRACTICE AREAS: Insurance Coverage Law; Insurance Bad Faith Litigation.
**Leung, Frankie Fook-Lun** ........................'49 '87 C&L.061 B.A., J.D. [Lewis,D.B.&B.]
*LANGUAGES: French, Japanese (reading), Chinese (Mandarin & Cantonese).
**Leung, Richard** ........................'66 '92 C.112 B.A. L.800 J.D. [Ⓐ Parker S.]
Leus, Hyacinth E. ........................'67 '93 [Vakili&L.]
Leutjen, Cheryl ........................'61 '93 C.1322 B.A. L.800 J.D. 444 S. Flower St.
**LeVee, Jeffrey A.** ........................'59 '84 C.228 B.A. L.597 J.D. [Jones,D.R.&P.]
**Levene, David W.**, (AV) ........................'45 '74 C.800 B.S. L.426 J.D. [Levene,N.&B.]
*PRACTICE AREAS: Bankruptcy.

**Levene, Neale & Bender L.L.P., (AV)** BB
**1801 Avenue of the Stars, Suite 1120, 90067**
**Telephone: 310-229-1234 Fax: 310-229-1244**
**Email: (attorneys initials)@LNBLAW.COM**
**David W. Levene; David L. Neale; Ron Bender. Associate: Craig M. Rankin; Nellwyn Voorhies; Monica Y. Kim.**
**Practice Limited to Bankruptcy Law, Insolvency Law and Business Reorganization.**
**Reference: 1st Business Bank.**
*See Professional Biographies, LOS ANGELES, CALIFORNIA*

Leventhal, Marc S. ........................'63 '89 C.112 A.B. L.1068 J.D. 1925 Century Park E.
**Leventhal, Robert C.** ........................'57 '85 C.1044 B.A. L.880 J.D. [Foley L.W.&A.]
*REPORTED CASES: Burton v. Security Pacific National Bank, 197 Cal. App. 3d 972 (1988).
*PRACTICE AREAS: Commercial Litigation; Construction Defects; Antitrust; Labor and Employment Litigation.
Leventhal, Stephen H. ........... '48 '76 C.1077 B.A. L.809 J.D. 11500 W. Olympic Blvd.

**Leventhal, S. Michael**
**(See Santa Monica)**

Leveton, David A. ........................'37 '63 C.112 A.B. L.1068 LL.B. 1880 Century Park E.
**Levey, Andrew S.** ........................'66 '92 C.112 B.A. L.464 J.D. [Ⓐ Bonne,B.M.O.&N.]
**Levey, Brian H.** ........................'67 '93 C&L.813 A.B., J.D. [Ⓐ Latham&W.]
**Levey, Jonathan R.** '70 '95 C.674 A.B. L.309 J.D.
(adm. in IL; not adm. in CA) [Ⓐ Munger,T.&O.]
*PRACTICE AREAS: Litigation.
**Levin, Adam** ........................'66 '91 C.154 B.A. L.1049 J.D. [Ⓐ Mitchell,S.&K.]
*PRACTICE AREAS: Employment Law; Labor Law; Litigation.
Levin, Alvin M. ........................'30 '58 C&L.910 A.B., J.D. 10639 Rochester
Levin, Arnold ........................'30 '61 C.112 A.B. L.309 LL.B. Comr. Supr. Ct.
Levin, Barry L., (AV) .......... '47 '80 C.1077 B.A. L.1095 J.D. 11661 San Vicente Blvd.
**Levin, C. James** ........................'54 '81 C.210 B.A. L.597 J.D. [O'Melveny&M.]
*PRACTICE AREAS: Corporate Law; Executive Compensation; Corporate Governance; Securities; Mergers, Acquisitions and Divestitures.
Levin, Daniel '56 '82 C.309 A.B. L.145 J.D.
(adm. in NY; not adm. in CA) U.S. Atty's Off.
**Levin, Fredrick S.** '63 '88 C.674 A.B. L.477 J.D.
(adm. in MI; not adm. in CA) [Ⓐ Mayer,B.&P.]
Levin, Harvey I. ........................'53 '78 C.112 B.A. L.426 J.D. 2049 Century Park E.
Levin, Herbert A. ........................'46 '71 C&L.112 A.B., J.D. Dep. Atty. Gen.
Levin, Ira S. '48 '73 C.1077 B.A. L.1068 J.D.
Sr. V.P. & Gen. Coun., The Decurion Corp.
**Levin, Jason** ........................'68 '92 C.668 B.A. L.1049 J.D. [Ⓐ Morris,P.&P.]
Levin, Jill S. '55 '82 C.1365 B.A. L.823 J.D.
Legal Recruiter & Atty., The Haffner Group, Inc.
**Levin, John P.**, (AV) ........................'48 '73 C.309 A.B. L.813 J.D. [Folger L.&K.]⊙
Levin, Judith B. ........................'— '78 C.339 B.S. L.1136 J.D. Dep. City Atty.
**Levin, Kenneth H.** ........................'53 '78 C.339 A.B. L.309 J.D. [Sidley&A.]
*PRACTICE AREAS: Corporate Law; Securities Law; Commercial Law.
Levin, Marilyn H. ........................'46 '80 C.339 B.A. L.767 J.D. Dep. Atty. Gen.
Levin, Mark Allen ........................'45 '71 C.112 B.A. L.1068 J.D. [Lewin&L.]
Levin, Mark Steven ............... '58 '83 C.800 B.S. L.1066 J.D. 1801 Century Park East
Levin, Nina ........................'54 '84 C.112 B.A. L.809 J.D. Research Atty., Ct. of App.
Levin, Paula D. ........................'53 '78 C.112 B.A. L.809 J.D. 10526 Wellworth Ave.
Levin, Richard H., (AV) ........................'36 '61 C.112 B.A. L.1066 LL.B. [Levin,S.C.&S.]
**Levin, Sandra J.** ........................'63 '87 C.112 B.A. L.1066 J.D. [Riordan&M.]
Levin, Sindee .................. '— '85 C.112 B.A. L.426 J.D. 10100 Santa Monica Blvd.
**Levin, Theodore D.** ........................'57 '86 C.174 B.S. L.767 J.D. [Morris,P.&P.]
**Levin, Victoria A.** ........................'67 '93 C.813 B.A. L.1068 J.D. [Ⓐ Orrick,H.&S.]
*LANGUAGES: Italian, French, Spanish.
*PRACTICE AREAS: Litigation.

**Levin & Freedman, LLP**
**(See Santa Monica)**

Levin, Stein, Chyten & Schneider, (AV) ........................ 12424 Wilshire Blvd.
**Levine, Andrea Trupin** ........................'49 '74 C.446 B.A. L.800 J.D. [Ⓐ J.Levine]
*LANGUAGES: French.
*REPORTED CASES: United States v. Miller, 874 F.2d 1255 (9th Cir. 1989); United States v. Gouveia, 704 F.2d 1116 (9th Cir. 1983); United States v. Gouveia, 467 U.S. 180.
*PRACTICE AREAS: White Collar Criminal Defense; General Criminal Defense; Business Civil Litigation.
**Levine, Arthur S.**, (AV) ........................'42 '67 C.112 A.B. L.1068 J.D. [A.S.Levine]
**Levine, Betty J.** ........................'47 '82 C.112 B.A. L.426 J.D. [Ⓐ Hooper,L.&B.]
*PRACTICE AREAS: Health Care; Litigation.
**Levine, Bruce H.** ........................'69 '95 C.569 B.S. L.426 J.D. [Ⓐ Mayer,B.&P.]
**Levine, C. Bruce**, (AV) ........................'45 '71 C.112 B.A. L.309 J.D. [Greenberg G.F.C.&M.]
*PRACTICE AREAS: Tax; Estate Planning; Business; Corporate.
**Levine, Edward** ........................'51 '78 C.112 B.A. L.597 J.D. [Sanders,B.G.S.&M.]
**Levine, Harmon B.** ........................'54 '80 C.112 B.A. L.1049 J.D. [Ⓐ Tuverson&H.]
Levine, Howard R. ........................'56 '82 C.1044 B.A. L.809 J.D. 445 S. Figueroa St.
**Levine, Howard S.** ........................'59 '88 C.102 B.A. L.978 J.D. [Ⓐ Weinstein&E.]
**Levine, Janet I.** ........................'55 '80 C.112 B.A. L.426 J.D. [Michaelson&L.]
**Levine, Jared Elliott** ........................'56 '81 C&L.309 A.B., J.D. [Nelson,G.F.&L.]
*PRACTICE AREAS: Entertainment Law.
Levine, Jeffrey L. ........................'51 '76 C.112 A.B. L.309 J.D. Pres., U.S. Container Co.
**Levine, Jerome L.**, (AV) ........................'40 '66 C.766 A.B. L.1065 J.D. [Levine&Assoc.]
*PRACTICE AREAS: Contract and Business Law; Licensing and Regulation; Litigation; Casino and Gaming Law; Indian Law.
**Levine, Joel**, (AV) ........................'45 '70 C.102 B.A. L.930 J.D. [J.Levine]
*REPORTED CASES: United States v. Miller, 874 F.2d 1255 (9th Cir. 1989); United States v. Gouveia, 704 F.2d 1116 (9th Cir. 1983); United States v. Gouveia, 467 U.S. 180.
*PRACTICE AREAS: White Collar Criminal Defense; General Criminal Defense; Business Civil Litigation.
Levine, John W. ........................'54 '78 C.1036 B.A. L.426 J.D. 11686 Darlington Ave.
Levine, Joseph ........................'46 '72 C.112 A.B. L.1068 J.D. Sr. Jud. Atty., Ct. of App.
**Levine, Kenneth A.** ........................'51 '88 C.035 M.A. L.426 J.D. [Ⓐ Serritella&P.]
Levine, Leonard B. ............ '46 '72 C.112 B.A. L.1068 J.D. 1901 Avenue of the Stars
**Levine, Lori M.** ........................'51 '87 C.112 B.A. L.426 J.D. [Ⓐ Schell&D.]
**Levine, Marci R.** ........................'62 '90 C.112 B.A. L.809 J.D. [Freid&G.]
*PRACTICE AREAS: Family Law.

Levine, Mark H. ........................'66 '92 C.309 A.B. L.976 J.D. 350 S. Grand Ave.
Levine, Mark S. ........................'57 '82 C&L.426 B.A., J.D. [Ⓐ J.R.Brown,Jr.]
Levine, Martin .....'39 '64 C.1036 A.B. L.976 J.D. Prof. of Law, Univ. of Southern Calif.
**Levine, Meldon E.**, (AV) '43 '70 C.112 A.B. L.309 J.D.
[Gibson,D.&C.] (⊙Wash., DC)
*LANGUAGES: Spanish.
*PRACTICE AREAS: International Transactions and Trade; Federal and State Administrative/Legislative and Governmental Advocacy.
Levine, Michael B. '55 '81 C.112 B.A. L.426 J.D.
CEO & Gen. Coun., Career Grp., Inc.
**Levine, Michael Cary** ........................'66 '91 C.188 A.B. L.659 J.D. [Ⓐ O'Melveny&M.]
*PRACTICE AREAS: Labor and Employment Law.
**Levine, Norman H.**, (AV) ........'49 '74 C.659 B.A. L.813 J.D. [Greenberg G.F.C.&M.]
*PRACTICE AREAS: Litigation.
Levine, Paul H. ........................'52 '78 C.800 A.B. L.426 J.D. [Rosin&L.]
Levine, Philip R. ........................'40 '65 C&L.94 A.B., LL.B. 1660 Roscomare Rd.
Levine, Richard A. ........................'51 '82 C.112 B.A. L.1148 J.D. 6500 Wilshire Blvd.
Levine, Saul R. ........................'26 '56 C.112 A.B. L.1068 LL.B. P.O. Box 250028
Levine, Tema A. ............ '55 '80 C.1169 B.A. L.426 J.D. 801 S. Grand Ave., 18th Fl.

**Levine, Arthur S., A Professional Corporation, (AV)**
**10390 Santa Monica Boulevard, 4th Floor, 90025-5058**
**Telephone: 310-557-1700 Fax: 310-557-0019**
**Arthur S. Levine (Certified Specialist, Estate Planning, Trust and Probate Law, The State Bar of California Board of Legal Specialization).**
**Business and Corporate Transactions, Real Estate and Estate Planning.**
*See Professional Biographies, LOS ANGELES, CALIFORNIA*

**Levine & Associates, (AV)** BB
**Suite 710, 2049 Century Park East, 90067**⊙
**Telephone: 310-553-8400 Fax: 310-553-8455**
**Jerome L. Levine. Associates: Mary L. Prevost (Resident, Seattle, Washington Office); Erin M. Copeland; Frank R. Lawrence. Of Counsel: Allan Albala.**
**General Business and Civil Trial and Appellate Practice in all State and Federal Courts. Complex Business Litigation, Corporation and Partnership Law, Real Estate, Contract and Business Law, Secured Transactions, International Law, Casino and Gaming Law, Intellectual Property, Advertising, Entertainment, Commercial and Indian Law.**
**Seattle, Washington Office: 999 Third Avenue, Suite 3210, 98104. Telephone: 206-626-5310. Fax: 206-626-5313.**
*See Professional Biographies, LOS ANGELES, CALIFORNIA*

**Levine, Joel, A Professional Corporation, (AV)**
**16000 Ventura Boulevard, Suite 500 (Encino), 91436**
**Telephone: 818-995-6052 Fax: 818-995-0407**
**Joel Levine;—Andrea Trupin Levine.**
**General Civil, Criminal and Appellate Practice in all State and Federal Courts. Corporate, Criminal and Commercial.**
*See Professional Biographies, LOS ANGELES, CALIFORNIA*

**Levinrad, Eric** ........................'66 '93 [Ⓐ Berman,B.M.&R.]
*PRACTICE AREAS: Commercial Litigation; Intellectual Property Litigation; Trademark; Copyrights; Trade Secrets.
Levinson, Donald E. ............... '48 '75 C.36 B.S. L.809 J.D. 11355 W. Olympic Blvd.
Levinson, Jeffrey A. ............... '61 '90 C.112 B.A. L.978 J.D. 1875 Century Park E.

**Levinson, Mark L., (AV) '40 '66 C.102 A.B. L.569 J.D.**
**1900 Avenue of the Stars, Suite 1700, 90067**
**Telephone: 310-277-3799**
**Music Law, Motion Pictures Law, Television Law, Copyright Law and General Entertainment Law.**
*See Professional Biographies, LOS ANGELES, CALIFORNIA*

**Levinson, Matthew** ........................'69 '94 C.188 B.A. L.112 J.D. [Ⓐ Thelen,M.J.&B.]
*PRACTICE AREAS: Litigation.
**Levinson, Paul**, (AV) ........................'31 '57 C.112 B.S. L.1068 J.D. [Levinson,M.J.&P.]
*PRACTICE AREAS: Taxation Law; Real Estate.
**Levinson, Ronald E.** ........................'58 '83 C.188 A.B. L.1068 J.D. [Ⓐ Kaye,S.F.H.&H.]
*PRACTICE AREAS: Real Estate; Business Transactions.
**Levinson, Tasha Dian** ........................'48 '77 L.1026 LL.B. [Ⓐ Fierstein&S.]
*PRACTICE AREAS: Estate Planning; Probate.
**Levinson, William Mark** ..........'53 '82 C.1036 A.B. L.978 J.D. [ⓒ Buchalter,N.F.&Y.]
*PRACTICE AREAS: Municipal Bond Financing Law; Corporate Law; Real Estate Law; Securities Law.

**Levinson & Kaplan**
**(See Encino)**

**Levinson, Lieberman & Maas, A Professional Corporation**
**(See Beverly Hills)**

**Levinson, Miller, Jacobs & Phillips, A Professional Corporation, (AV)**
**Suite 2000, 1875 Century Park East, 90067-2534**
**Telephone: 310-557-2455 Cable Address: "Levrom" Facsimile: 310-282-0472**
**Paul Levinson (Certified Specialist, Taxation Law, The State Bar of California Board of Legal Specialization); Gary S. Jacobs (Certified Specialist, Family Law, The State Bar of California Board of Legal Specialization); Stanton Lee Phillips; Samuel M. Robin;—Sharon Jill Sandler; J. Bennett Friedman; Fern S. Nisen; Erin L. Prouty. Of Counsel: Milton Louis Miller; Stephen I. Halper.**
**Real Estate, Corporation, Taxation, Estate Planning, Probate, Family and Tort Law. General Civil and Trial Practice in all State and Federal Courts.**
**References: First Charter Bank; Wells Fargo Trust (Trust Dept., Southern California Headquarters).**
*See Professional Biographies, LOS ANGELES, CALIFORNIA*

**Levit, William H., (P.C.)**, (AV) ......... '08 '30 C&L.813 A.B., J.D. [Stroock&S.&L.] ‡
Levitan, Jonathan M. ........................'54 '82 C&L.061 B.A. 12400 Wilshire Blvd.
Levitin, Sheldon L. ........................'35 '63 C.112 B.A. L.1068 J.D. Dep. Dist. Atty.
Leviton, Michael E. '31 '60 C.339 A.B. L.365 J.D.
(adm. in IL; not adm. in CA) Staff Atty., Levitt & Quinn Family Law Ctr.
**Leviton, Stuart L.** ........................'66 '93 C.659 B.S. L.846 J.D. [Ⓐ Latham&W.]
**Levitt, Dana N., (P.C.)** ........................'49 '77 C.454 B.A. L.228 J.D. [Alschuler G.&P.]
**Levitt, John S.**, (AV) ........................'56 '83 C.112 A.B. L.426 J.D. [ⓒ Firestein&F.]
*PRACTICE AREAS: Personal Injury Law; Civil Litigation; Insurance Defense.
Levitt, Judith A. ........................'— '78 C.494 B.A. L.426 J.D. 3314 Sunnynook Dr.
**Levitt, Meyer S.** ........................'38 '66 C.112 B.S. L.800 J.D. [Moss,L.&M.]
*PRACTICE AREAS: Family Law; General Trial Law; Civil Litigation; Construction Litigation.
**Levkowitz, Howard M.** ........................'67 '93 C.659 B.A.B.S. L.800 J.D. [Ⓐ Dewey B.]
*LANGUAGES: Spanish, Hebrew.
**Levun, Roy A.** ........................'51 '80 C.339 B.A. L.809 J.D. [Ⓐ D.B.Bloom]
**Levy, Amos M.** '62 '89 C.309 A.B. L.569 J.D.
(adm. in NY; not adm. in CA) [Ⓐ Latham&W.]
**Levy, Barry R., (A P.C.)**, (AV) ........................'43 '72 C.1077 B.A. L.426 J.D. [Horvitz&L.]
**Levy, C. Daniel**, (AV) ........................'53 '86 C&L.178 B.A., J.D. [Ⓐ B.P.Wolfsdorf]
*LANGUAGES: Spanish, French, German, Hebrew.
*PRACTICE AREAS: Immigration and Nationality Law.
**Levy, Charles M., (P.C.)**, (AV) ........................'37 '62 C&L.597 B.S.L., J.D. [Levy,S.&L.]
*PRACTICE AREAS: Commercial Law; Loan Documentation; Enforcement and Workouts.
Levy, David R. ........................'48 '81 L.809 J.D. 911 N. Kings Rd.
**Levy, David S.** ........................'66 '93 C.477 L.800 J.D. [Ⓐ Charlston,R.&W.]
*PRACTICE AREAS: Environmental Insurance Coverage; Litigation.
Levy, Harold J. ........................'40 '80 C.569 L.1095 J.D. [Stanbury,F.&L.]

Levy, Jeffrey H. ........................ '61 '87 C.1074 B.S. L.1067 J.D. Off. of Pub. Def.
**Levy, Margaret** ........................ '51 '75 C.475 B.A. L.1068 J.D. [Manatt,P.&P.]
*PRACTICE AREAS: Disability Insurance Litigation; Life Insurance Litigation; Health Insurance Litigation; Employment Litigation.
Levy, Maurice, Jr., (AV) ............... '10 '34 C.112 B.A. L.1068 J.D. 462 N. Highland‡

**Levy, Richard A. '56 '86 C.722 B.A. L.477 J.D.**
**10940 Wilshire Boulevard, Suite 1400, 90024**
**Telephone: 310-446-5377 Fax: 310-446-5379**
**Business Litigation emphasizing Trademark and Copyright Infringement.**
***See Professional Biographies, LOS ANGELES, CALIFORNIA***

**Levy, Richard B.** ........................ '68 '92 C.012 B.A. L.569 J.D. [▣ Gibson,D.&C.]
*PRACTICE AREAS: Labor and Employment Law; Entertainment and Sports Law.
**Levy, Richard Paul, (AV)** ............... '47 '72 C.966 B.A. L.477 J.D. [Gibson,D.&C.]
*PRACTICE AREAS: Securities Related Litigation; Class Action Defense Litigation; First Amendment Litigation; General Business Litigation; Plaintiffs/Contingent Fee Catastrophic Injury Litigation.
Levy, Robert J., (AV) ..................... '42 '68 C.684 B.A. L.1068 J.D. Dep. Pub. Def.
Levy, Stanley W., (AV) ............ '41 '66 C.112 A.B. L.1068 J.D. 1444 S. Alameda St.
**Levy, Steven E., (AV)** ..................... '48 '73 C.112 A.B. L.1068 J.D. [Sandler&R.]
**Levy, Steven Mark, (AV)** ............... '52 '77 C.154 B.A. L.1066 J.D. [Lewis,D.B.&B.]
*LANGUAGES: French.
Levy, Susan E. ..................... '50 '83 C.823 B.A. L.800 J.D. 1999 Ave. of the Stars

**Levy, Small & Lallas, (AV)**
**A Partnership of Professional Corporations**
**815 Moraga Drive, 90049-1633**
**Telephone: 310-471-3000 Telecopier: 310-471-7990**
**Charles M. Levy (P.C.); Steven G. Small (P.C.); Tom Lallas (P.C.); Leo D. Plotkin (P.C.); Walter R. Mitchell;—Mark D. Hurwitz; Theodore A. Cohen; Angel F. Castillo; Michael Mergenthaler.**
**Commercial and Secured Transactions Law, General Civil, Trial and Appellate Litigation. Banking, Corporate and Real Estate Law.**
***See Professional Biographies, LOS ANGELES, CALIFORNIA***

**Levyn, Thomas S.** ........................ '49 '74 C&L.800 B.S., J.D. [Agapay,L.&H.]
*PRACTICE AREAS: Real Estate; Risk Management; Business Law.
Lew, Bill W. .......................... '50 '76 C.112 B.A. L.1068 J.D. 865 S. Figueroa St.
Lew, Ronald S. W. ............................ '41 '72 C.426 B.A. L.809 J.D. U.S. Dist. J.
Lew, Stephen, (AV) ........................ '50 '76 C.112 A.B. L.178 J.D. [Costell&J.]
**Lew Powell, Amy** ......... '69 '94 C.800 B.S. L.809 J.D. [▣ Christensen,M.F.J.G.W.&S.]
*PRACTICE AREAS: Litigation.
**Lewand, Kimberly E.** ............ '66 '93 C.112 B.A. L.990 J.D. [▣ Demetriou,D.S.&M.]

**Lewellyn, Larry D., Law Offices of '55 '89 C&L.426 B.A., J.D.**
**3255 Wilshire Boulevard, Suite 1024, 90010**
**Telephone: 213-389-5582 Fax: 213-389-1143**
***PRACTICE AREAS: Probate Law; Personal Injury; Criminal Law.**
**Estate Planning, Probate Law, Elder Law, Elder Abuse Litigation, Conservatorship, Guardianship.**

**Lewi, Christopher C.** ..................... '62 '89 C.112 B.A. L.426 J.D. [▣ Booth,M.&S.]
Lewin, Henry ........................................ '36 '63 C.112 B.S. L.426 J.D. [Lewin&L.]
Lewin, Kurt J. .............................. '34 '64 C.112 B.A. L.1068 LL.B. Supr. Ct. J.

**Lewin, Lawrin S., (AV) '39 '64 C.112 B.A. L.1068 J.D.**
**10940 Wilshire Boulevard, Sixth Floor, 90024**
**Telephone: 310-443-7660 Fax: 310-443-7599**
**Probate, Estate Planning and Real Estate, Auditing Attorney Fees.**

Lewin, Noreen Spencer ............... '54 '79 C.597 B.A. L.424 J.D. 624 S. Grand Ave.
Lewin & Levin, A Partnership of Professional Corp. ............. 1925 Century Park East
**Lewis, Amy W.** .......................... '63 '92 C.101 B.A. L.426 J.D. [▣ Schaffer&L.]
Lewis, Arthur ............................ '25 '55 C.112 L.809 LL.B. 601 W. 5th St.
Lewis, Cheri Ann ................... '52 '84 C.1077 B.S. L.398 J.D. 12121 Wilshire Blvd.
**Lewis, Darren J.** ................ '65 '90 C.94 B.S. L.1068 J.D. [▣ Kleinberg L.L.B.&C.]
*PRACTICE AREAS: Music Recording Law.
**Lewis, David J.** ........................................................ '53 '78 L.061 LL.B. [D.Lewis]
Lewis, Edward G., (BV) ......................... '45 '71 C&L.800 B.A., J.D. [E.G.Lewis]
**Lewis, Floyd M.** ................. '27 '55 C.112 B.S. L.1068 LL.B. [▣ Parker,M.C.O.&S.]
*SPECIAL AGENCIES: Internal Revenue Service.
*TRANSACTIONS: Decedent Trust and probate court administration. I.R.S. Estate and Gift Tax Return examination procedures. Fiduciary income tax planning.
*PRACTICE AREAS: Trusts and Estates; Federal Estate and Gift Tax proceedings; Financial and Estate Planning; Trust and Estate Litigation; Charitable Trusts and Deferred Giving.
Lewis, Gina R. ........................... '69 '95 C.112 B.A. L.426 J.D. [▣ Liebert,C.&F.]
Lewis, Guy J. ........................................ '52 '79 C.940 B.A. L.426 J.D. [Lewis&S.]
Lewis, Honey A., (AV) ........................ '42 '69 C.112 B.A. L.426 Asst. City Atty.
**Lewis, James W.** .......................... '53 '89 C.170 B.A. L.1068 J.D. [Jackson&L.]
*PRACTICE AREAS: Environmental Law; Toxic Exposure; Employment Law; Civil Rights.
**Lewis, Jeffrey James** ................... '— '90 C.118 B.A. L.1066 J.D. [▣ Morgan,L.&B.]
**Lewis, Jennifer Cook** ........................ '59 '86 C.174 B.S. L.208 J.D. [Hill,F.&B.]
*LANGUAGES: French.
*PRACTICE AREAS: Business Litigation; Real Property Litigation; Eminent Domain; Prejudgement Remedies; Enforcement of Judgments.
Lewis, Joan ................. '51 '77 C.112 B.A. L.426 J.D. 3473 Manderville Canyon Rd.
**Lewis, Jodi M.** ................................ '61 '87 C.112 B.A. L.426 J.D. [▣ Wickwire G.]
*PRACTICE AREAS: Litigation; Construction and Business Law.
Lewis, Johanna ......................... '— '93 C.112 L.1136 J.D. 624 S Grand Ave., 27th Fl
Lewis, Joseph ................................ '10 '33 C&L.809 LL.B. 8484 Wilshire Blvd.
Lewis, Kenneth H. ......................... '52 '76 C.112 L.426 J.D. 601 W. 5th St.
**Lewis, Marjorie Ehrich, (AV)** ............ '54 '79 C.860 B.A. L.569 J.D. [Gibson,D.&C.]
*PRACTICE AREAS: General Business Litigation.
Lewis, Mason C. .......................... '35 '64 C&L.472 B.B.A., LL.B. Asst. U.S. Atty.
**Lewis, Matthew P.** ........................ '65 '91 C.605 A.B. L.426 J.D. [▣ White&C.]
**Lewis, Michael D.** ................... '68 '95 C.1281 B.A. L.1066 J.D. [▣ Latham&W.]
Lewis, Michael Richard ................... '54 '83 L.061 LL.B. 8827 Beverly Blvd.
**Lewis, Randi S.** ................... '55 '83 C.446 B.A. L.273 J.D. [Breidenbach,B.H.H.&H.]
**Lewis, Robert E.** .................... '44 '70 C.112 B.S. L.1068 J.D. [Anderson,A.L.&G.]©
*PRACTICE AREAS: Commercial and Secured Transactions; Real Estate; Corporate.
**Lewis, Robert F., (P.C.), (AV)** ....... '36 '62 C.112 B.A. L.1068 J.D. [Lewis,D.B.&B.]©
**Lewis, Robert P., Jr.** ................................ '44 '73 C.477 A.B. L.800 J.D. [Choate&C.]
*LANGUAGES: Chinese (Mandarin).
*PRACTICE AREAS: International; Agricultural.
**Lewis, Rosemarie Suazo** ...................... '63 '92 C.800 B.A. L.1137 [Borton,P.&C.]
*PRACTICE AREAS: Insurance; Personal Injury; Construction Defect.
**Lewis, Scott C.** .......................... '65 '91 C.112 B.A. L.477 J.D. [▣ Latham&W.]
*PRACTICE AREAS: Corporate Securities; Mergers and Acquisitions.
**Lewis, Steven R.** .......................... '61 '87 C.112 B.A. L.990 J.D. [Lewis,D.B.&B.]
Lewis, Terrance T. ...................... '57 '88 C.112 B.A. L.426 J.D. Dep. Pub. Def.
**Lewis, Toni** .......................... '56 '83 C.426 B.A. L.1068 J.D. [▣ Firestein&F.]
*PRACTICE AREAS: Personal Injury; Premise Liability; Casualty Claims.
Lewis, Walter H., (AV) .................. '36 '65 C.800 B.A. L.809 J.D. Dep. Dist. Atty.

**Lewis, D'Amato, Brisbois & Bisgaard, (AV) ▣**
**A Partnership including Professional Corporations**
**Suite 1200, 221 North Figueroa Street, 90012©**
**Telephone: 213-250-1800 Telex: 194508 Facsimile: 213-250-7900**

(This Listing Continued)

**Lewis, D'Amato, Brisbois & Bisgaard (Continued)**

**Members of Firm: Robert F. Lewis (P.C.); Christopher P. Bisgaard (P.C.); Roy M. Brisbois (P.C.); R. Gaylord Smith (Resident, San Diego Office); David E. Reynolds (P.C.); Duane C. Musfelt (Resident, San Francisco Office); Barry G. Kaiman (P.C.); Raul L. Martinez (P.C.); Steven Mark Levy; B. Casey Yim (P.C.); Alan E. Greenberg (Resident, San Diego Office); Mary G. Whitaker (P.C.); Scott Lichtig; Donald A. Ruston (Resident, Costa Mesa Office); James D. Fraser; David B. Paynter (Resident, San Francisco Office); Dennis R. Kasper; Ernest Slome (Resident, San Diego Office); Keith D. Taylor (Resident, Costa Mesa Office); Douglas R. Reynolds (Resident, San Diego Office); Marilyn R. Moriarty (Resident, San Diego Office); Jeffrey B. Barton (Resident, San Diego Office); Robert K. Wrede; Timothy R. Graves; Peter L. Garchie (Resident, San Diego Office); Steven R. Lewis; David N. Makous; Randall L. Mason (Resident, San Diego Office); Eric C. Castro; Lawrence N. Halperin; Jeffrey R. Kurtock (P.C.) (Resident, San Francisco Office); Gary M. Lape (Resident, Costa Mesa Office); Shawn K. Deasy (Resident, San Diego Office); Thomas Rittenburg; Bartley L. Becker; Lance A. Selfridge; Sharon S. Chandler (Resident, San Francisco Office); Nancy E. Zeltzer (Resident, Costa Mesa Office); John H. Shimada; Gary L. Effron; Kenneth T. Kreeble (Resident, San Bernardino Office); Joseph K. Hegedus; Judith A. Zipkin; Gordon J. Calhoun; Richard B. Wolf; Paul Y. Lee; David E. Long; Roger S. Raphael (Resident, San Francisco Office); Cathey A. Stricker; Thomas L. Vazakas (Resident, San Diego Office); Elise D. Klein; Joseph C. Owens; William John Rea, Jr.; Lee A. Wood (Resident, Costa Mesa Office); Dennis G. Seley (Resident, Sacramento Office); Jana I. Lubert; Judith M. Tishkoff; Thomas M. Diachenko (Resident, San Diego Office); R. Anthony Moya (Resident, San Diego Office); Thomas E. Francis (Resident, Costa Mesa Office); Susan E. Leonard (Resident, San Diego Office); H. Gilbert Jones (Resident, Costa Mesa Office); Howard G. Rath, Jr., (P.C.) (Certified Specialist, Taxation Law, The State Bar of California Board of Legal Specialization); Frankie Fook-Lun Leung; Michael W. Connally (Resident, Costa Mesa Office); Annie Verdries (Resident, Costa Mesa Office); Stephen T. Waimey; Mercedes Cruz; Armen Hairapetian; Claudia J. Robinson (Resident, Sacramento Office); Leon M. Cooper; James G. Bohm (Resident, Costa Mesa Office); George A. Boland (Resident, San Bernardino Office); Joan L. Danielsen (Resident, San Diego Office); Richard L. Antognini (Resident, Sacramento Office); Laura S. Inlow; Douglas R. Irvine; Scott W. Monson (Resident, Costa Mesa Office); Michael C. Olson (Resident, Costa Mesa Office); James J. Wallace (Resident, San Diego Office); Timothy J. Watson; Louis Robert De Stefano; David M. Reeder; Peter F. Harris; John F. Davis (Resident, Sacramento Office); David E. Isenberg (Resident, Costa Mesa Office); Russell J. Callison (Resident, Sacramento Office); Paul N. Phillips (Resident, Sacramento Office); Brad D. Krasnoff (Resident, Costa Mesa Office); Penny Paxton; Raul B. Garcia (Resident, Costa Mesa Office); Michael J. Lancaster (Resident, Costa Mesa Office); Bruce Legernes (Resident, San Francisco Office); Bruce L. Shaffer (Resident, Sacramento Office); Gregory P. Matzen (Resident, Sacramento Office); Joseph Arias (Resident, San Bernardino Office); Richard W. Bane (Resident, San Bernardino Office); Roger L. Bellows (Resident, San Bernardino Office); Henry W. Crowle (Resident, Sacramento Office); Charles S. Haughey, Jr. (Resident, San Diego Office); Janelle F. Garchie (Resident, San Diego Office); Robert V. Closson (Resident, San Diego Office); Thomas M. Correll (Resident, San Diego Office); Kenneth E. Goates (Resident, San Diego Office); Howard A. Slavin; Edward F. Morrison, Jr.; Jack D. Tomlinson (Resident, San Francisco Office); Kenneth D. Huston (Resident, San Diego Office); Gerald R Judson. Associates: Kelly D. Akins; Sarira D. Alexander; Norman E. Allen (Resident, San Francisco Office); Lee M. Amidon (Resident, San Bernardino Office); Paul Ellis Baron (Resident, San Francisco Office); Mark A. Birmingham (Resident, San Diego Office); Leslie S. Bowen (Resident, Costa Mesa Office); Larry J. Brock; Joseph C. Campo; Cindy Merten Cardullo (Resident, Sacramento Office); John S. Christopher; G. Russell Clark, Resident, San Diego Office); David S. Cohn (Resident, San Bernardino Office); Lori Creasey (Resident, Costa Mesa Office); Troy A. Edwards (Resident, Costa Mesa Office); Lawrence A. Eugenio; Karen A. Feld (Resident, San Bernardino Office); Tina Fisher; Kelly M. Flanagan (Resident, Costa Mesa Office); James E. Friedhofer (Resident, San Diego Office); J. Albert Garcia (Resident, San Diego Office); Robert H. Garnett; Christopher R. Green; Allison A. Greene (Resident, Costa Mesa Office); Christopher J. Greenleaf; Patrick P. Gunn; Jay D. Harker (Resident, Costa Mesa Office); Heather Anne Henderson (Resident, Costa Mesa Office); Paula F. Henry (Resident, Costa Mesa Office); Helen E. Hesse (Resident, Costa Mesa Office); Madonna L. Hultman (Resident, Costa Mesa Office); Charles J. Hyland (Resident, Costa Mesa Office); April M. Johnson (Resident, San Diego Office); Raimo H. Kaasik; Laura B. Kaliser; Jonathon Kaplan; Jenifer L. Kienle (Resident, San Diego Office); Catherine J. Kim (Resident, Costa Mesa Office); Harry T. Kozak (Resident, Costa Mesa Office); Jacqueline S. LaScala (Resident, San Diego Office); Sharon M. Lawrence (Resident, San Diego Office); Valerie L. Leatherwood; Douglas W. Lewis (Resident, San Diego Office); Judith A. Lewis (Resident, San Diego Office); Joan Creigh. Little (Resident, San Diego Office); Michael S. Little; Christopher D. Lockwood (Resident, San Bernardino Office); Dennis J. Mahoney (Resident, San Bernardino Office); Gregory P. Martin; James P. Mayo (Resident, Sacramento Office); John H. McCardle (Resident, Sacramento Office); Steven E. Meyer; Gail F. Montgomery (Resident, San Bernardino Office); Raffi A. Nahabedian; Paul F. O'Brien (Resident, San Diego Office); Terrell A. Quealy (Resident, San Diego Office); Catherine J. Quinn; Lisa K. Roberts (Resident, San Diego Office); James F. B. Sawyer; Larry R. Schmadeka; Robert M. Shannon (Resident, Sacramento Office); Christina M. Slatton; Christine Graves Thoene (Resident, San Diego Office); Karen E. Vaughey; Julie A. Veltkamp; Jamie E. Walters; Kenneth D. Watnick; Susan West; Cary L. Wood; Beth E. Yoffie; John Yong-Jin Yoon.**
**General Practice.**
**Lewis, D'Amato, Brisbois & Bisgaard California Offices:**
**Costa Mesa Office: 650 Town Center, Suite 1400, Costa Mesa, California, 92626. Telephone: 714-545-9200. Facsimile: 714-850-1030.**
**Sacramento Office: 2500 Venture Oaks Way, Sacramento, California 95833. Telephone: 916-564-5400. Facsimile: 916-564-5444.**
**San Bernardino Office: 650 East Hospitality Lane, Suite 600, San Bernardino, California 92408. Telephone: 909-387-1130. Facsimile: 909-387-1138.**
**San Diego Office: 550 West C Street, Suite 800, San Diego California 92101. Telephone: 619-233-1006. Facsimile: 619-233-8627.**
**San Francisco Office: 601 California Street, Suite 1900, San Francisco, California 94108. Telephone: 415-362-2580. Facsimile: 415-434-0882.**
**Affiliated Offices:**
**Jakarta, Indonesia Affiliated Office: Mulya Lubis and Partners, Wisma Bank Dharmala, 16th Floor, Jendral, Sudirman, Kav. 28, Jakarta 12920, Indonesia. Telephone: (62)(21) 521-1931/521-1932. Facsimile: (62)(21) 521-1930.**
**Bangkok, Thailand Affiliated Office: Kanung & Partners Law Offices, Raintree Office Garden, 272 Japanese School Lane, Rama IX Road, Bangkok 10310, Thailand. Telephone: (662) 319-7571/319-7574. Facsimile: (662) 319-6372.**
***See Professional Biographies, LOS ANGELES, CALIFORNIA***

**Lewis, David, Law Offices of, A Prof. Corp.**
**11400 West Olympic Boulevard Ninth Floor, 90064**
**Telephone: 310-575-0049 Fax: 310-444-9842**
**Email: lewislaw@ix.netcom.com**
**David J. Lewis.**
**Real Estate Transactional, Securities, Corporate, Business, Civil Trial.**
***See Professional Biographies, LOS ANGELES, CALIFORNIA***

Lewis, Edward G., A Professional Corporation, (BV) ................ 10100 Empyrean Way
Lewis & Scholnick ........................................................... 900 Wilshire Blvd.
**Lewiston, Jeffrey A.** ........................ '59 '86 C.20 B.A. L.1049 J.D. [▣ Grace,S.C.&S.]
*PRACTICE AREAS: Insurance Coverage Law; Insurance Defense Law; Product Liability Law; Appellate Law.

**Lewitt, Hackman, Hoefflin, Shapiro, Marshall & Harlan, A Law Corporation**
**(See Encino)**

Lewkowicz, Jennie F. ............ '57 '83 C.978 B.A. L.426 J.D. 1044 S. Robertson Blvd.
**Li, Jenny Y.** ........................... '66 '92 C.339 B.A. L.276 J.D. [▣ Quisenberry&B.]
Li, Luis ................................ '65 '91 C.976 B.A. L.1066 J.D. 355 S. Grand Ave., 35th Fl.
**Li, Mark K.** ........... '58 '86 C.112 B.S. L.767 J.D. [▣ Christensen,M.F.J.G.W.&S.]
*PRACTICE AREAS: Taxation; Estate Planning Law.
**Liang, Grace C.** ........................ '68 '94 C.112 B.A. L.178 J.D. [▣ Riordan&M.]
**Liang, Wu Hong** ................................................ '35 '85 [Arnberger,K.B.&C.]
*LANGUAGES: Chinese, English and Shanghai dialect.
*PRACTICE AREAS: Patent and Trademark Law; Intellectual Property.
**Libby, Gerold W., (AV)** ............. '42 '69 C.976 B.A. L.569 J.D. [Whitman B.A.&M.]
*PRACTICE AREAS: Business Law; Corporate Law; Project Finance; International Law.
**Libby, John F.** .............................. '58 '84 C.813 A.B. L.976 J.D. [Manatt,P.&P.]
*PRACTICE AREAS: Health Law; Business Litigation; White-Collar Criminal Defense.
**Libby, Patricia A.** ..................... '61 '87 C.813 B.A. L.1068 J.D. [▣ Arnold&P.]

CAA279P

CALIFORNIA—LOS ANGELES MARTINDALE-HUBBELL LAW DIRECTORY 1997

**Liberatore, Frank M.** ..................'59 '85 C&L.800 B.A., J.D. [🄰 Jackson,L.S.&K.]
*PRACTICE AREAS: Business Litigation; Employment Law.
Liberman, David ..................'48 '82 C.260 B.S. L.472 J.D. 2049 Century Park E.
**Liberman, Jason J.** ..................'67 '93 C.800 B.S. L.990 J.D. [🄰 Whitman B.A.&M.]
**Liberson, Howard S.** ..................'67 '95 C.112 B.A. L.426 J.D. [🄰 Morrison&F.]
**Liberson, Joel K.** ..................'63 '93 C.339 B.S. L.424 J.D. [🄰 Sidley&A.]
*PRACTICE AREAS: Litigation.
**Libertino, Teresa Anna** ..................'58 '87 C.483 B.A. L.464 J.D. [🄰 Murchison&C.]
*PRACTICE AREAS: General Insurance Defense Litigation.
**Libicki, Stuart,** (AV) ..................'49 '73 C.112 B.S. L.1066 J.D. [Schwartz,S.D.&S.]
*PRACTICE AREAS: Labor and Employment Law; Employee Benefits Litigation; Real Estate; Insurance.
**Libraty, Michael** ..................'— '92 C&L.112 B.A., J.D. [🄰 J.J.Gustin&Assoc.]
*PRACTICE AREAS: Commercial and Business Law.
**Licata, Francis P.** ..................'51 '76 C.112 B.A. L.990 J.D. [Lovich&P.]
Lichtenberg, Karen A. ..................'— '78 C.30 B.A. L.809 J.D. Sr. Dep. Co. Coun.
**Lichter, Linda,** (AV) ..................'51 '76 C.112 A.B. L.1066 J.D. [Lichter,G.N.&A.]
*PRACTICE AREAS: Entertainment Law.

**Lichter, Grossman, Nichols & Adler, Inc., (AV)**
**9200 Sunset Boulevard, Suite 530, 90069**
**Telephone: 310-205-6999 Fax: 310-205-6990**
**Email: lgninc@sure.net**
**Peter Grossman; Linda Lichter; Peter Nichols; Michael I. Adler; Carlos K. Goodman;—James J. Kershaw, III; Patricia L. Laucella; Cynthia Farrelly Gesner.**
**Practice Limited to Entertainment Law.**
***See Professional Biographies, LOS ANGELES, CALIFORNIA***

Lichtgarn, Eve ..................'58 '90 C.112 B.A. L.809 J.D. 4484 Wilshire Blvd., 2nd Fl.
**Lichtig, Scott** ..................'53 '78 C.154 B.A. L.1066 J.D. [Lewis,D.B.&B.]
Lichtman, Jay L. ..................'49 '74 C&L.107 B.A., J.D. 201 N. Figueroa St. Fl. 700
**Lichtman, Joanne** ..................'62 '88 C.882 B.A. L.309 J.D. [🄰 Howrey&S.]
*PRACTICE AREAS: Environmental Law.
**Lichtman, Joshua D.** ..................'68 '95 C.228 A.B. L.1068 [🄰 Fulbright&J.]
*PRACTICE AREAS: Litigation.
Licker, Mark D. ..................'53 '79 C.813 B.A. L.800 J.D. 10877 Wilshire Blvd.
Licker, Stephen S. ..................'39 '65 C&L.800 B.A., J.D. Dep. Dist. Atty.
Licker, William ..................'46 '72 C.112 B.A. L.1137 J.D. 11900 W. Olympic Blvd.
Liddell, Donald C. ..................'48 '75 C.763 A.B. L.1065 J.D. 633 W. 5th St.
**Lieb, Michael C.** ..................'— '86 C.1365 B.A. L.477 J.D. [🄰 Morgan,L.&B.]
Lieb, Robert D. ..................'53 '78 C.112 B.A. L.1049 J.D. [Gurewitz&L.]
**Lieb, William G.** ..................'54 '84 C.37 B.A. L.809 J.D. [🄰 Veatch,C.G.&N.]
*PRACTICE AREAS: Medical Malpractice Defense Law; General Casualty Defense Law.
**Liebeler, Eric C.** ..................'63 '90 C.453 B.S. L.228 J.D. [Kirkland&E.]
*PRACTICE AREAS: Litigation.

**Liebenbaum, Lawrence F., (AV) '35 '70 C.1097 B.A. L.426 J.D.**
**11766 Wilshire Boulevard, Suite 700, 90025-6538**
**Telephone: 310-471-0043 Fax: 310-445-2191**
**(Certified Specialist, Immigration and Nationality Law, The State Bar of California Board of Legal Specialization).**
**Immigration and Naturalization Law.**
***See Professional Biographies, LOS ANGELES, CALIFORNIA***

**Lieber, Deborah A.** ..................'64 '90 C.112 B.A. L.809 J.D. [🄰 Dennison,B.&P.]
Lieber, Enid I. ..................'53 '77 C.112 B.A. L.1068 J.D. 2419 Buckingham Ln.
**Lieberman, Marc A.** ..................'64 '91 C.103 A.B. L.1068 J.D. [Mayer,G.&G.]
*LANGUAGES: Spanish, French and Portuguese.
*REPORTED CASES: In re Barakat, 173 B.R. 672 (Bkrptcy. C.D. CAL. 1994).
*PRACTICE AREAS: Bankruptcy Litigation; Creditors Rights Law.
**Lieberman, Norman,** (BV) ..................'22 '68 C.112 B.A. L.1148 J.D. [🄲 Barbosa G.&B.]
*PRACTICE AREAS: Municipal Law; Land Use Law; Personnel Law; Eminent Domain Law.
Lieberman, Robert H. ..................'52 '77 C.112 B.A. L.800 J.D. 1925 Century Park E.
Liebert, Allan H., (BV) ..................'36 '62 C.999 L.809 LL.B. 1033 Gayley Ave.
Liebert, John, (AV) ..................'29 '66 C.112 B.S. L.1065 J.D. [Liebert,C.&F.]
Liebert, Cassidy & Frierson, A Professional Corporation, (AV)
6033 W. Century Blvd. (⊙San Francisco)
**Liebhaber, Jack M.** ..................'58 '84 C.1044 B.A. L.990 J.D. [Robinson,D.&W.]
*PRACTICE AREAS: General Litigation.
**Liebman, John R.,** (AV) ..................'35 '62 C.197 A.B. L.1068 J.D. [Tuttle&T.]
*LANGUAGES: German.
*PRACTICE AREAS: International Trade Regulation; International Trade Finance; Technology Transfer; International Joint Ventures; International Commercial Transactions.
Liebman, Joseph ..................'55 '83 C.1078 B.A. L.426 J.D. [J.Liebman]
**Liebman, Stuart J.,** (AV) ..................'45 '71 C.112 B.A. L.426 J.D. [Liebman&R.]
*PRACTICE AREAS: Personal Injury Defense Law; Insurance Law.
Liebman, Joseph, A Prof. Corp. ..................11150 Santa Monica Blvd.

**Liebman & Reiner, A Professional Law Corporation, (AV)**
**3255 Wilshire Boulevard 12th Floor, 90010⊙**
**Telephone: 213-387-0777 Fax: 213-383-6754**
**Stuart J. Liebman; John Reiner (Member of California Trial Lawyers Association, with recognized experience in the field of Trial Lawyer); Lane Quigley; James M. O'Brien (Resident, Roseville Office); John F. Distel (Resident, San Diego Office); Chad H. Pfeifer (Resident, San Francisco Office); Jack L. Sheppard; Solomon Soulema; James J. Rij (Resident, San Diego Office); Troy D. Wiggins (Resident, San Francisco Office); Marijo Kuperman (Certified Specialist, Workers Compensation Law, The State Bar of California Board of Legal Specialization) (Resident, San Diego Office);—Peter A. Karlin; John W. Evans; Craig D. Nelson; Arthur G. Lesmez; Russell M. Rubin; Michael P. Hollomon, Jr.; Maureen McCool; Leslie J. Eng; Bryan Reiner.**
**General Liability, Defense, Products Liability, Workers Compensation Defense, Insurance and Subrogation Law, Insurance Coverage and Bad Faith, Professional Liability. Trial Practice. Appellate Practice. Environmental and Industrial Disease Law.**
**Representative Clients: Southern California Rapid Transit District; Hertz Rent-A-Car; State Farm Insurance Co.**
**San Francisco, California Office: 100 First Street, Suite 2250. Telephone: 415-227-0777. Fax: 415-227-0537.**
**Roseville, California Office: 3017 Douglas Boulevard, Suite 300. Telephone: 916-852-0777. Fax: 916-852-8077.**
**San Diego, California Office: 225 Broadway, Suite 1500. Telephone: 619-232-0777. Fax: 619-238-5442.**
**San Jose, California Office: 95 South Market Street, Suite 300. Telephone: 408-993-0777. Fax: 408-993-0789.**
***See Professional Biographies, LOS ANGELES, CALIFORNIA***

**Liebster, Jeffrey R.** ..................'54 '81 C&L.477 B.A., J.D. [🄲 Wolf,R.&S.]
*PRACTICE AREAS: Commercial Law; Real Estate Law; Labor Law.
**Lien, Henry** ..................'70 '96 C.103 B.A. L.112 J.D. [🄰 Fenigstein&K.]
*PRACTICE AREAS: Litigation.
**Lieu, Marguerite T.** ..................'64 '89 C.911 B.A. L.990 J.D. [🄰 Manning,M.&W.]
Lifland, Carol M., (AV) ..................'55 '81 C.976 A.B. L.597 J.D. 218 Brownwood Ave.
**Lifland, Charles C.** ..................'57 '83 C.976 B.A. L.309 J.D. [O'Melveny&M.]
*PRACTICE AREAS: Antitrust; Securities; Mass Torts; Business Litigation; Appellate Practice.

**Liggins, Keith G. A. '56 '86 C.803 B.A.Eng. L.1065 J.D.**
**3550 Wilshire Boulevard, Suite 1750, 90010**
**Telephone: 213-382-4249 Facsimile: 213-385-0393**
**Email: kliggins@soho.ios.com**
**Civil Litigation including Personal Injury, Tort Law, Real Property and Business Litigation.**

Light, Edith Kornfeld ..................'— '79 C.1042 B.A. L.809 J.D. Dep. City Atty.
Light, Jeffrey Taylor ..................'58 '83 C&L.178 A.B., J.D. [Myman,A.F.G.&R.]
**Light, John R.,** (AV) ..................'41 '68 C&L.378 B.A., J.D. [Latham&W.]
**Light, William J.** ..................'63 '89 C.585 B.A. L.809 J.D. [🄰 Black C.H.&L.]
*PRACTICE AREAS: Insurance Coverage; Bad Faith Litigation; Insurance Guarantee Association Practice; Insurance Defense; Appellate Practice.
**Lightfoot, Mary P.** ..................'59 '88 C.112 B.A. L.1065 J.D. [🄰 Iverson,Y.P.&H.]
*PRACTICE AREAS: Employment Law; Civil Litigation; Products Liability.
**Lightfoot, Michael J.,** (AV) ..................'39 '64 C.262 A.B. L.893 LL.B. [Talcott,L.V.&S.]
*PRACTICE AREAS: Criminal Defense Law; Civil Litigation; Civil Rights Litigation; Appellate Law.

**Lightfoot & Northup, A Professional Corporation**
**(See Pasadena)**

**Ligorsky, Brenda** ..................'68 '93 C.860 B.A. L.800 J.D. [🄰 Michaelson&L.]
*LANGUAGES: French, Spanish and Italian.
**Ligorsky, Sharon A.** ..................'70 '95 C.860 B.A. L.426 J.D. [🄰 R.F.Hirschmann]
**Liguori, Paul E.** ..................'62 '87 C&L.276 B.S., J.D. [🄱 Fulbright&J.]
*PRACTICE AREAS: Bankruptcy.
Liker, Alan D., (AV) ..................'37 '61 C.563 B.B.A. L.569 LL.B. [A.D.Liker]
Liker, Alan D., P.C., (AV) ..................10560 Wyton Dr.
Liljedahl, Donald F. ..................'27 '57 C.546 B.S. L.936 J.D. Workers' Comp. Bd.
Lillard, Louise D. ..................'19 '85 C&L.112 B.A., J.D. 1629 Sunset Plz. Dr.‡
Lillie, Mildred L. ..................'15 '38 C.112 A.B. L.1066 J.D. Presiding Jus., Ct. of App.
**Lilly, J. Kevin** ..................'55 '85 C.1077 B.M. L.426 J.D. [🄰 Littler,M.F.T.&M.]
Lilygren, John A. ..................'16 '39 C.429 L.494 J.D. 6355 W. 79th St.
**Lim, John S. C.** ..................'57 '82 C.1077 B.S. L.1065 J.D. [Lim,R.&K.]
*LANGUAGES: Korean.
*PRACTICE AREAS: Real Estate; Corporate; Bankruptcy.
Lim, Maria Teresa M. ..................'63 '87 C.662 A.B. L.426 J.D. 221 N. Figueroa St.
Lim, S. Young ..................'61 '86 C.339 B.S. L.770 J.D. [Chang&L.]
Lim, Vincent A. ..................'63 '90 C.143 L.809 J.D. 501 Shatto Pl.
**Lim, Yvonne Janet** ..................'66 '94 C.103 B.A. L.1068 J.D. [🄰 Wilson,K.&B.]
*LANGUAGES: Korean.

**Lim, Ruger & Kim, LLP, (AV)**
**Arco Center, Suite 2800, 1055 West 7th Street, 90017**
**Telephone: 213-955-9500 Telecopier: 213-955-9511**
**Members of Firm: Christopher Kim; Richard M. Ruger; John S. C. Lim. Of Counsel: Franklin Michaels, Jr. Associates: Pio S. Kim; Henry M. Lee; Richard D. Henick; A. (John) F. Amer; Christine M. Chang.**
**Corporate, Real Estate, International, Bankruptcy, Business and Commercial Litigation, Tort Litigation, and Appellate.**
**Reference: City National Bank, Olympic-Burlington Branch.**
***See Professional Biographies, LOS ANGELES, CALIFORNIA***

**LiMandri, Gina** ..................'64 '90 C.112 B.A. L.1065 J.D. [🄰 Kaye,S.F.H.&H.]
*LANGUAGES: Spanish, Italian.
*PRACTICE AREAS: Litigation.
**Lin, David Swei-chuan** ..................'66 '91 C.188 B.A. L.94 J.D. [🄰 Schaffer&L.]
*LANGUAGES: Chinese (Mandarin), Taiwanese and Spanish.
*PRACTICE AREAS: Insurance Coverage/Bad Faith.
**Lin, George C.** ..................'70 '95 C.112 B.S. L.145 J.D. [🄰 O'Melveny&M.]
*LANGUAGES: Mandarin Chinese, Taiwanese.
*PRACTICE AREAS: Litigation.
**Lincenberg, Gary S.** ..................'60 '86 C.339 B.A. L.309 J.D. [Bird,M.B.W.&M.]
Lincoln, Thomas J., (AV) ..................'55 '80 C.999 B.A. L.1049 J.D. [Lincoln,G.&C.]⊙
Lincoln, Gustafson & Cercos, (AV)
2040 Ave. of the Stars, 4th Fl. (⊙San Diego, CA; Temecula, CA; Las Vegas, Nevada)
**Lind, Joan Thompson** ..................'63 '90 C&L.878 B.S., J.D. [Dale,B.&H.]
Lind, Kenneth C. ..................'52 '78 C.165 B.A. L.564 J.D. 10900 Wilshire Blvd.
**Lind, Laron J.** ..................'62 '90 C.1193 B.B.A. L.878 J.D. [🄰 Parker,M.C.O.&S.]
*PRACTICE AREAS: Commercial Litigation; Business Litigation.
Lind, Robert C. ..................'53 '80 C.494 B.E.S. L.273 J.D. Prof. of Law, Southwestern Univ.
**Lindahl, George M.,** (AV) ..................'49 '74 C.112 A.B. L.1065 J.D. [Hawkins,S.L.&B.]
**Lindborg, Peter F.** ..................'57 '81 C.754 B.A. L.560 J.D. [Gibbs,G.L.&A.]
*PRACTICE AREAS: Construction Law; Business Litigation; Bankruptcy.
**Lindeen, Gordon R., III** ..................'61 '87 C.112 B.A. L.61 J.D. Hughes Aircraft Co.
*LANGUAGES: Swedish.
**Lindemann, Barbara T.** ..................'35 '57 C.771 B.A. L.976 J.D. [🄲 Seyfarth,S.F.&G.]
*PRACTICE AREAS: Employment Law.
**Linden, Jeffrey L.,** (AV) ..................'42 '68 C.112 A.B. L.1068 J.D. [🄰 Cohen&L.]
*PRACTICE AREAS: Business Law; Securities Law; Real Estate Law.
**Linder, Wendy L.** ..................'58 '90 C.763 A.B. L.810 J.D. [🄰 Arter&H.]
**Lindgren, Laura** ..................'51 '78 C.589 B.A. L.1068 J.D. [Hennigan,M.&B.]
**Lindgren, Leslie Bigler** ..................'54 '80 C.668 B.A. L.1068 J.D. 555 Flower St.
Lindheim, William S., (AV) ..................'45 '70 C.112 B.S. L.1049 J.D. 1849 Sawtelle Blvd.

**Lindholm, Dwight H., (AV) '30 '54 C&L.494 B.B.A., LL.B.**
**3580 Wilshire Boulevard, 17th Floor, 90010**
**Telephone: 213-487-3330 Fax: 213-487-2706**
**General Civil, Civil Trial and Appellate Practice in all State and Federal Courts. Corporation, Healthcare Law, Real Property, Trust, Probate and Negligence Law.**

Lindley, F. Haynes, Jr. '45 '76 C.154 B.A. L.809 J.D.
The John Randolph Haynes & Dora Haynes Found.
Lindner, Bernard I. ..................'33 '79 C.563 B.S.E.E. L.1179 J.D. 6399 Wilshire Blvd.
**Lindon, Mark L.** ..................'60 '85 C.276 A.B. L.1068 J.D. [Schifino&L.]
*PRACTICE AREAS: Corporate Law; Securities Law; Acquisitions, Divestitures and Mergers Law.

**Lindquist, Eric Nelson, (AV) '36 '67 C.605 B.A. L.800 J.D.**
**445 South Figueroa Street, Suite 2600, 90071**
**Telephone: 213-612-7790 Fax: 213-612-7792**
***PRACTICE AREAS: Corporation Law; Business Law; Taxation Law.**
**Civil Litigation in all State and Federal Courts, Business, Transactions, Real Estate, Tax, Probate and Estate Planning, Commercial Litigation.**
***See Professional Biographies, LOS ANGELES, CALIFORNIA***

**Lindquist, Heather A.** ..................'50 '81 C.1077 B.A. L.809 J.D. [🄲 Knee&M.]
*PRACTICE AREAS: Employment Law; Labor Law; Discrimination; Sexual Harassment; Wrongful Termination.
Lindsay, Kevin W. ..................'47 '74 C.800 B.A. L.61 J.D. 4680 Wilshire Blvd.
**Lindsay, Michael R.** ..................'56 '83 C&L.101 B.A., J.D. [Graham&J.]
*LANGUAGES: French.
*PRACTICE AREAS: Employment Law; Litigation.
**Lindsay, William R.** ..................'59 '87 C.197 B.A. L.1066 J.D. [Gibson,D.&C.]
*PRACTICE AREAS: Real Estate Finance and Acquisition and Disposition.
**Lindsey, Michael K.** ..................'51 '76 C.839 B.S. L.813 J.D. [Paul,H.J.&W.]

CAA280P

**Lindsey, Rochelle M., (AV) '52 '79 C.839 B.A. L.1068 J.D.**
**12424 Wilshire Boulevard, Suite 900, 90025**
**Telephone: 310-207-8313 Fax: 310-442-6400**
**General Business, Corporate, Corporate Securities.**

**Liner, Scott K.** .................. '64 '89 C.112 B.S. L.426 J.D. [A Arnelle,H.M.W.&G.]
*PRACTICE AREAS: Products Liability; Insurance Coverage.
**Liner, Stuart A.** .......................... '62 '88 C.763 B.A. L.426 J.D. [Liner,Y.&S.]
*PRACTICE AREAS: Business Civil Litigation; Commercial Real Estate; Creditors' Rights; Insolvency; Construction.

**Liner, Yankelevitz & Sunshine LLP**
**11620 Wilshire Boulevard, Suite 400, 90025**
**Telephone: 310-478-3869 Fax: 310-445-3377**
**Partners: Steven B. Yankelevitz; Randall J. Sunshine; Stuart A. Liner. Associates: G. Frank Glabach (Certified Specialist, Taxation Law, Estate Planning, Trust and Probate Law The State Bar of California Board of Legal Specialization); David M. Cohen; Neil F. Radick; Peter J. Pitchess, II.**
**General Civil and Trial Practice in all State and Federal Courts, Real Estate, Corporate, Taxation, Estate Planning and Probate.**
***See Professional Biographies, LOS ANGELES, CALIFORNIA***

Linett, Stephen D. .................. '48 '74 C.299 B.A. L.569 J.D. 1900 Ave. of the Stars
Ling, Stella H. ........................................................... '62 '95 [A Seider&R.]
**Lingenbrink, David A.** .......................... '62 '88 C&L.911 B.A., J.D. [Galton&H.]
*REPORTED CASES: Shadoan v. Provident Life & Accident Ins. Co., 824 F.Supp. 907 (C.D.CA 1993); Qualls v. Blue Cross, 22 F.3d 839 (9th Cir. 1994); Redlands Community Hosp. v. New England Mutual, 28 Cal.Rptr.2d 582 (1994); Bellisario v. Lone Star Life Ins. Co., 871 F.Supp. 374 (C.D.CA 1994).
*PRACTICE AREAS: Civil Litigation.
Link, David F. .......................... '53 '90 C.1109 B.A. L.426 J.D. 1930 N. Vermont
**Link, George H.**, (AV) .................. '39 '65 C.112 A.B. L.309 LL.B. [Brobeck,P.&H.]
Linnetz, Jeffrey L., (AV) .............. '50 '77 C.415 B.A. L.1136 J.D. 3832 Wilsire Blvd.
**Linsley, Kristin A.** .......................... '60 '88 C.681 A.B. L.309 J.D. [Munger,T.&O.]
**Linstedt, Walter G.** ..... '33 '61 C.813 A.B. L.1065 J.D. Asst. Gen. Coun., Bank of Amer.
**Linstrom, Hugh A.** '49 '75 C.169 B.A. L.1068 J.D.
Sr. Corp. Coun., Farmers Grp., Inc.
*RESPONSIBILITIES: Property and Casualty Insurance; Litigation; Corporate and Regulatory Law.
**Linzer, Kenneth A.** .......................... '50 '85 C.860 B.S. L.1049 J.D. [Linzer&Assoc.]

**Linzer & Associates**
**12100 Wilshire Boulevard, 15th Floor, 90025**
**Telephone: 310-826-2627 Fax: 310-820-3687**
**Kenneth A. Linzer.**
**General Corporate, Business, Partnership, Intellectual Property, Trademarks, Copyrights, Entertainment, Franchise, Distribution, Internet, New Media and Multimedia, and Commercial Litigation.**
***See Professional Biographies, LOS ANGELES, CALIFORNIA***

Lipcsey, Erika .......................... '62 '91 C.1077 B.A. L.426 J.D. 221 N. Figueroa St.
Lipinski, Matthew S. .......................... '58 '85 C.112 A.B. L.809 J.D. Dept. of Transp.
Lipkin, Monica J. .......................... '51 '77 C.1044 B.S. L.178 J.D. 1742 Reedvale Ln.
**Lipman, Dana Hirsch** .............. '65 '90 C.276 B.A. L.426 J.D. [A Proskauer R.G.&M.]
Lipman, Jay A., (BV) .......................... '41 '68 C.415 B.S. L.770 J.D. Dep. Dist. Atty.
Lipman, Shelley .......................... '55 '86 C.061 L.054 LL.M. 6500 Wilshire Blvd.
**Lipner, Joseph M.** .......................... '64 '90 C.978 B.A. L.309 J.D. [A Irell&M.]
*LANGUAGES: Hebrew.
**Lippert, Teressa K.** .......................... '49 '82 C.560 B.A. L.1066 J.D. [Folger L.&K.]⊙
**Lippert, Tobin D.** .......................... '64 '90 C.112 B.A. L.426 J.D. [A Shearman&S.]
**Lippes, David S.** '67 '93 C.882 B.A. L.276 J.D.
(adm. in NY; not adm. in CA) [A Stroock&S.&L.]
*PRACTICE AREAS: Corporate Law.
Lippitt, Elizabeth A. .......................... '59 '87 C.170 B.A. L.208 J.D. Dep. Dist. Atty.
**Lippman, David S.** .............. '60 '89 C.813 B.S. L.1068 J.D. [A Proskauer R.G.&M.]
**Lippman, Peter I.**, (AV) '39 '82 C.111 B.S. L.809 J.D.
[Ashen,G.&L.] (See Pat. Sect.)⊙
Lipscher, Joel T. .......................... '38 '66 C.477 B.B.A. L.209 J.D. Int. Rev. Serv.
**Lipschultz, James D.** .......................... '58 '82 C.112 B.A. L.1065 J.D. [Gibbs,G.L.&A.]
*PRACTICE AREAS: Construction Law; Business Litigation; Commercial Law.
**Lipscomb, Laura Lyn** .......................... '62 '88 C.1077 B.A. L.1148 J.D. [Bivona&C.]
**Lipscomb, Lee G.**, (AV) .............. '39 '74 C.621 B.A. L.809 LL.B. [Engstrom,L.&L.]
*PRACTICE AREAS: Products Liability; Entertainment Insurance; Aviation; Trial Practice.
Lipscomb, Roderick C. .......................... '43 '69 C.112 A.B. L.1068 J.D. 767 N. Hill St.
**Lipscombe, Derek B.** '— '94 C.597 B.S.M.S. L.477 J.D.
(adm. in NJ; not adm. in CA) [A Morgan,L.&B.]
**Lipsig, Ethan**, (AV) .......................... '48 '74 C.668 B.A. L.1068 J.D. [Paul,H.J.&W.]
**Lipsman, Walter J.** .......................... '52 '77 C.112 B.A. L.426 J.D. [Morris,P.&P.]
**Lipstone, Douglas M.** .......................... '63 '89 C.112 B.S. L.1068 J.D. [Katz,H.S.&K.]
*PRACTICE AREAS: Transactional and Intellectual Property.
Lipstone, Ronald K., (AV) .............. '30 '55 C&L.800 B.S., LL.B. 1999 Ave. of the Stars
Lipton, Harold A. .............. '11 '34 C.563 B.S.S. L.309 J.D. 11377 W. Olympic Blvd.
Lipton, Laurie A .......................... '52 '87 C.1160 B.A. L.426 J.D. 1801 Century Park E.
**Lisenbery, John R.** .......................... '62 '88 C.800 B.A. L.426 J.D. [A Quisenberry&B.]
*REPORTED CASES: Simmons v. West Covina Medical Clinic, 212 Cal.App. 3d 696 (1989); Denny's, Inc. v. Chicago Ins. Co., 234 Cal.App. 3d 1786 (1991); American Arbitration Association v. Superior Court, 8 Cal.App. 4th 1131 (1992); Fireman's Fund Ins. Co. v. McDonald, Hecht & Solberg, 30 Cal. App. 4th 1371 (1994); General Star Indem. Co. v. Schools Excess Liability Fund, 888 F. Supp. 1022 (N.D. Cal. 1995).
*PRACTICE AREAS: Insurance Coverage; Insurance Defense; Commercial Litigation.
**Liset, J. Robert** .......................... '45 '70 C&L.276 A.B., J.D. [Musick,P.&G.]
*PRACTICE AREAS: Healthcare; Hospitals; Corporate Law; Litigation.
Lishner, Laurence H. .............. '47 '72 C.1097 B.A. L.464 J.D. 3000 S. Robertson Blvd.
Lisnow, Robert A., (A Professional Corporation) '50 '75
C.36 B.S. L.1095 J.D. 10866 Wilshire Blvd.
**List, Suzanne K.** .......................... '65 '92 C.112 B.A. L.770 J.D. [A Manatt,P.&P.]
*PRACTICE AREAS: Corporate Securities.
Litchman, John .......................... '56 '81 C.813 A.B. L.309 J.D. 1627 Pontius St.
Litchmann, Jean H. ........ '58 '85 C.813 A.B. L.1065 J.D. 221 N. Figueroa St., Ste., 1200
Litchmann, Marshall M. .............. '28 '56 C.112 A.B. L.1068 LL.B. 1627 Pontius Ave.
**Litman, Heather C.** .......................... '66 '91 C.112 B.A. L.861 J.D. [E.A.Pollack]
*LANGUAGES: French, Italian.
*PRACTICE AREAS: Customs Law; International Trade.
**Litovsky, Allan Z.** ........ '58 '96 C.061 B.S. L.36 J.D. [A Jones,D.R.&P.] (See Pat. Sect.)
Litt, Barrett S., (AV) .......................... '45 '69 C.112 B.A. L.1068 J.D. 3435 Wilshire Blvd.
**Litt, William M.** .......................... '67 '93 C.188 B.A. L.1068 J.D. [A S.L.Hartmann]
*PRACTICE AREAS: Civil Rights; Public Interest Law.
**Littell, John G.** .......................... '65 '91 C&L.893 B.S., J.D. [A Jeffer,M.B.&M.]
*PRACTICE AREAS: Corporate; Mergers and Acquisitions; Banking; Securities; Sports and Entertainment.
Little, David Wilfrid .......................... '45 '80 C.1097 B.A. L.1148 J.D. 4007 Division
**Little, Michael S.** .......................... '70 '96 C.112 B.A. L.93 J.D. [A Lewis,D.B.&B.]
*PRACTICE AREAS: Insurance Fraud Law.
Little, Wallace A. .............. '46 '77 C.766 B.A. L.767 J.D. Kenneth Leventhal & Co.
**Littlefield, Wayne B.**, (AV) .............. '46 '76 C.401 B.A. L.336 J.D. [Musick,P.&G.]
*PRACTICE AREAS: Litigation; Insurance.

**Littler, Mendelson, Fastiff, Tichy & Mathiason, A Professional Corporation, (AV)**
**2049 Century Park East, Suite 500, 90067**⊙
**Telephone: 310-553-0308 Facsimile: 310-553-5583**
**URL: http://www.littler.com**
**Robert F. Millman; Mark W. Robbins; Gordon A. Letter; Diane L. Kimberlin; Robert W. Feinstein; Ronald J. Cooke; Enrique L. Muñoz; W. Joseph Strapp; Shirley D. Deutsch; Jaffe D. Dickerson; Lawrence J. Song; Lester L. Jones; Connie L. Michaels; Allison R. Michael;—Ruth Benson; J. Kevin Lilly; Robert H. Taylor; Robert S. Blumberg; Jodi L. Kruger; Sheldon David Kasdan; Keith A. Jacoby; Lori B. Reber; Jack S. Bailey; Gordon F. Peery; Meghan A. White; Karen Lynn Scarborough Stanitz (Not admitted in CA).**
**Offices located in: California — Bakersfield, Fresno, Long Beach, Menlo Park, Oakland, Sacramento, San Diego, San Francisco, San Jose, Santa Maria, Santa Rosa and Stockton; Denver, Colorado; Washington, D.C.; Atlanta, Georgia; Baltimore, Maryland; Reno and Las Vegas, Nevada (a partnership with the Law Offices of Hicks & Walt); Morristown, New Jersey; New York, New York; and Dallas and Houston, Texas.**
***See Professional Biographies, LOS ANGELES, CALIFORNIA***

Littleton, Christine A. '52 '82 C.645 B.S. L.309 J.D.
Prof. of Law, U.C.L.A. Sch. of Law
**Littleworth, A. Todd** .......................... '55 '80 C.112 B.A. L.426 J.D. [C Pillsbury M.&S.]
**Littman, Barry** .......................... '69 '96 C.309 A.B. L.276 J.D. [A O'Melveny&M.]
Litvak, Alexander .......................... '48 '74 C.112 B.A. L.464 J.D. 1888 Century Park E.
Litvin, Milton J. .............. '27 '55 C.112 B.A. L.1068 LL.B. Div. Chief Asst. Co. Coun.
**Litz, Jennifer A.** .......................... '67 '92 C.763 B.A. L.1049 J.D. [A R.A.Litz&Assoc.]

**Litz, Ronald A., & Associates, (AV) '41 '66 C.823 B.A. L.569 J.D.**
**1901 Avenue of the Stars 18th Floor, 90067**
**Telephone: 310-201-0100 Fax: 310-201-0226**
***REPORTED CASES: Worton v. Worton, 234 Cal.App.3d 1638 (1991); Wright v. Johnston, 206 Cal.App. 3d 333 (1988).**
**Associates: Jennifer A. Litz.**
**Civil Litigation, Family Law, General Business Law, Entertainment Law.**
***See Professional Biographies, LOS ANGELES, CALIFORNIA***

**Liu, Brian P.Y.** .......................... '67 '96 C&L.112 A.B., J.D. [A Sullivan&C.]
**Liu, Jack Chi-Husan** .......................... '58 '88 L.061 LL.B. [C Morgan,L.&B.]
*LANGUAGES: Chinese.
**Liu, John Y.** .......................... '63 '83 C.112 B.A. L.1068 J.D. [Pillsbury M.&S.]
**Liu, Sally S.** .......................... '69 '95 C.112 B.A. L.1066 J.D. [A Kirkland&E.]
*PRACTICE AREAS: Litigation.
**Liu, Thomas T.** .......................... '57 '84 C.813 B.A. L.800 J.D. [Graham&J.]
*LANGUAGES: Mandarin and Spanish.
*PRACTICE AREAS: Employment Law; Labor Law.
**Liu, Wen** .......................... '58 '87 C.111 B.S. L.1068 J.D. [A Irell&M.] (Pat.)
*LANGUAGES: Chinese (Mandarin and Cantonese).
Livadary, Paul J., (AV) .............. '37 '65 C.813 A.B. L.1066 LL.B. 2029 Century Park E.
**Livdahl, David A.** .............. '47 '77 C.429 B.A. L.178 J.D. [Graham&J.] (⊙Beijing, ROC)
*LANGUAGES: Chinese and Japanese.
*PRACTICE AREAS: International Business Law; Corporate Law.
**Liversidge, Samuel G.** .......................... '69 '95 C.243 B.A. L.990 J.D. [A Gibson,D.&C.]
Livingston, Arthur, (AV) .............. '12 '36 C&L.800 A.B., LL.B. 10633 Kinnard Ave.‡
Livingston, Gary R. .............. '51 '86 C.112 A.B. L.809 J.D. 2029 Century Park E.
Livingston, James L. .............. '44 '79 C.112 B.A. L.800 J.D. 2184 N. Beverly GlenBlvd.
**Livingston, Katharine** .......................... '49 '86 C.112 B.A. L.1066 J.D. [Folger L.&K.]⊙
**Livornese, Don F.** .............. '60 '86 C.174 B.S.M.E. L.273 J.D. [Loeb&L.] (See Pat. Sect.)
*PRACTICE AREAS: Patent; Trademark; Copyright; Intellectual Property Litigation; Antitrust.
Llewellyn, Richard H., Jr. .............. '56 '82 C.228 B.A. L.309 J.D. Co. Bd. of Supervisors

**Lloreda, Carlos A., (AV) '47 '79 C.800 B.A. L.770 J.D.**
**4727 Wilshire Boulevard, Suite 402, 90010**
**Telephone: 213-965-0365; 965-0366 Facsimile: 213-965-0483**
***LANGUAGES: Spanish.**
***PRACTICE AREAS: Civil Litigation; Attorney Fee Disputes; Attorney Conduct; Personal Injury (Plaintiff and Defendant).**
**—James R. Balesh.**
**General Civil Litigation, Attorney Fees Disputes and Personal Injury (Plaintiff and Defendant).**
***See Professional Biographies, LOS ANGELES, CALIFORNIA***

Lloyd, Charles Earl, (AV) .......................... '34 '62 C.416 B.S. L.800 J.D. [C.E.Lloyd]
Lloyd, Charles Earl, A Law Corporation, (AV) .......................... 880 W. 1st St.
Lo, Cecily .......................... '57 '83 C.112 B.A. L.800 J.D. State Ct. of Apps.
LoBaugh, Leslie E., Jr. .......................... '45 '71 C.770 B.A. L.276 J.D. 633 W. 5th St.
Lobl, Rebecca .......................... '62 '91 C.881 B.A. L.426 J.D. 600 Wilshire Blvd.
Lobner, Breton K. .......................... '42 '71 C.112 B.A. L.464 J.D. Asst. City Atty.
LoCascio, Pamela Renee .... '61 '89 C.112 B.A. L.1137 J.D. 3255 Wilshire Blvd., 12th Fl.
Loch, Robert M. .......................... '31 '75 C.546 B.S. L.426 J.D. 810 S. Flower ST.
**Locher, William D.** .......................... '54 '79 C.36 B.S. L.990 J.D. [Gibbs,G.L.&A.]
*PRACTICE AREAS: Business Litigation; Commercial Law; Construction Law.
**Lochner, Scott J.** .......................... '56 '84 C.401 B.A. L.569 J.D. [C Sheppard,M.R.&H.]
*PRACTICE AREAS: Corporate Law, International Business Law and High Technology Law.
Locker, Paul E. .......................... '58 '84 C.178 A.B. L.309 J.D. Pres., Locker/Resource
Lockie, R. Thomas .......................... '31 '58 C&L.813 A.B., J.D. 146 N. Gunston Ave‡
**Locklin, James H.** .......................... '68 '92 C.158 B.S. L.800 J.D. [A Talcott,L.V.&S.]
*REPORTED CASES: California Men's Colony, Unit II Men's Advisory Council v. Rowland, 939 F2d 854 (9th Cir. 1991).
*PRACTICE AREAS: Appellate Law; Criminal Defense Law; Civil Litigation.

**Locko, Charles, (AV) '51 '80 C.112 B.A. L.800 J.D.**
**Suite 2610, 2029 Century Park East, 90067-3012**
**Telephone: 310-286-9908 Telecopier: 310-785-0027**
***PRACTICE AREAS: Real Estate Law.**
**Commercial Real Estate Law, Hotel, Multi-Family Residential and Shopping Center Law (Development, Financing, Acquisition and Management). Hazardous Materials Law (Compliance and Remediation).**
***See Professional Biographies, LOS ANGELES, CALIFORNIA***

**Lockwood, Clyde E., (A Professional Corporation)**, (AV) '32 '64
C.267 L.809 LL.B. [Patterson,R.L.G.&J.]
**Lockwood, James C.**, (AV) .......................... '37 '63 C.277 B.S. L.477 J.D. [Troy&G.]
*PRACTICE AREAS: Corporate Law; Securities Law.

**Loder, Lorraine L., (AV) '52 '77 C&L.800 B.A., J.D.**
**601 West Fifth Street Suite 1200, 90071**
**Telephone: 213-623-8774 Fax: 213-623-1409**
**General Business Practice, Corporate, Business Transactions, Business and Bankruptcy Litigation.**
***See Professional Biographies, LOS ANGELES, CALIFORNIA***

**Lodise, John P.** .......................... '61 '88 C.951 B.A. L.1068 J.D. [A Morrison&F.]
**Lodise, Margaret G.** .......................... '63 '88 C.668 B.A. L.1068 J.D. [A Ross,S.&G.]
*PRACTICE AREAS: Estate, Trust and Conservatorship Litigation; Appellate Practice; Business Litigation.
**Loeb, Ann** .......................... '55 '79 C.102 B.A. L.309 J.D. [Christa&J.]
*PRACTICE AREAS: Litigation; Media; Appeals.
**Loeb, Gary H.** .......................... '69 '96 C.813 B.A. L.178 J.D. [A Quinn E.U.&O.]
**Loeb, Jeffrey M.** .......................... '56 '81 C.112 B.A. L.1065 J.D. [Loeb&L.]
*PRACTICE AREAS: Trusts Law; Estates Law and Related Litigation.
**Loeb, Jonathan A.** .......................... '67 '92 C.112 B.A. L.800 J.D. [A Alschuler G.&P.]

CALIFORNIA—LOS ANGELES MARTINDALE-HUBBELL LAW DIRECTORY 1997

**Loeb, Lynn S.** ..................................'62 '88 C.112 B.A. L.273 J.D. [Baker&H.]
*PRACTICE AREAS: Intellectual Property Litigation.
Loeb, Ralph C. ............................'— '86 C.112 B.A. L.1065 J.D. [Edelstein,L.&S.]
**Loeb, Rodney W.**, (AV) .................. '28 '53 C.112 A.B. L.309 LL.B. [Ⓒ Daar&N.]
**Loeb, Ronald M., (P.C.)**, (AV) .............. '32 '60 C.112 A.B. L.309 LL.B. [Irell&M.]
Loeb, Steven S. ..................... '53 '79 C.1077 B.A. L.1095 J.D. 15233 Ventura Blvd.

**Loeb & Loeb LLP, (AV)** BR
**A Limited Liability Partnership including Professional Corporations**
**Suite 1800, 1000 Wilshire Boulevard, 90017-2475⊙**
**Telephone: 213-688-3400 Facsimile: 213-688-3460; 688-3461; 688-3462**
**Members of Firm: Joseph P. Loeb (1883-1974); Edwin J. Loeb (1886-1970); Mortimer H. Hess (1889-1968); Phillip E. Adler (A P.C.); Christopher K. Aidun (New York City Office); Kenneth B. Anderson (New York City Office); John Arao; Roger M. Arar (Century City Office); Donald L. B. Baraf (New York City Office); Robert S. Barry, Jr.; Harold A. Barza; Michael D. Beck (New York City Office); Carol Laurene Belfield; Kenneth R. Benbassat; Maribeth A. Borthwick (Century City Office); David H. Carlin (New York City Office); Marc Chamlin (New York City Office); Alex Chartove (Washington, D.C. Office); Andrew S. Clare (A P.C.); Richard J. Codding (Century City Office); Kenneth R. Costello; Terence F. Cuff; John J. Dellaverson (Century City Office); Lorenzo De Sanctis (Rome, Italy Office); David B. Eizenman (New York City Office); Frank E. Feder (A P.C.) (Century City and New York Offices); Martin D. Fern; David L. Ficksman; Evan Finkel (Century City Office); Jay M. Finkelstein (Washington, D.C. Office); David C. Fischer (New York City Office); John T. Frankenheimer (A P.C.) (Century City Office); Kenneth D. Freeman (New York City Office); James D. Friedman; Andrew S. Garb (A P.C.); David W. Grace; Fred B. Griffin; Philip J. Grosz (Century City Office); Lawrence B. Gutcho; Joseph P. Heffernan (A P.C.); Irv Hepner (New York City Office); Joyce S. Jun (Century City Office); Lance N. Jurich; Michael Bryce Kinney (New York City Office); William K. Konrad (Century City Office); Richard W. Kopenhefer (Century City Office); Mary D. Lane; John F. Lang (New York City Office); Michael Langs; Jerome L. Levine (New York City Office); Andrew E. Lippmann (New York City Office); Don F. Livornese (Century City Office); Jeffrey M. Loeb; Stuart Lubitz (Century City Office); Gary D. Mann (Century City Office); William J. Marlow (New York City Office); Michael A. Mayerson (Century City Office); Malissa Hathaway McKeith; Robert A. Meyer; Stephen R. Mick; Charles H. Miller (New York City Office); Malcolm L. Mimms, Jr. (Nashville, Tennessee Office); Douglas E. Mirell; Daniel G. Murphy; Anthony Murray; David C. Nelson; Susan V. Noonoo; Diane B. Paul; Alden G. Pearce (A P.C.); Robert L. Pelz (New York City Office); Martin R. Pollner (New York City Office); Guendalina Ponti (Rome, Italy Office); Shirley M. Price; Robert S. Reich (New York City Office); Victor A. Rodgers; Thomas E. Rohlf (A P.C.); Andrew M. Ross (New York City Office); Jonathan P. Roth; Stanford K. Rubin (A P.C.) (Century City Office); Stephen L. Saltzman (Century City Office); Fredric M. Sanders (New York City Office); David M. Satnick (New York City Office); David S. Schaefer (New York City Office); P. Gregory Schwed (New York City Office); Paul A. Sczudlo; Peter S. Selvin; David B. Shontz (New York City Office); Clark B. Siegel (Century City Office); David M. Simon (Century City Office); Michael F. Sitzer; Lee N. Steiner (New York City Office); Rebel R. Steiner, Jr. (Century City Office); Bruce M. Stiglitz (A P.C.) (Certified Specialist, Taxation Law, The State Bar of California Board of Legal Specialization); Richard P. Streicher (New York City Office); James D. Taylor (New York City Office); Raymond W. Thomas (Century City Office); Robert N. Treiman; William P. Wasserman (A P.C.) (Certified Specialist, Taxation Law, The State Bar of California Board of Legal Specialization); Ronald Weinstein (A P.C.); Bruce J. Wexler (New York City Office); Rebecca E. White (New York City Office); Alan W. Wilken; Roger R. Wise (Century City Office); Susan A. Wolf; William S. Woods, II; Richard H. Zaitlen (Century City Office); Michael P. Zweig (New York City Office). Of Counsel: Harold D. Berkowitz (A P.C.) (Century City Office); James R. Birnberg; Morton R. Field; Harry First (New York City Office); Howard I. Friedman (A P.C.); Marvin Greene (A P.C.); Abraham S. Guterman (New York City Office); Robert A. Holtzman (A P.C.); Harold I. Kahen (New York City Office); Gerald D. Kleinman (A P.C.) (Century City Office); Jay Adams Knight; Saul N. Rittenberg (A P.C.) (Century City Office); Alfred I. Rothman (A P.C.); Arthur A. Segall (New York City Office); Alan D. Shulman (Century City Office); Bernard M. Silbert (Century City Office); Harvey L. Silbert (Century City Office); Myron L. Slobodien (A P.C.) (Century City Office); John S. Warren (A P.C.). Senior Counsel: Miriam J. Golbert (Century City Office); Adrienne Halpern (New York City Office); Louis A. Mok (Century City Office); Laurie S. Ruckel (New York City Office); John P. Scherlacher (Century City Office). Associates: Paula G. Atkinson; Curtis W. Bajak (Century City Office); Jeremy W. Barber (Century City Office); Roberta S. Bell (New York City Office); Michele E. Beuerlein; Elana C. Bloom (New York City Office); Stephen Bongini (Century City Office); Marguerite L. Bui; Matthew Clark Bures; David A. Byrnes (Century City Office); Steve S. Chahine; Ying Chen (Century City Office); Paula K. Colbath (New York City Office); Marco D. Costales; Marita T. Covarrubias (Century City Office); Anne P. Donovan (New York City Office); Brant H. Dvëirin; Linda F. Edell (Nashville, Tennessee Office); Philippe O. Erwin (Century City Office); Jay Fenster (New York City Office); David A. Fleissig (New York City Office); Kenneth R. Florin (New York City Office); Richard J. Frey (Century City Office); Bruce Friedman; Daniel J. Friedman; Randall Collins Furlong (Century City Office); Raul Carl Galaz (Century City Office); Helen Gavaris (New York City Office); James P. Goodkind (Century City Office); Karen A. Greenstein (New York City Office); Kurtiss Lee Grossman; James R. Guerette (New York City Office); Karen Nielsen Higgins; Jonathan Y. Kang (Century City Office); David D. Kim (New York City Office); John W. Kittleson; Amir I. Kornblum (New York City Office); Paul H. Kovelman (Century City Office); Robert B. Lachenauer (New York City Office); Lynda C. Loigman (New York Office); Nina B. Luban; David L. Lubitz; Linda McCauley Mack (Century City Office); David Alan Makman (Century City Office); Sonya Makunga; Jonathan S. Marshall (Century City Office); Denise Marie McIntosh (Century City Office); Sharon S. Mequet; Beth R. Meyers (New York City Office); Paul G. Nagy (Century City Office); Lloyd Charles Nathan (Century City Office); Theotis F. Oliphant; Giovanni A. Pedde (Rome, Italy Office); Chris P. Perque (Century City Office); Harry S. Prawer (New York City Office); Ted Rittmaster (Century City Office); Allison Klayman Rosenthal (New York City Office); Michael E. Ross; Glen A. Rothstein; Michelle Oyler Saifer (New York City Office); Deborah L. Saltzman (New York City Office); Jay D. Sanders; Roni Schneider (New York City Office); Scott I. Schneider (New York City Office); Rachel Schwartz (New York City Office); Terri J. Seligman (New York City Office); Edward H. Shapiro (Nashville, Tennessee Office); Riccardo Siciliani (Rome, Italy Office); Brian R. Socolow (New York City Office); Adam F. Streisand; Gerald J. Strenio; Claudia M. Taylor (New York City Office); Arya Towfighi (Century City Office); David W. Victor (Century City Office); Joseph F. von Sauers (Century City Office); Courtney I. Williams (New York City Office); Susan Z. Williams (Century City Office); Weining Yang (Century City Office); Wendy W. Yang (Century City Office); Richard Kon Yoon; Maria L. Zanfini (New York City Office); Andrew D. Zuckerman (New York City Office); Richard S. Zuniga (Century City Office).**
**General Civil Practice.**
**Century City, California Office: Suite 2200, 10100 Santa Monica Boulevard, Los Angeles, 90067-4164. Telephone: 310-282-2000. Facsimile: 310-282-2191; 282-2192.**
**New York, N.Y. Office: 345 Park Avenue, 10154-0037. Telephone: 212-407-4000. Facsimile: 212-407-4990.**
**Washington, D.C. Office: Suite 601, 2100 M Street N.W., 20037-1207. Telephone: 202-223-5700. Facsimile: 202-223-5704.**
**Nashville, Tennessee Office: 45 Music Square West, 37203-3205. Telephone: 615-749-8300; Facsimile: 615-749-8308.**
**Rome, Italy Office: Piazza Digione 1, 00197. Telephone: 011-396-808-8456. Facsimile: 011-396-808-8288.**

***See Professional Biographies, LOS ANGELES, CALIFORNIA***

Loeffler, Lisa Wells, (AV) ............ '52 '84 C.679 B.A. L.809 J.D. 2049 Century Pk. E.
Loeffler, Robert M., (AV) ...........'23 '49 C.623 B.S. L.309 J.D. 10701 Wilshire Ave.‡
Loesberg, Michael J. ............... '67 '93 C.165 B.A. L.273 J.D. 1999 Ave. of the Stars
Loeser, Julius L. ......................... '45 '71 C&L.597 B.A., J.D. First Interstate Bank
Loeterman, Mark ......................... '53 '79 C.112 B.A. L.809 J.D. [Loeterman,S.&K.]
Loeterman, Nancy Cole ......................... '55 '82 C.112 A.B. L.426 J.D. [Cole&L.]
Loeterman, Shulkin & Kraemer ................................ 11611 San Vicente Blvd.
Loewen, Theodore A. ........................ '45 '72 C.684 A.B. L.1065 J.D. Dep. Dist. Atty.
**Loewy, Peter H.**, (AV) '55 '79 C.563 B.A. L.705 J.D.
[Fragomen,D.&B.] (⊙San Fran. & Palo Alto)
*LANGUAGES: French.
**Lofgren, Christine L.** ...................'67 '93 C&L.112 B.A., J.D. [Ⓐ Thelen,M.J.&B.]
*PRACTICE AREAS: Litigation.

**Lofgren, Douglas W. '46 '72 C.309 A.B. L.800 J.D.**
**One Bunker Hill, 12th Floor 601 West Fifth Street, 90071**
**Telephone: 213-623-8874 FAX: 213-623-9085**

(This Listing Continued)

**Lofgren, Douglas W. (Continued)**
**Civil and Criminal Litigation in State and Federal Courts, with Emphasis on Real Estate, Business, and Insurance Litigation and White Collar Criminal Defense.**

***See Professional Biographies, LOS ANGELES, CALIFORNIA***

**Loftin, Laura A., (A Professional Corporation)** '55 '81
C.228 A.B. L.309 J.D. [Mitchell,S.&K.]
*PRACTICE AREAS: Corporate Law; Securities Regulation Law; Mergers and Acquisitions Law.
**Lofton, Patricia** ................................ '47 '91 C.1077 B.A. L.990 J.D. [Ⓐ Horvitz&L.]
**Logan, Ben H., III**, (AV) .................. '51 '76 C.228 B.A. L.813 J.D. [O'Melveny&M.]
*PRACTICE AREAS: Creditors' Rights; Bankruptcy; Bankruptcy Workouts; Out of Court Debt Restructuring.
**Logan, Brenda J.** ................................'— '91 C.627 B.S. L.276 J.D. [Ⓐ Arter&H.]
*PRACTICE AREAS: Bankruptcy; Creditors Rights; Commercial Litigation.
**Logan, Jefferson K.** ........................... '60 '88 C&L.846 B.S., J.D. [Ⓐ Sidley&A.]
*PRACTICE AREAS: Business Litigation; Professional Liability; Products Liability Law.
**Logan-Stern, Michelle** .................'68 '95 C&L.112 B.A., J.D. [Ⓐ Thelen,M.J.&B.]
*PRACTICE AREAS: Business Litigation.
**Loh, Paul J.** ......................................'67 '92 C.112 A.B. L.309 J.D. [Ⓐ B.Tarlow]
*LANGUAGES: Mandarin and Taiwanese.
*PRACTICE AREAS: Criminal Law.
**Lohr, Noël C.** ...................................... '— '90 C&L.800 B.A., J.D. [Ⓐ Gibson,D.&C.]
Lohr-Schmidt, Berndt, (AV) ........... '43 '69 C.813 B.S. L.309 LL.B. 8033 Sunset Blvd.
Lombard, Russell J., (AV) ................ '43 '75 C.813 B.A. L.767 J.D. 550 S. Hope St.
Lombardero, David A. .................. '47 '76 C.674 A.B. L.813 J.D. 350 S. Grand Ave.
**Lombardo, John D.** ........................... '71 '96 C.154 B.A. L.1068 J.D. [Ⓐ Arnold&P.]
*PRACTICE AREAS: Litigation.
Lombardo, Vincent J. ................ '44 '72 C.426 B.A. L.809 J.D. 12400 Wilshire Blvd.
Lomeli, George R.G. ........................ '58 '88 C.800 M.S. L.1148 J.D. Dep. City Atty.
London, Judith M. ........................'63 '90 C.813 B.A. L.1068 J.D. 701 E. 3rd St.
London, Michael B. ....................... '54 '80 C.472 B.S. L.276 J.D. 10452 Olethaln
**Lonergan, James A.** ........................'53 '80 C.112 B.A. L.800 J.D. [Sheppard,M.R.&H.]
*PRACTICE AREAS: Real Estate Development Law; Finance Law; Landlord and Tenant Law.
**Long, Aimee D.** .................................. '69 '95 C.112 B.A. L.597 J.D. [Ⓐ Sidley&A.]
**Long, David E.** ............................ '58 '83 C.659 B.A. L.107 J.D. [Lewis,D.B.&B.]
Long, Ernest A., III .................'26 '57 C.112 B.A. L.426 LL.B. 130 S. Granville Ave.‡
**Long, Gregory A.**, (AV) ..............'48 '73 C.154 B.A. L.309 J.D. [Sheppard,M.R.&H.]
*PRACTICE AREAS: Civil Trial and Appellate Practice.
**Long, Jennifer L.** .................... '59 '87 C.309 A.B. L.1066 J.D. [Ⓒ Jeffer,M.B.&M.]
*PRACTICE AREAS: Federal, State and Local Taxation.
Long, John C. ..........................'53 '81 C.1097 B.S. L.101 J.D. Commonwealth Land Title Ins. Co.
Long, Leonard J. '51 '88 C.146 B.S. L.145 J.D.
(adm. in IL; not adm. in CA) Prof. of Law, Univ. of Southern Calif.
Long, Nira Hardon, (AVⓉ) .................'— '64 C.112 B.A. L.1068 J.D. [Ⓒ Moser&M.]
Long, Richard ........................'50 '79 C.112 B.A. L.809 J.D. 1888 Century Park E.
**Long, Robert A.**, (AV) .......................'45 '72 C.347 A.B. L.1119 J.D. [Latham&W.]
**Long, Thomas D.** ..................... '57 '82 C&L.813 A.B., J.D. [Nossaman,G.K.&E.]
*PRACTICE AREAS: Litigation; Environmental Law; Insurance Coverage.

**Long & Levit LLP, (AV)** BR
**A Limited Liability Partnership including a Professional Corporation**
**601 S. Figueroa, 25th Floor, 90071⊙**
**Telephone: 213-356-5900 Facsimile: 213-613-0664**
**Resident Partners: Randall A. Miller; Gretchen S. Carner; Cyril E. "Ted" Armbrister, Jr. Resident Associates: B. Gerard Cordelli; Patricia M. De La Peña; J. Andrew Douglas; Jeffrey A. Evans; Douglas H. Galt; Christina Katris-Michael; David M. Morrow; Susan Andrews O'Neal; JoLynn M. Pollard; Roni Reed; Stephen E. Ronk; Valerie J. Wiles.**
**Insurance Litigation (Environmental, Property, Casualty, Marine), Professional Liability, Products Liability, Toxic Torts, Securities and Commodities Litigation, Real Estate, Admiralty, Government, Entertainment and Election Law. General Civil Trial and Appellate Practice.**
**San Francisco, California Office: 101 California Street, Suite 2300. Telephone: 415-397-2222. Telex: 340924 HOME OFC SFO-LONG & LEVIT. Facsimile: 415-397-6392.**

***See Professional Biographies, LOS ANGELES, CALIFORNIA***

**Longaker, Richard P., II, Law Offices of**
**(See Santa Monica)**

**Longhetto, Loretto M.** .............'60 '90 C.550 B.A. L.1202 J.D. Coun., Teledyne, Inc.
Longjohn, Julia ......................... '67 '93 C.477 B.A. L.426 J.D. 600 N. Grand Ave.
Longo, Michael R., III .................................'54 '78 C&L.800 B.A., J.D. Univ. Park
**Longoria, Alice C.** .......................... '65 '91 C.1077 B.A. L.767 J.D. [Ⓐ Kirtland&P.]
**Lonnie, Dommond E.** .....................'64 '89 C.112 B.A. L.1068 J.D. [Ⓐ Grace,S.C.&S.]
*PRACTICE AREAS: Product Liability Law; Insurance Defense Law; Appellate Law.
**Loo, John**, (AV) ........................ '44 '76 C.851 B.S.E.E. L.426 J.D. [Moffitt,W.&L.]
*PRACTICE AREAS: Corporate Law; Commercial Law; Business Planning Law.
**Loo, Lori A.** ....................................... '64 '90 C.112 B.A. L.800 J.D. [Freid&G.]
*PRACTICE AREAS: Family Law.
**Loomis, C. Dennis** ....................'50 '78 C.112 B.A. L.1065 J.D. [Troop M.S.&P.]
*LANGUAGES: Italian.
*PRACTICE AREAS: Domestic and International; Copyright and Trademark Protection, Registration Enforcement Law; Intellectual Property Litigation; General Commercial Litigation.
**Loomis, Lloyd C.** ........'46 '72 C.178 B.A. L.502 J.D. Sr. Coun., Atlantic Richfield Co.
*RESPONSIBILITIES: Employment Law.
**Loomis, Roger D., Jr.**, (AV) .........'48 '74 C.112 B.A. L.178 J.D. [Buchalter,N.F.&Y.]
**Loomis, Tracy E.** ..................... '— '90 C.112 B.A. L.477 J.D. [Ⓐ King,P.H.P.&B.]
**Looney, Jeri Rouse** ......................'60 '85 C&L.477 B.A., J.D. [Ⓐ Lord,B.&B.]
Lopez, Donna Lee ....................... '60 '86 C.37 B.A. L.809 J.D. 444 S. Flower St.
Lopez, Leonard P. ..................... '— '95 C.112 B.A. L.813 J.D. 600 Wilshire Blvd.
Lopez, Manuel ........................'40 '67 C.1097 B.A. L.1114 J.D. 1526 W. Temple St.
**Lopez, Peter M.** ....................'49 '74 C.112 B.S. L.1068 J.D. [Kleinberg L.L.B.&C.]
*PRACTICE AREAS: Entertainment Law.
Lopez, Richard J. '35 '65 C.800 B.S. L.1068 LL.B.
Calif. Off. of Administrative Hearings
Lopez, Robert B. ..........................'33 '64 C.112 B.S. L.800 LL.B. Ret. Supr. Ct. J.
Lopez, Ruben M. .......................'43 '73 C.1042 B.A. L.1068 J.D. Depty. Co. Coun.
**Lopez, Tomás R.** ...........................'55 '81 C.1141 B.A. L.276 J.D. [Ⓐ Ochoa&S.]
*LANGUAGES: Spanish.
*PRACTICE AREAS: Civil Litigation; Labor; Environmental.
Lopker, John K. ......................'56 '87 C.112 B.A. L.273 J.D. Federal TransTel, Inc.
**LoPresti, Robert L.**, (BV) ......................'51 '76 C.1077 B.S. L.809 J.D. [Parker S.]
Loquvam, Joel J. ...............................'57 '87 C.273 B.A. L.464 J.D. [Duran,L.&R.]
Lord, Hilary G.D. '56 '81 C.112 B.S. L.145 J.D.
Sr. V.P. & Chf. Compl. Offr., Trust Company of the West
**Lord, Kenneth W.** '65 '95 C.95 B.A. L.861 J.D.
(adm. in NY; not adm. in CA) [Ⓐ Lane P.S.L.]
*PRACTICE AREAS: Maritime Law; Insurance Coverage; Fidelity and Surety Bonds; Commercial Litigation.
**Lord, Scott R.** .......................... '54 '79 C.1169 B.A. L.770 J.D. [Cohen&L.]
*REPORTED CASES: Regional Steel Corp. v. Superior Court (1994) 25 Cal.App.4th 525, 32 Cal.Rptr.2d 417.
*PRACTICE AREAS: Civil Litigation; Construction Law; Representation of Design Professionals; Wrongful Termination; Unfair Competition.

CAA282P

**Lord, Bissell & Brook, (AV)** [BB]
**300 South Grand Avenue, 90071-3200**⊙
**Telephone: 213-485-1500 Telecopy: 213-485-1200 Telex: 18-1135**
**Resident Partners: Charles A. Adamek; Gail M. Baev; C. Guerry Collins; Charles L. Crouch, III; David F. Hauge; Jeffrey S. Kravitz; Rudolf H. Schroeter; Keith G. Wileman. Of Counsel: Marguerite L. Brown. Resident Associates: Brenda Adams Bissett; Jacqueline C. Brown; John D. Buchanan; Stephen L. Cope; Charissa Dorian; Franklin T. Dunn; Mark Scott Fall; Cynthia M. Frey; John M. Hochhausler; Barbara J. Klass; Jacqueline Redin Klein; LouCinda Laughlin; Jeri Rouse Looney; George D. Lozano; Mitchell J. Popham; Karen A. Soomekh; Anthony F. Witteman.**
**General Practice.**
**Chicago, Illinois Office: Suites 2600-3600 Harris Bank Building, 115 South LaSalle Street, 60603. Telephone: 312-443-0700. Telecopy: 312-443-0570. Cable Address: "Lowirco". Telex: 25-0336.**
**Atlanta, Georgia Office: One Atlantic Center, 1201 West Peachtree Street, N.W., Suite 3700, 30309. Telephone: 404-870-4600. Telecopy: 404-872-5547.**
**Rockford, Illinois Office: 120 West State Street, Suite 200, 61101. Telephone: 815-963-8050.**
*See Professional Biographies, LOS ANGELES, CALIFORNIA*

**Lorig, Frederick A.**, (AV) ....................'46 '73 C.112 B.A. L.309 J.D. [Bright&L.]
*PRACTICE AREAS: Patent, Trade Secret and Antitrust Litigation.
**Losh, Stephen M.** ....................'39 '64 C&L.477 B.A., J.D. [C] J.M.Donovan]
*PRACTICE AREAS: Litigation.
Loshin, David G. ....................'35 '69 P.O. Box 480401
**Losk, Jonathan T.** ..........'58 '94 C.112 B.A. L.426 J.D. [A] Lyon&L.] (See Pat. Sect.)
*PRACTICE AREAS: Patent, Trademark, Contract and Unfair Competition; Intellectual Property.

**Loskamp, Alvin N., A Law Corporation**
**(See Burbank)**

**Loss, Theresa Ann** ....................'56 '90 C&L.36 B.A., J.D. [A] Selman B.]
Lossada, Juan ....................'60 '88 C&L.800 B.S., J.D. 600 N. Grand Ave.
**Lossing, Frances Elizabeth** .........'44 '78 C.477 B.A. L.1068 J.D. [C] O'Melveny&M.]
*PRACTICE AREAS: Banking and Finance; Public Utilities.
**Lotman, Michael A.**, (AV) ....................'46 '74 C.169 B.A. L.1065 J.D. [M.A.Lotman]

**Lotman, Michael A., A Prof. Corp., Law Office, (AV)**
**Third Floor 10100 Santa Monica Boulevard, 90067**
**Telephone: 310-286-6626 Fax: 310-286-2966**
**Michael A. Lotman. Of Counsel: Alan J. Diamond.**
**General Civil and Commercial Litigation, Title Insurance, Financial Institutions, Real Estate, Fidelity and Blanket Bond, Securities and Entertainment Litigation.**
*See Professional Biographies, LOS ANGELES, CALIFORNIA*

Lott, Chere D. ....................'— '78 C.118 B.A. L.1068 J.D. 6200 Willshire Blvd.
**Lott, Karl J.** ....................'60 '90 C.945 B.A. L.1068 J.D. [Lamb&B.]
*PRACTICE AREAS: Real Property Law; Entertainment Law.
**Lotts, Richard L.** ....................'41 '67 C.112 B.A. L.477 J.D. [Sheppard,M.R.&H.]
*PRACTICE AREAS: Labor Law; Employment Law.
**Loubier, Gregg J.** ....................'56 '86 C.1307 B.A. L.1067 J.D. [A] Andrews&K.]
*PRACTICE AREAS: Real Estate.
Loughran, Kenneth E. ..........'58 '84 C.112 A.B. L.770 J.D. Auburndale Properties, Inc.
Loughry, Daniel F. '51 '77 C.1057 B.A. L.818 J.D.
(adm. in MA; not adm. in CA) U.S. Admin. Law J., Soc. Sec. Admn.
**Loui, Warren R.** ....................'56 '82 C.453 B.S. L.813 J.D. [O'Melveny&M.]
*PRACTICE AREAS: Banking; Asset Securitization; Entertainment Finance.
**Louie, Jamie Ann** ....................'64 '92 C.1097 B.S. L.1137 J.D. [Prestholt,K.F.&V.]⊙
*PRACTICE AREAS: Personal Injury; Workers Compensation.
Louie, Judy '55 '82 C.705 B.A. L.1065 J.D.
Div. Coun. & Corp. V.P., PaineWebber, Inc.
**Louie, Kam C.** ............'50 '79 C.112 B.A. L.1067 J.D. [C] Ladas&P.] (See Pat. Sect.)
Louie, Linda G. ............'60 '86 C.112 B.A. L.800 J.D. 777 Figueroa St., 44th Fl.
**Louie, Winnie C.** ....................'64 '94 C.681 B.A. L.1068 J.D. [A] Sinnott,D.M.&P.]
*PRACTICE AREAS: Insurance Coverage Litigation.
**Loureiro, Karl R.** ....................'64 '92 C.1077 B.S. L.426 J.D. [A] Bottum&F.]
*LANGUAGES: Spanish.
Love, Christopher C. ....................'57 '83 C.1326 B.S. L.800 J.D. 221 N. Figueroa St.
**Love, Christopher E.** ....................'62 '92 C.502 B.J. L.494 J.D. [A] Foley L.W.&A.]
*PRACTICE AREAS: Health Care; Corporate Law.
**Love, Douglas E.** ....................'67 '96 C.800 B.S. L.464 J.D. [A] Orrick,H.&S.]

**Love, Richard A., Law Offices of, (AV) '47 '74 C.112 B.A. L.426 J.D.**
**11601 Wilshire Boulevard, Suite 2000, 90025**
**Telephone: 310-477-2070 Fax: 310-477-3922**
**Associates: Beth A. Shenfeld; Anne McWilliams; Eileen Spadoni; Neil J. Sheff; Marcy A. Pettitt.**
**Civil Trial and Appellate Practice in all State and Federal Courts. Discrimination and Employment, Business and Commercial Law, Securities, Product Liability, Negligence, and Insurance Bad Faith.**
*See Professional Biographies, LOS ANGELES, CALIFORNIA*

**Lovell, Carl E., III** ....................'67 '92 C.668 B.A. L.464 J.D. [A] Grace,S.C.&S.]
*PRACTICE AREAS: Insurance Defense Law; Product Liability Law; Insurance Bad Faith Law; Labor Law; Appellate Law.
Loveman, Peggy J. ....................'52 '85 C.1077 B.A. L.940 J.D. Dep. Pub. Def.
**Lovendosky, Keith A.** ....................'55 '80 C.472 B.A. L.1068 J.D. [Hart&W.]
*PRACTICE AREAS: Civil Litigation; Insurance Law; Corporate Litigation; Real Estate Litigation; Personal Injury Law.
**Loveridge, Lisa L.** ....................'63 '92 C.112 B.A. L.809 J.D. [Prestholt,K.F.&V.]
*PRACTICE AREAS: Premises Liability; Bad Faith; Insurance Defense Law.
Loversky, Thomas R. ....................'61 '89 C.746 B.A. L.426 J.D. Dep. Pub. Def.
Lovett, Michael A. ..........'58 '87 C.98 B.S. L.809 J.D. Assoc. Tax Coun., Unocal Corp.
**Lovich, Richard A.**, (AV) ....................'57 '84 C.1077 B.A. L.426 J.D. [Lovich&P.]

**Lovich & Penn, (AV)**
**777 South Figueroa, Suite 1507, 90017**
**Telephone: 213-689-3625 Fax: 213-689-3653**
**Staff Counsel American International Companies: Managing Attorney: Richard A. Lovich. Supervising Attorney: Francis P. Licata. Senior Trial Attorneys: Timothy W. Kaften; Ronald A. Mosher.**
**Products Liability, Professional Liability, Premises Liability, Medical Malpractice, Construction Liability, Workers' Compensation and Auto.**
*See Professional Biographies, LOS ANGELES, CALIFORNIA*

**Lovretovich & Karen**
**(See Woodland Hills)**

Low, Glenda M. ....................'62 '90 C.112 B.A. L.426 J.D. 1200 Wilshire Blvd.
Low, Ronald ..............'51 '85 C.112 B.A. L.329 J.D. 10866 Wilshire Blvd., 15th Fl.
**Lowary, Mark** ....................'66 '93 C.1109 B.A. L.809 J.D. [A] Berman,B.&B.]
Lowe, Howard E. ....................'40 '66 C&L.1068 B.A., J.D. 12011 San Vicente Blvd.
**Lowe, Michael S.** ....................'68 '94 C.918 B.A. L.569 J.D. [A] Irell&M.]
Lowe, Peter E. '41 '77 C.112 B.S. L.426 J.D.
Exec. V.P. & CEO, Mitsui Manufacturers Bk.
**Lowe, Robert J.**, (AV) ....................'54 '78 C.1044 B.A. L.1066 J.D. [R.J.Lowe]
Lowe, Sharon Mee-Yung ..........'54 '80 C.569 B.A. L.1068 J.D. 1171 Montecito Dr.

**Lowe, Steven T., (BV) '58 '84 C.880 B.S. L.184 J.D.**
**12424 Wilshire Boulevard, Suite 900, 90025**
**Telephone: 310-447-1727 Fax: 310-447-6485**
**Entertainment, Business, Corporate, Intellectual Property, Trademark, Copyright and Real Estate Litigation, Defamation, Investment Fraud.**
*See Professional Biographies, LOS ANGELES, CALIFORNIA*

**Lowe, Robert J., A Law Corporation, (AV)**
**2049 Century Park East Suite 900, 90067**
**Telephone: 310-551-6979 Fax: 310-551-6980**
**Email: ERISALAW@AOL.COM**
**Robert J. Lowe (Certified Specialist, Taxation Law, The State Bar of California Board of Legal Specialization).**
**Employee Benefits and Executive Compensation.**
*See Professional Biographies, LOS ANGELES, CALIFORNIA*

Lowenstein, Daniel H. ..........'43 '68 C.976 A.B. L.309 LL.B. Prof., UCLA Law Sch.
Lowenstein, Richard A., (AV) ..........'38 '65 C.999 L.809 J.D. Dep. Dist. Atty.
Lowenstein, Roger A., (AV Ⓣ) '43 '68 C.477 A.B. L.309 LL.B.
(adm. in NJ; not adm. in CA) 532 S. Windsor Blvd.
**Lower, James P.**, (AV) ....................'43 '69 C.154 A.B. L.426 J.D. [Hanna&M.]
*PRACTICE AREAS: Business and Corporate Practice; Civil Trial; Non-Profit and Private Foundations Representation.
**Lower, Judith A.** ....................'41 '85 C.813 A.B. L.426 J.D. [Hanna&M.]
*PRACTICE AREAS: Real Estate Law.
**Lowry, Michael L.**, (AV) ......'43 '68 C.228 A.B. L.902 J.D. [Ford&H.] (⊙Atlanta, GA)
**Lowry, Stephen M.** ....................'44 '80 C.950 B.A. L.659 J.D. [Morgan,L.&B.]
**Lowry, Walter S.** ..........'57 '84 C.103 A.B. L.569 J.D. [C] Skadden,A.S.M.&F.]
**Lowther, Joseph H.** ....................'61 '87 C.800 B.S. L.1148 J.D. [A] Ivanjack&L.]
*LANGUAGES: German.
*PRACTICE AREAS: Business Torts; Complex Litigation; Contract Law; Financial Institutions; Real Estate.
Lowy, Allan N. ........'49 '76 C.112 B.A. L.426 J.D. Pres., Pacific Prime Properties, Inc.
**Lowy, Dana** ....................'61 '92 C.112 B.A. L.809 J.D. [A] Zolla&M.]
*PRACTICE AREAS: Family Law.
**Lowy, Jeffrey M.** ....................'63 '92 C.37 B.A. L.809 J.D. [A] Mitchell,S.&K.]
*PRACTICE AREAS: Music Law; Entertainment Law; Intellectual Property Law.
Loya, Felix W. ....................'54 '79 C.111 B.S. L.800 J.D. 865 S. Figueroa St.
**Lozano, George D.** ....................'63 '90 C.112 B.A. L.276 J.D. [A] Lord,B.&B.]
Lozier, Selina K. ....................'64 '92 C.628 B.S. L.990 J.D. 633 W. 5th St.
**Lu, Eugene Y. C.**, (BV) ....................'42 '78 C.06 B.S. L.800 J.D. [Rogers&W.]
*PRACTICE AREAS: Banking and Project Finance.
**Lu, Samuel Kai** ....................'69 '94 C.813 B.A.B.S. L.178 J.D. [A] Irell&M.]
*PRACTICE AREAS: Intellectual Property Litigation.
**Lu, Shirley Sheau-Lih** ..........'66 '91 C&L.112 B.A., J.D. [A] Buchalter,N.F.&Y.]
*LANGUAGES: Mandarin Chinese and Korean.
*PRACTICE AREAS: Real Estate Transactions; Business.
**Luban, Nina B.** ....................'52 '90 C.1350 B.A. L.1068 J.D. [A] Loeb&L.]
*PRACTICE AREAS: Environmental Law.
**Lubega, Stephen K.** ....................'57 '86 C.267 B.S. L.809 J.D. [Asiedu&L.]
*LANGUAGES: Swahili.
*PRACTICE AREAS: Business Litigation; Family; Employment Litigation; Securities Litigation; Real Estate Litigation.
**Luber, David M.** ....................'50 '77 C.112 B.A. L.1066 J.D. [C] Case,K.B.&W.]
*PRACTICE AREAS: Real Estate; Real Estate Financing.
**Lubert, Jana I.** ....................'63 '88 C.112 B.A. L.426 J.D. [Lewis,D.B.&B.]
**Lubic, Michael B.** ....................'60 '86 C.976 B.S. L.145 J.D. [McCutchen,D.B.&E.]
*PRACTICE AREAS: Insolvency; Corporate Finance.
**Lubitz, David L.** ..........'66 '92 C.112 B.S. L.339 J.D. [A] Loeb&L.] (See Pat. Sect.)
*PRACTICE AREAS: Patent, Trademark and Copyright; International; Litigation.
**Lubitz, Stuart**, (AV) ........'34 '61 C.260 B.E.E. L.273 LL.B. [Loeb&L.] (See Pat. Sect.)
*PRACTICE AREAS: Trademark; Patent; Copyright.
**Lublinski, Michael** ....................'51 '76 C.563 B.A. L.276 J.D. [Kelley D.&W.]
*PRACTICE AREAS: Intellectual Property Law; Customs and International Trade Law; Corporate Law.
**Lucas, Carol Kurke** ....................'57 '83 C.696 B.A. L.569 J.D. [Ropers,M.K.&B.]
*PRACTICE AREAS: Health Care; Securities; Corporate.
**Lucas, Janice S.** ....................'65 '92 C.312 B.A. L.1049 J.D. [A] Wilson,E.M.E.&D.]
**Lucas, John R., Jr.** '45 '71
C.813 A.B. L.976 LL.B. Assoc. Gen. Coun., Atlantic Richfield Co.
*RESPONSIBILITIES: Corporate Law; Securities; Acquisitions, Divestitures and Mergers; Antitrust Law; General Practice.
Lucas, Michael W. ....................'45 '77 C.813 A.B. L.800 J.D. 10960 Wilshire Blvd.

**Lucas, Craig D.**
**(See Pasadena)**

**Luce, Matthew J.** ....................'68 '93 C.800 B.S. L.426 J.D. [Coleman&W.]

**Luce, Forward, Hamilton & Scripps LLP, (AV)**
**A Partnership including Professional Corporations**
**777 South Figueroa, Suite 3600, 90017**⊙
**Telephone: 213-892-4992 Fax: 213-892-7731**
**URL: http://www.luce.com**
**Resident Partners: Rex Heeseman; James E. Fitzgerald; Andrew J. Waxler; Daniel I. Simon. Associates: Teryl Murabayashi (Resident); Christina Bull Arndt (Resident); Matthew C. Elstein (Resident); Eric Todd Jorgensen (Resident); Greg R Groeneveld (Resident); Gregory H. King (Resident); David N. Ruben (Resident).**
**General Civil Practice and Litigation in all State and Federal Courts. Antitrust, Banking, Bankruptcy, Business, Commercial, Copyright, Corporate Finance, Corporations, Energy and Resource, Environmental, Estate Planning, Family, Fidelity and Surety, First Amendment, Foreign Investment, Health Care Organizations, Immigration and Naturalization, Insurance and Reinsurance, Intellectual Property, International Financial Transactions, Labor, Land Use, Mergers and Acquisitions, Municipal Finance, Partnership, Patent, Pension and Profit-Sharing, Probate, Probate Litigation, Product Liability and Warranty, Professional Responsibility, Public Utility, Real Property, Securities, Taxation, Trademark, Trust and Venture Financing Law, Water Law.**
**San Diego, California Office: 600 West Broadway, Suite 2600, 92101. Telephone: 619-236-1414. Fax: 619-232-8311.**
**La Jolla, California Office: 4275 Executive Square, Suite 800, 92037. Telephone: 619-535-2639. Fax: 619-453-2812.**
**San Francisco, California Office: 100 Bush Street, 20th Floor, 94104. Telephone: 415-395-7900. Fax: 415-395-7949.**
**New York, N.Y. Office: Citicorp Center, 153 East 53rd Street, 26th Floor, 10022. Telephone: 212-754-1414. Fax: 212-644-9727.**
**Chicago, Illinois Office: 180 North La Salle Street, Suite 1125, 60601. Telephone: 312-641-0580. Fax: 312-641-0380.**
*See Professional Biographies, LOS ANGELES, CALIFORNIA*

**Lucero, Gene A.** ....................'47 '73 C.813 B.A. L.1066 J.D. [Latham&W.]
*LANGUAGES: Spanish.
Lucero, Thomas Y. ....................'55 '80 C.112 B.A. L.309 J.D. 523 W. 6th St.
**Luchini, Eva M.** ....................'70 '96 C.112 B.A. L.178 J.D. [A] O'Melveny&M.]
Luckenbacher, Frank C. ..........'49 '76 C.1077 B.S. L.426 J.D. 740 N. LaBrea Ave.
**Luderer, R. Dennis**, (AV) ..........'45 '75 C.93 A.B. L.1049 J.D. [Ziffren,B.B.&F.]
*PRACTICE AREAS: Tax Law.
**Ludlam, James E.**, (AV) ..........'14 '40 C.813 A.B. L.309 J.D. [C] Musick,P.&G.]
**Ludwig, Michael L.** ..........'68 '94 C&L.800 B.S., J.D. [A] Sheppard,M.R.&H.]
Luedtke, Eric V. ..........'67 '94 C.1109 B.A. L.878 J.D. 888 S. Figueroa St.
Luevano, Daniel M. ....................'23 '59 C.112 A.B. L.765 LL.B. Off. of Dist. Atty.
Luevano, Mark ..........'55 '82 C.112 B.A. L.426 J.D. 12561 Indianapolis St.
**Luftman, Michael B.**, (AV) ....................'43 '73 C.659 B.S. L.426 J.D. [Reish&L.]
*PRACTICE AREAS: Tax, Estate Planning and Probate.
**Lui, Elwood**, (AV) ....................'41 '70 C.112 B.S. L.1068 J.D. [Jones,D.R.&P.]

CALIFORNIA—LOS ANGELES MARTINDALE-HUBBELL LAW DIRECTORY 1997

**Lukacsko, Shea H.** ....................'64 '91 C.990 B.S. L.1065 J.D. [Ⓐ Thelen,M.J.&B.]
*PRACTICE AREAS: Business Litigation and Construction.
**Lukas, Edward W., Jr.** ..........'63 '91 C.1042 B.S. L.1049 J.D. [Ⓐ Harrington,F.D.&C.]
**Luke, Michael S.** ..............................'70 '95 C&L.112 B.A., J.D. [Ⓐ Troop M.S.&P.]
*PRACTICE AREAS: Corporate.
Luke, Sherrill D. ...........................'28 '63 C.112 B.A. L.284 J.D. Supr. Ct. J.
**Lukehart, Catherine** ..................'66 '91 C.1049 B.A. L.809 J.D. [Ⓐ Gilbert,K.C.&J.]
Lukus, Frank W. ...................................'43 '70 C&L.37 B.A., J.D. 800 W. 1st
Lum, Jennifer T. ...............'61 '86 C.800 A.B. L.188 J.D. 312 N. Spring St., 12th Fl.

**Lum, Albert C.**
**(See South Pasadena)**

Lumb, David M. .........................'45 '76 C.597 B.A. L.94 J.D. 523 W. 6th St.
Luna, David A., (BV) ........................'49 '74 C.426 B.A. L.309 J.D. [Dobberteen&L.]
**Luna, Dennis R.** ...........................'46 '74 C.800 B.S. L.309 J.D. [Richman,L.K.&G.]
*PRACTICE AREAS: Corporate; Business Law; Real Estate; Taxation; Natural Resources.
**Lund, Eric James**, (AV) .........'59 '83 C.813 B.A. L.800 J.D. [Lund] (⊙Beverly Hills)
*LANGUAGES: French and Farsi.
*PRACTICE AREAS: Estate Planning; Trust and Probate Law.
Lund, Roger K. '39 '64 C.25 B.A. L.178 LL.B.
(adm. in NY; not adm. in CA) Amer. Bdcstg. Cos., Inc.

**Lund Law Corporation, (AV)**
**1901 Avenue of the Stars, Twentieth Floor, 90067**
**Telephone: 310-286-7485 Fax: 310-286-7486**
**Email: XLNT706@aol.com**
**Eric James Lund. Of Counsel: Theodore V. Kreps.**
**Estate Planning, Probate and Trust Law.**
***See Professional Biographies, LOS ANGELES, CALIFORNIA***

**Lundberg, G. Andrew** .........................'57 '83 C.813 A.B. L.309 J.D. [Latham&W.]
**Lundberg, Gregg D.** ................'57 '90 C.800 B.S. L.809 J.D. [Robinson,D.B.&K.]
*REPORTED CASES: In re Advent Management Corp., 178 B.R. 480 (Bankr. 9th Cir.).
*PRACTICE AREAS: Bankruptcy Law.
**Lundy, Robert W., Jr.** ................'50 '75 C.976 B.A. L.1068 J.D. [Hooper,L.&B.]
*PRACTICE AREAS: Healthcare Law; Hospital Law.
Luner, Sean Aaron .................'— '92 C.112 B.S. L.800 J.D. 1999 Ave. of the Stars
**Lunn, Gerald E., Jr.**, (AV) ..............'54 '80 C.1365 B.A. L.309 J.D. [G.E.Lunn,Jr.]

**Lunn, Gerald E., Jr., P.C., (AV)**
**1901 Avenue of the Stars, Twentieth Floor, 90067**
**Telephone: 310-277-6264; Mobile: 310-713-0504 Facsimile: 310-277-6271**
**Email: GLUNN@ix.netcom.com**
**Gerald E. Lunn, Jr. (Certified Specialist, Probate, Estate Planning and Trust Law, The State Bar of California Board of Legal Specialization).**
**Estate and Tax Planning with Emphasis in Prenuptial Agreements and Marital Contracts.**
***See Professional Biographies, LOS ANGELES, CALIFORNIA***

**Lunt, Gregory O.** .........................'67 '94 C.878 B.A. L.178 J.D. [Ⓐ Latham&W.]
*LANGUAGES: Korean.
Luppi, Henry M. ...............................'15 '47 C&L.93 J.D. 6118 Damask Ave.‡
Lupton, Ralph L. ...........................'06 '31 C&L.597 B.S., J.D. P.O. Box 761398‡
**Lurey, Michael S.**, (AV) ..................'46 '71 C.597 B.S. L.309 J.D. [Latham&W.]
*PRACTICE AREAS: Insolvency; Business Debtors (50%); Creditors (50%).
Lurie, Abraham M. ..........................'23 '57 C.608 B.S. L.426 5900 Wilshire Blvd.
**Lurie, Barry** ..........................'63 '89 C.813 B.A. L.1068 J.D. [Ⓐ Danning,G.D.&K.]
*LANGUAGES: French.
**Lurie, Bernard J.** ..........................'55 '80 C.112 B.A. L.1068 J.D. [Ⓐ R.Ehrenpreis]
**Lurie, Jonathan C.**, (AV) ...............'53 '86 C&L.061 B.A., LL.B. [Hoffman,S.&W.]
*PRACTICE AREAS: Estate Planning Law; Probate Law; Trust Law; International Estate Planning.
**Lurie, Robert A.** ......................'65 '91 C.112 B.S. L.1068 J.D. [Ⓐ Allen,M.L.G.&M.]
*PRACTICE AREAS: Real Estate.
**Lurie, Steven J.** ..................'62 '88 C.112 B.S. L.1066 J.D. [Greenberg G.F.C.&M.]
*PRACTICE AREAS: Real Estate; Corporate; Business.
Luros, Michael S. ..............................'47 '72 C.112 B.A. L.145 J.D. Mun. Ct. J.
**Lurvey, Ira H.**, (AV) ....................'35 '65 C.339 B.S. L.1066 J.D. [Lurvey&S.]
*PRACTICE AREAS: Family Law.

**Lurvey & Shapiro, (AV)**
**Fox Plaza, 2121 Avenue of the Stars, Suite 1550 (Century City), 90067**
**Telephone: 310-203-0711 Fax: 310-203-0610**
**Members of Firm: Ira H. Lurvey (Certified Specialist, Family Law, The State Bar of California Board of Legal Specialization); Judith Salkow Shapiro.**
**Family Law, Business and Civil Litigation in all State and Federal Courts.**
**Reference: City National Bank (Beverly Hills Main Office).**
***See Professional Biographies, LOS ANGELES, CALIFORNIA***

**Lussier, Kevin R.** ...................'64 '89 C.1109 B.A. L.1067 J.D. [Ⓐ Jones,D.R.&P.]
**Lustberg, Roger H.** ...........................'48 '73 C.976 A.B. L.309 J.D. [Riordan&M.]
Lustig, Jason P. ............................'62 '87 C.705 B.A. L.94 J.D. Dep. Dist. Atty.
**Luty, Robert L.**, (AV) ............................'48 '73 C.228 B.A. L.426 J.D. [R.L.Luty]

**Luty, Robert L., A Professional Corporation, (AV)**
**Suite 303, 11661 San Vicente Boulevard, 90049**
**Telephone: 310-207-4342 Fax: 310-207-5035**
**Robert L. Luty.**
**Personal Injury, Insurance Bad Faith, Products Liability, Medical and Legal Malpractice and General Liability.**
**Reference: Brentwood Savings Bank (Brentwood Branch).**
***See Professional Biographies, LOS ANGELES, CALIFORNIA***

Lutz, Ellen L. ................'55 '85 C.831 B.A. L.1066 J.D. Dir., Human Rights Watch
Lutz, Robert E., II '46 '73 C.800 A.B. L.112 J.D.
Prof. of Law, Southwestern Univ.School of Law
Lutz, William R. ...................'61 '87 C.112 B.A. L.629 J.D. 1800 Ave. of the Stars
**Lutzker, Wendy A.** ....................'69 '95 C&L.800 B.A., J.D. [Ⓐ Gibson,D.&C.]
**Luymes, Ted H.** ..........................'64 '90 C&L.101 B.A., J.D. [Ⓐ Kearney,B.&C.]
*LANGUAGES: Spanish.
Lybrand, A. Martin ...............'33 '73 C.800 B.S.C.E. L.1136 J.D. 888 S. Figueroa St.
**Lycoyannis, Christina** '64 '89 C.659 B.A. L.569 J.D.
(adm. in NY; not adm. in CA) [Ⓐ Kelley D.&W.]
Lyddan, Kathryn Mary ...............'55 '86 C.112 B.A. L.1065 J.D. 2049 Century Pk. E.
**Lykowski, Timothy S.** ...................'70 '95 C.597 B.A. L.800 J.D. [Ⓐ Gibson,D.&C.]
Lyman, David K. ..........'25 '54 C&L.800 B.S., LL.B. Sr. V.P., Pardee Construction Co.
**Lyman, Mary Ann** .....................'68 '94 C.112 A.B. L.976 J.D. [Ⓐ Munger,T.&O.]
Lyman, Ronald E. ....'48 '78 C.112 B.A. L.809 J.D. Mgr., Contracts, Hughes Aircraft Co.
**Lynberg, Charles A.**, (AV) ...................'29 '57 C&L.352 B.A., J.D. [Lynberg&W.]

**Lynberg & Watkins, A Professional Corporation, (AV)**
**Sixteenth Floor International Tower Plaza, 888 South Figueroa Street, 90017-2516⊙**
**Telephone: 213-624-8700 Fax: 213-892-2763**
**Charles A. Lynberg; Judith Gold; Norman J. Watkins; R. Jeff Carlisle; Dana J. McCune; Michael J. Larin; Randall J. Peters; Ric C. Ottaiano††; Dana A. Fox; Stephen M. Harber; Ruth Segal; Catherine L. Ferro; Heller-Ann C. Hancock; Louis E. Marino, Jr.; Douglas G. MacKay;—Christine H. Gosney; William F. Bernard††; Michael A. Cartelli; Pamela H. Roth; Claudia H. Hanzlick; Thomas G. Oesterreich; Peggy Kolkey; Wendy E. Schultz; Jason M. Booth; Jerome P. Doctors; Guy N. Webster;**

(This Listing Continued)



**Lynberg & Watkins, A Professional Corporation (Continued)**
**Jamie L. Vels; David K. Morrison; Timothy F. Rivers; Barry L. Bookbinder; Todd J. Wenzel; Mark F. Gamboa; Nicholas R. Andrea; Dina M. De Laurentis; Antonia M. Chan; Charles C. McKenna; Brian C. Plante; Mary E. Lynch††; Denah H. Yoshiyama; Michael T. Taurek; Kathy M. Gandara; Mark A. Hooper; Michael J. Pepek; Heather C. Jelensky; Lisa M. Baker; Alan Aghabegian; Kara J. Petreccia; Todd Harrison Stitt; Alex H. Cherin. Of Counsel: Martin D. Kaplan.**
**General Insurance Practice in all California and Federal Trial and Appellate Courts, including Defense of Bad Faith, Insurance Coverage, Excess Liability, Aviation, Product Liability, Casualty and Professional Liability Claims. Defense of Municipalities and Businesses. Environmental and Toxic Coverage and Defense Litigation.**
**Representative Clients: The American International Group of Companies (AIG); Universal Underwriters; National Home Life Insurance Co.; Gallagher-Bassett, Keenan & Associates (Third Party Administrators).**
**Santa Ana, California Office: Suite 101, 2020 E. 1st Street. Telephone: 714-973-1220. Fax: 714-973-1002.**
**††Santa Ana Office**
***See Professional Biographies, LOS ANGELES, CALIFORNIA***

**Lynch, Carol W.** .........................'51 '81 C.112 B.A. L.426 J.D. [Richards,W.&G.]
*PRACTICE AREAS: Public Law; Land Use Law.
**Lynch, Gregory G.** ...........................'— '85 C.1074 B.S. L.770 J.D. [Hillsinger&C.]
*LANGUAGES: French, Spanish and Italian.
**Lynch, Jeri Dye** ...........................'60 '86 C.800 B.A. L.809 J.D. [Ⓐ Weisman&R.]
*LANGUAGES: French and Spanish.
*PRACTICE AREAS: General Civil Litigation; Business Litigation; Insurance Coverage Litigation; Defense of Savings & Loan Executives; Professional Liability.
Lynch, John J. ..................................'33 '59 C&L.426 B.S., LL.B. Assessor, L.A. Co.
Lynch, Kimberle A. '55 '79 C.1077 B.A. L.426 J.D.
Sr. V.P., Worldwide Dist., Orion Pictures Corp.
Lynch, M. Joey ............'54 '82 C.208 B.S. L.809 J.D. 2029 Century Park E., Ste., 2700
**Lynch, Mark P.** ...........................'55 '86 C.112 B.A. L.809 J.D. [Weisman&R.]
*PRACTICE AREAS: Business Litigation; Construction Defect; Financial Institutions; Insurance Coverage; Real Estate Litigation.
**Lynch, Patrick**, (AV) ......................'41 '67 C&L.426 B.A., LL.B. [O'Melveny&M.]
*PRACTICE AREAS: General Civil Litigation; Antitrust Law; Trademarks; Copyrights; Intellectual Property.

**Lynch Rowin Novack Burnbaum & Crystal, P.C.**
**22nd Floor, 2121 Avenue of the Stars, 90067⊙**
**Telephone: 310-557-8422 Telex: 181 149 WEST LSA**
**Resident Counsel: David Paul Steiner (A Professional Corporation).**
**General Practice. Litigation, Corporate and Commercial, Products Liability, Environmental, Financing and Banking, Real Estate, Securities, Trusts and Estates, Trademark, Copyright, Art Business, International Transactions and Computer Law.**
**New York, New York Office: 300 East 42nd Street. Telephone: 212-682-4001. Telex: 220 883 TA UR. Telecopier: 212-986-2907.**
***See Professional Biographies, LOS ANGELES, CALIFORNIA***

Lynes, William H. '50 '76
C.732 B.A. L.398 J.D. Assoc. Reg. Coun., Chicago Title Ins. Co.
**Lyness, Audrey M.** ......................'61 '89 C.118 B.A. L.1065 J.D. [Ⓐ Barger&W.]
**Lynn, Jeffrey C.** ...........................'55 '81 C.940 B.A. L.809 J.D. [Ⓐ Tharpe&H.]
*PRACTICE AREAS: Insurance Coverage; Insurance Bad Faith.
Lynn, Julie G. '66 '92 C&L.893 B.A., J.D.
(adm. in VA; not adm. in CA) Parmount Pictures
Lynn, Katherine Lerner .........'47 '76 C.860 A.B. L.569 J.D. Sr. Jud. Atty., Ct. of App.
**Lynyak, Joseph T., III** ......................'51 '76 C.749 A.B. L.276 J.D. [Graham&J.]
*PRACTICE AREAS: Financial Service Law; Regulatory Practice.
**Lyon, Eileen** ............................'57 '87 C.112 B.A. L.800 J.D. [Manatt,P.&P.]
*PRACTICE AREAS: Corporate Law; Securities Law; Banking Law.
Lyon, John D. .......................................'37 '62 C.145 B.A. L.309 J.D. [Katsky&L.]
**Lyon, Richard E., Jr., (A Professional Corporation)**, (AV) '43 '70
C.813 B.S. L.878 J.D. [Lyon&L.] (See Pat. Sect.)
*PRACTICE AREAS: Patent, Trademark, Unfair Competition; Licensing of Intellectual Property; Intellectual Property.
**Lyon, Robert E., (A Professional Corporation)**, (AV) '36 '64
C&L.800 B.S., J.D. [Lyon&L.] (See Pat. Sect.)
*PRACTICE AREAS: Patent, Trademark, Copyright, Unfair Competition; Intellectual Property.

**Lyon & Lyon LLP, (AV)**
**A Limited Liability Partnership including Professional Corporations**
**First Interstate World Center, 47th Floor, 633 West Fifth Street, 90071-2066⊙**
**Telephone: 213-489-1600 Fax: 213-955-0440**
**Email: lyon@lyonlyon.com URL: http://www.lyonlyon.com**
**Members of Firm: Roland N. Smoot; Conrad R. Solum, Jr.; James W. Geriak (A Professional Corporation) (Costa Mesa Office); Robert M. Taylor, Jr. (Costa Mesa Office); Samuel B. Stone (A Professional Corporation) (Costa Mesa Office); Douglas E. Olson (A Professional Corporation) (La Jolla Office); Robert E. Lyon (A Professional Corporation); Robert C. Weiss (A Professional Corporation); Richard E. Lyon, Jr., (A Professional Corporation); John D. McConaghy (A Professional Corporation); William C. Steffin (A Professional Corporation); Coe A. Bloomberg (A Professional Corporation); J. Donald McCarthy (A Professional Corporation); Arnold Sklar; John M. Benassi (La Jolla Office); James H. Shalek; Allan W. Jansen (Costa Mesa Office); Robert W. Dickerson; Roy L. Anderson; David B. Murphy (Costa Mesa Office); James C. Brooks; Jeffrey M. Olson; Steven D. Hemminger (San Jose Office); Jerrold B. Reilly; Paul H. Meier; John A. Rafter, Jr.; Kenneth H. Ohriner; Mary S. Consalvi (La Jolla Office); Lois M. Kwasigroch; Lawrence R. LaPorte; Robert C. Laurenson (La Jolla Office); Carol A. Schneider. Associates: Hope E. Melville; Michael J. Wise; Kurt T. Mulville (Costa Mesa Office); Theodore S. Maceiko; Richard Warburg (La Jolla Office); James P. Brogan (Costa Mesa Office); Jeffrey D. Tekanic; Corrine M. Freeman (Costa Mesa Office); David A. Randall; Christopher A. Vanderlaan; Bruce G. Chapman; David T. Burse (San Jose Office); Charles R. Balgenorth; Wayne B. Brown (La Jolla Office); Jeffrey A. Miller (San Jose Office); Armand F. Ayazi; Jessica R. Wolff (La Jolla Office); Mark J. Carlozzi (Costa Mesa Office); Sheldon O. Heber (La Jolla Office); Jeffrey William Guise (La Jolla Office); Charles S. Berkman (La Jolla Office); Sheryl Rubinstein Silverstein (La Jolla Office); David E. Wang; Anthony C. Chen (La Jolla Office); Kenneth S. Roberts (Costa Mesa Office); Brent D. Sokol; Clarke W. Neumann, Jr. (La Jolla Office); John C. Kappos (Costa Mesa Office); Thomas J. Brindisi; Richard C. Hsu; Catherine Joyce; Charles Calvin Fowler (Costa Mesa Office); Lisa Ward Karmelich; Vicki Gee Norton (La Jolla Office); Jonathan T. Losk; Timothy J. Lithgow (La Jolla Office); Michael A. Tomasulo; Thomas R. Rouse; Edward M. Jordan; Charles A. Kertell; James K. Sakaguchi (Costa Mesa Office); Gary H. Silverstein (La Jolla Office); Amy Stark Hellenkamp (La Jolla Office); Richard H. Pagliery; William J. Kolegraff (La Jolla Office); Andrei Iancu; Jonathan Hallman (La Jolla Office); Lynn Y. McKernan (San Jose Office); Michael Bolan (San Jose Office); Farshad Farjami; Dmitry Milikovsy (San Jose Office); Gregory R. Stephenson; Howard N. Wisnia (La Jolla Office); Mary Agnes Tuck; Arlyn Alonzo; Neal Matthew Cohen (Costa Mesa Office). Of Counsel: Bradford J. Duft (La Jolla Office); Suzanne L. Biggs (La Jolla Office); F.T. Alexandra Mahaney (La Jolla Office); Stephen S. Korniczky (La Jolla Office).**
**Intellectual Property Law including Patent, Trademark, Copyright, Trade Regulation, Unfair Competition and Antitrust Law. Litigation.**
**Costa Mesa, California Office: Suite 1200, 3200 Park Center Drive. Telephone: 714-751-6606. Fax: 714-751-8209.**
**San Jose, California Office: Suite 1150, 303 Almaden Boulevard. Telephone: 408-993-1555. Fax: 408-287-2664.**
**La Jolla, California Office: Suite 660, 4250 Executive Square. Telephone: 619-552-8400. Fax: 619-552-0159.**
***See Professional Biographies, LOS ANGELES, CALIFORNIA***

**Lyons, Amy W.** .........................'53 '82 C.788 A.B. L.1049 J.D. [Veatch,C.G.&N.]
*LANGUAGES: Spanish.
*REPORTED CASES: Wilson v. Circus Circus Hotels, Inc., 101 Nev. 751-710 P.2d 77; Planet Insurance v. Transport Indemnity, 523 F.2d 285 (9th Cir. 1987).
*PRACTICE AREAS: Medical Malpractice Defense Law; General Casualty Defense Law.

Lyons, Bernard E. '34 '61 C.597 B.A. L.477 J.D.
V.P. & Gen. Coun., Consolidated Distributors, Inc.
**Lyons, John J.**, (AV) ..................... '51 '76 C.197 A.B. L.1066 J.D. [Latham&W.]
Lyons, Michael L. .................. '48 '77 C.112 B.S. L.1148 J.D. 12424 Wilshire Blvd.
**Lyons, N. David** ................ '50 '75 C.309 B.A. L.276 J.D. [Sedgwick,D.M.&A.]
Lyons, Sidney H. '27 '52 C.597 B.S. L.309 LL.B.
V.P., Bus. Affairs, CBS Entertainment
Lyster, Ronald W. .................. '50 '78 C.453 B.S. L.426 J.D. 1901 Ave. of the Stars
**Lytton, Sheldon H.**, (AV) ................ '42 '73 C.597 B.S. L.1068 J.D. [Kelly&L.]
Lytton, Stuart C. ........................ '50 '84 C.112 B.A. L.809 J.D. Dep. Dist. Atty.
Maas, Paul D. ........................ '52 '80 C.061 B.A. L.1148 J.D. [Maas&M.]
Maas & Marinovich .......................................... 3440 Wilshire Blvd.
Mabie, Thomas H. ................. '54 '79 C.112 B.A. L.1068 J.D. 801 S. Grand Ave.
**Mabrey, Kevin F.** ...................... '67 '96 C.36 B.S. L.800 J.D. [🄰 Gibson,D.&C.]
Macaluso, Stacey M. .................. '66 '92 C.1145 B.S. L.1019 J.D. 221 N. Figueroa
**Macaluso, Todd E.** ...................... '62 '87 C.93 B.S. L.215 J.D. [Schlothauer,C.&M.]
*LANGUAGES: Spanish.
**MacArthur, Frederick E.**, (AV) .... '24 '52 C&L.477 B.S.E., J.D. [MacArthur,U.H.&M.]
**MacArthur, Kenneth J.** ...................... '62 '95 C.112 B.S. L.800 J.D. [🄰 Troy&G.]
*PRACTICE AREAS: Business Litigation; Real Estate Litigation.
**MacArthur, William A.** ...................... '64 '91 C.1077 B.A. L.426 J.D. [🄰 Gibson,D.&C.]

**MacArthur, Uribe, Hicks & Mims, (AV)**
**626 Wilshire Boulevard, Suite 800, 90017-2900**
**Telephone: 213-538-1370 Fax: 213-538-1375**
**Members of Firm: Frederick E. MacArthur; J. A. Uribe; L. Westcott Hicks, Jr.; Stewart S. Mims; Stephen L. Kaplan.**
**General Civil, Trial and Appellate Practice in all Courts. Business Litigation, Arbitration, Real Estate, Corporation and General Business Law, State, Local, Federal and International Tax Planning, Tax Compliance, Tax Litigation, Estate Planning.**
**Reference: Wells Fargo Bank (Office, 707 Wilshire Boulevard).**
**Other Los Angeles Office: 10940 Wilshire Boulevard, Suite 1600. Telephone: 310-442-4855. Fax: 310-442-4858.**
*See Professional Biographies, LOS ANGELES, CALIFORNIA*

Macbeth, Arthur E. ........................ '29 '56 C.112 B.A. L.1068 3589 Glenalbyn Dr.‡
**MacCary, Karla Nefkens** ........ '65 '90 C.112 B.A. L.1068 J.D. [🄰 Nossaman,G.K.&E.]
*LANGUAGES: French.
*PRACTICE AREAS: Real Property Law; Corporations Law.
**MacCary, William T.** ................... '64 '90 C.813 A.B. L.1068 J.D. [🄰 Condon&F.]
**Maccoby, Matthew F.** ........................ '60 '88 C&L.976 B.A., J.D. [Kimball&W.]
*LANGUAGES: French and Russian.
*PRACTICE AREAS: General Business; Mergers and Acquisitions; Computer Software, Systems and Services; Real Property.
**MacCuish, David S.**, (AV) .... '47 '72 C.813 A.B. L.659 J.D. [McClintock,W.B.R.R.&M.]
*PRACTICE AREAS: Commercial Litigation; Oil and Gas Law; Trade Regulation; Environmental Litigation.
**MacDermott, Michael J.**, (AV) '50 '75
C.477 B.S. L.1068 J.D. [Pretty,S.&P.] (See Pat. Sect.)
*PRACTICE AREAS: Patents; Trademarks; Copyrights; Unfair Competition.
MacDonald, James C. .................. '63 '95 C.696 b.s. L.1137 J.D. 624 S. Grand Ave.
**MacDonald, Scott L.** ................... '67 '94 C.112 B.A. L.809 J.D. [🄰 Gilbert,K.C.&J.]
*PRACTICE AREAS: Insurance Defense.
**MacDonneil, Cori L.** ...................... '67 '92 C.112 B.A. L.990 J.D. [🄰 Gibson,D.&C.]
*LANGUAGES: Spanish.
*PRACTICE AREAS: Litigation; Health Care Fraud and Abuse.
Mace, Stephen G. .................. '41 '76 C.228 B.A. L.809 J.D. First Interstate Bancorp
**Maceiko, Theodore S.** ... '62 '90 C.158 B.S.M.E. L.426 J.D. [🄰 Lyon&L.] (See Pat. Sect.)
*PRACTICE AREAS: Patent, Trademark, Unfair Competition, Antitrust; Intellectual Property.
**Macellaro, Theresa J.** ...................... '62 '88 C.788 B.A. L.569 J.D. [Lavely&S.]
*REPORTED CASES: ASPCA v. Board of Trustees, 147 Misc. 2d 847, 556 N.Y.S. 2d 447 (S.Ct. 1990).
*PRACTICE AREAS: Entertainment Litigation; Sexual Harassment Litigation; Animal Rights Litigation; SLAPP Suit Expertise; Business Litigation.
**Macfarlane, Christine M.** ............ '64 '90 C&L.347 B.A., J.D. [🄰 Lesansky&Assoc.]
*LANGUAGES: Italian.
*PRACTICE AREAS: Aviation Law; Products Liability Law.
Machat, Michael ........................ '58 '83 C.228 BA L.112 JD 1875 Century Pk. E.
**Machida, Kenji, (A Professional Corporation)**, (AV) '43 '69
C.112 A.B. L.309 LL.B. [🄲 Berger,K.S.M.F.S.&G.]
**Machlovitch, Beth E.** ...................... '68 '92 C.012 B.A. L.569 J.D. [🄰 Troop M.S.&P.]
*PRACTICE AREAS: Litigation.
**Macht, Valarie H.** ................. '61 '89 C.893 B.A. L.276 J.D. [🄰 Thelen,M.J.&B.]
*PRACTICE AREAS: Bankruptcy Law and Commercial Litigation.
Machtinger, John F. .................. '63 '91 C.112 B.A. L.800 J.D. 2572 S. Centinela Ave.
**Machtinger, Leonard S.**, (AV) ............ '41 '65 C.563 B.A. L.309 LL.B. [Kenoff&M.]
*PRACTICE AREAS: Civil Litigation (business and entertainment).
**Machtinger, Sidney J.**, (AV) ......... '22 '50 C&L.597 B.S., J.D. [Greenberg G.F.C.&M.]
*PRACTICE AREAS: Federal and State Taxation; Tax Litigation; Estate Planning.
**Macias, Richard C.** ...................... '50 '76 C.668 B.A. L.309 J.D. [Bronson,B.&M.]
*PRACTICE AREAS: Federal and State Litigation; Commercial Law and Bankruptcy.
**Macias, Richard M.**, (BV) ................ '51 '76 C.112 A.B. L.1066 J.D. [Borton,P.&C.]
*PRACTICE AREAS: Business Litigation; Commercial Litigation; Tort Litigation Defense.
**MacIntosh, Susanne M.** ..................... '70 '95 C.773 B.A. L.597 J.D. [🄰 Sidley&A.]
Macintyre, Tuppence ................ '63 '91 C.914 B.A. L.276 J.D. 333 S. Hope St., 48th Fl.
MacIsaac, Vincent Peter ............. '57 '82 C.602 B.A. L.809 J.D. 2401 Colorado Blvd.
**Mack, Joan** ............................. '53 '95 C.813 B.A. L.426 J.D. [Hedges&C.]
**Mack, Linda McCauley** ...................... '63 '93 C.94 B.S. L.178 J.D. [🄰 Loeb&L.]
**MacKay, Douglas G.** ...................... '61 '87 C.112 B.S. L.809 J.D. [Lynberg&W.]
**Mackel, John E., III** .................. '59 '85 C.112 B.A. L.426 J.D. [Sullivan,W.&D.]
MacKenzie, David J. ..................... '33 '64 C.94 A.B. L.1068 LL.B. 300 Medio Dr.
MacKenzie, Timothy J. .............. '56 '84 C.112 B.A. L.990 J.D. 10866 Wilshire Blvd.
Mackey, Lesley E. .................. '65 '93 C.811 B.A. L.112 J.D. 801 S. Figueroa St.
**Mackey, Mary Devereaux** ..................... '61 '90 C.229 B.S. L.426 J.D. [🄰 Arter&H.]
*PRACTICE AREAS: Labor and Employment; Business Litigation.
Mackey, Robert D. ........................ '37 '76 C.112 B.A. L.1068 J.D. Supr. Ct. J.
**Mackey, Stuart J.** ...................... '69 '96 C.309 A.B. L.1066 J.D. [🄰 Folger L.&K.]⊙
**Mackey, Thomas G.** .................... '69 '94 C.1077 B.S. L.1065 J.D. [🄰 Gibson,D.&C.]
*PRACTICE AREAS: Labor and Employment Law.
**MacKinnon, Alexander F.** .............. '55 '82 C&L.477 B.S.C.E., J.D. [Kirkland&E.]
*PRACTICE AREAS: Litigation; Intellectual Property Law.
Macklin, Cerene .................. '67 '91 C.112 B.A. L.560 J.D. U.S. Dept. of Vet. Affs.
**Macklin, Meryl** ........................ '58 '84 C.976 B.A. L.1066 J.D. [Macklin T.]
*PRACTICE AREAS: Complex Business Litigation; Antitrust; Accountants Liability.

**Macklin Tatro, (AV)**
**1875 Century Park East, Suite 1220, 90067**
**Telephone: 310-229-2490 Fax: 310-229-2491**
**Members of Firm: René P. Tatro; Meryl Macklin; Craig S. Bloomgarden. Associate: Juliet A. Markowitz.**
**Complex Business Litigation including Environmental and Insurance Coverage Litigation, Real Estate, Construction Litigation, Antitrust, Accountants' Liability and Securities Fraud.**
*See Professional Biographies, LOS ANGELES, CALIFORNIA*

MacLaren, Ronni B. ..................... '55 '80 C.788 B.A. L.893 J.D. Asst. U.S. Atty.
**MacLean, Kurt A.**, (AV) '53 '82 C.1042 B.A. L.1068 J.D.
[Oppenheimer P.S.] (⊙Irvine)
*PRACTICE AREAS: Intellectual Property.
**MacLeod, Bruce R.**, (AV) ............ '48 '73 C.502 B.S. L.145 J.D. [Hennigan,M.&B.]
*PRACTICE AREAS: Securities; ERISA; Shareholders; Commercial Litigation.
**MacRae, Denise A.** ............ '60 '87 C.856 B.A. L.809 J.D. [🄰 Berger,K.S.M.F.S.&G.]
*LANGUAGES: Spanish.

**MacRae, Gerald C., (AV) '56 '87 C.02 B.A. L.809 J.D.** 🄱🄱
**1840 Century Park East, Suite 800, 90067-2109**
**Telephone: 310-553-6370 Fax: 310-553-4432**
**Civil Trial Practice in State and Federal Courts. Business Tort Litigation, False Claims Act Prosecution, Personal Injury, Professional Malpractice, Products Liability.**
*See Professional Biographies, LOS ANGELES, CALIFORNIA*

Macri, Dawne M. ............... '68 '93 C.112 B.A. L.424 J.D. 11100 Santa Monica Blvd.
**Mactavish, Heather A.** ............ '70 '95 C.1074 B.A. L.1068 J.D. [🄰 Heller E.W.&M.]
**Madans, Lawrence B.** ............. '46 '80 C.172 B.A. L.809 J.D. [Stockwell,H.W.&W.]
Madden, Erinn Marie '69 '94 C.893 B.A. L.763 LL.M.
(adm. in VA; not adm. in CA) Clk., U.S. Tax Ct.

**Madden, Jones, Cole & Johnson, A Professional Corporation**
**(See Long Beach)**

**Maddigan, Michael M.** .......... '67 '92 C.276 B.S.F.S. L.1066 J.D. [🄰 O'Melveny&M.]
**Maddux, David A.**, (AV) ........... '33 '60 C&L.800 B.S., LL.B. [Sheppard,M.R.&H.]
*PRACTICE AREAS: Labor and Employment Law.
Madhok, Sangeeta A. .................. '67 '94 C.061 B.A. L.978 J.D. 801 S. Figueroa St.
**Madison, Robert A.** ........... '63 '93 C.1074 B.A. L.1065 J.D. [🄰 Bonne,B.M.O.&N.]
**Madison, Steven G.** ...................... '55 '81 C.770 B.A. L.93 J.D. [Quinn E.U.&O.]
*PRACTICE AREAS: General Trial Practice; White Collar Crime; Appellate Litigation.
**Madison, Suzanne M.** ............ '65 '92 C.424 B.A. L.1068 J.D. [🄰 Kinsella,B.F.&T.]
*REPORTED CASES: Johnson v. Calvert, 5 Cal. 4th 84 (1993).
Madoff, Steven ............ '53 '79 C.107 B.A. L.472 J.D. V.P., Paramount Pictures Corp.
**Madok, Robert L.** ...................... '63 '91 C.276 B.A. L.800 J.D. [🄰 Paul,H.J.&W.]
Madrid, Rebecca M. ..................... '62 '90 C&L.560 B.A., J.D. Dep. Dist. Atty.
**Madris, Howard N.** ............. '66 '91 C.188 B.S. L.94 J.D. [🄰 Sulmeyer,K.B.&R.]
*PRACTICE AREAS: Bankruptcy Law; Business LItigation.
Maduke, Patricia J. ...................... '58 '88 C.02 B.A. L.809 J.D. 444 S. Flower St.
**Maeder, Gary W.**, (AV) .............. '49 '75 C.112 B.A. L.1068 J.D. [Heller E.W.&M.]
*PRACTICE AREAS: Federal Income and State and Local Taxation.
Magady, Terry M. .................. '56 '87 C.605 B.A. L.800 J.D. 1901 Ave. of the Stars
**Magaña, Brian R., (Professional Corporation)**, (AV) '48 '73
C.112 A.B. L.911 J.D. [Magaña,C.&M.]
*LANGUAGES: Spanish.
*PRACTICE AREAS: Automobile Product Law; Construction Accidents; FELA; Medical Malpractice Law; Railroad Personal Injury.
**Magaña, Raoul D.**, (AV) .......... '11 '36 C.112 A.B. L.1066 LL.B. [🄲 Magaña,C.&M.]

**Magaña, Cathcart & McCarthy, (AV)** 🄱🄱
**A Partnership including Professional Corporations**
**Suite 810 Gateway West Building, 1801 Avenue of the Stars (Century City), 90067-5899**
**Telephone: 310-553-6630; 213-879-2531 Fax: 310-785-9143**
**Brian R. Magaña (Professional Corporation); Peter T. Cathcart (Professional Corporation); William H. Wimsatt (Professional Corporation);—Richard L. Bisetti; Deborah Mitzenmacher; Kathleen A. McCarthy; Daniel A. Cribbs. Of Counsel: Daniel C. Cathcart (Professional Corporation). Retired: Raoul D. Magaña; James J. McCarthy.**
**Practice limited to Trials in all State and Federal Courts. Negligence Law. Appellate Practice. Aviation, Malpractice, Railroad, Products and Admiralty.**
**Reference: First Los Angeles Bank (1950 Avenue of the Stars, Los Angeles (Century City), California).**
*See Professional Biographies, LOS ANGELES, CALIFORNIA*

**Magaram, Philip S.**, (AV) ............ '37 '62 C.112 B.S. L.1068 LL.B. [Valensi,R.&M.]
*PRACTICE AREAS: Tax Planning Law; Estate Planning Law; General Business Law.
**Magasin, Michael R.** .................. '43 '69 C.112 B.A. L.1068 J.D. [🄲 Freeman,F.&S.]

**Magasinn & Magasinn, A Law Corporation**
**(See Marina Del Rey)**

Magdlen and Wenker, (AV) ................................ 1631 West Beverly Boulevard
**Magee, Howard L.** ...................... '70 '96 C.112 B.A. L.800 J.D. [🄰 Brobeck,P.&H.]
*PRACTICE AREAS: Labor Law.
Magee, James A., (AV) .................. '40 '67 C.976 B.A. L.477 J.D. 725 S. Figueroa St.
Magee, Katherine ........................ '43 '75 C.522 B.A. L.1148 J.D. P.O. Box 83202
**Magnanimo, Frank A.** ............. '69 '94 C.800 B.A. L.37 J.D. [🄰 Goldstein,K.&P.]
*LANGUAGES: Italian.
Magnuson, Charles H. ................. '29 '55 C&L.911 B.A., LL.B. 10866 Wilshire Blvd.
Magram, Richard O. '57 '84 C.860 B.A. L.61 J.D.
(adm. in PA; not adm. in CA) 831 Gretna Green Way
**Maguire, Everett W.**, (AV) .............. '28 '58 C.112 B.S. L.1068 J.D. [Maguire&O.]
*PRACTICE AREAS: Construction Law.
**Maguire, Perry E., (A Professional Corporation)** '43 '71
C.112 B.A. L.1068 J.D. [Farmer&R.]
*PRACTICE AREAS: Employee Benefit Law.

**Maguire, William E. '55 '81 C.112 B.A. L.1136 J.D.**
**10866 Wilshire Boulevard, Suite 300, 90024-4311**
**Telephone: 310-470-2929 Fax: 310-474-4710**
**Domestic and International Trademark Prosecution. Trademark, Copyright, Licensing and Product Placement Transactions. Entertainment and Intellectual Property Arbitration and Mediation.**

**Maguire & Orbach, Law Corporation, (AV)** 🄱🄱
**Suite 300, 10866 Wilshire Boulevard, 90024-4311**
**Telephone: 310-470-2929 Fax: 310-474-4710**
**Everett W. Maguire; David M. Orbach; Jeffrey D. Pearlman; David M. Huff; Michael D. Germain. Construction Law, Real Estate and Insurance. Civil Trial and Appellate Practice in State and Federal Courts.**
*See Professional Biographies, LOS ANGELES, CALIFORNIA*

**Mahaffa, Walt D.** ...................... '54 '80 C.426 B.A. L.990 J.D. [🄲 J.M.Donovan]⊙
*PRACTICE AREAS: Litigation; Business Law; Real Estate Law.
Mahan-Lamb, Nancy ...................... '57 '85 C.36 B.S. L.990 J.D. [Gibeaut,M.&B.]
**Maher, Pamela G.** ..... '59 '92 C.94 B.S. L.426 J.D. [🄰 Fulwider P.L.&U.] (See Pat. Sect.)
*PRACTICE AREAS: Intellectual Property Law.
Maher, Susan Brooks '52 '80
C.1055 B.A. L.861 J.D. Assoc. Legal Coun., Cedars-Sinai Med. Ctr.
**Mahlowitz, Robert M.** ........ '65 '92 C.659 B.A. L.93 J.D. [🄰 McClintock,W.B.R.R.&M.]
*PRACTICE AREAS: Civil Litigation; Federal Litigation; Franchise Termination; Contract Litigation; Environmental Law.
Mahmoodzadegan, Navid A. '69 '93 C.477 A.B. L.309 J.D.
1800 Ave. of the Stars, Suite 900 (Century City)
Mahmud, Diana '53 '78 C.112 B.A. L.1067 J.D.
Dep. Gen. Coun., Metropolitan Water Dist. of Southern Calif.
**Mahoney, James E., (P.C.)**, (AV) ... '40 '67 C.1042 A.B. L.1065 J.D. [Mahoney,C.J.&P.]
*PRACTICE AREAS: Real Estate; Business; Corporate; Commercial Litigation; Estate Planning.

**Mahoney, Coppenrath, Jaffe & Pearson LLP, (AV)** BB
**A Partnership including Professional Corporations**
**2049 Century Park East, Suite 2480, 90067-3283**
**Telephone: 310-557-1919 Telecopier: 310-277-6536**
**Members of Firm: James E. Mahoney (P.C.); Walter G. Coppenrath, Jr., (P.C.); Howard M. Jaffe (P.C.); Ronald C. Pearson; Daryl G. Parker; Charles L. Grotts; Arthur L. Martin. Of Counsel: Gerald Lee Tahajian.**
**General Civil, Trial and Appellate Practice. Commercial, Real Property, Insurance, Corporate, Probate, Trust, Estate Planning and Litigation, Admiralty, Marine and Inland Marine Insurance Law. Federal, State and Local Taxation, Guardianships and Conservatorships.**
**Reference: First Professional Bank, Santa Monica, California.**
*See Professional Biographies, LOS ANGELES, CALIFORNIA*

**Mahr, Thomas S.** ....'54 '81 C&L.472 B.M., J.D. [Katten M.&Z.] (⊙Irvine)
*PRACTICE AREAS: Business, Entertainment and Commercial Litigation.
Maiden, Hubert, (AV) ....'25 '52 C.112 L.800 J.D. 1925 Century Park E.‡
Maier, John L. ....'40 '66 C.477 A.B. L.813 LL.B. 1717 N. Highland Ave.
**Maile, Christopher S.** ....'58 '85 C.112 B.A. L.426 J.D. [Tharpe&H.]
*REPORTED CASES: Far West Financial Corp. vs. D & S Co., Inc., 46 Cal 3d 796, 1988.
*PRACTICE AREAS: Employment Litigation; Insurance Carrier/Agent Litigation; Employment Discrimination/Harassment; Construction Defect Litigation; Intellectual Property/Unfair Business Practices Litigation.
**Maile, Jonathan G.** ....'54 '79 C.112 B.A. L.809 J.D. [Tharpe&H.]
*PRACTICE AREAS: General Casualty Defense; Defense of Claims Against Truckers; Wrongful Termination; Sexual Harassment.
Main, Donovan M. ....'45 '70 C.605 B.A. L.800 J.D. Asst. Co. Coun.
**Mainland, Richard R.**, (AV) ....'39 '65 C.813 A.B. L.309 LL.B. [Fulbright&J.]
*PRACTICE AREAS: Intellectual Property Litigation; Securities Litigation; Antitrust; Unfair Trade; Alternative Dispute Resolution.
**Maire, Richard J., Jr.** ....'58 '83 C.112 B.A. L.800 J.D. [Ⓑ Morgan,L.&B.]
**Maisel, Christopher M., (P.C.)** ....'51 '77 C.842 B.B.A. L.846 J.D. [Cantilo,M.&H.]⊙
*PRACTICE AREAS: Insurance Insolvency; Regulatory; Litigation.
**Maisnik, M. Guy** ....'57 '84 C.112 B.A. L.426 J.D. [Paul,H.J.&W.]
**Maisonneuve, Mark D.** ....'52 '84 C.171 B.S. L.809 J.D. [Ⓐ J.M.Donovan]
**Maizel, Samuel R.** '55 '85 C.870 B.S. L.273 J.D.
(adm. in PA; not adm. in CA) [Ⓑ Pachulski,S.Z.&Y.]
*LANGUAGES: French.
*REPORTED CASES: In re Buckner, 66 F.3d 263 (10th Cir. 1995); United States Postal Service v. Dewey Freight Systems, Inc., 31 F.3d 620 (8th Cir. 1994); In re Trans World Airlines, Inc., 18 F.3d 208 (3d Cir. 1994); United States Agricultural Stabilization and Conservation Service v. Gerth, 991 F.2d 1428 (8th Cir. 1993); In re St. Johns Home Health Agency, Inc., 173 B.R. 238 (Bankr. S.D. Fla. 1994).
*PRACTICE AREAS: Bankruptcy; Government Contracts.
Maizlish, Leonard M., (BV) ....'32 '57 C&L.813 A.B., LL.B. 10573 W. Pico Blvd.
**Majcher, Thomas H.** '57 '83 C.816 B.E. L.809 J.D.
[Fulwider P.L.&U.] (See Pat. Sect.)
*PRACTICE AREAS: Patent, Trademark, Copyright and Unfair Competition Law; Litigation.
Majorell, Melanie ....'01 '23 C.571 L.705 J.D. 5959 W. Century Blvd., Ste. 100
**Makarewich, John A.** ....'56 '94 C.112 B.A. L.426 J.D. [Ⓐ Skadden,A.S.M.&F.]

**Maki, Lisa L. '65 '92 C.424 B.A. L.990 J.D.**
**815 Moraga Drive, 90049-1633**
**Telephone: 310-440-5575 Facsimile: 310-440-5576**
***REPORTED CASES: Fennessy v. Southwest Airlines, (1996) 91 F.3d 1359.**
***PRACTICE AREAS: Civil Practice; Civil Litigation.**
**Labor and Employment Law, including Plaintiff's Employment, Discrimination, Sexual Harassment, Disability Discrimination and Age Discrimination, Property Damage, Inverse Condemnation.**
*See Professional Biographies, LOS ANGELES, CALIFORNIA*

Makin, Cynthia C., (A Professional Corporation) '63 '88
C.1042 B.S. L.990 J.D. [Makin&M.]⊙
Makin & Masoner .... 10940 Wilshire Blvd., 16th Fl. (⊙Long Beach)
**Makman, David Alan** ....'63 '95 C.604 A.B. L.228 J.D. [Ⓐ Loeb&L.] (See Pat. Sect.)
*LANGUAGES: Japanese.
*PRACTICE AREAS: Intellectual Property.
**Makous, David N.** ....'51 '78 C.228 B.S. L.665 J.D. [Lewis,D.B.&B.] (Pat.)
**Makowsky, Sarah M.** ....'66 '91 C.347 B.A. L.426 J.D. [Ⓐ Yukevich&S.]
*PRACTICE AREAS: Products Liability Defense; Personal Injury Defense.
**Makunga, Sonya** ....'68 '96 C.951 B.A. L.1068 J.D. [Ⓐ Loeb&L.]
*LANGUAGES: Spanish.
Makuta, Celeste S. ....'48 '91 C.112 B.A. L.809 J.D. 633 W. 5th St.
Malamed, Daniel S., (AV) ....'12 '39 C&L.831 LL.B. 6331 Drexel Ave.‡
Malamud, Brad R. ....'53 '78 C.112 B.S. L.1065 J.D. 221 N. Figueroa St.
Malamud, Richard B. '53 '77 C.112 A.B. L.426 J.D.
Prof., Calif. State University Dominquez Hills
**Malanga, Gerald B.** ....'64 '93 C.800 B.A. L.990 J.D. [Ⓐ Ropers,M.K.&B.]
*LANGUAGES: Spanish.
*PRACTICE AREAS: General Civil Liability Defense.
**Malaret, Charles J.** ....'64 '89 C.767 B.A. L.1067 J.D. [Ⓐ Zevnik H.G.&M.]
*PRACTICE AREAS: Litigation; Insurance; Environmental.
**Malarney, Dana E.** ....'69 '96 C.823 B.A. L.809 J.D. [Ⓐ Manning,L.B.&B.]
*PRACTICE AREAS: Business Litigation; Bankruptcy.
Malatesta, Ian C., (AV) ....'52 '77 C.98 B.A. L.1136 J.D. 12400 Wilshire Blvd.
Malatt, Richard ....'50 '76 C.112 A.B. L.800 J.D. [Ⓐ Dumas&Assoc.]
**Malcolm, Joseph J.** '46 '76 C.705 B.A. L.776 J.D.
(adm. in NJ; not adm. in CA) [Grotta,G.&H.]⊙
**Malin, Allison L.** ....'65 '90 C.112 B.A. L.800 J.D. [Ⓐ Allen,M.L.G.&M.]
*PRACTICE AREAS: Real Estate; Natural Resources; Civil Trial; Environmental Law; General Practice.
**Malin, Ronald H.**, (AV) ....'34 '60 C.800 B.S. L.208 J.D. [Ⓑ Akre,B.&C.]
*PRACTICE AREAS: Real Estate Law; Real Estate Finance and Development Law; Syndications Law; Agricultural Law.
**Malingagio, Paul S.** ....'52 '79 C.112 B.A. L.426 J.D. [Sheppard,M.R.&H.]
*PRACTICE AREAS: Litigation; Civil Trials and Arbitrations; Creditors' Rights and Commercial Law.
**Maliniak, Abbie P.** ....'50 '82 C.112 B.A. L.705 J.D. [Ⓑ Epstein B.&G.]
*PRACTICE AREAS: Health Law.
**Malinowski, Joseph M.**, (AV) ....'47 '72 C&L.912 B.A., J.D. [Cadwalader,W.&T.]
**Malitz, Jeanne M.** ....'62 '90 C.1049 B.A. L.94 J.D. [Ⓐ Graham&J.]
*PRACTICE AREAS: Immigration.

**Malkus, Roger L.**
(See Torrance)

Mallano, Robert M. ....'38 '64 C.976 A.B. L.1066 LL.B. Presid. J.
**Mallen, Barry E.** ....'60 '85 C.112 B.A. L.464 J.D. [Manatt,P.&P.]
*PRACTICE AREAS: Entertainment; Copyright; Business Litigation.
**Mallen, Toby Rose** ....'55 '80 C.112 A.B. L.800 J.D. [Ⓐ Whitman B.A.&M.]

**Mallery, Daniel C. '60 '91 C.112 B.S. L.273 J.D.**
**1875 Century Park East, Suite 700, 90067**
**Telephone: 310-551-5252 Fax: 310-551-5251**
**Email: DCM100@concentric.net**
**Intellectual Property, Patent, Trademark, Copyright and Unfair Competition.**
*See Professional Biographies, LOS ANGELES, CALIFORNIA*

Mallery & Stern, (AV) .... 11835 W. Olympic Blvd.
Malley, Stephen A., (AV) ....'40 '65 C.696 A.B. L.1068 LL.B. 12424 Wilshire Blvd.
Mallory, Bobbi Tillmon, (AV) ....'52 '79 C&L.800 B.A., J.D. 3961 Mount Vernon Dr.
Mallory, George L., Jr., (AV) ....'52 '79 C.605 B.A. L.1137 J.D. [Mallory&B.]
**Mallory, Richard C.**, (AV) ....'45 '70 C.800 B.S. L.813 J.D. [Allen,M.L.G.&M.]
*PRACTICE AREAS: Real Estate.
**Mallory, Robert P.**, (AV) ....'43 '71 C.1060 B.S. L.1067 J.D. [McDermott,W.&E.]
*PRACTICE AREAS: Antitrust and Trade Regulation; Professional Liability; Unfair Competition.
Mallory, Sandra L. ....'57 '82 C.602 B.A. L.477 J.D. Coun., MS Mgmt. Servs.
Mallory & Brown-Curtis, (AV) .... 1925 Century Pk. E., 10th Fl.
**Mallya, Lynne E.** ....'57 '93 C.184 B.A. L.426 J.D. [Ⓐ Pillsbury M.&S.]
*PRACTICE AREAS: Civil Litigation; Automotive Products Liability; Commercial Litigation.
Malmo, David L. '58 '89 C.813 A.B. L.846 J.D.
Gen. Coun., Continental Graphics Corp.
Malone, Marion ....'23 '53 C&L.145 A.B., J.D. Int. Rev. Serv.
Malone, Terrance A., (AV) ....'39 '74 C.932 B.B.A. L.809 J.D. [Thompson,M.&F.]
**Maloney, Michael J.**, (AV) ....'39 '66 C.800 A.B. L.426 LL.B. [Gilbert,K.C.&J.]
**Maloney, Philip L.** ....'63 '90 C.860 B.A. L.813 J.D. [Ⓐ White&C.]
Malsbury, James W. ....'43 '69 C.605 B.A. L.477 J.D. 1875 Century Park, E.
**Maltin, Phillip R.** ....'59 '91 C.147 B.A. L.209 J.D. [Ⓐ Konowiecki&R.]
*LANGUAGES: Hebrew.
*PRACTICE AREAS: ERISA; Employment Litigation; Business Litigation.
Maltz, Ellen Marsha Mandel '47 '78 C.446 B.A. L.64 J.D.
(adm. in FL; not adm. in CA) 10433 Wilshire Blvd.‡
**Malynn, Todd M.** ....'65 '95 C.112 B.A. L.426 J.D. [Ⓐ Skadden,A.S.M.&F.]
Mamakos, James L., (AV) ....'28 '55 C.705 B.S. L.1066 LL.B. 5143 Sunset Blvd.
Mamer, Edmond B., (AV) ....'32 '61 C.1258 A.B. L.426 LL.B. Dep. Atty. Gen.
Manahan, Elsie, (BV) ....'18 '49 C&L.800 B.S., J.D. 6579 Firebrand St.
Manahan, Michael C. ....'35 '65 C.112 B.S. L.426 LL.B. 2149 Montana St.
Manar, Gerald T. '48 '76 C.476 B.S. L.213 J.D.
(adm. in MI; not adm. in CA) U.S. Dept. of Vets. Affairs
**Manason, Marc J.** ....'59 '84 C.477 B.A. L.1066 J.D. [Ⓐ Kane,B.&B.]
*PRACTICE AREAS: Redevelopment; Housing Law; Real Estate Law; Land Use Law; Environmental Law.
Manaster, Fred, (AV) ....'38 '63 C&L.597 B.A., LL.B Dep. Pub. Def.
**Manatt, Charles T., (P.C.)**, (AV) '36 '62
C.350 B.S. L.273 J.D. [Manatt,P.&P.] (⊙Wash., D.C.)
*PRACTICE AREAS: Government.

**Manatt, Phelps & Phillips, LLP, (AV)** BB
**A Limited Liability Partnership**
**Trident Center, East Tower, 11355 West Olympic Boulevard, 90064**⊙
**Telephone: 310-312-4000 Fax: 310-312-4224 Telex: 21-5653**
**Email: mpp@manatt.com**
**Members of Firm: Charles T. Manatt (P.C.); Thomas D. Phelps (P.C.); L. Lee Phillips (P.C.); Ronald S. Barak; Gordon M. Bava (P.C.).**
**Irwin P. Altschuler (Resident, Washington, D.C. Office); David R. Amerine (Resident, Washington, D.C. Office); George M. Belfield; Geoffrey A. Berkin; Ellen Berkowitz; Donna R. Black; Robert A. Blair (P.C.) (Resident, Washington, D.C. Office); Lawrence J. Blake; T. Hale Boggs; Diana K. Brown; Richard A. Brown; William S. Brunsten (P.C.); Alan M. Brunswick; Jack W. Buechner (Resident, Washington, D.C. Office); Cara R. Burns; Chris A. Carlson; Catherine A. Conway; Jay L. Cooper; June Langston (Walton) DeHart (Resident, Washington, D.C. Office); Neal Dittersdorf (Resident, Washington, D.C. Office); Gene R. Elerding; Roger Ellison; David Elson; Andrew Erskine; Diane L. Faber; Paul H. Falon (Resident, Washington, D.C. Office); Donald J. Fitzgerald (Certified Specialist, Taxation Law, The State Bar of California Board of Legal Specialization); Judith R. Forman (P.C.) (Certified Specialist, Family Law, The State Bar of California Board of Legal Specialization); Howard M. Frumes; Cynthia Futter; Peter R. Gilbert (Resident, Washington, D.C. Office); Donna Fields Goldstein; Andrea Jane Grefe; Rick L. Grossman (Certified Specialist, Taxation Law, The State Bar of California Board of Legal Specialization); Carl Grumer; Scott D. Harrington; Robert E. Hinerfeld; Paul S. Hoffman; Maria D. Hummer (P.C.); Phalen G. Hurewitz; Linda M. Iannone (Resident, Washington, D.C. Office); Paul H. Irving; Clarence L. James (Resident, Washington, D.C. Office); Rosalyn Evelyn Jones; Robert J. Kabel (Resident, Washington, D.C. Office); Andrew M. Katzenstein (Certified Specialist, Estate Planning, Trust and Probate Law, The State Bar of California Board of Legal Specialization); George David Kieffer; Sandra R. King; David M. Klaus (Resident, Washington, D.C. Office); Kenneth L. Kraus (Resident, Nashville, Tennessee Office); Barry S. Landsberg; David H. Larry (Resident, Washington, D.C. Office); John P. LeCrone; Mark S. Lee; Tin Kin Lee; Margaret Levy; John F. Libby; Edward L. Lublin (Resident, Washington, D.C. Office); Eileen Lyon; Barry E. Mallen; Laurence M. Marks; Gerald A. Margolis; Thomas J. McDermott Jr.; Thomas R. McMorrow; Sherwin L. Memel (P.C.); Peter M. Menard; Alan E. Morelli; James P. Mulkeen; Kevin O'Connell; Thomas P. Ondeck (Resident, Washington, D.C. Office); Robert H. Platt; William T. Quicksilver (P.C.); B. Michael Rauh (Resident, Washington, D.C. Office); John L. Ray (Resident, Washington, D.C. Office); Harold P. Reichwald; James H. Roberts III (Resident, Washington, D.C. Office); Christopher L. Rudd; Alan U. Schwartz; Brad William Seiling; Martin Shulman (Resident, Washington, D.C. Office); Laurie L. Soriano; Lisa Specht; Donald S. Stein (Resident, Washington, D.C. Office); Robert L. Sullivan (Resident, Nashville, Tennessee Office); Timothy M. Thornton; Ronald B. Turovsky; Leonard D. Venger; Vincent M. Waldman; Charles E. Washburn Jr.; H. Lee Watson; Nancy H. Wojtas; Shari Mulrooney Wollman; Steven J. Younger; Steven L. Zelinger (Resident, Washington, D.C. Office). Of Counsel: Dennis B. Franks; Joseph Horacek III, (P.C.); Arnold D. Kassoy; Kevin Keenan; Spencer L. Kimball (Not admitted in CA); Elliot B. Kristal; Robert A. Pallemon; Martin E. Steere; Abby B. Wayne; Gail Anderson Windisch (Firm General Counsel); Angela Wong; Thomas A. Zaccaro. Associates: Erin K. Atkins; Matthew D. Berger; Katrina L. Breuner; Donald Brown; Cynthia F. Catalino; Andrew Cushnir; Leah E. Delancey; Kathleen D. De Vaney; Katia T. Diehl; Dan Forman; Seth Gold; Marc P. Goodman; Jay R. Grant; Allison B. Gruettner; Daniel B. Hayes; Terri Donna Keville; Brian S. Keys; Coby A. King; John I. Lazar; Monte M. Lemann II; Suzanne K. List; Lisa Cathleen McArthur; Craig D. Miller; Jay M. Miller; Vibiana Molina; Eugene E. Mueller; Brenda B. Nelson; Seema L. Nene; John P. Phillips; Jill M. Pietrini; Adam Pines; Steven J. Plinio; Harvey Rochman; Ciema Lili Salem; Kelley L. Sbarbaro; Marlene R. Schwartz; Laurie Jill Slosberg; Allen Z. Sussman; Mary E. Wright; Candace Anne Younger.**
**General Civil and Trial Practice in all Courts. Banking and Financial Services; Bankruptcy and Creditors' Rights; Corporate Finance and Securities; Election and Campaign; Entertainment; Environmental; Estate Planning, Executive Compensation and Employee Benefits; Family; Fashion Industry; Federal, State and Local Government; Government Contracts; Healthcare; High Technology; Insurance; Intellectual Property; International Trade and Customs; Labor and Employment; Land Use; Legislative and Administrative; Motion Picture and Television; Music; New Media; Real Estate; Sports; Tax; White-Collar Criminal Defense.**
**Washington, D.C. Office: 1500 M Street, N.W., Suite 700. Telephone: 202-463-4300. Fax: 202-463-4394.**
**Nashville, Tennessee Office: 1233 17th Avenue South. Telephone: 615-327-2600. Fax: 615-327-2044.**
*See Professional Biographies, LOS ANGELES, CALIFORNIA*

**Mancini, Andrew** ....'44 '87 C.112 B.A. L.1136 J.D. [Ⓐ Bragg,S.S.&K.]
**Mancini, Maria Anna** ....'66 '94 C&L.426 B.A., J.D. [Ⓐ Radcliff,F.&D.]
*LANGUAGES: Italian, Spanish and French.
**Mancini, Stephen C.**, (BV) ....'57 '86 C.605 B.A. L.398 J.D. [Koletsky,M.&F.]
*PRACTICE AREAS: General Liability Defense Litigation; Construction Defect Defense Litigation; Wrongful Termination Defense Litigation; Sexual Harassment Defense Litigation; Toxic Tort Litigation.
**Mancino, Douglas M.**, (AV) ....'49 '74 C.381 B.A. L.608 J.D. [McDermott,W.&E.]
*PRACTICE AREAS: Health Care; Federal Tax.
Mandel, Carole Calkins ....'— '85 C.161 B.A. L.809 J.D. 1900 Ave. of the Stars
Mandel, Charles L. ....'51 '79 C.112 B.A. L.990 J.D. Dist. Atty. Off.
Mandel, Jonathan ....'51 '82 C.342 B.A. L.426 J.D. Dep. City Atty.
Mandel, M. Milo ....'36 '60 C&L.188 A.B., J.D. [Mandel&Mand.]
**Mandel, Marcy Jo** ....'55 '81 C.881 A.B. L.145 J.D. [Ⓑ O'Melveny&M.]
*PRACTICE AREAS: Tax Controversies and Litigation; State Taxation; Local Taxation.
**Mandel, Sam C.** ....'61 '87 C.1049 B.A. L.976 J.D. [Blanc W.J.&K.]
*PRACTICE AREAS: Entertainment; New Media Law; Technology; Corporate; Taxation.
**Mandel, Stuart R., (P.L.C.)**, (AV) ....'35 '62 C.112 B.A. L.1068 LL.B. [Mandel&Manp.]
Mandel & Mandel .... 1901 Ave. of the Stars, #1800

**Mandel & Manpearl, (AV)**
**A Partnership including a Professional Law Corporation)**
**1800 Avenue of the Stars, Suite 1000, 90067-4212**
**Telephone: 310-277-1313 FAX: 310-277-2626**
**Members of Firm: Gerald T. Manpearl; Stuart R. Mandel (P.L.C.).**
**State and Federal Civil Litigation. Personal Injury, Domestic Relations Law. Business and Corporate Litigation.**

**Mandel & Norwood**
**(See Santa Monica)**

**Mandelbaum, James C.** ... '59 '86 C.976 B.A. L.569 J.D. [Armstrong H.J.T.&W.]
*PRACTICE AREAS: Entertainment.
Mandell, Barbara J. ... '56 '82 C.4 B.S. L.426 J.D. 1200 Wilshire Blvd.
**Mandell, Lee Jay** ... '48 '91 C.688 M.E.E.E. L.809 J.D. [Freilich,H.&R.] (See Pat. Sect.)
*PRACTICE AREAS: Patent; Patent Applications.
**Mandell, Ronald J.**, (AV) ... '42 '68 C&L.800 B.S., J.D. [Moss,L.&M.]
*REPORTED CASES: J.A. Jones Construction Co. v. Superior Court, 27 Cal. App. 4th 1568 (1994).
*PRACTICE AREAS: Construction; Real Estate; General Business Law.
Mandell, Shelly M. ... '42 '88 L.809 J.D. [O'Donnell&M.]
**Manella, Arthur, (P.C.)**, (AV) ... '17 '41 C&L.800 B.S., LL.B. [🄲 Irell&M.]
Manella, David L. ... '49 '75 C.112 B.A. L.800 J.D. Dep. City Atty.
Manella, Nora M., (AV) ... '51 '76 C.914 B.A. L.800 J.D. U.S. Atty.
Manes, C. Renée ... '60 '86 C.597 B.S. L.309 J.D. 255 E. Temple St.
Manes, Hugh R. ... '24 '52 C.112 B.A. L.597 J.D. [Manes&W.]
Manes & Watson, (AV) ... 3435 Wilshire Blvd.
Manesh, Mike S. ... '55 '89 C.1341 B.S. L.998 J.D. 2049 Century Pk. E. Ste, 2680
**Manesis, Mary D.** ... '61 '90 C.112 B.A. L.1068 J.D. [🄰 Stroock&S.&L.]
*PRACTICE AREAS: Litigation.
**Manfredi, Christopher J.** ... '69 '95 C.668 B.A. L.569 J.D. [🄰 Paul,H.J.&W.]
Manfredi, George A., (AV) ... '44 '70 C.103 A.B. L.569 J.D. 1999 Ave. of the Stars
Mangels, Alan A. ... '47 '73 C.1109 M.P.A. L.1068 J.D. Dep. Atty. Gen.
**Mangels, Robert E., (P.C.)**, (AV) ... '43 '70 C.645 B.A. L.273 J.D. [Jeffer,M.B.&M.]
*PRACTICE AREAS: Civil Litigation; Trials.
Maniaci, Vincent M. '58 '88 C.112 B.A. L.767 J.D.
(adm. in PA; not adm. in CA) Occidental College
**Maniatis, Marina M.** ... '64 '91 C.145 B.A. L.365 J.D. [🄰 Barger&W.]
**Manibog, Darren A.** ... '70 '96 C.800 B.A. L.1066 J.D. [🄰 Allen,M.L.G.&M.]
Manibog, G. Monty ... '30 '61 C.602 A.B. L.426 LL.B. Mayor
**Manion, Brian G.**, (AV) ... '22 '51 C&L.208 B.S.L., J.D. [Weinstock,M.R.S.&N.] ‡
*PRACTICE AREAS: Civil Litigation; Corporations Law; Business Law.
**Maniscalco, James P.** ... '69 '95 C.112 B.A. L.800 J.D. [🄰 Gibson,D.&C.]
Manker, Meredith J. ... '56 '84 C.342 B.A. L.809 J.D. 4700 Wilshire Blvd.
Manlin, Roger A. S. ... '46 '72 C.475 B.A. L.477 J.D. 1870 N. Vermont Ave.
**Mann, David G.** ... '61 '88 C.112 B.A. L.800 J.D. [Musick,P.&G.]
*PRACTICE AREAS: Taxation; Corporate; Real Estate.
**Mann, Elizabeth D.** ... '57 '82 C.668 B.A. L.1068 J.D. [Hennigan,M.&B.]
*PRACTICE AREAS: Commercial; International; Securities.
**Mann, Gary D.** ... '50 '80 C.871 B.S. L.345 J.D. [Loeb&L.] (See Pat. Sect.)
*PRACTICE AREAS: Patent; Trademark; Copyright; Litigation.
Mann, Lewis T., III ... '60 '90 C.112 B.A. L.426 J.D. 620 Marie Ave.
**Mann, Lisa Girand** ... '67 '93 C.228 A.B. L.1068 J.D. [🄰 Orrick,H.&S.]
*PRACTICE AREAS: Litigation.
Mann, Richard L. ... '40 '84 C.1040 B.B.A. L.1137 Deputy Public Def.
Mann, Robert Steven, (AV) ... '52 '77 C.813 A.B. L.770 J.D. [Colton M.]
**Manning, A. Alan** ... '61 '86 C.800 B.S. L.1068 [🄲 Paul,H.J.&W.]
**Manning, Edward P.** ... '60 '85 C.693 B.A. L.426 J.D. [🄰 McClintock,W.B.R.R.&M.]
*PRACTICE AREAS: Environmental Compliance; Legislative and Regulatory Advocacy; Environmental Litigation; Environmental Criminal Defense.
**Manning, Steven D.** ... '53 '79 C.1097 B.S. L.1148 J.D. [Manning,M.&W.] (⊙San Diego)
*PRACTICE AREAS: Police Civil Liability Defense; Public Entity Defense Law; Complex Civil Litigation.

**Manning, Leaver, Bruder & Berberich, (AV)**
**Suite 655, 5750 Wilshire Boulevard, 90036**
**Telephone: 213-937-4730 Fax: 213-937-6727**
**Email: ManningLeaver@msn.com**
**Cameron B. Aikens (1916-1966); DeWitt M. Manning (1909-1992); George E. Leaver (Retired); Walter F. Bruder, Jr. (Retired). Partners: Joseph E. Berberich; Robert D. Daniels; Brent W. Smith; Penny L. Reeves; Michael D. Van Lochem; Halbert B. Rasmussen. Associates: Timothy D. Robinett; Rex L. Mills; Dana E. Malarney; Alan W. Forsley; Sean J. Ballard.**
**General Civil and Trial Practice, in all State and Federal Courts. Corporation, Insurance, Automobile Dealer Law, Probate and Estate Planning, Automotive Finance, Business Purchases and Sales, Real Property and Bankruptcy, Association and Commercial Law.**
**Representative Clients: General Motors Acceptance Corp.; Ford Dealers Advertising Assn.; Lincoln-Mercury Dealers Advertising Assn.; Motors Insurance Corp.; California Motor Car Dealers Assn.**
***See Professional Biographies, LOS ANGELES, CALIFORNIA***

**Manning, Marder & Wolfe, (AV)**
**45th Floor at First Interstate Tower, 707 Wilshire Boulevard, 90017⊙**
**Telephone: 213-624-6900 Fax: 213-624-6999**
**Email: rfs@mmw.com URL: http://www.mmw.com**
**Members of Firm: Steven D. Manning; John A. Marder; Dennis B. Kass; Anthony J. Ellrod; Eugene P. Ramirez; Martha A. Shen; Barry A. Bradley; Lawrence D. Esten. Associates: David C. Addison; Tina M. Alleguez; Anne E. Arvin; Steven D. Blades; Catherine Convy; Kevin E. Coventon; Alfred M. de la Cruz; Nicole M. Foos; Randel P. Friedman; Thomas R. Gill; Finola G. Halloran; Pamela S. Hicks; Kathleen A. Kelleher; Marguerite T. Lieu; Brian T. Moss; G. Andrew Nagle; Erwin A. Nepomuceno; M. Lauren Olander; Mildred K. O'Linn; David A. Peck; Uzzi O. Raanan; Steven J. Renick; John Revelli; Jonathan A. Ross; Patricia M. Scoles; Philip L. Soto; Barry G. Thorpe; James Urbanic; Christopher A. Wilson; David J. Wilson. Of Counsel: William J. Lopshire; Gerald F. Phillips.**
**Insurance Defense, Police Civil Liability, General Civil Litigation, Private Security Litigation, Corporate Law, Business Formation and Securities Offerings, Employment Litigation, Entertainment Law, Workers' Compensation Defense, Professional Liability (Medical Malpractice, Legal Malpractice, Construction Malpractice), Appellate Law, Health Law, Bad Faith, Insurance Coverage, Loss Prevention and Risk Management.**
**Irvine, California Office: 19800 MacArthur Boulevard, Suite 1450. Telephone: 714-556-0552. Facsimile: 714-724-4575.**
**San Diego, California Office: 964 Fifth Avenue, Suite 214. Telephone: 619-699-5933.**
***See Professional Biographies, LOS ANGELES, CALIFORNIA***

**Mannis, Joseph**, (AV) ... '44 '72 C.800 A.B. L.426 J.D. [Mannis&P.]
*PRACTICE AREAS: Family Law; Sports Law; Art Law.

**Mannis & Phillips, L.L.P., (AV)**
**2029 Century Park East, Suite 1200, 90067-2913**
**Telephone: 310-277-7117 Fax: 310-286-9182**
**Joseph Mannis; Stacy D. Phillips. Of Counsel: Gerald F. Phillips; Allan S. Morton;—Peter A. Lauzon; Jon S. Summers.**
**Family Law, Entertainment Law and General Civil Litigation.**
***See Professional Biographies, LOS ANGELES, CALIFORNIA***

Manns, George, (AV) ... '07 '30 C.112 B.A. L.809 LL.B. 106 S. Martel Ave.‡
**Manpearl, Gerald T.**, (AV) ... '37 '64 C.112 A.B. L.1068 J.D. [Mandel&Manp.]
Mansell, Robert W. ... '60 '85 C.1300 B.S. L.623 J.D. [Grayson,G.&M.]
**Mansfield, Andrew S.** ... '69 '94 C.859 B.A. L.1066 J.D. [🄰 O'Melveny&M.]
**Mansfield, Melanie K.** ... '70 '95 C&L.477 A.B., J.D. [🄰 Milbank,T.H.&M.]
Mansfield, Stephen A. ... '55 '82 C.690 B.A. L.1294 J.D. Asst. U.S. Atty.

**Manson, Richard P.** ... '49 '81 C.976 B.A. L.813 J.D. [🄲 Graham&J.]
*LANGUAGES: French.
*PRACTICE AREAS: Securities Law; Mergers and Acquisitions.
**Mansourian, Vick K.** ... '70 '95 C.1077 B.S. L.426 J.D. [🄰 Jones,D.R.&P.]
Mansueto, Daniel M. ... '59 '86 C.145 A.B. L.1068 J.D. 400 S. Hope St.
Mantalica & Treadwell ... 835 Wilshire Blvd.
**Mantovani, Bonni S.** ... '56 '82 C.4 B.S. L.823 J.D. [🄰 D.B.Bloom]
Manuel, A. Michael, (BV) '52 '79
C.940 B.A. L.1137 J.D. 2417 W. Beverly Blvd. (⊙Monterey Park)
Manulkin, Gary H. ... '42 '68 [Manulkin,G.&B.]
Manulkin, Glaser & Bennett, (AV) ... 3701 Wilshire Blvd.
**Manzanares, Jon N.**, (AV) ... '57 '82 C.112 B.A. L.800 J.D. [Konowiecki&R.]
*PRACTICE AREAS: General Business; Litigation.
**Manzano, Angel, Jr.** ... '50 '77 C.813 B.A. L.178 J.D. [Epstein B.&G.]
Manzella, Anthony C., (AV) ... '41 '67 C.705 B.A. L.276 J.D. Off. of Dist. Atty.
Manzo, Natalie S. ... '65 '91 C.309 B.A. L.813 J.D. 550 S. Hope St.
Manzo, Peter B. ... '63 '90 C.602 B.A. L.1066 J.D. Pub. Coun., Dir. Atty of Comm. Prog.
Mar, May Jin ... '66 '91 C.112 B.A. L.1065 J.D. Dep. Dist. Atty.
Marans, Michael D. ... '47 '73 C.112 A.B. L.1068 J.D. 12100 Wilshire Blvd., 15th Fl.
**Marasse, Richard L.** ... '48 '91 C.145 B.A. L.1040 J.D. [🄰 Skadden,A.S.M.&F.]
*LANGUAGES: French.
**Maravalli, Sharon** ... '53 '94 C.107 B.A. L.809 J.D. [🄰 R.L.Zukerman]
*PRACTICE AREAS: Family Law; Civil Litigation.
Marcella, Lucille K. ... '57 '84 C.472 B.Mus. L.800 J.D. First Interstate Bank
**Marcella, Susan M.** ... '— '88 C.178 B.S.N. L.800 J.D. [Gibson,D.&C.]
*PRACTICE AREAS: Litigation; Antitrust and Trade Regulation; Securities; Fraud and Deceit.
March, Jeremy G. ... '71 '91 C.112 B.A. L.800 J.D. Southern Calif. Assn. of Govts.
March, Kathleen P., (AV) ... '49 '75 C.170 B.A. L.976 J.D. U.S. Bkrptcy. J.
Marchand, Michele C. ... '— '80 C.475 B.A. L.1066 J.D. U.S. Atty. Off.
Marchand, Paul S. ... '63 '89 C.880 B.A. L.879 J.D. 109-203 7985 Santa Monica Blvd.
Marchese, William, Jr. ... '38 '76 C.229 B.A. L.1136 J.D. 2040 Ave. of the Stars
Marcin, John B. ... '63 '90 C.454 B.A. L.990 J.D. 1901 Ave. of the Stars, 20th Fl.
Marcinkus, James A. ... '48 '81 C.1077 B.A. L.1179 J.D. 13114 Wash. Blvd.
Marckese, Jeffrey N. ... '55 '82 C.610 B.S. L.1190 J.D. [🄰 Miller&M.]
Marconi, Dennis J. ... '46 '79 C.831 B.A. L.1136 J.D. 619 S. New Hampshire
**Marcus, Craig H.** ... '66 '91 C&L.426 B.B.A., J.D. [🄰 Stevens,K.A.&H.]
Marcus, David A. ... '68 '93 C.339 B.S. L.1066 J.D. 400 S. Hope St.
**Marcus, David G.** ... '52 '80 C.112 A.B. L.809 J.D. [Gray,Y.D.&R.]
**Marcus, David M.** ... '52 '79 C.112 B.A. L.426 J.D. [Marcus,W.S.&D.]
*PRACTICE AREAS: Title Insurance Law; Real Property and General Business; Litigation; Real Property Law; Commercial Law.
**Marcus, Fred J.**, (AV) ... '51 '81 C.999 B.A. L.426 J.D. [Freeman,F.&S.]⊙
*PRACTICE AREAS: Transactional Business; Tax Exempt Organizations; Estate Planning Law.
Marcus, Gregg ... '43 '72 C.208 B.S. L.61 J.D. Mun. Ct. J.
**Marcus, Jed L.** '53 '82 C.705 A.B. L.623 J.D.
(adm. in NJ; not adm. in CA) [Grotta,G.&H.]⊙
Marcus, Jeffrey L. ... '60 '90 C.306 B.S.B.A. L.1148 J.D. 3530 Wilshire Blvd.
Marcus, Kenneth J. '52 '79 C.112 A.B. L.426 J.D.
Dir., Equities Regul., Pacific Stock Exchange, Inc.
Marcus, Lyn H., (AV) ... '28 '54 C&L.477 B.A., J.D. 30 Driftwood St.
Marcus, Michael D., (AV) ... '41 '68 C.112 B.A. L.1068 J.D. 1801 Ave. of the Stars
**Marcus, Stephen H.** ... '45 '71 C.453 B.S. L.309 J.D. [Frandzel&S.]
*PRACTICE AREAS: Business Litigation; Banking and Finance.

**Marcus, Watanabe, Snyder & Dave, LLP**
**Suite 300, 1901 Avenue of the Stars, 90067-6005**
**Telephone: 310-284-2020 Facsimile: 310-284-2025**
**Members of Firm: David M. Marcus; Wendy Y. Watanabe; Patricia M. Snyder; Michael G. Dave; Justin E. Budare; Kathleen M. Collins; Richard I. Arshonsky.**
**Real Property, Business and Commercial Litigation, General Business Transactions, Title Insurance Claims and Litigation.**
***See Professional Biographies, LOS ANGELES, CALIFORNIA***

**Marder, John A.** ... '60 '85 C.67 B.A. L.61 J.D. [Manning,M.&W.] (⊙San Diego)
*PRACTICE AREAS: Civil Litigation Defense; Insurance Fraud Defense; Entertainment Law.
**Marder, Neal R.** ... '60 '86 C.112 B.A. L.426 J.D. [🄲 Sonnenschein N.&R.]
*PRACTICE AREAS: General Business and Commercial Litigation; Government Contracts; Labor.
**Marderosian, Jeff C.** ... '54 '79 C.1077 B.A. L.61 J.D. [🄰 Karns&K.]
*PRACTICE AREAS: Administrative Law; Education Law; Real Property; Labor Law.
Mardirossian, Garo, & Associates ... '56 '81 C.112 B.A. L.1148 J.D. 6311 Wilshire Blvd.
Mardirossian, Kathy Ann Volz ... '60 '89 C.1077 B.A. L.940 J.D. 6311 Wilshire Blvd.
**Marelich, Katherine M.** ... '67 '93 C.112 B.A. L.800 J.D. [🄰 Preston G.&E.]
*PRACTICE AREAS: Litigation.
**Marella, Vincent J.**, (AV) ... '46 '72 C&L.831 B.A., J.D. [Bird,M.B.W.&M.]
**Marenberg, Steven A.** ... '55 '81 C.918 B.A. L.145 J.D. [Irell&M.]
Marenstein, Alan B., (AV) ... '39 '70 2500 Wilshire Blvd.‡
**Marenus, Harold S.** ... '63 '89 C.112 B.A. L.1068 J.D. [Sheppard,M.R.&H.]
*PRACTICE AREAS: Commercial Law, Creditors' Rights Law and Bankruptcy Law.
**Margo, Roderick D.**, (AV) ... '50 '79 C&L.061 B.Com., LL.B. [Condon&F.]
Margolies, Dany ... '54 '79 C.112 B.A. L.800 J.D. P.O. Box 641127
Margolin, Bruce M., (A Prof. Law Corp.) '41 '67 C.800 L.809 LL.B.
8749 Holloway Dr.
Margolin, Richard A. ... '30 '60 C.112 B.S. L.1068 LL.B. Comr., Mun. Ct.
Margolis, Arthur L. ... '41 '73 C.112 B.A. L.767 J.D. [Margolis&M.]
**Margolis, Gerald A.**, (AV) ... '43 '69 C.309 B.A. L.262 J.D. [Manatt,P.&P.]
*PRACTICE AREAS: Entertainment; Intellectual Property Transactions; Litigation Matters.
**Margolis, Michael B.** ... '54 '79 C.1307 B.A. L.188 J.D. [Margolis&M.]
**Margolis, Naki B.** ... '56 '80 C.790 B.S. L.94 J.D. [Margolis&M.]
Margolis, Richard A. ... '60 '86 C.1077 B.S. L.809 J.D. Sr. Coun., Standard Mgmt. Co.
Margolis, Susan L. ... '54 '82 C.112 B.A. L.1066 J.D. [Margolis&M.]
Margolis & Margolis ... 2000 Riverside Dr.

**Margolis & Morin**
**444 South Flower Street, Sixth Floor, 90071**
**Telephone: 213-683-0300 Facsimile: 213-683-0303**
**Michael B. Margolis; Michael D. Morin; Karen Moskowitz; Naki B. Margolis; Michael D. Markovitch; Roger H. Gray; Edward C. Ho.**
**Civil Litigation, Employment, Construction, Unfair Competition, Corporate, Estate Planning, Probate, Professional Negligence and Business Law.**

Margulies, Harold P. ... '36 '66 C.112 B.S. L.809 LL.B. 10100 Santa Monica Blvd.
**Marino, Louis E., Jr.** ... '60 '87 C.800 B.S. L.809 J.D. [Lynberg&W.]
Marinovich, Adrian M. ... '52 '82 C.426 B.B.A. L.960 J.D. [Maas&M.]
Mark, Joel, (AV) ... '47 '72 C.112 A.B. L.1065 J.D. [🄰 Plotkin,M.&K.]
**Markel, Jeffrey D.** ... '62 '92 C.112 B.A. L.800 J.D. [🄲 A.A.Sigel]
*PRACTICE AREAS: Business Transactions; Civil; Appellate; Contracts; Interstate Law.
**Marken, Roger Erik**, (AV) ... '44 '72 C.911 B.S. L.809 J.D. [Ives,K.&D.] (⊙Santa Ana)
**Markenson, William D.**, (AV) '41 '67 C.112 A.B. L.1066 LL.B.
[🄲 Nossaman,G.K.&E.]
*PRACTICE AREAS: Corporations Law; Securities Law; Commercial Law.
Markey, Christian E., Jr., (AV) ... '29 '59 C.112 A.B. L.1068 J.D. University Park

**Markiles, Murray** ....................'61 '87 C.112 B.A. L.1068 J.D. [Troop M.S.&P.]
*PRACTICE AREAS: Corporate Securities; Mergers and Acquisitions; High Technology; Intellectual Property Law; Antitrust.
Markin, Terrence C. ..............'56 '82 C.605 A.B. L.1019 J.D. 2020 Ave. of the Stars‡
**Markle, R. Gerald**, (AV) .................. '50 '76 C.112 B.A. L.678 J.D. [Pansky&M.]
*REPORTED CASES: Grossman v. State Bar (1983) 34 Cal.3d 73; In Re Morales (1983) 35 Cal.3d 1; In re Possino (1984) 37 Cal.3d 163; Leoni v. State Bar (1985) 39 Cal.3d 609; In the Matter of Hagen (Rev. Dept. 192) 2 Cal. State Bar Ct.Rptr. 153.
*PRACTICE AREAS: Lawyer Disciplinary Defense and Admissions; Legal Malpractice; Ethics Consultations and Testimony.
Markman, Marla Kyle .................... '52 '77 C.763 B.A. L.61 J.D. Dep. Atty. Gen.
Markoff, Nancy Young ..............'58 '86 C.112 B.A. L.809 J.D. 2029 Century Park E.
**Markovitch, Michael D.** ..................................'41 '64 L.061 [Margolis&M.]
Markowitz, Jay ..........................'57 '82 C.1044 B.A. L.800 J.D. [Parker&M.]
**Markowitz, Joseph C.** ...............'54 '80 C.178 B.A. L.145 J.D. [Markowitz,F.&U.]
*PRACTICE AREAS: Litigation.
**Markowitz, Juliet A.** ....................'66 '93 C.1036 B.A. L.813 J.D. [🄰 Macklin T.]
*PRACTICE AREAS: Complex Business Litigation.

**Markowitz, Fernandez & Uriarte, (AV)**
**811 West Seventh Street Suite 1100, 90017**
**Telephone: 213-362-0350 Facsimile: 213-362-0359**
**Members of Firm: Joseph C. Markowitz; Josefina Fernandez McEvoy; Robert G. Uriarte.**
**Civil Trials, Appeals and Dispute Resolution including Commercial, Real Estate, Intellectual Property, Employment and Entertainment Law. Bankruptcy, Workouts, Debtor and Creditor. International Business Transactions and Litigation.**
***See Professional Biographies, LOS ANGELES, CALIFORNIA***

**Marks, Allan T.** ................ '64 '90 C.367 B.A. L.1066 J.D. [🄰 Milbank,T.H.&M.]
Marks, Donald B., (AV) ..................'42 '67 C.994 B.A. L.569 LL.B. [Marks&B.]
Marks, Keith H. ........................... '58 '85 C.36 B.S. L.809 J.D. Amsted Cos.
**Marks, Laurence M.** ..................'47 '78 C.112 B.A. L.1068 J.D. [Manatt,P.&P.]
*PRACTICE AREAS: Entertainment Law; Book Publishing; Motion Picture Finance.
**Marks, Lawrence D.** ...................'64 '91 C.112 B.A. L.464 J.D. [🄰 Murchison&C.]
*PRACTICE AREAS: Legal Malpractice Defense; Professional E & O Defense; General Liability Defense; Employment Litigation.
**Marks, Leslie Steven** ..................... '55 '80 C.112 B.A. L.426 J.D. [Wolf,R.&S.]
*PRACTICE AREAS: Civil Litigation; Construction Litigation; Entertainment Litigation; Real Estate Litigation.
Marks, Neison M. ........ '54 '88 C.259 B.A. L.990 J.D. Supervising Dep. Fed. Pub. Def.
**Marks, Paul S.** ...................'60 '88 C.103 A.B. L.800 J.D. [🄰 Whitman B.A.&M.]
Marks, Ronald A. ....................... '43 '72 C.112 B.S. L.809 J.D. [R.A.Marks]
**Marks, Scott A.** .....................'56 '90 C.112 B.A. L.426 J.D. [🄰 Mazursky,S.&A.]
*PRACTICE AREAS: Insurance Law; Bad Faith Law; Product Liability Law; Medical Malpractice Law; Business Torts.
**Marks, Stephen D., (A Professional Corporation)**, (AV) '41 '68
C.112 A.B. L.1065 J.D. [🄲 Mitchell,S.&K.]
Marks, Valerie E. ......................'59 '86 C.1044 B.A. L.809 J.D. 9255 Sunset Blvd.
Marks, Walter N. ........................... '30 '55 C&L.813 LL.B. 8758 Venice Blvd.‡
Marks & Brooklier, (AV) ........................................ 2029 Century Pk. E.

**Marks & Murase, L.L.P., (AV)** 🄱🅁
**The Wells Fargo Center, 333 South Grand Avenue Suite 1570, 90071-1535⊙**
**Telephone: 213-620-9690 FAX: 213-617-9109**
**Partners in Los Angeles, California: Shu Tokuyama; Matthew E. Digby. Associates in Los Angeles, California: Tanya K. Danforth (Not admitted in CA); John J. Del Propost; Craig L. Sheldon.**
**General Practice.**
**New York, New York Office: 399 Park Avenue. Telephone: 212-318-7700.**
**Washington, D.C. Office: Suite 750, 2001 L Street, N.W. Telephone: 202-955-4900.**
***See Professional Biographies, LOS ANGELES, CALIFORNIA***

Marks, Ronald A., A Law Corp. .....................................4221 Wilshire Blvd.
**Markson, Kenneth S.** ........................'54 '89 C.882 B.A. L.861 J.D. [Schell&D.]
*LANGUAGES: French.

**Markus, Mark J., Law Offices of '63 '91 C.1077 B.A. L.37 J.D.**
**11684 Ventura Boulevard, Suite 403 (Studio City), 91604-2613**
**Telephone: 818-509-1173 Facsimile: 818-509-1460**
**Email: bklawr@bklaw.com URL: http://www.bklaw.com/bklaw**
***PRACTICE AREAS: Bankruptcy; Debtor and Creditors Rights Remedies; Chapter 7, 11. 13; Consumer and Commercial Bankruptcy; Insolvency.**
**Practice Limited to Bankruptcy and Related Matters.**

Marley, Brett David '— '95 C.1036 B.A. L.978 J.D.
(adm. in FL; not adm. in CA) 121 South Swall Dr.
Marley, Patrick J. ................'39 '77 C.426 B.B.A. L.809 J.D. 1900 Ave. of the Stars
Marlis, Rand A. ..........'49 '74 C.597 B.A. L.1068 J.D. Pres., Creative Licensing Corp.
**Marmalefsky, Dan** ....................... '55 '80 C.112 A.B. L.976 J.D. [Morrison&F.]
*LANGUAGES: Spanish and French.
*PRACTICE AREAS: Criminal Defense; Civil Litigation; Appellate Litigation.
**Marmaro, Marc, (P.C.)**, (AV) ..........'48 '73 C.273 B.A. L.569 J.D. [Jeffer,M.B.&M.]
*PRACTICE AREAS: Business Litigation.
**Marmaro, Richard**, (AV) ......... '51 '76 C.273 B.A. L.569 J.D. [McCambridge,D.&M.]

**Marmon, Victor I., (AV) '51 '75 C.976 B.A. L.145 J.D.**
**Watt Plaza, 1875 Century Park East, Suite 1600, 90067**
**Telephone: 310-551-8120 Telecopier: 310-551-8113**
**Real Property, Business and Entertainment Law.**
***See Professional Biographies, LOS ANGELES, CALIFORNIA***

**Marmorstein, Victoria E.** ..................'53 '77 C.623 B.A. L.904 J.D. [Latham&W.]
*LANGUAGES: Spanish.
Marnell, Francis X. ............................ '21 '51 C.339 L.426 LL.B. Supr. Ct. J.
Maroko, Michael, (AV) .................... '50 '74 C.112 B.A. L.426 J.D. [Allred,M.&G.]
Maron, Max ....................................'14 '40 L.793 LL.B. 2029 Century Park E.
Maron, Milford A. '26 '55 C&L.800 A.B., LL.B.
Adm. Law J., Office of Admin. Hearings
Marpet, Jane R. .........................'44 '79 C.112 B.A. L.1136 J.D. Dep. Pub. Def.
**Marquardt, Joan M.** ................ '62 '87 C.145 A.B. L.846 J.D. [🄲 Brand F.D.F.&K.]
*PRACTICE AREAS: Finance; General Corporate; Real Estate.
Marquez, Mercedes ..................'59 '86 C.800 B.A. L.276 J.D. 3435 Wilshire Blvd.
Marquez, Monica ................ '60 '88 C.668 B.A. L.93 J.D. 1901 Ave. of The Stars

**Marquez & Teperson, P.C.**
**(See Pasadena)**

**Marquis, Charles K.** ....... '42 '68 C.813 B.A. L.477 J.D. [Gibson,D.&C.] (⊙N.Y., NY)
Marr, Cecil W. ......................... '45 '73 C.112 B.S. L.1068 J.D. 523 W. 6th St.
Marrero, Kathleen McColgan ...... '56 '91 C.999 B.A. L.940 801 S. Grand Ave., 18th Fl.
**Marriott, Anthony G.** ..............................'— '90 C&L.976 J.D. [🄰 Kern&W.]

**Marrone Robinson Frederick & Foster**
**(See Burbank)**

**Marsch, Susan M.** .........................'56 '93 C&L.477 B.A., J.D. [🄰 Latham&W.]
Marsel, Diane R. ............... '45 '76 C.112 B.A. L.426 J.D. Legal Aid Found. of L.A.
**Marsh, B. Richard**, (AV) ..............'27 '53 C.112 A.B. L.800 J.D. [Knapp,M.J.&D.]
*PRACTICE AREAS: Public Entity Law; Administrative Law.
Marsh, David D. ..........................'60 '88 C.112 B.A. L.1065 J.D. Dep. Pub. Def.
**Marsh, Greg W.**, (AVⓉ) '59 '81
C.426 B.B.A. L.809 J.D. [🄲 Grace,S.C.&S.] (⊙Las Vegas, NV)
*PRACTICE AREAS: General Civil Litigation Defense; Product Liability Law; Public Utility Defense Litigation; Drug Law; Premises Liability Defense.
**Marsh, Gregory M.** .......................... '68 '94 C.112 B.A. L.426 J.D. [🄰 Zolla&M.]
*PRACTICE AREAS: Family Law.

**Marsh, Harold, Jr., (AV) '18 '42 C.691 B.A. L.846 LL.B.**
**P.O. Box 251739, 90025**
**Telephone: 310-458-0433 Fax: 310-458-0433**
**Practice Limited to Consultation with other Law Firms and Acting as Co-Counsel, Expert Witness and Arbitrator in the Fields of Corporations, Securities and Commercial Law.**
***See Professional Biographies, LOS ANGELES, CALIFORNIA***

**Marsh, Jack A.** ......................... '64 '90 C.862 B.A. L.990 J.D. [🄰 Dale,B.&H.]
Marsh, Michele M.F. .................'68 '94 C.1042 B.A. L.809 J.D. 835 Wilshire Blvd.
Marshall, Arthur K. .........................'11 '37 C.563 B.S. L.724 LL.B. Ret. Supr. Ct. J.
**Marshall, Brooks P.** ...................'63 '88 C.473 B.S. L.477 J.D. [🄰 Thelen,M.J.&B.]
*PRACTICE AREAS: Business Litigation.
**Marshall, Christopher B.** '51 '82
C.112 B.A. L.426 J.D. [Bonne,B.M.O.&N.] (⊙Riverside)
Marshall, Consuelo B. ............................ '36 '62 C&L.329 B.A., J.D. U. S. Dist. J.
**Marshall, David D.** ..................'63 '89 C.605 A.B. L.220 J.D. [🄰 Morgan,L.&B.]
Marshall, Howard D. '30 '56 C.112 B.A. L.1068 LL.B.
V.P., First Interstate Bk. of Calif.
Marshall, James Fraser ................'60 '86 C.112 A.B. L.800 J.D. 221 N. Figueroa St.
Marshall, John A., (P.C.) ........................'57 '83 C.800 B.S. L.990 J.D. [Fuchs&M.]
**Marshall, Jonathan S.** .......................'63 '89 C&L.861 B.S.M., J.D. [🄰 Loeb&L.]
**Marshall, Lester D.** ..............'64 '90 C.800 B.S. L.426 J.D. [🄰 Stockwell,H.W.&W.]
Marshall, Marilee .......................'44 '81 C.1109 B.A. L.1068 J.D. 617 S. Olive St.
**Marshall, Richard A.** .........................'67 '96 C&L.800 A.B., J.D. [🄰 Kopple&K.]
**Marshall, Robert F.**, (AV) .......'48 '73 C.112 B.A. L.1068 J.D. [Greenberg G.F.C.&M.]
*PRACTICE AREAS: Entertainment; Communications; Litigation.
Marshall, Robert M. .......................'36 '63 C&L.426 B.S., LL.B. [Taecker,M.&N.]
Marshall, Sibyl .................. '65 '90 C.668 B.A. L.426 J.D. 1999 Avenue of the Stars
**Martell, Michele J.** ....... '62 '87 C.668 B.A. L.1068 J.D. Coun., Turner Bdcstg. Sys., Inc.
**Martens, Daniel L.** ...........................'68 '94 C&L.352 B.A., J.D. [🄰 Latham&W.]
*PRACTICE AREAS: Employment Litigation (75%); Litigation (25%).
**Martens, Erin E.** ..........................'69 '94 C.112 B.A. L.770 J.D. [🄰 Barger&W.]
*PRACTICE AREAS: Environmental Insurance Coverage; Insurance Bad Faith.
Martin, Areva Bell ......................... '62 '87 C.145 B.A. L.309 J.D. [Bolden&M.]
**Martin, Arthur L.**, (AV) '42 '73 C.667 B.S.Ch.E. L.767 J.D.
[🄰 Mahoney,C.J.&P.] (Pat.)
*PRACTICE AREAS: Business Litigation.
Martin, Arthur L., (AV) ............. '30 '55 C.31 A.B. L.1066 LL.B. 5143 Sunset Blvd.‡
**Martin, Benjamin R.** .............................'71 '96 C.800 B.A. L.893 J.D. [🄰 Irell&M.]
Martin, Bonnie Lee .......................... '30 '55 C.878 B.A. L.1068 LL.B. Supr. Ct. J.
**Martin, C. G. Gordon** ..................'50 '75 C.605 A.B. L.228 J.D. [Morgan,L.&B.]
**Martin, Clara Ruyan** ........................'64 '89 C.112 B.A. L.477 J.D. [Klein&M.]
**Martin, David H.** .................. '67 '92 C.339 A.B. L.309 J.D. [🄰 Hennigan,M.&B.]
**Martin, Dennis G.**, (AV) .............. '47 '72 C.112 B.A. L.976 J.D. [Blakely,S.T.&Z.]
**Martin, Diana Pfeffer** .......... '59 '90 C.966 B.S. L.1049 J.D. [🄲 McCutchen,D.B.&E.]
*PRACTICE AREAS: Environmental Regulatory Work.
Martin, Ella S. ......................... '51 '78 C.1077 B.A. L.1095 J.D. Dep. Co. Coun.
Martin, Elmer Dean, III, (AV) ........ '43 '68 C.602 B.B.A. L.966 J.D. [E.D.Martin III]⊙
**Martin, Felix M.** .................... '65 '95 C.340 B.A. L.990 J.D. [🄰 Negele&Assoc.]
*PRACTICE AREAS: Litigation; Business Law; Construction Law.
**Martin, Frederick, Jr.**, (AV) ..........'43 '68 C.976 B.A. L.623 J.D. [🄲 Foley L.W.&A.]
*PRACTICE AREAS: Real Estate.
**Martin, Gregg A.** ...................'62 '88 C.112 B.A. L.426 J.D. [Hamburg,H.E.&M.]
*PRACTICE AREAS: Real Estate Litigation; Business Litigation; Construction Law; Insurance Law; Employment Law.
**Martin, Gregory P.** ................. '51 '88 C.165 B.A. L.1179 J.D. [🄰 Lewis,D.B.&B.]
Martin, Hiram M. ...................'47 '72 C.112 B.A. L.1068 J.D. 10451 S. Figueroa St.
**Martin, James C.**, (BV) ..............'52 '78 C.170 B.A. L.770 J.D. [Crosby,H.R.&M.]
*PRACTICE AREAS: Appellate; Civil Writs; Post-Trial Motions.
**Martin, James R.**, (AV) ................ '37 '68 C.705 B.A. L.326 J.D. [Gibson,D.&C.]
*PRACTICE AREAS: Antitrust; Communications; Patent; Litigation.
**Martin, James Robertson** ..................'63 '94 C.454 B.A. L.426 J.D. [🄰 Simke C.]
*PRACTICE AREAS: Business Litigation; Civil Litigation; Criminal.
**Martin, John P.** .....................'58 '84 C.813 A.B. L.426 J.D. [Talcott,L.V.&S.]
*LANGUAGES: German.
*REPORTED CASES: United States v. Delgadillo-Velasquez, 856 F.2d 1292 (9th Cir. 1988).
*PRACTICE AREAS: Criminal Defense Law; Appellate Law; Civil Litigation.
Martin, Julieann '44 '80 C.112 B.A. L.809 J.D.
Tech. Coun., The MacNeal-Schwendler Corp.
Martin, Leroy A. ........................'52 '88 C.061 B.A. L.809 J.D. 643 S. Olive St.
**Martin, M. Kay** ..................... '62 '91 C.112 B.S. L.767 J.D. [🄰 Folger L.&K.]⊙
Martin, Neil B. ......................... '42 '72 C&L.800 A.B., J.D. First Interstate Bank
**Martin, Neil D.** ............................ '55 '80 C.147 B.A. L.800 J.D. [Hill,F.&B.]
*PRACTICE AREAS: Trade Secret; Copyright and Trademark Litigation; Unfair Competition; General Civil Litigation in State and Federal Courts.
**Martin, Paul T.** ........................'64 '91 C.31 B.A. L.800 J.D. [🄰 Orrick,H.&S.]
Martin, Susan J. '45 '73 C.210 B.A. L.770 J.D.
Prof. of Law, Southwestern Univ., School of Law
**Martin, Timothy J.** ............... '65 '90 C.276 A.B. L.477 J.D. [🄰 Brown R.M.F.&S.]
*LANGUAGES: French.
*PRACTICE AREAS: Litigation.
Martin, William J., Jr. ....... '46 '71 C.1031 B.A. L.823 J.D. Imm. & Naturalization Serv.
Martin, Elmer Dean, III, A Professional Corporation, (AV)
1880 Century Park E. (⊙Diamond Bar)

**Martin & Hudson**
**(See Pasadena)**

**Martineau, Marie L.** '59 '86 C.676 B.A. L.94 J.D.
[O'Melveny&M.] (⊙New York, N.Y.)
*PRACTICE AREAS: Asset Securitization; Corporate Finance; Public Finance.

**Martineau & Knudson**
**(See San Marino)**

**Martinelli, Lisa** ......................... '58 '83 C.560 B.A. L.809 J.D. [🄰 Hillsinger&C.]
Martinet, Leonard J. ......................'41 '81 C&L.1136 B.A., J.D. [Williams&M.]⊙
**Martinez, Darren R.** ............... '66 '91 C.602 B.A. L.1068 J.D. [🄰 Selvin&W.&W.]
*LANGUAGES: Spanish.
*PRACTICE AREAS: Bankruptcy; Business Litigation; Real Estate; Appeals.
**Martinez, Glenda E.** '64 '90 C.976 B.A. L.309 J.D.
Sr. Legal Coun., Univision Communication Grp.
*LANGUAGES: Spanish, Portuguese.
*RESPONSIBILITIES: Employment and Labor Law; Intellectual Property.

**Martinez, Joseph G.** ................ '58 '84 C.112 B.A. L.1067 J.D. [Parker,M.C.O.&S.]
*TRANSACTIONS: Initial and subsequent public offerings and public reports of several public companies; Acquisitions of several high technology companies; Organization of numerous corporations, limited liability companies and partnerships.
*PRACTICE AREAS: General Corporate Law; Securities Law; Commercial Law.
Martinez, Joseph R. ................ '32 '67 C.563 B.A. L.426 LL.B. Dep. Dist. Atty.
Martinez, Manny C. ................ '46 '88 C.112 B.A. L.1136 J.D. 2049 Century Park, E.
Martinez, Manuel S. ................ '23 '56 C.800 B.S. L.809 LL.B. 205 S. Bway.
**Martinez, Raul L., (P.C.)** ................ '51 '76 C.453 B.S. L.813 J.D. [Lewis,D.B.&B.]
**Martinez, Shannon Sullivan** ................ '67 '94 C.112 B.A. L.426 J.D. [Ⓐ Tuttle&T.]
**Martinez, Vilma S., (AV)** ................ '43 '68 C.846 B.A. L.178 LL.B. [Munger,T.&O.]
**Martini, Antonio D.** ................ '64 '91 C.867 B.A. L.178 J.D. [Ⓐ Orrick,H.&S.]
**Martis, Robert A.** ................ '63 '88 C.36 B.A. L.276 J.D. [Troop M.S.&P.]
*LANGUAGES: French.
*PRACTICE AREAS: Transactional Entertainment Law.
Martone, Roland A. ................ '16 '54 C.67 B.A. L.809 LL.B. Vet. Admn.
**Martyn, Daniel E., Jr., (AV)** ................ '52 '79 C.1019 B.A. L.564 J.D. [Danner&M.]
Marutani, Nancy O., (AV) ................ '53 '78 C.94 B.S. L.262 J.D. [Plotkin,M.&K.]
Marvin, Susan F. ................ '55 '88 C.347 B.S. L.426 J.D. 611 W. 6th St.
Marx, Ernest L. ..... '35 '61 C&L.597 B.S., J.D. Pres., Cohen & Marx Accountancy Corp.
**Marx, Michael S.** ................ '62 '88 C.800 B.S. L.1066 J.D. [Ⓐ Paul,H.J.&W.]
Marx, Pamela A. ............ '53 '78 C&L.800 A.B., J.D. Mental Health Advocacy Servs.
**Masago, Tohru** ................ '64 '93 L.061 LL.B. [Ⓐ Pillsbury M.&S.]
**Mase, John A., (A P.C.)** ................ '58 '83 C.690 B.S. L.94 J.D. [Fainsbert,M.&S.]
*PRACTICE AREAS: Taxation Law; Real Estate; Business Transactions; Corporate Law.
**Masenga, Thomas J., (AV)** ................ '52 '77 C.602 B.A. L.426 J.D. [Graham&J.]
*PRACTICE AREAS: Real Estate (Property) Law.
Maseredjian, David G., (AV) ............ '54 '79 C&L.800 B.S., J.D. 3360 Barham Blvd.
**Mashian, Bryan** ................ '60 '84 C.112 B.A. L.1068 J.D. [Buchalter,N.F.&Y.]
*PRACTICE AREAS: Real Estate Development; Acquisition Sales; Leasing, Exchange & Workouts.
Mashin, Alison R. ................ '62 '87 C.112 B.A. L.426 J.D. 1925 Century Pk. E.
Maskin, Leslie A. ................ '60 '86 C.94 B.S. L.262 J.D. 2112 Century Pk. Ln.
**Maslauski, Steven M.** ................ '59 '85 C.597 B.A. L.990 J.D. [Kirtland&P.]
**Mason, Belle C., (AV)** ................ '39 '79 C.112 B.A. L.1148 J.D. [Knee&M.]
*PRACTICE AREAS: Sexual Harassment; Wrongful Termination Defense; Employment Discrimination; Employment Litigation; Wage and Hour Law.
Mason, Carol C. ................ '58 '82 C.860 B.A. L.352 J.D. I.R.S.
Mason, Carolyn M. ................ '62 '88 C.174 B.A. L.1148 J.D. 801 S. Figueroa St.
**Mason, Cheryl White, (AV)** '52 '77
C.679 B.A. L.145 J.D. [O'Melveny&M.] (ⓒSan Francisco)
*PRACTICE AREAS: Public Utilities; Environmental and Civil Litigation; Litigation; Alternative Dispute Resolution.
Mason, Deborah A. ........... '60 '88 C.112 B.A. L.1136 J.D. 6222 Wilshire Blvd. 6th Fl.
Mason, George J. ................ '30 '68 C.800 L.1132 J.D. 801 S. Grand Ave., 10th Fl.
Mason, Guy A. ................ '62 '89 C.813 B.A. L.1068 J.D. 1709 S. Westgate #11
Mason, Lawrence E. ................ '36 '69 C.112 L.1095 LL.B. Dep. Dist. Atty.
Mason, Michael C. '60 '86
C&L.426 B.B.A., J.D. 1st V.P. & Coun., Shuwa Investments Corp.
**Mason, Peter H., (AV)** ................ '51 '76 C.112 B.A. L.904 J.D. [Fulbright&J.]
*PRACTICE AREAS: Antitrust; Insurance.
**Mason, Peter R.** ................ '59 '86 C.309 B.A. L.94 J.D. [Ⓒ Konowiecki&R.]
*PRACTICE AREAS: Health Care; Corporate; General Business.
Mason, Peter W. ................ '44 '77 C.550 B.A. L.1068 J.D. Dep. City Atty.
Mason, Richard K. ................ '47 '73 C.901 B.A. L.477 J.D. 450 N. Grand Ave.‡
**Mason, Robert M., III** ................ '55 '81 C.770 B.A. L.1067 J.D. [Bergman&W.]
*PRACTICE AREAS: Commercial Insurance; Civil Litigation; Civil Appeals.
**Mason, Stefan M., (AV)** ................ '39 '67 C.197 A.B. L.1068 J.D. [S.M.Mason]
*PRACTICE AREAS: Litigation; Negotiation and Mediation; Labor and Employment Law.
**Mason, Stephen G.** ................ '55 '89 C.999 B.M. L.724 J.D. [Ⓐ Coudert]
*PRACTICE AREAS: Property Taxation; Natural Resources; Civil Trial; Environmental Law.

**Mason, Stefan M., A Law Corporation, (AV)**
**27th Floor, 1999 Avenue of the Stars, 90067**
**Telephone: 310-553-3500 Fax: 310-553-3563**
**Stefan M. Mason. Of Counsel: Steven P. Krakowsky.**
**Management and Individual Labor Relations, Employment Discrimination, Wrongful Termination, Sexual Harassment, Wage and Hour, and Contracts Law. Mediation, Arbitration, Administrative, State and Federal Litigation and Appellate Practice.**
***See Professional Biographies, LOS ANGELES, CALIFORNIA***

Masoner, Leslie A. ................ '61 '88 C.1042 L.398 J.D. [Makin&M.]
Masry, Edward L. ................ '32 '61 C.112 A.B. L.426 LL.B. [Masry&V.]
Masry & Vititoe ................ 10850 Riverside Dr.
**Masse, Jeannie** ................ '69 '95 C.112 B.A. L.426 J.D. [Ⓐ Daniels,B.&F.]
**Massey, Desmond, (AVⓣ)** '39 '75 C&L.776 B.A., J.D.
(adm. in NJ; not adm. in CA) [Grotta,G.&H.]ⓒ
**Massey, Shalem A.** ................ '63 '89 C.112 B.A. L.1049 J.D. [Mendes&M.]
*LANGUAGES: Urdu, Hindi and Punjabi.
**Masters, Anna Segobia** ................ '59 '84 C.112 B.A. L.1068 J.D. [Crosby,H.R.&M.]
*PRACTICE AREAS: Employment Litigation.
**Masters, Jeffrey D.** ................ '54 '80 C.112 B.A. L.1068 J.D. [Cox,C.&N.]
*PRACTICE AREAS: Real Estate and Construction Litigation; Insurance Law.

**Masters & Ribakoff**
**(See Santa Monica)**

**Masterson, Stephen V.** ................ '64 '89 C.31 B.A. L.273 J.D. [Troop M.S.&P.]
*PRACTICE AREAS: Insurance Coverage Litigation.
Masterson, William A. ................ '31 '59 C.112 B.A. L.1068 J.D. Jus., Ct. of Appl.
**Mastras, George, Jr.** ................ '66 '93 C.976 B.A. L.112 J.D. [Ⓐ Katten M.&Z.]
Mastroianni, A. Douglas ................ '65 '90 C.36 B.S. L.659 J.D. 865 S. Figueroa St.
**Mastroianni, Douglas A.** ................ '65 '91 C.36 B.S. L.659 J.D. [Ⓐ Robins,K.M.&C.]
**Masuda, Kevin S.** ................ '67 '92 C.112 A.B. L.309 J.D. [Ⓐ Munger,T.&O.]
*PRACTICE AREAS: Corporate Finance; General Corporate.
**Masutani, David J.** ................ '65 '94 C&L.800 B.S., J.D. [Ⓐ Ginsburg,S.O.&R.]
Mathers, Todd W. ................ '62 '87 C&L.477 B.A., J.D. 11355 W. Olympic Blvd.
**Mathews, Carolyn A.** ....... '36 '88 C.846 B.F.A. L.1136 J.D. [Ⓐ Berger,K.S.M.F.S.&G.]
**Mathews, Christopher A.** ............ '62 '89 C.112 B.S. L.813 J.D. [Ⓐ Howrey&S.] (Pat.)
*PRACTICE AREAS: Intellectual Property; Commercial Litigation; Antitrust.
Mathews, Emet C. ................ '25 '60 C.605 B.A. L.426 LL.B. 6363 Wilshire Blvd.

**Mathias, Richard J., & Associates '63 '88 C&L.276 B.S.F.S., J.D.**
**611 West Sixth Street, Suite 2880, 90017**
**Telephone: 213-955-9700 Fax: 213-955-9711**
***LANGUAGES: Spanish.**
***PRACTICE AREAS: Labor and Employment Law; Wrongful Termination Litigation; Civil Rights; Gay and Lesbian Rights; Employee Benefits.**
**Labor and Employment Law, Commercial Litigation, Commercial Contracts, General Civil Litigation in all State and Federal Courts, Alternative Dispute Resolution.**
***See Professional Biographies, LOS ANGELES, CALIFORNIA***

Matison, Jason ................ '53 '80 C.112 B.A. L.1066 J.D. 2029 Century Park E.
**Matkins, Michael L., (AV)** ................ '45 '71 C.813 A.B. L.800 J.D. [Allen,M.L.G.&M.]
*PRACTICE AREAS: Real Estate.

Matlin, Dana '55 '88 C&L.767 B.S., J.D.
(adm. in NY; not adm. in CA) American Film Marketing Assn.‡
Matlof, David J. '67 '92 C.112 B.A. L.1066 J.D.
1800 Ave. of the Stars, Suite 900 (Century City)
**Matosich, Andrew J.** ................ '63 '93 C.508 B.A. L.893 J.D. [Ⓐ Stroock&S.&L.]
**Matson, Candace L.** ................ '55 '89 C.112 B.A. L.1068 J.D. [Ⓐ Sheppard,M.R.&H.]
*PRACTICE AREAS: Construction Law; General Business Law; Litigation.
**Matson, Greg K.** ................ '65 '90 C.112 B.A. L.276 J.D. [Ⓐ O'Melveny&M.]
**Matsumura, William E.** '56 '84
C.800 B.A. L.1066 J.D. Sr. Coun., Pacific Telesis Legal Group
Mattachione, Steven E. ......... '50 '76 C&L.426 B.S., J.D. Exec. V.P., Orthopaedic Hosp.

**Mattenson, Myles M., (AV) '41 '68 C.112 B.S. L.426 J.D.**
**Two Century Plaza Suite 1800, 2049 Century Park East, 90067**
**Telephone: 310-553-1160 Fax: 310-277-2755**
**Franchise Law. Corporate, Business, Uniform Commercial Code, Construction and Real Estate Law. Insurance Bad Faith, General Civil and Trial Practice.**
**Reference: Bank of America (Century City Branch).**
***See Professional Biographies, LOS ANGELES, CALIFORNIA***

**Mattes, Bradford E.** '56 '92
C.326 B.S.M.E. L.990 J.D. [Ⓐ Arant,K.L.&R.] (See Pat. Sect.)
*PRACTICE AREAS: Intellectual Property Litigation; Patent and Trademark Prosecution; Trade Secrets.
Matteson, Thomas R. ................ '64 '91 C.1074 B.A. L.426 J.D. 1900 Ave. of the Stars
**Matthai, Edith R., (AV)** ................ '50 '75 C.776 B.A. L.1065 J.D. [Robie&M.]
*PRACTICE AREAS: Legal Malpractice; Products Liability; Business Litigation.
Matthew, John Scott, (AV) ................ '36 '64 C.426 B.B.A. L.1068 J.D. [J.S.Matthew]
Matthew, John Scott, Law Offices of, (AV) ..... 15260 Ventura Boulevard (Sherman Oaks)
Matthews, Dennis ................ '48 '78 C.112 B.A. L.426 J.D. [Ⓐ Chase,R.D.&B.]
Matthews, Eulanda Lynn ................ '59 '85 C.112 B.A. L.1065 J.D. [Ⓐ Ivie,M.&W.]
**Matthias, Michael R., (AV)** ................ '47 '73 C.112 B.A. L.426 J.D. [Matthias&B.]
*PRACTICE AREAS: Securities Litigation; Tax Litigation; Business Litigation; Commercial.

**Matthias & Berg LLP, (AV)** BB
**Seventh Floor, 515 South Flower Street, 90071**
**Telephone: 213-895-4200 Telecopier: 213-895-4058**
**Michael R. Matthias; Jeffrey P. Berg; Stuart R. Singer; Kenneth M. H. Hoff; Michael D. Berger.**
**Corporate, Corporate Finance, Securities, Mergers and Acquisitions, Commercial Transactions, Asset Securitization, Municipal Finance, Securities Litigation, Tax Litigation, Business and Commercial Litigation, U.S. and International Taxation, including Expert Testimony.**
**Representative Clients: Synagro Technologies, Inc.; Mexalit, S.A.; Maxitile, Inc.; Allstar Inns; Chatsworth Products, Inc.; International Meta Systems, Inc.; Residential Resources, Inc.; AVIC Group International, Inc.; AutoBitter Group, Inc. National Quality Care, Inc.; Greater China Corp.; HBO Ole.**
**Reference: First Professional Bank.**
***See Professional Biographies, LOS ANGELES, CALIFORNIA***

Mattson, Marcus, (AV) ................ '04 '30 C.112 A.B. L.1066 LL.B. 700 S. Flower St.
Matuja, Jennifer A. ................ '64 '91 C.477 B.A. L.861 J.D. Dep. Dist. Atty.
**Matz, A. Howard, (AV)** ................ '43 '70 C.178 A.B. L.309 J.D. [Bird,M.B.W.&M.]

**Matz, Jeffrey A., Law Offices of, (AV) '42 '72 C.800 B.A. L.1095 J.D.** BB
**23822 Valencia Boulevard Suite 210, 91355ⓒ**
**Telephone: 805-222-9131**
**Trial and Civil Practice in Personal Injury, Toxic Chemical Contamination, Products Liability, Insurance Bad Faith, Employment Discrimination and Wrongful Discharge, Construction Accidents, Maritime Accidents, Air Crash Litigation, F.E.L.A. Litigation, Medical Malpractice and Business Fraud.**
**Scottsdale, Arizona Office: 6711 East Camelback Road, Suite 8. Telephone: 602-955-0900. Fax: 602-970-3172.**
***See Professional Biographies, LOS ANGELES, CALIFORNIA***

Matz, Laura A. ................ '53 '81 C.112 B.A. L.1068 J.D. 555 W. 5th St.
**Mauch, Carol M.** ................ '69 '94 C.918 B.A. L.569 J.D. [Ⓐ Latham&W.]
*LANGUAGES: French.
*PRACTICE AREAS: Health Care Transactional; Corporate.
Maupin, James C., (AV) ................ '29 '55 C.273 B.A. L.426 J.D. [Maupin,C.T.&W.]
Maupin, Cutler, Teplinsky & White, A Professional Corporation, (AV)
4929 Wilshire Blvd.
**Maurer, Randi** ................ '53 '88 C.112 B.A. L.426 J.D. [Ⓐ Perkins C.]
*PRACTICE AREAS: Litigation; Labor and Employment Law.
**Mausner, Jeffrey N., (AV)** ................ '50 '77 C.103 B.A. L.188 J.D. [Berman,B.M.&R.]
*REPORTED CASES: Tuchman v. Aetna, 44 Cal. App. 4th 1607 (1996); McCalden v. Simon Wiesenthal Center, 955 F.2d 1214 (9th Cir. 1992); McCalden v. Simon Wiesenthal Center, 919 F.2d 538 (9th Cir. 1990); U.S. v. Kowalchuk, 571 F. Supp. 72 (E.D. Pa. 199 3), affen banc, 773 F.2d 488 (3d Cir. 1985); Maikovskis v. I.N.S., 773 F.2d 435 (2d Cir. 1985).
*PRACTICE AREAS: Intellectual Property Litigation; Copyright; Trademark; Trade Secrets; Computer Law.
Mavridis, James C. ................ '— '56 L.809 LL.B. 15760 Ventura Blvd.‡
**MaWhinney, Ronald** ................ '60 '96 C.684 B.A. L.809 J.D. [Ⓐ Gilbert,K.C.&J.]
Maxie, Robert C., (BV) ................ '61 '91 C.612 B.S. L.623 J.D. [Maxie R.S.&V.]ⓒ
Maxie Rheinheimer Stephens & Vrevich, LLP, (BV)
555 S. Flower St. Ste. 4640 (ⓒSan Diego)
**Maxwell, Chris Ann** ................ '50 '75 C.112 B.A. L.61 J.D. [Ⓐ Troop M.S.&P.]
*PRACTICE AREAS: Entertainment.
Maxwell, Kimberly L. ................ '63 '90 C.1131 B.S. L.809 J.D. 2601 S. Figueroa St.

**Maxwell, Michael P. '49 '79 C&L.836 B.A., J.D.**
**10100 Santa Monica Boulevard, Suite 300, 90067**
**Telephone: 310-556-1511 Fax: 310-556-1513**
***REPORTED CASES: Aviall of Texas v. United States, 861 F.Supp. 100, CIT, 1994; Sulzer Escher Wyss, Inc. v. United States, 17 CIT, Slip Op. 93-113, June 22, 1993.**
**Customs and International Trade Law.**
***See Professional Biographies, LOS ANGELES, CALIFORNIA***

May, Bradford J. ................ '65 '92 C.802 B.A.B.S. L.178 J.D. 400 S. Hope St.
**May, Charles D.** ................ '54 '85 C.426 B.A. L.809 J.D. [Tharpe&H.] (ⓒOxnard)
May, Christopher N. ......... '43 '71 C.309 A.B. L.976 LL.B. Prof. of Law, Loyola Univ.
May, David ................ '56 '86 C.56 B.A. L.800 J.D. 9000 Sunset Blvd.‡
May, Gus T. ................ '64 '92 C.966 B.S. L.588 J.D. [Ⓐ Hall&Assoc.]
**May, John M.** ......... '41 '66 C.111 B.S. L.1068 LL.B. [Robbins,B.&C.] (See Pat. Sect.)
*LANGUAGES: French, German, Russian (reading only).
*PRACTICE AREAS: Patents; Trademarks; Copyrights; Licensing.
**May, Lawrence E., (AV)** ................ '47 '73 C.112 B.A. L.1068 J.D. [Ⓒ Kenoff&M.]
*PRACTICE AREAS: Corporate Law; Real Estate; Estate Planning; Business Planning Law.
**Maya, Charlotte R.** ................ '68 '93 C.691 B.A. L.112 J.D. [Ⓐ McKenna&C.]
*PRACTICE AREAS: Estate and Trust Planning; Probate and Estate Settlement.
Mayberry, Deborah Sue ................ '62 '91 C.1109 B.A. L.426 J.D. 510 W. 6th St.
**Mayeda, Daniel M.** ................ '57 '83 C.112 B.A. L.1068 J.D. [Leopold,P.&S.]
*PRACTICE AREAS: Entertainment; Civil Litigation; Copyright and Trademark; Libel and Slander; Unfair Competition.
Mayeda, Jon M. ................ '47 '72 C.684 A.B. L.1068 J.D. Mun. Ct. J.
**Mayer, Patrick W.** ................ '59 '84 C.446 B.A. L.990 J.D. [Fonda,G.H.&D.]
*LANGUAGES: Spanish.
*PRACTICE AREAS: Medical General Casualty Defense Law.
Mayer, Ralph, (BV) ................ '33 '64 C.112 B.S.Engr. L.426 LL.B. Dep. Dist. Atty.‡

**Mayer, Robert D., (P.C.)**, (AV) ........ '39 '67 C.112 B.S. L.1066 LL.B. [Mayer,G.&G.]
*PRACTICE AREAS: Real Estate Law; Insolvency Law.
**Mayer, Steven M.** ........................'68 '94 C.112 B.A. L.861 J.D. [Ⓐ Mayer,G.&G.]
*PRACTICE AREAS: Bankruptcy Law; Litigation; Creditor's Rights Law.

**Mayer, Brown & Platt, (AV)** BB
**350 South Grand Avenue, 25th Floor, 90071-1503**☉
**Telephone: 213-229-9500 Facsimile: 213-625-0248 Telex: 188089 Cable: LEMAYLA**
**URL: http://www.mayerbrown.com**
**Partners: Teresa A. Beaudet; Louis P. Eatman; L. Bruce Fischer; Michael F. Kerr; Kenneth E. Kohler; Alec G. Nedelman; Brian E. Newhouse; M. Ellen Robb; Kevin L. Shaw; Neil M. Soltman; Robert A. Southern (Not admitted in CA); James R. Walther; Don L. Weaver. Special Counsel: John Shepard Wiley, Jr. Counsel: Christopher P. Murphy. Associates: Andrei A. Baev; David C. Bolstad; Jacqueline R. Brady; Christopher D. Chen; Boise A. Ding; Henry Einar Fink; Douglas B. Frank; Anthony G. Graham; Richard Greta; Lorie S. Griffen; Jerome M.F.J. Jauffret; Fredrick S. Levin (Not admitted in CA); Bruce H. Levine; John Nadolenco; A. Ken Okamoto; Maria M. Rabassa; Mary Beth Rhoden; Nina E. Scholtz; Carl J. Thomas; Kimberly S. Winick.**
**General Practice.**
**Chicago, Illinois Office: 190 South La Salle Street, 60603-3441. Telephone: (312) 782-0600. Facsimile: (312) 701-7711. Telex: 190404. Cable: LEMAY.**
**Berlin, Germany Office: Spreeufer 5, 10178. Telephone: 011-49-30-247-3800. Facsimile: 011-49-30-247-38044.**
**Brussels, Belgium Office: Square de Meeûs 19/20, Bte. 4, 1050. Telephone: 011-32-2-512-9878. Facsimile : 011-3 2-2-511-3305.**
**Houston, Texas Office: 700 Louisiana Street, Suite 3600, 77002-2730. Telephone: (713) 221-1651. Facsimile: (723) 224-6410. Telex: 775809. Cable: LEMAYHOU.**
**London, England Office: 162 Queen Victoria Street, EC4V 4DB. Telephone: 011-44-171-248-1465. Facsimile: 011-44-171-329-4465. Telex: 8811095. Cable: LEMAYLDN.**
**New York, New York Office: 1675 Broadway, 10019-5820. Telephone: (212) 506-2500. Facsimile: (212) 262-1910. Telex: 701842. Cable: LEMAYEN.**
**Washington, D.C. Office: 2000 Pennsylvania Avenue, N.W., 20006-1882. Telephone: (202) 463-2000. Facsimile: (202) 861-0473. Telex: 892603. Cable: LEMAYDC.**
**Representative Offices:**
**Almaty, Republic of Kazakhstan: 162 Tulebaev Street #32. Telephone: 011-7-3272-636388. Facsimile: 011-7-3272-507828.**
**Bishkek, Kyrgyz Republic: Suite 405, Prospekt Manasa 55, 720001. Telephone: 011-7-3312-222970. Facsimile: 011-7-3312-620980.**
**Köln, Germany: An Lyskirchen 14, 50676. Telephone: 011-49-221-921-5210. Facsimile: 011-49-221-921-5514.**
**Tashkent, Republic of Uzbekistan: 5th Floor, 1 Turab Tula Street, 700003. Telephone: 011-7-3712-891179. Facsimile: 011-7-3712-891178.**
**Mexico City, Mexico, D.F., Independent Mexico Correspondent: Jáuregui, Navarrete, Nader y Rojas, S.C. Abogados, Paseo de la Reforma 199, Pisos 15, 16 y 17, 06500, Mexico. Telephone: 011-525-591-16-55. Facsimile: 011-525-535-80-62, 011-525-703-22-47. Cable: JANANE.**
*See Professional Biographies, LOS ANGELES, CALIFORNIA*

Mayer, Glassman & Gaines, (AV)
**A Partnership including Professional Corporations**
Suite 400, 11726 San Vicente Boulevard, 90049-5006
**Telephone: 310-207-0007 Telecopier: 310-207-3578**
**Frederick J. Glassman (P.C.); Robert D. Mayer (P.C.); Frederic N. Gaines; Richard P. Solomon; Marc A. Lieberman; Steven M. Mayer.**
**Entertainment, Corporate, Business, Civil Litigation, Real Estate, Insolvency and Family Law.**
**Reference: City National Bank, Brentwood Branch.**
*See Professional Biographies, LOS ANGELES, CALIFORNIA*

Mayersohn, Arnold L., Jr. '55 '81 C.174 B.S. L.45 J.D.
(adm. in AR; not adm. in CA) Coun., Westfield Corp., Inc.
Mayersohn, Paul F. ........................ '46 '79 C.112 B.A. L.809 J.D. [Surpin,M.&E.]
**Mayerson, Michael A.**, (AV) ............ '56 '81 C.659 B.S. L.178 J.D. [Loeb&L.]
*PRACTICE AREAS: Entertainment Law.
Mayerson, Saml. ................................ '22 '51 C.112 B.A. L.800 J.D. Mun. Ct. J.
**Mayes, Jeffrey C.** ......................'68 '93 C.800 B.S. L.823 J.D. [Ⓐ Radcliff,F.&D.]
Mayfield, Glenn E. ...................... '10 '50 C.112 L.809 LL.B. 1514 Sunset Plaza Dr.‡
Maylin, Kathleen G. .................. '53 '91 C.112 B.A. L.800 J.D. 6300 Wilshire Blvd.
Mayman, Linda Goldenberg ........ '48 '73 C.112 A.B. L.1068 J.D. 423 S. Bentley Ave.
Mayman, Robert M., (AV) .................. '45 '70 C.112 B.A. L.767 J.D. 423 S. Bentley St.
**Maynard, Jo-Ann Horn** ................ '49 '74 C.273 B.B.A. L.472 J.D. [Ⓐ Lane P.S.L.]
Maynard, Therese H. .....'55 '81 C.112 B.A. L.1068 J.D. Prof. of Law, Loyola Law School
**Mayo, Jennifer E.** ................'70 '95 C.112 B.A. L.1065 J.D. [Ⓐ Pillsbury M.&S.]

**Mayock, W. Michael**
(See Pasadena)

Mayorkas, Helena C. '57 '84 C.112 B.A. L.276 J.D.
Asst. Dir., Los Angeles Educational Partnership
**Mayuga, Sandor X.**, (AV) .................. '48 '74 C.112 A.B. L.659 J.D. [Tisdale&N.]
*PRACTICE AREAS: Banking and Financial Institutions; Regulatory Law; Corporations; Securities; General Business.
**Mazen, Brian K.** ........................'62 '87 C.1074 B.S. L.426 J.D. [Ⓐ Meserve,M.&H.]

**Mazirow, Arthur, (AV) '33 '59 C.112 B.S. L.1068 J.D.**
**3415 Sepulveda Boulevard Suite 1200, 90034**
**Telephone: 310-398-6227**
**Email: AM@FFSLAW.COM**
**(Also Of Counsel, Freeman, Freeman & Smiley, LLP).**
**Real Estate Development, Purchases, Sales, Leases, Financing and Joint Ventures.**
*See Professional Biographies, LOS ANGELES, CALIFORNIA*

Mazorow, Marc A. ......................'57 '90 C.1097 B.S. L.1148 J.D. [Ⓐ Morgan&W.]
Mazur, Stephen H. ..................................'60 '85 C.112 B.A. L.1068 J.D. Dist. Atty.
**Mazursky, Charles J.**, (AV) ............ '41 '70 C.966 B.A. L.1065 J.D. [Mazursky,S.&A.]
*PRACTICE AREAS: Insurance Bad Faith Law; Products Liability Law; Medical Malpractice.

**Mazursky, Schwartz & Angelo, (AV)**
**Suite 600, 10877 Wilshire Boulevard, 90024-4341**
**Telephone: 310-824-7725 Facsimile: 310-824-2735**
**Charles J. Mazursky; Arnold W. Schwartz; Christopher E. Angelo;—Scott A. Marks; Debra Jane Wegman.**
**Major Tort Litigation emphasizing Major Personal Injury, Insurance Bad Faith, Product Liability, Premise Liability, Professional Malpractice, Medical Malpractice and Business Torts. Civil Trial and Appellate Practice and Toxic Tort Litigation.**
*See Professional Biographies, LOS ANGELES, CALIFORNIA*

**McAchran, Kathleen L.** ................ '66 '90 C.840 B.A. L.309 J.D. [Ⓐ Paul,H.J.&W.]
**Mc Adam, Patrick M.**, (AV) ............ '46 '71 C&L.426 B.B.S., J.D. [Iverson,Y.P.&H.]
*PRACTICE AREAS: Civil Litigation and Appellate Practice; Corporation and Securities Law.
**McAdams, James M.**, (BV) .............. '45 '75 C.560 B.A. L.800 J.D. [Ⓐ Pierry&M.]
*PRACTICE AREAS: Admiralty/Maritime; Personal Injury; Products Liability (Plaintiff); Workmans Compensation.
**McAleenan, Sharon P.** ..................'60 '87 C.605 B.A. L.1049 J.D. [Ⓐ Borton,P.&C.]
*PRACTICE AREAS: Coverage Analysis; Products Liability; Construction Defect.
**McAllen, Peter G.** ....................'50 '82 C.674 A.B. L.1068 J.D. [Ⓐ Jones,D.R.&P.]
**McAllister, Brian D.** ..........................'59 '94 C.768 B.A. L.1065 J.D. [Ⓐ Dewey B.]
*PRACTICE AREAS: General Corporate.
McAllister, Bruce D. ............'43 '80 C.940 B.A. L.1148 B.A. 11661 San Vicente Blvd.
**McAloon, Michelle** .......................... '70 '95 C.112 B.A. L.1068 J.D. [Ⓐ Arter&H.]
*PRACTICE AREAS: Litigation.

**McAndrews, Michael A.**, (AV) ..........'47 '72 C.740 B.A. L.1068 J.D. [Orrick,H.&S.]
*PRACTICE AREAS: Real Property Law; Real Property Finance Law.
**McAniff, Edward J.**, (AV) '34 '61
C.321 A.B. L.569 LL.B. [O'Melveny&M.] (©San Francisco)
*PRACTICE AREAS: Banking Law; Securities Law.
**McArthur, Lisa Cathleen** ............'68 '93 C.112 B.A. L.1068 J.D. [Ⓐ Manatt,P.&P.]
*PRACTICE AREAS: Estate Planning; Probate; Taxation Law.
McAuliffe, Terry ..... '52 '89 C.494 B.E.S. L.990 J.D. 7060 Hollywood Blvd., Suite 1210
**McBirney, Bruce H.**, (AV) ............. '54 '79 C.426 B.A. L.1066 J.D. [McBirney&C.]
*PRACTICE AREAS: Real Estate; Commercial Leasing; Landlord/Tenant.

**McBirney & Chuck, P.C., (AV)**
**611 West Sixth Street, Suite 2500, 90017**
**Telephone: 213-236-2750 Telecopier: 213-236-2700**
**Bruce H. McBirney; Catherine Endo Chuck. Of Counsel: Michael E. Reznick.**
**Commercial Leasing, Corporate, Real Estate, Nonprofit Organizations, Estate Planning and Probate Practice, Civil Litigation.**
*See Professional Biographies, LOS ANGELES, CALIFORNIA*

**McBreen, Peter James**, (AV) .........'50 '76 C.112 A.B. L.1068 J.D. [McBreen,M.&K.]
*PRACTICE AREAS: Trial Law; Appellate Practice.

**McBreen, McBreen & Kopko, (AV)**
**Suite 922, 9841 Airport Boulevard, 90045**☉
**Telephone: 310-410-2887 Fax: 310-410-0735**
**Peter James McBreen (Resident); Brian J. Hogan (Not admitted in CA).**
**General Practice, Corporate, Mergers and Acquisitions, Securities, Commodities, Real Estate, Aviation, General and Commercial Litigation, Toxic Torts, Products Liability, Medical Malpractice and Environmental Law.**
**Chicago, Illinois: Suite 2520, 20 North Wacker Drive. Telephone: 312-332-6405. Fax: 312-332-2657.**
**Philadelphia, Pennsylvania Office: 1760 Market Street, Suite 900. Telephone: 215-864-2600. Fax: 215-864-2610.**
**Montvale, New Jersey Office: 110 Summit Avenue. Telephone: 201-573-1508. Fax: 201-573-0574.**
*See Professional Biographies, LOS ANGELES, CALIFORNIA*

**McBride, Kevin G.**, (AVⓉ) '54 '85 C.602 B.S. L.597 J.D.
(adm. in IL; not adm. in CA; See Pat. Sect.) [Jones,D.R.&P.]
**McBride, Patricia A.** ................ '63 '90 C.860 B.A. L.145 J.D. [Ⓐ Heller E.W.&M.]
McBurney, George W., (AV) ............... '26 '53 C&L.350 B.A., J.D. 555 W. Fifth St.
**McCabe, Michael E.** ..........................'63 '88 C.273 B.A. L.426 J.D. [Ⓐ Parker S.]
McCabe, Theodore A., (BV) ............ '26 '53 C.103 A.B. L.309 LL.B. P.O. Box 25336
**McCain, Kathleen Mary** .................'57 '84 C.607 B.A. L.879 J.D. [Rubinstein&P.]
*REPORTED CASES: Morgan Stanley Mortgage Capital, Inc. v. Insurance Commissioner of the State of California, 18 F.3d 790 (9th Cir. 1994), Bankr. L. Rep. (CCH) P.75, 755; Checker Motor Corp. v. Superior Court (Garamedi), 13 Cal. App. 4th 1007, (1993); Garamendi v. Executive Life, 17 Cal. App. 4th 504, Brookview Condominium Owners' Association v. Heltzer Enterprises - Brookview, 218 Cal. App. 3d 502, 267 Cal. Rptr. 76 (1990); Walton Insurance Company v. Chase Manhattan Bank, No. 90 Civ. 4714, 4715, 4797 & 4798 (JFK), 1990 U.S. Dist. LEXIS 10490, 1990 WL 121555 (S.D.N.Y. August 14, 1990); Prudential Reinsurance Company v. Superior Court (Gillespie), 265 Cal. Rptr. 386 (1989).
*PRACTICE AREAS: Litigation; Insurance Insolvency; Reinsurance; Real Estate.
McCall, John C., (AV) .......'18 '51 C.170 B.A. L.748 LL.B. 6055 E. Washington Blvd.‡
McCall, Melanie L. ....................'60 '94 C.150 B.F.A. L.426 J.D. 633 W. Fifth St.
McCall, Walter L., (AV) ............ '28 '69 C.112 B.A. L.809 LL.B. 224 N. Bundy Dr.‡
**McCambridge, George R.**, (AV) '45 '73 C.767 A.B. L.1068 J.D.
[McCambridge,D.&M.]
McCambridge, Gregory P. ................ '65 '91 C.112 B.A. L.800 J.D. Off. of Pub. Def.

**McCambridge, Deixler & Marmaro, (AV)**
**2029 Century Park East, Suite 2700, 90067**
**Telephone: 310-277-2650 Telecopier: 310-203-8304**
**Members of Firm: George R. McCambridge; Bert H. Deixler; Richard Marmaro; Lary A. Rappaport; Michael A. Firestein; Larry S. Greenfield. Associates: John W. Crumpacker; Melissa L. Burns; Hayes F. Michel; Natasha A. Kotto; Michael H. Weiss; Bryan C. Altman; Cameron J. Talley; David J. Becker. Of Counsel: Jonathan E. Rich.**
**Commercial and Entertainment related Litigation, White Collar Criminal Defense, General Corporate matters and Corporate and Regulatory matters for Banks and other Financial Institutions.**
*See Professional Biographies, LOS ANGELES, CALIFORNIA*

McCann, David T. ........................'57 '84 C.602 B.S. L.809 J.D. [Morgan&W.]
McCann, John R., (BV) ................ '17 '48 C.112 L.800 LL.B. 854 Thayer Ave.
**McCarthy, Ann Bridget** .........'55 '90 C.1077 B.A. L.809 J.D. [Ⓐ Whitman B.A.&M.]
**McCarthy, Brian J.** ....................'53 '79 C.860 B.A. L.262 J.D. [Skadden,A.S.M.&F.]
**McCarthy, Daniel J.** ............................ '57 '81 C.309 A.B. L.477 J.D. [Hill,F.&B.]
*REPORTED CASES: Old Town Historic Building, Ltd., 79 Bankr. 8 (Bankr. C.D. Cal. 1987); Howes, 89 Bankr. 77 (9th Cir. BAP 1988).
*PRACTICE AREAS: Creditor's Rights Law; Bankruptcy Law; Business Litigation.
McCarthy, David Martin ............'58 '88 C.415 B.A. L.262 J.D. 10900 Wilshire Blvd.
McCarthy, Gregory A. ............'46 '74 C.1109 B.A. L.1049 J.D. Princ. Dep. Co. Coun.
**McCarthy, J. Donald, (A Professional Corporation)**, (AV) '42 '68
C.188 B.M.E. L.309 J.D. [Lyon&L.] (See Pat. Sect.)
*PRACTICE AREAS: Patent, Trademark, Copyright, Trade Regulation; Unfair Competition, Antitrust; Intellectual Property.
McCarthy, J. Thomas, (AV) ....'32 '57 C&L.800 A.B., LL.B. 707 Wilshire Blvd., 51st Fl.
**McCarthy, James J.**, (AV) ........ '28 '62 C.424 Ph.B. L.426 LL.B. [Ⓑ Magaña,C.&M.]
*PRACTICE AREAS: Airplane Crash Litigation; Aviation Law; Motor Vehicle Litigation; Products Liability Law.
**McCarthy, Kathleen A.** ..............'63 '92 C.112 B.A. L.809 J.D. [Ⓐ Magaña,C.&M.]
*PRACTICE AREAS: Sexual Harassment and Discrimination; Personal Injury; Products Liability; Wrongful Death.
McCarthy, Michael E.S. '51 '79 C.321 B.A. L.178 J.D.
1999 Ave. of the Stars, Suite 1400
**McCarthy, Monika L.** ............'58 '90 C.1077 B.A. L.426 J.D. [Ⓐ Buchalter,N.F.&Y.]
*LANGUAGES: German.
*PRACTICE AREAS: Financial Institution Litigation; Banking; Patent Infringement.
McCarthy, Susan L. .................. '58 '86 C.112 B.A. L.800 J.D. 1801 Century Pk. E.
**McCarty, David J.**, (AV) ...................'— '77 C.154 B.A. L.309 J.D. [Sheppard,M.R.&H.]
*PRACTICE AREAS: Bankruptcy Law; Loan Workouts.
**McCashin, James P., II**, (AV) ......... '43 '75 C.31 B.A. L.61 J.D. [McCashin&Assoc.]

**McCashin & Associates, A Professional Corporation, (AV)**
**12400 Wilshire Boulevard, Suite 450, 90025-1061**
**Telephone: 310-207-0266 Fax: 310-207-8767**
**James P. McCashin, II.**
**Products Liability, Insurance Defense, Construction, Business, Real Estate, and Professional Malpractice Litigation, Motor Sports Law and Litigation.**
*See Professional Biographies, LOS ANGELES, CALIFORNIA*

McCaslin, Sharon ........................'49 '76 C.613 B.A. L.800 J.D. Asst. U.S. Atty.
McCauley, John W. ..................... '53 '79 C.1075 B.A. L.1065 J.D. Dep. Co. Coun.
**McCauley, Michael S.** .................. '71 '96 C.719 B.A. L.602 J.D. [Ⓐ Kirkland&E.]
*PRACTICE AREAS: Litigation.
McCawley, John M. .......................'27 '56 C.170 A.B. L.426 LL.B. [McCawley&Z.]
McCawley & Zovich ................................................6404 Wilshire Blvd.
McChesney, Richard '51 '76 C.112 B.A. L.101 J.D.
(adm. in UT; not adm. in CA) I.R.S.
**McClain, Russell A.** ...............'67 '95 C.329 B.A. L.446 J.D. [Ⓐ Skadden,A.S.M.&F.]
McClain-Hill, Cynthia ............ '57 '81 C.112 B.A. L.1068 J.D. 700 S. Flower, 11th Fl.

**McClaugherty & Associates**
(See Pasadena)

**McCleary, Mark** . . . . . . . . . . . '69 '95 C.112 B.S. L.426 J.D. [[A] Rodi,P.P.G.&C.]
*PRACTICE AREAS: Corporate Law; Taxation.
McClellan, Hollis McCray, (Ms.) . . . . '51 '85 C.705 B.A. L.339 J.D. 4050 Buckingham Rd.
**McClelland, Nancy P.** . . . . . . . . . . '44 '77 C.1097 B.A. L.800 J.D. [Gibson,D.&C.]
*PRACTICE AREAS: Labor and Employment Law.
**McClintock, Gregory R.**, (AV) '43 '69
C.1163 B.A. L.800 J.D. [McClintock,W.B.R.R.&M.]
*PRACTICE AREAS: Environmental Law; Hazardous Waste Law; Superfund; Antitrust Law; Trade Regulation Law.

**McClintock, Weston, Benshoof, Rochefort, Rubalcava & MacCuish LLP, (AV)**
**444 South Flower Street, 43rd Floor, 90071**
**Telephone: 213-623-2322 FAX: 213-623-0824**
**Gregory R. McClintock; Steven W. Weston; Ward L. Benshoof; John M. Rochefort; Sharon F. Rubalcava; David S. MacCuish; Jonathan M. Gordon; Vernon T. Meador, III; Samuel C. Taylor; John P. Zaimes; George C. Roux; Louis A. Karasik; Kurt V. Osenbaugh; Jocelyn Niebur Thompson; Malcolm C. Weiss; Thomas J.P. McHenry; Michael D. Young; Steven J. Vining; Thomas L. Van Wyngarden; Elaine M. Lemke; Edward J. Casey; Gerald E. Gosch; Barbara Biles; Edward P. Manning; Robert I. McMurry; Andrew M. Gilford. Associates: Eliot L. Teitelbaum; H. Elliott Heide; Martha Schreiber Doty; Clifton J. McFarland; Martin "Kelly" J. McTigue, Jr.; James J. Hevener; Nicki Marie Varyu Carlsen; Lawrence P. Brennan, Jr.; Eugene A. Burrus; John D. Arya; Kurt Weissmuller; Robert M. Mahlowitz; William E. Berner, Jr.; Joon-Soo Kim; Gideon Kracov; Nicole Rivas.**
**General Civil and Environmental Litigation and Environmental Law, including the Regulation of Air and Water Quality, Hazardous and Solid Waste, Land Use and California Environmental Quality Act/National Environmental Policy Act, Oil and Gas, Contracts, Construction, Labor, Products Liability, Toxic Torts, Real Estate, Banking and Insurance Disputes.**
***See Professional Biographies, LOS ANGELES, CALIFORNIA***

**McCloud, Janet S.** . . . . . . . . . . '47 '75 C.205 B.A. L.976 J.D. [Christensen,M.F.J.G.W.&S.]
*PRACTICE AREAS: Corporate.
**McClure, Jane** . . . . . . . . . . . '67 '95 C.893 B.S. L.1065 J.D. [[A] Christensen,M.F.J.G.W.&S.]
*PRACTICE AREAS: Litigation.
McClymonds, Susan E. '58 '84
C.1060 B.A. L.1068 J.D. V.P. & Sr. Coun., Wells Fargo Bk., N.A.
**McConaghy, John D., (A Professional Corporation)**, (AV) '43 '72
C.800 B.S.M.E. L.1068 J.D. [Lyon&L.] (See Pat. Sect.)
*PRACTICE AREAS: Patent, Trademark; Intellectual Property.
**McConnell, John W., III**, (AV) . . . . . . . . . '49 '74 C.800 B.A. L.61 J.D. [Meyers,B.&M.]
*PRACTICE AREAS: Litigation; Product Liability; Professional Liability; Environmental, Professional and CGL Coverage.
**McCool, Clinton T.** . . . . . . . . . . . . . . . . '— '86 C.649 B.A. L.809 J.D. [Biesty,M.&G.]
*PRACTICE AREAS: Insurance Defense Litigation; Insurance Coverage; Bad Faith Litigation; Errors and Omissions; Contract Litigation.
**McCool, Maureen** . . . . . . . . . . . . . . . . . . . '58 '90 C&L.426 B.S., J.D. [[A] Liebman&R.]
**McCormack, John J.** . . . . . '31 '62 C.93 B.S. L.273 J.D. Sr. Pat. Coun., Unisys Corp. (Pat.)
**McCormick, Charles E.** . . . . . . . . . . . . . '39 '69 C&L.477 B.A., J.D. [Sheppard,M.R.&H.]
*PRACTICE AREAS: Banking Law; Corporate Financing Law; Business Acquisitions Law.
McCormick, John Michael, Jr. '43 '84 C.800 B.S. L.426 J.D.
221 N. Figueroa St., 12th Fl.
**McCortney, Ryan D.** '59 '87 C.605 A.B. L.800 J.D.
[Sheppard,M.R.&H.] (⊙Costa Mesa)
*PRACTICE AREAS: Labor and Employment Law.
**McCortney, Susan Freeman** . . . . . . '62 '91 C.602 B.A. L.426 J.D. [[A] Sheppard,M.R.&H.]
*PRACTICE AREAS: Commercial Law and Bankruptcy.
**McCourt, C. Kelly** . . . . . . . . . . . . . . . . . . '61 '86 C.112 A.B. L.1065 J.D. [[A] B.S.Lemon]
*PRACTICE AREAS: Legal Malpractice; Commercial Litigation; Insurance Litigation.
McCoy, Janet A., (AV) . . . . . . . . . . . . '44 '82 C.112 B.A. L.809 J.D. 1801 Ave. of the Stars
**McCoy, John Milton, III** . . . . . . . . . . '68 '93 C.112 B.A. L.1066 J.D. [[A] Bird,M.B.W.&M.]
**McCoy, M. Scott** '65 '91 C.800 B.S. L.37 J.D.
(adm. in AZ; not adm. in CA) [[A] Kirkland&E.]
*PRACTICE AREAS: Litigation.
**McCoy, Richard T., III** . . . . . . . . . . . . . . '55 '79 C.475 B.S. L.228 J.D. [Blanc W.J.&K.]
*PRACTICE AREAS: Mergers and Acquisitions; Taxation; Partnerships; Business Law; Proprietary Rights.
McCoy, Robert E., (AV) . . . . . . . . . . . . . '29 '57 C.112 L.809 LL.B. 3530 Wilshire Blvd.‡
**McCrory, Darrell P.** . . . . . . . . . . . . . . '22 '49 C.966 Ph.B. L.813 LL.B. [[B] Monteleone&M.]⊙
**McCulloch, Kenneth J.** '43 '68 C.178 B.A. L.262 J.D.
(adm. in NY; not adm. in CA) [[B] Grotta,G.&H.]⊙
McCullough, Burton V., Law Offices of . . . . . . '41 '68 L.878 J.D. 601 S. Figueroa St.
**McCully, Barbara L.** . . . . . . . . . . . . . . '50 '85 C.763 B.A. L.1049 J.D. [[A] Murchison&C.]
*PRACTICE AREAS: Law and Motion Law; Appellate Practice.
**McCune, Dana J.** . . . . . . . . . . . . . . . . . . . . . . '53 '78 C.112 B.A. L.426 J.D. [Lynberg&W.]

**McCurnin, Thomas E. '50 '76 C.352 B.A. L.221 J.D.**
**333 South Grand Avenue, 37th Floor, 90071**
**Telephone: 213-626-5800 Fax: 213-626-5868**
***PRACTICE AREAS: Collections; Bank Operations; Real Estate; Lender Liability; Leasing Litigation.**
**General Civil Litigation in all State and Federal Courts, Banking and Finance, Bankruptcy, Commercial Law, Real Property.**
***See Professional Biographies, LOS ANGELES, CALIFORNIA***

**McCutchen, Doyle, Brown & Enersen, (AV)** [BR]
**355 South Grand Avenue Suite 4400, 90071-1560⊙**
**Telephone: 213-680-6400 Facsimile: 213-680-6499**
**Email: postmaster@mdbe.com URL: http://www.mccutchen.com**
**Members of Firm: Joseph R. Austin (Managing Partner); Colleen P. Doyle; James J. Dragna; Debra L. Fischer; Karla A. Francken; William H. Freedman; Melinda L. Hayes; Susan L. Hoffman; Michael B. Lubic; John C. Morrissey; James Franklin Owens; Rick R. Rothman; Patricia L. Shanks. Counsel: Karen A. Caffee; Peter Hsiao; Diana Pfeffer Martin; Douglas R. Painter; Clayton J. Vreeland. Associates: Jeffrey M. Anderson; P. Scott Burton; Greg A. Christianson; Jill F. Cooper; I-Fan Ching Go; Tiffany R. Hedgpeth; Heather Hoecherl; Asher D. Issacs; Micah R. Jacobs; Jerilyn López Mendoza; Neal A. Rubin; John D. Schlotterbeck; Allyson W. Sonenshine; Charles E. Shelton, II; Sandra Hughes Waddell; Cory Wurtzel; Kenneth J. Yood.**
**General Practice.**
**San Francisco, California Office: Three Embarcadero Center, 94111-4066. Telephone: 415-393-2000. Facsimile: 415-393-2286 (G I, II, III). Telex: 340817 MACPAG SFO.**
**San Jose, California Office: Market Post Tower, Suite 1500, 55 South Market Street, 95113-2327. Telephone: 408-947-8400. Facsimile: 408-947-4750. Telex: 910 250 2931 MACPAG SJ.**
**Walnut Creek, California Office: 1331 North California Boulevard, Post Office Box V, 94596-4502. Telephone: 510-937-8000. Facsimile: 510-975-5390.**
**Palo Alto, California Office: One Embarcadero Place, 2100 Geng Road, 94303-0913. Telephone: 415-846-4000. Fax: 415-846-4086.**
**Washington, D.C. Office: The Evening Star Building, Suite 800, 1101 Pennsylvania Avenue, N.W., 20004-2514. Telephone: 202-628-4900. Facsimile: 202-628-4912.**
**Taipei, Taiwan Republic of China Office: International Trade Building, Tenth Floor, 333 Keelung Road, Section 1, 110. Telephone: 886-2-723-5000. Facsimile: 886-2-757-6070.**
**Affiliated Offices In: Bangkok, Thailand; Beijing, China; Shanghai, China.**
***See Professional Biographies, LOS ANGELES, CALIFORNIA***

McDade, Robert J. . . . . . . . . . . . . . . . . . . . . . . . '68 '93 C.800 A.B. L.276 J.D. 633 W. 5th St.
McDaniel, Arthur J., (AV) . . . . '— '76 C.112 B.S. L.809 J.D. Tax Coun., Davis Companies
McDaniel, Glen '12 '37 C.802 A.B. L.178 LL.B.
(adm. in NY; not adm. in CA) 780 Linda Flora Dr.‡
**McDaniel, James R.**, (AV) . . . . . . . . . . . . . . . . . '53 '81 C.1060 B.A. L.1068 J.D. [Reish&L.]
*PRACTICE AREAS: Estate and Tax Planning; Probate; Tax Controversy; Employee Benefits.
**McDaniel, Katherine L.** '52 '80 C.605 A.B. L.1068 J.D.
Dir., Intel. Prop. & Assoc. Gen. Coun., The Times Mirror Co.
**McDaniel, M. Elizabeth** '— '84
C.880 B.A. L.1065 J.D. [Sheppard,M.R.&H.] (⊙San Francisco)
**McDaniel, Marcus A.** . . . . . . . . . . . . . . . . . . . '64 '90 C.937 B.A. L.309 J.D. [[A] Latham&W.]
McDaniel, Michael S., (AV) . . . . . . . . . . . . '49 '75 C.112 B.A. L.426 J.D. [Countryman&M.]
McDaniel, Stacy W. '60 '84
C.112 B.A. L.426 J.D. Assoc. Gen. Coun., Pacific Greystone Corp.
McDermott, Carol A. . . . . . . . . . . . . . . '64 '91 C.112 B.A. L.423 J.D. 355 S. Grand Ave.
**McDermott, John E.**, (AV) . . . . . . . . . '46 '72 C.611 B.A. L.309 J.D. [Cadwalader,W.&T.]
McDermott, John T. '34 '66 C.478 A.B. L.208 J.D.
(adm. in CO; not adm. in CA) Loyola Univ. Sch. of Law
**McDermott, Thomas J.** . . . . . . . . . . . . . . '56 '82 C.763 B.A. L.426 J.D. [[A] Bragg,S.S.&K.]
**McDermott, Thomas J., Jr.**, (AV) . . . . . . . . '31 '59 C.112 B.A. L.1068 J.D. [Manatt,P.&P.]
*PRACTICE AREAS: High Technology Litigation; Securities Litigation; Antitrust.

**McDermott, Will & Emery, (AV)** [BR]
**A Partnership including Professional Corporations**
**2049 Century Park East, 90067-3208⊙**
**Telephone: 310-277-4110 Facsimile: 310-277-4730**
**URL: http://www.mwe.com**
**Members of Firm: Chris M. Amantea; Paul A. Beck†; Joel M. Bernstein; Lee L. Blackman; Timothy P. Blanchard; Peter M. Branstein; Mark A. Conley; Marsha S. Croninger; John E. Curtis, Jr.; Kathleen L. Houston Drummy; Gary B. Gertler; Donald A. Goldman; Eric B. Gordon; Michael I. Gottfried; David Gould†; Daniel Grunfeld; Mary Ellen Hogan; Douglas A. Jaques; Ivan L. Kallick†; David L. Klatsky; Stephen A. Kroft; Lewis R. Landau; Rodger M. Landau; Jeffrey W. Lemkin; Robert P. Mallory; Douglas M. Mancino; Mark J. Mihanovic; Terese A. Mosher-Beluris; Denise G. Paully; Ira J. Rappeport; J. Peter Rich; Robert H. Rosenfield; Robert H. Rotstein; Thomas A. Ryan; Allan L. Schare; Richard K. Simon; Steven M. Spector†; Virginia Vance Sullivan. Counsel: Martin J. Schnitzer;—Allison Sher Arkin; Jane E. Boubelik; Alexander H. Bromley; Bryan T. Castorina; Juan Carlos Dominguez; David R. Gabor; James T. Grant; Genevieve M. Kelly; Hyong S. Koh; Daniel B. Lantry; Paul F. Lawrence; Michael L. Meeks; Ajay A. Patel; James B. Ryan; Theodore R. Schneck; Christina Anne Slawson; Jennifer L. Spaziano; Sarah Trimble; Anne H. West; Jane Chotard Wheeler.**
**General Practice (including Corporate, Employee Benefits, Estate Planning, Health, Litigation and Tax Law).**
**Chicago, Illinois Office: 227 West Monroe Street. Telephone: 312-372-2000. Facsimile: 312-984-7700.**
**Boston, Massachusetts Office: 75 State Street, Suite 1700. Telephone: 617-345-5000. Facsimile: 617-345-5077.**
**Miami, Florida Office: 201 South Biscayne Boulevard. Telephone: 305-358-3500. Facsimile: 305-347-6500.**
**Washington, D.C. Office: 1850 K Street, N.W. Telephone: 202-887-8000. Facsimile: 202-778-8087.**
**Newport Beach, California Office: 1301 Dove Street, Suite 500. Telephone: 714-851-0633. Facsimile: 714-851-9348.**
**New York, N.Y. Office: 50 Rockefeller Plaza. Telephone: 212-547-5508. Facsimile: 212-547-5444.**
**St. Petersburg, Russia Office: AOZT McDermott, Will & Emery, Griboyedova Canal 36, 191023, St. Petersburg, Russia. Telephone: (7) (812) 310-52-44; 310-55-44; 310-59-44; 850-20-45. Facsimile: (7) (812) 310-54-46; 325-84-50.**
**Vilnius, Lithuania Office: Smetonos 6, 2600 Vilnius, Lithuania. Telephone: 370 2 61-43-08. Facsimile: 370 2 22-79-55.**
**†Denotes a lawyer employed by a Professional Corporation which is a member of the Firm**
***See Professional Biographies, LOS ANGELES, CALIFORNIA***

McDonald, Brian M. '47 '74
C.940 B.A. L.426 J.D. Sr. V.P. & Gen. Coun., Sanwa Bk. Calif.
McDonald, Cheryl B. . . . . . . . . . . . . . . . . . '— '77 C.112 B.A. L.426 J.D. Chubb & Son, Inc.
McDonald, James W. . . . . . . . . . . . . . . . . . . '48 '79 C.112 L.1152 J.D. 2049 Century Pk. E.‡

**McDonald, Janis M., (AV) '29 '75 C.813 B.A. L.767 J.D.**
**Suite 2700, 1900 Avenue of the Stars, 90067**
**Telephone: 310-556-2028 Fax: 310-286-1728**
**(Certified Specialist, Family Law, The State Bar of California Board of Legal Specialization).**
**Family Law.**
**References: Wells Fargo Bank; First Interstate Bank; Great Western Bank.**
***See Professional Biographies, LOS ANGELES, CALIFORNIA***

**McDonald, Mark R.** . . . . . . . . . . . . . . . . . . . . '63 '88 C.674 A.B. L.309 J.D. [Morrison&F.]
*PRACTICE AREAS: Business Litigation; Securities Litigation.
**McDonald, Richard A.** . . . . . . . . . . . . . . . . '58 '86 C.112 B.A. L.426 J.D. [Reznik&R.]
*SPECIAL AGENCIES: Los Angeles County Metropolitan Transit Authority (MTA).
McDonald, Tracy Carolyn . . . . . . . . . . '59 '87 C.112 B.A. L.1137 J.D. 4700 Wilshire Blvd.
**McDonell, Jill P.** . . . . . . . . . . . . . . . . . '64 '92 C.112 B.A. L.809 J.D. [[A] Engstrom,L.&L.]
**McDonnell, George T.** . . . . . . . . . . . . . '53 '79 C.112 B.A. L.1065 J.D. [Allen,M.L.G.&M.]
*PRACTICE AREAS: Litigation.
**McDonnell, Thomas J.** . . . . . . . . . . . '59 '86 C.112 B.A. L.629 J.D. [Ericksen,A.K.D.&L.]
*PRACTICE AREAS: Insurance Defense Litigation; Insurance Coverage.
**McDonough, John R.**, (AV) . . . . . . . . . '19 '49 C.911 L.178 LL.B. [Carlsmith B.W.C.&I.]
*PRACTICE AREAS: Civil Litigation (100%).
McDowell, David F., Jr. . . . . . . . . . . . . '61 '86 C.103 A.B. L.145 J.D. 601 S. Figueroa St.
McDowell, James B. '35 '65 C.659 B.S. L.1017 LL.B.
Assoc. Reg. Coun., Prudential Ins. Co. of Amer., The
McDowell, John T. . . . . . . . . . . . . . . . . '60 '87 C.112 B.A. L.990 J.D. 12121 Wilshire Blvd.
**McDowell, Kathleen M.** . . . . . . . . . . . . . . . . . '54 '84 C.454 B.A. L.800 J.D. [Munger,T.&O.]
**McDowell, Marilyn G.** . . . . . . . . . . . . . . '53 '87 C.800 B.S. L.809 J.D. [[B] Gibson,D.&C.]
*PRACTICE AREAS: Litigation; Antitrust.
McElroy, Jeff Foster . . . . . . . . . . . . . '54 '83 C.1320 B.A. L.560 J.D. 1320 N. Cherokee Ave.
McElroy, Leslie P. . . . . . . . . . . . . . . . . . . '58 '87 C&L.1097 B.S., J.D. Dep. Atty. Gen.

**McElroy, Mary J.**
(See Templeton)

**McElvain, Randy M.** . . . . . . . . . . . . . . . '63 '88 C.990 B.A. L.1065 J.D. [Hawkins,S.L.&B.]
McEvilly, Eileen M. . . . . . . . . . . . . . '61 '89 C.112 B.A. L.426 J.D. 11900 W. Olympic Blvd.
**McEvoy, Josefina Fernandez** . . . . . . . . '60 '90 C&L.831 B.A., J.D. [Markowitz,F.&U.]
*LANGUAGES: Spanish.
*PRACTICE AREAS: Bankruptcy.
McFadden, Roger R. '38 '88 C.263 B.S. L.862 J.D.
(adm. in OK; not adm. in CA; Pat.) 2524 Canyon Dr.
McFall, Cynthia Anne . . . . . . . . . . . '58 '85 C.518 A.B. L.426 J.D. 10 Universal City Plaza
**McFall, Scott B.** . . . . . . . . . . . . . . . . . . . . . '51 '78 C.800 B.S. L.809 J.D. [Agajanian&M.]
**McFarland, Clifton J.** . . . . . . . '58 '89 C.453 B.S. L.178 J.D. [[A] McClintock,W.B.R.R.&M.]
*PRACTICE AREAS: Environmental Compliance; Environmental Litigation.
**McFarland, Elizabeth A.** . . . . . . . . . . . . . . '65 '93 C.112 B.A. L.276 J.D. [[A] Tisdale&N.]
*LANGUAGES: Italian.
*REPORTED CASES: Marriage of Heikes, California Supreme Court, 1995; Alleco Inc. v. Alfred, Maryland Court of Appeals, 1993; The Maxima Corporation v. 6933 Arlington Development Limited Partnership, Maryland Court of Special Appeals, 1993.
*PRACTICE AREAS: Commercial Litigation; Appellate Practice; Financial Institutions; General Business.
**McFarland, Jeffrey D.** . . . . . . . . . . . . . '63 '92 C.426 B.A. L.878 J.D. [[A] Milbank,T.H.&M.]
**McFarland, Larry W.** . . . . . . . . . . . . . . . . . . . '58 '87 C.846 B.A. L.326 J.D. [Baker&H.]
*PRACTICE AREAS: Intellectual Property; Litigation and Counseling.
**McFarland, Scotta E.**, (AV⊙) . . . . . . . . . . '47 '80 C.586 B.S.Ed. L.802 J.D. [[B] Dewey B.]
**McFarland, Theresa I.** . . . . . . . . . . . . . '64 '92 C.170 B.A. L.767 J.D. [[A] Folger L.&K.]⊙
**McFarlane, Robert A.** . . . . . . . . . . . . '67 '94 C.813 B.A.S. L.1065 J.D. [[A] Folger L.&K.]⊙
McGah, Edward R., Jr. . . . . . . . . . . . '54 '81 C.602 B.B.A. L.477 J.D. Exec. Asst. U.S. Atty.

McGahey, Shawn A. ..................... '— '91 C.629 B.A. L.188 J.D. Dep. Atty. Gen.
**McGannon, P. Casey** .................. '66 '93 C.813 B.A. L.800 J.D. [Ⓐ Paul,H.J.&W.]
McGarry, H. Patrick, Sr. ........... '30 '63 C.426 B.B.A. L.809 LL.B. 3237 Sunset Blvd.‡
Mc Garry, M. Eileen ................ '47 '88 C.502 B.A. L.1068 J.D. 11666 Gateway Blvd.

**McGarry & Laufenberg**
**(See El Segundo)**

**McGaughey & Spirito**
**(See Torrance)**

**McGeehan, C. Kevin**, (AV) ........................ '51 '78 C&L.976 B.A., J.D. [Irell&M.]
McGeever, Thomas D. ............... '54 '85 C.940 B.A. L.426 J.D. 4700 Wilshire Blvd.
**McGilvray, Alexander C., Jr.**, (AV) .............. '49 '74 C.813 A.B. L.1068 J.D. [Clark&T.]
*PRACTICE AREAS: General Corporate; Corporate Securities and Finance; Mergers and Acquisitions; Venture Capital.
McGinley, Wm. E. ...................................... '26 '53 C&L.800 B.S., LL.B. Supr. Ct. J.
**McGinnis, Carl L.** ................................... '20 '82 C.453 B.S. L.800 J.D. [Ⓐ Hoag&O.]
*PRACTICE AREAS: Probate; Tax.
**McGinnis, L. Susan** ........................ '56 '90 C.112 A.B. L.800 J.D. [Ⓐ Latham&W.]
McGinnis, Matthew L. ........................... '62 '91 C.112 A.B. L.93 J.D. 633 W. 5th St.

**McGinnis, Patrick E. '50 '76 C.112 B.S. L.36 J.D.**
**924 Westwood Boulevard, Suite 725, 90024**
**Telephone: 310-208-6625 Fax: 310-209-7444**
**(Certified Specialist, Taxation Law, California Board of Legal Specialization).**
***PRACTICE AREAS: Federal and State Taxation Law; Civil Tax Litigation; Tax Controversies Law; Tax Collection; Civil and Criminal Tax Fraud.**
**Tax Planning and Tax Litigation, Estate Planning and Bankruptcy.**
***See Professional Biographies, LOS ANGELES, CALIFORNIA***

**McGonagle, Erin K.** ........................... '65 '91 C.575 B.A. L.990 J.D. [Ⓐ Mendes&M.]
**McGonagle, Vincent A.** ........... '63 '88 C.397 B.A. L.990 J.D. [Ⓐ Wilson,E.M.E.&D.]
**McGonigle, Timothy D.** .................... '58 '84 C.602 B.B.A. L.990 J.D. [Ruben&M.]
*PRACTICE AREAS: Business Litigation; Securities Litigation; Insurance Bad Faith; Professional Liability.
**McGorrin, Denise Marie** .............. '59 '85 C.932 B.A. L.945 J.D. [Ⓐ Paul,H.J.&W.]
McGovern, David M. ....................... '69 '94 C.420 B.S. L.276 J.D. 333 S. Grand Ave.
**McGovern, Patrick Michael** '55 '86 L.061 LL.B.
(adm. in NY; not adm. in CA) [Zevnik H.G.&M.]⊙
*LANGUAGES: French.
*PRACTICE AREAS: International Law; Insurance Coverage; Commercial Litigation.
**McGowan, Vincent** ...................................... '66 '90 C.058 B.C L. [Harney]
*PRACTICE AREAS: Civil Trial; Medical Malpractice Law.
McGrail, Lawrence F.X. .................. '48 '77 C.565 B.S. L.1190 J.D. 5770 S. Eastern Ave.
McGregor, Kent D. '31 '58 C&L.878 B.S., J.D.
(adm. in UT; not adm. in CA) 4680 Wilshire Blvd.
**McGuinness, Joseph G.** .................. '58 '84 C.1077 B.A. L.809 J.D. [Wickwire G.]
*PRACTICE AREAS: Construction and General Business Litigation.
**McGuinness, Kathleen G.**, (AV) '48 '78 C.1044 B.A. L.1049 J.D.
V.P., Gen. Coun. & Secy., The Times Mirror Co.
**McGuinness, Michael G.** ................ '62 '88 C.911 B.A. L.426 J.D. [O'Melveny&M.]
*PRACTICE AREAS: Labor and Employment.
McGuire, James H. ........................ '48 '72 C.112 B.S. L.809 J.D. 1140 S. Robertson Blvd.
McGuire, John I. ....... '62 '87 C.178 B.A. L.569 J.D. Gen. Atty., Capital Cities/ABC, Inc.
**McGuire, Thomas P., (P.C.)** .......... '49 '75 C.112 B.A. L.1065 J.D. [Monteleone&M.]
*PRACTICE AREAS: Construction Law; OSHA; Environmental Law; Commercial Law.
**McGuirl, Maureen**, (AV) '50 '79
C.66 B.A. L.178 J.D. [Brown R.M.F.&S.] (⊙New York, NY.)
*REPORTED CASES: City of Anaheim v. Southern California Edison Co., 1990-2 Trade Cas. (CCH) 69426 (C.D. Cal. 1990), aff'd., 955 F.2d 1373 (9th Cir. 1992); City of Vernon v. Southern California Edison Co., 955 F.2d 1361 (9th Cir.), cert. denied, 121 L.Ed.2d 228 (1992); Eurim-Pharm GmbH v. Pfizer Inc., 593 F. Supp. 1102 (S.D.N.Y. 1984); Ikonen v. Hartz Mountain, 122 F.R.D. 258 (S.D. Cal. 1988); Kuhfeldt v. Liberty Mutual Insurance Co., (E.D. Mich).
*PRACTICE AREAS: Antitrust; Intellectual Property; Business Litigation.
McGurrin, Colleen M. ............ '61 '90 C.1077 B.A. L.809 J.D. 3865 Grandview Blvd.
**McHale, John R.** ....................... '60 '85 C.813 A.B. L.145 J.D. [Gipson H.&P.]
*PRACTICE AREAS: General Business; Corporate and Securities Law; Entertainment Transactions.
**McHale, Michael J.**, (AV) ................. '40 '65 C.363 A.B. L.477 LL.B. [McHale&C.]
*PRACTICE AREAS: Insurance Defense; Products Liability; Construction.

**McHale & Connor, A Professional Corporation, (AV)**
**Suite 300, 600 Wilshire Boulevard, 90017**
**Telephone: 213-629-1131 Fax: 213-627-9736**
**Michael J. McHale; Jan Allen Connor; Philip C. Allen; Bruce Janger; Kara Ann Pape;—Myrna Linett Strapp; Lawrence A. Walter; Sherry Grguric.**
**General Civil and Trial Practice in all State and Federal Courts. Insurance, Products Liability, Medical Legal and Malpractice Law.**
**Reference: First Interstate Bank, Los Angeles Main Office.**
***See Professional Biographies, LOS ANGELES, CALIFORNIA***

McHenry, James P. ......... '67 '95 C.112 B.A. L.426 J.D. 725 S. Figueroa St., Ste., 3750
**McHenry, Thomas J.P.** ........ '55 '85 C.976 B.A. L.569 J.D. [McClintock,W.B.R.R.&M.]
*LANGUAGES: French.
*SPECIAL AGENCIES: California Environmental Protection Agency; Regional Water Quality Control Boards; State Department of Toxic Substances Control; South Coast Air Quality Management District.
*PRACTICE AREAS: Environmental Law; Air Quality; Hazardous Waste; Forestry; International Natural Resources.
**McHugh, Joseph G.** .................... '62 '87 C.602 B.A. L.228 J.D. [Ⓑ O'Melveny&M.]
*PRACTICE AREAS: Real Estate Law.
McIlroy, John B. ..................................... '38 '63 C.347 A.B. L.208 J.D. 111 N. Hill
**McIlvery, John J.** ....................... '71 '95 C.800 B.S. L.1066 J.D. [Ⓐ Troop M.S.&P.]
*PRACTICE AREAS: Corporate Law; Securities.
McInerny, Kia W., (AV) ................. '47 '76 C.112 B.A. L.61 J.D. 1837 Kelton Ave.
**McIntire, Ronald A.** ........................... '60 '86 C.197 B.A. L.1068 J.D. [Perkins C.]
*PRACTICE AREAS: Airplane Crash Litigation; Asbestos Litigation; Business Torts; Product Liability Law; Tort Law.
**McIntosh, Daniel G.**, (AV) .......... '44 '72 C.112 A.B. L.1066 J.D. [Seyfarth,S.F.&G.]
*PRACTICE AREAS: Corporation Law; Real Estate Law; Business Law.
**McIntosh, Denise Marie** ..................... '67 '93 C.112 B.S. L.1065 J.D. [Ⓐ Loeb&L.]
*PRACTICE AREAS: Real Property (55%); General Practice (25%); Entertainment Law (15%); Family Law (5%).
McIntyre, Michael C. .................... '43 '74 C.1077 B.S. L.809 J.D. [Rotkin,S.&M.]
McIntyre, William E. ........... '28 '57 C.477 B.A. L.800 LL.B. 601 S. Saint Andrews Pl.
**McKain, R. Diane** ................. '51 '87 C.1077 B.S. L.426 J.D. [Ⓐ LeBoeuf,L.G.&M.]
*PRACTICE AREAS: Public Finance; Real Estate Finance.
**McKay, John K.** ......................... '53 '82 C.800 B.A. L.362 J.D. [Allen,M.L.G.&M.]
*PRACTICE AREAS: Real Estate Litigation; Land Use; Environmental Litigation; Employment Litigation.
**McKay, John P.**, (AV) ................ '40 '69 C.1109 B.A. L.990 J.D. [McKay,B.&G.]
*PRACTICE AREAS: Civil Trial; Insurance Defense; Personal Injury.
McKay, Klint James ......... '54 '83 C.477 B.A. L.912 J.D. 1801 Century Park E., 25th Fl.
McKay, Lequita J. .............. '30 '65 C.621 B.S. L.809 LL.B. 512 N. Larchmont Blvd.
McKay, Mitchell S. ................... '53 '83 C.112 B.A. L.809 J.D. 2650 W. Temple St.

**McKay, Byrne & Graham, (AV)**
**3250 Wilshire Boulevard, Suite 603, 90010**
**Telephone: 213-386-6900 Fax: 213-381-1762**

(This Listing Continued)

**McKay, Byrne & Graham (Continued)**
**John P. McKay; Michael A. Byrne; Robert L. Graham; Barry Hassenberg; Mark G. Cunningham; Paul A. de Lorimier;—Jeffrey Cabot Myers; Michael L. Fox. Of Counsel: Gail D. Solo (A Professional Corporation).**
**Insurance Law (Reinsurance and Excess Insurance Included), Personal Injury, Product Liability, Premises Liability, Construction, Land Subsidence, Motor Vehicle, Medical and Legal Malpractice and Intentional Torts Law. General Civil and Trial Practice in all State and Federal Courts.**
***See Professional Biographies, LOS ANGELES, CALIFORNIA***

McKean, Grover L. ........................... '49 '79 C&L.426 B.A., J.D. Lazard Freres & Co.
McKean, Nicholas F. '50 '78 C&L.878 B.A., J.D.
(adm. in AK; not adm. in CA) Dept. of Jus.-FBI
McKee, James J. ......................... '34 '62 C.061 B.A. L.309 LL.B. 1432 Barry Ave.
**McKee, Jennifer D.** .................... '67 '93 C.668 B.A. L.310 J.D. [Ⓐ Hancock R.&B.]
*LANGUAGES: Russian.
*PRACTICE AREAS: Insurance Coverage.
**McKeith, Malissa Hathaway**, (AV) ............ '59 '83 C.112 B.A. L.767 J.D. [Loeb&L.]
*PRACTICE AREAS: Environmental Law.
**McKelvey, Judy L.** .................... '57 '91 C.112 B.A. L.569 J.D. [Ⓐ Pollak,V.&F.]

**McKelvy, Carol L. '59 '90 C.800 B.S. L.426 J.D.**
**1925 Century Park East, Suite 2000, 90067**
**Telephone: 310-277-2236 Fax: 310-556-5653**
**Contracts, Civil Trial, Real Estate, Entertainment Law.**
***See Professional Biographies, LOS ANGELES, CALIFORNIA***

**McKenna, Charles C.** ................... '67 '93 C.112 B.A. L.426 J.D. [Ⓐ Lynberg&W.]
*PRACTICE AREAS: Governmental Entity Defense; General Liability Defense.
Mckenna, Kathleen M. ............... '53 '85 C.1042 B.A. L.426 J.D. 3550 Wilshire Blvd.
**McKenna, Kenneth G.** .... '53 '85 C.976 B.A. L.145 J.D. [Ⓑ Christensen,M.F.J.G.W.&S.]
*PRACTICE AREAS: Corporate Law; Finance Law; Bankruptcy Law.
McKenna, William F., (AV) ...... '14 '40 C.676 Ph.B. L.976 LL.B. 2400 Carman Crest Dr.

**McKenna & Cuneo, L.L.P., (AV)**
**444 South Flower Street, 90071⊙**
**Telephone: 213-688-1000 Telecopier: 213-243-6330**
**URL: http://www.mckennacuneo.com**
**Resident Partners: Thomas M. Abbott; John E. Cavanagh; Thomas Curtiss, Jr. (Certified Specialist, Estate Planning, Trust and Probate Law, The State Bar of California Board of Legal Specialization); James J. Gallagher; Michael T. Kavanaugh; Stanley W. Landfair; Robert L. Layton; Stephanie Berrington McNutt; Susan A. Mitchell; Robert Jon Newman; Marlo S. Oliver; Richard B. Oliver; Charles H. Pomeroy, IV; Mark R. Troy; Gail Frulla Zirkelbach. Resident Of Counsel: John A. Burkholder; Robert R. Plank. Resident Associates: Barbara J. Bacon; Cynthia Beckwith; Carol R. Brophy; Elizabeth Coppage Brown; Terry L. Brown; Tracey A. Calver; Edwin A. Carlson; Nicole Carson; Laura O. Doyle; N. Kemba Extavour; Dana Fitzgibbons; Tara A. Flanagan; Evelyn F. Heidelberg; R. Craig Holman; Karin L. Keutzer; Philip Bruno Kumpis; Pamela D. Launder; Charlotte R. Maya; Karen Poston Miller; Robert F. Miller; Kathleen A. Moran; Thomas A. Myers; Jin S. Park; Brian M. Regan; Karen Rinehart; Martin A. Rips; Michael R. Rizzo; Dawn Sellers; David A. Sonner; Elizabeth A. Stamper; Robert R. Valencia; Daniel E. Wax; Michael E. Weinsten.**
**General Civil, Criminal and Trial Practice in all State and Federal Courts, Federal Departments and Agencies. Government Contracts, White Collar Crime, Environmental, Labor and Employment and Health Care Law.**
**Washington, D.C. Office: 1900 K Street, N.W. Telephone: 202-496-7500.**
**San Francisco, California Office: One Market, Steuart Street Tower, Twenty-Seventh Floor. Telephone: 415-267-4000.**
**Denver, Colorado Office: 370 Seventeenth Street, Suite 4800. Telephone: 303-634-4000.**
**San Diego, California Office: Symphony Towers, Suite 3200, 750B Street. Telephone: 619-595-5400.**
**Dallas, Texas Office: 5700 Bank One Center, 1717 Main Street. Telephone: 214-746-5700.**
**Brussels, Belgium Office: 56, rue des Colonies, Box 14, B-1000. Telephone: 011-322-278-1211.**
***See Professional Biographies, LOS ANGELES, CALIFORNIA***

**McKenney, Steven D.** ....................... '65 '93 C.112 B.A. L.309 J.D. [Ⓐ Latham&W.]
*PRACTICE AREAS: International Joint Venture (80%); Corporate (20%).
**McKennon, Robert J.** .................. '59 '86 C.1109 B.A. L.800 J.D. [Barger&W.]
*PRACTICE AREAS: Business Litigation; Insurance Insolvency and Litigation; Bankruptcy Law.
McKenzie, Dwayne P. ................ '70 '94 C.112 B.A. L.1068 J.D. 601 S. Figueroa St.
**McKeon, Arthur J., III** ................ '52 '78 C&L.426 B.A., J.D. [Gilbert,K.C.&J.]
*PRACTICE AREAS: Insurance Defense; Employment Law; Business Litigation.
McKevitt, Jane A. ............................ '— '89 C&L.911 B.A., J.D. 725 S. Figueroa

**McKinley & Capeloto**
**(See Pasadena)**

McKinney, William L. ...................... '48 '75 C.990 B.A. L.426 J.D. 880 W. 1st St.
**McKinzie, Carl W.**, (AV) ............. '39 '67 C.845 B.B.A. L.802 J.D. [Riordan&M.]
McKittrick, Allan B. ........................ '38 '64 C.940 B.A. L.145 J.D. Asst. Co. Coun.
McKnight, Donald E., Jr. ............... '61 '87 C.285 B.A. L.276 J.D. 300 S. Grand Ave.
**McKnight, Frederick L.**, (AV) .......... '47 '73 C.674 A.B. L.1066 J.D. [Jones,D.R.&P.]
McLachlan, Michael D. .................. '68 '95 C.112 B.A. L.800 J.D. 624 S. Grand Ave.
**McLain, Michael A.** .................. '67 '92 C&L.426 B.A., J.D. [Ⓐ Cummins&W.]
*PRACTICE AREAS: Litigation; Insurance Coverage; Bankruptcy.
**McLain, Thomas E.**, (AV) ...................... '46 '74 C&L.228 B.A., J.D. [Perkins C.]
*LANGUAGES: Japanese.
*PRACTICE AREAS: International Business Transactions; Location Based Entertainment; Investments, Financings; Mergers and Acquisitions; Franchising.

**McLain, Richard W., A Professional Corporation**
**(See Glendale)**

McLane, David S. ..................... '58 '86 C.112 B.A. L.1068 J.D. Fed. Pub. Def. Off.
**McLane, Frederick B.**, (AV) .......... '41 '67 C.813 B.A. L.976 LL.B. [O'Melveny&M.]
*PRACTICE AREAS: Corporate Law; Banking; Securities.
McLarnon, Thomas P. ................ '61 '90 C.818 B.A. L.1136 J.D. Dep. Pub. Def.
**McLaughlin, Joseph M.**, (AV) ................ '28 '55 C.112 L.426 J.D. [McLaughlin&I.]
**McLaughlin, Lawrence J.**, (AV) ........ '52 '78 C.800 B.A. L.426 J.D. [McLaughlin&I.]
McLaughlin, Patrick W. .................. '50 '79 C&L.426 B.A., J.D. Asst. U.S. Atty.
McLaughlin, Pennie K. ....................... '61 '87 C.262 B.A. L.94 J.D. Pub. Def.

**McLaughlin and Irvin, (AV)**
**818 West Seventh Street, Suite 920, 90017**
**Telephone: 213-629-1414 Cable Address: "Loclinlaw" Telefacsimile: 213-629-3008**
**Members of Firm: Joseph M. McLaughlin; William B. Irvin; Lawrence J. McLaughlin.**
**General Business Matters. Litigation in State and Federal Courts. Labor and Employment Law. Employment Benefits Law, ERISA, Antitrust, Estates and Trusts.**
**Reference: Bank of America National Trust & Savings Assn. (Los Angeles Main Office).**
***See Professional Biographies, LOS ANGELES, CALIFORNIA***

McLean, Charles E., (A Law Corporation) .... '51 '76 C.112 B.A. L.809 J.D. [McLean&I.]
**McLean, David J.** ....................... '55 '82 C.902 B.A. L.276 J.D. [Latham&W.]
**McLean, Mark A.** ..................... '59 '87 C.94 B.A. L.602 J.D. [Ⓐ Troop M.S.&P.]
*PRACTICE AREAS: Labor and Employment Law.
McLean & Irvin ........................................... 23067 Ventura Blvd. Ste. 103
**McLean-Utley, Marsha**, (AV) ............... '— '65 C.112 A.B. L.1068 LL.B. [Daar&N.]
**McLeay, Margot I.** .......................... '60 '89 C&L.061 LL.B. [Barton,K.&O.]
*PRACTICE AREAS: General Civil Practice; Business Litigation; Banking Law; International Law; Insurance Coverage.
McLellan, Joseph F., (AV) ... '26 '51 C&L.477 B.S.M.E., J.D. 10877 Wilshire Blvd. (Pat.)

**McLeod, David S.** ............ '50 '75 C.800 B.A. L.767 J.D. [Dewey B.]
*PRACTICE AREAS: Litigation.
**McLoon, Daniel J.** ............ '56 '83 C.154 B.A. L.1068 J.D. [Jones,D.R.&P.]
**McLoughlin, John P.**, (AV) ............ '36 '63 C.363 B.S.S. L.309 LL.B. [Latham&W.]
McLurkin, Thomas C., Jr. ............ '54 '84 C.800 A.B. L.1095 J.D. Dep. City Atty.

**McMahan, Carl A., Law Offices of, (AV) '53 '83 C.763 B.A. L.464 J.D.**
**827 Moraga Drive, 90049**
**Telephone: 310-472-8078 Fax: 310-472-7014**
**(Also Of Counsel to Peter J. McNulty).**
***PRACTICE AREAS: Civil Trial; Product Liability Law; Medical Malpractice Law.**
**Of Counsel: Peter J. McNulty.**
**Medical Malpractice, Products Liability, Tort Law, Negligence, Complex Personal Injury Law. Civil Trials and Appeals in all State and Federal Courts.**
**Reference: City National Bank, Beverly Hills, California.**
*See Professional Biographies, LOS ANGELES, CALIFORNIA*

McMahon, Kathryn J. ............ '61 '86 C&L.800 B.S., J.D. 333 S. Hope St., 48th Fl.
**McMahon, M. Brian** ............ '42 '78 C.999 B.A. L.1068 J.D. [McMahon&S.]
*PRACTICE AREAS: Anti Trust; Complex Litigation; Oil; Energy; Pipeline Law.
**Mc Mahon, Raymond J.** ............ '67 '93 C.1109 B.A. L.1068 [A Bonne,B.M.O.&N.]
McMahon, Robert Coulfer ..... '12 '38 C.602 A.B. L.426 LL.B. 559 S. Beverly Glen Blvd.
**McMahon, Thomas M.** ............ '57 '82 C.93 B.A. L.1068 J.D. [Jones,D.R.&P.]

**McMahon & Spiegel**
**355 South Grand Avenue, Suite 3290, 90071-1591**
**Telephone: 213-628-9800 Fax: 213-628-9813**
**Members of Firm: M. Brian McMahon; Craig R. Spiegel; Marilyn K. Pace.**
**Business Litigation in Federal and State Courts and before Federal, State and Local Regulatory Agencies; Oil, Energy and Pipeline Law; Antitrust and Trade Regulation; Business Contracts.**
*See Professional Biographies, LOS ANGELES, CALIFORNIA*

McManus, Stephen M. ............ '54 '86 C.1077 B.A. L.426 J.D. Deputy Pub. Def.
**McMaster, Mary L.** ............ '60 '90 C.605 B.A. L.1066 J.D. [A Oliver,V.S.M.&L.]
*PRACTICE AREAS: Municipal Law; Land Use; Environmental; Eminent Domain.
**McMillan, Daniel D.** ............ '61 '88 C&L.426 B.S., J.D. [Jones,D.R.&P.]
McMillan, Leslie E. ............ '47 '72 C.426 B.A. L.1068 J.D. Dep. Pub. Def. IV
**McMorrow, Thomas R.** ............ '63 '89 C.112 B.A. L.273 J.D. [Manatt,P.&P.]
*PRACTICE AREAS: Government; Administrative Banking; General Corporate.
**McMurray, Randy H.** ............ '53 '86 C.1074 B.A. L.809 J.D. [A Robins,K.M.&C.]
*PRACTICE AREAS: Medical Malpractice; Product Liability Law; Professional Liability; Tort and Personal Injury.
**McMurry, Robert I.** ............ '47 '82 C.208 B.S. L.1068 J.D. [McClintock,W.B.R.R.&M.]
McNab, Cecil R. '58 '84 C.800 B.A. L.309 J.D.
(adm. in NY; not adm. in CA) 314 S. Muirfield Rd.‡

**McNally, H. Vincent, (AV) '41 '67 C&L.426 B.A., LL.B.**
**10920 Wilshire Boulevard Suite 650, 90024**
**Telephone: 310-208-7313 Fax: 310-824-1930**
**Insurance Bad Faith, Commercial and Business and Real Estate Litigation. Fidelity and Surety Law.**
*See Professional Biographies, LOS ANGELES, CALIFORNIA*

McNally, Kendra S. ............ '51 '77 C.597 B.A. L.37 J.D. Asst. U.S. Atty.
**McNamara, Edward J.** ............ '64 '91 C&L.800 B.A., J.D. [A Silver&F.]
*PRACTICE AREAS: General Civil Litigation; Employment; Probate.
McNamara, John J. (Jack) ............ '47 '74 C.116 B.A. L.800 J.D. 11752 San Vicente Blvd.
**McNamara, Kevin P.** ............ '68 '95 C.112 B.A. L.990 J.D. [A Berger,K.S.M.F.S.&G.]
**McNamara, Paul G.** ............ '56 '82 C.684 B.A. L.813 J.D. [O'Melveny&M.]
*PRACTICE AREAS: Civil Litigation; Defense Litigation; Federal Litigation.

**McNamara & Spira**
(See Santa Monica)

McNary, Carolyn L. ............ '44 '84 C.1077 B.A. L.809 J.D. Dep. Dist. Atty.
**McNatt, Christopher C., Jr.** ............ '66 '94 C.112 B.A. L.208 J.D. [A Berman,B.&B.]
**McNaughton, Kevin J.** ............ '52 '79 C.1138 B.A. L.1009 J.D. [Schaffer&L.]
McNeely, Milinda L. '57 '82 C.691 B.A. L.846 J.D.
Sr. V.P., Legal & Network TV Div., Paramount Pictures Corp.

**McNeil, Malcolm S., Law Offices of, (BV) '56 '83 C.1162 B.A. L.426 J.D.**
**5777 West Century Boulevard Suite 1475, 90045-7400**
**Telephone: 310-216-0747 Facsimile: 310-216-5736**
***LANGUAGES: French.**
***PRACTICE AREAS: Business Law; Dissolution of Marriage; Estate Planning; International Transactional Law; Emphasizing China.**
**—Alan M. O'Connor.**
**General Business, International Transactional Work, Corporate, Bankruptcy, Insurance, Real Estate, Commercial Court Litigation, Wills and Trusts and Family Law.**
*See Professional Biographies, LOS ANGELES, CALIFORNIA*

McNeill, Robert H., Jr. ............ '41 '79 C.887 B.A. L.809 J.D. [Ivie,M.&W.]
**McNevin, Christopher J.** ............ '58 '83 C.472 B.S. L.813 J.D. [Pillsbury M.&S.]
**McNicholas, Courtney Colleen** ............ '62 '87 C.112 B.A. L.464 J.D. [A Schaffer&L.]
**McNicholas, John P.**, (AV) ............ '36 '62 C.112 B.A. L.426 [McNicholas&M.]
*LANGUAGES: Spanish.
*REPORTED CASES: Rita M. v. Roman Catholic Archbishop (1986) 187 Cal. App. 1453; Spectrum Fin. Cos. v. Marconsult, Inc. (9th Cir. 1979) 608 F.2d 377, cert. den., 446 U.S. 936, 100 S.Ct. 2153, 64 L.Ed.2d 788; Deaile v. General Telephone Company (1974) 40 Cal.App.3d 841.
*PRACTICE AREAS: Jury Trials of Personal Injury and Business Tort Cases in State and Federal Courts.
**McNicholas, Patrick**, (BV) ............ '61 '86 C.767 B.M. L.464 J.D. [McNicholas&M.]
*PRACTICE AREAS: Bad Faith Law; Defective Products; Employment Discrimination; Malpractice Law; Personal Injury Law.

**McNicholas & McNicholas, (AV) BB**
**10866 Wilshire Boulevard, 90024**
**Telephone: 310-474-1582 FAX: 310-475-7871**
**Members of Firm: John P. McNicholas; Patrick McNicholas; David M. Ring. Associates: Mark K. Flores; Eric A. Gowey.**
**Jury Trials of Personal and Business Tort Cases in State and Federal Courts.**
*See Professional Biographies, LOS ANGELES, CALIFORNIA*

**Mc Niff, Terry**, (AV) ............ '54 '83 C.494 B.S. L.1068 J.D. [Goldman&K.]
*PRACTICE AREAS: Family Law; Palimony Defense; Premarital Planning; Civil Litigation.
McNitt, Robert C., Jr. ............ '65 '94 C.668 B.A. L.1065 J.D. 550 S. Hope St.
McNulty, James ............ '62 '88 C.719 B.A. L.1049 J.D. 11075 Santa Monica Blvd., 3rd Fl.
McNulty, Louisa J. ............ '51 '79 C.112 B.A. L.809 J.D. 3700 Wilshire Blvd.

**McNulty, Peter J., (AV) '54 '79 C.882 B.A. L.93 J.D. BB**
**827 Moraga Drive (Bel Air), 90049⊙**
**Telephone: 310-471-2707 Fax: 310-472-7014**
**(Also of Counsel to Carl A. McMahan).**
***REPORTED CASES: Herrera-Diaz vs. U.S. Department of Navy 845 F2d 1534 (9th Circuit 1988); Rodriguez vs. Superior Court of Kern County 221 Cal. App. 3d 1371.**
***PRACTICE AREAS: Civil Litigation; Trial Practice; Medical Malpractice; Products Liability Law; Personal Injury Law.**
**Associates: Michael L. Oran (A Professional Corporation). Of Counsel: John A. Alvarez (Resident, Gilroy Office); Robert M. Foote (Not admitted in CA); Robert P. Friedman; Carl A. McMahan.**
**Civil Litigation, Trial Practice, Medical Malpractice, Products Liability, Personal Injury and Commercial Torts.**

(This Listing Continued)

**McNulty, Peter J. (Continued)**
**Reference: City National Bank (Beverly Hills, California).**
**Gilroy, California Office: Suite F-2, 8352 Church Street. Telephone: 408-848-5900. Fax: 408-848-1391.**
**Aurora, Illinois Office: 8 East Galena Street.**
*See Professional Biographies, LOS ANGELES, CALIFORNIA*

**McNulty, Suzanne Naatz** ............ '60 '89 C.454 B.A. L.1049 J.D. [A Mendes&M.]
*LANGUAGES: Spanish.

**McNulty & Saacke**
(See Torrance)

**McNutt, Stephanie Berrington**, (AV) ..... '52 '81 C.112 B.A. L.809 J.D. [McKenna&C.]
**McNutt, Thomas B.**, (AV) ............ '49 '75 C.112 B.A. L.426 J.D. [Sedgwick,D.M.&A.]
**McOsker, John Erin** ............ '67 '93 C.602 B.A. L.770 J.D. [A Belcher,H.&B.]
**McOsker, Timothy B.** ............ '62 '87 C.602 B.A. L.1068 J.D. [Burke,W.&S.]
*PRACTICE AREAS: Municipal Law; Redevelopment Law; Planning Law; Airport Law.
**McPharlin, Eldon V.**, (AV) ............ '10 '37 C&L.352 B.A., J.D. [C Anderson,M.&C.]
McPhee, Karen J. ............ '51 '88 C.041 B.Comm. L.1068 J.D. [A Garfield,T.E.&T.]
**McPherson, Edwin F.**, (AV) ............ '57 '82 C.800 A.B. L.1049 J.D. [McPherson&K.]
*REPORTED CASES: People v. Von Villas, 10 Cal. App. 4th 201 (1992); Selleck v. Globe, 166 Cal. App. 3d 1123 (1985); Republic Corp. v. Superior Court (Delfino), 160 Cal.App. 3d 1253, 207 Cal.Rptr 241 (1984).
**McPherson, John E.** ............ '54 '86 C.763 B.A. L.1065 J.D. [Barger&W.]
*PRACTICE AREAS: General Corporate Law; Business Law; Insurance Regulation Law.
**McPherson, Mary E.** ............ '61 '86 C.914 B.A. L.602 J.D. [Tressler,S.M.&P.]

**McPherson & Kalmansohn, (AV)**
**1801 Century Park East, 24th Floor, 90067**
**Telephone: 310-553-8833 Fax: 310-553-9233**
**Members of Firm: Edwin F. McPherson; Mark E. Kalmansohn.**
**Entertainment and Business Litigation in all State and Federal Courts. Libel and Slander, Rights of Privacy and Publicity, Music, Copyright, Licensing, Sports, Insurance, Legal Malpractice.**
**Reference: City National Bank (Century City Office)**
*See Professional Biographies, LOS ANGELES, CALIFORNIA*

**McQueen, Carolyn Taylor** ............ '63 '89 C.811 B.A. L.1065 J.D. [A Gascou,G.&T.]
*PRACTICE AREAS: Fidelity; Suretyship; Construction Law.
McQueeney, Edward P. '— '78
C.107 B.A. L.569 J.D. Sr. Corp. Coun., Alpha Therapeutic Corp.
**McShane, James F.** ............ '54 '86 C.174 B.A. L.188 J.D. [Sheppard,M.R.&H.]
McShane, Kevin J. ............ '56 '84 C.260 B.S. L.809 J.D. 12100 Wilshire Blvd.
**McShane, Leslie J.** ............ '56 '89 C.103 B.A. L.426 J.D. [A Sheppard,M.R.&H.]
*PRACTICE AREAS: Commercial Finance Law; Secured Creditor Representation.
**McSwain, Valerie** ............ '— '95 C.911 B.A. L.112 J.D. [A Stevens,K.A.&H.]
**McSwiggin, Laura E.** ............ '58 '92 C.800 B.A L.426 J.D. [A Epport&R.]
**McTaggart, William V., Jr.** ............ '43 '78 C.588 A.B. L.426 J.D. [Parker,M.C.O.&S.]
*REPORTED CASES: Evans v. Safeco Life Ins. Co., 916 F.2d 1437 (9th Cir. 1990).
*PRACTICE AREAS: Business Litigation; Insurance Coverage/Bad Faith; ERISA; Banking and Finance Litigation.
McTernan, John T. ............ '10 '34 C.31 B.A. L.178 LL.B. 2226 Wayne Ave.‡
**McTigue, Martin "Kelly" J., Jr.** '59 '90
C.336 B.S. L.809 J.D. [A McClintock,W.B.R.R.&M.]
*SPECIAL AGENCIES: U.S. EPA; California Air Resources Board; Cal-EPA Department of Toxic Substances Control; South Coast Air Quality Management District; California Coastal Commission.
*PRACTICE AREAS: Environmental compliance; Air Quality; Hazardous Waste.
**McVeigh, Tanya S.** ............ '66 '92 C.800 B.A. L.1065 J.D. [A Gibson,D.&C.]
*PRACTICE AREAS: Antitrust; Real Estate Litigation.
**McVerry, Patricia A.**, (AV) ............ '53 '79 C.112 A.B. L.169 J.D. [C Katz,G.&F.]
*PRACTICE AREAS: Taxation; Estate Planning; Estate and Trust Administration.
McVey, David A., (BV) ............ '48 '74 C.193 B.A. L.665 J.D. [McVey&K.]⊙
McVey, Donald W., (AV) ............ '32 '63 C.112 B.S. L.1068 J.D. 10866 Wilshire Blvd.
McVey & Kim, A Prof. Corp., (BV) ............ 3700 Wilshire Blvd. (⊙Anaheim)
**McWatters, Thomas A., III** ............ '59 '86 C.827 B.S. L.851 J.D. [A Sidley&A.]
*PRACTICE AREAS: Commercial and Real Estate Litigation; Appellate Practice.
**McWilliams, Anne** ............ '59 '87 C.800 B.S. L.1065 J.D. [A R.A.Love]
**McWilliams, Timothy** ............ '63 '93 C.475 B.A. L.1148 J.D. [A Dennison,B.&P.]
**Meacham, Shelley R.** ............ '54 '94 C.1097 B.A. L.809 J.D. [A Gibson,D.&C.]
*PRACTICE AREAS: Legal Ethics and Professional Responsibility; Professional Liability.
**Mead, Leon F., II** ............ '62 '90 C.1232 B.A. L.426 J.D. [A Gibbs,G.L.&A.]
*PRACTICE AREAS: Commercial Litigation; Construction Law.
**Mead, Martin C.** ............ '65 '90 C.88 B.S. L.309 J.D. [A Paul,H.J.&W.]
**Mead, Roger B.** ............ '51 '79 C.309 A.B. L.569 J.D. [Folger L.&K.]⊙
**Meaders, Donald W.**, (AV) ............ '47 '73 C&L.309 A.B., J.D. [Pillsbury M.&S.]
**Meador, Vernon T., III** ..... '53 '78 C.112 B.A. L.1068 J.D. [McClintock,W.B.R.R.&M.]
*PRACTICE AREAS: Environmental Litigation; Toxic Torts; Insurance; Product Liability.
**Meadow, Cary M.** ............ '69 '94 C.846 B.B.A. L.800 J.D. [A Troop M.S.&P.]
*PRACTICE AREAS: Transactional Entertainment Law.
**Meadow, Judith L.** ............ '46 '79 C.1044 B.A. L.426 J.D. [A Russ,A.&K.]
*PRACTICE AREAS: Business Litigation; Trade Secrets; Unfair Competition; Trademark Infringement; Real Property.
**Meadows, David W.** ............ '57 '88 C.112 B.A. L.426 J.D. [A Andrews&K.]
*PRACTICE AREAS: Bankruptcy Law.
Meagher-Walker, Cynthia S. ............ '62 '91 C.05 B.A. L.809 J.D. Dep. Dist. Atty.
**Means, George M.** ............ '63 '88 C.999 B.A. L.1049 J.D. [Sidley&A.]
*PRACTICE AREAS: Real Estate and Business Transactions.
Mechanic, Harvey '48 '90 C.178 B.A. L.1009 J.D.
(adm. in NY; not adm. in CA) 3755 Watseka Ave., Apt. 10
Meck, John P. ............ '44 '72 C.426 B.A. L.1068 J.D. Sr. Coun., ARCO Products Co.
Mecom, William H. ............ '44 '80 C.112 A.B. L.1066 J.D. 1703 Armacost Ave.
Medearis, Miller, (AV) ............ '21 '49 C.999 L.192 J.D. [Medearis&G.]
Medearis & Grimm, (AV) ............ 1331 Sunset Boulevard
Medgyesy, Laura L. ..... '57 '89 C.597 B.A. L.800 J.D. Probate Div., Off. of the Co. Coun.
Medina, Agustin, Jr. ............ '46 '77 C.112 A.B. L.813 J.D. 221 N. Figueroa St.
**Medina, Maribel S.** '68 '96 C&L.112 B.A., J.D.
(adm. in NY; not adm. in CA) [A Fried,F.H.S.&J.]
**Medlen, William P.** ............ '59 '93 C.628 B.S. L.426 J.D. [Koslov&M.]
*PRACTICE AREAS: Civil Litigation; Construction Law; Insurance Law.
Mednick, Richard, (AV) ............ '33 '67 C.112 B.A. L.426 J.D. P.O. Box 241699
**Medvene, Edward M., (A Professional Corporation)**, (AV) '30 '57
C.831 A.B. L.659 LL.B. [Mitchell,S.&K.]
*PRACTICE AREAS: White Collar Crime Law; Antitrust Litigation; Securities Litigation.
Meehan, Richard J. ............ '37 '77 C.884 A.B. L.1221 J.D. 4477 Hollywood Blvd.
**Meeks, Larry M.** ............ '43 '68 C.902 B.A. L.178 LL.B. [Pircher,N.&M.]
*PRACTICE AREAS: Corporate Law; Securities Law.
**Meeks, Michael L.** ............ '68 '94 C.990 B.A. L.1068 J.D. [A McDermott,W.&E.]

**Meenan, Kevin**
(See Pasadena)

**Meer, Jon Douglas** ............ '63 '89 C.188 B.S. L.94 J.D. [A Paul,H.J.&W.]
**Meeske, William J.**, (AV) ............ '47 '72 C&L.477 B.A., J.D. [Latham&W.]
*PRACTICE AREAS: Securities; Antitrust; Commercial Litigation.
Meggelin, Maryann S. ............ '65 '90 C.674 A.B. L.1066 J.D. 11355 W. Olympic Blvd.

CAA293P

**Meghrouni, Michelle A.** . . . . . . . . . . '61 '87 C.112 B.A. L.767 J.D. [Hill,F.&B.]
*PRACTICE AREAS: Real Estate Finance; General Real Estate Law; Creditors' Rights.
**Mehlman, Gerald J.**, (AV) . . . . . '30 '54 C.477 B.A. L.976 LL.B. [C Stroock&S.&L.]
*PRACTICE AREAS: Estate Planning Law; Taxation; Probate Law; General Practice; Corporate Law.
**Mehlman, Rhonda H.** . . . . . . . . . . '63 '89 C.112 B.A. L.1068 J.D. [Shapiro,R.&C.]
*LANGUAGES: French.
*REPORTED CASES: Anaconda Minerals Co. v. Stoller Chemical Co., 990 F.2d 1175 (10th Cir. 1993).
*PRACTICE AREAS: Litigation; Franchise Law.
**Mehta, Steven G.** . . . . . . . . . . '67 '92 C.1077 B.A. L.464 J.D. [A Kussman&W.]
*REPORTED CASES: Fraker v. Sentry Life Insurance Co., 19 Cal.App. 4th 276 (1993).
*PRACTICE AREAS: Insurance Bad Faith Litigation; Products Liability; Medical Malpractice.
**Meier, Jennifer E.** . . . . . . . . . . '72 '96 C.378 B.S. L.1068 J.D. [A Irell&M.]
**Meier, Paul H.** . . . . . . . '57 '84 C.112 B.S. L.1066 J.D. [Lyon&L.] (See Pat. Sect.)
*PRACTICE AREAS: Intellectual Property.
Meiers, Barbara A. . . . . . . . . . . '42 '69 C.604 B.A. L.569 J.D. Mun. J.
**Meiers, Steven Alan**, (AV) . . . . . . '42 '69 C.800 B.A. L.569 J.D. [Gibson,D.&C.]
*PRACTICE AREAS: Corporate and Securities Law; General Limited and Limited Liability Partnerships; Mergers and Acquisitions; Consumer Product Safety Act.
Meigs, John V., Jr. . . . . . '69 '95 C.813 B.A. L.309 J.D. 300 S. Grand Ave., Suite 3000
**Meiners, Everett F.**, (AV) . . . . . '39 '65 C.112 B.A. L.1068 LL.B. [Parker,M.C.O.&S.]
*SPECIAL AGENCIES: National Labor Relations Board; Equal Employment Opportunity Commission; Agricultural Labor Relations Board; California Department of Fair Employment and Housing; American Arbitration Association.
*REPORTED CASES: (%italic; all Employment and Labor Law related cases %roman; ) Clayton v. UAW and ITT Gilfillan, United States Supreme Court, 451 U.S. 679 (1981); Bratton v. Bethlehem Steel Corp., 649 F.2d 658 (9th Cir. 1980); Sahara-Tahoe Corp. v. NLRB, 533 F. 2d 1125, (9th Cir. 1976).
*PRACTICE AREAS: Employment, Labor Law and Litigation on behalf of Management; Commercial UCC Law; International Law.
**Meinhardt, Robyn A.** . . . . . . . '53 '84 C.999 B.S.N. L.174 J.D. [A Foley L.W.&A.]
*PRACTICE AREAS: Health Care; Hospitals.
**Meisinger, Louis M.**, (AV) . . . . . '42 '68 C.112 B.A. L.1068 J.D. [Troop M.S.&P.]
*PRACTICE AREAS: Entertainment Litigation; Intellectual Property Litigation; Commercial Litigation.
**Mejia, Gabriela** . . . . . . . . . . '66 '92 C.112 B.A. L.1968 J.D. [A Andrews&K.]
*LANGUAGES: Spanish.
*PRACTICE AREAS: Litigation and International Law.
**Mejia, Susan Geier** . . . . . . . . '62 '89 C.1350 B.A. L.994 J.D. [A Burke,W.&S.]
*PRACTICE AREAS: Workers Compensation.
**Melamed, Agatha M.** . . . . . . . . . . '47 '72 C&L.966 B.A., LL.B. [Bryan C.]
*PRACTICE AREAS: Litigation Products Liability Law; Commercial Litigation; Labor.
**Melby, Donna D.**, (AV) . . . . . . '50 '79 C.112 B.A. L.426 J.D. [Sedgwick,D.M.&A.]
**Melden, Michele** . . . . . . . . . . '60 '88 C.914 B.A. L.309 J.D. [A Hooper,L.&B.]
*PRACTICE AREAS: Health Care Law.
Melendez, Martha L. . . . . . . . . '52 '87 C.976 B.A. L.1068 J.D. 700 S. Flower St.
Melgarejo, Monica S. . . . . . . . . '59 '85 C.813 B.A. L.800 J.D. Times Mirror Inc.
Meline, Ray, (BV) . . . . . . '33 '60 C.267 A.B. L.1066 LL.B. 12304 Santa Monica Blvd.
**Meline, Susanne L.** . . . . . . . . '67 '93 C.112 B.A. L.1065 J.D. [A Jones,D.R.&P.]
**Melissinos, C. John** . . . . . . . . '64 '90 C.188 B.A. L.1068 J.D. [A Weinstein&E.]
Melkonian, Harry G. . . . . . . '49 '75 C.696 B.A. L.569 J.D. 633 W. 5th St., Suite 1900
Meller, Sol . . . . . . . . . . . '46 '72 C.112 B.A. L.1068 J.D. 9000 W. Pico Blvd.‡
Mellinkoff, David, (AV) . . . . . '14 '39 C.813 B.A. L.309 LL.B. Univ. of Calif. Law School
Mells, Alexandra Kathryn '50 '84 C.112 B.A. L.426 J.D.
777 South Figueroa St., 37th Fl.
**Melnik, Roman** . . . . . . . . . . . '68 '95 C.309 A.B. L.178 J.D. [A Irell&M.]
*LANGUAGES: Russian, Belorussian.
Meloch, Lori Jo . . . . . . . . . '66 '91 C&L.800 B.S., J.D. 777 S. Figueroa St., 10th Fl.
Meloch, Sally Lynn . . . . . . . . . . '62 '87 C&L.800 B.S., J.D. Ass. U.S. Atty.
Melom, Halvor S. . . . . . . . . . . . . . . '51 '76 Sr. Dep. Co. Coun.
**Melton, Frank E.** . . . . . . . . . '54 '80 C.976 B.A. L.813 J.D. [Rintala,S.J.&R.]
Meltzer, Abraham C. . . . . . . . '— '92 C.309 A.B. L.1066 J.D. 445 S. Figueroa St.
**Meltzer, Laura J.** . . . . . . . . '56 '81 C.550 B.A. L.831 J.D. [Weiss,S.S.D.&S.]
*PRACTICE AREAS: Litigation; Civil Trials & Appeals; Negligence Law; Personal Injury Law; Products Liability Law.
Meltzer, Philip H. . . . . . . . . . . '10 '36 C&L.94 LL.B. 8844 S. Sepulveda Blvd.
**Meltzer, Stacey L.** . . . . . . . . '68 '95 C.112 B.A. L.426 J.D. [A Crosby,H.R.&M.]
**Melville, Hope E.** . . . . . . '51 '89 C.957 B.S. L.800 J.D. [A Lyon&L.] (See Pat. Sect.)
*PRACTICE AREAS: Patent, Trademark, Copyright, Unfair Competition; Intellectual Property.
**Memel, Sherwin L., (P.C.)**, (AV) . . . . '30 '55 C.112 B.A. L.1068 J.D. [Manatt,P.&P.]
*PRACTICE AREAS: Health Law.
**Menard, Ann Catherine** . . . . . . . '63 '91 C.112 B.A. L.426 J.D. [A O'Melveny&M.]
**Menard, Jean-Paul** . . . . . . . . . '59 '84 C.1077 B.A. L.426 J.D. [Stephens,B.&L.]
*LANGUAGES: French.
*PRACTICE AREAS: Business Litigation.
**Menard, Peter M.** . . . . . . . . . '53 '79 C.770 B.A. L.477 J.D. [Manatt,P.&P.]
*PRACTICE AREAS: Corporate Law; Securities Law; Technology Transfer.
Menaster, Albert J. . . . . . . . . . '48 '73 C&L.767 B.A., J.D. Dep. Pub. Def.
Mendelsohn, Aaron . . . . . . '51 '76 C.112 A.B. L.426 J.D. V.P., Bear, Stearns & Co., Inc.
**Mendelsohn, Lawrence S.** . . . . . '46 '74 C.1097 B.A. L.809 J.D. [Stockwell,H.W.&W.]
Mendelsohn, Phillip C. . . . . . . . '63 '90 C.976 B.A. L.1068 J.D. 1801 Century Park E.‡
**Mendelson, Jedd** '58 '83 C.188 B.S. L.477 J.D.
(adm. in NY; not adm. in CA) [Grotta,G.&H.]⊙
**Mendelson, Richard C.** . . . . . . . '54 '78 C.705 A.B. L.659 J.D. [Orrick,H.&S.]
*PRACTICE AREAS: Real Estate LAw.
Mendelson, Sanford H., (AV) . . . . . '40 '67 C.800 B.A. L.1068 J.D. 1509 Comstock Ave.
**Mendenhall, Kristin B.** . . . . . . '60 '92 C.813 A.B. L.425 J.D. [A Oliver,V.S.M.&L.]

**Mendes & Mount, L.L.P.**
**Citicorp Plaza, 725 South Figueroa Street Nineteenth Floor, 90017⊙**
**Telephone: 213-955-7700 Telecopy: 213-955-7725 Telex: 6831520 Cable Address: "MNDMT"**
**Members of Firm: William Blanc Mendes (1891-1957); Russell Theodore Mount (1881-1962); Charles G. Carluccio, III; James W. Hunt;—Joan E. Cochran; Mark S. Facer; Shalem A. Massey; Richard R. Nelson; Robert B. Schultz; Ty S. Vanderford. Associates: Garth W. Aubert; Felix Avila; John Francis Bazan; John G. Cahill; Alan H. Collier; Cory D. Esters; Jill Chiang Fung; Marlyn M. Gates; Renee A. Haupt; Lydia A. Hervatin; Mark R. Irvine; Charles S. Krolikowski; Kipp A. Landis; Erin K. McGonagle; Suzanne Naatz McNulty; Patrick T. Michael; Dennis Morris; David A. Robinson; Henry L. Sanchez; Yvonne T. Simon; Marla A. Smith.**
**General Practice. Insurance and Re-Insurance Law. Admiralty, Aviation and Space, Medical, Legal, Negligence, Products Liability and Public Utilities Law. Trials and Appeals.**
**New York, N.Y. Office: 750 Seventh Avenue. Telephone: 212-261-8000. Fax: 212-261-8750.**
**Newark, New Jersey Office: 1 Newark Center. Telephone: 201-639-7300. Fax: 201-639-7350.**

*See Professional Biographies, LOS ANGELES, CALIFORNIA*

**Mendez, John E.** . . . . . . . . . '57 '82 C.705 B.A. L.309 J.D. [Skadden,A.S.M.&F.]
Mendez, Robert G. . . . . . . . . '55 '80 C.668 B.A. L.1067 J.D. Paramount Pictures Corp.
**Mendler, Scott M.** . . . . . . . . . '57 '82 C.563 B.A. L.1068 J.D. [De Castro,W.&C.]
*PRACTICE AREAS: Taxation Law; Probate Law; Trusts Law; Estate Planning Law.

**Mendlin, Joyce S., Law Offices of, (AV) '54 '80 C.722 B.A. L.809 J.D.**
**1901 Avenue of the Stars Suite 1600, 90067-6080**
**Telephone: 310-553-5005 Telecopier: 310-553-5085**
**Federal and State Court Litigation and Civil Appeals, involving Business, Real Property, Insurance Coverage and Unfair Competition.**

*See Professional Biographies, LOS ANGELES, CALIFORNIA*

Mendonsa, John A. '40 '68 C.112 B.A. L.61 J.D.
Sr. Gen. Atty., Capital Cities/ABC, Inc.

Mendoza, Alberto C. . . . . . . . . . '34 '75 L.662 LL.B. 3545 Wilshire Blvd.‡
**Mendoza, Edward A.** . . . . . . . . . '56 '81 C.339 B.S. L.477 J.D. [Tuttle&T.]
*PRACTICE AREAS: Civil Litigation; Bankruptcy and Creditors' Rights; Accountants' Liability Litigation.
Mendoza, Gary S. . . . . . . . . . '55 '82 C.154 B.A. L.976 J.D. Calif. Dept. of Corp.
**Mendoza, Jerilyn López** . . . . . . '68 '96 C.813 A.B. L.112 J.D. [A McCutchen,D.B.&E.]
*PRACTICE AREAS: Commercial Litigation.
Mendoza, John A. . . . . . . . . '59 '89 C.112 B.A. L.398 J.D. 801 S. Grand Ave., 18th Fl.
**Mendoza, Lucy G.** . . . . . . . . . '66 '94 C.1097 B.S. L.809 J.D. [A Parker S.]
*LANGUAGES: Spanish and French.
*PRACTICE AREAS: General Practice.
**Mendoza, Robert G.** . . . . . . . . '53 '93 C.112 B.A. L.61 J.D. [A Robinson,D.&W.]
*LANGUAGES: Spanish.
*PRACTICE AREAS: Personal Injury; Insurance Defense; Product Liability.
Mendoza, Robert I. . . . . . . . . '63 '93 C.112 B.A. L.1066 J.D. 444 S. Flower St.
Mendoza, Ronald J. . . . . . . . . '41 '77 C.1077 B.A. L.1068 J.D. [Arredondo&M.]
**Menes, Barry A.**, (AV) . . . . . . . . '47 '73 C.1077 B.A. L.1049 J.D. [Menes]
*LANGUAGES: French.
*PRACTICE AREAS: Entertainment Law and Litigation; Business Law and Litigation; Intellectual Property Law.
**Menes, Paul I.** . . . . . . . . . . '55 '81 C.112 B.A. L.809 J.D. [Menes]
*PRACTICE AREAS: Entertainment Law and Litigation; Business Law; Intellectual Property Law.

**Menes Law Corporation, (AV) BB**
**1801 Century Park East, Suite 1560, 90067**
**Telephone: 310-286-1313 Cable Address: "Showlaw" Telex: 317948 MLC LSA Fax: 310-556-5695**
**Barry A. Menes; Paul I. Menes;—Marc M. Messineo. Of Counsel: John R. Climaco (Not admitted in CA); Edward M. Bernstein (Not admitted in CA).**
**Entertainment, Contracts, Entertainment and Business Litigation, Intellectual Property, Business and Corporate Law.**

*See Professional Biographies, LOS ANGELES, CALIFORNIA*

**Meneses, G. Arthur** . . . . . . . '58 '82 C.112 B.A. L.1068 J.D. [Berger,K.S.M.F.S.&G.]
**Meng, Eddy Ching-Liang** . . . . . . '67 '94 C&L.477 B.A., J.D. [A Milbank,T.H.&M.]
**Mengoli, Michael L.** . . . . . . . . '69 '94 C.112 B.A. L.1049 J.D. [A Selman B.]
*PRACTICE AREAS: Construction Defect; Casualty.
**Menjou, Christopher J.** . . . . . . . '66 '94 C&L.426 B.A., J.D. [A Brobeck,P.&H.]
*PRACTICE AREAS: Civil Litigation.
Menkel-Meadow, Carrie J. . . . . . '49 '74 C.66 A.B. L.659 J.D. Prof., U.C.L.A. Sch. of Law
**Menthe, Darrel C.** . . . . . . . . '71 '96 C.112 B.A. L.813 J.D. [A Fried,F.H.S.&J.]
*LANGUAGES: Russian, German, Spanish.
**Menton, James P., Jr.** . . . . . . . . '62 '92 C.597 B.A. L.112 J.D. [A Troy&G.]
*PRACTICE AREAS: Bankruptcy; Litigation.
**Menzer, Mitchell B.** . . . . . . . . '56 '84 C.31 B.A. L.1068 J.D. [O'Melveny&M.]
*PRACTICE AREAS: Real Estate Law; Environmental Law.
**Mequet, Sharon S.** . . . . . . . . . '65 '90 C.112 B.A. L.1065 J.D. [A Loeb&L.]
Mercado, Sonia . . . . . . . . . . '47 '84 C.54 B.A. L.1068 J.D. 777 S. Figueroa St.
Mercer, David T. . . . . . . . . '57 '83 C.112 B.S. L.1068 J.D. 11377 W. Olympic Blvd.
**Mercer, James W.**, (AV) . . . . . . '45 '71 C.477 A.B. L.145 J.D. [Hennigan,M.&B.]
Mercer, Thomas C., (AV) '40 '70 C.1077 B.A. L.426 J.D.
[Mercer&Z.] (⊙Orange, CA.)
Mercer and Zinder, A Professional Corporation, (AV)
4605 Lankershim Boulevard (North Hollywood) Penthouse Suite 840 (⊙Walnut Creek, Orange, San Diego & Ventura)

**Merchant & Gould, (AV)**
**Suite 400, 11150 Santa Monica Boulevard, 90025⊙**
**Telephone: 310-445-1140 Facsimile: 310-445-9031**
**Email: info@merchant-gould.com URL: http://www.merchant-gould.com**
**Raymond A. Bogucki; Gregory B. Wood; George Henry Gates, III; Charles Berman; Jai ho Rho;—Janice A. Sharp; Michael B. Farber; Sarah B. Adriano (Not admitted in CA); Victor G. Cooper; Ben M. Davidson; Albert F. Davis (Not admitted in CA); Karen S. Canady.**
**Patent, Trademark and Copyright Law, Licensing, Trade Secrets, Unfair Competition, Computer Law and Related Litigation.**
**Representative Clients: AT&T Global Information Solutions; Airtouch Communications; Bristol Myers Squibb Co.; University of California.**
**Minneapolis, Minnesota Office: Merchant, Gould, Smith, Edell, Welter & Schmidt, Professional Association, 3100 Norwest Center, 90 South 7th Street. Telephone: 612-332-5300. Facsimile: 612-332-9081.**
**St. Paul, Minnesota Office: Merchant, Gould, Smith, Edell, Welter & Schmidt, Professional Association, One Thousand Norwest Center, 55 E. 5th Street. Telephone: 612-298-1055. Facsimile: 612-298-1160.**

*See Professional Biographies, LOS ANGELES, CALIFORNIA*

**Meredith, Kristin E.** . . . . . . . . '57 '83 C.112 B.A. L.770 J.D. [Sedgwick,D.M.&A.]
**Mergenthaler, Michael** . . . . . . . . '60 '87 C.112 B.A. L.309 J.D. [A Levy,S.&L.]
*PRACTICE AREAS: Commercial Finance; Secured Transactions.
Meriwether, Charlotte G. . . . . . . '54 '80 C.1275 B.A. L.976 J.D. 13235 Old Oak Ln.
**Merkadeau, Stuart L.** . . . . . . . '61 '87 C.597 B.S.I.E. L.1068 J.D. [Graham&J.] (Pat.)
*PRACTICE AREAS: Intellectual Property Law.
Merkatz, Stephen Z. . . . . . . . . '46 '82 C.415 B.A. L.1136 Jewish Family Serv.
Merkin, Frederick N. . . . . . . . '46 '72 C.154 B.A. L.813 J.D. Sr. Asst. City Atty.
**Merliss, Joshua M.** . . . . . . . '51 '76 C.112 B.A. L.426 J.D. [A Gordon,E.K.G.F.&G.]
*PRACTICE AREAS: Personal Injury Law; Products Liability Law; Insurance Bad Faith Law.
**Merola, Frank A.** . . . . . . . . . '63 '88 C.276 B.S. L.1068 J.D. [Stutman,T.&G.]
*PRACTICE AREAS: Bankruptcy; Insolvency; Corporate Reorganization; Commercial Litigation.
Merrick, Jack C. . . . . . . . . '64 '89 C.178 B.A. L.800 J.D. 5820 Wilshire Blvd.
Merrick, Marc L. . . . . . . . . . '47 '74 C.112 B.A. L.1049 J.D. Dep. Dist. Atty.
**Merrick, Thomas R.** . . . . . . . . '64 '95 C.112 B.A. L.61 J.D. [A Murchison&C.]
*PRACTICE AREAS: Insurance Defense Litigation.
Merritt, Floyd I. . . . . . . . . . . '29 '54 C&L.981 LL.B. [Johnson,B.&M.]
Merritt, John B. . . . . . . '40 '68 C.112 A.B. L.911 J.D. Supvr. Atty., Atlantic Richfield Co.
**Merritt, Randy R.** . . . . . . . . . '57 '96 C.999 B.A. L.352 J.D. [A Latham&W.]
**Merritt, Sydney La Branche** . . . . '— '85 C.800 B.S. L.398 J.D. [La Follette,J.D.F.&A.]
*LANGUAGES: Spanish.
*PRACTICE AREAS: Medical Malpractice.
**Merritt, Tracy L.** . . . . . . . . . '62 '88 C.605 A.B. L.813 J.D. [A Arnold&P.]
*PRACTICE AREAS: Litigation.
**Merryman, Bryan A.** . . . . . . . . '62 '88 C.385 B.A. L.659 J.D. [C White&C.]
**Mersten, David R.** . . . . . . . '65 '90 C.112 B.A. L.1065 J.D. [A Greenberg G.F.C.&M.]
*PRACTICE AREAS: Civil Litigation.
**Mertens, Glen H.** . . . . . . . . . '56 '81 C.154 A.B. L.1066 J.D. [Ford&H.]
**Mesereau, Thomas A., Jr. (Professional Corporation)** '50 '79
C.309 B.A. L.1065 J.D. [Donahue&M.]
*PRACTICE AREAS: Complex Civil Litigation; Criminal; Healthcare Law.

**Meserve, Mumper & Hughes, (AV) BB**
**A Partnership**
**555 South Flower Street, 18th Floor, 90071-2319⊙**
**Telephone: 213-620-0300 Telecopier: 213-625-1930**
**Email: mmhla@ix.netcom.com**
**Members of Firm: Edwin A. Meserve (1863-1955); Shirley E. Meserve (1889-1959); Hewlings Mumper (1889-1968); Clifford E. Hughes (1894-1981); Dennett F. Kouri; Bernard A. Leckie (Irvine Office); Linda M. Lawson; David R. Eichten (San Diego and Irvine Offices); William E. von Behren; Joan E. Aarestad; Timothy A. Gravitt (Los Angeles, Irvine and San Diego Offices); E. Avery Crary (Irvine Office); Patricia A. Ellis; Lisa A. Roquemore (Irvine Office). Of Counsel: J. Robert Meserve (Irvine Office); Thomas E. Kellett; Julian Scheiner; Gary V. Spencer (Irvine Office). Associates: Joseph B.**

(This Listing Continued)

**Meserve, Mumper & Hughes (Continued)**
**McGinley (Irvine Office); Brian K. Mazen; Carol B. Burney; Geoffrey T. Tong; Christopher M. Stevens; Brian M. Holbrook; Matthew T. Currie; Kendra S. Meinert Hodson; Andrew L. Satenberg; Wendy C. Satuloff (Irvine Office); Becky J. Belke; Dennett F. Kouri, Jr.**
**General Civil and Trial Practice in all State and Federal Courts. Banking, Corporate, Real Estate, Labor, Life Insurance, Probate, Estate Planning, Family Law and Bankruptcy.**
**Irvine, California Office: 2301 Dupont Drive, Suite 410. Telephone: 714-474-8995. Telecopier: 714-975-1065.**
**San Diego, California Office: 701 "B" Street, Suite 1080. Telephone: 619-237-0500. Telecopier: 619-237-0073.**
*See Professional Biographies, LOS ANGELES, CALIFORNIA*

Meshack, Betty L. .............'58 '82 C.811 A.B. L.813 J.D. 210 W. Temple St., 19th Fl.
**Mesisca, Patrick A., Jr.**, (AV) ..........'48 '73 C.800 B.A. L.426 J.D. [Gilbert,K.C.&J.]
**Mesnick, Wendy M.** ..........'67 '93 C.112 B.A. L.1067 J.D. [A Greenberg G.F.C.&M.]
*PRACTICE AREAS: Litigation.

**Messina, Lalafarian & Manning**
**(See Glendale)**

**Messineo, Marc M.** .................................'68 '93 C.93 B.A. L.990 J.D. [A Menes]
*PRACTICE AREAS: Entertainment Law and Litigation; Intellectual Property Law; Business Law.
**Messinger, Leonard D.** ....................'53 '79 C.831 B.A. L.809 J.D. [Robbins,B.&C.]
*REPORTED CASES: Dolco Packaging Corp. v. Creative Industries, Inc. 1 USPQ 2d 1538 (C.D.CA. 1986) Gassaway v. Business Machine Security, 9 USPQ 2d 1572 (C.D.CA. 1988).
*PRACTICE AREAS: Trademark Law; Copyright Law; Transactions Law; Litigation; Unfair Competition Law.
**Messinger, Robert F.**......................'57 '94 C.29 B.A. L.339 J.D. [A Burke,W.&S.]
*PRACTICE AREAS: Municipal Law.
Meszaros, Liora ......................'44 '88 C.999 B.A. L.809 J.D. 4700 Wilshire Blvd.
Metson, Philip A. ..................'50 '75 C.112 B.A. L.800 J.D. 1901 Avenue of The Stars
Metter, Devera ........................'42 '79 C.1077 B.A. L.426 J.D. 1670 Corinth Ave.
Metzger, Paul ..................................'64 '91 C.112 B.A. L.426 J.D. Dep. Pub. Def.
**Metzger, Robert S.**, (AV) ................'50 '77 C.478 B.A. L.276 J.D. [Troop M.S.&P.]
*PRACTICE AREAS: Litigation; Government Contracts Law.
**Metzner, Margot A.**........................'51 '76 C.597 B.A. L.228 J.D. [Morrison&F.]
*PRACTICE AREAS: Business Litigation; Insurance Coverage; Environmental Litigation.
Mevis, Willis H. ..........................'21 '50 C.352 B.S.C. L.1065 LL.B. 314 W. 1st St.
Meyberg, Leonard J., Jr., (AV) ........'40 '66 C.154 B.A. L.1068 LL.D. [L.J.Meyberg,Jr.]
Meyberg, Leonard J., Jr., The Law Office of, (AV) ................ 2029 Century Park E.
**Meyer, Bruce D.**, (AV) ........................'45 '71 C&L.339 B.A., J.D. [Gibson,D.&C.]
*PRACTICE AREAS: Mergers and Acquisitions; Corporate and Securities; Banking and Savings and Loan Associations.
**Meyer, Catherine D.**, (AV) ............'51 '79 C.104 A.B. L.597 J.D. [Pillsbury M.&S.]
**Meyer, Charles D.**, (AV) ...............'56 '80 C.477 B.A. L.1068 J.D. [Goldman&K.]
*REPORTED CASES: Marvin v. Marvin, 122 Cal. App. 3d 871, 176 Cal. Rptr. 555 (1981); Watkins v. Watkins, 143 Cal. App. 3d 651, 192 Cal. Rptr. 54 (1983).
*PRACTICE AREAS: Real Estate; Cable Television; Premarital Planning; General Business.
**Meyer, David C.** ..............................'62 '89 C.112 B.A. L.800 J.D. [Gorry&M.]
*PRACTICE AREAS: Corporate Law; Entertainment and the Arts; Real Property.
**Meyer, David G.**.............................'57 '84 C.813 B.A. L.1068 J.D. [Howrey&S.]
*PRACTICE AREAS: White Collar Criminal Defense; Commercial Litigation.
**Meyer, David J.** ..................'51 '86 C.1350 B.S. L.112 J.D. [A Graham&J.] (Pat.)
Meyer, David S. ........................'57 '82 C.531 B.S. L.800 J.D. 660 S. Figueroa St.
**Meyer, Gary A.** ..........................'53 '80 C.112 B.A. L.1068 J.D. [Parker,M.C.O.&S.]
*REPORTED CASES: Los Angeles Chemical Company v. Superior Court, 226 Cal. App. 3d 703 (1990). Torrance Redevelopment Agency v. Solvent Coating Company, 763 F. Supp. 1060 (C.D. Cal. 1991).
*PRACTICE AREAS: Environmental Civil, Criminal and Administrative Litigation; Environmental/Hazardous Materials Management and Compliance.
Meyer, Irving .......................'41 '83 C&L.1190 B.S., J.D. 650 S. Grand Ave.
**Meyer, Jeffrey P.**, (AV) ..............'51 '77 C.569 B.A. L.1292 J.D. [Meyer&Assoc.]
*PRACTICE AREAS: Bankruptcy; Reorganization; Commercial Litigation.
**Meyer, Joshua A.** ......................'69 '95 C.1169 B.A. L.1068 J.D. [A Kinsella,B.F.&T.]
*LANGUAGES: Danish.
*PRACTICE AREAS: Litigation.
**Meyer, Keith A.** .........................'57 '82 C.154 B.A. L.426 J.D. [Shapiro,H.&M.]
Meyer, Kimberly Howland .....'58 '84 C.813 B.A. L.1068 J.D. 11377 W. Olympic Blvd.
**Meyer, Lisa Helfend**, (AV) .........................'57 '82 C.112 B.A. L.426 J.D. [Zolla&M.]
*LANGUAGES: Spanish.
*PRACTICE AREAS: Family Law.
**Meyer, Michael E.**, (AV) ..................'42 '68 C.966 B.S. L.145 J.D. [Pillsbury M.&S.]
**Meyer, Robert A.**, (AV) .........................'50 '75 C.30 B.A. L.276 J.D. [Loeb&L.]
*PRACTICE AREAS: Litigation.
**Meyer, Ronald K.** ...........................'51 '76 C&L.813 A.B., J.D. [Munger,T.&O.]
**Meyer, Steven E.** ...................'61 '89 C.112 B.A.B.S. L.770 J.D. [Lewis,D.B.&B.]
*PRACTICE AREAS: Civil Litigation; Real Estate; Bankruptcy Litigation.

**Meyer & Associates, (AV)**
**1875 Century Park East, Suite 600, 90067**
**Telephone: 310-551-2045 Facsimile: 310-551-1416**
**Jeffrey P. Meyer.**
**Bankruptcy, Litigation.**
*See Professional Biographies, LOS ANGELES, CALIFORNIA*

Meyerhoff, Samuel .........................'39 '65 C.112 L.426 LL.B. 13401 S. Main St.‡
Meyers, Barry M. ......................'53 '90 C.1077 B.A. L.940 J.D. 4700 Wilshire Blvd.
Meyers, Burton ....................'36 '62 C.112 A.B. L.1068 J.D. 1801 Ave. of the Stars
Meyers, Felicia R. ..................'64 '94 C.1077 B.A. L.1148 J.D. [A Garfield,T.E.&T.]
**Meyers, Herbert D.** ............................'52 '77 C.112 B.A. L.1068 J.D. [B Davis&F.]
*LANGUAGES: Swedish.
*PRACTICE AREAS: Real Estate; Corporate; Environmental.
**Meyers, Jeffrey A.** .........'66 '94 C.112 B.A. L.800 J.D. [Celebrezze&W.] (⊙San Fran.)
**Meyers, Jeffrey G.** ...............'43 '68 C.1019 B.A. L.1009 LL.B. [Meyers,B.&M.]⊙
*PRACTICE AREAS: Product Liability; Coverage; Reinsurance Issues; Professional Liability.
Meyers, John E., (BV) ...................'28 '68 C.999 L.809 LL.B. 2049 Century Park E.
**Meyers, Kenneth S.** ...................'56 '81 C.668 B.A. L.1066 J.D. [Alschuler G.&P.]
**Meyers, Myron, (P.C.)**, (AV) .......'28 '55 C.112 B.A. L.1068 J.D. [B Jeffer,M.B.&M.]
*PRACTICE AREAS: Real Estate Acquisition and Finance; Loan Documentation and Workouts; Joint Ventures; Foreign Investment in U.S.; Arbitration of Real Estate and Construction Disputes.
Meyers, Patrick T. ........................'42 '74 C.112 B.A. L.846 J.D. Princ. Dep. Co. Coun.

**Meyers, Bianchi & McConnell, A Professional Corporation, (AV)**
**11859 Wilshire Boulevard, Fourth Floor, 90025-6601⊙**
**Telephone: 310-312-0772 Cable Address: "Trialaw" Facsimile: 310-312-0656**
**Jeffrey G. Meyers; John W. McConnell III; Martin E. Pulverman; Elizabeth A. Kooyman;—Patrick D. Bingham; Frederick S. Reisz; Elizabeth S. Agmon; James M. Fowler; Carol J. Knoblow; Heidi M. Yoshioka. Of Counsel: James S. Bianchi; Harris Zeitzew; Andrew Feldman (Not admitted in CA); Carole D. Bos (Not admitted in CA).**
**General Civil and Trial Practice in all State and Federal Courts. Products Liability, Professional Malpractice Defense. Construction, Insurance, Reinsurance and Business Law.**
**Reference: Bank of America (Century City Branch).**
**New York, New York Office: 400 Madison Avenue. Telephone: 212-509-1663. Facsimile: 212-269-5927.**
*See Professional Biographies, LOS ANGELES, CALIFORNIA*

Meyerson, Lawrence C., (AV) ......'47 '72 C.112 B.A. L.426 J.D. 2121 Ave. of the Stars

Meymarian, Sharon L. ..................'68 '93 C.112 B.A. L.813 J.D. 601 S. Figueroa St.
**Meza, Matthew S.** ........................'62 '87 C.112 A.B. L.477 J.D. [A Shumaker&S.]
*PRACTICE AREAS: Real Property Law; Corporate Law; Insurance Regulation.
Mezzacappa, Ann L. ......................'51 '82 C.112 B.A. L.1137 J.D. [A Chase,R.D.&B.]
**Michael, Allison R.** .....................'60 '87 C.112 A.B. L.1068 J.D. [Littler,M.F.T.&M.]
*LANGUAGES: Spanish.
**Michael, Ann** ...................'60 '92 C.623 B.B.A. L.616 J.D. [A Harrington,F.D.&C.]
*PRACTICE AREAS: Civil Litigation; Construction Defect.

**Michael, Dale R. '42 '68 C.433 B.S. L.178 J.D.**
**6300 Wilshire Boulevard Suite 1630, 90048**
**Telephone: 213-782-1027 Fax: 213-651-4868**
***LANGUAGES: Spanish.**
**General Civil Litigation, Appellate Practice in all State and Federal Courts. Insurance Bad Faith, Employment Discrimination, Sexual Harassment, Wrongful Termination.**
*See Professional Biographies, LOS ANGELES, CALIFORNIA*

**Michael, Lisa Goodwin** ...............'63 '91 C.800 B.A. L.893 J.D. [A Foley L.W.&A.]
*PRACTICE AREAS: Civil Litigation; Labor and Employment Law.
**Michael, Patrick T.** ..........................'67 '93 C.112 B.A. L.990 J.D. [A Mendes&M.]

**Michaelis, Montanari & Johnson, A Professional Law Corporation**
**(See Westlake Village)**

**Michaels, Connie L.** .......................'61 '87 C.112 B.A. L.800 J.D. [Littler,M.F.T.&M.]
**Michaels, Franklin, Jr.**, (AV) ...............'53 '82 C.494 B.S. L.800 J.D. [B Lim,R.&K.]
*PRACTICE AREAS: Bankruptcy; Bankruptcy and Insolvency Law.
**Michaels, Janice M.** ........................'63 '90 C.112 B.A. L.990 J.D. [A Knopfler&R.]
*PRACTICE AREAS: Construction Defect Litigation; Insurance Coverage; Business Litigation.
**Michaels, Lawrence A., (A Professional Corporation)** '55 '82
C.112 B.A. L.800 J.D. [Mitchell,S.&K.]
*PRACTICE AREAS: Labor Law; Employment Law.
**Michaelson, Alvin S.**, (AV) ...............'39 '64 C.178 B.A. L.309 J.D. [Michaelson&L.]
*LANGUAGES: Spanish.
**Michaelson, Sherryl Elise** .....................'52 '85 C.846 B.A. L.569 J.D. [Hedges&C.]

**Michaelson & Levine, (AV)**
**1901 Avenue of the Stars, Suite 1708, 90067**
**Telephone: 310-278-4984 Fax: 310-286-9969**
**Members of Firm: Alvin S. Michaelson; Janet I. Levine. Associate: Brenda Ligorsky. Of Counsel: Roger L. Cossack.**
**Trials and Appeals in State and Federal Courts, specializing in White Collar Criminal Defense, and the representation of professionals accused of crimes.**
**Reference: City National Bank (Century City Branch).**
*See Professional Biographies, LOS ANGELES, CALIFORNIA*

**Michail, Maureen M.** .........................'71 '96 C.112 B.A. L.426 J.D. [A Daniels,B.&F.]
Michalski, James W. .............................'67 '95 C.112 B.A. L.309 J.D. [A Kindel&A.]
**Michel, Allen L.**, (AV) .........'50 '75 C.112 B.A. L.1068 J.D. [Berger,K.S.M.F.S.&G.]
**Michel, Hayes F.** ..................'63 '88 C.597 B.S. L.1068 J.D. [A McCambridge,D.&M.]
**Michel, Sydne Squire** ..................'— '95 C.112 B.A. L.426 J.D. [A Kirkland&E.]
*PRACTICE AREAS: Litigation; White Collar Criminal Defense.
**Michela, Patrick E.** ..................................'66 '94 C.112 B.A. L.990 J.D. [A Pick&B.]
Michelena, Nestor A. ...........................................'41 '70 L.1148 J.D. 523 W. 6th St.
**Michelena, Patricia M.** ..........................'66 '92 C.112 B.A. L.426 J.D. [A Cummins&W.]
*PRACTICE AREAS: Insurance Litigation; Insurance Subrogation.
**Michelena-Monroe, Mary T.** .........'64 '89 C.112 B.A. L.426 J.D. [A Pillsbury M.&S.]
Michels, Barry C. ..........................'54 '79 C.309 A.B. L.1066 J.D. 2211 Corinth Ave.
Michels, Philip ..........................'44 '73 C.112 B.A. L.1068 J.D. 924 Westwood Blvd.
**Michelson, Louis E.** ....................'56 '88 C.145 B.A. L.1068 J.D. [Sanders,B.G.S.&M.]

**Michino, Mitch Moriyasu, (AV) '42 '73 C.112 B.A. L.61 J.D.**
**Suite 313, 880 West First Street, 90012**
**Telephone: 213-680-2533 Telecopier: 213-680-3832**
***LANGUAGES: Japanese.**
***PRACTICE AREAS: International Corporate Law.**
**Of Counsel: James W. O'Neil.**
**International Corporate Law, Immigration and Naturalization.**
*See Professional Biographies, LOS ANGELES, CALIFORNIA*

**Michlovich, Lawrence A.** ...............'59 '86 C.339 B.S. L.477 J.D. Coun., Teledyne, Inc.
**Mick, Stephen R.** ...............'63 '87 C.688 B.S. L.659 J.D. [Loeb&L.] (See Pat. Sect.)
*PRACTICE AREAS: Intellectual Property; Litigation.
Mickell, Stacey C. ............................'58 '86 C.112 B.A. L.800 J.D. Jud. Atty., App. Ct.
**Mickelson, Angela A.**, (AV) ..............'53 '81 C.112 B.A. L.1068 J.D. [Hooper,L.&B.]
*PRACTICE AREAS: Hospital Law; Healthcare Law.
Micon, Gary ....................'57 '85 C.1077 B.A. L.1065 J.D. Sr. Jud. Atty., Ct. of App.
Midgley, Timothy J. ..............................................'49 '86 C&L.061 B.Sc [A Manes&W.]
Mietus, Edmund R. ..........................................'16 '40 C&L.436 B.S., LL.B. Dep. Dist. Atty.
**Migdal, Paul L.**, (AV) ..........................'36 '62 C.209 B.Sc. L.1068 J.D. [B Katz,G.&F.]
*PRACTICE AREAS: Entertainment Law; Motion Pictures and Television.
**Mihaly, Stephen A.** ........................'57 '84 C.813 B.S. L.1049 J.D. [A Mihaly,S.&M.]
**Mihaly, Zoltan M.**, (AV) ............................................'26 '62 C&L.061 J.D. [Mihaly,S.&M.]

**Mihaly, Schuyler & Mitchell, (AV)**
**An Association including Professional Corporations**
**Suite 1201, 1801 Century Park East, 90067**
**Telephone: 213-879-5600; 310-556-3500 Telecopier: 310-556-0413; 310-284-7982**
**Zoltan M. Mihaly; Rob R. Schuyler, A Professional Corporation; J. H. Mitchell, Jr., A Professional Corporation;—Stephen A. Mihaly; William R. Hess.**
**General Civil and Trial Practice. Tax, Corporation, Real Property, Oil and Gas, Estate Planning, Trust, Probate, Immigration, Nationality and International Business Law.**
**Representative Clients: Aerojet-General Corp.; Air France; American Hospital Supply Corp.; Applied Magnetics Corp.; Bell & Howell; Consulate General of Switzerland, Los Angeles; Elf Petroleum Corporation-U.S.A.; Exchange & Investment Bank, Geneva, Switzerland; U.T.A. French Airlines.**
*See Professional Biographies, LOS ANGELES, CALIFORNIA*

**Mihanovic, Mark J.** ..............................'60 '86 C&L.477 A.B., J.D. [McDermott,W.&E.]
*PRACTICE AREAS: Corporate Law; Securities; Finance.
Mihell, Monica Ariel ..................................'52 '84 C.1168 L.1148 J.D. [Farley&M.]
Mihlon, Sally A. .............................'51 '80 C.30 B.S. L.273 J.D. 355 S. Grand Ave.
**Mihlsten, George J.**, (AV) ..........................'53 '80 C&L.800 B.S., J.D. [Latham&W.]
Mikesell, Daniel D., Jr. ...................'39 '71 C.813 A.B. L.809 J.D. Princ. Dep. Co. Coun.
Mikulicich, Nikola M., Jr. ........'72 '93 C.1131 B.A. L.112 J.D. 1055 W. 7th St., 20th Fl.
Mikuni, Gary S. .........................................'51 '80 C.605 B.A. L.770 J.D. 200 S. San Pedro St.
**Milam, Margaret L.** ..........................'63 '88 C.112 B.A. L.1068 J.D. [A Pillsbury M.&S.]
**Milani, John F.** ..............................'68 '94 C.112 B.A. L.1065 J.D. [A O'Melveny&M.]
**Milani, Justine Witt** ....................'70 '95 C.112 B.A. L.1065 J.D. [A Sheppard,M.R.&H.]
*PRACTICE AREAS: Labor and Employment.
Milas, Martin H., (AV) .........................'42 '74 C.589 B.A. L.1065 J.D. Sr. Asst. Atty. Gen.

**Milbank, Tweed, Hadley & McCloy, (AV)** ⊞
**601 South Figueroa Street, 90017⊙**
**Telephone: 213-892-4000 Fax: 213-629-5063 ABA/net: MilbankLA**
**Resident Partners: Kenneth J. Baronsky; Paul S. Aronzon; Edwin F. Feo; David C. L. Frauman; C. Stephen Howard; David A. Lamb; Ted Obrzut; Eric H. Schunk; Peter P. Wallace; Karen B. Wong. Of Counsel: Alan M. Fenning. Senior Counsel: Neil J Wertlieb; Harry L. Usher. Resident Associates:**

(This Listing Continued)

CALIFORNIA—LOS ANGELES MARTINDALE-HUBBELL LAW DIRECTORY 1997

**Milbank, Tweed, Hadley & McCloy (Continued)**

**Taline A. Aharonian; Dino Barajas; Devan D. Beck; Amy Bersch; Scott M. Brown; Gregory L. Call; Veronica Davies; Michael Dayen; Jose M. Deetjan; Ada E. Ejikeme; R. Lee Garner III; Lawrence B. Gill; David J. Impastato (Not admitted in CA); Patricia K Jones; Nicholas L. Kondoleon; Melainie K. Mansfield; Allan T. Marks; Jeffrey D. McFarland; Eddy Ching-Liang Meng; John A. Mitchell; Fred Neufeld; Gloria M. Noh; William J. Peters; Eric R. Reimer; Kendrick F. Royer; Eileen Driscoll Rubens; Deborah Ruosch; Roger K. Smith; Scot Tucker; Scott Vick; Paul T. Wrycha; Andrew H.T. Wu.**
**General Practice.**
**New York, New York Office: 1 Chase Manhattan Plaza, 10005. Telephone: 212-530-5000. Fax: 212-530-5219. ABA/net: MilbankNY; MCI Mail: MilbankTweed.**
**Midtown Office: 50 Rockefeller Plaza, 10020. Telephone: 212-530-5800. Fax: 212-530-0158.**
**Washington, D.C. Office: International Square Building, Suite 1100, 1825 Eye Street, N.W., 20006. Telephone: 202-835-7500. Fax: 202-835-7586. ABA/net: MilbankDC.**
**Tokyo, Japan Office: Nippon Press Center Building, 2-1, Uchisaiwai-cho 2-chome, Chiyoda-ku, Tokyo 100. Telephone: 011-81-3-3504-1050. Fax: 011-81-3-3595-2790, 011-81-3-3502-5192.**
**London, England Office: Dashwood House, 69 Old Broad Street, London, EC2M 1Q5. Telephone: 011-44-171-448-3000. Fax: 011-44-171-448-3029.**
**Hong Kong Office: 3007 Alexandra House, 16 Charter Road. Telephone: 011-852-2571-4888. Fax: 011-852-2840-0792, 011-8522-845-9046. ABA/net: MilbankHK.**
**Singapore Office: 14-02 Caltex House, 30 Raffles Place, 048622. Telephone: 011-65-534-1700. Fax: 011-65-534-2733. ABA/net: EDNANG.**
**Moscow, Russia Office: 24/27 Sadovaya-Samotyochnya, Moscow, 103051. Telephone: 011-7-501-258-5015. Fax: 011-7-501-258-5014.**
**Jakarta, Indonesia Correspondent Office: Makarim & Taira S., 17th Floor, Summitmas Tower, Jl, Jend. Sudirman 61, Jakarta. Telephone: 011-62-21-252-1839 or 1272. Fax: 011-62-21-252-4740 or 2750.**

***See Professional Biographies, LOS ANGELES, CALIFORNIA***

Milberg, Jonathan P. ................ '45 '77 C.112 B.A. L.426 J.D. 3660 Wilshire Blvd.
Milberg Weiss Bershad Hynes & Lerach, LLP, (AV)
355 South Grand Avenue Suite 4170 (⊙San Diego & San Fran., Calif. & New York, N.Y.)
Milder, Alvin S. ..................... '32 '62 C.870 B.S. L.309 LL.B. 134 Greenfield Ave.
Milgrom, Daniel R. .................... '44 '69 C.477 B.A. L.1068 J.D. Off. of Pub. Def.
Milken, Lowell J., (AV) ................ '48 '73 C.112 B.S. L.1068 J.D. 844 Moraga Dr.
Milkowski, Louis '48 '76 C.93 B.S.B.A. L.564 J.D.
(adm. in NY; not adm. in CA) Brown, Kraft & Co.
**Millar, Sanford I.**, (AV) .................. '49 '75 C.800 A.B. L.809 J.D. [Rubinstein&P.]
*PRACTICE AREAS: Taxation Law; Real Property Law; Corporation Law; International Transactions.
**Millard, L. Raymond, (P.C.)**, (AV) .... '27 '58 C.112 A.B. L.1068 J.D. [Millard,P.H.&C.]
*PRACTICE AREAS: Insurance Defense; Civil Litigation.
**Millard, Mark Evans** ................ '60 '94 C.990 B.S. L.809 J.D. [🄰 Engstrom,L.&L.]
**Millard, Neal S.**, (AV) ..................... '47 '72 C.112 A.B. L.145 J.D. [White&C.]
Millard, Richard H., (AV) '41 '67 C.112 B.S. L.1068 LL.B.
12100 Wilshire Blvd., 15th Fl.

**Millard, Pilchowski, Holweger & Child, P.C., (AV)** BR
**A Partnership including Professional Corporations**
**12th Floor, 655 South Hope Street, 90017-3211**
**Telephone: 213-627-3113 Fax: 213-623-9237**
**Email: mphc@loop.com**
**L. Raymond Millard (P.C.); Thomas S. Pilchowski (P.C.); Marie Polizzi Holweger; Bradford T. Child;—Bradley P. Childers; Elizabeth T. Fitzgerald; Jeniffer A. Wilder; Russell W. Schatz, Jr.**
**General Civil Trial Practice in all Courts. Insurance, Personal Injury, Products Liability, Malpractice and Corporation Law.**

***See Professional Biographies, LOS ANGELES, CALIFORNIA***

Millen, Mathew L., (AV) ............ '47 '74 C.516 B.S. L.383 J.D. 10880 Wilshire Blvd.
**Miller, Adam D.** .................... '58 '85 C.966 B.S. L.209 J.D. [🄰 Engstrom,L.&L.]
**Miller, Angela C.** .................... '70 '96 C.112 B.A. L.813 J.D. [🄰 Folger L.&K.]⊙
**Miller, Bradley Scott** ................. '70 '96 C&L.477 B.A., J.D. [🄰 Orrick,H.&S.]
Miller, Bruce Joel .................... '56 '81 C.813 A.B. L.1068 J.D. 3601 Stewart Ave.
Miller, Carol G. ............... '49 '83 C.273 B.A. L.809 J.D. Sr. Jud. Atty., Ct. Of App.
**Miller, Craig D.** .......................... '68 '93 C.605 A.B. L.426 J.D. [🄰 Manatt,P.&P.]
*PRACTICE AREAS: Corporate Law; Financial Services.
**Miller, Cynthia C.** ................ '69 '96 C.112 B.A. L.800 J.D. [🄰 Bonne,B.M.O.&N.]
Miller, Dale S. ............................ '50 '78 C.112 A.B. L.990 J.D. [Miller&H.]
Miller, Dane Lee, (BV) ............ '49 '79 C.112 A.B. L.1066 J.D. 500 Citadel Dr.
**Miller, David H.**, (AV) ........ '53 '78 C.112 B.A. L.1068 J.D. Sr. Coun., Bank of Amer.
Miller, David R. '46 '72 C.112 B.A. L.426 J.D.
Chmn. of the Bd., Miller Entertainment Enterprises
**Miller, Donald C.** ......................... '62 '87 C.106 B.A. L.800 J.D. [🄰 Sandler&R.]
Miller, Donald P. ................ '42 '67 C.390 A.B. L.1009 LL.B. 4700 Wilshire Blvd.
Miller, Donn B., (AV) ................... '29 '54 C.611 B.A. L.477 J.D. 400 S. Hope St.
**Miller, Earle** ........................ '60 '84 C.309 A.B. L.145 J.D. [🄱 Brobeck,P.&H.]
*PRACTICE AREAS: Commercial Litigation; Banking Litigation; Employment Law.
Miller, Edward A. ..................... '60 '86 C.112 B.A. L.800 J.D. Dep. Dist. Atty.
**Miller, Elissa D.** .................. '55 '85 C.112 B.A. L.809 J.D. [🄱 Sulmeyer,K.B.&R.]
*PRACTICE AREAS: Bankruptcy Law; Business Litigation; Entertainment Litigation.
**Miller, Elizabeth J.** '66 '91
C.112 B.A. L.426 J.D. [🄰 Harrington,F.D.&C.] (⊙San Francisco)
**Miller, Emily B.** ...................... '46 '88 C.821 A.B. L.1068 J.D. [🄰 Pircher,N.&M.]
*LANGUAGES: French, German and Greek.
Miller, Gary N. ..................... '47 '78 C.1097 B.A. L.398 J.D. Princ. Dep. Co. Coun.
**Miller, Gavin**, (AV) ................... '26 '55 C&L.309 A.B., LL.B. [🄱 Heller E.W.&M.]
**Miller, Gerald J.** ................. '55 '85 C.112 A.B. L.1067 J.D. [🄰 Ginsburg,S.O.&R.]
*PRACTICE AREAS: Business Litigation.
Miller, Halvor T., Jr. ................... '32 '67 C.112 B.A. L.329 LL.B. 3307 W. 43rd Pl.
Miller, Ira J., (AV) ............................ '35 '65 C&L.800 B.S., LL.B. [Miller&C.]
**Miller, J. Clark** ..................... '65 '95 C.800 B.S. L.893 J.D. [🄰 Paul,H.J.&W.]
**Miller, James W.** ...................... '48 '74 C.112 B.A. L.426 J.D. [Musick,P.&G.]
*PRACTICE AREAS: Litigation.
**Miller, Jason T.** ...................... '71 '96 C.347 B.S. L.1068 J.D. [🄰 Latham&W.]
**Miller, Jay M.** ............................ '67 '93 C.477 B.A. L.1068 J.D. [🄰 Manatt,P.&P.]
*PRACTICE AREAS: Litigation.
**Miller, Jeffrey A.** ........................ '63 '89 C.831 B.A. L.569 J.D. [🄰 Jones,D.R.&P.]
Miller, Jeffrey A. ................. '69 '94 C.112 B.A. L.1068 J.D. 500 S. Grand Ave.
Miller, Jeremy N. ............................ '53 '77 C.339 B.A. L.597 J.D. [Miller&M.]
**Miller, Jesse D.**, (AV) ................... '30 '59 C.112 B.S. L.309 LL.B. [Fulbright&J.]
*PRACTICE AREAS: Antitrust; Securities Litigation; Products Liability; Litigation.
Miller, Joan M ....................... '50 '87 C.1131 B.A. L.46 J.D. 308 W. 54th St.
Miller, Joanne ............................ '64 '90 C.112 B.A. L.464 J.D. [Bolden&M.]
Miller, John R. .......................... '54 '93 C.1042 B.A. L.809 J.D. 505 Shatto Pl.
**Miller, John R.** ............... '64 '89 C.112 B.A. L.426 J.D. [🄰 Sonnenschein N.&R.]
*PRACTICE AREAS: Litigation; Insurance Coverage.
**Miller, John S., Jr.** ......................... '49 '77 C.1042 B.S. L.1068 J.D. [Cox,C.&N.]
*REPORTED CASES: Concrete Pipe and Products of California v. Construction Laborers Pension Trust for Southern California — U.S.— , 113 S.Ct. 2264 (1993); Tippett v. Terich, 37 Cal. App. 4th 1517 (1995).
*PRACTICE AREAS: Labor Relations Law; Employee Benefits Law; Construction Law.
**Miller, Joseph A., (P.C.)** ............ '55 '80 C.976 B.A. L.1065 J.D. [Monteleone&M.]
*PRACTICE AREAS: Litigation.

Miller, Joseph M., (AV) ............. '40 '65 C.309 A.B. L.1066 J.D. [Seyfarth,S.F.&G.]
**Miller, Judith E.** ..................... '59 '89 C.1036 A.B. L.800 J.D. [🄰 Robinson,D.B.&K.]
*PRACTICE AREAS: Bankruptcy Law.
**Miller, Karen Poston** ..................... '62 '90 C.763 B.S. L.476 J.D. [🄰 McKenna&C.]
*PRACTICE AREAS: Government Contracts; Litigation.
**Miller, Katharine Araujo** ............. '55 '87 C.678 B.S. L.1148 J.D. [Brown,W.&C.]
*PRACTICE AREAS: Municipal Law; Civil Litigation.
**Miller, Kenneth** .................. '60 '86 C.112 B.A. L.426 J.D. [Leland,P.S.F.M.&M.]
*PRACTICE AREAS: Creditor's Remedies, Bankruptcy; Business Litigation.

**Miller, Kimberly A. '53 '81 C.112 B.A. L.809 J.D.**
**10960 Wilshire Boulevard 10th Floor, 90024**
**Telephone: 310-445-4600 Fax: 310-444-6420**
**General Civil Trial, Personal Injury, Products Liability, Employment Law, Sexual Discrimination, FELA, Jones Act and Family Law.**

***See Professional Biographies, LOS ANGELES, CALIFORNIA***

Miller, Linda J. ..................... '49 '80 C.112 B.A. L.426 J.D. 10452 Lindbrook Dr.
Miller, Linda Landry ..................... '56 '85 C.766 B.A. L.464 J.D. 601 S. Figueroa
Miller, Lisa Clare Lerner ........... '61 '85 C.264 B.A. L.1338 J.D. Screen Actors Guild
Miller, Loren, Jr. ............................ '37 '63 C.629 B.A. L.426 LL.B. Supr. Ct. J.
**Miller, Louis R., III** .... '47 '72 C.208 B.S.B.A. L.1068 J.D. [Christensen,M.F.J.G.W.&S.]
*PRACTICE AREAS: Trials and Litigation.
**Miller, Marna F.** ..................... '64 '94 C.112 B.A. L.1148 J.D. [🄰 Shapiro,R.&C.]
Miller, Michael D., (AV) ............... '50 '76 C.1169 B.A. L.813 J.D. 3611 Motor Ave.
**Miller, Milton A.** ............................ '54 '79 C.813 A.B. L.309 J.D. [Latham&W.]
**Miller, Milton Louis**, (AV) ........ '32 '56 C.112 B.A. L.1068 J.D. [🄱 Levinson,M.J.&P.]
**Miller, Mona D.** ............................. '53 '77 C.188 A.B. L.813 J.D. [🄱 Blanc W.J.&K.]
*LANGUAGES: French, Russian.
*PRACTICE AREAS: Business Litigation.
**Miller, Nancy Kennerly** ................. '54 '80 C.813 B.A. L.1049 J.D. [Paul,H.J.&W.]
**Miller, O'Malley M.**, (AV) ............... '51 '76 C.813 B.A. L.800 J.D. [Munger,T.&O.]
**Miller, Patricia Y.** ....................... '53 '88 C.884 B.S.N. L.809 J.D. [🄰 Epstein B.&G.]
*PRACTICE AREAS: Health Law.
**Miller, Philip H.** ............................ '54 '94 C.882 B.S. L.262 J.D. [🄰 Irell&M.]
Miller, Philip S. .................... '40 '67 C&L.800 A.B., J.D. Principal Dep. Co. Coun.
**Miller, Randall A.** ............................ '58 '84 C.1044 B.S. L.464 J.D. [Long&L.]
**Miller, Richard T.** ................... '56 '91 C.705 B.A. L.809 J.D. [🄰 A.Wasserman]
*PRACTICE AREAS: Aviation Law; Insurance Law; Personal Injury/Insurance Defense.
**Miller, Rita J.**, (AV) ......................... '47 '79 C.183 A.B. L.426 J.D. [Munger,T.&O.]
**Miller, Rita Mongoven** .................. '63 '88 C.958 B.S. L.770 J.D. [🄰 Chapman&G.]
*PRACTICE AREAS: General Negligence; Products Liability; Insurance Bad Faith.
**Miller, Robert A., Jr.** ................... '54 '84 C.585 B.S.B.A. L.426 J.D. [Paul,H.J.&W.]
**Miller, Robert F.** ...................... '59 '86 C.154 B.A. L.464 J.D. [🄰 McKenna&C.]
*LANGUAGES: French.
*PRACTICE AREAS: Construction; Government Contracts.
Miller, Robert L., (AV) ..................... '40 '66 C.605 A.B. L.426 LL.B. [Miller&M.]
Miller, Robert Stephen ................ '56 '85 C.813 B.A. L.1068 J.D. Dep. Dist. Atty.
Miller, Robin M. ......................... '60 '87 C.112 B.A. L.464 J.D. Dep. City Atty.
Miller, Robyn L. '62 '87 C.668 B.A. L.1068 J.D.
Corp. Atty., Daniel, Mann, Johnson & Mendenhall
**Miller, Roy D.**, (AV) .................. '29 '55 C.668 B.A. L.813 J.D. [🄱 Gibson,D.&C.]
*PRACTICE AREAS: Taxation; Estate Planning; Trust and Estate Administration.
**Miller, Samuel R.**, (AV) ................ '48 '75 C.976 B.A. L.1066 J.D. [Folger L.&K.]⊙
*LANGUAGES: Spanish.
**Miller, Scott R.** ............................. '58 '83 C.546 B.S. L.800 J.D. [Riordan&M.]
**Miller, Seth A.** ...................... '61 '86 C.178 B.A. L.588 J.D. [🄰 Proskauer R.G.&M.]
**Miller, Stacey A.** ......................... '66 '92 C.605 A.B. L.990 J.D. [🄰 Tharpe&H.]
Miller, Stephen D., (AV) ............. '38 '63 C.902 B.A. L.276 LL.B. 550 S. Hope St.
Miller, Stephen K., (AV) ..................... '41 '67 C.112 B.S. L.1068 J.D. [Aran&M.]
**Miller, Steven L.** ......................... '64 '89 C.112 B.A. L.990 J.D. [🄰 White&C.]
**Miller, Terry L.** ............ '48 '79 C.1159 B.S. L.879 J.D. [Oppenheimer P.S.] (⊙Irvine)
*PRACTICE AREAS: Intellectual Property.
**Miller, Theodore N.**, (AV⊙) ............... '42 '67 C.477 B.A. L.976 LL.B. [Sidley&A.]
*PRACTICE AREAS: Antitrust Law; Securities Law; Complex and Commercial Litigation.
Miller, Thomas E. ......................... '39 '68 C&L.477 B.A., J.D. Dep. Dist. Atty.
**Miller, Warren K.**, (AV) ................. '44 '73 C.934 B.A. L.623 J.D. [Valensi,R.&M.]
*PRACTICE AREAS: Business; Business Tort Litigation; Real Estate Litigation; Construction Litigation.
Miller, Wayne J. ........................... '56 '82 C.813 B.A. L.608 J.D. [Miller&M.]
Miller, William McD., (AV) .......... '21 '49 C.813 A.B. L.800 LL.B. One Wilshire Blvd.
**Miller, William McD., III**, (AV) ......... '45 '71 C.629 B.A. L.426 J.D. [Musick,P.&G.]
*PRACTICE AREAS: Litigation.
Miller & Clearwaters, (AV) ........................................... 5250 W. Century Blvd.
Miller Gordon, Beth ..................... '62 '88 C.228 B.A. L.94 J.D. [🄰 Gittler,W.&B.]
Miller & Holguin ...................................... 1801 Century Park E., 7th Fl.

**Miller, Howard B.**
**(See El Segundo)**

**Miller Law Offices, The**
**(See Studio City)**

Miller & Miller, (AV) ........................................................ 3418 W. 6th St.
Miller & Miller, A Professional Corporation ...................... 2049 Century Park East

**Miller, Mitchell R.**
**(See Beverly Hills)**

**Miller & Nolan, Incorporated**
**(See Howrey & Simon)**

**Miller, Richard F., A Professional Corporation**
**(See Pasadena)**

**Millett, Patricia A.** .............. '65 '90 C.886 B.S. L.893 J.D. [🄰 Greenberg G.F.C.&M.]
*PRACTICE AREAS: General Commercial Litigation.
Millhouse, Keith F. ..................... '61 '86 C&L.990 B.S., J.D. 190 N. La Salle St.

**Millikan and Thomas**
**(See Pasadena)**

Milliken, Sarah C. ..................... '50 '82 C.668 B.A. L.1148 J.D. 2029 Century Park E.
Milliken, W. Dickerson, (AV) ....... '29 '54 C.197 A.B. L.174 LL.B. 2029 Century Pk., E.
**Millington, Kimberly A.** ....... '63 '93 C.112 B.A. L.809 J.D. [🄰 Breidenbach,B.H.H.&H.]
*LANGUAGES: French, Spanish and Italian.
Millington, Scott T. ...................... '60 '88 C.112 B.A. L.1068 J.D. Dep. Dist. Atty.
**Millman, Robert F.** ............... '49 '74 C.966 B.A. L.188 J.D. [Littler,M.F.T.&M.]
Mills, James A. '19 '54 C&L.912 B.A., LL.B.
(adm. in MI; not adm. in CA) 5330 Keniston Ave.‡
Mills, John W. ................... '49 '74 C&L.800 A.B., J.D. 8726 S. Sepulveda Blvd.
**Mills, John W., III** ........................... '60 '90 C.968 B.A. L.245 J.D. [Feder&M.]
*PRACTICE AREAS: Insolvency Law; Commercial Litigation; Debtor Creditor Law; Creditors Rights Law.
Mills, Linda G. ...................... '57 '83 C.112 B.A. L.1065 J.D. Univ. of Calif.
Mills, Michael E., (AV) ................... '45 '75 C.1077 B.A. L.809 J.D. [Mills&M.]
Mills, Patricia Hughes, (AV) ............... '57 '82 C&L.823 A.B., J.D. [Mills&M.]

CAA296P

**Mills, Rex L.** ..........'66 '95 C.112 B.A. L.426 J.D. [Ⓐ Manning,L.B.&B.]
Mills, Robert J. .......... '58 '91 C.1131 B.A. L.990 J.D. 2027 Harpers Way
**Mills, Robert Parker**, (AV) ....... '45 '71 C&L.502 B.A., J.D. [Bacon&M.] (⊙Pasadena)
*PRACTICE AREAS: General Civil Trial Litigation; Insurance Defense Law; Sexually Transmitted Disease (AIDS) Litigation; Employment Law; Construction Defect Litigation.
**Mills, Sherylle** ..........'69 '95 C.696 B.M. L.1066 J.D. [Ⓐ Katten M.&Z.]
*PRACTICE AREAS: General Civil Litigation; Copyright.
**Mills, Stephan A.** .......... '55 '80 C.112 B.A. L.1068 J.D. [Zemanek&M.]
*PRACTICE AREAS: Real Estate, Business and Construction Litigation (Trials and Appeals); Secured Transactions.
**Mills, William K.** .......... '58 '82 C.309 A.B. L.1068 J.D. [Ⓒ Shumaker&S.]
Mills & Mills, (AV) .......... 11755 Wilshire Blvd., 9th Fl.
**Milmeister, Dana** .......... '66 '93 C.112 B.A. L.800 J.D. [Ⓐ Alschuler G.&P.]
**Milner, Marla** .......... '67 '95 C&L.800 B.S., J.D. [Ⓐ Katz,H.S.&K.]
*PRACTICE AREAS: Corporate.
Milner, Marylin Jenkins, (AV) .......... '50 '79 C.914 A.B. L.426 J.D. 801 Figueroa St.
**Miloknay, Paul M.** .......... '65 '91 C.976 B.A. L.1068 J.D. [Ⓐ Sheppard,M.R.&H.]
**Milstead, Kathryn B.** ..........'59 '85 C.560 B.A. L.809 J.D. [Ivanjack&L.]
*PRACTICE AREAS: Real Estate; Commercial Litigation.
**Milstein, Mark** .......... '64 '91 C.112 B.A. L.1049 J.D. [Verboon,W.H.&P.]
*PRACTICE AREAS: Civil Litigation; Construction Defect Law.
**Mims, Stewart S.** ..........'47 '73 C.154 B.A. L.1065 J.D. [MacArthur,U.H.&M.]
*PRACTICE AREAS: Business Litigation; Professional Liability Litigation; Arbitration; Corporate Dissolutions; Partnership Dissolutions.
**Minaki, Haruki** .......... '62 '90 C.674 B.A. L.800 J.D. [Ⓐ Paul,H.J.&W.]
Minato, Susan M. ........ '62 '88 C.228 B.A. L.1068 J.D. Utility Workers Union-Local 132
**Minchella, Michael F., (P.C.)**, (AV) .......'45 '70 C&L.426 B.S., J.D. [Monteleone&M.]
*PRACTICE AREAS: Business Litigation; Commercial Litigation; Alternative Dispute Resolution; Construction Law; General Civil Trial Practice, State and Federal Courts.
**Mindel, Nancy J.** ..........'61 '87 C&L.800 B.S., J.D. [Harrington,F.D.&C.]
*REPORTED CASES: Span, Inc. v Associated International Insurance Co. 227 Cal. App. 3d 463 (1991).
*PRACTICE AREAS: Insurance Coverage Law; Appellate Law.
**Mindel, Steven A.** ..........'59 '85 C.112 B.A. L.800 J.D. [Weinstock,F.M.&K.]
*PRACTICE AREAS: Family Law; General Civil Litigation.
**Minden, Michael A.** .......'68 '95 C.112 B.A. L.426 J.D. [Ⓐ Christensen,M.F.J.G.W.&S.]
*PRACTICE AREAS: Civil Litigation; Entertainment Litigation.
**Mines, Amand K.** ..........'65 '91 C.945 B.A. L.990 J.D. [Ⓐ Sedgwick,D.M.&A.]
**Ming, Robert D.** ..........'— '96 C.1232 B.A. L.990 J.D. [Ⓐ Morgan,L.&B.]
Minikes, Morton .......... '38 '63 C.112 B.A. L.800 LL.B. [M.Minikes]
Minikes, Morton, A Law Corporation .......... 12100 Wilshire Blvd.
Mink, Allen, (AV) .......... '31 '57 C.861 B.A. L.1068 LL.B. [Mink&M.]

**Mink, Lyle R., Law Offices of, (AV) '44 '72 C.1077 B.S. L.426 J.D.**
**Suite 1700 2029 Century Park East, 90067**
**Telephone: 310-553-1010 Fax: 310-284-5743**
***REPORTED CASES: Kimmel v. Goland, 51 Cal. 3d 202 (1990); Hospital Building Co. v. Trustees of Rex Hospital, 425 U.S. 738 (1976); Fish v. Los Angeles Dodgers Baseball Club, 56 Cal. App. 3d 620 (1976); Paramount Convalescent Center, Inc. v. Department of Health Care Services, 15 Cal. 3d 489 (1975).**
**General Civil Trial and Appellate Practice in all State and Federal Courts.**
***See Professional Biographies, LOS ANGELES, CALIFORNIA***

Mink and Molloy, A Professional Corporation, (AV)
Suite 600, 12100 Wilshire Boulevard
**Minor, John A., III** .......... '51 '77 C.813 B.A. L.1066 J.D. [Ⓒ Arnelle,H.M.W.&G.]
*PRACTICE AREAS: Real Estate; Banking; Corporate Law.
Minsky, Bernard W. ..........'21 '49 C.112 B.S. L.800 J.D. 950 S. Grand Ave., 4th Fl.
Mintie, Nancy J. ..........'54 '79 C.1131 B.A. L.1068 J.D. Dir., Inner City Law Ctr.
**Minton, Carl**, (AV) ..........'28 '55 C.813 B.A. L.800 J.D. [Minton,M.&R.]
*PRACTICE AREAS: Corporation Law; Estate Planning; Trust and Probate Law; Real Estate Law; Business Law.

**Minton, Minton and Rand LLP, (AV) BB**
**510 West Sixth Street, 90014**
**Telephone: 213-624-9394 Fax: 213-624-9323**
**Members of Firm: Carl W. Minton (1902-1974); Carl Minton; David E. Rand.**
**Corporation Law, Estate Planning, Trust and Probate Law, Real Estate Law. General Business Practice.**
**Reference: Bank of America National Trust & Savings Assn. (Seventh & Flower Office, Los Angeles, Calif.).**
***See Professional Biographies, LOS ANGELES, CALIFORNIA***

Mintz, David ..........'59 '84 C.112 A.B. L.1065 J.D. Dep. Dist. Atty.
Mintz, Francis ..........'22 '54 C&L.966 B.B.A., J.D. 2751 Anchor Ave.‡
**Mintz, Jeffrey H.** ..........'70 '94 C.112 B.A. L.1068 J.D. [Ⓐ Alschuler G.&P.]
Mintz, Leslie S. ..........'63 '89 C.112 B.A. L.800 J.D. 11601 Wilshire Blvd.
**Mintz, Marshall G.**, (AV) .......... '47 '72 C.800 B.A. L.1068 J.D. [Kelly&L.]
*PRACTICE AREAS: Securities Law; Business Law; Real Estate Litigation.
Mintzer, Stewart A. .......... '40 '66 Dep. Pub. Def.
**Mira, Mary-Claire** ..........'— '86 C.426 L.809 J.D. [Gilbert,K.C.&J.]
*PRACTICE AREAS: Insurance Defense; Estate Planning.
Miranda, Roland ..........'58 '89 C.112 B.A. L.1097 J.D. 1055 W. 7th St.
**Mirell, Douglas E.**, (AV) ..........'56 '80 C.154 B.A. L.1067 J.D. [Loeb&L.]
*PRACTICE AREAS: Litigation; Constitutional and Civil Rights Law; Media Law; Entertainment; Intellectual Property and Franchising Litigation.
**Mirhashemi, Shervin** .......... '69 '95 C.112 B.A. L.800 J.D. [Ⓐ Charlston,R.&W.]
Mirisch, Donald I. '46 '72 C.1036 A.B. L.309 J.D.
V.P., Hanna-Barbera Productions, Inc.
Mirisch, Robert A. .......... '38 '67 C.659 B.S. L.800 J.D. 10940 Wilshire Blvd.
**Mirman, Alan M.**, (AV) ..........'51 '75 C.112 B.A. L.1068 J.D. [Horgan,R.B.&C.]
*PRACTICE AREAS: Business, Banking and Real Property Litigation; Secured Transactions; Bankruptcy.
Mirras, Joanne K. ..........'68 '92 C.112 B.S. L.1049 J.D. 355 S. Grand Ave., 31st Fl.
Misener, William A. ..........'48 '76 C.101 B.A. L.1137 J.D. Dep. Pub. Def.
**Mishik, Michael G.** .......... '64 '94 C.871 B.S. L.1068 J.D. [Ⓐ Latham&W.]
Misraje, Nathan ..........'53 '80 C.112 B.A. L.1065 J.D. 6500 Wilshire Blvd.
**Missan, Richard S.**, (AV) '33 '59 C&L.976 B.A., J.D.
(adm. in NY; not adm. in CA) [Ⓒ J.M.Donovan] (⊙New York)
*PRACTICE AREAS: Corporate Law; Securities Law; Litigation; Business Law.
**Mitchel, George C.**, (AV) ..........'27 '54 C&L.800 B.S., LL.B. [Ⓒ Booth,M.&S.]
**Mitchel, Steven M.** ..........'61 '87 C.112 B.A. L.464 J.D. [Booth,M.&S.]
**Mitchell, Briane Nelson** ..........'53 '78 C.178 A.B. L.336 J.D. [Shapiro,H.&M.]
Mitchell, Bruce E. ..........'50 '79 C.800 B.A. L.813 J.D. Comr., L.A. Supr. Ct.
**Mitchell, Burton A., (P.C.)**, (AV) ... '53 '78 C.1138 B.B.A. L.276 J.D. [Jeffer,M.B.&M.]
*PRACTICE AREAS: Taxation; Estate Planning; Closely-held Entities.
**Mitchell, C. Geoffrey** .......... '53 '79 C&L.575 B.A., J.D. [Brown,W.&C.]
*PRACTICE AREAS: Real Estate Law; Real Estate Finance; Business Law; Partnership Law.
**Mitchell, Dennis**, (AV) ..........'56 '84 C.813 B.A. L.1068 J.D. [Kirsch&M.]
*PRACTICE AREAS: Civil Litigation; Business Law; Real Estate Law.
Mitchell, Faith I. ..........'57 '84 C.36 B.A. L.767 J.D. State Dept. of Transp.
**Mitchell, J. H., Jr., A Professional Corporation**, (AV) '24 '51
C&L.800 B.S., LL.B. [Mihaly,S.&M.]
Mitchell, Jerrilavia Jefferson '59 '85
C.800 B.S.B.A. L.1068 J.D. Assoc. Coun., Auto. Club of Southern Calif.
**Mitchell, John A.** .......... '— '95 C.1365 B.A. L.145 J.D. [Ⓐ Milbank,T.H.&M.]
Mitchell, John Arai ..........'— '94 C.1365 B.A. L.145 J.D. 601 S. Figueroa St.
Mitchell, Johnnie M. .......... '42 '91 C.98 M.A. L.1136 J.D. Coun., Dept. of Indus. Rel.
**Mitchell, Judith M.** ..........'41 '77 C.679 B.A. L.426 J.D. [Huang&M.]
*LANGUAGES: German.
*REPORTED CASES: Aroney vs. California Horse Racing Board (1983) 145 Cal.App.3d 928; Valdez vs. Cory (1983) 140 Cal.App.3d 116; Jabola vs. Pasadena Redevelopment Agency (1981) 125 Cal.App.3d 931; Bunker vs. City of Glendale (1980) 111 Cal.App.3d 325.
*PRACTICE AREAS: Commercial Litigation; Arbitration; Appellate and Writ Practice; Litigation with Government Agencies.
**Mitchell, Larry W.** ..........'46 '76 C.1077 B.A. L.426 J.D. [Ⓒ Graham&J.]
*PRACTICE AREAS: Insurance Coverage Law; Primary and Excess Insurance; Reinsurance; Environmental Insurance; Civil Litigation.
Mitchell, Mark '65 '93 C.276 B.S. L.800 J.D.
Assoc. Coun., Writers Guild of Amer., West, Inc.
Mitchell, Michael R. .......... '42 '69 C.853 A.B. L.309 LL.B. 200 N. Larchmont
Mitchell, Milton, (AV) ..........'05 '28 C&L.800 LL.B. 1901 Ave. of the Star‡
Mitchell, Sandra K. .......... '59 '84 C.770 B.S.C. L.1097 J.D. Legal Aid Found. of L.A.
**Mitchell, Susan A.** ..........'54 '81 C&L.494 B.A., J.D. [McKenna&C.]
**Mitchell, Suzanne Harmatz** .......... '52 '80 C.813 B.A. L.1067 J.D. [Ⓐ Shapiro,H.&M.]
Mitchell, Theresa Eileen ..........'59 '88 C.800 B.A. L.809 J.D. Dep. Dist. Atty.
**Mitchell, Walter R.** .......... '55 '86 C.1044 B.A. L.1068 J.D. [Levy,S.&L.]
*PRACTICE AREAS: Commercial Finance; Secured Transactions; General Business Law.

**Mitchell, Robert E.**
**(See Norwalk)**

**Mitchell, Silberberg & Knupp LLP, (AV) BB**
**A Partnership including Professional Corporations**
**11377 West Olympic Boulevard, 90064**
**Telephone: 310-312-2000 Fax: 310-312-3100**
**Members of Firm: Shepard Mitchell (1908-1979); M. B. Silberberg (1908-1965); Guy Knupp (1907-1970); Arthur Groman (A Professional Corporation); Chester I. Lappen (A Professional Corporation); Harold Friedman (A Professional Corporation); Allan E. Biblin (A Professional Corporation); Edward M. Medvene (A Professional Corporation); Russell J. Frackman (A Professional Corporation); Thomas P. Lambert (A Professional Corporation); Eugene H. Veenhuis (A Professional Corporation); Philip Davis (A Professional Corporation); Roy L. Shults (A Professional Corporation); Steven M. Schneider (A Professional Corporation); Marvin Leon (A Professional Corporation); Patricia H. Benson (A Professional Corporation); Arthur Fine (A Professional Corporation); Hayward J. Kaiser (A Professional Corporation); Deborah P. Koeffler (A Professional Corporation); John M. Kuechle (A Professional Corporation); William L. Cole (A Professional Corporation); Richard S. Hessenius (A Professional Corporation); Joseph Ciasulli (A Professional Corporation); Frida Popik Glucoft (A Professional Corporation); Jean Pierre Nogues (A Professional Corporation); David Wheeler Newman (A Professional Corporation); Roger Sherman (A Professional Corporation); Alan L. Pepper (A Professional Corporation); John E. Hatherley (A Professional Corporation); Lawrence A. Ginsberg (A Professional Corporation); Daniel M. Petrocelli (A Professional Corporation); Mark A. Wasserman (A Professional Corporation); Allen J. Gross (A Professional Corporation); Anthony A. Adler (A Professional Corporation); Elia Weinbach (A Professional Corporation); Allan B. Cutrow (A Professional Corporation); Laura A. Loftin (A Professional Corporation); Peter B. Gelblum (A Professional Corporation); David P. Schack (A Professional Corporation); Lawrence A. Michaels (A Professional Corporation); Ronald A. DiNicola (A Professional Corporation); Andrew E. Katz (A Professional Corporation); James O. Thoma (A Professional Corporation); Kevin Gaut (A Professional Corporation); Danna L. Cook (A Professional Corporation); Larry C. Drapkin (A Professional Corporation); Steven E. Shapiro; Lucia E. Coyoca (A Professional Corporation); Regina T. Shanney-Saborsky (A Professional Corporation); Robert C. Welsh (A Professional Corporation); J. Eugene Salomon, Jr. (A Professional Corporation); John L. Segal (A Professional Corporation); George M. Borkowski (A Professional Corporation); David A. Steinberg (A Professional Corporation); Christopher B. Leonard (A Professional Corporation). Of Counsel: Edward Rubin (A Professional Corporation); William M. Kaplan (A Professional Corporation); Lessing E. Gold (A Professional Corporation); Douglas R. Ring (A Professional Corporation); Stephen D. Marks (A Professional Corporation); H. Wayne Taylor; Marvin A. Demoff (A Professional Corporation); Jeffrey B. Wheeler; Bernard Donnenfeld (A Professional Corporation); Douglas W. Bordewieck; A. Catherine Norian; Kim H. Swartz; Richard E. Ackerknecht. Associates: Scott H. Bauman; Yvette Molinaro; Richard B. Sheldon, Jr.; Yakub Hazzard; Mary Courtney Burke; Jeffrey H. Frankel; Jeffrey D. Goldman; Ann S. Lee; Brenda S. Barton; Brian S. Arbetter; Michelle Abend Bauman; Jeffrey L. Richardson; Matt J. Railo; Adam Levin; Tammy Cain Bloomfield; Michael Tsao; David J. Katz; Jeffrey D. Davine; Jeffrey K. Eisen; Tracy L. Thornburg; Howard D. Shapiro; Jeannette Hahm; Jeffrey M. Lowy; Timothy R. Collins, Jr.; Kim Y. Richardson; Jennifer Lightman Wessels; Wayne Kazan; Habib A. Balian; Harry H.W. Kim; Michael J. Zerman; Carolyn S. Javier; Roger A. Sandau; Sheri E. Cohen; Karl J. de Costa; Lee Anne Steinberg; Stefano G. Moscato; Stacie L. Feldman; Jason Krischer; Suzanne M. Steinke; Jeremy A. Lappen; D. James Chung.**
**General Civil, Appellate and Trial Practice. Corporation, Securities, Entertainment, Labor, Probate, Estate Planning, Trust, Federal and State Tax, Bankruptcy, Environmental, Antitrust, Financial Institutions, Administrative and International Law.**
**References: Wells Fargo Bank, N.A.; Merrill, Lynch.**
***See Professional Biographies, LOS ANGELES, CALIFORNIA***

**Mitidiere, Barry T.**, (AV) .......... '53 '79 C.112 B.A. L.426 J.D. [Wolf,R.&S.]
*PRACTICE AREAS: Civil Litigation; Real Estate; Business Law; Bankruptcy Law.
**Mitrovich, Robert P.** .......... '59 '88 C.605 A.B. L.800 J.D. [Ⓐ Charlston,R.&W.]
*PRACTICE AREAS: Insurance Defense; Construction Defect Coverage; Professional Liability.
Mitshell, John A. ..........'— '94 C.1365 L.145 J.D. 601 S. Figueroa St.
Mitsumori, Jas. K., (AV) .......... '21 '49 C&L.477 B.A., LL.B. 420 E. Third St.
**Mittelman, Alan Harvey** .......... '53 '82 C.910 A.B. L.809 J.D. [Bergman&W.]
*PRACTICE AREAS: Civil Litigation in both state and federal courts; Personal Injury Defense; Business Litigation; Insurance Coverage; Insurance Fraud.
**Mittermaier, Ingrid P.** .......... '67 '94 C.813 B.A. L.1066 J.D. [Ⓐ Runquist&Assoc.]
*LANGUAGES: German.
*PRACTICE AREAS: Non-Profit Organization Law; Corporate Law; Business Law.
Mittleman, David M. ..........'62 '87 C.1097 B.A. L.426 J.D. [Ⓐ Rohner&W.]
**Mittleman, Harry A.** ..........'69 '94 C.674 A.B. L.309 J.D. [Ⓐ Irell&M.]
**Mitzenmacher, Deborah** ..........'50 '81 C.1036 B.A. L.1068 J.D. [Ⓐ Magaña,C.&M.]
*PRACTICE AREAS: Trial Court and Appellate Litigation; Aircraft Accidents; Products Liability; Negligence; Wrongful Death.
**Mix, Corrine L.** ..........'66 '93 C.800 B.A. L.546 J.D. [Ⓐ Morris,P.&P.]
Miyahira, Janice R. ..........'61 '84 C.914 B.A. L.477 J.D. 281 S. Figueroa St.‡
**Miyake, Rie** .......... '— '95 L.1218 J.D. [Ⓐ Graham&J.]
Miyakoda, Mylene K. .......... '63 '90 C&L.112 B.A., J.D. 4700 Wilshire Blvd.
**Miyamoto, David T.** ..........'57 '81 C.112 B.S. L.1068 J.D. [Graham&J.]
*PRACTICE AREAS: Litigation.
Miyamoto, Gabriella Rehmann ..........'59 '86 C.813 B.S. L.1066 J.D. Sr. Atty., ARCO
**Miyamoto, Lynn** .......... '60 '87 C.112 B.A. L.1068 J.D. [Bonaparte&M.]
*LANGUAGES: Japanese.
*PRACTICE AREAS: Immigration and Nationality Law.
Miyoshi, David Masao .......... '44 '73 C.800 B.S. L.1065 J.D. 3250 Wilshire Blvd.
Mizel, Martin Lee ..........'44 '69 C.477 B.A. L.930 J.D. Dep. Pub. Def.
Mizel, Michael R., (AV) '51 '77 C.966 B.A. L.800 J.D.
[Simonsen&M.] (⊙Phoenix AZ)
Mizell, V. Tonik .......... '55 '82 C.309 A.B. L.813 J.D. 3474 Crestwold Ave.
Mizrahi, Edward Jack, (BV) ..........'31 '64 C.112 B.A. L.809 LL.B. 207 S. Bway.
Moacanin, Milan ..........'20 '52 C.061 L.564 LL.B. 6255 Sunset Blvd.
**Moak, James J.** .......... '53 '78 C.426 B.A. L.1068 J.D. [Thelen,M.J.&B.]
*PRACTICE AREAS: Life and Health Insurance; Disability Insurance; Extracontractual Insurance Claims; Unfair Insurance Practice; First Party Insurance Defense.
**Moberg, Marilyn A.** ..........'61 '86 C.112 B.A. L.770 J.D. [Crosby,H.R.&M.]
*PRACTICE AREAS: Business Litigation; Professional Liability; Insurance; Products Liability.

CAA297P

**Mobley, Todd M.** ....................... '66 '95 C.1060 B.S. L.809 J.D. [☒ Chapman&G.]
*PRACTICE AREAS: Product Liability; Professional Liability; Environmental Law; Construction Litigation; General Negligence.
**Mocciaro, Perry D.**, (AV) .................. '50 '75 C.800 A.B. L.1066 J.D. [Cox,C.&N.]
*PRACTICE AREAS: Civil Litigation; Real Property; Franchising Law.
Mocciaro, Rebecca B. .............. '52 '79 C.112 B.A. L.1068 J.D. 13174 Boca de Canon
Mochatel, Renée ....................... '57 '82 C.1074 B.A. L.990 J.D. 6300 Wilshire Blvd.
Mochkatel, Renee ...................... '57 '82 C.1075 B.A. L.990 J.D. [Allred,M.&G.]
**Modabber, Zia F.** ........................... '62 '88 C.112 B.A. L.426 J.D. [Katten M.&Z.]
*PRACTICE AREAS: Entertainment and General Business Litigation.
Moddelmog, Cecilia A. ............ '60 '88 C.1109 B.S. L.1068 J.D. 11766 Wilshire Blvd.
Modder, J. Joseph ........................... '64 '89 C.999 B.S. L.809 J.D. Dep. Pub. Def.
**Modisette, James P.**, (AV) .................. '44 '70 C.197 B.A. L.1065 J.D. [Hanna&M.]
*PRACTICE AREAS: Real Estate; Civil Trial; Probate; Estate Planning; Corporate.
**Modisette, Ruth**, (AV) .................. '46 '72 C.881 B.A. L.813 J.D. [Pillsbury M.&S.]
**Moe, John Arthur, II**, (AV) ..................... '50 '75 C&L.602 B.A., J.D. [Tuttle&T.]
*PRACTICE AREAS: Civil Litigation; Bankruptcy and Creditors' Rights.
Moe, Margaret J. ............................ '— '87 C.1077 B.A. L.426 J.D. Dep. Dist. Atty.
Moehlman, Denise B. ..................... '59 '86 C.475 B.A. L.426 J.D. Dist. Atty.'s Ofc.
Moeller, Elizabeth C. .................. '65 '91 C.477 B.A. L.426 J.D. 801 S. Figueroa St.
**Moeller, Paul H.** ................................ '47 '72 C.112 B.A. L.426 J.D. [☒ Tisdale&N.]
*PRACTICE AREAS: Mortgage; Banking; Real Estate Law.
**Moeller, Stephen F.** ......................... '45 '73 C.339 B.A. L.309 J.D. [Katten M.&Z.]
*PRACTICE AREAS: Entertainment Litigation; Business Litigation; General Business; Entertainment.
Moest, Robert C. .......................... '46 '74 C.31 B.A. L.1068 J.D. [Fleishman,F.&M.]
**Moffat, J. Kelly** ........................... '65 '91 C.112 B.A. L.1065 J.D. [☒ Fulbright&J.]
*PRACTICE AREAS: Corporate Law; Securities; Public Finance.
**Moffat, Jeffrey C.**, (AV) ................. '54 '81 C&L.101 B.A., J.D. [Bonne,B.M.O.&N.]
**Moffett, Carrie Ann** ................. '66 '94 C.436 B.A. L.209 J.D. [☒ Stevens,K.A.&H.]
*PRACTICE AREAS: Insurance Defense.
**Moffitt, John P.**, (AV) ....................... '42 '67 C.605 B.A. L.113 J.D. [Moffitt,W.&L.]
*PRACTICE AREAS: Civil Trial; Appellate Practice; Commercial Law; Real Estate; Business.

**Moffitt, Weagant & Loo LLP, (AV)**
**1900 Avenue of the Stars, Suite 1900, 90067**
**Telephone: 310-201-7575 Fax: 310-553-6437**
**Members of Firm: John P. Moffitt; Lance M. Weagant (Certified Specialist, Taxation Law and Probate, Estate Planning and Trust Law, The State Bar of California Board of Legal Specialization); John Loo.**
**General Civil and Trial Practice. Securities, Corporate Finance, Corporate, Commercial and Business Law, Real Property, Federal and State Taxation, Estate Planning, Trust and Probate Law.**
*See Professional Biographies, LOS ANGELES, CALIFORNIA*

Mohammed-Derzaph, Wendy ........... '57 '88 C.1138 B.B.A. L.1009 J.D. Dep. Dist. Atty.
Mohi, Gary ........................................ '31 '59 C&L.800 B.S., LL.B. P.O. Box 27730‡
**Mohn, Marvin D.** ....................... '65 '92 C.112 B.A. L.1065 J.D. [☒ Chadbourne&P.]
Mohr, Anthony J. ................................... '47 '72 C.918 B.A. L.178 J.D. Mun. J.
Moisa, Irma Rodriguez ........................ '66 '92 C.112 B.S. L.1066 J.D. [☒ Liebert,C.&F.]
**Mok, Louis A.**, (AV) ....... '32 '63 C.688 B.M.E. L.800 J.D. [☒ Loeb&L.] (See Pat. Sect.)
*PRACTICE AREAS: Patent; Trademark; Copyright.

**Mokhtarzadeh, Shahrokh, Law Offices of '61 '88 C.112 B.A. L.284 J.D.**
**2049 Century Park East, Suite 720, 90067-3283**
**Telephone: 310-788-0370 Fax: 310-788-0353**
***LANGUAGES: Persian/Farsi.**
***PRACTICE AREAS: Real Estate Litigation; Business Litigation; Insurance Defense Litigation; Family Law.**
**Business and Real Estate Litigation, Family Law, Insurance and Insurance Related Litigation.**
*See Professional Biographies, LOS ANGELES, CALIFORNIA*

Moktarian, Mark ...................... '58 '87 C.339 B.S. L.424 J.D. 2029 Century Park, E.
**Moldo, Byron Z.**, (BV) .................. '56 '83 C.112 B.A. L.809 J.D. [Saltzburg,R.&B.]
*PRACTICE AREAS: Receivership Law; Bankruptcy Law; Real Estate Law.
**Moley, Susan Frances** ............. '63 '92 C.426 B.S. L.276 J.D. [☒ Sulmeyer,K.B.&R.]
*PRACTICE AREAS: Bankruptcy.
Molho, Sonya Bekoff ................. '46 '77 C.1077 B.A. L.426 J.D. 12240 Venice Blvd.
Molidor, Mary Clare ............... '52 '78 C.602 A.B. L.1068 J.D. Supv. Asst. City Atty.
Molina, Pablo E. .............................. '39 '79 C.061 L.1114 J.D. 1824 Sunset Blvd.
**Molina, Vibiana** ........................ '67 '94 C.112 B.A. L.178 J.D. [☒ Manatt,P.&P.]
*PRACTICE AREAS: Entertainment Law; Music.
**Molinaro, Yvette** ........................ '63 '90 C.1139 B.A. L.809 J.D. [☒ Mitchell,S.&K.]
*PRACTICE AREAS: Civil Litigation; Criminal Defense.
Molino, Anthony A. .................. '58 '91 C.1131 B.A. L.1069 J.D. 137 N. Virgil Ave.
**Molinski, William A.** ...................... '64 '89 C&L.800 A.B., J.D. [☒ Fried,F.H.S.&J.]
**Molitz, Michael K.** ................... '65 '93 C.112 B.A. L.426 J.D. [☒ Fragomen,D.&B.]
**Molleur, Richard R.**, (AV) '32 '58 C.1107 A.B. L.276 LL.B.
Corp. V.P. & Gen. Coun., Northrop Grumman Corp.
*LANGUAGES: French.
*RESPONSIBILITIES: Federal Government Contracts and Procurement; Corporate and Environmental Law.
Molloy, C. Terrence ......................... '50 '76 C.103 B.A. L.800 J.D. [Mink&M.]
**Molloy, Frank W.** .......... '46 '72 C.197 A.B. L.659 J.D. [☒ Firm of R.M.Moneymaker]
*PRACTICE AREAS: Business Law and Litigation.
**Molloy, John J., III**, (AV) .................. '46 '72 C&L.800 B.S., J.D. [Walker,W.T.&W.]
*PRACTICE AREAS: Corporate; Tax; Real Estate.
**Mollrich, Stewart** ................................ '52 '79 C.800 B.A. L.990 J.D. [☒ Wewer]
*PRACTICE AREAS: Election Law; Legislation.
**Molodanof, Jack T.** ............................. '61 '87 C.768 B.S. L.464 J.D. [☒ Ochoa&S.]
*LANGUAGES: Greek.
*PRACTICE AREAS: Real Estate Litigation; Legislative Advocacy.
**Moloney, Stephen M.**, (AV) ............... '49 '75 C&L.770 B.S., J.D. [Gilbert,K.C.&J.]
*PRACTICE AREAS: Personal Injury Defense; Employment; Construction Defect; Contract and Business Litigation.
Moltar, Norman M., Jr. ................. '46 '72 C.112 B.S. L.800 J.D. 765 Linda Flora Dr.‡
**Momita, Craig S.** ........................ '61 '92 C.112 B.A. L.767 J.D. [☒ Daniels,B.&F.]
Mommaerts, Robert W. A., (AV) ........ '45 '72 C.112 B.S. L.1068 J.D. [Mommaerts&R.]
Mommaerts & Rutledge, (AV) ................................................... P.O. Box 761280
Momtahan, Dora A. ........................ '66 '92 C.597 B.S. L.1065 J.D. Co. Coun.
Monahan, Katherine E. ................ '65 '92 C.276 B.A. L.1065 J.D. 725 S. Figueroa St.
**Monahan, Marilyn A.** ....................... '59 '85 C.112 B.A. L.426 J.D. [Dorais&W.]
**Monahan, Michael A.** ..................... '52 '79 C.426 B.S. L.276 J.D. [Gibson,D.&C.]
*PRACTICE AREAS: Environmental; Administrative Law; Litigation.
**Moneymaker, Richard M.**, (AV) '36 '61
C.976 B.A. L.1066 J.D. [Firm of R.M.Moneymaker]
*PRACTICE AREAS: Bankruptcy.
**Moneymaker, Vincent B.** '64 '91 C.112 B.A. L.1067 J.D.
[☒ Firm of R.M.Moneymaker]
*PRACTICE AREAS: Bankruptcy.

**Moneymaker, Richard M., The Law Firm of, (AV) [BB]**
**Suite 2102 Broadway Plaza, 700 Flower Street, 90017**
**Telephone: 213-622-1088 Telecopier: 213-622-7002**
**Richard M. Moneymaker. Associates: Vincent B. Moneymaker; Sheri R. Handel. Of Counsel: Frank W. Molloy.**

(This Listing Continued)

**Moneymaker, Richard M., The Law Firm of (Continued)**
**Bankruptcy, Insolvency and Corporate Reorganization Law. General Commercial Litigation.**
**Reference: Bank of America (Los Angeles Main Office).**
*See Professional Biographies, LOS ANGELES, CALIFORNIA*

Monitz, Ronald M. ............. '54 '80 C.112 B.A. L.1068 J.D. 11355 W. Olympic Blvd.
**Monk, Michael W.** .......... '49 '74 C.309 B.A. L.659 J.D. [Musick,P.&G.] (⊙San Diego)
*PRACTICE AREAS: Labor and Employment.
Monkarsh, Brian M. ......................... '56 '83 C.112 B.A. L.813 J.D. [B.M.Monkarsh]
Monkarsh, Brian M., A Professional Corporation ........... 2049 Century Park E. Ste. 2050
Monroe, Bruce ................................................ '52 '88 C&L.990 B.A., J.D. Dep. City Atty.
**Monroe, Glenn E.** '45 '74 C.532 B.A. L.608 J.D.
(adm. in OH; not adm. in CA) [Howrey&S.]
*PRACTICE AREAS: Civil Litigation; Government Contract Law.
Monroe, Leonard H., (AV) .......... '27 '53 C.659 A.B. L.309 J.D. 2040 Ave. of the Stars
**Monroe, Sean A.** ............................. '70 '96 C.276 B.A. L.1066 J.D. [Munger,T.&O.]
**Monroe, Stephen S., (A Professional Corporation)** '47 '73
C.112 B.A. L.426 J.D. [☒ D.B.Bloom]
*LANGUAGES: German; Russian.
*REPORTED CASES: Burnett v. Natl. Enq., 144 CA 3d 991; Calder v. Jones Mueller v. Lacera, 8 CA 4th 41.
**Monroe, Theodore F.** ................. '62 '90 C.383 B.S. L.228 J.D. [☒ Crosby,H.R.&M.]
Montagna, Michael J. ........................ '34 '61 C&L.426 B.S., LL.B. Dep. Dist. Atty.
Monte, John D. ............................... '47 '76 C.112 B.A. L.398 J.D. [☒ Dumas&Assoc.]

**Monteleone & McCrory, (AV) [BB]**
**A Partnership including Professional Corporations**
**725 South Figueroa Street Suite 3750, 90017-5402⊙**
**Telephone: 213-612-9900 FAX: 213-612-9930**
**Members of Firm: Stephen Monteleone (1886-1962); G. Robert Hale (P.C.); Patrick J. Duffy, III (P.C.); Michael F. Minchella (P.C.); Thomas P. McGuire (P.C.); William J. Ingalsbe (P.C.) (Resident, Santa Ana Office); Philip C. Putnam (P.C.); Joseph A. Miller (P.C.); Diana M. Dron (Resident, Santa Ana Office); Donald J. Shields. Associates: David C. Romyn; Barry J. Jensen (Resident, Santa Ana Office); W. Jeffrey Burch; Andrew W. Hawthorne; Stephen L. Dubin; Erica S. Behrens. Of Counsel: Darrell P. McCrory.**
**Construction, Negligence and Product Defense, Environmental/OSHA, Federal, State and Municipal Government Contract Law. Transactional, International Business. General Civil and Trial Practice in all State and Federal Courts, Administrative Courts, Court of Claims, Arbitration and Alternative Dispute Resolution, Appellate Practice.**
**Santa Ana, California Office: Suite 750, 1551 North Tustin Avenue, 92705. Telephone: 714-565-3170. Fax: 714-565-3184.**
*See Professional Biographies, LOS ANGELES, CALIFORNIA*

**Montes, Joseph M.** ........................ '68 '94 C.770 B.A. L.426 J.D. [☒ Burke,W.&S.]
*PRACTICE AREAS: Municipal Law; Civil Litigation.
**Montes, Robert, Jr.** ......................... '65 '92 C.112 B.A. L.1068 J.D. [Coleman&W.]
*LANGUAGES: Spanish.
**Montesino, Braulio** ................... '52 '94 C.1097 B.A. L.426 J.D. [☒ Foley L.W.&A.]
*PRACTICE AREAS: Real Property Law; Corporate Law; Health Care Regulation; Integrated Health Care Delivery Systems.
**Montgomery, Duncan E.** ......... '— '85 C.112 B.A. L.208 J.D. [☒ Sonnenschein N.&R.]
*LANGUAGES: French.
*PRACTICE AREAS: Litigation; Appellate Law.
Montgomery, George, (AV) ........... '32 '60 C.800 B.S. L.426 J.D. 601 S. Figueroa St.
**Montgomery, James I., Jr.** ............. '56 '81 C.597 B.A. L.1068 J.D. [Daniels,B.&F.]
*PRACTICE AREAS: Trial Law; Insurance; Products Liability; Workers Compensation.
Montgomery, Jerome A. .............. '33 '65 C.1042 B.A. L.1065 LL.B. Asst. City Atty.
**Montgomery, Loren M.** ................... '— '96 C.674 B.A. L.228 J.D. [☒ Latham&W.]
**Montgomery, Robert K.**, (AV) .......... '38 '65 C.951 A.B. L.228 J.D. [Gibson,D.&C.]
*PRACTICE AREAS: Business and Corporate Finance; Mergers and Acquisitions.
Montgomery, Rochelle J. ..................... '57 '83 C.112 B.A. L.1068 J.D. NLRB
**Montgomery, Roxanne Diaz** ........ '67 '95 C.1109 B.A. L.1065 J.D. [☒ Richards,W.&G.]
*PRACTICE AREAS: Litigation; Municipal Law.
Montgomery, Susan E. .................... '60 '91 C.112 B.A. L.426 J.D. City Atty. Off.
**Montgomery, Susan I.**, (AV) ........... '58 '85 C.112 B.S. L.800 J.D. [Gumport,R.&M.]
*PRACTICE AREAS: Bankruptcy; Commercial and Business Litigation.
Montgomery, William McC. '49 '77 C.112 B.A. L.365 J.D.
1st V.P. & Assoc. Gen. Coun., PaineWebber, Inc.

**Montgomery, Michael B., A Law Corporation**
**(See El Monte)**

Montoya, Phil J., Jr. ........................ '60 '86 C&L.800 B.S., J.D. [☒ Rosner,O.&N.]
Montrose, Norman F., (BV) ............ '41 '66 C.112 B.A. L.426 LL.B. Dep. Dist. Atty.
Mood, George M. '40 '74 C.616 B.A. L.802 J.D.
(adm. in TX; not adm. in CA) 2607 Holt Ave.‡
Moog, Velda J. '40 '80 C.659 L.128 LL.B.
(adm. in DC; not adm. in CA) I.R.S.
**Moon, Albert I., Jr.** ...................... '31 '62 C.119 B.S. L.1068 J.D. [☒ Hancock R.&B.]
Mooney, C. Duane, (BV) ............... '23 '52 C.1042 L.809 LL.B. Prob. Atty., Supr. Ct.

**Mooney, F. Bentley, Jr., A Law Corportaion**
**(See North Hollywood)**

**Moonitz, Lois C. Jacobs** ................... '57 '82 C.66 A.B. L.145 J.D. [☒ Hughes H.&R.]
**Moonves, Jonathan D.** ...................... '59 '85 C&L.893 B.A., J.D. [Del,R.S.M.&D.]
*PRACTICE AREAS: Entertainment Law; Television Law; Motion Picture Law.
Moor, Carl H. ........................ '61 '88 C.821 B.A. L.976 J.D. Off. of U.S. Atty.
Moore, Albert J. ..................... '48 '78 C.454 B.A. L.1068 J.D. Prof. of Law, U.C.L.A.
**Moore, Catherine** ............................. '69 '94 C.951 B.A. L.813 J.D. [☒ Howrey&S.]
Moore, Charles J. ............... '45 '72 C.1097 B.A. L.1068 J.D. Principal Dep. Co. Coun.
**Moore, David C.** .......................... '66 '91 C.194 B.A. L.846 J.D. [☒ Hawkins,S.L.&B.]
Moore, Denise Donalda ................... '53 '78 C.932 B.S. L.112 J.D. [☒ Casterline&A.]
Moore, Eugene F. ..................... '23 '55 C.999 L.809 LL.B. 11000 Wilshire Blvd.
Moore, Everett C. ........................ '35 '89 C.1023 B.S. L.809 J.D. Dep. Pub. Def.
**Moore, Geoffrey T.** ...................... '55 '87 C.112 B.A. L.464 J.D. [☒ Tuverson&H.]
**Moore, Howard P.**, (AV) '28 '55 C.318 A.B. L.309 LL.B.
V.P. & Tr. Coun., Northern Tr. Bk. of Calif. N.A.
*RESPONSIBILITIES: Contracts; Estate Planning; Fiduciary Law; Real Estate; Probate.
Moore, Janet S. ......................... '53 '84 C.768 B.A. L.426 J.D. Dep. Dist. Atty.
**Moore, Joanna** ................................ '67 '93 C.112 B.A. L.426 J.D. [☒ Irell&M.]
Moore, Kathe R., (AV) .............. '47 '74 C.112 B.A. L.1049 J.D. 4929 Wilshire Blvd.
**Moore, Kenton E.** ...................... '58 '89 C.1077 B.S. L.999 J.D. [D.B.Parcells III]
*PRACTICE AREAS: Medical Malpractice; General Liability.
Moore, Kevin J. ................................ '61 '88 C.763 B.S. L.1137 J.D. 355 S. Grand
**Moore, Mark** ........................... '62 '90 C&L.846 B.B.A., J.D. [☒ Cox,C.&N.]
*PRACTICE AREAS: Insurance Law; Bad Faith; Commercial Litigation.
Moore, Michael E. ........................ '— '73 C.112 B.S. L.809 J.D. [Roquemore,P.&M.]
Moore, Richard C. ......... '56 '83 C.174 B.A. L.1065 J.D. 1875 Century Park E., 15th Fl.
**Moore, Robert Jay**, (AV) ................ '50 '77 C.575 A.B. L.1068 J.D. [Murphy,W.&B.]
*PRACTICE AREAS: Business Workouts; Bankruptcy Reorganizations; Creditors Remedies.
**Moore, Schuyler M.**, (AV) ............ '55 '81 C.112 B.A. L.1068 J.D. [Stroock&S.&L.]
*PRACTICE AREAS: Entertainment Contracts; Entertainment Finance; Entertainment Law; Taxation; Corporate Law.

**Moore, Scott J.** ....................'62 '87 C.426 B.S. L.1097 J.D. [Ⓐ Konowiecki&R.]
*PRACTICE AREAS: General Business; Corporate; Real Estate.
Moore, Stephen C. ....................'48 '73 C.800 B.A. L.426 J.D. 5939 Monterey Rd.
Moore, William A., Jr. ...... '43 '76 C.446 B.S. L.1049 J.D. V.P. & Sr. Coun., Union Bk.

**Moore, Christopher M., & Associates, A Law Corporation**
**(See Torrance)**

**Moore, Paul F.**
**(See Pasadena)**

**Moore, Rutter & Evans**
**(See Long Beach)**

**Moorehead, Carey B.** ..............'52 '79 C.112 B.A. L.426 J.D. [Ⓐ Wilson,E.M.E.&D.]
Moorhead, Dixon D. ....................'13 '41 C.339 B.S. L.146 J.D. 1801 Ave. of The Stars‡
**Moorhead, Michael D., (P.C.), (AV)** ........ '48 '75 C.940 B.A. L.426 J.D. [Pierry&M.]
*PRACTICE AREAS: Personal Injury; Medical Malpractice; Labor; Employment; Products Liability.
**Mootchnik, Marc D.** ...................'63 '89 C.1042 B.A. L.426 J.D. [Ⓐ Rintala,S.J.&R.]
Morales, Arturo J. ....................'50 '78 C.846 B.A. L.1068 J.D. [Ⓐ Liebert,C.&F.]

**Morales, Michael R.**
**(See Torrance)**

**Moran, Kathleen A.** .................. '67 '92 C.602 B.A. L.846 J.D. [Ⓐ McKenna&C.]
*PRACTICE AREAS: Business Litigation; Government Contracts Litigation.
Moran, Patrick D. ....................'40 '75 C.602 A.B. L.426 J.D. Dep. Dist. Atty.
**Moravec, Henry J., III** ..............'60 '90 C.1042 B.A. L.426 J.D. [Ⓐ Hoffman,S.&W.]
*PRACTICE AREAS: Estate Planning Law; Probate Law; Tax-Exempt Organizations; Charitable Planning.
Moray, Dean ....................'53 '79 C.112 B.A.Econ. L.426 J.D. [Moray&V.]
Moray and Vallette ....................6300 Wilshire Blvd.
Morehead, Christie L. ....................'57 '86 C.112 A.B. L.426 J.D. 555 W. 5th St.
**Morelli, Alan E.** ....................'61 '87 C.705 B.S. L.276 J.D. [Manatt,P.&P.]
*PRACTICE AREAS: Corporate Securities; Technology/Electronic Commerce.
Moremen, Philip M. ..........'61 '87 C.813 B.A. L.1068 J.D. 8th Fl., 515 S. Figueroa St.
Moreno, Carlos R. ....................'48 '75 C.976 A.B. L.813 J.D. Supr. Ct. J.
Moreno, Elizabeth A. ...... '58 '85 C.267 B.A. L.426 J.D. 1925 Century Park E., 22nd Fl.
**Moreno, Elizabeth G.** ..................'65 '93 C.112 A.B. L.309 J.D. [Ⓐ Jones,D.R.&P.]
Moreno, Leticia T. ...........'58 '89 C.112 B.A. L.1148 J.D. 520 S. Lafayette Pk. Pl. 204
Moreno, Luis '64 '93 C.326 B.A. L.426 J.D.
Corp. Atty., Law Engineering and Environmental Services, Inc.
Moret, Gilbert A. ....................'40 '66 5430 E. Beverly Blvd.
**Moret, Marisa A.** ........'69 '94 C.276 B.A. L.112 J.D. [Ⓐ Radcliff,F.&D.] (⊙San Fran.)
Morgan, Carol Jo ........'44 '82 C.446 B.A. L.426 J.D. Dep. Atty., State Dept. of Transp.
**Morgan, David F., (AV)** ....................'31 '61 C.821 B.A. L.309 J.D. [Barton,K.&O.]
*PRACTICE AREAS: Corporate Law; Securities; Mergers, Acquisitions & Divestitures; Finance.
**Morgan, Michael G.** ..............'68 '94 C.659 B.S. L.1068 J.D. [Ⓐ Sheppard,M.R.&H.]
*PRACTICE AREAS: Employment and Labor Litigation; Employment Law; Union Relations.
**Morgan, Nicolas** ............'67 '93 C&L.112 B.A., J.D. [Ⓐ Christensen,M.F.J.G.W.&S.]
*PRACTICE AREAS: Litigation.
**Morgan, R. Gregory** ....................'54 '81 C.112 B.A. L.477 J.D. [Munger,T.&O.]
Morgan, Richard LeBell ..............'48 '73 C.112 B.A. L.426 J.D. 3550 Wilshire Blvd.
**Morgan, Thomas C.** ....................'63 '91 C.112 B.A. L.426 J.D. [Girardi&K.]
*PRACTICE AREAS: Personal Injury.
**Morgan, Tonya L.** ....................'59 '90 C.112 B.A. L.426 J.D. [Ⓐ Chapin,F.&W.]
Morgan, Wm. Marshall, (AV) ..............'22 '50 C.665 B.A. L.800 J.D. [Morgan&W.]⊙

**Morgan, Lewis & Bockius LLP, (AV)**
**801 South Grand Avenue, 90017-4615⊙**
**Telephone: 213-612-2500 Telex: 67-3270 Fax: 213-612-2554**
**Email: postmaster@mlb.com URL: http://www.mlb.com**
**Members of Firm in Los Angeles: Jeffrey N. Brown; Anthony Ciasulli; Cynthia M. Cohen; Linda Van Winkle Deacon; Loyd P. Derby; Douglas A. Dodds; Peter Brown Dolan; William D. Ellis; David G. Ellsworth; William J. Emanuel; Stephen R. English; Barry V. Freeman; Jeffrey L. Grausam; John F. Hartigan; J. Dean Heller; Joseph E. Herman; Kathleen C. Johnson; Michael J. A. Karlin; Raymond R. Kepner; Jack Chi-Husan Liu; Stephen M. Lowry; C. G. Gordon Martin; Andrea Sheridan Ordin; Andrew C. Peterson; Mark S. Rapaport; Robert D. Redford; Paul A. Richler; Anthony Russo; John D. Shultz; Frank H. Smith, Jr.; Roseann C. Stevenson; Anne E. Stone; Thomas L. Taylor, III; Randolph C. Visser; James Wawro; Michael L. Wolfram; Kenneth B. Wright. Of Counsel in Los Angeles: John S. Battenfeld; Richard W. Esterkin; Y. Peter Kim; Richard J. Maire, Jr.; Michael A. Vacchio. Counsel in Los Angeles: Edward C. Cazier, Jr. Associates in Los Angeles: Edward T. Attanasio; Andre Y. Bates; Magara Lee Crosby; Lisa Ann Detrick; Susan R. Essex; Ann Haley Fromholz; Steven J. Glouberman; Keith D. Grossman; Robert Jon Hendricks; J. Michael Jack; Wendy K. Kilbride; Jeffrey James Lewis; Michael C. Lieb; Derek B. Lipscombe (Not admitted in CA); David D. Marshall; Robert D. Ming; Steven J. Oppenheimer; Raul Perez; Randi Paula Perry; Mark W. Pugsley; Jeffrey M. Reisner; Dawn Patrice Ross; Nancy M. Saunders; Theodore G. Spanos; Steven W. Spector; Eric M. Steinert; James R. Stewart; Mark J. Stubington; Adam Treiger; Jason Haruo Wilson; Joseph S. Wu.**
**General Practice.**
**Philadelphia, Pennsylvania Office: 2000 One Logan Square, 19103-6993. Telephone: 215-963-5000. Fax: 215-963-5299.**
**Washington, D.C. Office: 1800 M Street, N.W., 20036-5869. Telephone: 202-467-7000. Fax: 202-467-7176.**
**New York, New York Office: 101 Park Avenue, 10178-0060. Telephone: 212-309-6000. Fax: 212-309-6273.**
**Miami, Florida Office: 5300 First Union Financial Center, 200 South Biscayne Boulevard, 33131-2339. Telephone: 305-579-0300. Fax: 305-579-0321.**
**Harrisburg, Pennsylvania Office: One Commerce Square, 417 Walnut Street, 17101-1904. Telephone: 717-237-4000. Fax: 717-237-4004.**
**Pittsburgh, Pennsylvania Office: One Oxford Centre, 301 Grant Street, 32nd Floor, 15219-6401. Telephone: 412-560-3300. Fax: 412-560-3399.**
**Princeton, New Jersey Office: 100 Overlook Center, 08540-7814. Telephone: 609-520-6600. Fax: 609-520-6639.**
**London, England Office: Morgan, Lewis & Bockius, 4 Carlton Gardens, Pall Mall, London SW1Y 5AA. Telephone: 44-171-839-1677. Fax: 44-171-839-3650.**
**Frankfurt, Germany Office: Guiollettstraße 54, Frankfurt/Main 60325. Telephone: (49-69) 71 40 07-0. Fax: (49-69) 71 40 07-10.**
**Brussels, Belgium Office: 7 Rue Guimard, B-1040. Telephone: 32-2/512.55.01. Fax: 32-2/512.58.88.**
**Tokyo, Japan Office: Yurakucho Denki Building S-556, 7-1 Yurakucho 1-chome, Chiyoda-ku, Tokyo 100. Telephone: 81-03-3216-2500. Fax: 81-03-3216-2501.**
**Singapore Office: 80 Raffles Place, #14-20 UOB Plaza 2, Singapore, 048624. Telephone: 65-438-2188. Fax: 65-230-7100.**

***See Professional Biographies, LOS ANGELES, CALIFORNIA***

Morgan & Wenzel, Professional Corporation, (AV) ........ 3435 Wilshire Blvd. (⊙Irvine)
Morganstern, Myrna D. '46 '76 C.549 B.A. L.494 J.D.
U.S. Securities & Exchange Comm.
**Morgenthaler, Alisa M.** ...'60 '86 C.804 B.A. L.188 J.D. [Ⓐ Christensen,M.F.J.G.W.&S.]
*PRACTICE AREAS: Civil Litigation; Entertainment; Banking Law.
**Mori, Audra M.** ....................'67 '92 C.112 B.A. L.188 J.D. [Ⓐ Andrews&K.]
*PRACTICE AREAS: Litigation.
**Mori, Douglass H.** ....................'51 '78 C.668 B.A. L.880 J.D. [Parker S.]
**Mori, Jun, (AV)** ....................'29 '59 C.112 A.B. L.800 J.D. [Kelley D.&W.]
*PRACTICE AREAS: Corporate.
**Morin, Michael D.** ....................'52 '81 C.1307 B.A. L.61 J.D. [Margolis&M.]
*PRACTICE AREAS: Business Litigation; Contracts Law; Entertainment Law.
Morin, Volney F., (AV) ..............'19 '49 C.477 A.B. L.309 J.D. 1341 Cahuenga Blvd.
Morinaka, Barry S. ....................'47 '78 C.112 B.A. L.809 J.D. 3250 Wilshire Blvd.

Moring, David L. ....................'47 '78 C.112 B.A. L.426 J.D. [Ⓒ Herman&W.]
Morita, Carole Sei ....................'— '79 C.112 A.B. L.1065 J.D. 1055 Wilshire Blvd.
**Moritz, Luc** ....................'65 '95 C.061 L.1068 J.D. [Ⓐ O'Melveny&M.]
*PRACTICE AREAS: International Tax; Corporate Tax.
**Morner-Ritt, Mara** ....................'61 '88 C.800 B.A. L.1066 J.D. [Gipson H.&P.]
*PRACTICE AREAS: Corporate Law; Securities Law.
**Morof, Jeffrey W.** ....................'54 '79 C.477 A.B. L.910 J.D. [Bryan C.]
*PRACTICE AREAS: Civil Practice; Aviation Law; Products Liability Law.
Moroney, Carl V. ....................'33 '62 C.112 B.A. L.1068 LL.B. Supr. Ct. Comr.
**Moroney, E. Thomas, Jr.** ..............'59 '84 C.473 B.A. L.800 J.D. [Ⓒ Pircher,N.&M.]
*PRACTICE AREAS: Litigation.
**Morra, Linda Russano** ..................'52 '82 C.331 B.A. L.809 J.D. [Ⓐ A.M.Brucker]
*PRACTICE AREAS: Employee Benefits Law.
Morran, Kay Reiter ....................'36 '75 C.800 A.B. L.809 J.D. 5042 Wilshire Blvd.
Morris, Arthur O. ....................'31 '69 C.1043 A.B. L.809 LL.B. 4936 Crenshaw Blvd.

**Morris, David J., (AV) '41 '66 C.508 B.A. L.1066 J.D.**
**1900 Avenue of the Stars, Suite 2430, 90067**
**Telephone: 310-277-6244 Telecopier: 310-556-2366**
**General Civil Trial Practice, Business, Corporate and Real Estate Law.**

***See Professional Biographies, LOS ANGELES, CALIFORNIA***

**Morris, Dennis** ....................'63 '93 C.112 B.S. L.990 J.D. [Ⓐ Mendes&M.] (Pat.)
*LANGUAGES: Italian, Spanish and French.
Morris, Edward A. ....................'51 '76 C.426 B.A. L.809 J.D. [Early,M.&P.]
Morris, Herbert ....................'28 '58 C.051 Ph.D. L.976 LL.B. Prof., Univ. of Calif.
Morris, Janet ....................'56 '84 C.112 B.A. L.767 J.D. Bet Tzedek Legal Servs.
**Morris, Jean** ....................'54 '79 C.676 B.A. L.94 J.D. [Greenberg G.F.C.&M.]
*PRACTICE AREAS: Bankruptcy/Commercial Law.
Morris, John R. ....................'63 '88 C&L.426 B.A., J.D. Dist. Atty.'s Ofc.
**Morris, Leigh B.** ....................'46 '72 C.112 A.B. L.1068 J.D. [Troop M.S.&P.]
*PRACTICE AREAS: Real Estate Law; Real Estate and Commercial Finance Law; General Business; Franchising.
**Morris, Marcy S., (AV)** ........'55 '81 C.1044 B.A. L.1068 J.D. [Armstrong H.J.T.&W.]
*PRACTICE AREAS: Entertainment.
**Morris, Michael A., (AV)** ..............'54 '79 C.342 B.A. L.1066 J.D. [Stutman,T.&G.]
*PRACTICE AREAS: Bankruptcy; Insolvency; Corporate Reorganization; Commercial Litigation.
**Morris, Michael R., (AV)** ..............'53 '78 C.659 B.A. L.37 J.D. [Valensi,R.&M.]
*PRACTICE AREAS: Tax Law (Transactional and Litigation); Entertainment Law (Emphasizing Music, Copyright and related matters).
Morris, Peter '61 '86 C.188 B.A. L.309 J.D.
1800 Ave. of the Stars, Suite 900 (Century City)
Morris, Robert Lane ....................'57 '82 C.36 B.S. L.426 J.D. [Ⓐ Fuchs&M.]
**Morris, Stanley C.** ....................'63 '91 C.575 B.S. L.902 J.D. [Ⓐ Jones,D.R.&P.]
**Morris, Stephen J. M., (AV)** ........'34 '62 C.668 A.B. L.1066 LL.B. [Ⓒ Musick,P.&G.]
Morris, Stephen R. ....................'53 '81 C.309 A.B. L.1066 J.D. Princ. Dep. Co. Coun.
Morris, Timothy J. ....................'53 '78 C.800 B.S. L.426 J.D. 880 W. 1st St.
Morris, Ward A., (AV) ....... '31 '63 C.112 B.S. L.800 LL.B. 6222 Wilshire Blvd. 6th Fl.

**Morris, Polich & Purdy, (AV) [BB]**
**1055 West Seventh Street Suite 2400, 90017⊙**
**Telephone: 213-891-9100 Facsimile: 213-488-1178**
**Members of Firm: Jeffrey S. Barron; Anthony G. Brazil; James M. Chantland; Michael T. Colliau; Douglas J. Collodel; Steven M. Crane; Carol Ann Humiston; Marc S. Katz; Theodore D. Levin; Walter J. Lipsman; Landon Morris (1904-1991); Dean A. Olson; Theodore P. Polich, Jr.; Douglas C. Purdy; Donald L. Ridge; Nicholas M. Wieczorek. Associates: Michael F. Avila; Mark C. Carlson; Penelope D. Doherty; Philip M. Drewry; Michael A. Fox; Hal D. Goldflam; Brian G. Hanneman; Carla M. Hoffman; Christine A. Hull; Beth A. Kahn; Cynthia L. Keener; Katherine E. Klima Liner; Jason Levin; Corrine L. Mix; Marilyn Muir; Richard H. Nakamura Jr.; Derrick H. Nguyen; David B. Olson; Lee I. Petersil; Janet M. Richardson; Jeffrey T. Woodruff; Megan S. Wynne. Orange County Office Members of Firm: Gary L. Hoffman; Randall F. Koenig; John P. Miller; Steven C. Miller. Orange County Office Associates: William M. Betley; Kay Ann Connelly; Stephen J. McGreevy; Daniel J. McNamee; Thierry R. Montoya; Kristen Kay Nelson; Carlos A. Prietto, III; Paul S. Sienski. San Diego Office Members of Firm: Gary L. Jacobsen; Gerald P. Schneeweis. San Diego Office Associates: Diana L. Cuomo; William C. Getty; Mark Hellenkamp; Joseph C. Lavelle; Matthew J. Liedle; Margot Sanguinetti; William C. Wilson.**
**General Civil Trial and Appellate Practice in all State and Federal Courts. Construction Law, Insurance Law, Environmental Law, Products Liability, Architect and Engineer Liability, Government Tort Liability, Police Civil Liability, Pharmaceutical and Medical Device Liability, Toxic Tort Litigation and Commercial Litigation.**
**Reference: Security Pacific National Bank (6th & Flower Branch Office).**
**Orange County Office: 500 North State College Boulevard, 11th Floor, Orange, California. Telephone: 714-939-1100. Facsimile: 714-939-9261.**
**San Diego County Office: 501 W. Broadway, Suite 500, San Diego, California. Telephone: 619-557-0404. Facsimile: 619-557-0460.**

***See Professional Biographies, LOS ANGELES, CALIFORNIA***

Morrish, Robert G. ....................'56 '82 C.112 B.S. L.309 J.D. Libra Investments, Inc.
**Morrison, Carleton H., Jr.** ..............'42 '76 C.101 B.A. L.209 J.D. [Ⓐ Burke,W.&S.]
*LANGUAGES: Spanish.
*PRACTICE AREAS: Environmental Law; Public Law; Government Relations; Legislative Advocacy.
Morrison, Charles T., Jr., (AV) ........'25 '75 C.339 B.A. L.1136 J.D. [C.T.Morrison,Jr.]
**Morrison, David K.** ....................'57 '91 C.668 B.A. L.809 J.D. [Ⓐ Lynberg&W.]
*PRACTICE AREAS: Insurance Defense.
**Morrison, Edward F., Jr.** ..................'62 '87 C&L.880 B.A., J.D. [Lewis,D.B.&B.]
*PRACTICE AREAS: General; Civil; Construction; Errors and Omissions Litigation.
Morrison, J. Wayne ........'57 '84 C.839 B.B.A. L.845 J.D. Ct. Coun., State Bar of Calif.
Morrison, Lawrence C. ....................'46 '78 C.763 A.B. L.809 J.D. Dep. Dist. Atty.
**Morrison, Marina M.** ....................'60 '92 C.112 B.A. L.809 J.D. [Ⓐ Biesty,M.&G.]
**Morrison, Nancy G.** ....................'51 '77 C.112 B.A. L.767 J.D. [Pillsbury M.&S.]
**Morrison, Robert L., (AV)** ..............'47 '72 C.210 B.A. L.477 J.D. [Pillsbury M.&S.]
Morrison, Sarah E. ....................'63 '89 C.668 B.A. L.309 J.D. Off. of the Atty. Gen.
Morrison, Charles T., Jr., Inc., A Professional Law Corporation, (AV)
2100 N. Main St., Suite A2

**Morrison & Foerster LLP, (AV)**
**555 West Fifth Street, Suite 3500, 90013-1024⊙**
**Telephone: 213-892-5200 Facsimile: 213-892-5454**
**URL: http://www.mofo.com**
**Members of Firm: David B. Babbe; Charles S. Barquist; Donald I. Berger; Jerry R. Bloom; Michael J. Connell; Michèle B. Corash (Los Angeles and San Francisco Offices); Jerome H. Craig; R. Stephen Doan; Henry M. Fields; Thomas R. Fileti; Richard D. Fybel; Joseph Gabai; Marvin D. Heileson; Kathryn I. Johnstone; Gregory B. Koltun; Marc B. Leh; Dan Marmalefsky; Mark R. McDonald; Margot A. Metzner; J. Robert Nelson; Maren E. Nelson; Rena L. O'Malley; Dennis M. Perluss; John G. Petrovich; Marcia B. Pine; Anthony L. Press; Stephen P. Rothman; Susan E. Rule; Timothy F. Ryan; Darrell L. Sackl; Janie F. Schulman; John R. Shiner; B. Scott Silverman; Robert S. Stern; Pauline M. Stevens; Marcus A. Torrano; Laurie D. Zelon; Donna J. Zenor. Senior Of Counsel: Seth M. Hufstedler; Shirley M. Hufstedler; Patricia Dominis Phillips; Joseph L. Wyatt, Jr. Of Counsel: Burton J. Gindler; Jim G. Grayson; John P. Olson; J. Timothy Scott; John Sobieski; Michael V. Toumanoff. Associates: John W. (Jack) Alden Jr.; Lorie M. Alexander; Sarvenaz Bahar; David K. Barrett; Mark R. Bateman; Laura R. Boudreau; Laura D. Castner; Michael S. Chamberlin; Randall L. Clark; Thomas R. Davis; Elizabeth A. Deere; Andree D. Delgado; Yvonne D. Denenny; Steven J. Dettmann; Gavin Friedman; Hector G. Gallegos; Mark T. Gillett; Laurie B. Graniez; Richard W. Grime; Ronen Gross; Ann Haberfelde; Steven M. Haines; Saheli Datta Harvill; Amy A. Hoff; Shane Y. Kao; Michael Katz; Charles S. Kaufman; Howard S. Liberson; John P. Lodise; Lizabeth Rhodes; P. Rupert Russell; Kris G. Vyas; Derek H. Wilson; David C. Wright; Lester I. Yano; Rowena A. W. Yeung; Marc D. Young.**

(This Listing Continued)

CAA299P

CALIFORNIA—LOS ANGELES MARTINDALE-HUBBELL LAW DIRECTORY 1997

**Morrison & Foerster LLP (Continued)**

**Other offices located in: San Francisco, New York, Washington, D.C., London, Brussels, Hong Kong, Tokyo, Sacramento, Palo Alto, Walnut Creek, Orange County and Denver.**

***See Professional Biographies, LOS ANGELES, CALIFORNIA***

**Morrissey, J. Richard**, (AV) ........ '41 '66 C.770 A.B. L.1066 LL.B. [Pillsbury M.&S.]
**Morrissey, John C.** ................ '58 '85 C.976 B.A. L.145 J.D. [McCutchen,D.B.&E.]
*PRACTICE AREAS: Commercial Litigation; Intellectual Property Law.
**Morrow, Andrew M., III** .............. '62 '87 C.800 B.S. L.94 J.D. [Ⓐ Koletsky,M.&F.]
*PRACTICE AREAS: Construction Defect Defense Litigation; General Liability Defense Litigation.
**Morrow, David M.** ........................ '68 '94 C.112 B.A. L.426 J.D. [Ⓐ Long&L.]
*PRACTICE AREAS: Insurance Coverage Litigation; Insurance Defense.
Morrow, Dion G. .............................. '32 '57 C.990 L.426 J.D. Ret. Supr. Ct. J.
Morrow, Gregory J. ....................... '58 '91 C.878 B.S. L.464 J.D. Sr. Trial Atty., I.C.C.
**Morrow, Margaret M.**, (AV) ............... '50 '74 C.104 B.A. L.309 J.D. [Arnold&P.]
*REPORTED CASES: American States Insurance Co. v. Borbor, 826 F2d 888 (9th Cir. 1987); McKeown v. First Interstate Bank, 194 Cal App. 3d 1225 (1987); University of Southern California v. Superior Court, 222 Cal. App. 3d. 1028 (1990); The Crane v. The Arizona Republic, 972 F. 2d 1511 (9th Cir. 1992).
*PRACTICE AREAS: Appellate Practice; Arbitration and Mediation; Insurance Coverage Law; Commercial Litigation.
Morrow, Randall R., (AV) .................... '53 '78 C.800 B.S. L.426 J.D. 633 W. 5th St.
Morse, Ewin ................................ '14 '42 C.705 A.B. L.309 LL.B. 205 S Broadway
Morse, Frank P. ............................. '44 '70 C.813 B.A. L.309 J.D. [Sandler,R.&M.]
**Morse, Jonathan S.** ......................... '44 '77 C.674 B.S.E. L.477 J.D. [Ⓐ Kern&W.]
**Morse, Louise G.**, (BV) ................. '47 '74 C.1077 B.A. L.809 J.D. [Clopton,P.&B.]
Morse, Michael ............................... '41 '66 C&L.800 B.A., J.D. 205 S. Broadway
Morse, Richard C. ..................... '42 '67 C.112 A.B. L.1066 J.D. Atlantic Richfield Co.
**Mortimer, Ann Marie** ............. '66 '94 C.788 A.B. L.1066 J.D. [Ⓐ O'Donnell,R.&S.]
*PRACTICE AREAS: Litigation.

**Morton, Allan S., (AV) '44 '69 C.188 A.B. L.1068 J.D.**
**2029 Century Park East, Suite 1200, 90067**
**Telephone: 310-277-8946 Fax: 310-277-8944**
**Email: morton4law@aol.com**
**(Also of Counsel to Mannis & Phillips).**
**General Civil Practice. Business Litigation and Family Law. Arbitration and Mediation.**
***See Professional Biographies, LOS ANGELES, CALIFORNIA***

Morton, Rosalie L. ................................ '23 '65 C&L.800 B.S.L., J.D. Dep. Dist. Atty.
**Mortyn, Russell M.** ............... '63 '92 C.112 B.A. L.1065 J.D. [Ⓐ Bonne,B.M.O.&N.]
**Moscato, Stefano G.** ............... '70 '96 C.112 B.A. L.1068 J.D. [Ⓐ Mitchell,S.&K.]
*LANGUAGES: French, Italian.
*PRACTICE AREAS: Labor and Employment Law.
**Moscovitch, Eugene C.**, (AV) ........ '46 '73 C.940 B.A. L.1068 J.D. [Charlston,R.&W.]
Moser, Tom, (A Law Corporation), (BV) ......... '49 '76 C.597 B.A. L.802 J.D. [Moser&S.]
Moser & Moser
3460 Wilshire Boulevard, Suite 410 (⊙Albany & New York, NY , Washington D.C. and Prague, Czech Republic)
Moser & Sanders, (BV) ........................................ 16921 Parthenia St. (Sepulveda)
**Moses, Garry O.** ..................... '55 '89 C.800 B.A. L.809 J.D. [Ⓐ La Follette,J.D.F.&A.]
*PRACTICE AREAS: Medical Malpractice.
Moses, Stephen D. ..................... '34 '60 C.264 B.S. L.309 J.D. 1801 Ave. of the Stars
**Mosher, Robert D.**, (AV) .......... '46 '72 C.112 A.B. L.1068 J.D. [Nossaman,G.K.&E.]
*PRACTICE AREAS: Corporations Law; Securities Law; Commercial Law.
**Mosher, Ronald A.** ............................ '46 '73 C.502 B.S. L.1153 J.D. [Lovich&P.]
**Mosher-Beluris, Terese A.** ............ '58 '83 C.860 B.A. L.426 J.D. [McDermott,W.&E.]
*PRACTICE AREAS: Commercial Litigation; Arbitration.
**Mosk, Richard M.**, (AV) ........... '39 '64 C.813 A.B. L.309 J.D. [Sanders,B.G.S.&M.]
**Moskatel, Ira D.**, (AV) ............................ '50 '75 C.111 B.S. L.800 J.D. [Moskatel]

**Moskatel Law Corporation, (AV)**
**Suite 950, 10100 Santa Monica Boulevard, 90067**
**Telephone: 310-282-8383; 310-556-3847**
**Email: mlc@moskatel.com URL: http://www.moskatel.com/**
**Ira D. Moskatel (Certified Specialist, Taxation Law, The State Bar of California Board of Legal Specialization).**
**Taxation, Technology, Computer, Corporate Law.**
***See Professional Biographies, LOS ANGELES, CALIFORNIA***

Moskowitz, Joel S., (AV) ................ '47 '71 C.112 B.A. L.1068 J.D. 2049 Century Park
**Moskowitz, Karen** ............................ '57 '83 C.112 B.A. L.1065 J.D. [Margolis&M.]
**Moskowitz, Mark R.** .................... '46 '72 C.1036 B.A. L.309 J.D. [Hughes H.&R.]
*PRACTICE AREAS: Corporate Law; Securities Law; Gaming.
Moskowitz, Richard S. .................. '63 '88 C.659 B.A. L.1068 J.D. Dept. of Jus.
Mosley, Beverly E. .......................... '48 '77 C.627 B.S. L.426 J.D. Mun. Ct. Comr.
Mosley, Paul B. '46 '73 C&L.336 B.S., J.D.
(adm. in ID; not adm. in CA) Dept. of Jus., Immigration & Naturalization
**Moss, Brian T.** ........... '63 '91 C.763 B.A. L.1049 J.D. [Ⓐ Manning,M.&W.] (⊙Irvine)
Moss, Bruce A. ............. '53 '79 C.800 B.A. L.1095 J.D. Pres., Artwood Desk Design
Moss, Carol Sperry ................... '29 '77 C.145 B.A. L.809 J.D. 500 Crestline Dr.
**Moss, David Z.** ............................ '69 '95 C.112 A.B. L.1066 J.D. [Ⓐ Irell&M.]
Moss, Howard .................. '48 '77 C.112 B.A. L.1148 J.D. 1925 Century Pk. E.
**Moss, Jon Roger** ............. '37 '65 C.112 B.A. L.1068 J.D. [Berger,K.S.M.F.S.&G.]
Moss, Lawrence J. ............................ '53 '78 C.112 A.B. L.426 J.D. [L.J.Moss]
**Moss, Randy A.** .................... '66 '91 C.112 B.A. L.1065 J.D. [Ⓐ Cummins&W.]
*LANGUAGES: French.
*PRACTICE AREAS: Insurance Defense.
**Moss, Rodney**, (AV) .................. '35 '61 C.112 B.S. L.1068 LL.B. [Moss,L.&M.]
*PRACTICE AREAS: Real Property Law; Commercial Law; Construction Litigation.
Moss, Wendy J. ..................... '52 '78 C.823 B.S. L.426 J.D. Dep. Dist. Atty.

**Moss, Hovden & Lindsay, A Professional Corporation**
**(See Whittier)**

Moss, Lawrence J., P.C. ......................................... 1888 Century Pk. E.

**Moss, Levitt & Mandell, LLP, (AV)**
**1901 Avenue of the Stars 19th Floor, 90067**
**Telephone: 310-284-8900 Telecopier: 310-284-6660**
**Ronald J. Mandell; Meyer S. Levitt; Rodney Moss. Of Counsel: Howard B. Brown.**
**Construction, Real Estate, Surety, Commercial Corporate and Business Law. Family Law. Title Insurance Defense. General Civil and Trial Practice.**
***See Professional Biographies, LOS ANGELES, CALIFORNIA***

Mossawir, Harve H., Jr., (P.C.), (AV) '42 '70 C.16 B.A. L.145 J.D.
1800 Ave. of the Stars, Suite 900 (Century City)
**Most, Peter J.** ..................... '64 '89 C.112 B.A. L.273 J.D. [Hennigan,M.&B.]
*PRACTICE AREAS: Antitrust; Litigation; Securities Litigation.
**Mosten, Forrest S.**, (AV) ........................ '47 '72 C&L.112 A.B., J.D. [Mosten&T.]
*PRACTICE AREAS: Litigation and Mediation; Family Law; Real Estate; Business; Legal Malpractice.

**Mosten & Tuffias, (AV) BB**
**10990 Wilshire Boulevard, Suite 940, 90024**
**Telephone: 310-473-7611 Facsimile: 310-473-7422**
**Email: FMostenn@counsel.com**

(This Listing Continued)

**Mosten & Tuffias (Continued)**

**Members of Firm: Forrest S. Mosten (Certified Specialist, Family Law, The State Bar of California Board of Legal Specialization); Heidi S. Tuffias (Certified Specialist, Family Law, The State Bar of California Board of Legal Specialization).**
**Practice Concentrating on Family Law, Litigation Mediation.**
***See Professional Biographies, LOS ANGELES, CALIFORNIA***

**Mote, Julie A.** ........................ '65 '95 C.445 B.S. L.1065 J.D. [Ⓐ Hawkins,S.L.&B.]
**Motiey, Katayoun** ................. '68 '95 C&L.276 B.A., J.D. [Ⓐ Skadden,A.S.M.&F.]
*LANGUAGES: Farsi, French and Spanish.
Motley, Dale E. ............ '49 '76 C.800 B.A. L.809 J.D. 10100 Santa Monica Blvd., 8th Fl.
**Motooka, Marjorie E.** ........................ '— '88 C.312 B.A. L.629 J.D. [Ⓐ Schaffer&L.]
Motz, Barbara Manheimer ..................... '48 '75 C&L.1068 B.A., J.D. Atty. Gen. Off.
**Motzkin, Randee Schuster** ........... '66 '92 C.112 B.A. L.1068 J.D. [Ⓐ Katten M.&Z.]
*PRACTICE AREAS: Finance and Reorganization.
Mouhibian, Knar Kouleyan, (Ms.) ... '56 '83 C.112 B.A. L.426 J.D. 2121 Ave. of the Stars
Moulin, John M. .......................... '55 '80 C.107 B.A. L.809 J.D. Dep. Dist. Atty.
Mountain, James W. '30 '63 C&L.426 B.B.A., LL.B.
Dep. Gen. Coun., Metro. Water Dist. of So. Calif.
**Moura, John J.** ........................ '52 '78 C.112 A.B. L.1066 J.D. [Sinnott,D.M.&P.]
*PRACTICE AREAS: General Trial Practice; Insurance Coverage; Products Liability.
Moura, Lorraine B. '48 '78
C.112 B.A. L.1066 J.D. Sr. Corp. Coun. Litig., Farmers Group, Inc.
Mouser, Marlena J., (AV) ...................... '52 '81 C.112 B.A. L.426 J.D. [Guizot&M.]
**Moussouros, Elizabeth A.** ........... '63 '91 C.112 B.A. L.990 J.D. [Ⓐ Charlston,R.&W.]
*PRACTICE AREAS: Insurance Coverage and Bad Faith; Environmental Litigation.
**Moutes, Celia D.** ................. '— '92 C.1077 B.A. L.426 J.D. [Ⓐ Sedgwick,D.M.&A.]
Moutes, Eugene A. ................. '28 '56 C.112 A.B. L.426 LL.B. Div. Chief Pub. Def.
**Mouw, Allan R.** ..................... '69 '95 C.112 B.A. L.800 J.D. [Ⓐ Buchalter,N.F.&Y.]
*PRACTICE AREAS: Corporate; Securities.
Mowbray-d'Arbela, Melissa P. '66 '93 C.025 B.A. L.569 J.D.
(adm. in NY; not adm. in CA) 300 S. Grand Ave.
Moxon, Kendrick L ............................. '50 '84 C.30 B.A. L.1184 J.D. [Bowles&M.]
**Moyer, Craig A.**, (AV) ........... '55 '80 C.800 B.A. L.1068 J.D. [Demetriou,D.S.&M.]
*PRACTICE AREAS: Environmental Law; Energy Law; Administrative Law.
**Moyer, Michelle M.** ......................... '64 '91 C.112 B.A. L.800 J.D. [Ⓐ Kirtland&P.]
**Mudie, F. Patricia**, (AV) ......................... '40 '77 C.659 B.A. L.800 J.D. [F.P.Mudie]

**Mudie, F. Patricia, A Professional Corporation, (AV) BB**
**12100 Wilshire Boulevard, Suite 1900, 90025-1506**
**Telephone: 310-820-5505 Fax: 310-207-1030**
**F. Patricia Mudie.**
**Family Law, Divorce, Domestic Relations and Matrimonial Law.**
***See Professional Biographies, LOS ANGELES, CALIFORNIA***

Muehle, Maurice L. ............................ '33 '59 C.605 B.A. L.800 J.D. [Muehle&W.]
Muehle & Whitman ................................................ 12301 Wilshire Blvd.
**Mueller, Eugene E.** ........................ '64 '92 C&L.800 B.Sc., J.D. [Ⓐ Manatt,P.&P.]
*PRACTICE AREAS: Insurance.
Mueller, Frederick E., (AV) ... '23 '53 C.477 A.B. L.1068 LL.B. 650 S. Grand Ave. (Pat.)
**Mueller, Grace Ellen** ............ '63 '88 C.604 B.A. L.800 J.D. [Ⓒ Sonnenschein N.&R.]
*PRACTICE AREAS: Insurance Coverage; General Business Litigation.
**Mueller, John A.** ......................... '66 '91 C.112 B.A. L.477 J.D. [Ⓐ Konowiecki&R.]
*PRACTICE AREAS: General Business; Corporate; Health Care.
**Mueller, John C.** ............................ '52 '77 C.813 A.B. L.800 J.D. [Baker&H.]
*PRACTICE AREAS: Environmental and Natural Resources Law.
**Mueller, Kenneth N.**, (AV) ........ '35 '64 C.813 A.B. L.1065 LL.B [Bonne,B.M.O.&N.]
Mueller, Phillips W. ........................ '38 '65 C.976 B.A. L.597 J.D. Dep. Dist. Atty.
**Mueller, Thomas R.** ............................ '56 '79 C&L.930 B.A., J.D. [Jones,D.R.&P.]
Mueller, Walter H. ...................... '51 '83 C&L.1077 B.A., J.D. Dep. Dist. Atty.
**Muhlbach, Robert A.**, (AV) ..................... '46 '76 C.112 B.S. L.1065 J.D. [Kirtland&P.]
**Muhlestein, Randolph G.**, (AV) ...... '52 '79 C&L.101 B.S., J.D. [Carlsmith B.W.C.&I.]
*LANGUAGES: Spanish.
*PRACTICE AREAS: Latin American Trade (20%); Corporate Law (80%).
**Muir, Marilyn** .................................. '63 '89 C.877 B.S. L.878 J.D. [Ⓐ Morris,P.&P.]
**Muir, Mary L.** ......................... '55 '80 C.112 B.S. L.1068 J.D. [Langberg,C.&D.]
*PRACTICE AREAS: Estate Planning; Probate; Corporate Law; Taxation.
Mukai, Dennis ............................................................ '45 '74 [Nishiyama,M.L.E.&S.]
**Mukhey, Ashok W.** ........................... '59 '84 C.112 A.B. L.309 J.D. [Irell&M.]
**Mulkeen, James P.**, (AV) ..................... '45 '70 C.641 B.A. L.862 J.D. [Manatt,P.&P.]
*PRACTICE AREAS: Labor; Employment Litigation; Business Litigation.
**Mullender, Joseph D., Jr.**, (AV) '27 '54 C.605 B.A. L.800 LL.B.
[Carlsmith B.W.C.&I.]
Muller, Edward R. '52 '78 C.197 A.B. L.976 J.D.
(adm. in DC; not adm. in CA) 10880 Wilshire Blvd.
**Muller, F. Thomas, Jr.** ..................... '53 '82 C.976 B.A. L.569 J.D. [O'Melveny&M.]
*PRACTICE AREAS: Real Estate Finance; Land Use; Land Development.
Muller, James S. ............................. '60 '86 C.112 B.A. L.1067 J.D. 3435 Wilshire Blvd.
Muller, Mark D. .................... '59 '84 C.112 B.S. L.426 J.D. Deloitte, Haskins & Sells
**Muller, Robert J.** '58 '95 C.1349 B.A. L.851 J.D.
(adm. in NY; not adm. in CA) [Ⓐ Christensen,M.F.J.G.W.&S.]
*PRACTICE AREAS: Litigation.
**Mullin, J. Stanley**, (AV) ........ '07 '33 C.813 A.B. L.309 LL.B. [Ⓒ Sheppard,M.R.&H.] ‡
**Mullins, Michael M.** ............... '51 '76 C.103 A.B. L.893 J.D. [Ⓐ Parker,M.C.O.&S.]
*REPORTED CASES: Westinghouse v. Newman & Holtzinger, 46 Cal. Rptr. 2d 151 (Cal. App. 1995); Westinghouse v. Newman & Holtzinger, 992 F. 2d 932 (9th Cir. 1993); Canadian Commercial Bank v. Ascher Findley Co., 280 Cal. Rptr. 521 (Cal. App. 1991); In re City of Northfield, 386 N.W.2d 748 (Mn. App. 1986); Soo Line RR Co. v. Commissioner of Revenue, 377 N.W. 2d 453 (Mn. 1985).
*PRACTICE AREAS: Commercial and Business Litigation; Public Entities Litigation; Appellate Practice.
**Mulrooney, Michele M.** ............. '60 '85 C&L.800 B.S., J.D. [Armstrong H.J.T.&W.]
*PRACTICE AREAS: Probate and Estate Planning.
Mulvaney, Kahan & Barry, A Professional Corporation, (AV)
445 S. Figueroa St., Ste. 2600 (⊙San Diego, La Jolla, Orange)
Mulvey, Bernard M. ........................... '32 '65 C.569 B.S. L.724 J.D. [Mulvey&M.]
Mulvey, Michelle ........................... '39 '65 C.102 B.A. L.724 LL.B. [Mulvey&M.]
Mulvey & Mulvey ............................................................ 6255 Sunset Blvd.
**Mulvihill, Cynthia Coulter** ........... '64 '94 C.1069 B.A. L.1137 J.D. [Ⓐ Knopfler&R.]
*PRACTICE AREAS: Construction Litigation; Personal Injury Defense.
Mumford, John S. ...................... '56 '81 C.597 B.A. L.352 J.D. 1801 Century Pk., E.
Mumford, Thomas C. .................. '61 '87 C.350 B.B.A. L.800 J.D. 515 S. Flower St.‡
**Mumm, Frederick F.**, (AV) '53 '79
C.893 B.S. L.945 J.D. Asst. Gen. Coun., CBS Inc. (Pat.)
Mund, Alan M., (AV) .......................... '36 '64 C.112 L.800 J.D. 1267 Stoner Ave.
Mund, Geraldine ............................ '43 '77 C.1036 B.A. L.426 J.D. U.S. Bkrptcy. J.
Munger, Charles T., (AV) .............................. '24 '49 C.477 L.309 J.D. P.O. Box 55007‡
Munger, Molly, (AV) '48 '74
C.681 B.A. L.309 J.D. NAACP Legal Def. & Educ. Fund, Inc.

**Munger, Tolles & Olson, (AV)** [BB]
**A Law Partnership including Professional Corporations**
**355 South Grand Avenue 35th Floor, 90071⊙**
**Telephone: 213-683-9100 Cable Address: "Muntoll" Telex: 677574 Telecopier: 213-687-3702**
**Members of Firm: Richard D. Esbenshade (A Professional Corporation); Frederick B. Warder, Jr. (1932-1972); Peter R. Taft (A Professional Corporation); Robert K. Johnson (A Professional Corporation) (Certified Specialist, Taxation Law, The State Bar of California Board of Legal Specialization); Alan V. Friedman (A Professional Corporation); Ronald L. Olson (A Professional Corporation); Dennis E. Kinnaird (A Professional Corporation); Richard S. Volpert; Dennis C. Brown (A Professional Corporation); Jeffrey I. Weinberger; Melvyn H. Wald (1947-1992); Edwin V. Woodsome, Jr., (A Professional Corporation); Robert L. Adler; Cary B. Lerman; William L. Cathey; Charles D. Siegal; Ronald K. Meyer; Gregory P. Stone; Vilma S. Martinez; Lucy T. Eisenberg; Brad D. Brian; Bradley S. Phillips; George M. Garvey; Rita J. Miller; D. Barclay Edmundson; William D. Temko; Steven L. Guise (A Professional Corporation); Robert B. Knauss; R. Gregory Morgan; Stephen M. Kristovich; John W. Spiegel; Terry E. Sanchez; Steven M. Perry; Ruth E. Fisher; Mark B. Helm; Joseph D. Lee; Michael R. Doyen; Michael E. Soloff; Gregory D. Phillips; John B. Frank; Lawrence C. Barth; Kathleen M. McDowell; Glenn D. Pomerantz; Thomas B. Walper; Ronald C. Hausmann (Resident, San Francisco Office); Patrick J. Cafferty, Jr. (Resident, San Francisco Office); Jay Masa Fujitani; O'Malley M. Miller; Sandra A. Seville-Jones; Mark H. Epstein; Henry Weissmann; Kevin S. Allred; Marc A. Becker; Cynthia L. Burch; Bart H. Williams; Jeffrey A. Heintz; Judith T. Kitano; Kristin A. Linsley; Marc T. G. Dworsky; Jerome C. Roth (Resident, San Francisco Office); Steven D. Rose; Jeffrey L. Bleich (Resident, San Francisco Office); Garth T. Vincent; Ted Dane. Associates: Marsha Hymanson; Stuart N. Senator; Eva Orlebeke Caldera; Monica Wahl Shaffer; Leonard P. Leichnitz; Andrew J. Thomas; Robert L. DellAngelo; Bruce A. Abbott; Martin D. Bern (Resident, San Francisco Office); Margaret Elizabeth Deane (Resident, San Francisco Office); Deanne B. Kyle; Susan R. Szabo; Inez D. Hope; Bernardo Silva; Kristin Sherratt Escalante; Manuel A. Abascal; Jonathan E. Altman; Gregg W. Kettles; Steven B. Weisburd; Ilana B. Rubenstein; Mary Ann Lyman; Carla N. Jones; John C. Ulin; James H. Ellis; Burton A. Gross (Resident, San Francisco Office); Andrea J. Weiss; Steven W. Hawkins; David M. Rosenzweig; David C. Dinielli; Peter A. Detre; Elizabeth Earle Beske (Resident, San Francisco Office); Edward C. Hagerott, Jr.; Kevin S. Masuda; Daniel P. Collins; Robert E. Holo (Not admitted in CA); Michael J. O'Sullivan; Steven Usdan; Paul J. Watford; Timothy P. Grieve; Hojoon Hwang (Resident, San Francisco Office); Jennifer R. Scullion; Devon A. Gold; Jose F. Sanchez; Sean A. Monroe; Jonathan R. Levey (Not admitted in CA); Kelly M. Klaus (Resident, San Francisco Office); Dennis M. Woodside; Douglas A. Axel; Rachel M. Capoccia; Bruce Hamilton Searby.**
**General Practice. Corporation, Securities and Business Law. Litigation, Labor Relations, Antitrust Law, Taxation, Real Property, Trust and Probate Law, Savings and Loan Law, Environmental Law.**
**Reference: The Bank of California.**
**San Francisco, California Office: 33 New Montgomery Street, Suite 1900. Telephone: 415-512-4000. FAX: 415-512-4077.**

***See Professional Biographies, LOS ANGELES, CALIFORNIA***

Munisoglu, Elizabeth Mitchell ............ '35 '88 C.478 B.A. L.990 J.D. Dep. Dist. Atty.
Munnerlyn, Sherri Lynn '61 '86 C.1125 B.A. L.260 J.D.
(adm. in AR; not adm. in CA) I.R.S.
**Muñoz, Enrique L.**, (BV) .......... '52 '78 C.763 B.A. L.1049 J.D. [Littler,M.F.T.&M.]
Muñoz, J. David .................... '68 '95 C.940 L.1068 J.D. 555 S. Flower St., 18th Fl.
**Muñoz, Patricia M.** ............... '60 '88 C.112 B.A. L.1068 J.D. [Ⓐ Dwyer,D.B.&B.]
*PRACTICE AREAS: Personal Injury Claims.
**Munro, Andrew B.** ...................... '68 '94 C.112 B.A. L.309 J.D. [Ⓐ Latham&W.]
*PRACTICE AREAS: Corporate; Telecommunications; Healthcare.
**Munro, Pamela Harrington** ...... '66 '91 C.112 B.S. L.426 J.D. [Ⓐ Harrington,F.D.&C.]
Munson, C. Eric ........................ '49 '84 C.911 B.A. L.1068 J.D. 8457 Melrose Pl.
**Murabayashi, Teryl** .............. '62 '90 C.190 B.S.B.A. L.1065 J.D. [Ⓐ Luce,F.H.&S.]
*PRACTICE AREAS: Commercial Litigation; Bankruptcy; Secured Creditor Representation.
**Murakami, Melanie** .................. '70 '95 C.112 B.A. L.1065 J.D. [Ⓐ Orrick,H.&S.]
**Muramatsu, Hisako** ............... '61 '89 C.112 B.S. L.426 J.D. [Ⓐ Graham&J.] (Pat.)
*LANGUAGES: Japanese.
*PRACTICE AREAS: Intellectual Property Law; Patent Law.
Muramoto, Edward ..................... '62 '89 C.112 B.A. L.1068 J.D. 865 S. Figueroa St.
**Muramoto, Edward T.** ............. '62 '89 C.112 B.A. L.1068 J.D. [Ⓐ Robins,K.M.&C.]
*PRACTICE AREAS: Insurance; Construction Litigation; Fidelity and Surety Practice and Litigation.
Murase, Ichiro M. ...................... '47 '76 C.112 L.800 U.S. House of Representatives
**Murata, Michael M.** ........................ '61 '90 C.976 B.A. L.569 J.D. [Ⓐ Lane P.S.L.]
**Muravina, Elena** ....................— '92 C.061 B.S. L.426 J.D. [Ⓐ Sheppard,M.R.&H.]
*PRACTICE AREAS: Transactions with Russia and other CIS republics.

**Murawski, Roberta L. '58 '82 C.112 B.A. L.273 J.D.**
**Suite 900 2049 Century Park East, 90067-3111**
**Telephone: 310-551-6959 Fax: 310-556-5687**
**General Civil Litigation, including Family Law.**

***See Professional Biographies, LOS ANGELES, CALIFORNIA***

Murchison, Donald, (BV) .......... '18 '48 C&L.800 A.B., LL.B. 1801 Ave. of the Stars‡

**Murchison & Cumming, (AV)**
**Chase Plaza, 801 South Grand Avenue, 9th Floor, 90017⊙**
**Telephone: 213-623-7400 Telex: 350 290 Fax: 213-623-6336**
**Members of Firm: Michael D. McEvoy (Resident, Santa Ana Office); Friedrich W. Seitz; Michael B. Lawler; George V. Genzmer, III; Benjamin H. Seal, II; Tom Y. K. Mei (Resident, Santa Ana Office); Steven L. Smilay; Kenneth H. Moreno (Resident, San Diego Office); Richard M. Arias; Robert A. Grantham; Dan L. Longo (Resident, Santa Ana Office); Jean M. Lawler; Edmund G. Farrell III. Associates: Robert M. Scherk (Resident, San Diego Office); Richard D. Newman (Resident, Santa Ana Office); Barbara L. McCully; Russell S. Wollman; Mary Jane Dellafiora; Laura I. Baer; Kim Rodgers Westhoff; Victor A. Lee (Resident, Santa Ana Office); Teresa Anna Libertino; Elizabeth A. Pollock; George G. Romain; James D. Carraway; Thomas E. Dias (Resident, Santa Ana Office); Sydnee R. Singer; Bryan M. Weiss; Scott Hengesbach; Guy R. Gruppie; Lee Ann Kern; Michael J. Ryan; Nancy Morrow Norris; Jean A. Dalmore; Sharyn G. Alcaraz; Corine Zygelman; J. Lynn Feldner (Resident, San Diego Office); James S. Williams; Julie F. Smith; Hugh Jeffrey Grant; Lawrence D. Marks; Caroline M. Albert; Jefferson S. Smith (Resident, San Diego Office); Allison Rose; Thomas R. Merrick; Kasey A. Covert; Mary Ann Alsnauer; Gerhard S. Gackle.**
**General, Civil, Trial and Appellate Practice in all State and Federal Courts. Negligence, Product Liability, Professional Liability, Intellectual Property, Employment Law, Insurance Coverage, Bad Faith and Business Litigation.**
**Santa Ana, California Office: 801 Park Tower, 200 West Santa Ana Boulevard. Telephone: 714-972-9977. Fax: 714-972-1404.**
**San Diego, California Office: Symphony Towers, 750 B Street, Suite 2550. Telephone: 619-544-6836. Fax: 619-544-1568.**

***See Professional Biographies, LOS ANGELES, CALIFORNIA***

Murdoch, Robert R. ...................... '41 '68 C.198 A.B. L.659 LL.B. 840 N. Larrabee
**Murdock, Leslie N.** ........................ '43 '85 C.112 B.A. L.426 J.D. [Ⓐ Perkins C.]
*PRACTICE AREAS: Loan Modifications/Workout; Real Estate; General Corporate.
**Murdock, Nanci E.** ...................... '49 '83 C.800 B.A. L.426 J.D. [Ⓒ Agapay,L.&H.]
*REPORTED CASES: Musick, Peeler & Garrett v. Employers Insurance of Wausau, 113 S.Ct. 2085, 124 L.Ed. 2d 194, 61 U.S.L.W. 4520 (1993).
*PRACTICE AREAS: Appellate; Business Litigation; Intellectual Property.
Murdock, Susan E. '62 '87
C.228 A.B. L.178 J.D. Coun., New World Television Programming
**Murillo, Janet S.** ..................... '53 '78 C.770 B.A. L.1068 J.D. [Nossaman,G.K.&E.]
*PRACTICE AREAS: Corporations Law; Securities Law; Commercial Law.
Murphy, Allen W. ............................ '34 '77 C.724 B.B.A. L.809 J.D. 1830 Taft Ave.
Murphy, Barbara G. ....................... '54 '79 C.112 B.A. L.426 J.D. Dep. Dist. Atty.
**Murphy, Bennett J.** .......................... '57 '84 C.31 B.A. L.309 J.D. [Latham&W.]
*PRACTICE AREAS: Bankruptcy; Creditors Rights.
**Murphy, Brian A.** ........................ '64 '95 C.209 B.S. L.800 J.D. [Langberg,C.&D.]
Murphy, Brian J. ......................'59 '84 C.846 B.A. L.1049 J.D. 1137 W. Olympic Blvd.
**Murphy, Cheryl O'Connor** ............ '68 '94 C.112 B.A. L.800 J.D. [Ⓐ Howrey&S.]
**Murphy, Christopher P.** ................ '49 '85 C.061 B.A. L.1068 J.D. [Ⓒ Mayer,B.&P.]

**Murphy, Daniel G.** .............................. '52 '83 C.1100 B.A. L.1194 J.D. [Loeb&L.]
*PRACTICE AREAS: Litigation.
**Murphy, Dennis J.** ................ '55 '80 C.763 B.A. L.1065 J.D. [Schwartz,S.D.&S.]
*PRACTICE AREAS: ERISA; Employee Benefit Law; Labor and Employment Law.
**Murphy, Elizabeth H.** ................ '68 '94 C.112 B.A. L.800 J.D. [Ⓐ Buchalter,N.F.&Y.]
*PRACTICE AREAS: Litigation; Receiverships.
**Murphy, G. Wayne, (P.C.)** ........ '42 '69 C.1077 B.A. L.426 J.D. [Ⓐ Anderson,M.&C.]
*PRACTICE AREAS: Contract Law; Construction Law; Public Contract Law; Surety Law.
**Murphy, Hardy Ray** ........................ '68 '96 C.800 B.S. L.1068 J.D. [Ⓐ Fulbright&J.]
*PRACTICE AREAS: General Litigation.
**Murphy, James Duff** .................. '54 '82 C.800 A.B. L.426 J.D. [Oliver,V.S.M.&L.]
*PRACTICE AREAS: Eminent Domain; Inverse Condemnation; Civil Litigation.
**Murphy, James J.** '47 '74 C.1042 B.A. L.208 J.D.
V.P., Gen. Coun. & Secy., Transamerica Financial Servs.
**Murphy, James M.**, (AV) ............. '35 '63 C&L.309 A.B., LL.B. [Ⓒ Gibson,D.&C.]
Murphy, Judith .................................. '40 '81 C.525 B.A. L.336 J.D. 1531 W. Ninth St.
**Murphy, Kenneth J.**, (AV) ......................... '37 '64 C.770 B.S. L.800 J.D. [Arter&H.]
**Murphy, M. Laurie**, (BV) ................ '52 '85 C.1044 B.S. L.425 J.D. [Valensi,R.&M.]
*PRACTICE AREAS: Litigation; Real Estate Litigation; Construction Litigation; Business Litigation; Insurance Coverage and Litigation.
Murphy, Martin J. '— '87 C.999 M.B.A. L.426 J.D.
U.S. Securities & Exchange Comm.
**Murphy, Michael J.** ............... '57 '84 C.1148 B.A. L.813 J.D. [Ⓒ Allen,M.L.G.&M.]
*PRACTICE AREAS: Tax.

**Murphy, Michael M., (AV) '39 '64 C.602 B.B.A. L.1068 J.D.** [BB]
**555 South Flower Street, Suite 2850, 90071**
**Telephone: 213-488-3323 Fax: 213-689-0863**
**Practice Specializing in Real Estate Sales and Acquisitions, Commercial Leasing, Property Management, Real Estate Financing and Construction Law.**

***See Professional Biographies, LOS ANGELES, CALIFORNIA***

Murphy, Molly S. .......................... '65 '90 C&L.494 B.A., J.D. 221 N. Figueroa St.
Murphy, R. Dan, (AV) ................................ '44 '73 L.1148 J.D. Asst. Dist. Atty.
**Murphy, Randall L.** .................... '54 '89 C.546 B.A. L.976 J.D. [Ⓐ White O.C.&A.]
Murphy, Rena Carolyn ......................... '41 '70 C.612 B.S. L.1077 J.D. Juv. Ct. Ref.

**Murphy, Tamela J. '60 '92 C.610 B.B.A. L.117 J.D.**
**415 Washington Boulevard., Suite 504, 90292**
**Telephone: 310-822-4401 Fax: 310-822-4401**
**(Not admitted in CA).**
***PRACTICE AREAS: Entertainment Law (33%, 20); General Practice (66%, 50).**
**Entertainment, including Musicians and Film, Transactional and Litigation.**

***See Professional Biographies, LOS ANGELES, CALIFORNIA***

Murphy, Timothy M. ..................... '53 '77 C.1077 B.A. L.426 J.D. Comr., Supr. Ct.

**Murphy, Weir & Butler, A Professional Corporation, (AV)**
**2049 Century Park East, 21st Floor, 90067⊙**
**Telephone: 310-788-3700 FAX: 310-788-3777**
**Email: lawyer@mwblaw.com**
**Lawrence Bass; N. Dwight Cary; Spencer J. Helfen; Jean B. LeBlanc, II; Robert Jay Moore; Gary B. Rosenbaum; Adam G. Spiegel; Rolf S. Woolner; Mary L. Trokel Young;—Demetra V. Georgelos; Eric S. Kurtzman; William W. Neuschaefer; Paul P. Sagan; Eric E. Sagerman; Richard Villaseñor. Of Counsel: Bernard Shapiro; Robert L. Ordin.**
**Secured Financing and Commercial Lending, Real Estate Finance, Business Workouts and Bankruptcy Reorganizations, Creditors' Remedies. Trial Practice and Litigation.**
**San Francisco, California Office: 101 California Street, 39th Floor. Telephone: 415-398-4700. Telex: 705457 MWB UD. Telecopiers: 415-421-7879; 415-788-0783.**

***See Professional Biographies, LOS ANGELES, CALIFORNIA***

**Murray, Anthony**, (AV) ............................ '37 '65 C.1043 L.426 J.D. [Loeb&L.]
*PRACTICE AREAS: Civil, Criminal and Commercial Litigation.
**Murray, Christopher C.**, (AV) ......... '49 '75 C.339 B.A. L.800 J.D. [O'Melveny&M.]
*PRACTICE AREAS: Intellectual Property; Entertainment Law.
Murray, James D., (AV) .................... '36 '61 C.375 B.S. L.900 LL.B. [Murray&B.]
**Murray, Jason C.** ..................... '67 '94 C.549 B.A. L.800 J.D. [Ⓐ Gibson,D.&C.]
*PRACTICE AREAS: Entertainment Litigation; General Commercial Litigation.
Murray, Kevin '60 '87 C.1077 B.S. L.426 J.D.
8721 Santa Monica Blvd., West Hollywood
Murray, Marcia S. ...................... '44 '81 C.821 B.A. L.477 J.D. 1322 Killarney Ave.
**Murray, Margaret E.** ................. '58 '87 C.103 A.B. L.1065 J.D. [Folger L.&K.]⊙
*PRACTICE AREAS: Litigation; Employment Law.
**Murray, Robert C.** ..................... '59 '89 C.453 B.S. L.813 J.D. [Ⓐ O'Melveny&M.]
Murray & Bendel, (AV) .............................. 21031 Ventura Blvd. (Woodland Hills)

**Murray, Bradshaw & Budzyn, A Law Corporation**
(See Pasadena)

Murrin, Thomas L. ................ '39 '64 C.426 B.A. L.800 LL.B. 822 S. Tremaine Ave.
**Murtagh, Maurine M.** .................. '46 '96 C.276 B.S.B.A. L.228 J.D. [Ⓐ Irell&M.]
*LANGUAGES: Spanish.
**Musante, Thomas A.** ........ '65 '93 C&L.112 A.B., J.D. Assoc. Coun., SunAmerica Inc.
*RESPONSIBILITIES: General Corporate Practice.

**Musick, Peeler & Garrett LLP, (AV)**
**Suite 2000, One Wilshire Boulevard, 90017-3321⊙**
**Telephone: 213-629-7600 Cable Address: "Peelgar" Facsimile: 213-624-1376**
**Members of Firm: Elvon Musick (1890-1968); Joseph D. Peeler (1895-1991); Leroy A. Garrett (1906-1963); William L. Abalona (Resident at Sacramento Office; See Sacramento listing for full biographical information); Donald P. Asperger (Resident at Fresno Office; See Fresno listing for full biographical information); Willie R. Barnes; Graham E. Berry; James B. Bertero (Resident at San Diego Office; See San Diego listing for full biographical information); James B. Betts (Resident at Fresno Office; See Fresno listing for full biographical information); Hal G. Block (Resident at Irvine Office; See Irvine listing for full biographical information); Mary Catherine M. Bohen; Eduardo A. Guerini Bolt (Resident at Irvine Office; See Irvine listing for full biographical information); William A. Bossen; Geoffrey C. Brown; John R. Browning; Leonard E. Castro; Harry W. R. Chamberlain, II; Richard S. Conn; R. Joseph De Briyn (Chairman, Management Committee and Managing Partner); Dennis S. Diaz; Edsell M. Eady, Jr. (Resident at San Francisco Office; See San Francisco listing for full biographical information); Steven J. Elie; Philip Ewen; Susan J. Field; Martin L. Fineman (Resident at San Francisco Office; See San Francisco listing for full biographical information); Charles F. Forbes; Robert D. Girard; Mark J. Grushkin; Stephen A. Hansen (Resident at Fresno Office; See Fresno listing for full biographical information); Larry C. Hart; James M. Hassan; Susan J. Hazard; Paul D. Hesse; Michael J. Hickman (Resident at San Diego Office; See San Diego listing for full biographical information); Anne Yeager Higgins; Thomas T. Kawakami; Edward A. Landry; David M. Lester; J. Robert Liset; Wayne B. Littlefield; Seth B. Madnick (Resident at San Francisco Office; See San Francisco listing for full biographical information); David G. Mann; C. Donald McBride (Resident at San Francisco Office; See San Francisco listing for full biographical information); James W. Miller; William McD. Miller, III; Michael W. Monk; Robert Y. Nagata (Certified Specialist, Taxation Law, The State Bar of California Board of Legal Specialization); Lynn A. O'Leary; Gary F. Overstreet; Alan R. Perry (Resident at San Diego Office; See San Diego listing for full biographical information); David A. Radovich; Stuart W. Rudnick; Cheryl L. Schreck; Robert L. Schuchard; Brian J. Seery; Mary Beth Sipos; Charles E. Slyngstad; Gerard Smolin, Jr. (Resident at San Diego Office; See San Diego listing for full biographical information); W. Clark Stanton (Resident at San Francisco Office; See San Francisco listing for full biographical information); Robert M. Stone; David A. Tartaglio; Juan A. Torres; Eric L. Troff; Mark H. Van Brussel (Resident at Sacramento Office; See Sacramento listing for full biographical information); David L. Volk; Robert G. Warshaw; Steven D. Weinstein; J. Patrick Whaley (Certified Specialist, Taxation Law, The State Bar of California Board of Legal Specialization); Gary L. Wollberg (Resident at San Diego Office, See San Diego listing for full**

(This Listing Continued)

CAA301P

**Musick, Peeler & Garrett LLP (Continued)**

**biographical information); David C. Wright; Janet L. Wright (Resident at Fresno Office; See Fresno listing for full biographical information); Robert M. Zeller; Alan J. Zuckerman (Resident at San Diego Office; See San Diego listing for full biographical information). Of Counsel: Maryann Link Goodkind; Mark Kiguchi; James E. Ludlam; Stephen J. M. Morris; Lawrence E. Stickney. Associates: Amy C. Bloom (Resident at San Francisco Office); Lisa M. Burkdall; Heather Bussing (Resident at Fresno Office); Bethany A. Cook; Dennis M. P. Ehling; Lauren Erickson; Edward T. Fenno; John T. Gilbertson; Michael R. Goldstein; Spencer Hamer; Peter T. Haven; Robin L. Hayward (Resident at Irvine Office); Kevin D. Jeter; Michael F. Klein; Daniel H. Lee; Kathleen A. McKnight (Resident at Fresno Office); Daniel Penserini (Resident at Sacramento Office); Gail A. Regenstreif; Michael D. Rountree; Dori K. Rybacki (Resident at San Diego Office); John J. Selbak; Sharon A. Siefert; Samuel H. Stein; Lawrence A. Tabb; Etta A. Talbot; Jeffrey R. Thomas; Stuart D. Tochner; Danny W. Wan (Resident at San Francisco Office); Monica Seine Wong.**
**General Practice. Trial and Appellate Practice. Corporation, Securities and Antitrust Law. Healthcare, Hospital, College and University Law. Insurance, Excess, Reinsurance and Coverage. Labor, Real Estate, Land Use, Environmental, Eminent Domain, Oil and Gas and Mining Law. Taxation, Trust, Probate, Estate Planning, Bankruptcy and Pension and Profit Sharing Law.**
**San Diego, California Office: 1900 Home Savings Tower, 225 Broadway. Telephone: 619-231-2500. Facsimile: 619-231-1234.**
**San Francisco, California Office: Suite 1300, Steuart Street Tower, One Market Plaza. Telephone: 415-281-2000. Facsimile: 415-281-2010.**
**Sacramento, California Office: Wells Fargo Center, Suite 1280, 400 Capitol Mall. Telephone: 916-557-8300. Facsimile: 916-442-8629.**
**Fresno, California Office: 6041 North First Street. Telephone: 209-228-1000. Facsimile: 209-447-4670.**
**Irvine, California Office: 2603 Main Street, Suite 1025. Telephone: 714-852-5122. Facsimile: 714-852-5128.**

***See Professional Biographies, LOS ANGELES, CALIFORNIA***

**Mustafa, John W., II** ............ '63 '91 C.112 B.A. L.1068 J.D. [🄰 Sedgwick,D.M.&A.]
**Mutchnik, Allan G.** ................ '63 '88 C.112 B.A. L.188 J.D. [Skadden,A.S.M.&F.]
Muth, Dudley ..................... '39 '67 C.668 B.A. L.800 J.D. 61 S. Figuero St.‡

**Myer, Scott D. '61 '86 C.112 B.A. L.1068 J.D.**
**1900 Avenue of the Stars Suite 1070, 90067**
**Telephone: 310-277-3000 Fax: 310-277-3510**
**Business, Real Estate, Bankruptcy, Personal Injury, Estate Planning. General Civil and Trial Practice in all Courts.**

***See Professional Biographies, LOS ANGELES, CALIFORNIA***

Myers, Dale F. ..................... '43 '68 C.763 A.B. L.734 J.D. 9255 W. Sunset Blvd.
**Myers, David A.** .................. '63 '89 C.1042 B.A. L.426 J.D. [🄰 Chapin,F.&W.]
Myers, David J., (BV) .............. '57 '84 C.112 B.A. L.426 J.D. 1900 Ave. of the Stars
Myers, E. John ..................... '63 '89 C.112 B.A. L.426 J.D. Dep. Pub. Def.
**Myers, Jeffrey Cabot** ............. '61 '90 C.30 B.A. L.809 J.D. [🄰 McKay,B.&G.]
*PRACTICE AREAS: Appellate Practice; Insurance Defense; Personal Injury.
Myers, Jill Anne ................... '67 '94 C.1036 B.A. L.94 J.D. 725 S. Figueroa St.
Myers, Michael J. ......... '43 '69 C.763 B.A. L.1066 J.D. Coun., Atlantic Richfield Co.
Myers, Susan Baldwin ............... '61 '88 C.273 B.A. L.309 J.D. 444 S Flower St.
Myers, Thomas ............. '60 '85 C.696 B.A. L.800 J.D. 601 S. Figueroa St., 41st Fl.
**Myers, Thomas A.** ................ '64 '94 C.31 B.A. L.309 J.D. [🄰 McKenna&C.]
*PRACTICE AREAS: Labor and Employment Law.

**Myers & D'Angelo**
**(See Pasadena)**

Myman, Robert M., (AV) .......... '46 '71 C.1077 A.B. L.800 J.D. [Myman,A.F.G.&R.]
Myman, Abell, Fineman, Greenspan & Rowan, (AV) ........... 11777 San Vicente Blvd.
**Myricks, Randy J.** ............ '65 '93 C.966 B.B.A. L.494 J.D. [🄰 Allen,M.L.G.&M.]
*PRACTICE AREAS: Real Property.
**Nachman, David J.** ....... '68 '92 C.112 B.A. L.659 J.D. [🄰 Christensen,M.F.J.G.W.&S.]
*PRACTICE AREAS: Tax Law; Corporate Law; Business Law; Real Estate Law.
**Nachshin, Robert J., (A Professional Corporation),** (AV) '50 '77 C.105 B.A. L.178 J.D. [Nachshin&W.]
*PRACTICE AREAS: Family Law.

**Nachshin & Weston, (AV) BB**
**A Partnership including Professional Corporations**
**Suite 2240, 11755 Wilshire Boulevard, 90025**
**Telephone: 310-478-6868 Telefax: 310-473-8112**
**Robert J. Nachshin (A Professional Corporation) (Certified Specialist, Family Law, The State Bar of California Board of Legal Specialization); Scott N. Weston (A Professional Corporation). Associates: Joseph A. Langlois.**
**Practice Limited to Family, Domestic Relations, Divorce and Matrimonial Law.**

***See Professional Biographies, LOS ANGELES, CALIFORNIA***

Nachtigall, Ellen C. ...................... '66 '92 C.918 B.A. L.800 J.D. 444 S. Flower St.
Nadel, Paul J. ......................... '58 '83 C.800 B.A. L.597 J.D. 2121 Ave. of the Stars
Nadler, Robert A. .............. '62 '90 C.569 B.A. L.861 J.D. 1200 Wilshire Blvd., 6th Fl.
**Nadolenco, John** ...................... '70 '95 C.37 B.A. L.30 J.D. [🄰 Mayer,B.&P.]

**Naegele, Timothy D., & Associates, (AVⓉ) '41 '66 C.112 A.B. L.1066 LL.B. BB**
**Suite 2430, 1900 Avenue of the Stars, 90067⊙**
**Telephone: 310-557-2300 Facsimile: 310-457-4014**
**Email: naegelewdc@aol.com URL: http://www.naegele.com**
***SPECIAL AGENCIES: Federal Deposit Insurance Corporation, States of California and Maine (recodified state's banking laws).**
***REPORTED CASES: Downriver Community Federal Credit Union vs. Penn Square Bank, 879 F.2d 754 (10th Circuit, 1989); Bender vs. CenTrust Mortgage Corp., 833 F. Supp. 1525 (S.D. Fla. 1992); Bender v. CenTrust Mortgage Corp., 833 F. Supp. 1540 (S.D. Fla. 1992); Bender v. CenTrust Mortgage Corp., 51 F.3d 1027 (11th Cir. 1995).**
***TRANSACTIONS: Acquisition of Southern California Savings by The Securities Groups, 1982; Acquisitions by Household Bank, F.S.B., of Fidelity Federal Savings and Loan of Baltimore, 1984, American Heritage of Illinois, 1984, Fidelity Savings & Loan of Martins Ferry, Ohio, 1985, Brighton Federal of Colorado, 1985, and Century Savings of Kansas, 1985; and acquisition of United Bank of San Francisco by Hibernia Bancshares Corporation, 1986.**
***PRACTICE AREAS: Banks and Banking; Credit Unions; Bank Failures; Banking Litigation; Resolution Trust Corporation.**
**General Practice. Financial Institutions Law. Banking, Savings and Loan, Savings Bank and Credit Union Law.**
**Washington, D.C. Office: Suite 300, 1250 24th Street, N.W., 20037. Telephone: 202-466-7500. Facsimile: 202-466-3079 or 466-2888. Internet Web Site: http://www.naegele.com. Internet E-mail: naegelewdc@aol.com.**

***See Professional Biographies, LOS ANGELES, CALIFORNIA***

**Naegele, Tracy A.** .................. '54 '85 C.118 A.B. L.800 J.D. [🄰 J.W.E.Hoffmann]
Naftel, Nancy M., (BV) ................ '42 '80 C.112 A.B. L.1137 J.D. Dep. Dist. Atty.
**Nagai, John T.** ........................ '58 '82 C.813 A.B. L.309 J.D. [Graham&J.]
*LANGUAGES: Japanese.
*PRACTICE AREAS: Taxation Law; Corporate Law; International Business Law.
Nagano, Neil R. ........... '55 '83 C.112 A.B. L.1068 J.D. Screen Gems-EMI Music Inc.
**Nagata, Robert Y.,** (AV) ............... '45 '71 C.800 B.S. L.1049 J.D. [Musick,P.&G.]
*LANGUAGES: Japanese.
*PRACTICE AREAS: Taxation; Business Law.
Nagelberg, Larry ...................... '51 '79 L.1148 J.D. 10940 Wilshire Blvd.
**Nagle, G. Andrew** ........ '54 '83 C.1042 B.A. L.809 J.D. [🄰 Manning,M.&W.] (⊙Irvine)
**Nagle, Margaret A.** ................ '50 '75 C.93 A.B. L.178 J.D. [Stroock&S.&L.]
*PRACTICE AREAS: Litigation; Environmental Law; Products Liability.
Nagle, Robert E. ....... '48 '84 C.990 B.S. L.809 J.D. Sr. Corp. Coun., Farmers Group, Inc.
**Nagle, Theresa A.** .................. '57 '93 C.645 B.A. L.1066 J.D. [🄰 Folger L.&K.]⊙

**Nagler, Ellen Roth** ..................... '60 '86 C.112 B.A. L.800 J.D. [🄰 Jones,K.&A.]
*PRACTICE AREAS: Real Estate; Corporate.

**Nagler & Associates**
**(See Beverly Hills)**

**Nagy, John S.** ...... '51 '81 C.932 B.S.I.E. L.209 J.D. [Fulwider P.L.&U.] (See Pat. Sect.)
*PRACTICE AREAS: Patent, Trademark, Copyright and Unfair Competition Law; Litigation.
**Nagy, Paul G.** ............... '62 '94 C.112 B.S. L.426 J.D. [🄰 Loeb&L.] (See Pat. Sect.)
*PRACTICE AREAS: Patent Prosecution; Intellectual Property; Antitrust.
**Nahabedian, Raffi A.** ............... '65 '95 C.1077 B.S. L.990 J.D. [🄰 Lewis,D.B.&B.]
**Nahai, Behzad** ....................... '58 '84 C.054 LL.B. L.1066 LL.M. [Nahai]
*LANGUAGES: Persian and French.
*PRACTICE AREAS: Real Estate Law; Corporate Law; Civil Litigation.
**Nahai, Hamid** ................................... '52 '79 C&L.061 LL.B. [Nahai]
*LANGUAGES: French and Persian.
*PRACTICE AREAS: Real Estate Law; Business Law; Corporate Law; Environmental Law.

**Nahai Law Corporation, A Professional Corporation**
**Suite 800 1875 Century Park East, 90067**
**Telephone: 310-201-6800 Fax: 310-201-6811**
**Hamid Nahai; Behzad Nahai.**
**Real Estate, Environmental. Corporate and Business Law and Civil Litigation.**

***See Professional Biographies, LOS ANGELES, CALIFORNIA***

Nahin, Bruce A., (AV) ....................... '53 '77 C.112 B.A. L.426 J.D. [Nahin&N.]⊙
Nahin, Melville H. ................................ '29 '53 C.112 L.426 J.D. [Nahin&N.]
Nahin and Nahin, Law Corporation, (AV) ................ 6500 Wilshire Blvd. (⊙Valencia)
Nahmias, Edward B. '52 '81 C.588 B.S. L.724 J.D.
(adm. in NY; not adm. in CA) Capital Research Co.
Naiditch, Louis, (AV) ........................ '15 '37 C.112 L.809 LL.B. 1601 Blue Jay Way‡
Naiman, Loren M. ..................... '53 '78 C.112 B.A. L.426 LL.B. Dep. Dist. Atty.
**Naish, Dennis M.** .............................. '64 '89 C&L.911 B.A., J.D. [🄰 Thelen,M.J.&B.]
*PRACTICE AREAS: Construction and Government Contracts; Bankruptcy Law; General Commercial Litigation.
Najera, Carol Jane ........................... '60 '85 C&L.800 B.A., J.D. Dist. Atty. Off.
**Najfabadi, Elahe** ....................... '58 '91 L.1136 J.D. [🄰 C.Shusterman]
*LANGUAGES: Spanish, Farsi and Hindi.
*PRACTICE AREAS: Immigration and Naturalization Law.
Nakagawa, Robert Y. ........... '44 '71 C.339 B.S. L.1068 J.D. Workers Comp. App. Bd.
Nakagiri, Neal E. '54 '91 C.112 B.A. L.426 J.D.
Sr. V.P. & Gen. Coun., Associated Financial Grp., Inc.
Nakaki, Carolyn K. ........................... '57 '87 C&L.800 B.S., J.D. Dep. Dist. Atty.
**Nakamura, Richard H., Jr.** ............. '57 '82 C.112 B.A. L.1162 J.D. [🄰 Morris,P.&P.]
Nakamura, Robert Y. ..................... '51 '77 C.769 B.A. L.1065 J.D. 321 E. 2nd St.
Nakamura, Tetsujiro ............ '17 '56 C.112 A.B. L.809 LL.B. 321 E. 2nd St.‡
**Nakano, Nana** ............................ '— '96 C.426 B.A. L.990 J.D. [🄰 Bonne,B.M.O.&N.]
**Nakasone, Steven M.** .................. '46 '75 C.112 B.S. L.426 J.D. [🄲 Pillsbury M.&S.]
**Nakata, Stephen** .............................. '— '93 C.112 B.A. L.765 J.D. [🄰 Baker&H.]
*PRACTICE AREAS: Product Liability; Workers Compensation.
**Nakatani, Akiko** ......................... '69 '94 C.483 B.A. L.188 J.D. [🄰 Kelley D.&W.]
*PRACTICE AREAS: Corporate; International, Asia.
Nakazato, Arthur, (AV) ....................... '52 '78 C.665 B.A. L.831 J.D. U.S. Mag. J.
Nall, Theodore R., Jr. ............. '31 '74 C.695 B.A. L.398 J.D. Dep. Comm., Supr. Ct.
Nangle, John C. ........... '41 '66 C.145 B.A. L.597 J.D. Assoc. Reg. Solr., Dept. of Labor
Nangle, John J. '29 '56 C.276 B.S. L.734 LL.B.
(adm. in MO; not adm. in CA) U.S. Dept. of Labor
Nankivell, Paul H., II, (AV) .......... '48 '74 C.800 A.B. L.861 J.D. 4221 Wilshire Blvd.
Napoli, John W. ................ '46 '79 C.336 B.S.Bus. L.1179 J.D. Dep. Pub. Def.
Narayanan, Ash .............. '65 '91 C.879 B.S. L.426 J.D. Mgr., Arthur Andersen LLP
**Nardi, Denise A.** ........................... '58 '87 C.112 B.A. L.426 J.D. [🄰 Schell&D.]

**Nardoni, Silvio, (AV) '46 '71 C.684 B.A. L.477 J.D.**
**1925 Century Park East Suite 2000, 90067**
**Telephone: 310-277-2236 Fax: 310-788-9290**
**Business Litigation, Bankruptcy, Elder Law, Personal Injury, Elder Abuse Litigation.**

***See Professional Biographies, LOS ANGELES, CALIFORNIA***

**Narwitz, Norman S.,** (AV) ............. '38 '64 C.112 B.S. L.426 J.D. [Sands N.F.L.&L.]
**Nasatir, Iain A.W.** ................. '57 '83 C.178 B.A. L.978 J.D. [🄲 Pachulski,S.Z.&Y.]

**Nasatir, Hirsch & Podberesky**
**(See Santa Monica)**

Nash, Adrienne Elizabeth ........... '— '93 C.860 B.S. L.1068 J.D. 10880 Wilshire Blvd.
**Nash, Laura P.** ...................... '62 '88 C.426 B.A. L.1068 J.D. [🄰 Robins,K.M.&C.]
*PRACTICE AREAS: Litigation.
**Nash, Vicki A.** ...... '56 '93 C.112 B.S. L.426 J.D. [🄰 O'Melveny&M.] (⊙Newport Beach)

**Nash & Edgerton**
**(See Hermosa Beach)**

Naso, Michael A. .......... '62 '89 C.1044 B.A. L.809 J.D. 1901 Ave. of the Stars, 20th Fl.
**Nass, Menasche M.** ................ '49 '82 C.186 B.S. L.813 J.D. [De Castro,W.&C.]
*PRACTICE AREAS: Taxation Law; Business Law.
Nassif, George F. ................................ '57 '82 C.112 B.A. L.61 J.D. I.R.S.
Nassif, Nicholas S. ..................... '52 '87 C.350 B.S. L.221 J.D. 3055 Wilshire Blvd.
Nassiri, Kianoosh ............. '65 '89 C.1271 B.A. L.1194 J.D. 10850 Wilshire Blvd.
**Nathan, Lloyd Charles** ......................... '65 '91 C.054 LL.B. L.061 [🄰 Loeb&L.]
*LANGUAGES: French.
**Nathenson, Larry P.** .......... '58 '82 C.605 A.B. L.1068 J.D. [🄰 La Follette,J.D.F.&A.]
*PRACTICE AREAS: Insurance Coverage; Bad Faith Litigation.
**Nation, Robert** .................. '53 '83 C.112 B.A. L.1095 J.D. [🄰 Federman,G.&G.]
*PRACTICE AREAS: Complex Litigation; ADR; Insurance Coverage; Architectural; Engineering.
Natkin, Kenneth H., (AV) .... '37 '79 C.112 B.Arch. L.1066 J.D. 663 W. 5th (⊙San Fran.)
**Natsis, Anton N.** ...................... '58 '83 C&L.477 B.B.A., J.D. [Allen,M.L.G.&M.]
*PRACTICE AREAS: Real Estate Development Law; Finance Law.
**Natter, Janine S.** ......................... '65 '92 C.30 B.A. L.1065 J.D. [🄰 Codikow&C.]⊙
Nau, Robert M., (AV) ..................... '50 '77 C.347 B.S. L.800 J.D. [Alexander,H.N.&R.]
**Navarrette, Rick D.** ...................... '60 '86 C.37 B.A. L.1068 J.D. [Hong&C.]
*PRACTICE AREAS: Business Trials and Litigation; Bankruptcy; Commercial Law.
**Navarro, Ralph C.,** (AV) ........................ '49 '74 C.800 A.B. L.813 J.D. [Coudert]
Navarro, Rodolfo F. ............ '67 '92 C.112 B.A. L.1068 J.D. 210 W. Temple St., 19th Fl.
Navis, Patricia M. '48 '87 C.339 B.S. L.809 J.D.
Assoc. Gen. Coun. & V.P., Trust Company of the West
**Naylor, Christine** ................. '65 '94 C.1109 B.A. L.809 J.D. [🄲 Gibson,D.&C.]
Nayo, Lydia A. '51 '86 C.766 B.A. L.276 J.D.
(adm. in MD; not adm. in CA) Assoc. Prof., Loyola Univ. Law Sch.
Nazarian, John K. ........................... '23 '49 C&L.800 B.S., J.D. 10850 Wilshire Blvd.
**Neal, Dale K.,** (AV) ............................ '48 '74 C.309 B.A. L.813 J.D. [Latham&W.]
**Neal, Malena R.** .......................... '66 '91 C&L.329 B.A., J.D. [🄰 Fried,F.H.S.&J.]
Neal, Richard C. ........................... '47 '73 C.309 A.B. L.1066 J.D. Supr. Ct. J.

# PRACTICE PROFILES

## CALIFORNIA—LOS ANGELES

**Neale, David L.** .................. '62 '88 C.674 B.A. L.178 J.D. [Levene,N.&B.]
 *LANGUAGES: Chinese (Mandarin); Spanish.
 *REPORTED CASES: In re Oak Creek Energy Farms, Ltd., 107 B.R. 266 (Bkrptcy. E.D. Cal. 1989); Energrey Enterprises, Inc. v. Oak Creek Energy Systems, Inc., 119 B.R. 739 (E.D. Cal. 1990); In re Qintex Entertainment, Inc., 950 F.2d 1492 (9th. Cir. 1991); In re Oak Creek Energy Farms, Ltd., 99 B.R. 36 (Bkrptcy. E.D. Cal. 1989).
 *PRACTICE AREAS: Bankruptcy.
**Neale, Mary H.** ...................... '61 '89 C.112 B.A. L.178 J.D. [ⓒ Orrick,H.&S.]
 *PRACTICE AREAS: Public Finance; Banking; Project Finance.
Nearing, Henry L., Jr. ............................. '40 '71 C.884 B.E.E. L.94 J.D. I.R.S.
Nearing, Phoebe Lin ................ '55 '79 C.597 B.A. L.800 J.D. Asst. Dist. Coun.
**Nebenzahl, Bernard B., (A Professional Corporation)**, (AV) '33 '63
  C.112 B.A. L.1068 J.D. [Nebenzahl K.D.&L.]
 *PRACTICE AREAS: Banking; Financial Institutions Law; Real Property Law; Business Law.
Nebenzahl, Michael R. ................ '55 '83 C.112 B.A. L.426 J.D. [Ⓐ Pollak,V.&F.]
**Nebenzahl Kohn Davies & Leff, LLP, (AV)**
 **10940 Wilshire Boulevard 15th Floor, 90024**
 **Telephone:** 310-824-1700 Fax: 310-824-5676
 Bernard B. Nebenzahl, (A Professional Corporation); James A. Kohn (A Professional Corporation); M. Randel Davies; Randall S. Leff;—Gerald S. Frim; Trudi J. Lesser.
 General Civil Practice, Administrative, Real Estate, Financial Institutions, Legislative, Health Care, Employment, Secured Transactions, Shopping Centers, Commercial and Corporate Law. Trial and Appellate Practice.
 Reference: Bank of America (Beverly Wilshire Branch).
  *See Professional Biographies, LOS ANGELES, CALIFORNIA*

Neches, Bernard A. .............. '17 '41 C.112 A.B. L.1068 LL.B. 335 S. Bentley Ave.
Neco, Matthew A. ................ '61 '86 C.1044 B.A. L.966 J.D. 12424 Wilshire Blvd.
**Nedelman, Alec G.** ................ '55 '80 C.112 B.A. L.1068 J.D. [Mayer,B.&P.]
Needham, Robert J. ........ '53 '82 C.174 B.A. L.629 J.D. [Tharpe&H.] (◎Santa Barbara)
**Needle, Joshua C., (AV) '52 '77 C.1078 B.A. L.426 J.D.**
 **Suite 1800 1901 Avenue of the Stars, 90067**
 **Telephone:** 310-556-5676 FAX: 310-556-5654
 Email: jcneedle@aol.com
 Criminal Defense, Trials and Appeals in all State and Federal Courts.
  *See Professional Biographies, LOS ANGELES, CALIFORNIA*

Neel, Bradley J. '57 '83 C.659 B.A. L.276 J.D.
  Secy. & Corp. Real Estate Coun., The Decurion Corp.
Neel, Rebecca Potts ....... '— '85 C.477 B.A. L.426 J.D. V.P. & Coun., Sanwa Bk. Calif.
Neelley, Laura Moacanin, Law Offices of '62 '88
  C.800 B.A. L.940 J.D. 6255 Sunset Blvd.
**Neely, Sally Schultz, (AV)** .............. '48 '72 C&L.813 B.A., J.D. [Sidley&A.]
 *PRACTICE AREAS: Chapter 11 Reorganization Law.
Nees, William E. ............ '44 '77 C.174 B.S.E.E. L.1137 J.D. Dep. City Atty.
**Neff, Richard E.** .............. '54 '80 C.188 B.A. L.976 J.D. [Neff&Assoc.]◎
 *LANGUAGES: Spanish, Portuguese and French.
 *PRACTICE AREAS: Computers and Software; Licensing; International law; Copyright; Intellectual Property.
**Neff & Associates, A Professional Law Corporation**
 **11693 San Vicente Boulevard, Suite 550, 90049**◎
 **Telephone:** 310-540-6760 Fax: 310-540-0305
 Email: Richard@Nefflaw.com URL: http://www.Nefflaw.com
 Richard E. Neff; Susan E. Bunnell.
 Computers and Software, Licensing, International Law, Copyright, Intellectual Property, Corporate Transactions.
 Torrance, California Office: Union Bank Tower, Suite 650, 21515 Hawthorne Boulevard. Telephone: 310-540-6760. Fax: 310-540-0305.
  *See Professional Biographies, LOS ANGELES, CALIFORNIA*

**Negele, James R.** ............. '49 '81 C.339 B.S.C.E. L.426 J.D. [Negele&Assoc.]
 *REPORTED CASES: Teitel v. First Los Angeles Bank (1991) 231 Cal. App.3d 1593.
 *PRACTICE AREAS: Civil Litigation; Construction Law; Business Law; Wrongful Termination.
**Negele & Associates, A Law Corporation**
 **3800 Barham Boulevard, Suite 403, 90068**
 **Telephone:** 213-850-5100 Fax: 213-850-5505
 James R. Negele;—Thomas A. Ingram, Jr.; Adam D. H. Grant; Felix M. Martin.
 General Civil Litigation in all State and Federal Courts with Special Emphasis on Construction, Insurance, Corporate, Real Estate and Business Law.
  *See Professional Biographies, LOS ANGELES, CALIFORNIA*

Neher, Robert A. '31 '63 C.267 B.A. L.1065 J.D.
  Admin. Law J., Off. of Admin. Hearings
Neighbors, Slade J. ............... '57 '85 C.911 B.A. L.1148 J.D. 1925 Century Park East
**Neil, James C., (AV) '49 '74 C.112 B.A. L.426 J.D.**
 **Suite 670, 800 South Figueroa Street, 90017**
 **Telephone:** 213-689-1010 Facsimile: 213-622-9375
 Email: jcnesq@sprynet.com
 International Business and Tax Planning, International Commercial Law, Corporation and Real Estate Law.
  *See Professional Biographies, LOS ANGELES, CALIFORNIA*

Neilson, Jessica M. .................... '67 '92 C.941 B.A. L.629 J.D. [Ⓐ Quinn E.U.&O.]
Neilson, Richard R. ........ '54 '84 C.267 B.A. L.950 J.D. 725 S. Figueroa St., 19th Fl.
**Neiman, Allen I., (AV) '29 '55 C.112 B.S. L.800 LL.B.**
 **11111 Santa Monica Boulevard Suite 1840, 90025-3352**
 **Telephone:** 310-575-5555 Fax: 310-575-5550
 (Certified Specialist, Family Law, The State Bar of California Board of Legal Specialization).
 *PRACTICE AREAS: General Civil Litigation; Divorce; Domestic Relations; International Matrimonial; Civil Litigation.
 General Civil Litigation, Divorce, Matrimonial and Domestic Relations Law.
 Representative Clients: Republic of France; Americana Granitos do Brasil; Dabney/Resnick, Inc.; Cascade School; Sieroty Co.

Neiman, Phillip L. .............. '63 '90 C.821 B.A. L.1068 J.D. 11601 Wilshire Blvd.
Neiman, Phillip W., (AV) ........... '33 '62 C.112 B.A. L.1068 LL.B. 11755 Wilshire Blvd.
**Neinstein, Paul B.** ..................... '69 '94 C.112 B.A. L.423 J.D. [Ⓐ Troop M.S.&P.]
 *PRACTICE AREAS: Transactional Entertainment Law.
**Neistadt, Kim A.** .................... '58 '89 C.112 B.A. L.464 J.D. [Koletsky,M.&F.]
 *PRACTICE AREAS: General Liability Defense Litigation; Wrongful Termination Defense Litigation; Sexual Harassment Defense Litigation.
**Neistat, Douglas M., (AV)** ............ '46 '73 C.1077 B.A. L.1049 J.D. [Angel&N.]
 *PRACTICE AREAS: Bankruptcy; Corporate.
**Neiter, Gerald I., (AV)** ............ '33 '58 C&L.800 B.S.L., J.D. [G.I.Neiter]
 *PRACTICE AREAS: Civil Trial; Business Litigation; Matrimonial Law.
**Neiter, Richard M., (AV)** ............ '37 '63 C.112 B.S. L.800 LL.B. [Stutman,T.&G.]
 *TRANSACTIONS: Lead Bankruptcy Counsel to Debtors in Chapter 11 cases of Hamburger Hamlet Restaurants, Inc.; First City/Hunter's Ridge, the Doskocil Companies Incorporated; Wilson Foods Corporation; Sambo's Restaurants, Inc.; Federal Wholesale Toy Co.
 *PRACTICE AREAS: Bankruptcy; Insolvency; Corporate Reorganization; Commercial Litigation.
**Neiter, Gerald I., A Professional Corporation, (AV)**
 **Suite 2000, 1925 Century Park East (Century City), 90067**
 **Telephone:** 310-277-2236 Facsimile: 310-556-5653

*(This Listing Continued)*

**Neiter, Gerald I., A Professional Corporation** (Continued)
 Gerald I. Neiter.
 General Civil Trial Practice in all State and Federal Courts, and Family Law.
  *See Professional Biographies, LOS ANGELES, CALIFORNIA*

**Nelsen, Ned R., (AV)** ............. '20 '53 C&L.800 B.S., J.D. 444 S. Plymouth Blvd.‡
**Nelsen, Thompson, Pegue & Thornton, A Professional Corporation**
 (See Santa Monica)
**Nelson, Brenda B.** ........ '56 '92 C.1051 B.A. L.800 J.D. [Ⓐ Manatt,P.&P.]
 *PRACTICE AREAS: Corporate Securities.
**Nelson, Brian S.** .................... '62 '89 C.906 B.A. L.990 J.D. [Ⓐ Wilson,K.&B.]
 *REPORTED CASES: Pacific Estates v. American Speciality Ins. 13 CA4th, 561, 17 CR2d 434 (1993); Santa Patricia v. Murrissette Construction, 231 CA3d 113, 282 CR2d 209 (1991).
 *PRACTICE AREAS: Insurance Defense; Construction Defect; Personal Injury.
**Nelson, Craig D.** ............ '54 '79 C.966 B.A. L.910 J.D. [Ⓐ Liebman&R.]
**Nelson, David C.** ............... '59 '86 C.636 B.S. L.276 J.D. [Loeb&L.]
 *PRACTICE AREAS: Trusts and Estates Law and Related Litigation.
**Nelson, Glenn D.** ............ '51 '77 C.169 B.A. L.1068 J.D. [Nelson&B.]
 *LANGUAGES: Japanese.
 *PRACTICE AREAS: Business Litigation; Employment Law; Construction Litigation; Insurance Defense; Insurance Coverage.
Nelson, Grant S. '39 '63 C&L.494 B.A., J.D.
  (adm. in MN; not adm. in CA) Prof. of Law, UCLA
**Nelson, Gretchen M.** ............ '54 '84 C.788 B.A. L.276 J.D. [Ⓐ Corinblit&S.]
 *PRACTICE AREAS: Complex Civil Litigation; Antitrust; Securities.
**Nelson, J. Robert, (AV)** ............ '44 '72 C.112 B.A. L.1068 J.D. [Morrison&F.]
 *LANGUAGES: German.
 *PRACTICE AREAS: Bankruptcy; Debtor/Creditors Rights Law.
**Nelson, Jaleen** ............ '68 '94 C.101 B.A. L.1068 J.D. [Barton,K.&O.]
 *PRACTICE AREAS: General Civil Practice; Banking Litigation; Business Litigation; Insurance Coverage.
**Nelson, James** .................. '69 '95 C.112 B.A. L.809 J.D. [Ⓐ Sedgwick,D.M.&A.]
Nelson, James A. '44 '70 C.678 B.A. L.911 J.D.
  (adm. in WA; not adm. in CA) Dist. Coun., I.R.S.
**Nelson, Katy A.** ............ '54 '94 C.1077 B.A. L.426 J.D. [Ⓐ Selman B.] (◎San Diego)
**Nelson, Kay Neill** ............... '46 '78 C.37 B.A. L.809 J.D. [Nelson&N.]
 *PRACTICE AREAS: Litigation; Corporate; Real Estate.
**Nelson, Larry R., (AV)** .................... '47 '79 C.121 B.S. L.464 J.D. [Nelson G.]
 *PRACTICE AREAS: Legal Malpractice; Insurance Fraud; Construction Defect.
**Nelson, Maren E.** ............ '56 '81 C.605 A.B. L.800 J.D. [Morrison&F.]
 *PRACTICE AREAS: Securities Litigation.
**Nelson, Maria K.** .................. '59 '91 C.918 B.A. L.1049 J.D. [Ⓐ Jones,D.R.&P.]
**Nelson, Mark L.** ............ '54 '79 C.1079 B.A. L.1067 J.D. [Sheppard,M.R.&H.]
 *PRACTICE AREAS: Real Estate Development Law; Finance Law.
Nelson, Nicolle Renée ............... '63 '89 C&L.846 B.A., J.D. 555 S. Flower St.
**Nelson, Peter Martin, (AV)** ............ '54 '79 C.951 B.A. L.1065 J.D. [Nelson,G.F.&L.]
 *PRACTICE AREAS: Entertainment Law.
**Nelson, Peter R.** ............ '55 '84 C&L.426 B.A., J.D. [Gilbert,K.C.&J.]
 *PRACTICE AREAS: Workers' Compensation Law.
**Nelson, Rodney R.** ..................... '56 '87 C.999 B.S. L.1148 J.D. [Mendes&M.]
Nelson, Rodney E. ................. '34 '61 C.494 B.A. L.178 LL.B. Supr. Ct. J.
Nelson, Ronald L. ............... '61 '87 C.94 B.S. L.245 J.D. 11766 Wilshire Blvd.
Nelson, Shari Dennis, (AV) ............ '38 '63 C&L.800 B.A., LL.B. 11525 Bellagio Rd.‡
Nelson, Thelma G. '— '63 C.331 B.A. L.564 LL.B.
  (adm. in NY; not adm. in CA) U.S. Treasury
Nelson, Theresa L. ........................ '54 '90 C.846 B.A. L.61 J.D. [Ⓐ Kopesky&W.]
**Nelson, William L., (AV)** ............ '45 '70 C.37 B.A. L.569 J.D. [Nelson&N.]
 *PRACTICE AREAS: Corporate; Real Estate; Securities; Business Law; Litigation.
**Nelson & Brown**
 **550 South Hope Street Twentieth Floor, 90071-2604**
 **Telephone:** 213-891-9515 Fax: 213-689-7748
 Glenn D. Nelson; Lolita Brown Fletcher. Associate: Lorita M. Chan.
 General Civil Litigation in all State and Federal Courts, Insurance Defense, Construction, Real Estate, Labor and Employment including ERISA, Wrongful Termination, Discrimination and Employee Benefits.
 Representative Clients: Flagstar Corp.; Hughes Aircraft Corp.; McDonnell Douglas Corp.; Shell Oil Co.; Denny's, Inc.; State Farm Insurance; FDIC; RTC.
  *See Professional Biographies, LOS ANGELES, CALIFORNIA*

Nelson & Freedman ........................ 6701 Center Dr. W., Ste. 770
**Nelson • Griffin, (AV)**
 **350 South Figueroa Suite 903, 90071**
 **Telephone:** 213-626-4049 Fax: 213-626-4082
 Email: nglaw@so.ca.com
 Members of Firm: Larry R. Nelson; Thomas J. Griffin.
 Insurance Coverage Analysis, Defense of Legal Malpractice, Insurance Fraud, Personal Injury and Construction Defect Cases.
  *See Professional Biographies, LOS ANGELES, CALIFORNIA*

**Nelson, Guggenheim, Felker & Levine, (AV)**
 **10880 Wilshire Boulevard, Suite 2070, 90024**
 **Telephone:** 310-441-8000 Fax: 310-441-8010
 Members of Firm: Peter Martin Nelson; Alfred Kim Guggenheim; Patti C. Felker; Jared Elliott Levine. Associates: Warren D. Dern; George M. Davis.
 Entertainment Law.
  *See Professional Biographies, LOS ANGELES, CALIFORNIA*

**Nelson & Nelson, A Professional Corporation, (AV)**
 **2049 Century Park East, Suite 4060, 90067**
 **Telephone:** 310-556-1424 FAX: 310-556-1422
 William L. Nelson; Kay Neill Nelson;—E. Scott Fraser.
 Corporate, Real Estate, Securities and Business Law and Litigation.
 Reference: Wells Fargo Bank, Camden and Santa Monica Branch, Beverly Hills, California.
  *See Professional Biographies, LOS ANGELES, CALIFORNIA*

**Nemecek & Cole, A Professional Corporation**
 (See Sherman Oaks)
**Nemlaha, Beatrice H., (AV)** ............ '40 '79 C.477 B.A. L.1066 J.D. [B.H.Nemlaha]
 *LANGUAGES: Czech.
**Nemlaha, Beatrice H., P.C., (AV)** 🅱
 **11377 West Olympic Boulevard, 90064-1683**
 **Telephone:** 310-914-7911 Fax: 310-312-3787
 Beatrice H. Nemlaha (Certified Specialist, Family Law, The State Bar of California Board of Legal Specialization).
 Family Law. Prenuptial and Cohabitation Agreements, Dissolution Tax Planning. Inter-State, International Custody Disputes. Mediation.
  *See Professional Biographies, LOS ANGELES, CALIFORNIA*

**Nemschoff, Louise**
 (See Beverly Hills)
**Nene, Seema L.** ........................ '69 '94 C.930 B.A. L.1068 J.D. [Ⓐ Manatt,P.&P.]
 *PRACTICE AREAS: Corporate Securities.
Nenney, Milton J., (AV) ............ '15 '68 C.597 B.S.C. L.1068 J.D. [Williams&N.]

CALIFORNIA—LOS ANGELES MARTINDALE-HUBBELL LAW DIRECTORY 1997

**Nepomuceno, Erwin A.** '62 '89 C.112 B.A. L.426 J.D. [Manning,M.&W.]
Nesbitt, Patrick M. '44 '82 C.1070 B.S. L.1148 J.D. 11150 W. Olympic Blvd Ste 690‡
Ness, Timothy M. '53 '85 C.477 B.A. L.800 J.D. 4215 Glencoe Ave.
**Nessary, Richard** '69 '95 C.112 B.A. L.146 J.D. [Rodi,P.P.G.&C.]
*PRACTICE AREAS: Business Litigation; Environmental Litigation; Corporate Transactions.
**Nesset, Deborah M.** '51 '79 C.1077 B.A. L.809 J.D. [Robbins,B.&C.]
*PRACTICE AREAS: Entertainment; Commercial; Business Litigation.
**Nessim, Ronald J.** '55 '80 C.813 A.B. L.477 J.D. [Bird,M.B.W.&M.]
Netzer, Gary R. '35 '64 C.1077 B.S. L.800 LL.B. Sr. Asst. City Atty.
**Netzer, Linda A.** '54 '80 C.112 B.A. L.1068 J.D. [Epport&R.]
Neubauer, Diane R. '53 '80 C.112 A.B. L.809 J.D. 789 Westholme Ave.
**Neue, Mike D.** '69 '95 C.629 B.S. L.800 J.D. [Jeffer,M.B.&M.]
*PRACTICE AREAS: Insolvency Law.
**Neufeld, Fred** '48 '90 C.176 B.A. L.309 LL.B. [Milbank,T.H.&M.]
Neufeld, Marjorie Nieset '52 '84 C.172 B.A. L.861 J.D. 3000 W. Alameda Ave.
**Neufeld, Timothy L.** '47 '75 C.103 A.B. L.94 J.D. [Richards,W.&G.]
*PRACTICE AREAS: Business Litigation.
Neuman, Jerold B. '62 '87 C.37 B.A. L.178 J.D. 515 S. Figueroa St.
Neuman, Neva J. '52 '79 C.112 B.A. L.1095 J.D. [Krislov&N.]
**Neumann, Martin A.**, (AV) '57 '81 C.112 B.A. L.1068 [Weinstock,M.R.S.&N.]
*PRACTICE AREAS: Taxation Law; Estate Planning Law; Business Law.
**Neumeyer, Richard A.**, (AV) '44 '70 C.597 B.S. L.1068 J.D. [Neumeyer&B.]
*PRACTICE AREAS: Appellate Practice; Insurance Coverage; Insurance Bad Faith.

**Neumeyer & Boyd, LLP, (AV)**
**2029 Century Park East, Suite 1100, 90067**
**Telephone: 310-553-9393 Fax: 310-553-8437**
**Members of Firm: Richard A. Neumeyer; Carol Boyd; Lydia E. Hachmeister; Steven A. Freeman. Associates: Katherine Tatikian; Susie J. Kater; Daniel F. Sanchez; Stuart L. Brody; Reid L. Denham. Appellate, Law and Motion and Related Trial Court Practice in all California and Federal Courts. Insurance, Insurance Coverage, Insurance "Bad Faith."**
*See Professional Biographies, LOS ANGELES, CALIFORNIA*

**Neuschaefer, William W.** '69 '94 C.659 B.S. L.112 J.D. [Murphy,W.&B.]
**Neustadter, Jonathan P.** '69 '94 C.893 B.A. L.1068 J.D. [Hooper,L.&B.]
*PRACTICE AREAS: Health Care Law.
Neville, James, (AV) '23 '50 C.813 A.B. L.800 LL.B. 2500 Wilshire Blvd.
**Nevinny, Philip H. R.** '64 '90 C.178 B.A. L.94 J.D. [Epport&R.]
*LANGUAGES: German, French, Spanish.
Nevins, Richard F. '56 '88 C.597 B.S.J. L.426 J.D. Ernst & Young
**Nevis, Christopher J.** '67 '92 C.112 B.A. L.464 J.D. [Stevens,K.A.&H.]
Nevonen, Larry E. '54 '79 C.112 B.A. L.800 J.D. 4601 Wilshire Blvd.
Nevonen, Patricia A. '54 '79 C.1042 B.S. L.809 J.D. 1925 Century Pk. E., Ste., 920
New, Christina J. '22 '62
C.61 B.A. L.1068 LL.B. Admin. Law J., Off. of Admin. Hearings
**New, Lee** '57 '89 C.1097 B.A. L.426 J.D. [Thorpe&T.]
*PRACTICE AREAS: Business Litigation; Corporate Law.
**New, Pauline A.** '62 '86 C.604 B.A. L.477 J.D. [Selman B.]
Newbarr, David '47 '74 C.768 A.B. L.770 J.D. Dep. Dist. Atty.
**Newberry, Jodi M.** '65 '91 C.112 B.S. L.426 J.D. [Gibson,D.&C.]
*PRACTICE AREAS: Litigation.
**Newburry, Keith A.** '65 '93 C.477 B.S.M.E. L.800 J.D. [Pretty,S.&P.]
*PRACTICE AREAS: Patents; Trademarks; Copyrights; Unfair Competition; Litigation.
**Newby, Jon W.** '61 '86 C.112 B.A. L.309 J.D. [Sheppard,M.R.&H.]
*PRACTICE AREAS: Corporate Law; Securities Law; Mergers and Acquisitions.
Newcombe, Caroline B. '47 '81 C.174 B.A. L.893 J.D. 1901 Ave. of the Stars
**Newcombe, Mary** '55 '85 C.575 B.A. L.1068 J.D. [Hedges&C.]
**Newell, John M.** '60 '85 C.813 A.B. L.477 J.D. [Latham&W.]
**Newell, John P.** '63 '95 C.1350 B.A. L.810 J.D. [Barger&W.]
Newell, Robert M., (AV) '18 '46 C&L.813 A.B., J.D. 600 Wilshire Blvd., 17th Fl.
**Newell, Robert M., Jr.**, (AV) '44 '70 C&L.813 A.B., J.D. [Hanna&M.]
*PRACTICE AREAS: Civil Trial; White Collar Criminal Defense; Environmental Law; General Practice.
**Newhouse, Brian E.** '53 '78 C.207 B.A. L.477 J.D. [Mayer,B.&P.]
Newhouse, George B., Jr. '54 '82 C.309 B.A. L.1066 J.D. Asst. U.S. Atty.
**Newhouse-Porter, Nancy A.** '52 '78 C.800 B.A. L.1068 J.D. [Crosby,H.R.&M.]
*PRACTICE AREAS: Corporate; Entertainment Law.
**Newkirk, Colleen M. (Benedict)** '52 '81 C.436 B.S. L.1049 J.D. [Newkirk,N.&R.]
*PRACTICE AREAS: Medical Malpractice; Personal Injury Law.
**Newkirk, William H.**, (AV) '47 '75 C.112 B.A. L.809 J.D. [Newkirk,N.&R.]
*PRACTICE AREAS: Personal Injury Law (125); Medical Malpractice Law (70).

**Newkirk, Newkirk & Rolin, (AV)**
**11620 Wilshire Boulevard, Suite 460, 90025**
**Telephone: 310-477-7122**
**Members of Firm: Christopher Rolin; William H. Newkirk; Barry A. Drucker; Colleen M. (Benedict) Newkirk.**
**Personal Injury, Medical Malpractice, Professional Liability.**

Newman, Adam '67 '93 C.112 B.A. L.464 J.D. [Liebert,C.&F.]
**Newman, Bruce H.**, (AV) '35 '61 C.112 A.B. L.1068 LL.D. [Arter&H.]
**Newman, Carol L.** '49 '77 C.103 A.B. L.273 J.D. [Ruben&M.]
*PRACTICE AREAS: Business Law; Commercial Litigation; Antitrust Law.
**Newman, Dana P.** '52 '81 C.976 B.A. L.1066 J.D. [Pillsbury M.&S.]
**Newman, David Wheeler, (A Professional Corporation)**, (AV) '52 '78
C.154 B.A. L.1068 J.D. [Mitchell,S.&K.]
*PRACTICE AREAS: Taxation Law; Estate Planning Law; Business Planning Law.
**Newman, Elizabeth A.** '58 '92 C.309 A.B. L.800 J.D. [Bird,M.B.W.&M.]
**Newman, Gregory J.** '67 '93 C.112 B.A. L.810 J.D. [Sedgwick,D.M.&A.]
Newman, Homer B. '21 '54 C.112 B.S. L.809 LL.B. [Dixon,H.W.&N.]
Newman, Jay B. '56 '82 C.112 B.S. L.813 J.D. 1999 Ave. of the Stars
**Newman, Michael**, (AV) '48 '75 C.668 B.A. L.1065 J.D. [O'Melveny&M.]
*PRACTICE AREAS: Banking; Public Finance.
Newman, Michael F., (AV) '53 '78 C.208 B.A. L.426 J.D. [Dixon,H.W.&N.]
**Newman, Michael R.** '45 '71 C.208 B.A. L.365 J.D. [Daar&N.]
**Newman, Paul Andrew** '60 '87 C.354 B.S. L.426 J.D. [Newman&Assoc.]
*PRACTICE AREAS: Insurance Defense; Entertainment; Civil Litigation.
Newman, Robert D., Jr. '53 '78
C.813 B.A. L.976 J.D. Western Ctr. on Law & Poverty, Inc.
**Newman, Robert Jon** '50 '76 C.918 B.A. L.910 J.D. [McKenna&C.]
*PRACTICE AREAS: Government (Public) Contract Law; International Law; Environmental Law.
**Newman, Stephen J.** '70 '96 C.309 A.B. L.145 J.D. [Latham&W.]
Newman, William A., (AV©) '47 '74 C.976 B.A. L.477 J.D.
(adm. in NY; not adm. in CA) [Wyman,I.B.&L.] (©N.Y., NY)

**Newman & Associates**
**10100 Santa Monica, Suite 300, 90067**
**Telephone: 310-788-8937 Fax: 310-788-2709**
**Paul Andrew Newman.**
**Insurance Defense, Entertainment, Civil Litigation, Transactional Practice in Business.**
*See Professional Biographies, LOS ANGELES, CALIFORNIA*

**Newman, Nelson & Kawa, Inc.**
**(See Covina)**

Newmark, Linda A. '62 '88 C.112 B.A. L.813 J.D.
V.P., Bus. Affs., PolyGram Music Publishing Grp.
**Newsom, Ashley S.** '70 '95 C.112 B.A. L.1068 J.D. [Riordan&M.]
*PRACTICE AREAS: Corporate.
**Newton, Carl K.**, (AV) '31 '63 C.112 B.S. L.426 LL.B. [Burke,W.&S.]
*PRACTICE AREAS: Eminent Domain Law; Municipal Law; Litigation.
**Newton, Charles Isaac** '66 '95 C.103 B.A. L.1068 J.D. [Kirkland&E.]
*PRACTICE AREAS: Litigation.
**Newton, Mark A.** '58 '86 C.546 B.S. L.1065 J.D. [Barton,K.&O.]
*PRACTICE AREAS: General Business Litigation; Banking Litigation; Insurance Coverage; Professional Liability Defense; Real Estate Litigation.
**Newton, Meredith (MiMi)** '62 '89 C.659 B.A. L.276 J.D. [Zevnik H.G.&M.]
*PRACTICE AREAS: Environmental; Insurance.
**Newton, Michael D.** '70 '96 C&L.309 A.B., J.D. [Gibson,D.&C.]
**Newton, Stephen E.** '42 '68 C.188 A.B. L.1065 J.D. [Heller E.W.&M.]
*PRACTICE AREAS: Corporate Finance; Corporate Law; Mergers and Acquisitions; Securities Law; Banking.

**Newton, Richard B., A Professional Corporation**
**(See Pasadena)**

**Ney, Richard J.**, (AV©) '42 '68 C.228 A.B. L.273 J.D. [Chadbourne&P.]
**Ng, Daniel** '60 '95 C.112 B.A. L.1066 J.D. [Wolf,R.&S.]
*LANGUAGES: Cantonese, Mandarin.
*PRACTICE AREAS: Litigation.
**Ng, David Kam** '64 '88 L.1137 J.D. [Kroll&T.]
**Ng, Diana** '71 '96 C.112 B.A. L.800 J.D. [Reznik&R.]
Ng, Lawrence '62 '89 C&L.976 B.A., J.D. Off. of U.S. Atty.
**Nguyen, Beatrice B.** '70 '94 C.276 B.S.F.S. L.1066 J.D. [Folger L.&K.]©
*LANGUAGES: Vietnamese and French.
**Nguyen, Derrick H.** '64 '92 C.112 B.A. L.800 J.D. [Morris,P.&P.]
Nguyen, Jacqueline H. '65 '91 C.605 A.B. L.1068 J.D. One Wilshire Blvd.
**Nguyen, James D.** '72 '95 C.112 B.A. L.800 J.D. [Foley L.W.&A.]
*LANGUAGES: French.
*PRACTICE AREAS: Litigation.
Nguyen, Lauren T. '64 '91 C.477 B.A. L.1068 J.D. 555 W. 5th St.
**Nguyen, Tasha D.** '63 '86 C.800 A.B. L.309 J.D. [Whitman B.A.&M.]
Nibley, Robert, (AV) '13 '43 C.878 A.B. L.426 LL.B. 4860 Ambrose Ave.‡
**Niblock, John F.** '59 '94 C.198 B.A. L.1068 J.D. [O'Melveny&M.]
*PRACTICE AREAS: Litigation.
**Nicholas, William R.**, (AV) '34 '63 C.336 B.S. L.477 J.D. [Latham&W.]

**Nicholas, Frederick M.**
**(See Beverly Hills)**

**Nichols, James D.**, (AV) '44 '76 C.1 B.S. L.809 J.D. [Bonne,B.M.O.&N.]
Nichols, Paul W. '48 '79 C.112 B.A. L.1068 J.D. Dep. Pub. Def.
**Nichols, Peter**, (AV) '56 '81 C.597 B.Sc. L.813 J.D. [Lichter,G.N.&A.]
*PRACTICE AREAS: Entertainment Law.
**Nichols, Phillip G.**, (AV) '46 '74 C.605 A.B. L.1068 J.D. [Pircher,N.&M.]
*PRACTICE AREAS: Real Estate Law.
**Nichols, Robert F., Jr.**, (AV) '27 '66 C.1258 B.A. L.426 LL.B. [Ivanjack&L.]
*PRACTICE AREAS: Commercial Banking Law; Business Law; Real Estate Law; Corporate Law; Creditor's Rights.
**Nicholson, Guy C.** '55 '82 C.1077 B.A. L.426 J.D. [Tisdale&N.]
*PRACTICE AREAS: Financial Institutions Regulatory Litigation; Complex Business; Corporate and Real Estate Litigation; Appeals.
**Nicholson, John F.** '52 '79 C.589 B.A. L.597 J.D. [Cox,C.&N.]
*PRACTICE AREAS: Real Property Law; Land Use Law; Destination Resort and Country Club Law; Subdivisions and Real Estate Finance Law.
**Nicholson, Phillip R., (A Professional Corporation)**, (AV) '35 '62
C&L.800 B.S., J.D. [Cox,C.&N.]
*PRACTICE AREAS: Real Property Law.
Nicklin, H. Anthony '44 '73 C.112 B.A. L.426 J.D. Co. Coun.

**Nicolaysen, Gregory, A Professional Corporation**
**(See Beverly Hills)**

**Nicolette, Alan K.** '56 '85 C.27 B.A. L.809 J.D. [Nordstrom,S.N.&J.]
*PRACTICE AREAS: Plaintiffs Personal Injury.
Nida, Robert H. '40 '65 C.112 L.1068 LL.B.
V.P. & Gen. Coun., Auto. Club of Southern Calif.
Nieberg, Benjamin D. '63 '91 C.918 B.A. L.1066 J.D. 3939 Tracy St.‡
Nielsen, Gary W. '44 '70 C.112 A.B. L.1065 J.D.
8822 Cynthia St., West Hollywood (©Park City, UT)
Nielsen, Jorgen L. '45 '71 C.112 B.A. L.1065 J.D. 2049 Century Pk. E.
**Niemeth, Charles F.**, (AV) '39 '66
C.309 B.A. L.477 J.D. [O'Melveny&M.] (©New York, N.Y.)
*PRACTICE AREAS: Corporate Law; Mergers, Acquisitions and Divestitures; Securities.
**Niemiec, Peter J.** '51 '76 C.178 B.A. L.569 J.D. [Greenberg G.F.C.&M.]
*PRACTICE AREAS: Environmental Law.
**Niese, William A.** '36 '61 C.188 B.S. L.107 LL.B.
Sr. V.P., L.A. Times & Asst. Secy., The Times Mirror Co.
**Niesley, Robert C.** '62 '87 C&L.1049 B.A., J.D. [Booth,M.&S.]
Nieto, Patricia D. '51 '79 C.378 B.A. L.800 J.D. 1557 W. Beverly Blvd.
**Nieves, Tina Bailer** '61 '88 C.112 B.A. L.1067 J.D. [Chimicles,J.&T.]
Nigam, Hemanshu '64 '90 C.918 B.A. L.94 J.D. Dep. Dist. Atty.
Niles, Alban I. '33 '64 C&L.112 B.S., J.D. Presiding J., Mun. Ct.
Niles, Edward I., (AV) '26 '53 C&L.494 B.E.E., J.D. 2040 Ave. of the Stars
**Niles, John G.**, (AV) '43 '68 C.813 B.A. L.846 LL.B. [O'Melveny&M.]
*PRACTICE AREAS: General Business Litigation; Insurance Law; Insurance Regulation; Professional Malpractice.
**Nilsson, Byard G.**, (AV) '25 '54 C.878 B.S.E.E. L.273 J.D. [Darby&D.] (Pat.)
*REPORTED CASES: TOHO Co. Ltd. et al v. Sears, Roebuck & Co., 645 F.2d 788 (CA9 1981).
*TRANSACTIONS: First "Minitrial", ABA Journal, Dec. 1979. Early Computer Patents, 3,274,376; 3,212,062.
*PRACTICE AREAS: Patent Law; Trademark Law.
**Nilsson, Torgny R.** '65 '92 C.112 B.A. L.770 J.D. [Gartenberg J.G.&S.]
*LANGUAGES: Swedish and German.
**Nimmer, David**, (AV) '55 '80 C.813 A.B. L.976 J.D. [Irell&M.]
*LANGUAGES: French and Italian.
Nirenstein, Julius J. '44 '75 C.976 B.S. L.309 J.D. 11645 Chenault St.
**Nisen, Fern S.** '58 '92 C.188 B.S. L.426 J.D. [Levinson,M.J.&P.]
*PRACTICE AREAS: Civil Litigation.
Nishimoto, Cary H. '45 '72 C.112 B.A. L.61 J.D. Dep. City Atty.
**Nishimura, Alan B.** '46 '83 C.605 B.A. L.426 J.D. [Engstrom,L.&L.]
*PRACTICE AREAS: Governmental Agency Defense; Construction Litigation; Products Liability; General Trials.
Nishimura, Gilbert M. '47 '73 C.112 B.A. L.426 J.D. [Roquemore,P.&M.]
**Nishimura, Nanci E.** '53 '91 C.800 B.A. L.128 J.D. [Rossbacher&Assoc.]
*LANGUAGES: Japanese.

**Nishioka, Bruce Matsuo** '60 '91 C.629 B.S. L.1049 J.D. Coun., Transamerica Financial Servs.
Nishiura, Diana H. ... '42 '75 C.112 A.B. L.1067 J.D. Sr. Staff Coun., State Bkg. Dept.
Nishiyama, Daniel ... '44 '70 C.229 B.A. L.228 J.D. [Nishiyama,M.L.E.&S.]
**Nishiyama, Kristine M.** ... '70 '95 C.629 B.A. L.809 J.D. Coun., Capital Grp. Cos., Inc.
Nishiyama, Mukai, Leewong, Evans & Saldin ... 3435 Wilshire Blvd., 18th Fl.
Nison, Edward J. ... '57 '85 C.347 B.A. L.1065 J.D. Dep. Dist. Atty.
Nissman, Edward S. ... '45 '74 C.659 B.A. L.809 J.D. 5244 E. Beverly Blvd.
**Nitti, Wayne G.** ... '68 '94 C.112 B.A. L.309 J.D. [Ⓐ Latham&W.]
*PRACTICE AREAS: Litigation.
Nitz, Daren H. ... '63 '90 C.36 B.S. L.800 J.D. 725 S. Figueroa St.
**Nitzkowski, Greg M.** ... '57 '84 C.309 B.A. L.1068 J.D. [Paul,H.J.&W.]
**Nix, Maureen O'Grady** ... '66 '91 C.112 B.A. L.809 J.D. [Ⓐ Gilbert,K.C.&J.]
**Nixon, Christine A.** ... '64 '90 C.112 B.A. L.426 J.D. Assoc. Coun., SunAmerica Inc.
*RESPONSIBILITIES: General Corporate Practice.
Nizinski, Bernard L. ... '36 '63 C.1043 L.809 LL.B. 4988 N. Figueroa St.
Noble, Michael S '61 '88 C.1060 B.S. L.285 J.D. (adm. in WA; not adm. in CA) I.R.S.
Noble, Richard L., (AV) ... '39 '64 C&L.813 A.B., LL.B. [Noble&C.]⊙
**Noble, Susan Booth** ... '64 '91 C.813 B.A. L.1068 J.D. [Ⓐ Shearman&S.]
Noble & Campbell, (AV) ... 2222 Ave. of the Stars (⊙San Francisco)
**Noblin, James Robert** ... '59 '84 C.800 B.A. L.309 J.D. [Blecher&C.]
*PRACTICE AREAS: Antitrust; Business Litigation; Intellectual Property.
Nobumoto, Karen S. ... '52 '89 C.1033 B.A. L.809 J.D. Dep. Dist. Atty.
**Nocas, Andrew J.**, (AV) ... '41 '65 C&L.813 B.S., J.D. [Harney]
*PRACTICE AREAS: Civil Litigation.
**Nochimson, David**, (AV) ... '43 '70 C.976 B.A. L.178 LL.B. [Ziffren,B.B.&F.]
*PRACTICE AREAS: Entertainment Law.
**Noel, Gregg A.** ... '57 '82 C&L.426 B.B.A., J.D. [Skadden,A.S.M.&F.]
**Noelte, Heather M.** ... '64 '95 C.101 B.A. L.426 J.D. [Ⓐ Dempsey&J.]
*PRACTICE AREAS: Business Litigation; Securities Fraud; Officers and Directors Liability; Accountant's Liability; Employer Discrimination Defense.
**Nogues, Jean Pierre, (A Professional Corporation)** '53 '78 C.1075 B.A. L.1068 J.D. [Mitchell,S.&K.]
*PRACTICE AREAS: General Business Litigation; Securities Litigation; Accountant's Liability Law; Engineering and Construction Litigation.
**Noh, Gloria M.** ... '68 '94 C.112 B.A. L.426 J.D. [Ⓐ Milbank,T.H.&M.]
**Nojima, John A.** ... '65 '92 C.1131 B.S. L.990 J.D. [Ⓐ Callahan,M.&W.]
**Nolan, Erin E.** ... '69 '94 C.884 B.A. L.464 J.D. [Ⓐ Jones,D.R.&P.]
**Nolan, John J., III** ... '54 '87 C.1077 B.A. L.809 J.D. [Ⓐ Veatch,C.G.&N.]
Nolan, Rosanne M. ... '53 '79 C.312 B.A. L.426 J.D. 621 Sunset Blvd.
**Nolan, Thomas J.**, (AV) ... '48 '75 C&L.426 B.B.A., J.D. [Howrey&S.]
*PRACTICE AREAS: White Collar Criminal Defense; Complex Litigation; Directors and Officers Liability; Litigation.
Nollan, James P. ... '46 '72 C.800 B.S. L.426 J.D. Dep. City Atty.
**Noneman, Charles E.** ... '52 '78 C.112 B.A. L.1065 J.D. [Cox,C.&N.]
*PRACTICE AREAS: Civil Litigation; Employee Benefits Law; Labor and Employment Law; Construction Law.

**Noonan, W. Patrick, A Professional Corporation**
(See Woodland Hills)

**Noonen, Martin M.** ... '67 '93 C.172 B.S.E.E. L.208 J.D. [Ⓐ Graham&J.]
Noonoo, Robert E. '48 '75 C.309 A.B. L.831 J.D. (adm. in PA; not adm. in CA) 9528 Bolton Rd.
**Noonoo, Susan V.** ... '49 '75 C.105 B.A. L.831 J.D. [Loeb&L.]
*PRACTICE AREAS: Real Estate Law; Workout Law.
Nora, Suzanne Michael ... '57 '83 C.800 B.A. L.309 J.D. 10520 Wilshire Blvd.
**Norber, Samuel** ... '48 '81 C.102 B.A. L.1009 J.D. [Nossaman,G.K.&E.]
*PRACTICE AREAS: Municipal Finance Law; Taxation Law.
**Nordby, Erin L.** ... '71 '95 C&L.800 B.A., J.D. [Ⓐ Condon&F.]
Nordin, John Eric, II, (AV) ... '43 '71 C.763 B.A. L.1065 J.D. Asst. U.S. Atty.
Nordlinger, Stephanie ... '40 '75 C.112 B.A. L.426 J.D. 3933 S. Sycamore Ave.

**Nordman, Cormany, Hair & Compton**
(See Oxnard)

**Nordstrom, Lucia**, (AV) ... '59 '83 C.1042 B.S. L.800 J.D. [Nordstrom,S.N.&J.]
*LANGUAGES: Spanish and French.
*PRACTICE AREAS: Plaintiffs Personal Injury.
**Nordstrom, Russell E., (A Professional Corporation)**, (AV) '46 '74 C.800 B.A. L.426 J.D. [Nordstrom,S.N.&J.]
*LANGUAGES: Spanish.
*PRACTICE AREAS: Plaintiffs Trial Practice; Products Liability Law; General Negligence Trial Law; Appeals.

**Nordstrom, Steele, Nicolette and Jefferson, (AV)**
**A Partnership including a Professional Corporation**
**Fourteenth Floor, 12400 Wilshire Boulevard, 90025⊙**
**Telephone: 213-937-1000 Fax: 310-826-6968**
**Members of Firm: Russell E. Nordstrom (A Professional Corporation) (Recognized experience in the fields of General Personal Injury, Professional Negligence and Products Liability by the California Trial Lawyers Association); Joseph W. Steele, V; Jeffrey D. Jefferson (Not admitted in CA; Resident, Kenai, Alaska Office); Alan K. Nicolette; Lucia Nordstrom. Associates: Robert E. Blythe; Maria Iriarte-Abdo; Francis P. Papica (Resident, Orange Office); Timothy A. Black; Patrick DeBlase; Angela G. Kim.**
**Personal Injury and Wrongful Death. Professional Negligence, Aviation, Construction, Industrial and Asbestos Law.**
**Kenai, Alaska Office: Suite 201, 215 Fidalgo Avenue. Telephone: 907-283-9187.**
**Orange, California Office: 770 The City Drive South, Suite 3000. Telephone: 704-750-1010.**
*See Professional Biographies, LOS ANGELES, CALIFORNIA*

Nordwind, Betty L. '47 '71 C.1044 B.A. L.174 J.D. Exec. Dir., Harriett Bhuai Ctr. for Family Law
**Norgaard, Christopher** ... '48 '73 C.813 A.B. L.276 J.D. [Brown,W.&C.]
*PRACTICE AREAS: Litigation.
**Norian, A. Catherine** ... '48 '77 C.813 B.A. L.1068 J.D. [Ⓒ Mitchell,S.&K.]
*PRACTICE AREAS: Litigation.
Norlander, Lisa D. ... '58 '84 C.112 B.A. L.1065 J.D. 11601 Wilshire Blvd.
**Norman, Jan B.** ... '50 '84 C.112 B.A. L.800 J.D. [Ⓒ Hedges&C.]
**Norman, Mark W.** ... '62 '90 C.112 B.A. L.1049 J.D. [Ⓐ Harrington,F.D.&C.]
*PRACTICE AREAS: Construction Litigation.
Norman, Paula R. ... '57 '87 C.529 B.A. L.809 J.D. 11766 Wilshire Blvd.
**Norman, Thomas J.** '40 '65 C.381 B.A. L.608 J.D. (adm. in OH; not adm. in CA) Assoc. Gen. Coun., Farmers Grp., Inc.
*RESPONSIBILITIES: Labor and Employment Law; Litigation; Management.
**Norman, William K.**, (AV) ... '38 '67 C.112 B.A. L.1066 J.D. [Ord&N.]
**Norris, Edwin L.** ... '46 '73 C.228 B.A. L.976 J.D. [Sidley&A.]
*PRACTICE AREAS: Taxation Law.

**Norris, Floyd H., (AV) '08 '35 C.1013 B.S. L.623 LL.D.** BB
**Suite 405 Norris Building, 714 South Hill Street, 90014**
**Telephone: 213-624-4088 FAX: 213-624-4080**
**General Civil and Trial Practice in all State and Federal Courts. Corporation, Estate Planning, Trust and Probate Law.**

(This Listing Continued)

**Norris, Floyd H. (Continued)**
**References: Bank of America; Wells Fargo.**
*See Professional Biographies, LOS ANGELES, CALIFORNIA*

**Norris, Nancy Morrow** ... '62 '92 C.1077 B.A. L.809 J.D. [Ⓐ Murchison&C.]
*PRACTICE AREAS: General Liability.
**Norris, Stephen E.** ... '57 '82 C.674 B.A. L.767 J.D. [Horvitz&L.]
Norris, William A. ... '27 '55 C.674 A.B. L.813 J.D. U.S. Ct. of Apps. J.
North, Sally ... '44 '72 C.623 B.A. L.1065 J.D. 12220 Sunset Blvd.
**Northrup, Linda L.**, (AV) ... '56 '81 C.112 B.A. L.1065 J.D. [L.L.Northrup]

**Northrup, Linda L., A Prof. Corp., Law Offices of, (AV)**
**12424 Wilshire Boulevard, Suite 900, 90025**
**Telephone: 310-207-8300 Fax: 310-442-6400**
**Linda L. Northrup.**
**General Business Litigation and Appellate Practice concentrating in Business, Real Estate, Construction, Entertainment and Bankruptcy Litigation and General Legal advice in related areas.**
*See Professional Biographies, LOS ANGELES, CALIFORNIA*

**Norton, Constance E.** ... '61 '90 C.112 B.A. L.284 J.D. [Ⓐ Lane P.S.L.]
*PRACTICE AREAS: Litigation.
Norton, John M. ... '54 '92 C.549 B.A. L.809 J.D. 11766 Wilshire Blvd.
Norton, Marcy L. ... '52 '77 C.112 B.A. L.1068 J.D. 949 N. Kings Rd. #215
Norton, R. Lynn ... '61 '87 C.112 B.A. L.1067 J.D. Dep. Pub. Def.
**Norton, Robert C.** ... '48 '79 C.766 B.A. L.284 J.D. [Rodi,P.P.G.&C.]
*PRACTICE AREAS: General Business, Corporate and Securities Law.

**Norton & Fairman, (AV)**
**515 South Figueroa, Suite 1000, 90071**
**Telephone: 213-683-1561 Telecopier: 213-683-0409**
**Email: Fairlaw@Linkonline.net**
**Members of Firm: Thomas W. Norton (1910-1991); Robert L. Fairman. Associates: Richard J. Kellum.**
**Civil Trial and Appellate Practice in Federal and State Courts. Trial work involving Life, Health and Disability Insurance, ERISA matters, Casualty and Property Insurance, Real Property, Construction, Professional Liability, Wrongful Termination, Employment Law and Business Trial Law.**
**Representative Client: Equitable.**
**Reference: Bank of America.**
*See Professional Biographies, LOS ANGELES, CALIFORNIA*

**Noskin, Scott H.** ... '66 '91 C.477 B.B.A. L.424 J.D. [Ⓐ Epport&R.]

**Nossaman, Guthner, Knox & Elliott, LLP, (AV)**
**Thirty-First Floor, Union Bank Square, 445 South Figueroa Street, 90071-1672⊙**
**Telephone: 213-612-7800 Telefacsimile: 213-612-7801 Telex: 67-4908 Cable Address: "Nossaman"**
**Members of Firm: Walter L. Nossaman (1886-1964); William E. Guthner, Jr.; Alvin S. Kaufer; James C. Powers; Howard D. Coleman; Robert D. Mosher; Frederic A. Fudacz; Raymond J. Staton; Isidoro Berkman; Janet S. Murillo; Fredric W. Kessler; Geoffrey S. Yarema; Henry S. Weinstock; Barney A. Allison; Robert L. Toms, Sr.; Nancy C. Smith; Daniel M. Grigsby; Michael Heumann; Stephen P. Wiman; Allan H. Ickowitz; Samuel Norber; Thomas D. Long; John Ossiff; Jeffrey A. Stava; Mary Lou Byrne; Winfield D. Wilson; Sandra M. Kanter; Richard P. Bozof. Associates: Linda N. Cunningham; Karla Nefkens MacCary; Donna M. Gallarello; Brian G. Papernik; Scott N. Yamaguchi; Christine D. Ryan; Alfred E. Smith. Of Counsel: William D. Markenson; Karen J. Hedlund.**
**General Civil Practice, including Real Estate, Corporations and Litigation in all State and Federal Courts. Transportation, Bankruptcy, Municipal Finance, Land Use, Environmental, Hazardous Waste, Natural Resources, Health Care, Sports and Legislative Law.**
**Reference: Union Bank (Los Angeles Headquarters Office).**
**San Francisco, California Office: Thirty-Fourth Floor, 50 California Street. Telephone: 415-398-3600.**
**Orange County, California Office: Suite 1800, 18101 Von Karman Avenue, Irvine. Telephone: 714-833-7800.**
**Sacramento, California Office: Suite 1000, 915 L Street. Telephone: 916-442-8888.**
**Washington, D.C. Office: c/o French & Company, The Homer Building, Suite 370-S, 601 13th Street, N.W. Telephone: 202-783-7272.**
*See Professional Biographies, LOS ANGELES, CALIFORNIA*

Notaras, Peter Andrew ... '38 '62 C.112 A.B. L.1068 J.D. [P.A.Notaras]
Notaras, Peter Andrew, A Prof. Corp. ... 1800 Ave. of the Stars
Notkoff, Arnold M. ... '38 '70 C.688 B.S. L.1148 J.D. [Notkoff&C.]
Notkoff & Curran, A Prof. Corp. ... 700 S. Flower
Notre, Kevin ... '62 '88 C.1040 B.B.A. L.564 J.D. Jud. Research Atty, Supr. Ct.
Nott, Michael G. ... '40 '66 C.605 A.B. L.800 LL.B. Assoc. Jus., Ct of App.
**Notti, John C.** ... '49 '83 C.1077 B.A. L.398 J.D. [Ⓐ Hewitt&P.]
**Nourani, Leila** ... '67 '90 C&L.061 [Ⓐ Foley L.W.&A.]
*LANGUAGES: French and Persian.
*PRACTICE AREAS: Civil and Commercial Litigation; Antitrust.
Nourmand, H. Joseph ... '61 '86 C.112 B.A. L.800 J.D. 5455 Wilshire Blvd., Suite 1912

**Nouskajian & Cranert, Professional Corporation**
(See South Pasadena)

**Novack, Barry**
(See Beverly Hills)

Novak, Stephen Michael ... '55 '81 C.846 L.1137 J.D. Sr. Coun., Fox Bdcstg. Co.
**Novatt, Jeff M.**, (AV) ... '58 '83 C.228 B.S. L.260 J.D. [Walter,F.&R.]
*PRACTICE AREAS: Taxation Law; Business Law.
Novatt, Lon B. ... '60 '85 C.228 B.A. L.1068 J.D. Broadway Stores, Inc.
Novian, Farhad ... '60 '85 C.112 B.A. L.426 J.D. 1801 Century Pk. E.
**Novitski, David E.** ... '47 '73 C&L.597 B.S., J.D. [Ⓒ Latham&W.]
Novodor, Alan G. ... '45 '71 C.800 A.B. L.426 J.D. 1901 Ave. of the Stars
**Novotny, Ronald W., (P.C.)** ... '56 '81 C.112 B.A. L.1065 J.D. [Hill,F.&B.]
*SPECIAL AGENCIES: National Labor Relations Board.
*REPORTED CASES: Southern California Chapter ABC JAC v. State of California (1995) 4 Cal. 4th 422; General Truck Drivers Local 315 v. N.L.R.B., 20 F.3d 1017 (9th Cir. 1994); Inter-Modal Rail Employees Assoc. v. Santa Fe Railway, 80 F.3d 348 (9th Cir. 1996).
*PRACTICE AREAS: Labor and Employment Law; Apprenticeship Law; ERISA Litigation.

**Nowakoski, Edward J. '52 '77 C.262 B.A. L.705 J.D.**
**Union Bank Plaza, 445 South Figueroa Street, Suite 2700, 90071-1603⊙**
**Telephone: 213-680-1425 Fax: 213-489-6897**
***LANGUAGES: Mandarin Chinese, Spanish.**
**International Finance and Business Law, Immigration and Naturalization, Asset Protection and Bankruptcy, Business and Real Estate Transactions and Litigation, Eminent Domain.**
**Temecula, California Office: 27710 Jefferson Avenue, Suite 305. Telephone: 909-676-1424. Fax: 909-676-4796.**
*See Professional Biographies, LOS ANGELES, CALIFORNIA*

**Nowotny, Jane M.** ... '60 '90 C.112 B.A. L.862 J.D. [Ⓐ Jones,D.R.&P.]
**Nugent, Daniel W.** ... '68 '94 C.605 B.A. L.767 J.D. [Ⓐ Hancock R.&B.]
**Nugent, Gary W.** ... '66 '91 C.802 B.B.A. L.597 J.D. [Ⓐ Jones,D.R.&P.]
**Nunan, Terence S.**, (AV) ... '49 '74 C.668 B.A. L.1068 J.D. [Rutter,G.&H.]
*PRACTICE AREAS: Tax; Estate Planning; Probate.
Nunes, Robert F., Jr. ... '62 '87 C.112 B.A. L.770 J.D. 555 S. Flower St., 18th Fl.
**Nuñez, Michael J.** ... '65 '92 C.112 B.A. L.1065 J.D. [Ⓐ Tuverson&H.]
*PRACTICE AREAS: Civil Litigation.

**Nunnally, Robert H., Jr.** ........ '59 '84 C.45 B.A. L.42 J.D. [Rubinstein&P.]
*REPORTED CASES: In re Mission Insurance Company v. Imperial Casualty 41 Cal. App. 4th 828, (1995); Sunburst Bank v. Executive Life, 24 Cal. App. 4th 1156, (1994); Garamendi v. Mission Insurance Company (Appeal of Missouri Insurance Guaranty Association), 15 Cal. App. 4th 1277, (1993); Allegheny International Credit Corporation v. Segal, 735 S.W. 2d 552 (Texs. App.—Dallas 1987); Liquidation of Security Casualty Insurance Company, 127 Ill. 2d 434, 537 N.E.2d 775 (1989).
*PRACTICE AREAS: Insurance Insolvency; Intellectual Property.
Nunziato, Tom A. ........ '45 '77 C.318 B.A. L.930 J.D. [Rosner,O.&N.]
Nussbaum, Richard D. ........ '46 '72 C.112 B.A. L.426 J.D. [Stoll&N.]
**Nutter, Ralph H.**, (AV) ........ '20 '48 C&L.309 A.B., LL.B. [Ⓒ Hedges&C.]
Nutter, Steven T. ........ '49 '75 C.112 B.A. L.1065 J.D. V.P., U.N.I.T.E.
Nye, Robt. C. ........ '20 '48 C&L.426 A.B., LL.B. 6644 W. 87th St.‡
**Nyhan, Christina O.** ........ '67 '92 C.112 B.A. L.990 J.D. [Ⓐ Breidenbach,B.H.H.&H.]
**Nyhan, F. John**, (AV) ........ '44 '72 C.860 B.A. L.884 J.D. [Pillsbury M.&S.]
Nyhus, Ward R. ........ '14 '58 C.112 A.B. 414 Denslow Ave.
**Nykolyshyn, Roman Y.** ........ '50 '88 C.381 B.A. L.809 J.D. [Ⓐ Schell&D.]
**Nyquist, Peter Anders** ........ '68 '95 C.112 B.A. L.1067 J.D. [Ⓐ Daniels,B.&F.]
Oakes, David G. '48 '74 C.69 B.A. L.796 J.D.
Assoc. Dir. of Legal Affs., Twentieth Century Fox Film Corp.
**Oakes, Royal Forest** ........ '52 '78 C.112 B.A. L.1068 J.D. [Barger&W.]
*PRACTICE AREAS: Business Litigation; Wrongful Discharge Law; Employment Law; Reinsurance Law.
**Obel, Patrick R.** ........ '57 '84 C.800 B.S. L.309 J.D. [Troy&G.]
*PRACTICE AREAS: Real Estate; Finance Law; Environmental Law.
Ober, Matt D. ........ '59 '85 C.112 B.A. L.809 J.D. [Ⓐ Swedelson&G.]
**Oberbeck, D. Michael** ........ '71 '96 C.679 B.A. L.597 J.D. [Ⓐ Christensen,M.F.J.G.W.&S.]
*PRACTICE AREAS: Litigation.
Oberg, David L. ........ '62 '88 C.1077 B.S. L.809 J.D. 2049 Century Pk. E.
Oberman, Jeffrey T. ........ '38 '65 C.112 B.A. L.1068 J.D. 3580 Wilshire Blvd.
Oberscheven, Toni M. '53 '78
C.911 B.A. L.1065 J.D. Sr. Lit. Coun., Alpha Therapeutic Corp.
**Oberstein, Norman S., (A Professional Law Corporation)**, (AV) '40 '66
C.352 B.A. L.1066 J.D. [Oberstein,K.&H.]

**Oberstein, Kibre & Horwitz LLP, (AV)**
A Limited Liability Partnership
**1999 Avenue of the Stars Suite 1850, 90067**
Telephone: 310-557-1213 Facsimile: 310-557-2460
Norman S. Oberstein (A Professional Law Corporation); Joseph Kibre; Howard L. Horwitz. Of Counsel: Henry Pollard; Harold J. Stanton; Marian L. Stanton.
General Civil Trial and Appellate Litigation Practice; Entertainment, Family Law and General Business Litigation; Corporate, Mergers and Acquisitions.
*See Professional Biographies, LOS ANGELES, CALIFORNIA*

**O'Biecunas, Leo G., Jr.**, (AV) ........ '57 '81 L.809 J.D. [Zide&O.]
*PRACTICE AREAS: Commercial Collection; Construction Law.
**Oblath, Geoffry W.** ........ '49 '74 C.112 B.A. L.309 J.D. [Armstrong H.J.T.&W.]
*PRACTICE AREAS: Entertainment.
**O'Brien, Ann K.** ........ '64 '90 C&L.37 B.A., J.D. [Ⓐ Latham&W.]
**O'Brien, Christopher R.** ....'65 '91 C.30 B.A. L.800 J.D. [Ⓐ Christensen,M.F.J.G.W.&S.]
*PRACTICE AREAS: Corporate Law.
O'Brien, Joni C. ........ '48 '92 C.37 B.A. L.615 J.D. 12400 Wilshire Blvd. 13th Fl.
**O'Brien, Kathyleen A.** ........ '52 '78 C.242 B.A. L.276 J.D. [Sheppard,M.R.&H.]
*PRACTICE AREAS: Complex Business Counseling and Litigation; Intellectual Property; False Advertising; Unfair Trade Practices; Antitrust Law.
**O'Brien, Kenneth A., Jr.** '56 '81 C.976 B.A. L.178 J.D.
[Kelley D.&W.] (ⓞParsippany, NJ & N.Y., NY)
*PRACTICE AREAS: Litigation.
**O'Brien, Mark A.** ........ '55 '83 C.629 B.A. L.94 J.D. [Kane&O.]
*LANGUAGES: French and Japanese.
*PRACTICE AREAS: Civil Litigation; International Law.
O'Brien, Peter B. ........ '42 '70 C.800 B.A. L.809 J.D. 3350 Barham Blvd.
**O'Brien, Robert C., Jr.** ........ '66 '91 C.112 B.A. L.1066 J.D. [Ⓐ Skadden,A.S.M.&F.]
**O'Bryan, Rachel Charles** '67 '95 C.103 B.A. L.477 J.D.
(adm. in NY; not adm. in CA) [Ⓐ White&C.]
**Obrzut, Ted**, (AV) ........ '49 '74 C.112 B.A. L.1068 J.D. [Milbank,T.H.&M.]
**O'Callaghan, Michael T.** ........ '63 '93 C.800 B.S. L.426 J.D. [Ⓐ Ropers,M.K.&B.]
*PRACTICE AREAS: Construction Defect; Litigation.
**O'Callahan, James G.** ........ '56 '86 C.1169 A.B. L.1068 J.D. [Girardi&K.]
*PRACTICE AREAS: Products Liability; Medical and Professional Negligence; General Negligence; Business Torts.
**Ochoa, Arthur J.** ........ '68 '95 C.800 A.B. L.976 J.D. [Ⓐ O'Melveny&M.]
*PRACTICE AREAS: Corporate Law.
**Ochoa, Christopher Eric** ..... '69 '94 C&L.112 B.A., J.D. [Ⓐ Ochoa&S.] (ⓞSacramento)
*PRACTICE AREAS: Lobbying; Education; Hazardous Waste Land Acquisition.
Ochoa, Edward Henry ........ '63 '89 C.37 B.S. L.61 J.D. Dep. Atty. Gen.
**Ochoa, Ralph M.**, (BV) ..... '41 '70 C.112 B.A. L.1068 J.D. [Ochoa&S.] (ⓞSacramento)
*LANGUAGES: Spanish.
*PRACTICE AREAS: Legislative Advocacy; International Law.

**Ochoa & Sillas, (AV)** BB
**444 South, Flower Street, 18th Floor, 90071**ⓞ
Telephone: 213-362-1400 Fax: 213-622-0162
Members of Firm: Ralph M. Ochoa; Herman Sillas; Jesse M. Jauregui; Jacqueline Rich Moore. Associates: Jack T. Molodanof; Francisco Valles Lopez; Tomás R. Lopez; Rita A. Reyes; Carlos Hilario; Joyce E. Earl; Christopher Eric Ochoa; Christopher Gonzalez; Evan F. Hadnot (Certified Specialist, Workers Compensation Law, The State Bar of California Board of Legal Specialization); Thomas J. Joy; Mario Cordero. Of Counsel: Cochran & Lotkin, Washington, D.C.
General Civil Trial, Appellate Practice, Corporate, Administrative and Municipal Law, Products Liability, Insurance Defense and Legislative Practice. Municipal Finance, Construction Law, Workers Compensation Defense. International Law, Labor, Real Estate and Education.
Sacramento, California Office: Wells Fargo Center, 400 Capitol Mall, Suite 1850. Telephone: 916-447-3383. FAX: 916-447-3495.
Mexico City, Mexico Office: Bosques de Duraznos, No. 65-507-B, Bosques de Las Lomas, 11700 Mexico, D.F. Telephone: 905-596-68-48.
*See Professional Biographies, LOS ANGELES, CALIFORNIA*

**Ocon, Cary P.** ........ '61 '94 C.112 B.A. L.494 J.D. [Ⓐ Berman,B.M.&R.]
*LANGUAGES: Spanish.
*PRACTICE AREAS: Construction Litigation; Commercial Litigation.
O'Connell, Beverly R. ........ '65 '90 C.112 B.A. L.990 J.D. 555 W. 5th St.
**O'Connell, Christopher P.**, (AVⓣ) ..... '46 '73 C.321 A.B. L.178 J.D. [Hall D.K.F.&W.]
*LANGUAGES: French.
*PRACTICE AREAS: Corporate Law; Securities Law.
O'Connell, Daniel James ........ '60 '89 C.112 B.A. L.809 J.D. 2029 Century Park, E.
O'Connell, James L. ........ '43 '71 C.988 B.S. L.878 J.D. 2327 Moreno Dr.
**O'Connell, Kevin**, (AV) ........ '33 '61 C&L.309 A.B., J.D. [Manatt,P.&P.]
*PRACTICE AREAS: Litigation; Antitrust and Unfair Business Practices.
**O'Connor, Alan M.** ........ '63 '93 C.472 B.S. L.1148 J.D. [Ⓐ M.S.McNeil]
*PRACTICE AREAS: Bankruptcy Law; Commercial Law; Debt Recovery; Trademark and Copyright Law; Criminal Law.
O'Connor, Barbara E. ........ '50 '86 C.563 B.A. L.1040 J.D. Off. of Fed. Pub. Def.
**O'Connor, Edward F.** ........ '44 '71 C.477 B.S. L.347 J.D. [Oppenheimer P.S.] (ⓞIrvine)
*PRACTICE AREAS: Intellectual Property Litigation.
O'Connor, Kathleen M. ........ '51 '83 C.025 B.Sc. L.209 J.D. 3550 Wilshire Blvd.

**O'Connor, Maura B.** ........ '60 '88 C.118 B.A. L.494 J.D. [Ⓐ Arter&H.]
*PRACTICE AREAS: Real Estate Law; Corporate Law.
**O'Connor, Michael J.**, (AV) ........ '54 '79 C.112 A.B. L.1068 J.D. [White O.C.&A.]
*PRACTICE AREAS: Civil Litigation; Insurance Law.
**O'Connor, Michael J.** ........ '53 '79 C.602 A.B. L.228 J.D. [Ⓐ La Follette,J.D.F.&A.]
*PRACTICE AREAS: General Liability; Medical Malpractice.
**O'Connor, R. Timothy** ........ '62 '95 C.426 B.B.A. L.809 J.D. [Ⓐ Gilbert,K.C.&J.]
*PRACTICE AREAS: Personal Injury Defense in Vehicular, Premises and Products-Liability arenas.
**O'Connor, William V.**, (AV) ........ '42 '73 C.871 B.S. L.426 J.D. [Kern&W.]

**O'Connor, Bernard E., Jr., A Law Corporation**
**(See Torrance)**

Oda, Stanley Y., (AV) ........ '38 '71 C.312 B.B.A. L.1148 J.D. 3600 Wilshire Blvd.
O'Dea, Kathleen Maureen ........ '34 '88 C.1097 B.A. L.1190 J.D. 700 S. Flower St.
Odell, Robert B., Jr. '46 '74
C.813 A.B. L.1065 J.D. Assoc. Coun., Auto. Club of Southern Calif.
**Odendahl, John H.** ........ '61 '86 C.927 B.A. L.352 J.D. [Gabriel,H.&P.]
*REPORTED CASES: Concha v. London, 62 F.3d 1493 (9th Cir. 1995); Taylor Made Golf Company, Inc. v. Trend Precision Golf, Inc. 903 F.Supp. 1506 (M.D. Fla. 1995).
Oder, Kenneth W. ........ '47 '75 C&L.893 B.A., J.D. 633 W. 5th St.
Odom, Gary R. ........ '52 '77 C.940 B.A. L.809 J.D. 1331 Sunset Blvd.
**Odom, Richard S.**, (AV) ........ '44 '70 C&L.813 B.S., J.D. [Howrey&S.]
*PRACTICE AREAS: Complex Commercial Litigation; Products Liability.
O'Donnell, Joanne B. ........ '49 '83 C.112 B.A. L.426 J.D. 10100 Santa Monica Blvd.
O'Donnell, John L., Jr. ........ '62 '89 C.339 B.S. L.1049 J.D. [O'Donnell&M.]
**O'Donnell, Pierce**, (AV) ........ '47 '73 C&L.276 A.B., J.D. [O'Donnell,R.&S.]
*PRACTICE AREAS: Business Torts; Complex Litigation; Constitutional Law; Contract Law; Entertainment Law.
O'Donnell & Mandell ........ 12121 Wilshire Blvd.

**O'Donnell, Reeves & Shaeffer, LLP, (AV)**
**633 West Fifth Street, Suite 1700, 90071**
Telephone: 213-532-2000 Facsimile: 213-532-2020
Partners: Pierce O'Donnell; Rex T. Reeves, Jr.; John J. Shaeffer. Associates: Ann Marie Mortimer; Belynda Reck; Timothy J. Toohey; Lisa R. Brant; Brian J. Tucker. Of Counsel: Michael P. Flaherty (Not admitted in CA); Henry S. Rose; Suzanne Tragert.
Litigation, emphasis in areas of Antitrust, Complex Corporate, Complex Tort, Entertainment, Environmental, Intellectual Property, General Civil Litigation and Securities, Appellate in all Federal and State Courts.
*See Professional Biographies, LOS ANGELES, CALIFORNIA*

**Odou, Joel E. D.** ........ '67 '93 C.800 B.A. L.940 J.D. [Ⓐ La Follette J.D.F.&A.]
*PRACTICE AREAS: Insurance Defense Litigation.
**Odson, Robert J.** ........ '63 '92 C.605 B.A. L.800 J.D. [Ⓐ Paul,H.J.&W.]
**Oehmke, John C.** ........ '67 '96 C.276 B.A. L.309 J.D. [Ⓐ O'Melveny&M.]
*LANGUAGES: German.
Oelze, Lawrence A. ........ '42 '70 C.112 B.A. L.1095 LL.B. 4700 Wilshire Blvd.
**Oertel, Mark A.**, (AV) ........ '58 '85 C.101 B.S. L.809 J.D. [Bottum&F.]
*LANGUAGES: German.
*PRACTICE AREAS: Professional Malpractice Law; Civil Law; Trial Practice; Appellate Practice; Fidelity and Surety Law.
**Oesterreich, Thomas G.** ........ '61 '86 C.426 B.B.A. L.326 J.D. [Ⓐ Lynberg&W.]
*PRACTICE AREAS: Insurance Litigation and Coverage.
**Oetting, Richard F.**, (AV) ........ '31 '60 C.112 A.B. L.800 LL.B. [Barton,K.&O.]
*PRACTICE AREAS: Securities Litigation; Professional Liability Defense; Directors and Officers Insurance Defense; Banking Litigation; Federal Practice.
**Oetzell, Walter K.** ........ '49 '83 C.112 B.A. L.1068 J.D. [Thelen,M.J.&B.]
*PRACTICE AREAS: Bankruptcy Law; Commercial Law.
Offsay, Gerald R. ........ '53 '77 C.1044 B.A. L.178 J.D. Pres., RKO Pictures

**O'Flaherty & Belgum**
**(See Glendale)**

**Ogawa, Lisa A.** ........ '57 '82 C&L.800 B.S., J.D. [Frandzel&S.]
*PRACTICE AREAS: Loan Restructuring; Loan Workouts; Loans; Secured Transactions; Real Estate Finance.
Ogden, David A., (BV) ........ '45 '71 C.1097 B.A. L.1068 J.D. 1670 Corinth Ave.
Ogden, Gary L. ........ '62 '88 C.101 B.A. L.1066 J.D. Broadway Stores, Inc.
Ogden, J. Mark ........ '63 '91 C.36 B.S. L.990 J.D. U.S. Dept. of Labor
Ogden, Steven D. ........ '43 '69 C.605 B.A. L.1068 J.D. Dep. Dist. Atty.
Oghigian, Martin M. ........ '39 '67 C.112 A.B. L.800 J.D. Dep. Dist. Atty.
Ogilvie, Robert J. ........ '50 '76 C.31 B.A. L.813 J.D. Pres., Diversified Mgmt. Assocs., Inc.
Oglesby, Roger D. ........ '48 '78 C.502 B.J. L.1065 J.D. Times Mirror Sq.‡
Ogrin, Kenneth Dean ........ '65 '90 C.1077 B.A. L.1148 J.D. 6311 Wilshire Blvd.
**Oh, Angela E.** ........ '55 '86 C.112 B.A. L.1067 J.D. [Beck,D.D.B.&O.]
*LANGUAGES: Korean.
**Oh, Sam S.** ........ '63 '93 C.112 B.A. L.1068 J.D. [Ⓐ Tuttle&T.]
*LANGUAGES: Korean.
**O'Halloran, John** ........ '57 '88 C.061 B.A. L.569 J.D. [Ⓒ Gibson,D.&C.]
*PRACTICE AREAS: Probate; Trusts and Estates.
**O'Hanlon, Neil R.** ........ '50 '75 C&L.178 A.B., J.D. [Troop M.S.&P.]
*PRACTICE AREAS: Real Estate and Real Estate Finance Litigation; Financial Institutions Litigation; Bankruptcy Litigation; General Business Litigation.
**O'Hara, Callie C.** ........ '63 '92 C.877 B.S. L.990 J.D. [Dale,B.&H.]
O'Hara, Elizabeth M. ........ '59 '86 C.602 B.A. L.426 J.D. 4700 Wilshire Blvd.
**O'Hara, James F.** ........ '32 '59 C&L.724 B.A., LL.B. [Ⓒ Stein S.S.&O.]
*PRACTICE AREAS: Customs Law; International Trade Law.
**O'Hara, John F.**, (AV) ........ '17 '46 C.770 Ph.B. L.1065 J.D. [Ⓒ Parker,M.C.O.&S.]
*PRACTICE AREAS: Labor Relations; Employment Law.
**O'Hara, Lorraine H.** ........ '62 '88 C.937 B.A. L.150 J.D. [Ⓐ Seyfarth,S.F.&G.]
*PRACTICE AREAS: Employment Law; Labor Law.
O'Hara, Michael J. ........ '29 '65 C.426 L.809 LL.B. 10850 Wilshire Blvd.
O'Hara, Nancy ........ '51 '77 C.112 B.A. L.1068 J.D. Princ. Dep. Co. Coun.
O'Hare, Kathryn A. Sackett ........ '57 '81 C.597 B.S.J. L.800 J.D. Dep. City Atty.

**Ohashi & Priver**
**(See Pasadena)**

Ohata, Ronald N. ........ '51 '78 C.112 B.A. L.1065 J.D. U.S. Immig. J.
O'Heron, Joseph M. ........ '43 '72 C.112 B.A. L.1065 J.D. Dep. Atty. Gen.
**Ohlgren, Joel R.**, (AV) ........ '42 '69 C.112 B.A. L.1068 J.D. [Sheppard,M.R.&H.]
*PRACTICE AREAS: Bankruptcy Law; Commercial Law; Creditors Rights Law.
**Ohlson, Kate E.** ........ '68 '95 C.276 B.A. L.1067 J.D. [Ⓐ Troop M.S.&P.]
*PRACTICE AREAS: Insurance Coverage.
**Ohriner, Kenneth H.** ........ '56 '87 C.1044 B.E.M.E. L.724 J.D. [Lyon&L.] (See Pat. Sect.)
*PRACTICE AREAS: Intellectual Property.
**Okamoto, A. Ken** ........ '60 '91 C.1167 B.S. L.813 J.D. [Ⓐ Mayer,B.&P.]
*PRACTICE AREAS: Real Estate; Commercial; Corporate.
**O'Keefe, David J.**, (AV) ........ '39 '65 C.426 B.A. L.1068 LL.B. [Bonne,B.M.O.&N.]
**O'Keefe, Garet D.** ........ '66 '93 C.605 B.S. L.1355 J.D. [Ⓐ Crosby,H.R.&M.]
**O'Kelly, William P.** ........ '58 '84 C.1056 B.S. L.950 J.D. [Ⓐ Tharpe&H.]
Oken, Alan I. ........ '45 '72 C.1077 B.A. L.426 J.D. 1260 N. Kings Rd., W. Hollywood
**Oken, David H.** ........ '63 '94 C.1077 B.S. L.809 J.D. [Ⓐ Selman B.]
**Okuma, Mark T.** ........ '56 '84 C.339 B.S. L.597 J.D. [Sheppard,M.R.&H.]
*PRACTICE AREAS: Real Estate; Finance.

CAA306P

**Olander, M. Lauren** .................'66 '91 C.94 B.A. L.990 J.D. [Ⓐ Manning,M.&W.]
**O'Laughlin, Kathleen R.** .............'54 '82 C.602 B.S. L.426 J.D. [Ⓒ Bronson,B.&M.]
*PRACTICE AREAS: Business Litigation.
**Oldenkamp, David J.** ......... '50 '78 C.800 B.S. L.1148 J.D. [Oppenheimer P.S.] (Pat.)
*PRACTICE AREAS: Intellectual Property.
Older, Glenn E. .................... '28 '61 C.800 B.S. L.809 LL.B. 1631 Beverly Blvd.
**Oldman, Marshal A.**, (AV) ................. '51 '76 C&L.800 B.A., J.D. [Oldman&C.]
*PRACTICE AREAS: Probate and Trust Administration; Litigation; Conservatorships and Estate Planning.

**Oldman & Cooley, L.L.P., (AV)**
**Penthouse, Suite A, 16133 Ventura Boulevard (Encino), 91436**
**Telephone: 818-986-8080 Fax: 818-789-0947**
**Email: ILAL@AOL.COM**
**Members of Firm: Marshal A. Oldman; Susan J. Cooley; Susan R. Izenstark. Of Counsel: Michael L. Trope.**
**Probate, Conservatorships and Estate Planning, Tax, Trusts and Related Civil Trial and Appellate Practice in all State Courts.**
**References: City National Bank (Encino Office); Industrial Bank (Van Nuys).**
***See Professional Biographies, LOS ANGELES, CALIFORNIA***

**O'Leary, Kevin D.**, (BV) ................. '56 '83 C.478 B.A. L.276 J.D. [Padilla&O.]⊙
*LANGUAGES: Spanish.
*REPORTED CASES: State of Connecticut vs. Willie Milledge, 8 Conn. App. 119; 511 A.2d 366 (1986).
*PRACTICE AREAS: Business Litigation; Real Estate; Environmental; Admiralty; Maritime.
**O'Leary, Lynn A.** .....................'59 '83 C&L.770 B.S.C., J.D. [Musick,P.&G.]
*PRACTICE AREAS: Litigation; Insurance.
**O'Leary, Prentice L.**, (AV) ........ '42 '69 C.112 B.A. L.1068 J.D. [Sheppard,M.R.&H.]
*PRACTICE AREAS: Commercial Law; Creditors' Rights Law; Insolvency Law; Bankruptcy Law.
**O'Leary, Theodore H.**, (BV) ........'49 '82 C.494 B.A. L.809 J.D. [Bonne,B.M.O.&N.]
Olender, Terrys T. ...........................'— '31 C.486 L.800 450 N. Rossmore St.
O'Leno, Philip L. ..........................'12 '63 C&L.502 LL.B. 4929 Wilshire Blvd.
Oley, Jarlath .....'47 '72 C.112 A.B. L.1068 J.D. Sr. Dep. Gen. Coun., Metro. Water Dist.
Olian, Irwin A., Jr. ...............'48 '73 C.674 A.B. L.309 J.D. Bear, Stearns & Co., Inc.
Olin, Milton E., Jr. '48 '75 C.112 B.A. L.1068 J.D.
Sr. V.P., Bus. & Legal Affs., A & M Records, Inc.
**Olincy, J. Dan**, (AV) ........................ '29 '53 C&L.813 B.A., J.D. [Olincy&K.]
*PRACTICE AREAS: Tax; Estate Planning; Probate and Trust.

**Olincy & Karpel, (AV)** BB
**10960 Wilshire Boulevard, Suite 1111, 90024-3782**
**Telephone: 310-478-1213 FAX: 310-478-1215**
**Members of Firm: George R. Olincy (1904-1982); J. Dan Olincy (Certified Specialist, Taxation Law and Estate Planning, Trust and Probate Law, The State Bar of California Board of Legal Specialization); Philip Karpel (Certified Specialist, Taxation Law and Estate Planning, Trust and Probate Law, The State Bar of California Board of Legal Specialization). Associate: Joyce Riley.**
**Tax Law, Estate Planning, Probate and Trust.**
***See Professional Biographies, LOS ANGELES, CALIFORNIA***

**O'Linn, Mildred K.** ................... '60 '86 C.381 B.S. L.8 J.D. [Ⓐ Manning,M.&W.]
Olins, Jay S. .................... '35 '65 C.112 A.B. L.800 LL.B. 10118 Empyrean Way
**Oliphant, Theotis F.** .......................'70 '95 C.112 B.A. L.1066 J.D. [Ⓐ Loeb&L.]
*PRACTICE AREAS: Government Contracts; Litigation; International Law; Copyright.

**Oliphant, Jeffrey**
**(See Beverly Hills)**

**Oliva, Anthony J.** .................. '60 '86 C.674 B.A. L.1066 J.D. [Allen,M.L.G.&M.]
*PRACTICE AREAS: Litigation.
Oliva, Karin M. ....................... '67 '95 C.112 B.A. L.800 J.D. 355 S. Grand Ave.
Olivar, Harry A., (AV) ................... '38 '64 C.976 B.A. L.813 LL.B. [H.A.Olivar]
**Olivar, Harry A., Jr.** ........................ '63 '89 C.976 B.A. L.309 J.D. [Ⓐ Dewey B.]
*PRACTICE AREAS: Litigation.
Olivar, Harry A., (AV) ............................................. 426 S. Arden Blvd.
Olivas, David J ....................'60 '88 C.309 A.B. L.1097 J.D. 221 N. Figueroa St.
**Olive, Patricia A.** ................. '37 '72 C.623 B.A. L.990 J.D. [Stockwell,H.W.&W.]
**Oliver, Anthony T., Jr.**, (AV) ........... '29 '54 C&L.770 B.S., J.D. [Parker,M.C.O.&S.]
*SPECIAL AGENCIES: National Labor Relations Board; Department of Labor; Wage and Hour Administrator; Equal Employment Opportunity Commission; Office of Federal Contract Compliance.
*PRACTICE AREAS: Labor and Employment Law; Employment Discrimination; Wrongful Termination; Labor Arbitrations; Collective Bargaining Negotiations.
**Oliver, Dale H.** .......................'47 '73 C.475 B.A. L.309 J.D. [Quinn E.U.&O.]
*SPECIAL AGENCIES: Armed Services Board of Contract Appeal; U.S. Court of Federal Claims; General Services Board of Contract Appeals; London Court of International Arbitration; U.S. General Accounting Office.
*PRACTICE AREAS: Government Contracts and Regulations; General Commercial Litigation; White Collar Crime.
**Oliver, Kevin** .......................'70 '95 C.112 B.S. L.309 J.D. [Ⓐ O'Melveny&M.]
*PRACTICE AREAS: Real Estate.
**Oliver, Marlo S.** ........................'50 '80 C.1208 B.S. L.309 J.D. [McKenna&C.]
Oliver, Norman G., Jr., (AV) ...'23 '56 C&L.546 B.Sc., LL.B. 281 S Figueroa St., 2nd Fl.
**Oliver, Richard B.** .................... '51 '77 C.893 B.A. L.309 J.D. [McKenna&C.]
**Oliver, Robert** ......................'66 '95 C.940 B.A. L.426 J.D. [Ⓐ Heller E.W.&M.]
Oliver, Vincent J. ....................... '44 '71 C.502 B.S. L.426 J.D. 207 S. Broadway

**Oliver, Vose, Sandifer, Murphy & Lee, A Professional Corporation, (AV)** BB
**The Park, Second Floor, 281 South Figueroa Street, 90012**
**Telephone: 213-621-2000 Telecopier: 213-621-2211**
**Charles S. Vose; Connie Cooke Sandifer; James Duff Murphy; Edward W. Lee; Roger W. Springer;— Mary L. McMaster; Arthur J. Hazarabedian; Bradley E. Wohlenberg; Timothy J. Chung; Kristin B. Mendenhall. Of Counsel: William B. Barr.**
**Litigation and Appellate Matters, Eminent Domain and Inverse Condemnation, Municipal Law, General Redevelopment Counsel Services, Land Use and Real Estate Development Services, Administrative Law Practice and Municipal/Personal Injury Defense Work.**
**Representative Clients: Cities of Covina, Hermosa Beach, South Pasadena and Calabasas; Los Angeles County North Valley Building Corp.; Los Angeles County Coroner's Building Corp.; Los Angeles County Montrose Sheriff's Station Corp.**
**Special Counsel: Anaheim Redevelopment Agency; Arcadia Redevelopment Agency; City of Brea; Brea Redevelopment Agency; Calleguas Municipal Water District; City of Anaheim.**
***See Professional Biographies, LOS ANGELES, CALIFORNIA***

Oliverez, Peter E., Jr. .........................'60 '93 C.112 B.A. L.940 J.D. Pub. Def. Off.
Olivo, Eduardo ............................ '64 '90 C.800 B.A. L.426 J.D. [Bolden&M.]
**Olken, Scott M.** ......................'65 '90 C.112 B.A. L.597 J.D. [Ⓐ Knapp,M.J.&D.]
*PRACTICE AREAS: Business Acquisitions; Real Estate; Probate; Estate Planning.
O'Loughlin, John D. ......................'47 '72 C.436 B.A. L.1068 J.D. P.O. Box 34848
**Olpin, Owen**, (AV) ................ '34 '59 C.101 B.S. L.178 LL.B. [Ⓒ O'Melveny&M.]
*PRACTICE AREAS: Natural Resources; Environmental Law.
**Olsen, Cheryl Wright** ................. '65 '90 C.518 A.B. L.800 J.D. [Ⓐ Gibson,D.&C.]
*PRACTICE AREAS: Labor.
**Olsen, Chris D.** ........................... '65 '90 C.188 A.B. L.800 J.D. [Ⓐ Galton&H.]
*LANGUAGES: Spanish.
*PRACTICE AREAS: Civil Litigation.
**Olsen, Christine M.**, (AV) ...............'49 '76 C.518 A.B. L.94 J.D. [O'Melveny&M.]
*PRACTICE AREAS: Corporate Law; Banking.
**Olsen, Christopher T.** .................'64 '89 C.240 B.A. L.990 J.D. [Ⓐ Hornberger&C.]
*PRACTICE AREAS: Civil Litigation; Construction Defect; Commercial Law; Personal Injury; Premises Liability.

**Olsen, Gary K., (AV) '43 '70 C.770 B.A. L.112 J.D.**
**Suite 1800 2049 Century Park East, 90067**
**Telephone: 310-277-3603 Fax: 310-785-0506**
**(Certified Specialist, Family Law, The State Bar of California Board of Legal Specialization).**
***PRACTICE AREAS: Divorce Law.**
**Family Law**
***See Professional Biographies, LOS ANGELES, CALIFORNIA***

**Olsen, Roger Milton**, (AV) ................ '— '69 C.112 A.B. L.1066 J.D. [R.M.Olsen]

**Olsen, Roger M., A Professional Corporation, (AV)**
**Union Bank Plaza, 445 South Figueroa, 24th Floor, 90071**
**Telephone: 213-488-1870 Telecopy: 213-488-1861**
**Roger Milton Olsen.**
**Federal and State Taxation Law, Civil, Criminal and Tax Litigation.**
***See Professional Biographies, LOS ANGELES, CALIFORNIA***

**Olson, David B.** ....................... '62 '92 C.1075 B.S. L.800 J.D. [Ⓐ Morris,P.&P.]
Olson, David H. ....... '33 '59 C.112 A.B. L.1066 LL.B. Sr. Corp. Coun., Northrop Corp.
**Olson, David S.** ...................'61 '87 C.205 B.A. L.800 J.D. [Carlsmith B.W.C.&I.]
*PRACTICE AREAS: Corporate Litigation; Business Law; Commercial Law.
**Olson, Dean A.** ...........................'61 '86 C.36 B.S. L.809 J.D. [Morris,P.&P.]
**Olson, Doreen Marie** ....................'66 '93 C.112 B.A. L.1148 J.D. [Ⓐ Zolla&M.]
*LANGUAGES: Spanish.
*PRACTICE AREAS: Family Law.
**Olson, Elliott D.**, (AV) ............ '41 '68 C.112 B.S. L.1068 J.D. [Sedgwick,D.M.&A.]
**Olson, Gary**, (AV) ....................... '43 '69 C.377 B.S. L.378 J.D. [Latham&W.]
**Olson, Jeffrey M.**, (AV) ....... '55 '82 C.339 B.S. L.477 J.D. [Lyon&L.] (See Pat. Sect.)
*PRACTICE AREAS: Intellectual Property.
**Olson, John P.** ......................... '47 '72 C.112 B.A. L.800 J.D. [Ⓒ Morrison&F.]
*PRACTICE AREAS: Business Litigation; Environmental; Toxic Tort; Bad Faith Insurance Litigation.
**Olson, Kathryn E.** .......................'66 '94 C.659 B.A. L.1066 J.D. [Ⓐ Tuttle&T.]
**Olson, Milo V.**, (AV) .....................'07 '31 C.112 A.B. L.800 J.D. [Ⓒ Hanna&M.]
*PRACTICE AREAS: General Practice; Taxation; Real Estate; Natural Resources; Civil Trial.
**Olson, Ronald L., (A Professional Corporation)**, (AV) '41 '66
C.221 B.S. L.477 J.D. [Munger,T.&O.]
**Olson, Steven J.** .........................'68 '96 C.813 B.A. L.477 J.D. [Ⓐ Latham&W.]
**Olson, Susan Tandy**, (AV) ............'48 '83 C.1077 B.A. L.1068 J.D. [Grace,S.C.&S.]
*PRACTICE AREAS: Insurance Coverage and Bad Faith Law (including Environmental); Professional Liability; Appellate Law; Insurance; Product Liability Law.
**O'Malley, C. Timothy** ........... '55 '79 C.112 B.A. L.800 J.D. [Ⓒ Leland,P.S.F.M.&M.]
*PRACTICE AREAS: Financial Institutions; Creditor Bankruptcy; Business Litigation.
**O'Malley, John A.** ..................... '53 '81 C.1307 B.A. L.1066 J.D. [Fulbright&J.]
*PRACTICE AREAS: Litigation.
**O'Malley, John C.** ........................'64 '90 C.31 B.A. L.93 J.D. [Ⓐ Paul,H.J.&W.]
**O'Malley, Rebecca** ..................... '65 '90 C.976 B.A. L.178 J.D. [Ⓐ Andrews&K.]
*PRACTICE AREAS: General Business Litigation.
**O'Malley, Rena L.** ...................... '57 '83 C.813 A.B. L.1066 J.D. [Morrison&F.]
*PRACTICE AREAS: Business-Corporate Finance.
Omansky, Alfred W., (AV) ........... '37 '67 C.800 B.A. L.809 J.D. 3055 Wilshire Blvd.

**O'Melveny & Myers LLP, (AV)** BB
**400 South Hope Street, 90071-2899**⊙
**Telephone: 213-669-6000 Cable Address: "Moms" Facsimile: 213-669-6407**
**Email: omminfo@omm.com**
**Senior Partner: Warren Christopher (Century City Office; also in Los Angeles and Washington, D.C. Offices). Partners: Douglas W. Abendroth (Newport Beach Office); William G. Adams (Newport Beach Office); Wallace M. Allan; Russell G. Allen (Certified Specialist, Probate, Estate Planning and Trust Law, The State Bar of California Board of Legal Specialization) (Newport Beach Office); Kermit W. Almstedt (Washington, D.C. Office); John L. Altieri, Jr. (New York, N.Y. Office); Brian C. Anderson (Washington, D.C. Office); D. Stephen Antion; Dale M. Araki (Tokyo, Japan Office; may also be contacted at the Los Angeles Office); Seth Aronson; James R. Asperger; Gary Barnett (New York, N.Y. Office); George M. Bartlett; Thomas W. Baxter; John H. Beisner (Washington, D.C. Office); Charles W. Bender; Ben E. Benjamin (Washington, D.C. Office); Kendall R. Bishop (Century City and Los Angeles Offices); Leah Margaret Bishop (Century City Office); Robert D. Blashek, III (Century City Office); Donald T. Bliss, Jr. (Not admitted in CA; Washington, D.C. Office); Richard A. Boehmer; Daniel H. Bookin (San Francisco Office); Brian David Boyle (Washington, D.C. Office); Greyson Lee Bryan; Francis J. Burgweger, Jr. (New York, N.Y. Office); Joseph A. Calabrese (Century City Office); Jerry W. Carlton (Newport Beach Office); Cormac J. Carney (Newport Beach Office); David W. Cartwright (Century City Office); Dale M. Cendali (New York, N.Y. Office); Theresa A. Cerezola (New York, N.Y. Office); Howard Chao (Hong Kong and Shanghai Offices; may also be contacted at the Los Angeles Office); Martin S. Checov (San Francisco Office); Denise M. Clolery (New York, N.Y. Office and Century City, California Offices); Alan M. Cohen (New York, N.Y. Office); James W. Colbert, III; William N. Cooney; Bertrand M. Cooper; Stephen A. Cowan (San Francisco Office); Arthur B. Culvahouse, Jr. (Washington, D.C. Office); Michael A. Curley (New York, N.Y. Office); Brian S. Currey; John F. Daum (Washington, D.C. Office); F. Amanda DeBusk (Washington, D.C. Office); James H. De Meules; Daniel A. Deshon, IV (San Francisco Office); Charles P. Diamond (Century City Office); Thomas E. Donilon (Washington, D.C. Office); Robert S. Draper; Karen K. Dreyfus (Newport Beach Office); Scott H. Dunham; Robert N. Eccles (Washington, D.C. Office); Steven L. Edwards (Newport Beach Office); Michael J. Fairclough; Robert E. Ferdon (New York, N.Y. Office); José W. Fernandez (New York, N.Y. Office); Richard N. Fisher; Cliff H. Fonstein (New York, N.Y. Office); Andrew J. Frackman (New York, N.Y. Office); Patricia Frobes (Newport Beach and Los Angeles Offices); Travis C. Gibbs; Martin Glenn (New York, N.Y. Office); Richard B. Goetz; Gregory W. Goff; David E. Gordon; Kent V. Graham (Century City Office); Pamela C. Gray (Certified Specialist, Estate Planning, Trusts and Probate Law, The State Bar of California Board of Legal Specialization) (Newport Beach and Los Angeles Offices); Linda Boyd Griffey; Steven L. Grossman (New York, N.Y. Office); Catherine Burcham Hagen (Newport Beach and Los Angeles Office); Christopher D. Hall (London, England and New York Offices); Theodore C. Hamilton (Newport Beach Office); Marc P. Hanrahan (New York, N.Y. Office); Stephen J. Harburg (Washington, D.C. Office); John D. Hardy, Jr. (San Francisco Office and Los Angeles Office); Adam C. Harris (New York, N. Y. Office); Robert D. Haymer (Century City Office); Peter T. Healy (San Francisco Office); Howard M. Heitner; Joseph J. Herron (Newport Beach Office); Jack B. Hicks III; B. Boyd Hight; Bruce A. Hiler (Washington, D.C. Office); Michael S. Hobel (Century City Office); Gary N. Horlick (Washington, D.C. Office); Sandra Segal Ikuta; Robert S. Insolia (New York, N.Y. Office); Philip D. Irwin (Certified Specialist, Taxation Law, The State Bar of California Board of Legal Specialization); Wayne Jacobsen (Newport Beach Office); Tom A. Jerman (Washington, D.C. Office); Evan M. Jones; Richard M. Jones; Phillip R. Kaplan (Newport Beach Office); Peter C. Kelley (Century City Office); Holly E. Kendig; David E. Killough (San Francisco and Los Angeles Offices); Joseph K. Kim; Louis B. Kimmelman (New York, N.Y. Office); James H. Kinney (Century City Office); Matthew T. Kirby (Los Angeles, California and New York, N.Y. Offices); F. Curt Kirschner, Jr. (San Francisco Office); Paul R. Koepff (New York, N.Y. Office); Jeffrey I. Kohn (New York, N.Y. Office); C. Douglas Kranwinkle (New York, N.Y. and Los Angeles, California Offices); David A. Krinsky (Newport Beach Office); Gordon E. Krischer; Thomas J. Leary; Perry A. Lerner (New York, N.Y. and Century City, California Offices); C. James Levin; Douglas P. Ley (San Francisco Office); Charles C. Lifland; Ben H. Logan, III; Warren R. Loui (Century City Office); Patrick Lynch; Joseph M. Malkin (San Francisco Office); James P. Marlin (New York, N.Y. Office); Lowell C. Martindale, Jr. (Newport Beach Office); Marie L. Martineau (New York, N.Y. and Los Angeles California Offices); Cheryl White Mason (San Francisco and Los Angeles Offices); Jill H. Matichak (San Francisco and Los Angeles Offices); Edward J. McAniff (Los Angeles and San Francisco Offices); Michael G. McGuinness; Frederick B. McLane; Julie A. McMillan (San Francisco Office); Paul G. McNamara; Mitchell B. Menzer; Scott A. Meyerhoff (Newport Beach Office); Paul E. Mosley (Newport Beach Office); F. Thomas Muller, Jr.; Christopher C. Murray (Century City Office); Michael Newman; Charles F. Niemeth (New York, N.Y. and Century City, California Offices); John G. Niles; Jeffery L. Norton (New York, N.Y. Office); Christine M. Olsen; M. Randall Oppenheimer (Century City Office); Kenneth R. O'Rourke; Peter V. Pantaleo (New York, N.Y. Office); Richard G. Parker (Washington, D.C. Office); Stephen P. Pepe (Newport Beach and Los Angeles Offices); Donald V. Petroni (Century City Office); David G. Pommerening (Washington, D. C. Office); John B. Power; Laurence G. Preble (New York, N.Y. and Los Angeles, California Offices); Alan Rader (Century City Office); Ira H. Raphaelson (Washington, D.C. Office); Gilbert T. Ray; Charles C. Read; Frederick A. Richman (Century City Office); George A. Riley (San Francisco Office); Robert A. Rizzi (Washington, D.C.**

(This Listing Continued)

**O'Melveny & Myers LLP (Continued)**

**Office); Jeffrey J. Rosen (Washington, D.C. and New York, N.Y. Offices); Richard R. Ross (Century City Office); Frank L. Rugani (Newport Beach Office); Mark A. Samuels; Kathryn A. Sanders; William H. Satchell (Washington, D.C. and New York, N.Y. Offices); Stephen Scharf (Century City Office); Carl R. Schenker, Jr. (Washington, D.C. Office); Patricia A. Schmiege (San Francisco Office); Robert M. Schwartz (Century City Office); James V. Selna (Newport Beach Office); Ralph J. Shapira; Robert A. Siegel; Gary J. Singer (Newport Beach Office); Linda Jane Smith (Century City and Los Angeles Offices); Steven L. Smith (San Francisco Office); Darin W. Snyder (San Francisco Office); Masood Sohaili; Stephanie I. Splane (New York, N.Y. and Newport Beach, California Offices); John W. Stamper; Stephen J. Stern; Drake S. Tempest (New York, N.Y. Office); Gregory B. Thorpe; Henry C. Thumann; Stuart P. Tobisman (Century City and Los Angeles Offices); Lawrence P. Tu (Not admitted in CA; Hong Kong Office); Ko-Yung Tung (New York, N.Y. Office); Suzzanne Uhland; James R. Ukropina; Robert C. Vanderet; Framroze M. Virjee; Ulrich Wagner (New York, N.Y. Office); Diana L. Walker; Richard C. Warmer (San Francisco Office); Stephen H. Warren; David D. Watts; David I. Weil (Century City Office); Dean M. Weiner; Jacqueline A. Weiss (New York, N.Y. Office); John E. Welch (Washington, D.C. Office); Pamela Lynne Westhoff; Robert J. White; Robert E. Willett; Jonathan P. Williams (New York, N.Y. and Los Angeles, California Offices); Michael A. Wisnev; Charles C. Wolf; Thomas E. Wolfe (Newport Beach Office); W. Mark Wood; Michael G. Yoder (Newport Beach Office); Joel B. Zweibel (New York, N. Y. Office). Senior Counsellor: William T. Coleman, Jr. (Washington, D.C. Office). Senior Counsel: Edward W. Hieronymus. Of Counsel: Barton Beek (Newport Beach Office); R. Bradbury Clark; Owen Olpin; Lawrence J. Sheehan (Century City Office); Clyde E. Tritt (Certified Specialist, Taxation Law, The State Bar of California Board of Legal Specialization); William W. Vaughn. Special Counsel: Peter B. Ackerman; Susan E. Akens (Century City Office); Kevin Ray Baker (Newport Beach Office); David T. Beddow (Washington, D.C. Office); Stan Blumenfeld; Rosemary B. Boller (New York, N.Y. Office); Jennifer L. Borow (Century City Office); Mark L. Bradshaw (San Francisco and Los Angeles Offices); Avery R. Brown; Deborah J. Brown (Century City Office); Richard W. Buckner; Donald G. Carden (New York, N.Y. Office); Thomas G. Carruthers (New York, N.Y. Office); K. Leigh Chapman; Christine E. Coleman (Century City Office); Fiona M. Connell (Hong Kong Office); Steven M. Cooper; Reginam (Ginger) Covitt (Century City Office); John A. Crose, Jr.; George C. Demos (Newport Beach Office); Douglas E. Dexter (San Francisco Office); Marian J. Dillon (New York, N.Y. and Los Angeles, California Offices); Suzanne F. Duff; David P. Enzminger; David G. Estes (San Francisco Office); Thomas A. Ferrigno (Washington, D.C. Office); Charles W. Fournier (New York, N.Y. Office); Daniel M. Freedman (Not admitted in CA; Century City Office); David R. Garcia; James H. Gianninoto (New York, N.Y. Office); Joseph G. Giannola (New York, N.Y. Office); Robert A. Grauman (New York, N.Y. Office); Edward G. Gregory; Allan I. Grossman; Karen R. Growdon; Harold Henderson (Washington, D. C. Office); Margaret C. Henry (New York, N.Y. Office); David A. Hollander; Chris Hollinger; Mark C. Holscher; David I. Hurwitz (Not admitted in CA); Kenneth E. Johnson; Carol A. Johnston (Century City Office); Jeffrey M. Judd (San Francisco Office); Christopher N. Kandel (London, England Office); Jeffrey W. Kilduff (Washington, D.C. Office); Malcolm M. Kratzer (New York, N. Y. Office); Stanford G. Ladner (New York, N.Y. Office); Elizabeth A. Leckie (New York, N. Y. Office); David G. Litt (Washington, D.C. Office); Frances Elizabeth Lossing; Helen P. Mac Donald (London, England Office; may also be contacted at Los Angeles Office); Marcy Jo Mandel; Joseph G. McHugh; Gregory R. Oxford; Achilles M. Perry (New York, N.Y. Office); Diane E. Pritchard; Eric A. S. Richards; John A. Rogovin (Washington, D.C. Office); Tancred V. Schiavoni, III (New York, N.Y. Office); Peter O. Shinevar (New York, N.Y. Office); Edward J. Szczepkowski; Todd R. Triller (New York, N.Y. Office); Brett J. Williamson (Newport Beach Office); Alfred M. Wurglitz (Washington, D.C. Office). Associates: Christine M. Adams; Paul M. Alfieri (New York, N.Y. Office); Hubert L. Allen (San Francisco Office); Terrence R. Allen; Eric E. Amdursky; Iman Anabtawi (Century City Office); K. Allen Anderson (Newport Beach Office); Martine N. Apollon (Washington, D.C. Office); James D. Arbogast (New York, N.Y. Office); Barton S. Aronson (Washington, D.C. Office); Felipe J. Arroyo; Christine L. Bacon (New York, N.Y. Office); Linda A. Bagley (San Francisco Office); Patrick J. Bannon (San Francisco Office); Bernard C. Barmann, Jr.; Alfredo Barrios, Jr.; Steven Basileo; Evelyn Becker (Washington, D.C. Office); Angela M. Bellanca; Richard D. Beller; Carla J. Bennett; Laura B. Berger (Century City Office); Jay Blaivas (New York, N.Y. Office); Corey A. Boock; Michael G. Bosko (Newport Beach and San Francisco Offices); Lisa M. Bossetti; Debra L. Boyd; Laura C. Bremer (San Francisco and Los Angles Offices); Brian P. Brooks (Washington, D.C. Office); George H. Brown; J. Taylor Browning; Sharon Bunzel (San Francisco Office); Nadia St. George Burgard (New York, N.Y. Office); Walter R. Burkley, III; Andrea L. Campbell (New York, N.Y. Office); Bruce L. Campbell; Cannon Quigley Campbell; William A. Candelaria; Paul P. Canfield (New York, N.Y. Office); Jeffrey J. Carlisle (Washington, D.C. Office); Sean M. Carney; Christine L. Carr; Kevin B. Carter; Pinaki Chakravorty; John B. Chang (San Francisco Office); Gary A. Chodosh (New York, N.Y. Office); Apalla U. Chopra; Carla J. Christofferson (Century City Office); Peggy Ann Clarke (Washington, D.C. Office); Craig J. Coleman; Charles F. Connolly (Washington, D.C. Office); Craig A. Corman (Century City Office); Colleen Cox (Newport Beach Office); Frank M. Crance (Newport Beach Office); Andrea L. Crowe (New York, N.Y. Office); Brian Daly (New York, N.Y. Office); Scott J. Daruty (Newport Beach Office); Robert L. Davis (Newport Beach Office); Teresa E. Dawson (Washington, D.C. Office); Elizabeth A. Delaney (Washington, D.C. Office); Antonio A. Del Pino (New York, N.Y. Office); Ralph P. DeSanto (New York, N.Y. Office); Rafael Diaz-Granados (New York, N.Y. Office); Thomas J. Di Resta (New York, N.Y. Office); Mary P. Donlevy (Newport Beach Office); Erica K. Doran (New York, N.Y. Office); Kate W. Duchene; Bradford David Duea (Century City Office); Daniel M. Dunn (New York, N.Y. Office); Loryn D. Dunn; Martha Dye (Washington, D.C. Office); Mark C. Easton; Steven G. Eisner; John M. Farrell (Century City Office); Stephen P. Fattman (Washington, D.C. Office); Marcia A. Fay (San Francisco Office); John M. Fedorko (New York, N.Y. Office); Marc F. Feinstein; Aaron F. Fishbein (New York, N.Y. Office); Jeanne Morales Flynn (Century City Office); Suzanne Rich Folsom (Washington, D.C. Office); Michael Friedman (New York, N.Y. Office); Jess B. Frost; Lisa E. Funk (New York, N.Y. Office); Anne Elizabeth Garrett; Katherine E. Garrett; Neil K. Gilman (Washington, D.C. Office); John A. Gliedman (New York, N.Y. Office); Robin L. Gohlke; Gary R. Gold (Washington, D.C. Office); David B. Goldman; Jason P. Gonzalez (San Francisco Office); Victoria A. Graff; Todd A. Green (Newport Beach Office); Dionne C. Greene (New York, N.Y. Office); Jennifer G. Grenert (New York, N.Y. Office); Jonathan L. Griffith (Washington, D.C. Office); Alyssa A. Grikscheit (New York, N.Y. Office); Lawrence M. Hadley; Afshin Hakim; Andrea Hanneman (New York, N.Y. Office); Clint M. Hanni; Maria Snyder Hardy (Century City Office); Kevin M. Harr; David L. Hayes (Newport Beach Office); Judith A. Heinz; Krista Helfferich; David L. Herron; Lawrence J. Hilton (Newport Beach Office); Bruce R. Hirsh (Washington, D.C. Office); Mark Ho (Shanghai Office; China Counsel); Bonnie L. Hobbs (Hong Kong Office); Michael J. Holden (New York, N.Y. Office); Richard J. Holmstrom (New York, N.Y. Office); Carl D. Howard (New York, N.Y. Office); Lane Huang (Shanghai Office; China Counsel); Yongjin Im (New York, N.Y. and Los Angeles, California Offices); Mary A. Inman (San Francisco Office); Jill Irvin (New York, N.Y. Office); Bruce Gen Iwasaki; Neil Scot Jahss; Lynn A. Jansen; James Paul Jenal; Tonya Jenerette (Washington, D.C. Office); Nicholas G. Jenkins; Victor Jih (Century City Office); Teresa L. Johnson (London, England Office); Thomas J. Karr (Washington, D. C. Office); Allison M. Keller (Century City Office); Alice J. Kim (Not admitted in CA; Century City Office); Jonathan J. Kim; Patricia H. Kim (New York, N.Y. Office); Stuart Y. Kim; Susanna M. Kim (Newport Beach Office); Kathleen E. Kinney (Newport Beach Office); David S. Kitchen; Sandra R. Klein; Stephanie I. Klein (New York, N.Y. Office); Lonnie L. Kocontes; Hayley J. Kondon; Stephen V. Kovarik (New York, N.Y. Office); Peter Kozinets (San Francisco Office); Lisa E. Krim; Teresa Kwong (District of Columbia Office); John A. Laco; John M. Lambros; Jose Lau Dan (New York, N.Y. Office); Courtney A. Lederer (New York, N.Y. Office); James C. Lee; Mimi Lee (New York, N.Y. Office); Michelle M. Leonard (Century City Office); Michael Cary Levine; Barry P. Levinson (New York, N.Y. Office); Alfred P. Levitt (New York, N.Y. Office); Warren H. Lilien (San Francisco Office); George C. Lin; Barry Littman (Century City Office); Lisa Litwiller (Newport Beach Office); Robert G. Loewy (Newport Beach Office); Joseph C. Lombard (Washington, D.C. Office); Monique Janelle London (San Francisco Office); Eva M. Luchini; Michael M. Maddigan; Andrew S. Mansfield; Lisa H. Marino (Washington, D.C. Office); Dennis J. Martin (New York, N.Y. Office); Carlos M. Matos (Newport Beach Office); Greg K. Matson; Lori A. Mazur (New York, N.Y. Office); Marion K. McDonald (Washington, D.C. Office); Patricia A. McKenna (New York, N.Y. Office); Susan M. McNeill (New York, N.Y. Office); Ann Catherine Menard; Michael A. Meyer (Washington, D.C. Office); John F. Milani; Eric S. Miller (San Francisco Office); Jessica Davidson Miller (Washington, D.C. Office); Angela C. Mok (San Francisco Office); Luc Moritz; Robert C. Murray; Vicki A. Nash (Newport Beach Office); David B. Newdorf (San Francisco Office); John F. Niblock; Anthony R. G. Nolan (New York, N.Y. Office); Brent J. North (Newport Beach Office); Peter Obstler (San Francisco Office); Arthur J. Ochoa; John C. Oehmke; Geoffrey D. Oliver (Washington, D.C. Office); Kevin Oliver; David L. Orlic; Dean Pappas (Century City Office); Troy A. Paredes; Jeehye Park (New York, N.Y. Office); Kenneth G. Parker (Newport Beach Office); Lisa J. Parnell (Century City Office); Lynn E. Parseghian (Washington, D.C. Office); Gregory P. Patti, Jr. (New York, N.Y. Office); Mark D. Peterson (Newport Beach Office); George R. Phillips, Jr.; Claire J. Philpott (San Francisco Office); Steven Lee Pickering (San Francisco Office); Annette L. Poblete (New York, N.Y. Office); Stuart S. Poloner (New York, N.Y. Office); Karen Craig Poltrock (Newport Beach Office); Sean H. Porter (New York, N.Y. Office); Henry K. Prempeh (Washington, D.C. Office); Mark R. Pronk (New York, N.Y. Office); Yash A. Rana (New York, N.Y. Office); Anthony D. Ratner (San Francisco Office); Claudia E. Ray (New York, N.Y. Office); Michael C. Ray (Newport Beach Office); David J. Reis (San Francisco Office); Jendi B. Reiter**

(This Listing Continued)

**O'Melveny & Myers LLP (Continued)**

**(New York, N.Y. Office); Donald M. Remy (Washington, D.C. Office); Laurel A. Remington; Ramon E. Reyes, Jr. (New York, N.Y. Office); Thomas M. Riordan; Patrick R. Rizzi (Washington, D.C. Office); James Gerard Rizzo (New York, N.Y. Office); Deborah Rogers (Century City Office); Lori E. Romley (San Francisco Office); Allison M. Rose; Eric N. Roth (Century City Office); Valerie Granfield Roush (Washington, D.C. Office); Lynda M. Ruiz (San Francisco Office); Rogelio M. Ruíz (San Francisco Office); Carlos P. Salas; Deborah J. Saltzman; Paul Salvaty; Pamela D. Samuels; Philip C. Scheurer (Washington, D.C. Office); Christine A. Schnabel (Washington, D.C. Office); Scott Schrader (New York Office); Daniel A. Schulze (New York, N.Y. Office); Nancy L. Shackleton (Newport Beach Office); Nina Shafran (Washington, D.C. Office); Sam S. Shaulson (New York, N.Y. Office); Gregory B. Shean; Katherine Sieck (Newport Beach Office); James P. Sileneck (New York, N.Y. Office); Gulwinder S. Singh (Newport Beach Office); Thomas Singher (New York, N.Y. Office); John F. Slusher (Century City Office); Craig W. Smith; Ellen M. Smith (New York, N.Y. Office); Gary M. Smith (New York, N.Y. Office); Valerie A. Smith; Albert J. Solecki, Jr. (New York, N.Y. Office); Steven E. Soule; Geoffrey J. Spolyar; Irene E. Stewart; William J. Stuckwisch (Washington, D.C. Office); Christine H. Suh; Dean Sussman; Nancy E. Sussman (Century City Office); Janet I. Swerdlow; Christine Tam; Jadene M.W. Tamura (Newport Beach Office); Mark Christopher Teuton (Newport Beach Office); Mark E. Thierfelder (New York, N.Y. Office); Diana M. Torres; Glenn A. Trager; Gloria Trattles (New York, N.Y. Office); Dana S. Treister; Kenneth J. Turnbull (New York, N.Y. Office); George A.H. Turner (Newport Beach Office); Harry E. Turner (San Francisco Office); Mark T. Uyeda; Debra J. Vella; Scott M. Voelz; Karen Mary Wahle (Washington, D.C. Office); Kent D. Wakeford (Century City Office); Jeffrey W. Walbridge (Newport Beach Office); Ellen R. Waldorf (Washington, D.C. Office); Larry A. Walraven (Newport Beach Office); Stephanie M. Walter; Todd R. Watkins; Stephen J. Watson (New York, N.Y. Office); Aimee S. Weisner (Newport Beach Office); Kevin M. Wernick; Heather G. White; Molly M. White; Ronan M. Wicks (New York, N.Y. Office); Michael A. Williamson; David A. Wimmer; Robert Winter (New York, N.Y. Office); Jeffrey A. Wortman; Todd R. Wulffson (Newport Beach Office); Richard Xu (Hong Kong Office; China Counsel); Kevin Yamaga-Karns; Masami Yamamoto; Keith K. Yang (Century City Office); Stephanie K. Yonekura; Spencer H.C. Yu.**

**General Civil Litigation, Appellate Practice, and Criminal Trials Practice in all State and Federal Courts. Administrative; Antitrust; Banking; Bankruptcy; Commercial; Communications; Construction; Corporation and Corporate Financing; Environmental; Immigration and Naturalization; Insurance Coverage Defense; Intellectual Property; International Business; Labor and Employment; Employment Benefits; Media and Entertainment; Municipal, Municipal Zoning and Municipal Finance; Natural Resources; Oil and Gas; Patent, Trademark, Copyright and Unfair Competition; Probate, Trusts and Estate Planning; Public Utilities; Real Estate; Securities; and Tax Law.**

**Century City, California Office: 1999 Avenue of the Stars, 90067-6035. Telephone: 310-553-6700. Facsimile: 310-246-6779.**

**Newport Beach, California Office: 610 Newport Center Drive, 92660-6429. Telephone: 714-760-9600. Cable Address: "Moms". Facsimile: 714-669-6994.**

**San Francisco, California Office: Embarcadero Center West Tower, 275 Battery Street, 94111-3305. Telephone: 415-984-8700. Facsimile: 415-984-8701.**

**New York, New York Office: Citicorp Center, 153 East 53rd Street, 10022-4611. Telephone: 212-326-2000. Facsimile: 212-326-2061.**

**Washington, D.C. Office: 555 13th Street, N.W., 20004-1109. Telephone: 202-383-5300. Cable Address: "Moms". Facsimile: 202-383-5414.**

**London, England Office: 10 Finsbury Square, London, EC2A 1LA. Telephone: 0171-256-8451. Facsimile: 0171-638-8205.**

**Tokyo, Japan Office: Sanbancho KB-6 Building, 6 Sanbancho, Chiyoda-ku, Tokyo 102, Japan. Telephone: 03-3239-2900. Facsimile: 03-3239-2432.**

**Hong Kong Office: Suite 1905, Peregrine Tower, Lippo Centre, 89 Queensway, Central, Hong Kong. Telephone: 852-2523-8266. Facsimile: 852-2522-1760.**

**Shanghai, Peoples Republic of China Office: Shanghai International Trade Centre, Suite 2011, 2200 Yan An Road West, Shanghai, 200335, PRC. Telephone: 86-21-6219-5363. Facsimile: 86-21-6275-4949.**

***See Professional Biographies, LOS ANGELES, CALIFORNIA***

**Omens, Adryane R.** .................... '64 '90 C.112 B.A. L.426 J.D. [Ⓐ Danner&M.]
Omerberg, Maynard J. ....... '18 '43 C&L.966 Ph.B., LL.B. 8938 Wonderland Pk. Ave.‡
**Oncidi, Anthony J.** .................... '59 '85 C.668 B.A. L.145 J.D. [Troop M.S.&P.]
*PRACTICE AREAS: Labor and Employment Law; Litigation.
**O'Neal, Susan Andrews** .................... '62 '94 C.112 B.A. L.1148 J.D. [Ⓐ Long&L.]
**O'Neall, Cris K.** .................... '59 '86 C.154 B.A. L.1068 J.D. [Rodi,P.P.G.&C.]
*SPECIAL AGENCIES: County Assessment Appeals Boards; City Tax Boards.
*PRACTICE AREAS: State and Local Tax Counselling and Litigation; Environmental Litigation; Probate and Trust Litigation; Business and Commercial Litigation.
**O'Neil, James W.** .................... '31 '62 C.602 A.B. L.426 LL.B. [Ⓒ M.M.Michino]
*PRACTICE AREAS: Corporate Law; Banking Law.
**O'Neil, Stephen J.** .................... '60 '86 C.602 B.A. L.1068 J.D. [Sheppard,M.R.&H.]
*PRACTICE AREAS: Litigation.
**O'Neil, Thomas M.**, (AV) .......... '56 '82 C.1077 B.A. L.990 J.D. [Bonne,B.M.O.&N.]
**O'Neill, Mary L.** .................... '57 '81 C.112 B.A. L.809 J.D. [O'Neill,H.&A.]
*PRACTICE AREAS: Eminent Domain; Inverse Condemnation; Assessment Tax and Appeals; Probate; Civil Litigation.
**O'Neill, Michael J.** .................... '54 '82 C.112 B.A. L.464 J.D. [Robie&M.]
*REPORTED CASES: Smith v. Superior Court (1990) 217 Cal. App. 950; Orr v. Byers (1988) 198 Cal. App. 3d 666.
*PRACTICE AREAS: Insurance Bad Faith; Insurance Agency Malpractice; Insurance Coverage.
O'Neill, Robert B. '38 '63 C.602 B.A. L.262 LL.B.
V.P. & Gen. Coun., EMI Records Grp. North America

**O'Neill, Huxtable & Abelson, (BV)**
**800 West First Street, Suite 400, 90012**
**Telephone: 213-627-5017 Fax: 213-617-0196**
**Email: EmDOM@aol.com**
**Members of Firm: Francis H. O'Neill (1912-1992); Richard L. Huxtable (1927-1984); Leroy A. Abelson; Gavin M. Erasmus; Mary L. O'Neill. Associate: Christina E. Jackson.**
**Eminent Domain, Inverse Condemnation, Regulatory Takings, Property Taxation and Assessment Appeals, Real Property Litigation, Trusts and Estates, Probate and Probate Litigation, Civil Litigation and Trial Practice.**

***See Professional Biographies, LOS ANGELES, CALIFORNIA***

**O'Neill, Lysaght & Sun**
**(See Santa Monica)**

Ong, Tomson T. .................... '59 '84 C.800 B.A. L.426 J.D. Asst. U.S. Atty.
Ongkeko, Rafael A. ........... '53 '78 C.112 A.B. L.1066 J.D. Principal Dep. Co. Coun.
**Ono, Allan S.** .................... '61 '87 C.312 B.A. L.273 J.D. [Ⓐ Seyfarth,S.F.&G.]
*PRACTICE AREAS: Commercial Litigation; Bankruptcy/Creditors' Rights.
**Onstot, Stephen R.** .................... '59 '89 C.112 B.S.Ch. E. L.464 J.D. [Burke,W.&S.]
*PRACTICE AREAS: Environmental Law; Environmental Litigation; Regulatory Representation.
**Ontiveros, Aide C.** ............ '67 '94 C&L.112 B.A., J.D. [Ⓐ Breidenbach,B.H.H.&H.]
*LANGUAGES: Spanish.
*PRACTICE AREAS: Family Law; Criminal Defense; Insurance Defense.
**Ontiveros, Anthony M.** ............. '64 '91 C.560 B.A. L.1066 J.D. [Ⓐ R.E.Pfiester,Jr.]
*PRACTICE AREAS: Civil Litigation; FELA.
Onyejekwe, Moses O. .............. '59 '91 C.1357 B.A. L.1136 J.D. 3255 Wilshire Blvd.
Ooley, Michael D. .................... '54 '83 C.1163 B.A. L.800 J.D. 210 W. Temple St.
**Opdyke, T. William** .................... '48 '74 C.174 B.S. L.477 J.D. [Sheppard,M.R.&H.]
*PRACTICE AREAS: Corporate Trust Law; Public Finance Law; Corporate Securities Law; Mergers and Acquisitions.
**Opel, James C.**, (AV) .................... '45 '71 C.668 B.A. L.1066 J.D. [Gibson,D.&C.]
Opel, John E. .................... '63 '88 C.31 B.A. L.1068 J.D. 355 S. Grand Ave.‡
**Oppenheim, Charles B.** .................... '62 '88 C.188 B.A. L.262 J.D. [Foley L.W.&A.]
*PRACTICE AREAS: Health Care; Integrated Health Care Delivery Systems; Managed Care; Health Care Fraud.
Oppenheim, Nancy S. .................... '52 '81 C.112 B.A. L.426 J.D. 15260 Ventura Blvd.
**Oppenheim, Richard D., Jr.**, (AV) ........ '52 '77 C.112 B.A. L.426 J.D. [Sylvester&O.]
*PRACTICE AREAS: Trial Practice; Appellate Litigation; Insurance Defense Law; Public Entity Law.

Oppenheimer, Gregg .................... '51 '77 C.453 B.S. L.1066 J.D. 400 S. Hope St.

**Oppenheimer, M. Randall** ............. '52 '77 C.309 A.B. L.145 J.D. [O'Melveny&M.]

**Oppenheimer, Steven J.** ............... '44 '86 C.473 A.B. L.560 J.D. [Ⓐ Morgan,L.&B.]

**Oppenheimer Poms Smith, (AV)** BR

**2029 Century Park East, 38th Floor, 90067⊙**

**Telephone: 310-788-5000 FAX: 310-277-1297**

**Email: owdlaw.com**

**Richard L. Gausewitz (Resident, Irvine Office); Michael A. Kondzella (Resident, Irvine Office); Alan C. Rose; William Poms; Guy Porter Smith; Gary E. Lande; Louis J. Bovasso; Edward F. O'Connor (Resident, Irvine Office); Bernard R. Gans; Michael D. Harris; Jerry R. Potts; Mark P. Wine (Not admitted in CA); Christopher Darrow; Jane Shay Wald; Douglas N. Larson; David J. Oldenkamp; Marc E. Brown; Terry L. Miller (Resident, Irvine Office); Kurt A. MacLean (Resident, Irvine Office); J. Patrick Weir; Charles Rosenberg; James A. Henricks; Alan P. Block; James W. Inskeep; Steven W. Smyrski; Scott R. Hansen; Peter L. Holmes; Craig A. Slavin; Joel D. Voelzke.**

**Medical Device, Health Care, Business/Technology, Labor and Employment, Antitrust, professional Liability and Securities, Banking and Finance, Real Estate, Corporate Finance, Employee Benefits, International Corporate, Tax/Trust and Estate, Environmental Law and Toxic Torts, Insurance, Products Liability, Transportation, Dispute Resolution/Arbitration, European Community, International Tax.**

**Reference: City National Bank (Century Plaza Office, Century City).**

**Orange County Office: 1920 Main Street, Suite 1050, Irvine, California, 92714. Telephone: 714-263-8250. FAX: 714-263-8260.**

**San Jose, California Office: 333 West Santa Clara Street, Suite 1000, 95113. Telephone: 408-275-8790. FAX: 408-275-8793.**

**Oppenheimer Wolff & Donnelly:**

**Brussels, Belgium Office: Avenue Louise 250, Box 31, 1050. Telephone: 32-2-626-0500. FAX: 32-2-626-0510.**

**Chicago, Illinois Office: Two Prudential Plaza, 45th Floor, 180 North Stetson Avenue, 60601.**

**Minneapolis, Minnesota Office: 3400 Plaza VII, 45 South Seventh Street, 55401. Telephone: 612-344-9300. FAX: 612-344-9376.**

**New York, N.Y. Office: Citicorp Center, 153 East 53rd Street, 10022. Telephone: 212-826-5000. Telecopier: 212-486-0708.**

**Paris, France Office: 53 Avenue Montaigne, 75008. Telephone: (33/1) 44 95 03 50. FAX: (33/1) 44 95 03 40.**

**St. Paul, Minnesota Office: 1700 First Bank Building, 55101. Telephone: 612-223-2500. FAX: 612-223-2596.**

**Washington, D.C. Office: 1020 Nineteenth Street, N.W., Suite 400, 20036. Telephone: 202-293-6300. FAX: 202-293-6200.**

**Detroit, Michigan Office: Timberland Office Park, Suite 250, 5445 Corporate Drive, 48098. Telephone: 810-267-8500. FAX: 810-267-8559.**

**Affiliated Offices:**

**Goudsmit & Branbergen, J.J. Viottastraat, 46 Amsterdam 1071. Telephone: 31-20-662-30-31. FAX: 31-20-673-65-58.**

**Pisano, DeVito, Maiano & Catucci, Piazza Del Duomo, 20, Milan 20122. Telephone: 39-2-878281. FAX: 39-2-861275.**

**Pisano, DeVito, Maiano & Catucci, Via G. Borsi, 3, Rome 00197. Telephone: 39-6-8079087. FAX: 39-6-8078407.**

***See Professional Biographies, LOS ANGELES, CALIFORNIA***

**Opperman, Trudy D. Johnson** ......... '64 '89 C.106 B.A. L.352 J.D. [Chimicles,J.&T.]

**Oran, Michael L., (A Professional Corporation)** '57 '83 C.112 B.A. L.809 J.D. [Ⓐ P.J.McNulty]

*PRACTICE AREAS: Civil Litigation; Trial Practice; Medical Malpractice; Products Liability; Personal Injury.

**Orbach, David M.** ......................... '58 '83 C.112 B.A. L.426 J.D. [Maguire&O.]

*PRACTICE AREAS: Construction Law; Business Litigation.

Orchid, Harold L. ......................... '28 '56 C&L.623 A.B., LL.B. 11345 Dona Lola Dr.

**Ord & Norman, (AV)**

**1901 Avenue of the Stars, Suite 1250, 90067⊙**

**Telephone: 310-282-9900 Telecopier: 310-282-9917**

**Members of Firm: William K. Norman (Certified Specialist, Taxation Law, The State Bar of California Board of Legal Specialization); Edward O. C. Ord (Resident at San Francisco). Associates: Edi S. Stiles; Christian M. Winther (Resident at San Francisco).**

**Taxation (Federal, Foreign, State and Local), Tax Audits, International Business Transactions, Foreign Investment in the United States, Export Tax Incentives (FSC and DISC) Overseas Investment, NAFTA, Limited Liability Company, Corporation, Partnership and Statutory Trust Formations, Business Acquisitions, Technology Transfers, Business Startups, Family Owned Businesses, Real Estate, Cross Border Financing, Estate Planning, Foreign Trusts and Business and Investment Immigration and Expatriation.**

**San Francisco, California Office: 120 Montgomery Street, Suite 1055. Telephone: 415-274-3800. Telecopier: 415-274-3838.**

***See Professional Biographies, LOS ANGELES, CALIFORNIA***

**Ordin, Andrea Sheridan**, (AV) ....... '40 '66 C.112 B.A. L.1068 LL.B. [Morgan,L.&B.]

**Ordin, Robert L.** ........................ '24 '49 C.112 L.800 LL.B. [Ⓒ Murphy,W.&B.]

*PRACTICE AREAS: Business Workouts; Bankruptcy Reorganizations; Creditors Remedies.

**Ordonez, George E.** ............ '64 '92 C.426 B.B.A. L.1065 J.D. [Ⓐ Robinson,D.&W.]

*LANGUAGES: Spanish.

*PRACTICE AREAS: General Litigation; Insurance Coverage; Professional Errors and Omissions.

O'Reilly, Michael T. ...................... '59 '90 C.813 A.B. L.477 J.D. 601 Figueroa St.

O'Reilly, Terrence J., (AV) ....................... '50 '78 C&L.426 B.A., J.D. [Audet&O.]

**Orem, Belinda K.** ........................ '51 '81 C.508 B.A. L.1049 J.D. [Paul,H.J.&W.]

Oretzky, Perry S. .................... '46 '74 C.112 B.S. L.426 J.D. 10880 Wilshire Blvd.

Orfila, Stanford A., Jr. .................. '45 '70 C&L.800 B.S.L., J.D. 4700 Wilshire Blvd.

Orfirer, Dennis M. ...................... '56 '83 C.112 A.B. L.1067 J.D. 1818 Glendon Ave.

**Orgel, Robert B.** ..................... '55 '81 C.705 B.A. L.1068 J.D. [Pachulski,S.Z.&Y.]

Oring, Mark H. ............................ '40 '77 C.994 B.A. L.1065 J.D. [M.H.Oring]

Oring, Mark H., Law Offices of, A P.L.C. ................ 3580 Wilshire Blvd., 17th Fl.

**Oringher, Harvey T.**, (AV) ........ '49 '74 C.1019 B.A. L.1009 J.D. [Ginsburg,S.O.&R.]

**Orlanski, Ben D.** ......................... '67 '95 C.821 B.A. L.1068 J.D. [Ⓐ Irell&M.]

**Orlic, David L.** .................... '66 '94 C.197 B.A. L.659 J.D. [Ⓐ O'Melveny&M.]

**Orlik, Randy P.**, (AV) ....................... '52 '79 C.31 B.A. L.1066 J.D. [Cox,C.&N.]

*PRACTICE AREAS: Bankruptcy; Real Estate Finance; UCC Secured Transactions.

**Orloff, Lance D.** ........................ '59 '84 C.112 A.B. L.426 J.D. [Daniels,B.&F.]

*PRACTICE AREAS: Trial and Appellate Law; Insurance.

**Orlofsky, Michael J.** '63 '89 C.705 B.A. L.569 J.D. (adm. in NY; not adm. in CA) [Ⓒ Arnberger,K.B.&C.]

*PRACTICE AREAS: Trial and Appellate Litigation in all Courts.

Orman, Milton ................ '23 '52 C.273 A.B. L.966 LL.B. 420 S. Occidental Blvd.

Orme, Jane ............................ '— '32 C.813 L.986 LL.B. 328 N. Irving Blvd.

O'Rourke, John R. ................. '35 '63 C.800 A.B. L.426 LL.B. 4700 Wilshire Blvd.

**O'Rourke, Kenneth R.** ............... '59 '85 C.112 B.A. L.426 J.D. [O'Melveny&M.]

*PRACTICE AREAS: Business Litigation; Intellectual Property Litigation.

**O'Rourke, Allan & Fong**

**(See Glendale)**

Orozco, Francisco L. ...................... '45 '76 C.940 B.A. L.1067 J.D. Dep. City Atty.

Orozco, Sergio O. .................... '67 '94 C.112 B.A. L.1066 J.D. 777 S. Figueroa St.

Orr, David A. C. ........................ '46 '78 C.112 B.A. L.1188 J.D. 725 S. Figueroa

Orr, Diane L. ........................ '48 '77 C.178 B.A. L.564 J.D. P.O. Box 691324‡

**Orr, Gail L.** ..................... '55 '91 C.494 B.A. L.800 J.D. [Ⓐ Sinnott,D.M.&P.]

*PRACTICE AREAS: Insurance Coverage Litigation; Appellate Litigation.

**Orr, John M.** ................................ '65 '90 C&L.800 B.A., J.D. [Ⓐ Arter&H.]

Orr, Joseph B., (AV) ............. '30 '61 C.972 L.809 LL.B. 201 N. Figueroa St., 5th Fl.

**Orr, Ronald S.**, (AV) ................. '46 '72 C.813 B.S.E.E. L.800 J.D. [Gibson,D.&C.]

*PRACTICE AREAS: Debtor Creditor Relations; Bankruptcy; Corporate Reorganizations; Nonjudicial Debt Restructuring.

**Orr, Steven R.** ........................ '62 '88 C.800 A.B. L.309 J.D. [Richards,W.&G.]

*PRACTICE AREAS: Civil Litigation; Insurance Coverage; Dispute Resolution.

**Orrick, Herrington & Sutcliffe LLP, (AV)**

**777 South Figueroa Street, Suite 3200, 90017⊙**

**Telephone: 213-629-2020 Telecopier: 213-612-2499**

**URL: http://www.orrick.com**

**Resident Partners: Alan G. Benjamin; William W. Bothwell; Lori A. Bowman; William B. Campbell; Eugene J. Carron; Robert E. Freitas; Earl A. Glick; Todd E. Gordinier; Greg Harrington; W. Douglas Kari; Michael A. McAndrews; Richard C. Mendelson; Lawrence Peitzman; Gary D. Samson; Larry D. Sobel; Payne L. Templeton; Paul A. Webber; Howard J. Weg. Resident Of Counsel: Jeffrey S. Allen; John P. Kreis; Mary H. Neale; Michael E. Silver. Resident Associates: Ella L. Brown; Diana K. Chuang; Christopher L. Davis; Andrew D. Garelick; Margaret H. Gillespie; Owen P. Gross; Brett Healy; Victor Hsu; Alisa Jardine; Julie E. Knipstein; Linda S. Koffman; Scott G. Lawson; Victoria A. Levin; Douglas E. Love; Lisa Girand Mann; Paul T. Martin; Antonio D. Martini; Bradley Scott Miller; Melanie Murakami; William W. Oxley; Georgiana Rosenkranz; Christopher S. Ruhland; John P. Sharkey; David B. Shemano; Bridgette M. Smith; Winnie Tsien; Bradley S. White. Menlo Park, California Members of Firm: W. Reece Bader; G. Hopkins Guy, III; Lynne C. Hermle; Terrence P. McMahon; Christopher R. Ottenweller; Jon B. Streeter; Gary E. Weiss. Associates: David J. Anderman; Carl W. Chamberlin; Erin Farrell; Kenneth J. Halpern; Leslie Y. Kimball; Wendy Kosanovich; Amy L. Landers; Joseph C. Liburt; Sean A. Lincoln; Alexandra McClure; Peter C. McMahon; Matthew H. Poppe; Eve T. Saltman; Shelley J. Sandusky; Graeme Ellis Sharpe; Eric L. Wesenberg; Thomas H. Zellerbach. New York, New York Members of Firm: Paul B. Abramson; Charles W. Bradley; Bradford S. Breen; Peter R. Bucci; Charles N. Burger; Colman J. Burke; Fred C. Byers, Jr.; Richard Chirls; Katharine I. Crost; Bruce S. Cybul; Duncan N. Darrow; Michael Delikat; Edward M. De Sear; Rubi Finkelstein; Robert A. Fippinger; Lawrence B. Fisher; Adam W. Glass; Lawrence B. Goodwin; F. Susan Gottlieb; William A. Gray; Arnold Gulkowitz; Eileen B. Heitzler; Robyn A. Huffman; Laurence Bryan Isaacson; Robert M. Isackson; John J. Keohane; Alan M. Knoll; Peter J. Korda; Jeffrey A. Lenobel; Herbert J. Levine; Carl F. Lyon, Jr.; Daniel A. Mathews; Sam Scott Miller; Kathleen H. Moriarty; Barbara Moses; David Z. Nirenberg; Joshua E. Raff; Jill L. Rosenberg; Stephen K. Sawyier; Albert Simons, III; Louis H. Singer; Michael Voldstad; Richard Weidman; Neil T. Wolk. Special Counsel: Donald J. Robinson. Of Counsel: Stanley L. Amberg; Thomas Barr, IV; Susan L. Barry; Michael E. Emrich; William H. Horton, Jr.; John A. MacKerron; Robert B. Michel; Martin R. Miller; Amy Moskowitz; Richard H. Nicholls. Associates: Craig T. Beazer; Jonathan K. Bender; Thomas J. Benison; Leon J. Bijou; Colette Bonnard; Patti Lynn Boss; Eric R. Bothwell; Whitney R. Bradshaw; Karen M. Braun; Jarrett D. Bruhn; Juliet F. Buck; Benjamin C. Burkhart; Lawton M. Camp; Anthony Carabba, Jr.; Michael B. Carlinsky; Jennifer M. Clapp; Joseph M. Cohen; Caterina A. Conti; Robert A. Cote; Kyle W. Drefke; Joseph Evall; Marguerite J. Felsenfeld; Jeffrey J. Fessler; John D. Giansello, III; Michael A. Gilbert; Howard M. Goldwasser; Meryl A. Griff; Tzvi Hirshaut; Kiran J. Kamboj; René A. Kathawala; Joseph T. Kennedy; Jaemin Kim; Steven L. Kopp; Diane Krebs; Kenneth R. Linsk; Christopher Locke; Jonathan B. Lurvey; Michael D. Maline; Joseph E. Maloney; David A. Marple; Edward Mayfield; Lisa K. McClelland; Thomas N. McManus; James H. McQuade; Aimee B. Meltzer; Ronald Millet; Bradford E. Monks; Christopher J. Moore; C. Rochelle Moorehead; P. Quinn Moss; Bryan Jay Neilinger; William O'Brien; John F. Olsen; Edwin Gerard Oswald; Scott M. Pasternack; Marc J. Pensabene; Sheryl Lynn Pereira; Gail Pflederer; Nanci Prado; Ruth D. Raisfeld; Marlene Watts Reed; Marni J. Roder; Ira G. Rosenstein; Sidney M. Ruthenberg; Hooman Sabeti-Rahmati; David J. Sack; Al B. Sawyers; Martin L. Schmelkin; Patricia A. Seddon; William C. Seligman; Ronit Setton; Katherine A. Simmons; Corey A. Tessler; David M. Traitel; Sandra L. Tsang; Robert A. Villani; Steven I. Weinberger; Bradley E. Wolf; Michael J. Zeidel. Sacramento, California Members of Firm: R. Michael Bacon; Norman C. Hile; Perry E. Israel; Cynthia J. Larsen; Marc A. Levinson; Timothy J. Long; John R. Myers; Cynthia L. Remmers. Special Counsel: William E. Donovan. Of Counsel: E. Randolph Hooks; Iain Mickle. Associates: Jennifer P. Brown; Jordon Lee Burch; James T. Cahalan; Virginia M. Christianson; John P. Cook; William T. Darden; Stephen L. Davis; Edward P. Dudensing; Lynn T. Ernce; Eric J. Glassman; Kelcie M. Gosling; Trish Higgins; Christopher E. Krueger; Constance L. LeLouis; Kim Mueller; Charles W. Nugent; Andrew W. Stroud; Susan R. Thompson; Margaret Carew Toledo; Thomas J. Welsh. San Francisco, California Members of Firm: John E. Aguirre; William F. Alderman; Ralph H. Baxter, Jr.; Elaine R. Bayus; Daniel R. Bedford; Michael J. Bettinger; Steven A. Brick; Frederick Brown; Charles Cardall; Thomas Y. Coleman; Mary A. Collins; Dean E. Criddle; Roger L. Davis; Stanley J. Dirks; William M. Doyle; Raymond G. Ellis; Robert P. Feyer; Carlo S. Fowler; David S. Fries; Richard A. Gilbert; Robert J. Gloistein; Richard E. V. Harris; Richard D. Harroch; Gary A. Herrmann; Patricia K. Hershey; Richard I. Hiscocks; William L. Hoisington; Leslie P. Jay; John H. Kanberg; Lawrence T. Kane; Dana M. Ketcham; John H. Knox; Geoffrey P. Leonard; Mark R. Levie; Michael H. Liever; Peter Lillevand; Dora Mao; John E. McInerney, III; Michael R. Meyers; Thomas C. Mitchell; William G. Murray, Jr.; Noel W. Nellis; M. J. Pritchett; Greg R. Riddle; Marie B. Riehle; William L. Riley; Paul J. Sax; John F. Seegal; Thomas R. Shearer, Jr.; Gary R. Siniscalco; Richard V. Smith; Stephen A. Spitz; Alan Talkington; Ralph C. Walker; Jeffrey S. White; Kenneth G. Whyburn; Jeffrey D. Wohl; George G. Wolf; Cameron W. Wolfe, Jr.; George A. Yuhas. Of Counsel: Bruce S. Klafter; Philip C. Morgan; Catherine K. O'Connell; Douglas C. Sands; Samuel A. Sperry; Timothy P. Walker. Associates: Melody A. Barker; Pamela H. Bennett; Gregory D. Bibbes; Scott D. Blickenstaff; Paul C. Borden; Kerry Anne Bresnahan; Susan J. Briscoe; Jessica L. Cahen; David Malcolm Carson; David J. Castillo; Kevin Shih-Chun Chou; Brett E. Cooper; Robert E. Curry, III; Mark Davis; Kirsten J. Day; Ana Marie del Rio; Mary Patricia Dooley; Scott D. Elliott; Gabriela Franco; David K. Gillis; Carlos E. Gonzalez; Mary Elizabeth Grant; Maria Gray; Adam J. Gutride; John M. Hartenstein; Dolph M. Hellman; Mats F. Hellsten; Tanya Herrera; Lynne T. Hirata; Laura A. Izon; Stephen J. Jackson, Jr.; Andrew P. Johnson; Daniel Judge; Susan R. Kelley; Hera Lie Kim; Thomas P. Klein; William J. Kramer; Kathleen Hughes Leak; Nancy M. Lee; Gary Louie; Ashley E. Lowe; Steven C. Malvey; Douglas D. Mandell; Karen L. Marangi; George P. Miller; James W. Miller Jr.; Genevieve M. Moore; Lowell D. Ness; Mark F. Parcella; Anthony B. Pearsall; David C. Ritchey; Peter E. Root; Christian J. Rowley; Paul I. Rubin; Dave A. Sanchez; Michelle W. Sexton; Usha Rengachary Smerdon; David Sobul; Lawrence N. Tonomura; Adrienne Diamant Weil; Stephen E. Whittaker. Singapore Member of Firm: William R. Campbell. Associates: Kenneth S. Aboud; M. Tamara Box; Nicholas Chan Kei Cheong; Bruce R. Schulberg; David Z. Vance; Eleanor Wong. Washington, D.C. Members of Firm: Cameron L. Cowan; Felicia B. Graham; Keith W. Kriebel; Lorraine S. McGowen; Paul Weiffenbach. Of Counsel: David S. Katz; Dianne Loennig Stoddard. Associates: Michele E. Beasley; Mark S. Dola; Michael H. Freedman; Rohit H. Kirpalani; Douglas Madsen; Thomas D. Salus; Adam B. Tankel.**

**General Practice, including Corporate and Municipal Finance, Domestic and International Commercial Law, Banking and Commercial Finance, Project Finance, Structured Finance, Mergers and Acquisitions, Commercial Litigation, Insurance, Insurance Insolvency, White Collar Criminal Defense, Tax, Employee Benefits and Personal Estates, Antitrust, Distribution, and Trade Regulation, Intellectual Property, Real Estate, Environmental and Energy, Labor and Employment Law and Bankruptcy.**

**San Francisco, California Office: Old Federal Reserve Bank Building, 400 Sansome Street. Telephone: 415-392-1122. Telecopier: 415-773-5759.**

**New York, New York Office: 666 Fifth Avenue. Telephone: 212-506-5000. Telecopier: 212-506-5151.**

**Sacramento, California Office: 400 Capitol Mall. Telephone: 916-447-9200. Telecopier: 916-329-4900.**

**Washington, D.C. Office: Washington Harbour, 3050 K Street, N.W. Telephone: 202-339-8400. Telecopier: 202-339-8500.**

**Menlo Park, California Office: 1020 Marsh Road. Telephone: 415-833-7800. Telecopier: 415-614-7401.**

**Singapore Office: 10 Collyer Quay, #23-08 Ocean Building, Singapore. Telephone: 011-65-538-6116. Telecopier: 011-65-538-0606.**

***See Professional Biographies, LOS ANGELES, CALIFORNIA***

Ors, Rose D. ......................... '54 '83 C.112 B.A. L.1066 J.D. 7410 McCool Ave.

Ortega, Edward R., (BV) ..... '52 '77 C.112 B.A. L.1068 J.D. 801 S. Grand Ave., 18th Fl.

Ortega, Reuben A. ............................ '41 '67 C.560 B.A. L.276 J.D. Supr. Ct. J.

**Ortiz, Luz Aurora** ................ '67 '96 C.674 B.A. L.477 J.D. [Ⓐ Richman,L.K.&G.]

**Ortiz, Sandra M.** '58 '84 C&L.813 A.B., J.D. Gen. Coun., KCAL-TV, Walt Disney Co.

**Ortolano, Joan S.** '37 '80 C.1131 B.A. L.426 J.D. Sr. Coun., Pacific Telesis Legal Group

**Osaki, Keli N.** ......................... '— '95 C.112 B.A. L.990 J.D. [Resch P.A.&B.]

*PRACTICE AREAS: Business Litigation.

Osborn, Christopher J. ............. '47 '76 C.426 B.A. L.1137 J.D. 4700 Wilshire Blvd.

Osborn, Julia A. ............................ '40 '74 C.1130 B.A. L.426 J.D. N.L.R.B.

Osborn, Peter N. ...................... '54 '82 C.800 B.A. L.426 J.D. 801 S. Figueroa St.

CAA309P

Osborne, Carl K. ....'40 '68 L.809 J.D. 1157 South Beverly Drive
**Osborne, Jonathan L.**, (BV⊕) '61 '86 C.275 B.A. L.421 J.D.
(adm. in KY; not adm. in CA) [Zevnik H.G.&M.]
(⊙London, England, Wash., D.C., Palo Alto, CA., New York, NY.)
*PRACTICE AREAS: Insurance Coverage; Commercial Litigation.
**Osenbaugh, Kurt V.** ....'57 '82 C.813 B.A. L.1068 J.D. [McClintock,W.B.R.R.&M.]
*PRACTICE AREAS: Business Litigation; Environmental Litigation; Employment Litigation.
O'Shea, Brian ....'65 '94 C.321 B.A. L.128 J.D. Concorde-New Horizons Corp.
O'Shea, Michael D. ....'54 '79 C.940 B.A. L.276 J.D. 624 S. Grand Ave.
**O'Shea, Robert M.** ....'69 '95 C.692 B.A. L.93 J.D. [Ⓐ Latham&W.]
Osher, Irwin Spiegel, (AV) ....'29 '54 C&L.800 B.A., J.D. [I.O.Spiegel]
Osher, Irwin Spiegel, Law Corporation, (AV) ....9220 W. Sunset Blvd.
Oshiki, Alice M. ....'60 '84 C.1077 B.S. L.1065 J.D. 221 N. Figueroa St.
Oshiro, Arthur A. '52 '77 C&L.312 B.A., J.D.
(adm. in HI; not adm. in CA) I.R.S.
**Osias, David L.**, (AV) '54 '79 C.112 B.S. L.1066 J.D.
[Allen,M.L.G.&M.] (⊙San Diego)
*PRACTICE AREAS: Bankruptcy; Creditors' Rights; Water Rights and Resources.
**Osinoff, Peter R.**, (AV) ....'52 '76 C.976 B.A. L.813 J.D. [Bonne,B.M.O.&N.]
**Osman, Joel A.** ....'56 '82 C.112 B.A. L.1068 J.D. [Anderson,M.&C.]
*PRACTICE AREAS: Civil Litigation; Environmental Litigation.
**Osman, Randa A. F.** ....'64 '90 C.312 B.A. L.1065 J.D. [Ⓐ Quinn E.U.&O.]
**Ossentjuk, David A.** ....'61 '87 C.154 B.A. L.1068 J.D. [Hanna&M.]
*PRACTICE AREAS: Natural Resources; Civil Trial; Environmental Law; General Practice.
**Ossiff, John** ....'53 '85 C.1070 B.S. L.1068 J.D. [Nossaman,G.K.&E.]
*PRACTICE AREAS: Litigation.
Osteen, Jeffrey M. ....'61 '92 C.280 B.B.A. L.1066 J.D. 1900 Ave. of the Stars
**Oster, Bernard** ....'46 '81 C.102 B.A. L.1009 J.D. [Cohen P.&F.]
**Oster, Ronald M., (P.C.)**, (AV) ....'48 '73 C&L.813 A.B., J.D. [Paul,H.J.&W.]
Osteraas, Thomas L. ....'66 '93 C.309 A.B. L.494 J.D. 555 W. 5th St.
**Osterland, Gerry D.** '44 '69 C.801 B.A. L.502 J.D.
(adm. in MO; not adm. in CA) [Jones,D.R.&P.]
**Ostiller, Cathy** ....'70 '94 C&L.112 B.A., J.D. [Ⓐ Sidley&A.]
*LANGUAGES: French, Spanish.
**Ostiller, Patricia V.** ....'62 '89 C.597 B.S. L.426 J.D. [Ⓐ Sheppard,M.R.&H.]
Ostrin, Baker B. ....'62 '86 C.112 A.B. L.976 J.D. Dep. Pub. Def.

**Ostrin, Ronald E., (AV) '54 '79 C.112 B.A. L.1065 J.D.**
**11377 West Olympic Boulevard, Suite 900, 90064-1625**
**Telephone: 310-914-7991 Fax: 310-914-7907**
***PRACTICE AREAS: Bankruptcy Litigation; Business Litigation; Real Estate Litigation; Entertainment Law; General Civil Litigation.**
**General Civil Practice in all State and Federal Courts with emphasis on Bankruptcy, Real Estate and Entertainment Law.**
***See Professional Biographies, LOS ANGELES, CALIFORNIA***

**Ostroff, Peter I.**, (AV) ....'42 '67 C.112 B.A. L.1068 J.D. [Sidley&A.]
*PRACTICE AREAS: Complex Commercial Litigation; Intellectual Property; Employment and Computer Technology.
Ostrov, Frank E. ....'56 '87 C.112 B.A. L.1065 J.D. 12121 Wilshire Blvd.
**Ostrove, David**, (AV) ....'29 '60 C.112 B.A. L.809 LL.B. [Ostrove,K.&O.]
*REPORTED CASES: Edenfield v. Fane, 113 S. Ct. 1792, 1993; Sylvia S. Ibanez v. Florida Board of Accountancy, 114 Sup. Ct. 2084 (1994), Amicus Briefs, The American Association of Attorney CPAs in support of Commercial Free Speech.
*TRANSACTIONS: Tax Free Merger-Reorganization: System Parking and ABM, 1993-1994.
*PRACTICE AREAS: Taxation; Tax Litigation; Probate; Trusts; Business Litigation.
**Ostrove, Kenneth E.**, (AV) ....'57 '83 C.330 B.A. L.809 J.D. [Ostrove,K.&O.]
*PRACTICE AREAS: Probate; Estate Planning.

**Ostrove, Krantz & Ostrove, A Professional Corporation, (AV)** ▣
**(Successor To: Ostrove and Lancer, A Professional Corporation; David Ostrove, A Professional Corporation)**
**5757 Wilshire Boulevard, Suite 535, 90036-3600**
**Telephone: 213-939-3400 Fax: 213-939-3500**
**Email: OSTROVE@AOL.COM**
**David Ostrove; David S. Krantz; Kenneth E. Ostrove.**
**Complex Business Litigation, General Civil Litigation, Real Estate Transactions and Real Estate Litigation, Buying and Selling Businesses, Mergers, Consolidations, Tax-Free Reorganizations, Commercial Transactions, Civil RICO, Tax Matters and Tax Litigation, Probate, Wills, Trusts, Estate Planning, Litigation Support and Expert Testimony, Legal and Accounting Education. Maritime Law, Insurance Defense.**
**Reference: First Business Bank.**
***See Professional Biographies, LOS ANGELES, CALIFORNIA***

Ostrow, Kenneth A. '62 '88 C.188 B.A. L.1068 J.D.
V.P. & Gen. Coun., New World Television Programming
O'Sullivan, Daniel S. ....'63 '90 C.112 B.A. L.426 J.D. 1900 Ave of the Stars
O'Sullivan, Maureen S. ....'56 '81 C.112 B.A. L.1162 J.D. 1900 Ave of the Stars
**O'Sullivan, Michael J.** ....'65 '92 C.659 B.A. L.800 J.D. [Ⓐ Munger,T.&O.]
**O'Sullivan, Thomas E.**, (AV) ....'24 '55 C.800 B.S. L.426 J.D. [Ⓒ Sullivan,W.&D.]
*PRACTICE AREAS: Taxation Law; General Business Planning Law; Estate Planning Law; Probate Law.
**Oswald, Timothy J.** '59 '85 C.911 B.A. L.426 J.D.
Gen. Coun., Licensing, Guess?, Inc.
*RESPONSIBILITIES: Intellectual Property; Licensing; International Distribution.
**Oswalt, J. David**, (AV) ....'47 '76 C.37 B.A. L.1068 J.D. [Arnold&P.]
*PRACTICE AREAS: Commercial Litigation.
**Ota, Henry Y.**, (AV) ....'42 '70 C.197 B.A. L.800 J.D. [Pillsbury M.&S.]
**Otera, Richard H.** ....'68 '94 C.112 B.A. L.426 J.D. [Ⓐ Sheppard,M.R.&H.]
Otero, S. James ....'51 '77 C.1077 B.A. L.813 J.D. Mun. Ct.
Otis, Juliana ....'53 '82 C.112 B.A. L.426 J.D. V.P. & Corp. Coun., Jefferies & Co., Inc.
**Oto, Eric S.** ....'62 '87 C.112 B.S. L.1065 J.D. [Ⓐ Crosby,H.R.&M.]
O'Toole, Marilyn B., (AV) ....'44 '77 C&L.800 B.A., J.D. One Wilshire Blvd.
**O'Toole, Patricia M.**, (AV) ....'53 '82 C.605 B.A. L.1068 J.D. [O'Toole]
*LANGUAGES: French.
*SPECIAL AGENCIES: U.S. EPA (Environmental Protection Agency); Federal Occupational Safety and Health Administration (OSHA); California Occupational Safety and Health Administration (Cal OSHA); California OSH Appeals Board; South Coast Air Quality Management District (SCAQMD).

**O'Toole Law Firm, The, (AV)**
**601 South Figueroa Street, Suite 4100, 90017**
**Telephone: 213-630-4200 Facsimile: 213-683-1148**
**Patricia M. O'Toole.**
**Environmental and Worker Health and Safety Law.**
***See Professional Biographies, LOS ANGELES, CALIFORNIA***

Ott, Alan '61 '94 C&L.420 B.A., J.D.
(adm. in LA; not adm. in CA) 8655 Belford Ave. (Westchester)‡

**Ott & Horowitz**
**(See Glendale)**

**Otto, James D., (Professional Corporation)**, (AV) '49 '74
C.763 B.A. L.597 J.D. [Cummins&W.]
*PRACTICE AREAS: Business Litigation; Insurance Coverage Litigation; Professional Errors and Omissions; Reinsurance Law; Environmental Law.

Otto, James M. '61 '86 C.197 A.B. L.608 J.D.
(adm. in OH; not adm. in CA) Ernst & Young
**Otto, John Carpenter**, (AV) ....'30 '59 C.611 B.A. L.809 J.D. [Ⓒ Spray,G.&B.]
**Outcault, Richard F., Jr.**, (AV) ....'24 '51 C&L.813 A.B., LL.B. [Arter&H.]
Outlaw, Rondrew A. ....'46 '74 C.990 B.A. L.950 J.D. P.O. Box 35323
**Overfelt, Leslie** ....'55 '89 C.103 B.A. L.1068 J.D. [Ⓐ Konowiecki&R.]
*PRACTICE AREAS: Health Care; General Business.
**Overholt, David G.**, (AV) ....'35 '61 C.976 B.A. L.813 J.D. [Hoag&O.]⊙
*PRACTICE AREAS: Probate; Trust Administration; Tax.

**Overlander, Lewis & Russell**
**(See Pasadena)**

**Overstreet, Gary F.**, (AV) ....'42 '71 C.623 B.S. L.426 J.D. [Musick,P.&G.]
*PRACTICE AREAS: Labor and Employment.

**Overton, Lyman & Prince, LLP, (AV)**
**A Registered Limited Liability Partnership including Professional Corporations**
**777 South Figueroa Street, 37th Floor, 90017**
**Telephone: 213-683-1100 Cable Address: "Olap" Telecopier: 213-627-7795**
**Members of Firm: Eugene Overton (1880-1970); Edward Dean Lyman (1881-1962); George W. Prince, Jr. (1887-1971); Donald H. Ford; Dennis B. Hansen (P.C.); Roy E. Potts; Frederick W. Hill; Gregory C. Glynn; Gerald R. Whitt.**
**General Civil Trial and Appellate Practice in all State and Federal Courts. Corporation, Labor, Real Property and Construction Law, Employment, Literary Property, Trademark, Estate Planning, Trust and Probate Law. State and Federal Taxation, Water Rights, Business, Banking and International Business Law emphasizing Mexico and Japan. Bankruptcy and Creditors' Rights, Securities and Commodities Law.**
**References: Union Bank of California (550 S. Hope St., Los Angeles); Daiichi Kangyo Bank, Ltd.; Asahi Bank, Ltd.**
***See Professional Biographies, LOS ANGELES, CALIFORNIA***

Oviedo, Carlos '55 '91 C.846 B.A. L.848 J.D.
(adm. in TX; not adm. in CA) I.R.S.
Owen, Kenneth E., (AV) ....'38 '64 C.112 B.A. L.1068 LL.B. P.O. Box 27400
**Owen, Michael L.** ....'42 '68 C.813 A.B. L.309 LL.B. [Paul,H.J.&W.]
**Owen, Steven P.** ....'67 '94 C.839 B.A. L.940 J.D. [Ⓐ Borton,P.&C.]
*PRACTICE AREAS: Premises Liability; Personal Injury.
Owens, Andrew G., Jr., (AV) ....'45 '72 C.511 B.A. L.767 J.D. [Rosner,O.&N.]
**Owens, James Franklin** ....'61 '86 C.1365 B.A. L.362 J.D. [McCutchen,D.B.&E.]
*PRACTICE AREAS: Healthcare Law.
Owens, James M. ....'52 '78 C.800 A.B. L.426 J.D. Princ. Dep. Co. Coun.
**Owens, Joseph C.** ....'56 '84 C.112 B.A. L.1065 J.D. [Lewis,D.B.&B.]
*LANGUAGES: Spanish.
Owens, Michael L. ....'59 '86 C.1074 B.A. L.426 J.D. 3255 Wilshire Blvd.
**Owens, Robert B.**, (AV) ....'51 '77 C&L.800 B.S., J.D. [Owens&G.]
**Owens, Stephen T.** ....'48 '78 C.768 B.A. L.1068 J.D. [Graham&J.]
*LANGUAGES: French and Italian.
*PRACTICE AREAS: Commercial Litigation; Banking Litigation; Arbitration; Alternative Dispute Resolution.
Owens, Wilbert, Jr. ....'33 '72 C.85 B.S. L.809 J.D. Dep. Dist. Atty.

**Owens & Gach Ray, (AV)**
**10351 Santa Monica Boulevard, Suite 400, 90025**
**Telephone: 310-553-6611 Telecopier: 310-553-2179**
**Email: ogrlaw@aol.com**
**Members of Firm: Robert B. Owens; Linda Gach Ray.**
**General Civil Practice with emphasis on Commercial Litigation, Real Estate Litigation and Creditors' Rights in Bankruptcy Matters, Conservatorship Matters and Entertainment Litigation.**
***See Professional Biographies, LOS ANGELES, CALIFORNIA***

**Ownbey, Lloyd C., Jr.**
**(See Pasadena)**

Ownby, Gordon T. '56 '87 C.1077 B.A. L.426 J.D.
Gen. Coun., Cooperative of Amer. Physicians
Oxborough, Sharon K. ....'58 '85 C.300 B.A. L.309 J.D. 1410 West Blvd.
**Oxford, Gregory R.** ....'49 '74 C.477 B.A. L.813 J.D. [Ⓒ O'Melveny&M.]
*PRACTICE AREAS: Business Litigation.
**Oxley, William W.** ....'63 '88 C.147 B.A. L.464 J.D. [Ⓐ Orrick,H.&S.]
*LANGUAGES: Spanish.
**Oyakawa, Denis H.** ....'50 '74 C.112 B.A. L.976 J.D. [Graham&J.]
*PRACTICE AREAS: International Trade Law; Business Law; Commercial Law.
**Ozaki, DeAnne H.** ....'66 '91 C.112 B.A. L.1066 J.D. [Ⓐ Paul,H.J.&W.]
Ozell, Robert M. '53 '79 C.339 B.S. L.1068 J.D.
CEO & Gen. Coun., La Mancha Develop. Co.
**Ozello, Frank J., Jr.** ....'63 '89 C.178 B.A. L.724 J.D. [Ⓐ Gray,Y.D.&R.]
*PRACTICE AREAS: Insurance Coverage; Commercial Litigation; Tort Litigation.
**Ozeran, David J.** ....'62 '88 C.112 B.A. L.1067 J.D. [Ⓐ La Follette,J.D.F.&A.]
*PRACTICE AREAS: General Liability; Medical Malpractice.
**Ozzello, Mark A.** ....'56 '84 C.276 B.A. L.145 J.D. [Arias&O.]
*PRACTICE AREAS: Corporate Law; Business Litigation; Real Estate.
**Pabst, Thomas J.** ....'51 '78 C.112 B.A. L.426 J.D. [Ⓒ Chapman&G.]
*PRACTICE AREAS: Estate Planning Law; Estate Administration Law; Business; Corporate; Real Estate Law.
Pace, Dean Francis, (AV) ....'28 '55 C.524 B.S. L.128 J.D. [Pace&R.]
Pace, Joyce ....'58 '88 C.1042 B.A. L.1136 J.D. 1936 W. 79th St.
**Pace, Laura A.** ....'67 '92 C.112 B.A. L.426 J.D. [Ⓐ Harcock R.&B.]
**Pace, Marilyn K.** ....'49 '90 C.477 B.A. L.1068 J.D. [McMahon&S.]
**Pace, Richard R.** ....'40 '70 C.871 B.S. L.339 J.D. [Arter&H.]
*PRACTICE AREAS: Labor and Employment Law.
**Pace, Terrence R.** ....'66 '95 C&L.800 B.S., J.D. [Ⓐ Sonnenschein N.&R.]
*PRACTICE AREAS: Real Estate; Corporate Law.
Pace and Rose, (AV) ....1800 Avenue of the Stars (⊙Wash., D.C. & Paris, France)
Pachino, Barton P. '60 '84 C.228 B.A. L.597 J.D.
Sr. V.P. & Gen. Coun., Kaufman and Broad Home Corp.
**Pachter, Michael H.** '56 '81 C.1077 B.S. L.990 J.D.
Sr. Tax Coun., Atlantic Richfield Co.
*RESPONSIBILITIES: Taxation Law.
**Pachulski, Isaac M.**, (AV) ....'50 '74 C.112 B.A. L.309 J.D. [Stutman,T.&G.]
*PRACTICE AREAS: Bankruptcy; Insolvency; Corporate Reorganization.
**Pachulski, Richard M.**, (AV) ....'56 '79 C.112 B.A. L.813 J.D. [Pachulski,S.Z.&Y.]
*REPORTED CASES: In re F.A.B. Industries, 147 B.R. 763 (C.D. Cal. 1992).
*TRANSACTIONS: Represented the Creditors' Committees of Weintraub Entertainment, Inc. and First Executive Corporation; Represented or Representing the Debtors in TSL Holdings, Inc.; Penguin's Frozen Yogurt, Inc./Penguin's Place, Inc.; Commonwealth Equity Trust; and Sizzler International, Inc. and Affiliated Debtors.

**Pachulski, Stang, Ziehl & Young, Professional Corporation, (AV)**
**Suite 1100, 10100 Santa Monica Boulevard, 90067⊙**
**Telephone: 310-277-6910 Telecopier: 310-201-0760**
**Shareholders: Marc A. Beilinson; Andrew W. Caine; Linda F. Cantor; Larry W. Gabriel; Brad R. Godshall; Stanley E. Goldich; Richard J. Gruber; Ira D. Kharasch; Alan J. Kornfeld; Robert B. Orgel; Richard M. Pachulski; Jeffrey N. Pomerantz; Jeremy V. Richards; James I. Stang; Thomsen Young; Dean A. Ziehl;—Debra Grassgreen; Rachelle S. Visconte. Senior Counsel: Harry D. Hochman; Catherine A. Steiner. Of Counsel: Ellen M. Bender; Bradley E. Brook; James K. T. Hunter; George A. Juarez; Linda A. Kirios; Samuel R. Maizel (Not admitted in CA); Iain A.W. Nasatir; Arnold M. Quittner; William L. Ramseyer; Adrian F. Roscher; Don Willenburg.**

(This Listing Continued)

## PRACTICE PROFILES

## CALIFORNIA—LOS ANGELES

**Pachulski, Stang, Ziehl & Young, Professional Corporation** (Continued)
Bankruptcy, Corporate Reorganization, Debtor-Creditor Matters, Insurance Insolvency, Civil Litigation, Business, Commercial Law, General Real Estate, and Corporate and Entertainment Transactions.
San Francisco, California Office: 350 California Street, Suite 2020. Telephone: 415-263-7000. Facsimile: 415-263-7010.

*See Professional Biographies, LOS ANGELES, CALIFORNIA*

Paciulan, Richard J. '47 '77 C.588 B.S.E.E. L.818 J.D.
(adm. in MA; not adm. in CA; See Pat. Sect.) [A Ladas&P.]
Packard, Carlisle G. ................................ '56 '87 C&L.101 B.A., J.D. [A Cox,C.&N.]
Packard, Robert C., (AV) .................... '19 '48 C&L.800 B.S., J.D. [Kirtland&P.]
Packer, David L. .............................. '59 '85 C.276 B.A. L.893 J.D. [A Pircher,N.&M.]
  *PRACTICE AREAS: Real Estate Law; Real Estate Finance.
Packer, Donna ......................... '48 '77 C.1060 B.A. L.464 J.D. 1900 Ave. of the Stars
Packer, Rory A. '54 '80 C.339 B.A. L.365 J.D.
(adm. in IL; not adm. in CA) Westfield Corp., Inc.
Padilla, Jose L., Jr., (AV) ............'57 '82 C.112 B.A. L.770 J.D. [Gansinger,H.B.&P.]
  *LANGUAGES: Spanish.
  *PRACTICE AREAS: Construction Litigation; Business Litigation; Civil Litigation.
Padilla, Stephen M. ....................... '58 '86 C.800 B.S. L.477 J.D. [Padilla&O.]⊙
  *LANGUAGES: Spanish.
  *PRACTICE AREAS: Employment and Labor Law; Commercial Litigation; Business Litigation; Civil Litigation; Real Property Litigation.

**Padilla & O'Leary, (BV)**
**One Wilshire Boulevard, Suite 2100, 90017-3383**
Telephone: 213-489-2003 Fax: 213-489-2323
Members of Firm: Stephen M. Padilla; Kevin D. O'Leary.
Civil Litigation in all State and Federal Courts, Business and Commercial Law, Labor and Employment, Real Estate, Environmental and Casualty, Bankruptcy, Admiralty and Maritime, Insurance, Products Liability, Personal Injury and Toxic Torts.

*See Professional Biographies, LOS ANGELES, CALIFORNIA*

Padleschat, Joyce A. .................... '49 '83 C.112 B.A. L.1068 J.D. 633 W. 5th St.
Padova, Daniel J. ..................... '63 '96 C.990 B.S.M. L.1137 J.D. [A Engstrom,L.&L.]
Pagac, Christine A. ..................... '67 '91 C&L.477 B.A., J.D. [A Horvitz&L.]
Page, Dennis A. ........................ '40 '65 C.668 B.A. L.1066 LL.B. [Iverson,Y.P.&H.]
  *PRACTICE AREAS: Probate; Estate Planning; Unitary Tax; Tax Litigation.
Page, F. Scott ............................. '57 '83 C.705 B.A. L.94 J.D. [Seyfarth,S.F.&G.]
Page, Vincent C., (AV) ...................'26 '53 C&L.426 B.B.A., LL.B. [Hill,F.&B.] ‡
Paglia, Antoinette D. ............... '56 '91 C.1097 B.A. L.809 J.D. [A Gibson,D.&C.] (Pat.)
  *PRACTICE AREAS: Medical Malpractice and Health Law; General Civil Litigation; Intellectual Property; Patent Law.
Pagliery, Richard H. ................... '61 '96 C.1042 L.260 J.D. [A Lyon&L.]
  *LANGUAGES: Spanish.
  *PRACTICE AREAS: Intellectual Property.
Paguirigan, Cristeta S. ................. '59 '84 C.312 B.B.A. L.1066 J.D. 419 N. Croft Ave.
Pahl, Douglas J. ......................... '53 '78 C.228 A.B. L.802 J.D. [Kern&W.]
Paige, Ian D. ......................... '52 '82 L.398 J.D. 6222 Wilshire Blvd.
Paik, David J. ....................... '63 '92 C.665 B.S. L.347 J.D. 1 Wilshire Blvd.
Paine, Shirley J. ....................... '50 '90 C.813 A.B. L.800 J.D. [A Foley L.W.&A.]
  *REPORTED CASES: Mir v. Charter Suburban Hospital, 27 Cal. App. 4th 1471 (1994); Scripps Memorial Hospital v. Superior Court, 95 Daily Journal 11961, 1995.
  *PRACTICE AREAS: Health Care; Bioethics; Medical Staff Credentialing; Peer Review; Health Care Facility Licensing and Regulation.
Paine, Steven L. ......................... '48 '76 C.605 B.A. L.426 J.D. [Cotkin&C.]
  *PRACTICE AREAS: Insurance Coverage and Bad Faith Litigation; Reinsurance Disputes; Insurance Regulatory Matters; Professional Liability Litigation.
Painter, Christopher Martin Edward ........ '58 '86 C.367 B.A. L.813 J.D. Asst. U.S. Atty.
Painter, Douglas R. .................. '57 '88 C.446 B.S. L.1067 J.D. [C McCutchen,D.B.&E.]
  *LANGUAGES: Spanish.
  *PRACTICE AREAS: Litigation.
Paja, Salvador I. ................ '30 '56 C&L.999 B.B.A., LL.B. 339 N. Heliotrope Dr.‡
Pak, Jong Pil ........................ '62 '89 C.112 B.A. L.1065 J.D. 3600 Wilshire Blvd.
Pakula, Rina J. ...................... '67 '92 C.112 B.A. L.800 J.D. [A Shumaker&S.]
  *PRACTICE AREAS: Insurance Insolvency; Litigation; Healthcare.
Palarz, Herman S., (AV) ............'37 '63 C.112 B.A. L.800 LL.B. [Tyre K.K.&G.]⊙
Palazzo, Robert P., (AV) '52 '76 C.112 B.A. L.800 J.D. [icon]
**3002 Midvale Avenue, Suite 209, 90034**○
Telephone: 310-474-5483 Fax: 310-474-6736
  *REPORTED CASES: Soto v. Wisconsin Department of Revenue, WTAC, No. 88-I-16, August 29, 1989 CCH §203-092 (Wisconsin Tax Appeals Commission).
State, Local, Federal and International Taxation, Corporation, Entertainment, Church, Mining and Oil and Gas Law.
Inyo County Law Office: 230 South Main Street, Darwin, California 93522. Telephone: 619-876-5941.

*See Professional Biographies, LOS ANGELES, CALIFORNIA*

Paley, Andrew Marc ................... '65 '90 C.976 B.A. L.813 J.D. [A Latham&W.]
Pallemon, Robert A. ..................... '49 '76 C.602 A.B. L.1068 J.D. [A Manatt,P.&P.]
  *PRACTICE AREAS: Family Law; White Collar Criminal Defense; Litigation.
Paller, Joseph L., Jr. ................... '52 '78 C.112 B.A. L.1068 J.D. [Gilbert&S.]
Palmer, Charles F., (AV) .............. '46 '73 C.112 A.B. L.976 J.D. [Perkins C.]
Palmer, Curtis H. .................... '08 '32 C.112 L.1066 LL.B. 151 5th Anita Dr.‡
Palmer, Geoffrey H. ................. '50 '75 C.174 B.S. L.990 J.D. 11740 San Vicente Blvd.‡
Palmer, George M. .................... '38 '70 C.1042 B.A. L.800 J.D. Head Dep. Dist. Atty.
Palmer, Gerald W., (AV) ............. '40 '68 C.608 B.A. L.893 LL.B. [Jones,D.R.&P.]
Palmer, Harry D. ..................... '39 '68 C.813 B.A., LL.B. 2530 S. Bundy Dr.
Palmer, Helen Goldberger ........'66 '92 C.112 B.A. L.1068 J.D. [A Buchalter,N.F.&Y.]
  *LANGUAGES: Spanish.
  *PRACTICE AREAS: Commercial Litigation.
Palmer, John .................'— '90 C.976 B.A. L.893 J.D. [A Ladas&P.] (See Pat. Sect.)
Palmer, Pamela S. .................. '57 '83 C.112 B.A. L.800 J.D. [Latham&W.]
  *PRACTICE AREAS: Professional Liability and Securities Litigation.
Palmer, Robert L., (AV⊤) '46 '72
C.276 B.A. L.178 J.D. [Hennigan,M.&B.] (⊙Phoenix, AZ)
  *PRACTICE AREAS: Antitrust Law; Complex Litigation; False Claims Act; Securities Litigation.
Palmersheim, Karen R. .............. '66 '94 C.112 B.A. L.809 J.D. [A Robie&M.]
  *PRACTICE AREAS: Civil Litigation.
Palmieri, Ralph V., (AV) ................. '49 '77 C.102 B.S. L.276 J.D. 11755 Wilshire Blvd.
Palmieri, Ronald J. ......................... '— '81 911 Linda Flora Dr.
Palo, Margaret Reid-Alvarez ........'56 '83 C.112 B.A. L.1148 J.D. 4121 Beethoven St.
Palombo, Lisa A. ..................... '62 '90 C.912 B.A. L.94 J.D. [A Foley L.W.&A.]
  *LANGUAGES: Italian.
  *PRACTICE AREAS: Business and Commercial Litigation.
Palomino, Maria ...................... '58 '89 C&L.1049 B.A., J.D. Dep. Dist. Atty.
Paluga, Pamela J. ...................'63 '89 C.112 B.A. L.818 J.D. [A Agapay, L.&H.]
  *PRACTICE AREAS: Real Estate Litigation; Business Litigation.
Pancake, Jennifer L. ............... '62 '88 C.684 B.A. L.426 J.D. [Hill,F.&B.]
  *PRACTICE AREAS: Eminent Domain Law; Real Property and Land Use Litigation.
Pancione, Peter R., (AV) ............. '36 '64 C.573 B.S. L.107 LL.B. [Gipson H.&P.]
Paniccia, Patricia Lynn ............ '52 '81 C.312 B.A. L.990 J.D. KCOP-TV Channel 13
Panish, Howard R., (AV) ............ '27 '61 C.69 A.B. L.809 LL.B. [Greenberg&P.]

Pannell, Brenda J. ................ '65 '95 C.112 B.A. L.446 J.D. [A Chapin,F.&W.]
  *PRACTICE AREAS: Bad Faith Litigation.
Pannone, Joseph W. .................... '54 '80 C&L.426 B.A., J.D. [Kane,B.&B.]
  *SPECIAL AGENCIES: Special Counsel to City of Banning, City of Culver City, City of Glendale, City of Hawthorne, City of Pasadena.
  *REPORTED CASES: Ehrlich v. City of Culver City, 12 Cal.4th 854 (1996) (challenge to land use approval exactions).
  *TRANSACTIONS: Redevelopment Plan Adoptions/Amendments for the Cities of Banning, Glendale and Hawthorne; Sony Pictures Entertainment Developer Agreement for the City of Culver City.
  *PRACTICE AREAS: Municipal Law; Land Use Law; Redevelopment Law.
Pansegrau, Robert J. '48 '82 C.197 A.B. L.184 J.D.
(adm. in MA; not adm. in CA) PaineWebber Properties
Pansing, Gretchen C. ................. '— '92 C.112 B.A. L.426 J.D. 6300 Wilshire Blvd.
Pansky, Ellen A., (AV) .............. '53 '77 C.112 B.A. L.426 J.D. [A Pansky&M.]
  *REPORTED CASES: Rimel v. State Bar (1983) 34 Cal.3d 128; Greene v. Zank (1984) 158 Cal.App.3d 497; Palomo v. State Bar (1984) 36 Cal.3d 758; Tarver v. State Bar (1984) 37 Cal.3d 122; Leoni v. State Bar (1985) 39 Cal.3d 609.
  *PRACTICE AREAS: Lawyers Disciplinary Defense and Admissions; Legal Malpractice; Ethics Consultations and Testimony; Professional Licensure Defense.

**Pansky & Markle, (AV)**
**Suite 4050, 333 South Grand Avenue, 90071**
Telephone: 213-626-7300 Fax: 213-626-7330
Members of Firm: R. Gerald Markle; Ellen A. Pansky; Dennis W. Rihn.
Lawyer Disciplinary and Admissions Matters, Legal Malpractice, Professional Liability, General Civil Trial and Appellate Practice, Defense of Professional Licensing proceedings.

*See Professional Biographies, LOS ANGELES, CALIFORNIA*

Pantages, Sherry L. ................... '64 '88 C.800 B.A. L.464 J.D. [Cummins&W.]
  *PRACTICE AREAS: Environmental Coverage Litigation; Insurance Coverage Law; Bad Faith Litigation; Insurance Defense; Business Litigation.
Pantell, Lloyd S., (P.C.) ........... '51 '77 C.112 B.A. L.990 J.D. [Reinstein,P.&C.]
  *PRACTICE AREAS: Business Law; Commercial Law; Health Care Law; Partnership Law; Corporate Law.
Panunzio, Mindy Sheps '53 '82 C&L.705 B.S.W., J.D.
11400 W. Olympic Blvd., 9th Fl.
Panzer, Jonathan J. ................. '49 '81 C.1044 B.A. L.1068 J.D. [Shapiro,R.&C.]
Papageorge, Lee J. ................. '65 '95 C.674 A.B. L.813 J.D. [A Quinn E.U.&O.]
Papageorge, Thomas A., (AV) ........'54 '77 C.112 A.B. L.309 J.D. Dist. Atty's Off.
Papan, Virginia I. ......................... '62 '89 C.112 B.A. L.1043 J.D. Calif. Bar/BRI
Paparelli, Angelo A., (AV) ...... '49 '76 C.477 B.A. L.912 J.D. [Bryan C.] (⊙Irvine, Ca.)
  *LANGUAGES: Italian and Farsi (Persian).
Pape, Kara Ann ..................... '62 '87 C&L.426 B.A., J.D. [McHale&C.]
  *PRACTICE AREAS: Insurance Defense; Products Liability; Commercial Carriers.
Pape, Leonard ................... '49 '77 C.107 B.A. L.809 J.D. Dep. Atty. Gen.
Papell, Ronald M., (AV) .............. '47 '74 C.1077 L.809 J.D. [R.M.Papell]
  *LANGUAGES: French.
  *PRACTICE AREAS: Civil Litigation; Professional Liability; Personal Injury; Products Liability; Sexual Harassment.

**Papell, Ronald M., A Prof. Corp., Law Offices of, (AV)**
**Fifteenth Floor, 1875 Century Park East, 90067**
Telephone: 310-553-4767 Fax: 310-553-8002
Ronald M. Papell.
Civil Litigation, Professional Liability, Personal Injury, Products Liability, Sexual Harassment, Wrongful Termination, and Insurance Coverage Litigation.
Reference: City National Bank.

*See Professional Biographies, LOS ANGELES, CALIFORNIA*

Papenfuss, Herbert, (BV) '46 '72
C&L.477 B.A., J.D. 19725 Sherman Way (Canoga Pk.), Ste. 200
Papernik, Brian G. .................... '64 '91 C.867 B.S. L.178 J.D. [A Nossaman,G.K.&E.]
  *PRACTICE AREAS: Real Property Law.
Papiano, Neil, (AV) .............. '34 '61 C.813 B.A. L.880 LL.B. [Iverson,Y.P.&H.]
  *PRACTICE AREAS: Civil Litigation and Appellate Practice; Entertainment Law; Libel and Defamation Litigation; Corporation and Securities Law.
Papillon, Kimberly N. ............... '69 '96 C.112 B.A. L.178 J.D. [A Sheppard,M.R.&H.]
  *PRACTICE AREAS: Litigation.
Pappas, Dean ......................... '66 '91 C&L.800 B.S., J.D. [A O'Melveny&M.]
  *LANGUAGES: Greek.
  *PRACTICE AREAS: Real Estate.
Pappas, Louis W. ................ '57 '85 C.1074 B.A. L.809 J.D. [A Bonne,B.M.O.&N.]
Pappas, Michael E. ............... '61 '87 C.112 B.A. L.1065 J.D. [A Sonnenschein N.&R.]
  *PRACTICE AREAS: Insurance and Commercial Litigation; Creditor's Rights.
Pappy, George A., (AV) ................'31 '59 C.563 B.B.A. L.276 LL.B. [Pappy&D.]
**Pappy & Davis, A Prof. Corp., (AV)** ................................3424 Wilshire Blvd.
Papsdorf, Cynthia S. '57 '85
C.1214 B.A. L.564 J.D. [A Kelley D.&W.] (⊙Parsippany, NJ)
Paquette, Paul N. ................... '50 '83 C.1109 B.A. L.426 J.D. [Serritella&P.]
  *PRACTICE AREAS: Products Liability Defense; Public Entity Defense; General Civil Litigation.
Parada, Oswald .................... '63 '90 C.1078 B.A. L.426 J.D. Dep. Fed. Pub. Def.
Parandeh, Nayssan L. .................. '68 '95 C.112 B.A., J.D. [A Katten M.&Z.]
  *LANGUAGES: Farsi, German.
Parascandola, Anthony J. ........ '61 '89 C.234 B.A. L.734 J.D. [A Sedgwick,D.M.&A.]

**Parcells, Dayton B., III '60 '87 C.692 B.A. L.990 J.D.**
**2049 Century Park East Suite 2790, 90067**
Telephone: 310-201-9882 Fax: 310-201-9855
Kenton E. Moore.
Civil Trial and Appellate Practice in all State and Federal Courts. Emphasis in the Areas of Business Litigation, Products Liability, Personal Injury, Medical Malpractice Law and Employment.

*See Professional Biographies, LOS ANGELES, CALIFORNIA*

Parchman, Irving C. ...................... '58 '84 C&L.813 A.B., J.D. [A Pick&B.]
  *PRACTICE AREAS: Entertainment Law; Intellectual Property; Civil Litigation.

**Pardee, William R. '35 '61 C&L.770 B.S.C., LL.B.**
**6255 Sunset Boulevard Suite 2000, 90028**
Telephone: 213-464-6026
General Practice.

*See Professional Biographies, LOS ANGELES, CALIFORNIA*

Pardo, Robert ..................... '58 '87 C.112 B.S. L.426 J.D. [Jacob&P.]
Parducci, Pilar S. ................... '66 '93 C.112 B.A. L.188 J.D. [A Latham&W.]
Paredes, Roger F. ................. '62 '89 C.1077 B.A. L.1137 J.D. 3255 Wilshire Blvd.
Paredes, Troy A. .................. '71 '96 C.112 B.A. L.976 J.D. [A O'Melveny&M.]
Parga, Denise M. ................... '51 '82 C.569 B.A. L.846 J.D. [C Wolf,R.&S.]
  *PRACTICE AREAS: Construction Litigation; Civil Litigation.
Pargament, Michael .............. '39 '67 C.367 B.A. L.1009 LL.B. Dep. Dist. Atty.
Paris, Andrew E. .................. '67 '92 C.910 A.B. L.813 J.D. [A Kirkland&E.]
  *PRACTICE AREAS: Litigation.
Pariser, Wayne D. .................. '62 '87 C.605 A.B. L.1049 J.D. [Pollak,V.&F.]
Parisi, David C. .................. '66 '92 C.1109 B.S. L.94 J.D. [A Quisenberry&B.]
  *PRACTICE AREAS: Insurance Coverage.
Park, Ann I. ..................... '63 '87 C.309 A.B. L.1068 J.D. [A Heller E.W.&M.]
Park, Daniel E. ..................... '69 '94 C&L.112 B.A., J.D. [A Radcliff,F.&D.]
  *LANGUAGES: Korean.

**Park, David C.** ....'60 '86 C.112 B.A. L.93 J.D. [Barger&W.]
*PRACTICE AREAS: Business Litigation; Real Estate Litigation; Insurance Litigation; Banking Litigation; Architecture Law.
**Park, Francis Y.** ....'68 '94 C.112 B.A. L.178 J.D. [A Latham&W.]
Park, Heesok ....'56 '82 C.112 B.A. L.1066 J.D. [Hannon,P.&L.]
**Park, Jackie K.** ....'59 '86 C.103 B.A. L.597 J.D. [Pillsbury M.&S.]
**Park, Jacklyn J.** ....'70 '95 C.112 B.A. L.309 J.D. [A Latham&W.]
*LANGUAGES: Korean.
**Park, Jin S.** ....'68 '95 C.813 B.A. L.1068 J.D. [A McKenna&C.]
*LANGUAGES: Korean.
*PRACTICE AREAS: Litigation; Government Contracts; International Law.

**Park, John K., & Associates '60 '94 C.1167 B.S.E. L.809 J.D.**
**445 South Figueroa, Twenty-Seventh Floor, 90071-1603**
**Telephone: 213-612-7730 Fax: 213-426-2171**
***LANGUAGES: Korean.**
***PRACTICE AREAS: Patent; Trademark; Copyright; Trade Secrets; Contracts.**
**Intellectual Property, Patent, Trademarks, Copyright, Contracts and Licensing.**

***See Professional Biographies, LOS ANGELES, CALIFORNIA***

**Park, Maxine H.** ....'64 '94 C.1163 B.S. L.800 J.D. [A Parker S.]
*PRACTICE AREAS: Personal Injury; Government Benefits; Family Law.
**Parke, Margret G.** ....'59 '86 C.172 B.A. L.426 J.D. [A Sedgwick,D.M.&A.]
*LANGUAGES: German.
*PRACTICE AREAS: Insurance Fraud Law.
Parker, Barry S. ....'48 '76 C.763 B.S. L.809 J.D. 10880 Wilshire Blvd.
**Parker, Catherine Delarbre** ....'59 '90 C&L.061 LL.B. [C Golbert L.]
*LANGUAGES: French and Spanish.
*PRACTICE AREAS: Bankruptcy; Litigation.
**Parker, Daryl G.**, (AV) '44 '70
C&L.813 A.B., J.D. [Mahoney,C.J.&P.] (⊙Santa Moncica)
*PRACTICE AREAS: Real Estate, Insurance, Business and Maritime Litigation and Transactions.
**Parker, David B.**, (AV) ....'51 '76 C.112 B.A. L.1068 J.D. [C Shumaker&S.]
Parker, H. Craig ....'48 '76 C.112 B.A. L.809 J.D. 445 S. Figueroa
**Parker, Jeffrey J.** ....'65 '91 C.602 B.S. L.800 J.D. [A Sheppard,M.R.&H.]
*PRACTICE AREAS: Environmental Law.
Parker, Kenneth A. '42 '68
C.178 A.B. L.569 J.D. Univ. of Southern Calif. Sch. of Medicine
Parker, Lawrence B. '36 '61 C.188 B.A. L.569 J.D.
12366 Chandler Blvd., Valley Village
Parker, Mary S. ....'20 '71 L.809 J.D. Ret. Wkrs. Comp. J.
Parker, Rebekah L. ....'64 '89 C.118 B.A. L.1068 J.D. 350 S. Figueroa, Ste. 350
Parker, Ronald S. ....'47 '74 C.1077 B.A. L.809 J.D. [Parker&M.]
**Parker, Warrington S.** ....'64 '90 C.674 A.B. L.309 J.D. [A Quinn E.U.&O.]
Parker & Markowitz ....3550 Wilshire Blvd.

**Parker, Milliken, Clark, O'Hara & Samuelian, A Professional Corporation, (AV)**
**Twenty Seventh Floor, Security Pacific Plaza, 333 South Hope Street, 90071**
**Telephone: 213-683-6500 Telecopier: 213-683-6669**
**Claude I. Parker (1871-1952); John B. Milliken (1893-1981); Ralph Kohlmeier (1900-1976); Mark Townsend (1921-1989); Leslie W. Mullins (1951-1990); Frank W. Clark, Jr.; N. Matthew Grossman; Karl M. Samuelian; Anthony T. Oliver, Jr.; Everett F. Meiners; Richard A. Clark; Claire D. Johnson; Frank Albino; Nowland C. Hong; Carlo Sima; Stephen T. Holzer; Brenton F. Goodrich; Linda S. Klibanow; Richard D. Robins; William V. McTaggart, Jr.; Gary A. Meyer; William W. Reid; Cameron H. Faber; Rebecca M. Aragon; Joseph G. Martinez; Carl E. Kohlweck; Michael M. Mullins; Arsine B. Phillips; Michael S. Simon; Gregory M. Salvato;—Laron J. Lind; Marina Gatti; Faye Chen Barnouw; Asteghik Khajetoorians; Mark E. Elliott; Steven P. Heller; Michael D. Stevens; John Peter Schaedel; Paige E. Budd. Of Counsel: John F. O'Hara; Floyd M. Lewis; A. Albert Spar; Sidney I. Pilot; Richard L. Franck.**
**General Civil, Business, and Construction Litigation in State and Federal Courts. Environmental Civil, Criminal and Administrative Litigation, including government initiated and private party Superfund Litigation. Hazardous Materials Management and Compliance. Labor Relations and Employment Discrimination Law. Corporation, Partnership, Securities, Commercial and Business Law. Mergers and Acquisitions, Employee Benefits and Real Estate Law. Taxation (Federal, State and Local), Estate Planning, Probate, Banking, Government Contracts, Insurance and Eminent Domain Law. Bankruptcy/Reorganization, Creditors' Rights.**

***See Professional Biographies, LOS ANGELES, CALIFORNIA***

**Parker Stanbury, (AV)**
**A Partnership including a Professional Corporation**
**Thirty-Third Floor, 611 West Sixth Street, 90017-3101⊙**
**Telephone: 213-622-5124 Fax: 213-622-4858**
**Harry D. Parker (1891-1976); Raymond G. Stanbury (1904-1966). Members of Firm: Thomas Lee Waddell (A Professional Corporation); Douglass H. Mori; John D. Barrett, Jr.; Raymond F. Killion (Santa Ana Office); Robert L. LoPresti; Jack A. Lucas (Santa Ana Office); John W. Dannhausen; Ronald L. Smith; Graham J. Baldwin (San Bernardino Office); Timothy D. Lucas (San Diego Office); Douglas M. De Grave (Santa Ana Office); Richard A. Jones (Santa Ana Office); J. Luis Garcia. Associates: Craig J. Frilot (San Bernardino Office); Dana C. Clark (Santa Ana Office); Michael E. McCabe; Richard R. Therrien (Santa Ana Office); Walter Demyanek, Jr.; James M. Ledakis (San Diego Office); Michael Gould (Santa Ana Office); Patricia L. Blanton; Susan E. Price; Stanley A. Calvert (San Diego Office); Gerard L. Garcia-Barron; Gala E. Dunn; Karie E. Schroder; Nicole T. Saadeh; Evangelina P. Fierro Hernandez; Jenna Lea Grant (San Diego Office); Mary Crenshaw Tyler (San Diego Office); Gorman J. DeGrave (Santa Ana Office); Lucy G. Mendoza; Richard Leung; Maxine H. Park; Leonor C. Gonzales; Kate A. Willmore. Of Counsel: Robert H. Bergsten (Santa Ana Office).**
**General Civil, Trial and Appellate Practice in all State and Federal Courts. Insurance Law, Products Liability, Governmental Liability, Construction Accidents, Construction Defects; Land Subsidence, Toxic Torts, Wrongful Termination; Professional Malpractice, Coverage, Bad Faith, Transportation Law, Uninsured Motorist, First Party Claims, Vehicular Liability, Corporation, Family and Criminal Law.**
**Representative Clients: Allied Group Insurance; Allstate Insurance Co.; Nationwide/Wausau; Ohio Casualty Insurance Co.**
**Orange County Office: 888 North Main Street, Seventh Floor Santa Ana, California. Telephone: 714-547-7103. Fax: 714-547-3428.**
**San Bernardino, California Office: 290 North D Street, Suite 400. Telephone: 909-884-1256. Fax: 909-888-7876.**
**San Diego, California Office: 3131 Camino Del Rio North, Suite 1200. Telephone: 619-528-1259. Fax: 619-528-1419.**

***See Professional Biographies, LOS ANGELES, CALIFORNIA***

**Parkhurst, David G.**, (BV) '47 '73
C.112 B.A. L.800 J.D. [A Fulwider P.L.&U.] (See Pat. Sect.)
*PRACTICE AREAS: Patent, Trademark, Copyright and Unfair Competition Law; Litigation.
Parkin, Robert W. ....'32 '61 C.112 B.S. L.1001 LL.B. Supr. Ct. J.
**Parks, Michael W.** ....'65 '91 C.36 B.A. L.464 J.D. [A Ropers,M.K.&B.]
**Parminter, Steven R.** ....'53 '79 C.940 B.A. L.426 J.D. [Wilson,E.M.E.&D.]
**Parnell, Lisa J.** ....'65 '96 C.338 B.A. L.426 J.D. [A O'Melveny&M.]
Parnell, Lorna Kay ....'45 '72 C.679 B.S. L.345 J.D. Supr. Ct. J.
**Parris, Don**, (AV) ....'44 '68 C.112 B.S. L.1068 J.D. [Gibson,D.&C.]
*PRACTICE AREAS: Entertainment; Intellectual Property; Financing; Mergers and Acquisitions; Computers, Software and Technology.
**Parrish, D. Todd** ....'68 '94 C.1 B.B.A. L.990 J.D. [A Cummins&W.]
*PRACTICE AREAS: Litigation; Insurance Coverage; Bad Faith; Construction Defect.
**Parrish, J. Diane** ....'— '91 C.800 B.A. L.398 J.D. [C Runquist&Assoc.]
**Parry, David E.** ....'34 '69 C.77 B.A. L.809 J.D. [Hill,F.&B.]
*PRACTICE AREAS: Railroad Law; Personal Injury Law; Business Litigation; Medical Malpractice Defense Law; Property Damage Law.

**Parsons, Ann L.** ....'65 '94 C.112 B.A. L.145 J.D. [A Gipson H.&P.]
*PRACTICE AREAS: Corporate; General.
**Parsons, David W.**, (AV) ....'36 '69 C&L.284 J.D. [Parsons&D.]
*PRACTICE AREAS: Complex Coverage; Professional Liability; Reinsurance; General Insurance Litigation.

**Parsons and Destian, (AV) BR**
**1055 Wilshire Boulevard, Suite 1750, 90017⊙**
**Telephone: 213-975-0064 Telecopier: 213-975-1172**
**Email: dparsla@gnn.com**
**Members of Firm: David W. Parsons; Tony Destian. Of Counsel: G. David Rubin.**
**Litigation and General Insurance Practice. Coverage Excess and Reinsurance; Bad Faith Law; Fire Insurance Law; Products and Professional Liability; Asbestos, Hazardous Waste, Environmental Pollution and Other Toxic Tort Defense; Employment Wrongful Termination Liability; Equine Law, Mass Disaster Litigation; Municipal and Public Officials Liability; Landslide and Subsidence Law; Non-Marine, Marine and Inland Marine Insurance Law.**
**London, England Office: Guild House, 36-38 Fenchurch Street. EC3M 3DQ. Telephone: 071-929-5252. Telecopier: 071-283-4466. Telex: 914561.**

***See Professional Biographies, LOS ANGELES, CALIFORNIA***

Part, Marvin L., (BV) ....'31 '59 C.112 B.A. L.1068 LL.B. 6255 Sunset Blvd.
**Partain, Lisa N.** ....'67 '95 C.1239 B.A. L.809 J.D. [A Robbins,B.&C.]
*PRACTICE AREAS: Litigation; Patent, Trademark and Copyright.
Parton, Robert H. ....'64 '92 C.800 A.B. L.188 J.D. 555 W. 5th St.
Partos, Michael J. ....'64 '89 C.112 B.A. L.1049 J.D. 333 S. Grand Ave.
**Pascotto, Alvaro**, (AV) ....'49 '76 C.061 B.A. L.056 J.D. [Pascotto&G.]
*LANGUAGES: English, French, Spanish and Italian.
*PRACTICE AREAS: International; Entertainment; Real Estate; Aviation; Corporate.

**Pascotto & Gallavotti, (AV)**
**1800 Avenue of the Stars, 6th Floor, 90067-4276**
**Telephone: 310-203-7515 Facsimile: 310-284-3021**
**Alvaro Pascotto. Of Counsel: Mario Gallavotti, Avv.**
**International, Corporate, Business, Investment Taxation, Entertainment, Real Estate and Aviation Law. General Practice United States and Europe.**
**Rome, Italy Associated Office: Studio Legale Gallavotti Honorati & Pascotto, Via Po n. 9, 00198. Telephone: (06) 8530.1100. Facsimile: (06) 854.1323. E-Mail: MGAL@STAR.FLASHNET.IT**

***See Professional Biographies, LOS ANGELES, CALIFORNIA***

**Pash, David Andrew**, (BV) ....'58 '83 C.309 A.B. L.1066 J.D. [Kinsella,B.F.&T.]
**Pasich, Kirk A.**, (AV) ....'55 '80 C.112 B.A. L.426 J.D. [Troop M.S.&P.]
*PRACTICE AREAS: Insurance Coverage; Entertainment Litigation; Real Estate Litigation; Commercial Litigation.
Paskewitz, Donald P. ....'48 '78 C.494 B.A. L.1068 J.D. 555 W. 5th St.
Pass, Brian J. ....'64 '91 C.918 B.A. L.1068 J.D. 1800 Ave. of the Stars, Suite 900
**Passage, Daniel F.** '66 '92 C.112 B.A. L.178 J.D.
(adm. in NY; not adm. in CA) [A Andrews&K.]
*PRACTICE AREAS: Corporate Securitization; Securities.
**Passante, Anthony J., Jr.** ....'53 '80 C.112 B.A. L.1049 J.D. [Kaye,R.] (⊙San Diego)
Passin, Mark D. ....'54 '81 C.112 B.A. L.800 J.D. [Engel&E.]
Passman, Sanford M. ....'40 '77 C.339 L.1136 J.D. Physicians Labs., Inc.
Passovoy, Paul S. ....'55 '81 C.763 B.A. L.809 J.D. 6380 Wilshire Blvd.
**Pasternak, Cynthia F.** ....'52 '77 C.112 B.A. L.426 J.D. [Appleton,P.&P.]
**Pasternak, David J.**, (AV) ....'51 '76 C.112 B.A. L.426 J.D. [Appleton,P.&P.]
Pastirko-Kreins, Claudia T. '55 '82
C.763 B.A. L.1049 J.D. V.P. & Coun., Sanwa Bk. Calif.
Pastor, Bonnie ....'48 '78 C.112 A.B. L.426 J.D. 1901 Ave. of the Stars
Pastor, Dennis A. ....'43 '71 C.112 B.S. L.426 J.D. [C M.D.Pastor]
Pastor, Jerome, (AV) ....'23 '53 C.608 B.S. L.800 J.D. [J.Pastor]
Pastor, Mark D., (AV) ....'37 '63 C.347 B.A. L.309 J.D. [M.D.Pastor]
Pastor, Michael E. ....'49 '75 C.188 B.S. L.800 J.D. Mun. Ct. J.
Pastor, Jerome, A P.C., (AV) ....1901 Ave. of the Stars
Pastor, Mark D., Law Corporation, (AV) ....16830 Ventura Blvd. (Encino) Ste. 345
Pastore, Clare ....'60 '88 C.165 B.A. L.976 J.D. Western Ctr. on Law & Poverty, Inc.
Patalano, Anthony ....'52 '80 C.1042 B.A. L.809 J.D. Off. of Pub. Def.
**Patel, Ajay A.** ....'69 '94 C.112 B.A. L.800 J.D. [A McDermott,W.&E.]
**Patel, Jayesh** ....'62 '87 C.112 B.S. L.1066 J.D. [C Shumaker&S.]
*LANGUAGES: French, Latin and Gujarati.
**Patel, Vipal J.** ....'67 '91 C.381 B.S. L.273 J.D. [A Hancock R.&B.]
Patel-Sikora, Mona ....'62 '90 C.061 B.A. L.800 J.D. 777 S. Figueroa St.
**Paterno, Peter T.**, (AV) ....'51 '76 C.1167 B.S. L.112 J.D. [King,P.H.P.&B.]
**Paterson, Lee T.**, (AV) ....'41 '67 C.628 B.A. L.1068 J.D. [Sonnenschein N.&R.]
*PRACTICE AREAS: Management Employment Law; Labor (Private and Public Sector) Law.
Patrao, Raj C. ....'52 '81 C.112 B.S. L.1137 J.D. 4700 Wilshire Blvd., 3rd Fl.
Patrick, Kennett M., Inc., (BV) ....'42 '70 C.112 B.S. L.426 J.D. 3600 Wilshire Blvd.
**Patrick, Kirk A.** ....'48 '74 C.350 B.S. L.494 J.D. [Gibson,D.&C.]
*PRACTICE AREAS: Litigation; Insurance; Insurance Defense; Securities Litigation; Antitrust and Trade Regulation.
Patrick, Steven D. ....'49 '78 C.934 B.A. L.245 J.D. 633 W. 5th St.
Patrick, William B., (BV) ....'40 '67 C.608 B.S. L.813 LL.B. 849 S. Bway., 11th Fl.
Patronite, James M., Jr., (BV) ....'57 '83 C.112 B.A. L.426 J.D. P.O. Box 86021
Patrusky, Bernard, (AV) ....'30 '59 C&L.112 B.A., J.D. 5900 Wilshire Blvd.‡
**Patt, Mark S.**, (AV) ....'48 '74 C.112 B.A. L.477 J.D. [Trope&T.]
*PRACTICE AREAS: Family Law; Civil Litigation.
Patten, Dow W. ....'62 '88 C.101 B.A. L.878 J.D. 601 S. Figueroa

**Patten, Faith & Sandford**
**(See Monrovia)**

**Patterson, Charles E.** ....'41 '66 C.378 A.B. L.477 J.D. [Pillsbury M.&S.]
**Patterson, Gregory J.** ....'56 '88 C.740 B.A. L.809 J.D. [A Proskauer R.G.&M.]
*PRACTICE AREAS: Environmental Law.
**Patterson, Julie E.** ....'59 '93 C.608 B.S. L.800 J.D. [A Bryan C.]
*PRACTICE AREAS: Labor and Employment Law.
**Patterson, Richard H., Jr.** ....'58 '84 C.228 A.B. L.802 J.D. [C Poindexter&D.]
*PRACTICE AREAS: Insurance Defense; Civil Litigation; Probate Litigation.
**Patterson, Thomas E.** ....'60 '87 C.011 B.A. L.051 B.C.L. [Sidley&A.]
*PRACTICE AREAS: Bankruptcy Law; Reorganizations Law; Creditor's Rights Law.

**Patterson, Ritner, Lockwood, Gartner & Jurich, (AV)**
**A Partnership including Professional Corporations**
**Suite 900, 3580 Wilshire Boulevard, 90010⊙**
**Telephone: 213-487-6240 FAX: 213-380-8681**
**Members of Firm: Hobart G. Patterson (1922-1973); William F. Ritner (A Professional Corporation); Clyde E. Lockwood (A Professional Corporation); Harold H. Gartner, III, (A Professional Corporation); John A. Jurich (Resident, Bakersfield Office); Robert R. Scholl. Of Counsel: James F. McGahan (A Professional Corporation) (Resident, Ventura Office);—Carol J. Adams; Carolyn Wade Doran; Christopher W. Gardner; Ann Birgitta Gustafsson; Tobie B. Waxman.**
**Insurance, Personal Injury, Products Liability, Casualty and Medical Malpractice Law. Trials. Legal Malpractice.**
**Ventura, California Office: Suite 231, 260 Maple Court. Telephone: 805-644-1061.**
**Bakersfield, California Office: Suite 522, 1415 Eighteenth Street. Telephone: 805-327-4387.**
**San Bernardino, California Office: 325 Hospitality Lane, Suite 204. Telephone: 909-885-6063.**

***See Professional Biographies, LOS ANGELES, CALIFORNIA***

Patti, Anthony J. ....'49 '78 C.4 B.A. L.1095 J.D. Pub. Def. Off.

Patton, Aaron L. ........... '43 '78 C.906 B.S. L.809 J.D. Sr. Staff Coun., Northrop Corp.
Patton, Charles C., (BV) ................. '39 '70 C.1097 B.A. L.809 J.D. 880 W. First St.
**Patton, Cynthia M.** ................... '61 '86 C.881 A.B. L.273 J.D. [Ⓐ Brobeck,P.&H.]
*PRACTICE AREAS: Corporate; Securities; Healthcare.
**Patton, James H., Jr.**, (BV) ............. '36 '68 C.800 B.S. L.426 J.D. [Ⓐ Knopfler&R.]
*PRACTICE AREAS: Construction Law; Professional Malpractice Defense.
**Paturick, Charles** ......................... '43 '74 C.569 B.A. L.813 J.D. [Graham&J.]
*PRACTICE AREAS: Corporate Law; Business Law.
Patzakis, John M. ......................... '67 '92 C.800 B.A. L.770 J.D. [E.E.Corey]⊙
Paul, Cathy R. ......................... '59 '90 C.881 B.A. L.1068 J.D. 400 S. Hope St.
**Paul, Diane B.** ............................. '47 '82 C.691 B.A. L.800 J.D. [Loeb&L.]
*PRACTICE AREAS: Litigation; Bankruptcy.
**Paul, Holly R.** ....................... '59 '92 C.1077 B.A. L.1068 J.D. [Ⓐ Horvitz&L.]

**Paul, Jack, (AV) '28 '53 C.112 A.B. L.813 LL.B.**
**1801 Avenue of the Stars Suite 932, 90067**
**Telephone: 310-277-1322 Facsimile: 310-277-1333**
***TRANSACTIONS: Lead counsel for complex public construction claims litigation in Federal and State courts and arbitration; counsel for substantial recovery on behalf of contractor for changes and cost impact claims, Parsons of California, 82-1 BCA ¶15,659; estoppel against the Government, Inet Power, a Division of Teledyne, 68-1 BCA ¶7020; resolution of cost determination and damages claims and disputes.**
***PRACTICE AREAS: Government Contract Law; Construction Litigation.**
**Government Contract Law, Construction Litigation, Commercial and International Contract Disputes.**

***See Professional Biographies, LOS ANGELES, CALIFORNIA***

**Paul, James W.** '38 '79 C.608 B.S.M.E. L.1179 J.D.
[Fulwider P.L.&U.] (See Pat. Sect.)
*PRACTICE AREAS: Patent, Trademark, Copyright and Unfair Competition Law; Litigation.

**Paul, Hastings, Janofsky & Walker LLP, (AV)** BR
**A Limited Liability Partnership including Professional Corporations**
**Twenty-Third Floor, 555 South Flower Street, 90071-2371⊙**
**Telephone: 213-683-6000 FAX: 213-627-0705**
**Email: info@PHJW.com URL: http://www.phjw.com**
**Robert Pusey Hastings (1910-1996). Counsel: Oliver F. Green (Costa Mesa, California); Leonard S. Janofsky (Santa Monica, California); Lee G. Paul (Costa Mesa, California); Charles M. Walker (Santa Monica, California). Members of Firm: Nancy L. Abell (Santa Monica, California); Carl T. Anderson (Stamford, Connecticut); Toshiyuki Arai; Richard M. Asbill (Atlanta, Georgia); R. Lawrence Ashe, Jr., (P.C.) (Atlanta, Georgia); Mark W. Atkinson; Jesse H. Austin, III (Atlanta, Georgia); E. Lawrence Barcella, Jr. (Washington, D.C.); Christopher A. Barreca (Stamford, Connecticut); Alan J. Barton; Keith W. Berglund (Atlanta, Georgia); Daniel G. Bergstein (New York, New York); Stephen L. Berry; Woodson Toliver Besson (P.C.) (Santa Monica, California); Jonathan Birenbaum (Stamford, Connecticut); Thomas P. Brennan (P.C.); John H. Brinsley; Jamie Broder; Barry A. Brooks (New York, New York); Barbara Berish Brown (Washington D.C.); Daryl R. Buffenstein (Atlanta, Georgia); Thomas G. Burch, Jr. (Atlanta, Georgia); Siobhan McBreen Burke; Paul W. Cane, Jr.; Robert E. Carlson; Grace A. Carter; Eve Mary Coddon; Ronald T. Coleman, Jr. (Atlanta, Georgia); Kevin Conboy (Atlanta, Georgia); Paul J. Connell (Atlanta, Georgia); Douglas C. Conroy (Stamford, Connecticut); Stephen D. Cooke (Costa Mesa, California); James H. Cox (Atlanta, Georgia); Victoria A. Cundiff (New York, New York); Glenn D. Dassoff (Costa Mesa, California); Donald A. Daucher; Janet Toll Davidson (Costa Mesa, California); Barbra L. Davis; John F. Della Grotta (Costa Mesa, California); Nicholas DeWitt; Robert A. DeWitt (P.C.); R. Bruce Dickson (Washington. D.C. and New York, New York); Robert M. Dudnik (Santa Monica, California); William E. Eason, Jr. (Atlanta, Georgia); E. Donald Elliott (Washington, D.C.); Ralph B. Everett (Washington, D.C.); Zachary D. Fasman (Washington, D.C.); Philip N. Feder; Hydee R. Feldstein; Alfred G. Feliu (New York, New York); Esteban A. Ferrer, III (Stamford, Connecticut); Bruce W. Fraser; John C. Funk; Norman A. Futami; John J. Gallagher (Washington, D.C.); Jon A. Geier (Washington, D.C.); David L. Gersh; John S. Gibson; Michael Glazer; George L. Graff (New York, New York); Paul Grossman; William M. Hart (New York, New York); Lawrence J. Hass (Washington, D.C.); John D. Hawkins, Jr. (Stamford, Connecticut); Howard C. Hay (Costa Mesa, California); William B. Hill, Jr. (Atlanta, Georgia); Matthew A. Hodel (Costa Mesa, California); Michael A. Hood (Costa Mesa, California); Judith Richards Hope (Washington, D.C.); John P. Howitt (New York, New York); Mario J. Ippolito (Stamford, Connecticut); Nancy L. Iredale (P.C.); Euclid A. Irving (New York, New York); John Griffith Johnson, Jr. (Washington, D.C.); Weyman T. Johnson, Jr. (Atlanta, Georgia); Eric H. Joss (Santa Monica, California); Marguerite R. Kahn (New York, New York); James W. Kennedy (New York, New York); Ronald Kreismann (New York, New York); Thomas R. Lamia (New York, New York and Washington, D.C.); J. Al Latham, Jr.; Charles T. Lee (Stamford, Connecticut); Michael K. Lindsey; Ethan Lipsig; G. Hamilton Loeb (Washington, D.C.); Kevin C. Logue (New York, New York); M. Guy Maisnik; Philip J. Marzetti (Atlanta, Georgia); John S. McGeeney (Stamford, Connecticut); Roger M. Milgrim (New York, New York); Nancy Kennerly Miller; Robert A. Miller, Jr.; Chris D. Molen (Atlanta, Georgia); Donald L. Morrow (Costa Mesa, California); Julian D. Nealy (Atlanta, Georgia); Greg M. Nitzkowski; Carl W. Northrop (Washington, D.C.); Belinda K. Orem; Brendan J. O'Rourke (New York, New York); Charles B. Ortner (New York, New York); Kevin J. O'Shea (New York, New York); Ronald M. Oster (P.C.); Michael L. Owen; John G. Parker (Atlanta, Georgia); Charles A. Patrizia (Washington, D.C.); Paul L. Perito (Washington, D.C.); Thomas R. Pollock (New York, New York); John E. Porter; Patrick A. Ramsey; Clayton S. Reynolds (Stamford, Connecticut); David M. Roberts; Samuel D. Rosen (New York, New York); Bruce D. Ryan (Washington, D.C.); Leigh P. Ryan (New York, New York); Cheryl R. Saban (New York, New York); Douglas A. Schaaf (Costa Mesa, California); William A. Schmidt (Washington, D.C.); William F. Schwitter, Jr. (New York, New York); W. Andrew Scott (Atlanta, Georgia); Charles T. Sharbaugh (Atlanta, Georgia); Patrick W. Shea (Stamford, Connecticut); Robert L. Sherman (New York, New York); Andrew M. Short (New York, New York); Wayne H. Shortridge (Atlanta, Georgia); Marc L. Silverman (New York, New York); Joel M. Simon (New York, New York); William J. Simpson (Costa Mesa, California); David E. Snediker (Stamford, Connecticut); Robert S. Span (Santa Monica, California); John H. Steed (Tokyo, Japan); Alan K. Steinbrecher; George E. Stephens, Jr., (P.C.); Harvey A. Strickon (New York, New York); Kaoruhiko Suzuki; Peter J. Tennyson (Costa Mesa, California); Geoffrey L. Thomas (P.C.); Charles V. Thornton; Neil A. Torpey (New York, New York); Gary F. Torrell; John E. Trinnaman (Costa Mesa, California); Dennis H. Vaughn (Santa Monica, California); William Stewart Waldo; Elizabeth W. Walker; Paul R. Walker; Robert F. Walker (Santa Monica, California); Alan Wade Weakland; Lawrence I. Weinstein (New York, New York); C. Geoffrey Weirich (Atlanta, Georgia); Michael A. Wiegard (Washington, D.C.); Thomas S. Wisialowski; Seth M. Zachary (New York, New York); James A. Zapp; Harry A. Zinn (Santa Monica, California). Senior Counsel: Robert R. Burge (Costa Mesa, California); James W. Hamilton (Costa Mesa, California). Of Counsel: John M. Bergin (New York, New York); Theodore W. Browne, II (New York, New York); Roxanne E. Christ; Edwin I. Colodny (Washington, D.C.); Mary L. Cornwell (Costa Mesa, California); Jonathan C. Curtis; Julian B. Decyk; William D. DeGrandis (Washington, D.C.); Leslie A. Dent (Atlanta, Georgia); Brian J. Donnelly; Jane Elizabeth Eakins (Santa Monica, California); Jason O. Engel (Costa Mesa, California); Elliot K. Gordon (Santa Monica, California); Anna M. Graves; Kurt W. Hansson (Stamford, Connecticut); Andrew S. Holmes (Stamford Connecticut); Gage Randolph Johnson (Washington, D.C.); Steven D. Johnson (New York, New York); Rick S. Kirkbride; Thomas J. Knapp (Washington, D.C.); Peter W. LaVigne (New York, New York); Scott N. Leslie (Costa Mesa, California); A. Alan Manning; Deborah A. Marlowe (Atlanta, Georgia); Neal D. Mollen (Washington, D.C.); Robert C. Moot, Jr. (Atlanta, Georgia); Sean A. O'Brien (Costa Mesa, California); Tetsuya Ogawa (Tokyo, Japan); Craig K. Pendergrast (Atlanta, Georgia); Gloria C. Phares (New York, New York); David S. Phelps; Robert S. Plotkin (Washington, D.C.); Robert E. Pokusa (Washington, D.C.); Lucy Prashker (New York, New York); David E. Rabin (Stamford, Connecticut); William Thomas Reeder, Jr. (Washington, D.C.); Anthony J. Rossi; Christine A. Scheuneman; Charles A. Shanor (Atlanta, Georgia and Washington, D.C.); Margaret H. Spurlin (Washington, D.C.); Takashi Suzuki (Tokyo, Japan); Jeffrey G. Varga; William P. Wade; Philip R. Weingold (New York, New York); Patrick J. Whittle (Washington, D.C.); Kenneth M. Willner (Washington, D.C.); Michael S. Woodward; Gerald H. Yamada (Washington, D.C.); Darla L. Yancey (Costa Mesa, California); Clarisse W. J. Young. Associates: Leslie Abbott (Santa Monica, California); George W. Abele; Eliot J. Abt (Atlanta, Georgia); Elizabeth A. Adolff (Stamford, Connecticut); Terry Jon Allen (Costa Mesa, California); Steven D. Allison (Costa Mesa, California); Kenneth T. Araki; Peter Aronson; Elena R. Baca; Jennifer Stivers Baldocchi; Tracey T. Barbaree (Atlanta, Georgia); Michele L. Barber; Kirby D. Behre (Washington, D.C.); Brent J. Belnap (New York, New York); David S. Benyacar (New York, New York); Patricia M. Berry; James R. Bliss (Stamford, Connecticut); Stephanie A. Bohm (Atlanta, Georgia); Brent R. Bohn (Costa Mesa, California); David B. Booker (New York, New York); Robert L. Boyd (New York, New York); Deborah M. Bradley (Atlanta, Georgia); Marian L. Brancaccio (New York, New York); Glenn L. Briggs (Costa Mesa, California); Mark Bronson; Sheryl J. Brown (Washington, D.C.); Robert P. Bryant (Costa Mesa, California); David D. Burns (Washington, D.C.);**

(This Listing Continued)

**Paul, Hastings, Janofsky & Walker LLP (Continued)**

**Christine E. Cahill (Atlanta, Georgia); Joseph A. Callari (Stamford, Connecticut); Gwyneth A. Campbell; Robert R. Carlson; Dianne C. Carraway (Washington, D.C.); Patricia M. Carroll (New York, New York); Marie Censoplano (New York, New York); Sarka Cerna-Fagan (New York, New York); Veronica J. Cherniak (Atlanta, Georgia); Alpa Patel Chernof; TanYee Cheung (New York, New York); Justin C. Choi (New York, New York); John H. Clayton (New York, New York); A. Craig Cleland (Atlanta, Georgia); Michelle Weisberg Cohen (Washington, D.C.); Christopher H. Craig (Stamford, Connecticut); Sandra A. Crawshaw (New York, New York); Christine M. Crowe (Washington, D.C.); Kathleen O. Currey (Atlanta, Georgia); Marc A. Daniel (New York, New York); Barbara R. Danz (Costa Mesa, California); Cindy J.K. Davis (Atlanta, Georgia); Eric B. Davis (New York, New York); Jeanne R. Dawson; Behnam Dayanim (Washington, D.C.); Daniel P. Delaney; S. Mark Denham; Alejandro J. Diaz (Stamford, Connecticut); Kristina H. Dinerman; Mary C. Dollarhide (Stamford, Connecticut); Jessica S. Dorman-Davis (Costa Mesa, California); Patricia A. Driscoll (Stamford, Connecticut); Michael W. Dubus (Atlanta, Georgia); John C. Dworkin (New York, New York); Harold N. Eddy, Jr. (Stamford, Connecticut); Linda M. Edwards (Santa Monica, California); Susan Langley Elliot (Atlanta, Georgia); Dennis S. Ellis; Jewell L. Esposito (Washington, D.C.); William P. Ewing (Atlanta, Georgia); Malinda A. Faber (Costa Mesa, California); Wendell M. Faria (Washington, D.C.); Elizabeth A. Fealy (New York, New York); Alan M. Feld (New York, New York); Benjamin J. Ferron (New York, New York); Violet F. Fiacco (Costa Mesa, California); Regina M. Flaherty (Stamford, Connecticut); Scott M. Flicker (Washington, D.C.); Laura A. Forbes (Costa Mesa, California); Michele Freedenthal; Margo E. Freedman; Philip E. Fried (New York, New York); Intra L. Germanis (Washington, D.C.); David E. Gevertz (Atlanta, Georgia); Lisa M. Gigliotti (New York, New York); Ronald K. Giller; Margaret A. Gilleran (New York, New York); Mark A. Gloade (New York, New York); Karen K. Greenwalt; E. Jeffrey Grube; Delia Guevara; John W. Hamlin (Stamford, Connecticut); Andrew P. Hanson (Costa Mesa, California); Susan E. Himmer (Atlanta, Georgia); Eric J. Hoffman; Stacy M. Hopkins; Alan B. Horowitz (Washington, D.C.); James Che-Ming Hsu (New York, New York); Scott N. Hudson (New York, New York); Lisa G. Huffiness (New York, New York); James Judson Jackson (Stamford, Connecticut); Marcia N. Jackson (Santa Monica, California); Michael B. Jaffe (Stamford, Connecticut); Edward S. Johnson, Jr. (Atlanta, Georgia); Jarret L. Johnson (Costa Mesa, California); E. Ashton Johnston (Washington, D.C.); George R.A. Jones (Washington, D.C.); Karen E. Jorik (Atlanta, Georgia); Michael B. Kaufman (New York, New York); Deidre M. Kelly; Tara K. Kelly; Ann T. Kenny (New York, New York); Marc E. Kenny; Jong Han Kim; Ken Kimura (New York, New York); Eileen M. King (New York, New York); Rosemary Mahar Kirbach; Janet L. Kishbaugh (Atlanta, Georgia); Karen L. Kleiderman; Judith M. Kline; Cheryl L. Kopitzke (Santa Monica, California); Lisa M. LaFourcade (Costa Mesa, California); Douglas E. Lahammer; Gregory F. Lang (Stamford, Connecticut); Lisa J. Laplace (New York, New York); Aric H. Lasky; David S. Levin (New York, New York); Eric T. Levine (Stamford, Connecticut); Brigitte P. Lippmann (New York, New York); Katherine B. Lipton (New York, New York); Vincent D. Lowder (Costa Mesa, California); Robert L. Madok; Jenifer A. Magyar (Stamford, Connecticut); Christopher J. Manfredi; Paul C. Marazita (Stamford, Connecticut); Michael S. Marx; Andrew M. Mayer (New York, New York); Kathleen L. McAchran; P. Casey McGannon; Denise Marie McGorrin; Sarah M. McWilliams (Washington, D.C.); Martin C. Mead; Jon Douglas Meer; Michael T. Mervis (New York, New York); Ingrid M. Mesa (New York, New York); Cara D. Miller (Santa Monica, California); J. Clark Miller; Scott R. Miller (Costa Mesa, California); Haruki Minaki; Heather Morgan (Santa Monica, California); Jay A. Morrison (Washington, D.C.); Melinda L. Moseley (Atlanta, Georgia); John J. Neely, III (Atlanta, Georgia); Elizabeth A. Newell (New York, New York); Elizabeth Hardy Noe (Atlanta, Georgia); J. Yoheved Novogroder (New York, New York); Robert J. Odson; John C. O'Malley; Maureen E. O'Neill (Atlanta, Georgia); Joseph P. Opich (New York, New York); DeAnne H. Ozaki; Vincent J. Pasquariello (New York, New York); Susan M. Pavlin (Atlanta, Georgia); Joseph D. Penachio (New York, New York); Suzanne Marie Pepe-Robbins (Stamford, Connecticut); Bonnie Pierson-Murphy (Stamford, Connecticut); Alexis Pinto (New York, New York); Sara Rabinowitz Pinto (New York, New York Office); Leslie A. Plaskon (Stamford, Connecticut); Tracy S. Plott (Atlanta, Georgia); Lisa A. Popovich; Nancy E. Rafuse (Atlanta, Georgia); Philip J. Ragona (New York, New York); Lynne H. Rambo (Atlanta, Georgia); T. Robert Reid (Atlanta, Georgia); Ellen C. Rice (Washington, D.C.); Peter J. Roth; Joel H. Rothstein; Dena T. Sacco (Washington, D.C.); Alfred Sanchez, Jr.; Allyson G. Saunders; Mathew Anthony Schuh (Atlanta, Georgia); Glori J. Schultz; Susan E. Schwartz; Craig S. Seligman; Lee R. Seltman; Nancy E. Shallow (Washington, D.C.); Joseph C. Sharp (Atlanta, Georgia); Eric M. Sherbet (New York, New York); Glenn C. Shrader; Betty M. Shumener; Derek E. Smith; Naomi Weyand Smith (Atlanta, Georgia); Nancy L. Sommer (New York, New York); Stephen P. Sonnenberg; E. Gary Spitko (Atlanta, Georgia); David H. Steinberg (New York, New York); John B. Stephens (Costa Mesa, California); Joshua H. Sternoff (Washington, D.C.); Randall M. Stone (Washington, D.C.); Brian D. Sullivan (Atlanta, Georgia); Kristen K. Swartz (Atlanta, Georgia); Gregory J. Swedelson; Erin M. Sweeney (Washington, D.C.); Eric Jon Taylor (Atlanta, Georgia); Katherine A. Traxler; Michael W. Traynham; Richard M. Vicenzi (Stamford, Connecticut); Michael T. Voytek (Atlanta, Georgia); Stanley F. Wasowski (Atlanta, Georgia); L. Kent Webb (Atlanta, Georgia); Deborah S. Weiser (Santa Monica, California); Timothy J. Wellman (Washington, D.C.); Elise M. Whitaker (Atlanta, Georgia); Crystal L. Williams (Atlanta, Georgia); S. Reginald Williams (New York, New York); Jonathan B. Wilson (Atlanta, Georgia); Ivan J. Wolpert (New York, New York); Scott M. Wornow (New York, New York); Shannon P. Wright; Joshua G. Wrobel; Jenny C. Wu (Washington, D.C.); Stephen A. Yamaguchi; Julie Arias Young; Arthur L. Zwickel.**
**General Practice.**
**Orange County, California Office: Seventeenth Floor, 695 Town Center Drive, Costa Mesa. Telephone: 714-668-6200.**
**Washington, D.C. Office: Tenth Floor, 1299 Pennsylvania Avenue, N.W. Telephone: 202-508-9500.**
**Atlanta, Georgia Office: 24th Floor, 600 Peachtree Street, N.E. Telephone: 404-815-2400.**
**Santa Monica, California Office: Fifth Floor, 1299 Ocean Avenue. Telephone: 310-319-3300.**
**Stamford, Connecticut Office: Ninth Floor, 1055 Washington Boulevard. Telephone: 203-961-7400.**
**New York, New York Office: 31st Floor, 399 Park Avenue. Telephone: 212-318-6000.**
**Tokyo, Japan Office: Ark Mori Building, 30th Floor, 12-32 Akasaka, P.O. Box 577, 1-Chome, Minato-Ku. Telephone: (03) 3586-4711.**

***See Professional Biographies, LOS ANGELES, CALIFORNIA***

**Paul & Janofsky**
**(See Santa Monica)**

**Paully, Denise G.** ..................... '50 '76 C.881 A.B. L.262 J.D. [McDermott,W.&E.]
**Paulos, Nicholas** ........................ '65 '92 C.112 B.A. L.424 J.D. [Kane,W.&P.]
*PRACTICE AREAS: Insurance Defense; Civil Litigation.
Paxson, Mary Azzolina .............................. '38 '92 C.112 L.809 Pub. Def. Off.
Paxton, Mablean D. Ephriam, (Mrs.) '— '78 C.1168 B.S. L.1148 J.D.
3540 Wilshire Blvd.
**Paxton, Penny** ......................... '45 '78 C.294 B.A. L.229 J.D. [Lewis,D.B.&B.]
*PRACTICE AREAS: Workers Compensation; Employment Law.
**Payne, John A., Jr.**, (AV) ............. '48 '73 C.62 B.A. L.477 J.D. [Ⓒ Brobeck,P.&H.]
*PRACTICE AREAS: Tax.
**Payne, John R.** .................... '44 '75 C.1042 B.S. L.112 J.D. [Stockwell,H.W.&W.]
**Payne, Michael D.** ................ '66 '92 C.426 B.A. L.990 J.D. [Ⓐ Wilson,E.M.E.&D.]
Payton, Nolan H. .......... '19 '70 C.800 M.A. L.809 LL.B. 1728 W. Martin Luther King
**Pazos, James M.** ......................... '63 '92 C&L.112 B.A., J.D. [Ⓐ Knopfler&R.]
*PRACTICE AREAS: Construction Law; Insurance Coverage.
**Pearce, Alden G., (A P.C.)**, (AV) ........... '24 '50 C.112 A.B. L.228 LL.B. [Loeb&L.]
*PRACTICE AREAS: Corporate Law.
Pearl, Andrew J. ............... '59 '84 C.188 A.B. L.309 J.D. Dir., Fin., Relco Industries
**Pearl, Mark J.** ......................... '58 '84 C.112 A.B. L.1066 J.D. [Ⓒ Tisdale&N.]
*PRACTICE AREAS: Real Property; Community Development; Real Estate Exchanges; Real Estate Finance; Corporations.
**Pearl, Stephanie G.** ................ '60 '85 C.112 B.S. L.1068 J.D. [Ⓐ Fenigstein&K.]
*PRACTICE AREAS: Business, Employment and Health Care Litigation.
**Pearlman, Jeffrey D.** ...................... '60 '86 C&L.273 B.A., J.D. [Maguire&O.]
*PRACTICE AREAS: Construction Law; Public Contracts; Business Litigation.

**Pearlman, Borska & Wax**
**(See Encino)**

Pearlstein, Jonathan J. ............................................ '65 '90 [Hogan,B.&H.]
Pearman, Kim H., (AV) ....... '38 '65 C.800 B.S. L.1068 J.D. 14550 Friar St. (Van Nuys)
Pearman, Robert C., Jr. ...................... '— '77 C.659 B.S. L.976 J.D. [Robinson&P.]

CAA313P

**Pearson, Don M., (A Professional Corporation)**, (AV) '41 '69 C.101 B.S. L.309 J.D. [Argue P.H.&M.]
*PRACTICE AREAS: Business Law.
Pearson, Edward F., (AV) ....... '52 '78 C&L.800 B.A., J.D. 777 S. Figueroa St., 10th Fl.
Pearson, James H. ....... '34 '66 C.44 B.S. L.809 LL.B. Chief Asst. City Atty.
Pearson, Lennart Jon ....... '42 '74 C.101 B.S. L.30 J.D. Asst. U.S. Atty.
**Pearson, Mark** ....... '57 '91 C.1097 B.A. L.101 J.D. [🄰 Iverson,Y.P.&H.]
*LANGUAGES: Japanese and Mandarin Chinese.
*PRACTICE AREAS: Civil Litigation; Business Law.
**Pearson, Nicole Grattan** ....... '69 '95 C.273 B.A. L.800 J.D. [🄰 Shiotani&I.]
*PRACTICE AREAS: Business Law; Probate; Estate Planning; Real Estate Law; Tax Law.
Pearson, Richard C. '43 '69 C.112 B.S. L.813 J.D. Sr. V.P. & Gen. Coun., Security First Grp., Inc.
**Pearson, Ronald C.**, (AV) ....... '57 '85 C.636 B.S. L.1049 J.D. [Mahoney,C.J.&P.]
**Pearson, Scott M.** ....... '68 '94 [🄰 Stroock&S.&L.]
**Pease, Douglas C.** ....... '51 '81 C.112 B.A. L.1049 J.D. [🄰 Iverson,Y.P.&H.]
*PRACTICE AREAS: Civil Litigation.
Pech, Richard ....... '48 '76 C.1097 B.A. L.1148 J.D. 1800 Ave. of the Stars
**Pécheck, Mark S.** ....... '58 '84 C.112 B.A. L.1066 J.D. [Gibson,D.&C.]
*PRACTICE AREAS: Real Estate.
**Peck, Austin H., Jr.**, (AV) ....... '13 '38 C&L.813 A.B., J.D. [🄲 Latham&W.]
**Peck, David A.** ....... '68 '94 C.800 B.A. L.426 J.D. [🄰 Manning,M.&W.]
*PRACTICE AREAS: Insurance Defense Litigation.
Peck, Frank D. ....... '43 '72 C&L.336 B.A., J.D. 4055 Wilshire Blvd.
Peck, Kristine M. ....... '— '94 C.112 B.A. L.464 J.D. 801 S. Figueroa St.
Peck, Linda R. ....... '42 '77 C.112 B.A. L.1095 J.D. 706 Thayer Ave.
Peck, Mark W. ....... '65 '94 C.112 B.A. L.464 J.D. 1055 W. 7th St.
**Peck, Susan R.** ....... '58 '90 C.938 A.B. L.800 J.D. [🄰 Davis&F.]
*LANGUAGES: Spanish and French.
*PRACTICE AREAS: Business Litigation.
Peckham, John Henry, (AV) ... '13 '36 C.813 A.B. L.800 J.D. 801 S. Grand Ave., 11th Fl.
**Pedersen, Norman A.** ....... '46 '75 C.112 B.A. L.1068 LL.B. [Jones,D.R.&P.]
**Pedlar, Alan**, (AV) ....... '49 '76 C.112 B.S. L.1066 J.D. [Stutman,T.&G.]
*TRANSACTIONS: Attorney for Storage Technology Corporation, Chapter 11 Reorganization; Attorney for Carter Hawley Hale Stores, Inc., Chapter 11 Reorganization.
*PRACTICE AREAS: Bankruptcy; Insolvency; Corporate Reorganization; Commercial Litigation; Secured Transactions.
**Pedrick, Gregory J.** ....... '61 '93 C.1077 B.A. L.426 J.D. [🄰 Gilbert,K.C.&J.]
*PRACTICE AREAS: Business Planning; Estate Planning and Probate.
**Pedroz, Octavio A.** ....... '69 '95 C.813 B.A. L.309 J.D. [🄰 Sidley&A.]
*LANGUAGES: Spanish.
**Pedroza, Kenneth R.** ....... '70 '96 C.813 B.A. L.37 J.D. [🄰 Breidenbach,B.H.H.&H.]
**Peebles, Jane** ....... '51 '84 C.563 B.A. L.569 J.D. [Freeman,F.&S.] (⊙Irvine)
*PRACTICE AREAS: Estate Planning (Domestic and International); Charitable Giving.
Peel, Richard V. ....... '66 '94 C.112 B.A. L.276 J.D. 1900 Ave. of the Stars
**Peer, John E.**, (AV) ....... '49 '80 C.172 B.A. L.767 J.D. [Cummins&W.]
**Peery, Gordon F.** ....... '67 '96 C.800 B.A. L.880 J.D. [🄰 Littler,M.F.T.&M.]
*LANGUAGES: Japanese.
Peetris, Harry V. ....... '19 '51 L.800 J.D. Ret. Presid. J., Supr. Ct.
**Peikin, Roger B.** ....... '61 '91 C.884 B.S. L.809 J.D. [🄰 Trope&T.]
*PRACTICE AREAS: Family Law.
**Peim, David** ....... '57 '93 C.1044 B.A. L.426 J.D. [🄰 La Follette,J.D.F.&A.]
*PRACTICE AREAS: General Liability; Banking Law; Product Liability.
**Peitzman, Lawrence**, (AV) ....... '47 '74 C.112 B.A. L.1066 J.D. [Orrick,H.&S.]
*PRACTICE AREAS: Bankruptcy; Workouts.
**Pek, Jackson K.** ....... '70 '95 C.659 B.S. L.569 J.D. [🄰 White&C.]
Pelcin, Martin K. ....... '63 '89 C&L.107 B.A., J.D. [🄰 Schaffer&B.]
Pellegrini, Anthony A. ....... '31 '70 C.112 B.S. L.809 J.D. 2040 Ave. of the Stars‡
**Pelletier, Kristin** ....... '63 '91 C.112 B.A. L.800 J.D. [🄰 LeBoeuf,L.G.&M.]
*PRACTICE AREAS: Labor and Employment Litigation; Law Enforcement Litigation.
**Pelliccioni, Daniel M., (P.C.)**, (AV) ....... '46 '75 C.477 A.B. L.215 J.D. [Katten M.&Z.]
*PRACTICE AREAS: Bankruptcy Law; Finance and Reorganization Law.
Pellman, Amy M. ....... '60 '88 C.518 B.A. L.564 J.D. 606 S. Olive St., Suite 500
Pellman, Lloyd W. ....... '43 '72 C.608 B.Sc.Ed. L.426 J.D. Sr. Asst. Co. Coun.
Pelowski, Dennis P. ....... '63 '91 C&L.494 B.A., J.D. 505 Shatto Pl.
**Pelton, Annette A.** ....... '66 '93 C.800 B.A. L.809 J.D. [🄰 La Follette,J.D.F.&A.]
*PRACTICE AREAS: Litigation.
Peltyn, Ilona Z. ....... '47 '65 C.112 B.A. L.426 J.D. 1954 Rosodmare Rd.
**Peltz, Maxwell S.** ....... '66 '96 C.813 B.A. L.976 J.D. [🄰 Folger L.&K.]⊙
Pendell, Charles R. '29 '56 C.623 B.S. L.309 LL.B. (adm. in OK; not adm. in CA) 1745 Camino Palmero‡
**Pene, Katherine B.** ....... '46 '79 L.1095 J.D. [Schell&D.]
**Penhoet, Braden W.** ....... '65 '95 C.813 B.A. L.1068 J.D. [🄰 Brobeck,P.&H.]
*LANGUAGES: French.
*PRACTICE AREAS: Business; Technology.
**Penner, David J.** ....... '58 '84 C&L.800 B.S., J.D. [🄰 L.B.Trygstad]
**Penners, Ann K.** ....... '59 '92 C.668 B.A. L.426 J.D. [🄰 Chadbourne&P.]
**Pennington, John R.** ....... '52 '77 C.629 B.S. L.1068 J.D. [Sheppard,M.R.&H.]
*PRACTICE AREAS: Business Litigation.
**Penny, Patricia L.** ....... '52 '86 C.4 B.A. L.809 J.D. Sr. Coun., Bank of Amer.
Penny, Robert M. ....... '23 '50 L.999 LL.B. 1055 W. 7th St.
**Penny, Theodore A.**, (AV) ....... '50 '74 C.112 A.B. L.800 J.D. [Clopton,P.&B.]
*PRACTICE AREAS: Workers Compensation; Defense; Subrogation.
Pensig, Paul A., (AV) ....... '46 '70 C.569 B.A. L.1066 J.D. 333 S. Grand Ave.
Penso, Marc Gentry, (BV) ....... '60 '85 C.472 B.A. L.464 J.D. 1888 Century Park E.
**Penton, Janis S.** ....... '— '80 C.112 A.B. L.800 J.D. [🄰 Buchalter,N.F.&Y.]
**Pentoney, Stephen L.** ....'38 '73 C.763 B.S. L.800 Gen. Coun., De Anza Land & Leisure
**Pentz, Ada Rud** ....... '69 '95 C.112 B.A. L.426 J.D. [🄰 Hillsinger&C.]
**Pepe, Stephen P.**, (AV) '43 '69 C.555 B.A. L.228 J.D. [O'Melveny&M.] (⊙Newport Beach)
*PRACTICE AREAS: Labor and Employment.
**Pepek, Michael J.** ....... '69 '95 C.112 B.A. L.464 J.D. [🄰 Lynberg&W.]
**Pepper, Alan L., (A Professional Corporation)** '42 '73 C.112 B.S. L.1095 J.D. [Mitchell,S.&K.]
*PRACTICE AREAS: Corporate Law; Business Acquisitions Law; Telecommunication Law; Consumer Protection; Warranty Law.
**Pepperman, Donald R.** ....... '57 '83 C.1077 B.S. L.1148 J.D. [Blecher&C.]
*PRACTICE AREAS: Antitrust; Intellectual Property.
**Peraino, Laura G.** ....... '64 '89 C.880 B.A. L.846 J.D. [🄰 Crosby,H.R.&M.]
**Peraino, Vito C.** ....... '56 '81 C.912 B.A. L.477 J.D. [Hancock R.&B.]
Perea, Kenneth A. ....... '48 '73 C&L.767 B.A., J.D. Pub. Rel. Employ. Bd.
**Perea, Thomas V.** ....... '63 '89 C.1073 B.A. L.1065 J.D. [🄰 Chapin,F.&W.]
*LANGUAGES: Spanish.
**Pereira, Leslie A.** ....... '67 '95 C&L.477 B.A., J.D. [🄰 Latham&W.]
Perel, Liza Gail ....... '60 '87 C.05 B.A. L.018 LL.B. 9005 Burton Way
Perelman, Charles R. ....... '31 '55 C.659 B.S. L.930 LL.B. 1840 Century Park East
Perelman, Richard B. ....... '56 '81 C.112 B.A. L.426 J.D. Pres., Perelman, Pioneer & Co.
Perenchio, John Gardner '55 '82 C.103 A.B. L.1049 J.D. V.P., Chartwell Partnership Grp.

**Peretz, Avi S.**, (AV) ....... '52 '77 C.112 B.A. L.426 J.D. [Gabriel,H.&P.]
Pereyda, Lorenzo A., Jr. ....... '33 '66 C.999 B.S. L.809 LL.B. 5345 Olympic Blvd.
**Pereyra-Suarez, Charles**, (AV) ....... '47 '75 C.636 B.A. L.1066 J.D. [Davis W.T.]
*LANGUAGES: Spanish.
*PRACTICE AREAS: Civil Litigation; White Collar Defense; Health Law; Media and First Amendment.
**Perez, Cristina E.** ....... '68 '94 C.112 B.A. L.1148 J.D. [🄰 Blalock&G.]
*LANGUAGES: Spanish.
*PRACTICE AREAS: Immigration and Naturalization.
**Perez, Edith R.** ....... '54 '82 C.112 B.A. L.1066 J.D. [Latham&W.]
*LANGUAGES: Spanish.
Perez, Ida A. ....... '27 '84 C.768 B.A. L.1065 J.D. Legal Div., Dept. of Transp.
Perez, Ramona Godoy ....... '46 '72 C.112 B.A. L.1049 J.D. Assoc. Jus., Ct. of Appl.
**Perez, Raul** ....... '68 '94 C&L.309 B.A., J.D. [🄰 Morgan,L.&B.]
**Perez, Ronald E.** ..... '56 '90 C.608 B.S. L.966 J.D. [🄰 Fulwider P.L.&U.] (See Pat. Sect.)
*PRACTICE AREAS: Patent, Trademark, Copyright and Unfair Competition Law; Litigation.

**Perez, Albert, Jr.**
(See Covina)

**Perison, Eben Paul** ....... '65 '90 C.112 B.A. L.1065 J.D. [🄰 Gibson,D.&C.]
*PRACTICE AREAS: Corporate; Securities.
**Perkins, James J.** ....... '56 '86 C.1169 B.A. L.770 J.D. [Gilbert,K.C.&J.]
**Perkins, Robert E.**, (AV) ....... '44 '75 C.813 B.S. L.1066 J.D. [Cummins&W.]
*PRACTICE AREAS: Insurance Defense Litigation.

**Perkins Coie, (AV)**
**A Law Partnership including Professional Corporations**
**Strategic Alliance with Russell & DuMoulin**
**Strategic Alliance with So Keung Yip & Sin**
**1999 Avenue of the Stars, Ninth Floor, 90067-6109⊙**
**Telephone: 310-788-9900 Telex: 32-0319 PERKINS SEA Facsimile: 310-788-3399**
**URL: http://www.perkinscoie.com**
**Resident Members/Shareholders: David T. Biderman, A Prof. Corp.; Ronald A. McIntire; Thomas E. McLain; Charles F. Palmer; Bruce Eric Sherman; Douglas L. Thorpe. Of Counsel: Sandra J. Chan. Resident Associates: Wendy S. Albers; Mark Birnbaum; Karen M. Bray; Damon R. Fisher; Mark Jay Goldzweig; Elizabeth E. Kruis; Randi Maurer; Leslie N. Murdock; Colleen M. Regan; Benjamin E. Soffer; Michael I. Sorochinsky; Peter Stoughton.**
**General Trial and Appellate Practice in State and Federal Courts and before various Federal and State Administrative Tribunals. Corporate, Real Estate, Securities, General Business and Commercial, Corporate Finance, Taxation, Philanthropic Law, Aviation, Environmental, Natural Resources, Labor, Insolvency, Bankruptcy, Reorganization, Creditors' Rights, Administrative, Insurance and Antitrust Law.**
**Seattle, Washington Office: 1201 Third Avenue, 40th Floor. Telephone: 206-583-8888. Facsimile: 206-583-8500. Cable Address: "Perkins Seattle". Telex: 32-0319 PERKINS SEA.**
**Anchorage, Alaska Office: 1029 West Third Avenue, Suite 300. Telephone: 907-279-8561. Facsimile: 907-276-3108. Telex: 32-0319 PERKINS SEA.**
**Denver, Colorado Office: Mellon Financial Center, 1775 Sherman Street, Suite 2950. Telephone: 303-863-8686. Facsimile: 303-863-0423.**
**Washington, D.C. Office: 607 Fourteenth Street, N.W. Telephone: 202-628-6600. Facsimile: 202-434-1690. Telex: 44-0277 PCSO.**
**Portland, Oregon Office: 1211 Southwest Fifth Avenue, Suite 1500. Telephone: 503-727-2000. Facsimile: 503-727-2222. Telex: 32-0319 PERKINS SEA.**
**Bellevue, Washington Office: Suite 1800, One Bellevue Center, 411 - 108th Avenue N.E. Telephone: 206-453-6980. Facsimile: 206-453-7350, After April 29, 1997, Area Code will Change to 425. Telex: 32-0319 PERKINS SEA.**
**Spokane, Washington Office: North 221 Wall Street, Suite 600. Telephone: 509-624-2212. Facsimile: 509-458-3399. Telex: 32-0319 PERKINS SEA.**
**Olympia, Washington Office: 1110 Capitol Way South, Suite 405. Telephone: 360-956-3300. Facsimile: 360-956-1208.**
**Hong Kong Office: 23rd Floor Asia Pacific Finance Tower, Citibank Plaza, 3 Garden Road. Telephone: 852-2878-1177. Facsimile: 852-2524-9988.**
**London, England Office: 3/4 Royal Exchange Buildings, EC3V 3NL. Telephone: 171-369-9966. Facsimile: 171-369-9968.**
**Taipei, Taiwan Office: 8/F, TFIT Tower, 85 Jen Ai Road, Sec. 4, Taipei 106, Taiwan, R.O.C. Telephone: 011-886-2-778-1177. Facsimile: 011-886-2-777-9898.**
**Canada: Strategic Alliance with Russell & DuMoulin, 1700-1075 West Georgia Street, Vancouver, B.C. V6E 3G2. Telephone: 604-631-3131.**
**Strategic Alliance with, So Keung Yip & Sin, 1501 Edinburgh Tower, The Landmark, 15 Queen's Raod Central, Hong Kong. Telephone: 852-2810-8908. Facsimile: 852-2801-4148.**
**Revisers of the Washington Law Digest for this Directory.**

*See Professional Biographies, LOS ANGELES, CALIFORNIA*

**Perkins, Zarian & Duncan, P.C.**
**1801 Century Park East, Suite 1100, 90067⊙**
**Telephone: 310-203-4646 Fax: 310-203-4647**
**Adam D. Duncan, Jr.**
**Business Litigation including Securities, Real Estate, Construction, Insurance, Antitrust, Environmental and Commercial Disputes.**
**Irvine, California Office: 2030 Main Street, Suite 660. Telephone: 714-475-1700. Fax: 714-475-1800.**

*See Professional Biographies, LOS ANGELES, CALIFORNIA*

Perkovich, George R., Jr. ....... '25 '50 C&L.494 B.S., LL.B. Supr. Ct. J.
Perkowitz, Vicki W. '54 '81 C.112 B.A. L.770 J.D. (adm. in IL; not adm. in CA) Claims Coun., Commonwealth Land Title Ins. Co.
Perl, Iris Kate ....... '55 '83 C.112 B.A. L.809 J.D. 10880 Wilshire Blvd.
Perlberger, Martin, (AV) ....... '28 '54 C&L.813 B.A., J.D. 1267 Stoner Ave.
**Perlis, Michael F.**, (AV) ....... '47 '71 C&L.276 B.S.F.S., J.D. [Stroock&S.&L.]
*PRACTICE AREAS: Litigation; Insurance.
Perliss, Sanford H. ....... '58 '84 C.475 B.A. L.809 J.D. 900 Wilshire Blvd.
**Perlman, Dana M.** ....... '61 '86 C.112 B.A. L.800 J.D. [Stein P.&H.]
*PRACTICE AREAS: Business Litigation (75%); Bankruptcy (25%).
Perlman, Leonard S. ....... '65 '92 C.659 B.S. L.1068 J.D. 1888 Century Park E.
**Perlman, Rodney M., (P.C.)**, (AV) ....... '51 '76 C.273 B.A. L.245 J.D. [Wehner&P.]
Perlmutter, Sam, (AV) ....... '38 '64 C&L.800 B.S., J.D. 5757 Wilshire Blvd.
Perlmutter, Sharon ....... '— '91 C.112 A.B. L.976 J.D. 350 S. Grand Ave.
Perlo, Stanley, (AV) ....... '42 '74 C.112 B.A. L.809 J.D. Dep. Pub. Def.
Perlstein, Michael J., (P.C.) ....... '38 '63 C.477 B.A. L.1066 LL.B. 1925 Century Pk. E.
Perlsweig, Leon ....... '20 '55 L.1001 LL.B. 6300 Wilshire Blvd.
**Perluss, Dennis M.**, (AV) ....... '48 '73 C.813 B.A. L.309 J.D. [Morrison&F.]
*PRACTICE AREAS: Securities; Complex Business Litigation (Trial and Appellate).

**Perona, Langer & Beck, A Professional Corporation, (AV)**
**9255 Sunset Boulevard, Suite 920, 90069⊙**
**Telephone: 800-435-7542**
**Major A. Langer.**
**Personal Injury, Products Liability, Malpractice, Insurance (Bad Faith), Commercial Litigation and Trial Practice in all Courts and Administrative Agencies. Landslide and Subsidence Law.**
**Long Beach, California Office: 300 East San Antonio. Telephone: 310-426-6155. Facsimile: 310-490-9823.**

*See Professional Biographies, LOS ANGELES, CALIFORNIA*

**Perque, Chris P.** ....... '63 '91 C.420 B.S. L.861 J.D. [🄰 Loeb&L.] (See Pat. Sect.)
Perrell, Glenn M. ....... '50 '77 C.823 B.A. L.990 J.D. Title Ct. Servs.

**Perrin, Carol, (AV) '52 '77 C.1349 B.A. L.1048 J.D.**
**6300 Wilshire Boulevard, Suite 1850, 90048**
**Telephone: 213-651-1499 Fax: 213-651-1498**
**(Also Of Counsel, Law Offices of Rosaline L. Zuckerman and Tilles, Webb, Kulla & Grant, A Law Corporation, Beverly Hills).**
**Estate Planning, Business Law, Real Estate, Entertainment, Taxation, Probate and Trust Law.**

**Perrochet, Lisa** .......... '62 '87 C.112 B.A. L.426 J.D. [Horvitz&L.]
**Perron, Edward A.** .......... '54 '79 C&L.309 A.B., J.D. [Pillsbury M.&S.]
Perrone, Vincent L. '47 '73 C.861 B.A. L.569 J.D.
Exec. V.P. & Gen. Coun., Jobete Music Co., Inc.
**Perry, Charles R.** .......... '60 '86 C.112 A.B. L.1066 J.D. [[A] Folger L.&K.]⊙
Perry, Glen R. .......... '61 '88 C.659 B.S. L.910 J.D. Paramount Pictures Corp.
Perry, Ralph B., III, (AV) .......... '36 '64 C.309 A.B. L.813 LL.B. [Graven P.B.B.&Q.]
**Perry, Randi Paula** .......... '67 '93 C&L.260 B.A., J.D. [[A] Morgan,L.&B.]
Perry, Sheldon '38 '65 C.176 B.A. L.1009 J.D.
(adm. in NY; not adm. in CA) Pres., Take a Meeting Productions, Inc.
**Perry, Steven M.** .......... '56 '82 C.575 B.A. L.976 J.D. [Munger,T.&O.]
**Persaud, Veena D.** .......... '67 '96 C&L.112 B.S., J.D. [[A] Allen,M.L.G.&M.]
*LANGUAGES: French.
*PRACTICE AREAS: Land Use; Real Estate; Environmental Law.
Persky, Jerry .......... '49 '80 C.381 B.S. L.1238 J.D. 4221 Wilshire Blvd.
**Pertile, Cynthia L.** .......... '70 '95 C.612 B.A. L.802 J.D. [[A] Dummit,F.&B.]
Pestana, Frank S. .......... '13 '40 C.112 B.A. L.1066 LL.B. 7279 Mulholland Dr.
**Petak, Devera L.** .......... '53 '80 C.1079 B.A. L.1137 J.D. [[A] Zelle&L.]
*PRACTICE AREAS: Insurance Coverage; Medical Malpractice; Bad Faith Litigation.
**Petas, Marc E.** .......... '45 '71 C.112 B.S. L.800 J.D. [[C] Saltzburg,R.&B.]
**Peteler, David Kern** .......... '53 '81 C.118 B.A. L.178 J.D. [[C] Tisdale&N.]
*LANGUAGES: Russian.
*PRACTICE AREAS: Business Law; Securities; Corporate Finance; Mergers and Acquisitions; High Technology.
**Peter, Alois, Jr.** .......... '54 '87 C.1068 B.S. L.1026 J.D. [Verboon,W.H.&P.]
*PRACTICE AREAS: Construction Defect.
Peterka, Karin E. .......... '63 '91 C.36 B.A. L.339 J.D. 444 S. Flower St.
Peterka, Kristine M. .......... '64 '89 C.36 B.S. L.339 J.D. 221 N. Figueroa St.
Peters, Alec, Jr. '60 '88 C.4 B.A. L.575 J.D.
(adm. in NC; not adm. in CA) Univ. of Southern Calif.
Peters, Allen C. .......... '52 '80 C.499 B.A. L.861 J.D. Sr. Coun., Northrop Corp.
**Peters, Aulana L.**, (AV) ... '41 '74 C.562 B.A. L.800 J.D. [Gibson,D.&C.] (⊙Wash., DC)
*LANGUAGES: French; Italian.
*PRACTICE AREAS: Securities Litigation; Securities Law; SEC Regulatory Matters; Accountant's Liability; Commercial Litigation.
Peters, Clayburn H. .......... '47 '74 C.154 B.A. L.1068 J.D. Dep. Dist. Atty.
**Peters, Emily** .......... '68 '94 C.813 B.A. L.477 J.D. [[A] Rintala,S.J.&R.]
**Peters, Heather** .......... '65 '90 C.1206 B.S. L.809 J.D. [[A] Barger&W.]
*PRACTICE AREAS: Insurance Bad Faith; Employment Law.
**Peters, Paula J.** .......... '37 '68 C.112 B.A. L.1066 J.D. [Greenberg G.F.C.&M.]
*PRACTICE AREAS: Securities; Corporate; Corporate Reorganization.
**Peters, Randall J.** .......... '57 '82 C.112 B.A. L.809 J.D. [Lynberg&W.]
**Peters, Richard T.**, (AV) .......... '46 '72 C.770 B.A. L.1068 J.D. [Sidley&A.]
*PRACTICE AREAS: Bankruptcy Law; Chapter 11 Reorganization; Debtor-Creditors' Rights Law; Commercial Litigation.
Peters, Ronald F., (BV) .......... '36 '65 C.665 L.809 J.D. 34161 Crystal Lantern
**Peters, William J.** .......... '— '94 C.112 B.A. L.426 J.D. [[A] Milbank,T.H.&M.]

**Peters, Carol A.**
**(See Pasadena)**

Petersen, Michael W. .......... '61 '90 C.604 B.A. L.1068 J.D. V.P., Polygram USA
**Petersil, Lee I.** .......... '62 '88 C.112 B.A. L.426 J.D. [[A] Morris,P.&P.]
**Peterson, Andrew C.**, (AV) .......... '41 '72 C.918 A.B. L.145 J.D. [Morgan,L.&B.]
**Peterson, Carole C.** .......... '69 '94 C&L.800 B.A., J.D. [[A] White&C.]
**Peterson, Charles F.** .......... '56 '86 C.93 B.A. L.800 J.D. [[C] Sedgwick,D.M.&A.]
**Peterson, David T.** .......... '44 '71 C.112 B.S. L.276 J.D. [Troop M.S.&P.]
*PRACTICE AREAS: Environmental Litigation; Business and Entertainment Litigation.
**Peterson, George E.**, (AV) .......... '47 '72 C&L.426 B.A., J.D. [Bonne,B.M.O.&N.]
**Peterson, John A.**, (AV) .......... '49 '74 C.112 B.A. L.1065 J.D. [Veatch,C.G.&N.]
*PRACTICE AREAS: Vehicle Liability; General Casualty; Government Tort Liability; Coverage Issues and Uninsured Motorist Defense Law.
**Peterson, John W.** .......... '67 '95 C&L.800 B.S., J.D. [[A] White&C.]
**Peterson, Kurt C.**, (AV) .......... '53 '78 C.813 B.A. L.1065 J.D. [Crosby,H.R.&M.]
*PRACTICE AREAS: Commercial Litigation with special emphasis on Professional Liability; Securities; Insurance; Entertainment.
Peterson, Larry Alan .......... '62 '90 C.1110 B.A. L.61 J.D. Off. of the U.S. Trustee
Peterson, Laura L. .......... '59 '95 C.1032 B.A. L.809 J.D. 515 S. Figueroa St.
Peterson, Linda S. .......... '48 '77 C.1169 B.A. L.94 J.D. Coun., Occidental Petro. Corp.
**Peterson, Linda S.** .......... '52 '77 C.585 B.A. L.976 J.D. [Sidley&A.]
*PRACTICE AREAS: Civil Litigation.
Peterson, Mary .......... '65 '90 C.178 B.A. L.569 J.D. 400 S. Hope St.
**Peterson, Ronald C.**, (AV) .......... '45 '72 C.112 B.A. L.976 J.D. [Heller E.W.&M.]
*PRACTICE AREAS: Complex Civil Litigation.
Peterson, Stephen J., (BV) .......... '30 '63 C.112 A.B. L.1068 J.D. 4700 Wilshire Blvd.

**Peterson & Ross, (AV)**
**333 South Grand Avenue, Suite 1600, 90071-1520⊙**
**Telephone: 213-625-3500 Telecopy: 213-625-0210 Telex: 19-4545 EPALAW LSA**
**Member of Firm: Vivian Rigdon Bloomberg. Associates: Gina M. Brown; David T. Gluck; Laine T. Wagenseller; Brett P. Wakino.**
**General Civil Trial and Appellate Practice, Insurance (Corporate, Regulatory and Coverage Defense), Government Affairs, Antitrust, Aviation, Banking, Corporation, Employment Discrimination, Estate Planning, Insurance Law, International, Probate, Real Estate, Securities and Taxation Law.**
**Chicago, Illinois Office: 200 East Randolph Drive, Suite 7300, 60601-6969. Telephone: 312-861-1400.**
**New York, N.Y. Office: 33 Whitehall Street, 27th Floor, 10004. Telephone: 212-820-7700.**
**Springfield, Illinois Office: 600 South Second Street, Suite 400, 62704. Telephone: 217-525-0700.**
**Morristown, New Jersey Office: 55 Madison Avenue, Suite 200, 07960. Telephone: 201-993-9668.**
**Austin, Texas Office: 101 East Ninth Street, Suite 1000, 78701. Telephone: 512-472-5587.**
***See Professional Biographies, LOS ANGELES, CALIFORNIA***

**Petillon & Hansen**
**(See Torrance)**

**Petito, Deborah Hanna** .......... '59 '85 C.112 B.A. L.990 J.D. [Goldstein,K.&P.]
*PRACTICE AREAS: Labor and Employment; Civil Litigation.
**Petlak, Alan S.** .......... '70 '95 C.112 B.S. L.800 J.D. [[A] Jones,B.S.A.&F.]
Petrak, Jonathan .......... '59 '89 C.112 B.A. L.426 J.D. Dep. Pub. Def.
**Petreccia, Kara J.** .......... '70 '95 C.1077 B.B.A. L.809 J.D. [[A] Lynberg&W.]
**Petrich, Louis P.**, (AV) .......... '40 '66 C.112 A.B. L.1068 LL.B. [Leopold,P.&S.]
*PRACTICE AREAS: Entertainment; Civil Litigation; Copyright and Trademark; Libel and Slander; Unfair Competition.
**Petrides, Thomas H.** .......... '59 '84 C.93 A.B. L.800 J.D. [[C] Brobeck,P.&H.]
*PRACTICE AREAS: Labor and Employment.
**Petrocelli, Daniel M., (A Professional Corporation)**, (AV) '53 '81
C.112 B.S. L.809 J.D. [Mitchell,S.&K.]
*PRACTICE AREAS: Litigation.

**Petroff, Laura R.** .......... '55 '80 C.207 B.A. L.880 J.D. [Sonnenschein N.&R.]
*PRACTICE AREAS: Labor and Employment Litigation; Commercial Litigation.
**Petroni, Donald V.**, (AV) .......... '31 '59 C.549 B.A. L.813 LL.B. [O'Melveny&M.]
*PRACTICE AREAS: Entertainment Law; Communications and Media Law.
Petrossian, Alen .......... '59 '88 C.1077 B.S. L.1148 J.D. 2049 Century Park E.
**Petrovic, Christopher A.** .......... '69 '95 C.178 B.A. L.809 J.D. [[A] Selman B.]
*LANGUAGES: Serbo-Croatian.
*PRACTICE AREAS: Insurance.
**Petrovich, John G.** .......... '55 '85 C.800 B.S. L.1068 J.D. [Morrison&F.]
*PRACTICE AREAS: Corporate Finance; Multimedia.
**Petrulakis, Karen J.** '66 '93 C.1066 B.A. L.813 J.D.
[[A] Folger L.&K.] (⊙San Francisco)
**Petrullo, John P.** .......... '55 '88 C.1044 B.A. L.1148 J.D. [Preston G.&E.]
*PRACTICE AREAS: Products Liability Law.
Pettengill, Lori L. .......... '60 '87 C.1109 B.A. L.426 J.D. Dep. Dist. Atty.
**Petti, Russell G.** .......... '55 '88 C.401 B.A. L.245 J.D. [[A] Bannan,G.S.&F.]
**Pettigrew, Gregory M.** .......... '64 '90 C.477 B.A. L.597 J.D. [[A] Latham&W.]
Pettigrew, Judith Reif .......... '56 '88 C.66 B.A. L.809 J.D. Dep. Dist. Atty.
**Pettit, David** .......... '50 '75 C.112 B.A. L.1068 J.D. [Hedges&C.]
**Pettitt, Marcy A.** .......... '62 '88 C.326 B.S. L.990 J.D. [[A] R.A.Love]
*PRACTICE AREAS: Personal Injury Law.
Pettitt, Roger C., (AV) .......... '27 '55 C.112 A.B. L.1068 LL.B. [Brant&P.]
**Pettker, John D.**, (AV) .......... '42 '68 C&L.813 A.B., J.D. [Rodi,P.P.G.&C.]
*PRACTICE AREAS: Estate Planning and Probate Administration; Succession Planning for Family-Owned Businesses; Counseling Private Foundations.
Pettler, Robert J. .......... '52 '76 C.112 A.B. L.1066 J.D. 8033 Sunset Blvd.‡
Petty, Denis K. .......... '43 '69 C&L.800 A.B., J.D. Dep. Dist. Atty.‡
**Petty, Sarah E.** .......... '69 '94 C.112 B.A. L.800 J.D. [[A] Danning,G.D.&K.]
*PRACTICE AREAS: Bankruptcy; Insolvency.
Peugeot, Brad Jon .......... '51 '77 3400 W. 6th St.
Pevers, Marc W. .......... '39 '64 C.659 B.S.Econ. L.893 LL.B. 10501 Wilshire Blvd.
**Peyton, Robert W.** '51 '79 C.112 B.A. L.94 J.D.
V.P. & Sr. Coun., CB Coml. Real Estate Grp., Inc.
*RESPONSIBILITIES: Litigation; Business Advice/Contracts; Training.
Pfaeffle, Frederick W. .......... '62 '89 C.1222 B.B.A. L.800 J.D. 601 S. Figueroa St.
Pfaelzer, Mariana R. .......... '26 '58 C.112 A.B. L.1068 LL.B. U.S. Dist J.
**Pfaffmann, Carol A.** .......... '58 '84 C.473 B.A. L.188 J.D. [[C] Heller E.W.&M.]
*PRACTICE AREAS: Acquisitions, Divestitures and Mergers; Securities Law; Corporate Law.
**Pfahler, Stephen P.** .......... '64 '90 C&L.800 B.S., J.D. [[A] LeBoeuf,L.G.&M.]
*PRACTICE AREAS: Litigation; Public Law; Products Liability Law; Insurance Law.
Pfann, Susan D. .......... '49 '79 C.105 B.A. L.1148 J.D. Dep. City Atty.
Pfeffer, Andrew D. T. '44 '70
C.188 A.B. L.178 J.D. Pres., Epic Pictures Entertainment, Inc.
Pfeifer, Charles H. .......... '43 '76 C.906 B.A. L.285 J.D. 2601 S. Figueroa St.
Pfeiffer, William M. '42 '67 C.602 B.B.A. L.597 J.D.
Sr. V.P. & Gen. Coun., Calif. Assn. of Realtors
**Pfiester, R. Edward, Jr.**, (AV) .......... '43 '70 C&L.846 B.B.A., J.D. [R.E.Pfiester,Jr.]
*LANGUAGES: Spanish.
*PRACTICE AREAS: Personal Injury; FELA; Railroad Law.

**Pfiester, R. Edward, Jr., A Law Corporation, (AV)**
**2000 Riverside Drive, 90039-3707**
**Telephone: 213-384-0880 FAX: 213-669-8549**
**R. Edward Pfiester, Jr.;—Victor A. Russo; Anthony M. Ontiveros.**
**Personal Injury, Federal Employers Liability, Railroad, Products Liability, Bad Faith and Wrongful Death Litigation.**
**Reference: Sanwa Bank California (Headquarters Office).**
***See Professional Biographies, LOS ANGELES, CALIFORNIA***

**Pfister, Thomas L.**, (AV) .......... '48 '74 C.813 A.B. L.309 J.D. [Latham&W.]
**Pflaster, James** .......... '47 '73 C.112 B.A. L.1068 J.D. [[A] Schlothauer,C.&M.]
*LANGUAGES: Spanish.
*PRACTICE AREAS: Personal Injury Law (60%); Workers Compensation Law (40%).

**Pflug, Andrea J. '55 '80 C.112 B.A. L.809 J.D.**
**1875 Century Park East, Suite 1500, 90067**
**Telephone: 310-551-0199 Fax: 310-552-3228**
**Business Litigation, Real Estate, Corporate, Intellectual Property and Personal Injury Law.**
**Representative Clients: Travel Management Group, Inc.; Brana Publishing, Inc.; Gold's Gym, Huntington Beach.**

**Pflug, Christopher R.** ... '60 '87 C.1077 B.A. L.426 J.D. Corp. Coun., Farmers Grp., Inc.
*REPORTED CASES: Aragon v. Pappy, Kaplan, Vogel & Phillips, 214 Cal. App. 3d 451 (Cal. App. 2d Dist. 1989).
*RESPONSIBILITIES: Litigation and Discovery; Commercial; Corporate Organization.
**Pfrommer, Sara**, (AV) .......... '53 '78 C.112 B.A. L.1068 J.D. [Sheppard,M.R.&H.]
*PRACTICE AREAS: Bankruptcy Law; Creditors' Rights Law; Financial Institutions Litigation.
**Phan, Peter G.** .......... '69 '95 L.1066 [[A] Dewey B.]
Phansalkar, Mohan V. ..... '63 '87 C.910 A.B. L.178 J.D. V.P., Trust Company of the West
Pheffer, Jeffrey Ian .......... '54 '82 C.891 B.A. L.1137 J.D. 12121 Wilshire Blvd.
Phelps, Beauford H. .......... '26 '62 C.800 L.809 LL.B. Supr. Ct. J.
**Phelps, Carl B.**, (AV) .......... '39 '65 C.165 A.B. L.309 LL.B. [Andrews&K.]
*PRACTICE AREAS: Real Estate Law; Corporate Law.
**Phelps, David S.** .......... '60 '87 C.813 B.A. L.1068 J.D. [[C] Paul,H.J.&W.]
**Phelps, Kathy Bazoian** .......... '66 '91 C.668 B.A. L.1068 J.D. [Danning,G.D.&K.]
*LANGUAGES: Mandarin Chinese.
**Phelps, Thomas D., (P.C.)**, (AV) .......... '36 '63 C.350 B.S. L.273 J.D. [Manatt,P.&P.]
*PRACTICE AREAS: Corporate Securities; Financial Services.
Phelps, William H. '54 '80 C.170 B.A. L.1065 J.D.
V.P. & Assoc. Gen. Coun., Kidder, Peabody & Co., Inc.
Phelps, William R., Jr. '48 '74 C.579 B.A. L.976 J.D.
(adm. in WI; not adm. in CA) Prof., Whittier Coll. Sch. of Law
**Philibosian, Robert H.**, (AV) .......... '40 '68 C.813 A.B. L.809 LL.B. [Sheppard,M.R.&H.]
*PRACTICE AREAS: Government; Administrative Law.
Philip, Karen M. '65 '90 C.860 B.A. L.569 J.D.
Univ. Coun., University of Southern California
**Philips, Robert M.** .......... '55 '84 C.112 B.A. L.1066 J.D. [[A] Solish,A.&G.]
*PRACTICE AREAS: Commercial Litigation; Franchise Law; Intellectual Law; Property Law.
**Phillipp, James G.** .......... '42 '67 C.321 A.B. L.477 J.D. [Gibson,D.&C.]
*PRACTICE AREAS: Federal and State Tax Litigation; Transfer Pricing Issues.
Phillippay, Wendy J. .......... '54 '83 C.112 B.A. L.1065 J.D. 1900 Ave. of the Stars
**Phillips, Arsine B.** .......... '61 '86 C.112 B.A. L.800 J.D. [Parker,M.C.O.&S.]
*LANGUAGES: Armenian.
*PRACTICE AREAS: Business Litigation.
**Phillips, Bradley S.**, (AV) .......... '54 '79 C.813 B.A. L.976 J.D. [Munger,T.&O.]
Phillips, Clare S. .......... '59 '84 C.813 A.B. L.569 J.D. Asst. U.S. Atty.
Phillips, Clifford J. .......... '14 '40 C.112 B.A. L.800 LL.B. 914 Bluegrass Ln.

CALIFORNIA—LOS ANGELES MARTINDALE-HUBBELL LAW DIRECTORY 1997

**Phillips, Darlene Fischer, (P.C.)** .............'40 '78 C&L.800 B.A., J.D. [Hill,F.&B.]
*SPECIAL AGENCIES: Planning, zoning, and environmental boards and committees, California Coastal Commission; planning commissions, city councils and boards of supervisors for local public agencies; school boards and school district personnel commission.
*REPORTED CASES: T.M. Smith v. County of Los Angeles (1994) 24 Cal.App.4th 990; J.L. Thomas v. County of Los Angeles (1991) 232 Cal.App.3d 916; Friends of La Vina v. County of Los Angeles (1991) 232 Cal.App.3d 1446; William S. Hart Union High School District v. County of Los Angeles (1991) 226 Cal.App.3d 1612; Personnel Commission of the Lynwood Unified School District v. Board of Trustees (1990) 223 Cal.App.3d 1463.
*PRACTICE AREAS: Land Use Litigation; Environmental Litigation; Representation of School District Personnel Commissions.

**Phillips, Douglas C., (AV) '22 '54 C.36 L.809 J.D.**
**10880 Wilshire Boulevard, Suite 1800, 90024**
**Telephone: 213-879-3337 Facsimile: 310-470-9267**
**Probate and Estate Planning, General Civil Litigation, Arbitration and Mediation.**
**Bank Reference: Western Bank (Los Angeles, California).**

**Phillips, Gary R.** ..................................'58 '86 C&L.800 B.S., J.D. [Astor&P.]
*PRACTICE AREAS: Real Estate Law; Trial Practice; Business; Real Estate; Commercial.
Phillips, Gary S. ....................'51 '76 C.112 B.A. L.770 J.D. 11845 W. Olympic Blvd.
**Phillips, George R., (AV)** ..................'28 '57 C.112 B.S. L.1068 LL.B. [Astor&P.]
*PRACTICE AREAS: Taxation Law; Real Estate Law; Business Law; Estate Planning.
**Phillips, George R., Jr.** ..........................'63 '91 C&L.800 B.S.A., J.D. [O'Melveny&M.]
**Phillips, Gerald F.** ..........................'25 '50 C.197 A.B. L.178 LL.B. [Phillips&S.]
*PRACTICE AREAS: Entertainment Law; Family Law; General Commercial Litigation; Arbitration; Mediation.
**Phillips, Gregory D.** ......................'49 '85 C.813 B.A. L.976 J.D. [Munger,T.&O.]
Phillips, Jacqueline M. .... '47 '85 C.766 B.A. L.800 J.D. 2121 Ave. of the Stars, 22nd Fl.
**Phillips, John P.** ..........................'67 '94 C.197 B.A. L.1066 J.D. [Manatt,P.&P.]
*PRACTICE AREAS: Litigation.
**Phillips, L. Lee, (P.C.), (AV)** ..................'37 '59 C&L.188 A.B., J.D. [Manatt,P.&P.]
*PRACTICE AREAS: Entertainment (Music) Law.
**Phillips, Mark J., (AV)** .................'54 '80 C.112 B.A. L.1068 J.D. [Goldfarb,S.&A.]
*PRACTICE AREAS: Taxation Law; Estate Planning Law; Probate Law.
**Phillips, Martin W.** '56 '80
C.940 B.A. L.1068 J.D. Sr. Coun., Transamerica Financial Servs.
**Phillips, Michael C., (P.C.)** ........... '45 '71 C.174 B.A. L.426 J.D. [Anderson,M.&C.]
*PRACTICE AREAS: Toxic Torts; Products Liability Litigation; Construction Defect Litigation; Insurance Coverage; Maritime Litigation.
Phillips, Nina W. ......................................'42 '79 C&L.800 B.S., J.D. Dep. Co. Coun.
**Phillips, Patricia Dominis, (AV)** ........'34 '68 C.112 B.A. L.426 J.D. [Morrison&F.]
*PRACTICE AREAS: Family Law; Civil Litigation; Mediation and Arbitration.
Phillips, Samantha M. ...........'66 '91 C.813 A.B. L.1066 J.D. 333 S. Hope St., 48th Fl.
**Phillips, Stacy D., (AV)** ........................'58 '84 C.197 A.B. L.178 J.D. [Mannis&P.]
*PRACTICE AREAS: Family Law; Custody; Arbitration; Mediation.
**Phillips, Stanton Lee, (BV)** ..........'44 '70 C.1077 B.A. L.426 J.D. [Levinson,M.J.&P.]
*PRACTICE AREAS: Civil Litigation.
**Phillips, Thomas M.** ..................'55 '83 C.112 B.A. L.426 J.D. [Veatch,C.G.&N.]
*PRACTICE AREAS: Insurance Defense; Business Litigation.
**Phillips, Thomas P., (AV)** ..................'40 '66 C.668 B.A. L.165 J.D. [Phillips&B.]
Phillips, Virginia A. ....................'57 '82 C.112 A.B. L.1066 J.D. U.S. Mag. J.

**Phillips & Branch, (AV)**
**Eighteenth Floor, 1901 Avenue of the Stars (Century City), 90067**
**Telephone: 213-930-0986 Fax: 213-937-2964**
**Email: attyphil@aol.com**
**Members of Firm: Thomas P. Phillips; K. Christopher Branch.**
**Will Contests, Class Action Anti-trust and Securities Actions, Major Construction Cases, matters involving Charitable Foundations, Purchase and Sale of Businesses, Employment related matters, Commercial Disputes.**
*See Professional Biographies, LOS ANGELES, CALIFORNIA*

**Phillips & Salman**
**2029 Century Park East, Suite 1200, 90067-2957⊙**
**Telephone: 310-277-7117 Fax: 310-286-9182**
**Partners: Gerald F. Phillips; Robert R. Salman (Resident, New York City Office). Associate: Suzanne A. Salman (Resident, New York City Office).**
**Corporate and Commercial and Entertainment Law. Litigation in all Courts. Arbitration and Mediation.**
**Representative Clients: Amrep Corp.; Deloitte & Touche, LLP.; Sandvik, Inc.; Soap Opera Festivals, Inc.; Transamerica Insurance Finance Corporation.**
**New York, N.Y. Office: 111 Broadway, Thirteenth Floor. Telephone: 212-571-6500. Fax: 212-571-6533.**
*See Professional Biographies, LOS ANGELES, CALIFORNIA*

**Piano, John G.** .....................'67 '92 C.107 B.A. L.188 J.D. [Allen,M.L.G.&M.]
**Piccionelli, Gregory A.** .........................'54 '92 C.112 B.A. L.426 J.D. [Brull&P.]
*PRACTICE AREAS: Intellectual Property; Patent; Trademark; Copyright; Biotechnology Matters.
**Piccus, Todd Olen** .....................'65 '93 C.112 B.A. L.846 J.D. [Pircher,N.&M.]
*PRACTICE AREAS: Real Estate Law; Entertainment; Multimedia.
**Pichardo, Mario A.** ........................'58 '92 C&L.178 B.A., J.D. [Knapp,M.J.&D.]
*LANGUAGES: French, Spanish and Japanese.
*PRACTICE AREAS: Commercial Litigation; Corporate.
Picheny, Richard L. .........'46 '86 C.1029 B.S. L.426 J.D. 1801 Century Park E., 23rd Fl.
**Pick, Alan B., (AV)** .................................'45 '71 C.911 B.A. L.813 J.D. [Pick&B.]
Pick, Mark Laurence .........'53 '78 C.813 A.B. L.1066 J.D. Pres., Pick Productions, Inc.

**Pick & Boydston, (AV)**
**A Partnership including a Professional Corporation**
**800 West Sixth Street, Suite 400, 90017**
**Telephone: 213-624-1996 Telecopier: 213-624-9073**
**Alan B. Pick; Brian Boydston; Joan I. Samuelson; Irving C. Parchman; Patrick E. Michela; Trevor L. Alt; Mark K. Drew.**
**General Civil Trial and Appellate Practice. Antitrust, Business Regulation, Copyright and Trademark, Corporate, Real Estate, Securities, Taxation and Trust Law.**
*See Professional Biographies, LOS ANGELES, CALIFORNIA*

Pickard, Florence T. ..........................'34 '62 C.112 B.A. L.809 LL.B. Supr. Ct. J.
**Pickell, James B.** ....................'69 '94 C.112 B.A. L.426 J.D. [Katten M.&Z.]
*PRACTICE AREAS: Corporate; Securities.
Pickett, Angela R. ..........................'46 '73 C.112 B.A. L.1068 J.D. 325 S. Reno
Pickett, James R. ...........................'43 '68 C.299 B.A. L.188 J.D. 11377 Olympic Blvd.
**Pico, Timothy A.** ....................'— '95 C.112 B.A. L.990 J.D. [Sedgwick,D.M.&A.]
**Picone, Lawrence E.** ..............'58 '83 C.873 B.A. L.765 J.D. [Sedgwick,D.M.&A.]
Picone, Samuel B., (AV) ..........................'15 '42 C&L.809 J.D. 12910 Sunset Blvd.‡
Pidoux, Rae Fallon ...'68 '94 C.426 B.A. L.1068 J.D. Los Angeles Community Coll. Dist.
Piecuch, Stephen A. .........'40 '74 C.112 B.A. L.1068 J.D. 3575 Cahuenga Blvd., 2nd Fl.
**Piedrahita, Sandro F.** ...............'64 '90 C.976 B.A. L.309 J.D. [Robinson,D.B.&K.]
*LANGUAGES: French and Spanish.
*REPORTED CASES: In re Altabon Foods, Inc., 998 F. 2d 718 (9th Cir., 1993).
*PRACTICE AREAS: Commercial Litigation; Bankruptcy Law; Creditors' Rights Law; Real Estate.
**Pieper, Darold D.** .......................'44 '71 C.112 A.B. L.800 J.D. [Richards,W.&G.]
*PRACTICE AREAS: Public Law; Public Contracts Law; Public Transportation Law.
Pierce, David C. ................'61 '92 C.112 B.A. L.1137 J.D. 801 S. Grand Ave., 9th Fl.
**Pierce, Edward J., (AV)** ..................'51 '79 C.976 A.B. L.309 J.D. [Seyfarth,S.F.&G.]
*PRACTICE AREAS: Corporations Law; Securities Law; Real Estate Law.

**Pierce, Linda T.** ...........................'61 '92 C.1077 B.A. L.809 J.D. [Silver&F.]
*PRACTICE AREAS: Employment Law; General Business Litigation; Civil Litigation.
**Pierce, T. Peter** ..........................'64 '92 C.188 B.A. L.861 J.D. [Richards,W.&G.]
*PRACTICE AREAS: Municipal Law; Municipal Litigation.
**Pierovich, Michael** ...................'67 '96 C.276 B.S.F.S. L.228 J.D. [Gibson,D.&C.]
**Pierry, Joseph P.** ...........................'61 '86 C.93 B.A. L.776 J.D. [Pierry&M.]
*PRACTICE AREAS: Admiralty/Maritime; Personal Injury; Products Liability (Plaintiff); Workmans Compensation.
**Pierry, Thomas J., III** .....................'62 '87 C.911 B.A. L.800 J.D. [Pierry&M.]
*PRACTICE AREAS: Admiralty/Maritime; Personal Injury; Products Liability (Plaintiff); Workmans Compensation.
**Pierry, Thomas J., Sr., (AV)** ................'37 '65 C.679 B.S. L.800 LL.B. [Pierry&M.]
*PRACTICE AREAS: Maritime; Personal Injury; Products Liability (Plaintiff); Workmans Compensation.

**Pierry & Moorhead, LLP, (AV)**
**A Partnership including a Professional Corporation**
**301 North Avalon Boulevard, 90744-5888**
**Telephone: 310-834-2691, 213-775-8348, 714-636-2970 FAX: 310-518-5814**
**Members of Firm: Thomas J. Pierry, Sr.; Michael D. Moorhead (P.C.);—James M. McAdams; F. Joseph Ford, Jr.; Robert W. Ford; F. Javier Trujillo; Thomas J. Pierry, III; Joseph P. Pierry.**
**General Personal Injury Litigation, Maritime, Medical Malpractice, Products Liability.**
*See Professional Biographies, LOS ANGELES, CALIFORNIA*

Pierson, Carl A. .................................'20 '53 C.112 A.B. L.1065 J.D. Adm. Law J.
Pierson, David C., Professional Corporation, (AV) '35 '61
C.112 B.A. L.1065 J.D. 7401 Dunfield Ave.‡
**Pierson, Edward P.** '53 '78 C&L.208 B.A., J.D.
(adm. in CO; not adm. in CA) Sr. V.P., Legal & Bus. Affs., Warner/Chappell Music
Pierson, John C., (AV) .........................'41 '75 C.1077 B.A. L.426 J.D. [Pierson&P.]

**Pierson, John K. '63 '90 C.747 B.A. L.990 J.D.**
**The Gateway, 12424 Wilshire Boulevard, Suite 900, 90025-1043⊙**
**Telephone: 310-826-8009 Fax: 310-442-6400**
**Email: Pierson.law@aol.com**
***PRACTICE AREAS: Business Litigation; Bankruptcy; Entertainment; Criminal Defense; Negligence.**
**Of Counsel: Robert M. De Feo; Raymond Kirk Kolter; J. Eric Kirkland.**
**Civil and Trial Practice in all Courts. Business Litigation, Entertainment Law, Bankruptcy, Criminal Defense and Negligence.**
**Minneapolis, Minnesota Office: 5100 Gamble Drive, Suite 398. Telephone: 612-545-6326.**
*See Professional Biographies, LOS ANGELES, CALIFORNIA*

Pierson, Swan C. ..............................'14 '45 C.112 B.A. L.425 LL.B. [Pierson&P.] ‡
Pierson & Pierson, (AV) ..........................................11340 W. Olympic Blvd.
**Pietrini, Jill M.** ...................'61 '88 C.112 B.A. L.770 J.D. [Manatt,P.&P.] (Pat.)
*PRACTICE AREAS: Intellectual Property Litigation.
**Pigott, John T., (AV)** .....................'20 '50 C&L.976 B.A., LL.B. [Gibson,D.&C.]
*PRACTICE AREAS: Trusts and Estates; Real Property.
Pih, Jerri Hoi ...........................'61 '86 C.813 B.A. L.1068 J.D. 801 S. Grand Ave.
**Piibe, Anne-Marie P.** ..................'64 '90 C.112 B.A. L.426 J.D. [Jackson,L.S.&K.]
Pike, Donald W. ..........................................'24 '67 L.1095 LL.B. 111 N. Hill St.‡
Pilch, Howard D., (BV) .....'47 '72 C.112 B.A. L.1066 J.D. 2029 Century Park E., 6th Fl.
**Pilchowski, Thomas S., (P.C.), (AV)** '38 '74
C.214 B.S.E.E. L.1137 J.D. [Millard,P.H.&C.]
*PRACTICE AREAS: Insurance Defense; Civil Litigation.
**Pill, David M.** ....................'54 '79 C.112 B.A. L.426 J.D. Asst. Gen. Coun., CBS Inc.

**Pillsbury Madison & Sutro LLP, (AV)**
**Citicorp Plaza, 725 South Figueroa Street, Suite 1200, 90017-2513⊙**
**Telephone: 213-488-7100 Fax: 213-629-1033**
**Members of Firm: Lawrence D. Bradley, Jr.; John R. Cadarette, Jr.; Anthon S. Cannon, Jr.; Kenneth R. Chiate; Anthony R. Delling; William K. Dial; Blase P. Dillingham; John J. Duffy; Jerone J. English; Michael J. Finnegan; L. Gail Gordon; Kent B. Goss; T.J. (Mick) Grasmick; David L. Hayutin; Jeffrey W. Hill; Amy D. Hogue; Carolyn M. Huestis; Yuji Iwanaga; Sidney K. Kanazawa; Ralph D. Kirwan; Steven O. Kramer; Jennie L. La Prade; Thomas R. Larmore; Peter V. Leparulo; John Y. Liu; Christopher J. McNevin; Donald W. Meaders; Catherine D. Meyer; Michael E. Meyer; Ruth Modisette; Nancy G. Morrison; Robert L. Morrison; J. Richard Morrissey; Dana P. Newman; F. John Nyhan; Henry Y. Ota; Jackie K. Park; Charles E. Patterson; Edward A. Perron; Teresa M. Quinn; James M. Rishwain, Jr.; Patrick G. Rogan; Matthew R. Rogers; Kenneth N. Russak; Karl A. Schmidt; Faisal Shah; Robert V. Slattery Jr.; Sheryl E. Stein; William E. Stoner; Marshall M. Taylor; Reed S. Waddell; Robert L. Wallan; William S. Waller; Don R. Weigandt; John W. Whitaker; John G. Wigmore; Thomas E. Workman, Jr.; Gordon K. Wright. Of Counsel: Charles E. Anderson; Roland G. Simpson; Deborah S. Thoren-Peden. Senior Counsel: A. Todd Littleworth; Steven M. Nakasone. Associates: Keith A. Allen-Niesen; Farhad Bahar; Brett H. Bailey; Ian R. Barrett; J. Keith Biancamano; Dimitrios P. Biller; J. Douglas Bishop; Dawn S. Brookey; Jan H. Cate; J. Mark Childs; Barbara L. Croutch; Michael J. Crowley; Douglas H. Deems; Sybille Dreuth; Julie G. Duffy; Sheri F. Eisner; Douglas C. Emhoff; Jason R. Erb; Michael J. Erlinger; Alyssa First; Eric B. Foker; William B. Freeman; Jeffrey D. Frost; William T. Gillespie; Tracy Birnkrant Gray; Stewart S. Harrison; L. Keven Hayworth; Sabina A. Helton; Karen L. Hermann; Julia R. Johnson; Kelly A. Kightlinger; Lynne E. Mallya; Tohru Masago; Jennifer E. Mayo; Mary T. Michelena-Monroe; Margaret L. Milam; David S. Rauch; Jeffrey A. Rich; Julia Ellen Richards; Lori A. Ridley; Susan M. St. Denis; Kalman Steinberg; John T. Vangel; David J. Westgor; Marcus G. Whittle; Christopher T. Williams; Andrew M. Winograd.**
**General Civil Practice and Litigation in all State and Federal Courts. Business: Banking and Corporate Finance; Commercial Transactions/Energy; Corporate, Securities and Technologies; Creditors' Rights and Bankruptcy; Employee Benefits; Employment and Labor Relations; Environment, Health & Safety; Estate Planning; Finance and Commercial Transactions; Food and Beverage Regulation; Health Care; Political Law; Real Estate; Tax (domestic and international); and Telecommunications. Litigation: Alternative Dispute Resolution; Antitrust/Trade Regulation; Appellate; Banking/Financial Institutions; Commercial Disputes; Construction/Real Estate; Creditors' Rights, Bankruptcy and Insurance Insolvency; Energy Matters; Employment/Equal Opportunity; Environmental/Land Use; ERISA; Insurance; Intellectual Property; Maritime/Admiralty; Media/Entertainment/Sports; Securities; Tort/Product Liability; and White Collar Defense. Intellectual Property: Aesthetic Design & Trade Dress Protection; Biotechnology; Computer Law; Copyright Law; Intellectual Property Audits and Strategic Planning; International Trade Commission; Licensing and Technology Transfer; Procurement of Property Rights; Patent Prosecution; Trade Secrets and Unfair Competition; Trademark Law; Interference Practice; Mechanical/Biomed/Aeronautical; and Physics/Optics.**
**Costa Mesa, California Office: Plaza Tower, Suite 1100, 600 Anton Boulevard, 92626. Telephone: 714-436-6800. Fax: 714-662-6999.**
**Silicon Valley Office: 2700 San Hill Road, Menlo Park, 94025. Telephone: 415-233-4500. Fax: 415-233-4545.**
**Sacramento, California Office: 400 Capitol Mall, Suite 1700, 95814. Telephone: 916-329-4700. Fax: 916-441-3583.**
**San Diego, California Office: 101 West Broadway, Suite 1800, 92101. Telephone: 619-234-5000. Fax: 619-236-1995.**
**San Francisco, California Office: 235 Montgomery Street, 94104. Telephone: 415-983-1000. Fax: 415-983-1200.**
**Washington, D.C. Office: 1100 New York Avenue, N.W., Ninth Floor, 20005. Telephone: 202-861-3000. Fax: 202-822-0944.**
**New York, New York Office: 520 Madison Avenue, 40th Floor, 10022. Telephone: 212-328-4810. Fax: 212-328-4824. One Liberty Plaza, 165 Broadway, 51st Floor. Telephone: 212-374-1890. Fax: 212-374-1852.**
**Hong Kong Office: 6/F Asia Pacific Finance Tower, Citibank Plaza, 3 Garden Road, Central. Telephone: 011-852-2509-7100. Fax: 011-852-2509-7188.**
**Tokyo, Japan Office: Pillsbury Madison & Sutro, Gaikokuho Jimu Bengoshi Jimusho, 5th Floor, Samon Eleven Building, 3-1, Samon-cho, Shinjuku-ku, Tokyo 160 Japan. Telephone: 800-729-9830; 011-813-3354-3531. Fax: 011-813-3354-3534.**
*See Professional Biographies, LOS ANGELES, CALIFORNIA*

CAA316P

**Pilmer, Robert Alexander** . . . . . . . . '66 '93 C.605 A.B. L.426 J.D. [Ⓐ Buchalter,N.F.&Y.]
*PRACTICE AREAS: Financial Institutions Litigation; Real Property Litigation; Business Litigation.
Pilosof, Maurice B. . . . . . . . . . . . . . . . . . . . .'58 '84 C.112 B.A. L.809 J.D. 8797 Beverly Blvd.
**Pilot, Sidney I.**, (AV) . . . . . . . . . . .'33 '58 C.802 B.B.A. L.809 LL.B. [Ⓟ Parker,M.C.O.&S.]
*REPORTED CASES: Gardner v. Gardner - Domestic Relations; BMW of North American, Inc. v. New Motor Vehicle Board 209 Cal.Rept.50, 162 CA3d 980); Piano V. New Motor Vehicle Board, 163 Cal.Rptr. 41, 103 CA3d 412; American Isuzu Motors, Inc. v. New Motor Vehicle Board, 1986 230 Cal.Rept. 769 186 CA3d 464.
*PRACTICE AREAS: Automobile Dealerships.
**Pimstone, Gregory N.** . . . . . . . . . . . . . . . . . . .'64 '90 C.112 A.B. L.1066 J.D. [Ⓐ Latham&W.]
Pinchas, David E. . . . . . . . . . . . . . . . . . . . . . '59 '86 C.367 B.A. L.228 J.D. U.S. Attys. Off.
Pinchuk, Leslie, (AV) . . . . . . . . . . . . . . . . . . .'38 '65 C.112 A.B. L.1066 LL.B. Dep. City Atty.
Pinder, Jessalyn R. . . . . . . . . . . . . . . . . . . . . . '65 '91 C.112 B.A. L.208 J.D. City Atty.'s Ofc.
Pinder, Wilma W. . . . . . . . . . . . . . . . . . . . . . . . . . . . . . . . . . . . . . . . '41 '78 Asst. City Atty.
**Pine, Beverly Tillett** . . . . . . . . . . . . . . . . . . . . . . . . . .'48 '80 C.347 B.S. L.426 J.D. [Pine&P.]
**Pine, Marcia B.**, (AV) . . . . . . . . . . . . . . . . . . . '41 '79 C.188 B.A. L.426 J.D. [Morrison&F.]
*PRACTICE AREAS: Bankruptcy.
**Pine, Norman**, (AV) . . . . . . . . . . . . . . . . . . . . . . . . . . '49 '75 C.112 B.A. L.1066 J.D. [Pine&P.]

**Pine & Pine, (AV)**
**Suite 1520, 15760 Ventura Boulevard (Encino), 91436**
**Telephone: 818-379-9710 Fax: 818-379-9749**
**Members of Firm: Norman Pine; Beverly Tillett Pine.**
**Appellate and Related Trial Court Practice. Litigation Consulting and Brief-writing, Business Litigation in State and Federal Courts. False Claims Act (Whistleblowing), Antitrust Law, Unfair Trade Practices. Entertainment.**
***See Professional Biographies, LOS ANGELES, CALIFORNIA***

**Pines, Adam** . . . . . . . . . . . . . . . . . . . . . . . . . .'69 '94 C.659 B.A. L.569 J.D. [Ⓐ Manatt,P.&P.]
*PRACTICE AREAS: Banking Law; Litigation.
**Pines, Burt, (P.C.)**, (AV) . . . . . . . . . . . . . '39 '64 C.800 B.A. L.569 J.D. [Alschuler G.&P.]
**Pines, Daniel L.** . . . . . . . . . . . . . . . . . .'69 '94 C.276 B.S.F.S. L.1066 J.D. [Ⓐ Richards,W.&G.]
*PRACTICE AREAS: Litigation.

**Pines, David A., Law Offices of**
**(See Woodland Hills)**

Pinkerman, Connie Redbird . . . . . . . . . . . . . . .'— '80 C.45 M.D. L.1148 J.D. 616 N. Alvarado
Pinkner, Scott C. . . . . . . . . . . . . . . . .'62 '88 C.112 B.A. L.188 J.D. 7th Fl. 515 S. Figueroa St.
Pinkos, Cynthia '— '87 C.197 A.B. L.178 J.D.
(adm. in NY; not adm. in CA) Twentieth Century Fox Film Corp.
Pinkus, Roslyn . . . . . . . . . . . . . . . . . . . . . '42 '86 C.102 B.A. L.1095 J.D. 16830 Ventura Blvd.
**Pinsky, Scott D.** . . . . . . . . . . . . . . . . . . . . . '57 '85 C.668 B.A. L.1068 J.D. [Ⓐ Radcliff,F.&D.]
*LANGUAGES: French.
Pinto, Celeste, (AV) . . . . . . . . . . . . . . .'— '74 C.856 B.A. L.276 J.D. 515 N. Cliffwood Ave.
Pinto, J. Daniel '57 '86 C.421 B.A. L.940 J.D.
(adm. in IN; not adm. in CA) Mackey & Assoc.
**Pircher, Leo J.**, (AV) . . . . . . . . . . . . . . . . . . . .'33 '58 C.112 B.S. L.1066 J.D. [Pircher,N.&M.]
*PRACTICE AREAS: Real Estate Law; Tax Law.

**Pircher, Nichols & Meeks, (AV)**
**1999 Avenue of the Stars, 90067⊙**
**Telephone: 310-201-8900 FAX: 310-201-8922**
**Members of Firm: Stevens A. Carey; David E. Cranston; Alfred F. DeLeo; James L. Goldman; Sheldon A. Halpern; Kathleen M. Hogaboom; Jerry A. Katz; Gary M. Laughlin; Eugene J. M. Leone (Resident Partner, Chicago Office); Larry M. Meeks; Phillip G. Nichols; Leo J. Pircher (Certified Specialist, Taxation Law, The State Bar of California Board of Legal Specialization); Michael E. Scheinberg; Urban J. Schreiner; Randall C. Single. Associates: Marc A. Benjamin (Resident Associate, Chicago Office); Bruce J. Graham; John H. Irons, Jr.; William Howard Jackson; Robert D. Jaffe; Jay S. Laifman; Emily B. Miller; Ralph L. Olivi, Jr. (Resident Associate, Chicago Office); David L. Packer; Todd Olen Piccus; Michele A. Powers; Miryam Rosie Rees (Resident Associate, Chicago Office); Steven A. Rivers; Michael F. Smetana (Resident Associate, Chicago Office); Anne K. Smith (Resident Associate, Chicago Office); Valerie H. Wulf (Resident Associate, Chicago Office). Of Counsel: Steven B. Arbuss; Debra Spangler Barbanel; Erik C. Gould (Resident Of Counsel, Chicago Office); Barbara A. Kaye; Michael J. Kretzmer; E. Thomas Moroney, Jr.; Stephanie C. Silvers; Craig A. Smith; Daniel H. Willick.**
**Real Estate Law including Representation of Partnerships, Limited Liability Companies and Tax-Exempt Organizations in Acquisition, Development and Financing. Corporation, Federal and State Securities, Federal and State Taxation, Partnership, Municipal Finance, Environmental Law, Litigation, Bankruptcy and Limited Liability Company, Multimedia and Entertainment Law, Sports Law.**
**Chicago, Illinois Office: 900 North Michigan Avenue. Telephone: 312-915-3112. FAX: 312-915-3348; 312-915-3354.**
***See Professional Biographies, LOS ANGELES, CALIFORNIA***

Pirkey, Will Jay . . . . . . . . . . . . . . . . . . . . . . '51 '78 C.061 B.A. L.61 J.D. 3530 Wilshire Blvd.
Piro, Joseph N. . . . . . . . . . . . . . . . . . . . . . '44 '76 C.1042 B.A. L.990 J.D. Dep. City Atty.
Pirtle, William F. . . . . . . . . . . . . . . . . . . . . . . . .'48 '73 C.339 B.A. L.734 J.D. [Cochran&P.]
Pisano, A. Robert, (AV) . . . . . . . . . . . . . . . . .'43 '69 C.768 B.A. L.1066 J.D. 400 S. Hope St.
**Pisano, George A.** . . . . . . . . . . . . . . . . .'57 '83 C.426 B.A. L.1067 J.D. [Wilson,E.M.E.&D.]
*LANGUAGES: Italian.
**Pitchess, Peter J., II** . . . . . . . . . . . . . . . . '67 '93 C.800 B.S.B.A. L.426 J.D. [Ⓐ Liner,Y.&S.]
*PRACTICE AREAS: Commercial; Business Litigation.
**Pitre, Frank M.**, (AV) . . . . . . . . . . . . . . . . . . . . . .'55 '81 C&L.767 B.S., J.D. [Cotchett&P.]⊙
Pitt, Andrew S. . . . . . . . . . . . . . . . . . . . . . . . .'57 '84 C.473 B.S. L.209 J.D. Off. of U.S. Atty.
Pittluck, Norman . . . . . . . . . . . . . . . . . . . . . '20 '49 C.569 B.S. L.309 LL.B. Comr., Supr. Ct.
**Pittman, Dawn S.** . . . . . . . . . . . . . . . . . . . .'— '95 C&L.112 B.A., J.D. [Ⓐ Zevnik H.G.&M.]
*PRACTICE AREAS: Insurance Coverage Litigation; Environmental.
**Pitts, Deborah** . . . . . . . . . . . . . . . . . . . . . . . '54 '79 C.112 B.A. L.1068 J.D. [Hancock R.&B.]
Piuze, Michael J., (AV) . . . . . . . . . . . . . . . '44 '72 C.393 B.A. L.846 J.D. 11755 Wilshire Blvd.
**Pizer, Bradley J.**, (AV) . . . . . . . . . . . . . . . . . . . . '60 '86 C.813 B.A. L.770 J.D. [Pizer&M.]⊙
*PRACTICE AREAS: Business Litigation; Creditor Rights Law; Collections; Bankruptcy; Financial Institutions Law.

**Pizer & Michaelson Inc., (AV)** ⊞
**2029 Century Park East, Suite 600, 90067⊙**
**Telephone: 310-843-9729 Fax: 310-843-9619**
**Bradley J. Pizer.**
**General Civil Practice in all State and Federal Courts. Business Transactions and Litigation, Representing and Advising Financial Institutions, Credit Unions, Corporations and Partnerships, Creditor Rights in Bankruptcy, Collections, Real Estate, Family Law, Conservatorships, Estate Planning, Wills, Trusts, and Probate.**
**Santa Ana, California Office: 2122 North Broadway, Suite 100, 92706. Telephone: 714-558-0535. Telecopier: 714-550-0841.**
***See Professional Biographies, LOS ANGELES, CALIFORNIA***

Plafker, Stephen M. . . . . . . . . . . . . . . . . . . . . . . . . '40 '73 C.453 B.S. L.800 J.D. Dep. Dist. Atty.‡
**Plank, Robert R.** . . . . . . . . . . . . . . . . . . . . '28 '79 C.940 B.A. L.1224 J.D. [Ⓟ McKenna&C.]
**Plante, Brian C.** . . . . . . . . . . . . . . . . . . . . . '69 '94 C.690 B.S. L.990 J.D. [Ⓐ Lynberg&W.]
*PRACTICE AREAS: Insurance Coverage Litigation; General Civil Defense.
Plaskin, Kathryn Hall . . . . . . . . . . . . . . . . . .'51 '88 C.1136 B.S. L.809 J.D. [Ⓐ Herman&W.]
Platt, Alison R. . . . . . . . . . . . . . . . . . . . . . . . '59 '86 C.475 B.A. L.809 J.D. 1149 S. Hill St.
Platt, Daniel A. . . . . . . . . . . . . . . . . .'62 '87 C.188 B.S. L.262 J.D. 11355 W. Olympic Blvd.
Platt, Michael D. '60 '86
C.575 B.A. L.893 J.D. V.P. & Corp. Coun., Intl. Lease Fin. Corp.
**Platt, Robert H.** . . . . . . . . . . . . . . . . . . . . . . . '57 '83 C.188 B.S. L.262 J.D. [Manatt,P.&P.]
*PRACTICE AREAS: Labor/Employment Law; Sports; Litigation.

**Plattner, Glenn J.** . . . . . . . . . . . . . . . . . . . . . . . . .'63 '88 C.112 B.A. L.1067 J.D. [Solish,A.&G.]
*PRACTICE AREAS: Insurance Defense; Insurance Coverage; Business Litigation; Franchise Law; Real Estate Law.
**Plessala, Brian M.** . . . . . . . . . . . . . . . . '62 '89 C.1077 B.A. L.426 J.D. [Ⓐ Frederickson&Y.]
*PRACTICE AREAS: Business Litigation; Civil Litigation; Securities; Litigation.
Plevin, Toby L. . . . . . . . . . . . . . . . . . '48 '82 C.696 B.A. L.94 J.D. 10700 Santa Monica Blvd.
**Plinio, Steven J.** . . . . . . . . . . . . . . . . . . . . . . .'63 '88 C.165 B.A. L.597 J.D. [Ⓐ Manatt,P.&P.]
*PRACTICE AREAS: Music.
**Plonsker, Michael J.** . . . . . . . . . . . . . . . . . . . . . . '56 '81 C.477 B.B.A. L.339 J.D. [Lavely&S.]
*REPORTED CASES: Wood Newton v. Harry Thomason, et al., 22 F.3d 1455 (9th Cir. 1994).
*PRACTICE AREAS: Entertainment Litigation; Business Litigation; Right of Publicity and Privacy Law; Libel Law; Copyright Law.
**Ploscowe, Stephen A.**, (AVⓉ) '41 '65 C&L.188 B.S., LL.B.
(adm. in NJ; not adm. in CA) [Grotta,G.&H.]⊙
Plotkin, Jay J., (AV) . . . . . . . . . . . . . . . . . . .'38 '64 C.112 A.B. L.1066 LL.B. [Plotkin,M.&K.]
**Plotkin, Leo D., (P.C.)** . . . . . . . . . . . . . . . . . '56 '81 C.1044 B.A. L.1066 J.D. [Levy,S.&L.]
*PRACTICE AREAS: Creditors Rights Law; Real Estate Litigation; Copyright Litigation; Business and Commercial Litigation.
Plotkin, Michael M. . . . . . . . . . . . . . .'41 '66 C.112 B.S. L.1068 LL.B. 1801 Ave. of the Stars
**Plotkin, Steven** . . . . . . . . . . . . . . . . . '60 '86 C.112 B.A. L.1068 J.D. [Ⓐ Jeffer,M.B.&M.]
*PRACTICE AREAS: Trademark; Licensing; Copyright; Business Law.
Plotkin, Marutani & Kyriacou, Professional Corporation, (AV)
12650 Riverside Dr. (N. Hollywood)

**Plotkin, Michael E.**
**(See Pasadena)**

Plotkins, Albert C. . . . . . . . . . . . . . . . . . . . '45 '77 C.112 B.A. L.426 J.D. 3600 Wilshire Blvd.
**Plotkowski, Robert J.** . . . . . . . . . . . . . . . . . . .'62 '87 C.112 B.A. L.1066 J.D. [Troop M.S.&P.]
*PRACTICE AREAS: Real Estate Law; Environmental Law; General Business Law.
Pluim, Jan A. . . . . . . . . . . . . . . . . . . . . . . . . . '44 '74 C.800 B.S. L.426 J.D. Supr. Ct. J.
Plum, Stephen H., IV . . . . . . . . . . . . . . . . . . '57 '82 C&L.061 B.A. Paramount Pictures Corp.
**Plum, Timothy S.** . . . . . . . . . . . . . . . . . . . .'59 '85 C.800 B.A. L.770 J.D. [Ⓐ Sherwood&H.]
*PRACTICE AREAS: Real Estate Litigation; Business Litigation.
**Pluma, Gillian N.** . . . . . . . . . . . . . . . . . . . . . . .'63 '88 C.112 B.A. L.426 J.D. [Ⓐ Kirtland&P.]
**Poareo, Paul W.** . . . . . . . . . . . . . . . . . . . . .'50 '91 C.1131 B.A. L.1068 J.D. [Ⓐ Heller E.W.&M.]
**Pocaterra, Jan Long** . . . . . . . . . . . . . . . . . . . . .'50 '86 C.536 B.A. L.209 J.D. [Ⓐ Selman B.]
*PRACTICE AREAS: Insurance Coverage Law (including Environmental); Bad Faith; Appellate Law.
Pocrass, James L., (AV) . . . . . . . . . . . . . . . . .'47 '73 C.1077 B.S. L.426 J.D. [Shaffer,D.P.&G.]
Podbielski, Cheryl A. . . . . . . . . . . '58 '88 C.1097 B.A. L.809 J.D. 2121 Ave. of The Stars
Poe, Richard W. . . . . . . . . . . . . . . . . . . . . . '53 '78 C.893 B.A. L.309 J.D. 2144 Groveland Dr.
Poey, Dennis B. . . . . . . . . . . . . . . . . . . . . . . . '65 '90 C.112 B.A. L.809 J.D. Dep. Dist. Atty.
Poindexter, Gwendolyn Ryder . . . . . . . . . . . '54 '79 C.813 B.A. L.1065 J.D. Dep. City Atty.
Poindexter, Paul O. . . . . . . . . . . . . . . . . . . . . '45 '79 C.112 L.1137 J.D. Dep. City Atty.
**Poindexter, William M.**, (AV) . . . . . . . . . '25 '52 C.976 B.A. L.1066 J.D. [Poindexter&D.]
*PRACTICE AREAS: Probate; Trust Litigation; State and Local Tax.

**Poindexter & Doutré, Inc., (AV)**
**One Wilshire Building, Suite 2420, 624 South Grand Avenue, 90017-3325⊙**
**Telephone: 213-628-8297 Telecopier: 213-488-9890**
**William M. Poindexter; Alfred B. Doutré (1927-1980); Evan G. Williams; James P. Drummy; Jeffrey A. Kent; Bennett M. Sigmond; James W. Poindexter (Resident, San Francisco Office); Anthony J. Taketa;—Christine Kim; Mark A. Feldman. Of Counsel: Richard H. Patterson, Jr.**
**General Civil and Trial Practice. Corporation, Real Property, Insurance, Construction, Securities, Estate Planning, Trust, Probate, Federal, State and Local Tax Law.**
**Representative Clients: ASARCO; Braille Institute of America, Inc.; Westinghouse Electric.**
**Reference: Bank of California (Sixth/Flower).**
**San Francisco, California Office: 44 Montgomery Street, Suite 1300. Phone: 415-398-5811. Fax: 415-398-5808.**
***See Professional Biographies, LOS ANGELES, CALIFORNIA***

**Pointer, Karen E.** . . . . . . . . . . . . . '63 '94 C.426 B.S. L.1068 J.D. [Ⓐ Greenberg G.F.C.&M.]
*PRACTICE AREAS: Employment Law and Litigation.
**Poirier-Whitley, Kirstin D.** . . . . . . . . . . .'68 '94 C.112 B.A. L.1068 J.D. [Ⓐ Jones,D.R.&P.]
**Poitras, David M., (A Professional Corporation)** '62 '89
C.818 B.S.B.A. L.426 J.D. [Danning,G.D.&K.]
*LANGUAGES: French.
Polakov, Anthony S. . . . . . . . . . . . . . . . . . '56 '85 C.112 B.A. L.809 J.D. 11601 Wilshire Blvd.
**Polard, Steven G.** . . . . . . . . . . . . . . . . . . . . . . . . '54 '79 C.378 B.S.B. L.228 J.D. [Graham&J.]
*PRACTICE AREAS: Bankruptcy Law; Aviation Litigation; Business Litigation.
Polashuk, Robyn R. . . . . . . . . . . . . . . . . '65 '94 C.228 B.A. L.1068 J.D. 1800 Ave. of the Stars
**Polashuk, Stacie S.** . . . . . . . . . . . . . . .'70 '96 C.112 B.A. L.800 J.D. [Ⓐ Sonnenschein N.&R.]
**Pole, Debra E.**, (AV) . . . . . . . . . . . . . . . . '51 '77 C.216 B.A. L.260 J.D. [Brobeck,P.&H.]
*PRACTICE AREAS: Products Liability; Medical Devices; Pharmaceutical Litigation.
Polen, Jeri . . . . . . . . . . . . . . . . . . . . . . . . . . .'55 '82 C.1349 B.A. L.1067 J.D. Dep. Pub. Def.
**Polich, John E.** . . . . . . . . . . . . . . . . . . . . . . . '63 '95 C.684 B.A. L.800 J.D. [Ⓐ Sidley&A.]
**Polich, Theodore P., Jr.**, (AV) . . . . . . . . . . . '35 '61 C.813 B.A. L.800 J.D. [Morris,P.&P.]
Policzer, Milton A. . . . . . . . . '51 '75 C.597 B.S.J. L.1068 J.D. Los Angeles Herald Examiner

**Polin, Michael R. '59 '87 C.112 B.S. L.1136 J.D.**
**The Wilshire Landmark Building, 11755 Wilshire Boulevard Suite 1400, 90025-1520⊙**
**Telephone: 310-477-5455 Fax: 310-417-5058**
**Email: rmgn00a@prodigy.com**
***PRACTICE AREAS: International Business Law; Entertainment Law; Estate Planning; Business Law; Litigation.**
**International Business Law, Offshore Banking including the establishment of Foreign Corporation and Banking Relations, Estate Planning emphasizing Living Trusts and Wills, General Business Law, Entertainment Law, Sports Representation.**
**Santa Ana, California Office: 5 Hutton Centre, 11th Floor. Telephone: 714-445-9261. Fax: 714-825-8517.**
***See Professional Biographies, LOS ANGELES, CALIFORNIA***

Poliner, L. Joseph . . . . . . . . . . . . . . '34 '60 C.112 B.A. L.800 LL.B. 3055 Wilshire Blvd.
**Poliner, Phillip R.** . . . . . . . . . . . . . . . . . . . . . . '66 '91 C.112 B.A. L.809 J.D. [Ⓐ A.A.Sigel]
*PRACTICE AREAS: Civil Trial; Personal Injury; Medical Malpractice; Products Liability; Real Estate.

**Polinsky, David '61 '86 C.976 B.A. L.1068 J.D.**
**1901 Avenue of the Stars, Suite 200, 90067**
**Telephone: 310-553-0555 Fax: 310-203-8753**
***PRACTICE AREAS: Construction; General Business Litigation; Civil Litigation; Arbitration; Mediation.**
**Construction and General Business Litigation.**
***See Professional Biographies, LOS ANGELES, CALIFORNIA***

**Polish, James M.**, (AV) . . . . . . . . . . .'48 '73 C.112 A.B. L.1068 J.D. [Carlsmith B.W.C.&I.]
*PRACTICE AREAS: Commercial Litigation; Corporate Litigation; International Commercial Law.
**Polisoto, Catherine M.** . . . . . . . . . . . . . . . .'66 '91 C.188 B.S. L.112 J.D. [Ⓐ Konowiecki&R.]
*PRACTICE AREAS: Corporate; Health Care.
**Politis, John N.** . . . . . . . . . . . . . . . . . . . . . . . . '35 '69 C.870 B.S. L.1049 J.D. [Politis&P.]
*PRACTICE AREAS: Customs Law; International Trade.
**Politis, Nicholas J.** . . . . . . . . . . . . . . . . . . . . . .'58 '85 C.990 B.A. L.1148 J.D. [Politis&P.]
*PRACTICE AREAS: Customs Law; Commercial Insurance.

**Politis & Politis**
**865 S. Figueroa Street, Suite 1388, 90017**
**Telephone: 213-630-8800 Telecopier: 213-630-8818**

(This Listing Continued)

CAA317P

CALIFORNIA—LOS ANGELES MARTINDALE-HUBBELL LAW DIRECTORY 1997

**Politis & Politis (Continued)**

**Members of Firm: John N. Politis; Nicholas J. Politis.**
**Customs Law, International Trade Law, Insurance Defense, Business Litigation. General Civil Litigation, Commercial Litigation and Contracts.**
*See Professional Biographies, LOS ANGELES, CALIFORNIA*

Polito, Frank D. .................... '60 '86 C&L.276 B.A., J.D. [Gottesman&P.]
Polk, Michael S., (AV) .................... '50 '75 C.800 B.A. L.1068 J.D. [Polk,S.&P.]
Polk, Scheer & Prober, A Law Corp., (AV)
18425 Burbank Blvd. (Tarzana) (©San Rafael)
**Polkinghorn, William A., Jr.** '46 '71
C.813 B.A. L.1066 J.D. Sr. V.P. & Dep. Gen. Coun., Union Bk.
Pollack, Barry A. .................... '49 '75 C&L.107 B.A., J.D. [Adel&P.]
Pollack, Carol Wendelin .................... '48 '73 C.112 B.A. L.426 J.D. Sr. Asst. Atty. Gen.
**Pollack, Elon A.**, (AV) .................... '50 '73 C&L.861 B.A., J.D. [E.A.Pollack]
*PRACTICE AREAS: Customs Law; International Trade.
**Pollack, S. Thomas**, (AV) .................... '43 '70 C.103 A.B. L.569 J.D. [Irell&M.]

**Pollack, Elon A., Law Offices of, A Prof. Corp., (AV)**
**865 South Figueroa Street, Suite 1388, 90017**
**Telephone: 213-630-8888 Fax: 213-630-8890**
**URL: http://www.dutylaw.com**
**Elon A. Pollack;—Heather C. Litman.**
**Customs, International Trade Law and Related Matters.**
*See Professional Biographies, LOS ANGELES, CALIFORNIA*

Pollak, Howard A. .................... '65 '90 C.112 B.S. L.426 J.D. 2049 Century Park, E.
**Pollak, Michael M.**, (AV) .................... '53 '79 C.112 B.A. L.1067 J.D. [Pollak,V.&F.]

**Pollak, Vida & Fisher, (AV)**
**1801 Century Park East, 26th Floor, 90067**
**Telephone: 310-551-3400 Fax: 310-551-1036**
**Members of Firm: Michael M. Pollak; Scott J. Vida; Girard Fisher; Wayne D. Pariser; J. Susan Graham. Associates: Gerard A. Lafond, Jr.; Michael R. Nebenzahl; David A. Hadlen; Daniel P. Barer; Judy L. McKelvey; Lawrence J. Sher; Kathleen K. Andrews; Neil R. Anapol; Erica M. Broido; Nicole A. Greenwald.**
**Civil Litigation in State and Federal Trial and Appellate Courts, Insurance Coverage, Insurance Bad Faith, Casualty, Property, Governmental Tort Liability, Federal Civil Rights and Professional Negligence.**
**Representative Clients: Allstate Insurance Co.; Big Cities' Excess Pool ("BICEP"); City of Beverly Hills; Commercial Union Insurance Companies; County of Los Angeles.**
*See Professional Biographies, LOS ANGELES, CALIFORNIA*

**Pollard, Henry**, (AV) .................... '31 '54 C.563 A.B. L.178 J.D. [[C] Oberstein,K.&H.]
**Pollard, JoLynn M.** .................... '63 '88 C.1077 B.A. L.464 J.D. [[B] Long&L.]
Pollet, Andrew F., (AV) .................... '51 '77 C.800 B.S. L.1049 J.D. [Pollet&W.]
Pollet & Woodbury, A Law Corporation, (AV) .................... 10900 Wilshire Blvd.
**Polley, Terry L., (A Professional Corporation)**, (AV) '47 '73
C.112 A.B. L.945 J.D. [Ajalat,P.&A.]
*SPECIAL AGENCIES: Franchise Tax Board; Assessment Appeals Boards; State Board of Equalization; City Tax Boards; Employment Development Department.
*PRACTICE AREAS: State and Local Tax Law.
**Pollock, Elizabeth A.** .................... '56 '82 C.813 B.A. L.1068 J.D. [[B] Murchison&C.]
*LANGUAGES: German and Spanish.
*PRACTICE AREAS: Products Liability; Commercial Litigation.
**Pollock, John P.**, (AV) .................... '20 '49 C.813 A.B. L.309 J.D. [[C] Rodi,P.P.G.&C.]
**Pollock, Lorne M.** .................... '65 '92 C.012 B.A. L.029 LL.B. [[B] Wilson,E.M.E.&D.]
*PRACTICE AREAS: Civil Litigation; Real Estate Law; Premises Liability Law.
**Pollok, Julian A.**, (AV) .................... '42 '71 C.1077 B.A. L.1068 J.D. [J.A.Pollok]
Pollok, Stuart G. '63 '87 C.061 LL.B. L.276 LL.M.
(adm. in NY; not adm. in CA) V.P., Bus. Affairs & Spec. Proj., Prelude Pictures‡

**Pollok, Julian A., A Professional Corporation, (AV)**
**1000 Wilshire Boulevard, Suite 620, 90017**
**Telephone: 213-688-7795 Telecopier: 213-688-1080**
**Julian A. Pollok.**
**General Civil Trial, Commercial Litigation, Business Litigation including Contracts, Real Estate, and Unfair Competition in all State and Federal Courts.**
*See Professional Biographies, LOS ANGELES, CALIFORNIA*

Polsky, Barbara S. .................... '54 '79 C&L.477 B.A., J.D. 11355 W. Olympic Blvd.
**Polster, Lee M., (Professional Corporation)**, (AV) '48 '73
C.659 B.S. in Econ. L.809 J.D. [Resch P.A.&B.]
*PRACTICE AREAS: Corporate and Partnership Law; Securities Regulation; Business Law.
**Poltrock, Bruce D.** .................... '67 '92 C.800 B.S. L.767 J.D. [[B] Frandzel&S.]
Pomerance, Bradley E. .................... '65 '90 C.800 B.A. L.273 J.D. 333 S. Grand Ave.
Pomerance, Drew E. .................... '57 '81 C.112 B.A. L.1065 J.D. 10866 Wilshire Blvd.
**Pomerance, Jeffrey M.** .................... '61 '87 C.966 B.B.A. L.477 J.D. [[B] Foley L.W.&A.]
*PRACTICE AREAS: Business Law; Health Care Finance; Mergers and Acquisitions; Corporate Law.
Pomerantz, Andrew S. .................... '60 '90 C.112 B.A. L.809 J.D. 2049 Century Park E.
**Pomerantz, Glenn D.** .................... '58 '84 C.112 A.B. L.309 J.D. [Munger,T.&O.]
Pomerantz, Jason S. .................... '66 '91 C.112 B.A. L.426 J.D. [Dressler,R.&E.]
**Pomerantz, Jeffrey N.** .................... '65 '89 C&L.569 B.A., J.D. [Pachulski,S.Z.&Y.]
*REPORTED CASES: In re AEG Acquisition Corp.; In re F.A.B. Industries.
Pomerantz, Kimberly A. .................... '63 '88 C.800 B.A. L.809 J.D. 2049 Century Park E.

**Pomerantz, Leonard H., (AV) '28 '55 C.112 B.A. L.1068 J.D.**
**3700 Wilshire Boulevard, Suite 575, 90010**
**Telephone: 213-388-3253 Fax: 213-387-3348**
**Negligence and Products Liability Law. Civil and Trial Practice in all Courts.**

**Pomeroy, Charles H., IV** .................... '57 '88 C.1077 B.A. L.809 J.D. [McKenna&C.]
**Poms, William**, (AV) .................... '28 '59 C.128 B.S.M.E. L.276 J.D. [Oppenheimer P.S.] (Pat.)
*PRACTICE AREAS: Intellectual Property and International.

**Poms, Smith, Lande & Rose**
**(See Oppenheimer Poms Smith)**

**Ponce-Gomez, Diane S.** .................... '70 '96 C.112 B.A. L.1068 J.D. [[B] Arnold&P.]
*PRACTICE AREAS: Litigation.
**Poole, David S.** .................... '55 '80 C.112 B.A. L.800 J.D. [Danner&M.]
**Pope, Alexander H.**, (AV) .................... '29 '52 C&L.145 A.B., J.D. [Seyfarth,S.F.&G.]
*PRACTICE AREAS: Property Tax Law; Litigation; Administrative Law.
**Pope, Harold C.** .................... '41 '75 C.1042 B.A. L.602 J.D. [[B] Konowiecki&R.]
*PRACTICE AREAS: Health Care Law; Corporate Law; Real Estate Law.
**Popham, Mitchell J.** .................... '58 '86 C.112 B.A. L.426 J.D. [[B] Lord,B.&B.]
Popkin, Richard C. .................... '34 '64 C.705 B.S. L.800 LL.B. 5900 Wilshire Blvd.
**Popkoff, Burton R.**, (AV) .................... '42 '71 C.112 B.S. L.809 J.D. [Popkoff&S.]©

**Popkoff & Stern, (AV) [BB]**
**501 Shatto Place, Suite 100, 90020-1713©**
**Telephone: 213-389-1358; 389-2174 Fax: 213-380-4154**
**Members of Firm: Burton R. Popkoff (Certified Specialist, Estate Planning, Trust and Probate Law, The State Bar of California Board of Legal Specialization); Gary N. Stern.**
**Estate Planning, Probate, Tax and Business Litigation, Elder Law, Personal Injury and Malpractice Law.**
**Palm Springs, California Office: 225 South Civic Drive, Suite 212, 92262. Telephone: 619-322-8041.**

(This Listing Continued)

Popkoff & Stern (Continued)

**Poplawski, Edward G.** '57 '84 C.223 B.S.M.E. L.884 J.D.
[Pretty,S.&P.] (See Pat. Sect.)
*PRACTICE AREAS: Patents; Trademarks; Copyrights; Trade Secrets; Unfair Competition.
Popoola, Tayo A. .................... '55 '88 C.339 B.S. L.184 J.D. Dep. City Atty.
**Popovich, Jerry C.** .................... '65 '88 C&L.1137 B.S.L., J.D. [[B] Selman B.]
**Popovich, Lisa A.** .................... '60 '85 C.800 B.S. L.426 J.D. [[B] Paul,H.J.&W.]
Popper, Florence R. H. .................... '47 '72 C.659 B.A. L.1066 J.D. Calif. Appl. Project
**Porath, Sheri E.** .................... '65 '93 C.112 B.A. L.800 J.D. [[B] Greenberg G.F.C.&M.]
*PRACTICE AREAS: Litigation.
Porter, Calvin V., Jr. .................... '22 '52 C&L.215 LL.B. 3460 Wilshire Blvd.
Porter, Cary .................... '50 '80 C.112 B.A. L.809 J.D. U.C.L.A.
Porter, Gregory E. .................... '58 '88 C.112 L.990 J.D. 2056 Mandeville Canyon Rd.‡
Porter, Joann P. .................... '29 '59 C&L.800 B.A., LL.B. Dep. Dist. Atty.
**Porter, John E.** .................... '58 '83 C&L.813 B.S., J.D. [Paul,H.J.&W.]
**Porter, Paul M.** .................... '63 '91 C&L.426 B.A., J.D. [[B] Hill,F.&B.]
*PRACTICE AREAS: Business Litigation; Eminent Domain Litigation.
Porter, Verna L. .................... '41 '77 C.1097 B.A. L.809 J.D. 2500 Wilshire Blvd.
**Porterfield, Curtis D.** .................... '57 '81 C.280 A.B. L.880 J.D. [Troop M.S.&P.]
*PRACTICE AREAS: Insurance Coverage Litigation; Business & Entertainment Litigation.
Portillo, John A. .................... '54 '79 C&L.347 B.S., J.D. Dep. Dist. Atty.
**Posell, Richard E.**, (AV) .................... '41 '66 C.112 B.A. L.1066 J.D. [Greenberg G.F.C.&M.]
*PRACTICE AREAS: Entertainment; Litigation; Intellectual Property.
Posner, Ashley D. .................... '58 '82 L.1179 J.D. 10850 Wilshire Blvd.
**Posner, Harriet S.** .................... '60 '84 C.309 B.A. L.1068 J.D. [Skadden,A.S.M.&F.]
Posner, Laurence P. .................... '67 '94 C.1077 B.S. L.398 J.D. [[B] Posner&R.]
Posner, Michael P., (AV) .................... '40 '69 C.1043 B.A. L.426 J.D. [Posner&R.]
Posner & Rosen, P.C., (AV) .................... 3600 Wilshire Blvd.
Poss, Samuel, (AV) .................... '43 '79 C&L.569 B.A., J.D. 1154 Alvira St.
Post, Douglas F. .................... '57 '81 C.813 A.B. L.976 J.D. 1875 Century Pk. E.
**Post, J. Douglas** .................... '52 '78 C&L.813 B.A., J.D. [Arter&H.]
Potter, Howard F. .................... '30 '60 C.813 A.B. L.1068 LL.B. 5455 Wilshire Blvd.
**Potter, Katherine Cranston** '64 '90
C.112 B.A. L.800 J.D. [Celebrezze&W.] (©San Fran.)
**Potter, Kelley P.** .................... '66 '92 C.112 B.A. L.809 J.D. [[B] Arnold&P.]
**Potter, Nancy N.** .................... '54 '80 C.1168 B.A. L.813 J.D. [[B] Berger,K.S.M.F.S.&G.]
**Potts, Jerry R.** .................... '40 '74 C.1042 B.S.E. L.809 J.D. [Oppenheimer P.S.] (Pat.)
*PRACTICE AREAS: Patent Prosecution with emphasis on Computer and Integrated Circuit Technologies.
**Potts, Lee W.** .................... '— '86 C.768 B.A. L.1065 J.D. [Hennigan,M.&B.]
*PRACTICE AREAS: Commercial Litigation; Civil Rights; Defamation; First Amendment Litigation.
**Potts, Roy E.**, (AV) .................... '18 '52 C.679 B.S.M.E. L.976 LL.B. [Overton,L.&P.]
*PRACTICE AREAS: Labor Law; Literary Property Law; Business Litigation.
Poturica, Melanie M. .................... '54 '79 C.112 B.A. L.800 J.D. [Liebert,C.&F.]
**Poulson, Lynn O., (Mr.)**, (AV) .................... '38 '67 C.101 B.S. L.178 J.D. [Johnson,P.C.&S.]
*PRACTICE AREAS: Litigation; Corporate Law; Business; Real Estate.
**Powell, Barry E.**, (BV) .................... '48 '87 C.1077 B.A. L.426 J.D. [Grunfeld,D.L.&S.]
*PRACTICE AREAS: Customs Law.
Powell, Daniel P., (AV) .................... '52 '78 C.112 B.S. L.398 J.D. [West,P.&G.]
Powell, Elias, (AV) .................... '21 '46 C&L.472 J.D. 3225 Butler Ave.‡
**Power, John B.**, (AV) .................... '36 '62 C.605 A.B. L.569 J.D. [O'Melveny&M.]
*PRACTICE AREAS: General Corporate Law; Banking; Securities Law; Insolvency Matters; Mergers, Acquisitions and Divestitures.
**Powers, James C.**, (AV) .................... '30 '60 C.976 L.051 J.D. [Nossaman,G.K.&E.]
*PRACTICE AREAS: Litigation.
**Powers, John G., (A Professional Corporation)** '57 '80
C.763 B.S. L.770 J.D. [Farmer&R.]
*PRACTICE AREAS: Environmental; Corporate Real Estate; Land Use Law.
Powers, John M. .................... '54 '83 C.31 B.A. L.1009 J.D. Dep. Pub. Def.
**Powers, Michele A.** .................... '64 '94 C.604 B.A. L.966 J.D. [[B] Pircher,N.&M.]
*LANGUAGES: Spanish.
*PRACTICE AREAS: Civil Litigation; Water Law; Environmental Law.
Powers, Nancy A. .................... '53 '84 C.228 B.A. L.1068 J.D. 601 S. Figueroa St.
Powers, Robert C., (A Professional Corporation) '52 '78 C.1077 B.A. L.809 J.D.
4605 Lankershim Blvd., Ste 540 N. Hollywood
Powers, Susan M. .................... '57 '88 C.112 B.A. L.809 J.D. Dep. Dist. Atty.
Powers, Wm. C. .................... '13 '50 C.112 A.B. L.426 LL.B. 8330 Ramsgate Ave.
Poyourow, Robert, (AV) .................... '48 '74 C.112 B.A. L.1068 J.D. 600 Wilshire Blvd.
Pozorski, Edward G. .................... '38 '69 Principal Dep. Co. Coun.
Prager, Marvin, (AV) .................... '31 '59 C.112 B.S. L.1068 J.D. 11900 W. Olympic Blvd.
Prager, Susan Westerberg '42 '71
C.813 A.B. L.1068 J.D. Dean & Prof. of Law, Univ. of Calif.
**Praglin, Gary A.** .................... '55 '81 C.112 B.A. L.809 J.D. [Engstrom,L.&L.]
*PRACTICE AREAS: Products Liability; Professional Liability; General Trials.
Prague, Owen H. .................... '54 '81 C.183 B.A. L.818 J.D. 18425 Burbank Blvd. Suite, 622
**Praitis, Judith M.** .................... '62 '89 C.145 A.B. L.309 J.D. [Sidley&A.]
*LANGUAGES: Spanish.
*PRACTICE AREAS: Environmental Law.
**Prall, David S.** '63 '90 C.994 B.A. L.880 J.D.
(adm. in NY; not adm. in CA) [[B] Shearman&S.]
*LANGUAGES: Italian.
**Pramov, Henry P., Jr.** .................... '47 '74 C.276 A.B. L.128 J.D. [Rodi,P.P.G.&C.]
*PRACTICE AREAS: General Business, Tax and Real Estate.
**Prange, Lisa S.** .................... '70 '96 C.112 B.A. L.188 J.D. [[B] Latham&W.]
**Prata, Robert J.** .................... '65 '92 C.112 B.A. L.770 J.D. [[B] Hawkins,S.L.&B.]
Pratt, Catherine J. '62 '87 C.112 B.A. L.800 J.D.
V.P., Sr. Lit. Coun., PaineWebber, Inc.

**Pratt, Chad T-W '63 '90 C.770 B.A. L.426 J.D.**
**4929 Wilshire Boulevard, Suite 300, 90010©**
**Telephone: 213-936-9002 Fax: 213-938-6069**
**Civil Trial and Appellate Practice in State and Federal Courts. Landlord and Tenant Law, Uninhabitability, Labor Law, Family Law, Personal Injury, Premises Liability and Torts Law. Pasadena, California Office: 221 East Walnut Street, Suite 245. Telephone: 818-441-CHAD. Fax: 818-577-4561.**
*See Professional Biographies, LOS ANGELES, CALIFORNIA*

Praw, Albert Z., (AV) '48 '72
C.112 A.B. L.1068 J.D. Sr. V.P., Kaufman & Broad Home Corp.

**Pray, Price, Williams & Russell**
**(See Long Beach)**

**Preble, Laurence G.**, (AV) '39 '69
C.171 P.R.E. L.426 J.D. [O'Melveny&M.] (©New York, N.Y.)
*PRACTICE AREAS: Real Estate Law.
Pregerson, Dean D. .................... '51 '76 C.112 B.A. L.1067 J.D. U.S. Dist. J.
Preis, James J. .................... '52 '78 C.813 B.A. L.800 J.D. Mental Health Advocacy Servs., Inc.
**Prendergast, James D.** .................... '43 '74 C.112 A.B. L.1065 J.D. [Kelley D.&W.]
*PRACTICE AREAS: Commercial Law; Debtor-Creditor Law; Corporate Law.
**Prentice, Brian G.**, (AV) .................... '40 '66 C&L.800 A.B., LL.B. [[C] Sheppard,M.R.&H.]
*PRACTICE AREAS: Real Estate Law; Land Use; Finance Law; Environmental Law.

Prentice, Rebecca L. ....................'53 '82 C.267 B.A. L.188 J.D. 777 S. Figueroa St.
**Preonas, George E.** ....................'43 '68 C.813 B.A. L.477 J.D. [Seyfarth,S.F.&G.]
**Presant, Sanford C.**, (AVⓉ) ....................'52 '77 C.188 B.A. L.107 J.D. [Battle F.]
**Press, Anthony L.** ....................'58 '86 C.976 B.A. L.1068 J.D. [Morrison&F.]
*PRACTICE AREAS: Litigation.
**Press, Michelle R.** ....................'66 '92 C&L.94 B.S., J.D. [Ⓐ Daniels,B.&F.]
**Press, Stephen M.**, (AV) ....................'44 '75 C.112 B.S. L.809 J.D. [Dennison,B.&P.]
*PRACTICE AREAS: Insurance and Tort Defense; Business Litigation; Property Disputes; Uninsured Motorist Litigation.
**Prestholt, David A.** ....................'56 '83 C.112 B.A. L.1068 J.D. [Prestholt,K.F.&V.]⊙
*PRACTICE AREAS: Insurance Defense; Bad Faith; Trials.

**Prestholt, Kleeger, Fidone & Villasenor, (AV)** BR
**Suite 1600, 1055 West 7th Street, 90017⊙**
**Telephone: 213-895-4811 FAX: 213-895-4817**
**Members of Firm: David A. Prestholt; Kenneth S. Kleeger; Gary P. Fidone; Lisa A. Villasenor; Brian D. Holmberg; Willi H. Siepmann; David Crawford, III; Lisa L. Loveridge; Archie Chin; Robert J. Scott, Jr.; Avigal Horrow; Jamie Ann Louie; Robert S. Putnam; Arnie E. Goldstein; Brian J. Finn.**
**General Civil Trial Practice with emphasis on Insurance Litigation and Coverage Issues. Personal Injury, Casualty, Professional Negligence, Governmental Tort Liability and Insurance Company Practices and Procedures Law.**
**San Francisco, California Office: 989 Market Street, 6th Floor. Telephone: 415-267-6362. Fax: 415-267-6275.**

***See Professional Biographies, LOS ANGELES, CALIFORNIA***

**Prestidge, Myra J.** ....................'56 '84 C.1169 B.A. L.770 J.D. [W.D.Ross]⊙
*REPORTED CASES: City of Redwood City v. Dalton Construction Company, 221 Cal. App.3d 1570 (1990).
*PRACTICE AREAS: Municipal Law.
**Preston, John S.** ....................'47 '72 C.823 B.A. L.966 J.D. [Ⓒ J.M.Donovan]
*PRACTICE AREAS: Business Law; International Law.
Preston, Leslie J. ....................'43 '74 C.1077 B.A. L.1136 J.D. 2040 Ave of Stars
**Preston, Michael L.** ....................'64 '90 C.112 B.A. L.426 J.D. [Ⓐ Sullivan&C.]
**Preston, Scott** ....................'70 '95 C.477 A.B. L.309 J.D. [Ⓐ Sidley&A.]
*LANGUAGES: Spanish.

**Preston Gates & Ellis, (AV)**
**Suite 2100, 725 South Figueroa Street, 90017⊙**
**Telephone: 213-624-2395 Facsimile: 213-624-5924**
**Members of Firm: Jane H. Barrett; Roger Lane Carrick; Gregory Lawrence Evans; Howard A. Kroll; Philip Nelson Lee; John P. Petrullo; David B. Sadwick. Of Counsel: Elizabeth C. Green. Associates: Katherine M. Marelich; Gary Steven Sedlik; Mark B. Tuvim.**
**Languages: Chinese, French, German, Italian, Japanese, Portuguese, Russian, Spanish and Taiwanese.**
**General Practice.**
**Anchorage, Alaska Office: Suite 400, 420 L Street, 99501-1937. Telephone: 907-276-1969. Facsimile: 907-276-1365.**
**Coeur d'Alene, Idaho Office: 1200 Ironwood Drive, Suite 315. 83814. Telephone:208-667-1839. Facsimile: 208-765-2494.**
**Washington, D.C. Office: Preston Gates Ellis & Rouvelas Meeds, Suite 500, 1735 New York Avenue, N.W., 20006-4759. Telephone: 202-628-1700. Facsimile: 202-331-1024.**
**Portland, Oregon Office: 3200 US Bancorp Tower 111 S.W. Fifth Avenue, 97204-3688. Telephone: 503-228-3200. Facsimile: 503-248-9085.**
**Seattle, Washington Office: 5000 Columbia Seafirst Center, 701 Fifth Avenue. Telephone: 206-623-7580. Facsimile: 206-623-7022.**
**Spokane, Washington Office: 1400 Seafirst Financial Center, 601 West Riverside Avenue, 99201-0636. Telephone: 509-624-2100. Facsimile: 509-456-0146.**
**Hong Kong Office: 2901 Central Plaza, 18 Harbour Road, Hong Kong. Telephone: 852-2511-5100. Facsimile: 852-2511-9515.**

***See Professional Biographies, LOS ANGELES, CALIFORNIA***

**Pretsky, Helene E.** ....................'63 '87 C.112 B.A. L.1068 J.D. [Ⓐ Kinsella,B.F.&T.]
*PRACTICE AREAS: Corporate Law; Business Law; Intellectual Property Law.
**Pretty, Laurence H.**, (AV) '36 '69 C.054 B.S. L.273 J.D.
[Pretty,S.&P.] (See Pat. Sect.)
*PRACTICE AREAS: Patents; Trademarks; Copyrights; Unfair Competition; Litigation.

**Pretty, Schroeder & Poplawski, A Professional Corporation, (AV)** BR
**Suite 2000, 444 South Flower Street, 90071**
**Telephone: 213-622-7700 Telecopier: 213-489-4210**
**Laurence H. Pretty; Robert A. Schroeder; Edward G. Poplawski; Mark Garscia; Jeffrey F. Craft; Michael J. MacDermott; Suzanne R. Jones. Counsel: Richard A. Wallen. Of Counsel: Walton Eugene Tinsley;—Paul D. Tripodi, II; Marc H. Cohen; Keith A. Newburry; Sharon M. Fujita; J. Chris James; John A. Griecci; Anne Wang; Jeanine L. Hayes; Marc E. Hankin; Jeffrey A. Finn.**
**Patents, Trademarks, Copyrights and Unfair Competition Law. Litigation.**

***See Professional Biographies, LOS ANGELES, CALIFORNIA***

Price, Cornell J., (AV) ....................'43 '74 C.502 B.S.E.E. L.1068 J.D. [Ramsey&P.]
**Price, Ernest E.** ....................'62 '93 C.112 B.A. L.767 J.D. [Ⓐ Ropers,M.K.&B.]
*PRACTICE AREAS: General Civil Litigation; Environmental Coverage; Construction Defect; Real Property; Civil Rights.
Price, Jack T. ....................'18 '54 L.1001 LL.B. 304 S. Broadway
**Price, Kevin J.** ....................'69 '95 C&L.426 B.A., J.D. [Ⓐ La Follette,J.D.F.&A.]
*PRACTICE AREAS: Insurance Defense; General Product Liability.
Price, Michael G. ....................'37 '62 C.112 A.B. L.309 LL.B. Supr. Ct. Comr.
**Price, Phyllis Y.** ..... '61 '88 C.229 B.E.E. L.145 J.D. Sr. Pat. Atty., Hughes Aircraft Co.
*RESPONSIBILITIES: Trademark; Patent; Licensing; Copyright.
**Price, Scott** ....................'63 '89 C.877 B.S. L.188 J.D. [Ⓐ Cox,C.&N.]
**Price, Shirley M.** ....................'46 '83 C.112 B.A. L.800 J.D. [Loeb&L.]
*LANGUAGES: French and Russian.
*PRACTICE AREAS: Corporate; Banking; Finance Law.
Price, Stephen S. ....................'45 '78 C.557 B.A. L.1186 J.D. [Early,M.&P.]
**Price, Steven H.** ..... '62 '88 C.800 B.S. L.426 J.D. Assoc. Coun., Capital Grp. Cos., Inc.
*RESPONSIBILITIES: Trusts and Estates; General Corporate.
**Price, Susan E.** ....................'63 '89 C.222 B.A. L.464 J.D. [Ⓐ Parker S.]
**Price, William C.** ....................'56 '83 C.228 B.A. L.976 J.D. [Quinn E.U.&O.]
*REPORTED CASES: U.S. v. Pulido-Baquerizo, 800 F.2d 899 (9th Cir. 1986).
*PRACTICE AREAS: General Trial Practice; Employment; White Collar Crime; Appellate Litigation.
**Prickett, Pamela K.** ....................'54 '79 C&L.813 B.A., J.D. [Graham&J.]
*PRACTICE AREAS: Real Estate (Property) Law.
**Pridjian, John V.** ....................'64 '91 C&L.339 B.S., J.D. [Ⓐ Sidley&A.]
*LANGUAGES: French.
*PRACTICE AREAS: Tax.
Prietto, James Anthony ....................'59 '88 C.112 B.A. L.1065 J.D. 3255 Wilshire Blvd.
**Primiani, Marc S.**, (AV) ....................'54 '79 C.174 B.A. L.770 J.D. [Cohen P.&F.]
Prince, David L. ....................'58 '84 C.768 B.S. L.809 J.D. 1912 E. Vernon Ave.

**Prindle, Decker & Amaro**
**(See Long Beach)**

Pringle, John P. ....................'51 '76 C.800 B.S. L.809 J.D. [Roquemore,P.&M.]
**Pringle, Paul C.**, (AV) ..........'43 '69 C.197 A.B. L.477 J.D. [Brown&W.] (⊙San Fran.)
Prinz, Arno S. ....................'22 '60 C.800 L.809 LL.B. 3272 W. 6th St.
**Pritchard, Diane E.**, (AV) ..........'54 '81 C.588 B.A. L.569 J.D. [Ⓒ O'Melveny&M.]
*PRACTICE AREAS: Business Litigation.
**Pritchard, Peter Keith** ....................'64 '90 C.112 B.A. L.770 J.D. [Ⓐ Koletsky,M.&F.]
*PRACTICE AREAS: Construction Defect Insurance Defense.
Pritsker, Keith W., (AV) ....................'52 '79 C.112 B.A. L.809 J.D. Dep. City Atty.

Privett, Howard J., (AV) ....................'29 '58 C.990 L.1065 J.D. 600 Wilshire Blvd.
**Privette, Howard M.** ....................'64 '88 C.976 B.A. L.813 J.D. [Ⓐ Brobeck,P.&H.]
*PRACTICE AREAS: Securities Litigation; Commercial Litigation.
Prober, Dean R. ....................'56 '82 C.112 B.A. L.809 J.D. [Polk,S.&P.]
Probst, Robert R., (BV) ....................'16 '51 C.112 L.809 LL.B. 1901 Ave. of the Stars
Probstein & Weiner ....................1925 Century Pk., E.

**Proctor, Robert C., Jr., A Professional Corporation**
**(See Pasadena)**

**Propper, Grant E.**, (AV) ....................'33 '61 C.112 B.A. L.1068 LL.B. [Blum,P.&H.]
**Propper, Peggy A.** ....................'44 '88 C&L.1137 B.S., J.D. [Ⓐ Baker&H.]
*PRACTICE AREAS: Bankruptcy; Business.

**Proskauer Rose Goetz & Mendelsohn LLP, (AV)** BR
**2121 Avenue of the Stars, Suite 2700, 90067-3003⊙**
**Telephone: 310-557-2900 FAX: 310-557-2193**
**Email: info@proskauer.com URL: http://www.proskauer.com**
**Resident Partners: Howard D. Behar; Henry Ben-Zvi; Jeffrey A. Berman; Harold M. Brody; Scott P. Cooper; Thomas W. Dollinger; Howard D. Fabrick; Mitchell M. Gaswirth; Bernard D. Gold; Barry C. Groveman; Paul D. Rubenstein; David R. Scheidemantle; Marvin Sears; Lois D. Thompson; Martin S. Zohn. Special Counsel: Walter Cochran-Bond; Kenneth Krug; W. Herbert Young. Resident Associates: Aaron P. Allan; Christopher M. Brock; Yun Y. Choi; Nicholas P. Connon; James F. Dunn; Daniel E. Eaton; Steven J. Elkins; Alan H. Finkel; Maria E. Grecky; Gloria Ching-hua Jan; Elizabeth J. Kruger; Carol E. Kurtz; Erick Kwak; Dana Hirsch Lipman; David S. Lippman; Seth A. Miller; Gregory J. Patterson; Mary H. Rose; Jane E. Rudofsky; Lori E. Sambol; Christopher J. Tricarico; Tal O. Vigderson; Hao-Nhien Q. Vu; James M. Wakefield; Leslie A. Wederich; Scott J. Witlin.**
**General Practice.**
**New York, N.Y. Office: 1585 Broadway. Telephone: 212-969-3000.**
**Washington, D.C. Office: 1233 Twentieth Street, N.W., Suite 800. Telephone: 202-416-6800.**
**Boca Raton, Florida Office: One Boca Place, Suite 340 West, 2255 Glades Road. Telephone: 407-241-7400.**
**Clifton, New Jersey Office: 1373 Broad Street, P.O. Box 4444. Telephone: 201-779-6300.**
**Paris, France Office: Proskauer Rose Goetz & Mendelsohn, 9 rue Le Tasse. Telephone: (33-1) 44 30 25 30.**

***See Professional Biographies, LOS ANGELES, CALIFORNIA***

**Proudfoot, Don A., Jr.**, (AV) ....................'37 '64 C&L.813 A.B., J.D. [Graham&J.]
*PRACTICE AREAS: Litigation; Appellate Practice.
**Prough, Steven J.** ....................'66 '92 C.165 B.A. L.209 J.D. [Ⓐ Rexon,F.K.&H.]
*PRACTICE AREAS: Litigation.
**Prout, Maita Deal**, (AV) .......... '50 '81 C.112 B.A. L.1068 J.D. [Whitman B.A.&M.]
*PRACTICE AREAS: Bankruptcy; Commercial Law; Debtor and Creditor; Secured Transactions.
**Prouty, Erin L.** ....................'60 '86 C.800 B.A. L.1049 J.D. [Ⓐ Levinson,M.J.&P.]
Provencher, Lauri ....................'26 '77 L.1095 J.D. 2934 1/2 Beverly Glen Cir.‡
Provost, Norman J. ....................'38 '67 C&L.878 B.S., J.D. 633 W. 5th St.
Pruett, David P. ....................'62 '91 C.112 B.A. L.426 J.D. 3055 Wilshire Blvd.
**Pruetz, Adrian M.** ....................'48 '82 C.424 B.A. L.436 J.D. [Quinn E.U.&O.]
*REPORTED CASES: Constant v. Advanced Micro-Devices, Inc., 848 F.2d 1560 (Fed. Cir. 1988).
*PRACTICE AREAS: Intellectual Property, Complex Commercial and Construction Litigation.
Prusia, Tiffany J. ....................'67 '92 C.813 A.B. L.800 J.D. 801 S. Figueroa St.
**Prussin, Shari L.** '67 '93 C.188 B.S. L.659 J.D.
(adm. in NY; not adm. in CA) [Ⓐ Kelley D.&W.]
Pryce, Robert D. ....................'50 '84 C.112 M.P.A. L.61 J.D. [Barnes,M.&P.]
**Puebla, Debra R.** ....................'60 '86 C&L.188 B.A., J.D. [Sinnott,D.M.&P.]
*PRACTICE AREAS: Insurance Coverage Litigation; General Litigation.
Puette, Manning W., (BV) ....................'38 '71 C.885 B.S. L.284 J.D. 624 S. Grand Ave.
**Pugh, Jeffrey M.** ....................'61 '87 C.112 A.B. L.1065 J.D. [Kramer&G.]
*PRACTICE AREAS: Corporate Law; Art Law; Entertainment.
**Puglisi, Fred R.** ....................'60 '85 C.489 B.A. L.494 J.D. [Sheppard,M.R.&H.]
*PRACTICE AREAS: Litigation.
**Pugsley, Mark W.** ....................'66 '94 C.878 B.S. L.228 J.D. [Ⓐ Morgan,L.&B.]
Puig-Johnson, Elena M. ....................'— '80 C.1097 B.A. L.809 J.D. 205 S. Bway.
Pulliam, Karen A., (AVⓉ) ....................'50 '81 C.912 B.S. L.215 J.D. [Ⓒ Casterline&A.]
**Pulverman, Martin E.** ....................'53 '81 C.112 B.A. L.1065 J.D. [Meyers,B.&M.]
*PRACTICE AREAS: Litigation; Professional Liability; Product Liability; Appellate Practice.
Punter, Lawrence P. V. ....................'32 '73 C.415 B.A. L.329 J.D. Dep. City Atty.
Purcell, John G. ....................'32 '67 L.809 J.D. Claims Atty., Auto. Club of Southern Calif.
**Purcell, John S.** ....................'63 '92 [Quinn E.U.&O.]
**Purdy, Douglas C.**, (AV) ....................'44 '70 C.112 B.A. L.1068 J.D. [Morris,P.&P.]
Purdy, Geoffrey P. M. ....................'48 '75 C.426 B.S. L.1095 J.D. 2073 Grace Ave.
**Puretz, Dean M.** '56 '83 C.112 A.B. L.809 J.D.
Sr. Coun. & Asst. Secy., Transamerica Financial Servs.
*RESPONSIBILITIES: Compliance in US, UK and Canada.
**Purks, Darryl N.** ....................'62 '94 C.112 B.A. L.61 J.D. [Ibold&A.]
**Purtich, Richard R.**, (AV) .......... '— '77 C.112 A.B. L.1068 J.D. [King,P.H.P.&B.]
*PRACTICE AREAS: Business and Real Estate Litigation; Insurance Bad Faith; Unfair Insurance Practices.
Putkoski-Chodos, Gina Marie '57 '82 C.1097 B.A. L.426 J.D.
1559 S. Sepulveda Blvd.‡
**Putnam, Philip C., (P.C.)** ....................'54 '80 C&L.800 B.S., J.D. [Monteleone&M.]
*REPORTED CASES: Rain Bird Sprinkler Mfg. Corp. v. Franchise Tax Board (1991, 4th Dist.) 229 Cal. App. 3d 784, 280 Cal. Rptr. 362; Ronald v. 4'C's Electronic Packaging, Inc. (1985, 2d Dist.) 168 Cal. App. 3d 290, 214 Cal. Rptr. 225; County of Los Angeles v. Superior Court (T.G.I. Constr. Corp.) (1984, 2d Dist.) 155 Cal. App. 3d 798, 202 Cal. Rptr. 444.
*PRACTICE AREAS: Business/Corporate Law; Tax Law; Estate Planning; Employment Law; Construction.
**Putnam, Robert S.** ....................'53 '92 L.1026 J.D. [Prestholt,K.F.&V.]
*PRACTICE AREAS: Insurance Bad Faith; Construction Litigation; Civil Defense Litigation.
Pyes, Hugo H. ....................'16 '41 C&L.585 B.S.C., LL.B. 1259 S. Camden Dr.
**Pyke, Kathryn S.** ....................'58 '85 C.339 B.A. L.796 J.D. [Ⓐ Bonne,B.M.O.&N.]
**Pyon, Stevie** ....................'68 '95 C.154 B.A. L.800 J.D. [Ⓐ Sullivan&C.]
Qualls, Kriston D. ....................'57 '83 C.763 B.A. L.61 J.D. [Graven P.B.B.&Q.]
Quan, Carol ....................'52 '79 C.112 B.A. L.1067 J.D. Legal Div., Dept. of Transp.
**Quan, Richard K.**, (AV) ..........'36 '64 C.112 B.A. L.1068 LL.B. [Quan,C.K.Y.S.&H.]
*PRACTICE AREAS: Business Law; Real Estate; Banking.

**Quan, Cohen, Kurahashi, Yang, Scholtz & Hirano, A Professional Corporation, (AV)**
**777 South Figueroa Street, 38th Floor, 90017**
**Telephone: 213-892-7550 Telecopier: 213-892-7567**
**Richard K. Quan; Kenneth P. Scholtz; Arthur D. Cohen; Eileen Kurahashi; Richard P. Yang; Ronald M. Hirano.**
**General Civil and Trial Practice. Real Property, Banking, Commercial and Business Law and Related Litigation.**

***See Professional Biographies, LOS ANGELES, CALIFORNIA***

Quant, Kathy A. ....................'57 '85 C.1269 B.A. L.1238 J.D. Off. of Pub. Def.
Quarles, Alicia F. '49 '76 C.990 B.A. L.1068 J.D.
Exec. V.P. & Treas., EAC Construction Corp.
**Quateman, Lisa Greer**, (AV) ..........'53 '78 C.112 B.A. L.1068 J.D. [Quateman&Z.]

**Quateman & Zidell LLP, (AV)**
**1901 Avenue of the Stars, Suite 1505, 90067**
**Telephone: 310-556-7755 Fax: 310-556-7750**
**Lisa Greer Quateman; Steven H. Zidell;—Matthew P. Seeberger.**
**Corporate, Finance, Real Estate and Environmental. General Business.**

***See Professional Biographies, LOS ANGELES, CALIFORNIA***

CAA319P

CALIFORNIA—LOS ANGELES MARTINDALE-HUBBELL LAW DIRECTORY 1997

**Quattlebaum, Julian K., III**, (AVⓉ) '50 '77 C.1063 B.S. L.309 J.D.
(adm. in CO; not adm. in CA) Gen. Coun., Prime Ticket Networks, L.P.
**Quicksilver, William T., (P.C.)** ........... '52 '78 C.674 A.B. L.145 J.D. [Manatt,P.&P.]
*PRACTICE AREAS: Banking Law; Corporate Securities; Corporate Law.
**Quigley, Edward F., III** .................. '68 '94 C.112 B.A. L.1066 J.D. [Ⓐ Cox,C.&N.]
**Quigley, Lane**, (AV) .................. '49 '74 C.1077 B.S. L.426 J.D. [Liebman&R.]
*PRACTICE AREAS: Personal Injury Defense Law; Insurance Law; Trial Practice.
**Quillen, Gwyn** .................. '62 '88 C&L.800 B.A., J.D. [Alschuler G.&P.]
**Quinn, Carole A.** .................. '55 '91 C&L.608 B.A., J.D. [Ⓐ Hecker&H.]
**Quinn, Catherine J.** .................. '65 '95 C.1131 B.S. L.809 J.D. [Ⓐ Lewis,D.B.&B.]
Quinn, James H. .................. '09 '38 C.262 B.A. L.724 LL.B. 3333 Manning Ave.‡
Quinn, Jeffrey A. .................. '54 '79 C&L.477 A.B., J.D. 660 S. Figueroa St.
**Quinn, John B.**, (AV) .................. '51 '78 C.154 B.A. L.309 J.D. [Quinn E.U.&O.]⊙
*REPORTED CASES: Ficalora v. Lockheed Corp., 193 Cal. App. 3d 489 (1987); America's Cup Properties, Inc. v. America's Cup Club, Inc., 8 U.S.P.Q. 2d (BNA) 2025 (1988); Academy of Motion Picture Arts and Sciences v. Creative House Promotions, Inc., 944 F.2d 1446 (9th Cir. 1991) and 728 F. Supp. 1442 (C.D. Cal. 1989); Cinemateca Uruguaya v. Academy of Motion Picture Arts and Sciences, 826 F.Supp. 323 (C.D.Cal. 1993).
*PRACTICE AREAS: Employment; Intellectual Property; Unfair Competition; Real Estate; General Commercial Litigation.
**Quinn, John J.**, (AV) .................. '32 '59 C&L.800 A.B., J.D. [Arnold&P.]
*PRACTICE AREAS: Litigation.
**Quinn, John J.** '23 '59 C.285 A.B. L.276 J.D.
(adm. in DC; not adm. in CA) [Ⓒ Coleman&W.]
**Quinn, John J.**, (AVⓉ) .................. '50 '76 C.4 B.A. L.982 J.D. [Riordan&M.]
*PRACTICE AREAS: Trial Practice; White Collar Criminal Fraud.
**Quinn, Teresa M.**, (AV) .................. '52 '79 C.668 B.A. L.94 J.D. [Pillsbury M.&S.]
**Quinn, Tracey A.** .................. '66 '91 C.881 A.B. L.800 J.D. [Ⓐ Bryan C.]
*PRACTICE AREAS: Labor and Employment Law.

**Quinn Emanuel Urquhart & Oliver, LLP, (AV)**
**865 South Figueroa Street, 10th Floor, 90017⊙**
**Telephone: 213-624-7707 Telecopier: 213-624-0643**
**Members of Firm: John B. Quinn; Dale H. Oliver; A. William Urquhart; Gary A. Feess; Eric Emanuel; Steven G. Madison; Phyllis Kupferstein; David W. Quinto; Karen A. Rooney; William C. Price; Adrian M. Pruetz; Richard A. Schirtzer; Dominic Surprenant; Douglas A. Kuber; Scott B. Kidman; Ann Kotlarski; Charles K. Verhoeven; John P. D'Amato. Of Counsel: David C. Henri. Associates: Harold W. Hopp (Resident, Palm Desert, California); Kurt Michael Chen; Arpie Balekjian; Steven M. Anderson; Warrington S. Parker; Christopher Tayback; Randa A. F. Osman; William O. Stein; Kimberly S. Stenton; John S. Purcell; Jessica M. Neilson; Samuel Brooks Shepherd; Tricia J. Hartman; Rebecca Delfino; John R. Call; David J.P. Kaloyanides; Marshall M. Searcy; James J. Webster; Susan L. Barna; Grady Lee White; Lee J. Papageorge; Anna Y. Joo; Gary H. Loeb; Paul E. Van Horn (Not admitted in CA); Linda J. Kim; Nadia M. Bishop; Kristin L. Wetenkamp; Paul S. Chan; Scott R. Emery; Michael Ernest Williams; Adam D. Samuels.**
**Business Litigation and Trial Practice, including Antitrust; Banking; Construction; Copyright, Trademark and Patent Litigation; Employment; ERISA; Government Contracts; Health Care; Intellectual Property; Product Liability; Real Estate; Securities; Unfair Competition; White Collar Crime.**
**Representative Clients: Academy of Motion Picture Arts and Sciences; American Medical International, Inc.; Bell & Howell; Progressive Savings Assn.; Oak Tree Savings and Loan Association; Avery Dennison; Sizzler International, Inc.; Sumitomo Trust and Banking Co., Ltd.; Jupiter Hospital Corp.; Landmark Land Co., Inc.; Lockheed Corp.; Mattel, Inc.; The Ralph M. Parsons Co.**
**Reference: Citibank Corp.**
**Palm Desert, California Office: 74-090 El Paseo, Suite 101. Telephone: 619-340-2276. Telecopier: 619-346-1368.**

***See Professional Biographies, LOS ANGELES, CALIFORNIA***

Quinones, Connie R. .................. '64 '90 C.112 B.A. L.1137 J.D. Dep. Pub. Def.
Quint, Wilbur E., (AV) .................. '14 '38 C.860 A.B. L.309 LL.B. [W.E.Quint]
Quint, Wilbur E., P.C., (AV) .................. 530 Levering Ave.
**Quinto, David W.** .................. '55 '82 C.31 B.A. L.309 J.D. [Quinn E.U.&O.]⊙
*LANGUAGES: Spanish.
*REPORTED CASES: Quinto v. Legal Times of Washington, Inc., 506 F. Supp. 554 and 511 F. Supp. 579 (1981); Ficalora v. Lockheed Corp., 193 Cal. App. 3d 489 (1987); America's Cup Properties, Inc. v. America's Cup Club, Inc., 8 U.S.P.Q. 2d (BNA) 2025 (1988); Academy of Motion Picture Arts and Sciences v. Creative House Promotions, Inc., 944 F.2d 1446 (9th Cir. 1991) and 728 F. Supp. 1442 (C.D. Cal. 1989); Cinemateca Uruguay v. Academy of Motion Pictures Arts and Sciences, 826 F.Supp. 323 (C.D. Cal. 1993).
*PRACTICE AREAS: Copyright and Trademark; Real Property Litigation.
**Quisenberry, John N.**, (AV) .......... '42 '80 C.871 B.S. L.1068 J.D. [Quisenberry&B.]

**Quisenberry & Barbanel, (AV)**
**2049 Century Park East Suite 2200, 90067⊙**
**Telephone: 310-785-7966 FAX: 310-785-0254**
**John N. Quisenberry; Alan H. Barbanel; Stephen D. Treuer. Associates: Brian S. Kabateck; Amy Dantzler; Terry R. Bailey; Ora D. Kramer; Jenny Y. Li; David C. Parisi; Kathryn Paige Fletcher; Barbara Ciolino; Susan E. Abitanta; Phyllis J. Bersch; John R. Lisenbery; Carolyn Pierce Bell; Joshua A. Gratch; Derek W. Stark. Of Counsel: John A. Graniez.**
**Civil Litigation practice in State and Federal Courts, Trials and Appeals. Insurance Coverage and Litigation, including Casualty, Property and Environmental Claims. Business and Commercial Litigation. Unfair Competition and Business Torts Litigation.**
**San Diego, California Office: Emerald Shapery Center, 402 West Broadway, Suite 400. Telephone: 619-595-4866. Fax: 619-595-3166.**

***See Professional Biographies, LOS ANGELES, CALIFORNIA***

**Quittner, Arnold M.**, (AV) ....... '27 '52 C.1250 B.S. L.426 J.D. [Ⓒ Pachulski,S.Z.&Y.]
Quock, Kevin J. ............ '59 '88 C.1042 B.S. L.1137 J.D. 777 S. Figueroa St., 38th Fl.
**Raanan, Uzzi O.** .................. '66 '92 L.464 J.D. [Ⓐ Manning,M.&W.]
*LANGUAGES: Hebrew.
**Rabassa, Maria M.** .................. '64 '90 C.309 B.A. L.1066 J.D. [Ⓐ Mayer,B.&P.]
*LANGUAGES: Spanish.
*PRACTICE AREAS: Real Estate Law.
Rabaya, Violet C. .................. '49 '76 C.112 B.A. L.1066 J.D. 2029 Century Park E.
Rabichow, Phillip H., (BV) .................. '43 '72 C.339 B.S. L.1068 J.D. Dep. Dist. Atty.
**Rabin, Jeffrey A.** .................. '56 '81 C.112 B.A. L.1066 J.D. [Richards,W.&G.]
*PRACTICE AREAS: Real Property Law; Business Law.
**Rabinovitz, Joel, (P.C.)**, (AV) .................. '39 '63 C.188 A.B. L.309 LL.B. [Irell&M.]
**Rabkin, Michael W.** .................. '62 '88 C.112 B.A. L.800 J.D. [Wolf,R.&S.]
*PRACTICE AREAS: Community Association Law; Real Estate; Business Law.
Rabkin, Richard H. .................. '52 '80 C.112 B.A. L.1148 J.D. [Ⓐ Chase,R.D.&B.]
**Rabow, Jerome A.**, (AV) .................. '37 '61 C&L.309 A.B., J.D. [De Castro,W.&C.]
*PRACTICE AREAS: Probate Law; Trusts Law; Estate Planning Law.
**Racine, Scott H.**, (AV) ............ '51 '78 C.98 B.A. L.990 J.D. [Weinstein,B.R.H.&C.]
*PRACTICE AREAS: Tax; Business Law; Business Transactions.
**Rackliffe, Gail D.** .................. '55 '80 C.605 B.A. L.809 J.D. [Ⓐ Bragg,S.S.&K.]
*PRACTICE AREAS: Workers Compensation Law.
**Radcliff, Jules G., Jr.** .... '47 '76 C.1077 B.S. L.1068 J.D. [Radcliff,F.&D.] (⊙San Fran.)

**Radcliff, Frandsen & Dongell, (AV)** BR
**40th Floor, 777 South Figueroa Street, 90017⊙**
**Telephone: 213-614-1990 Facsimile: 213-489-9263**
**Members of Firm: Jules G. Radcliff, Jr.; Russell Mackay Frandsen; Richard A. Dongell. Of Counsel: Tal Clifton Finney. Associates: Francis P. Aspessi; Ruben A. Castellon; William W. Funderburk, Jr.; Jeffrey A. Gagliardi; David K. Lee; Maria Anna Mancini; Jeffrey C. Mayes; Marisa A. Moret; Daniel E. Park; Scott D. Pinsky; Eric H. Saiki; Steve R. Segura; Glenn M. White.**
**General Civil, Trial and Appellate Practice in all State and Federal Courts, Corporate, Environmental, Administrative, Regulatory, Telecommunications, Real Estate, Insurance, Professional Liability,**

(This Listing Continued)



**Radcliff, Frandsen & Dongell (Continued)**

**Trademark and Trade Name, Competitive Business Practices, Fiduciary, Financial Institutions, Securities and Finance, Commercial, International, Tax, Construction, Labor and Employment, Employment Benefits, Product Liability.**
**San Francisco, California Office: 88 Kearny Street, Suite 1475. Telephone: 415-399-8393. Facsimile: 415-989-5465.**
**Rome, Italy Office: Via Tacito, 7. Telephone: (39) 06-323-5588. Facsimile: (39) 06-324-3392.**

***See Professional Biographies, LOS ANGELES, CALIFORNIA***

**Rader, Alan**, (AV) .................. '44 '70 C.112 B.A. L.813 J.D. [O'Melveny&M.]
*PRACTICE AREAS: Intellectual Property Litigation; Music and General Business Litigation.
Rader, Robert H. G. .................. '67 '94 C&L.309 B.A., J.D. 555 W. 5th St.
Rader, Stephen P. .................. '55 '81 C&L.800 B.S., J.D. Bear, Stearns & Co., Inc.
**Raders, John M.**, (AV) ............ '53 '79 C&L.426 B.A., J.D. [Ⓒ Sedgwick,D.M.&A.]
**Radick, Neil F.** .................. '67 '93 C.597 B.A. L.800 J.D. [Ⓐ Liner,Y.&S.]
*PRACTICE AREAS: Financial Services; Insolvency.
Radin, Scott M. ........... '59 '89 C.112 B.A. L.809 J.D. 1999 Ave. of the Stars, 27th Fl.
Radon, Jenik .... '46 '72 C.178 B.A. L.813 J.D. 2029 Century Pk., E. (⊙New York, N.Y.)
**Radovich, David A.** .................. '57 '88 C.766 B.A. L.426 J.D. [Musick,P.&G.]
*PRACTICE AREAS: Litigation.
**Rae, Matthew S., Jr.**, (AV) ............ '22 '48 C&L.228 A.B., LL.B. [Darling,H.&R.]
*PRACTICE AREAS: Estate Planning Law; Trust Law; Probate Law.
Raeder, Myrna, (AV) .................. '47 '72 C.331 B.A. L.569 J.D. 15498 Hamner
Rafeedie, Edward .................. '29 '60 C&L.800 B.S.L., J.D. U.S. Sr. Dist. J.
**Rafeedie, Fredrick A.** .................. '62 '88 C.659 B.A. L.800 J.D. [Jones,B.S.A.&F.]
*PRACTICE AREAS: Securities; Business Litigation; Real Estate; Appellate Practice.
Raffalow, Richard E. .................. '49 '75 C.1029 B.A. L.767 J.D. [Silva,C.&R.]
**Rafferty, Gary L.** ........... '47 '72 C.800 A.B. L.1065 J.D. Coun., Hughes Aircraft Co.
Rafferty, John T. .................. '46 '74 C&L.823 A.B., J.D. Mun. Ct. Comr.
Rafferty, Owen P., (AV) .................. '20 '50 C&L.426 B.S. P.O. Box 90958
Rafferty, Susan Dianne .................. '61 '86 C.108 B.S. L.345 J.D. Coopers & Lybrand
Raft, David B. .................. '65 '89 C.112 B.A. L.809 J.D. [Frank,G.&S.]
**Rafter, John A., Jr.** ........... '56 '86 C.602 B.S. L.426 J.D. [Lyon&L.] (See Pat. Sect.)
*PRACTICE AREAS: Patent; Intellectual Property.
Ragsdale, Fred T. .................. '45 '72 C.426 B.A. L.1066 J.D. 3540 Wilshire Blvd.
Ragsdale, Noel M. '44 '77 C.681 A.B. L.1066 J.D.
Prof, of Law, Univ. of Southern Calif.
Rahmaty, Alireza .................. '40 '92 C.1137 B.A. L.1190 J.D. 3540 Wilshire Blvd.
Rahnama, Roshi .................. '67 '92 C.112 B.S. L.426 J.D. 3435 Wilshire Blvd.
**Raidy, Cherie S.** .................. '56 '81 C.800 B.A. L.809 J.D. [Ⓐ D.B.Bloom]
**Railo, Matt J.** .................. '69 '93 C.800 B.S. L.1068 J.D. [Ⓐ Mitchell,S.&K.]
*LANGUAGES: Finnish, German.
*PRACTICE AREAS: Litigation.
Raineri, Mark B .................. '61 '88 C.112 A.B. L.1068 J.D. U.S. S.E.C.
Raines, Andrew H. .................. '57 '84 C.674 A.B. L.276 J.D. [Jacob&P.]
Raisin, Bradley A. ............ '47 '75 C.112 B.A. L.1068 J.D. 10100 Santa Monica Blvd.
Raiskin, Daniel L., (AV) .................. '47 '72 C.1350 B.A. L.1009 J.D. [Raiskin&R.]
Raiskin & Revitz, (AV) .................. 10390 Santa Monica Blvd., 4th Fl.
Raizman, David H. '61 '87 C.881 A.B. L.178 J.D.
1800 Ave. of the Stars, Suite 900 (Century City)
Rake, Jeffrey P. .................. '68 '93 C.178 A.B. L.1066 J.D. 1800 Ave. of the Stars
**Rakow, J. Jay**, (AV) ........ '53 '78 C.569 B.A. L.188 J.D. [Christensen,M.F.J.G.W.&S.]
*PRACTICE AREAS: Entertainment Law; Litigation.
**Raleigh, John K.** .................. '61 '88 C.800 B.A. L.426 J.D. [Williamson,R.&D.]
*PRACTICE AREAS: Insurance Defense; Professional Malpractice; Construction Defect; Products Liability; Insurance Coverage.
**Rallis, Dean G., Jr.**, (BV) .................. '55 '80 C&L.800 B.S.B.A., J.D. [Baker&H.]
*PRACTICE AREAS: Insolvency Law; Bankruptcy Litigation; Reorganization Law; Secured Transactions; Real Estate Finance.
Ralph, Roberta .................. '26 '60 C.112 B.A. L.1068 LL.B. Supr. Ct. J.
**Ram, Michael J.** .... '40 '72 C.390 B.S.Ch.E. L.776 J.D. [Arant,K.L.&R.] (See Pat. Sect.)
*PRACTICE AREAS: Domestic and International Patent Prosecution; Domestic and International Trademark Prosecution; Trade Secrets; Medical Patents and Technology; Licensing.
**Ramer, Hayley E.** .................. '69 '94 C.1036 B.A. L.1292 J.D. [Wynne S.I.]
*PRACTICE AREAS: Bankruptcy.
**Ramey, John F.** .................. '63 '88 C.280 A.B. L.896 J.D. [Dale,B.&H.]
*PRACTICE AREAS: Medical Malpractice; Insurance Defense.
Ramirez, Bonnie C. ....... '42 '85 C.605 B.A. L.426 J.D. Constitutional Rights Foundation
Ramirez, Edith .................. '68 '93 C&L.309 A.B., J.D. 333 S. Grand Ave.
**Ramirez, Eugene P.** .................. '60 '88 C.1042 B.A. L.1148 J.D. [Manning,M.&W.]
*PRACTICE AREAS: Police Civil Liability Defense; Civil Litigation; Public Entity Defense; Police Canine Litigation.
Ramirez, Nancy '64 '91 C.112 A.B. L.309 J.D.
Mexican Amer. Legal Def. & Educ. Fund
**Ramirez, Nancy Sandberg** .......... '45 '87 C&L.1109 B.S.L., J.D. [Ⓐ Goldsmith&B.]
*PRACTICE AREAS: Probate; Guardianship and Conservatorship; Estate Planning; Wills; Trusts and Estates.
**Ramirez, Shirley D.** .................. '— '91 C.605 B.A. L.1068 J.D. [Ⓐ Frandzel&S.]
*LANGUAGES: Spanish.
*PRACTICE AREAS: Bankruptcy; Commercial Litigation.
**Ramniceanu, Nicolas** .................. '57 '84 C.31 B.A. L.813 J.D. [Resch P.A.&B.]
*LANGUAGES: French.
*PRACTICE AREAS: Real Estate; Business Law.
**Ramos, Andrea V.** .................. '66 '92 C.36 B.A. L.800 J.D. [Ⓐ Tuttle&T.]
*LANGUAGES: Spanish.
Ramos, Rene A. .................. '55 '81 C.112 B.A. L.1068 J.D. 3435 Wilshire Blvd.
Ramos, Robert Troy .................. '64 '94 444 S. Flower St., Ste. 2000
**Ramsden, Mary K.**, (AV) .......... '49 '81 C.112 A.B. L.426 J.D. [Ⓐ Hoffman,S.&W.]
*PRACTICE AREAS: Estate Planning Law; Probate Law; Trust Law.
**Ramsey, Christopher P.**, (AV) ......... '52 '77 C.112 B.A. L.1065 J.D. [Ramsey,B.&D.]
*PRACTICE AREAS: Municipality; Products Liability; General Negligence; Workers' Compensation Defense.
Ramsey, Edwin P. '17 '52 C&L.623 A.B., LL.B.
(adm. in OK; not adm. in CA) P.O. Box 49736‡
**Ramsey, Jerry A.**, (AV) ............ '36 '65 C.1097 B.A. L.1068 J.D. [Engstrom,L.&L.]
*PRACTICE AREAS: Insurance Casualty Defense; Insurance Policy Interpretation; Bad Faith Litigation; Civil Trials.
**Ramsey, Patrick A.** .................. '50 '76 C&L.800 B.A., J.D. [Paul,H.J.&W.]
Ramsey, Robert, Jr. .................. '40 '73 C.1042 B.A. L.1065 J.D. [Ramsey&P.]

**Ramsey, Bronstein & Dayton, (AV)**
**5959 West Century Boulevard, Suite 1410, 90045**
**Telephone: 310-641-8900 FAX: 310-641-7377**
**Members of Firm: Christopher P. Ramsey; John D. Bronstein; Lee W. Dayton. Associates: Alan L. Sobel. Of Counsel: Gregg H. Robin.**
**General Civil Litigation Practice, Products Liability, Tractor/Trailer Litigation, Construction Litigation, Drug Product Liability, Automotive Dealer Litigation, Workers' Compensation.**

***See Professional Biographies, LOS ANGELES, CALIFORNIA***

Ramsey & Price, (AV) .................. 727 W. 7th St.
Ramseyer, John Allen .................. '59 '88 C.37 B.S. L.940 J.D. Dep. Dist. Atty.

**Ramseyer, Lowell M.**, (AV) ...........'33 '65 C&L.800 B.S., J.D. [Harrington,F.D.&C.]
*PRACTICE AREAS: Professional Negligence Law (Medical Malpractice Law); Personal Injury Defense Law; Products Liability Law.
**Ramseyer, William L.** ...............'50 '80 C.112 B.S. L.800 J.D. [Pachulski,S.Z.&Y.]
**Rand, David E.**, (AV) ...................'36 '62 C.112 B.A. L.309 J.D. [Minton,M.&R.]
*PRACTICE AREAS: Corporation Law; Estate Planning; Trust and Probate Law; Real Estate Law; Business Law.
**Randall, David A.** .............'63 '91 C.37 B.S. L.36 J.D. [Lyon&L.] (See Pat. Sect.)
*PRACTICE AREAS: Patent, Trademark, Copyright, Unfair Competition; Intellectual Property.
Randall, Karen ...............'53 '76 C.881 B.A. L.1068 J.D. 1999 Ave. of the Stars
**Randolph, Jane Ellen** ............... '62 '88 C.172 B.A. L.464 J.D. [Anderson,M.&C.]
**Rank, Peter C.**, (AV) ...............'38 '63 C.813 A.B. L.1066 LL.B. [Konowiecki&R.]
*PRACTICE AREAS: Health Care Law; General Business; Government; Corporate; Environmental Law.
**Rankin, Craig M.** ................ '65 '91 C.959 B.S. L.436 J.D. [Levene,N.&B.]
*PRACTICE AREAS: Bankruptcy.
Ransohoff, Steven A. ...............'58 '83 C.881 A.B. L.1065 J.D. Film Finances, Inc.
**Ransom, Sonia J.** ...................'52 '92 C.112 B.A. L.426 J.D. [Kane,B.&B.]
*PRACTICE AREAS: Real Estate; Redevelopment Law; Administrative Law.
**Rapaport, Mark S.** ...................'47 '73 C&L.966 B.A., J.D. [Morgan,L.&B.]
**Rapoport, Gregg A.** ...................'62 '88 C.112 B.A. L.1068 J.D. [Baker&H.]
*LANGUAGES: Russian.
*PRACTICE AREAS: Business and Real Estate Litigation.

**Rapore and Lowe**
**(See Santa Monica)**

Rappaport, Andrew ......'55 '80 C.112 B.A. L.1068 J.D. 10 Universal City Plaza, 28th Fl.
**Rappaport, Lary A.**, (AV) ........'54 '79 C.112 A.B. L.1067 J.D. [McCambridge,D.&M.]
Rappaport, Michael D. '43 '68 C&L.966 B.S., J.D.
(adm. in WI; not adm. in CA) Asst. Dean, U.C.L.A. Sch. of Law
**Rappel, Marc W.** ...................'56 '81 C.802 B.A.S. L.145 J.D. [Latham&W.]
**Rappeport, Ira J.** ...............'54 '78 C.910 B.A. L.884 J.D. [McDermott,W.&E.]
Rasch, Edward B. ...................'34 '66 C.823 A.B. L.800 J.D. [E.B.Rasch]
Rasch, Edward B., A Professional Corporation ...............1464 Comstock Ave.
Rash, Carol ...................'59 '84 C.112 B.A. L.1065 J.D. Dep. Dist. Atty.
Rashman, Richard ...............'47 '71 C.112 B.A. L.1068 J.D. 3630 S. Sepulveda Blvd.
Raskin, Edw. M., (AV) ...................'10 '33 C.113 L.809 12851 Evanston St.
Raskin, Gary S. ...................'67 '93 C.112 B.A. L.770 J.D. [Plotkin,M.&K.]
**Raskin, Jeffrey S.** ...................'64 '93 C.112 B.A. L.770 J.D. [Reznik&R.]
*PRACTICE AREAS: Environmental Litigation; Real Estate Litigation; Business Litigation.
**Rasmussen, Denise Kabakow** ......'65 '91 C.112 B.A. L.426 J.D. [Wilson,E.M.E.&D.]
**Rasmussen, Halbert B.** ...............'59 '83 C.112 A.B. L.426 J.D. [Manning,L.B.&B.]
*PRACTICE AREAS: Automotive Dealer Law; Civil Trial; Business Purchase and Sales; Corporation; Association and Commercial Law.
**Rasmussen, Richard G.** ............... '58 '87 C.1259 B.A. L.426 J.D. [Argue P.H.&M.]
*PRACTICE AREAS: Real Estate; Finance; Business Transactions.
**Rath, Howard G., Jr., (P.C.)**, (AV) ..... '31 '59 C.112 B.S. L.800 J.D. [Lewis,D.B.&B.]
**Ratinoff, Joanne D.** ................... '53 '78 C.112 B.A. L.426 J.D. [Freid&G.]
*PRACTICE AREAS: Family Law.
**Ratinoff, Marisa S.** ...............'65 '91 C.770 Bs.C. L.602 J.D. [Jackson,L.S.&K.]
Ratliff, Barbara Kay ...................'45 '73 C.886 B.S. L.976 J.D. 880 W. 1st St.
**Rattet, Gary S.**, (AV) ...................'53 '79 C.154 B.A. L.93 J.D. [Gray,Y.D.&R.]
*PRACTICE AREAS: Business Law; Labor and Employment Law; Products Liability.
**Ratz, Kathleen M.** ................... '69 '94 C&L.494 B.S., J.D. [Sheppard,M.R.&H.]
*PRACTICE AREAS: Litigation.
Ratzky, Howard ................... '39 '81 C.1097 B.S. L.1148 J.D. 1359 W. Temple St.
**Rau, Robert W.**, (AV) ...................'36 '64 C.112 B.A. L.1068 J.D. [Gilbert,K.C.&J.]
**Rauch, David S.** ...................'64 '91 C.197 B.A. L.1068 J.D. [Pillsbury M.&S.]
**Rawles, Douglas C.** ................... '63 '91 C.170 B.A. L.767 J.D. [Brobeck,P.&H.]
*PRACTICE AREAS: Intellectual Property and Business Litigation.
**Rawlings, Douglas M.** ...................'47 '74 C.228 B.A. L.976 J.D. [Belin R.&B.]
*LANGUAGES: Finnish, German (Read).
**Rawls, John C., III** ................... '57 '82 C.178 A.B. L.846 J.D. [Blanc W.J.&K.]
*REPORTED CASES: Jeff Foxworthy v. Custom Tees, Inc., 879 F. Supp. 1200 (N.D. Ga. 1995).
*PRACTICE AREAS: Proprietary Rights Litigation; Business Litigation.
**Ray, David L.**, (AV) ................... '29 '71 C.112 B.S. L.1095 J.D. [Saltzburg,R.&B.]
*PRACTICE AREAS: State and Federal Court Receivership Practice; Bankruptcy Law; Partnership Law.
**Ray, Gilbert T.**, (AV) ...................'44 '72 C.49 B.A. L.329 J.D. [O'Melveny&M.]
*PRACTICE AREAS: Corporate Law and Public Finance.
Ray, Janet I. ...............'59 '85 C.1142 B.S. L.426 J.D. 10801 National Blvd., 4th Fl.
Ray, John S. ......'51 '76 C.188 A.B. L.309 J.D. Assoc. Gen. Coun., Capitol Records, Inc.
**Ray, Stephan M.**, (AV) ................... '54 '79 C.112 B.A. L.813 J.D. [Stutman,T.&G.]
*REPORTED CASES: Committee of Creditors Holding Unsecured Claims v. Citicorp Venture Capital, Ltd. (In re Papercraft Corp.); 187 B.R. 486 (Bankr. W.D. Pa. 1995); National Peregrine, Inc. v. Capital Fed. Sav. & Loan Ass'n (In re Peregrine Entertainment, Inc.), 116 B.R. 194 (C.D. Cal. 1990).
*PRACTICE AREAS: Bankruptcy; Insolvency; Corporate Reorganization; Commercial Litigation.
Raybould, Warren A. ...............'48 '76 C.339 B.S. L.365 J.D. Calif. Fed. Bk. FSB
Rayburn, Anthony W. ................... '64 '90 C.112 B.A. L.800 J.D. 400 S. Hope St.
**Raygor, Kent R.** ...................'52 '84 C&L.494 B.A., J.D. [Sheppard,M.R.&H.]
*PRACTICE AREAS: Intellectual Properties Law; Unfair Competition Law; Computer Law.
**Rayis, John D.** ...................'54 '81 C.475 B.A. L.912 J.D. [Skadden,A.S.M.&F.]
Raymer, Gregory P. '64 '92
(adm. in IL; not adm. in CA) 444 S. Flower St., Ste. 2000
**Raymond, Dion-Cherie** ............... '62 '90 C.112 B.A. L.1065 J.D. [J.L.Cochran,Jr.]
*PRACTICE AREAS: Personal Injury Law; Business Litigation.
Raynes, Alan S. ...............'64 '92 C.367 B.S. L.273 J.D. 1000 Wilshire Blvd. (Pat.)
Raynor, Richard Wayne ...............'66 '92 C.112 B.A. L.1049 J.D. 3250 Wilshire Blvd.
Ré, Donald M., (AV) ...............'46 '71 C.674 A.B. L.1068 J.D. 777 S. Figueroa St.
Rea, William J. ...................'20 '52 C.426 B.S. L.174 J.D. U.S. Dist. J.
**Rea, William John, Jr.**, (AV) ..........'53 '78 C.112 A.B. L.1068 J.D. [Lewis,D.B.&B.]
*PRACTICE AREAS: Civil Litigation; Errors and Omissions Defense; Insurance Coverage; Bad Faith Defense.
**Read, Charles C.** ................... '49 '75 C.309 A.B. L.1068 J.D. [O'Melveny&M.]
Read, Richard F. '34 '74 C.112 B.A. L.1148 J.D.
Sr. V.P., Brentwood Svgs. & Loan Assn.
**Reader, Anne-Marie** ...................'65 '92 C.347 B.S. L.800 J.D. [Cox,C.&N.]
*PRACTICE AREAS: Employment and Labor Law; Litigation.
Reader, Scot A. ...................'67 '93 C&L.800 B.S.A.E., J.D. 633 W. 5th St.

**Ready, Thomas J., (AV) '37 '66 C.112 A.B. L.813 LL.B.**
**333 South Grand Avenue, 33rd Floor, 90071-1504**
**Telephone: 213-229-9009 Facsimile: 213-229-9010**
**Email: TJRLA@AOL.com**
**Business Litigation.**
*See Professional Biographies, LOS ANGELES, CALIFORNIA*

**Reagin, Ronald W.**, (AV) '36 '62
C.502 B.S. L.273 LL.B. [Blakely,S.T.&Z.] (See Pat. Sect.)
Real, Manuel L. ...................'24 '52 C.800 B.S. L.426 LL.B. Dist. J.
Real, Teresa ...................'64 '93 C.1074 B.S. L.940 J.D. Group W Productions
**Reardon, Mark F.** '60 '86 C.36 B.S. L.190 J.D.
(adm. in AZ; not adm. in CA) Reg. Coun., CalMat Co.
**Reardon, Susan Erburu** ................... '56 '80 C.681 A.B. L.309 J.D. [Gibson,D.&C.]
*PRACTICE AREAS: Business Litigation; Media Law; Copyright Litigation; Eminent Domain and Land Use Litigation.
**Reaves, Rhonda M.** ...............'63 '92 C.976 B.A. L.813 J.D. [Heller E.W.&M.]
Reback, Sanford B., (BV) ............'50 '75 C.112 B.A. L.221 J.D. 3550 Wilshire Blvd.

**Reback, Hulbert, McAndrews & Kjar, LLP**
**(See Manhattan Beach)**

**Reber, Lori B.** ...................'70 '95 C.1042 B.A. L.990 J.D. [Littler,M.F.T.&M.]
Reber, M. Kenetta ...................'41 '76 C.1077 B.A. L.809 J.D. Dep. City Atty.
Rebhuhn, Harry J. ...................'54 '82 C.1044 B.A. L.800 J.D. 3580 Wilshire Blvd.

**Reboul, MacMurray, Hewitt, Maynard & Kristol, (AV)**
**Suite 1500, 1801 Century Park East, 90067**
**Telephone: 310-551-3070 Telecopier: 310-551-3071**
**Resident Partner: Andrew P. Tashman. Resident Associates: Joel J. Bernstein; Naomi A. Hentschel.**
**Staff Attorney: Kevin S. Wattles.**
**General Practice.**
**New York, N.Y. Office: 45 Rockefeller Plaza. Telephone: 212-841-5700.**
**Washington, D.C. Office: Suite 406, 1111 Nineteenth St., N.W., 20036. Telephone: 202-429-0004.**
*See Professional Biographies, LOS ANGELES, CALIFORNIA*

Recana, Mel Red ................... '39 '74 C&L.999 LL.B. Mun. Ct. J.
**Reck, Belynda** ...................'64 '92 C.338 B.S. L.800 J.D. [O'Donnell,R.&S.]
*PRACTICE AREAS: Litigation.
**Reck, R. Randolph**, (BV) ...................'53 '80 C.112 B.S. L.809 J.D. [Clopton,P.&B.]
**Redd, Janette M.** ................... '53 '89 C.112 B.A. L.1067 J.D. [Katten M.&Z.]
*PRACTICE AREAS: Real Estate Law.
**Reddick, C. N. Franklin, III** ...........'53 '80 C.768 B.A. L.1065 J.D. [Troop M.S.&P.]
*PRACTICE AREAS: Corporate Securities Law; Corporations Law.
**Reddock, Angela J.** ................... '69 '96 C.31 B.A. L.1068 J.D. [Gartner&Y.]
*PRACTICE AREAS: Labor and Employment Law.
**Redford, Robert D.**, (AV) ............... '32 '57 C&L.813 B.A., LL.B. [Morgan,L.&B.]
**Redlitz, Gregory V.** ...................'51 '77 C.976 B.A. L.178 J.D. [Thorne]
*PRACTICE AREAS: Entertainment Law.
**Redmond, John M.** ............ '50 '75 C.950 B.A. L.426 J.D. Sr. Coun., Bank of Amer.
Reed, Cathy R. '62 '91 C.112 B.A. L.1068 J.D.
Dir., Credits Admn., Writers Guild of Amer., West, Inc.
Reed, Dana W., (Mr.), (AV) ...................'44 '75 C.999 L.426 J.D. [Reed&D.]
Reed, Kevin S. ..... '64 '90 C.893 B.A. L.309 J.D. NAACP Legal Def. & Educ. Fund, Inc.
**Reed, Linda Buddenberg** ........'54 '80 C.813 A.B. L.800 J.D. Sr. Coun., Bank of Amer.
Reed, Martin S. ................... '47 '73 C.112 B.A. L.426 J.D. [Epstein&R.]
**Reed, Michael L.** ...................'66 '94 C.112 B.A. L.1068 J.D. [Gibson,D.&C.]
*PRACTICE AREAS: Corporate Law; Securities.
**Reed, Roni** ...................'66 '95 C.112 B.A. L.809 J.D. [Long&L.]
**Reed, Thomas F.** ...................'55 '80 C&L.800 A.B., J.D. [Hill,F.&B.]
**Reed, Wallace C.**, (AV) ...................'27 '55 C&L.800 A.B., J.D. [Hillsinger&C.]
*PRACTICE AREAS: Professional Liability; Medical Malpractice; Legal Malpractice; Arbitration - Medication.
Reed & Davidson, (AV) ...................777 S. Figueroa St. (Costa Mesa)
**Reeder, David M.** ...................'50 '88 C.513 B.A. L.221 J.D. [Lewis,D.B.&B.]
*PRACTICE AREAS: Bankruptcy Law; Debtor Creditor Law; Commercial Law.
Reedy, Kevin J. ...................'55 '89 C.112 B.A. L.1136 J.D. 8033 Sunset Blvd.
Reeks, Thomas E. ...................'31 '66 L.800 J.D. P.O. Box 27416
Reeks-Alden, Leslie ...................'63 '92 C.800 B.A. L.426 J.D. 6255 Sunset Blvd.
**Rees, Robert A.** ...................'55 '80 C.813 A.B. L.426 J.D. [Rintala,S.J.&R.]
**Rees, Samuel T.** ................... '46 '73 C&L.800 A.B., J.D. [Daar&N.]
**Reese, Gina** ...................'55 '92 C.1097 B.A. L.1148 J.D. [Hooper,L.&B.]
*LANGUAGES: Spanish.
*PRACTICE AREAS: Health Care Law.
Reese, James N. ................... '19 '46 Supr. Ct. J.
Reese, Paul D. ...................'63 '88 C.309 A.B. L.1068 J.D. 1888 Century Park E.
**Reeser, Edwin B., III** ...................'51 '77 C.309 A.B. L.1065 J.D. [Graham&J.]
*PRACTICE AREAS: Real Estate (Property) Law.
**Reeve, Derek Jon** ................... '70 '96 C&L.809 B.A., J.D. [Trope&T.]
*PRACTICE AREAS: Family Law.
**Reeves, Barbara A.**, (AV) ............'49 '73 C.1230 B.A. L.309 J.D. [Fried,F.H.S.&J.]
Reeves, David B. ................... '48 '73 C.367 A.B. L.1068 J.D. 633 W. 5th St.
**Reeves, Dean A.** ................... '61 '90 C.1077 B.A. L.800 J.D. [Hill,F.&B.]
*PRACTICE AREAS: General Civil and Business Litigation.
**Reeves, Penny L.** ...................'53 '82 C.112 B.A. L.426 J.D. [Manning,L.B.&B.]
*PRACTICE AREAS: Automotive Dealer Law; Probate; Business Purchase and Sales; Real Property; Commercial Law.
**Reeves, Rex T., Jr.** ................... '63 '88 C.103 A.B. L.309 J.D. [O'Donnell,R.&S.]
*PRACTICE AREAS: Litigation.
Reeves, Robert B. '52 '83
C.112 B.A. L.1068 J.D. Corp. Coun., Capitol Industries-EMI, Inc.
**Regan, Brian M.** ...................'65 '90 C.1042 B.S. L.426 J.D. [McKenna&C.]
*PRACTICE AREAS: Government Contracts; White Collar Criminal Defense; General Litigation.
**Regan, Colleen M.** ................... '56 '85 C.1320 B.A. L.426 J.D. [Perkins C.]
*PRACTICE AREAS: Civil Litigation.
Regan, Kristin A. ...................'63 '91 C.112 B.A. L.426 J.D. 444 S. Flower St.
**Regenstreif, Gail A.** ................... '69 '94 C.31 B.A. L.426 J.D. [Musick,P.&G.]
*PRACTICE AREAS: Business Litigation.
Regenstreif, Mitchell C. ...................'63 '89 C.178 B.A. L.569 J.D. 550 S. Hope St.
Reglos, Rose Fe Reyes ...................'63 '89 C.767 B.A. L.1065 J.D. Dep. Pub. Def.
Rehaut, Steven M. ...................'60 '85 C.112 B.A. L.1067 J.D. 6100 Wilshire Blvd.

**Rehwald Rameson Lewis & Glasner**
**(See Woodland Hills)**

**Reiber, Thomas E.** ...................'67 '92 C.893 B.A. L.1066 J.D. [Heller E.W.&M.]
Reich, Adam M. '66 '91 C.680 B.A. L.569 J.D.
Gen. Coun., Rabin Brothers Auctioneers & Appraisers
Reich, Cynthia D. ........'38 '87 C.112 B.A. L.426 J.D. Medicare Advocacy Project, Inc.
**Reich, Jonathan I.** ...................'58 '84 C.112 B.A. L.1068 J.D. [De Castro,W.&C.]
*PRACTICE AREAS: Business; Real Estate; Construction Defect; Corporate and Insurance Coverage Litigation.
Reich, Julius, (AV) ...................'33 '63 C&L.112 B.A., J.D. [Reich,A.C.&C.]
Reich, Peter L. ............ '55 '86 C.112 B.A. L.1066 J.D. Prof., Whittier Law Sch.
Reich, Adell, Crost & Cvitan, (AV) ...................501 Shatto Pl. (Orange)

**Reichard, Harvey, (AV) '37 '63 C.112 B.S. L.1068 LL.B.**
**501 Shatto Place, Suite 100, 90020**
**Telephone: 213-386-3860 Fax: 213-386-5583**
***PRACTICE AREAS: Worker's Compensation Law.**
**Workers Compensation Law.**
*See Professional Biographies, LOS ANGELES, CALIFORNIA*

Reichblum, Amalie Moses ..... '63 '92 C.860 B.A. L.178 J.D. 355 S. Grand Ave., 35th Fl.
Reiche, Gerald M. ...................'57 '93 C.1077 B.A. L.398 J.D. 3343 Wilshire Blvd.
**Reichenthal, Jason S.** ...................'70 '96 C.112 B.A. L.426 J.D. [Troop M.S.&P.]
*PRACTICE AREAS: Corporate; Financial Institutions; Securities Law.

CAA321P

CALIFORNIA—LOS ANGELES

MARTINDALE-HUBBELL LAW DIRECTORY 1997

**Reicher, Leland J.**, (AV) ... '49 '75 C.800 B.S. L.1068 J.D. [Reish&L.]
*PRACTICE AREAS: Real Estate; Business Law.
**Reichert, Thomas V.** ... '64 '94 C.276 B.S.F.S L.893 J.D. [Ⓐ Bird,M.B.W.&M.]
Reichert, William M. '50 '75
C.813 B.A. L.1068 J.D. V.P. & Sr. Coun., Wells Fargo Bk., N.A.
Reichman, Kenneth William '64 '89 C.112 B.A. L.809 J.D.
Law Clk. to U.S. Dist. Ct. J.
Reichmann, Joe ... '31 '59 C.112 B.S. L.1068 LL.B. U.S. Mag.
Reichstetter, Carol A. ... '50 '82 C.183 B.A. L.800 J.D. 1163 W. 27th St.
**Reichwald, Harold P.** ... '36 '62 C.994 B.A. L.569 LL.B. [Manatt,P.&P.]
*PRACTICE AREAS: Corporate Securities; Financial Services; Insurance Industry; Fashion Industry.
Reid, Dale C., (AV) ... '34 '61 C.112 B.S. L.813 J.D. 6500 Wilshire Blvd., 17th Fl.
Reid, John H. ... '53 '81 C&L.262 B.A., J.D. 700 S. Flower St.
Reid, John H. ... '48 '72 C.800 B.S. L.809 J.D. Supr. Ct. J.
**Reid, William W.** ... '54 '80 C.112 B.A. L.1067 J.D. [Parker,M.C.O.&S.]
*SPECIAL AGENCIES: Internal Revenue Service; California Franchise Tax Board; California Attorney General.
*REPORTED CASES: Clayton v. Automobile Workers, 451 U.S., 679 (1981); Wright v. Commissioner, 67 T.C.M. 3125 (1994).
*TRANSACTIONS: San Joaquin Hills Transportation Corridor; Harvard School/Westlake School for Girls Merger; I Have a Dream Foundation-Los Angeles; Galef Institute; California Tourism Corporation.
*PRACTICE AREAS: General Corporate Law; Taxation Law; Non-Profit Organizations; Employee Benefits Law; Executive Compensation Law.
Reif, Andrew '65 '91 C.893 B.S. L.659 J.D.
(adm. in NY; not adm. in CA) V.P., Bus. Affs., Intl. Creative Mgmt., Inc.
Reifman, Irving P., (AV) ... '39 '65 C&L.112 B.A., LL.B. State Prob. Ref. [Reifman&A.]
Reifman & Altman, (AV) ... 11601 Wilshire Blvd.
Reilly, Charles P. ... '42 '68 C.645 B.S. L.659 LL.B. Shamrock Invests.
Reilly, Cynthia Kittle ... '55 '93 C.767 B.A. L.560 J.D. 2121 Ave. of the Stars
Reilly, Edward G., Jr. '58 '85 C.112 B.A. L.1049 J.D.
V.P., Bus. & Legal Affs., Concorde-New Horizons Corp.
**Reilly, Jerrold B.** ... '47 '76 C.93 B.S. L.823 J.D. [Lyon&L.] (See Pat. Sect.)
*PRACTICE AREAS: Intellectual Property.
**Reilly, Kathleen A.** ... '50 '79 C&L.426 B.A., J.D. Sr. Corp. Coun., Farmers Grp., Inc.
*RESPONSIBILITIES: Insurance Regulatory and Administrative Law; Class Actions/Business/Commerical Litigation; Insurance Compliance Activity; General Corporate/Business/Insurance Agency/Employment Law.
**Reilly, Thomas H.** '46 '75 C.93 A.B. L.734 J.D.
Sr. Corp. Antitrust Coun., Atlantic Richfield Co.
*RESPONSIBILITIES: Antitrust Law.
**Reily, David H.**, (AV) ... '50 '81 C.446 B.A. L.800 J.D. [Irwin&R.]
*PRACTICE AREAS: Aviation; Products Liability; General Civil Practice; Trial Practice.
**Reimann, David W.**, (AV) ... '53 '82 C.951 B.A. L.1068 J.D. [Crawford&R.]
*PRACTICE AREAS: Business Litigation; Construction Litigation; Insurance Litigation.
**Reimann, Nancy Baldwin** ... '58 '83 C.770 B.S.C. L.1068 J.D. [Sheppard,M.R.&H.]
*PRACTICE AREAS: Banking and Finance Law; Secured Transactions Law; Estate Planning Law.
**Reimer, Eric R.** ... '61 '87 C.800 B.S. L.1065 J.D. [Ⓐ Milbank,T.H.&M.]
*PRACTICE AREAS: Banking Law; Finance Law.
Rein, Robert S., (AV) ... '44 '70 C.1036 B.A. L.309 J.D. [Saphier,R.&W.]
Rein, Scott J. ... '63 '88 C.1044 B.A. L.262 J.D. [Dressler,R.&E.]
Reinberg, Deborah B. ... '49 '76 C.112 B.A. L.1068 J.D. 2414 Nalin Dr.
Reiner, Andrew E. ... '61 '88 C.475 B.S.M.E. L.426 J.D. 11859 Wilshire Blvd.
**Reiner, Bryan** ... '66 '94 C.800 B.A. L.398 J.D. [Ⓐ Liebman&R.]
*PRACTICE AREAS: Liability; Workmans' Compensation.
**Reiner, John**, (AV) ... '47 '75 C.112 B.A. L.809 J.D. [Liebman&R.]
*PRACTICE AREAS: Personal Injury Defense Law; Insurance Law; Trial Practice.
Reiner, John J. ... '47 '77 C.112 A.B. L.800 J.D. 2049 Century Park East
Reinhardt, Stephen ... '31 '54 C.668 B.A. L.976 LL.B. U.S. Ct. of Apps. J.
**Reinis, Mitchell N.**, (AV) ... '39 '65 C.112 B.S. L.1066 LL.B. [Reinis&R.]
*REPORTED CASES: Russell vs. Price, 612 F.2d 1123,205 USPQ 206; Lew vs. Moss, 797 F.2d 747; McCaffrey vs. Diversified Land, 564 F.2d 1241; Southwestern Publishing vs. Simons, 651 F.2d 653; Golden West Melodies vs. Capitol Records, 274 CA2d 713.
*PRACTICE AREAS: Business Transactions; Litigation; Intellectual Property.
**Reinis, Richard G.**, (AV) ... '44 '70 C.674 B.A. L.800 J.D. [Reinis&R.]
*TRANSACTIONS: License agreements respecting trademarks "Bum Equipment", "Let's Get Ready to Rumble," Professional Sports and other national brands; quoted expert on apparel industry matters.
*PRACTICE AREAS: Licensing Law; Labor; Business Organization; Business Acquisitions; Real Estate.

**Reinis & Reinis, (AV)** BR
**550 South Hope Street, 20th Floor, 90071**
**Telephone: 213-624-4246 Facsimile: 213-624-4709**
**Members of Firm: Mitchell N. Reinis; Richard G. Reinis. Associates: Laura P. Worsinger; Steven M. Harrison; Gregory N. Weisman. Of Counsel: L. Douglas Brown.**
**General Corporate, Commercial, Litigation, Intellectual Property and Real Estate Law.**

***See Professional Biographies, LOS ANGELES, CALIFORNIA***

Reinjohn, Richard G., (AV) ... '39 '65 C.112 B.A. L.800 J.D. [R.G.Reinjohn]
Reinjohn, Richard G., P.C., (AV) ... 1 Wilshire Blvd.
**Reinke, Brent A.** ... '61 '88 C.605 A.B. L.426 J.D. [Clark&T.]
*PRACTICE AREAS: General Corporate; Mergers and Acquisitions; Corporate Securities and Finance.
**Reinstein, Todd Russell, (P.C.)**, (AV) '37 '63 C.112 B.S. L.1068 J.D.
[Reinstein,P.&C.]
*PRACTICE AREAS: Taxation Law; Real Estate Law; Health Care Law; Estate Planning and Probate Law; Commercial and Business Law.

**Reinstein, Pantell & Calkins, (AV)**
**A Partnership of Professional Corporations**
**10940 Wilshire, Suite 1600, 90024**
**Telephone: 310-443-4299**
**Partners: Todd Russell Reinstein (P.C.) (Certified Specialist, Taxation Law, The State Bar of California Board of Legal Specialization); Colleen Daphne Calkins (P.C.); Lloyd S. Pantell (P.C.). Of Counsel: William L. Feinstein; Jonathan B. Klinck.**
**Business and Commercial Transactions, Corporate and Partnership Law, Taxation, Real Estate, Health Care, Estate Planning, Trust, Probate, Civil and Criminal Tax Litigation, Employee Benefits and Relationships.**
**Reference: Wells Fargo Bank, San Diego, California.**

***See Professional Biographies, LOS ANGELES, CALIFORNIA***

Reisberg, Richard S. '41 '67 C.475 B.A. L.262 LL.B.
(adm. in NY; not adm. in CA) Reeves Entertainment Grp.
**Reish, C. Frederick**, (AV) ... '44 '69 C.36 B.S. L.37 J.D. [Reish&L.]
*REPORTED CASES: Amicus Briefs on behalf of the American Society of Pension Actuaries, Patterson v. Shumate, U.S. 112 S.Ct 2242 (1992); Citrus Valley Estates, Inc., et al. v. Commissioner of Internal Revenue, 99 T.C. 379 (1992).
*PRACTICE AREAS: Employee Benefits; ERISA Litigation.

**Reish & Luftman, A Professional Corporation, (AV)** BR
**11755 Wilshire Boulevard 10th Floor, 90025**⊙
**Telephone: 310-478-5656 Facsimile: 310-478-5831**
**URL: http://www.benefitslink.com/reish/**
**Bruce L. Ashton; Roland M. Attenborough; Joseph C. Faucher; Martin M. Heming; Jonathan A. Karp; Michael B. Luftman (Certified Specialist, Taxation Law, State Bar of California, Board of Legal Specialization); James R. McDaniel; Leland J. Reicher; C. Frederick Reish; Mark E. Terman; Michael A. Vanic; Lynn B. Witte;—Fernando L. Delmendo; Ilene Hirsch Ferenczy; Nelson J. Handy.**
**Corporate, Real Estate, Business and Real Estate Litigation, ERISA Litigation, Pension and Welfare Benefits, Taxation, Employment Law, Estate Planning and Probate. Civil Tax Controversies.**

(This Listing Continued)

**Reish & Luftman, A Professional Corporation (Continued)**

**Washington, D.C. Office: One Massachusetts Avenue, N.W., Suite 800, 20001. Telephone: 202-745-0024. Facsimile: 202-745-0005.**

***See Professional Biographies, LOS ANGELES, CALIFORNIA***

**Reisman, Ellen Kelly** '59 '84 C.93 B.A. L.145 J.D.
(adm. in DC; not adm. in CA) [Arnold&P.]
*PRACTICE AREAS: Food and Drug; Products Liability.
**Reisman, Louis A.**, (AV) ... '45 '70 C.339 B.S. L.597 J.D. [Weinstock,M.R.S.&N.]
*PRACTICE AREAS: Taxation Law; Business Law; Estate Planning Law.
**Reisner, Jeffrey M.** ... '63 '89 C.188 B.S. L.569 J.D. [Ⓐ Morgan,L.&B.]
**Reiss, Daniel H.** ... '62 '90 C.1077 B.S. L.426 J.D. [Angel&N.]
*PRACTICE AREAS: Bankruptcy Law.
**Reisz, Frederick S.** ... '64 '89 C.264 B.A. L.990 J.D. [Ⓐ Meyers,B.&M.]
*PRACTICE AREAS: Insurance Bad Faith; Environmental Pollution; Coverage.
Reisz, Michael ... '— '93 L.1068 J.D. 333 S. Hope St., 48th Fl.
Reisz, Willard M., (BV) ... '29 '53 C.112 B.S. L.1068 LL.B. 10880 Wilshire Blvd.
**Reiter, Ellis D., Jr.**, (AV) '38 '64 C.800 B.S. L.1065 J.D.
Exec. V.P. & Gen. Coun., Litig., CB Coml. Real Estate Grp., Inc.
*RESPONSIBILITIES: Department Administration; Litigation Management; Litigation; Real Estate.
**Reiter, Genise R., (A Professional Corporation)** '52 '78
C.112 B.A. L.809 J.D. [Saltzburg,R.&B.]
*PRACTICE AREAS: Litigation; Business Law; Real Estate Law; Entertainment Law.
Reiter, Stephen E. ... '50 '85 444 S. Flower St., Ste. 2000 (Pat.)
Reitkopp, Edward B. ... '52 '77 C.188 B.S. L.1068 J.D. [Ⓐ Liebert,C.&F.]
**Reitler, Paul M.**, (AV) ... '36 '64 C.813 A.B. L.309 LL.B. [Sheppard,M.R.&H.]
*PRACTICE AREAS: Business Litigation.
**Reitman, John P.**, (AV) ... '45 '78 C.1077 B.A. L.426 J.D. [Gumport,R.&M.]
*PRACTICE AREAS: Bankruptcy; Business and Commercial Law; Construction Law; Real Estate and Business Litigation; Litigation.
**Reitzenstein, Henry A.** ... '56 '81 C.112 B.A. L.1066 J.D. [De Castro,W.&C.]
*PRACTICE AREAS: Tax Law; Business Law.
Reizman, Neil M. ... '64 '90 C.112 B.S. L.1066 J.D. 633 W. Fifth St.
Relin, Milton M. ... '17 '54 C.112 B.S. L.800 J.D. 1701 Hill Dr.
**Remensperger, D. Eric** ... '57 '85 C.706 B.A. L.1009 J.D. [Ⓐ Gibson,D.&C.]
*PRACTICE AREAS: Finance; Real Estate; Commercial Real Estate; Partnerships.
**Remington, Laurel A.** ... '71 '97 C.112 B.A. L.659 J.D. [Ⓐ O'Melveny&M.]
**Remson, Kenneth A.** ... '56 '89 C.813 A.B. L.228 J.D. [Ⓐ Jones,D.R.&P.]
Renda, Dominic P., (AV) ... '13 '38 C&L.608 B.S., J.D. 2040 Ave. of the Stars‡
Rendon, Patrick L. ... '60 '86 C.311 B.A. L.800 J.D. 333 S. Grand Ave.
**René, James M.** ... '58 '87 C.605 B.A. L.188 J.D. [Ⓐ Sheppard,M.R.&H.]
**Renick, Steven J.** ... '56 '81 C.197 A.B. L.94 J.D. [Ⓐ Manning,M.&W.]
*LANGUAGES: Spanish.
**Renner, John Robert** ... '64 '90 C.197 A.B. L.1066 J.D. [Ⓐ Coudert]
*PRACTICE AREAS: Criminal Law (100%).
**Rennett, Allen E.**, (AV) ... '48 '73 C&L.659 B.A., J.D. [Richards,W.&G.]
*PRACTICE AREAS: Real Estate Law; Corporate Law; Partnership Law.
Rennick, Tamarra T. ... '65 '91 C.339 B.S. L.464 J.D. 777 S. Figueroa St., 10th Fl.
**Renshaw, Steven J.** ... '58 '85 C.160 B.S. L.602 J.D. [Ⓐ Brobeck,P.&H.]
*LANGUAGES: French and Polish.
*PRACTICE AREAS: Environmental Litigation; Antitrust Law.
Renton, William James, (AV) ... '43 '68 C.112 B.A. L.813 J.D. 333 S. Grand Ave.
**Renwick, Edward S., (A Professional Corporation)**, (AV) '34 '59
C&L.813 A.B., LL.B. [Hanna&M.]
*PRACTICE AREAS: Civil Trial and Appellate; Alternative Dispute Resolution; Natural Resources; Environmental Law; General Practice.

**Reppetto, Gerald G., (AV) '32 '63 C&L.800 B.S., LL.B.** BR
**Equitable Building, 3435 Wilshire Boulevard, Suite 640, 90010**
**Telephone: 213-388-4320 FAX: 213-383-1231**
**Personal Injury Defense, Products Liability Defense, Insurance Coverage.**

***See Professional Biographies, LOS ANGELES, CALIFORNIA***

**Resch, Ronald M., (Professional Corporation)**, (AV) '45 '70
C.112 B.A. L.61 J.D. [Resch P.A.&B.]
*PRACTICE AREAS: Real Estate; Business Law.

**Resch Polster Alpert & Berger LLP, (AV)**
**A Limited Liability Partnership including Professional Corporations**
**10390 Santa Monica Boulevard, Fourth Floor, 90025-5058**
**Telephone: 310-277-8300 FAX: 310-552-3209**
**Attorneys: Peter H. Alpert (Professional Corporation); Sheldon P. Berger (Professional Corporation); David Gitman (Professional Corporation); Keli N. Osaki; Lee M. Polster (Professional Corporation); Nicolas Ramniceanu; Ronald M. Resch (Professional Corporation). Of Counsel: Marvin G. Burns (Professional Corporation); Aaron A. Grunfeld; Nicholas T. Hariton; Lawrence R. Resnick (Professional Corporation); Charles S. Tigerman (Professional Corporation) (Certified Specialist, Estate Planning, Trust and Probate Law, California Board of Legal Specialization).**
**Business Law, Real Estate, Corporate, Financing, Securities Regulation, Federal, State and International Taxation and Commercial Litigation.**
**Reference: Imperial Bank, Beverly Hills, Calif.**

***See Professional Biographies, LOS ANGELES, CALIFORNIA***

**Resh, Dennis D.**, (BV) ... '51 '77 C.800 A.B. L.1065 J.D. [Ⓐ Borton,P.&C.]
*PRACTICE AREAS: Construction Litigation; Professional Liability.

**Resisa, Abraham '34 '57 C&L.37 B.A., LL.B.**
**1201 South Shenandoah Street, 90035**
**Telephone: 310-859-1216 Fax: 310-246-0715**
***PRACTICE AREAS: Research Federal Law; Title Insurance Law.**
**Legal Analysis Research of State and Federal Practice, Title Insurance, Real Property, Mortgage, Trusts, Deeds.**

**Resler, Jeffrey A.** ... '62 '88 C.918 B.A. L.569 J.D. [Robinson,D.B.&K.]
*PRACTICE AREAS: Bankruptcy Law; Corporate Reorganizations; Corporate Law.
**Resnick, Allen S.** ... '47 '84 C.112 B.A. L.800 J.D. [Jeffer,M.B.&M.]
*PRACTICE AREAS: Corporate, International.
Resnick, Barnet, (Law Corporation), (AV) ... '45 '73 C&L.1137 B.S.L., J.D. [White&R.]⊙
**Resnick, Lawrence R., (Professional Corporation)**, (AV) '34 '62
C.608 B.A. L.851 LL.B. [Ⓒ Resch P.A.&B.]
*PRACTICE AREAS: Business Litigation; Real Estate Litigation; Construction Industry Litigation.

**Resnick and Abraham, L.L.C.**
**2049 Century Park East, Suite 760, 90067**⊙
**Telephone: 310-557-2599**
**Bradford L. Treusch.**
**Commercial and Collection Law. Admiralty, Personal Injury, Bankruptcy Law.**
**Baltimore, Maryland Office: One East Franklin Street. Telephone: 410-539-6087; 1-800-638-7652. Fax: 410-576-0818.**
**Fairfax, Virginia Office: 4000 Legato Road. Suite 230. Telephone: 703-790-1776.**
**Washington, D.C. Office: Suite 700, 601 Pennsylvania Avenue, N.W. Telephone: 202-452-1411.**
**Hicksville, New York Office: 520 Old Country Road. Telephone: 516-938-1969.**
**Wilmington, Delaware Office: 100 East 14th Street. Telephone: 302-427-2247.**
**Philadelphia, Pennsylvania Office: 1608 Walnut Street, Suite 402. Telephone: 215-790-1010.**
**Burlington, New Jersey Office: 505 High Street, P.O. Box 1427. Telephone: 609-386-1911.**
**Norcross, Georgia Office: P.O. Box 921209. Telephone: 404-840-8482.**
**Pembroke Pines, Florida Office: 1000 N. Hiatus Road. Suite 140. Telephone: 305-432-6667.**
**Charlotte, North Carolina Office: P.O. Box 36798. Telephone: 704-332-1199.**

***See Professional Biographies, BALTIMORE, MARYLAND***

CAA322P

**Resser, Bernard M.**, (AV) ............'54 '80 C.112 B.A. L.1068 J.D. [Berman,B.M.&R.]
*PRACTICE AREAS: Business Litigation; Real Estate Litigation; Insurance Litigation; Creditor's Remedies; Competitive Business Practices.
**Ressler, Alison S.** ..........................'58 '84 C.103 B.A. L.178 J.D. [Sullivan&C.]
**Ressler, Kurt A.** ..............................................'66 '95 L.1066 [A Dewey B.]
Restivo, Roy S. ......................'66 '92 C.112 B.A. L.800 J.D. 12400 Wilshire Blvd.
Rettig, Albert A. ................'32 '56 C.569 B.S. L.1009 LL.B. 11777 San Vicente Blvd.
**Retz, Kirk J.** ...........................'62 '94 C.1077 B.S. L.426 J.D. [A Harrington,F.D.&C.]
*PRACTICE AREAS: Construction Litigation; Products Liability; Medical Malpractice; General Litigation.
**Retz, Linda J.** ........................'53 '93 C.1136 B.S. L.426 J.D. [A Hoffman,S.&W.]
*PRACTICE AREAS: Estate Planning Law; Probate Law; Trust Law.
Reuben, James A., (AV) '47 '76
C.1077 B.A. L.284 J.D. [Reuben,C.&A.] (⊙San Francisco)
**Reuben, Jeffrey L., (P.C.)** ...........'60 '85 C.918 B.A. L.145 J.D. [A Jeffer,M.B.&M.]
*PRACTICE AREAS: Federal and State Taxation.
Reuben, Cera & Alter, (AV)
9720 Wilshire Boulevard, Suite 500 (⊙San Francisco, CA, Reuben & Cera; New York, NY, Reub en, Cera & Alter)

**Reuben & Novicoff**
**(See Beverly Hills)**

**Revelli, John** ..........................'67 '94 C.1097 B.A. L.61 J.D. [A Manning,M.&W.]
Revere, Frank, (AV) ..................................'36 '62 C.767 L.426 LL.B. [Revere&W.]
Revere & Wallace, (AV) ..................................................900 Wilshire Blvd.
**Revich, Ira** ......................................'49 '74 C.477 B.S. L.912 J.D. [Charlston,R.&W.]
Revitz, Steven J., (AV) ......................'48 '74 C.112 B.S. L.1068 J.D. [Raiskin&R.]
**Rewinski, Jon L.** ...........................'59 '84 C.976 B.A. L.569 J.D. [Heller E.W.&M.]
*LANGUAGES: German.
*PRACTICE AREAS: Litigation; Appellate Practice; Securities Litigation; Securities Arbitration; Regulatory Investigations and Proceedings.
**Rexon, Brian L.**, (AV) ....................'43 '70 C.112 B.S. L.1068 J.D. [Rexon,F.K.&H.]
*PRACTICE AREAS: Labor Negotiation; Arbitration; National Labor Relations Board Proceedings.

**Rexon, Freedman, Klepetar & Hambleton, A Professional Corporation, (AV) BB**
**12100 Wilshire Boulevard, Suite 730, 90025**
**Telephone: 310-826-8300 FAX: 310-826-0333**
**Brian L. Rexon; Jeffrey C. Freedman; Ronald J. Klepetar; Debby R. Hambleton; Wendy K. Genz;— Steven J. Prough; Stephanie J. Hart.**
**Labor and Employment Relations Law, Wrongful Termination Litigation, Equal Opportunity Law and OSHA.**
**Reference: Santa Monica Bank.**
***See Professional Biographies, LOS ANGELES, CALIFORNIA***

Reyes, Adelaide E. ..................'32 '62 C&L.999 B.A., LL.B. 1605 W. Olympic Blvd.
**Reyes, Dorothy B.** ..................'52 '82 C.1177 B.S. L.426 J.D. [La Follette,J.D.F.&A.]
*PRACTICE AREAS: Bad Faith; General Liability.
Reyes, Janet Bloom ..........................'47 '88 C.112 M.A. L.809 J.D. Dep. City Atty.
**Reyes, Rita A.** ..............................'64 '92 C.112 B.A. L.1148 J.D. [A Ochoa&S.]
*LANGUAGES: Spanish.
*PRACTICE AREAS: Workers' Compensation; Civil Litigation; Employment Law.
Reyna, Mary E. ... '51 '92 C.844 B.S. L.1148 J.D. Asst. Coun., Metropolitan Trans. Auth.
Reynolds, Carolyn M. ......................'39 '64 C.800 L.426 LL.B. Asst. Chief U.S. Atty.
**Reynolds, David E., (P.C.)** ...............'48 '76 C.1077 B.A. L.1068 J.D. [Lewis,D.B.&B.]
Reynolds, James L. ..................'55 '84 C.1109 B.S. L.284 J.D. 2029 Century Pk. E.
Reynolds, Kenneth E. ........................'42 '67 C.976 A.B. L.309 J.D. Dep. Co. Coun.
**Reynolds, Margaret B.** ..................'57 '90 C.464 B.A. L.1148 J.D. [A Epstein B.&G.]
*PRACTICE AREAS: Health Law.
Reynolds, Mary Kay ................................'50 '79 C.770 B.A. L.426 J.D. [Seider&R.]
Reynolds, Patrick F. ........'62 '92 C.602 B.A. L.426 J.D. 1999 Ave. of the Stars, 28th Fl.
**Reynolds, Philip L.**, (AV) ...............'36 '66 C.111 B.S. L.309 LL.B. [C Latham&W.]
Reynolds, Roger D. '53 '78
C.800 B.A. L.426 J.D. V.P. & Sr. Coun., Wells Fargo Bk., N.A.
**Reynolds, Ronald D.** .........................'53 '81 C.174 B.A. L.564 J.D. [Troop M.S.&P.]
*PRACTICE AREAS: Securities and Antitrust Litigation; General Commercial Litigation.
Reynolds, Sara H. ...........................'60 '85 C.597 B.A. L.276 J.D. 777 S. Figueroa St.
Reynolds, Thomas C. ..........'58 '84 C.800 B.S. L.101 J.D. 1880 Century Park E. (Pat.)
**Reynoso, Cruz**, (AV) ...............'31 '59 C.668 B.A. L.1066 LL.B. [C Kaye,S.F.H.&H.]
*LANGUAGES: Spanish.
**Rezen, Randy L.** ...........................'55 '80 C.1044 B.A. L.107 J.D. [A Grace,S.C.&S.]
*PRACTICE AREAS: Insurance Coverage; Environmental; Real Estate Litigation.
**Reznick, Michael E.** ....................'53 '84 C.1077 B.A. L.426 J.D. [C McBirney&C.]
*PRACTICE AREAS: Civil Litigation.
**Reznik, Benjamin M.**, (AV) ..................'51 '76 C.112 B.A. L.800 J.D. [Reznik&R.]
*LANGUAGES: Hebrew.
*SPECIAL AGENCIES: Los Angeles County Metropolitan Transit Authority (MTA); Federal Deposit Insurance Corporation (FDR).
*REPORTED CASES: Jama Construction Co. v. City of Los Angeles, 938 F2d 1045 (9th Cir. 1991); Save Our Residential Environment v. City of West Hollywood, 9 Cal.App. 4th 1745 (1992).
*PRACTICE AREAS: Zoning, Land Use; Environmental Law; Utilities and Energy.
Reznik, Todd M. ........................'63 '87 C.112 B.A. L.1068 J.D. Deloitte & Touche

**Reznik & Reznik, A Law Corporation, (AV)**
**15456 Ventura Boulevard, Fifth Floor (Sherman Oaks), 91403-3023**
**Telephone: 213-872-2900; 818-907-9898 Telecopier: 818-907-8465**
**Benjamin M. Reznik; Janice M. Kamenir-Reznik; Penny Grosz-Salomon; Alan J. Kheel; Fred N. Gaines; Richard A. McDonald;—John M. Bowman; Kenneth A. Ehrlich; Jeffrey S. Raskin; L. Elizabeth Strahlstrom; Rebecca Ann Thompson; Robert B. Keeler; Kevin M. Kemper; Monica Witt; Andrew Vogel; Diana Ng. Of Counsel: Robert M. Hertzberg.**
**Environmental, Hazardous Waste, Zoning and Land Use, Real Estate Transactions and Litigation, Insurance Coverage, Utilities and Energy.**
**Representative Clients: MCA Development Company (subsidiary of MCA); Citicorp Real Estate, Inc. (subsidiary of Citicorp); Service Corporation International, New York Stock Exchange; BET Plant Services; Tokai Credit Corporation (subsidiary of Tokai Bank); Weyerhaeuser; RTC (Resolution Trust Corporation).**
***See Professional Biographies, LOS ANGELES, CALIFORNIA***

Rheuban, Steven Victor ..........'45 '71 C.37 B.S.B.A. L.426 J.D. 12301 Wilshire Blvd.
**Rho, Jai ho** .......................................'59 '86 C.309 B.A. L.1068 J.D. [Merchant&G.]
*PRACTICE AREAS: Intellectual Property.

**Rhoades, Rufus Von Thülen, (AV) '32 '60 C&L.813 A.B., LL.B. BB**
**633 West Fifth Street, 20th Floor, 90071**
**Telephone: 213-896-2491 Fax: 213-362-2957**
**Email: rufustax@ix.netcom.com**
**Federal and California Taxation Law.**
**Reference: City National Bank (3rd and Fairfax Branch).**
***See Professional Biographies, LOS ANGELES, CALIFORNIA***

**Rhoden, Mary Beth** ......................'69 '94 C.859 B.A. L.426 J.D. [A Mayer,B.&P.]
**Rhodes, Brian W.** ...............'66 '94 C.1335 B.S. L.809 J.D. [A Breidenbach,B.H.H.&H.]
*LANGUAGES: Spanish.
**Rhodes, Catherine L.** ....................'64 '91 C.813 B.A. L.809 J.D. [A Acker,K.&W.]
*LANGUAGES: French and Spanish.
*PRACTICE AREAS: Business Litigation; Conservatorships; Probate; Civil Litigation.
**Rhodes, J. Richard**, (AV) .............'29 '68 C.112 B.A. L.1095 J.D. [C Allen,R.S.&J.]
**Rhodes, Lizabeth** ........................'66 '91 C.788 A.B. L.1068 J.D. [A Morrison&F.]
**Rhodes, Randy** ...........................'57 '89 C.1077 B.A. L.1136 J.D. [C Gibson,D.&C.]
*PRACTICE AREAS: Medical Malpractice Defense; Bad Faith Defense.
**Rhody, R. Christopher** ...................'66 '92 C.276 B.A. L.767 J.D. [A Hancock R.&B.]
**Rhow, Ekwan E.** ...........................'69 '94 C.813 B.A. L.309 J.D. [A Bird,M.B.W.&M.]

**Ribet, Claudia, (AV) '53 '78 C.604 A.B. L.1162 J.D.**
**11661 San Vicente Boulevard, Suite 1015, 90049**
**Telephone: 310-826-2313 FAX: 310-826-8242**
**Email: Ribet@appellatelaw.com**
**(Also Of Counsel, Kulik, Gottesman & Mouton, L.L.P.).**
**Appellate Practice and Complex Civil Litigation.**
***See Professional Biographies, LOS ANGELES, CALIFORNIA***

**Ribner, Seth A.** ..........................................'58 '84 C.659 A.B. L.178 J.D. [Coudert]
Ricciardulli, Alex ....................'61 '87 C.112 A.B. L.1066 J.D. Dep. Pub. Def. II.
**Rice, Amy L.** ..................................'57 '83 C.112 B.A. L.800 J.D. [Gaims,W.W.&E.]
**Rice, Andrea Lynn**, (AV) ....................'47 '80 C.112 A.B. L.426 J.D. [Hollins&R.]⊙
*PRACTICE AREAS: Legal Malpractice Defense; Legal Malpractice; Insurance Coverage/Bad Faith; Real Estate/Brokers and Agents Errors & Omissions; Insurance Brokers and Agents Errors and Omissions.
Rice, David Lee ...........................................'52 '79 C.36 B.S. L.426 J.D. [D.L.Rice]
Rice, David Lee, A Prof. Law Corp., Law Offices of ............ 13101 Washington Blvd.
**Rich, J. Peter** .............................'53 '77 C.112 A.B. L.309 J.D. [McDermott,W.&E.]
*LANGUAGES: French.
*PRACTICE AREAS: Health Care; Hospitals; Corporate Law.
Rich, Janet R. ..........'63 '88 C.112 B.A. L.1068 J.D. Securities & Exchange Commission
**Rich, Jeffrey A.** ..........................'50 '83 C&L.472 B.A., J.D. [A Pillsbury M.&S.]
**Rich, Jonathan E.** '54 '80
C.319 B.A. L.145 J.D. [C McCambridge,D.&M.] (⊙Newtown, PA)
Rich, Leo S. ...........................................'27 '52 C.112 A.B. L.800 LL.B. Supr. Ct. Comr.
Rich, Randall B. .............................'61 '88 C.174 B.A. L.809 J.D. Off. of Pub. Def.
Rich, Richard P., (AV) ..............'24 '54 C.112 B.A. L.569 J.D. 1888 Century Park E.‡
**Rich, Robert A.** ................................'55 '81 C&L.446 B.S., J.D. [Wright,R.O.&T.]
*PRACTICE AREAS: Asbestos Litigation; Business Law; Translational Law; Personal Injury Law; Aviation Litigation.
**Rich, Steven M.** ...........................'64 '90 C.112 B.S. L.1066 J.D. [C P.J.Lesser]
*PRACTICE AREAS: Litigation.

**Rich & Ezer**
**(See Ezer & Williamson)**

**Richards, Eric A. S.** ...................'65 '89 C.976 B.A. L.309 J.D. [C O'Melveny&M.]
*LANGUAGES: Spanish.
*PRACTICE AREAS: Airport Project Finance; International Joint Ventures; Corporate and Securities.
**Richards, Jeremy V.** ...............'58 '82 C.051 B.A. L.309 LL.M. [Pachulski,S.Z.&Y.]
*REPORTED CASES: Carolco Television Inc. vs. National Broadcasting Co. (In re DeLaurentiis Entertainment Group, Inc.), 963 F.2d 1269 (9th Cir. 1992); In re Davey Roofing, Inc. 167 B.R. 604 (Bankr. C.D., 1994).
*TRANSACTIONS: Represented the Creditors Committees in Qintex Entertainment Inc.; Weintraub Entertainment, Inc.; Leisure Technology, Inc.; First Capital Holdings, Inc.; Represented or represents the Trustee in Triad America Corporation and Oppenheimer Industries, Inc.
**Richards, Julia Ellen** .................'62 '93 C.691 B.A. L.800 J.D. [A Pillsbury M.&S.]
**Richards, Laurie J.** ................................'43 '75 L.1148 J.D. [Coleman&R.]
**Richards, Peter C., (A Professional Corporation)** '52 '78
C.21 B.A. L.831 J.D. [C Langberg,C.&D.]
*PRACTICE AREAS: Entertainment Law; Taxation.
Richards-Johnson, Gloria M. ..............'50 '80 C&L.329 B.A., J.D. 333 S. Grand Ave.

**Richards, Watson and Gershon, Professional Corporation, (AV)**
**Thirty-Eighth Floor, 333 South Hope Street, 90071**
**Telephone: 213-626-8484 Telecopiers: 213-626-0078; 617-1144 Cable Address: "Richwat"**
**Richard Richards (1916-1988); Glenn R. Watson; Robert G. Beverly; Harry L. Gershon; Douglas W. Argue (Certified Specialist, Taxation Law, The State Bar of California Board of Legal Specialization); Mark L. Lamken; Erwin E. Adler; Darold D. Pieper; Allen E. Rennett; Steven Lee Dorsey; William L. Strausz; Anthony B. Drewry; Mitchell E. Abbott; Timothy L. Neufeld; Gregory W. Stepanicich; Rochelle Browne; Michael Jenkins; William B. Rudell; Quinn M. Barrow; Carol W. Lynch; Jeffrey A. Rabin; Gregory M. Kunert; Thomas M. Jimbo; Michele Beal Bagneris; Amanda F. Susskind; Robert C. Ceccon; Sayre Weaver; William K. Kramer; Steven H. Kaufmann; Gary E. Gans; John Joseph Harris; Kevin G. Ennis; Robin D. Harris; Michael Estrada; Laurence S. Wiener; Steven R. Orr; Michael G. Colantuono; C. Edward Dilkes; Peter M. Thorson; Brenda L. Diederichs; Deborah R. Hakman; B. Tilden Kim; Rubin D. Weiner; Saskia Tsushima Asamura; Kayser O. Sume; Saul Jaffe; Craig A. Steele; T. Peter Pierce; Benjamin Barnouw; Terence R. Boga; Daniel L. Pines; Lisa Bond; Diane Arkow Gross; Roxanne Diaz Montgomery.**
**The Firm Specializes in the Areas of Civil Litigation, Public Law, Municipal Finance, Insurance, Environmental Law, Oil and Gas, Corporation, Banking, Securities, State and Federal Tax, Estate Planning, Trust and Probate, Unfair Competition, Entertainment, Real Estate, Public Utilities, Administrative and Employment Law.**
**Reference: Bank of California, N.A. (Los Angeles Regional Main Office).**
***See Professional Biographies, LOS ANGELES, CALIFORNIA***

Richardson, Carol A. ......'51 '86 C.339 B.S. L.597 J.D. Dependency Ct. Legal Servs., Inc.
Richardson, Charles H. '46 '72 C.112 B.A. L.426 J.D.
Div. Mgr., Legal Claims, Auto. Club of Southern Calif.
**Richardson, Clare** ..........................'62 '86 C&L.800 A.B., J.D. [Foley L.W.&A.]
*PRACTICE AREAS: Corporate Law; Finance; Health Care; Hospitals.
**Richardson, D. Matthew**, (AV) ........'52 '84 C.911 B.A. L.1065 J.D. [Troop M.S.&P.]
*PRACTICE AREAS: Taxation Law; Estate Planning; General Business Law.
Richardson, Douglas F., (AV) .............'29 '54 C.112 A.B. L.309 J.D. 400 S. Hope St.‡
Richardson, Eric W. .....................'66 '92 C.800 A.B. L.477 J.D. 777 S. Figueroa St.
**Richardson, Janet M.** ....................'67 '92 C.597 B.A. L.1049 J.D. [A Morris,P.&P.]
**Richardson, Jeffrey L.** ....................'68 '93 C.950 B.S. L.800 J.D. [A Mitchell,S.&K.]
*PRACTICE AREAS: Litigation.
**Richardson, Kim Y.** ...........................'69 '95 C.112 B.A. L.309 J.D. [A Mitchell,S.&K.]
*PRACTICE AREAS: Civil Litigation.
**Richardson, Paul J.** '65 '91 C&L.800 B.A., J.D.
Asst. Gen. Coun., The Times Mirror Co. & Gen. Coun., Times Mirror Training
**Richardson, Tony L.** .......................'55 '86 C.309 B.A. L.813 J.D. [Kirkland&E.]
*PRACTICE AREAS: Litigation.
Richardson-Pelliccioni, Lori S. ..............'60 '86 C.509 B.S. L.365 J.D. Asst. U.S. Atty.
Richelson, Mark P. .........................'48 '73 C.1042 B.A. L.1049 J.D. Dep. Atty. Gen.
**Richey, Andria K.** ...................'55 '79 C.112 B.A. L.1066 J.D. [Sonnenschein N.&R.]
*PRACTICE AREAS: Commercial Litigation; Government Contracts Law; Intellectual Property Law.
Richey, Diane J. ..............'48 '82 C.105 A.B. L.426 J.D. V.P. & Sr. Coun., Union Bk.
Richey, Susan M. ...........................'50 '82 C.945 B.S. L.446 J.D. 300 S. Grand Ave.
Richland, Felipa Ruthe '57 '83 C.800 A.B. L.464 J.D.
11835 W. Olympic Blvd., E. Twr.
Richland, Robt. N., (BV) .........'25 '51 C.309 A.B. L.1066 LL.B. 10866 Wilshire Blvd.
**Richler, Paul A.** ..........................................'46 '74 C.012 L.029 LL.B. [Morgan,L.&B.]
Richlin, Stewart E. ...........................'60 '86 C.112 L.809 J.D. 9007 Melrose Ave.
**Richman, David S.**, (AV) ..............'52 '77 C.174 B.A. L.145 J.D. [Ginsburg,S.O.&R.]
**Richman, Frederick A.**, (AV) ..........'45 '71 C.309 A.B. L.569 J.D. [O'Melveny&M.]
*PRACTICE AREAS: State Taxation and Federal Taxation Litigation; Tax Planning for Technology Firms and Entertainment Clients.
**Richman, James D.**, (AV) ................'48 '74 C.605 B.A. L.1066 J.D. [Richman,L.K.&G.]
*PRACTICE AREAS: Real Estate; Taxation; Business Law; Finance.
Richman, Sheldon ..................'36 '62 C&L.800 B.S., LL.B. Partner, Deloitte & Touche
Richman, Stacey ..........................'66 '91 C.1036 B.A. L.978 J.D. 725 S. Figueroa St.

CAA323P

**Richman, Steven N.**, (AV) .................... '56 '81 C.800 B.A. L.426 J.D. [Epport&R.]

**Richman, Lawrence, Mann, Greene, Chizever, Friedman & Phillips, A Professional Corporation**
**(See Beverly Hills)**

**Richman, Luna, Kichaven & Glushon, (AV)**
**12424 Wilshire Boulevard, Suite 900, 90025**
**Telephone: 310-207-4880 Telecopier: 310-207-4889, 310-442-6400**
**Members of Firm: James D. Richman; Dennis R. Luna; Jeffrey G. Kichaven; Robert L. Glushon. Associate: Luz Aurora Ortiz.**
**General Business Transaction and Civil Litigation Practice, with special expertise in Corporate and Real Estate Transactions, Land Use, Natural Resource Matters and Federal and State Trial Practice.**
**References: Coast Federal Savings & Loan Assn. (Westwood Branch); City National Bank (Beverly Hills, Calif.).**

***See Professional Biographies, LOS ANGELES, CALIFORNIA***

**Richmond, Anthony J.** .................... '59 '88 C.112 B.S. L.1066 J.D. [Latham&W.]

Richmond, David L.S. .................... '45 '77 C.169 B.A. L.425 J.D. [Richmond&R.]

Richmond, Esther S. .................... '22 '65 C.994 B.A. L.426 J.D. [Richmond&R.]

**Richmond, Jeffrey A.** .............. '62 '91 C.309 A.B. L.1068 J.D. [🄰 Heller E.W.&M.]

**Richmond, John J.** .................... '51 '77 C.1042 B.A. L.426 J.D. [Barger&W.]
*PRACTICE AREAS: Real Estate Finance Law; Insurance Regulatory Law.

**Richmond, Paul J.** ................ '40 '69 C.1075 B.S. L.93 J.D. Atlantic Richfield Co.
*RESPONSIBILITIES: Corporate Law.

Richmond & Richmond, (AV) ................................ 12555 W. Jefferson Blvd.

Richter, Brooke K. .................... '65 '90 C.112 B.A. L.94 J.D. 600 Wilshire Blvd.

**Richter, David J.** .................... '68 '92 C.188 B.A. L.976 J.D. [🄰 Irell&M.]

**Richter, George R., Jr.**, (AV) .... '10 '33 C&L.800 A.B., LL.B. [🄲 Sheppard,M.R.&H.] ‡

**Richter, Jeffrey R.**, (AV) .................. '45 '71 C.112 A.B. L.846 J.D. [Walter,F.&R.]
*PRACTICE AREAS: Corporate Law; Commercial Transactions; Business Planning; Mergers and Acquisitions; Federal and State Securities Law.

**Richter, Robert V.** .................... '59 '87 C.800 B.S. L.426 J.D. [Hancock R.&B.]

Richter, Scott M. .................... '64 '89 C&L.472 B.A., J.D. 1400 Kelton Ave.

**Richter, Stuart M.** ............ '61 '86 C.893 B.S. L.990 J.D. [Katten M.&Z.] (⊙Irvine)
*PRACTICE AREAS: Litigation.

Rickershauser, Charles E., Jr., (AV) '28 '59
C.112 A.B. L.1068 LL.B. 355 S. Grand Ave., 34th Fl.

**Rickless & Wolf, (AV)**
**Suite 1900, 1900 Avenue of the Stars, 90067**
**Telephone: 310-201-7577 Telecopier: 310-277-5143**
**Michael B. Wolf.**
**General and International Law Practice. Entertainment, Corporate, Copyright and Tax Law.**
**London, England Office: Trafalgar House, ll Waterloo Place. Telephone: 071-839 3226. Telex: 917881 WITSOM G. Telecopier: 071-839-6741.**

***See Professional Biographies, LOS ANGELES, CALIFORNIA***

**Ridenour, Robert N.** .................... '59 '83 C.531 B.S. L.597 J.D. [Borton,P.&C.]
*PRACTICE AREAS: Casualty Litigation; Business Litigation.

Rider, Dennis J. .............. '52 '77 C.112 B.A. L.1068 J.D. 10345 W. Olympic Blvd.

**Rider, Julia J., (P.C.)** .............. '— '75 C.112 A.B. L.1068 J.D. [Jeffer,M.B.&M.]
*PRACTICE AREAS: General Civil Litigation; Professional Liability; Complex Tort Litigation; Insurance-Related Matters.

**Ridge, Donald L.** .................... '60 '87 C.605 A.B. L.800 J.D. [Morris,P.&P.]

**Ridley, Lori A.** .................... '58 '90 C.1077 B.S. L.809 [🄰 Pillsbury M.&S.]
*PRACTICE AREAS: Employee Benefits Law.

**Ridley, Robert W., (A Professional Corporation)**, (AV) '37 '63
C.1258 L.426 LL.B. [Farmer&R.]
*PRACTICE AREAS: ERISA.

Ridout, Christopher P. .................. '64 '89 C.309 B.S. L.464 J.D. 3699 Wilshire Blvd.

Riedel, Barry W. .................... '41 '77 C.605 B.A. L.809 J.D. P.O. Box 15448

Riedman, Kenneth L., Jr. ............ '36 '72 C.813 B.S. L.800 J.D. 461 S. Boylston St.‡

**Riegelhuth, Douglas H.** ................ '67 '93 C&L.112 B.A., J.D. [🄰 Crosby,H.R.&M.]

**Riekhof, Mark A.** .................... '69 '94 C.1049 B.B.A. L.770 J.D. [🄰 Galton&H.]

**Riera, Mark** .................... '57 '85 C.668 B.A. L.813 J.D. [Sheppard,M.R.&H.]
*PRACTICE AREAS: Antitrust and Trade Regulation; Condemnation Law.

**Rierdan, Valerie M.** .................. '69 '96 C&L.990 B.A., J.D. [🄰 Friedlander&W.]
*PRACTICE AREAS: Business Transactions.

**Rierson, Lee W.** .................... '67 '93 C.112 B.A. L.1068 J.D. [🄰 S.Drapkin]

**Ries, Donald Paul** .................... '59 '86 C.36 B.S. L.145 J.D. [Brown,W.&C.]
*PRACTICE AREAS: Real Estate; Finance.

Rifenbark, Neil, (AV) .................. '47 '73 C.813 A.B. L.426 J.D. [Johnson,R.&W.]

**Riff, Lawrence P.** .................... '55 '82 C.477 B.A. L.629 J.D. [Lane P.S.L.]
*PRACTICE AREAS: Chemical Products Liability, Railroad, Trucking and Transportation Law; Commercial Litigation; Insurance Defense.

**Riffer, Jeffrey K.** .................... '53 '78 C.347 B.S. L.1119 J.D. [Jeffer,M.B.&M.]
*PRACTICE AREAS: Antitrust; Defamation; Copyright; Trademark; Unfair Competition.

**Rifkin, Roy G.**, (AV) .................... '53 '78 C.188 A.B. L.659 J.D. [Wolf,R.&S.]
*PRACTICE AREAS: Civil Litigation; Real Estate; Entertainment Law.

**Rifkind, Robert Gore, Law Offices of, (AV) '28 '55 C.112 B.A. L.309 LL.B.**
**10100 Santa Monica Boulevard, Suite 215, 90067**
**Telephone: 310-552-0478 FAX: 310-552-0478**
**Corporate Securities and Real Estate and Related Litigation. Estate Planning and Probate.**

***See Professional Biographies, LOS ANGELES, CALIFORNIA***

Riggio, Joseph V. ........................................ '30 '53 L.724 LL.B. Mun. Ct. J.

Riggs, Brent D. .................... '42 '70 C.101 B.S. L.145 J.D. Dep. Dist. Atty.

Riggs, Stephen J. ............ '56 '82 C.112 B.A. L.1065 J.D. 777 S. Figueroa St., 10th Fl.

**Rihn, Dennis W.** .................... '57 '86 C.999 B.F.A. L.426 J.D. [Pansky&M.]
*REPORTED CASES: ITT v. Niles (1994) 9 Cal.4th 245.
*PRACTICE AREAS: Legal Malpractice; Professional Liability; General Civil Trial and Appellate Practice.

**Riley, David W.** .................... '56 '82 C.112 B.A. L.800 J.D. [Goodson&W.]
*PRACTICE AREAS: Tax; Business; Corporate; Partnership; Limited Liability Companies.

**Riley, Dennis P.** .................... '62 '88 C&L.770 B.S., J.D. [🄰 Serritella&P.]
*PRACTICE AREAS: Trial; Appellate Litigation.

**Riley, Grant K.**, (BV) .................. '56 '84 C.112 B.A. L.809 J.D. [Weinhart&R.]
*PRACTICE AREAS: Real Estate Litigation; Bankruptcy; Secured Creditors Rights.

**Riley, Joyce** .................... '61 '89 C.800 B.S. L.112 J.D. [🄰 Olincy&K.]
*PRACTICE AREAS: Tax Law; Estate Planning; Probate and Trust.

**Riley, Lynda M.** .................... '57 '86 C&L.061 B.A., LL.B. [🄰 Gabriel,H.&P.]

**Riley, Richard P.** .................... '63 '90 C.112 B.A. L.809 J.D. [🄰 Knopfler&R.]
*PRACTICE AREAS: Construction Defect Litigation; General Tort Litigation; Employment Law.

Riley, Sandra R. .................. '49 '80 C&L.398 B.A., J.D. Probate Atty., Supr. Ct.

**Riley, Sean** ................ '57 '86 C&L.061 B.Ec., LL.B. [Christensen,M.F.J.G.W.&S.]
*PRACTICE AREAS: Civil Litigation.

Riley, Timothy C. .................. '57 '83 C.1134 B.S. L.800 J.D. 725 S. Figueroa St.

Rincover, Neil B. .................. '54 '90 C.800 B.A. L.1148 J.D. 3600 Wilshire Blvd.

Rindge, Samuel F. .................... '43 '79 C.273 B.A. L.426 J.D. County Coun.

Rindge, Samuel H., (AV) ......... '13 '39 C.309 A.B. L.1065 J.D. 501 S. Plymouth Blvd.‡

**Rinehart, Karen** .............................. '— '96 L.426 J.D. [🄰 McKenna&C.]
*PRACTICE AREAS: Government Contracts.

**Ring, David M.** .................... '65 '90 C&L.800 B.S., J.D. [McNicholas&M.]

**Ring, Douglas R., (A Professional Corporation)**, (AV) '44 '77
C.398 B.A. L.1136 J.D. [🄲 Mitchell,S.&K.]
*PRACTICE AREAS: Real Estate Law; Land Use Law; Administrative Law.

**Ring, Michael W.**, (AV) .......... '43 '69 C.911 B.A. L.1066 J.D. [Sonnenschein N.&R.]
*PRACTICE AREAS: Real Estate and Real Estate Finance.

Ring, Peter S. '41 '66 C.708 B.A. L.276 J.D.
(adm. in CT; not adm. in CA) Loyola Marymount Univ.

Ring, Ricki C. .................... '46 '79 C.112 B.A. L.809 J.D. 2049 Century Park E.

**Ring, Robert A.**, (AV) .................... '55 '81 C.112 B.A. L.1049 J.D. [Ring&G.]
*PRACTICE AREAS: General Business; Commercial and Real Estate Litigation; General Business Transactions; Corporate Law.

**Ring & Green, (AV)**
**Suite 2300, 1900 Avenue of the Stars, 90067**
**Telephone: 310-201-0777 Fax: 310-556-1346**
**Members of Firm: Robert A. Ring; Susan H. Green.**
**Business, Commercial and Real Estate Litigation. General Business Transactions and Corporate Law. Trial Practice in all Courts.**
**Reference: Union Bank (Century City Office).**

***See Professional Biographies, LOS ANGELES, CALIFORNIA***

Ringold, Leslie Beth .................... '57 '85 C.966 B.A. L.800 J.D. Dep. Pub. Def.

Ringwald, Roland E. .................. '29 '62 C.1043 B.A. L.809 LL.B. Dep. City Atty.

**Ringwood, David K.** .................... '51 '84 C.165 B.A. L.809 J.D. [Howarth&S.]
*PRACTICE AREAS: Trial Practice; Complex and Multi-District Litigation; Products Liability Law; Business Litigation; Professional Liability.

Rini, Nicholas C. .................. '55 '80 C.1042 B.S. L.1049 J.D. Dep. Dist. Atty.

**Rintala, William T.**, (AV) ............ '38 '67 C.813 A.B. L.1066 J.D. [Rintala,S.J.&R.]

**Rintala, Smoot, Jaenicke & Rees, (AV)**
**10351 Santa Monica Boulevard, Suite 400, 90025-6937**
**Telephone: 310-203-0935 Facsimile: 310-556-8921**
**Members of Firm: William T. Rintala; Peter C. Smoot; J. Larson Jaenicke; Robert A. Rees; Melodie K. Larsen; Frank E. Melton. Associates: Robert W. Hodges; Marc D. Mootchnik; Michael B. Garfinkel; Emily Peters.**
**Civil Trial and Appellate Practice.**
**Representative Clients: William Morris Agency, Inc.; Broadcast Music, Inc.; Eaton Corp.**
**Reference: Western Bank.**

***See Professional Biographies, LOS ANGELES, CALIFORNIA***

**Riola, Jill Sarnoff** .................... '54 '80 C.696 B.A. L.569 J.D. [Baker&H.]
*PRACTICE AREAS: Trademark; Copyright; Advertising; Marketing Services.

**Riordan, Richard J.**, (AV) .............. '30 '57 C.674 A.B. L.477 J.D. [Riordan&M.] ‡

**Riordan, Thomas M.** ................ '57 '95 C.352 B.A. L.426 J.D. [🄰 O'Melveny&M.]
*PRACTICE AREAS: Litigation.

**Riordan & McKinzie, A Professional Law Corporation, (AV)**
**California Plaza, 29th Floor, 300 South Grand Avenue, 90071⊙**
**Telephone: 213-629-4824 FAX: 213-229-8550**
**Richard J. Riordan (Retired); Carl W. McKinzie; James A. Hamilton; Jeffrey L. DuRocher; Jeffrey L. Glassman; L. Andrew Gifford; Roger H. Lustberg; Martin J. Thompson (Resident, Orange County Office); Lawrence C. Weeks (Resident, Westlake Village Office); Kenneth D. Klein; Thomas L. Harnsberger; Richard J. Welch; Janis B. Salin; John J. Quinn; Angelo C. Falcone; William H. Emer; Kirk F. Maldonado (Resident, Orange County Office); James W. Loss (Resident, Orange County Office); Dana M. Warren (Resident, Westlake Village Office); Eugene G. Cowan; Scott R. Miller; Michael P. Whalen (Resident, Orange County Office); Cynthia M. Dunnett; Aaftab P. Esmail; Sandra J. Levin; Lance S. Bocarsly; Elaine R. Levin (Resident, Orange County Office); Donald J. Kula; Thomas M. Cleary;—Janine Y. Ariey; James H. Shnell (Resident, Orange County Office); Timothy F. Sylvester; Robert W. Stockstill, Jr.; Bart Greenberg (Resident, Orange County Office); Misara C. Shao; Gina M. Calvelli; Bruce C. Geyer; Brenda L. White; Robert N. Duran; Karen C. Goodin (Resident, Orange County Office); Reynolds T. Cafferata; Eric J. Smith; Pamela Smith Kelley; Thomas A. Waldman; David M. Janet; Sung Hui Kim; Diane M. Lambillotte; Eric Reed Hattler; Jonathan Gluck; Jacqueline A. Cookerly; Kyle B. Arndt; Douglas C. Carleton; Grace C. Liang; Michael G. McKinnon (Resident, Orange County Office); Ryan S. Hong; Amy E. Greenberg; Barbara A. Krieg; Ronn S. Davids; Jeanne Miller-Romero (Resident, Orange County Office); Ashley S. Newsom; Kristi L. Cobb. Of Counsel: Thomas L. Caps; Joseph A. Carbone; Patrick C. Haden.**
**General Civil and Trial Practice in all State and Federal Courts. Corporation, Corporate Securities, Real Estate, Antitrust, Patent, Trademark, Copyright and Unfair Competition Law. Taxation, Estate Planning, Trust and Probate Law.**
**Reference: Citibank, 333 S. Grand Avenue, Los Angeles, Calif.**
**Westlake Village, California Office: 5743 Corsa Avenue, Suite 116. Telephones: 818-706-1800; 805-496-4688. FAX: 818-706-2956.**
**Costa Mesa, California Office: 695 Town Center Drive, Suite 1500. Telephone: 714-433-2900. FAX: 714-549-3244.**

***See Professional Biographies, LOS ANGELES, CALIFORNIA***

Ripley, Audrey Y. .................... '47 '85 C.831 B.S. L.809 J.D. [Ripley&Assoc.]

Ripley & Associates ........................................ 4929 Wilshire Blvd.

**Rips, Martin A.** .................... '62 '89 C.596 B.A. L.273 J.D. [🄰 McKenna&C.]
*PRACTICE AREAS: Government Contracts Law; Litigation; International Arbitration.

Risen, Kenneth L. .............................. '37 '87 L.1190 LL.B. 2500 Wilshire Blvd.

**Rishwain, James M., Jr.** .............. '59 '84 C.112 B.A. L.990 J.D. [Pillsbury M.&S.]

**Riskin, Ira D.**, (AV) .................. '33 '62 C.112 B.A. L.1068 LL.B. [Hecht&R.]
*PRACTICE AREAS: Civil Trial; Trial Practice; Civil Appeals; Real Estate; Business Law.

**Ristaino, Kristine D.** .................. '66 '91 C.228 A.B. L.597 J.D. [🄰 Gibson,D.&C.]
*PRACTICE AREAS: Real Estate; General Corporate.

**Ritchie, Graham A.**, (AV) .......... '30 '56 C.112 B.A. L.1068 J.D. [🄲 Simmons,R.&S.]

Ritchie, Hugh J., (AV) ........ '21 '53 C&L.05 B.Com., LL.B. 6055 E. Washington Blvd.

**Ritchie, Richard G.** .................. '40 '72 C.1131 B.A. L.1068 J.D. [Inglis,L.&G.]
*PRACTICE AREAS: Business Litigation; Insurance Coverage; Arbitration; Mediation.

**Ritenour, David K.** .................. '69 '96 C.112 B.S. L.1068 J.D. [🄰 Graham&J.]
*PRACTICE AREAS: Real Estate; Securities; Banking.

**Ritner, William F., (A Professional Corporation)**, (AV) '37 '66
C.546 L.809 J.D. [Patterson,R.L.G.&J.] (⊙San Bernardino)

Rittenberg, Laurie .................... '54 '82 C.112 B.A. L.809 J.D. Dep. City Atty.

**Rittenberg, Saul N., (A P.C.)**, (AV) ......... '12 '35 C.112 A.B. L.597 J.D. [🄲 Loeb&L.]
*PRACTICE AREAS: Entertainment Law.

**Rittenburg, Thomas** .................. '53 '78 C.902 B.A. L.838 J.D. [Lewis,D.B.&B.]

Ritter, Laurence W., (BV) .......... '22 '53 C.197 A.B. L.976 J.D. 2040 Ave. of the Stars

**Rittmaster, Ted** .......... '61 '90 C.800 B.S.E.E. L.128 J.D. [🄰 Loeb&L.] (See Pat. Sect.)
*PRACTICE AREAS: Patent Prosecution.

**Ritz, T. Joshua** .................... '67 '92 C.800 B.A. L.1066 J.D. [🄰 Foley L.W.&A.]

**Rivard, Catherine L.** .................. '58 '86 C.605 A.B. L.597 J.D. [Troop M.S.&P.]
*PRACTICE AREAS: Insurance Coverage Litigation.

**Rivas, Nicole** .............. '69 '95 C&L.800 B.A., J.D. [🄰 McClintock,W.B.R.R.&M.]
*PRACTICE AREAS: Environmental and General Business Litigation.

Rivera, Lourdes A. .............. '65 '91 C&L.976 B.A., J.D. National Health Law Prog.

Rivera-Santander, Elizabeth G. ............ '56 '86 C.112 B.A. L.1068 J.D. 2606 E. 1st St.

**Rivers, Cheryl S.** .............. '54 '80 C.769 B.A. L.800 J.D. [🄰 Allen,M.L.G.&M.]
*PRACTICE AREAS: Real Estate.

Rivers, Donald P .............................. '51 '81 C.107 B.A. L.800 J.D. [Rivers&B.]

**Rivers, Steven A.** .................. '70 '95 C.112 B.A. L.1068 J.D. [🄰 Pircher,N.&M.]
*PRACTICE AREAS: Real Estate Law.

**Rivers, Timothy F.** .................. '65 '90 C.112 B.A. L.1049 J.D. [🄰 Lynberg&W.]
*PRACTICE AREAS: Insurance Defense; Construction Defect; Insurance Coverage.

Rivers & Bower ........................................ 10573 W. Pico Blvd.

Rivin, Kenneth A. .......... '47 '74 C.1169 B.A. L.426 J.D. 4250 Wilshire Blvd., 2nd Fl.

Riznyk, Stefano ......... '58 '88 C.02 B.Sc. L.61 J.D. [International L.e.a.] (⊙San Diego)
Rizzo, Karen ..................................'53 '77 C.573 B.A. L.472 J.D. Dep. Dist. Atty.
**Rizzo, Michael R.** ........................... '67 '92 C&L.276 B.S., J.D. [A McKenna&C.]
*LANGUAGES: Spanish.
*PRACTICE AREAS: Litigation; Government Contracts; White Collar Criminal Defense.
**Rizzo, Ronald S.**, (AV) '41 '65 C.746 B.S. L.276 LL.B.
[Jones,D.R.&P.] (⊙Chicago, IL)
Roadarmel, Paul M., Jr. ................... '60 '85 C.103 A.B. L.112 J.D. Dep. Atty. Gen.
**Roan, Peter**, (AV) .................. '59 '85 C.352 B.B.A. L.436 J.D. [C Konowiecki&R.]
*PRACTICE AREAS: Litigation and Environmental Law.
Roark, David L. ....................... '48 '73 C.112 B.A. L.464 J.D. 5939 Monterey Rd.
Roark, Paul R. ......................... '47 '72 C.112 B.A. L.1068 J.D. Fed. Trade Comm.
Robb, G. Charles ..................... '62 '92 C.976 B.A. L.309 J.D. 2049 Century Pk. E.
**Robb, M. Ellen** ................................ '51 '82 C.352 B.A. L.976 J.D. [Mayer,B.&P.]
**Robbins, Billy A.**, (AV) '26 '58
C.45 B.S.E.E. L.800 J.D. [Robbins,B.&C.] (See Pat. Sect.)
*PRACTICE AREAS: Patent Law; Trademark Law; Copyright Law; Trade Secret Law; Unfair Competition Law.

**Robbins, Clay, III '55 '81 C.112 B.A. L.426 J.D.**
**700 South Flower Street, Suite 500, 90017**
**Telephone: 310-553-6630 Fax: 310-785-9143**
**(Also of Counsel to Fish, Falkenhainer & Downer, Pasadena).**
***PRACTICE AREAS: Civil Litigation; Wrongful Discharge; Governmental Tort Liability; Premises Liability; Trademark Infringement.**
**General Civil Litigation.**
*See Professional Biographies, LOS ANGELES, CALIFORNIA*

Robbins, Daniel ............................'66 '91 C.880 B.A. L.1068 J.D. 801 S. Figueroa St.
**Robbins, David K.** ................................'57 '83 C.881 A.B. L.472 J.D. [Fried,F.H.S.&J.]
Robbins, Edward M., Jr. ..............'49 '78 C.608 B.S.E.E. L.284 J.D. Asst. U.S. Atty.
Robbins, Jill S., (AV) ........................'46 '71 C.112 B.A. L.800 J.D. P.O. Box 25926
**Robbins, Mark** ............................ '61 '88 C.112 B.A. L.426 J.D. [Epport&R.]
*PRACTICE AREAS: Commercial Litigation; Bankruptcy; Real Property; Banking Transactions.
**Robbins, Mark A.** ......................... '59 '89 C&L.273 B.A., J.D. [A Hancock R.&B.]
**Robbins, Mark W.** ........................ '51 '77 C.696 B.A. L.93 J.D. [Littler,M.F.T.&M.]

**Robbins, Berliner & Carson, (AV) BB**
**Fifth Floor, Figueroa Plaza, 201 North Figueroa Street, 90012-2628**
**Telephone: 213-977-1001 Telecopier: 213-977-1003**
**Members of Firm: Billy A. Robbins; Robert Berliner; John Carson; Michael S. Elkind; Leonard D. Messinger; John M. May; Clark D. Gross. Associates: Ying-Kit Lau; Horacio A. Farach; Sharon Wong; Deborah M. Nesset; Pete A. Smits; Wean Khing Wong; Lisa N. Partain. Of Counsel: John P. Spitals.**
**Patent, Trademark, Copyright and Unfair Competition Law. Trial and Appellate Practice in all Federal and State Courts.**
*See Professional Biographies, LOS ANGELES, CALIFORNIA*

Roberson, Robert L., Jr. ........................ '31 '59 C.990 B.A. L.800 J.D. Supr. Ct. J.
Roberts, A. James, III, (AV) ............'38 '67 C.871 B.S. L.1066 LL.B. 333 S. Hope St.
**Roberts, Carla M.** ..............'64 '91 C.800 A.B. L.976 J.D. [A Greenberg G.F.C.&M.]
*PRACTICE AREAS: Entertainment.
Roberts, Daniel K. ...................................'53 '79 C.112 B.S. L.800 J.D. [Roberts&R.]
**Roberts, David M.** ............................... '51 '76 C.112 A.B. L.464 J.D. [Paul,H.J.&W.]
Roberts, Florrie Young ................'49 '74 C.813 A.B. L.800 J.D. Loyola Law School
**Roberts, Gary M.** ................................ '62 '87 C.674 A.B. L.813 J.D. [C Gibson,D.&C.]
*PRACTICE AREAS: Litigation.
**Roberts, James C.**, (AV) ........................'45 '72 C.154 B.A. L.309 J.D. [Graham&J.]
*PRACTICE AREAS: Employment Law; Labor Law.
Roberts, James Francis '49 '81 C.112 B.A. L.426
Dep. Gen. Coun., Metropolitan Water Dist. of Southern Calif.
**Roberts, John W.** '29 '70 C.393 B.A. L.309 J.D.
(adm. in IL; not adm. in CA) [Zevnik H.G.&M.]⊙
*REPORTED CASES: Monsanto Company in Hines v. Vulcan, 658 F.Supp. 651 (N.D. Ill. 1988); Inland Steel Company in Inland Steel v. Koppers Company, 498 N.E.2d 1247 (Ind. App. 1986).
*PRACTICE AREAS: Commercial Litigation; Compensation and Liability; Environmental; Construction.
Roberts, Kimberly J. ...............'61 '89 C.112 B.A. L.1065 J.D. 1900 Ave. of the Stars
Roberts, Larry M. .... '57 '82 C.112 B.A. L.426 J.D. 3415 S. Sepulveda Blvd., Suite 1120
Roberts, Michael T. .......... '43 '68 C.265 B.A. L.1119 J.D. 2500 Wilshire Blvd., Pths. A
**Roberts, Michael W.**, (BV) .......... '38 '65 C.401 B.A. L.705 J.D. [C Simmons,R.&S.]
*REPORTED CASES: Williams v. American Casualty Insurance Co. (1971) 6 Cal. 3d 266, 491 p.2d 398, 98 Cal. Rptr. 814.
*PRACTICE AREAS: Business and Litigation (75%); Real Estate (20%); Estates and Estate Planning (5%).
**Roberts, Rebecca D.** '64 '92 C.813 B.A. L.276 J.D.
(adm. in PA; not adm. in CA) [A Latham&W.]
*PRACTICE AREAS: Health Care Law.
Roberts, Theodore K. ............................ '48 '82 C.112 B.A. L.705 J.D. [Roberts&R.]
**Roberts, Thomas G.** ......................... '49 '74 C&L.800 B.A., J.D. [Baker&H.]
*PRACTICE AREAS: Business Law; Real Estate Law.
Roberts, Vicki M. ........'59 '83 C.1077 B.A. L.809 J.D. 1100 Glendon Ave., West L.A.
Roberts, Virgil ...............'47 '72 C.112 B.A. L.309 J.D. Pres., Gen. Coun., Solar Records
**Roberts, William S.** ..............'45 '89 C.174 B.A. L.1049 J.D. [A Wilson,E.M.E.&D.]
Roberts & Roberts .................................................................510 W. 6th St.
**Robertson, Alexander, IV**, (AV) ............'59 '86 C&L.990 B.Sc., J.D. [Knopfler&R.]
*PRACTICE AREAS: Construction Law; Construction Defect Litigation; Real Estate Litigation.
Robertson, Andrew W., (AV) ............'49 '74 C.103 A.B. L.1068 J.D. 725 S. Figueroa
Robertson, Barton W., (AV) ...............'35 '69 C.112 B.S. L.426 J.D. [Tyre K.K.&G.]
Robertson, Carol A. .............. '52 '78 C.112 B.A. L.426 J.D. Sr. Coun., Calif. Fed. Bk.
**Robertson, Christina S.** .................. '63 '92 C.112 B.A. L.426 J.D. [A Knopfler&R.]
*PRACTICE AREAS: Construction Defect Litigation; General Tort Litigation.
Robertson, David A. ........................ '60 '89 C.399 B.A. L.911 J.D. 400 S. Hope St.
Robertson, Hugh Duff ......'57 '83 C.965 B.B.A. L.1148 J.D. 4727 Wilshire Blvd., 6th Fl.
Robertson, J. Bruce ........................... '57 '88 C.034 B.A. L.012 LL.B. [Duran,L.&R.]
**Robertson, James** ............................. '55 '95 C.1051 B.A. L.813 J.D. [A Sidley&A.]
*LANGUAGES: Japanese, Dutch.
*PRACTICE AREAS: Corporate Banking.
Robertson, John D. .................... '51 '76 C.112 B.A. L.1066 J.D. 1055 Wilshire Blvd.
**Robertson, Joy L.** ......................... '66 '93 C.112 B.A. L.809 J.D. [A Engstrom,L.&L.]
**Robertson, Kyle M.** ......................... '61 '88 C.914 B.A. L.93 J.D. [A Freeman,F.&S.]
Robertson, Lynn A. .......................... '57 '85 C.965 B.S. L.426 J.D. 550 S. Hope St.
**Robie, James R.**, (AV) ........................ '49 '75 C.154 B.A. L.426 J.D. [Robie&M.]
*REPORTED CASES: Allegro v. Superior Court; Austero v. National Casualty Co.; Omaha Paper Stock v. Harbor Ins. Co.; Prudential LMI v. Superior Court; von der Leith v. State Farm.
*PRACTICE AREAS: Insurance Bad Faith; Legal Malpractice.

**Robie & Matthai, A Professional Corporation, (AV) BB**
**Biltmore Tower, 500 South Grand, Suite 1500, 90071**
**Telephone: 213-624-3062 Fax: 213-624-2563**
**James R. Robie; Edith R. Matthai; Michael J. O'Neill; Kyle Kveton; Maria Louise Cousineau; Pamela E. Dunn (Certified Specialist, Appellate Law, The State Bar of California Board of Legal Specialization);—Craig W. Brunet; Kim W. Sellars; Teresa J. Friederichs; Bernadine J. Stolar; Claudia Sokol; Karen R. Palmersheim; Brian D. Huben; Wendy L. Schneider; Natalie A. Kouyoumdjian; Gabrielle M. Jackson.**

(This Listing Continued)

**Robie & Matthai, A Professional Corporation (Continued)**
**Products Liability, Insurance and Bad Faith Litigation, Legal Malpractice Defense, General Civil Litigation. Appellate Litigation.**
**Representative Clients: State Farm Fire & Casualty Co.; The Travelers; Fireman's Fund Ins. Co.; Lawyers Mutual Ins. Co.; Carrier Corp.**
**Reference: First Professional Bank.**
*See Professional Biographies, LOS ANGELES, CALIFORNIA*

Robin, Ellis Paul ........................................'57 '81 C.112 B.A. L.809 J.D. [Hoffman&R.]
**Robin, Gregg H.**, (AV) ............................ '51 '80 C.112 B.A. L.809 J.D. [C Ramsey,B.&D.]
*PRACTICE AREAS: Workers Compensation Defense Law (100%).
**Robin, Samuel M.**, (AV) ...........'45 '71 C.112 B.A. L.1068 J.D. [Levinson,M.J.&P.]
*PRACTICE AREAS: Civil Litigation; Employment Law.
**Robinett, Timothy D.** ..................'67 '93 C.112 B.A. L.426 J.D. [A Manning,L.B.&B.]
*PRACTICE AREAS: Civil Trial.
**Robinow, Robert W.** ......... '33 '61 C.112 A.B. L.106 LL.B. Sr. Coun., Bank of Amer.
**Robins, Richard D.**, (AV) .......... '51 '77 C.112 A.B. L.1066 J.D. [Parker,M.C.O.&S.]
*TRANSACTIONS: Represent major parking companies, real estate development, medical related companies and computer reseller in Tax Law, General Corporate, Real Estate and Litigation.
*PRACTICE AREAS: Tax; General Corporate; Real Estate; Litigation.
**Robins, Thomas M., III**, (AV) .............'46 '72 C.112 B.A. L.800 J.D. [Frandzel&S.]

**Robins, Kaplan, Miller & Ciresi, (AV)**
**2049 Century Park East, Suite 3700, 90067⊙**
**Telephone: 310-552-0130 Fax: 310-229-5800**
**Members of Firm: Steven D. Archer; Roman M. Silberfeld; J. Kevin Snyder; David C. Veis. Associates: Joseph C. Cane, Jr.; Bernice Conn; Michael Geibelson; Douglas A. Greer; Douglas A. Mastroianni; Randy H. McMurray; Edward T. Muramoto; Laura P. Nash; Shann D. Winesett.**
**Trials and Appeals in all Federal and State Courts. Administrative, Antitrust, Appellate, Banking, Bankruptcy and Reorganization, Construction, Communications, Corporate, Employment and Employee Benefits, Environmental, Estate Planning and Probate, Franchising, Finance, Health, Insurance Law, Intellectual Property, International Litigation and Trade, Medical Malpractice, Personal Injury, Products Liability, Real Estate, Securities, Tax, Transportation.**
**Atlanta, Georgia Office: 2600 One Atlanta Plaza, 950 East Paces Ferry Road NE. Telephone: 404-233-1114. Fax: 404-233-1267.**
**Boston, Massachusetts Office: Suite 2200, 222 Berkeley Street. Telephone: 617-267-2300. Fax: 617-267-8288.**
**Chicago, Illinois Office: Suite 1400, 55 West Wacker Drive. Telephone: 312-782-9200. Fax: 312-782-7756.**
**Costa Mesa Office: 600 Anton Boulevard, Suite 1600. Telephone: 714-540-6200. Fax: 714-545-6915.**
**Minneapolis, Minnesota Office: 2800 LaSalle Plaza, 800 LaSalle Avenue. Telephone: 612-349-8500. Fax: 612-339-4181.**
**San Francisco, California Office: Suite 2700, 444 Market Street. Telephone: 415-399-1800. Fax: 415-391-1968.**
**Washington, D.C. Office: Suite 1200, 1801 K Street, N.W. Telephone: 202-775-0725. Fax: 202-223-8604.**
*See Professional Biographies, LOS ANGELES, CALIFORNIA*

**Robinson, Angela D., Law Offices of '60 '96 C.1097 B.A. L.325 J.D.**
**Century Plaza Towers, 2049 Century Park East, Suite 1100, 90067**
**Telephone: 310-286-9547 Fax: 310-286-9549**
**Email: ADRLaw@aol.com**
**Entertainment Contracts, Entertainment Litigation, Corporate, Merchandising, Business (Joint Venture Agreements) and General Business Litigation for Representation of Artist, Producers, Record Companies and Sports.**
**Representative Clients: Loud/RCA; Priority Records, Sony Music, California Record Distributors; M.S. Distribution; Cisum/Next Plateau; Tommy Boy; East West/Atlantic; Lenchmob/Priority Records; Motown.**

Robinson, Carl C. ..................... '46 '77 C.477 B.S.E. L.1068 J.D. [Robinson&P.]
**Robinson, David A.** ..............................'67 '92 C.684 B.A. L.426 J.D. [A Mendes&M.]
*LANGUAGES: French.
**Robinson, David M.** ............. '67 '95 C.878 B.S.B.A. L.990 J.D. [A Engstrom,L.&L.]
*LANGUAGES: Spanish, German.
Robinson, Dianne ............................ '46 '73 C.112 B.A. L.800 J.D. 6401 Colgate Ave.
Robinson, Edward N. ...............'45 '74 C.477 B.A. L.659 J.D. The First Boston Corp.
**Robinson, James D.** .................................'59 '84 C.884 B.S. L.1049 J.D. [Kelly&L.]
*PRACTICE AREAS: Administrative Law; Business; Real Estate.
**Robinson, Keith A.** ............................ '58 '86 C.813 A.B. L.800 J.D. [Bergman&W.]
*PRACTICE AREAS: Business Litigation; Contract Litigation; Real Estate Litigation; Environmental Liability; Federal Taxation.

**Robinson, Mark P., Law Offices of, (AV) '24 '50 C&L.426 LL.B. BB**
**One Wilshire Boulevard, 22nd Floor, 90017-3383**
**Telephone: 213-485-1798 FAX: 213-236-0791**
***PRACTICE AREAS: Civil Litigation; Torts; Business Litigation.**
**General Civil and Criminal Litigation, Business, Personal Injury, Legal and Medical Malpractice and Products Liability Litigation, Trial and Appellate Practice, Family Law.**
*See Professional Biographies, LOS ANGELES, CALIFORNIA*

Robinson, Martha S. '14 '40 C&L.900 A.B., LL.B.
Prof. of Law, Emeritus, Loyola Univ.
**Robinson, Michael C., Jr.** .......... '56 '85 C.1097 B.A. L.426 J.D. [Robinson,D.&W.]⊙
*PRACTICE AREAS: Professional Errors and Omissions; Products Liability; Insurance Coverage.
**Robinson, Michael S.** ................... '59 '84 C.413 B.A. L.426 J.D. [Anderson,M.&C.]

**Robinson, Peter E., (AV) '43 '77 C.112 B.A. L.800 J.D.**
**2049 Century Park East, 26th Floor, 90067**
**Telephone: 310-556-9200 Fax: 310-556-9229**
**Email: per@protonet.com**
***PRACTICE AREAS: Real Estate Law; Corporate Law; Business Law.**
**Real Estate Law, Corporate Law, Business Law.**
*See Professional Biographies, LOS ANGELES, CALIFORNIA*

Robinson, Richard E. ..................... '52 '79 C.1169 A.B. L.1066 J.D. Asst. U.S. Atty.
**Robinson, Robert E.** ................................'67 '92 C&L.426 B.A., J.D. [Ibold&A.]
Robinson, Roosevelt, Jr. ................... '27 '56 C.852 L.329 LL.B. 4580 Mt. Vernon Dr.
Robinson, Sara R. '49 '83 C&L.472 B.A., J.D.
(adm. in FL; not adm. in CA) 300 N. Los Angeles St.‡
**Robinson, William J.**, (AV) ........'51 '78 C.112 B.S.E.E. L.426 J.D. [Graham&J.] (Pat.)
*PRACTICE AREAS: Intellectual Property Law; Litigation.

**Robinson, Di Lando & Whitaker, A Professional Law Corporation, (AV)**
**800 Wilshire Boulevard Suite 1300, 90017-2687⊙**
**Telephone: 213-229-0100 Facsimile: 213-229-0114**
**Michael C. Robinson, Jr.; Michael A. Di Lando; Ronald S. Whitaker; Jack M. Liebhaber;—George E. Ordonez; Steve H. Yu; Kevin K. Broerman; Kenneth W. Johnson; Mark Kane; Leslie Anne Denny; Robert G. Mendoza. Of Counsel: Timothy L. Salazar (Not admitted in CA).**
**General Insurance Defense Practice Including Civil, Business and Insurance Litigation in both State and Federal Courts, Self Insured, Professional Liability and Products Liability, Entertainment and Sports, Employment and Labor, Corporations and Coverage.**
**San Francisco, California Office: 465 California Street. Suite 510. 94104. Telephone: 415-391-9475. Fax: 415-391-3799.**
*See Professional Biographies, LOS ANGELES, CALIFORNIA*

**Robinson, Diamant, Brill & Klausner, A Professional Corporation, (AV) BB**
**Suite 1500, 1888 Century Park East (Century City), 90067**
**Telephone: 310-277-7400 Telecopier: 310-277-7584**
**Gilbert Robinson (1927-1991); Elliott Lisnek (1939-1992); Lawrence A. Diamant; Martin J. Brill; Edward M. Wolkowitz; Gary E. Klausner; Irving M. Gross; Douglas D. Kappler; Philip A. Gasteier;**

(This Listing Continued)

CAA325P

**Robinson, Diamant, Brill & Klausner, A Professional Corporation (Continued)**
Karl E. Block; Leslie A. Cohen; Gregg D. Lundberg; Sandford L. Frey; Jeffrey A. Resler;—Judith E. Miller; Sandro F. Piedrahita; Christopher E. Jones; Nicole D. Lance; Robyn B. Sokol; Jeffrey W. Dulberg; Seth D. Garland.
Bankruptcy, Insolvency, Reorganization and Commercial Litigation Law. General Civil and Trial Practice in all State and Federal Courts.
References: Fidelity & Deposit Co.; Home Savings of America (Century City Office); Metrobank (Los Angeles Regional Office); Wells Fargo Bank (Century City Office).
*See Professional Biographies, LOS ANGELES, CALIFORNIA*

Robinson & Pearman ....1055 W. 7th St.

**Robinson, Phillips & Calcagnie**
(See Laguna Niguel)

**Robison, Clinton Davis** ....'64 '92 C.112 B.A. L.990 J.D. [Ⓐ Booth,M.&S.]
*LANGUAGES: Spanish.
Robison, William R. ....'47 '74 C.94 A.B. L.588 J.D. 2546 Amherst Ave.
**Roche, Robert J.** ....'64 '92 C.112 B.A. L.1068 J.D. [Ⓐ Hanna&M.]
*LANGUAGES: Spanish.
*PRACTICE AREAS: Natural Resources; Environmental Law; Oil and Gas.
**Rochefort, John M.** ....'47 '73 C.800 B.A. L.1065 J.D. [McClintock,W.B.R.R.&M.]
*PRACTICE AREAS: Business and Commercial Litigation; Antitrust and Franchise Law; Construction Law; Environmental Litigation; Toxic Tort.
Rochlin, Judith ....'48 '74 C.112 B.A. L.37 J.D. 10846 Missouri
**Rochman, Harvey** ....'64 '92 C.112 B.A. L.800 J.D. [Ⓐ Manatt,P.&P.]
Rochman, Jeri L. ....'64 '91 C.36 B.S. L.990 J.D. Dep. Pub. Def.
**Rochmes, Paul H.** ....'46 '77 C&L.145 B.A., J.D. [Alschuler G.&P.]
**Rockey, Jay D.** ....'58 '86 C.878 B.A. L.61 J.D. [Ⓐ Sidley&A.]
*PRACTICE AREAS: Real Estate; Land Use; Leasing.
Rockwell, Lisa M. ....'60 '86 C.813 A.B. L.477 J.D. V.P. & Sr. Coun., Union Bk.
**Rodarte, Daniel D.** ....'54 '79 C.1169 A.B. L.309 J.D. [Rodarte&G.]
*PRACTICE AREAS: Products Liability; Medical Device Litigation.

**Rodarte & Geringer**
**10880 Wilshire Boulevard Suite 1050, 90024**
Telephone: 310-441-8020 Fax: 310-441-8021
Email: 104457.513@compuserve.com
Daniel D. Rodarte; Aylene M. Geringer.
Product Liability, Medical Device and Toxic Tort Litigation.
*See Professional Biographies, LOS ANGELES, CALIFORNIA*

Rodda, Clinton ....'15 '41 C&L.800 A.B., LL.B. Comr., Supr. Ct.
Roddy, Kevin P. ....'55 '80 C&L.575 B.A., J.D. [Milberg W.B.H.&L.]

**Rodenborn, Michelle M., Law Offices of**
(See Long Beach)

**Rodgers, Ronald L., Jr.**, (AV) ....'56 '82 C.800 B.A. L.273 J.D. [Rodgers&G.]
*PRACTICE AREAS: General Business Law; Real Estate; International; Land Use and Development; Corporate.
**Rodgers, Victor A.** ....'58 '81 C.800 B.S. L.1066 J.D. [Loeb&L.] (See Pat. Sect.)
*PRACTICE AREAS: Trademark; Patent; Copyright.

**Rodgers & Greenfeld, (AV)** BR
**660 South Figueroa Street 23rd Floor, 90017**
Telephone: 213-955-4850 Fax: 213-955-4851
Members of Firm: Ronald L. Rodgers, Jr.; J. Steven Greenfeld.
General Business Law, Real Estate, Land Use and Development, Corporate, International, Antitrust, General Civil, Trial and Appellate Practice in all State and Federal Courts.
*See Professional Biographies, LOS ANGELES, CALIFORNIA*

**Rodi, Pollock, Pettker, Galbraith & Cahill, A Law Corporation, (AV)** BR
**Suite 400 801 South Grand Avenue, 90017**
Telephone: 213-895-4900; 680-0823 Telecopiers: 213-895-4921; 895-4922; 895-4750
Karl B. Rodi (1908-1982); John D. Cahill; John D. Pettker (Certified Specialist, Probate, Estate Planning and Trust Law, The State Bar of California Board of Legal Specialization); Daniel C. Bond (1942-1977); William R. Christian; Henry P. Pramov, Jr.; Robert A. Yahiro; Elizabeth B. Blakely; Robert C. Norton; John F. Cermak, Jr.; Tim G. Ceperley; Coralie Kupfer; Cris K. O'Neall; John S. Cha; Scott E. Adamson;—Sonja A. Inglin; Thomas J. Yoo; Richard Nessary; Mark McCleary. Of Counsel: John P. Pollock; Margaret Rosenthal.
General Civil and Trial Practice, State and Federal Courts. Corporate, Securities, Business, Taxation, Real Estate and Banking Law. Estate Planning, Probate, Products Liability and Environmental and Employment Law.
*See Professional Biographies, LOS ANGELES, CALIFORNIA*

**Rodiger, Georgiana G.** ....'53 '80 C.1168 B.A. L.990 J.D. [Ⓐ Gibson,D.&C.]
*PRACTICE AREAS: Litigation; Bankruptcy.
Rodolf, Robert W. ....'33 '60 C.813 A.B. L.1068 LL.B. Dep. Co. Coun.
**Rodríguez, Albert R.**, (AV) ....'51 '78 C.112 B.A. L.976 J.D. [Rodríguez,H.&C.]
**Rodriguez, Denise R.** ....'51 '79 C.912 B.A. L.477 J.D. [Foley L.W.&A.]
*SPECIAL AGENCIES: Provider Reimbursement Review Board.
*PRACTICE AREAS: Health Care; Hospitals; Medicare and Medicaid; Administrative Law.
**Rodriguez, Eddie** ....'67 '94 C.112 B.A. L.813 J.D. [Ⓐ Brobeck,P.&H.]
*LANGUAGES: Chinese (Cantonese).
*PRACTICE AREAS: Corporate; Business; Technology.
Rodriguez, Isabel H. ....'50 '82 C.1168 L.1238 J.D. 5312 E. Beverly Blvd.
Rodriguez, Rey M. ....'63 '93 C.188 B.A. L.1066 555 S. Flower St.
Rodriguez, Rose E. '39 '86 C.112 A.B. L.1184 J.D.
(adm. in VA; not adm. in CA) 5810 W. Gregory‡
Rodriguez, Susan A. ....'64 '90 C.976 B.A. L.477 J.D. 221 N. Figueroa St.
Rodriguez, Victor M. ....'59 '91 C.1077 B.A. L.1068 J.D. Dep. Dist. Atty.

**Rodríguez, Horii & Choi, (AV)**
**777 South Figueroa Street, Suite 4207, 90017**
Telephone: 213-892-7700 Fax: 213-892-7777
Members of Firm: Albert R. Rodríguez; Dwayne M. Horii; William C. Choi.
Tax Law including California State and Local Taxation, Tax Exempt Organizations, Tax Litigation and International Taxation.
*See Professional Biographies, LOS ANGELES, CALIFORNIA*

Roe, Susan ....'61 '91 C.112 B.A. L.1068 J.D. 1055 Wilshire Blvd.
**Roeb, Craig A.** ....'61 '87 C.112 B.A. L.426 J.D. [Chapman&G.]
*PRACTICE AREAS: Professional Liability Law; Business and Commercial Litigation; Products Liability Law.
**Rogal, Melissa A.** ....'71 '96 C.659 B.S.B.A. L.569 J.D. [Ⓐ Troop M.S.&P.]
*PRACTICE AREAS: Entertainment.
**Rogan, Patrick G.**, (AV) ....'44 '72 C.154 B.A. L.426 J.D. [Pillsbury M.&S.]
Rogen, Richard D. ....'47 '75 L.1095 [Kaplan,K.&R.]
Rogers, Carol Leah ....'63 '89 C.112 B.A. L.276 J.D. The State Bar of Calif.
**Rogers, Dani H.** ....'62 '87 C.112 B.A. L.767 J.D. [Bronson,B.&M.]
*LANGUAGES: Spanish.
*PRACTICE AREAS: Product Liability and Personal Injury Litigation.
**Rogers, David Booth** ....'58 '83 C&L.813 A.B., J.D. [Latham&W.]
**Rogers, Deborah** ....'48 '94 C.1077 B.A. L.309 J.D. [Ⓐ O'Melveny&M.]
Rogers, J. Earl ....'42 '74 C.763 B.A. L.61 J.D. 3664 Wasatch Ave.
Rogers, James F., (AV) ....'28 '57 C.112 B.S. L.1065 J.D. 6820 La Tijera Blvd.
Rogers, John J. ....'15 '49 C.911 B.A. L.1001 LL.B. Dep. City Atty.
**Rogers, John T., Jr.**, (AV) ....'55 '81 C.813 B.S. L.1068 J.D. [Ross,S.&G.]
*PRACTICE AREAS: Trusts and Estates; Taxation Law.
**Rogers, Lila E.** ....'68 '94 C.66 B.A. L.800 J.D. [Ⓐ Gibson,D.&C.]
*PRACTICE AREAS: Real Estate; Finance.
**Rogers, Matthew R.** ....'61 '87 C.299 B.A. L.94 J.D. [Pillsbury M.&S.]
**Rogers, Michael C.** ....'70 '95 C&L.1049 B.A., J.D. [Ⓐ Callahan,M.&W.]
*PRACTICE AREAS: Civil Litigation; Insurance Defense.
Rogers, Robin N. ....'64 '90 C.112 B.A. L.1066 J.D. 355 S. Grand Ave., 35th Fl.
**Rogers, Stanley**, (AV) ....'34 '60 C.674 A.B. L.1068 J.D. [Rogers&H.]
*PRACTICE AREAS: Civil Practice; Real Property; Probate and Business Law; Trusts.
**Rogers, Steven M.** ....'70 '95 C.112 B.A. L.426 J.D. [Ⓐ Tuttle&T.]

**Rogers & Harris, (AV)**
**Suite 404, 9200 Sunset Boulevard, 90069**
Telephone: 310-278-3142 Fax: 310-271-3649
Members of Firm: Stanley Rogers; Michael Harris.
General Civil and Trial Practice in all State and Federal Courts. Real Property, Entertainment, Corporation, Estate Planning, Trusts, Probate and Business Law.
Reference: Union Bank (Beverly Hills Main Office).

**Rogers & Wells, (AV)** BR
**444 South Flower Street, 90071-2901**⊙
Telephone: 213-689-2900 Facsimile: 213-689-2999
Partners: Michael D. Berk; Allan E. Ceran; John I. Forry; John A. Karaczynski; John K. Keitt, Jr. (Not admitted in CA); Terry O. Kelly; Eugene Y. C. Lu; Richard A. Shortz; Carl W. Sonne; I. Bruce Speiser. Associates: Christopher R. Baker; David B. Cohen; Alan H. Fairley; Richard C. Jun (Not admitted in CA); Steven M. Ruskin; Julie A. Shepard; Steven S. Spitz.
General Practice.
New York, N.Y. Office: Two Hundred Park Avenue, New York, N.Y. 10166-0153. Telephone: 212-878-8000. Facsimile: 212-878-8375. Telex: 234493 RKWUR. E-Mail: email@rw.com.
Washington, D.C. Office: 607 Fourteenth Street, N.W., Washington, D.C. 20005-2018. Telephone: 202-434-0700. Facsimile: 202-434-0800.
Paris, France Office: 47, Avenue Hoche, 75008-Paris, France. Telephone: 33-1-44-09-46-00. Facsimile: 33-1-42-67-50-81. Telex: 651617 EURLAW.
London, England Office: 40 Basinghall Street, London EC2V 5DE, England. Telephone: 44-171-628-0101. Facsimile: 44-171-628-6111.
Frankfurt, Germany Office: Westendstrasse 16-22, 60325 Frankfurt/Main, Federal Republic of Germany. Telephone: 49-69-97-14-78-0. Facsimile: 49-69-97-14-78-33.
Hong Kong: One Exchange Square, 8 Connaught Place, Central, Hong Kong. Telephone: 852-2844-3500. Facsimile: 852-2844-3555.
Revisers of the New York Law Digest for this Directory.
*See Professional Biographies, LOS ANGELES, CALIFORNIA*

**Rogier, Alain G., (AV) '47 '75 C.112 B.A. L.426 J.D.**
**12100 Wilshire Boulevard, Suite 1900, 90025-1722**
Telephone: 310-207-0421 Fax: 310-826-3210
*LANGUAGES: French.
Family Law Dissolutions, Domestic and International Custody, Paternity, Support.
Reference: French Consulate, Beverly Hills, California.
*See Professional Biographies, LOS ANGELES, CALIFORNIA*

**Rognlien, Carrie J.** ....'66 '94 C.112 B.S. L.426 J.D. [Girardi&K.]
Rohaly, Julie Claire '53 '92 L.1148 J.D.
(adm. in OR; not adm. in CA) 2833 Greenfield Ave.
**Rohatiner, Marc E.**, (AV) ....'53 '78 C.112 B.A. L.1068 J.D. [Wolf,R.&S.]
Rohde, Stephen F., (AV) ....'44 '70 C.597 B.A. L.178 J.D. 1880 Century Pk. E.
**Rohlf, Thomas E., (A P.C.)** ....'46 '71 C&L.813 A.B., J.D. [Loeb&L.]
*PRACTICE AREAS: Corporate Law.
Rohner, Franklin B. ....'27 '55 C&L.813 A.B., LL.B. [Rohner&W.]
Rohner & Walerstein, (AV) ....11111 Santa Monica Blvd.
Roit, Natasha ....'60 '86 C.112 B.A. L.426 J.D. 116 N. Robertson Blvd.
**Rojas, Valerie D.** ....'70 '95 C.1110 B.A. L.809 J.D. [Ⓐ Hillsinger&C.]
**Rokaw, Sue Carol** ....'49 '85 C.696 B.A. L.767 J.D. [Ropers,M.K.&B.]
*PRACTICE AREAS: Insurance Coverage and Bad Faith Litigation; Business Litigation.
Roland, George P., (BV) ....'48 '75 C.112 B.A. L.208 J.D. 6922 Hollywood Blvd.
**Roland, Yvette D.** ....'51 '85 C.112 B.A. L.1068 J.D. [Hancock R.&B.]
**Rolin, Christopher**, (AV) ....'40 '66 C.112 B.A. L.800 J.D. [Newkirk,N.&R.]
*PRACTICE AREAS: Real Estate; Legal Malpractice; Estate and Trust Litigation.
**Roll, Richard D.** ....'66 '95 C.813 A.B. L.188 J.D. [Ⓐ Christensen,M.F.J.G.W.&S.]
*PRACTICE AREAS: General Civil Litigation.
**Rollman, Fredric A.** ....'55 '80 C.659 B.S. L.228 J.D. [Donfeld,K.&R.]
*PRACTICE AREAS: Real Estate; General Business Transactions.
Rolnick, Harriet M. ....'51 '79 C.472 B.A. L.809 J.D. U.S. Atty's. Off.
Rolnick, Ronald G., (AV) ....'49 '75 C.112 A.B. L.1068 J.D. [Sandler,R.&M.]
Rolon, Millicent L. ....'65 '88 C.1044 B.A. L.982 J.D. Dep. Trial Coun., Calif. State Bar
**Rolston, Arthur L., (A Professional Law Corporation)**, (AV) '42 '67
C.800 A.B. L.1066 J.D. [Billet&K.]
*PRACTICE AREAS: Commercial; Bankruptcy; Equipment Leasing; Business Law; Litigation.
**Romain, George G.** ....'61 '89 C.1044 B.A. L.94 J.D. [Ⓐ Murchison&C.]
*LANGUAGES: French.
*PRACTICE AREAS: Errors and Omissions; Liability of Directors and Officers; Attorney Malpractice.
**Roman, Dennis N.** ....'44 '75 C.608 B.S. L.1148 J.D. [Clopton,P.&B.]

**Romano, Daniel, Law Offices of**
(See Santa Monica)

**Rombro, S. Roger** ....'44 '73 C.659 B.A. L.861 J.D. [S.R.Rombro]

**Rombro, S. Roger, A Law Corporation**
**10866 Wilshire Boulevard, Suite 500, 90024**
Telephone: 310-475-4088 Fax: 310-475-5543
S. Roger Rombro.
Business and Family Law and Civil Litigation
*See Professional Biographies, LOS ANGELES, CALIFORNIA*

Romero, Cynthia B. ....'43 '76 C.112 B.A. L.1068 J.D. 11910 Avon Way
Romero, Enrique ....'46 '77 C.112 B.A. L.765 J.D. Supr. Ct. J
Romero, Frederick A. ....'48 '80 C.1097 B.A. L.1068 J.D. 1125 N. Ditman Ave.
**Romero, Richard F.** ....'70 '95 C.309 B.A. L.1068 J.D. [Ⓐ Gibson,D.&C.]
**Romey, Michael G.** ....'62 '88 C.178 B.A. L.1066 J.D. [Latham&W.]
*PRACTICE AREAS: Environmental Litigation.
Romeyn, Thomas A. ....'41 '67 C.1042 B.S. L.1065 J.D. Dep. Dist. Atty.
Romig, Susan ....'55 '82 C.112 B.A. L.809 J.D. 9200 Sunset Blvd.
**Romyn, David C.** ....'61 '89 C.112 B.A. L.1065 J.D. [Ⓐ Monteleone&M.]
*PRACTICE AREAS: Construction Litigation; Construction Defects.
Ronce, Thomas M. '49 '75 C.112 B.A. L.1049 J.D.
2nd V.P. & Asst. Gen. Coun., Transamerica Occidental Life Ins. Co.
Roney, John H., (AV) ....'32 '60 C.605 B.A. L.1068 LL.B. 400 S Hope St.

**Ronge, John R. '48 '84 C.46 B.S. L.426 J.D.**
**10866 Wilshire Boulevard, 15th Floor, 90024**
Telephone: 310-441-4100 Fax: 310-470-1360
Email: RONGEJOHN@aol.com
Tax, Probate and Estate Planning, Real Estate, Business.
*See Professional Biographies, LOS ANGELES, CALIFORNIA*

**Ronk, Stephen E.** ....'65 '93 C.1074 B.S. L.1148 J.D. [Ⓐ Long&L.]

Ronzio, Frank E. '51 '90
C.818 B.S.,M.B.A. L.398 J.D. 5900 Wilshire Blvd. (⊙Montebello)
Roofian, Michael .................... '62 '89 C.112 B.S. L.426 J.D. 12400 Wilshire Blvd.
Rooney, Daniel G. .................... '48 '75 C.912 B.A. L.276 J.D. 12121 Wilshire Blvd.
**Rooney, Karen A.**, (AV) ................ '55 '80 C.112 B.A. L.1049 J.D. [Quinn E.U.&O.]
*PRACTICE AREAS: General Commercial Litigation; Employment; Securities.
Root, Bennett W., Jr. ............................ '45 '70 C.477 A.B. L.309 J.D. 633 W. 5th St.
**Root, Jane H.** ................................ '65 '91 C.103 B.A. L.1068 J.D. [▣ Arter&H.]
*PRACTICE AREAS: Litigation.
**Roper, James L.**, (AV) .................... '35 '61 C.112 A.B. L.1068 J.D. [Roper&F.]
*PRACTICE AREAS: Agent E & O; Construction Defect Litigation; Legal Malpractice Law; Excess Insurance Law; Real Estate Errors and Omissions.
Roper, Margaret Ann .................... '70 '95 C.602 B.A. L.426 J.D. 515 S. Figueroa St.
**Roper, Theodore J.** ........................ '51 '81 C.768 B.A. L.284 J.D. [Kelley D.&W.]
*LANGUAGES: Japanese.
*PRACTICE AREAS: Corporate; International Transactional Law; Mergers and Acquisitions.

**Roper & Folino, (AV)**
**Suite 1700, 3255 Wilshire Boulevard, 90010-1420**
**Telephone: 213-388-3181 Telecopier: 213-388-2600**
**Email: legalkix@ix.netcom.com**
**Members of Firm: James L. Roper; Domenic Folino; Michael J. Irwin; John B. Larson; Joseph L. Stark; Raymond J. Fargo; Michael A. Kruppe; John M. Bergerson; Tamar D. Tujian.**
**Insurance, Trial and Appellate Practice in all State and Federal Courts. Negligence, Products Liability, Malpractice, Casualty and Fire Insurance Law, Professional Negligence, Landslide and Subsidence Law, Construction Litigation, Municipality and Public Entities, Excess and Surplus Lines, Bad Faith and Wrongful Termination, Insurance, Coverage and Litigation and Reinsurance Law, Toxic Torts, Construction Defect Defense, Subrogation Law.**
**Reference: First Interstate Bank (Wilshire Blvd. at Catalina Office).**
***See Professional Biographies, LOS ANGELES, CALIFORNIA***

**Ropers, Majeski, Kohn & Bentley, A Professional Corporation, (AV)** ▣
**550 South Hope Street, Suite 1900, 90071⊙**
**Telephone: 213-312-2000 Fax: 213-312-2001**
**Stephen J. Erigero; Frank T. Sabaitis (Resident); Marta B. Arriandiaga; Sue Carol Rokaw; Carol Kurke Lucas; Allan E. Anderson (Resident);—Michael W. Parks; Sean S. Varner; Ernest E. Price; Andrew D. Castricone; Charlene Rudio Culver; I. Paul Bae (Resident); Bradley P. Boyer; Michael T. O'Callaghan; Robin L Jacobs; Gerald B. Malanga; Robin J. Devereux.**
**Arbitration and Mediation, Appellate Services, Banking and Financial Institutions Services, Bankruptcy, Commercial Litigation, Construction Litigation, Employment Law, Environmental Compliance and Litigation, Estate Planning, Trusts Probate and Elder Law, Fidelity and Surety Law, Health Care Law, Insurance Coverage and Litigation, Insurance Regulatory and Reinsurance, Intellectual Property Protection and Litigation, Products Litigation, Professional Malpractice Litigation, Real Estate Law, Trials and Antitrust.**
**Redwood City, California Office: 1001 Marshall Street. Telephone: 415-364-8200. Fax: 415-367-0997.**
**San Jose, California Office: 80 North 1st Street. Telephone: 408-287-6262. Fax: 408-297-6819.**
**San Francisco, California Office: 670 Howard Street. Telephone: 415-543-4800. Fax: 415-512-1574.**
**Santa Rosa, California Office: Fountaingrove Center, Suite 300, 3558 Round Barn Boulevard. Telephone: 707-524-4200. Fax: 707-523-4610.**
**Sacramento, California Office: 1000 G. Street, Suite 400. Telephone: 916-556-3100. Fax: 916-442-7121.**
***See Professional Biographies, LOS ANGELES, CALIFORNIA***

Roquemore, Thomas L. ................ '23 '54 C&L.800 B.S., LL.B. [Roquemore,P.&M.]
Roquemore, Pringle & Moore, Inc., (BV) ..... 6055 East Washington Boulevard Suite 430
Rorie, William E. ........................ '50 '82 C.45 B.S.Ch.E. L.809 J.D. [Wilson&B.]
Rosa, Edouard V., (BV) .................. '49 '83 C.1042 B.A. L.1179 J.D. [Huebner&R.]
Rosales, Olivia .......................... '66 '92 C.112 B.A. L.1068 J.D. Dep. Atty. Gen.
Rosales, Terso R. ........................ '48 '75 C.112 B.A. L.1068 J.D. Asst. City Atty.
Rosario, Dexter B. ..................... '45 '90 C&L.061 B.A., LL.B. 3660 Wilshire Blvd.
Rosch, Thomas Lee ............ '62 '89 C.309 A.B. L.813 J.D. The Boston Consulting Grp.
**Roscher, Adrian F.** ................ '60 '85 C.178 B.A. L.813 J.D. [▣ Pachulski,S.Z.&Y.]
*LANGUAGES: German.
*PRACTICE AREAS: Entertainment and Business Transactions; Motion Picture Production and Distribution.
**Rose, Alan C.**, (AV) ............ '22 '52 C.453 B.S. L.273 J.D. [Oppenheimer P.S.] (Pat.)
*PRACTICE AREAS: Patents, Trademarks, Copyrights, Licensing, Unfair Competition.
**Rose, Allison** ........................ '64 '89 C.1168 B.A. L.990 J.D. [▣ Murchison&C.]
*PRACTICE AREAS: Professional Liability; Environmental Coverage; Appellate Practice.
**Rose, Allison M.** .................... '69 '94 C.659 B.A. L.426 J.D. [▣ O'Melveny&M.]
Rose, Billy ........................ '61 '86 C.112 B.A. L.800 J.D. [Alexander,H.N.&R.]
**Rose, Bradley M.** ................................ '60 '85 C&L.623 B.A., J.D. [Kaye,R.]
*REPORTED CASES: Trinidad Corp. v. S/S KEIYOH MARU, 845 P.2d 818 (9th Cir, 1988).
Rose, Carol L. .......................... '49 '77 C.260 B.A. L.1048 J.D. Dep. Dist. Atty.
Rose, Cirina ............................ '63 '90 C.112 B.A. L.809 J.D. [Bolden&M.]
**Rose, David V.** ........................ '54 '83 C.531 B.S. L.893 J.D. [Wright,R.O.&T.]
*PRACTICE AREAS: Insurance Coverage Litigation; Commercial Litigation.
**Rose, Flavio** ........................................ '55 '95 C.061 L.1066 J.D. [▣ Irell&M.]
*LANGUAGES: Spanish.
**Rose, Henry S.** ...................... '24 '49 C&L.800 A.B., J.D. [▣ O'Donnell,R.&S.]
*PRACTICE AREAS: International Law; Environmental Law.
Rose, I. Nelson ... '50 '79 C.112 B.A. L.309 J.D. Prof. of Law, Whittier Coll. Sch. of Law
**Rose, Mary H.** ...................... '54 '78 C.103 A.B. L.569 J.D. [▣ Proskauer R.G.&M.]
Rose, Reid A. ........................ '54 '79 C.112 B.A. L.1065 J.D. Dep. Dist. Atty.
Rose, Robert S., (AV) ...................... '21 '55 C&L.426 B.B.A., J.D. [Pace&R.]
**Rose, Sidney R.**, (AV) .................... '27 '52 C.112 L.800 J.D. [Valensi,R.&M.]
*PRACTICE AREAS: General Business Law; Real Estate Law.
**Rose, Steven D.** ........................ '61 '91 C.112 B.A. L.1065 J.D. [Munger,T.&O.]
Rose, Valerie Scott .................. '64 '91 C.75 B.F.A. L.809 J.D. Dep. Dist. Atty.
Rose, Klein & Marias, (AV)
18th Fl., 801 S. Grand Ave. (⊙Long Beach, Pomona, San Bernardino, San Diego, Santa Ana & Ventura)
Rosebrock, Elizabeth Ashley .............. '58 '88 C.37 B.A. L.809 J.D. 624 S. Grand Ave.
Roseman, Bernard .................... '35 '74 C.426 B.S. L.1190 J.D. 8027 Yorktown Ave.
Roseman, Joyce A. ................ '49 '81 C.1097 B.S. L.1136 J.D. 2916 W. Florence Ave.
Roseman, Martin G. .......... '55 '79 C.659 B.A. L.273 J.D. 1520 Wilshire Blvd., 6th Fl.

**Roseman, Steven A., Law Offices of '63 '93 C&L.061 B.S., J.D.**
**12011 San Vincente Boulevard, Suite 600, 90049-4948**
**Telephone: 310-440-3144 Fax: 310-440-3140**
**Email: sarinla@aol.com**
***PRACTICE AREAS: Construction Litigation; Real Estate Litigation; Community Association Law.**
**Construction, Real Estate, Community Associations, Landlord-Tenant, Business, Civil Litigation.**
***See Professional Biographies, LOS ANGELES, CALIFORNIA***

**Rosemblat, Raphael A.** ................ '58 '83 C.112 B.A. L.767 J.D. [▣ D.B.Bloom]
Rosen, Adam J. ...................... '64 '90 C.446 B.S. L.978 J.D. 2121 Ave. of the Stars
Rosen, Alan L. ........................ '50 '75 C.112 B.A. L.800 J.D. 15233 Ventura Blvd.
Rosen, David L. ............ '18 '49 C.112 A.B. L.800 J.D. Ret. Wkrs. Comp. App. Brd. J.
Rosen, David S. .................. '41 '66 C&L.472 B.B.A., LL.B. 1617 Pontius Ave., 3rd Fl.
Rosen, Elaine S. ...................... '46 '81 C.112 B.A. L.809 J.D. 545 W. Ave. Twenty-Six
**Rosen, Ellen Resinski** .................. '60 '85 C.397 B.A. L.884 J.D. [▣ Simke C.]
*PRACTICE AREAS: Business Litigation; Entertainment Litigation; Fiduciary Malpractice.
Rosen, Harvey H., (AV) ........ '41 '67 C.563 B.A. L.273 J.D. 601 S. Figueroa St., 24th Fl.
Rosen, Howard Z., (AV) .................... '47 '72 C.112 B.A. L.1065 J.D. [Posner&R.]
Rosen, Joshua L. .................. '56 '80 C.4 B.A. L.145 J.D. 11377 W. Olympic Blvd.
**Rosen, Kevin S.** .......................... '62 '88 C.197 A.B. L.178 J.D. [Gibson,D.&C.]
*PRACTICE AREAS: Litigation, including Securities; Real Estate; Consumer Lender and Broker Liability; Bad Faith; Unfair Competition.
**Rosen, Leon D.**, (AV) '37 '62 C.145 B.A. L.178 LL.B.
[Freilich,H.&R.] (See Pat. Sect.)
*PRACTICE AREAS: Patent Law; Trademark Law; Patent Applications; Licensing Law.
**Rosen, Martin E.** ........................ '57 '83 C.112 B.A. L.1068 J.D. [Barger&W.]
*PRACTICE AREAS: Business Litigation; Insurance Bad Faith.
**Rosen, Peter K.**, (AV) .................. '54 '78 C.112 B.A. L.800 J.D. [Weisman&R.]
*REPORTED CASES: Nicolet, Inc. v. Superior Court (Insurance Co. of North America) 188 Cal. App.3d 28 (Cal. Ap. 1d 1986); Estate of Linnick 171 Cal. App. 3d 752 (Cal. Ap. 2 Dist. 1985); Blue Chip Properties v. Permanent Rent Control Bd. of City of Santa Monica, 170 Cal. App.3d 648 (Cal. Ap. 2 Dist. 1985); Santa Monica Pines, Ltd. v. Rent Control Bd. of City of Santa Monica, 35 Cal.3d 858 (Cal. 1984); Williams v. Hartford Ins. Co., 147 Ca. App.3d 893 (Cal.Ap. 2 Dist. 1983).
*PRACTICE AREAS: Directors & Officers Litigation; Securities Litigation; Financial Institutions Litigation; Insurance Coverage; General Litigation.
Rosen, Phillip L. '55 '79 C.881 A.B. L.813 J.D.
Sr. V.P., Bus. & Legal Affairs, New Line Cinema Corp.
**Rosen, Robert A.** .................... '64 '91 C&L.276 A.B., J.D. [▣ Charlston,R.&W.]
*LANGUAGES: Spanish and Italian.
*PRACTICE AREAS: Environmental Law.
**Rosen, Robert C.** '45 '70 C.494 B.S. L.229 J.D.
(adm. in PA; not adm. in CA) [Rosen&Assoc.]
*PRACTICE AREAS: Business Law; Securities.
Rosen, Roger J., (AV) ......... '44 '71 C.800 B.S. L.1095 J.D. 10000 Santa Monica Blvd.
Rosen, Ronald D., (AV) ............ '44 '69 C.112 B.A. L.1066 J.D. 5750 Wilshire Blvd.
Rosen, Ronald M. ........................................ '48 '81 C.112 B.A. L.1067 J.D. I.R.S.
**Rosen, Ronald S.**, (AV) ........................ '32 '58 C&L.813 A.B., LL.B. [Troy&G.]
*PRACTICE AREAS: Entertainment Litigation; Business Litigation; Real Estate Litigation.
**Rosen, S. Alan, (A Professional Corporation)**, (AV) '48 '74
C.112 B.A. L.1068 J.D. [Horgan,R.B.&C.]
*PRACTICE AREAS: Administration; Banking; Corporate; Corporate Securities and Finance.

**Rosen & Associates**
**Suite 5850 633 West Fifth Street, 90071**
**Telephone: 213-362-1025 Fax: 213-362-1026**
**Robert C. Rosen (Not admitted in CA). Of Counsel: David E. Kronemyer.**
**General Civil Practice, Commercial Litigation, Mergers and Acquisitions, Real Estate, Legal Malpractice.**
***See Professional Biographies, LOS ANGELES, CALIFORNIA***

**Rosenbaum, Gary B.** .................. '62 '88 C.597 B.A. L.1068 J.D. [Murphy,W.&B.]
*PRACTICE AREAS: Secured Financing; Commercial Lending; Business Workouts.
**Rosenbaum, John E.** .................. '58 '95 C.659 B.A. L.767 J.D. [▣ White&C.]
**Rosenbaum, Lee N.**, (AV) ............ '54 '79 C.813 A.B. L.309 J.D. [▣ Wyman,I.B.&L.]
**Rosenbaum, Mark J.** .................. '68 '94 C.978 B.S. L.426 J.D. [▣ Wolf,R.&S.]
*PRACTICE AREAS: Community Association Law; Civil Litigation.
**Rosenbaum, Paul R.** ....... '64 '93 C.112 B.S. L.800 J.D. [▣ Christensen,M.F.J.G.W.&S.]
*PRACTICE AREAS: Real Estate; Business Law.
**Rosenberg, Alicia G.** .................... '61 '85 C.914 B.A. L.1068 J.D. [Blecher&C.]
*PRACTICE AREAS: Antitrust; Intellectual Property.
**Rosenberg, Charles** ........... '48 '83 C.339 B.S. L.365 J.D. [Oppenheimer P.S.] (Pat.)
*PRACTICE AREAS: Intellectual Property.

**Rosenberg, Charles B., (AV) '45 '72 C.33 B.A. L.309 J.D.**
**1901 Avneue of the Stars Suite 1600, 90067**
**Telephone: 310-286-3002 Fax: 310-286-3032**
***LANGUAGES: French.**
**Complex civil and business litigation in state and federal courts. Litigation Management, including selection of counsel. Commercial arbitration. Expert witness on reasonableness of legal fees in large cases.**
***See Professional Biographies, LOS ANGELES, CALIFORNIA***

Rosenberg, Daniel C. .............. '54 '79 C.112 A.B. L.1066 J.D. 10940 Wilshire Blvd.
**Rosenberg, David S.** .................... '59 '86 C&L.659 B.S., J.D. [▣ Cox,C.&N.]
Rosenberg, Edward A. '25 '49 C&L.813 A.B., J.D.
(adm. in OR; not adm. in CA) 7949 Woodrow Wilson Dr.‡
Rosenberg, Edwin M. .................. '31 '60 C.112 B.A. L.809 LL.B. 3435 Wilshire St.
Rosenberg, James L. .................. '49 '78 C.424 B.A. L.1190 J.D. 3250 Wilshire Blvd.
Rosenberg, Mark I., (AV) ............ '47 '72 C.112 A.B. L.1065 J.D. 2049 Century Park E.
Rosenberg, William H. .................. '48 '88 C.994 B.A. L.809 J.D. 2049 Century Park E.
Rosenblatt, Richard M. .................. '— '94 C.112 B.A. L.800 J.D. 550 S. Hope St.
Rosenblood, Kenneth L. ............ '62 '87 C.028 B.A. L.809 J.D. 12235 Gorham Ave.
Rosenblum, Michael S. ............ '61 '86 C.659 B.S. L.1068 J.D. 10866 Wilshire Blvd.
Rosencrans, Suzanne .................. '62 '90 C.103 A.B. L.178 J.D. New Line Cinema
**Rosendahl, Roger W.**, (AV) ............ '43 '73 C.800 A.B. L.276 J.D. [Cadwalader,W.&T.]
*LANGUAGES: German.
Rosene, Robert B. ...................... '34 '63 C&L.352 B.A., J.D. 166 Little Park Lane
Rosenfeld, Betty, (AV) ..... '28 '79 C.37 B.A. L.1136 J.D. 1875 Century Park E. Ste. 1400
**Rosenfeld, Edward M.**, (AV) .............. '40 '64 C.659 B.S. L.178 J.D. [Shapiro,R.&C.]
*PRACTICE AREAS: Litigation.
**Rosenfeld, Jeffrey A.** .................. '62 '88 C.1077 B.A. L.990 J.D. [Troop M.S.&P.]
*PRACTICE AREAS: Business and Entertainment Litigation; Insurance Coverage Litigation.
**Rosenfeld, John D.** ........................ '64 '92 C&L.800 B.S., J.D. [▣ Cox,C.&N.]
*PRACTICE AREAS: Construction Defect Litigation; Insurance Coverage Litigation; Real Estate Litigation; General Business Litigation.
**Rosenfeld, Morton M.**, (AV) ............ '48 '72 C.674 A.B. L.477 J.D. [Rosenfeld&W.]
*PRACTICE AREAS: Corporate Law; Corporate Securities.

**Rosenfeld, Andrew M.**
**(See Torrance)**

**Rosenfeld, Meyer & Susman, LLP**
**(See Beverly Hills)**

**Rosenfeld & Wolff, A Professional Corporation, (AV)** ▣
**2049 Century Park East, Suite 600, 90067**
**Telephone: 310-556-1221 Fax: 310-556-0401**
**Morton M. Rosenfeld; Steven G. Wolff; Alan D. Aronson.**
**Corporate, Corporate Securities, Real Estate, General Business.**
***See Professional Biographies, LOS ANGELES, CALIFORNIA***

Rosenfelt, Frank E. .................... '21 '50 C&L.188 B.S., LL.B. 948 Bel Air Rd.
**Rosenfield, Michael L.** ...................... '58 '87 C.36 B.A. L.990 J.D. [Barger&W.]
*PRACTICE AREAS: Insurance Regulatory Law; General Corporate Law.
**Rosenfield, Robert H.**, (BV) ........ '42 '76 C.966 B.S. L.309 LL.B. [McDermott,W.&E.]
**Rosenkranz, Georgiana** .............. '66 '93 C.605 B.A. L.4268 J.D. [▣ Orrick,H.&S.]
*PRACTICE AREAS: Public Finance; School District Debt Finance.
Rosenman, Shari Cohen .............. '62 '88 C.788 B.A. L.1065 J.D. 2121 Ave. of the Stars
**Rosenson, S. David**, (AV) .............. '36 '62 C.112 B.A. L.813 LL.B. [Wasser,R.&C.]
*PRACTICE AREAS: Family Law.
Rosenstein, Earl '26 '58 C.597 B.B.A. L.209 J.D.
(adm. in IL; not adm. in CA) Sr. V.P., Prism Entertainment Corp.
Rosenstein, Larry D., (AV) ........ '51 '76 C.347 B.A. L.1049 J.D. 11766 Wilshire Blvd.
**Rosenthal, Allan M.**, (AV) .............. '46 '73 C.112 A.B. L.426 J.D. [Wolf,R.&S.]
*PRACTICE AREAS: Products Liability Law; Civil Litigation.

CALIFORNIA—LOS ANGELES MARTINDALE-HUBBELL LAW DIRECTORY 1997

**Rosenthal, Edward S.** ....................'54 '81 C.118 B.A. L.178 J.D. [Fried,F.H.S.&J.]
**Rosenthal, Jill** ....................'63 '91 C.112 B.A. L.276 J.D. [[A] Kinsella,B.F.&T.]
*PRACTICE AREAS: Litigation.
**Rosenthal, Margaret** ....................'56 '79 C.994 B.A. L.146 J.D. [[B] Rodi,P.P.G.&C.]
*LANGUAGES: French, Hungarian and Romanian.
*PRACTICE AREAS: Employment Law; Health Care Law.
Rosenthal, Mark Alan '59 '86
C.112 B.S. L.800 J.D. V.P. & Gen. Coun., Raleigh Enterprises
**Rosenthal, Mark M.** ....................'48 '73 C.918 B.A. L.477 J.D. [Jeffer,M.B.&M.]
*PRACTICE AREAS: Business; Sports, Copyright, Trademark and Entertainment Litigation.
Rosenthal, Marvin R. '35 '59 C.563 B.B.A. L.472 J.D.
(adm. in FL; not adm. in CA) 622 Barrington‡
Rosenthal, Robert M. ....... '36 '76 C.659 B.S. L.809 J.D. 2040 Ave. of the Stars, 4th Fl.
**Rosenthal, Shari L.** ....................'60 '86 C.823 B.A. L.809 J.D. [Breidenbach,B.H.H.&H.]
**Rosenthal, Sol**, (AV) ....................'34 '59 C.674 A.B. L.309 J.D. [[B] Blanc W.J.&K.]
*PRACTICE AREAS: Entertainment Law.
Rosentswieg, Suzanne, (AV) '41 '76
C.112 B.A. L.1148 J.D. 1669 N. Crescent Heights Blvd.
**Rosenwasser, Lisa G.** .................... '58 '85 C.112 B.A. L.809 J.D. [Dennison,B.&P.]
*PRACTICE AREAS: Insurance and Tort Defense; Business Litigation; Property Disputes; Uninsured Motorist Litigation.
**Rosenzweig, David M.** ....................'64 '95 C.309 A.B. L.276 J.D. [[A] Munger,T.&O.]
*LANGUAGES: French.
Rosett, Arthur I. ....................'34 '60 C&L.178 B.A., LL.B. Prof. of Law, U.C.L.A.
Rosin, Richard M., (AV) ....................'42 '67 C.154 B.A. L.1066 J.D. [Rosin&L.]
Rosin & Levine, A Professional Corporation, (AV) .....10390 Santa Monica Blvd., 4th Fl.
**Roski-Amendola, Reon** ....................'64 '94 C.800 B.A. L.426 J.D. [[A] Allen,M.L.G.&M.]
*LANGUAGES: Chinese.
*PRACTICE AREAS: Real Estate.
Roslin, Matthew I. ....................'68 '91 C.659 B.S. L.1068 J.D. 333 S. Hope St.
**Roslin, Sophia Friedman** ....................'67 '93 C.659 B.A. L.597 J.D. [Jones,D.R.&P.]
Rosman, David M. .........'53 '78 C.976 B.A. L.1068 J.D. 1900 Ave. of the Stars, 17th Fl.
**Rosmann, David J.** ....................'58 '96 C.350 B.S.E.Sc. L.426 J.D. [[A] Irell&M.]
Rosner, David L., (A Professional Law Corporation), (AV) '37 '63
C.800 B.S. L.426 LL.B. [Rosner,O.&N.]
Rosner, Leland S. ............. '45 '72 C.1077 B.A. L.464 J.D. 10866 Wilshire Blvd. (Pat.)
Rosner, Owens & Nunziato, (AV) .................... 1925 Century Park E.
Rosoff, Howard L., (P.C.), (AV) ...........'39 '63 C.569 B.S. L.1068 J.D. [Rosoff,S.&B.]
Rosoff, Schiffres & Barta, (AV) .................... 11755 Wilshire Blvd.
Ross, Adam ....................'— '96 C.112 B.A. L.426 J.D. 6230 Wilshire Blvd.
Ross, Alan, Jr. ....................'22 '49 C&L.188 A.B., LL.B. 316 W. 2nd St.
**Ross, Bradley D.** ....................'56 '81 C.112 B.A. L.426 J.D. [Kendig&R.]
*PRACTICE AREAS: Employment/Labor Law; Business Litigation; Real Estate Litigation.
**Ross, Bruce S.**, (AV) .................... '47 '72 C.604 A.B. L.1066 J.D. [Ross,S.&G.]
*PRACTICE AREAS: Estate, Trust and Conservatorship Litigation; Professional Responsibility Litigation; Probate; Appellate Practice; Mediation.
Ross, David R. ....................'42 '69 C.1044 B.A. L.823 J.D. Dep. Dist. Atty.
**Ross, Dawn Patrice** ....................'— '90 C.912 B.S. L.309 J.D. [[A] Morgan,L.&B.]
Ross, Edward M. ....................'33 '60 C.112 A.B. L.1068 J.D. Supr. Ct. J.
**Ross, Elise A.** ....................'57 '84 C.112 B.A. L.1067 J.D. [[A] Ivanjack&L.]
*LANGUAGES: Spanish and French.
*REPORTED CASES: Bank of America National Trust and Savings Association v. Sanati, 11 Cal. App. 4th 1079 (1992).
*PRACTICE AREAS: Regulatory Compliance; Operations and Transactional Advice to Financial Institutions.
**Ross, Jonathan A.** ....................'60 '87 C.30 B.S. L.273 J.D. [[A] Manning,M.&W.]
**Ross, Julia L.** ....................'62 '89 C.299 B.A. L.309 J.D. [[B] Gipson H.&P.]
*LANGUAGES: French.
*PRACTICE AREAS: Litigation.
Ross, Leo J. ....................'18 '39 C&L.724 LL.B. 5757 Wilshire Blvd.
**Ross, Melanie C.** ....................'65 '90 C.1365 B.A. L.800 J.D. [[A] Knee&M.]
*PRACTICE AREAS: Employment Litigation; Employment Discrimination; Wrongful Termination Defense; Sexual Harassment; Labor Arbitration.
**Ross, Michael E.** ....................'64 '94 C.813 A.B. L.1068 J.D. [[A] Loeb&L.]
**Ross, Richard R.**, (AV) .................... '46 '74 C.112 B.A. L.426 J.D. [O'Melveny&M.]
*PRACTICE AREAS: Entertainment Law.
Ross, Robert M. .................... '48 '73 C.800 L.426 J.D. [Klass,H.&R.]
Ross, Sari Stabler .................... '60 '86 C.112 A.B. L.800 J.D. Bet Tzedek Legal Servs.
Ross, Sheri E. ....................'51 '78 C.188 B.S. L.426 J.D. 1660 Roscomare Rd.
**Ross, Steven A.** ....................'57 '82 C.311 B.A. L.976 J.D. [Sheppard,M.R.&H.]
**Ross, Steven U.** ....................'55 '81 C.112 B.A. L.426 J.D. [[B] B.R.Bailey]
*PRACTICE AREAS: Business Litigation; Real Estate Law.
**Ross, Susan Kohn**, (AV) .................... '45 '78 C.112 B.A. L.809 J.D. [S.K.Ross&Assoc.]
*SPECIAL AGENCIES: U.S. Customs Service; Food and Drug Administration; Department of State; Department of Commerce and U.S. Trade Representative.
*PRACTICE AREAS: International Trade Law; Customs Law; Transportation Law; Business Law.
**Ross, William D.**, (AV) .................... '48 '75 C.813 B.A. L.770 J.D. [W.D.Ross]⊙
*REPORTED CASES: William S. Hart Union High School Dist. v. Regional Planning Commission, 226 Cal.App.3d 1612 (1991); Long Beach Unified School District v. State of California, 225 Cal.App.3d 155 (1990), Petition for Review denied February 28, 1991; City of Sacramento v. State of California, 50 Cal.3d 51, 266 Cal.Rptr. 139 (1990); American River Fire Protection Dist. v. Board of Supervisors, 211 Cal.App.3d 1076, 259 Cal.Rptr. 858 (1989); Carmel Valley Fire Protection Dist. v. State of California, 190 Cal.App.3d 521, 234 Cal.Rptr. 795 (1987).
*PRACTICE AREAS: Land Use; Municipal and Zoning; Real Estate.

**Ross, Ivanjack, Lambirth & Aranoff**
**(See Ivanjack & Lambirth)**

**Ross, S. K., & Assoc., P.C., (AV)**
**5777 West Century Boulevard, Suite 520, 90045-5659**
**Telephone: 310-410-4414 FAX: 310-410-1017**
**Email: skohnxro@counsel.com URL: http://www.skralaw.com**
**Susan Kohn Ross;—John W. Shi.**
**Languages: German, Mandarin Chinese.**
**Customs, International Trade, Transportation, Admiralty and Maritime, Business and Commercial Law.**
**Representative Clients and References available upon request.**
***See Professional Biographies, LOS ANGELES, CALIFORNIA***

**Ross, Sacks & Glazier, (AV)**
**Suite 3900 300 South Grand Avenue, 90071**
**Telephone: 213-617-2950 Fax: 213-617-9350**
**Members of Firm: Bruce S. Ross (Certified Specialist, Estate Planning, Trust and Probate Law, The State Bar of California Board of Legal Specialization); Kenneth M. Glazier; Robert N. Sacks; John T. Rogers, Jr. (Certified Specialist, Estate Planning, Trust and Probate Law, The State Bar of California Board of Legal Specialization); Terrence M. Franklin. Counsel: Christina M. Jacobs; Jeryll S. Cohen. Associates: Margaret G. Lodise; Jana W. Bray; John F. Eyrich.**
**Estate, Trust and Conservatorship Litigation. Business Litigation. Professional Responsibility Litigation. Appellate Practice. Probate and Estate Planning.**
***See Professional Biographies, LOS ANGELES, CALIFORNIA***

**Ross, William D., Law Offices of, A Prof. Corp., (AV)**
**520 South Grand Avenue, Suite 300, 90071**⊙
**Telephone: 213-892-1592 Telecopier: 213-892-1519**

(This Listing Continued)

**Ross, William D., Law Offices of, A Prof. Corp. (Continued)**
**William D. Ross; Diane C. DeFelice; Myra J. Prestidge. Of Counsel: Carol B. Sherman; Lisabeth D. Rothman.**
**Civil Trial and Appellate Practice in State and Federal Courts. Business Litigation, Employment Rights, Land Use, Real Property, Environmental, Water Rights, Public Finance, State and Local Administrative Law.**
**Palo Alto, California Office: 425 Sherman Avenue, Suite 310. Telephone: 415-617-5678. Fax: 415-617-5680.**
***See Professional Biographies, LOS ANGELES, CALIFORNIA***

**Rossbacher, Henry H.**, (AV) ....'43 '69 C.659 B.S.Ec. L.893 LL.B. [Rossbacher&Assoc.]
*PRACTICE AREAS: Civil Litigation; Criminal Litigation; Appellate Litigation; Securities Litigation; Constitutional Law.

**Rossbacher & Associates, (AV)** [B]
**Union Bank Plaza, Twenty-Fourth Floor, 445 South Figueroa Street, 90071**
**Telephone: 213-895-6500 Fax: 213-895-6161**
**Members of Firm: Henry H. Rossbacher. Of Counsel: George M. Snyder. Associates: James S. Cahill; Linda L. Griffis; Karen D. Kerner; Nanci E. Nishimura; Tracy W. Young; Julie A. Langslet; David F. Desmond.**
**Civil, Criminal and Appellate Litigation in all State and Federal Courts and Administrative Tribunals.**
***See Professional Biographies, LOS ANGELES, CALIFORNIA***

**Rossi, Angela M.** .................... '60 '87 C.1044 B.A. L.990 J.D. [[A] Stevens,K.A.&H.]
**Rossi, Anthony J.**, (AV) ....................'32 '61 C&L.800 B.A., J.D. [[B] Paul,H.J.&W.]
**Rossi, Michael A.** ....................'65 '91 C.112 B.A. L.1066 J.D. [[A] Troop M.S.&P.]
*PRACTICE AREAS: Risk Management Consulting; Insurance Coverage: Advice, Claims Presentation, Alt. Dispute Resolution & Litigation.
**Rossman, Adam S.** .................... '66 '95 C.112 B.A. L.426 J.D. [[A] Aronoff&S.]
*LANGUAGES: French.
*PRACTICE AREAS: Commercial Litigation; Bankruptcy; Real Estate Litigation; Transactions.
Rostagno, Juan A. ....................'36 '67 C.055 L.809 LL.B. 770 Tigertail Rd.
Roston, Ellsworth R., (AV) .............. '22 '49 C&L.976 B.E., LL.B. [Roston&S.] (Pat.)
Roston and Schwartz, A Professional Corporation, (AV) ........5900 Wilshire Blvd. (Pat.)
**Rosvall, Wallace L.** '46 '72 C.112 B.A. L.800 J.D.
Sr. V.P. & Asst. Gen. Coun., CB Coml. Real Estate Grp., Inc.
*RESPONSIBILITIES: Litigation; Employment; Contracts; Real Estate.
**Rotell, Cynthia A.** ....................'60 '90 C.66 B.A. L.1009 J.D. [[A] Latham&W.]
**Roten, Russell W.** ....................'49 '77 C&L.575 B.A., J.D. [Lane P.S.L.]
*PRACTICE AREAS: International Practice; Business Law; Corporate Law; Commercial Litigation.
Roth, Alan M. '43 '69 C.994 B.A. L.1009 J.D.
(adm. in NY; not adm. in CA) Dir., Tax, Northrop Corp.
Roth, Amil, (AV) ....................'27 '61 C.112 B.A. L.1068 LL.B. 1875 Century Park E.
**Roth, Carl A.** ....................'61 '90 C.112 A.B. L.309 J.D. [[A] Skadden,A.S.M.&F.]
Roth, David, P.C., (AV) .................... '46 '73 C.1097 B.S. L.426 J.D. 1901 Ave. of the Stars
Roth, Debra J. ........ '57 '81 C.260 B.A. L.813 J.D. V.P., Bus. Affs., Orion Pictures Corp.
**Roth, Eric N.** .................... '67 '95 C.112 B.A. L.813 J.D. [[A] O'Melveny&M.]
*PRACTICE AREAS: Tax Law.
Roth, H. I. ....................'16 '41 C.113 B.S. L.800 LL.B. 357 S. Curson Ave.
Roth, Herbert L. '37 '62 C.823 A.B. L.976 LL.B.
Exec. V.P. & Gen. Coun., Karsten Realty Advisors
**Roth, Jonathan P.** ....................'62 '88 C.112 B.A. L.426 J.D. [Loeb&L.]
**Roth, Mark S.** .................... '51 '78 C.800 B.A. L.809 J.D. [Cozen&O.]
*PRACTICE AREAS: Subrogation; Products Liability; Negligence; Construction Defects; Trials.

**Roth, Michael Dundon, Law Offices of, (AV) '52 '77 C.454 B.A. L.93 J.D.**
**The Wilshire Landmark Building, 11755 Wilshire Boulevard, Suite 1400, 90025-1520**
**Telephone: 310-477-5455 Facsimile: 310-477-1979**
***PRACTICE AREAS: Health Care Law.**
**—Sharon F. Roth.**
**Practice Limited to Health Care and Related General Practice Areas.**
**Reference: Marathon National Bank.**
***See Professional Biographies, LOS ANGELES, CALIFORNIA***

Roth, Mitchell W. ....................'50 '77 C.1044 B.A. L.724 J.D. [Schmid&V.]
**Roth, Pamela H.** ....................'61 '85 C.401 B.A. L.273 J.D. [[A] Lynberg&W.]
**Roth, Peter J.** ....................'68 '93 C&L.228 A.B., J.D. [[A] Paul,H.J.&W.]
Roth, Robert A., (BV) ............'41 '68 C.112 B.S. L.145 J.D. 12304 Santa Monica Blvd.
**Roth, Sharon F.** ....................'58 '89 C.150 B.A. L.426 J.D. [M.D.Roth]
*PRACTICE AREAS: Health Care Law.
Roth, Virgil L. ....................'45 '76 C.228 B.A. L.602 J.D. 801 S. Figueroa St.
Roth, W. Norman, (AV) ....................'40 '67 C.46 B.S.C.E. L.802 J.D. [Roth&G.] (Pat.)
Roth, William Mark .......... '63 '89 C.112 A.B. L.426 J.D. 221 N. Figueroa St., Ste., 1200
Roth & Goldman, A Professional Association, (AV) .................... 523 W. Sixth St. (Pat.)
Rothans, Steven J. ....................'57 '82 C&L.426 B.A., J.D. [Carpenter&R.]

**Rothbard, William I., Law Offices of, (AV) '50 '76 C.477 B.A. L.1065 J.D.**
**12424 Wilshire Boulevard, Suite 900, 90025-1043**
**Telephone: 310-207-4603 Facsimile: 310-442-6400**
**Business and Civil Litigation in all State and Federal Trial and Appellate Courts, Antitrust, Unfair Competition, Advertising, Trade Regulation, Copyright, Trademark, Election Law, Legislative and Regulatory Representation.**
***See Professional Biographies, LOS ANGELES, CALIFORNIA***

**Rothenberg, Alan I.**, (AV) ....................'39 '64 C&L.477 B.A., J.D. [Latham&W.]
Rothenberg, Oscar, (A Professional Corporation) '31 '59
C.800 B.S. L.809 LL.B. 1157 S. Beverly Dr.
Rothenbucher, Tom W. ....................'64 '89 C.813 A.B. L.1068 J.D. 5757 Wilshire Blvd.
**Rothman, Alfred I., (A P.C.)**, (AV) .......... '17 '41 C&L.477 A.B., J.D. [[B] Loeb&L.] ‡
*PRACTICE AREAS: Litigation; Arbitration and Mediation.
Rothman, Barry K. ....................'20 '71 C.563 L.1095 J.D. 1880 Century Park E.
Rothman, Barry K. .................... '42 '70 C.112 B.S. L.809 J.D. 1880 Century Park E.
**Rothman, Daniel L.**, (AV) ....... '25 '51 C.426 B.B.A. L.809 LL.B. [[B] Karpman&Assoc.]
**Rothman, Don**, (AV) .................... '36 '66 C.162 B.A. L.800 J.D. [Sulmeyer,K.B.&R.]
*PRACTICE AREAS: Bankruptcy.
**Rothman, Frank**, (AV) .............. '26 '52 C&L.800 A.B., LL.B. [Skadden,A.S.M.&F.]
**Rothman, Lisabeth D.** ....................'57 '82 C.668 B.A. L.178 J.D. [[B] W.D.Ross]
*PRACTICE AREAS: Appellate Practice; Business; Civil Trial; Commercial Litigation; Securities.
Rothman, Louis P. ....................'36 '60 C.178 A.B. L.188 LL.B. [[B] H.L.Thomas]
**Rothman, Matthew** ....................'65 '91 C.668 B.A. L.426 J.D. [[A] Sulmeyer,K.B.&R.]
*PRACTICE AREAS: Bankruptcy; Insolvency.
**Rothman, Michael J.** ....................'62 '88 C.118 B.A. L.494 J.D. [[A] Barger&W.]
**Rothman, Rick R.** .................... '63 '89 C.477 B.A. L.276 J.D. [McCutchen,D.B.&E.]
*PRACTICE AREAS: Environmental.
Rothman, Shelley T. '41 '69 C.788 B.A. L.569 J.D.
Contracts Supvr., Los Angeles Unified Sch. Dist.
Rothman, Stanley ....................'35 '66 C.563 B.E.E. L.800 LL.B. [S.Rothman]
**Rothman, Stephen P.** .................... '57 '85 C.976 B.A. L.309 J.D. [Morrison&F.]
*PRACTICE AREAS: Corporate Finance; Mergers and Acquisitions; Business Law; Sports; Retail.
Rothman, Stanley, A Prof. Corp. .................... 11601 Wilshire Blvd.
Rothschild, Frances .................... '41 '67 C.112 B.A. L.1068 LL.B. Supr. Ct. J.
**Rothschild, Shelly**, (AV) .................... '49 '77 C.788 B.A. L.94 J.D. [Andrews&K.]
*PRACTICE AREAS: Bankruptcy Law.

**Rothstein, Gary D.** .................... '57 '89 C.763 A.B. L.770 J.D. [Ⓐ Brobeck,P.&H.]
*PRACTICE AREAS: Trusts and Estates; Estate Planning; Probate.
**Rothstein, Glen A.** .................... '70 '95 C.112 B.A. L.1068 J.D. [Ⓐ Loeb&L.]
**Rothstein, Joel H.** .................... '63 '90 C.1097 B.A. L.569 J.D. [Ⓐ Paul,H.J.&W.]

**Rothstein, Larry A.**
**(See Woodland Hills)**

Rotkin, Schmerin & McIntyre .................... 2222 S. Broadway (⊙Palm Springs)
**Rotstein, Robert H.**, (AV) .................... '51 '76 C.112 A.B. L.1068 J.D. [McDermott,W.&E.]
*PRACTICE AREAS: Complex Business Litigation; Intellectual Property Law; Copyright Law; Entertainment Litigation.
Rouda, Ronald Lee .................... '47 '74 C.112 B.A. L.426 J.D. 11664 National Blvd.
**Rountree, Michael D.** .................... '65 '94 C.154 B.A. L.770 J.D. [Ⓐ Musick,P.&G.]
*LANGUAGES: French.
*PRACTICE AREAS: Corporate/Business Litigation.

**Roup, Loomis & Johnson LLP**
**(See Lake Forest)**

**Rouse, Ming-Chu C.** .................... '51 '84 C.061 B.A. L.596 J.D. [Ⓐ Sandler&R.]
*LANGUAGES: Mandarin Chinese.
**Rouse, Thomas R.** .................... '63 '95 C.112 B.S. L.426 J.D. [Ⓐ Lyon&L.]
*LANGUAGES: French, Spanish.
*PRACTICE AREAS: Patent; Trademark; Copyright; Trade Secret; Unfair Competition.
Rouse, William J. .................... '66 '92 C&L.800 B.S., J.D. 6300 Wilshire Blvd.
**Roux, George C.** .................... '55 '81 C.112 B.A. L.893 J.D. [McClintock,W.B.R.R.&M.]
*PRACTICE AREAS: Hazardous Waste and Environmental Litigation; Construction Litigation; Business Litigation; Trials and Appeals.
Rouzbehani, Fariborz .................... '52 '92 C.800 B.A. L.1136 J.D. 1925 Century Park E.
Rowan, Thomas Patrick .................... '47 '74 C.770 B.A. L.426 J.D. [Myman,A.F.G.&R.]
**Rowe, Brian F.** .................... '62 '93 C.112 B.S. L.426 J.D. [Ⓐ Beckman,D.S.&R.]
*PRACTICE AREAS: Insurance; Bankruptcy; General Practice.
**Rowen, Eric V.** .................... '57 '82 C.112 B.A. L.426 J.D. [Jones,D.R.&P.]
Rowse, Gary T. .................... '45 '73 C.112 A.B. L.800 J.D. Off. of City Atty.
Roxborough, Nicholas P. .................... '55 '83 C.112 B.S. L.809 J.D. 10866 Wilshire Blvd.
**Roy, Dennis S.** .................... '54 '81 C.103 A.B. L.1068 J.D. [Brown,W.&C.]
*PRACTICE AREAS: Real Estate; Redevelopment Law.
**Roy, Guy M.** .................... '62 '92 C.112 B.A. L.990 J.D. [Ⓐ Charlston,R.&W.]
**Roybal, Scott F.** .................... '59 '87 C.878 B.A. L.178 J.D. [Sheppard,M.R.&H.]
*PRACTICE AREAS: Litigation; Government Contracts Law.
Royce, George R., (AV) .................... '38 '64 C.668 B.A. L.1068 LL.B. [Royce&I.]
Royce & Inferrera, (AV) .................... 2049 Century Park, East
**Royer, Kendrick F.** .................... '64 '91 C.674 B.S.E. L.880 J.D. [Ⓐ Milbank,T.H.&M.]
*LANGUAGES: Japanese.
Roylance, Richard C. ...... '54 '81 C.198 A.B. L.893 J.D. Trial Coun., State Bar of Calif.
Rozanski, Stanley H. .................... '52 '78 C.331 B.A. L.1095 J.D. 11601 Wilshire Blvd.
**Rozansky, Daniel A.** .................... '65 '92 C.112 B.A. L.423 J.D. [Ⓐ Hewitt&P.]
*PRACTICE AREAS: Insurance Defense; General Liability; Medical and Dental Malpractice.
**Rozell, Kenneth D.** .................... '62 '91 C.999 B.A. L.426 J.D. [Ⓐ Burke,W.&S.]
*PRACTICE AREAS: Municipal and Public Law; Land Use; Redevelopment; Litigation.
Rozenberg, Wayne .................... '65 '91 C.763 B.S. L.426 J.D. 3926 Wilshire Blvd.
**Rozwood, Benjamin** .................... '68 '96 C.112 L.309 [Ⓐ Troy&G.]
*LANGUAGES: Spanish.
*PRACTICE AREAS: Securities Law; Corporate Law.
Rub, Martin H. .................... '49 '74 C.112 B.A. L.809 J.D. [M.H.Rub]
Rub, Martin H., A Professional Corporation .................... 10940 Wilshire Blvd.
**Rubalcava, Sharon F.**, (AV) '46 '75 C.112 B.A. L.1068 J.D.
[McClintock,W.B.R.R.&M.]
*PRACTICE AREAS: Environmental Law; Air Pollution; Water Quality; Administrative Law; CEQA.
**Rubanowitz, Daniel B.** .................... '62 '90 C.112 B.A. L.426 J.D. [Ⓐ Trope&T.]
*PRACTICE AREAS: Family Law.
Rubaum, Lawrence S .................... '59 '84 C.112 B.A. L.426 J.D. [Shaffer,G.&R.]
**Rubel, Michael A.**, (AV) .................... '49 '76 C.103 A.B. L.1068 J.D. [Del,R.S.M.&D.]
*PRACTICE AREAS: Real Estate Law; Partnership Law; Corporation Law.
Ruben, Charles E., (AV) ...... '44 '72 C.112 B.S. L.1049 J.D. 11111 Santa Monica Blvd.
**Ruben, David N.** .................... '65 '91 C.112 B.A. L.809 J.D. [Ⓐ Luce,F.H.&S.]
*PRACTICE AREAS: Product Litigation; Warranty.
**Ruben, Steven A.** .................... '60 '86 C.1077 B.S. L.1068 J.D. [Gibson,D.&C.]
*PRACTICE AREAS: Trusts and Estates.
**Ruben, Steven J.**, (AV) .................... '44 '70 C.112 A.B. L.426 J.D. [Ruben&M.]
*PRACTICE AREAS: Business Litigation; Professional Liability; Insurance Law.

**Ruben & McGonigle LLP, (AV)**
**1999 Avenue of the Stars, 15th Floor, 90067-6045**
**Telephone: 310-772-2950 Fax: 310-772-2955**
**Steven J. Ruben; Timothy D. McGonigle; Judith R. Seligman; Mark Jones; Russell W. Clampitt; Peter M. Kunstler; Angeli Cuesta Aragon. Of Counsel: Bryan J. Axelrood (Certified Specialist, Taxation Law, State Bar of California Board of Legal Specialization); Robert M. Silverman; George J. Wang; Carol L. Newman.**
**General Civil Litigation, Professional Liability, Securities, Trial Appellate, Corporations, Insurance, Probate, Family and Entertainment Law, Administrative and Legislative Practice in all State and Federal Courts.**

*See Professional Biographies, LOS ANGELES, CALIFORNIA*

**Rubens, Eileen Driscoll** .................... '62 '93 C.843 B.B.A. L.426 J.D. [Ⓐ Milbank,T.H.&M.]
**Rubens, Jack H.** .................... '57 '82 C.112 B.A. L.1068 J.D. [Sheppard,M.R.&H.]
*PRACTICE AREAS: Land Use Law; Real Estate Law; Secured Transactions.
**Rubenstein, Ilana B.** .................... '68 '94 C.945 B.A. L.477 J.D. [Ⓐ Munger,T.&O.]
**Rubenstein, Paul D.**, (AV) .................... '46 '71 C.112 B.A. L.309 J.D. [Proskauer R.G.&M.]
*PRACTICE AREAS: Real Estate; Partnership Law.
**Rubenstein, Steven M.** .................... '53 '78 C.477 B.A. L.112 J.D. [Rubenstein&F.]
*PRACTICE AREAS: Civil Litigation; Entertainment Litigation; Real Estate Litigation; Business Litigation; Insurance Defense.

**Rubenstein & Finch**
**2049 Century Park East, Suite 1200, 90067-3114**
**Telephone: 310-277-1646 FAX: 310-277-4259**
**Steven M. Rubenstein; Roxanne P. Finch.**
**Litigation Practice in the areas of Real Estate, Entertainment, Business and Personal Injury Law. Insurance Defense.**

*See Professional Biographies, LOS ANGELES, CALIFORNIA*

**Rubin, Alan** .................... '50 '76 C.367 B.A. L.477 J.D. [Epstein,A.&R.]
*PRACTICE AREAS: Criminal Law.
**Rubin, Cynthia Lu** .................... '53 '85 C.112 B.A. L.426 J.D. [Goldfarb,S.&A.]
*PRACTICE AREAS: Real Estate Law; Business Litigation.
Rubin, Dale M. .................... '50 '75 C.1077 B.A. L.1095 J.D. [Rubin&R.]
**Rubin, Edward, (A Professional Corporation)**, (AV) '12 '37
C.112 A.B. L.228 LL.B. [Ⓒ Mitchell,S.&K.]
*PRACTICE AREAS: Entertainment Law; Copyright Law; Intellectual Property Law.
**Rubin, G. David** .................... '70 '95 C.112 B.A. L.426 J.D. [Ⓒ Parsons&D.]
*LANGUAGES: Spanish.
*PRACTICE AREAS: Complex Coverage; Excess and Reinsurance Litigation; General Insurance Litigation.
Rubin, Howard M. .................... '47 '72 C.112 B.A. L.1068 J.D. 445 S. Figueroa St.
Rubin, Irving I. M. .................... '52 '78 C.30 B.S. L.1095 J.D. P.O. Box 241958
Rubin, Jay T. .................... '53 '78 C.112 B.A. L.426 J.D. 3600 Wilshire Blvd.
**Rubin, Jennifer A.** '62 '86
C.112 B.A. L.1066 J.D. Asst. Gen. Coun., Turner Bdcstg. Sys., Inc.
Rubin, L. Anthony .................... '51 '77 C.112 B.S. L.990 J.D. 2161 Manoeville Canyon Rd.
Rubin, Lael R. .................... '42 '78 C.477 B.A. L.1136 J.D. Dep. Dist. Atty.
**Rubin, Miles J., (A Professional Corporation)**, (AV) '29 '54
C.945 B.A. L.1009 LL.B. [Deutsch&R.]
*PRACTICE AREAS: Family Law; Domestic Relations Law; Matrimonial Law; Divorce Law.
**Rubin, Neal A.** .................... '67 '94 C.31 B.A. L.800 J.D. [Ⓐ McCutchen,D.B.&E.]
*LANGUAGES: Spanish.
*PRACTICE AREAS: Commercial Litigation; Employment Litigation.
Rubin, Norman A. .................... '29 '55 C.112 B.S. L.1068 LL.B. 2525 Sawtelle Blvd.
Rubin, Philip .................... '46 '72 C.112 B.A. L.629 J.D. 10100 Santa Monica Blvd.
Rubin, Rand S. .................... '53 '79 C.112 B.A. L.1095 J.D. [Rubin&R.]
**Rubin, Renee M.** .................... '65 '92 C.1349 B.S. L.813 J.D. [Ⓐ White&C.]
Rubin, Robert J. .................... '11 '33 C&L.809 J.D. 611 W. Sixth St.
Rubin, Robert S. .................... '47 '74 C.112 B.A. L.284 J.D. 3600 Wilshire Blvd.
**Rubin, Russell M.** .................... '58 '86 C.112 B.A. L.809 J.D. [Ⓐ Liebman&R.]
**Rubin, Stanford K., (A P.C.)**, (AV) .................... '37 '62 C.339 B.A. L.813 LL.B. [Loeb&L.]
*PRACTICE AREAS: Trusts and Estates.
Rubin, Steven D. .................... '58 '90 C.112 B.A. L.990 J.D. 2029 Century Park, E.
**Rubin, Thomas S.** .................... '68 '95 C.309 A.B. L.1068 J.D. [Ⓐ Kenoff&M.]
*PRACTICE AREAS: Entertainment Law; Litigation.

**Rubin & Eagan, P.C.**
**(See Beverly Hills)**

**Rubin-Elbaz, Betty** .................... '57 '84 C.112 B.A. L.809 J.D. Corp. Coun., Guess ?, Inc.
*LANGUAGES: French.
*RESPONSIBILITIES: Corporate.
Rubin & Rubin .................... 1519 W. Temple St.
Rubiner, John K. .................... '66 '90 C.339 B.S. L.112 J.D. Off. of U.S. Atty.
**Rubinfeld, Alyce Ann** .................... '55 '83 C.1077 B.A. L.1065 J.D. [Ⓐ Epstein B.&G.]
*PRACTICE AREAS: Labor and Employment Law; Litigation.
**Rubinfeld, Amy L.** .................... '64 '89 C.1049 B.A. L.800 J.D. [Ⓐ Buchalter,N.F.&Y.]
*PRACTICE AREAS: Commercial Business Litigation; Banking Law; Financial Institutions; Insurance Coverage; Prejudgment Remedies including Receivership Actions.
**Rubinroit, Howard J.**, (AV) .................... '44 '69 C.705 B.A. L.659 LL.B. [Sidley&A.]
*PRACTICE AREAS: Business Litigation; Real Estate and Construction Litigation; Insurance Coverage Disputes; Product Liability.
Rubinstein, Boris .................... '65 '91 C.112 B.S. L.426 J.D. [Korbatov,R.&R.]
**Rubinstein, Karl L.**, (AV) .................... '43 '68 C.839 B.A. L.744 J.D. [Rubinstein&P.]
*REPORTED CASES: Quackenbush California Insurance Commissioner v. Allstate Ins. Co. 116 S.Ct. 1712 (1996); Sunburst Bank, N.A. v. Executive Life, 24 Cal. App. 4th 1156 (1994); Garamendi v. Executive Life, 17 Cal. App. 4th 504 (1993); Checkers Motor Corporation v. Superior Court (Garamendi), 13 Cal. App. 4th 1007 (1993); Commercial National Bank v. Superior Court (Garamendi), 14 Cal. App. 4th 393 (1993).
*TRANSACTIONS: Final Liquidation Dividend Plan For Mission Insurance Companies (1996); Rehabilitation Plan for Executive Life Insurance Company (1994); Rehabilitation Plan for Mission American Insurance Company (1986); Rehabilitation Plan for Baldwin-United Insurance Companies (1984).
*PRACTICE AREAS: Business and Commercial Litigation; Intellectual Property; Workouts; Insurance; Reinsurance.

**Rubinstein & Perry, A Professional Corporation, (AV)**
**355 South Grand Avenue, 31st Floor, 90071⊙**
**Telephone: 213-346-1000 Fax: 213-680-3275**
**Email: info@rplaw.com URL: http://www.rplaw.com**
**Dana Carli Brooks; Melissa S. Kooistra; Kathleen Mary McCain; Robert H. Nunnally, Jr.; Karl L. Rubinstein; Sanford I. Millar (Certified Specialist, Taxation Law, The State Bar of California Board of Legal Specialization);—David Wayne Johnson, Jr.; Shannon M. Keane; Donald B. Serafano.**
**General Civil Practice, Insolvencies, General Corporate, Insurance, Reinsurance Litigation, Real Estate, Real Estate Litigation, Workouts and Reorganization, Intellectual Properties, Bankruptcy and Taxation.**
**San Francisco, California Office: 101 California Street, Suite 4090. Telephone: 415-658-0800. Fax: 415-399-1407.**

*See Professional Biographies, LOS ANGELES, CALIFORNIA*

**Ruby, Steven N.** .................... '60 '87 C.1049 B.A. L.990 J.D. [Ⓐ Saltzburg,R.&B.]
*PRACTICE AREAS: Bankruptcy Law; Litigation; Business Law.

**Rucker, Fred, Law Offices of '53 '78 C.154 B.A. L.93 J.D.**
**10100 Santa Monica Boulevard, Suite 300, 90067**
**Telephone: 310-203-9330 Fax: 310-203-9332**
**Complex Commercial, Securities, Real Estate and Insurance Coverage Litigation, White Collar Criminal Defense.**

*See Professional Biographies, LOS ANGELES, CALIFORNIA*

Rud-Pentz, Ada ...... '69 '95 C.112 B.A. L.426 J.D. Assoc. Gen. Coun., Plott Mgmt. Corp.
**Rudd, Christopher L.** .................... '62 '87 C.659 B.A. L.228 J.D. [Manatt,P.&P.]
*PRACTICE AREAS: Entertainment Law; General Business Litigation.
**Ruddy, Catherine Hunt**, (AV) .................... '53 '77 C&L.800 B.S., J.D. [Beckman,D.S.&R.]
*PRACTICE AREAS: Life, Health and Disability Insurance Law; ERISA; Contract Dispute Resolution; Employment.
**Rudell, William B.** .................... '39 '68 C.674 A.B. L.976 LL.B. [Richards,W.&G.]
*PRACTICE AREAS: Municipal Law; Municipal Finance; Aviation Law; Land Use Law.
Rudich, David, (AV) ....... '42 '70 C.1077 B.S. L.112 J.D. 9255 W. Sunset Blvd., Fl. 920
Rudin, Milton A., (AV) .................... '20 '47 C.112 B.A. L.309 J.D. 12121 Wilshire Blvd.
**Rudman, Jamie** .................... '68 '93 C.112 B.A. L.1068 J.D. [Ⓐ Katten M.&Z.]
*PRACTICE AREAS: Employment; Labor; Litigation.
**Rudman, Norman G.**, (AV) .................... '30 '56 C.112 A.B. L.1066 J.D. [Slaff,M.&R.]
*PRACTICE AREAS: Motion Picture; Entertainment; Television; Copyright and Trademark; Transactions and Litigation.
Rudnick, Ben H. .................... '08 '35 15171 Mulholland Dr.‡
**Rudnick, Dana M.** .................... '69 '93 C.446 B.S. L.1068 J.D. [Ⓐ Gibbs,G.L.&A.]
*PRACTICE AREAS: Commercial; Business Law.
**Rudnick, Stuart W.** .................... '46 '72 C.966 B.A. L.477 J.D. [Musick,P.&G.]
*PRACTICE AREAS: Labor and Employment.
**Rudnicki, Robert Michael** .... '56 '81 C.1044 B.A. L.1068 J.D. Sr. Coun., Bank of Amer.
**Rudofsky, Jane E.** .................... '62 '93 C.112 B.A. L.1068 J.D. [Ⓐ Proskauer R.G.&M.]
*PRACTICE AREAS: Real Estate; Corporate.
Rudolph, Michael H. .................... '60 '86 C.893 B.A. L.276 J.D. 1840 Century Park E. 8th Fl.
Rudy, Abraham M. ...... '61 '91 C.112 B.A. L.800 J.D. 1999 Ave. of the Stars, Suite 1400
**Rudy, Mark M.** .................... '61 '86 C.770 B.A. L.1065 J.D. [Ⓐ Veatch,C.G.&N.]
*LANGUAGES: French.
*PRACTICE AREAS: Medical Malpractice; General Casualty Defense Law.
**Ruf, Kevin F.** .................... '61 '88 C.112 A.B. L.477 J.D. [Ⓒ R.L.Corbin]
*REPORTED CASES: Teitel v. First Los Angeles Bank, 91 Daily Journal D.A.R., 79 79 (1991).
Ruff, Marilyn K. .................... '40 '81 L.1190 J.D. 10866 Wilshire Blvd.
**Ruffalo, Robert S.** .................... '53 '80 C.112 B.A. L.809 J.D. [Hillsinger&C.]
**Rufflo, Suzanne M.** .................... '61 '88 C.770 B.S. L.426 J.D. [Ⓐ Sinnott,D.M.&P.]
*PRACTICE AREAS: General Business Litigation; Insurance Coverage Litigation.
Ruffolo, Anthony J., Jr. '33 '59
C.112 A.B. L.426 LL.B. Dep. Chief Coun., Dept. of Transp.‡
Ruffra, Robin A. .................... '53 '79 C.421 B.A. L.426 J.D. Dep. Co. Coun.
**Rufus-Isaacs, Alexander G.** .................... '57 '88 C.061 B.A. [Ⓐ Arter&H.]
*LANGUAGES: French, German and Portuguese.

**Rugendorf, David Scott** ................... '65 '90 C.966 B.A. L.477 J.D. [▣ R.F.Seone]
*PRACTICE AREAS: Criminal Law (100%, 350); Felonies (12); Appellate Practice (5).
**Ruger, Richard M.** ........................... '55 '80 C.426 B.S. L.659 J.D. [Lim,R.&K.]
*LANGUAGES: Korean.
*PRACTICE AREAS: Corporate; International; Real Estate.
**Ruhl, Mary B.** ..................................... '48 '77 C.954 B.A. L.966 J.D. [Latham&W.]
*LANGUAGES: Swedish.
*PRACTICE AREAS: Finance Transactions.
**Ruhland, Christopher S.** ............... '70 '94 C.112 B.A. L.1068 J.D. [▣ Orrick,H.&S.]
**Ruiz, Christopher P.** ...................... '54 '82 C.800 B.A. L.1068 J.D. [Tharpe&H.]
*PRACTICE AREAS: Construction Defect Litigation; Community/Homeowners Association.
Ruiz, James P., (BV) ..................................... '36 '77 L.426 J.D. 10866 Wilshire Blvd.
Ruiz, Jerry J. '55 '80 C.1169 B.A. L.1066 J.D.
V.P. & Sr. Coun., Wells Fargo Bk., N.A.
Ruiz, Vincent A., (AV) ............. '54 '80 C.112 B.A. L.1066 J.D. [Gutierrez&Assoc.]©
**Rule, Susan E.** ................................. '64 '90 C.103 A.B. L.178 J.D. [Morrison&F.]
*PRACTICE AREAS: Litigation.
**Rummler, William F.** ............................................ '43 '70 C&L.878 J.D. [Booth,M.&S.]
**Runk, Thomas A.** ..... '48 '81 C.422 B.S. L.1137 J.D. [Fulwider P.L.&U.] (See Pat. Sect.)
*PRACTICE AREAS: Patent, Trademark, Copyright and Unfair Competition Law; Litigation.
**Runquist, Lisa A.**, (AV) .............. '52 '77 C.300 B.A. L.494 J.D. [Runquist&Assoc.]
*PRACTICE AREAS: Nonprofit Organization Law; Corporate Law; Business Law; Securities.

**Runquist & Associates, (AV)** ▣
**10821 Huston Street (North Hollywood), 91601-4613**
**Telephone: 818-760-8986 Fax: 818-760-8314**
**Email: RUNQUIST@silicon.net**
**Lisa A. Runquist;—Ingrid P. Mittermaier. Of Counsel: J. Diane Parrish.**
**Nonprofit Organizations, also as it relates to Health Care Law, Corporate Law and Securities.**
***See Professional Biographies, LOS ANGELES, CALIFORNIA***

**Ruosch, Deborah** ..................... '67 '91 C.972 B.A. L.494 J.D. [▣ Milbank,T.H.&M.]
Rusch, Wesley ......................... '56 '82 C.94 B.A. L.426 J.D. 837 Traction Ave.

**Rushfeldt, Shelley & Drake**
**(See Sherman Oaks)**

Rushforth, Marjorie ................. '43 '78 C.112 M.A. L.1137 J.D. 118 Gateway Blvd.‡
Rushiddin, Candace L. '50 '83 C.1077 B.A. L.1068 J.D.
(adm. in PA; not adm. in CA) I.R.S.
Rushton, Ann ................................ '49 '74 C.813 B.A. L.112 J.D. Dep. Atty. Gen.
**Ruskey, John A.**, (AV) ................ '39 '67 C.831 B.S. L.569 LL.B. [Gibson,D.&C.]
*PRACTICE AREAS: Litigation; Trusts and Estates; Family Law.
Ruskin, Alfred B. ................... '22 '59 C.477 B.A. L.1068 LL.B. 2326 Midvale Ave.‡
**Ruskin, Steven M.** ................................ '65 '90 C&L.477 A.B., J.D. [▣ Rogers&W.]
**Ruskus, Geniveve Joan** ................... '71 '96 C.813 B.A. L.1068 J.D. [▣ Trope&T.]
*PRACTICE AREAS: Family Law; Civil Trial.
**Russ, Larry C.**, (AV) ................. '53 '78 C.112 B.A. L.1065 J.D. [Russ,A.&K.]
*PRACTICE AREAS: Unfair Competition Litigation; Trademark; Trade Secret; Antitrust Law; Real Property.

**Russ, August & Kabat, A Professional Corporation, (AV)**
**Suite 1200, 12424 Wilshire Boulevard, 90025**
**Telephone: 310-826-7474 Fax: 310-826-6991**
**Larry C. Russ; Richard Lee August; Jules L. Kabat; Laura K. Stanton; Evan M. Kent; D. John Hendrickson;—Judith L. Meadow; Efrat M. Cogan; France D. Lemoine; Robyn K. Johnson; Barry D. Kaye. Of Counsel: Steven M. Siemens.**
**Intellectual Property Litigation, Trademark, Copyright, Patent, Trade Secret, Product Licensing, Antitrust, Unfair Competition, Business Litigation, Real Estate Litigation and Transactions, Environmental, Entertainment Law.**
***See Professional Biographies, LOS ANGELES, CALIFORNIA***

**Russak, Kenneth N.** ...................... '57 '82 C.31 B.A. L.800 J.D. [Pillsbury M.&S.]
Russell, Barry ..................................... '40 '67 C.112 B.S. L.1068 LL.B. U.S. Bkrptcy. J.
Russell, Dennis ........................ '56 '85 C.280 A.B. L.809 J.D. 12121 Wilshire Blvd.
Russell, Dorothy Miller '54 '79
C.112 B.A. L.1068 J.D. V.P. & Sr. Coun., Wells Fargo Bk., N.A.
**Russell, Jason D.** ..................... '68 '93 C.605 B.A. L.178 J.D. [▣ Skadden,A.S.M.&F.]
*LANGUAGES: Spanish.
*PRACTICE AREAS: General Corporate Law; Securities Litigation.
**Russell, L. Michael** '47 '73 C.813 A.B. L.976 J.D.
Gen. Coun., Chf. Intl. Coun. & Asst. Secy., Teledyne, Inc.
*LANGUAGES: French.
**Russell, P. Rupert** ........................................ '58 '95 C.061 B.A. [▣ Morrison&F.]
**Russell, Theodore A.** ................... '70 '94 C.188 B.A. L.800 J.D. [▣ Gibson,D.&C.]
*PRACTICE AREAS: Labor and Employment; Litigation.
**Russell, Theodore A.**, (AV) '43 '70
C.112 A.B. L.1066 J.D. [Sheppard,M.R.&H.] (©San Francisco)
*PRACTICE AREAS: Business Litigation.
Russell, Thomas Hunter ................... '40 '65 C&L.800 B.S.L., J.D. 6290 Sunset Blvd.
**Russell, Thomas O., III** ............. '50 '83 C.112 A.B. L.426 J.D. [Harrington,F.D.&C.]
*PRACTICE AREAS: Personal Injury Defense Law; Construction Defect Law; Products Liability Law.

**Russell, Hancock & Jeffries**
**(See Pasadena)**

**Russell & Mirkovich**
**(See Long Beach)**

**Russo, Anthony** ......................... '50 '80 C.1077 B.A. L.426 J.D. [Morgan,L.&B.]
**Russo, John J.** ............................. '52 '79 C.800 B.A. L.426 J.D. [Gilbert,K.C.&J.]
*PRACTICE AREAS: Insurance Defense; Estate Planning.
Russo, Robert John ........................................ '47 '81 L.1221 9000 W. Sunset Blvd.
Russo, Ron ....................................... '42 '68 C&L.426 B.S., J.D. Sr. Asst. Atty. Gen.
**Russo, Victor A.** ............................ '59 '84 C.112 B.A. L.36 J.D. [▣ R.E.Pfiester,Jr.]
*PRACTICE AREAS: Civil Litigation; FELA.
Russum, John C., Jr. ..................... '52 '79 C.610 B.G.S. L.851 J.D. 5870 W. 75th St.
**Rust, Neil W.** ........................................ '57 '87 C.054 B.Sc. L.659 J.D. [White&C.]
**Rustand, Kay** ............................. '48 '78 C.112 B.A. L.1068 J.D. [Arter&H.]
*PRACTICE AREAS: Securities; Corporate and Commercial Law; Real Estate.
**Rustum, William M.** ................. '65 '94 C.692 B.S. L.569 J.D. [▣ Gibson,D.&C.]
*PRACTICE AREAS: Corporate.

**Rutan & Tucker, LLP**
**(See Costa Mesa)**

**Ruth, David C.** ............................ '56 '84 C.154 B.A. L.309 J.D. [De Castro,W.&C.]
*PRACTICE AREAS: Taxation Law; Real Estate Law; Business Law.
Ruth, Steven ............................. '61 '90 C.659 B.A. L.1068 J.D. 221 N. Figueroa St.
**Ruthberg, Miles N.** ........................ '52 '79 C.976 B.A. L.309 J.D. [Latham&W.]
*PRACTICE AREAS: Professional Liability and Securities Litigation; Class Actions; Complex Litigation.
**Rutledge, Arthur D.**, (AV) ............ '41 '69 C.112 B.S. L.61 J.D. [▣ Chapin,F.&W.]
*PRACTICE AREAS: Insurance Defense Law; General Tort Litigation.
Ruttenberg, Bernard, (AV) .......... '28 '72 C.800 Phar. D. L.1136 J.D. 3225 Woodbine St.
**Ruttenberg, Brenda H.** .......... '47 '72 C.112 B.A. L.426 J.D. Sr. Coun., Bank of Amer.

**Ruttenberg, Edward A.**, (AV) ........... '50 '75 C.976 B.A. L.309 J.D. [Leopold,P.&S.]
*PRACTICE AREAS: Entertainment; Civil Litigation; Copyright and Trademark; Libel and Slander; Unfair Competition.
Ruttenberg, Gary M., (AV) ........................... '45 '71 C.112 B.S. L.426 J.D. [Bloom&R.]
**Ruttenberg, Kenneth G.** ................ '67 '93 C.112 B.A. L.426 J.D. [▣ Weisman&R.]
*PRACTICE AREAS: Civil Litigation; Business Litigation.
**Rutter, Marshall A.**, (AV) ................... '31 '60 C.31 B.A. L.659 J.D. [Rutter,G.&H.]
*PRACTICE AREAS: Business Litigation; Family Law; Environmental Law.

**Rutter, Greene & Hobbs, Incorporated, (AV)**
**1900 Avenue of the Stars, Suite 2700, 90067**
**Telephone: 310-286-1700 Telecopier: 310-286-1728**
**Christine H. Belgrad; Brian L. Davidoff; Geoffrey M. Gold; Olivia Goodkin; Curtis A. Graham; Warren G. Greene; Franklin D. Hobbs, III; Sharon I. Juhn; Brandon L. Kirk; Terence S. Nunan (Certified Specialist, Probate, Estate Planning and Trust Law, The State Bar of California Board of Legal Specialization); Marshall A. Rutter; Joel Weinstein.**
**General Civil and Trial Practice. Corporation, Securities, Partnership, Financial Institutions, Bankruptcy, Family, Taxation (International, Domestic, Litigation), Environmental, Probate, Estate Planning and Real Property Law.**
***See Professional Biographies, LOS ANGELES, CALIFORNIA***

Ryals, James W. ...................... '60 '88 C.178 B.A. L.426 J.D. 2121 Ave. of the Stars
**Ryan, Christine D.** ................ '65 '92 C.112 B.A. L.800 J.D. [▣ Nossaman,G.K.&E.]
*LANGUAGES: French and German.
*PRACTICE AREAS: Litigation.
Ryan, Colleen ........................... '65 '90 C.352 B.A. L.800 J.D. 350 S. Grand Ave.
Ryan, E. Christopher .......... '51 '83 C.813 A.B. L.1068 J.D. Dir., Bus. Affs., CBS, Inc.
Ryan, Gregory R., (AV) ................. '56 '81 C.112 A.B. L.426 J.D. 600 Wilshire Blvd.
**Ryan, James B.** ............................ '68 '93 C.112 B.A. L.1068 J.D. [▣ McDermott,W.&E.]
**Ryan, James P.** ...... '63 '89 C.602 B.A. L.1066 J.D. Assoc. Coun., Capital Grp. Cos., Inc.
Ryan, John L. ......................................... '38 '72 C.1097 L.426 J.D. Ct. of App.
**Ryan, Kerry T.** ............................................ '59 '87 C.347 B.S. L.260 J.D. [Clark&T.]
*PRACTICE AREAS: General Business Litigation; Commercial Litigation; Unfair Competition Litigation; Trade Secrets Litigation.
**Ryan, Michael D.**, (AV) ................. '44 '72 C.911 B.A. L.309 J.D. [Gibson,D.&C.]
*LANGUAGES: German.
*PRACTICE AREAS: Labor and Employment Law.
**Ryan, Michael J.** ...................... '63 '92 C.112 B.A. L.809 J.D. [▣ Murchison&C.]
*PRACTICE AREAS: General Liability.
**Ryan, Paul M., Jr.** ..................... '49 '86 C.893 B.A. L.1136 J.D. [▣ Kegel,T.&T.]
**Ryan, Thomas A.** .................. '64 '89 C.674 A.B. L.1066 J.D. [McDermott,W.&E.]
*PRACTICE AREAS: Litigation.
**Ryan, Timothy F.** ........................ '46 '72 C.112 B.A. L.426 J.D. [Morrison&F.]
*PRACTICE AREAS: Labor and Employment.
Ryan, William C. ......................................... '51 '86 C.1044 B.S. L.809 J.D. Mun. Ct. J.
**Rybicki, Richard C.** .................. '67 '92 C.112 B.A. L.188 J.D. [▣ Thelen,M.J.&B.]
*PRACTICE AREAS: Labor and Employment Law; Appellate Law.
Ryburn, Jack T. ........................................ '23 '50 C&L.800 A.B., J.D. Supr. Ct. J.
Ryeom, Raymond H. ........................ '69 '94 C.659 B.A. L.273 J.D. 1 Wilshire Blvd.
**Rykoff, Stephen R.**, (AV) .................. '36 '61 C&L.813 B.A., J.D. [S.R.Rykoff]
*REPORTED CASES: Pierce v. Lyman (1991) 3 Cal. Rptr. 2d 236.
*PRACTICE AREAS: Attorney Malpractice; Probate Litigation.

**Rykoff, Stephen R., Professional Law Corporation, (AV)**
**Suite 1400 11755 Wilshire Boulevard, 90025**
**Telephone: 310-477-5455 Fax: 310-477-1966**
**Stephen R. Rykoff.**
**General Civil Trial and Appellate Practice, Attorney Malpractice Defense and Probate Litigation.**
***See Professional Biographies, LOS ANGELES, CALIFORNIA***

**Saadeh, Nicole T.** ........................ '63 '89 C.112 B.A. L.426 J.D. [▣ Parker S.]
*LANGUAGES: Spanish.

**Saakvitne, Nicholas L., A Law Corporation**
**(See Santa Monica)**

**Sabaitis, Frank T.** ...................... '54 '80 C.93 A.B. L.209 J.D. [Ropers,M.K.&B.]
*PRACTICE AREAS: Construction Litigation; Products and General Civil Litigation; Bad Faith Litigation.
**Sabarsky, Martin A.** ............................ '70 '95 C.103 A.B. L.309 J.D. [▣ Latham&W.]
*LANGUAGES: Spanish.
*PRACTICE AREAS: Tax; Corporate.
Sabatini, Catherine A. ..................... '49 '80 C.555 B.A. L.1068 J.D. 300 Esplanade Dr.
**Sabban, Nina Madden**, (AV) .......... '44 '78 C.112 A.B. L.426 J.D. [Hoffman,S.&W.]
*PRACTICE AREAS: Estate Planning Law; Probate Law; Trust Law.
**Sabin, Edward N.** .............. '66 '91 C.112 B.A. L.1068 J.D. [▣ Greenberg G.F.C.&M.]
*PRACTICE AREAS: Litigation.
**Sable, Joshua M.** .................................. '68 '93 C.860 B.A. L.1068 J.D. [Wilson,K.&B.]
Sabo, Gerard E. ..................... '50 '77 C.1077 B.A. L.426 J.D. 2401 Colorado Blvd.
**Sabo, Gregory** ............................. '67 '93 C.112 B.A. L.426 J.D. [▣ Chapman&G.]
*PRACTICE AREAS: Professional Liability; General Negligence; Construction Litigation.
**Sabo, Helen A.** ........................................ '62 '88 C.112 B.A. L.813 J.D. [▣ Arter&H.]

**Sabo & Green, A Professional Corporation**
**(See Calabasas)**

**Sachs, Adam** .......................... '59 '86 C.1036 B.A. L.1066 J.D. [Folger L.&K.]©
**Sachs, Joel**, (AV) .......................................... '41 '66 C&L.260 B.A., J.D. [Silver&F.]
*PRACTICE AREAS: Estate Planning Law; Trust Law; Probate Law; Tax Law.
**Sackl, Darrell L.** .............................. '48 '73 C.747 B.A. L.813 J.D. [Morrison&F.]
*PRACTICE AREAS: Real Estate; Commercial Finance; Secured Transactions.
Sackman, J. David ........................ '56 '82 C.1169 B.A. L.1066 J.D. [Reich,A.C.&C.]
Sackman, Julie I. '51 '76
C.112 A.B. L.800 J.D. Asst. Gen. Atty., The Flying Tiger Line, Inc.
Sackman, Kenneth J. ......................... '51 '76 C.1036 B.A. L.800 J.D. [Gilbert&S.]
**Sacks, Janet** ............................... '63 '89 C.800 B.A. L.426 J.D. [▣ Daniels,B.&F.]
Sacks, Melvyn Douglas, (BV) ......... '38 '65 C.112 A.B. L.1068 LL.B. 1901 Ave. of Stars
**Sacks, Robert A.** ................................... '57 '83 C.309 A.B. L.847 J.D. [Sullivan&C.]
**Sacks, Robert N.** ............................ '60 '86 C.966 B.A. L.1068 J.D. [Ross,S.&G.]
*LANGUAGES: Spanish.
*PRACTICE AREAS: Estate, Trust and Conservatorship Litigation; Business Litigation; Appellate Practice.
Sacks, Stefan Eric .................. '68 '94 C.112 B.A. L.94 J.D. 1901 Ave. of the Stars

**Sacks, Rivera & Zolonz**
**(See Culver City)**

**Sacks Zweig & Burris, LLP**
**(See Santa Monica)**

Sadd, Steven S. ........................ '46 '73 C.1097 B.A. L.426 J.D. 1901 Ave. of the Stars
Sadeghi, Reza ................................... '61 '91 C.608 B.S. L.285 J.D. [▣ Vakili&L.]
Sadighpour, Kourosh ............. '62 '89 C.1188 B.A. L.398 J.D. 1801 Century Park, E.
Sadler, Richard B., III ................................... '40 '66 C&L.420 B.S., J.D. F.B.I.
**Sadler, Thomas C.** ............................ '54 '82 C.813 A.B. L.1068 J.D. [Latham&W.]
**Sadler, Walter R.** ...................... '56 '83 C.112 B.A. L.1067 J.D. [Leopold,P.&S.]
*PRACTICE AREAS: Entertainment; Civil Litigation; Copyright and Trademark; Libel and Slander; Unfair Competition.
**Sadlon, Holly J.** .......................... '69 '94 C.705 B.A. L.1068 J.D. [▣ White O.C.&A.]
*PRACTICE AREAS: Civil Litigation.

**Sadowsky, Stephen B.**, (AV) .......... '48 '79 C.978 B.A. L.1066 J.D. [Talcott,L.V.&S.]
*REPORTED CASES: United States v. City of Rancho Palos Verdes, 841 F.2d 329 (9th Cir. 1988); U.S. v. Helmandollar, 852 F.2d 498 (9th Cir. 1988); Chizen v. Hunter, 809 F.2d 560 (9th Cir. 1986); United States v. Duz-Mor Diagnostic Laboratory, Inc., 650 F.2d 223 (9th Cir. 1981).
*PRACTICE AREAS: Criminal Defense Law; Civil Litigation; Appellate Law.
**Sadwick, David B.** .................... '61 '86 C.112 B.A. L.813 J.D. [Preston G.&E.]
*PRACTICE AREAS: Environmental Law; Pharmaceutical; Technology.
**Saferstein, Harvey I.**, (AV) .......... '43 '69 C.112 B.A. L.309 LL.B. [Chadbourne&P.]
**Saffer, Sherry M.** .................... '58 '83 C.112 B.A. L.809 J.D. [Steiner&S.]
*REPORTED CASES: Gribin v. Hammer Galleries, a Division of Hammer Holdings, 793 F.Supp. 233 (C.D. Cal. 1992).
Saffir, Cynthia R. '54 '80 C.112 B.A. L.426 J.D.
Dir., Legal Servs., Writers Guild of America, West, Inc.
Safford, Robert C. .................... '47 '75 12400 Wilshire Blvd.
Safran, Bruce R. .................... '45 '73 L.1049 J.D. 5195 Lindley Ave.
**Sagan, Paul P.** .................... '62 '91 C.103 B.A. L.112 J.D. [Murphy,W.&B.]
Sagar, Alka Khosla .................... '59 '84 C.112 B.A. L.1068 J.D. Off. of U.S. Atty.
**Sager, Kelli L.** .................... '60 '85 C.1223 B.A. L.878 J.D. [Davis W.T.]
*PRACTICE AREAS: Media Law; Constitutional Law; Civil Appeal; Copyright/Trademark.
**Sagerman, Eric E.** .................... '66 '91 C.112 B.A. L.1068 J.D. [Murphy,W.&B.]
**Saggese, Nicholas P.** .................... '47 '80 C.112 B.A. L.426 J.D. [Skadden,A.S.M.&F.]

**Sagheb, S. Shane '58 '83 C.112 B.A. L.426 J.D.**
**15760 Ventura Boulevard, 91436**
**Telephone: 818-981-3136**
**Business Law including Trial and Appellate practice in all State and Federal Courts. Labor and Employment, Litigation of Business Disputes, Arbitration.**

**Sahn, Victor A.**, (AV) .................... '54 '80 C.823 B.A. L.1049 J.D. [Sulmeyer,K.B.&R.]
*PRACTICE AREAS: Bankruptcy; Business Litigation.
**Saifer, Michelle Oyler** .................... '68 '94 C.112 B.A. L.1194 J.D. [Loeb&L.]
*PRACTICE AREAS: Environmental Law.
**Saiki, Eric H.** .................... '65 '91 C.112 B.A. L.1065 J.D. [Radcliff,F.&D.]
St. Clair, H. Spencer, (AV) .................... '13 '36 C&L.800 B.S.B.A., LL.B. 888 S. Figuerda St.

**St. Clair, Grace Greer**
**(See Hermosa Beach)**

**St. Denis, Michael J.** .................... '58 '90 C.112 B.A. L.426 J.D. [Sheppard,M.R.&H.]
**St. Denis, Susan M.** .................... '59 '90 C.911 B.A. L.426 J.D. [Pillsbury M.&S.]
St. John, John R., (AV) .................... '47 '72 C.605 A.B. L.1066 J.D. 333 S. Grand
**St. John, Ronald R.**, (AV) .................... '56 '81 C&L.800 A.B., J.D. [Barton,K.&O.]
*PRACTICE AREAS: Real Estate; Environmental Law; Taxation; Estate Planning; Probate.
**St. Marie, Ronald M.** .................... '56 '81 C.1077 B.A. L.800 J.D. [Chan]
*REPORTED CASES: Clamp Mfg. Co., Inc. v. Enco Mfg. Co., 5 U.S.P.Q. 2d 1643 (C.D. Cal. 1987) aff'd 870 F.2d 512 (9th Cir. 1989); Indiana Plumbing Supply v. Standard of Lynn, Inc., 880 F.Supp. 743 (C.D. Cal. 1995); San Francisco Mercantile Co., Inc. v. Beebas Creations, Inc., 704 F.Supp. 1005 (C.D. Cal.1988); Dorman v. DWLC Corp., 35 Cal.App.4th 1808 (2d Dist. 1995).
*PRACTICE AREAS: Business Litigation emphasizing Intellectual Property; Unfair Competition; Trade Secrets.
St. Pierre, Kraig Stephen .................... '66 '91 C.184 B.A. L.477 J.D. Dep. Dist. Atty.
**St. Pierre-Kumar, Jeanine M.** .................... '64 '90 C&L.990 B.A., J.D. [Knopfler&R.]
*PRACTICE AREAS: Construction Litigation; Wrongful Termination Litigation.
**Sakai, Susan** .................... '60 '86 C.770 B.S.C. L.1068 J.D. [Irell&M.]
Sakamoto, Chiyoko, (Miss) .................... '12 '38 L.29 LL.B. 4940 1/2 McConnell Ave.
Sakamoto, Larry K. .................... '57 '83 C.800 B.S. L.809 J.D. 1055 Wilshire Blvd.
**Sakamoto, Sandra L.** '53 '83
C.878 B.A. L.426 J.D. Sr. Coun., Pacific Telesis Legal Group
Sakir, Kelly A. .................... '61 '93 C.37 B.A. L.426 J.D. Dep. Dist. Atty.
Sakiyama, Ann .................... '48 '77 C.112 B.A. L.800 J.D. [Tan&S.]
**Salamone, Mary A.** .................... '62 '87 C.696 B.A. L.188 J.D. [Gibbs,G.L.&A.]
*PRACTICE AREAS: Commercial Law; Business Litigation; Construction Law.
**Salamunovich, Joseph M.** .................... '59 '86 C&L.426 B.A., J.D. [Gibson,D.&C.]
*PRACTICE AREAS: Securities; Mergers, Acquisitions and Divestitures; Corporate Law; Contracts; Business Law.
**Salandra, Anthony R.** .................... '55 '80 C.529 A.B. L.990 J.D. [Kaye,S.F.H.&H.]
*PRACTICE AREAS: Real Estate.
**Salas, Carlos P.** .................... '71 '96 C.569 B.A. L.145 J.D. [O'Melveny&M.]
*LANGUAGES: Spanish.
**Salazar, Timothy L.**, (BV) '57 '84 C.1077 B.A. L.1068 J.D.
(adm. in NM; not adm. in CA) [Robinson,D.&W.] (Albuquerque, NM)
*PRACTICE AREAS: Labor Law; Employment Law.
**Salcido, Richard** .................... '50 '77 C.426 B.A. L.284 J.D. [Crosby,H.R.&M.]
*PRACTICE AREAS: Civil Litigation; Products Liability; Pharmaceutical Litigation; Insurance.
**Saldaña, Manuel** .................... '63 '88 C.813 A.B. L.1065 J.D. [Bronson,B.&M.]
*LANGUAGES: Spanish.
*PRACTICE AREAS: Civil Litigation; Product Liability.
Saldin, Thomas N. .................... '49 '74 C.763 B.A. L.1049 J.D. [Nishiyama,M.L.E.&S.]
**Salem, Ciema Lili** .................... '— '92 C.112 B.A. L.809 J.D. [Manatt,P.&P.]
*PRACTICE AREAS: Intellectual Property.
Salem, Leslie A. .................... '61 '91 C.951 B.A. L.1049 J.D. 777 S. Figueroa St., 10th Fl.
**Salem, Linda Margolies** .................... '59 '84 C.668 B.A. L.1065 J.D. [Crosby,H.R.&M.]
*PRACTICE AREAS: Business Litigation; Insurance; Intellectual Property.
Saler, Alan G. .................... '59 '84 C.867 B.A. L.178 J.D. [Jones H.C.&B.]
Salerno, Paul R., Jr. .................... '49 '74 C.976 B.A. L.1068 J.D. [Salerno&D.]
Salerno, Victor M. .................... '52 '77 C.112 B.A. L.1049 J.D. 880 W. 1st St.
Salerno & Dassoff .................... 700 S. Flower St.
**Sales, Michael W.** .................... '50 '77 C.602 B.S.E.E. L.472 J.D. Hughes Aircraft Co. (Pat.)
Sales, Sassoon, (AV) .................... '44 '74 C.061 B.A. L.054 LL.B. [S.Sales]
Sales, Sassoon, A Professional Corporation, (AV) .................... 1801 Century Park E.
Saliman, Brian L. .................... '70 '95 C.188 B.A. L.309 J.D. 555 W. 5th St.
**Salin, Janis B.** .................... '53 '79 C.112 B.A. L.1068 J.D. [Riordan&M.]
**Salinas, Arturo T.** .................... '61 '88 C&L.426 B.A., J.D. [Wilson,K.&B.]
*LANGUAGES: Spanish.
**Salinas, Raúl F.** .................... '60 '86 C.426 B.B.A. L.276 J.D. [Alvarado,S.V.&S.]
*LANGUAGES: Spanish.
*PRACTICE AREAS: Commercial Law; Business Litigation.
Salinsky, Robert A. .................... '50 '79 C.912 B.S. L.1095 J.D. 5840 York Blvd.
Sallas, Linda Ann .................... '54 '82 C.966 B.A. L.800 J.D. 110 S. Citrus Ave.
**Salley, Robert B.** .................... '59 '88 C.112 B.A. L.1148 J.D. [Tharpe&H.]
**Sallus, Marc L.**, (AV) .................... '54 '79 C.154 B.A. L.1065 J.D. [Weinstock,M.R.S.&N.]
*PRACTICE AREAS: Civil Litigation; Probate; Trust Litigation.
Sally, Ronald O. .................... '63 '89 C.228 B.A. L.1068 J.D. 700 S. Flower St.
Salmas, George C. .................... '49 '74 C.1042 B.A. L.1068 J.D. 1901 Ave. of the Stars
Salmas, Kathleen M. .................... '53 '83 C.446 B.S.N. L.1137 J.D. Staff Coun., Northrop Corp.
**Salmen, Cynthia L.** .................... '56 '89 C&L.494 B.A., J.D. [Gibson,D.&C.]
*PRACTICE AREAS: Antitrust and Trade Regulation; Insurance.
**Salomon, J. Eugene, Jr. (A Professional Corporation)** '62 '87
C.659 B.S. L.800 J.D. [Mitchell,S.&K.]
*LANGUAGES: Spanish.
*PRACTICE AREAS: Music Law; Entertainment Law.
Salseda, Gerald C. .................... '60 '85 C.426 B.A. L.112 J.D. Dep. Fed. Pub. Def.
Salter, C. Robert .................... '22 '54 C.684 B.A. L.800 J.D. 720 W. 8th St.
Salter, Eric B. '54 '81 C.112 B.A. L.809 J.D.
V.P. & Reg. Underwriting Coun., Commonwealth Land Title Insurance Company
Salter, Janice A. .................... '41 '79 C.477 B.A. L.284 J.D. 9200 Sunset Ave.
Salter, John L. '47 '74 C.477 B.B.A. L.912 J.D.
(adm. in MI; not adm. in CA) Pres., Independent Med. Evaluators, Inc.
Salter, Leon M. .................... '33 '59 C.112 B.A. L.1068 LL.B. Dep. Pub. Def.
Salter, Randall G. .................... '65 '91 C.605 B.A. L.809 J.D. 4700 Wilshire Blvd.
Saltz, Beverly I. .................... '34 '77 C.112 B.S. L.1095 J.D. State Dept. of Transp.‡
**Saltzburg, Damon G.** .................... '67 '92 C.112 B.A. L.94 J.D. [Saltzburg,R.&B.]
*PRACTICE AREAS: Bankruptcy; Debtor and Creditor Law; Litigation.
**Saltzburg, Henley L.**, (AV) .................... '37 '63 C.112 B.A. L.1068 J.D. [Saltzburg,R.&B.]
*PRACTICE AREAS: Litigation; Commercial Transactions; Bankruptcy Law; Real Estate Law.

**Saltzburg, Ray & Bergman, LLP, (AV)**
**A Partnership including Professional Corporations**
**Tenth Floor, 10960 Wilshire Boulevard, 90024**
**Telephone: 213-879-8733; 310-473-8405 Fax: 310-473-3689; 310-444-9205**
**Members of Firm: David L. Ray; Henley L. Saltzburg; Alan M. Bergman; Genise R. Reiter (A Professional Corporation); Peter A. Davidson; Eric F. Edmunds, Jr.; Sandra L. Stevens; Paul T. Dye; Byron Z. Moldo. Associates: Norman A. Fagin; Jenny Van Le; Sara T. Harris; Deirdre Hughes Hill; Steven N. Ruby; David A. Greene; Karrin Feemster; Nancy R. Binder; Damon G. Saltzburg; Gordon P. Stone, III. Of Counsel: Arthur M. Katz; Marc E. Petas.**
**Commercial Litigation, Bankruptcy, Federal and State Court Receiverships, Real Estate, Financial Institutions, Commercial Transactions and Financing, Mortgage Banking, Entertainment Industry, Insurance Defense, Probate and Estate Planning.**
***See Professional Biographies, LOS ANGELES, CALIFORNIA***

**Saltzman, Deborah J.** .................... '70 '96 C.31 B.A. L.893 J.D. [O'Melveny&M.]
Saltzman, Robert M. '54 '79 C.197 A.B. L.309 J.D.
Assoc. Dean & Adjunct Assoc. Prof., U.S.C. Law Ctr.
**Saltzman, Stephen L.** .................... '60 '86 C.276 B.S. L.178 J.D. [Loeb&L.]
*LANGUAGES: German and Spanish.
**Salute, Gregory J.** .................... '66 '93 C.112 B.A. L.809 J.D. [Dwyer,D.B.&B.]
*PRACTICE AREAS: Insurance Defense.
**Salvato, Gregory M.** .................... '54 '86 C.154 B.A. L.426 J.D. [Parker,M.C.O.&S.]
*PRACTICE AREAS: Bankruptcy/Reorganization; Creditors' Rights; Real Estate Litigation.
**Salvaty, Benjamin B.** .................... '40 '66 C.602 B.B.A. L.800 J.D. [Hill,F.&B.]
*REPORTED CASES: Centerview/Glen Avalon Homeowners Association v. Volpe (C.D. Cal., 1976) 424 F. Supp. 626; Atchison, Topeka and Santa Fe Ry. Co. v. Stockton Port District (1983) 140 CA 3d 111, 189 Cal.Rptr. 208; People v. Home Trust Investment Co. (1970) 8 CA3d 1022, 87 Cal.Rptr. 722; Litigation: Represented one of the California Highway Patrol officers in the Rodney King case.
*TRANSACTIONS: Represented Santa Fe Railway Company in the sale of its First Street Yard to the Metro Rail for its maintenance yard, involving a total consideration of $43,000,000.00.
*PRACTICE AREAS: Eminent Domain; Inverse Condemnation; Land Use; Environmental; Defense of Police Officers in Civil Rights Cases.
**Salvaty, Paul** .................... '67 '94 C.602 B.A. L.1065 J.D. [O'Melveny&M.]

**Salvo, Alice A., (AV) '55 '82 C.1044 B.A. L.809 J.D.**
**18801 Ventura Boulevard, Suite 312 (Tarzana), 91356-3372**
**Telephone: 818-705-1100 Fax: 818-705-0943**
**(Certified Specialist, Estate Planning, Trust and Probate Law, The State Bar of California Board of Legal Specialization).**
***PRACTICE AREAS: Elder Law; Conservatorship; Probate; Estate Planning; Conservatorship Probate.**
**Probate, Estate Planning and Trust Law. Elder Law, Conservatorship, Probate, Trust Litigation.**
***See Professional Biographies, LOS ANGELES, CALIFORNIA***

**Salz, Mark S.** .................... '69 '95 C.1049 B.A. L.990 J.D. [Bonne,B.M.O.&N.]
*PRACTICE AREAS: Medical Malpractice.

**Salzman, Ira M.**
**(See Pasadena)**

Samarghachian, Haroutioun H. .................... '63 '92 C.112 B.A. L.398 J.D. 11835 W. Olympic Blvd.
**Sambol, Lori E.** .................... '65 '90 C.112 B.A. L.1068 J.D. [Proskauer R.G.&M.]
**Samek, Carol K.** .................... '58 '83 C.112 B.A. L.1066 J.D. [Christa&J.] (Pat.)
*LANGUAGES: Slovak and Czech.
*PRACTICE AREAS: Business Litigation.
**Samel, Charles H.** .................... '61 '85 C.446 B.A. L.276 J.D. [Howrey&S.]
*PRACTICE AREAS: Complex Litigation; Construction Litigation; Environmental Law; Insurance Coverage.
Samelson, Lawrence D. .................... '45 '74 C.1077 B.A. L.809 J.D. 3255 Wilshire Blvd. 12th Fl.
**Samet, Jack I.**, (AV) .................... '40 '65 C.178 B.A. L.309 J.D. [Baker&H.]
*REPORTED CASES: Holmes vs. S.I.P.C., U.S. Supreme Court, 1991; S.E.C. vs. Korocorp, 9th Circuit, 1978; Hanly vs. S.E.C., 2nd Circuit, 1969; Rollins Burdick Hunter vs. Alexander & Alexander, Cal. Ct. of Appeal, 1988; In Re ZZZZ Best Litigation, Cal. Dist. Court, 1995.
*PRACTICE AREAS: Securities Litigation; Corporate Control Disputes; Legal Malpractice; Business; Unfair Competition.
Samoian, Robert P., (AV) .................... '40 '65 C&L.800 A.B., LL.B. Dep. Dist. Atty.
Samovar, Kerry R. .................... '68 '93 C.112 B.A. L.1066 J.D. 633 W. 5th St.
**Sampson, David C.** .................... '52 '85 C.763 B.S.B.A. L.1068 J.D. [Baker&H.]
*LANGUAGES: German and Czech.
*PRACTICE AREAS: Land Use; Real Estate.
**Sampson, Linda A.** .................... '68 '93 C.426 B.A. L.990 J.D. [Jeffer,M.B.&M.]
*PRACTICE AREAS: Land Use Entitlement Law; Business Litigation; Real Estate Litigation; Construction Defect Litigation.

**Sampson, William A., II & Associates**
**(See Pacific Palisades)**

**Samsel, Christine A.** .................... '64 '90 C.788 B.A. L.893 J.D. [Troop M.S.&P.]
*PRACTICE AREAS: Employment; General Litigation; Appellate.
**Samson, Gary D.**, (AV) .................... '48 '74 C.800 A.B. L.1065 J.D. [Orrick,H.&S.]
*PRACTICE AREAS: Secured Transactions; Banking; Commercial Law; Bankruptcy.
Samson, Louis S. .................... '48 '76 C.800 B.A. L.809 J.D. 1990 Westwood Blvd., 3rd Fl.
Samson, Marc. L. .................... '53 '80 C.1042 B.S. L.1136 J.D. 500 Citadel Dr.
**Samuelian, Karl M.**, (AV) .................... '32 '57 C.112 B.A. L.1068 LL.B. [Parker,M.C.O.&S.]
*TRANSACTIONS: Counsel For Belridge Oil Company in $3.65 Billion dollar merger with Shell Oil Company.
*PRACTICE AREAS: Corporate and General Business; General Taxation; Real Estate; Political Campaign Contribution Law.
**Samuels, Adam D.** .................... '71 '95 C.112 B.A. L.273 J.D. [Quinn E.U.&O.]
**Samuels, David M.** .................... '63 '91 C.112 B.A. L.990 J.D. [Fonda,G.H.&D.]
**Samuels, Donald L.** .................... '61 '86 C.103 B.A. L.178 J.D. [Samuels&S.]
*PRACTICE AREAS: Employment Law; Civil Litigation; Intellectual Property Law.
**Samuels, Jack D.**, (AV) .................... '35 '60 C.103 A.B. L.178 LL.B. [Samuels&S.]
*PRACTICE AREAS: Business Law; Corporation Law; Business Litigation; Entertainment Law.
Samuels, Jeffrey P. .................... '45 '70 C.930 B.A. L.339 J.D. 6535 Wilshire Blvd.
**Samuels, Joel G.**, (AV) .................... '59 '84 C.674 A.B. L.813 J.D. [Sidley&A.]
*PRACTICE AREAS: Bankruptcy Law; Corporate Reorganizations Law; Insolvency Law; Debtor-Creditor Relations Law.
**Samuels, Karen E.** .................... '64 '92 C.893 B.A. L.309 J.D. [Small L.&K.]
*LANGUAGES: French.
*PRACTICE AREAS: Trademark; Copyright; Litigation.
**Samuels, Mark A.** .................... '57 '82 C.112 A.B. L.1068 J.D. [O'Melveny&M.]
*PRACTICE AREAS: Litigation; Intellectual Property.
Samuels, Michael W. .................... '41 '64 L.1065 J.D. 2500 Silver Lake Terr.
**Samuels, Pamela D.** .................... '58 '90 C.800 B.A. L.1066 J.D. [O'Melveny&M.]

CAA331P

CALIFORNIA—LOS ANGELES MARTINDALE-HUBBELL LAW DIRECTORY 1997

**Samuels, S. Zachary, (P.C.), (AV)** ..........'45 '69 C.112 B.S. L.800 J.D. [Dolman&S.]
*PRACTICE AREAS: Tax Law; Probate Law; Trust Law; Estate Planning; Real Estate.
**Samuels, Sherwin L., (AV)** ...............'35 '60 C.309 A.B. L.1066 LL.B. [Sidley&A.]
*PRACTICE AREAS: Corporate Law; Mergers and Acquisitions; Corporate Securities Law; Real Estate Law.

**Samuels & Samuels, (AV)**
**2029 Century Park East, Suite 2718, 90067**
**Telephone: 310-201-0101 Facsimile: 310-201-0166**
**Members of Firm: Jack D. Samuels; Donald L. Samuels.**
**General Business, Labor and Employment, Corporate and Entertainment Law, Business, Employment and Entertainment Litigation.**
***See Professional Biographies, LOS ANGELES, CALIFORNIA***

**Samuelson, C. Ransom, II, (AV)** ........'46 '71 C.197 A.B. L.800 J.D. [Gibson,D.&C.]
*PRACTICE AREAS: Real Estate Law.
**Samuelson, Joan I.** ..........................'50 '77 C.112 B.A. L.1066 J.D. [Pick&B.]
Sanabria, Eufemio ........................'45 '75 C&L.1127 B.S., J.D. 3008 Wilshire Blvd.
**Sanchez, Alfred, Jr.** ...................'66 '95 C.1109 B.A. L.800 J.D. [Ⓐ Paul,H.J.&W.]
**Sanchez, Arturo D.** .....................'65 '94 C.112 B.A. L.1137 J.D. [Ⓐ Alexander&Y.]
*LANGUAGES: Spanish.
*PRACTICE AREAS: Civil Litigation; Business and Real Estate Litigation; Insurance Fraud.
**Sanchez, Daniel F.** ....................'52 '77 C.112 B.A. L.1119 J.D. [Ⓐ Neumeyer&B.]
*PRACTICE AREAS: Appellate Practice; Insurance Coverage; Insurance Bad Faith.
**Sanchez, David, (AV)** .....................'62 '87 C&L.813 B.A., J.D. [Sanchez&A.]
*PRACTICE AREAS: Corporate Finance; Securities Law; Partnerships; Limited Liability Companies.
Sanchez, Eduardo G. ..................'64 '89 C.1131 B.S. L.1049 J.D. 500 Citadel
**Sanchez, Henry L.** ......................'67 '95 C.560 B.A. L.602 J.D. [Ⓐ Mendes&M.]
*LANGUAGES: Spanish.
**Sanchez, Jose F.** ......................'67 '92 C.309 B.A. L.813 J.D. [Ⓐ Munger,T.&O.]
*LANGUAGES: Spanish.
Sanchez, Lou ..................................................'28 '61 125 W. 4th St.
**Sanchez, Terry E.** ......................'56 '81 C.154 B.A. L.813 J.D. [Munger,T.&O.]

**Sanchez & Amador, LLP, (AV)**
**601 South Figueroa Street, Suite 2300, 90017**
**Telephone: 213-891-1822 Facsimile: 213-891-1808**
**Richard S. Amador; David Sanchez. Of Counsel: Delynn Y. Arneson; Elizabeth Brandon-Brown.**
**Corporate, Securities and General Business Transactions, Employment, Trademark and General Business Litigation.**
***See Professional Biographies, LOS ANGELES, CALIFORNIA***

**Sandau, Roger A.** ......................'66 '92 C.112 B.A. L.1065 J.D. [Ⓐ Mitchell,S.&K.]
*PRACTICE AREAS: Music Law; Entertainment Law; Music Publishing.
**Sandelmann, Frank** ..........................'64 '96 C.112 B.A. L.94 J.D. [Ⓐ Gorry&M.]
*LANGUAGES: German.
*PRACTICE AREAS: Commercial Litigation.
**Sanders, Barry A., (AV)** ..................'45 '71 C.659 A.B. L.976 LL.B. [Latham&W.]
**Sanders, Edward, (AV)** ..........'22 '50 C.112 A.B. L.800 LL.B. [Sanders,B.G.S.&M.]
Sanders, Eric L. ........'60 '87 C.112 B.A. L.1068 J.D. Coun., Wells Fargo Bk., N.A.
Sanders, J. Stanley, (AV) ................'42 '69 C.940 B.A. L.976 LL.B. [Barnes,M.&P.]
**Sanders, James L.** ....................'48 '74 C.221 B.S. L.862 J.D. [Sheppard,M.R.&H.]
*PRACTICE AREAS: Criminal Law; Securities Regulation Law and Litigation; Criminal Trial Practice.
**Sanders, Jay D.** ..................................'68 '95 C.37 B.A. L.221 J.D. [Ⓐ Loeb&L.]
*PRACTICE AREAS: Insolvency and Workout.
**Sanders, Kathryn A.** ..................'58 '85 C.112 B.A. L.800 J.D. [O'Melveny&M.]
*PRACTICE AREAS: General Corporate Law; Securities; Public Finance; Project Finance.
**Sanders, Michael, (AV)** ..........'52 '77 C.597 B.S. L.1066 J.D. [Sanders,B.G.S.&M.]
Sanders, Salvador ...................................'34 '74 C.1042 B.A. L.990 J.D. N.L.R.B.
Sanders, Sharon G. ..................'41 '85 C.1077 B.A. L.1186 J.D. Dep. Co. Coun.
Sanders, Teresa M. .....................................'54 '87 C.1077 B.A. L.809 J.D. [Moser&S.]

**Sanders, Barnet, Goldman, Simons & Mosk, A Professional Corporation, (AV)**
**Suite 850, 1901 Avenue of the Stars (Century City), 90067**
**Telephone: 310-553-8011 Telecopier: 310-553-2435**
**Irwin G. Barnet; James R. Eskilson; Jerry Fine; Kenneth A. Goldman; Deborah L. Gunny; Ruth N. Holzman; Edward Levine (Certified Specialist, Estate Planning, Trust and Probate Law, The State Bar of California Board of Legal Specialization); Louis E. Michelson; Richard M. Mosk; Edward Sanders; Michael Sanders; Bernard P. Simons; Russell L. Van Patten, Jr. Of Counsel: Louis M. Brown; Lazare F. Bernhard; Gordon R. Kanofsky.**
**Corporation, Securities, Business and Real Estate Law, Business and Commercial Litigation, Alternate Dispute Resolution, Federal and State Taxation Law, Administrative Law, International Arbitration, Estate Planning, Trust and Probate Law.**
***See Professional Biographies, LOS ANGELES, CALIFORNIA***

**Sandifer, Connie Cooke** ...........'52 '78 C.112 B.A. L.1049 J.D. [Oliver,V.S.M.&L.]
*PRACTICE AREAS: Eminent Domain; Inverse Condemnation; Civil Litigation.
Sandler, Irwin E., (AV) ......................'32 '59 C.112 A.B. L.1068 J.D. [Sandler&B.]
**Sandler, Raymond C., (AV)** ..................'13 '37 C&L.623 B.A., LL.B. [Sandler&R.]
**Sandler, Richard V.** ......'48 '73 C.112 B.S. L.1068 J.D. [Ⓒ Sandler&R.] & [Ⓒ Victor&S.]
Sandler, Robert A. ........................'44 '70 C.112 A.B. L.800 J.D. [Sandler,R.&M.]
**Sandler, Sharon Jill** .................'62 '90 C.061 B.C. L.800 J.D. [Ⓐ Levinson,M.J.&P.]
*LANGUAGES: Afrikaans.
*PRACTICE AREAS: Domestic Relation and Family Law.
Sandler & Breier, (AV) ................................................ 10850 Wilshire Blvd.
Sandler, Rolnick & Morse, (AV) ......................... 10000 Santa Monica Boulevard

**Sandler and Rosen, (AV)**
**Suite 510 Gateway West, 1801 Avenue of the Stars (Century City), 90067**☉
**Telephone: 310-277-4411; 213-879-9161 Cable Address: "Raynels" Fax: 310-277-5954**
**Members of Firm: Nelson Rosen (1910-1985); Raymond C. Sandler; Charles L. Birke; Steven E. Levy; William F. Tisch; Craig C. Birker. Associates: Ming-Chu C. Rouse; Virginia A. Johnson; Ivar E. Leetma (Resident, San Diego Office); Donald C. Miller. Of Counsel: Richard V. Sandler.**
**Business Law, Real Estate, Land Use, Construction, and Environmental Law. Corporate Law, Employment Law, Estate Planning, Trust and Probate Law. General Civil and Trial Practice in all State and Federal Courts.**
**Reference: First Interstate Bank (Century City Office, Los Angeles).**
**San Diego, California Office: 701 B Street, 92101. Telephone: 619-231-0340. Facsimile: 619-231-8752.**
***See Professional Biographies, LOS ANGELES, CALIFORNIA***

**Sandlin, Ava M.** ......................................'55 '93 L.809 J.D. [Ⓐ Serritella&P.]
**Sandona, Ray** ...................'53 '78 C.231 A.B. L.1068 J.D. [Ⓐ Skadden,A.S.M.&F.]
Sandoz, John H. .................................'33 '71 C.112 A.B. L.800 J.D. Supr. Ct. J.
**Sands, David H.** ......................'62 '87 C.604 B.A. L.94 J.D. [Troop M.S.&P.]
*PRACTICE AREAS: Financial Institutions Law; Corporate and Securities Law; Secured Transactions.
**Sands, Donald J.** .............................'39 '74 C&L.1136 B.S.L., J.D. [Sands N.F.L.&L.]
Sands, Edward I., (AV) ..............'40 '64 C.112 A.B. L.178 LL.B. 835 S. Lucerne Blvd.
**Sands, Eugene P.** .....................................'53 '94 C.722 B.A. L.426 J.D. [Lavely&S.]
*PRACTICE AREAS: Litigation.

**Sands Narwitz Forgie Leonard & Lerner, Professional Corporation, (AV)**
**11100 Santa Monica Boulevard Suite 1770, 90025**
**Telephone: 310-479-8826 Facsimile: 310-479-8834**
**Norman S. Narwitz; Donald J. Sands; Peter S. Forgie; Arthur A. Leonard; Neil S. Lerner;—Kelly Bennett Honig; Howard L. Jacobs; Danielle F. Furman.**

(This Listing Continued)

**Sands Narwitz Forgie Leonard & Lerner, Professional Corporation (Continued)**
**General Civil Litigation Practice in State and Federal Courts. Trials and Appeals. Admiralty and Maritime, Business Litigation, Personal Injury, Transportation, Inland Marine, Insurance Coverage and Defense.**
***See Professional Biographies, LOS ANGELES, CALIFORNIA***

Sanes, Frank, Jr. ...................'39 '76 C.1097 B.S. L.1068 J.D. 5777 W. Century Blvd.
Saney, Parviz '36 '87 L.178 M.C.L
(adm. in NY; not adm. in CA) 451 S. Barrington Ave.
Sanfilippo, T. Anthony ............'34 '63 C&L.426 B.S., LL.B. 5012 Eagle Rock Blvd.‡
**Sanford, Thomas C.** ....................'47 '75 C.1097 B.S. L.809 J.D. [Williams,B.&S.]
*PRACTICE AREAS: Negligence; Products Liability; Medical Malpractice; Insurance; Arbitration.
Sanford, Thomas F. ..............'39 '66 C.426 B.A. L.1068 LL.B. Liberty Mut. Ins. Co.
**Sang, Bin Xue** .............................'59 '91 C.061 B.A. L.228 J.D. [Ⓐ Graham&J.]
*LANGUAGES: Mandarin Chinese.
*PRACTICE AREAS: General Business Law; International Business Transaction Law.
San Juan, Del C. ..........................'64 '90 C.112 B.A. L.1148 J.D. Dep. City Atty.
Sannes, Brenda K. ..........................'58 '83 C.118 B.A. L.966 J.D. Asst. U.S. Atty.
Sanowski, Deborah A. ............'61 '88 C.37 B.A. L.1067 J.D. Atty., Calif. Fed. Bk.
Sansing, Emma '50 '74 C.498 B.A. L.500 J.D.
V.P., Bus. Affs., Intl. Creative Mgmt., Inc.
**Santana, Arturo, Jr.** ..........................'60 '86 C.112 B.A. L.1068 J.D. [Clark&T.]
*LANGUAGES: Spanish.
*PRACTICE AREAS: General Business Litigation; Commercial Litigation; Unfair Competition Litigation; Trade Secrets Litigation; Insurance Defense and Personal Injury Litigation.
**Santoro, Michael A.** ...................'54 '79 C.800 B.S. L.426 J.D. [Cadwalader,W.&T.]
**Santos, Laura L. '54 '90 C.112 B.A. L.1067 J.D.**
**900 Wilshire Boulevard Suite 1012, 90017-4711**
**Telephone: 213-689-9941 Fax: 213-589-9945**
**Email: LLS98775@AOL.com**
***LANGUAGES: Spanish.**
**Family Law, Bankruptcy, Probate including Trusts and Wills, Real Estate.**
***See Professional Biographies, LOS ANGELES, CALIFORNIA***

Santos, Virna L. ..........................'65 '90 C.112 B.A. L.309 J.D. Dep. Atty. Gen.

**Santwier, Rickard**
**(See Pasadena)**

**Sanz, Parris J.** ..........................'68 '93 C.112 A.B. L.309 J.D. [Ⓐ Latham&W.]
*PRACTICE AREAS: Taxation.
Sanzo, Frank A. ...................'37 '74 C.1043 B.A. L.809 J.D. 5232 E. Beverly Blvd.
**Saperstein, Israel, (AV)** ..........'45 '78 C.1097 B.S. L.1148 J.D. [Sulmeyer,K.B.&R.]
*PRACTICE AREAS: Bankruptcy; Commercial Litigation.
**Saphier, Michael D., (AV)** ..................'42 '68 C.112 A.B. L.477 J.D. [Saphier&H.]
*LANGUAGES: Spanish.
*PRACTICE AREAS: Health Care Law.
Saphier, Michael S., (AV) ...............'42 '68 C.860 B.A. L.569 J.D. [Saphier,R.&W.]

**Saphier and Heller, Law Corporation, (AV)**
**Suite 1900, 1900 Avenue of the Stars, 90067-4410**
**Telephone: 310-201-7555 Telecopier: 310-286-7821**
**Michael D. Saphier; Dona L. Heller;—Beth A. Kase.**
**Hospital, Health Care and General Business Law.**
***See Professional Biographies, LOS ANGELES, CALIFORNIA***

Saphier, Rein & Walden, (AV) ...................................10000 Santa Monica Blvd.
Sapire, Dennis H. .........................'54 '86 C&L.061 B.A., LL.B. P.O. Box 691868
Sapone, Mary Ann ..........................'48 '84 C.766 B.A. L.426 J.D. [Ⓐ Pollet&W.]
Sapp, Karen E. .........................'58 '83 C.197 A.B. L.846 J.D. 10521 Cheviot Dr.
Sarantes, Mary Papadopoulos, (AV) .........'62 '87 C.112 B.A. L.990 J.D. 815 Moraga Dr.
**Sarcone, Francis X.** ......................'47 '72 C.698 A.B. L.221 J.D. [Cummins&W.]
*LANGUAGES: Italian.
*PRACTICE AREAS: Property Coverage; First Party Coverage; Fraud and Errors Investigation; Personal Injury Defense; Bad Faith.
Sarfaty, Joseph, (AV) ......................'22 '60 C.112 B.S. L.426 J.D. [Kurtzman&S.]
Sargrad, Gita D. '59 '87 C.705 B.A. L.1292 J.D.
Dir., Bus. & Legal Affs., Orion Pictures Corp.
**Sarian, Ronald N.** ..............................'57 '86 C.112 B.A. L.426 J.D. [Ⓐ Astor&P.]
*PRACTICE AREAS: Business, Real Estate, Tort and Construction Litigation.
Sarin, Garish ...............................'56 '82 C.061 B.A. L.1238 J.D. 1541 Wilshire Blvd.
**Sarkis, Anthony J.** ........'64 '90 C.112 B.A. L.1066 J.D. [Ⓐ Christensen,M.F.J.G.W.&S.]
*LANGUAGES: Persian, Assyrian and German.
*PRACTICE AREAS: Civil Litigation; Securities Litigation.
Sarkisian, Ruben N. ....................'56 '83 C.800 B.A. L.426 J.D. 3550 Wilshire Blvd.
Sarmiento, Ellen Ann ..................'55 '81 C.1349 B.A. L.1067 J.D. Dep. City Atty.
**Sarmiento Knowlton, Janette** .........'60 '86 C.800 B.A. L.426 J.D. [Knapp,M.J.&D.]
*PRACTICE AREAS: Litigation; Public Entity Law; Environmental Law.
Sarna, Raymond L. ......................'45 '71 C.800 A.B. L.813 J.D. 632 N. Harper Ave.
**Sarno, Cynthia N.** ........'— '83 C.112 A.B. L.209 J.D. Corp. Coun., Farmers Grp., Inc.
*RESPONSIBILITIES: Property and Casualty Insurance; General Corporate Law; Appellate Supervision.
Sarnoff, Laurence M. ..............'42 '67 C.112 B.A. L.1066 LL.B. Dep. Pub. Def.
Sarnoff, Wm. M., (BV) ..........................'15 '46 L.800 LL.B. 12400 Wilshire Blvd.
**Saroians, Vahan** ..........................'67 '94 C.1077 B.S. L.426 J.D. [Ⓒ N.J.Williams]
*PRACTICE AREAS: Real Estate; Lending; Bankruptcy.
Sartorius, Sharon C. ..............'65 '93 C.276 B.S. L.800 J.D. 777 S. Figueroa St., 10th Fl.
Sarup, Raj Prem ......................'23 '91 C.061 B.A. L.145 LL.M. 350 S. Figueroa St.
**Sasaki, Judith M.** ........................'58 '85 C&L.312 B.A., J.D. [Bucksbaum&S.]
*PRACTICE AREAS: Financial Institution Litigation; Real Estate Litigation; Business Litigation.
Saslow, Edward ..............'41 '67 C.1044 B.A. L.178 LL.B. Associated Financial Corp.
**Sassoe, Albert L., Jr.** .........................'57 '82 C.112 B.A. L.426 J.D. [Golob,B.&S.]
*PRACTICE AREAS: Business Litigation; Insurance Coverage Law; Mobile Home Park Litigation.
**Satenberg, Andrew L.** ..............'69 '94 C.575 B.A. L.569 J.D. [Ⓐ Meserve,M.&H.]
**Sater, Gregory J.** ....................'66 '92 C.813 B.A. L.309 J.D. [Ⓐ Greenberg G.F.C.&M.]
*PRACTICE AREAS: Business Litigation; Intellectual Property Litigation; Entertainment Litigation; Copyright Law; Trademark Law.
**Sather, Kelly L.** .................'69 '95 C.674 A.B. L.228 J.D. [Ⓐ Greenberg G.F.C.&M.]
*PRACTICE AREAS: Transactional Entertainment.
Sato, Ann Atsuko .................................'— '91 C.112 B.A. L.426 J.D. Dep. Dist. Atty.
Sato, Vincent B. ...........................'57 '83 C.1109 B.A. L.426 J.D. Dep. City Atty.
**Satrom, Thomas** ..........................'53 '84 C.951 A.B. L.1119 J.D. [Gibson,D.&C.]
*PRACTICE AREAS: Litigation.
**Satter, Lisa A.** ........................'56 '84 C.763 B.A. L.1049 J.D. [Ⓒ Gilbert,K.C.&J.]
**Satz, Steven L.** ..............................'50 '78 C.347 B.A. L.502 J.D. [Ⓐ Andrews&K.]
*PRACTICE AREAS: Real Estate.
**Sauer, Gerald L.** ...................'57 '84 C.112 B.A. L.1065 J.D. [Greenberg G.F.C.&M.]
*PRACTICE AREAS: Business Litigation; Real Estate Litigation; Labor Law; Entertainment Litigation.
Sauer, Lynda M. ............................'60 '85 C.145 B.A. L.209 J.D. 1055 W. 7th St.
**Sauer, Russell F., Jr.** ...........................'55 '80 C.597 B.A. L.813 J.D. [Latham&W.]
**Saunders, Allyson G.** ....................'54 '87 C.107 B.A. L.426 J.D. [Ⓐ Paul,H.J.&W.]
Saunders, Anne-Marie, (AV) ................'45 '74 C.273 B.A. L.809 J.D. 624 S. Grand Ave.
Saunders, Daniel A. '62 '92 C.674 A.B. L.1066 J.D.
1800 Ave. of the Stars, Suite 900 (Century City)

CAA332P

**Saunders, Jennifer Upham** ... '60 '90 C.1169 B.A. L.1066 J.D. [Ⓐ Latham&W.]
*PRACTICE AREAS: Finance.
Saunders, Lauren K. ... '60 '89 C.813 B.A. L.309 J.D. 10951 W. Pico Blvd.
**Saunders, Matthew J.** ... '58 '85 C.112 B.A. L.809 J.D. [Engstrom,L.&L.]
*PRACTICE AREAS: Governmental Agency Defense; Construction Litigation; General Trials.
Saunders, Myra K. ... '50 '79 C.112 B.A. L.1049 J.D. Univ. of Calif.
**Saunders, Nancy M.** ... '58 '83 C.668 B.A. L.1065 J.D. [Ⓐ Morgan,L.&B.]
**Sausser, Gordon F.**, (AV) ... '33 '66 C.112 B.S. L.809 LL.B. [Veatch,C.G.&N.]
*PRACTICE AREAS: Civil Litigation; Insurance Defense.
Savage, Janet M. ... '60 '86 C.813 A.B. L.309 J.D. 5515 Melrose Ave.
Savage, Kim K. ... '54 '83 C.629 B.A. L.1065 J.D. National Sr. Citizens Law Ctr.
**Savard, Glenn L.** ... '58 '87 C.1110 B.A. L.426 J.D. [Ⓐ Buchalter,N.F.&Y.]
Saver, Matthew H. ... '53 '78 C.112 B.A. L.1068 J.D. [Ⓒ Myman,A.F.G.&R.]
**Savikas, Victor G.**, (AVⓉ) ... '41 '68 C&L.209 B.A., J.D. [Jones,D.R.&P.]
Savino, Mona B. ... '— '90 C.893 B.A. L.1184 J.D. 525 S. Virgil Ave.
**Saviola, Georgia P.** ... '59 '90 C.228 B.A. L.893 J.D. [Ⓐ Howrey&S.]
*LANGUAGES: Greek.
*PRACTICE AREAS: White Collar Criminal Defense; Commercial Litigation.
Savitch, Leon ... '23 '49 C.659 B.S. L.309 LL.B. Supr. Ct. J.
Savitt, Robert E. ... '42 '68 C.112 A.B. L.1065 J.D. Dep. Dist. Atty.
**Savva, John L.** ... '60 '88 C.1168 B.A. L.426 J.D. [Sullivan&C.]
**Sawkar, Suhasini S.** ... '54 '87 C.061 B.A. L.398 J.D. [Ⓐ Herzfeld&R.]
Sawyer, Eric C. ... '64 '89 C.112 B.A. L.1068 J.D. Dep. Atty. Gen.
**Sawyer, James F. B.** ... '55 '90 C.454 B.A. L.1049 J.D. [Lewis,D.B.&B.]
Sawyer, Robert E. '43 '69 C.321 A.B. L.309 J.D.
Assoc. Gen. Coun., Occidental Petroleum Corp.
Sax, Eugene E. ... '07 '31 C&L.800 A.B., LL.B. Ret. Supr. Ct. J.
Sax, Hilary H. ... '18 '45 C.851 B.B.A. L.309 LL.B. 8568 Burton Way
Sax, Jeffrey F. ... '58 '83 C.354 B.S. L.426 J.D. [Ⓐ Soller,S.&H.]
Sax, Jodi L. ... '65 '92 C.112 B.A. L.426 J.D. 11355 W. Olympic Blvd.
**Saxe, Deborah Crandall** ... '49 '78 C.645 B.A. L.1068 J.D. [Heller E.W.&M.]
**Saxton, Roger S.** '52 '80 C.930 B.A. L.607 J.D.
(adm. in PA; not adm. in CA) [Ⓒ Arnberger,K.B.&C.]
*LANGUAGES: English, Swedish and Japanese.
*PRACTICE AREAS: Litigation and Business Transactions between Australia, U.S. and Asia.
Sayer, Andrew Fenning ... '59 '86 [Sayer&S.]
Sayer, Floyd ... '26 '50 C&L.569 B.A., J.D. [Sayer&S.]
Sayer & Sayer ... 10960 Wilshire Blvd.
**Sayre, Mark D.** ... '57 '83 C.112 B.A. L.990 J.D. [Schaffer&L.]
**Sbarbaro, Kelley L.** ... '65 '93 C.112 B.A. L.800 J.D. [Ⓐ Manatt,P.&P.]
**Scalabrini, Gary Edward** ... '61 '92 C.800 B.S. L.1065 [Ⓐ Gibbs,G.L.&A.]
*PRACTICE AREAS: Construction Law; Business Litigation; Labor and Employment Law.
Scales, Anne ... '51 '80 C.668 B.A. L.800 J.D. Sr. Coun., Sanwa Bk. Calif.
**Scali, Lois J.** ... '48 '86 C.102 B.A. L.1068 J.D. [Irell&M.]
*LANGUAGES: Italian.
**Scalzo, Ralph J.** ... '35 '67 C.401 B.S.I.E. L.800 J.D. [Grace,S.C.&S.]
*PRACTICE AREAS: Employment Law; Labor Law; Litigation.
**Scarlett, Gregory B.** ... '52 '87 C.259 A.B. L.1068 J.D. [Ⓐ Barger&W.]
*PRACTICE AREAS: General Litigation.
Scarpellino, Tina, (AV) ... '36 '75 L.1095 J.D. Dep. Co. Coun.
Schaaf, Charles E. ... '16 '40 C.197 A.B. L.309 LL.B. 1730 Reedvale Lane‡
Schaap, Robert J., (AV) ... '35 '60 C.910 B.S. L.734 LL.B. [R.J.Schaap]⊙
Schaap, Robert J., P.C., (AV) ... 5601 W. Slauson Blvd. (⊙Woodland Hills)
**Schachter, David M.** ... '59 '85 C.112 B.A. L.1049 J.D. [Fried,B.&C.]
*PRACTICE AREAS: Financial Institutions Law - Corporate Securities; General Corporate and Regulatory Representation; Mergers and Acquisitions; Bank Applications and Organizations.
**Schachter, Robin M., (P.C.)** ... '52 '77 C.30 B.A. L.128 J.D. [Jeffer,M.B.&M.]
*PRACTICE AREAS: Employee Benefits; Taxation.
**Schack, David P., (A Professional Corporation)** '57 '82
C.813 B.A. L.1068 J.D. [Mitchell,S.&K.]
*PRACTICE AREAS: Litigation; Insurance; Real Estate Law.
**Schaedel, John Peter** ... '70 '95 C.188 B.S. L.1068 J.D. [Ⓐ Parker,M.C.O.&S.]
*LANGUAGES: Spanish, French, German.
*PRACTICE AREAS: Labor and Employment; Labor Relations.
**Schaefer, Kathryn** ... '69 '95 C.276 B.S.F.S. L.145 J.D. [Ⓐ Irell&M.]
**Schaefer, Sheila E.** ... '61 '87 C.95 B.A. L.802 J.D. [Ⓐ Dennison,B.&P.]
Schaertel, Arthur T., (A Professional Corporation) '39 '74
C.895 B.A. L.426 J.D. 1800 Ave. of the Stars
**Schafer, Terrence J.** ... '65 '90 C&L.426 B.A., J.D. [Kirtland&P.]
**Schaffer, Clifford L.**, (AV) ... '39 '67 C.800 B.S. L.1066 LL.B. [Schaffer&L.]
Schaffer, Doris, (AV) ... '34 '80 C.112 B.A. L.426 J.D. [Ⓒ Schaffer&B.] ‡
**Schaffer, Edmund S.**, (AV) ... '45 '71 C.112 A.B. L.309 J.D. [Goldman&K.]
Schaffer, Gregory Paul ... '63 '88 C.273 B.A. L.800 J.D. 11355 W. Olympic Blvd.
Schaffer, Robert L., (AV) ... '33 '59 C&L.800 B.S.L., LL.B. [Schaffer&B.]
Schaffer & Baumer, (AV) ... 2049 Century Park E.

**Schaffer & Lax, A Professional Corporation, (AV)**
**Suite 600, 5757 Wilshire Boulevard, 90036-3664**
**Telephone: 213-934-4300 Fax: 213-931-5680**
**Clifford L. Schaffer; Stephen A. Lax; Kevin J. McNaughton; Barbara C. Fasiska; Alexander J. Chen; Mark D. Sayre; Jill A. Franklin; John H. Horwitz;—Marjorie E. Motooka; G. Calvin Hutchinson; Michael M. Walsh; David M. Frishman; Courtney Colleen McNicholas; Suzanne R. Feffer; Amy W. Lewis; Marshall Zelaznik; Steven M. Dailey; Julie A. August; David Swei-chuan Lin; R. Bret Beattie; Sharyl B. Zimmerman.**
**General Insurance Practice. Insurance Coverage, Products Liability, Medical Products, Bad Faith Litigation, Construction Litigation, Professional Liability, Environmental Law, State and Federal Courts.**
**Reference: Union Bank, Downtown Los Angeles, California.**
***See Professional Biographies, LOS ANGELES, CALIFORNIA***

Schafler, Norman L. ... '36 '75 L.1148 J.D. 10590 Wilshire Blvd.
**Schalow, Thomas** ... '49 '82 C.976 B.A. L.800 J.D. [Ⓐ Argue P.H.&M.]
*PRACTICE AREAS: Civil Litigation.

**Schapira, Leonard L., Law Office of**
**(See Hermosa Beach)**

**Schare, Allan L.** ... '61 '86 C.112 A.B. L.1066 J.D. [McDermott,W.&E.]
*PRACTICE AREAS: Litigation.
**Scharf, Stephen** ... '49 '75 C.165 B.A. L.813 J.D. [O'Melveny&M.]
*PRACTICE AREAS: Entertainment Law; Intellectual Property Law.
Scharfer, James A. ... '53 '81 C.118 B.A. L.494 J.D. 906 Masselin Ave.
**Schatz, Russell W., Jr.** ... '60 '91 C.426 B.S. L.1137 J.D. [Ⓐ Millard,P.H.&C.]
*PRACTICE AREAS: Insurance Defense; Civil Litigation.

**Schauer, Nancy R., (AV) '50 '76 C&L.477 A.B., J.D.**
**5601 West Slauson, Suite 282, 90230**
**Telephone: 310-338-6670 Fax: 310-338-6673**
**Business Law and Receivership Law.**
***See Professional Biographies, LOS ANGELES, CALIFORNIA***

**Schauer, Richard** ... '29 '55 C.605 B.A. L.1068 J.D. [Ⓒ Sidley&A.]
*PRACTICE AREAS: Judicial Administration Litigation.

Schauerman, Anne M. ... '55 '80 C.112 B.A. L.809 J.D. [Smith&S.]
Schechet, David A. ... '60 '86 C.112 B.A. L.1068 J.D. 1901 Ave. of the Stars
Schechter, Dan S. ... '52 '77 C.426 B.A. L.1068 J.D. Prof., Loyola Univ. Law Sch.
Schechter, Harry L. ... '15 '38 C.102 A.B. L.178 LL.B. 7760 Hollywood Blvd.‡
**Schechter, Minda R.**, (AV) ... '51 '75 C.788 B.A. L.813 J.D. [Graham&J.] (Pat.)
*PRACTICE AREAS: Antitrust Law; Intellectual Property Law; International Joint Ventures and Distribution Law; Franchise Law.
Scheck, Naomi M. ... '55 '81 C.112 B.A. L.1066 J.D. 12424 Wilshire Blvd.
**Schecter, Daniel Scott** ... '66 '93 C.112 B.A. L.800 J.D. [Ⓐ Latham&W.]
**Schecter, Jill R.** ... '68 '93 C.112 B.A. L.1068 J.D. [Ⓐ Gibbs,G.L.&A.]
*PRACTICE AREAS: Construction Litigation.
**Scheer, Marilyn S.** ... '54 '79 C.793 B.A. L.221 J.D. [Ⓒ Sulmeyer,K.B.&R.]
*PRACTICE AREAS: Bankruptcy; Creditor's Rights; General Litigation.
Scheerer, Thomas M. ... '44 '72 C.112 A.B. L.1068 J.D. Dep. Atty. Gen.
**Scheffel, Evan** ... '69 '96 C.1111 B.A. L.1187 J.D. [Beck,D.D.B.&O.]
**Scheidemantle, David R.** ... '60 '88 C.999 B.Mus. L.262 J.D. [Proskauer R.G.&M.]
*PRACTICE AREAS: Securities; Banking; Antitrust Litigation.
Scheifly, John E., (AV) ... '25 '48 C.103 Sc.B. L.902 J.D. 801 S. Grand Ave.
Schein, Daniel B. '59 '90 C.301 B.A. L.30 J.D.
(adm. in PA; not adm. in CA; Pat.) 10877 Wilshire Blvd.
**Scheinberg, Michael E.**, (AV) ... '57 '83 C&L.597 B.A., J.D. [Pircher,N.&M.]
*PRACTICE AREAS: Real Estate Finance.
**Scheiner, Julian** ... '37 '72 C&L.910 B.S.E.E., J.D. [Ⓒ Meserve,M.&H.]
Scheinman, Ronald L., (AV) ... '33 '58 C.112 B.S. L.1068 J.D. 1800 Ave. of the Stars

**Schell & Delamer, LLP, (AV)** BB
**A Partnership including Professional Corporations**
**865 South Figueroa Street Suite 2750, 90017⊙**
**Telephone: 213-622-8181 Fax: 213-627-5252**
**Gerald F. H. Delamer (1892-1955); Walter O. Schell (1895-1981); Roland R. Kaspar (Professional Corporation); Garrin James Shaw (Professional Corporation); Robert S. Hamrick (Professional Corporation); Jeffrey F. Briskin; Katherine B. Pene. Associates: Candace E. Ahrens Kallberg; Denise A. Nardi; Randy A. Berg; Kenneth S. Markson; Joseph P. Sepikas; Gregory J. Amantia (Resident at Thousand Oaks Office); John J. Latzanich, II. (Resident at Thousand Oaks Office); Lori M. Levine; Sylvia Havens; Roman Y. Nykolyshyn.**
**Products Liability, Premise Liability and Security Issues, Insurance Coverage and Bad Faith, Public Entity and Government Liability, Automobile and Transportation, Truck and Heavy Equipment, Restaurant and Club Liability, Medical and Dental Malpractice, Wrongful Termination and Employers Liability, Defamation and Invasion of Privacy, Environmental (including EMF and RFI Exposure and Toxic Torts), Construction Defect and Land Subsidence, Business and Commercial Law, Professional Liability, Pharmaceutical Liability.**
**Representative Clients: Hartford Insurance Group; Liberty Mutual Group; Travelers Insurance Co.**
**References: Los Angeles: First Interstate Bank; Merrill-Lynch.**
**Thousand Oaks, California Office: 100 East Thousand Oaks Boulevard, Suite 142. Telephone: 805-496-9533. Fax: 805-496-3424.**
***See Professional Biographies, LOS ANGELES, CALIFORNIA***

Schelly, Paul A. ... '42 '72 C.112 B.A. L.426 J.D. 3255 Wilshire Blvd.
Schenck, John D., (AV) ... '34 '60 C.319 B.A. L.1068 LL.B. [Schenck&E.]
Schenck & Edelman, (AV) ... 10866 Wilshire Blvd.
**Schenz, Gregory R.** ... '65 '93 C.273 B.A. L.426 J.D. [Ⓐ B.R.Bailey]
Scheper, David C. ... '58 '85 C.309 A.B. L.602 J.D. U.S. Dept. of Jus.
**Scher, Stephanie R.** ... '48 '76 C.112 B.A. L.1068 J.D. [Kane,B.&B.]
*SPECIAL AGENCIES: Special Counsel to City of Bell Gardens, West San Gabriel Valley Consortium.
*PRACTICE AREAS: Municipal Law; Land Use Law; Redevelopment Law; Election Law.
**Scherago, Michael A.** ... '67 '93 C.273 B.A. L.426 J.D. [Ⓐ Dummit,F.&B.]
**Scherby, Stephanie H.** ... '66 '91 C.66 B.A. L.767 J.D. [Ⓐ Charlston,R.&W.]
*PRACTICE AREAS: Environmental Insurance Coverage; Tort Litigation.
Scherer, Stephen E. ... '48 '73 C.339 B.S. L.36 J.D. [Scherer&B.]
Scherer & Bradford ... 1901 Ave. of the Stars
**Scherlacher, John P.**, (AV) '38 '66
C.923 B.S.B.E. L.273 LL.B. [Ⓒ Loeb&L.] (See Pat. Sect.)
*PRACTICE AREAS: Patent; Trademark.
**Scherzer, Stephen G.** ... '48 '73 C.629 B.S. L.770 J.D. [Tharpe&H.] (⊙Newport Beach)
*PRACTICE AREAS: Personal Injury Defense; Commercial Business Litigation; Construction Litigation (Defense); Intellectual Property Litigation (Defense).
**Schetina, Gregory D.** ... '55 '81 C.112 A.B. L.426 J.D. [Tuttle&T.]
*PRACTICE AREAS: Civil and Professional Liability Litigation; White-Collar Criminal Defense.

**Scheuer, Keith, Law Offices of, (AV) '49 '78 C.813 B.A. L.800 J.D.**
**1875 Century Park East, Suite 1760, 90067**
**Telephone: 310-286-9157 Fax: 310-552-3437**
**Email: kscheuer@aol.com**
**Real Estate Litigation and Business Litigation.**

**Scheuneman, Christine A.** ... '50 '81 C.378 B.A. L.209 J.D. [Ⓒ Paul,H.J.&W.]
Schewatz, Mary '50 '79 C.477 B.A. L.213 J.D.
(adm. in MI; not adm. in CA) Dist. Coun., I.R.S.
**Schewe, Edward C.** ... '57 '89 C.36 B.S. L.990 J.D. [Ⓐ Bright&L.] (See Pat. Sect.)
*PRACTICE AREAS: Intellectual Property Law.
Schey, Peter A. '47 '73 C.112 A.B. L.61 J.D.
Center For Human Rights & Constitutional Law
**Schiada, Paul** ... '62 '87 C.112 B.A. L.800 J.D. [Ⓐ Katten M.&Z.]
*LANGUAGES: Italian.
*PRACTICE AREAS: Corporate.
Schiavelli, George P. ... '48 '74 C.813 A.B. L.1068 J.D. Supr. Ct. J.
**Schibel, Robert L.**, (AV) ... '38 '70 C.494 B.B.A. L.800 J.D. [R.L.Schibel]

**Schibel, Robert L., A Professional Corporation, (AV)**
**Suite 1000, 11111 Santa Monica Boulevard, 90025**
**Telephone: 310-473-6888 Fax: 310-473-0906**
**Robert L. Schibel (Certified Specialist, Family Law, The State Bar of California Board of Legal Specialization).**
**General Civil and Trial Practice in all State and Federal Courts. Family, Domestic Relations, Corporate, Real Property, Business and Entertainment Law.**
**Representative Clients: Inco Homes; XIV Karats, Gallery Judaica; Dryer Productions, Inc .**
**Reference: City National Bank (Beverly Hills Branch).**
***See Professional Biographies, LOS ANGELES, CALIFORNIA***

**Schield, Brian E.** ... '54 '79 C.966 B.A. L.990 J.D. [Graham&J.]
*LANGUAGES: French.
*PRACTICE AREAS: Immigration and Nationality or Naturalization Law.
**Schienberg, Randy M.** ... '58 '85 C.813 B.A. L.1068 J.D. [Armstrong H.J.T.&W.]
*PRACTICE AREAS: Entertainment.
Schiewe, Jon A. ... '44 '72 C&L.208 B.A., J.D. 6380 Wilshire Blvd.
**Schiff, Adam B.** ... '60 '86 C.813 A.B. L.309 J.D. [Ⓒ Foley L.W.&A.]
*PRACTICE AREAS: Litigation; Fraud and Abuse Compliance Plans.
Schiff, Anthony Hunter, (AV) ... '52 '77 C.1051 B.S. L.809 J.D. [Schiff&B.]

**Schiff, Joel P., Law Offices of, (AV) '42 '66 C&L.188 A.B., J.D.**
**1801 Century Park East Twenty Third Floor, 90067**
**Telephone: 310-201-2550 Fax: 310-201-2551**
**Appellate Practice and Business Litigation, State and Federal, Mediation and Arbitration, Business Law.**
***See Professional Biographies, LOS ANGELES, CALIFORNIA***

**Schiff, Michael J., (P.C.)**, (AV) ... '38 '63 C&L.477 B.B.A., J.D. [Easton&S.]

CAA333P

**Schiff, Scott A.** ........................ '63 '88 C.112 B.A. L.1065 J.D. [Ⓐ Aronoff&S.]
*PRACTICE AREAS: Real Estate; Business Transactional; Bankruptcy Law; Civil Litigation.
Schiff & Bernstein, A Professional Corporation, (AV) .............. 2049 Century Park E.
Schiffmacher, Mark D., (AV) ....... '46 '72 C.169 A.B. L.1066 J.D. 1801 Century Park E.‡

**Schiffmacher, Weinstein, Boldt & Racine, Professional Corporation**
**(See Weinstein, Boldt, Racine, Halfhide & Camel)**

Schiffman, Robyn M., (AV) '59 '87
C.174 B.A. L.1148 J.D. Coun., Taisho Claims Servs. Corp.
Schiffres, H. Steven, (P.C.), (AV) ............ '50 '76 C&L.597 B.A., J.D. [Rosoff,S.&B.]
**Schifino, Paul G.** ........................ '61 '89 C.425 B.B.A. L.276 J.D. [Schifino&L.]
*PRACTICE AREAS: Corporate Law; Securities Law; Acquisitions, Divestitures and Mergers Law.

**Schifino & Lindon**
**1901 Avenue of the Stars, Suite 251, 90067**
**Telephone: 310-553-2600 Fax: 310-553-2625**
**Members of Firm: Paul G. Schifino; Mark L. Lindon. Of Counsel: Jolie L. Busch (Not admitted in CA). Corporate, Securities and General Business.**
***See Professional Biographies, LOS ANGELES, CALIFORNIA***

**Schildkraut, Bruce S.** .................. '63 '88 C.529 B.A. L.831 J.D. [Ⓐ Weinstein&E.]
**Schimbor, Patricia Shuler**, (AV) ...... '49 '76 C.1169 A.B. L.1067 J.D. [Hancock R.&B.]
**Schimley, Paul F.** .................... '55 '81 C.573 B.A. L.1049 J.D. [Anderson,M.&C.]
*PRACTICE AREAS: Employment Litigation; Real Estate Litigation.

**Schimmel, Hillshafer & Loewenthal**
**(See Sherman Oaks)**

Schindler, Rose M. ..... '52 '85 C.502 B.A. L.209 J.D. U.S. Securities & Exchange Comm.
**Schirm, Barry R.** ........................ '55 '80 C.1189 B.A. L.809 J.D. [Grace,S.C.&S.]
*PRACTICE AREAS: Product Liability Law; Insurance Coverage Law; Insurance Defense Law; Professional Liability Law; Appellate Law.
Schirn, Robert, (AV) .................. '41 '66 C.674 B.A. L.1068 LL.B. Dep. Dist. Atty.
**Schirtzer, Richard A.** .................. '57 '85 C.1044 B.A. L.477 J.D. [Quinn E.U.&O.]
*PRACTICE AREAS: Securities; Banking.
**Schlaff, John A.** .............................. '59 '88 C.112 A.B. L.309 J.D. [Ⓐ Belin R.&B.]
Schlang, Setha '51 '76 C&L.112 B.A., J.D.
Dep. Gen. Coun., Metropolitan Water Dist. of Southern Calif.
**Schlegel, Richard J.**, (BV) .............. '45 '74 C.473 B.S. L.809 J.D. [Ⓐ Sylvester&O.]
*PRACTICE AREAS: Insurance Defense.
Schleimer, Joseph D. ......................'— '86 C.1169 B.A. L.678 J.D. 2029 Century Park E.
Schlesinger, Alfred W., (AV) .......... '27 '59 C.494 B.A. L.426 LL.B. 6255 Sunset Blvd.
**Schlesinger, Diane L.** ...'63 '88 C.112 B.A. L.1066 J.D. [Ⓐ Faustman,C.D.&F.] (⊙Irvine)
*PRACTICE AREAS: Employment Law; Labor Law; Business Litigation.
**Schlessinger, Gary A.**, (AV) ............ '31 '60 C.563 B.A. L.1066 J.D. [Ⓑ Frye,A.&M.]
*PRACTICE AREAS: Insurance Coverage Law; Litigation; Partnership Dissolutions Law; Legal Malpractice.
**Schlichter, Kurt A.** .................... '64 '94 C.112 B.A. L.426 J.D. [Ⓐ Grace,S.C.&S.]
*PRACTICE AREAS: Products Liability; Consumer Warranty; Insurance; Labor; Business Litigation.

**Schlifkin, Robert S., (AV) '39 '69 C.1016 B.S. L.1095 J.D.**
**1925 Century Park East, Suite 1250, 90067-2713**
**Telephone: 310-553-5151 FAX: 310-553-7204**
**(Member of California Trial Lawyers Association, with recognized experience in the fields of General Personal Injury, Product Liability and Professional Negligence).**
**Practice limited to Civil Litigation. Professional Liability, Personal Injury, Products Liability and Business Fraud.**
**Reference: First Los Angeles Bank.**
***See Professional Biographies, LOS ANGELES, CALIFORNIA***

**Schloss, Leonora M.** ............ '61 '87 C.734 A.B. L.178 J.D. [Ⓐ Sonnenschein N.&R.]
*LANGUAGES: Russian and German.
*REPORTED CASES: Local 21, International Federation of Professional & Technical Engineers, AFL-CIO, v. Thornton C. Bunch, Jr., Waldemar Rojas, et al.
*PRACTICE AREAS: Labor and Employment.
Schlosser, Susan G. .................. '60 '90 C.1042 B.S. L.425 J.D. 1200 Wilshire Blvd.
**Schlothauer, Thomas L.**, (AV) '42 '73 C.172 B.S.C.E. L.770 J.D.
[Schlothauer,C.&M.]
*PRACTICE AREAS: Torts (100%, 200); Products Liability Law; Professional Liability Law.

**Schlothauer, Collins & Macaluso, (AV)**
**11661 San Vicente Boulevard, Suite 303, 90049**
**Telephone: 310-820-8606 Fax: 310-820-7057**
**Partners: Thomas L. Schlothauer; Mark Scott Collins (Member of California Trial Lawyers Association, with recognized experience in the fields of Trial Lawyer, Professional Negligence, Product Liability, General Personal Injury and Insurance Bad Faith); Todd E. Macaluso. Associate: James Pflaster. Of Counsel: Malcolm G. Heib.**
**Civil Litigation in all State and Federal Courts, Personal Injury, Medical Malpractice, Aviation Law including Plane Crashes, Products Liability.**
**Affiliated San Jose California Office: Collins & Schlothauer, 60 South Market Street, Suite 1100. Telephone: 408-298-5161. Fax: 408-297-5766.**
***See Professional Biographies, LOS ANGELES, CALIFORNIA***

Schlotman, Edward A. ......................... '39 '66 C&L.426 B.A., J.D. Asst. City Atty.
Schlotter, Charles J. '49 '74 C&L.665 B.A., J.D.
(adm. in PA; not adm. in CA) 1387 Midvale Ave.
**Schlotterbeck, John D.** .......... '61 '93 C.770 B.S. L.1065 J.D. [Ⓐ McCutchen,D.B.&E.]
*PRACTICE AREAS: Environmental Law.
Schmadeka, Larry ......................... '65 '92 C.154 B.A. L.810 J.D. 221 N. Figueroa St.
**Schmadeka, Larry R.** .................. '65 '92 C.154 B.A. L.809 J.D. [Ⓐ Lewis,D.B.&B.]
Schmale, Neal E. ........................ '46 '74 C.179 B.S. L.426 J.D. Sr. V.P., Unocal Corp.

**Schmeltzer, Aptaker & Shepard, P.C.**
**1999 Avenue of the Stars Twenty-Seventh Floor, 90067-4095⊙**
**Telephone: 310-557-2966 FAX: 310-286-6610**
**Email: sas@saslaw.com URL: http://www.saspc.com**
**—Daniel P. Ben-Zvi.**
**Labor and Employment Law, Maritime, Equal Employment Opportunity, Civil Litigation, Employee Benefits, Franchise, Criminal, Health Care Law, Antitrust, Interstate Commerce and Corporate Law. Washington, D.C. Office: The Watergate, Suite 1000, 2600 Virginia Avenue, N.W., 20037-1905. Telephone: 202-333-8800. Facsimile: 202-342-3434.**
***See Professional Biographies, LOS ANGELES, CALIFORNIA***

**Schmelz, Ronie M.** ........................ '61 '87 C.112 B.A. L.1065 J.D. [Sidley&A.]
*LANGUAGES: Hebrew.
*PRACTICE AREAS: Civil Litigation; Health Care Litigation.
Schmerin, H. David .................. '34 '61 C.112 B.A. L.1068 LL.B. [Rotkin,S.&M.]
Schmid, Susan H., (AV) ........................ '51 '74 C.37 B.A. L.800 J.D. [Schmid&V.]
Schmid & Voiles, (AV) ................................. 333 S. Hope St., 8th Fl. (⊙Orange)
**Schmidt, Deborah** .................. '58 '87 C.66 B.A. L.978 J.D. [Ⓐ Gabriel,H.&P.]
*LANGUAGES: Hebrew.
*PRACTICE AREAS: Business Transactions; Real Estate; Loan Workouts and Lending Transactions.
Schmidt, Juliet ......................... '63 '88 C.112 A.B. L.1068 J.D. Dep. Dist. Atty.
**Schmidt, Karl A.**, (AV) .............. '47 '74 C.112 B.S. L.1066 J.D. [Pillsbury M.&S.]
**Schmidt, Roy J., Jr.**, (AV) .................. '41 '66 C&L.813 A.B., J.D. [Gibson,D.&C.]
*PRACTICE AREAS: Corporate and Corporate Securities; Mergers and Acquisitions; Real Estate.
**Schmidt, Thomas P.** ........................ '62 '91 C.999 B.S. L.426 J.D. [Ⓐ Graham&J.]
Schmier, Eric S. ...................... '46 '74 C.477 B.A. L.1065 J.D. 2034 Cotner Ave.
Schmier, Kenneth J. .................. '50 '74 C.112 B.B.A. L.1065 J.D. 2034 Cotner Ave.
Schmier, Michael K., (P.C.), (AV) ........... '45 '70 C&L.477 B.B.A., J.D. [Schmier&S.]
Schmier & Schmier, (AV) ....................................................... 2034 Cotner Avenue
Schmit, Lucien A., III ........................ '60 '84 C.112 A.B. L.1066 J.D. [Albright,Y.&S.]
Schmitt, Michael A. ........ '47 '74 C.424 B.A. L.976 J.D. Southwestern Univ. Sch. of Law
**Schmutz, Arthur W.**, (AV) ........... '21 '53 C.367 A.B. L.309 LL.B. [Ⓑ Gibson,D.&C.]
**Schnabel, Laurence H.**, (AV) ........ '41 '68 C.813 B.A. L.1068 J.D. [Hawkins,S.L.&B.]
**Schnaider, Guillermo W.**, (AV) .............. '44 '70 C&L.426 B.A., J.D. [Kinkle,R.&S.]
**Schnapp, Lawrence P.** ........................ '62 '88 C.659 B.S. L.1068 J.D. [Ⓐ Troy&G.]
*PRACTICE AREAS: Corporate Securities; General Corporate.
**Schneck, Theodore R.** ............ '64 '91 C.311 B.A. L.477 J.D. [Ⓐ McDermott,W.&E.]
**Schnegg, Patricia M.**, (AV) .............. '52 '77 C&L.426 B.A., J.D. [Knapp,M.J.&D.]
*SPECIAL AGENCIES: Interstate Commerce Commission; California Public Utilities Commission.
*PRACTICE AREAS: Litigation; Financial and Estate Planning Law; Business Law; Employment Law; Transportation Law.
**Schneider, Carol A.** .............. '51 '88 C.112 B.A. L.800 J.D. [Lyon&L.] (See Pat. Sect.)
*PRACTICE AREAS: Patent; Intellectual Property.
**Schneider, Eric A.** .................. '54 '80 C.112 B.A. L.1068 J.D. [Anderson,M.&C.]
*PRACTICE AREAS: Personal Injury Defense; Business Torts; Construction Litigation.
Schneider, Gary M. .................. '50 '76 C.112 B.A. L.1095 J.D. 12100 Wilshire Blvd.
Schneider, Jenny ........................... '66 '92 C.112 B.A. L.426 J.D. 555 S. Flower St.
**Schneider, Rochelle J.** ... '51 '79 C.112 B.A. L.809 J.D. Staff Coun., Hughes Aircraft Co.
*LANGUAGES: Spanish, French and Italian.
**Schneider, Scott A.** .................. '63 '89 C&L.352 B.A., J.D. [Ⓐ Gaims,W.W.&E.]
**Schneider, Spencer A.** .................. '69 '94 C&L.112 B.A., J.D. [Ⓐ Daniels,B.&F.]⊙
**Schneider, Steven M., (A Professional Corporation)**, (AV) '48 '73
C.188 B.S. L.309 J.D. [Mitchell,S.&K.]
*PRACTICE AREAS: Labor Law; Litigation; Employment Discrimination Law; Litigation; Wrongful Discharge Litigation.
Schneider, Stuart I. ...................... '56 '82 C.112 B.A. L.426 J.D. [Levin,S.C.&S.]
**Schneider, Wendy L.** ...................... '67 '95 C.945 B.A. L.1068 J.D. [Ⓐ Robie&M.]
*LANGUAGES: Italian and French.
*PRACTICE AREAS: Civil Litigation.
Schneirow, Burton J. ........................ '32 '68 C.112 B.A. L.426 J.D. Dep. Dist. Atty.
**Schnitzer, Alan M** ............ '59 '87 C.112 B.A. L.426 J.D. [Ⓐ Harrington,F.D.&C.]
*LANGUAGES: French and German.
*PRACTICE AREAS: Litigation; Products Liability Law; Medical Malpractice Law.
**Schnitzer, Martin J.**, (AV) ..... '28 '53 C.112 B.A. L.1068 LL.B. [Ⓑ McDermott,W.&E.]
*PRACTICE AREAS: Alternative Dispute Resolution; Health Care; Insurance.
Schoch, Edward D. .................. '43 '75 C.813 B.S. L.426 J.D. 8009 Kentwood Ave.
**Schoenberg, E. Randol** ................ '66 '91 C.674 A.B. L.800 J.D. [Ⓐ Katten M.&Z.]
*PRACTICE AREAS: Litigation.
Schoenberg, E. Randol ............. '66 '91 C.674 A.B. L.800 J.D. 1999 Ave. of the Stars
Schoenberg, Ronald R. ............................ '37 '65 C.602 A.B. L.1066 LL.B. Mun. Ct. J.
**Schoenburg, Patrick S.** .............................................. '65 '92 L.800 [Ⓐ Dewey B.]
Schoenburg, Robert B. ........ '36 '72 C.1075 B.S. L.990 J.D. Legal Div., Dept. of Transp.
**Schoenfield, James R.**, (AV) ............ '51 '76 C.112 B.A. L.1068 J.D. [J.R.Schoenfield]

**Schoenfield, James R., A Professional Corporation, (AV)**
**1801 Century Park East, Suite 2400, 90067**
**Telephone: 310-556-9605 FAX: 310-551-2814**
**James R. Schoenfield.**
**Business Transactions, Licensing, Real Estate and Entertainment Law.**
***See Professional Biographies, LOS ANGELES, CALIFORNIA***

**Schoenholz, William** ...................... '55 '81 C.112 B.A. L.800 J.D. [Katz,H.S.&K.]
*PRACTICE AREAS: Real Estate; Commercial; Secured Transactions; Corporate.
**Schoenleber, Michael W.** .......... '49 '80 C.813 B.A. L.1068 J.D. [Ⓐ Korshak,K.K.&S.]
*LANGUAGES: Spanish.
*PRACTICE AREAS: Immigration and Naturalization.
**Scholl, Robert R.** .................. '46 '81 C.846 B.A. L.809 J.D. [Patterson,R.L.G.&J.]
**Scholl, Wendy Anne** .................. '67 '92 C.112 B.A. L.426 J.D. [Ⓐ Hawkins,S.L.&B.]
**Schollenberger, Julia** .................. '57 '87 C.1077 B.A. L.1068 J.D. [Ⓐ Hooper,L.&B.]
*PRACTICE AREAS: Health Care Law.
Scholnick, Eric Nils ............................ '55 '81 C.112 B.A. L.93 J.D. [Lewis&S.]
Scholnick, Seymour A. .......... '25 '54 C.696 B.S. L.276 J.D. 1906 S. Roxbury Dr. (Pat.)
**Scholtz, Kenneth P.** .............. '38 '64 C.111 B.S. L.1066 LL.B. [Quan,C.K.Y.S.&H.]
*PRACTICE AREAS: Administrative Law; Business; Commercial; Insurance; Real Estate Litigation.
**Scholtz, Michael W.** ............ '64 '92 C.800 B.A. L.1066 J.D. [Ⓐ Greenberg G.F.C.&M.]
*PRACTICE AREAS: Bankruptcy; Commercial Law.
**Scholtz, Nina E.** ........................ '67 '92 C.112 B.A. L.1066 J.D. [Ⓐ Mayer,B.&P.]
**Schomer, Scott P.** .................. '62 '90 C.932 B.S. L.94 J.D. [Ⓐ Allen,M.L.G.&M.]
*PRACTICE AREAS: Commercial Litigation.
**Schonbuch, Michael N.** .................. '65 '90 C.1044 B.A. L.94 J.D. [Ⓐ Daniels,B.&F.]
Schooler, John T. ............................................ '51 '80 C.112 B.A. L.1136 J.D. I.R.S.
**Schoor, Charles D.** .................. '47 '75 C.659 B.S. L.800 J.D. [Hughes H.&R.]
*PRACTICE AREAS: Bankruptcy; Receiverships; Real Property and Business Litigation.

**Schoth, Karl W., & Associates**
**(See Pasadena)**

Schotland, Marvin I. '47 '73 C&L.150 B.A., J.D.
(adm. in OH; not adm. in CA) Exec. V.P., Jewish Community Found. of Greater L.A.
**Schrader, David L.** ...................... '62 '90 C.205 B.S. L.94 J.D. [Ⓐ Brobeck,P.&H.]
*PRACTICE AREAS: Litigation.
**Schreck, Cheryl L.** ...................... '59 '85 C.880 B.A. L.838 J.D. [Musick,P.&G.]
*PRACTICE AREAS: Labor and Employment.
**Schreiber, Edwin C.**, (AV) .............. '43 '67 C.112 B.A. L.1068 J.D. [Schreiber&S.]
*REPORTED CASES: Cadillac-Fairview California, Inc. v. Dow Chemical Company, 840 F.2d 691 (9th cir 1988) (Client - Shell Oil Company); Klotz v. United States, 602 F.2d 921 (9th cir 1979); NLRB v. Big Bear Supermarket, 640 F.2d 924 (9th cir 1980) cert denied 449 U.S. 919; Benefield v. Exxon Shipping Co., 959 F.2d 805 (9th cir 1922); Davis v. Air Technical Industries, (1978) 22 Cal. 3d 1.
**Schreiber, Jeffrey D.** .............. '53 '83 C.878 B.S. L.1358 J.D. [Ⓐ Tuverson&H.]⊙

**Schreiber, Mark**
**(See Encino)**

**Schreiber & Schreiber, Inc., (AV)**
**Suite 401, 16501 Ventura Boulevard (Encino), 91436**
**Telephone: 818-789-2577 Fax: 818-789-3391**
**Edwin C. Schreiber;—Robert G. Klein.**
**Civil and Appellate Practice. Corporate, Business, Finance, Real Estate, Environmental, Tax, and Exempt Organizations, Estate Planning, Trust and Probate Law.**
**Representative Clients: Shell Oil Co.; Nature's Best; Richard S. Staley Racing Stables; Perceptronics, Inc.; Acutek Adhesive Specialities; California Truck Trailer Finance Co.; Western Diesel, Inc.; All Post, Inc.**

Schreier, Douglas B. .................. '59 '84 C.800 B.S. L.1066 J.D. 1840 Century Park E.
**Schreier, James S.** .............. '50 '75 C.477 B.A. L.976 J.D. [Christensen,M.F.J.G.W.&S.]
*PRACTICE AREAS: Civil Litigation.
**Schreier, Konrad F., III** .......... '55 '95 C.800 B.S./B.A. L.426 J.D. [Ⓐ Brobeck,P.&H.]
*PRACTICE AREAS: Financial Services; Insolvency; Secured Transactions.
Schreiner, Steven P. ........................ '57 '86 C.112 B.A. L.770 J.D. Dep. Dist. Atty.
**Schreiner, Urban J.**, (BV) .............. '31 '59 C.197 A.B. L.1068 J.D. [Pircher,N.&M.]
*PRACTICE AREAS: Municipal Bond Law; Finance Law.
**Schrieffer, Paul K.** ........................ '65 '90 C.112 B.A. L.809 J.D. [Ⓐ Bottum&F.]

CAA334P

**Schroder, Karie E.** ... '63 '88 C.112 B.A. L.426 J.D. [Ⓐ Parker S.]
*PRACTICE AREAS: Insurance Defense.
**Schroeder, Beth Ackerman** ... '59 '85 C.966 B.A. L.1068 J.D. [Ⓐ Silver&F.]
*PRACTICE AREAS: Management Employment Relations Law; Labor Law; General Business Litigation.
**Schroeder, Bill E.**, (AV) ... '42 '67 C.813 B.A. L.1066 LL.B. [Baker&H.]
*PRACTICE AREAS: Litigation.
**Schroeder, Douglas W.** ... '65 '88 L.1137 J.D. [Ⓐ Dwyer,D.B.&B.]
*TRANSACTIONS: Trial of in Re December 7, 1987, Air Crash Cases.
*PRACTICE AREAS: Tort Defense; Civil Appeals; Products Liability; Insurance Coverage; Construction Litigation.
**Schroeder, J. Conrad** ... '66 '92 C.800 B.A. L.861 J.D. [Ⓐ Kirtland&P.]
**Schroeder, Robert A.**, (AV) '42 '69 C.158 B.S. L.188 J.D.
[Pretty,S.&P.] (See Pat. Sect.)
*PRACTICE AREAS: Patents; Trademarks; Copyrights; Unfair Competition; Litigation.
**Schroeder, Stephanie Ann** ... '63 '91 C.112 B.A. L.800 J.D. [Ⓐ Cox,C.&N.]
*PRACTICE AREAS: Commercial Litigation.
**Schroeter, Rudolf H.**, (AV) ... '32 '64 L.809 J.D. [Lord,B.&B.]
*PRACTICE AREAS: Product Liability Litigation; Toxic Tort Litigation; Insurance Coverage Litigation; General Litigation.
Schube, Peter H. '59 '87 C.918 B.A. L.569 J.D.
(adm. in NY; not adm. in CA) 4911 Ben Ave., Valley Village
**Schuchard, Robert L.** ... '52 '77 C.813 B.A. L.770 J.D. [Musick,P.&G.]
*PRACTICE AREAS: Healthcare; Hospitals; Corporate Law; Mergers, Acquisitions and Divestitures.

**Schuchman, Alan, Law Offices of '47 '76 C.415 B.A. L.1009 J.D.**
**1901 Avenue of the Stars 20th Floor, 90067**
**Telephone: 310-556-2889 Fax: 310-556-0065**
**Personal Injury, Medical Malpractice, Products Liability, Civil Litigation, Family Law.**
*See Professional Biographies, LOS ANGELES, CALIFORNIA*

Schuck, Edwin G., Jr. ... '44 '71 C&L.178 B.S., J.D. 355 S. Grand Ave.
Schuele, Donna C. ... '57 '85 C.930 B.A. L.1066 J.D. Whittier Coll. Sch. of Law
**Schufreider, Charles J.**, (AV) ... '45 '70 C.597 B.A. L.339 J.D. [Barton,K.&O.]
*PRACTICE AREAS: Trial Practice; Employment Law; Commercial Banking Litigation; Professional Liability Defense; Insurance Coverage.
Schuit, Robert J. ... '54 '79 C.112 B.A. L.809 J.D. Dep. Dist. Atty.
Schulcz, Fred E. ... '58 '85 C.766 B.A. L.464 J.D. 3550 Wilshire Blvd.
Schuler, Jack M. ... '51 '79 C.1077 B.A. L.809 J.D. 3435 Wilshire Blvd.
Schuller, Earl ... '30 '62 L.809 LL.B. 8317 W. Fourth St.‡
Schulman, David I. ... '51 '79 C.813 B.A. L.1068 J.D. Dep. City Atty.
**Schulman, George E., (A Professional Corporation)** '47 '72
C.994 B.A. L.569 J.D. [Danning,G.D.&K.]
*PRACTICE AREAS: Litigation; Receivership Law; Bankruptcy Law; Antitrust Law; Trade Regulation Law.
Schulman, Irwin ... '34 '60 C.112 A.B. L.1068 LL.B. Legal Div., Dept. of Transp.

**Schulman, J. Brin, (AV) '34 '59 C.112 B.A. L.800 J.D.**
**10866 Wilshire Boulevard Suite 970 Westwood Place, 90024**
**Telephone: 310-234-1933 Fax: 310-234-1943**
**General Civil, Criminal, Trial and Appellate Practice in all State and Federal Courts. Business, Commercial, Entertainment, Real Estate, Conservatorship, Trust and Probate Litigation. White Collar Criminal Defense, Organ Transplantation and Family Law.**
*See Professional Biographies, LOS ANGELES, CALIFORNIA*

**Schulman, Janie F.** ... '62 '87 C.112 A.B. L.1066 J.D. [Morrison&F.]
*PRACTICE AREAS: Labor and Employment Law.
**Schulman, Michael T.** ... '55 '80 C.893 B.A. L.178 J.D. [Wolf,R.&S.]
*PRACTICE AREAS: Corporate Law; Securities; Entertainment Law.
**Schulman, Robert S.**, (AV) ... '41 '67 C&L.705 A.B., J.D. [Crosby,H.R.&M.]
*PRACTICE AREAS: Commercial Litigation; Insurance and Reinsurance.
**Schultz, Daniel J.** ... '56 '89 C.870 B.S. L.966 J.D. [Troop M.S.&P.]
*PRACTICE AREAS: Insurance Coverage Litigation.
**Schultz, David Keith** ... '65 '90 C.112 B.A. L.426 J.D. [Ⓐ Grace,S.C.&S.]
*PRACTICE AREAS: Insurance Defense Law; Product Liability Law; Insurance Coverage Law; Professional Liability Law; Appellate Law.
**Schultz, Glori J.** ... '70 '95 C.477 B.S. L.800 J.D. [Ⓐ Paul,H.J.&W.]
Schultz, Joel R. ... '36 '67 C.659 B.S. L.426 LL.B. P.O. Box 64243
**Schultz, Robert B.** ... '47 '83 C.33 B.S. L.107 J.D. [Mendes&M.]
**Schultz, Steven Mark** ... '62 '87 C.112 B.A. L.1068 J.D. [Gibson,D.&C.]
**Schultz, Thomas A.** ... '65 '90 C.112 B.A. L.426 J.D. [Harney]
*PRACTICE AREAS: Civil Trial; Products Liability Law; Medical Malpractice Law.
**Schultz, Wendy E.** ... '63 '90 C.668 B.A. L.426 J.D. [Ⓐ Lynberg&W.]
Schumann, Elena Freshman ... '59 '84 C.112 B.A. L.426 J.D. 6151 W. Century Blvd.
**Schunk, Eric H.** ... '55 '81 C.276 B.S. L.1068 J.D. [Milbank,T.H.&M.]
Schupler, Robert J. ... '57 '83 C.223 B.S. L.809 J.D. 9255 Sunset Blvd.
Schur, Dara L. ... '53 '79 C.429 B.A. L.1066 J.D. Western Ctr. on Law & Poverty, Inc.
**Schuster, John S.** ... '64 '89 C.112 A.B. L.1065 J.D. [Ⓐ Howrey&S.]
*PRACTICE AREAS: White Collar Criminal Defense; Commercial Litigation.
Schuster, Robert J. ... '43 '68 C&L.966 B.S., J.D. 11150 Santa Monica Blvd.
**Schutz, Scott M.** ... '59 '86 C&L.878 B.S., J.D. [Kirtland&P.]
**Schuyler, Rob R., A Professional Corporation**, (AV) '32 '58
C.800 B.A. L.477 J.D. [Mihaly,S.&M.]
*LANGUAGES: French.
*PRACTICE AREAS: International Business Clients doing Business in United States and Europe; Visa and Immigration Law; Trial Practice; Estate Planning; Airline Law.

**Schwab, Douglas B. '44 '70 C.951 B.A. L.309 J.D.**
**11845 West Olympic Boulevard, Suite 1000, 90064**
**Telephone: 310-444-5929 FAX: 310-312-8189**
**Civil Litigation, Health Care, Business, Securities and Real Estate.**
*See Professional Biographies, LOS ANGELES, CALIFORNIA*

**Schwab, Richard J.** ... '51 '76 C.112 B.A. L.426 J.D. [Ⓐ L.B.Trygstad]
**Schwaber, Steven A.**, (AV) ... '42 '69 C.112 B.A. L.426 J.D. [Angel&N.]
*PRACTICE AREAS: Bankruptcy; Receiverships.
Schwappach, Nancy S. ... '61 '87 C.170 B.A. L.893 J.D. Asst. Gen. Coun., Roll Intl. Corp.
Schwarcz, David R. ... '63 '89 C&L.978 B.A., J.D. [Schwarcz&Y.]
Schwarcz & Yoshino ... 2040 Avenue of the Stars, Suite 400
**Schwartz, Alan U.**, (AV) ... '33 '57 C.188 B.A. L.976 LL.B. [Manatt,P.&P.]
*PRACTICE AREAS: Entertainment; Financing.
**Schwartz, Arnold W.**, (AV) ... '45 '74 C.1044 B.S. L.809 J.D. [Mazursky,S.&A.]
*PRACTICE AREAS: Products Liability Law; Major Personal Injury; Insurance Bad Faith Law; Business Torts; Professional Liability Law.
Schwartz, Bradley D. ... '59 '85 C.763 B.S. L.1049 J.D. 333 S. Grand Ave.
Schwartz, Charles H., (AV) '35 '62 C.223 B.S.E.E. L.273 J.D.
5900 Wilshire Blvd. (Pat.)
Schwartz, David S. ... '59 '87 C&L.976 B.A., J.D. ACLU
Schwartz, David S. ... '32 '65 C.24 B.A. L.800 J.D. 6222 Wilshire Blvd.
**Schwartz, Douglas W.** ... '60 '85 C.674 A.B. L.813 J.D. [Ⓐ Kopple&K.]
**Schwartz, Elan R.** ... '69 '94 C.37 B.A. L.464 J.D. [Ⓐ Danning,G.D.&K.]
*PRACTICE AREAS: Bankruptcy.
Schwartz, Francis ... '17 '41 C&L.494 B.S., LL.B. 11755 Wilshire Blvd.
Schwartz, Harold D. ... '19 '54 C.112 B.A. L.426 LL.B. 1214 S. Westgate
Schwartz, Herbert E., (AV) ... '36 '64 C.112 B.S. L.1068 LL.B. [Schwartz&S.]
Schwartz, Jack L. ... '51 '75 C.1044 B.A. L.904 J.D. 11901 Santa Monica Blvd.
Schwartz, Justin ... '63 '89 C.918 B.A. L.1065 J.D. Ste. 655, 5750 Wilshire Blvd.
**Schwartz, Karen L.** ... '51 '86 C.1079 B.A. L.990 J.D. [Ⓐ Sedgwick,D.M.&A.]
Schwartz, Lawrence I. ... '42 '66 C.112 B.A. L.1068 LL.B. 12424 Wilshire Blvd.
Schwartz, Mark R. ... '48 '79 C.94 B.A. L.809 J.D. 2049 Century Park E., 11th Fl.
**Schwartz, Marlene R.** ... '— '93 C.645 B.S. L.904 J.D. [Ⓐ Manatt,P.&P.]
*PRACTICE AREAS: Health Law.
**Schwartz, Martin S.**, (AV) ... '35 '61 C.563 B.B.A. L.569 LL.B. [Ⓒ Belin R.&B.]
Schwartz, Merton L. ... '25 '51 C.112 L.809 LL.B. 10575 Lindbrook Dr.‡
Schwartz, Patricia Gorner ... '40 '66 C.112 B.A. L.1068 LL.B. Comr., Mun. Ct.
**Schwartz, Peter**, (AV) ... '57 '83 C.112 B.A. L.426 J.D. [Gabriel,H.&P.]
*REPORTED CASES: Berg v. Leason, 32 F.3d 422 (9th Cir, 1994); Trulis v. Barton, 67 F.3d 779 (9th Cir. 1995); Taub v. First State, 44 Cal.App.4th 811 (1995).
Schwartz, Randall B., (BV) ... '53 '78 C.112 B.A. L.426 J.D. 10866 Wilshire Blvd.
**Schwartz, Robert David** ... '64 '93 C.112 B.S. L.464 J.D. [Ⓐ Anderson,A.L.&G.]
**Schwartz, Robert M.**, (AV) ... '59 '84 C.112 B.A. L.800 J.D. [O'Melveny&M.]
*PRACTICE AREAS: Litigation; Entertainment and Intellectual Property Litigation.
Schwartz, Sheri M. ... '68 '95 [Ⓐ Seider&R.]
Schwartz, Stephen L. ... '40 '66 C&L.800 J.D. 1901 Ave. of the Stars
Schwartz, Stephen M., (AV) ... '43 '73 C.1077 B.A. L.426 J.D. 9721 Cashio St.
Schwartz, Steven H. ... '55 '80 C.1077 B.A. L.1049 J.D. 1900 Ave. of the Stars
Schwartz, Stewart J. ... '52 '77 C.1077 B.S. L.1066 J.D. 1880 Century Park E.
**Schwartz, Susan E.** ... '62 '94 C.645 B.A. L.426 J.D. [Ⓐ Paul,H.J.&W.]
Schwartz, Theodore F. '35 '62 C&L.910 LL.B.
11755 Wilshire Blvd. (⊙Clayton, Mo. & San Fran., Calif.)
Schwartz, Victoria Winkler ... '59 '89 C.1049 B.A. L.426 J.D. 221 N. Figueroa St.
Schwartz, William H. ... '48 '78 C.112 B.A. L.809 J.D. Dep. Dist. Atty.
Schwartz & Siegel, (AV) ... 11755 Wilshire Blvd.

**Schwartz, Steinsapir, Dohrmann & Sommers, (AV)**
**6300 Wilshire Boulevard, Suite 2000, 90048⊙**
**Telephone: 213-655-4700 Fax: 213-655-4488**
**Members of Firm: Laurence D. Steinsapir; Robert M. Dohrmann; Richard D. Sommers; Stuart Libicki; Michael R. Feinberg; Michael D. Four; Margo A. Feinberg; Henry M. Willis; Dennis J. Murphy; D. William Heine, Jr.; Claude Cazzulino; Dolly M. Gee; William T. Payne (Resident at Pittsburgh, Pennsylvania Office). Associates: Brenda E. Sutton; Erika A. Zucker.**
**Labor Law, Trust and Employee Benefit Law (ERISA). Libel and Slander, General Civil and Trial Practice in all State and Federal Courts and Arbitrations, Real Estate Law, Credit Unions, Nonprofit Corporations, Political Campaign Finance Law.**
**Pittsburgh, Pennsylvania Office: 3600 One Oxford Centre. Telephone: 412-456-2008. Fax: 412-456-2020.**
*See Professional Biographies, LOS ANGELES, CALIFORNIA*

**Schwartz, Wisot & Wilson, LLP**
**(See Beverly Hills)**

Schwartzman, Jack, (AV) ... '32 '59 C.112 B.S. L.1068 LL.B. 10730 Bellagio Rd.
**Schwarz, David A.** ... '60 '92 C.178 B.A. L.228 J.D. [Ⓐ Irell&M.]
*LANGUAGES: French.
**Schwarzmann, Michael D.** ... '63 '95 C.800 B.S. L.426 J.D. [Ⓐ Arter&H.]
*PRACTICE AREAS: Bankruptcy; Corporate Reorganization; Creditors Rights.
**Schweikert, Claudia** ... '71 '95 C.228 A.B. L.813 J.D. [Ⓐ Hennigan,M.&B.]
*LANGUAGES: Spanish and French.
*PRACTICE AREAS: Litigation.
**Schwenk, Steven X.** '57 '89 C.831 B.A. L.659 J.D.
[Ⓒ Celebrezze&W.] (⊙San Francisco)
Schwerdtfeger, Michael B. ... '65 '89 C.800 B.S.Ch.E. L.1068 J.D. ARCO
**Schwigen, Leonard R.** ... '61 '93 C.927 B.A. L.352 J.D. [Ⓐ Gabriel,H.&P.]

**Schwimmer, Arthur E., (AV) '41 '64 C.178 A.B. L.1009 LL.B.**
**2049 Century Park East, Suite 1800, 90067**
**Telephone: 310-277-8448**
**Appellate Practice in State and Federal Courts.**
*See Professional Biographies, LOS ANGELES, CALIFORNIA*

Schwimmer, Bertram '10 '32 C.569 L.1009 LL.B.
(adm. in NY; not adm. in CA) 2300 Fox Hills Dr.‡
**Schwimmer, John A.** ... '58 '83 C.103 B.A. L.1066 J.D. [Alschuler G.&P.]
**Scoles, Patricia M.** ... '58 '88 C.1077 B.A. L.426 J.D. [Ⓐ Manning,M.&W.]
Scoll, David L. ... '48 '76 C.101 B.A. L.800 J.D. First Interstate Bank
**Scollan, Francis N.** ... '69 '96 C.112 B.A. L.1066 J.D. [Ⓐ Allen,M.L.G.&M.]
*PRACTICE AREAS: Litigation.
**Scolney, Peter N.**, (AV) ... '48 '79 C.112 B.A. L.425 J.D. [Weiss,S.S.D.&S.]
*PRACTICE AREAS: Litigation.
**Scott, A. Timothy** ... '52 '77 C&L.813 A.B., J.D. [Heller E.W.&M.]
*PRACTICE AREAS: State and Federal Income Taxation.
Scott, Francis E. ... '42 '68 C&L.426 B.S., J.D. Sr. Dep. Co. Coun.
**Scott, J. Timothy** ... '57 '85 C.754 B.S. L.262 J.D. [Ⓒ Morrison&F.]
*PRACTICE AREAS: Corporate Finance; Corporate; Real Estate.
Scott, Jack D., (AV) ... '25 '58 C&L.800 B.S., J.D. 1000 Wilshire Blvd.
**Scott, Jeff E.** ... '61 '86 C.918 B.A. L.477 J.D. [Goldberg&S.]
*PRACTICE AREAS: Commercial Litigation; Entertainment Litigation; Real Estate Litigation.
Scott, Jill Baran ... '60 '86 C.788 A.B. L.910 J.D. 777 S. Figueroa St., 10th Fl.
Scott, John H., (AV) ... '47 '73 C.112 A.B. L.800 J.D. Dep. Pub. Def.
**Scott, Myrl R.**, (AV) ... '28 '56 C.112 A.B. L.813 J.D. [Ⓒ Sheppard,M.R.&H.]
*PRACTICE AREAS: Corporate Law; Real Estate Law.
Scott, Neale ... '22 '55 C.112 B.A. L.426 LL.B. 6300 Wilshire Blvd.
Scott, Peter ... '38 '65 C&L.846 B.A., LL.B. 4841 Bonvue Ave.
**Scott, Robert J., Jr.** ... '61 '90 C.112 A.B. L.770 J.D. [Prestholt,K.F.&V.]⊙
*PRACTICE AREAS: General Civil Litigation; Insurance Coverage; Insurance Bad Faith.
Scott, Terrence V. ... '55 '78 C.112 B.A. L.1068 J.D. 9119 Sunset Blvd.
Scott, W. Roger ... '51 '78 C.385 A.B. L.150 J.D. 1125 Oban Dr.
**Scott, William M., IV** ... '60 '85 C.197 A.B. L.982 J.D. [Sheppard,M.R.&H.]
*PRACTICE AREAS: Commercial Law and Banking Law.
**Scoular, Robert F.**, (AV) ... '42 '68 C&L.734 B.S.A.E., J.D. [Sonnenschein N.&R.]
*PRACTICE AREAS: Litigation; Government Contracts Litigation; Intellectual Property Law.
**Scouton, Roger O.** ... '51 '77 C.584 B.A. L.585 J.D. [Dale,B.&H.]
**Scouton, Susan R.** ... '64 '91 C.426 B.A. L.809 J.D. [Dale,B.&H.]

**Scroggie, Robin R. '57 '83 C&L.352 B.A., J.D.**
**333 South Grand Avenue, 37th Floor, 90071**
**Telephone: 213-620-9576 Facsimile: 213-625-1832**
***PRACTICE AREAS: Criminal Law.**
**Criminal Trial and Appellate Practice in all State and Federal Courts.**
*See Professional Biographies, LOS ANGELES, CALIFORNIA*

**Scullion, Jennifer R.** ... '— '95 C.94 B.A. L.112 J.D. [Ⓐ Munger,T.&O.]
*PRACTICE AREAS: Litigation.
Scully, Marcia '48 '78 C.477 B.G.S. L.426 J.D.
Dep. Gen. Coun., Metropolitan Water Dist. of Southern Calif.
**Sczudlo, Paul A.**, (AV) ... '55 '80 C.976 B.A. L.1066 J.D. [Loeb&L.]
*PRACTICE AREAS: Taxation; International Law.
Seaborne, John K. '23 '51 C&L.966 Ph.B., LL.B.
(adm. in WI; not adm. in CA) O & R Engines, Inc.

**Seal, Benjamin H., II**, (AV) .......... '39 '75 C.1077 B.A. L.1095 J.D. [Murchison&C.]
*PRACTICE AREAS: General Insurance Defense Litigation.
**Searby, Bruce Hamilton** .............. '68 '96 C.674 B.A. L.477 J.D. [[A] Munger,T.&O.]
*LANGUAGES: Spanish.
*PRACTICE AREAS: Litigation.
Searcy, David Joe .................. '33 '85 C.1097 B.A. L.398 J.D. Ref., L.A. Supr. Ct.‡
Searcy, Harley A. '49 '75 C.112 B.A. L.813 J.D.
Dep. Gen. Coun., Metropolitan Water Dist. of Southern Calif.
**Searcy, Marshall M.** .................. '68 '93 C.846 B.A. L.309 J.D. [[A] Quinn E.U.&O.]
Searle, Peter J. .................... '59 '87 C.1109 B.A. L.809 J.D. [[A] Chase,R.D.&B.]
**Sears, Craig F.** .................. '49 '75 C.679 B.S. L.800 J.D. [Harrington,F.D.&C.]
*PRACTICE AREAS: Personal Injury Defense Law; Products Liability Law; Construction Defects Law; Professional Negligence Law.
**Sears, Marvin**, (AV) .................. '27 '53 C.569 A.B. L.309 LL.B. [Proskauer R.G.&M.]
*PRACTICE AREAS: Corporate; Real Estate; Entertainment Law.
Sears, William T. .................... '54 '88 C.871 B.S. L.813 J.D. 221 N. Figueroa St.
**Seaton, Barry C.** .................. '62 '87 C.112 B.A. L.800 J.D. [[A] Small L.&K.]
*PRACTICE AREAS: Trademark and Copyright.
**Seaver, Laura Stern**, (AV) .................. '50 '75 C.112 B.A. L.813 J.D. [Seaver&G.]
*PRACTICE AREAS: Estate Planning; Charitable Organizations.
**Seaver, R. Carlton**, (AV) .................. '47 '75 C.674 A.B. L.813 J.D. [Seaver&G.]
*PRACTICE AREAS: Business Law; Civil Litigation; Probate and Trust Litigation.
Seaver, Richard C. .......... '22 '50 C.668 A.B. L.1066 J.D. Chmn. of the Bd., Hydril Co.

**Seaver & Gill, LLP, (AV)**
**444 South Flower Street, Suite 2300, 90071**
**Telephone: 213-689-4700 Facsimile: 213-689-0330**
**Members of Firm: Michael J. Gill; Laura Stern Seaver; R. Carlton Seaver.**
**General Business Practice, Probate and Trust Administration, Conservatorship Law, Probate, Trust, Conservatorship and Elder Abuse Litigation, Civil Litigation, Estate Planning and Charitable Organizations.**

***See Professional Biographies, LOS ANGELES, CALIFORNIA***

Sebastian, Armen .................... '60 '91 C.1097 B.A. L.809 J.D. 210 S. Spring St.

**Sebghati, Saviz, Law Offices of '61 '86 C.112 A.B. L.94 J.D.**
**Wilshire Bundy Plaza, 12121 Wilshire Boulevard Suite 401, 90025**
**Telephone: 310-207-9706 Facsimile: 310-826-6696**
***LANGUAGES: Persian.**
**Business, Corporate and Real Estate Law.**

***See Professional Biographies, LOS ANGELES, CALIFORNIA***

**Secof, Howard S.**, (AV) .................... '53 '78 C.112 B.A. L.426 J.D. [Honn&S.]
*PRACTICE AREAS: Litigation; Torts; Business Law; Real Property; Entertainment Law.
**Sedach, Steven W.** .................. '59 '87 C.112 B.A. L.464 J.D. [[A] Veatch,C.G.&N.]
Sedgwick, Mary A. .................... '60 '87 C.1077 B.S. L.426 J.D. Asst. U.S. Atty.

**Sedgwick, Detert, Moran & Arnold, (AV)**
**A Partnership including Professional Corporations**
**801 South Figueroa Street, 18th Floor, 90017-5556⊙**
**Telephone: 213-426-6900 Fax: 213-426-6921**
**Email: E-Mail@SDMA.com**
**Members of Firm: Lane J. Ashley; David M. Humiston; N. David Lyons; Michael R. Velladao; Michael R. Davisson; Edward T. Stork; T. Emmet Thornton; Craig S. Barnes; Robert F. Helfing; Thomas B. McNutt; Kristin E. Meredith; Elliott D. Olson; William A. Boeck; Donna D. Melby; Tod I. Zuckerman; Rebecca R. Weinreich. Special Counsel: Mark A. Graf; John M. Raders; Jeffrey M. Smith; Bruce G. Shanahan; Lawrence E. Picone; Jordon E. Harriman; Kathryn M. Trepinski; James J. S. Holmes; Gary K. Kwasniewski; Charles F. Peterson; Kathleen Caswell Vance. Associates: Susan F. Hannan; Bruce S. Bolger; Janice Rourke Hugener; Margret G. Parke; Karen L. Schwartz; Jeanette L. Viau; Lisa A. Clark; H. Alix Evans; Douglas L. Stuart; Richard A. Janisch; Anthony J. Parascandola; Marco P. Ferreira; Birgit A. Huber; Amand K. Mines; John W. Mustafa, II; Thomas A. Delaney; Steven D. Di Saia; Jay E. Framson; Wynn Cross Kaneshiro; Celia D. Moutes; Gregory J. Newman; Tracey N. Broadhead; Victor A. Bullock; Spencer A. Krieger; Brandon D. Smith; James Nelson; Timothy A. Pico; Eric L. Tanezaki.**
**General Civil Litigation and Trial Practice. Aviation, Business, Construction, Directors and Officers Liability, Employment and Labor, Entertainment, Environmental, Fidelity and Surety, General Liability, Health Care, Pharmaceuticals, Insurance and Reinsurance, Intellectual Property, Products Liability and Professional Malpractice.**
**San Francisco, California Office: 16th Floor, One Embarcadero Center. Telephone: 415-781-7900. Cable Address: "Sedma". Fax: 415-781-2635.**
**Irvine, California Office: 3 Park Plaza, 17th Floor. Telephone: 714-852-8200. Fax: 714-852-8282.**
**New York, New York Office: 41st Floor, 59 Maiden Lane. Telephone: 212-422-0202. Fax: 212-422-0925.**
**Chicago, Illinois Office: The Rookery Building, Seventh Floor, 209 South La Salle Street. Telephone: 312-641-9050. Fax: 312-641-9530.**
**London, England Office: Lloyds Avenue House, 6 Lloyds Avenue, EC3N 3AX. Telephone: 0171-929-1829. Fax: 0171-929-1808. Telex: 927037.**
**Zurich, Switzerland Office: Spluegenstrasse 3, CH-8002. Telephone: 011-411-201-1730. Fax: 011-411-201-4404.**

***See Professional Biographies, LOS ANGELES, CALIFORNIA***

**Sedin, Tammy L.** .................... '58 '86 C.800 B.A. L.1065 J.D. [Houlé&S.]
*PRACTICE AREAS: Public Entity Defense; Insurance Defense; Personal Injury Litigation.
**Sedlik, Gary Steven** .................. '68 '95 C.478 B.A. L.904 J.D. [[A] Preston G.&E.]
*LANGUAGES: Japanese and Spanish.
*REPORTED CASES: Makell v. State, 104 Md.App. 334, 656 A.2d 348 (Md. Ct. Spec. App. 1995).
*PRACTICE AREAS: Litigation.
**Sedor, Dan P.** .................... '60 '88 C.112 B.A. L.426 J.D. [[A] Jeffer,M.B.&M.]
*PRACTICE AREAS: General Business and Securities Litigation.
See, Ramona G. ............ '59 '86 C.477 B.A. L.93 J.D. 8th Fl., 515 S. Figueroa St.
Seebach, Alice A. ............ '48 '85 C&L.477 B.B.A., J.D. 633 W. 5th St., Suite 1900
**Seeberger, Matthew P.** .................. '60 '88 C.821 B.A. L.608 J.D. [Quateman&Z.]
Seeman, Stanley S. .................. '39 '72 C.1077 B.A. L.426 J.D. Dep. Dist. Atty.
**Seery, Brian J.** .................... '43 '69 C&L.724 B.A., J.D. [Musick,P.&G.]
*PRACTICE AREAS: Taxation; Tax Controversy.
**Seferian, Anthony V.** .................. '64 '89 C.659 B.A. L.1097 J.D. [[A] Hewitt&P.]
Segal, Bernard I. .................... '32 '60 C.112 B.A. L.1066 J.D. [Segal&K.]
Segal, Jay '27 '55 C.102 A.B. L.1009 LL.B.
(adm. in NY; not adm. in CA) 300 N. Los Angeles St.
**Segal, Jeffrey C.** .................... '59 '86 C.605 A.B. L.904 J.D. [Selman B.]
Segal, Jeffrey D. .................... '56 '82 C.813 B.A. L.800 J.D. [J.D.Segal]
**Segal, John L., (A Professional Corporation)** '60 '88
C.951 B.A. L.800 J.D. [[A] Mitchell,S.&K.]
*PRACTICE AREAS: Litigation; Appeals.
Segal, Lloyd M. .................. '48 '76 C.94 B.A. L.809 J.D. 11900 W. Olympic Blvd.
Segal, Martin N. .................. '34 '68 C.1097 B.S. L.809 LL.B. 5757 Wilshire Blvd.
**Segal, Milton** .................... '27 '54 C.112 A.B. L.800 J.D. [[A] Langberg,C.&D.]
**Segal, Ruth** .................... '60 '86 C.112 B.A. L.809 J.D. [Lynberg&W.]
**Segal, William D.**, (AV) .................. '34 '64 C.112 B.S. L.1066 J.D. [Simmons,R.&S.]
*PRACTICE AREAS: Corporate Law; Business Law.
Segal, Jeffrey D., A Professional Corporation .................. 10390 Santa Monica Blvd.
Segal & Klar, A Professional Corporation .................. 12400 Wilshire Blvd.
**Sege, Alan D.** .................... '66 '95 C.604 B.A. L.276 J.D. [[A] Irell&M.]
*LANGUAGES: Hebrew.
**Segel, Alvin G.** .................... '45 '71 C.94 B.A. L.178 J.D. [Irell&M.]
**Segura, Steve R.** .................. '65 '91 C.112 B.A. L.1068 J.D. [[A] Radcliff,F.&D.]
Seide, David Z. .................... '56 '84 C.659 B.A. L.569 J.D. Asst. U.S. Atty.

Seideman, Stephen A. .............. '55 '81 C.112 B.S. L.1068 J.D. 12424 Wilshire Blvd.
**Seiden, Richard F.**, (AV) .................. '49 '74 C.659 B.A. L.1066 J.D. [Foley L.W.&A.]
*PRACTICE AREAS: Corporate Law; Business Law; Health Care; Hospitals; Financing.
Seider, Dennis J., (AV) .................... '42 '67 C.112 B.A. L.1068 J.D. [Seider&R.]
Seider & Reynolds, A Law Corporation, (AV) .................. 1800 Ave. of the Stars
Seidner, Mordechai .............. '54 '80 C.831 A.B. L.365 J.D. Associated Financial Corp.
**Seifert, Norbert M.** .................. '56 '81 C.659 B.S. L.569 J.D. [Sonnenschein N.&R.]
*PRACTICE AREAS: Real Estate and Real Estate Finance.
Seigel, Anita Rose .................. '48 '73 C.112 B.A. 10434 Ravenwood Ct.
**Seigel, Benjamin S., (P.C.)**, (AV) .......... '36 '74 C.502 B.S. L.1136 J.D. [Katz,H.S.&K.]
*REPORTED CASES: In Re Confections by Sandra, Inc. 83 BR 729; In Re: Tr-3 Industries 41 BR 128.
*PRACTICE AREAS: Corporate Reorganizations; Debtor/Creditor Rights; Chapter 11 Representations; Bankruptcy; Business Reorganization.
Seigel, Darren D. .............. '66 '91 C.37 B.A. L.809 J.D. 11111 Santa Monica Blvd.
**Seigel, Karen S.** .................. '54 '92 C.112 B.A. L.424 J.D. [[B] Hill,F.&B.]
*PRACTICE AREAS: Business Litigation; Labor and Employment Law (Management); Wrongful Discharge and Discrimination Litigation.
Seigel, Mark D. '49 '76 C.623 B.S. L.37 J.D.
(adm. in OK; not adm. in CA) 10518 Holman Ave.‡
**Seigle, Laura A.** .................... '67 '94 C.309 A.B. L.976 J.D. [[A] Irell&M.]
**Seiling, Brad William** .............. '64 '89 C.276 B.S.F.S. L.1068 J.D. [Manatt,P.&P.]
*PRACTICE AREAS: Commercial Litigation; Election Law.
**Seine, Anthony D.**, (BV) .............. '38 '68 C.800 B.S. L.809 LL.B. [Veatch,C.G.&N.]
*PRACTICE AREAS: Vehicle and Homeowner's Liability; Commercial Claims; Coverage Issues; Medical Malpractice; Products Liability Defense Law.
Seinfeld, Sandra Lee .................. '56 '86 C.112 B.A. L.426 J.D. Dep. Dist. Atty.
**Seitz, Friedrich W.**, (AV) .................. '41 '72 C.800 B.A. L.809 J.D. [Murchison&C.]
*LANGUAGES: German.
*PRACTICE AREAS: Domestic and International Products Liability Litigation; Catastrophic Injury Litigation; Toxic and Environmental Law.
Seitz, Rick .................... '51 '77 C&L.426 B.A., J.D. 8421 Lincoln Blvd.
**Selan, Fred**, (AV) .................. '39 '66 C.800 B.A. L.1068 J.D. [[B] Jeffer,M.B.&M.]
*PRACTICE AREAS: General Business; Real Estate and Taxation; Start-up Companies, Finance and Operations.
**Selbak, John J.** .................... '69 '95 C.1109 B.A. L.990 J.D. [[A] Musick,P.&G.]
*PRACTICE AREAS: Insurance Coverage; Commercial Litigation; Regulatory Licensing; Professional Defense.
Selber, Bernard S. .................... '19 '42 C.113 L.800 LL.B. Supr. Ct. J.
Seledee, Craig A. .............. '51 '76 C.813 B.A. L.976 J.D. 725 S. Figueroa St., 5th Fl.
SeLegue, Roger .................. '33 '85 C.1097 B.A. L.398 J.D. 4700 Wilshire Blvd.
**Selfridge, Lance A.** .................. '56 '81 C.112 B.A. L.1068 J.D. [Lewis,D.B.&B.]
**Selgrath, Ronald J.** .................. '45 '72 C.112 A.B. L.1068 J.D. [Akre,B.&C.]
*REPORTED CASES: Beaudreau v. Superior Court 14 C 3 448, 121 CR 585; Cole v. Los Angeles Community College District 137 CR 588, 68 CA 2 26; In re. Larry P 201 CA 3 888, 247 CR 472; In re. Marianne R 113 CA 3 423, 169 CR.
*PRACTICE AREAS: Litigation; Insurance Coverage.
**Seliger, Mary A.** .................. '44 '82 C.1077 B.A. L.426 J.D. [[A] Bonne,B.M.O.&N.]
**Seligman, Craig S.** .................. '60 '90 C.197 B.A. L.809 J.D. [[A] Paul,H.J.&W.]
*PRACTICE AREAS: Corporate Law; Securities Law; Acquisitions, Divestitures and Mergers Law.
Seligman, Hyatt E. .................. '49 '77 C.112 B.A. L.426 J.D. Dep. Dist. Atty.
**Seligman, Judith R.** .................. '44 '84 C.610 B.S. L.1068 J.D. [Ruben&M.]
*PRACTICE AREAS: Family Law; Civil Litigation; Professional Liability.
Seligman, Manuel .................. '22 '48 C.112 A.B. L.800 J.D. P.O. Box 241929
**Seligman, Marc A.** .................. '57 '94 C.1044 B.S. L.1019 J.D. [[A] Chimicles,J.&T.]
*PRACTICE AREAS: Commercial Litigation; Consumer Litigation; Securities Litigation; Antitrust Litigation.
Seligman, Robert Z. ........ '51 '76 C.112 B.A. L.1068 J.D. 1900 Ave. of the Stars, 19th Fl.

**Seligmann, William A., (AV) '25 '74 C.966 B.Comm. L.1049 J.D.**
**One Wilshire Building, 624 South Grand Avenue Suite 2420, 90017**
**Telephone: 213-892-1122 Fax: 213-488-9890**
**Estate Planning, Wills, Trusts, Corporate, Tax, Corporate Organization, Mergers and Acquisitions, Qualified and Non Qualified Retirement Plans.**

***See Professional Biographies, LOS ANGELES, CALIFORNIA***

**Seligsohn, Henry N.**, (AV) .............. '39 '65 C.112 B.A. L.426 LL.B. [[A] Stone,D.&W.]
*LANGUAGES: Swedish.
*PRACTICE AREAS: Personal Injury; Legal Malpractice.
**Sellars, Kim W.** .................... '49 '89 C.112 B.A. L.426 J.D. [[A] Robie&M.]
*PRACTICE AREAS: Litigation.
**Sellers, Dawn** .................... '66 '94 C.773 B.A. L.1068 J.D. [[A] McKenna&C.]
Sellers, Dylan Karl .................. '59 '85 C.112 B.A. L.1066 J.D. 344 Delfern Ave.
Sellers, Pamela C. .................. '46 '74 C.112 B.A. L.426 J.D. Admin. J., EEOC
**Sellers, Stuart K.** .................. '54 '84 C.966 B.A. L.1136 J.D. [[A] Tharpe&H.]
Sellung, Elizabeth Abrams ..... '65 '90 C.112 B.A. L.477 J.D. 355 S. Grand Ave., 35th Fl.
**Selman, Neil H.**, (AV) .................. '49 '74 C&L.800 B.A., J.D. [Selman B.]

**Selman • Breitman, (AV) [BR]**
**11766 Wilshire Boulevard, Sixth Floor, 90025-6538⊙**
**Telephone: 310-445-0800 Fax: 310-473-2525**
**Members of Firm: Neil H. Selman; Craig R. Breitman; Robert A. Steller (Partner, San Diego Office); Alan B. Yuter; Nancy W. Shokohi; Jeffrey C. Segal; A. Scott Goldberg; Elaine K. Fresch; Nicholas Banko; Brad D. Bleichner; David L. Jones; Mark L. Jubelt; Monica Cruz Thornton; David T. Bamberger; Sterling Tao (Partner, San Francisco Office);—Lynette Klawon; Ramon Z. Bacerdo (Resident, San Francisco Office); John S. Knowlton; Murray M. Sinclair; Jeffrey A. Simmons; Mark S. Gruskin; Anthony L. Cione; Christopher J. Harrington; Sheryl W. Leichenger; Theresa Ann Loss; Jerry C. Popovich; Lisa Hannah Kahn; David H. Oken; Katy A. Nelson; Jan Long Pocaterra; Kim Karelis; Asim K. Desai; Pauline A. New; Dianne M. Costales; Eldon S. Edson; James B. Kamanski; Michael L. Mengoli; Rita H. Issagholian; Sarah F. Burke (Resident, San Diego Office); Darcy D. Jorgensen; Linda S. Wendell (Resident, San Francisco Office); Jeffrey S. Bolender; Jeffrey T. Briggs; Marcie A. Keenan; Lisa M. Dyson (Resident, San Francisco Office); Aimee Y. Wong; Grace Horoupian; Kathleen T. Deeley; Christopher A. Petrovic; Kimberly D. Allario (Resident, San Diego Office); Wendy Wen Yun Chang; Jack M. Zakariaie. Of Counsel: Thomas A. Leary (Of Counsel, San Diego Office).**
**General Civil and Trial Practice in all State and Federal Courts. Insurance, Products Liability and Toxic Substance Law.**
**Reference: City National Bank (Beverly Hills Branch).**
**San Diego, California Office: Emerald Plaza, 402 W. Broadway, Suite 400. Telephone: 619-595-4880. Facsimile: 619-595-4890.**
**San Francisco, California Office: Citicorp Center, One Sansome Street, Suite 1900. Telephone: 415-951-4646. Fax: 415-951-4676.**

***See Professional Biographies, LOS ANGELES, CALIFORNIA***

Selsky, Ira B. .................... '42 '68 C.4 B.A. L.569 LL.B. [[C] Myman,A.F.G.&R.]
**Seltman, Lee R.** .................... '68 '94 C.243 B.A. L.800 J.D. [[A] Paul,H.J.&W.]
**Seltz, Thomas P.** .................. '64 '91 C.436 B.S. L.424 J.D. [[A] Crosby,H.R.&M.]
**Seltzer, Marc I.** .................... '62 '92 C.112 B.A. L.94 J.D. [[A] Baker&H.]
*PRACTICE AREAS: Intellectual property; National and International Anticounterfeiting Enforcement and Litigation; Internet Monitoring and Enforcement.
**Seltzer, Marc M.**, (AV) .............. '47 '72 C.112 A.B. L.1068 J.D. [Corinblit&S.]
*REPORTED CASES: Wool v. Tandem Computers, Inc., 818 F.2d 1433 (9th Cir. 1987); In re ZZZZ Best Securities Litigation, 864 F.Supp. 960 (C.D. Cal. 1994); In re Corrugated Container Antitrust Litigation 752 F.2d 137 (5th Cir.), cert. denied, 473 U.S. 911 (1985); In re Taxable Municipal Bonds Litigation (1994-1995 Transfer Binder) Fed.Sec.L.Rep. (CCH) 98,405 (E.D. La. 1994).
*PRACTICE AREAS: Complex Civil Litigation; Antitrust; Securities.

**Seltzer, Maryann** '47 '72 C.112 B.A. L.809 J.D.
Asst. Corp. Secy. & Sr. Corp. Coun., Farmers Grp., Inc.
*LANGUAGES: Romanian, Hungarian and French.
*RESPONSIBILITIES: Corporate Organization; Life Insurance Operations; General Corporate.
Seltzer, Richard K., (AV) ........ '41 '68 C.112 Phar.D. L.1068 J.D. 2050 S. Beverly Dr.‡
**Selvin, Peter S.** .............................'53 '80 C.112 B.A. L.1068 J.D. [Loeb&L.]
*PRACTICE AREAS: Litigation.

**Selvin & Weiner & Weinberger, (AV)**
**A Partnership of Professional Corporations**
**12401 Wilshire Boulevard, Second Floor, 90025**
**Telephone: 310-207-1555 Fax: 310-207-3666**
**Paul P. Selvin (1917-1987); Beryl Weiner (Professional Corporation); William E. Weinberger (Professional Corporation). Associates: Kathryn M. Stanton; Darren R. Martinez; David M. De Castro. General Civil, Trial, Appellate, Administrative and Legislative Practice in all State and Federal Courts. Corporation, Commercial, Real Property, Taxation, Health Care, Libel and Slander, Estate Planning, Probate, Family and Entertainment Law.**
***See Professional Biographies, LOS ANGELES, CALIFORNIA***

Selvo, Gerald V. ................................ '47 '76 C&L.339 B.S., J.D. [De Carlo,C.&S.]
**Selwood, Pierce T.**, (AV) ..........'39 '65 C.674 A.B. L.309 LL.B. [Sheppard,M.R.&H.]
*PRACTICE AREAS: Litigation; Class Actions; RICO.
Selzer, Susan Weiss ................ '35 '75 C.112 A.B. L.1148 J.D. 634 N. Mccadden Pl.
**Semien, Ralph M.** .................'49 '92 C.1136 B.S. L.426 J.D. [🄰 Epstein B.&G.]
*PRACTICE AREAS: Labor and Employment Law; Education Law; Litigation.
**Semmel, Amy** ......................... '57 '84 C.659 B.A. L.1066 J.D. [🄰 Donfeld,K.&R.]
*LANGUAGES: Spanish.
*PRACTICE AREAS: Business Litigation; Employer/Employee Dispute Resolution; Family Law; Real Property Litigation.
**Sencer, Robert D.**.........................'61 '88 C.112 B.A. L.800 J.D. [🄰 Gelfand&G.]
*LANGUAGES: Spanish.
*PRACTICE AREAS: Products Liability Law; Litigation.
Sendowski, Michael H. ............. '54 '80 C.809 B.A. L.426 J.D. 6601 Lindenhurst St.
**Sendra, Maria** ....................... '61 '92 C.976 B.A. L.1066 J.D. [🄰 Jeffer,M.B.&M.]
*LANGUAGES: Spanish, French and Valenciano.
*PRACTICE AREAS: Corporate; Securities.
Senen, Sanford ............................ '52 '83 C.260 B.A. L.809 J.D. 6006 Wilshire Blvd.
**Senet, Theodore L.**........................'51 '78 C.112 B.A. L.426 J.D. [Gibbs,G.L.&A.]
*PRACTICE AREAS: Real Property Law; Insurance Law; Construction Law.
Senior, David A. .................. '57 '83 C.840 B.S. L.809 J.D. 1900 Ave. of the Stars
Senior, Teresa R. ........................'60 '87 C.112 B.A. L.800 J.D. 4215 Glencoe Ave.

**Seone, Richard F. '58 '94 C.1042 B.A. L.1148 J.D.**
**1801 Avenue of the Stars, Suite 640, 90067**
**Telephone: 310-788-0477 Fax: 310-788-0923**
***PRACTICE AREAS: Immigration and Naturalization; Family Law; Criminal Law.**
**Associate: David Scott Rugendorf.**
**Family Law, Immigration, Criminal and Personal Injury.**
***See Professional Biographies, LOS ANGELES, CALIFORNIA***

**Sepikas, Joseph P.** ....................... '52 '87 C.1077 B.A. L.1095 J.D. [🄰 Schell&D.]
Sepkowitz, Irv ....................'36 '63 C.112 B.S. L.1068 J.D. Universal Television (MCA)
**Serafano, Donald B.** ...................'67 '93 C.154 B.A. L.112 J.D. [🄰 Rubinstein&P.]
*PRACTICE AREAS: Civil Litigation.
**Serafine, Mary Louise** ..................'48 '92 C.705 B.A. L.976 J.D. [🄰 Chadbourne&P.]
Seretan, L. Glen ............................'— '91 C.112 B.A. L.809 J.D. Dep. Atty. Gen.
Sermons, Sylvia ......................... '54 '80 C.112 B.A. L.809 J.D. 5249 Vincent Ave.
Seror, David ..............................'50 '75 C.112 B.A. L.1188 J.D. 1879 Century Pk. E.
**Serota, Todd B.**.........................'58 '83 C.453 S.B. L.1017 J.D. [Brobeck,P.&H.] (Pat.)
*PRACTICE AREAS: Intellectual Property; Litigation; Licensing.
Serratore, Steven J. ...........'64 '89 C.763 B.A. L.770 J.D. 801 S. Figueroa St., 18th Fl.
**Serritella, Anthony P.**, (BV) ...................'51 '76 C&L.800 A.B., J.D. [Serritella&P.]
*PRACTICE AREAS: Trials; Appellate Litigation.

**Serritella & Paquette, A Professional Corporation, (BV)**
**201 North Figueroa Street, Suite 1050, 90012**
**Telephone: 213-250-1600 Facsimile: 213-250-0949**
**Anthony P. Serritella; Paul N. Paquette;—Dennis P. Riley; Gloria Cardenas Conn; Alarice M. Garcia; Ava M. Sandlin; Kenneth A. Levine.**
**Municipal Liability, Products Liability, Employment, Construction Defect and Appellate Practice.**
***See Professional Biographies, LOS ANGELES, CALIFORNIA***

**Serviss, Claudia J.** .............................'47 '92 C.562 B.A. L.1137 J.D. [🄰 Ford]
Serviss, Jerald B., (AV) ..................'49 '73 C.831 A.B. L.884 J.D. 555 W. 5th St.
**Sessa, Stephen E.** ....................... '67 '93 C.728 B.A. L.1148 J.D. [🄰 Spray,G.&B.]
Sestanovich, Thomas R. ........'62 '88 C&L.112 B.A., J.D. 1800 Century Park E., 10th Fl.
**Setaro, Renu Mago** ........................ '68 '95 C.893 B.A. L.94 J.D. [🄰 Epport&R.]
*LANGUAGES: French.
**Sethi, Muira K.**...............................'70 '94 C.112 B.A. L.426 J.D. [Brown,W.&C.]
*LANGUAGES: Spanish and Hindi.
*PRACTICE AREAS: Litigation.
**Sethuraman, Anand** ............'70 '96 C.597 B.S.E.E. L.602 J.D. [🄰 Blakely,S.T.&Z.]
**Seto, Karen B.**...........................'65 '94 C.659 B.S. L.1068 J.D. [🄰 Fried,F.H.S.&J.]
**Seto, Stephen C.** .......................'67 '94 C.165 B.A. L.800 J.D. [🄰 Sulmeyer,K.B.&R.]
*PRACTICE AREAS: Bankruptcy Law; Business Litigation.
Seto, Theodore P., (AVⓉ) '51 '77 C&L.309 B.A., J.D.
(adm. in MA; not adm. in CA) Assoc. Prof., Loyola Law School
Seton, Gilbert D., (AV) .................. '27 '50 C.813 A.B. L.309 J.D. 919 S. Albany St.
**Settelmayer, Daniel K.** ...................'61 '87 C.800 A.B. L.770 J.D. [🄲 Latham&W.]
**Sevell, Robert D.** ...........................'48 '73 C.112 B.A. L.426 J.D. [Foley L.W.&A.]
*PRACTICE AREAS: Business Law; Health Care Finance; Corporate Law.
Severo, Michael V. ........................'47 '76 C.1097 B.A. L.1148 J.D. [Severo&S.]
Severo & Severo ...................................411 West 5th Street, Suite 850
**Seville-Jones, Sandra A.** ................ '60 '86 C.309 B.A. L.1068 J.D. [Munger,T.&O.]

**Seyfarth, Shaw, Fairweather & Geraldson, (AV)**
**2029 Century Park East, 90067-3063⊙**
**Telephone: 310-277-7200 Facsimile: 310-201-5219**
**URL: http://www.seyfarth.com**
**Partners: Stephen A. Bauman (Certified Specialist, Taxation Law, The State Bar of California Board of Legal Specialization) (Resident); Robert E. Buch (Certified Specialist, Workers' Compensation Law, The State Bar of California Board of Legal Specialization); Georgeanne Henshaw (Resident); Jerry M. Hill; David D. Kadue (Resident); Steven J. Kmieciak; David J. Kuckelman; Daniel G. McIntosh (Resident); Joseph M. Miller (Certified Specialist, Workers' Compensation Law, The State Bar of California Board of Legal Specialization) (Resident); F. Scott Page (Resident); Edward J. Pierce (Resident); George E. Preonas (Resident); Stacy D. Shartin (Resident); Kenneth D. Sulzer (Resident); Diana Tabacopoulos; Thomas Larry Watts; Thomas J. Weiss (Resident); Mitchel D. Whitehead (Resident); Kenwood C. Youmans (Resident). Of Counsel: Barbara T. Lindemann; Alexander H. Pope; Conward E. Williams. Resident Associates: Brian T. Ashe; W. Michael Battle; Jeffrey L. Braker; James A. Breslo; John G. Correnti; Barbara A. Fitzgerald; Sean J. Gallagher; Judith A. Gordon; David M. Gruenberg; Philecia L. Harris; Gaye E. Hertan; David D. Jacobson; Steven B. Katz; Thomas R. Kaufman; Patricia Kinaga; Lorraine H. O'Hara; Allan S. Ono; Laura Wilson Shelby; David T. Van Pelt; Jan A. Yoss.**
**Labor and Employment Law, Employee Benefits, Employment Discrimination, Employment-at-Will, Health Care, Occupational, Safety and Health, Worker's Compensation. Government Contracts. White-Collar Criminal. Litigation, Administrative Law, Business Contract Disputes, Construction, Corporations and Partnerships, General Tort, Insurance, Intellectual Property, Product Liability,**

(This Listing Continued)

**Seyfarth, Shaw, Fairweather & Geraldson (Continued)**

**Professional Liability, Securities and Commodities. Corporate, Acquisitions, Antitrust, Bankruptcy and Creditors' Rights, Commercial and Financial Transactions, Contracts, Divestitures, Joint Ventures, Mergers, Real Estate, Tax Law, Trust and Probate. Environmental, Safety and Health.**
**Chicago, Illinois Office: 55 E. Monroe Street, Suite 4200. Telephone: 312-346-8000. Facsimile: 312-269-8869.**
**Washington, D.C. Office: 815 Connecticut Avenue, N.W. Telephone: 202-463-2400. Facsimile: 202-828-5393.**
**New York, N.Y. Office: 900 Third Avenue, 16th Floor. Telephone: 212-715-9000. Facsimile: 212-752-3116.**
**San Francisco, California Office: Suite 2900, 101 California Street. Telephone: 415-397-2823. Facsimile: 415-397-8549.**
**Sacramento, California Office: 400 Capitol Mall, Suite 2350. Telephone: 916-558-4828. Facsimile: 916-558-4839.**
**Houston, Texas Office: 700 Louisiana Street, Suite 3900. Telephone: 713-225-2300. Facsimile: 713-225-2340.**
**Atlanta, Georgia Office: One Atlantic Center, 1201 West Peachtree Street, Suite 3260. Telephone: 404-892-6412. Facsimile: 404-892-7056.**
**Brussels, Belgium Office: Avenue Louise 500, Box 8. Telephone: (32) (2) 647.60.25. Fax: (32) (2) 640.70.71.**
**Affiliated Law Firm:**
**Matray, Matray et Hallet: 34/24, Boulevard Frère-Orban, 4000, Liege, Belgium. Telephone: (32) (41) 52 70 68. Telex: macoha 42330. Telecopier: (32) (41) 52 08 57.**
***See Professional Biographies, LOS ANGELES, CALIFORNIA***

Sezna, Edward W. ................. '47 '77 C.1070 B.S. L.800 J.D. 2170 Century Park E.
**Sfregola, Michael F.** .................'54 '79 C.112 B.A. L.800 J.D. [Allen,M.L.G.&M.]
*PRACTICE AREAS: Tax and Real Estate.
**Shabaik, Nadia A.** ..........................'71 '96 C.112 B.A. L.1068 J.D. [🄰 Latham&W.]
Shabanian, Victoria S. ................. '57 '93 C.914 B.A. L.1068 J.D. 312 N. Spring St.
Shabel, Scott Lee, (BV) ............. '54 '78 C.188 B.A. L.145 J.D. 12100 Wilshire Blvd.
Shabo, Harold E. ........................................ '41 '67 C.112 A.B. L.1068 LL.B. Supr. Ct. J.
**Shackelford, Ricky L.** ....................'63 '90 C.309 B.A. L.36 J.D. [🄰 Jones,D.R.&P.]
Shade, Patricia ..........................'45 '83 C.112 B.A. L.1136 J.D. 200 N. Main St.
**Shadur, Ellen J.** ........................... '60 '86 C.914 B.A. L.976 J.D. [🄰 Gipson H.&P.]
*LANGUAGES: French.
**Shaeffer, John J.** ..................................'— '88 C&L.770 B.S., J.D. [O'Donnell,R.&S.]
*PRACTICE AREAS: Litigation.
Shaff, Carl, II ..................................'48 '77 C.330 B.A. L.1095 J.D. 5455 Wilshire Blvd.
Shaffer, Butler D. '35 '62 C.546 B.A. L.145 J.D.
(adm. in NE; not adm. in CA) Prof., Southwestern Univ. Sch. of Law
Shaffer, David M., (AV) ......................... '40 '66 C.800 L.809 LL.B. [Shaffer,D.P.&G.]
**Shaffer, K. John** .............................'64 '91 C.813 A.B. L.1066 J.D. [Stutman,T.&G.]
*PRACTICE AREAS: Bankruptcy; Insolvency; Corporate Reorganization; Commercial Litigation.
Shaffer, Marcy ..........................'55 '80 C.681 A.B. L.309 J.D. 10724 Wilshire Blvd.
**Shaffer, Monica Wahl** ...................'61 '91 C.472 B.S. L.145 J.D. [🄰 Munger,T.&O.]
**Shaffer, Robert H., Jr.** ..................... '66 '91 C&L.990 B.A., J.D. [🄰 Booth,M.&S.]
Shaffer, Robert W., Jr. ...................... '43 '74 C.800 B.A. L.61 J.D. [Shaffer,G.&R.]
Shaffer, Doble, Pocrass & Gam, (AV) ....................................... 12301 Wilshire Blvd.
Shaffer, Gold & Rubaum .......................................................... 12011 San Vicente Blvd.
**Shaffery, John** .......................................'— '92 C.1210 B.S. L.809 J.D. [Feldman&S.]
*PRACTICE AREAS: Environmental Litigation; Groundwater Contamination; Environmental Cleanup; Underground Storage Tanks; Proposition 65.
Shafiroff, Cynthia L. ......................'— '86 C.112 B.A. L.809 J.D. 4700 Wilshire Blvd.
**Shafran, J. A.**, (AV) ............... '38 '64 C.112 B.S. L.1066 J.D. [Sonnenschein N.&R.]
*PRACTICE AREAS: Real Estate; Corporate; General Business.
**Shafton, Anthony E.**, (AV) ....'41 '67 C.112 A.B. L.1068 LL.B. [Berger,K.S.M.F.S.&G.]
Shafton, Lester B. '05 '28 C.339 B.S. L.309 J.D.
(adm. in IL; not adm. in CA) 2300 Fox Hills Dr.‡
Shafton, Lori A. ...................... '65 '92 C.112 B.A. L.426 J.D. 801 S. Grand Ave.
**Shafton, Robert M.**, (AV) ................ '31 '55 C&L.37 B.A., J.D. [Stroock&S.&L.] ‡
*PRACTICE AREAS: Arbitrator-Mediator; Expert Witness.
Shah, Bharati ...........................................'60 '92 C&L.061 B.S., LL.B. 444 S. Flower St.
**Shah, Faisal** ............................................'60 '87 C.174 B.S. L.767 J.D. [Pillsbury M.&S.]
**Shah, Preeti G.** .............................................................'58 '88 L.061 LL.B. [Kegel,T.&T.]
Shahalayi, Chaye F. ...............'45 '79 C.645 B.S. L.1148 J.D. 5331 E. Olympic Blvd.
**Shahar, Martine Safran** ............... '57 '82 C.112 B.A. L.1065 J.D. Home Box Office
Shahin, Robert S., (AV) ................ '45 '70 C.112 B.A. L.1068 J.D. 10544 Wyton Dr.
Shaikh, Ayaz R. ........................... '65 '93 C.976 B.A. L.276 J.D. 355 S. Grand Ave.
Shakur, Nyisha Mbalia ..............'51 '87 C.331 B.A. L.309 J.D. 2049 Century Park E.
Shalant, Joseph L., (AV) .......... '39 '67 C.112 A.B. L.1068 LL.B. 3580 Wilshire Blvd.
**Shalek, James H.** ..............'53 '78 C.659 B.A. L.94 J.D. [Lyon&L.] (See Pat. Sect.)
*PRACTICE AREAS: Patent, Trademark, Copyright; Intellectual Property.
**Shallman, Daniel N.** ...................... '70 '95 C.339 B.S. L.145 J.D. [🄰 Gibson,D.&C.]
Shamir, Ruth ........................................................ '36 '65 5900 Wilshire Blvd.
**Shanahan, Angela** .................'55 '85 C.800 B.A. L.426 J.D. [Demetriou,D.S.&M.]
*PRACTICE AREAS: Probate; Trust Administration; Estate Planning; Business Transactions.
**Shanahan, Bruce G.** .............. '50 '81 C.846 B.S. L.800 J.D. [🄲 Sedgwick,D.M.&A.]
Shanahan, Edmond F., (AV) '12 '42 C.111 B.S. L.800 LL.B.
725 S. Norton Ave. (Pat.)‡
Shanahan, Maureen G. .......'61 '86 C.228 B.A. L.426 J.D. Securities & Exchange Comm.
Shane, Joseph ................................ '07 '30 C.628 L.809 LL.B. Mun. Ct. Comr.
Shane and Paolillo, P.C. .... 2049 Century Park E., 12th Fl. (ⓞNewton, Mass., N.Y., N.Y.)
Shankman, Ned N. .................... '41 '70 C.800 B.A. L.1095 J.D. 740 N. La Brea Ave.
**Shanks, Patricia L.**, (AV) '40 '78
C.813 B.A. L.174 J.D. [McCutchen,D.B.&E.] (ⓞSan Fran.)
*PRACTICE AREAS: Environmental Law.
**Shanney-Saborsky, Regina T., (A Professional Corporation)** '49 '80
C.800 B.A. L.1148 J.D. [Mitchell,S.&K.]
*PRACTICE AREAS: Employee Benefits/ERISA; Business Planning Law; Succession Planning Law.
**Shanying, Lei** ..................................................'73 '95 [Arnberger,K.B.&C.]
*LANGUAGES: Mandarin, Cantonese and English.
*PRACTICE AREAS: Economic Law; Contracts; Real Estate Dispute.
**Shao, Misara C.** ............................'— '90 C.813 B.A. L.800 J.D. [🄰 Riordan&M.]
*PRACTICE AREAS: Litigation.
**Shapira, Ralph J.**, (AV) ............... '46 '75 C.604 B.A. L.1066 J.D. [O'Melveny&M.]
**Shapiro, Bernard**, (AV) ........... '17 '46 C.112 A.B. L.1066 LL.B. [🄲 Murphy,W.&B.]
*PRACTICE AREAS: Business Workouts; Bankruptcy Reorganizations; Creditors Remedies.
Shapiro, Bernard S., (A Law Corp.), (AV) '33 '60
C.112 B.A. L.1068 J.D. 12304 Santa Monica Blvd.
Shapiro, Burton J. '47 '72 C.1350 B.A. L.326 J.D.
(adm. in TX; not adm. in CA) 2147 N. Beachwood Dr.‡
**Shapiro, Carl W.** ....................... '49 '76 C.976 B.A. L.309 J.D. [Shapiro,H.&M.]
**Shapiro, Daniel C.** ....................... '54 '79 C.112 B.A. L.809 J.D. [Wolf,R.&S.]
*PRACTICE AREAS: Community Association Law; Real Estate.
Shapiro, Daniel M. .................. '46 '75 C.154 B.A. L.309 J.D. 333 S. Grand Ave.
**Shapiro, David B.**.........................'59 '82 C.112 B.A. L.1068 J.D. [Cummins&W.]
*PRACTICE AREAS: Premises Liability; Insurance Defense; Personal Injury.
Shapiro, Haskell ........................... '15 '54 C.800 L.809 LL.B. 3660 Wilshire Blvd.

CAA337P

CALIFORNIA—LOS ANGELES MARTINDALE-HUBBELL LAW DIRECTORY 1997

**Shapiro, Howard D.** ........ '66 '92 C.691 B.A. L.1051 J.D. [Ⓐ Mitchell,S.&K.]
*LANGUAGES: Mandarin.
*PRACTICE AREAS: Immigration; Employment Immigration; Immigration Discrimination.
**Shapiro, Jeffrey N.** ........ '70 '96 C.112 A.B. L.145 J.D. [Ⓐ Irell&M.]
Shapiro, Jonathan S. ........ '63 '90 C.309 A.B. L.1066 J.D. Asst. U.S. Atty.
**Shapiro, Judith Salkow, (AV)** ........ '38 '76 C.112 B.A. L.1068 J.D. [Lurvey&S.]
*PRACTICE AREAS: Family Law.
Shapiro, Laurence J. ........ '60 '90 C.659 B.A. L.477 J.D. 400 S. Hope St.
Shapiro, Lawrence D. ........ '35 '61 C.339 B.S. L.209 J.D. 2029 Century Pk. E.
**Shapiro, Lynn A.** ........ '69 '94 C&L.800 B.S., J.D. [Ⓐ Skadden,A.S.M.&F.]
Shapiro, Marvin N., (AV) ........ '36 '62 C.112 A.B. L.1066 LL.B. [Rose,K.&M.]
**Shapiro, Marvin S., (P.C.), (AV)** ........ '36 '59 C&L.178 A.B., LL.B. [Irell&M.]
Shapiro, Michael H. '38 '65 C.112 B.A. L.145 J.D.
Prof. of Law, Univ. of Southern Calif.
**Shapiro, Mitchell S., (AV)** ........ '40 '65 C.823 B.A. L.145 J.D. [Shapiro,R.&C.]
Shapiro, Norman J. ........ '43 '70 C.112 B.A. L.1095 J.D. Dep. Dist. Atty.
Shapiro, Ralph ........ '50 '77 C.800 B.S. L.809 J.D. Dist. Atty. Off.
**Shapiro, Robert L., (AV)** .... '42 '69 C.112 B.S. L.426 J.D. [Christensen,M.F.J.G.W.&S.]
*REPORTED CASES: Lead Counsel in United States of America v. Samango (607 Fed. 2d 877); People v. Christian Brando; People v. O.J. Simpson.
*PRACTICE AREAS: Criminal Defense; Litigation Law.
**Shapiro, Steven E.** ........ '58 '83 C&L.178 B.S.E.E., J.D. [Mitchell,S.&K.] (Pat.)
Shapiro, Vicki G. '49 '78 C.788 B.A. L.426 J.D.
Asst. Exec. Dir., Legal Affs., Screen Actors Guild

**Shapiro, Hinds & Mitchell LLP**
**11100 Santa Monica Boulevard Suite 900, 90025**
**Telephone: 310-445-9888 Fax: 310-445-9899**
**Carl W. Shapiro; James Andrew Hinds, Jr.; Briane Nelson Mitchell; Norman A. Dupont; Keith A. Meyer. Of Counsel: Cindy F. Forman; Leora D. Freedman. Associate: Suzanne Harmatz Mitchell; Colleen E. Curtin.**
**Alternative Dispute Resolution, Appellate, Commercial Litigation, Commercial Policyholders Mass Tort Exposure Dispute Resolution, Environmental, First Amendment, Insolvency, Insurance Coverage, Intellectual Property and Partnership and Shareholder Disputes.**
*See Professional Biographies, LOS ANGELES, CALIFORNIA*

**Shapiro, Rosenfeld & Close, A Professional Corporation, (AV)** BB
**Suite 2600, One Century Plaza, 2029 Century Park East, 90067**
**Telephone: 310-277-1818 Telecopier: 310-201-4776**
**Email: src_law@ix.netcom.com**
**Mitchell S. Shapiro; Edward M. Rosenfeld; Richard H. Close; Helmut F. Furth; Rochelle Buchsbaum Spandorf; Douglas L. Carden; Jonathan J. Panzer; Cathryn S. Gawne; Julie J. Bisceglia; Lisa K. Skaist; Rhonda H. Mehlman; Marna F. Miller; Jennifer A. DeMarrais. Of Counsel: Alan D. Jacobson; Alan G. Dowling; Barry Kurtz.**
**General Business Practice. Franchising, Entertainment, Copyright, Corporation, Bankruptcy and Reorganization, Taxation, Estate Planning and Real Estate Law. Antitrust, Trade Regulation, Land Use, Unfair Competition and Administrative Law. Civil Litigation.**
*See Professional Biographies, LOS ANGELES, CALIFORNIA*

Shapkin, John S. ........ '42 '76 C.1044 B.A. L.1136 J.D. 8220 Waring Ave.
**Shapnick, Wendy K.** ........ '67 '92 C.112 B.A. L.1066 J.D. [Ⓐ Epport&R.]
Shardlow, Paul Jeffrey ........ '55 '82 C.101 B.S. L.284 J.D. 3600 Wilshire Blvd.
**Share, Karen A.** ........ '49 '75 C.112 A.B. L.1065 J.D. [Stegman&C.]
*PRACTICE AREAS: Business Litigation; Arbitration.
**Share, Richard Hudson, (AV)** ........ '38 '64 C.112 B.S. L.800 J.D. [Frandzel&S.]

**Sharenow, Leonard, (AV) '44 '70 C.696 A.B. L.569 J.D.**
**1901 Avenue of the Stars, 20th Floor, 90067**
**Telephone: 310-203-8100 Fax: 310-277-9430**
***PRACTICE AREAS: Business Crimes; Criminal Trial Practice; Civil Trial; Environmental; Tax Fraud.**
**White Collar Crime, Criminal Tax, Environmental Defense, Securities Litigation, Complex Civil Trials.**
*See Professional Biographies, LOS ANGELES, CALIFORNIA*

**Sharer, John H., (AV)** ........ '32 '62 C.112 B.A. L.1068 LL.B. [Gibson,D.&C.]
**Sharf, Jesse** ........ '62 '86 C.659 B.A. L.569 J.D. [Gibson,D.&C.]
*PRACTICE AREAS: Real Estate; Finance; Leases and Leasing.
Sharif, Said "Sid" M. ........ '48 '80 C.061 B.Sc. L.1137 J.D. [Gesvi-S.&Assoc.]
**Sharkey, John P.** ........ '54 '91 C.790 B.A. L.809 J.D. [Ⓐ Orrick,H.&S.]
**Sharp, J. Daniel** ........ '59 '87 C.893 B.A. L.1065 J.D. [Folger L.&K.]⊙
**Sharp, Janice A.** ....... '51 '90 C.061 B.Sc. L.1137 J.D. [Ⓐ Merchant&G.] (See Pat. Sect.)
*PRACTICE AREAS: Patent Law; Trademark Law; Copyright Law; Biotechnology Law.
**Sharp, Keith A., (AV)** ........ '58 '83 C.605 A.B. L.426 J.D. [Falk&S.]
*PRACTICE AREAS: Labor; Corporate.
Sharp, Wendy C. ........ '53 '88 C.112 B.A. L.809 J.D. 11726 San Vicente Blvd.
Sharpe, Alan A. ........ '42 '82 Off. of Pub. Def.
**Sharpe, Kirk H.** ........ '67 '93 C.628 B.B.A. L.809 J.D. [Ⓐ Buchalter,N.F.&Y.]
*PRACTICE AREAS: Corporate; Banking; Finance.
**Shartin, Stacy D., (AV)** ........ '49 '73 C.112 A.B. L.1068 J.D. [Seyfarth,S.F.&G.]
Shashaani, Ramona ........ '57 '86 C.112 B.A. L.1049 J.D. 12100 Wilshire Blvd.
**Shatz, Benjamin G.** ........ '69 '92 C.112 L.990 J.D. [Ⓐ Crosby,H.R.&M.]
**Shaub, David R.** ........ '35 '62 C&L.477 B.S., LL.B. [Shaub&W.]
*PRACTICE AREAS: Transnational and Domestic Business; Intellectual Property; International Investment and Tax Related Matters; Pacific Basin Trade and Investment; Offshore Trusts and Corporations.

**Shaub & Williams**
**12121 Wilshire Boulevard, Suite 205, 90025**
**Telephone: 310-826-6678 Telefax: 310-826-8042 Email: 74577.1544@compuserve.com**
**Email: dshaub@earthlink.net**
**David R. Shaub; Leslie Gail Williams; Edward Everett Vaill; Alan M. Kindred. Of Counsel: Ingo Leetsch (Not admitted in the United States); Hong Sun.**
**General and International Practice. Business and Investment Transactions. Business and Transnational Litigation in all Courts. E.U. Law, Intellectual Property Protection and Licensing, Computer Software and Telebroadcast Law, Entertainment. Foreign Companies and Trusts. Real Estate. International Insurance Transactions, Foreign Joint Ventures. Immigration.**
**Associated With: Hurt, Sinisi & Papadakis in San Diego, Atlanta, Rome and Milan, Italy, Athens, Greece.**
*See Professional Biographies, LOS ANGELES, CALIFORNIA*

Shaw, Curtis M. ........ '44 '75 C.560 B.S. L.426 J.D. 6255 Sunset Blvd.
Shaw, Deborah G. ........ '63 '89 C.914 B.A. L.426 J.D. Dep. Dist. Atty.
Shaw, Douglas A. ........ '44 '70 C.813 B.A. L.112 J.D. 12400 Wilshire Blvd.
**Shaw, Garrin James, (Professional Corporation), (AV)** '43 '69
C.684 B.A. L.1065 J.D. [Schell&D.]
**Shaw, John W., (AV)** ........ '53 '78 C.1042 B.A. L.426 J.D. [Kern&W.]
**Shaw, Kevin L.** ........ '55 '80 C.846 B.A. L.326 J.D. [Mayer,B.&P.]
**Shaw, Nina L., (AV)** ........ '— '81 C.66 B.A. L.178 J.D. [Del,R.S.M.&D.]
*PRACTICE AREAS: Entertainment Law; Television Law; Motion Picture Law; Theater Law.
Shawaf, Raad K. ........ '65 '92 C.112 B.A. L.1068 J.D. 3164 Stoner Ave.

**Shawn, Mann & Niedermayer, L.L.P.**
**2029 Century Park East Suite 1690⊙**
**Telephone: 310-553-8065 Fax: 310-557-0729**
**Gregory S. Abrams.**

(This Listing Continued)

**Shawn, Mann & Niedermayer, L.L.P. (Continued)**
**Business Law and Litigation before Courts and Government Agencies. Legislative Advocacy, Corporate, Intellectual Property, International, Procurement, Real Estate, Trade Association, Transactional and Transportation Law.**
**Washington, D.C., Government Affairs Office: 499 S. Capitol Street, S.W., Suite 420. Telephone: 202-842-3000. Fax: 202-547-7161.**
**Washington, D.C. Office: 1850 M Street, N.W., Suite 280. Telephone: 202-331-7900. Fax: 202-331-0726.**
**San Diego, California Office: 401 West "A" Street, Suite 1850. Telephone: 619-236-0303. Fax: 619-238-8181.**
**San Francisco, California Office: The Fox Plaza, 1390 Market Street, Suite 1204. Telephone: 415-982-0150. Fax: 415-522-0513.**
**Bloomington, Minnesota Office: 2090 West 98th Street. Telephone: 612-881-6577. Fax: 612-881-6894.**
*See Professional Biographies, LOS ANGELES, CALIFORNIA*

**Shbaro, Suzanne Z.** ........ '66 '94 C.112 B.A. L.809 J.D. [Ⓐ Bergman&W.]
*LANGUAGES: American Sign Language.
**Shea, Edith Sanchez** ........ '66 '91 C.188 B.A. L.94 J.D. [Ⓐ Galton&H.]
*LANGUAGES: Spanish.
*PRACTICE AREAS: Civil Litigation.
Shea, Robert M. ........ '32 '60 C.112 B.A. L.309 LL.B. 449 N. Las Palmas Ave.
Shead, Lori J. ........ '70 '95 C&L.800 B.A., J.D. 333 S. Hope St., 48th Fl.
Sheahen, Robert ........ '45 '73 C.608 B.A. L.930 J.D. 2049 Century Park E.
**Shean, Gregory B.** ........ '67 '95 C.95 A.B. L.1068 J.D. [Ⓐ O'Melveny&M.]
*PRACTICE AREAS: Real Estate Law.
**Shearer, Bernard, (AV)** ........ '35 '60 C.112 B.A. L.309 LL.B. [Greenberg G.F.C.&M.]
*PRACTICE AREAS: Corporate; Business.

**Shearman & Sterling, (AV)** BB
**777 South Figueroa Street, 34th Floor, 90017-5418⊙**
**Telephone: (213) 239-0300 Fax: (213) 239-0381, 614-0936**
**Resident Partners: Ronald M. Bayer (Managing Partner); Jaculin Aaron; Richard B. Kendall; Darryl Snider. Resident Associates: James B. Bucher; J. Patrick Frey; Charles M. Grant; Scott P. Jacobs; Mir Saied Kashani; Tobin D. Lippert; Susan Booth Noble; David S. Prall (Not admitted in CA); Michael H. Strub, Jr.; Richard B. Vilsoet; Steven D. Winegar.**
**General Practice.**
**New York, N.Y. Office: 599 Lexington Avenue, New York, New York 10022-6069 and Citicorp Center, 153 East 53rd Street, New York, New York 10022-4676. Telephone: (212) 848-4000. Telex: 667290 Num Lau. Fax: 599 Lexington Avenue: (212) 848-7179. Citicorp Center: (212) 848-5252.**
**Abu Dhabi, United Arab Emirates Office: P.O. Box 2948. Telephone: (971-2) 324477. Fax: (971-2) 774533.**
**Beijing, People's Republic of China Office: Suite #2205, Capital Mansion, No. 6, Xin Yuan Nan Lu. Chao Yang District, Beijing, 100004. Telephone: (86-10)6465-4574. Fax: (86-10) 6465-4578.**
**Budapest, Hungary Office: Szerb utca 17-19, 1056 Budapest. Telephone: (36-1) 266-3522. Fax: (36-1) 266-3523.**
**Düsseldorf, Federal Republic of Germany Office: Couvenstrasse 8 40211 Düsseldorf. Telephone: (49 211) 178 88-0. Fax: (49 211) 178 88-88. Telex: 8588294 NYLO.**
**Frankfurt, Federal Republic of Germany Office: Bockenheimer Landstrasse 55, 60325 Frankfurt am Main. Telephone: (49-69) 97107-0. Fax: (49-69) 97107-100.**
**Hong Kong Office: Standard Chartered Bank Building, 4 Des Voeux Road, Central. Telephone: (852) 2978-8000. Fax: (852) 2978-8099.**
**London, England Office: 199 Bishopsgate, London EC2M 3TY. Telephone: (44-171) 920-9000. Fax: (44-171) 920-9020.**
**Paris, France Office: 114 avenue des Champs-Elysées, 75008. Telephone: (33-1) 53-89-7000. Fax: (33-1) 53-89-7070. Telex: 282964 ROYALE.**
**San Francisco, California Office: 555 California Street, 94104-1522. Telephone: (415) 616-1100. Fax: (415) 616-1199.**
**Singapore Office: 80 Raffles Place #16-21, UOB Plaza 2. Singapore 048624. Telephone (65) 230-3800. Fax: (65) 230-3899.**
**Tokyo, Japan Office: Shearman & Sterling (Grant Finlayson Gaikokuho-Jimu-Bengoshi Jimusho), Fukoku Seimei Building, 5th Fl. 2-2-2, Uchisaiwaicho, Chiyoda-ku, Tokyo 100, Japan. Telephone: (81 3) 5251-1601. Fax: (81 3) 5251-1602.**
**Toronto, Ontario, Canada Office: Commerce Court West, Suite 4405, P.O. Box 247, M5L 1E8. Telephone: (416) 360-8484. Fax: (416) 360-2958.**
**Washington, D.C. Office: 801 Pennsylvania Avenue, N.W., 20004-2604. Telephone: (202) 508-8000. Fax: (202) 508-8100.**
*See Professional Biographies, LOS ANGELES, CALIFORNIA*

**Shebby, David P.** ........ '68 '94 C.112 B.A. L.813 J.D. [Ⓐ Kinsella,B.F.&T.]
*PRACTICE AREAS: Litigation; Employment; Entertainment.
**Sheehan, Joseph J., (AV)** ........ '54 '81 C.1169 A.B. L.976 J.D. [Del Tondo&S.]
*PRACTICE AREAS: Complex Litigation; Civil Trial; Insurance Defense; Insurance Coverage.
**Sheehan, Lawrence J., (AV)** ........ '32 '60 C&L.813 A.B., LL.B. [Ⓒ O'Melveny&M.]
*PRACTICE AREAS: Mutual Funds; Investment Management.

**Sheehy, Kevin D.**
**(See Santa Monica)**

**Sheff, Neil J.** ........ '61 '89 C.112 B.A. L.426 J.D. [Ⓐ R.A.Love]
*LANGUAGES: Spanish, Hebrew.
**Sheffield, Chaney M., (AV)** ........ '51 '76 C.112 B.A. L.61 J.D. [Iwasaki&S.]
*PRACTICE AREAS: General Practice; Business; Real Estate; Entertainment; Personal Injury.
Shegerian, Carney R. ........ '64 '90 C.1019 B.B.A. L.426 J.D. 2049 Century Park E.
**Shehabi, Soroush Richard** '65 '95
C.309 A.B. L.1065 J.D. [Ⓐ Christensen,M.F.J.G.W.&S.]
*LANGUAGES: Persian and French.
*PRACTICE AREAS: Environmental Law; Land Use Law; Civil Litigation.
**Shekou, Sally** ........ '70 '95 C.112 B.A. L.1066 J.D. [Ⓐ Latham&W.]
*LANGUAGES: Farsi, Spanish and Italian.
**Shelby, Eric J.** ........ '66 '92 C.112 B.A. L.1067 [Ⓐ Allen,M.L.G.&M.]
*PRACTICE AREAS: Real Estate.
**Shelby, Laura Wilson** ........ '64 '91 C.112 B.A. L.1067 J.D. [Ⓐ Seyfarth,S.F.&G.]
Shelby, Stuart ........ '35 '58 C.299 A.B. L.575 LL.B. P.O. Box 711
Sheldon, Betty Jo ........ '17 '42 C&L.800 A.B., LL.B. Supr. Ct. J.

**Sheldon, Bryan King, (AV) '58 '84 C.966 B.S. L.809 J.D.**
**11400 West Olympic Boulevard, 9th Floor, 90064**
**Telephone: 310-575-4111 FAX: 310-575-1520**
**Civil Litigation in State and Federal Courts. Trials, Appeals and Administrative Agency Practice. Emphasizing Litigation of Complex Business Disputes, Unfair Trade Practices, Intellectual Property, Entertainment and Real Estate Disputes.**
*See Professional Biographies, LOS ANGELES, CALIFORNIA*

**Sheldon, Craig L.** ........ '53 '78 C.188 B.S. L.1065 J.D. [Ⓐ Marks&M.]
*LANGUAGES: Japanese.
**Sheldon, Richard B., Jr.** ........ '64 '90 C.420 B.A. L.990 J.D. [Ⓐ Mitchell,S.&K.]
*PRACTICE AREAS: Litigation.
Shelley, John A. ........ '48 '79 C&L.629 B.S., J.D. 12121 Wilshire Blvd.
**Shelton, Charles E., II** ........ '63 '92 C.893 B.A. L.976 J.D. [Ⓐ McCutchen,D.B.&E.]
*LANGUAGES: Spanish.
*PRACTICE AREAS: Environmental Law; Litigation.
**Shelton, Dominique R.** ........ '67 '91 C.103 B.A. L.276 J.D. [Ⓐ Hancock R.&B.]
*LANGUAGES: French.
Shelton, Elliot L. ........ '50 '75 C.24 B.A. L.990 J.D. 11377 West Olympic Blvd.
**Shemano, David B.** ........ '65 '92 C.112 B.A. L.1065 J.D. [Ⓐ Orrick,H.&S.]
Shemaria, Victoria R. ........ '42 '76 C.112 B.A. L.184 J.D. 8350 Santa Monica Blvd.
**Shen, Martha A.** ........ '62 '87 C.112 B.A. L.1148 J.D. [Manning,M.&W.]
*PRACTICE AREAS: Police Civil Liability Defense; Medical Malpractice; Public Entity Defense.
**Shenfeld, Beth A.** ........ '59 '84 C.1036 B.A. L.1068 J.D. [Ⓐ R.A.Love]

**Shenoi, Allan A.** ...........................'58 '82 C.691 B.A. L.846 J.D. [Graham&J.]
*PRACTICE AREAS: Maritime Law and Litigation.
Shepard, David J. ......................'50 '78 C.112 B.A. L.1049 J.D. 1990 S. Bundy Dr.
**Shepard, Julie A.** ...........................'65 '94 C.112 B.A. L.464 J.D. [Ⓐ Rogers&W.]
**Shephard, Charles N.** ............'51 '77 C.112 B.A. L.1068 J.D. [Greenberg G.F.C.&M.]
*PRACTICE AREAS: Litigation.
**Shepherd, Samuel Brooks** ...........'66 '92 C.95 B.A. L.145 J.D. [Ⓐ Quinn E.U.&O.]⊙
Sheppard, Albert M. .................'23 '47 C.999 B.A. L.596 LL.B. 865 Comstock Ave.
Sheppard, Gerald A., (AV) .................'26 '54 C&L.800 B.A., LL.B. 800 S. Figueroa
**Sheppard, Jack L.** ........................ '49 '80 C.112 B.A. L.1136 J.D. [Liebman&R.]
*PRACTICE AREAS: Personal Injury Defense Law; Insurance Law; Subrogation Law; Trial Practice.
**Sheppard, Thomas R.**, (AV) ........'34 '62 C.813 A.B. L.309 LL.B. [Sheppard,M.R.&H.]
*PRACTICE AREAS: Real Estate Law; Taxation Law.

**Sheppard, Mullin, Richter & Hampton LLP, (AV)** BB
**A Limited Liability Partnership including Professional Corporations**
**Forty-Eighth Floor, 333 South Hope Street, 90071-1448⊙**
**Telephone: 213-620-1780 Telecopier: 213-620-1398 Cable Address: "Sheplaw"**
**Email: info@smrh.com URL: http://www.smrh.com**
**Counsel: Gordon F. Hampton (1912-1996); J. Stanley Mullin (Retired); George R. Richter, Jr. (Retired); James C. Sheppard (1898-1963); Myrl R. Scott†; Frank Simpson, III (1926-1993). Members of Firm: Charles F. Barker; Robert S. Beall (Orange County Office); John D. Berchild, Jr.; Anthony J. Bishop; John R. Bonn (San Diego Office); Barbara L. Borden (San Diego Office); David M. Bosko (Orange County Office); Lawrence M. Braun; Arthur Wm. Brown, Jr.; James R. Brueggemann; Richard W. Brunette, Jr.; Steven W. Cardoza (Orange County Office); James J. Carroll, III†; Michael J. Changaris (San Diego Office); Dennis Childs (San Diego Office); Gary A. Clark; John D. Collins†; Joseph F. Coyne, Jr.; André J. Cronthall; Joseph A. Darrell (San Francisco Office); Phillip A. Davis; Dean A. Demetre (Orange County Office); Polly Towill Dennis; Domenic C. Drago (San Diego Office); Juliette M. Ebert (San Francisco Office); Frank Falzetta; Robert B. Flaig; Merrill R. Francis†; Geraldine A. Freeman (San Francisco Office); Richard M. Freeman†; Marsha D. Galinsky; John J. Giovannone (Orange County Office); Randolph B. Godshall (Orange County Office); Gerald N. Gordon; Joseph G. Gorman, Jr.†; Gordon A. Greenberg; Andrew J. Guilford (Orange County Office); Guy N. Halgren (San Diego Office); Gary L. Halling (San Francisco Office); Harold E. Hamersmith; Douglas R. Hart; Don T. Hibner, Jr.; James Blythe Hodge†; Robert Joe Hull†; John D. Hussey†; Brent R. Liljestrom (Orange County Office); James A. Lonergan; Gregory A. Long†; Richard L. Lotts†; James M. Lowy (San Francisco Office); Charles H. MacNab, Jr. (San Francisco Office); David A. Maddux†; Paul S. Malingagio; Alan H. Martin (Orange County Office); David J. McCarty; Charles E. McCormick; Ryan D. McCortney; M. Elizabeth McDaniel; James F. McShane; James J. Mittermiller (San Diego Office); Christopher B. Neils (San Diego Office); Mark L. Nelson; Jon W. Newby; Wesley L Nutten, III†; Kathyleen A. O'Brien; Joel R. Ohlgren; Mark T. Okuma; Prentice L. O'Leary†; Stephen J. O'Neil; T. William Opdyke; John R. Pennington; Joseph E. Petrillo (San Francisco Office); Sara Pfrommer; Robert H. Philibosian; Fred R. Puglisi; Kent R. Raygor; Nancy Baldwin Reimann; Paul M. Reitler†; Mark Riera; Scott F. Roybal; Jack H. Rubens; John F. Runkel, Jr. (San Francisco Office); Theodore A. Russell; D. Ronald Ryland (San Francisco Office); James L. Sanders; William M. Scott IV; Pierce T. Selwood†; Thomas R. Sheppard†; Randal B. Short (San Francisco Office); Richard J. Simmons; John R. Simon†; James J. Slaby, Jr.; Mark K. Slater (San Francisco Office); Ann Kane Smith; Dianne Baquet Smith; Martin J. Smith (Certified Specialist, Taxation Law, The State Bar of California Board of Legal Specialization); Richard L. Sommers; Mark A. Spitzer; Richard L. Stone; Joan H. Story (San Francisco Office); R. Marshall Tanner (Orange County Office); Finley L. Taylor†; Laura S. Taylor (San Diego Office); Stephen C. Taylor†; Timothy B. Taylor (San Diego Office); Robert A. Thompson (San Francisco Office); Carlton A. Varner†; Victor A. Vilaplana (San Diego Office); Perry Joseph Viscounty (Orange County Office); Edward D. Vogel (San Diego Office); L. Kirk Wallace; Michael J. Weaver†; William V. Whelan (San Diego Office); Robert E. Williams; Darryl M. Woo (San Francisco Office); Roy G. Wuchitech; William R. Wyatt (San Francisco Office); John A. Yacovelle (San Diego Office). Special Counsel: Fredric I. Albert (Orange County Office); Philip F. Atkins-Pattenson (San Francisco Office); Thomas M. Brown; Frederick V. Geisler; Laurence K. Gould, Jr.; Rebecca V. Hlebasko (San Francisco Office); Scott J. Lochner; Steven C. Nock (Orange County Office); Ethna M. S. Piazza (San Diego Office); Maria C. Pracher (San Francisco Office); Brian G. Prentice; David A. Pursley (San Francisco Office); Paul F. Rafferty (Orange County Office). Senior Attorneys: David M. Beckwith (San Diego Office); Donna L. Hueckel; Harold S. Marenus; Renée Louise Robin (San Francisco Office); Steven A. Ross; Betty J. Santohigashi (San Diego Office); Sheldon M. Siegel (San Francisco Office); Alan Van Derhoff (San Diego Office); Karin A. Vogel (San Diego Office); Loretta A. Wider (San Francisco Office). Associates: Nancy McAniff Annick; Cindy Thomas Archer (Orange County Office); Karin L. Backstrom (San Diego Office); John O. Beanum; Scott A. Brutocao; James M. Burgess; Dennis A. Calderon (San Diego Office); Justine Mary Casey (Orange County Office); David B. Chidlaw (San Diego Office); Gene R. Clark (Orange County Office); Ronald S. Cohen; Araceli K. Cole; Sharli Colladay; Thomas A. Counts (San Francisco Office); S. Ellen D'Arcangelo; Brian M. Daucher (Orange County Office); Wendi J. Delmendo; Julie A. Dunne (San Diego Office); Teresa F. Elconin; Phillip J. Eskenazi; Grant P. Fondo (San Francisco Office); Linda D. Fox (San Diego Office); Travis M. Gemoets; Robert S. Gerber (San Diego Office); Anna E. Goodwin (San Francisco Office); Kurt L. Gottschall; Kelly L. Hensley; Paula A. Hobson; Frank W. Iaffaldano; Kristen A. Jensen (San Francisco Office); Beverly A. Johnson (Orange County Office); Frank J. Johnson, Jr. (San Diego Office); Mark D. Johnson; Sarah D. Keller; Tracey A. Kennedy; Jay T. Kinn; Greg S. Labate (Orange County Office); James F. Lam; Bub-Joo S. Lee; Steven J. Lehrhoff; Ted C. Lindquist, III (San Francisco Office); Michael L. Ludwig; Philip A. Magen (San Diego Office); I. Kenneth Magid (San Diego Office); Aaron J. Malo (Orange County Office); Candace L. Matson; Susan S. Matsui (Orange County Office); Susan Freeman McCortney; Leslie J. McShane; Michael Paul Mihalek (San Francisco Office); Justine Witt Milani; Paul M. Miloknay; Michael G. Morgan; Elena Muravina; Christie M. Musser (San Francisco Office); Thomas D. Nevins (San Francisco Office); Patricia V. Ostiller; Richard H. Otera; Tyler M. Paetkau (San Francisco Office); Kimberly N. Papillon; Jeffrey J. Parker; Kathleen M. Ratz; Felicia R. Reid (San Francisco Office); James M. René; Michael J. St. Denis; Lara A. Saunders (Orange County Office); Michael J. Shea (San Diego Office); Michelle Sherman; Robert M. Shore; Angela Dahl Sisney (San Diego Office); Michael D. Stewart (Orange County Office); Robert T. Sturgeon; Barry Sullivan; Turner Swan; Stanley Sze; Amy L. Tranckino (San Diego Office); Lei K. Udell (San Diego Office); David A. Urban; Holly O. Whatley; Tara L. Wilcox (San Diego Office); Tawnya R. Wojciechowski (Orange County Office); Timothy J. Yoo.**
**General Civil Trial and Appellate Practice in all State and Federal Courts; Financial Institutions Law; Commercial Law; Banking; Bankruptcy and Reorganization; Corporate; Securities; Antitrust; Intellectual Property; Unfair Competition; Labor and Employment; Pension and Employee Benefits; Federal, State and Local Taxation; Real Estate; Land Use; Environmental; White Collar Criminal Defense; International Business; Administrative; Probate; Trust; and Estate Planning.**
**Orange County, California Office: 650 Town Center Drive, 4th Floor, Costa Mesa. Telephone: 714-513-5100. Telecopier: 714-513-5130. Home Page Address: http://www.smrh.com.**
**San Francisco, California Office: Seventeenth Floor, Four Embarcadero Center. Telephone: 415-434-9100. Telecopier: 415-434-3947. Home Page Address: http://www.smrh.com.**
**San Diego, California Office: Nineteenth Floor, 501 West Broadway. Telephone: 619-338-6500. Telecopier: 619-234-3815. Home Page Address: http://www.smrh.com.**
**†Professional Corporation**

***See Professional Biographies, LOS ANGELES, CALIFORNIA***

**Sheps, Mindy** ..............................'53 '82 C&L.705 B.A., J.D. [Wolf,R.&S.]
*PRACTICE AREAS: Real Estate.
**Sher, Jonathon F.** ....................'49 '73 C.112 B.A. L.800 J.D. [Wilson,E.M.E.&D.]
**Sher, Lawrence J.** ....................'55 '92 C.994 B.A. L.999 J.D. [Ⓐ Pollak,V.&F.]
Sher, Robert B. ....................'44 '75 C.1097 B.A. L.800 J.D. 3151 Arrowhead Dr.
**Sherak, Barbra E.** ....................'70 '95 C.1036 B.A. L.426 J.D. [Ⓐ Troop M.S.&P.]
*PRACTICE AREAS: Financial Services; Corporate; Securities.
Sherick, Jack .............................'23 '79 L.1224 J.D. 1269 Sunset Blvd.
**Sheridan, Peter C.** ..........'60 '88 C.1077 B.A. L.970 J.D. [Christensen,M.F.J.G.W.&S.]
*PRACTICE AREAS: Civil Litigation.

**Sherin and Lodgen LLP, (AVⓉ)**
**11300 West Olympic Boulevard Suite 700, 90064⊙**
**Telephone: 310-914-7891 Fax: 310-552-5327**
**Email: lawyers@sherin.com**
**George Waldstein (Not admitted in CA).**
**General Civil Practice. Banking, Business, Computer, Construction, Creditors' Rights and Bankruptcy, Environment, Estate Planning and Probate, Labor, Litigation and Appeals in all Courts, Products Liability, Real Estate, Commercial Leasing and Lending, Securities, Taxation, Maritime Law, Trade Regulation and Antitrust Law.**

(This Listing Continued)

**Sherin and Lodgen LLP (Continued)**

**Boston, Massachusetts Office: 100 Summer Street. Telephone: 617-426-5720. Telecopier: 617-542-5186.**

***See Professional Biographies, LOS ANGELES, CALIFORNIA***

**Sherman, Bruce Eric** ......................'56 '82 C.112 B.A. L.1065 J.D. [Perkins C.]
**Sherman, Carol B.** ..........................'51 '81 C.705 B.A. L.426 J.D. [⊠ W.D.Ross]
Sherman, Carole Runcie ..........................'49 '78 C.112 B.A. L.809 J.D. [Sherman&S.]
Sherman, Dana ..................'53 '78 C.112 B.A. L.426 J.D. 2049 Century Park E.
**Sherman, Eric Michael** ...'71 '96 C.112 B.A. L.477 J.D. [Ⓐ Christensen,M.F.J.G.W.&S.]
*LANGUAGES: Spanish.
*PRACTICE AREAS: Litigation.
**Sherman, Glenn T.**, (AV) ..............'54 '79 C.112 B.A. L.809 J.D. [Freeman,F.&S.]
*PRACTICE AREAS: Commercial Real Estate Transactions; Construction and Franchise Law.
**Sherman, Jeffrey Adam** ..........................'61 '87 C.260 B.S. L.809 J.D. [Tax C.]
**Sherman, Kenneth L.** ..........................'64 '88 C.800 B.S.E.E. L.273 J.D. [Tax C.]
Sherman, Kenneth P. ..................'51 '76 C.112 B.A. L.809 J.D. 3825 San Rafael Ave.
Sherman, Laura R. ..........................'67 '94 C.112 B.A. L.1065 J.D. [Ⓐ Sherman&K.]
**Sherman, Lisa G.** ..........................'68 '93 C.696 B.A. L.910 J.D. [Knee&M.]
*PRACTICE AREAS: Employment Discrimination; Wrongful Termination Defense; Sexual Harassment; Personnel Policies; Employment Contracts.
**Sherman, Michael A.** ....................'56 '80 C.178 B.A. L.1066 J.D. [Alschuler G.&P.]
**Sherman, Michael S., (P.C.)**, (AV) ....'46 '71 C.112 A.B. L.1066 J.D. [Jeffer,M.B.&M.]
*PRACTICE AREAS: Entertainment; General Business; Advertising; Intellectual Property.
**Sherman, Michelle**, (AV) ........'61 '88 C.788 B.A. L.1068 J.D. [Ⓐ Sheppard,M.R.&H.]
Sherman, Paul D. ..................................................'46 '78 [Sherman&S.]
**Sherman, Roger, (A Professional Corporation)**, (AV) '32 '60
C&L.976 B.A., LL.B. [Mitchell,S.&K.]
*PRACTICE AREAS: Entertainment Law; Copyright Law.

**Sherman, Dan & Portugal, A Professional Corporation**
**(See Beverly Hills)**

Sherman & Kurtz ..................................................4727 Wilshire Blvd.
Sherman & Sherman, A Prof. Law Corp. ..........................860 S. Bronson Ave.

**Shernoff, Bidart & Darras**
**(See Claremont)**

**Sherrell, John B.**, (AV) ..........................'51 '77 C.976 B.A. L.477 J.D. [Latham&W.]
Sherrick, Richard D., II ........'50 '80 C.1097 B.A. L.809 J.D. 5203 Highland View Ave.
Sherter, Jeffrey H. ..................'53 '82 C.112 B.A. L.1148 J.D. 4071 McLaughlin Ave.
Sherwin, Gregory J. ..................'51 '76 L.999 LL.B. 11755 Wilshire Blvd., 15th Fl.
Sherwood, A. Joseph, (AV) ............'09 '33 C&L.800 A.B., J.D. 12424 Wilshire Blvd.
**Sherwood, Arthur L.**, (AV) ..............'43 '69 C.1066 B.A. L.309 J.D. [Gibson,D.&C.]
*PRACTICE AREAS: Civil Litigation; Antitrust; Securities; Regulatory Law; Environmental.
**Sherwood, Don C., (P.C.)**, (AV) ..........'47 '71 C.682 B.A. L.846 J.D. [Sherwood&H.]
*PRACTICE AREAS: Real Estate Litigation; Business Litigation; Negotiation and Drafting of Real Property Leases.
Sherwood, Richard E., (AV) ............'28 '53 C.976 B.A. L.309 LL.B. 400 S. Hope St.

**Sherwood and Hardgrove, (AV)** BB
**A Partnership including a Professional Corporation**
**Suite 240, 11990 San Vicente Boulevard, 90049-5004**
**Telephone: 310-826-2625 FAX: 310-826-6055**
**Don C. Sherwood (P.C.); Kenneth M. Hardgrove. Associates: Charles G. Brackins; Timothy S. Plum; Chet A. Cramin; Darlene R. David.**
**Real Estate and Business Litigation. General Civil, Trial and Appellate Practice in all State and Federal Courts.**

***See Professional Biographies, LOS ANGELES, CALIFORNIA***

Shevin, Eric D. ........................'64 '92 C.763 B.S. L.1049 J.D. 8749 Holloway Dr.
**Sheybani, Mithra** ..................'61 '88 C.483 B.A. L.426 J.D. [Ⓐ Donovan L.N.&I.]
**Shi, John W.** ..........................'63 '95 C.061 B.A. L.101 J.D. [Ⓐ S.K.Ross&Assoc.]
*LANGUAGES: Mandarin.
*PRACTICE AREAS: International Trade; Customs Law; Transportation Law; Business Law.

**Shibley, William H.**
**(See Long Beach)**

Shibuya, Patrick K. ......................'55 '84 C.112 B.A. L.426 J.D. Dep. City Atty.
**Shields, Carolyn J.** ..............................................'45 '83 L.184 J.D. [Lane P.S.L.]
*PRACTICE AREAS: Maritime Law; Civil Litigation; Insurance; Products Liability.
**Shields, Donald J.** ..........'33 '62 C.112 B.S.E.E. L.1066 LL.B. [Monteleone&M.] (Pat.)
*PRACTICE AREAS: Construction Law; Construction Litigation; Business Litigation; Alternative Dispute Resolution.
**Shields, Henry, Jr., (P.C.)**, (AV) ..............'45 '74 C.801 B.S. L.1066 J.D. [Irell&M.]
Shields, James M. .......'34 '66 C.1073 B.S. L.1065 J.D. Mng. Atty., Continental Ins. Co.
**Shiffrin, Steven H.** ..........................'41 '75 C&L.426 B.A., J.D. [⊠ Irell&M.]
**Shih, Bruce J.** ..........................'62 '89 C.910 A.B. L.1068 J.D. [Ⓐ Jones,D.R.&P.]
**Shih, Eric** ..........................'62 '91 C.401 B.S. L.597 J.D. [Ⓐ Graham&J.]
*PRACTICE AREAS: Patent Infringement; Patent Counseling.
**Shilliday, Robert James, III** '67 '93
C.280 B.A. L.494 J.D. [Ⓐ Christensen,M.F.J.G.W.&S.]
*PRACTICE AREAS: Litigation.
Shilub, Michael J. ......................'55 '83 C.112 B.A. L.426 J.D. 1840 Century Park E.
Shim, Casey T. ..........................'53 '84 C.112 B.S. L.426 J.D. 6500 Wilshire Blvd.
**Shimada, John H.** ..........................'57 '82 C.267 B.S. L.659 J.D. [Lewis,D.B.&B.]
Shimaji, Michael R. ..................'52 '86 C.112 B.S. L.426 J.D. 5757 Wilshire Blvd.
**Shimasaki, Susan D.** ..........'54 '78 C&L.800 B.A., J.D. Coun., Atlantic Richfield Co.
**Shimato, Nao S.** ..........................'65 '96 C.800 B.A. L.809 J.D. [Ⓐ Graham&J.]
*LANGUAGES: Japanese.
*PRACTICE AREAS: Intellectual Property Litigation; Civil Litigation; Corporate Transactions.
Shimmel, Joan C. ..........................'24 '79 C.1109 B.S. L.809 J.D. I.R.S. App. Off.
**Shimomura, Ruby P.** ..........................'64 '91 C.312 B.A. L.426 J.D. [Chan]
*LANGUAGES: Ilocano (Filipino dialect).
*PRACTICE AREAS: General Litigation.
Shin, Brian Y. '64 '91 C.976 B.A. L.178 J.D.
1800 Ave. of the Stars, Suite 900 (Century City)
**Shin, Sung H.** ..........................'66 '91 C.112 B.A. L.178 J.D. [Ⓐ Tuttle&T.]
*LANGUAGES: Korean.
**Shinderman, Mark** ..........................'63 '88 C.276 B.S.B.A. L.309 J.D. [Weiss,S.S.D.&S.]
*PRACTICE AREAS: Bankruptcy Law; Civil Litigation.
**Shiner, John R.**, (AV) ..........................'43 '69 C.800 B.A. L.1049 J.D. [Morrison&F.]
*PRACTICE AREAS: Litigation; Labor; Business.
Shiner, Philip, (AV) ..........................'38 '70 C.112 B.S. L.426 J.D. Asst. City Atty.
**Shinmoto, Lynn A.** ..........................'55 '80 C&L.800 B.A., J.D. [Devirian&S.]
*PRACTICE AREAS: General Trial Law; Civil Litigation; Construction Law.
Shintani, Scott K. ..........................'63 '89 C.339 B.A. L.966 J.D. 333 S. Hope St.
**Shiotani, Barney B.**, (AV) ..........................'34 '69 C.312 B.B.A. L.800 J.D. [Shiotani&I.]
*PRACTICE AREAS: Tax; Corporate; Real Estate; Oil and Gas Law.

**Shiotani & Inouye, (AV)** BB
**11100 Santa Monica Boulevard, Suite 1820, 90025**
**Telephone: 310-575-3688 Telecopier: 310-575-4095**
**Members of Firm: Barney B. Shiotani; Lawrence G. Inouye. Associate: Nicole Grattan Pearson.**

(This Listing Continued)

**Shiotani & Inouye (Continued)**

**General Business Practice. Real Estate, Corporate, Tax, Estate Planning, Probate and Oil and Gas Law.**
**References: First Los Angeles Bank (Airport Office); Bank of California.**

*See Professional Biographies, LOS ANGELES, CALIFORNIA*

**Shipman, Alexander** ....................'58 '87 C.112 A.B. L.426 J.D. [Ⓐ Knapp,M.J.&D.]
*PRACTICE AREAS: Corporate; Securities; Real Property; Environmental and Tax Law.

**Shipow, Mark S.**, (AV) .............'54 '79 C.112 B.A. L.1068 J.D. [Whitman B.A.&M.]
*PRACTICE AREAS: Business Litigation; Intellectual Property Infringement; Complex Commercial Litigation.

Shirani, Lee Ali ..............'64 '90 C.112 B.A. L.1065 J.D. 7th Fl., 515 S. Figueroa St.

Shirinian, Arletta ..........................'53 '83 C.112 B.A. L.809 J.D. 700 S. Flower St.

Shirley, Edward G., (AV) '38 '65
C.813 A.B. L.1066 J.D. Exec. V.P. & Gen. Coun., RCI Industries

**Shishido, Keith M.** ..............................'60 '86 C.112 B.A. L.426 J.D. [Ives,K.&D.]

**Shivers, Cassandra C.** ..................'65 '94 C.112 B.A. L.426 J.D. [Ⓐ Troop M.S.&P.]
*PRACTICE AREAS: Insurance Coverage; Litigation.

**Shladovsky, David J.** ....................'60 '85 C.1036 A.B. L.94 J.D. [Ⓐ Hughes H.&R.]

Shockley, Brenda Yvonne, (P.C.) ... '46 '72 C.605 B.A. L.426 J.D. 1234 S. Tremaine Ave.

Shockley, Ernest V. ..................'23 '53 C.112 L.809 LL.B. 5255 Santa Monica Blvd.

**Shockro, Michael J.**, (AV) ..................'42 '67 C.813 B.A. L.178 LL.B. [Latham&W.]

**Shohet, George A.** ......................'60 '83 C.112 B.A. L.426 J.D. [Ⓐ Corinblit&S.]
*PRACTICE AREAS: Complex Civil Litigation; Antitrust; Securities.

**Shokohi, Nancy W.** ..............................'59 '86 C.112 B.A. L.426 J.D. [Selman B.]

**Sholkoff, Jack S.** .........................'64 '89 C.860 B.A. L.800 J.D. [Ⓐ Whitman B.A.&M.]

Sholley, Susan R. ..................'43 '81 C.178 M.A. L.1068 J.D. 1324 3/4 Carroll Ave.

Sholomson, Stephen L. '41 '69 C.112 A.B. L.1068 J.D.
(adm. in FL; not adm. in CA) 11810 Mayfield Ave.‡

**Shore, Michael D.** ..........................'67 '93 C.112 B.A. L.426 J.D. [Ⓐ Epport&R.]
*PRACTICE AREAS: Real Property; Banking; Finance.

**Shore, Robert M.** ....................'61 '93 C.111 B.S. L.1066 J.D. [Ⓐ Sheppard,M.R.&H.]

Shore, Samuel, (AV) ..................'24 '64 C.397 B.S. L.800 J.D. 2650 W. Temple St.

**Shore, Sussan H.**, (AV) ...........'52 '76 C.112 B.A. L.426 J.D. [Weinstock,M.R.S.&N.]
*PRACTICE AREAS: Estate and Trust Administration; Estate Planning Law; Probate Litigation; Pre Marital Planning.

Shorr, Margo Alison ....................'64 '89 C.477 B.A. L.930 J.D. 4215 Glencoe Ave.

**Shorr, Matthew S.** ......................'53 '82 C.1077 B.A. L.809 J.D. [Ⓐ Berman,B.&B.]

**Short, Dale E.** ..........................'55 '80 C.350 B.S. L.800 J.D. [Troy&G.]
*PRACTICE AREAS: Corporate Law; Securities Law; Partnership Law.

**Short, George G.**, (AV) .....................'50 '74 C.112 B.A. L.61 J.D. [G.G.Short]⊙

**Short, George G., A Professional Corporation, (AV)**
**815 Moraga Drive, 90049**⊙
**Telephone: 310-440-4299 Telecopier: 805-564-6646**
**George G. Short (Certified Specialist, Taxation Law, State Bar of California Board of Legal Specialization).**
**Tax, Estate and Retirement Planning. Corporate, Partnership and Limited Liability Company Law. Tax Dispute Resolution. Closely-Held Business Planning. Financial Planning.**
**Santa Barbara, California Office: 1421 State Street, Suite A. Telephone: 805-564-6644. Fax: 805-564-6646.**

*See Professional Biographies, LOS ANGELES, CALIFORNIA*

**Shortz, Richard A.** ..........................'45 '71 C.347 B.S. L.309 J.D. [Rogers&W.]

**Shoss, Ricki J.** ..................'66 '91 C.477 B.B.A. L.326 J.D. [Ⓐ Breidenbach,B.H.H.&H.]
*PRACTICE AREAS: General Litigation; Insurance Bad Faith; Construction Defect.

**Shostak, Marjorie M.**, (AV) ..........................'14 '45 C&L.546 A.B. [Stein S.S.&O.]
*REPORTED CASES: United States v. Winkler-Koch Engineering, 209 F.2d 758, 41 CCPA 121, C.A.D. 540 (1953); United States v. Baltimore & Ohio RR a/c United China & Glass Co., 47 CCPA 1, C.A.D. 719 (1959); United States v. Quon Quon Co., 46 CCPA 70, C.A.D. 699 (1959); Mattel, Inc. v. United States, 926 F.2d 1116, 9 Fed. Cir. (T) 63 (1991).
*PRACTICE AREAS: Customs Law; International Trade Law.

**Shostak, S. Richard**, (AV) ............'31 '56 C.112 A.B. L.1068 J.D. [Stein S.S.&O.]⊙
*REPORTED CASES: Superscope v. United States, 727 F.Supp. 629, 13 CIT 997 (1989); Bushnell International v. United States, 49 Cust. Ct. 123, CD 2370 (1962); Rudolph Miles v. United States, 567 F.2d 979, 65 CCPA 32, CAD 1202 (1978); Authentic Furnituera Products, Inc. v. United States, 486 F.2d 1062, 61 CCPA 5, CAD 1109 (1974); O.L. Electronics, Inc. Arrow Sales, Inc. v. United States, 49 CCPA 111, CAD 804 (1962).
*PRACTICE AREAS: Customs Law; International Trade Law.

Showers, Bicknell J. ............'23 '50 C&L.800 LL.B. Adm. Law J., State Personnel Bd.

Shpall, R. William ..............................'43 '70 C.112 B.A. L.426 J.D. 880 W. 1st St.

**Shrader, Glenn C.** ......................'60 '89 C.112 B.A. L.276 J.D. [Ⓐ Paul,H.J.&W.]

Shrader, Patricia ..............................'38 '80 C.112 B.A. L.809 J.D. Dep. Dist. Atty.

Shraibati, Malek H. ...........'60 '88 C.769 B.A. L.426 J.D. 3325 Wilshire Blvd., 9th Flr.

Shrenger, Erlinda G. ..............'64 '91 C.112 B.S. L.1068 J.D. 333 S. Hope St., 48th Fl.

**Shrenger, Justin J.** ..........................'63 '90 C.112 B.S. L.178 J.D. [Hausmann&S.]
*LANGUAGES: Chinese (Mandarin).
*REPORTED CASES: Cal. Cosmetology Coalition v. Riley, Secy. of Ed., 871 F.Supp. 1263 ((C.D.Cal. 1994).

**Shreve, Patrick L.**, (AV) ..................'40 '66 C.426 B.S. L.1066 LL.B. [Tuttle&T.]
*PRACTICE AREAS: Real Estate; Business; Natural Resources.

Shtofman, Robert Scott ..............................'58,'85 C.397 B.A. 445 S. Figueroa

**Shuck, Thomas E., (P.C.)** ....................'53 '79 C.473 A.B. L.1003 J.D. [Ivanjack&L.]
*REPORTED CASES: In Re Kruger, 77 B.R. 785 (Bankr. C.D.Cal. 1987).
*PRACTICE AREAS: Bankruptcy; Equipment Leasing; Business Litigation; Construction Litigation.

**Shukan, David Scott** ............'64 '89 C.674 A.B. L.846 J.D. [Ⓐ Skadden,A.S.M.&F.]

**Shukiar, Lisa S.** ..............................'— '92 C.112 B.A. L.800 J.D. [Ⓐ Bergman&W.]
*PRACTICE AREAS: Complex Litigation.

Shulkin, Robert J. ......................'55 '81 C.966 B.A. L.659 J.D. [Loeterman,S.&K.]

**Shulman, Alan D.**, (AV) ......................'30 '53 C&L.597 B.S., J.D. [Ⓑ Loeb&L.]
*PRACTICE AREAS: Probate; Estate Planning; Individual Taxation.

Shulman, Edith I. ......................'59 '87 C.1036 B.A. L.800 J.D. 1441 Federal Ave.‡

**Shults, Roy L., (A Professional Corporation)**, (AV) '48 '73
C.112 B.A. L.309 J.D. [Mitchell,S.&K.]
*PRACTICE AREAS: Federal and State Antitrust and Trade Regulation Litigation and Counseling; Trademark and Unfair Competition Litigation and Counseling; Business Tort and Contract Litigation.

**Shultz, John D.** ..........................'39 '68 C.37 A.B. L.1066 J.D. [Morgan,L.&B.]

**Shumaker, Charles M., III**, (AV) ..........'55 '82 C.860 B.A. L.477 J.D. [Shumaker&S.]

**Shumaker & Sragow, LLP, (AV)**
**865 South Figueroa, Suite 850, 90017**
**Telephone: 213-622-4441 Fax: 213-622-1444**
**Email: shumaker@pmplaw.com**
**Members of Firm: Charles M. Shumaker III; Darry A. Sragow. Associate: Matthew S. Meza. Of Counsel: David B. Parker; William K. Mills; Jayesh Patel; Rina J. Pakula.**
**General Practice, Business and Commercial Transactions, Employee Relations, Real Estate Development and Finance, Hospitality Law, Non-Profit Law, Election Law and the Law of Politics, Complex Commercial Litigation in all Courts.**

*See Professional Biographies, LOS ANGELES, CALIFORNIA*

**Shuman, Steven C.** ....................'54 '78 C.112 B.A. L.1068 J.D. [Engstrom,L.&L.]
*PRACTICE AREAS: Jewelers Block Litigation; Insurance Policy Interpretation; Bad Faith Defense; Complex Business Litigation; Professional Liability Claims.

**Shumener, Betty M.** ....................'52 '88 C.112 B.A. L.426 J.D. [Ⓐ Paul,H.J.&W.]

Shumsky, Ellen B. ....................'49 '76 C.112 B.A. L.800 J.D. Dep. Pub. Def.

Shuster, Gary S. .......................'67 '92 C.112 B.A. L.309 J.D. 333 S. Hope St., 30th Fl.

**Shusterman, Carl, Law Offices of, (AV) '49 '73 C.112 B.A. L.1068 J.D.** BB
**One Wilshire Building, 624 South Grand Avenue, Suite 1608, 90017**
**Telephone: 213-623-4592 Fax: 213-623-3720**
**Email: visalaw@ix.netcom.com URL: http://websites.earthlink.net/~visalaw**
**(Certified Specialist, Immigration and Nationality Law, The State Bar of California Board of Legal Specialization).**
***PRACTICE AREAS: Immigration and Naturalization Law.**
**Associates: Elahe Najfabadi; Claire H. Kim; Ellen Ma Lee.**
**Immigration and Naturalization.**

*See Professional Biographies, LOS ANGELES, CALIFORNIA*

Shutan, Peter H. ..............................'56 '86 C.112 B.A. L.809 J.D. Dep. City Atty.

Shutan, Robert H., (AV) ....................'18 '43 C.605 B.A. L.1066 J.D. 555 W. Fifth St.

**Shuter, Richard K.** ....................'68 '94 C.860 B.A. L.831 J.D. [Ⓑ Crosby,H.R.&M.]

**Shymansky, Julia Marie** ..........'62 '87 C.923 B.A. L.228 J.D. [Ⓑ Brand F.D.F.&K.]
*PRACTICE AREAS: Commercial Litigation.

**Shyn, Henry** ..............................'63 '89 C.112 B.A. L.93 J.D. [Ⓐ Cummins&W.]
*LANGUAGES: Korean.
*PRACTICE AREAS: Business Law.

Sias, William C. ......................'56 '84 C.1168 B.A. L.1068 J.D. 221 N. Figueroa St.

Siciliano, Jill ..........................'60 '90 C.1077 B.A. L.809 J.D. State Dept. of Trans.

**Siciliano, Loretta** ....................'49 '77 C.813 B.A. L.1065 J.D. [Ⓐ Hoffman,S.&W.]
*PRACTICE AREAS: Taxation Law.

**Sidle, Kenneth I.**, (AV) ....................'45 '71 C.112 B.A. L.976 J.D. [Gipson H.&P.]
*REPORTED CASES: Fogerty vs. Fantasy, Inc. - U.S. -, 114 S.Ct. 1023 (1994); Fantasy, Inc. vs. John Fogerty, 654 F.Supp. 1129 (N.D. Cal. 1986), 664 F.Supp. 1345 (N.D. Cal. 1987); Goldberg vs. Dolly Parton, Jane Fonda, Tom Hayden, 924 F.2d 1062 (9th Cir., 1991) (Unpublished).
*PRACTICE AREAS: Civil and Business Litigation; Entertainment Law; Copyright Law; Defamation Law.

**Sidley, Michael I., (AV) '61 '88 C.112 A.B. L.464 J.D.** BB
**1900 Avenue of the Stars, Suite 1450, 90067**
**Telephone: 310-551-1295 Fax: 310- 277-5953**
**Criminal, Civil Trial, Personal Injury, Business Litigation and Employment Law.**

Sidley, Milton ..............................'31 '58 C&L.494 B.A., J.D. 11925 Goshen‡

**Sidley & Austin, (AV)** BB
**A Partnership including Professional Corporations**
**555 West Fifth Street, 40th Floor, 90013-1010**⊙
**Telephone: 213-896-6000 Telecopier: 213-896-6600**
**Resident Partners: Amy L. Applebaum; Philip M. Battaglia; David W. Burhenn; Gary J. Cohen; Ronald C. Cohen; Stephen G. Contopulos; M. Scott Cooper; George Deukmejian; Lori Huff Dillman; Edward D. Eddy III; Bradley H. Ellis; Robert Fabrikant; Howard D. Gest; Richard J. Grad; Johnny D. Griggs; Larry G. Gutterridge; Jennifer C. Hagle; Kent A. Halkett; Adam M. Handler; Thomas P. Hanrahan; James M. Harris; Richard W. Havel; Marc I. Hayutin; Michael C. Kelley; Moshe J. Kupietzky; Perry L. Landsberg; Kenneth H. Levin; George M. Means; Theodore N. Miller; Sally Schultz Neely; Edwin L. Norris; Peter I. Ostroff; Thomas E. Patterson; Richard T. Peters; Linda S. Peterson; Judith M. Praitis; Howard J. Rubinroit; Joel G. Samuels; Sherwin L. Samuels; Ronie M. Schmelz; D. William Wagner; Michael D. Wright. Counsel: James F. Donlan; Stuart L. Kadison; Richard Schauer; Yee-Yoong Yong. Resident Associates: Mark Anchor Albert; Alan Au; Lee L. Auerbach; Randee J. Barak; Leslie Kent Beckhart; Ellie Mask Bertwell; Jonathan M. Brenner; Steven A. Ellis; Adam G. Engelskirchen; Jeffrey M. Fisher; Lisa A. Fontenot; John E. Friedrichs; Stephen W. Geary; Marlo Ann Goldstein; Robert A. Holland; Robert W. Kadlec; Jennifer Landau; Kevin T. Lantry; Joel K. Liberson; Jefferson K. Logan; Aimee D. Long; Susanne M. MacIntosh; Thomas A. McWatters III; Cathy Ostiller; Octavio A. Pedroz; John E. Polich; Scott Preston; John V. Pridjian; James Robertson; Jay D. Rockey; Matthew E. Sloan; Glenn E. Solomon; Sarah V. J. Spyksma; Sonya Sud; Laurine E. Tuleja; Catherine M. Valerio Barrad; Stanley J. Wallach; Daron Watts.**
**General Practice.**
**Chicago, Illinois Office: One First National Plaza 60603. Telephone: 312-853-7000. Telecopier: 312-853-7036.**
**New York, New York Office: 875 Third Avenue 10022. Telephone: 212-906-2022. Telecopier: 212-906-2021.**
**Washington, D.C. Office: 1722 Eye Street, N.W. 20006. Telephone: 202-736-8000. Telecopier: 202-736-8711.**
**Dallas, Texas Office: 4500 Renaissance Tower, 1201 Elm Street 75270. Telephone: 214-939-4500. Telecopier: 214-939-4600.**
**London, England Office: Royal Exchange, EC3V 3LE. Telephone: 011-44-171-360-3600. Telecopier: 011-44-171-626-7937.**
**Tokyo, Japan Office: Taisho Seimei Hibiya Building, 7th Floor, 9-1, Yurakucho, 1 Chome, Chiyoda-ku, 100. Telephone: 011-81-3-3218-5900. Facsimile: 011-81-3-3218-5922.**
**Singapore Office: 36 Robinson Road, #18-01 City House, Singapore 0106. Telephone: 011-65-224-5000. Telecopier: 011-65-224-0530.**

*See Professional Biographies, LOS ANGELES, CALIFORNIA*

**Siefert, Sharon A.** ......................'65 '93 C.112 B.A. L.1049 J.D. [Ⓐ Musick,P.&G.]
*PRACTICE AREAS: Professional Liability; Insurance Coverage.

**Siegal, Charles D.** ..........................'46 '76 C.119 B.S. L.813 J.D. [Munger,T.&O.]

Siegal, Zola ......................'21 '67 C.1019 B.A. L.809 J.D. 800 S. Ridgeley Dr.

**Siegel, Brian** ..... '46 '72 C.823 B.A. L.178 J.D. Legal Recruiter, The Haffner Group, Inc.

Siegel, Christine H. ....'51 '86 C.112 B.A. L.1238 J.D. Equal Employ. Opportunity Comm.

**Siegel, Clark B.** ..............................'58 '84 C.813 A.B. L.145 J.D. [Loeb&L.]
*LANGUAGES: French and Spanish.
*PRACTICE AREAS: Entertainment Law; Banking Law; Corporate Law; Creditors Rights; Interactive and Multi-Media Technology.

**Siegel, David** ..............................'56 '81 C.260 B.A. L.1065 J.D. [Irell&M.]

**Siegel, Ira M.**, (AV) ......'49 '77 C.563 B.E.E.E. L.472 J.D. [Ⓑ Ladas&P.] (See Pat. Sect.)

**Siegel, Jay A.** ..............................'51 '88 C.259 B.A. L.809 J.D. [Clopton,P.&B.]

**Siegel, Jeffrey P.** ....................'65 '93 C.860 B.A. L.978 J.D. [Ⓐ R.F.Hirschmann]
*PRACTICE AREAS: Business Litigation; Criminal Law.

**Siegel, Joel D.** ......................'66 '91 C.112 B.A. L.1065 J.D. [Ⓐ Solish,A.&G.]
*PRACTICE AREAS: Business Litigation; Real Estate Litigation; Trademark Law; Franchise Law.

Siegel, M. Roy ......................'43 '70 C.766 B.A. L.1049 J.D. 3540 Wilshire Blvd.

Siegel, Mark S. '51 '76 C.165 A.B. L.1066 J.D.
Pres., Remy Investors & Consultants, Inc.

Siegel, Phyllis A. ..........................'48 '79 C.860 B.A. L.1068 J.D. [Schwartz&S.]

**Siegel, Robert A.** ..........................'49 '75 C.112 A.B. L.477 J.D. [O'Melveny&M.]
*PRACTICE AREAS: Litigation; Labor and Employment Law.

Siegel, Terri I. ..............................'48 '79 C.112 B.A. L.426 J.D. Dep. City Atty.

Siegel, Tom M. ......................'30 '77 C.1097 B.A. L.1136 J.D. 4250 Wilshire Blvd.

**Siegel, Tristan B.L.** ......................'66 '96 C.573 B.A. L.893 J.D. [Ⓐ Jones,D.R.&P.]

Siegler, Adam ..............................'57 '84 C.112 B.A. L.426 J.D. 555 W. 5th St.

Siegler, Edward J. ....................'49 '76 C.1077 B.A. L.426 J.D. 11755 Wilshire Blvd.

**Sieke, Eric T.** ..................'54 '78 C.679 B.S. L.1066 J.D. Sr. Coun., Bank of Amer.

**Sieke, Mark R., (P.C.)** ....................'57 '84 C.112 B.A. L.1066 J.D. [Jeffer,M.B.&M.]
*PRACTICE AREAS: International and Domestic Taxation; Estate and Trust Administration; Business Transactions.

**Siemens, Reynold L.** ..................'62 '95 C.051 B.Phil. L.309 J.D. [Ⓐ Heller E.W.&M.]

**Siemens, Steven M.** ......................'54 '82 C.813 B.A. L.1065 J.D. [Ⓑ Russ,A.&K.]
*PRACTICE AREAS: Real Estate Law; Administrative; Land Use.

**Siener, Gary J.**
**(See Woodland Hills)**

**Siepmann, Willi H.** ....................'46 '81 C.101 B.A. L.878 J.D. [Prestholt,K.F.&V.]
*PRACTICE AREAS: Personal Injury; General Practice.

Sierra, Cristina L. ..........'56 '82 C.1075 B.S. L.800 J.D. 777 S. Figueroa St., 10th Fl.

Sierra-Winn, Leticia ..............'62 '89 C.976 B.A. L.101 J.D. 650 Calif. St., 20th Fl.

# PRACTICE PROFILES

# CALIFORNIA—LOS ANGELES

Sies, Jerry ....................... '41 '83 C.1313 L.1238 J.D. 1605 W. Olympic Blvd.
Sieveke, Patricia A. ........ '60 '86 C.112 B.A. L.1049 J.D. [Ⓐ Mulvaney,K.&B.] (⊙Orange)
Sievert, Richard D. .......... '47 '75 C.174 B.A. L.1068 J.D. 11726 San Vicente Blvd.
**Sigel, Allan A., Law Offices of,** (AV) '27 '53 C.999 L.426 J.D.
  Gayley Center - Westwood, 1125 Gayley Avenue, 90024
  Telephone: 310-824-4070 Telecopier: 310-208-7271
  *PRACTICE AREAS: Corporate Transactions; Civil Trial; White Collar Criminal Litigation; Officer and Director Liability; Real Estate.
  —Phillip R. Poliner. Of Counsel: Jeffrey D. Markel.
  Civil Trial and Criminal Litigation. Corporate, Business, Personal Injury, Medical Malpractice, Legal Malpractice, Product Liability, Real Estate, Family Law and Appellate Practice.
  Reference: Western Bank, Los Angeles, California.

        *See Professional Biographies, LOS ANGELES, CALIFORNIA*

**Sigelman, Kenneth M., and Associates**
  (See San Diego)
Sigg, Eric W. ....................... '52 '85 C&L.112 B.A., J.D. Resch. Atty., Ct. of App.
Sigler, Richard ........ '45 '71 C.112 B.A. L.800 J.D. V.P., Hanna-Barbera Productions, Inc.
Sigman, Harry C., (AV) ............... '39 '64 C.112 A.B. L.309 LL.B. [H.C.Sigman]
Sigman, Harry C., Professional Corporation, (AV) ................ P.O. Box 67E08
**Sigmond, Bennett M.** ............ '57 '83 C.339 A.B. L.1068 J.D. [Poindexter&D.]
  *PRACTICE AREAS: Commercial Litigation; Bankruptcy; Real Estate; Secured Transactions.
Sikand, Renee C., (AV) .................. '57 '84 C.800 B.A. L.426 J.D. [Thrush&S.]
**Silane, Frank A.,** (AV) ............... '45 '74 C&L.262 A.B., J.D. [Condon&F.]
Silas, Martina A. ............... '55 '85 C.825 B.S. L.1148 J.D. 4215 Glencoe Ave.
Silberberg, Fred ...................... '60 '86 C.339 B.A. L.209 J.D. [F.Silberberg]
**Silberberg, Henry J.,** (AV) '44 '68
          C.563 B.S. L.569 J.D. [Brown R.M.F.&S.] (⊙New York, NY)
  *PRACTICE AREAS: Litigation; Arbitration; Business Divorce.
Silberberg, Fred, P.C. ............................ 2029 Century Park, E., 17th Fl.
**Silberfeld, Roman M.,** (AV) .......... '49 '74 C.112 B.A. L.426 J.D. [Robins,K.M.&C.]
  *LANGUAGES: German.
  *PRACTICE AREAS: Commercial and Business Litigation; Medical Malpractice; Product Liability Law; Professional Liability; Tort and Personal Injury.
Silberg, David A. '43 '68 C.477 B.B.A. L.446 LL.B.
          (adm. in MD; not adm. in CA) 128 S. Orange Dr.
**Silbergeld, Arthur F.** ............... '42 '76 C.477 B.A. L.831 J.D. [Sonnenschein N.&R.]
  *PRACTICE AREAS: Employment Law; Labor Law.
Silbermann, Barry D. ............ '42 '76 C.679 B.S.I.E. L.1095 J.D. 2121 Ave. of the Stars
**Silbert, Bernard M.,** (AV) ............ '14 '38 C&L.800 A.B., J.D. [Loeb&L.]
  *PRACTICE AREAS: Probate and Trust Administration; Trusts and Estates.
**Silbert, Harvey L.,** (AV) ............ '12 '36 C&L.809 J.D. [Loeb&L.]
  *PRACTICE AREAS: Trusts and Estates.
**Silbert, Stephen D., (A Professional Corporation),** (AV) '42 '68
          C.154 B.A. L.1066 J.D. [Christensen,M.F.J.G.W.&S.]
  *PRACTICE AREAS: Corporate; Securities; Transactions.
Silbiger, Gary, (AV) ............ '47 '74 C.1097 B.A. L.809 J.D. [Silbiger&H.]
Silbiger & Honig, (AV) ............................ 3765 Motor Ave.
**Silfen, Jill H.** ............... '66 '91 C.1044 B.A. L.800 J.D. [Ⓐ Latham&W.]
**Sillas, Herman,** (AV) ............ '34 '60 C.112 B.A. L.1068 J.D. [Ochoa&S.] (⊙Sacramento)
  *LANGUAGES: Spanish.
  *PRACTICE AREAS: Civil Litigation; Government Law; Education Law; Legislative Advocacy.
Sills, Robert L., (BV) ............... '38 '67 C.170 L.809 J.D. 6500 Wilshire Blvd.
Sills, Steven D. ............... '47 '87 C.1077 B.S. L.809 J.D. Pres., Sills & Adelmann
**Silva, Bernardo** ............... '66 '93 C&L.813 A.B., J.D. [Ⓐ Munger,T.&O.]
  *LANGUAGES: Spanish.
Silva, John M., (AV) ............... '37 '64 C.426 B.S. L.809 LL.B. [Silva,C.&R.]
Silva, Roy Z. ....................... '62 '88 C.101 B.A. L.178 J.D. [Anderson&W.]
**Silva, Tiffany Doon** ............... '66 '95 C.813 B.A. L.809 J.D. [Ⓐ Gibson,D.&C.]
Silva, Clasen & Raffalow, (AV) ............................ 4484 Wilshire Blvd., 2nd Fl.
Silver, Barry Lee ............ '44 '80 C.112 B.A. L.809 J.D. 2049 Century Pk. E.
Silver, Bernard, (AV) ................... '26 '54 L.800 LL.B. 12121 Wilshire Blvd.
Silver, Donald P. ......... '49 '74 C.112 A.B. L.1068 J.D. 11661 San Vicente Blvd., Bldg, 210
Silver, Emanuel M. ................... '10 '53 C.16 B.A. L.809 LL.B. 520 S. Burnside Ave.
Silver, Henry ........................ '11 '47 C.057 LL.D. 3809 Amersburg Rd.‡
**Silver, Michael E.** ............ '58 '84 C.309 A.B. L.569 J.D. [Ⓐ Orrick,H.&S.]
  *PRACTICE AREAS: Secured Transactions; Real Estate Law.
**Silver, Perry S.,** (AV) ............... '46 '71 C.112 B.A. L.426 J.D. [Silver&F.]
  *PRACTICE AREAS: Business Law; Real Property Law; Commercial Law.
**Silver, Robert Scott** ............ '66 '92 C.1036 B.A. L.112 J.D. [Ⓐ Dennison,B.&P.]
**Silver, Steven A.** ............... '56 '89 C.1077 B.A. L.809 J.D. [Ⓐ Wolf,R.&S.]
  *PRACTICE AREAS: Products Liability Law; Civil Litigation.
**Silver & Freedman, A Professional Law Corporation,** (AV)
  1925 Century Park East, Suite 2100, 90067
  Telephone: 310-556-2356 Telecopier: 310-556-0832
  Neil H. Freedman; Perry S. Silver; Joel Sachs; Margaret McDonald Kane; Mitchell B. Stein;—Edward J. McNamara; Bruce H. Leiserowitz; Beth Ackerman Schroeder; Linda T. Pierce.
  General Civil, Trial and Appellate Practice in State and Federal Courts and Administration Agencies. Business, Corporate, Partnership, LLC, Commercial and Tax Law, Real Property Acquisitions, Sales, Exchanges, Leases and Development, Business Acquisitions, Sales and Mergers, Estate Planning and Probate, Management Employment Relations, Labor Law and Family Law.

        *See Professional Biographies, LOS ANGELES, CALIFORNIA*

**Silverberg, Charles D., (A Professional Corporation),** (AV) '32 '56
          C&L.813 A.B., J.D. [Katz,G.&F.]
  *PRACTICE AREAS: Entertainment Law; Motion Pictures and Television.
Silverman, Ami L. ............... '51 '87 C.800 B.A. L.426 J.D. N.L.R.B.
Silverman, Arden B. ............... '56 '82 C.994 B.A. L.809 J.D. [Burg&S.]
**Silverman, B. Scott** ............... '49 '75 C.813 B.A. L.1065 J.D. [Morrison&F.]
  *PRACTICE AREAS: Labor and Employment.
**Silverman, Bennett L.,** (AV) ............ '42 '72 C.800 B.S.C.E. L.426 J.D. [Gibson,D.&C.]
Silverman, David A. ............... '68 '95 C.112 B.A. L.569 J.D. 350 S. Grand Ave.
**Silverman, Irene L.** '42 '71 C.112 L.1095 J.D.
  1840 Century Park East, Eighth Floor, 90067-2101
  Telephone: 310-553-4999 Fax: 310-553-2033
  Email: ILS101@AOL.COM
  (Certified Specialist, Estate Planning, Trust and Probate Law, The State Bar of California Board of Legal Specialization).
  Estate Planning, Trusts and Probate Law. Conservatorships and Guardianships, Elder Law, Health Care and Elder Abuse Litigation. Probate Litigation.

        *See Professional Biographies, LOS ANGELES, CALIFORNIA*

**Silverman, Lora** ............... '64 '91 C.453 S.B. L.426 J.D. [Ⓐ Knee&M.]
  *PRACTICE AREAS: Employment Discrimination; Wrongful Termination Defense; Sexual Harassment; Personnel Policies; Employment Contracts.
Silverman, Mark J. ............ '46 '75 C.1097 B.A. L.1068 J.D. 3550 Wilshire Blvd.
Silverman, Marvin ............ '35 '75 C.188 B.S. L.426 J.D. 8021 Okean Terr.
Silverman, Michael G. ............... '60 '87 C.112 B.A. L.1065 J.D. [Ⓦ W.G.Glenn]
Silverman, Philip ............... '20 '56 C.262 B.S. L.809 LL.B. 221 S. Beverly Glen Blvd.
Silverman, Rick '58 '88 C.800 B.F.A. L.477 J.D.
          1800 Ave. of the Stars, Suite 900 (Century City)

Silverman, Robert Lewis ............ '53 '80 C.339 B.S. L.809 J.D. Transamerica Ins. Co.
**Silverman, Robert M.** ............ '46 '73 C.966 B.A. L.273 J.D. [Ⓡ Ruben&M.]
  *PRACTICE AREAS: Antitrust Law; Securities Litigation; White Collar Criminal Defense.
**Silverman, Ronald I., (A Professional Corporation),** (AV) '39 '67
          C.112 B.A. L.1068 J.D. [Cox,C.&N.]
  *PRACTICE AREAS: Real Property Law; Land Use Law; Vested Rights Law; Development Agreements and Real Estate Finance Law.
Silverman, Seymour ............... '34 '78 L.1095 J.D. Dist. Coun., Vet. Admn.
**Silverman, Steven H.** ............ '53 '91 C.1044 B.A. L.809 J.D. [Ⓐ Berger,K.S.M.F.S.&G.]
Silvers, Aimée Domínguez ............ '57 '89 C.342 B.A. L.800 J.D. 660 S. Figueroa St.
Silvers, Lorraine A. ............ '50 '78 C.112 B.A. L.809 J.D. Dep. Dist. Atty.
Silvers, Michael H. ............ '49 '75 C.994 B.A. L.831 J.D. [M.H.Silvers]
**Silvers, Stephanie C.** ............ '52 '77 C.994 B.A. L.1068 J.D. [Ⓒ Pircher,N.&M.]
  *PRACTICE AREAS: Real Estate Law.
Silvers, Michael H., A Law Corp. ............................ 10100 Santa Monica Blvd.
**Silverstein, Robert P.** ............ '68 '96 C.112 B.A. L.1065 J.D. [Demetriou,D.S.&M.]
  *PRACTICE AREAS: Eminent Domain; Environmental Law; General Civil Litigation.
Silverstein, Seymour ............ '24 '51 C&L.800 B.S., J.D. 1880 Century Pk., E.
Silverton, Ron ............ '31 '58 L.112 LL.B. 2244 Beverly Blvd.
**Sim, Ashley S.H.** ............ '70 '95 C.813 B.A. L.309 J.D. [Ⓐ Jones,D.R.&P.]
**Sim, Steven P.,** (AV) ............ '51 '76 C.347 A.B. L.813 J.D. [Irell&M.]
**Sima, Carlo** ............ '48 '73 C&L.800 A.B., J.D. [Parker,M.C.O.&S.]
  *PRACTICE AREAS: Real Property Law; Estate Planning and Probate Law.
**Simantob, David** ............ '66 '91 C.103 B.A. L.1068 J.D. [Ⓐ Sonnenschein N.&R.]
  *LANGUAGES: Persian, French.
  *PRACTICE AREAS: Litigation; Insurance Law.
Simenon, Pierre N. ............ '59 '92 C.061 L.94 J.D. 1000 Wilshire Blvd.
**Simke, Stuart A.,** (AV) ............ '35 '61 C.112 B.A. L.1068 LL.B. [Simke C.]
  *PRACTICE AREAS: Business Litigation; Entertainment Litigation; Administrative Law; Contract Litigation.
**Simke Chodos,** (AV) [Ⓑ]
  A Partnership of Professional Corporation
  Suite 1511, 1880 Century Park East, 90067
  Telephone: 310-203-3888 Fax: 310-203-3866
  Stuart A. Simke; David M. Chodos;—Richard A. Fond; Ellen Resinski Rosen; James Robertson Martin. Of Counsel: James L. Keane.
  Civil and Business Litigation, Entertainment, Commercial, Real Estate, Personal Injury, Malpractice and Insurance Defense Law, Criminal Trial.
  Reference: City National Bank (Wilshire-La Cienega Branch).

        *See Professional Biographies, LOS ANGELES, CALIFORNIA*

Simkin, Michael Jay ........................ '— '89 C.112 B.A. L.809 J.D. [Simkin&B.]
Simkin & Blaine ........................ 1901 Ave. of the Stars
Simmes, David R. ............ '36 '74 C&L.1137 B.S.L., J.D. Legal Div., Dept. of Trans.
**Simmons, Frederick L.,** (AV) ............ '28 '58 C.112 B.A. L.1068 J.D. [Simmons,R.&S.]
  *PRACTICE AREAS: Federal Taxation; State Taxation; Estate Planning; Trust Probate; Taxation.
**Simmons, Jeffrey A.** ............ '56 '92 C.1073 B.A. L.809 J.D. [Ⓐ Selman B.]
**Simmons, Jonathan L.** ............ '67 '93 C.112 B.A. L.990 J.D. [Simmons,R.&S.]
  *PRACTICE AREAS: Estate Planning; Estate Probate; Corporate Law; Litigation; General Practice.
Simmons, Joy A. ............ '42 '77 Sr. Atty., Legal Aid Found.
**Simmons, Richard J.,** (AV) ............ '51 '76 C.454 B.A. L.1066 J.D. [Sheppard,M.R.&H.]
Simmons, Robert L., Jr. ............ '61 '89 C.197 B.A. L.893 J.D. 11100 Santa Monica Blvd.
Simmons-Brill, Sabrina ............ '63 '92 C.112 B.A. L.1148 J.D. [Ⓐ Koslov&M.]
  *PRACTICE AREAS: Civil Litigation; Insurance Litigation.
**Simmons, Ritchie & Segal,** (AV) [Ⓑ]
  555 South Flower Street Suite 4640, 90071
  Telephone: 213-624-7391 FAX: 213-489-7559
  Members of Firm: Frederick L. Simmons (Certified Specialist, Taxation Law and Probate, Trusts and Estate Planning, The State Bar of California Board of Legal Specialization); Jonathan L. Simmons; William D. Segal. Of Counsel: Graham A. Ritchie; Lee E. Stark; Michael W. Roberts.
  General Civil and Trial Practice in all State and Federal Courts and Administrative Agencies. Corporations, Municipal, Corporate Securities, Eminent Domain, Real Estate, State and Federal Tax, Estate Planning, Trust and Probate Law.
  Reference: South Bay Bank, Los Angeles.

        *See Professional Biographies, LOS ANGELES, CALIFORNIA*

Simon, Albert ............ '22 '48 C&L.800 A.B., LL.B. 4116 Verdugo View Dr.
Simon, Arnold ............ '24 '67 C.976 B.S. L.426 J.D. 333 S. Hope St.
**Simon, Brette S.** ............ '71 '94 C.112 B.A. L.1068 J.D. [Ⓐ Gibson,D.&C.]
  *PRACTICE AREAS: Corporate Law.
Simon, Brian P. ............ '58 '85 C.1168 B.A. L.809 J.D. [Haile&S.]
Simon, Bruce S. ............ '53 '82 C.477 B.B.A. L.213 J.D. 2876 Wood Wardia Dr.
Simon, Carroll M. ............ '21 '62 L.1001 LL.B. Claims Atty., Auto. Club of Southern Calif.
**Simon, Daniel I.,** (AV) ............ '40 '68 C.1077 B.A. L.1068 J.D. [Luce,F.H.&S.]
  *PRACTICE AREAS: Captive Insurance; Business Insurance; Reinsurance; Insurance Products; Reinsurance Arbitration.
Simon, David Henry ............ '38 '63 C&L.966 B.S., LL.B. 924 Westwood Blvd.
**Simon, David M.** ............ '57 '82 C.453 S.B. L.276 J.D. [Loeb&L.] (See Pat. Sect.)
  *PRACTICE AREAS: Trademark; Patent; Copyright; Intellectual Property.
Simon, Harry W. ............ '61 '87 777 S. Figueroa St.
Simon, Howard L. ............ '60 '85 C.339 B.A. L.94 J.D. Gleason Corp.
Simon, James M. ............ '57 '83 C.112 B.A. L.426 J.D. [Gross,G.&S.]
Simon, Jerome M. ............ '20 '50 C.426 B.A., LL.B. Paramount Pictures Corp.
Simon, Jules F. ............ '53 '83 C.771 B.A. L.178 J.D. 10880 Wilshire Blvd.
**Simon, Michael S.** ............ '63 '89 C.112 B.A. L.1061 J.D. [Parker,M.C.O.&S.]
  *PRACTICE AREAS: Litigation; Government Benefits; Construction Litigation; Insurance.
**Simon, Richard K.,** (AV) ............ '44 '70 C.154 B.A. L.659 LL.B. [McDermott,W.&E.]
Simon, Robert S. ............ '40 '69 C.800 B.A. L.809 J.D. 3250 Wilshire Blvd.
Simon, Wayne ............ '56 '81 C.472 A.B. L.813 J.D. 10390 Santa Monica Blvd., 4th Fl.
Simon, William H., Jr., (AV) ............ '29 '55 C.112 B.S. L.1068 J.D. 10940 Wilshire Blvd.
**Simon, Yvonne T.** ............ '66 '95 C.112 B.A. L.426 J.D. [Ⓐ Mendes&M.]
**Simon, McKinsey, Miller, Zommick, Sandor & Dundas, A Law Corporation**
  (See Long Beach)
**Simon & Simon, Ltd.**
  (See Manhattan Beach)
Simone, Lisa Marie ............ '66 '95 C.112 B.A. L.1137 J.D. [Ⓐ Frank,G.&S.]
Simone, Martin ............ '46 '72 C&L.426 B.A., J.D. [Frank,G.&S.]
**Simonetti, Lisa M.** ............ '— '93 C.112 B.A. L.1068 J.D. [Ⓐ Stroock&S.&L.]
  *PRACTICE AREAS: Litigation.
Simonian, Mark S. ............ '55 '81 C.813 B.A. L.477 J.D. 777 S. Figueroa St.
Simonis, Julian A. ............ '59 '84 C.112 B.A. L.809 J.D. 11601 Wilshire Blvd.
**Simonoff, Rachael A.** ............ '71 '96 C.145 B.A. L.178 J.D. [Ⓐ Gibson,D.&C.]
  *LANGUAGES: French.
**Simons, Bernard P.,** (AV) ............ '42 '67 C.705 B.A. L.1065 J.D. [Sanders,B.G.S.&M.]
**Simons, Cynthia K.** ............ '61 '88 C.112 B.A. L.1068 J.D. [Ⓐ Cox,C.&N.]
  *PRACTICE AREAS: Land Use; Environmental.
**Simons, Donald S.,** (AV) ............ '29 '55 C.800 B.S. L.1068 LL.B. [Tyre K.K.&G.]
**Simons, Steven A.** ............ '56 '87 C.1077 B.A. L.809 J.D. [Ⓐ Callahan,M.&W.]
Simonsen & Mizel, L.L.P., ............ 2049 Century Park E. (⊙Phoenix AZ & Farmington Hills MI)

CAA341P

CALIFORNIA—LOS ANGELES
MARTINDALE-HUBBELL LAW DIRECTORY 1997

Simpkins, Mark B. .............. '64 '94 C.800 B.A. L.426 J.D. 624 S Grand Ave., 27th Fl

Simpson, Allyson B. ......................'51 '76 C&L.800 B.S., J.D. 601 S. Figueroa St.

**Simpson, C. Edward**, (AV) .......... '37 '64 C.880 B.A. L.800 LL.B. [Jones,B.S.A.&F.]
*PRACTICE AREAS: Securities Litigation; Class Actions; Trial Practice.

**Simpson, Derek A.** ......................'71 '96 C.692 B.A. L.802 J.D. [Ⓐ Gilbert,K.C.&J.]

**Simpson, Douglas K.** ...............'56 '85 C.112 B.A. L.767 J.D. [Ⓐ Whitman B.A.&M.]

Simpson, James R. '40 '72
C.367 B.A. L.575 J.D. Sr. V.P., Human Res., The Times Mirror Co.

**Simpson, Kimberly A.** .................'66 '95 C.16 B.A. L.112 J.D. [Ⓐ Folger L.&K.]⊙
*LANGUAGES: Spanish.

**Simpson, Randolph C.** ............. '69 '94 C.112 B.A. L.276 J.D. [Ⓐ Charlston,R.&W.]

**Simpson, Roger W.** ......................... '52 '83 C.330 B.A. L.1137 J.D. [Cotkin&C.]
*PRACTICE AREAS: Insurance Coverage and Bad Faith Litigation.

**Simpson, Roland G.**, (AV) .......... '50 '75 C.602 B.A. L.1068 J.D. [Ⓒ Pillsbury M.&S.]

Simpson, Sharon J. ............ '63 '92 C.94 B.S. L.813 J.D. 445 S. Figueroa St., 31st Fl.

Simpson, Stephen W. ..................................'37 '62 C&L.174 A.B., LL.B. I.R.S.

Sims, Alexandra J. ................. '67 '92 C.276 A.B. L.569 J.D. 1999 Ave. of the Stars

Sims, Edward S. ...................'17 '52 C.861 B.A. L.767 LL.B. 909 S. Stanley Ave.‡

**Simshauser, Peter** ................ '57 '84 C.57 A.B. L.339 J.D. [Skadden,A.S.M.&F.]

Sinanian, Zaven V. ........................ '60 '89 C.589 B.A. L.146 J.D. Dep. Atty. Gen.

Sinay, Florence T. ............... '49 '74 C.112 B.A. L.1068 J.D. 8400 De Longpre Ave.

**Sinclair, Murray M.** ........................'50 '90 C.112 B.A. L.809 J.D. [Ⓐ Selman B.]

**Sinclair, Patricia Timko** ...................'60 '86 C.575 B.A. L.309 J.D. [Latham&W.]

**Sinclair Tenenbaum Olesiuk & Emanuel**
**(See Beverly Hills)**

**Sinclitico, Dennis J.**, (AV) ....... '47 '71 C.1049 B.A. L.966 J.D. [La Follette,J.D.F.&A.]
*PRACTICE AREAS: Medical Malpractice.

**Sinderbrand, Gregory M.** ..... '70 '95 C.37 B.A. L.809 J.D. [Ⓐ Breidenbach,B.H.H.&H.]
*PRACTICE AREAS: Insurance Coverage; Bad Faith Litigation.

Sinetar, Raymond J., (AV) ........ '34 '63 C.112 B.A. L.1068 LL.B. Sr. Atty., Ct. of App.

**Singer, Lisa D.** ........... '69 '94 C.260 B.S. L.659 J.D. [Ⓐ Christensen,M.F.J.G.W.&S.]
*PRACTICE AREAS: Real Estate Law.

**Singer, Martin D.**, (AV) ..................... '52 '77 C.563 B.A. L.1009 J.D. [Lavely&S.]
*SPECIAL AGENCIES: California Labor Commissioner.
*REPORTED CASES: Harris v. EMI Television Programs, 102 Cal.App.3d 214, 162 Cal.Rptr. 357 (1980); Page v. Something Wierd Video, 908 E. Supp. 714 (C.D. Cal. 1995).
*PRACTICE AREAS: Entertainment Litigation; Business Litigation; Right of Publicity and Privacy Law; Libel Law; Copyright Law.

Singer, Michael S. ................... '44 '79 C.1097 B.A. L.809 J.D. 329 N. Rowen Ave.

Singer, Nathan D. ..................... '48 '85 C.025 B.S. L.426 J.D. 3055 Wilshire Blvd.

Singer, Sheldon F. .................... '47 '72 C.112 B.A. L.426 J.D. 3345 Wilshire Blvd.

**Singer, Stuart R.**, (AV) ....................'41 '68 C.197 A.B. L.178 LL.B. [Matthias&B.]
*LANGUAGES: French and Spanish.
*PRACTICE AREAS: U.S. and International Tax; Estate Planning.

**Singer, Sydnee R.** ...................... '55 '88 C.472 B.M. L.347 J.D. [Ⓐ Murchison&C.]
*PRACTICE AREAS: Civil Litigation.

**Single, Randall C.** .........................'63 '88 C.340 B.A. L.813 J.D. [Pircher,N.&M.]
*PRACTICE AREAS: Real Estate Law.

Singleton, David M. ............ '58 '85 C.267 B.S. L.990 J.D. 11520 San Vincente Blvd.

**Singleton, Diane A.** .................. '55 '91 C.768 B.A. L.1137 J.D. [Ⓐ Dwyer,D.B.&B.]
*LANGUAGES: French.

Singleton, Kimberlee ............................................'62 '89 333 S. Grand Ave.

**Sinnott, Randolph P.**, (AV) .............'54 '82 C.477 A.B. L.800 J.D. [Sinnott,D.M.&P.]
*PRACTICE AREAS: Insurance Coverage Litigation; General Litigation; Trial Practice.

**Sinnott, Dito, Moura & Puebla, (AV)**
**550 South Hope Street Twentieth Floor, 90071⊙**
**Telephone: 213-312-1470 Fax: 213-892-8322**
**Members of Firm: Randolph P. Sinnott; John A. Dito; John J. Moura; Debra R. Puebla. Associates: Suzanne M. Rufflo; David M. Harris; Gail L. Orr; Shane C. Youtz; Winnie C. Louie.**
**Insurance Coverage Litigation, Bank and Finance Litigation, General Business Litigation and Trial and Appellate Practice.**
**San Francisco, California Office: 1 Post Street, Suite 2680, 94104. Telephone: 415-352-6200. Fax: 415-352-6224.**

*See Professional Biographies, LOS ANGELES, CALIFORNIA*

Sinsheimer, Richard, (AV) ..... '22 '56 C.112 B.A. L.1068 J.D. 11759 San Vincente Blvd.

Sinykin, H. Robert ......................'25 '59 C.494 L.1035 LL.B. 10490 Wilshire Blvd.‡

**Sipos, Mary Beth** ........................ '60 '86 C.788 A.B. L.94 J.D. [Musick,P.&G.]
*LANGUAGES: French.
*PRACTICE AREAS: Litigation; Insurance.

Sipprelle, Keith A. ......................'61 '89 C.154 B.A. L.1068 J.D. 725 S. Figueroa St.

Siqueiros, John A. .............'63 '89 C.674 A.B. L.112 J.D. Coun., Dept. of Indus. Rel.

**Siracuse, Philip L.**, (AV) ..............'40 '67 C.112 B.A. L.426 J.D. [Crosby,H.R.&M.]
*PRACTICE AREAS: General Litigation including Product Liability; Intellectual Property; Commercial and Insurance Litigation.

Sisco, Eric A. ......................... '49 '78 C.282 B.A. L.1049 J.D. 801 S. Grand Ave.

Siskel, Howard B. ..............'15 '40 C&L.800 B.S., J.D. Pres., Surety Ins. Servs. Co.‡

**Siskind, Ira L.** ...................... '55 '90 C.112 B.A. L.1179 J.D. [Ⓐ Koletsky,M.&F.]
*PRACTICE AREAS: Construction Defect; General Liability.

Siskind, Lawrence A. ............... '34 '60 C.1036 B.A. L.309 LL.B. 3760 Boise Ave.

Sisman, Hyman ..............................'52 '77 C.112 B.A. L.809 J.D. Dist. Atty. Off.

Sitzer, Harvey Allan, (BV) .......'32 '59 C.112 B.S. L.800 LL.B. 2049 Century Park East

**Sitzer, Michael F.** ...............................'57 '82 C.813 B.A. L.800 J.D. [Loeb&L.]
*LANGUAGES: German.
*PRACTICE AREAS: Insolvency Law; Creditors Rights.

Sivesind, James A. ..................................................'61 '94 [Ⓐ Reed&D.]

Size, George G. ........................ '53 '83 C.674 A.B. L.309 J.D. Dist. Atty's. Off.

**Sjoholm-Sierchio, Kristi Anne** .......... '58 '87 C.1307 B.A. L.800 J.D. [Bergman&W.]
*PRACTICE AREAS: Business Litigation; Governmental Law; Contract Litigation; Bankruptcy Litigation.

**Skacevic, Stephen M.**, (AV) ...............'53 '80 C.112 B.A. L.990 J.D. [Frandzel&S.]
*PRACTICE AREAS: Bankruptcy.

**Skadden, Arps, Slate, Meagher & Flom LLP, (AV)**
**300 South Grand Avenue, 90071⊙**
**Telephone: 213-687-5000 Fax: 213-687-5600**
**Partners: Jerome L. Coben; Rand S. April; Joseph J. Giunta; John A. Donovan; Frank Rothman; Douglas B. Adler; Brian J. McCarthy; Edward E. Gonzalez; Nicholas P. Saggese; Rodrigo A. Guerra, Jr.; Darrel J. Hieber; Thomas C. Janson, Jr.; John D. Rayis; Raymond W. Vickers (Not admitted in CA); Gregg A. Noel; Eric S. Waxman; Jeffrey B. Valle; Jeffrey H. Dasteel; Harriet S. Posner; Peter Simshauser; Michael A. Woronoff; Michael A. Lawson; Jeffrey H. Cohen; Karen Leili Corman; Allan G. Mutchnik; John E. Mendez. Counsel: Peter W. Clapp; Lori Anne Czepiel; Moshe J. Kushman; Walter S. Lowry; Garrett J. Waltzer. Of Counsel: Warren Ettinger. Associates: Aisha H. Abdur-Rahman (Not admitted in CA); Victoria Lynn Anderson (Not admitted in CA); Jennifer A. Bensch; Jodi Birk (Not admitted in CA); David Y. Chen; Sharon L. Cohen; Janet L. Dhillon; George M. Eshaghian; Lee B. Essner; Jonathan L. Friedman; Gary S. Glickman; Jonathan H. Grunweig; Stephen J. Helwig; Leonard W. Hersh; Elizabeth Horton; Thomas J. Ivey; Daniel Ko; John A. Makarewich; Todd M. Malynn; Richard L. Marasse; Russell A. McClain; Katayoun Motiey; Robert C. O'Brien, Jr.; Carl A. Roth; Jason D. Russell; Ray Sandona; Lynn A. Shapiro; David Scott Shukan; Mark A. Snyder; Daniel J. Weiser; Ben D. Whitwell; Douglas A. Wickham; Stanley M. Yukevich.**
**General Practice.**
**Firm/Affiliate Offices:**
**New York, New York: 919 Third Avenue, 10022. Telephone: 212-735-3000. Fax: 212-735-2000; 212-735-2001. Telex 645899 Skarslaw.**

(This Listing Continued)

**Skadden, Arps, Slate, Meagher & Flom LLP** (Continued)
**Boston, Massachusetts: One Beacon Street, 02108. Telephone: 617-573-4800. Fax: 617-573-4822.**
**Washington, D.C.: 1440 New York Avenue, N.W., 20005 Telephone: 202-371-7000. Fax: 202-393-5760.**
**Wilmington, Delaware: Skadden, Arps, Slate, Meagher & Flom (Delaware), One Rodney Square, P.O. Box 636, 19899. Telephone: 302-651-3000. Fax: 302-651-3001.**
**Chicago, Illinois: Skadden, Arps, Slate, Meagher & Flom (Illinois), 333 West Wacker Drive, 60606. Telephone: 312-407-0700. Fax: 312-407-0411.**
**San Francisco, California: Four Embarcadero Center, 94111. Telephone: 415-984-6400. Fax: 415-984-2698.**
**Houston, Texas: 1600 Smith Street, Suite 4460, 77002. Telephone: 713-655-5100. Fax: 713-655-5181.**
**Newark, New Jersey: One Newark Center, 07102. Telephone: 201-639-6800. Fax: 201-639-6858.**
**Tokyo, Japan: Skadden, Arps, Slate, Meagher & Flom (International), 403, ABS Building, 2-4-16 Kudan Minami, Chiyoda-ku, Tokyo 102. Telephone: 81-3-3221-9738. Fax: 81-3-3221-9753.**
**London, England: 25 Bucklersbury EC4N 8DA. Telephone: 011-44-171-248-9929. Fax: 011-44-171-489-8533.**
**Hong Kong: Skadden, Arps, Slate, Meagher & Flom (International), 30/F Peregrine Tower, Lippo Centre, 89 Queensway, Central. Telephone: 011-852-2820-0700. Fax: 011-852-2820-0727.**
**Sydney, New South Wales, 2000, Australia: Skadden, Arps, Slate, Meagher & Flom (International), Level 26-State Bank Centre, 52 Martin Place. Telephone: 011-61-2-9224-6000. Fax: 011-61-2-9224-6044.**
**Toronto, Ontario: Skadden, Arps, Slate, Meagher & Flom (International), Suite 1820, North Tower, P.O. Box 189, Royal Bank Plaza, M5J 2J4. Telephone: 416-777-4700. Fax: 416-777-4747.**
**Paris, France: 105 rue du Faubourg Saint-Honoré, 75008. Telephone: 011-33-1-40-75-44-44. Fax: 011-33-1-49-53-09-99.**
**Brussels, Belgium: 523 avenue Louise, Box 30, 1050. Telephone: 011-32-2-639-0300. Fax: 011-32-2-639-0339.**
**Frankfurt, am Main, Germany: MesseTurm, 27th Floor, 60308. Telephone: 011-49-69-9757-3000. Fax: 011-49-69-9757-3050.**
**Beijing, China: Skadden, Arps, Slate, Meagher & Flom (International), East Wing Office, Level 4, China World Trade Center, No. 1 Jian Guo Men Wai Avenue, 100004. Telephone: 011-86-10-6505-5511. Fax: 011-86-10-6505-5522.**
**Moscow, Russia: Pleteshkovsky Pereulok 3/2, 107005. Telephone: 011-7-501-940-2304. Fax: 011-7-501-940-2511.**
**Singapore, Singapore: Skadden, Arps, Slate, Meagher & Flom (International), 9 Temasek Boulevard, Suite 29-01, Suntec City Tower Two, Singapore, 038989. Telephone: 011-65-434-2900. Fax: 011-65-434-2988.**

*See Professional Biographies, LOS ANGELES, CALIFORNIA*

**Skaist, Lisa K.** .........................'61 '87 C.860 B.A. L.426 J.D. [Shapiro,R.&C.]
*PRACTICE AREAS: Business Litigation; Franchising Law.

**Skeen, Spencer C.** ......................'68 '92 C.112 B.A. L.464 J.D. [Ⓐ Chapin,F.&W.]

**Skinner, Robert L.** ............................ '63 '90 C&L.800 B.S., J.D. [Ⓐ White&C.]

**Skitzki, Paul J.** ..........................'63 '90 C.37 B.A. L.190 J.D. [Ⓐ Williams,B.&S.]

Skjeie, David F. ........................ '52 '77 C.112 B.A. L.464 J.D. Dep. Co. Coun.

Sklansky, David A. ...................... '59 '84 C.112 A.B. L.309 J.D. Asst. U.S. Atty.

**Sklar, Arnold** ..................................'46 '72 C.112 B.A. L.800 J.D. [Lyon&L.]
*PRACTICE AREAS: Antitrust, Franchise, Licensing; Intellectual Property.

**Sklar, Daniel M.**, (AV) ..........................'26 '53 C.174 A.B. L.309 LL.B. [D.M.Sklar]
*PRACTICE AREAS: Entertainment; Civil Litigation.

Sklar, Leonard M. ................'26 '63 C.569 B.M.E. L.426 J.D. 3550 Wilshire Blvd.‡

**Sklar, Daniel M., A Professional Law Corporation, (AV)**
**1900 Avenue of the Stars, Suite 1450**
**Telephone: 310-277-2582 FAX: 310-277-5953**
**Daniel M. Sklar.**
**General Practice. Entertainment and Copyright Law. Litigation.**

*See Professional Biographies, LOS ANGELES, CALIFORNIA*

**Skocypec, Ronald J.** ..................... '46 '76 C.705 B.S. L.1068 J.D. [Grace,S.C.&S.]
*PRACTICE AREAS: Insurance Coverage and Bad Faith Law (including Environmental); Professional Liability Law; Appellate Law; Insurance Defense Law; Product Liability Law.

Skuris, Stephen J. ....................... '54 '80 C.112 A.B. L.1065 J.D. 633 W. 5th St.

Slabach, Frederick G. '56 '82 C.496 B.S. L.500 J.D.
(adm. in MS; not adm. in CA) Assoc. Dean, Whittier Law School

**Slaby, James J., Jr.**, (AV) ...........'40 '68 C.793 B.S. L.494 J.D. [Sheppard,M.R.&H.]
*PRACTICE AREAS: Corporate Law; Securities Law; Mergers and Acquisitions.

**Slade, Andrea Y.** ............................ '43 '78 C.112 A.B. L.809 J.D. [Arter&H.]

**Slaff, Mosk & Rudman, (AV)**
**Suite 825, 9200 Sunset Boulevard, 90069**
**Telephone: 310-275-5351 Telecopier: 310-273-8706**
**George Slaff (1906-1989); Edward Mosk (1916-1989). Members of Firm: Norman G. Rudman; Marc R. Stein; Valerie V. Flugge.**
**Motion Picture, Entertainment, Television, Copyright and Trademark Law. Trials and Appeals in Federal and State Courts.**
**Reference: City National Bank.**

*See Professional Biographies, LOS ANGELES, CALIFORNIA*

**Slate, Daniel H.**, (AV) ................. '52 '77 C.684 B.A. L.1068 J.D. [Hughes H.&R.]
*PRACTICE AREAS: Bankruptcy; Out of Court Debt Restructuring; Workouts.

Slate, Houston H., (AV) ........................'— '47 C.838 B.S. L.800 LL.B. [Slate&L.]

Slate & Leoni, (AV) ......................................... 201 N. Figueroa St.

Slater, Felix ..................... '35 '64 C.112 B.S. L.809 LL.B. 1605 W. Olympic Blvd.

Slater, Franklin J. ...............'35 '76 C.112 B.S. L.1095 J.D. 1605 W. Olympic Blvd.

Slater, Gary M. .......................'45 '72 C.800 B.A. L.1049 J.D. 5757 Wilshire Blvd.

**Slater, Martin R.**, (AV) ............ '55 '82 C.1042 B.S. L.101 J.D. [Ⓒ Johnson,P.C.&S.]
*LANGUAGES: Thai.
*PRACTICE AREAS: Corporate Law; Real Estate Transactions; Estate Planning.

Slater, Robert I. ........................'49 '74 C.37 B.S. L.472 J.D. 5455 Wilshire Blvd.

**Slates, Ronald P.**, (AV) ........................'43 '69 C.112 B.A. L.1068 J.D. [R.P.Slates]
*LANGUAGES: German and French.
*PRACTICE AREAS: Creditors' Rights; Bankruptcy; Commercial Debt Collection; Business Litigation; Real Estate.

**Slates, Ronald P., A Professional Corporation, (AV)**
**548 South Spring Street, Suite 1012, 90013-2309**
**Telephone: 213-624-1515; 213-654-1461 Fax: 213-624-7536; 213-654-1463**
**Ronald P. Slates;—G. Michael Jackson.**
**Bankruptcy (Creditor), Commercial Debt Collection with Pre-Judgment Writs of Attachment and Possession, General Business and Commercial Litigation and Real Estate Transactional Litigation, Business Contractual Negotiations.**

*See Professional Biographies, LOS ANGELES, CALIFORNIA*

Slaton, Melanie V. .........................'63 '88 C.267 B.A. L.1066 J.D. 6399 Wilshire

**Slattery, Robert V., Jr.** ................ '50 '77 C.813 A.B. L.178 J.D. [Pillsbury M.&S.]

**Slatton, Christina M.** ................'62 '89 C.1176 B.A. L.990 J.D. [Ⓐ Lewis,D.B.&B.]

**Slaughter, Daniel K.** ...............'61 '88 C.188 B.A. L.1068 J.D. [Ⓒ Heller E.W.&M.]

Slaughter-Bormann, Ovette ...... '62 '89 C.112 B.A. L.446 J.D. Paramount Pictures Corp.

**Slavin, Craig A.** .........'65 '94 C.1074 B.S.M.E. L.1184 J.D. [Oppenheimer P.S.] (Pat.)
*PRACTICE AREAS: Patent and Trademark Prosecution, Litigation and Licensing.

**Slavin, Howard A.**, (AV) .............. '41 '67 C.800 B.S. L.1127 J.D. [Lewis,D.B.&B.]
*PRACTICE AREAS: Trials and Appeals Emphasizing Defense of Physicians; Health Care Providers in Malpractice Matters.

Slavkin, Wendy L. .........................'54 '79 C.112 B.A. L.464 J.D. 11700 Iowa Ave.

**Slawson, Christina Anne** ..........'69 '93 C.685 B.A. L.054 J.D. [Ⓐ McDermott,W.&E.]

Slawson, W. David '31 '59 C.31 A.B. L.309 LL.B.
(adm. in CO; not adm. in CA) Prof. of Law, Univ. of Southern Calif.

Sleisenger, Thomas P. ..................'55 '81 C.309 B.A. L.1065 J.D. Asst. U.S. Atty.★

CAA342P

**Sletten, Steven Eugene** .................'57 '82 C.1077 B.A. L.1068 J.D. [Gibson,D.&C.]
*PRACTICE AREAS: Commercial Litigation with concentration in Antitrust, Entertainment; Insurance/ Reinsurance; Alternative Dispute Resolution.
Sliskovich, Joseph V. ..............'54 '78 C.800 A.B. L.426 J.D. Prof., Loyola Law Sch.
Slivkin, Richard H. ..................'50 '77 C.696 B.A. L.982 J.D. 2040 Ave. of the Stars
**Slizewski, Edward J.** ................'62 '92 C.145 A.B. L.1068 J.D. [B Heller E.W.&M.]
Sloan, Harry E. ...................'50 '76 C.112 B.A. L.426 J.D. 1440 S. Sepulveda Blvd.
**Sloan, Jacqueline H.** .........................'68 '95 C.309 B.A. L.809 J.D. [Wynne S.I.]
**Sloan, Matthew E.** ...........................'64 '93 C.976 B.A. L.309 J.D. [A Sidley&A.]
**Sloan, Norman D.**, (AV) ..................'47 '73 C.1077 B.S. L.426 J.D. [B Gipson H.&P.]
*PRACTICE AREAS: Real Property Law; Corporate Law; General Business Law.
Sloan, Peter M., (AV) ............'48 '74 C.112 B.A. L.426 J.D. 11845 W. Olympic Blvd.

**Sloan, Sheldon H., (AV) '35 '62 C.112 B.S. L.800 J.D.**
**1801 Avenue of the Stars, Suite 417, 90067**
**Telephone: 310-201-0622 Fax: 310-556-1620**
**Email: SSloanlaw@aol.com**
**Governmental Affairs, Administrative and Legislative Advocacy, Business and Real Estate.**
*See Professional Biographies, LOS ANGELES, CALIFORNIA*

**Sloan, Todd M., Law Offices of**
(See Malibu)

**Sloane, Owen J.**, (AV) ..........'41 '66 C.188 B.A. L.976 J.D. [Berger,K.S.M.F.S.&G.]
**Slobodien, Myron L., (A P.C.)**, (AV) ......'23 '50 C.112 B.S. L.800 LL.B. [B Loeb&L.]
*PRACTICE AREAS: Entertainment Law.
**Sloca, Steven L.**, (AV) ........................'44 '70 C.197 B.A. L.976 LL.B. [Irell&M.]
**Slome, Troy H.** ..........................'65 '95 C.112 B.A. L.464 J.D. [A Engstrom,L.&L.]
**Slominski, James M.** ..................'60 '93 C.546 B.S.C.E. L.36 J.D. [A Hornberger&C.]
*PRACTICE AREAS: Intellectual Property; General Civil Litigation; Products Liability; Construction Defect; Negligence.
**Slon, Sandra G.** ............................'48 '84 C.473 B.A. L.1066 J.D. [Alschuler G.&P.]
**Slosberg, Laurie Jill** ......................'68 '93 C.860 B.A. L.94 J.D. [A Manatt,P.&P.]
*PRACTICE AREAS: Bankruptcy; Creditor's Rights; Commercial Litigation.
**Slusher, John F.** ......................'68 '95 C.197 B.A. L.800 J.D. [A O'Melveny&M.]
**Slyngstad, Charles E.** ..................'54 '79 C.112 A.B. L.1065 J.D. [Musick,P.&G.]
*PRACTICE AREAS: Litigation.
**Small, Bradley** ................'68 '94 C.103 B.A. L.1068 J.D. [A Greenberg G.F.C.&M.]
*PRACTICE AREAS: Banking; Sports and Entertainment.
**Small, Steven G., (P.C.)** ...........................'47 '72 C&L.309 B.A., J.D. [Levy,S.&L.]
*PRACTICE AREAS: Secured Transactions; Commercial Law; General Business Law.
**Small, Thomas M.**, (AV) '33 '57 C.679 B.S. L.1119 J.D.
[Small L.&K.] (See Pat. Sect.)
*PRACTICE AREAS: Trademark, Patent and Copyright; Arbitration; Mediation.
**Small, William S., (P.C.)** ..................'49 '77 C.309 A.B. L.1068 J.D. [Alschuler G.&P.]

**Small Larkin & Kiddé, (AV)** BB
**10940 Wilshire Boulevard, Eighteenth Floor, 90024**
**Telephone: 310-209-4400 Fax: 310-209-4450 Cable Address: SLK MARK Telex: 49616151**
**Email: SLK@SLKlaw.com URL: http://www.lainet.com/legal/**
**Members of Firm: Thomas M. Small; Joan Kupersmith Larkin; Thomas S. Kiddé; Christopher C. Larkin; Jon E. Hokanson; Janet A. Kobrin;—Kenneth L. Wilton; Barry C. Seaton; Karen E. Samuels; Donald J. Cox, Jr.; Michelle A. Cooke; Sasha E. Farrah (Not admitted in CA).**
**Domestic and International Intellectual Property Law, including Counseling, Due Diligence Investigations, Litigation and Licensing in Trademark, Patent, Copyright, Unfair Competition, Trade Secrets and related matters and Business and Commercial Litigation.**
*See Professional Biographies, LOS ANGELES, CALIFORNIA*

Smalstig, Ronald L. ......................'55 '83 C.470 B.A. L.990 J.D. Dep. Dist. Atty.
**Smaltz, Donald C.**, (AV) ..............'37 '61 C.645 B.A. L.1017 LL.B. [Smaltz,A.&F.]
*PRACTICE AREAS: Complex Business Litigation; Antitrust; Environmental; White Collar Criminal Defense.

**Smaltz, Anderson & Fahey, A Professional Law Corporation, (AV)**
**333 South Grand Avenue, Suite 3580, 90071**
**Telephone: 213-625-1666 Telex: 213-625-8010**
**Donald C. Smaltz; Leighton M. Anderson; William F. Fahey; James D. Kowal; Leland A. Wahl;—Lisa M. Kerr.**
**Complex Business Litigation including Antitrust, Environmental, Intellectual Property, Securities and White Collar Criminal Defense. Trial and Appellate Practice in State and Federal Courts.**
*See Professional Biographies, LOS ANGELES, CALIFORNIA*

**Smario, Leslie M.** ..................'60 '85 C.154 B.A. L.800 J.D. [Demetriou,D.S.&M.]
*PRACTICE AREAS: General Business Litigation; Complex Civil Litigation; Environmental Law.
**Smason, Tami S.** .........................'59 '85 C.112 B.S. L.1066 J.D. [Foley L.W.&A.]
*PRACTICE AREAS: Commercial Litigation; Health Care Litigation; Business Torts.
Smathers, Joy Ellen ...................'49 '75 C.362 B.A. L.260 J.D. 1888 Century Pk. E.

**Sment, Michael R., Law Offices of, (AV) '54 '79 C.800 B.A. L.1049 J.D.**
**1800 Avenue of the Stars, Suite 1000, 90067-4212⊙**
**Telephone: 310-277-6361; 310-277-6362 Fax: 310-277-6517**
**Email: rockjr@aol.com**
***LANGUAGES: Spanish.**
***PRACTICE AREAS: Bankruptcy; Real Estate; Business Litigation; Litigation; Appeals.**
**Bankruptcy Litigation in Bankruptcy and Federal Courts, Creditors Rights and Insolvency, Business and Real Estate Litigation in State and Federal Courts. Bankruptcy, State and Federal Appellate Matters. Arbitrations, Mediations.**
**Ventura, California Office: 674 County Square Drive, Suite 108. Telephone: 805-654-0311. Telecopier: 805-984-2399.**
*See Professional Biographies, LOS ANGELES, CALIFORNIA*

Smerling, Terry ..............................'45 '71 C.112 A.B. L.178 J.D. Supr. Ct. J.
**Smersfelt, Kenneth N.** ..................'68 '93 C.112 B.A. L.770 J.D. [A Crosby,H.R.&M.]
**Smiland, William M.**, (AV) ....................'42 '68 C.813 A.B. L.1066 J.D. [Smiland&K.]
*REPORTED CASES: O'Neill v. U.S., 50 F 3d 677 (9th Cir. 1995) affirming Barcellos & Wolfsen v. Westlands Water District, 849 F. Supp. 717 (E.D. Cal. 1993); Westlands Water District v. U.S., 850 F. Supp. 1388 (E.D. Cal. 1994); Sumner Peck Ranch v. Bureau of Reclamation, 823 F. Supp. 715 (E.D. Cal. 1993); Dunn-Edwards Corp. v. South Coast Air Quality Management Dist., 19 Cal. App. 4th 519 (1993); Dunn-Edwards Corp. v. South Coast Air Quality Management Dist., 19 Cal. App. 4th 536 (1993).
*PRACTICE AREAS: Public Law; Air Pollution; Water Resources; Commercial Litigation; Corporate Law.

**Smiland & Khachigian, (AV)**
**Seventh Floor One Bunker Hill, 601 West Fifth Street, 90071⊙**
**Telephone: 213-891-1010 Facsimile: 213-891-1414**
**Members of Firm: Joseph W. Swanwick (1858-1932); Charles E. Donnelly (1890-1973); Ernest M. Clark, Jr. (Emeritus); William M. Smiland; Kenneth L. Khachigian; Theodore A. Chester, Jr.; Christopher G. Foster. Of Counsel: Charles H. Chase.**
**General Civil Trial and Appellate Practice in all State and Federal Courts, Corporation, Commercial and General Business Practice. Water Resources, Air Pollution, Environmental and Government Regulation Practice.**
**San Clemente, California Office: 209 Avenida Del Mar, Suite 203, 92672. Telephone: 714-498-3879. Facsimile: 714-498-6197.**
*See Professional Biographies, LOS ANGELES, CALIFORNIA*

**Smilay, Steven L.** ......................'53 '79 C.1077 B.A. L.426 J.D. [Murchison&C.]
*PRACTICE AREAS: Intellectual Property; Litigation; Construction Litigation; General Business Tort Litigation.
**Smiles, Joan E.** ..................'— '92 C.881 B.A. L.800 J.D. [A Greenberg G.F.C.&M.]
*PRACTICE AREAS: Employment Law.

**Smiley, Bruce M.**, (AV) ..................'49 '74 C.112 B.A. L.809 J.D. [Freeman,F.&S.]
*PRACTICE AREAS: Real Property Law; Shopping Center Law.
Smiley, Robert W., Jr. .....................'43 '84 C.813 B.A. L.981 LL.B. P.O. Box 49422
Smiley, Stanley R. ..............................'47 '71 C.1044 B.A. L.724 J.D. 333 S. Grand
**Smith, Alfred E.** ......................'72 '96 C.112 B.A. L.309 J.D. [A Nossaman,G.K.&E.]
*PRACTICE AREAS: Litigation.
**Smith, Ann Kane** ...........................'45 '76 C.706 B.A. L.809 J.D. [Sheppard,M.R.&H.]
*PRACTICE AREAS: Labor/Employment; Litigation.
**Smith, Barry A.**, (AV) ..........'43 '71 C.1077 B.S. L.809 J.D. [B Buchalter,N.F.&Y.]
**Smith, Blithe Ann** .....................'66 '92 C.145 B.A. L.1068 J.D. [A Bergman&W.]
*LANGUAGES: French.
*PRACTICE AREAS: Federal and State Contract Procurement; Contract Litigation; Civil Rights Defense; Business Litigation.
Smith, Bonnie M. .........................'— '79 C.494 B.A. L.426 J.D. 6006 Wilshire Blvd.‡
**Smith, Brandon D.** ................'67 '94 C.112 B.A. L.767 J.D. [A Sedgwick,D.M.&A.]
**Smith, Brent W.** .......................'54 '79 C.112 B.A. L.1068 J.D. [Manning,L.B.&B.]
*PRACTICE AREAS: Automotive Dealer Law; Civil Trial; Business Purchase and Sales; Association and Commercial Law.
**Smith, Brian P.** ............................'65 '95 C.800 B.M. L.809 J.D. [A Koletsky,M.&F.]
*LANGUAGES: Spanish.
*PRACTICE AREAS: Construction Defect; General Liability.
**Smith, Bridgette M.** ......................'68 '94 C.112 B.A. L.800 J.D. [A Orrick,H.&S.]
Smith, Byron O., (P.C.), (AV) ...'16 '40 C&L.813 A.B., J.D. 777 S. Figueroa St., 10th Fl.
Smith, Carol K. ..............................................'33 '61 Legal Aid Found. of L.A.
Smith, Carolynne .....................'48 '79 C.800 B.A. L.1065 J.D. 11615 Moraga Ln.
**Smith, Carrie F.** ..........................'62 '90 C.112 B.S. L.940 J.D. [A Cotkin&C.]
*PRACTICE AREAS: Family Law; General Business and Civil Litigation; Municipal Liability Defense; Civil Rights Litigation.
**Smith, Charles G.** ........................'60 '84 C.813 A.B. L.426 J.D. [Kinsella,B.F.&T.]
*LANGUAGES: French.
*PRACTICE AREAS: Civil Litigation; Directors and Officers Liability; Insurance Law.
Smith, Christopher Lane ...............'66 '93 C.1049 B.B.A. L.770 J.D. [Schmid&V.] ‡
Smith, Clifton S., Jr., (AV) ...............'52 '76 C&L.800 A.B., J.D. 777 S. Figueroa St
Smith, Cortez ..............................'65 '90 C.674 B.A. L.659 J.D. 1999 Ave. of the Stars
Smith, Craig A. ........................'49 '79 C.1109 B.A. L.1137 J.D. 4700 Wilshire Blvd.
**Smith, Craig A.** ......................'52 '79 C.330 A.B. L.1068 J.D. [B Pircher,N.&M.]
*PRACTICE AREAS: Real Estate Law.
**Smith, Craig W.** ........................'66 '93 C.112 B.A. L.976 J.D. [A O'Melveny&M.]
**Smith, Dean J.** ...........................'62 '87 C&L.426 B.A., J.D. [A Ginsburg,S.O.&R.]
**Smith, Derek E.** ..............................'64 '91 C.101 B.S. L.188 J.D. [A Paul,H.J.&W.]
Smith, Diana L. ...............................................'59 '87 C.763 L.1137 J.D. Co. Dist. Atty.
**Smith, Dianne Baquet** ...............'55 '80 C.813 A.B. L.1066 J.D. [Sheppard,M.R.&H.]
Smith, Douglas D. '44 '74 C&L.37 B.S.C.E., J.D.
Assoc. Gen. Coun. & Dir., Risk Mgmt., AECOM Tech. Corp.
Smith, Edward B., III, (AV) '24 '53 C.112 B.A. L.1068 LL.B.
707 Wilshire Blvd., 51st Fl.
Smith, Edwin M., Jr. ..................................'50 '76 C&L.309 A.B., J.D. USC Law Ctr.
**Smith, Eric J.** ...........................'62 '91 C.1331 B.A. L.112 J.D. [A Riordan&M.]
*LANGUAGES: Spanish.
*PRACTICE AREAS: International and Domestic Corporate Law and Taxation.
**Smith, Frank H., Jr.**, (AV) ....................'43 '69 C&L.602 B.A., J.D. [Morgan,L.&B.]
Smith, Frank R. ..................................'21 '56 C.112 B.A. L.426 LL.B. 11116 Ophir Dr.‡
Smith, Frederick E. '32 '62 C.976 B.A. L.477 LL.B.
(adm. in MI; not adm. in CA) Libr., Univ. of Calif.
Smith, Gaillen R. ..........................'48 '76 C.112 B.A. L.1224 J.D. 128 S. Serrano Ave.
**Smith, Glen A.** .............................'55 '82 C.112 B.A. L.426 J.D. [Baker&H.]
**Smith, Glenn D.** ......................'64 '89 C.878 B.S. L.188 J.D. [A Stroock&S.&L.]
*LANGUAGES: Dutch and German.
*PRACTICE AREAS: Corporate Law; Securities Law; Finance Law; Mergers and Acquisitions Law; Banking Law.
**Smith, Gregory R.**, (AV) ........................'44 '69 C.154 B.A. L.309 J.D. [Irell&M.]
**Smith, Guy Porter**, (AV) ..........'33 '59 C&L.597 B.S., J.D. [Oppenheimer P.S.] (Pat.)
*PRACTICE AREAS: Intellectual Property Litigation and Prosecution.
Smith, Herman T. .......................'15 '56 C.671 B.A. L.809 LL.B. 5535 Bedford Ave.
Smith, Hiram E. ........................'58 '92 C.499 B.S. L.500 J.D. 6255 Sunset Blvd.
**Smith, Howard** .............................'68 '93 C.107 B.S. L.940 J.D. [A Chapin,F.&W.]
*PRACTICE AREAS: Insurance Litigation; Medical Malpractice; Civil Appeals.
Smith, James E. (Jay) ....................'58 '83 C.309 B.A. L.16 J.D. 6100 Wilshire Blvd.
Smith, Janine A. ...............'61 '87 C.264 A.B. L.659 J.D. 1901 Ave. of the Stars
**Smith, Jay E.** .................................'65 '92 C.97 B.S.B.A. L.800 J.D. [A Lane P.S.L.]
*PRACTICE AREAS: Litigation.
Smith, Jeffrey Carlin '51 '79 C.1051 B.S. L.1065 J.D.
Planning & Develop., Times Mirror Company, The
**Smith, Jeffrey M.** ..........'47 '79 C.588 B.S.Ch.E. L.146 J.D. [B Sedgwick,D.M.&A.]
**Smith, Jeffrey P.** ....................'47 '76 C.668 B.A. L.800 J.D. [Beckman,D.S.&R.]
*PRACTICE AREAS: Life, Health and Disability Insurance Law; ERISA; Civil Litigation; General Practice.
**Smith, Jeriel C.** ......................'45 '74 C.112 B.A. L.1068 J.D. [Gibbs,G.L.&A.]
*PRACTICE AREAS: Construction Law; Business Litigation.
**Smith, Jessica Cullen** '63 '92 C.881 B.A. L.94 J.D.
(adm. in MA; not adm. in CA) [A Troop M.S.&P.]
*PRACTICE AREAS: Corporate; Corporate Securities; Intellectual Property; Entertainment.
**Smith, Joel McCabe**, (AV) ...............'45 '72 C.112 B.A. L.1068 J.D. [Leopold,P.&S.]
*PRACTICE AREAS: Entertainment; Civil Litigation; Copyright and Trademark; Libel and Slander; Unfair Competition.
Smith, Julie A. '63 '90 C.856 B.A. L.309 J.D.
1800 Ave. of the Stars, Suite 900 (Century City)
**Smith, Julie F.** ............................'68 '95 C&L.101 B.S., J.D. [A Murchison&C.]
*LANGUAGES: Spanish.
*PRACTICE AREAS: Personal Injury; Construction Defect.
Smith, Kevin D. ..................................'57 '84 C&L.990 B.A., J.D. 624 S. Grand Ave.
**Smith, Kimberly A.** ......................'66 '91 C.112 B.A. L.823 J.D. [A Yukevich&S.]
*PRACTICE AREAS: Products Liability Defense; Personal Injury Defense; Employment Law.
**Smith, Lauren A.** ......................'55 '80 C.112 B.A. L.1066 J.D. [Hennigan,M.&B.]
**Smith, Laurie E.** ..........................'71 '96 C.112 B.A. L.893 J.D. [A Troop M.S.&P.]
*PRACTICE AREAS: Litigation.
Smith, Lawrence Ronald ............'66 '93 C.112 B.A. L.1148 J.D. 3699 Wilshire Blvd.
**Smith, Linda Jane**, (AV) '52 '77
C.188 B.A. L.1068 J.D. [O'Melveny&M.] (⊙Century City)
Smith, Lloyd M. ..........................'06 '33 C.813 A.B. L.309 LL.B. 2333 High Oak Dr.‡
**Smith, Marci L.** ..............................'65 '92 C&L.101 B.A., J.D. [A Latham&W.]
**Smith, Mark Halliwell**, (AV) ..............'56 '81 C.112 B.S. L.309 J.D. [Valensi,R.&M.]
*LANGUAGES: Spanish.
*PRACTICE AREAS: Corporate Law; Securities Law; Real Estate Law; General Business Law.
**Smith, Marla A.** ..............................'62 '93 C.378 B.A. L.800 J.D. [A Mendes&M.]
Smith, Marla Ann .........'62 '93 C.378 B.F.A. L.800 J.D. 12400 Wilshire Blvd. 13th Fl.
**Smith, Martin J.** .......................'56 '81 C.800 A.B. L.1068 J.D. [Sheppard,M.R.&H.]
*PRACTICE AREAS: Employee Benefits; ERISA.
**Smith, Matthew A.** ......................'64 '93 C.1077 B.S. L.800 J.D. [A Crosby,H.R.&M.]
**Smith, Michael T.** .....................'65 '94 C.1075 B.A. L.809 J.D. [A Arant,K.L.&R.]
*PRACTICE AREAS: Trademark; Copyright; Intellectual Property; Litigation Support.

CAA343P

Smith, Nancy ... '50 '80 C.800 B.A. L.809 J.D. 4605 Lakershim Blvd.
Smith, Nancy Anne ... '— '88 C.477 B.A. L.339 J.D. 11377 W. Olympic Blvd.
**Smith, Nancy C.** ... '56 '81 C.260 B.A. L.976 J.D. [Nossaman,G.K.&E.]
*PRACTICE AREAS: Real Property Law; Transportation Law.
Smith, Patrick N. ... '62 '91 C.170 B.A. L.990 J.D. Dep. Pub. Def.
Smith, Patrick S. ... '59 '85 C.35 B.S. L.809 J.D. 11766 Wilshire Blvd.
**Smith, Paul K.** ... '58 '86 C.426 B.B.A. L.800 J.D. [Smith&K.]
*PRACTICE AREAS: Business Litigation; Insurance Coverage; Estate Planning; Small Business Formation.
Smith, Peter S. ... '33 '61 C.112 A.B. L.426 J.D. Ret. Supr. Ct. J.
**Smith, R. David** ... '50 '79 C.112 A.B. L.800 J.D. [Ⓒ Gradstein,L.&V.]
**Smith, Rebecca J.** ... '58 '90 C.1042 B.A. L.809 J.D. [Ⓐ Gilbert,K.C.&J.]
Smith, Reid B. ... '45 '77 C.112 B.A. L.1095 J.D. [Ⓐ Gittler,W.&B.]
**Smith, Richard C.**, (AV) ... '43 '69 C.154 A.B. L.1065 J.D. [Arnold&P.]
*PRACTICE AREAS: Real Estate Law; Airport Law.
Smith, Richard D. ... '43 '81 C.1136 L.809 J.D. Sr. Law Clk.
**Smith, Richard K., Jr.** ... '55 '81 C&L.339 B.A., J.D. [White&C.]
Smith, Robert Borthwick ... '24 '49 C&L.800 LL.B. 5191 Franklin Ave.
**Smith, Robert M.** ... '53 '81 C.1097 B.A. L.1066 J.D. [Dewey B.]
*PRACTICE AREAS: Corporate.
Smith, Robin M. ... '56 '85 C.197 B.A. L.178 J.D. 10585 Santa Monica Blvd.
**Smith, Roger K.** ... '60 '95 C.201 B.A. L.1068 J.D. [Ⓐ Milbank,T.H.&M.]
**Smith, Ronald L.** ... '54 '80 C.112 B.A. L.809 J.D. [Parker S.]
**Smith, Sandra J.** ... '59 '87 C.918 B.A. L.1068 J.D. [Horvitz&L.]
**Smith, Scott O.**, (AV) ... '48 '74 C.800 B.S. L.426 J.D. [Ⓒ Buchalter,N.F.&Y.]
*PRACTICE AREAS: Insolvency; Commercial Litigation; Creditor Rights.
Smith, Shelley Ilene ... '47 '73 C.112 B.A. L.1068 J.D. Asst. City Atty.
Smith, Sherman W. ... '22 '49 C.922 A.B. L.329 LL.B. 4061 San Luis Dr.
Smith, Sidney O., III '57 '85 C.309 A.B. L.280 J.D.
(adm. in GA; not adm. in CA) 6201 Sunset Blvd.‡
Smith, Spurgeon E. ... '54 '82 C.061 B.S. L.329 J.D. Asst. U.S. Atty.
**Smith, Stephen S.** ... '69 '93 C.691 B.A. L.846 J.D. [Ⓐ Greenberg G.F.C.&M.]
*PRACTICE AREAS: Litigation; Entertainment.
Smith, Steven E., (AV) ... '37 '77 C.1097 B.A. L.1148 J.D. 650 S. Grand Ave.
**Smith, Steven E., (A Professional Corporation)** '55 '80
C.800 B.A. L.426 J.D. [Danning,G.D.&K.]
**Smith, Steven I.**, (AV) ... '54 '80 C.112 B.A. L.809 J.D. [Ⓐ Herzfeld&R.]
**Smith, Steven R.** ... '61 '89 C.878 B.A. L.94 J.D. [Ⓐ Sonnenschein N.&R.]
*PRACTICE AREAS: Litigation.
**Smith, Suzelle M.**, (AV) ... '53 '83 C.94 B.A. L.893 J.D. [Howarth&S.]
*PRACTICE AREAS: Trial Practice; Commercial Litigation; Complex and Multi-District Litigation; Products Liability Law; Appellate Practice.
**Smith, T. Edward** ... '70 '96 C.976 B.A. L.228 J.D. [Ⓐ Latham&W.]
**Smith, T. Mark** ... '66 '92 C.154 B.A. L.1068 J.D. [Ⓐ Sonnenschein N.&R.]
**Smith, Tamara C.** ... '64 '89 C&L.800 B.A., J.D. [Ⓐ Crosby,H.R.&M.]
**Smith, Terry Lynn** ... '52 '94 C.398 A.A. L.809 J.D. [Ⓐ Gilbert,K.C.&J.]
*PRACTICE AREAS: Insurance Defense; Workers' Compensation Law.
Smith, Theodore J., III ... '57 '84 C.808 B.S.B.A. L.803 J.D. Dep. City Atty.
Smith, Toxey Hall ... '15 '37 L.500 J.D. 6255 Sunset Blvd.
Smith, V. James ... '55 '82 C.668 B.A. L.1068 J.D. First Interstate Bank
**Smith, Valerie A.** ... '63 '90 C.112 B.A. L.426 J.D. [Ⓐ O'Melveny&M.]
**Smith, Ward D.**, (AV) ... '53 '81 C.112 A.B. L.464 J.D. [Bannan,G.S.&F.]
*PRACTICE AREAS: Environmental Law; Products Liability; Commercial Law.
**Smith, Wayne C.** ... '59 '86 C.112 B.S. L.464 J.D. [Ⓐ Charlston,R.&W.]
*PRACTICE AREAS: Professional Liability Defense.
**Smith, Wayne M.** ... '59 '84 C&L.477 B.S.E., J.D. [Graham&J.]
*PRACTICE AREAS: Intellectual Property; Patent Law; Commercial Litigation.
**Smith, Wayne W.**, (AV) ... '42 '72 C.1042 B.A. L.1068 J.D. [Gibson,D.&C.] (ⓞIrvine)
*PRACTICE AREAS: Business and Securities Litigation; Entertainment Litigation.
Smith, Wesley J., (AV) ... '49 '75 C.1077 B.A. L.1095 J.D. 2263 S. Harvard Blvd.
Smith, William E., Jr. ... '45 '80 C.112 B.A. L.426 J.D. Dep. Dist. Atty.
Smith, William G. ... '33 '64 C.112 B.S. L.800 J.D. P.O. Box 42247
Smith, Woodrow D. ... '49 '76 C.1070 B.S. L.426 J.D. 633 W. 5th St.
**Smith-Hess, Iris** ... '— '82 L.1136 J.D. [Ⓐ Ladas&P.] (See Pat. Sect.)

**Smith & Hilbig LLP**
**(See Torrance)**

**Smith & Kaufman LLP**
**601 South Figueroa Street, 41st Floor, 90017**
**Telephone: 213-623-9704 Fax: 213-623-4619**
**Paul K. Smith; Stephen J. Kaufman.**
**Business Litigation (Unfair Competition, Contract Disputes and Business Torts), Insurance Litigation, Environmental Coverage, Directors' and Officers' Coverage, Surety and Fidelity, Reinsurance, Political Campaign Finance and Election Law. Wills, Trusts and Estate Planning and Small Business Entity Formation.**

***See Professional Biographies, LOS ANGELES, CALIFORNIA***

Smith & Smith ... 888 S. Figueroa
**Smithson, David M.** ... '57 '85 C.629 B.S. L.93 J.D. [Ⓐ Cummins&W.]
*PRACTICE AREAS: Insurance Coverage; Environmental Defense; Business Litigation.
Smithson, Jennifer A. ... '61 '92 C&L.1137 B.S.L., J.D. 5670 Wilshire Blvd.
**Smits, Pete A.** ... '61 '90 C.475 B.S.E.E. L.846 J.D. [Ⓐ Robbins,B.&C.] (See Pat. Sect.)
*LANGUAGES: Latvian and Spanish.
*PRACTICE AREAS: Litigation; Trademark Law; Copyright Law; Patent Law; Intellectual Property.
**Smoller, Jonathan L.** ... '61 '88 C.112 B.A. L.1068 J.D. [Carlsmith B.W.C.&I.]
*PRACTICE AREAS: Commercial Litigation; Corporate Litigation.
**Smooke, Michael G.**, (AV) ... '45 '71 C.112 A.B. L.309 J.D. [Fulbright&J.]
*PRACTICE AREAS: Real Estate; Finance.
**Smoot, Peter C.**, (AV) ... '45 '71 C.112 B.A. L.800 J.D. [Rintala,S.J.&R.]
**Smoot, Roland N.**, (AV) ... '25 '55 C.111 B.S. L.276 J.D. [Lyon&L.] (See Pat. Sect.)
*PRACTICE AREAS: Patent, Trademark, Trade Regulation, Unfair Competition; Intellectual Property.
Smuckler, Elizabeth L. ... '60 '89 C.112 B.A. L.426 J.D. 11859 Wilshire Blvd.
Smurr, Douglas P. ... '59 '88 C.112 B.A. L.464 J.D. [Frank,G.&S.]
Smyle, Sue Ellen ... '43 '84 C.860 B.A. L.426 J.D. 221 N. Figueroa St.
Smylie, Robert O., (AV) ... '48 '77 C.112 B.A. L.809 J.D. [R.Smylie&Assoc.]
Smylie, Robert & Associates, (AV) ... 2049 Century Pk. E.
**Smyrski, Steven W.** ... '60 '92 C.679 B.S.M.E. L.809 J.D. [Oppenheimer P.S.] (Pat.)
*PRACTICE AREAS: Intellectual Property.
**Smyth, Bruce T.** ... '53 '79 C.813 B.A. L.893 J.D. [Ⓐ Charlston,R.&W.]
*PRACTICE AREAS: Business Litigation; Insurance Coverage.
Snader, Robert M. ... '25 '63 C.966 B.S.E.E. L.1068 J.D. 11791 Chenault St.
**Sneed, Tracy L.** ... '68 '93 C.893 B.A. L.846 J.D. [Ⓐ Friedlander&W.]
*PRACTICE AREAS: Business Transactions.
Sneider, Carolyn M. ... '66 '91 C.446 B.S. L.426 J.D. 10990 Wilshire Blvd.
**Sneiderman, Hayley L.** ... '66 '94 C&L.112 B.A., J.D. [Ⓐ Bronson,B.&M.]
**Snider, Darryl**, (AV) ... '49 '74 C&L.477 B.A., J.D. [Shearman&S.]
Snipper, Stephen J. ... '43 '76 1880 Century Park E.
Snow, Hugh J., (AV) ... '26 '55 C.813 B.A. L.1068 LL.B. [Snow&S.]
Snow & Snow, (AV) ... 11661 San Vicente Blvd.
Snowden, Pamela E. ... '45 '76 C.477 B.A. L.800 J.D. Dep. City Atty.‡

Snyder, Arthur K. ... '32 '60 C.990 B.A. L.800 J.D. 355 S. Grand Ave.
Snyder, Brent C. ... '64 '93 C.774 B.A. L.846 J.D. 555 S. Flower St.
**Snyder, Christina A.**, (AV) ... '47 '73 C.668 B.A. L.813 J.D. [Corinblit&S.]
*REPORTED CASES: Norman Williams v. Baxter Rice, 458 U.S. 654 (1982); Jedwab v. MGM Grand Hotels, Inc., 509 A.2d 584 (Del. Ch. 1986); Medallion Television Enterprises, Inc. v. SelecTV, 833 F.2d 1360 (9th Cir. 1987); Inforex Corp. v. MGM/UA Entertainment Co., 608 F.Supp. 129 (C.D. Cal. 1984).
*PRACTICE AREAS: Complex Civil Litigation; Antitrust; Securities.
Snyder, Deborah J. '53 '85
C.605 B.A. L.426 J.D. V.P. & Sr. Coun., Wells Fargo Bk., N.A.
**Snyder, Douglas P.** ... '54 '81 C.112 B.A. L.1068 J.D. [Cox,C.&N.]
*PRACTICE AREAS: Real Property Law.
**Snyder, George M.** ... '39 '80 C.911 B.S. L.426 J.D. [Ⓒ Rossbacher&Assoc.]
*PRACTICE AREAS: Civil Litigation; D&O; Insurance; Warranty; ERISA.
**Snyder, J. Kevin** ... '56 '82 C&L.800 B.A., J.D. [Robins,K.M.&C.]
*PRACTICE AREAS: Construction Law; Insurance Defense; Intellectual Property; Business Litigation.
**Snyder, Lawrence A., (A P.C.)** ... '53 '81 C.112 B.A. L.426 J.D. [Fainsbert,M.&S.]
*PRACTICE AREAS: Taxation Law; Estate Planning; Business Transactions; Real Estate.
Snyder, Linda R. ... '48 '77 C.112 B.A. L.1066 J.D. 1801 Century Park E.
Snyder, M. J. ... '42 '67 C.112 A.B. L.659 J.D. 2207 Maricopa Dr.‡
**Snyder, Mark A.** ... '64 '93 C.112 A.B. L.426 J.D. [Ⓐ Skadden,A.S.M.&F.]
Snyder, Mark R. ... '59 '83 C.147 B.S. L.1068 J.D. 4700 Wilshire Blvd.
**Snyder, Martin B.**, (BV) ... '51 '77 C.112 B.A. L.1049 J.D. [Goldfarb,S.&A.]
*PRACTICE AREAS: Civil Litigation; Real Estate Law; Business Litigation.
**Snyder, Patricia M.** ... '57 '82 C&L.426 B.A., J.D. [Marcus,W.S.&D.]
*PRACTICE AREAS: Real Property Litigation; General Business Litigation.
**Snyder, Ross D.** ... '66 '92 C.453 B.S. L.112 J.D. [Ⓐ Hecker&H.]
Snyder, Stanton J. ... '54 '80 C.112 B.A. L.1049 J.D. Dep. City Atty.
Snyderman, W. Dennis ... '44 '70 C.112 B.S. L.425 J.D. 11755 Wilshire Blvd.
**Sobel, Alan L.** ... '63 '88 C.156 B.A. L.904 J.D. [Ⓐ Ramsey,B.&D.]
*PRACTICE AREAS: Tractor-Trailer Litigation; General Products Negligence.
**Sobel, Larry D.** ... '51 '76 C.223 B.S. L.659 J.D. [Orrick,H.&S.]
*PRACTICE AREAS: Taxation Law; Public Finance Law.
Sobel, Lionel S., (AV) ... '46 '70 C.112 A.B. L.1068 J.D. Prof., Loyola Univ. Law Sch.
Sobel, William R. ... '58 '83 C.025 B.A. L.029 LL.B. [Edelstein,L.&S.]
Sobelle, Richard E., (AV) ... '35 '61 C&L.813 B.A., J.D. 600 Wilshire Blvd.
**Sobelsohn, Bernard**, (AV) ... '43 '68 C&L.178 A.B., LL.B. [Allen,R.S.&J.]
Sobelsohn, Daniel ... '71 '95 C&L.176 B.A., J.D. 601 S. Figueroa St.
**Sobelsohn, Daniel E.** ... '71 '95 C&L.178 B.A., J.D. [Ⓐ Sullivan&C.]
Sobhani, Paree M. ... '64 '89 C.112 B.A. L.809 J.D. 350 S. Figueroa St.
Sobieski, James L. ... '36 '61 C&L.813 B.A., J.D. Sr. V.P., Jardine Insurance Brokers, Inc.
**Sobieski, John**, (AV) ... '32 '58 C&L.813 A.B., LL.B. [Ⓒ Morrison&F.]
*PRACTICE AREAS: Appellate Practice and Business Litigation.
Sobo, Steven M. ... '46 '72 C.1077 B.A. L.809 J.D. 11835 W. Olympic Blvd.
**Socransky, Lisa E.** ... '— '91 C.112 B.A. L.426 J.D. [Ⓐ King,P.H.P.&B.]
*LANGUAGES: French.
Sofelkanik, Victor R. ... '55 '89 C.757 B.S. L.1148 J.D. Dep. City Atty.
**Sofen, Ronald S.** ... '48 '75 C.112 L.1068 [Gibbs,G.L.&A.]
*PRACTICE AREAS: Construction; Business Litigation.
**Soffer, Benjamin E.** ... '— '95 C.645 B.S. L.426 J.D. [Ⓐ Perkins C.]
*PRACTICE AREAS: Bankruptcy; Litigation.
**Sohagi, Margaret Moore** ... '55 '86 C.112 B.A. L.426 J.D. [Freilich,K.F.&S.]
**Sohaili, Hushmand** ... '54 '79 C.801 B.A. L.800 J.D. [Kaye,S.F.H.&H.]
*PRACTICE AREAS: Acquisitions; Joint Ventures; Real Estate; Real Estate Finance; Sales.
**Sohaili, Masood** ... '58 '82 C.112 B.A. L.800 J.D. [O'Melveny&M.]
*PRACTICE AREAS: Bond Counsel; Multi-Family Housing.
Sohigian, Ronald M. ... '37 '62 C.976 A.B. L.309 LL.B. Supr. Ct. J.
**Soiret, Jacques E.**, (AV) ... '42 '68 C.426 B.A. L.800 J.D. [Kirtland&P.]
**Sokol, Brent D.** ... '64 '93 C.597 B.S. L.94 J.D. [Ⓐ Lyon&L.] (See Pat. Sect.)
*PRACTICE AREAS: Patent, Trademark, Copyright, Antitrust; Trade Secret, Unfair Competition; Intellectual Property.
**Sokol, Claudia** ... '63 '93 C.569 L.809 J.D. [Ⓐ Robie&M.]
*LANGUAGES: Spanish.
*PRACTICE AREAS: Appellate Practice; Civil Litigation.
**Sokol, Robyn B.** ... '64 '92 C.174 B.S. L.94 J.D. [Robinson,D.B.&K.]
**Sokol, Ronald J., (A Professional Corporation)** '50 '78
C.112 B.A. L.770 J.D. [Billet&K.]
**Sokol, Steven A.** ... '50 '78 C.112 B.A. L.809 J.D. [Ⓐ Agapay,L.&H.]
**Sokoloff, Stanley W.**, (AV) '38 '66
C.971 B.S.Ch.E. L.818 J.D. [Blakely,S.T.&Z.] (See Pat. Sect.)
Sokolow, Norman H., (AV) ... '19 '49 C.112 A.B. L.800 J.D. Dep. Atty. Gen.‡
Soladar, Gordon D. ... '50 '79 C.569 L.809 J.D. 3200 Wilshire Blvd.
**Solares, Erick L.** ... '62 '89 C.112 B.A. L.1049 J.D. [Ⓐ Barbosa G.&B.]
*LANGUAGES: Spanish.
*PRACTICE AREAS: Personal Injury Law; Tort Liability; Civil Rights.
Solarz, M. Neil, (AV) ... '52 '77 C.112 B.A. L.767 J.D. [Borofsky&S.]
**Solarz, M. Neil**, (AV) ... '52 '77 C.112 B.A. L.767 J.D. [Ⓒ Weinstock,M.R.S.&N.]
*PRACTICE AREAS: Estate Planning; Probate/Trusts; Corporate; Business; Tax.
**Solberg, Mary K.** ... '56 '81 C.679 B.S. L.145 J.D. [Gipson H.&P.]
*PRACTICE AREAS: Corporate Securities.
**Soldate, S. Stuart** ... '51 '76 C.309 B.A. L.813 J.D. [Barger&W.]
*PRACTICE AREAS: Insurance Regulatory Law; Securities Law; Corporate Tax Law.
**Soldwedel, Cynthia T.** ... '63 '89 C.112 B.A. L.1066 J.D. [Ⓐ Lane P.S.L.]
*PRACTICE AREAS: Employment Law; Education Law.
Soleimani, Shahram ... '62 '95 C.112 B.A. L.1136 J.D. 1801 Century Pk. E.
Soleymani, David B. ... '63 '88 C.477 B.S. L.178 J.D. Sr. V.P., MSS Capital Corp.
Soli, Peter Andrew ... '50 '79 C.112 B.A. L.1127 J.D. 2049 Century Park E., 18th Fl.
**Solis, Carlos**, (AV) ... '45 '70 C&L.767 A.B., J.D. [Heller E.W.&M.]
*PRACTICE AREAS: Complex Litigation; Creditor Bankruptcy Law; Real Estate Litigation; Creditors Rights; Intellectual Property Litigation.
**Solish, Jonathan Craig**, (AV) ... '49 '75 C.1169 B.A. L.1068 J.D. [Solish,A.&G.]
*REPORTED CASES: Strang v. Cabrol, 37 Cal.3d 720, 209 Cal.Rptr. 347 (1984); Nelson v. Tiffany Industries, Inc. 778 F.2d 533 (9th Cir. 1985); 6th & K Ltd., v. Ramada Franchise Systems, Inc., Bus. Franchise Guide (CCH) 10,721 (S.D. Cal. 1995); O'Leary v. Mid Wilshire Associates, 7 Cal. App. 4th 1450 (1992); 6th & K v. RFS, Inc., Bus. Franchise Guide (CCH) ¶10,721 (S.D.Cal). 1995).
*PRACTICE AREAS: Franchise Law; Antitrust; Intellectual Property; Civil Trials; Appellate.

**Solish, Arbiter & Gehring, LLP, (AV)**
**12100 Wilshire Boulevard 15th Floor, 90025**
**Telephone: 310-826-2255 FAX: 310-207-3230**
**Jonathan Craig Solish; Ross Arbiter; Steven D. Wiener; Judith B. Gitterman; Thomas G. Gehring;— Robert M. Philips; Glenn J. Plattner; Joel D. Siegel.**
**Franchise, Intellectual Property, Labor, Insurance, Business, Real Estate, Corporate, Tort, Administrative Law and Litigation and Appellate Practice in all State and Federal Courts before Municipal Administration and Regulatory Boards, Agencies and Elected Councils, Banking and Finance.**

***See Professional Biographies, LOS ANGELES, CALIFORNIA***

Soll, Arthur, (AV) ... '31 '59 C.112 B.A. L.1068 J.D. 11835 W. Olympic Blvd.
Soll, Kathleen L. ... '67 '93 C.112 B.A. L.800 J.D. 2121 Ave. of the Stars
Sollami, Paul F. ... '46 '74 C.728 B.S. L.800 J.D. 12304 Santa Monica Blvd.
Soller, Shayne & Horn ... 624 South Grand Avenue (ⓞNew York, NY; Boston, MA.)

**Solner, Michael C.**
(See Encino)

**Solo, Gail D., (A Professional Corporation)** '50 '75
C.112 B.A. L.1068 J.D. [Ⓑ McKay,B.&G.]
*LANGUAGES: Spanish.
*PRACTICE AREAS: Labor and Employment; Civil Trial; Personal Injury; Medical Malpractice.
**Soloff, Michael E.** ........................'58 '84 C.103 B.A. L.309 J.D. [Munger,T.&O.]
**Solomon, Amy Fisch** ....................'60 '89 C.1077 B.A. L.426 J.D. [Girardi&K.]
*PRACTICE AREAS: Professional Liability; Toxic Torts.
**Solomon, Glenn E.** ....................'67 '91 C.112 B.A. L.309 J.D. [Ⓐ Sidley&A.]
*PRACTICE AREAS: Complex Business Litigation; Employment Law; Real Estate Law.
Solomon, Kay S. ....................'62 '87 C.800 B.S. L.426 J.D. 333 S. Hope St., 48th Fl.
Solomon, Mark B. ....................'50 '77 C.823 B.A. L.765 J.D. 6255 Sunset Blvd.
**Solomon, Richard P.** ....................'50 '83 C.280 B.A. L.61 J.D. [Mayer,G.&G.]
*PRACTICE AREAS: Entertainment Law; Television Law; Motion Picture Law; Intellectual Property Law.

**Solomon, Stephen E., (AV) '39 '66 C.477 B.B.A. L.813 LL.B.** BR
**1801 Century Park East Suite 2400, 90067**
**Telephone: 310-556-0360 Fax: 310-556-0462**
**Federal and state income tax planning and controversy matters.**
***See Professional Biographies, LOS ANGELES, CALIFORNIA***

Solomon, Steven ....................'50 '76 C.1029 B.S. L.1095 J.D. 6922 Hollywood Blvd.‡
Solov, Lessing C., (AV) ..........'32 '59 C.112 B.A. L.1065 J.D. 1625 W. Olympic Blvd.
**Soloway, Howard B.**, (AV) ..........'46 '72 C.112 A.B. L.309 J.D. [Donovan L.N.&I.]
Soltis, Stephen J. '30 '56 C.1258 L.426 LL.B.
2nd V.P. & Asst. Gen. Coun., Transamerica Occidental Life Ins. Co.
**Soltman, Neil M.**, (AV) ....................'49 '75 C.831 B.A. L.128 J.D. [Mayer,B.&P.]
**Solum, Conrad R., Jr.**, (AV) ....'35 '60 C&L.800 B.E., LL.B. [Lyon&L.] (See Pat. Sect.)
*PRACTICE AREAS: Patent, Trademark, Copyright, Unfair Competition; Intellectual Property.
Somer, Abraham, (AV) ..........'38 '63 C&L.800 B.A., LL.B. 11377 W. Olympic Blvd.
Somer, Stuart '62 '91 C.880 B.S. L.802 J.D.
(adm. in TX; not adm. in CA) 221 N. Figueroa St.
Somerfeld, Henry ....................'53 '79 C&L.472 B.B.A., J.D. 2029 Century Park East
Somers, Harold M. '15 '56 C.025 B.Com. L.107 LL.B.
(adm. in NY; not adm. in CA) 152 N. Kenter Ave‡
Somers, Margery ....................'48 '94 C.112 B.A. L.940 J.D. 6300 Wilshire Blvd.
Somers, Pamela ....................'51 '79 C.1169 B.A. L.426 J.D. 12121 Wilshire Blvd.
**Sommer, John R.** ....................'58 '82 C.347 B.A. L.1068 J.D. [Ⓑ Baker&H.]
*LANGUAGES: Spanish.
*REPORTED CASES: Acuson Corp. v. Aloka Co., Ltd., 10 USPQ 1814 (Cal. App., 6th Dist. 1989).
*PRACTICE AREAS: Intellectual Property Litigation; Business Advice and Litigation.
**Sommers, Howard N.** '42 '67
C.124 B.S.E.E. L.569 J.D. [Ⓑ Fulwider P.L.&U.] (See Pat. Sect.)
*REPORTED CASES: Raceway Components, Inc. v. Butler Mfg. Co., F.Supp. 856; 11 USPQ2d 1799 (USDC, SDWVa, 1989) MW; Cento Group, S.p.A. v. OroAmerica, Inc., 822 F.Supp 1058 (USDC, SDNY, 1993).
*PRACTICE AREAS: Patent Law; Trademark Law; Copyright Law; Unfair Competition Law.
**Sommers, Richard D.**, (AV) ..........'45 '71 C.1068 A.B. L.426 J.D. [Schwartz,S.D.&S.]
*PRACTICE AREAS: ERISA; Employee Benefit Law; Labor and Employment Law.
**Sommers, Richard L.** ....................'52 '77 C.339 B.S. L.477 J.D. [Sheppard,M.R.&H.]
*PRACTICE AREAS: Commercial Law; Banking Law; Real Estate Finance Law.
Sommerstein, Gary ....................'65 '90 C.112 B.A. L.800 J.D. [Ⓐ Pollet&W.]
Sondheim, Harry B., (AV) ..........'35 '57 C&L.145 A.B., J.D. Head Dep., Appellate Div.
**Sonenshine, Allyson W.** '71 '96
C.659 B.A. L.800 J.D. [Ⓐ McCutchen,D.B.&E.] (☉San Francisco)
*LANGUAGES: French.
*PRACTICE AREAS: Litigation and Employment Law.
Sonfield & Sonfield, A Prtnship incl. Prof. Corps.
1888 Century Pk. E. (☉Houston, Texas & Fairfax, Va.)
**Song, Joon W.** ....................'67 '95 C.112 B.A. L.1068 J.D. [Ⓐ Frandzel&S.]
*LANGUAGES: Korean.
*PRACTICE AREAS: Commercial Litigation; Municipal Law.
**Song, Lawrence J.** ....................'52 '77 C.679 B.A. L.128 J.D. [Littler,M.F.T.&M.]
**Sonne, Carl W.** ....................'58 '84 C&L.101 B.A., J.D. [Rogers&W.]
Sonnenberg, Andrea L. ..........'61 '86 C.800 B.S. L.426 J.D. Paramount Pictures Corp.
**Sonnenberg, Glenn A.** '56 '80 C&L.800 A.B., J.D.
Pres., ING Real Estate Investors, Inc.
**Sonnenberg, Stephen P.** ....................'52 '92 C.1349 B.A. [Ⓐ Paul,H.J.&W.]
**Sonnenschein, Edward, Jr.**, (AV) ..........'54 '79 C&L.309 A.B., J.D. [Latham&W.]

**Sonnenschein Nath & Rosenthal, (AV)** BR
**601 South Figueroa Street, Suite 1500, 90017**☉
**Telephone: 213-623-9300 Telecopier: 213-623-9924**
**Percy Anderson; Michael J. Bayard; Ernest P. Burger; Charles R. Campbell, Jr.; Martin J. Foley; Matthew C. Fragner; Brent Matthew Giddens; Peter J. Gurfein; Elliott J. Hahn; Mark T. Hansen; Sue L. Himmelrich; Ronald D. Kent; Lee T. Paterson; Laura R. Petroff; Andria K. Richey; Michael W. Ring; Robert F. Scoular; Norbert M. Seifert; J. A. Shafran; Arthur F. Silbergeld; Susan M. Walker. Of Counsel: Neal R. Marder; Grace Ellen Mueller; Henry S. Zangwill. Associates: Jeffry Butler; Anthony Capobianco; Nargis Choudhry; Stephen J. Curran; Weston A. Edwards; Jonathan F. Golding; Charles W. Hokanson; Bryan C. Jackson; Scott L. Jones; Suzanne Cate Jones; Matthew I. Kaplan; Namyon Kim; Jessie A. Kohler; Pauline Ng Lee; John R. Miller; Duncan E. Montgomery; Terrence R. Pace; Michael E. Pappas; Stacie S. Polashuk; Leonora M. Schloss; David Simantob; Steven R. Smith; T. Mark Smith; David W. Tufts; John E. Walker; Vivian L. Williams; Lauren M. Yu; Consuelo A. Zermeno.**
**Antitrust, Aviation Litigation, Banking, Bankruptcy, Commercial Financing, Construction, Corporate, Employee Benefits, Environmental, Estate Planning, Executive Compensation, First Amendment, Franchising, Government Contracts, Health Care, Insurance, Intellectual Property, International Trade, Labor and Employment, Land Use, Litigation, Media, Municipal Bonds, Probate, Product Liability, Professional Liability, Real Estate, Securities, Taxation, Trade Regulation, Venture Capital, White Collar Criminal Defense, Workouts, Zoning.**
**Chicago, Illinois Office: Suite 8000 Sears Tower, 233 South Wacker Drive. Telephone: 312-876-8000. Cable Address: "Sonberk". Telex: 25-3526. Facsimile: 312-876-7934.**
**New York, N.Y. Office: 1221 Avenue of the Americas, 24th Floor. Telephone: 212-768-6700. Facsimile: 212-391-1247.**
**Washington, D.C. Office: 1301 K Street, N.W., Suite 600 East Tower. Telephone: 202-408-6400. Fax: 202-408-6399.**
**San Francisco, California Office: 685 Market Street, 10th Floor. Telephone: 415-882-5000. Facsimile: 415-543-5472.**
**St. Louis, Missouri Office: One Metropolitan Square, Suite 3000. Telephone: 314-241-1800. Facsimile: 314-259-5959.**
**Kansas City, Missouri Office: Suite 1100, 4520 Main Street, 64111. Telephone: 816-932-4400. Facsimile: 816-531-7545.**
**London, England Office: Sonnenscheins, Royex House, Aldermanbury Square, EC2V 7HR. Telephone: 0171-600-2222. Facsimile: 0171-600-2221.**
***See Professional Biographies, LOS ANGELES, CALIFORNIA***

**Sonner, David A.** ....................'57 '88 C.1167 B.S. L.809 J.D. [Ⓐ McKenna&C.]
*PRACTICE AREAS: Government Contracts Law; Litigation.
**Sonnett, Anthony E.** ....................'60 '86 C.881 B.A. L.1019 J.D. [Yukevich&S.]
*PRACTICE AREAS: Products Liability Defense; Personal Injury Defense; Commercial Litigation.
Soo Hoo, Bentley M. ....................'62 '90 C.1097 B.S. L.426 J.D. 201 N. Figueroa St.
Soo Hoo, Mona C. ..........'57 '83 C.112 B.S. L.1066 J.D. 660 S. Figueroa St., 21st Fl.

**Soodik, Michael J.**
(See Pasadena)

**Soomekh, Karen A.** ....................'42 '93 C.959 B.S. L.809 J.D. [Ⓐ Lord,B.&B.]
**Soosman, Barry F.** ....................'60 '84 C&L.800 B.S., J.D. [Ⓑ Buchalter,N.F.&Y.]
*PRACTICE AREAS: Real Estate; Bank and Finance.
**Soper, Robert G.** ....................'57 '84 C.112 A.B. L.1068 J.D. [Ⓐ Arter&H.]
**Soref, Randye B.** ....................'55 '81 C.1019 B.A. L.61 J.D. [Buchalter,N.F.&Y.]
*PRACTICE AREAS: Insolvency; Chapter 11; Commercial Litigation.
Sorenson, Richard G. ....................'33 '76 C.112 B.S. L.464 J.D. Dep. City Atty.
**Soriano, Laurie L.** ....................'61 '86 C.659 B.S. L.1067 J.D. [Manatt,P.&P.]
*PRACTICE AREAS: Entertainment Law.
**Sorochinsky, Michael I.** ....................'68 '93 C&L.112 B.A., J.D. [Ⓐ Perkins C.]
*LANGUAGES: Russian.
*PRACTICE AREAS: Bankruptcy; Litigation.
**Sorrell, Paul N.** ....................'61 '86 C.940 B.A. L.1068 J.D. [Belin R.&B.]
*PRACTICE AREAS: Business Litigation; Real Estate; Construction Defect; Financial Institution Litigation.
**Sorrell, Todd M.** ....................'69 '94 C.112 B.A. L.1068 J.D. [Ⓐ Fulbright&J.]
*LANGUAGES: Spanish.
*PRACTICE AREAS: Litigation.
Sorrentino, Joseph N. ....................'37 '68 C.112 B.A. L.309 J.D. Co. Pros.
Sosa, R. Thomas ....................'48 '73 C.112 B.A. L.426 J.D. 2241 Lyric Ave.
**Soskin, Stephen P.** ....................'56 '81 C&L.339 B.S., J.D. [Charlston,R.&W.]
**Sosnow, Kelly J.** ....................'70 '95 C.659 B.A. L.309 J.D. [Ⓐ Latham&W.]
**Soto, Philip L.** ....................'59 '87 C.813 B.A. L.426 J.D. [Ⓐ Manning,M.&W.]
Sotomayor, Rande Sherman ...'58 '84 C.228 A.B. L.910 J.D. 777 S. Figueroa St., 10th Fl.
Soudry, Roslyn, (BV) ....................'47 '76 C.445 B.A. L.64 J.D. 1675 Century Park E.
**Soukup, John F.** ....................'48 '74 C&L.800 B.A., J.D. [Aronoff&S.]
*PRACTICE AREAS: Real Estate - Transactional; Business - Transactional.
Soule, Matthew D. ....................'57 '83 C.911 B.A. L.629 J.D. 201 N. Figueroa St.
**Soule, Steven E.** ....................'68 '95 C.813 B.S. L.112 J.D. [Ⓐ O'Melveny&M.]
**Soulema, Solomon**, (AV) ....................'50 '75 C.1077 B.A. L.1095 J.D. [Liebman&R.]
*LANGUAGES: Spanish and Greek.
*PRACTICE AREAS: Workers Compensation Defense Law.
Souras, Louis G. '59 '87 C.893 B.A. L.228 J.D.
(adm. in FL; not adm. in CA) 668 Echo Park Ave.

**Sousa, Angela M. '54 '80 C.112 A.B. L.309 J.D.**
**1840 Century Park East Eighth Floor, 90067**
**Telephone: 310-553-1390 Telecopier: 310-553-1392**
**Business Litigation, Construction and Public Utilities Litigation.**
***See Professional Biographies, LOS ANGELES, CALIFORNIA***

Sousa, Anthony J. ....................'50 '84 C.112 A.B. L.284 J.D. Dep. Dist. Atty.
Sousa, Barbara C. ....................'63 '94 C.112 B.A. L.426 J.D. 555 S. Flower St.
**Southern, Robert A.**, (AV Ⓣ) '30 '55 C&L.597 B.S., LL.B.
(adm. in IL; not adm. in CA) [Mayer,B.&P.]
**Southern, Tawnya L.** ....................'67 '94 C.112 B.A. L.809 J.D. [Ⓐ Acker,K.&W.]
*PRACTICE AREAS: Civil Litigation; Construction Defect.
Southers, Eleanor K. ....................'38 '83 C.766 B.A. L.398 J.D. 10866 Wilshire Blvd.
Southworth, John F. ....................'44 '70 C.976 B.A. L.893 LL.B. [Ⓐ Miller&H.]
**Souveroff, Michael W.** ....................'61 '86 C.813 A.B. L.800 J.D. [Ⓐ Bryan C.]
*PRACTICE AREAS: Corporate.
Souza, William Joseph ....................'51 '84 C.763 B.A. L.809 J.D. First Interstate Bank
Soven, Abby ....................'36 '69 C.102 B.A. L.800 J.D. Supr. Ct. J.
Sowa, Paul F. ....................'45 '72 C.339 B.S. L.1068 J.D. 1520 Wilshire Blvd., 6th Fl.
Sowders, Steven A., (AV) ....................'47 '73 C.37 B.A. L.809 J.D. Dep. Dist. Atty.
**Sowers, Donald G.** ....................'53 '86 C.999 A.S. L.809 J.D. [Takakjian&S.]☉
*PRACTICE AREAS: Criminal Defense.
**Soza, Jeffrey C.** ....................'62 '87 C.800 B.S. L.1065 J.D. [Christensen,M.F.J.G.W.&S.]
*PRACTICE AREAS: Corporate; Securities Law.
**Spackman, Paul** ....................'48 '90 C.763 B.A. L.426 J.D. [R.Iungerich]
*REPORTED CASES: Silva v. Superior Court, (1993) 14 Cal.App. 4th 562.
*PRACTICE AREAS: Administrative Law; Civil Trial; Physicians Licensing.
**Spadoni, Eileen** ....................'59 '87 C.112 B.A. L.1068 J.D. [Ⓐ R.A.Love]
*LANGUAGES: Spanish, French.
Spahn, John C. ....................'50 '82 C.112 A.B. L.1148 J.D. 4295 Via Arbolada★
**Spalding, William F.**, (AV) ........'19 '48 C.602 B.S.C. L.309 LL.B. [Ⓑ Gibson,D.&C.] ‡
*PRACTICE AREAS: Labor and Employment Law; Administrative Law.
**Spandorf, Rochelle Buchsbaum** ..........'51 '76 C.188 B.S. L.910 J.D. [Shapiro,R.&C.]
*PRACTICE AREAS: Domestic and international franchising and licensing matters in all industries.
Spangenberg, Erich Lawson '60 '85 C.787 B.A. L.930 J.D.
(adm. in TX; not adm. in CA) 555 W. 5th St.
Spangler, Lore K. ....................'45 '81 C.112 B.A. L.809 J.D. 2148 1/2 Sunset Blvd.
Spann, Calvin D. ....................'25 '62 C.1043 B.A. L.426 LL.B. 2323 Buckingham Rd.
**Spanos, Theodore G.** ....................'61 '86 C.112 B.A. L.1065 J.D. [Ⓐ Morgan,L.&B.]
**Spar, A. Albert** ....................'16 '39 C&L.472 B.A., J.D. [Ⓑ Parker,M.C.O.&S.]
*REPORTED CASES: In re Arstein (Probate); Buck v. Buck - Domestic Relations; Participation in recent automobile appellate cases: BMW of North America, Inc. v. New Motor Vehicle Board (Hal Watkins Chevrolet Inc. 209 Cal.Rept.50, 162 CA3d 980); Piano v. New Motor Vehicle Board, 163 Cal.Rept.41, 103 CA3d 412; Champian Motorcycles v. New Motor Vehicle Board (Yamaha).
*PRACTICE AREAS: General Civil Litigation; Automobile Dealer Transactions and Litigation.
**Sparks, Jerry R.** ....................'68 '93 C.475 B.A. L.423 J.D. [Ⓐ Hewitt&P.]
**Spatz, Alan B.** ....................'54 '79 C.477 B.A. L.1066 J.D. [Troop M.S.&P.]
*PRACTICE AREAS: Financial Institutions Law; Corporate and Securities Law.
Spaulding, Anthony A. ..........'34 '60 C.800 B.A. L.1068 LL.B. 12301 Wilshire Blvd.
**Spaziano, Jennifer L.** ....................'71 '95 C.93 A.B. L.990 J.D. [Ⓐ McDermott,W.&E.]
Speaks, Denise D. ....................'53 '78 C.411 B.A. L.665 J.D. Univ. Park
Spear, Alison D. ....................'66 '93 C.309 A.B. L.464 J.D. 11355 W. Olympic Blvd.
Spear, Bradley H. ....................'59 '88 C.112 B.S. L.398 J.D. 1126 Wilshire Blvd.
**Spear, Martin J.** ....................'43 '71 C.1077 B.A. L.809 J.D. [Barton,K.&O.]
*PRACTICE AREAS: Trial Practice; Corporate Law; Banking; Loan Restructuring; Commercial Finance.
**Specht, Lisa**, (AV) ....................'45 '76 L.1095 J.D. [Manatt,P.&P.]
*PRACTICE AREAS: Government.
**Spector, Steven M.**, (AV) ..........'47 '72 C.112 A.B. L.426 J.D. [McDermott,W.&E.]
*PRACTICE AREAS: Bankruptcy; Banks and Banking; Debtor and Creditor.
**Spector, Steven W.** ....................'65 '91 C&L.659 B.A., J.D. [Ⓐ Morgan,L.&B.]
Spector, William D., (AV) ..........'25 '51 C.112 L.809 LL.B. [Spector,B.H.&B.]
Spector, Buter, Hoberman & Buzard, A Law Corp., (AV) .......... 11611 San Vicente Blvd.
**Spees, Sherry D.** ....................'56 '81 C.659 B.A. L.831 J.D. [Weiss,S.S.D.&S.]
*PRACTICE AREAS: Tax Law; Bankruptcy Law; Corporate Law.
**Speiser, I. Bruce**, (AV) ....................'48 '74 C.705 B.A. L.273 J.D. [Rogers&W.]
*PRACTICE AREAS: Bankruptcy Litigation; Foreclosures; Receiverships; Loan Workouts; Business Litigation.
Spence, John C., III ....................'43 '68 C.813 A.B. L.1068 J.D. Dep. Dist. Atty.
**Spencer, Bud** ....................'68 '94 C.112 B.S. L.809 J.D. [Ⓐ Ericksen,A.K.D.&L.]
*PRACTICE AREAS: Insurance Defense Litigation.
Spencer, Kenneth F. ....................'60 '85 C&L.705 B.A., J.D. 10940 Wilshire Blvd.

CAA345P

**Spencer, Richard C., Law Offices of,** (AV) '43 '69 C.823 A.B. L.107 J.D. [BB]
**One Wilshire Boulevard, Suite 2100, 90017**
**Telephone: 213-629-7900 Fax: 213-629-7990**
***PRACTICE AREAS: Civil Litigation; Business Law.**
**Civil Litigation, Business Law.**
***See Professional Biographies, LOS ANGELES, CALIFORNIA***

Spencer, Steven E. .................... '56 '85 C.705 B.A. L.1049 J.D. 3600 Wilshire Blvd.
Spencer, Vaino H. ............................ '20 '52 L.809 LL.B. Pres. Jus., Ct. of Appls.
Spensley, W. Robert, (AV) '25 '51 C.494 B.M.E. L.502 LL.B.
1880 Century Pk. E. (Pat.)
Spero, Nancy E., (AV) ...................... '49 '74 C&L.112 B.A., J.D. P.O. Box 49834

**Spero, Peter, Professional Corporation**
**(See Santa Monica)**

**Speyer, James F.** ................................ '59 '87 C.951 B.A. L.273 J.D. [Arnold&P.]
**Spiegel, Adam G.** .............................'64 '89 C.112 B.A. L.276 J.D. [Murphy,W.&B.]
*PRACTICE AREAS: Secured Financing; Commercial Lending; Business Workouts.
Spiegel, Albert A. ..........................'16 '40 C.665 B.A. L.309 LL.B. 2050 S. Bundy Dr.‡
**Spiegel, Bennett L.**, (AV) ......................'59 '85 C.705 B.A. L.976 J.D. [Wynne S.I.]
**Spiegel, Craig R.** ............................. '53 '80 C.747 B.A. L.309 J.D. [McMahon&S.]
*PRACTICE AREAS: Business Litigation; Antitrust Law; Securities; Class Actions.
Spiegel, Harry, A Professional Law Corporation '50 '79
C.766 B.A. L.1136 J.D. 6100 Wilshire Blvd.
**Spiegel, Jody L.** ...................... '60 '85 C.914 B.A. L.800 J.D. [[A] Brobeck,P.&H.]
*PRACTICE AREAS: General Civil Litigation; Products Liability.
**Spiegel, John W.** ................................'48 '77 C.813 A.B. L.976 J.D. [Munger,T.&O.]
Spiegel, Mark A. ......................... '47 '72 C.228 A.B. L.309 J.D. 2050 S. Bundy Dr.
Spiegel, Michael ..........................'46 '73 C.1077 B.S. L.809 J.D. [Spiegel,V.&Y.]
**Spiegel, Ronald L.** ........................'58 '87 C.1077 B.S. L.426 J.D. [Feingold&S.]
*PRACTICE AREAS: Civil Trial; Real Property Litigation; Construction and Tort Litigation.
Spiegel, Stephen Jay ......................... '52 '77 C.398 B.A. L.1095 J.D. [Einstein&S.]
Spiegel, Vitabile & Yochelson ............................................4221 Wilshire Blvd.
Spiegelman, Jack ........................ '27 '60 C.112 B.S. L.809 LL.B. [Spiegelman&E.]
Spiegelman, Steve J. '53 '92 C.426 B.A. L.221 J.D.
(adm. in SD; not adm. in CA) P.O. Box 48271
Spiegelman & Edwards ...................................... 1642 Westwood Blvd., 3rd Fl.

**Spile & Siegal, LLP**
**(See Encino)**

**Spillane, Jay M.** ...................................'60 '86 C.112 B.A. L.1065 J.D. [Fox&S.]
*PRACTICE AREAS: Litigation.
Spillane, John K. ................................. '53 '78 C&L.426 B.A., J.D. Dep. Dist. Atty.
Spillane, Suzanne V. ............................'63 '93 C.112 A.B. L.188 J.D. 515 S. Flower St.
Spinks, Lynwood L. ........'52 '79 C.10 B.A. L.309 J.D. Exec. V.P., Carolco Pictures Inc.
Spinrad, Frederick L. .....................'48 '74 C.800 B.S. L.426 LL.B. 12400 Wilshire Blvd.
**Spira, Immanuel I.** ..........................'63 '90 C.228 B.S. L.597 J.D. [[A] Katten M.&Z.]
*PRACTICE AREAS: Entertainment Finance Law.
**Spira, Samuel R.** ......................................'64 '94 C.112 B.A. L.999 J.D. [[A] Klein&M.]
**Spira, Susan G.** ...........................'63 '90 C.112 B.A. L.426 J.D. [[A] Allen,M.L.G.&M.]
*PRACTICE AREAS: Bankruptcy/Creditors' Rights (80%, 40); Receiverships (20%, 10).
Spirito, Kim Thurman ............................'57 '82 C.800 B.A. L.426 J.D. 221 N. Figueroa St.
**Spitals, John P.** ........'53 '80 C.103 Sc.B. L.564 J.D. [[C] Robbins,B.&C.] (See Pat. Sect.)
*LANGUAGES: French, German, Italian, Spanish.
*PRACTICE AREAS: Patent Prosecution Law (Biological and Chemical).
Spitser, James L. .................................'38 '65 C.112 B.S. L.1068 J.D. Asst. City Atty.
**Spitz, Jeffrey** ...........................'56 '85 C.659 B.A. L.1067 J.D. [Greenberg G.F.C.&M.]
*PRACTICE AREAS: Entertainment Litigation; Intellectual Property Litigation; Real Estate Litigation; Bankruptcy Litigation; General Business Litigation.
**Spitz, Jill A.** .............................................'64 '92 C.1077 B.S. L.800 J.D. [[A] Dale,B.&H.]
Spitz, Richard A. ..................................'60 '86 C.1077 B.S. L.861 J.D. 555 S. Flower St.
**Spitz, Steven S.** ........................................'68 '94 C.103 A.B. L.178 J.D. [[A] Rogers&W.]
**Spitzer, Mark A.** ............................'60 '86 C.942 B.A. L.228 J.D. [Sheppard,M.R.&H.]
Spitzer, Matthew L. ................................ '52 '77 C.112 B.A. L.800 J.D. USC Sch. of Law
**Spitzer, Susan Michelle** ........'57 '82 C&L.426 B.A., J.D. [Bovitz&S.] & [[C] Dixon&D.]
*PRACTICE AREAS: Bankruptcy Law; Finance.
**Spitzer, Susan Michelle** ...................................'57 '82 C&L.426 B.A., J.D. [[C] Dixon&J.]
*PRACTICE AREAS: Bankruptcy Law; Creditor's Rights.
Spivack, Mona Sedky .......................'66 '93 C.813 A.B. L.276 J.D. 333 S. Grand Ave.
Spivak, Joel A. ..............................'58 '82 C.112 B.A. L.1137 J.D. 3555 Keystone Ave.
Spivak, William B., Jr., (AV) ........... '35 '62 C.112 B.A. L.1068 LL.B. Asst. U.S. Atty.
**Spivey, Corey J.** ............................... '69 '94 C.691 B.A. L.976 J.D. [[A] Gipson H.&P.]
*PRACTICE AREAS: Litigation.
Spivey, Reuben A. ............... '41 '89 C.112 B.S. L.999 J.D. 5200 W. Century Blvd FL. 900
Spizer, S. W. ................................. '07 '30 C.112 L.809 J.D. 11722 Darlington Ave.‡
**Spoeri, James C.**, (BV) ...........................'52 '77 C.436 B.A. L.424 J.D. [Clopton,P.&B.]

**Spolin & Silverman**
**(See Santa Monica)**

**Spolyar, Geoffrey J.** .......................... '70 '96 C.477 B.A. L.800 J.D. [[A] O'Melveny&M.]
*LANGUAGES: Japanese, German.
**Spooner, Mark J.**, (AV) .............................. '45 '70 C.276 A.B. L.893 J.D. [Arnold&P.]
*PRACTICE AREAS: Complex Civil Litigation; Antitrust; Franchising/Distribution.
Spradlin, Thomas Richard, (AV) '37 '63 C&L.273 B.A., J.D.
(adm. in VA; not adm. in CA) 10992 Ashton Ave.‡
Spratt, James T. ..............................'58 '86 C.112 B.A. L.398 J.D. 2049 Century Park E.

**Spray, Gould & Bowers, A Professional Corporation, (AV)**
**Suite 1655, 3530 Wilshire Boulevard, 90010**
**Telephone: 213-385-3402**
**Joseph A. Spray (1899-1971); Charles W. Bowers (1904-1974); Robert M. Dean (Tustin Office); Bruce Alan Finck (Ventura Office); Keith E. Walden (Tustin Office); Richard C. Turner; Joseph G. Young (Ventura Office); Steven Tobin; Michael W. Champ; Robert D. Brugge; Joey P. Moore (Tustin Office); W. Glenn Johnson (Tustin Office); Michael D. Cortson. Of Counsel: Charles P. Gould; Robert A. Von Esch, III (Tustin Office); John Carpenter Otto;—Linda L. Adams (Tustin Office); Donald R. Wood (Ventura Office); J. Jane Fox (Ventura Office); Francis M. Drelling (Tustin Office); David H. Pierce (Ventura Office); Michael P. Farrell (Tustin Office); Stephen E. Sessa; Carlos C. Cabral; Nicole M. Kilgore (Ventura Office).**
**General Civil Trial and Appellate Practice, State and Federal Courts. Insurance Law including Coverage and Bad Faith, Casualty and Products Liability, Construction Defect, Premises Liability and Motor Carrier. Commercial Litigation including Contract Disputes, Employment, Professional Liability, Franchise, Environmental, Taxation and Estate Planning.**
**Representative Clients: State Farm Mutual Automobile Insurance Co.; State Farm Fire and Casualty Co.**
**Ventura, California Office: Suite 300, 1000 Hill Road. Telephone: 805-642-8400.**
**Tustin, California Office: 17592 Seventeenth Street, Third Floor. Telephone: 714-544-7200.**
***See Professional Biographies, LOS ANGELES, CALIFORNIA***

**Sprecher, Max J.** ........................ '63 '93 C.112 B.A. L.809 J.D. [[A] Lavely&S.]
*REPORTED CASES: Page v. Something Weird Video, 908 E. Supp. 714 (C.D. Cal. 1995).
*PRACTICE AREAS: Business and Entertainment Litigation; Right of Publicity; Privacy; Defamation; Copyright.

**Springer, Jeffrey Z. B.**, (AV) ........'53 '79 C.112 A.B. L.800 J.D. [Demetriou,D.S.&M.]
*PRACTICE AREAS: Eminent Domain; Environmental Law; Commercial Law; General Civil Litigation.
Springer, Kenneth D. ................................'60 '94 C.277 B.E.E. L.276 J.D. 633 W. 5th St.
**Springer, Kristi Miki** ...........................'66 '91 C.197 B.A. L.1068 J.D. [[A] Graham&J.]
Springer, Pamela Davis ............................'51 '77 C.35 B.S. L.809 J.D. Dep. Dist. Atty.
Springer, Paul D. '42 '68 C.1029 B.A. L.1009 J.D.
Sr. V.P. & Asst. Gen. Coun., Paramount Pictures Corp.
**Springer, Roger W.** .................... '45 '73 C.763 B.A. L.1049 J.D. [Oliver,V.S.M.&L.]
*PRACTICE AREAS: Personal Injury; Appeals.
Spronz, Steven C. ............................'54 '79 C.569 B.A. L.1019 J.D. 6534 Withworth Dr.
Sprowl, Arthur V. '20 '56 C.679 B.S. L.345 J.D.
(adm. in IN; not adm. in CA) Sr. V.P., Secy. & Gen. Coun., Transamerica Ins. Co.
Sprung, Susan P. ......................................... '60 '85 C.1044 B.S. L.94 J.D. 400 S. Hope St.
Spuehler, Donald R., (AV) ....................'34 '65 C&L.309 A.B., LL.B. 400 S. Hope St.
**Spyksma, Sarah V. J.** .................................'62 '87 C.112 B.A. L.309 J.D. [[A] Sidley&A.]
*PRACTICE AREAS: Real Estate Transactions.
**Sragow, Darry A.** ...........................................'46 '83 C.188 B.S. L.276 J.D. [Shumaker&S.]
**Srinivasan, Jay P.** ...................................'69 '96 C.339 B.S. L.569 J.D. [[A] Gibson,D.&C.]
*LANGUAGES: Tamil.
Stack, Richard G. ..................................'62 '89 C.352 B.A. L.1068 J.D. Dist. Coun., I.R.S.
**Stack, Richard L.**, (AV) ..........................'47 '73 C.112 B.A. L.426 J.D. [Darling,H.&R.]
*PRACTICE AREAS: Trusts and Estates; Corporate; Real Property; Non-Profit Organizations.
**Stackel, Dean** ................................'64 '89 C&L.569 B.S., J.D. [[A] Buchalter,N.F.&Y.]
*PRACTICE AREAS: Real Estate Law; Environmental Law.

**Stacker, Patrick C.**
**(See Long Beach)**

**Staenberg, Marc R.** ......................... '47 '73 C.966 B.A. L.705 J.D. [M.R.Staenberg]

**Staenberg, Marc R., A Prof. Corp., Law Offices of**
**1801 Century Park East, Twenty-Third Floor, 90067**
**Telephone: 310-201-2550 Fax: 310-201-2551**
**Marc R. Staenberg.**
**Business and Transactions, Entertainment and Sports Law. Civil Litigation.**
***See Professional Biographies, LOS ANGELES, CALIFORNIA***

Stafford, Kathi Jean ......... '54 '79 C.1 B.A. L.846 J.D. Assoc. Gen. Coun., SunSoft, Inc
**Stafford, Walter V.**, (AV) '40 '66 C.112 B.A. L.1066 LL.B.
Sr. Exec. V.P. & Gen. Coun., CB Commercial Real Estate Grp., Inc.
*RESPONSIBILITIES: Mergers and Acquisitions; General Corporate Advice.

**Stafford, Michael N.**
**(See Glendale)**

**Stagg, Regina A.** ...............................'56 '82 C.112 A.B. L.1066 J.D. [Blanc W.J.&K.]
*REPORTED CASES: Mitchell v. Superior Court, 37 Cal. 3d 268.
*PRACTICE AREAS: Commercial, Copyright and Proprietary Rights Litigation; Employment and Discrimination Law.
**Staggs-Wilson, Elizabeth** ..................'66 '91 C.309 B.A. L.597 J.D. [[A] Davis W.T.]
*PRACTICE AREAS: Commercial Litigation; Media Law; Copyright; Employment Law.
**Staines, Joseph J.** '45 '77 C&L.262 B.S., J.D.
Sr. Staff Tax Coun., Atlantic Richfield Co.

**Staitman, Snyder & Tannenbaum**
**(See Encino)**

**Stall, Richard J., Jr.**, (AV) ..................'41 '67 C.679 B.S. L.813 J.D. [Stall,A.&G.]
*PRACTICE AREAS: General Business; Real Estate; Civil Litigation.

**Stall, Astor & Goldstein, (AV)**
**Pico Law Building, 10507 West Pico Boulevard Suite 200, 90064**
**Telephone: 310-470-6852 Facsimile: 310-470-3673**
**Email: StAsGo@msn.com**
**Richard J. Stall, Jr.; Sanford Astor; Don W. Goldstein. Associates: Cynthia C. Lam; Constance E. Boukidis.**
**General Civil Trial and Appellate Practice in all State and Federal Courts. Transactional Services in Business, Real Estate, Labor, Entertainment Matters, Family Law, Insurance Defense, Intellectual Property, Patents, Trademarks and Copyrights.**
***See Professional Biographies, LOS ANGELES, CALIFORNIA***

**Stamato, Juliana** ........................... '56 '84 C.705 B.A. L.426 J.D. [[A] Arter&H.]
*PRACTICE AREAS: Secured Transactions; Real Estate Transactions; Affordable Housing.
Stambler, Errol H., (BV) ............ '46 '73 C.280 B.A. L.623 J.D. 10880 Wilshire Blvd.
Stambul, Richard A., (AV) ........... '47 '72 C.112 A.B. L.426 J.D. 2049 Century Pk., E.
**Stamey, Susanne E.** ......................... '66 '95 C.154 B.A. L.426 J.D. [[A] Jones,D.R.&P.]
Stamm, Alan, (AV) ...........'31 '57 C.976 A.B. L.309 J.D. 1840 Century Park E., 8th Fl.
Stamm, Ronald W. '54 '80
C.1349 B.A. L.1194 J.D. Assoc. Coun., L.A. Co. Metro. Transp. Auth.
Stamos, Gregory, (AV) ....................................'46 '72 [Rose,K.&M.] ([C]Long Beach)
**Stamper, Elizabeth A.** ..........................'65 '92 C.473 B.A. L.94 J.D. [[A] McKenna&C.]
**Stamper, John W.**, (AV) ........................ '46 '74 C.347 B.A. L.597 J.D. [O'Melveny&M.]
*PRACTICE AREAS: Litigation; Mediation; International Arbitration; Alternative Dispute Resolution.

**Stanard, Blender & Schwartz**
**(See Woodland Hills)**

Stanbury, George R., (A P.C.) ........... '46 '74 C.112 B.A. L.800 J.D. [Stanbury,F.&L.]
Stanbury, Fishelman & Levy, A Professional Corporation
9200 Sunset Blvd., Penthouse Suite 30
**Standish, Gail J.** ............................... '63 '93 C.453 S.B. L.1068 J.D. [[A] Irell&M.]
Standish, William J. .....................'39 '74 C.477 A.B. L.426 J.D. [Standish&B.]
Standish and Birmingham ........................................ 2049 Century Pk. E.
**Standlee, Michael C.** ..................... '68 '94 C.154 B.A. L.800 J.D. [[A] Stutman,T.&G.]
*PRACTICE AREAS: Bankruptcy; Insolvency; Corporate Reorganization.
**Stanfield, Diane C.** ..........................'56 '82 C.1077 B.A. L.1068 J.D. [Baker&H.]
*PRACTICE AREAS: Real Estate Litigation.
**Stanford, Paul** '42 '81 C&L.145 A.B., J.D.
Exec. V.P., Gen. Coun. & Secy., CalMat Co.
**Stang, Harry R.**, (AV) ............................ '36 '63 C.604 A.B. L.813 LL.B. [Bryan C.]
*PRACTICE AREAS: Employment and Labor Relations.
**Stang, James I.**, (AV) ................... '55 '80 C.112 B.A. L.1065 J.D. [Pachulski,S.Z.&Y.]
*TRANSACTIONS: Represented Official Subcommittee of Employee Organizations in Orange County chapter 9 Case; Debtor Representation of Gateway Educational Products, Ltd., Manufacturer of Hooked on Phonics.
**Stanitz, Karen Lynn Scarborough** '67 '92 C&L.312 B.A., J.D.
(adm. in HI; not adm. in CA) [[A] Littler,M.F.T.&M.]
*PRACTICE AREAS: Litigation.
**Stankevich, Mark** ................'53 '80 C.390 B.A. L.1066 J.D. [Greenberg G.F.C.&M.]
*PRACTICE AREAS: Entertainment Law; Intellectual Property.
**Stankowski, James A.** ..............'57 '82 C.262 B.A. L.990 J.D. [Wilson,E.M.E.&D.]
**Stanley, Anya** .......................... '49 '75 C.763 B.A. L.823 J.D. [Gibbs,G.L.&A.]
*PRACTICE AREAS: Title Insurance Law; Real Property Law.
Stanley, Edmund C. ................................ '30 '72 L.981 LL.B. 1155 N. Fuller Ave.
Stanley, Harold M. ....................'33 '61 C.112 A.B. L.1066 LL.B. 4837 E. 3rd St.
Stanley, Steven M. ...................'61 '90 C.112 B.A. L.940 J.D. 12100 Wilshire Blvd.
Stanley, Walter Jerome ..................'58 '89 C&L.800 B.S., J.D. 12100 Wilshire Blvd.

**Stanton, Harold J.**, (AV) .......................... '40 '66 C.112 B.S. L.1068 J.D. [Stanton]
*PRACTICE AREAS: Family Law; Personal Injury; Business Litigation; Business Law; Mediation and Arbitration (Family Law).
**Stanton, Kathryn M.** .................. '62 '89 C.112 B.A. L.800 J.D. [A Selvin&W.&W.]
*PRACTICE AREAS: Estate Planning; Appeals; Business Litigation; Real Estate; Family Law.
**Stanton, Laura K.** ................................ '55 '80 C.1077 B.A. L.426 J.D. [Russ,A.&K.]
*PRACTICE AREAS: Intellectual Property Litigation; Trade Secrets; Securities Litigation; Unfair Competition; Real Estate Litigation.
**Stanton, Marian L.**, (AV) ........................ '— '81 C.112 B.A. L.1148 J.D. [Stanton]
*PRACTICE AREAS: Family Law; Business Litigation.

**Stanton, Paul L., (AV) '47 '73 C.156 A.B. L.1068 J.D.**
**11111 Santa Monica Boulevard Suite 1840, 90025-3352**
**Telephone: 310-444-1840 Fax: 310-268-8444**
***LANGUAGES: Spanish.**
***PRACTICE AREAS: Fiduciary Litigation.**
**Associates: Shannon H. Burns.**
**Fiduciary Litigation including Probate and Trust Litigation, Elder Abuse, Legal Malpractice. Estate Planning, Probate and Trust Administration, Alternative Dispute Resolution.**
*See Professional Biographies, LOS ANGELES, CALIFORNIA*

Stanton, Roger L., (AV) .... '40 '67 C.112 B.A. L.1068 LL.B. Div. Chf., Off. of Pub. Def.

**Stanton Law Corporation, (AV)**
**1999 Avenue of the Stars Suite 1850, 90067**
**Telephone: 310-789-1994 Fax: 310-282-0328**
**Harold J. Stanton; Marian L. Stanton. Of Counsel: Oberstein, Kibre & Horwitz, Los Angeles, California.**
**Family Law, Personal Injury, Business Litigation, Business Law, Mediation and Arbitration.**
*See Professional Biographies, LOS ANGELES, CALIFORNIA*

**Stanwyck, Steven J., (AV) '44 '71 C.208 B.A. L.1066 J.D. BB**
**1900 Avenue of the Stars, Suite 1700, 90067-4403**
**Telephone: 310-557-8390 Telecopier: 310-557-8391**
**Arbitration, Mediation and Litigation in Financial Matters, Computers, Business Information Systems and Telecommunications.**
*See Professional Biographies, LOS ANGELES, CALIFORNIA*

**Stapke, Mark R.** .......................................... '55 '83 C.112 A.B. L.629 J.D. [Thorpe&T.]
*PRACTICE AREAS: Construction Litigation; Business Litigation.
Staples, Gregory W. .................. '56 '91 C.112 B.A. L.1065 J.D. Fed. Trade Comm.
**Star, Linda** ........................................ '53 '80 C.112 B.A. L.809 J.D. [Hillsinger&C.]
**Stark, Derek W.** ........................ '67 '94 C.112 B.A. L.426 J.D. [A Quisenberry&B.]
*PRACTICE AREAS: Business Litigation; Real Estate Litigation; Insurance Coverage.
**Stark, Joseph L.** ........................................ '58 '84 C.112 B.A. L.809 J.D. [Roper&F.]
*PRACTICE AREAS: Appellate Practice; Insurance Coverage; Public Entity Law; Nursing Home; Administrative Hearings and Appeals.
**Stark, Lee E.**, (AV) .................... '27 '56 C&L.800 A.B., LL.B. [C Simmons,R.&S.]
Stark, Todd Evan '57 '82
C.112 B.A. L.426 J.D. Assoc. Gen. Coun., TCW Realty Advisors

**Stark, Rasak & Clarke**
**(See Torrance)**

Starks, Cammy C. ........................................ '67 '95 C.112 B.A. L.800 J.D. [A Pollet&W.]
Starler, Michael H., (AV) ..................... '49 '75 C.1077 B.S. L.809 J.D. [M.H.Starler]
Starler, Michael H., Law Corp., (AV) ........................................ 12100 Wilshire Blvd.
Starr, David S. ........................................ '64 '90 C.569 B.A. L.228 J.D. 633 5th St.
Starr, Debra Hope .......................... '52 '78 C.112 B.A. L.770 J.D. Dep. Dist. Atty.
**Starr, Ephraim** ........................................ '71 '96 C.31 B.A. L.228 J.D. [A Kirkland&E.]
*LANGUAGES: Russian.
*PRACTICE AREAS: Intellectual Property Litigation; Litigation.
Starre, Gary A. ........................ '51 '76 C.112 B.A. L.426 J.D. 12100 Wilshire Blvd.
**Starrett, Lucinda** .................................. '57 '86 C.674 A.B. L.659 J.D. [Latham&W.]
*LANGUAGES: French.
**Stashower, Arthur L.**, (AV) .................. '30 '53 C&L.477 A.B., J.D. [C Chrystie&B.]
*PRACTICE AREAS: Entertainment Law; Labor Arbitration Law.
**Stathas, James A.** ............................. '66 '92 C.966 B.A. L.602 J.D. [Kinkle,R.&S.]
Statman, Jay ........................ '54 '80 C.112 A.B. L.426 J.D. 12121 Wilshire Blvd.
**Staton, Raymond J.** ................. '43 '74 C.1105 B.A. L.802 J.D. [Nossaman,G.K.&E.]
*PRACTICE AREAS: Trusts Law; Estates Law.
Staub, D. Joshua .......... '67 '94 C.154 B.A. L.861 J.D. 2121 Ave. of the Stars, 22nd Fl.
**Staub, Jerry K.**, (AV) ........................ '42 '67 C&L.800 B.A., J.D. [Argue P.H.&M.]
*PRACTICE AREAS: Civil Litigation.
**Staub, Keith M.** ................................ '56 '88 C.107 B.S. L.1049 J.D. [A Hewitt&P.]
*PRACTICE AREAS: Medical and Dental Malpractice; Professional Negligence; Insurance Defense.
**Staub, Michael K.** .................. '65 '95 C.1074 B.S. L.800 J.D. [A Charlston,R.&W.]

**Stauber, Ronald J., (AV) '40 '67 C.851 B.A. L.608 J.D.**
**1840 Century Park East, 8th Floor, 90067**
**Telephone: 310-556-0080 Telecopier: 310-556-3687**
**General Civil Practice. Real Estate, Corporation, Securities and Business Law. Litigation.**
*See Professional Biographies, LOS ANGELES, CALIFORNIA*

**Stava, Jeffrey A.** ........................... '58 '83 C&L.426 B.A., J.D. [Nossaman,G.K.&E.]
*PRACTICE AREAS: Municipal Finance Law.

**Stavin, Richard A., and Associates '49 '75 C.1046 B.A. L.564 J.D.**
**1840 Century Park East, Suite 800, 90067⊙**
**Telephone: 310-553-1144**
**Business and Fraud Litigation, Insurance Defense, Unfair Competition, Wrongful Termination, Discrimination Litigation.**
**Representative Clients: State Farm Insurance Co.; Allstate Insurance Co.; Farmers Insurance Group; California Casualty Group; Metro-Goldwyn Mayer, Inc.; Sizzler International, Inc.; AVI Entertainment Group, Inc.; Metropolitan Property Casualty Insurance Co.; Mercury Insurance Group.**
**Reference: Merchantile National Bank.**
**Encino, California Office: 15760 Ventura Boulevard, Suite 1600. Telephone: 818-385-1144. Fax: 818-385-1149.**
*See Professional Biographies, LOS ANGELES, CALIFORNIA*

**Stazer, Alan K.** .................................. '36 '80 C.112 B.A. L.809 J.D. [C Cummins&W.]
*PRACTICE AREAS: Environmental Law.
Stearns, Mary ........................................ '52 '79 C.1042 B.A. L.426 J.D. [Stearns&C.]
Stearns, Ronald A. ........... '47 '91 C.1042 B.A. L.597 J.D. 777 S. Figueroa St., 10th Fl.
Stearns & Clemons ........................................................ 3250 Wilshire Blvd.
Stechel, Howard J., P.C. .................. '42 '67 C.188 B.A. L.976 LL.B. [H.J.Stechel]
Stechel, Louis '13 '38 C.563 L.724 LL.B.
(adm. in NY; not adm. in CA) 3654 Barham Blvd.‡
Stechel, Howard J., P.C. ........................................................ 3325 Wilshire Blvd.
**Steckbauer, William W.** .......................... '58 '84 C.112 B.A. L.809 J.D. [Weinhart&R.]
*PRACTICE AREAS: Civil Litigation.
Steckmest, Lawrence D. '50 '76
C.813 B.A. L.228 J.D. Litig. Coun., Occidental Petroleum Corp.
**Stedman, J. Russell** ........... '59 '84 C.112 B.A. L.800 J.D. [Barger&W.] (⊙San Fran.)
*PRACTICE AREAS: General Business Litigation; Commercial Tort Litigation; Employment Litigation; Administrative Law.
Steel, Sari J. ........................ '60 '91 C.112 B.A. L.1148 J.D. Off. of Co. Coun.
**Steele, Bruce J.** .................. '47 '76 C.174 B.A. L.1068 J.D. Sr. Coun., Bank of Amer.

Steele, Corey Leon ............ '52 '78 C.112 A.B. L.809 J.D. 12304 Santa Monica Blvd.
**Steele, Craig A.** ........................................ '62 '92 C&L.800 B.A., J.D. [Richards,W.&G.]
*PRACTICE AREAS: Litigation; Public Law; Political Law.
**Steele, Eugenia L.** ................ '65 '90 C.426 B.A. L.809 J.D. [A Gordon,E.K.G.F.&G.]
*PRACTICE AREAS: Personal Injury Law; Products Liability Law; Insurance Bad Faith Law.
Steele, George L. ........................ '— '96 C.277 B.S. L.112 J.D. 801 S. Figueroa St.
**Steele, John C.** ........................................ '67 '95 C&L.101 B.A., J.D. [Wehner&P.]
*LANGUAGES: Korean.
**Steele, Joseph W., V** '49 '75 C.35 B.S. L.878 J.D.
[Nordstrom,S.N.&J.] & [C Guizot&M.]
*PRACTICE AREAS: Products Liability Law; Professional Malpractice Law; General Negligence Trials and Appeals.
Steele, Ray M. ........................ '13 '48 C.547 A.B. L.477 LL.B. State Dept. of Transp.
**Steere, Martin E.** ........................ '56 '80 C&L.893 B.A., J.D. [C Manatt,P.&P.]
*PRACTICE AREAS: Real Estate Law.
Steeves, Myron S. ................ '59 '90 C.1259 B.A. L.276 J.D. 777 S. Figueroa St.
Stefanski, Thomas J. ........................ '53 '80 C.1044 B.A. L.398 J.D. [Frank,G.&S.]
Steffen, Zona ........................ '40 '75 C.1097 B.A. L.800 J.D. Dep. Pub. Def.
**Steffin, William C., (A Professional Corporation)**, (AV) '45 '72
C.966 B.S.Ch.E. L.1065 LL.B. [Lyon&L.] (See Pat. Sect.)
*PRACTICE AREAS: Patent, Trademark, Copyright, Unfair Competition; Intellectual Property.
Steffy, Paul M. '23 '48 C.423 A.B. L.276 J.D.
(adm. in MD; not adm. in CA) 10328 Cresta Dr.‡
Stegall, Daniel R. ........................ '46 '73 C.277 B.S. L.893 J.D. 725 S. Figueroa St.
Steger, Michael D. ........................ '66 '93 C&L.893 B.A., J.D. 444 S. Flower St.
**Stegman, Daphne M.**, (AV) ........................ '48 '75 C.856 A.B. L.1068 J.D. [Stegman&C.]
*PRACTICE AREAS: Antitrust; Intellectual Property; Business Litigation; Construction Disputes; Employment Law.
Stegman, Edwin B., (BV) ........................ '21 '52 C&L.800 J.D. 2049 Century Park E.

**Stegman & Caragozian, (AV)**
**1900 Avenue of the Stars, Suite 1750, 90067**
**Telephone: 310-843-9338 Fax: 310-843-0438**
**Daphne M. Stegman; John S. Caragozian; Karen A. Share. Of Counsel: Donald E. Warner, Jr.**
**General Civil Trial and Appellate Practice in all State and Federal Courts and Administrative Agencies.**
*See Professional Biographies, LOS ANGELES, CALIFORNIA*

Stehr, Judith I. ........................ '— '79 C.1077 B.A. L.1095 J.D. 930 S. La Brea Ave.
Steiger, Walt A., (AV) ........................ '12 '36 C&L.378 A.B., LL.B. 5640 Sherbourne Dr.‡
Stein, Alec C. ........................ '14 '39 C.550 L.94 LL.B. 11740 Wilshire Blvd.
Stein, Carol E. ................ '52 '78 C.112 B.A.Econ. L.464 J.D. 15600 Mulholland Dr.
**Stein, Craig J.** ........................ '52 '79 C.1145 B.S. L.1019 J.D. [Gartenberg J.G.&S.]
*PRACTICE AREAS: Business Litigation.
Stein, Ellyn Jill ............. '58 '85 C.813 A.B. L.569 J.D. 1901 Ave. of the Stars, 7th Fl.
Stein, Jay R. ........................ '48 '73 C.1077 B.A. L.426 J.D. 2049 Century Park E.
Stein, Jerry H., (BV) ........................ '51 '77 C.1044 B.A. L.1068 J.D. [Levin,S.C.&S.]
Stein, Larry I. ........................ '50 '75 C.112 A.B. L.1066 J.D. 633 W. 5th St.
**Stein, Marc R.**, (AV) ........................ '47 '76 C.112 A.B. L.1068 J.D. [Slaff,M.&R.]
*PRACTICE AREAS: Entertainment Transactions; General Business Litigation; Copyright and Trademark.
**Stein, Michael D.** ........................ '62 '87 C.112 B.A. L.1066 J.D. [A Bryan C.]
*PRACTICE AREAS: General Civil Practice; Contract Law.
**Stein, Mitchell B.** ........................ '52 '78 C.112 B.A. L.426 J.D. [Silver&F.]
*PRACTICE AREAS: Commercial Insurance; General Civil Litigation; General Business Law; Real Property Law.
**Stein, Mitchell J.** ........................ '58 '85 C&L.665 B.A., J.D. [Stein P.&H.]
*PRACTICE AREAS: Business Litigation; Corporate Organization.
**Stein, Mitchell Reed** ........................ '66 '91 C.800 B.A. L.990 J.D. [Kreger&S.]
*PRACTICE AREAS: General Practice; Entertainment and the Arts.
Stein, ReneéE. ........................ '54 '89 C&L.940 B.A., J.D. 633 W. 5th St., 31st Fl.‡
**Stein, Samuel H.** ........................ '62 '89 C.339 B.S. L.846 J.D. [A Musick,P.&G.]
**Stein, Scott A.** ........................ '66 '91 C.245 B.B.A. L.800 J.D. [Armstrong H.J.T.&W.]
*PRACTICE AREAS: Entertainment Law.
**Stein, Sheryl E.** ........................ '52 '79 C.472 B.A. L.809 J.D. [Pillsbury M.&S.]
**Stein, Tamar C.**, (AV) ........................ '48 '77 C.112 B.A. L.1068 J.D. [Cox,C.&N.]
*SPECIAL AGENCIES: All city councils and planning commissions; California Coastal Commission; California services districts.
*PRACTICE AREAS: Land Use Law; Land Use and Real Estate Litigation; Business Litigation.
Stein, William L. ........................ '34 '59 C.659 B.S. L.309 J.D. 10720 Woodbine St.
**Stein, William O.** ........................ '64 '90 C.112 B.A. L.426 J.D. [A Quinn E.U.&O.]

**Stein & Kahan, A Law Corporation**
**(See Santa Monica)**

**Stein Perlman & Hawk**
**9000 Sunset Boulevard, Suite 500, 90069**
**Telephone: 310-247-9500 Telecopier: 310-247-0109**
**Mitchell J. Stein; Dana M. Perlman; Dennis J. Hawk. Associates: Daniel L. Krishel.**
**Business Litigation and Bankruptcy Law.**
*See Professional Biographies, LOS ANGELES, CALIFORNIA*

**Stein Shostak Shostak & O'Hara, A Professional Corporation, (AV) BB**
**515 South Figueroa Street, Suite 1200, 90071-3329⊙**
**Telephone: 213-486-0010 Fax: 213-486-0011**
**Philip Stein (1899-1955); Marjorie M. Shostak; S. Richard Shostak; Joseph P. Cox; Steven B. Zisser. Of Counsel: James F. O'Hara.**
**Customs and International Trade Law. Practice before Federal Administrative Agencies. Trials and Appeals.**
**Washington, D.C. Office: Suite 807, 1620 L Street, N.W. Telephone: 202-223-6270. Fax: 202-659-4237.**
**San Diego, California Office: 2675 Customhouse Court, Suite B. Telephone: 619-661-6317. Fax: 619-661-1448.**
*See Professional Biographies, LOS ANGELES, CALIFORNIA*

Steinberg, Andrew D. ........................ '56 '82 C.112 B.A. L.809 J.D. 11355 W. Olympic Blvd.
Steinberg, Charles J. .... '60 '86 C.674 A.B. L.569 J.D. V.P. & Gen. Coun., UNIVISA, Inc.
**Steinberg, David A., (A Professional Corporation)** '62 '87
C.1044 B.A. L.1068 J.D. [Mitchell,S.&K.]
*PRACTICE AREAS: Litigation.
Steinberg, Ellis ........................ '53 '79 C.112 B.A. L.1148 J.D. 3600 Wilshire Blvd.
Steinberg, Eric S. ........................ '47 '74 C.112 B.S. L.1065 J.D. 2710 S. Yates Ave.
Steinberg, H. Arthur ........ '26 '53 C.563 B.B.A. L.178 LL.B. 221 S. Barrington Ave.‡
**Steinberg, Howard J.** ........................ '54 '79 C.454 B.A. L.93 J.D. [Irell&M.]
**Steinberg, Jonathan H.** ........................ '52 '81 C.112 A.B. L.1068 J.D. [Irell&M.]
**Steinberg, Kalman** ........................ '66 '93 C.354 B.S. L.1068 J.D. [A Pillsbury M.&S.]
*LANGUAGES: French.
**Steinberg, Lee Anne** ........................ '65 '96 C.951 B.A. L.1066 J.D. [A Mitchell,S.&K.]
*PRACTICE AREAS: Labor and Employment Law.
**Steinberg, Marjorie S.**, (AV) ........................ '46 '75 C.813 A.B. L.1068 J.D. [Tuttle&T.]
*PRACTICE AREAS: Bankruptcy; Corporate Law; Real Estate.
Steinberg, Maxine B. ........................ '37 '79 C.107 B.A. L.803 J.D. 2934 1/2 Beverly Glen Cir.
**Steinberg, Michael H.** ........................ '62 '88 C.112 A.B. L.813 J.D. [Sullivan&C.]
**Steinberg, Robert** ........................ '60 '86 C.659 B.S.S.E. L.276 J.D. [Irell&M.] (Pat.)
**Steinberg, Robert** ........................ '64 '89 C&L.309 B.A., J.D. [A Jeffer,M.B.&M.]
*PRACTICE AREAS: Securities; Corporate Finance; Mergers and Acquisitions; General Corporate.

CAA347P

CALIFORNIA—LOS ANGELES | MARTINDALE-HUBBELL LAW DIRECTORY 1997

**Steinberg, Robert A.** ........'52 '77 C.477 A.B. L.228 J.D. [Davis W.T.]
*PRACTICE AREAS: Business Transactions; Taxation; Corporate and Securities Law.
Steinberg, Robert B., (AV) ........'28 '54 C.112 B.S. L.1068 LL.B. [Rose,K.&M.]
**Steinberg, Robert H.** ........'58 '83 C.347 B.S. L.1068 J.D. [Gipson H.&P.]
*PRACTICE AREAS: Secured Lending; Motion Picture Finance; Real Estate; General Business.
Steinberg, Robert K. ........'37 '63 C.112 B.S. L.426 J.D. 2029 Century Park E., 6th Fl.

**Steinberg Barness Glasgow & Foster LLP**
**(See Manhattan Beach)**

**Steinberg, Nutter & Brent**
**(See Santa Monica)**

**Steinberger, Mitchell J.** ........'67 '93 C.813 A.B. L.1066 J.D. [[A] Kaye,S.F.H.&H.]
*LANGUAGES: German.
*PRACTICE AREAS: Litigation.
**Steinbrecher, Alan K.**, (AV) ........'46 '77 C.575 A.B. L.228 J.D. [Paul,H.J.&W.]
Steindler, Curt S. ........'62 '89 C.1131 B.A. L.1066 J.D. 523 W. 6th St.
**Steiner, Catherine A.** ........'62 '87 C.112 A.B. L.1068 J.D. [[C] Pachulski,S.Z.&Y.]
**Steiner, David Paul**, (AV) ........'49 '75 C.813 B.A. L.1065 J.D. [Steiner&S.]
**Steiner, Jeffrey E., (P.C.)** ........'50 '75 C.976 B.S. L.659 J.D. [Jeffer,M.B.&M.]
*PRACTICE AREAS: General Real Estate; Commercial Leasing; Real Estate Lending and Loan Workouts; Real Estate Joint Ventures.
Steiner, Jonathan B. ........'44 '70 C.112 A.B. L.1068 J.D. Dir., Calif. Appellate Project
**Steiner, Matt** ........'55 '81 C.112 B.A. L.426 J.D. [[C] Kamine,S.&U.]
*PRACTICE AREAS: Construction.
**Steiner, Rebel R., Jr.** ........'60 '86 C.16 B.A. L.976 J.D. [Loeb&L.]
*PRACTICE AREAS: Entertainment Law.

**Steiner & Saffer, A Professional Law Corporation, (AV)**
**2121 Avenue of the Stars Twenty-Second Floor, 90067-5010⊙**
**Telephone: 310-557-8422 FAX: 310-556-0336**
**David Paul Steiner; Sherry M. Saffer.**
**Art, Entertainment, Intellectual Property and Commercial Litigation in all State and Federal Courts. Artist, Publisher, Gallery and Art Collector Transactions, Domestic and International Business, Insurance Coverage, Real Estate Litigation.**
**Reference: Mercantile National Bank (Century City Branch).**
**New York, New York Affiliated Office: Lynch Rowin Novack Burnbaum & Crystal, 300 East 42nd Street, 10th Floor. Telephone: 212-682-4001. Fax: 212-986-2907.**

***See Professional Biographies, LOS ANGELES, CALIFORNIA***

**Steinert, Eric M.** ........'67 '93 C.691 B.A. L.1066 J.D. [[A] Morgan,L.&B.]
Steinfeld, Susan Frances ........'60 '89 C&L.280 B.S., J.D. Dep. Dist. Atty.
Steingard, Richard M. ........'57 '82 C.112 B.A. L.426 J.D. 800 Wilshire Blvd.

**Steinhart, Terran T., (AV) '39 '65 C.112 B.A. L.309 LL.B.**
**4311 Wilshire Boulevard, Suite 405, 90010-3708**
**Telephone: 213-933-8263 FAX: 213-933-2391**
***REPORTED CASES: Frances T. vs. Village Green Owners' Association, 42 C.3d 490 (California Supreme Court 1986); Columbia Record Productions vs. Hot Wax Records, Inc., 966 F.2d 515 (9th Cir. 1992).**
**General Practice with emphasis on Business, Entertainment and Personal Injury Litigation. Appeals in State and Federal Courts and Dispute Resolution for Christian Ministries.**

***See Professional Biographies, LOS ANGELES, CALIFORNIA***

**Steinke, Suzanne M.** ........'69 '96 C.813 A.B. L.966 J.D. [[A] Mitchell,S.&K.]
*PRACTICE AREAS: Labor and Employment Law.
**Steinman, Peter L.** ........'63 '89 C.446 B.A. L.276 J.D. [[A] Gaims,W.W.&E.]
**Steinmann, Joan M.** ........'61 '89 C&L.494 B.A., J.D. [Beck,D.D.B.&O.]
Steinmetz, Fred H. ........'09 '36 C.112 A.B. L.1066 LL.B. 6333 Ivarene Ave.
**Steinsapir, Laurence D.**, (AV) ........'35 '59 C.610 B.S.C. L.930 J.D. [Schwartz,S.D.&S.]
*PRACTICE AREAS: Labor Law; Education Law; Arbitration Law; Real Estate.
**Steitz, Nelson P.**, (AV) ........'19 '53 C.855 A.B. L.800 LL.B. [[C] Anderson,M.&C.]
**Steller, Robert A.** ........'54 '77 C.986 B.B.A. L.1066 J.D. [Selman B.] (⊙San Diego)
Stempel, Dyanne L. ........'64 '91 C.881 B.A. L.273 J.D. 444 S. Flower St.
Stenson, Robert E. '64 '91 C.276 B.S.B.A. L.1068 J.D.
V.P., Regulatory & Legal Affs., GE Capital- ResCom
**Stenton, Kimberly S.** ........'65 '92 C.112 B.A. L.426 J.D. [[A] Quinn E.U.&O.]
**Stepanicich, Gregory W.** ........'51 '77 C.112 A.B. L.1065 J.D. [Richards,W.&G.]
*PRACTICE AREAS: Public Law; Land Use Law.
**Stephan, George J.**, (AV) ........'50 '75 C.800 B.S. L.809 J.D. [Ginsburg,S.O.&R.]
Stephens, Albert Lee, Jr. ........'13 '39 C&L.800 A.B., LL.B. U.S. Sr. Dist. J.
**Stephens, George E., Jr., (P.C.)**, (AV) ........'36 '63 C.174 L.813 LL.B. [Paul,H.J.&W.]
**Stephens, John F.** ........'68 '95 C&L.705 B.S., J.D. [[A] Bronson,B.&M.]
**Stephens, John H.**, (AV) ........'38 '68 C&L.800 B.S., J.D. [[C] Gibbs,G.L.&A.]
*PRACTICE AREAS: Labor and Employment Law; Employee Benefits Law; Litigation.
**Stephens, R. Wicks, II**, (AV) ........'34 '63 C.112 B.S. L.813 LL.B. [Stephens,B.&L.]
*PRACTICE AREAS: Business Litigation; Professional Liability Litigation; Antitrust and Trade Regulation; Alternate Dispute Resolution.
Stephens, Sean D., (BV) ........'65 '90 C&L.623 B.B.A., J.D. [Maxie R.S.&V.]⊙
**Stephens, Thaddeus G.** ........'69 '96 C.604 B.A. L.813 J.D. [[A] Sullivan&C.]
Stephens, William A. ........'39 '72 C.1042 B.A. L.426 J.D. 3253 Benda St.

**Stephens, Berg & Lasater, A Professional Corporation, (AV) [BB]**
**1055 West Seventh Street, Twenty-Ninth Floor, 90017**
**Telephone: 213-629-3111 Telecopy: 213-629-2302; 213-624-4734**
**Lawrence M. Berg (1947-1995); R. Wicks Stephens II; Richard W. Lasater II; Mark G. Ancel; Dudley M. Lang (Certified Specialist, Taxation Law, The State Bar of California Board of Legal Specialization); Joseph F. Butler; Frederick A. Clark; Joel A. Goldman; C. Stephen Davis; Kenneth A. Feinfield (Certified Specialist, Estate Planning, Trust and Probate Law, The State Bar of California Board of Legal Specialization); Jean-Paul Menard; Michael J. Kaminsky; John A. Dragonette. Of Counsel: Louis R. Baker; J. Lane Tilson.**
**General Civil Litigation Practice in State and Federal Courts, Alternate Dispute Resolution. Antitrust, Business and Commercial, Insurance, Environmental, Real Estate and Construction Litigation. Corporate, Securities and Real Estate Transactions. Federal, State and Local and International Taxation. Estate Planning, Trust and Probate.**

***See Professional Biographies, LOS ANGELES, CALIFORNIA***

Stephenson, George D. ........'14 '38 C.945 L.893 LL.B. 12342 Montana Ave.‡
**Stephenson, Gregory R.** ........'64 '96 C.477 B.S.M.E. L.94 J.D. [[A] Lyon&L.]
*PRACTICE AREAS: Intellectual Property.

**Stephenson & Stephenson**
**(See San Pedro)**

**Stepp, John Edd, Jr.**, (AV) ........'43 '68 C.846 B.B.A. L.326 LL.B. [Gibson,D.&C.]
*PRACTICE AREAS: Antitrust Litigation; Antitrust Counseling; Business Litigation.
**Steres, Mark** ........'59 '84 C.112 A.B. L.800 J.D. [Brown,W.&C.]
*PRACTICE AREAS: Zoning; Municipal Law.
Sterling, Bonnie L. ........'43 '87 C&L.1137 B.S., J.D. 621 Sunset Blvd.
**Sterling, Graham L., III**, (AV) ........'29 '57 C.605 B.A. L.813 J.D. [[C] J.M.Donovan]
*PRACTICE AREAS: Securities Law; Corporate Law.
Sterling, William N. ........'48 '73 C.831 A.B. L.569 J.D. Dep. City Atty.
Stern, Ana Marie, (AV) ........'43 '70 C&L.846 B.B.A., J.D. 1960 Rockford Rd.‡
**Stern, Charles M.**, (AV) ........'43 '69 C&L.309 A.B., LL.B. [Katten M.&Z.]
*PRACTICE AREAS: Business Litigation.
**Stern, Dean**, (AV) ........'38 '64 C.112 B.S. L.1068 LL.B. [Gibson,D.&C.]
*PRACTICE AREAS: General Litigation.

Stern, Donald ........'36 '78 C.111 B.S. L.800 J.D. 333 S. Hope St.
Stern, Donald J. ........'29 '56 C.112 B.S. L.1068 LL.B. 6253 Hollywood Blvd.
**Stern, Douglas W.**, (AV) ........'53 '78 C.112 A.B. L.1068 J.D. [Fulbright&J.]
*PRACTICE AREAS: Antitrust; Business Litigation.
Stern, Eugene B. ........'48 '74 C.228 B.A. L.800 J.D. V.P. & Sr. Coun., Sanwa Bk. Calif.
Stern, Fredric W. ........'55 '91 C.1077 B.A. L.426 J.D. 17525 Ventura Blvd.
Stern, Gary M. ........'51 '76 C.339 B.S. L.1068 J.D. 1801 Century Park E., Ste. 1900
**Stern, Gary N.** ........'55 '80 C.112 B.A. L.809 J.D. [Popkoff&S.]⊙
Stern, Harvey H. ........'49 '76 C.1036 B.A. L.1009 J.D. I.R.S.
Stern, Helen F. ........'55 '83 C.112 B.A. L.1148 J.D. 2049 Century Pk. E.
**Stern, Jeffrey S.** ........'54 '81 C.1077 B.A. L.426 J.D. [Gray,Y.D.&R.]
*PRACTICE AREAS: Civil Litigation; Workers' Compensation.
Stern, Joanne B. ........'45 '71 C.103 A.B. L.976 J.D. Whittier Coll. Sch. of Law
Stern, Lawrence F. ........'44 '72 C&L.112 B.S., J.D. Chf. Fin. Offr., Westwood Fin. Corp.
Stern, Lawrence I., (AV) ........'47 '74 C.112 B.A. L.426 J.D. [Mallery&S.]
Stern, Lisa ........'59 '84 C.684 B.A. L.990 J.D. 602 S. Hudson Ave.
**Stern, Marc M.**, (AV) ........'59 '86 C.813 B.S. L.800 J.D. [[A] Greenberg G.F.C.&M.]
*PRACTICE AREAS: Estate Planning; Probate; Trust Administration.
Stern, Michael L. ........'45 '73 C.813 A.B. L.309 J.D. 445 S. Figueroa St.
Stern, Paul G. ........'52 '92 C.685 B.A. L.976 J.D. Off. of U.S. Atty.
Stern, Robert M. ........'44 '70 C.668 B.A. L.813 J.D. Ctr. for Governmental Studies
**Stern, Robert S.** ........'50 '75 C.339 B.S. L.145 J.D. [Morrison&F.]
*PRACTICE AREAS: Accountants' Liability; Securities Litigation; Financial Institutions Litigation.
Stern, Roger C., (AV) ........'27 '52 C.112 B.A. L.426 J.D. [Kahn,S.&B.]
Stern, Stanley ........'37 '71 C.563 B.E.E. L.426 J.D. 12100 Wilshire Blvd.
**Stern, Stephen J.**, (AV) ........'40 '66 C.112 A.B. L.767 LL.B. [O'Melveny&M.]
*PRACTICE AREAS: Public Finance; Project Finance.

**Stern & Goldberg**
**(See Beverly Hills)**

**Sternberg, Stacey** ........'71 '96 C.112 B.A. L.477 J.D. [[A] Latham&W.]
**Sternberg, Terence M.** ........'50 '79 L.1148 J.D. [Vittal&S.]
*SPECIAL AGENCIES: Malibu City Council; Malibu Planning Commission.
*PRACTICE AREAS: Unfair Business Practices Litigation; Business Litigation; Real Estate Litigation; Land Use Litigation.
Sternfeld, William M. ........'27 '55 C.112 A.B. L.1068 LL.B. 5668 W. 63rd St.
Stettin, Jacob J. ........'53 '79 C.012 B.A. L.031 LL.B. [Stettin&C.]
Stettin & Cass ........3055 Wilshire Blvd.

**Stettner, Eisenberg & Morris**
**(See Glendora)**

**Steuber, David W.**, (AV) ........'49 '73 C.855 B.A. L.893 J.D. [Troop M.S.&P.]
*PRACTICE AREAS: Insurance Coverage Litigation; Business and Corporate Litigation; Environmental and Toxic Tort Litigation.
**Stevanovich, Milo M.** ........'62 '91 C.339 B.S.A. L.589 J.D. [[A] Graham&J.]
*LANGUAGES: Russian; Serbo-Croatian.
*PRACTICE AREAS: Bankruptcy Law; Creditors Rights.
**Stevens, Carl R.** ........'53 '78 C.800 B.A. L.1188 J.D. [Stevens,K.A.&H.]⊙
*PRACTICE AREAS: Defense of Legal and Medical Malpractice; General Insurance Defense Law; Insurance Coverage; Bad Faith; Wrongful Termination.
**Stevens, Christopher M.** ........'65 '91 C.94 B.A. L.823 J.D. [[A] Meserve,M.&H.]
Stevens, Kelly H. ........'21 '51 C.112 A.B. L.800 LL.B. 801 Warner Ave.‡
Stevens, Lillian M. ........'29 '55 C&L.800 A.B., J.D. Supr. Ct. J.
**Stevens, Lisa** ........'68 '94 C.269 B.A. L.800 J.D. [[A] Lane P.S.L.]
Stevens, Mark J., (BV) ........'53 '83 C.659 B.S. L.426 J.D. 1010 Wilshire Blvd.
**Stevens, Michael D.** ........'63 '91 C.112 B.S. L.1065 J.D. [[A] Parker,M.C.O.&S.]
*PRACTICE AREAS: Environmental Law; Environmental Insurance Coverage; Litigation.
Stevens, Norman E., (AV) ........'28 '56 C.112 B.A. L.1068 J.D. [N.E.Stevens]
**Stevens, Pauline M.** ........'47 '73 C.881 A.B. L.659 J.D. [Morrison&F.]
*PRACTICE AREAS: Financial Transactions; Derivatives; Workouts; Entertainment Finance.
Stevens, Robt. S. ........'16 '43 C&L.813 A.B., LL.B. Ret. Supr. Ct. J.
**Stevens, Sandra L.** ........'50 '78 C.1077 B.A. L.426 J.D. [Saltzburg,R.&B.]
*PRACTICE AREAS: Litigation; Debtor Creditor Law; Commercial Law.
**Stevens, Steven B.** ........'56 '81 C.118 B.A. L.339 J.D. [Watkins&S.]
*PRACTICE AREAS: Appellate Practice; Insurance Bad Faith; Professional Malpractice; Employment Discrimination.

**Stevens, Kramer, Averbuck & Harris, A Professional Corporation, (AV) [BB]**
**1990 South Bundy Drive, Suite 340, 90025⊙**
**Telephone: 310-442-8435 Fax: 310-442-8441**
**Carl R. Stevens; Jeffrey S. Kramer; Clayton C. Averbuck; Charles L. Harris (Resident Partner, Irvine Office);—Angela M. Rossi; Craig H. Marcus; Valerie McSwain (Resident Irvine Office); Christopher J. Nevis; Lee E. Burrows (Resident, Irvine Office); Monica A. Blut; Angie Y. Yoon; Carrie Ann Moffett; Lydia R. Bouzaglou (Resident, Irvine Office); John R. Marking (Resident, Irvine Office); Robert A. Fisher, II (Resident, Irvine Office); Jeanne E. Pepper (Resident, Irvine Office); Ada Berman; Marissa R. Arrache.**
**General Civil Litigation Defense in all State and Federal Courts. Commercial and Personal Lines, Construction Defect, Bad Faith, Insurance Coverage and Declaratory Relief, Medical Malpractice, Environmental Law, Legal Malpractice, Wrongful Termination, Governmental Entity Defense.**
**Irvine, California Office: 18400 Von Karman Avenue, Suite 615, 92612. Telephone: 714-253-9553. Fax: 714-253-9643.**

***See Professional Biographies, LOS ANGELES, CALIFORNIA***

Stevens, Norman E., Professional Corporation, (AV) ........16611 Park Lane Circle
**Stevenson, Clinton R.**, (AV) ........'23 '51 C.611 B.A. L.309 LL.B. [[C] Latham&W.]
Stevenson, Michael ........'49 '84 C.112 B.A. L.564 J.D. 445 S. Figueeroa St.
**Stevenson, Roseann C.** ........'54 '79 C.705 B.A. L.800 J.D. [Morgan,L.&B.]
Stevenson, Scot B., (AV) ........'49 '74 C.800 A.B. L.809 J.D. 1200 Wilshire Blvd.
Steward, Evelyne R. ........'39 '78 C.1097 B.A. L.1190 J.D. 6290 Sunset Blvd.
Stewart, Alison L. ........'67 '93 C.112 B.A. L.1067 J.D. 801 S. Grand Ave.
**Stewart, Cameron A.** ........'60 '88 C.285 B.A. L.990 J.D. [[A] J.L.Cochran,Jr.]
*PRACTICE AREAS: Personal Injury; Employment Litigation; Civil Rights Litigation.
Stewart, Daniel L. ........'37 '62 C.112 B.A. L.309 J.D. Prof., Loyola Univ. Law Sch.
**Stewart, David K.** ........'65 '90 C.769 B.A. L.990 J.D. [[A] Tharpe&H.]
*PRACTICE AREAS: Automobile Accident; Construction Defect.
Stewart, Eliza ........'54 '76 C&L.878 B.A., J.D. [Stewart&S.]

**Stewart, Hunsdon Cary '43 '70**
**7377 West 85th Street, 90045-2456**
**Telephone: 310-641-7320 Fax: 310-641-7320**
***LANGUAGES: Spanish.**
***PRACTICE AREAS: Civil Trial; Business Real Estate; Professional Negligence; Family Law.**
**Civil Trial, Business, Real Estate, Professional Negligence and Family Law.**

***See Professional Biographies, LOS ANGELES, CALIFORNIA***

**Stewart, Irene E.** ........'58 '91 C.112 B.A. L.800 J.D. [[A] O'Melveny&M.]
Stewart, J. Frank ........'51 '80 C.280 B.A. L.893 J.D. 446 1/2 Landfair Ave.
Stewart, James J. ........'18 '54 C.999 L.809 LL.B. 361 S. Clark Dr. Beverly Hills, CA‡
**Stewart, James R.** ........'45 '82 C.768 B.A. L.1068 J.D. [[A] Morgan,L.&B.]
Stewart, Lorrie S. ........'52 '77 C.112 B.A. L.284 J.D. Dep. Dist. Atty.
**Stewart, Mark M.** ........'53 '81 C.241 B.S. L.734 J.D. [La Follette,J.D.F.&A.]
*PRACTICE AREAS: Medical Malpractice.
**Stewart, Marla M.** ........'52 '79 C.990 B.A. L.851 J.D. [Bivona&C.]⊙

CAA348P

Stewart, Michael P. ........................'56 '81 C.112 B.A. L.809 J.D. Dep. Dist. Atty.
**Stewart, Sandra C.** ..........................'— '84 C.112 B.A. L.426 J.D. [Cox,C.&N.]
*PRACTICE AREAS: Real Estate and Construction Litigation.
**Stewart, Thomas A.** ..................................'46 '85 L.1137 J.D. [Dennison,B.&P.]
*PRACTICE AREAS: Construction Defect Litigation; Earth Movement Litigation; Products Liability; Business Litigation; Tort Defense.
Stewart, Vilate D. ....................................'55 '79 C&L.878 B.S., J.D. [Stewart&S.]
Stewart, William F. ....................................'36 '62 L.1068 Sr. Asst. Co. Coun.
Stewart & Stewart ............................................11664 National Blvd.
**Stickney, Lawrence E.** ..............'43 '69 C&L.800 B.S.B.A., J.D. [Ⓒ Musick,P.&G.]
Stidman, Valerie H. ......................'68 '95 C&L.800 B.S., J.D. 2029 Century Pk. E.
Stieg, Edward C. ...........................'52 '77 C.477 A.B. L.800 J.D. Coun., Itochu Inter. Inc.
**Stiffelman, Gary S.**, (AV) ..........'52 '79 C.378 B.G.S. L.1068 J.D. [Ziffren,B.B.&F.]
*PRACTICE AREAS: Entertainment Law.
**Stiglitz, Bruce M., (A P.C.)**, (AV) ..............'35 '63 C&L.477 B.B.A., J.D. [Loeb&L.]
*PRACTICE AREAS: Taxation of Entertainment Industry; International Taxation; Estate Planning.
**Stiles, Edi S.** ......................................'61 '93 C.890 B.S. L.990 J.D. [Ⓐ Ord&N.]
*PRACTICE AREAS: Taxation; Estate Planning; General Business.
**Stilz, Richard A.**, (AV) ..........................'45 '71 C.112 B.A. L.426 J.D. [Stilz&B.]

**Stilz & Boyd, A Professional Corporation, (AV)**
**Suite 1000, Westside Towers, 11845 West Olympic Boulevard, 90064**
**Telephone: 310-312-8100 Telecopy: 310-312-8189**
**Richard A. Stilz; Earl E. Boyd.**
**General Civil, Criminal and Appellate Practice in all State and Federal Courts. Corporate, Commercial and Family Law Practice.**
***See Professional Biographies, LOS ANGELES, CALIFORNIA***

**Stindt, Thomas E.**, (AV) ..............'43 '71 C.112 B.A. L.1068 J.D. [Gilchrist&R.]⊙
*PRACTICE AREAS: Contested Trusts and Estates; Family Wealth Transactions; Estate Planning.
**Stinehart, William, Jr.**, (AV) ............'43 '70 C.813 B.A. L.1068 J.D. [Gibson,D.&C.]
*PRACTICE AREAS: Personal Tax Planning.
**Stitt, Todd Harrison** ....................'69 '95 C.112 B.A. L.809 J.D. [Ⓐ Lynberg&W.]
*PRACTICE AREAS: Insurance Coverage.
Stock, Linda M. ..........................'48 '89 C.1077 B.A. L.809 J.D. Fed. Trade Comm.
Stockdale, John E., (AV) ..........................'24 '55 C.112 L.426 J.D. [J.E.Stockdale]
Stockdale, John E., P.C., (AV) ..................................1520 Wilshire Blvd., 6th Fl.
Stockel, Susan R. ..................................................'38 '77 159 N. Cliffwood Ave.
**Stockley, Jeffery E.** ....................'68 '93 C.800 B.A. L.426 J.D. [Ⓐ Koletsky,M.&F.]
*PRACTICE AREAS: Construction Defect Defense; General Liability Defense.
Stockman, Michael I. .........................'60 '87 C&L.426 B.A., J.D. 400 S. Hope St.
**Stockstill, Robert W., Jr.** ......................'62 '87 C&L.420 B.A., J.D. [Ⓐ Riordan&M.]
Stockwell, Eugene L., Jr., (AV) '19 '49
C.813 B.A. L.800 LL.B. 6222 Wilshire Blvd. 6th Fl.

**Stockwell, Harris, Widom & Woolverton, A Professional Corporation, (AV)** BR
**6222 Wilshire Boulevard, Sixth Floor, P.O. Box 48917, 90048-0917⊙**
**Telephone: 213-935-6669; 818-784-6222; 310-277-6669 Fax: 213-935-0198**
**Steven I. Harris (Managing Attorney); Patricia A. Olive; David L. Slucter (Resident, San Bernardino Office); Richard M. Widom (Managing Attorney); Jeffrey T. Landres (Resident, Ventura Office); Linda S. Freeman (Santa Ana and San Diego Offices); Michael L. Terry (Resident, Grover Beach Office); William M. Carero; Brian R. Horan; David F. Grant (Resident, Santa Office Office); Edward S. Muehl (Santa Ana and San Diego Offices); Lawrence S. Mendelsohn; Edwin H. McKnight, Jr. (Resident, Santa Ana Office); Steven A. Meline (Resident, Santa Ana Office); Ted L. Hirschberger; Theodore G. Schneider, Jr. (Resident, San Bernardino Office); Lawrence B. Madans; Lester D. Marshall; John R. Payne; George Woolverton; James C. Shipley (Resident, Ventura Office); Jeffrey Eugene Lowe (Resident, Santa Ana Office).**
**Workers Compensation Insurance and Employment Matters.**
**Santa Ana, California Office: Suite 500, 1551 N. Tustin Avenue, P.O. Box 11979. Telephone: 714-479-1180. Fax: 714-479-1190.**
**Ventura, California Office: 2021 Sperry Avenue, Suite 46. Telephone: 805-654-8994; 213-617-7290. Fax: 805-654-1546.**
**San Bernardino, California Office: Suite 303, 215 North "D" Street. Telephone: 909-381-5553. Fax: 909-384-9981.**
**San Diego, California Office: Suite 400, 402 West Broadway. Telephone: 619-235-6054. Fax: 619-231-0129.**
**Grover Beach, California Office: Suite 307, 200 South 13th Street. Telephone: 805-473-0720. Fax: 805-473-0635.**
***See Professional Biographies, LOS ANGELES, CALIFORNIA***

**Stoddard, Marshall C., Jr.**, (AV) '51 '76
C.319 B.A. L.1048 J.D. [Kelley D.&W.] (⊙N.Y., N.Y.)
*PRACTICE AREAS: Commercial Law; Banking Law; Bankruptcy Law.
Stoddard, Wilcox R., (AV) ....................'26 '54 C&L.800 B.S., LL.B. Asst. Co. Coun.
Stodden, Ann E. ...........................'28 '52 C&L.800 B.S., LL.B. Prob. Dept., Supr. Ct.
**Stodder, Seth M. M.** ......................'70 '95 C.311 B.A. L.800 J.D. [Ⓐ Gibson,D.&C.]
**Stodel, Jeffrey C.** ..........................'47 '74 C.800 B.A. L.426 J.D. [Ⓒ Chapin,F.&W.]
Stogel, Lauren Dale ..................'61 '87 C.228 B.A. L.245 J.D. 11738 Mayfield Ave.
**Stokdyk, Steven B.** ..........................'67 '91 C.813 A.B. L.1068 J.D. [Sullivan&C.]
**Stoke, H. Randall**, (AV) ....................'28 '55 C.112 B.S. L.1066 J.D. [Ⓒ Latham&W.]
**Stolar, Bernadine J.** ..............................'52 '87 C&L.426 B.A., J.D. [Ⓐ Robie&M.]
*PRACTICE AREAS: Insurance Defense.
Stoll, Estie R. ..................'45 '80 C.66 B.A. L.1009 J.D. 725 S. Figueroa St., 19th Fl.
Stoll, Robert J., Jr. .............................................'44 '70 C.769 B.A. L.61 J.D. [Stoll&N.]
Stoll & Nussbaum, A Professional Corporation ......................11601 Wilshire Blvd.
Stoller, Irving ............................'28 '52 C.112 B.S. L.809 LL.B. 405 N. Wilton Pl.
Stoller, Melinda F. ..........................................'— '90 L.809 J.D. 1200 Wilshire Blvd.
**Stolman, Theodore B.**, (AV) ...........'41 '67 C&L.884 B.S.E., LL.B. [Stutman,T.&G.]
*PRACTICE AREAS: Bankruptcy; Insolvency; Corporate Reorganization; Commercial Litigation.
**Stolpman, Thomas G., (Inc.)**, (AV) '49 '76
C.112 B.A. L.800 J.D. [Stolpman K.E.M.&K.]⊙
*PRACTICE AREAS: Products Liability Law; Professional Negligence Law; Maritime Accidents Law.

**Stolpman • Krissman • Elber • Mandel & Katzman LLP, (AV)**
**A Partnership including Professional Corporations**
**Suite 1800, 10880 Wilshire Boulevard (Westwood), 90024⊙**
**Telephone: 310-470-8011**
**Members of Firm: Thomas G. Stolpman (Inc.).**
**Tort Litigation, Trials, Appeals and Workers Compensation.**
**Long Beach, California Office: Nineteenth Floor, 111 West Ocean Boulevard. Telephone: 310-435-8300. Telecopier: 310-435-8304.**
***See Professional Biographies, LOS ANGELES, CALIFORNIA***

**Stomel, Alan J.** ............................................'56 '86 C.668 B.A. L.426 J.D. [Angel&N.]
*PRACTICE AREAS: Bankruptcy.
**Stone, Anne E.** ..........................'61 '86 C.188 A.B. L.477 J.D. [Morgan,L.&B.]
Stone, Christopher D. '37 '64 C.309 A.B. L.976 LL.B.
(adm. in NY; not adm. in CA) Univ. of Southern Calif. Sch. of Law
**Stone, Elizabeth A.** ....................'63 '88 C.112 B.A. L.464 J.D. [Ⓐ Jeffer,M.B.&M.]
*LANGUAGES: Japanese, Spanish.
*PRACTICE AREAS: Real Estate; Corporations; Civil Litigation.
Stone, Elmer J. ............................'19 '49 C.112 L.800 J.D. 801 S. Grand Ave.
**Stone, Ethan G.** ..............................'68 '96 C.309 A.B. L.178 J.D. [Ⓐ Irell&M.]
*LANGUAGES: Hebrew.

**Stone, Gordon P., III** ......................'65 '93 C.893 B.S. L.990 J.D. [Ⓐ Saltzburg,R.&B.]
*PRACTICE AREAS: Bankruptcy; Debtor and Creditor Law; Litigation.
**Stone, Gregory P.** ............................'52 '77 C.111 B.S. L.976 J.D. [Munger,T.&O.]
**Stone, Jean**, (BV) ..................................'34 '77 C.800 L.1095 J.D. [Hillsinger&C.]
**Stone, Jonathan B.** .......................'58 '85 C.112 A.B. L.1066 J.D. [Barbosa G.&B.]
*PRACTICE AREAS: Municipal Law; Planning, Zoning and Land Use Law; Bonds and Securities Law.
**Stone, Lawrence H.** ..................'58 '86 C.1036 B.A. L.978 J.D. [Jackson,L.S.&K.]
**Stone, Lawrence M., (P.C.)**, (AV) ..............'31 '56 C&L.309 A.B., LL.B. [Ⓒ Irell&M.]
Stone, Linda May, (Mrs.) ..............'43 '67 C&L.800 B.S.L., J.D. 1051 S. Beacon Ave.
**Stone, Lois A.** ..........................'— '89 C.1097 B.S. L.809 J.D. [Ⓐ Bright&L.]
*PRACTICE AREAS: Intellectual Property Law; Litigation.
Stone, Marcia ......................'39 '64 C.665 B.A. L.477 J.D. 3014 N. Beachwood Dr.
Stone, Pamela K. ..........................'62 '93 C.456 B.S. L.1049 J.D. 3580 Wilshire Blvd.
**Stone, R. Timothy** ..................'61 '86 C.472 B.B.A. L.276 J.D. [Hawkins,S.L.&B.]
**Stone, Rena Denton** ..................'55 '84 C.112 B.A. L.800 J.D. [Hawkins,S.L.&B.]
**Stone, Richard J.**, (AV) ........................'45 '71 C.145 B.A. L.1068 J.D. [Zelle&L.]
**Stone, Richard L.** .....................'59 '83 C.112 B.A. L.426 J.D. [Sheppard,M.R.&H.]
*PRACTICE AREAS: Commercial Law; Investment Fraud Law; Litigation.
Stone, Robert M. ..........................................'34 '63 C.994 B.A. L.569 LL.B. U.S. Mag.
**Stone, Robert M.** ..........................'48 '74 C.918 B.A. L.94 J.D. [Musick,P.&G.]
*PRACTICE AREAS: Labor and Employment.
**Stone, Robert N.**, (AV) ..................'30 '55 C.112 A.B. L.1066 J.D. [Stone,D.&W.]
*PRACTICE AREAS: Personal Injury; Malpractice; Products Liability; Aviation; Civil Trial.
Stone, Robert W. ...............'68 '93 C.684 B.A. L.145 J.D. 1901 Avenue of the Stars
**Stone, Rodney J.** ..........................'61 '88 C.801 B.S. L.339 J.D. [Ⓐ Gibson,D.&C.]
*PRACTICE AREAS: Antitrust and Trade Regulation; Litigation.
Stone, Ronit M. ..............'61 '86 C.112 B.A. L.800 J.D. 12401 Wilshire Blvd., 2nd Fl.

**Stone, Dolginer & Wenzel, A Law Corporation, (AV)**
**6500 Wilshire Boulevard Suite 2060, 90048**
**Telephone: 213-653-2244 FAX: 213-658-1155**
**Robert N. Stone; Charles I. Dolginer; Mark D. Wenzel;—Henry N. Seligsohn. Of Counsel: A. J. Connick Doran.**
**Practice limited to Personal Injury, Malpractice, Products Liability and Aviation Law. Civil Trial Practice in all Courts.**
**Reference: Union Bank (Head Office, 900 South Main Street, Los Angeles).**

**Stone & Doyle**
**(See Pasadena)**

**Stone & Feeley, P.C.**
**(See Law Offices of Thomas J. Feeley, P.C.)**

**Stone & Hiles**
**(See Beverly Hills)**

**Stone & Rosenblatt, A Professional Corporation**
**(See Encino)**

**Stoner, William E.** ..........................'56 '81 C.967 B.S. L.228 J.D. [Pillsbury M.&S.]
**Stork, Edward T.** ......................'51 '78 C.588 B.A. L.982 J.D. [Sedgwick,D.M.&A.]
**Stoughton, Peter** ..........................'66 '93 C.112 B.A. L.1068 [Ⓐ Perkins C.]
*PRACTICE AREAS: Real Estate.
**Stout, Reed A.**, (AV) ..........................'11 '37 C.878 A.B. L.273 J.D. [Arter&H.]
Stovitz, Laura K. ...............'61 '86 C.605 B.A. L.1068 J.D. 11611 San Vicente Blvd.
Stowe, John R. ..............................'34 '79 C.627 B.G.E. L.1179 J.D. 2653 Patricia Ave.
**Stowell, David T.** ..........................'55 '81 C.344 B.A. L.990 J.D. [De Castro,W.&C.]
**Straatsma, B. Derek**, (AV) ..............'55 '81 C.112 B.A. L.1136 J.D. [Burke,W.&S.]
*PRACTICE AREAS: Workers Compensation Law; Civil Litigation; Labor Law; Municipal Law.
Strage, Michael M. ..................'59 '86 C.178 B.A. L.800 J.D. 515 S. Figueroa St.
**Strahlstrom, L. Elizabeth** ..................'68 '94 C.112 B.A. L.464 J.D. [Ⓐ Reznik&R.]
*LANGUAGES: Spanish.
*PRACTICE AREAS: Land Use; Environmental Law; Administrative Law; Water Law.
Straight-Gagnon, Kimberly ................'58 '84 C&L.608 B.S., J.D. 255 S. Grand Ave.

**Strain & Rosenberger, A Law Corporation**
**(See Long Beach)**

Stralka, William F. ......................'42 '73 C.497 B.A. L.1136 J.D. State Bar of Calif.
**Strand, Helen E.** ..........................'41 '89 C.37 B.A. L.426 J.D. [Ⓐ Tharpe&H.]
*LANGUAGES: Chinese, Japanese, French.
*PRACTICE AREAS: Civil Litigation.
Strange, Brian R., (AV) ....................'56 '82 C.112 B.A. L.1065 J.D. [Strange&H.]
**Strange, Owen W.**, (AV) ..............'28 '53 C.605 A.B. L.800 LL.B. [Ⓒ Booth,M.&S.]
Strange, Robert F. .... '37 '61 C&L.966 B.B.A., LL.B. 3324 Castle Heights Ave. Apt. 303
Strange & Hoey, (AV) ..........................................12100 Wilshire Blvd. (⊙San Diego)
Strantz, Eugene R. ..............'— '72 C.494 B.A. L.1127 J.D. 5900 Wilshire Blvd.‡
**Strapp, Myrna Linett** ........................'48 '75 C.608 B.S. L.117 J.D. [Ⓐ McHale&C.]
**Strapp, W. Joseph** ..................'48 '73 C&L.608 B.A., J.D. [Littler,M.F.T.&M.]

**Strassman, Harvey, (AV) '33 '59 C.112 A.B. L.800 LL.B.** BR
**1875 Century Park East, 15th Floor, 90067**
**Telephone: 310-277-6775 Fax: 310-552-3228**
**Practice Limited to Family Law and Civil Litigation.**
***See Professional Biographies, LOS ANGELES, CALIFORNIA***

Stratman, Victoria Dagy ......................'51 '83 C.502 B.A. L.352 J.D. 400 S. Hope St.
Stratton, Maria E., (AV) ....................'52 '79 C.800 B.A. L.1066 J.D. Fed. Pub. Def.
Straughn, Carol J. ..........................'46 '82 C&L.1179 B.S.L., J.D. 210 W. Temple St.
Strauss, Deborah C. '56 '81 C.659 B.A. L.178 J.D.
(adm. in NY; not adm. in CA) 654 Woodruff Ave.‡
Strauss, Howard T. ............................'51 '76 C.112 B.A. L.426 J.D. Dep. Dist. Atty.
Strauss, Leigh R. ..................'61 '90 C.1077 B.A. L.1068 J.D. 12121 Wilshire Blvd.
**Strauss, Robert E.** ..........'64 '90 C.309 A.B. L.1068 J.D. [Weinstock,M.R.S.&N.]
*PRACTICE AREAS: Corporate; Business; Tax; Estate Planning.
**Strauss, Stephen J.** ..........'56 '83 C.30 B.A. L.809 J.D. [Fulwider P.L.&U.] (See Pat. Sect.)
*PRACTICE AREAS: Patent, Trademark, Copyright and Unfair Competition Law; Litigation.
**Strausz, William L.** ..................'46 '73 C.911 B.A. L.426 J.D. [Richards,W.&G.]
*PRACTICE AREAS: Public Finance Law; Public Law.
Strawbrich, Robert C. '58 '92
C.94 B.S.B.M.E. L.846 J.D. 1800 Ave. of the Stars, Suite 900 (Pat.)
Strayhan, Dennis C. '46 '72 C.884 B.A. L.425 J.D.
(adm. in LA; not adm. in CA) Div. Mgr., U.S. Bkrptcy. Ct.
**Streeter, John W.**, (AV) ....................'52 '79 C.906 B.A. L.426 J.D. [Kern,S.&G.]
*PRACTICE AREAS: Construction Defects.
Streich, Robert M. ..................'58 '88 C.112 B.A. L.1065 J.D. 4318 Victoria Park Pl.
**Streisand, Adam F.** ..........................'63 '91 C.855 B.A. L.29 J.D. [Ⓐ Loeb&L.]
*PRACTICE AREAS: Litigation.
Strenger, Laurence N. '44 '69 C.178 A.B. L.145 J.D.
399 Park Ave. (⊙New York, N.Y.)
**Strenio, Gerald J.** ..........................'68 '95 C.846 B.B.A. L.477 J.D. [Ⓐ Loeb&L.]
*LANGUAGES: Spanish.
*PRACTICE AREAS: Bankruptcy; Commercial Litigation.
Strick, Laurence D. ...........'50 '77 C.767 A.B. L.800 J.D. 1857 Century Park E., 6th Fl.
**Strick, Susan P.** ..........................'54 '82 C.112 B.A. L.809 J.D. [Ⓒ Geragos&G.]
*PRACTICE AREAS: Civil Rights; Criminal Defense; Civil Litigation.

**Stricker, Cathey A.** ....................'57 '85 C.528 B.A. L.575 J.D. [Lewis,D.B.&B.]
**Strickland, Julia B.** ....................'54 '78 C.112 B.A. L.1068 J.D. [Stroock&S.&L.]
*PRACTICE AREAS: Securities Litigation.

**Strickstein, Herbert J., (AV) '32 '57 C&L.800 B.S.L., J.D.**
**2049 Century Park East, Suite 1200, 90067**
Telephone: 310-553-4888 FAX: 213-879-5459
Real Estate, Condominium, Planned Development and Cooperative Housing Law.
*See Professional Biographies, LOS ANGELES, CALIFORNIA*

**Stringfellow, Walter A.**, (AV) ....... '45 '71 C&L.228 B.A., J.D. [Stringfellow&Assoc.]

**Stringfellow & Associates, A Law Corporation, (AV)**
**444 South Flower Street, 31st Floor, 90071**
Telephone: 213-538-3880 Fax: 213-538-3890
Walter A. Stringfellow;—Manuel J. Diaz; David A. Keisner. Of Counsel: Lisa Schwartz Tudzin.
Litigation, Business, Construction, Environmental and Real Estate, and Representation of Doctors and Hospitals in Workers' Compensation.
*See Professional Biographies, LOS ANGELES, CALIFORNIA*

Strnad, Jeff .........'52 '80 C.309 A.B. L.976 J.D. Prof. of Law, Univ. of Southern Calif.
Strom, Cindy M. .................... '61 '93 C.1175 B.A. L.546 J.D. 624 S. Grand Ave.
**Strom, Robb Michael** ....................'59 '85 C.112 B.A. L.1049 [▣ Frandzel&S.]
*LANGUAGES: Spanish.
*PRACTICE AREAS: Civil Litigation.
**Stromberg, G. Thomas, Jr.** ............'55 '82 C.309 B.A. L.878 J.D. [Heller E.W.&M.]
*PRACTICE AREAS: International, Corporate and Project Finance.
**Stromberg, Ross E.**, (AV) ....................'40 '66 C.330 B.A. L.1066 J.D. [Jones,D.R.&P.]
Strong, George G., Jr. ....................'47 '74 C.976 B.A. L.1049 J.D. Price Waterhouse
**Strong, Peter H.**, (AV) ................'52 '75 C.37 B.A. L.813 J.D. [▣ Augustini,W.&D.]
**Strong, Richard A.**, (AV) ..............'43 '69 C.878 B.S. L.309 J.D. [Gibson,D.&C.]
*PRACTICE AREAS: General Corporate; Securities; Mergers and Acquisitions.

**Stroock & Stroock & Lavan LLP, (AV)** BB
**Suite 1800, 2029 Century Park East, 90067-3086**⊙
Telephone: 310-556-5800 Telecopier: (310) 556-5959 Cable Address: "Plastroock, L.A." Telex: Plastroock LSA 677190 (Domestic and International)
Resident Partners: Richard S. Forman; Schuyler M. Moore; Margaret A. Nagle; Michael F. Perlis; Julia B. Strickland; Michael M. Umansky. Of Counsel: Gerald J. Mehlman. Retired Partners: Merrill E. Jenkins; William H. Levit (P.C.); Robert M. Shafton;—Judith L. Anderson; Maryanne Carson; Wrenn E. Chais; James W. Denison; Karen R. Dinino; Joseph W. Dung; D. Wayne Jeffries; Nicholas F. Klein; David S. Lippes (Not admitted in CA); Mary D. Manesis; Andrew J. Matosich; Scott M. Pearson; Lisa M. Simonetti; Glenn D. Smith; Chauncey M. Swalwell; Matthew C. Thompson; Karynne G. Weiss.
New York, N.Y. Office: 180 Maiden Lane, New York, N.Y., 10038. Telephone: 212-806-5400. Telecopiers: (212) 806-5919; (212) 806-6006; (212) 806-6086; (212) 425-9509; (212) 806-6176.
New York Conference Center: 767 Third Avenue, New York, N.Y., 10017-2023. Telephone: 212-806-5767; 5768; 5769; 5770. Telecopier: (212) 421-6234.
Boston, Massachusetts Office: 100 Federal Street, 02110. Telephone: 617-482-6800. Fax: 617-330-5111.
Budapest, Hungary Office: East-West Business Center, Rákóczi ut 1-3, H-1088. Telephone: 011-361-266-9520 or 011-361-266-7770. Telecopier: 011-361-266-9279.
Miami, Florida Office: 200 South Biscayne Boulevard, Suite 3300, First Union Financial Center, 33131-2385. Telephone: 305-358-9900. Telecopier: (305) 789-9302.
Washington, D.C. Office: 1150 Seventeenth Street, N.W., Suite 600, 20036-4652. Telephone: 202-452-9250. Telecopier: (202) 293-2293.
*See Professional Biographies, LOS ANGELES, CALIFORNIA*

**Strother, James F.** '38 '66 C&L.893 B.S.M.E., LL.B.
(adm. in VA; not adm. in CA) Assoc. Gen. Coun., Ernst & Young LLP
Strotz, R. J. Rodriguez ....................'50 '76 C.800 B.A. L.1068 J.D. 857 S. Bronson Ave.
Stroud, Dan L., (AV) ....................'31 '57 C.112 B.A. L.1068 LL.B. 888 S. Figuerda St.
**Stroud, Zahava Aroesty** ..............'58 '85 C.112 B.A. L.1067 J.D. [▣ Bragg,S.S.&K.]
*PRACTICE AREAS: Insurance Defense Litigation.
Strouse, David James ...........'55 '82 C.477 B.S. L.1068 J.D. CBS Television Network
**Strub, Michael H., Jr.** ................'65 '91 C.276 B.S.F.S. L.846 J.D. [▣ Shearman&S.]
**Strug, Jeffrey N.** ....................'69 '95 C.028 B.A. L.06 LL.B. [▣ Allen,M.L.G.&M.]
*PRACTICE AREAS: Tax.
Strugo, Robin D. ....................'59 '84 C.668 B.A. L.1066 J.D. Clk., Supr. Ct.
**Strulson, Richard D.** ....................'68 '95 C.893 B.A. L.228 J.D. [▣ Latham&W.]
**Struman, Dale M.** ....................'54 '89 C.763 B.A. L.809 J.D. [Lamb&B.]
Struthers, Alex, Jr. '38 '75 C.426 B.A. L.809 J.D.
Los Angeles Unified School Dist./Garfield High School
**Stuart, Colbern C.** ....................'68 '95 C.802 B.A. L.61 J.D. [▣ Cozen&O.]
*PRACTICE AREAS: Insurance Subrogation; Insurance Coverage-Defense.
Stuart, David W. ....................'65 '94 C.1077 B.S. L.426 J.D. Dep. Dist Atty.
**Stuart, Douglas L.** ...............'62 '87 C.112 B.A. L.464 J.D. [▣ Sedgwick,D.M.&A.]
Stuart, James D. ....................'30 '58 C.154 A.B. L.800 J.D. 428 S. June St.‡
**Stubbs, V. Joseph** ....................'49 '75 C.804 B.A. L.986 J.D. [Brobeck,P.&H.]
**Stubington, Mark J.** ...............'65 '92 C.112 B.A. L.477 J.D. [▣ Morgan,L.&B.]
**Stuckey, Karen M.** ....................'64 '89 C.502 B.J. L.1049 J.D. [▣ Arter&H.]
Stulberg, Jeffrey D. ....................'57 '88 C&L.629 B.S., J.D. 835 Wilshire Blvd.
**Stulberg, Robert** ...............'59 '86 C.103 A.B. L.309 J.D. [Armstrong H.J.T.&W.]
*PRACTICE AREAS: Entertainment.
**Stull, Paul M.** .........'52 '77 C.967 B.A. L.477 J.D. [▣ Fulwider P.L.&U.] (See Pat. Sect.)
*PRACTICE AREAS: Patent, Trademark, Copyright and Unfair Competition Law; Litigation.
Stuller, Erwin L. .................... '26 '53 C.339 B.S. L.209 J.D. P.O. Box 2031

**Stuimreiter, John J., Law Offices of**
(See Pasadena)

**Sturgeon, John A.**, (AV) ....................'36 '63 C&L.813 A.B., J.D. [White&C.]
**Sturgeon, Robert T.** ...............'63 '95 C&L.800 B.A., J.D. [▣ Sheppard,M.R.&H.]
*PRACTICE AREAS: Litigation.
**Sturges, Jennifer L.** ...............'66 '91 C.1165 B.S. L.61 J.D. [▣ Bonne,B.M.O.&N.]
**Sturman, Herbert D.**, (AV) ...............'36 '61 C&L.178 A.B., LL.B. [Fierstein&S.]
*PRACTICE AREAS: Corporate Law; Tax Planning Law; Litigation and Probate Law.
**Sturman, Jeff M.** ....................'61 '90 C.911 B.A. L.629 J.D. [▣ Trope&T.]
*PRACTICE AREAS: Family Law; Civil Litigation; Tax Law.
**Sturman, Martin L., (A Professional Corporation)**, (AV) '33 '58
C.1016 L.424 J.D. [Goldfarb,S.&A.]
*PRACTICE AREAS: Taxation Law; Corporate Law; Estate Planning Law.
**Sturrock, Michael W.** ...............'65 '91 C.800 B.S. L.276 J.D. [▣ Latham&W.]
*PRACTICE AREAS: Corporate.
**Sturtevant, Jill M.** ............'53 '79 C.112 B.A. L.602 J.D. Sr. Coun., Bank of Amer.
Sturzenegger, Lisa H. ...........'60 '87 C&L.893 B.A., J.D. 333 S. Hope St., 48th Fl.
**Stutman, Jack**, (AV) ....................'14 '42 C&L.309 A.B., LL.B. [Stutman,T.&G.] ‡

**Stutman, Treister & Glatt, Professional Corporation, (AV)** BB
**3699 Wilshire Boulevard, Suite 900, 90010**
Telephone: 213-251-5100 FAX: 213-251-5288
Jack Stutman (Retired Founder); George M. Treister; Herman L. Glatt; Richard M. Neiter; Robert A. Greenfield; Charles D. Axelrod; Theodore B. Stolman; Isaac M. Pachulski; Kenneth N. Klee; Alan Pedlar; George C. Webster, II; Stephan M. Ray; Michael A. Morris; Jeffrey C. Krause; Michael H. Goldstein; Lee R. Bogdanoff; Frank A. Merola; K. John Shaffer; Mareta C. Hamre; Michael L. Tuchin; Jeffrey H. Davidson; Ronald L. Fein; Mark S. Wallace; Eric D. Goldberg; Eve H. Karasik; Thomas R. Kreller; Martin R. Barash; James O. Johnston Jr.; Michael C. Standlee.
(This Listing Continued)

**Stutman, Treister & Glatt, Professional Corporation (Continued)**
Bankruptcy, Insolvency, Corporate Reorganization and Commercial Litigation.
*See Professional Biographies, LOS ANGELES, CALIFORNIA*

**Stylides, Bonnie** ....................'— '94 C.860 B.A. L.813 J.D. [▣ Kaye,S.F.H.&H.]

**Styskal, Wiese & Melchione**
(See Glendale)

**Su, Henry M.** ...............'69 '94 C.112 B.A. L.809 J.D. [▣ La Follette,J.D.F.&A.]
*LANGUAGES: Chinese.
*PRACTICE AREAS: Construction Liability.
**Suarez, Kathryn Ellen** ............'68 '94 C.112 B.A. L.1066 J.D. [▣ Jeffer,M.B.&M.]
*PRACTICE AREAS: Business and Labor Litigation.
Suchy, Thomas J. ....................'59 '84 C.476 B.A. L.215 J.D. 505 Shatto Pl.
**Sud, Sonya** ....................'70 '95 C.145 B.S. L.597 J.D. [▣ Sidley&A.]
**Suddleson, M. Kenneth**, (AV) ......'49 '69 C.112 A.B. L.1068 J.D. [▣ Kaye,S.F.H.&H.]
*PRACTICE AREAS: Entertainment Law.
**Sudmann, Andrea B.** ............'58 '83 C.918 B.A. L.262 J.D. Sr. Coun., Bank of Amer.
Suehiro, Amy F. ....................'49 '85 C.1097 B.A. L.426 J.D. Dep. Dist. Atty.
Suemori, Garrett H. ....................'49 '77 C.800 B.S. L.1049 J.D. 624 S. Grand Ave.
Sufrin, Ronald K. '52 '78 C.112 B.A. L.1067 J.D.
Spec. Coun., U.S. Sec. & Exch. Comm.
Sugar, Philip J., (AV) ...............'46 '73 C.1060 A.B. L.1065 J.D. Asst. City Atty.‡
Sugawara, Joyce, Ms. ....................'56 '81 C.475 B.A. L.1067 J.D. I.R.S.
**Sugimoto, Douglas K.** ....................'71 '96 C.112 B.S. L.309 J.D. [▣ Irell&M.]
**Suh, Christine H.** ....................'69 '94 C.813 A.B. L.1066 J.D. [▣ O'Melveny&M.]
Suh, Patricia M. ...............'60 '84 C.112 B.A. L.1065 J.D. 3435 Wilshire Blvd.
Suhr, Tong S. ....................'35 '78 C.629 B.A. L.809 J.D. [T.S.Suhr]
Suhr, Tong S., P.C. ....................3600 Wilshire Blvd.
**Sulat, Genalin Y.** ...............'69 '96 C.705 B.S.N. L.1068 J.D. [▣ R.I.Fine&Assoc.]
*LANGUAGES: Tagalog.
*PRACTICE AREAS: General Litigation; Class Actions; Antitrust; Government.
**Sulla, Jennifer** ....................'60 '94 C.93 B.A. L.893 J.D. [▣ Hennigan,M.&B.]
*PRACTICE AREAS: Litigation.
**Sullivan, Barry** ....................'— '88 L.1066 J.D. [▣ Sheppard,M.R.&H.]
*PRACTICE AREAS: Contract Law, Litigation, Real Property Law.
**Sullivan, Brian A.** ....................'53 '84 C.145 B.A. L.1066 J.D. [Graham&J.]
*PRACTICE AREAS: Securities Law; Corporate Law.
Sullivan, Daniel M. ("R.D.") ...............'60 '87 C.1111 B.S. L.260 J.D. 633 W. 5th St.
Sullivan, Deirdre Ann ...............'59 '89 C.788 A.B. L.1009 J.D. 515 S. Figueroa St.
**Sullivan, Douglas W.**, (AV) ...............'53 '79 C.347 B.A. L.893 J.D. [Folger L.&K.]⊙
Sullivan, Glen J. ....................'51 '76 C&L.813 A.B., J.D. 633 W. 5th St.
Sullivan, James R. ....................'39 '79 C.839 B.S. L.1068 J.D. Asst. U.S. Atty.
Sullivan, Jane E. ....................'47 '91 C.347 B.A. L.990 J.D. Pub. Def. Off.
**Sullivan, Mary E.** ....................'62 '87 C.423 B.S. L.276 J.D. [Katz,G.&F.]
*PRACTICE AREAS: Entertainment Law; Motion Picture Finance; Corporate Law.
**Sullivan, Mary L.** ...............'40 '69 C&L.585 B.S., J.D. Coun., Hughes Aircraft Co.
**Sullivan, Michael R.**, (AV) ...............'47 '73 C.112 A.B. L.1068 J.D. [Sullivan]
*SPECIAL AGENCIES: National Transportation Safety Board, State Bar of California.
*PRACTICE AREAS: Aviation; Business; Corporation.
Sullivan, Michael Ward ...............'66 '92 C.426 B.A. L.1065 J.D. 1200 Wilshire Blvd.
**Sullivan, Paul F.** ...............'65 '90 C.763 B.S. L.464 J.D. [▣ Williamson,R.&D.]
*PRACTICE AREAS: Insurance Defense; Professional Malpractice; Intellectual Property; Business Litigation; Construction Defect.
**Sullivan, Peter** ....................'52 '78 C.178 A.B. L.262 J.D. [Gibson,D.&C.]
*PRACTICE AREAS: Antitrust Litigation and Counseling (U.S. and International); Unfair Competition; Intellectual Property; Government Investigations; General Commercial Litigation.
**Sullivan, Roger M., (A Professional Corporation)**, (AV) '26 '52
C.605 L.426 J.D. [Sullivan,W.&D.]
*PRACTICE AREAS: Eminent Domain Law; Land Use Regulation Law.
**Sullivan, Stacey A.** ....................'68 '96 C.112 B.A. L.1065 J.D. [▣ Hill,F.&B.]
**Sullivan, Virginia Vance** ............'61 '86 C.259 B.S. L.260 J.D. [McDermott,W.&E.]
*PRACTICE AREAS: Health Care; Hospitals; Mergers, Acquisitions and Divestitures.

**Sullivan & Cromwell, (AV)** BB
**444 South Flower Street, 90071-2901**⊙
Telephone: 213-955-8000 Telecopier: 213-683-0457
Partners in Los Angeles: Stanley F. Farrar; Frank H. Golay, Jr.; Robert A. Sacks; Alison S. Ressler; Michael H. Steinberg; John L. Savva. Associates in Los Angeles: Elizabeth S. Bluestein; Patrick S. Brown; Julius G. Christensen; Valerie C. Edwards; Ken Ikari; Brian P.Y. Liu; Michael L. Preston; Stevie Pyon; Daniel E. Sobelsohn; Thaddeus G. Stephens; Steven B. Stokdyk; Steven W. Thomas. General Practice.
New York City Office: 125 Broad Street, 10004-2498. Telephone: 212-558-4000. Telex: 62694. Telecopier: 212-558-3588.
Washington, D.C. Office: 1701 Pennsylvania Avenue, N.W., 20006-5805. Telephone: 202-956-7500. Telecopier: 202-293-6330.
Paris Office: 8, Place Vendôme, Paris 75001, France. Telephone: (011)(331)4450-6000. Telex: 240654. Telecopier: (011)(331)4450-6060.
London Office: St. Olave's House, 9a Ironmonger Lane, London EC2V 8EY, England. Telephone: (011)(44171)710-6500. Telecopier: (011)(44171)710-6565.
Melbourne Office: 101 Collins Street, Melbourne, Victoria 3000, Australia. Telephone: (011)(613)9654-1500. Telecopier: (011)(613)9654-2422.
Tokyo Office: Sullivan & Cromwell, Gaikokuho Jimu Bengoshi Jimusho, Akai Law Offices (Registered Associated Offices), Tokio Kaijo Building Shinkan, 2-1, Marunouchi 1-chome, Chiyoda-ku, Tokyo 100, Japan. Telephone: (011)(813)3213-6140. Telecopier: (011)(813)3213-6470.
Hong Kong Office: 28th Floor, Nine Queen's Road, Central, Hong Kong. Telephone: (011)(852)2826-8688. Telecopier: (011)(852)2522-2280.
Frankfurt Office: Oberlindau 54-56, 60323 Frankfurt am Main, Germany. Telephone: (011)(4969)7191-260. Telecopier: (011)(4969)7191-2610.
*See Professional Biographies, LOS ANGELES, CALIFORNIA*

**Sullivan Law Corporation, (AV)** BB
**545 South Figueroa Street, Suite 1216, 90071-1599**
Telephone: 213-488-9200 Telecopier: 213-488-9664
Michael R. Sullivan;—Douglas G. Carroll.
Corporation, Taxation, Environmental, Commercial, Aviation, Insurance, Government Contracting and Litigation in all State and Federal Courts, Internal Revenue Service, National Transportation Safety Board, and Federal Government Boards of Contract Appeals.
*See Professional Biographies, LOS ANGELES, CALIFORNIA*

**Sullivan, Workman & Dee, (AV)** BB
A Partnership including a Professional Corporation
**Twelfth Floor, 800 Figueroa Street, 90017**
Telephone: 213-624-5544 Fax: 213-627-7128
Partners: Roger M. Sullivan (A Professional Corporation); Henry K. Workman; John J. Dee; Charles D. Cummings; Charles F. Callanan; Gary A. Kovacic; Joseph S. Dzida, Jr.; John E. Mackel, III; Paul C. Epstein; Christopher K. Cooper;—Susan Mapel Kahn; Emil J. Wohl. Of Counsel: Henry G. Bodkin, Jr.; Thomas E. O'Sullivan.
General Civil Practice including Trial and Appellate Litigation. Eminent Domain, Land Use and Real Property, Business, Securities and Corporate Matters, Entertainment Law, Probate, Trust and Estate Planning Law.
Reference: First Business Bank.
*See Professional Biographies, LOS ANGELES, CALIFORNIA*

**Sulmeyer, Irving**, (AV) ...............'27 '52 C.111 B.S. L.813 J.D. [Sulmeyer,K.B.&R.]
*PRACTICE AREAS: Bankruptcy.

**Sulmeyer, Kupetz, Baumann & Rothman, A Professional Corporation, (AV)** [BB]
**300 South Grand Avenue, 14th Floor, 90071**
Telephone: 213-626-2311 Fax: 213-629-4520
Irving Sulmeyer; Arnold L. Kupetz; Richard G. Baumann; Don Rothman; Alan G. Tippie; Israel Saperstein; Victor A. Sahn; Steven R. Wainess; David S. Kupetz; Howard M. Ehrenberg; Kathryn Kerfes;—Nathan H. Harris; Susan Frances Moley; Matthew Rothman; Wesley Avery; Mark S. Horoupian; Stephen C. Seto; Howard N. Madris; Tanya M. Vince. Of Counsel: Marilyn S. Scheer; Frank Vram Zerunyan; Suzanne L. Weakley; Elissa D. Miller.
Bankruptcy, Insolvency, Corporate Reorganization, Commercial Law and Creditor's Rights. General Civil and Trial Practice.
Representative Clients: General Electric Capital Corp.; Continental Insurance Co.; Litton Industries; North American Phillips Corp.; Ventura Port District; Northwest Financial; Heller Financial Inc.; Transamerica Occidental Life Insurance Co.; Transamerica Realty Services, Inc.; Body Glove International.
*See Professional Biographies, LOS ANGELES, CALIFORNIA*

**Sultan, Jeffrey E., (P.C.)** ... '48 '73 C.112 B.A. L.1068 J.D. [Jeffer,M.B.&M.]
*PRACTICE AREAS: Corporate; Securities; Partnerships; Oil and Gas; Nonprofit Religious Corporations.
**Sulzer, Kenneth D.** ... '60 '85 C.605 A.B. L.309 J.D. [Seyfarth,S.F.&G.]
**Sume, Kayser O.** ... '66 '91 C.813 A.B. L.93 J.D. [Richards,W.&G.]
*PRACTICE AREAS: Insurance Coverage; Civil Litigation.
Summer, Mary C. ... '49 '84 C.801 B.A. L.809 J.D. 12350 W. Olympic Blvd.
Summerhayes, Diana L. ... '50 '83 C.187 B.A. L.426 J.D. Dep. Dist. Atty.
**Summers, Jon S.** ... '64 '89 C.800 B.A. L.809 J.D. [A] Mannis&P.]
*PRACTICE AREAS: Family Law; Custody.
Summers, Stacy L. ... '62 '89 C.800 B.S.N. L.990 J.D. 10 Universal City Plaza
Sumner, Jas. D., Jr. ... '19 '48 C.968 A.B. L.893 LL.B. 10513 Rocca Pl.
Sumpter, Gail M. ... '55 '80 C.112 B.A. L.1049 J.D. 11845 W. Olympic Blvd.
Sumpter, Jeffrey L. ... '56 '85 C.932 B.B.A. L.464 J.D. 205 S. Barrington Ave.
Sumrow, Matthew A. ... '69 '94 C.112 B.A. L.1065 J.D. 555 S. Flower St.
Sumski, Bill J. ... '66 '91 C.990 B.A. L.1068 J.D. 2029 Century Park E.
**Sun, Hong** ... '— '94 C.061 B.A. L.1148 J.D. [B] Shaub&W.]
*LANGUAGES: Chinese-Mandarin, Shanghai, Sichuan, Tianjing, Hubei, Yunnan, Hunan.
*PRACTICE AREAS: Immigration; Trademarks; Copyright; International Business; Litigation.
Sun, John L. ... '46 '74 C.1097 B.S. L.1049 J.D. 3550 Wilshire Blvd., Ste. 1250
**Sun, Lazarus N.** ... '60 '87 C.178 B.A. L.930 J.D. [A] Jeffer,M.B.&M.]
*LANGUAGES: Mandarin Chinese.
*PRACTICE AREAS: Employee Benefits.
**Sunderland, Allison M.** ... '69 '94 C.112 B.A. L.1065 J.D. [A] Troy&G.]
*PRACTICE AREAS: Financial Institutions; Real Estate Litigation.
Sundstedt, Frank E., Jr., (AV) ... '46 '72 C.1042 B.S. L.809 J.D. Dep. Dist. Atty.
**Sung, Raymond T.** ... '65 '90 C.813 B.A. L.1068 J.D. [A] Brobeck,P.&H.]
*LANGUAGES: Chinese, German and French.
*PRACTICE AREAS: Commercial Law; Secured Transactions; Banking and Finance.
**Sunkin, Neil M.** ... '59 '85 C.1036 B.A. L.245 J.D. [A] Arter&H.]
*REPORTED CASES: Federal Deposits Insurance Corp. v. Claycomb, 945 F.2d 853 (5th Cir. 1991), cert. den'd, 504 U.S. 955; Federal Deposit Insurance Corp. v. Selaiden Builders, Inc., 973 F.2d 1249 (5th Cir. 1992), cert. den'd, 507 U.S. 1051.
**Sunshine, Randall J.** ... '55 '86 C.103 B.A. L.262 J.D. [Liner,Y.&S.]
*PRACTICE AREAS: Business; Civil Litigation.
**Supanich, Dennis M., (AV)** ... '53 '78 C.436 B.S. L.800 J.D. [Aikenhead,C.&S.]
**Supnik, Paul D.**
(See Beverly Hills)
**Supowit, Stuart E.** ... '53 '85 C.645 B.A. L.809 J.D. [A] Federman,G.&G.]
*PRACTICE AREAS: Products Liability; Premises Liability; Business Torts.
Sure, Jane G. ... '21 '45 C.112 B.A. L.800 J.D. 7349 Pacific View Dr.
Surlin, Matthew Tobias ... '45 '81 C.1077 B.A. L.1068 J.D. 11601 Wilshire Blvd.
**Surman, Gregory L.** ... '62 '87 C.112 B.A. L.1066 J.D. [A] Gibson,D.&C.]
*PRACTICE AREAS: Corporations; International.
Surpin, Shelley H., (AV) ... '49 '76 C.813 B.A. L.1066 J.D. [Surpin,M.&E.]
Surpin, Mayersohn and Edelstone, (AV) ... 1880 Century Pk. E.
**Surprenant, Dominic** ... '55 '86 C.338 B.A. L.309 J.D. [Quinn E.U.&O.]
*PRACTICE AREAS: Complex Commercial Litigation; Antitrust; Intellectual Property.
Surtees, Suzanne P. ... '63 '88 C&L.800 B.A., J.D. 10501 Wilshire Blvd.‡
Susnow, Robert L. ... '47 '74 C.112 B.A. L.809 J.D. 1423 S. Grand Ave.
Sussin, Robert D. ... '43 '71 C.150 B.B.A. L.1068 J.D. [R.D.Sussin]
Sussin, Robert D., A Professional Corporation ... 12100 Wilshire Blvd.
**Susskind, Amanda F.** ... '57 '82 C.813 B.S. L.1065 J.D. [Richards,W.&G.]
*LANGUAGES: French and German.
*PRACTICE AREAS: Public Law; Public Finance; Redevelopment Law; Litigation.
**Sussman, Allen Z.** ... '64 '88 C.188 B.S. L.94 J.D. [A] Manatt,P.&P.]
*PRACTICE AREAS: Corporate Securities; Financial Services and Banking.
**Sussman, Dean** ... '69 '96 C.813 A.B. L.309 J.D. [A] O'Melveny&M.]
*LANGUAGES: Italian.
Sussman, Jerome J. ... '36 '59 C.674 A.B. L.309 LL.B. 1875 Century Park, E.
Sussman, Lisa Ann ... '60 '86 C.112 B.A. L.809 J.D. 5670 Wilshire Blvd.
**Sussman, Nancy E.** ... '— '90 C.112 B.S. L.1068 J.D. [A] O'Melveny&M.]
Sutcliffe, Robert J., (AV) ... '51 '76 C.112 A.B. L.309 J.D. 601 S. Figueroa St.
**Sutherland, Kevin R.** ... '65 '92 C.112 B.A. L.823 J.D. [A] Condon&F.]
**Suttle, Mark Oneal** ... '50 '90 C.112 B.A. L.309 J.D. [B] Gibson,D.&C.]
*PRACTICE AREAS: Business Litigation.
**Sutton, Brenda E.** ... '61 '93 C.221 B.A. L.112 J.D. [A] Schwartz,S.D.&S.]
*PRACTICE AREAS: Labor Law; Employment Discrimination; Civil Rights Law.
**Suzuki, Kaoruhiko** ... '47 '75 C&L.309 A.B., J.D. [Paul,H.J.&W.] (©Tokyo, Japan)
Suzuki, Paul T. ... '— '74 C.112 B.A. L.1068 J.D. 1055 Wilshire Blvd.
Suzuki, Takehiko ... '64 '89 C.228 A.B. L.94 J.D. 725 S. Figueroa St.
Suzumoto, Mark K. ... '54 '83 C.112 B.S. L.107 J.D. 725 S. Figueroa St.
**Swain, Philip C., (AV©)** ... '57 '84 C.860 B.A./B.S.M.E. L.597 J.D. [Kirkland&E.] (Pat.)
*PRACTICE AREAS: Litigation; Intellectual Property Law.
**Swain & Dipolito**
(See Long Beach)
**Swainston, Howard D., (AV)** ... '26 '65 C.877 L.878 J.D. [B] Breidenbach,B.H.H.&H.] ‡
**Swalwell, Chauncey M.** ... '64 '90 C.112 B.A. L.42 J.D. [A] Stroock&S.&L.]
*PRACTICE AREAS: Real Estate Law; Real Estate Litigation.
**Swan, Turner** ... '61 '89 C.309 A.B. L.800 J.D. [A] Sheppard,M.R.&H.]
*PRACTICE AREAS: Business Law and Litigation.
Swanigan, Vivienne A. ... '56 '85 C.1097 B.S. L.1068 J.D. Dep. City Atty.
**Swank, William K.** ... '51 '76 C.668 B.A. L.813 J.D. [Brobeck,P.&H.]
**Swanson, Daniel G.** ... '57 '84 C.112 A.B. L.309 J.D. [Gibson,D.&C.]
*PRACTICE AREAS: Antitrust; International Competition Law; Communications/Entertainment; Intellectual Property; Business Litigation.
**Swanson, Elizabeth L.** ... '55 '90 C&L.878 B.S., J.D. [Ashen,G.&L.]
*PRACTICE AREAS: Litigation.
Swanson, Joel D., (BV) ... '35 '73 C.112 B.A. L.426 J.D. 10 Universal City Plaza, 28th Fl.
**Swanson, Julia S.** ... '46 '92 C.061 B.S. L.564 J.D. [A] Howarth&S.]
*LANGUAGES: Japanese.
**Swanson, Stephen T.** ... '42 '70 C.112 A.B. L.426 J.D. [Arter&H.]
**Swanson, Todd E.** ... '58 '85 C.494 B.A. L.800 J.D. [Hooper,L.&B.]
*PRACTICE AREAS: Health Care Law; Hospital Law.
**Swartz, David Adam** ... '66 '91 C.659 B.S. L.1068 J.D. [A] Allen,M.L.G.&M.]
*PRACTICE AREAS: Litigation; Transactional Real Estate; Leasing.

Swartz, Jacob, (AV) ... '15 '41 C.347 A.B. L.309 J.D. [Swartz&S.]
**Swartz, Kim H.** ... '54 '81 C.280 B.A. L.245 J.D. [B] Mitchell,S.&K.]
*PRACTICE AREAS: Entertainment Law.
Swartz, Louis, (BV) ... '23 '66 C.347 B.S. L.809 J.D. [Swartz&S.]
**Swartz, Michael** ... '66 '92 C&L.976 B.A., J.D. [A] Hennigan,M.&B.]
**Swartz, Richard W.** ... '50 '76 C.112 B.A. L.809 J.D. [Hong&C.]
*PRACTICE AREAS: Business Trials; Litigation.
Swartz & Swartz, (AV) ... 523 W. 6th St.
Swasey, Robt. L. ... '27 '54 C.800 L.809 LL.B. Mun. Ct.J.
**Swe, Sana** ... '64 '94 C.605 B.A. L.426 J.D. [A] Irell&M.]
Swearinger, Bill ... '53 '80 C.990 L.999 J.D. 6922 Hollywood Blvd.
Swearinger, Ronald E. ... '26 '58 C.911 B.A. L.800 J.D. Supr. Ct. J.
Swedelson, David C. ... '53 '78 C.112 B.A. L.1148 J.D. [Swedelson&G.]
**Swedelson, Gregory J.** ... '66 '94 C.112 B.A. L.800 J.D. [A] Paul,H.J.&W.]
Swedelson & Gottlieb ... 11900 W. Olympic Blvd.
**Swedlow, Nathan** ... '28 '71 L.1114 J.D. [B] Zide&O.]
Sweeney, Bonny E. '59 '88 C.940 B.A. L.930 J.D.
[A] Milberg W.B.H.&L.] (©New York & San Francisco)
Sweeney, Ronald E. ... '53 '79 C.112 B.A. L.800 J.D. Tabu Productions
Sweeney, Timothy J. ... '58 '83 C.339 B.S. L.477 J.D. 725 S. Figueroa St.
Sweet, Judith A. ... '46 '75 C&L.426 B.A., J.D. 2220 Century Hill
Sweeters, Julianne M. ... '53 '85 C.112 B.S. L.426 J.D. State Sr. Resch. Atty.
Swegles, William H. ... '47 '77 C.763 B.A. L.813 J.D. 245 S. Wilton Pl.
Swendeman, Dalton '43 '81
C.1077 B.S. L.1095 J.D. Claims Atty., Auto. Club of Southern Calif.
**Swenson, John J., (AV)** ... '42 '68 C&L.494 B.A., J.D. [Gibson,D.&C.]
*PRACTICE AREAS: Bad Faith Defense; Punitive Damage Litigation; Insurance; General Commercial Litigation; Antitrust.
Swenson, Kenneth W. ... '59 '87 C.378 B.A. L.800 J.D. 601 S. Figueroa St.
**Swerdloff, Arthur J.** ... '39 '64 C.154 B.A. L.1066 LL.B. [Berger,K.S.M.F.S.&G.]
**Swerdlow, Janet I.** ... '62 '91 C.763 B.S. L.800 J.D. [A] O'Melveny&M.]
**Swerdlow, Florence & Sanchez, A Law Corporation**
(See Beverly Hills)
Swift, Malcolm S. ... '49 '75 C.684 B.A. L.464 J.D. Sr. Coun., Intl., Northrop Corp.
Swift, Susan R. ... '64 '91 C.112 B.A. L.990 J.D. 777 S. Figueroa St.
Swing, Ross G. ... '46 '72 C.112 B.S. L.800 Asst. Gen. Coun., Caesars World, Inc.
Switzer, Jill, (AV) '48 '76
C.112 A.B. L.1148 J.D. V.P. & Sr. Coun., Sanwa Bank California
Sydney, Jeffrey M. ... '47 '73 C.178 A.B. L.813 J.D. Sr. V.P., Polygram & Polydor, Inc.
Sykes, David F. '47 '79
C.1097 B.S. L.1148 J.D. Claims Atty., Auto. Club of Southern Calif.
**Sylva, Julia E.** ... '55 '83 C.1042 B.A. L.426 J.D. [Frandzel&S.]
*LANGUAGES: Spanish.
*PRACTICE AREAS: Municipal Law; Municipal Finance Law.
**Sylvester, Lee, (AV)** ... '30 '55 C.696 A.B. L.309 J.D. [Sylvester&O.]
*PRACTICE AREAS: Trial Practice; Appellate Litigation; Insurance Defense Law; Public Entity Law.
**Sylvester, Timothy F.** ... '59 '84 C.860 B.A. L.1068 J.D. [A] Riordan&M.]

**Sylvester & Oppenheim, (AV)**
**15260 Ventura Boulevard, Suite 1500 (Sherman Oaks), 91403**
Telephone: 818-905-5200 FAX: 818-789-6078
Members of Firm: Lee Sylvester; Richard D. Oppenheim, Jr. Associates: Richard J. Schlegel; Gary R. Kaplan.
General Trial and Appellate Litigation, Insurance Defense, Public Entity Defense, Entertainment and Intellectual Property Law.
*See Professional Biographies, LOS ANGELES, CALIFORNIA*

Szabadi, Peter, (AV) ... '42 '69 C.563 B.A. L.569 J.D. 1800 Century Park E.
**Szabo, Susan R.** ... '57 '91 C.1169 B.A. L.1066 J.D. [A] Munger,T.&O.]
*LANGUAGES: Spanish.
Szczepanski, Peter G. ... '63 '94 C.190 B.A. L.546 J.D. 624 S. Grand Ave.
**Szczepkowski, Edward J.** ... '62 '88 C.659 B.S.E. L.94 J.D. [B] O'Melveny&M.]
*PRACTICE AREAS: Litigation.
**Sze, Hoyt** ... '70 '95 C.112 B.A. L.188 J.D. [A] Latham&W.]
*LANGUAGES: Chinese and Spanish.
**Sze, Stanley** ... '67 '94 C.813 B.S. L.276 J.D. [A] Sheppard,M.R.&H.]
**Sze, Victor S.** ... '67 '95 C.112 B.A. L.426 J.D. [A] Ku,F.L.&C.]
*LANGUAGES: Chinese (Mandarin).
*PRACTICE AREAS: Business; Corporate.
Szkolnik, Fred M. ... '55 '80 C.800 B.A. L.61 J.D. 12100 Wilshire Blvd.
Ta, Trang-Thuy Thi '— '90 C.846 B.A. L.1292 J.D.
(adm. in NJ; not adm. in CA) 1625 W. Olympic Blvd.‡
Taam, David M.S. ... '61 '86 C.154 B.A. L.426 J.D. 12400 Wilshire Blvd. 13th Fl.

**Tabachnick, Erica, (AV) '53 '80 C.112 B.A. L.426 J.D.**
**1200 Wilshire Boulevard, Suite 400, 90017**
Telephone: 213-482-1600 Facsimile: 213-482-0515
*REPORTED CASES: Read vs. State Bar, 53 Cal.3rd 394; Stanley vs. State Bar, 50 Cal.3rd 555; Billings vs. State Bar, 50 Cal.3rd 358; Farnham vs. State Bar, 47 Cal.3rd 429; Greenbaum vs. State Bar, 43 Cal.3rd 543.
*PRACTICE AREAS: Lawyer Disciplinary and Admissions Defense; Legal Malpractice; Mental Health Therapists Licensure Defense; Ethics Consultations and Testimony.
Lawyer Disciplinary and Admissions Matters, Reinstatements, Ethics Consultations, Legal Malpractice, Professional Liability, Defense of Professional Licensing Proceedings.
*See Professional Biographies, LOS ANGELES, CALIFORNIA*

Taback, Joseph, (AV) ... '33 '58 C.339 B.S. L.426 J.D. [J.Taback]
Taback, Marci A. ... '64 '90 C.112 B.A. L.426 J.D. [A] J.Taback]
Taback, Joseph, P.C., (AV) ... 2029 Century Park East (Century City)
Tabacopoulos, Barbara '63 '89 C.800 B.S. L.597 J.D.
V.P. & Assoc. Tax Coun., First Interstate Bancorp
**Tabacopoulos, Diana** ... '60 '87 C.800 B.A. L.597 J.D. [Seyfarth,S.F.&G.]
*PRACTICE AREAS: Business Litigation; ERISA Litigation; Employment Litigation.
**Tabb, David A.** ... '67 '93 C.112 B.A. L.260 J.D. [A] A.R.Hamrick,III]
**Tabb, Lawrence A.** ... '61 '88 C.882 B.A. L.990 J.D. [A] Musick,P.&G.]
**Tabor, Stephen H., (AV)** ... '46 '72 C.112 A.B. L.1065 J.D. [Armstrong&T.]©
*REPORTED CASES: Hilb, Rogal and Hamilton Insurance Services of Orange County, Inc. vs. Stanley P. Robb; Schwalbe vs. Jones (1976) 16 Cal.3d 514, 516 (546 P.2d 1033; 128 Cal. Rptr. 321); Daar vs. Alvord (1980) 101 Cal.App.3d 480, 481-482 (161 Cal.Rptr. 658).
*PRACTICE AREAS: Civil Trial; Commercial; Corporate; Insurance; Surety.
Tachiki, Karen L. ... '53 '79 C.112 B.A. L.1068 J.D. Asst. Gen. Coun., Metro. Water Dist.
Tackett, Charles V. ... '36 '66 Principal Dep. Co. Coun.
**Tady, Brandon K.** ... '53 '78 C&L.800 B.A., J.D. [A] Tharpe&H.]
*PRACTICE AREAS: Insurance Coverage; Insurance Bad Faith; First Party Property; Liability Defense.
Taecker, Henry R., Jr., (AV) ... '17 '42 C&L.597 B.S., J.D. [Taecker,M.&N.]
Taecker, Marshall & Neuhoff, A Prof. Corp., (AV) ... 11661 San Vicente Blvd.
Taft, Leroy B., (AV) ... '30 '60 C&L.800 B.S., LL.B. 11661 San Vicente Blvd.
**Taft, Peter R., (A Professional Corporation)**, (AV) '36 '63
C&L.976 B.A., LL.B. [Munger,T.&O.]
Taggart, Deborah S. ... '53 '80 C.112 B.A. L.426 J.D. [Schmid&V.]

CAA351P

**Taggart, Jennifer T.** ..............'68 '95 C.1074 B.S. L.809 J.D. [Demetriou,D.S.&M.]
*PRACTICE AREAS: Environmental Law.
**Tahajian, Gerald Lee,** (BV) '41 '70
C.267 B.S. L.767 J.D. [Mahoney,C.J.&P.] (⊙Fresno & Anaheim)
*PRACTICE AREAS: Estate Planning and Probate.
**Taitelman, Michael A.** ..............'66 '91 C.112 B.A. L.1066 J.D. [🄰 Alschuler G.&P.]
Taitz, Emanuel ..................'51 '92 C.94 B.S. L.1009 J.D. 2040 Avenue of The Stars
**Takács, Cynthia M.** ........'64 '90 C.696 B.A. L.800 J.D. [🄰 Christensen,M.F.J.G.W.&S.]
*LANGUAGES: Hungarian.
*PRACTICE AREAS: Civil Litigation; Intellectual Property; Entertainment.
Takahashi, Ben K. ..............................'21 '67 C.061 L.809 LL.B. 420 E. 3rd St.
**Takakjian, Paul,** (BV) '53 '79 C.112 B.A. L.426 J.D.
[Takakjian&S.] (⊙Encino, Orange & Oxnard)
*LANGUAGES: French.
*REPORTED CASES: P. v. Tamborrino (1989) 215 Cal. App. 3d 575 263 Ca. RPTR. 731.
*PRACTICE AREAS: Criminal Defense.

**Takakjian & Sowers, (BV)**
**Westside Towers, Suite 1000, 11845 West Olympic Boulevard, 90064⊙**
**Telephone: 310-312-8055 Telecopier: 310-312-8189**
**Members of Firm: Paul Takakjian (Certified Specialist, Criminal Law, The State Bar of California Board of Legal Specialization); Donald G. Sowers.**
**Criminal Law.**
**San Fernando Valley, California Office: 16501 Ventura Blvd, Encino, California. Telephone: 818-379-8588. Fax: 818-789-3391.**
**Ventura County, California Office: 300 Esplanade Drive, Oxnard, California. Telephone: 805-522-0720. Fax: 805-988-0570.**
**Orange County, California Office: 333 City Boulevard West, Suite 1700, Orange, California. Telephone: 714-456-9955. Fax: 714-938-3255.**
**San Gabriel Valley, California Office: 225 South Lake Avenue, 9th Floor, Pasadena, California. Telephone: 818-242-0042. Fax: 818-795-6321.**
**South Bay, California Office: World Trade Center, Suite 800, Long Beach, California. Telephone: 310-424-7337. Fax: 310-983-8199**
*See Professional Biographies, LOS ANGELES, CALIFORNIA*

Takasugi, Jon R. ...............................'63 '90 C.1169 B.A. L.800 J.D. Dep. Pub. Def.
Takasugi, Robert M. ..........................'30 '60 C.112 B.S. L.800 J.D. U.S. Sr. Dist. J.
Takata, Timothy D. ..........................'49 '74 C.112 B.S. L.426 J.D. 3435 Wilshire Blvd.

**Takehara, Ronald M., Law Offices of '62 '87 C.1077 B.A. L.464 J.D.**
**2049 Century Park East, Suite 1100, 90067**
**Telephone: 310-785-3880 Fax: 310-785-3882**
**Email: rmtlaw@aol.com**
**(Associate, Sedgwick, Detert, Moran & Arnold, 1992-1994).**
**General Civil Litigation. Business, Entertainment, Insurance, Subrogation, Bad Faith and Personal Injury Law.**
*See Professional Biographies, LOS ANGELES, CALIFORNIA*

**Takesh, Fahi** ...............................'69 '96 C.112 B.A. L.426 J.D. [🄰 Trope&T.]
*LANGUAGES: French, Farsi.
**Taketa, Allyson S.** ..................'69 '93 C.813 A.B. L.800 J.D. [🄰 LeBoeuf,L.G.&M.]
*PRACTICE AREAS: Litigation.
**Taketa, Anthony J.** ......................'58 '83 C.426 B.A. L.1068 J.D. [Poindexter&D.]
*PRACTICE AREAS: Insurance Defense; Construction Law; Civil Litigation; Probate Litigation.
**Takeuchi, Derrick K.** ........................'51 '81 C.813 A.B. L.276 J.D. [Graham&J.]
*LANGUAGES: Japanese.
*PRACTICE AREAS: International Business Law; Corporate Law.
**Takeuchi, Robert H., (P.C.),** (AV) ........'37 '64 C.112 A.B. L.800 LL.B. [🄲 Arndt&V.]
*PRACTICE AREAS: International Business Law.
Talaie, Mohammad Ali .............'50 '86 C.1077 B.S. L.1190 J.D. 4221 Wilshire Blvd.
**Talbot, Etta A.** ...........................'47 '95 C.33 B.A. L.990 J.D. [🄰 Musick,P.&G.]
*PRACTICE AREAS: Real Property Finance; General Real Property; Corporate.
**Talcott, Robert M.,** (AV) ................'32 '59 C.184 B.A. L.276 J.D. [Talcott,L.V.&S.]
*PRACTICE AREAS: Criminal Defense Law; Civil Litigation; Appellate Law.

**Talcott, Lightfoot, Vandevelde & Sadowsky, (AV)** 🄱🄱
**Thirteenth Floor 655 South Hope Street, 90017**
**Telephone: 213-622-4750 Fax: 213-622-2690**
**Members of Firm: Robert M. Talcott; Michael J. Lightfoot; John D. Vandevelde; Stephen B. Sadowsky; John S. Crouchley; John P. Martin; Melissa N. Widdifield. Associate: James H. Locklin.**
**General Civil and Criminal Trial and Appellate Practice in all State and Federal Courts.**
**Reference: Sterling Bank, Los Angeles, California.**
*See Professional Biographies, LOS ANGELES, CALIFORNIA*

Talifer, Henry ...........................'39 '69 C.112 B.A. L.770 J.D. Dep. City Atty.‡
**Tallent, Stephen E.,** (AV) '37 '63 C.813 A.B. L.145 J.D.
[Gibson,D.&C.] (⊙Wash., DC)
*PRACTICE AREAS: Labor; Employee Benefits; Employment and Discrimination Litigation; International Labor Law.
**Talley, Cameron J.** ...........'59 '93 C.112 B.A. L.1066 J.D. [🄰 McCambridge,D.&M.]
**Talley, Kimberly M.** .........................'— '90 C.790 B.A. L.309 J.D. [🄰 Gartner&Y.]
*PRACTICE AREAS: Labor and Employment Law.
**Tallman, Karen A.** '57 '84 C.473 B.A. L.273 J.D.
V.P. & Sr. Coun., CB Coml. Real Estate Grp., Inc.
*RESPONSIBILITIES: Corporate; Business; Contracts.
Talmas, Bernard W. ..........'46 '71 C.401 B.S. L.262 J.D. 3435 Wilshire Blvd., 30th Fl.
**Talwani, Rajeev M.** ........................'59 '86 C.178 B.A. L.309 J.D. [🄰 Barbosa G.&B.]
*PRACTICE AREAS: Commercial Law; Corporate Law; General Business Law.
**Tam, Christine** .........................'70 '96 C.112 B.A. L.178 J.D. [🄰 O'Melveny&M.]
**Tamborelli, John V.** ..................'61 '88 C.676 B.S. L.990 J.D. [🄰 Bergman&W.]
*PRACTICE AREAS: Products Liability Defense; Tort Defense; Real Estate Litigation; Commercial Litigation; Toxic Exposure.
**Tamin, Alex O.** ....................'70 '95 C.367 B.A. L.1068 J.D. [🄰 Jeffer,M.B.&M.]
*PRACTICE AREAS: Litigation.
**Tamiya, Sharon L.** ...............................'— '88 C.112 B.A. L.426 J.D. [🄰 Cox,C.&N.]
*PRACTICE AREAS: Real Estate Finance Law; Subdivision Development; Regulatory Compliance.
**Tamkin, Gregory S.** .........................'69 '94 C.197 B.A. L.893 J.D. [🄰 Howarth&S.]
*LANGUAGES: Spanish.
Tamkin, Priscilla M. ..............'49 '75 C.813 B.A. L.1065 J.D. 1230 Stone Canyon Rd.
Tamman, David M. ..........................................'67 '94 L.800 J.D. 515 S. Flower St.
Tamura, Kaoru ..............'66 '93 C.112 B.A. L.809 J.D. 200 S. San Pedro St., Ste. 403
Tan, Diane M. L. '51 '79 C&L.800 A.B., J.D.
Staff Atty., Dept. of Fair Employ. & Housing
Tan, Lawrence ................................................'51 '77 1021 S. Union Ave.
Tan, Robert Lew ..........................'— '78 C.800 B.S. L.1065 J.D. [🄲 Tan&S.]
Tan, William L., (AV) ..................'49 '75 C.659 B.A. L.1065 J.D. [Tan&S.]
Tan & Sakiyama, (AV) ...................................................300 S. Grand Ave.
**Tan-Sanchez, Charisma T.** ..........'71 '95 C.112 B.S. L.1066 J.D. [🄰 Barbosa G.&B.]
*PRACTICE AREAS: Litigation; Education Law.
**Tanaka, Gary Y.** .......................'63 '91 C&L.1137 B.S., J.D. [🄰 Astor&P.]
*PRACTICE AREAS: Real Estate Law; Corporate Law; Estate Planning.
**Tanaka, Jean E.** .......................'58 '84 C.112 B.A. L.1068 J.D. [Del,R.S.M.&D.]
*PRACTICE AREAS: Entertainment Law; Television Law; Motion Picture Law.
Tanenbaum, Fred L., (AV) ..............'41 '67 C.112 A.B. L.1065 J.D. [Tanenbaum&D.]
Tanenbaum & Dempster, (AV) ..............................................4801 Wilshire Blvd.
**Tanezaki, Eric L.** ..................'— '96 C.800 B.S. L.464 J.D. [🄰 Sedgwick,D.M.&A.]

Tang, Angel K. ..........................'45 '73 C.061 LL.B. L.884 J.D. Atlantic Richfield Co.
Tang, Deborah J. ......'61 '86 C.276 B.A. L.273 J.D. Immigration and Naturalization Serv.
Tani, Diana K. ...........................'63 '88 C.769 B.A. L.426 J.D. U.S. Sec. & Exch. Comm.
**Tanji, Kenneth K., Jr.** .........................'65 '92 C.112 B.S. L.464 J.D. [Coleman&W.]
*PRACTICE AREAS: Civil Litigation; Torts; Insurance Defense; Products Liability.

**Tankel, Frederic B., (AV) '29 '54 C.494 B.A. L.309 J.D.**
**10507 West Pico Boulevard, Suite 200, 90064**
**Telephone: 310-470-6852 Fax: 310-470-3673**
**General Civil and Trial Practice in all State and Federal Courts, Corporation, Real Estate, Trust and Probate Law.**
*See Professional Biographies, LOS ANGELES, CALIFORNIA*

Tannatt, Michael B. ..................'47 '84 C.112 B.A. L.800 J.D. Coun., Bank of Amer.
Tannenbaum, Saml. R. ..............'19 '50 C.339 B.S. L.209 J.D. 1642 Westwood Blvd.
Tannenbaum, Susan C. ..................'55 '84 C.1036 B.A. L.426 J.D. Dep. Dist. Atty.
**Tanner, Colin J.** ..................'65 '90 C.1049 B.A. L.1065 J.D. [🄰 Fainsbert,M.&S.]
*PRACTICE AREAS: Commercial Litigation; Real Estate Litigation; Tort Litigation; Insurance Bad Faith Litigation; Products Liability Litigation.
Tao, Cathy H. .........................'64 '91 C.112 B.A. L.426 J.D. 1200 Wilshire Blvd.
Tapanes, Mario A. ...................'60 '85 C&L.426 B.A., J.D. 12304 Santa Monica Blvd.
Tapanes, Mario U. ..........................'32 '76 C.525 M.D. L.809 2827 Glendon St.
Tapper, Lawrence R., (AV) ...............'34 '63 C.112 B.S. L.800 LL.B. Dep. Atty. Gen.
Tappert, Sheryl A. ......................'65 '93 C.31 B.A. L.800 J.D. 700 S. Flower St.
Tarduno, Mary E. ..................'57 '82 C.401 B.S. L.309 J.D. 333 S. Hope St., 48th Fl.

**Tarkanian, William V., Law Offices of**
**(See Pasadena)**

**Tarlow, Barry,** (AV) .................................'39 '65 C&L.94 B.A., LL.B. [B.Tarlow]
*PRACTICE AREAS: Criminal Law.

**Tarlow, Barry, A Prof. Corp., Law Offices of, (AV)** 🄱🄱
**9119 Sunset Boulevard, 90069**
**Telephone: 310-278-2111 Cable Address: "Habeas" Fax: 310-550-7055**
**Email: lobt@earthlink.net**
**Barry Tarlow (Certified Specialist, Criminal Law, The State Bar of California Board of Legal Specialization);—Mark O. Heaney; A. Blair Bernholz; Evan A. Jenness; Paul J. Loh.**
**Criminal Trial and Appellate Practice, all State and Federal Courts.**
*See Professional Biographies, LOS ANGELES, CALIFORNIA*

**Tarr, Ralph W.** ...............................'48 '76 C.197 A.B. L.1065 J.D. [Andrews&K.]
*PRACTICE AREAS: General Practice; Natural Resources Law; Environmental Law.
Tarsey, Patrice T. .................'53 '75 C.112 B.A. L.1068 J.D. 10501 Wilshire Blvd.
**Tartaglio, David A.** ....................'58 '84 C.112 B.A. L.800 J.D. [Musick,P.&G.]
*LANGUAGES: Spanish.
*PRACTICE AREAS: Litigation; Insurance.
Tashjian, Vatche D. ..........................'65 '89 C.676 B.A. L.776 J.D. [🄰 Garber&G.]
**Tashman, Andrew P.,** (AV) .........'44 '68 C&L.178 A.B., LL.B. [Reboul,M.H.M.&K.]
**Tashman, Henry J.** ..........................'48 '74 C.184 A.B. L.276 J.D. [Davis W.T.]
*PRACTICE AREAS: Litigation; Copyright; Trademark; Antitrust; Entertainment.
Tashnek, Gary ..................'55 '81 C.112 B.S. L.809 J.D. 11111 Santa Monica Blvd.
**Tasker, John J.** ..........................'53 '78 C&L.879 B.S., J.D. [Callahan,M.&W.]
**Tassone, Marlene C.** ....................'41 '76 C.763 A.B. L.809 J.D. [Clopton,P.&B.]
**Tate, John R.** ..............................'51 '76 C.197 A.B. L.880 J.D. [Arter&H.]
**Tate, Maj-Le R.** ......................'70 '95 C.112 B.A. L.1049 J.D. [🄰 Burke,W.&S.]
*PRACTICE AREAS: Litigation.
**Taten, Mary** ..........................'59 '94 C.276 B.S.B.A. L.1068 J.D. [🄰 Katten M.&Z.]
*PRACTICE AREAS: Firm Financing.
**Tatikian, Katherine** .......................'49 '90 C.773 B.A. L.809 J.D. [🄰 Neumeyer&B.]
*PRACTICE AREAS: Appellate Practice; Insurance Coverage; Insurance Bad Faith.
**Tatro, René P.,** (AV) ..........................'53 '77 C.375 B.S. L.309 J.D. [Macklin T.]
*PRACTICE AREAS: Complex Commercial Litigation; Environmental; Insurance Coverage.
Tatsugi, Kenji ...........................'60 '88 C.154 B.A. L.1065 J.D. 6310 San Vicente Blvd.
Tatsui, Kiyoko .....................'— '77 C.112 A.B. L.1066 J.D. 1652 3/4 Sawtelle Blvd.
**Tatum, Franklin M., III,** (AV⑦) '46 '73
C.840 B.A. L.880 J.D. [Wright,R.O.&T.] (⊙Richmond, VA)
*PRACTICE AREAS: Products Liability Law.
**Taub, David M.** ..........................'69 '95 C.228 B.A. L.1068 J.D. [🄰 Latham&W.]
**Taubenfeld, Elaine M.** ..............'55 '92 C.350 B.S. L.1066 J.D. [🄰 Jeffer,M.B.&M.]
*PRACTICE AREAS: Estate Planning; Taxation.
Tauber, Raymond R. ...........................'13 '36 C&L.800 B.A., LL.B. 3261 Edith St.

**Taubman, Simpson, Young & Sulentor**
**(See Long Beach)**

**Taue, Patricia I.** .......................'64 '90 C.112 A.B. L.276 J.D. [🄰 Charlston,R.&W.]
*PRACTICE AREAS: Environmental Insurance Coverage.
**Tauger, Debra J.** ................'57 '88 C.112 B.A. L.818 J.D. [🄰 M.B.F.Biren&Assoc.]
**Taurek, Michael T.** ......................'68 '94 C.112 B.A. L.990 J.D. [🄰 Lynberg&W.]
**Taurino, T.A.** ......................'59 '88 C.311 B.S. L.813 J.D. [🄰 Gansinger,H.B.&P.]
*PRACTICE AREAS: Business Litigation; Civil Litigation; Insurance Coverage.
Taussig, John E. ..................'44 '80 C.309 B.A. L.1148 J.D. 8271 Beverly Blvd.
**Tavera, Leonard M** ..................'60 '86 C.976 B.A. L.112 J.D. [🄲 Kinsella,B.F.&T.]
*PRACTICE AREAS: Product Liability; Commercial Litigation; Personal Injury; Transactional.
**Tavetian, Gary E.** ....................'57 '84 C.112 B.A. L.800 J.D. [🄰 Wilson,E.M.E.&D.]
Tawatao, Rau Mona ..............'61 '87 C.112 B.A. L.1068 J.D. Law Clk. to U.S. Dist. Ct.

**Tax Consulting Group**
**2029 Century Park East Seventeenth Floor, 90067**
**Telephone: 310-789-3250 Facsimile: 310-789-3210**
**Jeffrey Adam Sherman;—Kenneth L. Sherman; John A. Harbin; Victor J. Yoo; Norman J. Kreisman.**
**Tax Law, Bankruptcy, Intellectual Property, Employee Benefits, Patent, Trademark, Copyright and Trade Secrets. Corporate Structuring, Estate and Business Planning.**
*See Professional Biographies, LOS ANGELES, CALIFORNIA*

**Tayback, Christopher** .................'63 '89 C.602 B.A. L.309 J.D. [🄰 Quinn E.U.&O.]
*PRACTICE AREAS: Criminal Law (100%).
**Taylor, Amalia L.** ....................'42 '74 C.1097 B.A. L.426 J.D. [🄰 Gray,Y.D.&R.]
*PRACTICE AREAS: Insurance Defense; Construction Law; Product Liability.
Taylor, Barry A. ..........................'42 '69 C.1077 A.B. L.1068 J.D. Dep. Pub. Def.
Taylor, Cathryn M. '57 '82 C&L.352 B.B.A., J.D.
Sr. V.P. & Assoc. Gen. Coun., Trust Company of the West
Taylor, Charles E. '48 '75 C.69 B.B.A. L.273 J.D.
(adm. in VA; not adm. in CA) Chf. Coun., Contract Rights, Northrop Grumman Corp.
**Taylor, Diane F.** ......................'70 '95 C.112 B.A. L.1049 J.D. [🄰 Tharpe&H.]
*PRACTICE AREAS: Construction Defect; Insurance Defense.
Taylor, Edward D. ..................'33 '63 C.112 B.A. L.1066 LL.B. 628 N. Laurel Ave.‡
Taylor, Elenor Rita ............'59 '85 C.154 B.A. L.273 J.D. Constitutional Rights Found.
Taylor, Eric C. ............................'62 '89 C.197 B.A. L.893 J.D. 500 W. Temple St.
**Taylor, Frieda A.** ....................'60 '91 C.103 A.B. L.1068 J.D. [🄰 Folger L.&K.]⊙
**Taylor, Gail W.** ..........'45 '75 C.577 B.A. L.912 J.D. Sr. Tax Coun., Atlantic Richfield Co.
*RESPONSIBILITIES: Taxation Law.
Taylor, Gerald, Jr. ..........................................'39 '72 C.1042 B.S. L.809 J.D. I.R.S.
**Taylor, H. Wayne,** (AV) .................'45 '71 C.813 A.B. L.309 J.D. [🄲 Mitchell,S.&K.]
*PRACTICE AREAS: Securities Law; Mergers and Acquisitions; Corporate Law.

Taylor, James M. ... '29 '60 C.1097 B.A. L.1068 J.D. 11516 Thurston Circle‡
**Taylor, John A., Jr.** ... '58 '87 C.101 B.A. L.309 J.D. [Horvitz&L.]
Taylor, Katharyne B. ... '59 '92 C.347 B.M. L.861 J.D. Dep. Dist. Atty.
Taylor, Kenneth Hymes ... '66 '93 C.659 B.S. L.1068 J.D. Pub. Def.
Taylor, Leigh H. '41 '66 C&L.862 B.A., J.D.
(adm. in OK; not adm. in CA) Dean, Southwestern Univ. Sch. of Law
**Taylor, Marshall M.** ... '47 '74 C.976 B.A. L.1068 J.D. [Pillsbury M.&S.]
**Taylor, Michael L.** ... '49 '75 C&L.770 B.A., J.D. [Antin&T.]
*PRACTICE AREAS: Employee Benefit Law; Tax Exempt Organizations; Taxation; Estate Planning; Probate Law.
Taylor, Minna ... '47 '77 C.1350 B.A. L.800 J.D. V.P., Legal Affs., Fox, Inc.
**Taylor, N. Denise**, (AV) ... '57 '81 C.636 B.A. L.990 J.D. [Bonne,B.M.O.&N.]
Taylor, N. Gregory '35 '61 C.800 B.A. L.569 LL.B.
Gen. Coun., Metropolitan Water Dist. of Southern Calif.
Taylor, Robert D. ... '61 '86 C.1077 B.S. L.813 J.D. 5002 Pendleton Ct.‡
**Taylor, Robert G.**, (AV) ... '23 '49 C.937 A.B. L.813 J.D. [Tuttle&T.]
*PRACTICE AREAS: Agricultural Cooperatives; Cooperative Taxation; Business.
**Taylor, Robert H.** ... '64 '92 C.674 A.B. L.1068 J.D. [[A] Littler,M.F.T.&M.]
**Taylor, Samuel C.** ... '52 '79 C.813 B.A. L.309 J.D. [McClintock,W.B.R.R.&M.]
*PRACTICE AREAS: Environmental Litigation; Product Law; Toxic Torts; Business Litigation; Construction Law.
**Taylor, Stephen C.**, (AV) ... '32 '61 C.674 A.B. L.1068 LL.B. [Sheppard,M.R.&H.]
*PRACTICE AREAS: Business Law; Environmental Law.
Taylor, Terry G. ... '48 '72 C.605 A.B. L.800 J.D. 333 S. Hope St., 48th Fl.
**Taylor, Thomas L., III** ... '46 '73 C.188 A.B. L.846 J.D. [Morgan,L.&B.]
*PRACTICE AREAS: Litigation of Securities, Commodities and Corporate Matters; Securities and Commodities Regulatory and Enforcement Matters.

**Taylor Kupfer Summers & Rhodes**
**(See Pasadena)**

**Taylor, Lawrence**
**(See Long Beach)**

**Tebbetts, Allan Edward**, (AV) ... '40 '72 C.800 B.A. L.426 J.D. [Carlsmith B.W.C.&I.]
*PRACTICE AREAS: Environmental Law; Commercial Litigation; Corporate Litigation; Government Law; Municipal Law.
Tecimer, Dina ... '55 '82 C.112 B.A. L.426 J.D. 12180 Greenock Lane
Tegnazian, Terry A. ... '52 '77 C.103 A.B. L.976 J.D. 1145 Gayley Ave.
Teisher, Sheila A. ... '50 '75 C.776 B.S. L.893 J.D. Touche Ross & Co.
Teitel, Richard D. ... '50 '77 C.605 A.B. L.276 J.D. 11835 W. Olympic Blvd.
**Teitelbaum, Eliot L.** ... '61 '87 C.156 B.A. L.273 J.D. [[A] McClintock,W.B.R.R.&M.]
*PRACTICE AREAS: Construction and Environmental Litigation; General Business and Commercial Litigation.
Teitelbaum, Melvin ... '49 '81 C.102 B.A. L.809 J.D. 1800 S. Robertson Blvd.
**Tekanic, Jeffrey D.** ... '66 '91 C.111 B.S. L.145 J.D. [[A] Lyon&L.] (See Pat. Sect.)
*PRACTICE AREAS: Patent, Trademark, Trade Regulation; Unfair Competition, Antitrust; Intellectual Property.
**Tekosky, Steven R.** ... '54 '82 C.112 A.B. L.809 J.D. [Heller E.W.&M.]
*PRACTICE AREAS: Environmental Litigation and Regulation.
Tekulsky, Joseph D. ... '22 '49 C.309 B.A. L.178 LL.B. 13570 Bayliss Rd.‡
Telerant, David ... '46 '80 C.1097 B.S. L.1136 J.D. 6380 Wilshire Bldg.
**Teller, Stephen L.** ... '50 '75 C.112 A.B. L.1067 J.D. [[C] J.A.Joannes]
**Temko, William D.** ... '54 '79 C.951 B.A. L.178 J.D. [Munger,T.&O.]
Tempereau, Margot ... '58 '82 C.112 B.A. L.1067 J.D. 1801 Ave. of the Stars
Temple, John M. ... '54 '82 C.352 B.G.S. L.1066 J.D. 333 S. Hope St., 48th Fl.
Temple, Mark S. ... '47 '79 C.645 B.A. L.705 J.D. 1440 S. Sepulveda Blvd., 2nd Fl.
**Templeton, G. Cresswell, III** ... '59 '85 C&L.800 A.B., J.D. [Hill,F.&B.]
*PRACTICE AREAS: Trade Secret Litigation; Construction Law; ERISA Litigation; Entertainment Law.
**Templeton, Payne L.** ... '57 '87 C.309 A.B. L.1066 J.D. [Orrick,H.&S.]
*PRACTICE AREAS: Complex Litigation.
Ten Brink, Kent H. ... '36 '65 C.937 A.B. L.1068 LL.B. 6476 San Marco Circle
**Tencer, Philip C.** ... '67 '94 C.112 B.A. L.1066 J.D. [[A] Howrey&S.]
Tenner, Jack ... '20 '42 C&L.209 LL.B. Supr. Ct. J.
Tenner, Michael A. ... '59 '89 C.112 B.A. L.426 J.D. 4215 Glencoe Ave.
Tenner, Paul A. ... '63 '88 C.112 B.A. L.1065 J.D. Dep. Trial Coun., State Bar of Calif.
**Tenzer, Mitchell C.** ... '53 '80 C.367 B.A. L.309 J.D. [[A] Ziffren,B.B.&F.]
*PRACTICE AREAS: Entertainment Law.
**Teplin, Lawrence**, (AV) ... '36 '64 C.1097 B.A. L.1068 LL.B. [Cox,C.&N.]
*PRACTICE AREAS: Civil Litigation; Construction Litigation; Real Property Law; Hazardous and Toxic Substances Law.
Teplinsky, Allan ... '42 '67 C.966 B.B.A L.436 J.D. [Maupin,C.T.&W.]
Tepper, Foster, (AV) ... '37 '63 C.112 A.B. L.1068 LL.B. 11461 Sunset Blvd.
**Tepper, R. Bruce, Jr.** ... '49 '76 C.197 A.B. L.734 J.D. [Kane,B.&B.]
*REPORTED CASES: Dusek v. Anaheim Redevelopment Agency, 173 Cal. App. 3d 1029 (1985) (CEQA); Redevelopment Agency of Burbank v. Gilmore, 38 Cal. 3d 790 (1985) (amicus-eminent domain-interest on deposits); Creighton v. Revitsky, 171 Cal. App. 3d 1225 (1985) (elections); Kane v. Hidden Hills, 179 Cal. App. 3d 899 (1986) (exhaustion of administrative remedies); Community Redevelopment Agency v. Bloodgood, 182 Cal. App. 3d 342 (1986) (tax increment allocation of penalties and interest).
*TRANSACTIONS: Earthquake Emergency Redevelopment Plans Adopted by the City of Las Angeles.
*PRACTICE AREAS: Litigation; Land Use Law; Environmental Law; Eminent Domain Law.
Tepper, Scott J., (AV) ... '45 '72 C.112 A.B. L.309 J.D. [Garfield,T.E.&T.]
Terakawa, Alan K. ... '43 '77 C.1097 B.A. L.426 J.D. Princ. Dep. Co. Coun.
Teran, Diana M. ... '63 '88 C.1168 B.A. L.61 J.D. Dep. Dist. Atty.
Terauchi, Terrence S. ... '48 '73 C.766 B.A. L.1066 J.D. Dist. Atty. Off.
**Tercero, Napoleon G., III** ... '51 '89 C.112 B.A. L.398 J.D. [[A] Herzfeld&R.]
*LANGUAGES: Spanish, Italian, French and Russian.
**Teren, Pamela McKibbin** ... '63 '90 C.112 B.A. L.426 J.D. [Abrolat&T.]
**Terhar, Michael J.**, (AV) ... '53 '79 C.911 B.S. L.426 J.D. [Kern&W.]
**Terman, Mark E.** ... '58 '83 C.112 B.S. L.426 J.D. [Reish&L.]
*PRACTICE AREAS: ERISA Litigation; Employment; Business; Unfair Competition Litigation.
**Terrazone, Rodney L.** ... '51 '78 C.684 B.A. L.809 J.D. [Gilbert,K.C.&J.]
**Terris, Sharon R.** ... '64 '89 C.112 B.A. L.424 J.D. [[A] Tressler,S.M.&P.]
**Terry, William Burks** '50 '76 C.112 B.A. L.602 J.D.
V.P. & Asst. Gen. Coun., Northrop Grumman Corp.
*RESPONSIBILITIES: Legal Support to all Company Operations; Acquisitions and Divestitures.
**Terzian, Richard R.**, (AV) ... '34 '60 C.197 A.B. L.800 LL.B. [LeBoeuf,L.G.&M.]
*PRACTICE AREAS: Litigation.
**Tesar, Christopher** ... '50 '78 C.112 B.A. L.1068 J.D. [Walter,F.&R.]
*PRACTICE AREAS: General Real Estate Law; Business Law.
Teschendorf, Lynn '51 '76 C.966 B.A. L.560 J.D.
V.P. & Gen. Coun., Wedbush Morgan Securities, Inc.
**Tesh, Mary C.** ... '66 '94 C.881 B.A. [[A] Latham&W.]
Teske, Paula S., (AV) ... '51 '80 C.679 B.A. L.426 J.D. 3415 S. Sepulveda Blvd.
**Tesser, Brandon M.** ... '68 '93 C.112 B.A. L.426 J.D. [[A] Arnelle,H.M.W.&G.]
*PRACTICE AREAS: Civil Litigation; Business Litigation.
**Test, Mary Lawrence** ... '42 '90 C.788 B.A. L.809 J.D. [[A] Bonne,B.M.O.&N.]
*LANGUAGES: French.
Tether, Ivan J. ... '— '75 C.867 B.A. L.276 J.D. 633 W. 5th St.
**Tetreault, Nancy L.** ... '55 '90 C.112 B.A. L.426 J.D. [[A] Bronson,B.&M.]
**Tetreault, Paul L.** ... '55 '84 C.990 B.A. L.809 J.D. [[A] Agajanian&M.]
Tevis, Gregory C. ... '48 '76 C.446 B.A. L.880 J.D. Reg. Coun., Smith Barney Shearson
Tevrizian, Dickran, Jr. ... '40 '66 C&L.800 B.S., J.D. U.S. Dist. Ct. J.
Thaller, Robert S. ... '38 '62 C&L.910 A.B., J.D. 1999 Ave. of the Stars
Tharp, Michael B. '49 '83 C.112 B.A.,M.R.A. L.809 J.D.
(adm. in OR; not adm. in CA) Pres., Michael Tharp & Assoc., Inc.
**Tharp, Ronny R.**, (AV) ... '44 '70 C&L.352 B.M., J.D. [Tharp&B.]
*PRACTICE AREAS: Probate, Trust, Guardianship and Conservatorship Administration; Wills, Trusts and other Methods of Estate Planning; Litigation of Will Contests and other Contested Fiduciary Proceedings.

**Tharp & Berg, (AV)**
**555 South Flower Street, Suite 2850, 90071-2404**
**Telephone: 213-627-6227 Telecopier: 213-689-4651**
**Ronny R. Tharp; Richard G. Berg.**

***See Professional Biographies, LOS ANGELES, CALIFORNIA***

**Tharpe, Edgar A., III** ... '45 '73 C&L.800 B.A., J.D. [Tharpe&H.]
*PRACTICE AREAS: Construction Defect Litigation; Professional Malpractice; Product Liability.

**Tharpe & Howell, (AV)**
**15th Floor, 12400 Wilshire Boulevard, 90025⊙**
**Telephone: 310-826-4240 Fax: 310-207-1301**
**Members of Firm: Todd R. Howell; Edgar A. Tharpe, III; Jonathan G. Maile; Timothy D. Lake; Paul V. Wayne; Stephen G. Scherzer; Christopher S. Maile; Christopher P. Ruiz; Robert B. Salley; Charles D. May; Robert J. Needham. Associates: William P. O'Kelly; Paul W. Burke; Stuart K. Sellers; Robert M. Freedman; David Breitburg; Mitchell I. Cohen; Brian J. Ferber; Robert L. Cardwell; Helen E. Strand; David B. Wasson; Louis K. Tsiros; Warren J. Higgins; J. June Chang; Jeffrey C. Lynn; Paul H. Lasky; Carole A. Busch; Diane F. Taylor; Brandon K. Tady; Richard A. Ferch; David K. Stewart; Stacey A. Miller. Santa Barbara Office Resident Associates: Paul M. Bielaczyc; Heather A. Sciacca; Steven Patrick Lee; Eric B. Kunkel; P. Mark Kirwin; Jill Renee Markota; Erik B. Feingold; Denise M. Kale. Oxnard, California Office Resident Associates: Gene B. Sharaga; Deborah Meyer-Morris.**
**Civil Trial and Arbitration Practice. Insurance, Casualty, Malpractice and Products Liability Law. Business Litigation. Wrongful Termination/Employment Litigation, Construction Litigation.**
**Santa Barbara, California Office: 25 East Anapamu Street, Third Floor. Telephone: 805-962-4000. Fax: 805-965-5121.**
**Newport Beach, California Office: 4400 MacArthur Boulevard, Suite 500. Telephone: 714-261-8000. Fax: 714-955-4990.**
**Santa Maria, California Office: 910 East Stowell Road, Suite F. Telephone: 805-928-8600. Fax: 805-928-3550.**
**Oxnard, California Office: 300 Esplanade Drive, Suite 1820. Telephone: 805-485-2275. Fax: 805-988-7897.**

***See Professional Biographies, LOS ANGELES, CALIFORNIA***

Thedens, Edgar O. ... '24 '56 C&L.309 A.B., LL.B. 507 N. Detroit St.

**Thelen, Marrin, Johnson & Bridges LLP, (AV)**
**Suite 3400, 333 South Grand Avenue, 90071⊙**
**Telephone: 213-621-9800 Fax: 213-623-4742**
**Email: postmaster@tmjb.com**
**David L. Bacon; Charles S. Birenbaum; Robert G. Campbell; John B. Clark; Curtis A. Cole; W. Glenn Cornell; Christine C. Franklin; Thomas E. Hill; Linda S. Husar; Remy Kessler; Helen J. Lauderdale; James J. Moak; Walter K. Oetzell; Timothy M. Truax; John L. Viola; Lonnie E. Woolverton (P.C.). Of Counsel: William F. Holbrook. Associates: John N. Childers; Gary H. Green, II; Lisa S. Haleblian; Michael D. Holtz; Gayle I. Jenkins; Matthew Levinson; Christine L. Lofgren; Michelle Logan-Stern; Shea H. Lukacsko; Valarie H. Macht; Brooks P. Marshall; Dennis M. Naish; Richard C. Rybicki; Teri L. Vasquez; Jason G. Wilson.**
**Representative Clients: The Bechtel Group of Companies; Hydril Co.; Industrial Indemnity Co.; Kaiser Aluminum & Chemical Corp.**
**San Francisco Office: Two Embarcadero Center. Telephone: 415-392-6320. Fax: 415-421-1068.**
**San Jose Office: 17th Floor, 333 West San Carlos Street. Telephone: 408-292-5800. Fax: 408-287-8040.**
**New York, New York Office: Suite 1100, 330 Madison Avenue. Telephone: 212-297-3200. Fax: 212-972-6569.**

***See Professional Biographies, LOS ANGELES, CALIFORNIA***

Theodore, Jasmina A. ... '55 '80 C.1172 B.A. L.966 J.D. Assoc. Gen. Coun., Unocal Corp.
**Theodosopoulos, Randi J.** ... '63 '88 C&L.502 B.J., J.D. [Breidenbach,B.H.H.&H.]
**Therrien, Scott J.** ... '62 '88 C.645 B.B.A. L.809 J.D. [[A] Barger&W.]
**Thibodo, Todd D.** ... '63 '93 C.763 B.A. L.188 J.D. [[A] Davis W.T.]
**Thiesmeyer, Kirtley M.**, (AV) ... '38 '67 C.303 A.B. L.1066 J.D. [[C] G.C.Carter]
*LANGUAGES: French and German.
*PRACTICE AREAS: Banking; International Trade; Commercial Law and Real Estate; General Corporate.
Thole, Margo ... '63 '89 C&L.569 B.A., J.D. 400 S. Hope St.
**Thoma, James O., (A Professional Corporation)** '56 '81
C.1142 B.A. L.846 J.D. [Mitchell,S.&K.]
*LANGUAGES: Portuguese.
**Thomas, Andrew J.** ... '58 '87 C.112 B.A. L.1049 J.D. [Thomas&W.]
*PRACTICE AREAS: Business; Real Estate Litigation.
**Thomas, Andrew J.** ... '65 '92 C.813 B.A. L.309 J.D. [[A] Munger,T.&O.]
**Thomas, Carl J.** ... '60 '87 C.347 B.S. L.1119 J.D. [[A] Mayer,B.&P.]
Thomas, Christopher D. ... '49 '84 C.1097 L.325 J.D. 3660 Wilshire Blvd.
Thomas, Christopher J. ... '56 '87 C.945 B.A. L.809 J.D. 922 N. Mariposa Ave.
**Thomas, David A.**, (AV) ... '22 '49 C.605 B.A. L.309 LL.B. [[C] Hanna&M.]
Thomas, Earl E. ... '49 '77 C.976 B.A. L.800 J.D. Asst. City Atty.
**Thomas, Geoffrey L., (P.C.)**, (AV) ... '44 '72 C.309 A.B. L.813 J.D. [Paul,H.J.&W.]
Thomas, Hardy L., (AV) ... '39 '66 C.813 B.A. L.309 LL.B. [H.L.Thomas]
**Thomas, J. Nicholson** ... '52 '78 C&L.37 B.S., J.D. [Gibson,D.&C.]
*PRACTICE AREAS: Business Tax; Real Estate.
Thomas, James B. ... '44 '69 C.976 B.A. L.1066 J.D. Computax Corp.
**Thomas, Jeffrey R.** ... '70 '95 C.174 B.S. L.800 J.D. [[A] Musick,P.&G.]
Thomas, Jeffrey S. ... '60 '87 C&L.378 B.S., J.D. [Wells&T.]
Thomas, Jonathan Y. '54 '83
C&L.976 B.A., J.D. Chmn. of the Bd., Saybrook Capital Corp.
Thomas, Kirk C. ... '65 '94 C.1165 B.S. L.1051 J.D. [[A] H.L.Thomas]
**Thomas, Mary Sikra** ... '69 '94 C.205 B.A. L.309 J.D. [[A] Gibson,D.&C.]
*PRACTICE AREAS: Litigation; Environmental Law.
Thomas, Maxine F. ... '47 '71 C.1097 B.A. L.352 J.D. L.A. Mun. Ct.
Thomas, Ralph C. '56 '85 C.473 B.A. L.607 J.D.
(adm. in OH; not adm. in CA) Special Agent, F.B.I.
**Thomas, Raymond W.** ... '50 '76 C.112 B.A. L.976 J.D. [Loeb&L.]
*PRACTICE AREAS: Labor and Employment Law.
**Thomas, Reba W.** ... '46 '85 C.813 B.A. L.1068 J.D. [Latham&W.]
Thomas, Sally A. ... '50 '82 C.1042 B.S. L.1068 J.D. Dep. Dist. Atty.
Thomas, Stephen L., (AV) ... '48 '74 C.103 A.B. L.910 J.D. [Thomas&E.]
**Thomas, Steven E.** ... '60 '87 C.260 B.A. L.976 J.D. [Irell&M.]
**Thomas, Steven W.** ... '67 '93 C.502 B.A. L.228 J.D. [[A] Sullivan&C.]
Thomas, Thomas D. ... '53 '80 C.800 B.S. L.188 J.D. 1999 Ave. of the Stars
**Thomas, Wendy L.** ... '63 '91 C&L.945 B.A., J.D. [[A] Jones,D.R.&P.]
Thomas & Elliott, (AV) ... 12400 Wilshire Blvd.
Thomas, Hardy L., A Prof. Corp., Law Offices of, (AV) ... Ste. 340, 11620 Wilshire Blvd.

**Thomas & Price**
**(See Glendale)**

**Thomas & Walton LLP**
**550 South Hope Street, Suite 1000, 90071**
**Telephone: 213-488-1600 Fax: 213-228-0256**
**Members of Firm: John R. Walton; Andrew J. Thomas.**
**General Practice.**

***See Professional Biographies, LOS ANGELES, CALIFORNIA***

**Thompson, Barry J.** .... '63 '90 C&L.1049 B.A., J.D. [Ⓐ Crosby,H.R.&M.]
Thompson, Cary H. .... '56 '82 C.112 B.A. L.800 J.D. 11355 W. Olympic Blvd.
Thompson, Clifton W. .... '58 '91 C.101 B.S. L.336 J.D. [Roth&G.] (Pat.)
Thompson, Craig E. '55 '81 C.906 B.A. L.911 J.D.
(adm. in WA; not adm. in CA) Security Pacific Burns Fry
Thompson, Darrell .... '65 '90 C&L.477 B.A., J.D. 1516 Hi Point St.
Thompson, Diane A. .... '56 '87 C.1042 B.A. L.426 J.D. Sr. Tax Atty., ARCO
Thompson, Douglas A. .... '65 '91 C.860 B.A. L.990 J.D. [Ⓐ Garfield,T.E.&T.]
**Thompson, E. Bruce** .... '45 '74 C.36 B.A. L.800 J.D. [Ⓒ Ibold&A.]
**Thompson, Jocelyn Niebur** '56 '82 C.112 B.A. L.1068 J.D.
[McClintock,W.B.R.R.&M.]
*LANGUAGES: Spanish.
*PRACTICE AREAS: Environmental Law; Air Quality; Water Quality; California Environmental Quality Act (CEQA); Proposition 65.
Thompson, Joseph T., (AV) .... '22 '49 C.871 B.S. L.426 J.D. [Thompson,M.&F.]
**Thompson, Julio A.** .... '64 '90 C.912 B.A. L.477 J.D. [Tuttle&T.]
*PRACTICE AREAS: Labor and Employment Law; Trade Secrets; Unfair Business Practices; Commercial Litigation; Appellate Law.
Thompson, Katherine M. .... '65 '91 C.860 B.A. L.990 J.D. 11755 Wilshire Blvd.
**Thompson, Lawrence H.** .... '47 '75 C.112 B.A. L.1068 J.D. [Ⓐ Dolle&D.]
*PRACTICE AREAS: Condemnation Law; Inverse Condemnation Law; Zoning and Land Use Law.
**Thompson, Lois D.** .... '46 '70 C.788 B.A. L.178 J.D. [Proskauer R.G.&M.]
*PRACTICE AREAS: Litigation; Alternative Dispute Resolution.
**Thompson, Lynn K.** .... '52 '77 C.813 A.B. L.1065 J.D. [Bryan C.]
*PRACTICE AREAS: Labor and Employment Law.
**Thompson, Matthew C.** .... '65 '91 C.112 B.A. L.1065 J.D. [Ⓐ Stroock&S.&L.]
*PRACTICE AREAS: Corporate Law; Corporate Entertainment Law; General Civil Litigation.
**Thompson, Rebecca Ann** .... '61 '92 C.800 B.A. L.602 J.D. [Ⓐ Reznik&R.]
*SPECIAL AGENCIES: Los Angeles County Metropolitan Transit Authority (MTA).
*PRACTICE AREAS: Environmental Litigation; Environmental Compliance; Energy.
Thompson, Shari A. .... '60 '88 C.800 B.A. L.990 J.D. 865 S. Figueroa St., #3100
Thompson, Ted E. .... '50 '85 C.229 B.A. L.1068 J.D. 1310 Barry Ave.
**Thompson, Timothy N.** .... '51 '91 C.911 B.B.A. L.1148 J.D. [Ⓐ Koletsky,M.&F.]
*PRACTICE AREAS: Construction Litigation.
Thompson, Malone & Ferry, (AV) .... 15260 Ventura Blvd., (Sherman Oaks)

**Thompson & Waldron**
**1901 Avenue of the Stars, Suite 1901, 90067⊙**
**Telephone: 310-553-7310 Facsimile: 310-553-6843**
**Jeffrey B. Krashin.**
**General Civil Practice, Government Contract, Construction and Contract Law, Suretyship, Federal Administrative and Legislative Practice.**
**Alexandria, Virginia Office: 4th Floor. 1055 North Fairfax Street. 22314-1541. Telephone: 703-684-3340. Facsimile: 703-684-6225.**
*See Professional Biographies, LOS ANGELES, CALIFORNIA*

**Thomson, Gregory A.** .... '— '90 C&L.976 B.A., J.D. [Ⓐ King,P.H.P.&B.]
**Thomson, William E., Jr.**, (AV) '35 '63
C.105 B.S.Ch. E. L.276 J.D. [Kaye,S.F.H.&H.] (Pat.)

**Thomson & Nelson, A Professional Law Corporation**
**(See Whittier)**

**Thon, Beck, Vanni, Phillipi & Nutt, A Professional Corporation**
**(See Pasadena)**

**Thoren-Peden, Deborah S.** .... '58 '82 C.477 B.A. L.800 J.D. [Ⓒ Pillsbury M.&S.]
**Thorland, Karen R.** .... '68 '94 C.112 B.A. L.1068 J.D. [Ⓐ Jones,D.R.&P.]
**Thorn, Christopher Adams** .... '59 '84 C.966 B.B.A. L.800 J.D. [Ⓐ Gartner&Y.]
*PRACTICE AREAS: Labor and Employment Law.
**Thornburg, Tracy L.** .... '64 '92 C.976 B.A. L.800 J.D. [Ⓐ Mitchell,S.&K.]
*PRACTICE AREAS: Employment Litigation; Management Labor Relations; Wage and Hour Law.
Thorndal, Mary .... '47 '82 C.585 B.S.N. L.809 J.D. 10940 Wilshire Blvd.
**Thorne, Robert**, (AV) .... '54 '80 C.112 B.A. L.1065 J.D. [Thorne]
*PRACTICE AREAS: Entertainment Law.

**Thorne and Company, A Professional Law Corporation, (AV)**
**1801 Century Park East, Twelfth Floor, 90067**
**Telephone: 310-553-9000 Facsimile: 310-201-9190**
**Robert Thorne; Gregory V. Redlitz; Michael R. Fuller.**
**Entertainment Law.**
*See Professional Biographies, LOS ANGELES, CALIFORNIA*

**Thornhill, Michael C.** .... '51 '76 C.881 A.B. L.94 J.D. [Ginsburg,S.O.&R.]
**Thornton, Bruce M.**, (AV) .... '51 '76 C.846 B.A. L.1068 J.D. [Gascou,G.&T.]
*PRACTICE AREAS: Trials and Appeals; Insurance Coverage; Construction; Fidelity; Suretyship.
**Thornton, Charles V.**, (AV) .... '42 '69 C.188 A.B. L.477 J.D. [Paul,H.J.&W.]
**Thornton, John T.** '55 '80 C.602 B.A. L.1049 J.D.
1st V.P. & Sr. Coun., CB Coml. Real Estate Grp., Inc.
*RESPONSIBILITIES: Litigation; Business Advice/Contract; Training.
**Thornton, Monica Cruz** .... '59 '87 C.112 B.A. L.1067 J.D. [Selman B.]
*LANGUAGES: Spanish.
**Thornton, Robert R.**, (AV) '29 '57
C.674 B.S.E. L.309 LL.B. [Ⓒ Carlsmith B.W.C.&I.] (Pat.)
*PRACTICE AREAS: Intellectual Property; Artistic Properties; Literary Properties; Commercial Law.
**Thornton, T. Emmet** .... '48 '78 C.906 B.S. L.464 J.D. [Sedgwick,D.M.&A.]
**Thornton, Timothy M.**, (AV) .... '29 '55 C&L.93 B.S., J.D. [Manatt,P.&P.]
*PRACTICE AREAS: Litigation.
**Thornton, William H.** .... '46 '74 C&L.659 B.A., J.D. Sr. Coun., Bank of Amer.
Thorpe, Andrew J. .... '50 '76 C.112 B.A. L.1137 J.D. 3754 Wasatch Ave.
**Thorpe, Barry G.** .... '60 '86 C.1042 B.A. L.809 J.D. [Ⓐ Manning,M.&W.]
**Thorpe, Brendan J.** .... '60 '88 C&L.426 B.A., J.D. [Thorpe&T.]
*PRACTICE AREAS: Business Litigation; Real Estate Litigation.
**Thorpe, Douglas L.**, (AV) .... '37 '69 C.546 B.S.C.E. L.802 J.D. [Perkins C.]
**Thorpe, Gregory B.** .... '53 '82 C.112 B.A. L.426 J.D. [O'Melveny&M.]
**Thorpe, John G.**, (AV) .... '24 '52 C&L.426 B.B.A., LL.B. [Thorpe&T.]
*PRACTICE AREAS: Real Estate Law.
**Thorpe, Vincent W.**, (AV) .... '33 '60 C&L.426 B.S., J.D. [Thorpe&T.]
*PRACTICE AREAS: Business Litigation; Corporate Law.

**Thorpe and Thorpe, Professional Corporation, (AV)**
**One Bunker Hill, Suite 800, 601 West 5th Street, 90071**
**Telephone: 213-680-9940 Telecopier: 213-680-4060**
**Timothy D. Kevane; Rebecca Hairston Lessley; Lee New; Mark R. Stapke; Brendan J. Thorpe; John G. Thorpe; Vincent W. Thorpe. Of Counsel: John C. Carpenter; Sanford Holo; Jennifer Harris.**
**Civil, Trial and Appellate Practice. Business, Corporate, Securities, Real Property, Estate Planning, Trusts and Probate, Taxation, Construction Insurance, Trade Regulation and Unfair Competition Law.**
**Reference: Sanwa Bank.**
*See Professional Biographies, LOS ANGELES, CALIFORNIA*

**Thorson, Peter M.** .... '51 '78 C.112 B.A. L.426 J.D. [Ⓐ Richards,W.&G.]
*PRACTICE AREAS: Municipal Law; Redevelopment Law; Land Use Law.
**Thrasher, Thomas N., Jr.** .... '67 '95 C.112 B.A. L.1137 J.D. [Ⓐ Koletsky,M.&F.]
*PRACTICE AREAS: Construction Defect Litigation; General Civil Litigation.

**Throckmorton, Beckstrom, Oakes & Tomassian LLP**
**(See Pasadena)**

Thrush, Dale A. .... '42 '78 C.800 B.Arch. L.426 J.D. [Thrush&S.]
Thrush & Sikand, (AV) .... 10850 Wilshire Blvd.
**Thumann, Henry C.**, (AV) .... '35 '61 C.339 B.A. L.309 LL.B. [O'Melveny&M.]
*PRACTICE AREAS: General Business Litigation; Antitrust; Securities.
**Thurmond, Karl S.** .... '60 '86 C.197 A.B. L.309 J.D. [Ⓐ Fenigstein&K.]
*PRACTICE AREAS: Business Litigation; Business and Commercial Law.
**Thurston, Adam J.** .... '66 '92 C.94 B.A. L.880 J.D. [Ⓐ Bryan C.]
**Tibbetts, Deborah J.** .... '66 '93 C.1103 B.S. L.178 J.D. [Ⓐ Jeffer,M.B.&M.]
*PRACTICE AREAS: Labor and Employment.
**Tiberend, Diane E.** '60 '86 C.1042 B.S. L.426 J.D.
Coun., Transamerica Financial Servs.
**Tichon, Michael John** .... '42 '69 C.602 B.A. L.145 J.D. [Ⓒ Davis W.T.]
Ticker, Neil .... '47 '76 C.112 B.A. L.1179 J.D. Security First Grp., Inc.
Tidus, Jeffrey A., (AV) .... '56 '79 C.112 B.A. L.1066 J.D. 444 S. Flower St.
**Tiedt, John E.** .... '61 '88 C.112 B.A. L.990 J.D. [Ⓐ Dummit,F.&B.]
**Tierney, James P.**, (AV) .... '42 '68 C.705 B.S. L.564 J.D. [J.P.Tierney]
*REPORTED CASES: Sid & Marty Krofft Television Productions, Inc. v. McDonald's Corp., 562 F.2d 1152 (9th Cir, 1977); Lutz v. De Laurentis, 211 Cal. App. 3d, 1317, 260 Cal. Rptr. 106 (1989).
*PRACTICE AREAS: Entertainment Litigation; Commercial Litigation.
Tierney, John N. .... '43 '68 C.321 A.B. L.145 J.D. 1140 N. La Brea Ave.

**Tierney, James P., P.C., The Law Offices of, (AV)**
**800 Tarcuto Way, 90077**
**Telephone: 310-576-1260 Fax: 310-576-1270**
**James P. Tierney; Susan Clary.**
**Business and Entertainment Litigation.**
*See Professional Biographies, LOS ANGELES, CALIFORNIA*

**Tigerman, Charles S., (Professional Corporation)**, (AV) '42 '69
C.502 B.A. L.734 J.D. [Ⓒ Resch P.A.&B.]
*PRACTICE AREAS: Computer Law; Estate Planning; Business Law.
Tiggs, Marcus Gregory .... '63 '88 C.990 B.A. L.1136 J.D. 201 N. Figueroa St.
Tighe, Barry .... '32 '62 C.426 B.S. L.809 LL.B. Dep. Dist. Atty.
Tighe, Maureen A., (AV) .... '57 '85 C&L.705 B.A., J.D. Asst. U.S. Atty.
Tijerina, Roland R. .... '60 '87 C.1097 B.S. L.1137 J.D. [Ⓐ Morgan&W.]

**Tilem White & Weintraub LLP**
**(See Glendale)**

**Tilles, David F.** .... '55 '80 C.112 B.A. L.1068 J.D. [Fenigstein&K.]
*PRACTICE AREAS: Corporate, Real Estate, Business, and Commercial Law; Business Litigation.

**Tillipman, James M.**
**(See Santa Monica)**

**Tilner, Mitchell C.**, (AV) .... '53 '80 C.976 B.A. L.426 J.D. [Horvitz&L.]
**Tilson, J. Lane**, (AV) .... '34 '60 C.112 A.B. L.1068 LL.B. [Ⓒ Stephens,B.&L.]
*PRACTICE AREAS: Business Litigation; Professional Liability Litigation.
**Timms, Charles F., Jr.** .... '48 '77 C.668 B.A. L.477 J.D. [Ⓒ LeBoeuf,L.G.&M.]
*PRACTICE AREAS: Environmental.
Ting, Sandee .... '62 '92 C.103 B.A. L.1066 J.D. 550 S. Hope St.
**Tinsley, Walton Eugene**, (AV) '21 '54
C.150 E.E. L.800 J.D. [Ⓒ Pretty,S.&P.] (See Pat. Sect.)
*PRACTICE AREAS: Patents; Trademarks; Unfair Competition.
**Tipler, James Harvey** .... '51 '78 C.976 B.A. L.813 J.D. [Tipler]⊙

**Tipler Law Firm, The, (BV)**
**8224 Blackburn Avenue, Suite 100, 90048-4216⊙**
**Telephone: 213-651-3590 Fax: 213-651-4273**
**Email: TiplerFL@aol.com**
**James Harvey Tipler; Mal Duncan.**
**Trial Practice, Negligence Law.**
**Andalusia, Alabama Office: The Tipler Building. P.O. Drawer 1397. Telephone: 334-222-4148. Fax: 334-222-4086.**
**Fort Walton Beach, Florida Office: 348 Miracle Strip Parkway, Suite 18. Telephone: 904-664-0600. Fax: 904-664-6990.**
**Atlanta, Georgia Office: Garland Law Building. 3151 Maple Drive, N.E. Telephone: 404-814-9755. Fax: 404-365-5041.**
**London, England Office: 31 Bedford Square. WC1B 3SG. Telephone: 44-071-323-2722. Fax: 44-071-631-4659.**
*See Professional Biographies, LOS ANGELES, CALIFORNIA*

**Tippie, Alan G.**, (AV) .... '53 '79 C.608 B.A. L.426 J.D. [Sulmeyer,K.B.&R.]
*PRACTICE AREAS: Financial Restructuring; Bankruptcy; Business Litigation.
**Tipton, John M.** .... '62 '88 C.473 A.B. L.309 J.D. [Allen,M.L.G.&M.]
*PRACTICE AREAS: Real Estate Development Law; Finance Law.
**Tisch, William F.** .... '44 '70 C.668 B.A. L.426 J.D. [Sandler&R.]
**Tischler, Ronald B., (P.C.)**, (AV) .... '44 '69 C.216 B.A. L.309 J.D. [Irell&M.]
**Tisdale, Jeffrey A.** .... '49 '78 C.112 B.A. L.61 J.D. [Tisdale&N.]
*PRACTICE AREAS: Financial Institutions Regulatory Counseling; Corporate and Securities Law; Entertainment Law; International Business.
**Tisdale, Jon H.** .... '54 '80 C.1075 B.A. L.800 J.D. [Gilbert,K.C.&J.]
Tisdale, Raphael E. '45 '70
C.800 B.A. L.1066 J.D. Sr. Dir., Bus. Affs., Capitol Records, Inc.

**Tisdale & Nicholson, (AV)**
**Suite 755 2049 Century Park East, 90067**
**Telephone: 310-286-1260 Facsimile: 310-286-2351**
**Members of Firm: Jeffrey A. Tisdale; Guy C. Nicholson; Sandor X. Mayuga. Associates: Paul S. Cooley; Elizabeth A. McFarland. Of Counsel: Richard A. Kolber; David Kern Peteler; Mark J. Pearl; Kenneth S. Fields; Paul H. Moeller.**
**General Civil Trial and Administrative Practice before all State and Federal Courts and Regulatory Agencies. Civil Appeals, Banking, Corporate, Regulatory, Real Estate, Entertainment, International Business, Finance and Litigation Matters, Including Real Estate Workouts and Receiverships, Mergers and Acquisitions. Complex Business, Bankruptcy and Insolvency, Directors and Officers and Other Professional Liability, Trials and Appeals.**
*See Professional Biographies, LOS ANGELES, CALIFORNIA*

**Tishkoff, Judith M.** .... '57 '88 C.1042 B.S.N. L.800 J.D. [Lewis,D.B.&B.]
**Tissot, Jeremy L.** .... '69 '94 C.454 B.A. L.990 J.D. [Ⓐ Callahan,M.&W.]
*PRACTICE AREAS: Insurance Defense; Real Estate Litigation.

**Tistaert, Lawrence C., (AV) '42 '67 C.112 B.A. L.1068 J.D.** 🅱
**11766 Wilshire Boulevard, Suite 1580, 90025-6537**
**Telephone: 310-312-0874 Fax: 310-312-1034**
**Email: lctist@ix.netcom.com**
**Business, Real Estate, Probate/Trust and Trial Practice.**
**Representative Clients: Bell Foundry Co.; Brendan Tours; Franklin Telecommunications Corp.; Munro Properties; United States Tour Operators Association.**
**Reference: Bank of America.**
*See Professional Biographies, LOS ANGELES, CALIFORNIA*

**Titcher, Paul J.** .... '65 '90 C.112 B.A. L.1066 J.D. [Ⓐ Cox,C.&N.]
*PRACTICE AREAS: Real Property Law; Subdivision Development Law; Resort and Country Club Law; Real Estate Finance Law.
Title, David M. .... '51 '87 C.112 B.A. L.426 J.D. 1801 Century Park, E.

**Title, Gail Migdal**, (AV) ................ '46 '71 C.914 A.B. L.1066 J.D. [Katten M.&Z.]
*LANGUAGES: French.
*PRACTICE AREAS: Entertainment Litigation; Intellectual Property; General Commercial Litigation; Business Crimes.
**Title, Julius M.**, (AV) ...................... '15 '41 C&L.800 B.A., LL.B. [🄲 Troy&G.]
*PRACTICE AREAS: Alternative Dispute Resolution.

**Title, Lawrence H., Law Office of, (AV) '45 '71 C&L.813 A.B., J.D.**
**2029 Century Park East Suite 2750, 90067-3099**
**Telephone: 310-284-8583 Telecopier: 310-284-7953**
***PRACTICE AREAS: Business Law; Real Estate Law; Corporate and Corporate Finance.**

Titus, Patricia Jo ........................ '60 '85 C.813 A.B. L.1068 J.D. Dep. Dist. Atty.
**Tobey, Bruce D.** ........................'59 '84 C.112 B.A. L.1068 J.D. [Troop M.S.&P.]
*PRACTICE AREAS: Transactional; Entertainment Law.
Tobin, Gale ........................'63 '91 C.659 B.A. L.025 LL.B. 2049 Century Pk. E.
**Tobin, John J.**, (AV) '35 '69 C&L.1114 B.A., J.D.
[Kegel,T.&T.] (©Rancho Cucamonga)
**Tobin, Stanley E., (P.C.)**, (AV) ...........'30 '59 C.309 B.A. L.976 LL.B. [Hill,F.&B.]
*PRACTICE AREAS: Labor (Management) Law.
**Tobin, Steven** ................................'50 '76 C.476 B.A. L.1095 J.D. [Spray,G.&B.]
Tobin, W. Paul, (BV) ......................'51 '81 C.763 B.A. L.1068 J.D. 9200 Sunset Blvd.
**Tobisman, Stuart P.**, (AV) '42 '70
C.112 A.B. L.1066 J.D. [O'Melveny&M.] (©Century City)
*PRACTICE AREAS: Tax Law; Estate Planning; Trusts and Estates.
Tobor, Cheryl ..............'— '87 C.1077 B.A. L.426 J.D. 6701 Center Dr., W., 12th Fl.
**Tochner, Stuart D.** ....................'59 '86 C.112 A.B. L.800 J.D. [🄰 Musick,P.&G.]
**Toczauer, Tyrone I.** ....................'59 '86 C.1077 B.A. L.398 J.D. [🄰 Hillsinger&C.]
*LANGUAGES: Hungarian.
Todd, Marsha ....................... '69 '94 C.112 B.A. L.1066 J.D. 444 S. Flower St.
Todd, Matthew P. ..................'59 '87 C.1077 B.A. L.398 J.D. 1126 Wilshire Blvd.
**Todd, S. Thomas** ...............................'50 '75 C.112 B.A. L.813 J.D. [Horvitz&L.]
**Toder, Jeffrey A.**, (AV) ...............'57 '82 C.674 A.B. L.659 J.D. [Troop M.S.&P.]
*PRACTICE AREAS: Government Contracts Law.
Toews, Ronald ........................'57 '81 C.1163 B.S. L.800 J.D. P.O. Box 36776
Tohl, Bernard G. ................'19 '70 C.800 B.S. L.1095 J.D. 848 N. La Cienega Blvd.
Toister, Tamar Rachel ........................'57 '84 C.112 B.A. L.426 J.D. Dep. Pub. Def.
**Tokumori, Gary** .........................'62 '90 C.1097 B.A. L.426 J.D. [🄰 Ivanjack&L.]
*PRACTICE AREAS: Business Litigation; Commercial Litigation; Bankruptcy.
**Tokuyama, Shu** ........................................ '48 '79 C&L.178 B.A., J.D. [Marks&M.]
*LANGUAGES: Japanese.
Tolbert, James L. ..................'26 '60 C.1043 B.A. L.1114 LL.B. 6363 Sunset Blvd.
Toll, Arthur ...............................'27 '50 C&L.930 A.B., LL.B. 2029 Century Pk., E.
Toll, Daniel M. ....................'54 '82 C&L.1137 B.S.L., J.D. 2029 Century Park E.
**Tolles, Stephen L.** .....................'46 '82 C.674 A.B. L.1066 J.D. [Gibson,D.&C.]
*PRACTICE AREAS: Federal Income Taxation; California Income, Property and Sales Taxation.
Tolmas, Ed ......................... '37 '64 C.112 A.B. L.809 LL.B. 523 W. 6th St.
Tolnai, Lester J. ......................'46 '74 C.112 B.A. L.426 J.D. Sr. Dep. Co. Coun.
Tom, Franklin, (AV) '41 '68 C.112 B.S. L.1068 J.D.
V.P. & Gen. Coun., Managed Health Network, Inc.
Tom, Suzanne Prevot ..........................'58 '84 C.659 B.A. L.861 J.D. Dep. City Atty.
**Tomasulo, Michael A.** ........................ '68 '95 C.112 B.S. L.800 J.D. [🄰 Lyon&L.]
*LANGUAGES: Spanish.
*PRACTICE AREAS: Intellectual Property.
Tombak, Ivy ..............................'56 '82 C.659 B.A. L.273 J.D. 1629 Rising Glen Rd.
**Tomin, Harold J.**, (AV) ..................'40 '65 C.273 B.A. L.597 J.D. [Fenigstein&K.]
*PRACTICE AREAS: Complex Business Litigation; Antitrust Counseling and Litigation; Securities Litigation; Employment Litigation.
Tomlinson, Janet M. ...................... '60 '86 C.1077 B.A. L.990 J.D. [Schmid&V.] ‡
**Toms, Robert L., Sr.**, (AV) .......... '35 '65 C.92 B.A. L.228 J.D. [Nossaman,G.K.&E.]
*PRACTICE AREAS: Corporation Law; Securities Law; Business Law; Regulatory Law; International Trade Law.
**Tong, Geoffrey T.** ...................'62 '88 C.112 B.A. L.426 J.D. [🄰 Meserve,M.&H.]
**Tooch, Daron L.** .......................'63 '88 C.112 B.A. L.309 J.D. [🄰 Foley L.W.&A.]
Tooch, Melinda J., (BV) ............'52 '78 C.1077 B.A. L.426 J.D. 11766 Wilshire Blvd.
**Toohey, Timothy J.** ..................'49 '87 C.813 B.A. L.1066 J.D. [🄰 O'Donnell,R.&S.]
*PRACTICE AREAS: Litigation.
**Toor, Bruce A.**, (AV) ..................'34 '67 C.112 B.A. L.1068 J.D. [🄲 Gibson,D.&C.]
*PRACTICE AREAS: Civil Litigation; Medical Malpractice; Alternative Dispute Resolution.
Topel, Eugene ...........................'36 '66 C.999 B.S. L.426 LL.B. 1010 Wilshire Blvd.
Toppila, W. Brian ......................'60 '89 C.112 A.B. L.259 J.D. 12301 Wilshire Blvd.
**Torem, Shana T.** .........................'69 '94 C.112 B.A. L.1068 J.D. [🄰 Foley L.W.&A.]
*LANGUAGES: Hebrew.
*REPORTED CASES: Summit Technology, Inc. v. High-Line Medical Instruments Company, Inc. et al., 922 F.Supp. 299 (C.D. Cal. 1996).
*PRACTICE AREAS: Litigation.
Torgow, Martha A. '54 '79
C.112 B.A. L.1068 J.D. Gen. Coun., Los Angeles Comm. Coll. Dist.
Torok, Andrew F. ......................'61 '86 C.112 B.A. L.1065 J.D. 801 S. Grand Ave.
Torpy, Gary B. ........................................'51 '77 C.823 A.B. L.734 J.D. [Torpy,G.B.]
Torpy, Gary B., A Prof. Corp., Law Offices of .......................... 12100 Wilshire Blvd.
Torrance, Calvin W. ..................... '34 '61 C.299 A.B. L.309 LL.B. Dep. Atty. Gen.
**Torrano, Marcus A.** ......................... '61 '88 C.636 B.S. L.1066 J.D. [Morrison&F.]
*PRACTICE AREAS: Labor.
**Torre, Christine M.** ...........................'58 '92 C.788 B.A. L.426 J.D. [🄰 Bryan C.]
*PRACTICE AREAS: Employment; Labor Relations.
**Torrell, Gary F.** ...........................'55 '83 C.1044 B.S. L.893 J.D. [Paul,H.J.&W.]
**Torres, Diana M.** ....................'65 '92 C.674 A.B. L.976 J.D. [🄰 O'Melveny&M.]
**Torres, Juan A.** .........................'60 '87 C.112 B.A. L.1066 J.D. [Musick,P.&G.]
*LANGUAGES: Spanish.
*PRACTICE AREAS: Litigation.
Torres, Ricardo A. ..........................'29 '66 C.426 B.B.A. L.809 LL.B. Supr. Ct. J.
**Torrey, Rebecca L.** ...................'61 '91 C.246 B.A. L.228 J.D. [🄰 Jeffer,M.B.&M.]
*PRACTICE AREAS: Labor and Employment Litigation.
Torribio, John A. ..............................'40 '66 C.813 B.A. L.800 LL.B. Supr. Ct. J.
Tortorici, Peter F. '49 '75 C.608 B.A. L.724 J.D.
(adm. in NY; not adm. in CA) President, CBS Entertainment
**Tosetti, Paul D.** .............................'54 '82 C&L.309 B.A., J.D. [Latham&W.]
**Totino, Edward D.** .....................'68 '93 C.800 B.A. L.188 J.D. [🄰 Brobeck,P.&H.]
*PRACTICE AREAS: Litigation.
**Toumanoff, Michael V.** ...............'52 '82 C.309 A.B. L.1066 J.D. [🄲 Morrison&F.]
*PRACTICE AREAS: Public Pension Law; Business Litigation.
**Tourtelot, Robert H.**, (AV) ............'34 '65 C.770 B.Sc. L.1065 J.D. [Tourtelot&B.]
*PRACTICE AREAS: Civil Litigation; Personal Injury Litigation; Product Liability Litigation; Corporate; Real Estate.

**Tourtelot & Butler, A Professional Law Corporation, (AV)**
**Suite 1090, 11835 West Olympic Boulevard, 90064-5001**
**Telephone: 310-575-5600 Fax: 310-575-5626**
**Robert H. Tourtelot; Laurie J. Butler (P.C.);—Marlena M. Blankenship. Of Counsel: Peter J. Wilke.**

(This Listing Continued)

**Tourtelot & Butler, A Professional Law Corporation (Continued)**

**General Civil and Trial Practice with special emphasis on Real Estate, Business, Partnership, Intellectual Property, Unfair Competition, Construction Litigation, Product Liability and Personal Injury Litigation, Geothermal Energy and Oil and Gas Related Matters, Labor and Employment Law.**
***See Professional Biographies, LOS ANGELES, CALIFORNIA***

Toussaint, Claudia S. ........................'63 '91 C.112 B.A. L.1065 J.D. 555 W. 5th St.
**Touton, Louis L.** .......'55 '82 C.453 S.B.E.E. L.178 J.D. [Jones,D.R.&P.] (See Pat. Sect.)
Tovar, Rene ...........................'62 '88 C.1042 B.S. L.990 J.D. 5959 W. Century Blvd.
**Tovmassian, Henry** ........................ '62 '89 C.569 B.A. L.1068 J.D. [Kehr,C.T.&F.]
*LANGUAGES: Armenian.
*PRACTICE AREAS: Real Estate; Corporate Litigation; Business Litigation; Civil Litigation.
**Towfighi, Arya** .................................'68 '94 C.659 B.A. L.990 J.D. [🄰 Loeb&L.]
**Towle, Edmund J., III, (Professional Corporation)**, (AV) '48 '74
C.276 A.B. L.178 J.D. [Kinsella,B.F.&T.]
**Towne, Richard P.**
**(See Woodland Hills)**

Townsend, Richard E. ................... '48 '76 C.154 M.A. L.1068 J.D. Asst. Co. Coun.
Townsend, Vince M., Jr. ...............'06 '42 C.943 B.A. L.329 LL.B. 3662 Arlington Ave.
Toyama, Lori A. ..............................'56 '83 C.800 B.A. L.426 J.D. 2550 Federal Ave.
Trachman, Lester E., (AV) ...........'31 '59 C.112 B.S. L.1068 J.D. 1875 Century Pk. E.
**Trachtenberg, Jordan** ......................'57 '84 C.183 B.A. L.1068 J.D. [🄰 Billet&K.]
**Tracy, Suzanne E.** ..........................'58 '89 C.69 B.A. L.802 J.D. [🄰 Kirkland&E.]
*PRACTICE AREAS: Litigation; Real Estate; Arbitration.
**Tracy, Teresa R.** ...........................'52 '79 C.1077 B.A. L.426 J.D. [Baker&H.]
*PRACTICE AREAS: Management Labor and Employment Law (Private and Public).
**Trager, Glenn A.** ...........................'— '96 C.112 B.A. L.813 J.D. [🄰 O'Melveny&M.]
**Tragert, Suzanne** ....................'63 '88 C.94 B.A. L.276 J.D. [🄲 O'Donnell,R.&S.]
*PRACTICE AREAS: Litigation.
**Traina, Paul A.** ...............................'64 '91 C.494 L.990 J.D. [🄰 Engstrom,L.&L.]

**Trainotti, D. Michael, A Professional Law Corporation**
**(See Long Beach)**

Trammell, George W., III ...................... '36 '63 C&L.800 B.S., LL.B. Supr. Ct. J.
**Tran, Tina M.** ..............................'71 '96 C.800 B.A. L.1066 J.D. [🄰 Troop M.S.&P.]
*PRACTICE AREAS: Litigation.
**Trapp, Janet E.** ........................'61 '89 C.112 B.S. L.1148 J.D. [🄰 Dummit,F.&B.]
Trask, Gordon W. ..............................'47 '76 C.112 B.A. L.809 J.D. Sr. Dep. Co. Coun.
Trattner, Ira ................................'47 '75 C.978 B.A. L.1009 J.D. Ira Trattner Prod.
Travis, Karen J. ....................'50 '87 C.1044 B.S. L.112 J.D. 3926 Wilshire Blvd.
**Travis, Ted L.** ............................... '61 '89 C.972 B.A. L.546 J.D. [Dale,B.&H.]
*PRACTICE AREAS: Personal Injury Defense Law; Insurance Coverage Law; Municipal Entity Defense Law.
**Traxler, Katherine A.** ......................'65 '90 C.602 B.A. L.1068 J.D. [🄰 Paul,H.J.&W.]
Traylor, Michael S. ..................'62 '88 C.477 B.A. L.426 J.D. 3660 Wilshire Blvd.
**Traynham, Michael W.** ..................'58 '91 C.890 B.A. L.1274 J.D. [🄰 Paul,H.J.&W.]
Treadwell, Mark A. ...................... '49 '74 C.112 B.A. L.4238 J.D. [Mantalica&T.]

**Tredway, Lumsdaine & Doyle, LLP**
**(See Downey)**

**Tregub, Susan H.** .....................................'67 '93 C.800 B.A. L.426 J.D. [Donahue&M.]
*PRACTICE AREAS: Securities Arbitration; Business Law; Corporate Law.
**Treiger, Adam** .....................................'— '94 C.112 B.A. L.276 J.D. [🄰 Morgan,L.&B.]
**Treiman, Robert N.** ..................................'62 '88 C.951 B.A. L.1068 J.D. [Loeb&L.]
**Treister, Dana S.** ....................'65 '94 C.813 B.A. L.800 J.D. [🄰 O'Melveny&M.]
*PRACTICE AREAS: Labor and Employment; General Litigation.
**Treister, George M.**, (AV) ..............'23 '50 C.112 B.S. L.976 LL.B. [Stutman,T.&G.]
*PRACTICE AREAS: Bankruptcy; Insolvency; Corporate Reorganization.
Trendacosta, Anthony A., (BV) '50 '75
C.1077 B.A. L.1095 J.D. Gen. Coun., Rent Control Bd.
**Trendacosta, Patricia Yamamoto** ..........'51 '86 C.112 B.A. L.426 J.D. [Frandzel&S.]
**Trepanier, Lisa Dearden** ............................................ '68 '91 L.188 [🄰 Dewey B.]
**Trepinski, Kathryn M.** ..........'59 '85 C.473 A.B. L.809 J.D. [🄲 Sedgwick,D.M.&A.]

**Tressler, Soderstrom, Maloney & Priess**
**2049 Century Park East, Suite 2140, 90067-3283©**
**Telephone: 310-226-7460 Fax: 310-226-7461**
**Resident Partner: Mary E. McPherson. Associate: Jeffrey J. Christovich; Sharon R. Terris.**
**General Civil Trial and Appellate Practice. Trusts and Estate Planning, Property and Casualty Insurance, Corporation, Real Estate, Health Care, Employment, Professional Liability, Environmental, Securities Law and Drug and Medical Device Litigation.**
**Chicago, Illinois Office: 233 Wacker Drive, 22nd Floor. Telephone: 312-627-4000. FAX: 312-627-1717.**
**Wheaton, Illinois Office: 2100 Manchester Road, Suite 950. Telephone: 630-668-2800. FAX: 630-668-3003.**
**Waukegan, Illinois Office: 415 Washington Street, Suite 203. Telephone: 847-623-2100. FAX: 847-623-9695.**
**New York, New York Office: 655 Madison Avenue, Suite, 1900. Telephone: 212-593-5050. FAX:212-593-5404.**

***See Professional Biographies, LOS ANGELES, CALIFORNIA***

**Trester, Fredric W.** ...................'54 '80 C.37 B.A. L.770 J.D. [Wilson,E.M.E.&D.]
*PRACTICE AREAS: Construction Law; Real Estate Law; Products Liability.
**Treuer, Stephen D.** ......................'54 '84 C.1307 B.A. L.1066 J.D. [Quisenberry&B.]
*REPORTED CASES: North Star Reinsurance Corporation v. Superior Court, 10 Cal. App. 4th 1815 (1992).

**Treusch, Bradford L., Law Offices of, (AV) '49 '75 C.112 B.A. L.426 J.D.**
**Suite 760, Two Century Plaza, 2049 Century Park East, 90067**
**Telephone: 310-557-2599 Fax: 310-557-9986**
**Family Law, Divorce, Negligence, Real Estate, Commercial Collections, Corporate, Tax, Estate Planning, Wills and Probate. General Civil Trial Practice.**
**A List of Representative Clients Furnished Upon Request.**
**Reference: Bank of America (Century Plaza Office).**

Treusch, Paul E. '— '35 C&L.145 Ph.B., J.D.
(adm. in IL; not adm. in CA) Prof. of Law, Southwestern Univ. Law School
Trevithick, Ronald L., (AV) .........'34 '60 C.112 B.S. L.1068 LL.B. 800 Wilshire Blvd.
**Tricarico, Christopher J.** ..........'64 '92 C.800 B.A. L.659 J.D. [🄰 Proskauer R.G.&M.]
*LANGUAGES: Spanish, Italian.
*PRACTICE AREAS: Entertainment Law; Motion Pictures and Television.
**Tricarico, Vincent**, (AV) ..........................'42 '72 C&L.724 B.A., J.D. [Clark&T.]
*PRACTICE AREAS: General Business Litigation; Commercial Litigation; Antitrust Litigation; Unfair Competition Litigation; Securities Litigation.
Trice, Terra Y. ........................'63 '89 C.436 B.A. L.809 J.D. 12400 Wilshire Blvd.
Tricker, Richard P. ..............................'57 '81 C.112 B.A. L.1066 J.D. [Kopesky&W.]
**Trimarche, Gregory D.** ................'63 '89 C&L.378 B.A., J.D. [Demetriou,D.S.&M.]
*PRACTICE AREAS: Environmental Law; Civil Litigation; Insurance Law.
**Trimble, Sarah** ......................'69 '95 C.859 B.A. L.420 J.D. [🄰 McDermott,W.&E.]
Trinkaus, Walter R., (AV) '13 '38
C.740 A.B. L.800 LL.B. Prof., Emeritus, Loyola Univ. Law Sch.
Triplett, Dennis R. ........................'63 '89 C.221 B.A. L.569 J.D. 3580 Wilshire Blvd.
Triplett, Susan J. ............................'47 '77 C.801 B.A. L.228 J.D. 444 S. Flower St.
**Tripodi, Paul D., II** ........................ '66 '92 C.645 B.S. L.112 J.D. [🄰 Pretty,S.&P.]
*PRACTICE AREAS: Patents; Trademarks; Copyrights; Unfair Competition; Litigation.

Tripp, Pamela R. ............ '59 '92 C.1190 B.S.L. L.1068 J.D. 2040 Ave. of the Stars
**Tripp, Paula G.** ............ '58 '84 C.800 B.A. L.464 J.D. [Ⓐ Anderson,M.&C.]
*PRACTICE AREAS: Aviation; Motor Carrier and Truck Liability; Premises Liability; Construction Defect and Accident Litigation.
**Tritt, Clyde E.**, (AV) ............ '20 '49 C.170 A.B. L.813 J.D. [Ⓒ O'Melveny&M.]
Troe, Charles H. ............ '47 '72 C.352 B.B.A. L.145 J.D. 777 S. Figueroa St., 10th Fl.
**Troff, Eric L.** ............ '52 '83 C.477 B.A. L.426 J.D. [Musick,P.&G.]
*PRACTICE AREAS: Litigation.
**Troop, Richard E.**, (AV) ............ '41 '70 C.260 B.E.E. L.426 J.D. [Troop M.S.&P.]
*PRACTICE AREAS: Corporate Securities Law; Corporate Law; Entertainment Law.

**Troop Meisinger Steuber & Pasich, LLP, (AV)**
**A Partnership including a Professional Corporation**
**10940 Wilshire Boulevard, 90024-3902**
**Telephone: 310-824-7000 Orange County: 714-953-6221 Telecopier: 310-443-7599**
**Members of Firm: Scott W. Alderton; Martin S. Appel (Certified Specialist, Taxation Law, The State Bar of California Board of Legal Specialization); Mary K. Barnes; Anthony M. Basich; Mary Craig Calkins; Elizabeth A. Casey; Tyrone R. Childress; James J. Ciccone; Harrison J. Dossick; Robert E. Duffy; John M. Genga; Marc J. Graboff; Blaine Eric Greenberg; David Halberstadter; Fred D. Heather; Clyde M. Hettrick, III; Robert M. Jason; Martin D. Katz; Thomas Glen Leo; C. Dennis Loomis; Murray Markiles; Robert A. Martis; Louis M. Meisinger; Robert S. Metzger; Leigh B. Morris; Neil R. O'Hanlon; Anthony J. Oncidi; Kirk A. Pasich; David T. Peterson; Robert J. Plotkowski; Curtis D. Porterfield; C. N. Franklin Reddick III; Ronald D. Reynolds; D. Matthew Richardson; Jeffrey A. Rosenfeld; David H. Sands; Alan B. Spatz; David W. Steuber; Bruce D. Tobey; Jeffrey A. Toder; Richard E. Troop; Rita L. Tuzon. Principal Attorneys: Michael T. Anderson; Bryan B. Arnold; Eric A. Barron; Amy L. Kincaid Berry; Samuel E. Bramhall; Karen Palladino Ciccone; Jon E. Drucker; Cindy Zimmerman Dubin; Joseph B. Hershenson; Louis M. Kaplan; Stephen V. Masterson; Catherine L. Rivard; Daniel J. Schultz; Susan Page White. Associates: Mehran Arjomand; Whitney E. Bakley (Not admitted in CA); Jessica R. Bass; William F. Bly; Mylene J. Brooks; Antony E. Buchignani; Matthew F. Burke; Kenneth L. Burry; Richard A. Chapkis; Alisa M. Chevalier; Michael R. Chiappetta; Bert C. Cozart; Kristina M. Diaz; Hilari Hanamaikai Elson; Amy J. Fink; Howard A. Fishman; Scott D. Galer; Danielle L. Gilmore; Linda M. Giunta; Laurence L. Gottlieb; G. Karl Greissinger; Joy K. Gumpert; Kathleen M. Hallinan; Jacqueline Jourdain Hayes (Not admitted in CA); Jeffrey M. Jacobberger; John D. Jenkins; Julie M. Kaufer; Alyssa Tara Kennedy; John C. Kirke; Abigail Klem; Lauri S. Konishi; Linda D. Kornfeld; Aneeta Kumar; Greg R. Langer; Michael S. Luke; John J. McIlvery; Mark A. McLean; Beth E. Machlovitch; Cary M. Meadow; Paul B. Neinstein; Kate E. Ohlson; Jason S. Reichenthal; Melissa A. Rogal; Michael A. Rossi; Christine A. Samsel; Barbra E. Sherak; Cassandra C. Shivers; Jessica Cullen Smith (Not admitted in CA); Laurie E. Smith; Tina M. Tran; William T. Um; Alissa L. Vradenburg; Eric A. Wannon; James D. Weiss; Mark A. Wiesenthal; Lori M. Yankelevits; Julie S. Zimmerman. Of Counsel: Peter M. Eichler; Dennis D. Hill; Paul R. Katz; Chris Ann Maxwell; Glenn Warner.**
**Corporate Law, including Corporate Securities and Finance, Entertainment, Financial Services, Institutional Finance, International Transactions, Insurance Coverage Advice, Labor and Employment Law, Real Estate, Tax, and Litigation including, General Business and Securities Litigation, Environmental and Insurance Coverage Litigation.**

***See Professional Biographies, LOS ANGELES, CALIFORNIA***

Troost, Frank W. ............ '16 '39 C&L.800 B.S., LL.B. Ret. Mun. Ct. J.
**Trope, Eugene L.**, (AV) ............ '16 '46 C.800 A.B. L.1001 LL.B. [Trope&T.]
*PRACTICE AREAS: Family Law; Civil Litigation; White Collar Defense.
Trope, Konrad L. ... '55 '87 C.668 B.A. L.1068 J.D. 4215 Glencoe Ave. (Marina Del Rey)
**Trope, Michael L.** ...... '51 '87 C.800 B.A. L.426 J.D. [Ⓒ Oldman&C.] (⊙Beverly Hills)
*PRACTICE AREAS: Probate Litigation; Child Custody.
**Trope, Roland L.** '47 '82 C.800 B.A. L.976 J.D.
(adm. in NY; not adm. in CA) [Trope&T.] (⊙New York)
**Trope, Sorrell**, (AV) ............ '27 '49 C&L.800 A.B., J.D. [Trope&T.]
*REPORTED CASES: Sokolow v. City of Hope, 41 Cal.2d 556, 1953; Arsenian v. Meketarian, 138 Cal. App.2d 627, 1956; Wunch v. Wunch, 184 Cal. App.2d 527, 1960; Rheuban v. Rheuban, 238 Cal. App.2d 552, 1965; Buck v. Superior Court of Orange, 232 Cal. App.2d 153, 1965.
*PRACTICE AREAS: Family Law.

**Trope and Trope, (AV)** BR
**12121 Wilshire Boulevard, Suite 801, 90025**
**Telephone: 310-207-8228 Fax: 310-826-1122**
**Members of Firm: Sorrell Trope (Certified Specialist, Family Law, The State Bar of California Board of Legal Specialization); Eugene L. Trope; Maryanne La Guardia; Steven Knowles (Certified Specialist, Family Law, The State Bar of California Board of Legal Specialization); Mark S. Patt; Bruce E. Cooperman (Certified Specialist, Family Law, The State Bar of California Board of Legal Specialization); Mark Vincent Kaplan (Certified Specialist, Family Law, The State Bar of California Board of Legal Specialization). Associates: Thomas Paine Dunlap; Donna Beck Weaver (Certified Specialist, Family Law, The State Bar of California Board of Legal Specialization); Carolyn J. Kozuch; Anne Campbell Kiley; Roger B. Peikin; Salvador P. Laviña; Lori A. Howe; Warren D. Camp; Robert B. Clayton; Leslie M. Jordon; Nancy Cronenwalt; Andrea A. Fugate; Jeff M. Sturman; Susan E. Wiesner; Fahi Takesh; Derek Jon Reeve; Geniveve Joan Ruskus; Daniel B. Rubanowitz. Of Counsel: Roland L. Trope (Not admitted in CA).**
**Family Law and General Civil Trial Work. Appellate, Custody.**

***See Professional Biographies, LOS ANGELES, CALIFORNIA***

**Tropp, Deborah S.** ............ '67 '92 C.112 B.A. L.464 J.D. [Ⓐ Ericksen,A.K.D.&L.]
*LANGUAGES: Spanish.
*PRACTICE AREAS: Insurance Defense; Personal Injury.
Tropp, Stephen W. ............ '55 '85 L.464 J.D. 11355 W. Olympic Blvd.
**Trost, Glenn W.** ............ '56 '84 L.809 J.D. [Ⓐ Coudert]
*PRACTICE AREAS: Patent Litigation.
Trost, Scott T. ............ '54 '82 C.1265 B.S. L.352 J.D. 543 Sycamore
Trostler, Flora, (AV) ............ '46 '74 C.112 B.A. L.809 J.D. Dep. City Atty.
**Trotter, Rhonda Renee** ............ '62 '93 C.813 B.A. L.1066 J.D. [Ⓐ Kaye,S.F.H.&H.]
*PRACTICE AREAS: Litigation; Entertainment Transactions.
Trotti, Isabelle ............ '34 '58 C.424 B.S. L.597 J.D. 12828 Marlboro
Troy, Brigitta B., (Mrs.) ............ '40 '70 C.681 A.B. L.800 J.D. 350 S. Bristol Ave.
**Troy, Joseph F.**, (AV) ............ '38 '64 C.976 B.A. L.309 LL.B. [Troy&G.]
*LANGUAGES: French.
*PRACTICE AREAS: Corporate Finance; Securities; Mergers and Acquisitions; Structured Finance.
**Troy, Mark R.** ............ '60 '85 C.112 B.A. L.426 J.D. [McKenna&C.]
Troy, Susan J. ............ '55 '80 C.604 B.A. L.273 J.D. Federated Linen Grp.

**Troy & Gould, Professional Corporation, (AV)**
**16th Floor, 1801 Century Park East, 90067**
**Telephone: 310-553-4441 Facsimile: 310-201-4746 Cable Address: "Tromalaw"**
**Istvan Benko; Kenneth R. Blumer; Yvonne E. Chester; Thomas Henry Coleman; Gary O. Concoff; Alan M. Dettelbach; William J. Feis; Russ M. Fukano; Martin T. Goldblum (Certified Specialist, Taxation Law, The State Bar of California Board of Legal Specializations); William D. Gould; Sanford J. Hillsberg; Derek W. Hunt; Jeffrey W. Kramer; Allyn O. Kreps; James C. Lockwood; Patrick R. Obel; Ronald S. Rosen; Dale E. Short; Joseph F. Troy. Of Counsel: Frank V. Calaba; David Y. Handelman; Julius M. Title; David J. Wohlberg;—Jennifer L. Gentin; Sharon R. Gold; Young J. Kim; William O. Knox; Kenneth J. MacArthur; James P. Menton, Jr.; Benjamin Rozwood; Lawrence P. Schnapp; Allison M. Sunderland; Natasha Wazzan.**
**Corporate, Securities, Real Property, Taxation, International, Bankruptcy and Entertainment Law. General Civil Trial and Appellate Litigation, including Financial Institutions, Intellectual Property, Employment and Environmental Litigation.**

***See Professional Biographies, LOS ANGELES, CALIFORNIA***

**Truax, Timothy M.** ............ '60 '85 C.768 B.A. L.800 J.D. [Thelen,M.J.&B.]
*PRACTICE AREAS: Construction Law; Government Contracts Law.

**Truby, Phyllis Alden, (AV) '47 '76 C.112 B.A. L.426 J.D.**
**12100 Wilshire Boulevard, Suite 1600, 90025**
**Telephone: 310-826-8136 Fax: 310-826-6715**
***PRACTICE AREAS: Business and Commercial Law; Franchise and Distribution Law; Real Property Law.**

(This Listing Continued)



**Truby, Phyllis Alden (Continued)**
**Business Law, Real Estate Law and Franchise Law.**

***See Professional Biographies, LOS ANGELES, CALIFORNIA***

Truce, W. Joseph, (AV) .... '43 '71 C.911 B.A. L.284 J.D. [Kegel,T.&T.] (⊙Long Beach)
Trueblood, Alexander ............ '62 '90 C.112 B.A. L.1068 J.D. 11601 Wilshire Blvd.
**Trujillo, F. Javier** ............ '52 '83 C.1046 B.A. L.564 J.D. [Ⓐ Pierry&M.]
*LANGUAGES: Spanish.
*PRACTICE AREAS: Admiralty/Maritime; Personal Injury; Products Liability (Plaintiff); Workmans Compensation.
**Trujillo, Sylvia J.** ............ '69 '96 C.104 B.A. L.1066 J.D. [Ⓐ Barbosa G.&B.]
**Truman, Kathleen M. O'Prey** ............ '66 '92 C.112 B.A. L.1065 J.D. [Ⓐ Latham&W.]
**Trupiano, Martin J.** ............ '46 '76 C.477 B.A. L.912 J.D. [Graham&J.]
*PRACTICE AREAS: Antitrust Litigation; Trade Regulation Litigation; Commercial Litigation.
**Trussell, Elizabeth S.** ............ '46 '78 C.112 A.B. L.426 J.D. [Ⓒ Buchalter,N.F.&Y.]
*PRACTICE AREAS: Commercial Law; Finance Law; Secured Transactions Law.
Truszkowski, Henry C. ....... '52 '93 C.549 B.S. L.809 J.D. 725 S. Figueroa St., Ste., 2200
**Tryfman, Donna** ............ '67 '95 C.1036 B.A. L.398 J.D. [Ⓐ M.J.Werksman]
*LANGUAGES: Spanish, Hebrew.
*PRACTICE AREAS: Criminal Defense.
**Trygstad, Lawrence B.**, (AV) ............ '37 '68 C.477 B.A. L.800 J.D. [L.B.Trygstad]
**Trygstad, Shanon** ............ '67 '94 C.112 B.A. L.800 J.D. [Ⓐ L.B.Trygstad]
*LANGUAGES: Spanish.

**Trygstad, Lawrence B., A Law Corporation, (AV)**
**Fourth Floor, 1880 Century Park East, 90067-1600**
**Telephone: 310-552-0500 Fax: 310-552-1306**
**Lawrence B. Trygstad;—Richard J. Schwab; David J. Penner; Rosemary O. Ward; Shanon Trygstad.**
**General Civil and Criminal Trial Practice. Labor, Negligence and Family Law. Estate Planning and Probate, School Law and Administrative Practice.**
**Representative Clients: United Teachers-Los Angeles; South Bay United Teachers.**
**Reference: City National Bank, Century City Branch.**

***See Professional Biographies, LOS ANGELES, CALIFORNIA***

Trzcinski, Diane M. ............ '46 '77 C.121 B.A. L.1190 J.D. [Johnson,R.&W.]
**Tsang, Jarlon** ............ '— '96 C.112 B.S. L.94 J.D. [Ⓐ Fulbright&J.]
*LANGUAGES: Mandarin Chinese.
*PRACTICE AREAS: Corporate Law; Public Finance.
**Tsao, Jennifer M.** ............ '66 '92 C.112 B.A. L.426 J.D. [Ⓐ Graham&J.]
**Tsao, Michael** ............ '69 '94 C.197 A.B. L.1068 J.D. [Ⓐ Mitchell,S.&K.]
*PRACTICE AREAS: Litigation.
**Tseng, George G.C.** ............ '69 '96 C.112 B.S.E.E. L.426 J.D. [Ⓐ Blakely,S.T.&Z.]
**Tsien, Winnie** ............ '68 '94 C.1168 B.A. L.1067 J.D. [Ⓐ Orrick,H.&S.]
*LANGUAGES: Chinese.
*PRACTICE AREAS: Litigation; Municipal Law; Public Finance.
**Tsiros, Louis K.** ............ '62 '90 C.178 A.B. L.94 J.D. [Ⓐ Tharpe&H.]
*LANGUAGES: French and Spanish.
*PRACTICE AREAS: General Commercial Litigation; Insurance Coverage; Construction Law.
Tso, Jack B. ............ '31 '61 C.1043 B.A. L.426 LL.B. Supr. Ct. J.
Tso, Kerrin I. ............ '58 '83 C.605 A.B. L.426 J.D. Dep. City Atty.
**Tsuboi, Dahni K.** ............ '67 '92 C.914 B.A. L.976 J.D. [Ⓐ Tuttle&T.]
*LANGUAGES: Spanish.
Tsuda, Naomi C. ............ '58 '82 C.1109 B.A. L.1148 J.D. Atty., F.A.A.
Tsujimoto, Trude A. '53 '81 C.800 B.S. L.802 J.D.
Sr. V.P. & Assoc. Gen. Coun., Calif. Fed. Bk. FSB
**Tu, Lawrence P.** '54 '83 C&L.309 A.B., J.D.
(adm. in DC; not adm. in CA) [O'Melveny&M.] (⊙Hong Kong)
*LANGUAGES: Chinese (Mandarin).
*PRACTICE AREAS: Securities; Finance; Corporate Law; Project Finance; International Finance and Joint Ventures.
Tuan, Kuang-Sheng '52 '85 L.802 J.D.
(adm. in PA; not adm. in CA) Coun., Dossy Intl. Corp.
Tubert, Patricia V. ............ '52 '77 C.112 L.809 J.D. Mng. Asst. City Atty.
Tuch, Robert I. ............ '47 '74 C.112 B.A. L.1068 J.D. 840 Glenmere Way
**Tuchin, Michael L.** ............ '65 '90 C.813 A.B. L.1066 J.D. [Stutman,T.&G.]
*PRACTICE AREAS: Bankruptcy; Insolvency; Corporate Reorganization; Commercial Litigation.
Tuchman, Aviv L. ............ '62 '88 C.112 A.B. L.426 J.D. 12121 Wilshire Blvd.
**Tuck, Mary Agnes** ............ '71 '96 C.112 B.A. L.1068 J.D. [Ⓐ Lyon&L.]
*PRACTICE AREAS: Intellectual Property.
**Tucker, Brian J.** ............ '60 '93 C.602 B.A. L.426 J.D. [Ⓐ O'Donnell,R.&S.]
*PRACTICE AREAS: Litigation.

**Tucker, John A., Jr., (AV) '32 '61 C.813 A.B. L.208 J.D.**
**12th Floor, 800 Wilshire Boulevard, 90017**
**Telephone: 213-629-0060 FAX: 213-624-9441**
**(Also Of Counsel to Clark & Trevithick, A Professional Corporation).**
**Real Property, Estate Planning and Probate Law.**

***See Professional Biographies, LOS ANGELES, CALIFORNIA***

**Tucker, Robert M. '54 '81 C.112 A.B. L.809 J.D.**
**10940 Wilshire Boulevard, Suite 1500, 90024-3942**
**Telephone: 310-209-1000 Fax: 310-824-6400**
**Civil Litigation. Personal Injury, Negligence, Product Liability, Insurance, Subrogation and Business Litigation. Trials.**
**Reference: Metro Bank.**

**Tucker, Scot** ............ '60 '91 C.911 B.A. L.878 J.D. [Ⓐ Milbank,T.H.&M.]
**Tudzin, Lisa Schwartz** ............ '62 '87 C.112 B.A. L.800 J.D. [Ⓒ Stringfellow&Assoc.]
**Tudzin, Michael** ............ '61 '93 C.1077 B.S. L.1148 J.D. [Ⓐ Dennison,B.&P.]
**Tuffias, Heidi S.** ............ '66 '90 C.112 B.A. L.800 J.D. [Mosten&T.]
*PRACTICE AREAS: Family Law; Child Custody; Mediation; Representation of Children.
**Tufts, David W.** ............ '67 '95 C&L.101 B.S., J.D. [Ⓐ Sonnenschein N.&R.]
Tuggle, James H. ............ '42 '74 C.112 A.B. L.1068 J.D. 12400 Wilshire Blvd.
**Tuggy, Stephen A.** ............ '59 '85 C.937 B.A. L.1068 J.D. [Heller E.W.&M.]
*PRACTICE AREAS: Complex Commercial Litigation.
**Tujian, Tamar D.** ............ '67 '93 C.112 B.A. L.426 J.D. [Roper&F.]
*PRACTICE AREAS: Construction and Design; Insurance Defense Law; Public Entity Law; Litigation Defense; Wrongful Death Law.

**Tulac, John W.**
**(See Claremont)**

**Tuleja, Laurine E.** ............ '57 '91 C.309 A.B. L.1066 J.D. [Ⓐ Sidley&A.]
*PRACTICE AREAS: Environmental Law.
Tuller, Ronald A. ............ '39 '65 C.112 B.S. L.1068 LL.B. Asst. City Atty.
**Tully, W. Bradley**, (AV) ............ '57 '82 C.112 B.S. L.1068 J.D. [Hooper,L.&B.]
*PRACTICE AREAS: Healthcare Law; Hospital Law.
Tumonis, Elaine F. ............ '58 '86 C.976 B.A. L.1068 J.D. Dep. Atty. Gen.
**Tumpson, Albert J.** ............ '53 '77 C.112 A.B. L.1065 J.D. [Gabriel,H.&P.]
*LANGUAGES: French.
*PRACTICE AREAS: Banking, Commercial and Real Estate Litigation; Trials and Appeals; Receivership Law; Loan Workouts and Lending Transactions.
**Tune, Kenneth S.** ............ '45 '72 C.112 B.A. L.309 J.D. [Howarth&S.]
*PRACTICE AREAS: Appellate Practice; Complex Litigation.
Tunick, David C. ............ '40 '72 C.112 B.A. L.1068 J.D. Loyola Law School
Turchin, Carolyn ............ '45 '79 C.112 B.A. L.426 J.D. Chf. U.S. Mag. J.

Turetsky, Carol N. .............. '43 '82 C.1046 B.A. L.1148 J.D. 11340 W. Olympic Blvd.
**Turigliatto, Jon A.** .............................'66 '93 C.112 B.A. L.802 J.D. [Ⓐ Chapman&G.]
*PRACTICE AREAS: General Negligence; Professional Liability; Construction Litigation; Business Litigation; Commercial Litigation.
Turkat, Jennifer .............................'64 '90 C.103 A.B. L.424 J.D. Dep. Pub. Def.
Turkel, Dorothy G. '11 '35 C&L.477 B.A., J.D.
(adm. in MI; not adm. in CA) 11143 Montana‡
Turkell, Jeffrey A. ....................'60 '86 C.112 B.A. L.1065 J.D. 11766 Wilshire Blvd.
**Turken, James H.**, (AV) ..............'52 '79 C.426 B.S. L.809 J.D. [Buchalter,N.F.&Y.]
*PRACTICE AREAS: Civil Litigation.
**Turkowitz, Steven M.** ....................'46 '72 C.976 B.A. L.178 J.D. [S.M.Turkowitz]

**Turkowitz, Steven M., A Professional Corporation**
**1900 Avenue of the Stars, Suite 1800, 90067**
**Telephone: 310-788-0074 Telecopier: 310-788-0141**
**Steven M. Turkowitz.**
**Retail Development and Leasing, Land Use, Entitlements, Governmental Assistance, Environmental, Equity and Debt Financing, Joint Ventures, Partnerships and Limited Partnerships, Real Property Acquisition and Disposition, Commercial, Tenant Leases, Shopping Center Development and Corporate and Securities Law.**
***See Professional Biographies, LOS ANGELES, CALIFORNIA***

Turley, Paul W. ............................'38 '73 C.1259 B.A. L.966 J.D. Dep. Dist. Atty.
**Turnbull, Steven W.** ..........................'60 '89 C.101 B.S. L.911 J.D. [Ⓐ White&C.]
Turner, Barbara ..........................'50 '77 C.112 B.A. L.426 J.D. Deputy Dist. Atty.
Turner, Bonnie Kaye ..................'55 '79 C.112 B.A. L.800 J.D. First Interstate Bank
Turner, Cheryl C. ........................'— '87 C&L.800 J.D. 2049 Century Park E., 12th FL.
Turner, Ezra, Jr. ........................'27 '64 C.112 A.B. L.809 LL.B. 8700 S. Haas Ave.
**Turner, Glenn E., III** ......................'53 '80 C.36 B.S. L.990 J.D. [Gibbs,G.L.&A.]
*PRACTICE AREAS: Business Litigation; Commercial Law; Construction Law.
Turner, James C. '45 '70 C.659 B.S. L.884 J.D.
(adm. in PA; not adm. in CA) V.P., Taxation, Security First Grp., Inc.
**Turner, Jeffrey S.**, (AV) ..............'55 '79 C.383 B.A. L.228 J.D. [Ⓐ Brobeck,P.&H.]
*PRACTICE AREAS: Commercial Law; Banking Law; Financial Services Law; Loan Restructuring Law; Workouts Law.
Turner, Jonathan M. ....................'55 '81 C.147 B.A. L.1067 J.D. [Garfield,T.E.&T.]
Turner, Lawrence J. ....................'57 '84 C.1077 B.S. L.426 J.D. 9200 Sunset Blvd.
**Turner, Michael S.** ..........................'61 '87 C.112 B.A. L.426 J.D. [Hill,F.&B.]
*PRACTICE AREAS: Litigation; Mechanics Lien Law; Construction Law; Construction Litigation; Representation of Pest Control Operators.
Turner, Paul ............................'47 '73 C.1042 B.A. L.1068 J.D. Ct. of App. J.
**Turner, Richard C.** ........................'51 '77 C.112 B.A. L.426 J.D. [Spray,G.&B.]
Turner, Ronald S. ..................'59 '85 C.112 B.A. L.800 J.D. 11727 Barrington Ct.
Turner, Steven M. ....................'60 '86 C.112 B.A. L.426 J.D. 9200 Sunset Blvd.‡

**Turner, Gerstenfeld, Wilk, Aubert & Young, LLP**
**(See Beverly Hills)**

**Turovsky, Ronald B.** ......................'57 '83 C.112 B.A. L.1066 J.D. [Manatt,P.&P.]
*PRACTICE AREAS: Election and Governmental Litigation.
**Tuso, Tracy Michelle** ................'69 '95 C.426 B.A. L.809 J.D. [Ⓐ Engstrom,L.&L.]
Tussey, Linda Ann ....................'52 '77 C.112 B.A. L.809 J.D. Dep. Dist. Atty.
Tuttle, Kathleen J. ....................'53 '83 C.112 A.B. L.1066 J.D. Dist. Atty. Off.

**Tuttle & Taylor, A Law Corporation, (AV)** BB
**355 South Grand Avenue Fortieth Floor, 90071-3102**⊙
**Telephone: 213-683-0600 Facsimile: 213-683-0225**
**Edward W. Tuttle (1877-1960); Edward E. Tuttle (1907-1996); Robert G. Taylor; Merlin W. Call; Frank C. Christl; Patrick L. Shreve; C. David Anderson; Richard S. Berger; John R. Liebman; Alan E. Friedman; Timi Anyon Hallem; Charles L. Woltmann; Marjorie S. Steinberg; Douglas W. Beck; John Arthur Moe, II; Robert L. Shuler (Resident, Sacramento, California Office); Mark A. Borenstein; Nancy E. Howard; Marc L. Brown; Michael H. Bierman; Louis E. Kempinsky; Gordon A. Goldsmith; Gregory D. Schetina; Diann H. Kim; Marla J. Aspinwall; Robin D. Wiener (Resident, Sacramento, California Office); Laura J. Carroll; Edward A. Mendoza; Jeffrey D. Wexler; Julio A. Thompson;—John R. Dent; Sung H. Shin; Marnie S. Carlin; Kate Schneider Gold; Dahni K. Tsuboi; Andrea V. Ramos; Sam S. Oh; Sherry L. Appel; Malissia R. Lennox; Kathryn E. Olson; Thomas I. Dupuis; Shannon Sullivan Martinez; Dean A. Bochner; Steven M. Rogers; Jeffrey S. Karr. Of Counsel: Julian B. Heron, Jr. (Resident, Washington, D.C. Office); Phillip L. Fraas (Resident, Washington, D.C. Office); Pamela G. Bothwell.**
**General Practice. Corporation, Securities, Real Property, Bankruptcy and Insolvency, Taxation and Antitrust Law. General Civil Litigation in all State and Federal Courts. Agricultural and Cooperative Law. Administrative and Labor Relations Practice. Estate Planning, Probate and Trust Law. Environmental and Natural Resources and Insurance Law. International Law.**
**Reference: Union Bank, 455 South Figueroa Street, Main Office (Los Angeles, California).**
**Washington, D.C. Office: Tuttle, Taylor & Heron, 1025 Thomas Jefferson Street, N.W. 20007-5201. Telephone: 202-342-1300. Facsimile: 202-342-5880.**
**Sacramento, California Office: 1521 I Street, 95814-2016. Telephone: 916-441-2249. Facsimile: 916-441-2910.**
***See Professional Biographies, LOS ANGELES, CALIFORNIA***

**Tuverson, Arthur W., (P.C.)**, (AV) ..........'47 '70 C&L.800 A.B., J.D. [Tuverson&H.]
*PRACTICE AREAS: Managed Care Litigation; Medical and Legal Malpractice Defense; Insurance Defense Law; Casualty Insurance Law; General Negligence Trials and Appeals.

**Tuverson & Hillyard, (AV)**
**A Limited Liability Partnership, including Professional Corporations**
**12400 Wilshire Boulevard, Suite 900, 90025**⊙
**Telephone: 310-826-7855; 625-1234 Fax: 310-826-8738**
**Managing Partners of the Firm: Arthur W. Tuverson (P.C.) (Managing Partner, Los Angeles Office); Steven D. Hillyard (P.C.) (Managing Partner, Newport Beach Office); Jeffrey G. Keane (Managing Partner, Palm Springs Office); John T. Farmer (Managing Partner, San Diego Office). Partners of the Firm: Deborah deBoer (Resident Partner, Palm Springs Office); Jerry Wayne Howard (Resident Partner, Palm Springs Office); Richard G. Harris; Mark S. Siegel (Resident Partner, San Diego Office). Los Angeles Associates: Michael A. Coletti; Christopher A. Datomi; Mitchell L. Fenton; Bradley N. Gibson; Kevin Pauley Hillyer; Mario A. Iorillo; Harmon B. Levine; Michael J. Nuñez. Newport Beach Associates: Patricia Ann Carmichael; Peter A. Herzog; Margaret Krinsky; Brian M. Meadows; Geoffrey T. Moore; Charles J. Norek. Palm Springs Associates: Raymond E. Brown; Gregory E. Deetman; JoAnna D. Gorsage; Jennifer R. Johnson; Jack M. LaPedis (Palm Springs Office); Alexander R. Martinez (Palm Springs Office); Daniel P. Martz; Jennifer F. Swiller. San Diego Associates: Anthony T. Case; Marci S. Daniels; Mary Agnes Matyszewski; Renee J. Palermo; Jeffrey D. Schreiber; Jonathan M. Shiff; David C. Weber.**
**General Civil and Trial Practice in all State and Federal Courts. Medical and Legal Malpractice Defense, Public Entity Defense, Construction Defect and Construction Site Injury Defense, Personal Lines, Transactional Services, Asset Management, Lender Liability and Director's and Officer's Liability.**
**Newport Beach, California Office: 4675 MacArthur Court, Suite 650, Newport Beach, California 92660. Telephone: 714-752-7855. Fax: 714-752-5437.**
**Palm Springs, California Office: 1800 Tahquitz Canyon Way, Palm Springs, California 92263. Telephone: 619-322-7855. Fax: 619-322-5121.**
**San Diego, California Office: 4365 Executive Drive, Suite 700, San Diego, California 92121. Telephone: 619-452-7855. Fax: 619-452-2153.**
***See Professional Biographies, LOS ANGELES, CALIFORNIA***

**Tuvim, Mark B.** ........................'55 '92 C.575 B.A. L.1068 J.D. [Ⓐ Preston G.&E.]
*PRACTICE AREAS: Labor and Employment Law; General Litigation.
**Tuzon, Rita L.** ............................'59 '84 C.813 A.B. L.1066 J.D. [Troop M.S.&P.]
*PRACTICE AREAS: Entertainment Litigation; Commercial Litigation; Securities/Banking Litigation.
Twining, Joseph P. ....................'53 '78 C.951 B.A. L.818 J.D. 633 W. 5th St.
Twomey, Joseph G. ....................'26 '51 C&L.93 A.B., LL.B. 400 S. Hope St.
Twomey, Russell D., Jr. '29 '56
C&L.800 B.S., LL.B. Dep. Gen. Coun., Metro. Water Dist.
Twu, Jimmie Chin ....................'69 '94 C.112 B.A. L.1067 J.D. 1901 Ave. of the Stars
**Tyerman, Barry W.**, (AV) ........'47 '72 C.112 B.S. L.1068 J.D. [Armstrong H.J.T.&W.]
*PRACTICE AREAS: Motion Pictures; Music; Interactive Media.
**Tyler, Don F.**, (AV) ....................'06 '30 C.605 B.A. L.309 LL.B. [Walker,W.T.&W.] ‡
Tyler, Elizabeth Plott '62 '90 C.112 B.A. L.880 J.D.
Gen. Coun. & V.P. of Operations, Plott Mgmt. Corp.
Tyler, Sherie A. ....................'38 '77 C.763 L.1148 J.D. 1343 Kellam Ave.‡
Tyre, Milton S., (AV) ....................'17 '40 C.112 B.A. L.309 LL.B. [Tyre K.K.&G.]
Tyre Kamins Katz & Granof, A Law Corporation, (AV)
1840 Century Park, E. (⊙Nevada City, CA)
Tyrrell, Thomas M. ..................'48 '76 C.976 B.A. L.426 J.D. Princ. Dep. Co. Coun.
Tyson, Allan S. ..........................'47 '72 C.1077 B.A. L.1068 J.D. Dep. Dist. Atty.
**Tyson, Robert F., Jr.** ..........................'64 '90 C&L.884 B.S., J.D. [Ⓐ Booth,M.&S.]
Tyson, Rosalind R. '48 '79 C.276 B.S. L.813 J.D.
Assoc. Reg. Dir. for Regul., Secs. & Exch. Comm.
Tyson, Sandra Lee ..........................................'34 '79 L.1136 LL.B. [S.L.Tyson]
**Tyson, Timothy T.** ........'43 '77 C.880 B.A. L.809 J.D. [Freilich,H.&R.] (See Pat. Sect.)
*PRACTICE AREAS: Patent, Trademark and Copyright Law; Trademark Law; Copyright Law; Litigation; Licensing Law.
Tyson, Sandra Lee, A Law Corporation ................2049 Century Park East Suite 2050
**Tyukody, Daniel J.** ..........................'56 '86 C.228 B.S. L.145 J.D. [Brobeck,P.&H.]
*PRACTICE AREAS: Litigation; Securities Law; Antitrust Law; Patent Law; Insurance Law.
Uchima, Kei ..........................'25 '51 C.112 B.S. L.800 LL.B. 321 E. 2nd St.
**Udell, Jonathan** ..........................'44 '83 C.112 B.A. L.426 J.D. [Ⓐ D.B.Bloom]
**Udovic, Kimberly Ann** ..................'68 '93 C.659 B.S. L.145 J.D. [Ⓐ Gibson,D.&C.]
*PRACTICE AREAS: Litigation; Copyright and Trademark Litigation.
**Udovic, Michael S.** ....................'66 '91 C.605 A.B. L.426 J.D. [Ⓐ Gibson,D.&C.]
Uhl, Robert A., (AV) ....................'46 '76 C.665 B.A. L.262 J.D. [R.A.Uhl]
Uhl, Robert A., Inc., (AV) ..........................................9255 Sunset Blvd., Ste. 411
**Uhland, Suzzanne** ....................'62 '88 C.813 A.B. L.976 J.D. [O'Melveny&M.]
*LANGUAGES: Spanish, Italian and Latin.
*PRACTICE AREAS: Bankruptcy Law.
Ukai, Clara A. M. ....................'61 '85 C.800 B.A. L.1066 J.D. Paramount Pictures Corp.
**Ukropina, James R.**, (AV) ..............'37 '66 C.813 A.B. L.800 LL.B. [O'Melveny&M.]
*PRACTICE AREAS: Corporate Law.
**Ulin, John C.** ..........................'65 '93 C.103 A.B. L.1068 J.D. [Ⓐ Munger,T.&O.]
*LANGUAGES: French.
Ullerich, Henry G. ....................'31 '60 C.352 B.A. L.1066 LL.B. Dep. Atty. Gen.
**Ullman, Ian C.** ..........................'68 '94 C.112 B.A. L.426 J.D. [Ⓐ Cummins&W.]
*PRACTICE AREAS: Insurance Coverage; Subrogation.
Ullman, Richard A. ....................'46 '71 C.800 B.A. L.426 J.D. Int. Rev. Serv.
Ulman, Edward S. ....................'36 '63 C.112 B.A. L.1068 LL.B. 3738 Degman Blvd.
**Ulman, Lawrence J.**, (AV) ..............'50 '75 C&L.800 A.B., J.D. [Gibson,D.&C.]
*PRACTICE AREAS: Entertainment; Banking; Commercial Law.
**Um, William T.** ..........................'67 '93 C.112 B.A. L.94 J.D. [Ⓐ Troop M.S.&P.]
*LANGUAGES: Korean.
*PRACTICE AREAS: Commercial Litigation; Insurance Coverage Litigation; General Business Litigation.
Umanoff, Adam S. ....................'59 '83 C.188 B.S. L.178 J.D. Gen. Coun., Zond Corp.
**Umansky, Michael M.**, (AV) ..............'41 '67 C.659 B.S.E. L.309 J.D. [Stroock&S.&L.]
*PRACTICE AREAS: Corporate Law; Securities Law; Acquisitions, Divestitures and Mergers Law.
**Ung, Diane** ..........................'63 '93 C.668 B.A. L.426 J.D. [Ⓐ Foley L.W.&A.]
*PRACTICE AREAS: Hospitals; Health Care Legislation; Medicare and Medicaid.
Ung, Sheree S. ..........................'55 '85 C.112 B.S. L.93 J.D. 400 S. Hope St.
**Ungerer, Phyllis**, (AV) ..............'46 '73 C.289 A.B. L.1065 J.D. [Kamine,S.&U.]
*REPORTED CASES: Wang v. Division of Labor (1990) 219 CA3d 1152.
*PRACTICE AREAS: Construction.
Unickel, Sidney J. ....................'07 '31 C&L.800 B.A., LL.B. 10501 Wilshire Blvd.‡
Unruh, Janet Carr '50 '81
C.112 B.A. L.809 J.D. Coun., Transamerica Occidental Life Ins. Co.
Unterberger, Howard J. ..............'55 '80 C.659 B.A. L.309 J.D. 1801 Century Park, E.
Unterman, Thomas, (AV) '44 '70
C.674 A.B. L.145 J.D. Sr. V.P. & CFO, The Times Mirror Co.
**Upton, Christine S.** ....................'45 '80 C.112 B.A. L.809 J.D. [Ⓐ King,W.E.&B.]
*PRACTICE AREAS: Civil Trials; Real Estate.
Urbach, Alex S., (AV) ........'36 '62 C.112 B.A. L.800 LL.B. Prob. Atty., L.A. Supr. Ct.
**Urban, David A.** ....................'65 '92 C.228 B.S. L.1068 J.D. [Ⓐ Sheppard,M.R.&H.]
**Urbanic, James** ....................'64 '92 C.112 B.A. L.990 J.D. [Ⓐ Manning,M.&W.]
*PRACTICE AREAS: Insurance Defense.
Urgo, John Francis ..........................'54 '80 C.1139 B.A. L.809 J.D. Dep. Dist. Atty.
**Uriarte, Robert G.**, (AV) ..............'55 '83 C.426 A.B. L.1068 J.D. [Markowitz,F.&U.]
*LANGUAGES: Spanish.
*PRACTICE AREAS: Creditor's Rights; Bankruptcy; Commercial Litigation.
**Uribe, J. A.**, (AV) ....................'42 '67 C.178 A.B. L.1065 J.D. [MacArthur,U.H.&M.]
**Uribe, Steven C.** ....................'67 '95 C.1168 B.A. L.178 J.D. [Ⓐ Hancock R.&B.]
Urick, Lisa G. ..........................'58 '91 C.914 B.A. L.426 J.D. 633 W. 5th St.
**Urquhart, A. William**, (AV) ..............'47 '79 C&L.262 B.A., J.D. [Quinn E.U.&O.]
*PRACTICE AREAS: Intellectual Property; Unfair Competition; General Commercial Litigation; Government Contracts and Regulations; Antitrust Law.
**Urwin, Gary L.** ..........................'55 '82 C.604 B.A. L.1068 J.D. [Ⓐ White&C.]
**Usdan, Steven** ..........................'72 '95 C.978 B.A. L.112 J.D. [Ⓐ Munger,T.&O.]
**Usher, Harry L.**, (AV) ..............'39 '65 C.103 A.B. L.813 LL.B. [Ⓐ Milbank,T.H.&M.]
**Usher, Richard S.** ....................'52 '77 C.473 B.A. L.1068 J.D. [Furman U.]
*PRACTICE AREAS: General Corporate; Acquisitions and Mergers; Environmental; Real Estate; Employment Benefits.
**Uwechue-Akpati, Chinye** ....................'62 '93 L.054 LL.B. [Ⓐ Cummins&W.]
*PRACTICE AREAS: Environmental Coverage.
Uyeda, James A. ....................'47 '72 C.112 B.A. L.1068 J.D. Calif. Appl. Project

**Uyeda, James S. '59 '85 C.112 B.A. L.1068 J.D.**
**Suite 2700, 445 South Figueroa Street, 90071**
**Telephone: 213-489-6873 Fax: 213-489-6891**
***LANGUAGES: Japanese.**
**Civil Litigation, Real Estate, Construction, Commercial Law, Corporate Formation and Transactions, Personal Injury, Wills and Trusts.**

**Uyeda, Mark T.** ..........................'70 '95 C.276 B.S.B.A. L.228 J.D. [Ⓐ O'Melveny&M.]
Uyekawa, Karen C. ....................'50 '79 C.1042 B.A. L.112 J.D. Law Clk. to Dist. Ct. J.
Vacca, John J., (AV) ....................'43 '69 C.1077 B.A. L.426 J.D. Pub. Def. Off.
**Vacchio, Michael A.** ....................'58 '83 C.940 B.A. L.1065 J.D. [Morgan,L.&B.]
**Vadon, Michele R.** ....................'52 '82 C.112 B.A. L.426 J.D. [Burke,W.&S.]
*PRACTICE AREAS: Civil Rights Litigation; Municipal Law; Municipal Litigation; Tort Litigation.
Vahan, Randolph K. ..............'42 '67 C&L.813 B.A., LL.B. 11661 San Vicente Blvd.
Vahid-Tehrani, Guita '62 '92 C.112 B.A. L.1148 J.D.
(adm. in PA; not adm. in CA) U.S. Dept. of Jus.
Vahradian, Mark H. ..............'67 '92 C.228 B.A. L.1068 J.D. 10454 Ashton Ave.‡

CAA357P

**Vaill, Edward Everett** ......................'40 '66 C.165 A.B. L.145 J.D. [Shaub&W.]
*REPORTED CASES: Scranton v. Litton Industries Leasing Corporation, 494 F.2d 778 (5th Cir., 1974), cert. den., 95 Sup. Ct. 774 (1975).
*TRANSACTIONS: Successfully concluded 23 negotiations with the Federal Trade Commission or the Antitrust Division, including all Hart-Scott-Rodino Premerger Notification filings.
*PRACTICE AREAS: Litigation; Insurance Coverage; Tax; International Insurance Transactions; Foreign Joint Venture Laws.
**Vaisbort, Edward D.**, (AV) ............. '64 '88 C.1077 B.S. L.1065 J.D. [Knopfler&R.]
*LANGUAGES: Spanish.
*PRACTICE AREAS: Business Litigation; Real Estate Litigation and Transactions; Environmental law; Construction Litigation; Insurance Law.
Vakili, Sa'id ..................................'63 '94 C.1040 B.A. L.1325 J.D. [Vakili&L.]
Vakili & Leus .............................................................3701 Wilshire Blvd.
**Valayre, Roland** .........................'50 '92 C.053 B.A. L.569 J.D. [Ⓐ Folger L.&K.]⊙

**Valdivia, Jeannette E., Law Offices of**
(See Pasadena)

**Vale, Stephen E.** '53 '81 C.1103 B.B.A. L.184 J.D.
(adm. in CT; not adm. in CA) Mng. Dir. & Reg. Coun., Kroll Assocs., Inc.
Valencia, M. Guadalupe ................ '56 '89 C.426 B.A. L.1065 J.D. 444 S. Flower St.
**Valencia, Robert R.** ............... '65 '94 C.1074 B.S.B.A. L.990 J.D. [Ⓐ McKenna&C.]
*PRACTICE AREAS: Litigation; Health Care.
**Valencia, Vicente, Jr.** .....................'58 '91 C&L.462 B.A., J.D. [Ⓐ Black C.H.&L.]
*LANGUAGES: Spanish.
*PRACTICE AREAS: Insurance Coverage; Coverage Litigation; Bad Faith Litigation.
**Valensi, Stephen G.**, (AV) .............. '18 '49 C.112 A.B. L.426 J.D. [Valensi,R.&M.]
*PRACTICE AREAS: Real Estate Law; General Business Law.

**Valensi, Rose & Magaram, Professional Law Corporation, (AV)**
**Suite 1000, 1800 Avenue of the Stars, 90067-4212**
**Telephone: 310-277-8011 Cable Address: "Valerose" Telecopier: 310-277-1706**
**Kenneth L. Heisz; Margaret E. Lennon; Philip S. Magaram (Certified Specialist, Taxation Law, The State Bar of California Board of Legal Specialization); Warren K. Miller; Michael R. Morris (Certified Specialist, Taxation Law, The State Bar of California Board of Legal Specialization); M. Laurie Murphy; Sidney R. Rose; Mark Halliwell Smith; Stephen G. Valensi; Elizabeth Allen White;—David Halm; Geraldine A. Wyle.**
**General Business, Corporate, Real Estate, Tax, Labor and Entertainment Law, Related Civil Trial, Appellate, Arbitration and Administration Hearing Practice concerning: Mergers and Acquisitions, Business Agreements and Licenses, Corporate Securities and Corporate Finance, Real Estate Purchases, Sales, Development and Finance, Federal, State and Local Taxation, Estate, Gift and Asset Protection Planning, Trusts and Probate, Secured Transactions, Creditors Rights, Employer and Employee Representation, Wrongful Termination and Discrimination Matters, Music and Copyright Law and Related Entertainment Matters.**
***See Professional Biographies, LOS ANGELES, CALIFORNIA***

**Valenzuela, Jacqueline I.**, (BV) .............. '52 '76 C.112 B.A. L.1049 J.D. [Arter&H.]
Valenzuela, Manuel A., Jr. ............. '55 '87 C.112 B.A. L.809 J.D. Sr. Dep. Co. Coun.
**Valeriano, Gary J.** ................... '52 '79 C.1077 B.A. L.426 J.D. [Anderson,M.&C.]
**Valerio Barrad, Catherine M.** ........... '60 '93 C.112 B.A. L.597 J.D. [Ⓐ Sidley&A.]
*LANGUAGES: Spanish.
*PRACTICE AREAS: Litigation; Appellate.
Valinoti, James R. ................ '64 '93 C.1019 B.B.A. L.809 J.D. 1200 Wilshire Blvd.
**Valle, Jeffrey B.** ........................'55 '83 C.112 B.A. L.1066 J.D. [Skadden,A.S.M.&F.]
**Vallejos, William A.** .................'58 '89 C.1168 B.A. L.1068 J.D. [Ⓐ Burke,W.&S.]
*PRACTICE AREAS: Municipal Law; Land Use Law; Police Malpractice Defense.
**Vallens, Howard S.** ................... '60 '86 C.154 B.A. L.464 J.D. [Celebrezze&W.]⊙
*LANGUAGES: Danish.
Vallette, Diane Lynn ........................'54 '81 C.553 B.A. L.1148 J.D. [Moray&V.]
Vallier, Thomas R. .................'55 '85 C.112 B.A. L.426 J.D. 2049 Century Park E.
Valner, Rudy ..................... '60 '89 C.112 B.A. L.426 J.D. 10100 Santa Monica Blvd.
Van Antwerp, L. Walker, III ............ '59 '84 C.878 B.A. L.800 J.D. 3325 Wilshire Blvd.
**Vance, Kathleen Caswell** ........... '61 '87 C&L.426 B.A., J.D. [Ⓒ Sedgwick,D.M.&A.]
**Van Dalsem, Bruce E.** ........................... '61 '86 L.999 LL.B. [Gradstein,L.&V.]
van Dam, M. Nicole ..................... '62 '89 C.659 B.A. L.800 J.D. 1055 W. 7th St.
Van De Bunt, Bennet M. ........'62 '87 C.112 B.A. L.309 J.D. 8th Fl., 515 S. Figueroa St.
**Van De Kamp, John K.**, (AV) ............. '36 '60 C.197 B.A. L.813 LL.B. [Ⓒ Dewey B.]
*PRACTICE AREAS: Litigation.
**Vandenburg, Thomas F.** ..................'66 '92 C&L.893 B.A., J.D. [Ⓐ Howarth&S.]
**Vanderbilt, Christine L.** ...............'53 '77 C.293 B.A. L.800 J.D. [Ⓐ Chapman&G.]
*PRACTICE AREAS: Professional Liability; Insurance Coverage Litigation; Business and Commercial Litigation.
**Vanderet, Robert C.**, (AV) ........... '47 '73 C.112 A.B. L.813 J.D. [O'Melveny&M.]
*REPORTED CASES: Crane vs. Arizona Republic, 729 F.Supp. 698 (C.D.Cal.1989); Fresno Rifle and Pistol Club vs. Van de Kamp, 965 F.2d 723 (9th Cir. 1992); Galloway vs. CBS, 18 Med.L.Rep. 1161 (Cal. App. 1987); Kruse vs. Bank of America, 202 Cal.App.3d 38 (1988); Maheu vs. CBS, 201 Cal.App.3d 662 (1988).
*PRACTICE AREAS: First Amendment Litigation; Securities Litigation; Media Law; Libel, Slander and Defamation.
Vanderford, Maile P. ..................'62 '87 C.112 B.A. L.464 J.D. [Ⓐ Chase,R.D.&B.]
**Vanderford, Ty S.** ..............................'63 '87 C.800 B.A. L.464 J.D. [Mendes&M.]
*LANGUAGES: French and Russian.
Vanderhorst, Joseph A. '56 '82 C.112 A.B. L.426 J.D.
Dep. Coun., Metropolitan Water Dist. of Southern Calif.
**Vanderlaan, Christopher A.** '65 '91 C.112 B.S. L.1065 J.D.
[Lyon&L.] (See Pat. Sect.)
*PRACTICE AREAS: Intellectual Property.
Vandernat, Ray F. .................. '50 '78 C.1109 B.A. L.1137 J.D. 1626 Beverly Blvd.
**Vanderziel, Kathleen M.** ................ '64 '92 C.112 B.A. L.93 J.D. [Ⓐ Gibson,D.&C.]
*PRACTICE AREAS: Labor and Employment.
**Vandevelde, John D.**, (AV) ............'46 '75 C.1075 B.S. L.426 J.D. [Talcott,L.V.&S.]
*PRACTICE AREAS: Criminal Defense Law; Civil Litigation; Appellate Law.
Vandever, James D. '50 '75
C.112 B.A. L.1068 J.D. V.P. & Tax Coun., The Decurion Corp.
Van Dueck, Ralph A. .................. '57 '85 C.112 B.A. L.990 J.D. 4700 Wilshire Blvd.
**Van Dyke, Patricia A.** ................. '58 '83 C.645 B.S. L.910 J.D. [Ⓒ Jones,D.R.&P.]
**Vane, Jennifer A.** ......................'65 '90 C.602 B.A. L.800 J.D. [Ⓐ Hancock R.&B.]
Van Etten, David B. .................. '56 '81 C.424 B.A. L.276 J.D. 725 S. Figueroa St.
**Vangel, John T.** ..................... '61 '96 C.309 A.B. L.178 J.D. [Ⓐ Pillsbury M.&S.]
**Van Gelderen, Michele R.** ..................'68 '94 C.813 L.1066 J.D. [Goldberg&S.]
*PRACTICE AREAS: Commercial Litigation; Entertainment Litigation; Real Estate Litigation.
**van Ginkel, Eric**, (AV⊕) ....................... '39 '73 L.061 J.D. [Ⓒ Alschuler G.&P.]
*LANGUAGES: Dutch, French, German, Italian.
**Van Horn, Paul E.** '66 '95 C.976 B.A. L.178 J.D.
(adm. in NY; not adm. in CA) [Ⓐ Quinn E.U.&O.]
**Van Horn, Thomas H.** '63 '89 C.586 B.A. L.744 J.D.
(adm. in TX; not adm. in CA) [Ⓐ Lane P.S.L.]
*PRACTICE AREAS: Litigation.
**Van Horst, Jeannette Lynne** ....... '54 '93 C.267 B.S. L.809 J.D. [Ⓐ Bonne,B.M.O.&N.]
**Vanic, Michael A.**, (AV) ......................'48 '76 C.800 A.B. L.426 J.D. [Reish&L.]
*REPORTED CASES: Swoboda vs. Pala Min., Inc. 844 F.2d 654 (9th Cir. 1988); Seedman vs. U.S. District Court for the Cent. Dist. of California, 837 F.2d 413 (9th Cir. 1988); Columbus Line, Inc. vs. Gray Line Sight-Seeing Companies Associated, Inc., 120 Cal. App. 3d 622, 174 Cal. Rptr. 527 (1981); and Merry vs. Coast Community College Dist., 97 Cal. App. 3d 214, 158 Cal. Rptr. 603 (1979).
*PRACTICE AREAS: Appellate; Business; ERISA Litigation.

**van Krieken, Lisa McCabe** ............'57 '85 C.112 B.A. L.1066 J.D. [Folger L.&K.]⊙
Van Kula, George, III .............................'63 '88 C.602 B.A. L.477 J.D. 633 W. 5th St.
**Van Le, Jenny** ........................... '61 '85 C&L.813 B.A., J.D. [Ⓐ Saltzburg,R.&B.]
*LANGUAGES: French and Vietnamese.
*PRACTICE AREAS: Business Transactions; Real Estate Law.
**Van Lochem, Michael D.** ..............'59 '83 C.112 B.A. L.426 J.D. [Manning,L.B.&B.]
*PRACTICE AREAS: Automotive Dealer Law; Civil Trial; Bankruptcy; Commercial Law.
**Vann, Bruce P.** ....................................'55 '80 C.910 A.B. L.228 J.D. [Kelly&L.]
*PRACTICE AREAS: Corporate Law; Securities Offerings; Secured Lending.
**Van Oosterhout, Lori A.** ..................'60 '91 C.37 B.S. L.1067 J.D. [Ⓐ Wolf,R.&S.]
*LANGUAGES: French.
*PRACTICE AREAS: Real Estate Litigation; Business Litigation.
**Van Patten, Anthony J., (P.C.)**, (AV) ..... '32 '63 C.112 A.B. L.1066 LL.B. [Arndt&V.]
*LANGUAGES: Japanese, Chinese.
*REPORTED CASES: Ministry of Defense of Islamic Republic of Iran v. Gould, Inc. 969 F.2d 764, 9th Cir., 1992. Counsel for Republic of Iran.
*PRACTICE AREAS: Intellectual Property; Corporate Law; International Law.
**Van Patten, Russell L., Jr.** ......... '60 '87 C.813 B.S. L.976 J.D. [Sanders,B.G.S.&M.]
**Van Pelt, David T.** ................. '64 '93 C.189 B.A. L.228 J.D. [Ⓐ Seyfarth,S.F.&G.]
Van Petten, H. O, (AV) ....................'20 '50 C&L.813 A.B., LL.B. [Van Petten&H.]
Van Petten & Holen, (AV) ...................................................900 Wilshire Blvd.
**VanRiper, Michele** .......... '67 '92 C.1049 B.A. L.426 J.D [Ⓐ Breidenbach,B.H.H.&H.]
**Van Sickle, Barry** ..................................'51 '78 C.490 B.S. L.1035 J.D. [Hill,F.&B.]
*PRACTICE AREAS: FELA; Railroad Accidents and Injuries; Commercial Litigation; Contract Litigation; Professional Liability.
Van Sloten, Richard R. ............. '47 '77 C.1097 B.A. L.426 J.D. 6675 Northside Dr.
Van Steenburg, Mark '55 '84 C.546 B.S. L.1187 J.D.
(adm. in MI; not adm. in CA) FBI
**Van Steenwyk, Cheryl L.** ............... '58 '85 C.112 B.A. L.464 J.D. [Ⓐ Katten M.&Z.]
*PRACTICE AREAS: Litigation; Real Estate.
**Van Vleck, Brian** .................................'66 '91 C.112 B.A. L.1065 J.D. [Ⓐ Graham&J.]
**Van Wyngarden, Thomas L.** '62 '87
C.112 B.A. L.1065 J.D. [McClintock,W.B.R.R.&M.]
*PRACTICE AREAS: Environmental and Commercial Litigation; Toxic Torts; Environmental Insurance Coverage Litigation.
**Van Zyl, Leslie G.** ....................... '61 '91 C.1074 B.A. L.1065 J.D. [Ⓐ Hill,F.&B.]
*PRACTICE AREAS: Federal Employers Liability Act Defense; Rail Freight Damage/Loss Defense; Business Litigation.
Varat, Jonathan .........................'45 '73 C&L.659 B.A., J.D. Prof. of Law, U.C.L.A.
Varela, Jose H. ..................................'56 '87 C.740 B.A. L.1066 J.D. Pub. Def.‡
**Varga, Jeffrey G.**, (AV) ................ '50 '78 C.112 B.A. L.1049 J.D. [Ⓒ Paul,H.J.&W.]
Varga, Stephen A. ......................'54 '80 C.813 B.A. L.426 J.D. 221 N. Figueroa St.
Vargas, Fernando D. .................'60 '87 C.209 B.A. L.464 J.D. 1625 W. Olympic Blvd.
Vargas-Rodriguez, Maria C. ........'48 '79 C.112 B.A. L.426 J.D. 1605 W. Olympic Blvd.
**Varnen, Craig** ...............................'68 '94 C.112 B.A. L.1066 J.D. [Ⓐ Irell&M.]
**Varner, Carlton A.**, (AV) ............'47 '72 C.352 B.A. L.494 J.D. [Sheppard,M.R.&H.]
*PRACTICE AREAS: Business Litigation; Antitrust Law.
**Varner, Sean S.** ........................'66 '93 C.112 B.A. L.990 J.D. [Ⓐ Ropers,M.K.&B.]
*PRACTICE AREAS: Corporate Transactions.
Vasegh, Donna ............. '63 '89 C.112 B.A. L.990 J.D. 16633 Ventura Blvd. (Encino)
**Vasquez, Aurora** ......................................... '61 '88 C.426 B.A. L.1137 J.D. [Ibold&A.]
*LANGUAGES: Spanish.
**Vasquez, Teri L.** ..................... '67 '94 C.112 B.A. L.1068 J.D. [Ⓐ Thelen,M.J.&B.]
*PRACTICE AREAS: Insurance Litigation; Civil Litigation.
Vassallo, Stephanie C. .................. '64 '91 C&L.846 B.A., J.D. 10940 Wilshire Blvd.
Vassolo, Ruben A. ..................... '60 '87 C.112 A.B.Ec. L.309 J.D. 550 S. Hope St.
Vastano, Patrick G. ...................... '58 '85 C.994 B.S. L.990 J.D. [Vastano&A.]
Vastano & Angarella ........................................................ 12121 Wilshire Blvd.
**Vaughan, Barry C.** ...................... '50 '81 C.174 B.A. L.145 J.D. [Ⓒ Gibbs,G.L.&A.]
*PRACTICE AREAS: Business Litigation; Construction Litigation; Environmental.
**Vaughey, Karen E.** ........................ '66 '95 C.813 B.A. L.426 J.D. [Ⓐ Lewis,D.B.&B.]
*LANGUAGES: French.
Vaughn, Bari L. ........................ '56 '85 C.112 B.A. L.800 J.D. 1900 Ave. of the Stars
**Vaughn, James D.** ................... '67 '93 C.276 B.S. L.1066 J.D. [De Castro,W.&C.]
*PRACTICE AREAS: Business Litigation; Real Estate Litigation.
**Vaughn, William W.**, (AV) ........'30 '56 C.813 A.B. L.1068 LL.B. [Ⓒ O'Melveny&M.]
*PRACTICE AREAS: Litigation.
**Vaynerov, Maxim** ......................'69 '95 C&L.112 B.A., J.D. [Ⓐ Berger,K.S.M.F.S.&G.]
*LANGUAGES: Russian.
Vazquez, Mario F. .....................'46 '80 C.1097 B.S. L.1068 J.D. 1557 W. Beverly Blvd.
Veatch, Wayne, (AV) .................. '05 '35 C.629 B.A. L.1065 J.D. 3926 Wilshire Blvd.

**Veatch, Carlson, Grogan & Nelson, (AV)** BB
**A Partnership including a Professional Corporation**
**3926 Wilshire Boulevard, 90010**
**Telephone: 213-381-2861 Telefax: 213-383-6370**
**Members of Firm: James C. Galloway, Jr. (A Professional Corporation); Anthony D. Seine; Mark A. Weinstein; John A. Peterson; Gordon F. Sausser; Thomas M. Phillips; Amy W. Lyons; Michael Eric Wasserman; Michael A. Kramer. Associates: Hollis O. Dyer; Mark M. Rudy; D. Michael Bush; André S. Goodchild; Kevin L. Henderson; Gilbert A. Garcia; William G. Lieb; Dawn M. Costello; Daniel R. Brown; Stephen D. Enerle; John J. Nolan, III; Steven W. Sedach; Joan E. Hewitt; Joanne M. Andrew. Of Counsel: David J. Aisenson (Judge Retired); Lyn A. Woodward.**
**General Civil and Trial Practice, State and Federal Courts. Insurance and Healthcare Law.**
***See Professional Biographies, LOS ANGELES, CALIFORNIA***

Veenhuis, Diana .................. '48 '79 C.112 B.A. L.800 J.D. 800 S. Robertson Blvd.
**Veenhuis, Eugene H., (A Professional Corporation)**, (AV) '44 '71
C.494 B.S. L.813 J.D. [Mitchell,S.&K.]
*PRACTICE AREAS: Taxation Law; ERISA; Business Planning Law.
**Vega, Mark A.** ...................................'63 '92 C&L.37 B.A., J.D. [Ⓒ Daniels,B.&F.]
*PRACTICE AREAS: Entertainment Litigation; Intellectual Property; Media and First Amendment.
Vega, Xavier J. .......................................... '55 '80 C.813 B.A. L.770 J.D. I.R.S.
**Veis, David C.** .............................'53 '78 C.112 B.A. L.800 J.D. [Robins,K.M.&C.]
*PRACTICE AREAS: General Corporate; Insurance; Intellectual Property Law; Litigation.
**Veis, Susan J.** .......................... '55 '88 C.112 B.A. L.990 J.D. [Ⓐ Dummit,F.&B.]
Velarde, Carlos E. ......................................'29 '60 C.1043 L.800 J.D. Supr. Ct. J.
**Velarde, Jasmin A.** ..........................'68 '93 C.112 B.A. L.904 J.D. [Ⓐ Ives,K.&D.]
Velasco, Rolando N. ............................. '38 '92 L.061 LL.B. 3325 Wilshire Blvd.
Velazquez, Sharyn ................'43 '88 C.1163 B.S. L.1137 J.D. 210 W. Temple St.
Velkei, Steven A. .................'65 '92 C.674 B.A. L.1065 J.D. 725 S. Figueroa St.
**Vella, Debra J.** ......................... '65 '96 C.763 A.B. L.112 J.D. [Ⓐ O'Melveny&M.]
**Vella, Vivienne Angela** ................'64 '89 C.112 B.A. L.1066 J.D. [Ⓐ Gibson,D.&C.]
*PRACTICE AREAS: Intellectual Property/Media Law.
**Velladao, Michael R.** .................'58 '83 C.767 B.A. L.990 J.D. [Sedgwick,D.M.&A.]
**Vels, Jamie L.** ............................ '65 '91 C.112 B.S. L.426 J.D. [Ⓐ Lynberg&W.]
*LANGUAGES: Spanish.
*PRACTICE AREAS: Insurance Coverage; Insurance Defense (Bad Faith).
**Veltkamp, Julie A.** ......................'64 '91 C.879 B.A. L.990 J.D. [Ⓐ Lewis,D.B.&B.]
**Vena, David H.**, (AV) .....................'38 '65 C.112 A.B. L.309 LL.B. [Latham&W.]
**Venderbush, David R.** ................ '63 '89 C.976 B.A. L.813 J.D. [Ⓐ Brobeck,P.&H.]
*PRACTICE AREAS: Appellate; Mass Tort Litigation.

**Vendler, Xianchun J.** ....................'63 '95 L.426 J.D. [[A] Christensen,M.F.J.G.W.&S.]
*LANGUAGES: Mandarin Chinese.
*PRACTICE AREAS: Corporate Law; Securities Law.
**Venegas, Patricia** ........................'58 '88 C.1097 B.S. L.1068 J.D. [[A] Argue P.H.&M.]
*PRACTICE AREAS: Civil Litigation.
**Venger, Leonard D.**, (AV) ...............'42 '67 C.112 B.A. L.1068 J.D. [Manatt,P.&P.]
*PRACTICE AREAS: Business Litigation.
Venturi, Greg J. ..........................'40 '65 C.112 A.B. L.1068 J.D. Mission Ins. Co.
Vera, Hernan D. ...........................'70 '94 C.813 A.B. L.112 J.D. 400 S. Hope St.
**Verboon, Gary W.** ..................'57 '81 C.1232 B.A. L.990 J.D. [Verboon,W.H.&P.]
*PRACTICE AREAS: Construction Defect Litigation.

**Verboon, Whitaker, Hartmann & Peter, LLP**
**11100 Santa Monica Boulevard, Suite 1950, 90025-3384**
**Telephone: 310-445-5447 Facsimile: 310-445-9176**
**Gary W. Verboon; Michael T. Whitaker; Ronald A. Hartmann; Alois Peter, Jr.; M. Thereza Braga (Not admitted in CA); Fred Adelman; Mark Milstein.**
**Construction Defect Litigation.**
*See Professional Biographies, LOS ANGELES, CALIFORNIA*

**Veregge, Peter S.** ............................'58 '91 C.112 B.A. L.425 J.D. [[A] Howrey&S.]
*PRACTICE AREAS: Environmental.
Ver Halen, Peter C., (Law Corporation) '42 '68 C.426 B.A. L.1068 J.D.
[Crahan,J.&V.H.]
**Verhoeven, Charles K.** ..................'63 '89 C&L.352 B.B.A., J.D. [Quinn E.U.&O.]
*PRACTICE AREAS: General Commercial Litigation; Intellectual Property; Unfair Competition; Real Property Litigation; Antitrust Law.
Vernon, James F. ...................................'49 '75 C&L.813 B.S., J.D. 607 S. Hill St.‡
Veron, Juaneita M. .............................'25 '51 C&L.800 B.A., J.D. Mun. Ct. J.‡
Verrone, Patric M. ..............................'59 '84 C.309 B.A. L.93 J.D. 6466 Odin St.
Vertun, Alan S. ...................................'51 '76 C.112 A.B. L.809 J.D. [A.S.Vertun]
Vertun, Alan S., A Prof. Law Corp. ...................................4250 Wilshire Blvd.
Vezzani, Diane L. ..................................'44 '80 C.489 L.1136 Dep. Dist. Atty.
**Viau, Jeanette L.** ...................'60 '86 C.112 B.A. L.426 J.D. [[A] Sedgwick,D.M.&A.]
**Vick, Jonathan S.** ...................................'60 '87 C&L.990 B.A., J.D. [Knopfler&R.]
*PRACTICE AREAS: Construction Law; Wage and Hour Law; Occupational Safety and Health Law; Oil and Gas Litigation.
**Vick, Scott** ..............................'67 '94 C.267 B.A. L.426 J.D. [[A] Milbank,T.H.&M.]
**Vickers, Raymond W.** '43 '69 C&L.309 A.B., LL.B.
(adm. in NY; not adm. in CA) [Skadden,A.S.M.&F.]
Vickers, Thomas H. ...........................'35 '85 C.930 B.A. L.426 J.D. [Morgan&W.]
Vickman, James A. ...............'59 '87 C.112 B.A. L.800 J.D. 11845 West Olympic Blvd.
Victor, Alan E. .................'54 '87 C.012 B.A. L.426 J.D. 12410 Santa Monica Blvd.
**Victor, Carol R.** ................................'65 '92 C.276 B.S. L.1065 J.D. [[A] Burke,W.&S.]
*PRACTICE AREAS: Litigation; Employment Law.
**Victor, David W.** .................'65 '93 C.112 B.A. L.800 J.D. [[A] Loeb&L.] (See Pat. Sect.)
Victor, Edward G., (AV) ..........................'40 '69 C.339 B.S. L.597 J.D. [Victor&S.]
**Victor, JoAnn Ellen** ......................'47 '85 C.112 B.A. L.1068 J.D. [[A] Jackson&L.]
*PRACTICE AREAS: Directors and Officers Liability; Employment Law; Civil Appeals.
**Victor, Leon A.** ..............'65 '90 C.112 B.A. L.1049 J.D. [[A] Breidenbach,B.H.H.&H.]⊙

**Victor, Robert M.**
**(See Encino)**

Victor & Sandler, (AV) ..................................................844 Moraga Dr., 2nd Fl.
**Victorino, Louis D.** .... '45 '71 C.813 B.A. L.1068 J.D. [Fried,F.H.S.&J.] (⊙Wash. D.C.)
Victoroff, Gregory T. ...........................'54 '79 C.72 B.A. L.1003 J.D. 1880 Century Pk. E.
**Vida, Scott J.**, (AV) ..........................'56 '82 C.112 B.A. L.978 J.D. [Pollak,V.&F.]
**Vidano, Thomas A.** .................'62 '92 C.813 B.A. L.112 J.D. [[A] Leland,P.S.F.M.&M.]
*LANGUAGES: German.
*PRACTICE AREAS: Business Litigation; Bankruptcy.
Vidor, Robert W. '31 '60 C.112 B.A. L.1068 LL.B.
Asst. Chief Coun., Dept. of Transp.‡
**Vienna, Anthony M.**, (AV) ...............'43 '70 C.1042 B.S. L.800 J.D. [Argue P.H.&M.]
*PRACTICE AREAS: Probate and Estate Planning; Tax.
Vieri, Albert, (AV) ......'23 '48 C&L.976 B.A., J.D. Coun., State Dept. of Industrial Rel.
**Vigderson, Tal O.** ......................'64 '95 C.763 B.S. L.426 J.D. [[A] Proskauer R.G.&M.]
**Vigil, Carmen** ..........................'44 '86 C.525 B.S. L.426 J.D. [[A] Bonne,B.M.O.&N.]
**Villa, Fernando** ...............................'57 '85 C.112 B.A. L.1066 J.D. [Alvarado,S.V.&S.]
*LANGUAGES: Spanish.
*SPECIAL AGENCIES: California Department of Health Services; Los Angeles County Department of Public Works; Community Redevelopment Agency of Los Angeles; City of Los Angeles Fire Commission.
*PRACTICE AREAS: Environmental Law; Land Use Law; Local Government Law; Commercial Litigation; Real Estate Litigation.
Villalobos, Michael ............................'52 '83 C.1097 B.A. L.426 J.D. Dep. Dist. Atty.
**Villalpando, Daniel J.** .........................'69 '94 C.31 B.A. L.1068 J.D. [[A] Cox,C.&N.]
*PRACTICE AREAS: Real Estate Transactions.
**Villapando, Daniel I.** .........................'69 '94 C.31 B.A. L.1068 J.D. [[A] Brobeck,P.&H.]
*LANGUAGES: Spanish.
*PRACTICE AREAS: Real Estate Transactions.
Villarreal, Jose G. ....................................'26 '61 C.999 L.809 LL.B. 4585 Lexington Ave.
**Villasenor, Lisa A.** ......................'58 '88 C.1042 B.S. L.426 J.D. [Prestholt,K.F.&V.]⊙
*PRACTICE AREAS: Insurance Defense Litigation; Special Investigations Unit Trials.
**Villaseñor, Richard** .......................'67 '92 C.966 B.A. L.112 J.D. [[A] Murphy,W.&B.]
*LANGUAGES: Chinese, French, German and Spanish.
**Villegas, Daniel R.** ..........................'60 '90 C.684 B.A. L.596 J.D. [[A] Arter&H.]
**Vilsoet, Richard B.** ..........................'53 '89 C.684 B.A. L.426 J.D. [[A] Shearman&S.]
**Vince, Tanya M.** ..........................'69 '94 C.112 B.S. L.464 J.D. [[A] Sulmeyer,K.B.&R.]
*PRACTICE AREAS: Bankruptcy Law; Business Litigation.
**Vincent, Dirk L.** ......................'67 '92 C.1058 B.B.A. L.178 J.D. [Fairbank&V.]
*PRACTICE AREAS: Complex Business Litigation; Securities; Consumer Class Actions; Competitive Business Torts; Trial Practice.
**Vincent, Garth T.** ...............................'61 '90 C.309 B.A. L.91 J.D. [Munger,T.&O.]
*LANGUAGES: Spanish.
**Vincenti, Ross D.** '60 '88 C.112 B.A. L.800 J.D.
Asst. Gen. Coun. & Asst. Secy., Transamerica Financial Servs.
*RESPONSIBILITIES: Commercial Law; Real Estate Law; Finance and Banking Law.
Vining, Douglas L. ...........................'66 '93 C.1110 B.A. L.1068 J.D. 601 S. Figueroa St.
Vining, Julia Baughman ...................'60 '88 C.914 B.A. L.800 J.D. 515 S. Figueroa St.
**Vining, Steven J.** ...............'57 '85 C.454 B.A. L.800 J.D. [McClintock,W.B.R.R.&M.]
*PRACTICE AREAS: Land Use Counseling and Litigation; CEQA and NEPA Counseling and Litigation; Hazardous Waste Litigation; General Business Litigation.
Vinnick, Jeffrey A. ..........'61 '88 C.112 B.A. L.426 J.D. 12100 Wilshire Blvd., 15th Fl.
Vinnicof, Cecil ..................'14 '37 C&L.800 B.A., LL.B. 600 S. San Vicente Blvd.‡
Vinnicof, Paul .....................'43 '70 C&L.813 B.S., J.D. 600 S. San Vicente Blvd.‡
**Viola, John L.** .............................'54 '80 C.178 B.A. L.569 J.D. [Thelen,M.J.&B.]
*PRACTICE AREAS: Appellate Practice; ERISA Law; Life and Health Insurance; Insurance Bad Faith; Employment Claims.
**Viola, Thomas J.**, (AV) ...................'36 '62 C&L.426 B.S., LL.B. [Gilbert,K.C.&J.]
Virgo, Paul J. '46 '75 C.1077 B.A. L.1148 J.D.
Asst. Chf. Trial Coun., State Bar of Calif.

**Virjee, Framroze M.** ...................'60 '84 C.112 B.A. L.1065 J.D. [O'Melveny&M.]
*PRACTICE AREAS: Labor and Employment.
**Virsik, Sylvia M.** ...........................'65 '92 C.112 B.A. L.800 J.D. [[A] Gaims,W.W.&E.]
**Visconte, Rachelle S.** ...............'71 '95 C.112 B.A. L.1066 J.D. [[A] Pachulski,S.Z.&Y.]
*PRACTICE AREAS: Bankruptcy.
**Visser, Randolph C.** ..........................'49 '75 C.597 B.A. L.1068 J.D. [Morgan,L.&B.]
Vitabile, Steven ..................................'50 '77 C.999 B.A. L.1095 J.D. [Spiegel,V.&Y.]
Vititoe, James W. '47 '77 C.945 B.A. L.809 J.D.
(adm. in IA; not adm. in CA) [Masry&V.]
**Vitsut, Ullar** .... '35 '63 C.112 B.S. L.1068 J.D. V.P. & Asst. Gen. Coun., Bank of Amer.
**Vittal, J. Anthony**, (AV) ..........................'43 '74 C.813 A.B. L.1068 J.D. [Vittal&S.]
*LANGUAGES: German.
*SPECIAL AGENCIES: Beverly Hills City Council; California Senate and Assembly.
*REPORTED CASES: Garstang v. Superior Court, 39 Cal. App. 4th 526 (1995).
*PRACTICE AREAS: Business Litigation; Unfair Business Practices Litigation; Real Estate Litigation; Construction Litigation; Civil RICO Litigation.

**Vittal and Sternberg, (AV) [BB]**
**2121 Avenue of the Stars, 22nd Floor, 90067-5010⊙**
**Telephone: 310-551-0900 Facsimile: 310-551-2710**
**Email: javittal@ix.netcom.com**
**J. Anthony Vittal (Resident); Terence M. Sternberg (Resident, Woodland Hills Office).**
**Resolution of Complex Business and Real Estate Disputes Through Litigation in the State and Federal Trial and Appellate Courts and ADR Techniques.**
**Woodland Hills, California Office: 21700 Oxnard Street. Suite 1640. 91367-7326. Telephone: 818-710-7801. Facsimile: 818-593-6192.**
*See Professional Biographies, LOS ANGELES, CALIFORNIA*

Vitti, Anthony M. ..............'43 '71 C.472 B.B.A. L.1095 J.D. 11835 W. Olympic Blvd.
Vitzthum, Barbara J. '63 '88 C.190 B.A. L.378 J.D.
(adm. in NE; not adm. in CA) Assoc. Dir., Planned Gifts, Univ. of Calif.
Vletas, Gus G., (AV) ...........'29 '56 C.839 B.S. L.846 LL.B. 11845 W. Olympic Blvd.
Vodnoy, Joseph T., (BV) ......................'35 '60 C&L.659 B.S.Ec., LL.B. 316 W. 2nd St.
**Voelz, Scott M.** .......................'71 '95 C.610 B.A. L.976 J.D. [[A] O'Melveny&M.]
*PRACTICE AREAS: Litigation.
**Voelzke, Joel D.** ...............'61 '95 C.1167 B.S. L.800 J.D. [Oppenheimer P.S.] (Pat.)
*PRACTICE AREAS: Intellectual Property; Litigation.
**Vogel, Andrew** ......................................'71 '96 C.197 B.A. L.112 J.D. [[A] Reznik&R.]
*PRACTICE AREAS: Environmental.
Vogel, Miriam A. ...........................................'40 '75 C.999 L.1148 J.D. Ct. of App. J.
Vogel, Rachel Terner '64 '91 C.178 B.A. L.309 J.D.
1800 Ave. of the Stars, Suite 900 (Century City)
Vogel, Richard T., Jr. ..........'46 '73 C.112 B.A. L.1068 J.D. Tax Coun., Northrop Corp.
**Vogel, Robert D.**, (AV) ......................................................'50 '74 [Bryan C.]
*PRACTICE AREAS: Employment Law; Civil Litigation.
**Vogelenzang, Pierre, (P.C.)**, (AV) ........................'— '72 L.861 LL.M. [Alschuler G.&P.]
Voiles, Douglas B. ....................................'56 '81 C&L.623 B.A., J.D. [Schmid&V.] ‡
**Volk, David L.**, (AV) ..........................'45 '77 C.33 B.A. L.276 J.D. [Musick,P.&G.]
*PRACTICE AREAS: Healthcare Law; Hospitals; Corporate Law; Medicare and Medicaid.
Volk, Martin I. ........'53 '78 C.569 B.A. L.94 J.D. Assoc. Gen. Tax Coun., Unocal Corp.
**Volpert, Richard S.**, (AV) ................'35 '60 C.31 B.A. L.178 LL.B. [Munger,T.&O.]
Volpert, Samuel A. .....................'61 '87 C.112 B.A. L.990 J.D. 1999 Ave. of the Stars
**Volz, John C.** ....................................'62 '89 C.763 B.S. L.940 J.D. [[A] Koletsky,M.&F.]
*PRACTICE AREAS: Construction Defect; Product Liability; Personal Injury.
**von Behren, William E.** ...............'55 '80 C.910 B.A. L.734 J.D. [Meserve,M.&H.]
VonBlum, Warren P. ...........................'43 '69 C.763 A.B. L.1066 J.D. 3605 Ashwood Ave.
**Von Eschen, Lisa A.** ................................'64 '91 C.945 B.A. L.569 J.D. [[A] Latham&W.]
**Von Helmolt, Kenneth M.** .................'58 '94 C.112 B.A. L.426 J.D. [[A] Agajanian&M.]
**von Kalinowski, Julian O.**, (AV) ........'16 '40 C.496 B.A. L.893 J.D. [[C] Gibson,D.&C.]
*PRACTICE AREAS: Antitrust Law; Business Litigation; Complex Litigation.
**von Leden, Jon E.** .........................................'49 '79 C.1077 B.A. L.809 J.D. [Kegel,T.&T.]
von Sauer, James A., (BV) ...............'50 '78 C.112 B.A. L.809 J.D. 4132 Wawona St.
**von Sauers, Joseph F.** .....'59 '92 C.433 B.E.E.E. L.809 J.D. [[A] Loeb&L.] (See Pat. Sect.)
*PRACTICE AREAS: Intellectual Property; Entertainment Law.
von Wittenburg, Davis H., (AV) ....................'26 '56 C.112 B.S. L.809 J.D. U.S. Trustee
**Voorhies, Nellwyn** ..................'68 '93 C.276 B.A. L.1066 J.D. [[A] Levene,N.&B.]
*PRACTICE AREAS: Bankruptcy.
**Voorhies, Richard C.**, (AV) ...............................'28 '67 C&L.800 B.A. [Voorhies&K.]
*PRACTICE AREAS: Civil Trial; Insurance; Product Liability; Medical Malpractice; Negligence Law.

**Voorhies & Kramer, A Professional Corporation, (AV)**
**1122 Wilshire Boulevard, 90017**
**Telephone: 213-250-1122**
**Richard C. Voorhies; R. Brian Kramer.**
**General Civil and Trial Practice in all State and Federal Courts. Insurance, Products Liability, Medical Malpractice and Negligence Law.**
**Reference: Western Bank (Beverly Hills Branch).**
*See Professional Biographies, LOS ANGELES, CALIFORNIA*

Vorenberg, Eliza .................................'60 '90 C.104 B.A. L.178 J.D. 6426 Hayes Dr.
**Vorkink, Marshall W.**, (AV) ..................'27 '55 C.112 B.A. L.1068 J.D. [Cummins&W.]
*PRACTICE AREAS: Personal Injury Litigation Defense; Railroad Law; Complex Fire; Subrogation; Third Party Tortfeasor Litigation.

**Vorzimer, Garber, Masserman & Ecoff**
**(See Beverly Hills)**

**Vose, Charles S.**, (AV) ..............'47 '77 C.1042 B.A. L.1137 J.D. [Oliver,V.S.M.&L.]
*PRACTICE AREAS: Municipal; Land Use and Real Estate Development Services; General Redevelopment Counsel Services; Real Estate.
Vossman, Laura A. '64 '88
C.1016 B.A. L.276 J.D. Branch Chf., U.S. Sec. & Exch. Comm.
**Vradenburg, Alissa L.** ..................'71 '96 C.188 B.A. L.309 J.D. [[A] Troop M.S.&P.]
*PRACTICE AREAS: Corporate; Entertainment.
**Vradenburg, George, III**, (AV⑦) ..............'43 '68 C.604 A.B. L.309 LL.B. [Latham&W.]
*PRACTICE AREAS: Entertainment; Sports; Media; Communications.
**Vreeland, Clayton J.** ..................'55 '83 C.800 B.S. L.1068 J.D. [[B] McCutchen,D.B.&E.]
*PRACTICE AREAS: Healthcare; Tax.
**Vroom, Cynthia A.** ......................................'49 '87 C.768 B.A. L.813 J.D. [Fox&S.]
*LANGUAGES: French and Italian.
*PRACTICE AREAS: Litigation; Intellectual Property; Infringement.
**Vu, Hao-Nhien Q.** ..............................................'— '95 L.1068 J.D. [[A] Proskauer R.G.&M.]
*PRACTICE AREAS: Litigation.
**Vyas, Kris G.** ..................................'66 '92 C.112 B.A. L.1068 J.D. [[A] Morrison&F.]
Wachs, Joel S. ...................................'39 '65 C.112 B.A. L.309 J.D. City Councilman
Wachs, Julius .....................................'47 '85 C.994 B.A. L.809 J.D. 15260 Ventura Blvd.
**Wachtel, Edward W.**, (AV) ..................'48 '73 C.763 B.S. L.1049 J.D. [Goodson&W.]
*PRACTICE AREAS: Tax Planning; Tax Controversies; Estate Planning; ERISA; Business Acquisitions and Dispositions.
**Wachtell, Michael L.**, (AV) '42 '67 C.563 B.E.E. L.273 J.D.
[Buchalter,N.F.&Y.] (Pat.)
*PRACTICE AREAS: Banking; Commercial Litigation; Patent and Trademark.
Wacker, Ellen Gorman ...............'57 '82 C.112 A.B. L.1068 J.D. 10742 Rochester Ave.
**Waddell, Reed S.** .............................'57 '82 C.112 B.A. L.1068 J.D. [Pillsbury M.&S.]

**Waddell, Sandra Hughes** .............. '58 '93 C.260 L.178 J.D. [Ⓐ McCutchen,D.B.&E.]
*PRACTICE AREAS: Environmental Law.
**Waddell, Thomas Lee, (A Professional Corporation)**, (AV) '33 '62 C.197 A.B. L.1065 LL.B. [Parker S.]
Waddington, Lawrence C. .................. '31 '57 C.170 B.A. L.1068 LL.B. Supr. Ct. J.
**Wade, William P.** ........................ '47 '72 C.800 B.S. L.1068 J.D. [Ⓒ Paul,H.J.&W.]
Wadsworth, Fraser & Dahl, (AV) .......................................3580 Wilshire Blvd.
Waecker, Mark ............. '49 '78 C.705 B.A. L.1077 J.D. 6500 Wilshire Blvd., 16th Fl.
**Wagenseller, Laine T.** ....................... '68 '93 C.228 A.B. L.800 J.D. [Ⓐ Peterson&R.]
*LANGUAGES: French.

**Wager, Donald R., (AV) '36 '63 C.800 B.A. L.950 LL.B.**
**10960 Wilshire Boulevard, Suite 1000, 90024**
**Telephone: 310-235-3939 Fax: 310-325-3949**
**State and Federal Criminal Defense. Administrative Law.**
**Reference: Bank of America, Santa Monica, California.**
***See Professional Biographies, LOS ANGELES, CALIFORNIA***

**Waggoner, Ellen C.** ............................ '67 '95 C.813 A.B. L.309 J.D. [Ⓐ Latham&W.]
**Waggoner, Kenneth L.**, (AV) .......... '48 '73 C.1042 B.A. L.426 J.D. [Brobeck,P.&H.]
*PRACTICE AREAS: Environmental Law; Petroleum Marketing Litigation; Insurance Coverage Litigation.
Wagle, Sanjay ........................ '65 '92 C.145 B.A. L.800 J.D. 33rd. Fl. 611 W. 6th St.
**Wagner, Christopher R.** ............. '66 '92 C&L.770 B.S., J.D. [Ⓐ Charlston,R.&W.]
*LANGUAGES: Spanish.
*PRACTICE AREAS: Insurance Coverage; Civil Litigation.
**Wagner, D. William**, (AV) ..................... '43 '68 C&L.597 B.A., J.D. [Sidley&A.]
*PRACTICE AREAS: Real Estate Law.
**Wagner, Eve H.** ................. '60 '86 C.1136 B.S. L.800 J.D. [Greenberg G.F.C.&M.]
*PRACTICE AREAS: Entertainment Litigation; Employment Litigation; Business Litigation.
Wagner, Fera M. .......... '48 '82 C.1016 B.S.B.A. L.146 J.D. Paramount Pictures Corp.
Wagner, Frank M., Jr. ........................... '40 '65 C.244 B.A. L.923 J.D. N.L.R.B.
**Wahl, Leland A.** ........................... '59 '87 C.951 B.A. L.880 J.D. [Smaltz,A.&F.]
*PRACTICE AREAS: Complex Business Litigation; Environmental; Intellectual Property; Construction.
**Waimey, Stephen T.**, (AV) ............. '48 '76 C.797 B.A. L.569 J.D. [Lewis,D.B.&B.]
*PRACTICE AREAS: Litigation; Commercial; Product Liability.
Wainer, Ivan R., (AV) ............... '26 '52 C.112 B.S. L.426 J.D. 2049 Century Pk. E.
**Wainess, Steven R.** ............................ '50 '82 L.1127 J.D. [Sulmeyer,K.B.&R.]
*PRACTICE AREAS: Bankruptcy; Commercial Litigation.
**Wainfeld, Gabriel H.** .................. '61 '88 C.112 B.A. L.1148 J.D. [Ⓐ Gray,Y.D.&R.]
*PRACTICE AREAS: Insurance Defense; Premises Liability.
Wainman, R. Michael .......... '46 '73 C.112 B.A. L.1049 J.D. 11500 W. Olympic Blvd.
Waisbren, Suzanne D. ...... '53 '89 C.112 B.A. L.1136 J.D. [Ⓐ Williams&M.] (⊙San Fco.)
**Waite, David P., (P.C.)** .................. '60 '87 C.569 B.A. L.276 J.D. [Jeffer,M.B.&M.]
*PRACTICE AREAS: Environmental; Litigation; Real Estate Transactional.
Waite, Nicholas B. ......................... '45 '74 C&L.477 B.A., J.D. Ralphs Grocery Co.
**Wakefield, James M.** ............ '57 '91 C.297 B.A. L.1068 J.D. [Ⓐ Proskauer R.G.&M.]
*LANGUAGES: German.
**Wakeford, Kent D.** ................. '69 '96 C.112 B.A. L.800 J.D. [Ⓐ O'Melveny&M.]
**Wakino, Brett P.** ..................... '67 '92 C.112 B.A. L.1065 J.D. [Ⓐ Peterson&R.]
Walch, Richard ........ '50 '76 C.112 A.B. L.800 J.D. Exec. Dir., L.A. County Bar Assn.
**Walcher, Alan E.**, (AV) ....................... '49 '74 C&L.878 B.S., J.D. [Epstein B.&G.]
Walcroft, Deborah Ann ........ '47 '89 L.1179 J.D. Sr. Staff Coun., ITT Hartford Ins. Co.
**Wald, Jane Shay** .......................... '— '76 C&L.209 B.A., J.D. [Oppenheimer P.S.]
*PRACTICE AREAS: Intellectual Property.
**Wald, Stuart J.** ............................. '66 '94 C.112 B.A. L.861 J.D. [Wynne S.I.]
Waldeck, Patricia S., (AV) '45 '78 C.741 B.A. L.809 J.D. 624 S. Grand Ave. (⊙Las Vegas)
Walden, Richard E. ...................... '58 '83 C.840 B.A. L.846 J.D. [Saphier,R.&W.]
Walden, Richard M. ................. '46 '72 C&L.659 A.B., J.D. Pres., Operation USA
**Waldinger, Lawrence J.** ................ '68 '94 C.860 B.A. L.273 J.D. [Ⓐ Weisman&R.]
*PRACTICE AREAS: Business Litigation; Corporate; Transactional Law.
**Waldman, Carl R.** ......................... '57 '83 C.668 B.A. L.1068 J.D. [C.R.Waldman]
*PRACTICE AREAS: Estate Planning Law; Tax Planning Law; General Business Law.
Waldman, Gary A. .................. '46 '74 C.800 B.A. L.1095 J.D. Service Packing Co.
**Waldman, Ira J.**, (AV) ....................... '51 '76 C.67 B.A. L.1294 J.D. [Cox,C.&N.]
*PRACTICE AREAS: Real Property Law; Bankruptcy Law; Creditors Rights Law.
**Waldman, Irwin, (A P.C.)**, (AV) ........ '35 '59 C.569 A.B. L.178 J.D. [Ⓒ Chapin,F.&W.]
**Waldman, Thomas A.** ................. '65 '93 C.309 B.A. L.1068 J.D. [Ⓐ Riordan&M.]
*PRACTICE AREAS: Corporate.
Waldman, Valerie R. ................. '65 '90 C.668 B.A. L.1066 J.D. [Ⓐ Wyman,I.B.&L.]
**Waldman, Vincent M.** ...................... '59 '84 C.674 A.B. L.813 J.D. [Manatt,P.&P.]
*PRACTICE AREAS: Entertainment and Intellectual Property Law; Closely-Held Business; Strategic Business Planning.

**Waldman, Carl R., A Law Corporation**
**18th Floor, 1901 Avenue of the Stars, 90067**
**Telephone: 310-785-9090 FAX: 310-201-0226**
**Carl R. Waldman.**
**Estate Planning, Tax Planning, General Business and Estate Administration Law.**
***See Professional Biographies, LOS ANGELES, CALIFORNIA***

**Waldo, William Stewart**, (AV) ........... '51 '77 C.276 A.B. L.477 J.D. [Paul,H.J.&W.]
Waldorf, Michael E. ....... '42 '67 C.112 B.A. L.1068 J.D. Pres., Waldorf Associates, Inc.
**Waldstein, George**, (AVⓉ) '25 '57 C&L.309 A.B., LL.B. (adm. in MA; not adm. in CA) [Sherin&L.]⊙
Walerstein, Donald P., (AV) ................. '50 '76 C.112 B.A. L.809 J.D. [Rohner&W.]
**Wales, Kathy TeStrake** ..................... '45 '78 C.966 B.S. L.1068 J.D. [Dewey B.]
*PRACTICE AREAS: Corporate.
Walfield, Paul ....................... '52 '90 C.415 B.A. L.1136 J.D. 3660 Wilshire Blvd.
**Walizer, Michael H.** ................... '43 '88 C.1044 B.A. L.1068 J.D. [Ⓐ Arnold&P.]
*PRACTICE AREAS: Real Estate and Banking Litigation; Bankruptcy; Legal Ethics and Discipline; Construction Defects; General Business Litigation.
Walizer, Nancy J. '50 '76 C.932 B.A. L.879 J.D. Asst. V.P., Corp. Prop. Dept., First Interstate Bk. of Calif.
**Walker, Diana L.**, (AV) .............. '41 '70 C.477 A.B. L.1068 J.D. [O'Melveny&M.]
*PRACTICE AREAS: Corporate Finance; Securities Disclosure; Financial Institutions Law; Corporate Governance; Executive Compensation.
**Walker, Elizabeth W.** ..................... '55 '84 C.629 B.S. L.1049 J.D. [Paul,H.J.&W.]
Walker, Greta Backstrom ............. '57 '83 C.800 B.S. L.1068 J.D. Co. Dep. Dist. Atty.
Walker, Grover P. ..................... '41 '69 C.986 B.A. L.1068 J.D. 2012 Rimpau Blvd.
**Walker, John E.** ............. '68 '93 C.112 B.A. L.569 J.D. [Ⓐ Sonnenschein N.&R.]
*LANGUAGES: German.
*PRACTICE AREAS: Litigation.
**Walker, John F., Jr.**, (AV) ................. '42 '72 C.602 B.S. L.309 J.D. [Latham&W.]
**Walker, Kathleen M.** ............. '65 '91 C.112 B.S. L.809 J.D. [Ⓐ Bonne,B.M.O.&N.]
Walker, Leroy S. ..................... '41 '77 C.659 B.S. L.569 J.D. 6300 Wilshire Blvd.
Walker, Lynn, (Mr.) '29 '52 C&L.846 B.A., LL.B. (adm. in TX; not adm. in CA) 1264 N. Kings Rd.‡
Walker, Marcia J. .......... '61 '86 C.1074 B.A. L.800 J.D. 1925 Century Park E., 22nd Fl.
**Walker, Monica J.** ...................... '68 '93 C.112 B.A. L.426 J.D. [Ⓐ Cummins&W.]
*LANGUAGES: Japanese.
*PRACTICE AREAS: Insurance Defense; Litigation; Insurance Coverage; Insurance Bad Faith.

**Walker, Paul R.**, (AV) ....................... '45 '70 C.602 A.B. L.659 LL.B. [Paul,H.J.&W.]
Walker, Richard L. ............................ '53 '79 C.309 A.B. L.1068 J.D. Dep. Atty. Gen.
**Walker, Robert D.**, (AV) ................... '37 '63 C.800 B.A. L.1068 J.D. [R.D.Walker]
*PRACTICE AREAS: Professional Negligence; Products Liability; Medical-Legal Law; Unfair Competition; Defamation Law.
Walker, Robt. E. ..................... '17 '41 C&L.190 A.B., J.D. Asst. Dist. Coun., Vet. Admn.
**Walker, Susan M.** ....................... '51 '87 C.112 B.A. L.1067 J.D. [Sonnenschein N.&R.]
*PRACTICE AREAS: Litigation.
Walker, Thomas M. ........... '64 '91 C.154 B.A. L.629 J.D. 601 S. Figueroa St., 24th Fl.
**Walker, Todd W.** ............... '68 '95 C.1056 B.S.B.A. L.880 J.D. [Ⓐ Brobeck,P.&H.]
*PRACTICE AREAS: Litigation; Insurance; Securities.
**Walker, William M.** ........................ '63 '90 C.112 B.A. L.569 J.D. [Ⓐ Coudert]
*LANGUAGES: German, Mandarin and Chinese.

**Walker, Robert D., A Professional Corporation, (AV)**
**Suite 1208, One Park Plaza, 3250 Wilshire Boulevard, 90010-1606**
**Telephone: 213-382-8010 Fax: 213-388-1033**
**Robert D. Walker;—Delia Flores.**
**Civil Trial Practice in all State and Federal Courts. Professional Negligence, Products Liability and Medical-Legal Law, Unfair Competition and Defamation Law, Hospital Staff Privilege Law.**
**Reference: Bank of America (Los Angeles Main Office)**
***See Professional Biographies, LOS ANGELES, CALIFORNIA***

**Walker, Wright, Tyler & Ward, (AV)**
**A Partnership**
**Suite 900, 626 Wilshire Boulevard, 90017**
**Telephone: 213-629-3571 Telecopier: 213-623-5160**
**Members of Firm: Irving M. Walker (1885-1969); Howard W. Wright (1892-1977); J. Randolph Huston; Robert J. Witt; John M. Anglin; Robin C. Campbell; Mark T. Flewelling. Retired: Don F. Tyler; Shirley C. Ward, Jr.; Stevens Weller, Jr. Associates: John S. Ward; Robert A. Ackermann; Katherine E. Adkins; Charles J. Kao. Of Counsel: John J. Molloy, III.**
**General Civil and Trial Practice. Banking, Corporation, Real Estate, Estate Planning, Taxation and Probate Law.**
**Representative Clients: McDonald's Corp.; The Hong Kong & Shanghai Banking Corp.; ; Farmer Bros Corp.; Santa Catalina Island Co.; Higgins Brick Co.; Thor Industries West, Inc.; Forest City Management, Inc.; General Bank; Dahsing Bank; First Union Mortgage Corp.; LTV Energy Products Co.; Penhall Co.**
***See Professional Biographies, LOS ANGELES, CALIFORNIA***

Wall, Anthony J. ............... '55 '81 C.170 B.A. L.800 J.D. 2121 Ave. of the Stars, 10th Fl.

**Wall, Thomas Edward**
**(See Culver City)**

**Wallace, Gary R.** ............................... '61 '87 C.94 B.A. L.800 J.D. [Angel&N.]
*PRACTICE AREAS: Civil Litigation.
**Wallace, L. Kirk**, (AV) ............. '48 '73 C.813 B.A. L.1068 J.D. [Sheppard,M.R.&H.]
*PRACTICE AREAS: Real Estate Law; Secured Transactions.
Wallace, LaDonna .................... '43 '79 C.112 B.A. L.426 J.D. 4215 Glencoe Ave.
Wallace, Leslie R. ...................... '53 '79 C.813 B.A. L.37 J.D. First Interstate Bank
**Wallace, Mark S.** ............................ '54 '77 C.674 A.B. L.178 J.D. [Stutman,T.&G.]
*SPECIAL AGENCIES: California Franchise Tax Board and State Board of Equalization; Internal Revenue Service.
*PRACTICE AREAS: Bankruptcy; Insolvency; Corporate Reorganization; Bankruptcy Tax.
**Wallace, Peter P.** ........................ '46 '83 C.870 B.S. L.309 J.D. [Milbank,T.H.&M.]
**Wallace, Richard G.** ............................. '49 '78 C.674 A.B. L.178 J.D. [Coudert]
*LANGUAGES: Japanese.
Wallace, William M. ........................... '10 '32 C.724 L.732 LL.B. 601 S. Arden Blvd.
Wallace, Wilma B. ......... '62 '89 C.103 A.B. L.893 J.D. 28th Fl., 1900 Ave. of the Stars

**Wallace, Brennan & Folan**
**(See Torrance)**

Wallach, Aleta J. .................. '45 '72 C.112 B.A. L.1068 J.D. 12694 Montana Ave.
Wallach, Jason, (AV) ....................... '50 '75 C.659 B.A. L.569 J.D. [Herman&W.]
**Wallach, Stanley J.** ........................ '65 '92 C.228 A.B. L.145 J.D. [Ⓐ Sidley&A.]
*LANGUAGES: Russian.
Wallack, Gordon Reid, (AV) .............. '54 '78 C.800 B.A. L.1137 J.D. [G.R.Wallack]
Wallack, Gordon Reid, A Law Corp., (AV) .......... 1914 S. Selby Ave., W. Los Angeles
Wallack-Roselli, Rina E. .... '— '83 C.234 B.S. L.912 J.D. V.P., Paramount Pictures Corp.
**Wallan, Robert L.** ...................... '60 '86 C.112 B.A. L.1049 J.D. [Pillsbury M.&S.]
**Wallen, Richard A.**, (AV) '37 '63 C.112 B.A. L.800 J.D. [Pretty,S.&P.] (See Pat. Sect.)
*PRACTICE AREAS: Patents; Trademarks; Copyrights; Unfair Competition.
Wallen, Roy L. ............................ '47 '75 C.1142 B.S. L.1221 J.D. Dep. Pub. Def.
Wallenstein, Joel M. ...................... '60 '89 C.426 B.A. L.1136 J.D. Dep. Pub. Def.
Wallenstein, Raymond, (AV) .......... '11 '34 C.339 B.S. L.145 J.D. 133 S Glenroy Ave.

**Waller, David G., (AV) '35 '62 C.112 B.S. L.1068 LL.B.**
**600 Wilshire Boulevard, Suite 300, 90017-3215**⊙
**Telephone: 213-627-3141 FAX: 213-627-5938**
**General Civil and Trial Practice in all State and Federal Courts. Family Law, Mediation, Corporation, Probate and Real Property Law.**
**Reference: Bank of America.**
**Torrance, California Office: 24520 Hawthorne Boulevard, Suite 110. Telephone: 310-375-0077.**
***See Professional Biographies, LOS ANGELES, CALIFORNIA***

**Waller, John J., Jr.** ........................ '55 '80 C.112 A.B. L.1065 J.D. [Walter,F.&R.]
*PRACTICE AREAS: General Business Litigation; Antitrust Litigation and Counseling.
**Waller, William S.** ....................... '57 '84 C.112 B.A. L.800 J.D. [Pillsbury M.&S.]
Wallerstein, Robert H. ..................... '26 '62 C.112 L.809 J.D. Mun. Ct. J.
**Wallerstein, Robert S.** ............. '48 '73 C.800 B.A. L.464 J.D. [Armstrong H.J.T.&W.]
*PRACTICE AREAS: Entertainment.
Wallis, Douglas J. '50 '75 C.934 B.A. L.477 J.D. Gen. Coun. & Exec. V.P., Calif. Fed. Bk FSB
**Wallis, Leslie E.** ............................ '58 '87 C.347 B.S. L.1068 J.D. [Fierstein&S.]
*LANGUAGES: German.
*PRACTICE AREAS: Civil Trial; Appellate Practice; Trademark; Copyright.
Walls, Darlene C. ........................... '60 '89 C.477 B.A. L.1136 J.D. Dep. Pub. Def.
Walls, W. Casey .......................... '— '90 C.112 B.S. L.602 J.D. 1999 Ave. of the Stars
**Walper, Thomas B.** ......................... '54 '80 C.800 B.S. L.426 J.D. [Munger,T.&O.]
**Walsh, Angela Lui** '67 '93 C.112 B.A. L.1066 J.D. [Ⓐ Harrington,F.D.&C.] (⊙San Diego)
*LANGUAGES: Mandarin and Cantonese Chinese, Spanish.
Walsh, Arthur B. ............................ '43 '79 C.426 B.A. L.1148 J.D. Dep. City Atty.
**Walsh, David M.** ..................... '61 '85 C.112 B.A. L.800 J.D. [Bronson,B.&M.]
*PRACTICE AREAS: Commercial and Environmental Litigation; Commercial Law.
Walsh, Dennis J. ..................... '57 '82 C.880 B.A. L.990 J.D. 3255 Wilshire Blvd.
Walsh, Douglas L. ..................... '42 '76 C.766 B.A. L.809 J.D. 3345 Wilshire Blvd.
**Walsh, Gerard J.** ....................... '53 '78 C.659 B.A. L.1066 J.D. [Brobeck,P.&H.]
*PRACTICE AREAS: Real Estate Law; Banking Law; Financial Services Law.
Walsh, James P., Jr., (AV) .................. '40 '73 C.705 B.A. L.1049 J.D. Asst. U. S. Atty.
**Walsh, James R.**, (AV) ............. '47 '72 C.768 B.A. L.1066 J.D. [Walsh,D.L.&K.]⊙
Walsh, Joseph F., (BV) ..................... '49 '75 C.112 A.B. L.809 J.D. 316 W. 2nd St.
**Walsh, Joseph M., Jr.** '53 '82 C.712 B.A. L.426 J.D. [Ives,K.&D.] (⊙Rancho Cucamonga)

**Walsh, Matthew M.** ....'67 '94 L.1065 [Ⓐ Dewey B.]
**Walsh, Michael M.** ....'63 '90 C.112 B.S. L.426 J.D. [Ⓐ Schaffer&L.]
*REPORTED CASES: Goldrich v. Natural Y. Surgical Specialties, Inc. (1994) 25 Cal.App 4th 772.
*PRACTICE AREAS: Products Liability; Construction Defect; General Negligence.
**Walsh, Patrick W.**, (AV) ....'49 '74 C.813 B.A. L.1066 J.D. [Case,K.B.&W.]
*PRACTICE AREAS: Civil Trial; Real Estate; Health.
**Walsh, Rondi Jan** ....'65 '92 C.112 B.A. L.426 J.D. [Ⓐ Cummins&W.]
*PRACTICE AREAS: Coverage Litigation; Bad Faith Litigation.

**Walsh, Donovan, Lindh & Keech, (AV)**
**Suite 2600, 445 South Figueroa Street, 90071-1630**⊙
**Telephone: 213-612-7757 Telefax: 213-612-7797 Telex: WU 401760 WADINH LSA ESL 62949341**
**James R. Walsh.**
**General Civil and Trial Practice. Admiralty, Commercial, Construction, Bankruptcy, Franchising, International Practice and Insurance Law.**
**San Francisco, California Office: Suite 2000, 595 Market Street. Telephone: 415-957-8700. Telefax: 415-543-9388. Telex: WU 384831 WADINH SFO; RCA 286833 WDL UR; ESL 62756007.**
**Long Beach, California Office: 301 East Ocean Boulevard, Suite 1200. Telephone: 310-901-4848. Telefax: 310-901-4850. Telex: 384-831.**
*See Professional Biographies, LOS ANGELES, CALIFORNIA*

**Walsleben, Jennifer L.** ....'65 '96 C.846 B.J. L.990 J.D. [Ⓐ Breidenbach,B.H.H.&H.]
**Walter, John F.**, (AV) ....'44 '70 C&L.426 B.A., J.D. [Walter,F.&R.]
*PRACTICE AREAS: Civil Litigation.
**Walter, Lawrence A.** ....'51 '86 C.112 B.A. L.1137 J.D. [Ⓐ McHale&C.]
**Walter, Stephanie M.** ....'69 '94 C.1032 B.A. L.276 J.D. [Ⓐ O'Melveny&M.]
*PRACTICE AREAS: Environmental Law; Natural Resources Law; Water Law.

**Walter, Finestone & Richter, A Professional Corporation, (AV)**
**Suite 1900, 11601 Wilshire Boulevard, 90025**
**Telephone: 310-575-0800 Fax: 310-575-0170**
**Email: WFRLAW@Primenet.com**
**John F. Walter; William Finestone; Jeffrey R. Richter; Christopher Tesar; Jeff M. Novatt; John J. Waller, Jr.;—Nancy R. Benveniste; Joseph L. Greenslade.**
**General Civil and Trial Practice in all State and Federal Courts. Corporation, Estate Planning, Probate, Real Property, Franchise, Securities, Taxation, Exempt Organizations. Commercial, Anti-trust and Unfair Competition Law.**
*See Professional Biographies, LOS ANGELES, CALIFORNIA*

**Walters, Jamie E.** ....'64 '90 C.112 B.A. L.502 J.D. [Ⓐ Lewis,D.B.&B.]
Walther, Deborah S. ....'54 '78 C.112 B.A. L.813 J.D. 1033 Hilgard Ave.‡
**Walther, James R.**, (AV) ....'45 '72 C.813 A.B. L.1068 J.D. [Mayer,B.&P.]
Walthers, Kal J. ....'62 '89 C.112 B.A. L.1066 J.D. 10940 Wilshire Blvd.
Walton, Brian, (AV) '47 '74 C.101 B.A. L.878 J.D.
Exec. Dir., Writers Guild of Amer., West, Inc.
Walton, Donald D ....'63 '88 C.154 B.A. L.309 J.D. 4236 Don Mariano Dr.
**Walton, John R.** ....'62 '87 C.813 A.B. L.477 J.D. [Thomas&W.]
*LANGUAGES: Japanese.
*PRACTICE AREAS: Business; International Litigation.
Walton, Richard A., (AV) ....'28 '59 L.809 LL.B. 880 W. 1st St.
**Waltzer, Garrett J.** ....'61 '87 C.170 B.A. L.1068 J.D. [Ⓒ Skadden,A.S.M.&F.]

**Walzer, Peter M., Law Offices of, (AV) '53 '81 C.112 B.A. L.809 J.D.** BV
**Suite 2610, 2029 Century Park East, 90067**
**Telephone: 310-557-0915**
**Email: peterlaw@aol.com**
**(Certified Specialist, Family Law, State Bar of California Board of Legal Specialization).**
***PRACTICE AREAS: Family Law.**
**Practice Limited to Family Law.**
*See Professional Biographies, LOS ANGELES, CALIFORNIA*

Walzer, Stuart B., (AV) ....'24 '52 C.112 B.S. L.309 LL.B. 2029 Century Park East
**Wang, Anne** ....'62 '90 C.112 B.S. L.800 J.D. [Ⓐ Pretty,S.&P.] (See Pat. Sect.)
*LANGUAGES: Chinese (Mandarin).
*PRACTICE AREAS: Patent Law; Trademark Law.
**Wang, David E.** ....'64 '93 C.800 B.S.E.E. L.1066 J.D. [Ⓐ Lyon&L.] (See Pat. Sect.)
*LANGUAGES: German and Chinese.
*PRACTICE AREAS: Patent, Trademark, Copyright, Unfair Competition, Antitrust; Intellectual Property.
**Wang, George J.** ....'58 '86 C.569 B.A. L.990 J.D. [Ⓒ Ruben&M.]
*LANGUAGES: Chinese.
*PRACTICE AREAS: Civil Litigation; Securities; International Transactions.
**Wang, Grace I.** ....'68 '93 C.112 B.A. L.1067 J.D. [Ⓐ Chapin,F.&W.]
*LANGUAGES: Taiwanese.
**Wang, Willie** ....'61 '91 C.112 B.A. L.1148 J.D. [Dale,B.&H.]
Wank, Harry B. ....'05 '62 C.178 L.981 LL.B. [Wank&W.]
Wank, Jordon M. ....'34 '59 C.112 B.S. L.426 LL.B. [Wank&W.]
Wank, Michael H. ....'39 '63 C.102 B.A. L.1009 LL.B. [Wank&W.]
Wank & Wank ....1800 N. Highland Ave.
Wanner, Kathrin A. '68 '94 C&L.178 B.A., J.D.
(adm. in NY; not adm. in CA) 11355 W. Olympic Blvd.
**Wannon, Eric A.** ....'66 '91 C.446 B.S. L.426 J.D. [Ⓐ Troop M.S.&P.]
*LANGUAGES: French.
*PRACTICE AREAS: Insurance Coverage; General Litigation.
Wanzo, Marion M. ....'17 '58 C&L.912 A.B., LL.B. 3907 W. 60th St.‡
Wapner, Frederick N. ....'49 '75 C.112 B.A. L.464 J.D. Mun. J.
Wapner, Joseph A. ....'19 '49 C&L.800 A.B., LL.B. Ret. Supr. Ct. J.
Wapnick, Mark S., (AV) ....'47 '72 C&L.800 B.S., J.D. [Wapnick&A.]
Wapnick & Alvarado, (AV) ....11300 W. Olympic Blvd.
Ward, Cheryl J. ....'44 '75 C.589 B.S. L.1066 J.D. Sr. Asst. City Atty.
**Ward, Diane A.** .... '46 '77 C.802 B.A. L.1068 J.D. Sr. Fin. Coun., Atlantic Richfield Co.
*RESPONSIBILITIES: Corporate Securities Law; Corporate Financing Law.
Ward, Francine D. '53 '91 C.331 B.A. L.276 J.D.
(adm. in NY; not adm. in CA) 11750 W. Sunset Blvd.
**Ward, John S.** ....'58 '86 C.183 B.A. L.800 J.D. [Ⓐ Walker,W.T.&W.]
*PRACTICE AREAS: Civil Practice.
**Ward, Julie M.** ....'55 '84 C.1169 B.A. L.1066 J.D. [Arnold&P.]
*PRACTICE AREAS: Commercial Litigation; Employment Law Litigation.
**Ward, Kelly A.** ....'62 '90 C.112 B.A. L.809 J.D. [Harrington,F.D.&C.]
*PRACTICE AREAS: Civil Litigation.
**Ward, Marc R.** ....'59 '85 C&L.426 B.A., J.D. [Federman,G.&G.]⊙
*PRACTICE AREAS: General Civil Litigation, Property and Casualty Emphasis.
Ward, R. Jeffery ....'59 '86 C.1044 B.S. L.477 J.D. [Bosco,B.W.&N.]
**Ward, Rosemary O.** ....'49 '91 C.999 B.A. L.990 J.D. [Ⓐ L.B.Trygstad]
**Ward, Scott P.** ....'67 '95 C.911 B.A. L.1068 J.D. [Ⓐ Cotkin&C.]
*PRACTICE AREAS: General Civil and Business Litigation; Professional Liability Litigation; Insurance Coverage and Defense.
**Ward, Shirley C., Jr.**, (AV) ....'07 '32 C.112 A.B. L.813 J.D. [Walker,W.T.&W.] ‡
**Ward, Ted S.** ....'62 '89 C.174 B.S. L.1068 J.D. [Ⓐ White&C.]
Ward, Ted T. ....'28 '54 C.339 B.S. L.209 J.D. 6500 Wilshire Blvd.
**Ward Karmelich, Lisa** ....'70 '94 C.1075 B.S.E.E. L.426 J.D. [Ⓐ Lyon&L.]
*PRACTICE AREAS: Patent, Trademark, Copyright; Intellectual Property.
Wardlaw, Brian T. ....'45 '74 C.112 B.A. L.426 J.D. [Wardlaw&J.]
Wardlaw, Kim McLane ....'54 '79 C.112 B.A. L.1068 J.D. U.S. Dist. J.
Wardlaw & Jones, A Professional Law Corporation ....650 S. Grand Ave.
Ware, Bernard ....'58 '92 C.112 B.A. L.1068 J.D. 3255 Wilshire Blvd.

**Warfel, Debra Hartman** ....'60 '85 C.112 B.A. L.809 J.D. [Ⓐ Federman,G.&G.]
Wargo, Robert P. ....'66 '94 C.228 B.A. L.112 J.D. 911 Linda Flora Dr.
Warheit, Neil A. ....'54 '83 C.477 B.A. L.36 J.D. National Labor Relations Board
Warmsley, Beulow W. ....'19 '50 C.511 A.B. L.724 LL.B. 3756 Santa Rosalia Dr.
**Warner, Bruce, (P.C.)**, (AV) ....'44 '70 C.112 B.A. L.800 J.D. [Alschuler G.&P.]
**Warner, Donald E., Jr.**, (AV) ....'41 '74 C.112 A.B. L.1068 J.D. [Ⓒ Stegman&C.]
*PRACTICE AREAS: Labor Law; Employment Law.
**Warner, Glenn**, (AV) ....'24 '51 C&L.813 B.A., J.D. [Ⓒ Troop M.S.&P.]
*PRACTICE AREAS: Insurance Coverage Litigation; Business Litigation.
Warner, Harry P. ....'13 '37 C&L.477 A.B., J.D. 6455 Hayes Dr.
Warner, Julian R. ....'43 '69 C.112 A.B. L.1065 J.D. 11601 Wilshire Blvd.
**Warner, Ronald**, (AV) ....'44 '69 C.861 B.A. L.569 J.D. [Arter&H.]
**Warren, Bruce M.** ....'57 '82 C.112 B.A. L.61 J.D. [Berger,K.S.M.F.S.&G.]
**Warren, John S., (A P.C.)**, (AV) ....'22 '51 C.494 B.S.L. L.1065 J.D. [Ⓒ Loeb&L.] ‡
*PRACTICE AREAS: Taxation.
**Warren, Judith**, (AV) ....'49 '79 C.813 A.B. L.1068 J.D. [Warren&H.]
*PRACTICE AREAS: Estate Planning Law; Probate Law; Professional Corporations; General Corporate Practice.
**Warren, Linwood, Jr.** ....'58 '89 C.951 B.A. L.893 J.D. [Ⓐ Bottum&F.]
*PRACTICE AREAS: Litigation.
**Warren, Robert S.**, (AV) ....'31 '56 C&L.800 B.A., LL.B. [Gibson,D.&C.]
*PRACTICE AREAS: Litigation, including Communications and Securities and Business cases.
Warren, Scott K. ....'62 '86 C.112 B.A. L.464 J.D. 2029 Century Park E.
**Warren, Sheldon J.** ....'48 '80 C.112 B.A. L.767 J.D. [Bronson,B.&M.]
*PRACTICE AREAS: Product Liability; Personal Injury.
**Warren, Stephen H.** ....'61 '88 C&L.813 B.A., J.D. [O'Melveny&M.]
*PRACTICE AREAS: Bankruptcy Law.
Warren, Stuart M., (AV) ....'42 '68 C.674 A.B. L.309 LL.B. 612 N. Sepulveda Blvd.
**Warren, William D.** '24 '50 C&L.339 B.A., J.D.
(adm. in IL; not adm. in CA) [Ⓒ Irell&M.]

**Warren & Herman, (AV)**
**1901 Avenue of the Stars, Suite 300, 90067-6005**
**Telephone: 310-843-9030 Telecopier: 310-843-9034**
**Members of Firm: Michael G. Herman; Judith Warren.**
**Real Estate, Estate Planning, Probate and Corporations. General Civil Practice.**
*See Professional Biographies, LOS ANGELES, CALIFORNIA*

**Warshaw, Robert G.** ....'61 '89 C.1077 B.A. L.426 J.D. [Musick,P.&G.]
*PRACTICE AREAS: Litigation.

**Warwick, Katherine Butts '41 '80 C.914 A.B. L.345 J.D.**
**300 South Grand Avenue 14th Floor, 90071**
**Telephone: 213-346-9067 Fax: 213-346-9069**
**Bankruptcy Litigation specializing in Creditors Rights.**
*See Professional Biographies, LOS ANGELES, CALIFORNIA*

Wash, J. Lauchlan ....'60 '88 C.383 B.A. L.30 J.D. S.E.C.
**Washburn, Charles E., Jr.** ....'52 '79 C.112 B.A. L.1068 J.D. [Manatt,P.&P.]
*PRACTICE AREAS: Banking Law; Consumer Compliance Law.
**Washton, Martin Carl**, (AV) ....'47 '72 C.415 B.A. L.178 J.D. [Gibson,D.&C.]
*PRACTICE AREAS: Complex Business Litigation; Federal Securities; Class Action; Financial Institution Litigation.
**Wasilczyk, John J.** ....'49 '77 C.1108 B.S. L.1066 J.D. [Brobeck,P.&H.]
*PRACTICE AREAS: Environmental Law; Employment Law; Petroleum Marketing Litigation; Insurance Coverage Litigation; General Business Litigation.

**Wasmund, H. Andrew**
**(See Manhattan Beach)**

**Wasser, Bonnie Stern, (AV) '57 '84 C.112 B.A. L.809 J.D.**
**12121 Wilshire Boulevard, Suite 205, 90025**
**Telephone: 310-447-1684 Fax: 310-207-9374**
**Email: bwasser@earthlink.net URL: http://www.ilw.com/wasser**
**(Certified Specialist, Immigration Law, The State Bar of California Board of Legal Specialization).**
***LANGUAGES: French.**
**Immigration and Nationality Law and Employment Law.**
*See Professional Biographies, LOS ANGELES, CALIFORNIA*

**Wasser, Dennis M.**, (AV) ....'42 '68 C.112 B.A. L.800 J.D. [Wasser,R.&C.]
**Wasser, Laura Allison** ....'68 '94 C.112 B.A. L.426 J.D. [Ⓐ Wasser,R.&C.]

**Wasser, Rosenson & Carter, (AV)** BV
**Suite 1200, One Century Plaza, 2029 Century Park East (Century City), 90067**
**Telephone: 310-277-7117 Fax: 310-553-1793**
**Members of Firm: Dennis M. Wasser (Certified Specialist, Family Law, The State Bar of California Board of Legal Specialization); S. David Rosenson (Certified Specialist, Family Law, The State Bar of California Board of Legal Specialization); Susan K. Carter. Associates: John A. Foley (Certified Specialist, Family Law, The State Bar of California Board of Legal Specialization); Laura Landesman (Certified Specialist, Family Law, The State Bar of California Board of Legal Specialization); Laura Allison Wasser.**
**Family Law, Divorce, Domestic Relations, Matrimonial Law.**
*See Professional Biographies, LOS ANGELES, CALIFORNIA*

**Wasserman, Arthur, Law Offices of, (AV) '28 '51 C.604 L.800 LL.B.**
**16380 Roscoe Boulevard, Suite 120, (Van Nuys), 91406**
**Telephone: 818-895-8234 Fax: 818-895-0675**
**Associate: Richard T. Miller.**
**Aviation, Civil Litigation, Insurance and General Civil Trial Practice in all State and Federal Courts.**

**Wasserman, Glenn F.** ....'49 '75 C.184 B.A. L.1068 J.D. [Kane,B.&B.]
*SPECIAL AGENCIES: Special Counsel to City of Carlsbad; Special Counsel to the Housing Authority of the City of Glendale; Special Counsel to the Redevelopment Agency of the Cities of Los Angeles, San Diego, Redondo Beach, Carlsbad, Santa Ana, Santa Clara, Palmdale, Orange, Pasadena and Santa Clara.
*REPORTED CASES: Norfolk Development & Housing Authority v. Chesapeake & Potomac Telephone, 464 U.S. 30, 78 L.Ed.2d 29 (1983) (Amicus brief-relocation); Westport Taxi Service v. Adams, 571 F2d 697 (2d Cir. 1978) (challenge to federal grant project); United Handicapped Federation v. Andre, 558 F.2d 413 (8th Cir. 1977) (challenge to federal grant project); Leary v. Crapsey, 566 F.Supp. 863 (2d Cir. 1977) (challenge to federal grant project); Vanko v. Finley, 440 F.Supp. 656 (N.D. Ohio, 1977) (challenge to federal grant project).
*TRANSACTIONS: Grand Central Square Mixed Use Project (Los Angeles), Horton Plaza-4th Avenue Apartments (San Diego); Villa Santiago Affordable Housing Development (Orange); Baldwin Hills Crenshaw Shopping Center (Los Angeles); Convention Center Expansion (Los Angeles); Japanese American National Museum (Los Angeles).
*PRACTICE AREAS: Redevelopment; Affordable Housing; Land Use; Public Financing Law.
**Wasserman, Mark A., (A Professional Corporation)** '55 '81
C.112 A.B. L.145 J.D. [Mitchell,S.&K.]
*PRACTICE AREAS: Employment Law Litigation; Equal Employment Law; Labor Law.
**Wasserman, Michael Eric** ....'53 '81 C.112 B.A. L.629 J.D. [Veatch,C.G.&N.]
*REPORTED CASES: Hector v. Cedars-Sinai Medical Center 180 Cal. App. 3d 493.
*PRACTICE AREAS: Dental Malpractice; General Casualty Defense Law.
Wasserman, Milton, (P.C.) ....'26 '59 C.112 A.B. L.809 LL.B. 6535 Wilshire Blvd.
Wasserman, Susan R. ....'52 '76 C.112 B.A. L.809 J.D. 5750 Wilshire Blvd.
**Wasserman, William P., (A P.C.)**, (AV) ....'45 '71 C.112 B.A. L.1065 J.D. [Loeb&L.]
*PRACTICE AREAS: Taxation.

**Wasserman, Comden & Casselman L.L.P.**
**(See Tarzana)**

Wasserstrom, Sara E. ....'59 '83 C.112 B.A. L.770 J.D. 10990 Wilshire Blvd.

CAA361P

**Wasson, David B.** ....................'59 '88 C.1109 B.A. L.990 J.D. [Tharpe&H.]
*PRACTICE AREAS: Personal Injury Defense; Construction Defect Defense; ERISA; Labor.
Watai, Madge S., (Mrs.) ....................'27 '68 C.696 B.Mus. L.426 J.D. Supr. Ct. J.
**Watanabe, Shigeru** ....................'44 '72 C.112 B.A. L.426 J.D. [Kelley D.&W.]
*PRACTICE AREAS: Litigation.
**Watanabe, Wendy Y.** ....................'55 '80 C.112 B.A. L.426 J.D. [Marcus,W.S.&D.]
*PRACTICE AREAS: Title Insurance Law; Real Property and General Business Litigation.
**Watenmaker, Alan S.**, (AV) ..........'46 '72 C.112 B.S. L.1066 J.D. [Hoffman,S.&W.]
*PRACTICE AREAS: Estate Planning Law; Probate Law; Trust Law.
Waterhouse, William L. .........'47 '76 C.112 B.A. L.1067 J.D. 11355 W. Olympic Blvd.
**Waterman, Mark W.** ..........'67 '94 C&L.112 B.S., J.D. [Breidenbach,B.H.H.&H.]
Waters, Frank J., (AV) ....................'10 '34 C.113 L.809 108 North Orange Dr.‡
Waters, Laughlin E. ....................'14 '46 C.112 A.B. L.800 J.D. U.S. Sr. Dist. J.
Waters, Ronald '40 '74 C.347 B.S. L.345 J.D.
(adm. in IN; not adm. in CA) 1451 S. Ogden Dr.‡
Waters, Voula D. ....................'25 '50 C.112 A.B. L.767 LL.B. 112 N. June St.

**Waters, McCluskey & Boehle**
**(See Santa Monica)**

**Watford, Paul J.** ....................'67 '96 C&L.112 B.A., J.D. [Munger,T.&O.]
*PRACTICE AREAS: Litigation.
**Watkins, Laura M.** ....................'68 '93 C.800 B.A. L.1049 J.D. [Engstrom,L.&L.]
**Watkins, Norman J.** ....................'45 '71 C.1047 B.A. L.665 J.D. [Lynberg&W.]
**Watkins, Shirley K.**, (AV) ....................'57 '82 C.112 B.A. L.61 J.D. [Watkins&S.]
*PRACTICE AREAS: Employment Discrimination; Medical Malpractice; Product Liability.
**Watkins, Todd R.** ....................'65 '94 C.309 A.B. L.477 J.D. [O'Melveny&M.]

**Watkins & Stevens, (AV)**
**A Law Partnership**
**Suite 600 10877 Wilshire Boulevard, 90024**
**Telephone: 310-824-5624 FAX: 310-824-2735**
**Members of Firm: Shirley K. Watkins; Steven B. Stevens.**
**Major Tort Litigation emphasizing Substantial Personal Injury, Employment Discrimination, Insurance Bad Faith, Product Liability, Professional Malpractice, Medical Malpractice and Business Torts. Civil Trial and Appellate Practice.**
*See Professional Biographies, LOS ANGELES, CALIFORNIA*

**Watnick, Kenneth D.** ....................'65 '90 C.188 B.S. L.228 J.D. [Lewis,D.B.&B.]
**Watson, Alan J.** ....................'68 '95 C.112 B.A. L.209 J.D. [Whitman B.A.&M.]
Watson, Carol A., (AV) ....................'42 '78 C.475 B.S. L.1137 J.D. [Manes&W.]
**Watson, Elizabeth** ....................'55 '81 C.597 B.S.J. L.800 J.D. [Greenberg G.F.C.&M.]
*PRACTICE AREAS: Real Estate.
**Watson, Glenn R.**, (AV) ....................'17 '39 C.618 A.B. L.623 LL.B. [Richards,W.&G.]
*PRACTICE AREAS: Oil and Gas Law; Public Law; Litigation; Environmental.
**Watson, H. Lee** ....................'38 '75 C.597 B.S. L.1066 J.D. [Manatt,P.&P.]
*PRACTICE AREAS: Litigation.
**Watson, H. Thomas** ....................'60 '92 C.336 B.S. L.112 J.D. [Horvitz&L.]
Watson, James B. '52 '77 C&L.800 B.A., J.D.
Asst. Gen. Coun., Transamerica Occidental Life Ins. Co.
Watson, John E. ....................'50 '84 C.1097 B.A. L.426 J.D. 3255 Wilshire Blvd.
Watson, Keith H. ....................'63 '90 C.112 B.A. L.426 J.D. 865 S. Figueroa St. #3100
Watson, Nancy J. ....................'53 '79 C.112 B.A. L.809 J.D. State Bar of Calif.
**Watson, Stevphen A.** ....................'59 '88 C.339 B.A. L.1049 J.D. [Zelle&L.]
**Watson, Timothy J.** ....................'60 '87 C.1253 B.A. L.990 J.D. [Lewis,D.B.&B.]
Watson, William D. ....................'49 '92 C.1333 B.S. L.426 J.D. 1900 Ave. of the Stars
Watt, Lucile ....................'17 '49 C.112 A.B. L.1001 LL.B. 2528 Elsinore St.‡
**Watters, Thomas L.**, (AV) ....................'47 '75 C.679 B.S.I.E. L.1340 J.D. [Hart&W.]
*REPORTED CASES: Trope v. Katz 11 Cal. 4th 274, 45 Cal. Rptr. 2d 241 (S. Ct. In Bank 1995).
*PRACTICE AREAS: Trial and Appellate Practice; Business Litigation; Real Estate Litigation; Civil Litigation; Insurance Defense and Coverage.
Wattles, Joshua S. '51 '79 C.483 B.A. L.276 J.D.
Sr. V.P. & Dep. Gen. Coun., Paramount Pictures Corp.
**Wattles, Kevin S.** ....................'62 '90 C.309 B.A. L.990 J.D. [Reboul,M.H.M.&K.]
**Watts, Daron** ....................'68 '94 C.1049 B.A. L.800 J.D. [Sidley&A.]
*LANGUAGES: Spanish.
*PRACTICE AREAS: Litigation.
**Watts, David D.**, (AV) ....................'41 '67 C.806 B.A. L.569 J.D. [O'Melveny&M.]
*PRACTICE AREAS: Trusts and Estates.
Watts, Robert B., Jr. ........'30 '59 C&L.813 B.A., J.D. Asst. Gen. Coun., Northrop Corp.
Watts, Ronald E. ....................'20 '73 C.025 L.1127 J.D. 1109 W. 30th St.‡
**Watts, Thomas Larry**, (AV) ..........'39 '72 C.154 B.A. L.1068 J.D. [Seyfarth,S.F.&G.]
*PRACTICE AREAS: Litigation; Financial Institution Litigation; Securities Litigation; Insurance Coverage; Environmental Litigation.
Wawra, Steven A. '40 '68 C.112 B.A. L.1068 J.D.
Sr. V.P. & Gen. Coun., Mitsui Real Estate Sales U.S.A. Co., Ltd.
**Wawro, James**, (AV) ....................'44 '69 C.1031 A.B. L.188 J.D. [Morgan,L.&B.]
Wawro, Mary F. ....................'45 '77 C.1031 A.B. L.809 J.D. Sr. Asst. Co. Coun.
**Wax, Daniel E.** ....................'40 '89 C.667 B.S.Ch.E. L.464 J.D. [McKenna&C.]
Wax, Nancy E. ....................'52 '78 C.112 B.A. L.809 J.D. 1500 Camden Ave.
**Waxler, Andrew J.** ....................'58 '84 C.112 B.A. L.426 J.D. [Luce,F.H.&S.]
*PRACTICE AREAS: Insurance Coverage; Professional Liability.
**Waxman, Eric S.** ....................'57 '82 C.112 B.A. L.1067 J.D. [Skadden,A.S.M.&F.]
Waxman, Henry A. ....................'39 '65 C.112 B.A. L.1068 J.D. U.S. House of Rep.
**Waxman, J. Mark**, (AV) '50 '73
C.112 B.A. L.1066 J.D. [Foley L.W.&A.] (©Washington, D.C.)
*REPORTED CASES: Summit Health Ltd. v. Pinhas, 111 S.Ct. 1842 (1991).
*PRACTICE AREAS: Health Care; Hospitals; Commercial Litigation; Administrative Law; Antitrust and Trade Regulation.
**Waxman, Tobie B.** ....................'63 '93 C.273 B.A. L.426 J.D. [Patterson,R.L.G.&J.]
**Way, Donald A.**, (AV) ......'34 '65 C.112 A.B. L.426 LL.B. [Breidenbach,B.H.H.&H.]
**Wayne, Abby B.** ....................'57 '86 C.1169 B.A. L.94 J.D. [Manatt,P.&P.]
*PRACTICE AREAS: Health Law.
Wayne, Diane ....................'44 '68 C.112 B.A. L.800 J.D. Supr. Ct. J.
Wayne, Elisa Levin '57 '81
C.477 B.A. L.809 J.D. Sr. Staff Atty., Off. of Hearings & App.
Wayne, Michael I. ....................'— '94 C.426 B.A. L.809 J.D. [Roquemore,P.&M.]
**Wayne, Paul V.** ....................'55 '81 C.112 B.A. L.1049 J.D. [Tharpe&H.]
*PRACTICE AREAS: Toxic Tort Litigation; Products Liability; Construction Defect Litigation; Personal Injury Litigation; Insurance Coverage.
**Wayte, Alan**, (AV) ....................'36 '61 C&L.813 A.B., J.D. [Dewey B.]
*PRACTICE AREAS: Real Estate.
**Wazzan, Natasha** ....................'69 '95 C.112 B.A. L.800 J.D. [Troy&G.]
*LANGUAGES: French, Japanese.
*PRACTICE AREAS: Corporate; Securities.
**Weagant, Lance M.**, (AV) ....................'50 '76 C&L.800 A.B., J.D. [Moffitt,W.&L.]
*PRACTICE AREAS: Estate Planning; Taxation Law; Probate, Trust and Tax Litigation.
**Weakland, Alan Wade** ....................'58 '83 C.228 B.A. L.800 J.D. [Paul,H.J.&W.]
**Weakley, Caren R.** ....................'68 '93 C.112 B.A. L.426 J.D. [La Follette,J.D.F.&A.]
*PRACTICE AREAS: Medical Malpractice.
**Weakley, Suzanne L.** ....................'45 '79 C.813 A.B. L.208 J.D. [Sulmeyer,K.B.&R.]
*PRACTICE AREAS: Bankruptcy; Financial Transactions.
**Weaver, Don L.**, (AV) ....................'51 '77 C.112 B.A. L.800 J.D. [Mayer,B.&P.]
**Weaver, Donna Beck**, (BV) ....................'52 '77 C.112 A.B. L.284 J.D. [Trope&T.]
*REPORTED CASES: Glade v. Glade (1995) 38 CA 4th 1441.
*PRACTICE AREAS: Family Law.
**Weaver, Elizabeth M.** ....................'54 '81 C&L.228 B.A., J.D. [Howrey&S.]
*PRACTICE AREAS: Environmental Law.
**Weaver, Kristina E.** ....................'71 '94 C.112 B.A. L.426 J.D. [Bannan,G.S.&F.]
*PRACTICE AREAS: Insurance Defense Litigation; Products Liability Litigation; Commercial Litigation.
Weaver, Melissa Weeks ....................'55 '82 C.170 B.A. L.276 J.D. 6276 Drexel Ave.
**Weaver, Michael J.**, (AV) '46 '73
C.1042 A.B. L.1049 J.D. [Sheppard,M.R.&H.] (©San Diego)
Weaver, Richard W. ......'32 '68 C.800 L.397 Claims Atty., Auto. Club of Southern Calif.
**Weaver, Robert L., (A Professional Corporation)** '43 '69
C.813 A.B. L.178 LL.B. [Farmer&R.]
*PRACTICE AREAS: Estate Planning; Probate Law; Taxation.
**Weaver, Sayre** ....................'52 '84 C&L.976 B.A., J.D. [Richards,W.&G.]
*PRACTICE AREAS: Civil Rights and Land Use Litigation; Eminent Domain.
**Webb, Jeffrey F.** ....................'64 '90 C.659 B.S. L.893 J.D. [Gibson,D.&C.]
*PRACTICE AREAS: Labor and Employment Law.
**Webb, Robin A.** ....................'67 '92 C&L.800 B.A., J.D. [Daniels,B.&F.]
**Webber, Eric A.** ....................'57 '88 C.347 B.Sc. L.145 J.D. [Irell&M.]
Webber, Karen '55 '90 C.464 B.A. L.809 J.D.
(adm. in HI; not adm. in CA) 9600 S. Sepulveda Blvd.
**Webber, Paul A.**, (AV) ....................'34 '62 C&L.911 B.A., LL.B. [Orrick,H.&S.]
*PRACTICE AREAS: Public Finance Law; Corporate Law.

**Webber, Stephen E., (BV) '42 '74 C.1097 B.A. L.1065 J.D.**
**3435 Wilshire Boulevard Suite 1800, 90010**
**Telephone: 213-386-2505 Fax: 213-386-4440**
***PRACTICE AREAS: Mental Health Law; Criminal Defense.**
**Criminal Defense specializing in Sanity Issues, Mental Health Law.**
*See Professional Biographies, LOS ANGELES, CALIFORNIA*

Weber, Alan ....................'32 '59 C.902 A.B. L.477 J.D. 625 N. Flores St.
Weber, David M. ....................'53 '78 C.112 B.A. L.1068 J.D. 1020 N. Jolla Ave.
**Weber, Mark E.** ....................'56 '80 C.273 B.A. L.339 J.D. [Gibson,D.&C.]
*PRACTICE AREAS: Antitrust Law; Appellate Practice; Litigation.
**Weber, Robert, Jr.**, (AV) ....................'51 '76 C.800 B.A. L.309 J.D. [Bronson,B.&M.]
*PRACTICE AREAS: Real Estate Law; Real Estate Finance Law; Corporate Law; Securities Law; Business and Commercial Law.
Weber, Robert J. ....................'38 '74 C.197 B.A. L.184 J.D. 8350 Santa Monica Blvd.
**Webster, George C., II**, (AV) ....................'53 '78 C.112 B.A. L.309 J.D. [Stutman,T.&G.]
*PRACTICE AREAS: Bankruptcy; Insolvency; Corporate Reorganization; Commercial Litigation.
**Webster, Guy N.** ....................'62 '89 C&L.1137 B.S., J.D. [Lynberg&W.]
*REPORTED CASES: People v. Mark Edwin Taylor (1992) 6 Cal. App. 4th 1084.
*PRACTICE AREAS: Insurance.
**Webster, James J.** ....................'67 '92 C&L.061 B.Com., LL.B. [Quinn E.U.&O.]
Webster, LeeAnn M. '68 '94 C.610 B.S. L.117 J.D.
(adm. in OH; not adm. in CA) 11933 Darlington, #1
**Webster, Martin H.**, (AV) ......'17 '41 C.111 B.S. L.309 LL.B. [Greenberg G.F.C.&M.]
*PRACTICE AREAS: Tax; Corporate; Estate Planning.
**Webster, Pamela Kohlman**, (AV) '55 '82 C.768 B.A. L.1067 J.D.
[Buchalter,N.F.&Y.]
*PRACTICE AREAS: Bankruptcy; Insurance Insolvency.
Wechsler, Nick ....................'49 '74 C.800 B.S. L.426 J.D. 955 S. Carrillo Dr.
Wedeen, Joseph I. ....................'30 '65 C.31 A.B. L.1066 LL.B. 2049 Century Park E.
**Wederich, Leslie A.** ....................'60 '85 C.945 B.A. L.309 J.D. [Proskauer R.G.&M.]
**Wedner, Gregory A.**, (AV) ....................'50 '75 C.112 B.A. L.809 J.D. [Bergman&W.]
*PRACTICE AREAS: Computer Law; Professional Liability Defense; Securities Litigation; Commercial Insurance; Business Litigation.
**Wedner, Jacob A.** ....................'19 '49 C.665 B.S. L.800 J.D. [Bergman&W.]
Weedin, Jack T., Jr. ....................'50 '76 C.1077 B.A. L.1148 J.D. Dep. Pub. Def.
**Weg, Howard J.**, (AV) ....................'54 '79 C.112 B.A. L.809 J.D. [Orrick,H.&S.]
*PRACTICE AREAS: Bankruptcy; Commercial; Creditor Bankruptcy; Debtor Creditor Law; Lender Rights.
**Wegman, Debra Jane** ....................'54 '83 C.112 B.A. L.426 J.D. [Mazursky,S.&A.]
*REPORTED CASES: National & International Brotherhood, etc. et al vs. Superior Court, 215 Cal. App. 3d 934, 264 Cal. Rptr. 44.
*PRACTICE AREAS: Insurance Coverage and Bad Faith; Professional Liability Law; Major Tort Litigation.
Wegner, Lorraine Daly '62 '87 C.262 B.A. L.800 J.D.
V.P. & Sr. Tr. Admr., Sanwa Bank
Wegner, Mary Lee ......'61 '87 C.965 B.A. L.494 J.D. Gen. Atty., Capital Cities/ABC, Inc.
**Wegner, William Edward** ....................'50 '80 C.770 B.A. L.678 J.D. [Gibson,D.&C.]
*PRACTICE AREAS: General Commercial Trial Law; Antitrust Law; Construction Law; Intellectual Property Law; Entertainment Law.
**Wehner, Charles C., (P.C.)**, (AV) ....................'48 '73 C&L.923 B.A., J.D. [Wehner&P.]

**Wehner and Perlman, (AV)**
**A Partnership of Professional Corporations**
**11100 Santa Monica Boulevard, Suite 800, 90025-3384**
**Telephone: 310-478-3131 Facsimile: 310-312-0078**
**Members of Firm: Charles C. Wehner (P.C.); Rodney M. Perlman (P.C.). Associates: Steven M. Cohen; Steven A. Berliner; David Eum; Stephen T. Hodge; John C. Steele.**
**General Civil Litigation. Trial and Appellate Practice in Federal and State Courts including Business, Securities, Insurance, Construction, Professional Liability, Business Crimes and Federal Criminal Fraud Defense.**
*See Professional Biographies, LOS ANGELES, CALIFORNIA*

Wehrli, Martin G. ....................'37 '65 C.174 A.B. L.1068 LL.B. 1900 Ave. of the Stars
Weidman, Leon W. ........'44 '71 C.1068 B.S. L.229 J.D. Asst. U.S. Atty., Chf. Civil Div.
**Weigandt, Don R.** ....................'47 '75 C.976 B.A. L.178 J.D. [Pillsbury M.&S.]
Weikum, Amanda ....................'42 '79 C.879 B.A. L.1136 J.D. Off. of Pub. Def.
**Weil, Alan Jay**, (AV) ....................'48 '73 C&L.846 B.A., J.D. [Gaims,W.W.&E.]
**Weil, David I.** ....................'50 '80 C.813 B.A. L.276 J.D. [O'Melveny&M.]
*PRACTICE AREAS: Media Law; Entertainment Law; Intellectual Property Law.
**Weil, Diane C.** ....................'56 '81 C.605 A.B. L.800 J.D. [Andrews&K.]
*PRACTICE AREAS: Bankruptcy Law; Debtor Creditor Law; Real Estate Law.
**Weil, Peter M.**, (AV) ..........'48 '74 C&L.966 B.A., J.D. [Christensen,M.F.J.G.W.&S.]
*PRACTICE AREAS: Real Estate; Corporate Law.
Weil, Robert ....................'22 '51 C.112 B.A. L.800 J.D. Ret. Supr. Ct. J.
Weil, Ruth M. ....................'42 '78 C.773 B.A. L.1068 J.D. Vets. Admn.
**Weinbach, Elia, (A Professional Corporation)**, (AV) '45 '73
C.569 B.A. L.309 J.D. [Mitchell,S.&K.]
*PRACTICE AREAS: Securities Litigation; Employment Litigation; Business Litigation.
Weinberg, A. Brian ....................'20 '49 C.112 B.A. L.800 J.D. P.O. Box 64459
**Weinberg, Herbert L.** ....................'33 '81 C.112 L.1136 J.D. [King,W.E.&B.]
*PRACTICE AREAS: Business Law; Transactional Law; Pharmacy Law.
Weinberg, Jack ....................'33 '60 C.1043 B.A. L.1068 LL.B. 2856 Forrester Dr.
Weinberg, Lee M. ....................'62 '87 C.696 B.A. L.976 J.D. 300 S. Grand Ave.
Weinberg, Leonard D., (AV) .....'24 '51 C.339 B.S. L.800 J.D. 10450 Charing Cross Rd.‡

**Weinberg, Lisa A.** ......................'62 '87 C.103 A.B. L.1066 J.D. [[A] Cox,C.&N.]
*SPECIAL AGENCIES: Appearances before County Board of Supervisors, City Councils, Planning Commissions and Rent Control Boards.
*REPORTED CASES: %italic; Arroyo Vista Partners v. County of Santa Barbara, %roman; 732 F. Supp. 1046, (C.D.Cal., 1990).
*PRACTICE AREAS: Land Use Law; Real Estate Litigation; Commercial Litigation.
**Weinberg, Steven L.** ..............'63 '92 C.112 B.A. L.426 J.D. [[A] Lesansky&Assoc.]
*PRACTICE AREAS: Civil Defense; Professional Liability; Intellectual Property; Computer Law.
Weinberger, Brian S. ................'57 '92 C.724 B.A. L.1148 J.D. 4311 Wilshire Blvd.
**Weinberger, Jeffrey I., (AV)** ............'47 '71 C.563 B.A. L.178 J.D. [Munger,T.&O.]
**Weinberger, Peter** ..................'61 '91 C.112 A.B. L.425 J.D. [[A] Ginsburg,S.O.&R.]
**Weinberger, William E., (Professional Corporation)** '55 '82
C.188 B.A. L.813 J.D. [Selvin&W.&W.]
*REPORTED CASES: Paramount General Hospital Company vs. Jay, 1989, 213 Cal.App.3d 360; Long Beach Lesbian and Gay Pride, Inc. v. City of Long Beach, 1992, 14 Cal.App. 4th 312.
*PRACTICE AREAS: Business Litigation; Appeals; Professional Liability; First Amendment Law.
**Weinblatt, Henry J.** .........................'41 '85 C.831 B.A. L.809 J.D. [Dale,B.&H.]
**Weiner, Beryl, (Professional Corporation), (AV)** '43 '70
C.112 A.B. L.426 J.D. [Selvin&W.&W.]
*LANGUAGES: Hebrew and Spanish.
*REPORTED CASES: Orient Handel v. United States Fidelity & Guaranty Company, 192 Cal.App.3d 684, (1987); Artesia Medical Development Company v. Regency Associates, Inc., 214 Cal.App.3d 957 (1989); Paramount General Hospital Company v. Jay, 213 Cal.App.3d 360 (1989); Marriage of Diller, Court of Appeal Case No. B035205 (1991), U.S. cert. den. at 112 S.Ct. 657, 116 L.Ed.2d 748, rehearing denied at 112 S.Ct. 1248, (1992); Gertz v. Unger, Court of Appeal Case No. B056074 (1992).
*PRACTICE AREAS: Civil Litigation; Appeals; Family Law; Entertainment Law; Health Care.
**Weiner, Dean M., (AV)** .................'47 '76 C.112 B.S. L.464 J.D. [O'Melveny&M.]
*PRACTICE AREAS: Municipal Finance and Derivatives; Taxation; Corporate Law; Low Income Housing Tax Credits; Mortgage Securitization.
Weiner, Gerald B. ......................'44 '70 C.911 B.A. L.1065 J.D. [Probstein&W.]
**Weiner, Jeffrey M., (AV)** .................'51 '76 C.112 B.A. L.569 J.D. [Kimball&W.]
*PRACTICE AREAS: General Business; Securities; Mergers and Acquisitions.
**Weiner, Joel R.** ...........................'62 '88 C.112 B.A. L.1066 J.D. [Katten M.&Z.]
*PRACTICE AREAS: Litigation.
Weiner, Nathaniel I. ..................'47 '72 C.188 B.A. L.309 J.D. Off. of Corp. Coun.
Weiner, Nicholas ...........'48 '76 C.502 B.A. L.809 J.D. 2040 Ave. of the Stars, 4th Fl.
**Weiner, Perrie M.** .................'61 '88 C.112 B.A. L.426 J.D. [[A] Brobeck,P.&H.]
*LANGUAGES: Hebrew.
*PRACTICE AREAS: General Civil Litigation.
Weiner, Robert E. .................'38 '62 C.918 A.B. L.178 LL.B. 2265 Westwood Blvd.
**Weiner, Rubin D.** ......................'64 '91 C.209 A.B. L.659 J.D. [Richards,W.&G.]
*PRACTICE AREAS: Municipal Law; Municipal Finance.

**Weiner, Richard S.**
**(See Beverly Hills)**

Weingart, Gail C., (BV) ...................'44 '79 C.174 B.S. L.1148 J.D. Asst. City Atty.
Weingart, Gregory J. ..........'65 '92 C.668 B.A. L.309 J.D. 355 S. Grand Ave., 35th Fl.
Weinglass, Leonard I. '33 '59 C.273 B.A. L.976 LL.B.
3550 Wilshire Blvd (©N.Y., N.Y.)
**Weinhart, Brian S.**..........................'60 '85 C&L.800 B.A., J.D. [Weinhart&R.]
*PRACTICE AREAS: Real Estate Transactions; Business Transactions.

**Weinhart & Riley, (BV)**
**12424 Wilshire Boulevard Suite 1200, 90025**
**Telephone: 310-207-1234 Fax: 310-207-3775**
**Grant K. Riley; Brian S. Weinhart; Linda Randlett Kollar; William W. Steckbauer. Associates: Daria A. Dub; Anthony E. Goldsmith; Margaret W. Wolfe; Susan M. Freedman.**
**Real Estate Litigation, Real Estate and Business Transactions, Commercial Litigation, Secured Creditors Rights, Bankruptcy, Administrative Law and Title Insurance Defense.**
***See Professional Biographies, LOS ANGELES, CALIFORNIA***

Weinhouse, Gary D. ....................'68 '93 C.112 B.A. L.426 J.D. 12121 Wilshire Blvd.
**Weinman, Glenn A.** ............'55 '81 C.112 B.A. L.800 J.D. Gen. Coun., Guess ?, Inc.
*RESPONSIBILITIES: Corporate; Finance; Corporate Securities; Commercial Transactions; Labor and Employment Law.
Weinman, Kenneth M. ...........'47 '73 C.569 B.A. L.262 J.D. 11400 W. Olympic Blvd.
Weinreb, Marnin ........................'67 '92 C.112 B.A. L.426 J.D. 9023 W. Alcott St.
**Weinreich, Rebecca R.** ..............'62 '86 C.477 B.A. L.94 J.D. [Sedgwick,D.M.&A.]
**Weinstein, David A., (AV)** ....... '47 '73 C.1044 B.A. L.823 J.D. [Weinstein,B.R.H.&C.]
*PRACTICE AREAS: Tax; Estate Planning.
Weinstein, David M. ...........................'45 '76 C&L.309 A.B., J.D. 3676 Lowry Rd.
**Weinstein, David R., (AV)** ..................'52 '78 C.823 B.S. L.800 J.D. [Weinstein&E.]
**Weinstein, Henry G.** .......................'62 '89 C.112 B.A. L.426 J.D. [[A] Frandzel&S.]
*LANGUAGES: Spanish.
**Weinstein, Joel** ..................................'56 '81 C.8 B.A. L.188 J.D. [Rutter,G.&H.]
*PRACTICE AREAS: Corporate Law; Securities; Banking and Commercial/Finance Law.
Weinstein, Julia L. ...........'51 '81 C.914 B.A. L.724 J.D. 3110 Mandeville Canyon Rd.‡
**Weinstein, Karen R.** ...............'61 '94 C.112 B.A. L.1068 J.D. [[A] Foley L.W.&A.]
*PRACTICE AREAS: Health Care; Corporate Law; Medical Staff Credentialing; Health Care Facility Regulation.
**Weinstein, Les J., (AV)** ..........'34 '59 C.659 B.S.M.E. L.273 J.D. [Graham&J.] (Pat.)
*PRACTICE AREAS: Litigation; Antitrust; Patent, Trademark and Copyright.
Weinstein, Lisa .........................'55 '88 C.477 B.A. L.112 J.D. 1801 Century Pk. E.
**Weinstein, Mark A., (AV)** .............'50 '75 C.112 B.A. L.426 J.D. [Veatch,C.G.&N.]
*REPORTED CASES: Hacker (Eleanor) v. City of Glendale, Cal.Rptr.2d, 1993 WL 231478 (Cal.App. 2 Dist., Jun 29, 1993) (NO. B047989); Hacker v. City of Glendale, 7 Cal.App. 4th 120, 279 Cal.Rptr.371 (Cal.App. 2 Dist., Mar 22, 1991) (NO. B047989); Chevlin v. Los Angeles Community College Dist., 212 Cal.App.3d 382, 260 Cal.Rptr. 628, 54 Ed. Law Rep. 920 (Cal.App. 2 Dist., July 06, 1989) (NO. B031967); Leader v. State, 182 Cal.App.3d 1079, 226 Cal.Rptr. 207 (Cal.App. 2 Dist., May 19, 1986) (NO. CIV B009187); Kuykendall v. State, 178 Cal.App.3d 563, 223 Cal.Rptr. 763 (Cal.App. 2 Dist., Mar 06, 1986) (NO. B014924).
*PRACTICE AREAS: Government Tort Liability; Police Misconduct; Vehicle Liability; Medical Malpractice Defense Law.
Weinstein, Robert ...................'— '88 C.569 B.A. L.426 J.D. 2029 Century Park E.
**Weinstein, Ronald, (A P.C.)** ...............'45 '70 C.674 A.B. L.976 LL.B. [Loeb&L.]
*PRACTICE AREAS: Insolvency Law; Workout Law; Real Estate Law.
Weinstein, Sara A. ...............'58 '84 C.1019 B.B.A. L.809 J.D. 2049 Century Pk., E.
**Weinstein, Stacy J.**...................'69 '94 C.112 B.A. L.1068 J.D. [[A] Fried,F.H.S.&J.]
**Weinstein, Steven D.** .......................'48 '73 C.112 B.A. L.800 J.D. [Musick,P.&G.]
*PRACTICE AREAS: Labor and Employment.
**Weinstein, Steven H.** ...............................'53 '79 C.112 B.A. L.809 J.D. [Barger&W.]
*PRACTICE AREAS: Insurance Regulatory Litigation; Environmental Law; Litigation; Business Litigation; Construction Law.
Weinstein, Stuart '63 '89 C.951 B.A. L.178 J.D.
(adm. in NY; not adm. in CA) 2034 Cotner Ave.
Weinstein, Susan ......................'58 '83 C.112 B.A. L.426 J.D. 865 S. Figueroa St.
**Weinstein, Toni** .......................'56 '91 C.823 B.S. L.800 J.D. [[A] Irell&M.]

**Weinstein, Boldt, Racine, Halfhide & Camel, Professional Corporation, (AV)** [BB]
**1801 Century Park East, Suite 2200, 90067-2336**
**Telephone: 310-203-8466 Cable Address: "Swbrtax" Telex: 701-793 Telecopy: 310-552-7938**
**David A. Weinstein; Ronald M. Boldt; Scott H. Racine; Roger G. Halfhide; David J. Camel; M. Katharine Davidson. Of Counsel: Thomas N. Lawson.**
**Federal and State Taxation, Employee Benefits, Estate Planning and Business Transactions.**
(This Listing Continued)

**Weinstein, Boldt, Racine, Halfhide & Camel, Professional Corporation (Continued)**
**Reference: City National Bank (Los Angeles, Calif.).**
***See Professional Biographies, LOS ANGELES, CALIFORNIA***

**Weinstein & Eisen, A Professional Corporation, (AV)**
**1925 Century Park East Suite 1150, 90067-2712**
**Telephone: 310-203-9393 Fax: 310-203-8110**
**David R. Weinstein; Deborah H. Eisen;—Howard S. Levine; Bruce S. Schildkraut; C. John Melissinos.**
**Bankruptcy, Insolvency, Reorganization and Creditors Rights.**
***See Professional Biographies, LOS ANGELES, CALIFORNIA***

**Weinsten, Michael E.** ..........................'65 '91 C.861 B.A. L.273 J.D. [[A] McKenna&C.]
*PRACTICE AREAS: Government Contracts; Litigation; White Collar.
**Weinstock, Bruce J.**..................'51 '77 C.174 B.A. L.861 J.D. [Weinstock,F.M.&K.]
*PRACTICE AREAS: Business Law; Real Estate; Entertainment Law; Civil Practice.
**Weinstock, Harold, (AV)** .........'25 '50 C.569 B.S. L.309 J.D. [Weinstock,M.R.S.&N.]
*PRACTICE AREAS: Estate Planning Law; Probate Law; Taxation Law.
**Weinstock, Henry S.** ...................'51 '79 C.112 B.A. L.1068 J.D. [Nossaman,G.K.&E.]
*PRACTICE AREAS: Litigation.
Weinstock, Judith Gross .............'52 '80 C.112 B.A. L.1095 J.D. 945 Schumacher Dr.
**Weinstock, Mark S.**...................'66 '92 C.112 B.A. L.597 J.D. [[A] Greenberg G.F.C.&M.]
*PRACTICE AREAS: Real Estate.

**Weinstock, Feinberg, Mindel & Kline**
**12400 Wilshire Boulevard, 4th Floor, 90025-1023**
**Telephone: 310-447-8675 Facsimile: 310-447-8678**
**Members of Firm: Irwin Feinberg; Bruce J. Weinstock; Steven A. Mindel; Jeremy B. Kline. Associates: Maritoni Acosta; Linda Fenton.**
**General Civil Litigation, Family Law.**
***See Professional Biographies, LOS ANGELES, CALIFORNIA***

**Weinstock, Manion, Reisman, Shore & Neumann, A Law Corporation, (AV)** [BB]
**Suite 800, 1888 Century Park East (Century City), 90067**
**Telephone: 310-553-8844 Los Angeles: 213-879-4481 Fax: 310-553-5165**
**Brian G. Manion (Retired); Harold Weinstock (Certified Specialist, Taxation Law and Probate, Estate Planning and Trust Law, The State Bar of California Board of Legal Specialization); Louis A. Reisman; Sussan H. Shore (Certified Specialist, Probate, Estate Planning and Trust Law, The State Bar of California Board of Legal Specialization); Martin A. Neumann; Marc L. Sallus; Robert E. Strauss; Susan Abraham;—Gordon H. Einstein. Of Counsel: Gary M. Borofsky (Certified Specialist, Taxation Law, The State Bar of California Board of Legal Specialization); M. Neil Solarz (Certified Specialist, Estate Planning, Trust and Probate Law, The State Bar of California Board of Legal Specialization).**
**Estate Planning, Trust and Probate, Taxation, Corporate, Partnership, Real Property, General Business Law, Civil and Trust Litigation.**
**References: City National Bank (Century City); Wells Fargo Bank (Beverly Hills Main Office); Security Pacific National Bank (Century Plaza Office); Sanwa Bank California.**
***See Professional Biographies, LOS ANGELES, CALIFORNIA***

Weintraub, David B. ...........'61 '90 C.705 B.A. L.117 J.D. 832 N. Orange Grove Ave.
Weintraub, Debre Katz ......................................'55 '79 C.112 B.A. L.800 J.D. Mun. J.
Weintraub, Lori ............'55 '80 C.66 B.A. L.1068 J.D. 9229 W. Sunset Blvd., 8th Fl.
**Weintraub, William M., (P.C.)** ........'52 '78 C.659 B.S. L.1292 J.D. [Jeffer,M.B.&M.]
*PRACTICE AREAS: Civil Tax Litigation; Partnership and Individual Taxation; Real Estate Transactions.
**Weir, J. Patrick** ...........................'54 '82 C.112 B.S. L.1065 J.D. [Oppenheimer P.S.]
*PRACTICE AREAS: Intellectual Property.
**Weirick, Bradford P.** ..............................'60 '87 C.197 A.B. L.1066 J.D. [Gibson,D.&C.]
*PRACTICE AREAS: Corporate and Securities Practice, Specializing in Mergers and Acquisitions; High Technology Company Acquisitions and Financings; Public and Private Securities Offerings; Joint Venture Capital Financings.
Weis, Lauren L. ..........................................'50 '77 C.112 B.A. L.426 J.D. Dep. Dist. Atty.
**Weisberg, Daniel** ......................'63 '89 C.178 B.A. L.569 J.D. [[A] Brobeck,P.&H.]
**Weisberg, Gene A.** ......................'54 '79 C.1044 B.A. L.800 J.D. [Cummins&W.]
*PRACTICE AREAS: Insurance Coverage; Business Litigation; Construction; Insurance Fraud; Subrogation.
Weisberg, Jason L. ......'62 '90 C.1077 B.A. L.809 J.D. Ste. 403, 1300 W. Olympic Blvd.
Weisberg, William R. ......................'52 '77 C.939 B.A. L.1136 J.D. 2139 Stoner Ave.
**Weisburd, Steven B.** ...........................'66 '94 C.112 B.A. L.813 J.D. [[A] Munger,T.&O.]
**Weise, Steven O., (AV)** ...............'49 '74 C.976 B.A. L.1066 J.D. [Heller E.W.&M.]
*PRACTICE AREAS: Corporate Transactions and Work-Outs.
**Weisel, Jessica** ..............................................'70 '94 C.293 B.A. L.976 J.D. [[A] Irell&M.]
Weisel, Lee D. ...............................'39 '66 C.293 B.A. L.976 LL.B. 1722 Westwood Blvd.
**Weiser, Daniel J.** ...............'59 '85 C.605 A.B. L.1066 J.D. [[A] Skadden,A.S.M.&F.]
Weiser, Frank A. ......................'53 '79 C.112 B.A. L.809 J.D. 7941 1/2 Blackburn Ave.
**Weiser, Herbert M., (AV)** ................'31 '55 C&L.208 B.S.L., J.D. [King,W.E.&B.]
**Weishart, Sandra I.** ...........................'54 '79 C.112 B.A. L.1068 J.D. [Barger&W.]
*PRACTICE AREAS: Business Litigation; Insurance Coverage Law; Banking Law.
**Weisman, Dana E., (AV)** .................'56 '80 C.845 B.B.A. L.846 J.D. [Weisman&R.]
*LANGUAGES: Spanish.
*PRACTICE AREAS: State and Federal Court Litigation; Intellectual Property and Entertainment; Unfair Competition; Real Estate; Corporate Law.
**Weisman, Gregory N.** ...................'68 '94 C.112 B.A. L.1049 J.D. [[A] Reinis&R.]
*TRANSACTIONS: Trademark, Copyright and License Agreements.
*PRACTICE AREAS: Medical Malpractice; Insurance Litigation; Construction Defect Litigation; Product Liability; Business Litigation.
**Weisman, Mark L., (AV)** .......................'44 '70 C&L.800 B.A., J.D. [Weisman&R.]
*LANGUAGES: Spanish.
*PRACTICE AREAS: Business Litigation; Intellectual Property; Financial Institutions; Real Estate; Environmental.
Weisman, Roger D. ..........................................'34 '60 C&L.494 B.A., LL.B. Asst. City Atty.

**Weisman, Paul H., Law Offices of**
**(See Sherman Oaks)**

**Weisman & Rosen, (AV)**
**1900 Avenue of the Stars, Suite 1800, 90067**
**Telephone: 310-788-7000 Fax: 310-788-7010**
**Mark L. Weisman; Peter K. Rosen; Dana E. Weisman; Mark P. Lynch. Associates: Jeri Dye Lynch; Brad S. Kane; Kenneth G. Ruttenberg; Lawrence J. Waldinger.**
**Business Litigation.**
***See Professional Biographies, LOS ANGELES, CALIFORNIA***

**Weiss, Andrea J.** ......................'69 '96 C.228 A.B. L.813 J.D. [[A] Munger,T.&O.]
*PRACTICE AREAS: Litigation.
**Weiss, Andrew L.** ....................'56 '91 C.107 B.S. L.1040 J.D. [[A] Jackson,L.S.&K.]
Weiss, Barry R., (AV) ..... '36 '62 C.112 A.B. L.800 J.D. 2121 Ave of the Stars, 10th Fl.
**Weiss, Bryan M.** ..........................'60 '87 C.861 B.S. L.940 J.D. [[A] Murchison&C.]
*PRACTICE AREAS: Insurance Coverage and Litigation.
Weiss, Charles F. ............................'63 '88 C.674 B.S.E. L.477 J.D. 633 W. 5th St.

**Weiss, David, (AV) '35 '65 C.112 B.S. L.1068 J.D.**
**2551 Colorado Boulevard, 90041**
**Telephone: 213-254-5020 Telecopier: 213-254-4538**
**Technology, Patent, Trademark, and Copyright Law, Unfair Competition and Intellectual Property Law.**
***See Professional Biographies, LOS ANGELES, CALIFORNIA***

Weiss, Edward J. ..............'63 '88 C.112 A.B. L.1066 J.D. 11355 W. Olympic Blvd.

**Weiss, Eric P.** ... '64 '92 C.205 B.A.A.S. L.1148 J.D. [Ⓐ Koletsky,M.&F.]
*PRACTICE AREAS: Insurance Defense; Automobile Fraud Defense; Landlord-Tenant.
Weiss, Harry E. ... '16 '40 C.109 A.B. L.999 LL.B. 9000 Sunset Blvd.
Weiss, Jack S. '64 '92 C.674 A.B. L.1068 J.D. 1800 Ave. of the Stars, Suite 900 (Century City)
**Weiss, James D.** ... '68 '93 C.112 B.S. L.347 J.D. [Ⓐ Troop M.S.&P.]
*PRACTICE AREAS: General Litigation; Insurance Coverage Litigation.
**Weiss, Jeffrey E.** ... '63 '89 C.1138 B.B.A. L.978 J.D. [Ⓐ Kegel,T.&T.]
*LANGUAGES: Yiddish.
Weiss, Jody M. ... '66 '92 C.112 B.A. L.978 J.D. [Allred,M.&G.]
**Weiss, Karynne G.** ... '60 '86 C.569 B.S. L.1009 J.D. [Ⓐ Stroock&S.&L.]
*LANGUAGES: Spanish.
*PRACTICE AREAS: Bankruptcy; Commercial Litigation.
**Weiss, Malcolm C.** ... '56 '83 C.112 B.A. L.1051 J.D. [McClintock,W.B.R.R.&M.]
*SPECIAL AGENCIES: South Coast Air Quality Management District; Department of Toxic Substances Control; California Regional Water Quality Control Board; U.S. EPA; Cal-EPA.
*PRACTICE AREAS: Environmental Law; Air Quality Issues; Environmental Due Diligence; Environmental Auditing; Lease Disputes.
**Weiss, Marco F.**, (AV) ... '31 '57 C.112 A.B. L.145 J.D. [Goldman&K.]
*PRACTICE AREAS: International Transactions; Financing; Banking; Joint Ventures.
Weiss, Mark A. ... '42 '68 C.112 B.S.E.E. L.1068 J.D. Supr. Ct. Comr.
**Weiss, Mark F.** ... '54 '79 C.112 B.A. L.800 J.D. [Weiss&H.] (⊙Newport Beach)
*PRACTICE AREAS: Healthcare; Corporate; Real Property; Business Law.
Weiss, Marvin H. ... '35 '59 C.563 B.B.A. L.569 LL.B. 6605 Eleanor Ave.
Weiss, Michael ... '52 '84 C.426 B.A. L.1190 J.D. 2049 Century Park E.
Weiss, Michael ... '27 '62 C.112 B.S. L.800 LL.B. 1122 S. Robertson Blvd.
**Weiss, Michael H.** ... '56 '83 C.112 A.B. L.1066 J.D. [Ⓐ McCambridge,D.&M.]
**Weiss, Michael H.**, (AV) ... '51 '82 C.569 B.A. L.767 J.D. [Weiss,S.S.D.&S.]
*PRACTICE AREAS: Bankruptcy Law.
Weiss, Morris ... '42 '67 C&L.912 B.S.B.A., J.D. 2029 Century Park E., 6th Fl.
Weiss, Myron A. ... '36 '61 C.930 B.A. L.309 LL.B. [M.A.Weiss]
Weiss, Noel ... '51 '76 C.112 B.S. L.426 J.D. 1925 Century Park E.
**Weiss, Philip D.** ... '61 '88 C.1077 B.A. L.426 J.D. [Ⓐ Agajanian&M.]
Weiss, Philip E. '57 '91 C.766 B.A. L.767 J.D. 333 S. Grand Ave, 33rd Fl. (⊙San Diego)
Weiss, Ralph M. ... '55 '85 C.1077 B.S. L.398 J.D. 1801 Century Park E.
Weiss, Richard D. ... '54 '79 C.112 B.A. L.1068 J.D. Princ. Dep. Co. Coun.
**Weiss, Robert C., (A Professional Corporation)**, (AV) '40 '67 C.112 B.S.M.E. L.800 J.D. [Lyon&L.] (See Pat. Sect.)
*PRACTICE AREAS: Patent, Trademark, Copyright, Trade Regulation; Unfair Competition, Antitrust, Litigation; Intellectual Property.
**Weiss, Samuel H.**, (AV) ... '55 '78 C.112 B.A. L.1068 J.D. [Weiss]
*LANGUAGES: French.
Weiss, Samuel M., (A Professional Law Corporation) '48 '74 C.583 B.A. L.1095 J.D. 9000 Sunset Blvd.
Weiss, Stephen H., (AV) ... '48 '74 C.112 B.A. L.1068 J.D. Gen. Coun., Sanwa Bk. Calif.
**Weiss, Steven M.** ... '61 '90 C.112 B.S. L.800 J.D. [Ⓐ Jeffer,M.B.&M.] (Pat.)
*PRACTICE AREAS: Patent Law; Trademark; Trade Secrets; Antitrust.
**Weiss, Thomas J.**, (AV) ... '41 '74 C.602 A.B. L.309 J.D. [Seyfarth,S.F.&G.]
*PRACTICE AREAS: Litigation; Healthcare Law.

**Weiss, Walter S., (AV) '29 '52 C&L.705 A.B., J.D.**
**12424 Wilshire Boulevard, Ninth Floor, 90025**
**Telephone: 310-207-6679 Fax: 310-207-6830**
**Litigation Practice including Professional Negligence, Securities and Insurance Coverage Law.**
***See Professional Biographies, LOS ANGELES, CALIFORNIA***

Weiss, William D. ... '46 '72 C.112 A.B. L.800 J.D. Pub. Def. Off.

**Weiss, David J., Law Offices of**
**(See Santa Monica)**

**Weiss & Humphries, A Professional Corporation**
**2049 Century Park East, Suite 880, 90067-3110⊙**
**Telephone: 310-843-2800; 714-548-4700 Facsimile: 310-843-2820**
**Email: weiss@weisslaw.com**
**Mark F. Weiss; Robin J. Humphries.**
**Health Care, Business, Corporation, Commercial, Real Property.**
**Newport Beach, California Office: 610 Newport Center Drive, Suite 1010, 92658-7920. Telephone: 714-548-4700.**
***See Professional Biographies, LOS ANGELES, CALIFORNIA***

**Weiss Law Corporation, (AV) [BR]**
**1901 Avenue of the Stars, 20th Floor, 90067**
**Telephone: 310-282-8600 Fax: 310-785-0010**
**Samuel H. Weiss.**
**Real Estate, Corporate, Bankruptcy, Civil Litigation, Estate Planning, Tax, Business and Commercial.**
***See Professional Biographies, LOS ANGELES, CALIFORNIA***

Weiss, Myron A., Inc. ... 10850 Wilshire Blvd.

**Weiss, Robert E., Incorporated**
**(See Covina)**

**Weiss, Scolney, Spees, Danker & Shinderman, (AV)**
**1875 Century Park East, Suite 800, 90067-4104**
**Telephone: 310-785-1313 Fax: 310-785-1301**
**Michael H. Weiss; Sherry D. Spees; Peter N. Scolney; Ashleigh A. Danker; Mark Shinderman; Laura J. Meltzer.**
**General Civil and Trial Practice, Bankruptcy, Corporate, Tax, Business and Commercial Law.**
***See Professional Biographies, LOS ANGELES, CALIFORNIA***

**Weissbard, Samuel H.**, (AV) '47 '70 C.930 B.A. L.273 J.D. (adm. in DC; not adm. in CA) [Foley L.W.&A.]
*PRACTICE AREAS: Commercial Real Estate; Commercial Leasing; Financial Transactions; Workouts and Creditor's Rights.
**Weissburg, Adam B.** ... '64 '90 C.112 A.B. L.800 J.D. [Ⓐ Cox,C.&N.]
*PRACTICE AREAS: Bankruptcy; Workouts; Secured Finance Law.
**Weissburg, Carl**, (AV) ... '30 '58 C.112 B.A. L.1066 J.D. [Foley L.W.&A.]
*PRACTICE AREAS: Health Care Corporate Law; Health Care Legislation; Integrated Health Care Delivery Systems; Medicare Fraud and Abuse; Administrative Agency Law.
**Weissler, Eric C.** ... '54 '81 C.976 B.A. L.309 J.D. [Armstrong H.J.T.&W.]
*PRACTICE AREAS: Entertainment.
**Weissman, Barry Leigh**, (AV) ... '48 '73 C.112 B.A. L.770 J.D. [Graham&J.]
Weissman, Bernard '15 '39 C&L.477 A.B., J.D. (adm. in MI; not adm. in CA) 11909 Foxboro Dr.‡
**Weissman, Carol A.** ... '49 '76 C.1097 B.A. L.426 J.D. [Ⓐ R.Weissman]
Weissman, Donna Sue Levit '54 '79 C.112 B.A. L.1067 J.D. Dep. Atty. III, Dept. of Transp.
**Weissman, Richard** ... '47 '72 C.112 A.B. L.426 J.D. [R.Weissman]
*PRACTICE AREAS: Receivership Law; Real Estate Law; Corporate Law; Commercial Law; Litigation.
**Weissman, Seth I.** ... '69 '95 C.112 B.A. L.800 J.D. [Brown,W.&C.]
*PRACTICE AREAS: Real Estate; Business; Corporate Law.

**Weissman, Richard, Inc., A Prof. Corp., Law Offices of**
**Suite 255, 5959 Topanga Canyon Boulevard (Woodland Hills), 91367**
**Telephone: 818-226-5434 Fax: 818-226-9105**
**Email: RichW7616@aol.com**

(This Listing Continued)

CAA364P

**Weissman, Richard, Inc., A Prof. Corp., Law Offices of (Continued)**
**Richard Weissman; Carol A. Weissman.**
**Receiverships.**
***See Professional Biographies, LOS ANGELES, CALIFORNIA***

**Weissmann, Henry** ... '62 '87 C.154 B.A. L.976 J.D. [Munger,T.&O.]

**Weissmann, Wolff, Bergman, Coleman & Silverman**
**(See Beverly Hills)**

**Weissmuller, Kurt** ... '58 '84 C.1077 B.A. L.426 J.D. [Ⓐ McClintock,W.B.R.R.&M.]
*PRACTICE AREAS: Environmental Litigation; Environmental Compliance.
**Weisz, Barry M.**, (AV) ... '53 '78 C.112 A.B. L.1068 J.D. [Jeffer,M.B.&M.]
*PRACTICE AREAS: Corporate; Real Estate; Creditor's Rights.
Weisz, Michael B. ... '44 '70 C.705 A.B. L.1066 J.D. 2049 Century Pk. E.
Weisz, Richard A. ... '44 '70 C.705 A.B. L.659 LL.B. [Klein&W.]
Weisz, Vera A., (AV) ... '52 '78 C.112 B.A. L.1068 J.D. 9911 W. Pico Blvd.
Weitz, Andrew M. ... '57 '87 C.1077 B.A. L.1148 J.D. 4700 Wilshire Blvd.
Weitzman, Donna B. ... '— '63 C&L.912 B.S., J.D. 4700 Wilshire Blvd.
Welborne, John H., (AV) ... '47 '77 C.112 A.B. L.1067 J.D. 777 S. Figueroa St., 10th Fl.
**Welch, Harriet M.**, (AV) ... '54 '78 C.425 B.A. L.128 J.D. [Ⓒ Buchalter,N.F.&Y.]
*PRACTICE AREAS: Municipal Finance; Corporate.
Welch, Jack ... '52 '81 C.309 A.B. L.846 J.D. 777 S. Figueroa St., 10th Fl.
**Welch, John S.**, (AV) ... '20 '49 C.877 B.S. L.309 LL.B. [Ⓒ Latham&W.]
**Welch, Richard J.** ... '52 '77 C.228 A.B. L.813 J.D. [Riordan&M.]
**Welch, Susan Paulsrud** ... '64 '90 C.108 B.S. L.145 J.D. [Latham&W.]
Weld, N. Brooks ... '39 '76 C.1097 B.A. L.1137 J.D. 3055 Wilshire Blvd.
**Welin, Craig A.** ... '63 '88 C&L.800 B.A., J.D. [Frandzel&S.]
*PRACTICE AREAS: Bankruptcy; Banks and Banking; Business Law; Commercial Law; Collections.
Welke, Dale A., (AV) ... '38 '64 C.494 B.A. L.178 LL.B. [Kopesky&W.]
**Weller, Stevens, Jr.**, (AV) ... '25 '51 C&L.813 A.B., J.D. [Walker,W.T.&W.] ‡
**Wells, Amy H.** ... '57 '88 C.605 B.A. L.1068 J.D. [Cox,C.&N.]
*PRACTICE AREAS: Real Property Law.
Wells, Anne ... '58 '91 C.1097 B.A. L.426 J.D. 601 S. Figueroa St.
Wells, David F. ... '39 '70 C.112 B.S. L.1148 J.D. Dep. Dist. Atty.
Wells, Donna Cox ... '45 '92 C&L.112 B.A., J.D. [Ⓐ Wells&T.]
**Wells, Karen Labat** ... '61 '86 C.1131 B.S. L.426 J.D. [Ⓐ Atkins&E.]
*PRACTICE AREAS: Civil Litigation; Commercial Litigation.
**Wells, Kimberly R.** ... '68 '93 C.668 B.A. L.1068 J.D. [Ⓐ Fulbright&J.]
*PRACTICE AREAS: Litigation.
**Wells, Lisalee Anne** ... '48 '75 C.914 B.A. L.813 J.D. [LeBoeuf,L.G.&M.]
*PRACTICE AREAS: Public Finance.
Wells, Richard L. ... '21 '51 C.813 A.B. L.309 LL.B. Supr. Ct. J.
Wells, Samuel J. ... '45 '71 C.813 B.A. L.378 J.D. [Wells&T.]
**Wells, William W.** ... '43 '73 C.813 B.S. L.800 J.D. [Ⓒ Graham&J.]
*LANGUAGES: Korean.
Wells & Thomas ... 11661 San Vicente Blvd.
**Welpton, Sherman Seymour, Jr.**, (AV) ... '08 '31 C&L.546 J.D. [Ⓒ Gibson,D.&C.]
**Welsh, John J.** ... '62 '89 C.602 B.B.A. L.982 J.D. [Burke,W.&S.]
*PRACTICE AREAS: Education Law; Business Transactions; Corporate Litigation.
**Welsh, Robert C., (A Professional Corporation)** '47 '87 C.112 B.A. L.1068 J.D. [Mitchell,S.&K.]
*PRACTICE AREAS: Business Litigation; Copyright Law; Trademark Law; Antitrust Law.
**Welter, Gerald G.**, (AV) ... '40 '66 C.966 B.S. L.1068 LL.B. [Welter&G.]
*PRACTICE AREAS: Business Litigation; Real Estate; Probate.

**Welter and Greene, (AV)**
**Suite 817 1880 Century Park East, 90067**
**Telephone: 310-552-5252 Fax: 310-552-1006**
**Gerald G. Welter; Richard J. Greene.**
**Business and Corporate Litigation and Transactions, Real Estate and Probate.**
***See Professional Biographies, LOS ANGELES, CALIFORNIA***

**Weltman, Stephen F.** ... '41 '67 C.976 A.B. L.659 LL.B. [Ⓐ Freeman,F.&S.]
Wender, Faith ... '52 '77 C.994 B.A. L.1019 J.D. 11377 W. Olympic Blvd.
Wenderoff, Lori A. ... '58 '84 C.1097 B.A. L.61 J.D. 10866 Wilshire Blvd.
**Wenger, Nancy J.** ... '65 '90 C.112 B.A. L.1067 J.D. [Ⓐ Wilson,K.&B.]
Wenger, Raymond J., Jr. '26 '51 C.321 B.S. L.309 J.D. (adm. in PA; not adm. in CA) 1154 Roberto La.‡
Weniz, Martin P. ... '52 '80 C.112 A.B. L.809 J.D. 10850 Wilshire Blvd.
Wenker, Randall W., (AV) ... '37 '65 C&L.426 B.A., J.D. [Magdlen&W.]
Wentworth, Diane Nissim ... '45 '76 C.94 B.A. L.426 J.D. Asst. City Atty.
**Wenzel, Mark D.** ... '55 '80 C.112 B.A. L.426 J.D. [Stone,D.&W.]
*PRACTICE AREAS: Personal Injury; Malpractice; Products Liability; Aviation; Civil Trial.
**Wenzel, Todd J.** ... '66 '92 C.112 B.A. L.809 J.D. [Ⓐ Lynberg&W.]
*PRACTICE AREAS: Insurance Coverage Defense; Insurance Defense; Products Liability Defense.

**Werksman, Mark J., Law Offices of, (AV) '59 '85 C.976 B.A. L.800 J.D. [BR]**
**601 West Fifth Street, Twelfth Floor, 90071**
**Telephone: 213-688-0460 Fax: 213-624-1942**
**Associate: Donna Tryfman.**
**Criminal Litigation in all State and Federal Courts.**
***See Professional Biographies, LOS ANGELES, CALIFORNIA***

Werlich, John M. ... '45 '70 C.1042 B.A. L.426 J.D. Asst. City Atty.
**Werlin, Leslie M.** ... '50 '75 C.112 B.A. L.1068 J.D. [Friedlander&W.]
*PRACTICE AREAS: Business and Commercial Litigation.
**Werner, Gary F.** ... '62 '94 C.112 B.A. L.426 J.D. [Ⓐ Bottum&F.]
**Wernick, Kevin M.** ... '69 '96 C.813 B.A. L.112 J.D. [Ⓐ O'Melveny&M.]
Wernik, Bruce A. ... '56 '81 C.705 B.A. L.61 J.D. 1800 N. Highland Ave.
**Werre, Gregory D.** ... '64 '90 C.911 B.A. L.809 J.D. [Ⓐ Bonne,B.M.O.&N.]
Wertheim, Jay P. ... '52 '79 C.813 B.S. L.1065 J.D. 1999 Ave. of The Stars
**Wertheimer, Alan S.**, (AV) ... '48 '72 C&L.813 A.B., J.D. [Armstrong H.J.T.&W.]
*PRACTICE AREAS: Entertainment.
**Wertlieb, L. Scott** ... '68 '95 C.966 B.A. L.1148 J.D. [Ⓐ Koletsky,M.&F.]
*PRACTICE AREAS: Construction Defect; General Liability; Insurance.
**Wertlieb, Neil J.** ... '58 '84 C.112 B.S. L.1066 J.D. [Ⓒ Milbank,T.H.&M.]

**Wesierski & Zurek**
**(See Irvine)**

Wesley, David S., (AV) ... '46 '73 1149 S. Hill St.
**Wesley, Nancy M.** ... '45 '89 C.1058 B.A. L.767 J.D. [Celebrezze&W.] (⊙San Fran.)
**Wessel, Bruce A.**, (AV) ... '56 '84 C.855 B.A. L.976 J.D. [Irell&M.]
**Wessels, Jennifer Lightman** ... '70 '95 C.659 B.A. L.309 J.D. [Ⓐ Mitchell,S.&K.]
*PRACTICE AREAS: Labor and Employment.
Wessling, Donald M., (AV) ... '36 '62 C.597 B.S. L.145 J.D. 400 S. Hope St.
**Wessling, Robert B.**, (AV) ... '37 '63 C.209 A.B. L.477 J.D. [Ⓒ Latham&W.]
Wesson, Julius C. ... '45 '75 C.1130 B.A. L.1068 J.D. 4629 Northridge Dr.
**West, Anne H.** ... '68 '93 C.178 B.A. L.1068 J.D. [Ⓐ McDermott,W.&E.]
**West, Barry G.**, (AV) ... '43 '67 C.994 B.A. L.724 LL.B. [Gaims,W.W.&E.]
**West, David** ... '52 '80 C.401 B.S. L.262 J.D. [Gibson,D.&C.]
*PRACTICE AREAS: Employee Benefits; Executive Compensation; Exempt Organizations; Federal and California Political and Election Law.

West, George O., (AV) .......................... '19 '48 C.999 L.724 LL.B. [West,P.&G.]
West, John S. ........................................'57 '82 C&L.426 B.A., J.D. [Allred,M.&G.]
**West, Kim W.**, (AV) ..............................'50 '77 C.923 B.S. L.228 J.D. [Arter&H.]
West, Nina E., (BV) ............... '39 '75 C.813 A.B. L.990 J.D. 10311 Eastborne Ave.
West, Roger E. ................................ '46 '73 C.112 B.A. L.426 J.D. Asst. U.S. Atty.
**West, Susan** ............................. '62 '93 C.112 B.A. L.426 J.D. [[A] Lewis,D.B.&B.]
*PRACTICE AREAS: Surety Law; Construction Litigation; Bankruptcy Creditors Rights.
West, Powell & Glass, (AV) ........................................... 2650 W. Temple St.
Westbrook, Robert William ................'52 '82 C.577 B.A. L.61 J.D. [[A] Jackson&W.]
Westfall, Alfred R. ........................ '15 '61 C.172 B.S. L.426 LL.B. Int. Rev. Serv.
**Westfall, Curtis A.** ......................... '60 '87 C.800 B.A. L.1049 J.D. [Hill,F.&B.]
*PRACTICE AREAS: Commercial Litigation; Creditors' Rights Litigation; Plaintiffs Personal Injury Practice.
**Westgor, David J.** ..................... '53 '93 C.747 B.A. L.426 J.D. [[A] Pillsbury M.&S.]
Westhoff, Christopher M. .................... '49 '74 C.112 B.A. L.809 J.D. Asst. City Atty.
**Westhoff, Kim Rodgers** ...............'57 '82 C.800 B.A. L.809 J.D. [[A] Murchison&C.]
*REPORTED CASES: In Re Bittelman, Debtor (Bankr. 9th Cir., 1988) 107 Bankr. 230; In Re Marvin A. Hartenaka Marvin Arthur Harten, Debtor (Bankr. 9th Cir., 1987) 7 8 Bankr. 252, 16 Bankr. Ct. Dec. (CRR) 686; Silbrico Corp. v. Raanan (1985) 170 Cal. App. 3d 202.
*PRACTICE AREAS: Law and Motion; Appellate.
**Westhoff, Pamela Lynne** ......... '60 '86 C.426 B.B.A. L.800 M.B.A. [O'Melveny&M.]
**Westman, Steven J.** ..........................'70 '96 C.112 B.A. L.477 J.D. [[A] Davis W.T.]
*PRACTICE AREAS: Media Law; General Civil Litigation.
**Weston, Richard C.** .................... '60 '86 C.645 B.A. L.1068 J.D. [Hawkins,S.L.&B.]
**Weston, Scott N., (A Professional Corporation)** '62 '87
C.112 B.A. L.426 J.D. [Nachshin&W.]
*PRACTICE AREAS: Family Law.
**Weston, Steven W.**, (AV) ....'46 '72 C.112 B.A. L.1066 J.D. [McClintock,W.B.R.R.&M.]
*PRACTICE AREAS: Land Use; Environmental Litigation; Commercial Litigation; Trials and Appeals; California Environmental Quality Act (CEQA).
Weston, William S. .................. '51 '78 C.768 B.A. L.809 J.D. 3600 Wilshire Blvd.
Westover, Dorothy W. ...................... '24 '64 C.500 B.A. L.809 LL.B. Int. Rev. Serv.
Westphal, Wesley B. ...........................'65 '90 C.1163 B.B.A. L.990 J.D. [J.S.Matthew]
**Westreich, Benzion J.**, (AV) .......... '52 '79 C.563 B.A. L.178 J.D. [Brown R.M.F.&S.]
**Wetenkamp, Kristin L.** ...............'64 '96 C.878 B.A. L.101 J.D. [[A] Quinn E.U.&O.]
*LANGUAGES: Arabic.
Weterrings, Jorgen W. ................... '59 '87 C.183 B.A. L.818 J.D. 801 S. Figueroa St.
Wetzel, William A., (AV®) '40 '66 C.321 B.S. L.569 LL.B.
(adm. in NY; not adm. in CA) Reeves Teletape Corp.
**Wewer, William**, (AV®) .........................'47 '77 C.668 B.A. L.273 J.D. [Wewer]⊙
*SPECIAL AGENCIES: U.S. Postal Service; Internal Revenue Service; all state charitable solicitation regulatory agencies.
*PRACTICE AREAS: Nonprofit & Charitable Organizations; Postal Law.

**Wewer Law Firm, (AV®)**
**777 South Figueroa Street, Suite 3700, 90017⊙**
**Telephone: 213-622-7021 Toll-free: 888-449-2700 Fax: 213-622-8781**
**Email: wewerlaw@ixi.net**
**Members of Firm: William Wewer. Counsel: Stewart Mollrich.**
**Nonprofit Organizations, Postal, Tax, Corporate and Election Law, Administrative and Legislative Practice.**
**Helena, Montana Office: 21 North Last Chance Gulch. P.O. Box 555. 59624. Telephone: 406-449-2700. Fax: 406-449-0942.**
**Washington, D.C. Office: 4401 Connecticut Avenue, N.W. Suite 292A. 20008. Telephone: 202-393-9575. Fax: 202-363-5672.**
***See Professional Biographies, LOS ANGELES, CALIFORNIA***

Wexler, Gary A., (AV) .................... '47 '73 C.112 B.A. L.1068 J.D. [Gittler,W.&B.]
**Wexler, Jeffrey D.** ............................ '62 '87 C.112 B.A. L.309 J.D. [Tuttle&T.]
*PRACTICE AREAS: Civil Litigation; Patent, Trademark, Copyright; Agricultural Litigation; Franchisor-Franchisee Litigation; False Claims Litigation.
**Weyer, Frank M.** ......... '57 '87 C.999 B.E. L.1066 J.D. [[A] Hecker&H.] (See Pat. Sect.)
Whalen, Alison M. '57 '82 C.668 B.A. L.145 J.D.
1800 Ave. of the Stars, Suite 900 (Century City)
**Whalen, Daniel G.** ..................... '61 '86 C.154 B.A. L.426 J.D. [[A] Engstrom,L.&L.]
**Whalen, Eileen M.** .........................'64 '89 C.228 A.B. L.800 J.D. [[A] Knapp,M.J.&D.]
*PRACTICE AREAS: General Business Litigation.
**Whalen, Michael S.**, (AV) .............'54 '79 C.1109 B.A. L.1066 J.D. [Brobeck,P.&H.]
**Whaley, J. Patrick**, (AV) ............... '34 '60 C.668 A.B. L.813 J.D. [Musick,P.&G.]
*PRACTICE AREAS: Taxation; Non-Profit and Charitable Organizations.
**Whatley, Holly O.** .......................................'— '92 L.846 [[A] Sheppard,M.R.&H.]
*PRACTICE AREAS: General Business Litigation, Unfair Competition, Antitrust.
**Wheat, Francis M.**, (AV) ............. '21 '49 C.668 A.B. L.309 LL.B. [[C] Gibson,D.&C.]
Wheat, Jerald E. ................'33 '61 C.112 B.A. L.1068 LL.B. Principal Dep. Co. Coun.
Wheatley, Diana M. ............................... '49 '74 C.813 A.B. L.1066 J.D. Mun. Ct.
Wheaton, O. Andrew ....................'64 '90 C.511 B.A. L.309 J.D. 445 S. Figueroa St.
Wheeler, Charles H. '50 '77 C.893 B.A. L.446 J.D.
Exec. Dir., National Immig. Law Ctr.
**Wheeler, David C.**, (AV) ................'47 '74 C.347 B.A. L.597 J.D. [Augustini,W.&D.]
Wheeler, David E. ........ '51 '78 C.1185 B.A. L.1065 J.D. 1801 Century Park E., 26th Fl.
**Wheeler, Jane Chotard** ............'52 '90 C.37 B.A. L.1097 J.D. [[A] McDermott,W.&E.]
**Wheeler, Jeffrey B.**, (AV) ............. '52 '78 C.112 B.A. L.990 J.D. [[C] Mitchell,S.&K.]
*PRACTICE AREAS: Estate Planning Law; Probate Law; Trust Administration Law; Non-Profit Organizations Law.
Wheeler, Sara M. ............................'— '88 C&L.846 B.A., J.D. 221 N. Figueroa St.
Whelan, Dennis E. ........................ '36 '69 C.112 B.A. L.809 LL.B. Dep. Dist. Atty.
**Whipple, Anthony Henry** ............... '48 '79 C.112 B.A. L.1148 J.D. [Acker,K.&W.]
*PRACTICE AREAS: Tort and Insurance Coverage Litigation.
Whisman, Linda A. '54 '83 C.112 B.A. L.809 J.D.
Dir., Law Libr., Southwestern Univ. School of Law
**Whitaker, John W.**, (AV) ............. '42 '68 C.813 A.B. L.800 J.D. [Pillsbury M.&S.]
**Whitaker, Mary G., (P.C.)** ............. '47 '78 C.118 B.A. L.813 J.D. [Lewis,D.B.&B.]
**Whitaker, Michael T.** ............... '58 '84 C.1074 B.A. L.809 J.D. [Verboon,W.H.&P.]
*PRACTICE AREAS: Bad Faith Litigation; Professional Liability; Construction Litigation; Commercial Litigation.
**Whitaker, Michael W.** '70 '96 C.1109 B.A. L.1066 J.D.
[[A] Christensen,M.F.J.G.W.&S.]
*PRACTICE AREAS: Litigation.
**Whitaker, Ronald S.** ............... '57 '83 C.112 B.A. L.1068 J.D. [Robinson,D.&W.]⊙
*PRACTICE AREAS: Professional Errors and Omissions; Products Liability; Insurance Coverage; General Litigation.
**Whitaker, Seth W.** ......................'50 '78 C.228 B.A. L.1065 J.D. [Booth,M.&S.]
Whitby, Roger M. ........................'39 '69 C.101 B.S. L.309 LL.B. Sr. Asst. Co. Coun.
Whitcomb, Michael L. '50 '76 C.642 B.A. L.208 J.D.
Gen. Solr., Union Pacific R.R. Co.
**White, Andrew M.**, (AV) ..................'47 '74 C.976 B.A. L.813 J.D. [White O.C.&A.]
*PRACTICE AREAS: Civil Litigation; Entertainment.
**White, Bradley S.** .........................'57 '83 C.800 B.A. L.426 J.D. [[A] Orrick,H.&S.]
**White, Brenda L.** ...........................'65 '90 C.378 B.A. L.309 J.D. [[A] Riordan&M.]
White, Brooke Erin ...................'61 '86 C.367 B.S. L.1068 J.D. City Atty's. Off.

**White, David S., Law Offices of, (AV) '50 '77 C.156 B.A. L.1067 J.D.**
**10960 Wilshire Boulevard, Suite 1225, 90024**
**Telephone: 301-479-4222 Telecopier: 301-479-3008**
***PRACTICE AREAS: Real Estate; Business and Entertainment Litigation; Alternate Dispute Resolution; Arbitration.**
**Associates: John R. Winandy.**
**Business, Real Estate, Entertainment and Family Law. General Civil Trial and Appellate Practice in all State and Federal Courts.**
**Representative Clients: Mar International Records, Inc.; Union Home Loan, Inc.; Disco Azteca.**
**Reference: California Independent Mortgage Brokers Assn.**
***See Professional Biographies, LOS ANGELES, CALIFORNIA***

**White, Debra Alligood** ...............'60 '93 C.309 A.B. L.1068 J.D. [[A] Gibson,D.&C.]
*PRACTICE AREAS: General Corporate.
White, Denis ........................... '42 '70 C.813 A.B. L.1068 J.D. 835 Wilshire Blvd.
**White, Elizabeth Allen**, (AV) ........... '55 '82 C.112 B.A. L.426 J.D. [Valensi,R.&M.]
*LANGUAGES: French and Spanish.
*PRACTICE AREAS: Employment Litigation; General Business Litigation.
White, George, Jr. ......................... '62 '89 C.802 B.A. L.309 J.D. 5900 Wilshire Blvd.
**White, Glenn M.** .......................... '58 '88 C&L.846 B.S., J.D. [[A] Radcliff,F.&D.]
**White, Grady Lee** ......................'63 '93 C.597 B.S. L.1068 J.D. [[A] Quinn E.U.&O.]
*PRACTICE AREAS: High-tech Intellectual Property; Computer Law.
**White, Heather G.** .................. '68 '95 C.112 B.A. L.309 J.D. [[A] O'Melveny&M.]
**White, Jack R., (P.C.)**, (AV) ....................'36 '62 C&L.800 A.B., LL.B. [Hill,F.&B.]
*PRACTICE AREAS: Business and Tax Litigation; Appellate Practice.
**White, James O., Jr.**, (AV) ............ '20 '48 C&L.813 A.B., LL.B. [[C] Cummins&W.]
White, Jimmie D. ................................'47 '77 C.1131 B.A. L.1068 J.D. U.C.L.A.
White, John A., (AV) ................ '15 '42 L.1065 J.D. 1763 Mandeville Canyon Rd.‡

**White, Mary Dinius '55 '91 C&L.426 B.S., J.D.**
**Howard Hughes Center, 6601 Center Drive West, Suite 500, 90045**
**Telephone: 310-641-2939 Fax: 310-348-8129**
***PRACTICE AREAS: Domestic Relations Law (40%); Criminal Appellate Practice (20%); Estate Planning and Trust Law (20%); Wills (10%); Probate Law (10%).**
**Family Law, Estate Planning and Probate, Conservatorship and Guardianship.**

**White, Meghan A.** .................'65 '91 C.800 B.S. L.426 J.D. [[A] Littler,M.F.T.&M.]
**White, Michael J.** ............................ '42 '85 C.453 B.S. L.1068 J.D. [Daar&N.]
**White, Molly M.** .................. '65 '94 C.276 B.S.F.S. L.426 J.D. [[A] O'Melveny&M.]
White, Pamela L. ............... '48 '73 C.112 B.A. L.426 J.D. Legal Aid Found. of L.A.
**White, Robert J.**, (AV) ..................'46 '72 C.339 B.S. L.477 J.D. [O'Melveny&M.]
*PRACTICE AREAS: Bankruptcy; Loan Restructuring; Out of Court Debt Restructuring.
**White, Roger T.** ........................ '31 '59 C.962 A.B. L.966 LL.B. [[C] Sonfield&S.]
**White, Susan Page** .................... '61 '88 C.937 B.A. L.426 J.D. [Troop M.S.&P.]
*PRACTICE AREAS: Insurance Coverage Litigation; Entertainment Law.
White, Timothy J. '53 '79 C.767 B.A. L.1068 J.D.
V.P., The CIT Grp./Equipment Financing, Inc.
White, Wayne N., Jr. '53 '86
C.139 B.A. L.1067 J.D. Assoc. Campus Coun., Univ. of Calif.
**White, William A.** ........................... '60 '85 C.188 B.S. L.800 J.D. [Hill,F.&B.]
*REPORTED CASES: Best Brands Beverage, Inc. v. Falstaff Brewing Corp., 842 F.2d 578 (2d Cir. 1987).
*PRACTICE AREAS: Business Litigation; Antitrust; Insurance Coverage Disputes; Land Use and Condemnation Law.
**White, William F., Jr.** ........................ '35 '60 C&L.309 A.B., LL.B. [[C] Daar&N.]

**White & Case, (AV)**
**633 West Fifth Street, Suite 1900, 90071-2007⊙**
**Telephone: 213-620-7700 Telex: 277823 WHCS UR Facsimile: 213-687-0758; 213-617-2205; 213-617-0376 Additional information on White & Case and our lawyers is available on our home page URL: http://www.whitecase.com/**
**Partners: C. Randolph Fishburn; Burton H. Fohrman; Brian L. Holman; Neal S. Millard; Neil W. Rust; Richard K. Smith, Jr.; John A. Sturgeon; Travers D. Wood; Daniel J. Woods. Partner Of Counsel: Jay H. Grodin. Counsel: Bryan A. Merryman. Associates: David H. Bate; James R. Cairns; Jordan S. Cohen; James R. Cowan; Susan J. De Witt; John D. Early; Amber N. Hartgens; Christopher W. Kelly; Matthew P. Lewis; Philip L. Maloney; Steven L. Miller; Rachel Charles O'Bryan (Not admitted in CA); Jackson K. Pek; Carole C. Peterson; John W. Peterson; John E. Rosenbaum; Renee M. Rubin; Robert L. Skinner; Steven W. Turnbull; Gary L. Urwin; Ted S. Ward; Robert L. Wilkerson; Mark A.H. Young.**
**General Practice.**
**New York, New York: Telephone: 212-819-8200. Facsimile: 212-354-8113.**
**Miami, Florida: Telephone: 305-371-2700. Facsimile: 305-358-5744; 305-358-5745.**
**Washington, D.C.: Telephone: 202-626-3600. Facsimile: 202-639-9355.**
**Brussels, Belgium: Telephone: (32-2) 647-05-89. Facsimile: (32-2) 647-16-75.**
**Budapest, Hungary: Telephone: (36-1) 269-0550. Facsimile: (36-1) 269-1199.**
**Helsinki, Finland: Telephone: (358-9) 631-100. Facsimile: (358-9) 179-477.**
**Istanbul, Turkey: Telephone: (90-212) 275-75-33; (90-212) 275-68-98. Facsimile: (90-212) 275-75-43.**
**Ankara, Turkey: Telephone: (90-312) 446-2180. Facsimile: (90-312) 446-9871.**
**London, England: Telephone: (44-171) 726-6361. Facsimile: (44-171) 726-4314; (44-171) 726-8558.**
**Moscow, Russia: Telephone: (7-095) 961-2112. Satelite Telephone: (7-501) 961-2112. Facsimile: (7-095) 961-2121. Satelite Facsimile: (7-501) 961-2121.**
**Paris, France: Telephone: (33) 01-42-60-34-05. Facsimile: (33) 01-42-60-82-46.**
**Prague, Czech Republic: Telephone: (42-2) 2481-1796. Facsimile: (42-2) 232-5522; (42-2) 232-5585.**
**Stockholm, Sweden: Telephone: (46-8) 679-80-30. Facsimile: (46-8) 611-21-22.**
**Warsaw, Poland: Telephone: (48-22) 625-33-33; (48-22) 622-67-67; (48-39) 12-19-06. Facsimile: (48-22) 628-22-28.**
**Almaty, Kazakhstan: Telephone: (7-3272) 50-74-91/2; (7-3272) 50-78-71. Facsimile: (7-3272) 50-74-93.**
**Tashkent, Republic of Uzbekistan: Telephone: (7-3712) 32-00-59; (7-3712) 32-01-49. Satellite Telephone: (7-3712) 40-61-18; (7-3712) 40-61-24. (7-3712) 40-61-32. Facsimile: (7-3712) 40-61-81.**
**Bangkok, Thailand: White & Case (Thailand) Limited. Telephone: (662) 236-6154/7. Facsimile: (662) 237-6771.**
**Bombay, India: Liaison Office, (91-22) 282-6300/01/02/03. Facsimile: (91-22) 282-6305.**
**Hanoi, Vietnam: Representative Office, Telephone: (84-4) 822-7575. Facsimile: (84-4) 822-7297.**
**Hong Kong: Telephone: (852) 2822-8700. Facsimile: (852) 2845-9070.**
**Singapore, Republic of Singapore: Telephone: (65) 225-6000. Facsimile: (65) 225-6009.**
**Tokyo, Japan: White & Case Gaikokuho Jimu Bengoshi Jimusho. Telephone: (81-3) 3239-4300. Facsimile: (81-3) 3239-4330.**
**Jeddah, Saudi Arabia: Law Office of Hassan Mahassni, Telephone: (966-2) 665-4353. Facsimile: (966-2) 669-2996.**
**Riyadh, Saudi Arabia: Law Office of Hassan Mahassni, Telephone: (966-1) 464-4006; (966-1) 462-1626. Facsimile: (966-1) 465-1348.**
**Johannesburg, Republic of South Africa: Telephone: 27 (11) 333-1584. Facsimile: 27 (11) 333-0310.**
**Mexico City, Mexico: Telephone: (52-5) 540-9600; (52-5) 520-4770. Facsimile: (52-5) 520-4656; (52-5) 520-7262; (52-5) 520-1271; (52-5) 540-9698; (52-5) 540-9699.**
**Jakarta, Indonesia Office: Telephone: (62-21) 231-1965; (62-21) 381-8805. Facsimile: (62-21) 231-1778.**
***See Professional Biographies, LOS ANGELES, CALIFORNIA***

**White O'Connor Curry & Avanzado LLP, (AV)**
**10900 Wilshire Boulevard Suite 1100, 90024-3959**
**Telephone: 310-443-0222 Fax: 310-443-0233**
**Email: whiteo.com**
**Andrew M. White; Michael J. O'Connor; James E. Curry; Melvin N.A. Avanzado; John M. Gatti;—Jonathan H. Anschell; David E. Fink; Holly J. Sadlon; Lee S. Brenner; Randall L. Murphy; James W. Irey.**
**General Civil and Trial Practice in all States and Federal Courts.**
***See Professional Biographies, LOS ANGELES, CALIFORNIA***

White & Resnick, (AV) ........ 2040 Avenue of the Stars, 4th Fl. (⊙Newport Beach, CA)

CALIFORNIA—LOS ANGELES
MARTINDALE-HUBBELL LAW DIRECTORY 1997

**Whitefield, Derek S.** '60 '85 C.475 B.A. L.912 J.D. [Grace,S.C.&S.]
*PRACTICE AREAS: Product Liability Law; Insurance Coverage Law; Insurance Defence Law; Appellate Law.
Whiteford, Wendy A. '64 '90 C.112 B.S. L.1065 J.D. 444 S. Flower St., Ste. 2000
**Whitehead, Charles G.** '64 '90 C.588 B.S. L.990 J.D. [Ⓐ Berman,B.&B.]
Whitehead, Frank H., III '58 '87 C.800 B.A. L.426 J.D. 3255 Wilshire Blvd., 12th Fl.
Whitehead, Glenn A. '55 '78 C.112 B.A. L.1068 J.D. Bus. Affs. Dept., Home Box Office, Inc.
**Whitehead, Mitchel D.** '53 '78 C.112 B.A. L.426 J.D. [Seyfarth,S.F.&G.]
Whitehill, Jess '21 '50 C.112 B.A. L.800 LL.B. Supr. Ct. J.
**Whitehill, Michael H.**, (AV) '56 '81 C.112 A.B. L.1066 J.D. [Kussman&W.]
*PRACTICE AREAS: Insurance Bad Faith Law; Personal Injury; Products Liability Law; Medical Malpractice.
Whitehouse, Timothy A. '37 '67 C.154 B.A. L.426 L.A. Co. Supr. Ct.
Whitesell, Thomas C. '58 '83 C.427 B.A. L.352 J.D. 500 S. Grand Ave.
Whitlo, Richard C. '44 '79 C.800 B.S. L.1136 LL.B. 801 S. Grand Ave.
Whitman, Scott L. '58 '83 C.464 B.A. L.1148 J.D. [Muehle&W.]
**Whitman, Todd E.** '67 '94 C.477 B.B.A. L.800 J.D. [Ⓐ Allen,M.L.G.&M.]
*PRACTICE AREAS: Litigation.

**Whitman Breed Abbott & Morgan, (AV)**
**633 West Fifth Street, 90071⊙**
**Telephone: 213-896-2400 Cable Address: "Whitsom LSA" Telex: 68-6157 (WU) Telecopier: 213-896-2450**
**URL: http://www.financelaw.com**
**Resident Partners: Christopher A. Burrows; Francis W. Costello; Joseph P. Dailey (Not admitted in CA); Richard A. Eastman; James C. Hughes; Robert L. Ivey; Gerold W. Libby; Maita Deal Prout; Mark S. Shipow; Richard T. Williams; Paul C. Workman. Resident Associates: Alex R. Baghdassarian; Donald M. Clary; Vito A. Costanzo; Roger B. Coven; Daniel W. Lee; Jason J. Liberman; Toby Rose Mallen; Paul S. Marks; Ann Bridget McCarthy; Tasha D. Nguyen; Jack S. Sholkoff; Douglas K. Simpson; Alan J. Watson.**
**General Practice including International Commercial Law.**
**New York, New York Office: 200 Park Avenue. Telephone: 212-351-3000.**
**Greenwich, Connecticut Office: 100 Field Point Road. Telephone: 203-869-3800.**
**Sacramento, California Office: Senator Hotel Building, 1121 L Street. Telephone: 916-441-4242.**
**Newark, New Jersey Office: One Gateway Center. Telephone: 201-621-2230.**
**Palm Beach, Florida Office: 220 Sunrise Avenue. Telephone: 407-832-5458.**
**London, England Office: 11 Waterloo Place. Telephone: 71-839-3226. Telex: 917881.**
**Tokyo, Japan Office: Suite 450, New Otemachi Building, 2-2-1 Otemachi, Chiyoda-Ku, Tokyo 100. Telephone: 81-3-3242-1289.**
**Associated with: Tyan & Associes, 22, La Sagesse Street-Rmeil, Beirut, Lebanon. Telephone: 337968. Fax: 200969. Telex: 43928.**

***See Professional Biographies, LOS ANGELES, CALIFORNIA***

Whitmire, Robert L., (P.C.), (AV) '42 '67 C.309 B.A. L.150 J.D. 555 S. Flower St.
**Whitney, George H.**, (AV) '14 '40 C.951 A.B. L.813 LL.B. [Ⓒ Gibson,D.&C.]
*LANGUAGES: French.
*PRACTICE AREAS: Corporation Finance; Real Property.
**Whitney, Tracey M.** '69 '94 C.228 B.A. L.800 J.D. [Ⓐ Gibson,D.&C.]
**Whitt, Gerald R.** '50 '76 C.228 B.S.E.E. L.813 J.D. [Overton,L.&P.]
*PRACTICE AREAS: Business Law; Commercial Law; Creditors Rights; Bankruptcy Law.
**Whittle, Marcus G.** '52 '91 C.990 B.S. L.1068 J.D. [Ⓐ Pillsbury M.&S.]
**Whitwell, Ben D.** '57 '88 C.112 B.A. L.800 J.D. [Ⓐ Skadden,A.S.M.&F.]

**Whitworth, Valerie C., Law Offices of '52 '80 C.112 B.A. L.1068 J.D.**
**10850 Wilshire Boulevard, Suite 819, 90024-4305**
**Telephone: 310-446-5836 Fax: 310-446-5838**
**Complex Business Litigation, Entertainment, Transactional, Bankruptcy. Appellate Law.**

***See Professional Biographies, LOS ANGELES, CALIFORNIA***

Wick, Charles Z. '17 '43 C.477 B.M. L.930 LL.B. 120 S. Mapleton Dr.
Wickens & Lebow 1801 Century Pk. E. (⊙Washington, D.C. & Boca Raton, Fla.)
**Wickers, Alonzo B., IV** '68 '93 C.309 A.B. L.112 J.D. [Ⓐ Jones,D.R.&P.]
**Wickham, Douglas A.** '60 '86 C.112 B.A. L.276 J.D. [Ⓐ Skadden,A.S.M.&F.]
Wickline, Richard P. '62 '90 C.665 B.A. L.1068 J.D. 333 S. Grand Ave.

**Wickwire Gavin LLP**
**35th Floor 777 South Figueroa Street, 90017-5831⊙**
**Telephone: 213-688-9500 Telecopier: 213-627-6342**
**Email: wgca@wickwire.com**
**David P. Dapper; Joseph G. McGuinness. Associates: Kayhan M. Fatemi; Elizabeth M. Lascheid; Jodi M. Lewis.**
**General Civil, Administrative and Legislative Practice before all Federal and Local Courts, Departments, Agencies and the Congress. Construction, Public Contract, Fidelity and Surety, Federal Grant, Environmental, Bankruptcy, Corporate and Commercial Syndication.**
**Vienna, Virginia Office: Wickwire Gavin, P.C., International Gateway, 8100 Boone Boulevard, Suite 700. Telephone: 703-790-8750. Telecopier: 703-448-1801.**
**Washington, D.C. Office: Wickwire Gavin, P.C., Two Lafayette Centre, Suite 450, 1133 21st Street, N.W. Telephone: 202-887-5200. Cable Address: "WireGG". FAX: 202-223-0120.**
**Madison, Wisconsin Office: Wickwire Gavin, P.C., Suite 300, 2 East Gilman Street, P.O. Box 1683. Telephone: 608-257-5335. Fax: 608-257-2029.**
**Greenbelt, Maryland Office: Wickwire Gavin, P.C., Suite 220, 6411 Ivy Lane. Telephone: 301-441-9420.**
**Minneapolis, Minnesota Office: Wickwire Gavin, P.A., 4700 Norwest Center, 90 South Seventh Street. Telephone: 612-347-0408. Telecopier: 612-673-0720.**

***See Professional Biographies, LOS ANGELES, CALIFORNIA***

Widdifield, Ann Migden '53 '87 C.112 B.A. L.426 J.D. Asst. Exec. Dir., Writers Guild of Amer., West, Inc.
**Widdifield, Melissa N.** '58 '87 C.112 B.A. L.426 J.D. [Talcott,L.V.&S.]
*PRACTICE AREAS: Criminal Defense Law; Civil Rights Law; Civil Litigation.
Widelitz, Kenneth S. '50 '75 C.659 B.S. L.1068 J.D. 10519 Lauriston Ave.
**Widom, Richard M.**, (AV) '52 '77 C&L.1077 J.D. [Stockwell,H.W.&W.]
**Wieczorek, Nicholas M.** '58 '83 C.800 B.A. L.1068 J.D. [Morris,P.&P.]

**Wiederschall, James S., Law Offices of**
**(See Woodland Hills)**

**Wien, Howard, (AV) '51 '77 C.674 A.B. L.800 J.D.**
**18th Floor 2049 Century Park East, 90067**
**Telephone: 310-553-3332 Fax: 310-553-8700**
**Publishing, Copyrights, Trademarks and Litigation.**

Wiener, Gerald H. '41 '67 C.112 A.B. L.1068 LL.B. The Richland Grp.
**Wiener, Ian C.** '61 '92 C.197 A.B. L.276 J.D. [Ⓐ Irell&M.]
**Wiener, Laurence S.** '61 '87 C.674 A.B. L.1068 J.D. [Richards,W.&G.]
*PRACTICE AREAS: Public Law; Municipal Law; Land Use Law; California Environmental Quality Act.
Wiener, Robert A. '51 '79 C.273 B.A. L.616 J.D. 6255 Sunset Blvd.
**Wiener, Steven D.**, (AV) '40 '75 C.197 B.A. L.1068 J.D. [Solish,A.&G.]
*PRACTICE AREAS: Franchise Law; Business Litigation.
**Wiesenthal, Mark A.** '55 '96 C.112 B.A. L.426 J.D. [Ⓐ Troop M.S.&P.]
*PRACTICE AREAS: Real Estate.
**Wiesner, Susan E.** '61 '87 C&L.190 B.A., J.D. [Ⓐ Trope&T.]
*LANGUAGES: French.
*PRACTICE AREAS: Family Law.
Wiggen, Ralph E. '33 '61 C&L.145 B.A., J.D. 3345 Wilshire Blvd.
Wiggin and Co. 2121 Avenue of the Stars (⊙Cheltenham)
Wiggins, David '52 '85 C.668 B.A. L.1065 J.D. 1999 Ave. of the Stars, 27th Fl.
**Wiggins, Herbert N.** '59 '86 C.197 A.B. L.1066 J.D. [Ⓐ Atkins&E.]
*LANGUAGES: Spanish and Portuguese.
*REPORTED CASES: G. Monchette v. Oakland Unified School District, 217 Cal.App. 3d 303, 266 Cal. P.appl. (1990).
*PRACTICE AREAS: Government Liability; Premises Liability; Automobile Accidents and Injuries; International; Products Liability (10%).
Wiggins, J. Brad '56 '83 C&L.101 B.A., J.D. 1801 Century Park East, 7th Fl.
**Wigmore, John G.**, (AV) '28 '58 C.813 B.S. L.1068 LL.B. [Pillsbury M.&S.]
Wilbur, William '44 '83 C.976 B.A. L.1136 J.D. 1605 W. Olympic Blvd.
**Wilcott, Scott J**, (AV) '38 '67 C.112 B.S. L.800 J.D. Exec. V.P., Law & Prop., CalMat Co.
**Wilcox, Deanna M.** '61 '94 C.1163 B.A. L.145 J.D. [Ⓐ Heller E.W.&M.]
**Wilder, Jeniffer A.** '67 '93 C.475 B.A. L.1187 J.D. [Ⓐ Millard,P.H.&C.]
*PRACTICE AREAS: Insurance Defense; Civil Litigation.
Wildermuth, Michael S. '63 '89 C.112 B.A. L.1049 J.D. 1055 W. 7th St.
**Wileman, Keith G.** '58 '83 C.276 B.S.F.S. L.800 J.D. [Lord,B.&B.]
*PRACTICE AREAS: Products Liability Defense; Railroad Liability Defense; Insurance Coverage; Architect Liability Defense; Business Litigation.
Wilen, Daniel B. '40 '65 C.107 B.A. L.569 J.D. Coun., Barkley Court Reporters
**Wiles, Alexander F.** '52 '77 C.112 A.B. L.1066 J.D. [Irell&M.]
**Wiles, Valerie J.** '59 '89 C.970 B.A. L.1068 J.D. [Ⓐ Long&L.]
Wiley, Jerry '33 '67 C.866 B.A. L.800 J.D. Vice Dean & Prof., Univ. of Southern Calif.
**Wiley, John Shepard, Jr.** '53 '81 C.112 A.B. L.1066 J.D. [Ⓒ Mayer,B.&P.]
**Wilke, Peter J.** '48 '77 C.112 B.A. L.285 J.D. [Ⓒ Tourtelot&B.]
*PRACTICE AREAS: Business Litigation; Entertainment Law; Corporate Law; Securities (public filings and private offerings); Real Estate.
**Wilken, Alan W.**, (AV) '47 '74 C.31 A.B. L.1068 J.D. [Loeb&L.]
*PRACTICE AREAS: Litigation.
**Wilkening, Raquel L.** '67 '92 C.112 B.S. L.309 J.D. [Ⓐ Folger L.&K.]⊙
**Wilkerson, Robert L.** '61 '89 C.112 B.A. L.1066 J.D. [Ⓐ White&C.]
**Wilkinson, Kirk A.** '59 '86 C.473 B.A. L.1119 J.D. [Latham&W.]
*PRACTICE AREAS: Environmental Litigation.
Wilkinson, Michael R. '50 '82 C.112 B.A. L.426 J.D. Dep. City Atty., Spec. Operations Div.
Wilkof, Arthur M., (A Prof. Corp.), (BV) '37 '67 C.381 B.S. L.426 LL.B. 1925 Century Pk. E.
Willcockson, Kleber '37 '65 (adm. in IA; not adm. in CA) 1809 Armacost Ave.‡
Willd, John A. '24 '53 C.112 B.A. L.800 J.D. 314 W. 1st St.
**Willenburg, Don**, (AV) '56 '84 C.424 B.A. L.813 J.D. [Ⓒ Pachulski,S.Z.&Y.]
*REPORTED CASES: In re Pub. Serv. Co. of N.H., 884 F. 2d 11 (1st Cir. 1989); Greyhound Real Estate Finance Co. v. Official Unsecured Creditors' Committee (In re Northview Corp.) 130 B.R. 543 (9th Cir. BAP 1991).
*TRANSACTIONS: Sale of Ticor Title Co. to Chicago Title Co.; 21st Century Film Library.
**Willens, Earl P.**, (AV) '35 '60 C.112 A.B. L.1066 LL.B. [Ⓒ Corinblit&S.]
*PRACTICE AREAS: Complex Civil Litigation; Antitrust; Securities.
**Willett, Robert E.**, (AV) '43 '74 C.1077 B.A. L.1066 J.D. [O'Melveny&M.]
*PRACTICE AREAS: Antitrust Law; Patent Litigation; Trade Secrets; Securities Litigation; General Commercial Litigation.
Williams, Alexander H., III '44 '69 C.976 B.A. L.893 LL.B. Supr. Ct. J.
**Williams, Allan S.** '69 '95 C.1042 B.A. L.61 J.D. [Ⓐ Fierstein&S.]
*PRACTICE AREAS: Business Litigation; Tort Litigation; Trusts and Estates; Construction Defect Litigation.

**Williams, Arnold F. '55 '87 C.813 A.B. L.1068 J.D.**
**800 Wilshire Boulevard 12th Floor, 90017**
**Telephone: 213-688-7523 Fax: 213-688-2771**
**Email: arnofwms@netcom.com**
**Wills, Trusts and Estate Planning, Probate, Charitable Tax Planning and Elder Law.**

***See Professional Biographies, LOS ANGELES, CALIFORNIA***

**Williams, Bart H.** '62 '88 C&L.976 B.A., J.D. [Munger,T.&O.]
*PRACTICE AREAS: Commercial Litigation; White Collar Criminal Defense.
Williams, Brian K. '63 '89 C.112 B.A. L.1068 J.D. 611 W. 6th St., 16th Fl.
Williams, Cameron '42 '70 C.112 B.A. L.1068 J.D. [Tyre K.K.&G.]
Williams, Carol Cavan '53 '80 C.813 B.A. L.1068 J.D. Capitol Records, Inc.
Williams, Cassandra L. '68 '94 C&L.800 B.A., J.D. 15456 Ventura Blvd., 5th Fl. (Sherman Oaks)
**Williams, Christopher T.** '67 '94 C.112 B.A. L.1065 J.D. [Ⓐ Pillsbury M.&S.]
**Williams, Conward E.** '37 '61 C&L.923 A.B., J.D. [Ⓒ Seyfarth,S.F.&G.]
*PRACTICE AREAS: Government Contract Law; International Law; Litigation; Boards of Contract Appeals.
Williams, Countess C. '59 '85 C.103 A.B. L.309 J.D. (adm. in MA; not adm. in CA) Assoc. Coun., Writers Guild of Amer., West, Inc.
**Williams, Cranston J.** '63 '92 C.999 B.S. L.112 J.D. [Ⓐ Baker&H.]
Williams, Damien E. '38 '85 L.1137 J.D. Dep. City Atty.
Williams, David W. '10 '37 C.113 B.A. L.800 LL.B. U.S. Sr. Dist. J.‡
Williams, Donald A. '56 '84 C&L.990 B.S., J.D. [Williams&N.]
**Williams, Donald C.** '39 '67 C.267 B.A. L.950 J.D. [Carlsmith B.W.C.&I.]
*PRACTICE AREAS: Commercial Law; Commercial Real Estate Development; Pacific Rim Trade.
Williams, Elliott L. '40 '70 C.112 B.A. L.284 J.D. Gen. Coun., Directors Guild of Amer.
Williams, Ernest G. '25 '54 C.1097 L.426 J.D. Supr. Ct. J.
**Williams, Evan G.** '43 '69 C.112 B.A. L.1068 J.D. [Poindexter&D.]
*PRACTICE AREAS: Corporate; Securities; Alternative Energy; Real Estate.
Williams, George H. '41 '73 C.1077 B.A. L.809 J.D. 10 Universal City Plaza, 28th Fl.
**Williams, Harley J., (P.C.)**, (AV) '50 '76 C.352 B.B.A. L.976 J.D. [Blanc W.J.&K.]
**Williams, James P.** '52 '89 C&L.705 B.A., J.D. [Jeffer,M.B.&M.]
*PRACTICE AREAS: Trademark and Unfair Competition; Copyright; Advertising.
**Williams, James S.**, (AV) '49 '77 C.112 B.A. L.284 J.D. [Ⓐ Murchison&C.]
*REPORTED CASES: %italic; United States v. Wickland %roman; (1980) 619 F.2d 75; %italic; Pacific Service Stations 6 v. Mobil Oil Corp. %roman.
*PRACTICE AREAS: Insurance Coverage; Insurance Bad Faith Litigation; Insurance Defense.
Williams, Jerry L., (Mrs.) '33 '75 C&L.1127 B.S.L., J.D. L.A. Housing Authority
Williams, Jimmie L., Jr. '62 '89 C.112 B.S. L.941 J.D. 865 S. Figueroa St. #3100
**Williams, Jonathan P.** '49 '81 C.976 B.A. L.1065 J.D. [O'Melveny&M.] (⊙New York)
*LANGUAGES: Korean.
Williams, Judith A. '47 '74 C.242 B.A. L.426 J.D. Univ. Park
**Williams, Kenneth** '59 '85 C.893 B.A. L.94 J.D. [Cox,C.&N.]
*PRACTICE AREAS: Construction Law; Real Property Law.
Williams, Larry E. '44 '72 C.112 B.A. L.178 J.D. 1060 Crenshaw Blvd.
**Williams, Lawrence D.**, (AV) '38 '64 C.1042 B.A. L.1068 J.D. [Williams&B.]⊙
*PRACTICE AREAS: Estate Planning Law; Tax Planning Law; Corporate Law.
**Williams, Lee D.**, (AV) '50 '77 C.112 B.A. L.1068 J.D. [Williams&K.]
**Williams, Leslie Gail** '— '80 C.605 B.A. L.112 J.D. [Shaub&W.]
*LANGUAGES: French, German and Spanish.
*PRACTICE AREAS: European Union; International Business and Intellectual Property Transactions; and Related Litigation.
Williams, Lynn A. '56 '82 C.112 B.A. L.800 J.D. V.P., Cushman Realty Corp.
**Williams, Michael Ernest** '70 '95 C.800 B.A. L.309 J.D. [Ⓐ Quinn E.U.&O.]

CAA366P

**Williams, Michael T.** ........................ '53 '82 C.354 B.A. L.1049 J.D. [Andrews&K.]
*PRACTICE AREAS: Civil Litigation; Appellate; Aviation; Antitrust; Bankruptcy.
**Williams, Nedy A.** ........................ '71 '96 C.1042 B.A. L.1062 J.D. [A Burke,W.&S.]
*PRACTICE AREAS: Civil Litigation.

**Williams, Norma J., Law Offices of '52 '77 C.918 B.A. L.1066 J.D.**
**600 Wilshire Boulevard, Ninth Floor, 90017-3212**
**Telephone: 213-975-1845 Facsimile: 213-975-1833**
***PRACTICE AREAS: Real Estate; Bankruptcy Law; Commercial Law.**
**Of Counsel: Vahan Saroians.**
**Real Estate Transactions and Real Estate Litigation.**
*See Professional Biographies, LOS ANGELES, CALIFORNIA*

**Williams, Ralph O., III,** (AV) ........................ '45 '72 C&L.1190 B.S., J.D. [King&W.]
Williams, Raymond H. ........................ '32 '64 C.800 A.B. L.809 LL.B. Dep. City Atty.
**Williams, Richard D.,** (AV) ........ '46 '73 C.906 B.A. L.1068 J.D. [Charlston,R.&W.]
**Williams, Richard T.,** (AV) ........ '45 '72 C&L.813 A.B., J.D. [Whitman B.A.&M.]
*PRACTICE AREAS: Antitrust; Business Litigation; Intellectual Property Litigation.
**Williams, Robert E.** ........................ '51 '76 C.112 B.A. L.309 J.D. [Sheppard,M.R.&H.]
*PRACTICE AREAS: Real Estate Law; Secured Transactions.
**Williams, Sandra K.** ........ '54 '78 C.788 A. B. L.477 J.D. Asst. Gen. Coun., CBS Inc.
Williams, Stanley P. ........................ '52 '82 C.112 B.A. L.809 J.D. 4228 Creed Ave.
**Williams, Susan J.,** (AV) ........................ '52 '78 C.674 B.A. L.309 J.D. [Hennelly&G.]
*LANGUAGES: Spanish.
*PRACTICE AREAS: Litigation.
**Williams, Susan Z.** ........................ '60 '86 C.860 A.B. L.800 J.D. [A Loeb&L.]
*LANGUAGES: French.
Williams, Teresa A., (AV) ............ '55 '81 C.112 B .A. L.464 J.D. [Williams&Assoc.]
**Williams, Vivian L.** ............ '65 '94 C.309 B.A. L.569 J.D. [A Sonnenschein N.&R.]
*PRACTICE AREAS: Labor and Employment.
Williams & Associates, Law Offices of, (AV) ........ 15300 Ventura Blvd. (Sherman Oaks)

**Williams and Ballas, (AV) BB**
**1800 Century Park East, Suite 510, 90067⊙**
**Telephone: 310-557-8383 Fax: 310-557-8380**
**Members of Firm: Lawrence D. Williams (Certified Specialist, Estate Planning, Trust and Probate Law, The State Bar of California Board of Legal Specialization); Stephen B. Ballas (Certified Specialist, Taxation Law, The State Bar of California Board of Legal Specialization). Of Counsel: Stanley P. Graham. Associates: Melissa Hamilton.**
**Estate Planning, Tax Planning, Probate and Corporate Law.**
**San Francisco, California Office: 160 Sansome Street, Suite 1200. Telephone: 415-296-9904. Fax: 415-981-0898.**
*See Professional Biographies, LOS ANGELES, CALIFORNIA*

**Williams, Berges & Sanford, (AV)**
**Suite 511, 10850 Riverside Drive, 91602**
**Telephone: 818-769-6622 Fax: 818-769-9632**
**Email: wbs1@lawnt.com**
**Members of Firm: Ronald A. Berges; Thomas C. Sanford. Associates: Stephen M. Kalpakian; Paul J. Skitzki.**
**General Civil and Trial Practice. Negligence, Products Liability, Probate, Malpractice and Insurance Law.**
*See Professional Biographies, LOS ANGELES, CALIFORNIA*

**Williams & Kilkowski, (AV)**
**22nd Floor, 2121 Avenue of the Stars, 90067**
**Telephone: 310-282-8995 Facsimile: 310-282-8930**
**Lee D. Williams; James M. Kilkowski.**
**Civil Litigation. Bankruptcy, Secured Transactions, Corporate, Business, Real Estate and Entertainment Law.**
**Reference: Santa Monica Bank.**
*See Professional Biographies, LOS ANGELES, CALIFORNIA*

Williams & Martinet, P.C. ........................ 221 N. Figueroa St. (⊙San Francisco)
Williams & Nenney, (AV) ........................ 11520 San Vicente Blvd.

**Williams Woolley Cogswell Nakazawa & Russell**
**(See Long Beach)**

Williamson, Joanne '52 '80
C.347 B.A. L.912 J.D. Asst. Reg. Coun., Chicago Title Ins. Co.
**Williamson, Marcus R.** ............ '41 '76 C.390 B.S. L.469 J.D. [Williamson,R.&D.]
*PRACTICE AREAS: Insurance Defense; Business Litigation; Products Liability; Construction Defect; Professional Malpractice.
**Williamson, Michael A.** ............ '64 '92 C.668 B.A. L.426 J.D. [A O'Melveny&M.]
**Williamson, Richard E.** ........................ '60 '85 C.36 B.S. L.464 J.D. [Ezer&W.]
*PRACTICE AREAS: Partnership; Real Estate; Business; Commercial; Construction Litigation.

**Williamson, Raleigh & Doherty, A Law Corporation, (BV)**
**801 South Grand Avenue, 11th Floor, 90017**
**Telephone: 213-629-3480 Facsimile: 213-688-0057**
**John J. Doherty; John K. Raleigh; Marcus R. Williamson;—Jeffrey S. Bretoi; Paul F. Sullivan. Of Counsel: James T. Catlow.**
**General Civil Litigation in all State and Federal Courts, Insurance Defense, Business Litigation, Products Liability, Construction Defect, Professional Malpractice, Insurance Coverage, Catastrophe and Land Subsidence Losses, Insurance Fraud, Premise Liability, Governmental/Municipality Defense, Environmental Liability.**
*See Professional Biographies, LOS ANGELES, CALIFORNIA*

**Willick, Daniel H., (AV) '42 '73 C.112 A.B. L.1068 J.D.**
**1999 Avenue of the Stars Twenty-Seventh Floor, 90067**
**Telephone: 310-286-0485 Facsimile: 310-286-0487**
**(Also of Counsel Pircher, Nichols & Meeks).**
**Associate: Marc I. Willick.**
**General Civil Litigation Practice in all State and Federal Courts. Health Care Law. Administrative Law.**
*See Professional Biographies, LOS ANGELES, CALIFORNIA*

**Willick, Marc I.** ........................ '68 '94 C.112 B.A. L.426 J.D. [A D.H.Willick]

**Willing, Andrew Russell, (AV) '41 '66 C.31 B.A. L.309 J.D. BB**
**Promenade West, 880 West First Street Suite 302, 90012**
**Telephone: 213-626-6600 Facsimile: 213-626-0488**
***LANGUAGES: Spanish.**
**Criminal Defense in State and Federal Courts. Appellate Practice. Municipal Law. Land Use. Administrative Law (Emphasizing Medical License Defense).**
**Reference: Wells Fargo Bank (Pasadena Main Office).**
*See Professional Biographies, LOS ANGELES, CALIFORNIA*

Willis, Dean A. ........................ '63 '88 C.112 B.A. L.426 J.D. 400 S. Hope St.
**Willis, Henry M.** ........................ '52 '78 C.918 B.A. L.1066 J.D. [Schwartz,S.D.&S.]
*PRACTICE AREAS: Labor and Employment Law; Public Employment Relations Law; Employment Discrimination Law.
Willis, Jack R. ........................ '40 '61 C.112 B.A. L.1068 J.D. 7060 Hollywood Blvd.
Willis, Jeffrey L., (A Prof. Law Corp.) '46 '71
C.994 B.A. L.800 J.D. 639 S. New Hampshire Ave.
Willman, Mark T. ........................ '54 '81 C.154 B.A. L.426 J.D. 110 N. Grand Ave.
Willman, William P., (BV) ........ '18 '48 C&L.800 A.B., LL.B. 14342 Mulholland Dr.

**Willmore, Kate A.** ........................ '47 '91 C.112 B.A. L.763 J.D. [A Parker S.]
*PRACTICE AREAS: Civil Litigation; Bankruptcy; General Civil.
**Willner, Arthur I.** ........................ '55 '82 C.178 B.A. L.724 J.D. [Wright,R.O.&T.]
*PRACTICE AREAS: Products Liability Litigation; Insurance Defense Litigation; Aviation Law.
**Willner, Robert A.** ........................ '56 '91 C.112 B.A. L.426 J.D. [A Buchalter,N.F.&Y.]
*PRACTICE AREAS: Secured and Unsecured Financing and Lending; General Corporate and Transactional Practice.
Wills, Charles E., (AV) ........................ '— '48 C&L.910 B.S.E.E., J.D. [C.E.Wills] (Pat.)
Wills, Charles E., Law Corp., (AV) ........................ 801 S. Figueroa St., 14th Fl. (Pat.)
Wills-Thomas, Barbara J. ........ '51 '77 C.112 B.A. L.800 J.D. Legal Div., Dept. of Transp.

**Willsey Law Offices, Owned by a Prof. Corp.**
**(See Pasadena)**

Wilmore, John D. ............ '65 '92 C.674 B.A. L.800 J.D. Univ. of Southern California
Wilner, Michael R. ..... '66 '91 C.197 B.A. L.659 J.D. U.S. Securities & Exchange Comm.

**Wilner, Robert D., Law Offices of, (AV) '36 '64 C.1097 L.809 LL.B.**
**601 West 5th Street, Room 203, 90071-2000**
**Telephone: 213-624-4223**
**(Certified Specialist, Estate Planning, Trust and Probate Law, The State Bar of California Board of Legal Specialization).**
**Probate and Estate Planning, Trusts and Wills.**
*See Professional Biographies, LOS ANGELES, CALIFORNIA*

**Wilner, Klein & Siegel, A Professional Corporation**
**(See Beverly Hills)**

Wilsbacher, Mary Anne Banks '65 '90
C.923 B.S.J. L.851 J.D. Atty. Advsr., Off. of U.S. Trustee
Wilson, A. Charles, (AV) ........ '24 '51 C.112 L.800 J.D. 1801 Century Pk. E., 17th Fl.‡
**Wilson, Beth Mezoff** ........................ '62 '88 C.103 A.B. L.1068 J.D. [A Fulbright&J.]
*PRACTICE AREAS: Corporate Law.
Wilson, Christine J. ............ '55 '86 L.1148 J.D. Assoc. Gen. Coun., Plott Mgmt. Corp.
**Wilson, Christopher A.** ............ '67 '93 C.228 B.A. L.426 J.D. [A Manning,M.&W.]
**Wilson, David J.** ........................ '55 '88 C.112 B.A. L.800 J.D. [A Manning,M.&W.]
*PRACTICE AREAS: Writs and Appeals; Business Litigation; Insurance Bad Faith; Employment and Disability.
**Wilson, Deborah J.** ........................ '66 '91 C.636 B.S. L.1068 J.D. [A Gascou,G.&T.]
Wilson, Delph R. ............ '46 '73 C.831 B.B.A. L.262 J.D. 1520 Wilsire Blvd., 6th Fl.
**Wilson, Dennis L.** ........................ '66 '91 C.267 B.A. L.800 J.D. [A Baker&H.]
*PRACTICE AREAS: Intellectual Property.
**Wilson, Derek H.** ........................ '59 '87 C.966 B.A. L.309 J.D. [A Morrison&F.]
**Wilson, Donald D.** ........................ '45 '71 C.112 B.A. L.1068 J.D. [Grace,S.C.&S.]
*PRACTICE AREAS: Automobile and Premises Liability; Complex Litigation; Product Liability; Medical Malpractice; Construction Claims.
**Wilson, Donald K., Jr.** ........................ '54 '79 C.800 B.S. L.569 J.D. [C J.L.Cochran,Jr.]
*PRACTICE AREAS: Entertainment and Sports Law.
**Wilson, Elta M.** ..... '47 '80 C.112 B.A. L.629 J.D. Sr. Coun., Pacific Telesis Legal Group
Wilson, Franklin H., (AV) ............ '34 '65 C.112 B.A. L.178 LL.B. 600 Wilshire Blvd.
**Wilson, James J.** ........................ '46 '72 C.838 B.S. L.1119 J.D. [Diamond&W.]
*PRACTICE AREAS: Entertainment Law; Music Recording Law; Motion Picture Law; Television Law.
**Wilson, Jason G.** ........................ '69 '94 C.674 A.B. L.112 J.D. [A Thelen,M.J.&B.]
*LANGUAGES: French.
*PRACTICE AREAS: Business Litigation.
**Wilson, Jason Haruo** ........................ '— '89 C.668 B.A. L.309 J.D. [A Morgan,L.&B.]
Wilson, John R. ........................ '40 '70 C.1075 B.S. L.809 J.D. Dep. City Atty.
Wilson, Koh Siok Tian ........................ '42 '66 L.061 LL.B. 1342 N. Haywood Ave.
Wilson, Laurie L. ........................ '66 '91 C.966 B.S. L.800 J.D. 333 S. Grand Ave.
Wilson, Michael A. ........................ '42 '70 C.112 A.B. L.1065 J.D. Dep. Dist. Atty.
**Wilson, Molly** '51 '76 C.112 B.A. L.1068 J.D.
V.P. & Sr. Coun., W. Coast Film Programming, Home Box Office
Wilson, Patricia M. ........................ '57 '83 C.112 B.A. L.1065 J.D. [Shane&P.]
**Wilson, Robert G.,** (AV) ........................ '48 '74 C.112 B.A. L.813 J.D. [Cotkin&C.]
*PRACTICE AREAS: Antitrust; Bankruptcy; Business; Commercial and Securities Litigation.
Wilson, Robert L. ................ '33 '60 C.25 A.B. L.659 LL.B. 2040 Ave. of the Stars
**Wilson, Robert L., (Professional Corporation),** (AV) '31 '59
C.112 A.B. L.1068 J.D. [Wilson,K.&B.]
Wilson, Ronald N. ........................ '48 '73 C.813 B.A. L.309 J.D. [Wilson&B.]
Wilson, Stephen V. ........................ '42 '67 C.401 B.A. L.1009 J.D. U.S. Dist. J.
Wilson, Steven J. ........................ '49 '84 C.112 B.A. L.426 J.D. 33rd Fl. 611 W. 6th St.
**Wilson, Suzanne V.** ........................ '62 '91 C.112 B.A. L.309 J.D. [A Blanc W.J.&K.]
*REPORTED CASES: Jeff Foxworthy v. Custom Tees, Inc., 879 F. Supp. 1200 (N.D. Ga. 1995).
*PRACTICE AREAS: Commercial Litigation; Proprietary Rights Litigation; Employment Law; Discrimination Law.
Wilson, Terry ............ '46 '79 C.623 B.A. L.1066 J.D. 221 N. Figueroa St., Ste., 1200
Wilson, Veronica M. '58 '91
C.766 B.A. L.809 J.D. Coun., Twentieth Century Fox Film Corp.
**Wilson, William G.,** (AV) ........................ '41 '65 C&L.846 B.B.A., LL.B. [Jones,D.R.&P.]
**Wilson, Winfield D.,** (AV) ........................ '47 '72 C.112 A.B. L.1068 J.D. [Nossaman,G.K.&E.]
*PRACTICE AREAS: Real Property Law; Litigation.
Wilson & Becks, (BV) ........................ 5900 Wilshire Blvd.

**Wilson, Elser, Moskowitz, Edelman & Dicker, (AV)**
**Suite 2700, 1055 West Seventh Street, 90017⊙**
**Telephone: 213-624-3044 Telex: 17-0722 Facsimile: 213-624-8060**
**Resident Partners: Patrick M. Kelly; Jonathon F. Sher; Robert M. Young, Jr.; L. Victor Bilger, Jr.; Steven R. Parminter; Otis D. Wright, II; Vincent P. D'Angelo; James A. Stankowski; Martin K. Deniston; Roland L. Coleman, Jr.; Jack A. Janov; George A. Pisano; Stephen R. Knapp (Resident); Fredric W. Trester; E. Paul Dougherty, Jr. (Not admitted in CA; Resident, Tokyo Office); Mark K. Worthge. Resident Associates: Robert M. Anderson; Jonathan C. Balfus; Bradley R. Blamires; Vernon A. Fagin; Terry Lees Higham; Jordan T. Jones; Herbert P. Kunowski; Robert A. Latham III; Jeffrey M. Lenkov; Janice S. Lucas; Vincent A. McGonagle; Carey B. Moorehead; Michael D. Payne; Lorne M. Pollock; Denise Kabakow Rasmussen; William S. Roberts; Gary E. Tavetian.**
**General Insurance and Reinsurance Practice and Litigation. Commercial, Corporate and Securities Law. Domestic and International Property and Casualty Insurance and Reinsurance. Products and Professional Liability, Toxic Tort Defense, Environmental Impairment Liability, Medical and Hospital Malpractice, Municipal and Public Officials Liability, Trusts and Estates. Aviation, Marine and Inland Marine. Securities and Fiduciary Liability and General Subrogation.**
**New York, N.Y. Office: 150 East 42nd Street, 10017. Telephone: 212-490-3000. Telex: 177679. Facsimile: 212-490-3038; 212-557-7810.**
**San Francisco, California Office: 650 California Street, 94108. Telephone: 415-433-0990. Telex: 16-0768. Facsimile: 415-434-1370.**
**Washington, D.C. Office: The Colorado Building, Fifth Floor, 1341 "G" Street, N.W., 20005. Telephone: 202-626-7660. Telex: 89453. Facsimile: 202-628-3606.**
**Newark, New Jersey Office: Two Gateway Center, 07102. Telephone: 201-624-0800. Telex: 6853589. Facsimile: 201-624-0808.**
**Philadelphia, Pennsylvania Office: The Curtis Center, Independence Square West, 19106. Telephone: 215-627-6900. Telex: 6711203. Facsimile: 215-627-2665.**
**Baltimore, Maryland Office: 250 West Pratt Street, 21201. Telephone: 410-539-1800. Telex: 19-8280. Facsimile: 410-539-1820.**
**Miami, Florida Office: International Place, 100 Southeast Second Street, 33131. Telephone: 305-374-4400. Telex: 810845940. Facsimile: 305-579-0261.**
**Chicago, Illinois Office: 120 N. LaSalle Street, 26th Floor, 60602. Telephone: 312-704-0550. Telex: 1561590. Facsimile: 312-704-1552.**
**White Plains, N.Y. Office: 925 Westchester Avenue, 10604. Telephone: 914-946-7200. Facsimile: 914-946-7897.**

(This Listing Continued)

**Wilson, Elser, Moskowitz, Edelman & Dicker (Continued)**

**Dallas, Texas Office: 5000 Renaissance Tower, 1201 Elm Street, 75270. Telephone: 214-698-8000. Facsimile: 214-698-1101.**
**Albany, New York Office: One Steuben Place. Telephone: 518-449-8893. Fax: 518-449-8927.**
**London, England Office: 141 Fenchurch Street, EC3M 6BL. Telephone: 01-623-6723. Telex: 885741. Facsimile: 01-626-9774.**
**Tokyo, Japan Office: AIU Building, 1-3 Marunouchi 1-chome, Chiyoda-Ku, 100. Telephone: 011-813-216-6551. Facsimile: 011-(813) 3216-6965.**
**Affiliate Office in Paris, France: Honig Buffat Mettetal. 21 rue Clément Marot, 75008. Telephone: 33 (1) 44.43.88.88. Fax: 33 (1) 44.43.88.77.**
**Affiliate Offices in Germany: Munich, Germany: Bach, Langheid Dallmayr Pacellistrasse 8, 80333. Telephone: (49) 89 296 259. Facsimile: (49) 89 290 4756.**
**Cologne, Germany: Bach, Langheid Dallmayr Wilhelm-Waldeyer-Strasse 14, 50937. Telephone: (49) 221 944 027 0. Facsimile: (49) 221 944 027 8.**
**Frankfurt/Main, Germany: Bach, Langheid Dallmayr Schutzenstrasse 4, 60313. Telephone: (49) 69 920 740 0. Facsimile: (49) 69 920 740 40.**
**Wiesbaden, Germany: Bach, Langheid Dallmayr Robert-Koch, Ste. 6. Telephone(49) 611 56 42 38. Facsimile: (49) 611 564232.**

*See Professional Biographies, LOS ANGELES, CALIFORNIA*

**Wilson, Kenna & Borys, LLP, (AV)**
**A Limited Liability Partnership including Professional Corporations**
**Third Floor, 11075 Santa Monica Boulevard, 90025-3556**
**Telephone: 310-478-4285 FAX: 310-478-4351**
**Email: WKBLAW@AOL.COM**
**Members of Firm: Lawrence Borys (Professional Corporation); Timothy W. Kenna (Professional Corporation); Garth Goldberg; Christopher A. Kanjo; Jeffrey C. Burt. Associates: Ronald W. Ito; Arturo T. Salinas; Brian S. Nelson; Sylvia Anne Dyal; Lisa K. Garner; Charles N. Hargraves; Nancy J. Wenger; Joshua M. Sable; Shenne J. Hahn; Kristin M. Kubec; Yvonne Janet Lim. Of Counsel: Robert L. Wilson (Professional Corporation).**
**Professional Malpractice, Errors and Omissions, Product Liability, General Liability, Insurance Coverage, Bad Faith, Surety, Casualty and Fidelity Law. General Litigation in all State and Federal Courts.**

*See Professional Biographies, LOS ANGELES, CALIFORNIA*

**Wilton, Kenneth L.** ....... '61 '86 C.112 B.A. L.1065 J.D. [Ⓐ Small L.&K.]
*PRACTICE AREAS: Intellectual Property; Unfair Competition; Trade Secrets; Computer Law; Commercial Litigation.
**Wiman, Stephen P.**, (AV) ....... '47 '72 C.112 B.A. L.1065 J.D. [Nossaman,G.K.&E.]
*PRACTICE AREAS: Commercial Litigation.
**Wimmer, David A.** ....... '66 '91 C.659 B.A. L.880 J.D. [Ⓐ O'Melveny&M.]
**Wimsatt, William H., (Professional Corporation)**, (AV) '43 '75
C.734 B.A. L.426 J.D. [Ⓐ Magaña,C.&M.]
*PRACTICE AREAS: Airplane Crash Litigation; Aviation Law; Defective Products; Medical Malpractice Law; Products Liability Law.
**Winandy, John R.** ....... '64 '89 C.178 B.A. L.800 J.D. [Ⓐ D.S.White]
*PRACTICE AREAS: Real Estate; Business and Entertainment Litigation; Alternative Dispute Resolution; Arbitration.
Windham, Mark E., (AV) ....... '59 '84 C.112 A.B. L.1065 J.D. Dep. Pub. Def. IV
**Windisch, Gail Anderson** ....... '52 '80 C.1169 B.A. L.1068 J.D. [Ⓒ Manatt,P.&P.]
**Windisch, Mark S.** ....... '49 '75 C.228 A.B. L.1068 J.D. [Foley L.W.&A.]
*PRACTICE AREAS: Health Care; Hospitals; Administrative Law; State and Federal Legislative Practice; Managed Care.
Windle, Melville P. '26 '52 C&L.945 A.B., B.C.L.
(adm. in VA; not adm. in CA) Sr. V.P., Transamerica Ins. Co.
**Windler, Katherine M.** ....... '63 '92 C.174 B.A. L.112 J.D. [Ⓐ Kelley D.&W.]
*PRACTICE AREAS: Bankruptcy; Commercial Litigation.
**Windust, Paul W.** ....... '68 '93 C&L.800 B.S., J.D. [Ⓐ Wolf,R.&S.]
*PRACTICE AREAS: Commercial Litigation.
**Wine, Mark P.**, (AVⓉ) '49 '74 C.674 A.B. L.352 J.D.
(adm. in IA; not adm. in CA) [Oppenheimer P.S.]
*PRACTICE AREAS: Intellectual Property; Business and Commercial Litigation.
**Winegar, Steven D.** ....... '67 '94 C.976 B.A. L.112 J.D. [Ⓐ Shearman&S.]
**Winer, Kimberly G.** ....... '66 '91 C.259 B.A. L.426 J.D. [Ⓐ Graham&J.]
**Winesett, Shann D.** ....... '66 '93 C.549 B.A. L.426 J.D. [Ⓐ Robins,K.M.&C.]
*LANGUAGES: German.
*PRACTICE AREAS: Medical Malpractice; Product Liability Law; Professional Liability; Tort and Personal Injury.
**Winfield, Thomas F., III**, (AV) ....... '42 '68 C&L.705 B.A., J.D. [Brown,W.&C.]
*PRACTICE AREAS: Litigation; Real Estate; Environmental; Land Use.
**Wingfield, Jane Lindsey** ....... '44 '77 C.174 B.A. L.800 J.D. [Gibson,D.&C.]
*LANGUAGES: French.
*PRACTICE AREAS: Real Estate and Business Transactions.
**Winick, Kimberly S.** ....... '58 '85 C.478 B.A. L.846 J.D. [Ⓐ Mayer,B.&P.]
*LANGUAGES: Spanish.
Winn, Donald D. ....... '32 '56 C&L.623 B.B.A., LL.B. 330 Ocean Dr.
**Winn, Ross E.** ....... '54 '83 C.112 B.A. L.426 J.D. [Winn&F.]

**Winn & Fields**
**1801 Century Park East, Suite 1150, 90067**
**Telephone: 310-772-0800 Fax: 310-552-4760**
**Ross E. Winn; Stacey B. Fields.**
**Estate Planning including Charitable Gift and Tax Planning. General Business Law.**

*See Professional Biographies, LOS ANGELES, CALIFORNIA*

Winne, William Lawrence ....... '46 '75 C.813 B.A. L.809 J.D. 3540 Wilshire Blvd.
Winner, Zachary ....... '65 '92 C.800 B.A. L.464 J.D. 624 S Grand Ave., 27th Fl
**Winnick, Janet A.** ....... '61 '86 C.813 B.A. L.1068 J.D. [Allen,M.L.G.&M.]
*PRACTICE AREAS: Real Estate.
**Winograd, Andrew M.** ....... '69 '94 C&L.477 B.B.A., J.D. [Ⓐ Pillsbury M.&S.]
**Winograd, Risa B.** ....... '64 '91 C.112 B.A. L.426 J.D. [Ⓒ Christensen,M.F.J.G.W.&S.]
*PRACTICE AREAS: Real Estate.
Winograde, Jana ....... '64 '90 C.112 B.A. L.1066 J.D. Gen. Atty., Capital Cities/ABC, Inc.
Winslow, Robert L., (P.C.), (AV) '26 '49 C&L.813 A.B., LL.B.
1800 Ave. of the Stars, Suite 900 (Century City)
**Winslow, William L.**, (AV) ....... '50 '74 C.112 A.B. L.1068 J.D. [Ⓒ Goldfarb,S.&A.]
*PRACTICE AREAS: Structured Settlements; Estate Planning; Special Needs Trusts.
Winston, Warren M. ....... '42 '78 [Davis&W.]
Winter, Ralph C. ....... '37 '72 C.766 A.B. L.1065 J.D. P.O. Box 35481
**Winterman, Craig L.**, (AV) ....... '50 '77 C.629 B.S. L.809 J.D. [Herzfeld&R.]
*PRACTICE AREAS: Product Liability Law; Trial Practice.
**Winthrop, Rebecca J.** ....... '59 '84 C.800 B.A. L.426 J.D. [Ⓐ Kelley D.&W.]
Winthrop-Michel, Ellen ....... '55 '79 C.112 B.A. L.1068 J.D. 3056 Greentree Ct.
Wintrob, Jay S. ....... '57 '82 C.112 A.B. L.1066 J.D. 1 SunAmerica Ctr., Century City
**Wintroub, David L.**, (AV) ....... '41 '67 C.546 B.S. L.477 LL.B. [Wintroub&F.]
*PRACTICE AREAS: Estate Planning; Probate; Taxation; Real Estate.

**Wintroub & Fridkis, (AV)**
**A Partnership including a Professional Corporation**
**1875 Century Park East, 20th Floor, 90067**
**Telephone: 310-277-0440 Telecopier: 310-277-7994**
**David L. Wintroub; Cliff Fridkis (P.C.).**
**Civil Trial and Appellate Practice. Arbitration, Mediation, Corporation, Business, Government Contracts, Real Property, Secured Financing, Title Insurance, Taxation, Probate, Insurance, Estate Planning.**

*See Professional Biographies, LOS ANGELES, CALIFORNIA*

**Wippler, Michael P.** ....... '64 '91 C.112 B.A. L.1065 J.D. [Ⓐ Hanna&M.]
*PRACTICE AREAS: Real Estate; Civil Trial; General Practice.
**Wirta, Henry A., Jr.** '55 '83
C.800 B.A. L.1049 J.D. [Harrington,F.D.&C.] (ⓞSan Francisco)
*PRACTICE AREAS: Personal Injury Defense; Products Liability Law; General Civil Litigation Defense.
Wirth, Mary Catherine ....... '66 '92 C.112 A.B. L.1065 J.D. 400 S. Hope St.
**Wirthlin, Richard C.** ....... '63 '88 C.101 B.A. L.145 J.D. [Irell&M.]
Wirtschafter, David ....... '57 '85 C.112 B.A. L.800 J.D. Intl. Creative Mgmt., Inc.
**Wise, Michael J.** ....... '61 '89 C.112 B.S. L.426 J.D. [Ⓐ Lyon&L.] (See Pat. Sect.)
*PRACTICE AREAS: Patent, Trademark, Copyright, Unfair Competition; Antitrust; Intellectual Property.
Wise, Richard C., II ....... '62 '91 C.426 B.B.A. L.990 J.D. [Ⓐ Fuchs&M.]
**Wise, Roger R.** ....... '56 '84 C.339 B.S.E.E. L.365 J.D. [Loeb&L.] (See Pat. Sect.)
*PRACTICE AREAS: Trademark; Patent; Copyright.

**Wise, Wiezorek, Timmons & Wise, A Professional Corporation**
**(See Long Beach)**

Wiseman, Diane J. ....... '49 '84 C.112 B.A. L.809 J.D. Dep. Pub. Def.
Wiseman, Oscar, (AV) ....... '08 '32 C&L.800 B.A., LL.B. 9200 Sunset Blvd.
**Wish, Ernest Allen**, (AV) ....... '51 '76 C.112 B.A. L.1065 J.D. [E.A.Wish]

**Wish, Ernest Allen, A Professional Law Corporation, (AV)**
**2121 Avenue of the Stars, 22nd Floor, 90067-5010**
**Telephone: 310-277-0785 Fax: 310-203-0599**
**Ernest Allen Wish.**
**Business, Entertainment, Sports, Real Estate Litigation.**

*See Professional Biographies, LOS ANGELES, CALIFORNIA*

Wishingrad, Annie ....... '55 '87 C.061 B.S. L.809 J.D. 1801 Century Park E.
Wishman, Jeffrey N., (AV) ....... '55 '80 C.259 B.S. L.809 J.D. 201 N. Figueroa
**Wisialowski, Thomas S.** ....... '60 '85 C.965 B.B.A. L.813 J.D. [Paul,H.J.&W.]
**Wisnev, Michael A.** ....... '56 '80 C.502 B.S. L.813 J.D. [O'Melveny&M.]
**Wisnicki, Norman S.** ....... '53 '80 C.978 B.A. L.426 J.D. [Wolf,R.&S.]
*PRACTICE AREAS: Civil Litigation; Construction Litigation; Business and Commercial Litigation; Real Estate Litigation.
Wisot, G. Keith ....... '42 '67 C.668 B.A. L.1068 LL.B. Supr. Ct. J.‡
Wissner, Peter A. ....... '48 '74 C.112 B.A. L.1068 J.D. P.O. Box 491455
**Witham, Jeffrey R.** ....... '59 '84 C.1097 B.A. L.1066 J.D. [Dewey B.]
*PRACTICE AREAS: Litigation.
Withem, Michael L. ....... '52 '78 C.1077 B.A. L.990 J.D. 11500 W. Olympic Blvd.
Withers, Arlene Falk ....... '51 '78 C.184 B.A. L.1068 J.D. 1150 S. Olive St.
**Witlin, Scott J.** ....... '63 '88 C.188 B.S. L.813 J.D. [Ⓐ Proskauer R.G.&M.]
**Witt, Monica** ....... '64 '92 C.112 B.A. L.426 J.D. [Ⓐ Reznik&R.]
*PRACTICE AREAS: Real Estate Litigation; Eminent Domain; Inverse Condemnation; Land Use.
**Witt, Robert J.** ....... '41 '66 C.209 B.S.C. L.1068 J.D. [Walker,W.T.&W.]
*PRACTICE AREAS: Probate and Estate Planning; Taxation; Banking.
**Wittbrodt, Richard J.** ....... '57 '88 C.477 B.B.A. L.990 J.D. [Gibbs,G.L.&A.]
*PRACTICE AREAS: Real Estate Construction Law; Commercial Law.
**Witte, Lynn B.**, (AV) ....... '51 '79 C.675 B.A. L.1051 J.D. [Reish&L.]
*PRACTICE AREAS: Employee Benefits Consulting and Litigation; Taxation.
**Witteman, Anthony F.** ....... '59 '87 C.112 B.A. L.426 J.D. [Ⓐ Lord,B.&B.]
*PRACTICE AREAS: Environmental Insurance Coverage.
**Witteman, Teri L.** ....... '68 '93 C.112 B.A. L.1068 J.D. [Ⓐ Latham&W.]
Wittenberg, Jess S. ....... '52 '77 C.188 A.B. L.309 J.D. Nelson Entertainment

**Witter and Harpole**
**(See Pasadena)**

Wittorff, H. John, (BV) ....... '33 '64 C.768 B.A. L.426 LL.B. Asst. City Atty.
Witz, Rosalie C. ....... '— '79 C.1097 B.A. L.1148 J.D. 4477 Hollywood Blvd.
**Wixon, Clarke A.** ....... '68 '94 C.112 B.S. L.800 J.D. [Ⓐ Darby&D.] (Pat.)
*PRACTICE AREAS: Patent Law; Trademark Law.
Wodinsky, Peter H. ....... '54 '82 C.1078 B.A. L.809 J.D. 3000 S. Robertson Blvd.
**Wofford, Michael K.** ....... '59 '86 C.800 B.S. L.426 J.D. [Clark&T.]
*PRACTICE AREAS: General Corporate; Corporate Securities and Finance; Mergers and Acquisitions.
**Wogoman, Susan E.** ....... '50 '93 C.101 B.A. L.800 J.D. [Ⓐ Davis W.T.]
*PRACTICE AREAS: Health Law.
**Wohl, Emil J.** ....... '68 '94 C.800 B.A. L.1049 J.D. [Ⓐ Sullivan,W.&D.]
*PRACTICE AREAS: Real Estate Litigation; Eminent Domain Law; Land Use Regulation Law.
Wohl, James P., (BV) ....... '37 '64 C&L.813 A.B., J.D. 1901 Ave. of the Stars
**Wohlberg, David J.**, (AV) ....... '53 '79 C.1169 B.A. L.976 J.D. [Ⓒ Troy&G.]
*PRACTICE AREAS: Corporate Law; Securities Law; Entertainment Law; Business Litigation.
**Wohlenberg, Bradley E.** ....... '66 '94 C.112 B.A. L.426 J.D. [Ⓐ Oliver,V.S.M.&L.]
*PRACTICE AREAS: Municipal; General Redevelopment.
Wohn, Kathleen M. ....... '58 '90 C.112 B.S. L.426 J.D. 355 S. Grand Ave.
Wojciak, Edward J. ....... '47 '80 C.363 B.S. L.1095 J.D. 800 W. 6th St.
**Wojtas, Nancy H.** ....... '51 '76 C.477 B.A. L.912 J.D. [Manatt,P.&P.]
*PRACTICE AREAS: Corporate Law; Securities Law; Health Law.

**Wolas, Herbert, Law Offices of, (AV) '33 '61 C.112 B.A. L.1068 J.D.**
**1875 Century Park East, Suite 2000, 90067**
**Telephone: 310-277-0408 Fax: 310-282-0843**
***REPORTED CASES: Union Bank v. Wolas, Trustee, 112 S.Ct. 632.**
***PRACTICE AREAS: Bankruptcy; Insolvency; Reorganization; Commercial Litigation; Restructuring.**
**Chapter 11 Reorganizations, Bankruptcy, Insolvency, Creditor-Debtor Relations, Commercial Law and Business Related Matters.**

*See Professional Biographies, LOS ANGELES, CALIFORNIA*

Wolcott, Justine ....... '65 '94 C.426 B.S.F.S. L.276 J.D. 555 S. Flower St.
**Wold, James G.** ....... '65 '90 C.800 B.A. L.990 J.D. [Ⓐ La Follette,J.D.F.&A.]
*PRACTICE AREAS: Medical Malpractice; General Liability.
Woldman, Donald N. '38 '64
C.1016 B.S.B.A. L.146 LL.B. 2049 Century Park E. (Century City)
**Wolen, Alan R.**, (AV) ....... '41 '66 C.112 B.S. L.800 J.D. [Ⓒ Barger&W.]
*PRACTICE AREAS: General Corporate Law; Insurance Law; Real Estate Law.
**Wolf, Ann Luotto** ....... '62 '88 C.1051 B.A. L.1065 J.D. [Ⓐ Carlsmith B.W.C.&I.]
*LANGUAGES: French and Spanish.
*PRACTICE AREAS: Commercial Litigation; Corporate Litigation; Latin American Trade.
**Wolf, Brian G.** ....... '57 '85 C.477 B.A. L.326 J.D. [Lavely&S.]
*PRACTICE AREAS: General Civil and Business Litigation; Entertainment Litigation.
**Wolf, Charles C.** ....... '52 '80 C.94 B.S. L.93 J.D. [O'Melveny&M.]
*REPORTED CASES: In re Maxicare Health Plans; In re Drexel Burnham Lambert Group, Inc.; In re Prime Motor Inns; In re Phar-Mor, Inc.; In re Orange County.
*PRACTICE AREAS: Bankruptcy; Municipal Finance.
Wolf, David M. ....... '53 '78 C.112 A.B. L.597 J.D. [Wolf&W.,9000 Sunset Blvd.]
Wolf, Diane E. ....... '45 '87 C.112 B.A. L.809 J.D. 2029 Century Park E., Ste. 1200
Wolf, Ellen K. ....... '59 '83 C.112 B.A. L.813 J.D. [Wolf&W.,11755 Wilshire Blvd.]
Wolf, John H. ....... '41 '67 C&L.260 B.S.B.A., J.D. [Wolf&W.,11755 Wilshire Blvd.]
Wolf, Joseph, (AV) ....... '27 '55 C.861 B.B.A. L.569 J.D. [Wolf&W.,9000 Sunset Blvd.]
**Wolf, Kenneth S.**, (AV) ....... '43 '69 C.150 B.A. L.309 J.D. [Ⓒ Hoffman,S.&W.]
*PRACTICE AREAS: Estate Planning Law; Probate Law; Trusts Law; Beneficiary Rights Disputes.
Wolf, Lawrence ....... '50 '75 C.1077 B.A. L.770 LL.B. 2049 Century Park East
**Wolf, Lesley Sara**, (AV) ....... '53 '78 C.771 B.A. L.893 J.D. [Gibson,D.&C.]
*PRACTICE AREAS: Real Estate Development and Finance (Workouts and Foreclosures included).

CAA368P

Wolf, Marvin L. ....................'51 '76 C.1077 B.A. L.809 J.D. 2049 Century Pk. E.
**Wolf, Michael, (A Professional Corporation),** (AV) '52 '76
C.112 B.A. L.1068 J.D. [Wolf,R.&S.]
*PRACTICE AREAS: Entertainment Law; Corporate Law.
**Wolf, Michael B.**, (AV) ....................'42 '69 C.112 A.B. L.1066 J.D. [Rickless&W.]
**Wolf, Richard B.**, (AV) ....................'44 '70 C.112 A.B. L.1068 J.D. [Lewis,D.B.&B.]
Wolf, Rosalind D. ...... '47 '79 C.766 B.A. L.1065 J.D. Staff Coun., Calif. Teachers Assn.
**Wolf, Susan A.** ....................'56 '81 C&L.477 B.G.S., J.D. [Loeb&L.]
*PRACTICE AREAS: Corporate, Banking and Finance Law.
**Wolf, Wendy A.** ....................'60 '86 C.112 B.A. L.976 J.D. [Irell&M.]

**Wolf, Rifkin & Shapiro, LLP, (AV)**
**A Partnership including a Professional Corporation**
**11400 West Olympic Boulevard Ninth Floor, 90064-1565**
**Telephone: 310-478-4100 FAX: 310-479-1422**
**Members of Firm: Michael Wolf (A Professional Corporation); Daniel C. Shapiro; Roy G. Rifkin; Michael T. Schulman; Leslie Steven Marks; Allan M. Rosenthal; Mindy Sheps; Norman S. Wisnicki; Barry T. Mitidiere; Marc E. Rohatiner; Charles H. Baren; Michael W. Rabkin. Associates: Andrew S. Gelb; Matthew L. Grode; Matthew Fladell; Steven A. Silver; Mark J. Rosenbaum; Kelly Marie Allegra; Richard S. Grant; Karin E. Freeman; Lori A. Van Oosterhout; Paul W. Windust; Daniel Ng; Laura S. Blint. Of Counsel: Gerald Lloyd Friedman; Jeffrey R. Liebster; Denise M. Parga.**
**General Civil Practice in State and Federal Courts. Trials and Appeals. Corporate, Real Estate, Community Associations, Entertainment, Taxation, Estate Planning and Probate, Construction, Products Liability and Related Litigation Matters.**
***See Professional Biographies, LOS ANGELES, CALIFORNIA***

Wolf & Wolf ....................................... 11755 Wilshire Blvd., 15th Fl.
Wolf & Wolf, P.C., (AV) ....................................... 9000 Sunset Blvd.
**Wolfe, Charles W.**, (AV) ....................'08 '33 C&L.426 A.B., J.D. [Larwill&W.]
*PRACTICE AREAS: Probate; Estate Planning; Real Property.
Wolfe, Elisa B. ....................'59 '85 C.112 B.S. L.809 J.D. Dep. Atty. Gen.
**Wolfe, Herbert N., (P.C.)**, (AV) ....... '39 '65 C.1077 B.A. L.1066 J.D. [Jeffer,M.B.&M.]
*PRACTICE AREAS: Business Law and Litigation.
Wolfe, Kenneth N. ....................'52 '78 C.1077 B.A. L.809 J.D. 1400 Colorado Blvd.
Wolfe, Laurence N. ....................'29 '72 C.1097 B.A. L.398 J.D. 2020 Paramount Dr.
**Wolfe, Margaret W.** ....................'45 '90 C.846 B.A. L.800 J.D. [Weinhart&R.]
**Wolfe, Michelle McCoy** ......... '64 '91 C.112 B.A. L.809 J.D. [La Follette,J.D.F.&A.]
*PRACTICE AREAS: General Liability; Medical Malpractice.
Wolfe, Patricia M. ............'32 '78 C.054 B.A. L.1066 J.D. 11111 Santa Monica Blvd.
**Wolfe, Robert J.** ....................'61 '87 C.1042 B.S. L.809 J.D. [Engstrom,L.&L.]
*PRACTICE AREAS: Construction Litigation; Real Estate; Title Insurance Matters; Bad Faith; Professional Liability.
Wolfe, Stephen G. ....................'48 '78 C.112 A.B. L.262 J.D. U.S. Attys. Off.
**Wolfen, Karen Africk** ....................'60 '86 C.112 B.A. L.1068 J.D. [Alschuler G.&P.]
**Wolfen, Werner F., (P.C.)**, (AV) ....................'30 '53 C.112 B.S. L.1066 J.D. [Irell&M.]
**Wolff, Claudio O.** ....................'58 '83 C.112 B.A. L.1068 J.D. [B.R.Bailey]
*PRACTICE AREAS: General Corporate and Securities Law; Real Estate Law; International Transactions.
Wolff, Cynthia L. .............. '60 '86 C.1365 B.A. L.1049 J.D. 611 W. 6th St., Ste. 2650
**Wolff, Joan A.** ....................'57 '83 C.103 A.B. L.1068 J.D. [Alschuler G.&P.]
**Wolff, Steven G.** .................... '56 '81 C.112 B.A. L.1066 J.D. [Rosenfeld&W.]
*PRACTICE AREAS: Real Estate Law.

**Wolflick & Simpson**
**(See Glendale)**

**Wolfram, Michael L.** ....................'45 '71 C.309 A.B. L.846 J.D. [Morgan,L.&B.]
**Wolfsdorf, Bernard P.**, (AV) ....................'54 '81 C&L.061 B.A., LL.B. [B.P.Wolfsdorf]

**Wolfsdorf, Bernard P., A Professional Corporation, (AV)**
**17383 Sunset Boulevard, Suite 120 (Pacific Palisades), 90272**
**Telephone: 310-573-4242 FAX: 310-573-5093**
**Email: visalaw@wolfsdorf.com URL: http://ilw.com/wolfsdorf**
**Bernard P. Wolfsdorf (Certified Specialist, Immigration and Nationality Law, The State Bar of California Board of Legal Specialization).;—Michele A. Buchanan; C. Daniel Levy; Stephen M. Dewar (Not admitted in CA); Michael S. Greenbaum (Not admitted in CA); Mitchell Berenson.**
**Specializes in the exclusive practice of Immigration and Nationality Law, with an emphasis on Business and Entertainment related Immigration Matters. Asylum/Refugee, Deportation, Family-Based Immigration, Nationality and Appellate Matters are also handled.**
***See Professional Biographies, LOS ANGELES, CALIFORNIA***

Wolfson, Bruce L. ....................'29 '55 C&L.112 B.A., J.D. 9000 Sunset Blvd.
Wolfson, Harold M. '13 '37 L.436 LL.B.
(adm. in WI; not adm. in CA) Wolfson Bros. Realty Co.
Wolfson, Tina ....................'69 '94 C.178 B.A. L.309 J.D. 555 W. 5th St.
**Wolin, Les J.** ....................'56 '85 C.423 B.A. L.770 J.D. [Goldfarb,S.&A.]
*LANGUAGES: Hebrew.
*PRACTICE AREAS: Probate Law; Taxation Law; Business Law.
Wolinsky, Iris C. ....................'53 '84 C.112 B.A. L.809 J.D. 13674 Bayliss Rd.
**Wolkowitz, Edward M.**, (AV) ......'49 '76 C.1077 B.A. L.809 J.D. [Robinson,D.B.&K.]
*PRACTICE AREAS: Bankruptcy Law; Reorganization; Commercial Transactions.
**Woll, Robert** ....................'56 '85 C.674 A.B. L.813 J.D. [Dewey B.]
*PRACTICE AREAS: Banking Law; Corporate and Securities; International; Financial Transactions; Telecommunications Law.
Wollan, Dennis E. ....................'41 '71 C.309 A.B. L.813 J.D. 5740 Spring Oak Terr.
**Wollitz, Howard N.**, (AV) ..........'48 '73 C.1049 B.A. L.1068 J.D. [Charlston,R.&W.]
**Wollman, Russell S.** ....................'58 '87 C.112 B.A. L.809 J.D. [Murchison&C.]
*PRACTICE AREAS: Products Liability Law.
**Wollman, Shari Mulrooney** ..............'63 '88 C.112 B.A. L.800 J.D. [Manatt,P.&P.]
*PRACTICE AREAS: Intellectual Property; Computer Law; Entertainment; Commercial Litigation.
**Wolman, Philip J.**, (AV) ...........'50 '76 C.112 A.B. L.1068 J.D. [Buchalter,N.F.&Y.]
*PRACTICE AREAS: Taxation (100%).
**Wolontis, Nikki** ....................'53 '78 C.569 B.A. L.813 J.D. [Fried,B.&C.]
*PRACTICE AREAS: Financial Institutions Law - General Corporate and Regulatory Representation; Mergers and Acquisitions; Bank Applications and Organizations; Corporate Securities.
Woloz, Leslie Ann ....................'49 '75 C.1060 B.A. L.1095 J.D. 10866 Wilshire Blvd.
**Wolpert, Dorothy**, (AV) ..............'34 '76 C.659 B.A. L.1068 J.D. [Bird,M.B.W.&M.]
Wolpow, Laura D. ....................'67 '92 C.112 B.A. L.809 J.D. 700 S. Flower St.
**Woltmann, Charles L.** ....................'47 '74 C&L.976 B.A., J.D. [Tuttle&T.]
*PRACTICE AREAS: Commercial Law; Agricultural Cooperatives.
**Won, Eugene Y. T.** ....................'44 '91 C.477 B.A. L.1068 J.D. [Jones,D.R.&P.]
**Won, Grace** ....................'67 '95 C.309 B.A. L.276 J.D. [Latham&W.]
**Wong, Aimee Y.** ....................'70 '95 C.112 B.A. L.800 J.D. [Selman B.]
*LANGUAGES: Cantonese.
**Wong, Angela** ....................'51 '79 C.112 B.A. L.276 J.D. [Manatt,P.&P.]
*PRACTICE AREAS: Health Law; Estates and Trusts.
**Wong, Christopher F.** ....................'64 '89 C.112 A.B. L.976 J.D. [Irell&M.]
**Wong, Daniel C.** ....................'63 '96 L.101 J.D. [Buchalter,N.F.&Y.]
*PRACTICE AREAS: General Commercial Litigation; Financial Institution and Insolvency Litigation.
Wong, Delbert E. ....................'20 '49 C.112 B.S. L.813 LL.B. Supr. Ct. J.
**Wong, Doreena** ....................'51 '88 C.1169 B.A. L.569 J.D. [S.L.Hartmann]
*PRACTICE AREAS: Civil Rights; Constitutional Law.
Wong, H. Deane, (AV) ..............'45 '83 C.813 B.A. L.1068 J.D. 10940 Wilshire Blvd.
**Wong, Karen B.** ....................'61 '86 C&L.800 B.S., J.D. [Milbank,T.H.&M.]
Wong, Kent D. ..................'56 '84 C.112 L.1238 J.D. Dir., Labor Ctr., Univ. of Calif.
Wong, Linda Jeanne ..........'49 '77 C&L.800 B.A., J.D. Exec. Dir., Calif. Tommorrow

**Wong, Monica Seine** ....................'69 '95 C.112 B.A. L.1065 J.D. [Musick,P.&G.]
*PRACTICE AREAS: Healthcare; Corporate.
**Wong, Norman Y.** .........'71 '96 C&L.112 B.S., J.D. [Christensen,M.F.J.G.W.&S.]
*PRACTICE AREAS: Litigation.
**Wong, Regina R.** ....................'71 '96 C&L.112 B.A., J.D. [Anderson,M.&C.]
Wong, Richard ....................'35 '83 C.37 B.A. L.1148 J.D. Dep. City Atty.
Wong, Rosanne ....................'57 '84 C.1097 B.S. L.426 J.D. 10866 Wilshire Blvd.
**Wong, Sharon** .........'64 '92 C.112 B.S. L.426 J.D. [Robbins,B.&C.] (See Pat. Sect.)
*LANGUAGES: Chinese (Cantonese).
*PRACTICE AREAS: Patent Law; Trademark Law; Copyright Law; Unfair Competition Law.
Wong, Stevan F. ....................'53 '88 C.178 B.A. L.309 J.D. 2049 Century Park E.
Wong, Thomas A., Jr., (AV) ....................'42 '67 C.813 A.B. L.1065 J.D. [T.Wong,Jr.]
Wong, Wallace M. ....................'51 '79 C.976 B.A. L.770 J.D. Dept. of Corporations
**Wong, Wean Khing** ....'60 '87 C.453 B.S. L.809 J.D. [Robbins,B.&C.] (See Pat. Sect.)
*LANGUAGES: Mandarin, Cantonese and Malay.
*PRACTICE AREAS: Patent Law; Trademark Law; Copyright Law.
Wong, Thomas A, Jr., P.C., (AV) ........................................333 S. Grand Ave.
**Woo, Arnold D.** ....................'58 '92 C&L.800 A.B., J.D. [Hill,F.&B.]
*PRACTICE AREAS: Civil Litigation; Business Litigation.
**Woo, C. Craig** ....................'60 '87 C.112 B.A. L.169 J.D. [Jackson,L.S.&K.]
Woo, Christie E. '66 '92 C.518 A.B. L.273 J.D.
(adm. in DC; not adm. in CA) Dept. of Immig. & Nat.

**Woo, David Bow, (AV) '39 '65 C.674 A.B. L.1066 J.D.**
**700 South Flower Street, Suite 1100, 90017-4113**
**Telephone: 213-892-6309 FAX: 213-892-2215**
**Business Law, Real Estate and Banking. General Civil Trial Practice.**

Woo, Frankie En-Long ....................'66 '90 C.659 B.S. L.911 J.D. 225 S. Olive St.
Woo, Richard E. ....................'47 '77 C.800 B.A. L.426 J.D. Sr. Litig. Coun., ARCO
Woo, Sarah Suzuki ....................'36 '72 L.1136 LL.B. 3866 Cochran Ave.
Wood, Carey M. ....................'67 '94 C.668 B.A. L.1067 J.D. 1900 Ave. of the Stars
**Wood, Cary L.** ....................'59 '90 C.475 B.A. L.1049 J.D. [Lewis,D.B.&B.]
Wood, David E. ....................'57 '85 C.951 B.A. L.1065 J.D. [Anderson&W.]
Wood, David E. ....................'40 '72 C.112 B.A. L.1068 J.D. 1801 Ave. of the Stars
Wood, David F. ....................'45 '75 C.478 B.A. L.809 J.D. 624 S. Grand Ave.
**Wood, Douglas J.** '50 '76 C.690 B.A. L.1170 J.D.
(adm. in NJ; not adm. in CA) [Hall D.K.F.&W.] (©N.Y., N.Y. & Bucharest, Romania)
*PRACTICE AREAS: Advertising Law; Media and Entertainment Law; Marketing Law; International Law; Trade Regulation Law.
**Wood, Gregory B.**, (AV) '45 '75 C.112 B.S. L.1095 J.D.
[Merchant&G.] (See Pat. Sect.)
Wood, Judith L. ............... '47 '77 C.112 B.A. L.1068 J.D. Security Pacific Natl. Bk.
**Wood, Kathleen M.** ....................'61 '87 C.378 B.A. L.178 J.D. [Bucksbaum&S.]
*PRACTICE AREAS: Intellectual Property; General Corporate Commercial; Securities; Antitrust.
Wood, Lester T., III ........... '41 '78 C.724 B.B.A. L.1136 J.D. Fund Servs. Assoc., Inc.
Wood, Richard A. ....................'54 '81 C.763 A.B. L.1049 J.D. 3926 Wilshire Blvd.
**Wood, Travers D.**, (AV) ....................'43 '70 C.112 B.A. L.800 J.D. [White&C.]
**Wood, W. Mark**, (AV) ....................'42 '68 C.770 B.A. L.800 J.D. [O'Melveny&M.]
*PRACTICE AREAS: Civil Litigation; Aviation; Insurance Coverage Defense.

**Wood, J. Kirk**
**(See Santa Monica)**

Woodard, Cheryl Anne, (BV) ......'— '72 C&L.800 B.A., J.D. 12304 Santa Monica Blvd.
Woodbury, John M., Jr. ....................'55 '84 C.1077 B.S. L.809 J.D. [Pollet&W.]
Wooden, John H. ....................'27 '60 C.1043 B.A. L.809 LL.B. 6363 Sunset Blvd.
Woodhead, Consuelo S., (AV) ............'48 '74 C.821 B.A. L.659 J.D. Asst. U.S. Atty.
**Woodland, Irwin F.**, (AV) ....................'22 '61 C.178 A.B. L.608 J.D. [Gibson,D.&C.]
*PRACTICE AREAS: Antitrust; Securities Litigation; Accountants Liability; Administrative Law.
Woodmansee, Charles H. ....................'23 '52 C.273 L.800 J.D. Ret. Supr. Ct. J.
**Woodruff, Jeffrey T.** ....................'64 '90 C.174 B.A. L.1065 J.D. [Morris,P.&P.]
Woods, Arleigh M. ............'29 '53 C.139 B.S. L.809 LL.B. Presiding Jus., Ct. of App.
**Woods, Daniel J.** ....................'52 '77 C&L.800 A.B., J.D. [White&C.]
**Woods, Donald F., Jr.**, (AV) ....................'46 '72 C.276 B.S. L.178 J.D. [Dewey B.]
*PRACTICE AREAS: Litigation.
Woods, Gabrielle C. .........'56 '88 C.605 A.B. L.329 J.D. Coun., Calif. Assn. of Realtors
Woods, George T. ....................'34 '59 C.705 A.B. L.976 J.D. 302 N. La Brea Ave.
**Woods, Julie L.** ....................'64 '89 C.502 B.S.B.A. L.309 J.D. [Horvitz&L.]
Woods, Norvell Fred, Jr. ............ '35 '64 C.691 B.A. L.426 J.D. Jus., State Ct. of App.
Woods, Pamela ....................'54 '81 C.813 B.A. L.1066 J.D. 405 Hilgard Ave.
Woods, Willard L. ....................'18 '50 C.403 A.B. L.426 LL.B. 3847 Crenshaw Blvd.
Woods, William ....................'51 '86 C.763 B.A. L.809 J.D. Deputy Dist. Atty.
**Woods, William S., II**, (AV) ....................'55 '80 C.154 B.A. L.1068 J.D. [Loeb&L.]
*PRACTICE AREAS: Taxation.
Woods, William T. ....................'26 '60 3660 Wilshire Blvd. Penthouse
**Woodside, Dennis M.** ....................'69 '96 C.188 B.S. L.813 J.D. [Munger,T.&O.]
**Woodsome, Edwin V., Jr., (A Professional Corporation)**, (AV) '46 '72
C.321 A.B. L.309 J.D. [Munger,T.&O.]
**Woodward, Lyn A.** ....................'62 '90 C.112 B.A. L.426 J.D. [Veatch,C.G.&N.]
*PRACTICE AREAS: General Casualty Defense; Coverage Disputes; Government Tort Liability Defense Law.
**Woodward, Michael S.** ....................'50 '76 C.112 B.A. L.276 J.D. [Paul,H.J.&W.]
Wooldridge, Brian L. ....................'47 '72 C.940 B.A. L.800 J.D. D.A. Dept.
**Wooley, M. Eugene**, (AV) ....................'33 '65 C&L.800 B.A., J.D. [Kern&W.]
**Woollacott, Cynthia A. R.** ..........'58 '83 C.112 B.S. L.1068 J.D. [Woollacott J.&W.]
*PRACTICE AREAS: Business Litigation; Commercial Litigation; Complex Litigation.
**Woollacott, Jay A., (A Law Corp.)** '54 '78 C.426 B.A. L.1068 J.D.
[Woollacott J.&W.]
*PRACTICE AREAS: Business Litigation; Commercial Litigation; Corporate Law; Real Property Law.

**Woollacott Jannol & Woollacott**
**A Partnership including Professional Corporations**
**1875 Century Park East, Suite 1400, 90067**
**Telephone: 310-277-5504 Telecopier: 310-552-7552**
**Members of Firm: Jay A. Woollacott (A Law Corp.); Martin B. Jannol (A Prof. Corp.); Cynthia A. R. Woollacott. Associates: Janet L. Karkanen.**
**General and Complex Business, Real Estate and Construction Litigation in Federal and State Courts and Arbitration, General Business and Real Estate Transactions, Corporate and Partnership Law.**
***See Professional Biographies, LOS ANGELES, CALIFORNIA***

**Woolley, Susan M.** ....................'59 '90 C&L.813 A.B., J.D. [S.L.Hartmann]
*LANGUAGES: Spanish.
*PRACTICE AREAS: Civil Rights; Litigation; Immigration and Naturalization.
**Woolner, Rolf S.** ....................'57 '83 C.037 B.A. L.976 J.D. [Murphy,W.&B.]
**Woolverton, George**, (BV) ..........'50 '75 C.1130 B.A. L.809 J.D. [Stockwell,H.W.&W.]
**Woolverton, Lonnie E., (P.C.)**, (AV) ....'32 '63 C.112 B.A. L.800 J.D. [Thelen,M.J.&B.]

**Woolway, Gilbert, (AV) '19 '49 C&L.800 B.S., LL.B.**
**1631 West Beverly Boulevard, 90026**
**Telephone: 213-482-8425 Fax: 213-482-8250**

(This Listing Continued)

**CAA369P**

**Woolway, Gilbert (Continued)**

**General Civil Practice in all State and Federal Courts. Probate, Trusts, Corporation and Real Property Law.**
**Reference: Bank of America, Larchmont Branch.**

**Woosley, Clifford H.** .................'51 '79 C.966 B.A. L.426 J.D. [Ⓒ Gilbert,K.C.&J.]
Wooster, Mark A. .......'59 '86 C.472 A.B. L.309 J.D. 1999 Ave. of the Stars, Suite 1400
**Wooten, Robert A., Jr.**, (AV) ..............'47 '73 C.112 A.B. L.1068 J.D. [Bottum&F.]
*PRACTICE AREAS: Professional Malpractice Law; Civil Law; Trial Practice; Appellate Practice; Fidelity and Surety Law.
**Wootton, Chad B.** .................. '65 '90 C.276 B.A. L.800 J.D. [Ⓐ Charlston,R.&W.]
*LANGUAGES: French.
*PRACTICE AREAS: Insurance Coverage; Professional Liability; Civil Litigation.
Work, Michael L., (AV) '56 '85 C.259 B.S. L.192 J.D.
(adm. in LA; not adm. in CA) 6310 San Vicente Blvd.
Workeneh, Debra '55 '87
C.512 B.A. L.1066 J.D. Asst. V.P. & Assoc. Coun., Sanwa Bk. Calif.
Workman, David A. ..........................'30 '58 C&L.813 A.B., LL.B. Supr. Ct. J.
**Workman, Douglas J.** ...............'58 '83 C.893 B.S. L.597 J.D. [Ⓐ Hartman&Assoc.]
*TRANSACTIONS: Real Estate Acquisitions, Dispositions, Financing, Leasing, Public Land Private Offerings of Securities, Partnership and Limited Liability Company Agreements General Corporate.
*PRACTICE AREAS: Corporate and Real Estate Law.
**Workman, Henry K.**, (AV) ........... '26 '57 C.800 B.S. L.426 LL.B. [Sullivan,W.&D.]
*PRACTICE AREAS: Estate Planning Law; Administration Law; Civil Appeals; Condemnation Law.
**Workman, Paul C.**, (AV) ...............'54 '80 C.112 A.B. L.426 J.D. [Whitman B.A.&M.]
*PRACTICE AREAS: Business Litigation.
**Workman, Thomas E., Jr.**, (AV) ........ '27 '58 C&L.426 B.B.A., J.D. [Pillsbury M.&S.]
**Woronoff, Michael A.** ........... '60 '85 C.679 B.S.I.M. L.477 J.D. [Skadden,A.S.M.&F.]
Worrell, Robert K., (AV) .............. '32 '61 C.112 B.A. L.800 J.D. 333 S. Grand Ave.
**Worsinger, Laura P.** ..................... '47 '72 C.1109 B.A. L.1068 J.D. [Ⓐ Reinis&R.]
*PRACTICE AREAS: Business Litigation; Commercial Litigation; Insurance Law; Antitrust; Trade Regulation.
Worth, Robert J. ............................'50 '89 C.1095 B.A. L.1136 J.D. [Ⓐ J.R.Brown,Jr.]
**Worthge, Mark K.** ...................'57 '85 C.112 B.S. L.1068 J.D. [Wilson,E.M.E.&D.]
**Wortman, Jeffrey A.** ....................'63 '95 C.597 B.S. L.846 J.D. [Ⓐ O'Melveny&M.]
*PRACTICE AREAS: Litigation.
Wotring, Dorothy L. ................ '20 '57 C&L.800 B.S., J.D. 215 N. Bowling Green Way‡
**Wrede, Robert K.**, (AV) ........................ '39 '70 C&L.188 B.A., J.D. [Lewis,D.B.&B.]
*REPORTED CASES: Purex/PJG -419 F. Supp 931; 596 F2d 881; 664 F 2d 1105; Masterson v Onion, 485 F 2d 252; API v EPA 661 F 2d 340.
*PRACTICE AREAS: Commercial Disputes; Entertainment; Antitrust; Professional Liability; Products Liability.
**Wright, Adam A.** ..........................'63 '89 C.112 B.A. L.809 J.D. [Kane,W.&P.]
*PRACTICE AREAS: Insurance Defense; Civil Litigation.
Wright, Daniel E. '56 '81 C.930 B.A. L.93 J.D.
(adm. in MA; not adm. in CA) 467 Crane Blvd.
**Wright, David C.** ..........................'68 '94 C.54 B.S. L.990 J.D. [Ⓐ Morrison&F.]
**Wright, David C.**, (AV) ...................'46 '72 C.112 B.A. L.426 J.D. [Musick,P.&G.]
*PRACTICE AREAS: Employee Benefits; Business Law.
**Wright, David M.** .............. '58 '86 C.1074 B.A. L.809 J.D. [Ⓐ La Follette,J.D.F.&A.]
*PRACTICE AREAS: Medical Malpractice.
Wright, Denise E. ........................'52 '79 C.800 B.A. L.1148 J.D. 4727 Wilshire Blvd.
**Wright, Gordon K.**, (AV) ...............'20 '48 C&L.800 A.B., LL.B. [Pillsbury M.&S.]
Wright, Jac O'Delle Grier .....'52 '77 C.112 B.A. L.1068 J.D. The Flying Tiger Line, Inc.
**Wright, Jennifer L.** ........................'68 '93 C.112 B.A. L.800 J.D. [Ⓐ Folger L.&K.]⊙
Wright, John J. ...................'58 '90 C.602 B.S.Ch.E. L.228 J.D. 333 S. Hope St., 48th Fl.
Wright, Jonathan A. .....'48 '73 C.112 B.A. L.1068 J.D. V.P. & Mng. Sr. Coun., Union Bk.
**Wright, Kenneth B.**, (AV) ....................'34 '61 C.668 B.A. L.813 J.D. [Morgan,L.&B.]
**Wright, Leslie E., III.** ...................'62 '92 C&L.37 B.Arch., J.D. [Ⓐ Daniels,B.&F.]
**Wright, Mary E.** ........................'54 '89 C.1291 B.A. L.767 J.D. [Ⓐ Manatt,P.&P.]
*PRACTICE AREAS: Labor and Employment.
**Wright, Michael D.** ...........................'62 '88 C.679 B.S. L.347 J.D. [Sidley&A.]
*PRACTICE AREAS: Banking and Commercial Law.
**Wright, Michael F.** ..........................'54 '79 C&L.813 B.A., J.D. [Case,K.B.&W.]
**Wright, Otis D., II** ....................'44 '80 C.1097 B.S. L.809 J.D. [Wilson,E.M.E.&D.]
Wright, Pamela A. ................. '65 '91 C.553 B.S. L.1292 J.D. Wells Fargo Bk., N.A.
**Wright, Patricia E.** ...........................'54 '85 C.529 B.A. L.800 J.D. [Coleman&W.]
*PRACTICE AREAS: Civil Litigation; Torts; Insurance Defense; Products Liability.
**Wright, Robert H.** ..................... '64 '91 C.893 B.A. L.347 J.D. [Ⓐ Gibson,D.&C.]
**Wright, Robert M.** '44 '71 C.112 B.A. L.1068 J.D.
V.P. & Gen. Coun., Auto. Club of Southern Calif.
*RESPONSIBILITIES: General Business; Insurance.
Wright, Robyn D. ..............................'64 '90 C.860 B.A. L.94 J.D. [Ⓐ Brookwell K.]
**Wright, Shannon P.** ..................... '71 '95 C.112 B.A. L.426 J.D. [Ⓐ Paul,H.J.&W.]
**Wright, Simon D.** .......................................'64 '88 L.061 LL.B. [Lane P.S.L.]
*PRACTICE AREAS: Insurance Coverage; Insurance Defense; Maritime Law.
Wright, William H. .......'61 '92 C.111 B.S. L.1068 J.D. 10100 Santa Monica Blvd. (Pat.)
Wright, Wyndell J. ......................'61 '86 C.800 B.A. L.309 J.D. 201 N. Figueroa St.

**Wright, Robinson, Osthimer & Tatum, (AV)**
**Suite 1800 888 South Figueroa Street, 90017⊙**
**Telephone: 213-488-0503 Telefax: 213-624-3755**
**Resident Principals: Franklin M. Tatum, III; Paul H. Burleigh; Kenneth G. Katel; Michael J. Belcher; Nancy E. Fitzhugh; Robert A. Rich; Arthur I. Willner; David V. Rose. Resident Associates: Brian S. Inamine; Robert G. Harrison; Colin J. Gibson; Taylor L. Clark.**
**General Civil and Trial Practice. Products Liability, Construction, Corporate, Insurance and Environmental Law.**
**Richmond, Virginia Office: Suite 400, 411 East Franklin Street. Telephone: 804-783-1100.**
**San Francisco, California Office: Suite 1800, 44 Montgomery Street. Telephone: 415-391-7111.**
**Washington, D.C. Office: Suite 920, 5335 Wisconsin Avenue, N.W. Telephone: 202-244-4668. Telefax: 202-244-5135.**
**Norfolk, Virginia Office: 1600 Nationsbank Center, One Commercial Place. Telephone: 757-623-0035. Telefax: 757-623-4160.**
***See Professional Biographies, LOS ANGELES, CALIFORNIA***

**Wrobel, Joshua G.** ............................ '70 '96 C.154 B.A. L.477 J.D. [Ⓐ Paul,H.J.&W.]
**Wruble, Jeffrey S.** ...................'55 '80 C.112 B.A. L.1049 J.D. [Buchalter,N.F.&Y.]
*PRACTICE AREAS: Commercial Litigation; Real Estate Litigation; Banking and Bank Operations; Business Litigation.
**Wrycha, Paul T.** .......................'65 '92 C.966 B.S. L.436 J.D. [Ⓐ Milbank,T.H.&M.]
**Wu, Andrew H.T.** ...................'63 '89 C.112 B.S. L.1067 J.D. [Ⓐ Milbank,T.H.&M.]
*LANGUAGES: Chinese.
*PRACTICE AREAS: Contracts; Immigration and Naturalization; Small Business Law; Family Law; Real Estate.
**Wu, Daisy C.** ........................ '74 '96 C.945 B.A. L.893 J.D. [Ⓐ Gibson,D.&C.]
*LANGUAGES: Mandarin Chinese.
**Wu, Joseph S.** ...........................'— '90 C.112 B.A. L.1068 J.D. [Ⓐ Morgan,L.&B.]
Wu, Patrick A. ..................................... '49 '75 C.112 B.A. L.426 J.D. Dep. Co. Coun.
**Wu, Raymond** .......................... '67 '92 C.156 B.A. L.94 J.D. [Ⓐ Katten M.&Z.]
*PRACTICE AREAS: Litigation.
**Wuchitech, Roy G.** ......................'46 '72 C.145 B.A. L.846 J.D. [Sheppard,M.R.&H.]
*PRACTICE AREAS: Environmental Law.

**Wulfe, Kym R.** ......................... '66 '93 C.800 B.A. L.276 J.D. [Ⓐ Kaye,S.F.H.&H.]
*PRACTICE AREAS: Entertainment Transactional.
Wuliger, Frank ............................ '49 '77 C.800 B.A. L.426 J.D. 2054 Fox Hills Dr.
**Wurst, Harold E.**, (AV) ........... '39 '65 C.602 B.S.E.E. L.276 J.D. [Darby&D.] (Pat.)
*REPORTED CASES: Windsurfing International, Inc. v. BIC Leisure Products, Inc., AMF, Inc. and James Drake, Intervenor, 613 F. Supp. 933 (S.D.N.Y 1985); 231 U.S.P.Q. 19 (S.D.N.Y 1986); 782 F.2d 995 (CAFC 1986); cert. den., 477 U.S. 905 (1986); 828 F.2d 755 (CAFC 1987).
*PRACTICE AREAS: Litigation.
**Wurst, John E.** '65 '94 C.112 B.A. L.190 J.D.
(adm. in NE; not adm. in CA; Pat.) [Ⓐ Darby&D.]
*PRACTICE AREAS: Patent Law.
**Wurtzel, Cory** '69 '96 C.112 B.A. L.1066 J.D.
[Ⓐ McCutchen,D.B.&E.] (⊙San Francisco)
*PRACTICE AREAS: Environmental.
**Wyatt, Joseph L., Jr.**, (AV) ........... '24 '50 C.597 A.B. L.309 LL.B. [Ⓒ Morrison&F.]
*PRACTICE AREAS: Tax; Trust; Probate; Ethics; Public Pension.
**Wyatt, Marva Jo** ........................................'— '87 C&L.861 B.A., J.D. [Ⓐ Kaye,R.]
Wyatt, W. Keith ..................................'53 '78 C.103 B.A. L.112 J.D. [Ivie,M.&W.]
**Wyle, Geraldine A.** ..................... '53 '79 C.112 B.A. L.1068 J.D. [Ⓐ Valensi,R.&M.]
*PRACTICE AREAS: Commercial Litigation; Probate.
Wyler, Paul .....'29 '53 C.563 B.S.S. L.569 LL.B. Adm. Law J., Unemploy. Ins. App. Bd.
**Wyles, Kelvin T.** ...........................'63 '94 C&L.050 B.A., LL.M. [Ⓐ Folger L.&K.]⊙
Wylie, Thomas B. ................................'45 '75 C&L.1077 B.A., J.D. [Johnson,R.&W.]
**Wyman, Mathew A.** ...............................'61 '86 C.668 B.A. L.178 J.D. [Cox,C.&N.]
Wyman, Robert A. ............................'60 '84 C.597 B.S. L.276 J.D. [Wyman,I.B.&L.]
**Wyman, Robert A., Jr.** ...........................'54 '80 C.674 A.B. L.893 J.D. [Latham&W.]
Wyman, Scott A. ...................'46 '72 C.597 B.A. L.1068 J.D. 7060 Hollywood Blvd.
Wyman, Isaacs, Blumenthal & Lynne, (AV) ............................. 2029 Century Park E.
Wyner, Steven Marcus ..............................'49 '77 C.454 B.B.A. L.1067 J.D. [Wyner]
Wyner Law Corporation ..............................................10390 Santa Monica Blvd.
Wynn, Philip H. ....................................... '41 '68 C&L.37 B.A., J.D. Dep. Dist. Atty.
**Wynne, Megan S.** ........................... '68 '93 C.367 B.A. L.93 J.D. [Ⓐ Morris,P.&P.]
**Wynne, Richard L.**, (AV) ............................'57 '82 C.347 B.A. L.178 J.D. [Wynne S.I.]
**Wynne, Suzanne Kahn** ......................'68 '93 C.112 B.A. L.425 J.D. [Ⓐ Frandzel&S.]
*PRACTICE AREAS: Litigation; Commercial Litigation.

**Wynne Spiegel Itkin, A Law Corporation, (AV)** 🅱🅻
**1901 Avenue of the Stars, Suite 1600, 90067-6080**
**Telephone: 310-551-1015 Fax: 310-551-3059**
**Richard L. Wynne; Bennett L. Spiegel; Robbin L. Itkin; Eve Jaffe; Christopher W. Combs; Stuart J. Wald; Hayley E. Ramer; Jacqueline H. Sloan.**
**Practice Limited to Bankruptcy Law, Insolvency Law and Business Reorganization.**
***See Professional Biographies, LOS ANGELES, CALIFORNIA***

**Xanders, Julie Kusske** '64 '89
C.976 B.A. L.1066 J.D. Asst. Gen. Coun., The Times Mirror Co.
Yachzel, Joel S. ............................'47 '76 C.1077 B.S. L.1148 J.D. 10850 Wilshire Blvd.
**Yacoubian, Talin V.** .........'— '93 C.668 B.A. L.273 J.D. [Ⓐ Christensen,M.F.J.G.W.&S.]
*LANGUAGES: Armenian; Arabic; French.
*PRACTICE AREAS: Business; Entertainment Litigation.
Yacoubian, Vahe ......................'60 '84 C&L.112 B.A., J.D. 11355 W. Olympic Blvd.
Yacullo, Victor F., (P.C.), (AV) ................ '38 '64 C.800 B.A. L.569 LL.B. [Kindel&A.]
Yaffe, David P. ........................................'33 '59 C&L.112 B.S., LL.B. Supr. Ct. J.
**Yaffe, Nancy E.** ...........................'64 '95 C.112 B.A. L.800 J.D. [Ⓐ Folger L.&K.]⊙
Yager, Thomas C. ................................'18 '49 C.112 A.B. L.800 J.D. Sr. J., Supr. Ct.
Yagjian, Anita P. '54 '80
C.813 B.A. L.770 J.D. Assoc. Coun., Auto. Club of Southern Calif.
Yagjian, Michael A. '49 '73
C&L.800 B.A., J.D. Pres. & Gen. Coun., Gourmet's Fresh Pasta
**Yahiro, Robert A.**, (AV) ....................'50 '76 C.112 A.B. L.800 J.D. [Rodi,P.P.G.&C.]
*PRACTICE AREAS: Corporate; Taxation; Employee Benefits; Environmental Law.
Yakura, Elaine K. ......................... '54 '80 C.976 B.A. L.1066 J.D. 405 Figueroa Ave.
**Yamaga-Karns, Kevin** ......................'69 '95 C&L.846 B.A., J.D. [Ⓐ O'Melveny&M.]
*LANGUAGES: Japanese.
*PRACTICE AREAS: Corporate Law.
**Yamaguchi, Scott N.** ................. '66 '91 C&L.112 B.A., J.D. [Ⓐ Nossaman,G.K.&E.]
*PRACTICE AREAS: Litigation.
**Yamaguchi, Stephen A.** ................... '64 '89 C.813 B.A. L.178 J.D. [Ⓐ Paul,H.J.&W.]
Yamaki, Michael R., (AV) .... '47 '77 C.112 B.A. L.1136 J.D. 333 S. Grand Ave., 37th Fl.
Yamamoto, Andrew J. ...................'61 '88 C.976 B.A. L.112 J.D. [Yamamoto&Y.]
Yamamoto, Eric R. .................................'48 '75 C.800 B.S. L.426 J.D. [Yamamoto&Y.]
Yamamoto, Kevin M. ........'63 '93 C.112 B.S. L.1049 J.D. 1801 Century Park E. # 1250
**Yamamoto, Masami** ................... '65 '91 C.104 B.A. L.569 J.D. [Ⓐ O'Melveny&M.]
*LANGUAGES: Japanese.
Yamamoto & Yamamoto, LLP. ....................................................... 12100 Wilshire Blvd.
Yan, James S. '52 '87 C.569 B.A. L.966 J.D.
(adm. in WI; not adm. in CA) I.R.S.
**Yanagizawa, Koichi M.** .............................'46 '79 C.763 B.A. L.61 J.D. [Iwasaki&S.]
*LANGUAGES: Japanese.
*PRACTICE AREAS: Immigration; General Practice.
Yang, Edward C. '57 '88 C.112 B.S. L.1148 J.D.
(adm. in PA; not adm. in CA) 1093 Broxton Ave.
**Yang, Keith K.** ............................ '66 '94 C.112 B.A. L.179 J.D. [Ⓐ O'Melveny&M.]
Yang, Lee C. ....................................... '64 '91 C.145 A.B. L.800 J.D. 4215 Glencoe Ave.
Yang, Lyndane ......'58 '85 C.800 B.A. L.1068 J.D. Transamerica Occidental Life Ins. Co.
**Yang, Michele Yeun** ..........................'65 '92 C.813 A.B. L.1068 J.D. Capital Grp. Cos., Inc.
**Yang, Mina S.** ...................................'69 '96 C.112 B.A. L.1068 J.D. [Ⓐ Arnold&P.]
*LANGUAGES: Korean.
*PRACTICE AREAS: Corporate; Real Estate.
**Yang, Richard P.** .................. '49 '74 C.112 A.B. L.1068 J.D. [Quan,C.K.Y.S.&H.]
*PRACTICE AREAS: Real Estate; Banking; Debtor and Creditor Remedies; Business Law.
Yang, Stan K. ......................................'59 '85 C.597 B.A. L.1066 J.D. 777 S. Figueroa St.
**Yang, Vivian W.** ............................ '67 '95 C.645 B.S. L.276 J.D. [Ⓐ Latham&W.]
*LANGUAGES: Chinese (Mandarin).
**Yang, Weining** ............... '63 '95 C.061 M.S. L.426 J.D. [Ⓐ Loeb&L.] (See Pat. Sect.)
*LANGUAGES: Chinese.
*PRACTICE AREAS: Patent Prosecution.
**Yang, Wendy W.** ............ '68 '95 C.112 B.A. L.94 J.D. [Ⓐ Loeb&L.] (See Pat. Sect.)
*LANGUAGES: Taiwanese and Mandarin.
*PRACTICE AREAS: Intellectual Property.
Yankelevits, Daniel M. .......... '67 '91 C.1349 B.A. L.309 J.D. 1901 Avenue of the Stars
**Yankelevits, Lori M.** ......................'66 '91 C.112 A.B. L.597 J.D. [Ⓐ Troop M.S.&P.]
*PRACTICE AREAS: Insurance Coverage Litigation.
**Yankelevitz, Steven B.** ........................ '52 '80 C.415 B.S. L.990 J.D. [Liner,Y.&S.]
*PRACTICE AREAS: Corporate; Partnership; Limited Liability Companies; Business Law; Securities Law.
**Yanney, Fred G.** ...................... '52 '77 C&L.546 B.S., J.D. [Ⓒ Fulbright&J.]
*PRACTICE AREAS: Public Finance; Electric Utility Regulation.
**Yanni, Rami S.** ..............................'63 '93 C.112 B.A. L.426 J.D. [Ⓐ Graham&J.]
*LANGUAGES: Arabic.
Yanny, Joseph A., (P.C.) ......... '52 '78 C&L.201 B.E., J.D. 1925 Century Pk., E. (Pat.)
**Yano, Lester I.** .......................... '57 '94 C.910 B.S.C.E. L.1068 J.D. [Ⓐ Morrison&F.]

Yarber, Sharon '51 '76 C.112 B.A. L.809 J.D.
V.P., Assoc. Reg. Coun. & Legal Dept. Mgr., Chicago Title Ins. Co.
Yarc, Mariellen . . . . . . . . . . '54 '86 C.112 B.A. L.809 J.D. 1200 Wilshire Blvd.
Yardum-Hunter, Alice M., (BV) . . . '53 '80 C.1019 B.A. L.1049 J.D. 11601 Wilshire Blvd.
**Yarema, Geoffrey S.** . . . . . . . . . '53 '78 C.260 B.S. L.893 J.D. [Nossaman,G.K.&E.]
*PRACTICE AREAS: Natural Resources Law; Real Property Law; Transportation Law; Project Finance Law.
Yaris, Greg . . . . . . . . . . '57 '82 C.1044 B.A. L.276 J.D. 1801 Century Park East
**Yariv, Amir** . . . . . . . . . . '67 '94 C.112 B.A. L.426 J.D. [🄰 Epport&R.]
*LANGUAGES: Hebrew and Spanish.
*PRACTICE AREAS: Real Property; Contract; Bankruptcy.
Yarosh, Laurence . . . . . . . . . . '52 '78 C&L.494 B.Phys., J.D. CCH Incorporated

**Yaroslow, Gerald M., (AV) '47 '76 C.659 A.B. L.800 J.D.**
**Suite 950, Century City North Building, 10100 Santa Monica Boulevard, 90067-4013**
**Telephone: 310-277-8863 Fax: 310-556-3847**
**Certified Specialist, Probate, Estate Planning and Trust Law, The State Bar of California Board of Legal Specialization.**
**Estate Planning, Estate and Trust Administration, Probate, Estate and Trust Dispute Resolution.**
***See Professional Biographies, LOS ANGELES, CALIFORNIA***

Yasui, Robert K. . . . . . . . . . . '61 '87 C.112 B.A. L.569 J.D. 555 S. Flower St., 28th Fl.
**Yates, Gary S.** . . . . . . . . . . '54 '79 C.112 B.A. L.426 J.D. [🄰 Herzfeld&R.]
**Yates, Pamela J.** . . . . . . . . . . '63 '88 C.143 B.S. L.809 J.D. [🄰 Brobeck,P.&H.]

**Yates, Gregory A., A Prof. Corp., Law Offices of**
**(See Beverly Hills)**

**Yeager, Neil F.** . . . . . . . . . . '48 '74 C.154 B.A. L.800 J.D. [Burke,W.&S.]
*PRACTICE AREAS: Corporate and Corporate Finance Law; Real Estate Law; Securities Law; Commercial Law.
Yeam, Kevin W. . . . . . . . . . . '61 '86 C.800 B.S. L.990 J.D. 12121 Wilshire Blvd.
Yee, Andrea . . . . . . . . . . '52 '78 C.112 B.A. L.1137 J.D. Dep. City Atty.
**Yee, Carol** '66 '94 C.94 B.A. L.464 J.D.
(adm. in MA; not adm. in CA) Staff Coun., SunAmerica Inc.
*RESPONSIBILITIES: General Corporate Practice.
Yee, Carolyn M. . . . . . . . . . . '49 '76 C.112 A.B. L.1066 J.D. 611 W. 6th St.
Yee, Derek S. . . . . . . . . . . '62 '87 C.174 B.A. L.93 J.D. [Albright,Y.&S.]
Yee, Donald H. . . . . . . . . . . '— '87 C.112 B.A. L.893 J.D. 11377 W. Olympic Blvd.
Yee, Hermen Y. '— '87 C.1097 B.S. L.1292 J.D.
(adm. in NJ; not adm. in CA) U.S. Securities & Exchange Comm.
**Yee, Steven R.** . . . . . . . . . . '66 '91 C.112 B.A. L.1065 J.D. [🄰 Anderson,M.&C.]
**Yeh, Jack S.** . . . . . . . . . . '69 '94 C.112 B.A. L.1049 J.D. [🄰 Ku,F.L.&C.]
*LANGUAGES: Chinese (Mandarin).
*PRACTICE AREAS: Civil Trial; Litigation.
**Yeh, Julie** . . . . . . . . . . '63 '93 C.914 B.A. L.1068 J.D. [Jackson&L.]
*LANGUAGES: Chinese (Mandarin).
*PRACTICE AREAS: Employment; Underground Storage Tank Litigation.
Yellin, Ira E., (AV) . . . . . . . . . . '40 '66 C.674 A.B. L.309 LL.B. The Yellin Co.
Yelsky, Jerome A. . . . . . . . . . . '47 '77 C.1077 B.A. L.809 J.D. [Cherin&Y.]
Yeomans, E. D., (AV) . . . . . . . . . . '10 '35 C.575 A.B. L.309 J.D. 515 N. Lillian Way‡
Yep, Stanley . . . . . . . . . . '26 '63 C.112 B.A. L.809 LL.B. P.O. Box 861116
**Yeruhim, Yelena** . . . . . . . . . . '66 '92 C.112 B.A. L.800 J.D. [🄲 Brand F.D.F.&K.]
*PRACTICE AREAS: Real Estate Law; Corporate Law.
**Yeung, Rowena A. W.** . . . . . . . . . . '66 '91 C.821 B.A. L.178 J.D. [🄰 Morrison&F.]
*LANGUAGES: Cantonese.
Yglecias, Michael A. . . . . . . . . . . '57 '82 C.112 B.A. L.1068 J.D. Dep. Dist. Atty.
**Yguico, Carlos V.** . . . . . . . . . . '62 '87 C.112 B.A. L.800 J.D. [🄰 Gascou,G.&T.]
*LANGUAGES: Filipino.
*REPORTED CASES: FSR Brokerage, Inc. v. Superior Court (1995) 35 Cal. App. 4th 6a, 41 Cal. Rptr. 2d 404.
*PRACTICE AREAS: Trials and Appeals; Insurance Coverage; Construction; Fidelity; Suretyship.
Yi, Michael Y. . . . . . . . . . . '61 '95 C.112 B.S. L.1136 J.D. [🄰 Bloom&R.]
**Yi, Miwon** . . . . . . . . . . '65 '92 C&L.893 B.A., J.D. [🄰 Jones,D.R.&P.]
**Yim, B. Casey, (P.C.)** . . . . . . . . . . '48 '75 C.763 A.B. L.1003 J.D. [Lewis,D.B.&B.]
Yip, Jeffrey S. . . . . . . . . . . '48 '74 C.112 B.S. L.426 J.D. 9841 Airport Blvd.
**Yobski, James B.** . . . . . . . . . . '64 '89 C.992 B.A. L.801 J.D. [🄰 Bronson,B.&M.]
**Yocca, Christine M.** . . . . . . . . . . '64 '88 C&L.426 B.A., J.D. [🄰 Agajanian&M.]
Yochelson, Alan S. . . . . . . . . . . '55 '80 C.112 B.A. L.809 J.D. Dep. Dist. Atty.
Yochelson, David A. . . . . . . . . . . '50 '77 C.318 B.A. L.1095 J.D. [Spiegel,V.&Y.]
**Yoffie, Beth E.** . . . . . . . . . . '60 '85 C.112 A.B. L.1065 J.D. [🄰 Lewis,D.B.&B.]
Yoka, Walter M. . . . . . . . . . . '55 '80 C.1097 B.A. L.809 J.D. [Morgan&W.]
Yokomizo, Douglas . . . . . . . . '60 '85 C.154 B.A. L.1065 J.D. 725 S.Figueroa St., Ste., 3750
**Yokoyama, Frank A.** . . . . . . . . . . '68 '94 C.112 B.S. L.309 J.D. [🄰 Hancock R.&B.]
**Yonekura, Stephanie K.** . . . . . . . . . . '70 '96 C&L.112 B.A., J.D. [🄰 O'Melveny&M.]
**Yong, Jeffrey S.** . . . . . . . . . . '61 '88 C.112 B.A. L.1065 J.D. [Alexander&Y.]
*LANGUAGES: Mandarin Chinese.
*PRACTICE AREAS: Business and Real Property Litigation; Environmental Law; Bankruptcy; Securities; China Trade.
**Yong, Yee-Yoong** . . . . . . . . . . '56 '87 C&L.061 LL.B. [🄲 Sidley&A.]
*LANGUAGES: Chinese.
**Yoo, Mary J.** . . . . . . . . . . '69 '96 C.681 B.A. L.145 J.D. [🄰 Latham&W.]
*LANGUAGES: Korean.
**Yoo, Thomas J.** . . . . . . . . . . '68 '94 C.112 B.A. L.1068 J.D. [🄰 Rodi,P.P.G.&C.]
*LANGUAGES: Korean.
*PRACTICE AREAS: Business Litigation; Products Liability; Professional Errors and Omissions.
**Yoo, Timothy J.** . . . . . . . . . . '— '91 L.426 J.D. [🄰 Sheppard,M.R.&H.]
**Yoo, Victor J.** . . . . . . . . . . '— '94 C.05 B.A. L.809 J.D. [Tax C.]
*PRACTICE AREAS: Tax Bankruptcy; Real Estate; Business.
**Yood, Kenneth J.** . . . . . . . . . . '63 '89 C.311 B.A. L.1044 J.D. [🄰 McCutchen,D.B.&E.]
*LANGUAGES: Spanish.
*PRACTICE AREAS: Healthcare Law.
**Yoon, Angie Y.** . . . . . . . . . . '70 '95 C.112 B.A. L.426 J.D. [🄰 Stevens,K.A.&H.]
*PRACTICE AREAS: General Civil Litigation; Personal Injury; Construction Defect.
**Yoon, John Yong-Jin** . . . . . . . . . . '61 '87 C.309 A.B. L.1068 J.D. [🄰 Lewis,D.B.&B.]
*LANGUAGES: Korean, Japanese and Spanish.
**Yoon, Richard Kon** . . . . . . . . . . '70 '96 C.112 B.S. L.800 J.D. [🄰 Loeb&L.]
*LANGUAGES: Korean.
*PRACTICE AREAS: Intellectual Property.
**Yoong, Dominic K.L.** . . . . . . . . . . '67 '94 C.668 B.A. L.188 J.D. [🄰 Latham&W.]
Yorizane, Ronald A. . . . . . . . . . . '48 '75 C.1097 B.S. L.426 J.D. Dep. Pub. Def.
**York, Gary A.**, (AV) . . . . . . . . . . '43 '69 C.668 B.A. L.813 LL.B. [Buchalter,N.F.&Y.]
*PRACTICE AREAS: Real Estate.
**York, James R.**, (AV) . . . . . . . . . . '45 '78 C.1077 B.A. L.1221 J.D. [Gray,Y.D.&R.]
*PRACTICE AREAS: Insurance Law; Workers Compensation; Products Liability; Public Entity Law.

**Yoshida, Gerald T.**
**(See Santa Monica)**

Yoshinaga, Paul I. . . . . . . . . . . '59 '87 C.112 B.A. L.352 J.D. 500 W. Temple St.
Yoshino, Denise L. . . . . . . . . . . '54 '80 C.312 B.A. L.800 J.D. [Schwarcz&Y.]
**Yoshioka, Heidi M.** . . . . . . . . . . '64 '90 C.426 B.A. L.809 J.D. [🄰 Meyers,B.&M.]
*PRACTICE AREAS: Insurance Defense.

**Yoshiyama, Denah H.** . . . . . . . . . . '68 '94 C.112 B.A. L.809 J.D. [🄰 Lynberg&W.]
**Yoss, Jan A.** . . . . . . . . . . '63 '89 C.339 B.A. L.1068 J.D. [🄰 Seyfarth,S.F.&G.]
*PRACTICE AREAS: Commercial, Tort and Employment Litigation.
Youhne, Young . . . . . . . . . . '35 '75 C.990 B.S. L.1068 J.D. 4311 Wilshire Blvd.
**Youmans, Kenwood C.** . . . . . . . . . . '46 '74 C.112 B.A. L.477 J.D. [Seyfarth,S.F.&G.]
*PRACTICE AREAS: Labor and Employment.
**Young, Beth Ann R.** . . . . . . . . . . '64 '89 C.112 B.A. L.426 J.D. [🄰 Epport&R.]
*PRACTICE AREAS: Commercial Litigation; Bankruptcy; Real Property; Banking Transactions.
Young, Brian P. . . . . . . . . . . '51 '76 C.112 A.B. L.809 J.D. Sr. V.P., Amer. Life League‡
Young, Christina Ann . . . . . . . . . . '62 '87 C.605 B.A. L.1065 J.D. Dep. Dist. Atty.
**Young, Christina L.** . . . . . . . . . . '68 '94 C.228 B.A. L.426 J.D. [🄰 Kern,S.&G.]
*PRACTICE AREAS: Premises Liability; Medical Malpractice; Products Liability; Defamation; Contracts.
**Young, Clarisse W. J.** . . . . . . . . . . '57 '82 C.312 B.A. L.477 J.D. [🄲 Paul,H.J.&W.]
Young, David . . . . . . . . . . '38 '65 C.309 A.B. L.188 LL.B. 11766 Wilshire Blvd.
**Young, Debbie L.** . . . . . . . . . . '58 '83 C.112 B.A. L.1068 J.D. Sr. Coun., Bank of Amer.
Young, Eric R. . . . . . . . . . . '47 '72 C.800 B.A. L.1068 J.D. Princ. Dep. Co. Coun.
**Young, Jamie** . . . . . . . . . . '56 '82 C.910 B.A. L.569 J.D. [Ziffren,B.B.&F.]
*PRACTICE AREAS: Entertainment Law.
Young, Jaye A. . . . . . . . . . . '60 '83 C.699 B.A. L.813 J.D. 1800 S. Robertson Blvd.
Young, Judith L. . . . . . . . . . . '59 '83 C.112 B.A. L.800 J.D. 633 W. 5th St.
**Young, Julie Arias** . . . . . . . . . . '68 '93 C.112 B.A. L.276 J.D. [🄰 Paul,H.J.&W.]
**Young, Lee R., Jr.** . . . . . . . . . . '37 '66 C.1097 B.A. L.809 J.D. [🄲 Atkins&E.]
*PRACTICE AREAS: Entertainment Law.
**Young, Lesley D.** . . . . . . . . . . '70 '95 C&L.800 B.A., J.D. [🄰 Bryan C.]
**Young, Marc D.** . . . . . . . . . . '63 '93 C&L.878 B.S., J.D. [🄰 Morrison&F.]
**Young, Mark A.H.** . . . . . . . . . . '69 '95 C.112 B.A. L.800 J.D. [🄰 White&C.]
Young, Mark T. . . . . . . . . . . '55 '79 C.112 B.A. L.1067 J.D. 11726 San Vicente Blvd.
**Young, Mary L. Trokel** . . . . . . . . . . '62 '89 C.976 B.A. L.569 J.D. [Murphy,W.&B.]
*PRACTICE AREAS: Business Workouts; Bankruptcy Reorganizations; Creditors Remedies.
**Young, Michael D.** . . . . . . . . . . '60 '85 C.112 B.A. L.800 J.D. [McClintock,W.B.R.R.&M.]
*REPORTED CASES: United States v. Rogers, 769 F 2d 1418 (9th Cir. 1985); Cose v. Getty Oil Co., 4 F.3d 700 (9th Cir. 1993).
*PRACTICE AREAS: Environmental Litigation; Commercial and General Business Litigation; Employment Litigation; Mediation; ADR.
**Young, Mona H.** . . . . . . . . . . '64 '91 C.326 B.S. L.494 J.D. [🄰 Gascou,G.&T.]
*PRACTICE AREAS: Litigation; Suretyship.
**Young, Naomi**, (AV) . . . . . . . . . . '50 '74 C.734 B.A. L.770 J.D. [Gartner&Y.]
*PRACTICE AREAS: Labor and Employment Law.
**Young, Philip** . . . . . . . . . . '67 '91 C.602 B.A. L.494 J.D. [🄰 Lane P.S.L.]
*PRACTICE AREAS: Labor and Employment; Toxic Torts.
**Young, Robert E.**, (AV) . . . . . . . . . . '47 '72 C.112 B.A. L.1065 J.D. [Frederickson&Y.]
*REPORTED CASES: State of Trynin 49 Cal 3rd 868 1989.
*PRACTICE AREAS: Business Litigation; Conservatorships; Securities Litigation; Civil Litigation; Unlawful Detainers.
**Young, Robert M., Jr.** . . . . . . . . . . '48 '74 C.112 B.S. L.1065 J.D. [Wilson,E.M.E.&D.]
**Young, Rufus C., Jr.** . . . . . . . . . . '40 '65 C&L.1049 B.A., J.D. [Burke,W.&S.]
*LANGUAGES: Japanese, Spanish and Vietnamese.
*SPECIAL AGENCIES: E.P.A., California Regional Water Quality Control Boards, California Department of Health Services, California Integrated Waste Management Board, South Coast Air Quality Management District.
*PRACTICE AREAS: Environmental Law; Hazardous Waste and Toxic Substances; Solid Waste Law; Endangered Species; Contaminated Property Cleanup Law.
**Young, Stephen N.** '58 '86
C.473 B.A. L.273 J.D. Assoc. Gen. Coun., Ernst & Young LLP
**Young, Stuart H., Jr., (P.C.)**, (AV) . . . . . . . . . . '43 '68 C.154 B.A. L.813 LL.B. [Hill,F.&B.]
*PRACTICE AREAS: Labor Law; Employee Benefit Law; Employment Discrimination Law; Wrongful Discharge Law; Trust Law.
Young, Thad D. . . . . . . . . . . '42 '71 C.1097 B.S. L.800 J.D. Dep. Dist. Atty.
**Young, Thomsen**, (AV) . . . . . . . . . . '46 '74 C.112 B.A. L.1068 J.D. [Pachulski,S.Z.&Y.]
*REPORTED CASES: In re Madison Associates, 183 B.R. 206 (Bankr. C.D. California 1995).
*TRANSACTIONS: Represented Creditors Committee in Qintex Entertainment, Inc., Madison Associates (Formerly Pannell Kerr Forster), represented the chapter 11 Trustee in 21st Century Film Corporation and NSB Film Corporation (formerly Hemdale Entertainment).
**Young, Tracy W.** . . . . . . . . . . '55 '84 C.569 B.A. L.978 J.D. [🄰 Rossbacher&Assoc.]
*REPORTED CASES: People v. Kramer, 132 A.D.2d 708, 518 N.Y.S.2d 189 (N.Y.A.D. 2 Dept. 1987); Sosinsky v. Grant, 6 Cal.App.4th 1548 (Cal.App. 5 Dist. 1992); U.S. v. Blaylock, 20 F.3d 1458 (9th Cir. 1994).
*PRACTICE AREAS: Appellate Law; Litigation.
**Young, W. Herbert**, (AV) . . . . . . . '37 '63 C.112 B.S. L.1068 J.D. [🄲 Proskauer R.G.&M.]
*PRACTICE AREAS: Environmental Law.

**Young, Henrie, Humphries & Mason**
**(See Pomona)**

**Young & Thompson**
**(See Arlington, Virginia)**

**Youngblood, Juliette** . . . . . . . . . . '63 '90 C.456 B.A.B.S. L.426 J.D. [🄰 Irell&M.]
Youngdahl, Bonnie S. . . . . . . . . . . '39 '86 C.112 B.A. L.809 J.D. Dept. of Corps.
Youngdahl, Laurie C. . . . . . . . . . . '63 '89 C.705 B.A. L.800 J.D. 11693 San Vicente Blvd.
**Younger, Candace Anne** . . . . . . . . . . '68 '93 C.881 B.A. L.1068 [🄰 Manatt,P.&P.]
*PRACTICE AREAS: Business and Insurance Litigation.
**Younger, Eric E.**, (AV) . . . . . . . . . . '43 '69 C.800 B.A. L.309 LL.B. [🄲 Graham&J.]
*LANGUAGES: Spanish and French.
*PRACTICE AREAS: Alternative Dispute Resolution.
**Younger, Steven J.** . . . . . . . . . . '62 '87 C.426 B.A. L.1068 J.D. [Manatt,P.&P.]
*PRACTICE AREAS: Entertainment Law.
Younger, Timothy M. . . . . . . . . . . '64 '90 C.940 B.A. L.426 J.D. 400 S. Hope St.
Younglove, Sonia M. '— '90 C.112 B.A. L.1068 J.D.
Staff Atty., Calif. Assn. of Realtors

**Youngman, Hungate & Leopold, A Professional Corporation**
**(See Leopold, Petrich & Smith)**

Yousefzadeh, Faramarz . . . . . . . . . . '64 '87 C.800 B.S. L.809 J.D. [F.Yousefzadeh]
Yousefzadeh, Faramarz, A Professional Law Corporation . . . . . . . . . . P.O. Box 49272
**Youssefmir, Jacques** . . . . . . . . . . '71 '95 C.36 B.A. L.309 J.D. [🄰 Latham&W.]
*LANGUAGES: Farsi.
**Youth, Thomas B.** . . . . . . . . . . '64 '90 C.112 B.A. L.309 J.D. [🄰 Brobeck,P.&H.]
**Youtz, Shane C.** . . . . . . . . . . '66 '91 C.972 B.A. L.494 J.D. [🄰 Sinnott,D.M.&P.]
*PRACTICE AREAS: Insurance Coverage Litigation; Business Litigation.
Yowell, Margaret A. . . . . . . . . . . '62 '89 C.802 B.A. L.846 J.D. 355 S. Grand Ave.
**Yslas, Stephen D.** '47 '72 C&L.1068 B.A., J.D.
V.P. & Asst. Gen. Coun., Northrop Grumman Corp.
**Yu, Lauren M.** . . . . . . . . . . '55 '88 C.012 B.Sc. L.029 J.D. [🄰 Sonnenschein N.&R.]
*LANGUAGES: Chinese (Mandarin).
*PRACTICE AREAS: Litigation.
**Yu, Spencer H.C.** . . . . . . . . . . '68 '94 C.691 B.A. L.846 J.D. [🄰 O'Melveny&M.]
*LANGUAGES: Chinese.
**Yu, Steve H.** . . . . . . . . . . '67 '92 C.112 B.A. L.36 J.D. [🄰 Robinson,D.&W.]
**Yu-Cheng Chang, John Andrew** . . . . . . . '65 '90 C.674 A.B. L.276 J.D. [🄰 Gibson,D.&C.]
Yuen, Roger . . . . . . . . . . '60 '88 C.1097 B.A. L.1065 J.D. 808 N. Spring St.
Yuen, Victoria A.M. . . . . . . . . . . '48 '81 C.477 B.A. L.809 J.D. William M. Mercer, Inc.
**Yukevich, James J.** . . . . . . . . . . '53 '78 C&L.93 B.A., J.D. [Yukevich&S.]
*PRACTICE AREAS: Products Liability Defense; Personal Injury Defense.

CAA371P

CALIFORNIA—LOS ANGELES MARTINDALE-HUBBELL LAW DIRECTORY 1997

**Yukevich, Stanley M.** ...........'64 '93 C.309 B.A. L.1068 J.D. [🄰 Skadden,A.S.M.&F.]

**Yukevich & Sonnett**
**601 South Figueroa Street Seventeenth Floor, 90017**
**Telephone: 213-362-7777 Telecopier: 213-362-7788**
**Members of Firm: James J. Yukevich; Anthony E. Sonnett. Associates: H. David Henry; Alexander G. Calfo; Sarah M. Makowsky; Kimberly A. Smith; Abdalla J. Innabi.**
**Litigation and Products Liability.**
***See Professional Biographies, LOS ANGELES, CALIFORNIA***

Yum, Chris C. ...............'61 '89 C&L.446 B.A., J.D. 7700 Little River Tpke., Ste. 502
**Yung, Steven C.** .................'66 '94 C.1097 B.S. L.800 J.D. [🄰 Alvarado,S.V.&S.]
*PRACTICE AREAS: Civil Litigation; Business Transactional.
**Yurosko, Michael E.** .................'43 '73 C&L.608 B.A., J.D. Atlantic Richfield Co.
**Yuter, Alan B.** ............................'56 '81 C.188 B.A. L.276 J.D. [Selman B.]
Yuter, Arthur '44 '69 C.563 B.B.A. L.273 J.D.
(adm. in NY; not adm. in CA) N.L.R.B.
**Yuwiler, Ken** ..........................'61 '86 C.1077 B.A. L.809 J.D. [🄰 R.Edwards]
Yzurdiaga, John, (AV) .................'40 '71 C.112 B.A. L.426 J.D. 800 Wilshire Blvd.
**Zaccaro, Thomas A.** ...................'59 '84 C.276 B.A. L.93 J.D. [🄲 Manatt,P.&P.]
*PRACTICE AREAS: General Business Litigation.
**Zackrison, John A.** .....................'52 '79 C.101 B.A. L.309 J.D. [Kirkland&E.]
*PRACTICE AREAS: Environmental Litigation and Counseling.
Zacks, Arthur H, ....................'42 '68 C.112 B.A. L.309 LL.B. 9000 Sunset Blvd.
Zacky, Hayden A. ......................'64 '92 C.112 B.A. L.809 J.D. Dist. Attys Off.
**Zaelke, Edward W.** ......................'58 '83 C.1042 B.A. L.1068 J.D. [Arnold&P.]
*PRACTICE AREAS: Real Estate.
**Zafman, Norman**, (AV) '34 '70
C.563 B.E.E. L.809 J.D. [Blakely,S.T.&Z.] (See Pat. Sect.)
Zager, Raymond L. .........................'24 '55 C.877 L.809 LL.B. 464 N. Kilkea Dr.
Zahler, Pamela Gregg ..............'61 '86 C.861 B.A. L.260 J.D. 9255 W. Sunset Blvd.
**Zaif, Samuel M.** ........................'48 '84 C.112 A.B. L.1067 J.D. [🄲 Frye,A.&M.]
**Zaimes, John P.** .............'49 '80 C.112 A.B. L.276 J.D. [McClintock,W.B.R.R.&M.]
*LANGUAGES: Spanish.
*SPECIAL AGENCIES: Cal/OSHA Appeals Board; Cal/OSHA Standards Board.
*REPORTED CASES: Meghrig v. KFC Western, Inc., 1996 U.S. Lexis 1955; 1996 Westlaw 117012; KFC Western, Inc. v. Meghrig, 49F3d5186 (9th Cir. 1995); Cory v. Western Oil & Gas Assn., 471 U.S. 81, 105 S.Ct. 1859 (1985); Western Oil & Gas Assn. v. Cory, 726 F. 2d 1340 (9th Cir. 1984).
*PRACTICE AREAS: Environmental Litigation; Labor and Employment Counseling and Litigation; Oil and Gas Litigation; Business Litigation; Trials and Appeals.
**Zaitlen, Richard H.**, (AV) '46 '73 C.679 B.S.Ch.E. L.273 J.D.
[Loeb&L.] (See Pat. Sect.)
*PRACTICE AREAS: Trademark; Patent; Copyright.
**Zakariaie, Jack M.**.........................'68 '93 C.112 B.A. L.426 J.D. [🄰 Selman B.]
*LANGUAGES: Persian.
*REPORTED CASES: Amex Life Assurance Company v. Slome Capital Corp., 43 CalApp 4th 1588.
*PRACTICE AREAS: Civil Litigation; Insurance Defense; Insurance Coverage.
Zakheim, Rosalyn S. ...........'47 '72 C.788 A.B. L.1066 J.D. Sr. Jud. Atty., Ct. of App.
Zakson, Laurence S. ...............................'61 '85 C.846 B.A. L.1065 J.D. 501 Shatto Pl.
**Zalba, Julia** ..............................'68 '93 C.112 B.A. L.1068 J.D. [🄰 Kelley D.&W.]
Zamel, Stanley A. ..........................'52 '80 C.800 A.B. L.809 J.D. [Wilson&B.]
**Zamora, Anthony N.R.**.................'61 '90 C.309 A.B. L.800 J.D. [Zamora&H.]
*LANGUAGES: Spanish.
*PRACTICE AREAS: Corporate; Commercial Transactions; Litigation; Real Estate.

**Zamora & Hoffmeier, A Professional Corporation**
**520 South Grand Avenue, Suite 675, 90071**
**Telephone: 213-488-9411 Fax: 213-488-9418**
**Anthony N.R. Zamora; Nancy Hoffmeier Zamora.**
**Corporate, Bankruptcy, Real Estate, Commercial Transactions, Business Litigation, Land Use, Employment and Public Law.**
***See Professional Biographies, LOS ANGELES, CALIFORNIA***

Zamost, Nanette Brown ....................'56 '83 C.976 B.A. L.800 J.D. 333 S. Grand
**Zangwill, Henry S.**, (AV) .........'44 '70 C.16 B.S. L.846 J.D. [🄲 Sonnenschein N.&R.]
*PRACTICE AREAS: Insurance Coverage; Business Litigation.
Zank, Gloria A. ..................'37 '74 C.1097 L.809 J.D. Staff Atty., State Bar of Calif.
Zankich, L. Frank ....................'61 '86 C.1042 B.S. L.809 J.D. 3250 Wilshire Blvd.
Zapf, Jacqueline Trzaska ..............'50 '76 C.739 B.A. L.597 J.D. First Interstate Bank
**Zapf, Robert J.**, (AV🅃) '50 '76 C&L.93 B.A., J.D.
(adm. in NY; not adm. in CA) [Lane P.S.L.]
*PRACTICE AREAS: Admiralty and Maritime; International Commercial Law; Commercial Litigation and Arbitration.
**Zapp, James A.**..................................'46 '80 C.813 B.S. L.426 J.D. [Paul,H.J.&W.]
Zappia, Edward P. ........................'64 '94 C.112 B.A. L.809 J.D. [🄰 Liebert,C.&F.]
Zar, Parham ...............'66 '94 C.112 B.A. L.1148 J.D. 5455 Wilshire Blvd. Suite 1912
**Zarefsky, Ralph** .................................'50 '76 C.597 B.A. L.813 J.D. [Baker&H.]
*PRACTICE AREAS: Litigation.
Zaret, Thomas C. ....................'59 '84 C.475 B.S. L.721 J.D. 11755 Wilshire Blvd.
**Zaro, David R.** .....................'59 '86 C.813 B.A. L.1065 J.D. [Allen,M.L.G.&M.]
*PRACTICE AREAS: Litigation; Bankruptcy; Creditors Rights.
**Zarro, Michael T.** .........................'55 '83 C.112 B.A. L.1068 J.D. [Brobeck,P.&H.]
*PRACTICE AREAS: General Civil Litigation.
**Zarrow, Joshua D.**...............'60 '87 C.605 A.B. L.904 J.D. Sr. Coun., Teledyne, Inc.
Zarrow, Stanton H., (AV) .........'34 '60 C.454 B.A. L.309 LL.B. TCW Realty Advisors
Zatolokin, James R. .....................'45 '76 C.475 B.A. L.477 J.D. 11755 Wilshire Blvd.
Zawadzki, Roman J. ..........'47 '76 C.112 B.S. L.809 J.D. Principal Asst. Dist. Counsel
Zax, Frederick M., (AV) '38 '64 C.112 B.A. L.800 LL.B.
Pres. & Gen. Coun., Paper Moon Graphics, Inc.
**Zax, Lauren E.** ......................'67 '94 C.860 B.A. L.477 J.D. [🄰 Korshak,K.K.&S.]
*PRACTICE AREAS: Labor and Employment Law; Equal Opportunity Law; Public Employment Law; Civil Litigation.
Zayachak, Joseph J. ............'53 '80 C.426 B.A. L.1095 J.D. 11340 W. Olympia Blvd.
**Zbur, Richard S.** ..............................'57 '85 C.976 B.A. L.309 J.D. [Latham&W.]
Zebrowski, John ................................'48 '75 C.659 B.A. L.276 J.D. Ct. App. J.
**Zebrowski, John R.** ....................'53 '80 C.1044 B.A. L.1019 J.D. [Hughes H.&R.]
*PRACTICE AREAS: Environmental.
**Zecca, John A.** .....................'67 '93 C.188 B.S. L.1065 J.D. [🄰 Kaye,S.F.H.&H.]
*PRACTICE AREAS: Securities Law; Corporate Law.
Zee, Elizabeth W. '51 '79
C.518 A.B. L.982 J.D. V.P., Legal Affs., Paramount Pictures Corp.
Zeidler, D. Zeke .......'64 '91 C.1077 B.A. L.426 J.D. Dependency Ct. Legal Servs., Inc.
Zeidman, Scott C. ...........................'61 '90 C.426 B.S. L.1067 J.D. [🄰 Morgan&W.]
Zeidner, Robert B., (AV) ..............'52 '78 C.174 B.A. L.64 J.D. 10866 Wilshire Blvd.
Zeigler, Elisabeth E. ..............................'17 '42 C&L.800 B.A., J.D. Ret. Supr. Ct. J.‡
**Zeilenga, Richard S.** .....................'62 '87 C&L.597 B.S., J.D. [De Castro,W.&C.]
*PRACTICE AREAS: Business Litigation; Land Use; CEQA Planning and Litigation; Entitlement Disputes; Environmental/Insurance Coverage Litigation.
**Zeitinger, Rob C.** ..............................'57 '86 C.893 B.S. L.976 J.D. [Irell&M.]
Zeitsoff, P. Vernon, (AV) ......'45 '71 C.112 B.A. L.1068 J.D. 11845 W. Olympic Blvd.
**Zeitzew, Harris** ..................'25 '76 C.800 B.S. L.426 J.D. [🄲 Meyers,B.&M.] (Pat.)
*PRACTICE AREAS: Product Liability; Consumer Protection.
**Zelaznik, Marshall** .......................'65 '92 C.1042 B.A. L.767 J.D. [🄰 Schaffer&L.]

**Zeldow, Edward** ...........................'— '88 C.1293 B.M. L.1066 J.D. [Irell&M.]
**Zelen, Garrett J., (BV) '52 '78 C.1169 B.A. L.426 J.D.**
**12100 Wilshire Boulevard, Suite 1500, 90025**
**Telephone: 310-820-0077 FAX: 310-820-1205**
**(Certified Specialist, Criminal Law, The State Bar of California Board of Legal Specialization).**
***PRACTICE AREAS: Criminal Trial (State and Federal); Appellate Law; Forfeiture Law; Juvenile Law.**
**Criminal Trial, Appellate, Forfeiture, and Juvenile Practice State and Federal Courts.**
**Reference: Santa Monica Bank, West Los Angeles Branch.**
***See Professional Biographies, LOS ANGELES, CALIFORNIA***

Zelin, M. Jason ..........'50 '76 C.860 B.A. L.1068 J.D. Pres., Happy Entertainment, Inc.

**Zelle & Larson, (AV)**
**Oppenheimer Tower, 10990 Wilshire Boulevard, 90024⊙**
**Telephone: 310-478-7877 Telecopier: 310-478-5420**
**Members of Firm: Bryan M. Barber; Richard J. Stone. Counsel: Elizabeth D. Lear. Resident Associates: Jennifer A. Chmura; Desiree De Lisle; René I. Gamboa, IV; Craig C. Hunter; Devera L. Petak; Stevphen A. Watson.**
**Trials and Appeals in all Federal and State Courts. Insurance Law, Environmental Law, International Litigation, Antitrust, Corporate, Securities, Reinsurance, Alternative Dispute Resolution, Equine Law, Employment, Intellectual Property and Product Liability.**
**Minneapolis, Minnesota Office: 33 South Sixth Street, City Center, Suite 4400. Telephone: 612-339-2020.**
**Waltham, Massachusetts Office: 3 University Office Park, 95 Sawyer Road, Suite 500. Telephone: 617-891-7020.**
**Dallas, Texas Office: 1201 Main Street, Suite 3000. Telephone: 214-742-3000.**
**San Francisco, California Office: One Market Plaza, Steuart Street Tower, 15th Floor. Telephone: 415-978-9788.**
**Miami, Florida Office: 200 South Biscayne Boulevard, Suite 4670. Telephone: 305-373-5000.**
***See Professional Biographies, LOS ANGELES, CALIFORNIA***

Zelleke, Andargachew S. ........................'61 '87 C&L.309 A.B., J.D. Univ. of CA
**Zeller, Robert M.** ......................'50 '75 C.112 A.B. L.1068 J.D. [Musick,P.&G.]
*PRACTICE AREAS: Real Property Law; Real Estate Law.
**Zellers, Michael C.** ...............................'55 '80 C.294 A.B. L.608 J.D. [Arter&H.]
**Zelon, Laurie D.**, (AV) .....................'52 '77 C.188 A.B. L.309 J.D. [Morrison&F.]
*PRACTICE AREAS: Environmental Litigation; Geotechnical Litigation; Business Litigation.
Zeltonoga, William L. ...................'41 '69 C.112 A.B. L.309 J.D. 753 N. Croft Ave.
**Zemanek, John D.**, (AV) ...................'51 '77 C.688 B.A. L.1066 J.D. [Zemanek&M.]
*REPORTED CASES: Joffe v. United California Bank, 141 Cal.App.3d 541, 190 Cal.Rptr.443 (1983).
*PRACTICE AREAS: Real Estate, Business and Construction Litigation (Trials and Appeals); Real Property Financing; Secured Transactions.

**Zemanek & Mills, A Professional Corporation, (AV)**
**11845 West Olympic Boulevard, Suite 625, 90064**
**Telephone: 310-473-8100 Fax: 310-445-3166**
**John D. Zemanek; Stephan A. Mills.**
**Business, Real Estate and Construction Litigation. State and Federal Civil Trial and Appellate Practice, Creditors' Rights, Trade Secrets, Corporate and Partnership Law.**
***See Professional Biographies, LOS ANGELES, CALIFORNIA***

**Zenor, Donna J.**, (AV) ......................'45 '73 C.36 B.A. L.188 J.D. [Morrison&F.]
*PRACTICE AREAS: Banking Transactions; Structured Finance; Asset Securitization.
**Zerman, Michael J.** ....................'60 '94 C.918 B.A. L.37 J.D. [🄰 Mitchell,S.&K.]
*PRACTICE AREAS: Commercial Real Estate Law; Mortgage Finance Law; Corporate Law.
**Zermeno, Consuelo A.** ..........'68 '94 C.112 B.S. L.813 J.D. [🄰 Sonnenschein N.&R.]
*PRACTICE AREAS: Labor and Employment.
Zerner, David M., (BV) ...........'20 '51 C.563 B.B.S. L.809 LL.B. 954 Schumacher Dr.
**Zerner, Lawrence J.** ...............................'63 '91 C.1077 B.A. L.426 J.D. [🄰 Kirsch&M.]
**Zerunyan, Frank Vram** .........'59 '89 C.1042 B.A. L.1137 J.D. [🄲 Sulmeyer,K.B.&R.]
*LANGUAGES: Armenian, French and Turkish.
*PRACTICE AREAS: Real Estate; Litigation; Loan Workouts; Reorganizations; Bankruptcy Litigation.
Zervas, George J. ........'33 '62 C.867 A.B. L.1066 J.D. Prof. of Law, Southwestern Univ.
Zettas, Carol A. .........................'59 '84 C.112 B.A. L.800 J.D. State Bar of Calif.

**Zeutzius & LaBran**
**(See Pasadena)**

**Zevnik, Paul Anton**, (AV🅃) ...........'50 '77 C&L.309 A.B., J.D. [Zevnik H.G.&M.]⊙
*PRACTICE AREAS: Insurance Coverage; Environmental Law; Toxic Tort Litigation.

**Zevnik Horton Guibord & McGovern, P.C., (AV🅃)**
**333 South Grand Avenue Twenty First Floor, 90071⊙**
**Telephone: 213-437-5200 Telefax: 213-437-5222**
**Paul Anton Zevnik; Michel Yves Horton; Barbara B. Guibord (Not admitted in CA); Patrick Michael McGovern (Not admitted in CA); Joseph G. Homsy (Not admitted in CA); John W. Roberts (Not admitted in CA); John K. Crossman (Not admitted in CA); Jonathan L. Osborne (Not admitted in CA);—K. Eric Adair; Kristen C. Boling; David S. Cox; Carol A. Crotta; Mark B. Hartzler; Nick P. Karapetian; Steven E. Knott; Jason B. Komorsky; Charles J. Malaret; Meredith (MiMi) Newton; Dawn S. Pittman.**
**Commercial Litigation, Environmental Law, Insurance Coverage, Toxic Tort Litigation, International Law, Practice before State and Federal Courts and Administrative Tribunals.**
**Chicago, Illinois Office: Thirty Third Floor, 77 West Wacker Drive. Telephone: 312-977-2500. Fax: 312-977-2560.**
**Washington, D.C. Office: Ninth Floor, 1299 Pennsylvania Avenue, N.W. Telephone: 202-824-0950. Fax: 202-824-0955.**
**New York, N.Y. Office: 745 Fifth Avenue, Twenty-Fifth Floor. Telephone: 212-935-2735. Telefax: 212-935-0614.**
**Palo Alto, California Office: 5 Palo Alto Square, 3000 El Camino Real. Telephone: 415-842-5900. Facsimile: 415-855-9226.**
**London, England Office: 4 Kings Bench Walk, Temple, London, EC4Y 7DL. Telephone: 071-353-0478. Facsimile: 071-583-3549.**
**Norfolk, Virginia Office: Main Street Tower, 300 Main Street, 13th Floor. Telephone: 757-624-3480. Fax: 757-624-3479.**
***See Professional Biographies, LOS ANGELES, CALIFORNIA***

Zhang, Huijie ...........................................'53 '90 L.061 S.J.D. 11835 W. Olympic Blvd.
**Zhang, Jinshu** .........................'59 '93 C.061 B.A. L.1066 J.D. [🄰 Jones,D.R.&P.]
Zia-Zarifi, Saman ...........................'68 '93 C&L.188 B.A., J.D. 444 S. Flower St.
Zide, Gay ..........................'47 '92 C.112 B.A. L.1049 J.D. 2049 Century Park, E.
**Zide, Thomas**, (AV) ..............................'35 '60 C.1097 B.A. L.800 J.D. [Zide&O.]
*PRACTICE AREAS: Commercial Collection; Insolvency; Business.

**Zide & O'Biecunas, (AV) 🄱🄱**
**Suite 403, 1300 West Olympic Boulevard, 90015⊙**
**Mailing Address: P.O. Box 15363, Del Valle Station**
**Telephone: 213-487-7550 Fax: 213-382-6095**
**Email: leoatzano@aol.com**
**Thomas Zide; Leo G. O'Biecunas, Jr. Associates: Douglas M. Kaye; Nathan Swedlow.**
**Commercial, Insolvency, Business and Construction Law.**
**Ventura, California Office: 101 South Victoria Avenue. Telephone: 805-642-2426. Fax: 805-642-8881.**
***See Professional Biographies, LOS ANGELES, CALIFORNIA***

**Zidell, Steven H.** .............................'60 '85 C.112 B.A. L.1068 J.D. [Quateman&Z.]
**Ziegler, Jay R.**, (AV) ...............'47 '72 C.112 B.A. L.1066 J.D. [Buchalter,N.F.&Y.]
*PRACTICE AREAS: Business Litigation.
**Ziegler, Peter F.**, (AV) ...................'45 '74 C.976 B.S. L.800 J.D. [Gibson,D.&C.]
*PRACTICE AREAS: Business Practice; Securities Offerings/Public and Private Companies; Mergers and Acquisitions; Finance and General Corporate Matters.

**Ziehl, Dean A.**, (AV) '52 '78 C.112 B.A. L.426 J.D. [Pachulski,S.Z.&Y.]
Zier, Larry A. '63 '91 C&L.061 B.A., LL.B. 3580 Wilshire Blvd.
**Zieve, Les** '60 '86 C.800 B.A. L.1065 J.D. [Huron,Z.&K.]
*PRACTICE AREAS: Bankruptcy; Creditors Rights; Foreclosure and Real Estate Litigation.
Ziff, Norman D. '44 '82 C.129 L.1148 J.D. 6404 Wilshire Blvd.
Ziff, Ronald A. '50 '74 C.112 B.A. L.809 J.D. 11111 W. Olympic Blvd.
**Ziffren, Kenneth**, (AV) '40 '67 C.597 B.A. L.1068 J.D. [Ziffren,B.B.&F.]
*PRACTICE AREAS: Entertainment Law.
**Ziffren, Leo G.**, (AV) '22 '50 C&L.352 B.A., J.D. [Ⓒ Gibson,D.&C.]
*PRACTICE AREAS: Copyright/Trademark; Entertainment; General Corporate; Real Estate.
**Ziffren, Lester**, (AV) '25 '53 C.112 B.A. L.1068 J.D. [Ⓒ Gibson,D.&C.]
*PRACTICE AREAS: General Corporate; Real Estate.

**Ziffren, Brittenham, Branca & Fischer, (AV) BR**
**Thirty Second Floor, 2121 Avenue of the Stars, 90067**
**Telephone: 310-552-3388 Fax: 310-553-7068; 553-1648**
**Members of Firm: Kenneth Ziffren; Harry M. Brittenham; John G. Branca; Samuel N. Fischer; Paul L. Brindze; R. Dennis Luderer; David Nochimson; Gary S. Stiffelman; Clifford W. Gilbert-Lurie; Kathleen Hallberg; Jamie Young; Mitchell C. Tenzer; Kenneth A. August; Steven H. Burkow; David Lande; Jamey Cohen.**
**Entertainment and Tax Law.**
***See Professional Biographies, LOS ANGELES, CALIFORNIA***

Zigman, Louis '44 '70 C.569 B.S. L.273 J.D. 473 South Holt Ave.
Zimbert, Richard '29 '50 C&L.339 B.S.
Sr. V.P. & Gen. Coun., Paramount Pictures Corp.
Zimel, Jeffrey M. '66 '91 C.112 B.A. L.1065 J.D. Dep. Pub. Def.
**Zimmerman, Julie S.** '68 '95 C.112 B.A. L.273 J.D. [Ⓐ Troop M.S.&P.]
*PRACTICE AREAS: Insurance Coverage.
Zimmerman, Kurt F. '63 '91 C.813 B.A. L.1068 J.D. Off. of U.S. Atty.
**Zimmerman, Sharyl B.** '66 '94 C.112 B.A. L.464 J.D. [Ⓐ Schaffer&L.]
*PRACTICE AREAS: Products Liability; Medical Products.
Zimmerman, Shelley A. '56 '82 C.112 B.A. L.1065 J.D. 1801 Century Park East
**Zimmermann, Scott Z.**, (AV) '53 '77 C.112 A.B. L.1068 J.D. [Zimmermann,K.&C.]
*PRACTICE AREAS: Business Litigation; Torts; Equine Law.

**Zimmermann, Koomer & Connolly LLP, (AV)**
**10960 Wilshire Boulevard, Suite 1225, 90024**
**Telephone: 310-231-6565 Fax: 310-231-6566**
**Members of Firm: Scott Z. Zimmermann; Michael D. Koomer; John G. Connolly.**
**Representation and Counseling in the areas of Business and Real Estate Litigation, Employment Law, Torts and Equine Law.**
***See Professional Biographies, LOS ANGELES, CALIFORNIA***

**Zimring, Stuart D., (AV) '46 '72 C.112 B.A. L.1068 J.D. BR**
**12650 Riverside Drive (North Hollywood), 91607-3492**
**Telephone: 818-755-4848 Fax: 818-508-0181**
**(Certified Specialist, Estate Planning, Probate and Trust Law, The State Bar of California Board of Legal Specialization).**
***PRACTICE AREAS: Estate Planning; Probate and Trust; Real Estate Law; Business; Elder Law.**
**Associate: Dena L. Klotz.**
**Estate Planning, Trust and Probate Law, Elder Law, Business and Banking, Real Estate, Condominiums and Homeowners Associations.**
**Representative Clients: TransWorld Bank; Cytec Industries Inc.; Huntington Palisades Property Owners Assn.; Buff, Smith & Hensman Architects, Inc.**
***See Professional Biographies, LOS ANGELES, CALIFORNIA***

Zinger, Charles, (AV) '31 '64 C.809 L.981 4609 Russell Ave.
Zinman, Marvin, (AV) '26 '54 C.112 A.B. L.1068 LL.B. 315 W. 9th St.
Zinman, Roberta Scharlin '49 '78 C.112 A.B. L.1137 J.D. Dep. City Atty.
Ziontz, Mitch C. '65 '90 C.112 B.A. L.1068 J.D. 444 S. Flower St.
**Zipkin, Judith A.** '54 '85 C.477 B.A. L.426 J.D. [Lewis,D.B.&B.]
Zipperman, Barbara J. '53 '80 C.674 A.B. L.1067 J.D.
V.P., Bus. & Legal Affs., Interscope Communications, Inc.
Zipperstein, Steven E., (AV) '59 '83 C.112 B.A. L.1067 J.D. Chf. Asst. U.S. Atty.
Zipser, Stanley, (AV) '23 '52 C.871 B.S. L.426 J.D. 10866 Wilshire Blvd.
**Zirkelbach, Andrew E.** '59 '91 C.839 B.S. L.276 J.D. [Ⓐ Howrey&S.]
*PRACTICE AREAS: Government Contract Law.
**Zirkelbach, Gail Frulla** '62 '86 C.674 B.A. L.893 J.D. [McKenna&C.]
Ziskin, Jay H. '20 '46 C&L.800 A.B., LL.B. 1830 Westholme Ave.‡
Ziskind, Gregg M. '44 '72 C.112 A.B. L.1068 J.D. 2566 Overland Ave.
Ziskrout, David A. '35 '62 C.112 B.A. L.1068 LL.B. Comr., Supr. Ct.
**Zisser, Bruce R.** '61 '95 C.112 B.S.E.E. L.426 J.D. [Ⓐ Bright&L.]
*PRACTICE AREAS: Intellectual Property Law; Litigation.
**Zisser, Steven B.** '59 '88 C.112 B.A. L.426 J.D. [Stein S.S.&O.] (⊙San Diego)
*PRACTICE AREAS: Customs Law; International Trade Law; Administrative Law.
**Ziven, Steven L.**, (AV) '53 '78 C.659 B.S. L.966 J.D. [Ⓒ Freeman,F.&S.]
*PRACTICE AREAS: Corporations Law; Business Transactions; Real Estate Law.
Zlatkoff, Michael '51 '78 C.112 B.A. L.809 J.D. 601 W. 5th St.
Zlotnik, Arna H. '54 '83 C.1077 B.A. L.398 J.D. 2049 Century Park East
**Zobler, Andrew E.** '61 '88 C.1044 B.A. L.1009 J.D. [Ⓐ Dewey B.]
*LANGUAGES: Spanish, Hebrew.
**Zobrist, Duane H.**, (AV) '40 '69 C.878 A.B. L.800 J.D. [Carlsmith B.W.C.&I.]
*LANGUAGES: Spanish, Portuguese.
*PRACTICE AREAS: International Law; Business Law; North American Free Trade Agreement; Commercial Law; Mexico Trade.
Zoeller, Jean E. '55 '81 C.959 B.A. L.976 J.D. Sr. Gen. Atty., Capital Cities/ABC, Inc.
**Zohar, Daniel Y.** '68 '93 C.228 B.A. L.112 J.D. [Ⓐ Hanna&M.]
*PRACTICE AREAS: Civil Trial; General Practice.
**Zohn, Martin S.**, (AV) '47 '72 C.347 A.B. L.309 J.D. [Proskauer R.G.&M.]
*PRACTICE AREAS: Bankruptcy; Corporate; Litigation.
**Zoida, Salvatore A.** '66 '92 C.178 B.A. L.276 J.D. [Ⓐ Hooper,L.&B.]
*LANGUAGES: Italian.
*PRACTICE AREAS: Health Care Litigation.
**Zolkin, David B.** '65 '91 C.112 B.A. L.800 J.D. [Ⓐ Arter&H.]
**Zolla, Marshall S., (A P.C.)**, (AV) '39 '64 C.112 A.B. L.1066 J.D. [Zolla&M.]
*PRACTICE AREAS: Family Law.

**Zolla and Meyer, (AV) BR**
**A Partnership including a Professional Corporation**
**Suite 1020, 2029 Century Park East, 90067**
**Telephone: 310-277-0725 Facsimile: 310-277-3784**
**Email: familylaw@zmlalaw.com URL: http://www.zmlalaw.com/familylaw**
**Members of Firm: Marshall S. Zolla (A P.C.) (Certified Specialist, Family Law, The State Bar of California Board of Legal Specialization); Lisa Helfend Meyer (Certified Specialist, Family Law, The State Bar of California Board of Legal Specialization). Associates: Doreen Marie Olson; Dana Lowy; Gregory M. Marsh.**
**Family Law.**
**Reference: Bank of California, Beverly Hills.**
***See Professional Biographies, LOS ANGELES, CALIFORNIA***

Zolt, Eric M. '52 '78 C.659 B.S. L.145 J.D.
(adm. in IL; not adm. in CA) Univ. of Calif. Sch. of Law
**Zomber, Peter J.** '51 '80 C.800 B.A. L.884 J.D. [La Follette,J.D.F.&A.]
*PRACTICE AREAS: General Liability; Medical Malpractice; Products Liability; Construction Litigation.
Zorick, Stephen B., Jr. '44 '70 C.112 B.A. L.1068 J.D. IRS
Zovich, Thomas M. '43 '70 C&L.426 B.B.A., J.D. [McCawley&Z.]
Zubieta, Charles A. '26 '53 C.112 B.A. L.1068 J.D. 600 Wilshire Blvd.
**Zubrzycki, Charles R.** '50 '94 C.602 B.A. L.273 J.D. [Ⓐ Foley L.W.&A.]
*PRACTICE AREAS: Intellectual Property; Environmental.
**Zucker, David C.** '46 '71 C&L.502 B.A., J.D. [Ⓒ Jones,D.R.&P.]
**Zucker, Erika A.** '65 '93 C.604 B.A. L.588 J.D. [Ⓐ Schwartz,S.D.&S.]
*PRACTICE AREAS: Labor and Employment.
**Zucker, Gregg** '67 '93 C.260 B.A. L.1068 J.D. [Ⓐ Brobeck,P.&H.]
*PRACTICE AREAS: Products Liability Defense.
Zucker, Jody C. '61 '87 2121 Ave. of the Stars
Zuckerman, Stephen D. '42 '70 C.674 A.B. L.800 J.D. 12400 Wilshire Blvd.
**Zuckerman, Tod I.** '54 '80 C.800 B.A. L.1065 J.D. [Sedgwick,D.M.&A.]⊙
Zuckman, Mark, (BV) '55 '80 C.800 B.A. L.1067 J.D. Dep. Pub. Def.
Zufelt, Karl D. '47 '74 C.877 B.S. L.878 J.D. I.R.S.

**Zugsmith, George S., A Professional Corporation**
**(See Long Beach)**

**Zuk, Michael A.**, (AV) '52 '78
C.1077 B.A. L.809 J.D. [Herzfeld&R.] (⊙Newport Beach, CA)
*PRACTICE AREAS: Medical Malpractice; Product Liability Law; Trial Practice.

**Zukerman, Rosaline L., Law Offices of, (AV) '30 '81 C.339 B.A. L.809 J.D.**
**1888 Century Park East Suite 1100, 90067**
**Telephone: 310-277-5277 Fax: 310-277-5276**
***PRACTICE AREAS: Family Law; Real Estate; Business Law; Criminal Law.**
**Associates: Deborah L. Graboff; Sharon Maravalli; Deborah Davis; Rachel S. Jacoby. Of Counsel: Carol Perrin.**
**Family, Business, Corporate and Real Estate Law. Criminal Defense, Litigation.**
***See Professional Biographies, LOS ANGELES, CALIFORNIA***

**Zukin, Helen E., The Law Offices of '58 '85 C.1169 B.A. L.426 J.D.**
**11755 Wilshire Boulevard, Suite 1400, 90025-1520**
**Telephone: 310-477-5455 Facsimile: 310-477-8531**
**Civil Litigation, specializing in Products Liability, Complex Personal Injury, Property Damage Litigation and Toxic Exposure Matters.**
***See Professional Biographies, LOS ANGELES, CALIFORNIA***

Zukor, Susie A. '— '91 C.112 B.A. L.809 J.D. Dep. Pub. Def.
**Zuniga, Juan E.** '64 '92 C&L.309 A.B., J.D. [Ⓐ Katten M.&Z.]
*LANGUAGES: Spanish.
*PRACTICE AREAS: Real Estate; International Transactions; Litigation.
**Zuniga, Richard S.** '53 '82 C.112 A.B. L.1066 J.D. [Ⓐ Loeb&L.]
**Zurzolo, Debby R.** '56 '82 C.112 B.A. L.1068 J.D. [Greenberg G.F.C.&M.]
*PRACTICE AREAS: Real Estate.
Zurzolo, Vincent P. '56 '82 C.112 B.A. L.1067 J.D. U.S. Bkrptcy. J.
Zusman, Marina '47 '89 C.061 B.A. L.1136 J.D. 8556 Gregory Way
Zussman, Marc I. '48 '73 C.1077 B.A. L.800 J.D. 5900 Wilshire Blvd.
Zussman, Marilyn '46 '82 C.112 B.A. L.1136 J.D. 5900 Wilshire Blvd.
Zuzga, Cynthia A. '54 '82 C.475 B.A. L.213 J.D. Dep. Dist. Atty.
**Zweig, Bertram R.**, (AV) '34 '62 C.659 A.B. L.178 LL.B. [Jones,D.R.&P.]
**Zweighaft, Peter K.** '70 '96 C.787 B.A. L.472 J.D. [Ⓐ Friedlander&W.]
*PRACTICE AREAS: Business Litigation; Commercial Litigation.
Zwelling, Jeffrey M. '66 '94 C.112 B.A. L.767 J.D. 10100 Santa Monica Blvd. (Pat.)
**Zwickel, Arthur L.** '64 '93 C&L.426 B.S., J.D. [Ⓐ Paul,H.J.&W.]
**Zwicker, Laura A.** '66 '91 C.910 B.A. L.347 J.D. [Ⓐ Gibson,D.&C.]
*PRACTICE AREAS: Trusts and Estates; Tax.
**Zygelman, Corine** '65 '95 C.1077 B.A. L.398 J.D. [Murchison&C.]
*PRACTICE AREAS: Litigation.
Zygmunt, Jay A. '52 '78 C.602 B.B.A. L.597 J.D. Sr. V.P. & Gen. Coun., L.A. Rams
**Zylberglait, Pablo M.** '68 '94 C.1077 B.S. L.276 J.D. [Ⓐ Barger&W.]

## NICARAGUAN LAWYERS RESIDENT IN LOS ANGELES

**Minnella, Mendieta & Associates**
**(See Managua, Nicaragua)**

## LOS BANOS, 14,519, *Merced Co.*

**Amaral, Edward M.**, (BV) '53 '80 C.1074 B.S. L.426 J.D. [Germino,R.A.J.C.&M.]⊙
*PRACTICE AREAS: Real Estate Law; Agricultural Law; Probate and Estate Planning; Elder Care Law; Business Law.
**Carpenter, Glenn C.** '55 '81 C.174 B.A. L.813 J.D. [Germino,R.A.J.C.&M.]⊙
*PRACTICE AREAS: Business Law; Real Property Law; Probate and Estate Planning; Trust Administration.
Castellucci, Philip R. '36 '63 C.813 A.B. L.1065 J.D. J., Mun. Ct.
Falasco, Robt. M. '22 '52 C&L.770 B.S., J.D. 1828 7th St.‡
**Germino, Donald O.**, (BV) '39 '65 C.800 A.B. L.1066 J.D. [Germino,R.A.J.C.&M.]⊙
*PRACTICE AREAS: Transactional; Civil Litigation; Estate Planning; Probate.
**Germino, John O.**, (AV) '36 '62 C&L.813 A.B., J.D. [Germino,R.A.J.C.&M.]⊙
*PRACTICE AREAS: Civil Litigation.

**Germino, Runte, Amaral, Jordan, Carpenter & MacKay, A Professional Law Corporation, (AV)**
**1120 West I Street, Suite B, P.O. Box 591, 93635⊙**
**Telephone: 209-826-5024 Fax: 209-826-3164**
**D. Oliver Germino (1903-1972); John O. Germino; Donald O. Germino.**
**John A. Runte; Edward M. Amaral; J. Scott Jordan; Glenn C. Carpenter; Norman E. MacKay; Susan R. F. Solomon; Paul J. McDonald.**
**General Civil and Trial Practice in State and Federal Courts. Personal Injury, Probate, Water Rights, Corporation, Taxation, Agricultural, Condemnation, Family and Corporate Law.**
**Palo Alto, California Office: 2500 El Camino Real, Suite 210. Telephone: 415-857-9211. Fax: 415-852-9256.**
***See Professional Biographies, LOS BANOS, CALIFORNIA***

Hunter, William C. '47 '80 L.1186 J.D. Dep. Dist. Atty.
**Jordan, J. Scott** '54 '79 C&L.770 B.S., J.D. [Germino,R.A.J.C.&M.]⊙
*PRACTICE AREAS: Family Law; Bankruptcy; Transactional; Litigation.

**Linneman, Burgess, Telles, Van Atta & Vierra, (AV)**
**654 K Street, P.O. Box 1364, 93635⊙**
**Telephone: 209-826-4911 FAX: 209-826-4766**
**Email: 1btvv@aol.com**
**Members of Firm: Eugene J. Vierra; Alfred L. Whitehurst.**
**General Civil and Trial Practice. Water District and Rights Law. Real Property, Probate, Negligence, Products Liability, Agricultural Law and Personal Injury.**
**Merced, California Office: 312 West 19th Street, P.O. Box 2263. Telephone: 209-723-2137. Fax: 209-723-0899.**
**Dos Palos, California Office: 1820 Marguerite Street, P.O. Box 156. Telephone: 209-392-2141. Fax: 209-392-3964. E-Mail: drathmann@aol.com**
***See Professional Biographies, LOS BANOS, CALIFORNIA***

Lower, Roy '18 '50 C.112 A.B. L.1065 J.D. 610 W. Pacheco Blvd.‡
**MacKay, Norman E.**, (BV) '43 '75 C.813 B.A. L.770 J.D. [Germino,R.A.J.C.&M.]⊙
*PRACTICE AREAS: Business Litigation; Real Estate Transactions; Toxic or Hazardous Materials Litigation.
**McDonald, Paul J.** '55 '89 C.959 B.S. L.765 J.D. [Germino,R.A.J.C.&M.]⊙

CALIFORNIA—LOS BANOS MARTINDALE-HUBBELL LAW DIRECTORY 1997

**Runte, John A.**, (BV) .......... '38 '73 C.436 B.S. L.770 J.D. [Germino,R.A.J.C.&M.]⊙
*PRACTICE AREAS: Real Property; Trusts; Commercial Transactions; Taxation; Probate.
**Solomon, Susan R. F.**, (BV) ....'47 '80 C.659 B.A. L.770 J.D. [Germino,R.A.J.C.&M.]⊙
*PRACTICE AREAS: Real Property Law; Civil Litigation; Appellate Practice.
Vaughn, William A., (CV) ....................'54 '81 C.767 B.S. L.464 J.D. 525 J St.
**Vierra, Eugene J.**, (BV) ......... '35 '66 C.112 A.B. L.1065 J.D. [Linneman,B.T.V.&V.]
*LANGUAGES: Portuguese.
*PRACTICE AREAS: Agricultural Law; Probate Law; Personal Injury Law.
**Whitehurst, Alfred L.** ........... '58 '84 C.770 B.A. L.1049 J.D. [Linneman,B.T.V.&V.]
*PRACTICE AREAS: Personal Injury; Product Liability; Criminal Law; Real Property.

## LOS GATOS, 27,357, *Santa Clara Co.*

Anderson, Larry E., (AV) ..................... '51 '79 C.813 B.A. L.770 J.D. Town Atty.

**Ashworth, Christopher, Law Offices of, (AV) '42 '73 C.112 B.A. L.1065 J.D.**
**540 North Santa Cruz Avenue Suite 270, 95030⊙**
**Telephone: 408-867-1573 Fax: 408-867-4387**
***PRACTICE AREAS: Interstate Commercial Litigation; Commercial Constitutional Litigation. Interstate Commerce, Public Utilities, Transportation and Complex Civil Litigation.**
**Los Angeles, California Office: 1925 Century Park East, Suite 1250.**

Bays, Michael S., (BV) ........'51 '77 C.477 B.A. L.770 J.D. 19A North Santa Cruz Blvd.

**Bicknell, David G., (BV) '51 '79 C.112 B.A. L.770 J.D.**
**15951 Los Gatos Boulevard, Suite 1A, P.O. Box 536, 95031-0536**
**Telephone: 408-358-4900 Facsimile: 408-356-2638**
***PRACTICE AREAS: Real Property; Construction Litigation.**
**Real Estate and Construction Litigation.**
***See Professional Biographies, LOS GATOS, CALIFORNIA***

Bondelie, Rolf Marcus, (AV) ................ '22 '56 C.768 A.B. L.1066 196 W. Main St.
**Bosomworth, Bradley D.** ................'62 '88 C.629 B.S. L.770 J.D. [Sweeney,M.&W.]
*PRACTICE AREAS: Business Law; Corporate Law; Real Estate Law.
Branch, Susan Konecny ......................'45 '83 C.37 B.A. L.1065 J.D. 7 Central Ct.
Carney, Janis A. ...........................'50 '90 C.768 B.A. L.770 J.D. 16450 Los Gatas Blvd.
Crawford, Philip John .......'45 '87 C.768 B.A. L.770 J.D. 18602 Saratoga Los Gatos Rd.
Danell, Albin E. ................................'34 '62 C.208 B.S. L.809 LL.B. P.O. Box DL
Davies, Olivia C. ..........................'21 '49 C&L.813 A.B., LL.B. 16070 Matilija Dr.‡
DeCaro, Barbara Morlan .........'40 '70 C.813 B.A. L.1065 J.D. 225 N. Santa Cruz Ave.
**Dempster, J. Robert** ................'32 '61 C.508 B.S. L.208 LL.B. [Dempster,S.&R.] ‡

**Dempster, Seligmann & Raineri, (BV)**
**La Cañada Building, 3 1/2 North Santa Cruz Avenue, Suite A, 95030**
**Telephone: 408-399-7766 Fax: 408-399-7767**
**Email: Joe@Southbaylaw.com URL: http://www.Southbaylaw.com**
**Members of Firm: J. Robert Dempster (Retired 1985); William R. Seligmann; Joseph Raineri.**
**Litigation, Personal Injury, Land Use, Construction Law, Real Estate, Business, Products Liability and Other Civil Matters.**
***See Professional Biographies, LOS GATOS, CALIFORNIA***

Dermer, Martin D., (CV) .........'34 '75 C.1027 B.S. L.770 J.D. 15720 Winchester Blvd.
Diemer, Harvey H. ...............'35 '70 C.846 B.S.M.E. L.770 J.D. 202 Altura Vista‡
Dorhout, Kevin L. ......................'66 '92 C&L.770 B.S., J.D. Amer. Consulting Grp.
Fadem, B. J. ....................'55 '85 C.768 B.S. L.284 J.D. 14103 Winchester Blvd.
Feldman, Martin S., (BV) ......................'50 '77 C.446 B.A. L.770 J.D. P.O. Box 537
Ferrito, Thomas J., (AV) ..........'42 '70 C.768 B.S. L.770 J.D. 101 Church St.; Suite 14
Frisch, Floyd C., (BV) ...............'38 '66 C.107 B.S. L.767 J.D. 2 N. Santa Cruz Ave.
Fusco, Holly C. ....................'61 '92 C.831 B.A. L.284 J.D. 236 N. Santa Cruz Ave.
Gerbino, Fred W., Jr. .............'54 '81 C.768 B.A. L.770 J.D. 14103 Winchester Blvd.
Gifford, James M., (BV) ..........'29 '59 C.813 A.B. L.1066 J.D. 16275 Los Gatos Blvd.
Gifford, Suzanne Balaze, (AV) .........'38 '64 C&L.477 B.A., LL.B. 18400 Overlook Rd.
Gordon, Gene M. ......................'44 '77 C.766 B.A. L.765 J.D. 18195 La Verne Dr.
Hartman, Lloyd C. ..................'14 '38 C&L.569 A.B., LL.B. 800 Blossom Hill Rd.‡
Hill, Preston W., (BV) .........................'33 '60 C.605 B.A. L.800 LL.B. City Atty.
Hopkins, Joyce Kettren .....'51 '83 C.665 B.S.N. L.426 J.D. Secy., Forest Med. Grp., Inc.
Hover, Wade H., (BV) ........................'23 '51 C.813 B.A. L.893 LL.B. [W.H.Hover]
Hover-Smoot, Julia G. ...................'56 '83 C.112 B.A. L.770 J.D. 101 Church St.
Hover, Wade H., P.C., (BV) ................................................... 101 Church St.
Jones, Michael J. ..........................................'58 '83 19-A N. Santa Cruz Blvd.
Jones, Rebecca Sue ....................'61 '87 C&L.770 B.S., J.D. 19A N. Santa Cruz Ave.
Judd, Evan V., (BV) ..................'30 '59 C.101 B.S. L.273 LL.B. 409 Alberto Way
Kahn, Robert S., (BV) ...........'51 '77 C.477 B.S. L.770 J.D. 25263 Terrace Grove Rd.
Kesselman, Leo .......................'38 '64 C.629 B.S. L.1065 J.D. 200 Glenridg Ave.
Ladd, Patricia E. ...................................................'37 '71 P.O. Box 1540
Lindberg, Ralph D. '21 '49 C&L.878 B.S., J.D.
(adm. in UT; not adm. in CA) 14560 Clearview Dr.‡
Lowman, Thomas E., (BV) ..................'41 '69 C.375 B.A. L.900 J.D. 101 Church St.
**Manzagol, Allan James** ............. '67 '93 C.112 B.A. L.770 J.D. [Ⓐ Sweeney,M.&W.]
*PRACTICE AREAS: Business Litigation; Construction Law; Landlord-Tenant Law.
**Mason, Roger M.**, (AV) ............. '56 '82 C.1044 B.A. L.767 J.D. [Sweeney,M.&W.]
*PRACTICE AREAS: Labor and Employment Law; Wage and Hour Law; Prevailing Wage Litigation.
Morgenthaler, Mark P. '52 '78 C.813 B.S. L.765 J.D.
Pres. & CEO, Crystal River Group
**Neider, Le Roy J.**, (AV) ..................'37 '65 C.336 B.S.B.A. L.813 J.D. [L.J.Neider]
*PRACTICE AREAS: Taxation Law; Corporate Law; Estate Planning Law.

**Neider, Le Roy J., A Professional Law Corporation, (AV)**
**16275 Los Gatos Boulevard, 95032-4519**
**Telephone: 408-358-1831 Facsimile: 408-358-3349**
**Le Roy J. Neider (Certified Specialist, Taxation Law, The State Bar of California Board of Legal Specialization).**
**Business, Corporation and Partnership, Estate Planning, Real Property and Taxation Law.**
**Representative Clients: Better Care, Inc., d/b/a/ Willow Glen Convalescent Hospital; California Independent Oil Marketers Assn.; Investment Equity Exchange; Karnan Associates, Inc.; Nora Lam Ministries; Pacific Oil Conference; San Tomas Hospital, Inc.; Data Recall; Alloy Hard Surfacing, Inc.; Watsonville Manor, Inc.**

Oldham, Nina Davis ............ '53 '81 C.454 B.A. L.813 J.D. 16500 Soda Springs Rd.‡
Pagano, James L., (BV) ......................... '55 '81 C.273 B.A. L.770 J.D. [Toothman&P.]
Paul, Philip S. ...............'38 '67 C.813 A.B. L.809 LL.B. Chmn. of the Bd., Ventures Inc.
Pfeiffer, Theresa L., (BV) ..................'50 '79 C&L.770 B.A., J.D. 202 University Ave.

**Poyner, Roger W., (BV) '35 '66 C.112 A.B. L.408 J.D.**
**16450 Los Gatos Boulevard, Suite 216, 95032⊙**
**Telephone: 408-358-1900 FAX: 408-358-1225**
**(Certified Specialist, Probate, Estate Planning and Trust Law, The State Bar of California Board of Legal Specialization).**
***PRACTICE AREAS: Probate; Estate Planning Law; Trust Law.**
**Trust Law, Estate Planning and Probate.**
**Monterey, California Office: 232 Madison Street, The Panetta Building. Telephone: 408-649-3131. FAX: 408-649-1934.**
***See Professional Biographies, LOS GATOS, CALIFORNIA***

**Raineri, Joseph** ............................................................ '60 '88 [Dempster,S.&R.]
*PRACTICE AREAS: Personal Injury; Products Liability; Construction Law; Business Litigation; Real Estate.

Raineri, Joseph C. ..........'60 '88 C.36 B.S. L.770 J.D. 3 1/2 N. Santa Cruz Ave. Ste. A
Reedy, Randall D. ..................................................'48 '74 19-A N. Santa Cruz Blvd.
Rosenberg, Jeffrey P. ...........................'55 '82 C.112 B.A. L.1137 J.D. [Rosenberg&R.]
Rosenberg, Milton D., (BV) ..............'30 '55 C.112 A.B. L.1066 J.D. [Rosenberg&R.]
Rosenberg and Rosenberg, (BV) ........................................16275 Los Gatos Blvd.
**Sacks, Mason J.**, (AV) ...........................'51 '74 C.813 A.B. L.309 J.D. [M.J.Sacks]
*PRACTICE AREAS: Contested Trusts and Estates; Will Contests; Probate; Living Trust Law; Beneficiary Rights Disputes.

**Sacks, Mason J., Inc., A Prof. Law Corp., (AV)**
**Suite 101, 16615 Lark Avenue, 95030**
**Telephone: 408-358-4400 Fax: 408-358-2487**
**Mason J. Sacks.**
**Trusts, Estate Planning, Estate and Trust Administration, Probate, and Disputed Inheritance Matters.**
***See Professional Biographies, LOS GATOS, CALIFORNIA***

Sandall, Kenneth W. ................'45 '82 C.1073 B.A. L.464 J.D. 983 University Ave.
Schatzel, Thomas E., (AV) ........'36 '63 C&L.174 B.S.E.E., LL.B. [T.E.Schatzel] (Pat.)
Schatzel, Thomas E., Law Offices of, A Prof. Corp., Law Offices of, (AV)
16400 Lark Ave. (Pat.)
**Seligmann, William R.**, (BV) ..........'56 '83 C.112 B.A. L.770 J.D. [Dempster,S.&R.]
*PRACTICE AREAS: Land Use; Public Entity Law; Personal Injury; Eminent Domain; Construction Law.
Smith, Delman W., (BV) .....................'45 '74 C.112 B.A. L.770 J.D. [Smith&V.]
Smith, Donald L. ...............................'48 '75 C.174 B.S. L.770 J.D. [D.L.Smith]
Smith, Donald L., A Prof. Corp. ..................................................983 Univ. Ave.
Smith & Ventura, (BV) ..........................................................405 Alberto Way
Snyder, Lynne R., (BV) ................'44 '70 C.112 B.A. L.1065 J.D. 101 Church St.
Steele, Paul M., (BV) ....................'45 '74 C.755 B.A. L.1035 J.D. 101 Church St.
Sullivan, James M., (BV) ...........'41 '70 C&L.770 B.S.C., J.D. 225 N. Santa Cruz Ave.
**Sweeney, Joseph M.**, (BV) .......... '52 '77 C.602 B.B.A. L.767 J.D. [Sweeney,M.&W.]
*LANGUAGES: Spanish.
*PRACTICE AREAS: Construction Law; Real Estate Law; Business Litigation.

**Sweeney, Mason & Wilson, A Professional Law Corporation, (AV)**
**983 University Avenue, Suite 104C, 95030**
**Telephone: 408-356-3000 Fax: 408-354-8839**
**Joseph M. Sweeney; Roger M. Mason; Kurt E. Wilson; Bradley D. Bosomworth; Allan James Manzagol.**
**Business and Corporate Law and Litigation, Labor and Employment Law, Wage and Hour Law, Prevailing Wage Law, Construction, Insurance and Real Estate.**
***See Professional Biographies, LOS GATOS, CALIFORNIA***

Teerlink, Heber N., (AV) ................. '24 '52 C.112 L.1065 J.D. 16101 Matilija Dr.‡
Tobin, Lauren C. ........................'66 '92 C&L.575 B.S., J.D. [Ⓐ Toothman&P.]
Toothman, James E., (BV) ..................'46 '73 C.767 B.S. L.770 J.D. [Toothman&P.]
Toothman & Pagano, (BV) ................................................................61 E. Main St.
Triplett, John R., (BV) ...............'34 '67 C.1056 B.S. L.770 J.D. 240 Old Adobe Rd.
Valor, Scott H. '— '91 C.768 B.A. L.1065 J.D.
Envir. Studies Dept., San Jose State Univ.
Van Bruggen, Elaine T., (BV) ........'26 '69 C.685 B.A. L.813 LL.B. 103 Amanda Lane
Ventura, Brent N., (BV) .............................'54 '79 C.605 B.A. L.770 J.D. [Smith&V.]
Voyles, Stanley R. ...............'47 '73 C&L.813 B.A., J.D. 16167 Redwood Lodge Rd.
Wax, Elliot ...........................'12 '52 C.563 B.S. L.284 LL.B. 15720 Winchester Blvd.
Webb, Robt. L. .....................'17 '52 C.112 A.B. L.284 J.D. 19640 Redberry Dr.‡
Weber, Michael C., (AV) ....... '39 '71 C.112 B.S. L.1065 J.D. 14103-G Winchester Blvd.

**Whittington, Michael T., (CV) '58 '84 C&L.770 B.S., J.D.**
**15425 Los Gatos Boulevard, Suite 120, 95032⊙**
**Telephone: 408-369-9655 Fax: 408-369-0355**
**Real Estate, Business, General Civil Litigation and Trials.**
**Bakersfield, California Office: Commonwealth Plaza, 3300 Truxtun Avenue, Suite 390, 93303. Telephone: 805-327-2294. Fax: 805-323-8731.**
**Newport Beach, California Office: 4590 MacArthur, Suite 550, 92660. Telephone: 714-833-2370. Fax: 714-833-0949.**
***See Professional Biographies, BAKERSFIELD, CALIFORNIA***

Whyte, Ann von Weise ................'44 '70 C.788 B.A. L.426 J.D. 220 Prospect Ave.‡
**Wilson, Kurt E.**, (BV) ................'59 '85 C.112 B.A. L.1065 J.D. [Sweeney,M.&W.]
*PRACTICE AREAS: Business Litigation.
Wilson, Kurt E., (BV) ................'31 '78 C.766 A.B. L.408 J.D. 150 Longmeadow Rd.
Zoller, William G. .......... '40 '66 C.502 A.B. L.1068 LL.B. Pres., Falcon Financial, Inc.

## LOS OLIVOS, —, *Santa Barbara Co.*

Bruce, Greg ......................................'48 '75 C.813 B.A. L.1065 J.D. P.O. Box 390
Bruce, Kay Smith ................................'50 '76 C.813 B.A. L.1065 J.D. P.O. Box 390
Dullea, Peter A., (BV) ..........................'46 '77 C.112 B.A. L.61 J.D. P.O. Box 126
Kornblum, Sheila M., (CV) .....'35 '83 C.112 A.B. L.1186 J.D. 2963 Grand Ave., Suite 8
Tillman, Jonathan A., (BV) ...................'44 '72 C.112 B.A. L.1095 J.D. [Tillman&G.]
Tillman, Wendy Gaster ......................'55 '82 C.112 B.A. L.1049 J.D. [Tillman&G.]
Tillman & Gaster, (BV) ........................... 2445 Alamo Pintado Ave., Suite 202

## LOS OSOS, —, *San Luis Obispo Co.*

Booth, William A., (CV) ...................'49 '74 C.800 B.A. L.1065 J.D. P.O. Box 6942
Burnham, John T. ......................'26 '51 C&L.608 B.A., J.D. 1432 Las Encinas Dr.

**Collins, Michael**
**(See San Luis Obispo)**

Coray, Howard F. '19 '43 C.1085 L.878 LL.B.
(adm. in UT; not adm. in CA) 2891 Rodman Dr.‡
**Corcoran, Claire M.** .........................'57 '89 C&L.061 B.C.L. [Ⓐ George,G.&S.]⊙
*LANGUAGES: Irish, French and Dutch.
*PRACTICE AREAS: Civil Litigation.
**Cyr, Anne C.** ........................ '69 '93 C.112 B.A. L.464 J.D. [Ⓐ George,G.&S.]⊙
*PRACTICE AREAS: Estate Planning and Probate; Business Transactions.
**Gallo, Ray A.**, (BV) ......................'35 '63 C.309 A.B. L.880 LL.B. [George,G.&S.]⊙
*LANGUAGES: Spanish.
*PRACTICE AREAS: Tort and Business Litigation; Real Estate.
**George, J. K.**, (AV) ....................'43 '70 C.813 A.B. L.767 J.D. [George,G.&S.]⊙
*PRACTICE AREAS: Estate Planning and Administration; Taxation; Trust Administration and Litigation; Business Transactions.

**George, Gallo & Sullivan, A Law Corporation, (AV)** BB
**2238 Bayview Heights Drive, P.O. Box 6129, 93402⊙**
**Telephone: 805-528-3351 Telecopier: 805-528-5598**
**Email: jgeorgeggs@aol.com**
**J. K. George (Certified Specialist, Probate, Estate Planning, and Trust Law, The State Bar of California Board of Legal Specialization).; Ray A. Gallo; Shaunna L. Sullivan;—Anne C. Cyr; Claire M. Corcoran.**
**Probate, Estate Planning and Trust Administration, Business and Corporate Transactions, Taxation, Real Property and Construction, Civil Litigation.**
**Reference: Mid State Bank, Los Osos, California.**
**San Luis Obispo, California Office: 694 Santa Rosa, P.O. Box 12710. Telephone: 805-544-3351. Facsimile: 805-528-5598.**
***See Professional Biographies, LOS OSOS, CALIFORNIA***

Grove, Roger E., (BV) ....................'38 '69 C.336 B.S. L.284 J.D. 671 Highland Dr.
Havlena, Thomas J. ....................'45 '73 C.1109 B.A. L.800 J.D. P.O. Box 6699
Kramer, Wendy W. ............'41 '82 C.112 B.A. L.1095 J.D. 900 Los Osos Valley Rd.
Leddy, Albert M. ....................'25 '50 C.112 B.A. L.1066 J.D. Bd. of Prison Terms‡
Lucero, Luis A., (CV) ....................'52 '79 C.560 B.A. L.1137 J.D. 1660 15th St.
Malykont, Paul ....................'44 '70 C.800 B.S. L.1095 J.D. 2335 Oak Ridge Dr.
McElhinney, Susan ....................'— '71 C.813 L.1068 457 Lilac
Ray, Chas. P. '21 '53 C.623 B.S. L.616 LL.B.
(adm. in OK; not adm. in CA) P.O. Box 6135‡
**Sullivan, Shaunna L., (BV)** ............'55 '80 C.1074 B.A. L.464 J.D. [George,G.&S.]⊙
*REPORTED CASES: Phillips v. State Personnel Bd. (1986) 184 Cal. App. 3d 651; 229 Cal.Rptr. 502.
*PRACTICE AREAS: Real Estate Transactions; Land Use; Civil Litigation; Appellate Practice.
Tevis, Lloyd ....................'20 '51 C.112 B.S. L.426 LL.B. 90 Costa Azul Dr.‡

## LOWER LAKE, —, *Lake Co.*

Green, Ronald C. ....................'46 '71 C.401 B.S. L.659 J.D. 16085 Florence St.
Tulanian, Stephen D. ....................'50 '77 C.112 A.B. L.767 J.D. 16285-A Main St.
Wall, Jay J. ....................'26 '51 C.800 B.A. L.809 LL.B. P.O. Box 1395

## LYNWOOD, 61,945, *Los Angeles Co.*

Chick, Eva E. ..........'— '90 C.112 B.A. L.809 J.D. 3737 Martin Luther King Jr. Blvd.

## MADERA, * 29,281, *Madera Co.*

Bandy, Frederick E. ....................'49 '76 C.112 A.B. L.464 J.D. Research Atty.
Barker, John A. ............'45 '81 C.267 B.A. L.999 J.D. 210 S. "D" St. (⊙Fresno)
Bartow, Herbert E., (AV) ....................'26 '53 C.766 L.1065 J.D. [H.E.Bartow]
Bartow, Herbert E., Inc., (AV) .................... 123 E. 4th St.
Christiansen, Axel E., (BV) ....................'29 '54 C.112 A.B. L.1065 J.D. 123 E. 4th St.
Dahman, Victor C. ....................'39 '68 C.112 B.A. L.1065 J.D. 121 North R. St.

**Dowling, Aaron & Keeler, Incorporated**
(See Fresno)

Frank, William R. ....................'47 '87 C.267 B.A. L.1189 J.D. 41264 Ave. 11
Gendron, Lester J. ....................'25 '53 C.267 L.1065 J.D. 106 N. Gateway Dr.
Green, Denslow B., (AV) ....................'22 '47 C&L.813 A.B., J.D. [Green,G.&R.]
Green, Green & Rigby, (AV) ....................219 South "D" Street
Griffith, George W. ............'33 '81 C.1097 B.S. L.1186 J.D. Assoc. Dist. Atty.
Hernandez, David O. ....................'52 '79 C.267 B.S. L.770 J.D. 123 S. Lake St.
Hitchcock, Douglas J. ..........'48 '73 C.112 B.A. L.1067 J.D. Calif. Rural Legal Assist.
Hoffman, Charles J. ....................'32 '62 C.976 B.A. L.813 J.D. Asst. Dist. Atty.

**Kimble, MacMichael & Upton, A Professional Corporation**
(See Fresno)

**Lang, Richert & Patch, A Professional Corporation**
(See Fresno)

Licalsi, Ernest J. ....................'58 '84 C.267 B.S. L.1065 J.D. Dep. Dist. Atty.

**Linn, Lindley & Blate, A Professional Association**
(See Oakhurst)

Mar, William F., Jr. ....................'53 '84 C.1097 B.A. L.770 J.D. Dep. Dist. Atty.
Martin, Paul R. ....................'28 '69 C.267 L.1132 J.D. Supr. Ct. J.
Martin, Robert C. ............'63 '91 C.112 B.A. L.464 J.D. Dep. Dist. Atty.
Minier, David D. ....................'34 '61 C.674 A.B. L.813 LL.B. Dist. Atty.
Moffat, Edward P., II ....................'46 '72 C.740 B.S. L.284 J.D. Supr. Ct. J.
**Mortimer, Steven R.** ....................'46 '72 C.112 B.A. L.1067 J.D. [Mortimer&O.]
*PRACTICE AREAS: Domestic Relations; Collections; Landlord Tenant; Probate and Estate Planning; Real Property.

**Mortimer and Oakley**
**110 North D Street, 93638**
**Telephone: 209-674-8712 Fax: 209-674-4160**
**Steven R. Mortimer; James E. Oakley; Eric Wyatt.**
**General Practice.**
***See Professional Biographies, MADERA, CALIFORNIA***

**Oakley, James E.** ....................'53 '77 C.112 B.A. L.990 J.D. [Mortimer&O.]
*PRACTICE AREAS: Family Law; General Litigation; Estate Planning/Probate; Real Property Law; Probate.
Rigby, Mitchell C., (BV) ....................'52 '77 C.112 A.B. L.1065 J.D. [Green,G.&R.]
Scoleri, Joseph J., III ....................'66 '93 C&L.770 B.A., J.D. Dep. Public Def.
Staggs, Nancy C. ....................'54 '84 C.800 B.A. L.284 J.D. 2000 N. Schnoor St.

**Stammer, McKnight, Barnum & Bailey**
(See Fresno)

Wayne, Roger L. ....................'34 '69 C.932 B.S. L.1114 J.D. Dep. Dist. Atty.

**Wild, Carter & Tipton, A Professional Corporation**
(See Fresno)

**Wyatt, Eric** ....................'66 '92 C.112 L.770 J.D. [Mortimer&O.]
*PRACTICE AREAS: Criminal Defense; Civil Litigation; Family Law.

## MAGALIA, —, *Butte Co.*

Anderson, David F. ....................'23 '49 C&L.878 B.S., J.D. P.O. Box 1457‡
Snider, Ray F., Jr., (BV) ....................'22 '54 C.768 A.B. L.1066 LL.B. 6558 Lesley Ct.

## MALIBU, 2,328, *Los Angeles Co.*

Allgreen, Chris A. ............'59 '86 C.763 B.S. L.1137 J.D. 5859 Deerhead Rd., 2nd Fl.
Beisman, Mickey ............'43 '83 C.483 B.A. L.1068 J.D. 23326 Paloma Blanca Dr.
Benton, Andrew K. '52 '79 C.1315 B.S. L.616 J.D.
(adm. in OK; not adm. in CA) Exec. V.P., Pepperdine Univ.
Berman, Abraham ....................'26 '60 C.569 B.S. L.800 LL.B. [Millstone&B.]
Berns, Gerald P. '44 '70 C.690 B.S. L.94 J.D.
(adm. in MO; not adm. in CA) 6740 Wildlife Rd.

**Biava, James E., (AV) '31 '60 C.659 B.S. L.309 LL.B.**
**22526 Pacific Coast Highway, 90265**
**Telephone: 310-456-3330**
**General Civil Practice. Trust, Probate, Real Estate, Corporation and Business Law.**
**Reference: Bank of America National Trust & Savings Assn., Malibu, California.**
***See Professional Biographies, MALIBU, CALIFORNIA***

Bigham, W. Harold '32 '60 C.797 B.A. L.880 J.D.
(adm. in TN; not adm. in CA) Prof. of Law, Pepperdine University
Birch, Thomas A. ....................'50 '83 C&L.1136 B.S., J.D. 5940 Filaree Heights
Birenbaum, Sam ....................'48 '74 C.112 A.B. L.1065 J.D. 22933 Pacific Coast Hwy.
**Birkel, Julia L.** ....................'57 '84 C.813 A.B. L.1068 J.D. [⊠ T.M.Sloan]
*PRACTICE AREAS: Civil Litigation.
Brain, Robert Donald '54 '80
C.813 B.S. L.1066 J.D. Assoc. Prof. of Law, Pepperdine Univ.
Brekke, Edgar A., (BV) ........'33 '65 C.999 L.809 J.D. Gen. Coun., Sunglass Safari Inc.

**Chaleff & English**
(See Santa Monica)

Cheadle, Elizabeth A. '54 '82 C.112 B.A. L.1068 J.D.
Staff Coun., Mts. Recreation & Conserv. Auth.
Chopin, Paul Dean ....................'— '87 C&L.990 B.A., J.D. P.O. Box 804
Coben, William A. ....................'32 '63 C.33 B.A. L.1068 J.D. 21390 Rambla Vista St.
Cochran, Robert F., Jr. '51 '76 C.122 B.A. L.893 J.D.
(adm. in WV; not adm. in CA) Pepperdine Univ. Sch. of Law
Cosentino, John ....................'62 '88 C.112 B.A. L.1136 J.D. Cosentino Inc.
Davenport, David ....................'50 '78 C.813 B.A. L.378 J.D. Pres., Pepperdine Univ.
Dealey, David J., (AV) ............'33 '61 C.112 B.S. L.1066 J.D. 18111 Sandy Cape Dr.‡
Dexter, Robert F., (AV) ............'13 '38 C.112 A.B. L.276 J.D. 20940 Pacific Coast Hwy.‡
Dunaway, G. Baxter '28 '60 C.10 B.S. L.273 J.D.
(adm. in TX; not adm. in CA) Prof., Pepperdine Univ. Sch. of Law
Erickson, Yolande P. .................... '55 '83 [Ross&E.]
Estes, R. Wayne '31 '56 C.1064 B.A. L.880 J.D.
(adm. in TN; not adm. in CA) Prof., Pepperdine Univ., Sch. of Law
Fener, Diane ....................'50 '81 C.94 A.B. L.276 J.D. [Seaboard]
Ferris, Barbara O'Neill ............'55 '85 C.766 B.A. L.426 J.D. 6744 Wandermere Rd.
Foster, Erin L. ............'62 '88 C.112 B.A. L.425 J.D. 23805 Stuart Ranch Rd.
**Frye, Douglas J., (Professional Corporation)** '48 '75 C.354 B.S. L.823 J.D.
[Frye&H.]
*PRACTICE AREAS: Corporations; Business; Taxation; Estate Planning; Health Care.

**Frye & Hsieh LLP**
**A Partnership including A Professional Corporation**
**23955 Pacific Coast Highway Suite A201, 90265⊙**
**Telephone: 310-456-0800 Fax: 310-456-0808**
**Douglas J. Frye (Professional Corporation); Stewart Hsieh.**
**General Civil and Trial Practice in all Courts. Corporation, Business, State, Federal and International Taxation, Estate Planning, Real Estate, Securities, Administrative, Professional Liability, Negligence Law and Government Finance.**
**Los Angeles, California Office: 626 Wilshire Boulevard, Suite 800. Telephone: 310-820-5545.**
***See Professional Biographies, MALIBU, CALIFORNIA***

Girard, Joseph M., (AV) ....................'29 '55 C.112 A.B. L.800 J.D. P.O. Box 6648
Gotfredson, E. Jay ....................'— '72 C.112 L.1095 3600 La Paz Lane
Gradisher, Michael R. '60 '86
C.1097 B.A. L.990 J.D. Pepperdine University School of Law
Graves, Arthur A., III ....................'51 '78 C.911 B.A. L.990 J.D. [Pratter&G.]⊙
Greiner, Robert P. ....................'30 '65 C.696 B.A. L.1068 LL.B. Dep. Pub. Def.
Griffith, Michael W. ....................'59 '89 C.208 B.A. L.990 J.D. P.O. Box 2502
Haney, William P., Jr. '41 '67 C.1111 B.A. L.192 J.D.
(adm. in AL; not adm. in CA) Prof. of Law, Pepperdine Univ.
Hanson, Gary A. ..........'54 '80 C.878 B.S. L.990 J.D. Gen. Coun., Pepperdine Univ.
Howe, Marlynn P. ........'58 '85 C&L.990 B.A., J.D. Assoc. Gen. Coun., Pepperdine Univ.
Howlett, Richd. H., (AV) ....'14 '37 C&L.174 A.B., LL.B. 31427 W. Pacific Coast Hwy.‡
**Hsieh, Stewart** ....................'53 '88 C.1097 B.S. L.809 J.D. [Frye&H.]⊙
*PRACTICE AREAS: Business Transactions; Estate Planning; Probate; Corporations.
Kabo, Dorianne Joy '53 '87 C.94 B.A. L.990 J.D.
(adm. in PA; not adm. in CA) 3949 1/2 Las Flores Canyon Rd.
Kagon, Robert L. ....................'51 '84 C.763 B.A. L.767 J.D. 101 Loma Metisse
Karpuk, Robert A. ....................'52 '80 C.94 B.A. L.809 J.D. 1557 Monte Viento Dr.
Kelsey, Ingrid N. ....................'23 '72 C.112 L.809 J.D. 5792 Calpine Dr.‡
Kerr, William A. ....................'42 '68 C.112 B.S. L.1068 J.D. [W.A.Kerr]
Kerr, William A., A Prof. Corp. .................... 23410 Civic Center Way
Keyes, W. Noel ............'21 '48 C&L.178 B.A., LL.B. Prof. of Law, Pepperdine Univ.
Lardizabal, Carlos A. '35 '58 C&L.662 B.A., LL.B.
(adm. in NY; not adm. in CA) 33002 Pacific Coast Hwy.
Leanse, David V. ............'29 '55 C.112 A.B. L.309 LL.B. 23440 Civic Center Way
Leemon, Darryl M. ....................'46 '72 C.800 A.B. L.426 J.D. 6938 Grasswood
Lemieux, Ronald J. ....................'36 '71 C.800 L.966 J.D. P.O. Box 6767
Levin, Marc, (AV) ....................'40 '70 C.659 B.S. L.426 J.D. 22203 Pacific Cst. Hwy.
Liebeler, Susan Wittenberg .....'42 '67 C.477 B.A. L.1068 LL.B. Lexpert Research Servs.
Linder, Milton, (AV) ....................'21 '51 C.112 L.809 LL.B. 28034 Sea Ln.‡
Lobel-Angel, Meredith A. ..........'56 '83 C&L.813 A.B., J.D. Dir., Legal Affs., Inscape
Lowry, L. Randolph '51 '86 C.990 B.A. L.300 J.D.
(adm. in ID; not adm. in CA) Pepperdine Univ. Sch. of Law
Mann, Stanley K. ............'32 '67 C&L.174 B.S., J.D. Prof./Dir., Pepperdine Univ.
McCausland, Timothy J. ............'61 '87 C.36 B.S. L.990 J.D. 29500 Heathercliff Rd.
McGoldrick, James M. .....'44 '70 C.990 B.A. L.145 J.D. Prof. of Law, Pepperdine Univ.
McIntosh, Robert H. ....................'27 '82 C.871 B.S. L.464 J.D. Mun. Ct. Comr.
McKibbin, David, III ........'12 '36 C.659 A.B. L.309 LL.B. Prof., Pepperdine Law Sch.
Medove, Jack, (AV) ....................'29 '67 C.1043 B.A. L.426 P.O. Box 4362
Merrick, John J. ....................'19 '57 L.809 29245 Sea Lion Pl.‡
Metscher, Joseph G. ............'43 '71 C.1046 B.A. L.537 J.D. 18174 Kingsport Dr.
Miller, Jay C. ....................'14 '72 C.912 L.1136 LL.B. 24142 Malibu Rd.‡
Miller, Mary E. ............'51 '77 C.112 B.A. L.309 J.D. Prof. of Law, Pepperdine Univ.
Millstone, B. Allen ....................'27 '61 C.112 B.S. L.809 LL.B. [Millstone&B.]
Millstone & Berman ....................6637 Zumirez Dr.
Morse, H. Newcomb '19 '46 C.597 L.861 LL.B.
(adm. in GA; not adm. in CA) Law Prof., Pepperdine Univ.
Murgatroyd, George W., III, (AV) ........'48 '83 C.112 B.A. L.809 J.D. P.O. Box 422B‡
Murphy, Edward W. ............'36 '61 C&L.884 B.C.E., J.D. 20710 Pacific Coast Hwy.
Nelson, Charles I. '41 '65 C.1 B.S. L.846 J.D.
(adm. in TX; not adm. in CA) Prof. of Law, Pepperdine Univ.
Nelson, Kit L. ....................'23 '51 C&L.800 B.S., J.D. 33740 Pacific Coast Hwy.‡
Noll, Marianne B., (BV) ............'38 '67 C.800 B.A. L.1068 J.D. 20450 Roca Chica Dr.
O'Neal, Mike E. ....................'46 '74 C.305 B.A. L.813 J.D. 24255 Pacific Coast Hwy.
Perman, Gerald A. ....................'35 '64 C.107 B.A. L.800 LL.B. 28870 Gray Fox St.
Phillips, Phil E. .....'66 '92 C&L.990 B.A., J.D. Dir., Regulatory Compl., Pepperdine Univ.
Phillips, Ronald F. '34 '65 C.1 B.S. L.846 J.D.
Dean & Prof., Pepperdine Univ. Law Sch.
Pick, Bernard J. ....................'48 '73 C.813 A.B. L.800 J.D. 29528 Haruester Rd.
Pratter, Michael S., (BV) ....................'41 '67 C.347 B.A. L.912 J.D. [Pratter&G.]⊙
Pratter & Graves, (BV) .................... 23852 Pacific Coast Hwy., #772 (⊙Irvine)
Raiford, John D. ....................'28 '66 C.871 B.S. L.188 LL.B. 3011 Malibu Canyon Rd.
Ridley, Pamela Miller ............'54 '79 C.800 B.A. L.813 J.D. 28860 W. Selfridge Dr.
Ritter, Minton, (AV) ....................'39 '69 C.659 B.A. L.472 J.D. 7237 Birdview Ave.
Robinson, Peter R. .....'55 '80 C.112 B.A. L.1065 J.D. Asst. Prof., Pepperdine Law School
Ross, Daniel J. ....................'53 '78 C.821 B.A. L.767 J.D. [Ross&E.]
Ross & Erickson ....................Suite 203, 23440 Civic Ctr. Way
Sampson, William W. ........'47 '75 C.112 B.A. L.1068 J.D. 28990 Pacific Coast Hway.
Sangster, Claudia B. '54 '81 C.990 B.A. L.326 J.D.
Sr. Coun. Estate & Gift Planning, Pepperdine Univ.
Sapiro, Stanley M. ....................'18 '44 C.112 A.B. L.1065 J.D. 1566 Monte Viento

CAA375P

CALIFORNIA—MALIBU MARTINDALE-HUBBELL LAW DIRECTORY 1997

Scarberry, Mark Stephen '53 '78 C.605 A.B. L.1068 J.D.
Prof. of Law, Pepperdine Univ.
Scott, Richard N. ................'40 '69 C.112 B.A. L.1068 J.D. 24955 Pacific Coast Hwy.
Seaboard Land Group ........................................1045 Tottenham Lane
Shoop, Paul ......................'47 '72 C.69 B.A. L.846 J.D. 23805 Stuart Ranch Rd.
Silk, Sherrill M. ..................'49 '91 C.112 B.S. L.990 J.D. 11906 Beach Club Way

**Sloan, Todd M., Law Offices of, (AV) '39 '72 C.659 B.A. L.893 J.D.**
**22601 Pacific Coast Highway, Suite 240, 90265**
**Telephone: 310-456-7900 Facsimile: 310-317-6266**
***LANGUAGES: Spanish.**
***PRACTICE AREAS: General Litigation; Unfair Competition Law; Banking Regulatory Litigation.**
**Associate: Julia L. Birkel.**
**General Litigation, Unfair Competition Law, Banking Litigation.**
***See Professional Biographies, MALIBU, CALIFORNIA***

Smith, F. LaGard '44 '68 C&L.950 B.S., J.D.
(adm. in OR; not adm. in CA) Prof. of Law, Pepperdine Univ.
Sobelman, Karen A. '54 '80 C.112 B.A. L.990 J.D.
Assoc. Prof. of Law, Pepperdine Univ.
Talbott, James N. ...............'56 '85 C.999 B.S. L.1338 J.D. 11077 Pacific View Dr.
Trabish, Michael S. ...............'53 '78 C.112 B.A. L.426 J.D. 23715 W. Malibu Rd.
Valdman, Lilya ..................................'39 '63 L.426 29329 Bluewater Rd.
Weedman, Charles V. ..................'27 '59 C&L.800 B.A., LL.B. 20771 Big Rock Dr.
Weingarten, Myrna M. ..............'36 '71 C&L.800 B.S., J.D. 3653 Maliba Vista Dr.‡
Willhardt, E. Gail ...................'42 '75 C.97 B.S. L.213 J.D. 6208 Tapia Dr., Apt. D
Wright, Paul J. ...........................'55 '87 L.061 LL.B. 24955 Pacific Coast Hway.
York, Arnold G., (AV) '37 '65
C.102 B.A. L.1068 LL.B. Publisher, The Malibu Times, Inc.
York, Kenneth H. '16 '41 C&L.174 A.B., LL.B.
(adm. in CO; not adm. in CA)
Prof. of Law, Emeritus, Pepperdine Univ. and Univ. of Calif., Los Angeles

## MAMMOTH LAKES, 4,785, *Mono Co.*

Bassage, James D., (CV) ....................'43 '68 C.945 B.A. L.276 J.D. P.O. Box 621
**Baumwohl, David S.** ....................'55 '80 C.1077 B.S. L.464 J.D. [D.S.Baumwohl]
*PRACTICE AREAS: Real Property (Transaction and Litigation); Business (Transaction and Litigation); General Litigation.

**Baumwohl, David S., A Prof. Corp., Law Offices of**
**The Mammoth Mall, Suite 220, P.O. Box 1188, 93546**
**Telephone: 619-934-2000 Fax: 619-934-2600**
**Email: MAMMOTHLAW@QNET.COM**
**David S. Baumwohl.**
**General Business, Real Estate and Litigation.**
***See Professional Biographies, MAMMOTH LAKES, CALIFORNIA***

**Berger, Michael, Law Offices of, (BV) '48 '73 C.112 B.A. L.1067 J.D.**
**4 Oak Tree Place, P.O. Box 1768, 93546**
**Telephone: 619-934-6215 Fax: 619-934-4063**
***LANGUAGES: Spanish.**
***PRACTICE AREAS: Civil Litigation; Criminal Law.**
**Associate: Robert S. Hanna.**
**Criminal and Civil Litigation.**
***See Professional Biographies, MAMMOTH LAKES, CALIFORNIA***

Blumberg, Myron, (AV) ....................'19 '54 C.494 B.B.A. L.800 J.D. [Blumberg]⊙
Blumberg Law Corporation, (AV) ...............1196 Majestic Pines Dr. (⊙Long Beach)
Boone, David L. ..........................................'39 '72 C&L.999 J.D. Rincon Center
Bornfeld, Michael J. ...................'39 '65 C.605 A.B. L.1065 J.D. P.O. Box 2975
**Carney, R. Mark** ..................'58 '85 C&L.602 B.A., J.D. [Liebersbach,M.C.&R.]
*LANGUAGES: Spanish.
*PRACTICE AREAS: Commercial and Real Estate Litigation and Transactions; Land Use Development Law; Education Law.
Cooper, Lee E., Jr. ......................'31 '61 C.112 B.S. L.1068 J.D. Ret. Mun. Ct. J.
Dwyer, Kip ................................'56 '84 C.112 B.A. L.1065 J.D. P.O. Box 3567
Forstenzer, Edward ...........................'46 '72 C.477 B.A. L.1065 J.D. Jus. Ct. J.
**Hanna, Robert S.** ..................................'64 '92 C.840 B.S. L.1065 J.D. [Ⓐ M.Berger]
*PRACTICE AREAS: Civil Litigation; Criminal Law.
Heflin, Mary L. ..............................'47 '78 C.800 B.A. L.809 J.D. P.O. Box 8742
Hess, Linda D. ..................................'54 '83 C.63 B.S. L.1068 J.D. P.O. Box 351
Kappos, Stephen N. ..............'53 '86 C.330 B.A. L.464 J.D. 325 Old Mammoth Rd.
**Liebersbach, Richard W.** ..............'52 '77 C.800 B.A. L.426 J.D. [Liebersbach,M.C.&R.]
*PRACTICE AREAS: Real Estate Litigation; Land Use Development Law; Condominium and Homeowners Association; Business Law; Corporate Law.

**Liebersbach, Mohun, Carney & Reed, (AV)**
**Sherwin Professional Plaza, 2nd Floor, Old Mammoth Road, P.O. Box 3337, 93546**
**Telephone: 619-934-4558 Facsimile: 619-934-2530**
**Richard W. Liebersbach; Gerald Fitzgibbon Mohun, Jr.; R. Mark Carney; James S. Reed.**
**General Civil Practice in State Courts, Trials and Appeals, Real Estate, Condominium/Homeowners' Association, Criminal Defense, Negligence, Commercial and Business Law, Land Use Development Law, Environmental Law, Public and Administrative Law.**
***See Professional Biographies, MAMMOTH LAKES, CALIFORNIA***

Magid, James M. ................................'45 '73 C.800 B.A. L.426 J.D. P.O. Box 8510
Medina, Sandra E. ........................'33 '77 C.1097 B.A. L.1221 J.D. P.O. Box 1118
**Mohun, Gerald Fitzgibbon, Jr.** '56 '83 C.112 B.A. L.1065 J.D.
[Liebersbach,M.C.&R.]
*PRACTICE AREAS: Civil Litigation; Criminal Law; Tort and Insurance Law.
Purnell, Sandra E. ..................'43 '85 C.912 B.S. L.112 J.D. 126 Old Mammoth Rd.
**Reed, James S., (AV)** ..........'38 '66 C.763 B.A. L.1065 J.D. [Liebersbach,M.C.&R.]
*PRACTICE AREAS: Public Land Law (10%); Environmental Law (20%); Public Law (60%).
Rudder, Paul S. ..............'46 '73 C.264 B.A. L.1065 J.D. Sherwin Prof. Plaza, 2nd Fl.
Saari, Roy A. ......................................'45 '73 C.800 B.A. L.426 J.D. P.O. Box 7086‡
Wood, Frederick G., (BV) '51 '76
C.112 B.A. L.770 J.D. 126 Old Mammoth Rd., Suite 203

## MANHATTAN BEACH, 32,063, *Los Angeles Co.*

Allen, Robert E. ..........................'68 '93 C.112 B.A. L.1068 J.D. 2120 The Strand
**Andersen, G. Steven, (AV)** ............'42 '82 C.112 A.B. L.426 J.D. [Andersen,K.&S.]

**Andersen, Keleher & Spata, (AV)**
**1332 Park View Avenue, Suite 102, 90266**
**Telephone: 310-546-6662 Fax: 310-546-5707**
**Members of Firm: G. Steven Andersen; James F. Keleher; Michael C. Spata; Dennis Neil Jones. Of Counsel: Robert C. Littlejohn.**
**General Civil Litigation and Trial Practice, Eminent Domain, Inverse Condemnation, Land Use, Zoning, Environmental and Mobile Home Park Law, Real Property Litigation, General Liability and Insurance Law.**
***See Professional Biographies, MANHATTAN BEACH, CALIFORNIA***

Anderson, Walter N., (AV) .........'09 '37 L.1251 LL.B. 340 S. Sepulveda Blvd., Ste. 1
Baer, Joseph R. .......'57 '86 C.1109 B.A. L.809 J.D. 317 Rosecrans 2nd (⊙310-939-1350)
Bain, Robert G. ......'53 '80 C.347 B.A. L.800 J.D. V.P., Specials, Fox Broadcasting Co.
Barger, Bill Dale ............'25 '81 C.378 B.S. L.1136 J.D. 806 Manhattan Beach Blvd.
**Barness, Daniel I.** '55 '82
C.112 B.A. L.1065 J.D. [Steinberg B.G.&F.] (⊙New York, N.Y.)
*LANGUAGES: French, Spanish and Hebrew.
*PRACTICE AREAS: Bankruptcy Law; Creditors Rights Law; Commercial Law; Business Law.
**Barness, Jordan G.** ..................'57 '84 C.112 B.A. L.809 J.D. [Steinberg B.G.&F.]
*LANGUAGES: Portuguese, Spanish, French and Hebrew.
*PRACTICE AREAS: Corporate; Entertainment; Real Estate Law.
Blanke, Beverly A. ..................................................'— '78 807 Crest Dr.
**Blut, Elliot S.** ......................'67 '92 C.112 B.A. L.1065 J.D. [Reback,H.M.&K.]
Bohl, Robert D. .....................'47 '76 C.800 A.B. L.809 J.D. 3701 Highland Ave.
Bowman, Stanley D. ..............................................'48 '77 1141 Highland Ave.
**Bradley, Marcus J.** ..................'62 '94 C.112 B.A. L.767 J.D. [Ⓐ Reback,H.M.&K.]

**Carico, Christopher D. '61 '88 C.605 A.B. L.426 J.D.**
**1141 Highland Avenue, Suite 201, 90266**
**Telephone: 310-545-8199 Fax: 310-546-8540**
**(Certified Specialist, Estate Planning, Trust and Probate Law, The State Bar of California Board of Legal Specialization).**
***PRACTICE AREAS: Estate Planning; Trusts and Estates; Probate; Elder Law.**
**Estate Planning, Trust, Probate and Elder Law.**
***See Professional Biographies, MANHATTAN BEACH, CALIFORNIA***

Carpini-Pace, Laura ......................'62 '89 C.112 B.A. L.1065 J.D. 931 1st. St.
Chettle, A. B., Jr., (AV) ..........................................'37 '62 C&L.276 B.S., J.D. P.O. Box 7
Clark, Sarah E. .......................................'55 '85 C.326 B.A. L.846 J.D. 326 28th St.
Contratto, Anthony M. ..............'53 '88 C.112 B.A. L.426 J.D. 3701 Highland Ave.
Corcovelos, Thomas C. ...................'50 '76 C.426 B.A. L.1066 J.D. [Corcovelos&F.]
Corcovelos & Forry ..................................................................1001 6th St.
Crosner, Albert L. ....................'38 '78 C.502 B.B.A. L.1136 J.D. 1501 Gates Ave.
Da Silva, Gary N. ......................'53 '79 C.674 A.B. L.569 J.D. 616 Highland Ave.
Davis, B. Martin, III, (AV) .............'51 '76 C&L.800 B.S., J.D. 1201 Morningside Dr.
Davis, John E. ..........................................'42 '67 C.378 B.A. L.900 J.D. 337 3rd St.
Dixon, Kathleen F. ...........................'52 '77 C.800 B.A. L.809 J.D. 2617 Bell Ave.

**DuRoss, Daniel V., Law Offices of, (BV) '47 '76 C.426 B.A. L.809 J.D.**
**1001 Sixth Street Suite 150, 90266-6750**
**Telephone: 310-374-3336 Fax: 310-318-3832**
**Email: DeweyDur@aol.com**
***PRACTICE AREAS: Wills and Trusts; Probate; Estate Planning; Elder Law.**
**Associate: Kaysie A. Fitzpatrick.**
**Probate and Estate Planning.**
***See Professional Biographies, MANHATTAN BEACH, CALIFORNIA***

Enochs, Duane C. ................................'31 '56 C.911 B.A. L.800 LL.B. 3208 Strand
**Ferrante, David M.** ..............................'64 '92 C.420 B.A. L.425 J.D. [Ⓐ Reback,H.M.&K.]

**Fierberg, Ira M., Law Office of '62 '89 C.112 B.A. L.426 J.D.**
**1334 Park View Avenue, Suite 100, 90266**
**Telephone: 310-546-8181 Fax: 310-546-8180**
**Email: tiburon27@aol.com**
**Personal Injury, including Vehicular, Slip and Fall, Major Bodily Injury, Dog Bites, Wrongful Death. General Civil Litigation in all State and Federal Courts, Trial, Business Litigation, Sports Law, Motor Racing Sports Representation and Motor Racing Consulting.**
***See Professional Biographies, MANHATTAN BEACH, CALIFORNIA***

**Fitzpatrick, Kaysie A.** ....................'67 '93 C.112 B.A. L.464 J.D. [Ⓐ D.V.DuRoss]
*PRACTICE AREAS: Estate Planning; Probate; Elder Law.
**Foley, Shannon M.** ...........................'60 '86 C.36 B.S. L.273 J.D. [Steinberg B.G.&F.]
*PRACTICE AREAS: Business Litigation.
Forry, Craig B. .............................'56 '84 C.902 B.A. L.990 J.D. [Corcovelos&F.]
**Foster, Douglas B.** ......................'59 '87 C.945 B.A. L.426 J.D. [Steinberg B.G.&F.]
*PRACTICE AREAS: Civil Litigation; General Business Practice.
Gallon, Mark M. .....................'34 '59 C.477 B.A. L.813 J.D. 4301 Strand St.
Gennaco, Michael J. ..................'53 '84 C.197 B.A. L.813 J.D. U.S. Attys. Off.
**Glasgow, Donna**, (AV⊕) '51 '78 C.156 B.A. L.1292 J.D.
(adm. in NY; not adm. in CA) [Steinberg B.G.&F.]
*LANGUAGES: French.
*PRACTICE AREAS: Commercial and Real Estate Transactions; Litigation; Real Estate Foreclosures; Domestic Relations; Probate.
Gold, Paul Eric ......................'57 '82 C.112 A.B. L.464 J.D. 1334 Park View Ave.
Gordon, Joan Tremblay ..........................................'26 '79 L.1136 J.D. [Gordon&G.]
Gordon, Joseph T. ..................................'57 '81 C.112 B.A. L.426 J.D. [Gordon&G.]
Gordon, Warren M., (BV) ....................'19 '49 C.16 B.S. L.309 LL.B. [Gordon&G.]
Gordon & Gordon, (BV) ..............................................1601 N. Sepulveda Blvd.
Gould, George ..........................................'25 '76 C.112 L.1221 J.D. 131 40th St.
Grant, Melinda E. .........................'50 '76 C.800 B.A. L.1068 J.D. 619 18th St.
Griffiths, Barry G. ..........................'46 '92 C.205 B.S. L.770 J.D. 616 8th St.
Guimera, Irene M., (AV) ..................'53 '78 C.569 B.A. L.178 J.D. [Guimera&G.]
Guimera, Joseph E., (AV) ..................'53 '78 C.331 B.A. L.178 J.D. [Guimera&G.]
Guimera & Guimera, A Law Corporation, (AV) ..........................225 S. Sepulveda Blvd.
Hall, George V., (AV) ..............'22 '60 C.688 B.Ch.E. L.1068 J.D. 201 El Porto St.‡
Hallett, James M., (AV) .........................'47 '72 C.976 B.A. L.1066 J.D. 1001 6th St.
**Harari, Roanld D.** '57 '82 C&L.178 A.B., J.D.
(adm. in NY; not adm. in CA) [Ⓒ Steinberg B.G.&F.]
*LANGUAGES: Spanish.

**Harvey, Kenneth L., (AV) '47 '73 C.112 B.A. L.770 J.D.**
**818 Manhattan Beach Boulevard, 90266**
**Telephone: 310-545-6445; 376-1857 Fax: 310-376-9008**
**Email: kharvey333@aol.com**
**General Civil Trial. Family and Real Estate Law.**
***See Professional Biographies, MANHATTAN BEACH, CALIFORNIA***

Harwell, John D., (AV) ......................'49 '78 C.1188 A.B. L.1065 J.D. 225 27th St.
Hilby, Gerald M. ..........................'29 '60 C.906 B.A. L.426 LL.B. 3504 The Strand‡
Hindenlang, Walter J. '44 '78
C.800 B.S. L.426 J.D. V.P., Hughes Electronics Telecom. & Space
Homan, Robert W. ..................................'27 '73 C.112 A.B. L.990 J.D. P.O. Box 3681
Hoover, Marlene L. ................................................'45 '78 C.546 L.426 J.D. 1207 10th St.
**Horrow, Michael B.** ............................'66 '92 C.645 B.S. L.61 J.D. [Ⓐ Reback,H.M.&K.]
**Hulbert, Donna P.** ..................'59 '84 C.112 B.A. L.1068 J.D. [Ⓐ Reback,H.M.&K.]
**Hulbert, Gregory M.** .....................'57 '83 C.1077 B.A. L.426 J.D. [Reback,H.M.&K.]
Ingram, Timothy H. ..................................'45 '72 C.813 A.B. L.800 J.D. P.O. Box 189
**Jones, Dennis Neil** ..........................'54 '84 C.800 B.A. L.1049 J.D. [Ⓐ Andersen,K.&S.]
*REPORTED CASES: Valentino v. Elliott SAV-ON-GAS, Inc., (1988) 201 Cal. App. 3d 692; People ex rel Goramendi v. American Autoplan, Inc., (1993) 20 Cal. App. 4th 710; Adler v. Western Home Insurance Co., 878 F.Supp. 1329 (C.D. Cal. 1995).
Kandell, Michael D. ..................'50 '79 C.1029 B.S. L.1136 J.D. P.O. Box 453
**Keleher, James F.** ..............................'50 '82 C.589 B.S. L.426 J.D. [Andersen,K.&S.]
*REPORTED CASES: Tenants Association of Park Santa Anita vs. Beverly Southers, et al. (1990) 222 CA 3d 1293, 272 CR 361.
Kelly, Donald N., (BV) ........'42 '79 C.800 B.A. L.809 J.D. 818 Manhattan Beach Blvd.
**Kinnier, Russell D.** ..................................'64 '93 C.446 B.A. L.30 J.D. [Reback,H.M.&K.]

**Kirkpatrick, William R. (Randy)** '47 '74 C.918 B.A. L.800 J.D. [Steinberg B.G.&F.]
*PRACTICE AREAS: Real Estate; General Business Practice.
**Kjar, James J.** '55 '80 C.800 B.S. L.426 J.D. [Reback,H.M.&K.]
Klein, Melvin A. '34 '64 C.871 B.S. L.273 J.D. (adm. in DC; not adm. in CA) 8 San Miguel Ct.
Kohn, Roger L. '41 '83 C.311 B.A. L.1068 J.D. 524 Eleventh St.
**Laurin, Paul J.** '62 '88 C.112 B.A. L.1065 J.D. [Steinberg B.G.&F.]
*PRACTICE AREAS: Bankruptcy Law; Creditors Rights Law; Commercial Law; Entertainment Law.
Lawrence, William R. '25 '54 C.800 B.S. L.1065 J.D. 230 16th St.‡
**Lee, Jeffrey Michael** '66 '96 C&L.112 B.A., J.D. [Steinberg B.G.&F.]
*PRACTICE AREAS: Estates and Trusts; Commercial Law.
Leonard, Michael J. '46 '74 C.670 B.A. L.809 J.D. 317 Rosecrans Ave., 2nd Fl.
**Lew, Jin N.** '62 '88 C.112 B.A. L.426 J.D. [Reback,H.M.&K.]
Linsley, Philip R. '50 '76 C.112 B.A. L.809 J.D. 1334 Park View Ave.
**Littlejohn, Robert C.** '49 '78 C.112 B.A. L.809 J.D. [Andersen,K.&S.]
Long, George E. '23 '49 C.524 L.273 LL.B. (adm. in DC; not adm. in CA) 1447 2nd St.‡
Lovejoy, John E. '38 '66 C.871 B.S.E.E. L.1068 J.D. 1201 Morningside Dr.
Lowerre, George H., III, (AV) '21 '49 C.112 A.B. L.800 LL.B. 704 Manhattan Ave.‡
Lowerre, Mark '51 '87 C.112 A.B. L.809 J.D. 1220 Highland Ave.
**Luke, Nancy A.** '57 '83 C.838 B.A. L.426 J.D. [Reback,H.M.&K.]
Mahar, Francis X. '41 '69 C.602 B.A. L.982 LL.B. 504 Dianthus St.
Maloney, John F., (AV) '46 '77 C.1042 B.S. L.1148 J.D. 317 Rosecrans Ave.
**Manko, Teri E.** '63 '92 C.112 B.A. L.809 J.D. [Reback,H.M.&K.]
Maxwell, Eugenia B. '43 '68 C.259 B.A. L.362 J.D. P.O. Box 3003
**McAndrews, Thomas F.** '54 '85 C.770 B.S. L.426 J.D. [Reback,H.M.&K.]
McCarroll, Orville W., (AV) '20 '51 C.906 B.A. L.426 J.D. 1019 Duncan Ave.‡
McCormick, James L. '44 '78 C.309 B.A. L.981 545 Third St.
McDonald, Daniel S. '30 '61 C.800 A.B. L.809 LL.B. 216 Manhattan Ave.
Meisenholder, Lynda '53 '78 C.1042 B.A. L.426 J.D. 1405 Lynngrove Dr.
Mendelsberg, Ronald L. '37 '75 C.124 B.S.E.E. L.809 J.D. 25 Fairway Dr.‡
Muenzer, Franklin B. '41 '76 C.813 B.S. L.809 J.D. 820 Manhattan Ave.
Mullen, Gerald E., (AV) '37 '67 C.112 A.B. L.1066 LL.B. 1334 Park View Ave.
Munson, J. D. '62 '94 C.1042 B.A. L.426 J.D. 417 Bayview Dr.
Myers, Loring M., Jr., (BV) '32 '63 C&L.150 B.A., J.D. 880 Manhattan Beach Blvd.‡
Neu, John H. '38 '66 C&L.190 A.B., J.D. Assoc. Prof., Whittier Coll.
Nichols, Russell A. '46 '77 C.112 B.S. L.426 J.D. 1750 11th St.
Parachini, Maria N. '54 '84 C.787 B.S. L.1009 J.D. 2709 Maple Ave.
**Paritzky, Ethan** '68 '95 C.659 B.A. L.800 J.D. [Reback,H.M.&K.]
*PRACTICE AREAS: Business Transactions.
Partridge, Wayne E., (AV) '40 '65 C.112 A.B. L.309 J.D. 1734 9th St.
Piantadosi, Richard N., (AV) '42 '72 C.1097 B.A. L.426 2609 N. Sepulveda Blvd.
Pullen, Myron D. '37 '75 C.112 B.A. L.809 J.D. 1406 19th St.
Ralls, Morgan S., Jr., (BV) '38 '65 C&L.800 B.S., LL.B. 1001 6th St., Ste. 150
**Reback, Robert C.** '43 '73 C.112 B.S. L.1068 J.D. [Reback,H.M.&K.]

**Reback, Hulbert, McAndrews & Kjar, LLP**
**1230 Rosecrans Avenue Suite 450, 90266**
**Telephone: 310-297-9900 Facsimile: 310-297-9800**
**Robert C. Reback; Gregory M. Hulbert; Thomas F. McAndrews; James J. Kjar;—Jin N. Lew; Donna P. Hulbert; Teri E. Manko; Russell D. Kinnier; David M. Ferrante; Marcus J. Bradley; Elliot S. Blut; Patrick E. Stockalper; Michael B. Horrow; Nancy A. Luke; Ethan Paritzky.**
**Civil Litigation Defense, Insurance Defense, Professional Liability, Personal Injury, Product Liability, Business Litigation, Real Estate, Commercial Litigation, Risk Management, Loss Prevention, Mediation, Legal and Medical Malpractice.**
*See Professional Biographies, MANHATTAN BEACH, CALIFORNIA*

Rice, Gary D. '51 '77 C.136 B.S. L.213 J.D. 880 Manhattan Beach Blvd.
Ringgold, Wm. K., Jr. '40 '72 C.586 B.S. L.796 J.D. 2609 Sepulveda
Rothman, Ron '33 '71 1219 Morningside Dr.
Sarabia, Antonio R., II, (AV) '51 '79 C.605 A.B. L.145 J.D. 1632 Mathews
Schoettler, R. William, Jr. '36 '65 C.813 L.809 LL.B. Ret. Supr. Ct. J.
Scully, William S., Jr., (AV) '36 '61 C.800 B.S. L.1068 LL.B. 2322 Ardmore
Shalvoy, James A. '51 '79 C.276 A.B. L.213 J.D. 1201 Morningside Dr. Ste. 215
Siegelman, Burt A. '61 '87 C.37 B.A. L.61 J.D. 835 2nd St.
**Simon, Carol Bremer** '51 '81 C.1060 B.A. L.464 J.D. [Simon&S.]
*PRACTICE AREAS: Family Law.
**Simon, David E.** '43 '69 C.112 B.S. L.800 J.D. [Simon&S.]⊙
*PRACTICE AREAS: Estate Planning; Wills; Trusts; Probate; Civil Litigation.

**Simon & Simon, Ltd.**
**1500 Rosecrans Avenue Suite 360, 90266**⊙
**Telephone: 310-536-9393 Fax: 310-536-9351**
**David E. Simon; Carol Bremer Simon (Certified Specialist, Family Law, The State Bar of California Board of Legal Specialization).**
**General Civil Litigation, Family Law, Real Property, Probate, Estate Planning, Personal Injury, Business.**
**Hawthorne, California Office: 4477 W. 118th Street, Suite 101. Telephone: 319-973-0474.**
*See Professional Biographies, MANHATTAN BEACH, CALIFORNIA*

**Spata, Michael C., (AV)** '51 '77 C.446 B.A. L.1137 J.D. [Andersen,K.&S.]
Stabile, Gary D., (AV) '42 '68 C.112 B.A. L.1068 J.D. 1334 Park View Ave.
**Steinberg, Alex, (AV)** '33 '61 C.112 B.A. L.800 J.D. [Steinberg B.G.&F.]
*PRACTICE AREAS: General Business; Real Property; Estate Planning; Trusts and Probate Administration.

**Steinberg Barness Glasgow & Foster LLP, (AV)** 
**1334 Park View Avenue, Suite 100, 90266**
**Telephone: 310-546-5838 Telecopier: 310-546-5630**
**Email: SGBF@ix.netcom.com**
**Members of Firm: Alex Steinberg; Daniel I. Barness; Donna Glasgow (Not admitted in CA); Douglas B. Foster; Jordan G. Barness; Paul J. Laurin; Shannon M. Foley; Richard L. Weiner; William R. (Randy) Kirkpatrick; Jeffrey Michael Lee. Of Counsel: Roanld D. Harari (Not admitted in CA).**
**General Business Practice, Corporation, Real Estate, Estate Planning, Trust and Probate Law, Civil Litigation, Bankruptcy, Creditor's Rights and Commercial Law.**
**References: Home Bank; Imperial Bank; Citizens Commerical Trust & Savings Bank; Bank of America.**
*See Professional Biographies, MANHATTAN BEACH, CALIFORNIA*

Stelter, Susan L. '55 '82 C.502 B.S. L.597 J.D. 105 N. Meadows Ave.
**Stockalper, Patrick E.** '62 '91 C.112 B.A. L.1049 J.D. [Reback,H.M.&K.]
Stubbs, John R. '46 '83 C.740 B.S. L.426 J.D. 515 Dianthus St.
Sublette, Camm '52 '89 C.259 B.A. L.1136 J.D. 820 Manhattan Ave.
Sweeney, William R., (AV) '26 '53 C.878 L.1065 LL.B. 317 Rosecrans Ave., 2nd Fl.‡
Tobias, Alvin S., (BV) '36 '67 L.464 J.D. 3701 Highland Ave.
Urban, Walter R. '45 '74 C.112 B.A. L.800 J.D. 2609 N. Sepulveda Blvd.

**Valentine, Robert S., (BV) '38 '67 C.112 B.A. L.426 J.D.**
**1334 Park View Avenue, Suite 100, P.O. Box 8, 90267-0008**
**Telephone: 310-545-6565 Fax: 310-546-8151**
**Probate, Estate Planning, Real Estate and Personal Injury Practice.**
*See Professional Biographies, MANHATTAN BEACH, CALIFORNIA*

von Glahn, Christopher G. '40 '68 C.164 B.A. L.94 LL.B. 1141 Highland Ave.

**Wasmund, H. Andrew '46 '72 C.112 A.B. L.426 J.D.**
**1334 Park View Avenue, Suite 100, 90266**
**Telephone: 310-545-3243 Fax: 310-545-4782**
**General Civil and Criminal Litigation with emphasis in Federal Court. Arbitration and Mediation, Family Law, Personal Injury.**
*See Professional Biographies, MANHATTAN BEACH, CALIFORNIA*

Wasserman, Terry K. '51 '78 C.112 B.A. L.809 J.D. 3800 Highland Ave.
Wattles, Frank '33 '66 C.36 B.S.E.E. L.800 J.D. P.O. Box 3514
**Weiner, Richard L.** '60 '86 C.37 B.A. L.61 J.D. [Steinberg B.G.&F.]
*PRACTICE AREAS: Business Litigation; Entertainment Litigation.
Weinstein, Craig D. '60 '85 C.112 B.A. L.809 J.D. 820 Manhattan Ave.
Zavidow, Robert M. '53 '79 C.112 B.A. L.1148 J.D. 1746 2nd St.
Ziemann, Timothy H., (AV) '47 '74 C.112 B.A. L.426 J.D. 1334 Park View Ave.; Suite 100

## MANTECA, 40,773, *San Joaquin Co.*

Alcorn, Mark D. '57 '84 C.1060 B.S. L.464 J.D. Indy Electronics, Inc.
Barkley, Michael James '45 '86 L.1197 J.D. 161 N. Sheridan Ave.
Brinton, John D., (BV) '49 '76 C.147 B.A. L.1132 J.D. [McFall,B.&B.]
Brown, Michael M., (A Professional Law Corporation), (BV) '43 '70 C.906 B.A. L.1065 J.D. 1150 W. Center St.
Frederick, John A. '51 '80 C.169 B.A. L.1132 J.D. [McFall,B.&B.]
Hackett, Grace G. '24 '77 L.1026 LL.B. 13039 S. Hwy. 99
Haynes, Priscilla H. '22 '52 C.112 A.B. L.1065 J.D. Ret. Mun. Ct. J.
Holmes, Ronald L. '42 '77 C.605 B.A. L.336 J.D. 212 W. Yosemite Ave.
Lupul, Donald K. '46 '75 C.999 L.1132 [McFall,B.&B.]
McFall, John J. '18 '41 C.112 A.B. L.1066 LL.B. 165 St. Dominic Dr.
McFall, Burnett & Brinton, (BV) 165 St. Dominic Dr.

**Neumiller & Beardslee, A Professional Corporation**
**(See Stockton)**

Ridge, Samuel B. '33 '74 C.766 A.B. L.1065 J.D. 130 S. Union Rd.

## MARINA, 26,436, *Monterey Co.*

Herbert, Clarke E. '44 '69 C.112 B.S. L.426 J.D. Secy., Del Monte Furniture Rental, Inc.
McLeod, Daniel D., (CV) '58 '86 C.112 B.A. L.1226 LL.B. 218 Reservation Rd.

## MARINA DEL REY, —, *Los Angeles Co.*

(Part of the incorporated City of Los Angeles)

Adams, Thomas M., (AV) '35 '60 C&L.910 A.B., J.D. 4676 Admiralty Way
Altshuler, David R. '47 '73 C.112 B.A. L.61 J.D. 520 Wash. Blvd.
Amato, Leonard M., (AV) '39 '65 C&L.800 B.S., LL.B. 4720 Lincoln Blvd.
Anderson, Craig H. '42 '67 C.309 B.A. L.494 J.D. P.O. Box 9728
Anderson, T. Valfrid '60 '86 C.766 B.A. L.1066 J.D. Western Fed. Svgs. & Loan Assn.
Barrett, Robert M. '48 '81 C&L.276 A.B., J.D. Asst. Prof. of Law, Univ. of Laverne School of Law
Ben-Yehuda, Ron C. '61 '87 C.976 B.A. L.813 J.D. Assoc. Gen. Coun., Quarterdeck Corp.

**Bernick, Kathy F. '42 '79 C.494 B.A. L.426 J.D.**
**520 Washington Boulevard Suite 663, 90292**
**Telephone: 310-578-6116 Fax: 310-827-4545**
***PRACTICE AREAS: Employment Discrimination; Civil Rights; Sexual Harassment; Disability Discrimination; Intellectual Property.**
**Employment Discrimination, Civil Rights, Sexual Harassment, Disability Discrimination, Intellectual Property only Computer, Software and Hardware, Copyrights, Trademarks and Trade Secrets.**

Boelter, Allen B. '56 '82 C.477 B.A. L.800 J.D. [Boelter&P.]
Boelter and Perry 330 Washington Blvd.
Boston, Lucille J. '27 '68 C.800 L.1095 LL.B. [L.J.Boston]
Boston, Lucille J., Inc., A Prof. Law Corp. 4724 Lincoln Blvd., Suite 230

**Brandon-Brown, Elizabeth, Law Office of '48 '91 C.260 B.S. L.128 J.D.**
**8055 West Manchester Avenue, Suite 405, 90293**
**Telephone: 310-302-0035**
***PRACTICE AREAS: Securities; Corporate; Business Law.**
**Securities and Corporate Law.**
*See Professional Biographies, MARINA DEL REY, CALIFORNIA*

Brandow, Wayne R., (BV) '44 '70 C.722 B.A. L.426 J.D. 520 Washington Blvd.
Breakstone, Jeffrey L. '54 '89 C.112 B.A. L.398 J.D. 4151 Via Marina
Buckner, Alan G., (AV) '39 '67 C.112 A.B. L.1068 J.D. [A.G.Buckner]
Buckner, Alan G., A Professional Corporation, (AV) 4215 Glencoe Ave.
Cadoo, Donald G., (AV) '25 '55 C.990 B.A. L.800 J.D. 4560 S. Admiralty Way‡
Carlin, Cindy '54 '79 C.1077 B.S. L.809 J.D. [Rousso&C.]
Chasan, Roslyn P. '32 '68 C.999 L.809 LL.B. 4676 Admiralty Way‡
Coplan, Daniel Jonathan '55 '85 C.569 B.F.A. L.809 J.D. 330 Washington St.
Crum, Stephen B. '60 '90 C.112 B.A. L.426 J.D. 4676 Admiralty Way
Dahle, Scott L. '63 '91 C.300 B.S.B.A. L.477 J.D. 4676 Admiralty Way
Dallas, Traci A. '63 '89 C.605 A.B. L.178 J.D. 13950 N.W. Passage
Dey, Stephen G., (AV) '46 '76 C.426 B.A. L.809 J.D. 4676 Admiralty Way
Di Giulio, Joseph, (AV) '36 '70 C.1043 L.800 J.D. 4720 Lincoln Blvd.
Dinerstein, Maurice '14 '71 L.809 J.D. 117 Privateer Mall‡
Dormer, Scott Bradley '66 '91 C&L.426 B.A., J.D. 4676 Admiralty
Eakin, Alan Jay '44 '70 C.1042 A.B. L.1065 J.D. 4519 Admiralty Way
Estrada, Nicolas J. '48 '85 C.426 B.S. L.809 J.D. 4676 Admiralty Way
Evans, Hugh H., Jr. '31 '59 C.813 B.A. L.1068 LL.B. Chmn. of the Bd. & CEO, Western Fed. Svgs. & Loan Assn.
**Feldman, Jonathan M.** '54 '81 C.112 B.A. L.767 J.D. [Magasinn&M.]
*PRACTICE AREAS: Business Law; Real Estate.
Fine, Martin A. '50 '83 C.813 B.A. L.990 J.D. 4346 Redwood Ave.
Fontaine, Lucille C. '— '79 C.139 B.A. L.1136 J.D. 13428 Maxella Ave.
Frank, Morton '25 '50 C.260 L.472 LL.B. (adm. in FL; not adm. in CA) 4139 Via Marina‡
Fraser, Robert H., (AV) '27 '51 C&L.352 B.S., LL.B. 3812 Via Dolce (Pat.)‡
Friedemann, John F. '58 '84 C.112 A.B. L.464 J.D. [Friedemann&M.]
Friedemann & Maurer 4676 Admiralty Way
Girard, Joseph C. '44 '72 C.770 B.A. L.426 J.D. 4560 Admiralty Way
Glembockie, James J. '51 '91 C.646 B.A. L.809 J.D. 119 Driftwood
Goldenberg, Max '16 '42 C.352 L.309 J.D. 4346 Redwood Ave.
Goldklang, Ira C. '66 '90 C.978 B.A. L.659 J.D. Dir., Legal Affs., North Communications, Inc.
Gordon, Ellen Gittel '44 '70 C.446 B.A. L.276 J.D. 3215 Ocean Front Walk
Gordon, Gittel, (AV) '44 '70 C.446 B.A. L.276 J.D. 3215 Ocean Front Walk
Gould, Harold I., (A P.C.) '29 '56 C.112 A.B. L.1068 J.D. [H.I.Gould]
Gould, Harold I., A Professional Corporation 4300 Promenade Way

Grossman, Eugene .......................... '36 '70 C&L.1095 B.A., J.D. P.O. Box 9547
Gruber, Ira L. .............................. '40 '77 C.1097 B.A. L.1095 J.D. 4335 Alla Rd.
Hall, William Duane .............................................. '46 '76 4640 Admiralty Way
Havens, Robert S. .................. '43 '79 C.1077 B.A. L.1136 J.D. 4324 Promenade Way
Hobart, G. Dana, (P.C.), (AV) .... '32 '64 C.1043 B.A. L.800 LL.B. 4676 Admiralty Way
Howard, Alvin F., (A L.C.), (AV) '14 '38
C.113 A.B. L.1066 LL.B. 13082 Mindanad Way‡
Kaplan, Richard S. ......................... '44 '76 C.1097 B.A. L.426 J.D. [Tanzman&K.]
Keating, Thomas J. ........................ '61 '86 C.473 B.S. L.150 J.D. P.O. Box 9579
Kiss, Richard M. ........... '50 '78 C.1068 A.B. L.813 J.D. 13221 Admiral Ave., Unit D.
Klein, Richard S. ........................ '55 '80 C.597 B.A. L.813 J.D. 337 Washington Blvd.
Klugman, Ellen ........................ '56 '84 C.222 B.A. L.1068 J.D. 13930 Old Harbor Lane
Knight, Stephen ............................................ '41 '78 L.1136 J.D. 2554 Lincoln Blvd.
Korn, Lloyd P. .................... '55 '84 C.260 B.S.B.A. L.472 J.D. 4616 Glencoe Ave.
Lanning, Michael K., (A Professional Law Corporation) '32 '58
C.112 B.A. L.1068 LL.B. 4676 Admiralty Way
Lavi, Donald L. ........................ '61 '86 C.112 B.A. L.93 J.D. 4676 Admiralty Way
Lebow, Ronald M., (AV) ............ '53 '78 C.112 B.A. L.426 J.D. 4676 Admiralty Way
Leeds, A. James .................................................. '41 '71 C.112 L.809 J.D. [Leeds&L.]
Leeds, Wm. A. ................................................ '08 '36 C.178 L.1009 LL.B. [Leeds&L.]
Leeds & Leeds ..................................................................... 13237 Fiji Way
Leib, Charles R. ...................... '44 '71 C.112 A.B. L.426 J.D. 330 Washington St.
Levin, Michael A. ...................... '40 '74 C.800 Phar.D. L.809 J.D. 4519 Admiralty Way
Levin, Michael A. ...................... '42 '68 C.112 B.S. L.1068 J.D. 4519 Admiralty Way
Levy, David L. ........................... '38 '63 C.112 B.A. L.1068 LL.B. 13235 Fiji Way‡
Lipman, Annette '54 '81 C.1077 B.S. L.1049 J.D.
V.P. & Coun., Western Fed. Svgs. & Loan Assn.
Lockton, Andrew W., III, (AV) .......................... '25 '50 C.951 L.477 J.D. P.O. Box 9160‡
Lovett, Steven R. ....................................... '53 '78 C.112 A.B. L.809 J.D. [Lovett&O.]
Lovett & Obrenski, A Professional Law Corporation .................... 4551 Glencoe Ave.
Lysle, Richard S. .................. '47 '72 C.188 A.B. L.800 J.D. 330 Washington Blvd.
**Magasinn, Arnold W., (AV)** .......... '35 '67 C.112 B.S. L.1095 LL.B. [Magasinn&M.]
*PRACTICE AREAS: Business Law; Taxation Law; Trust and Estate Planning.
**Magasinn, Michael L.** ...................... '65 '95 C.1077 B.S. L.809 J.D. [Ⓐ Magasinn&M.]
*PRACTICE AREAS: Estate Planning; Probate; Business Law.
**Magasinn, Vicki Fisher**, (AV) ........... '49 '77 C.112 B.A. L.809 J.D. [Magasinn&M.]
*PRACTICE AREAS: Estate Planning; Trusts; Probate; Business.

**Magasinn & Magasinn, A Law Corporation, (AV)**
**4640 Admirality Way, Suite 402, 90292**
**Telephone: 310-301-3545 Telecopier: 310-301-0035**
**Jonathan M. Feldman; Arnold W. Magasinn (Certified Specialist, Taxation Law, The State Bar of California Board of Legal Specialization); Vicki Fisher Magasinn (Certified Specialist, Estate Planning, Trust and Probate Law, The State Bar of California Board of Legal Specialization);—Michael L. Magasinn.**
**Specializing in Taxation, Estate Planning, Probate, Trusts, Charitable Organizations, Real Estate, Business, Corporate and Partnership Law and Business Secession Planning.**
***See Professional Biographies, MARINA DEL REY, CALIFORNIA***

Masada, Linda Scasserra '43 '80 C.706 B.A. L.426 J.D.
Western Fed. Svgs. & Loan Assn.
Maurer, Michael T. ..................................... '59 '84 C.350 B.S. L.477 J.D. [Friedemann&M.]
McCullough, Thomas B., Jr. .......... '43 '68 C.216 B.A. L.260 J.D. 4676 Admiralty Way
McGookin, Ralph J., (BV) ............ '31 '60 C.112 B.A. L.809 LL.B. 13900 Tahiti Way
Merrill, Burton ....................... '33 '66 C.1097 B.S. L.800 J.D. 4324 Promenade Way
Miller, Michael H. ................................ '43 '74 C.994 B.A. L.809 J.D. P.O. Box 10694
Mitchell, Charles K. ................ '39 '84 C.347 A.B. L.809 J.D. 4676 Admiralty Way
Moe, Michael A. ........................ '43 '76 C.628 B.S. L.1190 J.D. 4551 Glencoe Ave.
Monk, Alonzo ........................................ '58 '83 C.112 B.A. L.990 J.D. 24 Yawl St.
Moore, Donald Hugh, (AV) ......... '46 '72 C.684 B.A. L.1068 J.D. 4640 Admirality Way
Moss, Ellen S. ........................... '35 '78 C.1077 B.A. L.1095 J.D. 4351 Alla Rd.
Mott-Simpson, Kathleen P., (AV) ..................... '47 '77 L.1136 J.D. 13160 Mindanao Way
Murez, Libbe R. ...................................... '— '77 C.976 Mus.B. L.1136 J.D. 4600 Via Dolce
Myers, Adam J., III ..................... '51 '86 C.645 B.S. L.309 J.D. 330 Washington Blvd.
Newman, Alan B. ................. '36 '61 C.188 B.S. L.309 LL.B. 4334 Promenade Way
Obrenski, Timothy V. ............................... '51 '79 C.679 B.S. L.809 J.D. [Lovett&O.]
Perkins, Richard A., (AV) .......... '10 '34 C.339 A.B. L.477 J.D. 13909 Old Harbor Ln.
Perry, Michael J. .................................... '59 '86 C.477 B.A. L.809 J.D. [Boelter&P.]
Potts, Allen J. '31 '59 C&L.659 A.B., J.D.
(adm. in IL; not adm. in CA) Pres., Pavia Properties, Inc.
Ramey, William J., (BV) ................... '36 '65 C.999 L.809 LL.B. 330 Washington Blvd.
Reber, Joseph E. ................................ '40 '65 C&L.508 B.A., J.D. 4143 Via Marina
Riet, Anne E. Van der .............................. '62 '89 C&L.426 B.S., J.D. 337 Wash. St.
Rooney, Keith E. '64 '92 C.813 B.A. L.178 J.D.
(adm. in NY; not adm. in CA) 932 Dickson St.
Rousso, Jeffrey I. ..................................... '53 '79 C.800 A.B. L.809 J.D. [Rousso&C.]
Rousso & Carlin, A Law Corp. .............................................................. 944 Oxford Ave.
Russo, Frederick ........................... '51 '76 C.1077 B.A. L.1148 J.D. 330 Wash. Blvd.
Sandler, Merle H., (BV) ......... '28 '53 C.800 L.426 J.D. 13078 Mindanao Way, Apt. 214
Sarafopoulos, John ....................................... '49 '76 C&L.477 A.B., J.D. 4215 Roma Ct.
Sasamori, Norman Cousins .......... '62 '95 C.990 B.A. L.1188 J.D. 4676 Admiralty Way
Schiffer, Douglas J. .................... '53 '82 C.112 B.A. L.61 J.D. 330 Washington St.
Schwartz, Jonathan .................... '43 '68 C.65 B.A. L.659 LL.B. 4676 Admiralty Way
Shanahan, Joseph P., Jr., (BV) .... '36 '66 C&L.884 B.S., J.D. 5111 Ocean Front Walk
Shcolnek, Richard P. ............................ '48 '73 C&L.477 A.B., J.D. 4109 Via Marina St.
Shoeps, Bernard S., (AV) ............ '45 '72 C.1077 B.A. L.426 J.D. 4560 Admiralty Way
Simon, Barry J. .......................... '51 '79 C.1042 B.A. L.426 J.D. 4676 Admiralty Way
Snyder, Harold W., (BV) ........................ '22 '50 C.112 B.S. L.426 LL.B. [Snyder&S.] ‡
Snyder, Theda, (AV⊕) .... '48 '77 C.107 B.A. L.424 J.D. Legal Cost Coun., Legalard, Inc.
Snyder & Snyder .......................................................................... 4337 Marina City Drive
Solitare, David A. ............................ '56 '83 C.112 B.A. L.1068 J.D. [Solitare,D.A.]
Solitare, David A., Law Offices of ........................................................... 4215 Glencoe Ave.
Stearns, John F., (AV) .............................. '36 '75 L.809 J.D. 13900 Tahiti Way
Stuppler, Anita R. ................................... '46 '78 C.446 B.A. L.64 J.D. 4139 Via Marina‡
Swanger, Alfred L. .................... '29 '59 C.629 B.S. L.1068 LL.B. 2554 Lincoln Blvd.
Swanson, Otto F. ....................................... '32 '71 C.843 L.1136 J.D. [Swanson&S.]
Swanson, Steven F. ............................ '52 '82 C.774 B.A. L.1136 J.D. [Swanson&S.]
Swanson and Swanson ................................................................ 4676 Admiralty Way
Tanzman, Susan D., (BV) ......................... '45 '71 C.800 B.A. L.426 J.D. [Tanzman&K.]
Tanzman & Kaplan, (BV) ........................................................... 330 Washington St.
Thompson, Dorothy ...................................... '— '78 C.36 B.S. L.809 J.D. 13900 N.W. Passage
Wickes, Donald J. ................................ '31 '80 L.1148 J.D. 13065 Mindanao Way
Zachary, George C., (AV) ................ '31 '56 C.563 A.B. L.976 LL.B. 20 Ironside St.‡

## MARIPOSA, * —, *Mariposa Co.*

**Allen, Polgar, Proietti & Fagalde, (AV)**
**A Partnership including a Professional Corporation**
**5079 Highway 140, P.O. Box 1907, 95338⊙**
**Telephone: 209-966-3007 Fax: 209-742-6353**
**Michael A. Fagalde; F. Dana Walton (Resident).**
**General Civil and Criminal Trial Practice. Personal Injury, Wrongful Termination, Family Law, Corporation, Business, Condemnation, Taxation, Estate Planning, Probate, Real Property, Bankruptcy and Creditors' Rights Law.**
**Merced, California Office: 1640 "N" Street, Suite 200. P.O. Box 2184. Telephone: 209-723-4372. Fax: 209-723-7397.**
***See Professional Biographies, MARIPOSA, CALIFORNIA***

Campbell, Ralph J. ...................................................... '21 '68 C.999 L.1132 J.D. Dist. Atty.
Eckerson, James B. ........................................ '43 '72 C.312 B.A. L.770 J.D. P.O. Box 748
**Fagalde, Michael A.**, (BV) ................ '53 '83 C.768 B.S. L.770 J.D. [Allen,P.P.&F.]⊙
*PRACTICE AREAS: Criminal Law; Employment Law; Family Law.
Fletcher, Kimberly Ann ........................................................ '58 '87 Dep. Dist. Atty.
Gimblin, Richard S. ......................... '37 '63 C.766 B.A. L.1065 J.D. 4980 10th St.
Green, Jeffrey G. .......................................... '41 '72 C.769 B.A. L.770 J.D. Co. Coun.
Johnson, Christine A. ................................ '51 '77 C.1042 B.A. L.1137 J.D. Dist. Atty.
Kimball, Frank C. '11 '39 C.30 L.273 J.D.
(adm. in DC; not adm. in CA) 4501 Bridgeport Dr.‡
Lindstedt, James B. .......................... '33 '72 C.686 B.A. L.809 LL.B. 4613 Hwy. 49,. S.

**Linn, Lindley & Blate, A Professional Association**
**(See Oakhurst)**

McMechan, Richard L. .............................. '37 '72 C.1042 B.S. L.1137 LL.B. Supr. Ct. J.
McNally, Francis W. ................................ '47 '72 C.112 A.B. L.767 J.D. Dep. Dist. Atty.
Moser, Richard L. ........................................ '38 '68 C.426 B.S. L.809 LL.B. P.O. Box 899
Mueller, Egon W. ........................................... '23 '50 C&L.966 B.S., LL.B. Jud. Dist. J.
Parrish, Wayne R. ........................ '38 '66 C&L.800 B.S., LL.B. 2160 Hwy. 49 South
Starchman, Donald J. ........................ '43 '77 C.377 B.S. L.1049 J.D. 5320 Hwy. 49 N.
Turkington, William W., III .................... '31 '86 C.1097 B.S. L.1336 J.D. Dep. Dist. Atty.
**Walton, F. Dana** .............................................. '50 '79 C.267 L.1132 J.D. [Allen,P.P.&F.]
*PRACTICE AREAS: Probate; Trusts; Estate Planning; Family Law; Civil Litigation.

## MARKLEEVILLE, * —, *Alpine Co.*

Bradford, Harold F. ........................................ '35 '63 C&L.813 A.B., J.D. 18 Hawkside Ct.
Cook, J. Hilary ................................ '29 '59 C.112 A.B. L.1065 LL.B. (Ret.) Supr. Ct. J.
Murdock, Henry G. ....................................... '35 '73 C.575 B.A. L.767 J.D. Dist. Atty.
Rogers, David A. ........................... '42 '81 C.112 B.S. L.765 J.D. 54 Canon View Rd.

## MARSHALL, —, *Marin Co.*

Hurwitz, Steven S. .......................................... '46 '72 C.608 B.A. L.30 J.D. P.O. Box 714

## MARTINEZ, * 31,808, *Contra Costa Co.*

**Adams, Jonathan Daniel** ........................ '43 '76 C.1097 B.S. L.464 J.D. [Turner,H.&A.]
*REPORTED CASES: Moore v. R.G. Industries Inc., 789 F2d 1326.
*PRACTICE AREAS: Real Estate Litigation; Construction Litigation; Environmental Law; Insurance Coverage; Personal Injury.
Anderson, Sharon L. ...................................... '55 '80 C.118 B.A. L.464 J.D. Dep. Co. Coun.
Antoon, Thomas M. ........................ '49 '76 C.112 B.A. L.1026 J.D. 1261 Bear Creek Rd.
Arnason, Richard E. .................... '21 '45 C.585 B.S. L.1066 LL.B. Ret. Supr. Ct. J.
Baker, Brian S., (BV) ............................ '54 '83 C.1044 B.A. L.284 J.D. Dep. Dist. Atty.
Barker, Elizabeth Kaye ............................ '63 '89 C.659 B.A. L.188 J.D. Dep. Pub. Def.
Barker, Terri D .......................................... '63 '89 C.267 B.A. L.770 J.D. Dep. Dist. Atty.
Baum, Brandon Drew ............................ '60 '85 C.112 A.B. L.1065 J.D. Dep. Co. Coun.
Berkow, Josanna ........................................... '51 '77 C.445 B.S. L.64 J.D. Supr. Ct. Ref.
Bialik, Leslie J. ............................... '51 '89 C.112 B.A. L.1153 J.D. Dep. Pub. Def.
Bolen, Steven C. ............................ '64 '89 C.740 B.A. L.1065 J.D. Dep. Dist. Atty.
Bonis, Peter H. ................................ '55 '85 C.1213 B.S. L.464 J.D. Dist. Atty. Off.
Bradley, Jeffrey C., (BV) ...................... '48 '73 C.569 B.S. L.1065 J.D. Asst. Pub. Def.

**Brans, Kenneth R., (BV) '45 '73 C.112 B.A. L.1067 J.D.**
**2530 Arnold Drive, Suite 125, P.O. Box 2490, 94553**
**Telephone: 510-228-3595 Fax: 510-228-8086**
**Real Estate, Landlord and Tenant Law (Commercial, Residential, and Mobile Home), Litigation, Estate Planning.**

**Bray, A. F., Jr.**, (AV) ........................................ '18 '49 C.813 A.B. L.800 J.D. [Bray&B.]
*PRACTICE AREAS: Estate Planning; Probate Law; Guardianship and Conservatorship.
**Bray, Oliver W.** ................................................. '54 '85 C.1060 B.S. L.1153 J.D. [Bray&B.]
*PRACTICE AREAS: Probate Law; Estate Planning; Trust Administration; Trust Litigation; Guardianship and Conservatorship.

**Bray and Bray, (AV)**
**736 Ferry Street, 94553**
**Telephone: 510-228-2550 FAX: 510-370-8558**
**A. F. Bray, Jr.; Oliver W. Bray.**
**Estate Planning, Probate, Trust Administration and Litigation, Conservatorships and Guardianships.**
***See Professional Biographies, MARTINEZ, CALIFORNIA***

**Breitwieser, Richard J., (BV) '34 '66 C.116 B.S. L.1065 J.D.**
**736 Ferry Street, 94553**
**Telephone: 510-838-8430 Fax: 510-370-8558**
***PRACTICE AREAS: Family Law; Uniform Child Custody Jurisdiction Act; Civil Litigation; Business Law; Estate Planning and Probate Law.**
**Court appearances for out of area attorneys. Family Law, Interstate Support (URESA, UCCJA), Civil Litigation, Business, Estate Planning, Probate and Taxation Law. Guardianship and Conservatorship.**
***See Professional Biographies, MARTINEZ, CALIFORNIA***

Brookman, Raymond C. ............................. '33 '60 C.549 B.A. L.1065 J.D. 535 Main St.
Brown, David Glenn ................................. '57 '86 C.98 B.S. L.879 J.D. Co. Dist. Atty.
**Bruno, Richard S.**, (BV) ........................ '55 '84 C.740 B.S. L.1197 J.D. [Gordon,D.W.&P.]
*PRACTICE AREAS: Land Use Litigation; Real Property Law; Personal Injury Law.
Cannelora, Louis ................................ '15 '39 C.767 L.1065 LL.B. 115 Fountainhead Ct.
Chang, W. Gerald ........................... '63 '91 C.112 B.A. L.464 J.D. Dep. Dist. Atty.
Chapot, Suzanne J., (Ms.), (BV) ........................ '45 '76 C.800 B.A. L.284 J.D. Pub. Def.
Cook, Daniel E. ........................................ '56 '85 C.112 B.A. L.767 J.D. Dep. Pub. Def.
Cope, John C. ................................................ '63 '91 C&L.101 B.A., J.D. Dep. Dist. Atty.
Costanza, Angelo J., (BV) ............................ '48 '74 C.112 A.B. L.1065 J.D. 706 Ferry St.
Couch, Georgia Kaye Wisner ......................... '39 '89 C.766 L.1153 J.D. P.O. Box 1533

**Cummins, Bernard F., (AV) '31 '61 C.740 A.B. L.767 LL.B.** ⊞
**917 Las Juntas Street, P.O. Box 351, 94553**
**Telephone: 510-228-3001 Fax: 510-228-6825**
***REPORTED CASES: Los Angeles Metropolitan Transit Authority v. Public Utilities Commission (1963) 59 Cal. 2d 863; People v. Estrada (1965) 234 Cal.App.2d 136; 11 ALR 3d 1307; Pleasant Hill v. First Baptist Church (1969) 1 Cal. App. 3d 384; Estate of Wochos (1972) 23 Cal.App.3d 47.**
**General Civil, Trial and Appellate Practice in all Courts. Business, Probate, Real Property and Condemnation Law.**
***See Professional Biographies, MARTINEZ, CALIFORNIA***

Davi, Jerome A., (BV) '28 '71 C.871 B.S. L.284 J.D. Dep. Dist. Atty.
Davidson, Virginia Hollins '44 '74 C.351 B.A. L.912 J.D. Dep. Pub. Def.
Dawes, Vickie L. '53 '78 C.1077 B.A. L.1095 J.D. Dep. Co. Coun.
**DeFraga, Allan**, (BV) '41 '66 C.813 A.B. L.1065 J.D. [Gordon,D.W.&P.]
*PRACTICE AREAS: Personal Injury Law; Real Property Law; Probate Law.
Dolgin, David A. '25 '51 C.112 B.S. L.1065 J.D. Ret. Supr. Ct. J.
Easton, Stephen K. '45 '71 C.112 A.B. L.1065 J.D. Juv. Ct. Ref.
Engelbart, Joan E. '53 '88 C.112 A.B. L.312 J.D.
Medical Social Worker & HIV/AIDS Coord., Kaiser Permanente
Farr, Michael D., (AV) '39 '67 C.101 B.A. L.1066 J.D. Dep. Co. Coun.
Filice, J. H., (AV) '28 '55 C.112 A.B. L.1065 LL.B. 970 W. Green St.‡
Firestone, Jacob '47 '73 C.763 B.A. L.1065 J.D. 204 Augustine Dr.
Fischer, David R. '60 '89 C.999 L.1153 J.D. 0117 Green St.
Fleming, Margaret M. '59 '86 C.112 B.A. L.770 J.D. Dep. Dist. Atty.
Flier, Richard S. '45 '72 C.112 B.A. L.1065 J.D. Supr. Ct. J.
Franks, Phyllis M. '53 '81 C.112 B.A. L.770 J.D. Dep. Dist. Atty.
Funk, John Nelson '55 '80 C.112 B.A. L.1066 J.D. Dep. Pub. Def. IV
Garcia, Luis V. '62 '91 C.309 A.B. L.1068 J.D. Off. of Pub.Def.
George, Virginia M. '59 '86 C.112 B.A. L.767 J.D. Dep. Dist. Atty.
Georgiou, Nancy '62 '87 C.800 A.B. L.1065 J.D. Dep. Dist. Atty.
Goodmacher, Maxine '34 '76 C.112 A.B. L.767 J.D. [M.Goodmacher]
Goodmacher, Maxine, Inc., A Professional Corporation 1721 Alhambra Ave.

**Gordon, DeFraga, Watrous & Pezzaglia, A Law Corporation, (AV)**
**611 Las Juntas Street, P.O. Box 630, 94553**
**Telephone: 510-228-1400 Fax: 510-228-3644**
**Allan DeFraga; Thomas A. Watrous; James A. Pezzaglia; Timothy John Ryan; Peter D. Langley; Richard S. Bruno; Bruce C. Paltenghi;—Gregory D. Rueb.**
**Civil and Trial Practice before all Federal, State and Local Courts and Administrative Agencies, Business, Corporate, Real Property and Land Use Matters, Landslide and Soil Subsidence, Inverse Condemnation and Municipal Law, Civil Rights, Environmental, Air Pollution and Toxic Torts, Estate Planning and Probate Law, Insurance Defense.**
**Representative Clients: Martinez Sanitary Service; Plant Maintenance; Lippow Development Co.**
***See Professional Biographies, MARTINEZ, CALIFORNIA***

Graham, Gayle Elaine, (BV) '57 '82 C.112 B.A. L.464 J.D. Dep. Dist. Atty.
Graves, Dennis C. '42 '72 C.585 B.S. L.767 J.D. Dep. Co. Coun.
Green, William H '62 '87 C.112 A.B. L.1065 J.D. Dep. Pub. Def.
Grout, Daniel A. '66 '93 C.309 B.A. L.1065 J.D. 535 Main St., 3rd Fl.
Hall, Sam W., Jr. '21 '47 C.112 B.A. L.1066 LL.B. Ret. Supr. Ct. J.
Harvey, Gregory C., (AV) '44 '71 C.112 B.A. L.1065 J.D. Dep. Co. Coun.
Hast, Julie Ann, (BV) '59 '84 C.112 B.A. L.61 J.D. Dep. Dist. Atty.
Hatzenbuhler, John D. '28 '62 C.169 A.B. L.1065 J.D. Ret. Mun. J.
Haynes, Brian F. '64 '88 C.808 B.A. L.1188 J.D. Dep. Dist. Atty.
**Highsmith, Teresa L.** '55 '91 C.549 B.A. L.1153 J.D. [C.J.Williams]
*REPORTED CASES: City of Lafayette v. East Bay Municipal Utility District, (1993) 16 CA4th 1005, 20 CR2d 658.
Hinton, Barbara C. '65 '92 C&L.813 B.A., J.D. Dep. Pub. Def.
Hoffman, Curtis R., (BV) '37 '69 C.112 B.S. L.1065 J.D. Dep. Dist. Atty.
**Huguet, Maurice E., Jr.**, (AV) '36 '62 C.112 A.B. L.1065 J.D. [Turner,H.&A.]
*PRACTICE AREAS: Probate; Trusts; Estate Planning; Municipal; Real Estate.
James, Ellen S. '43 '70 C.771 B.A. L.1066 J.D. Supr. Ct. J.
Judnick, Jesse L. '54 '87 C.766 B.A. L.1065 J.D. Research Atty., Supr. Ct.
Katague, Diosdado D. '58 '85 C&L.112 A.B., J.D. Dep. Dist. Atty.
Katz, Lawrence G. '45 '72 C.112 A.B. L.1065 J.D. Juv. Ct. Ref.
Kenney, Laura R. '60 '85 C.918 B.A. L.800 J.D. Co. Supr. Ct. Atty.
Kensok, Thomas J '58 '87 C.740 B.S. L.1065 J.D. Dep. Dist. Atty.
Kerr, Kevin T. '56 '82 C.766 B.A. L.990 J.D. Co. Coun.
Kerridge, Kathy J. '52 '82 C.477 B.G.S. L.1065 J.D. 535 Main St.
Lamphere, Paul O., (AV) '33 '61 C&L.767 B.S., J.D. 1320 Arnold Dr., Ste 271
Lane, Edward V., Jr., (BV) '39 '66 C.112 B.S. L.1065 LL.B. Dep. Co. Coun.
**Langley, Peter D.**, (AV) '44 '72 C.966 B.S. L.273 J.D. [Gordon,D.W.&P.]
*PRACTICE AREAS: Real Property Law; Family Law; Business Law; Homeowner Association Law; Public Entity Defense.
**Lawrence, Judith E.** '48 '89 C.112 A.B. L.284 J.D. [Willis&L.]
*PRACTICE AREAS: Family; Civil Litigation; Juvenile (Dependency).
Lee, George I. '48 '77 C.103 B.A. L.659 J.D. 235 Whitehaven Way
Levine, Michael M. '40 '80 L.1153 J.D. 1721 Alhambra Ave.
Libbey, James H., (AV) '42 '69 C.197 A.B. L.767 J.D. Supr. Ct. Comr.
MacMaster, Doug '60 '87 C.112 B.S. L.1066 J.D. Dep. Dist. Atty.
Madonne, Marjorie, (BV) '40 '69 C.112 B.A. L.1066 J.D. Dep. Pub. Def.
Marchesi, Silvano B., (AV) '43 '68 C&L.767 B.A., J.D. Asst. Co. Coun.
Marchiano, James J. '43 '70 C.999 A.B. L.1066 J.D. Supr. Ct. J.
Marks, Robert C., (BV) '35 '63 C.112 B.S. L.1065 LL.B. Zeta Graphics Corp.
Martinez, Freddie L. '55 '82 C.560 B.A. L.767 J.D. Dep. Dist. Atty.
McClure, George W. '19 '50 C.112 A.B. L.1066 J.D. 3761 Canyon Way‡
McCormick, Kenneth W. '60 '88 C.112 B.A. L.464 J.D. Dep. Dist. Atty.
McCowen, Cecily E. '63 '90 C.939 B.A. L.1066 J.D. Dep. Pub. Def.
McGrath, Robert G. '43 '69 C.112 A.B. L.1065 J.D. Supr. Ct. J.
Merrill, Edward L. '26 '51 C.112 A.B. L.1066 J.D. Supr. Ct. J.
Miller, Dale A., (AV) '41 '70 C.940 B.A. L.1026 J.D. Sr. Dep. Dist. Atty.
Mockler, Terri A. '57 '82 C.112 B.A. L.1065 J.D. Dep. Pub. Def.
Morken, John S. '33 '59 C.112 A.B. L.1065 LL.B. 1221 Thomas Dr.
Motta, Joseph A. '62 '88 C.740 B.S. L.464 J.D. Dep. Dist. Atty.
Murphy, Dennis N., (BV) '41 '70 C.767 B.S. L.1065 J.D. Sr. Dep. Dist. Atty.
Murphy, Patrick R., (BV) '28 '55 C.999 L.464 LL.B. Pub. Def.
Nix, Brad '56 '82 C.800 B.S. L.1065 J.D. Dep. Dist. Atty.
Nolan, Denise M. '53 '80 C.1289 B.A. L.1066 J.D. Asst. Pub. Def.
Oda, John S., (BV) '32 '64 C.112 A.B. L.1065 J.D. Asst. Dist. Atty.
Olmsted, Kenneth A., (AV) '54 '80 C.65 B.A. L.1067 J.D. P.O. Box 1992
O'Malley, William A. '24 '62 C.262 A.B. L.284 LL.B. Supr. Ct. J.
**Paltenghi, Bruce C.**, (BV) '50 '78 C.267 B.A. L.1231 J.D. [Gordon,D.W.&P.]
*PRACTICE AREAS: Probate and Estate Administration; Environmental Law; Toxic Torts; Estate Planning Law; Administration Law.
Patsey, Richard L. '35 '61 C.118 B.A. L.1066 LL.B. Supr. Ct. J.
Pettis, John A. '46 '72 C.112 A.B. L.1066 J.D. 1830 Pacheco Blvd.
**Pezzaglia, James A.**, (AV) '41 '68 C.112 B.S. L.1065 J.D. [Gordon,D.W.&P.]
*PRACTICE AREAS: Administrative Law; Environmental Law; Estate Planning Law.
Phillips, Carolyn D. '42 '75 L.1065 J.D. P.O. Box 1979
Pipes, L. Douglas, (AV) '43 '68 C.169 B.A. L.309 J.D. Sr. Dep. Dist. Atty.
Poling, Kathleen U. '38 '82 C.923 B.S. L.1153 J.D. 815 Marina Vista, Ste. F
Rinner, Margaret E. '48 '74 C.788 B.A. L.276 J.D. 2229 Lake Oaks Ct.‡
Romero, Thomas C., (BV) '44 '72 C.1073 B.A. L.1066 J.D. Off. of Dist. Atty.
**Rueb, Gregory D.** '66 '91 C&L.464 B.S., J.D. [[illegible] Gordon,D.W.&P.]
*PRACTICE AREAS: General Litigation and Trial Practice; Criminal Law; Personal Injury; Medical Malpractice; Environmental Law.
**Ryan, Timothy John**, (AV) '52 '78 C.770 B.S. L.1026 J.D. [Gordon,D.W.&P.]
*PRACTICE AREAS: Tort Litigation; Landslide Law; Homeowner Association Law; Inverse Condemnation Law; Insurance Defense Law.

**Sanders, Dodson, Rives & Cox**
**(See Pittsburg)**

**Schlegel, Leanne '42 '93 C.1073 B.A. L.1153 J.D.**
**736 Ferry Street, 94553**
**Telephone: 510-228-6225 Fax: 510-228-5663**
**Family Law including Custody and Visitation, Business, Corporations, Non-Profit Organizations.**
***See Professional Biographies, MARTINEZ, CALIFORNIA***

Schmidt, David F. '51 '78 C.37 B.A. L.1065 J.D. Dep. Co. Coun.
Schuman, Jeanne M. '50 '79 C.608 B.A. L.1197 J.D. Dep. Pub. Def.
Scott, McGregor W. '62 '89 C.770 B.A. L.1065 J.D. Dep. Dist. Atty.
Sequeira, Paul D., (BV) '58 '84 C.112 B.A. L.950 J.D. Dep. Dist. Atty.
Spinetta, Peter L. '41 '69 C.740 B.A. L.976 J.D. Supr. Ct. J.
Stirling, Robert B. '43 '69 C.766 B.A. L.1065 J.D. Juvenile Ct. Ref.
Swager, Douglas E. '45 '70 C.112 B.S. L.1065 J.D. Supr. Ct. J.
Taylor, Lauren S. '64 '89 C.112 B.A. L.1065 J.D. P.O. Box 323
Taylor, Wakefield '12 '37 C.112 B.A. L.1066 LL.B. 1270 Escobar St.‡
Trembath, James R. '40 '65 C.112 B.A. L.1065 J.D. Supr. Ct. J.
Turnbaugh, Albert J., A Prof. Corp., (CV) '46 '74 C.147 B.A. L.284 J.D. 706 Main St.

**Turner, Huguet & Adams, (AV)**
**924 Main Street, P.O. Box 110, 94553**
**Telephone: 510-228-3433 Fax: 510-228-3596**
**Members of Firm: Maurice E. Huguet, Jr.; Jonathan Daniel Adams.**
**General Civil and Trial Practice. Property and Casualty Insurance, Probate, Trusts, Estate Planning, Real Estate, Business, Municipal, Environmental, Land Use and Corporation Law.**
***See Professional Biographies, MARTINEZ, CALIFORNIA***

Waddell, John N., (BV) '38 '68 C.118 B.A. L.1065 J.D. Dep. Dist. Atty.
Wagner, Ann I. '45 '75 C.1066 A.B. L.1065 J.D. P.O. Box 1979
Walenta, Arthur W., Jr., (AV) '35 '61 C.112 B.S. L.309 J.D. Asst. Co. Coun.
**Watrous, Thomas A.**, (AV) '38 '64 C.112 A.B. L.1066 J.D. [Gordon,D.W.&P.]
*PRACTICE AREAS: Personal Injury Law; Business Litigation; Civil Rights Law.
Wayne, Linda A. '54 '80 C.112 B.A. L.770 J.D. Dep. Dist. Atty.

**Weiler, Leonard D., A Professional Corporation**
**(See San Ramon)**

Westman, Victor J., (AV) '37 '63 C.766 A.B. L.1065 J.D. Co. Coun.
Westover, Wayne A., Jr. '27 '51 L.1065 J.D. Supr. Ct. J.
Wheeler, Robert C. '47 '85 C.284 B.A. L.1066 J.D. 1340 Arnold Dr., Suite 120
**Williams, Charles J.**, (AV) '30 '55 C.112 A.B. L.1066 LL.B. [C.J.Williams]
*PRACTICE AREAS: Appellate Law; Civil Trial Law; Administrative Law; Land Use Law; Condemnation Law.
Williams, Lynda D. '62 '88 C.267 B.A. L.464 J.D. Dep. Dist. Atty.
Williams, Victoria T. '44 '89 C.878 B.S. L.767 J.D. Dep. Co. Coun.

**Williams, Charles J., A Professional Corporation, (AV)** BB
**1320 Arnold Drive Suite 160, 94553**
**Telephone: 510-228-3840 Fax: 510-228-1703**
**Charles J. Williams; Teresa L. Highsmith.**
**Civil Trial and Appellate Practice in all State and Federal Courts. Land Use, Municipal, Planning Zoning and Subdivision, Civil Rights, Environmental, Condemnation and Administrative Law.**

**Willis, Stuart W.**, (BV) '43 '71 C.112 A.B. L.1066 J.D. [Willis&L.]
*PRACTICE AREAS: Criminal Trial; Family; Civil Litigation; Juvenile (Criminal).

**Willis & Lawrence, (BV)**
**615 Green Street, P.O. Box 830 (Court Station), 94553**
**Telephone: 510-229-1230 Fax: 510-229-1232**
**Stuart W. Willis; Judith E. Lawrence.**
**Criminal Trial Practice. Family, (Interstate Support-RURESA, UCCJA), Civil Litigation, Juvenile, Business, Personal Injury and Negligence Law.**
***See Professional Biographies, MARTINEZ, CALIFORNIA***

Wilner, Sarah Beth '55 '81 C.112 B.A. L.1065 J.D. Dep. Pub. Def.
Wyllie-Pletcher, Jennifer '68 '93 C.112 B.A. L.284 J.D.
Dir., BWA Legal Advocacy Prog.
Yamaguchi, Jon F. '61 '88 C.112 B.A. L.767 J.D. Dep. Dist. Atty.
Zichichi, Joseph T. '42 '69 C.112 A.B. L.1065 J.D. 1134 Alhambra Ave.

## MARYSVILLE, * 12,324, *Yuba Co.*

Anderson, David R., (BV) '47 '73 C.112 A.B. L.1067 J.D. [Sanders&A.]
**Berrier, Stephen W.**, (BV) '56 '84 C.112 B.S. L.464 J.D. [Rich,F.M.&I.]
*PRACTICE AREAS: Insurance Defense; Personal Injury; Insurance Coverage; General Litigation.
**Bordsen, Brant J.**, (CV) '55 '81 C.112 B.S. L.464 J.D. [Rich,F.M.&I.]
*PRACTICE AREAS: Civil Litigation; Landlord/Tenant; Bankruptcy; Land Use Planning; Municipal Law.
Castellanos, John J. '49 '80 C.1060 B.A. L.1026 J.D. Dep. Pub. Def.
Cook, Robert J. '23 '54 L.464 LL.B. P.O. Box 2447
Crall, Debra L. '65 '91 C.112 B.A. L.990 J.D. Dep. Pub. Def.
Curry, James L., (BV) '44 '75 C.147 B.A. L.464 J.D. 613 "D" St.
Davis, Eugene J., (BV) '48 '76 C.1060 A.B. L.464 J.D. 322 "B" St.
Dawson, James F. '40 '74 C.767 B.S.B.A. L.464 J.D. Mun. Ct. J.
Gee, Pauline W. '49 '77 C.112 B.A. L.1065 J.D.
Reg. Coun., Calif. Rural Legal Assistance
Gibbons, Frederick J. '37 '78 L.1026 LL.B. 501 "B" St.
Guthrie, Joel T., (BV) '39 '66 C.768 B.S. L.1065 LL.B. 425 "C" St.
Hadley, Harold D., (BV) '10 '41 C.273 L.904 LL.B. P.O. Box 1308
Hadley, Sheldon C., (CV) '52 '82 C.112 B.A. L.464 J.D. 230 Fifth St.
**Hall, Jill Ceruda** '64 '91 C&L.112 B.A., J.D. [Rich,F.M.&I.]
*LANGUAGES: Spanish.
*PRACTICE AREAS: Domestic Relations; Civil Litigation and Practice; Immigration.
Hennessy, Michael E. '42 '80 C.502 B.S. L.809 J.D. 1129 D. Street
Hewitt, Arthur E., (BV) '15 '38 C.999 L.1065 LL.B. [A.E.Hewitt]
Hewitt, Arthur E., Inc., A Prof. Corp., (BV) 716 D St.
Islip, Robert W., (BV) '37 '64 C.740 A.B. L.767 J.D. 630 B St.
**Iverson, Roland K., Jr.**, (BV) '42 '70 C.112 B.A. L.1065 J.D. [Rich,F.M.&I.]
*PRACTICE AREAS: Construction Law; Personal Injury; Products Liability (Plaintiff and Defendant); Medical Malpractice.
Johanson, Julise M. '54 '84 C.140 B.S. L.284 J.D. Calif. Rural Legal Assistance
Johnson, Keith C. '48 '83 C.347 B.A. L.770 J.D. Off. of Co. Coun.
**Lane, David R.**, (BV) '47 '73 C.147 B.A. L.1067 J.D. [Rich,F.M.&I.]
*PRACTICE AREAS: Civil Litigation; Criminal Law; Family Law.
Lee, Gina Osburn '66 '91 C.147 B.A. L.464 J.D. 423 4th St.
Lenhard, Robert C. '34 '62 C.112 A.B. L.1066 J.D. Supr. Ct. J.
Leri, Craig A., (CV) '48 '75 C.1074 B.A. L.285 J.D. 1101 D St.
Marquez, Arturo A., (CV) '46 '74 C.147 B.A. L.464 J.D. 306 B Street
Marquez, Roberto '62 '87 C.147 B.A. L.464 J.D. 1129 "D" Street
Mathews, Thomas F. '35 '69 C.767 B.S. L.1026 J.D. Supr. Ct. J.
McGrath, Patrick J. '56 '81 C.1060 B.A. L.464 J.D. Dep. Dist. Atty.
**Morris, Chester**, (AV) '32 '62 C.112 L.1065 J.D. [Rich,F.M.&I.]
*PRACTICE AREAS: General Tort & Insurance Litigation; Business Litigation; Medical & Legal Malpractice; Crop Damage Cases; Alternative Dispute Resolution.
Nash, John S., Jr. '51 '76 C.1077 B.A. L.809 J.D. Dep. Dist. Atty.

CALIFORNIA—MARYSVILLE MARTINDALE-HUBBELL LAW DIRECTORY 1997

O'Connor, Kathleen R., (CV) ... '47 '73 C.813 B.A. L.1067 J.D. Dep. Dist. Atty.
O'Rourke, Charles F. ... '45 '75 C&L.1049 Dist. Atty.
Orr, William R., (BV) ... '49 '78 C.347 L.1026 LL.B. Dep. County Coun.
Parker, H. Earl, Jr., (CV) ... '48 '77 C.549 B.S. L.464 J.D. P.O. Box 2441

**Rich, Fuidge, Morris & Iverson, Inc., (AV) BB**
**1129 D Street, P.O. Box "A", 95901**
**Telephone: 916-742-7371 Fax: 916-742-5982**
**William P. Rich (1880-1965); Richard H. Fuidge (1906-1976); Chester Morris; Roland K. Iverson, Jr.; David R. Lane (Certified Specialist, Family Law, The State Bar of California Board of Legal Specialization); Brant J. Bordsen; Stephen W. Berrier; Jill Ceruda Hall.**
**General Civil and Trial Practice. Corporation, Water Rights, Insurance, Real Estate, Crop Damage, Estate Planning, Family and Probate Law. Medical and Legal Malpractice, Personal Injury, Employment Law, Criminal Law, Alternative Dispute Resolution.**
**General Counsel: Linda Fire Protection District; City of Yuba City; County of Yuba; City of Live Oak.**
**Local Counsel: California State Automobile Assn.; State Farm Insurance Cos.**
***See Professional Biographies, MARYSVILLE, CALIFORNIA***

Robert, Jean-Baptiste ... '56 '92 C.112 B.A. L.426 J.D. Dep. Pub. Def.
Sager, Laurence J. ... '43 '80 C.1077 B.A. L.1095 J.D. Dep. Dist. Atty.
Sanbrook, John, (BV) ... '35 '60 C&L.770 B.A., J.D. 1129 D St., Drawer A
Sanders, Charles W., Jr., (CV) ... '46 '72 C.112 A.B. L.464 J.D. [Sanders&A.]
Sanders & Anderson, (BV) ... 716 D St.
Sasaki, Carolyn A. ... '60 '89 C.112 B.A. L.1026 J.D. Drawer 1512
Schoenig, Richd. A. ... '20 '50 C.112 A.B. L.1065 J.D. Ret. Supr. Ct. J.
Shaw, George C. ... '46 '80 C.1074 B.S.M.E. L.1136 J.D. 2312 Hammonton Rd.
Speck, Christian A. ... '63 '90 C.1074 B.S. L.1067 J.D. 1129 D St.
Wahlberg, D. Karl ... '35 '68 C.800 B.S. L.809 LL.B. 310 First St.
Wahlberg, Donna J. ... '53 '88 L.999 J.D. 310 1st St.
Wasilenko, David E. ... '46 '76 C.147 B.A. L.464 J.D. Mun. Ct. J.
Williams, Bartley C. ... '33 '65 C.768 B.A. L.767 LL.B. [Williams&W.]
Williams, Minna, (Mrs.) ... '39 '72 C&L.061 [Williams&W.]
Williams & Williams ... 320 4th St.

## MATHER, 4,885, *Sacramento Co.*

Bailey & Marzano, (AV) ... 3745 Whitehead St., Suite 5 (⊙Santa Monica)
Durham, J. Douglas, (AV) ... '51 '82 C.578 B.A. L.365 J.D. [A Bailey&M.]
Nelson, Stephen L., (AV) ... '47 '77 C&L.1137 B.S.L., J.D. [Bailey&M.]
Okun, Lori T. ... '61 '88 C.112 B.A. L.1067 J.D. [Yim,O.&W.]
Yim, Randall A., (BV) ... '52 '77 C.813 B.A. L.659 J.D. [Yim,O.&W.]
Yim, Okun & Watson, (BV) ... 3745 Whitehead St.

## MAYWOOD, 27,850, *Los Angeles Co.*

Flack, Milton W. ... '28 '55 C.112 A.B. L.426 LL.B. 5110 District Blvd.
Forde, E. Charles, (BV) ... '24 '48 C&L.800 B.A., LL.B. 4520 E. Slauson Ave.
Martinez, Manuel J. ... '52 '79 C.426 B.A. L.1068 J.D. H.U.D.

## McARTHUR, 21,661, *Lassen Co.*

Mc Alerney, Matthew J., (BV) ... '52 '77 C&L.770 B.A., J.D. 545-000 EMA LU Ln.

## McKINLEYVILLE, —, *Humboldt Co.*

Armstrong, Thomas K., (AV) ... '27 '60 C.679 B.S.E.E. L.800 J.D. 2720 Central Ave.
Wagner, Eris Hawley, (CV) ... '48 '83 C.330 B.A. L.1067 J.D. P.O. Box 2147

## MEADOW VISTA, —, *Placer Co.*

Calfee, David W. ... '21 '50 C.813 A.B. L.1065 J.D. 17201 Creek Side Dr.‡
Palenko, John M., (BV) ... '38 '74 L.1152 J.D. P.O. Box 1329

## MENDOCINO, —, *Mendocino Co.*

Ayres, Robert E. ... '37 '78 C.766 B.A. L.981 LL.B. P.O. Box 842‡
Bederman, Henriet T. '27 '76 C.339 B.A. L.46 J.D.
(adm. in IL; not adm. in CA) P.O. Box 1687‡
Cone, Allan E., (AV) ... '34 '57 C.339 A.B. L.813 LL.B. [Graham,C.M.&R.]
Files, Thomas T. ... '18 '49 C.112 B.S. L.813 J.D. 45101 Heeser Dr.‡
Graham, Anthony E., (BV) ... '46 '74 C.767 B.A. L.464 J.D. [Graham,C.M.&R.]
Graham, Cone, McKinney & Roberts, (AV) ... 45060 Ukiah St.
Graubard, Phoebe ... '43 '89 C.766 B.A. L.284 J.D. P.O. Box 4
Green, Karen ... '57 '89 L.061 LL.B. P.O. Box 1460
Hardy, John, (AV) ... '35 '65 C.112 A.B. L.1066 LL.B. 45160 Main St. (⊙San Francisco)
Jackson, James A. ... '56 '85 C.555 B.A. L.273 J.D. 45100 Main St.
Jones, Rodney R. ... '46 '71 C&L.800 A.B., J.D. P.O. Box 802
Lintott, Meredith J. ... '57 '85 C.112 B.A. L.61 J.D. 40560 Ukiah St.
McKinney, E. Melville, (AV) ... '39 '64 C.999 A.B. L.1065 J.D. [Graham,C.M.&R.]
O'Rourke, Margaret Mary, (BV) ... '47 '81 C.1073 B.A. L.284 J.D. 45160 Main St.
Roberts, Harvey L., Jr. ... '54 '84 C.1069 B.A. L.464 J.D. [Graham,C.M.&R.]
Rodseth, James D. ... '51 '88 C.1060 B.A. L.464 J.D. P.O. Box 1912

## MENLO PARK, 28,040, *San Mateo Co.*

Alexander, Myron D. ... '09 '33 C&L.597 B.S.L., J.D. 750 Menlo Ave.‡
Allen, Anthony M. ... '66 '92 C.976 B.A. L.1067 J.D. [A Gunderson D.S.V.F.&H.]
**Almirantearena, Evangelina** ... '63 '88 C.813 B.A. L.1066 J.D. [A Howrey&S.]
*LANGUAGES: Spanish.
*PRACTICE AREAS: Antitrust; Criminal Litigation.
Altman, Ronald E. ... '59 '84 [White&A.]
**Anagnostou, Stephanie A.** ... '67 '94 C.112 B.A. L.767 J.D. [A Cooley G.]
*PRACTICE AREAS: Corporate and Securities; Mergers and Acquisitions; Emerging Growth Companies; Venture Capital.
**Anderman, David J.** ... '69 '94 C&L.659 B.A., J.D. [A Orrick,H.&S.]
Aptekar, Joanna R. ... '68 '93 C.659 B.A. L.1068 2800 Sandhill Rd.
Arewa, Olufunmilayo (Funmi) B. '64 '95 C&L.309 A.B., J.D.
(adm. in NY; not adm. in CA) [A Gunderson D.S.V.F.&H.]
Arnheim, Ralph L. (Buddy), III '67 '92 C.659 B.S. L.339 J.D.
[A Gunderson D.S.V.F.&H.]

**Arnold, White & Durkee, A Professional Corporation, (AV) BB**
**155 Linfield Drive, 94025-3741⊙**
**Telephone: 415-614-4500 Facsimile: 415-614-4599**
**Email: info@awd.com URL: http://www.awd.com**
**Gerald P. Dodson; Glenn W. Rhodes; David L. Bilsker; James F. Valentine; Mark K. Dickson; Thomas C. Mavrakakis; Emily A. Evans; Erica D. Wilson; Karen J. Kramer (Not admitted in CA); John R. Moore (Not admitted in CA); Chun-Pok "Roger" Leung; David West; Daniel T. Shvodian.**
**Intellectual Property including Patent, Trademark, Copyright, Trade Secret, Unfair Competition, Licensing and Related Government Agency Proceedings, Antitrust and International Trade Matters. Trials and Appeals in Federal and State Courts.**
**Houston, Texas Office: 750 Bering Drive, 77057-2198; P.O. Box 4433, 77210-4433. Telephone: 713-787-1400. Facsimile: 713-789-2679. Telex: 79-0924.**
**Austin, Texas Office: 1900 One American Center, 600 Congress Avenue, 78701-3248. Telephone: 512-418-3000. Facsimile: 512-474-7577.**
**Arlington, Virginia Office: 2001 Jefferson Davis Highway, Suite 401, 22202-3604. Telephone: 703-415-1720. Facsimile: 703-415-1728.**
**Chicago, Illinois Office: 800 Quaker Tower, 321 North Clark Street, 60610-4714. Telephone: 312-744-0090. Facsimile: 312-755-4489.**

(This Listing Continued)

CAA380P

**Arnold, White & Durkee, A Professional Corporation (Continued)**
**Minneapolis, Minnesota Office: 4850 First Bank Place, 601 Second Avenue South, 55402-4320. Telephone: 612-321-2800. Facsimile: 612-321-9600.**
***See Professional Biographies, MENLO PARK, CALIFORNIA***

Aronstam, Kirk L. ... '47 '75 C.629 B.A. L.1049 J.D. 1075 Curtis St.
Arthur, Lynne Lampros ... '67 '92 C.276 B.A. L.770 J.D. 4400 Bohannon Dr.
**Bader, W. Reece**, (AV) ... '41 '67 C.951 B.A. L.228 J.D. [Orrick,H.&S.]
*PRACTICE AREAS: Securities; Commodities Law; Environmental Law.
**Baer, Marc H.** ... '64 '92 C.813 A.B. L.426 J.D. [A Clapp,M.B.D.&V.]
*LANGUAGES: French and Italian.
Baldwin, Patrick ... '50 '80 C.424 B.A. L.1065 J.D. 350 Sharon Park Dr.
**Barkan, David M.** ... '65 '92 C.309 A.B. L.1066 J.D. [A Fish&R.]
*PRACTICE AREAS: Patent Litigation.
Baroumand, Cynthia ... '66 '94 C.112 B.S. L.767 J.D. [A Gunderson D.S.V.F.&H.]
**Barr, Robert** ... '47 '74 C.453 S.B.E.E. L.94 J.D. [Weil,G.&M.] (See Pat. Sect.)
*PRACTICE AREAS: Intellectual Property.
**Barry, Patrick R.** ... '66 '95 C.176 B.A. L.1065 J.D. [Venture]
*PRACTICE AREAS: Corporate; Securities.
Barton, Reneé L. ... '62 '87 C.112 B.A. L.602 J.D. [A Gunderson D.S.V.F.&H.]
Bauer, Fred A. M. ... '52 '77 C&L.309 A.B., J.D. Raychem Corp.
**Bautista, John V.** ... '66 '91 C.112 B.A. L.309 J.D. [Venture]
*LANGUAGES: French and Spanish.
*PRACTICE AREAS: Corporate Law; Securities.
**Bauz, N. Thane** '63 '91 C&L.46 B.S.M.E., J.D.
(adm. in IL; not adm. in CA) [A Howrey&S.]
*PRACTICE AREAS: Intellectual Property Litigation; Patent Prosecution.
Bayer, Gary G. ... '42 '68 C.976 B.A. L.813 LL.B. 1326 Hoover St., #1
Beard, Brian K. ... '64 '90 C.339 B.A. L.352 J.D. [A Gunderson D.S.V.F.&H.]
**Becker, Daniel M.** ... '59 '95 C.309 B.A. L.813 J.D. [A Pennie&E.] (See Pat. Sect.)
*PRACTICE AREAS: Intellectual Property; Patent Law.
**Beckford, Joseph G.**, (AV) ... '37 '65•C.31 B.A. L.976 J.D. [Enterprise]
**Bellagamba, Robert A.**, (AV) ... '47 '73 C.112 B.A. L.765 J.D. [Clapp,M.B.D.&V.]⊙
Beltramo, John R. ... '35 '62 C.813 A.B. L.1065 J.D. Secy. & Gen. Mgr., Beltramo's Inc.
**Benz, William H.**, (AV) '42 '71 C.25 B.S.C. L.767 J.D.
[Burns,D.S.&M.] (See Pat. Sect.)

**Bergeson, Eliopoulos, Grady & Gray**
(See San Jose)

Berghouse, Jack D. ... '51 '81 C.1073 B.A. L.765 J.D. 1190 Chestnut St.
Bergquist, Joel R. '43 '68 C.951 B.A. L.477 J.D.
(adm. in NE; not adm. in CA) U.S. Geological Survey
Berrett, John R. ... '20 '49 C.878 B.S. L.813 LL.B. 699 Menlo Oaks Dr.‡
**Bertram, Bruce M.** '42 '79
C.1070 B.S. L.1095 J.D. Div. Pat. Coun., Raychem Corp. (Pat.)
Billings, Lucy J. '— '90 C.37 B.S. L.966 J.D.
(adm. in WI; not adm. in CA; Pat.) 2200 Sand Hill Rd.
**Bilsker, David L.** ... '62 '90 C.178 B.S.Ch.E. L.260 J.D. [Arnold,W.&D.] (See Pat. Sect.)
**Blawie, Elias J.** ... '58 '83 C.112 A.B. L.1066 J.D. [Venture]
*PRACTICE AREAS: Corporate Law; Securities.
**Bobrow, Jared** ... '62 '88 C.911 B.A. L.178 J.D. [Weil,G.&M.]
*PRACTICE AREAS: Intellectual Property Litigation.
Boenig, Leonard D. ... '25 '69 C.823 B.S. L.770 J.D. 28 Palm Ct.
**Boley, Leslie J.** ... '67 '96 C.112 B.A. L.146 J.D. [A Burns,D.S.&M.]
**Bonnel, Julie E.** ... '66 '94 C.770 B.S. L.767 J.D. [Clapp,M.B.D.&V.]
*PRACTICE AREAS: Personal Injury; Commercial Litigation.
**Bonwick, Catherine M.** ... '64 '90 C.436 B.S. L.813 J.D. Corp. Coun., Raychem Corp.
**Boom, Steve J.** ... '68 '94 C.813 B.S. L.309 J.D. [Venture]
*LANGUAGES: French, German and Spanish.
*PRACTICE AREAS: Corporate; Securities; Technology.
Borak, Peter W. ... '45 '76 C&L.813 A.B., J.D. 308 Santa Rita Ave.
**Borden, Gale Heuman** ... '57 '85 C.813 A.B. L.1067 J.D. [Schachter,K.O.&B.]
*PRACTICE AREAS: Labor and Employment Law and Litigation.
**Borovoy, Roger S.**, (AV) ... '35 '60 C.453 B.S. L.309 LL.B. [C Fish&R.] (See Pat. Sect.)
*PRACTICE AREAS: Intellectual Property; Patent.
**Boselli, Kathryn Louise**, (BV⑦) '57 '83
C.105 B.A. L.659 J.D. Corp. Coun., Raychem Corp.

**Boyarsky, Jeffery L., (BV) '47 '72 C.112 A.B. L.767 J.D.**
**Suite 200, 800 Oak Grove Avenue, 94025**
**Telephone: 415-325-7000**
**Criminal and Civil Trial Practice in all Courts. Misdemeanor and Felony, Criminal Appeals, Juvenile, Guardianship and Conservatorship Law.**
***See Professional Biographies, MENLO PARK, CALIFORNIA***

**Bozicevic, Karl**, (AV) ... '52 '78 C.861 B.S. L.1206 J.D. [Fish&R.] (See Pat. Sect.)
*PRACTICE AREAS: Medical Devices and Biotechnology; Cell and Molecular Biology; Biochemistry; Molecular Genetics; Biomedical Sciences.
Brady, Robert J., (BV) ... '42 '80 C.112 B.A. L.1231 J.D. 849 Menlo Ave.
Breckenridge, John P. ... '57 '82 C.813 B.A. L.1068 J.D. 2200 Sand Hill Rd.
**Bright, Earl A., II** ... '65 '93 C&L.623 B.S.M.E., J.D. [A Burns,D.S.&M.] (See Pat. Sect.)
**Brill, Wayland M.** ... '48 '77 C.813 B.A. L.1065 J.D. [Enterprise]
*PRACTICE AREAS: General Business Law; Securities Law; International Transactions; Joint Ventures; Mergers and Acquisitions.
Britton, Brent C.J. ... '66 '94 C.453 S.M. L.94 J.D. 2882 Sand Hill Rd.
**Brock, James Lee** ... '62 '87 C.154 B.A. L.145 J.D. [Venture]
*PRACTICE AREAS: Corporate Law; Securities; Mergers; Acquisitions.
**Brown, Arnold E., II** ... '67 '93 C.309 B.A. L.1066 J.D. [Venture]
*PRACTICE AREAS: Corporate and Securities; Entertainment Transactions.
**Brown, Dennis M.** ... '60 '86 C.112 B.A. L.770 J.D. [Littler,M.F.T.&M.]
**Brown, J. Melissa** ... '40 '81 C.972 B.S. L.813 J.D. Corp. Coun., Raychem Corp.
**Bruguera, Carolyn M.** ... '66 '93 C.309 A.B. L.1066 J.D. [Venture]
**Bucek, Michelle L.** ... '67 '95 C.1073 B.S. L.494 J.D. [A Littler,M.F.T.&M.]
Buechner, Paul E., III ... '28 '55 C.112 B.S. L.1066 LL.B. 530 Grace Dr.‡
**Burkard, Herbert G.** '34 '69 C.31 B.A. L.776 J.D.
Asst. Gen. Coun. & Corp. Pat. Coun., Raychem Corp. (Pat.)
*LANGUAGES: German and Spanish.
Burke, James H. ... '26 '55 C.112 L.1065 LL.B. 2420 Sandhill Rd.
**Burke, Melissa A.** ... '64 '94 C.309 A.B. L.1065 J.D. [A Pillsbury M.&S.]

**Burns, Doane, Swecker & Mathis, L.L.P., (AV)**
**Building 4, Suite 160, 3000 Sand Hill Road, 94025⊙**
**Telephone: 415-854-7400 Facsimile: 415-854-8275**
**Email: burnsdoane.com**
**Ralph L. Freeland, Jr.; James W. Peterson; Robert E. Krebs; T. Gene Dillahunty (Not admitted in CA); William H. Benz; Gerald F. Swiss. Associates: Michael J. Ure; Leslie A. Mooi; Earl A. Bright II; Charles H. Jew; Leslie J. Boley.**
**Patent, Trademark, Copyright, Trade, Unfair Competition and Related, Antitrust Law. Litigation. Practice before State and Federal Courts and U.S. International and Administrative Agencies.**
**Alexandria, Virginia Office: Suite 100, 699 Prince Street, 22314, P.O. Box 1404, 22313. Telephone: 703-836-6620. Facsimile: 703-836-2021; 836-7356; 836-3503; Group 4: 703-836-0028.**

(This Listing Continued)

**Burns, Doane, Swecker & Mathis, L.L.P. (Continued)**
**Research Triangle Park, North Carolina Office: P.O. Box 14846, Research Triangle Park, 27709-4846, 1009 Slatter Road, Suite 210, Durham, 27703. Telephone: 919-941-9240. Facsimile: 919-941-1515.**
*See Professional Biographies, MENLO PARK, CALIFORNIA*

Cahill, John M. .......................... '51 '82 C.112 B.A. L.765 J.D. 1190 Chestnut St.
**Cale, Edgar B. "Chip"** .......................'63 '92 C.659 B.A. L.1066 J.D. [Venture]
*PRACTICE AREAS: Corporate Law; Securities Law.
**Caraccio, L. William** .................'58 '86 C.112 B.A. L.1066 J.D. [Pillsbury M.&S.]
*PRACTICE AREAS: Securities Law; Mergers and Acquisitions Law; Corporate Law.
**Carlson, Alan B.**, (AV) '46 '72 C.112 B.A. L.1067 J.D.
[Littler,M.F.T.&M.] (⊙San Jose)
Cerrone, Kimberlie L. '52 '89 C.339 B.S. L.1065 J.D.
[⊠ Gunderson D.S.V.F.&H.] (Pat.)
Cervantez, Thomas J. ..................'64 '92 C.426 B.B.A. L.309 J.D. 2700 San Hill Rd.
**Chamberlin, Carl W.** .............'58 '85 C.813 A.B. L.1065 J.D. [⊠ Orrick,H.&S.]
**Chao, Bernard H.** ...... '65 '90 C.679 B.S.E.E. L.228 J.D. [⊠ Pennie&E.] (See Pat. Sect.)
*PRACTICE AREAS: Intellectual Property; Litigation.
**Chao, Yuan** ........'47 '87 C.813 B.S. L.770 J.D. Div. Pat. Coun., Raychem Corp. (Pat.)
*LANGUAGES: Chinese and Portuguese.
Chapman, Colin Daniel .........'59 '88 C.112 A.B. L.477 J.D. [Gunderson D.S.V.F.&H.]
Charlton, Clyde H. ...........'61 '86 C.605 B.A. L.767 J.D. 4400 Bohannon Dr., Ste. 100
Chavez, Paula N. ......................'55 '90 C.112 B.A. L.426 J.D. 2180 Sand Hill Rd.
Chen, Nancy M. ..............'68 '93 C.813 A.B. L.309 J.D. [⊠ Gunderson D.S.V.F.&H.]
**Cherensky, Steven S.** ...............'58 '93 C.367 B.S.E. L.1066 J.D. [⊠ Weil,G.&M.]
Chernick, Clifford Ross, (BV) ...........'46 '72 C.112 B.A. L.1065 J.D. 770 Menlo Ave.
Chielpegian, Michael Seymour '69 '96
C.7700 B.S. L.813 J.D. [⊠ Gunderson D.S.V.F.&H.]
Chillag, Nancy A. .........................'57 '83 C.347 A.B. L.770 J.D. 413 Willow Rd.
**Chinn, Cathryn S.** ...........................'57 '84 C&L.813 B.A., J.D. [Venture]
*PRACTICE AREAS: Corporate Law; Securities.
**Clapp, Duane E., Jr.**, (AV) ............ '43 '69 C.813 A.B. L.1065 J.D. [Clapp,M.B.D.&V.]

**Clapp, Moroney, Bellagamba, Davis and Vucinich, (AV)**
**4400 Bohannon Drive, Suite 100, 94025⊙**
**Telephone: 415-327-1300 Fax: 415-327-3707**
**Members of Firm: Duane E. Clapp, Jr.; Carl J. Moroney; Robert A. Bellagamba; Timothy C. Davis; Jeffrey M. Vucinich; Christopher W. Wood; Gregory J. Sebastinelli; Mark O'Connor; P. Christian Scheley; Donald L. Sullivan; Gregory C. Simonian; Jane A. Corning. Associates: Seth E. Watkins; Timothy L. Yoshida; Terilynn T. Perez; Bruce N. Furukawa; Andrew R. Pollack; L. Theodore Scheley, III; Marc H. Baer; Tracy C. Neistadt; Merrilee Hague; Robert L. Rosenthal; Carol J. Stair; Patricia Anna Kantor; Norman C. Escover; Steven M. Cvitanovic; James S. Thielmann; Julie E. Bonnel; Mary Kaela Kozlovsky; Dawson G. Crawford; Jessica L. Grant; Robert Shatzko; Mark L. Weaver; Paul V. Lankford; Daniela Davidian; Matthew A. Schenone.**
**General Insurance Law and Civil Trial Practice. Casualty Insurance (Automobile and Fire), Aviation, Professional Liability, Medical and Legal Malpractice Law. Real Estate and Insurance Liability (Agent Errors and Omissions), Construction Litigation, Environmental and Toxic Tort, Products Liability Law, Employment Discrimination, Wrongful Termination, Discrimination Law (Sex and Housing) Insurance Coverage, Declaratory Relief and Bad Faith Litigation.**
**Pleasanton, California Office: 6140 Stoneridge Mall Road, Suite 545. Telephone: 510-734-0990. Fax: 510-734-0888.**
**San Francisco, California Office: One Sansome Street, Suite 1900. Telephone: 415-398-6045. Fax: 415-327-3707.**
*See Professional Biographies, MENLO PARK, CALIFORNIA*

Clark, Michael J. ...............................'46 '71 C&L.767 B.S., J.D. 356 Hedge Rd.
Clasgens, Joseph H., III '48 '74 C.976 B.A. L.813 J.D.
Exec. V.P. & Dir., Brownson, Rehmus & Fosworth, Inc.
Claus, Rachel Lehmer ........ '44 '80 C.766 B.A. L.767 J.D. Univ. Coun., Standord Univ.
Cloud, Roger Allen '49 '89 C.260 B.S. L.770 J.D.
Sr. Coun., Intell. Prop., Informix Software., Inc.
**Clough, James P.** ...................'50 '76 C.1021 B.S. L.982 J.D. [Pillsbury M.&S.]
**Coats, William S.**, (AV) ..................'50 '80 C.767 A.B. L.1065 J.D. [Howrey&S.]
*PRACTICE AREAS: Intellectual Property; Licensing; General Litigation; Bankruptcy.
**Cobey, Christopher E.**, (AV) ...... '49 '74 C.813 B.A. L.1067 J.D. [Schachter,K.O.&B.]
*PRACTICE AREAS: Labor and Employment Law; Civil Litigation.

**Coddington, Hicks & Danforth, A Professional Corporation**
**(See Redwood City)**

**Cohn, Peter** .........................................'56 '82 C.112 B.S. L.1066 J.D. [Venture]
*PRACTICE AREAS: Securities; Mergers and Acquisitions; Venture Capital; Corporate.
Colburn, David M. ......................'59 '83 C.477 B.A. L.966 J.D. 2882 Sand Hill Rd.

**Cole, George S., (BV) '55 '81 C.813 A.B. L.477 J.D.**
**793 Nash Avenue, 94025**
**Telephone: 415-322-7760 Fax: 415-322-6117**
**Email: gscdlawyer@aol.com**
***PRACTICE AREAS: Computer Law; Intellectual Property.**
**Computer Law and Intellectual Property.**
*See Professional Biographies, MENLO PARK, CALIFORNIA*

**Collins, James P.**, (AV) ......................'52 '80 C.112 B.S. L.767 J.D. [O'Reilly&C.]
*PRACTICE AREAS: Plaintiff Personal Injury; Aviation; Products Liability; Medical Malpractice; Legal Malpractice.

**Cooley Godward LLP, (AV)**
**3000 Sand Hill Road, Building 3, Suite 230, 94025⊙**
**Telephone: 415-843-5000 Telex: 380816 COOLEY PA Fax: 415-854-2691**
**Email: webmaster@cooley.com URL: http://www.cooley.com**
**Members of Firm: Craig E. Dauchy; Eric C. Jensen; David R. Lee; Mark P. Tanoury. Special Counsel: John E. Cummerford. Associates: Stephanie A. Anagnostou; John A. Dado; Catherine A. Dring; Lawrence J. Fassler; Matthew P. Fisher (Not admitted in CA); James F. Fulton, Jr.; Vincent P. Pangrazio; Erika F. Rottenberg; Mark G. Seneker.**
**General Practice.**
**San Francisco, California Office: 20th Floor, One Maritime Plaza. Telephone: 415-693-2000. Telex: 380815 COOLEY SFO Fax: 415-951-3698 or 415-951-3699.**
**Palo Alto, California Office: Five Palo Alto Square, 3000 El Camino Real. Telephone: 415-843-5000. Telex: 380816 COOLEY PA Fax: 415-857-0663.**
**San Diego, California Office: 4365 Executive Drive, Suite 1100. Telephone: 619-550-6000. Fax: 619-453-3555.**
**Boulder, Colorado Office: 2595 Canyon Boulevard, Suite 250. Telephone: 303-546-4000. Fax: 303-546-4099.**
**Denver, Colorado Office: One Tabor Center, 1200 17th Street, Suite 2100. Telephone: 303-606-4800. Fax: 303-606-4899.**
*See Professional Biographies, MENLO PARK, CALIFORNIA*

**Corning, Jane A.** ...................'56 '82 C.169 B.A. L.464 J.D. [Clapp,M.B.D.&V.]
Cosgrove, John R., (AV) ................'31 '60 C&L.813 A.B., LL.B. 295 East Creek Dr.
**Cottle, Karen O.**, (AV) .......'49 '76 C.668 A.B. L.1066 J.D. Gen. Coun., Raychem Corp.
**Cotton, Patricia L.** ......................'66 '91 C.464 B.A. L.770 J.D. [Pillsbury M.&S.]
**Crandall, Nelson D.**, (BV) ......................'54 '79 C.112 A.B. L.1067 J.D. [Enterprise]
*PRACTICE AREAS: Corporate Law; Partnership Law; Limited Liability Companies; Securities Law; Business Law.
**Crawford, Dawson G.** ..................'67 '95 C.668 B.A. L.770 J.D. [Clapp,M.B.D.&V.]
*PRACTICE AREAS: Environmental Law; Toxic Tort; Products Liability; Auto; Construction Defect.
Craze, Charles E., (AV) .... '40 '73 C.401 B.S. L.1003 J.D. [Gibbs&C.] (⊙Seminole, FL.)

**Creager, Stephen E.** ........'53 '85 C.1331 B.A. L.976 J.D. Corp. Coun., Raychem Corp.
**Cummerford, John E.** ....................................'58 '84 C.36 B.A. L.178 J.D. [⊠ Cooley G.]
*LANGUAGES: Spanish.
*PRACTICE AREAS: Technology Law; Corporate.

**Curtis & Daschbach**
**(See Thoits, Love, Hershberger & McLean, Palo Alto, California)**

**Custalow, Amy L.** ......................................'68 '94 C.228 B.A. L.813 J.D. [Venture]
**Cvitanovic, Steven M.** ...................'67 '93 C.37 B.A. L.284 J.D. [Clapp,M.B.D.&V.]
*PRACTICE AREAS: Personal Injury; Construction.
**Dado, John A.** .........................................'62 '90 C&L.112 B.S., J.D. [⊠ Cooley G.]
*PRACTICE AREAS: Venture Capital; Emerging Companies.
**Daiuto, Brian J.** ........ '64 '95 C.8 B.S.E.E. L.1066 J.D. [⊠ Pennie&E.] (See Pat. Sect.)
*PRACTICE AREAS: Intellectual Property; Patent Prosecution; Patent Litigation.
Daley, Linda B. ..............'57 '84 C.813 A.B. L.1066 J.D. [⊠ Gunderson D.S.V.F.&H.]
**Danko, Michael** ........................'58 '83 C.197 A.B. L.893 J.D. [⊠ O'Reilly&C.]
*PRACTICE AREAS: Personal Injury/Wrongful Death; Business Litigation; Aviation Litigation; Environmental Litigation; Insurance Bad Faith.
Daschbach, Howard M., Jr., (AV) .........'24 '51 C.229 A.B. L.813 J.D. 1075 Curtis St.‡
**Dauchy, Craig E.** .......................................'49 '75 C.976 B.A. L.813 J.D. [Cooley G.]
*PRACTICE AREAS: Venture Capital Law; Emerging Company Law.
**Davidian, Daniela** ....................'69 '94 C.112 B.A. L.1049 J.D. [⊠ Clapp,M.B.D.&V.]
*PRACTICE AREAS: Civil Litigation.
Davis, Philippe G. ..............................'61 '90 C.112 B.A. L.770 J.D. 1075 Curtis St.
**Davis, Timothy C.**, (AV) ....................'46 '74 C&L.893 B.A., J.D. [Clapp,M.B.D.&V.]
Daye, Robert E., (BV) ............................'43 '69 C.549 B.A. L.767 J.D. 849 Menlo Ave.
Dearborn, Nancy Lawver ................'54 '79 C.103 B.A. L.846 J.D. Pres., Ivy Assocs.
**del Calvo, Jorge A.**, (AV) '55 '82 C.813 B.A. L.309 J.D.
[Pillsbury M.&S.] (⊙San Jose)
**Deming, Renée Raimondi** ............................'53 '81 C.813 A.B. L.1067 J.D. [Venture]
*PRACTICE AREAS: Tax; Employee Benefits.
**Derwin, Douglas K.** ........................'57 '83 C.112 B.A. L.309 J.D. [Weil,G.&M.]
*PRACTICE AREAS: Intellectual Property Law and Litigation; Commercial Litigation.
**De Stefano, Paul R.** ...........'50 '75 C.216 B.A. L.800 J.D. [Pennie&E.] (See Pat. Sect.)
*LANGUAGES: German and French.
*PRACTICE AREAS: Intellectual Property; International Transactional Work related to the Biological Sciences.
Dettmer, Scott C. ...................'57 '82 C.112 B.A. L.800 J.D. [Gunderson D.S.V.F.&H.]
Devine, William F., Jr. ............................'56 '90 C.197 B.A. L.94 J.D. 1052 Sonoma Pl.
Dibble, Ann E. ...............................'63 '89 C.659 B.S. L.1068 J.D. 2882 Sand Hill Rd.
**Dickson, Mark K.** ....... '55 '88 C.1196 B.S. L.326 J.D. [Arnold,W.&D.] (See Pat. Sect.)
Dillahunty, Mary Ann ............'49 '94 C.475 B.S. L.813 J.D. 3000 Sand Hill Rd. (Pat.)
**Dillahunty, T. Gene** '42 '69 C.612 B.S.Ch.E. L.273 J.D.
(adm. in VA; not adm. in CA; See Pat. Sect.) [Burns,D.S.&M.]
Dilworth, Lucienne F. ..........................'55 '89 C.112 B.A. L.813 J.D. 2700 San Hill Rd.
**Dodson, Gerald P.**, (AV) '47 '72
C.390 B.S.M.E. L.446 J.D. [Arnold,W.&D.] (See Pat. Sect.)

**Draeger, James M., (BV) '53 '80 C.670 B.A. L.765 J.D.**
**770 Menlo Avenue, Suite 101, 94025**
**Telephone: 415-324-0964 Fax: 415-327-0619**
**Real Estate Law; Estate Planning Law, Probate Law; Business Associations.**
**Representative Client: Draeger Supermarkets.**

Dran, Robert J. ............................................'47 '73 C.813 A.B. L.309 J.D. 2700 Sand Hill Rd.
**Dring, Catherine A.** ...........................'63 '91 C.112 B.S. L.800 J.D. [⊠ Cooley G.]
*PRACTICE AREAS: Corporate Law; Emerging Companies.
**Dunkley, Patrick H.** .........................'60 '90 C.768 B.S. L.770 J.D. [⊠ Pillsbury M.&S.]
**Dyer, Charles A.**, (AV) .............................'40 '71 C.502 B.J. L.1065 J.D. [Dyer&W.]

**Dyer & White, (AV) ⊞**
**Suite 200, 800 Oak Grove Avenue, 94025**
**Telephone: 415-325-7000 Fax: 415-325-3116**
**Members of Firm: Charles A. Dyer; Rand N. White.**
**Civil and Trial Practice. Personal Injury, Products Liability, Professional Negligence, Labor and Employment Law, Securities, Trade Secret and Corporate Litigation.**
*See Professional Biographies, MENLO PARK, CALIFORNIA*

Eastling, John R. ............................'—'80 C.309 A.B. L.494 J.D. Pres., Liticom Ltd.
**Efron, Boris E.**, (AV) ..................................'48 '78 C.628 B.S. L.61 J.D. [B.E.Efron]
*PRACTICE AREAS: Personal Injury Law; Insurance Law; Business Law.

**Efron, Boris E., A Professional Corporation, (AV)**
**3351 El Camino Real, Suite 200 (Atherton), 94027**
**Telephone: 415-369-1900 Telecopier: 415-363-1117**
**Boris E. Efron;—Karen M. Platt; Yani D. Sakel.**
**Languages: Russian, Greek and Korean.**
**General Civil and Trial Practice in State and Federal Courts. Personal Injury, Insurance, Business Litigation and Construction Law.**
*See Professional Biographies, MENLO PARK, CALIFORNIA*

**Egan, William J., III** ....... '47 '75 C.420 B.S.E.E. L.861 J.D. [Fish&R.] (See Pat. Sect.)
*PRACTICE AREAS: Intellectual Property; Patents; Trademarks; Copyrights; Trade Secrets.
**Eisler, Barry M.** '64 '89 C&L.188 B.A., J.D.
(adm. in PA; not adm. in CA) [⊠ Weil,G.&M.]
**Elliott, R. Hollis**, (BV) .....................'35 '63 C&L.813 A.B., J.D. [Flickinger&E.]
*PRACTICE AREAS: Civil Trial; Eminent Domain; Criminal; Family Law; Probate Law.
Emerick, Susan Peters .........................'46 '80 C.347 B.A. L.596 J.D. 420 Claire Pl.
**Enayati, Elizabeth F.** ..........................'60 '89 C&L.770 B.S., J.D. [Venture] (Pat.)
**Engers, Scott** '53 '79 C.112 B.A. L.770 J.D.
V.P. & Corp. Coun., Con-Way Transp. Servs., Inc.

**Enterprise Law Group, Inc., (AV) ⊞**
**Menlo Oaks Corporate Center, 4400 Bohannon Drive, Suite 280, 94025-1041**
**Telephone: 415-462-4700 Facsimile: 415-462-4747**
**Email: info@enterpriselaw.com**
**Wayland M. Brill; Nelson D. Crandall; Sherwood M. Sullivan; William B. Walker. Of Counsel: William D. Sauers; Thomas S. Jordan, Jr.; Joseph G. Beckford.**
**Business Transactional, Intellectual Property and Business Litigation, Practice Representing Domestic Technology Clients and Technology and Other Clients Headquartered Outside of the U.S.**
*See Professional Biographies, MENLO PARK, CALIFORNIA*

**Erickson, Sonya F.** .......................'65 '90 C.990 B.A./B.S. L.911 J.D. [Venture]⊙
*PRACTICE AREAS: Securities/Corporate Finance; Licensing; General Corporate.
**Ericson, William W.** ............................'58 '90 C.276 B.S.F.S. L.597 J.D. [Venture]⊙
*LANGUAGES: Japanese.
*PRACTICE AREAS: Business Transactions.
**Escover, Norman C.** ..........'64 '95 C.1074 B.S.ARCE L.767 J.D. [Clapp,M.B.D.&V.]
*PRACTICE AREAS: Construction Litigation; Civil Litigation.
**Esselstein, William D.**, (AV) ........'38 '69 C.870 B.S. L.1065 J.D. [Esselstein,W.J.&G.]
*PRACTICE AREAS: Local Government; Commercial Law; Civil Litigation.

**Esselstein, Wright, Jones & Greenberg, A Professional Corporation, (AV)**
**750 Menlo Avenue, Suite 250, 94025**
**Telephone: 415-614-0160 Fax: 415-321-0198**
**Kingsford F. Jones (1941-1996); William D. Esselstein; Timothy C. Wright (Certified Specialist, Family Law, The State Bar of California Board of Legal Specialization); Diane Stein Greenberg;—Susan D. Flax; Golnar Yazdi Moghimi.**

(This Listing Continued)

CALIFORNIA—MENLO PARK MARTINDALE-HUBBELL LAW DIRECTORY 1997

**Esselstein, Wright, Jones & Greenberg, A Professional Corporation (Continued)**
**Estate Planning, Trust Administration and Probate, Family Law Mediation and Litigation, Local Government Law, Real Property and Business Law, General Trial Practice.**
**References: Wells Fargo Bank, Menlo Park; Bank of America, Menlo Park.**
***See Professional Biographies, MENLO PARK, CALIFORNIA***

**Ettinger, Adam T.** ........ '66 '94 C.112 B.A. L.94 J.D. [[A] Pillsbury M.&S.]
*PRACTICE AREAS: Intellectual Property; Litigation; Corporate Transactions.
**Evans, Emily A.** ........ '60 '92 C.178 B.S. L.262 J.D. [[A] Arnold,W.&D.] (See Pat. Sect.)
Everett, Michael T. ........ '49 '75 C.197 A.B. L.659 J.D. Sr. V.P., Raychem Corp.

**Faisant, Robin D., (AV) '31 '58 C.336 B.A. L.813 J.D.** BB
**1550 El Camino Real, Suite 220, 94025**
**Telephone: 415-328-6333 Telecopier: 415-324-1031**
***PRACTICE AREAS: Estate Planning; Probate Law; Land Use Law.**
**Litigation in State and Federal Courts. Business, Land Use Law. Municipal, Planning and Zoning Law. Estate Planning, Wills, Trusts and Probate Law.**
***See Professional Biographies, MENLO PARK, CALIFORNIA***

**Farrell, Erin** ........ '67 '93 [[A] Orrick,H.&S.]
**Fassler, Lawrence J.** ........ '60 '91 C.112 B.S. L.178 J.D. [[A] Cooley G.]
*LANGUAGES: Italian, French.
*PRACTICE AREAS: Corporate; Mergers and Acquisitions; Securities; Partnerships; Licensing.
Feirman, Robert I. ........ '42 '68 C.563 B.B.A. L.1009 LL.B. The Fierman Corp.
Ferris, Robert A. ........ '42 '67 C.93 A.B. L.262 J.D. 3000 Sand Hill Rd., Bldg. 2‡
Field, Charles D., Jr. ........ '49 '85 C.813 B.A. L.770 J.D. 224 C Oak Court‡
Field, Winston L. ........ '08 '35 C.112 A.B. L.1066 J.D. 2325 Eastridge Ave.‡
Fielding, Judith L., (AV) ........ '38 '78 C.569 B.A. L.767 J.D. P.O. Box 718‡
**Filler, Andrew L.** ........ '66 '95 C.188 B.S.M.E. L.767 J.D. [[A] Weil,G.&M.]
**Finch, Laurel** '56 '94 C&L.813 B.A., J.D.
(adm. in AZ; not adm. in CA) [Venture]
*PRACTICE AREAS: Corporate Transactions; Securities Law; Private and Public Company Representation.

**Fish & Richardson P.C., (AV)** BB
**2200 Sand Hill Road Suite 100, 94025⊙**
**Telephone: 415-322-5070 Fax: 415-854-0875**
**Email: info@fr.com URL: http://www.fr.com**
**Frederick P. Fish (1855-1930); W.K. Richardson (1859-1951); James H. A. Pooley; Hans R. Troesch; John E. Gartman; John R. Schiffhauer; Karl Bozicevic; Jack L. Slobodin; William J. Egan, III; Reginald J. Suyat; Jodi L. Sutton. Of Counsel: Mark A. Lemley; Roger S. Borovoy;—Frank E. Scherkenbach; Shelley K. Wessels; Wayne P. Sobon; Howard G. Pollack; David M. Shaw (Not admitted in CA); David J. Goren; David M. Barkan; Mark D. Kirkland; Timothy A. Porter; Audrey M. Sugimura.**
**Intellectual Property Law: Trials, Transactions, Patents, Trademarks, Copyrights, Trade Secrets, Entertainment Law, Telecommunications Law, Drug and Medical Device and Antitrust Law.**
**Washington, D.C. Office: 601 13th Street, N.W. Telephone: 202-783-5070. Fax: 202-783-2331.**
**Houston, Texas Office: One Riverway, Suite 1200. Telephone: 713-629-5070. Fax: 713-629-7811.**
**Boston, Massachusetts Office: 225 Franklin Street. Telephone: 617-542-5070. Fax: 617-542-8906. Telex: 200154.**
**Minneapolis, Minnesota Office: Fish & Richardson P.C., P.A., 60 South Sixth Street, Suite 3300. Telephone: 612-335-5070. Fax: 612-288-9696.**
**La Jolla, California Office: 4225 Executive Square, Suite 1400. Telephone: 619-678-5070. Fax: 619-678-5099.**
**New York, N.Y. Office: 45 Rockefeller Plaza, Suite 2800. Telephone: 212-765-5070. Fax: 212-258-2291.**
***See Professional Biographies, MENLO PARK, CALIFORNIA***

**Fisher, Matthew P.** '62 '90 C.976 B.A. L.276 J.D.
(adm. in NY; not adm. in CA) [[A] Cooley G.]
*PRACTICE AREAS: Mergers and Acquisitions; Leveraged Buyouts; Venture Capital.
**Flax, Susan D.**, (BV) ........ '46 '84 C.741 B.A. L.284 J.D. [[A] Esselstein,W.J.&G.]
*PRACTICE AREAS: Family Law; Mediation.
**Flegel, John L.**, (BV) ........ '48 '73 C.154 B.A. L.770 J.D. [Jorgenson,S.M.&F.]
*PRACTICE AREAS: Litigation; Civil and Business Law.
**Flickinger, Chandler**, (BV) ........ '25 '59 C.37 B.S. L.813 J.D. [Flickinger&E.]
*LANGUAGES: German and Spanish.
*PRACTICE AREAS: Corporate; Real Property; Probate Law.

**Flickinger & Elliott, (BV)**
**841 Menlo Avenue, 94025-4771**
**Telephone: 415-321-8460 Fax: 415-321-8466**
**Members of Firm: Chandler Flickinger; R. Hollis Elliott.**
**General Civil and Trial Practice. Eminent Domain, Corporate, Real Property, Criminal, Family and Probate Law.**

Fotenos & Suttle, P.C., (AV) ........ 713 Santa Cruz Ave. (⊙San Francisco)
**Fourr, Robert C.**, (AV) ........ '47 '75 C&L.813 A.B., J.D. [Venture]
*LANGUAGES: German.
*PRACTICE AREAS: Intellectual Property.
**Fowler, Kathleen** ........ '60 '95 C.188 J.D. L.1065 J.D. [[A] Pennie&E.] (See Pat. Sect.)
*PRACTICE AREAS: Patent Prosecution; Opinion Work; Intellectual Property; Biotechnology.
Fox, Saul A. ........ '53 '78 C.831 B.S. L.659 J.D. 2800 Sand Hill Rd.
Frank, Robert E., (BV) '36 '64 C.1254 B.S. L.1026 LL.B.
1550 El Camino Real, Ste. 220
Franklin, Steven R. ........ '57 '84 C.339 B.S. L.813 J.D. [Gunderson D.S.V.F.&H.]
Free, Ledger D. ........ '21 '51 C.309 A.B. L.813 J.D. 970 Monte Rosa Dr.‡
**Freeland, Ralph L., Jr.**, (AV) '17 '47
C.813 B.A. L.273 J.D. [Burns,D.S.&M.] (See Pat. Sect.)
**Fulton, James F., Jr.** ........ '66 '95 C&L.276 B.S.F.S., J.D. [[A] Cooley G.]
*PRACTICE AREAS: General Corporate; Venture Capital; Securities Regulation.
**Furukawa, Bruce N.** ........ '65 '91 C.178 B.A. L.770 J.D. [[A] Clapp,M.B.D.&V.]
Garcia, David A. ........ '67 '92 C.813 A.B. L.309 J.D. 2800 Sandhill Rd.
**Gartman, John E.** ........ '60 '86 C&L.846 B.S., J.D. [Fish&R.]
*PRACTICE AREAS: Intellectual Property; Litigation and Counseling.
**Gavenman, Jon E.** ........ '67 '91 C.668 B.A. L.1065 J.D. [Venture]
*PRACTICE AREAS: Corporate Law; Securities.
Gelles, Henry '26 '55 C.823 B.S. L.982 J.D.
(adm. in NY; not adm. in CA) 2280 Eastridge Ave.‡
**Gerstner, Marguerite E.** '53 '93
C.732 B.S. L.770 J.D. Div. Pat. Coun., Raychem Corp. (Pat.)
Gibbs, Greta E. ........ '52 '87 C.352 B.A. L.1051 J.D. 2200 Sand Hill Rd.
Gibbs & Craze, P.A., (AV)
1550 El Camino Real, Suite 220 (⊙Seminole, FL, Cleveland, OH.)
Gilburne, Miles R., (AV) ........ '51 '75 C.674 A.B. L.309 J.D. 2882 Sand Hill Rd.
Glenn, Michael A., (AV) ........ '51 '80 C.37 B.S. L.1231 J.D. P.O. Box 7831 (Pat.)
Glynn, John W., Jr. ........ '40 '66 C.602 A.B. L.893 LL.B. 3000 Sandhill Rd., Bldg. 4
Goldberg, Nicole, (AV) '53 '77
C.112 B.A. L.1065 J.D. V.P. & Gen. Coun., Liposome Tech., Inc.
**Gordon, Laura A.** ........ '67 '92 C.112 B.A. L.813 J.D. [Venture]
*PRACTICE AREAS: Corporate Law; Securities.
**Goren, David J.** ........ '— '94 C.112 B.A. L.276 J.D. [[A] Fish&R.] (See Pat. Sect.)
*PRACTICE AREAS: Intellectual Property; Patents; Trademarks.
Goth, O. A. John, (AV) ........ '25 '52 C.112 A.B. L.1066 J.D. [Goth&S.]
Goth & Silvestri, A Professional Corporation, (AV) ........ 1010 El Camino Real

Goyle, Sanjoy K. '67 '93 C.228 B.A. L.94 J.D.
(adm. in CT; not adm. in CA) [[A] Gunderson D.S.V.F.&H.]
Grant, Frank Alexander, IV '70 '96 C.1064 B.A. L.813 J.D.
[[A] Gunderson D.S.V.F.&H.]
**Grant, Jessica L.** ........ '68 '95 C.112 B.A. L.767 J.D. [Clapp,M.B.D.&V.]
*PRACTICE AREAS: Personal Injury Defense; Coverage (Bad Faith); Environmental Toxic Tort.
Grant, William J. ........ '36 '69 C.912 B.S., Engr. L.1065 J.D. 15 Shasta Lane
**Green, Joshua L.**, (AV) ........ '56 '80 C.112 B.A. L.1068 J.D. [Venture]
*PRACTICE AREAS: General Securities Law; Emerging Growth Companies Law; Venture Capital Law.
**Greenberg, Diane Stein** ........ '47 '71 C.66 B.A. L.569 J.D. [Esselstein,W.J.&G.]
*PRACTICE AREAS: Estate Planning, Trust and Probate Law.
**Greenwald, Bradley A.** ........ '62 '93 C.352 B.A. L.309 J.D. [[A] Pennie&E.] (See Pat. Sect.)
*PRACTICE AREAS: Intellectual Property.
Gregg-Emery, Valeta A. ........ '52 '92 C.112 B.S. L.174 J.D. 2200 Sand Hill Rd. (Pat.)

**Gregory, John M., (BV) '47 '73 C.813 B.A. L.770 J.D.**
**1550 El Camino Real, Suite 220, 94025-4111**
**Telephone: 415-328-6335 Facsmile: 415-324-1031**
***PRACTICE AREAS: Products Liability Law (40%); Insurance Law (40%); Legal Malpractice Law (20%).**
**Litigation in State and Federal Courts.**
***See Professional Biographies, MENLO PARK, CALIFORNIA***

Grey, Richard G. '29 '80 C.112 M.B.A. L.767 J.D.
HMS Grp.-Venture Capital Investors
Growney, William E., Jr. ........ '70 '95 C.112 B.A. L.309 J.D. [[A] Gunderson D.S.V.F.&H.]
Gunderson, Robert V., Jr., (AV) '51 '79 C.378 A.B. L.145 J.D.
[Gunderson D.S.V.F.&H.]
Gunderson Dettmer Stough Villeneuve Franklin & Hachigian, LLP, (AV)
155 Constitution Dr.
**Guy, G. Hopkins, III** ........ '57 '82 C.893 B.S. L.692 J.D. [Orrick,H.&S.]
*PRACTICE AREAS: Intellectual Property Litigation; Patent and Trade Secret Litigation.
Hachigian, Jay K. ........ '58 '85 C.112 B.S. L.800 J.D. [Gunderson D.S.V.F.&H.]
**Hadidi, Frederick F.** ........ '67 '92 C.188 B.S.E.E. L.813 J.D. [[A] Pennie&E.] (See Pat. Sect.)
*PRACTICE AREAS: Intellectual Property; Patent Prosecution; Patent Litigation.
**Haffner, F. Kinsey**, (AV) ........ '48 '74 C&L.813 B.A., J.D. [Pillsbury M.&S.]
**Hague, Merrilee** ........ '66 '91 C.112 B.A. L.770 J.D. [[A] Clapp,M.B.D.&V.]
**Hall, Michael W.** ........ '48 '82 C.1078 B.A. L.1066 J.D. [Venture]
*PRACTICE AREAS: Corporate Law; Securities.
**Halluin, Albert P.** ........ '39 '70 C.420 B.A. L.64 J.D. [Pennie&E.] (See Pat. Sect.)
*PRACTICE AREAS: Intellectual Property.
**Halpern, Kenneth J.** ........ '66 '95 C.103 B.A. L.309 J.D. [[A] Orrick,H.&S.]
**Handley, Laura A.** ........ '63 '91 C.732 B.S. L.309 J.D. [[A] Weil,G.&M.]
Haverty, Alan W., (AV) ........ '33 '63 C.767 B.S. L.1065 J.D. 1260 Trinity Dr.
Healy, Timothy W. ........ '59 '86 C.112 A.B. L.767 J.D. 4400 Bohannon Dr.
Heibein, Alan N. '48 '75 C&L.107 B.A., J.D.
(adm. in NY; not adm. in CA) 725 Evergreen St.
**Heit, Warren S.** ........ '65 '90 C.860 B.S.E.E. L.262 J.D. [[A] Pennie&E.] (See Pat. Sect.)
*PRACTICE AREAS: Intellectual Property.
**Hendricks, Sharon** ........ '64 '92 C.228 A.B. L.145 J.D. [Venture]
*PRACTICE AREAS: Corporate Law; Securities.
**Hermle, Lynne C.** ........ '56 '81 C.112 B.A. L.1065 J.D. [Orrick,H.&S.]
*PRACTICE AREAS: Employment and General Litigation.
Hills-Walecka, B. Alison ........ '61 '89 C.112 B.A. L.767 J.D. 1795 Oak Ave.‡
**Hohenwarter, Catherine A.** ........ '63 '90 C.478 B.A. L.336 J.D. [[A] R.P.Kahn]
*PRACTICE AREAS: Personal Injury; Insurance Defense; Real Estate Litigation; Elder Abuse.
Holmes, Will ........ '92 '96 C.1068 B.A. L.767 J.D. [[A] Gunderson D.S.V.F.&H.]

**Howrey & Simon, (AV)**
**301 Ravenswood Avenue, 94025⊙**
**Telephone: 415-463-8100 Fax: 415-463-8400**
**Members of Firm: William S. Coats; Stephen J. Rosenman; Robert P. Taylor; Edwin H. Wheeler (Not admitted in CA). Resident Associates: Evangelina Almirantearena; N. Thane Bauz (Not admitted in CA); Christopher Kelley.**
**General and Trial Practice including Antitrust, Commercial Litigation, Corporate and Transactional, Environmental, Government Contracts, Insurance Coverage, Intellectual Property, International Trade, Products Liability, Securities Litigation, Supreme Court and Appellate and White Collar Criminal Defense.**
**Washington, D.C. Office: 1299 Pennsylvania Avenue, N.W., 20004-2402. Telephone: 202-783-0800. Fax: 202-383-6610.**
**Los Angeles, California Office: Suite 1400, 550 South Hope Street, 90071-2604. Telephone: 213-892-1800. Fax: 213-892-2300.**
***See Professional Biographies, MENLO PARK, CALIFORNIA***

**Hoyng, Charles F.** ........ '50 '89 C.473 B.S. L.1066 J.D. [[C] Pennie&E.] (See Pat. Sect.)
*PRACTICE AREAS: Licensing; Intellectual Property.
Hoyt, Elizabeth E. '45 '79
C.431 B.A. L.260 J.D. Asst. Gen. Coun., Informix Software., Inc.
**Huntwork, Vicki L.** ........ '65 '91 C.472 B.S. L.575 J.D. [[A] Pennie&E.] (See Pat. Sect.)
*PRACTICE AREAS: Intellectual Property; Corporate.
Ingebritsen, Samuel A. ........ '31 '58 C.966 B.B.A. L.996 LL.B. 1930 Camino A Los Cerros
**Ishimoto, Lance K.** ........ '59 '94 C.112 B.A. L.813 J.D. [[A] Pennie&E.] (See Pat. Sect.)
*PRACTICE AREAS: Intellectual Property.
**Jargiello, David M.** ........ '60 '89 C.930 B.A. L.1066 J.D. [Venture]
*PRACTICE AREAS: Corporate Law; Securities.
**Jensen, Eric C.** ........ '62 '88 C.813 A.B. L.1068 J.D. [Cooley G.]
*PRACTICE AREAS: Corporate and Securities Law; Venture Capital Law.
Jerome, Roy ........ '14 '49 C.112 A.B. L.813 LL.B. 1580 Middle Ave.‡
**Jew, Charles H.** ........ '56 '85 C.178 B.A. L.569 J.D. [[A] Burns,D.S.&M.] (See Pat. Sect.)
**Johnson, Craig W.**, (AV) ........ '46 '74 C.976 B.A. L.813 J.D. [Venture]
*PRACTICE AREAS: Corporate Law; Securities.
**Johnston, Frances** ........ '57 '94 C&L.813 B.A., J.D. [Venture]
*PRACTICE AREAS: Corporations; Securities.
**Jordan, Thomas S., Jr.**, (AV) ........ '33 '61 C.674 A.B. L.309 J.D. [[C] Enterprise]
*PRACTICE AREAS: Real Estate Law; Environmental Law.
**Jorgenson, John D.**, (AV) ........ '25 '51 C&L.813 A.B., LL.B. [Jorgenson,S.M.&F.]
*PRACTICE AREAS: Estate Planning; Probate and Trust Administration.

**Jorgenson, Siegel, McClure & Flegel, (AV)** BB
**Suite 210, 1100 Alma Street, 94025-3392**
**Telephone: 415-324-9300 Fax: 415-324-0227**
**Members of Firm: John D. Jorgenson; Marvin S. Siegel; William L. McClure; John L. Flegel; Margaret A. Sloan. Associates: Dan K. Siegel.**
**General Civil and Trial Practice, Estate Planning, Probate and Trust Administration, Business, Real Property, Land Use and Municipal Law.**
**Counsel for: City of Menlo Park.**
**References: Mid-Peninsula Bank (Palo Alto); Bank of America National Trust & Savings Assn.**
***See Professional Biographies, MENLO PARK, CALIFORNIA***

Joyce, William T. ........ '26 '53 C&L.767 LL.B. P.O. Box 674‡
Jung, Michael K. ........ '69 '96 C.1066 B.A. L.477 J.D. [[A] Gunderson D.S.V.F.&H.]
Kahn, Michelle D. ........ '58 '86 C.112 B.A. L.767 J.D. 2200 Sand Hill Rd.
**Kahn, Robert P., (P.C.)**, (AV) ........ '45 '69 C&L.945 B.A., J.D. [R.P.Kahn]
*PRACTICE AREAS: Personal Injury; Insurance Defense; Real Estate Litigation; Elder Abuse.

**Kahn, Robert P., A Prof. Corp., Law Offices of, (AV)**
**3351 El Camino Real, Suite 200 (Atherton), 94027**
**Telephone: 415-369-1900 Telecopier: 415-363-1117**
**Robert P. Kahn (P.C.);—Catherine A. Hohenwarter.**
**General Civil and Business and Construction Law, Trial Practice in all State and Federal Courts, Personal Injury, Insurance, Landslide and Subsidence, Products Liability Law, and Public Entity Defense Law. Elder Rights Law.**
***See Professional Biographies, MENLO PARK, CALIFORNIA***

**Kaile, Davina K.** .................... '— '94 C.813 A.B. L.276 J.D. [Ⓐ Pillsbury M.&S.]
**Kantor, Patricia Anna** ............ '71 '96 C.770 B.A. L.767 J.D. [Ⓐ Clapp,M.B.D.&V.]
*PRACTICE AREAS: Insurance Defense.
Karel, Steven '50 '80 C.813 B.S. L.309 J.D.
V.P., Gen. Coun. & Secy., Robert Half Intl. Inc.
Keeler, Davis E. '39 '66 C.608 B.A. L.597 J.D.
(adm. in IL; not adm. in CA) P.O. Box 772‡
**Keller, Donald M., Jr.** .......................... '57 '82 C.197 A.B. L.93 J.D. [Venture]
*PRACTICE AREAS: Corporate Law; Securities.
**Kelley, Christopher** .................. '63 '93 C.453 B.S.E.E. L.1068 J.D. [Ⓐ Howrey&S.]
Kelly, John M., (AV) '39 '66 C.112 B.S. L.1065 LL.B.
Exec. V.P. & Gen. Coun., SRI Intl.
Kendall, Cheryl Ann ... '— '90 C.112 B.A. L.770 J.D. Assoc. Coun., Robert Half Intl. Inc.
Kennedy, Michael Patrick ...... '69 '94 C.37 B.A. L.276 J.D. [Ⓐ Gunderson D.S.V.F.&H.]

**Kennelly, Dennis Lawrence, Law Office of, (BV) '48 '73 C.321 A.B. L.228 J.D.**
**1030 Curtis Street, Suite 200, 94025-4501**
**Telephone: 415-853-1291 Fax: 415-328-4715**
**Employment Law and General Civil Trial Practice.**
***See Professional Biographies, MENLO PARK, CALIFORNIA***

Kerwin, Melvin C., (BV) .................... '32 '62 C.908 A.B. L.1065 J.D. [Kerwin&K.]
Kerwin, Patrick C. .......................... '60 '87 C.112 B.A. L.1065 J.D. [Kerwin&K.]
Kerwin & Kerwin, (BV) ...................................................545 Middlefield Rd.
**Khare, Sanjay K.** ...................................... '67 '95 C.145 B.A. L.813 J.D. [Venture]
*PRACTICE AREAS: Corporate; Securities.
Kiem, Barbara J. ......................'47 '80 C.906 B.A. L.767 J.D. 1550 El Camino Real
Kieser, Chas. W. .......................... '18 '50 C.112 B.S. L.1065 J.D. P.O. Box 7616
**Kim, Edward Y.** ........................................ '67 '95 C.95 A.B. L.477 J.D. [Venture]
*PRACTICE AREAS: Corporate; Securities.
Kim, Nancy S. ...................'66 '90 C.112 B.A. L.1066 J.D. [Ⓐ Gunderson D.S.V.F.&H.]
**Kimball, Leslie Y.** ..........................'59 '87 C.1060 B.A. L.767 J.D. [Ⓐ Orrick,H.&S.]
**Kipnis, Jason D.** ..............................'67 '93 C.453 B.S. L.813 J.D. [Ⓐ Weil,G.&M.]
Kirk, Cassius L., Jr. .......................... '29 '55 C.813 A.B. L.1066 LL.B. 1330 University Dr.‡
**Kirkland, Mark D.** ........ '62 '94 C.602 B.S.E.E. L.770 J.D. [Ⓐ Fish&R.] (See Pat. Sect.)
*PRACTICE AREAS: Patent; Technology Licensing; Trademark; Copyright.
**Kleinman, Marlene S.** ............. '66 '91 C.112 B.A. L.494 J.D. [Ⓐ Littler,M.F.T.&M.]
**Kohler, Thomas D.** '61 '90 C.158 B.S.M.E. L.945 J.D.
(adm. in NY; not adm. in CA; See Pat. Sect.) [Ⓒ Pennie&E.]
*PRACTICE AREAS: Intellectual Property; Medical and Mechanical Patents; Patent Litigation.
**Kosanovich, Wendy** ......................'62 '96 C.683 B.A. L.1355 J.D. [Ⓐ Orrick,H.&S.]
**Kozlovsky, Mary Kaela** ................. '69 '94 C&L.770 B.S., J.D. [Clapp,M.B.D.&V.]
**Kramer, Karen J.** '64 '89 C.228 A.B. L.910 J.D.
(adm. in NY; not adm. in CA; See Pat. Sect.) [Ⓐ Arnold,W.&D.]
**Krebs, Robert E.** '43 '69 C&L.174 B.S., J.D.
[Burns,D.S.&M.] & [Ⓒ Pezzola&R.] (See Pat. Sect.)
Lafranchi, Robert J. ........................... '37 '73 C.770 B.Sc. L.767 J.D. 849 Menlo Ave.
Lampron, Shawn E. ............'57 '83 C.309 B.A. L.569 J.D. [Ⓒ Gunderson D.S.V.F.&H.]
**Landers, Amy L.** ........................ '60 '94 C.1213 B.F.A. L.1065 J.D. [Ⓐ Orrick,H.&S.]
**Lankford, Paul V.** .................. '69 '95 C.112 B.A. L.767 J.D. [Ⓐ Clapp,M.B.D.&V.]

**Latta, Kurt A., (BV) '43 '69 C.674 A.B. L.813 LL.B.**
**750 Menlo Avenue, Suite 250, 94025**
**Telephone: 415-324-0622 Fax: 415-322-8485**
***PRACTICE AREAS: Business Transactions; Real Estate; Taxation.**
**Business Practice (excluding Litigation) with emphasis on Transactions and Securities Law.**
***See Professional Biographies, MENLO PARK, CALIFORNIA***

Law, Benjamin B. ......................... '13 '38 C.506 L.1065 LL.B. 7 Campbell Lane‡
**Lee, David C.** ............................................. '63 '91 C.112 B.A. L.813 J.D. [Venture]
*LANGUAGES: Cantonese.
*PRACTICE AREAS: Corporate Law; Securities Law; Intellectual Property Law.
**Lee, David R.** .............................................. '57 '87 C.112 A.B. L.276 J.D. [Cooley G.]
*PRACTICE AREAS: Emerging Growth Companies; Corporate Law; Computer Law.
**Lee, Dennis Y.** ......... '64 '93 C.477 B.S.E.E. L.352 J.D. [Ⓐ Weil,G.&M.] (See Pat. Sect.)
**Lee, Michael D.** ......................... '70 '95 C.112 B.S. L.464 J.D. [Ⓐ Pillsbury M.&S.]
*LANGUAGES: Cantonese and Mandarin.
**Lee, Victor K.** '58 '96 C.908 B.Sc. L.1009 J.D.
(adm. in NY; not adm. in CA; See Pat. Sect.) [Ⓐ Pennie&E.]
*LANGUAGES: Chinese.
*PRACTICE AREAS: Biotechnology Patent Law; Intellectual Property.
**Lemkin, Jason M.** ........................................ '69 '96 C.309 B.A. L.1066 J.D. [Venture]
*PRACTICE AREAS: Corporate; Securities Law.
**Lemley, Mark A.** ................ '66 '91 C.813 A.B. L.112 J.D. [Ⓒ Fish&R.] (See Pat. Sect.)
*PRACTICE AREAS: Intellectual Property; Antitrust.
**Leung, Chun-Pok "Roger"** ...... '61 '95 C.1243 B.S.M.E. L.1066 J.D. [Ⓐ Arnold,W.&D.]
*LANGUAGES: Cantonese Chinese, Mandarin Chinese.
Lewis, Keith W. ......................................... '53 '80 C&L.767 B.A., J.D. 545 Middlefield Rd.
**Liburt, Joseph C.** ...................................... '65 '91 C.311 B.A. L.1066 J.D. [Ⓐ Orrick,H.&S.]
Likens, George B. ...................... '10 '34 C.813 A.B. L.767 LL.B. 321 Sherwood Way‡
**Lincoln, Sean A.** ...................................... '63 '88 C.1275 B.A. L.309 J.D. [Ⓐ Orrick,H.&S.]

**Littler, Mendelson, Fastiff, Tichy & Mathiason, A Professional Corporation, (AV)**
**750 Menlo Avenue, Suite 300, 94025⊙**
**Telephone: 415-326-5732 Facsimile: 415-326-1351**
**URL: http://www.littler.com**
**Resident Attorney: J. Richard Thesing; Alan B. Carlson; Brian T. McMillan; Dennis M. Brown;—Marlene S. Kleinman; Michelle L. Bucek.**
**Offices located in: California — Bakersfield, Fresno, Long Beach, Los Angeles, Oakland, Sacramento, San Diego, San Francisco, San Jose, Santa Maria, Santa Rosa and Stockton; Denver, Colorado; Washington, D.C.; Atlanta, Georgia; Baltimore, Maryland; Reno and Las Vegas, Nevada (a partnership with the Law Offices of Hicks & Walt); Morristown, New Jersey; New York, New York; and Dallas and Houston, Texas.**
***See Professional Biographies, MENLO PARK, CALIFORNIA***

LLoyd, David B. '56 '82 C.770 B.S. L.1065 B.S.
Chf. Admin. Offr., American Tech., Inc.
Long, Mark P. ..................'67 '95 C.37 B.A. L.477 J.D. [Ⓐ Gunderson D.S.V.F.&H.]
Luther, James ................................ '22 '58 C.352 B.Sc. L.813 LL.B. 750 Menlo Ave.‡
**Lyons, Michael J.** '66 '93 C.645 B.S. L.276 J.D.
(adm. in NY; not adm. in CA; See Pat. Sect.) [Ⓐ Pennie&E.]
*PRACTICE AREAS: Intellectual Property.
**MacMillan, Bruce E.** ........ '51 '81 C.112 B.A. L.1065 J.D. Corp. Coun., Raychem Corp.
**Manaster, Kenneth A.** ................ '42 '67 C&L.309 A.B., LL.B. [Ⓒ Pillsbury M.&S.]
**Mandel, SaraLynn** ......... '56 '84 C.112 B.A. L.678 J.D. [Ⓒ Pennie&E.] (See Pat. Sect.)
*PRACTICE AREAS: Intellectual Property; Biotechnology.
Mandelbrot, David R. .............. '67 '92 C.112 B.S.B.A. L.228 J.D. 2800 Sandhill Rd.
Margolis, Adele P., (BV) ....................... '60 '84 C&L.770 B.S., J.D. 183 E. Creek Dr.
Markham, James R. '66 '93 C.311 B.A. L.145 J.D.
(adm. in VA; not adm. in CA) [Ⓐ Gunderson D.S.V.F.&H.]
Martin, Elton F., (BV) ..................................... '17 '50 C.169 A.B. L.813 LL.B. 805 Wallea Dr.
**Martin, Katharine A.** .................. '62 '87 C.112 B.A. L.464 J.D. [Pillsbury M.&S.]
Martino, Paul G. ...............'69 '94 C.276 A.B. L.1066 J.D. [Ⓐ Gunderson D.S.V.F.&H.]
Matteson, Duncan L., Jr. ............ '58 '84 C.800 B.S. L.813 J.D. 1000 El Camino Real
**Mavrakakis, Thomas C.** '64 '94
C.667 B.S.E.E. L.724 J.D. [Ⓐ Arnold,W.&D.] (See Pat. Sect.)
Maynor, Donald H. ........................................'45 '74 C.37 B.A. L.930 J.D. [D.H.Maynor]
Maynor, Donald H., A Professional Law Corporation ...................3220 Alpine Rd.
McCandless, Jett A. ....... '57 '83 C.112 A.B. L.1065 J.D. Pres., McCandless Capital Corp.
**McClure, Alexandra** ......................... '69 '96 C.1074 B.A. L.770 J.D. [Ⓐ Orrick,H.&S.]
**McClure, William L., (BV)** .......... '52 '78 C.112 B.A. L.770 J.D. [Jorgenson,S.M.&F.]
*PRACTICE AREAS: Real Estate Law; Land Use Law; Business Law; Municipal Law.
McCormick, Thomas L. ................................ '44 '73 C.494 B.A. L.767 J.D. 1155 Crane St.
McCunn, Drummond F. ................................ '41 '74 C.813 B.S. L.765 J.D. 700 Harvard Ave.
McCusker, Anthony J. ..............'69 '95 C.112 B.A. L.1065 J.D. [Ⓐ Gunderson D.S.V.F.&H.]
McDonough, Louis E. ..................... '14 '38 C.178 A.B. L.1009 LL.B. 455 San Mateo Dr.‡
**McIntire, John P.** ........................................ '69 '94 C.154 B.A. L.976 J.D. [Venture]
*PRACTICE AREAS: Corporate Law.
**McMahon, Peter C.** ..................... '64 '92 C.446 B.A. L.128 J.D. [Ⓐ Orrick,H.&S.]
**McMahon, Terrence P., (BV)** ................ '50 '76 C&L.770 B.S.C., J.D. [Orrick,H.&S.]
*PRACTICE AREAS: Intellectual Property Litigation.
**McMillan, Brian T.** ..................... '57 '83 C.112 B.A. L.770 J.D. [Littler,M.F.T.&M.]
**Medearis, Mark A.** ........................................ '54 '79 C.174 B.S. L.813 J.D. [Venture]
*PRACTICE AREAS: Corporate Law; Securities; Intellectual Property.
**Mendelsohn, Susan R.** .......................'46 '80 C.645 B.S. L.767 J.D. [Ⓒ Pillsbury M.&S.]
Merchant, John C. ..................'64 '92 C.112 B.A. L.770 J.D. 4400 Bohannon Dr., Ste. 100
Michelson, Michael W. ...................... '51 '76 C&L.309 A.B., J.D. 2800 Sand Hill Rd.
**Miller, Keith A.** ........................................... '64 '93 C.101 B.A. L.145 J.D. [Venture]
*LANGUAGES: Japanese.
*PRACTICE AREAS: Corporate Securities; Technology Licensing.
**Miller, Lynn L.** ............................. '50 '74 C.112 B.A. L.1068 J.D. [Pillsbury M.&S.]
**Miller, Robert E., (AV)** ......................... '47 '72 C.367 B.A. L.846 J.D. [R.E.Miller]
*PRACTICE AREAS: Business Law.

**Miller, Robert E., Inc., A Professional Corporation, (AV) BR**
**1550 El Camino Real, Suite 220, 94025-4111**
**Telephone: 415-326-6135 Fax: 415-324-1031**
**Email: 73532.77@compuserve.com**
**Robert E. Miller.**
**Business Law.**
**Representative Clients: Aeroground, Inc.; Hussmann Corp.; International Scientific Products, Inc.; Space Power, Inc.; Tiburon Systems, Inc.; Walt & Company Communications, Inc.; Western Multiplex Corp.; Z-Tech Sales, Inc.**
***See Professional Biographies, MENLO PARK, CALIFORNIA***

Minalga, Maryanne ..........'63 '93 C.767 B.A. L.051 M.A. [Ⓐ Gunderson D.S.V.F.&H.]
Mitchell, Kimberly S. ......................'59 '83 C.813 A.B. L.1068 J.D. 75 La Loma Dr.
**Moghimi, Golnar Yazdi** ...........'66 '92 C.112 B.A. L.770 J.D. [Ⓐ Esselstein,W.J.&G.]
*LANGUAGES: Farsi and French.
*PRACTICE AREAS: Estate Planning, Trust and Probate Law.
**Monroe, Richard E.**, (AVⓉ) '43 '74 C.477 B.A. L.813 J.D.
(adm. in WA; not adm. in CA) [Venture]⊙
**Mooi, Leslie A.** ....... '59 '90 C&L.025 B.Sc., LL.B. [Ⓐ Burns,D.S.&M.] (See Pat. Sect.)
**Moore, Charles L.** .............................. '66 '96 C.871 B.S. L.1066 J.D. [Venture]
*PRACTICE AREAS: Corporate Law; Securities Law; Venture Capital Transactions; Technology Transactions.
**Moore, John R.** '64 '92 C&L.953 B.S., J.D.
(adm. in NY; not adm. in CA; See Pat. Sect.) [Arnold,W.&D.]
Moore, Walter T. ......................'63 '92 C.112 B.A. L.1065 J.D. 3000 Sand Hill Rd.
**Moroney, Carl J., (AV)** ............'42 '68 C.602 B.A. L.765 J.D. [Clapp,M.B.D.&V.]⊙
**Morrissey, Michael A.** ..............................'64 '92 C.813 B.A. L.1066 J.D. [Venture]
*PRACTICE AREAS: Corporate Law; Securities.
Mosbacher, R. Bruce ......................... '53 '79 C&L.813 B.A., J.D. 2200 Sand Hill Rd.
Moses, William P., (AV) ...........'17 '47 C.112 L.1065 LL.B. 1250 Sharon Park Dr. #60‡
**Nahm, Tae Hea** ........................................ '60 '85 C.309 A.B. L.145 J.D. [Venture]
*LANGUAGES: Korean.
*PRACTICE AREAS: Corporate Law; Securities.
**Nakagawa, Christine F.** ............. '65 '95 C.112 B.A. L.770 J.D. [Ⓐ Pillsbury M.&S.]
Nakata, Christine M. ..........'59 '95 C.112 B.A. L.767 J.D. [Ⓐ Gunderson D.S.V.F.&H.]
Narayan, Beverly Elaine .....'61 '87 C.112 B.A. L.1065 J.D. 4400 Bohannon Dr., Ste. 100
**Neistadt, Tracy C.** ............... '60 '89 C.112 B.A. L.1065 J.D. [Ⓐ Clapp,M.B.D.&V.]
Nelson, M. John ............................... '57 '87 C.768 B.S. L.770 J.D. 845 Oak Grove Ave.

**Newcomb, Brian W., (AV) '47 '73 C.560 B.A. L.1065 J.D.**
**770 Menlo Avenue, Suite 101, 94025**
**Telephone: 415-322-7780 Telefax: 415-327-0619**
**General Civil and Trial Practice. Business Litigation, Construction, Real Estate and Mechanics Lien Law.**
***See Professional Biographies, MENLO PARK, CALIFORNIA***

Newell, Carla S. ................'60 '85 C.145 B.A. L.477 J.D. [Gunderson D.S.V.F.&H.]
**Nguyen, Patrick P.** ...................... '66 '91 C.112 B.S. L.1068 J.D. [Ⓐ Weil,G.&M.]
Nibbi, Margaret E. ..........'61 '87 C.813 B.A. L.276 J.D. [Ⓐ Gunderson D.S.V.F.&H.]
Niehans, Daniel J., (AV) ........'49 '74 C.367 B.A. L.445 J.D. [Gunderson D.S.V.F.&H.]
Nolan, J. Michael '45 '72 C.712 B.A. L.276 J.D.
Sr. V.P., Gen. Coun. & Secy., Argonaut Ins. Co.
Norback, Ernest H., (AV) ................ '13 '50 C.112 L.767 LL.B. 1145 Rosefield Way‡
**Novack, Sheri M.** ... '60 '87 C.112 B.S. L.904 J.D. Div. Pat. Coun., Raychem Corp. (Pat.)
Nygren, Karl F. ............................................... '27 '50 C.209 L.145 J.D. [K.F.Nygren]
Nygren, Karl F., A Professional Corporation ..................................... 360 Encinal Ave.
**Ocker, Jonathan M.** ................... '53 '78 C.966 B.A. L.910 J.D. [Pillsbury M.&S.]
O'Connor, Daniel E. ...........'61 '90 C.112 B.S. L.1066 J.D. [Gunderson D.S.V.F.&H.]
**O'Connor, Mark** .................... '60 '86 C.436 B.A. L.770 J.D. [Clapp,M.B.D.&V.]
O'Donnell, Matthew C. .............. '55 '81 C.740 B.S.B.A. L.765 J.D. 1190 Chestnut St.
O'Donnell, Philip J. ........................ '22 '49 C&L.813 A.B., J.D. 510 Sand Hill Circle‡
Olson, Debra A. ................................ '52 '77 C.846 B.A. L.802 J.D. 937 Cotton St.
Olson, Perry V. '48 '75 C&L.966 B.B.A., J.D.
(adm. in WI; not adm. in CA) Dir., The Portola Grp., Inc.‡
**O'Reilly, Terry, (AV)** ...................... '45 '70 C.426 B.A. L.1066 J.D. [O'Reilly&C.]
*PRACTICE AREAS: Plaintiff Personal Injury; Aviation; Products Liability; Medical Malpractice; Legal Malpractice.

**O'Reilly & Collins, A Professional Corporation, (AV) BR**
**2500 Sand Hill Road, Suite 201, 94025**
**Telephone: 415-854-7700 Fax: 415-854-8350**
**Terry O'Reilly; James P. Collins;—James P. Tessier; Michael Danko.**

(This Listing Continued)

CALIFORNIA—MENLO PARK MARTINDALE-HUBBELL LAW DIRECTORY 1997

**O'Reilly & Collins, A Professional Corporation (Continued)**

**Civil Trial Practice. Plaintiff Personal Injury, Aviation, Products Liability, Medical and Legal Malpractice, Bad Faith and Consumer Fraud Law.**

***See Professional Biographies, MENLO PARK, CALIFORNIA***

**Orrick, Herrington & Sutcliffe LLP, (AV)**
**1020 Marsh Road, 94025⊙**
**Telephone: 415-833-7800 Telecopier: 415-614-7401**
**URL: http://www.orrick.com**
**Members of Firm: W. Reece Bader; G. Hopkins Guy, III; Lynne C. Hermle; Terrence P. McMahon; Christopher R. Ottenweller; Jon B. Streeter; Gary E. Weiss. Associates: David J. Anderman; Carl W. Chamberlin; Erin Farrell; Kenneth J. Halpern; Leslie Y. Kimball; Wendy Kosanovich; Amy L. Landers; Joseph C. Liburt; Sean A. Lincoln; Alexandra McClure; Peter C. McMahon; Matthew H. Poppe; Eve T. Saltman; Shelley J. Sandusky; Graeme Ellis Sharpe; Eric L. Wesenberg; Thomas H. Zellerbach. Los Angeles, California Members of Firm: Alan G. Benjamin; William W. Bothwell; Lori A. Bowman; William B. Campbell; Eugene J. Carron; Robert E. Freitas; Earl A. Glick; Todd E. Gordinier; Greg Harrington; W. Douglas Kari; Michael A. McAndrews; Richard C. Mendelson; Lawrence Peitzman; Gary D. Samson; Larry D. Sobel; Payne L. Templeton; Paul A. Webber; Howard J. Weg. Of Counsel: Jeffrey S. Allen; John P. Kreis; Mary H. Neale; Michael E. Silver. Associates: Ella L. Brown; Diana K. Chuang; Christopher L. Davis; Andrew D. Garelick; Margaret H. Gillespie; Owen P. Gross; Brett L. Healy; Victor Hsu; Alisa Jardine; Julie E. Knipstein; Linda S. Koffman; Scott G. Lawson; Victoria A. Levin; Douglas E. Love; Lisa Girand Mann; Paul T. Martin; Antonio D. Martini; Bradley Scott Miller; Melanie Murakami; William W. Oxley; Luan Phan; Georgiana Rosenkranz; Christopher S. Ruhland; John P. Sharkey; David B. Shemano; Bridgette M. Smith; Winnie Tsien; Bradley S. White. New York, New York Members of Firm: Paul B. Abramson; Charles W. Bradley; Bradford S. Breen; Peter R. Bucci; Charles N. Burger; Colman J. Burke; Fred C. Byers, Jr.; Richard Chirls; Katharine I. Crost; Bruce S. Cybul; Duncan N. Darrow; Michael Delikat; Edward M. De Sear; Rubi Finkelstein; Robert A. Fippinger; Lawrence B. Fisher; Adam W. Glass; Lawrence B. Goodwin; F. Susan Gottlieb; William A. Gray; Arnold Gulkowitz; Eileen B. Heitzler; Robyn A. Huffman; Laurence Bryan Isaacson; Robert M. Isackson; John J. Keohane; Alan M. Knoll; Peter J. Korda; Jeffrey A. Lenobel; Herbert J. Levine; Carl F. Lyon, Jr.; Daniel A. Mathews; Sam Scott Miller; Kathleen H. Moriarty; Barbara Moses; David Z. Nirenberg; Joshua E. Raff; Jill L. Rosenberg; Stephen K. Sawyier; Albert Simons, III; Louis H. Singer; Michael Voldstad; Richard Weidman; Neil T. Wolk. Special Counsel: Donald J. Robinson. Of Counsel: Stanley L. Amberg; Thomas Barr, IV; Susan L. Barry; Michael E. Emrich; William H. Horton, Jr.; John A. MacKerron; Robert B. Michel; Martin R. Miller; Amy Moskowitz; Richard H. Nicholls. Associates: Craig T. Beazer; Jonathan K. Bender; Thomas J. Benison; Leon J. Bijou; Colette Bonnard; Patti Lynn Boss; Eric R. Bothwell; Whitney R. Bradshaw; Karen M. Braun; Jarrett D. Bruhn; Juliet F. Buck; Benjamin C. Burkhart; Lawton M. Camp; Anthony Carabba, Jr.; Michael B. Carlinsky; Jennifer M. Clapp; Joseph M. Cohen; Caterina A. Conti; Robert A. Cote; Kyle W. Drefke; Joseph Evall; Marguerite J. Felsenfeld; Jeffrey J. Fessler; John D. Giansello, III; Michael A. Gilbert; Howard M. Goldwasser; Meryl A. Griff; Tzvi Hirshaut; Kiran J. Kamboj; René A. Kathawala; Joseph T. Kennedy; Jaemin Kim; Steven L. Kopp; Diane Krebs; Kenneth R. Linsk; Christopher Locke; Jonathan B. Lurvey; Michael D. Maline; Joseph E. Maloney; David A. Marple; Edward Mayfield; Lisa K. McClelland; Thomas N. McManus; James H. McQuade; Aimee B. Meltzer; Ronald Millet; Bradford E. Monks; Christopher J. Moore; C. Rochelle Moorehead; P. Quinn Moss; Bryan Jay Neilinger; William O'Brien; John F. Olsen; Edwin Gerard Oswald; Scott M. Pasternack; Marc J. Pensabene; Sheryl Lynn Pereira; Gail Pflederer; Nanci Prado; Ruth D. Raisfeld; Marlene Watts Reed; Marni J. Roder; Ira G. Rosenstein; Sidney M. Ruthenberg; Hooman Sabeti-Rahmati; David J. Sack; Al B. Sawyers; Martin L. Schmelkin; Patricia A. Seddon; William C. Seligman; Ronit Setton; Katherine A. Simmons; Corey A. Tessler; David M. Traitel; Sandra L. Tsang; Robert A. Villani; Steven I. Weinberger; Bradley E. Wolf; Michael J. Zeidel. Sacramento, California Members of Firm: R. Michael Bacon; Norman C. Hile; Perry E. Israel; Cynthia J. Larsen; Marc A. Levinson; Timothy J. Long; John R. Myers; Cynthia L. Remmers. Special Counsel: William E. Donovan. Of Counsel: E. Randolph Hooks; Iain Mickle. Associates: Jennifer P. Brown; Jordon Lee Burch; James T. Cahalan; Virginia M. Christianson; John P. Cook; William T. Darden; Stephen L. Davis; Edward P. Dudensing; Lynn T. Ernce; Eric J. Glassman; Kelcie M. Gosling; Trish Higgins; Christopher E. Krueger; Constance L. LeLouis; Kim Mueller; Charles W. Nugent; Andrew W. Stroud; Susan R. Thompson; Margaret Carew Toledo; Thomas J. Welsh. San Francisco, California Members of Firm: John E. Aguirre; William F. Alderman; Ralph H. Baxter, Jr.; Elaine R. Bayus; Daniel R. Bedford; Michael J. Bettinger; Steven A. Brick; Frederick Brown; Charles Cardall; Thomas Y. Coleman; Mary A. Collins; Dean E. Criddle; Roger L. Davis; Stanley J. Dirks; William M. Doyle; Raymond G. Ellis; Robert P. Feyer; Carlo S. Fowler; David S. Fries; Richard A. Gilbert; Robert J. Gloistein; Richard E. V. Harris; Richard D. Harroch; Gary A. Herrmann; Patricia K. Hershey; Richard I. Hiscocks; William L. Hoisington; Leslie P. Jay; John H. Kanberg; Lawrence T. Kane; Dana M. Ketcham; John H. Knox; Geoffrey P. Leonard; Mark R. Levie; Michael H. Liever; Peter Lillevand; Dora Mao; John E. McInerney, III; Michael R. Meyers; Thomas C. Mitchell; William G. Murray, Jr.; Noel W. Nellis; M. J. Pritchett; Greg R. Riddle; Marie B. Riehle; William L. Riley; Paul J. Sax; John F. Seegal; Thomas R. Shearer, Jr.; Gary R. Siniscalco; Richard V. Smith; Stephen A. Spitz; Alan Talkington; Ralph C. Walker; Jeffrey S. White; Kenneth G. Whyburn; Jeffrey D. Wohl; George G. Wolf; Cameron W. Wolfe, Jr.; George A. Yuhas. Of Counsel: Bruce S. Klafter; Philip C. Morgan; Catherine K. O'Connell; Douglas C. Sands; Samuel A. Sperry; Timothy P. Walker. Associates: Melody A. Barker; Pamela H. Bennett; Gregory D. Bibbes; Scott D. Blickenstaff; Paul C. Borden; Kerry Anne Bresnahan; Jessica L. Cahen; David Malcolm Carson; David J. Castillo; Kevin Shih-Chun Chou; Brett E. Cooper; Robert E. Curry, II; Mark Davis; Kirsten J. Day; Ana Marie del Rio; Mary Patricia Dooley; Scott D. Elliott; Gabriela Franco; David K. Gillis; Carlos E. Gonzalez; Mary Elizabeth Grant; Maria Gray; Adam J. Gutride; John M. Hartenstein; Dolph M. Hellman; Mats F. Hellsten; Tanya Herrera; Lynne T. Hirata; Laura A. Izon; Stephen J. Jackson, Jr.; Andrew P. Johnson; Daniel Judge; Susan R. Kelley; Hera Lie Kim; Thomas P. Klein; William J. Kramer; Kathleen Hughes Leak; Nancy M. Lee; Gary Louie; Ashley E. Lowe; Steven C. Malvey; Douglas D. Mandell; Karen L. Marangi; George P. Miller; James W. Miller Jr.; Genevieve M. Moore; Lowell D. Ness; Mark F. Parcella; Anthony B. Pearsall; David C. Ritchey; Peter E. Root; Christian J. Rowley; Paul I. Rubin; Dave A. Sanchez; Michelle W. Sexton; Usha Rengachary Smerdon; David Sobul; Lawrence N. Tonomura; Adrienne Diamant Weil; Stephen E. Whittaker. Singapore Member of Firm: William R. Campbell. Associates: Kenneth S. Aboud; M. Tamara Box; Nicholas Chan Kei Cheong; Bruce R. Schulberg; David Z. Vance; Eleanor Wong. Washington, D.C. Members of Firm: Cameron L. Cowan; Felicia B. Graham; Keith W. Kriebel; Lorraine S. McGowen; Paul Weiffenbach. Resident Of Counsel: David S. Katz; Dianne Loennig Stoddard. Associates: Michele E. Beasley; Mark S. Dola; Michael H. Freedman; Rohit H. Kirpalani; Douglas Madsen; Thomas D. Salus; Adam B. Tankel.**
**General Practice, including Corporate and Municipal Finance, Domestic and International Commercial Law, Banking and Commercial Finance, Project Finance, Structured Finance, Mergers and Acquisitions, Commercial Litigation, Insurance, Insurance Insolvency, White Collar Criminal Defense, Tax, Employee Benefits and Personal Estates, Antitrust, Distribution, and Trade Regulation, Intellectual Property, Real Estate, Environmental and Energy, Labor and Employment Law and Bankruptcy.**
**San Francisco, California Office: Old Federal Reserve Bank Building, 400 Sansome Street. Telephone: 415-392-1122. Telecopier: 415-773-5759.**
**Los Angeles, California Office: 777 South Figueroa Street. Telephone: 213-629-2020. Telecopier: 213-612-2499.**
**New York, New York Office: 666 Fifth Avenue. Telephone: 212-506-5000. Telecopier: 212-506-5151.**
**Sacramento, California Office: 400 Capitol Mall. Telephone: 916-447-9200. Telecopier: 916-329-4900.**
**Singapore Office: 10 Collyer Quay, #23-08 Ocean Building, Singapore. Telephone: 011-65-538-6116. Telecopier: 011-65-538-0606.**
**Washington, D.C. Office: Washington Harbour, 3050 K Street, N.W. Telephone: 202-339-8400. Telecopier: 202-339-8500.**

***See Professional Biographies, MENLO PARK, CALIFORNIA***

Ott, Charles W. ....................... '62 '88 C&L.494 B.S.B., J.D. 2700 Sand Hill Rd.
**Ottenweller, Christopher R.** ............... '48 '77 C.659 B.A. L.276 J.D. [Orrick,H.&S.]
*PRACTICE AREAS: Intellectual Property Litigation.
Palermo, Christopher J. ................ '64 '89 C.426 B.A. L.1065 J.D. 2200 Sand Hill Rd.
**Palmer, Kara Diane** ....................... '67 '93 C.112 B.A. L.1066 J.D. [Venture]⊙
*PRACTICE AREAS: Business and Technology; General Corporate Practice.
**Pangrazio, Vincent P.** ..................... '63 '93 C&L.426 B.S.E.E., J.D. [🄰 Cooley G.]
*PRACTICE AREAS: Securities; Emerging Growth Companies; Licensing.
**Park, Marina H.** ....................... '56 '82 C.112 B.A. L.477 J.D. [Pillsbury M.&S.]
**Pease, Ann M. Caviani** ..... '63 '95 C.966 B.S. L.813 J.D. [🄰 Pennie&E.] (See Pat. Sect.)
*PRACTICE AREAS: Intellectual Property.
Pederson, Lee M. '57 '92 C.494 B.S. L.1035 J.D.
(adm. in MN; not adm. in CA) Pat. Coord., Liposome Tech., Inc.

**Pennie & Edmonds LLP**
**2730 Sand Hill Road, 94025⊙**
**Telephone: 415-854-3660 Fax: 415-854-3694**
**Email: pennie.com URL: http://www.pennie.com**
**Resident Partners: Jon R. Stark; Paul R. De Stefano; Albert P. Halluin. Resident Counsel: Charles F. Hoyng; SaraLynn Mandell. Resident Associates: Thomas D. Kohler (Not admitted in CA); Warren S. Heit; Michael J. Lyons (Not admitted in CA); Bernard H. Chao; Frederick F. Hadidi; Victor K. Lee (Not admitted in CA); Lance K. Ishimoto; Mark R. Scadina; William L. Wang; Daniel M. Becker; Brian J. Daiuto; Kathleen Fowler; Ann M. Caviani Pease; Vicki L. Huntwork; Bradley A. Greenwald.**
**Intellectual Property and Technology Litigation including Patent, Trademark, Trade Secrets, Copyright and Unfair Competition Causes, Computer and Communication Law and Related Government Agency Proceedings, Licensing, Arbitration and International Trade Matters. Trials and Appeals in all Federal and State Courts.**
**New York, N.Y. Office: 1155 Avenue of the Americas. Telephone: 212-790-9090. Telex: (WUI) 66141-Pennie. Cable Address: "Penangold." Facsimile: GII/GII/GIII (212) 869-9741; GIII (212) 869-8864.**
**Washington, D.C. Office: 1667 K Street, N.W., Suite 1000. Telephone: 202-496-4400. Facsimile: 202-496-4444.**

***See Professional Biographies, MENLO PARK, CALIFORNIA***

**Perez, Terilynn T.** ................. '60 '87 C.112 B.S. L.770 J.D. [🄰 Clapp,M.B.D.&V.]
*LANGUAGES: Spanish.
Perret, Paul F. ................ '43 '75 C.597 B.S. L.813 J.D. 1177 Johnson St., Suite 200‡
**Peterson, James W.**, (AV) '44 '72
C.446 B.S. L.128 J.D. [Burns,D.S.&M.] (See Pat. Sect.)
Peterson, Sheila J. ...................... '— '89 C.768 B.S. L.770 J.D. 4400 Bohannon Dr.
**Pezzola, Stephen P.**, (AV) ............... '56 '81 C.112 B.S. L.1066 J.D. [Pezzola&R.]⊙
*PRACTICE AREAS: Business Planning; Corporate Law; Venture Capital Law; Healthcare Law; Non-Profit Representation.

**Pezzola & Reinke, A Professional Corporation, (AV)**
**Building 4, 3000 Sand Hill Road, Suite 160, 94025⊙**
**Telephone: 415-854-8797**
**Stephen P. Pezzola.**
**Corporate, Partnership, Emerging Growth Companies, Health Care, Mergers and Acquisitions, State and Federal Securities Law, Computer Law, Venture Capital, Intellectual Property, Real Estate, Nonprofit Representation and State, Federal and International Taxation.**
**Oakland, California Office: Suite 1300, Lake Merritt Plaza, 1999 Harrison Street, 94612, Telephone: 510-273-8750. Fax: 510-834-7440.**
**San Francisco, California Office: 650 California Street, 32nd Floor, 94111. Telephone: 415-989-9710.**

***See Professional Biographies, MENLO PARK, CALIFORNIA***

**Pickus, Joshua W. R.** ......................... '61 '86 C.674 A.B. L.145 J.D. [Venture]
*PRACTICE AREAS: Corporate Law; Securities; Intellectual Property.
**Pierson, Stanley F.** ........................... '59 '85 C.813 B.A. L.1068 J.D. [Venture]
*LANGUAGES: French and Portuguese.
*PRACTICE AREAS: Corporate; Securities.

**Pillsbury Madison & Sutro LLP, (AV)**
**2700 Sand Hill Road, 94025-7020⊙**
**Telephone: 415-233-4500 FAX: 415-233-4545**
**Members of Firm: James P. Clough; Jorge A. del Calvo; F. Kinsey Haffner; Katharine A. Martin; Lynn L. Miller; Jonathan M. Ocker; Marina H. Park; Scott T. Smith; Michael J. Sullivan; Allison M. Leopold Tilley; Georgia K. Van Zanten; Wayne M. Whitlock; Debra L. Zumwalt. Of Counsel: Kenneth A. Manaster. Senior Counsel: Susan R. Mendelsohn; Barbara R. Shufro; John S. Wesolowski. Associates: Melissa A. Burke; L. William Caraccio (Resident); Patricia L. Cotton; Patrick H. Dunkley; Adam T. Ettinger; Davina K. Kaile; Michael D. Lee; Christine F. Nakagawa; Betsy G. Stauffer; John E. Wood.**
**General Civil Practice and Litigation in all State and Federal Courts. Business: Banking and Corporate Finance; Commercial Transactions/Energy; Corporate, Securities and Technologies; Creditors' Rights and Bankruptcy; Employee Benefits; Employment and Labor Relations; Environment, Health & Safety; Estate Planning; Finance and Commercial Transactions; Food and Beverage Regulation; Health Care; Political Law; Real Estate; Tax (domestic and international); and Telecommunications. Litigation: Alternative Dispute Resolution; Antitrust/Trade Regulation; Appellate; Banking/Financial Institutions; Commercial Disputes; Construction/Real Estate; Creditors' Rights, Bankruptcy and Insurance Insolvency; Energy Matters; Employment/Equal Opportunity; Environmental/Land Use; ERISA; Insurance; Intellectual Property; Maritime/Admiralty; Media/Entertainment/Sports; Securities; Tort/Product Liability; and White Collar Defense. Intellectual Property: Aesthetic Design & Trade Dress Protection; Biotechnology; Computer Law; Copyright Law; Intellectual Property Audits and Strategic Planning; International Trade Commission; Licensing and Technology Transfer; Procurement of Property Rights; Patent Prosecution; Trade Secrets and Unfair Competition; Trademark Law; Interference Practice; Mechanical/Biomed/Aeronautical; and Physics/Optics.**
**Costa Mesa, California Office: Plaza Tower, Suite 1100, 600 Anton Boulevard, 92626. Telephone: 714-436-6800. Fax: 714-662-6999.**
**Los Angeles, California Office: Citicorp Plaza, 725 South Figueroa Street, Suite 1200, 90017. Telephone: 213-488-7100. Fax: 213-629-1033.**
**New York, New York Office: 520 Madison Avenue, 40th Floor, 10022. Telephone: 212-328-4810. Fax: 212-328-4824.**
**Sacramento, California Office: 400 Capitol Mall, Suite 1700, 95814. Telephone: 916-329-4700. Fax: 916-441-3583.**
**San Diego, California Office: 101 West Broadway, Suite 1800, 92101. Telephone: 619-234-5000. Fax: 619-236-1995.**
**San Francisco, California Office: 235 Montgomery Street, 94104. Telephone: 415-983-1000. Fax: 415-983-1200.**
**Washington, D. C. Office: 1100 New York Avenue, N.W., Ninth Floor, 20005. Telephone: 202-861-3000. Fax: 202-822-0944. 1050 Connecticut Avenue, N.W., Suite 1200, 20036-5303. Telephone: 202-887-0300. Fax: 202-296-7605.**
**Hong Kong Office: 6/F Asia Pacific Finance Tower, Citibank Plaza, 3 Garden Road, Central. Telephone: 011-852-2509-7100. Fax: 011-852-2509-7188.**
**Tokyo, Japan Office: Pillsbury Madison & Sutro, Gaikokuho Jimu Bengoshi Jimusho, 5th Floor, Samon Eleven Building, 3-1, Samon-cho, Shinjuku-ku, Tokyo 160 Japan. Telephone: 800-729-9830; 011-813-3354-3531. Fax: 011-813-3354-3534.**

***See Professional Biographies, MENLO PARK, CALIFORNIA***

Pitnick, Brian J. .................... '59 '84 C.1169 B.A. L.188 J.D. 3351 El Camino Real
Pizzoli, Maria L. ..................... '65 '93 C.112 B.A. L.1065 J.D. 2700 Sand Hill Rd.
**Platt, Karen M.**, (BV) .................... '51 '84 C.446 B.A. L.966 J.D. [🄰 B.E.Efron]
*PRACTICE AREAS: Personal Injury Law; Insurance Law; Real Estate Law.
Poggi, John J., Jr. ..................... '46 '74 C.674 A.B. L.659 J.D. 181 Constitution Dr.
**Pollack, Andrew R.** .............. '64 '90 C.112 B.A. L.770 J.D. [🄰 Clapp,M.B.D.&V.]
**Pollack, Howard G.** ......................... '66 '92 C.813 A.B. L.276 J.D. [🄰 Fish&R.]
*PRACTICE AREAS: Intellectual Property; Litigation; Patents; Computer Science.
Pollock, Donald W. '26 '51 C.872 L.221 LL.B.
(adm. in IA; not adm. in CA) 825 Olive St.
**Pooley, James H. A.**, (AV) ...................... '48 '73 C.390 B.A. L.178 J.D. [Fish&R.]
*PRACTICE AREAS: Intellectual Property; Litigation; Trade Secrets.
**Poppe, Matthew H.** ..................... '68 '95 C.813 A.B. L.145 J.D. [🄰 Orrick,H.&S.]
*LANGUAGES: French.
**Porter, Timothy A.** ....................... '65 '93 C.674 A.B. L.1066 J.D. [🄰 Fish&R.]
*PRACTICE AREAS: Patent Prosecution and Litigation.
**Potter, Scott P.** ............................. '68 '95 C.112 B.A. L.1066 J.D. [Venture]
*PRACTICE AREAS: Securities; General Corporate; Venture Capital.
**Powers, Matthew D.** ....................... '59 '82 C.597 B.S. L.309 J.D. [Weil,G.&M.]
*PRACTICE AREAS: Intellectual Property Law; International Litigation.
**Rader, Elizabeth H.** '65 '93 C.104 A.B. L.494 J.D.
(adm. in NY; not adm. in CA; See Pat. Sect.) [🄰 Weil,G.&M.]
Raissinia, Abdolreza ("Abdy") '62 '92
C.768 B.S.E.E. L.770 J.D. 4400 Bohannon Dr. (Pat.)

CAA384P

Ray, Steve R. .................. '56 '81 C&L.800 B.S., J.D. [🄲 Gunderson D.S.V.F.&H.]
**Reich, Ariel** .................. '61 '93 C.025 B.Sc. L.178 J.D. [🄰 Weil,G.&M.]
**Reines, Edward** .................. '63 '88 C.1044 B.A. L.178 J.D. [🄰 Weil,G.&M.]
**Reutens, Patrick G.** .................. '58 '91 C.061 B.Sc. L.976 J.D. [Venture]
*PRACTICE AREAS: Intellectual Property; Technology Development and Transfer.
**Rhodes, Glenn W.** ........ '56 '85 C.947 B.A. L.326 J.D. [Arnold,W.&D.] (See Pat. Sect.)

**Richardson, George B. '47 '73 C.674 B.A. L.813 J.D.**
**750 Menlo Avenue, Suite 250, 94025**
**Telephone: 415-614-0160 Fax: 415-321-0198**
**Email: DissoLawGR@aol.com**
***PRACTICE AREAS: Family Law; Pre-Marital Law; Dissolution; Post-Dissolution Matters. Litigation and Mediation Involving Family Law, Dissolution and Post-Dissolution Matters.**
***See Professional Biographies, MENLO PARK, CALIFORNIA***

**Risberg, Robert L., Jr.** '57 '90 C&L.966 B.S.E.E., J.D.
[🄰 Weil,G.&M.] (See Pat. Sect.)
Roberts, Bruce B., (BV) .................. '46 '74 C.112 B.S. L.284 J.D. 2200 Sand Hill Rd.
Robertson, Jack, (AV) .................. '16 '52 C.871 B.S. L.813 LL.B. 750 Menlo Ave.‡
**Robertson, John W.** '68 '95 C.228 A.B. L.893 J.D.
(adm. in WA; not adm. in CA) [Venture]⊙
*LANGUAGES: Mandarin.
*PRACTICE AREAS: Securities; Mergers and Acquisitions; Venture Capital; International Commercial Transactions.

**Robertson, Alexander, Luther, Esselstein, Shiells & Wright, A Professional Corporation**
**(See Esselstein, Wright, Jones & Greenberg, A Professional Corporation)**

**Robinson, Charles F.** ......... '57 '84 C.309 B.A. L.976 J.D. Corp. Coun., Raychem Corp.
*RESPONSIBILITIES: Financial Institutions and Real Estate Litigation.
**Rosenman, Stephen J.**, (AV) ...... '55 '80 C.453 B.S.E.E. L.273 J.D. [Howrey&S.] (Pat.)
*PRACTICE AREAS: International Trade; Intellectual Property.
**Rosenthal, Robert L.** .................. '66 '94 C.012 B.A. L.767 J.D. [Clapp,M.B.D.&V.]
*LANGUAGES: French.
Rothert, Harlow P., (AV) .................. '08 '37 C&L.813 A.B., LL.B. 2372 Branner Dr.‡
**Rottenberg, Erika F.** .................. '62 '92 C.1044 B.S. L.1066 J.D. [🄰 Cooley G.]
*PRACTICE AREAS: Employer-Employee Relations; Labor Law.
**Ruffin, Edmund S., Jr.** .................. '62 '90 C.846 B.A. L.945 J.D. [Venture]
*PRACTICE AREAS: Corporate Law; Mergers and Acquisitions; Securities.
Saffo, Paul L., III .................. '54 '81 C.309 A.B. L.813 J.D. IFTF
**Sakel, Yani D.** .................. '55 '89 C.768 B.A. L.770 J.D. [🄰 B.E.Efron]
*LANGUAGES: Greek.
*PRACTICE AREAS: Personal Injury Law; Insurance Law; Product Liability Law.
**Saltman, Eve T.** .................. '64 '90 C.188 B.A. L.276 J.D. [🄰 Orrick,H.&S.]
**Sandusky, Shelley J.** .................. '66 '91 C.813 A.B. L.1066 J.D. [🄰 Orrick,H.&S.]
**Saraceni, Paul M.** ......... '64 '92 C.105 B.S. L.575 J.D. [🄰 Weil,G.&M.] (See Pat. Sect.)
Sasaki, Linda A. .................. '63 '88 C.112 B.A.S. L.477 J.D. 2730 Sand Hill Rd.
**Sauers, William D.**, (AV) .................. '26 '53 C.267 A.B. L.813 J.D. [🄲 Enterprise]
*LANGUAGES: German.
*PRACTICE AREAS: Corporate Law; Business Law.
**Scadina, Mark R.** ...... '69 '94 C.770 B.S.E.E. L.1066 J.D. [🄰 Pennie&E.] (See Pat. Sect.)
*PRACTICE AREAS: Intellectual Property, Patent Litigation and Prosecution.

**Schachter, Kristoff, Orenstein & Berkowitz, L.L.P., (AV)**
**90 Middlefield Road, Suite 201, 94025⊙**
**Telephone: 415-473-1400 Telecopier: 415-463-0346**
**Gale Heuman Borden; Christopher E. Cobey.**
**Labor Relations and Employment Law and Litigation on Behalf of Employers. Legislative Law.**
**San Francisco, California Office: 505 Montgomery Street, 14th Floor. Telephone: 415-391-3333. Telecopier: 415-392-6589.**
**Sacramento, California Office: 980 9th Street, Suite 1760. Telephone: 916-442-3333. Telecopier: 916-442-2348.**
***See Professional Biographies, MENLO PARK, CALIFORNIA***

**Scheley, L. Theodore, III** ......... '62 '90 C.112 B.A. L.1026 J.D. [🄰 Clapp,M.B.D.&V.]
**Scheley, P. Christian** .................. '61 '86 C.112 B.A. L.464 J.D. [Clapp,M.B.D.&V.]
**Schenone, Matthew A.** .................. '91 '96 C.112 B.A. L.767 J.D. [🄰 Clapp,M.B.D.&V.]
**Scherkenbach, Frank E.** .................. '63 '90 C.813 B.S. L.309 J.D. [🄰 Fish&R.]
*PRACTICE AREAS: Intellectual Property; Litigation.
**Schiffhauer, John R.** .................. '59 '85 C.453 S.B. L.982 J.D. [Fish&R.] (See Pat. Sect.)
*PRACTICE AREAS: Intellectual Property; Litigation; Patents; Trademarks.
Schlegel, Frank G. .................. '30 '59 C&L.966 B.B.A., LL.B. 132 Stone Pine Ln.
Schmitz, Craig M. .................. '69 '94 C.112 B.A. L.1066 J.D. [🄰 Gunderson D.S.V.F.&H.]
**Sebastinelli, Gregory J.** .................. '57 '82 C&L.767 B.S., J.D. [Clapp,M.B.D.&V.]
Sellers, Cameron .................. '69 '95 C.112 B.S. L.1355 J.D. [🄰 Gunderson D.S.V.F.&H.]
**Sellers, John H.** .................. '66 '94 C.813 A.B. L.145 J.D. [Venture]
*PRACTICE AREAS: Corporate; Securities.
Semion, John W. .................. '46 '72 C&L.813 B.A., J.D. P.O. Box 569
**Seneker, Mark G.** .................. '68 '94 C.188 B.A. L.1068 J.D. [🄰 Cooley G.]
*PRACTICE AREAS: Venture Capital; Emerging Companies; Corporate Law.
**Shaffer, John C., Jr.**, (AV) .................. '43 '69 C.605 A.B. L.1066 J.D. [J.C.Shaffer,Jr.]
*PRACTICE AREAS: Labor and Employment; Personal Injury; Insurance Law.

**Shaffer, John C., Jr., A Prof. Law Corp., Law Offices of, (AV)**
**750 Menlo Avenue, Suite 250, 94025**
**Telephone: 415-324-0622 Fax: 415-321-0198**
**John C. Shaffer, Jr.**
**Civil Trial Practice. Labor Employment Law Issues including Discrimination, Sexual Harassment and Wrongful Termination from Employment, Business and Personal Injury Litigation, Insurance Bad Faith and Coverage Issues.**
***See Professional Biographies, MENLO PARK, CALIFORNIA***

**Sharpe, Graeme Ellis** .................. '66 '91 C.188 B.A. L.477 J.D. [🄰 Orrick,H.&S.]
Sharples, Kenneth K. '59 '92 C.164 A.B. L.262 J.D.
(adm. in NY; not adm. in CA; Pat.) 2730 Sand Hill Rd.
**Shatzko, Robert** .................. '64 '92 C.426 B.A. L.464 J.D. [Clapp,M.B.D.&V.]
*LANGUAGES: Japanese.
*PRACTICE AREAS: Civil Litigation.
**Shaw, David M.** '66 '92 C.576 B.S.Ch.E. L.228 J.D.
(adm. in NY; not adm. in CA; See Pat. Sect.) [🄰 Fish&R.]
*PRACTICE AREAS: Intellectual Property; Patents; Litigation.
Shea, Denise M. .................. '63 '87 C.813 A.B. L.1066 J.D. 2730 Sand Hill Rd.
Sheehy, Douglas T. .................. '66 '94 C.197 B.A. L.904 J.D. [🄰 Gunderson D.S.V.F.&H.]
**Sherman, Craig E.** '63 '90 C.813 A.B. L.309 J.D.
(adm. in NY; not adm. in CA) [Venture]⊙
*LANGUAGES: French, Italian, Spanish, Korean.
*PRACTICE AREAS: Corporate Finance; Securities.
Shiells, Leon E. .................. '27 '53 C&L.813 A.B., J.D. 750 Menlo Ave.‡
Shinn, Paul B. .................. '66 '95 [White&A.]
Shiraishi, Ann S. ...... '47 '88 C.312 B.Ed. L.770 J.D. Assoc. Coun., Robert Half Intl. Inc.
**Shufro, Barbara R.** .................. '57 '83 C.1307 B.A. L.588 J.D. [🄲 Pillsbury M.&S.]
**Shvodian, Daniel T.** .................. '65 '96 C.105 B.S.E.E. L.893 J.D. [🄰 Arnold,W.&D.]
**Siegel, Dan K.** .................. '67 '92 C.112 B.A. L.188 J.D. [🄰 Jorgenson,S.M.&F.]
**Siegel, Daniel R.** .................. '58 '83 C.103 B.S. L.178 J.D. [🄰 Weil,G.&M.]

**Siegel, Marvin S.**, (AV) .................. '36 '62 C.477 B.A. L.813 J.D. [Jorgenson,S.M.&F.]
*PRACTICE AREAS: Business Law; Estate Planning; Probate and Trust Administration.
**Silverman, Mark L.** .................. '64 '91 C.112 B.A. L.1068 J.D. [Venture]
Silvestri, Philip S., (AV) .................. '44 '70 C&L.767 B.A., J.D. [Goth&S.]
**Simonian, Gregory C.** .................. '59 '87 C.267 B.S. L.770 J.D. [Clapp,M.B.D.&V.]
**Sloan, Margaret A.** .................. '43 '79 C.228 B.A. L.813 J.D. [Jorgenson,S.M.&F.]
*PRACTICE AREAS: Real Estate Law; Land Use Law; Municipal Law.
**Slobodin, Jack L.**, (AV) ...... '35 '63 C.188 B.S. L.1066 LL.B. [Fish&R.] (See Pat. Sect.)
*PRACTICE AREAS: Civil Litigation; Patent Law; Intellectual Property Law.
**Smith, Scott T.** .................. '54 '81 C.1164 B.A. L.1066 J.D. [Pillsbury M.&S.]
Smithline, Todd P. .................. '68 '93 C.860 B.A. L.1068 J.D. [🄰 Gunderson D.S.V.F.&H.]
**Sobon, Wayne P.** ........ '62 '92 C.813 B.A.B.S. L.1066 J.D. [🄰 Fish&R.] (See Pat. Sect.)
*LANGUAGES: German.
*PRACTICE AREAS: Intellectual Property; Patents.
Solomon, Bradley A. .................. '63 '89 C.918 B.A. L.245 J.D. 600 Sharon Park Dr.
Soqui, Shannon .................. '67 '94 C.112 B.A. L.770 J.D. [🄰 Gunderson D.S.V.F.&H.]
Spanner, Robert A., (AV) .................. '48 '74 C&L.813 B.A., J.D. [R.A.Spanner]
Spanner, Robert A., A Prof. Corp., Law Offices of, (AV)
545 Middlefield Road, Suite 220
**Spataro, Carl L., Jr.** .................. '59 '96 C.880 M.B.A. L.813 J.D. [Venture]
*PRACTICE AREAS: Corporate Finance; Licensing.
Specker, Robert G. .................. '67 '93 C&L.112 B.A., J.D. [🄰 Gunderson D.S.V.F.&H.]
Sproat, Barbara J. '48 '77 C.604 A.B. L.818 J.D.
(adm. in MA; not adm. in CA) 754 Gilbert Ave.‡
Spurlock, Steven M. .................. '60 '89 C.112 A.B. L.1066 J.D. [Gunderson D.S.V.F.&H.]
**Stair, Carol J.** .................. '63 '93 C&L.770 B.A., J.D. [Clapp,M.B.D.&V.]
Stanley, David H. '46 '76 C.197 A.B. L.767 J.D.
V.P., Legal Gen. Coun. & Secy., Informix Corp.
**Stark, Jon R.** .................. '51 '82 C.560 B.S. L.813 J.D. [Pennie&E.] (See Pat. Sect.)
*PRACTICE AREAS: Intellectual Property; Litigation.
**Stauffer, Betsy G.** .................. '65 '90 C.747 B.A. L.494 J.D. [🄰 Pillsbury M.&S.]
Stone, David J. .................. '18 '48 C.309 M.B.A. L.813 LL.B. 217 Town & Country Vil.‡
Stough, Brooks, (AV) .................. '54 '80 C&L.813 B.A., J.D. [Gunderson D.S.V.F.&H.]
**Streeter, Jon B.** .................. '56 '81 C.813 A.B. L.1066 J.D. [Orrick,H.&S.]
*PRACTICE AREAS: Intellectual Property Litigation.
**Sugimura, Audrey M.** ......... '68 '94 C.112 B.A. L.276 J.D. [🄰 Fish&R.] (See Pat. Sect.)
*PRACTICE AREAS: Patent Prosecution.
**Sullivan, Donald L.** .................. '61 '87 C.112 B.A. L.770 J.D. [Clapp,M.B.D.&V.]
**Sullivan, Michael J.** ........ '59 '84 C.951 B.A. L.477 J.D. [Pillsbury M.&S.] (⊙San Fran)
**Sullivan, Sherwood M.**, (AV) .................. '32 '61 C&L.846 B.B.A., J.D. [Enterprise]
*REPORTED CASES: Shahvar v. Superior Court, 25 Cal. App. 4th 653, 30 Cal. Rptr. 2 597 (statements by attorney outside of court proceeding not privileged).
*PRACTICE AREAS: Litigation of Corporation and Shareholder and Partnership and Partner Relations; Commercial Litigation; Commercial Property Tax Litigation.
**Suto, Jeffrey Y.** .................. '61 '88 C.813 A.B. L.1068 J.D. [Venture]
*PRACTICE AREAS: Securities Law; General Corporate Law; Venture Capital Law.
Suttle, John C., (AV) .................. '46 '80 C.813 B.A. L.1065 J.D. [Fotenos&S.]⊙
**Sutton, Jodi L.** .................. '61 '88 C.813 B.A. L.878 J.D. [Fish&R.]
*PRACTICE AREAS: Intellectual Property; Litigation.
**Suyat, Reginald J.** .................. '46 '76 C.911 B.S. L.276 J.D. [Fish&R.] (See Pat. Sect.)
*PRACTICE AREAS: Intellectual Property.
**Swiss, Gerald F.** ......... '53 '81 C.602 B.S. L.776 J.D. [Burns,D.S.&M.] (See Pat. Sect.)
**Tanoury, Mark P.** .................. '54 '82 C.608 B.S. L.477 J.D. [Cooley G.]
*PRACTICE AREAS: Corporate Law; Partnerships; Venture Capital Law.
Taviss, Michael L. .................. '60 '91 C.453 B.S. L.150 J.D. [🄰 Gunderson D.S.V.F.&H.]
**Taylor, Robert P.**, (AV) .................. '39 '70 C.37 B.S.E.E. L.276 J.D. [Howrey&S.]
Tedrow, James W. .................. '21 '47 C&L.145 A.B., J.D. 344 Felton Dr.‡
Terman, Donna L. .... '54 '79 C.679 B.A. L.813 J.D. Exec. Dir., Walter S. Johnson Found.
**Tessier, James P.** .................. '62 '88 C.966 B.B.A. L.1066 J.D. [🄰 O'Reilly&C.]
*PRACTICE AREAS: Plaintiff Personal Injury; Aviation; Products Liability; Medical Malpractice; Legal Malpractice.
**Thesing, J. Richard**, (AV) '39 '67
C.426 B.S. L.813 LL.B. [Littler,M.F.T.&M.] (⊙San Francisco)
**Thielmann, James S.** .................. '65 '94 C.768 B.S. L.770 J.D. [Clapp,M.B.D.&V.]
*PRACTICE AREAS: Litigation; Defense; Medical Malpractice; Personal Injury.
Thornburgh, John W. ........ '65 '91 C.691 B.A. L.813 J.D. 2200 Sand Hill Rd., Suite 100
Thurston, Peter J., (BV) .................. '34 '72 C&L.800 B.A., J.D. 3000 Sand Hill Rd.
**Tilley, Allison M. Leopold** .................. '63 '88 C.112 B.A. L.1066 J.D. [Pillsbury M.&S.]
**Tobiason, Thomas H.** .................. '66 '92 C.103 A.B. L.477 J.D. [Venture]
*PRACTICE AREAS: Corporate; Securities.
**Tomomatsu, Christine A.** .................. '54 '90 C.878 B.A. L.1065 J.D. [Venture]
**Tonsfeldt, Steven J.** .................. '60 '87 C.352 B.B.A. L.1066 J.D. [Venture]
*PRACTICE AREAS: General Corporate Law; Securities Law; Banking Law.
Torrey, Lorin A. .................. '10 '41 C.597 B.S.C. L.424 J.D. 671 Oak Grove Ave.‡
**Troesch, Hans R.** .................. '49 '82 C.800 B.A. L.813 J.D. [Fish&R.] (See Pat. Sect.)
*PRACTICE AREAS: Intellectual Property; Patents; Copyrights; Trade Secrets.
**Ure, Michael J.** '60 '90 C.101 B.S.E.E. L.1184 J.D.
[🄰 Burns,D.S.&M.] (See Pat. Sect.)
*LANGUAGES: Mandarin Chinese.
**Valentine, James F.** '61 '90 C.608 B.S.E.E. L.424 J.D.
[Arnold,W.&D.] (See Pat. Sect.)
**VanBuskirk, Anne M.** .................. '65 '95 C.802 B.S.E.E. L.846 J.D. [🄰 Weil,G.&M.]
**Van Ligten, Glen R.** .................. '63 '90 C.112 B.S. L.1065 J.D. [Venture]
*PRACTICE AREAS: Securities Law; Corporate Law; Venture Capital Law; Intellectual Property Law.
Van Zandt, Peter J. .................. '61 '91 C.1168 B.A. L.765 J.D. 4400 Bohannon Dr.
**Van Zanten, Georgia K.** .................. '43 '84 C.906 B.A. L.770 J.D. [Pillsbury M.&S.]
Veltman, Ross B. .................. '54 '78 C.674 A.B. L.813 J.D. 1053 Sierra Dr.‡

**Venture Law Group, (AV)**
**2800 Sand Hill Road, 94025⊙**
**Telephone: 415-854-4488 Fax: 415-854-1121**
**URL: http://www.venlaw.com**
**Directors: Elias J. Blawie; James Lee Brock; Cathryn S. Chinn; William W. Ericson (Resident at Kirkland, Washington Office); Joshua L. Green; Michael W. Hall; Craig W. Johnson; Donald M. Keller, Jr.; Mark A. Medearis; Tae Hea Nahm; Joshua W. R. Pickus; Craig E. Sherman (Not admitted in CA; Resident at Kirkland Washington Office); Jeffrey Y. Suto; Steven J. Tonsfeldt; Mark B. Weeks; Mark Windfeld-Hansen; Robert v. W. Zipp. Senior Attorneys: John V. Bautista; Edgar B. "Chip" Cale; Peter Cohn; Renée Raimondi Deming; Elizabeth F. Enayati; Sonya F. Erickson (Resident at Kirkland, Washington Office); Jon E. Gavenman; Michael A. Morrissey; David C. Lee; Stanley F. Pierson; Patrick G. Reutens; Edmund S. Ruffin, Jr.; Mark L. Silverman; Glen R. Van Ligten. Attorneys: Patrick R. Barry; Steve J. Boom; Arnold E. Brown, II; Carolyn M. Bruguera; Amy L. Custalow; Laurel Finch (Not admitted in CA); Robert C. Fourr; Laura A. Gordon; Sharon Hendricks; David M. Jargiello; Frances Johnston; Sanjay K. Khare; Edward Y. Kim; Jason M. Lemkin; John P. McIntire; Keith A. Miller; Charles L. Moore; Kara Diane Palmer (Resident at Kirkland, Washington Office); Scott P. Potter; John W. Robertson (Not admitted in CA; Resident at Kirkland, Washington Office); John H. Sellers; Carl L. Spataro, Jr.; Thomas H. Tobiason; Christine A. Tomomatsu; Heayoon J. Woo; Deann K. Wright; Mitchell Stanton Zuklie. Of Counsel: Richard E. Monroe (Not admitted in CA; Resident at Kirkland, Washington Office).**
**Securities Law, Mergers and Acquisitions, Intellectual Property, Complex Corporate Transactions and Relationships.**

(This Listing Continued)

CALIFORNIA—MENLO PARK

MARTINDALE-HUBBELL LAW DIRECTORY 1997

**Venture Law Group (Continued)**

**Kirkland, Washington Office: 4750 Carillan Point, 7th Floor. Telephone: 206-739-8700. Fax: 206-739-8750.**

*See Professional Biographies, MENLO PARK, CALIFORNIA*

Victor, Marc B. ....... '51 '76 C.197 B.A. L.813 J.D. Pres., Litigation Risk Analysis, Inc.
Villeneuve, Thomas F. ....... '57 '83 C.1169 B.A. L.1066 J.D. [Gunderson D.S.V.F.&H.]
Vu, Nancy M. .......................... '68 '93 C.813 B.A. L.309 J.D. 2700 Sand Hill Rd.
**Vucinich, Jeffrey M.**, (BV) ........... '50 '75 C.813 B.S. L.765 J.D. [Clapp,M.B.D.&V.]
Walker, Patricia L. ...................... '47 '85 C.164 B.A. L.770 J.D. 300 Arlington Way
**Walker, William B.** ....... '35 '64 C.838 B.S.Ch.E. L.276 J.D. [Enterprise] (See Pat. Sect.)
*PRACTICE AREAS: Patent Law; Trademark; Copyright; Unfair Competition; Licensing.
**Wang, William L.** .... '65 '94 C.112 B.S.E.E. L.1066 J.D. [🄰 Pennie&E.] (See Pat. Sect.)
*PRACTICE AREAS: Intellectual Property; Patent Prosecution; Patent Litigation.
**Watkins, Seth E.** ................ '55 '91 C.1036 B.A. L.1065 J.D. [🄰 Clapp,M.B.D.&V.]
*LANGUAGES: Hebrew and French.
**Weaver, Mark L.** .................. '67 '95 C.763 B.S. L.284 J.D. [🄰 Clapp,M.B.D.&V.]
*PRACTICE AREAS: Construction Defect; Auto Insurance Defense.
**Weeks, Mark B.** .............................. '61 '87 C.951 B.A. L.770 J.D. [Venture]
*LANGUAGES: Japanese.
*PRACTICE AREAS: Corporate Law; Securities; Intellectual Property.
Weil, Arthur S. ........................... '50 '75 C.112 A.B. L.1065 J.D. 1100 Alma

**Weil, Gotshal & Manges LLP**
**A Limited Liability Partnership including Professional Corporations**
**Silicon Valley Office**
**2882 Sand Hill Road, Suite 280, 94025-7022⊙**
**Telephone: 415-926-6200 Telecopier: 415-854-3713**
**Resident Partners: Robert Barr; Jared Bobrow; Douglas K. Derwin (Resident); Matthew D. Powers (Resident). Resident Associates: Steven S. Cherensky; Barry M. Eisler (Not admitted in CA); Andrew L. Filler; Laura A. Handley; Jason D. Kipnis; Dennis Y. Lee; Patrick P. Nguyen; Elizabeth H. Rader (Not admitted in CA); Ariel Reich; Edward Reines; Robert L. Risberg, Jr.; Paul M. Saraceni; Daniel R. Siegel; Anne M. VanBuskirk; Peter A. Wenzel; Jack Yang.**
**General Practice.**
**New York, N.Y. Office: 767 Fifth Avenue. Telephone: 212-310-8000. Cable Address: "Wegoma". Telex: 424281; 423144. Telecopier: 212-310-8007.**
**Dallas, Texas Office: 100 Crescent Court, Suite 1300. Telephone: 214-746-7700. Fax: 214-746-7777.**
**Houston, Texas Office: 700 Louisiana Street, Suite 1600. Telephone: 713-546-5000. Telecopier: 713-224-9511.**
**Miami, Florida Office: 701 Brickell Avenue, Suite 2100. Telephone: 305-577-3100. Telecopier: 305-374-7159.**
**Washington, D.C. Office: 1615 L Street, N.W., Suite 700. Telephone: 202-682-7000. Telecopier: 202-857-0939; 857-0940. Telex: 440045.**
**Brussels, Belgium Office: 81 avenue Louise, Box 9-10, 1050 Brussels. Telephone: 011-32-2-543-7460. Telecopier: 011-32-2-543-7489.**
**Budapest, Hungary Office: Bank Center, Granite Tower, H-1944 Budapest. Telephone: 011 36 1 302-9100. Fax: 011 36 1 302-9110.**
**London, England Office: 99 Bishopsgate, London EC2M 3XD. Telephone: 44-171-426-1000. Telecopier: 44-171-426-0990.**
**Prague, Czechoslovakia Office: Charles Bridge Center, Krizovnicke nam. 1, 110 00 Prague 1, Czech Republic. Telephone: 011-42-2-24-09-73-00. Telecopier: 011-42-2-24-09-73-10.**
**Warsaw, Poland Office: ul. Zlota 44/46, 00-120 Warsaw. Telephone: 011-48-22-622-1300. Telecopier: 011-48-22-622-1301.**

*See Professional Biographies, MENLO PARK, CALIFORNIA*

**Weiss, Gary E.** ................................ '57 '84 C.188 B.A. L.178 J.D. [Orrick,H.&S.]
*PRACTICE AREAS: Securities and Intellectual Property Litigation.
**Wenzel, Peter A.** ......................... '65 '92 C.112 B.A. L.770 J.D. [🄰 Weil,G.&M.]
**Wesenberg, Eric L.** ..................... '60 '87 C.112 B.A. L.273 J.D. [🄰 Orrick,H.&S.]
**Wesolowski, John S.** ................ '48 '86 C.112 B.A. L.770 J.D. [🄲 Pillsbury M.&S.]
**Wessels, Shelley K.** ...................... '59 '91 C.623 B.A. L.813 J.D. [🄰 Fish&R.]
*PRACTICE AREAS: Intellectual Property; Litigation.
**West, David** .............................. '59 '96 C.768 B.A. L.813 J.D. [🄰 Arnold,W.&D.]
**Wheeler, Edwin H.** '57 '83 C.880 B.A. L.145 J.D.
(adm. in DC; not adm. in CA) [Howrey&S.]
*PRACTICE AREAS: Antitrust; Complex Litigation; Intellectual Property.
White, Mark Cameron ........................ '55 '88 C.705 B.A. L.1066 J.D. [White&A.]
**White, Rand N.**, (AV) ...................... '50 '76 C&L.813 B.A., LL.B. [Dyer&W.]
White & Altman ................................................ 750 Menlo Ave.
**Whitlock, Wayne M.** ...................... '55 '83 C.877 B.S. L.101 J.D. [Pillsbury M.&S.]
Wilcox, Jonathan J., (AV) ....... '43 '69 C.705 B.A. L.1066 J.D. Pres., Menai Corporation
Williams, Schuyler L., (AV) ........... '43 '78 C.228 B.A. L.767 J.D. 2700 Sand Hill Rd.
**Wilson, Erica D.** ...................... '62 '92 C.112 B.S.C.E. L.1065 J.D. [🄰 Arnold,W.&D.]
Wilson, Mark G. .... '48 '76 C.112 B.S. L.813 J.D. TVI Mgmt and August Capital Mgmt.
**Windfeld-Hansen, Mark** ........................ '56 '83 C.31 B.A. L.976 J.D. [Venture]
*PRACTICE AREAS: Tax.
Winnike, Sharon C. .............................. '55 '80 C.602 B.A. L.477 J.D. 1 Frederick Ct.
Wong, Alan C. ...................... '62 '89 C.813 A.B. L.1066 J.D. 2730 Sand Hill Rd.
**Woo, Heayoon J.** .............................. '64 '92 C.309 B.A. L.813 J.D. [Venture]
*LANGUAGES: Korean.
*PRACTICE AREAS: Corporate Securities; Intellectual Property Licensing.
**Wood, Christopher W.**, (BV) ....... '52 '79 C.659 B.A. L.1218 J.D. [Clapp,M.B.D.&V.]
**Wood, John E.** .......................... '65 '91 C.228 B.A. L.309 J.D. [🄰 Pillsbury M.&S.]
*LANGUAGES: German.
*PRACTICE AREAS: General Business; Corporate/Securities.
**Wright, Deann K.** ............................ '61 '92 C.966 B.S. L.1065 J.D. [Venture]
*PRACTICE AREAS: Corporate Law; Biotechnology; Emerging Growth Companies.
**Wright, Timothy C.**, (AV) .......... '40 '70 C.763 B.A. L.1188 J.D. [Esselstein,W.J.&G.]
*PRACTICE AREAS: Family Law; Civil Litigation.
**Yang, Jack** ............................................. '67 '92 C.67 B.S. [🄰 Weil,G.&M.]
Yao, David K. ........................ '66 '91 C.659 B.A.B.S. L.178 J.D. 2700 Sand Hill Rd.
Yee, Bennett Lyle ............... '64 '91 C&L.112 B.A., J.D. [🄰 Gunderson D.S.V.F.&H.]
Yelland, Janet S., (BV) ...................... '35 '83 C.763 A.B. L.999 J.D. 1301 Crane St.
**Yoshida, Timothy L.** ............. '55 '84 C.766 B.A. L.1065 J.D. [🄰 Clapp,M.B.D.&V.]
Young, David T. ................ '59 '85 C.937 B.A. L.309 J.D. [Gunderson D.S.V.F.&H.]
Younger, Maribeth ........................ '66 '94 C.473 B.A. L.309 J.D. 2800 Sand Hill Rd.
**Zellerbach, Thomas H.** .................. '49 '91 C.170 B.A. L.659 J.D. [🄰 Orrick,H.&S.]
**Zipp, Robert v. W.** ............................. '62 '88 C.839 B.A. L.228 J.D. [Venture]
*PRACTICE AREAS: Corporation Law.
**Zuklie, Mitchell Stanton** ...................... '69 '96 C.95 A.B. L.1066 J.D. [Venture]
*PRACTICE AREAS: Corporate Law; Securities.
**Zumwalt, Debra L.** .......................... '55 '79 C.36 B.S. L.813 J.D. [Pillsbury M.&S.]

## MENTONE, 5,675, *San Bernardino Co.*

Watson, Andrew A. ....................... '38 '79 C.37 B.A. L.809 J.D. 1820 Mentone Blvd.

## MERCED, * 56,216, *Merced Co.*

**Allen, Terry L., (P.C.)**, (AV) .................. '38 '64 C.1056 L.765 J.D. [Allen,P.P.&F.]
*PRACTICE AREAS: Personal Injury Law; Business Litigation and Criminal Law.

**Allen, Polgar, Proietti & Fagalde, (AV)** 🅱🅱
**A Partnership including a Professional Corporation**
**1640 "N" Street, Suite 200, P.O. Box 2184, 95344⊙**
**Telephone: 209-723-4372 Fax: 209-723-7397**

(This Listing Continued)

CAA386P

**Allen, Polgar, Proietti & Fagalde (Continued)**

**Members of Firm: Terry L. Allen (P.C.); Gary B. Polgar; Donald J. Proietti; Michael A. Fagalde; Jeffrey S. Kaufman; F. Dana Walton (Resident, Mariposa Office); Brian L. McCabe; Paul C. Lo.**
**General Civil and Criminal Trial Practice. Personal Injury, Wrongful Termination, Family Law, Corporation, Business, Condemnation, Taxation, Estate Planning, Probate, Real Property, Bankruptcy and Creditors' Rights Law.**
**Mariposa, California Office: 5079 Highway 140. P.O. Box 1907. Telephone: 209-966-3007. Fax: 209-742-6353.**

*See Professional Biographies, MERCED, CALIFORNIA*

Asturias, Daniel H., (BV) ...................... '46 '74 C&L.770 B.A., J.D. 650 W. 20th St.
Atkinson, Paul G. ........ '30 '90 C.1074 B.S. L.1132 J.D. Stoddard Bldg., 708 W. 20th St.
Barnett, James M., (BV) ................. '46 '72 C.112 B.A. L.1068 LL.B. Dep. Pub. Def.
Berrey, Allen R. ............................ '57 '85 C.112 B.S. L.464 J.D. Dep. Co. Coun.
Brantley, Samuel K., Jr., (CV) ............................ '11 '38 C.267 B.A. 557 W. 17th St.
Brown, Geraldine, (CV) .................... '46 '79 C.766 B.A. L.1189 J.D. 640 W. 20th St.
Brown, Marvin J., (BV) ................... '43 '71 C.768 B.A. L.770 LL.B. 720 W. 19th St.
**Browning, Corbett J.** ............ '62 '89 C.1239 B.A. L.923 J.D. [Flanagan,M.R.G.&C.]
*PRACTICE AREAS: Employment Law; Municipal Law; Civil Litigation.

**Brunn & Flynn, A Professional Corporation**
**(See Modesto)**

Bultena, David A., (CV) ...... '39 '72 C.112 B.A. L.1137 J.D. Supervising Dep. Dist. Atty.
Callister, Jerry E., (AV) ................ '42 '71 C.101 B.S. L.1066 J.D. [Callister,H.&C.]
Callister, Hendricks & Capron, A Professional Law Corporation, (AV) ..... 544 W. 20th St.
**Canelo, Adolph B., III**, (AV) ............ '25 '54 C.770 L.767 LL.B. [Canelo,H.W.W.&P.]
*PRACTICE AREAS: Personal Injury Law; Products Liability Law; Malpractice Law.

**Canelo, Hansen, Wilson, Wallace & Padron, Professional Corporation, (AV)**
**548 West 21st Street, P.O. Box 2165, 95344-0165**
**Telephone: 209-383-0720 Fax: 209-383-4213**
**Adolph B. Canelo, III; Ronald W. Hansen; Charles Rayburn Wilson; James H. Wilson; Rickey D. Wallace; James P. Padron; Shelly A. Seymour.**
**General Trial and Appellate Practice. Personal Injury, Workers Compensation, Business, Real Property, Partnership, Probate and Family Law.**

*See Professional Biographies, MERCED, CALIFORNIA*

Capron, David, (BV) ........................ '52 '80 C.112 A.B. L.101 J.D. [Callister,H.&C.]
Checketts, Blair H. ........................... '30 '71 C.1109 B.A. L.1137 J.D. 2222 M St.‡
Collins, Arthur R., (CV) ............................................ '43 '76 L.464 J.D. 655 W. 19th St.
Cone, Douglas B. ................................. '42 '85 C.878 B.S. L.1132 J.D. 2040 M. St.
Cook, Ralph J. ............................ '47 '73 C.1073 B.A. L.1065 J.D. Mun. Ct. Comr.
**Corman, Gerald W.**, (BV) ......... '48 '74 C.911 B.A. L.950 J.D. [Flanagan,M.R.G.&C.]
*PRACTICE AREAS: Family Law.
Courtney, Haven P., (CV) .................. '28 '56 C&L.813 A.B., LL.B. [Courtney&W.]
Courtney & Whiting, (CV) ............................................................. 928 W. 18th St.
**Crist, Kathleen** ............................... '64 '90 C.238 B.S. L.426 J.D. [Silveira,M.&L.]
*LANGUAGES: German.
*REPORTED CASES: Koch v. Hankins.
*PRACTICE AREAS: Securities Litigation; General Law; Commercial Litigation.
**Curry, Ben**, (AV) .............................. '23 '51 C.267 B.A. L.1065 J.D. [Curry&C.]
*REPORTED CASES: Merced Irrigation District v. Woolstenhulme 4 Cal.3d 478, 93 CR 833, 483 P.2d 1.
*PRACTICE AREAS: Estate Planning; Real Estate (Property) Law; Probate.
**Curry, Thomas M.** ............................. '65 '91 C.112 B.A. L.1065 J.D. [Curry&C.]
*PRACTICE AREAS: Estate Planning; Civil Litigation; Probate; Trusts; Criminal Defense.

**Curry and Curry, (AV)**
**530 West 21st Street, P.O. Box 2287, 95344-0287**
**Telephone: 209-722-8081 Facsimile: 209-722-5957**
**Thomas M. Curry; Ben Curry.**
**Estate Planning, Probate, Living Trusts, Wills, Trust and Estate Litigation, Asset Protection, Elder Law, General Civil Litigation, Personal Injury and Real Property Law.**

Dawson, Betty L., (BV) ...................... '48 '78 C.766 B.A. L.1065 J.D. [Haden&D.]
Deutsch, David E. '60 '90 C.1097 B.A. L.284 J.D.
Staff Atty., Central Calif. Legal Servs.
Dougherty, Frank ............................... '45 '77 C.398 B.A. L.1186 J.D. Mun. Ct. J.
**Fagalde, Michael A.**, (BV) .................. '53 '83 C.768 B.S. L.770 J.D. [Allen,P.P.&F.]⊙
*PRACTICE AREAS: Criminal Law; Employment Law; Family Law.
**Flanagan, Hugh M.**, (BV) '39 '71
C.679 B.S.M.E. L.426 J.D. [Flanagan,M.R.G.&C.] (Pat.)
*PRACTICE AREAS: Real Estate Law; Business Law; Landlord-Tenant Law.

**Flanagan, Mason, Robbins, Gnass & Corman, (BV)**
**3351 North "M" Street, Suite 100, P.O. Box 2067, 95344-0067**
**Telephone: 209-383-9334 Fax: 209-383-9386**
**Email: FMRGC@cell2000.com**
**Members of Firm: Hugh M. Flanagan; Michael L. Mason; Kenneth M. Robbins; William E. Gnass; Gerald W. Corman; Corbett J. Browning; Philip R. Golden (Certified Specialist, Estate Planning, Trust and Probate Law, The State Bar of California Board of Legal Specialization). Associates: Sharon E. Williams.**
**General Civil and Trial Practice. Real Estate, Business, Corporation, Family, Personal Injury, Estate Planning and Probate Law. Tax, Labor, Municipal, Water, Eminent Domain, Land Use/Zoning.**

*See Professional Biographies, MERCED, CALIFORNIA*

**Fromson, Paul D.**, (BV) ............. '46 '75 C.1042 B.A. L.61 J.D. [Tenenbaum,L.&F.]
*PRACTICE AREAS: Trial; Criminal Law; Family Law.
Galvin, Stephen P., (BV) ........... '13 '38 C.770 B.S. L.1066 LL.B. 627 W. Donna Dr.‡
**Gnass, William E.**, (BV) .......... '42 '72 C.280 B.S. L.1049 J.D. [Flanagan,M.R.G.&C.]
*SPECIAL AGENCIES: City of Waterford, City of Turlock, Madera Civil Service Commission.
*REPORTED CASES: Merced County Taxpayers' Association, et. al. v. County of Merced, et al., 218 Cal. App. 3d 396.
*PRACTICE AREAS: Land Use including CEQA; Municipal Law including Public Financing; Eminent Domain Law; Air and Water Quality.
**Golden, Philip R.** ................. '58 '85 C.813 A.B. L.770 J.D. [Flanagan,M.R.G.&C.]
*PRACTICE AREAS: Estate Planning; Trusts and Estates; Business Law.
Goul, Dudley J., (AV) ............................ '22 '51 C&L.813 B.A., LL.B. 530 W. 21st St.‡
Gwin, Melbourne N., Jr. ........................ '33 '77 C.131 B.A. L.1153 J.D. 2111 K St.
Haden, Robert H. ............................................. '19 '49 C&L.893 LL.B. 2241 N St.
Haden, Robert T., (CV) ....................................................... '46 '80 [Haden&D.]
Haden and Dawson, Professional Corporation, (BV) ................................ 2241 N St.
**Hansen, Ronald W.**, (AV) ............... '47 '72 C&L.770 B.A., J.D. [Canelo,H.W.W.&P.]
*REPORTED CASES: Irwin v. Irwin, G9 CA 3d 317 (1977); Segoviano v. Housing Authority, 143 CA3d 162 (1983).
*PRACTICE AREAS: Personal Injury Law; Probate Law; Business Litigation.
Hendricks, Bruce J., (BV) ................. '45 '73 C.101 B.S. L.767 J.D. [Callister,H.&C.]
Hider, Michael S. ................................ '36 '73 C.151 B.S. L.770 J.D. Supr. Ct. J.
Howard, Roland V., Sr. ................ '37 '64 C.112 A.B. L.1065 LL.B. 708 W. 20th St.
Ivey, William T. .............................. '28 '58 C.790 A.B. L.273 LL.B. Supr. Ct. J.
Jacobs, Harry L., (BV) ................ '45 '78 C.767 B.A. L.1026 J.D. P.O. Box 3904
Kathka, Alvin R. ................................ '50 '77 C.1079 B.A. L.464 J.D. Pub. Def. III
**Kaufman, Jeffrey S.** ...................... '60 '86 C.112 B.A. L.1065 J.D. [Allen,P.P.&F.]
*PRACTICE AREAS: Real Property Law; Business Transactions; Business Litigation.
Kelley, Ann L., (CV) ................................................ '41 '82 L.770 J.D. 2040 "M" St.

**Kimble, MacMichael & Upton, A Professional Corporation**
**(See Fresno)**

**King, Keith C., (BV) '31 '61 C.112 B.A. L.1066 J.D.**
**510 West 21st Street, 95340**
**Telephone: 209-722-5746 Fax: 209-725-0803**
**(Certified Specialist, Estate Planning, Trust and Probate Law, The State Bar of California Board of Legal Specialization).**
***PRACTICE AREAS: Estate Planning and Probate; Trusts; Business Law; Conservatorships; Will Contests.**
**Estate Planning, Trust and Probate Law, Elder Law, Medi-Cal Planning, Real Estate and Business Law, Probate Litigation.**
*See Professional Biographies, MERCED, CALIFORNIA*

Kirihara, John D., (CV) ... '50 '80 C.112 B.A. L.1067 J.D. [Ⓐ Morse,M.&M.]
Koehler, Clytie ... '46 '86 C&L.1049 B.A., J.D. Mng. Atty., Central Calif. Legal Servs.
**Lampe, Christopher W.**, (BV) ... '50 '75 C.112 A.B. L.1065 J.D. [Tenenbaum,L.&F.]
*PRACTICE AREAS: Civil Trials; Negligence Law; Business Law.

**Lang, Richert & Patch**
**(See Fresno)**

Lawrence, Cyril L. ... '42 '72 C.1042 B.A. L.284 J.D. 2111 "K" St.
**Lewis, Thomas E.**, (BV) ... '55 '82 C.112 B.A. L.464 J.D. [Silveira,M.&L.]
*PRACTICE AREAS: Litigation; Real Estate; Business Law.
**Linneman, James E.**, (AV) ... '33 '60 C&L.813 B.A., J.D. [Linneman,B.T.V.&V.]
*PRACTICE AREAS: Personal Injury Litigation; Agricultural Law; Real Property Law.

**Linneman, Burgess, Telles, Van Atta & Vierra, (AV)**
**312 West 19th Street, P.O. Box 2263, 95344⊙**
**Telephone: 209-723-2137 FAX: 209-723-0899**
**Members of Firm: James E. Linneman; Jeffrey A. Nelson.**
**General Civil and Trial Practice. Water District and Rights Law. Real Property, Probate, Negligence, Products Liability, Agricultural Law and Personal Injury.**
**Representative Clients: Panoche Water District; Panoche Drainage District; San Luis Water District; Redfern Ranches, Inc.; Spain Air.**
**Reference: The Bank of America National Trust & Savings Assn.**
**Dos Palos, California Office: 1820 Marguerite Street, P.O. Box 156. Telephone: 209-392-2141. Fax: 209-392-3964. E-Mail: drathmann@aol.com**
**Los Banos, California Office: 654 K Street, P.O. Box 1364. Telephone: 209-826-4911. FAX: 209-826-4766. E-Mail: 1btvv@aol.com**
*See Professional Biographies, MERCED, CALIFORNIA*

**Lo, Paul C.** ... '68 '94 C&L.112 B.S., J.D. [Ⓐ Allen,P.P.&F.]
*LANGUAGES: Hmong.
*PRACTICE AREAS: Personal Injury; Criminal Defense; General Civil Litigation.
Marks, Ronald H., (BV) ... '45 '72 C.1060 B.A. L.1066 J.D. 2025 "K" St.
**Mason, Michael L.**, (BV) ... '44 '69 C.940 B.A. L.623 J.D. [Flanagan,M.R.G.&C.]
*PRACTICE AREAS: Personal Injury Law; Civil Litigation.
**Mattos, Weldon J., Jr.**, (BV) ... '48 '73 C.112 A.B. L.1067 J.D. [Silveira,M.&L.]
*PRACTICE AREAS: Personal Injury; Business; Probate; Mediation Services.
**McCabe, Brian L.** ... '61 '89 C.112 B.S. L.1148 J.D. [Allen,P.P.&F.]
*PRACTICE AREAS: Family Law; Labor Law; Civil Litigation.
McKechnie, C. Logan, (BV) ... '42 '77 C.061 LL.B L.1137 J.D. 305 E. 21stSt.
Miller, Jeffrey L., (BV) ... '50 '78 C.112 B.S. L.1095 J.D. Dep. Pub. Def.
Morse, Brian D., (BV) ... '49 '77 C.285 B.A. L.1136 J.D. [Morse,M.&M.]
Morse, Larry D., (BV) ... '27 '55 C.999 L.809 J.D. [Morse,M.&M.]
Morse, R. Neil, (BV) ... '51 '76 C.336 B.A. L.285 J.D. [Morse,M.&M.]
Morse, Morse & Morse, A Law Corporation, (BV) ... 760 W. 20th St.
**Nelson, Jeffrey A.** ... '51 '77 C.911 B.A. L.1065 J.D. [Linneman,B.T.V.&V.]
*PRACTICE AREAS: Personal Injury Litigation; Insurance Law; Criminal Law.
Newman, William A., III, (CV) ... '50 '76 C.1365 B.B.A. L.280 J.D. 2103 "O" St.
Nord, Steven F., (BV) ... '47 '74 C.112 A.B. L.1065 J.D. City Atty.

**Oliver, Casey A. '62 '89 C.1079 L.1189 J.D.**
**2040 M Street, Suite C, 95340**
**Telephone: 209-725-0770**
***PRACTICE AREAS: Personal Injury, Juvenile Law and Family Law; Insurance Disputes.**
**Personal Injury, Juvenile Law, Insurance Disputes and Family Law.**
*See Professional Biographies, MERCED, CALIFORNIA*

Ortega, David Richard ... '57 '84 C.763 B.A. L.1049 J.D. Dep. Co. Coun.
**Padron, James P.**, (CV) ... '48 '84 C.267 B.A. L.1065 J.D. [Canelo,H.W.W.&P.]
*LANGUAGES: Spanish.
*PRACTICE AREAS: Personal Injury Law; Workers Compensation Law; Family Law.
**Polgar, Gary B.**, (BV) ... '49 '74 C.112 B.A. L.1065 J.D. [Allen,P.P.&F.]
*PRACTICE AREAS: Creditor, Debtor and Trustee Bankruptcy Law; Commercial Law; Real Estate Law.
Pro, Michael L., (BV) ... '49 '78 C.1073 B.A. L.464 J.D. Dep. Pub. Def.
**Proietti, Donald J.**, (BV) ... '54 '79 C.37 B.A. L.1137 J.D. [Allen,P.P.&F.]
*PRACTICE AREAS: Personal Injury Law; Civil Law; Business Litigation; Probate Litigation.

**Quigley, William P. (Pat), (AV) '37 '65 C.112 A.B. L.1066 LL.B.**
**650 West 20th Street, P.O. Box 1229, 95341**
**Telephone: 209-383-4444 Fax: 209-383-5989**
**General Trial Practice. Business, Real Estate, Estate Planning, Probate.**
**Representative Clients: Wainwright Development Co.; Black Rascal Estates; Riggs Ambulance Service; Riggs Communications; Merced Transportation; Isenberg Motors; Pierre Perrett Farming; Yosemite Motels.**
*See Professional Biographies, MERCED, CALIFORNIA*

**Robbins, Kenneth M.**, (BV) ... '50 '76 C.112 B.A. L.990 J.D. [Flanagan,M.R.G.&C.]
*PRACTICE AREAS: Tax; Business; Agriculture; Water Law.
Sanders, Victor D. ... '33 '74 L.1132 LL.B. Dep. Dist. Atty.
Saude, Fernanda A. ... '46 '82 C.767 B.S.B.A. L.1026 LL.B. Dep. Co. Coun.
**Seymour, Shelly A.** ... '60 '86 C.177 B.A. L.352 J.D. [Canelo,H.W.W.&P.]
*PRACTICE AREAS: Family Law.
Shrum, Wesley M. '25 '50 C&L.623 B.A., J.D.
(adm. in OK; not adm. in CA) 1404 San Gabriel Way‡

**Silveira, Mattos & Lewis, (BV)**
**530 West 21st Street, P.O. Box 2287, 95344-0287**
**Telephone: 209-722-3815 Fax: 209-722-5957**
**F.A. Silveira (1907-1989); Weldon J. Mattos, Jr.; Thomas E. Lewis; Kathleen Crist.**
**General Civil and Trial Practice. Personal Injury Defense, Insurance, Real Property and Real Estate Law.**
*See Professional Biographies, MERCED, CALIFORNIA*

Simonet, Ross A., (CV) ... '43 '79 C.169 B.A. L.1132 J.D. Dep. Dist. Atty.
Solmonson, Sheldon C. ... '22 '55 C&L.809 LL.B. Asst. Co. Coun.
Spencer, Gordon J., (BV) ... '49 '75 C.911 B.A. L.464 J.D. Dist. Atty.

**Stodolka, Julie E. Furman '49 '87 C.188 A.B. L.1068 J.D.**
**800 W. 20th Street, Suite C-1, 95348**
**Telephone: 209-725-2025 Fax: 209-725-2620**
***PRACTICE AREAS: Bankruptcy Law; Real Estate; Tax Workouts.**
**Bankruptcy Law, Real Estate and Tax Workouts.**
*See Professional Biographies, MERCED, CALIFORNIA*

Suydam, John H. ... '13 '40 C.508 L.180 LL.B. 3052 Sequoia Ct.‡
Tarhalla, James B., (CV) ... '50 '79 C.267 L.1189 710 W. 18th St., Suite 15
Temple, Ralph S., Jr., (BV) ... '40 '66 C.951 A.B. L.1065 LL.B. 650 W. 20th St.
**Tenenbaum, Samuel S.**, (BV) ... '45 '71 C.112 A.B. L.770 J.D. [Tenenbaum,L.&F.]
*PRACTICE AREAS: Trial; Criminal Law; Family Law.

**Tenenbaum, Lampe & Fromson, (BV)**
**2005 "O" Street, 95340**
**Telephone: 209-384-7887 Fax: 209-384-5865**
**Members of Firm: Samuel S. Tenenbaum; Christopher W. Lampe; Paul D. Fromson.**
**General Civil and Criminal Trial Practice in State and Federal Courts. Negligence, Criminal and Family Law. Business Litigation.**
*See Professional Biographies, MERCED, CALIFORNIA*

Umbarger, Alice J., (BV) ... '41 '74 C.112 B.A. L.1067 J.D. Dep. Pub. Def.
**Wallace, Rickey D.**, (BV) ... '51 '77 C.770 B.S. L.464 J.D. [Canelo,H.W.W.&P.]
*REPORTED CASES: Buhlert Trucking v. WCAB (1988) 199 CA 3d 1530.
*PRACTICE AREAS: Personal Injury; General Civil Litigation.
Whiting, John E. ... '25 '53 C.813 L.1065 J.D. 1045 Emory Way
Whiting, Russell G., (CV) ... '45 '73 C.999 L.169 J.D. [Courtney&W.]

**Wild, Carter & Tipton, A Professional Corporation**
**(See Fresno)**

**Williams, Sharon E.** ... '66 '94 C.36 B.S. L.464 J.D. [Ⓐ Flanagan,M.R.G.&C.]
*PRACTICE AREAS: Land Use; Corporate; Municipal; Trusts; Taxation.
**Wilson, Charles Rayburn**, (BV) ... '45 '70 C&L.966 B.S., J.D. [Canelo,H.W.W.&P.]
*REPORTED CASES: Mullen v. Glens Falls Insurance Co., 73 CA 3d 163 (1977); In re Marriage of Spengler, 5 CA 4th 288 (1992).
*PRACTICE AREAS: Personal Injury Law; Probate Law; Civil Litigation.
**Wilson, James H.**, (BV) ... '43 '73 C.867 B.A. L.770 J.D. [Canelo,H.W.W.&P.]
*REPORTED CASES: Elston v. City of Turlock, 38 C3d 227 (1985); Mendez v. Superior Court, 206 CA3 557 (1988); Baker v. Walker & Walker, 133 CA3 746 (1982).
*PRACTICE AREAS: Personal Injury Law; Workers Compensation Law; General Civil Litigation; Family Law.
Winton, Gordon H., Jr. ... '13 '46 C.112 A.B. L.765 LL.B. 143 W. 20th St.‡

## MIDDLETOWN, —, *Lake Co.*

Downing, James C., (AV) ... '24 '53 C.112 B.S. L.1065 LL.B. P.O. Box 398‡
Kemp, Maurice, (BV) '32 '61 C.674 A.B. L.813 LL.B.
21208 Calistoga Rd. (⊙Palo Alto)
Tallyn, William L. ... '35 '71 C.705 B.A. L.1068 J.D. P.O. Box 425

## MILLBRAE, 20,412, *San Mateo Co.*

Agosta, Steven S., (BV) ... '42 '68 C.768 B.A. L.1065 J.D. [Wexler,W.&A.]
Barrett, C. Patrick ... '50 '87 C.1069 B.A. L.770 J.D. 119 Park Blvd.

**Church, Mark M., (BV) '51 '76 C.169 B.A. L.464 J.D.**
**Bay View Federal Bank Building, 475 El Camino Real, Suite 300, 94030**
**Telephone: 415-697-2400**
**—Robert G. Zelenka.**
**General Civil and Trial Practice. Business, Corporate, Real Property, Probate, Estate Planning, Personal Injury and Family Law.**

**Church, Mark M.**, (BV) ... '51 '76 C.169 B.A. L.464 J.D. [Church&Assoc.]

**Church & Associates, (BV)**
**Bay View Federal Bank Building, 475 El Camino Real, Suite 300, 94030**
**Telephone: 415-697-2400**
**Mark M. Church;—Robert G. Zelenka.**
**General Civil and Trial Practice. Business, Corporate, Real Property, Probate, Estate Planning, Personal Injury and Family Law.**
*See Professional Biographies, MILLBRAE, CALIFORNIA*

Coleman, Sharon A. ... '46 '72 C&L.767 B.A., J.D. 300 El Bonito Way
**Corey, George R.**, (AV) ... '33 '64 C.477 B.A. L.1065 LL.B. [Corey,L.M.&P.]
*PRACTICE AREAS: Business Litigation; Municipal Law; Civil Litigation.

**Corey, Luzaich, Manos & Pliska, LLP, (AV)**
**700 El Camino Real, P.O. Box 669, 94030**
**Telephone: 415-871-5666 Fax: 415-871-4144**
**George R. Corey; Stevan N. Luzaich; Jeffrey D. Manos; Edward W. Pliska; Dario B. deGhetaldi; Leticia G. Toledo.**
**General Civil and Criminal Trial Practice. Probate, Estate Planning, Business, Corporate, Personal Injury, Negligence, Real Estate and Municipal Law.**
*See Professional Biographies, MILLBRAE, CALIFORNIA*

Curl, Cathleen M., (BV) ... '53 '79 C.813 B.A. L.770 J.D. [Manos&C.]
**deGhetaldi, Dario B.** ... '50 '86 C.813 B.A. L.1065 J.D. [Corey,L.M.&P.]
*PRACTICE AREAS: Business Litigation; Real Estate Litigation; Municipal Law; Civil Appeals and Writs.
Eichelmann, Norman F. ... '33 '88 C.284 B.B.A. L.765 J.D. 219 El Camino Real

**Erskine, Morse, (AV) '15 '41 C.813 A.B. L.309**
**700 El Camino Real, 94030-2009**
**Telephone: 415-871-5666 Fax: 415-871-4144**
***PRACTICE AREAS: Corporate Law; Real Estate Law; Title Insurance Law.**
**General Practice.**

Hall, Donna L. ... '50 '84 C.766 B.A. L.1230 J.D. P.O. Box 1442
Jenkinson, Daryl W. ... '13 '39 C.999 L.1065 J.D. 1041 Vista Grande Ave.
Johnson, J. Leland ... '38 '83 C.838 B.S. L.767 J.D. 440 Millbrae Ave.
Laubscher, Lawrence R. ... '31 '57 C&L.813 A.B., LL.B. 301 Ashton Ave.
Litwin, Jack L. '36 '61 C.178 B.A. L.893 LL.B.
(adm. in VA; not adm. in CA) 911 Sequoia Ave.‡
**Luzaich, Stevan N.**, (BV) ... '50 '75 C.112 B.A. L.1065 J.D. [Corey,L.M.&P.]
*PRACTICE AREAS: Probate; Commercial Law; Real Estate; Elder Law.
**Manos, Jeffrey D.** ... '55 '81 C.767 B.A. L.1065 J.D. [Corey,L.M.&P.]
*PRACTICE AREAS: Civil Practice; Personal Injury; Business Litigation.
Manos, Jerry R., (BV) ... '55 '81 C.767 B.A. L.1065 J.D. [Manos&C.]
Manos & Curl, (BV) ... 700 El Camino Real
Mitchell, Glen T. ... '24 '52 C.112 B.A. L.1066 LL.B. 1140 Helen Dr.‡
Parker, George W. ... '33 '66 C.766 B.A. L.767 LL.B. 1214 Frontera Way
**Pliska, Edward W.**, (BV) ... '35 '65 C.674 A.B. L.184 LL.B. [Corey,L.M.&P.]
*PRACTICE AREAS: Criminal Law; Civil Litigation.
Pollak, Steven L., (AV) ... '49 '75 C.629 B.S. L.284 J.D. 700 ElCamino Real, Suite 201
Robinson, Barbara M. '52 '85 C.602 B.A. L.912 J.D.
(adm. in MI; not adm. in CA) Best Western El Rancho Inn
Smith, A. Randall ... '50 '80 C.88 B.A. L.1026 J.D. 1699 El Camino Real
Smith, Maureen O'Hara ... '42 '86 C.112 A.B. L.770 J.D. 219 Barclay Ave.‡
Sobiloff, Elfriede F. ... '— '64 C.057 L.765 LL.B. 220 Magnolia Ave.
Steiner, Stephen D. ... '49 '92 C.112 B.A. L.770 J.D. 700 El Camino Real, Suite 201
Stern, Milton, Jr. ... '19 '54 C.930 B.B.A. 231 E. Millbrae Ave.
**Toledo, Leticia G.** ... '61 '89 C.740 B.A. L.1065 J.D. [Corey,L.M.&P.]
*LANGUAGES: Spanish.
*PRACTICE AREAS: Estate Planning; Probate Administration; Trust Administration; Guardianship and Conservatorship.
Walker, John M. ... '42 '79 C.475 B.A.Econ. L.1026 J.D. 1050 Pinehurst Ct.
Wentworth, Kathleen A. ... '49 '73 C&L.767 B.S., J.D. 1180 Millbrae Ave.‡
Wexler, David D., (BV) ... '17 '45 C&L.851 LL.B. 485 Broadway
Wexler, Wexler & Agosta, (BV) ... 485 Bway.

CALIFORNIA—MILLBRAE MARTINDALE-HUBBELL LAW DIRECTORY 1997

**Zelenka, Robert G.** .....................'49 '79 C.506 B.S. L.285 J.D. [A M.M.Church]
*PRACTICE AREAS: Tax; Probate; Estate Planning; Pension Law; Corporate Law.
**Zelenka, Robert G.** ..................'49 '79 C.506 B.S. L.285 J.D. [A Church&Assoc.]
*PRACTICE AREAS: Tax; Probate; Estate Planning; Pension Law; Corporate Law.

## MILL VALLEY, 13,038, *Marin Co.*

Advice & Counsel Incorporated, (AV⊙) ................ 70 Lomita Dr. (⊙San Francisco)
Baird, Mariah ....................................'54 '86 C.112 B.A. L.1066 J.D. P.O. Box 2180
Balmes, Vernon R. ...............................'32 '56 C&L.597 B.S., J.D. 20 Stanton Way
Barnes, Catharine S. ...........................'52 '79 C.918 B.A. L.893 J.D. 85 Helens Lane
Baumbach, Charles R. ......................'33 '64 C&L.145 B.A., J.D. 339 Cardinal Court
Becker, Jonathan L. ...........................'54 '79 C.813 B.A. L.1067 J.D. 924 Ventura Way
Becker, Nance F. ...........................'57 '81 C.1349 B.A. L.813 J.D. 108 Richardson Dr.
Becker, Reuben J. ..............'41 '71 C.860 B.A. L.893 LL.B. 591 Redwood Highway
Begley, Robert J. ...............................'46 '72 C.473 B.A. L.665 J.D. 271 Miller Ave.
Bernstein, Cassandra B. ..................'51 '78 C.549 B.A. L.1065 J.D. 20 Jackson Terrace
Bjorklund, Christian C. '42 '67 C.36 B.S.E.E. L.37 J.D.
(adm. in AZ; not adm. in CA) 419 La Verne Ave.‡
Blau, Allan I. ...................................'33 '59 C.831 B.S. L.339 LL.B. 311 Miller Ave.
Blonder, Nicholas .............................'49 '75 C.766 B.A. L.767 J.D. P.O. Box 5513
Brewer, W. Dennis, (BV) ...........'50 '80 C.112 B.A. L.767 J.D. 725 E. Blithedale Ave.
Brown, David P., (AV) ...............'24 '49 C&L.767 B.S., LL.B. 150 Seminary Dr., 3E.‡
Bushman, Ronald M. ....................'33 '57 C.339 B.S. L.502 J.D. 40 Harbor Cove Way
Cahill, Daniel M., (BV) ............................'48 '76 C.767 B.A. L.285 J.D. 50 Shell Rd.
**Cameron, James K.**, (AV) ........'52 '77 C.813 A.B. L.309 J.D. [J.K.Cameron&Assoc.]
*LANGUAGES: French, Italian and Spanish.
*PRACTICE AREAS: Commercial Bankruptcy and Loan Restructuring Law; Entertainment Law.

**Cameron, James K., & Associates, A Prof. Corp., (AV)**
**223 Meda Lane, 94941**
**Telephone: 415-380-3783 Fax: 414-388-6219**
**James K. Cameron.**
**Commercial Bankruptcy, Loan Restructuring and Entertainment Law.**

Christison, Kenneth M. ...................'42 '72 C.506 B.S. L.273 J.D. 601 Glenwood Ave.
Clarke, Cheryl A. ....................'55 '82 C.597 B.S.J. L.767 J.D. 478 Green Glen Way
Coren, Kenneth A. ..........................'49 '77 C.273 B.A. L.724 J.D. 265 Miller Ave.
Coulston, Clifford G. '42 '67 C.472 B.B.A. L.564 LL.B.
(adm. in NY; not adm. in CA) 66 Mirabel Ave.‡
Crosland, Royda ...................'47 '84 C.560 B.A. L.767 J.D. 133 E. Blithedale Ave.
Dale, Richard R. ..........................'58 '84 C.276 B.A. L.1066 J.D. 1239 Lattie Ln.
Dear, Maureen B. ...................'59 '84 C.112 B.A. L.1067 J.D. 591 Redwood Hwy.
Desmarais, Josee ...................'48 '79 C.999 B.A. L.014 LL.L. 111 Columbia Ave.‡

**Donahue, Gallagher, Woods & Wood, (AV)**
**Shelter Point, 591 Redwood Highway, Suite 1200, 94941⊙**
**Telephone: 415-381-4161 Facsimile: 415-381-7515**
**Members of Firm: Eric W. Doney; Jonathan G. Wong. Associates: Robyn Renée Newcomb; Jonathan N. Osder; Jonas W. Kant (Not admitted in CA).**
**General Civil and Trial Practice in all State and Federal Courts. Corporate, Real Property, Intellectual Property, Insurance, Immigration, Labor and Employment, Tax, Probate and Estate Planning Law.**
**Oakland, California Office: 300 Lakeside Drive, Suite 1900. Telephone: 415-451-0544. Facsimile: 415-832-1486.**
**Walnut Creek, California Office: 1646 North California Boulevard, Suite 310. Telephone: 510-746-7770. Facsimile: 510-746-7776.**
***See Professional Biographies, MILL VALLEY, CALIFORNIA***

**Doney, Eric W.** .......'52 '77 C.112 B.A. L.1065 J.D. [Donahue,G.W.&W.] (⊙Oakland)
*PRACTICE AREAS: Computer Law; Computer Software; Copyright.
Dyer, Gregory C. ........................'47 '72 C&L.813 B.A., J.D. 103 E. Blithedale Ave.
Eissler, Ellen R. .......................'61 '87 C.1320 B.A. L.1066 J.D. 185 Magee Ave.
Ellis, Alan, (AV⊙) '43 '68 C.645 B.A. L.884 J.D.
(adm. in PA; not adm. in CA) [A.Ellis]
Ellis, Alan, P.C., Law Offices of, (AV⊙) ................................ 265 Miller Ave.
Fabric, Elliot A. ....................................'48 '75 C&L.472 B.A., J.D. 79 S. Knoll Rd.
Farrow, Laura E. Hammond ................'54 '80 C.668 B.A. L.1066 J.D. 34 Forrest St.
Ferguson, Douglas P., (AV) ................'39 '63 C.309 L.813 LL.B. 591 Redwood Hwy.
Fields, Gary B., (AV) ............'34 '60 C.309 A.B. L.813 LL.B. 103 E. Blithedale Ave.
Fiene, Laura M. ...................'61 '85 C.801 B.S. L.846 J.D. 440 Throckmorton Ave.
Flaxman, Peter F. .......................'45 '70 C.1077 B.S. L.800 J.D. 591 Redwood Hwy.
Foust, Rebecca Jane .....................'57 '82 C.788 B.A. L.813 J.D. 112 Lomita Dr.
Friscia, Steven J. .........................'51 '76 C.112 B.A. L.809 J.D. P.O. Box 1657
Fuller, D. Ward ..........................'45 '71 C.800 B.S. L.1066 J.D. 210 Tamalpais Ave.
Gage, John C., (AV) .....................'42 '68 C.668 B.A. L.178 LL.B. 109 Hillside Ave.
Georgeson, Adamont Nicholas ...........'46 '73 C&L.477 B.A., J.D. 591 Redwood Hwy.
Giacomini, Edward D. ..............'31 '61 C.602 A.B. L.1066 J.D. 311 Vista Linda Dr.‡
Goldsholle, Gerry H., (AV⊙) ..................'40 '64 C.945 A.B. L.178 J.D. [Advice&C.]⊙
Gordon, Larry M. ....'48 '79 C.103 A.B. L.1065 J.D. Land Organizer, Indus. Areas Found.
Graham, Richard W., (AV) ....................'30 '55 C&L.813 A.B., J.D. P.O. Box 1907‡
Granett, Gabriel L. ........................'42 '72 C.112 A.B. L.1026 J.D. 232 Manor Dr.‡
Green, Jerry A. ...........................'43 '68 C.112 B.A. L.1066 J.D. P.O. Box 5094
Greenberg, Arnold M., (BV) ..........'28 '57 C.347 B.S. L.1066 LL.B. 228 Oakdale Ave.
Groth, William I. '27 '53 C.674 B.A. L.494 LL.B.
(adm. in IL; not adm. in CA) 4 Starboard Ct.‡
Harmon, Robert L., (AV) .......'30 '55 C&L.813 A.B., LL.B. Pres. & CEO, Moana Corp.
Harriman, William M. E. ....................'23 '64 C.112 B.A. L.1066 J.D. P.O. Box 189‡

**Helmenstine, Robert A., (AV) '39 '67 C.966 B.S.M.E. L.1065 J.D.**
**591 Redwood Highway, 94941**
**Telephone: 415-388-7181 Fax: 415-383-2074**
**General Practice with special emphasis on Civil Litigation, Business Contracts, Torts, Construction, Environmental, Personal Injury and Property Damage.**
***See Professional Biographies, MILL VALLEY, CALIFORNIA***

Higgins, Tara .........................'58 '86 C.112 B.A. L.770 J.D. 150 Shoreline Hwy.
Hirsch, Susan L. ...................................'54 '82 C.208 B.S. L.285 J.D. 15 Lee St.
Horn, Lawrence R. .......................'43 '73 C.494 B.A. L.284 J.D. 825 Autumn Ln.
Hurvich, Fred A. Rico ....'37 '63 C.659 B.A. L.477 LL.B. P.O. Box 1704 (⊙San Rafael)
Jackson, Jay, (AV) ..........................'25 '52 C.112 A.B. L.1065 J.D. [J.Jackson]
Jackson, Jay, P.C., (AV) ..........................................100 Shoreline Hwy., Bldg. B
Jordan, Andrew C. ...................'56 '81 C.112 B.A. L.767 J.D. 66 W. Blithedale Ave.‡
**Kant, Jonas W.** '65 '96 C.112 B.A. L.117 J.D.
(adm. in NY; not adm. in CA) [A Donahue,G.W.&W.] (⊙Oakland)

**Karpman, Valerie Ansel, (AV) '43 '76 C.994 B.A. L.284 J.D.**
**103 East Blithedale Avenue, 94941**
**Telephone: 415-381-8887 Facsimile: 415-381-8888**
**Civil Litigation in all Courts. Business Litigation, Personal Injury, Professional Liability, Products Liability, Insurance Bad Faith Litigation, Women's Health Litigation.**
***See Professional Biographies, MILL VALLEY, CALIFORNIA***

Keel, Susan I. ...................................'48 '77 C.112 B.S. L.809 J.D. 34 Forrest St.
Keener, William H. ..................................'52 '77 398 S. Morning Sun Ave.
Kemp, George W., Jr. '17 '46 C&L.215 A.B., LL.B.
(adm. in MI; not adm. in CA) 225 Tennessee Valley Rd.‡
Khourie, Michael N., (AV) ..........'22 '49 C&L.608 B.S., LL.B. 450 E. Strawberry Dr.
King, Cynthia A. ..........................'52 '85 C.938 B.A. L.1067 J.D. 100 Sycamore Ave.‡
Korican, Peter M. ..............'37 '63 C.178 A.B. L.1066 LL.B. 367 S. Morningsun Ave.
Kunzig, Anne E. ........................'52 '81 C.260 B.A. L.1065 J.D. 100 Shoreline Hwy.
Kutler, Robert M. ...........................'49 '80 C.846 B.A. L.285 J.D. 211 Melrose Ave.
Licht, Louis ..............................................'15 '44 C.112 L.809 1 Ralston Ave.
Lindberg, Theodore L., Jr. ................'43 '74 C.1060 B.S.E.E. L.767 J.D. 11 Swift Ct.
Litman, Craig A. ............................'46 '75 C.494 B.A. L.1035 J.D. 101 Walnut Ave.
**Lucas, Steven S.** .....................'65 '92 C.112 B.A. L.309 J.D. [A Nielsen,M.P.M.&N.]⊙
*PRACTICE AREAS: Political Law.
Lybrand, Anna R. ........................'42 '76 C.69 B.A. L.284 J.D. 427 County View‡
Lyons, Timothy K. ..............................'43 '72 C&L.477 A.B.Ec., J.D. 81 Circle Ave.
McCubbin, Susan Brubeck ...............................'48 '77 L.1137 LL.B. 36 Tiburon Blvd.‡
Moore, Linda W. ....................'45 '87 C.112 B.A. L.999 J.D. 165 Marguerite Ave.‡
Nakano, Douglas K., (BV) ..........'45 '74 C.1073 B.A. L.1065 J.D. 233 Cleveland Ave.
Nemir, Donald, (BV) ..........................'31 '61 C.112 A.B. L.1066 J.D. P.O. Box 1089
**Newcomb, Robyn Renée** '66 '93
C.112 B.A. L.767 J.D. [A Donahue,G.W.&W.] (⊙Oakland)
**Nielsen, Vigo G., Jr., (P.C.)**, (AV) '42 '72 C.976 B.A. L.464 J.D.
[Nielsen,M.P.M.&N.]⊙

**Nielsen, Merksamer, Parrinello, Mueller & Naylor, LLP, (AV)**
**A Partnership including a Professional Corporation**
**591 Redwood Highway, Building 4000, 94941⊙**
**Telephone: 415-389-6800**
**Email: nmpmn@aol.com**
**Vigo G. Nielsen, Jr., (P.C.). Associates: Steven S. Lucas; John A. Ramirez.**
**Government, Administrative, Constitutional, Civil Rights, Election and Legislative Law. Civil Trial and Appellate Practice in all State and Federal Courts.**
**Reference: Wells Fargo, San Francisco, Personal Banking.**
**San Francisco, California Office: 120 Montgomery Street, Suite 1055, 94104. Telephone: 415-389-6800.**
**Sacramento, California Office: One City Centre, 770 L Street, Suite 800, 95814. Telephone: 916-446-6752.**
***See Professional Biographies, MILL VALLEY, CALIFORNIA***

**Osder, Jonathan N.** '67 '94 C.112 B.A. L.1355 J.D.
[A Donahue,G.W.&W.] (⊙Oakland)
*LANGUAGES: Spanish.
Parker, David M. ...................'55 '84 C.147 B.A. L.464 J.D. 133 E. Blithedale Ave.
Pinto, Radovan Z. ..........................'45 '72 C.766 B.A. L.1065 J.D. P.O. Box 202
Plath, Robert W. .........................'26 '58 C.477 B.A. L.1065 LL.B. P.O. Box 2022
Pollak, John H. ........................'42 '70 C.477 B.A. L.339 J.D. 655 Redwood Hwy.
Pollak, William T. '18 '47 C.477 A.B. L.813 J.D.
(adm. in OH; not adm. in CA) 2 Salt Creek Ln.‡
Pratt, Kenneth ........................'27 '78 C.813 B.A. L.1227 J.D. 191 Throckmorton Ave.
Prensky, Harriet P., (AV) .........................'57 '81 C.1349 B.A. L.112 J.D. [Prensky&T.]
Prensky & Tobin, (AV) ..........................................................655 Redwood Hwy.
Purcell, Jack B., (AV) ............................'21 '51 C&L.309 A.B., LL.B. 333 Summit Ave.‡

**Rabin, Susan '41 '86 C.597 B.S. L.284 J.D.**
**219 East Blithedale Avenue, Suite 4, 94941-2033**
**Telephone: 415-381-5252 Fax: 415-381-5222**
**Entertainment, Business, Copyright and Trademark Law.**
***See Professional Biographies, MILL VALLEY, CALIFORNIA***

**Ramirez, John A.** ..............'70 '96 C.112 B.A. L.1065 J.D. [A Nielsen,M.P.M.&N.]⊙
*PRACTICE AREAS: Election and Political Law.
Reilly, James T. ...............................'45 '75 C.870 B.S. L.990 J.D. P.O. Box 1338
**Robb, Joseph W., Jr.**, (BV) ..................'26 '52 C.112 A.B. L.1065 J.D. [Robb&R.]
*PRACTICE AREAS: Business Organization; Estate Planning.
**Robb, Philip A.** .......................................'62 '90 C.112 B.A. L.284 J.D. [Robb&R.]
*PRACTICE AREAS: Business Law; Estate Planning and Probate Law.

**Robb & Ross, (AV)**
**A Partnership including Professional Corporations**
**591 Redwood Highway, Suite 2250, 94941**
**Telephone: 415-332-3831 Fax: 415-383-2074**
**Joseph W. Robb, Jr.; Sterling L. Ross (Certified Specialist, Estate Planning, Trust and Probate Law, The State Bar of California Board of Legal Specialization); Alan J. Titus; Philip A. Robb.**
**Estates and Trusts, General Business and Real Estate.**
***See Professional Biographies, MILL VALLEY, CALIFORNIA***

Robertson, Stephen M., (BV) ..............'43 '70 C.112 B.A. L.1065 J.D. P.O. Box 550
Rosanelli, Carol Egan '56 '89 C.112 B.S. L.362 J.D.
(adm. in FL; not adm. in CA) 421 Marion Ave.‡
Rose, M. Fred, (AV) ..........................'35 '64 C.768 B.S. L.1065 LL.B. P.O. Box 719
Rosenberg, Steven J. ........................'44 '69 C&L.352 B.A., J.D. 591 Redwood Hwy.
**Ross, Sterling L.**, (AV) ..............................'46 '72 C.813 B.A. L.477 J.D. [Robb&R.]
*PRACTICE AREAS: Estate Planning; Trust Law; Probate Law; Business Law.
Sandmann, Peter B., (AV) ........................'41 '66 C.216 A.B. L.659 LL.B. [Tesler&S.]⊙
Seaver, Martin H. ...........................'16 '53 C.813 A.B. L.1065 J.D. 47 Circle Ave.‡
Seidler, Patrick M. ..................'59 '84 C.112 B.S. L.1066 J.D. 187 E. Blithedale Ave.
Shroyer, Lee E. .....................................'36 '66 C&L.767 B.S., J.D. 33 Dorset Lane
Soffer, Jonathan H. ....................'57 '82 C.966 B.A. L.1137 J.D. 311 Ricardo Rd.
Sprague, Robert M., (AV) .................'42 '67 C.118 B.A. L.846 J.D. 423 Pixie Trail
States, Linda D. ..................'66 '94 C.112 B.A. L.1065 J.D. 20A Sunnyside Ave., #239
Swor, Stacy W. ...............................'42 '68 C&L.508 B.A., J.D. 591 Redwood Hway.
Synchef, Richard M. .......................'50 '75 C.966 B.A. L.597 J.D. 16 Midway Ave.
Tesler, Pauline H., (AV) ..........................'42 '74 C.681 B.A. L.966 J.D. [Tesler&S.]⊙
Tesler & Sandmann, (AV) ........................................ 16 Buena Vista (⊙San Francisco)
**Titus, Alan J.** ......................................'56 '83 C.112 A.B. L.1067 J.D. [Robb&R.]
*PRACTICE AREAS: Business Law; Real Estate; Estate Planning and Probate Law; Business Litigation.
Tobin, Patricia, (AV) ........................'51 '78 C.1350 B.A. L.188 J.D. [Prensky&T.]
Toler, Eugene J. ...........................'45 '74 C.923 B.S.B.A. L.61 J.D. S & P Co.
Van Kirk, H. Spencer, III ...............'44 '75 C.401 B.S. L.309 J.D. 193 Greenwood St.
Wagner, Robert H. ..........................'49 '78 C.112 B.S. L.765 J.D. P.O. Box 362
Ware, William D. .............................'54 '83 C.112 B.A. L.464 J.D. 25 Escalon Dr.
Weisman, Diana R. '70 '96 C.477 B.A. L.629 J.D.
(adm. in NM; not adm. in CA) 29 Portola Lane
Werner, Jan O. ..........................'44 '75 C.867 A.B. L.1065 J.D. 820 Edgewood Ave.
Whelan, John W. '22 '48 C.363 A.B. L.276 J.D.
(adm. in DC; not adm. in CA) 306 Bristol Pl.‡
Willis, Harry M., Law Office of, (AV) '48 '77
C.112 B.A. L.1065 J.D. 187 E. Blithedale Ave.
**Wong, Jonathan G.** ..............'59 '83 C.668 B.A. L.1067 J.D. [Donahue,G.W.&W.]
*LANGUAGES: French, German, Spanish and Mandarin Chinese.
*PRACTICE AREAS: Litigation; Immigration and Nationality Law; Employment Law.

## MILPITAS, 50,686, *Santa Clara Co.*

Anderson, Francis A. ............ '44 '72 C.197 A.B. L.813 J.D. Pres., Peco Controls Corp.
Backman, Richd. F., (CV) ............ '25 '53 C.112 B.A. L.1066 LL.B. 1 N. Main St.
Berry, Lisa C. .........'58 '83 C&L.472 B.B.A., J.D. Assoc. Gen. Coun., LSI Logic Corp.
Chan, Ted W. ............ '60 '90 C.112 B.A. L.770 J.D. Quantum Corp.
Cox, Barton J. ............ '58 '83 C.602 B.S. L.1068 J.D. 300 Woodruff Way
Go, Justin Q. H. ............ '52 '79 C.838 B.S. L.770 J.D. Analyst, LSI Logic Corp.
Harrison, David B., (AV) '42 '69
C.169 A.B. L.1065 J.D. Chf. Pat. Coun., Quantum Corp. (Pat.)
Jackson, Rex S. ....... '60 '85 C.228 B.A. L.813 J.D. V.P. & Gen. Coun., Read-Rite Corp.
Kryder, Andrew L. '52 '77 C&L.770 B.Com., J.D.
V.P., Fin. & Corp. Gen. Coun., Quantum Corp.
Ladden, Richard M. ............ '38 '74 C.102 B.A. L.770 J.D. 1404 Acadia Ave.
Mills, Edward F. ............ '51 '76 C.813 B.A. L.770 J.D. 830 Hillview Ct.
Moore, Alicia J. .........'60 '86 C.813 A.B. L.1068 J.D. V.P. & Gen. Coun., Adaptec, Inc.
Moore, Cliff G. ............ '53 '90 C.112 B.A. L.477 J.D. Corp. Coun., Quantum Corp.
Niven, Kenneth W. ..... '53 '79 C.813 B.S. L.1066 J.D. Asst. Gen. Coun., LSI Logic Corp.
Pursel, David G. '45 '79 C.911 B.S.E.E. L.678 J.D.
(adm. in WA; not adm. in CA; Pat.) Assoc. Gen. Coun., Intell. Prop., LSI Logic Corp.
Rostoker, Michael D. '58 '84 C.665 B.S. L.1218 J.D.
(adm. in NH; not adm. in CA; Pat.) V.P., LSI Logic Corp.
Sanders, David E. '47 '76 C.768 B.S. L.678 J.D.
(adm. in WA; not adm. in CA) V.P., Gen. Coun. & Secy., LSI Logic Corp.
Shpizner, Michael J. ............ '49 '85 C.103 B.A. L.1068 Assoc. Coun., Adaptec Inc.
**Skjerven, Morrill, MacPherson, Franklin & Friel LLP**
(See San Jose)
Smith, Barton A. ......... '48 '79 C.475 B.S.Ch.E. L.770 J.D. Corp. Coun., Quantum Corp.
Sommer, Richard F. ......'61 '92 C.674 B.A. L.813 J.D. CEO & Pres., Dela Cruz Med. Ctr.
Tanner, David R. ............ '41 '81 C.1069 B.S. L.770 J.D. 45 S. Park Victoria Dr.
Toepfer, R. Elizabeth ......... '66 '94 C.112 B.A. L.770 J.D. Legal Asst., Read-Rite Corp.
**Tsai, Michael I.** ............ '60 '90 C.309 A.B. L.659 J.D. D.J. Digital, Inc.
Weiss, Franklyn C. '38 '66 C.645 B.S.E.E. L.128 J.D.
Pat. Coun., LSI Logic Corp. (Pat.)
Wellman, Mary Anne C. .......'56 '95 C.768 B.S. L.770 J.D. Corp. Coun., Quantum Corp.
Williams, Michael J. ... '57 '83 C.112 B.S. L.1137 J.D. Asst. Gen. Coun., LSI Logic Corp.

## MIRANDA, —, *Humboldt Co.*

Hoffman, Frederick C. ............ '28 '67 C.112 A.B. L.1066 J.D. P.O. Box 334‡
Sinoway, Ronald M. ............ '45 '72 C.645 B.A. L.276 J.D. P.O. Box 603

## MISSION HILLS, —, *Los Angeles Co.*

(Part of the incorporated City of Los Angeles)

Draper, Thomas N., (AV) ............ '32 '58 C&L.426 B.S., LL.B. P.O. Box 8119
Friedman, Steven L. '50 '78 C.1077 B.A. L.1221 J.D.
15455 San Fernando Mission Blvd.
Heublein, Vincent W., (AV) ............ '— '50 C.642 L.800 LL.B. P.O. Box 8119
Jackman, Richard ............ '44 '83 C.112 B.A. L.426 J.D. 15545 Devonshire St.
Laing, John B. ............ '53 '88 C.112 B.A. L.809 J.D. 10550 Sepulveda Blvd.
Larson, Timothy A. ............ '50 '75 C.112 B.A. L.809 J.D. 15545 Devonshire St.
Levine, Jeffrey E. ............ '47 '72 C.1077 B.A. L.1049 J.D. 15545 Devonshire St.
McConville, Terence N. ............ '46 '76 C.112 A.B. L.1095 J.D. 10545 Cedros Ave.
Moran, William M. ............ '46 '72 L.1137 J.D. 15455 San Fernando Mission Blvd.
Nelson, Bruce L., (AV) ............ '36 '64 C.112 B.S. L.1068 LL.B. P.O. Box 8119
Schummer, Allan R., (AV) ............ '31 '62 C.112 B.A. L.809 LL.B. 15545 Devonshire St.
Stearns, Robert S., (AV) ............ '23 '57 C.800 B.S. L.809 LL.B. P.O. Box 8119‡

## MISSION VIEJO, 72,820, *Orange Co.*

Allen, Shirli C. ............ '19 '77 C.800 B.E.M.E. L.1137 J.D. John Wayne Airport
Bailey, Robert G. ............ '24 '49 C.112 L.309 LL.B. P.O. Box 2700
**Baur, Maureen E.** ............ '63 '94 C.112 B.A. L.1137 J.D. [Ⓐ T.J.Borchard]
*PRACTICE AREAS: Business Litigation.
**Blackburn, Gregory V.** '51 '77 C.112 B.A. L.809 J.D.
Sr. V.P., Gen. Coun. & Secy., Coldwell Banker Corp.
**Blanchard, John T.** ............ '48 '74 C.475 B.A. L.597 J.D. [Ⓒ Cavett&Assoc.]
*PRACTICE AREAS: Real Estate Litigation; Title Insurance; Intellectual Property; Construction; Real Estate and Mortgage Banking Defense.
Boehmer, Clifford B. ............ '27 '74 C.910 B.S.E.E. L.981 LL.B. 25266 Pacifica
**Boothby, J. Lee** ............ '— '79 C&L.838 B.A., J.D. [Ⓒ T.J.Borchard]
*LANGUAGES: Greek.
*PRACTICE AREAS: General Civil Litigation.
**Borchard, Thomas J.**, (AV) '54 '82
C.475 B.A. L.1187 J.D. [T.J.Borchard] (ⓄSaginaw, MI)
*PRACTICE AREAS: Business; Real Estate Litigation; Civil Litigation; Intellectual Property Litigation.

**Borchard, Thomas J., Inc., A Professional Corporation, (AV)**
**25909 Pala, Suite 380, 92691**Ⓞ
Telephone: 714-457-9505 Facsimile: 714-457-1666
Thomas J. Borchard;—David S. Nichol; Maureen E. Baur; Anna M. Camarena; Nancy Christine Green. Of Counsel: Charles B. Flood, III (Resident, Vista, California Office); J. Lee Boothby.
Business and Real Estate Practice, including Corporate, Partnerships, Estate Planning, Real Property and Construction Law. Civil Trial and Appellate Litigation.
Vista, California Office: 510 Escondido Avenue, Suite E. Telephone: 619-758-3500. Fax: 619-758-0545.
Saginaw, Michigan Office: 2604 West Genesee.
*See Professional Biographies, MISSION VIEJO, CALIFORNIA*

**Boyd, John Roberts, Law Offices of, (AV) '37 '71 C.1097 B.S. L.809 J.D.**
**Los Altos Plaza, 26691 Plaza Drive, Suite 250, 92691**
Telephone: 714-582-8188 Telecopier: 714-582-5902
—Shannon Roberts Boyd.
Civil and Real Estate Litigation, Family Law, Wills, Trusts and Probate Related Matters.
References: Bank of America; ABKO Corp., Wichita, Kansas.
*See Professional Biographies, MISSION VIEJO, CALIFORNIA*

**Boyd, Shannon Roberts** ............ '65 '94 C.800 B.S. L.999 J.D. [Ⓐ J.R.Boyd]
*PRACTICE AREAS: Real Estate; Probate; Wills; Trusts and Estates.
Bracken, Linda J. ............ '51 '80 C.763 B.A. L.809 J.D. 27271 Las Ramblas
**Bruno, Gino J.** '36 '62 C&L.800 B.S., LL.B.
V.P. & Corp. Coun., Coldwell Banker Corp.
**Buckley, Lawrence J.**, (AV) .....'51 '76 C.801 B.A. L.990 J.D. [Buckley] (ⓄPhoenix AZ)
*PRACTICE AREAS: Real Estate, Commercial and Business Litigation; Creditor Representation; Bankruptcy and Insolvency Litigation; Foreclosures.
Buckley, Stephen S. ............ '39 '69 C&L.339 B.S., J.D. 22911 Via Santa Maria‡

**Buckley Firm, The, P.C., (AV)** BB
**Suite 200, 26522 La Alameda, 92691**
Telephone: 714-348-8300 Facsimile: 714-348-8310 Email: TBF_law@ix.netcom.com
Email: 73321.331@compuserve.com
Lawrence J. Buckley; John Thomas Callan; Jeffrey W. Griffith; Stephen J. Kane; John W. Klein; Paula Scotland; Edgar C. Smith, III; Adam H. Springel. Of Counsel: Timothy D. Carlyle; Jonathan C. Cavett.

(This Listing Continued)

**Buckley Firm, The, P.C. (Continued)**

Real Estate, Commercial and Business Litigation. Creditor Bankruptcy, Title Insurance Litigation, Real Estate Foreclosures and Related Litigation; Construction Defect and Employment Litigation.
Reference: Bank of California.
*See Professional Biographies, MISSION VIEJO, CALIFORNIA*

Butler, Michael V. ............ '51 '83 C.112 B.S. L.1137 J.D. 24832 Lagrima St.
**Callan, John Thomas** ............ '55 '91 C.767 B.S. L.800 J.D. [Buckley] (ⓄPhoenix AZ)
*PRACTICE AREAS: Real Estate Transactions and Litigation; Business Litigation.
**Camarena, Anna M.** ............ '58 '94 C.1078 L.1186 J.D. [Ⓐ T.J.Borchard]
*PRACTICE AREAS: Business Transactional; Estate Planning; Family Law; Business Litigation.
Carey, Rodger M., (BV) ....... '47 '78 C.112 B.A. L.1137 J.D. 26421 Crown Valley Pkwy.
**Carlyle, Timothy D.**, (AV) ............ '48 '74 C.112 B.A. L.1065 J.D. [Ⓒ Buckley]
*PRACTICE AREAS: Real Estate; Business Law; Finance.
**Cavett, Jonathan C.**, (BV) '40 '77
C.1077 B.A. L.1095 J.D. [Cavett&Assoc.] & [Ⓒ Buckley]
*PRACTICE AREAS: Real Estate Litigation; Title Insurance; Intellectual Property; Construction Law; Mortgage Banking Defense.

**Cavett & Associates, (BV)**
**26522 La Alameda, Suite 200, 92691**
Telephone: 714-348-7144 Fax: 714-348-8310
Jonathan C. Cavett. Of Counsel: John T. Blanchard.
Real Estate Litigation, Title Insurance, Intellectual Property, Construction, Real Estate and Mortgage Banking Defense.

Chou, Donald ............ '52 '77 C.45 B.A. L.93 J.D. Professional Fin. Advisors, Inc.
Connors, Donald E. ............ '52 '78 C.454 B.A. L.1202 J.D. 25291 Terreno
Cover, James N. ............ '— '88 L.1137 J.D. 27758 Santa Margarita Pkwy., #282
Cozad, Ronald J. ............ '55 '84 C.112 B.A. L.426 J.D. [Cozad&K.]
Cozad & Krutcik ............ 26691
Davis, Dorothy K., (AV) ............ '28 '53 C.112 A.B. L.1066 J.D. 23722 Via Potes‡
DeLorenzo, Kenneth L. ............ '45 '77 C.1109 B.S. L.1137 J.D. 27001 LaPaz Rd.
Doherty, Martin J. ............ '38 '75 C.1041 B.A. L.1137 J.D. 27442 Almendra
Dougherty, Frank ............ '17 '41 C&L.145 A.B., J.D. 27812 Via Granados
Douglass, Willis B. '50 '78 C.691 B.A. L.796 J.D.
(adm. in CO; not adm. in CA) 25402 Campina Dr.
Dumhart, Anton ............ '33 '63 C.336 B.S. L.1068 J.D. 21497 Bastia‡
Farrell, Jodeane Barlow, (BV) ............ '45 '76 C.37 B.A. L.426 J.D. [J.B.Farrell]
Farrell, Jodeane Barlow, A Professional Corporation, (BV) ....26921 Crown Valley Pkwy.
**Faust, Robert V., II**, (BV) ............ '51 '78 C.1109 B.A. L.1137 J.D. [Faust&F.]Ⓞ

**Faust & Faust, (BV)**
**Suite 200, 27281 Las Ramblas, 92691**Ⓞ
Telephone: 714-582-3540 Fax: 714-582-5300
Members of Firm: Robert V. Faust (1921-1988); Robert V. Faust, II.
Custody Support, Family, Personal Injury Law, Probate and Estates.
Orange, California Office: 500 North State College Boulevard, Suite 780. Telephone: 714-582-3540.
*See Professional Biographies, MISSION VIEJO, CALIFORNIA*

Fleming, Jeff. A. ............ '55 '82 C.169 B.A. L.1137 J.D. 23166 Los Alisos Blvd.
Foulke, Maria May ............ '67 '92 C.112 B.A. L.1065 J.D. Ceramic Creations
Friedman, David ............ '36 '72 L.1001 J.D. 27758 Santa Margarita Pkwy.
Gould, Richard B. ..... '47 '74 C.846 B.A. L.365 J.D. Litig. Coun., Coldwell Banker Corp.
Greco, Cosmo C. '14 '40 C&L.705 LL.B.
(adm. in NJ; not adm. in CA) 27866 Via Sarasate‡
**Green, Nancy Christine** ............ '67 '94 C.1042 B.S. L.1137 J.D. [Ⓐ T.J.Borchard]
*LANGUAGES: Spanish.
*PRACTICE AREAS: Business Litigation; Corporate Litigation/Transaction; Civil Transaction/Litigation.
Greenberg, Arthur R. '14 '38 C.867 L.1009 LL.B.
(adm. in NY; not adm. in CA) 27392 Via Cortez
Greenstreet, Max L. '10 '33 C.1042 L.862
(adm. in OK; not adm. in CA) 25511 Classic Dr.‡
**Griffith, Jeffrey W.** ............ '50 '76 C.112 B.A. L.1068 J.D. [Buckley]
*PRACTICE AREAS: Business Litigation; Bankruptcy Law; Real Estate Law; Creditor's Rights; Anti Competitive Practices.
Harms, Michael S. ............ '59 '86 C.800 B.S. L.770 J.D. 26141 Las Flores
Harrison, David M. ............ '53 '95 C.999 B.A. L.1137 J.D. 23456 Madero
Heller, Frank ............ '23 '54 27832 Via Sarasate
Henson, Barbara A. ............ '26 '50 C.242 A.B. L.94 J.D. 26591 Lira Circle
Hull, Michael B. '45 '81
C.800 B.S. L.276 J.D. V.P. & Litig. Coun., Coldwell Banker Corp.
Jackson, James T. ............ '57 '91 C.1042 B.S. L.1137 J.D. 25909 Pala
Jacobs, Barry J. ............ '47 '73 C.679 B.S.A.E. L.990 J.D. 23762 Calle Salvador
**Johnson, Max B.** '42 '72
C.800 M.S.C.E. L.1137 J.D. Asst. Gen. Coun., Mission Viejo Co.
**Kane, Stephen J.** ............ '67 '93 C.36 B.S. L.1049 J.D. [Ⓐ Buckley]
*PRACTICE AREAS: Construction; Real Estate; Business; Commercial Litigation.
Kaye, Stuart M. ............ '46 '80 C.36 B.S. L.1137 J.D. 23456 Madero
Kirby, Paula G. '50 '83 C.1204 B.S. L.838 J.D.
(adm. in AZ; not adm. in CA) 25231 Mistyridge‡
**Klein, John W.** ............ '56 '86 C.178 B.A. L.273 J.D. [Buckley]
*LANGUAGES: German.
*PRACTICE AREAS: Real Estate; Commercial and Business Litigation; Bankruptcy; Insolvency.
Krogh, David L. .......'54 '88 C.768 B.S. L.1137 J.D. Litig. Coun., Coldwell Banker Corp.
Krutcik, James A. ............ '61 '89 C.800 B.A. L.990 J.D. [Cozad&K.]
Lampel, Eric P. .........'55 '80 C.112 B.A. L.426 J.D. 26421 Crown Valley Pkwy., 2nd Fl.
LeSourd, Peter '38 '66 C.813 B.A. L.309 J.D.
(adm. in WA; not adm. in CA) Assoc. Prof., Saddleback Coll.
Linsenbard, William E. ............ '31 '61 C.112 B.A. L.809 LL.B. 27271 Las Ramblas
Martens, Eric W., (AV) ............ '40 '65 C.112 B.A. L.1068 LL.B. 26861 Trabaco Rd.
Martin, Janet S. ..............'59 '84 C.1042 B.S. L.426 J.D. Gen. Coun., Sir Speedy, Inc.
Mellenger, Richard E. ............ '44 '71 C.116 B.S. L.107 J.D. 26691 Plaza
Merritt, Thomas R. ............ '58 '85 C.1109 B.A. L.1065 J.D. 27271 Las Ramblas
Million, Gary E. ............ '51 '94 C.398 B.S. L.1137 J.D. 23456 Madero
Moore, Terrence Jay ............ '58 '91 C.1232 B.A. L.809 J.D. 25909 Pala
Mount, Larry C. ............ '55 '82 C.1109 B.A. L.464 J.D. 22561 Summerfield
Murphy, Edward J. '18 '49 C.579 L.585 LL.B.
(adm. in ND; not adm. in CA) 27561 Cenajo‡
Nestor, Paul J., (AV) ............ '45 '69 C.749 B.S. L.262 J.D. [P.J.Nestor]
Nestor, Paul J., A P.C., (AV) ............ 27772 Vista Del Lago
**Nichol, David S.** ............ '62 '92 C.381 B.S. L.1187 J.D. [Ⓐ T.J.Borchard]
*PRACTICE AREAS: Real Estate; Business Litigation; Environmental Hazard Litigation Matters; Intellectual Property Litigation.
Osborne, Paul R. ............ '36 '75 C.921 L.1137 J.D. 24541 Artemia Ave.
Pfingst, Joseph P. ............ '24 '78 C&L.724 B.A., LL.B. 24043 Silvestre
Pocock, T. Keith ............ '36 '63 C.208 B.S.B.A. L.1068 J.D. 23761 Via Fabricante
Quiel, Frederick G. ............ '45 '95 C.1073 B.S. L.1137 J.D. 23456 Madero
Resnik, Leona '16 '45 C&L.800 A.B., J.D.
(adm. in DC; not adm. in CA) 27642 Via Turina‡

Richebourg, J. Ronald '39 '76
C.768 B.S. L.1026 J.D. Asst. Gen. Coun., Unisys Corp. (Pat.)
**Rose, Ronald W.** '46 '72
C.1077 B.A. L.1065 J.D. V.P. & Dir., Litig., Coldwell Banker Corp.
Ruben, Audrey H. '26 '77 C.569 B.A. L.724 J.D.
(adm. in NY; not adm. in CA) 21285 Amora‡
Ruben, Robert J., (AVⓉ) '23 '54 C.178 B.S. L.262 LL.B.
(adm. in NY; not adm. in CA) 21285 Amora‡
Sammons, Donald E. '32 '59 C.610 B.S. L.150 LL.B. 26895 LaSierra Dr.
**Scotland, Paula** '49 '87 C.475 B.S. L.426 J.D. [Buckley]
*REPORTED CASES: In Re Thomas K. Morgan, 149 B.R. 147 (9th Cir. BAP (Cal.), Jan 12, 1993).
*PRACTICE AREAS: Bankruptcy Law.
Selski, Berl H., (AV) '46 '72 C.1097 B.S. L.426 J.D. [Selski&S.]
Selski & Sturgeon, (AV) 26471 Crown Valley Pky.
Sessions, Don D., (AV) '49 '76 C.101 B.S. L.426 J.D. [D.D.Sessions]
Sessions, Don D., A Prof. Law Corp., (AV) 23456 Madero
Shapiro, Barnett '10 '36 C.112 L.809 24091 Ankara St.
**Smith, Edgar C., III** '57 '86 C.397 B.A. L.809 J.D. [Buckley]
*PRACTICE AREAS: Business Commercial and Real Estate Litigation; Bankruptcy.
**Smith, William K.** '44 '70 C.684 B.A. L.1068 J.D.
Sr. V.P., Gen. Coun. & Secy., Mission Viejo Co.
Spackman, Randall P. '44 '74 C.101 B.A. L.228 J.D. 27271 Las Ramblas
**Springel, Adam H.** '68 '93 C.477 B.A. L.1049 J.D. [Ⓐ Buckley]
*PRACTICE AREAS: Construction, Real Estate and Business Litigation.
Stuart, Louise J. '49 '80 C.112 B.A. L.1068 J.D. 26932 Oso Pkwy.
Sturgeon, E. Allen '42 '74 C&L.1137 B.S.L., J.D. [Selski&S.]
Sweeney, James S., (BV) '51 '77 C.276 B.S.F.S. L.1009 J.D. 26300 La Almeda St.
Valk, Alec '52 '77 C.112 B.A. L.596 J.D. [A.Valk]
Valk, Alec, A Prof. Corp. 25909 Pala
Von der Ahe, Vincent M. '46 '72 C.800 B.S. L.813 J.D. 26440 La Alameda
Wallace, Bruce D., (AV) '41 '65 C&L.813 B.A., J.D. 27929 Trocadero‡
Warde, Deirdre '36 '81 C.999 B.S. L.1137 J.D. 27405 Puerta Real
Watson, Eugene B., (CV) '42 '72 C.420 B.A. L.1137 J.D. 24722 Spadra Lane
**Webster, Walter D.** '37 '65 C.645 B.S.E.E. L.61 J.D.
Sr. V.P., Mun. Legal Affs. & Govt. Rel., Mission Viejo Co.
Weston, Robert G. '22 '51 L.607 J.D.
(adm. in OH; not adm. in CA) 25286 Aldea Ct.‡
Wolcott, Dixon R., (BV) '46 '73 C.112 B.A. L.1065 J.D. 27046 Pacific Terr. Dr.
Yemen, Arpo '22 '64 C&L.912 B.S.C.E., LL.B.
(adm. in MI; not adm. in CA) 24902 Via Santa Cruz‡

## MODESTO, * 164,730, *Stanislaus Co.*

Abbott, Michael L., (CV) '55 '90 L.464 J.D. [Rein&A.]
Aguilar, Charles E. '26 '61 Mun. Ct. J.
Aguilar, Kathleen '56 '82 C&L.813 B.A., J.D. Small Clms. Advsr., Co. Coun.
Aguirre, Mary Ann '54 '81 C.112 B.A. L.1065 J.D. 1130 12th St.
Alonso, George '52 '83 C.1222 B.A. Ec. L.770 J.D. [Alonso]
Alonso Law Firm, The 2031 D Yosemite Blvd.
Ameral, Ann Q., (BV) '54 '80 C.1079 B.A. L.1065 J.D. 919 15th St.
Andersen, Richard Lee '52 '78 C.112 B.A. L.990 J.D. 1301 K St.
**Anderson, Erik R.**, (CV) '50 '78 C.112 A.B. L.770 J.D. [Ⓐ Curtis&A.]
*PRACTICE AREAS: Business Planning Law; Business Litigation; General Civil Litigation.
Anderson, George E., (BV) '44 '74 C.1079 B.A. L.1132 J.D. [Rushing,L.&A.]
**Anderson, Thomas L.**, (BV) '45 '74 C.101 B.A. L.878 J.D. [Strauss,N.A.&R.]
*PRACTICE AREAS: Negligence; Products Liability; Workers Compensation; Civil Trial.
**Arata, George S.**, (BV) '50 '76 C.169 B.A. L.113 J.D. [Curtis&A.]
*PRACTICE AREAS: Insurance Defense Law; Workers Compensation Law; Personal Injury Law.

**Askew & Archbold**
**(See Stockton)**

**Augustine, Rodney A.** '60 '87 C.112 B.A. L.464 J.D. [Colaw&A.]
*PRACTICE AREAS: Estate Planning; Business Law; Tax; Civil Litigation.
Avila, Philip B., (BV) '53 '83 C.267 B.A. L.464 J.D. 900 "H" St.
Azevedo, Arthur, (BV) '43 '67 C.112 A.B. L.1066 J.D. 1316 "K" St.
Azevedo, Eugene M. '35 '60 C&L.770 B.S., J.D. Supr. Ct. J.
Ball, John R., (BV) '42 '67 C.169 A.B. L.1065 J.D. [Duncan,B.E.&U.]⊙
Barakatt, James '30 '64 C.1060 B.A. L.1132 Mun. Ct. J.
**Barringer, Bart W.**, (BV) '57 '85 C.169 B.A. L.464 J.D. [Mayol&B.]
*PRACTICE AREAS: Civil Litigation; Real Estate Law; Business Transactions.
**Bartow, Brian J.** '55 '89 C.112 A.B. L.1067 J.D. [Ⓐ Damrell,N.S.P.&L.]
*PRACTICE AREAS: Healthcare and Hospital Law; Litigation; Business Law.
**Beal, Richard M.** '47 '72
C.472 B.B.A. L.966 J.D. V.P. & Spec. Coun., E. & J. Gallo Winery
*RESPONSIBILITIES: Taxation; General Business.
Beauchesne, Roger M. '47 '76 C.823 B.A. L.1065 J.D. Mun. Ct. J.
Beaver, Lawrence C., (CV) '52 '78 C.169 B.A. L.1132 J.D. 429 15th St.
Beck, Stephen R., (CV) '50 '79 C.112 A.B. L.1067 J.D. 1124 11th St.
Begen, Gerard John, (BV) '49 '85 C.573 B.S. L.809 J.D. Dep. Dist. Atty.
Benincasa, Stephanie '61 '93 C.459 B.S. L.990 J.D. 1014 16th St.
**Betker, Judy A.** '66 '91 C.1042 B.S. L.770 J.D. [Ⓐ Curtis&A.]
*PRACTICE AREAS: Estate Planning; Business Planning; Taxation; Business Law.
Bonte, Thomas H., (CV) '52 '85 C.112 B.A. L.770 J.D. 1301 K St.

**Borton, Petrini & Conron, (AV)**
**The Turner Building, 900 "H" Street, Suite D, 95354⊙**
**Telephone: 209-576-1701 Fax: 209-527-9753**
**Email: bpcmod@bpclaw.com**
**Members of Firm: Bradley A. Post; Michael J. Macko; Samuel L. Phillips.**
**Commercial/Real Estate Litigation, Insurance Law, General Civil Trial and Appellate Practice in State and Federal Courts, Personal Injury and Casualty Defense Litigation, Insurance Bad Faith and Coverage, Labor and Employment, Toxic Torts, Real Estate, Land Use Planning, Zoning, Municipal, Professional Errors and Omissions, Healthcare Provider Malpractice Defense, Products Liability, Oil and Gas, Water, Natural Resources, Environmental, Public Entity, Administrative, Agricultural, Banking, Contracts, Corporations, Partnerships, Taxation, Creditor's Remedies, Bankruptcy, Probate, Estate Planning, Family Law.**
**Bakersfield, California Office: The Borton, Petrini & Conron Building, 1600 Truxtun Avenue, P.O. Box 2026. Telephone: 805-322-3051. Fax: 805-322-4628. Email: bpcbak@bpclaw.com.**
**San Luis Obispo, California Office: 1114 Marsh Street. Telephone: 805-541-4340. Fax: 805-541-4558. Email: bpcslo@bpclaw.com.**
**Visalia, California Office: 206 South Mooney Boulevard, P.O. Box 1028. Telephone: 209-627-5600. Fax: 209-627-4309. Email: bpcvis@bpclaw.com.**
**Fresno, California Office: T. W. Patterson Building, 2014 Tulare Street, Suite 830. Telephone: 209-268-0117. Fax: 209-237-7995. Email: bpcfrs@bpclaw.com.**
**Sacramento, California Office: 2233 Watt Avenue, Suite 290. Telephone: 916-484-3555. Fax: 916-484-3550. Email: bpcsac@bpclaw.com.**
**Santa Barbara, California Office: 211 East Victoria Street, Suite D. Telephone: 805-564-2404. Fax: 805-564-2176. Email: bpcsb@bpclaw.com**
**Los Angeles, California Office: 707 Wilshire Boulevard, Suite 5100. Telephone: 213-624-2869. Fax: 213-489-3930. Email: bpcla@bpclaw.com.**
**San Diego, California Office: John Burnham Building, 610 West Ash Street, 9th Floor. Telephone: 619-232-2424. Fax: 619-531-0794. Email: bpcsd@bpclaw.com.**

(This Listing Continued)

**Borton, Petrini & Conron (Continued)**
**Newport Beach, California Office: 4675 MacArthur Court, Suite 1150. Telephone: 714-752-2333. Fax: 714-752-2854. Email: bpcnb@bpclaw.com.**
**San Francisco, California Office: 111 Pine Street, Suite 730. Telephone: 415-981-4415. Fax: 415-391-5538. Email: bpcsf@bpclaw.com.**
**Redding, California Office: 280 Hemsted Drive, Suite 100. Telephone: 916-222-1530. Fax: 916-222-4498. Email: bpcred@bpclaw.com.**
**San Bernardino, California Office: 290 North "D" Street, Suite 500. Telephone: 909-381-0527. Fax: 909-381-0658. Email: bpcsbdo@bpclaw.com.**
**San Jose, California Office: 2 North Second Street. Telephone: 408-298-3997. Fax: 408-298-3365. Email: bpcsj@bpclaw.com.**
**Ventura, California Office: 1000 Hill Road, Suite 310. Telephone: 805-650-9994. Fax: 805-650-7125. Email: bpcvta@bpclaw.com.**
**Santa Rosa, California Office: 50 Santa Rosa Avenue, Suite 300. Telephone: 707-527-9477. Fax: 707-527-9488. Email: bpcsr@bpclaw.com.**
***See Professional Biographies, MODESTO, CALIFORNIA***

**Boyd, Katherine R.**, (CV) '60 '89 C&L.836 B.S., J.D. [Trimbur D.E.&B.]
*PRACTICE AREAS: Civil Litigation; Personal Injury; Insurance Defense; Employment Law.
Boyland, William E. '40 '66 C&L.608 B.A., J.D. Dep. Pub. Def.
Brennan, Francis W. '19 '47 C.674 A.B. L.309 LL.B. 1812 Camden Dr.‡
**Brereton, Hugh E.**, (BV) '43 '74 C.112 B.A. L.464 J.D. [Curtis&A.]
*PRACTICE AREAS: Family Law; Probate Law.
**Brew, Richard Douglas**, (AV) '47 '72 C.112 B.A. L.426 J.D. [R.D.Brew]
*PRACTICE AREAS: Business; Corporation and Corporate Financing; International Business; Real Estate; Taxation.

**Brew, Richard Douglas, A Professional Law Corporation, (AV) BB**
**Suite 350 / Judge Frank C. Damrell Building, 1601 I Street, 95354-1110**
**Telephone: 209-572-3157 Telefax: 209-572-4641**
**Email: interleg.com**
**Richard Douglas Brew.**
**Sophisticated Business, Financial, and Transactional Legal Service.**
***See Professional Biographies, MODESTO, CALIFORNIA***

**Brink, Karin Smith**, (CV) '63 '90 C.800 A.B. L.464 J.D. [Israels,B.&G.]
*PRACTICE AREAS: Estate Planning; Elder Rights; Guardianships; Conservatorships; Trusts and Probate Matters.
Brody, Alton A., Jr. '46 '76 C.763 L.61 J.D. 304 Greenwich Lane‡
Brondyke, Donald V. '19 '51 C&L.912 B.A., LL.B.
(adm. in MI; not adm. in CA) P.O. Box 4938‡
Brooks, Guy Allen '34 '70 C.1079 B.A. L.1132 J.D. 920 15th St.
**Brunn, Charles K.**, (AV) '31 '57 C&L.767 B.S., J.D. [Brunn&F.]
**Brunn, Gerald E.**, (BV) '57 '82 C&L.767 B.A., J.D. [Brunn&F.]

**Brunn & Flynn, A Professional Corporation, (AV) BB**
**928 12th Street, P.O. Box 3366, 95353**
**Telephone: 209-521-2133 Fax: 209-521-7584**
**Email: brunnfly@ix.netcom.com**
**Charles K. Brunn; Timothy T. Flynn; Gerald E. Brunn; Roger S. Matzkind;—Michael G. Donovan; Andrew N. Eshoo.**
**Insurance Defense, Civil Defense. General Civil Trial Practice. Real Estate, Construction Law, Probate, Trust, Estate Planning, Corporate, Family and Workers Compensation Law, Personal Injury. Trials in all Courts.**
***See Professional Biographies, MODESTO, CALIFORNIA***

Buchler, Robert L., (CV) '48 '82 C.112 B.S. L.464 J.D. 1024 J St.
Budin, Jerome N. '46 '79 C.112 B.A. L.1067 J.D. 1316 K St.
Burch, Marjorie A. '58 '86 C.464 B.A. L.1026 J.D. [Ⓐ Cunningham&L.]
**Burks, Kristine L.** '67 '96 C.112 B.S. L.284 J.D. [Ⓐ Damrell,N.S.P.&L.]
*PRACTICE AREAS: Business Litigation; Commercial Litigation; Antitrust.
Burns, Susan E., (CV) '62 '88 C.112 B.A. L.1065 J.D. 318 McHenry Ave.
Bush, Diedre Jane Josephine, Law Offices of '47 '89
C.139 B.A. L.861 J.D. 1301 K. St., Ste C.
**Byrd, Timothy A.** '60 '87 C.112 A.B. L.1066 J.D. Atty., E. & J. Gallo Winery
*RESPONSIBILITIES: Environmental; Real Estate; Contracts.
**Cabral, Ted M.** '66 '93 C.112 B.A. L.770 J.D. [Ⓐ Curtis&A.]
*LANGUAGES: Portuguese.
**Calverley, Helen M.** '64 '91 C.475 B.A. L.215 J.D. [Ⓐ Crabtree,S.Z.J.&F.]
*PRACTICE AREAS: Business Law; Employment Litigation; Health Care.
Camacho, Timothy M. '66 '91 C.1073 B.S. L.112 J.D. [Ⓐ Moorad,C.&G.]
Canant, Fred C. '29 '53 C&L.69 A.B., LL.B. [Canant&W.]
Canant & Woodall 621 Fourteenth St., Suite A
Cardenas, David '54 '82 C.267 B.A. L.770 J.D. 821 13th St., Suite A
**Cardozo, A. A., Jr.**, (AV) '36 '61 C.813 A.B. L.1065 J.D. [Cardozo&C.]
*PRACTICE AREAS: Insurance Defense; Personal Injury; Railroad Law; Medical Malpractice; Employment Litigation.
**Cardozo, Richard A.**, (BV) '50 '76 C.1079 B.A. L.1137 J.D. [Cardozo&C.]
*PRACTICE AREAS: General Civil Litigation; Insurance Defense Law; Personal Injury Law.

**Cardozo & Cardozo, (AV) BB**
**1101 Sylvan Avenue, #B-4, 95350**
**Telephone: 209-571-3600 FAX: 209-571-1553**
**Members of Firm: A. A. Cardozo, Jr.; Richard A. Cardozo.**
**Civil and Trial Practice, Insurance Defense, F.E.L.A., Personal Injury, Labor/Employment Law and Sexual Harassment.**
***See Professional Biographies, MODESTO, CALIFORNIA***

**Carlson, Jonathan A.** '62 '88 C.1288 B.A. L.464 J.D. [Ⓐ Curtis&A.]
*PRACTICE AREAS: Business Litigation; Construction Law; Commercial Litigation; Creditor Bankruptcy; Public Entity Defense Litigation.
Carner, Bert M., Jr. '12 '38 P.O. Box 828‡
Cash-Dudley, E.F., (CV) '44 '82 C.1079 L.1065 J.D. 1608 F St.
**Cashman, Wylie P.**, (BV) '47 '81 C.182 B.A. L.770 J.D. [Normoyle&N.]
*PRACTICE AREAS: Civil Litigation; Real Estate Transactions; Business Transactions; Construction Law.
Cassidy, Alan K. '57 '89 C.112 B.A. L.1097 J.D. [Ⓐ Perry&W.]
Chamness, Christopher L. '50 '81 C.668 B.A. L.809 J.D.
2312 Ustick Rd. (⊙Claremont)
Champion, Darrell F., (BV) '49 '74 C&L.464 J.D. [Champion,W.&N.]
Champion, Walker & Niermeyer, A Prof. Law Corp., (BV) 419 Tully Rd.
Chartrand, Cory B. '65 '93 C.101 B.A. L.464 J.D. [Ⓐ Thayer,H.H.&G.]
Chase, Robert D. '44 '73 C.802 B.A. L.61 J.D. Chf. Dep. Pub. Def.
**Christian, Michelle Luisa** '71 '96 C.112 B.A. L.1065 J.D. [Ⓐ Damrell,N.S.P.&L.]
**Cipponeri, Terri L.**, (CV) '61 '89 C.1079 B.S. L.1065 J.D. [Ⓐ Curtis&A.]
*PRACTICE AREAS: Litigation; Insurance Defense; Personal Injury.
Clark, Albert G., Jr., (BV) '38 '64 C.112 A.B. L.1065 J.D. [Moorad,C.&G.]
**Cochrane, Kenneth C.**, (BV) '48 '72 C.112 B.S. L.1065 J.D. [Jones,C.H.N.&Z.]
*PRACTICE AREAS: Family Law.
**Colaw, Curtis D.**, (CV) '60 '87 C.267 B.S. L.464 J.D. [Colaw&A.]
*PRACTICE AREAS: Collections; Business Law; Family Law; Civil Litigation.

**Colaw & Augustine, (CV)**
**717 16th Street, Suite 3, 95354**
**Telephone: 209-549-0933 Fax: 209-549-2357**
**Curtis D. Colaw; Rodney A. Augustine.**

(This Listing Continued)

CAA390P

**Colaw & Augustine (Continued)**

**Commercial Collections, Creditors, Bankruptcy, Estate Planning, Business Law, Personal Injury, Family Law, Taxation Law and Civil Trial Practice.**

*See Professional Biographies, MODESTO, CALIFORNIA*

Cole, Dallas J. ....................'39 '68 L.1132 J.D. Co. Pub. Def.
Cole, Terry K. ....................'38 '68 C.36 B.S. L.284 J.D. Mun. Ct. J.
Collins, Carl W., (BV) ..........'51 '83 C.645 B.S. L.1338 J.D. 1127-12th St., Suite 202
**Combs, Carl E.**, (CV) ....................'60 '90 C.101 B.A. L.37 J.D. [Mayol&B.]
*LANGUAGES: Spanish.
*PRACTICE AREAS: Business Law; Civil Litigation; Insurance Law.
Conway, Thomas B., (BV) ....................'24 '52 C.112 A.B. L.1065 819 10th St.
Cook, Jeremy C., Jr., (CV) ..............'48 '76 C.112 A.B. L.1132 J.D. 1119 12th St.
Cordova, Ricardo ..........'54 '79 C.426 B.A. L.1067 J.D. Calif. Rural Legal Assistance
Cousins, Patricia Melugin ....................'43 '79 C.112 A.B. L.770 J.D. 1500 J St.
**Crabtree, Robert W.**, (AV) ........'40 '67 C.112 B.S. L.1065 J.D. [Crabtree,S.Z.J.&F.]
*PRACTICE AREAS: Probate; Estate Planning; Corporate; Business Transactions.

**Crabtree, Schmidt, Zeff, Jacobs & Farrar, (AV) BB**
**1100 14th Street, Second Floor, P.O. Box 3307, 95353**
**Telephone: 209-522-5231 Fax: 209-526-0632**
**Members of Firm: Robert W. Crabtree; Walter J. Schmidt; Thomas D. Zeff; Nan Cohan Jacobs; E. Daniel Farrar. Associate: Helen M. Calverley.**
**General Civil and Criminal Trial Practice. Probate, Estate Planning, Insurance, Real Property, Commercial Law, Secured Transactions, Bankruptcy (Debtor and Creditor), Banking, Insurance Defense, Family Law, Adoptions and Corporation Law.**
**Counsel for: Great American Insurance Co.; United Pacific/Reliance Insurance Co.; Hahn Property Management Corp.; Kemper Insurance Co.; State Farm Fire & Casualty; National Can Co.; Central Valley Production Credit Assn.; WestAmerica Bank.**

*See Professional Biographies, MODESTO, CALIFORNIA*

Critzer, Stephen A., (CV) ....................'58 '86 C.1051 B.S. L.464 J.D. [Critzer&M.]
Critzer & McDade, (CV) ....................1031 15th St., Ste 4
Cummins, Nancy Ashley, (BV) ..........'59 '90 C.1077 B.S. L.769 J.D. Dep. Dist. Atty.
Cunningham & Lansden, (BV)
605 Standiford Ave., #N (⊙Simi Valley, Victorville, Lancaster, Fresno, Modesto & Oxnard)
**Curtis, Ralph S.**, (BV) ....................'48 '74 C.740 B.A. L.1067 J.D. [Curtis&A.]
*PRACTICE AREAS: General Civil Litigation; Insurance Defense Law; Personal Injury Law; Employment Law; Professional Liability.

**Curtis & Arata, A Professional Corporation, (BV)**
**1300 K Street, Second Floor, P.O. Box 3030, 95353**
**Telephone: 209-521-1800 Fax: 209-572-3501**
**A. A. Cardozo (1910-1985); Ralph S. Curtis; George S. Arata; D. Lee Hedgepeth; Michael B. Ijams; Edgar H. Hayden, Jr.; Hugh E. Brereton;—Erik R. Anderson; Jonathan A. Carlson; Terri L. Cipponeri; Richard J. Sordello, Jr.; Ross W. Lee; Jack M. Jacobson; Ted M. Cabral; Sabrina Tourtlotte; Judy A. Betker; Andrew S. Mendlin; Kimberly W. Ringer.**
**General Civil, Trial and Appellate Practice. Corporation, Business, Real Property, Tax, Bankruptcy, Insurance and Insurance Defense, Estate Planning, Probate, Trusts, Family Law, Workers' Compensation Defense, Personal Injury, Employment Law, Environmental Law, Products Liability, Guardianships, Conservatorships and Adoptions.**
**Representative Clients: California State Automobile Assn.; State Farm Mutual Insurance Co.**
**Reference: Modesto Banking Co. (Main Branch-Modesto).**

*See Professional Biographies, MODESTO, CALIFORNIA*

**Damrell, Frank C., Jr.**, (AV) '38 '65
C.112 A.B. L.976 LL.B. [Damrell,N.S.P.&L.] (⊙Sacramento)
*PRACTICE AREAS: Complex Litigation; Business Litigation; Government Law; Administrative Law.

**Damrell, Nelson, Schrimp, Pallios & Ladine, A Professional Corporation, (AV) BB**
**1601 I Street, Fifth Floor, 95354⊙**
**Telephone: 209-526-3500 Fax: 209-526-3534**
**Email: dnsp1@ix.netcom.com**
**Frank C. Damrell (1898-1988); Frank C. Damrell, Jr.; Duane L. Nelson; Roger M. Schrimp; Steven G. Pallios; Wray F. Ladine; Matthew O. Pacher; Fred A. Silva;—Craig W. Hunter; John K. Peltier; Brian J. Bartow; Jefferey A. Wooten; C. Kelley Evans; Wendelin Z. Warwick; Lisa L. Gillispie; Amy E. Elliott; Kristine L. Burks; Michelle Luisa Christian. Of Counsel: Surendra J. Sood, M.D.; Cressey H. Nakagawa.**
**Civil Trial and Appellate Practice in all State and Federal Courts. General Business Practice, Complex Business Litigation, Government, Administrative and Legislative Practice, Business Planning and Dissolution, Personal Injury and Insurance Law, Corporate, Environmental, Resource Recovery, Water and Agricultural Law, Land Use, Real Estate Development, Zoning and Construction Law, Healthcare and Hospital Law, Taxation, Estate Planning and Probate and Trust Administration.**
**Representative Clients: American Honda Motor Co., Inc.; Bronco Wine Co.; E. & J. Gallo Winery; Gallo Glass Co.; The Luckey Co.; Norfolk Southern Corp.; Pep Boys of California, Inc.; W. R. Grace & Co.; National Medical Enterprises, Inc.; Ogden Corp.**
**Sacramento, California Office: Suite 200, 1100 K Street. Telephone: 916-447-2909. Fax: 916-447-0552.**
**Oakdale, California Office: 703 West "F" Street, P.O. Drawer C. Telephone: 209-848-3500. Fax: 209-848-3400.**

*See Professional Biographies, MODESTO, CALIFORNIA*

Daniel, Christopher G. ..............'66 '92 C.112 B.S.M.E. L.861 J.D. 1601 I St. 5th Fl.
Davis, Brian C., (CV) ....................'48 '78 C.560 B.A. L.464 J.D. 802 14th St.
**Davis, Gary S.**, (AV) ....................'39 '65 C.37 B.S. L.1065 J.D. [Trimbur D.E.&B.]
*PRACTICE AREAS: Civil Litigation; Personal Injury; Insurance Defense; Employment Law.
de Camp, Donald T., (BV) ....................'48 '73 C.210 B.A. L.767 J.D. Dep. Pub. Def.
**Dinkler, Sara Church** .......'57 '83 C.112 B.A. L.1066 J.D. Atty., E. & J. Gallo Winery
*RESPONSIBILITIES: Litigation; Labor/Employment; Contracts; Intellectual Property.
Donahue, Michael Wayne ....................'50 '86 L.1132 J.D. 2401 Van Pelt Pl.
**Donovan, Michael G.** ....................'50 '92 C.1060 B.A. L.1153 J.D. [A Brunn&F.]
Drabkin, Harry P. ....................'36 '70 C.766 B.A. L.1026 J.D. Dep. Co. Coun.
Duncan, Jerry M., (AV) ............'42 '67 C.112 B.A. L.1065 J.D. [Duncan,B.E.&U.]⊙
Duncan, Ball, Evans & Ubaldi, A Professional Corporation, (AV)
909 14th St. (⊙Sacramento)
**Dunn, John M.** ....................'68 '93 C&L.602 B.A., J.D. [A McCormick,B.S.W.&C.]
**Dyer, Michael J.**, (BV) '54 '83
C.1060 B.S. L.1067 J.D. [Neumiller&B.] (⊙Stockton, CA.)
*PRACTICE AREAS: Personal Injury Law; Products Liability Law; Real Estate Litigation; Business Litigation.
**Dyke, James R.**, (BV) '41 '66 C.911 B.A. L.950 J.D.
[Neumiller&B.] (⊙Stockton, CA.)
*PRACTICE AREAS: Estate Planning; Wills; Trust Law; Probate Law; Estate Taxation Law.
**Echols, Paul E.**, (CV) ....................'60 '89 C.1073 B.A. L.169 J.D. [Trimbur D.E.&B.]
*PRACTICE AREAS: Corporate; Business Law; Business Litigation; Real Estate; Civil Litigation.
Eiser, George H., III, (CV) ..............'48 '75 C.1077 B.A. L.809 J.D. Asst. City Atty.
Elledge, Ernest T., (CV) ....................'49 '83 C.112 L.464 J.D. 1012 11th St.
Elledge, Robt. R. ....................'20 '49 C.112 A.B. L.1065 J.D. 1301 K St.
**Elliott, Amy E.** ....................'70 '96 C.112 B.A. L.608 J.D. [A Damrell,N.S.P.&L.]
*PRACTICE AREAS: Business Litigation; Insurance Defense.
**Eshoo, Andrew N.** ....................'47 '84 C.112 A.B. L.1132 J.D. [Brunn&F.]
*REPORTED CASES: Pacific Gas & Electric Co. v. County of Stanislaus, 35 Cal.App.4th 908, review granted 9/28/95.
**Evans, C. Kelley** ....................'64 '90 C.051 B.A. L.1067 J.D. [A Damrell,N.S.P.&L.]
*LANGUAGES: French, German and Welsh.
*PRACTICE AREAS: Labor and Employment Law; Business Litigation; Probate and Trust Administration and Litigation.

Evans, Mathew D., (BV) ....................'47 '77 C.549 B.S. L.464 J.D. [Duncan,B.E.&U.]⊙
Fairfield, Bernard V ....................'48 '86 C.1077 B.A. L.1132 J.D. Dep. Pub. Def.
**Farrar, E. Daniel** ....................'64 '91 C.999 B.A. L.972 J.D. [Crabtree,S.Z.J.&F.]
*PRACTICE AREAS: Insurance Defense; Civil Litigation.
Faulkner, Kent M., (BV) ....................'42 '79 C.97 B.B.A. L.809 J.D. 1301 "K" St.
Fernwood, Stanley M. ....................'18 '49 C.768 L.1065 LL.B. 2805 Keller St.
Fischer, Randolph A ....................'61 '87 C.1060 B.A. L.1067 J.D. Dep. Dist. Atty.
Flores, Armando M., (BV) ....................'51 '78 C.768 B.A. L.1067 J.D. 429 13th St.
**Flynn, Timothy T.**, (BV) ....................'49 '76 C.112 B.A. L.767 J.D. [Brunn&F.]
Fontan, Douglas T., (BV) ....................'47 '73 C.112 B.A. L.767 J.D. Dep. Dist. Atty.
Ford, Mahlon, (BV) ....................'38 '70 C.1079 B.A. L.1132 J.D. 225 E. Granger
**Fores, Robert P.**, (BV) ....................'58 '85 C.112 B.A. L.464 J.D. [Gianelli&F.]
*PRACTICE AREAS: Civil Litigation; Debt Collection; Personal Injury and Negligence; Construction.
Frailing, John B., (BV) ....................'47 '77 C.112 B.A. L.284 J.D. [Froba,F.&R.]
Freeland, John D. ....................'56 '83 C.112 A.B. L.770 J.D. 1101 Sylvan Ave.
**Friedman, Louis** '39 '67 C.37 B.S. L.426 LL.B.
Exec. V.P., Fin. & Admin., E. & J. Gallo Winery
**Friedrich, Matthew I.** '68 '93
C.770 B.S. L.1065 J.D. [A Neumiller&B.] (⊙Stockton, CA.)
*PRACTICE AREAS: Business Law, Real Estate Taxation, Estate Planning.
Froba, David J., (BV) ....................'39 '77 C.999 B.A. L.284 J.D. [Froba,F.&R.]
Froba, Frailing & Rockwell, (BV) ....................821 13th St.
Fulfer, E. Paul, (BV) ....................'17 '55 C.328 B.A. L.1065 LL.B. 821 13th St.
Fulfer, Richard L., (CV) ....................'54 '80 C.112 B.A. L.770 821 13th St., Ste. E
Gaarde, Ralph E., (BV) ........'38 '67 C.112 B.S. L.1132 1130 Coffee Rd. (⊙Groveland)
Gant, Vernon F., (BV) ....................'48 '78 C.813 B.A. L.1026 J.D. [Gant&G.]
Gant, Warren F., (BV) ....................'27 '55 C.976 B.A. L.813 LL.B. [Gant&G.]
Gant and Gant, (BV) ....................1130 12th Street, Suite E
**Gianelli, David L.**, (BV) ....................'60 '85 C.112 B.A. L.464 J.D. [Gianelli&F.]
*PRACTICE AREAS: Estate Planning, Probate and Trusts; Business and Corporate Planning; Taxation.
**Gianelli, Louis F.**, (AV) ....................'28 '72 C.112 B.S. L.1132 J.D. [Gianelli&F.]
*PRACTICE AREAS: Estate Planning, Probate and Trusts; Business and Corporate Planning.
**Gianelli, Michael L.**, (BV) ....................'51 '76 C.112 B.A. L.464 J.D. [Gianelli&F.]
*PRACTICE AREAS: Bankruptcy (Creditor); Commercial; Debt Collection; Civil Litigation; Estate Planning, Probate and Trusts.

**Gianelli & Fores, A Professional Law Corporation, (AV) BB**
**1014 16th Street, P.O. Box 3212, 95353**
**Telephone: 209-521-6260 Telecopier: 209-521-5971**
**Louis F. Gianelli; Michael L. Gianelli (Certified Specialist, Probate, Estate Planning and Trust Law, The State Bar of California Board of Legal Specialization); Robert P. Fores; David L. Gianelli (Certified Specialist, Probate, Estate Planning and Trust Law, The State Bar of California Board of Legal Specialization); Lisa B. Williams.**
**Business and Corporate Planning, Estate Planning, Probate and Trusts, Bankruptcy (Creditor), Commercial, Debt Collection, Civil Litigation, Personal Injury and Negligence, Construction, Taxation, Discrimination Defense, Adoption, Guardianships, Conservatorships and Juvenile Dependency.**

*See Professional Biographies, MODESTO, CALIFORNIA*

Gillease, Dennis B., (CV) ..........'44 '82 C.871 B.S. L.1132 J.D. 1320 Standiford Ave.
**Gillispie, Lisa L.** ....................'68 '93 C.112 B.A. L.94 J.D. [A Damrell,N.S.P.&L.]
*LANGUAGES: German.
*PRACTICE AREAS: Business Litigation; Securities Litigation; Complex Litigation.
Gilroy, Christine ....................'44 '84 C.112 B.A. L.1153 J.D. Dist. Atty's Off.
Girolami, Aldo ....................'39 '71 C&L.770 B.S.C., J.D. Supr. Ct. J.
Gleason, Sean F., (CV) ....................'53 '81 C.188 B.A. L.284 J.D. [Moorad,C.&G.]
Gonsalves, Victor A. ....................'43 '74 C.112 B.S. L.1065 J.D. 515 13th St.
Goodwin, Gregory J., (CV) ..........'56 '83 C.1060 B.A. L.464 J.D. [A Thayer,H.H.&G.]
Goss, Michael A., (BV) ....................'47 '78 C.490 B.A. L.1132 J.D. 1119 12th St.
Goulart, John B. ....................'55 '86 C.112 B.A. L.1132 J.D. Dep. Dist. Atty.
Gregerson, Byron A., (BV) ..............'42 '86 C.494 B.A. L.999 J.D. [Thayer,H.H.&G.]
Griffin, John E. ....................'10 '36 C.813 A.B. L.767 J.D. 1015 Brady Ave.‡
Griffin, John E., Jr. ....................'39 '66 C.112 A.B. L.767 J.D. Supr. Ct. J.
**Griffith, David R.** ....................'65 '94 L.999 J.D. [Israels,B.&G.]
*PRACTICE AREAS: Complex Business Litigation; Civil Litigation; Bankruptcy (Creditor).
Grisez, John P. ....................'43 '73 C.112 B.S. L.1067 J.D. 724 10th St.‡
Gross, Malcolm D., (BV) ....................'42 '84 C.350 B.S. L.1132 J.D. 1127 12th St.
Haight, Gerald A. W. ..............'42 '69 C.112 B.A. L.1065 J.D. 605 15th St., Ste. A
Halley, Francis W. ....................'12 '38 C.112 B.A. L.1066 J.D. Ret. Supr. Ct. J.
Halley, William Michael, (A Prof. Corp.), (BV) '42 '71
C.767 B.A. L.765 J.D. 1101 15th St.
Hanna, Mitchell J., (BV) '54 '79 C.112 B.A. L.1049 J.D.
Gen. Coun. & Chf. Admin. Offr., Memorial Hosp. Assn.
**Harrell, Brett R.** ..............'55 '83 C.112 A.B. L.602 J.D. Atty., E. & J. Gallo Winery
*RESPONSIBILITIES: Products Liability; Employment/Labor; Commercial/Contracts; Safety Workers.
**Harrigfeld, Karna E.** '66 '92 C.112 B.A. L.464 J.D.
[A Neumiller&B.] (⊙Stockton, CA.)
*PRACTICE AREAS: Environmental Compliance and Cost Recovery; Water Law; Real Estate Acquisition and Development.
**Harris, George P.** ....................'51 '78 C.674 A.B. L.818 J.D. [A Strauss,N.A.&R.]
*PRACTICE AREAS: Civil Litigation.
Hawkins, Lewis N., (BV) ....................'13 '37 L.1065 J.D. 1119 12th St.
**Hawkins, Matthew K.**, (BV) ........'62 '87 C&L.101 B.A., J.D. [McCormick,B.S.W.&C.]
*LANGUAGES: Spanish.
**Hayden, Edgar H., Jr.** ....................'45 '71 C.61 B.A. L.1049 J.D. [Curtis&A.]
*PRACTICE AREAS: Insurance Defense; Subrogation; Collections; Personal Injury; Products Liability.
**Hedgepeth, D. Lee**, (BV) ....................'53 '79 C.1079 B.A. L.464 J.D. [Curtis&A.]
*PRACTICE AREAS: Insurance Defense Law; Workers Compensation Defense; General Civil Litigation.
**Herum, Steven A.**, (BV) '53 '79
C.813 B.A. L.1065 J.D. [Neumiller&B.] (⊙Stockton, CA.)
*REPORTED CASES: L.I.F.E. Committee v. City of Lodi (1989) 213 Cal. App.3d 1139, 262 Cal. Rptr. 1665; Save Stanislaus Area Farm Economy v. Board of Supervisors (1993) 13 Cal.App.4th 141, 16 Cal.Rptr.2d 408; Bright Development v. City of Tracy, (1993) 20 Cal.App.4th 783, 24 Cal.Rptr.2d 618; Stanislaus Audubon Society v. County of Stanislaus (Willms Ranch) (1995) 33 Cal.App.4th 144, 39 Cal.Rptr.2d 54; California Trout v. Schaefer (Stockton-East Water District) 58 F.3d 469 (9th Cir. 1995).
*PRACTICE AREAS: Real Property Acquisition and Development; Land Use Law; Zoning Law; Environmental Law.
Hodder, Janet B., (CV) ....................'38 '82 C.184 B.A. L.1132 J.D. [Thayer,H.H.&G.]
**Hollenback, John J., Jr.**, (BV) ........'50 '75 C.1060 B.A. L.846 J.D. [Jones,C.H.N.&Z.]
*PRACTICE AREAS: Family Law; Business Litigation; Civil Litigation; Writs and Appeals.
Hollingsworth, Gordon, (CV) ....................'48 '74 C.103 B.A. L.284 J.D. 821 13th St.
**Hunter, Craig W.** ....................'55 '80 C.766 B.A. L.1066 J.D. [A Damrell,N.S.P.&L.]
*PRACTICE AREAS: Real Estate; Workouts; Banking.
Hutcheson, Geoffrey C., (BV) ....................'47 '76 C.623 B.A. L.464 J.D. 1124 13th St.
**Ijams, Michael B.**, (BV) ....................'52 '78 C.112 A.B. L.1067 J.D. [Curtis&A.]
*PRACTICE AREAS: Business Law; Civil Litigation; Insurance Defense Law; Employment Law.
Ingersoll, David, (CV) ....................'52 '84 C.112 B.S. L.1065 J.D. Dep. Dist. Atty.
**Israels, Sidney A.**, (AV) ....................'43 '71 C.112 A.B. L.1068 J.D. [Israels,B.&G.]⊙

**Israels, Brink & Griffith, A Professional Law Corporation, (AV)**
**1500 J Street, P.O. Box 1637, 95353⊙**
**Telephone: 209-572-1130 Fax: 209-572-1134**
**Email: ibg@Sonnet.com URL: http://www.sonnet.com:80/modesto/ibg/**

(This Listing Continued)

CAA391P

**Israels, Brink & Griffith, A Professional Law Corporation (Continued)**

Sidney A. Israels; Karin Smith Brink; David R. Griffith.
Civil Practice including Business Litigation, Real Estate Law, Estate Planning, Elder Rights, Guardianships and Conservatorships, Trusts and Probate Matters, Agribusiness Law, Health Care, Bankruptcy, Creditor Representation, Administrative Law, Trademark Law, Business Acquisition and Sale, Zoning, Commercial Law and Assistance to General Counsel, including local litigation referral and establishment of business area location.
San Francisco, California Office: 353 Sacramento Street, Suite 1500, 94111. Telephone: 415-576-1130. Fax: 415-362-1776.

*See Professional Biographies, MODESTO, CALIFORNIA*

**Jacobs, Nan Cohan**, (BV) ........... '51 '77 C.347 A.B. L.345 J.D. [Crabtree,S.Z.J.&F.]
*PRACTICE AREAS: Business; Commercial; Banking; Bankruptcy (Creditor); Real Estate.
**Jacobson, Jack M.** ........................'53 '78 C.339 B.A. L.1049 J.D. [A Curtis&A.]
*PRACTICE AREAS: Insurance Defense; Family Law; Personal Injury.

**Jacobson, Hansen, Najarian & Flewallen, A Professional Corporation**
(See Fresno)

Jensen, J. Wilmar, (AV) ...................... '27 '52 C&L.813 B.A., J.D. [Jensen&J.]⊙
Jensen, Mark R. ............................'60 '87 C.1169 B.A. L.464 J.D. [Jensen&J.]⊙
Jensen & Jensen, (AV) ..................................1514 H St. (⊙Newman & Oakdale)
Johnson, Elwyn L. ...................'30 '55 C.112 A.B. L.1066 J.D. 1518 Edgebrook Dr.‡
Johnson, Hurl W., III ........................... '51 '77 C.1073 B.A. L.1049 J.D. Mun. Ct. J.
Johnston, David C., (CV) ............................'51 '76 C.636 L.1132 J.D. P.O. Box 3010
**Jones, Jack R.**, (AV) ......................'28 '52 C&L.813 B.A., J.D. [Jones,C.H.N.&Z.]
*PRACTICE AREAS: Estate Planning; Probate; Transactional Business Law.

**Jones, Cochrane, Hollenback, Nelson & Zumwalt, (AV)**
**819 Tenth Street, P.O. Box 3209, 95353**
Telephone: 209-577-6100 Fax: 209-577-1038
Members of Firm: Jack R. Jones (Certified Specialist, Probate, Trust and Estate Planning Law, The State Bar of California Board of Legal Specialization); Kenneth C. Cochrane (Certified Specialist, Family Law, The State Bar of California Board of Legal Specialization); John J. Hollenback, Jr. (Certified Specialist, Family Law, The State Bar of California Board of Legal Specialization); Gary C. Nelson; Frank T. Zumwalt.
General Civil and Trial Practice. Family, Domestic Relations, Business, Corporate, Real Estate, Estate Planning, Probate, Trust, Personal Injury, Insurance Law, Agricultural and Bankruptcy Law, Workers Compensation.
References: Union Safe Deposit Bank.

*See Professional Biographies, MODESTO, CALIFORNIA*

**Kanai, Mark A.**, (BV) ......................'45 '71 C.112 A.B. L.1066 J.D. [M.A.Kanai]

**Kanai, Mark A., A Professional Corporation, (BV)**
**1101-15th Street, P.O. Box 791, 95353**
Telephone: 209-527-3650 Facsimile: 209-527-5518
Mark A. Kanai.
Business, Corporate, Estate Planning, Probate, Elder Law, Real Estate and Communications Law.

*See Professional Biographies, MODESTO, CALIFORNIA*

Kell, George W. ............................. '24 '52 C&L.966 B.A., J.D. 201 E. Rumble Rd.
Krajewski, Lance J., (BV) .............. '43 '73 C.851 B.S.M.E. L.426 J.D. 1214 11th St.
Kroll, James J., Jr., (AV) ......................... '43 '76 C.766 B.A. L.767 J.D. 611 13th St.
Lacey, Thomas A., A Professional Corporation, (BV) '33 '61
C.112 A.B. L.1066 J.D. 1522 H St.
Lacy, Edward M., Jr. ............................. '42 '68 C.112 B.A. L.1065 J.D. Supr. Ct. J.
**Ladine, Wray F.**, (BV) .............'50 '76 C.112 B.A. L.809 J.D. [Damrell,N.S.P.&L.]
*PRACTICE AREAS: Administrative Law; Civil Litigation; Alcoholic Beverage Licensing Law.
LaForce, Ronald L., (BV) ......................... '36 '62 C.800 A.B. L.1065 J.D. 1025 16th St.

**Lamb & Michael, A Professional Corporation**
**1314 G Street, 95354**
Telephone: 209-578-4111 Fax: 209-578-4969
Jack B. Lamb (1924-1992); William H. Michael; Linda S. Leong.
Representation of Collection agencies, manufacturers, insurance companies and other enterprises in the collection of money, credit reporting and collection practices. Suits in all California Courts and creditor representation in bankruptcy.

*See Professional Biographies, MODESTO, CALIFORNIA*

**Lee, Ross W.** ......................................'62 '92 C.1079 B.S. L.464 J.D. [A Curtis&A.]
*PRACTICE AREAS: Business Law; Civil Litigation; Corporate Law; Business Litigation; Business Transactions.
**Leong, Linda S.** ............................................ '57 '91 L.1132 J.D. [Lamb&M.]
*LANGUAGES: Cantonese.
*PRACTICE AREAS: Commercial Law; Civil Trial Practice.
Lewis, James F., (CV) .................. '64 '90 C.770 B.S. L.464 J.D. 1601 I St. 5th Fl.
Loeffler, Michael G., (BV) ............... '50 '75 C.112 B.A. L.464 J.D. [Waggoner&L.]
Louis, Robert S., (CV) ..................................... '35 '64 L.1065 J.D. 1630 "I" St.
Luse, Steven M., (A Professional Corporation), (BV) ..........'20 '69 L.1132 821 13th St.
Lustri, Philip R. ............................'32 '86 C.667 B.Ch.E. L.1132 J.D. 309 El Rio Dr.
Lyions, Michael L., (BV) ...................'43 '70 C.768 B.A. L.1065 J.D. [Rushing,L.&A.]
Machado, John J., (BV) ........................ '49 '75 C.112 A.B. L.1065 J.D. 1500 J St.
**Macko, Michael J.**, (BV) .....................'59 '86 C.112 B.A. L.940 J.D. [Borton,P.&C.]
*PRACTICE AREAS: Bankruptcy; Personal Injury; Public Entity Defense; Products Liability; Employment Law.

**Marderosian, Swanson & Oren**
(See Fresno)

Martelli, Paul L., (AV) ..................'24 '55 C.145 A.B. L.1065 LL.B. 1300 K Street
**Martin, Laurence H.**, (BV) '38 '64 C.813 A.B. L.1065 J.D.
V.P., Govt. Affs., & Assoc. Gen. Coun., E. & J. Gallo Winery
*RESPONSIBILITIES: Political/Government Affairs.
**Mastache, Jorge**, (CV) .................'59 '90 C.112 B.A. L.1065 J.D. [Strauss,N.A.&R.]
*LANGUAGES: Spanish.
*PRACTICE AREAS: Workers Compensation.
**Matzkind, Roger S.**, (BV) ......................'53 '77 C.768 B.A. L.809 J.D. [Brunn&F.]

**Mayall, Hurley, Knutsen, Smith & Green, A Professional Corporation**
(See Stockton)

Mayhew, William A. ..........................'40 '65 C.112 B.S. L.1068 J.D. Mun. J.
Maylen, Charles E., III, (CV) ............... '48 '89 C.112 B.A. L.1132 J.D. 914 13th St.
**Mayol, James D.**, (BV) ........................ '57 '84 C.169 B.A. L.464 J.D. [Mayol&B.]
*PRACTICE AREAS: Employment Law; Civil Litigation; Construction Law; Real Estate; Business Law.

**Mayol & Barringer, (BV)**
**1324 "J" Street, P.O. Box 3049, 95353**
Telephone: 209-544-9555 Fax: 209-544-9875
Members of Firm: James D. Mayol; Bart W. Barringer; Carl E. Combs.
General Civil Litigation, Real Estate, Business, Personal Injury, Employment and Construction Law.

*See Professional Biographies, MODESTO, CALIFORNIA*

**McAllister, Jane E.**, (BV) .............'61 '88 C.813 B.A. L.1132 J.D. [McAllister&M.]
*LANGUAGES: French and Italian.
*PRACTICE AREAS: Estate Planning Law; Business Law; Alcoholic Beverage Control Law.
**McAllister, Kirk W.**, (AV) ............ '44 '70 C.813 B.A. L.800 J.D. [McAllister&M.]
*PRACTICE AREAS: Criminal Law; Equine Law.

**McAllister & McAllister, (AV)**
**City Mall Building, Suite 32, 948 11th Street, 95354**
Telephone: 209-575-4844 FAX: 209-575-0240

(This Listing Continued)

**McAllister & McAllister (Continued)**

Members of Firm: Kirk W. McAllister (Certified Specialist, Criminal Law, The State Bar of California Board of Legal Specialization); Jane E. McAllister.
Civil and Criminal Trial Practice, Estate Planning and Probate Law, Business Law, Alcoholic Beverage Control Practice, Equine Law.

*See Professional Biographies, MODESTO, CALIFORNIA*

**McCormick, Barstow, Sheppard, Wayte & Carruth LLP, (AV)**
**Centre Plaza Office Tower, 1150 Ninth Street, Suite 1510, 95354⊙**
Telephone: 209-524-1100 Fax: 209-524-1188
Matthew K. Hawkins. Associate: John M. Dunn.
General Civil and Trial Practice. Agricultural and Water Law, Banking Law, Bankruptcy and Reorganization, Civil Rights Litigation, Civil Practice, Commodities Law, Condemnation Law, Construction Law, Corporate Law, Employment Law, Environmental Law, Estate Planning, Family Law, Franchise Law, Health Care Law, Insurance Law Legal Malpractice, Medical Malpractice, Municipal Law, Probate, Public Entity, Real Estate Agent Malpractice, Real Estate Law, Securities and Taxation Law.
Counsel for: Aetna Life & Casualty Co.; California State Automobile Assn.; Firemen's Fund Insurance Co.; Bank of Fresno; Kings River State Bank; Glendale Federal Bank; Hartford Accident & Indemnity Co.; Kemper Insurance Group; The Travelers Insurance Co.; United Pacific/Reliance Insurance Co.
Fresno, California Office: Five River Park Place East, 93-720-1501. Telephone: 209-433-1300. Mailing Address: P.O. Box 28912, 93729-8912.

*See Professional Biographies, MODESTO, CALIFORNIA*

McDade, James R. ..........................................'62 '91 C.101 B.A. L.61 J.D. [Critzer&M.]
**McGrath, Patrick M.** ............ '62 '93 L.464 J.D. [A Neumiller&B.] (⊙Stockton, CA.)
*PRACTICE AREAS: Real Estate; Land Use and Development Law; Environmental Law; Business Transactions; Governmental Relations.
McGrew, Spencer P., (BV) ................... '46 '73 C.276 B.S. L.1065 J.D. 1301 "K" St.
Mckenna, Charles R. ......................... '41 '81 C.768 B.S. L.1132 J.D. Off. of Dist. Atty.
McManus, Michael S., (AV) .......... '53 '78 C.112 B.A. L.1068 J.D. U.S. Bankruptcy J.
McSparin, Cheryl K., (CV) .............'49 '81 C.1079 B.A. L.1067 J.D. Dep. Dist. Atty.
Mello, Kenneth M., (BV) ............. '52 '77 C.770 B.S. L.1067 J.D. 318 McHenry Ave.
**Mendlin, Andrew S.** ........................'66 '96 C.112 B.A. L.464 J.D. [A Curtis&A.]
*PRACTICE AREAS: Insurance Defense.
Meredith, Lynne R., (BV) .......... '56 '82 C.610 B.S. L.770 J.D. Family Support Comr.
**Michael, William H.** ...................................'47 '73 C&L.347 A.B., J.D. [Lamb&M.]
*PRACTICE AREAS: Collections.
Milam, James J., (BV) ............................ '42 '67 C&L.767 A.B., J.D. 1211 K St.
**Mitchell, William R.** ......................... '19 '47 C&L.813 A.B., LL.B. [Mitchell&V.] ‡

**Mitchell & Vance, (BV)**
**Suite G, 821 Thirteenth Street, P.O. Box 3166, 95353**
Telephone: 209-524-9331 Fax: 209-524-5501
Email: DVANCEESQ@aol.com
Members of Firm: William R. Mitchell (Retired); Donald L. Vance.
Estate Planning, Probate and Trust Administration, General Civil and Trial Practice, Elder Care, Real Estate, Personal Injury and Business.
Reference: Bank of America National Trust and Savings Assn., Modesto Branch.

*See Professional Biographies, MODESTO, CALIFORNIA*

Mitterling, Allen R. ..........................................'44 '74 C.282 A.B. L.464 J.D. 1130 L St.
Moorad, Calvin, (BV) .................. '35 '64 C.768 A.B. L.1065 J.D. [Moorad,C.&G.]
Moorad, Clark & Gleason, (BV) ....................................................1020 15th St.
**Morrison, Robert C.**, (BV) '46 '72
C.112 B.A. L.1067 J.D. [Neumiller&B.] (⊙Stockton, CA)
*PRACTICE AREAS: Business Planning, Organizations, Operations & Transactions; Formation of Capital and Taxation; Business Sales and Acquisitions; Bankruptcy and Reorganization.
Mower, James P., (CV) ...................... '26 '53 C.112 B.S. L.309 LL.B. 928 12th St.
Munson, Stephen E. ......................'57 '89 C.1079 B.A. L.312 J.D. 121 Downey Ave.
Murphy, John T. ............................................ '32 '57 C&L.793 LL.B. 1012 11th St.
**Murray, Daniel T.** ......... '45 '70 C.884 A.B. L.178 J.D. Tax Coun., E. & J. Gallo Winery
*RESPONSIBILITIES: Tax; ERISA/Benefits; General Corporate.
**Nakagawa, Cressey H.** '43 '69
C.813 B.A. L.1065 J.D. [B Damrell,N.S.P.&L.] (⊙San Fran.)
Neal, Janet B. ...........................'43 '85 C.813 A.B. L.1067 J.D. 5712 Chenault Dr.
**Neibauer, Douglas L.**, (BV) ...............'40 '64 C&L.508 B.S., LL.B. [Strauss,N.A.&R.]
*PRACTICE AREAS: Civil Trial; Corporate Law; Probate.
**Nelson, Duane L.**, (AV) .............'42 '67 C.112 B.A. L.1065 J.D. [Damrell,N.S.P.&L.]
*PRACTICE AREAS: Civil Litigation; Personal Injury Law.
**Nelson, Gary C.**, (CV) ................ '58 '86 C.1079 B.A. L.464 J.D. [Jones,C.H.N.&Z.]
*PRACTICE AREAS: Personal Injury; Workers' Compensation; Family Law.
Netzer, Jonathan G. .................'66 '91 C.1169 B.A. L.1049 J.D. [A Cunningham&L.]

**Neumiller & Beardslee, A Professional Corporation, (AV)** BB
**611 Thirteenth Street, 95354-2435⊙**
Telephone: 209-577-8200 Fax: 209-577-4910
Thomas J. Shephard, Sr.; Robert C. Morrison; James R. Dyke; Steven A. Herum; Michael J. Dyer; Jeanne Marie Zolezzi; Thomas H. Terpstra;—Clifford W. Stevens; Karna E. Harrigfeld; Matthew I. Friedrich; Patrick M. McGrath.
General Civil Practice and Litigation in all State and Federal Courts. Real Property, Condominium, Land Use, Natural Resources, Environmental, Water and Water Rights, Mining, Agricultural, Corporation, Partnership, Business Planning, Securities, Creditor's Rights in Bankruptcy, Taxation, Employee Benefits, Insurance, Administrative, Health Care, Governmental and Legislative, Trusts, Estate Planning, Probate and Municipal Law.
Representative Clients: Roman Catholic Bishop of Stockton; Doctors Medical Center of Modesto; Farmland Management Services; J.C. Williams Co.; Kaufman & Broad Central Valley, Inc.; Morrison Homes; Stanislaus Area Association of Governments; Stanislaus Food Products; Teichert Aggregate; The Westside Irrigation District.
Stockton, California Office: 5th Floor, Waterfront Office Towers II, 509 West Weber Avenue, P.O. Box 20, 95201-3020. Telephone: 209-948-8200. Fax: 209-948-4910.

*See Professional Biographies, MODESTO, CALIFORNIA*

**Newman, Russell A.**, (BV) ..............'51 '78 C.813 B.A. L.1065 J.D. [Normoyle&N.]
*SPECIAL AGENCIES: Board of Supervisors, City Councils Planning Commissions, LAFCO, for Stanislaus, San Joaquin, Merced, Tuolumne, Calaveras and surrounding counties. School Boards on developer fee issues.
*PRACTICE AREAS: Real Estate Transactions; Business Transactions; Land Use; Zoning and Development Law.
Nickerson, Robert L., (AV) ..................'26 '51 C.190 A.B. L.767 J.D. 1300 K Street
Niermeyer, Lawrence Timothy, (CV) .... '62 '91 C.63 B.S. L.284 J.D. [Champion,W.&N.]
**Normoyle, Michael C.**, (BV) ............. '48 '76 C.169 B.A. L.188 J.D. [Normoyle&N.]
*SPECIAL AGENCIES: State Water Resources Control Board (SWRCB); Regional Water Quality Control Boards (RWQCBs); San Joaquin Valley Unified Air Pollution Control District (SJVUAPCD); California Integrated Waste Management Board (CIWMB); Board of Supervisors, City Councils and Planning Commissions in Stanislaus, San Joaquin, Merced, Tuolumne, Calaveras and surrounding Counties.
*PRACTICE AREAS: Civil Litigation; Environmental Law; Business Transactions.

**Normoyle & Newman, A Professional Law Corporation, (BV)**
**801-10th Street, Fifth Floor, Suite 1, 95354**
Telephone: 209-521-9521 Telecopier: 209-521-4968
Michael C. Normoyle; Russell A. Newman; Wylie P. Cashman; John T. Resso; George A. Petrulakis; Michael S. Warda.

(This Listing Continued)

**Normoyle & Newman, A Professional Law Corporation (Continued)**
**General Business Practice. Civil Trial and Appellate Practice. Real Estate Development and Zoning, Real Estate and Business Transactions, Corporation, Construction, Administrative, Environmental, Solid Waste, Toxic and Hazardous Waste, Resource Recovery, Government and Legislative Law, Estate Planning and Probate.**
*See Professional Biographies, MODESTO, CALIFORNIA*

**Ochsner, Barbara L.** ................. '59 '90 C.897 B.S. L.464 J.D. [Trimbur D.E.&B.]
*PRACTICE AREAS: Insurance Coverage; Insurance Defense; Personal Injury; Employment Law.

**Ogden, Ralph C., III, (BV) '53 '79 C.990 B.A. L.464 J.D.**
**1535 J Street, Suite A, P.O. Box 1867, 95353**
**Telephone: 209-524-4466 Fax: 209-524-1660**
**Collections, Real Estate and Business Transactions, Environmental and Hazardous Waste Law, Corporate Law, Wills/Trusts/Estate Planning and Probate.**
*See Professional Biographies, MODESTO, CALIFORNIA*

Ottoboni, Jeffrey A ................ '61 '88 C.602 B.B.A. L.1068 J.D. 600 Yosemite Blvd.
**Owens, Jack B.**, (AV) '44 '70 C&L.813 A.B., J.D.
Exec. V.P. & Gen. Coun., E. & J. Gallo Winery
*RESPONSIBILITIES: Litigation; Antitrust; General Commercial; Trademark; Product Liability.
**Pacher, Matthew O.**, (BV) ..........'54 '83 C.1160 B.A. L.464 J.D. [Damrell,N.S.P.&L.]
*PRACTICE AREAS: Civil Litigation; Real Estate Law; Corporation Law.
**Pallios, Steven G.**, (AV) ............'50 '75 C.267 B.S. L.1068 J.D. [Damrell,N.S.P.&L.]
*PRACTICE AREAS: Real Estate Law; Corporation Law; Estate Planning Law.
Palmer, Richard J., (CV) ................. '42 '77 C.37 B.A. L.1137 J.D. 1024 J St.
Palmisano, Nick, (CV) ........................'46 '83 C.1190 L.1137 J.D. 1100 I St.
Parke, Area J.M., (CV) ...................'52 '88 C.476 B.F.A. L.1230 J.D. Pub. Def.
**Peltier, John K.**, (CV) .................'53 '91 C&L.05 B.A., LL.B. [A Damrell,N.S.P.&L.]
*PRACTICE AREAS: Civil Litigation; Complex Litigation.
Peluso, Charles J., (BV) ........................ '43 '67 C.770 B.A. L.1066 J.D. [C.J.Peluso]
Peluso, Charles J., Law Office of, A Professional Corporation, (BV) ..........631 15th St.
Perry, Bruce R. ..................................................'47 '76 [Perry&W.]
Perry & Wildman, (BV) ........................................... 948 11th St., Suite 16
**Petrulakis, George A.** ......................'63 '91 C.309 A.B. L.1068 J.D. [Normoyle&N.]
*SPECIAL AGENCIES: Board of Supervisors, City Councils, Planning Commissions, LAFCO, School Boards on developer fee issues; Property Tax Assessment Appeals Boards; Emergency Medical Services Agencies; County Committees on School District Organization; Community Services Districts, Irrigation Districts and other special districts in Stanislaus, San Joaquin, Merced, Tuolumne and surrounding counties.
*REPORTED CASES: Save Stanislaus Area Farm Economy vs. Board of Supervisors (1993) 13 Cal.App.4th 191, 16 Cal.Rept.2d 408.
*PRACTICE AREAS: Zoning, Planning and Land Use; Subdivisions; Real Estate Law; Property Rights; Emergency Medical Services Law.
**Phillips, Samuel L.** ...........................'60 '87 C.767 B.A. L.1065 J.D. [Borton,P.&C.]
*LANGUAGES: Spanish.
*PRACTICE AREAS: Civil Litigation; Agricultural Law; Construction Law.
Phipps, Arral A. ....................................... '47 '75 C&L.734 B.A., J.D. Dep. Dist. Atty.
Pierson, Frank S. ........................ '23 '51 C.169 A.B. L.809 LL.B. Ret. Supr. Ct. J.
Pimentel, Philip A., (BV) ...................'55 '84 C.1079 B.A. L.770 J.D. 1200 G St.
Pomper, Robert F. ......................'67 '94 C.112 B.A. L.602 J.D. 1601 I St. 5th Fl.
**Post, Bradley A.**, (BV) ......................'59 '86 C.169 B.A. L.464 J.D. [Borton,P.&C.]
*PRACTICE AREAS: Agricultural Litigation; Civil Rights Violations; Public Entity Law; Products and Premises Liability.
Poston, John M. '46 '72 C.691 B.A. L.846 J.D.
(adm. in TX; not adm. in CA) 524 Cormorant Dr.‡
Quinlan, Thomas J., (BV) ................ '43 '74 C.339 B.S. L.284 J.D. Dep. Dist. Atty.

**Quinn, Daniel F.**
**(See Stockton)**

**Ramirez, Mina**, (CV) ................'56 '85 C.1169 B.A. L.1066 J.D. [Strauss,N.A.&R.]
*LANGUAGES: Spanish.
*PRACTICE AREAS: Civil Trial; Negligence; Products Liability; Medical Malpractice; Sexual Harassment.
Ramsey, Bruce E., (CV) ........................'52 '88 C.112 B.A. L.770 J.D. [Ulrich&R.]
Rancano, Juan C. ......................'61 '88 C.112 B.S. L.1066 J.D. 3136 Sherwood Ave.
Reed, Betty Ann ............................................'43 '79 C.705 B.A. 804 Fourteenth St.
**Reidl, Paul W.** ...................'55 '80 C&L.273 B.A., J.D. Atty., E. & J. Gallo Winery
*RESPONSIBILITIES: Intellectual Property and Litigation; Federal Regulatory and Litigation; International Regulatory.
Rein, Michael A., (BV) ...........................'55 '83 C.1079 B.A. L.37 J.D. [Rein&A.]
Rein, Teresa Vig .............................................'57 '82 C&L.37 B.A., J.D. [Rein&A.]
Rein & Abbott, (BV) ................................................................715 14th St.
**Resso, John T.** ......................................'66 '91 C.112 B.A. L.770 J.D. [Normoyle&N.]
*PRACTICE AREAS: Civil Litigation; Business Transactions; Real Estate Law; Estate Planning; Probate.
Reynolds, Donald R., (BV) ..................'44 '78 C.1079 B.A. L.1132 J.D. 910 11th St.
Ries, Catherine A., (BV) ............'50 '77 C.112 B.A. L.1067 J.D. 205 Magnolia Ave.
**Ringer, Kimberly W.** ......................'65 '93 C.990 B.A. L.426 J.D. [A Curtis&A.]
*PRACTICE AREAS: Insurance Defense; Public Agency Law; Family Law.

**Ringhoff, Stephen '44 '75 L.1132 J.D.**
**1500 J. Street, P.O. Box 3009, 95354**
**Telephone: 209-527-5360 Fax: 209-527-1727**
**Email: ringhoff@S2.Sonnet.com**
**Personal Injury, Commercial Litigation.**
*See Professional Biographies, MODESTO, CALIFORNIA*

Ritchey, Glenn A., Jr. ...............................'37 '72 C.112 B.S. L.1340 J.D. Supr. Ct. J.
Rockwell, David N., (BV) ......................'47 '72 C.1100 A.B. L.309 J.D. [Froba,F.&R.]
Rose, Hugh, III ......................................'38 '65 C.1254 B.S. L.1065 J.D. Supr. Ct. J.
Rose, Kathryn H. .............................'49 '80 C.665 B.A. L.1026 J.D. P.O. Box 1827
Ruggieri, Francis R., (BV) ...................'26 '56 C.665 A.B. L.1065 J.D. 1115 Eye St.
Rushing, Lyions & Anderson, (BV) .............................................. 125 McHenry
**Sadler, James L.**, (BV) ..........................'46 '73 C&L.878 B.S., J.D. [Stockton&S.]
*PRACTICE AREAS: Trials; Crop Damage Law; Real Property Law; Personal Injury Law; Negligence Law.
**Sadler, Karen Tall**, (CV) ......................'47 '78 C&L.878 B.S., J.D. [A Stockton&S.]
Salter, Timothy W., (BV) ......................'47 '72 C.770 B.S.C. L.767 J.D. [Salter&S.]
Salter & Struck, (BV) ............................................................1025 14th Street
Schechter, Jeanne E., (BV) ..........'63 '90 C.608 B.S.B.A. L.426 J.D. Dep. Dist. Atty.
Schmidt, Carol A., (CV) .......................'46 '89 C.273 B.S. L.1026 J.D. 928 12th St.
Schmidt, Frank J. ....................................'59 '89 C.112 B.A. L.1065 J.D. 1025 14th St.
**Schmidt, Walter J.**, (BV) ...........'46 '71 C.112 A.B. L.1065 J.D. [Crabtree,S.Z.J.&F.]
*PRACTICE AREAS: Agricultural Law; Commercial; Banking; Bankruptcy (Creditor); Business.
**Schrimp, Roger M.**, (AV) '41 '66
C.112 A.B. L.1066 J.D. [Damrell,N.S.P.&L.] (⊙Oakdale)
*PRACTICE AREAS: Business Law; Real Estate Law; Complex Business Litigation.
Sconyers, Alison A. ...........................'62 '92 C.999 A.S. L.464 J.D. 1014 16th St.
Seeley, Mark V. ........'60 '85 C.112 B.S.Ch.E. L.326 J.D. 3116 Williamsburg Way (Pat.)
Shailor, Nancy J., (CV) ................................'47 '88 L.1132 J.D. 609 14th St.
Sharp, Paul F., Jr., (CV) ......................'25 '66 C.112 B.S. L.1132 1220 Karen Way
Shastid, Jon B. ................................................'14 '59 600 Yosemite Blvd.

**Shephard, Thomas J., Sr.**, (AV) '34 '59
C.112 A.B. L.1066 LL.B. [Neumiller&B.] (⊙Stockton, CA)
*PRACTICE AREAS: Water Agencies and Water Rights Law; Flood Control Law; Mining Law; Health Care Law; Church Law.
Shumar, Mark C., (CV) ..................'64 '90 C.1060 B.A. L.950 J.D. 605 StaniforAve.
Siefkin, Susan D., (BV) ...........................'43 '83 C.112 B.A. L.1132 J.D. Mun. Ct. J.
**Silva, Fred A.**, (CV) ....'58 '87 C.169 B.A. L.1067 J.D. [Damrell,N.S.P.&L.] (⊙Oakdale)
*LANGUAGES: Portuguese.
*PRACTICE AREAS: Complex Litigation; Business Litigation.
Silveira, Marie Sovey, (BV) ...............'55 '81 C.800 A.B. L.1065 J.D. 217 Mensinger
Silveira, Michael J. '55 '81 C.112 B.A. L.1065 J.D.
Secy. & Corp. Coun., Save Mart Supermarkets
**Skol, Armand G.** '43 '68 C.156 A.B. L.276 J.D.
V.P. & Dep. Gen. Coun., E. & J. Gallo Winery
*REPORTED CASES: U.S. v. The Gillette Co.; U.S. v. Hercules & Matsui; In Re: Fine Paper Antitrust Litigation; In Re: Corrugated Container Antitrust Litigation; EEC Pulp Cartel Proceedings.
*RESPONSIBILITIES: Employment and Labor; International; Litigation; Law Office Management; Antitrust.
Sloan, Gregory Brandon .......................'50 '82 C.766 B.A. L.284 J.D. Dep. Pub. Def.
Smith, Peter H. .............................'42 '67 C.950 A.B. L.1066 J.D. 1535 J St.; Suite A
Smith, Steven A., (BV) .....................'50 '87 C.629 B.S. L.1132 J.D. 909 15th St.
Solano, Stephen, (BV) ........................'44 '78 C.1079 B.A. L.1132 J.D. 1119 12th St.
Solorio, Esequiel ...............................'65 '91 C&L.112 B.S., J.D. 1300 K St., 2nd Fl.
**Sood, Surendra J., M.D.** .........'45 '95 C.999 M.D. L.1132 J.D. [B Damrell,N.S.P.&L.]
*LANGUAGES: Hindi and Punjabi.
*PRACTICE AREAS: Personal Injury.
**Sordello, Richard J., Jr.** .....................'64 '91 C&L.112 B.S., J.D. [A Curtis&A.]
*PRACTICE AREAS: Insurance Defense; Business Litigation.
Stahl, Donald N., (BV) ....................................'34 '66 C.734 A.B. L.1066 LL.B. Dist. Atty.
Steffen, Scott T., (BV) '49 '77
C.267 B.S. L.464 J.D. Asst. Gen. Coun., Modesto Irrigation Dist.
**Stevens, Clifford W.**, (BV) '61 '90
C.1109 B.A. L.464 J.D. [A Neumiller&B.] (⊙Stockton, CA.)
*PRACTICE AREAS: Bankruptcy and Civil Litigation.
**Stockton, Cleveland J.**, (AV) ............'20 '49 C.597 B.A. L.309 LL.B. [Stockton&S.]
*REPORTED CASES: Riddle vs Leushner (1959) 51 Cal 2nd 574; Estate of Neilson (1962) 57 Cal 2nd 733; Sunset-Sterneau vs Bonzi (1964) 60 Cal 2nd 834; Sanders Construction Co., Inc. vs San Joaquin First Federal Savings and Loan Association (1982) 136 Cal App. 3rd 387; Quigley vs Pet (1984) 162 Cal. App. 3rd 877.
*PRACTICE AREAS: Trials; Banking Law; Personal Injury Law; Estate Planning Law; Corporate Law.

**Stockton & Sadler, (AV) [BR]**
**1034 Twelfth Street, P.O. Box 3153, 95353**
**Telephone: 209-523-6416 Fax: 209-523-2315**
**Members of Firm: Cleveland J. Stockton; James L. Sadler. Associates: Karen Tall Sadler.**
**Civil Trial and Appellate Practice. Agriculture, Business, Corporate, Estate Planning, Probate, Partnerships, Real Estate, Personal Injury.**
**Representative Clients: Dan Mellis Liquors; American Lumber Co.; Paul's Rexall Drug Stores; American Distributing Co.; Tro-Pic-Kal Mfg. Co.; Pete Pappas Broadcasting Co.; Pete Pappas Broadcasting, Inc.; Sanders Construction Co.; Goldrush Broadcasting, Inc.; Paul M. Zagaris Realtor, Inc.**
*See Professional Biographies, MODESTO, CALIFORNIA*

Stolpe, Shana Angela Bagley .........'68 '93 C.112 B.A. L.770 J.D. [A Thayer,H.H.&G.]
Stone, Charles V. ...........................................'29 '57 C.942 L.1065 LL.B. Supr. Ct. J.
Stone, Michael R., (BV) .....................'53 '79 C.112 B.A. L.1065 J.D. Off. of Dist. Atty.
**Strauss, Alan H.** ..........................'32 '56 C.477 B.A. L.309 J.D. [B Strauss,N.A.&R.]
*PRACTICE AREAS: Family Law; Civil Trial; Criminal Trial; Bankruptcy.
**Strauss, Randall Edward** ...........'66 '93 C.112 B.A. L.1066 J.D. [A Strauss,N.A.&R.]
*PRACTICE AREAS: Civil Litigation; Business Law; Environmental Law.

**Strauss, Neibauer, Anderson & Ramirez, A Professional Corporation, (BV)**
**620 12th Street, 95354**
**Telephone: 209-526-2211 Fax: 209-526-0244**
**Douglas L. Neibauer (Member of California Trial Lawyers Association, with recognized experience in the field of Trial Lawyer); Thomas L. Anderson (Member of California Trial Lawyers Association, with recognized experience in the fields of Trial Lawyer, General Personal Injury and Workers' Compensation); Mina Ramirez (Member of California Trial Lawyers Association, with recognized experience in the fields of General Personal Injury, Workers' Compensation and Family Law); Randall Edward Strauss; George P. Harris; Jorge Mastache. Of Counsel: Alan H. Strauss (Member of California Trial Lawyers Association, with recognized experience in the fields of Family Law and Criminal Defense - Misdemeanor).**
**Civil and Criminal Trial Practice. Negligence, Products Liability, Workers Compensation, Corporate and Probate Law. Bankruptcy and Family Law.**
*See Professional Biographies, MODESTO, CALIFORNIA*

Struck, James D., (BV) .................................'55 '80 C.800 B.A. L.464 J.D. [Salter&S.]
Tangle, Howard ...........................................'39 '68 C&L.809 J.D. 1400 K St.‡
Taylor, Carson N. ...................................................'24 '52 C.174 L.767 LL.B. Mun. J.
Taylor, Edward T., Jr. ...........................'20 '49 C.112 A.B. L.767 LL.B. P.O. Box 4650‡
**Terpstra, Thomas H.** ..........'63 '89 C.595 B.A. L.464 J.D. [Neumiller&B.] (⊙Stockton)
*LANGUAGES: Spanish.
*PRACTICE AREAS: Land Use Law; Endangered Species Law; Municipal Law.
Thayer, Dale H., (BV) .......................'44 '70 C&L.339 B.S., J.D. [Thayer,H.H.&G.]
Thayer, Harvey, Hodder & Gregerson, A Professional Law Corporation, (BV)
1100 14th St., Ste., F
**Tourtlotte, Sabrina** ............................'66 '93 C.1079 B.A. L.464 J.D. [A Curtis&A.]
Trimble, Gene F. ..............................'40 '70 C.800 M.B.A. L.16 J.D. Off. of Pub. Def.
**Trimbur, John M.**, (BV) ....................'20 '48 C&L.767 B.S., J.D. [Trimbur D.E.&B.]
*PRACTICE AREAS: Estate Planning; Probate.

**Trimbur Davis Echols & Boyd, A Professional Corporation, (AV)**
**Suite One, 1301 "L" Street, P.O. Box 3464, 95353-3464**
**Telephone: 209-521-2040 Fax: 209-521-2634**
**Kevin L. Clark (1950-1994); John M. Trimbur; Gary S. Davis; Paul E. Echols; Katherine R. Boyd; Barbara L. Ochsner.**
**General Civil Trial Practice. Personal Injury and Insurance Defense, Elder, Probate, Real Estate, Employment Law and Corporation Law.**
*See Professional Biographies, MODESTO, CALIFORNIA*

Trott, Larry J. .........................................'57 '90 C.112 B.A. L.1067 J.D. 1300 K St.
Ulrich, Carl E., Jr., (BV) .......................'38 '66 C.813 A.B. L.1065 J.D. [Ulrich&R.]
Ulrich & Ramsey, (BV) ................................................................1124 11th St.
Underwood, Gerald V. ..............................'25 '50 C&L.813 A.B., J.D. Ret. Supr. Ct. J.
**Vance, Donald L.**, (BV) ......................'43 '74 C.112 A.B. L.1065 J.D. [Mitchell&V.]
Vander Wall, David G. ..............................'49 '74 C.165 B.A. L.1068 J.D. Supr. Ct. J.
Van Konynenburg, Frank A. ..............'40 '65 C.112 B.S. L.1066 LL.B. 2485 Ladd Rd.
Waggoner, Carl O., (BV) ........................'43 '69 C.112 B.A. L.61 J.D. [Waggoner&L.]
Waggoner & Loeffler, Law Offices of, (BV) ................................ 318 McHenry Ave.
Walker, David B., (BV) .......................'52 '79 C.813 B.A. L.61 J.D. [Champion,W.&N.]
**Warda, Michael S.** ..........................'67 '95 C.1079 B.A. L.1132 J.D. [Normoyle&N.]
*PRACTICE AREAS: Land Use; Real Estate Law; Business Transactions; Governmental Relations.
**Warwick, Wendelin Z.** ............'62 '91 C.112 B.A. L.464 J.D. [B Damrell,N.S.P.&L.]
*PRACTICE AREAS: Business and Corporation.
Watts, Gary W., (BV) ..............'46 '74 C.147 B.A. L.464 J.D. [A Duncan,B.E.&U.]⊙

CALIFORNIA—MODESTO MARTINDALE-HUBBELL LAW DIRECTORY 1997

Wesley, Jane J. ............................'40 '86 C.347 B.M.E. L.1132 J.D. 1031 15th St.
Wesselius, Sharon L., (BV) ..............'52 '79 C.112 A.B. L.770 J.D. P.O. Box 578243
**Weston-Dawkes, Matthew** '52 '77
C.976 B.A. L.309 J.D. Sr. Assoc. Gen. Coun., E. & J. Gallo Winery
*RESPONSIBILITIES: Anti-trust/Trade Regulation; Administrative Law; Alcohol Beverage Law; Litigation; Commercial Law.
Whitlock, Daniel E., Jr., (CV) .................'45 '78 C.112 B.A. L.1132 J.D. 418 13th St.
Whitlock, Dorrie E., (CV) .........'48 '76 C.112 A.B. L.1068 J.D. 819 W. Roseburg Ave.
Wiegand, Cort V. ...........................'50 '76 C.112 B.S. L.464 J.D. 1301 "K" St.
Wildman, Robert M., (BV) ...........................................'48 '81 [Perry&W.]
**Williams, Lisa B.** .................................'63 '89 C.112 B.S. L.1067 J.D. [Gianelli&F.]
*PRACTICE AREAS: Litigation.
Williamsen, Nancy Barnett .............................'54 '84 L.765 J.D. 1101 Sylvan Ave.
Winger, Elmer L. ..........................................'15 '46 C&L.813 A.B., J.D. 1130 Coffee Rd.‡
Winston, Robert J., (BV) .........................'48 '77 C.999 L.1095 J.D. 950 10th St.
Wolfe, Alexander M. ..................'30 '56 C.112 A.B. L.1066 LL.B. 2209 Coffee Rd.
Woodall, Clifford L. ...........................'53 '87 C.1079 B.A. L.1132 J.D. [Canant&W.]
**Wooten, Jefferey A.** ......................'63 '91 C&L.112 B.A., J.D. [Ⓐ Damrell,N.S.P.&L.]
*PRACTICE AREAS: Business Law; Real Estate; Business Litigation; Personal Injury.
Wright, Wm. Dean, (CV) .....................'49 '78 C.112 B.A. L.1065 J.D. Dep. Co. Coun.
**Zeff, Thomas D.**, (AV) ..............'51 '76 C.629 B.S. L.1065 J.D. [Crabtree,S.Z.J.&F.]
*PRACTICE AREAS: Insurance Defense; Civil Litigation.
Zeff, William ...............................................'11 '35 L.1065 J.D. Ret. Supr. Ct. J.
**Zolezzi, Jeanne Marie**, (BV) '60 '85
C.813 A.B. L.770 J.D. [Neumiller&B.] (⊙Stockton, CA.)
*PRACTICE AREAS: Environmental Compliance, Regulation and Cost Recovery; Toxics; Real Estate Transactions Water Law; Water Rights Law (including Reclamation Reform Act); Eminent Domain.
**Zumwalt, Frank T.** ......................'60 '87 C.147 B.A. L.464 J.D. [Jones,C.H.N.&Z.]
*PRACTICE AREAS: Personal Injury Law; Insurance Law; Civil Litigation.

## MOJAVE, 2,573, *Kern Co.*

Burns, Jack D. .............................................'34 '75 C.872 B.A. L.1188 J.D. 15825 K St.

## MONARCH BEACH, —, *Orange Co.*

Jaffray, Ernst A. '14 '42 C.061 A.B. L.51 LL.B.
(adm. in GA; not adm. in CA) 32402 Ascension Rd.‡
Moraitis, Theodore, (BV) ......'43 '73 C.912 B.A. L.1137 J.D. 32241 Crown Valley Pkwy.
Scoville, Harmon G. ..........'22 '52 C.112 A.B. L.813 J.D. (Ret.) Pres. Jus., Ct. of App.

## MONROVIA, 35,761, *Los Angeles Co.*

Burgett, Timothy S. ..........'63 '89 C.802 B.S.B.A. L.893 J.D. Coun., World Vision Intl.
Dab, John M. ......'58 '82 C.112 B.A. L.1068 J.D. Gen. Coun., American Tech. Grp., Inc.
Daines, Scott N. ................'55 '85 C.877 B.S. L.809 J.D. 1044B Royal Oaks Dr.
Donnelly, Michael J. ...........................'60 '86 C.763 B.A. L.1148 J.D. [Holland&D.]
Duffy, Charles R., (BV) ..............'43 '72 C.1075 B.S. L.809 J.D. 316 W. Foothill Blvd.
**Faith, Eric**, (BV) ..........................'44 '70 C.605 A.B. L.1066 J.D. [Patten,F.&S.]
*PRACTICE AREAS: Family Law; Negligence; Civil Litigation.
Faith, Lyle H., (BV) ..........................'30 '61 C.112 B.A. L.426 LL.B. 134 W. Lime
**Faith, William E.**, (AV) ...........................'20 '50 C.605 B.A. L.426 J.D. [Patten,F.&S.]
*PRACTICE AREAS: Estate Planning and Probate.
Faust, Robert H. ...........................'52 '78 C.112 B.S. L.464 J.D. Mun. Ct. Comr.
Gonzales, Ernest S. ......................'55 '81 C.1042 B.S. L.770 J.D. 112 E. Lemon Ave.
**grindstaff, Lorraine** ........................'49 '83 C.1097 B.A. L.426 J.D. [Patten,F.&S.]
*REPORTED CASES: Rojo vs. Kliger (1990) 52 Cal. 3d 65; Ensworth vs. Mullvain (1990) 224 Cal. App. 3d 1105; Estate of Falco (1987) 188 Cal. App. 3d 1004.
*PRACTICE AREAS: Appeals; Litigation; Real Estate; Business.
Hanley, Robt. R., (BV) .................'07 '31 C&L.597 B.S., J.D. 316 W. Foothill Blvd.
Hansen, Robert J. ....................'29 '55 C&L.813 A.B., LL.B. 915 W. Hillcrest Blvd.
Hegarty, Patrick J. ..........................................'48 '73 C.629 B.S. L.426 J.D. Mun. Ct. J.
Hoffman, Peter C. ......................'50 '81 C.602 B.S. L.1068 J.D. Sierra Autocars Inc.
**Hoffman, Thomas Oliver** ..................'56 '81 C.112 B.S. L.1068 J.D. [Ⓐ Patten,F.&S.]
*PRACTICE AREAS: Litigation; Real Estate; Business; Corporate.
Holland, Kenneth D., (BV) ...................'26 '52 C&L.800 A.B., LL.B. [Holland&D.]
Holland & Donnelly, (BV) ................................................814 W. Foothill Blvd.
**Hudson, Raymond W.**, (AV) ....................'18 '54 C.112 B.S. L.426 [Hudson&K.] ‡

**Hudson & Kooiman**
**635 West Foothill Boulevard, 91016-2038**
**Telephone: 818-359-9335; 818-357-3204 Fax: 818-303-2391**
**Email: g_kooiman@msn.com**
**Raymond W. Hudson (Retired); Gerrit P. Kooiman.**
**Tax Law, Probate and Estate Planning, Conservatorship, Business and Real Estate.**
**Reference: Granite State Bank, Monrovia, CA.**

Hyde, Sheral A. ..............................'57 '87 C.101 B.A. L.809 J.D. 210 E. Walnut, Unit J
**Kooiman, Gerrit P.** .............................'46 '72 C.684 B.A. L.1067 J.D. [Hudson&K.]
*PRACTICE AREAS: Probate; Estate Planning; Taxation; Estate and Gift Taxation; Trust Administration.
Lawrence, Lewis D. ......................'20 '49 C.604 A.B. L.309 J.D. 525 S. Myrtle Ave.‡
Mc Kay, William R. ....'54 '82 C&L.800 A.B.,M.B.A., J.D. Pres., Southwest Products Co.
McManamon, William T., (BV) ............'20 '49 C&L.424 B.S., J.D. 525 S. Myrtle Ave.
Meaglia, Richard, (BV) .................'54 '79 C&L.426 B.A., J.D. 688 W. Foothill Blvd.
Moore, S. Clark ...........................................'24 '57 C.763 B.A. L.800 J.D. Mun. Ct. J.
Naiditch, Barry S. ....................'47 '80 C.1077 B.S. L.1136 J.D. 417 Cloverleaf Way
Parker, William L. ...........................'31 '79 C.642 B.A. L.426 J.D. 789 Ridgeside Dr.‡

**Patten, Faith & Sandford, (AV)**
**635 West Foothill Boulevard, 91016-2097**
**Telephone: 818-359-9335 Fax: 818-303-2391**
**William E. Faith; Jules Sandford; Eric Faith; Kevin Welch; Lorraine grindstaff; Thomas Oliver Hoffman.**
**General Civil Practice in State and Federal Courts. Trials and Appeals. Litigation, Real Estate, Business and Corporate, Estate Planning and Probate. Negligence and Family Law.**

Rellas, Chris S., (AV) ...........................................'22 '52 C.602 L.809 LL.B. P.O. Box 948
Rutherford, Jenice L. ..........'55 '80 C.645 B.S. L.1017 J.D. Coun., World Vision Intl.
**Sandford, Jules**, (AV) ..............................'28 '61 C.800 B.S. L.426 J.D. [Patten,F.&S.]
*REPORTED CASES: Estate of Collins (1968) 268 Cal. App. 2d 86; In re Marriage of Stratton (1975) 46 Cal. App. 3d 173; Hainey vs. Norman (1966) 247 Cal. App. 2d 528.
*PRACTICE AREAS: Litigation; Real Estate; Business; Corporate.
Sheriff, Thomas M. .........'41 '66 C.453 B.S. L.623 J.D. Gen. Coun., World Vision Intl.
Stern, Glenn E. ......................'46 '78 C.1097 B.S. L.1148 J.D. 417 Cloverleaf Way
**Welch, Kevin** ..........................................'51 '76 C.112 B.S. L.426 J.D. [Patten,F.&S.]
*PRACTICE AREAS: Litigation; Real Estate; Business and Corporate.
Wilson, Paul G., Jr. ..........................'25 '57 C.446 B.A. L.273 J.D. 635 W. Foothill Blvd.‡

## MONTAGUE, 1,415, *Siskiyou Co.*

Walker, Robert Z. ............'43 '68 C.112 B.A. L.1068 J.D. 11834 Ager Beswick Rd.‡

## MONTARA, —, *San Mateo Co.*

Briody, Joan E. ..................................'33 '70 C.330 A.B. L.1026 J.D. 314 Third St.

## MONTCLAIR, 28,434, *San Bernardino Co.*

Flores, Christina ..........................'59 '91 C.1168 B.A. L.426 J.D. 4732 Evart St.

## MONTEBELLO, 59,564, *Los Angeles Co.*

**Adams, Richard L.** ...................'50 '77 C.1097 B.A. L.116 J.D. [Ⓐ Alvarez-Glasman&C.]
*PRACTICE AREAS: Land Use, Zoning and Planning; Transactional Contracts; Personnel Matters; Estate Planning; Family Law.
Ajemian, Van Ralph ...........................................'54 '81 L.1068 J.D. 331 N. Vail Ave.‡
**Alvarez-Glasman, Arnold M.** .....'53 '78 C.1075 B.A. L.426 J.D. [Alvarez-Glasman&C.]
*PRACTICE AREAS: Municipal Law; Redevelopment Law; Public Agency Law; Real Estate Law.

**Alvarez-Glasman & Colvin, (BV)**
**200 East Beverly Boulevard, 2nd Floor, 90640**
**Telephone: 213-727-0870 Fax: 213-727-0878**
**Members of Firm: Arnold M. Alvarez-Glasman; Roger A. Colvin. Associates: Scott S. Widitor; Richard L. Adams; Gregory A. Docimo; Martha E. Romero.**
**Sole Practice Public Agency, Land Use, Redevelopment, Litigation and Bankruptcy.**
*See Professional Biographies, MONTEBELLO, CALIFORNIA*

Benavidez, Roland ..................'55 '80 C.1097 B.A. L.1137 J.D. 109 W. Madison Ave.
Colon, Jose ..........................'58 '86 C.674 A.B. L.1068 J.D. 3114 W. Beverly Blvd.
**Colvin, Roger A.**, (BV) .........'48 '76 C.800 B.A. L.1095 J.D. [Alvarez-Glasman&C.]
*PRACTICE AREAS: Municipal Law; Tort Defense Litigation; Real Estate.
**Docimo, Gregory A.** ...........'56 '82 C.426 B.A. L.424 J.D. [Ⓐ Alvarez-Glasman&C.]
*PRACTICE AREAS: Municipal Tort Liability Defense; Insurance Defense (Personal Injury); Construction Defect Defense; Products Liability Defense.
Ferr, James J. ..................................................'30 '55 C.102 L.426 J.D. P.O. Box 701‡
Fleishman, Leon ........................'35 '68 C.1097 B.S. L.809 LL.B. 869 N. Garfield Ave.
Garcia, William R. ...............'52 '77 C.1097 B.A. L.1066 J.D. 2637 W. Beverly Blvd.
Gonzalez, Mario P. ...........................................'26 '66 L.809 LL.B. 111 S. Garfield Ave.
Guerrero, Michael A., (AV) ..........'52 '77 C.1077 B.A. L.426 J.D. 3500 Beverly Blvd.
Guillen, Marin A. ......................'23 '63 C.112 B.A. L.809 LL.B. 2509 W. Beverly Blvd.
Malanca, Frank N. .........................'44 '70 C.800 B.A. L.426 J.D. 917 W. Beverly Blvd.
Mora, Ramon A. ...................'51 '80 C.112 B.A. L.1095 J.D. 3500 W. Beverly Blvd.
Moreno, Gregory W. .....................'45 '73 C.1042 B.A. L.426 J.D. 3500 Beverly Blvd.
Nguyen, Nho-Trong ......................'38 '88 C.1075 M.B.A. L.1137 J.D. P.O. Box 96
O'farrill, Anthony J. ..................'64 '92 C&L.426 B.S., J.D. 130 S. Montebello Blvd.
Orozco, Richard E. ...............................'29 '70 L.809 J.D. 1607 Paramount Blvd.
**Romero, Martha E.** ..............'57 '87 C.112 B.A. L.426 J.D. [Alvarez-Glasman&C.]
*REPORTED CASES: 17 CAL App. 4th 1240 Mann v. Board of Retirement.
*PRACTICE AREAS: Bankruptcy Creditor; Municipal Law; Municipal Taxation.
Ronzio, Frank E. '51 '90
C.818 B.S.,M.B.A. L.398 J.D. 111 S. Garfield Ave. (⊙Los Angeles)
Solorzano, Edward F. ................'36 '76 C.426 B.S.E.E. L.1190 J.D. 816 N. 16th St.
Stern, Herman ................................'14 '41 C.563 B.S. L.309 LL.B. 900 W. Bunker Hill
Trageman, Albert ..........................'31 '60 C&L.112 B.S., LL.B. 111 S. Garfield Ave.
Ucuzoglu, Nathan .....................'51 '76 C.800 B.A. L.426 J.D. 111 S. Garfield Ave.
Urban, John M. ...................'51 '76 C.800 B.A. L.809 J.D. 420 N. Montebello Blvd.
**Widitor, Scott S.** ..................'56 '87 C.951 B.A. L.1068 J.D. [Ⓐ Alvarez-Glasman&C.]
*PRACTICE AREAS: Municipal Litigation; Real Estate Litigation; Tort Litigation; Business Litigation.

## MONTECITO, —, *Santa Barbara Co.*

Bagdasarian, Ross ..........................'49 '75 C.813 B.A. L.809 J.D. 1192 E. Mountain Dr.
Hay, John, (A Professional Law Corporation), (BV) '24 '51
C.215 A.B. L.477 J.D. 1482 E. Valley Rd.
Hodges, Lauder W. ................'— '28 C.813 A.B. L.178 LL.B. 300 Hot Springs Rd.‡
Sotos, Victor H. '24 '50 L.146 LL.B.
(adm. in IL; not adm. in CA) 462 Cota Ln.‡
Towers, George E. .......................'35 '64 C.1043 B.A. L.800 LL.B. 759 Picacho Ln.
Tuthill, A. R. .............................'07 '31 C.113 B.A. L.800 LL.B. 300 Hot Springs Rd.‡

## MONTEREY, 31,954, *Monterey Co.*

**Albov, Michael A.**, (BV) ..................'49 '76 C.112 B.A. L.1067 J.D. [Hudson,M.F.&S.]
*PRACTICE AREAS: Real Property Law; Environmental Law; Maritime Law; Administrative Law.
Antoncich, Michael A., (BV) ............'42 '68 C.112 A.B. L.1065 J.D. 457 Webster St.
**Archer, Daniel F.** ..............................'63 '89 C.1060 B.S. L.770 J.D. [Ⓐ Fenton&K.]
**Arnold, Robert E., III** ..........'62 '96 C.477 B.A. L.284 J.D. [Ⓐ Horan,L.K.D.S.L.&C.]
*PRACTICE AREAS: Business Transactions; Corporate Law; Securities Law; Real Estate; Civil Litigation.

**Ascher, Yvonne A.** '58 '85 C.999 B.A. L.1226 J.D.
**2100 Garden Road, Suite C307, 93940**
**Telephone: 408-641-9019 Fax: 408-641-9018**
**Estate Planning, Estate Administration, Trusts, Long Term Care and Medicaid Planning.**
*See Professional Biographies, MONTEREY, CALIFORNIA*

Baker, Diana C. ....'48 '78 C.112 A.B. L.284 LL.B. Exec. Dir., Monterey Co. Legal Servs.
Baker, Paul W., (AV) ..........................'37 '67 C.336 B.A. L.1066 J.D. 80 Garden Ct.
Barelli, D. Richard, (BV) ....................'37 '66 C.602 B.S. L.1065 J.D. 2100 Garden Rd.
**Barron, Gerald V., III**, (AV) ...........................'45 '72 C&L.767 B.A., J.D. [Fenton&K.]
Barton, Jo C., (Mrs.) '31 '55 C&L.623 B.A., LL.B.
(adm. in OK; not adm. in CA) Coast Rte.‡
Basista, Michael, (CVⓉ) '22 '73 C.754 B.A. L.1017 LL.B.
(adm. in PA; not adm. in CA) 883 Belden St.‡
Battey, Jonathan C. ..................................'54 '79 C.112 B.A. L.1065 J.D. [Gray&B.]
Bebermeyer, Robert R., (BV) ...............'40 '65 C.791 B.S. L.472 LL.B. 444 Pearl St.
**Beers, William M.** ..............'40 '69 C.950 L.596 J.D. Assoc. Gen. Coun., DPIC Cos.
Berry, Douglas A., (CV) .........'46 '80 C.763 B.A. L.1137 J.D. 2100 Garden Rd., Ste. H
**Blum, Mark A.** ..............'54 '86 C.766 B.A. L.1065 J.D. [Horan,L.K.D.S.L.&C.]
*PRACTICE AREAS: Land Use; Planning; Zoning; Subdivision; Inverse Condemnation.
**Bohnen, Thomas P.**, (AV) .......................'43 '69 C.988 B.S. L.767 J.D. [Bohnen,R.&D.]
*PRACTICE AREAS: Taxation; Estate Planning; Wills; Trusts; Probate.

**Bohnen, Rosenthal & Dusenbury, (AV)**
**555 Abrego Street, Second Floor, P.O. Box 1111, 93942-1111**
**Telephone: 408-649-5551 Fax: 408-649-0272**
**Members of Firm: Thomas P. Bohnen (Certified Specialist, Taxation Law, The State Bar of California Board of Legal Specialization); Robert E. Rosenthal; Douglas K. Dusenbury. Of Counsel: Roger D. Bolgard; Harry Finkle.**
**Business and Civil Litigation, Insurance Defense, Personal Injury, Family Law, Business, Corporation, Real Property, Taxation, Estate Planning and Probate, Creditor's Rights, Environmental and Employment Law.**
*See Professional Biographies, MONTEREY, CALIFORNIA*

**Bolgard, Roger D.**, (BV) '39 '76 C.674 A.B. L.1026 J.D.
[Ⓒ Bohnen,R.&D.] (⊙Redwood)
*PRACTICE AREAS: Business Law; Construction Law; Partnership; Corporations Law; Business Litigation.
Bomberger, Russell B. ..................'34 '70 C.831 B.S. L.981 LL.B. P.O. Box 8741★
**Bouhaben, Sarah J.** .................................'62 '90 C.284 B.A. L.770 J.D. [Ⓐ Low,B.&L.]
**Boustani, Eric Bakri** ...........................'69 '96 C.766 B.S. L.770 J.D. [Ⓐ Davis&S.]
*PRACTICE AREAS: Intellectual Property; Litigation.
Bowersox, Kim C. ...................'54 '83 C.112 B.A. L.273 J.D. Mahoney Tancredi Co.
**Boyns, Sara B.** .................................................'57 '88 C.878 B.S. L.1226 J.D. [Call&B.]
*PRACTICE AREAS: Business Litigation; Civil Litigation; Civil Appeals; Employment Litigation; Estate Planning.

**Brandwein, William A.**, (AV) ................ '36 '67 C&L.209 J.D. [W.A.Brandwein]⊙
*PRACTICE AREAS: Civil and Criminal Tax Litigation; Estate Planning.

**Brandwein, William A., A Professional Law Corporation, (AV)**
**215 West Franklin Street, P.O. Box LAW, 93942⊙**
**Telephone: 408-372-3266 Fax: 408-372-0812**
**William A. Brandwein (Certified Specialist, Taxation Law, The State Bar of California Board of Legal Specialization).**
**Tax Law, Individual, Corporate and Estate Taxation. Civil and Criminal Tax Litigation, Probate and Estate Planning.**
**Columbus, Ohio Office: 42 East Gay Street, 11th Floor. Telephone: 614-461-1352. Fax: 614-221-0816.**
***See Professional Biographies, MONTEREY, CALIFORNIA***

Brehmer, George W., (BV) ............'35 '65 C.610 A.B. L.608 J.D. Prof. Bldg., 5th Flr.
**Bridges, John S.** ....................... '58 '85 C.506 B.S. L.1067 J.D. [Fenton&K.]
Brown, David W., (CV) ........................'49 '81 C.813 B.S. L.770 J.D. 1201 9th St.
Bruning, Fred W., Jr. ............... '51 '77 C.668 B.A. L.426 J.D. 23707 Determine Ln.
**Buchert, Kenneth D.** ................ '37 '87 C.150 B.S. L.1226 J.D. [⊠ R.R.Wellington]
*PRACTICE AREAS: Municipal and Administrative Law; Public Employment and Personnel Law.
**Buck, Gwendolen S.**, (BV) ..........................................................'42 '76 [Zerbe,B.&L.]
*PRACTICE AREAS: Family Law; Civil Litigation; Personal Injury Law; Intellectual Property Law; Trademark Law and Copyright Law.
Burnett, James T. '42 '67 C.1021 B.S. L.262 LL.B.
(adm. in NY; not adm. in CA) F.B.I.
Busch, Douglas G. ......................................... '28 '69 631 S. Atlantic Blvd.
**Call, Brian D.**, (BV) ................................ '55 '81 C.1051 B.A. L.809 J.D. [Call&B.]
*PRACTICE AREAS: Business Transactions; Real Estate Transactions; Business Litigation.

**Call & Boyns, (BV)**
**500 Camino El Estero, Suite 200, 93940**
**Telephone: 408-649-3218 FAX: 408-649-4705**
**Members of Firm: Sara B. Boyns; Brian D. Call.**
**Real Estate and Business Transactions, Civil Litigation and Appeals, Probate and Estate Planning.**
***See Professional Biographies, MONTEREY, CALIFORNIA***

**Cameron, Mark A.**, (CV) ..................'57 '83 C.1110 B.A. L.1065 J.D. [Fenton&K.]
Capestro, Andrew J., (CV) ................'41 '67 C.112 A.B. L.1065 J.D. 1088 Cass St.
**Casey, Patrick S. M.** ............... '66 '93 C.20 B.A. L.426 J.D. [⊠ Noland,H.E.&H.]⊙
*PRACTICE AREAS: Corporate; Partnership; Taxation; Estate Planning.
**Clifford, Robert C.**, (AV) .......'26 '52 C&L.813 A.B., LL.B. [⊠ Horan,L.K.D.S.L.&C.]
**Coniglio, Peter J.**, (BV) ............ '29 '56 C.770 B.S. L.767 LL.B. [Hudson,M.F.&S.]
*PRACTICE AREAS: Estate Planning; Family Law; Business Litigation.
Conners, William B. ...................................'48 '77 C.549 B.S. L.770 J.D. City Atty.
Cook, George R., Law Offices of ........... '41 '80 C.112 A.B. L.1026 J.D. 460 Alma St.
**Cook, James J.**, (BV) ...........'48 '73 C.649 B.A. L.1017 J.D. [Horan,L.K.D.S.L.&C.]
*PRACTICE AREAS: Personal Injury; Business Litigation.
Cooper, Joseph D., (CV) ................'60 '89 C.112 B.S. L.1189 J.D. [Cooper&H.]⊙
Cooper & Hoppe, (BV) ......................................... 1088 Cass St. (⊙Fresno)
Curtis, William D. ...........................................'30 '58 L.1065 J.D. Supr. Ct. J
**Dalton, Gerald B.**, (BV) ................'31 '60 C&L.767 B.S., LL.B. [Hudson,M.F.&S.]
*PRACTICE AREAS: Real Property Law; Corporations; Partnerships; Estate Planning.
Daniels, William B., (BV) ............... '41 '67 C.197 A.B. L.1066 J.D. [Heisler,S.&D.]
Daunt, Philip J. ..................................'51 '80 C.477 A.B. L.851 J.D. 2100 Garden Rd.
**Daunt, Robert T.** ......................................'49 '77 C.477 B.A. L.851 J.D. [Davis&S.]
*PRACTICE AREAS: Computer Law; Intellectual Property Law; Corporate Law.
**Dauphiné, Susan M.**, (BV) ..................'44 '69 C.813 B.A. L.178 J.D. [Fenton&K.]
**Davis, G. Gervaise, III**, (AV) ..................'32 '58 C&L.276 B.S., J.D. [Davis&S.]
*PRACTICE AREAS: Computer Law; Intellectual Property Law and Litigation; General Business Law.

**Davis & Schroeder, P.C., (AV)**
**4th Floor, Professional Building, 215 West Franklin Street Post Office Box 3080, 93942-3080**
**Telephone: 408-649-1122 FAX: 408-649-0566**
**URL: http://www.iplawyers.com**
**G. Gervaise Davis III; George L. Schroeder; John D. Laughton; Robert T. Daunt;—Catherine Mccauley-Libert; Eric Bakri Boustani.**
**Internet, Computer and High Technology Law, Estate Planning, Probate, Real Property, Business and Computer Litigation, Corporation, Tax Law and Patent, Trademark, Trade Secret, and Copyright Law.**
**Reference: First National Bank of Central California, Monterey, California.**
***See Professional Biographies, MONTEREY, CALIFORNIA***

**DeLay, Paul R.**, (BV) ...........'19 '49 C.602 A.B. L.276 LL.B. [⊠ Lozano S.S.W.&B.]
*REPORTED CASES: Monterey County Deputy Sheriff's Association v. County of Monterey (1979) 23 Cal. 3d 296; CSEA v. King City Unified School District (1981) 116 Cal. App. 3d 695; MPUSD v. Certificated Employees Council (1974) 42 Cal. App. 3d 328; Sheehan v. Eldridge (1970) 5 Cal. App. 3d 77.
*PRACTICE AREAS: Government Law; Litigation.
Demmon, William M., Jr. '54 '81 C.347 B.S. L.879 J.D.
(adm. in IN; not adm. in CA) Sr. V.P. & Gen. Mgr., Design Professionals Ins. Co.
**de Villiers, P. Francois** ............'67 '96 C&L.999 B.S.M.E., J.D. [⊠ LaRiviere,G.&P.]
*LANGUAGES: Afrikaans.
*PRACTICE AREAS: Patent, International and Domestic; Trademarks; Copyrights.
**Dewar, Roderick L.**, (BV) ..................'29 '55 C&L.813 A.B., LL.B. [Dewar&R.]
*PRACTICE AREAS: Real Property Law; Mortgage Law; Wills Law; Probate Law; Estate Planning Law.

**Dewar and Rockwood, A Professional Corporation, (BV)**
**587 Hartnell Street, P.O. Box 1027, 93940**
**Telephone: 408-373-4463; 800-200-8515 Fax: 408-373-2566**
**Roderick L. Dewar; Terry G. Rockwood; Brian C. McCoy.**
**General Civil and Trial Practice in all Courts. Personal Injury, Government Tort Claims, Family, Real Property and Mortgage Law, Business, Estate Planning and Probate Law.**
***See Professional Biographies, MONTEREY, CALIFORNIA***

Dixon, Leslie E. '18 '47 C&L.420 B.A., LL.B.
(adm. in LA; not adm. in CA) P.O. Box 342
Drucker, George W., Jr. ..............'30 '55 C.597 B.S. L.309 LL.B. 700 Cannery Row‡
**Duffy, Thomas R.**, (BV) ......................'49 '75 C.813 A.B. L.1066 J.D. [Duffy&G.]
*PRACTICE AREAS: Commercial and Real Estate Litigation; Creditor's Remedies in Insolvency Matters; Real Property and Commercial Transactions.

**Duffy & Guenther, (BV)**
**419 Webster Street, 93940**
**Telephone: 408-649-5100 Fax: 408-649-5102**
**Email: dglaw@mbay.net**
**Members of Firm: Thomas R. Duffy; Ralph P. Guenther;—John E. Kesecker.**
**Commercial Litigation, Bankruptcy, Secured Transactions, Commercial Law and Business Reorganization.**
***See Professional Biographies, MONTEREY, CALIFORNIA***

Dunnion, Thomas J. ....................'45 '75 C.763 B.A. L.1049 J.D. 2711 Garden Rd.
**Dusenbury, Douglas K.** ..................'43 '68 C.375 B.A. L.378 J.D. [Bohnen,R.&D.]
*PRACTICE AREAS: Business and Civil Litigation; Personal Injury; Family Law.
**Dyer, Stephen W.**, (BV) ..........'46 '74 C.112 A.B. L.767 J.D. [Horan,L.K.D.S.L.&C.]
Ehrman, Kenneth A., (AV) ................'17 '61 C.309 B.S. L.981 LL.B. 80 Garden Ct.
**Etienne, Myron E., Jr.**, (AV) ...... '24 '53 C.1027 B.S. L.1065 J.D. [Noland,H.E.&H.]⊙
*PRACTICE AREAS: Civil Litigation; Real Estate Law; Land Use Law; Development Law.

Evans, William E., (CV) '50 '79
C.800 B.A. L.809 J.D. Pres., Evan-Moor Publishing Corp.
Evers, Sharyn F. ..........................'61 '85 C.500 B.B.A. L.472 J.D. 2100 Garden Rd.
Farzan, Manoucher ........................'24 '54 C.112 B.A. L.1065 J.D. 631 Abrego St.
Feavel, Patrick M. ..........................'50 '83 C.1080 B.A. L.426 J.D. 2711 Garden Rd.
**Fenton, Lewis L.**, (AV) ..........'25 '51 C&L.813 B.A., LL.B. [Fenton&K.] (⊙San Jose)

**Fenton & Keller, (AV)**
**2801 Monterey-Salinas Highway, P.O. Box 791, 93942-0791⊙**
**Telephone: 408-373-1241 Telecopier: 408-373-7219**
**Members of Firm: J. Hampton Hoge (1899-1977); Lewis L. Fenton; Charles R. Keller; Gerald V. Barron, III; Nolan M. Kennedy; Ronald F. Scholl; Thomas H. Jamison; Susan M. Dauphiné; Larry E. Hayes; Nancy P. Tostevin; Mark H. Johnson (Certified Specialist, Estate Planning, Trust and Probate Law, The State Bar of California Board of Legal Specialization); Mark A. Cameron; John S. Bridges; Frances R. Gaver (Certified Specialist, Estate Planning, Trust and Probate Law, The State Bar of California Board of Legal Specialization); Dennis G. McCarthy; Daniel F. Archer; Jacqueline P. McManus; Donald Forrest Leach; David C. Sweigert; Lorie A. Kruse; Lonnie Truax; Virginia H. Lauderdale; Christopher E. Panetta.**
**General Civil, Trial and Appellate Practice in State and Federal Courts, Administrative, Agribusiness, Commercial, Corporation, Insurance, Land Use Planning, Probate, Real Estate, Taxation, Trust and Estates Law.**
**Salinas, California Office: 132 West Gabilan Street. Telephone: 408-757-8937. Facsimile: 408-574-0621.**
***See Professional Biographies, MONTEREY, CALIFORNIA***

**Finkle, Harry**, (AV) ................. '48 '72 C.112 B.A. L.1066 J.D. [⊠ Bohnen,R.&D.]
*PRACTICE AREAS: Labor and Employment; Litigation.
Fischer, Todd A. ................................'61 '89 C.494 B.S. L.809 J.D. [Fischer,N.&S.]
Fischer, Norris & Schrader ......................................Ryan Ranch, 6 Harris Ct.

**Flavin, Sean, (AV) '24 '50 C.813 A.B. L.309 LL.B.**
**500 Camino El Estero, Suite 200, P.O. Box 2229, 93942-2229**
**Telephone: 408-372-7535 Fax: 408-372-2425**
***PRACTICE AREAS: Estate Planning; Probate Law; Real Estate Law; Corporate Law; Partnership Law.**
**General Civil Practice, Corporations and Partnerships, Estate Planning, Probate and Real Property Law, State and Local Taxation.**
***See Professional Biographies, MONTEREY, CALIFORNIA***

**Flores, Victor**, (BV) '43 '82 C.556 B.S.E.E. L.208 J.D.
(adm. in AZ; not adm. in CA; See Pat. Sect.) [⊠ LaRiviere,G.&P.]
*LANGUAGES: Spanish.
*PRACTICE AREAS: Patents; Trademarks; Copyrights; Licensing.
Folsom, Ann A. ......................................... '39 '77 C.684 B.A. L.1226 J.D. 128 Seafoam‡
Fors, Geoffrey C. .......................................'57 '84 C&L.770 B.S., J.D. 769 Pacific St.
Foster, Richd. H. ............................'27 '52 C.112 A.B. L.1066 LL.B. 2100 Garden Rd.

**Fox, Dennis W. '46 '74 C.112 B.A. L.809 J.D.**
**2100 Garden Road, Suite H, 93940**
**Telephone: 408-646-9898 Telecopier: 408-646-0720**
**Email: dwfox@redshift.com**
**(Certified Specialist, Estate Planning, Trust and Probate Law, The State Bar of California Board of Legal Specialization).**
***REPORTED CASES: Estate of Stevenson, 14 Cal. Rptr. 2d 250.**
***PRACTICE AREAS: Living Trusts; Estate Planning; Trust Administration; Probate.**
**Estate Planning, Probate, Trust Administration, Estate Litigation.**
***See Professional Biographies, MONTEREY, CALIFORNIA***

**Freiman, Harold M.** ..............'64 '90 C.112 A.B. L.178 J.D. [⊠ Lozano S.S.W.&B.]
*PRACTICE AREAS: Litigation; Education Law.
**Freska, Anna M.** .........................'61 '91 C.31 B.A. L.770 J.D. [Hudson,M.F.&S.]
*LANGUAGES: Polish, English and German.
**Gaver, Frances R.**, (BV) ................'29 '86 C.914 B.A. L.1226 J.D. [⊠ Fenton&K.]
Gayle, Dennis A. .......................... '41 '72 C.112 B.A. L.1148 J.D. 1340 Munras Ave.
Gerstl, Hugo N. .............................'41 '66 C.112 A.B. L.1068 LL.B. [Gerstl&G.]
Gerstl & Gorman, Inc. ......................................................... 33 Soledad Dr.
**Gianascol, Christine P.** ............'51 '88 C.1169 A.B. L.1126 J.D. [Noland,H.E.&H.]⊙
*PRACTICE AREAS: Civil Litigation; Land Use Law.
Gilles, Jeffrey R. .........................'54 '79 C.770 B.A. L.464 J.D. [Gilles,M.&S.]⊙
Gilles, Minor & Sullivan ........................................30 Ragsdale Dr. (⊙Salinas)
Gorman, Richard D. ..................................'40 '66 C.321 B.S. L.184 J.D. [Gerstl&G.]
Gray, Gary E., (BV) .................................'46 '73 C.546 B.A. L.464 J.D. [Gray&B.]
Gray & Battey, (BV) ........................................................... 149 Bonifacio Pl.
**Grubman, Ronald E.** .............'43 '74 C.223 B.S. L.813 J.D. [⊠ LaRiviere,G.&P.] (Pat.)
*PRACTICE AREAS: Business; Intellectual Property Interface; Licensing; Due Diligence.

**Grunsky, Ebey, Farrar & Howell, A Professional Corporation**
**(See Watsonville)**

**Guenther, Ralph P.**, (BV) .................'61 '86 C.1077 B.S. L.1067 J.D. [Duffy&G.]
*PRACTICE AREAS: Creditor's Remedies; Bankruptcy; Commercial and Real Estate Litigation; Real Property and Commercial Transactions.
Gunter, Roy C., III, (BV) .......'47 '75 C.951 B.A. L.1067 J.D. 580 Calle Principal, Ste 2
Guy, J. Michael .......................'46 '74 C.375 A.B. L.1068 J.D. 126 Bonifacio Place
Ham, Albert S., (BV) ............'30 '54 C.112 B.A. L.1066 LL.B. 470 Camino El Estero
Ham, Marti Anne .........................'67 '92 C&L.770 B.A., J.D. 470 Camino El Estero
**Hamerly, Paul M.**, (AV) ................'20 '48 C&L.813 B.A., J.D. [Noland,H.E.&H.]⊙
*PRACTICE AREAS: General Business Law; Estate Planning Law; Probate Law.
Hanson, Murlie C. ................................'53 '79 C&L.972 B.A., J.D. 2100 Garden Rd.
**Harray, Richard K.**, (AV) .............'42 '68 C.597 A.B. L.813 LL.B. [Harray,M.&L.]
*LANGUAGES: French and Spanish.
*PRACTICE AREAS: General Insurance Including Casualty and Malpractice; Employment Law; Personal Injury; Property Damage; Products Liability.

**Harray, Masuda & Linker, (AV)** ⊞
**80 Garden Court, Suite 260, 93940**
**Telephone: 408-373-3101 Fax: 408-373-6712**
**Richard K. Harray; Michael P. Masuda; Stan L. Linker.**
**Civil Litigation and Appellate Practice in all State and Federal Courts. Casualty, Insurance, Public Entity, Employment, Medical and Professional Malpractice.**
***See Professional Biographies, MONTEREY, CALIFORNIA***

Harrow, Barry R., (BV) ....................'49 '80 C.1350 B.A. L.1136 J.D. [Harrow&C.]
Harrow and Cayce, (BV) ...................................200 E. Franklin Street, Suite 250
**Hayes, Larry E.**, (BV) ......................'46 '80 C.1253 B.S. L.770 J.D. [Fenton&K.]

**Heisinger, Buck, Morris & Rose**
**(See Carmel)**

Heisler, Stewart & Daniels, Inc., (BV) ..................................... 563 Figueroa Street
Hendry, John L., (BV) .... '38 '65 C.813 A.B. L.1065 LL.B. 2801 Monterey-Salinas Hwy.
Hollingsworth, David M., (CV) ........'37 '65 C.198 B.A. L.950 LL.B. 126 Bonifacio Pl.
Hoot, Willard D. '15 '42 C.645 A.B. L.477
(adm. in OH; not adm. in CA) United Calif. Bk.
Hoppe, Theodore W., (BV) ................'63 '88 C.859 B.A. L.546 J.D. [Cooper&H.]⊙
Horan, Kevin W., (BV) ................'54 '79 C.668 B.A. L.1065 J.D. 499 Van Buren St.

**Horan, Laurence P.**, (AV) ....... '29 '55 C.112 A.B. L.1066 J.D. [Horan,L.K.D.S.L.&C.]
*LANGUAGES: Spanish.
*PRACTICE AREAS: Civil Litigation; Professional Negligence Law; Eminent Domain Law.

**Horan, Lloyd, Karachale, Dyer, Schwartz, Law & Cook, Incorporated, (AV)**
**499 Van Buren Street, P.O. Box 3350, 93942-3350**
Telephone: 408-373-4131 FAX: 408-373-8302
Laurence P. Horan; Francis P. Lloyd (Certified Specialist, Estate Planning, Trust and Probate Law, The State Bar of California Board of Legal Specialization); Anthony T. Karachale (Certified Specialist, Taxation Law, The State Bar of California Board of Legal Specialization); Dennis M. Law; Gary D. Schwartz (Certified Specialist, Taxation Law, The State Bar of California Board of Legal Specialization); James J. Cook; Stephen W. Dyer; Mark A. Blum;—Mark A. O'Connor; Sonia S. Sharma; Robert E. Arnold, III. Of Counsel: William C. Marsh; Robert C. Clifford.
Language: Spanish.
General Civil and Trial Practice, Corporation, Taxation, Employee Benefit, Real Estate, Personal Injury, Professional Negligence, Wrongful Termination, Condemnation, Land Use, Environmental, Commercial, Trusts, Estate Planning, Probate, Trust and Estate Litigation.
References: Wells Fargo Bank; Bank of America National Trust & Savings Assn.; First National Bank of Monterey; Monterey County Bank.
*See Professional Biographies, MONTEREY, CALIFORNIA*

**Hoss, Peter T.**, (AV) ............... '34 '59 C.188 B.A. L.813 J.D. [Noland,H.E.&H.]⊙
*PRACTICE AREAS: Construction Law; Business Litigation; Real Estate Law.
**Hubbard, Alexander F.** ............... '65 '91 C.112 B.A. L.1065 J.D. [Thompson&H.]
*PRACTICE AREAS: Litigation; Real Property; General Business; Estate Planning; Probate.
**Hubbard, Donald G.**, (AV) ........... '34 '62 C.768 B.A. L.1066 LL.B. [Thompson&H.]
*PRACTICE AREAS: Real Property; Land Use; General Business; Administrative Law and Estate Planning.

**Hudson, Martin, Ferrante & Street, (BV)** BB
**490 Calle Principal, P.O. Box 112, 93940**
Telephone: 408-375-3151 Telecopier: 408-375-0131
Email: hmfs@aol.com
W. G. Hudson (1877-1954); Carmel Martin (1879-1965); Peter J. Ferrante (1903-1975); William L. Hudson (1907-1982); Webster Street (1898-1984). Of Counsel: John F. Martin. Members of Firm: Carmel Martin, Jr.; Peter J. Coniglio; Gerald B. Dalton; Michael A. Albov; Peter R. Williams; Anna M. Freska.
General Civil and Trial Practice. Banking, Real Property, Commercial, Cable and Communications, Corporation, Construction, Personal Injury, Estate Planning, and Probate Law.
Representative Clients: California-American Water Co.; Monterey County Bank; Fisherman's Wharf Property Owners Assn.; Monterey Peninsula TV Cable; Granite Construction Co., Inc.; CTB-MacMillan/McGraw-Hill; Cypress Coast Bank.
References: Bank of America National Trust & Savings Assn. (Monterey and Pacific Grove Offices); Wells Fargo Bank (Monterey Branch).
*See Professional Biographies, MONTEREY, CALIFORNIA*

**Isbill, Ute M.** ....................................... '59 '93 C.999 L.1226 J.D. [Ⓐ G.R.Walker]
*PRACTICE AREAS: Estate Planning; Probate; Trusts; Real Property Law.
Jacobs, Arthur B. ............................ '41 '67 C.994 B.A. L.659 LL.B. 555 Abrego St.
**Jahn, Ellen M.** ................................ '53 '88 C.347 B.S. L.1189 J.D. [Lozano S.S.W.&B.]
*REPORTED CASES: Belanger v. Madera, Unified School District 963 F. 2d 248 (9th Cir. 1992).
*PRACTICE AREAS: Personnel; Employment Discrimination; Collective Bargaining; Federal Litigation.
**Jamison, Thomas H.**, (AV) ............... '47 '75 C.951 B.A. L.1065 J.D. [Fenton&K.]⊙
Johnson, Chris P., (CV) .................. '47 '72 C&L.767 B.S., J.D. 215 W. Franklin St.
**Johnson, Mark H.**, (BV) ................. '56 '81 C.309 B.A. L.1065 J.D. [Fenton&K.]
Jones, Arthur T., (BV) ...................................... '26 '49 C&L.800 J.D. [Jones&J.]⊙
Jones, Carol J. ................................ '44 '86 C.1075 B.S. L.1226 J.D. 1340 Munras Ave.
Jones, W. Montgomery, (BV) ........................................ '29 '52 L.426 LL.B. [Jones&J.]⊙
Jones and Jones, (BV) .................................................. 1340 Munras Ave. (⊙Glendale)
Jordan, Gary L., (AV) '36 '62 C.378 B.S.Ch.E. L.273 J.D.
(adm. in KS; not adm. in CA; Pat.) Monterey Institute of Intl. Studies
**Jordan, Judd L.** ................... '50 '76 C.112 B.A. L.1068 J.D. [Ⓒ Lozano S.S.W.&B.]
*PRACTICE AREAS: Litigation.
Joyce, John R., (CV) ............................. '41 '73 C.911 B.A. L.94 J.D. 2600 Garden Rd.
Kadushin, Karen D., (AV) '43 '77 C.112 B.A. L.284 J.D.
Dean, Monterey College of Law
Kaplan, Allen C. .......................................... '38 '76 C.529 B.A. L.477 J.D. 33 Soledad Dr.
**Karachale, Anthony T.**, (AV) ...... '39 '65 C&L.813 A.B., LL.B. [Horan,L.K.D.S.L.&C.]
**Keeler, Christopher D.** ............... '66 '94 C.813 B.A. L.101 J.D. [Lozano S.S.W.&B.]
*LANGUAGES: Spanish.
*PRACTICE AREAS: Education Law; Construction Law; Public Entity Law.
Keeley, Carolyn I. ........................................ '49 '79 C.339 B.A. L.770 J.D. Dep. Dist. Atty.
Keiley, Anthony J., III, (BV) .................. '57 '82 C.112 B.A. L.770 J.D. [A.J.Keiley,III]
Keiley, Anthony J. III, A Professional Law Corporation, (BV)
215 W. Franklin St., Fifth Floor (⊙San Jose)
**Keller, Charles R.**, (AV) ................. '40 '66 C&L.813 B.A., LL.B. [Fenton&K.]⊙
Kelly, Joanne ................................ '38 '79 C.219 B.A. L.1226 J.D. 700 Cass St.
Kelly, Robert B. ......................... '35 '80 C.188 B.M.E. L.1226 J.D. McGraw-Hill, Inc.
Kendall, Prescott J., III ...................... '49 '77 C.1169 B.A. L.1066 J.D. 2100 Garden Rd.
**Kennedy, Michele C.**, (CV) ............. '51 '82 C.112 B.A. L.1065 J.D. [Spiering,S.&K.]
*LANGUAGES: Spanish, German and Italian.
*PRACTICE AREAS: Personal Injury; Civil Litigation.
**Kennedy, Nolan M.**, (AV) ................... '43 '73 C.69 B.A. L.1065 J.D. [Fenton&K.]⊙
Kennifer, Frederick L. .......... '54 '82 C.112 A.B. L.770 J.D. Pres., Kennifer Property Co.
**Kesecker, John E.** ................................... '67 '93 C.1075 B.S. L.464 J.D. [Ⓐ Duffy&G.]

**Koontz, Robert J., (BV) '47 '76 C.112 B.A. L.1065 J.D.**
**631 Abrego Street, 93940**
Telephone: 408-644-9232 Fax: 408-644-9405
Estate Planning, Probate, Conservatorship Law, Business, Real Property and Civil Practice.
*See Professional Biographies, MONTEREY, CALIFORNIA*

Kroopf, Kenneth J., (A P.C.) ............ '49 '75 C.112 B.A. L.800 J.D. 787 Munras Ave.
**Kruse, Lorie A.** ..................................... '65 '93 C.112 B.A. L.770 J.D. [Ⓐ Fenton&K.]
LaBarbera, Dennis G. ........................ '48 '73 C.569 B.A. L.477 J.D. Dist. Atty. Off.
**LaRiviere, F. David**, (AV) ........ '39 '73 C.813 B.S.E.E. L.770 J.D. [LaRiviere,G.&P.]⊙
*PRACTICE AREAS: Patents, Trademarks and Copyrights; Contracts and Licensing; Business; Intellectual Property Interface; Litigation Support.

**LaRiviere, Grubman & Payne, (AV)**
**4 Justin Court, P.O. Box 3140, 93942⊙**
Telephone: 408-649-8800 Facsimile: 408-649-8835
Members of Firm: F. David LaRiviere; Robert W. Payne. Of Counsel: Ronald E. Grubman. Associates: P. Francois de Villiers; Victor Flores (Not admitted in CA).
Patent, Trademark, Trade Secrets, Trade Dress, Copyright and Multi-National High Technology Law. Commercial, Industrial, Agricultural and Aerospace/defense Contracts and Licensing and related Litigation. Due Diligence Studies, Validity and Patentability Searches and Opinions.
San Jose, California Office: 160 West Santa Clara Street, Suite 1400.
*See Professional Biographies, MONTEREY, CALIFORNIA*

Larson, Amy M. ........................ '63 '88 C.886 B.S. L.945 J.D. 201 Glenwood Circle
Lauderdale, James M., Jr., (CV) .......... '48 '74 C&L.770 B.A., J.D. 150 Carmelito Ave.
**Lauderdale, Virginia H.** .................... '60 '86 C.31 B.A. L.569 J.D. [Ⓐ Fenton&K.]
*PRACTICE AREAS: Corporate Law; Securities Law; Real Estate Law.
**Laughton, John D.**, (BV) ..................... '48 '78 C.112 B.A. L.1065 J.D. [Davis&S.]
*PRACTICE AREAS: Real Estate Law; General Business Law.
**Law, Dennis M.**, (BV) ............... '44 '70 C.813 A.B. L.1068 J.D. [Horan,L.K.D.S.L.&C.]
*PRACTICE AREAS: Civil, Commercial and Real Estate Litigation; Real Property Transactions.

**Leach, Donald Forrest** ........................ '59 '91 C.732 B.A. L.276 J.D. [Ⓐ Fenton&K.]
**Lewis, Rose-Eve K.**, (CV) .................. '49 '80 C.643 B.A. L.1065 J.D. [Zerbe,B.&L.]
*LANGUAGES: French.
*PRACTICE AREAS: Real Estate Law; Business Law; Partnership Law; Corporation Law.
Lichtenegger, Larry J., (CV) ................... '42 '68 C.375 B.A. L.376 J.D. P.O. Box 2686

**Lindsey, Bruce**
(See Salinas)

**Linker, Stan L.**, (BV) ...................... '49 '74 C.267 B.A. L.464 J.D. [Harray,M.&L.]
*PRACTICE AREAS: General Insurance Including Casualty and Malpractice; Employment Law; Personal Injury; Property Damage; Products Liability.
**Llewellyn, Kathleen** ...................... '49 '92 C.740 B.A. L.1226 J.D. [Ⓐ G.R.Walker]
*PRACTICE AREAS: Estate Planning; Probate; Trusts; Real Property Law.
**Lloyd, Francis P.**, (BV) ............ '35 '60 C.112 A.B. L.1066 J.D. [Horan,L.K.D.S.L.&C.]
*PRACTICE AREAS: Trust Law; Estate Planning Law; Probate Law; Estate Law; Estate and Trust Litigation.
Lombardo, Julie Culver ........................ '60 '85 C&L.770 B.S.C., J.D. Dep. Dist. Atty.

**Lombardo, Anthony, & Associates**
(See Salinas)

**Long, Jay B. '53 '82 C.112 B.S. L.1067 J.D.**
**500 Camino El Estero, Suite 200, 93940⊙**
Telephone: 408-649-3877; Fax: 408-649-4705
Email: jayblong@ix.netcom.com
Environmental and Energy Law, including Regulatory and Legislative Matters; Insurance Coverage Law; Construction and Design Law; Sports, Sponsorship and Event Law; Advertising, Marketing and Distribution Law; Select Business, Real Estate, other Civil Litigation and Trial Practice in all State and Federal Courts; Alternate Dispute Resolution.
Long Beach, California Office: Greater Los Angeles World Trade Center, One World Trade Center, Suite 800, 90831-0800. Telephone: 310-983-8146. Fax: 310-983-8199.
*See Professional Biographies, MONTEREY, CALIFORNIA*

Loop, Loretta L. ........................................... '55 '87 L.1226 J.D. 2100 Garden Rd.
Love, Cheri D. ................................ '63 '89 C.112 A.B. L.1065 J.D. 1 Harris Ct.

**Low, Ball & Lynch, A Professional Corporation, (AV)**
**10 Ragsdale Drive, Suite 175, 93940⊙**
Telephone: 408-655-8822 Fax: 408-655-8881
Sarah J. Bouhaben.
General Civil and Trial Practice, Insurance, Environmental Law, Land Use, Real Estate, Corporate, Professional Malpractice, Products Liability, Securities, Commercial Litigation and Appellate Practice.
Redwood City, California Office: 10 Twin Dolphin Drive, Suite B-500, 94065. Telephone: 415-591-8822. Fax: 415-591-8884.
San Francisco, California Office: 601 California Street, Suite 2100, 94108. Telephone: 415-981-6630.
*See Professional Biographies, MONTEREY, CALIFORNIA*

**Lowrey, Lloyd W., Jr.**, (BV) ........... '46 '72 C.112 B.S. L.813 J.D. [Noland,H.E.&H.]⊙
*PRACTICE AREAS: Water Law; Real Estate Law; Environmental Law; Business Law.
**Lozano, Louis T.**, (AV) ............... '48 '75 C.112 B.A. L.1066 J.D. [Lozano S.S.W.&B.]
*LANGUAGES: French and Armenian.
*REPORTED CASES: Trend v. Central Unified School Dist (1990) 220 Cal. App. 3d 102; N. State v. Pittsburg Unified School Dist. (1990) 220 Cal. App. 3d 1418; San Francisco Unified S.D. v. Superior Court (1981) 116 Cal. App. 3d 231.
*PRACTICE AREAS: Public Facilities Finance; Labor Relations; Employment; Education Law.

**Lozano Smith Smith Woliver & Behrens, A Professional Corporation, (AV)**
**Building A, Suite 200, One Harris Court, 93940⊙**
Telephone: 408-646-1501 Fax: 408-646-1801
Louis T. Lozano (Resident); Ellen M. Jahn (Resident);—Harold M. Freiman (Resident); Christopher D. Keeler (Resident); Karen Segar Salty (Resident). Of Counsel: Paul R. DeLay (Resident); Judd L. Jordan (Resident).
Education, Labor and Employment, Civil Rights and Disability, Local Government, Land Use, Eminent Domain, Public Finance, Business and Insurance Litigation.
Fresno, California Office: 2444 Main Street, Suite 260. Telephone: 209-445-1352. Fax: 209-233-5013.
San Rafael, California Office: 1010 B Street, Suite 200. Telephone: 415-459-3008; 800-648-3435. Fax: 415-456-3826.
San Luis Obispo, California Office: 987 Osos Street. Telephone: 805-549-9541. Fax: 805-549-0740.
*See Professional Biographies, MONTEREY, CALIFORNIA*

Lunding, Franklin J., Jr. .................. '38 '63 C.976 B.A. L.1066 LL.B. 215 W. Franklin
MacPherson, John J. ............................ '28 '81 C.871 B.S. L.767 J.D. 108 Webster St.

**Mallery, Terry M. '47 '79 C.147 B.S. L.464 J.D.**
**215 West Franklin Street, Fifth Floor, 93940**
Telephone: 408-655-2020 Fax: 408-655-2030
Email: tmallery@mbay.net
Business and Real Estate Transactions, including Corporations, Partnerships and Leases, Business and Real Estate Sales and Exchanges, Tax Collection Defense, Mediation of Business Disputes.
*See Professional Biographies, MONTEREY, CALIFORNIA*

**Mallett, Thomas E.** ........................ '58 '84 C.112 B.S. L.1067 J.D. [Ⓐ Zerbe,B.&L.]
*PRACTICE AREAS: Taxation; Estate Planning.
Malone, James L. .......................... '31 '61 C.668 B.A. L.813 J.D. 2600 Garden Rd.
Marr, Randall L. ......................... '55 '90 C.112 B.S. L.1226 J.D. P.O. Box 2652
**Marsh, William C.**, (BV) ..... '30 '59 C.112 B.S. L.1065 LL.B. [Ⓒ Horan,L.K.D.S.L.&C.]
**Martin, Carmel, Jr.**, (BV) ........... '20 '50 C.112 B.S. L.813 LL.B. [Hudson,M.F.&S.]
*PRACTICE AREAS: Estate Planning; Probate; Real Property Law.
**Martin, John F.**, (AV) ............. '16 '40 C.112 B.A. L.1066 LL.B. [Ⓒ Hudson,M.F.&S.]
*PRACTICE AREAS: Estate Planning; Probate; Elder Law.
**Masuda, Michael P.**, (BV) ................. '56 '81 C&L.585 B.A., J.D. [Harray,M.&L.]
*PRACTICE AREAS: General Insurance Including Casualty and Malpractice; Employment Law; Personal Injury; Property Damage; Products Liability.
**May, Martin J.**, (AV) .................. '29 '61 C.508 B.S. L.767 J.D. [Noland,H.E.&H.]⊙
*PRACTICE AREAS: Taxation Law; Probate Law; Estate Planning Law; Corporation Law.
McCann, Thomas P. .......................... '35 '85 C.723 B.A. L.1226 J.D. 33 Soledad Dr.
**McCarthy, Dennis G.** ...................... '51 '85 C.768 B.A. L.569 J.D. [Ⓐ Fenton&K.]
**Mccauley-Libert, Catherine** ............. '54 '90 C.112 A.B. L.1226 J.D. [Ⓐ Davis&S.]
*PRACTICE AREAS: Trademark and Copyright Law.

**McCleerey, Terrance K., (BV) '37 '63 C.350 B.S. L.352 J.D.**
**457 Webster Street, 93940**
Telephone: 408-373-0933 Fax: 408-373-3172
*PRACTICE AREAS: Criminal Law; Military Criminal Law; Personal Injury; Family Law.
Criminal Law, Military Criminal Law, D.U.I./D.W.I. Defense, Personal Injury and Family Law.
*See Professional Biographies, MONTEREY, CALIFORNIA*

**McClure, C. Micheal, (AV) '43 '69 C.1097 B.A. L.426 J.D.**
**631 Abrego Street, P.O. Box 3315, 93942-3315**
Telephone: 408-649-6161 Fax: 408-649-1384
Email: CMM3315@AOL.COM
*LANGUAGES: Spanish.
General Civil Trial Practice. Real Property, Business, Family and Personal Injury Law.
*See Professional Biographies, MONTEREY, CALIFORNIA*

**McCoy, Brian C.** ................................ '53 '78 C.112 B.A. L.426 J.D. [Dewar&R.]
*PRACTICE AREAS: Personal Injury; Family; Real Property; General Civil Litigation.
McCrone, Willard P., (CV) ................. '46 '74 C.870 B.S. L.893 J.D. 587 Hartnell St.
**McManus, Jacqueline P.**, (CV) .......... '61 '86 C&L.1049 B.A.,J.D. [Ⓐ Fenton&K.]

Meheen, M. Michael, (CV) ................ '39 '65 C.628 B.S. L.1065 J.D. 631 Abrego St.
**Meyenberg, Werner D. ("Randy")** '63 '89 C.112 B.A. L.770 J.D. [Ⓐ Noland,H.E.&H.]⊙
*PRACTICE AREAS: Real Estate Law; Land Use Law; Development Law; General Business Law.
Milani, Louis J. ................................... '29 '57 C&L.813 B.A., J.D. 209 Pearl St.
Minor, Timothy J. ...................... '55 '81 C.813 B.A. L.809 J.D. [Gilles,M.&S.]
Moore, Julie E., (CV) ..................... '57 '81 C.112 A.B. L.1067 J.D. 142 Carmelito
Moraz, Michaeleen ...................... '53 '81 C.464 B.A. L.767 J.D. 550 Figueroa St.
Mounteer, Carl A. ........... '47 '88 C.800 Ph.D. L.1226 J.D. 215 W. Franklin S., 5th Fl.
**Nakata, Lisa**, (CV) ................ '65 '91 C.112 B.A. L.770 J.D. [Ⓐ Noland,H.E.&H.]⊙
*PRACTICE AREAS: Creditor Bankruptcy; Environmental Law; Real Property Transaction; General Business.

**Newhouse, James H., (AV) '38 '66 C.112 B.A. L.1066 J.D.**
**631 Abrego Street, 93940**
**Telephone: 408-655-2000 FAX: 408-649-1384**
**(Certified Specialist, Criminal Law, The State Bar of California Board of Legal Specialization).**
**Criminal Law and Appeals.**

***See Professional Biographies, MONTEREY, CALIFORNIA***

Newman, Michael L., (CV) .................. '47 '73 C.112 B.A. L.1067 J.D. 539 Hartnell
Noble, James E. ................... '29 '62 C.859 B.S. L.616 J.D. 1176 Harrison St. (Pat.)

**Noland, Hamerly, Etienne & Hoss, A Professional Corporation, (AV)**
**Heritage Harbor, 99 Pacific Street Building 200, Suite C, 93940⊙**
**Telephone: 408-373-4427 Fax: 408-373-4797**
**Paul M. Hamerly; Myron E. Etienne, Jr.; Peter T. Hoss; James D. Schwefel, Jr.; Martin J. May; Stephen W. Pearson; Lloyd W. Lowrey, Jr.; Anne K. Secker; Paula Robinson; Jerome F. Politzer, Jr.; Christine P. Gianascol; Werner D. ("Randy") Meyenberg; Lisa Nakata; Patrick S. M. Casey.**
**Business and Commercial Litigation. Construction Litigation. General Business, Corporation, Probate, Estate Planning, Real Property, Land Use, Administrative Law, Tax Law and Family Law.**
**Salinas, California Office: Civic Center Building, 333 Salinas Street. Telephones: 408-424-1414; 372-7525. Fax: 408-424-1975.**
**King City, California Office: 104 South Vanderhurst, Suite D, 93930. Telephone: 408-386-1080. Fax: 408-386-1083.**

***See Professional Biographies, MONTEREY, CALIFORNIA***

Nordstrom, Vincent Alexander .............. '66 '92 C.754 B.S. L.564 J.D. 125 Seeno St.
Norris, Geoffrey A. ............................ '62 '89 C.1169 B.A. L.767 J.D. [Fischer,N.&S.]
**O'Connor, Mark A.** ............ '59 '90 C.169 B.S. L.464 J.D. [Ⓐ Horan,L.K.D.S.L.&C.]
*PRACTICE AREAS: Civil Litigation; Insurance Law.
**Ometer, Jo Marie**, (BV) ................... '46 '72 C.608 B.A. L.767 J.D. [Zerbe,B.&L.]
*PRACTICE AREAS: Probate; Estate Planning; Conservatorships and Trusts.

**Ontiveros & Kreeft**
**(See Salinas)**

Orliss, Theodore E., (AV) ................. '36 '61 C.911 A.B. L.309 LL.B. 790 Colton St.
Ottman, Janna L. ............. '30 '80 C.377 B.S. L.1226 J.D. 215 W. Franklin St., 5th Fl.
Page, Charles H., (AV) .... '29 '59 C&L.813 A.B., LL.B. 2801 Monterey-Salinas Highway
Palmer, Albert J. ..................................... '20 '46 C&L.597 B.S., LL.B. 450 Pacific St.
Panelli, Michael R., (BV) .................... '19 '49 C&L.770 J.D. 1062 Cass St., Suite B
**Panetta, Christopher E.** ................... '63 '94 C.112 B.A. L.1068 J.D. [Ⓐ Fenton&K.]
*PRACTICE AREAS: General Litigation; Employment Litigation.

**Panetta, Joseph R., (BV) '33 '59 C&L.770 B.S., J.D.**
**The Panetta Building, Madison at Pacific, P.O. Box 1709, 93940**
**Telephone: 408-646-0916**
***LANGUAGES: Italian.**
**Associates: Dennis E. Powell.**
**Civil and Criminal Trial Practice. Real Property, Probate, Business, Construction, Family and Personal Injury Law. State and Federal Taxation.**

***See Professional Biographies, MONTEREY, CALIFORNIA***

Panetta, Leon E., (BV) .............................. '38 '65 C&L.770 B.A., J.D. (M.C.)

**Parnie, A. David, (AV) '39 '65 C.95 A.B. L.813 LL.B.**
**Suite I, 2100 Garden Road, 93940**
**Telephone: 408-649-4802 Fax: 408-649-1306**
***PRACTICE AREAS: General Litigation; Family; Business.**
**General Litigation, Family and Business Law.**

***See Professional Biographies, MONTEREY, CALIFORNIA***

Parravano, Ronald A., (BV) ........................ '48 '76 C&L.426 B.A., J.D. 1045 Cass St.
Pavlet, Jennifer Mahnke .................... '64 '92 C.813 A.B. L.1068 J.D. 80 Garden Ct.
**Payne, Robert W.**, (AV) ............ '50 '76 C.813 B.A. L.1067 J.D. [LaRiviere,G.&P.]⊙
*PRACTICE AREAS: Intellectual Property; Business Litigation; Licensing.
**Pearson, Stephen W.**, (AV) ......... '44 '71 C.668 A.B. L.1065 J.D. [Noland,H.E.&H.]⊙
*PRACTICE AREAS: Construction Law; Commercial Law; Real Estate Litigation.
Peckinpah, Denver C. ........ '16 '40 C.267 J.C. L.1065 J.D. Bixby Canyon Coast, Rte. #1
Penn, Marian R. ..................... '46 '72 C.188 A.B. L.309 J.D. Monterey Coll. of Law
Pierce, Jacqueline M., (BV) ............... '57 '83 C.788 B.A. L.585 J.D. 2340 Garden Rd.
**Politzer, Jerome F., Jr.**, (CV) ......... '57 '82 C.112 A.B. L.767 J.D. [Noland,H.E.&H.]⊙
*PRACTICE AREAS: Taxation Law; Business Law.
Ponce, Carmen A. .............................. '64 '91 C.112 B.A. L.276 J.D. 1 Harris Ct.
Ponce, Robert D., (CV) .................... '53 '83 C.112 B.A. L.1065 J.D. 411 Pacific St.
**Powell, Dennis E.** ........................... '46 '76 C&L.1051 B.A., J.D. [Ⓐ J.R.Panetta]

**Poyner, Roger W., (BV) '35 '66 C.112 A.B. L.408 LL.B.**
**The Panetta Building, 232 Madison Street, 93940⊙**
**Telephone: 408-649-3131 FAX: 408-649-1934**
**(Certified Specialist, Probate, Estate Planning and Trust Law, The State Bar of California Board of Legal Specialization).**
**Trust Law, Estate Planning and Probate.**
**Los Gatos, California Office: 16450 Los Gatos Boulevard, Suite 216. Telephone: 408-358-1900. FAX: 408-358-1225.**

***See Professional Biographies, LOS GATOS, CALIFORNIA***

Pryer, Rex A., (CV) .......................... '30 '59 C.330 B.A. L.813 J.D. 457 Webster St.
**Rathie, Robert W.** .................. '50 '94 C.147 B.A. L.1226 J.D. [Ⓐ R.R.Wellington]
*PRACTICE AREAS: Municipal Law; Administrative Law; Personnel Policies; Real Property.
Reimann, Kathryn ... '54 '81 C.197 A.B. L.1067 J.D. 101 Camino Agua Jito Ave., Suite 2

**Reith, Daniel I., (AV) '39 '65 C.197 A.B. L.1066 LL.B.**
**457 Webster Street, 93940-3220**
**Telephone: 408-372-6999 FAX: 408-373-3172**
**(Certified Specialist, Family Law, The State Bar of California Board of Legal Specialization).**
***PRACTICE AREAS: Family Law; Personal Injury; Civil Litigation.**
**General Civil Practice, including Family Law, Personal Injury, Civil Litigation, Probate and Trust.**

***See Professional Biographies, MONTEREY, CALIFORNIA***

Roberson, Donald E. ................... '52 '78 C.1073 B.A. L.1065 J.D. 587 Hartnell St.
**Robinson, Paula**, (BV) ............ '53 '82 C.1060 B.A. L.1226 J.D. [Noland,H.E.&H.]⊙
*PRACTICE AREAS: Civil Litigation; Employment Litigation.
**Rockwood, Terry G.**, (BV) ................. '46 '74 C.112 B.A. L.767 J.D. [Dewar&R.]
*LANGUAGES: Spanish.
*PRACTICE AREAS: General Civil Litigation; Personal Injury Law; Insurance Law; Family Law.
Rodriguez, Leigh ....................... '57 '91 C.112 B.A. L.1230 J.D. 499 Calle Principal
Rogers, Harry Ellis, (CV) ................ '43 '71 C.767 B.A. L.284 J.D. 2100 Garden Rd.

Romberg, Steven F. ......................................... '46 '78 C.966 B.A. L.1226 J.D. 975 Cass St.
Romig, Harold J., Jr., (BV) ............................ '28 '57 C.529 L.1065 J.D. 633 Grove St.
**Rosenthal, Robert E.**, (CV) ............... '49 '75 C.147 B.A. L.464 J.D. [Bohnen,R.&D.]
*PRACTICE AREAS: Business and Civil Litigation; Personal Injury; Insurance Defense; Contract Negotiation.
Russell, Joseph P. ................... '32 '65 C.112 A.B. L.1026 LL.B. 34 Los Encinos Dr.
**Salty, Karen Segar** .................... '61 '94 C.861 B.A. L.767 J.D. [Ⓐ Lozano S.S.W.&B.]
*LANGUAGES: French.
Scarlett, Teri Elaine ........... '59 '87 C.147 B.A. L.1226 J.D. Monterey Co. Legal Servs.
Schnal, Richard M., (BV) ............. '31 '59 C.112 A.B. L.1066 J.D. 587 Hartnell St.
**Scholl, Ronald F.**, (BV) ........................ '42 '74 C.846 B.S. L.426 J.D. [Fenton&K.]
Schrader, Daniel P. ......................... '62 '89 C.1042 B.A. L.809 J.D. [Fischer,N.&S.]
**Schroeder, George L.**, (BV) ................ '31 '59 C.112 A.B. L.1066 J.D. [Davis&S.]
*PRACTICE AREAS: Estate Planning Law; Probate Law; Real Property Law.
**Schwartz, Gary D.**, (BV) ......... '44 '73 C.347 B.S. L.426 J.D. [Horan,L.K.D.S.L.&C.]
*PRACTICE AREAS: Estate Planning; Taxation; International Tax; Probate and Trust Law; Business.
**Schwefel, James D., Jr.**, (BV) ....... '36 '64 C.112 A.B. L.1066 J.D. [Noland,H.E.&H.]⊙
*PRACTICE AREAS: Real Estate Law; Agricultural Law; Business Law.
**Secker, Anne K.**, (BV) .............. '55 '80 C.589 B.A. L.339 J.D. [Noland,H.E.&H.]⊙
*LANGUAGES: German.
*PRACTICE AREAS: Commercial Law; Business Litigation; Civil Litigation; Construction Law.
**Sharma, Sonia S.** .............. '69 '94 C.1109 B.A. L.1065 J.D. [Ⓐ Horan,L.K.D.S.L.&C.]
*PRACTICE AREAS: Taxation; Estate Planning; Probate and Trust Law; Business Law; Corporate Law.
Shaules, James .......................... '51 '85 C&L.426 B.A., J.D. 215 W. Franklin St.
Siegel, Jonathan P. .......................... '42 '70 C&L.966 B.S., J.D. Dep. Pub. Def.
Smaage, Beth C., (BV) ...................... '57 '86 C.1060 L.1226 J.D. 555 Abrego St.
Smith, Patrick C. ............................ '44 '72 C&L.911 B.A., J.D. Calif. Ins. Grp.

**Soskin, William H., Law Offices of, (AV) '42 '69 C.33 B.A. L.145 J.D.**
**Suite F, 2100 Garden Road, 93940**
**Telephone: 408-649-8006**
**Corporate, Business, Taxation, Real Estate, Estate Planning and Probate Law.**

***See Professional Biographies, MONTEREY, CALIFORNIA***

Sosnowski, Michael S., (BV) ......... '48 '74 C.1169 B.A. L.770 J.D. 490 Calle Principal
**Spiering, James F.**, (BV) ............... '48 '74 C.629 B.A. L.767 J.D. [Spiering,S.&K.]
*PRACTICE AREAS: Personal Injury; Civil Litigation.

**Spiering, Swartz & Kennedy, (BV)**
**550 Hartnell Street, 93940-2890**
**Telephone: 408-373-3235; 800-624-9911 Facsimile: 408-373-8211**
**Members of Firm: James F. Spiering; Andrew H. Swartz; Michele C. Kennedy.**
**General Civil Trial and Appellate Practice. Personal Injury, Real Property, Administrative Law, Banking Law and Employment Law.**
**Reference: First National Bank of Monterey County (Monterey Branch).**

***See Professional Biographies, MONTEREY, CALIFORNIA***

Stamp, Michael W., Law Offices of, (AV) '50 '76
C.112 A.B. L.1066 J.D. 500 Camino El Estero Ste 200
Staples, John N., III, (BV) '46 '76 C.855 B.A. L.990 J.D.
V.P. & Mgr., Bank of America
Stupar, James R. .................................. '49 '75 C.877 B.S. L.464 J.D. 2100 Garden Rd.
Sullivan, James W. ..................... '48 '75 C.309 B.A. L.813 J.D. [Gilles,M.&S.]⊙
**Swartz, Andrew H.**, (BV) .............. '48 '73 C.665 B.A. L.770 J.D. [Spiering,S.&K.]
*PRACTICE AREAS: Civil Litigation; Banking Litigation; Personal Injury; Employment Law.
**Sweigert, David C.**, (CV) .................. '53 '91 C.1060 B.A. L.1067 J.D. [Ⓐ Fenton&K.]
**Thompson, Ralph W.**, (AV) ........... '19 '48 C.165 A.B. L.813 LL.B. [Thompson&H.]
*PRACTICE AREAS: Litigation; General Business; Real Property; Estate Planning; Probate.
**Thompson, Ralph W., III**, (AV) ............ '42 '68 C.1163 B.A. L.61 J.D. [Thompson]
*PRACTICE AREAS: Business; Commercial Litigation; Personal Injury; Wrongful Death; Sexual Harassment.

**Thompson & Hubbard, A Law Corporation, (AV)**
**Aguajito Building, 400 Camino Aguajito, 93940**
**Telephone: 408-372-7571 Fax: 408-372-1700**
**Ralph W. Thompson; Donald G. Hubbard; Timothy J. Walsh; Alexander F. Hubbard.**
**General Civil, Trial and Appellate Practice in State and Federal Courts. Corporation, General Business, Real Property, Land Use, Construction, Estate Planning, Probate, Conservatorships and Trusts, Personal Injury, Product Liability, Domestic, Administrative and Taxation Law.**

***See Professional Biographies, MONTEREY, CALIFORNIA***

**Thompson Law Office, The, (AV) [BB]**
**580 Calle Principal, First Floor, 93940-2818**
**Telephone: 408-646-1224 Fax: 408-646-1225**
**Ralph W. Thompson, III (Recognized Experience as a Trial Lawyer and in the fields of General Personal Injury, Products Liability, Professional Negligence, Insurance Bad Faith and Public Entity Liability Law, California Trial Lawyers Association).**
**General Civil and Trial Practice, Arbitration and Mediation Services.**

***See Professional Biographies, MONTEREY, CALIFORNIA***

Thomson, Russell A., (BV) ......... '30 '64 C.790 B.A. L.1065 J.D. 470 Camino El Estero
**Tostevin, Nancy P.**, (BV) ........................ '38 '78 C.813 B.A. L.770 J.D. [Fenton&K.]
**Truax, Lonnie** ............................................ '49 '94 C.823 B.S. L.770 J.D. [Ⓐ Fenton&K.]

**Walker, George R., (AV) '28 '52 C&L.608 B.S., J.D. [BB]**
**5th Floor, Professional Building, 215 West Franklin Street, P.O. Box Law, 93942**
**Telephone: 408-649-1100 Fax: 408-649-6805**
***PRACTICE AREAS: Estate Planning; Probate; Trusts; Real Property Law.**
**Associates: Ute M. Isbill; Kathleen Llewellyn.**
**Civil Practice. Estate Planning, Probate, Trust and Real Property Law.**
**Representative Clients: A. F. Victor Foundation, Carmel, California; The Carmel Foundation, Carmel, California; Robert Louis Stevenson School, Pebble Beach, California; Brintons Consolidated, Inc.; C & E Farms, Inc.; The Mildred Hitchcock Huff Charitable Trust.**

***See Professional Biographies, MONTEREY, CALIFORNIA***

**Walsh, Timothy J.** ........................ '51 '84 C.321 B.A. L.770 J.D. [Thompson&H.]
*PRACTICE AREAS: Litigation; Family Law.

**Warner, Charles G., Law Offices of, (AV) '41 '66 C.813 A.B. L.1066 LL.B. [BB]**
**2340 Garden Road, Suite 208, 93940**
**Telephone: 408-375-0203 Facsimile: 408-375-4159**
**Civil Litigation.**

***See Professional Biographies, MONTEREY, CALIFORNIA***

Warner, Molly Abel, (CV) ............. '52 '83 C.1078 B.A. L.1226 J.D. 2100 Garden Rd.

**Wellington, Robert R., Law Offices of, (BV) '40 '66 C.813 B.A. L.1065 LL.B.**
**857 Cass Street, Suite D, 93940**
**Telephone: 408-373-8733 Facsimile: 408-373-7106**
**Email: robwlaw@aol.com**
**Associates: Kenneth D. Buchert; Robert W. Rathie.**
**Municipal and Administrative Law, Public Employment and Personnel, General Civil, Trial and Appellate Practice. Real Property, Condemnation, Land Use and Construction Law.**

***See Professional Biographies, MONTEREY, CALIFORNIA***

**Wieben, John S.**, (BV) ..................... '47 '73 C.112 A.B. L.1067 J.D. [Wieben&W.]
*PRACTICE AREAS: Family Law.

**CAA397P**

**Wieben, Pamela Shea**, (AV⓪) '48 '74
C.788 B.A. L.477 J.D. [Wieben&W.] (⊙Bloomfield Hills, MI)
*PRACTICE AREAS: Personal Injury Law; Civil Litigation; Employment Law.

**Wieben & Wieben, (AV⓪)**
**444 Pearl Street, Suite C, 93940**
**Telephone: 408-375-0577 Fax: 408-375-0580**
**Members of Firm: John S. Wieben (Certified Specialist, Family Law, The State Bar of California Board of Legal Specialization); Pamela Shea Wieben.**
**A General Civil Trial Practice, Specializing in Complex Family Law Litigation and Mediation; Personal Injury, Medical Malpractice, Municipal and Employment Law.**
*See Professional Biographies, MONTEREY, CALIFORNIA*

**Williams, Peter R.**, (CV) '49 '85 L.1226 J.D. [Hudson,M.F.&S.]
*PRACTICE AREAS: Real Property Law; Construction Law; Negligence Litigation.
Williams, Robert E. '47 '73 C.112 B.A. L.37 J.D. 215 Franklin St.
Willoughby, David A., (BV) '56 '81 C.112 B.A. L.1066 J.D. 2100 Garden Rd.
Wilsdon, Richard T. '34 '59 C.668 B.A. L.813 J.D. 2100 Garden Rd.
Yudin, Jon '49 '78 C.415 B.S. L.1224 J.D. Asst. Dist. Atty.
**Zerbe, Carl**, (BV) '46 '71 C.210 B.A. L.813 J.D. [⊡ Zerbe,B.&L.]
*PRACTICE AREAS: Estate Planning Law; Business Law; Real Estate Law; Partnership Law; Corporation Law.

**Zerbe, Buck & Lewis, Professional Law Corporation, (BV)**
**400 Camino El Estero, 93940**
**Telephone: 408-646-1733 Fax: 408-646-8484**
**Gwendolen S. Buck; Rose-Eve K. Lewis; Thomas E. Mallett; Jo Marie Ometer (Certified Specialist, Probate, Estate Planning and Trust Law, The State Bar of California Board of Legal Specialization).**
**Of Counsel: Carl Zerbe.**
**Business, Real Property, Estate Planning, Taxation, Family, Civil Litigation, Personal Injury, Partnership, Corporation, Probate, Trademark and Copyright Law.**
*See Professional Biographies, MONTEREY, CALIFORNIA*

Zikan, Karel John '32 '88 C.139 M.A. L.1226 J.D. 643 Larkin St.

## MONTEREY PARK, 60,738, *Los Angeles Co.*

**Bacon, Marilyn J.** '63 '90 C.112 B.A. L.426 J.D. Atty., Southern Pacific Lines
Bamberger, Lawrence K. '36 '62
C.112 B.A. L.800 LL.B. Legal Dept., State Comp. Ins. Fund
Bayer, Judith H. '39 '83 C.129 B.A. L.809 J.D. Co. Coun. Off. of L.A.
Belda, Rosemarie '60 '86 C.770 B.A. L.1066 J.D. Dep. Co. Coun.
Bloom, Steven E. '45 '72 C.112 B.S. L.1065 J.D.
Asst. Chf. Coun., State Comp. Ins. Fund
Carrillo, Luis A. '46 '76 C.112 B.A. L.1066 J.D. 939 S. Atlantic Blvd.
Clark, Laurence E., (P.C.) '29 '62 C.602 B.S. L.426 LL.B. 631 S. Atlantic Blvd.
Creskoff, Doram & Hume L.L.P., (AV)
2501 Davidson Dr., Ste. 301 (⊙Washington, DC)
Davidson, J. Valerie '49 '91 C.763 B.A. L.1137 J.D.
Legal Coun., State Comp. Ins. Fund
Davidson, Timothy T. '55 '80 C.112 L.1095 J.D. 900 Corporate Ctr. Dr.
Doram, Michael R., (AV) '40 '67 C.813 A.B. L.276 J.D. [Creskoff,D.&H.]⊙
Dunn, Gloria Y. '— '77 C.353 B.A. L.1065 J.D. P.O. Box 412
Estep, David F. '61 '93 C.1042 B.A. L.426 J.D. DCLS, Inc.
Godfrey, Jane A. '51 '82 C.587 B.S.Ed. L.809 J.D. 201 Centre Plaza Dr.
Goldsmith, Jack O. '14 '39 C.112 A.B. L.800 LL.B. 2063 S. Atlantic Blvd.‡
Graves, Joseph L. '16 '49 C.112 B.A. L.426 LL.B. 329 W. Emerson Ave.‡
Guizar, Humberto M. '56 '86 C.1077 B.A. L.1095 J.D. Jerry B. Peek, Inc.
Hayden, Kathryn A. '50 '92 C.208 B.A. L.1137 J.D. Staff Atty., State Comp. Ins. Fund
Hershenson, Arthur '29 '60 C.1043 B.A. L.809 LL.B. State Comp. Ins. Fund
Horowitz, Elizabeth M., (AV) '29 '55 C.813 B.A. L.800 LL.B.
Juv. Ct. Mediator & Ref.‡
Huebsch, Maurice O. '15 '37 C&L.145 B.A., J.D. 320 De la Fuente Ave.
Hume, Robert T. '46 '72 C.976 B.A. L.30 J.D.
(adm. in DC; not adm. in CA) [Creskoff,D.&H.]
Hunt, Brenda L. '63 '90 C.911 B.A. L.678 J.D. Staff Atty., State Comp. Ins. Fund
Hwang, Andrew B. '51 '87 L.378 J.D.
(adm. in ID; not adm. in CA) 328 S. Atlantic Blvd.
Jenkins, Patricia H. '47 '78 C.112 B.A. L.1136 J.D. Co. Coun., Children's Servs. Div.
Klein, Paul '28 '60 C.112 B.A. L.800 J.D. State Comp. Ins. Fund
Lebecki, Alexander N. '63 '91 C.112 B.A. L.705 J.D. 223 N. Garfield Ave.
Lee, David W. '49 '92 C.045 B.S. L.1190 J.D. 108 N. Ynez Ave.
Leventer, Robert E. '55 '79 C.477 L.1238 J.D. Supr. Ct. Comr.
Lewis, Jacqueline Honovich '64 '90 C.426 B.B.A. L.1066 J.D.
Auxiliary Legal Servs., Inc.
Li, Kenneth S. '52 '80 C&L.285 B.S., J.D. 300 S. Alantic Blvd.
Liao, Abraham C. '48 '83 C.061 B.S. L.1148 J.D. 300 S. Garfield Ave.
Liou, May F. '53 '86 C.061 B.A. L.809 J.D. 400 S. Atlantic Blvd.
Lou, Elizabeth '40 '77 C.025 B.Sc. L.426 J.D. 826 S. Atlantic Blvd.
Maisner, Linda J. '43 '77 C.1077 A.B. L.1068 J.D. 415A N. Sierra Vista St.
Malouf, Jeanette '52 '78 C&L.878 B.A., J.D. Atty., Auxiliary Legal Servs., Inc.
Manuel, A. Michael, (BV) '52 '79
C.940 B.A. L.1137 J.D. 231 W. Garvey Ave. (⊙Los Angeles)
Mason, Anna M. '44 '80 C.1042 B.A. L.1137 J.D. Dep. Co. Coun.
May-Rucker, Rhonda '59 '87 C.112 B.A. L.426 J.D. Crim. Ct. Juv. Adm. Off.
McIntosh, Howard A. '16 '66 C.593 B.S. L.426 LL.B. 1440 Ridgecrest St.
Michelson, Harry L. '25 '63 C.102 B.A. L.800 J.D. 1871 Ash Dr.‡
Morelli, Stephen M. '60 '87 C&L.184 B.A., J.D. 300 S. Atlantic Blvd.
**Moret, Glenn C.** '66 '91 C.112 B.S. L.1066 J.D. Atty., Southern Pacific Lines
Morgan, Glyn D. '51 '79 C.1077 B.A. L.1095 J.D. Dep. Sheriff
Pacheco, Randall '49 '78 C.112 L.1065 J.D. 201 Centre Plz. Dr.
Peek, Jerry B. '34 '69 C.1163 B.A. L.810 J.D. Pres., Jerry B. Peek, Inc.
**Pohle, William H., Jr.**, (AV) '43 '69
C.112 A.B. L.770 J.D. Assoc. Gen. Coun., Southern Pacific Lines
Poon, William '40 '84 C.763 B.S. L.1136 J.D. Poon & Wong
Quarles, Betty R. '58 '91 C.112 B.A. L.426 J.D. Staff Coun., State Comp. Ins. Fund
Rentzer, Nona '64 '92 C.800 B.A. L.398 J.D. Coun., State Comp. Ins. Fund
Resnick, Tracey Felton '56 '82 C.938 B.A. L.1170 J.D. 201 Centre Plaza Dr.
Salazar, Michael A. '46 '86 C.1097 B.A. L.1179 J.D. 807 S. Atlantic Blvd.
Sanchez, Leopoldo G. '26 '54 C.740 L.809 LL.B. Ret. Supr. Ct. J.
Schicker, David '46 '87 C.112 B.A. L.1136 J.D. State Comp. Ins. Fund
Schiff, Jo Ann R. '34 '80 C.771 B.A. L.1136 J.D. Supr. Ct.
Strauss, Jeffrey E. '57 '85 C.112 B.A. L.426 J.D. 108 N. Ynez Ave.
Tennison, Mary Christine '57 '83
C.383 B.A. L.990 J.D. Southern Pacific Transportation Company
Tu, John Y. '49 '90 C.846 L.1179 J.D. 119 S. Atlantic Blvd.
Tucker, Marcus O. '34 '62 C.800 A.B. L.329 J.D. Juv. Ct. J.
Waddington, Michael J. '64 '89 C.425 B.B.A. L.861 J.D. 400 S. Atlantic Blvd.
Weekes, Martin E. '33 '62 C.433 B.S. L.800 J.D. Asst. Co. Coun.
Whitaker, Jerome P. '40 '80 C.112 B.S. L.809 J.D. State Comp. Ins. Fund

## MONTE RIO, —, *Sonoma Co.*

Averbuck, David S., (BV) '43 '67 C.112 B.A. L.1066 J.D. Sonoma State Univ.

## MONTE SERENO, 3,287, *Santa Clara Co.*

Allan, Lionel M. (Lon), (AV) '43 '69 C.477 A.B. L.813 J.D. Pres., Allan Advisors, Inc.
Lively, Patricia D., (BV) '51 '77 C.1176 B.A. L.770 J.D. 15500 Kavin Ln.
Schneider, Isabel S. '44 '76 C.289 B.A. L.770 J.D.
(adm. in CO; not adm. in CA) 15676 Oak Knoll Dr.‡

## MONTROSE, —, *Los Angeles Co.*

Ashen, Robert M., (AV) '34 '58 C.679 B.S.M.E. L.309 J.D. [Ashen,G.&L.] (Pat.)⊙
Ashen, Golant & Lippman, (AV) 4385 Ocean View Blvd. (Pat.)
Barta, Faye C. '44 '79 C.980 B.A. L.1068 J.D. 2339 Honolulu St., 2nd Fl.
Golant, Joseph H., (AV) '41 '66 C.399 B.S.M.E. L.145 J.D. [Ashen,G.&L.] (Pat.)⊙
Jeffers, Thomas J., Jr. '29 '54 C&L.426 B.B.A., LL.B. [T.J.Jeffers,Jr.]
Jeffers, Thomas J., Jr., Professional Corporation 2528 Honolulu Ave.
Kimber, Donald C., (AV) '18 '52 C&L.800 J.D. 4415 Rockland Pl.‡
Lippman, Peter I., (AV) '39 '82 C.111 B.S. L.809 J.D. [Ashen,G.&L.] (Pat.)⊙
Petrovits, James J. '41 '75 C.855 B.S. L.1190 J.D. 2339 Honolulu Ave., 2nd Fl.
Potter, Shanley & Shanley, (BV) 2317 Florencita Dr.
Shanley, Barry E., (BV) '50 '76 C.800 B.A. L.1068 J.D. [Potter,S.&S.]
Shanley, Susan Potter, (CV) '52 '77 C.773 B.A. L.1068 J.D. [Potter,S.&S.]
Sill, Richard A., (CV) '50 '76 C.605 B.A. L.228 J.D. 2528 Honolulu Ave.
Torres, Patricia Hughes '50 '80 C.37 B.S. L.1095 J.D. 2339 Honolulu Ave., 2nd Fl.
Waters, Duane E. '45 '71 C.112 B.S. L.1068 J.D. 2229 Crescent Ave.
Widdis, Lawrence A. '49 '82 L.1190 LL.B. 2168 Glenada Ave.

## MOORPARK, 25,494, *Ventura Co.*

Campeau, Joseph O. '30 '88 C.930 B.S.E.E. L.769 J.D. 484 E. Los Angeles Ave.
Haynes, Douglas B. '48 '73 C.112 B.A. L.1068 J.D. [D.B.Haynes]
Haynes, Douglas B., Law Office of 13612 Deering Lane
McNamara, James E. '63 '90 C.1077 B.A. L.398 J.D. 484 E. Los Angeles Ave.
Mogul, Martin H. '51 '82 C.1036 B.A. L.809 J.D. Dept. of Defense
Moody, Karl L. '41 '80 L.398 J.D. 530 New Los Angeles St.
Quarnstrom, Ellen M. '12 '36 L.800 LL.B. 4627 Bella Vista Dr.
Tobin, Timothy B. '51 '78 C.980 B.A. L.7 J.D.
(adm. in OH; not adm. in CA) 14834 Marquette St.‡
Young, Victoria E. '33 '74 C&L.1136 B.S., J.D. 4359 Brookdale Lane‡

## MORAGA, 15,852, *Contra Costa Co.*

Adams, Roy W., Jr. '50 '80 C.112 B.S.E.E. L.1068 J.D. 1024 Country Club Dr.
Bannister, John G., Jr. '41 '66 C&L.813 A.B., LL.B. 24 Brandt Dr.
Barbour, Sandra I. '51 '77 C.813 B.A. L.767 J.D.‡
Bolen, James B., Jr. '24 '53 C&L.813 A.B., LL.B. 411 Kingsford Dr.‡
Burch, Charles B. '48 '73 C.813 A.B. L.145 J.D. U.S. Atty. Off.
Burch, James L. '29 '54 C.686 B.S. L.174 LL.B. 3 Merrill Dr.‡
Butler, Leland E. '32 '63 C.112 A.B. L.1066 LL.B. 1758 Donald Dr.‡
Coburn, Wm. H., Jr., (AV) '25 '53 C.112 L.1065 J.D. 832 Country Club Dr.‡
Cooper, John S. '31 '57 C.112 A.B. L.1066 LL.B. P.O. Box 395
Coward, Robert, (AV) '25 '52 C.112 L.1065 LL.B. 152 Walford Dr.
Duda, Frederick R. '28 '60 C.339 B.S. L.767 LL.B. 2101 Donald Dr.‡
Epstein, Edwin M. '37 '62 C.659 A.B. L.976 LL.B. St. Mary's Coll.
Falconer, Virginia G. '48 '74 C.813 B.A. L.1066 J.D. 119 Selborne Way‡
Goldeen, Barbara, (BV) '27 '65 C.112 B.A. L.284 J.D. P.O. Box 6007
Harrington, Charles L. '32 '64 C.112 B.S. L.1065 LL.B. 1620 School St.; Suite 104
Henry, Robert W., Jr. '38 '67 C.1258 B.A. L.426 LL.B. 1030 Country Club Dr., Ste. E
Hickman, Richard A. '24 '53 C.112 A.B. L.1065 LL.B. 126 Brookfield Dr. E.‡
Karlin, Jeffrey H., (AV⓪) '55 '80 C.1044 B.S. L.1065 J.D.
[Karlin,J.H.] (⊙Los Angeles)
Karlin, Jeffrey H., A Professional Corporation, (AV⓪) P.O. Box 6118
Kennedy, Rosalie O. '55 '83 C.705 B.A. L.276 J.D. 300 Donald Dr.
Kilbourne, George W., (BV) '24 '52 C.477 B.S.E. L.1066 J.D. 661 Augusta Dr.
Loewenthal, Nancy Sokol '48 '78 C.339 B.A. L.1003 J.D.
(adm. in OH; not adm. in CA) 6 Gleneagle Ct.‡
McGhee, Matthew A. '39 '82 C.061 M.A. L.1153 J.D. Diablo Valley Coll.
Murtha, John R., (BV) '24 '55 C.971 B.S.M.E. L.724 LL.B. 1253 Larch Ave. (Pat.)
Mussman, Robert C., Sr. '24 '50 C&L.494 B.S.L., J.D.
(adm. in MN; not adm. in CA) 1056 Sanders Dr.‡
Niehans, Patricia Lazowska '52 '78 C.918 B.A. L.477 J.D. 22 Harrington Rd.‡
Nilson, Norman F. '40 '69 C.878 B.S. L.273 J.D. 71 Lambeth Sq.
Parker, Joseph R. '15 '39 C&L.494 B.A., LL.B.
(adm. in MN; not adm. in CA) Member Assessment Appeals Board, Marin
Peizer, Donna M. '40 '86 C.174 B.S. L.1066 J.D. P.O. Box 438
Peterson, Thomas A. '37 '81 C.589 B.S. L.1153 J.D. 1015 Larch Ave.
Powlan, Roy K. '55 '82 C.112 B.A. L.1177 J.D. P.O. Box 6312
Radcliffe, Martha Clark '25 '75 C.112 B.A. L.1065 J.D. 920 Country Club Dr.
Rankin, William J. '50 '76 C.112 B.A. L.145 J.D. 21 Tia Pl.‡
Schaus, Margaret E. '56 '84 C.911 B.A. L.1065 J.D. 205 Fernwood Dr.‡
Strom, Harold L., (AV) '15 '39 C.112 A.B. L.1066 LL.B. 1735 St. Andrews Dr.‡
Wilson, Kirk Randolph '50 '77 C.112 B.A. L.1065 J.D. 1635 School St.

## MORENO VALLEY, 118,779, *Riverside Co.*

Blaisdell, David F. '46 '75 C.1097 B.A. L.809 J.D. 22690 Cactus Ave.
Burnette, Marbi L. '56 '85 C.1109 B.a. L.770 J.D. 14212 Woodpark Dr.
Cherniss, David A. '54 '79 C.112 B.A. L.61 J.D.
23025 Atlantic Cir. (⊙Half Moon Bay)
Condas, Thomas M. '57 '84 C.878 B.S. L.1137 J.D. [Hollins,S.&F.] (⊙Orange, CA.)
Hayes, Roderick D. '32 '57 C.475 B.A. L.477 J.D. 24060 Postal Ave.
Hirst, Albert E. '53 '80 C.1163 B.S. L.61 J.D. 24490 Sunnymead Blvd.
Hollins, Schechter & Feinstein, A Professional Corporation, (AV)
22690 Cactus Ave. Ste. 240 (⊙San Diego, Orange, Palm Springs, California)
Katz, Eli M. '16 '47 C.102 B.A. L.1009 J.D.
(adm. in NY; not adm. in CA) 24780 Early Morn Lane‡
Martinez, Paula E. '49 '83 C.103 B.A. L.1137 J.D. 10930 Shady Glade Rd.‡
Morris, M. Conway, (BV) '29 '56
C&L.878 B.A., J.D. Moreno Valley Law Ctr. (⊙Anaheim)
Patterson-Musser, Colleen Sue '62 '89 C.398 B.A. L.1137 J.D. 24490 Sunnymead Blvd.
Reikes, Joyce Manulis, (BV) '36 '76 C&L.1198 B.S., J.D.
13800 Heacock Ave., Bldg. D
Snyder, Jack H. '58 '83 C.112 B.A. L.1067 J.D. [Hollins,S.&F.] (⊙Orange, Ca.)
Spala, Gerald A., (BV) '54 '80 C.112 B.A. L.809 J.D. 23318 Olivewood Plaza Dr.
Stewart, Richard A. '42 '83 C.1077 B.A. L.1198 J.D. 23236 Harland Dr.‡

## MORGAN HILL, 23,928, *Santa Clara Co.*

Andersen, Candace Jane Kay ..............'60 '85 C&L.101 B.A., J.D. 275 Tennant Ave.
Bassett, Craig J. ............................'55 '82 C&L.101 B.S., J.D. 275 Tennant Ave.
Baum, Gary M. ..............................'60 '84 C.940 B.A. L.800 J.D. City Atty.
Chalfant, Peter S. ........ '47 '76 C.871 B.S. L.1065 J.D. Gen. Coun. & Secy., Wiltron Co.
Courtney, Kevin Patrick, (BV) '52 '77
C&L.770 B.S., J.D. 17415 Monterey Rd. (©San Jose)
Courtney, Kevin Patrick, (BV) '52 '77
C&L.770 B.S., J.D. 17415 Monterey Rd. (©Morgan Hill)
Crawford, Francis N., (BV) ............'22 '56 C.112 B.A. L.1065 J.D. 16145 Sunset Ave.
Crossen, James R. ..........................'50 '83 C.112 B.A. L.770 J.D. ESL Inc.
Dowdle, Michael D. .....................'45 '80 C.172 B.S. L.284 J.D. 700 Count Fleet Ct.

**Falk, Vestal & Fish, L.L.P.**
**16590 Oak View Circle, 95037©**
**Telephone: 408-778-3624 Fax: 408-776-0426 Pager: 408-683-1839 Cellular: 408-781-3145**
**Email: Rcfpatlaw@aol.com**
**Ronald C. Fish.**
**Matters of Intellectual Property and Trade Regulation. Patent, Trademark and Copyright Prosecution and Trial Practice. Trade Secret Protection. Related matters of Antitrust Law and Deceptive Trade Practices.**
**Reference: Provident Bank, Dallas, Texas.**
**Dallas, Texas Office: Plaza of the Americas, 700 North Pearl, Suite 970. Telephone: 214-954-4400.**
*See Professional Biographies, MORGAN HILL, CALIFORNIA*

**Fish, Ronald C.** ........'47 '77 C.597 B.S.E.E. L.1065 J.D. [Falk,V.&F.] (See Pat. Sect.)©
*PRACTICE AREAS: Intellectual Property Law.
**Foster, J. Robert**, (AV) ............'40 '65 C.768 B.A. L.1065 LL.B. [Rusconi,F.T.&W.]
*PRACTICE AREAS: Business Law; Estate Planning Law.
**Foster, John Crandall** ..............'64 '90 C.1169 B.A. L.464 J.D. [Ⓐ Rusconi,F.T.&W.]
Johnson, Christina L. ...........'51 '86 C.608 B.S.N. L.770 J.D. 2355 Willow Springs Rd.
Johnson, Tracey '65 '91 C.519 B.A. L.436 J.D.
(adm. in WI; not adm. in CA) 331 Wright Ave.‡
Knapp, Gregory J., (BV) ..................'47 '72 C.768 B.A. L.770 J.D. 17800 Casa Lane
Nielsen, Steen C. '53 '78 C.976 B.A. L.678 J.D.
(adm. in WA; not adm. in CA) P.O. Box 635‡
Perry, Laura A. ...............................'51 '92 C.768 B.S. L.770 J.D. 275 Tennant Ave.
Quinn, Robin S. .......................... '51 '79 C.608 B.A. L.1095 J.D. 2192 Windemere Ct.
Rusconi, Ernest, (BV) ..................'22 '50 C.598 B.S. L.309 LL.B. 30 Keystone Ave.

**Rusconi, Foster, Thomas & Wilson, A Professional Corporation, (AV)**
**30 Keystone Avenue, P.O. Box 10, 95038**
**Telephone: 408-779-2106 Fax: 408-779-1553**
**Email: rftw@garlic.com URL: http://www.garlic.com/~rftw**
**J. Robert Foster (Certified Specialist, Probate, Estate Planning and Trust Law, The State Bar of California Board of Legal Specialization); George P. Thomas, Jr. (Certified Specialist, Family Law, The State Bar of California Board of Legal Specialization); Susan VicklundWilson;—John Crandall Foster.**
**General Civil and Trial Practice. Probate, Real Property, Negligence, Business, Corporate, Family Law, Estate Planning and Environmental Law.**
**Representative Clients: Simonsen Laboratories, Inc.; Farotte Construction, Inc.; Sierra Bioresource, Inc.**
**References: Wells Fargo Bank; South Valley National Bank.**

Smereski, Nancy Lee '— '83 C&L.705 B.A., J.D.
(adm. in NJ; not adm. in CA) 16745 Jackson Oaks Dr.‡
Testaguzza, Louis .................'28 '79 C.1179 B.S.A.E. L.767 J.D. 281 Summer Circle
**Thomas, George P., Jr.**, (BV) ........'48 '73 C.112 B.S. L.1065 J.D. [Rusconi,F.T.&W.]
*PRACTICE AREAS: Family Law; Business Law; Real Estate Law.
Tichinin, Bruce, (BV) ...............'45 '72 C.112 A.B. L.1066 J.D. 17775 Monterey St.
van Keulen, Craig C., (BV) ..............'55 '81 C.770 B.A. L.734 J.D. 17600 Monterey
van Keulen, Scott D. ...................'56 '83 C.800 B.S. L.734 J.D. 17600 Monterey Rd.
**VicklundWilson, Susan** ...............'57 '88 C.846 B.S. L.796 J.D. [Rusconi,F.T.&W.]
*PRACTICE AREAS: Environmental Law; Business Litigation; Family Law.

**Warnock, W. Matthew '58 '86 C&L.101 B.A., J.D.**
**60 West Main Avenue, Suite 12-A, 95037**
**Telephone: 408-778-7273 Fax: 408-778-7989**
**Email: mwarnock@mhl.com**
***LANGUAGES: French.**
***PRACTICE AREAS: Bankruptcy (30%); Estate Planning (20%); Litigation (20%); Real Estate (15%); Commercial Law (15%).**
**Estate Planning, Probate, Real Property, Transactions, Litigation and Bankruptcy.**

Wright, James L. .....................'49 '74 C.1067 B.A. L.1068 J.D. 490 La Baree Dr.
Wright, Janet Gaffaney ................'52 '77 C&L.770 B.S., J.D. 18665 Castle Lake Dr.

## MORRO BAY, 9,664, *San Luis Obispo Co.*

Bradstreet, Robert E. ..................'31 '55 C&L.378 A.B., J.D. 209 Dunes St., Unit 7‡

**Cook, C. Randall, Law Offices of, (CV) '54 '80 C.112 B.A. L.1065 J.D.**
**780 Piney Way, 93442-1926**
**Telephone: 805-772-4431 FAX: 805-772-5134**
***PRACTICE AREAS: Civil Litigation - Plaintiff and Defendant; Personal Injury; General Real Property; General Business/Corporate; Probate and Estates/Wills.**
**General Civil and Trial Practice, Personal Injury, Real Property, Business Law, Probate and Trusts, Unlawful Detainers and Creditors and Debtors Rights.**
*See Professional Biographies, MORRO BAY, CALIFORNIA*

Finn, John E., (AV) ..........................'29 '53 C&L.426 LL.B. 1163 Main Street

**George, Gallo & Sullivan, A Law Corporation**
**(See San Luis Obispo)**

**Kirschner, Charles G.** ......................'56 '84 C.112 B.S. L.770 J.D. [Ⓐ Ogle&M.]
*PRACTICE AREAS: Family Law; Civil Litigation.
McKown, Daniel C. ...................'31 '73 C.665 B.S. L.990 J.D. 355 Fairview Dr. (Pat.)
**Merzon, James B.**, (BV) ..................'42 '69 C.267 B.A. L.1068 J.D. [Ogle&M.]
*PRACTICE AREAS: Real Estate Law; Business Litigation; Probate Estate Planning and Administration.
**Ogle, Charles E., (A Professional Corporation)**, (AV) '25 '52
C.910 L.809 LL.B. [Ogle&M.]©
*PRACTICE AREAS: Condemnation Law; Business Litigation; Probate Estate Planning and Administration.
**Ogle, Charles Patrick** ....................'56 '82 C.112 A.B. L.767 J.D. [Ⓐ Ogle&M.]
*PRACTICE AREAS: Real Property Law; Estate Administration; Creditors Rights.

**Ogle & Merzon, (AV)** ⒷⒷ
**A Partnership including a Professional Corporation**
**770 Morro Bay Boulevard, P.O. Box 720, 93443-0720©**
**Telephone: 805-772-7353 Fax: 805-772-7713**
**Charles E. Ogle (A Professional Corporation); James B. Merzon;—Charles G. Kirschner; Charles Patrick Ogle.**
**General Civil and Trial Practice. Real Property, Business Law, Probate, Estate Planning, Trusts, Negligence, Condemnation, Family Law and Creditors Rights.**
**San Luis Obispo, California Office: P.O. Box 1855, 93406. Telephone: 805-543-0295.**
*See Professional Biographies, MORRO BAY, CALIFORNIA*

Ortiz, Ginger T. ..............................'66 '91 C.208 B.A. L.464 J.D. P.O. Box 94

Sheehy, John F. '28 '74 C.1060 B.A. L.280 J.D.
(adm. in GA; not adm. in CA) P.O. Box 1331‡
Skousen, Judy ....................................'47 '71 C&L.36 B.S., J.D. P.O. Box 834

## MOSS BEACH, —, *San Mateo Co.*

Petsas, Kosta J. .................................'45 '76 C.767 B.A. L.809 J.D. P.O. Box 3200
Pritchard, William R. ........................'48 '79 C.347 B.A. L.767 J.D. P.O. Box 714

## MOSS LANDING, —, *Monterey Co.*

Hansen, Richard G. ...............................'25 '58 C.174 L.424 LL.B. P.O. Box 310

## MOUNTAIN CENTER, —, *Riverside Co.*

Wied, Wilson W. ....................'10 '39 C.494 B.S. L.813 61202 Devils Ladder Rd.‡

## MOUNTAIN VIEW, 67,460, *Santa Clara Co.*

Abdollahi, O. Antony ..........................'66 '91 C.112 B.S. L.1066 J.D. [Ⓐ Newton,K.&R.]
**Aikins, Deborah Churton** ..................'54 '84 C.112 B.A. L.1065 J.D. [General C.]
*PRACTICE AREAS: Real Estate; Land Use.
**Aikins, Douglas B.**, (AV) ...................'50 '78 C.623 B.A. L.767 J.D. [General C.]
*SPECIAL AGENCIES: Redevelopment Agencies; City Councils and Planning Commissions; U.S. Army Corps of Engineers; California Fish & Game Commission; LAFCO's.
*PRACTICE AREAS: Land Use Law; Redevelopment Law; California Environmental Law; Municipal Law.
**Alonzi, Christopher H.** ............'64 '92 C.1077 B.A. L.1065 J.D. [Ⓐ Whitmore J.&B.]
*PRACTICE AREAS: Labor and Employment (100%).
Alvarado, Kathleen Bernadette ........'66 '93 C.477 B.A. L.990 J.D. [Ⓐ Newton,K.&R.]
Anderson, Paul R. '59 '84 C.813 B.A. L.1068 J.D.
Dir., Intl. Products Div., Adobe Systems, Inc.
Atkinson • Farasyn, (BV) ..................................................660 W. Dana St.
Baird, Steven G. ...................................'52 '80 C.813 A.B. L.770 J.D. [Atkinson F.]
**Baker, Alisa J.** ......................................'57 '84 C.659 B.A. L.276 J.D. [General C.]
*PRACTICE AREAS: Corporate Law; Multimedia Law; Technology Licensing; Intellectual Property; Executive Compensation.

**Baker, J. Norman, (AV) '33 '63 C.659 A.B. L.93 LL.B.** ⒷⒷ
**San Antonio Center, 2570 El Camino Real West, Suite 504, 94040**
**Telephone: 415-941-0604 Fax: 415-941-4697**
**(Certified Specialist, Family Law, The State Bar of California Board of Legal Specialization).**
***REPORTED CASES: In Re Marriage of Hug 154 Cal. App. 3rd 780 (1984).**
**General Civil and Trial Practice. Family Law, Personal Injury, Real Property, Business Litigation and Arbitration.**
**Reference: Bank of the West (Los Altos Branch).**
*See Professional Biographies, MOUNTAIN VIEW, CALIFORNIA*

Barnard, Kathryn A. .........................'62 '89 C&L.813 B.A., J.D. El Camino Hosp.
Barnett, Carol .......'63 '94 C.112 B.A. L.284 J.D. Support Network for Battered Women
Bartlett, Bruce ..................................'27 '57 C.112 A.B. L.1065 J.D. P.O. Box 427B
Bass, Lewis .......................'47 '76 C.563 B.S.M.E. L.770 J.D. 1110 San Antonio Rd.
Baugh, Bradford, (AV) ..........................'50 '75 C&L.813 A.B., J.D. [Baugh&G.]
Baugh & Goodley, (AV) ......................................... 2570 El Camino Real, W.
**Bayha, Betsy E.**, (BV) ......................'51 '77 C.1154 B.A. L.309 J.D. [General C.]
*PRACTICE AREAS: Corporate Law; Technology Licensing; Technology Transfers; Intellectual Property; Business Law.
Behm, R. Scott ...........................'59 '85 C&L.546 B.A., J.D. Sun Microsystems, Inc.
Bergmann, Sandra J. .....................'54 '84 C.259 B.A. L.188 J.D. Silicon Graphics, Inc.
**Berry, Sally F.** ..........................'— '89 C.208 B.A. L.770 J.D. [Ⓐ Luce&Q.]
*PRACTICE AREAS: Estate Planning Law; Probate Administration Law; Conservatorship and Guardianship; Trust Administration Law.
Bojack, Audrey D. .........................'50 '75 C&L.966 B.A., J.D. 1451 Grant Rd.
**Bolanos, Richard C.** ..................'55 '83 C.766 B.A. L.770 J.D. [Whitmore J.&B.]
*REPORTED CASES: Barner v. City of Novato (9th Cir. 1994) 17 F.3d 1256; Zazueta v. San Benito County (1995) 38 Cal.App.4th 106.
*PRACTICE AREAS: Labor and Employment Law (100%).
Bonner, Angelene '68 '94 C.97 B.S.B.A. L.608 J.D.
(adm. in OH; not adm. in CA) Silicon Graphics, Inc.
Booth, Robert K., Jr. ........................'40 '66 C.112 A.B. L.1065 J.D. [Atkinson F.]
Bravard, Wyman N. '53 '80 C.347 B.A. L.1119 J.D.
(adm. in IN; not adm. in CA) 2525 Charleston Rd.
Brill, Gerow D. '35 '92 C.158 B.S.E.E. L.1218 J.D.
(adm. in NY; not adm. in CA; Pat.) Corp. Pat. Coun., Macrovision Corp.
Buell, Thor E. ............................'52 '80 C.112 B.A. L.1066 J.D. 613 Moorpark Way
Burdick, Laura Annette '60 '86
C.147 B.S. L.770 J.D. Assoc. Gen. Coun., Sun Microsystems, Inc.
**Burke, Kathryn J.** ......................'50 '76 C.966 B.A. L.1066 J.D. [Ⓐ Whitmore J.&B.]
*REPORTED CASES: Relyea v. Ventura County Fire Protection District (1992) 2 Cal. App. 4th 875; Zuzueta V. San Benito County (1995) 38 Cal.App. 4th 106; Gauthier v. City of Red Bluff (1995) 34 Cal.App. 4th 1441; Barner v. City of Novato (1994) 17 F.3d 1256.
*PRACTICE AREAS: Labor and Employment Law (100%).
**Burriss, Richard S.**, (AV) .....................'40 '67 C.401 B.S. L.770 J.D. [Burriss&M.]
*PRACTICE AREAS: Business Law; Business Litigation; Intellectual Property; Marketing Communications.
**Burriss, Susan Howie**, (BV) ..............'42 '79 C.1209 B.A. L.770 J.D. [Burriss&M.]
*LANGUAGES: French.
*PRACTICE AREAS: Estate Planning; Probate; Tax; Civil Litigation.

**Burriss & Monahan, A Professional Corporation, (AV)**
**Old Mill Office Center, Suite 160, 201 San Antonio Circle, 94040**
**Telephone: 415-948-7127 Fax: 415-941-6709**
**Richard S. Burriss; Susan Howie Burriss; William J. Monahan; Alan T. Foster; Stephanie A. Casper.**
**General Practice. Civil Litigation, Corporate, Copyright/Trademark, Securities, Business, Employment Law, Taxation, Exempt Organizations, Real Estate, Bankruptcy, Estate Planning, Probate, Family and Pension Law, Toxic Substances, Legislative Advocacy, Marketing Communications.**
*See Professional Biographies, MOUNTAIN VIEW, CALIFORNIA*

Caparas, Armando T. ..............................'23 '75 L.662 LL.B. 1266 Lubich Dr.
Capitina, Michael F. ........................'61 '89 C.112 B.A. L.770 J.D. 1372 Castro St.
Capitina, Nevo F., (BV) ..................'21 '54 C.608 B.Sc. L.813 J.D. 372 Castro St.
**Casper, Stephanie A.** ......................'67 '93 C.112 B.A. L.770 J.D. [Burriss&M.]
*PRACTICE AREAS: Business Law; Business Litigation; Labor Law.
Chambliss, Marque C. ...............'61 '87 C.309 A.B. L.1066 J.D. Silicon Graphics, Inc.
Chasuk, Alfred P., (BV) ..............................'23 '51 C.768 L.770 J.D. [Chasuk&C.]
Chasuk, John C., (BV) ........................'56 '81 C.111 B.S. L.1067 J.D. [Chasuk&C.]
Chasuk & Chasuk, A Professional Law Association, (BV) ..................384 Castro St.
Choy, Peter M. C., (AV) '48 '73
C&L.976 B.A., J.D. Dep. Gen. Coun., Sun Microsystems, Inc.
**Clark, Nancy J.** ..................'59 '92 C.352 B.B.A. L.1065 J.D. [Ⓐ Whitmore J.&B.]
*PRACTICE AREAS: Labor and Employment Law (100%).
**Clausing, Vivian Metzger** ..............'62 '87 C.813 B.A. L.1068 J.D. [Ⓒ General C.]
*PRACTICE AREAS: Environmental; Real Estate Law.
Clayton, Stephen F. ....................'51 '77 C.061 B.A. L.464 J.D. 2550 Garcia Ave.
Cole, Patricia E. '46 '76
C.1188 B.A. L.1065 J.D. Assoc. Gen. Coun., Sun Microsystems, Inc.
Coté, Emily J. .....................................'56 '82 C.773 B.A. L.770 J.D. [Atkinson F.]

Covey, Jo Amanda '55 '78 C.181 B.S.Ed. L.923 J.D.
Corp. Coun., NEC Electronics, Inc.
Cox, Chip ........................ '60 '92 C.878 B.S. L.477 J.D. [Ⓐ Newton,K.&R.]
Curotto, Alexis Joseph ........................ '69 '94 C.602 B.A. L.770 J.D. [Ⓐ Newton,K.&R.]
Dearborn, Charles H., III ....... '52 '79 C.228 B.A. L.846 J.D. Gen. Coun., Acuson Corp.
**Duffy, Maureen M.** ........................ '59 '93 C.352 B.G.S. L.477 J.D. [Ⓐ Whitmore J.&B.]
*LANGUAGES: French and Swahili.
*PRACTICE AREAS: Labor and Employment Law (100%).
Ekroot, Bryn ........................ '62 '93 C.112 B.A.B.S. L.813 J.D. Synopsys (Pat.)
Elwell, Suzanne E. '60 '89 C.488 B.S. L.352 J.D.
Support Network for Battered Women
Falcon, Glynn P., (BV) ........................ '47 '74 C.768 B.S. L.284 J.D. 384 Castro St.
Fernandez, Irene H. ............ '60 '92 C.813 B.S.E.E. L.588 J.D. Silicon Graphics, Inc.
Finneran, Ann M. ........................ '60 '85 C.228 B.A. L.477 J.D. 1451 Grant Rd.
**Foster, Alan T.** ........................ '52 '78 C.1074 B.S. L.426 J.D. [Burriss&M.]
*PRACTICE AREAS: Business Law; Intellectual Property; Mergers and Acquisitions; Nonprofit Corporations; Real Estate.
Fuelleman, Cheryl .......... '50 '84 C.150 B.A. L.999 J.D. Coun., Sun Microsystems, Inc.
Gazzera, Stephen P., Jr., (BV) .......... '28 '54 C&L.770 LL.B. 1134 W. El Camino Real
Gee, Nancy Ann, (CV) ........................ '53 '78 C.112 B.S. L.770 J.D. 774 W. Dana

**General Counsel Associates, (AV)**
**1891 Landings Drive, 94043**
**Telephone: 415-428-3900 Fax: 415-428-3901**
**Partners: Deborah Churton Aikins; Douglas B. Aikins; Alisa J. Baker; Betsy E. Bayha; Paul C. Graffagnino; John W. Hollingsworth; Robert W. Luckinbill; John B. Montgomery; Anne L. Neeter; Clifford S. Robbins; Elizabeth Roth; Roger Royse; Robert H. Sloss; Samuel L. Wright, III. Of Counsel: Vivian Metzger Clausing; Naomi A. Vargas.**
*See Professional Biographies, MOUNTAIN VIEW, CALIFORNIA*

Giusti, Gerald G., (BV) .......... '37 '62 C.766 B.A. L.770 J.D. 800 W. El Camino Real
Golzen, Frank R. ........................ '16 '75 L.981 LL.B. 2672 Bayshore Frontage Rd.
Goodley, Elizabeth ........................ '57 '82 C.112 B.A. L.770 J.D. [Baugh&G.]
**Graffagnino, Paul C.** ........................ '58 '83 C.951 B.A. L.276 J.D. [General C.]
*PRACTICE AREAS: Corporate; Securities; Venture Capital; Corporate Finance.
Greene, Patricia M. ........................ '61 '90 C.914 B.A. L.813 J.D. 1505 Alison Ave.
Grussing, Joleen M. ........................ '65 '89 C.154 B.A. L.178 J.D. [Ⓐ Newton,K.&R.]
Harris, Matthew S. ........................ '58 '88 C.645 B.A. L.602 J.D. 801 Church St.
Hawes, Brian E. ........................ '56 '82 C.636 B.S. L.770 J.D. 1079 Mercy St.
Hayes, Chester F. '39 '74 C.588 B.S.B.A. L.818 J.D.
(adm. in MA; not adm. in CA) Western Reg. Coun., GTE Govt. Systems Corp.
**Hollingsworth, John W.** ........................ '58 '84 C.112 B.A. L.1065 J.D. [General C.]
*PRACTICE AREAS: Corporate Law; Technology Licensing; Technology Transfers; Multimedia Law; Commercial Law.
**Honig, Nancy** '54 '81 C.966 B.A. L.770 J.D.
Assoc. Gen. Coun., Knight-Ridder Information, Inc.,
**Hughes, Jack W.** ........................ '70 '96 C.112 B.A. L.228 J.D. [Whitmore J.&B.]
*PRACTICE AREAS: Labor and Employment Law (100%).
Hulst, Jary J. ........................ '61 '87 C.350 B.A. L.352 J.D. [Ⓐ Newton,K.&R.]
Hynes, Marc G., (BV) ........................ '45 '71 C.112 B.A. L.1066 J.D. [Atkinson F.]
Iriadomi, Elizabeth Ann ........................ '60 '85 C.112 A.B. L.1067 J.D. NASA
**Johnson, Janice E.** ........................ '49 '81 C.766 B.A. L.1065 J.D. [Whitmore J.&B.]
*LANGUAGES: Spanish.
*PRACTICE AREAS: Labor and Employment Law (90%); Municipal Law (5%); Education Law (5%).
**Johnson, Melissa C.** ........................ '52 '87 C.378 B.G.S. L.464 J.D. [Luce&Q.]
*PRACTICE AREAS: Civil, Commercial and Trust Litigation; Administrative Law.
Kandel, Minouche ...'65 '91 C.976 B.A. L.309 J.D. Support Network for Battered Women
Karas, David B ........... '60 '88 C.184 B.A. L.1040 J.D. Coun., Sun Microsystems, Inc.
Kastner, Eric C., (AV) ........................ '47 '72 C.112 B.S. L.1067 J.D. [Newton,K.&R.]
Kershner, Cheryl R. ........................ '59 '87 C.766 B.A. L.767 J.D. 2570 W. El Camino Real
Kleinberg, Judith G. ........ '— '72 C.477 B.A. L.1066 J.D. Exec. Dir., Kids in Common
Korn, Paul A. ........................ '37 '64 C.659 B.S. L.575 J.D. Sytek, Inc.
Kostrzewa, Kate ........................ '62 '90 C.112 B.A. L.1068 J.D. 1636 Yale Dr.
Kukasawa, John F., Jr. .......... '43 '74 C.1239 B.A. L.770 J.D. 1134 W. El Camino Real
Kwartler, Kenneth M. '56 '84 C.1044 B.A. L.94 J.D.
Coml. Coun., Silicon Graphics, Inc.
Lambert, Carl L. ........................ '38 '66 C.112 B.A. L.1065 J.D. Cornish & Carey
Laub, Sam E. .....'38 '67 C.608 B.Met.E. L.911 LL.B. Gen. Coun., Silicon Graphics, Inc.
Leib, Gerald B. ........................ '45 '75 C.112 A.B. L.765 J.D. P.O. Box 390127‡
Leichter, Helene L. ............ '61 '89 C.813 A.B. L.770 J.D. 2570 W. El Camino Real
Lim, Kang S. ........................ '56 '92 C.061 B.Sc. L.1065 J.D. Sun Microsystems, Inc.
Liontas, James A. ........................ '26 '80 C.550 B.S. L.999 J.D. 436 Dell Ave.
London, J. A.(Jack) .............. '25 '52 C.1021 L.770 LL.B. 1134 W. El Camino Real‡
**Luce, James G.**, (AV) ........................ '45 '74 C.976 B.A. L.770 J.D. [Luce&Q.]
*REPORTED CASES: Stephenson v. Calpine Conifers II, 652 F. 2d 808 (1981) (9th Circuit); Bank of America v. Salinas Nissan, Inc., 207 Cal. App. 3d 260 (Sixth Dist., 1989); In Re Hoffmeister I, 161 Cal. App. 3d 1163 (First Dist., 1984); In Re Hoffmeister II, 191 Cal. App. 3d 351 (First Dist., 1987).
*PRACTICE AREAS: General Business; Corporate and Real Estate Litigation; Arbitration.

**Luce & Quillinan, (AV)** ▣
**444 Castro Street, Suite 900, 94041-2073**
**Telephone: 415-969-4000 FAX: 415-969-6953**
**Members of Firm: James G. Luce; James V. Quillinan (Certified Specialist, Estate Planning, Trust and Probate Law, The State Bar of California Board of Legal Specialization); Melissa C. Johnson. Associate: Sally F. Berry.**
**Business and Commercial Transactions, Estate and Tax Planning, Probate Estate and Trust Administration, Conservatorships, Guardianships, Tax, Real Estate, Land Use and Development and Environmental Law, Contracts, Business Entity Structuring and Tax Planning and Securities. Litigation and Appellate Practice with emphasis in the areas of Estate and Trust Litigation, Commercial Disputes, Trade Secrets, Employer Defense, Personal Injury, Construction and Insurance Matters. Arbitration, Mediation and Special Master Services. Preventive Law Counseling to Businesses.**
*See Professional Biographies, MOUNTAIN VIEW, CALIFORNIA*

**Luckinbill, Robert W.** ........................ '62 '87 C.1079 B.A. L.770 J.D. [General C.]
*PRACTICE AREAS: Business Law; Employment Litigation; Intellectual Property.
Luebkeman, Theodore C. .......... '52 '79 C.112 B.A. L.950 J.D. 1134 El Camino Real W.
MacKinnon, Sandra E. '59 '86 C.788 A.B. L.1065 J.D.
Sec. Coun., Silicon Graphics, Inc.
Martin, J. Philip ........................ '46 '70 C&L.623 B.B.A., J.D. [Ⓐ Newton,K.&R.]
Mayo, Frank E. ........................ '43 '69 C&L.767 B.A., J.D. P.O. Box 521
McCrory, Charles, (AV) ........................ '31 '60 C.930 B.A. L.1065 P.O. Box 4277
**Monahan, William J.** ........................ '57 '83 C.112 B.A. L.770 J.D. [Burriss&M.]
*PRACTICE AREAS: Civil Litigation; Business Litigation; Civil Appeals; Commercial Law; Real Property.
**Montgomery, John B.** ........................ '57 '85 C.813 A.B. L.596 J.D. [General C.]
*PRACTICE AREAS: Corporate Law; Securities; Venture Capital; Business Law.
Moran, Cathleen C., (BV) ........................ '49 '78 C.813 A.B. L.1065 J.D. 444 Castro St.
**Morgan, Michael R.**, (BV) ........................ '41 '72 C.766 B.A. L.767 J.D. [Morgan&P.]
*PRACTICE AREAS: Business Law; Tax Planning Law; Estate Planning.

**Morgan & Posilippo, (AV)**
**444 Castro Street, Suite 900, 94041-2073**
**Telephone: 415-969-4000 Fax: 415-969-6953**
**Michael R. Morgan; Richard Posilippo.**

(This Listing Continued)



**Morgan & Posilippo (Continued)**
**General Civil Trial Practice including Business Law, Construction Contract Law, Insurance Litigation, Tax Planning Law, Estate Planning, Torts and Personal Injury.**
*See Professional Biographies, MOUNTAIN VIEW, CALIFORNIA*

**Mould, Susanna L.** ........................ '58 '91 C.112 B.A. L.1065 J.D. [Ⓐ Whitmore J.&B.]
*LANGUAGES: Spanish.
*PRACTICE AREAS: Labor and Employment Law (100%).
Murray, Gwyn Firth .......... '61 '87 C.976 B.A. L.813 J.D. Coun., Silicon Graphics, Inc.
**Neeter, Anne L.** ........................ '50 '78 L.188 J.D. [General C.]
*LANGUAGES: Dutch and German.
*PRACTICE AREAS: Computer Law; Multimedia Law; Commercial Law; Equipment Finance and Leasing; Corporate Law.
Nelson, Douglas J. ........................ '58 '86 C.878 B.S. L.770 J.D. Sun Microsystems, Inc.
Neuwald, Edward R. ........................ '19 '37 C.767 A.B. L.1065 LL.B. 1633 Montalto Dr.
Newman, John H. '50 '77 C.112 B.A. L.1065 J.D.
V.P., Legal Affs., Gen. Coun. & Secy., Scios Nova Inc.
Newton, Stephen L., (AV) ........................ '46 '73 C.98 B.S. L.767 J.D. [Newton,K.&R.]
Newton, Kastner & Remmel, A Professional Corporation, (AV)
Second Floor, 1451 Grant Road
Nimer, Jonathan B. ........................ '58 '85 C.918 B.A. L.1066 J.D. Sun Microsystems, Inc.
O'Grady, Brian J., (BV) .......... '52 '77 C.112 B.A. L.464 J.D. 1134 W. El Camino Real
**O'Neill, Cynthia** ........................ '59 '87 C.112 B.A. L.770 J.D. [Whitmore J.&B.]
*PRACTICE AREAS: Labor and Employment Law (100%).
Peters, Steven D. '59 '86 C.499 B.A. L.813 J.D.
Assoc. Gen. Coun., Adobe Systems, Inc.
**Posilippo, Richard**, (AV) ........................ '43 '69 C.770 B.A. L.1066 J.D. [Morgan&P.]
*PRACTICE AREAS: Construction Contract Law; Insurance Litigation; Personal Injury; Torts.
Pouliot, Colleen M. '58 '83 C.770 B.S. L.1067 J.D.
V.P., Gen. Coun. & Secy., Adobe Systems, Inc.‡
**Quillinan, James V.**, (AV) ........................ '48 '74 C.813 B.A. L.770 J.D. [Luce&Q.]
*PRACTICE AREAS: Estate Planning Law; Probate Administration Law; Conservatorship and Guardianship; Trust Administration Law and related Litigation.
Rebagliati, Steve F. ........................ '64 '90 C&L.770 B.S.C., J.D. [Ⓐ Newton,K.&R.]
Remmel, Ronald F., (BV) ........................ '49 '79 C.112 B.A. L.999 J.D. [Newton,K.&R.]
Resnick, Nancy E. ............ '59 '86 C.112 B.A. L.1065 J.D. 2570 W. El Camino Real
**Robbins, Clifford S.** ........................ '56 '82 C.846 B.A. L.309 J.D. [General C.]
*PRACTICE AREAS: Corporate Law; Venture Capital; Corporate Finance; Technology Licensing; Technology Transfers.
Robinson, Russell ........................ '62 '93 C.112 B.A. L.284 J.D. 372 Castro St.
Rock, Martha .......... '— '85 C&L.112 B.A., J.D. Sr. Corp. Coun., Adobe Systems, Inc.
Rose, Denise McIntyre .......... '54 '81 C.679 B.A. L.1068 J.D. El Camino Hosp. Found.
Rosenberg, Marilyn ......... '58 '88 C&L.813 A.B., J.D. Div. Coun., Silicon Graphics, Inc.
**Roth, Elizabeth** ........................ '46 '82 C.188 B.A. L.228 J.D. [General C.]
*PRACTICE AREAS: Employment Litigation.
Rowan, Gail ........................ '60 '92 C.1350 B.A. L.1065 J.D. 2570 W. El Camino
**Royse, Roger** ........................ '59 '84 C&L.585 B.A., J.D. [General C.]
*PRACTICE AREAS: Taxation.
Schneider, Michael E., (A P.C.), (BV) '44 '70
C.112 B.A. L.770 J.D. 444 Castro St., Ste. 900
Sears, Michael E. ........................ '56 '89 C.871 B.S. L.813 J.D. Sun Microsystems, Inc.
Serrao, Claire E. ........................ '65 '91 C.768 B.S. L.770 J.D. 11451 Grant Rd.
Shearer, Peter R. '48 '75 C.816 B.E. L.776 J.D.
(adm. in NJ; not adm. in CA; Pat.) Scios Nova Inc.
Siegal, Leonard J., (BV) ........................ '48 '75 C.838 B.S. L.365 J.D. [Atkinson F.]
**Simons, Robert A.** '47 '72
C.801 B.S. L.424 J.D. Gen. Coun., Knight-Ridder Information, Inc.

**Skjerven, Morrill, MacPherson, Franklin & Friel LLP**
**(See San Jose)**

**Sloss, Robert H.** ........................ '54 '79 C.813 A.B. L.1065 J.D. [General C.]
*PRACTICE AREAS: Business; Employment; Intellectual Property Litigation.
Smith, Robert J. ........................ '32 '56 C&L.424 B.S.C., J.D. 1134 W. El Camino Real
Smullin, Wm. David, (AV) ....... '43 '68 C.813 A.B. L.1066 J.D. 201 San Antonio Circle
Solomon, Lee E. ........................ '20 '53 C.813 A.B. L.1065 J.D. 181 Ana Ave.
Teasdale, Russell E. '31 '58
C.665 B.B.A.,M.A. L.813 J.D. Exec. V.P., DDI Pharmaceuticals, Inc.
Tompkins, Julie F. ............ '64 '91 C.112 B.A. L.426 J.D. 2570 W. Camino Real Ste 600
Toppel, Harold S., (BV) ........................ '41 '67 C.912 Ph.B. L.477 J.D. [Atkinson F.]
Toth, Liza K., (BV) ........................ '59 '83 C.33 B.S. L.608 J.D. 1220 Charleston Rd. (Pat.)
Tramz, Stephanie C. ..... '45 '77 C.112 B.A. L.1066 J.D. Div. Coun., Raytheon Company
Traub, Jean R., (Mr.) ........................ '22 '52 C.339 B.S. L.813 LL.B. 1963 Amalfi Way‡
**Vargas, Naomi A.** ........................ '54 '80 C.112 B.A. L.1066 J.D. [© General C.]
*PRACTICE AREAS: Real Estate; Land Use.
Wang, Daphne L. ........................ '59 '87 C.999 LL.B. L.770 J.D. 49 W. Camono Real
Webster, James R. '16 '39 C.59 L.846 LL.B.
(adm. in TX; not adm. in CA) 3384 Truman Ave.‡
Weiner, Steven S. ............ '63 '90 C.659 B.S. L.309 J.D. Silicon Graphics, Inc. (Pat.)
Weinert, Barry J. ........................ '54 '81 C.112 B.S. L.208 J.D. Silicon Graphics, Inc.
Wheeler, Ellen ........................ '52 '92 C.768 B.A. L.770 J.D. P.O. Box 4181
**Whitmore, Richard S.**, (AV) ........................ '42 '67 C&L.813 B.A., J.D. [Whitmore J.&B.]
*REPORTED CASES: Sunnydale Public Safety Officers Assoc. v. City of Sunnydale (1976) 55 Cal.App. 3d 732; Vernon Firefighters v. City of Vermon (1980) (107 Cal.App.3f 802; ULAC v. City of Salinas (1981) 654 F.2d 557; Relyea v. Ventura County Fire Protection District (1992) 2 Cal. App. 4th 875; Gauthier v. City of Red Bluff (1995) 34 Cal.App. 4th 1441.
*PRACTICE AREAS: Labor and Employment Law (90%); Municipal Law (10%).

**Whitmore Johnson & Bolanos, (AV)**
**2570 West El Camino Real, Suite 600, 94040**
**Telephone: 415-941-9333; 800-585-4529 Fax: 415-941-9476**
**Members of Firm: Richard S. Whitmore; Janice E. Johnson; Richard C. Bolanos; Cynthia O'Neill. Associates: Kathryn J. Burke; Nancy J. Clark; Christopher H. Alonzi; Susanna L. Mould; Maureen M. Duffy; Jack W. Hughes.**
**Labor and Employment Law.**
*See Professional Biographies, MOUNTAIN VIEW, CALIFORNIA*

**Wright, Samuel L., III** ........................ '55 '84 C.951 B.A. L.1065 J.D. [General C.]
*PRACTICE AREAS: Real Estate.
Zaorski, James M. '58 '84 C.453 B.S. L.1292 J.D.
(adm. in NJ; not adm. in CA) 2361 Laura Ln.‡
Zolt, Nina B. ........................ '52 '76 C.659 B.A. L.94 J.D. Kaleida Labs., Inc.

## MOUNT LAGUNA, —, *San Diego Co.*

Sada, Gary E., (BV) ........................ '35 '63 C.763 A.B. L.1049 LL.B. P.O. Box 146

## MOUNT SHASTA, 3,460, *Siskiyou Co.*

Aiello, Frank V., (BV) ........................ '47 '73 C.112 A.B. L.1065 J.D. P.O. Box 337
Boston, Robert B., (CV) ........................ '53 '79 C.112 B.A. L.770 J.D. [Kirsher,W.&B.]⊙

**Breyer, Arnold David, (BV) '42 '67 C.339 B.A. L.426 J.D.**
**112 Siskiyou Avenue, P.O. Box 201, 96067⊙**
**Telephone: 916-926-3134 Fax: 916-926-8607**
**(Certified Specialist, Family Law, The State Bar of California Board of Legal Specialization).**
**Practice Limited to Personal Injury and Family Law.**
**Redding, California Office: 1721 Court Street. Telephone: 916-244-3690. Fax: 916-244-0923.**

*See Professional Biographies, MOUNT SHASTA, CALIFORNIA*

Kirsher, Winston & Boston, Law Corp., (CV) ..........205 N. Mt. Shasta Blvd. (⊙Weed)
Masunaga, Laura Jean ................. '48 '82 C.813 B.A. L.1066 J.D. 1009 Ream Ave.
McCarthy, Elizabeth K. ......................... '54 '79 C.976 B.A. L.94 J.D. City Atty.
Stearns, Timothy H. .................... '47 '75 C.446 B.S. L.284 J.D. 505 S. Shasta Blvd.
Winston, Robert D., (CV) ............ '49 '78 C.1077 B.S. L.809 J.D. [Kirsher,W.&B.]⊙

## MURRIETA, 2,769, *Riverside Co.*

Boots, Clydene ..................... '37 '89 C.378 B.S./B.A. L.1198 J.D. Westview Farm
Borie, John D. ...................... '26 '52 C.112 A.B. L.1065 J.D. 38329 Aberdeen Dr.‡
Dickson, Kenneth C. ................... '48 '73 C.378 B.A. L.228 J.D. 41486 Serrai Ct.★
Feinstein, Eloise Hock .............. '57 '82 C.1109 B.A. L.1068 J.D. 39902 Milkmaid La.‡

## NAPA, * 61,842, *Napa Co.*

Amendola, Stephen A. ............ '52 '92 C.767 B.S. L.770 J.D. Pres., Eldex Labs., Inc.
Andres, Thomas M. ...................... '51 '79 C.602 B.B.A. L.284 J.D. 3318 David Dr.
Balcher, Alan M. ............................ '50 '79 C.112 B.A. L.1095 J.D. [Gravett&B.]
**Baldwin, Robyn L.** ............... '65 '93 C.112 B.A. L.1065 J.D. [[A] Gaw,V.S.M.&M.]
*PRACTICE AREAS: Litigation; Employment; Environmental; Trademark; Copyright.
**Bardwell, Paul A.**, (BV) ............. '51 '76 C.767 B.A. L.464 J.D. [Murphy,L.B.&L.]
*PRACTICE AREAS: Family Law; Personal Injury Law.
Barwick, Jill E., (CV) ................... '57 '84 C.169 B.A. L.464 J.D. 2800 Jefferson St.
Beckon, Brian J. .............................. '64 '90 C.999 B.A. L.464 J.D. 944 Main St.
Bernstein, Joel J. ......................... '47 '75 C.259 B.A. L.112 J.D. P.O. Box 6134
**Berryman, Kelly Jayne** .......... '65 '90 C.597 B.A. L.1065 J.D. [[A] Gaw,V.S.M.&M.]
*PRACTICE AREAS: Business Transactions; Real Estate Transactions; Secured Finance; Commercial Leasing.
Beutler, Gloria M. ..................... '23 '45 C&L.813 A.B., LL.B. 312 Deer Hollow‡
Beyer, Michael K. '49 '76 C.309 A.B. L.1066 J.D.
Sr. V.P., Gen. Coun. & Secy., Robert Mondavi Winery
Blanckenburg, Wm. L. .................. '15 '39 C.112 B.A. L.1066 LL.B. 60 Oak Crest‡
Blevans, Robert E., (AV) .................. '50 '77 C&L.1137 B.S., J.D. [Fershko,L.&B.]
Block, Alvin L. .......................... '29 '77 C.1365 A.B. L.981 LL.B. 3230 Beard Rd.
Block, Harold A., (AV) ............ '11 '36 C.813 A.B. L.1066 J.D. 31 Gleneagle Circle‡
**Blyth, Stanley D.** .................... '58 '93 C.1078 B.A. L.112 J.D. [Dickenson,P.&F.]
*PRACTICE AREAS: Civil Litigation; Personal Injury; Taxation.
Boitano, James D., (AV) ................ '27 '52 C.770 L.767 J.D. 1001 2nd St., Ste 315
**Buehl, Stephen T.** ..................... '47 '74 C.976 B.A. L.813 J.D. [Gagen,M.M.&A.]
*PRACTICE AREAS: Commercial Litigation; Business Law; Land Use Law; Wine Industry Regulatory Matters.
**Carey, Paul G.**, (BV) ................. '56 '82 C.112 B.A. L.1066 J.D. [Dickenson,P.&F.]
*PRACTICE AREAS: Civil Litigation; Personal Injury Law; Real Property Litigation.
**Carey, Thomas F.** ..................... '68 '95 C.813 B.A. L.228 J.D. [Dickenson,P.&F.]
*PRACTICE AREAS: Land Use Planning; Alcoholic Beverage Regulation.
Carlson, Terrence, (BV) ........................ '42 '72 C.136 B.S. L.284 J.D. 33 Lynn Dr.
Carter, Scott H. ....................... '52 '78 C.112 B.A. L.464 J.D. 2180 Jefferson St.
Champlin, Philip A. ........................ '39 '65 C.976 B.A. L.1066 J.D. Supr. Ct. J.
Chan, Wilbert F. ......................... '34 '71 C.800 B.S. L.1049 J.D. 1227 Coombs St.

**Chester, Daniel, The Law Office of '59 '89 C.1060 B.A. L.767 J.D.**
**1001 2nd Street, Suite 345, 94559**
**Telephone: 707-257-5378 Fax: 707-257-5399**
**Email: ChesterDK@AOL.COM**
***PRACTICE AREAS: Civil Litigation; Construction Law; Real Estate Litigation; Business Law; Evictions.**
**Civil Litigation, Construction Law, Real Estate Litigation, Business Law, Evictions, Estate Planning, Living Trusts and Wills.**

*See Professional Biographies, NAPA, CALIFORNIA*

**Collin, Francis J., Jr.**, (AV) ......... '42 '67 C.112 A.B. L.1066 J.D. [Dickenson,P.&F.]
*PRACTICE AREAS: Estate Law; Tax Planning Law; Trust Law; Estate Administration Law.
Cook, John L. ................................ '43 '68 C.112 A.B. L.1068 J.D. City Atty.

**Coombs & Dunlap, (AV) [BB]**
**1211 Division Street, 94559⊙**
**Telephone: 707-252-9100 Fax: 707-252-8516**
**Frank L. Coombs (1853-1934); Nathan F. Coombs (1881-1973); Frank L. Dunlap (1913-1984). Members of Firm: Malcolm A. Mackenzie (Certified Specialist, Family Law, The State Bar of California Board of Legal Specialization); C. Preston Shackelford (Certified Specialist, Family Law, The State Bar of California Board of Legal Specialization); Diane M. Price; Diane L. Dillon; L. Randolph Skidmore; Charles P. Kuntz;—Donald M. Davis; Rafael Rios, III. Of Counsel: June E. Moroney.**
**General Civil, Trial and Appellate Practice, all State and Federal Courts. Business, Real Property, Municipal, Personal Injury, Family, Estate Planning and Probate Law.**
**Representative Clients: City of St. Helena; Napa Sanitation District; Saintsbury; Napa Valley Family Medical Group, Inc.; California Council of the Blind; Havens Wine Cellars; Coldwell-Banker, Brokers of the Valley; ZD Winery; Anderson's Conn Valley Vineyards; Corison Wines.**
**St. Helena, California Office: 1110 Adams Street. Telephone: 707-963-5202; 944-8779.**

*See Professional Biographies, NAPA, CALIFORNIA*

**Craig, Christine L.** ................. '65 '92 C.112 B.A. L.770 J.D. [[C] Gaw,V.S.M.&M.]
*PRACTICE AREAS: Trust Administration; Probate; Estate Planning.
**Davis, Donald M.** ......................... '61 '93 C.896 B.A. L.112 J.D. [[A] Coombs&D.]
*LANGUAGES: Arabic, French.
*PRACTICE AREAS: Business Law; Real Estate Law; Civil Litigation; Municipal Law.

**Diamond, David A., (BV) '59 '84 C.37 B.A. L.1067 J.D.**
**816 Brown Street, 94559**
**Telephone: 707-254-8100 Fax: 707-254-8147**
**Email: diamond@napanet.net URL: http://www.trustwizard.com**
**(Certified Specialist, Estate Planning, Trust and Probate Law, The State Bar of California Board of Legal Specialization).**
***PRACTICE AREAS: Estate Planning, Trust and Probate Law; Estate and Gift Taxation.**
**Estate Planning, Administration of Estates and Trusts, Estate and Gift Taxation, Inheritance Disputes, Business and Tax Planning, Family Partnerships, Charitable Trust Planning.**

*See Professional Biographies, NAPA, CALIFORNIA*

**Dickenson, Charles H.**, (BV) ........ '53 '78 C.112 A.B. L.1065 J.D. [Dickenson,P.&F.]
*PRACTICE AREAS: Civil Litigation; Personal Injury Law.
**Dickenson, Howard G.**, (AV) ..... '23 '51 C.112 B.S. L.1065 LL.B. [Dickenson,P.&F.] ‡
*PRACTICE AREAS: Probate Law; Trust Administration Law; Estate Planning Law.

**Dickenson, Peatman & Fogarty, A Professional Law Corporation, (AV) [BB]**
**809 Coombs Street, 94559-2977**
**Telephone: 707-252-7122 Telecopier: 707-255-6876**
**Joseph G. Peatman; David W. Meyers; C. Richard Lemon; Francis J. Collin, Jr., Certified Specialist, Probate, Estate Planning and Trust Law, California Board of Specialization; David B. Gilbreth; Charles H. Dickenson; Paul G. Carey; Richard P. Mendelson; Joseph M. Keebler; Cathy A. Roche; Jonathan P. Dyer; James W. Terry; Katherine Ohlandt; Stanley D. Blyth; Linda Emerson; Thomas F. Carey; Grace Goodman Ross. Of Counsel: Walter J. Fogarty, Jr.; Howard G. Dickenson (Retired).**

(This Listing Continued)

**Dickenson, Peatman & Fogarty, A Professional Law Corporation (Continued)**
**General Civil and Trial Practice in all State and Federal Courts. Personal Injury, Real Estate, Alcohol Beverage Law and Related Trade Regulations, Land Use Planning and Local Government Law. Estate Planning and Probate Administration, Business, Corporate, Construction, Personal Taxation Law.**

*See Professional Biographies, NAPA, CALIFORNIA*

**Dillon, Diane L.**, (BV) ......................... '52 '81 C.112 B.A. L.1067 J.D. [Coombs&D.]⊙
*PRACTICE AREAS: Estate Planning Law; Probate Law.
Drago, Frank J., (BV) .................. '50 '75 C&L.767 B.A., J.D. 1001 2nd St., Ste 255
Dunlap, John F. ........................ '22 '50 C.112 A.B. L.1065 J.S.D. 2111 3rd Ave.‡
**Dyer, Jonathan P.** ..................... '57 '89 C.446 B.A. L.1067 J.D. [[A] Dickenson,P.&F.]
*LANGUAGES: Russian.
*PRACTICE AREAS: Civil Litigation.
**Elliott, Joyce L.** ....................... '59 '88 C.147 B.S. L.767 J.D. [[A] Gaw,V.S.M.&M.]
*PRACTICE AREAS: Family Law.
Ellwein, Lola C. ................................. '52 '85 C.766 B.A. L.1065 J.D. 1040 Main St.
**Emerson, Linda** .................... '58 '93 C.1060 B.A. L.1067 J.D. [Dickenson,P.&F.]
*PRACTICE AREAS: Land Use Planning; Local Government Law.
**Fanucci, Robert M.** ..................... '56 '82 C.766 B.A. L.284 J.D. [Gagen,M.M.&A.]
*LANGUAGES: Italian.
*PRACTICE AREAS: Tax Law; Business Law; Real Estate Law; Estate Planning Law; Tax Law.
Ferguson, Jack L., (BV) ............................ '31 '61 C.267 L.981 LL.B. 585 Coombs St.
Fershko, Victor A. .................. '42 '69 C.569 B.S. L.1009 J.D. [Fershko,L.&B.]⊙
Fershko, Lewis & Blevans, (AV) .......................................... 1005 Coombs St.
Flax, Joseph D., (BV) ..................... '44 '70 C.112 A.B. L.1065 J.D. 563 Jefferson St.
Flores, Louis F. ............................ '31 '76 C.112 B.S. L.1065 J.D. P.O. Box 2686
**Fogarty, Walter J., Jr.**, (AV) ........ '39 '65 C.112 B.S. L.1066 J.D. [[C] Dickenson,P.&F.]
*PRACTICE AREAS: Estate Planning; Estate Administration Law.
Footman, Duncan, (BV) '41 '69 C.976 B.A. L.145 J.D.
1211 Division St. (⊙Sacramento)
Fort, Allen Keys ........................ '43 '71 C.629 B.A. L.770 J.D. 2180 Jefferson St.
Fortes, Melvin F., (CV) ................ '55 '81 C.770 B.S. L.1066 J.D. 1005 Jefferson St.
Freed, David I., (AV) ............................ '42 '67 C.112 A.B. L.1066 J.D. [D.I.Freed]
Freed, David I., P.C., (AV) ..................................................... P.O. Box 6230
Fretz, Donald R. ............................. '22 '51 C.210 B.A. L.767 J.D. Ret. Supr. Ct. J.
Friedman, Alan H. '42 '68 C.112 A.B. L.1066 J.D.
Exec. Dir., The Center for Govt. Dispute Resolution
Frisch, John F., (CV) ................... '45 '77 C.1060 B.S. L.1026 J.D. 1114 Frankin St.

**Gagen, McCoy, McMahon & Armstrong, A Professional Corporation, (AV)**
**1001 Second Street, Suite 315, 94559⊙**
**Telephone: 707-224-8396 FAX: 707-224-5817**
**Robert M. Fanucci; Stephen T. Buehl (Resident).**
**Real Estate, Business, Estate Planning, Federal and State Income Taxation, General Civil and Criminal Trial Practice, Insurance, Probate, Family and Corporation Law, Wine Industry Regulatory Matters, Sales, Leases, Mergers and Acquisitions of Vineyards and Wineries.**
**Danville, California Office: 279 Front Street P.O. Box 218. Telephone 510-837-0585. Fax: 510-838-5985.**

*See Professional Biographies, NAPA, CALIFORNIA*

Gately, Wm. F. ....................................... '20 '53 C.112 L.1065 J.D. 389 Bluejay Way‡
**Gaw, David B.**, (BV) ..................... '45 '71 C.174 A.B. L.1065 J.D. [Gaw,V.S.M.&M.]⊙
*PRACTICE AREAS: Estate Planning Law; Trust and Probate Law; Elder Law.

**Gaw, Van Male, Smith, Myers & Miroglio, A Professional Law Corporation, (AV)**
**944 Main Street, 94559-3045⊙**
**Telephone: 707-252-9000 Telecopier: 707-252-0792**
**URL: http://www.gvmsmm.com**
**David B. Gaw (Certified Specialist, Probate, Estate Planning and Trust Law, State Bar of California, Board of Legal Specialization); Nicholas R. Van Male; Wyman G. Smith, III; Bruce A. Myers; Bruce A. Miroglio;—Joyce L. Elliott; Kelly Jayne Berryman; Christine L. Craig; Robyn L. Baldwin; Rhonda Lee Savitch.**
**General Civil Trial Practice in all State and Federal Courts. Land Use, Planning and Local Government Law, Business and Corporate Law, Real Estate, Estate Planning and Probate Administration, Elder Law, Family Law, Criminal Law, Corporate and Personal Taxation, Pension and Profit Sharing, Agricultural Law, Alcohol Beverage Law and Personal Injury.**
**Reference: The Vintage Bank.**
**Fairfield, California Office: Corporate Plaza. 1261 Travis Boulevard, Suite 350. Telephone: 707-425-1250. Fax: 707-425-1255.**

*See Professional Biographies, NAPA, CALIFORNIA*

**Gilbreth, David B.**, (BV) ............... '47 '76 C.112 B.A. L.208 J.D. [Dickenson,P.&F.]
*PRACTICE AREAS: Real Estate Law; Land Use Law; Tax Law.
Gravett, Charles Lewis ............................ '47 '75 C&L.893 B.A., J.D. [Gravett&B.]
Gravett & Balcher ...................................................... 1125 Jefferson St.
Griffiths, George W., (BV) ................................................ '34 '72 P.O. Box 5567
Grupp, Leal A. .................... '39 '66 C.112 B.A. L.1065 J.D. 2367 Soda Canyon Rd.
Guadagni, Raymond A., (BV) ........... '46 '71 C.112 B.S. L.1065 J.D. [Guadagni G.&F.]
Guadagni Gasper & Flax, (BV) ............................................... 563 Jefferson St.
Guidotti, Joanna R. ........................ '53 '77 C.740 B.A. L.765 J.D. 485 Brown St.
Haas, Michael J. ................................. '42 '75 C.966 B.B.A. L.284 J.D. [Haas&P.]
Haas & Pahlmeyer ............................................................ P.O. Box 2410
Hamilton, H. Trevor .................. '31 '73 C.990 B.A. L.1049 J.D. 2800 Jefferson St.
**Hoff, Paul M.**, (AV) ................... '46 '72 C.112 B.A. L.1065 J.D. [Zeller,H.&Z.]
*REPORTED CASES: Mavroudis vs. Superior Court (1980) 102 Cal.App.3d 594; Molien vs. Kaiser Foundation Hospitals (1980) 27 Cal.3d 916; Dinong vs. Superior Court (1980) 102 Cal.App.3d 845.
*PRACTICE AREAS: Civil Litigation; Personal Injury; Governmental Affairs; Real Property Litigation.

**Jones, James V., (AV) '39 '67 C.112 A.B. L.1065 J.D.**
**1564 First Street, 94559**
**Telephone: 707-252-8644 Fax: 707-252-0852**
***LANGUAGES: Spanish.**
***REPORTED CASES: Roads v. Superior Court 275 Cal. App. 2d 593; People v. Mentzer 163 Cal. App. 3d 482.**
**General Civil and Criminal Trial Practice. Probate, Real Property, Family, Personal Injury, Municipal and Corporate Law.**
**Reference: Napa National Bank.**

*See Professional Biographies, NAPA, CALIFORNIA*

**Jordan, Kim H.** ............................ '53 '95 C.1049 B.A. L.770 J.D. [[C] B.S.Leonard]
*PRACTICE AREAS: Civil Litigation; Family Law; Intellectual Property; Estate Planning; Probate.
**Keebler, Joseph M.**, (AV) ............. '42 '67 C.684 B.A. L.1066 J.D. [Dickenson,P.&F.]
*PRACTICE AREAS: Real Property; Land Use Planning; Estate Planning; Wills and Trust; Litigation.
Ketron, Bruce D. ............................ '45 '70 C.112 B.A. L.1065 J.D. [Ketron&Z.]⊙
Ketron & Zatman ............................................... 810 Brown St. (⊙Santa Rosa)
Kirlin, Anne M., (BV) ................... '44 '77 C.914 B.A. L.800 J.D. 3460 Villa Lane
Klein, Larry M., (AV) ........................... '46 '72 C.502 A.B. L.426 J.D. [L.M.Klein]
Klein, Larry M., Inc., (AV) ................................................... 1792 Second St.
Knudson, Alvin J. ............................ '38 '72 C.766 B.A. L.767 J.D. 944 Main St.⊙
Kongsgaard, Thos. ......................... '21 '50 C.112 B.S. L.813 LL.B. Ret. Supr. Ct. J.
Kozlowski, David J. ...................... '48 '75 C.1060 B.S. L.464 J.D. 560 Hoover St.
Kriens, Cameron L. ........................ '60 '87 C.267 B.S. L.398 J.D. 8 Rockrose Ct.
Kroyer, Stephen T. ........................ '50 '78 C.691 B.A. L.1137 J.D. Dep. Dist. Atty.
**Kuntz, Charles P.** ............................... '44 '70 C&L.813 B.A., J.D. [Coombs&D.]
*PRACTICE AREAS: Civil Litigation; Personal Injury Law; Probate Law; Trust Law; Litigation.

CAA401P

**Lann, Kelly A.** ............................'66 '93 C.112 A.B. L.910 J.D. [Murphy,L.B.&L.]
*PRACTICE AREAS: Family Law; Civil Litigation.
Laughridge, Don E. ........................'48 '79 C.446 B.A. L.05 LL.B 833 Franklin St.
Leister, Leslie R., (BV) ......................'46 '79 C.112 A.B. L.770 J.D. 2139 1st St.
**Lemon, C. Richard**, (AV) ............'43 '69 C.112 A.B. L.1066 J.D. [Dickenson,P.&F.]
*PRACTICE AREAS: Corporate Law; Real Estate Law; Tax Law.

**Leonard, Beverly Saxon '52 '91 C.1078 B.A. L.284 J.D.**
**1001 2nd Street, Suite 345, 94559**
**Telephone: 707-257-5378 Facsimile: 707-257-5399**
**Email: bsleonard@aol.com**
**Associate: Kim H. Jordan.**
**Civil Trial Practice, Business, Family, Land Use, Environmental and Employment Law.**
*See Professional Biographies, NAPA, CALIFORNIA*

Lewis, Roger J., (AV) ....................'51 '76 C.911 B.A. L.426 J.D. [Fershko,L.&B.]
Lieberstein, Gary A. ....................'55 '80 C.112 B.A. L.1065 J.D. Dep. Dist. Atty.
Linden, David J. ........................'42 '67 C.112 A.B. L.1065 J.D. 531 Jefferson St.
**Logan, Donald J.** ....................'54 '81 C.636 B.S. L.1049 J.D. [Murphy,L.B.&L.]
*PRACTICE AREAS: Real Estate Law; Tax Law; Business Law; Estate Planning.
**Loomis, Paul** ........................'54 '83 C.112 B.A. L.426 J.D. [Murphy,L.B.&L.]
*PRACTICE AREAS: Construction Litigation; Personal Injury; Commercial Torts; Insurance Law.
**Mackenzie, Malcolm A.**, (AV) ............'45 '71 C.813 A.B. L.1066 J.D. [Coombs&D.]
*PRACTICE AREAS: Civil Litigation; Family Law; Probate Law; Municipal Law.
Marshall, James M., (CV) ..................'53 '81 C.112 B.A. L.284 J.D. 1210 Pearl St.
Mc Intyre, Linda J. S. ....................'60 '92 C.959 B.S. L.436 J.D. 816 Brown St.
McNeely, Henry E. ..........'13 '65 C.912 A.B. L.1066 LL.B. 2001 Hillcrest Dr.‡
Meibeyer, Charles W., (BV) ............'51 '82 C.477 B.G.S. L.1066 J.D. 1001 2nd. St.
**Mendelson, Richard P.**, (AV) ..........'53 '82 C.309 B.A. L.813 J.D. [Dickenson,P.&F.]
*LANGUAGES: French.
*PRACTICE AREAS: Alcohol Beverage Law; Land Use Planning.
**Meyers, David W.**, (AV) ............'42 '68 C.684 B.A. L.1066 J.D. [Dickenson,P.&F.]
*PRACTICE AREAS: Civil Litigation; Local Government Law; Environmental Law; Real Estate Law.
**Miroglio, Bruce A.**, (CV) ..........'57 '82 C.112 B.A. L.464 J.D. [Gaw,V.S.M.&M.]⊙
*REPORTED CASES: Vianna v. Doctors' Management Company (1994) 27 Cal.App.4th 1186.
*PRACTICE AREAS: Civil Litigation; Personal Injury Law; Medical Malpractice Defense; Probate Litigation; Employment Litigation.
Moore, John G. ......................'38 '64 C.604 A.B. L.1066 LL.B. General Delivery‡
Morhar, Lee D. ..............................'51 '81 C.1077 B.A. L.1065 J.D. Dist. Atty.
**Moroney, June E.** ....................'47 '75 C.813 A.B. L.1065 J.D. [⊠ Coombs&D.]
*LANGUAGES: Spanish and Italian.
*PRACTICE AREAS: Civil Litigation; Appeals.
Mowinckel, Larry E. '43 '66
C.766 B.A. L.1065 LL.B. Napa Co. Human Servs. Develop. Sys.
Mulhern, Paul C., (CV) ..........................'36 '72 C.1049 L.464 J.D. 845 Jefferson St.
**Murphy, J. Michael**, (AV) ..............'50 '77 C.112 A.B. L.464 J.D. [Murphy,L.B.&L.]
*PRACTICE AREAS: General Civil Litigation; Real Estate Law; Business Law; Personal Injury Law; Construction Law.

**Murphy, Logan, Bardwell & Loomis, A Professional Corporation, (AV)**
**2350 First Street, P.O. Box 5540, 94581-0540**
**Telephone: 707-257-8100 Fax: 707-257-6479**
**J. Michael Murphy; Donald J. Logan; Paul A. Bardwell; Paul Loomis; Kelly A. Lann.**
**General Civil and Trial Practice. Real Estate, Construction, Land Use, Taxation, Business, Corporate, Commercial, Family, Personal Injury, Bankruptcy, Labor, Criminal, Estate Planning and Probate Law.**
*See Professional Biographies, NAPA, CALIFORNIA*

**Myers, Bruce A.** ....................'51 '81 C.112 B.S. L.464 J.D. [Gaw,V.S.M.&M.]⊙
*PRACTICE AREAS: Taxation Law; Business Transactions; Pension Law; Profit Sharing Law.
Nelson, Vincent E. ..............................'59 '89 C.766 B.A. L.999 J.D. [L.M.Klein]
Neumiller, Paul A. ....................'55 '84 C.112 A.B. L.1067 J.D. 1411 King Ave.
**Ohlandt, Katherine** ..................'51 '91 C.813 B.A. L.846 J.D. [Dickenson,P.&F.]
*PRACTICE AREAS: Estate Planning; Business Succession; Trust Administration; Probate.
Pahlmeyer, Jayson L. ........................'44 '74 C.766 B.A. L.284 J.D. [Haas&P.]
Paradis, Maurice L. ....................'24 '51 C&L.93 B.S., LL.B. 244 Kaanapali Dr.‡
**Peatman, Joseph G.**, (AV) ..............'34 '59 C&L.813 A.B., J.D. [Dickenson,P.&F.]
*PRACTICE AREAS: Land Use Law; Zoning Law; Real Estate Law.
Peter, Bradley S., (CV) ....................'44 '78 C.629 B.S. L.765 J.D. 1040 Main St.
**Price, Diane M.**, (BV) ..............'53 '79 C.112 B.A. L.1065 J.D. [Coombs&D.]⊙
*PRACTICE AREAS: General Civil Litigation; Personal Injury Law; Municipal Law; Family Law.
Quigley, John J. ..........................'26 '52 C.112 B.S. L.1065 LL.B. Ret. Mun. J.
Ramos, David G. ........................'56 '84 C.112 B.A. L.284 J.D. 1040 Main St.

**Rendleman, James D. '56 '85 C.575 B.S. L.1148 J.D.**
**3273 Claremont Way #206, 94558**
**Telephone: 707-258-6234 Fax: 707-258-6264**
***LANGUAGES: German.**
***PRACTICE AREAS: Labor Law; Business Law; General Litigation; Political and Community Affairs.**
**Labor and Employment Law, Corporate and Business, Insurance Defense, Insurance Coverage, Tax.**
*See Professional Biographies, NAPA, CALIFORNIA*

**Rios, Rafael, III** ........................'66 '94 C.1067 B.S. L.770 J.D. [⊠ Coombs&D.]
*LANGUAGES: Spanish.
*PRACTICE AREAS: General Practice.
Roberts, Daryl A. ....................'57 '83 C.112 B.S.B.A. L.464 J.D. Dep. Dist. Atty
Robertson, William A., III, (BV) ............'47 '80 C.112 A.B. L.464 J.D. 743 Wilson St.
**Roche, Cathy A.** ....................'— '88 C.1110 B.A. L.1065 J.D. [Dickenson,P.&F.]
*PRACTICE AREAS: Land Use Law; Real Estate Law.
Rodde, Stephen S. ....................'49 '80 C.813 M.B.A. L.1068 J.D. 1500 3rd St.
Rodeno, R. Gregory, (BV) '45 '71 C.813 B.A. L.1067 J.D.
1040 Main St. (⊙St. Helena)
**Ross, Grace Goodman** ..............'58 '83 C.112 B.A. L.800 J.D. [⊠ Dickenson,P.&F.]
*LANGUAGES: Spanish.
*PRACTICE AREAS: Estate Planning; Trust Administration; Land Use.
Rosson, Elise W. ....................'— '78 C.813 B.A. L.1065 J.D. 4294 Big Ranch Rd.
Rossy, Mary A. ........................'37 '83 C.999 A.S. L.1153 J.D. 907 Jefferson St.
Ryan, S. Katelin ............ '46 '88 C.447 B.A. L.1065 J.D. 1370 Trancas St. (⊙Fairfield)
**Savitch, Rhonda Lee** ............'52 '93 C.112 A.B. L.1065 J.D. [⊠ Gaw,V.S.M.&M.]
*LANGUAGES: French and Italian.
*PRACTICE AREAS: Civil Litigation; Land Use; Insurance Coverage; Bad Faith Litigation.
Schetter, Carl F. ..................'32 '59 C&L.436 B.S., J.D. 1040 Main St., Suite 303
Sellers, Eldon ......................'21 '72 C.999 B.M. L.284 J.D. 1246 Olive Hill Ln.
**Shackelford, C. Preston**, (AV) ..........'48 '74 C.1044 B.A. L.1066 J.D. [Coombs&D.]
*PRACTICE AREAS: Family Law; Municipal Law; Probate Law.
Silver, Brian R., (BV) ........................'42 '69 C&L.309 A.B., LL.B. 816 Brown St.
**Skidmore, L. Randolph** ..............'46 '76 C.112 A.B. L.1188 J.D. [Coombs&D.]⊙
*PRACTICE AREAS: Business Law; Real Estate Law.
Smith, Douglas N., (BV) ................'48 '77 C.1078 B.A. L.464 J.D. 1207 Coombs St.
**Smith, Wyman G., III**, (BV) ..........'50 '76 C.174 B.A. L.464 J.D. [Gaw,V.S.M.&M.]⊙
*PRACTICE AREAS: Business; Corporate; Real Estate Transactions.
Snowden, Randolph F. '49 '74
C.112 A.B. L.1067 J.D. Admr., Adolescent Treatment Center, Inc.
Snowden, W. Scott ......................'46 '72 C.902 A.B. L.1066 J.D. Supr. Ct. J.

Spencer, Stephen C. ....................'50 '79 C.221 B.A. L.1137 J.D. 372 Blue Jay Way
Spohn, Vincent M., (BV) ..................'48 '80 C&L.602 A.B., J.D. 1005 Jefferson St.
Stanton, Richard C. ..............................'26 '51 C&L.813 A.B., J.D. 21 Syar Dr.‡
Stanton, Stephen G. ......................'39 '65 C.668 B.A. L.1065 J.D. 301 River St.
Stevens, Hjordis C. '24 '51 C.061 L.94 LL.B.
(adm. in MA; not adm. in CA) 118 Valley Club Cir.‡
Stone, Rodney G., (BV) ....................'48 '80 C.1060 B.S. L.1026 J.D. 822 Brown St.
Strauss, Elizabeth A., (BV) ..............'49 '74 C.112 B.A. L.1068 J.D. 1595 King Ave.
**Terry, James W.**, (BV) ..............'49 '76 C.112 A.B. L.770 J.D. [⊠ Dickenson,P.&F.]
*LANGUAGES: French.
*PRACTICE AREAS: Corporate; Business Law; Banking Law; Real Property; Estate Planning and Administration.
Thomas, Brad S. ..........................'58 '89 C.101 B.A. L.1065 J.D. 1031 Jefferson St.
Thomas, Stephen J. ......................'61 '89 C.1074 B.S. L.1065 J.D. 1031 Jefferson St.
Tisher, Francisca P. ......................'52 '80 C.112 B.A. L.1227 J.D. 3920 Hagen Rd.
Toller, Frank G. ..............................'43 '69 C&L.767 B.A., J.D. 809 Coombs St.
**Van Male, Nicholas R.**, (AV) ...... '38 '71 C.112 A.B. L.1067 J.D. [Gaw,V.S.M.&M.]⊙
*PRACTICE AREAS: Civil Litigation; Family Law; Land Use Planning Law.
Vieira, Marc W. ..........................'48 '74 C.766 B.A. L.767 J.D. Mun. Ct. Comr.
Wagner, J. Roland, (AV) ..................'37 '69 C.999 L.765 J.D. [J.R.Wagner]
Wagner, J. Roland, A P.C., (AV) ..................................P.O. Box 3248
Walker, Herbert W. ..........................'33 '59 C.813 B.A. L.800 J.D. Supr. Ct. J.
Walzl, L. Jody '55 '84 C.445 B.S. L.64 J.D.
(adm. in MD; not adm. in CA) 2521 Aspen Way‡
Westmeyer, Robert, (AV) ..................'45 '72 C.229 B.S. L.878 J.D. Co. Coun.
Worthington, Frank, (BV) ............'38 '65 C.112 A.B. L.1066 LL.B. 2040 Jefferson St.
York, Ellen M., (BV) ..........................'50 '75 C.112 B.A. L.1065 J.D. [York&Y.]
York & York, (BV) ..................................................822 Brown St.
Yost, Rebecca Anne ..................'60 '88 C.147 B.A. L.284 J.D. [⊠ Fershko,L.&B.]
Young, Ronald T. L. ..................'48 '73 C.351 B.A. L.36 J.D. Mun. Ct. J.
Zaltsman, David L. ......................'57 '84 C.273 B.A. L.597 J.D. Dep. Co. Coun.
**Zeller, Cathy A.** ......................'52 '82 C.112 A.B. L.765 J.D. [Zeller,H.&Z.]
*PRACTICE AREAS: Estate Planning; Probate; Guardianships; Conservatorship; Business and Corporations.
**Zeller, Robert H.**, (AV) ..................'24 '52 C.112 A.B. L.1065 J.D. [Zeller,H.&Z.]
*PRACTICE AREAS: Estate Planning; Probate Law; Living Trusts and Wills; Corporate Law; Real Estate Transactions.

**Zeller, Hoff & Zeller, Inc., (AV)**
**929 Randolph Street, 94559-2997**
**Telephone: 707-252-6633 FAX: 707-252-9204**
**Robert H. Zeller; Paul M. Hoff; Cathy A. Zeller.**
**General Civil and Trial Practice. Probate, Wills, Trusts, Estate Planning and Administration, Construction, Real Property, Corporate, Family Law. Commercial and Banking, Municipal Law, Insurance Law, Negligence, Personal Injury, Tort Law, Real Property and Governmental Entity Litigation.**
**Reference: Napa Valley Bank.**
*See Professional Biographies, NAPA, CALIFORNIA*

## NATIONAL CITY, 54,249, *San Diego Co.*

Binkle, Michael K. ....................'60 '85 C.602 B.A. L.1067 J.D. 2727 Hoover Ave.
Dewell, Ernest P. ..........................'39 '74 C.475 B.S. L.61 J.D. 2732 Grove St.
Gonzales, Jorge O. ....................'49 '79 C.763 A.B. L.477 J.D. 1810 Palm Ave.
Harter, Linda Kaye, (BV) ............'48 '75 C.1097 B.A. L.1049 J.D. Sr. Asst. City Atty.
Hlawatsch, Alfred G., (BV) ................'40 '67 C.668 B.A. L.208 J.D. 711 E. 16th St.
Moore, Robert G., (AV) ....................'36 '70 C.1074 B.S. L.1026 J.D. [R.G.Moore]
Moore, Robert G., A Professional Corporation, (AV) ................ 2414 Hoover Ave.
Teyssier, Paul ......................'52 '81 C.112 B.A. L.809 J.D. 3200 Highland Ave.
Winter, Jeffrey M. ........................'59 '87 C.877 B.A. L.61 J.D. 212 W. 24th St.

## NEEDLES, 5,191, *San Bernardino Co.*

George, Ralph F., Jr. ..........................'52 '86 L.1137 J.D. 119 F Street
Sherman, Margaret T., (Mrs.) '27 '51 C&L.150 B.A., LL.B.
(adm. in OH; not adm. in CA) Route 4, Box 321‡

**Welebir & McCune, A Professional Law Corporation**
**(See Redlands)**

## NEVADA CITY, * 2,855, *Nevada Co.*

Anderson, Jim, (BV) ......................'47 '74 C.588 B.S.M.E. L.1065 J.D. City Atty.
Andrew, Francis E. '38 '68 C.221 B.A. L.597 J.D.
(adm. in IA; not adm. in CA) 14618 Tyler Foote Rd.‡
Bass, Alvin S. ........................'41 '68 C.563 B.S. L.273 J.D. 14327 Sunrock Rd.‡
Bass, Joleen B. ..................................................'51 '81 510 Main St.
Bergman, Robert J. ......................'47 '77 C.112 B.A. L.800 J.D. P.O. Box 1924
**Berliner, Eric L.**, (CV) ..........................'63 '91 C.285 B.A. L.767 J.D. [Berliner]
**Berliner, Harold A.**, (AV) ......................'23 '51 C.767 L.602 J.D. [Berliner]

**Berliner Law Offices, (AV)** ⊞
**224 Main Street, 95959**
**Telephone: 916-265-5585 Fax: 916-478-0303**
**Email: berlinlw@nccn.net**
**Harold A. Berliner; Eric L. Berliner. Associate: Lawrence D. Sanders.**
**General Civil Practice emphasizing Corporate Law and Civil Litigation, Taxation.**
*See Professional Biographies, NEVADA CITY, CALIFORNIA*

Berry, Kristina Gayle ....................'62 '90 C.147 B.A. L.818 J.D. Dep. Dist. Atty.
Brick, Brian E., (AV) ......................'54 '79 C.112 B.A. L.426 J.D. P.O. Box 787
Bryan, Carl F., II ..............................'48 '74 C.112 B.A. L.426 J.D. Sup. Ct. J.
Burton, Richard ........................'44 '70 C.763 B.S. L.1068 J.D. 301 Broad St.
Butz, M. Kathleen, (AV) ......................'50 '82 C.112 B.A. L.1067 J.D. Cthse.
Campbell, Richard N., (BV) ................'43 '72 C.475 B.S. L.477 J.D. Pub. Def.
**Clinch, Nanci G.**, (BV) ........................'50 '77 C.37 B.A. L.1049 J.D. [N.G.Clinch]

**Clinch, Nanci G., A Professional Corporation, (BV)**
**Suite 204, 401 Spring Street, 95959**
**Telephone: 916-265-8690 Fax: 916-265-8694**
**Nanci G. Clinch (Certified Specialist, Family Law, The State Bar of California Board of Legal Specializations).**
**Family Law.**
*See Professional Biographies, NEVADA CITY, CALIFORNIA*

Darlington, John ..........................'44 '70 C.1077 B.A. L.426 J.D. Supr. Ct. J.
De Graw, Harold E. ....................'43 '69 C.623 B.A. L.1065 J.D. Asst. Co. Coun.
Di Lorenzo, Robert J. ....................'48 '81 C.766 B.A. L.61 J.D. P.O. Box 206
Dodds, James M. ......................'35 '63 C.813 B.A. L.800 LL.B. P.O. Box 832‡
Dover, Albert P. ..............................'48 '74 C&L.37 B.S., J.D. Mun. Ct. J.
Dowling, Sean P., (BV) ............'49 '74 C&L.767 B.S., J.D. 103 Providence Mine Rd.
Dremann, James E. ....................'43 '73 C&L.112 B.A., J.D. 234 Commercial St.
Edwards, Ersel L., (BV) ..............................'41 '74 C&L.1186 J.D. Mun. Ct. J.
Ellers, Richard F., A Professional Corporation, (BV) '44 '71
C.629 B.A. L.1065 J.D. P.O. Box 927
Esrey, Denise L. ..........................'59 '90 C.267 B.S. L.464 J.D. Dep. Dist. Atty.

**Farrar, Charles R., Jr., Law Offices of**
(See Grass Valley)

Ferguson, Michael W. . . . . '46 '72 C.112 B.A. L.1065 J.D. Dist. Atty.
Filipps, David A. . . . '57 '83 C.1163 B.S. L.800 J.D. Corp. Coun., Ridgewood Assocs., Inc.
Francis, Frank D. . . . . '34 '63 C&L.767 B.S., J.D. Supr. Ct. J.
Frishman, Richard A., (BV) . . . . '48 '74 C.112 B.A. L.800 J.D. 206 Sacramento St.
Gabrielli, Warren D. . . . . '26 '55 C.768 A.B. L.1026 LL.B. 12305 Valley View Rd.‡
Geffner, Daniel M. . . . . '49 '75 C.910 A.B. L.30 J.D. Co. Pub. Def.
Haas, Stephen C. . . . . '47 '72 C.1042 B.A. L.426 J.D. P.O. Box 1740
Haley, Allan S., (AV) . . . . '44 '70 C&L.309 A.B., J.D. 1710 (©Sacramento)
Hamilton, Patricia C., (BV) . . . . '46 '79 C.112 B.A. L.464 J.D. Research Atty., Supr. Ct.
Hart, John E. '39 '64 C.684 B.A. L.800 J.D.
Secy., Treas. & Gen. Coun., Creative Medical Develop., Inc.
Hartman, Linda M. . . . . '47 '80 C.1060 B.A. L.464 J.D. Dep. Co. Coun.
Kaufman, Steven R., (BV) . . . . '45 '71 C.112 B.S. L.1068 J.D. 103 Providence Mine Rd.
Kottcamp, Glenn M. . . . . '46 '80 C.267 B.A. L.1189 J.D. 308 Main St.
**Kraemer, Holly**, (BV) . . . . '44 '84 C.112 B.A. L.878 J.D. [Spiller,M.&K.]
*LANGUAGES: French.
*PRACTICE AREAS: Business and Real Estate Transactions; General Civil Litigation.
Kroeker, Dennis W. . . . . '46 '72 C.112 B.A. L.1065 J.D. 531 Uren St.
Krumm, Jeffrey D. '52 '78 C.1169 A.B. L.1065 J.D.
Chief Dep. Dist. Atty., Nevada Cty. Dist. Atty's Office
Malott, Richard A. . . . . '33 '57 C.330 A.B. L.1066 J.D. 10099 Ridgewood Rd.‡
Malott, Russell E. . . . . '66 '92 C.636 B.B.A. L.990 J.D. CEO, Ridgewood Assoc. Inc.
Manka, Paul J. . . . . '52 '79 C.112 B.A. L.398 J.D. 107 Court St.
McCall, Cheryl . . . . '50 '90 C.976 M.S.L. L.1066 J.D. 205 N. Pine St.
McPherson, King G., (BV) . . . . '45 '76 C.911 B.S. L.765 J.D. 439 Coyote St.
**McProud, Clarence H.**, (BV) . . . . '54 '79 C.112 B.S. L.1067 J.D. [Spiller,M.&K.]
*REPORTED CASES: Neighborhood Action Group v. County of Calaveras, 156 Cal. App. 3d. 1176 (1984).
*PRACTICE AREAS: Property Law; Probate and Estate Planning; Business Law.
Minch, Janet A. . . . . '45 '80 C.768 B.A. L.464 J.D. 206 Sacramento St.
Morrison, John M. . . . . '22 '53 C.768 A.B. L.767 LL.B. 11133 Ridge Rd.‡

**Munkelt, Stephen A., (BV) '50 '78 C.112 B.A. L.1049 J.D.**
**107 Court Street, 95959**
Telephone: 916-265-8508 Fax: 916-265-0881
Email: smunk@gv.net
*REPORTED CASES: People v. Aldridge (1984) 35 Cal. 3d 473; People v. Schroeder (1991) 227 Cal. App. 3d 784.
*PRACTICE AREAS: Criminal Defense Law; Civil Litigation; Personal Injury-Plaintiff. Civil and Criminal Litigation, and Family Law.
*See Professional Biographies, NEVADA CITY, CALIFORNIA*

**Oleson, Raymond C.**, (AV) . . . . '50 '76 C.813 A.B. L.597 J.D. [Oleson]©
*REPORTED CASES: CNA Casualty v. Seaboard Surety 176 Cal. App. 3d 598 (1986); Lunsford v. American Guarantee and Liability, 18 F.3d 653 (9th Cir. 1994).

**Oleson Law Corporation, (AV)**
**11931 Willow Valley Road, 95959©**
Telephone: 916-478-0415 Fax: 916-478-0184
Email: olelaw@oro.net
Raymond C. Oleson.
General Civil Litigation emphasizing Insurance Coverage, Environmental, Real Estate, Business and Construction Litigation.
San Francisco, California Office: 601 California Street, Suite 800. Telephone: 415-392-0415. Fax: 415-392-0372.
*See Professional Biographies, NEVADA CITY, CALIFORNIA*

Palarz, Herman S., (AV) . . . . '37 '63 C.112 B.A. L.800 LL.B. [Tyre K.K.&G.]©
Palley, David B., (BV) . . . . '46 '75 C.309 A.B. L.1066 J.D. 103 Providence Mine Rd.
Rathe, Mark W. . . . . '58 '85 C.1169 B.A. L.767 J.D. Co. Coun.
Ray, Susan Ellenbogen . . . . '45 '77 C.112 B.A. L.1095 J.D. 308 Main St.
Reich, Lorraine A., (CV) . . . . '49 '81 L.809 J.D. 207 N. Pine St.

**Rich, Fuidge, Morris & Iverson, Inc.**
(See Marysville)

**Roach, Terry A., (AV) '38 '66 C.813 B.A. L.1065 LL.B.**
**14137 Banner Mountain Lookout Road, P.O. Box 1558, 95959**
Telephone: 916-265-2475 FAX: 916-265-3198
Email: terryr@treehouse.org
Real Property, Land Use, Environmental, Business Law, Estate Planning and Probate, Computer Law, General Civil Trial and Appellate Practice and Alternative Dispute Resolution.
*See Professional Biographies, NEVADA CITY, CALIFORNIA*

Roberts, George A., (BV) . . . . '48 '77 C.1077 B.A. L.1095 J.D. [Roberts,R.&R.]
Roberts, Roberts & Roberts, (BV) . . . . 301 Broad St.
Rollin, Bonnie L. . . . . '41 '89 C.766 B.S. L.284 J.D. P.O. Box 239
**Sanders, Lawrence D.** . . . . '67 '94 C.145 B.A. L.629 J.D. [A Berliner]

**Shine, Compton & Nelder-Adams**
(See Grass Valley)

Simmons, Duncan M. . . . . '52 '82 C.112 B.A. L.1026 J.D. State Lands Comm.
**Spiller, Steven T.**, (BV) . . . . '46 '76 C.605 B.A. L.420 J.D. [Spiller,M.&K.]
*REPORTED CASES: Moylan v. Dykes, 181 Cal.App. 3d. 561 (1986).
*PRACTICE AREAS: Commercial Litigation; Real Property; Business Transactions.

**Spiller, McProud & Kraemer, (AV)**
**505 Coyote Street, Suite A, 95959**
Telephone: 916-265-5831 Telecopier: 916-265-5836
URL: http://www.SMBK.COM
Steven T. Spiller; Clarence H. McProud; Holly Kraemer.
General Civil Trial Practice. Real Property, Land Use and Environmental Law, Commercial Litigation, Probate, Administrative, Corporate, Mediation and Arbitration.
*See Professional Biographies, NEVADA CITY, CALIFORNIA*

Thomsen, Lynn A. . . . . '62 '87 C.112 L.464 J.D. 241 Commercial St.
Tyre Kamins Katz & Granof, (AV) . . . . 419 Broad St. (©Los Angeles, CA)
Walters, David M. . . . . '47 '77 C.112 B.A. L.763 J.D. Courthouse
Wellner, Melanie K. . . . . '— '84 C.112 L.410 J.D. Dep. Co. Coun.
Wetherall, Wm. B., (AV) . . . . '11 '37 C&L.336 B.A., LL.B. 222 Church St.
Wilson, Jeffrey R. . . . . '49 '81 C.1074 B.S. L.464 J.D. 107 Court St.
Wolfson, Ronald A., (CV) . . . . '44 '75 C.112 B.A. L.809 J.D. Asst. Dist. Atty.

## NEWARK, 37,861, *Alameda Co.*

Abel, Timothy, (BV) . . . . '29 '57 C.112 L.1065 J.D. 3900 New Park Mall, 3rd Fl.
Allen, Sydney M., (Mrs.) . . . . '28 '52 C&L.813 A.B., LL.B. 6031 Joaquin Murieta Ave.‡
Bernard, Steven M., (BV) . . . . '46 '73 C.563 B.A. L.1009 J.D. 3900 Newpark Mall, 3rd Fl.
Brill, Jennifer L. . . . . '65 '92 C.477 B.A. L.209 J.D. 3900 New Park Mall, 3rd Fl.
Johnson, Robert Lowell, (BV) . . . . '49 '80 C.112 B.S. L.770 J.D. 5800 Thorton Ave.
Knutsen, Thomas E., (BV) . . . . '52 '77 C.950 B.S. L.285 J.D. 3900 Newpark Mall, 3rd Fl.
Lawrence, Raymond P., (BV) '20 '56 C.352 B.S. L.765 LL.B.
6100 Joaquin Murieta Ave.
MacKenzie, Stuart I. . . . . '52 '80 C.1066 B.A. L.284 J.D. 3900 New Park Mall Rd., 3rd Fl.

Schechter, Paul B. '44 '70 C.46 B.S. L.424 J.D.
(adm. in IL; not adm. in CA) Gingiss Formalwear

## NEWBURY PARK, —, *Ventura Co.*

Custodio, Laura Lee . . . . '51 '91 17 San Lucas Ave.
Rogers, Robert K., Jr. . . . . '44 '77 C.763 A.B. L.101 J.D. 587F N. Ventu Park Rd.
Thomas, John C. . . . . '42 '78 C.1077 B.A. L.1095 J.D. 2696 Lavery Ct.‡
Watkins, Russell T. . . . . '44 '79 C.999 B.S. L.1190 J.D. 376 S. Havenside Ave.

## NEW CASTLE, —, *Placer Co.*

**Schnetz, Karl J., (CV) '35 '77 C.1060 A.B. L.1026 J.D.**
**671 Newcastle Road, Suite 1, P.O. Box 291, 95658**
Telephone: 916-663-1100 Fax: 916-663-2602
*LANGUAGES: Spanish, German and French.
*PRACTICE AREAS: Personal Injury; Civil Litigation; Insurance Law; Real Estate; Contracts. Personal Injury, Civil Litigation, Insurance Law, Real Estate, Contracts and Criminal Law.
*See Professional Biographies, NEW CASTLE, CALIFORNIA*

## NEWHALL, 9,651, *Los Angeles Co.*

Abdallah, Ahmed M. . . . . '37 '79 L.061 LL.B. 24932 High Spring Ave.
Adams, Adrian W. . . . . '23 '51 C.605 L.426 LL.B. 24201 Colwyn Ave.‡
Carabino, Joseph C., (BV) . . . . '47 '77 C.1044 B.A. L.1137 J.D. P.O. Box 220939
Delnero, David S., A Professional Law Corporation, (BV) '48 '75
C.112 B.A. L.800 J.D. 24273 San Fernando Rd., 2nd Fl.
Kotler, Richard L. . . . . '52 '80 C.1078 B.A. L.809 J.D. 23942 Lyons Ave.
Lynn, Spencer W. . . . . '21 '50 C.800 B.S. L.616 LL.B. 6209 N. Barnes‡
Phelan, Michael J. . . . . '38 '67 C.426 B.B.A. L.1065 LL.B. 24509 Walnut St.
Vogel, Willard B. . . . . '22 '62 C.800 L.809 LL.B. 25207 Atwood Blvd.
Wolfe, Edward E. . . . . '07 '41 C.569 L.1009 LL.B. 19825 Avenue of the Oaks

## NEWMAN, 4,151, *Stanislaus Co.*

Densmore, Harold R. . . . . '18 '52 C.112 A.B. L.1065 J.D. City Atty.‡
Jensen, J. Wilmar, (AV) . . . . '27 '52 C&L.813 B.A., LL.B. [Jensen&J.]©
Jensen, Mark R. . . . . '60 '87 C.1169 B.A. L.464 J.D. [Jensen&J.]©
Jensen & Jensen, (AV) . . . . 1031 Fresno St. (©Modesto & Oakdale)
Stephens, Carrie Maureen . . . . '64 '90 C&L.464 B.S., J.D. 1107 "S" St.

## NEWPORT BEACH, 66,643, *Orange Co.*

**Abendroth, Douglas W.** . . . . '52 '82 C.112 B.A. L.426 J.D. [O'Melveny&M.]
Abney, Michael L. . . . . '61 '88 C.421 B.A. L.309 J.D. 4675 MacArthur Ct.
Adams, Mark S. . . . . '55 '86 C.112 B.S. L.426 J.D. 610 Newport Center Dr.
Adams, William C., (AV) . . . . '28 '55 C&L.800 B.A., J.D. 1800 Kings Rd.‡
**Adams, William G.**, (AV) . . . . '39 '69 C.813 A.B. L.878 J.D. [O'Melveny&M.]
*LANGUAGES: French.
*PRACTICE AREAS: Corporate Securities; International Law.
**Adkinson, Don R.**, (AV) . . . . '28 '56 C.668 B.A. L.1066 LL.B. [Barger&W.]
*PRACTICE AREAS: Real Property Law; Estate Planning Law; Probate Law; Municipal Law.
Adler, Kenneth S. . . . . '44 '78 C&L.1137 B.S.L., J.D. [Adler&S.]
Adler & Stauffer, A P.C. . . . . 2022 Quail St.
**Aires, Timothy Carl** . . . . '62 '88 C.763 B.S. L.464 J.D. [Bruck&P.]
*PRACTICE AREAS: Commercial Litigation; Creditor's Rights; Enforcement of Judgments.
**Akhtar, Adeel S.** . . . . '70 '94 C.06 B.Sc. L.309 J.D. [Knobbe,M.O.&B.]
*LANGUAGES: French, Urdu, Arabic.
**Akins, Julie McCoy** . . . . '58 '83 C.69 B.A. L.802 J.D. [Stradling,Y.C.&R.]

**Alcorn, John R., Law Offices of, (AV) '49 '75 C.813 B.A. L.770 J.D.**
**500 Newport Center Drive, Suite 300, 92660**
Telephone: 714-721-1100 Fax: 714-721-9700
(Certified Specialist, Immigration and Nationality Law, The State Bar of California Board of Legal Specialization).
*LANGUAGES: German.
*PRACTICE AREAS: Deportation; Asylum; Immigration; U.S. Work Visas; Appeals. U.S. Immigration and Nationality Law.
*See Professional Biographies, NEWPORT BEACH, CALIFORNIA*

**Alcser, Marc G.** . . . . '69 '96 C.800 B.S. L.1067 J.D. [A Stradling,Y.C.&R.]
**Alexander, Craig C.**, (AV) . . . . '52 '77 C.35 B.S. L.1065 J.D. [© Self&B.]
*PRACTICE AREAS: Estate Planning; Probate; Estate Administration; Pension and Profit Sharing Plans; Taxation.
**Allen, Robert F., Jr.**, (AV) . . . . '49 '74 C.112 B.S. L.464 J.D. [Allen&F.]
*PRACTICE AREAS: Civil Trial Practice; Appellate Practice; Personal Injury Law; Products Liability Law; Insurance Coverage.
**Allen, Russell G.**, (AV) . . . . '46 '71 C.293 B.A. L.813 J.D. [O'Melveny&M.]

**Allen & Flatt, Incorporated, (AV)**
**Suite 370, 4400 MacArthur Boulevard, 92660**
Telephone: 714-752-7474 FAX: 714-752-1645
Robert F. Allen, Jr.; John C. Flatt;—James E. Ballidis; Suzanne Boyer Leslie; John A. El-Farra.
General Civil Trial and Appellate Practice. Personal Injury, Products Liability, Insurance Coverage, Insurance Defense, Negligence, Bad Faith and Business Litigation. Trials in all State and Federal Courts.
Reference: Bank of America, Newport Beach.
*See Professional Biographies, NEWPORT BEACH, CALIFORNIA*

**Altman, Daniel E.** . . . . '58 '89 C.339 B.S. L.1066 J.D. [Knobbe,M.O.&B.] (See Pat. Sect.)

**Alvarado, Smith, Villa & Sanchez, A Professional Corporation, (AV) BB**
**Suite 800, 4695 MacArthur Court, P.O. Box 8677, 92658-8677©**
Telephone: 714-955-1433 Fax: 714-955-1704
URL: http://www.Alvarado-Smith.com
Raymond G. Alvarado (Resident, Los Angeles Office); Ruben A. Smith; Maurice Sanchez; Fernando Villa (Resident, Los Angeles Office); John M. Sorich; Barbara L. Tang; Raúl F. Salinas (Resident Los Angeles Office);—J. Michelle Hickey (Resident, Los Angeles Office); John B. Carmichael, III; Frances Q. Jett (Resident, Los Angeles Office); Susan Bade Hull (Resident, Los Angeles Office); Christopher M. Leo; Amy Toboco Dibb; Steven M. Lawrence (Resident, Los Angeles Office); Robert W. Brown, Jr. (Resident, Los Angeles Office); Steven C. Yung (Resident, Los Angeles Office); Thomas A. Zeigler; Roger E. Borg.
Sophisticated Business Transactions and Complex Litigation.
Los Angeles, California Office, 611 West Sixth Street, Suite 2650. Telephone: 213-229-2554. Fax: 213-617-8966.
*See Professional Biographies, NEWPORT BEACH, CALIFORNIA*

**Amundsen, Roland J.** . . . . '53 '87 C.1042 B.A. L.1137 J.D. [Young&A.]
*PRACTICE AREAS: General; Real Estate; Construction Litigation; General Tort Law.
Andersen, R. Lee '47 '76 C.477 B.A. L.260 J.D.
(adm. in FL; not adm. in CA) 1300 Dove St.‡

**Andersen & Waldron, (AV)**
**610 Newport Center Drive Suite 750, 92660©**
Telephone: 714-760-0204 Telecopier: 714-760-2507
Partners: Gary A. Waldron; Kyle L. Crenshaw. Associates: Carol Foster; Janet L. Callister; Sherry S. Bragg.
Real Property, Business and Commercial Litigation, including Civil Trial and Appellate Practice in all State and Federal Courts, with special emphasis on Title Insurance Defense, Bankruptcy and Lender Liability. Real Estate and Business Transactions including Acquisition and Development Agreements, Partnership, Joint Venture and Construction Contracts and Loan Documentation.

(This Listing Continued)

**Andersen & Waldron (Continued)**
San Diego, California Office: 350 West Ash Street, Suite 700. Telephone: 619-233-8292. Telecopier: 619-233-8636.

**Anderson, Eric G.** ... '61 '89 C.1074 B.S. L.800 J.D. [Davis,P.K.&W.]
*PRACTICE AREAS: Business Litigation.
**Anderson, Lowell** '50 '82 C.546 B.S.M.E. L.1065 J.D. [Knobbe,M.O.&B.] (See Pat. Sect.)
Anderson, Margaret R. ... '33 '78 C&L.1137 B.S.L., J.D. Mun. Ct. J.
Andres, James B. ... '50 '76 C.636 B.A. L.1065 J.D. 207 La Jolla Dr.
Angelo, Joseph, (BV) ... '45 '74 C.1042 B.S. L.61 J.D. 23 Corp. Plaza Dr.
Anslow, Robert E. ... '59 '84 C.605 B.A. L.1148 J.D. 4920 Campus Dr.
Arabian, Allison A. ... '65 '90 C.112 B.A. L.1065 J.D. 3501 Jamboree Rd. Ste 6000
Ardon, Karen ... '65 '90 C.94 B.S. L.800 J.D. 4675 MacArthur Ct.
Arneson, Joan C. ... '52 '77 C.112 B.A. L.1067 J.D. [Bowie A.K.W.&G.]
**Arnold, Larry M., (Professional Corporation)**, (AV) '49 '74 C.800 B.A. L.61 J.D. [Cummins&W.]
*PRACTICE AREAS: Civil Litigation; Insurance; Real Estate; Environmental; Business.
**Arrington, R. Patrick**, (AV) ... '42 '68 C.560 B.A. L.309 LL.B. [Brobeck,P.&H.]
*PRACTICE AREAS: Corporate Securities.
Arthur, David J. '56 '81 C.112 B.S. L.950 J.D. Intell. Prop. Atty., Rockwell International Corporation (Pat.)
Ashin, Robert W. ... '52 '78 C.800 B.S. L.426 J.D. 390 Seawind Dr.
Ashlock, Howard J. ... '52 '91 C.1075 B.S. L.1137 J.D. 4695 MacArthur Ct., Ste., 840
**Ashton, Helaine S.** ... '53 '88 C&L.1137 B.S.L., J.D. [Kimball,T.&S.] (⊙San Diego)
*PRACTICE AREAS: Landlord/Tenant.
**Ashworth, Mark S.**, (BV) ... '51 '78 C.101 B.S. L.1137 J.D. [Ashworth&M.]
*PRACTICE AREAS: Professional Liability; General Civil Litigation; Insurance Defense; Chiropractic Malpractice Law; Medical Malpractice Law.

**Ashworth & Moran, (AV)**
**18 Corporate Plaza, Suite 114, 92660⊙**
**Telephone: 714-720-1477 Fax: 714-720-1478**
**Mark S. Ashworth.**
**General Civil, Trial and Appellate Practice. State and Federal Courts, Corporation, Business and Real Estate Law, Estate Planning.**
**Laguna Niguel, California Office: 28202 Cabot Road, Suite 300. Telephone: 714-365-5776. Fax: 714-365-5720.**
*See Professional Biographies, NEWPORT BEACH, CALIFORNIA*

**Atzen, Jonathan F.** ... '65 '91 C.112 B.A. L.426 J.D. [Ⓐ Brobeck,P.&H.]
*LANGUAGES: Spanish.
*PRACTICE AREAS: Corporate Law; Securities Law; Venture Capital Law; Health Care Law.
Audick, Mary D. ... '54 '80 C.66 B.A. L.776 J.D. F.D.I.C.
Austero, Wayne J., (AV) ... '45 '71 C.800 A.B. L.426 J.D. 3 Civic Plaza
**Auw, Pierre E.**, (BV) ... '29 '64 C.642 L.809 [Ⓐ H.E.Westover&Assoc.]
*PRACTICE AREAS: Trust Law; Probate Law; Estate Planning Law.
Avey, Victoria C., (AV) ... '— '78 C.378 B.S. L.734 J.D. 4340 Campus Dr.
Baade, David R., (AV) ... '42 '70 C.800 B.A. L.1049 J.D. 3501 Jamboree
**Babcock, Brenton R.** ... '64 '92 C.112 B.S.M.E. L.276 J.D. [Knobbe,M.O.&B.]
**Babcock, Richard J.** ... '63 '89 C&L.879 B.S., J.D. [Ⓐ Brobeck,P.&H.]
*PRACTICE AREAS: Health Care Law.
**Baik, Steven S.** ... '68 '96 C.1074 B.S.E.E. L.1065 J.D. [Ⓐ Howard,R.N.C.F.&R.]
*PRACTICE AREAS: Patents; Copyright; Trademark; General Litigation.
Baker, John H. ... '51 '79 C.339 B.A. L.1148 J.D. [Ⓐ Barclay]
**Baker, John S.** ... '60 '89 C.1214 B.S. L.494 J.D. [Ⓐ Brobeck,P.&H.]
*PRACTICE AREAS: General Corporate Law; Securities Law.
**Baker, Kevin Ray** ... '61 '89 C.154 B.A. L.309 J.D. [Ⓒ O'Melveny&M.]
*PRACTICE AREAS: Mergers and Acquisitions; Securities Offerings; Franchise Law and General Corporate Matters.
Baker, Robert M.L., III '65 '92 C.112 B.A. L.809 J.D. 4750 Von Karman Ave. (⊙Santa Monica)

**Baldikoski, Charles & Kane**
**4695 MacArthur Court, Suite 860, 92660**
**Telephone: 714-852-8868 Facsimile: 714-852-9878**
**Thomas H. Baldikoski (1937-1993); Bruce H. Charles; Stephen M. Kane.**
**General Business, Corporate, Business Finance, and Real Property Law and Transactions.**
*See Professional Biographies, NEWPORT BEACH, CALIFORNIA*

**Balfour MacDonald Mijuskovic & Olmsted, A Professional Corporation**
(See Costa Mesa)

**Ballidis, James E.**, (BV) ... '55 '85 C.1042 B.S. L.809 J.D. [Ⓐ Allen&F.]
*PRACTICE AREAS: Civil Trial Practice; Appellate Practice; Personal Injury Law; Products Liability Law; Negligence Law.
**Balog, Timothy A.** ... '62 '94 C.161 B.B.A. L.1137 J.D. [Balog&R.]
*PRACTICE AREAS: Sports Law; Estate Planning; Probate; Corporate; Family Law.

**Balog & Rasch**
**1601 Dove Street, Suite 184, 92660**
**Telephone: 714-851-2500 Fax: 714-851-2520**
**Members of Firm: Timothy A. Balog; Robert M. Rasch.**
**Sports, Transactions, Estate Planning, Probate, Corporate, Family and Real Property Law.**
*See Professional Biographies, NEWPORT BEACH, CALIFORNIA*

**Bancroft, Ellen S.** ... '65 '90 C.347 B.S. L.880 J.D. [Ⓐ Brobeck,P.&H.]
*PRACTICE AREAS: Corporate; Securities.
Barclay, John A., (AV) ... '51 '75 C&L.800 B.A., J.D. [Barclay]
Barclay Law Corporation, (AV) ... 5000 Birch Street, Suite 2900

**Barger & Wolen, (AV)**
**19800 MacArthur Boulevard, Suite 800 (Irvine), 92715⊙**
**Telephone: 714-757-2800 FAX: 714-752-6313**
**Email: barwol@ix.netcom.com**
**Members of Firm: Don R. Adkinson (Resident); Dennis W. Harwood (Resident); John M. Meindl (Resident); Edwin A. Oster (Resident). Associates: Eric M. Crowe; J. Ronald Ignatuk (Resident); Robert K. Renner (Resident).**
**General Civil Practice. Banking, Municipal, Tax, Corporation, Securities, Real Property, Construction, Family, Estate Planning, Probate, Business and Bankruptcy Law. Trial and Appeals.**
**References: Bank of America (Los Angeles Main Office); Security Pacific National Bank (Los Angeles Main Office).**
**Los Angeles, California Office: 515 South Flower Street, 34th Floor, 90071. Telephone: 213-680-2800. Cable Address: "Barwol". Facsimile: 213-614-7399.**
**San Francisco, California Office: 47th Floor, 101 California Street, 94111. Telephone: 415-434-2800. FAX: 415-434-2533.**
**New York, N.Y. Office: 100 Park Avenue, 23rd Floor, 10017. Telephone: 212-557-2800. FAX: 212-213-1199.**
**Sacramento, California Office: 925 "L" Street, Suite 1100, 95814. Telephone: 916-448-2800. FAX: 916-442-5961.**
*See Professional Biographies, NEWPORT BEACH, CALIFORNIA*

Barnes, Stephen G. ... '61 '90 C.1001 B.A. L.1137 J.D. [Barnes&F.]
Barnes & Farrell ... 1301 Dove St.
**Barney, Johnathan A.** ... '65 '93 C.886 B.S.M.E. L.477 J.D. [Knobbe,M.O.&B.]
Barone, James P., (AV) ... '54 '80 C.1122 B.A. L.990 J.D. [J.P.Barone]
Barone, James P., A Professional Law Corporation, (AV) ... One Corporate Plz.
Barrett, Brett Aaron ... '64 '92 C.608 B.S.B.A. L.1137 J.D. 1300 Dove St.
Barsamian, Walter ... '26 '70 C.103 A.B. L.809 J.D. 3990 Westerly Pl.
**Barton, Robert M.**, (AV) ... '22 '45 C.378 A.B. L.477 J.D. [Barton,K.&O.]⊙
*PRACTICE AREAS: Business Law; Taxation; Estate Planning; Estate Administration.

**Barton, Klugman & Oetting, (AV)**
**A Partnership of Professional Corporations**
**Suite 700, 4400 MacArthur Boulevard, P.O. Box 2350, 92660⊙**
**Telephone: 714-752-7551 Telecopier: 714-752-0288**
**Counsel to Firm: Robert M. Barton†.**
**General Civil and Trial Practice. Taxation, Corporation, Banking, Probate and Trust Law. Antitrust, Corporate Securities, Real Property, Environmental, Oil and Gas, Labor and International Business Law. Professional Liability Defense, Insurance Coverage, Directors and Officers Insurance Defense and Coverage.**
**Los Angeles, California Office: 37th Floor, 333 South Grand Avenue, 90071-1599. Telephone: 213-621-4000. Telecopier: 213-625-1832.**
**†Denotes a lawyer whose Professional Corporation is a member of the partnership or is Counsel to the Firm**
*See Professional Biographies, NEWPORT BEACH, CALIFORNIA*

**Basile, Lena A.** ... '— '96 C.331 B.A. L.326 J.D. [Ⓐ Knobbe,M.O.&B.]
**Basista, Joseph J.** ... '66 '97 C.867 B.S.M.E. L.273 J.D. [Ⓐ Knobbe,M.O.&B.]
**Baskin, Scott D., (P.C.)**, (AV) ... '53 '78 C.813 B.A. L.976 J.D. [Irell&M.]
**Baum, Cari S.** ... '61 '90 C.112 B.A.B.S. L.809 J.D. [Ⓐ Borton,P.&C.]
*PRACTICE AREAS: Insurance Defense.
Beadleston, Thomas Scott '50 '75 C.188 B.A. L.339 J.D. V.P., Individual Compl., Pacific Mut. Life Ins. Co.
**Bear, James B.**, (AV) '41 '69 C.112 B.S.E. L.1068 J.D. [Knobbe,M.O.&B.] (See Pat. Sect.)
Beatty, Kirk D., (BV) ... '45 '72 C&L.1137 J.D. 130 Newport Ctr. Dr.
Beck, David A. '53 '78 C.546 B.A. L.190 J.D. (adm. in NE; not adm. in CA) Coun./Sect. Chief, Fed Deposit Ins. Corp.
Beckley, John K. ... '60 '89 C.112 B.A. L.1065 J.D. 4695 MacArthur Ct.
**Beek, Barton**, (AV) ... '24 '55 C.111 B.S. L.426 LL.B. [Ⓒ O'Melveny&M.]
*PRACTICE AREAS: Corporate Finance; Mergers and Acquisitions; Emerging hi-tech companies.
Behnam, Esther M. ... '31 '83 C.685 B.A. L.1137 J.D. 18 Rue Deauville
**Bekken, Robert J.**, (AVⓉ) ... '51 '76 C.20 B.A. L.245 J.D. [Fisher&P.]
*PRACTICE AREAS: Labor (Management) Laws; Employment Law; Wrongful Discharge Law.
**Bemis, Larry R.**, (AV) ... '44 '72 C.800 B.S. L.809 J.D. [Millar,H.&B.]
*PRACTICE AREAS: Taxation Law; Estate Planning Law; Corporate Law.
Benner, Barbara A. ... '59 '85 C&L.339 B.S., J.D. 4695 Macarthur Ct., 7th Fl.
Benson, Robert J. ... '66 '91 C.768 B.S. L.1066 J.D. 840 Newport Center Dr., Suite 500
Berger, Jay L. ... '64 '88 C.1044 B.A. L.464 J.D. 5120 Campus Dr.
Berglund & Johnson, (AV) ... 4340 Campus Dr., Ste. 100 (⊙Woodland Hills)
Berman, Myles L., Law Offices of, (AVⓉ) '54 '80 C.339 B.A. L.146 J.D. 4630 Campus Dr. (⊙Los Angeles & Thousand Oaks)
Bernard, Robert B. ... '17 '62 C.800 A.B. L.809 LL.B. 300 Amethyst Ave.
**Bernauer, Thomas A.**, (AV) ... '42 '68 C&L.800 B.A., J.D. [T.A.Bernauer]

**Bernauer, Thomas A., A Professional Corporation, (AV)** BB
**500 Newport Center Drive, Suite 950, 92660**
**Telephone: 714-720-1313 Fax: 714-720-7457**
**Thomas A. Bernauer (Certified Specialist, Family Law, The State Bar of California Board of Legal Specialization).**
**Practice Limited to Family Law, Custody, Division of Property, Spouse Support, Child Support.**
*See Professional Biographies, NEWPORT BEACH, CALIFORNIA*

**Bernstein, Neila R.**, (AV) ... '55 '80 C.112 B.A. L.1068 J.D. [Ⓐ Stradling,Y.C.&R.]
**Berretta, Frederick S.** ... '57 '89 C.453 B.S.M.E. L.309 J.D. [Knobbe,M.O.&B.]
Bethel, George F., A Professional Corporation, (AV) '37 '63 C.871 L.30 J.D. 610 Newport Ctr. Dr. (Pat.)
**Beuerle, Stephen C.** '70 '96 C.477 B.S.M.E. L.997 J.D. [Ⓐ Knobbe,M.O.&B.] (See Pat. Sect.)
Beuglet, Charles P. ... '— '79 C.028 B.A. L.012 LL.B. 470 Vista Trucha
**Beutler, Ernest A., Jr.**, (AV) '33 '61 C.597 B.S.M.E. L.273 LL.B. [Ⓐ Knobbe,M.O.&B.] (See Pat. Sect.)
**Bhamre, Hema Christine**, (BV) ... '62 '87 C.112 B.A. L.464 J.D. [Self&B.]
*PRACTICE AREAS: Civil Litigation; Professional Negligence; Employment Litigation.
**Bidna, Howard M.**, (AV) ... '53 '78 C.112 B.A. L.1068 J.D. [Bidna&K.]

**Bidna & Keys, A Professional Law Corporation, (AV)**
**5120 Campus Drive, 92660**
**Telephone: 714-752-7030 Telecopier: 714-752-8770**
**Howard M. Bidna; Richard D. Keys; Harvey M. Moore; Jon A. Longerbone.**
**Business, Commercial, Financial and Real Estate Transactions and Litigation. Creditor-Debtor Relations. Business Bankruptcy and Insolvency Law.**
**Reference: The Bank of California (Newport Beach Branch).**
*See Professional Biographies, NEWPORT BEACH, CALIFORNIA*

Bierman, Philip M. ... '66 '94 C.800 B.S. L.809 J.D. 3501 Jamboree Rd., S. Tower
Bilello, Thomas C. ... '64 '90 C.112 B.A. L.309 J.D. Pacific Mutual Life Ins. Co.
Bisnar, John P. ... '48 '78 C.1042 B.S. L.990 J.D. [Bisnar&Assoc.]
Bisnar & Associates ... 4590 Macarthur Blvd.
Bissell, William G. ... '51 '80 C.763 B.A. L.990 J.D. 1200 Quail St.
**Black, Bradley V.** ... '60 '86 C.350 B.A. L.352 J.D. [Ⓐ Cummins&W.]
*PRACTICE AREAS: Civil Litigation.
**Black, William A.** ... '57 '90 C.966 B.S. L.1137 J.D. [Pedersen&B.]
**Blackie, Jeffrey A.** ... '60 '90 C.112 B.A. L.1065 J.D. [Ⓐ Call,C.&J.]
*PRACTICE AREAS: Litigation.

**Blank, Christopher L., (AV) '57 '84 C.112 B.S. L.273 J.D.**
**4695 MacArthur Court, Suite 1200, 92660**
**Telephone: 714-250-4600 Facsimile: 714-250-4604**
**Email: clblank@aol.com**
***PRACTICE AREAS: Business Litigation; Business Law.**
**Business Law, Business Litigation, Bankruptcy, Equipment Finance and Leasing, Commercial Law.**
*See Professional Biographies, NEWPORT BEACH, CALIFORNIA*

Blied, Timothy J., (BV) ... '53 '79 C.1259 B.A. L.990 J.D. [Schmiesing&B.]
Blush, Susan A. ... '48 '81 C.1246 B.A. L.426 J.D. 2801 W. Coast Hwy.
Bohan, Anthony ... '44 '82 C.112 A.B. L.1137 J.D. 320 Superior Ave.
Bojarski, Jill M. ... '53 '81 C.1109 B.A. L.1137 J.D. 1300 Dove St.
**Bollar, Robert W.** ... '61 '86 C.800 B.A. L.464 J.D. [Cummins&W.]
*PRACTICE AREAS: Insurance Coverage.
Bonaparte, Ronald H., (AV) ... '35 '59 C.668 A.B. L.813 J.D. [Bonaparte&M.]⊙
Bonaparte & Miyamoto, A Professional Law Corporation, (AV) 5030 Campus Dr. (⊙L.A.)
**Bonner, Richard W.**, (AV) ... '47 '74 C.1109 B.A. L.990 J.D. [R.W.Bonner]

**Bonner, Richard W., A Professional Corporation, (AV)**
**(Formerly Crosby, Gary & Bonner)**
**Suite 200, 1300 Dove Street, 92660**
**Telephone: 714-752-8266 Fax: 714-752-7967**
**Richard W. Bonner.**
**Criminal Trial Practice.**

(This Listing Continued)

**Bonner, Richard W., A Professional Corporation (Continued)**
Reference: Bank of America, Newport Beach.
*See Professional Biographies, NEWPORT BEACH, CALIFORNIA*

Boortz, Donald L., (AV) ...........'46 '73 C.112 A.B. L.1068 J.D. 610 Newport Ctr. Dr.
**Borg, Roger E.** .......................'56 '85 C.101 B.A. L.1068 J.D. [Ⓐ Alvarado,S.V.&S.]
*LANGUAGES: Italian.
*PRACTICE AREAS: Litigation.
Borgen, Richard L., (BV) .........'39 '66 C.112 B.S. L.1068 J.D. 610 Newport Center Dr.
Borges, Fredrick M. ........................ '60 '92 C.1109 B.A. L.1137 J.D. 4675 Macarthur Ct.

**Borton, Petrini & Conron, (AV)**
**4675 MacArthur Court, Suite 1150, 92660☉**
Telephone: 714-752-2333 Fax: 714-752-2854
Email: bpcnb@bpclaw.com
Members of Firm: William H. Cantrell; Phillip B. Greer; Michael F. Long. Associates: Donald A. Diebold; Paul T. McBride; Cari S. Baum; Carolyn M. Kern.
Commercial/Real Estate Litigation, Insurance Law, General Civil Trial and Appellate Practice in State and Federal Courts, Personal Injury and Casualty Defense Litigation, Insurance Bad Faith and Coverage, Labor and Employment, Toxic Torts, Real Estate, Land Use Planning, Zoning, Municipal, Professional Errors and Omissions, Healthcare Provider Malpractice Defense, Products Liability, Oil and Gas, Water, Natural Resources, Environmental, Public Entity, Administrative, Agricultural, Banking, Contracts, Corporations, Partnerships, Taxation, Creditor's Remedies, Bankruptcy, Probate, Estate Planning, Family Law.
Bakersfield, California Office: The Borton, Petrini & Conron Building, 1600 Truxtun Avenue, P.O. Box 2026. Telephone: 805-322-3051. Fax: 805-322-4628. Email: bpcbak@bpclaw.com.
San Luis Obispo, California Office: 1114 Marsh Street. Telephone: 805-541-4340. Fax: 805-541-4558. Email: bpcslo@bpclaw.com.
Visalia, California Office: 206 South Mooney Boulevard, P.O. Box 1028. Telephone: 209-627-5600. Fax: 209-627-4309. Email: bpcvis@bpclaw.com.
Fresno, California Office: T. W. Patterson Building, 2014 Tulare Street, Suite 830. Telephone: 209-268-0117. Fax: 209-237-7995. Email: bpcfrs@bpclaw.com.
Sacramento, California Office: 2233 Watt Avenue, Suite 290. Telephone: 916-484-3555. Fax: 916-484-3550. Email: bpcsac@bpclaw.com.
Santa Barbara, California Office: 211 East Victoria Street, Suite D. Telephone: 805-564-2404. Fax: 805-564-2176. Email: bpcsb@bpclaw.com
Los Angeles, California Office: 707 Wilshire Boulevard, Suite 5100. Telephone: 213-624-2869. Fax: 213-489-3930. Email: bpcla@bpclaw.com.
San Diego, California Office: John Burnham Building, 610 West Ash Street, 9th Floor. Telephone: 619-232-2424. Fax: 619-531-0794. Email: bpcsd@bpclaw.com.
Modesto, California Office: The Turner Building, 900 "H" Street, Suite D. Telephone: 209-576-1701. Fax: 209-527-9753. Email: bpcmod@bpclaw.com.
San Francisco, California Office: 111 Pine Street, Suite 730. Telephone: 415-981-4415. Fax: 415-391-5538. Email: bpcsf@bpclaw.com.
Redding, California Office: 280 Hemsted Drive, Suite 100. Telephone: 916-222-1530. Fax: 916-222-4498. Email: bpcred@bpclaw.com.
San Bernardino, California Office: 290 North "D" Street, Suite 500. Telephone: 909-381-0527. Fax: 909-381-0658. Email: bpcsbdo@bpclaw.com.
San Jose, California Office: 2 North Second Street. Telephone: 408-298-3997. Fax: 408-298-3365. Email: bpcsj@bpclaw.com.
Ventura, California Office: 1000 Hill Road, Suite 310. Telephone: 805-650-9994. Fax: 805-650-7125. Email: bpcvta@bpclaw.com.
Santa Rosa, California Office: 50 Santa Rosa Avenue, Suite 300. Telephone: 707-527-9477. Fax: 707-527-9488. Email: bpcsr@bpclaw.com.
*See Professional Biographies, NEWPORT BEACH, CALIFORNIA*

Bosché, Thomas S. ............... '58 '84 C.602 A.B. L.770 J.D. 610 Newport Center Dr.
**Botta, Bartholomew M.** ......................'68 '93 C.776 B.A. L.900 J.D. [Ⓐ Rynn&J.]
Bowie, Alexander, (AV) ..................'32 '56 C&L.174 LL.B. [Bowie A.K.W.&G.]
Bowie Arneson Kadi Wiles & Giannone, (AV) ..........................4920 Campus Dr.

**Bradford, Peter C., (AV) '35 '61 C&L.813 A.B., LL.B.** BB
**Suite 1250, 610 Newport Center Drive, 92660**
Telephone: 714-640-1800 FAX: 714-721-9923
(Certified Specialist, Estate Planning, Trust and Probate Law, The State Bar of California Board of Legal Specialization).
*LANGUAGES: French.
Estate Planning, Trust and Probate Law.
References: Wells Fargo Bank; Bank of America, Trust Department.
*See Professional Biographies, NEWPORT BEACH, CALIFORNIA*

**Brady, Celeste Stahl**, (AV) ..........'55 '80 C.763 B.S. L.1049 J.D. [Stradling,Y.C.&R.]
**Bragg, Robert A.**, (AV) ................'51 '81 C.767 B.A. L.765 J.D. [Bragg,S.S.&K.]☉
**Bragg, Sherry S.** ............................ '61 '87 C&L.112 B.A., J.D. [Ⓐ Andersen&W.]
*LANGUAGES: Spanish.

**Bragg, Short, Serota & Kuluva, (AV)**
**4695 MacArthur Court, Suite 530, 92660-1860☉**
Telephone: 714-442-4800 Fax: 714-442-4816
Robert A. Bragg; Patricia D. Short; Lori D. Serota. Associates: Cody Dale Lund; Marvin A. Martinez.
Insurance Defense Practice.
San Francisco, California Office: Bragg & Dziesinski, Two Embarcadero Center, Suite 1400. Telephone: 415-954-1850. Fax: 415-434-2179.
Los Angeles, California Office: 801 South Figueroa Street, Suite 2100. Telephone: 213-612-5335. Fax: 213-612-5712.
*See Professional Biographies, NEWPORT BEACH, CALIFORNIA*

**Brainerd, John H. '43 '70 C.112 B.S. L.800 J.D.**
**4100 Newport Place, Suite 800, 92660**
Telephone: 714-252-2824 Facsimile: 714-863-0164
Business, Estate and Individual Tax and Transaction Planning and Related Matters. Drafting of Legal Documents. Related Court and Administrative Tax Representation. Business Acquisitions and Dispositions.
*See Professional Biographies, NEWPORT BEACH, CALIFORNIA*

**Branse, Debra B.** ......................... '69 '95 C.112 B.A. L.477 J.D. [Ⓐ Newmeyer&D.]
Branstine, Daniel L. ........................... '54 '90 C.800 B.A. L.347 J.D. 1300 Dove St.
Brawner, Barbara M. ..................'62 '89 C.112 B.A. L.426 J.D. 4675 MacArthur Dr.
**Breckenridge, John E.**, (AV) ... '34 '59 C.976 B.A. L.1066 LL.B. [Ⓒ Stradling,Y.C.&R.]
**Brennan, James S.** ........................'67 '91 C.112 B.A. L.188 J.D. [Ⓐ Brobeck,P.&H.]
*PRACTICE AREAS: Business; Technology.
**Brewer, Burleigh J.**, (AV) ........................ '42 '67 C.800 B.S. L.426 J.D. [Obegi&B.]
*PRACTICE AREAS: Estate Planning; Trust Law; Probate; Tax Law.
Bridgford, Richard K. .........................'60 '85 C&L.813 B.A., J.D. [Bridgford,K.&G.]
Bridgford, Knottnerus & Gleason ..........................................620 Newport Center Dr.
Briesacker, Russell P., Jr. ..............'49 '80 C.1109 B.A. L.1137 J.D. 4590 Macarthur Blvd.

**Briggs, Steven E., (AV) '42 '71 C&L.1049 B.S., J.D.**
**2700 Newport Boulevard, Suite 172, 92663**
Telephone: 714-673-7410
(Certified Specialist, Family Law, The State Bar of California Board of Legal Specialization).
*PRACTICE AREAS: Family Law.
Family Law and Related Litigation.
*See Professional Biographies, NEWPORT BEACH, CALIFORNIA*

Briles, Tracy D. ...........................'67 '95 C.1109 B.A. L.1137 J.D. 4675 MacArthur Ct.
Brinckloe, William B., Jr., (AV) ......'55 '83 C.1214 B.A. L.809 J.D. 500 Newport Ctr. Dr.
Bringgold, Donald R., (AV) ...... '27 '55 C.112 B.A. L.1068 LL.B. 17 Rue Chateau Royal
Brizendine, Richard C., (BV) .........'55 '81 C.763 A.B. L.61 J.D. 4400 MacArthur Blvd.

**Brobeck, Phleger & Harrison LLP, (AV)** BB
A Partnership including a Professional Corporation
**4675 MacArthur Court, Suite 1000, 92660☉**
Telephone: 714-752-7535 Facsimile: 714-752-7522
Managing Partner: Bruce R. Hallett. Resident Partners: R. Patrick Arrington; Roger M. Cohen; Richard A. Fink; Laura B. Hunter; Kathlene W. Lowe; Frederic Alport Randall, Jr.; Gabrielle M. Wirth. Of Counsel: Jeffrey S. Rovner. Associates: Jonathan F. Atzen; Richard J. Babcock; John S. Baker; Ellen S. Bancroft; James S. Brennan; Susan N. Cayley; Kevin D. DeBré; Scott S. Draeker; Ethan D. Feffer; R. Scott Feldmann; Dana E. Frost; Lisa Schechter Goon; Neel Grover; Anita Gruettke; Elizabeth T. Hall; Lee J. Leslie; Gregory T. May; Barbara J. Miller; Daniel E. Roston; Matthew V. Waterman; Greg T. Williams.
General Practice, including Business and Technology, Litigation, Securities Litigation, Technology Litigation, Environmental Litigation, Product Liability Litigation, Labor Law, Financial Services and Insolvency (including Bankruptcy and Loan Workout), Real Estate, and Tax/Estate Planning.
San Francisco, California Office: Spear Street Tower, One Market. Telephone: 415-442-0900. Facsimile: 415-442-1010.
Palo Alto, California Office: Two Embarcadero Place, 2200 Geng Road. Telephone: 415-424-0160. Facsimile: 415-496-2885.
Los Angeles, California Office: 550 South Hope Street. Telephone: 213-489-4060. Facsimile: 213-745-3345.
San Diego, California Office: 550 West C Street, Suite 1300. Telephone: 619-234-1966. Facsimile: 619-236-1403.
Austin, Texas Office: Brobeck, Phleger & Harrison LLP, 301 Congress Avenue, Suite 1200. Telephone: 512-477-5495. Facsimile: 512-477-5813.
Denver, Colorado Office: Brobeck, Phleger & Harrison LLP, 1125 Seventeenth Street, 25th Floor. Telephone: 303-293-0760. Facsimile: 303-299-8819.
New York, N.Y. Office: Brobeck, Phleger & Harrison LLP, 1633 Broadway, 47th Floor. Telephone: 212-581-1600. Facsimile: 212-586-7878.
Brobeck Hale and Dorr International Office:
London, England Office: Veritas House, 125 Finsbury Pavement, London EC2A 1NQ. Telephone: 44 071 638 6688. Facsimile: 44 071 638 5888.
*See Professional Biographies, NEWPORT BEACH, CALIFORNIA*

Broderick, Daniel P., (AV) ..................................'42 '73 C.1049 B.S. L.276 J.D. [Howser&B.]
**Broker, Jeffrey W.**, (AV) ....................'47 '72 C.112 A.B. L.1068 J.D. [Broker&O.]

**Broker & O'Keefe, Professional Corporation, (AV)** BB
**4695 MacArthur Court Suite 1200, 92660**
Telephone: 714-222-2000 Fax: 714-222-2022
Email: chpter11@aol.com URL: http://wwwbroker-okeefe.com
Jeffrey W. Broker; Sean A. O'Keefe;—Lauren B. Lessler; David D. Piper.
Bankruptcy and Insolvency Law, Corporate Reorganizations and Related Commercial Litigation.
*See Professional Biographies, NEWPORT BEACH, CALIFORNIA*

**Brown, Douglas S.** .................. '57 '83 C.674 A.B. L.178 J.D. [Stradling,Y.C.&R.]
Brown, Eric R. ..........................'56 '89 C.1074 B.A. L.464 J.D. [Ⓐ Saxon,B.G.&K.]
Brown, F. Mackenzie, (AV) '36 '64 C.112 B.A. L.800 LL.B.
1151 Dove St. (☉San Diego)
Brown, Richard A., Jr., (AV) ................ '40 '68 C.813 A.B. L.383 J.D. [Howser&B.]
**Brown, Ronald K., Jr., (A Professional Corporation)** '56 '81
C.1042 B.A. L.1137 J.D. [Good,W.H.&W.]
*PRACTICE AREAS: Landlord-Tenant Transaction and Litigation; General Business Litigation.
Brown, Steven W. '44 '72
C.112 A.B. L.426 J.D. V.P. & Ins. Coun., Pacific Mut. Life Ins. Co.
**Brown, Thomas K.**, (AV) ............... '50 '78 C&L.770 B.A., J.D. [McDermott,W.&E.]
*PRACTICE AREAS: Corporate Law; Real Estate.
**Bruck, Richard H.**, (AV) ......................'48 '72 C.112 B.A. L.1068 J.D. [Bruck&P.]
*PRACTICE AREAS: Corporate Law; Securities Law; Commercial Transactions.

**Bruck & Perry, A Professional Corporation, (AV)**
**500 Newport Center Drive, 92660**
Telephone: 714-719-6000 Telecopier: 714-719-6040
Richard H. Bruck; David J. Perry; Karen Nicolai Winnett; Paul C. Nyquist; Daniel K. Donahue; Timothy Carl Aires; Teresa Tormey Fineman; Rick L. Raynsford; Kevin W. Kirsch; Dana M. Zeigler.
Corporate, Securities, Finance, Mergers and Acquisitions, Domestic and International Commercial Transactions, Real Estate and Civil Litigation in all State and Federal Courts including Business, Securities, Commercial Insurance, and Legal Malpractice Defense.
*See Professional Biographies, NEWPORT BEACH, CALIFORNIA*

Bryant, Jackson C. ............................'18 '50 C.113 A.B. L.800 LL.B. 1535 Superior

**Buchalter, Nemer, Fields & Younger, A Professional Corporation, (AV)** BB
**Suite 1450, 620 Newport Center Drive, 92660☉**
Telephone: 714-760-1121 Fax: 714-720-0182
Email: buchalter@earthlink.net URL: http://www.buchalter.com
Clifford John Meyer; Debra Solle Healy; Kirk S. Rense;—Lori S. Ross; Mark M. Scott.
References: City National Bank; Wells Fargo Bank; Metrobank.
Los Angeles, California Office: 24th Floor, 601 South Figueroa Street. Telephone: 213-891-0700. Fax: 213-896-0400.
New York, New York Office: 15th Floor, 605 Third Avenue. Telephone: 212-490-8600. Fax: 212-490-6022.
San Francisco, California Office: 29th Floor, 333 Market Street. Telephone: 415-227-0900. Fax: 415-227-0770.
*See Professional Biographies, NEWPORT BEACH, CALIFORNIA*

**Buchanan, Vicki Marolt**, (AV🅣) ..........'49 '84 C.174 B.S. L.208 J.D. [Cox B.P.&S.]
*PRACTICE AREAS: Complex Commercial Litigation; Insurance Bad Faith; Creditor Bankruptcy; Appellate Advocacy.
Bugna, LaVerne June, (Mrs.) .......... '19 '70 C.112 B.S. L.990 J.D. 47 Seabrook Cove‡
**Bunker, William B.**, (AV) '51 '78 C.1075 B.S. L.101 J.D.
[Knobbe,M.O.&B.] (See Pat. Sect.) (☉Riverside)
Burnham, Janice L. ........................'51 '78 C.164 B.A. L.1202 J.D. 1300 Dove St.
Burton, Marvin O., (AV) ........................'37 '66 C.801 L.809 LL.B. 333 Bayside Dr.
**Burton, Thomas W.** .........................'46 '73 C.154 B.S. L.1049 J.D. [Ⓒ Cummins&W.]
*PRACTICE AREAS: Business Law; Trusts and Estates; Technology and Science; Real Estate; Computers and Software.
**Busch, Jerome A.**, (BV) ...........................'46 '81 C.1109 B.A. L.990 J.D. [White&R.]
*PRACTICE AREAS: Taxation; Civil and Criminal Law; IRS Representation; Financial Crimes; Environmental Crimes.
**Buxbaum, David A.**, (AV) ...............'— '70 C.605 B.A. L.1068 J.D. [Buxbaum&C.]☉
*PRACTICE AREAS: Corporate; Business Banking; Estate Planning; Commercial; Real Estate.

**Buxbaum & Chakmak, A Law Corporation, (AV)**
**5160 Campus Drive, 92660☉**
Telephone: 714-833-3107 Fax: 714-833-2466
David A. Buxbaum; John Chakmak; Charles L. Zetterberg; Betty O. Yamashiro;—John P. Howland; Joan Penfil.
Business, Commercial, Banking, Insurance (Coverage and Defense), Corporate, Real Estate, Bankruptcy (Creditors' Rights), Estate Planning, Administrative Law, and Family Law. Trials in all State and Federal Courts.
Claremont, California Office: 414 Yale Avenue. Telephone: 909-621-4707. Fax: 909-621-7112.
*See Professional Biographies, NEWPORT BEACH, CALIFORNIA*

**Byun, Ann A.** ................................................'— '92 L.426 J.D. [Knobbe,M.O.&B.]
**Call, Wayne W.**, (AV) ........................'47 '73 C.877 B.A. L.878 J.D. [Call,C.&J.]
*PRACTICE AREAS: Litigation.

**Call, Clayton & Jensen, A Professional Corporation, (AV)**
**Suite 700, 610 Newport Center Drive, 92660**
Telephone: 714-717-3000 FAX: 714-717-3100
Email: ccj@ix.netcom.com

(This Listing Continued)

**Call, Clayton & Jensen, A Professional Corporation (Continued)**
Wayne W. Call; L. Whitney Clayton, III; Jon E. Jensen; Troy L. Tate; Seth L. Liebman;—Michael R. Overly; Maryam Shokrai; Jeffrey A. Blackie. Of Counsel: Peter N. Kalionzes.
Business and Real Estate Litigation, State and Federal Courts. Corporate, Securities and Real Estate Matters.
*See Professional Biographies, NEWPORT BEACH, CALIFORNIA*

**Callahan, Craig A.** .................. '59 '86 C.112 B.A. L.1067 J.D. [Newmeyer&D.]
*PRACTICE AREAS: Construction Litigation; Insurance Litigation; General Business Litigation.
**Callahan, Rebecca**, (AV) ............ '52 '82 C.800 B.A. L.1066 J.D. [Callahan&Assoc.]
*PRACTICE AREAS: Insolvency; Business Litigation; Bankruptcy Litigation; Appellate Practice.

**Callahan & Associates, (AV)** BB
**5120 Campus Drive, 92660**
Telephone: 714-476-2898 Facsimile: 714-752-8770
Rebecca Callahan. Associate: Katherine T. Corrigan.
*See Professional Biographies, NEWPORT BEACH, CALIFORNIA*

**Callister, Janet L.** ........................ '48 '80 C.112 B.A. L.426 J.D. [A Andersen&W.]
Callister, Thomas K. ............... '— '71 C&L.800 B.S., J.D. Resource Mgmt. Solutions
Cameron-Kelley, Susan, (BV) ............... '52 '80 C.1042 B.S. L.1137 J.D. 1101 Dove St.
Campbell, William D. ......'38 '64 C.910 B.S. L.800 LL.B. CEO, Value Line Financial Co.
**Campf, Darren M.** .............................. '65 '92 C&L.990 B.A., J.D. [A White&R.]
*PRACTICE AREAS: Business Litigation.
**Cannon, John F.** ..........................'64 '90 C&L.426 B.A./B.A., J.D. [A Stradling,Y.C.&R.]

**Cano, Kristin M., (AV) '51 '78 C.645 B.S. L.809 J.D.** BB
**One Corporate Plaza, 92660**
Telephone: 714-759-1505 FAX: 714-640-9535
Email: KristinCanoLawOffice@internetMCI.com
Corporate Securities, Business, Corporate, Corporate Finance, Securities Regulation, Securities Litigation, Mergers and Acquisitions, Venture Capital, and Commodities Law. Partnership, Contract, Class Actions Law. Complex and Multi District Litigation, and State and Federal Government Contracts.
*See Professional Biographies, NEWPORT BEACH, CALIFORNIA*

**Cantrell, William H.**, (CV) ............. '52 '76 C.1212 B.S. L.1068 J.D. [Borton,P.&C.]
*PRACTICE AREAS: Casualty Litigation; Commercial Litigation; Employment Law; Professional Liability; Environmental Law.
Canty, Cheryl Ann .........'61 '86 C.112 B.A. L.990 J.D. 4675 Macarthur Ct., Suite 1000
**Canuso, Vito A., III** '58 '90 C.884 B.S. L.1049 J.D.
[Knobbe,M.O.&B.] (See Pat. Sect.)
Capaldi, Michael D. ......................... '60 '87 C&L.800 B.A., J.D. 4695 MacArthur Ct.
**Capretz, James T.**, (AV) ................... '39 '63 C&L.425 B.B.A., LL.B. [Capretz&R.]
*PRACTICE AREAS: International Law; Commercial Litigation; Medical Product Liability; Mediation.

**Capretz & Radcliffe, (AV)** BB
**5000 Birch Street, West Tower Suite 2500, 92660-2139**
Telephone: 714-724-3000 Fax: 714-757-2635
Email: CRLAWYERS@AOL.CON URL: http://www.CAPRETZ.com
James T. Capretz; Richard J. Radcliffe. Associates: Peter A. Martin. Of Counsel: William B. Lawless (Not admitted in CA).
General Civil and Trial Practice, State and Federal Courts, Business, International, Medical, Product Liability, Mass Tort Litigation, Corporate and Construction Law.
*See Professional Biographies, NEWPORT BEACH, CALIFORNIA*

**Caput, Frank A.**, (AV) ................................'40 '66 C.800 B.S. L.309 LL.B. [Irell&M.]
**Cardoso, Linda T.** ................................'57 '89 C.1131 B.S. L.1137 J.D. [Kimball,T.&S.]
*PRACTICE AREAS: Landlord Tenant.
**Carlson, C. Craig**, (AV) ........................'42 '69 C&L.800 B.S., J.D. [Stradling,Y.C.&R.]
Carlson, John E. ........................ '43 '68 C.747 B.A. L.878 J.D. Pacific Mut. Life Ins. Co.
**Carlton, Jerry W.**, (AV) ...........'41 '68 C.586 B.B.A. L.846 LL.B. [O'Melveny&M.]
*PRACTICE AREAS: Taxation.
Carlton, Karen Kelly ......................'61 '86 C.1083 B.A. L.896 J.D. [Carlton&C.]⊙
Carlton, Terry J. ..........................'61 '86 C.475 B.A. L.896 J.D. [Carlton&C.]
Carlton & Carlton, P.L.L.C. ......................... 20311 S.W. Birch St. (⊙Raleigh, N.C.)

**Carman, E. Day, (AV) '— '57 C.800 B.A. L.767 J.D.**
**567 San Nicolas Drive Suite 206, 92660**⊙
Telephone: 714-729-3300 Fax: 714-760-3024
*PRACTICE AREAS: Wrongful Termination; Discrimination; Sexual Harassment; Defamation; General Civil Trial and Appellate Practice.
Wrongful Termination, Discrimination, Sexual Harassment, Defamation, General Civil Trial and Appellate Practice, Corporate and Business Representation and Litigation.
Reference: Wells Fargo, Newport Beach.
San Jose, California Office: 13th Floor, 50 West San Fernando. Telephone: 408-275-0501.

Carmichael, David R. '42 '68 C.112 B.S. L.1068 J.D.
Sr. V.P. & Gen. Coun., Pacific Mut. Life Ins. Co.
**Carmichael, John B., III** ........... '56 '82 C&L.800 B.S., J.D. [A Alvarado,S.V.&S.]
*PRACTICE AREAS: Mortgage Banking; Real Estate Transactions and Lending; Commercial Corporate Law.
**Carmichael, Patricia Ann** ............ '47 '90 C&L.1137 B.S.L., J.D. [A Tuverson&H.]
**Carney, Cormac J.** ........................ '59 '87 C.112 B.A. L.309 J.D. [O'Melveny&M.]
**Carollo, David Lee** ........................ '59 '86 C.912 B.A. L.276 J.D. [Cummins&W.]
*PRACTICE AREAS: Bad Faith Litigation; Real Estate Litigation; Bankruptcy Adversary Litigation; Business Litigation; Coverage Analysis.
Carr, John L. .............................'32 '60 C&L.426 B.S., LL.B. CEO, RTC-Gibralter Svgs.
Carrick, John M. '64 '90 C.105 B.A. L.128 J.D.
(adm. in MD; not adm. in CA) R.T.C.
Carstens, Donald ..................'46 '72 C.911 B.A. L.950 J.D. 3 Upper Newport Plaza
**Carter, Kathleen A.** .................................'61 '90 C&L.352 B.A., J.D. [Remer,D.&G.]
Carver, Lori Suzanne ...................... '63 '91 C&L.347 B.S., J.D. 620 Newport Ctr. Dr.
Cary, George S. ........'51 '76 C.112 A.B. L.1066 J.D. 840 Newport Center Dr., Suite 500
**Casey, Michelle M.** ................................ '71 '96 C.188 B.S. L.273 J.D. [A Fisher&P.]
Casoria, John B. .....................'56 '83 C.790 B.A. L.1137 J.D. 20271 S.W. Birch St.

**Casselberry, Steven, (AV) '50 '77 C.112 B.A. L.904 J.D.**
**One Newport Place, 1301 Dove Street, Suite 940, 92660-2473**
Telephone: 714-476-9999 Fax: 714-476-0175
Email: steve@speed.net
*PRACTICE AREAS: Banking Law; Litigation; Bankruptcy Law; Commercial Law; Real Estate (Property) Law.
Of Counsel: Richard A. Harvey.
Financial Institutions, Mortgage Banking, Bankruptcy and Foreclosure, Business and Commercial Litigation, Real Estate, Commercial Financing and General Civil Trial in all State and Federal Courts.
Representative Clients: El Camino National Bank; First National Bank of Portsmouth; Huntington National Bank; Inland Empire National Bank; Landmark Bank; Omni Bank; Pioneer Savings and Loan Assn.; Queen City Bank.
*See Professional Biographies, NEWPORT BEACH, CALIFORNIA*

Cassidy, Michael J. ............... '53 '86 C&L.1137 B.S., J.D. 2424 S.E. Bristol, Ste 250
Caston, Michael E., (AV) .................... '43 '75 C.1077 B.A. L.1148 J.D. 1300 Dove St.
**Caulfield, James D.** ............'46 '70 C&L.878 B.S., J.D. Gen. Coun., Galardi Grp., Inc.
**Causey, Ingrid M.** ............................ '68 '93 C.881 B.A. L.800 J.D. [A Newmeyer&D.]
Cavanaugh, Diana, (BV) ................ '42 '77 C.763 B.A. L.1137 J.D. 5140 Birch St.

**Cayley, Susan N.** ........................... '64 '93 C.112 B.A. L.426 J.D. [A Brobeck,P.&H.]
*LANGUAGES: French, Farsi.
*PRACTICE AREAS: Corporate.
**Celotti, Janice L.**, (AV) ........................'53 '78 C.112 B.A. L.1068 J.D. [Wolf&P.]
*PRACTICE AREAS: Creditors Rights Litigation (Commercial/Multi-Family and Residential).
Chabre, Gustave S. ........................ '38 '75 C.800 B.S. L.990 J.D. 1130 E. Balboa Blvd.
Chaix, John E. ......... '64 '91 C.763 B.A. L.1137 J.D. 4000 Mac Arthur Blvd., Ste. 6800
**Chakmak, John**, (BV) ...................'45 '71 C.813 B.A. L.1068 J.D. [Buxbaum&C.]⊙
*PRACTICE AREAS: Civil Litigation; Insurance; Commercial; Banking.
Chamberlain, John P. ......................'43 '68 C.102 B.A. L.174 J.D. [Chamberlain&V.]
Chamberlain, Suzanne Viau ............'54 '81 C.112 B.A. L.426 J.D. [Chamberlain&V.]
Chamberlain & Viau, A Prof. Law Corp. ............................................1000 Quail St.
**Chandler, Katherine M.** '53 '78 C.112 B.A. L.1049 J.D.
Sr. Coun., Chevron Land & Development Co.
**Chandler, Linda Hart** ..........................'38 '74 C.659 B.A. L.1137 J.D. [Chandler&V.]
*PRACTICE AREAS: Business Law; Employment Law; Related Civil Litigation.

**Chandler & Vatave**
**3 Corporate Plaza Drive Suite 204, 92660**
Telephone: 714-721-0580 Facsimile: 714-721-0981
Members of Firm: Linda Hart Chandler; Sunil Lewis Vatave.
Business and Employment Law with related Civil Litigation including Contracts, Real and Personal Properties, Wrongful Termination and related Tort actions.
*See Professional Biographies, NEWPORT BEACH, CALIFORNIA*

Chapman, Charles Michael ......... '49 '82 C.805 B.B.A. L.616 J.D. 100 Bayview Circle
Charamza, Walter W. ............'21 '52 C.605 A.B. L.1066 LL.B. 2224 Port Durness Pl.‡
Charest, Suzanne J. ................. '46 '86 C.383 B.A. L.596 J.D. 4650 von Karman Ave.
**Charles, Bruce H.** .....................'51 '77 C.800 B.A. L.1068 J.D. [Baldikoski,C.&K.]
Cheadle, C. Tucker, (AV) ................................................'— '78 [Cheadle&G.]
Cheadle & Garrett, (AV) ........................................................1151 Dove St.
Cheever, Sharon A. '55 '83 C.763 B.S.B.A. L.1049 J.D.
V.P. & Invest. Coun., Pacific Mut. Life Ins. Co.
Chelius, George L., (AV) ........................... '40 '75 C.208 L.809 J.D. 3600 Birch St.
Chen, Raymond T. .....................'68 '94 C.112 B.S.E.E. L.569 J.D. 620 Newport Ctr. Dr.
Chiboucas, James, (AV) .............. '59 '84 C&L.800 B.S., J.D. 4343 Von Karman Ave.
Cho, Mona Y. ................ '70 '95 C.112 B.A. L.1068 J.D. 4695 Macarthur Ct., 7th Fl.
Choy, Ivette Santaella ................................................'56 '89 C.262 B.A. L.30 J.D. R.T.C.
**Christianson, Michael J.**, (AV) .........................'41 '65 C&L.352 LL.B. [White&R.]
Christy, John C. ...................................'54 '80 C.1109 B.A. L.1137 J.D. 4063 Birch
Chwalek, Bernadine E. '55 '81 C.454 B.A. L.1048 J.D.
Asst. V.P. & Invest. Coun., Pacific Mut. Life Ins. Co.

**Claire, Colleen M., (AV) '31 '57 C&L.800 B.S., LL.B.**
**Suite 1, 3800 Pacific Coast Highway (Corona Del Mar), 92625**
Telephone: 714-675-0755 Fax: 714-675-7536
Estate Planning, Probate, Trusts and Taxation Law.
*See Professional Biographies, NEWPORT BEACH, CALIFORNIA*

**Clark, Christopher R.** ..........................'59 '86 C.112 B.S. L.464 J.D. [Fingal,F.&C.]
*PRACTICE AREAS: Real Estate Litigation; Construction Defects; Insurance Bad Faith; Business Litigation.
Clark, Teresa P. ........................ '45 '74 C.112 B.S. L.426 J.D. 508 Redlands Ave. (Pat.)
**Clark, Thomas P., Jr.**, (AV) ........... '43 '73 C.602 A.B. L.502 J.D. [Stradling,Y.C.&R.]
**Clayton, L. Whitney, III**, (AV) .............'50 '78 C.878 B.A. L.464 J.D. [Call,C.&J.]
*LANGUAGES: Spanish.
*PRACTICE AREAS: Litigation.
Clohan, William C., Jr. '48 '76 C.1070 B.S. L.276 J.D.
(adm. in DC; not adm. in CA) Willdex Advisory Group
Cobb, John B., (AV) ..............'34 '66 C.871 B.S. L.1068 LL.B. 250 Newport Ctr. Dr.

**Cohen, Ivan P. '52 '79 C&L.061 B.A., J.D.**
**1301 Dove Street, Suite 670, 92660**
Telephone: 714-851-8494 Facsimile: 714-851-8499 714-660-1462
*LANGUAGES: Dutch and Afrikaans.
Domestic and International, Commercial and Consumer Collections Law, Corporate Finance and Business Law, General Civil Practice and Litigation in all State and Federal Courts.
Representative Clients: Available Upon Request.
Reference: Wells Fargo Bank, Irvine, California.
Johannesburg, South Africa Office: 1, 14th Street, Corner Louis Botha Avenue, Orange Grove, 2192. Telephone: 011-2711-485-2270. Facsimile: 011-2711-485-1453.
*See Professional Biographies, NEWPORT BEACH, CALIFORNIA*

Cohen, Robert Lawrence ....... '65 '91 C.94 B.S. L.426 J.D. 270 Newport Beach Ctr. Dr.
**Cohen, Roger M.** .................................'56 '81 C.112 B.A. L.1066 J.D. [Brobeck,P.&H.]
*PRACTICE AREAS: Corporate Finance; Leverage Buyouts; Banking.
**Cohn, Lawrence B.** ................. '49 '84 C.1169 A.B. L.426 J.D. [Stradling,Y.C.&R.]
Colby, Stephen A. .............................'40 '74 C.492 B.A. L.1240 J.D. 1107 Quail St.
**Collins, John J.**, (AV) ......................'36 '62 C.770 B.A. L.426 LL.B. [Collins,C.M.&T.]⊙
*PRACTICE AREAS: General Trial Practice; Public Liability; Insurance Bad Faith; Products Liability; Construction Litigation.

**Collins, Collins, Muir & Traver, (AV)**
**333 Bayside Drive, 92660**⊙
Telephone: 714-723-6284 Fax: 714-723-7701
John J. Collins.
Casualty, Products Liability, Construction, Malpractice Insurance, Employment Termination, Sexual Abuse, and Personal Injury Law. General Trial Practice.
Pasadena, California Office: Suite 300, 265 North Euclid, 91101. Telephone 818-793-1163. Fax: 818-793-5982.
*See Professional Biographies, NEWPORT BEACH, CALIFORNIA*

**Colvin, Christopher A.** ........... '66 '95 C.674 B.S.A.E. L.273 J.D. [Knobbe,M.O.&B.]
*LANGUAGES: French.
Combs, Kenneth H., (BV) ..........'46 '74 C.763 B.A. L.800 J.D. 4400 MacArthur Blvd.
**Combs, Leigh Taylor** ...........................'72 '94 C.1097 B.A. L.800 J.D. [A Irell&M.]
Comer, Roy L., (BV) ..................................'53 '78 C.112 B.A. L.1137 J.D. [Berglund&J.]
Conn, Robert L. ..........................'55 '80 C.1239 B.A. L.426 J.D. 4100 Newport Place Dr.
Conner, Jeffrey S. ............................ '59 '84 C.112 B.A. L.767 J.D. J.S. Conner Co.
Connors, John J. ................ '39 '65 C.755 B.S. L.365 J.D. 1401 Dove St. Ste. 390 (Pat.)
**Cook, Bruce V., P.C.**, (AV) ........................'47 '75 C.101 B.S. L.878 J.D. [Voss,C.&T.]
*PRACTICE AREAS: Construction Law; Real Estate Development Law; Commercial Leasing; Business Law; Property Management.
Copenbarger, Lloyd G. ......................... '41 '71 C&L.623 B.S., J.D. 4675 Macarthur Ct.
Cordova, Ron, (BV) ........'46 '72 C.197 A.B. L.800 J.D. 130 Newport Ctr. Dr., Ste 100
Corfield, Michael A. ....................'62 '88 C.1109 B.A. L.1049 J.D. 3501 Jamboree Rd.
**Corrigan, Katherine T.** ............ '62 '87 C.112 B.A. L.990 J.D. [A Callahan&Assoc.]
*LANGUAGES: French.
*PRACTICE AREAS: Bankruptcy; Commercial Real Estate; Business Litigation; Appellate Practice.
Coss, Edward G. .............................'52 '79 C.1078 B.A. L.1095 J.D. [Lazof&C.]
Cossman, Harry ..................................'22 '52 C.229 L.800 J.D. 3121 W. Coast Hwy.‡
Cote, George J. B. .................................'27 '79 C.734 B.S. L.1137 J.D. 5 Civic Plaza
Coté, Lance R. ......................................'53 '80 C.112 B.A. L.800 J.D. [Sainick&C.]
Cotora, Craig, (P.C.) ..............................'51 '76 C.813 A.B. L.1068 J.D. [C.Cotora]⊙

Cotora, Craig, Inc., A Professional Law Corporation
1300 Dove St. Ste., 200 (©Los Angeles)
**Couchot, Paul J.** ........................'61 '87 C.112 B.A. L.1067 J.D. [Winthrop C.]
*TRANSACTIONS: Rusty Pelican Restaurants; Sherwood Shutter Corporation; Chen-Tech Industries, Inc.; Baldwin Park Town Center; Rancho Mirage Bob Hope Associates.
*PRACTICE AREAS: Bankruptcy Law; Reorganization.
Courtney, Alan W. ........................'54 '80 C.398 B.A. L.464 J.D. [A.W.Courtney]©
Courtney, Alan W., A Professional Corporation ........366 San Miguel Dr. (©Santa Ynez)

**Cox Buchanan Padmore & Shakarchy, (AV®)**
**840 Newport Center Drive, Suite 700, 92660-6310©**
**Telephone: 714-720-9100 Fax: 714-720-1508**
**Email: cbpssocal@aol.com**
**Vicki Marolt Buchanan.**
**Trial and Appellate Practice in State and Federal Courts. Corporation, Contracts, Business, International Business Transactions and Natural Resources Law.**
**Palo Alto Office: 755 Page Mill Road, Suite A280. Telephone: 415-424-0600. Fax: 415-493-9408.**
**Denver, Colorado Office: 1775 Sherman Street, Suite 2500. Telephone: 303-839-9191. Fax: 303-839-9318.**
**New York, New York Office: 630 Third Avenue. Telephone: 212-953-6633. Fax: 212-576-1614.**
***See Professional Biographies, NEWPORT BEACH, CALIFORNIA***

Coyle, Francis J., Jr. ............'50 '79 C.105 B.A.Econ. L.990 J.D. 3700 Newport Blvd.
**Coyne, Jeffrey B.** ..................'66 '91 C.228 A.B. L.800 J.D. [Ⓐ Stradling,Y.C.&R.]
Crain, E. Gene, (AV) ..................'34 '59 C.668 B.A. L.145 J.D. 5030 Campus Dr.
Cramin, Corey S. ..............'60 '84 C.112 B.A. L.464 J.D. 7th Fl., 4695 MacArthur Ct.
**Crenshaw, Kyle L.** ..........................'54 '82 C.147 B.A. L.273 J.D. [Andersen&W.]
Cristin, Michael ..........................'46 '76 C.112 B.A. L.1148 J.D. 1300 Dove St.
Crockett, David L., (BV) ....................'43 '70 C.112 B.S. L.1068 J.D. 1301 Dove St.
**Crowe, Eric M.** ..........................'51 '88 C.273 B.A. L.410 J.D. [Ⓐ Barger&W.]
Crowley, R. Terrence .....'57 '83 C.800 A.B. L.426 J.D. 4675 MacArthur Ct., Suite 1000
Crowther, Geoffrey D. ..................'50 '79 C.1077 B.A. L.1095 J.D. 149 Via Waziers
**Cucchissi, Michael S.**, (AV) ..............'53 '78 C.453 S.B. L.659 J.D. [Newmeyer&D.]
*PRACTICE AREAS: Real Estate Law.
Cullen, Philip J. ..............'21 '54 C.573 B.B.A. L.705 LL.B. 1875 Port Wheeler Pl.‡

**Cummins & White, LLP, (AV)**
**Limited Liability Partnership, including Professional Corporation**
**2424 S.E. Bristol Street, Suite 300, P.O. Box 2513, 92660-0757©**
**Telephone: 714-852-1800 Telecopier: 714-852-8510**
**Larry M. Arnold (Professional Corporation); James R. Wakefield; David Lee Carollo; Robert W. Bollar; Karen L. Taillon; Annabelle Moore Harris. Of Counsel: Thomas W. Burton; Marshall T. Hunt; Jay F. Stocker; William Bruce Voss. Associates: Lawrence E. Johnson; Laura N. MacPherson; Bradley V. Black; Patti L. Whitfield; Jeffrey Daniel Mansukhani; Susan M. Oglesby; Heather Skinner Nevis.**
**General Practice.**
**Los Angeles, California Office: 865 South Figueroa Street, 24th Floor. Telephone: 213-614-1000. Telecopier: 213-614-0500.**
**Affiliated Taipei, Taiwan Office: Chang & Associates, No. 12 Jen-Ai Road, Section 2, Seventh Floor, Taipei, Taiwan, Republic of China. Telephone: (02) 341-4602. Fax: (02) 321-6388.**
***See Professional Biographies, NEWPORT BEACH, CALIFORNIA***

**Curry, Randy D., Law Offices of '53 '85 C&L.398 B.A., J.D.**
**660 Newport Center Drive, Suite 950, 92660**
**Telephone: 714-760-3836 Fax: 714-644-0840**
**Insurance Bad Faith.**
***See Professional Biographies, NEWPORT BEACH, CALIFORNIA***

Cusic, Sharon L. ..................'54 '84 C.1147 B.B.A. L.616 J.D. 23 Corporate Plz. Dr.
Dahl, David D. ....................'46 '75 C.1042 B.A. L.1137 J.D. Prin., Dahl Co. (The)
Daily, James D. ..........................'65 '90 C.965 B.S. L.990 J.D. 4100 Newport Pl.
**Daly, Charles Dion**, (AV) ..........................'40 '70 C.813 B.A. L.1065 J.D. [C.D.Daly]

**Daly, C D, Law Corporation, (AV)**
**500 Newport Center Drive, Suite 630, 92660**
**Telephone: 714-644-9083 FAX: 714-720-3790**
**Charles Dion Daly.**
**Business, Real Estate Law and Related Litigation.**
***See Professional Biographies, NEWPORT BEACH, CALIFORNIA***

**Damon, Eric P.** ..................'65 '95 C.65 B.S.E.E. L.800 J.D. [Howard,R.N.C.F.&R.]
**Damon, James G., III** ......................'57 '84 C.367 B.A. L.426 J.D. [Voss,C.&T.]
*PRACTICE AREAS: Litigation; Complex Litigation; Lender Liability; Directors and Officers Liability; Landlord and Tenant Law.
Daniell, John R. ..........................'18 '69 C.668 L.1117 J.D. P.O. Box 8163‡
**Dapelo, Gary A., (A Professional Corporation)**, (AV) '52 '80
C.112 B.A. L.1137 J.D. [Good,W.H.&W.]
*PRACTICE AREAS: Business Litigation; Wrongful Termination; Real Estate Litigation; Intellectual Property Litigation.
Darnell, Roger D. ..................'43 '69 C&L.800 B.S., J.D. 1613 E. Bay Ave., Balboa
Davenport, Deborah L. ..........'54 '85 C&L.990 B.A., J.D. 4100 Newport Pl. Dr., Ste 700
David, George H. ..........................'45 '75 C.112 B.S. L.426 J.D. 15 Crestwood Dr.
**Davidson, Donald R., III** ..........................'46 '72 C.197 B.A. L.273 J.D. [Wolf&P.]
*PRACTICE AREAS: Mortgage Banking; Real Estate Litigation; Unlawful Detainers.
Davidson, Lawrence H., (BV) ..........'46 '73 C&L.800 B.S., J.D. 300 Newport Center Dr.

**Davies, Stanton W., II, (AV) '46 '72 C.800 B.S. L.61 J.D.**
**2700 Newport Boulevard, Suite 172, 92663**
**Telephone: 714-723-9000**
***PRACTICE AREAS: Family Law.**
**Practice Limited to Family Law. Divorce, Property Settlement, Support Issues.**
***See Professional Biographies, NEWPORT BEACH, CALIFORNIA***

Davis, G. Kay ..........................'— '86 C.844 B.S. L.1137 J.D. P.O. Box 2471
**Davis, Ryan E.** ....................'69 '96 C.112 B.A. L.800 J.D. [Ⓐ Stradling,Y.C.&R.]
**Davis, S. Eric**, (BV) ....................'42 '68 C.705 A.B. L.477 J.D. [Davis,P.K.&W.]©
*PRACTICE AREAS: Bankruptcy; Corporate; Real Estate Transactions.

**Davis, Punelli, Keathley & Willard, (AV) BB**
**610 Newport Center Drive, Suite 1000, P.O. Box 7920, 92658-7920©**
**Telephone: 714-640-0700 Telecopier: 714-640-0714**
**Members of Firm: Robert E. Willard; S. Eric Davis; Frank Punelli, Jr.; H. James Keathley; Eric G. Anderson; Katherine D. Keathley. Of Counsel: Lewis K. Uhler.**
**Real Estate and Mortgage Banking, Corporate, Partnership, Construction, Commercial, Bankruptcy, Business Litigation, Creditor's Rights Law, Environmental Law. Including Trial and Appellate Practice in all State and Federal Courts.**
**San Diego, California Office: 501 West Broadway, Suite 900, 92101. Telephone: 619-558-2581.**
***See Professional Biographies, NEWPORT BEACH, CALIFORNIA***

Davitt, Sean A., Law Offices of '58 '89
C.1042 B.S. L.1137 J.D. 3501 Jamboree Rd. Ste 600 S. Tower
Dawson, Keith A., (BV) ..............'48 '77 C.684 B.A. L.1137 J.D. Five Civic Plaza
Dean, Warren C., Jr. (Professional Corporation), (AV) '47 '73
C.1109 B.A. L.800 J.D. [Rigg&D.]
Deans, William C., (AV) ....................'37 '61 C&L.813 A.B., LL.B. [W.C.Deans]
Deans, William C., A Professional Corporation, (AV) ................ 1801 Buttonshell Lane

**DeBré, Kevin D.** ..............'60 '90 C.112 B.S. L.1065 J.D. [Ⓐ Brobeck,P.&H.] (Pat.)
*PRACTICE AREAS: Intellectual Property Licensing.
**Delli Paoli, William M.** ..............'54 '93 C.1109 B.A. L.1148 J.D. [Wentworth&P.]©
*PRACTICE AREAS: Personal Injury; Wrongful Death; Products Liability; Insurance Bad Faith; Civil Appeals.
Delsack, Kurt ..........................'33 '85 C.563 B.B.A. L.128 J.D. [Fisher&D.]
**Demos, George C.** ..............'62 '89 C.112 B.A. L.800 J.D. [© O'Melveny&M.]
*PRACTICE AREAS: Health Care.
Dempsey, John R. ..........................'55 '82 C.426 B.A. L.809 J.D. 5 Civic Plz.
Desatnik, Colyn B. ..................'55 '84 C&L.061 B.Com., LL.B. 450 Newport Dr.
Deveraux, Valerie J. ..............'60 '91 C.112 B.S. L.1137 J.D. 130 Newport Center Dr.
Dewhirst, Nancy J. ..........'66 '92 C.846 B.A. L.1068 J.D. 4675 Macarthur Ct., Suite 1000
Dey, Jeffrey R. '53 '79 C.267 B.S. L.1049 J.D.
Asst. V.P. & Invest. Coun., Pacific Mut. Life Ins. Co.
Dial, Stephen F. ....................'53 '79 C.178 A.B. L.309 J.D. 620 Newport Ctr. Dr.
**Dibb, Amy Toboco** ..................'65 '90 C.208 B.A. L.426 J.D. [Ⓐ Alvarado,S.V.&S.]
*PRACTICE AREAS: Business Litigation; Civil Litigation; Commercial Litigation.
**Dibb, Michael G.** ..................'64 '91 C&L.426 B.A., J.D. [Ⓐ Newmeyer&D.]
*PRACTICE AREAS: Insurance; Construction; Business Litigation.
Dickerson, Joe A., (BV) ............'30 '63 C.112 A.B. L.1066 J.D. 20101 S.W. Birch St.
Dickinson, Margie R. ..................'46 '88 C.112 B.A. L.1137 J.D. [Hawes&F.] (Pat.)
Dickson, Richard K., II ....................'46 '76 C.112 B.S. L.464 J.D. 1100 Quail St.
**Diebold, Donald A.** ..................'63 '90 C.228 B.S. L.910 J.D. [Ⓐ Borton,P.&C.]
*PRACTICE AREAS: Construction Defect; Personal Injury; General Liability Defense.
Dillion, Cynthia Shimon ....'57 '82 C.112 B.S. L.800 J.D. V.P., Pacific Mut. Life Ins. Co.
**Dillion, Gregory L.**, (AV) ..............'54 '80 C.188 B.A. L.846 J.D. [Newmeyer&D.]
*PRACTICE AREAS: Litigation involving Real Estate; Lender Liability; Construction and Insurance Coverage.
Diner, Helena G. .....'59 '87 C.994 B.A. L.659 J.D. 1 Monterey Pine Dr., Newport Coast
Di Noto, Frank J. ..........................'24 '50 C&L.800 B.S., J.D. 11 Bordeaux‡
**DiVincenzo, Joseph P.**, (AV) ..............'50 '75 C&L.800 B.A., J.D. [Remer,D.&G.]
*PRACTICE AREAS: Personal Injury; Corporate; Litigation.
Dixon, Ralph F. ..........................'07 '31 C&L.608 A.B., LL.B. 2503 E. Bluff Dr.‡
**Donahue, Daniel K.** ..........................'54 '80 C&L.190 B.A., J.D. [Bruck&P.]
*PRACTICE AREAS: Corporate Law; Securities Law; Commercial Transactions.
**Doss, Dennis H., (A Professional Corporation)**, (BV) '52 '78
C.1077 B.A. L.61 J.D. [Doss&P.]

**Doss & Page, (BV)**
**A Partnership including a Professional Corporation**
**Suite 590, 4695 MacArthur Court, 92660**
**Telephone: 714-752-5370 Fax: 714-752-2521**
**Dennis H. Doss (A Professional Corporation); Gregory S. Page. Associate: Daniel A. Nassie.**
**Banking, Corporate, Title Insurance, Business, Real Estate and Civil Litigation.**
***See Professional Biographies, NEWPORT BEACH, CALIFORNIA***

Dougherty, James E., (BV) ..............'30 '63 C.112 B.S. L.1068 J.D. 4100 Newport Pl.
**Draeker, Scott S.** ..................'66 '96 C.768 B.A. L.94 J.D. [Ⓐ Brobeck,P.&H.]
*PRACTICE AREAS: Intellectual Property.
**Draffin, Jill M.**, (AV) ..............'53 '78 C.112 B.A. L.1065 J.D. [McDermott,W.&E.]
*PRACTICE AREAS: Finance; Real Estate; Banks and Banking.
Dreeben, Helen L. ..........'61 '86 C.93 B.A. L.818 J.D. Gen. Coun., H & H Agency Inc.
**Dreyfus, Karen K.** ..................'61 '87 C.188 B.A. L.1065 J.D. [O'Melveny&M.]
*PRACTICE AREAS: Corporate Law.
**Drummond, William H.**, (AV) ...'31 '61 C&L.502 B.S.C.E., J.D. [Drummond&D.] (Pat.)
*PRACTICE AREAS: Patent, Trademark, Copyright and Unfair Competition Law; Litigation.

**Drummond & Duckworth, (AV) BB**
**4590 MacArthur Boulevard, Suite 500, 92660**
**Telephone: 714-724-1255 Fax: 714-724-1139**
**Email: patent_lawyer@msn.com**
**William H. Drummond; David G. Duckworth.**
**Patent, Trademark, Copyright and Unfair Competition Law, Litigation.**
***See Professional Biographies, NEWPORT BEACH, CALIFORNIA***

**Drummy King White & Gire, A Professional Corporation**
**(See Costa Mesa)**

**Drysdale, Don M., Law Offices of, (AV) '47 '76 C.1077 B.A. L.1068 J.D. BB**
**Suite 700, 610 Newport Center Drive, 92660-6442**
**Telephone: 714-760-9677 Fax: 714-760-9551**
**Email: 75722.164@compuserve.com**
**Franchise Law, Business, Corporate Law and International Domestic and Regulatory Compliance.**
***See Professional Biographies, NEWPORT BEACH, CALIFORNIA***

DuBois, Joseph E. ..........................'44 '74 C.870 B.S. L.1049 J.D. 1300 Dove St.
Du Bose, Guy '54 '79 C.800 A.B. L.1148 J.D.
Sr. V.P. & Gen. Coun., Mercury Svgs. RTC
**Duckworth, David G.** ..............'66 '93 C.770 B.S.M.E. L.426 J.D. [Drummond&D.] (Pat.)
*PRACTICE AREAS: Patent; Trademark; Unfair Competition; Related Litigation.
**Duncan, Anne Heller** ............'55 '86 C.112 B.A. L.1049 J.D. [Ⓐ McDermott,W.&E.]

**Duncan, John A., A Professional Corporation**
**(See Orange)**

Duryea, Leslie N., II, (AV) ..............'26 '50 C.679 B.S. L.813 LL.B. 1151 Dove St.
**Dyess, Robert W., Jr.** ..........................'50 '75 C.880 B.E. L.37 J.D. [Good,W.H.&W.]
*PRACTICE AREAS: Taxation; Real Estate; Business; Estate Planning.
Eadie, Scott James ........'56 '83 C.1109 B.A. L.1137 J.D. 4400 MacArthur Blvd., 5th Fl.
**Eadington, George**, (AV) ..................'50 '76 C&L.770 B.S., J.D. [Eadington,M.&E.]

**Eadington, Merhab & Eadington, A Professional Corporation, (AV) BB**
**Suite 600, South Tower, 3501 Jamboree Road, P.O. Box 9408, 92658-9408**
**Telephone: 714-854-5000 Telecopier: 714-854-5138**
**George Eadington; Marla Merhab Robinson; Debra L. Klevatt.**
**General Business, Corporate and Partnership, State and Federal Securities, Finance, Real Estate and Commercial, Employment, Taxation, Business and Commercial Litigation in all State and Federal Courts, Trust and Estate Planning and Probate and Trust Litigation.**
**References: Orange National Bank.**
***See Professional Biographies, NEWPORT BEACH, CALIFORNIA***

**Eber, Loraine P.** ..........................'55 '81 C.766 B.A. L.1065 J.D. [Severson&W.]©
Edwards, Ray H. ..........................'37 '78 C.1042 B.S. L.1137 J.D. 5 Civic Plz.
**Edwards, Steven L.**, (AV) ..............'47 '73 C.401 B.A. L.569 J.D. [O'Melveny&M.]
*PRACTICE AREAS: Real Estate.

**Edwards, Sooy & Byron, A Professional Corporation, (AV)**
**660 Newport Center Drive, Suite 465, 92660©**
**Telephone: 714-717-5000 Fax: 714-717-5001**
**URL: http://sdclaw.com/ews**
**Scott L. Ghormley.**
**Civil Litigation and Trial Practice in all State and Federal Courts with emphasis on Commercial, Governmental, Insurance and Professional Liability Defense in all Fields. Architect and Engineering Defense, Accountant Liability, Legal and Medical Defense, Municipal Corporations and Related Issues, Land Use Law, Real Estate and Construction, Delay Damage Claims, Heavy Construction Claims, Insurance Coverage, Bad Faith Litigation, Products Liability, Torts and Negligence, Wrongful Death Law, Securities Arbitration, Wrongful Termination, Employment Law.**

(This Listing Continued)

**Edwards, Sooy & Byron, A Professional Corporation (Continued)**
San Diego, California Office: 101 West Broadway, Ninth Floor, 92101. Telephone: 619-231-1500. Fax: 619-231-1588.
*See Professional Biographies, NEWPORT BEACH, CALIFORNIA*

**El-Farra, John A.** ... '69 '95 C.112 B.A. L.809 J.D. [Allen&F.]
*PRACTICE AREAS: Civil Trial Practice; Personal Injury Law; Product Liability Law; Negligence Law.
Ellingson, John R. ... '46 '74 C.1042 B.S. L.1049 J.D. [Howser&B.]
**Ellis, Holly A.** ... '63 '93 C.112 B.A. L.800 J.D. [Ⓐ Stradling,Y.C.&R.]
**Ellis, Karen A.** ... '38 '80 C.1209 B.A. L.128 J.D. [Stradling,Y.C.&R.]
Ellis, Tracee L. ... '69 '94 C&L.800 B.S., J.D. 4675 MacArthur Ct.

**Ellowitz, Jonathan R. '46 '79 C.112 B.A. L.809 J.D.**
**One Corporate Plaza, Suite 110, 92660**
Telephone: 714-640-8441 Telefax: 714-640-9009
Small Business and Bankruptcy Law.
*See Professional Biographies, NEWPORT BEACH, CALIFORNIA*

Emard, Bruce A. '53 '81
C.112 B.A. L.990 J.D. 840 Newport Ctr. Rd., Ste 700 (⊙Santa Ana)
**Engelhardt, Carol L.** ... '45 '70 C.112 B.A. L.1068 J.D. Coun., Coldwell Banker
**Ermer, Michael G.** ... '58 '83 C.910 A.B. L.309 J.D. [Irell&M.]
Ertz, Julian S. ... '19 '53 C.831 B.S.C. L.560 J.D. 1617 Westcliff Dr.‡
Esnard, R. Paul ... '24 '54 C&L.800 B.A., J.D. 319 Marine Ave.
Evans, John Franklin, (P.C.), (AV) ... '43 '69 C&L.800 B.S., J.D. 4000 MacArthur Blvd.
Evans, Mark D. ... '51 '88 C.1049 B.S. L.398 J.D. 4675 Macarthur Ct.
**Evertz, Douglas J.** ... '60 '86 C.1049 B.A. L.464 J.D. [Ⓐ Stradling,Y.C.&R.]
Eyrich, Keith C. ... '52 '77 C.1042 B.A. L.990 J.D. V.P., Develop., The Irvine Co.
**Fahrney, Richard L., II**, (AV) ... '52 '77 C.112 B.A. L.1049 J.D. [Fingal,F.&C.]
*PRACTICE AREAS: Litigation; Real Estate; Business; Health Care; Insurance.
Fait, Kenneth E. ... '43 '70 C.813 A.B. L.61 J.D. P.O. Box 1960‡
Farnell, R. Richard, (AV) ... '43 '68 C.605 B.A. L.37 J.D. [R.R.Farnell]
Farnell, R. Richard, A Prof. Corp., (AV) ... 4675 MacArthur Ct., 12th Floor
Farrell, David J. ... '61 '90 C.1109 B.A. L.1137 J.D. [Barnes&F.]
Farrin, James S. ... '62 '90 C.855 B.A. L.228 J.D. 840 Newport Ctr. Dr.
Faulkner, D. Scott ... '51 '76 C.911 B.A. L.378 J.D. Santa Barbara Svgs. & Loan Assn.
Fedrick, Michael F. ... '65 '91 C.813 B.S. L.1068 J.D. 620 Newport Ctr. Dr. (Pat.)

**Feeley, Thomas J., P.C., Law Office of**
(See Los Angeles)

**Feffer, Ethan D.** ... '66 '92 C.112 A.B. L.1065 J.D. [Ⓐ Brobeck,P.&H.]
Fehrmann, Kevin M. ... '49 '77 C.774 B.A. L.809 J.D. 4425 Jamboree Blvd.
**Feick, Douglas P.** ... '65 '91 C.473 B.S. L.800 J.D. [Ⓐ Stradling,Y.C.&R.]
Feinberg, Ross W. ... '58 '85 C.800 B.S. L.1049 J.D. [Feldsott L.&F.]
Feld, Richard G. ... '60 '85 C.112 B.S. L.1065 J.D. [Rodarti,F.&G.]
Feldman, Melvin S., (AV) ... '35 '61 C&L.659 B.S., LL.B. 1300 Dove St.
**Feldmann, R. Scott** ... '61 '93 C.880 B.E. L.1066 J.D. [Ⓐ Brobeck,P.&H.]
*LANGUAGES: Portuguese.
*PRACTICE AREAS: Intellectual Property Litigation; Intellectual Property Counseling; Business Litigation.
Feldsott, Stanley, (BV) ... '41 '70 C.1077 B.S. L.800 J.D. [Feldsott L.&F.]
Feldsott Lee & Feinberg, (BV) ... 4 Civic Plz. Ste. 300
Fell, Richard M. ... '55 '80 C&L.800 B.S., J.D. Pres., Fell Capital Mgmt.
Ferentz, Jeff D., (P.C.), (AV) '52 '79
C.112 B.A. L.1137 J.D. 500 Newport Ctr. Dr., 2nd Fl.
**Ferrentino, Joseph A.** ... '67 '92 C.1075 B.A. L.426 J.D. [Ⓐ Newmeyer&D.]
*PRACTICE AREAS: Business Litigation; Construction Litigation; Insurance.
**Feuchter, Bruce**, (AV) ... '53 '79 C.112 B.A. L.1065 J.D. [Stradling,Y.C.&R.]
Fick, Robert C. ... '45 '76 C&L.502 B.S.M.E., J.D. Sr. Atty., F.D.I.C.
**Fields, David M.** '57 '83 C.976 B.A. L.309 J.D.
V.P. & Gen. Coun., Irvine Retail Properties Co.
Finch, Judith Malone, (AV) '44 '76 C.326 B.A. L.262 J.D.
Exec. V.P. & Gen. Coun., Imperial Corp. of Amer.
**Fineman, Teresa Tormey** ... '64 '89 C.112 B.A. L.990 J.D. [Bruck&P.]
*PRACTICE AREAS: Corporate Law; Securities Law; Commercial Transactions.
Finerty, James P. ... '42 '84 C.770 B.S. L.426 J.D. [Ⓐ Barclay]
**Fingal, Stephen L.** ... '50 '77 C.1109 B.A. L.1067 J.D. [Fingal,F.&C.]
*PRACTICE AREAS: Real Estate Law; Corporations Law; Estate Planning Law.

**Fingal, Fahrney & Clark, LLP, (AV)**
**333 Bayside Drive, 92660**
Telephone: 714-557-7676 Fax: 714-755-1276
Email: FCC@PACBELL.NET
Stephen L. Fingal; Richard L. Fahrney II; Christopher R. Clark.
Full service Business and Litigation practice. General Civil and Trial practice in State and Federal Courts. Real Estate, Corporate, Business Transactions, Estate Planning, Sports Law, Health Law, Construction Defect, Insurance Bad Faith, and Complex Litigation.

**Fink, Leonard T.** ... '67 '94 C.36 B.S. L.1049 J.D. [Ⓐ Sims,M.&M.]
**Fink, Richard A.** ... '55 '81 C.347 B.A. L.597 J.D. [Brobeck,P.&H.] (⊙Denver, CO)
*PRACTICE AREAS: General Corporate Law; Securities Law; Venture Capital Law.
Finnegan, Jeffrey C. ... '49 '79 C.945 B.S. L.809 J.D. R.T.C.
Fisher, Paul E. ... '59 '86 C.112 B.A. L.1065 J.D. [Fisher&D.]
Fisher & Delsack ... 3501 Jamboree Rd., 6th Fl.

**Fisher & Phillips, (AV)** Ⓑ
A Partnership including Professional Corporations and Associations
**4675 MacArthur Court, Suite 550, 92660**⊙
Telephone: 714-851-2424 Telecopier: 714-851-0152
Resident Members: Robert J. Bekken; James J. McDonald, Jr.; Karl R. Lindegren; Robert V. Schnitz.
Resident Associates: Georgia V. Ingram; Robert Yonowitz; John M. Polson; Lyne A. Richardson; Cynthia Walker Lane; Jeffrey B. Freid; Warren Lee Nelson; Anne M. Terra; Christopher C. Hoffman; Nancy E. McAllister; Michelle M. Casey; Christina T. Nguyen.
Atlanta, Georgia Office: 1500 Resurgens Plaza, 945 East Paces Ferry Road, N.E., 30326. Telephone: 404-231-1400. Telecopier: 404-240-4249. Telex: 54-2331.
Fort Lauderdale, Florida Office: Suite 2300 NationsBank Tower, One Financial Plaza, 33394. Telephone: 954-525-4800. Telecopier: 954-525-8739.
Redwood City, California Office: Suite 345, Three Lagoon Drive, 94065. Telephone: 415-592-6160. Telecopier: 415-592-6385.
New Orleans, Louisiana Office: 3710 Place St. Charles, 201 St. Charles Avenue, 70170. Telephone: 504-522-3303. Telecopier: 504-529-3850.
*See Professional Biographies, NEWPORT BEACH, CALIFORNIA*

**Flatt, John C.**, (BV) ... '44 '70 C.692 B.A. L.64 J.D. [Allen&F.]
*PRACTICE AREAS: Negligence Law; Business Litigation; Insurance Coverage.

**Fleischli, Jack A., (BV) '49 '75 C.112 B.A. L.990 J.D.**
**1300 Dove Street, Suite 200, 92660**
Telephone: 714-660-7200 Fax: 714-660-0308
Constuction Defects, Real Estate and Business Litigation.
*See Professional Biographies, NEWPORT BEACH, CALIFORNIA*

Flicker, Martin L. ... '51 '78 C.608 B.A. L.208 J.D. 4650 Von Karman Ave.
**Florman, Martin P.** ... '63 '89 C.112 B.A. L.809 J.D. [Ⓐ McDermott,W.&E.]
**Flynn, Michael E.**, (AV) ... '60 '85 C.602 B.B.A. L.426 J.D. [Stradling,Y.C.&R.]

Fogarty, Kimberly V. ... '59 '92 C.37 B.A. L.1137 J.D. [Hawes&F.]
Fohrman, Jeffrey W. ... '58 '89 C.1077 B.S. L.1137 J.D. [Ⓐ Mozingo&P.]
Foley, Thomas R. ... '66 '94 C.546 B.S. L.800 J.D. 840 Newport Center Dr., Suite 500
**Fossum, John C., (P.C.)**, (AV) ... '41 '67 C.112 B.A. L.1066 LL.B. [Irell&M.]
**Foster, Carol** ... '42 '93 C.802 B.A. L.112 J.D. [Ⓐ Andersen&W.]
*PRACTICE AREAS: Business Litigation; Real Property Litigation; Bankruptcy.
Foster, Robert A., (AV) ... '22 '50 C&L.900 A.B., J.D. 404 E. Oceanfront‡
Fowler, Larned B. ... '54 '80 C.674 B.A. L.262 J.D. 4675 MacArthur Ct.
**Fox, Melissa J.** ... '68 '93 C.1036 B.A. L.861 J.D. [Ⓐ Greenbaum&K.]⊙
*LANGUAGES: Hebrew.
*PRACTICE AREAS: Collections; Probate; Trusts and Estates; Criminal Law.
**Freeman, Stephen T.** ... '58 '84 C.477 B.B.A. L.215 J.D. [Stradling,Y.C.&R.]
**Freid, Jeffrey B.** ... '68 93 C.846 B.B.A. L.426 J.D. [Ⓐ Fisher&P.]
Friedenberg, Mildred M. ... '21 '60 L.809 58 Sea Pine Lane
Friedland, Jennifer M. ... '68 '92 C.813 A.B. L.309 J.D. 610 Newport Beach Ctr. Dr.
**Friedland, Michael K.** '66 '91 C.112 B.A. L.309 J.D.
[Knobbe,M.O.&B.] (See Pat. Sect.)
*LANGUAGES: Spanish and Russian.
Friend, Susan B. ... '61 '86 C.112 B.A. L.61 J.D. 1839 Highland Dr.
**Fritz, Linda C.**, (BV) ... '52 '83 L.1137 J.D. [Kimball,T.&S.] (⊙San Diego)
*LANGUAGES: Spanish.
*PRACTICE AREAS: Real Estate Litigation; Business Litigation.
**Frobes, Patricia**, (AV) ... '47 '78 C.33 B.A. L.878 J.D. [O'Melveny&M.]
**Frost, Dana E.** ... '70 '96 C.112 B.A. L.1067 J.D. [Ⓐ Brobeck,P.&H.]
*LANGUAGES: Spanish.
*PRACTICE AREAS: Corporate; Securities.
**Frydman, Ben A.**, (AV) ... '47 '73 C.112 A.B. L.309 J.D. [Stradling,Y.C.&R.]
Fujimoto, Daniel K. ... '65 '92 C.112 B.A. L.1067 J.D. 1301 Dove St., Ste 850
Fundenberg, William C., Jr., (BV) ... '32 '60 C&L.813 A.B., LL.B. 3 Civil Plaza‡
Gabrielson, N. Brooke, (AV) ... '44 '68 C&L.800 B.A., J.D. [Howser&B.]
**Gale, Paul L.**, (AV) ... '50 '75 C.112 A.B. L.1068 J.D. [Stradling,Y.C.&R.]
Gallagher, Maureen A., (BV) ... '51 '83 C.800 B.S. L.426 J.D. R.T.C.
**Gallagher, Shannon** ... '57 '82 C.770 B.S.C. L.426 J.D. [Ⓐ Gardner&Q.]
*PRACTICE AREAS: Taxation.
**Gallo, Joseph P.** ... '65 '94 C.605 A.B. L.1148 J.D. [Kelegian&T.]
*PRACTICE AREAS: Construction Defect; Premises Liability.
Galvin, John Patrick, Sr., (AV) '33 '72
C&L.215 B.S., J.D. 610 Newport Ctr. Dr. Ste 1240‡
Gammill, Victor L. ... '54 '78 C.1109 B.A. L.426 J.D. 20301 S.W. Birch St.
**Gardner, David H.**, (AV) ... '46 '73 C.112 A.B. L.1068 J.D. [Gardner&Q.]
*PRACTICE AREAS: Taxation.
Gardner, Jeffrey B. '56 '84
C.745 B.S. L.61 J.D. [Saxon,B.G.&K.] (⊙San Dimas & Riverside)

**Gardner and Quan, Incorporated, (AV)**
**5000 Birch Street, Suite 4400, 92660**
Telephone: 714-851-9025 FAX: 714-752-7132
David H. Gardner; Judy A. Quan; Shannon Gallagher.
Federal, State and International Taxation, General Business, Corporations, Pension and Profit Sharing. Estate Planning, Probate, Real Property, Health Care, Securities, ERISA and Tax Litigation.
Reference: Marine National Bank.
*See Professional Biographies, NEWPORT BEACH, CALIFORNIA*

Garon, Jon ... '63 '88 C.494 B.A. L.178 J.D. [Ⓒ Hawes&F.]
Garretson, Robert A. ... '42 '72 C&L.426 B.A., J.D. 1201 Dove St.
Garrett, Thomas B., (AV) ... '53 '78 C.112 B.A. L.1049 J.D. [Cheadle&G.]
**Garrett, William E.** ... '65 '93 C.659 B.S. L.1065 [Ⓐ Stradling,Y.C.&R.]
**Garris, Christian J.** ... '68 '94 C.154 B.A. L.770 J.D. [Ⓐ R.K.Scott]
Gefis, Carol A. ... '60 '89 C.963 B.S. L.300 J.D. 4675 MacArthur Ct.
Geib, Richard J. '39 '67 C.309 A.B. L.1066 J.D.
Asst. V.P. & Invest. Coun., Pacific Mut. Life Ins. Co.
**Geiger, Paul J.**, (AV) ... '49 '75 C&L.426 B.B.A., J.D. [Geiger&W.]
*PRACTICE AREAS: Real Estate; General Business; Franchise.

**Geiger & Weber, (AV)**
**Westerly Place, 1500 Quail Street, Suite 200, 92660**
Telephone: 714-756-0100 Facsimile: 714-756-0137
Paul J. Geiger; Marc Lindsey Weber. Associate: Nicola J. Trigg.
Real Estate, Franchise, Corporate and General Business; Litigation in areas of Franchise, Real Estate, Business and ERISA; Tax, Probate and Estate Planning.
*See Professional Biographies, NEWPORT BEACH, CALIFORNIA*

Gelfer, Scott H. ... '60 '85 C.1042 B.S. L.426 J.D. [Rodarti,F.&G.]
Generaux, Arthur P., Jr., (AV) ... '34 '61 C.986 B.B.A. L.374 LL.B. [A.P.Generaux]
Generaux, Arthur P., A Law Corporation, (AV) ... 4400 MacArthur Blvd., Ste. 500
**Genova, Gina L.** ... '67 '92 C.112 B.A. L.464 J.D. [Ⓐ Remer,D.&G.]
**Genovese, C. Timothy** ... '62 '88 L.61 J.D. [Kimball,T.&S.]
*PRACTICE AREAS: Landlord/Tenant; Real Estate.

**Genovese, Michael J., (AV) '48 '76 C.35 B.S. L.1137 J.D.**
**2123 San Joaquin Hills Road, 92660**
Telephone: 714-729-8000 FAX: 714-729-1580
General Business, Real Estate, Corporate, Partnership and Taxation Law.
*See Professional Biographies, NEWPORT BEACH, CALIFORNIA*

Geocaris, James A., (AVⓉ) ... '49 '75 C.309 B.A. L.813 J.D. 100 Bayview Ct.
**George, Paul B.**, (AV) ... '47 '73 C.629 B.S. L.767 J.D. [McDermott,W.&E.]
Gertner, Michael Avey, (AV) ... '39 '65 C.659 B.S. L.178 J.D. 4340 Campus Dr.
**Ghormley, Scott L.** ... '50 '76 C.813 B.A. L.1065 J.D. [Ⓐ Edwards,S.&B.]
*LANGUAGES: French.
Giannone, Patricia B. ... '55 '84 C.1042 B.A. L.809 J.D. [Bowie A.K.W.&G.]
Gibeaut, Randy A. ... '46 '73 C.112 B.A. L.284 J.D. 1117 W. Bay Ave.‡
**Gibson, Darryl S.** ... '64 '89 C&L.800 B.S., J.D. [Ⓐ Stradling,Y.C.&R.]
Gibson, Julia A. ... '61 '92 C&L.1137 B.S.L., J.D. 4675 MacArthur Ct., Ste. 900

**Gibson, Dunn & Crutcher LLP**
(See Irvine)

**Giezentanner, John P.** ... '64 '94 C.112 B.S. L.309 J.D. [Knobbe,M.O.&B.]
Gifford, Anne K. ... '42 '77 C.014 B.A. L.1137 J.D. 705 W. Bay Ave.
Gillette, George C., (AV) ... '21 '49 C.696 L.309 J.D. 412 62nd St.‡
**Gilmore, Richard C.** ... '65 '93 C&L.878 B.S., J.D. [Knobbe,M.O.&B.]
Glasier, Richard L. ... '27 '56 C.999 L.1001 LL.B. 3409 Finley Ave.‡
**Glassman, Daniel** ... '70 '95 C.105 B.S. L.800 J.D. [Ⓐ Stradling,Y.C.&R.]
Gleason, John S. ... '57 '84 C.112 B.A. L.1065 J.D. 620 Newport Ctr. Dr.
Gleason, John S. ... '57 '85 C.112 B.A. L.1065 J.D. [Bridgford,K.&G.]
Glenn, Everett L. ... '52 '77 C.604 B.A. L.930 J.D. 4695 MacArthur Court
Godbey, Dexter W. ... '47 '72 C.112 B.A. L.1068 J.D. 213 Via Cordova
**Goetz, Jon E.** ... '60 '87 C.112 B.A. L.309 J.D. [Stradling,Y.C.&R.]

**Gold, Philip John, (BV) '29 '77 C.112 B.S. L.990 J.D.**
**1301 Dove Street, Suite 440, 92660**
Telephone: 714-752-0800 Fax: 714-752-0313
Practice Limited To Probate, Estate Planning, Guardianship, Conservatorship, Wills, Trusts and Elder Law.

(This Listing Continued)

**Gold, Philip John (Continued)**
Reference: Union Bank (Sunny Hills Branch).
*See Professional Biographies, NEWPORT BEACH, CALIFORNIA*

**Goldstock, Barry P., (AV) '41 '68 C.112 B.A. L.1068 J.D.**
**Suite 200, 1300 Dove Street, 92660**
Telephone: 714-955-0200 Fax: 714-955-3682
*PRACTICE AREAS: Family Law (100%).
Family Law.

**Golubow, Richard H.** ....................'64 '92 C.1044 B.S. L.809 J.D. [Winthrop C.]
*TRANSACTIONS: Tam's Stationers, Inc.; BHI Dover XI; BHI Dover Fund IVII; Sunrise Growers, Inc.
*PRACTICE AREAS: Bankruptcy Law; Corporate Reorganization; Workouts.

**Good, Wildman, Hegness & Walley, (AV)**
A Partnership including Professional Corporations
**5000 Campus Drive, 92660**
Telephone: 714-955-1100 Fax: 714-833-0633
Members of Firm: Thomas J. O'Keefe (A Professional Corporation) (Certified Specialist, Taxation Law, The State Bar of California Board of Legal Specialization); John A. Stillman; Thomas E. Walley; Paul C. Hegness, A Professional Corporation; Robert W. Dyess, Jr. (Certified Specialist, Taxation Law, The State Bar of California Board of Legal Specialization); Gary A. Dapelo (A Professional Corporation); Richard L. Seide; Ronald K. Brown, Jr., (A Professional Corporation); Kristine A. Thagard; Heidi Stilb Lewis; Nancy E. Raney; Paul W. Wildman (1924-1983).
General Civil Litigation and Commercial Trial Practice, Real Estate, Acquisition, Development and Financing, Construction, Commercial Landlord-Tenant, Business and Commercial Transactions, Securities, Taxation, Estate Planning, Probate and Trusts, Intellectual Property and Licensing, Family Law, Labor and Employment Law, Alternative Dispute Resolution and White Collar Criminal Defense.
*See Professional Biographies, NEWPORT BEACH, CALIFORNIA*

**Gooding, Martha K.** ............'54 '81 C.1042 B.A. L.1066 J.D. [Howard,R.N.C.F.&R.]
*PRACTICE AREAS: Business Litigation; Securities Litigation; Arbitration; Alternative Dispute Resolution.
**Gooding, Robert E., Jr.**, (AV) .....'44 '69 C.597 B.S. L.477 J.D. [Howard,R.N.C.F.&R.]
*PRACTICE AREAS: Trials and Appellate Practice; Securities and Antitrust Litigation; Business Litigation; Professional Responsibility Litigation.
**Goodman, Richard C.**, (AV) .........'45 '71 C.112 B.A. L.1068 J.D. [Stradling,Y.C.&R.]
**Goon, Lisa Schechter** ...............'64 '91 C.112 B.S. L.1068 J.D. [⊠ Brobeck,P.&H.]
*PRACTICE AREAS: Securities; General Corporate Representation.
**Goossens, Dorit** ......................'68 '94 C.1259 B.S. L.809 J.D. [⊠ Winthrop C.]
**Gordon, Lee M.** ...................'69 '94 C.112 B.A. L.309 J.D. [⊠ Howard,R.N.C.F.&R.]
Gordon, Stanley M., (AV) ..........'46 '72 C.112 B.A. L.1068 J.D. 610 Newport Ctr. Dr.

**Gorman, James R. '44 '76 C.645 B.S. L.1049 J.D.**
**4041 McArthur Boulevard, Suite 400, 92660-2554**
Telephone: 714-752-2266 Fax: 714-756-0625
(Also Of Counsel, Barnes, Crosby & FitzGerald).
*PRACTICE AREAS: Business Litigation; General and Civil Litigation; Estate Planning.
Business Litigation, General and Civil Litigation, Estate Planning.
*See Professional Biographies, NEWPORT BEACH, CALIFORNIA*

Goseco, Frank E. ..........'60 '87 C.112 B.A. L.1137 J.D. 4675 MacArthur Ct., Ste. 900
Gowdy, J. David '54 '82
C.375 B.A. L.101 J.D. 4695 MacArthur Ct., Ste., 840 (⊙Irving, TX)
Gradishar, Rudolph L. ....................'16 '55 C.494 B.B.A. L.800 J.D. 118 Via Lorca‡
**Grant, Devon D.** ........................'64 '95 C.937 B.S. L.1137 J.D. [⊠ White&R.]
*PRACTICE AREAS: Business Law; Estate Planning; Probate; Conservation.
Gray, John S. ................................'— '75 C.763 B.A. L.284 J.D. 5160 Birch St.
**Gray, Pamela C.**, (AV) '44 '76 C.914 B.A. L.426 J.D.
[O'Melveny&M.] (⊙Los Angeles)
**Gray, Veronica M., (Law Corporation)**, (BV) '48 '76
C.1044 B.A. L.990 J.D. [White&R.]
*PRACTICE AREAS: Business and Real Estate Litigation.
**Greek, Susan E.** ................................'58 '86 C.112 B.A. L.61 J.D. [Kimball,T.&S.]
*PRACTICE AREAS: Landlord/Tenant.
Green, Philip W. ........................'54 '79 C.112 B.A. L.1068 J.D. 100 Bayview Cir.
**Green, Todd A.** .........................'67 '95 C.674 A.B. L.178 J.D. [⊠ O'Melveny&M.]
**Greenbaum, Martin B., (P.C.)**, (AV) '45 '69 C.112 B.A. L.1068 J.D.
[Greenbaum&K.]⊙
*PRACTICE AREAS: Collections; Mechanics Lien Law; Enforcement of Judgement Law; Construction Collection.

**Greenbaum & Katz, (AV)**
An Association including a Professional Corporation
**359 San Miguel Drive, 92660**
Telephone: 714-760-1400 Fax: 714-760-1300
URL: http://www.collectionlaw.com
Martin B. Greenbaum (P.C.); Stuart A. Katz;—Melissa J. Fox.
Collection, Enforcement of Judgments, Mechanics Liens, Construction Payment Law.
*See Professional Biographies, NEWPORT BEACH, CALIFORNIA*

**Greene, Andra Barmash** ......................'57 '81 C.103 B.A. L.309 J.D. [Irell&M.]
Greene, Donald L. ...................................................'29 '69 211 Nata
**Greer, Phillip B.** ............................'53 '80 C.112 B.A. L.809 J.D. [Borton,P.&C.]
*PRACTICE AREAS: Business Litigation; Construction Litigation.
Gribben, Walter P. '33 '62 C&L.800 B.A., J.D.
Chmn. of the Bd., The Royal Intl. Partners Ltd.
Grierson, R. Scot ....................'65 '93 C.312 B.A. L.1188 J.D. 500 Newport Ctr. Dr.
**Griffith, Dwight J.**, (AV) .......................'50 '75 C&L.800 B.A., J.D. [Remer,D.&G.]
*PRACTICE AREAS: Estate Planning; Trust; Transactional.
Grimwade, Richard L. '45 '71 C.399 B.A. L.966 J.D.
4400 MacArthur Blvd., 7th Fl. (⊙Los Angeles)
**Grover, Neel** ..........................'71 '95 C.112 B.A. L.1049 J.D. [⊠ Brobeck,P.&H.]
**Gruettke, Anita** ......................'58 '96 C.1075 B.A. L.800 J.D. [⊠ Brobeck,P.&H.]
*PRACTICE AREAS: Litigation; Employment.
Grumman, Barry Jon ......................'51 '75 C.112 B.A. L.1095 J.D. [Grumman&M.]
Grumman & Mazura ........................................................ 4041 MacArthur Blvd.
**Gudmestad, Terje** ........'54 '83 C.1109 B.S.E.E. L.426 J.D. Hughes Aircraft Co. (Pat.)
**Gunn, Marguerite L.** ...................'60 '87 C.339 B.S. L.146 J.D. [Knobbe,M.O.&B.]
Gurwell, Karin Easter .....................'48 '79 C.112 B.A. L.809 J.D. 1300 Dove St.
Gustafson, John M. .....................'44 '71 C.303 B.A. L.345 J.D. 4590 Macarthur Blvd.
**Gustafson, Kay Virginia** ......................'52 '77 C&L.813 A.B., J.D. [⊠ Wolf&P.]
*PRACTICE AREAS: Mortgage Banking; Regulatory Matters; Real Estate; General Business Transactions.
Guze, Jennifer L. .................'54 '79 C.813 B.A. L.800 J.D. Pacific Mut. Life Ins. Co.
**Habel, James P.** ..........................'62 '88 C.349 B.S. L.93 J.D. [Kelegian&T.]
*PRACTICE AREAS: Personal Injury Defense; Civil Litigation.
Hacker, Kerry V. ..................................'44 '78 C.112 B.S. L.1137 J.D. P.O. Box 5918
Hackett, Terry C., (AV) ...........'48 '73 C&L.800 B.S., J.D. 3 Upper Newport Plaza Dr.
Hackler, Walter A. ...............'37 '74 C.966 B.S. L.990 J.D. 2372 S.E. Bristol St. (Pat.)
**Haddan, Jon R.**, (AV) .........................'52 '77 C.800 B.S. L.1068 J.D. [Phillips&H.]
*PRACTICE AREAS: Corporate Law; Securities.
Hafer, Stanley J. ...........................'29 '61 C.502 B.S. L.809 LL.B. P.O. Box 10246
Hafif, Herbert, (AV) ........................'29 '56 C.668 B.A. L.800 J.D. [H.Hafif]⊙
Hafif, Herbert, A Professional Corporation, (AV) ..............3 Civic Plz. (⊙Claremont)

**Hagen, Catherine Burcham**, (AV) '43 '78
C.605 B.A. L.426 J.D. [O'Melveny&M.] (⊙Los Angeles)
*PRACTICE AREAS: Labor and Employment; Sexual Harassment and Disability Discrimination.
**Hagler, James T.** ..................'65 '95 C.871 B.S.E.E. L.1049 J.D. [Knobbe,M.O.&B.]
Hahn, Thomas G., A Professional Law Corporation, (BV) '47 '72
C.813 B.A. L.61 J.D. 1301 Dove St.
**Hall, Elizabeth T.** ......................'67 '92 C.103 A.B. L.184 J.D. [⊠ Brobeck,P.&H.]
*PRACTICE AREAS: Corporate; Securities; Venture Capital.
**Hallett, Bruce R.** .........................'56 '81 C.112 B.A. L.1068 J.D. [Brobeck,P.&H.]
*PRACTICE AREAS: Corporate Finance and Securities Law.
Halloran, Robert L., (AV) ..........................................'36 '67 L.809 LL.B. 333 Bayside Dr.
**Halpern, Stacey R.** .......................'64 '93 C.690 B.A. L.464 J.D. [Knobbe,M.O.&B.]
Hamer, W. Spencer ....................'69 '96 C.477 B.A. L.800 J.D. 4675 MacArthur Ct.
**Hamilton, Theodore C.**, (AV) ..............'56 '83 C&L.813 A.B., J.D. [O'Melveny&M.]
Hammad, Michael ..........................................'39 '75 C.1097 B.S. L.1190 J.D. 1201 Dove St.
**Hamman, Donald J.** ........................'55 '80 C.112 B.A. L.1065 J.D. [Stradling,Y.C.&R.]
**Hampton, George L., IV** ...........'64 '89 C.691 B.A. L.846 J.D. [⊠ McDermott,W.&E.]
Handel, Arthur Mark ....................'50 '77 C.659 B.S. L.800 J.D. 250 Newport Ctr. Dr.
Handweiler, Martin C., (AV) ...................................'40 '72 L.990 J.D. [M.C.Handweiler]
Handweiler, Martin C., Inc., (AV) ...................................................1201 Dove St.

**Hankin, Theodore M., (AV) '52 '77 C.112 A.B. L.1065 J.D.** ⊠
**Suite 900, One Newport Place, 92660**
Telephone: 714-752-8840 FAX: 714-851-1732
Corporate, Business, Tax, Probate and Estate Planning Law. Civil Litigation, Business Transactions, Banking, Real Estate, Partnership.
*See Professional Biographies, NEWPORT BEACH, CALIFORNIA*

**Hanle, Steven M.** ..........................'63 '93 C.112 B.S. L.426 J.D. [⊠ Stradling,Y.C.&R.]
**Hansen, Loren P., (P.C.)**, (AV) ..............'50 '79 C.112 B.A. L.426 J.D. [Knecht&H.]
*PRACTICE AREAS: Banking Law; Securities Law; Corporate Law.
Hanson, Rondell B., (AV) ........'37 '63 C.813 B.A. L.1066 J.D. 190 Newport Center Dr.
Hardiman, Gráinne W. ..................'43 '85 C.061 B.A. L.1137 J.D. 5120 Campus Dr.

**Hargan, Mark C., (AV) '51 '78 C.1254 B.S.B.A. L.1137 J.D.**
**1300 Dove Street, Suite 200, 92660**
Telephone: 714-851-1229 Fax: 714-851-5014
*REPORTED CASES: National Marble Co. v. Bricklayers and Allied Craftsmen (1986) 184 Cal. App. 3d 1057.
Construction Litigation, Civil Litigation, Business, Corporate, Real Estate Law, Bankruptcy, Insolvency and Creditor's Rights.
*See Professional Biographies, NEWPORT BEACH, CALIFORNIA*

Harker, James G. ...............................'47 '77 C.966 B.A. L.1137 J.D. 2422 Santiago Dr.
Harkins, Daniel M. .............'49 '74 C&L.378 B.A., J.D. 4695 MacArthur Ct., Ste., 840
Harlan, Nancy M. '46 '75 C.1073 B.S. L.1066 J.D.
Sr. V.P., Pres. & Gen. Coun., The Presley Cos.
**Harle, Jakob S.** ..................................................'62 '87 C.112 B.A. L.1068 J.D. [Harle,J.&K.]
*LANGUAGES: German.
*PRACTICE AREAS: Community Association Law; Real Estate; General Corporate.

**Harle, Janics & Kannen**
**1300 Dove Street, Suite 200, 92660**
Telephone: 714-756-2170 Fax: 714-756-2171
Jakob S. Harle; Kathleen A. Janics; Karen A. Kannen.
Community Association Law, Real Estate, General Corporate, Civil Litigation.
*See Professional Biographies, NEWPORT BEACH, CALIFORNIA*

**Harpole, Myron E.**, (AV) ....................'27 '50 C.112 B.A. L.309 J.D. [Witter&H.]⊙
Harriman, Harold C. ........................'33 '65 C.112 B.A. L.1026 LL.B. P.O. Box 3605
Harrington, Bruce E., (AV) ..................'44 '70 C.154 B.A. L.1068 J.D. 1301 Dove St.
**Harris, Annabelle Moore** ....................'61 '87 C.1109 B.A. L.464 J.D. [Cummins&W.]
*PRACTICE AREAS: Insurance Coverage and Bad Faith.
**Harris, Rhonda R.** ............................'66 '93 C.1074 B.A. L.770 J.D. [⊠ R.K.Scott]
Harrison, Dean W. '31 '59 C.674 A.B. L.178 LL.B.
Sr. V.P., Secy. & Gen. Coun., RTC-Gibraltar Svgs.
Hartley, Les J. ......................'36 '61 C.112 B.S. L.426 LL.B. 1301 Dove St., Ste 450
Hartman, Jeffrey A., (BV) ...................'49 '75 C.61 B.A. L.990 J.D. 4 Corporate Plaza
Harvey, Donald W. ...................'32 '75 C.688 B.S. L.990 J.D. 2039 Port Weybridge Pl.
**Harvey, Richard A.** ......................'44 '74 C.1042 B.S. L.1065 J.D. [⊠ S.Casselberry]
*PRACTICE AREAS: Real Estate Law; Commercial Law; Litigation; Contractor's Law.
**Harwood, Dennis W.**, (AV) .................'38 '65 C.668 B.A. L.800 LL.B. [Barger&W.]
*PRACTICE AREAS: Real Property Law; Corporate Law; Securities Law.

**Harwood, Adkinson & Meindl**
(See Barger & Wolen)

Hawekotte, John W., Jr. .........'48 '78 C.770 B.S.C. L.1068 J.D. 4400 MacCarthur Blvd.
Hawes & Fischer ................................................... 660 Newport Center Dr. (Pat.)

**Hawkins, Robert C., Law Offices of '51 '87 C.763 B.A. L.629 J.D.**
**110 Newport Center Drive Suite 200, 92260**
Telephone: 714-650-5550 FAX: 714-650-1181
Email: rhawkins@earthlink.net
Water Law, Municipal Law, Condemnation/Land Use and Environmental Law.
*See Professional Biographies, NEWPORT BEACH, CALIFORNIA*

Hawley, Dale E. .....'43 '75 C.763 B.S. L.1188 J.D. Asst. V.P., Pacific Mut. Life Ins. Co.
Hays, William T. ........................................'21 '49 C.190 L.767 LL.B. 3700 Campus Dr.

**Hayton, Arthwell C., (AV) '20 '49**
**200 Paris Lane, Suite 114, 92663**
Telephone: 714-646-0775 Fax: 714-646-1776
Court Appointed Referee, Arbitrator and Judge Pro Tem.

**Healy, Debra Solle** ...................'54 '79 C.1075 B.A. L.426 J.D. [Buchalter,N.F.&Y.]
*PRACTICE AREAS: Bank & Finance Litigation.
Heaton, Richard L. ..........................................'50 '76 C.112 B.A. L.383 J.D. [Cheadle&G.]
Heffernan, John B., (AV) ..................'50 '75 C.813 B.A. L.1049 J.D. [J.B.Heffernan]
Heffernan, John B., A Law Corp., (AV) .......................................... 610 Newport Ctr. Dr.
**Hegness, Paul C., A Professional Corporation**, (AV) '47 '73
C&L.37 B.S.B.A., J.D. [Good,W.H.&W.]
*PRACTICE AREAS: Business Transactions.
**Henderson, Lee W.** .............'55 '96 C.608 B.S.E.E. L.117 J.D. [⊠ Knobbe,M.O.&B.]
Henderson, Mark J. ...........................................'63 '88 C.188 B.S. L.800 J.D. [Hines&H.]

**Henderson, Thomas W., (AV) '34 '61 C.668 B.A. L.1068 LL.B.** ⊠
**5030 Campus Drive, 92660**
Telephone: 714-252-8544 Fax: 714-252-8548
(Certified Specialist, Probate, Estate Planning, Trust Law, The State Bar of California Board of Legal Specialization).
General Civil and Trial Practice. Probate, Estate Planning and Personal Injury Law.
Reference: Bank of America, Westcliff Branch, Newport Beach.
*See Professional Biographies, NEWPORT BEACH, CALIFORNIA*

CALIFORNIA—NEWPORT BEACH MARTINDALE-HUBBELL LAW DIRECTORY 1997

**Hepps, Steven M.** .................... '61 '87 C.800 B.A. L.990 J.D. [Kelegian&T.]
*PRACTICE AREAS: Civil Litigation; Construction Defect; Insurance Defense; Personal Injury; Product Liability.
**Hering, Denise Harbaugh** ........... '50 '87 C.502 B.S. L.1049 J.D. [Stradling,Y.C.&R.]
**Herron, Joseph J.** .................... '54 '80 C.112 B.S. L.813 J.D. [O'Melveny&M.]
Herzfeld & Rubin, (AV)
620 Newport Ctr. Dr. (⊙N.Y. NY, Los Angeles CA, Miami & Fort Lauderdale FL)
**Herzog, Peter A.** .................... '55 '81 C.684 B.A. L.464 J.D. [▣ Tuverson&H.]
**Heston, Halli B.** .................... '55 '79 C.112 B.A. L.809 J.D. [Heston&H.]
*PRACTICE AREAS: Bankruptcy Law; Probate; Wills; Estate Planning.
**Heston, Richard G.**, (AV) .............. '54 '79 C.112 B.A. L.809 J.D. [Heston&H.]
*REPORTED CASES: In re Kullgren, 109 B.R. 949 (Bankruptcy C.D.Cal 1990); In re Marriage of McCann, 27 Cal.App 4th 102 (1996).
*PRACTICE AREAS: Family Law; Bankruptcy Law.

**Heston & Heston, (AV)**
**4041 MacArthur Boulevard Suite 400, 92660**
**Telephone: 714-222-1041 FAX: 714-222-1043**
**Richard G. Heston (Certified Specialist, Family Law, The State Bar of California Board of Legal Specialization); Halli B. Heston (Certified Specialist, Personal and Small Business Bankruptcy Law, The State Bar of California Board of Legal Specialization).**
**Bankruptcy Law, Family Law, Probate, Wills and Estate Planning.**
*See Professional Biographies, NEWPORT BEACH, CALIFORNIA*

Heumann, Linda Shannon .................... '53 '79 C&L.36 B.S., J.D. 610 Newport Ctr.
Hicken, Michael B. .................... '53 '83 C.101 B.S. L.1137 J.D. 901 Dover Dr. #100
Hicks, H. Thomas .................... '54 '80 C.112 B.S. L.1065 J.D. [Slocumb&H.]
Hile, Donald L. .................... '59 '86 C.886 B.A. L.990 J.D. 4000 MacArthur Blvd.
Hill, George R. .................... '31 '55 L.37 J.D. 1100 Quail St.
**Hillyard, Steven D., (P.C.)**, (AV) .................... '49 '75 L.1137 J.D. [Tuverson&H.]
Hilton, Alex .................... '53 '90 C.276 B.S. L.1137 J.D. 2611 Bayshore Dr.
**Himelfarb, Elisa** .................... '65 '95 C.112 B.A. L.1066 J.D. [Kimball,T.&S.]
*PRACTICE AREAS: Landlord and Tenant Law.
Hines, Marc S. .................... '63 '89 C.502 B.A. L.800 J.D. [Hines&H.]
Hines & Henderson .................... 4700 Teller Ave., 2nd Fl.
**Hirsh, Dwight C.** .................... '69 '94 C.770 B.A. L.464 J.D [▣ Newmeyer&D.]
*PRACTICE AREAS: Construction Litigation; Business Litigation; Insurance Coverage.
**Hoag, Hallack W.**, (AV) .................... '05 '32 C.347 A.B. L.976 LL.B. [Hoag&O.]⊙
*PRACTICE AREAS: Probate; Trust Law; Tax.

**Hoag & Overholt, (AV)**
**5030 Campus Drive, 92660⊙**
**Telephone: 714-955-2260**
**Members of Firm: Hallack W. Hoag; David G. Overholt.**
**Probate and Trust Law. Federal and State Taxation. General Civil Practice.**
**Reference: Bank of America (Fashion Island Branch).**
**Los Angeles, California Office: Suite 1902, Wilshire Financial Tower. Telephone: 213-386-7848. Fax: 213-386-0194.**
*See Professional Biographies, NEWPORT BEACH, CALIFORNIA*

**Hodges, Kenneth R.**, (AV) .................... '40 '66 C.940 B.A. L.1068 LL.B. [Millar,H.&B.]
*PRACTICE AREAS: Real Estate Law; Real Estate Litigation; Business Litigation.
**Hoffer, David A.** .................... '63 '88 C.813 A.B. L.1066 J.D. [▣ Stradling,Y.C.&R.]
**Hoffman, Christopher C.** .................... '69 '95 C.770 B.S. L.1049 J.D. [▣ Fisher&P.]
Hoffner, Donna W. .................... '45 '87 C.112 A.B. L.1137 J.D. 1048 Irvine Ave.
**Holbrook, Peter D.** .................... '56 '82 C.93 B.S. L.884 J.D. [McDermott,W.&E.]
*PRACTICE AREAS: Civil Rights; Labor and Employment; Unfair Competition.
**Holland, Catherine J.** .................... '62 '87 C.602 B.A. L.767 J.D. [Knobbe,M.O.&B.]
Holland, J. Mark .................... '60 '86 C&L.623 B.S., J.D. 20271 S.W. Birch St. (Pat.)
**Holland, Steven N.** .................... '61 '88 C.112 B.A. L.426 J.D. [McDermott,W.&E.]
*PRACTICE AREAS: Commercial Litigation.
**Hollander, Teri N.** .................... '68 '96 C.104 A.B. L.426 J.D. [▣ Stradling,Y.C.&R.]
*LANGUAGES: German, French, Italian.
**Hopkins, Steven W.** .................... '67 '96 C.878 B.S. L.145 J.D. [▣ Irell&M.]
*LANGUAGES: Japanese.
Hopper, J. Steven '45 '74 C.216 B.A. L.1017 J.D.
(adm. in PA; not adm. in CA) 4063 Birch St.‡
Horan, Glenn M. .................... '57 '83 C.282 B.A. L.809 J.D. Horian Industries
Horlick, Lisa L. .................... '69 '94 C.94 B.A. L.276 J.D. 4675 Macarthur Ct., Suite 1000
Horton, Whiteley & Cooper, (AV) .................... 4590 MacArthur Blvd. Ste. 500 (⊙Oakland)
**Howald, Walter G.**, (BV) .................... '39 '66 C.112 A.B. L.1066 J.D. [W.G.Howald]

**Howald, Walter G., Incorporated, (BV)**
**1500 Quail Street, Suite 440, Suite 440, 92660**
**Telephone: 714-851-7770 FAX: 714-851-2173**
**Walter G. Howald.**
**Real Estate, Business Litigation, Family Law, Civil Litigation, Estate Planning.**
**Reference: Wells Fargo Bank.**

**Howard, Jeffrey M.**, (BV) .................... '46 '74 C.165 B.A. L.1065 J.D. [Howard&Assoc.]
*REPORTED CASES: Hadley v. Krepel, 167 Cal.App. 3d 677 (1985).
*PRACTICE AREAS: Business Litigation; Securities and Investment Fraud; Real Estate Litigation; Complex Litigation.

**Howard & Associates, P.C., (BV)**
**One Corporate Plaza, 92660**
**Telephone: 714-759-1477 FAX: 714-640-9009**
**Jeffrey M. Howard.**
**Business and Real Estate Litigation, Securities and Investment Fraud.**
*See Professional Biographies, NEWPORT BEACH, CALIFORNIA*

**Howard, Rice, Nemerovski, Canady, Falk & Rabkin, A Professional Corporation, (AV)**
**610 Newport Center Drive Suite 450, 92660-6435⊙**
**Telephone: 714-721-6900 Telecopier: 714-721-6910**
**URL: http://www.hrice.com**
**Robert E. Gooding, Jr.; Fay E. Morisseau; Martha K. Gooding; William C. Rooklidge; Matthew Francis Weil; Stacy J. May (Not admitted in CA); Eric P. Damon; Lee M. Gordon; Steven S. Baik.**
**General Practice including Trial and Appellate Litigation. General Corporate; Finance; Securities; Mergers and Acquisitions; Administrative; Municipal; Public Utility; Banking; Constitutional; Entertainment; Estate Planning; International Business; Real Estate, Land Use and Environmental; Bankruptcy and Reorganization; Trade Secret; Intellectual Property; Taxation; Trade Regulation Law; Alternative Dispute Resolution including Arbitration, Mediation and Early Neutral Evaluation.**
**San Francisco, California Office: 7th Floor, Three Embarcadero Center, 94111. Telephone: 415-434-1600. Telecopy: 415-399-3041.**
*See Professional Biographies, NEWPORT BEACH, CALIFORNIA*

**Howland, John P.** .................... '41 '67 C.197 B.A. L.659 LL.B. [▣ Buxbaum&C.]⊙
*PRACTICE AREAS: Estate Planning; Corporate; Business; Bankruptcy (Creditor's Rights).
Howser, Fred A., (AV) .................... '36 '61 C&L.800 B.S., LL.B. [Howser&B.]
Howser & Brown, A Professional Corporation, (AV) .................... 4340 Campus Dr. Ste., 100
**Hubbard, Kim R. '53 '79 C.112 B.S.L. L.1137 J.D.**
**1301 Dove Street Suite 440, 92660**
**Telephone: 714-752-0800 Fax: 714-752-0313**
***PRACTICE AREAS: Probate Law; Conservatorship Law; Elder Law.**
**Probate Law, Conservatorship Law, Elder Law.**
*See Professional Biographies, NEWPORT BEACH, CALIFORNIA*

Huddleston, Dona J. .................... '34 '83 C.449 B.A. L.1068 J.D. Coun., R.T. C.
**Huebsch, Mark J.** .................... '51 '76 C&L.800 A.B., J.D. [Stradling,Y.C.&R.]
Hueston, John C. .................... '64 '93 C.197 B.A. L.976 J.D. 610 Newport Ctr. Dr., Ste. 1700
Hughes, David A. .................... '44 '83 C.1042 B.S.M.E. L.1137 J.D. 441 N. Newport Blvd.
Hughes, William W., Jr. .................... '40 '67 C&L.800 B.S., J.D. Chmn., Hughes/Purcell
Hugill, Steven E. .................... '41 '67 C.674 A.B. L.1066 LL.B. 50 Baycrest Ct.
Hultman, Kenneth W. '42 '74
C.169 B.A. L.1137 J.D. V.P. & Sr. Atty., Gibraltar Money Ctr., Inc.
Humphreys, James A., Jr., (AV) '29 '59
C.861 B.B.A. L.477 LL.B. 4590 MacArthur Blvd., Ste. 260
Humphries, Robin J. .................... '56 '84 C.112 B.A. L.800 J.D. [Weiss&H.] (⊙Los Angeles)
**Hunt, Marshall T.**, (AV) .................... '20 '49 C.112 B.A. L.800 LL.B. [▣ Cummins&W.]
*PRACTICE AREAS: Manufacturers Products Liability; Construction Litigation; Insurance Company Defense; Libel; Professional Errors and Omissions.
**Hunter, Laura B.** .................... '60 '87 C.1049 B.B.A. L.1067 J.D. [Brobeck,P.&H.]
*PRACTICE AREAS: Venture Capital; Corporate and Securities Law; Mergers and Acquisitions.
Hurley, Stephen R. .................... '58 '92 C.1241 B.B.A. L.61 J.D. 4695 Macarthur Ct. Ste. 530
Hurst, Royce Orleans .................... '47 '79 C.994 B.A. L.1137 J.D. 3901 MacArthur Blvd.
Huston, Robert J., III .................... '44 '70 C.813 B.A. L.188 J.D. 4299 Macarthur Blvd.
**Hutchins, Michael Paul** .................... '62 '95 C.884 B.C.E. L.494 J.D. [▣ Newmeyer&D.]
*PRACTICE AREAS: Construction Law; Environmental Law; Products Liability; Public Works; Insurance.
**Ignatuk, J. Ronald** .................... '53 '90 C.645 B.A. L.426 J.D. [▣ Barger&W.]
**Ingram, Georgia V.** .................... '58 '88 C.228 B.A. L.1049 J.D. [▣ Fisher&P.]
**Ireland, John D.** .................... '62 '88 C.112 B.A. L.1068 J.D. [▣ Stradling,Y.C.&R.]
**Ireland, Victor C.** .................... '54 '81 C.1109 B.A. L.1049 J.D. [McDermott&T.]
*PRACTICE AREAS: Health Care Law; Tax; Corporate; Securities.

**Irell & Manella LLP, (AV)**
**A Law Partnership including Professional Corporations**
**Suite 500, 840 Newport Center Drive, 92660-6324⊙**
**Telephone: 714-760-0991 Telecopier: 714-760-0721**
**Resident Members: Scott D. Baskin (P.C.); Frank A. Caput; Michael G. Ermer; John C. Fossum (P.C.); Andra Barmash Greene; Thomas W. Johnson, Jr.; Kyle S. Kawakami; Richard J. McNeil; Layn R. Phillips; Anthony W. Pierotti; Richard M. Sherman, Jr.,(P.C.). Resident Of Counsel: Robert W. Stedman (P.C.). Resident Associates: Leigh Taylor Combs; Steven W. Hopkins; Francine J. Lipman; Marc S. Maister; John M. Nakashima; Elizabeth K. Penfil; Noah B. Salamon; Mary-Christine (M.C.) Sungaila.**
**General Civil Practice and Litigation in all State and Federal Courts and Arbitration Tribunals. Administrative, Antitrust, Aviation, Computer, Corporate, Corporate Securities and Finance, Mergers and Acquisitions, Election and Redistricting, Entertainment, Estate Planning, Trusts and Probate, Federal, State and Local Taxation, First Amendment and Media, International Business and Taxation, Insolvency, Bankruptcy, Reorganization and Creditors Rights, Insurance, Labor Relations, Wrongful Termination and Discrimination, Pension and Profit Sharing, Real Estate, Real Estate Finance, Banking and Secured Transactions Law. Patent, Trademark and Copyright Law. Intellectual Property and Trade Secrets. High Technology Litigation, Including Intellectual Property, Trade Secrets and Unfair Competition Litigation. Selected Criminal Defense.**
**Los Angeles, California Offices: Suite 900, 1800 Avenue of the Stars, 90067-4276. Telephone: 310-277-1010. Cable Address: "Irella LSA". Telecopier: 310-203-7199 and Suite 3300, 333 South Hope Street, 90071-3042. Telephone: 213-620-1555. Telecopier: 213-229-0515.**
*See Professional Biographies, NEWPORT BEACH, CALIFORNIA*

**Ivey, Christopher D.** .................... '68 '94 C.1042 B.S. L.1049 J.D. [▣ Stradling,Y.C.&R.]
*LANGUAGES: Spanish.
**Jacobsen, Wayne** .................... '56 '82 C.112 A.B. L.800 J.D. [O'Melveny&M.]
*PRACTICE AREAS: ERISA; Employee Benefits.
**Janics, Kathleen A.** .................... '61 '90 C.800 B.S. L.1049 J.D. [Harle,J.&K.]
*PRACTICE AREAS: Community Association Law; Real Estate; General Corporate.
**Janowsky, Lewis P.**, (AV) .................... '51 '77 C.107 B.A. L.146 J.D. [Rynn&J.]
*PRACTICE AREAS: Employment Law; Agricultural Law.
Jeffries, George J., (AV) '36 '62 C.112 A.B. L.800 LL.B.
500 Newport Ctr. Dr., Ste 520
**Jennings, Joseph F.** .................... '62 '90 C.223 B.S. L.602 J.D. [Knobbe,M.O.&B.]
**Jensen, Jon E.**, (AV) .................... '47 '75 C.101 B.A. L.813 J.D. [Call,C.&J.]
*PRACTICE AREAS: Corporate Law; Securities Law.
**Jensen, Stephen C.** ...... '63 '90 C.101 B.S. L.112 J.D. [Knobbe,M.O.&B.] (See Pat. Sect.)
*LANGUAGES: Dutch.
**Johnson, Eric E.** .................... '55 '80 C.684 B.A. L.950 J.D. [McDermott&T.]
*PRACTICE AREAS: Medicare Reimbursement; Medicare Fraud and Abuse; Hospital and Medical Practice Acquisitions; Medical Staff Issues and Service Agreements.
Johnson, Ernest R. .................... '43 '74 C.1042 B.S. L.809 J.D. P.O. Box 7976
Johnson, Gerald S. .................... '29 '60 C&L.37 J.D. Corp. V.P. & Sr. Coun., Gibraltar Svgs.
Johnson, Kelly S. ....... '60 '88 C.800 B.S. L.990 J.D. [▣ Feldsott L.&F.] & [K.S.Johnson]

**Johnson, Kelly S., Law Offices of '60 '88 C.800 B.S. L.990 J.D.**
**160 Newport Center Drive, Suite 110, 92660**
**Telephone: 714-729-8014 Fax: 714-729-8050**
**Bankruptcy, Debtor Rights, Business and Real Estate Litigation.**
*See Professional Biographies, NEWPORT BEACH, CALIFORNIA*

**Johnson, Lawrence E.** .................... '56 '95 C.012 B.Comm. L.014 LL.B. [▣ Cummins&W.]
*LANGUAGES: English, French and Spanish.
*PRACTICE AREAS: Corporate Law; Securities Law; Technology Law; International Trade.
**Johnson, Thomas W., Jr.**, (AV) .................... '41 '69 C.347 B.S. L.345 J.D. [Irell&M.]
Johnson, Tracy D. .................... '— '93 C.1060 B.S. L.112 J.D. 610 Newport Dr.
Johnston, Jenifer L. .................... '64 '93 C.112 B.A. L.1049 J.D. 840 Newport Ctr. Dr.
Jones, Stanley R., (AV) .................... '39 '66 C.668 B.A. L.1068 LL.B. 4695 MacArthur Ct.

**Jones, Day, Reavis & Pogue**
**(See Irvine)**

Joseff, Mark F. .................... '22 '52 C&L.800 B.A., LL.B. 1728 Bedford Ln.
Kadi, William J. .................... '46 '72 C.112 B.S. L.464 J.D. [Bowie A.K.W.&G.]
Kagan, Matthew H. '62 '89 C.139 B.S. L.770 J.D.
[▣ Herzfeld&R.] (⊙Los Angeles, CA.)
**Kalionzes, Peter N.**, (BV) .................... '45 '74 C.800 B.A. L.990 J.D. [▣ Call,C.&J.]
*PRACTICE AREAS: Residential Real Estate Development, Sale and Financing; General Corporate Business Matters; Construction Defect Litigation.
**Kane, Robert J.** .................... '46 '72 C.724 B.A. L.569 J.D. [Stradling,Y.C.&R.]
**Kane, Stephen M.** .................... '56 '82 C.813 B.A. L.800 J.D. [Baldikoski,C.&K.]
**Kannen, Karen A.** .................... '63 '90 C.188 B.S. L.1049 J.D. [Harle,J.&K.]
*PRACTICE AREAS: Civil Litigation; Community Association Law; Real Estate; General Corporate.
**Kaplan, Phillip R.**, (AV) .................... '51 '77 C.976 B.A. L.800 J.D. [O'Melveny&M.]
Karch, J. Frederick .................... '44 '78 C.674 B.S.E. L.800 J.D. 1300 Dove
Karger, Patti S. .................... '18 '52 C.112 L.809 3027 Carob St.
Karssen, Paul M., (AV) .................... '56 '81 C.1109 B.A. L.800 J.D. 610 Newport Ctr.
**Katayama, Arthur S.**, (AV) .................... '27 '59 C.513 A.B. L.1001 LL.B. [Katayama,A.S.]
*LANGUAGES: Japanese.

**Katayama, Arthur S., A Professional Corporation, (AV)**
**Suite 700, 4400 MacArthur Boulevard, P.O. Box 2350, 92660**
**Telephone: 714-851-5851 FAX: 714-752-0288**
**Arthur S. Katayama.**

(This Listing Continued)

**Katayama, Arthur S., A Professional Corporation (Continued)**
**Taxation, Probate, Real Property, Antitrust, International Business and Corporate Law. Business Litigation.**

Katz, M. Taylor .................. '59 '87 C.605 B.A. L.940 J.D. 610 Newport Center Dr.
**Katz, Stuart A.**, (BV) ..............'57 '85 C.347 B.A. L.1119 J.D. [Greenbaum&K.]⊙
*PRACTICE AREAS: Collections; Creditors Rights; Enforcement of Judgments; Construction Remedies; Commercial Litigation.
Kaufman, Joseph Q. '59 '87 C.628 B.A. L.596 J.D.
(adm. in OR; not adm. in CA) Gen. Coun., GemChem, Inc.
Kaufman, Marcus M. ............ '29 '56 C.112 B.A. L.800 J.D. 620 Newport Center Dr.
**Kawakami, Kyle S.** ........................... '59 '86 C.112 B.A. L.813 J.D. [Irell&M.]
Kays, John H. ................. '45 '75 C.801 B.A. L.1119 J.D. 4000 MacArthur Blvd. E.
**Keathley, H. James** ..................'55 '83 C.139 B.A. L.1137 J.D. [Davis,P.K.&W.]
*PRACTICE AREAS: Business Litigation.
**Keathley, Katherine D.** .........................'59 '90 L.1137 J.D. [Ⓐ Davis,P.K.&W.]
*PRACTICE AREAS: Business Litigation.
**Kelegian, Mark A.** ......................... '60 '87 C&L.1049 B.A., J.D. [Kelegian&T.]
*PRACTICE AREAS: Premises Liability; Products Liability; Construction Defect; Fraudulent (S.I.U.) Claims; Civil Litigation.

**Kelegian & Thomas, (AV)** BR
**4685 MacArthur Court, Suite 400, 92660**
**Telephone: 714-553-1200 Fax: 714-553-1013**
**Email: KelThomLaw@aol.com**
**Mark A. Kelegian; Michael Paul Thomas; Joseph P. Gallo; Bruce A. Thomason; Steven M. Hepps; James P. Habel; Jeri E. Tabback; Dean H. McVay; Erik R. Musurlian; William N. Villard.**
**Civil Litigation, Insurance Defense, Personal Injury, Premises Liability, Products Liability, Construction Defect, Insurance Law, Automobile Liability, Business Torts and Disputes, Landlord Tort Liability, Copyright and Trademark Infringement, Fraudulent (S.I.U.) Claims.**
***See Professional Biographies, NEWPORT BEACH, CALIFORNIA***

Kellogg, John C. ........................... '58 '84 C.800 B.A. L.426 J.D. 1300 Dove St.

**Kemble, Donn, (AV) '28 '59 C.112 B.S. L.1068 J.D.**
**Suite 6000, 4000 MacArthur Boulevard, 92660**
**Telephone: 714-833-3335 Fax: 714-752-8170**
***LANGUAGES: German.**
**General Trial and Appellate Practice in all Courts, Business, Corporation, Estate Planning, Real Estate and Taxation Law.**
***See Professional Biographies, NEWPORT BEACH, CALIFORNIA***

Kennedy, Craig P., (BV) ...................... '52 '77 C.800 A.B. L.809 J.D. 1300 Dove St.
Kennedy, Paul, Jr., (AV) .................. '22 '71 C.800 B.A. L.809 J.D. 1048 Irvine Ave.
**Kern, Carolyn M.** ............................ '62 '94 C.98 B.S. L.931 J.D. [Ⓐ Borton,P.&C.]
*PRACTICE AREAS: Construction Defect Litigation.
**Kester, Steven L.**, (AV) .................... '50 '78 C.1077 B.A. L.809 J.D. [Kester&Q.]
*PRACTICE AREAS: Banking; Business Law; Environmental Law; Real Estate.

**Kester & Quinlan, (AV)**
**1470 Jamboree Road, Suite 200, 92660**
**Telephone: 714-759-7760 FAX: 714-760-8156**
**Email: F.E.Quinlan@aol.com**
**Francis E. Quinlan; Steven L. Kester; Dale K. Quinlan.**
**Business Litigation, Banking, Real Estate, Taxation, Insurance Defense, Medical Malpractice, Environmental Law, Estate and Business Planning.**
***See Professional Biographies, NEWPORT BEACH, CALIFORNIA***

Kettley, Richard M., (BV) ................... '40 '71 C.101 B.S. L.339 J.D. P.O. Box 8164
Keup, Erwin J., (AV) '30 '58 C&L.436 B.S., J.D.
4400 Macarthur Blvd. (⊙Los Angeles)
**Keys, Richard D.** ..............................'57 '82 C.112 B.A. L.1066 J.D. [Bidna&K.]
*PRACTICE AREAS: Business Litigation.
**Kilpatrick, Christopher J.** ........... '57 '82 C.112 B.A. L.1068 J.D. [Stradling,Y.C.&R.]
**Kimball, Theodore C.**, (AV) '51 '77
C.36 B.S. L.1137 J.D. [Kimball,T.&S.] (⊙San Diego)
*PRACTICE AREAS: Landlord/Tenant Law (85%, 600).

**Kimball, Tirey & St. John, (AV)**
**1600 Dove Street, Suite 450, 92660⊙**
**Telephone: 714-476-5585; 800-564-6611 Fax: 714-476-5580**
**Email: ktsud@evict-collect.com URL: http://www.evict-collect.com/~ktsud/**
**Theodore C. Kimball; Patricia H. Tirey; Wendy St. John; Robert C. Thorn; Helaine S. Ashton (Managing Partner, Newport Beach Office); Linda C. Fritz; Mark A. Brody (Resident, San Diego Office); Susan E. Greek; Theodore E Owens; Linda T. Cardoso; C. Timothy Genovese; Sherri S. Shafizadeh; Elisa Himelfarb; Danielle T. Kussler.**
**Residential and Commercial Landlord/Tenant Law, Collections, Real Estate, Business, Banking and Finance Litigation.**
**San Diego, California Office: 1202 Kettner Boulevard, Fifth Floor, 92101. Telephone: 619-234-1690; 800-338-6039. Fax: 619-237-0457.**
**San Mateo, California Office: 1900 South Norfolk Street, Suite 320, 94403. Telephone: 415-525-1690; 800-525-1690. Fax: 415-525-2120.**
***See Professional Biographies, NEWPORT BEACH, CALIFORNIA***

Kincannon, Gary L. ......................'50 '80 C.1073 B.A. L.1049 J.D. [Saxon,B.G.&K.]⊙
**King, John R.** ..................... '60 '93 C.101 B.S.E.E. L.846 J.D. [Knobbe,M.O.&B.]
**King, Raymond**, (AV) .....................'55 '80 C.112 B.A. L.1067 J.D. [King&Assoc.]
*PRACTICE AREAS: Civil Trials; Banking Litigation; Commercial Litigation; Business; Construction.

**King & Associates, (AV)**
**620 Newport Center Drive, Suite 1425, P.O. Box 10071, 92658**
**Telephone: 714-644-1355 Facsimile: 714-644-1366**
**Raymond King.**
**Civil Trials, Banking and Commercial Litigation, Receivership, Business, Construction and Real Estate Litigation, Creditor's Rights in Bankruptcy.**
***See Professional Biographies, NEWPORT BEACH, CALIFORNIA***

Kinney, Michael W., (P.C.) .......... '56 '82 C.112 B.A. L.426 J.D. 500 Newport Ctr. Dr.
**Kirsch, Kevin W.** ............................ '67 '93 C.112 B.A. L.426 J.D. [Ⓐ Bruck&P.]
*PRACTICE AREAS: Business and Commercial Litigation; Creditor's Rights and Enforcement of Judgments; Construction Defect; Insurance Defense; Employment Law.
Kiser, Steven C. ........................ '50 '81 C.259 B.S. L.1068 J.D. 220 Newport Ctr. Dr.
**Klevatt, Debra L.** ...................... '67 '93 C.1109 B.A. L.426 J.D. [Eadington,M.&E.]
*PRACTICE AREAS: Business; Corporate; Employment Law; Civil Litigation.
Klingensmith, Allen .................. '24 '52 C.112 B.A. L.1065 J.D. 453 Via Lido Soud‡
**Knecht, Richard E., (P.C.)**, (AV) ............'48 '73 C.112 B.A. L.61 J.D. [Knecht&H.]
*PRACTICE AREAS: Banking Law; Corporate Law; Real Estate Law.

**Knecht & Hansen, (AV)**
**A Partnership of Professional Corporations**
**Suite 900, 1301 Dove Street, 92660**
**Telephone: 714-851-8070 FAX: 714-851-1732**
**Members of Firm: Richard E. Knecht (P.C.); Loren P. Hansen (P.C.).**
**General Business Practice. Banking, Corporate, Commercial and Real Estate Law.**
***See Professional Biographies, NEWPORT BEACH, CALIFORNIA***

**Knight, Nancy Morse**, (BV) ......... '31 '74 C.788 B.A. L.1068 J.D. [Wentworth&P.]⊙
*PRACTICE AREAS: Personal Injury; Wrongful Death; Professional Negligence; Products Liability; Business Fraud.

**Knobbe, Louis J., (P.C.)**, (AV) '32 '60
C.350 B.S. L.426 J.D. [Knobbe,M.O.&B.] (See Pat. Sect.)

**Knobbe, Martens, Olson & Bear, LLP, (AV)** BR
**A Limited Liability Partnership including Professional Corporations**
**620 Newport Center Drive, 16th Floor, 92660⊙**
**Telephone: 714-760-0404 Fax: 714-760-9502**
**Louis J. Knobbe (P.C.); Don W. Martens (P.C.); Gordon H. Olson (P.C.); James B. Bear; Darrell L. Olson (P.C.); William B. Bunker; William H. Nieman; Lowell Anderson; Arthur S. Rose; James F. Lesniak; Jerry T. Sewell; John B. Sganga, Jr.; Edward A. Schlatter; W. Gerard von Hoffmann, III; Joseph R. Re; Catherine J. Holland; Karen J. Vogel (Not admitted in CA); Andrew H. Simpson; Jeffrey L. Van Hoosear; Daniel E. Altman; Ernest A. Beutler, Jr.; Marguerite L. Gunn; Stephen C. Jensen; Vito A. Canuso III; William H. Shreve; Lynda J. Zadra-Symes; Steven J. Nataupsky; Paul A. Stewart; Joseph F. Jennings; Craig S. Summers; Brenton R. Babcock; Diane M. Reed; Johnathan A. Barney; John R. King; Ronald J. Schoenbaum; Richard C. Gilmore; John P. Giezentanner; Adeel S. Akhtar; Frederick S. Berretta; Christopher A. Colvin; James T. Hagler; Stephen M. Lobbin; Douglas G. Muehlhauser; David N. Weiss; Lori L. Yamato; Glenn R. Smith; Ann A. Byun; Stacey R. Halpern; R. Scott Weide; Michael K. Friedland; Stephen C. Beuerle; John C. Wilson; Joseph J. Basista; Lee W. Henderson; Chad W. Miller; Lena A. Basile.**
**Intellectual Property Law including Patent, Trademark, Copyright, Unfair Competition, Trade Secret, Licensing, Computer Law, Antitrust Law, and related litigation.**
**Representative Clients: AST Research Inc., Irvine; ASM America-Phoenix; NIH Washington, D.C.; Microsoft Corp.**
**San Diego, California Office: 501 West Broadway, Suite 1400. Telephone: 619-235-8550. Fax: 619-235-0176.**
**Riverside, California Office: 3801 University Avenue, Suite 710. Telephone: 909-781-9231. Fax: 909-781-4507.**
***See Professional Biographies, NEWPORT BEACH, CALIFORNIA***

Knottnerus, Wilfred O. ................ '60 '85 C.508 B.A. L.1049 J.D. [Bridgford,K.&G.]
Knuth, June C. '46 '72 C.800 B.A. L.426 J.D.
V.P. & Invest. Coun., Pacific Mut. Life Ins. Co.
**Kolodny, H. Lee** ................ '67 '94 C.426 B.B.A. L.800 J.D. [Ⓐ Stradling,Y.C.&R.]

**Koontz, Betty L., (AV) '30 '80 C.990 B.A. L.1148 J.D.**
**Suite 320, 5 Civic Plaza, 92660-5915**
**Telephone: 714-721-8730 Facsimile: 714-720-1232**
**(Certified Specialist, Estate Planning, Trust and Probate Law, The State Bar of California Board of Legal Specialization).**
**Practice limited to Estate Planning, Probate and Trust Law.**
**Reference: Glendale Federal Bank.**
***See Professional Biographies, NEWPORT BEACH, CALIFORNIA***

Koontz, Walter G., Jr. ................'54 '81 C.823 B.A. L.1137 J.D. 4675 MacArthur Ct.
Kray, Steven B., (BV) ..........................'52 '77 C.763 B.S. L.800 J.D. [Stephens&K.]
**Krinsky, David A.**, (AV) ...................'48 '73 C&L.800 B.A., J.D. [O'Melveny&M.]
*PRACTICE AREAS: Corporate Law; Securities Law; Business Law.
**Krinsky, Margaret** ...............................'69 '95 C.112 B.A. L.770 J.D. [Ⓐ Tuverson&H.]
*PRACTICE AREAS: Medical Malpractice; Insurance Defense.
Kroesche, Thomas R. .......................................... '51 '82 C&L.878 B.A., J.D. [Ⓐ Barclay]
Kroll, Allan I. .......................................'55 '80 C.477 B.S. L.309 J.D. P.O. Box 9431
Krup, Robert J. .............................'46 '73 C.426 B.S. L.1049 J.D. 1301 Dove St.
**Kussler, Danielle T.** ........................'70 '95 C.1042 B.S. L.426 J.D. [Kimball,T.&S.]
*PRACTICE AREAS: Landlord and Tenant Law.
Kuzelka, Timothy C. ........................'52 '79 C.35 B.S. L.1137 J.D. 333 Bayside Dr.
Kwong, Bennette .......................................... '47 '81 C.112 B.S. L.1137 J.D. F.D.I.C.
Labbe, Robert L. ................. '59 '87 C.732 D.E.C. L.012 B.C.L. 3018 Corte Hermosa
**Lafitte, David E.** ..................'64 '91 C.174 B.A. L.861 J.D. [Ⓐ Stradling,Y.C.&R.]
**Laird, Edward L.**, (BV) .........................'55 '82 C.112 B.S. L.990 J.D. [Voss,C.&T.]
*PRACTICE AREAS: Litigation; Construction Law; Mechanics Lien Law; Insurance Coverage/Bad Faith Law; Commercial Law.
Laird, Peter J., (BV) ............. '41 '69 C.112 A.B. L.1065 J.D. 4350 Von Karman St.
Lam, Nam-Yeng Mark ................ '57 '89 C.299 B.A. L.1065 J.D. 1103 Quail Street
Lamoreaux, Betty Lou .............. '— '57 C.1097 B.A. L.765 J.D. 1818 Port Ashley‡
**Lane, Cynthia Walker** ......................'54 '87 C.966 B.A. L.990 J.D. [Ⓐ Fisher&P.]
Lang, Judith I., (BV) ......................................'51 '82 L.1137 J.D. 4675 MacArthur Ct.
Lapin, Michael L. ..........'39 '63 C&L.339 B.A., LL.B. 19 Valore Dr. (Newport Coast)
**La Porte, Donna L.** ...............................'50 '79 C&L.878 B.S., J.D. [Ⓐ Wolf&P.]
*PRACTICE AREAS: Secured Real Property Creditor Rights.
Larkin, Thomas B., Jr. ........ '18 '42 C&L.893 B.A., J.D. 1573 E. Ocean Blvd., Balboa‡
Larsen, Howard M., (BV) ................... '44 '74 C.1042 B.S. L.990 J.D. [H.M.Larsen]
Larsen, Howard M., Incorporated, (BV) ..........................4 Upper Newport Plaza

**Latham & Watkins**
**(See Costa Mesa)**

LaTorre, Joseph S. ......................................................'48 '74 C.800 B.S. Lok-Fast, Inc.
Launer, Leland C., (AV) ................................'18 '48 C.684 A.B. L.800 J.D. 419 Onda‡
Lauridsen, Jeffrey T. ....................... '49 '88 C&L.1198 B.A., J.D. 4675 MacArthur Ct.
**Lautsch, John C.**, (AV) ......................'— '72 C.813 B.S. L.1067 J.D. [J.C.Lautsch]

**Lautsch, John C., A Professional Corporation, (AV)** BR
**1200 Quail Street, Suite 140, 92660**
**Telephone: 714-955-9095 Telefax: 714-955-2978**
**John C. Lautsch.**
**Business Litigation and Appeals, Trade Secret and Copyrights, General Business and Corporate, Estate Planning.**
***See Professional Biographies, NEWPORT BEACH, CALIFORNIA***

LaVerne, R. George ........................... '47 '76 C.112 B.A. L.1049 J.D. 1300 Dove St.
Lawless, William B., (AVⓥ) '22 '46 C.107 A.B. L.602 J.D.
(adm. in NY; not adm. in CA) Pres., Judges Mediation Network
(⊙Orleans & Barnstable, MA)

**Lawrence, C. Stephen '48 '84 C.431 B.A. L.128 J.D.**
**4675 MacArthur Court, Suite 670, 92660**
**Telephone: 714-250-4550 Fax: 714-833-0976**
**(Partner, Hogan & Hartson L.L.P.).**
***PRACTICE AREAS: Food, Drug and Medical Device Law.**
**Food, Drug and Medical Device Law.**
***See Professional Biographies, NEWPORT BEACH, CALIFORNIA***

Lawrence, Frank ................... '59 '91 C.362 B.A. L.1137 J.D. 4340 Campus Dr.
Lawrence, Philip B. .......... '63 '91 C.112 B.A. L.990 J.D. Eugene Burger Mgmnt. Corp.
Lazarus, Joel D. '50 '76 C.339 B.S. L.365 J.D.
(adm. in AZ; not adm. in CA) F.D.I.C.
Lazof, Ronald C., (BV) ....................... '47 '72 C.1077 B.S. L.1068 J.D. [Lazof&C.]
Lazof & Coss, (BV) ..............................................4590 Macarthur Blvd.
Lee, Martin L., (BV) ..................................'46 '73 C.112 B.A. L.1065 J.D. [Feldsott L.&F.]
Leeds, Richard F. ........................'48 '78 C.112 B.A. L.809 J.D. 4695 MacArthur Ct.
Leguay, Allan P. ....................... '50 '76 C.112 A.B. L.273 J.D. 100 Bayview Circle
Leibold, Barbara Zeid .................'61 '87 C.112 B.A. L.1065 J.D. 660 Newport Ctr. Dr.
**Leo, Christopher M.** ..................'66 '93 C.112 B.A. L.285 J.D. [Alvarado,S.V.&S.]
*PRACTICE AREAS: General Corporate; International.
Leonard, Steven C. ...................... '58 '84 C&L.800 B.A., J.D. 610 Newport Ctr. Dr.
**Leslie, Lee J.** ...................................'66 '92 C.188 B.A. L.1068 J.D. [Ⓐ Brobeck,P.&H.]
*PRACTICE AREAS: Emerging Growth Companies; Venture Capital; Multimedia; Corporate Finance.

CALIFORNIA—NEWPORT BEACH MARTINDALE-HUBBELL LAW DIRECTORY 1997

**Leslie, Suzanne Boyer** .................... '62 '87 C.1042 B.A. L.1137 J.D. [🄰 Allen&F.]
*PRACTICE AREAS: Civil Trial Practice; Personal Injury Law; Negligence Law.
**Lesniak, James F.** ... '43 '69 C&L.477 B.S.E.E., J.D. [Knobbe,M.O.&B.] (See Pat. Sect.)
**Lessler, Lauren B.** ...................... '65 '93 C.112 B.A. L.800 J.D. [🄰 Broker&O.]
Levin, Brian ............'63 '92 C.659 B.A. L.813 J.D. 840 Newport Center Dr., Suite 500
Levy, David '32 '58 C.659 B.S. L.976 J.D.
(adm. in CT; not adm. in CA) V.P. & Tax Coun., Pacific Mut. Life Ins. Co.
**Lew, Carol L.** .......................... '62 '86 C.1077 B.A. L.1065 J.D. [Stradling,Y.C.&R.]
**Lewin, James F.** .............................. '57 '89 C.174 B.A. L.809 [🄰 Wolf&P.]
*PRACTICE AREAS: Secured Real Property Creditor Rights.
**Lewis, Heidi Stilb** .......................... '54 '81 C.37 B.A. L.1137 J.D. [Good,W.H.&W.]
*LANGUAGES: Spanish.
*PRACTICE AREAS: Civil Litigation.
**Lianides, Peter** ............................'65 '92 C.1169 B.A. L.770 J.D. [🄰 Winthrop C.]
**Liebman, Seth L.** ............................ '60 '85 C.280 B.B.A. L.846 J.D. [🄰 Call,C.&J.]
*LANGUAGES: Spanish and French.
*REPORTED CASES: Mansour v. Superior Court, 38 Cal. App. 4th 1750 (1995); Barber v. Rancho Mortgage Investment Corp., 26 Cal. App. 4th 1819 (1994).
*PRACTICE AREAS: Litigation.
Liebrader, David ................................... '66 '93 C.112 B.A. L.61 J.D. 4921 Birch St.

**Liechty, Douglas C., (AV) '34 '61 C.629 B.A. L.1065 J.D. 🄱🄱**
**Suite 520 Newport Financial Plaza, 500 Newport Center Drive, 92660-7005**
**Telephone: 714-644-8600 Fax: 714-759-6832**
**Family, Civil Litigation, Personal Injury Law and Mediation.**
*See Professional Biographies, NEWPORT BEACH, CALIFORNIA*

Liechty, Jean Singleton, (BV) ....'35 '79 C.629 B.B.A. L.1137 J.D. 500 Newport Ctr. Dr.‡
**Lindegren, Karl R.** ................................. '60 '86 C&L.800 A.B., J.D. [Fisher&P.]
**Lipman, Francine J.** ........................... '59 '94 C.112 B.A. L.1067 J.D. [🄰 Irell&M.]
**Lipsky, David I.** ............................... '39 '72 C.112 B.A. L.426 J.D. [🄰 R.K.Scott]
Little, Robert W., (A Law Corp.), (BV) '33 '60
C.966 B.S. L.1068 J.D. 4675 MacArthur Ct.
**Livingston, Lori Winder** ...................'53 '79 C.112 B.S. L.990 J.D. [🄲 Voss,C.&T.]
*PRACTICE AREAS: Estate Planning, Probate and Trust Administration; Conservatorship Law; Elder Care Law; Wills Contests; Charitable Trusts and Foundations.
Livingston, William J., (P.C.) '49 '74 C.800 B.A. L.990 J.D.
1st V.P., Merrill Lynch, Pierce, Fenner & Smith, Inc.
**Lobbin, Stephen M.** .............. '70 '95 C.893 B.S.E.E. L.1068 J.D. [Knobbe,M.O.&B.]
Lofland, Kurt T. .................................... '51 '82 C.1042 B.A. L.1137 J.D. [Hawes&F.]
Long, David M., (AV) ................ '40 '77 C.1097 B.S. L.1137 J.D. 3300 Irvine Ave.
Long, John J. '13 '38 C.546 L.190 J.D.
(adm. in NE; not adm. in CA) 97 Linda Isle‡
**Long, Michael F.** ............................ '58 '84 C.36 B.S. L.365 J.D. [Borton,P.&C.]
*PRACTICE AREAS: Construction Defect and Accidents; Professional Malpractice; Commerical Litigation.
**Longerbone, Jon A.**, (AV) ..................'49 '79 C.1077 B.A. L.1065 J.D. [Bidna&K.]
*PRACTICE AREAS: Business Litigation.
Lorman, Jonathan ...................................'43 '68 C&L.976 B.A., LL.B. P.O. Box 7519
Lovell, Gary B., (AV) ............'26 '54 C.112 A.B. L.1065 LL.B. 1242 W. Ocean Front
**Lowe, Kathlene W.** ........................... '49 '76 C&L.878 B.A., J.D. [Brobeck,P.&H.]
*PRACTICE AREAS: Employment Law; Commercial and Real Property Litigation.
Lowe, Russell H. '49 '76 C&L.878 B.S., J.D.
(adm. in UT; not adm. in CA) Irvine Retail Properties Co.
**Lund, Cody Dale** ...................... '61 '88 C.999 A.A. L.1137 J.D. [🄰 Bragg,S.S.&K.]
**Lurker, David A.**, (AV) ..................... '54 '79 C.1042 B.A. L.464 J.D. [Voss,C.&T.]
*PRACTICE AREAS: Real Estate (Property) Law; Commercial Leasing; Construction Law; Real Estate Development Law.
MacMillin, Carrie, (BV) .....................'37 '77 C.112 B.S. L.990 J.D. 450 Newport Ctr.
**MacPherson, Laura N.** ................ '62 '88 C&L.1049 B.B.A., J.D. [🄰 Cummins&W.]
*PRACTICE AREAS: Insurance Defense.
MacSporran, James M. .............'48 '77 C.313 B.S. L.990 J.D. 130 Newport Center Dr.
Madigan, Peter J., (A P.C.), (BV) ... '39 '67 C.549 B.S. L.767 J.D. 20301 S.W. Acacia St.
Magilavy, David ..............................'21 '77 C.145 M.B.A. L.1225 J.D. 1617 Westcliff Dr.

**Maher, Lee & Goddard, LLP**
**(See Newport Beach)**

Mahoney, James J. ....................... '39 '64 C.112 B.S. L.1066 J.D. 1470 Jamboree Rd.
Mahoney, Thomas P., (AV) .................'15 '51 C.262 B.S. 4000 MacArthur Blvd. (Pat.)
**Mainero, Mario W., Jr.**, (AV) .........'55 '80 C.154 B.A. L.560 J.D. [M.W.Mainero,Jr.]
*LANGUAGES: Italian.
*REPORTED CASES: Spellis v. Lawn, 200 Cal. App. 3d 1075, 246 Cal. Rptr. 385 (1988).

**Mainero, Mario W., Jr., Inc., (AV) 🄱🄱**
**Suite 201, 5160 Birch Street, 92660**
**Telephone: 714-851-7763 FAX: 714-851-8188 (7765)**
**Email: mwmlaw@aol.com**
**Mario W. Mainero, Jr.; Jan A. Zemanek.**
**Business, Real Estate and Probate Litigation, Civil Trial.**
**Reference: Bank of Newport.**
*See Professional Biographies, NEWPORT BEACH, CALIFORNIA*

**Maister, Marc S.** ........................ '64 '91 C.061 B.Comm. L.1066 J.D. [🄰 Irell&M.]
*LANGUAGES: English and Afrikaans.
Malik, M. Alim .......................... '58 '89 C.061 B.S. L.309 LL.M. 4675 MacArthur Ct.
Mamey, Nelson G. .........................'54 '80 C.800 B.S. L.809 J.D. 5160 Birch St.
Mancillas, Marshall A. ........................'50 '78 C&L.800 B.S., J.D. 21 Augusta Ln.‡
Mandel, Joshua H. .......................'68 '93 C.25 B.A. L.1065 J.D. 4675 Macarthur Ct.
Mandel, Maurice, II ....................'— '80 C.800 B.S. L.1137 J.D. 160 Newport Ctr. Dr.
**Mann, David H.** .................. '60 '88 C.1060 B.S. L.1065 J.D. [🄰 Stradling,Y.C.&R.]
**Manning, Patrick John** ........................'53 '85 C&L.1051 B.S., J.D. [Sims,M.&M.]
*PRACTICE AREAS: Insurance Defense Law; Legal Malpractice Law.
**Mansukhani, Jeffrey Daniel** ..........'65 '91 C.1049 B.A. L.259 J.D. [🄰 Cummins&W.]
*PRACTICE AREAS: Insurance Coverage; Civil Litigation; Bad Faith Litigation.
Marhoefer, Gordon J. .................'32 '73 C&L.426 B.A., J.D. Mass. Mut. Life Ins. Co.
Marks, Linda S. ..........................'57 '85 C.112 B.A. L.809 J.D. One Newport Place
Marrison, M. Patricia ..........................'48 '78 C.112 B.A. L.1068 J.D. 5160 Birch
Marshall, Douglas M. ........................'47 '73 C.112 B.S. L.1065 J.D. 4100 Newport Pl.
**Martens, Don W., (P.C.)**, (AV) '34 '64
C.966 B.S.Eng. L.273 J.D. [Knobbe,M.O.&B.] (See Pat. Sect.)
Martin, John D. ....................................'53 '80 C.112 B.A. L.425 J.D. [Martin&M.]
**Martin, Peter A.** ....................... '63 '93 C.1232 B.A. L.1137 J.D. [🄰 Capretz&R.]
*LANGUAGES: Spanish and German.
*PRACTICE AREAS: Construction Defect; Business Litigation; Medical Product Liability.
Martin & McCormick ................................................... 5000 Birch St., Ste. 440
**Martindale, Lowell C., Jr.**, (AV) ...... '40 '69 C.1042 B.A. L.800 J.D. [O'Melveny&M.]
**Martinez, Marvin A.** ......................'46 '79 C.679 B.S. L.1137 J.D. [🄰 Bragg,S.S.&K.]
Mast, Paul G. ............................................'32 '58 C&L.813 A.B., J.D. [Mast&M.]
Mast, Steven D. ............................ '59 '85 C.813 B.A. L.1068 J.D. [Mast&M.]
Mast and Mast ...................................................................... 1300 Dove St.
Matcha, Morrie, (BV) ..................... '21 '54 C.668 A.B. L.800 J.D. P.O. Box 976

**Matheis, Mary Aileen '26 '82 C.703 B.A. L.1137 J.D.**
**1300 Dove Street, Suite 200, 92660-2710**
**Telephone: 714-476-4488 FAX: 714-476-2878**
**General Law, Wills, Trust, Probate, Real Estate, Dissolutions, Civil Law, Business Litigation, Trial.**

**Matsen, Jeffrey R., & Associates**
**(See Santa Ana)**

Matten, Bradley K. ............ '48 '73 C.339 B.S. L.1068 J.D. Shorecliff Financial Corp.
**Matthews, Robert J.** ............................'55 '81 C.800 B.S. L.893 J.D. [🄲 Stradling,Y.C.&R.]
**May, Bruce D.** ....................................'54 '79 C.112 A.B. L.1068 J.D. [Stradling,Y.C.&R.]
*REPORTED CASES: Todd Shipyards v. City of Los Angeles (1982) 130 Cal. App. 3d 222, 181 Cal. App. 3d 222, 181 Cal. Rptr. 652, hrng. denied; Santos v. Todd Pacific Shipyards Corporation, 585 F.Supp. 482 (C.D. Cal. 1984) Todd Pacific Shipyards Corporation, 81 L.A. 1095 (1983) (E. Jones, Arb.).
**May, Gregory T.** ..............................'60 '92 C.871 B.S. L.464 J.D. [🄰 Brobeck,P.&H.]
**May, Stacy J.** '65 '93 C&L.352 B.B.A., J.D.
(adm. in AZ; not adm. in CA) [🄰 Howard,R.N.C.F.&R.]
*PRACTICE AREAS: Commercial Litigation.
Mazura, Terrence A. ................................'50 '81 C.339 B.S. L.46 J.D. [Grumman&M.]
Mazurek, Ralph R. ...................'54 '81 C.800 B.A. L.426 J.D. 100 Bayview Cir., Suite 6000
**McAllister, Nancy E.** ................................'67 '94 C.1176 B.A. L.426 J.D. [🄰 Fisher&P.]
**McBride, Paul T.** ................................'56 '81 C.477 B.A. L.188 J.D. [🄰 Borton,P.&C.]
*PRACTICE AREAS: Casualty Defense; Construction Defects.
**McCamish, Larry O.** '53 '80 C.763 B.A. L.1137 J.D.
Sr. Coun., Chevron Land & Development Co.
**McCarty, John C.** ............................'63 '88 C.1042 B.A. L.1137 J.D. [🄰 R.K.Scott]
McClary, Paul D., Jr. ...............................'33 '59 C&L.426 B.S., LL.B. P.O. Box 3081‡
McClellan, Robert M. '51 '79 C.800 A.B. L.1137 J.D.
Pres., McClellan Sports Mgmt. Grp.
**McCormick, James (Kimo) E., III**, (AV) '48 '74
C.813 A.B. L.276 J.D. [J.E.McCormick III]
McCormick, Kathy J. ..............................'55 '81 C.112 B.A. L.426 J.D. [Martin&M.]

**McCormick, James E., III, (AV)**
**4100 Newport Place, Suite 455, 92660-2437**
**Telephone: 714-252-8100 Fax: 714-252-8300**
**James (Kimo) E. McCormick, III.**
**Corporate and Corporate Securities, Limited liability Company Practice, Mergers and Acquisitions, Real Estate, Real Estate Leasing Practice, International Business, Venture Capital and Finance.**
*See Professional Biographies, NEWPORT BEACH, CALIFORNIA*

**McDermott, John A., II**, (AV) .......'43 '70 C.602 B.B.A. L.1068 J.D. [McDermott&T.]
*PRACTICE AREAS: Health Care; Capital Financing; Commercial Transactions; Real Estate Law; Civil Litigation.
**Mc Dermott, Michael A.** ............ '49 '75 C.602 B.S. L.1065 J.D. [🄰 McDermott&T.]
*LANGUAGES: French.
*PRACTICE AREAS: Charitable Trust Law; Nonprofit Corporate; Tax; Pension Plans; Civil Litigation.

**McDermott & Trayner, Professional Law Corporation, (AV)**
**One Newport Place, 1301 Dove Street, Suite 1050, 92660⊙**
**Telephone: 714-851-0441 Telecopier: 714-851-1735**
**John A. McDermott, II; Ronald G. Trayner (Resident, Pasadena Office); Eric E. Johnson; Victor C. Ireland; Ralph J. Morgan. Of Counsel: Thomas M. Collins (Resident, Pasadena Office);—Michael A. Mc Dermott.**
**Health Care, Hospital, Corporate and Administrative Law and Civil Litigation.**
**Pasadena, California Office: 225 South Lake Avenue, Suite 410. Telephone: 818-792-8242. Telecopier: 818-449-2458.**
*See Professional Biographies, NEWPORT BEACH, CALIFORNIA*

**McDermott, Will & Emery, (AV) 🄱🄱**
**A Partnership including Professional Corporations**
**1301 Dove Street, Suite 500; 92660-2444⊙**
**Telephone: 714-851-0633 Facsimile: 714-851-9348**
**URL: http://www.mwe.com**
**Members of Firm: Thomas K. Brown; Jill M. Draffin; Paul B. George; Peter D. Holbrook; Steven N. Holland; John B. Miles; Gregory W. Preston; Stuart W. Price; Bernard E. Schneider; Michael Schulman; Joseph E. Thomas; J. Russell Tyler, Jr.;—Anne Heller Duncan; Martin P. Florman; George L. Hampton IV; Robert I. Newton; Renée M. Raithel; Tambra L. Raush.**
**General Practice (including Corporate, Employee Benefits, Estate Planning, Health, Litigation and Tax Law).**
**Chicago, Illinois Office: 227 West Monroe Street. Telephone: 312-372-2000. Facsimile: 312-984-7700.**
**Boston, Massachusetts Office: 75 State Street, Suite 1700. Telephone: 617-345-5000. Facsimile: 617-345-5077.**
**Miami, Florida Office: 201 South Biscayne Boulevard. Telephone: 305-358-3500. Facsimile: 305-347-6500.**
**Washington, D.C. Office: 1850 K Street, N.W. Telephone: 202-887-8000. Facsimile: 202-778-8087.**
**Los Angeles, California Office: 2049 Century Park East. Telephone: 310-277-4110. Facsimile: 310-277-4730.**
**New York, N.Y. Office: 50 Rockefeller Plaza. Telephone: 212-547-5508. Facsimile: 212-547-5444.**
**St. Petersburg, Russia Office: AOZT McDermott, Will & Emery, Griboyedova Canal 36, 191023 St. Petersburg, Russia. Telephone: (7) (812) 310-52-44; 310-55-44; 310-59-44; 850-20-45. Facsimile: (7) (812) 310-54-46; 325-84-50.**
**Vilnius, Lithuania Office: Smetonos 6, 2600 Vilnius, Lithuania. Telephone: 370 2 61-43-08. Facsimile: 370 2 22-79-55.**
*See Professional Biographies, NEWPORT BEACH, CALIFORNIA*

**McDonald, James J., Jr.** ..............................'60 '84 C.1275 B.A. L.276 J.D. [Fisher&P.]
*PRACTICE AREAS: Labor (Management) Laws; Employment Law; Wrongful Discharge Law.
McDonald, Patricia A. .........'55 '80 C.1042 B.S. L.800 J.D. 2121 E. Pacific Coast Hwy.
McDonnell, Robert J. ...................................'40 '75 C&L.999 LL.B. 1300 Quail St.
**McEvers, Duff S.** ....................................'54 '81 C.800 B.A. L.1137 J.D. [🄲 Walker]
*PRACTICE AREAS: International Law; Litigation; Business Law.
**McEwen, David R.** ............................'46 '75 C.112 B.A. L.426 J.D. [Stradling,Y.C.&R.]
McGee, James F. ..........................'50 '80 C.659 B.S. L.1137 J.D. 23 Corporate Plz. Dr.
McGinnis, Felix H., (AV) ..............................'10 '35 C&L.426 LL.B. 864 W. 16th St.‡
McGraw, Phillip R. ......................................'25 '54 C&L.800 B.S., LL.B. Ret. Mun. J.
McIntosh, Gail H. '46 '82 C.1109 B.A. L.426 J.D.
Asst. V.P. & Ins. Coun., Pacific Mut. Life Ins. Co.
**McKee, Michael D.** '46 '79
C.1232 B.A. L.1068 J.D. Exec. V.P. & Chf. Legal Off., The Irvine Co.
McKeever, Joseph E. '51 '77 C.1031 A.B. L.378 J.D.
Asst. V.P., Invest. Coun., Pacific Mut. Life Ins. Co.
McKinney, Julia C. '56 '81 C.112 B.A. L.426 J.D.
Asst. V.P. & Ins. Coun., Pacific Mut. Life Ins. Co.
McLaughlin, Michael T., (AV) '33 '72 C.1097 B.A. L.426 J.D.
Asst. V.P. & Ins. Coun., Pacific Mut. Life Ins. Co.

**McMillen, Jeffrey B. '65 '92 C.1109 B.S. L.1137 J.D.**
**One Newport Place, 1301 Dove Street, Suite 670, 92660-2468**
**Telephone: 714-660-0119 Fax: 714-660-1462**
***PRACTICE AREAS: Consumer Law (35%, 50); Criminal Law (20%, 20); Family Law (10%, 10); Bankruptcy (10%, 10); Business (10%, 10).**
**Consumer Law, Criminal Law, Family Law, Bankruptcy, Business and Real Estate Litigation.**
*See Professional Biographies, NEWPORT BEACH, CALIFORNIA*

McMurray, Kimberly A. ......................... '61 '90 C.112 L.990 J.D. 4920 Campus Dr.
**McNeil, Richard J.** ..............................'59 '84 C.976 B.A. L.1066 J.D. [Irell&M.]

**McQueen, Matthew** ............... '67 '93 C.951 B.A. L.477 J.D. [Ⓐ Stradling,Y.C.&R.]
**McVay, Dean H.** ..................... '63 '90 C.477 B.A. L.880 J.D. [Kelegian&T.]
*PRACTICE AREAS: General Liability Defense; Fraudulent (S.I.U.) Claims; Construction Defects.
Mead, Alice N., (BV) ........................ '40 '65 C.787 B.A. L.800 J.D. [Mead&M.]
Mead, Frank F., III, (BV) ..................... '29 '72 C&L.800 B.A., J.D. [Mead&M.]
Mead and Mead, (BV) ....................................... 4100 Newport Pl. Dr.
**Meadows, Brian M.** ................ '66 '94 C.1109 B.A. L.1137 J.D. [Ⓐ Tuverson&H.]
*PRACTICE AREAS: Medical Malpractice; General Liability Defense.
Meghrouni, Alexis D. ................ '57 '90 C.112 B.A. L.426 J.D. [Ⓐ Saxon,B.G.&K.]
**Meindl, John M.**, (AV) ..................... '44 '72 C.112 B.A. L.426 J.D. [Barger&W.]
*LANGUAGES: German.
*PRACTICE AREAS: Real Property Law; Construction Law; Business Law.
Melum, Tony ..................... '44 '79 C.112 B.A. L.1137 J.D. 2315 Margaret Dr.
Menkes, Roslyn, (BV) ............................................ '28 '77 1101 Dove St.
**Menter, Timothy S.** ..................... '61 '87 C.886 B.A. L.902 J.D. [Ⓐ Newmeyer&D.]
*PRACTICE AREAS: Environmental Law; Insurance Law.

**Merring, Robert A. '51 '77 C.813 A.B. L.178 J.D.**
**369 San Miguel Drive Suite 305, 92660**
**Telephone: 714-760-6655 Fax: 714-760-9292**
**Email: rmerring@counsel.com**
***PRACTICE AREAS: Business; Commercial; Real Property Litigation; Alternative Dispute Resolution; Intellectual Property.**
**Business, Commercial and Real Property Litigation. Alternative Dispute Resolution. Intellectual Property, Trade Regulation. Bankruptcy and Debtor-Creditor Rights, Real Property and Transactional Matters.**
*See Professional Biographies, NEWPORT BEACH, CALIFORNIA*

**Meyer, Clifford John** ................ '32 '61 C&L.309 A.B., LL.B. [Buchalter,N.F.&Y.]
*PRACTICE AREAS: Financial Institutions; General Business Litigation.
**Meyerhoff, Scott A.** ........................ '58 '84 C.1077 B.S. L.426 J.D. [O'Melveny&M.]
Michel, Michael L., (BV) ..................... '39 '65 C&L.861 B.A., LL.B. [Michel&R.]
Michel & Rhyne, (BV) ....................................... 4041 MacArthur Blvd.
Michelman, Eric I. ........... '58 '83 C.103 B.A. L.94 J.D. 4695 MacArthur Ct., Ste., 840
Michelsen, Erik B. ..................... '61 '87 C.684 B.S. L.990 J.D. 5000 Campus Dr.

**Mickelson, Wendy J., (AV) '49 '80 C.1078 B.A. L.1137 J.D.**
**5120 Campus Drive, 92660**
**Telephone: 714-724-1872 Fax: 714-752-8770**
***PRACTICE AREAS: Family Law.**
**Family Law.**
*See Professional Biographies, NEWPORT BEACH, CALIFORNIA*

**Miles, John B.**, (AV) ..................... '43 '73 C.228 B.A. L.1292 J.D. [McDermott,W.&E.]
*PRACTICE AREAS: Corporate Law; Real Estate.
**Millar, Richard W., Jr.**, (AV) ................ '38 '67 C.605 L.767 LL.B. [Millar,H.&B.]
*REPORTED CASES: Shearer v. Superior Court (1977) 70 Cal.App.3d 424, 138 Cal.Rptr. 824; Canal-Randolph Anaheim, Inc. v. Moore (1978) 78 Cal.App.3d 477, 143 Cal.Rptr. 789, 144 Cal.Rptr. 474; Canal-Randolph Anaheim, Inc. v. Wilkoski (1980) 103 Cal.App.3d 282, 163 CalRptr. 30; Askew v. Askew (1994) 22 Cal.App.4th 942, 28 Cal.Rptr.2d 284.
*PRACTICE AREAS: Business Litigation; Real Estate Litigation.

**Millar, Hodges & Bemis, (AV)**
**One Newport Place, Suite 900, 1301 Dove Street, 92660-2448**
**Telephone: 714-752-7722 FAX: 714-752-6131**
**Members of Firm: Richard W. Millar, Jr.; Kenneth R. Hodges; Larry R. Bemis. Associates: David A. St.Clair.**
**General Trial and Appellate Practice in all Courts. Business, Corporation, Estate Planning, Real Estate and Taxation Law.**
**Reference: Manufacturers Bank, Newport Beach, California.**
*See Professional Biographies, NEWPORT BEACH, CALIFORNIA*

Miller, Allan ..................................... '38 '66 C.184 B.A. L.426 J.D. [Miller&M.]
**Miller, Barbara J.** ..................... '66 '92 C.813 B.S. L.383 J.D. [Ⓐ Brobeck,P.&H.]
*LANGUAGES: German.
*PRACTICE AREAS: Employment Litigation; Business Litigation.
**Miller, Chad W.** ................ '68 '96 C.549 B.S.E.E. L.596 J.D. [Ⓐ Knobbe,M.O.&B.]
Miller, James L.I. ..................... '52 '86 C.1097 B.A. L.809 J.D. 212 33rd St.

**Miller, John Andrew, (AV) '40 '66 C.197 A.B. L.800 LL.B.**
**South Tower, Suite 600, 3501 Jamboree Road, 92660**
**Telephone: 714-725-6311 Fax: 714-725-6340**
***PRACTICE AREAS: Employment Law; Business Transactions; Business Litigation; Corporate and Partnership Formation.**
**Employment Law for Employers and Executives. Corporate and Transactional Law.**
*See Professional Biographies, NEWPORT BEACH, CALIFORNIA*

Miller, Thomas E., (BV) ............ '48 '73 C.1042 B.A. L.1065 J.D. 4695 McArthur Ct.
Miller & Miller ................................................ 4041 MacArthur Blvd.
Milman, Jeffrey A., (BV) .......... '56 '81 C.1109 B.A. L.1049 J. D. 2424 S.E. Bristol St.
Minna, Dennis F. ..................... '51 '87 C.684 B.A. L.1137 J.D. 2424 S.E. Bristol
Mirecki, Kevin J. ..................... '58 '89 C.800 B.S. L.1137 J.D. 3501 Jamboree Rd.
Mischel, Laurence, Jr., (BV) ................. '34 '63 C&L.575 A.B., LL.B. 1300 Dove St.
**Mishow, M. Edward**, (AV) ................ '55 '81 C.910 B.S.B.A. L.309 J.D. [Voss,C.&T.]
*PRACTICE AREAS: Individual and Corporate Tax Planning; Taxation (Local, Personal Property, State, Federal or International) Law; Federal Income, Estate and Gift Taxation Law; Partnership Law.
Misner, Michael D. .......... '48 '85 C.378 B.A. L.326 J.D. 4695 MacArthur Ct., Ste., 840
Mitchell, Craig A. ..................... '56 '93 C.1131 B.A. L.1137 J.D. [Horton,W.&C.]
Mitchell, Wallace L., II ....................................... '39 '66 4299 MacArthur Blvd.
Mitchell, William R. ..................... '54 '81 C.800 B.A. L.464 J.D. P.O. Box 7489
Moad, Michael B. ..................... '53 '79 C.1109 B.A. L.1137 J.D. 1617 Westcliff Dr.
**Mohney, D. Scott** ....................................... '53 '86 C.1097 L.398 J.D. [Ⓐ R.K.Scott]
Molseed, Michael C. ..................... '42 '79 C.1131 B.A. L.1127 J.D. 400 Colton St.
Moorad, Jeffrey S. ..................... '55 '82 C.112 B.A. L.884 J.D. [Steinberg&M.]
Moore, Frederick C. ..................... '56 '86 C.1074 B.S. L.1065 J.D. 5000 Birch St.
**Moore, Geoffrey T.** ..................... '55 '87 C.112 B.A. L.464 J.D. [Ⓐ Tuverson&H.]
**Moore, Harvey M.** ..................... '55 '81 C.112 A.B. L.1068 J.D. [Bidna&K.]
Morgan, James Norman, (AV) ... '25 '54 C.112 L.1065 J.D. 1303 Avocado Ave., Ste 280‡
**Morgan, Ralph J.** ..................... '43 '70 C.112 A.B. L.1068 J.D. [McDermott&T.]
*PRACTICE AREAS: Civil Litigation; Corporate; Municipal Law; Real Estate Law.
**Morisseau, Fay E.**, (AV) ..... '51 '78 C.623 B.S. L.326 J.D. [Howard,R.N.C.F.&R.] (Pat.)
*PRACTICE AREAS: Intellectual Property Litigation and Counseling; Business and Commercial Litigation.
Morningstar, W. W., (AV) ................ '24 '53 C.684 B.A. L.1065 J.D. 240 Nice Lane‡
Morrell, Gregory R. ..................... '45 '73 C.800 B.A. L.426 J.D. 113 G St.
Morrison, Robert H., (AV) ........... '39 '65 C.800 B.S. L.1065 J.D. 2138 Vista Laredo‡
**Morrow, William D.** ..................... '54 '82 C.154 B.A. L.990 J.D. [Sims,M.&M.]
*PRACTICE AREAS: Construction Defect Litigation; Land Subsidence.
Mosler, Damon Craig .... '64 '90 C.112 B.A. L.1049 J.D. 660 Newport Ctr. Dr., Ste. 1600
**Mosley, Paul E.** ..................... '59 '86 C&L.101 B.A., J.D. [O'Melveny&M.]
*LANGUAGES: Spanish.
**Mounedji, Selim** ..................... '59 '94 C.800 B.S. L.426 J.D. [Ⓐ Sims,M.&M.]
*LANGUAGES: French and Arabic.
Mozingo, Glen R., (AV) ............ '46 '79 C.1042 B.S. L.1137 J.D. [Mozingo&P.]ⓞ
Mozingo & Price, (AV) ............................ 1 Newport Place, Ste 900 (ⓞSacramento)
Mudge, Carter A. ..................... '64 '90 C.112 B.A. L.1049 J.D. 450 Newport Ctr. Dr.
**Muehlhauser, Douglas G.** ..... '60 '95 C.112 B.A. L.1049 J.D. [Knobbe,M.O.&B.]
Mulichak, Hydee J. ..................... '66 '92 C.800 B.A. L.426 J.D. [Ⓐ Neben&S.]
**Mulroy, Michael Hennessey** ....... '66 '93 C.145 B.A. L.1068 J.D. [Ⓐ Stradling,Y.C.&R.]
**Murphy, John J.**, (AV) ..................... '44 '70 C.116 B.S. L.893 LL.B. [Stradling,Y.C.&R.]
**Murphy, Michael E.** ..................... '68 '94 C&L.990 B.S., J.D. [Ⓐ Sims,M.&M.]
Murray, David D. ..................... '43 '78 C.63 B.S. L.1137 J.D. 1201 Dove St.
**Musurlian, Erik R.** ..................... '69 '95 C.1049 B.S. L.112 J.D. [Kelegian&T.]
*PRACTICE AREAS: Civil Litigation; Construction Defect; Premises Liability.

**Myers, Frank B., (AV) '41 '66 C.154 B.A. L.426 LL.B.**
**Suite 720, 4400 MacArthur Boulevard, 92660**
**Telephone: 714-752-2001 Facsimile: 714-955-3670**
**International Business Law, Mining and Ore Processing Facilities Development, Natural Resource Development, Engineering, Construction, Electronics and General Business and Corporate Law.**
*See Professional Biographies, NEWPORT BEACH, CALIFORNIA*

Myers, Laura A. ..................... '53 '78 C.112 B.A. L.1065 J.D. 1301 Dove St.
**Nakashima, John M.** ..................... '54 '87 C.1042 B.A. L.800 J.D. [Ⓐ Irell&M.]
Nanko, James R. ..................... '60 '85 C.800 B.S. L.426 J.D. 1300 Dove St.
**Nassie, Daniel A.** ..................... '52 '90 C.147 B.A. L.999 J.D. [Ⓐ Doss&P.]
**Nataupsky, Steven J.** '66 '91
C.860 B.S.E.S. L.569 J.D. [Knobbe,M.O.&B.] (See Pat. Sect.)
Neary, Robert V. '53 '78 C.800 B.A. L.426 J.D.
Sr. V.P. & Gen. Coun., WCB Properties
Neben, Marvin, (AV) ................ '25 '48 C&L.930 B.A., J.D. 270 Newport Ctr. Dr.
Neben & Starrett, Inc., (AV) ....................................... 270 Newport Center Dr.
**Needham, Richard T.** ................ '64 '90 C.112 B.S. L.426 J.D. [Ⓐ Stradling,Y.C.&R.]
*LANGUAGES: German.
Nelson, David H., (AV) ................ '35 '60 C.494 B.A. L.309 LL.B. 450 Newport Ctr.
Nelson, John C. ..................... '51 '77 C.108 B.A. L.1179 J.D. 1201 Dove St.
Nelson, Terry A. ............ '45 '74 C.112 L.1137 J.D. 1000 Quail St. Ste 125
**Nelson, Warren Lee** ..................... '47 '95 C.1169 B.A. L.966 J.D. [Ⓐ Fisher&P.]
Neu, Roger L. ..................... '51 '78 C.1032 B.A. L.426 J.D. [R.L.Neu]
Neu, Roger L., Inc. ............................................. 500 Newport Center Dr.
**Neue, Karyn S.** ..................... '67 '95 C.112 B.A. L.800 J.D. [Walker]
*PRACTICE AREAS: Business Litigation; Corporations; Bankruptcy; Wills; Trusts.
**Nevis, Heather Skinner** ................ '67 '92 C.112 B.A. L.464 J.D. [Ⓐ Cummins&W.]
*PRACTICE AREAS: Business Litigation; Insurance Defense.
Newman, Jill ..................... '68 '94 C.112 B.A. L.1067 J.D. 660 Newport Ctr. Dr.
**Newmeyer, Thomas F.**, (AV) ............ '53 '78 C.763 B.S. L.426 J.D. [Newmeyer&D.]
*PRACTICE AREAS: Litigation involving Business; Unfair Competition; Trade Secrets; Partnership Dissolutions; Wrongful Termination.

**Newmeyer & Dillion, (AV)**
**North Tower, Suite 6000, 3501 Jamboree Road, 92660**
**Telephone: 714-854-7000 Telecopier: 714-854-7099**
**Members of Firm: Thomas F. Newmeyer; Gregory L. Dillion; John A. O'Hara; Madison S. Spach Jr.; John E. Pope; Michael S. Cucchissi; Craig A. Callahan. Associates: Gene M. Witkin; Timothy S. Menter; R. Brad Sevier; Sandra Schaeffer; Ingrid M. Causey; Joseph A. Ferrentino; Michael G. Dibb; Dwight C. Hirsh; Debra B. Branse; Michael Paul Hutchins.**
**Real Estate, Real Estate Finance, Corporate, Bankruptcy, Partnerships, General Civil Litigation.**
**Reference: Marine National Bank.**
*See Professional Biographies, NEWPORT BEACH, CALIFORNIA*

**Newton, Robert I.** ..................... '65 '90 C&L.846 B.B.A., J.D. [Ⓐ McDermott,W.&E.]
**Nguyen, Christina T.** ..................... '71 '96 C.800 B.S. L.1066 J.D. [Ⓐ Fisher&P.]
**Nicholas, Frank**, (AV) ..................... '50 '77 C.1044 B.S. L.800 J.D. [F.Nicholas]

**Nicholas, Frank, A Law Corporation, (AV)**
**610 Newport Center Drive, Suite 1010, 92660-6419**
**Telephone: 714-760-6760**
**Frank Nicholas.**
**General Civil Trial Practice, Plaintiff's Personal Injury, Medical Malpractice, Legal Malpractice, Products Liability, Negligence and Tort Law, Insurance Bad Faith, Insurance Coverage, Wrongful Employment Termination and Discrimination.**
**References: Bank of America; Union Bank; California Federal Savings and Loan; American States Savings and Loan.**
*See Professional Biographies, NEWPORT BEACH, CALIFORNIA*

**Nieman, William H.**, (BV) '42 '80 C.910 B.S.E.E. L.1049 J.D.
[Knobbe,M.O.&B.] (See Pat. Sect.) (ⓞRiverside)
Nienow, Harvey C., A Law Corporation, (AV) '22 '50
C.966 B.S.M.E. L.436 J.D. 1300 Dove St. (Pat.)
Noble, Jeffrey J. ..................... '61 '94 C.1042 B.A. L.1137 J.D. [Ⓢ Sainick&C.]
Nokes, Beau James ..................... '60 '85 C.878 B.A. L.464 J.D. 2424 S.E. Bristol
**Norek, Charles J.**, (AV) ..................... '47 '78 C.927 B.S. L.365 J.D. [Ⓐ Tuverson&H.] ‡
*PRACTICE AREAS: Medical Malpractice Law (100%).
Norman, Ronald E. ..................... '54 '82 C.112 B.A. L.1049 J.D. 4675 MacArthur Ct.
Nuutinen, Arto Juhani ..................... '60 '90 C.112 BS. L.1049 J.D. 4920 Campus Dr.
**Nyquist, Paul C.** ..................... '45 '72 C.800 B.A. L.1068 J.D. [Bruck&P.]
*PRACTICE AREAS: Business and Commercial Litigation; Employment Law; Insurance Defense; Legal Malpractice Defense.
**Obegi, Joseph C.**, (AV) ..................... '45 '71 C&L.800 B.S., J.D. [Obegi&B.]
*PRACTICE AREAS: Estate Planning; Trust Law; Probate; Tax Law.

**Obegi & Brewer, P.C., (AV)**
**Suite 350, 4041 MacArthur Boulevard, 92660**
**Telephone: 714-833-7824 Fax: 714-833-3133**
**Burleigh J. Brewer; Joseph C. Obegi.**
**Estate Planning, Trust, Probate and Tax Law.**
*See Professional Biographies, NEWPORT BEACH, CALIFORNIA*

O'Connell, Katherine B. ..................... '50 '76 C.36 B.A. L.1137 J.D. 333 Bayside Dr.
OConnell, Mark A. ..................... '49 '76 C.36 B.S. L.1137 J.D. 333 Bayside Dr.

**Officer, Philip N. '38 '70 C.112 B.S. L.1066 J.D.**
**1300 Dove Street, Suite 200, 92660**
**Telephone: 714-261-8322**
***PRACTICE AREAS: Construction Law (60%); Products Liability (5%); Contracts (10%); Criminal Law (10%); Personal Injury (15%).**
**Construction Law, Products Liability, Contracts, Criminal Law, Personal Injury.**
*See Professional Biographies, NEWPORT BEACH, CALIFORNIA*

**Oglesby, Susan M.** ..................... '66 '92 C.112 B.A. L.1049 J.D. [Ⓐ Cummins&W.]
*PRACTICE AREAS: Civil Litigation; First Party Insurance Property Coverage; Bad Faith.
Oh, Susie H. '64 '91 C.112 B.S.E.E. L.1065 J.D.
Intell. Prop. Atty., Rockwell International Corporation (Pat.)
**O'Hara, John A.** ..................... '60 '85 C.112 B.A. L.180 J.D. [Newmeyer&D.]
*PRACTICE AREAS: Litigation involving Construction; Real Estate; Insurance Coverage; Business Litigation.
**O'Keefe, Sean A.** ..................... '58 '84 C.197 B.A. L.282 J.D. [Broker&O.]
**O'Keefe, Thomas J., (A Professional Corporation)**, (AV) '36 '62
C.426 B.B.A. L.813 J.D. [Good,W.H.&W.]
*PRACTICE AREAS: Estate Planning Law; Wills Law; Trusts Law; Probate Law; Taxation Law.
Olsen, Dan G. ..................... '54 '81 C&L.101 B.S., J.D. 190 Newport Ctr. Dr.

**Olsen, Debra M.**, (AV) '54 '79 C.112 B.A. L.1137 J.D. [Witter&H.]
*PRACTICE AREAS: Federal and State Tax; Tax Litigation; Estate Planning; Trust and Probate Law.
**Olson, Darrell L., (P.C.)**, (BV) '52 '77
C.894 B.A. L.273 J.D. [Knobbe,M.O.&B.] (See Pat. Sect.)
**Olson, Gordon H., (P.C.)**, (AV) '33 '62
C.597 B.S. L.273 J.D. [Knobbe,M.O.&B.] (See Pat. Sect.)
Olson, John S. '54 '81 C&L.378 B.A., J.D. 610 Newport Ctr. Dr.

**O'Melveny & Myers LLP, (AV)**
**610 Newport Center Drive, 92660-6429⊙**
**Telephone: 714-760-9600 Cable Address: "Moms" Facsimile: 714-669-6994**
**Email: ommifo@omm.com**
**Members of Firm: Douglas W. Abendroth; William G. Adams; Russell G. Allen (Certified Specialist, Probate, Estate Planning and Trust Law, The State Bar of California Board of Legal Specialization); Jerry W. Carlton; Cormac J. Carney; Karen K. Dreyfus; Steven L. Edwards; Patricia Frobes; Pamela C. Gray; Todd A. Green; Catherine Burcham Hagen; Theodore C. Hamilton; Joseph J. Herron; Wayne Jacobsen; Phillip R. Kaplan; David A. Krinsky; Lowell C. Martindale, Jr.; Scott A. Meyerhoff; Paul E. Mosley; Stephen P. Pepe; Frank L. Rugani; James V. Selna; Gary J. Singer; Stephanie I. Splane; Thomas E. Wolfe; Michael G. Yoder. Of Counsel: Barton Beek. Special Counsel: Kevin Ray Baker; George C. Demos; Brett J. Williamson.**
**General Civil Litigation, Appellate Practice, and Criminal Trials Practice in all State and Federal Courts. Administrative; Antitrust; Banking; Bankruptcy; Commercial; Communications; Construction; Corporation and Corporate Financing; Environmental; Immigration and Naturalization; Insurance Coverage Defense; Intellectual Property; International Business; Labor and Employment; Employment Benefits; Media and Entertainment; Municipal, Municipal Zoning, and Municipal Finance; Natural Resources; Oil and Gas; Patent, Trademark, Copyright, and Unfair Competition; Probate, Trusts, and Estate Planning; Public Utilities; Real Estate; Securities; and Tax Law.**
**Los Angeles, California Office: 400 South Hope Street, 90071-2899. Telephone: 213-669-6000. Cable Address: "Moms". Facsimile: 213-669-6407. E-mail: omminfo@omm.com.**
**Century City, California Office: 1999 Avenue of the Stars, 90067-6035. Telephone: 310-553-6700. Facsimile: 310-246-6779.**
**San Francisco, California Office: Embarcadero Center West Tower, 275 Battery Street, 94111-3305. Telephone: 415-984-8700. Facsimile: 415-984-8701.**
**New York, New York Office: Citicorp Center, 153 East 53rd Street, 10022-4611. Floor. Telephone: 212-326-2000. Facsimile: 212-326-2061.**
**Washington, D.C. Office: 555 13th Street, N.W., 20004-1109. Telephone: 202-383-5300. Cable Address: "Moms". Facsimile: 202-383-5414.**
**London, England Office: 10 Finsbury Square, London, EC2A 1LA. Telephone: 0171-256-8451. Facsimile: 0171-638-8205.**
**Tokyo, Japan Office: Sanbancho KB-6 Building, 6 Sanbancho, Chiyoda-ku, Tokyo 102, Japan. Telephone: 03-3239-2800. Facsimile: 03-3239-2432.**
**Hong Kong Office: Suite 1905, Peregrine Tower, Lippo Centre, 89 Queensway, Central, Hong Kong. Telephone: 852-2523-8266. Facsimile: 852-2522-1760.**
**Shanghai, People's Republic of China Office: Shanghai International Trade Centre, Suite 2011, 2200 Yan An Road West, Shanghai, 200335, PRC. Telephone: 86-21-6219-5363. Facsimile: 86-21-6275-4949.**
***See Professional Biographies, NEWPORT BEACH, CALIFORNIA***

O'Neill, Patricia '46 '80 C.800 B.A. 610 Newport Ctr. Dr.
**Oster, Edwin A.**, (AV) '50 '76 C.813 B.A. L.1067 J.D. [Ⓐ Barger&W.]
*PRACTICE AREAS: Business Litigation; Insurance Coverage; ERISA; Professional Liability.
Oster, Robert M., (AV) '32 '56 C.569 A.B. L.309 LL.B. P.O. Box 9587
Otis, Glen M. '55 '84 C.112 B.A. L.1137 J.D. 567 San Nicoles
**Otsuki, Joy Heuser** '61 '96 C.112 B.A. L.426 J.D. [Ⓐ Stradling,Y.C.&R.]
**Otuteye, Maxy Rush** '49 '95 C.309 B.A. L.1066 J.D. [Voss,C.&T.]
*PRACTICE AREAS: Corporate; Real Estate; Financial.
**Outwater, David E.** '70 '95 C.1074 B.S. L.1067 J.D. [Ⓐ Stradling,Y.C.&R.]
**Overholt, David G.**, (AV) '35 '61 C.976 B.A. L.813 J.D. [Hoag&O.]⊙
*PRACTICE AREAS: Probate; Trust Administration; Tax.
**Overly, Michael R.** '60 '89 C.839 B.S. L.426 J.D. [Ⓐ Call,C.&J.]
*PRACTICE AREAS: Litigation.
**Overton, Thomas W.** '66 '95 C.800 B.A. L.1068 J.D. [Ⓐ Sims,M.&M.]
**Owens, Theodore E** '43 '88 C.990 B.S. L.61 J.D. [Kimball,T.&S.]
*PRACTICE AREAS: Landlord/Tenant.
**Page, Gregory S.** '56 '86 C.1042 B.S. L.809 J.D. [Doss&P.]

**Paone, Callahan, McHolm & Winton**
**(See Irvine)**

**Park, Jee Hi** '61 '90 C.66 B.A. L.1065 J.D. [Ⓐ Stradling,Y.C.&R.]

**Parker, James M., (AV) '34 '66 C.426 B.S. L.809 J.D.** BB
**4695 MacArthur Court, Suite 1290, 92660**
**Telephone: 714-752-2408 Fax: 714-752-2464**
***PRACTICE AREAS: Real Estate; Corporate Law; Construction Defects; Litigation.**
**General Civil, Trial and Appellate Practice, State and Federal Courts. General Corporate, Real Estate, Commercial, Land Use and Administrative.**
***See Professional Biographies, NEWPORT BEACH, CALIFORNIA***

Parker, Stuart M., (BV) '47 '74 C.112 B.A. L.1068 J.D. 160 Newport Ctr. Dr.
Parks, William R., III '41 '76 C.768 B.S. L.990 J.D. Prof. of Law, Orange Coast Coll.
Patrick, Lisa Mitts '63 '88 C.1109 B.A. L.1137 J.D. 20311 Acacia St., Ste 140
Patterson, Bradley A. '57 '91 C.549 B.A. L.1067 J.D. 1301 Dove St.
Paul, Richard S. '44 '79 C.232 B.S.B.A. L.1137 J.D. 177 Riverside Dr.

**Paul, Hastings, Janofsky & Walker LLP**
**(See Costa Mesa)**

**Pearlman, Marshall M.**, (AV) '36 '67 C.1046 B.A. L.564 [M.M.Pearlman]

**Pearlman, Marshall M., A Prof. Corp., Law Offices of, (AV)**
**Suite 600, South Tower, 3501 Jamboree Road, 92660**
**Telephone: 714-854-0890 Facsimile: 714-854-0891**
**Email: 75671.1771@compuserve.com**
**Marshall M. Pearlman.**
**Litigation: Environmental, Toxic Tort, Product Liability, General Business, Due Diligence: Environmental.**
**Representative Clients: Uniroyal Chemical Co., Inc.; Cooper Tire & Rubber Co.; Chevron Chemical Co.; Valent U.S.A. Corp.; Amana Refrigeration, Inc.**
***See Professional Biographies, NEWPORT BEACH, CALIFORNIA***

**Pedersen, Neil**, (AV) '57 '89 C&L.1137 B.S., J.D. [Pedersen&B.]

**Pedersen & Black, A Professional Law Corporation, (AV)**
**1300 Dove Street, Suite 200, 92660**
**Telephone: 714-263-9955 Fax: 714-263-0575**
**Neil Pedersen; William A. Black.**
**Business Litigation, Trials and Appeals, Insurance Coverage and Bad Faith Litigation, Construction Defect Litigation, Entertainment Law, General Corporate, Business Entity Formation.**
***See Professional Biographies, NEWPORT BEACH, CALIFORNIA***

**Pemberton, Gary A.** '55 '86 C.112 B.A. L.1066 J.D. [Stradling,Y.C.&R.]
**Penfil, Elizabeth K.** '66 '95 C.914 A.B. L.800 J.D. [Ⓐ Irell&M.]
**Penfil, Joan** '38 '85 C.477 B.A. L.1137 J.D. [Ⓐ Buxbaum&C.]⊙
*PRACTICE AREAS: Family Law.
Penney, John C., (AV) '27 '54 C.605 B.A. L.800 LL.B. 1025 Bayside Cove E.‡
**Pepe, Stephen P.**, (AV) '43 '69 C.555 B.A. L.228 J.D.
[O'Melveny&M.] (⊙Los Angeles)
*PRACTICE AREAS: Labor and Employment.
Perez, Hector C. '45 '72 C&L.846 B.B.A., J.D. 567 San Nicholas Dr.
**Perry, David J.**, (AV) '50 '76 C.1042 B.S. L.809 J.D. [Bruck&P.]
*PRACTICE AREAS: Real Estate Law; Finance Law; Commercial Transactions.
Person, James C., Jr. '45 '72 C.800 A.B. L.1065 J.D. 507 29th St.
**Peters, Donald**, (AV) '32 '65 C.602 B.S.C. L.809 J.D. [D.Peters]

**Peters, Donald, A Law Corporation, (AV)** BB
**1300 Dove Street, Suite 200, 92660**
**Telephone: 714-955-3818 Fax: 714-955-1341**
**Donald Peters.**
**General Civil Trial Practice. Personal Injury, Medical Malpractice, Elder Law, Elder Abuse, Estate Planning, Estate Supervision, Public Entity Liability, Maritime, Aviation and Insurance Law.**
***See Professional Biographies, NEWPORT BEACH, CALIFORNIA***

Pethick, Linda '51 '77 C.773 B.A. L.800 J.D. 1 Corporate Plza.
**Pfeifer, Michael R.**, (AV) '50 '76 C.154 B.A. L.188 J.D. [Wolf&P.]
*PRACTICE AREAS: Real Estate; Commercial and Bankruptcy Litigation; Mortgage Servicing and Secondary Market Transactions; Mortgage-Backed Securities; Creditor Rights.
Pfund, Peter J. '52 '80 C.229 B.A. L.1137 J.D. 2382 S.E. Bristol St.
**Phillips, James M., Jr.** '48 '77 C&L.575 A.B., J.D. [Phillips&H.]
*PRACTICE AREAS: Corporate Law; Securities.
**Phillips, Layn R.**, (AV) '52 '77 C&L.862 J.D. [Irell&M.]

**Phillips & Haddan, (AV)**
**4695 MacArthur Court, Suite 840, 92660**
**Telephone: 714-752-6100 Fax: 714-752-6161**
**Members of Firm: James M. Phillips, Jr.; Jon R. Haddan. Associate: Robert J. Zepfel.**
**Business, Corporate and Securities, Franchising, Real Estate, Municipal Finance, Investment Management and Financial Services, Mergers and Acquisitions.**

Pickell, Robert J., (BV) '27 '56 C&L.208 A.B., J.D. [R.J.Pickell]⊙
Pickell, Robert J., A Law Corporation, (BV) 1300 Dove St., Ste. 200 (⊙Riverside)
**Pierotti, Anthony W.** '60 '87 C.1042 B.S. L.1067 J.D. [Irell&M.]
**Piper, David D.** '68 '95 C.112 B.A. L.464 J.D. [Ⓐ Broker&O.]
**Pitts, Robert W.** '63 '89 C.36 B.S. L.273 J.D. [Winthrop C.]
*TRANSACTIONS: Debtor-Go Vacations America, Inc., and Go Vacations California, Inc.; Debtor-La Jolla Building Associates, A California Limited Partnership; Trustee-Glen Ivy Resorts, Inc., and Affiliated Entities; Debtor-Besteel Industries, Inc.; Debtor-Pleion Corporation.
*PRACTICE AREAS: Reorganization; Bankruptcy Law; Corporate Insolvency Law.
Platt, Richard Stephen, (BV) '37 '66 C&L.800 B.A., LL.B. 4675 MacArthur Ct.
Playdon, Pamela J. '39 '86 C.061 B.S. L.284 J.D.
(adm. in IL; not adm. in CA) F.D.I.C.
Plummer, Mark B. '57 '85 C.1042 B.S. L.426 J.D. 3 Civic Plaza
Polos, Peter J. '64 '90 C.112 B.A. L.426 J.D. 2424 S.E. Bristol
**Polson, John M.** '65 '91 C.1111 B.S. L.426 J.D. [Fisher&P.]
**Pope, John E.**, (AV) '42 '77 C.112 B.S. L.1068 J.D. [Newmeyer&D.]
*PRACTICE AREAS: Real Estate Law.
**Popelar, Ralph F., Jr.** '52 '83 C.1077 B.A. L.398 J.D. [Ⓐ Sims,M.&M.]
**Porter, Julie M.**, (AV) '59 '85 C&L.426 B.S., J.D. [Stradling,Y.C.&R.]
**Powell, Carolyn** '68 '92 C.112 B.A. L.1066 J.D. [Ⓐ Severson&W.]
*LANGUAGES: French, German.
*PRACTICE AREAS: Auto Finance Defense; Professional Malpractice; Insurance Defense; Insurance Coverage.

**Powell, Thomas L., (AV) '— '74 C.940 B.A. L.800 J.D.**
**3501 Jamboree Road, Suite 6000, 92660**
**Telephone: 714-721-7287 Fax: 714-721-7388**
**Real Estate Development, Subdivisions, Real Estate Transactions, Land Use and Redevelopment.**
***See Professional Biographies, NEWPORT BEACH, CALIFORNIA***

**Preston, Gregory W.** '55 '82 C.165 B.A. L.809 J.D. [McDermott,W.&E.]
*PRACTICE AREAS: General Corporate Law; Securities Law; Mergers and Acquisitions; Corporate Finance; Venture Capital Law.
Preston, Victor H. '40 '75 C.1042 B.S. L.990 J.D. 5000 Birch St.
Price, Don G., (BV) '46 '73 C.813 A.B. L.464 J.D. [Mozingo&P.]⊙
**Price, Stuart W.** '62 '86 C.112 B.A. L.1068 J.D. [McDermott,W.&E.]
Price, William F., (AV) '24 '49 C&L.800 B.S., J.D. 4650 Von Karman Ave.
Prince, Philip M. '53 '79 C.1044 B.S. L.107 J.D. 20301 Acacia
Probst, Janet H. '39 '90 C.823 B.A. L.1137 J.D. 2424 S.E. Bristol St.
**Punelli, Frank, Jr.**, (AV) '43 '67 C&L.352 B.A., J.D. [Davis,P.K.&W.]⊙
*PRACTICE AREAS: Business Litigation; Real Estate Transactions; Mortgage Banking; Environmental Law.
Purcell, D. Paul '54 '81 C.112 A.B. L.1067 J.D. 4675 Macarthur Ct.
Purcell, Ted M. '60 '87 C.36 B.S. L.800 J.D. 620 Newport Ctr. Dr.
**Purdy, Court Bryant** '69 '95 C.174 B.A. L.1049 J.D. [Wentworth&P.]
*PRACTICE AREAS: Personal Injury; Environmental.
Purnell, Larry W. '47 '83 C.1165 B.S. L.893 J.D.
(adm. in WA; not adm. in CA) 213 Promontory Dr. W.‡
**Puzder, Andrew F.**, (AV Ⓣ) '50 '78 C.161 B.A. L.910 J.D. [Stradling,Y.C.&R.]
**Quan, Judy A.** '55 '81 C.770 B.S. L.1068 J.D. [Gardner&Q.]
*PRACTICE AREAS: Business Corporations.
Queen, Stephen, (BV) '40 '71 C.569 B.E.E. L.990 J.D. 3501 Jamboree Rd.
**Quinlan, Dale K.** '50 '82 C.871 B.S. L.260 J.D. [Kester&Q.]
**Quinlan, Francis E.**, (AV) '48 '79 C.966 B.A. L.809 J.D. [Kester&Q.]
*SPECIAL AGENCIES: Federal Bureau of Investigation, 1979-1982.
*PRACTICE AREAS: Banking; Commercial Litigation; Taxation; Estate Planning; White Collar Crime (Civil and Criminal).
**Quiogue, Manuel**, (BV) '49 '76 C.477 B.S.E. L.273 J.D. [Roberts&Q.] (See Pat. Sect.)
*PRACTICE AREAS: Patent; Trademark; Intellectual Property.
**Radcliffe, Richard J.** '66 '91 C.1259 B.S. L.426 J.D. [Capretz&R.]
*PRACTICE AREAS: Business Litigation; Construction Law; Corporate Law; Real Property; Medical Product Liability.
**Rahmes, Mary T.** '56 '85 C.475 B.A. L.61 J.D. [Ⓐ R.K.Scott]
**Raithel, Renée M.** '68 '93 C.800 B.A. L.569 J.D. [Ⓐ McDermott,W.&E.]
**Ramiza, Gerald J.** '66 '94 C.659 B.S. L.1067 J.D. [Ⓐ Stradling,Y.C.&R.]
**Randall, Frederic Alport, Jr.** '56 '84 C.477 B.A. L.767 J.D. [Brobeck,P.&H.]
*PRACTICE AREAS: General Corporate Law; Securities Law; Venture Capital Law.
**Raney, Nancy E.** '58 '83 C.813 B.A. L.426 J.D. [Good,W.H.&W.]
*PRACTICE AREAS: Civil Litigation.
Rapillo, John P., (BV) '52 '78 C.763 A.B. L.61 J.D. 2700 Newport Blvd.
Rapp, Dieter K., & Associates '53 '86 C.112 B.A. L.809 J.D. 1101 Dove St.
**Rasch, Robert M.** '53 '78 C.800 B.S. L.426 J.D. [Balog&R.]
*PRACTICE AREAS: Estate Planning; Business Law; Tax Planning; Non-Profit Tax Law; Corporate Law.
Raskin, S. Robert, Jr. '63 '90 C.197 B.A. L.309 J.D. 840 Newport Center Dr., Suite 500
Rasmussen, Eric B. '44 '78 C.112 B.S. L.284 J.D. 4400 MacArthur Blvd.
**Raush, Tambra L.** '66 '91 C.112 B.A. L.1049 J.D. [Ⓐ McDermott,W.&E.]
**Rauth, William R., III**, (AV) '44 '70 C.112 A.B. L.1066 J.D. [Stradling,Y.C.&R.]
Ray, Milton L. '21 '50 C.696 B.A. L.145 J.D. 840 Newport Center Dr.

**Raymond, Paul W., (BV) '53 '83 C.112 B.A. L.1137 J.D.**
**Suite 950, 1301 Dove Street, 92660-2473**
**Telephone: 714-476-2197 Fax: 714-955-2886**
***PRACTICE AREAS: Taxation-Civil and Criminal, Federal and State.**
**Federal and State Taxation. Civil and Criminal Tax Litigation and Tax Controversy.**
***See Professional Biographies, NEWPORT BEACH, CALIFORNIA***

**Raynsford, Rick L.** ... '56 '82 C.112 B.A. L.464 J.D. [Bruck&P.]
*PRACTICE AREAS: Mediation; Business Litigation; Wrongful Termination; Real Estate Litigation; Trade Secrets.
**Re, Joseph R.** ... '60 '86 C.705 B.S.C.E. L.724 J.D. [Knobbe,M.O.&B.] (See Pat. Sect.)
Read, James W., Jr. ... '34 '61 C.112 B.S. L.1065 J.D. P.O. Box 780, Balboa
**Read, Randal Jason** ... '57 '85 C.267 B.A. L.990 J.D. [🄰 Rynn&J.]
Reavis, H. Clay, Jr., (BV) ... '22 '59 C.154 B.A. L.800 J.D. 4650 Von Karman Ave.
**Reed, Diane M.** ... '62 '90 C.477 B.G.S. L.1049 J.D. [Knobbe,M.O.&B.]
**Reeves, Andrea Levitan** ... '67 '93 C.188 B.S. L.659 J.D. [🄰 Stradling,Y.C.&R.]
**Reich, Marc** ... '65 '92 C.1044 B.S. L.1067 J.D. [🄰 Voss,C.&T.]
Reichmann, F. Joseph ... '46 '79 C.1246 B.S. L.1095 J.D. 4000 MacArthur Blvd.
**Reilly, Thomas H.** ... '57 '83 C.976 B.A. L.800 J.D. [Scott,R.&W.]
Reiss, Brian R. ... '53 '79 L.1095 J.D. 3700 Campus Dr.
**Remer, Franklin I.**, (AV) ... '29 '51 C.102 L.1009 LL.B. [Remer,D.&G.]
*PRACTICE AREAS: Litigation; Personal Injury.

**Remer, DiVincenzo & Griffith, A Professional Corporation, (AV)**
**2121 East Pacific Coast Highway, Suite 280 (Corona Del Mar), 92625**
**Telephone: 714-759-0781 Fax: 714-759-0788**
**Max Hurwitz (1914-1974); Robert R. Hurwitz (1921-1990); Franklin I. Remer; Joseph P. DiVincenzo; Dwight J. Griffith; Kathleen A. Carter; Gina L. Genova.**
**General Trial and Appellate Practice in all State and Federal Courts. General Business, Agri-Business, Corporation, Real Property, Estate Planning, Trust, Probate, Negligence, Taxation, Complex Litigation, Products Liability and Insurance Law.**
**References: First American Trust Co., Newport Beach; Sanna Trust, Newport Beach; Northern Trust, Newport Beach, California; Bank of Newport, Newport Beach.**
***See Professional Biographies, NEWPORT BEACH, CALIFORNIA***

**Renner, Robert K.** ... '65 '91 C.339 B.S. L.1068 J.D. [🄰 Barger&W.]
**Rense, Kirk S.**, (AV) ... '47 '80 C.1097 B.A. L.800 J.D. [Buchalter,N.F.&Y.]
*PRACTICE AREAS: Creditor and Trustee Representation; Receivership Administration; Financial Litigation.
**Resnick, Barnet, (Law Corporation)**, (AV) '45 '73
C.209 Ph.B. L.1137 J.D. [White&R.]⊙
*PRACTICE AREAS: Business Law (25%); Tax Planning (20%); Estate Planning (20%); Corporate (20%); Tax Controversy (15%).
Restaino, John M., Jr. ... '53 '88 C.1046 B.S. L.1137 J.D. 2424 S.E. Bristol
**Reynolds, Roland P.** ... '65 '90 C.197 A.B. L.464 J.D. [🄰 Wolf&P.]
*PRACTICE AREAS: Mortgage Banking; Real Estate and Commercial Litigation; Creditors' Rights.
Rhodes, Herbert B. ... '28 '56 C.112 B.A. L.426 LL.B. P.O. Box 7094
Rhyne, Karen A. ... '58 '85 C.1109 B.A. L.1137 J.D. [Michel&R.]
**Rich, Robert E.**, (AV) ... '50 '75 C.112 B.A. L.1068 J.D. [Stradling,Y.C.&R.]
**Richards, Melissa L.** ... '63 '89 C.112 B.S. L.767 J.D. [Wolf&P.]
*PRACTICE AREAS: Regulatory Compliance; Lending Transactions.
**Richardson, Lyne A.** ... '64 '89 C.800 B.S. L.426 J.D. [🄰 Fisher&P.]
Richley, M. A., Jr. ... '28 '58 C&L.800 B.S., LL.B. 809 Via Lido Soud‡
Rickard, Ronald G. ... '46 '71 C.1042 B.A. L.339 J.D. 601 Lido Park Dr.
Ridge, Raymond L., (BVⓣ) '43 '71 C&L.878 B.A., J.D.
(adm. in UT; not adm. in CA) P.O. Box 8036‡
Ridgeway, Tod ... '45 '72 C.800 B.S. L.426 J.D. Pres., Ridgeway Develop.
Rigg, Robert R., (Professional Corporation), (AV) '42 '67 C&L.800 B.A., J.D.
[Rigg&D.]
Rigg and Dean, (AV) ... 333 Bayside Dr.
Riley, Leonard A. '43 '75 C&L.1137 B.S., J.D.
Chf. Exec. Offr., United States Juice Corp.
Roberson, Pamela M. ... '65 '90 C.1109 B.A. L.1068 J.D. 4675 Macarthur Ct., Suite 1000
Roberts, Christine Karol ... '48 '86 C.1271 B.G.S. L.802 J.D. P.O. Box 9827
**Roberts, James A.** ... '50 '76 C.154 B.S. L.1065 J.D. [🄱 R.K.Scott]
**Roberts, Larry K.**, (AV) '49 '76 C.339 B.S.E.E. L.426 J.D.
[Roberts&Q.] (See Pat. Sect.)
*PRACTICE AREAS: Patent; Trademark; Intellectual Property.
Roberts, Terence W. ... '42 '76 C.169 B.A. L.464 J.D. 3901 MacArthur Blvd.

**Roberts and Quiogue, A Law Corporation, (AV)**
**660 Newport Center Drive, Suite 710, P.O. Box 8569, 92658**
**Telephone: 714-640-6200 Facsimile: 714-640-1206**
**Manuel Quiogue; Larry K. Roberts.**
**Intellectual Property Law, Patent, Trademark and Trade Secret and Related Matters.**
***See Professional Biographies, NEWPORT BEACH, CALIFORNIA***

**Robinson, Marla Merhab** ... '60 '87 C.1049 B.B.A. L.1137 J.D. [🄰 Eadington,M.&E.]
*PRACTICE AREAS: Labor and Employment; General Corporate Matters; Business Litigation.

**Robinson, Phillips & Calcagnie**
**(See Laguna Niguel)**

Robison, Craig ... '51 '79 L.1137 J.D. Mun. J.
Rodarti, Josef M., (AV) ... '59 '85 C&L.426 B.A., J.D. [Rodarti,F.&G.]
Rodarti, Feld & Gelfer, (AV) ... 4675 MacArthur Court, Ste., 930
Rodda, George, Jr. ... '30 '73 C.800 A.B.M.S. L.1137 J.D. 359 San Miguel Dr.
Roger Leung, Chun-Pok ... '61 '95 C.45 B.S.M.E. L.1066 J.D. 620 Newport Ctr. Dr.
**Rogoff, Joseph A.** ... '59 '86 C.1077 B.S. L.1068 J.D. [White&R.]
*PRACTICE AREAS: Real Estate.
**Rooklidge, William C.** '57 '85 C.670 B.S.M.E. L.596 J.D.
[Howard,R.N.C.F.&R.] (Pat.)
*PRACTICE AREAS: Intellectual Property Litigation and Counselling.
**Rose, Arthur S.** ... '51 '81 C.112 B.S. L.273 J.D. [Knobbe,M.O.&B.] (See Pat. Sect.)
**Roseman, Leslie R.** ... '49 '90 C.608 B.S. L.1137 J.D. [White&R.]
*PRACTICE AREAS: Sexual Harassment; Discrimination; Wrongful Termination; Personal Injury.
**Rosen, Daniel, (Law Corporation)** ... '47 '73 C.699 B.S. L.472 J.D. [White&R.]
*PRACTICE AREAS: Corporate and Business Law (40%); Health Care (30%); Mergers and Acquisitions (10%); Employment and Labor (10%); Estate Planning (10%).
Rosenthal, Deborah M. ... '52 '81 C.477 B.A. L.976 J.D. 100 Bayview Circ.
**Ross, Lori S.** ... '61 '86 C.112 A.B. L.1068 J.D. [🄰 Buchalter,N.F.&Y.]
*LANGUAGES: French.
*PRACTICE AREAS: Insolvency.
Ross, Roger F., II ... '60 '93 C.174 B.S. L.383 J.D. 4675 MacArthur Ct., Suite 1000
**Roston, Daniel E.** ... '65 '94 C.112 B.S.,B.A. L.464 J.D. [🄰 Brobeck,P.&H.]
Rothman, Larry, Law Offices of, (BV) '50 '76
C.112 A.B. L.29 J.D. 1301 Dove St., Ste 850
**Rovens, Douglas J.** ... '56 '82 C.112 B.A. L.809 J.D. [🄱 Stradling,Y.C.&R.]
**Rovner, Jeffrey S.** ... '57 '82 C.446 B.S. L.273 J.D. [🄱 Brobeck,P.&H.]
*PRACTICE AREAS: Corporate Finance; Municipal Finance; Real Estate.
Rowen, Jane ... '68 '92 C.800 B.A. L.1067 J.D. 4675 Macarthur Ct., Suite 1000
Rubel, James L., Jr., (AV) ... '28 '54 C.112 A.B. L.800 LL.B. 3432 Via Oporto
Rubin, David M. ... '60 '86 C&L.861 B.A., J.D. 620 Newport Ctr. Dr.
**Rubin, Lois E.**, (BV) ... '54 '80 C.112 B.A. L.426 J.D. [🄰 Rynn&J.]
Rubino, Michael J. ... '60 '87 C.112 B.S. L.1065 J.D. 4 Civic Plaza

**Rudolph Law Group, The, A Professional Corporation**
**(See Costa Mesa)**

Rue, Michael M. ... '51 '76 C&L.426 B.B.A., J.D. Marketplace Properties
**Rugani, Frank L.**, (AV) ... '48 '78 C.605 A.B. L.1067 J.D. [O'Melveny&M.]

Russ, James P., (P.C.) ... '42 '76 C.882 B.A. L.1137 J.D. P.O. Box 7668
**Russell, Anthony R.** ... '47 '74 C.645 B.S. L.1049 J.D. [Seely&R.]
*PRACTICE AREAS: Limited Liability Companies; Business Organization; Buying and Selling of Businesses; Corporate Contracts; Partnership and Commercial.
Russell, Christopher E. ... '58 '85 C.1042 B.A. L.61 J.D. 5015 Birch St.
Russey, Edward W., III ... '55 '93 C.69 B.A. L.846 J.D. 4921 Birch St.

**Rutan & Tucker, LLP**
**(See Costa Mesa)**

Rutter, J. Edgar T., II ... '31 '55 C.674 A.B. L.800 LL.B. 941 Via Lido Soud‡
Ruzicka, Gregory V. ... '55 '81 C.112 B.A. L.990 J.D. 130 Newport Ctr. Dr.
**Rynn, Patricia J.**, (AV) ... '55 '80 C.763 B.A. L.1049 J.D. [Rynn&J.]
*PRACTICE AREAS: Agricultural Law; Employment Law.

**Rynn & Janowsky, (AV)**
**4100 Newport Place Drive, Suite 700, 92660**
**Telephone: 714-752-2911 Telecopier: 714-752-0953**
**Members of Firm: Lewis P. Janowsky; Patricia J. Rynn;—Randal Jason Read; Lois E. Rubin (Certified Specialist, Family Law, The State Bar of California Board of Legal Specialization); Bartholomew M. Botta.**
**Employment Law, Agricultural Law and Commercial Law.**
***See Professional Biographies, NEWPORT BEACH, CALIFORNIA***

**Sable, Martin J. '53 '79 C.273 B.A. L.1137 J.D.**
**1300 Dove Street, Suite 200, 92660-2416**
**Telephone: 714-474-2380 Facsimile: 714-474-1516**
**Email: 71271.1656@compuserve.com**
***PRACTICE AREAS: Civil Litigation; Personal Injury; Corporate Law; Business Law; Construction Defects.**
**Civil Litigation, Personal Injury, Corporate Law, Business.**
***See Professional Biographies, NEWPORT BEACH, CALIFORNIA***

Sainick, Frederick B. ... '52 '77 C.112 B.A. L.1068 J.D. [Sainick&C.]
Sainick & Coté ... 190 Newport Center Dr., 2nd Fl.
**St. John, Wendy**, (AV) ... '58 '83 C.477 B.A. L.1049 J.D. [Kimball,T.&S.] (⊙San Diego)
*PRACTICE AREAS: Landlord/Tenant Law.
**Salamon, Noah B.** ... '71 '96 C.821 B.A. L.145 J.D. [🄰 Irell&M.]
Salinas, Sandra I. ... '65 '92 C.139 B.A. L.1137 J.D. 1201 Dove St.
Sallee, S. Hilary ... '65 '93 C.112 B.A. L.93 J.D. 1600 Dove St. Ste. 450
**Saltarelli, Thomas R.**, (BV) ... '47 '81 C.645 B.S. L.1137 J.D. [Saltarelli]
*PRACTICE AREAS: Real Estate Litigation; Business Litigation; Business Transactions; Real Estate Transactions; Civil Litigation.

**Saltarelli Law Corporation, (BV)**
**4400 McArthur Boulevard, Suite 900, P.O. Box 10367, 92658-0367**
**Telephone: 714-833-9200 Fax: 714-833-9486**
**Thomas R. Saltarelli.**
**Real Estate Transactions and Litigation, Business and Civil Litigation, Corporate and Transactional.**
**Representative Clients: Pan West Financial, Inc.; Pacific Gas Specialties Corporation; Bixby Plaza Carpets, Inc.; Orange Tree Realty, Inc.; Rancon Financial Corporation; California Oaks Development Company; Kulberg Ltd.; EBR Escrow Corp.; U.S. Carpentry, Inc.; Merit Property Management, Inc.**

**Saltzburg, Ray & Bergman, LLP**
**(See Los Angeles)**

**Salzman, Ira M.**
**(See Pasadena)**

**Samini, Babak** ... '70 '95 C.800 B.A. L.608 J.D. [Voss,C.&T.]
*PRACTICE AREAS: Corporate; Federal Taxation; Real Estate.
**Sanchez, Maurice** ... '56 '81 C.112 B.A. L.1066 J.D. [Alvarado,S.V.&S.]
*LANGUAGES: Spanish.
*PRACTICE AREAS: Automotive Franchise; Labor and Employment; General Business Litigation.
**Sanford, David T.** ... '57 '90 C.112 B.A. L.1137 J.D. [🄱 Walker]
*LANGUAGES: Spanish and French.
*PRACTICE AREAS: Business and Real Property Litigation; Corporations; Real Estate; Business and Transactional Law; Civil Litigation.
Sanner, David L., (BV) ... '49 '74 C&L.800 B.A., J.D. [Howser&B.]
Satin, Kenneth A. ... '46 '73 C.1097 B.A. L.426 J.D. 5015 Birch St.
Sauer-Swensson, Barbara, (BV) ... '41 '66 C.768 B.A. L.1065 J.D. Dept.-Head, F.D.I.C.‡
Savage, Christopher R. ... '46 '73 C.178 B.A. L.1049 J.D. 4041 MacArthur Blvd.
Saxon, Barry, Gardner & Kincannon, A Prof. Corp., (AV)
4400 MacArthur Blvd. (⊙San Diego, Riverside & San Dimas)
**Schaaf, K. C.**, (AV) ... '48 '73 C.174 B.S.E.E. L.813 J.D. [Stradling,Y.C.&R.]
**Schaeffer, Sandra** ... '66 '91 C.36 B.S. L.1049 J.D. [🄰 Newmeyer&D.]
*PRACTICE AREAS: Business Litigation.
Schechter, Lisa Anne ... '64 '91 C&L.112 B.S., J.D. 4675 Macarthur Ct., Suite 1000
Scherzer, Stephen G. ... '48 '73 C.629 B.S. L.770 J.D. [Tharpe&H.] (⊙Los Angeles)
**Schilling, John R.**, (AV) ... '42 '68 C.112 B.A. L.1068 J.D. [J.R.Schilling]

**Schilling, John R., A Professional Corporation, (AV)** 🄱🄱
**4675 MacArthur Court Suite 590, Tower One, 92660-1839**
**Telephone: 714-833-8833 Fax: 714-833-3883**
**John R. Schilling (Certified Specialist, Family Law, The State Bar of California Board of Legal Specialization).**
**Practice Limited to Family Law.**
**References: Union Bank (Airport Branch); City National Bank (Newport Beach); Bank of America (Newport Beach).**
***See Professional Biographies, NEWPORT BEACH, CALIFORNIA***

**Schlatter, Edward A.** '59 '85 C.277 B.I.E. L.477 J.D.
[Knobbe,M.O.&B.] (See Pat. Sect.)
Schmidt, William V., (AV) ... '34 '59 C.668 B.A. L.813 LL.B. [W.V.Schmidt]
Schmidt, William V., A Professional Corporation, (AV) ... 5030 Campus Dr.
Schmiesing, James A., (AV) ... '38 '63 C&L.426 LL.B. [Schmiesing&B.]
Schmiesing & Blied, (AV) ... 4100 Newport Place
**Schnapp, Roger H.**, (AV) ... '46 '70 C.188 B.S. L.309 J.D. [R.H.Schnapp]

**Schnapp, Roger H., A Professional Corporation, (AV)**
**4041 MacArthur Boulevard, Suite 160, 92660-2513**
**Telephone: 714-752-0491 Fax: 714-752-1102**
**Email: RHS@SCHNAPP.COM URL: HTTP://WWW.SCHNAPP.COM**
**Roger H. Schnapp.**
**Employment Law. Government Relations.**
***See Professional Biographies, NEWPORT BEACH, CALIFORNIA***

**Schneider, Bernard E.**, (AV) ... '46 '73 C.940 B.A. L.800 J.D. [McDermott,W.&E.]
*PRACTICE AREAS: Corporate Law; Banks and Banking; Real Property.
**Schnitz, Robert V.** ... '62 '88 C.597 B.A. L.424 J.D. [Fisher&P.]
**Schoenbaum, Ronald J.** '65 '93
C.861 B.S. L.260 J.D. [Knobbe,M.O.&B.] (See Pat. Sect.)
Schrank, Stephen C. ... '47 '78 C.112 B.S.C.E. L.809 J.D. 1945 Port Chelsea Pl.
Schroeder, Reinhold ... '56 '94 C&L.879 B.S., J.D. 20311 Birch
**Schulman, Michael** ... '51 '78 C.112 B.A. L.770 J.D. [McDermott,W.&E.]
*PRACTICE AREAS: Trusts and Estates; Taxation; Charitable Organizations.
Schwartz, Ronald B., (AV) ... '45 '72 C.112 B.A. L.61 J.D. [R.B.Schwartz]
Schwartz, Ronald B., A Professional Corporation, (AV) ... 202 Newport Center Dr. 2nd Fl.

CAA415P

CALIFORNIA—NEWPORT BEACH                                                    MARTINDALE-HUBBELL LAW DIRECTORY 1997

Schwarzstein, Richard J., (AV) '34 '60 C.178 A.B. L.309 J.D.
 Second Floor, Redstone Plaza, 1300 Dove Street, 92660
 Telephone: 714-752-9152 Fax: 714-752-0651
 Corporation, Securities, Real Property, International Business and Computer Law.
   See Professional Biographies, NEWPORT BEACH, CALIFORNIA
Scott, Mark M. . . . . . . . . . . . . . . . . . . . . . '63 '88 C.36 B.S. L.800 J.D. [A Buchalter,N.F.&Y.]
 *PRACTICE AREAS: Financial Institutions Litigation.
Scott, R. Craig . . . . . . . . . . . . . . . . . . . . . . . . . . . . '53 '78 C.&L.878 B.S., J.D. [Scott,R.&W]
Scott, Robert K., (AV) . . . . . . . . . . . . . . . . . . . . '49 '75 C.1188 B.A. L.61 J.D. [R.K.Scott]⊙
Scott, Reilly & Whitehead
 1301 Dove Street, Suite 1000, 92660
 Telephone: 714-222-0166 Facsimile: 714-222-0113
 URL: http://www.employerlaw.com
 R. Craig Scott; Thomas H. Reilly; Nancy Rader Whitehead;—Diane Desfor Stalder; Pamela L. Whitesides.
   See Professional Biographies, NEWPORT BEACH, CALIFORNIA
Scott, Robert K., A Prof. Corp., The Law Offices of, (AV)
 660 Newport Center Drive, Suite 950, 92660⊙
 Telephone: 714-644-1301 Fax: 714-644-0840
 URL: http://www.robertkscott.com
 Robert K. Scott;—David I. Lipsky; D. Scott Mohney; John C. McCarty; Rhonda R. Harris; Mary T. Rahmes; Christian J. Garris. Of Counsel: William M. Shernoff (P.C.); James A. Roberts.
 Practice limited to Plaintiffs Insurance Bad Faith, Automobile Insurance, Fire Insurance, Commercial Liability Insurance, Homeowners Insurance, Accident and Health Insurance. Catastrophic Personal Injury, Wrongful Death, Wrongful Termination, Lender's Liability and Consumer Law, Litigation.
 San Francisco, California Office: 100 Van Ness Avenue, 19th Floor, 94102. Telephone: 415-437-0673.
 Associate Office: Mart & DeVries, Sacramento, California
   See Professional Biographies, NEWPORT BEACH, CALIFORNIA
Seely, Hall, (AV) . . . . . . . . . . . . . . . . . . . . . . . . . . '36 '63 C.813 B.A. L.309 LL.B. [Seely&R.]
 *PRACTICE AREAS: Business Litigation; Closely Held Businesses; Family Law; Estate Planning; Estate Litigation.
Seely & Russell, (AV)
 Suite 140, 4631 Teller Avenue, 92660
 Telephone: 714-955-3575; 955-3570 FAX: 714-851-2722
 Members of Firm: Hall Seely (Certified Specialist, Family Law, The State Bar of California Board of Legal Specialization); Anthony R. Russell.
 General Civil and Administrative Agency Practice. Business, Real Estate, Family Law, Business Litigation, Arbitration and Estate Planning.
   See Professional Biographies, NEWPORT BEACH, CALIFORNIA
Seide, Richard L. . . . . . . . . . . . . . . . . . . . . . . '54 '80 C&L.800 B.S., J.D. [Good,W.H.&W.]
 *PRACTICE AREAS: Commercial Landlord/Tenant Law; Leases and Leasing; Receivership Law; Civil Litigation.
Seidenberg, Peter A., (BV) . . . . . . . . . . . . . . . . . . '55 '80 C.1044 B.A. L.990 J.D. 5000 Birch St.
Self, Michael C., (AV) . . . . . . . . . . . . . . . . . . . . . . . . . '58 '87 C.112 B.S. L.464 J.D. [Self&B.]
 *PRACTICE AREAS: Corporate Law; Contract; Commercial Law; Securities; Transactional.
Self & Bhamre, (AV)
 4400 MacArthur Boulevard, Suite 320, 92660
 Telephone: 714-955-0230 Fax: 714-955-0240
 Michael C. Self; Hema Christine Bhamre;—George D. Straggas. Of Counsel: Craig C. Alexander.
 General Business Transactional and Litigation including Civil and Trial Practice, State and Federal Courts, Corporations, Contract, Transactional, Securities, Employment, Commercial, Professional Negligence, Taxation, Estate Planning, Probate and Trust Administration and Wills.
   See Professional Biographies, NEWPORT BEACH, CALIFORNIA
Selna, James V., (AV) . . . . . . . . . . . . . . . . . . . . . '45 '71 C&L.813 A.B., J.D. [O'Melveny&M.]
 *PRACTICE AREAS: Antitrust; Complex Commercial Litigation.
Semeta, Richard K. . . . . . . . . . . . . . . . . . . . . . . . . . '58 '84 C.516 B.S. L.744 J.D. [A White&R.]
 *PRACTICE AREAS: Securities; Taxation; Business Law.
Serota, Lori D. . . . . . . . . . . . . . . . . . . . . . . . . . . . . . '58 '84 C.800 B.A. L.809 J.D. [Bragg,S.S.&K.]
Sessa, Anthony . . . . . . . . . . . . . . . . . . . . . . . . . . '35 '86 C.415 B.S. L.1225 J.D. 4650 Von Karman
Severson & Werson, A Professional Corporation, (AV)
 4675 MacArthur Court, Suite 370, 92660⊙
 Telephone: 714-442-7110 Facsimile: 714-442-7118
 Loraine P. Eber;—Carolyn Powell; Kimberly D. Taylor.
 General Civil Practice in State and Federal Courts and Administrative Agencies, Appeals, Commercial and Consumer Lending Transactions, Work-outs and Bankruptcy, Construction, Professional Liability, Environmental, Insurance, Publishing, Employment Relations, Real Estate, Securities, Franchising, Corporate, Tax, Estate Planning and Probate.
 San Francisco, California Office: Twenty-Fifth Floor, 1 Embarcadero Center. Telephone: 415-398-3344. Telecopier: 415-956-0439.
   See Professional Biographies, NEWPORT BEACH, CALIFORNIA
Sevier, R. Brad . . . . . . . . . . . . . . . . . . . . . . '63 '89 C.112 B.A. L.426 J.D. [A Newmeyer&D.]
 *PRACTICE AREAS: Real Estate Law; Finance; General Business Law.
Sewell, Jerry T. . . . . . . . '49 '80 C.502 B.S. L.494 J.D. [Knobbe,M.O.&B.] (See Pat. Sect.)
Sganga, John B., Jr. . . . . . . . . . '60 '84 C.390 B.S. L.569 J.D. [Knobbe,M.O.&B.] (See Pat. Sect.)
Shafizadeh, Sherri S. . . . . . . . . . . . . . . . . . . . . . '59 '96 C.112 B.A. L.1137 J.D. [Kimball,T.&S.]
 *PRACTICE AREAS: Landlord and Tenant Law.
Shaw, Susanne S. . . . . . . . . . . . . . . . . . . . . . . . . . . '46 '72 C.112 B.A. L.61 J.D. Mun. Ct. J.
Shea, Patrick C. . . . . . . . . . '50 '77 C.112 B.A. L.1049 J.D. V.P., Beacon Bay Enterprises, Inc.
Shechter, Morris . . . . . . . . . . . . . . . . . . . . . . . . . . . '27 '55 C.112 B.A. L.809 J.D. 5000 Birch St.
Shepard, Rudolph C. . . . . . . . . . . . . . . . . . . . . '41 '70 C.800 B.S. L.1068 J.D. [Stradling,Y.C.&R.]
Sherman, Randall J. . . . . . . . . . . . . . . . . . . . . . . . '54 '79 C.112 B.A. L.800 J.D. [Stradling,Y.C.&R.]
Sherman, Richard M., Jr.,(P.C.), (AV) . . . . . . . '47 '75 C.154 B.A. L.1066 J.D. [Irell&M.]
Shernoff, William M., (P.C.) '37 '62
 C.472 B.B.A. L.966 J.D. [R.K.Scott] (⊙Palm Desert)
Shoffner, Gary E., (AV) . . . . . . . . . '50 '77 C.112 B.A. L.477 J.D. 4041 Macarthur Blvd.
Shokrai, Maryam . . . . . . . . . . . . . . . . . . . . . . . '63 '90 C.112 B.A. L.1068 J.D. [A Call,C.&J.]
 *LANGUAGES: Farsi, French.
 *PRACTICE AREAS: Litigation.
Short, Patricia D. . . . . . . . . . . . . . . . . . . . . . . . . . '52 '79 C.800 B.S. L.990 J.D. [Bragg,S.S.&K.]
Shreiar, Barry R. . . . . . . . . . . . . . . . . . . . . . . . . . . . . . '62 '94 C.112 B.A. L.809 J.D. [A Lazof&C.]
Shreve, William H. . . . . '63 '90 C.112 B.S. L.1273 J.D. [Knobbe,M.O.&B.] (See Pat. Sect.)
Siddiqi, Numan J. . . . . . . . . . . . . . . . . '72 '95 C.112 B.A. L.1066 J.D. [A Stradling,Y.C.&R.]
 *LANGUAGES: Hindi/Urdu.
Silldorf, Burdman, Duignan & Eisenberg, (AV)
 4000 Mac Arthur Blvd., Ste. 6800 (⊙San Diego, Ontario)
Simmons, Anderson M. . . . . . . . . . . . . . . . . . . . '63 '95 C.846 B.A. L.930 J.D. [A Sims,M.&M.]
Simmons, Kathleen D. '55 '82 C.1042 B.A. L.1049 J.D.
                                  Asst. V.P. & Invest. Coun., Pacific Mut. Life Ins. Co.
Simmons, Raymond H. . . . . . . '58 '82 C.112 B.A. L.1065 J.D. 366 San Miguel Dr.
Simpson, Andrew H. . . . . '48 '91 C.61 B.S. L.426 J.D. [Knobbe,M.O.&B.] (See Pat. Sect.)
Simpson, C. Robert . . . . . . . . . . . . . . . . . . . . . '57 '84 C.112 B.A. L.228 J.D. [Wolf&P.]
 *PRACTICE AREAS: Mortgage Fraud.
Simpson, Kendall C. . . . . . . . . . '36 '61 C&L.900 B.B.A., LL.B. 4 Upper Newport Plaza
Sims, Wayne R., (A Professional Corporation, (AV) '41 '66
                                  C.605 B.A. L.1066 J.D. [Sims,M.&M.]
 *PRACTICE AREAS: Insurance Defense Law; Railroad Law; Legal Malpractice Law.

Sims, Morrow & Manning, (AV)
 A Partnership including a Professional Corporation
 450 Newport Center Drive, Suite 250, 92660-7612
 Telephone: 714-721-8101 Fax: 714-721-8661
 Members of Firm: Wayne R. Sims (A Professional Corporation); Patrick John Manning; William D. Morrow;—David A. Sprowl; Ralph F. Popelar, Jr.; Selim Mounedji; Leonard T. Fink; Michael E. Murphy; Christopher A. White (Resident); Anderson M. Simmons; Thomas W. Overton.
 Insurance, Personal Injury, Railroad, Legal Malpractice, Products and Premises Liability, Construction, Business, Insurance Agent Broker Law, General Civil Litigation.
   See Professional Biographies, NEWPORT BEACH, CALIFORNIA
Singer, Gary J., (AV) . . . . . . . . . . . . . . . . '52 '77 C.112 B.A. L.426 J.D. [O'Melveny&M.]
 *PRACTICE AREAS: Corporate; Securities; Mergers and Acquisitions.
Skaist, Mark L. . . . . . . . . . . . . . . . . . . '65 '91 C.112 B.A. L.426 J.D. [A Stradling,Y.C.&R.]
Slaughter, Donald E., (AV) . . . . . . . . . . . . . '50 '75 C.770 B.S.C. L.426 J.D. [Slaughter&S.]
Slaughter, W. James, (AV) . . . . . . . . . . . . . '56 '82 C.770 B.S.C. L.94 J.D. [Slaughter&S.]
Slaughter & Slaughter, (AV) . . . . . . . . . . . . . . . . . . . . . . . . . . 1470 Jamboree Road, Suite 200
Slocumb, Laura A. . . . . . . . . . . . . . . . . . . . . . . . . . . '50 '82 C.1044 B.A. L.990 J.D. [Slocumb&H.]
Slocumb & Hicks . . . . . . . . . . . . . . . . . . . . . . . . . . . . . . . . . . . . . . . 4 Corporate Plaza, Ste. 215
Smith, Alton J., (AV) . . . . . . . . . . . . . . . . . . . . '48 '78 C.169 B.A. L.1137 J.D. [A.J.Smith]
Smith, Glenn R. '51 '92 C.172 B.S.E.E. L.1068 J.D.
                                  [Knobbe,M.O.&B.] (See Pat. Sect.)
Smith, Kevin L. . . . . . . . . . . . . . . . . . . . '56 '81 C.473 B.A. L.477 J.D. 4700 Teller Ave., 2nd Fl.
Smith, Leonard, (AV) . . . . . . . . . . . . . . . . . . . . . . '18 '47 C.113 B.A. L.1001 LL.B. 2512 Crestview Dr.
Smith, Robert W. '51 '80 C.645 B.S. L.128 J.D.
                                  (adm. in PA; not adm. in CA) V.P., Pulte Home Corp.
Smith, Ruben A., (AV) . . . . . . . . . . . . . . . . '57 '85 C.800 B.S. L.976 J.D. [Alvarado,S.V.&S.]
 *LANGUAGES: Spanish.
 *PRACTICE AREAS: Real Estate; Commercial and Financial Transactions; U.S./Mexico Transactions.
Smith, W. Bailey, (BV) . . . . . . . . . . . . . . . . . '44 '70 C.813 B.A. L.1065 J.D. 4041 MacArthur Blvd.
Smith, Alton J., A Professional Corporation, (AV)
 610 Newport Center Drive, Suite 700, 92660
 Telephone: 714-760-8800 Fax: 714-760-9204
 Alton J. Smith.
 General Civil and Trial Practice. Medical Malpractice, Insurance, Bad Faith Litigation, Personal Injury, and Products Liability.
   See Professional Biographies, NEWPORT BEACH, CALIFORNIA
Snyder, Paul E. . . . . . . . . . . . . . . . . . . . . '49 '80 C.116 B.A. L.1049 J.D. 130 Newport Center Dr.
Sontag, Richard . . . . . . . . . . . . . . . . . . . . . '56 '83 C.112 B.A. L.629 J.D. 130 Newport Center Dr.
Sorich, John M. . . . . . . . . . . . . . . . . . . . . . . . . '60 '86 C.309 B.A. L.818 J.D. [Alvarado,S.V.&S.]
 *PRACTICE AREAS: Secured Transaction Litigation; Business Litigation; Environmental Litigation; Construction Defect Litigation.
Soroy, H. Michael . . . . . . . . . . . . . . . . . . . . '50 '91 C.061 B.A. L.1179 J.D. 537 Newport Ctr. Dr.
Space, Richard T. '47 '75 C.935 B.A. L.229 J.D.
                                  (adm. in CT; not adm. in CA) Capitol Financial
Spach, Madison S., Jr., (AV) . . . . . . . . . . . . '51 '80 C&L.228 B.A., J.D. [Newmeyer&D.]
 *PRACTICE AREAS: Bankruptcy; Litigation involving Real Estate Development and Construction.
Spencer, Patricia V. . . . . . . . . . . . . . . . . . . . . . . '59 '90 C.112 A.B. L.1137 J.D. [A.W.Courtney]
Spertus, James W. . . . . . . . . . . . . . . . . . . '65 '91 C.112 B.A. L.800 J.D. 840 Newport Center Dr.
Spielman, M. Roy, (AV) . . . . . . . . . '24 '55 C.124 B.S. L.564 LL.B. 220 Via Eboli (Pat.)‡
Spiezia, John J. . . . . . . . . . . . . . . . . . . . . . . . . . . . '48 '78 C.870 B.A. L.990 J.D. Coldwell Banker
Splane, Stephanie I. '56 '86
                                  C.684 B.A. L.976 J.D. [O'Melveny&M.] (⊙New York, N.Y.)
 *PRACTICE AREAS: Banking; Securities; General Corporate Law; Mergers and Acquisitions.
Sprowl, David A., (BV) . . . . . . . . . . . . . . . . . '54 '79 C&L.990 B.A., J.D. [A Sims,M.&M.]
Stalder, Diane Desfor . . . . . . . . . . . . . . . . . . '55 '91 C&L.800 B.A., J.D. [A Scott,R.&W.]
Starrett, William C., II, (AV) . . . . . . . . . . . . '41 '67 C&L.800 A.B., J.D. [Neben&S.]
Stauffer, Gerald M. . . . . . . . . . . . . . . . . . . . . . . . . . . . . . . . . . . . . . . . . '37 '69 [Adler&S.]
St.Clair, David A. . . . . . . . . . . . . . . . . . . . . . . '68 '93 C.112 B.S. L.1137 J.D. [A Millar,H.&B.]
Stedman, Robert W., (P.C.), (AV) . . . . . . '38 '67 C.966 B.B.A. L.1066 LL.B. [A Irell&M.]
Steinberg, Gary R. . . . . . . . . . . . . . . . . . . . . . . '49 '74 C.112 B.A. L.7 J.D. 4675 MacArthur Ct.
Steinberg, Leigh W., (AV) . . . . . . . . . . . . '49 '74 C.112 A.B. L.1066 J.D. [Steinberg&M.]
Steinberg, Stanley R., (BV) . . . . . . . . . . . . '49 '74 C.1097 B.A. L.36 J.D. 4041 Mac Arthur Blvd.
Steinberg & Moorad, (AV) . . . . . . . . . . . . . . . . . . . . . . . . . . . . . . . . 500 Newport Center Dr.
Stellhorn, Cisca . . . . . . . . . . . . . . . . . . . . . '51 '76 C.112 B.S. L.1137 J.D. 1500 Quail St.
Stephens, Lon T., (BV) . . . . . . . . . . . . . . . . . '55 '80 C.1109 B.A. L.990 J.D. [Stephens&K.]
Stephens & Kray, A Prtnrshp. of Prof. Corp., (BV) . . . . . . . . . . . . . . . . . . . . . 5000 Birch St.
Sterling, Ann M. . . . . . . . '63 '89 C.1075 B.A. L.1065 J.D. 4675 Macarthur Ct., Suite 1000
Sterling, Lisa D. . . . . . . . . . . . . . . . . . . . . . . . . '65 '89 C.267 B.S. L.770 J.D. 1001 Dove St.
Stern, Steven L., (BV) '43 '69 C.813 B.A. L.309 J.D.
 610 Newport Center Drive, Suite 1000, 92660
 Telephone: 714-640-9193 Fax: 714-640-0714
 *LANGUAGES: German.
 *PRACTICE AREAS: Business; Real Estate Litigation; Construction Law.
 General Business, Corporate and Partnership, Finance, Real Estate and Commercial Employment, Business and Commercial Litigation in all State and Federal Courts, Probate and Trust Litigation, Employment Law and Creditor's Rights.
   See Professional Biographies, NEWPORT BEACH, CALIFORNIA
Stern, Wolf H. . . . . . . . . . . . . . . . . . '23 '51 C&L.800 B.A., J.D. 170 Newport Center Dr.
Stevens, Christine E. . . . . . . . . . . . . . . . . . . . '47 '85 C.1077 B.A. L.1137 J.D. 5120 Campus Dr.
Stewart, Michael J. . . . . . . . . . . . . . . . . . . . . . . . '47 '77 C.1109 B.A. L.1137 J.D. NPA Systems
Stewart, Paul A. . . . . . . . . . . . . . . . . . . . . . . . '65 '91 C.668 B.A. L.893 J.D. [Knobbe,M.O.&B.]
Stiepan, James L., (AV) '51 '76 C.228 A.B. L.309 J.D.
                                  V.P. & Gen. Coun., Irvine Off. Co. & Irvine Bus. Props. Co.
Stillman, John A. . . . . . . . . . . . . . . . . . . . . '40 '69 C.766 B.A. L.800 J.D. [Good,W.H.&W.]
 *PRACTICE AREAS: Business; Real Estate; Litigation; White Collar Criminal.
Stocker, Jay F. . . . . . . . . . . . . . . . . . . . . . . . . . . '60 '87 C.911 B.A. L.990 J.D. [C Cummins&W.]
 *PRACTICE AREAS: Business Law; Real Estate Law.
Stocker, John M., Jr. '47 '74 C.813 B.A. L.1068 J.D.
                                  Asst. V.P. & Invests. Coun., Pacific Mut. Life Ins. Co.
Stone, Edward H., (AV) . . . . . . . . . . . . . . . . . . . '39 '67 C.339 B.S. L.365 J.D. [E.H.Stone]
 *REPORTED CASES: Estate of Pittman, 104 CAL. APP. 3d 288.
Stone, James D. . . . . . . . . . . . . . . . . . . . . . '42 '82 C&L.1137 B.S., J.D. 4490 Von Karman Ave.
Stone, Rena C., (AV) . . . . . . . . . . . . . . . . . . . . . '53 '78 C.112 B.A. L.426 J.D. [C Stradling,Y.C.&R.]
Stone, Edward H., P.C., (AV)
 270 Newport Center Drive, 92660-7535
 Telephone: 714-640-2812 Fax: 714-640-9951
 Edward H. Stone (Certified Specialist, Probate, Estate Planning and Trust Law, The State Bar of California Board of Legal Specialization).
 Estate Planning, Probate and Business Planning.
   See Professional Biographies, NEWPORT BEACH, CALIFORNIA
Stradling, Fritz R., (AV) . . . . . . . . . . . . . . . . . '26 '50 C&L.966 B.B.A., LL.B. [Stradling,Y.C.&R.]
Stradling, Yocca, Carlson & Rauth, A Professional Corporation, (AV)
 660 Newport Center Drive, Suite 1600, 92660-6441⊙
 Mailing Address: P.O. Box 7680, 92658-7680
 Telephone: 714-725-4000 Facsimile: 714-725-4100
 Fritz R. Stradling; Nick E. Yocca; C. Craig Carlson; William R. Rauth III; K. C. Schaaf; Richard C. Goodman; John J. Murphy; Thomas P. Clark, Jr.; Ben A. Frydman; David R. McEwen; Paul L. Gale;

(This Listing Continued)

**Stradling, Yocca, Carlson & Rauth, A Professional Corporation (Continued)**

**Rudolph C. Shepard; Robert J. Kane; Bruce C. Stuart; E. Kurt Yeager; Robert J. Whalen; Robert E. Rich; Randall J. Sherman; Bruce Feuchter; Mark J. Huebsch; David G. Casnocha (Resident, San Francisco Office); Karen A. Ellis; Bruce D. May; Andrew F. Puzder; Donald J. Hamman; John J. Swigart, Jr. (Certified Specialist, Probate, Estate Planning and Trust Law, The State Bar of California Board of Legal Specialization); Celeste Stahl Brady; Christopher J. Kilpatrick; Douglas S. Brown; Julie McCoy Akins; Lawrence B. Cohn; Stephen T. Freeman; Carol L. Lew; Michael E. Flynn; Julie M. Porter; Gary A. Pemberton; Denise Harbaugh Hering; Jon E. Goetz; Russell A. Miller (Resident, San Francisco Office);—Michael A. Zablocki; Neila R. Bernstein; Nicholas J. Yocca; J. Michael Vaughn; John D. Ireland; David H. Mann; Douglas J. Evertz; Sean Tierney (Resident, San Francisco Office); Darryl S. Gibson; Jee Hi Park; Richard T. Needham; Robert Craig Wallace; John F. Cannon; David A. Hoffer; Douglas P. Feick; Mark L. Skaist; Jeffrey B. Coyne; John E. Woodhead, IV; Matthew P. Thullen; Andrea Levitan Reeves; John David Vaughan; Steven M. Hanle; Michael Hennessey Mulroy; Mary Anne Wagner; Matthew McQueen; Holly A. Ellis; William E. Garrett; Christopher D. Ivey; H. Lee Kolodny; Gerald J. Ramiza; Daniel Glassman; David E. Outwater; Joy Heuser Otsuki; Numan J. Siddiqi; David E. Lafitte; Teri N. Hollander; Marc G. Alcser; Ryan E. Davis; Brent N. Triff; Michele McCormick Troyan; Gary J. Vyneman; Thomas M. Williams. Of Counsel: John E. Breckenridge; Rena C. Stone; Douglas J. Rovens; Robert J. Matthews.**
**General Business, Corporate and Partnership, Corporate Securities, Finance, Taxation, Real Estate and Real Estate Finance, Banking, Commercial, Labor, Administrative, Estate Planning, Trusts, Probate, ERISA, Municipal, Municipal Finance, Water Law and Redevelopment Law. General Civil Practice and Litigation in all State and Federal Courts.**
**San Francisco, California Office: 44 Montgomery Street, Suite 2950, 94104-4803. Telephone: 415-765-9180. Facsimile: 415-765-9187.**

***See Professional Biographies, NEWPORT BEACH, CALIFORNIA***

**Straggas, George D.** ... '60 '87 C.112 B.A. L.464 J.D. [Ⓐ Self&B.]
*PRACTICE AREAS: Civil Litigation; Financial Services; Commercial Litigation.
**Strecker, Marc S.** ... '63 '89 C.145 A.B. L.477 J.D. [Ⓐ Voss,C.&T.]
*PRACTICE AREAS: General and Complex Business Litigation; Estate Litigation; Real Property Law; Foreclosures; Partition of Real Property.
Strople, Christopher W. ... '43 '69 C.426 A.B. L.1068 J.D. Mun. Ct. J.
Stroud, David ... '46 '73 C.1042 B.A. L.1225 J.D. 4695 Macarthur Ct.
**Stuart, Bruce C.**, (AV) ... '52 '76 C.197 A.B. L.1068 J.D. [Stradling,Y.C.&R.]
Stuhley, Jon R., (AV) ... '40 '68 C.112 B.S. L.800 J.D. [J.R.Stuhley]
Stuhley, Jon R., A Prof. Corp., (AV) ... Ste. 100, 270 Newport Ctr. Dr.
Sullivan, Gregory ... '47 '89 C.1042 B.A. L.1137 J.D. 1301 Dove St.
**Summers, Craig S.**, (AV) '56 '83
C.800 B.S. L.426 J.D. [Knobbe,M.O.&B.] (See Pat. Sect.)
Sundstedt, Michael J. ... '54 '81 C.1042 B.A. L.1137 J.D. 1107 Quail St.
**Sungaila, Mary-Christine (M.C.)** ... '67 '91 C.813 B.A. L.1068 J.D. [Ⓐ Irell&M.]
Sussman, Andrew M. ... '49 '83 C.893 B.A. L.208 J.D. 5000 Birch St.
**Swigart, John J., Jr.**, (AV) ... '47 '80 C.674 B.A. L.1065 J.D. [Stradling,Y.C.&R.]
Sylvester, April Louise ... '67 '94 C.112 B.A. L.800 J.D. 1600 Dove St. Ste. 450
**Tabback, Jeri E.** ... '54 '92 C&L.1137 B.S.L., J.D. [Kelegian&T.]
*PRACTICE AREAS: General Liability Defense; Insurance Bad Faith; Civil Rights Defense.
Tachner, Leonard, (AV) '44 '73
C.563 B.S.E.E. L.1137 J.D. 3990 Westerly Pl., Ste 295 (Pat.)
**Taillon, Karen L.**, (AV) ... '47 '83 C&L.1137 B.S.L., J.D. [Cummins&W.]
*PRACTICE AREAS: Real Estate Law; Hospital and Health Care Law; Commercial Law; Contracts Law; Employment Law.
Takamine, Gene ... '46 '80 C.208 B.A. L.1137 J.D. 3901 MacArthur Blvd.
Talbert, Tamra ... '52 '83 C.1042 B.A. L.931 J.D. 5000 Birch St.
Talbot, J. Thomas ... '35 '64 C.813 A.B. L.1065 J.D. P.O. Box 7322‡
**Tang, Barbara L.** ... '58 '88 C.112 B.A. L.426 J.D. [Alvarado,S.V.&S.]
*PRACTICE AREAS: Public Utilities; Corporate.
**Tate, Troy L.**, (AV) ... '56 '82 C.878 B.A. L.1068 J.D. [Call,C.&J.]
*PRACTICE AREAS: Litigation.
Taub Corrigan, Katherine T. ... '62 '87 C.112 B.A. L.990 J.D. Dep. Dist. Atty.
Taylor, Alicia D. ... '60 '90 C&L.800 B.A., J.D. 4100 Newport Pl. Ste 800
**Taylor, Kimberly D.** ... '67 '92 C&L.184 B.S., J.D. [Ⓐ Severson&W.]
*PRACTICE AREAS: Business Litigation; Automobile Finance Law; Creditor's Rights.

**Taylor, Lawrence**
**(See Long Beach)**

Teachey, Suzanne M. ... '61 '89 C.608 B.A. L.426 J.D. 840 Newport Center Dr., Suite 500
Teal, John C., Jr., (AV) ... '47 '73 C.112 A.B. L.426 J.D. 20311 Birch St., Ste., 150
Tedder, David H. ... '46 '74 C.1075 B.S. L.426 J.D. 1100 Quail St.
Tennant, Milton ... '41 '79 C.112 B.S. L.1137 J.D. 4000 MacArthur Blvd.
**Terra, Anne M.** ... '66 '94 C.112 B.A. L.1049 J.D. [Ⓐ Fisher&P.]
Terreri, Frank J., (BV) ... '22 '72 C.980 B.S. L.1137 J.D. 3857 Birch St.
Terrill, G. Sherman ... '43 '80 C.1208 B.S. L.1240 J.D. 314 62nd St.
TeWinkle, Garrett J. ... '39 '73 C.475 B.A. L.426 J.D. 4650 Von Karman
**Thagard, Kristine A.** ... '57 '80 C.1254 B.S. L.800 J.D. [Good,W.H.&W.]
*PRACTICE AREAS: Civil Litigation; Construction Defect Litigation; Wrongful Termination; Real Estate.
Tharpe & Howell, (AV)
4400 MacArthur Blvd., Suite 500 (⊙Los Angeles, Santa Barbara, Santa Maria & Oxnard)
**Thel, Albert J., Jr.**, (AV) ... '49 '78 C&L.893 B.A., J.D. [Voss,C.&T.]
*PRACTICE AREAS: Real Estate (Property) Law; Corporate Law; Corporate (Corporation) Financing Law; Secured Transactions; Business Acquisitions.
Thomas, Janet M. C. ... '56 '93 C.732 B.S. L.276 J.D. 110 Newport Ctr. Dr.
Thomas, Joseph A. ... '29 '58 C&L.800 B.S., J.D. 19800 MacArthur Blvd.
**Thomas, Joseph E.** ... '55 '81 C.401 B.A. L.990 J.D. [McDermott,W.&E.]
*PRACTICE AREAS: Securities; Real Estate; General Business Litigation.
Thomas, Keith ... '55 '83 C.1109 B.A. L.426 J.D. 4685 MacArthur Ct.
**Thomas, Michael Paul**, (AV) ... '56 '86 C.1109 B.A. L.1066 J.D. [Kelegian&T.]
*REPORTED CASES: Radcliff v. Landau (1991) 883 F.2d 1481; Elder v. Rice (1994) 21 Cal.App. 4th 1604.
*PRACTICE AREAS: Civil Litigation; Premises Liability Law; Insurance Law; Appellate Law.
**Thomason, Bruce A.** ... '61 '89 C.1169 A.B. L.602 J.D. [Kelegian&T.]
*PRACTICE AREAS: Construction Defect Litigation; General Civil Litigation.
**Thorn, Robert C.**, (AV) ... '55 '81 C.763 B.A. L.61 J.D. [Kimball,T.&S.] (⊙San Diego)
*PRACTICE AREAS: Landlord/Tenant; Real Estate.

**Throckmorton, Beckstrom, Oakes & Tomassian LLP**
**(See Pasadena)**

Thrower, Tracy L. ... '62 '90 C.911 B.A. L.1049 J.D. R.T.C.
**Thullen, Matthew P.** ... '62 '93 C&L.477 B.A., J.D. [Ⓐ Stradling,Y.C.&R.]
Thyen, Delane J. ... '36 '75 C.755 B.S. L.1137 J.D. 351 Hospital Rd.‡
Tingler, David S., (AV) ... '33 '60 C.813 A.B. L.800 J.D. P.O. Box 1938‡
**Tirey, Patricia H.**, (BV) '57 '83 C.112 B.A. L.1049 J.D.
[Kimball,T.&S.] (⊙San Diego)
*PRACTICE AREAS: Landlord/Tenant Law.
Tomalas, Roger P. ... '47 '76 C.112 B.A. L.1095 J.D. 5 Civic Plz.
Toretto, Stephen J. '56 '88 C.1044 B.S. L.184 J.D.
(adm. in CT; not adm. in CA) Dir.-Staff Atty., Pacific Mut. Life Ins. Co.
Tow, Marc R. ... '51 '77 C.1044 B.A. L.1137 J.D. 3900 Birch St.
**Trebler, Per H.**, (AV) ... '38 '71 C.668 B.A. L.1127 J.D. [P.H.Trebler]
*PRACTICE AREAS: Trusts and Estates; Probate; Guardianship and Conservatorships; Aged and Aging.

**Trebler, Per H., P.C., (AV)**
**2121 East Pacific Coast Highway, Suite, 280 (Corona Del Mar), 92625**
**Telephone: 714-640-5969**

(This Listing Continued)

**Trebler, Per H., P.C. (Continued)**

**Per H. Trebler.**
**Trust and Estate, Probate, Guardianships and Conservatorships, Aged and Aging.**

Treska, Edward J. ... '65 '92 C.172 B.S.E.E. L.1049 J.D. 620 Newport Ctr.Dr.
**Triff, Brent N.** ... '70 '96 C.112 B.A. L.1049 J.D. [Ⓐ Stradling,Y.C.&R.]
**Trigg, Nicola J.** ... '61 '90 C&L.061 LLB. [Ⓐ Geiger&W.]
*PRACTICE AREAS: Real Estate; Corporate Law; Business Law; Finance; Contracts.
**Troyan, Michele McCormick** ... '71 '96 C&L.426 B.S., J.D. [Ⓐ Stradling,Y.C.&R.]
Tucker, Larry ... '48 '75 C.112 B.A. L.426 J.D. P.O. Box 7974‡

**Tulac, John W.**
**(See Claremont)**

Turner, James K. ... '28 '55 C.800 B.S. L.426 LL.B. Ret. Supr. Ct. J.
Turner, Sandy L. ... '51 '82 C.560 B.A. L.1137 J.D. 324 Canal St.

**Tuverson & Hillyard, (AV)**
**A Limited Liability Partnership, including Professional Corporations**
**4675 MacArthur Court, Suite 650, 92660⊙**
**Telephone: 714-752-7855 Fax: 714-752-5437**
**Resident Partners: Steven D. Hillyard (P.C.). Resident Associates: Patricia Ann Carmichael; Peter A. Herzog; Margaret Krinsky; Brian M. Meadows; Geoffrey T. Moore; Charles J. Norek.**
**General Civil and Trial Practice in all State and Federal Courts. Medical and Legal Malpractice Defense, Public Entity and Insurance Defense.**
**Los Angeles, California Office: 12400 Wilshire Boulevard, Suite 900, Los Angeles, California 90025. Telephones: 310-826-7855; 625-1234. Fax: 310-826-8738.**
**Palm Springs, California Office: 1800 Tahquitz Canyon Way, Palm Springs, California 92263. Telephone: 619-322-7855. Fax: 619-322-5121.**
**San Diego, California Office: 4365 Executive Drive, Suite 700, San Diego, California 92121. Telephone: 619-452-7855. Fax: 619-452-2153.**

***See Professional Biographies, NEWPORT BEACH, CALIFORNIA***

Tweed, Randy '61 '93 C&L.585 B.B.A., J.D.
(adm. in CO; not adm. in CA) 4675 MacArthur Ct.
**Tyler, J. Russell, Jr.** ... '59 '87 C&L.878 B.A., J.D. [McDermott,W.&E.]
*LANGUAGES: Spanish.
*PRACTICE AREAS: Lender Liability Securities; Litigation; Real Property Litigation.
**Uhler, Lewis K.** ... '33 '58 C.976 B.A. L.1066 LL.B. [Ⓒ Davis,P.K.&W.]
*PRACTICE AREAS: Governmental Affairs; International Law.
Unsworth, Charles W. ... '42 '68 C.97 B.A. L.477 J.D. [C.W.Unsworth]
Unsworth, Charles W., A Prof. Corp. ... P.O. Box 688
Urtnowski, J. Brian ... '55 '85 C.763 B.S. L.1065 J.D. [Waier&U.]
van der Capellen, Adriaan F. ... '54 '91 C.1042 B.A. L.1137 J.D. 4685 McArthur Court
**Van Hoosear, Jeffrey L.** ... '60 '86 C.72 B.A. L.94 J.D. [Knobbe,M.O.&B.]
VanLeeuwen, Jessica A. ... '57 '91 C.843 B.A. L.1148 J.D. R.T.C.
**Van Wert, Ronald K.**, (AV) ... '43 '69 C.112 B.A. L.1065 J.D. [R.K.Van Wert]

**Van Wert, Ronald K., A Professional Corporation, (AV)** BR
**One Newport Place, Suite 900, 1301 Dove Street, 92660**
**Telephone: 714-752-7964**
**Ronald K. Van Wert (Certified Specialist, Taxation Law, The State Bar of California Board of Legal Specialization).**
**Federal and State Business Tax Litigation, including Criminal Tax Litigation, Estate Planning and Corporate.**

***See Professional Biographies, NEWPORT BEACH, CALIFORNIA***

**Vatave, Sunil Lewis** ... '68 '95 C.112 B.A. L.1148 J.D. [Chandler&V.]
*PRACTICE AREAS: Busines Torts; NASD Arbitration; Employment Litigation; Civil Litigation.
**Vaughan, John David** ... '64 '93 C.309 A.B. L.800 J.D. [Ⓐ Stradling,Y.C.&R.]
**Vaughn, J. Michael** ... '61 '87 C.36 B.S. L.800 J.D. [Stradling,Y.C.&R.]
**Verdon, Jeffrey M.**, (AV) ... '54 '78 C&L.1221 B.S.L., J.D. [J.M.Verdon]

**Verdon, Jeffrey M., P.C., (AV)**
**2801 W. Pacific Coast Highway, Suite 380, 92663**
**Telephone: 714-631-3500; 800-521-0464 Fax: 714-631-0355**
**Email: jmvstaff@earthlink.net**
**Jeffrey M. Verdon.**
**Advanced Asset Protection Strategies, Advanced Estate Planning Strategies and International Trusts.**

***See Professional Biographies, NEWPORT BEACH, CALIFORNIA***

Vestermark, Gary D., (AV) ... '41 '72 C.112 A.B. L.273 J.D. [G.D.Vestermark]
Vestermark, Gary D., A Law Corporation, (AV) ... Ste. 200, 1300 Dove St.
**Villard, William N.** ... '67 '94 C.896 B.S. L.61 J.D. [Kelegian&T.]
*PRACTICE AREAS: Civil Litigation; Premises Liability Law; Construction Defect.
Virtue, John, (AV) ... '29 '59 C.112 B.A. L.1068 J.D. 3737 Birch St.
**Vogel, Karen J.** '58 '84 C.112 B.A. L.273 J.D.
(adm. in DC; not adm. in CA) [Knobbe,M.O.&B.]
**Vogt, James D., (Law Corporation)** ... '44 '70 C.629 B.A. L.1068 J.D. [Ⓒ White&R.]
*PRACTICE AREAS: Personal Injury Law; Business Litigation.

**Vollmer, Michael V., (AV) '45 '72 C.112 B.A. L.426 J.D.** BR
**4340 Campus Drive, Suite 100, 92660-1892**
**Telephone: 714-852-0833 Fax: 714-852-8731**
**Email: mvollmer@aol.com**
***PRACTICE AREAS: Estate Planning Law; Probate Law; Trust Law.**
**Practice limited to Estate Planning, Probate, Trust and Taxation Law.**
**References: Bank of America NT&SA (Newport Beach, California); First American Trust Co. (Newport Beach, California).**

***See Professional Biographies, NEWPORT BEACH, CALIFORNIA***

**von Hoffmann, W. Gerard, III** '56 '84
C.605 A.B. L.1049 J.D. [Knobbe,M.O.&B.] (See Pat. Sect.)
**Voss, William Bruce**, (BV) ... '48 '75 C.1109 B.A. L.990 J.D. [Ⓒ Cummins&W.]

**Voss, Cook & Thel, (AV)**
**A Partnership including Law Corporations**
**Suite 700, 840 Newport Center Drive, 92660**
**Telephone: 714-720-0300 Telecopier: 714-720-1508**
**Email: VossCook@aol.com**
**Members of Firm: Bruce V. Cook, P.C.; James G. Damon III; Edward L. Laird; David A. Lurker; M. Edward Mishow; Albert J. Thel, Jr. Associates: Marc Reich; Marc S. Strecker; Maxy Rush Otuteye; Babak Samini. Of Counsel: Lori Winder Livingston.**
**Real Estate, Construction, Land Use, Partnerships, Federal and State Taxation, Financial Institutions, Mortgage Banking, Secured Financing, Commercial, General Business, Corporations, Securities Syndications, Bankruptcy, Advertising and Estate Planning Law. General Civil and Trial Practice in all State and Federal Courts.**

***See Professional Biographies, NEWPORT BEACH, CALIFORNIA***

**Vyneman, Gary J.** ... '59 '93 C.339 B.S.G.E. L.1148 J.D. [Ⓐ Stradling,Y.C.&R.]
*PRACTICE AREAS: Taxation.
**Wagner, Mary Anne** ... '65 '93 C.763 A.B. L.1065 J.D. [Ⓐ Stradling,Y.C.&R.]
Wagner, William O., (AV) ... '38 '66 C&L.426 B.B.A., LL.B. [W.O.Wagner]
Wagner, William O., Inc., A Law Corporation, (AV) ... 3400 Irvine Ave.
Waier, Randall S. ... '47 '77 C.208 B.S. L.426 J.D. [Waier&U.]
Waier & Urtnowski ... 1301 Dove St.
**Wakefield, James R.** ... '52 '81 C.1109 B.A. L.464 J.D. [Cummins&W.]
*PRACTICE AREAS: Construction Law; Insurance Defense.
Waldo, Georgia J. ... '24 '71 C.112 B.S. P.O. Box 1933

**Waldron, Gary A.**, (AV) ... '49 '80 C&L.378 B.A., J.D. [Andersen&W.]⊙
Walker, Anthony ... '52 '85 C.112 B.A. L.464 J.D. 1300 Dove St.
**Walker, Joseph A.**, (AV) ... '45 '70 C.339 B.A. L.800 J.D. [Walker]
*PRACTICE AREAS: Business and Real Property Litigation; Business Law; Employment Law; Bankruptcy.

**Walker Law Firm, The, A Professional Corporation, (AV)** BR
**Suite 450, 1301 Dove Street, 92660-2464**
**Telephone: 714-752-2522 Telecopier: 714-752-0439**
**Email: JWALKER208@AOL.COM**
**Joseph A. Walker. Of Counsel: Duff S. McEvers; David T. Sanford; Karyn S. Neue.**
**Civil Litigation in all State and Federal Courts. Employment Litigation for Employers, Commercial U.D.'s and Appeals, Real Property, Business, Partnership and Corporate Law and Bankruptcy; Arbitration and Mediation Representation.**
**Reference: Marine National Bank.**
***See Professional Biographies, NEWPORT BEACH, CALIFORNIA***

Wallace, Douglas K., (BV) ... '30 '60 C.605 A.B. L.800 LL.B. 5030 Campus Dr.
Wallace, Earl ... '67 '94 C.112 B.A. L.426 J.D. 130 Newport Center Dr.
Wallace, Jay B. ... '66 '94 C.112 B.A. L.464 J.D. 4675 Macarthur Ct.
**Wallace, Jeffrey J.** '52 '77 C.605 A.B. L.800 J.D.
V.P. & Gen. Coun., Irvine Coml. Land Sales Co./Irvine Indus. Co.
**Wallace, Robert Craig** ... '65 '90 C.999 B.A. L.800 J.D. [A Stradling,Y.C.&R.]
**Walley, Thomas E.**, (AV) ... '44 '70 C&L.800 B.A., J.D. [Good,W.H.&W.]
*PRACTICE AREAS: Civil Litigation; Family Law; Construction.
Walling, Robert J. ... '45 '72 C.112 A.B. L.1065 J.D. 100 Bayview Circle
Walsh, Michael T. ... '46 '74 C.728 B.S. L.659 J.D. 4425 Jamboree Blvd.
Walsworth, James H., (BV) ... '34 '59 C.112 B.S. L.1065 LL.B. 4340 Campus Dr.
Waltuch, Joseph L. '48 '72
C.112 B.A. L.1065 J.D. V.P. & Sr. Coun., Imperial Corp. of Amer.
Ward, Kathleen M. ... '61 '90 C.426 B.A. L.1065 J.D. 4695 MacArthur Ct.
**Waterman, Matthew V.** ... '64 '92 C.36 B.A. L.1066 J.D. [A Brobeck,P.&H.]
*PRACTICE AREAS: Corporate.
**Weber, Marc Lindsey** ... '53 '78 C.112 B.A. L.1068 J.D. [Geiger&W.]
*PRACTICE AREAS: Real Estate; Franchise; Taxation.
**Weide, R. Scott** ... '65 '91 C.546 B.S. L.190 J.D. [Knobbe,M.O.&B.] (See Pat. Sect.)
**Weifenbach, Diane** ... '59 '92 C&L.1137 B.S.L., J.D. [A Wolf&P.]
*PRACTICE AREAS: Secured Real Property Creditor Rights.
**Weil, Matthew Francis** ... '61 '92 C.112 A.B. L.1066 J.D. [A Howard,R.N.C.F.&R.]
*LANGUAGES: Russian.
*PRACTICE AREAS: Litigation; Intellectual Property.
Weiner, Christine C. ... '44 '90 C.906 B.A. L.1137 J.D. 1300 Dove St.
**Weiss, David N.** ... '58 '94 C.112 B.S.E.E. L.705 J.D. [Knobbe,M.O.&B.]
Weiss, Mark F. ... '54 '79 C.112 B.A. L.800 J.D. [Weiss&H.] (⊙Los Angeles)
Weiss & Humphries, A Professional Corporation
610 Newport Ctr. Dr., Ste. 1010 (⊙Los Angeles)
Wells, Thomas, (AV) ... '39 '70 C.940 B.A. L.1117 J.D. 3501 Jamboree
**Wentworth, Theodore S.**, (AV) ... '38 '63 C.999 L.1065 J.D. [Wentworth&P.]⊙
*PRACTICE AREAS: Personal Injury; Wrongful Death; Products Liability; Professional Malpractice; Business Fraud.

**Wentworth & Paoli, P.C., (AV)** BR
**4631 Teller Avenue, Suite 100, 92660**
**Telephone: 714-752-7711 Fax: 714-752-8339**
**Theodore S. Wentworth (Member of California Trial Lawyers Association, with recognized experience in the fields of Trial Lawyer, General Personal Injury, Professional Negligence, Product Liability, Appellate Law and Motion, Public Entity Liability and Insurance Bad Faith); William M. Delli Paoli; Nancy Morse Knight; Court Bryant Purdy.**
**Practice Limited to Personal Injury, including Wrongful Death, Professional Liability and Products Liability Litigation, Business and Estate Fraud, Fire Loss and Human Rights Violations.**
**Reference: Wells Fargo Bank, Newport Beach, Calif.**
***See Professional Biographies, NEWPORT BEACH, CALIFORNIA***

Werksman, Gerald M., (AV(T)) ... '35 '61 C&L.178 B.A., LL.B. 1300 Dove St.
**Westover, Alyssa C.** ... '66 '91 C.800 B.S. L.990 J.D. [A H.E.Westover&Assoc.]
*PRACTICE AREAS: General Civil Litigation; Probate Litigation; Probate Administration; Estate Planning and Trust Law.
**Westover, Barrett E.** ... '63 '91 C.800 B.A. L.1137 J.D. [A H.E.Westover&Assoc.]
*PRACTICE AREAS: General Civil Litigation; Probate Litigation; Probate Administration; Estate Planning; Trust Law.

**Westover, Harry E., & Associates, Law Offices of, (AV) '31 '57**
**C.37 B.S.M.E. L.1068 J.D.**
**901 Dover Drive, Suite 100, 92660**
**Telephone: 714-646-7200 Fax: 714-646-7665**
**(Certified Specialist, Estate Planning, Trust and Probate Law, The State Bar of California Board of Legal Specialization).**
***PRACTICE AREAS: Probate Law; Probate Litigation; Estate Planning Law; Trust Law.**
**Associates: Pierre E. Auw (Certified Specialist, Estate Planning, Trust and Probate Law, The State Bar of California Board of Legal Specialization); Barrett E. Westover; Alyssa C. Westover.**
**Probate and Trust Litigation and Administration, Estate Planning, Probate and Trust Law.**
***See Professional Biographies, NEWPORT BEACH, CALIFORNIA***

**Whalen, Robert J.**, (AV) ... '53 '78 C.309 A.B. L.1066 J.D. [Stradling,Y.C.&R.]
**White, Bruce David**, (AV) ... '48 '73 C&L.546 B.S., J.D. [White&R.]
*PRACTICE AREAS: Bankruptcy.
**White, Christopher A.** ... '64 '91 C.112 B.A. L.426 J.D. [A Sims,M.&M.]
White, Eugene C. ... '52 '77 C.36 B.S. L.990 J.D. 4301 Birch St.
White, James D., (P.C.) ... '47 '75 C.475 B.S. L.213 J.D. 500 Newport Ctr. Dr.
**White, Paul J., (Law Corporation)** ... '56 '82 C.999 B.A. L.809 J.D. [White&R.]
*PRACTICE AREAS: Tax Planning and Business Transactions (60%); Estate Planning (20%); Employee Benefits (10%); Retirement Plans.
White, Richard C., (AV) ... '33 '63 C&L.813 A.B., LL.B. 610 Newport Ctr.

**White & Resnick, (AV)**
**A Partnership of Law Corporations**
**4400 MacArthur Boulevard, Suite 900, P.O. Box 7849, 92658-7849**⊙
**Telephone: 714-851-9001 Telecopier: 714-833-3445**
**Email: barlaw@deltanet.com**
**Partners: Barnet Resnick (Law Corporation); Paul J. White (Law Corporation); Daniel Rosen (Law Corporation); Veronica M. Gray (Law Corporation). Associates: Jerome A. Busch; Darren M. Campf; Devon D. Grant; Richard K. Semeta. Of Counsel: Michael J. Christianson; Joseph A. Rogoff; James D. Vogt (Law Corporation).**
**Los Angeles, California Office: ABC Entertainment Center. Fourth Floor. 2040 Avenue of the Stars. 90067-4703. Telephone: 213-583-1439.**

**White & Roseman, (AV)**
**1201 Dove Street, Suite 480, 92660**
**Telephone: 714-622-6100 Fax: 714-852-2141**
**Members of Firm: Bruce David White; Leslie R. Roseman.**
**Bankruptcy, Sexual Harassment, Discrimination, Wrongful Termination, Personal Injury**
***See Professional Biographies, NEWPORT BEACH, CALIFORNIA***

**Whitehead, Nancy Rader** ... '57 '82 C.1075 B.A. L.800 J.D. [Scott,R.&W.]
**Whitesides, Pamela L.** ... '46 '91 C&L.800 B.S., J.D. [A Scott,R.&W.]
**Whitfield, Patti L.** ... '65 '91 C.112 B.A. L.464 J.D. [A Cummins&W.]
*PRACTICE AREAS: Business Law.

Whitney, Richard P. ... '52 '94 C.112 B.A. L.1137 J.D. [A Sainick&C.]

**Whittington, Michael T., (CV) '58 '84 C&L.770 B.S., J.D.**
**4590 MacArthur, Suite 550, 92660**⊙
**Telephone: 714-833-2370 Fax: 714-833-0949**
**Real Estate, Business, General Civil Litigation and Trials.**
**Bakersfield, California Office: Commonwealth Plaza, 3300 Truxtun Avenue, Suite 390, 93303. Telephone: 805-327-2294. Fax: 805-323-8731.**
**Los Gatos, California Office: 15425 Los Gatos Boulevard, Suite 120, 95032. Telephone: 408-369-9655. Fax: 408-369-0355.**
***See Professional Biographies, BAKERSFIELD, CALIFORNIA***

Wiles, Wendy H., (AV) ... '55 '80 C.990 B.S. L.1148 J.D. [Bowie A.K.W.&G.]
**Willard, Robert E.**, (AV) ... '29 '59 C.906 B.A. L.309 J.D. [Davis,P.K.&W.]
*PRACTICE AREAS: Business Litigation; Construction; Real Estate; Environmental Law.
Willford, Sandford R. ... '25 '52 C&L.800 A.B., J.D. 62 Linda Isle‡
**Williams, Greg T.** ... '64 '90 C&L.494 B.I.S., J.D. [A Brobeck,P.&H.]
*PRACTICE AREAS: Corporate; Securities.
**Williams, Thomas M.** ... '69 '96 C.855 B.A. L.800 J.D. [A Stradling,Y.C.&R.]
**Williamson, Brett J.** ... '63 '89 C.112 B.A. L.800 J.D. [C O'Melveny&M.]
*PRACTICE AREAS: Litigation.
**Wilson, John C.** ... '71 '96 C.112 B.A. L.273 J.D. [A Knobbe,M.O.&B.]
Wilson, Mark B. ... '63 '88 C.800 B.S. L.426 J.D. 4100 Newport Pl., Ste., 520
Wind, Kimberly J., (BV) ... '66 '92 C.645 B.A. L.1049 J.D. [A Silldorf,B.D.&E.]
**Winnett, Karen Nicolai** ... '53 '79 C.1042 B.A. L.800 J.D. [Bruck&P.]
*PRACTICE AREAS: Corporate Law; Securities Law; Commercial Transactions.
**Winthrop, Marc J.**, (AV) ... '48 '74 C.112 A.B. L.1068 J.D. [Winthrop C.]
*PRACTICE AREAS: Bankruptcy Reorganization; Commercial Bankruptcy; Workouts.

**Winthrop Couchot Professional Corporation, (AV)** BR
**3 Civic Plaza, Suite 280, 92660**
**Telephone: 714-720-4100 Fax: 714-720-4111**
**Marc J. Winthrop; Paul J. Couchot; Robert W. Pitts;—Richard H. Golubow; Dorit Goossens; Peter Lianides.**
**Bankruptcy, Insolvency, Corporate Reorganization and Commercial Litigation.**
***See Professional Biographies, NEWPORT BEACH, CALIFORNIA***

**Wirth, Gabrielle M.** ... '57 '82 C.112 B.A. L.1067 J.D. [Brobeck,P.&H.]
*PRACTICE AREAS: Labor Law; Employment Litigation; Insurance Coverage Litigation; Unfair Competition.
**Witkin, Gene M.** ... '65 '90 C.112 B.A. L.1068 J.D. [A Newmeyer&D.]
*PRACTICE AREAS: Litigation involving Insurance Coverage; Business; Construction; Bankruptcy.

**Witter and Harpole, (AV)**
**610 Newport Center Drive, Suite 1050, 92660**⊙
**Telephone: 714-644-7600 Fax: 714-759-1014**
**Myron E. Harpole (Certified Specialist, Taxation Law, The State Bar of California Board of Legal Specialization); Debra M. Olsen (Resident).**
**Federal and State Tax, Tax Litigation, Estate Planning, Trust and Probate Law.**
**Reference: Union Bank (Newport Beach, Calif.).**
**Pasadena, California Office: Wells Fargo Building, 350 W. Colorado Boulevard, Suite 400. Telephone: 213-624-1311; 818-440-1111. FAX: 213-620-0430.**
***See Professional Biographies, NEWPORT BEACH, CALIFORNIA***

**Wolf, Alan S.**, (AV) ... '55 '80 C.197 B.A. L.809 J.D. [Wolf&P.]
*PRACTICE AREAS: Mortgage Banking; Creditors Rights in Bankruptcy Proceedings; Real Estate Law.

**Wolf & Pfeifer, A Law Corporation, (AV)** BR
**500 Newport Center Drive Suite 800, 92660**
**Telephone: 714-720-9200 Fax: 714-720-9250**
**URL: http://www.wolfpfeifer.com**
**Alan S. Wolf; Michael R. Pfeifer; Melissa L. Richards; Janice L. Celotti; Donald R. Davidson, III;—Roland P. Reynolds; Donna L. La Porte; C. Robert Simpson; Diane Weifenbach; James F. Lewin. Of Counsel: Kay Virginia Gustafson.**
**Real Estate Finance and Mortgage Banking (Residential and Commercial/Multi-Family), Regulatory Compliance, Multistate Licensing, Corporate and Loan Origination/Servicing Matters, Securitization and Secondary Marketing (MBS/CMBS), Federal and State Court Litigation including Complex and Class Action Defense Litigation, Default Servicing (Residential and Commercial/Multifamily), Mortgage Fraud Resolution, Foreclosures, Deeds-in-Lieu, Bankruptcy Representation (Freddie Mac Approved), REO Management and Evictions.**
***See Professional Biographies, NEWPORT BEACH, CALIFORNIA***

**Wolfe, Thomas E.** ... '52 '81 C.112 A.B. L.426 J.D. [A O'Melveny&M.]
*PRACTICE AREAS: Corporate Law.
**Woodhead, John E., IV** ... '60 '92 C.112 B.S. L.426 J.D. [A Stradling,Y.C.&R.]
Worley, Jesse D. '23 '49 C.244 B.A. L.893 LL.B.
(adm. in TN; not adm. in CA) 811 Baywood Dr.‡
Wright, Hugh L., (BV) ... '21 '57 C.112 A.B. L.809 LL.B. Sr. Atty., R.T.C.
**Yamashiro, Betty O.** ... '— '85 C.312 B.Ed. L.1137 J.D. [Buxbaum&C.]⊙
*PRACTICE AREAS: Banking; Bankruptcy; Creditors Rights; Civil Litigation.
**Yamato, Lori L.** ... '70 '95 C.800 B.S.E.E. L.477 J.D. [Knobbe,M.O.&B.]
**Yeager, E. Kurt**, (AV) ... '53 '78 C.112 A.B. L.1066 J.D. [Stradling,Y.C.&R.]
**Yocca, Nicholas J.**, (AV) ... '57 '86 C.309 A.B. L.1049 J.D. [A Stradling,Y.C.&R.]
**Yocca, Nick E.**, (AV) ... '29 '59 C.665 A.B. L.477 J.D. [Stradling,Y.C.&R.]
**Yoder, Michael G.**, (AV) ... '53 '78 C.800 A.B. L.813 J.D. [O'Melveny&M.]
*PRACTICE AREAS: Complex Business Litigation; Land Use Litigation; Business Torts; Trade Secrets.
Yonis-Sandlaufer, Robin S. '54 '80 C.1044 B.A. L.978 J.D.
Asst. V.P. & Invest. Coun., Pacific Mut. Life Ins. Co.
**Yonowitz, Robert** ... '62 '87 C.705 B.A. L.273 J.D. [A Fisher&P.]
York, Michael G., (BV) ... '54 '79 C.112 B.A. L.426 J.D. 1300 Dove St.
Young, Dennis M. '47 '74 C.197 B.A. L.1049 J.D.
Assoc. Gen. Coun., Deutsche Financial Services Corp.
**Young, Steven R.**, (AV) ... '54 '80 C.878 B.A. L.990 J.D. [Young&A.]
*PRACTICE AREAS: Trials; Real Estate Law; Construction Disputes.

**Young & Amundsen, (AV)** BR
**620 Newport Center Drive, Suite 420, 92660**
**Telephone: 714-640-4400 Fax: 714-717-4862**
**Members of Firm: Steven R. Young; Roland J. Amundsen.**
**Construction and Real Estate Litigation, Real Estate, Bankruptcy, Broker Liability, Subsidence Law. General Litigation in all Courts, Trade and Customs Law.**
***See Professional Biographies, NEWPORT BEACH, CALIFORNIA***

Youngman, Arn K. ... '32 '60 C&L.800 B.S., LL.B. Pacific Develop. Grp.
Yu, Philip K. '61 '91 C.112 B.S. L.273 J.D.
Intell. Prop. Atty., Rockwell International Corporation (Pat.)
Yuskis, Michael J. ... '— '78 C&L.800 A.B., J.D. 950 Cagney Ln.‡
**Zablocki, Michael A.** ... '44 '69 C.102 B.A. L.273 J.D. [A Stradling,Y.C.&R.]
**Zadra-Symes, Lynda J.** ... '62 '89 [Knobbe,M.O.&B.]
*LANGUAGES: French, German.
Zech, Eugene V. ... '47 '76 C.112 B.A. L.990 J.D. 1201 Dove St.
**Zeigler, Dana M.** ... '— '89 C.112 B.A. L.1065 J.D. [A Bruck&P.]
*PRACTICE AREAS: Securities Law; Corporate Law.
**Zeigler, Thomas A.** ... '60 '89 C.1025 B.S. L.596 J.D. [A Alvarado,S.V.&S.]
*PRACTICE AREAS: Corporate/Business; Public Utilities; Intellectual Property.
**Zemanek, Jan A.** ... '64 '93 C.112 B.S. L.800 J.D. [M.W.Mainero,Jr.]
*LANGUAGES: Czech.

Zepfel, Robert J., (AV) .................. '52 '77 C.112 B.A. L.1066 J.D. [▣ Phillips&H.]
Zetterberg, Charles L., (AV) .......... '43 '71 C.918 B.A. L.178 LL.B. [Buxbaum&C.]ⓒ
*PRACTICE AREAS: Civil Litigation; Insurance; Real Estate; Business.
Zeughauser, Peter D., (AV) ............ '50 '75 C.966 B.A. L.734 J.D. 550 Newport Ctr. Dr.
Zinn, Harold M. '12 '35 C&L.724 LL.B.
(adm. in NY; not adm. in CA) 310 Vista Trucha‡
Zuk, Michael A., (AV) '52 '78
C.1077 B.A. L.809 J.D. [Herzfeld&R.] (ⓒLos Angeles, CA)

## NICASIO, —, *Marin Co.*

Lewis, Mimi Reichert ............ '51 '79 C.1169 A.B. L.1065 J.D. 5899 Lucas Valley Rd.

## NIPOMO, 3,642, *San Luis Obispo Co.*

Brantingham, Paul J. .................... '43 '69 C&L.178 A.B., LL.B. 1541 Los Padres Dr.
Frederick, Jacqueline Vitti ................ '55 '80 C.1077 L.398 J.D. 111 N. Oakglen Ave.
Lacey, Hugh J., Jr. ......................... '22 '49 C.152 A.B. L.94 LL.B. 350 Via Vicente‡

**Murray, Guy W. '54 '87 C.101 B.A. L.1148 J.D.**
**671 West Tefft Street, Suite 9, P.O. Box 180, 93444**
**Telephone: 805-929-7150 Fax: 805-929-7151**
**Email: NIPOMOLAW@AOL.COM**
**General Civil Trial Practice in all State and Federal Courts, Civil Litigation, Casualty Defense, Real Estate and Construction Law.**
*See Professional Biographies, NIPOMO, CALIFORNIA*

## NORCO, 23,302, *Riverside Co.*

Davis, Linn .............................. '— '67 C.112 B.S. L.424 J.D. 3000 N. Corona Ave.
Kastner, Joseph C., (BV) ................ '33 '71 C.642 L.1148 LL.B. P.O. Box 369
Keefer, Patricia L. .......................... '41 '86 L.1137 J.D. 2350 Temescal Ave.
King-Jeffers, Sharon W., (CV) ....... '40 '78 C&L.1137 B.S.L., J.D. 2399 Mountain Ave.
McBride, Leonard H. ...................... '21 '54 C.813 L.767 LL.B. 815 E. River Dr.‡
Rinehart, Robert L., (BV) ................ '39 '74 C&L.1137 B.L., J.D. 1809 Lampton Ln.
Selby, Louis L. .............................. '26 '62 C&L.145 A.B., J.D. 4000 Corona Ave.‡

## NORTH FORK, —, *Madera Co.*

Bashore, Glen T. ............................ '13 '54 C.477 B.S. L.16 LL.B. 34675 Rd. 274‡
Flanagan, James H., Jr., (BV) '34 '62
C&L.813 A.B., J.D. Pres., American Benefit Development Corp.
Levy, Gordon P. .................. '31 '59 C.112 A.B. L.426 LL.B. 31863 Oak Junction Rd.

## NORTH HIGHLANDS, 31,854, *Sacramento Co.*

Bowe, Debra A. .................................... '51 '81 C.446 B.A. L.30 J.D. I.R.S.
Gibson, Bridgette M. '63 '88 C.811 B.A. L.803 J.D.
(adm. in LA; not adm. in CA) Spec. Asst. U.S. Atty., U.S. Treasury Dept.
Jacobs, Steven ..................................................... '54 '87 L.790 J.D. I.R.S.
Monty, Roger B. .......................... '37 '81 C.184 B.A. L.464 J.D. I.R.S.
Parent, Daniel J. '54 '81 C&L.508 B.A., J.D.
(adm. in MT; not adm. in CA) I.R.S.
Rohall, Thomas M. '55 '81 C.999 B.A. L.285 J.D.
(adm. in WA; not adm. in CA) I.R.S.
Temple, John E. .............................. '37 '80 L.1026 J.D. 6929 Bismarck Dr.

## NORTH HOLLYWOOD, —, *Los Angeles Co.*

Abel, Richard .................. '50 '80 C.112 B.A. L.1095 J.D. Van den Bergh Foods Co.
Abraham, Thomas J. ......................... '46 '84 C.1077 B.A. L.1148 J.D. 4089 Beck Ave.
Abrams, Paul '10 '34 C.563 B.S. L.178 LL.B.
(adm. in NY; not adm. in CA) 12840 Riverside Dr.
Andrus, Lesley A., (AV) ... '46 '75 C.813 A.B. L.800 J.D. 12001 Ventura Pl., Studio City
Bandgren, Jimmie B. ................ '35 '90 C&L.1137 B.S.L., J.D. Robinson May Co.
Becker, Emanuel ................................ '11 '34 C.999 L.1251 LL.B. 6858 Atoll Ave.‡
Berger, Leon H. ................... '10 '35 C.112 A.B. L.800 J.D. 3645 Wrightwood Dr.‡
Berman, Gary M. ................. '42 '82 C.112 B.A. L.1148 J.D. 12653 Cumpston St.
Bilson, Michael, (AV) ........... '35 '61 C.188 B.S. L.1066 LL.B. 4640 Lankershim Blvd
Blue, Barbara P. ..................... '46 '73 C&L.260 B.S.J., J.D. 4149 Wilkinson Ave.
Bornstein, Alfred ..................................... '26 '59 L.809 6608 Clybourn Ave.‡
Braun, Jennifer ............ '61 '87 C.668 B.A. L.1066 J.D. Bet Tzedek Legal Servs.
**Brito, Eduardo A.** .......................... '62 '91 C&L.112 B.A., J.D. [▣ Rosato&S.]
*LANGUAGES: Spanish.
**Brotman, David B.** ........ '55 '81 C.1036 A.B. L.426 J.D. [L.Tobin&Assoc.]
*PRACTICE AREAS: Workers Compensation Law (100%, 200).
Budinger, Jerome M., (AV) ........... '23 '49 C.112 L.800 LL.B. 4605 Lankershim Bldg.‡
Buhan, Elaine, (AV) .......................... '35 '72 L.1095 J.D. 12399 Erwin St.
Burkenheim, Marie Sabath ........ '46 '78 C.1077 B.A. L.1221 J.D. 6109 Wilkinson Ave.
Carter, Maxine L. ......................... '19 '70 C.426 L.1127 J.D. 5551 Biloxi Ave.‡
Casale, William S. ..................... '49 '80 C.923 B.A. L.809 J.D. 12407 LaMaida St.‡
Caylor, Michele D. ......................... '48 '84 C.999 L.809 J.D. 13040 Sarah St.
Cerveris, Steven R. ................. '57 '85 C.112 B.A. L.426 J.D. 12650 Riverside Dr.
Clarke, Thomas W., (AV) ......................... '11 '37 4605 Lankershim Blvd., Ste 721
Clifford, Richard R., A P.C., (AV) '37 '63 C.477 A.B. L.813 J.D.
4605 Lankershim Blvd.
Cooper, Phyllis N., (AV) .............. '15 '38 C&L.800 B.A., J.D. 3447 Wrightview Dr.‡
Crisler, Ted R. ........................ '56 '89 C.312 B.A. L.398 J.D. 16921 Parthenia St.
Cronin, Thos. R. ........................... '26 '54 C.209 L.426 J.D. 4605 Lankershim Bl.
De Silva, Rohini P. .................. '43 '79 C.1133 B.F.A. L.178 J.D. 3624 Berry Dr.
Dezen, Phillip M. ....... '39 '89 C.112 B.A. L.426 J.D. 4329 Wilkinson Ave., Studio City‡
Donahue, Daniel J. ..................... '59 '85 C.1075 B.A. L.940 J.D. [G.K.Jackson]
Dresser, Glen, (BV) ..................... '49 '74 C&L.800 B.A., J.D. 12650 Riverside Dr.
Dreufus, Bethany ........................ '68 '95 C.188 B.A. L.1066 Bet Tzedek Legal Servs.
Duryea, Thomas E. .............. '49 '76 C.608 B.S. L.1003 J.D. 6160 Laurel Canyon Blvd.
Earley, James P. ...................... '25 '55 C.112 A.B. L.1065 J.D. 4605 Lankershim Blvd.
Edmisten, Lawrence F., Jr., (AV) .... '10 '37 C.800 B.A. L.309 LL.B. 12427 Ventura Blvd.
Engel, Harold L. ......................... '26 '69 C.111 L.981 LL.B. 13074 Greenleaf St.
Engel, Shirley A. '28 '67 C.112 B.A. L.1077 J.D.
Prof., Univ. of West L.A. Sch. of Law
Fitzgerald, Paul D. ..................... '64 '89 C.107 B.S. L.990 J.D. P.O. Box 590
Freund, Benni H. ...................... '35 '64 C.112 B.A. L.809 LL.B. 11424 Burbank Blvd.
Frick, James J. ...................... '57 '89 C.1075 B.A. L.398 J.D. 11300 Weddington St.
Galen, Suzanne E. ...................... '36 '79 C.823 B.S. L.1136 J.D. 12650 Riverside Dr.
Geldin, Max ........................ '16 '45 C.696 B.S. L.692 J.D. 3386 Canton Way (Pat.)
Gillette, Paul .............................................. '27 '67 6167 Lankershim Blvd.
Glaser, Jerome ....................... '30 '64 C.415 B.S. L.809 LL.B. 4650 Whitsett St.
Glickman, Stuart I. ................. '40 '68 4024 Radford Ave., Bldg. #3, Studio City
Gold, Jack J. ......................... '41 '71 C.999 L.1148 LL.B. 4109 Farmdale Ave.
Goldberg, Jerome L., (AV) '33 '58 C&L.813 A.B., LL.B.
12001 Ventura Pl. (Studio City)
Graf, Justin ...................... '24 '52 C.112 B.A. L.426 LL.B. 12650 Riverside Dr.
Grossman, Edward ........................ '47 '80 C.174 B.A. L.208 J.D. 5531 Corteen Pl.
Haddix, Lance ........................ '39 '65 C.145 B.A. L.912 J.D. 4605 Lankershim Blvd.
Halpern, H. Russell ................. '47 '71 C.999 L.1148 LL.B. 6180 Laurel Canyon Blvd.

**Harris, Rand F., A Prof. Corp., Law Offices of**
**(See Los Angeles)**

**Harwick, Maurice, (AV) '33 '58 C.999 L.809 J.D.**
**P.O. Box 16119, 91615**
**Telephone: 310-829-0231 Facsimile: 310-828-1811**
**Reference: Union Bank, Santa Monica Office.**

Helm, Ralph B. ............................ '21 '50 C.472 L.800 LL.B. 4605 Lankershim Blvd.‡
Henrikson, Harold L. ..................... '17 '58 C.502 A.B. L.309 LL.B. 12145 Hessy St.‡
Hilsen, Linda Teal, (AV) ......... '50 '79 C.1109 B.A. L.1137 J.D. 11300 Weddington St.
Hoiby, Glenn W. ........................ '37 '65 C.112 B.S. L.800 J.D. 11240 Magnolia Blvd.
Holland, Thomas L. ........................ '43 '74 C.112 B.A. L.1068 J.D. 12952 Blairwood
Hurley, Andrew J. ...................... '17 '42 C.757 B.A. L.128 LL.B. 1130 Weddington St.
Hurley, Joseph G., (AV) ........................ '27 '53 C.757 L.128 J.D. P.O. Box 590
Jackson, Glenn K., (AV) .................... '47 '76 C.112 B.S. L.1095 J.D. [G.K.Jackson]
Jackson, Theodore ................... '35 '62 C.1043 L.426 LL.B. 3051 Dona Marta St.
Jackson, Glenn K., A Prof. Law Corp., (AV) .................. 12034 Riverside Dr., 2nd Fl.
**Johanson, Erick T.** ....................... '47 '82 C.871 B.S. L.1127 J.D. [L.Tobin&Assoc.]
*PRACTICE AREAS: Workers Compensation (100%, 100).
Johnson, Gary R. '55 '79 C&L.352 B.B.A., J.D.
(adm. in IA; not adm. in CA) 13011 Woodbridge, Studio City
Kagan, Benjamin ......................... '31 '58 C.112 B.A. L.1068 J.D. 6527 Morse Ave.
Kalb, Marcus .............. '18 '56 C.112 B.S. L.426 LL.B. 12403 Ventura Ct., Studio City‡
**Kamon, Ellen B.**, (AV) ........................ '51 '82 C.112 A.B. L.1095 J.D. [Rosato&S.]
*PRACTICE AREAS: Commercial Litigation; Prosecution Insurance Defense Law; Bad Faith Law.
Katz, Jay Lawrence ................. '41 '77 C.339 B.A. L.398 J.D. 12650 Riverside Dr.
Kendall, Jack L. ........................ '43 '74 L.1095 J.D. 5320 Laurel Canyon Blvd.
Kenealy, Barry H., (AV) ................ '28 '64 C.259 L.426 LL.B. 4605 Lankershim
Kenealy, James N., Jr., (AV) ........... '26 '53 C.1097 L.426 J.D. 4605 Lankershim Blvd.
Kirshenbaum, William B. '59 '84
C.659 B.S. L.1068 J.D. V.P. & Gen. Coun., Aviation Equip., Inc.
Klinger, Tobias G., (AV) ........... '11 '39 C.112 A.B. L.178 J.D. 4605 Lankershim Blvd.
Kobrin, Helena Kempner ............ '48 '78 C.1019 B.A. L.776 J.D. 7629 Fulton Ave.
Kreger, Melvin J., (AV) ............................ '37 '78 L.1221 J.D. [M.J.Kreger]
Kreger, Melvin J., A Law Corporation, (AV) ........................ 11424 Burbank BLvd.
Kulick, Andrew Jay '58 '88
C.800 B.A. L.1136 J.D. Corp. Coun., HHL Financial Servs., Inc.
Lang, Michael J. ......................... '— '84 C.846 B.S. L.809 J.D. 13047 Ventura Blvd.
Langman, Wendell '34 '61 C&L.966 B.S., J.D.
(adm. in WI; not adm. in CA) Century Natl. Ins. Co.
Lee, Edward R. ......................... '29 '57 C.112 L.426 7135 Coldwater Canyon Ave.
Leitner, Anthony U. ....................... '34 '58 C.145 B.A. L.569 LL.B. P.O. Box 9819
**Lerman, Jeffrey E.** ...................... '61 '87 C.112 B.A. L.426 J.D. [▣ Rosato&S.]
*PRACTICE AREAS: Defense Personal Injury; Defense Professional Liability; Plaintiff Personal Injury.
Levin, Asher A. ...................... '50 '76 C.112 A.B. L.1188 J.D. 12650 Riverside Dr.
**Liebherr, Donald P.**, (AV) ............ '48 '76 C.1097 B.A. L.1095 J.D. [L.Tobin&Assoc.]
*PRACTICE AREAS: Workers Compensation Law.
Lipton, Harley L. ............................... '52 '79 L.1221 J.D. 12427 Ventura Blvd.
Lipton, Hugh A., (AV) ................. '43 '70 C.1095 L.809 J.D. 11320 Magnolia Blvd.
Long, Doris J. .......................... '42 '76 C.112 B.A. L.809 J.D. 6663 Ethel Ave.
Loo, Jack R. ............................... '46 '78 C.763 B.A. L.1068 J.D. P.O. Box 16376
**Louie, Peter E.** ........................ '64 '91 C.112 B.S. L.990 J.D. [▣ L.Tobin&Assoc.]
*PRACTICE AREAS: Workers Compensation (100%, 100).
Magaram, Teresa R. ................... '55 '79 C.112 B.A. L.426 J.D. 12115 Magnolia Blvd.
**Magloff, Michael B.**, (AV) ............. '40 '66 C.1036 B.A. L.1066 LL.B. [Rosato&S.]
*PRACTICE AREAS: Commercial Litigation; Prosecution Insurance Defense Law; Bad Faith Law.
Malone, John Anthony .............. '57 '88 C&L.02 B.Sc., LL.B. 11300 Weddington St.
McCaul, Paul F. ........... '41 '67 C.569 B.E.E. L.273 J.D. 4605 Lankershim Blvd. (Pat.)
McCurdy, John D., (A Professional Corporation), (AV) '44 '72
C.768 B.A. L.1066 J.D. 4605 Lamkershim Blvd.
Mestad, John B. ........... '21 '61 C.55 L.809 LL.B. 3748 Wrightwood Dr. (Studio City)‡
Meyer, Douglas O. '50 '78 C.1209 B.A. L.1095 J.D.
Asst. V.P. & Coun., Pierce Bros. Mortuaries & Cemeteries
Miller, Philip G. .................... '46 '72 C.112 B.S. L.178 J.D. 12650 Riverside Dr.‡
**Mooney, F. Bentley, Jr.**, (AV) .......... '36 '72 C&L.1095 B.A., LL.B. [F.B.Mooney,Jr.]
*PRACTICE AREAS: Business Law; Estate Planning; Medicaid Eligibility Planning; Asset Protection.

**Mooney, F. Bentley, Jr., A Law Corporation, (AV) ▣**
**4605 Lankershim Boulevard, Suite 718, 91602**
**Telephone: 818-769-4221 213-877-3902 FAX: 818-769-5002**
**F. Bentley Mooney, Jr.**
**Practice limited to Business Law, Estate Planning and Probate Law.**
*See Professional Biographies, NORTH HOLLYWOOD, CALIFORNIA*

Morrow, Robert E. ................. '08 '48 C.813 A.B. L.1001 LL.B. 4623 Cartwright Ave.‡
Myhrvold, Alton A., (BV) ................. '28 '62 C.791 L.809 LL.B. 4635 Bellflower
Nesh, William ...................... '50 '78 C.705 B.A. L.1137 J.D. 10933 Camarillo St.
Nichols, Roger J., (AV) .................. '30 '58 C.112 B.A. L.1066 J.D. [R.J.Nichols]
Nichols, Roger J., A Prof. Corp., Law Offices of, (AV) ......... 5100 Riverton Ave. Ste. 12
Oakley, Robert D. ...................... '27 '72 C.208 L.809 J.D. 6140 Fulcher Ave.
**Oliphant, John H.** '43 '73 C&L.477 B.S., J.D.
Sr. V.P., Legal Affs. & Gen. Coun., Technicolor, Inc.
Oliver, Aaron ............................ '13 '38 C.309 A.B. L.665 LL.B. 11507 Moorpark‡
Oliver, Leavy W. ....................... '48 '78 C.747 B.A. L.1066 J.D. 11470 Cumpston St.
Ostrin, Benjamin B. .................... '16 '40 C.102 L.1009 LL.B. 11313 Weddington St.‡
Paley, Alvin ........................ '22 '56 C.906 B.S. L.1001 LL.B. 12650 Riverside Dr.‡
Pierce, Justin W. ........................ '54 '84 C.112 B.A. L.426 J.D. 12505 Hesby St.
Potter, Lee, (Miss) ................................ '— '67 C.999 L.809 6167 Lankershim Blvd.
Prelock, Edward P. '34 '64 C&L.378 LL.B.
(adm. in KS; not adm. in CA) Dir., Legal Contract Affs., Teamsters Local 399
Pucker, Amy L. .......................... '64 '89 C.112 B.A. L.1066 J.D. Film Roman
Rainer, I. Warren ....................... '14 '38 C.46 B.S. L.36 LL.B. 11472 Laurel Crest Rd.
Reff, Herbert L. ........................ '30 '62 C.112 B.S. L.809 LL.B. 12650 Riverside Dr.
**Robbins, Peter** ........................ '53 '80 C.112 B.A. L.426 J.D. [▣ L.Tobin&Assoc.]
*LANGUAGES: Spanish.
*PRACTICE AREAS: Workers Compensation (100%).
Robinson, Morris ...................... '15 '39 C.563 L.880 LL.B. 5914 Wilkinson Ave.‡
Roller, Barbara Rose ................. '52 '78 C.174 B.A. L.426 J.D. 12350 Addison St.
**Rosato, Ralph L.**, (AV) ................... '48 '74 C.426 B.A. L.1068 J.D. [Rosato&S.]
*PRACTICE AREAS: Commercial Litigation; Prosecution Insurance Defense Law; Bad Faith Law.

**Rosato & Samuels, A Professional Corporation, (AV)**
**R & S Plaza, 11650 Riverside Drive, 91602-1066**
**Telephone: 818-753-9200 Telecopier: 818-766-2507**
**Ralph L. Rosato; Cary S. Samuels; Ellen B. Kamon; Michael B. Magloff;—Jeffrey E. Lerman; Pamela Sirkin; Ann C. Schneider; Eduardo A. Brito; Cameron H. Totten; Nathan D. Wirtschafter.**
**General Civil Trial and Appellate Practice in all Courts. Life, Health and Disability Insurance Claims and Defense including Managed Care and ERISA, Professional Liability, Errors and Omissions**

(This Listing Continued)

**Rosato & Samuels, A Professional Corporation (Continued)**

**Insurance Coverage and Legal Malpractice, General and Commercial Property and Casualty Defense, Employment Law, Business Litigation, Commercial Litigation, Entertainment Litigation, Products Liability, Surplus Lines and Special Risk Insurance Defense, Real Estate Litigation, including the Representation of Brokers and Real Estate Agents, Property Law, Escrow and Title Matters, Structural Defense and Premises Liability, Partnership Disputes and Breaches of Fiduciary Duties as between partners.**

*See Professional Biographies, NORTH HOLLYWOOD, CALIFORNIA*

Rosenthal, Robert F. '37 '63 C.112 B.S. L.800 LL.B. 4535 Radford Ave.
Rubin, Gene L. '26 '52 C.112 B.A. L.426 LL.B. 3301 Laurel Canyon Blvd.
Said, Patricia H. '48 '85 C&L.061 B.S., L.L.B. 6454 Coldwater Canyon
Samson, Lawrence A., (BV) '58 '83 C.112 B.A. L.1148 J.D. [G.K.Jackson]
**Samuels, Cary S.**, (AV) '48 '74 C.112 B.A. L.809 J.D. [Rosato&S.]
*PRACTICE AREAS: Commercial Litigation; Prosecution Insurance Defense Law; Bad Faith Law.
Sauer, John A. '40 '76 C.999 B.A. L.809 J.D. 6906 Bluebell Ave.
**Schlosberg, Phillip**, (AV) '46 '71 C.112 B.A. L.1065 J.D. [P.Schlosberg]

**Schlosberg, Phillip, A Professional Corporation, (AV)**
**12650 Riverside Drive, 91607-3492**
**Telephone: 818-755-4848 Fax: 818-760-2583**
**Phillip Schlosberg.**
**Real Property, Business Litigation, Domestic Relations Law and Personal Injury.**
*See Professional Biographies, NORTH HOLLYWOOD, CALIFORNIA*

Schmidt, Rocky '58 '83 C.585 B.A. L.1068 J.D. 4640 Vantage Ave.
**Schneider, Ann C.** '62 '91 C.1097 B.A. L.112 J.D. [Rosato&S.]
*PRACTICE AREAS: Civil Trial; Family Law.
Schnoebelen, Michael '16 '51 C.112 A.B. L.426 J.D. 4240 Bluebell Ave.‡
Schonfeld, Arthur D., (BV) '41 '68 C.112 B.A. L.1068 J.D. 6350 Laurel Canyon Blvd.
Schwartz, Robert A., (AV) '50 '76 C.966 B.A. L.809 J.D. 11650 Riverside Dr.
Selimos, Dean J. '54 '82 C.112 B.A. L.1127 J.D. 4920 Lankershim Blvd.
Silverton, Lawrence E., (AV) '25 '53 C.293 B.A. L.477 J.D. 12650 Riverside Dr.
**Sirkin, Pamela** '— '90 C.1077 B.A. L.809 J.D. [Rosato&S.]
*PRACTICE AREAS: Civil Litigation.
Solomon, Davia '50 '84 C.1097 B.S.N. L.1136 J.D. P.O. Box 590
Steed, Michael R. '49 '74 C&L.426 B.A., J.D. 3838 Vantage
**Stettler, David M.** '59 '90 C.589 B.A. L.999 J.D. [L.Tobin&Assoc.]
Straw, Bill '40 '68 C.383 B.S. L.1066 J.D. 11715 Blix St.
Streimer, Laura Ann '57 '86 C.112 B.A. L.446 J.D.
Dir., Valley Rights Proj., Bet Tzedek Legal Servs.
Struck, MaryAnn K. '36 '79 L.1127 J.D. 4318 Bellingham Ave.
Susman, Benjamin L., (AV) '24 '51 C.999 L.800 J.D. 12843 Sarah St., Studio City‡
Tenner, James L., (P.C.), (BV) '31 '58 C.112 A.B. L.809 LL.B. 11733 Victory Blvd.
**Tobin, Lawrence L.**, (BV) '47 '80 C.679 B.S. L.809 J.D. [L.Tobin&Assoc.]
*PRACTICE AREAS: Workers Compensation law (100%).

**Tobin, L., & Associates, A Law Corporation, (AV)**
**11300 Weddington Street, P.O. Box 978, 91603-0978**
**Telephone: 818-760-8100 Fax: 818-760-8132**
**Lawrence L. Tobin; Donald P. Liebherr; David B. Brotman; Erick T. Johanson; David M. Stettler; Peter E. Louie;—Peter Robbins; Jeffrey R. Ward.**
**Workers Compensation Defense.**

**Totten, Cameron H.** '69 '95 C.1349 B.A. L.861 J.D. [Rosato&S.]
*PRACTICE AREAS: Health Care Litigation; Professional Liability.
VanGelder, Edward S. '42 '68 C.112 B.A. L.1068 J.D. 5818 Wilkinson Ave.
Vein, Jon F. '63 '89 C.112 B.S. L.309 J.D. Film Roman, Inc.
**Ward, Jeffrey R.** '61 '92 C.112 B.S. L.1049 J.D. [L.Tobin&Assoc.]
*PRACTICE AREAS: Worker's Compensation Law.
Wasserman, Larry E. '50 '76 C.112 B.A. L.426 J.D. 11650 Riverside Dr.
Waters, B. Nolan '50 '80 C.800 B.A. L.809 J.D. 11483 Killion St.
Weisel, Ben '14 '56 C.597 B.S. L.809 LL.B. 12752 Califa St.‡
Wildes, Clarence A. '30 '78 C.1179 M.S. L.1114 J.D. 10621 Burbank Blvd.

**Williams, Berges & Sanford**
**(See Los Angeles)**

**Wirtschafter, Nathan D.** '— '95 C.367 B.A. L.426 J.D. [Rosato&S.]
*PRACTICE AREAS: Litigation; Professional Liability; Insurance Defense; Exempt Organization Tax Law.
Wohl, Leila L. '34 '78 C.1097 B.A. L.809 J.D. 12722 Riverside Dr.‡
Ziff, Sheldon M. '30 '52 C.112 B.S. L.800 LL.B. 12512 Chandler Blvd.

**Zimring, Stuart D.**
**(See Los Angeles)**

Zugelter, Frank L. '28 '58 C&L.150 B.S., LL.B.
(adm. in OH; not adm. in CA; Pat.) 10221 Riverside Dr.

## NORTH PALM SPRINGS, —, *Riverside Co.*

Coulter, Ray R. '33 '64 C&L.800 Phar.D., LL.B. Chf. Fin. Offr., Wintec, Ltd.
Noble, Frederick W. '39 '67 C.112 B.A. L.1068 LL.B. 19020 N. Indian Dr.‡

## NORTHRIDGE, —, *Los Angeles Co.*

(Part of the incorporated City of Los Angeles)

Abell, Jeffrey M. '47 '72 C.112 A.B. L.800 J.D. 9425 Balcom Ave.‡
Agan, Shirley A., (BV) '48 '77 C.112 B.A. L.426 J.D. 19360 Rinaldi St., Porter Ranch
Alexander, Norman D., Jr. '30 '56 C&L.623 B.B.A., LL.B. 10100 Topeka Dr.
Anderson, Michael H. '40 '66 C.763 B.S. L.61 J.D. 1011 Vanalden Ave.‡
Arnall, Christina M. '49 '79 C.909 B.A. L.1095 J.D. 9420 Reseda Blvd.
Batson, Terrilyn '57 '84 C.1075 B.A. L.1068 J.D. Coun., Great Western Bk.
Beal, James E., (BV) '34 '71 C.870 B.S. L.426 J.D. 9045 Corbin Ave., 2nd Fl.
Berman, Alan B. '58 '83 C&L.228 A.B., J.D. 9828 Sylvia Ave.
Boehm, H. G. '30 '75 C.112 B.S. L.1077 10329 Melvin Ave.‡
Bohl, Phillip W. '24 '52 C.494 L.1035 LL.B. West Publishing Co.
Bricker, Elizabeth Anne '— '63 C.341 A.B. L.262 LL.B. 8421 Nestle Ave.
Chadwick, Donald E. '34 '72 C.755 L.1095 J.D. 9003 Reseda Blvd.
Chagnon, Andre J. '44 '76 C.321 A.B. L.765 J.D. 18645 Gledhill St.‡
Chambers, Marks S. '48 '77 C.112 A.B. L.990 J.D. 10126 Reseda Blvd.
Cohen, Howard I. '35 '76 C.453 B.S. L.1095 J.D. 19601 Nordhoff St.‡
Cohen, Sheldon, (AV) '32 '73 C.112 B.S. L.1095 J.D. 8363 Reseda Blvd.
Cole, Peggy S. '26 '50 C&L.813 A.B., LL.B. 17545 Sunburst St.‡
Consiglio, Michael E. '40 '73 C.1077 B.S. L.426 LL.B. 18606 Dearborn St.
**Dambach, James J.**, (AV) '31 '58 C.112 B.S. L.1068 LL.B. [Dambach&D.]

**Dambach & Dambach, (AV)**
**9322 Lasaine Avenue, 91327**
**Telephone: 818-886-4632 Fax: 818-886-4527**
**Members of Firm: James J. Dambach.**
**Estate Planning, Probate and Trust Law.**
**References: Bank of America National Trust & Savings Assn. (Canoga Park Main Office); American Savings (Canoga Park Office).**

Davis, Lawrence H. '55 '85 C.112 B.S. L.809 J.D. 11344 Quail Creek Rd.
Degerman, David C. '52 '82 C.494 B.A. L.1066 J.D. 8550 Balboa Blvd.
Dersh, Irving '29 '74 C&L.1095 B.A., J.D. 19012 Kingsbury St.
Docan, Carol A. '48 '73 C.112 B.A. L.426 J.D. Prof. of Bus. Law, Calif. State Univ.
Dudor, Walter J. '54 '79 C.1077 B.S. L.800 J.D. 19559 Vintage St.
Econom, Kim '60 '91 C.1077 B.S. L.426 J.D. 8828 Reseda Blvd.
Ferreri, Carlo, (BV) '27 '53 C&L.608 B.A., J.D. 8932 Reseda Blvd.‡
Field, Theodore '23 '58 C.112 B.S. L.809 LL.B. 9420 Reseda Blvd.
Fleming, Leslie L. '49 '75 C.112 B.A. L.809 J.D. 9036 Reseda Blvd.
Fred, Arthur W. '06 '28 C&L.107 LL.B. 10666 Beckford Ave.‡
Garon, Myron L. '20 '47 C.494 L.426 LL.B. 19420 Business Center Dr.
Gavron, Denise H. '57 '83 C.112 B.A. L.426 J.D. 12050 Dunblane Ave.
Geissler, Paul R. '52 '80 C.800 B.A. L.1221 J.D. 8520 Balboa Blvd.
Hanson, L. Thaxton '20 '54 C.339 B.S. L.477 J.D. 9816 Belmar Ave.
Hart, Mark A. '50 '75 C.1077 B.A. L.426 J.D. 19360 Rinaldi St.
Hast, Patrick J., (AV) '40 '69 C.1097 B.S. L.1114 J.D. 9420 Reseda Blvd.
Hultman, Jeffrey J. '46 '75 C.184 B.S.E.E. L.809 J.D. Sr. Coun., Great Western Bk.
James, Barbara Law '32 '89 C.914 A.B. L.426 J.D. 11400 Edenburg Ave.
Katz, Howard F. '50 '77 C.1077 B.A. L.1095 J.D. 19214 Romar St.
Kaufman, Elizabeth, (BV) '48 '78 C.665 B.S. L.1095 J.D. 19350 Business Center Dr.
Keary, Merle '25 '55 C.846 B.A. L.809 LL.B. 8801 Reseda Blvd.
Kosasky, Mel J. '47 '79 L.765 J.D. 17423 Napa St.
Kriensky, Joseph '27 '75 C.588 B.S.E.E. L.1148 J.D. 10214 Topeka Dr.‡
Leland, Bonita Marie '52 '79 C.112 B.A. L.1095 J.D. 17210 Parthenia St.
Levun, Loretta K. '51 '78 C.273 B.A. L.809 J.D. P.O. Box 7275
Levy, Marvin '53 '81 C.1077 B.A. L.1095 J.D. 12251 Shady Hollow Ln.
Levy, Stuart '67 '92 C.112 B.A. L.276 J.D. 9839 Canby Ave.
Linger, Alexander '38 '80 C.331 B.A. L.1221 J.D. 8935 Garden Grove Ave. (Pat.)
Malak, Pamela Croft '52 '83 C&L.426 B.A., J.D. 17438 Chase St.
Mandell, Laurence H., (BV) '53 '78 C.1077 B.A. L.1095 J.D. 19400 Business Ctr. Dr.
Mandell, Robert J. '56 '87 C.330 B.A. L.809 J.D. 19400 Business Center Dr.
McLean, James Lankford '50 '76 C.945 A.B. L.692 J.D. P.O. Box 104
Miller, Gerald F. '30 '64 C.112 B.S. L.426 LL.B. [Miller&W.]
Miller & Wilets 17446 Napa St.
Niesen, Mark, (BV) '19 '54 C.563 B.S.S. L.809 J.D. 18950 San Jose St.
Obrien-Holcomb, Diane J. '64 '89 C.884 B.S. L.1009 J.D. 8550 Balboa Blvd.
O'Neal, Steven M., (BV) '49 '74 C.347 B.S. L.809 J.D. 8550 Balboa Blvd.
Pagan, John M. '53 '81 C.112 B.A. L.1136 J.D.
V.P., Claims & Asst. Chf. Coun., Surety Co. of Pacific
Pratt, William K. '39 '74 C.504 B.A. L.1095 J.D. 17420 Nordhoff St.
Reilly, Francis R. '24 '52 C.128 B.A.E. L.276 J.D.
(adm. in DC; not adm. in CA) 19000 Merridy St.‡
Richardson, Michael Gilles '57 '90 L.398 J.D. 8619 Reseda Blvd.
Riley, Dennis L. '40 '68 C&L.426 B.A., J.D. 9810 Amestoy Ave.
Sabatasse, H. James, (AV) '43 '70 C.999 L.809 J.D. 9420 Reseda Blvd.
Saltzman, Barbara R. '40 '92
C.339 B.S.N. L.424 J.D. Los Angeles Co. Dept. of Mental Health
Schatz, Gerald '24 '62 C.112 B.A. L.809 LL.B. 19420 Business Center Dr.‡
Scheppers, Ruth Clement '32 '76 C.800 B.S. L.1095 J.D. 18615 Dearborn St.
Slee, Dennis '38 '76 C.800 B.S. L.1095 J.D. 9036 Reseda Blvd.
Smith, Francis E., (AV) '23 '55 C.800 A.B. L.426 J.D. 9020 Reseda Blvd.
Smith, R. Milton, (AV) '25 '51 C.800 L.809 LL.B. 9440 Shoshone Ave.
Snoke, Robin S. D. '— '76 C&L.1077 B.A., J.D. 9010 Corbin St.
Sprouse, Kenneth M. '52 '86 C.112 M.S. L.426 J.D. 18213 Osborne St.
Stern, George '50 '77 C.112 B.A. L.1148 J.D. 9123 White Oak Ave.
Strumpf, Susan Feinberg '55 '81 C.112 B.A. L.426 J.D. 11800 Eddleston Dr.
Swenson, James S. '21 '50 C&L.494 B.S.L., LL.B.
(adm. in MN; not adm. in CA) 17500 Kinzie St.‡
Termini, Michael, (BV) '52 '80 C.1109 B.A. L.809 J.D. Pres., GDI Technologies
Thale, Melvin B. '16 '47 C&L.494 B.S.L., J.D. 7875 Texhoma Ave.
Turner, Perry E., (AV) '21 '59 C.679 B.S.E.E. L.800 J.D. P.O. Box 280880‡
Tyler, Robert F., (AV) '14 '40 C&L.174 B.A., LL.B. 9020 Reseda Blvd.
Van Valkenburg, Thomas D. '46 '76 C.642 L.1137 LL.B. 9020 Reseda Blvd., Ste. 206
Velasco, Dan O., (AV) '39 '65 C.770 L.426 LL.B. 11260 Wilbur Ave.
Victor, Toni L. '47 '75 C&L.546 A.B., J.D.
(adm. in NE; not adm. in CA) 10115 Donna Ave.
Volchok, Lester B. '23 '68 C.102 L.1095 LL.B. 8727 Tampa Ave., 2nd Fl.
Volchok, Paul M. '46 '74 C.1077 B.A. L.809 J.D. [Volchok,V.&Z.]
Volchok, Volchok & Zayon 8727 Tampa Ave., 2nd Fl.
Warnberg, Alvin H. '13 '42 C.999 L.809 LL.B. 19318 Lemarsh St.
Waterstone, Stuart I. '42 '76 C.1097 B.A. L.426 J.D. 18937 Olympia St.
Weinreb, Lawrence A., (BV) '24 '51 C.112 L.809 LL.B. 19400 Business Center Dr.
Weisberger, Gerald L. '32 '72 C.1040 B.B.A. L.1095 J.D. 12252 High Glen Way‡
Whittingham, David K. '42 '81 9045 Corbin Ave., 2nd Fl.
Wilets, Jacquelyn G. '33 '64 C.966 B.S. L.426 LL.B. [Miller&W.] ‡
Williger, Sheldon, (BV) '23 '50 L.146 LL.B. 9521 Geyser Ave.‡
Zayon, Herman '46 '74 C.1077 B.A. L.809 J.D. [Volchok,V.&Z.]

## NORTH SHERMAN OAKS, —, *Los Angeles Co.*

(See Van Nuys)

## NORWALK, 94,279, *Los Angeles Co.*

Barnett, Burt, (AV) '39 '66 C.1042 A.B. L.1066 J.D. [B.Barnett]
Barnett, Burt, A Law Corporation, (AV) 12749 Norwalk Blvd.
Birney, William J., Jr. '31 '61 C.712 B.A. L.809 LL.B. Supr. Ct. J.
Blye, Steven P., (AV) '55 '84 C.112 B.A. L.809 J.D. 12749 Norwalk Blvd.
**Brau, Paul D.**, (BV) '52 '77 C.112 B.A. L.990 J.D. [C.R.Weldon]
*PRACTICE AREAS: Personal Injury; Medical Malpractice; Legal Malpractice; Products Liability; Workers Compensation.
Conway, Chris R. '41 '67 C.605 A.B. L.800 J.D. Supr. Ct. J.
**Daley, E. Neal** '51 '76 C.112 B.A. L.990 J.D. [C.R.Weldon]
*PRACTICE AREAS: Personal Injury; Medical Malpractice; Legal Malpractice; Product Liability; Workers Compensation.
Deyo, Richard N., (AV) '40 '74 C.766 B.A. L.1097 J.D. 12749 Norwalk Blvd.
Di Loreto, Joseph E. '41 '67 C.670 B.A. L.426 J.D. Supr. Ct. J.
**Dixon, Paul R.**, (BV) '53 '78 C.940 B.A. L.61 J.D. [C.R.Weldon]
*PRACTICE AREAS: Personal Injury; Medical Malpractice; Legal Malpractice; Product Liability; Workers Compensation.
Edson, James W. '31 '60 C.684 A.B. L.800 J.D. Supr. Ct. J.
Einstein, Robert '24 '52 C.800 A.B. L.809 LL.B. Supr. Ct. J.
Elliott, Forest L., Jr. '40 '72 C.587 B.S.B.A. L.426 J.D. Dep. Pub. Def. IV
Frisco, Charles E. '22 '51 C&L.426 LL.B. Supr. Ct. J.
Fukushima, Paul J., (BV) '50 '75 C.668 B.A. L.228 J.D. 12749 Norwalk Blvd.
Gibson, Leonard W., (BV) '31 '61 C.112 B.S. L.1068 LL.B. 12749 Norwalk Blvd.
Gomez, Marcus '53 '79 C.668 B.A. L.1068 J.D. 12440 Firestone Blvd.
Goza, Harry V., Jr., (BV) '18 '47 C.813 A.B. L.1065 J.D. 12749 S. Norwalk Blvd.
Holmes, Douglas R., (AV) '52 '78 C.1097 B.A. L.809 J.D. [Hopper&H.]
Hopper, James R., (AV) '45 '79 C.1109 B.A. L.1137 J.D. [Hopper&H.]

CAA420P

Hopper & Holmes, (AV) .......................14714 Carmenita Rd.
**Jacobsma, Laila Havre** ............... '58 '93 C&L.1137 B.S.L., J.D. [ⓐ C.R.Weldon]
*PRACTICE AREAS: Personal Injury Law; Medical Malpractice; Legal Malpractice; Product Liability Law; Workers' Compensation.
Kramer, Randy, (AV) ............ '49 '75 C.1044 B.A. L.1049 J.D. [R.Kramer]
Kramer, Randy, A Law Corporation, (AV) ............ 12749 Norwalk Blvd.
Marotta, Alfred E., (AV) ............ '41 '69 C.1077 B.A. L.1148 J.D. [Marotta&R.]
Marotta & Ramos, (AV) ............ 12440 E. Firestone, Suite 208
McDaniel, Robert C. ............ '36 '65 C.112 A.B. L.1066 LL.B. 12749 Norwalk Blvd.
McKnew, Thomas I., Jr. ............ '36 '60 C.711 A.B. L.446 J.D. Supr. Ct. J.
Miller-Pasewark, Judith L. ............ '53 '78 C&L.990 B.A., J.D. Women's Law Ctr.

**Miller, Paul H.**
**(See Santa Fe Springs)**

**Mitchell, Robert E., (BV) '28 '56 C&L.800 B.S., LL.B.**
**13915 South San Antonio Drive, P.O. Box 365, 90650**
**Telephone: 310-863-8736 Fax: 310-868-7266**
***PRACTICE AREAS: Corporate Law; Estate Planning; Real Estate Law; Business Litigation. Corporate, Estate Planning, Real Estate and Business Litigation Law.**
*See Professional Biographies, NORWALK, CALIFORNIA*

Mitchell, Susan A. ............ '56 '92 C.800 L.1137 J.D. 13915 S. San Antonio Dr.
Nguyen, Catherine T. ............ '52 '91 C.616 B.S. L.1136 J.D. [ⓐ Hopper&H.]
Nunes, Joseph G. ............ '20 '60 C.112 B.S. L.426 LL.B. 12440 Firestone Blvd.
Pratt, Daniel J. ............ '50 '77 C.1042 B.A. L.1137 J.D. 12720 Norwalk Blvd.
Prukop, Harold K. ............ '33 '59 C&L.426 B.S., LL.B. Dep. Dist. Atty.
Ramirez, Javier B. ............ '43 '73 C.763 B.A. L.800 J.D. 12749 Norwalk Blvd.
Ramos, Manuel ............ '53 '80 C.668 B.A. L.800 J.D. [Marotta&R.]
Ringwalt, Charles C., (AV) ............ '31 '59 C.674 A.B. L.1065 LL.B. 12440 Firestone Blvd.
Rodriguez, Carlos ............ '37 '66 C.112 B.S. L.1068 LL.B. Wkrs. Comp. J.
Saria, Robert J. ............ '60 '87 C.800 B.A. L.809 J.D. 16323 S. Graystone Ave.
Schuster, Dennis M. ............ '48 '80 C.426 B.A. L.990 J.D. 12749 Norwalk Blvd.
Seymour, Ernest J., (AV) ............ '22 '50 C.611 L.800 J.D. 12749 Norwalk Blvd.
Simpson, C. Robert, Jr. ............ '25 '50 C.503 B.S. L.188 LL.B. Supr. Ct. J.
Stark, Ronald M. ............ '43 '75 C.1042 B.A. L.809 J.D. 12749 Norwalk Blvd.
Stevens, Peter H. ............ '22 '51 C&L.800 J.D. Ret. Supr. Ct. J.
Stone, Morris ............ '30 '57 C.800 B.S. L.1068 J.D. 12749 Norwalk Blvd.
Sutton, James M., Jr. ............ '32 '61 C&L.800 A.B., LL.B. Supr. Ct. J.
Tarle, Norman P. ............ '50 '76 C.563 B.A. L.1068 J.D. Supr. Ct. Comr.
Taylor, H. George ............ '30 '57 C.800 B.S. L.1068 J.D. Ct. Comr., Supr. Ct.
**Turner, Jerry D.**, (BV) ............ '37 '72 C.999 L.809 J.D. [ⓐ C.R.Weldon]
*PRACTICE AREAS: Personal Injury; Medical Malpractice; Legal Malpractice; Product Liability.
Walker, J. Kimball ............ '24 '49 C&L.972 J.D. Supr. Ct. J.‡

**Weldon, Charles R., (AV) '33 '57 C.1042 B.A. L.800 J.D. BB**
**Suite 104 Southeast Law Center, 12749 Norwalk Boulevard, P.O. Box 1110, 90651**
**Telephone: 310-864-3737 FAX: 310-863-9962**
***PRACTICE AREAS: Personal Injury; Medical Malpractice; Legal Malpractice; Product Liability. —Jerry D. Turner; E. Neal Daley; Paul R. Dixon; Paul D. Brau; Laila Havre Jacobsma.**
**General Civil and Trial Practice in all State and Federal Courts. Personal Injury, Products Liability, Medical and Legal Malpractice and Negligence Law.**
*See Professional Biographies, NORWALK, CALIFORNIA*

**Wieder, Catherine Grant**
**(See Cerritos)**

Zandona, Anthony ............ '49 '78 C.415 B.A. L.1137 J.D. 14125 San Antonio Dr.
Zeitountsian, Patricia A. ............ '47 '78 C.112 B.A. L.1136 J.D. Women's Law Center

## NOVATO, 47,585, *Marin Co.*

Ash, Robert Michael ............ '44 '72 C.373 B.A. L.326 J.D. P.O. Box 1567
Auwbrey, Robert G. ............ '29 '63 C.766 L.310 J.D. 1108 Clayton St.
Bates, Richard A. '61 '87 C&L.190 B.S.B.A., J.D.
(adm. in IN; not adm. in CA) Sr. Coun., Fireman's Fund Ins. Co.

**Berger, Kahn, Shafton, Moss, Figler, Simon & Gladstone, (AV)**
**A Professional Corporation including a Professional Corporation**
**Suite 304, 1701 Novato Boulevard, 94947⊙**
**Telephone: 415-899-1770 Telecopier: 415-899-1769**
**Robert W. Mehr; Roger M. Vosburg.**
**General Civil and Trial Practice in all State and Federal Courts. Corporation, Real Estate, Music and Entertainment Law and Intellectual Property, Labor and Insurance Law.**
**Los Angeles, California Office: 4215 Glencoe Avenue (Marina L.C. Del Rey), 90292-5634. Telephone: 310-821-9000. Telecopier: 310-578-6178.**
**Irvine, California Office: Suite 650, 2 Park Plaza, 92614. Telephone: 714-474-1880. Telecopier: 714-474-7265.**
**San Diego, California Office: 402 W. Broadway, Suite 400, 92101. Telephone: 619-236-8602. Telecopier: 619-236-0812.**
**Bend, Oregon Office: P.O. Box 1407, 97709. Telephone: 541-388-1400. Telecopier: 541-388-4731.**
*See Professional Biographies, NOVATO, CALIFORNIA*

Bragman, Lawrence Wayne ............ '54 '82 C.659 B.A. L.765 J.D. 1202 Grant Ave.
Brayton, Alan R. ............ '49 '77 C.1070 B.S. L.1066 J.D. [Brayton H.C.]
Brayton Harley Curtis ............ 222 Rush Landing Rd.
Carter, Edwin F. (Ted) ............ '37 '78 C.188 B.A. L.284 J.D. 1450 Grant Ave.
Cincotta, Antone G., Jr. ............ '30 '57 C.767 B.S. L.1065 J.D. 790 McClay Rd.
Cleek, Robert J. ............ '49 '78 C.767 B.A. L.284 J.D. [Whitener&C.]
Cohen, Molly E. ............ '35 '60 C.104 A.B. L.976 LL.B. 43 Caribe Isle‡
Cooke, Theodore ............ '29 '89 C.1016 B.A. L.1227 J.D. Marin Mun. Water Dist.
Corey, Joseph P. ............ '66 '91 C.767 B.A. L.588 J.D. 999 Grant Ave.
Crist, Shelia K. ............ '65 '92 L.284 J.D. 999 Grant Ave.
Crocker, Katherine H. ............ '55 '80 C.112 A.B. L.1066 J.D. Asst. V.P. & Asst. Gen. Coun.
Curtis, Francine S. ............ '36 '82 C.145 L.765 J.D. [Brayton H.C.]
Daly, Jeffrey N. ............ '41 '66 C.813 A.B. L.178 LL.B. 352 Ignacio Blvd.
Davis, Charles A., (P.C.) ............ '43 '74 C.1097 B.S. L.284 J.D. 7100 Redwood Blvd.
DeGeller, Donald J. ............ '25 '53 C.768 A.B. L.770 LL.B. 2725 Topaz Dr.‡
Dobson, Richard E. '46 '72 C.112 A.B. L.1066 J.D.
V.P. & Gen. Coun., The Fund American Cos., Inc. (⊙Greenwich, Conn.)
Donadio, David R. ............ '63 '91 C.659 B.A. L.767 J.D. 999 Grant Ave.
DuFort, George H., (A P.C.) ............ '29 '60 C.112 B.A. L.767 J.D. 313 Fairway Dr.
Elin, Catherine A. '50 '92 C.569 B.A. L.564 J.D.
(adm. in NJ; not adm. in CA) 346 School Rd.‡
Engelberg, Claire ............ '21 '54 C.102 L.1066 4 Birdie Dr.‡
Esquivel, Teodoro F. '44 '79 C.112 B.A. L.796 J.D.
(adm. in TX; not adm. in CA) Pres., Escolta Corp.
Farmer, Robert ............ '36 '79 C.623 B.L.S. L.981 LL.B. 639 Midway Blvd.
Fish, Michael J. ............ '55 '81 C.1078 B.A. L.1065 J.D. [Fish&S.]
Fish & Snell, P.C., (BV) ............ 365 Bel Marin Keys Blvd., Ste., 102
Fleischman, Robert L. '49 '75 C.208 B.A. L.564 J.D.
Asst. V.P. & Assoc. Gen. Coun., Fireman's Fund Ins. Co.
Freitas, David M. '51 '78 C&L.767 B.A., J.D.
Asst. V.P. & Asst. Gen. Coun., Fireman's Fund Ins. Co.

Geagan, James, (AV) ............ '47 '76 C.602 B.A. L.767 J.D. 222 Rush Landing Rd.
Gildea, James B. ............ '48 '75 C.112 B.A. L.1065 J.D. 42 Washington St.‡
Glusman, Paul '47 '75 C.112 B.A. L.284 J.D.
Asst. V.P. & Asst. Gen. Coun., Fireman's Fund Ins. Co.
Grijalva, Beth Nanninga '58 '86 C.840 B.F.A. L.846 J.D.
(adm. in TX; not adm. in CA) Sr. Coun.
Grijalva, Douglas Cole '49 '80 C.766 B.A. L.1066 J.D.
Asst. V.P. & Asst. Gen. Coun., Fireman's Fund Ins. Co.
Grinnell, Daniel V. ............ '46 '80 C.31 A.B. L.1019 J.D. 934 Bel Marin Keys Blvd.
Grundstrom, Ed V., (BV) ............ '26 '56 C.800 A.B. L.813 LL.B. 1682 Novato Blvd.
Gunheim, Erik S. ............ '59 '88 C.1078 B.A. L.767 J.D. [Gunheim,P.&G.]
Gunheim, Gunnar G., (AV) ............ '25 '59 C.112 B.A. L.765 J.D. [Gunheim,P.&G.]
Gunheim, Phillips & Gunheim, (AV) ............ Ste., 350, 1682 Novato Blvd.
Hand, James L. ............ '46 '81 C.112 B.A. L.813 J.D. 999 Grant Ave.
Harley, Philip A. '47 '74 C&L.900 B.A., J.D.
(adm. in KS; not adm. in CA) [Brayton H.C.]
**Hawkins, Laura Tracy** ............ '51 '86 C.112 A.B. L.1227 J.D. [Palmer,J.H.&S.]⊙
*PRACTICE AREAS: Family Law; Bankruptcy Law.
Heon, Larry L. ............ '33 '66 C.766 B.S. L.284 LL.B. 118 Wild Horse Valley Dr.

**Hirsch, Richard A. '42 '69 C.309 B.A. L.602 J.D.**
**7665 Redwood Boulevard, Suite 200, 94945**
**Telephone: 415-898-9979 FAX: 415-897-5316**
**Real Estate, Transactional, Constructional-Transactional and Litigation. Real Estate Litigation.**

Holland, Janet M. '46 '72 C&L.767 B.A., J.D.
Asst. V.P. & Asst. Gen. Coun., Fireman's Fund Ins. Co.
Hopkins, Linda M. ............ '48 '86 C.112 B.A. L.1227 J.D. 999 Grant Ave.
Huffman, Darlene A. ............ '56 '89 C.1036 A.B. L.1066 J.D. Coun., Fireman's Fund Ins. Co.
Jennings, Hal Douglas ............ '— '84 C.112 B.A. L.767 J.D. 10 Germaine Pl.
Johnson, Dean L. ............ '54 '82 C.145 M.B.A. L.879 J.D. 95 Half Moon Rd.
**Jones, David Price**, (AV) ............ '35 '62 C.112 B.A. L.1066 J.D. [Palmer,J.H.&S.]
*PRACTICE AREAS: Business Law; Corporate Law; Estate Planning; Probate Law; Real Estate Law.
Jordan, Richard H. ............ '46 '74 C.911 B.A. L.1065 J.D. 250 Bel Marin Keys Blvd.
Karr, Denise M. ............ '61 '88 C.112 B.A. L.1065 J.D. 1150 East Ct.
Langan, Keith E. '55 '82 C.767 B.S. L.284 J.D.
Asst. V.P. & Gen. Coun., Fireman's Fund Ins. Co.
Lebell, Jeanette L. ............ '58 '89 C.112 B.A. L.1067 J.D. 750 Grant Ave.
Lee, Charles F., (BV) ............ '43 '69 C.267 B.S. L.1065 J.D. 505-A San Marin Dr.
Lee, Tommy R., (CV) ............ '48 '78 C.1078 B.A. L.1026 J.D. 1450 Grant Ave.
Lehmann, Harry V. ............ '47 '77 1450 Grant Ave.
Lewin, Werner S., Jr. ............ '54 '81 C.188 B.S. L.1065 J.D. 55 Cavalla Cay
Lewis, Jean Price ............ '41 '77 L.1026 LL.B. 1450 Grant Ave.
Lines, Kal W. ............ '16 '52 C.37 B.S. L.284 LL.B. 1 Goldfinch Ct.‡
Lueders, Scott W. ............ '51 '77 C.112 B.A. L.284 J.D. 750 Grant Ave.
MacKay, Robert F., (CV) ............ '32 '62 C.976 B.A. L.1066 LL.B. 1683 Novato Blvd.
Mahoney, Dorothy ............ '54 '88 C&L.1137 B.S., J.D. 999 Grant Ave.
Major, John F. ............ '46 '72 C.178 A.B. L.309 J.D. 377 San Luis Way
Marcus, Thomas L. ............ '53 '78 C.976 A.B. L.1066 J.D. Broderbund Software, Inc.
Meeker, Charles A. '25 '53 L.734 LL.B.
(adm. in MO; not adm. in CA) 72 Salvatore‡
**Mehr, Robert W.** ............ '61 '87 C.147 B.A. L.809 J.D. [Berger,K.S.M.F.S.&G.]
Miller, Margaret A. ............ '61 '86 C.112 B.A. L.284 J.D. 1173 Bel Marin Keys Blvd.
Mitlyng, Linda S. ............ '50 '84 C.446 B.A. L.831 J.D. 999 Grant Ave.
Murano, Gabriel S. ............ '46 '78 C.312 L.1095 J.D. 2549 Topaz Dr.
Noah, Oren P. ............ '57 '88 C.112 B.S. L.1065 J.D. 365 Bel Marin Keys Blvd.
Obninsky, Victor P., (CV) ............ '44 '70 C.178 B.A. L.1065 J.D. Two Commercial Blvd.
O'Keefe, Patrick F. '47 '78 C.986 B.A. L.1137 J.D.
V.P. & Assoc. Gen. Coun., Fireman's Fund Ins. Co.
**Palmer, Bruce M.**, (BV) ............ '48 '76 C.813 A.B. L.1065 J.D. [Palmer,J.H.&S.]
*PRACTICE AREAS: Real Estate Law; Business Law; Mobilehome Park Law.
**Palmer, Clark M.**, (BV) ............ '24 '51 C&L.813 A.B., LL.B. [Palmer,J.H.&S.]
*PRACTICE AREAS: Estate Planning; Probate Law.

**Palmer, Jones, Hawkins & Strong, (AV)**
**Suite 200, 7665 Redwood Boulevard, 94948⊙**
**Telephone: 415-892-1616 Fax: 415-897-5316**
**Email: LawPalmer@AOL.COM**
**Clark M. Palmer; David Price Jones; Bruce M. Palmer; Laura Tracy Hawkins; Kenneth F. Strong; E. Mark Zunino.**
**General Civil and Trial Practice. Construction Law and Litigation, Business, Corporations, Partnerships, Real Estate, Mobilehome Park Law, Landlord Representation, Bankruptcy, Trusts, Wills, Probate, Insurance Defense, and Family Law.**
**Santa Rosa, California Office: 50 Santa Rosa Avenue, 95404. Telephone: 707-576-7182. Fax: 707-578-3943.**
*See Professional Biographies, NOVATO, CALIFORNIA*

Panza, Frank N. '42 '67 C.712 B.A. L.262 J.D.
V.P. & Gen. Tax Coun., Fireman's Fund Ins. Co.
Peak, John A., (AV) ............ '45 '70 C.546 B.A. L.174 J.D. 999 Grant Ave.
Phillips, Daniel E. ............ '48 '75 C.767 B.S. L.1065 J.D. [Gunheim,P.&G.]
Pinkerton, Ernest E. ............ '33 '61 C&L.813 B.A., J.D. 250 D-1 Bel Marin Keys Blvd.
Pollak, Robert K. ............ '53 '80 C.800 B.A. L.426 J.D. 725 Sun Ln.
Pose, Walter E. ............ '22 '50 C&L.494 B.S.L., J.D. 61 Club View Dr.‡
Postel, Waldo F., Jr. ............ '24 '50 C.112 A.B. L.1065 J.D. 513 Village Circle
Purver, Jonathan M. ............ '39 '67 C.112 B.A. L.1068 LL.B. 205 Scotia Lane
Ricca, John A. '45 '76 C.477 B.A. L.776 J.D.
Asst. V.P. & Asst. Gen. Coun., Fireman's Fund Ins. Co.
Ritzinger, David P. ............ '49 '78 C.763 B.S. L.1137 J.D. 2215 Laguna Vista Dr.
Rush, Richard E., Jr. ............ '41 '67 C.112 A.B. L.276 J.D. 107 Wild Horse Valley Dr.‡
Scarborough, Paul ............ '35 '59 C&L.893 LL.B. 197 San Andreas Dr.
Schaefer, Frederic L. ............ '36 '66 C.112 B.A. L.1065 LL.B. 115 Thunderbird Ct.
Schoen, William R. ............ '45 '70 C.684 A.B. L.1068 J.D. 5 Kenilworth Ct.
Schweizer, Deborah F. ............ '60 '86 C.112 B.A. L.564 J.D. P.O. Box 2109
Scott, Michael P. ............ '58 '83 C&L.36 B.A., J.D. Coun.
Shaw, Leonard, (AV) ............ '32 '56 C.597 B.S. L.502 J.D. 595 Fairway Dr.‡
Shipsey, Thomas E. ............ '53 '78 C.147 B.A. L.408 J.D. 125 Thunderbird Ct.

**Silvestri, George J., Jr., (AV) '41 '69 C.740 B.A. L.1065 J.D.**
**365 Bel Marin Keys Boulevard, Suite 102, 94949-5654**
**Telephone: 415-883-8800 Fax: 415-883-8818**
**General Civil, Municipal, Real Estate, Land Use, Personal Injury, Landslide and Subsidence, Redevelopment, Environmental, Business, Legislative, Probate, Mediation, Arbitration and Appeals.**
*See Professional Biographies, NOVATO, CALIFORNIA*

Smith, Margaret '42 '76 C.273 B.A. L.1026 J.D.
Asst. V.P. & Asst. Gen. Coun., Fireman's Fund Ins. Cos.
Smith, Timothy P. '54 '78 C.209 B.A. L.339 J.D.
Asst. V.P. & Asst. Gen. Coun., Fireman's Fund Ins. Co.
Snell, Philip C., (BV) ............ '48 '79 C.767 B.S. L.765 J.D. [Fish&S.]

CAA421P

Sonenstein, David M. '47 '72 C.154 B.A. L.1065 J.D.
V.P. & Assoc. Gen. Coun., Fireman's Fund Ins. Co.
Stevens, John P. '49 '77 C&L.776 B.A., J.D.
(adm. in NJ; not adm. in CA) Asst. V.P. & Asst. Gen. Coun., Fireman's Fund Ins. Co.
Strohecker, Albert J., III '46 '71 C.659 B.S. L.94 J.D.
(adm. in PA; not adm. in CA) Asst. V.P. & Asst. Gen. Coun., Fireman's Fund Ins. Co.
**Strong, Kenneth F.** ... '52 '79 C.112 B.A. L.1065 J.D. [Palmer,J.H.&S.]
*PRACTICE AREAS: Litigation; Construction Law; Environmental Law.
Tenery, Cecile A. '40 '79 C&L.767 B.A., J.D.
Asst. V.P. & Asst. Gen. Coun., Fireman's Fund Ins. Co.
Thornsjo, Douglas F., (AV⊙) ... '27 '51 C&L.494 B.S., LL.B. 1085 Bel Marin Keys Blvd.
Tolles, Lois V. McKenna ... '32 '89 C.766 B.A. L.767 J.D. 15 Winged Foot Dr.
Torgovitsky, Harry ... '40 '66 C.766 B.S. L.1065 J.D. Pres., T Grp., Ltd.
Trumbull, John A. ... '37 '63 C.813 B.A. L.309 LL.B. 1122 Grant Ave.
Volkart, Judith H. '47 '84 C.1078 B.A. L.1065 J.D.
Asst. V.P. & Asst. Gen. Coun., Fireman's Fund Ins. Co.
**Vosburg, Roger M.** ... '52 '80 C.1042 B.A. L.809 J.D. [Berger,K.S.M.F.S.&G.]
Wallis, Kai A. '40 '73 C.932 B.A. L.209 J.D.
(adm. in IL; not adm. in CA) State Farm Ins. Agcy.
Walsh, Morgan ... '48 '78 C.112 B.A. L.770 J.D. Sr. Coun., Fireman's Fund Ins. Co.
Weinroth, Daryl J. ... '55 '80 C.112 B.S. L.1065 J.D. 750 Grant Ave.
Wertheimer, Warren, (AV) ... '33 '60 C.477 A.B. L.309 LL.B. 351 San Andreas Dr.
Whitener, Tommie W. ... '42 '72 C.112 B.A. L.1065 J.D. [Whitener&C.]
Whitener & Cleek ... 7120 Redwood Blvd.
Wiechers, Anthony J., (AV) ... '19 '44 C.112 A.B. L.1066 LL.B. 39 Eagle Dr.‡
Wilson, Joseph G. ... '18 '47 C.939 A.B. L.813 LL.B. 108 Paper Mill Cres. Ct.‡
Wolfe, Jonathan S. ... '50 '77 C.813 A.B. L.309 J.D. 1701 Novato Blvd.
**Zunino, E. Mark** ... '60 '87 C.112 A.B. L.767 J.D. [Palmer,J.H.&S.]
*PRACTICE AREAS: Construction Law; Insurance Law; Construction Litigation.

## NUEVO, 1,628, *Riverside Co.*

Schelling, Robbie ... '51 '86 C&L.1137 B.S.L., J.D. P.O. Box 442

## OAKDALE, 11,961, *Stanislaus Co.*

Bush, Hartley H., (BV) ... '22 '54 C.33 A.B. L.1066 J.D. City Atty. [Bush,A.M.&H.]
Bush, Ackley, Milich & Hallinan, (BV) ... 366 West F St.

**Damrell, Nelson, Schrimp, Pallios & Ladine, A Professional Corporation, (AV)**
**703 West "F" Street, P.O. Drawer C, 95361⊙**
**Telephone: 209-848-3500 Fax: 209-848-3400**
**Email: dnsp1@ix.netcom.com**
**Roger M. Schrimp; Fred A. Silva.**
**Civil Trial and Appellate Practice in all State and Federal Courts, General Business Practice, Complex Business Litigation, Government, Administrative and Legislative Practice, Business Planning and Dissolution, Personal Injury and Insurance Law, Corporate, Environmental, Resource Recovery, Water and Agricultural Law, Land Use, Real Estate Development, Zoning and Construction Law, Health Care and Hospital Law, Taxation, Estate Planning and Probate and Trust Administration.**
**Modesto, California Office: 1601 I Street, Fifth Floor. Telephone: 209-526-3500. Fax: 209-526-3534.**
**Sacramento, California Office: Suite 200, 1100 K Street. Telephone: 916-447-2909. Fax: 916-447-0552.**
***See Professional Biographies, OAKDALE, CALIFORNIA***

Dodge, Julie C. ... '66 '95 L.1132 J.D. 315 West "F" St.
Gorman, John L., III, (CV) ... '53 '89 C.1109 B.A./B.S. L.770 J.D. 332 W. F St.
Hallinan, Thomas N., (BV) '35 '59 C&L.629 B.S., J.D.
Asst. City Solr. [Bush,A.M.&H.]
Jensen, J. Wilmar, (AV) ... '27 '52 C&L.813 B.A., J.D. [Jensen&J.]⊙
Jensen, Mark R. ... '60 '87 C.1169 B.A. L.464 J.D. [Jensen&J.]⊙
Jensen & Jensen, (AV) ... 128 S. Third Ave. (⊙Modesto & Newman)
Leap, James P. ... '39 '79 C.1120 B.S. L.1095 J.D. 730 E. "F" St., Suite E
Minor, William O. ... '30 '57 C.112 A.B. L.1066 LL.B. 13730 Lancaster Rd.‡
**Schrimp, Roger M.**, (AV) '41 '66
C.112 A.B. L.1066 J.D. [Damrell,N.S.P.&L.] (⊙Modesto)
*PRACTICE AREAS: Business Law; Real Estate Law; Complex Business Litigation.
**Silva, Fred A.**, (CV) ... '58 '87 C.169 B.A. L.1067 J.D. [Damrell,N.S.P.&L.] (⊙Modesto)
*LANGUAGES: Portuguese.
*PRACTICE AREAS: Business Litigation; Complex Litigation.
Smith, Frederick W., (CV) ... '53 '82 C.1109 B.A. L.1137 J.D. 332 W. F St.

**Stockton & Sadler**
**(See Modesto)**

## OAKHURST, —, *Madera Co.*

Ballard, Kenneth R. ... '38 '72 C&L.800 B.S., J.D. 40327 Rd. 425A
**Blate, Gary T.** ... '50 '79 C.112 B.A. L.1137 J.D. [Linn,L.&B.]
*REPORTED CASES: Duckett v. Pistoresi Ambulance Service, Inc., 19 Cal. App. 4th 1525-Cal Rptr 2d Nov. 1993.
*PRACTICE AREAS: Personal Injury; Business and Collections; Family; Criminal.
Blea, Dale J. ... '60 '93 C&L.1137 B.S., J.D. 40061 49 Highway
Chappel, Gregory M. ... '51 '84 C.112 A.B. L.464 J.D. 49430 Rd. 426
Clay, Helen P., (Mrs.) ... '10 '36 L.809 LL.B. P.O. Box 31‡
Clay, John E. ... '12 '36 L.809 LL.B. P.O. Box 31‡
Collings, Gary L., (BV) ... '42 '73 C.1097 L.809 J.D. P.O. Box 2730
Cummings, Richard G. ... '42 '84 C.813 B.A. L.770 J.D. 40327 Stagecoach Rd.
Jamison, John O. ... '48 '74 C.267 B.A. L.464 J.D. P.O. Box 1249
**LaLonde, John P.** ... '53 '95 C.477 B.S. L.1227 J.D. [Linn,L.&B.]
*PRACTICE AREAS: Family Law; Juvenile Court; Criminal; Business Litigation; Mediation.
**Lindley, Robert B.** ... '50 '76 C.813 B.A. L.1068 J.D. [Linn,L.&B.]
*PRACTICE AREAS: Probate and Estate Administration; Estate Planning; Taxation; Corporate; Real Estate.
**Linn, David A.** ... '48 '76 C.679 B.S. L.990 J.D. [Linn,L.&B.]
*REPORTED CASES: LDG Timber Enterprises Incorporated v. United States U.S. Claims Court Reporter, 8 Cl. Ct. 445 (1985).
*PRACTICE AREAS: Personal Injury Litigation; Banking Litigation; Natural Resources Law; Business Litigation; Criminal Law.

**Linn, Lindley & Blate, A Professional Association**
**Yosemite Bank Building, 40061 49 Highway, Suite 101, P.O. Box 2347, 93644**
**Telephone: 209-683-7333; 209-642-2555 FAX: 209-683-3634**
**David A. Linn; Robert B. Lindley; Gary T. Blate; John P. LaLonde.**
**General Civil and Trial Practice including Personal Injury, Probate and Estate Planning, Corporate, Business, Taxation, Natural Resources Law, Banking Litigation, Criminal Law and Family Law.**
**Representative Clients: Yosemite Bank; L.D.G. Timber, Inc.; H & L Lumber Co., Inc.; Disabled Veterans of America; Interwest Corp., Salt Lake City, Utah; Golden Oak Bank, Oakhurst, Calif.; Madera Newspapers Incorporated; Suburban Propane of Morristown, New Jersey; J.R. Forest Products, Inc.; Butler Logging, Inc.**
***See Professional Biographies, OAKHURST, CALIFORNIA***

McReynolds, Clayton W. ... '58 '90 C.999 B.S. L.990 J.D. P.O. Box 517
Smothers, David A. ... '51 '85 C.112 B.A. L.1049 J.D. 49269 Golden Oak Dr.
Thomas, Bren K. ... '59 '91 C.628 B.S. L.629 J.D. P.O. Box 517
Watkins, James H. ... '41 '78 C.112 B.A. L.1148 J.D. 49370 Road 426

## OAKLAND, * 372,242, *Alameda Co.*

Abdul-Rahim, Lila M., (BV) ... '58 '83 C.483 B.A. L.1065 J.D. 385 Grand Ave.
Abramowitz, Marc L. ... '53 '78 C.112 A.B. L.309 J.D. Monterey Labs., Inc.‡
**Abrams, Denise** ... '50 '86 C.690 B.A. L.1066 J.D. [Kazan,M.E.S.&A.]
**Adams, Dirk S.** '51 '76 C.846 B.S. L.309 J.D.
Grp. Sr. V.P., Corp. Devel., World Savings & Loan Assoc.
Adams, Philip Victor ... '51 '77 C.1169 B.A. L.112 J.D. Off of Pub. Def.
Adauto, Gilbert C. ... '49 '84 C.112 A.B. L.1066 J.D. 645 El Dorado Ave.
Ader, James S., (AV) ... '44 '72 C.178 B.A. L.1066 J.D. 1616 Franklin St.
Adler, Barry, (BV) ... '46 '74 C.154 B.A. L.767 J.D. [Eskanos&A.]
Agate, James D. ... '56 '84 C&L.061 B.A. Univ. of Calif.
Agretelis, Demetrios P. ... '33 '65 C.112 B.A. L.1066 LL.B. Supr. Ct. J.
**Aguilar-Guerrero, Brenda** ... '64 '90 C.112 B.A. L.1068 J.D. [🄰 Erickson,B.H.&W.]
*LANGUAGES: Spanish.
**Ahn, Joseph Y.** ... '61 '89 C.112 B.A. L.1065 J.D. [🄰 Haims,J.M.&M.]
*LANGUAGES: Korean.
*PRACTICE AREAS: Insurance Defense Law; Insurance Coverage; Litigation.
**Aiken, Benj. R., Jr.**, (AV) ... '11 '36 C.813 B.A. L.1066 J.D. [Aiken,K.&C.] ‡

**Aiken, Kramer & Cummings, Incorporated, (AV)** BB
**Suite 550 Ordway Building, One Kaiser Plaza, 94612**
**Telephone: 510-834-6800 Fax: 510-834-9017**
**Email: aikenkrame@aol.com**
**Benj. R. Aiken (1879-1955); Bauer E. Kramer (Retired); Benj. R. Aiken, Jr. (Retired); Fred V. Cummings (Retired); John A. Harkavy; Elizabeth M. Engh (Certified Specialist, Probate, Estate Planning and Trust Law, State Bar of California Board of Legal Specialization); Matthew F. Graham; Steven J. Cramer; Richard A. Sipos. Of Counsel: Russell L. Barlow; Bruce G. Herold; Michael A. Coan;—Ellen Suzanne Wyatt; Michael S. Treppa.**
**General Business and Real Estate, Transactional Practice, General Civil Litigation Practice, Corporate, Commercial, Environmental, Employment, Construction, Insurance, Intellectual Property, Estate Planning, Probate and Tax.**
**Reference: Union Bank of California, Oakland, California.**
***See Professional Biographies, OAKLAND, CALIFORNIA***

Aikin, Roger L. '47 '88
C.20 B.A. L.770 J.D. V.P. & Gen. Coun., CivicBank of Commerce
**Ainsworth, David V.** '40 '72
C.378 A.B. L.284 J.D. V.P. & Gen. Coun., Amer. Pres. Lines, Ltd.
**Akawie, Alice L.**, (AV) ... '54 '79 C.112 A.B. L.1065 J.D. [Marshall,A.&L.]
*PRACTICE AREAS: Real Estate Law; Financing Law.
**Aker, Gregory R.** ... '53 '82 C.477 B.A. L.1065 J.D. [Lempres&W.]
*PRACTICE AREAS: Business and Commercial Litigation; Banking Law; Construction Law; Real Estate; Insurance Law.
Albers, Dennis M. ... '48 '73 C.169 A.B. L.1065 J.D. 1433 Webster St.‡
Alcabes, Jaime A. ... '49 '74 C.569 B.A. L.767 J.D. 80 Grand Ave.
Alderson, Richard L. '47 '77 C.197 A.B. L.309 J.D.
V.P. & Gen. Coun., Oakland A's Baseball Co.
Alex, Ken ... '57 '83 C.1169 B.A. L.309 J.D. Dep. Atty. Gen.
**Alexander, David L.**, (AV) ... '48 '74 C.112 B.A. L.1066 J.D. Port Atty., Port of Oakland
*RESPONSIBILITIES: Public Finance.
**Alexander, Gary S.** ... '66 '93 C.309 A.B. L.767 J.D. [🄰 Hardin,C.L.E.&B.]
*REPORTED CASES: Medina v. Hillshore Partners 40 Cal App 4th 477.
*PRACTICE AREAS: Civil Litigation; Environmental Law; Product Liability.
Alexander, Michael D. ... '49 '77 C.112 A.B. L.273 J.D. 300 Lakeside Dr., Ste. 1900
**Alexander, Michelle** ... '67 '95 C.880 B.A. L.813 J.D. [🄰 Saperstein,G.D.&B.]
*PRACTICE AREAS: Civil Rights.
**Allard, Anthony J.**, (AV) ... '50 '77 C.763 B.A. L.284 J.D. [Bennett,S.R.&A.]
*PRACTICE AREAS: Litigation; Landslide Law; Subsidence Law; Construction Law.
**Allen, A. Clifford** ... '56 '84 C.112 B.A. L.1065 J.D. [🄰 Donahue,G.W.&W.]
*PRACTICE AREAS: Civil Litigation; Computer Software Law; Employment Law; Trade Secrets Law.
Allen, Bruce E. '45 '73 C.112 B.A. L.770 J.D.
Assoc. Gen. Coun., ICF Kaiser Engineers, Inc.
**Allen, James E., Jr.** ... '43 '67 C&L.1065 A.B., J.D. Dep. Port Atty. II, Port of Oakland
**Allen, Jeffrey**, (AV) ... '48 '73 C.112 B.A. L.1066 [Graves&A.]
*PRACTICE AREAS: Real Estate; Bankruptcy; Litigation; Receiverships; General Practice.
Allen, Pamela '58 '86 C.475 B.A. L.912 J.D.
(adm. in PA; not adm. in CA) 1330 Broadway
**Allen, Robert G.**, (BV) ... '46 '71 C.768 A.B. L.1065 J.D. [Knox R.]
*PRACTICE AREAS: Corporate; Real Estate and Probate Law.
**Allen, Roger F.**, (AV) ... '45 '77 C.768 B.A. L.284 J.D. [Morton,L.&A.]
*PRACTICE AREAS: Civil Trial; Insurance Defense; Personal Injury; Mediation; Arbitration.
**Alloway, Willard L.**, (AV) ... '46 '72 C.112 A.B. L.1066 J.D. [Hardin,C.L.E.&B.]
*PRACTICE AREAS: Civil Trials; Toxic Torts; Governmental Liability.
**Allswang, David**, (AV) ... '40 '77 C.112 A.B. L.767 J.D. [Allswang,S.&W.]

**Allswang, Smith & Walsh, (AV)**
**7700 Edgewater Drive, Suite 215, 94621⊙**
**Telephone: 510-567-1010 Fax: 510-567-1020**
**David Allswang; Anne Schmitz.**
**Civil Litigation specifically utilizing Alternative Dispute Resolution in the following areas: Construction, Land Use, Commercial, Environmental, Real Estate Errors and Omissions, Products Liability, Professional Liability, Premises Liability, Insurance Defense, Insurance Fraud, Bad-Faith Defense and Insurance Coverage.**
**San Francisco, California Office: 180 Montgomery Street, Suite 2000, 94104. Telephone: 415-291-8844. Fax: 415-291-8855.**
***See Professional Biographies, OAKLAND, CALIFORNIA***

Alschuler, George A., (BV) ... '35 '67 C&L.813 B.A., J.D. 45 Embarcadero Cove‡
Altemus, Daniel F., Jr. ... '48 '74 C.154 A.B. L.770 J.D. N.L.R.B.
**Altura, Judith B.** ... '45 '81 C.102 B.A. L.767 J.D. [Strickland&H.]
*PRACTICE AREAS: Auto Medical Fraud; Personal Injury; Premises Liability; Products Liability.
Alvarez, Jose, (BV) ... '46 '75 80 Grand Ave.
Amateau, Susan ... '46 '74 C.112 B.A. L.1066 J.D. The Regents of Univ. of Calif.
**Amenta, Janice** ... '65 '92 C.112 B.A. L.1065 J.D. [🄰 Boornazian,J.&G.]
*PRACTICE AREAS: Maritime; Insurance; Civil Litigation.
Ammon, Barry D. ... '53 '80 C.112 B.A. L.800 J.D. 1430 Franklin St.
Amspoker, Todd A. ... '58 '83 C.112 B.A. L.1065 J.D. [Rinehart&A.]
Anders, Gideon, (AV) '45 '77 C.112 B.A. L.128 J.D.
National Econ. Develop. & Law Ctr.
Andersen, Benjamin O., (AV) ... '40 '66 C.174 B.A. L.1065 J.D. 385 Grand Ave.
Andersen, David L., (AV) ... '45 '72 C.112 B.A. L.1066 J.D. [Andersen&Z.]
Andersen & Zimmer, (AV) ... 385 Grand Ave.
Anderson, Bebe J. ... '52 '82 C.112 B.A. L.178 J.D. 491 9th St.
Anderson, Elisabeth Olney, (AV) ... '27 '72 C.112 A.B. 150 Grand Ave.
Anderson, Jack F. ... '40 '70 C.549 B.S. L.329 J.D. [Webster&A.]
Anderson, James H. ... '54 '90 C.1111 B.A. L.770 J.D. 1999 Harrison St.
Anderson, Lucinda E. ... '48 '79 C.768 B.S. L.1065 J.D. 235 W. Macarthur Blvd.
Anderson, Mary-Margaret, (BV) ... '51 '78 C.112 A.B. L.765 J.D. 166 Santa Clara Ave.
**Anderson, Paul C.** ... '64 '89 C.602 B.A. L.426 J.D. [🄰 McDonough,H.&A.]
*PRACTICE AREAS: Real Estate Law; Land Use Law; Municipal Law.

**Andrada, J. Randall**, (AV) ...............'51 '76 C.740 B.A. L.1065 J.D. [Ryan,A.&L.]
*PRACTICE AREAS: Civil Trial; Insurance Defense Law; Malpractice Defense; Sexual Abuse Litigation; Premises Liability.
Andrews, Jorgan K. ........................ '68 '94 C.174 B.A. L.893 J.D. 1999 Harrison St.
**Andrews, Paulette G.** ...................'58 '89 C.740 B.A. L.1065 J.D. [🄰 Lempres&W.]
*LANGUAGES: Spanish.
*PRACTICE AREAS: Litigation.
Angelides, Stephen P. .....................'52 '78 C.112 A.B. L.1066 J.D. P.O. Box 29291
**Angress, Rachel K.** ...............'69 '94 C.1060 B.S. L.1065 J.D. [🄲 Hardin,C.L.E.&B.]
*PRACTICE AREAS: Family Law.
**Angstadt, Eric P.**, (BV) ................... '59 '85 C.36 B.S. L.464 J.D. [Hoyt,M.&A.]⊙
*REPORTED CASES: Trevice v. Blue Cross of California, (1989) 209 Ca.App.3rd 878; Angell v. Peterson Tractor Company, Inc. (1994) 21 Cal.App. 4th, 981.
*PRACTICE AREAS: Wage and Hour Law; Litigation; Employment Discrimination Law; Labor Relations Law and Litigation; Unlawful Termination Law and Litigation.
**Ankenman, C. Gregg** .............. '60 '88 C.101 B.A. L.1066 J.D. [Wendel,R.B.&D.]
*LANGUAGES: Spanish.
*PRACTICE AREAS: Real Estate Law; Business Law.
**Anthony, Steven R.**, (AV) ................'40 '66 C.36 B.A. L.1065 LL.B. [Anthony&C.]
*PRACTICE AREAS: Civil Trial Law; Insurance Law; Medical Liability Defense Law; Wrongful Termination; Legal Malpractice.

**Anthony & Carlson, (AV)**
**1999 Harrison Street, Suite 1750, 94612**
**Telephone: 510-835-8400 Fax: 510-835-5566**
**Members of Firm: Steven R. Anthony; Richard H. Carlson. Associates: Barbara L. Vankoll. Of Counsel: Jane L. Trigero.**
**General Civil Trial Practice, Professional Negligence, Insurance Bad Faith, Wrongful Termination/ Discrimination, Commercial Litigation.**
***See Professional Biographies, OAKLAND, CALIFORNIA***

Anton, John M., (BV) ....................'47 '72 C.112 B.A. L.1067 J.D. [🄰 Boxer,E.&G.]
Aracic, Nicholas, (AV) ....................'44 '74 C.602 A.B. L.1066 J.D. Dep. Co. Coun.‡
Arakaki, Joanne Y.Y.L. .......................'58 '84 C.312 B.B.A. L.310 J.D. 350 20th St.
Arguedas, Cristina C., (AV) ..............'53 '79 C.550 B.A. L.705 J.D. [Cooper,A.&C.]
**Arias, Cathy L.** ................................'64 '89 C.112 B.A. L.1067 J.D. [Larson&B.]
Armstrong, James L., Jr. '51 '79
C.813 A.B. L.767 J.D. Supvr. Trial Atty.; Off. of City Atty.
Armstrong, Saundra B. ......................'47 '77 C.267 B.A. L.767 J.D. U.S. Dist. J.
**Armstrong, Thomas C.** ......................'59 '85 C.668 B.A. L.1065 J.D. [Pezzola&R.]
Arne, Courtland D. ..............................'29 '55 C.112 B.A. L.1065 J.D. 25 Rydal Ct.‡
Arnold, Sandra Burns, (AV) ..................'52 '77 C.70 B.A. L.262 J.D. 456 Eighth St.
Aronson, Elliot B. ..................'43 '80 C.197 A.B. L.1218 J.D. 1 Kaiser Plaza (Pat.)
Ashburne, Michael R., (AV) .........'45 '72 C.475 B.A. L.1066 J.D. 8300 Golf Links Rd.
Ashby, Marilyn A. ..........................'33 '75 C.101 B.S. L.1197 J.D. 290 Crestmont Dr.
**Ashley, Eugene G.** ..................'67 '94 C.112 B.A. L.464 J.D. [Rankin,S.M.T.&R.]
**Aspedon, Beth E.** ........................'58 '86 C.208 B.A. L.188 J.D. [Fitzgerald,A.&B.]
*PRACTICE AREAS: Labor and Employment Law.
Astle, Ruth ...........'47 '75 C.766 B.A. L.284 J.D. Adm. Law J., Off. of Adm. Hearings
Auer, Andrea ......................................'64 '89 C.188 B.A. L.1065 J.D. Asst. Pub. Def.
Aure, Kathleen D. '46 '76 C.438 A.B. L.862 J.D.
Assoc. Reg. Coun., Kaiser Found. Health Plan, Inc.
Axell, Elyse ..................... '57 '85 C.112 B.S. L.976 J.D. Univ. Coun., Univ. of Calif.
Ayer, Thomas M. '34 '61 C.112 B.S. L.1065 LL.B.
Sr. Invest. Strategist, A.M. Howells & Co., Inc.
Babington, Carol G., (BV) '43 '76 C.112 B.A. L.1065 J.D.
Asst. Gen. Coun., Alameda-Contra Costa Transit Dist.
Bachand, Clifford B. .......................'20 '52 C.156 B.B.A. L.767 LL.B. Mun. Ct. J.
Bachrach, William H., (AV) .................'39 '66 C.976 B.A. L.477 J.D. [W.H.Bachrach]
Bachrach, William H., A Professional Corporation, (AV) ................ 1 Kaiser Plz. St.
Backers, Angela C. .........................'58 '84 C.740 B.A. L.767 J.D. Dep. Dist. Atty.
Badger, George R. ...................'29 '80 C.477 M.B.A. L.767 J.D. 414 13th St.
Baier, Carl A. ..............................'61 '87 C.813 A.B. L.597 J.D. Dep. Atty. Gen.
**Baier, Molly J.** ..........................'58 '84 C.187 B.A. L.1067 J.D. [Lempres&W.]
*LANGUAGES: German, Spanish.
*REPORTED CASES: Corman c. Morgan (In re Morgan), 197 B.R. 892 (N.D. Cal. 1996).
*PRACTICE AREAS: Bankruptcy; Creditors' Rights; Real Estate; Commercial Litigation.
Bailey, Gregory A., (BV) ..................'56 '83 C.112 A.B. L.464 J.D. Off. of Dist. Atty.
**Bailey, Jolene K.** '62 '92 C.1060 B.A. L.770 J.D.
Coun., World Savings & Loan Assoc.
**Bairey, Jeffrey G.**, (BV) ..........................'57 '83 C.112 A.B. L.1065 J.D. [Larson&B.]
Baizer, Robert D. ......................'49 '75 C.112 B.A. L.284 J.D. [Yonemura,Y.&B.]
**Baker, Lawrence A.** ........................'48 '78 C.112 B.A. L.765 J.D. [Haims,J.M.&M.]
*PRACTICE AREAS: Insurance; Personal Injury Defense; Bad Faith Law; Construction Litigation; Appellate Practice.
**Baker, Scott D.**, (AV) ................. '53 '79 C.103 A.B. L.1065 J.D. [Crosby,H.R.&M.]
*PRACTICE AREAS: Business Litigation; Intellectual Property Litigation.
**Baldwin, Edward D.** ........................ '61 '93 C.871 L.284 J.D. [🄰 Haims,J.M.&M.]
*PRACTICE AREAS: Personal Injury Law; Environmental Insurance Litigation; Construction Defect Litigation.
**Baldwin, Elsa M.** ................... '57 '90 C.668 B.A. L.1065 J.D. [🄰 Hardin,C.L.E.&B.]
*PRACTICE AREAS: Environmental Law; Civil Litigation; Labor Law.
Baldwin, John C., (AV) ..................'25 '54 C.813 A.B. L.1066 LL.B. Asst. Dist. Atty.
Baldwin, William M., (BV) ..............'41 '69 C.813 A.B. L.1066 J.D. Asst. Dist. Atty.
Ballachey, Michael E. ......................'37 '64 C.112 A.B. L.1066 LL.B. Supr. Ct. J.
**Baller, Morris J.**, (AV) ............... '44 '70 C&L.309 B.A., J.D. [Saperstein,G.D.&B.]
*LANGUAGES: French.
*PRACTICE AREAS: Litigation; Employment Law.
Ballinger, Maria Chan .................'62 '87 C.112 A.B. L.309 J.D. Asst. U.S. Trustee
**Ban, Daniel J.** ..............................'67 '94 C&L.112 B.A., J.D. [🄰 Gassett,P.&F.]
*PRACTICE AREAS: Workers Compensation.
**Banister, John H.** ..............................'56 '81 C.154 B.A. L.990 J.D. [Bell,R.&H.]
*PRACTICE AREAS: Construction Law; Business Litigation; Environmental Law.
**Banke, Kathy M.**, (AV) ............ '53 '79 C.1060 B.A. L.1067 J.D. [Crosby,H.R.&M.]
*PRACTICE AREAS: Appellate.
Banks, Sharon D. '45 '82 C.801 B.S. L.1065 J.D.
Gen. Coun., Alameda-Contra Costa Transit Dist.
**Barack, Rachel L.** ................. '69 '94 C.112 B.A. L.1065 J.D. [🄰 Hardin,C.L.E.&B.]
*PRACTICE AREAS: Products Liability; Civil Litigation.
Baranco, Gordon S. ............................ '48 '73 C.112 B.A. L.1067 J.D. Supr. Ct. J.
**Barany, Gizelle A.** ........................ '58 '90 C.112 A.B. L.1066 J.D. [🄰 Pezzola&R.]
Bard, George T. .............. '29 '65 C.477 B.A. L.1026 LL.B. The Sherwin-Williams Co.
**Barlow, Russell L.**, (AV) .................. '36 '61 C.813 A.B. L.1066 LL.B. [Aiken,K.&C.]
Barnard, John, (BV) '47 '75 C.674 A.B. L.1066 J.D.
Pres. & Gen. Coun., Equitec Financial Grp., Inc.
Barnes, Robert ...............'48 '76 C.569 B.A. L.767 J.D. Univ. Coun., Univ. of Calif.
Barni, Thomas J., (BV) .....................'49 '76 C.112 B.A. L.1049 J.D. Dep. Dist. Atty.
**Barrett, William A.** ........................'41 '69 C.767 B.S. L.284 J.D. [McInerney&D.]
*PRACTICE AREAS: Construction; Business Litigation; Athlete Representation.

**Barron, David W. '53 '79 C.112 B.A. L.1066 J.D.**
**6250 Merced Avenue, 94611**
**Telephone: 510-339-7330 Fax: 510-339-7337**
**Email: 71722.3454@compuserve.com**
***PRACTICE AREAS: Real Estate Law; Financing Law; General Business Law.**
**Real Estate, Real Estate Finance and Commercial Leasing Law.**
***See Professional Biographies, OAKLAND, CALIFORNIA***

**Barron, George J.**, (AV) '47 '72
C.767 B.A. L.1068 J.D. [Donahue,G.W.&W.] (⊙Walnut Creek)
*PRACTICE AREAS: Employment Law; Insurance Defense Law; Labor (Management or Employees) Law.
**Barron, Vikki L.** .......................'66 '93 C.112 B.A. L.767 J.D. [Ryan,A.&L.]
Barrueta, Anthony A. '65 '91 C.93 A.B. L.846 J.D.
(adm. in MD; not adm. in CA) Coun., Kaiser Found. Health Plan, Inc.
Barsotti, Mario H. ......................'24 '56 C.112 B.S. L.1065 J.D. Ret. Mun. Ct. J.
Bartlett, Robert S. ....................'51 '78 C.112 B.A. L.383 J.D. 3540 Grand Ave.
Barton, Robert R., (AV) ...............'27 '54 C.112 B.S. L.1066 LL.B. 1901 Harrison St.
**Baskin, Richard J.**, (BV) ............'52 '83 C.112 B.A. L.767 J.D. [Van Blois,K.S.&B.]
*LANGUAGES: German.
*PRACTICE AREAS: Personal Injury; Wrongful Death; Products Liability; Construction Accidents; Class Actions.
**Bates, Christopher T.** .............'64 '94 C.112 B.A. L.1065 J.D. [🄰 Boornazian,J.&G.]
Baylis, Owen E. ...............................'55 '88 C.813 B.A. L.770 J.D. 200 Webster St.
Bazile, Leo .......................................'43 '74 C.813 B.A. L.1066 J.D. [Harrison,T.&B.]
Beal, Melvin W. .................'43 '79 C.696 Ph.D. L.477 J.D. Univ. Coun., Univ. of Calif.
Beasley, Adrionne D. ......................'43 '78 C.112 M.P.H. L.1066 J.D. Dep. Dist. Atty.
**Beasley, Alice M.**, (AV) ............'45 '73 C.441 B.A. L.1066 J.D. [Erickson,B.H.&W.]
Beaupre, Dean A., (AV) ....................'43 '70 C.215 B.A. L.477 J.D. Asst. Pub. Def.
Beccar-Varela, Gabriel .............'48 '85 C.061 S.T.L. L.1153 J.D. 625 Mariposa Ave.

**Becherer Beers Murphy Kannett & Schweitzer**
**(See Emeryville)**

Becker, Edwin I. .......................'13 '39 C.112 A.B. L.1066 LL.B. 3437 Fruitvale Ave.
**Beckett, Jennifer** .......................'61 '91 C.66 A.B. L.1065 J.D. [🄰 Crosby,H.R.&M.]
*PRACTICE AREAS: Litigation.
Bedrick, Stephen B. ...........................'46 '74 C.976 B.A. L.178 J.D. 1440 Bway.
Beers, Roger, (AV) .................................. '43 '70 C.69 B.A. L.309 LL.B. 1300 Clay St.
Beesley, Phyllis A. ........................'50 '77 C.112 B.A. L.284 J.D. 1551 Excelsior Ave.‡
Beeson, Donald L. ...........................'44 '73 C.112 B.S.E.E. L.284 J.D. [Collins&B.] (Pat.)
**Behrendt, Daniel E., Esq.** ................'69 '95 C.1066 B.A. L.1067 J.D. [🄲 General C.]
*PRACTICE AREAS: Business Litigation; Employment/Labor.
Behrens, Eric K., (AV) '48 '78
C.309 A.B. L.1066 J.D. Univ. Coun., Regents of the Univ. of Calif.
Belcourt, Dennis L. .......................'59 '85 C.549 B.A. L.1065 J.D. 200 Webster St.

**Beles, Robert J., (AV) '42 '68 C.610 A.B. L.1065 J.D.**
**#1 Kaiser Plaza, Suite 1750, 94612**
**Telephone: 510-836-0100 FAX: 510-832-3690**
**(Certified Specialist, Criminal Law, The State Bar of California Board of Legal Specialization).**
**Criminal Trials in State and Federal Courts.**
***See Professional Biographies, OAKLAND, CALIFORNIA***

Belinkoff, Dena R. '55 '83 C.112 A.B. L.1066 J.D.
Coun., Kaiser Found. Health Plan, Inc.
**Bell, Howard H.**, (AV) ................'24 '51 C.823 A.B. L.813 LL.B. [🄲 Bell,R.&H.]
*PRACTICE AREAS: Business Law; Real Estate Law.

**Bell, Rosenberg & Hughes LLP, (AV)**
**1300 Clay Street, Suite 1000, P.O. Box 70220, Station "D", 94612-0220**
**Telephone: 510-832-8585 Fax: 510-839-6925**
**Members of Firm: Robert Rosenberg (Certified Specialist, Estate Planning, Trust and Probate Law, The State Bar of California Board of Legal Specialization); Roger M. Hughes; James C. Nelson; Catherine M. Fisher; John H. Banister; Roland Nikles. Of Counsel: Howard H. Bell. Retired Member: James Dunlavey. Associates: Teresa Jenkins Main; Howard G. Curtis, II; Jennifer M. Fergusson; John A. Russo.**
**General Civil and Trial Practice. Business, Estate Planning, Taxation, Probate, Construction Litigation and Real Estate Law.**
***See Professional Biographies, OAKLAND, CALIFORNIA***

Bender, Susan A., (AV) .......................'40 '70 C.994 B.A. L.284 J.D. 1 Kaiser Plz.
**Bendes, Charles N.** ..........................'51 '76 C.33 B.A. L.770 J.D. [Wald&B.]
*REPORTED CASES: Roffinella v. Sherinian 179 Cal App 3d 230 (1986).
*PRACTICE AREAS: Real Estate Law and Litigation; Corporate and Business Law and Litigation; Probate Litigation.
**Beneville, Susan P.** ..................'65 '91 C.94 B.A. L.276 J.D. [🄰 Crosby,H.R.&M.]
Bengtson, John D. ...................'57 '83 C.112 B.S. L.1068 J.D. 1842 Leimert Blvd.
Benjamin, Kathleen D. ........'50 '81 C.411 B.A. L.426 J.D. Asst. Mgr., NRS Mgmt. Grp.
**Bennett, Bryant M.**, (AV) ........ '19 '44 C.112 A.B. L.1066 LL.B. [Bennett,S.R.&A.] ‡
*PRACTICE AREAS: Litigation; Insurance Defense Law; Insurance Law.

**Bennett, Samuelsen, Reynolds and Allard, A Professional Corporation, (AV)**
**1951 Webster Street, Suite 200, 94612**
**Telephone: 510-444-7688; 510-987-8001 Fax: 510-444-5849**
**Bryant M. Bennett (Retired); David J. Samuelsen; Richard L. Reynolds; Anthony J. Allard; John G. Cowperthwaite;—Roger Blake Hohnsbeen; Don Henry Schaefer; Thomas S. Gelini; Frederick W. Gatt; Rodney Ian Headington; Candace Smith-Dabney.**
**General Civil Trial and Appellate Practice in all State and Federal Courts. Casualty Insurance, Personal Injury, Insurance Coverage, Construction and Landslide/Subsidence Law.**
**Representative Clients: Allstate Insurance Co.; California State Automobile Assn.; The Continental Insurance Cos.; County of Alameda.**
***See Professional Biographies, OAKLAND, CALIFORNIA***

Benson, Howard R. ...........................'26 '56 C.112 B.S. L.1065 J.D. [Munck,B.&S.] ‡
**Benson, Marc R.** ..........................'63 '90 C.165 B.A. L.94 J.D. [🄰 Crosby,H.R.&M.]
**Benson, Sandra Rae** ............. '49 '85 C.112 B.A. L.1066 J.D. [Van Bourg,W.R.&R.]
*PRACTICE AREAS: Labor Law.
Berger, Michael R., (BV) ..................'48 '75 C.846 B.S. L.1065 J.D. 3306 Harrison St.
**Bergez, Raymond J.**, (AV) .......... '38 '64 C.112 A.B. L.1066 J.D. [Hardin,C.L.E.&B.]
*PRACTICE AREAS: Civil Litigation; Toxic Torts; Products Liability Law.
Bergman, Alan R. ...................'45 '74 C.112 B.A. L.1065 J.D. 166 Santa Clara Ave.
**Berke-Dreyfuss, Elizabeth** ...........'53 '84 C.608 B.A. L.767 J.D. [🄰 Wendel,R.B.&D.]
*PRACTICE AREAS: Bankruptcy.
Berkeley, Rhodes & Schwartz, (BV) ..................................1540 San Pablo Ave.
Berkley, Thomas L., (BV) .................................'15 '42 L.1065 J.D. [Berkeley,R.&S.]
**Berman, Bruce A.** ...........................'63 '94 C.112 B.A. L.464 J.D. [🄰 Gassett,P.&F.]
*PRACTICE AREAS: General Civil Litigation; Insurance Defense; Defense of Self Insureds.
**Berman, Stephanie L.** ....................'65 '91 C.477 B.A. L.273 J.D. [🄰 Crosby,H.R.&M.]
Bernard, Peter '36 '61 C.363 A.B. L.477 J.D.
(adm. in MI; not adm. in CA) Chf. Coun., Dept. of Energy
**Berris, Ellen D.** ....................................'63 '88 C.260 B.S. L.767 J.D. [🄰 Berry&B.]
**Berry, Phillip S.**, (AV) ........................... '37 '62 C&L.813 A.B., J.D. [Berry&B.]
Berry, Theodore O. ...................'35 '64 C.1043 B.A. L.1065 LL.B. 484 Lake Park Ave.
Berry, Xanthe M. ...............'60 '87 C.112 B.A. L.284 J.D. East Bay Mun. Utility Dist.

CAA423P

**Berry & Berry, A Professional Corporation, (AV)**
**1300 Clay Street, Ninth Floor, P.O. Box 70250, Station D, 94520**
**Telephone: 510-835-8330 Fax: 510-835-5117**
**Samuel H. Berry (1904-1990); Phillip S. Berry; Carolyn Collins; Leonardo J. Vacchina; Peter R. Gilbert; Lynne P. Blair;—Evanthia Spanos; Gregory D. Meronek; Ellen D. Berris; Laura Przetak.**
**Civil Litigation. Casualty Insurance Law. Professional Liability, Personal Injury, Torts, Products Liability, Asbestos and Toxic Tort Defense, and Pharmaceutical and Medical Device Liability Law.**
**Representative Clients: Parke-Davis; Warner-Lambert; St. Paul Insurance Co.; Fireman's Fund Insurance Co.; American International Underwriters; Lloyd's of London; Celina Insurance Group; American Optical; Biomet, Inc.**
***See Professional Biographies, OAKLAND, CALIFORNIA***

Bethards, Laureen A. '58 '89 C.112 B.A. L.1065 J.D. 1 Kaiser Plz.
**Bevan, John P.** '54 '94 C.336 B.Arch. L.767 J.D. [⊠ Larson&B.]
Bezemek, Robert J. '48 '74 C.112 B.A. L.1066 J.D. 1611 Telegraph Ave.
Bianchi, George R., (AV) '36 '64 C&L.767 A.B., J.D. 5903 Margarido Dr.‡
**Biatch, Joel A.** '56 '83 C.1169 A.B. L.1066 J.D. [Cooper,M.&B.]
*PRACTICE AREAS: Business Law; Architect Law; Estate Planning.
**Bickham, J. David** '62 '90 C.174 B.A. L.273 J.D. [⊠ Crosby,H.R.&M.]
*PRACTICE AREAS: Commercial and Real Estate Litigation.
Bigelow, Glenn D., (A Prof. Corp.) '45 '74 L.765 J.D. 3577 Fruitvale Ave.
Bigelow, Katherine J. '49 '75 C.112 B.A. L.426 J.D. 5949 Leona St.
Billups, Darryl J., (BV) '48 '75 C.1073 B.A. L.1067 J.D. Dist. Atty. Off.
Biren, Andrea L. '50 '77 C.914 B.A. L.1066 J.D. Unemp. Ins. App. Bd.
Bischoff, LeAnn G. '66 '92 C.494 B.A. L.1066 J.D. Calif. Indian Legal Servs.
Bishop, Catherine M., (AV) '42 '73 C.787 B.A. L.128 J.D. 6215 Hillegass Ave.
Bittner, Gayle E., (AV) '53 '81 C.1145 B.S. L.990 J.D. [Schmit,M.B.&S.]
**Bjonerud, Deborah T.** '63 '89 C.768 B.A. L.1065 J.D. [⊠ Liccardo,R.S.&M.]
*PRACTICE AREAS: Real Estate; Litigation.
**Bjork, Robert D., Jr.**, (AV) '46 '74 C.966 B.A. L.861 J.D. [Bjork,L.P.&K.]
*PRACTICE AREAS: Admiralty Law; Drug and Medical Device Litigation; Products Liability Law; Toxic Torts.

**Bjork, Lawrence, Poeschl & Kohn, (AV)**
**The Ross House, 483 Ninth Street, 94607**
**Telephone: 510-832-8134 FAX: 510-832-0461**
**Email: home@bjorklaw.com**
**Members of Firm: Robert D. Bjork, Jr.; Robert K. Lawrence; Thomas F. Poeschl, Jr.; Dorine Ruiz Kohn. Associates: Elizabeth K. Ryan; Mark P. Epstein; Patricia H. Perry; Susan J. Sherrill; Lilly M. Omid.**
**General Civil Litigation. Trials, Business and Construction Litigation, Insurance Coverage and Defense, Professional and Products Liability Litigation, Employment Law.**
***See Professional Biographies, OAKLAND, CALIFORNIA***

**Blair, Lynne P.** '59 '83 C.112 B.A. L.1065 J.D. [Berry&B.]
Blakely, Joseph A. '50 '76 C.112 A.B. L.1065 J.D. Off. of Pub. Def.
Blakely, Richard S. '44 '69 C&L.260 B.S.B.A., J.D.
(adm. in FL; not adm. in CA) Dept. of Energy
Blau, H. Andre, (BV) '26 '67 C.112 B.S. L.1026 J.D. 4075 Norton Ave.
Blazer, Lawrence C., (BV) '54 '80 C.813 A.B. L.228 J.D. Dep. Dist. Atty.
**Blitch, Stephen G.**, (AV) '47 '76 C.112 A.B. L.1066 J.D. [Crosby,H.R.&M.]
*PRACTICE AREAS: Civil Litigation; Business Litigation; Product Liability; State and Local Government Law.
Blockton, Gilbert B. '53 '79 C.597 B.A. L.1066 J.D. 1970 Broadway
Bloom, Susan L. ... '47 '74 C.665 B.A. L.107 J.D. Admin. Law J., Unemp. Ins. Appls. Bd.

**Blum, Edward L., (AV) '46 '72 C.112 B.A. L.1067 J.D.**
**1999 Harrison Street, Suite 1333, 94612**
**Telephone: 510-452-4400 Fax: 510-452-4406**
***PRACTICE AREAS: Real Estate Law; Commercial Litigation.**
**Associate: Anne Tremaine.**
**Real Estate and Commercial Litigation.**
***See Professional Biographies, OAKLAND, CALIFORNIA***

**Blum, Lorin B., Law Offices of, (AV) '38 '63 C.112 B.A. L.1065 J.D.**
**1939 Harrison Street, Suite 618, 94612-3533⊙**
**Telephone: 510-465-3927 Fax: 510-465-4222**
**Email: lbblum@ix.netcom.com**
**(Certified Specialist, Family Law, The State Bar of California Board of Legal Specialization).**
***PRACTICE AREAS: Family Law.**
**Associates: Sharon M. Braz (Certified Specialist, Family Law, The State Bar of California Board of Legal Specialization).**
**Family Law.**
**Walnut Creek, California Office: 1850 Mt. Diablo Boulevard, Suite 605, 94596. Telephone: 510-933-6125.**
***See Professional Biographies, OAKLAND, CALIFORNIA***

Blumenfeld, Michael J., (BV) '48 '75 C.112 B.A. L.284 J.D. [Sher,B.]
**Boat, John S.** '67 '92 C.802 B.B.A. L.464 J.D. [Knox R.]
*PRACTICE AREAS: Corporate, Business, Zoning and Real Estate.
**Bodden, Tara D.** '67 '94 C.276 A.B. L.770 J.D. [⊠ Larson&B.]
Boehm, Kathleen B. '48 '88 C.339 B.S.N. L.999 J.D. 490 Grand Ave.
Bonini, Griffin M. J. '65 '91 C.154 B.A. L.770 J.D. 1999 Harrison St.
Bonitz, Richard E. '38 '65 C.767 B.S. L.1065 J.D.
V.P. & Assoc. Gen. Coun., ICF Kaiser Engineers, Inc.
**Boone, W. Daniel**, (AV) '43 '68 C.31 B.A. L.276 J.D. [Van Bourg,W.R.&R.]
*PRACTICE AREAS: Labor Law.
Boornazian, James G., (AV) '21 '59 C.112 B.S. L.765 J.D. 1800 Harrison St.‡

**Boornazian, Jensen & Garthe, A Professional Corporation, (AV)**
**1800 Harrison Street, 25th Floor, P.O. Box 12925, 94604⊙**
**Telephone: 510-834-4350 Telecopier: 510-839-1897**
**David J. Garthe; Andrew R. Adler (Resident, Walnut Creek Office); Charles I. Eisner; Gregory J. Rockwell; Robert G. Crow; William T. Mulvihill; Robert B. Lueck (Resident, Walnut Creek Office); Gail C. Trabish; Kathleen E. Hegen; David R. Sidran (Resident, Walnut Creek Office); Bruce H. Winkelman; Colette F. Stone (Resident, Walnut Creek Office); Alan E. Swerdlow;—Steven G. Lanum; Paul G. Minoletti; Marjorie J. Heinrich (Resident, Walnut Creek Office); Kathy M. Katano-Lee; Paul A. Giacoletti; Dennis P. Fitzsimons; Joan M. Saupé (Resident, Walnut Creek Office); Jacqueline Jordan Leung; Janice Amenta; Benjamin T. Reyes, II; Jonathan Talbot Rodriguez (Resident, Walnut Creek Office); Kristin L. Jenny (Resident, Walnut Creek Office); Kelly T. Nugent; Christopher T. Bates; Brenda M. Lillington (Resident, Walnut Creek Office); Jordan A. Rodman; John S. Huster; Jennifer E. McEneaney (Resident, Walnut Creek Office). Of Counsel: Robert E. Jensen.**
**Insurance, Trial, Appellate Practice and General Business. Legal, Medical, Dental, Real Estate Malpractice and Products Liability Law.**
**Walnut Creek, California Office: Suite 550, 2121 North California Boulevard. Telephone 510-934-8400. Telecopier: 510-934-3635.**
***See Professional Biographies, OAKLAND, CALIFORNIA***

Booty, Kelvin H., Jr., (BV) '34 '60 C.112 A.B. L.309 LL.B. Co. Coun.
**Boranian, Steven J.** '67 '94 C.309 A.B. L.597 J.D. [⊠ Crosby,H.R.&M.]
**Borgen, David** '52 '81 C.705 B.A. L.1065 J.D. [⊠ Saperstein,G.D.&B.]
Born, Stephen M. '62 '91 C.367 B.A. L.94 J.D. 1999 Harrison St.
Bort, Jos. P. '15 '42 C.112 B.S. L.1066 LL.B. 6316 Bullard Dr.
**Bortnick, Caryn** '56 '85 C.98 B.A. L.809 J.D. [⊠ Larson&B.]
*REPORTED CASES: Industrial Indemnity v. Superior Court (1989), 209 Cal. App. 3d 1093.
Bostick, Bradley L. '55 '83 C.112 B.A. L.284 J.D. 55 Samaria Lane

**Bostick, Mark S.** '53 '83 C.112 A.B. L.767 J.D. [Wendel,R.B.&D.]
*PRACTICE AREAS: Bankruptcy Law; Commercial Litigation.
Bouba, Janice L '47 '86 C.454 B.A. 2101 Webster St.
**Bouret, Marc P.**, (BV) '53 '78 C.169 B.A. L.61 J.D. [⊠ Haims,J.M.&M.]
*PRACTICE AREAS: Civil Litigation; Insurance Defense; Negligence; Torts; Products Liability.
**Bova, Anthony M.** '63 '92 C.770 B.A. L.93 J.D. [⊠ Crosby,H.R.&M.]
**Boven, Douglas G.**, (AV) '43 '70 C&L.477 B.S.E., J.D.
[Crosby,H.R.&M.] (⊙San Fran. & Santa Rosa)
*PRACTICE AREAS: Finance and Commercial Law; Reorganization and Workouts; Creditor and Debtors Rights; Bankruptcy; Secured Transactions.
**Bowden, SusanBeth** '64 '93 C.999 A.B. L.770 J.D. [⊠ Crosby,H.R.&M.]
Boxer, Lawrence A. '40 '71 L.284 J.D. [Patton,W.&B.]
Boxer, Stewart N., (AV) '39 '66 C.102 B.A. L.262 LL.B. [Boxer,E.&G.]
Boxer, Elkind & Gerson, (AV) 171 12th St.
Brady, Lois I. '45 '87 C.665 B.A. L.1066 J.D. 1221 Broadway
Brandes, H. Paul '33 '62 C.37 B.S. L.813 LL.B.
Sr. Coun., Kaiser Found. Health Plan, Inc.
Brandt, Craig A. '57 '88 L.1230 J.D. 370 Grand Ave.
Braner, Matthew Curt '58 '85 C.112 B.A. L.1065 J.D. 4157 Emerald St.
**Branson, FitzGerald & Howard, A Professional Corporation**
**(See Redwood City)**
Bratcher, Gerald T. '43 '75 C.766 A.B. L.1065 J.D. 421 Bellevue Ave.
Bratter, Susanne '52 '79 C.763 B.A. L.1065 J.D. [Paoli&B.]
Brauer, William J., (AV) '44 '69 C.674 A.B. L.976 J.D. 5000 MacArthur Blvd.
Braverman, Robert A., (BV) '40 '66 C.1066 B.S. L.1065 J.D. 1611 Telegraph Ave.
**Braz, Sharon M.** '46 '87 C.112 B.S. L.765 J.D. [⊠ L.B.Blum]⊙
*PRACTICE AREAS: Family Law; Family Law Mediation.
**Brecher, Joseph J.** '41 '66 C.31 B.A. L.569 J.D. [Kennedy,G.M.&C.]
*LANGUAGES: Spanish.
*PRACTICE AREAS: Environmental Law; Land Use Law; Consumer Law; High Technology Law.
Breecker, Robert E. '45 '70 C.112 B.A. L.1066 J.D. 440 Grand Ave.
Brennan, Peter T., (BV) '43 '70 C.112 A.B. L.1066 J.D. Asst. Pub. Def.
Bressler, Sandra E. '43 '76 C.112 A.B. L.1066 J.D. 3837 Woodruff Ave.
**Bret, Thomas V.** '49 '77 C.767 B.S. L.284 J.D. [Knox R.]
*PRACTICE AREAS: Taxation; Estate Planning and Probate, Trust Law.
**Brewer, Steven J.**, (BV) '54 '80 C.112 B.A. L.1026 J.D. [Gwilliam,I.C.C.&B.]
*PRACTICE AREAS: General Negligence; Professional Malpractice; Product Liability; Construction Accidents.
Brindle, Thomas J., (AV) '48 '76 C.768 A.B. L.767 J.D. [Hanna,B.M.M.&J.]
**Brinley, Thomas E.** '64 '90 C.112 B.A. L.770 J.D. [⊠ Crosby,H.R.&M.]
Brockman, Robert J. '51 '79 1300 Clay St.
Brodie, Michael J. '45 '71 C.112 A.B. L.1065 J.D.
Sr. Staff Coun., State Compensation Ins. Fund‡
Brodie, Terrie B. '56 '90 C.112 B.S. L.284 J.D. Off. of Gen. Coun., Dept. of Navy

**Brody & Satz, (AV)**
**405 Fourteenth Street, Suite 1100, 94612**
**Telephone: 510-763-0600 Telex: WUI 650-250-5965 MCI MAIL: 250-5965 FAX: 510-763-0668**
**Members of Firm: Richard B. Satz; Mary M. Rudser.**
**Civil and Trial Practice. Business, Business Formation, Operation and Dissolution, Commercial Practice, Commercial and Retail Leases, Tax, Bankruptcy, Real Property, Estate Planning, Probate.**
***See Professional Biographies, OAKLAND, CALIFORNIA***

Brooks, Michael S. '44 '76 C.475 B.A. L.282 J.D. 7335 Skyline Blvd.
Brooks, W. Keith '46 '82 C.112 L.1197 J.D. 1440 Bway.
Brophy, D. Richard, (P.C.), (AV) '34 '62 C.267 B.A. L.767 LL.B. [Hanna,B.M.M.&J.]
Brower, Robert W. '46 '80 C.705 A.B. L.1026 J.D. 200 Webster St.
Brown, Elissa J. '55 '83 C.112 B.A. L.1066 J.D. 914 Bayview Ave.
**Brown, Eugene, Jr.**, (AV) '47 '78 C.112 A.B. L.767 J.D. [Hardin,C.L.E.&B.]
*PRACTICE AREAS: Products/Toxic Tort Liability; Governmental Tort Liability Law; Civil Trials.
**Brown, Gregory D.**, (AV) '49 '75 C.112 B.A. L.284 J.D. [Larson&B.]
Brown, H. Barksdale '63 '92 C.174 B.A. L.765 J.D. 180 Grant Ave.
Brown, Janet E. '65 '93 C.339 B.A. L.1066 J.D. [⊠ Sigman,L.&F.]
Brown, Joanne M., (AV) '47 '73 C.112 B.A. L.1066 J.D. Supr. Ct. Comr.
Brown, Judith T. '46 '77 C.705 A.B. L.1066 J.D. 407 Orange St.
**Brown, Lisa M.** '68 '93 C.112 B.A. L.494 J.D. [⊠ Hardin,C.L.E.&B.]
*PRACTICE AREAS: Civil Litigation; Products Liability; Toxic Torts.
Brown, Lorna Patton '46 '88 C.112 B.A. L.1065 J.D. 1970 Bway.
**Brown, Paula A.** '62 '89 C.588 B.S. L.1202 J.D. [⊠ L.C.Cavin,Jr.]
*PRACTICE AREAS: Maritime Personal Injury; Products Liability; Negligence; Medical Malpractice; Longshoreman and Harborworkers Compensation Act.
Brown, Terry G. '46 '78 C.145 B.S.B.A. L.1066 J.D. Dep. City Atty.
**Brown, Timothy N.**, (AV) '42 '68 C&L.309 A.B., LL.B.
[Crosby,H.R.&M.] (⊙San Fran.)
*PRACTICE AREAS: Real Estate; Environmental Law.
Brown, Victor Emmanuel '45 '88 C.982 B.S. L.284 J.D. 580 Grand Ave.
Brown, Walter A., Jr., (BV) '41 '68 C.112 B.A. L.1065 J.D. Dep. Dist. Atty.
Bruce & McCoy, (AV) One Kaiser Plz. (Pat.)
Brummer, George L. '54 '80 C.1044 B.A. L.665 J.D. [Hanna,B.M.M.&J.]
**Brunn, McKnight**, (AV) '19 '50 C.145 Ph.B. L.144 J.D. [⊠ Crosby,H.R.&M.]
Brunsell, Clayton W., (BV) '20 '51 C.112 A.B. L.1066 LL.B. 105 Jackson St.
**Brunson, Fatima Michon** '70 '96 C.1068 B.A. L.1066 J.D. [⊠ Fitzgerald,A.&B.]
*PRACTICE AREAS: Family Law; Probate Administration; Estate Planning.
Brush, Murray P., III, (BV) '29 '69 C.674 B.A. L.1066 LL.B. Dep. Dist. Atty.
**Bruzzone, Richard A.** '55 '82 C.813 B.S. L.770 J.D. [Crosby,H.R.&M.]
*PRACTICE AREAS: Real Estate.
Bryant, Barbara S., (AV) '49 '80 C.112 B.A. L.284 J.D. 492 9th St.
Bryson, David B., (AV) '41 '66
C.674 A.B. L.178 LL.B. National Econ. Develop. & Law Ctr.
Buccat, Betty O. '49 '76 C.112 B.A. L.1068 J.D. 3516 Rhoda Ave.
**Buckley, Mike C.**, (AV) '44 '70
C.112 A.B. L.1066 J.D. [Crosby,H.R.&M.] (⊙Santa Rosa)
*PRACTICE AREAS: Bankruptcy; Creditor and Debtor Rights; Secured Transactions.
Bukowski, Kenneth A. '64 '89 C&L.546 B.S., J.D. 1951 Webster St.
Buller, Terry D., (AV) '50 '76 C.766 B.A. L.767 J.D. [T.D.Buller]
Buller, Terry D., Professional Corporation, (AV) 1418 Lakeside Dr.
**Bupp, C. Randall**, (AV) '50 '75 C.188 B.A. L.1065 J.D. [Kornfield,P.&B.]
*PRACTICE AREAS: Bankruptcy Practice; Commercial Litigation; Financial Institution Representation Law.
Burgess, Peggy Anne '64 '90 C.93 B.A. L.767 J.D. 1221 Bway.
Burke, Bruce T. H. '50 '78 C.112 B.A. L.1065 J.D. 11 Embarcadero W.
**Burke, Georgia H.** '— '83 C.706 B.A. L.276 J.D. [⊠ Zackler&Assoc.]
*LANGUAGES: Japanese.
*PRACTICE AREAS: Food, Drug and Cosmetic Law; International Sales; Customs Law; Trademarks; Administrative Law.
Burke, Thomas F., (BV) '51 '83 C&L.770 B.A., J.D. Dep. Dist. Atty.
**Burnham, Clark J.**, (AV) '42 '68 C.112 B.A. L.1068 J.D. [Larson&B.]
Burnhill, Clifford, (AV) '07 '32 C&L.813 A.B., LL.B. 7211 Snake Rd.‡
**Burnison, Boyd E.**, (AV) '34 '62 C.350 B.S. L.1066 J.D. [Crosby,H.R.&M.]
*PRACTICE AREAS: Labor and Employment.

Burr, Anne Michelle . . . . . '63 '92 C.112 B.S. L.284 J.D. [Ⓐ Kazan,M.E.S.&A.]
Burr, Kenneth M., (AV) . . . . . '44 '74 C.1077 B.A. L.809 J.D. Dist. Atty. Off.
Burris, John L., (AV) . . . . . '45 '74 C.284 B.S. L.1066 J.D. 1212 Broadway
Burroughs, John Robert . . . . . '53 '86 C.309 A.B. L.1066 J.D. 1430 Franklin St.
**Burrows, Matthew H.** . . . . . '68 '94 C.112 B.A. L.1065 J.D. [Ⓐ Corbett&K.]⊙
**Bush, Philip L.**, (AV) . . . '49 '74 C.813 B.A. L.1065 J.D. [Crosby,H.R.&M.] (⊙San Fran.)
*PRACTICE AREAS: Business; Real Estate Finance and Acquisitions; Securities Regulation; Corporate and Partnership.
Byrnes, B. Rebecca . . . . . '49 '81 C.112 A.B. L.1067 J.D. Dep. Co. Coun.
Byrnes, Bryant H. . . . . . '51 '79 C.112 B.A. L.767 J.D. 180 Grand Ave.
Caftel, Brad J. . . . . . '52 '76 C.475 B.A. L.1066 J.D. National Econ. Develop. & Law Ctr.
Cahalan, Geo. M. . . . . . '13 '38 C.334 B.Sc. L.494 LL.B. 5656 LaSalle Ave.‡
Cake, Lee W., (BV) . . . . . '32 '64 C.112 B.A. L.1068 J.D. 270 Grand Ave.‡
Caldecott & Phillips, (AV) . . . . . Ste. 800, 405 14th St.
**Caleo, Paul D.** . . . . . '62 '86 C&L.061 B.A., LL.B. [Ⓐ Larson&B.]
Calhoun, Robert K., Jr. . . . . . '42 '71 C.696 A.B. L.976 LL.B. Asst. Pub. Def.
**Cali, Stephen L.** . . . . . '59 '88 C.112 B.A. L.284 J.D. [Ⓐ Lempres&W.]
*PRACTICE AREAS: Commercial; Construction; Legal Malpractice; Personal Injury; Property Damage.
**Cambray, Joan M.** . . . . . '56 '89 C.1154 B.S.N. L.1049 J.D. [Ⓐ Wendel,R.B.&D.]
*PRACTICE AREAS: Litigation.

**Camp, Priscilla, (AV) '41 '78 C.378 B.S. L.284 J.D.**
**The Arlington, 492 Ninth Street, Suite 300, 94607**
**Telephone: 510-465-3885 Fax: 510-839-9800**
***PRACTICE AREAS: Elder Law; Conservatorship; Probate; Long Term Care.**
**Elder Law, including Powers of Attorney, Probate, Conservatorship and MediCal Eligibility for Nursing Home Patients.**
*See Professional Biographies, OAKLAND, CALIFORNIA*

**Campbell, Joseph W.**, (AV) . . . . . '48 '72 C.197 A.B. L.1066 J.D. [Digardi&C.]
*PRACTICE AREAS: Motor Vehicle; Civil Litigation; Personal Injury; Wrongful Death; Claims and Government Torts.
Campbell, Karen D., (BV) . . . . . '50 '76 C.112 B.A. L.284 J.D. Dep. Dist. Atty.
Campbell, Richard M. '42 '67 C&L.884 A.B., J.D.
(adm. in PA; not adm. in CA) V.P., Krieger-Campbell, Inc.
Campbell, Robert F. . . . . . '58 '88 C.112 B.S. L.169 J.D. 1221 Broadway
Canning, Marcia Joan '48 '76
C.166 B.A. L.1065 J.D. Univ. Coun., Regents of the Univ. of Calif.
**Carbone, Michael P.**, (AV) . . . . . '42 '66 C&L.767 B.S., J.D. [Wendel,R.B.&D.]
*PRACTICE AREAS: Commercial Leasing; Real Property Development; Alternative Dispute Resolution.
**Carlson, Richard H.**, (AV) . . . . . '41 '67 C.112 A.B. L.1065 LL.B. [Anthony&C.]
*REPORTED CASES: Morris vs. County of Marin (1977) 18 Cal 3d 901; Sunseri vs. Camperos DeValle (1986) 185 Cal App 3d 559.
Carmine, Colton C., (BV) . . . . . '53 '79 C.1073 L.1197 J.D. Dep. Dist. Atty.
Carnagey, Roger A. . . . . . '52 '78 C.112 B.A. L.767 J.D. 1 Kaiser Plaza
**Carne, John E.**, (AV) . . . . . '46 '72 C.112 B.A. L.1066 J.D. [Crosby,H.R.&M.]
*PRACTICE AREAS: Media; Business Litigation; Property Taxation; Land Use and Condemnation Litigation.
Caro, Marie-Louise . . . . . '— '83 C.112 A.B. L.1065 J.D. U.S. Dist. Ct.
**Carolan, Duffy** . . . . . '62 '91 C.1075 B.S. L.767 J.D. [Ⓐ Crosby,H.R.&M.]
**Caron, Martha Louise**, (AV) . . . . . '51 '75 L.1067 J.D. [Liccardo,R.S.&M.]
*SPECIAL AGENCIES: California Association of Brokers.
*PRACTICE AREAS: Real Estate Law: Litigation, Arbitration & Mediation.
Carpenter, Christopher G., (AV) . . . . . '41 '67 C.112 B.A. L.1066 J.D. Asst. Dist. Atty.
**Carringer, Christine A.** . . . . . '54 '87 C.645 B.A. L.464 J.D. [Ⓐ Knox R.]
*PRACTICE AREAS: Civil Trial; Insurance Defense.
Carson, Susan M. . . . . . '58 '87 C.112 A.B. L.978 J.D. 1729 Wellington St.
Carter, Callan G. . . . . '67 '94 C.880 B.A. L.29 J.D. Staff Atty., Calif. Ctr. for Law & Deaf
Carter, Geoffrey N. . . . . . '44 '70 C&L.734 A.B., J.D. Mun. Ct. Comr.
Carter, Renée . . . . . '57 '89 C.112 B.S. L.767 J.D. P.O. Box 24653
Carter, Ronald W. . . . . . '55 '83 C.499 B.A. L.893 J.D. 630 20th St.
Cartwright, Joan S. . . . . . '43 '79 C.475 B.A. L.352 J.D. Mun. J.
Casalina, C. Stephen . . . . . '13 '44 L.765 LL.B. 418 3rd St.
Casetta, Jack . . . . . '57 '90 C.112 B.A. L.940 J.D. 492 Ninth St.
Casey, John C., (CV) . . . . . '48 '75 C.763 B.A. L.284 J.D. 1970 Bway.
Cassady, John J., (BV) . . . . . '37 '71 C.602 B.A. L.1153 J.D. 339 15th St.
Cassidy, Jane, (AV) . . . . . '50 '87 C.36 M.A. L.770 J.D. 6250 Merced Ave.
Cassman, Ted W. . . . . . '55 '81 C.813 B.S. L.1066 J.D. [Cooper,A.&C.]
Castellanos, Cecilia P. . . . . . '45 '74 C&L.37 B.A., J.D. 1300 Clay St.
**Castillo, Avalyn Y.** . . . . . '64 '91 C.309 A.B. L.846 J.D. [Ⓐ Crosby,H.R.&M.]
*LANGUAGES: Spanish.
Castillo, Felipe C. . . . . . '52 '77 C.112 B.A. L.800 J.D. 1611 Telegraph Ave.
Cate, Claudia . . . . . '44 '76 C.112 A.B. L.1066 J.D. Univ. of Calif.‡
**Caton, Kevin D.** . . . . . '65 '91 C.951 B.A. L.112 J.D. [Ⓐ Crosby,H.R.&M.]
**Cattani, Maryellen B.**, (AV) '43 '69 C.881 A.B. L.1066 J.D.
Exec. V.P. & Gen. Coun., Amer. Pres. Cos., Ltd.
Caudle, Welch, Politeo & Bovee, LLP, (AV) . . . . . 383 Fourth St., Ste. 201 (⊙Concord)
**Cavallero, Robert J.**, (BV) . . . . . '51 '77 C.770 B.S. L.767 J.D. [Mullen&F.]
**Cavalli, Steven R.**, (AV) . . . . . '48 '81 C.112 B.A. L.765 J.D. [Gwilliam,I.C.C.&B.]
*PRACTICE AREAS: Product Liability; Construction Accidents; Highway Design.
**Cavin, Lyle C., Jr.**, (AV) . . . . . '44 '70 C.740 B.A. L.284 J.D. [L.C.Cavin,Jr.]⊙
*PRACTICE AREAS: Maritime Personal Injury Law; Products Liability Law; Negligence Law; Medical Malpractice; Longshoreman and Harborworkers Compensation Act.

**Cavin, Lyle C., Jr., A Professional Corporation, (AV)**
**1432 Martin Luther King, Jr. Way, 94612**
**Telephone: 510-444-2501; 800-484-6044 Code 2501**
**Lyle C. Cavin, Jr.;—Paula A. Brown.**
**Maritime Personal Injury, Products Liability, Negligence, Medical Malpractice, Longshoreman and Harbor Workers Compensation Act.**

Ceasar, Sharon L. . . . . . '54 '92 C.112 B.A. L.310 J.D. 200 Webster St.
**Cederborg, Mark L.**, (BV) . . . . . '51 '79 C.774 B.A. L.464 J.D. [Knox R.]
*PRACTICE AREAS: Estate Planning; Probate and Trust Law; Conservatorships; Civil Trial Law and Asbestos Land Probate Litigation.
Cederborg, Timothy S., (BV) . . . . . '43 '69 C.112 A.B. L.1065 J.D. [Mullally&C.]
**Celestre, W. Michael** . . . . . '45 '73 C.112 B.A. L.1066 LL.B. 2101 Webster St. Ste. 1590
Chalik, John P. . . . . . '44 '72 C.170 B.A. L.1066 J.D. 308 63rd St.‡
**Chamberlain, Brad A.** . . . . . '54 '87 C.763 B.A. L.1065 J.D. [Crosby,H.R.&M.]
*PRACTICE AREAS: Business Law; Corporate Law.
Chambers, Robert F., (BV) . . . . . '47 '72 C.112 A.B. L.464 J.D. Dep. Dist. Atty.
Chambliss, Lorenzo E. . . . . . '41 '66 C.766 B.A. L.1066 LL.B. Sr. Dep. Co. Coun.
Chandler, Stephen M., (AV) '30 '54
C&L.813 A.B., LL.B. Pres., Wayne & Gladys Valley Found.
**Chang, Eun-Hee** . . . . . '55 '85 C.681 A.B. L.309 J.D. [Crosby,H.R.&M.]
*PRACTICE AREAS: Real Estate.

**Chapman, Marian C., (AV) '45 '76 C.112 A.B. L.770 J.D.**
**1939 Harrison Street, Suite 290, 94612-3532**
**Telephone: 510-444-0599 Fax: 510-238-5100**
***PRACTICE AREAS: Family Law; Mediation.**
*See Professional Biographies, OAKLAND, CALIFORNIA*

Chapuis & Ramsaur . . . . . 440 Grand Ave.
Chapuis Ramsaur, Rose C. . . . . . '46 '84 C.061 L.1153 J.D. [Chapuis&R.]
Chase, Douglas S., (BV) . . . . . '18 '50 C.112 A.B. L.1066 LL.B. [Chase&C.]
Chase, Jonathan S. . . . . . '52 '79 C.112 A.B. L.1065 J.D. [Chase&C.]
Chase, Martha M. '49 '76
C.112 A.B. L.1065 J.D. Univ. Coun., Regents of the Univ. of Calif.
Chase & Chase, (BV) . . . . . 11 Embarcadero W.
**Chen Fung, Jean Buo-lin** . . . . . '69 '95 C.813 B.S., A.B. L.1066 J.D. [Ⓐ Fitzgerald,A.&B.]
*LANGUAGES: Cantonese.
*PRACTICE AREAS: Environmental Law; Hazardous Waste.
Cherrin, Mervin N. . . . . . '43 '68 C&L.477 B.A., J.D. 180 Grand Ave.

**Cherry, James J., (AV) '44 '70 C.112 B.S. L.1067 J.D.**
**2030 Franklin Street, Fifth Floor, 94612**
**Telephone: 510-444-4033 Facsimile: 510-444-3667**
**General Real Estate, Real Estate Development, Construction, Public and Regulatory Approvals, Commercial Property Management, Franchise Operations, and General Business.**

Chesir, Daniel A. '42 '82 C.978 B.A. L.1065 J.D.
Coun., Kaiser Found. Health Plan, Inc.
Chester, Peter M. . . . . . '61 '87 C.771 B.A. L.978 J.D. 2000 Powell St. Ste. 1450
Chew, Hon, (BV) . . . . . '29 '55 C.112 B.S. L.1066 J.D. 822 Franklin St.
Chick, Warren H. . . . . . '45 '81 C.112 B.S. L.1066 J.D. 718 Grizzly Terrace Dr.
**Chilvers, Robert M.** . . . . . '42 '75 C.112 A.B. L.309 J.D. [Chilvers&T.]

**Chilvers & Taylor, P.C., (AV)**
**2030 Franklin Street, Fifth Floor, 94612**
**Telephone: 510-444-7744 Fax: 510-444-4713**
**Robert M. Chilvers; William "Zak" Taylor;—Leila Clark-Riddell.**
**Antitrust, Complex Business and Commercial Litigation and Health Care Industry Litigation, including Trials, Appeals, Mediation, Arbitration and Private Judging.**
**Representative Clients: Omni Healthcare, Inc.; San Francisco IPA; Saatchi & Saatchi Advertising, N.A., Inc.; United Broadcasting Co.any.**
*See Professional Biographies, OAKLAND, CALIFORNIA*

Chin, Francis F. '48 '74 C.112 A.B. L.1066 J.D.
Gen. Coun., Metropolitan Transp. Comm.
**Chinchilla, Hector J.** '53 '86
C.112 A.B. L.1065 J.D. [Crosby,H.R.&M.] (⊙San Francisco)
*PRACTICE AREAS: Business; Real Estate; Land Use; Commercial Litigation.
Ching, Lynn K. . . . . . '— '90 C.312 B.A. L.767 J.D. 483 Ninth St.
**Chiosso, James R.**, (AV) . . . . . '42 '75 C.767 B.A. L.1026 J.D. [Gwilliam,I.C.C.&B.]
*PRACTICE AREAS: Trials; Personal Injury; Product Liability; Governmental Torts; Employment Discrimination.
Chiu, Louise L. '33 '78 C.112 M.D. L.464 J.D.
Dir., Reg. Risk Mgmt. Dept., The Permanente Med. Grp., Inc.
Chiu, Nancy K. . . . . . '46 '75 C.94 B.A. L.426 J.D. Dep. Atty. Gen.
Chong, Oy-Lene . . . . . '52 '79 C.800 A.B. L.1065 J.D. 120 11th, 1st Fl.
Chorney, Christine A. . . . . . '48 '76 C.569 B.A. L.1065 J.D. 418 3rd St.
**Chow, Gareth M.** . . . . . '65 '94 C.112 B.S. L.770 J.D. [Ⓐ Kornfield,P.&B.]
*PRACTICE AREAS: Bankruptcy Practice; Business Law; Commercial Law; Real Estate Law.
Choy, Cheryl Y. K. . . . . . '53 '79 C.813 A.B. L.569 J.D. 2938 Millsbrae Ave.
Christensen, Pamela C. . . . . . '47 '77 C.172 B.S. L.767 J.D. 1999 Harrison St.
Chu, Norbert . . . . . '54 '81 C.477 B.A. L.767 J.D. Dep. Dist. Atty.
Ciullo, Virgilio . . . . . '41 '71 C.823 B.A. L.128 J.D. 1719 Clemens Rd.
Clancy, Edwin A., Jr., (AV) . . . . . '22 '52 C.112 A.B. L.765 LL.B. 405 14th St.
Clancy, Michael R. . . . . . '51 '78 C.311 B.A. L.1292 J.D. 491 9th St.
**Clark, Gail Prebil** '47 '81
C.770 B.A. L.1065 J.D. [Donahue,G.W.&W.] (⊙Walnut Creek)
*LANGUAGES: French.
*PRACTICE AREAS: Corporate Law; Securities; Computer Software.
Clark, Harriett W. '39 '65 C.254 B.A. L.329 J.D.
V.P. & Asst. Gen. Coun., Kaiser Found. Health Plan, Inc.
**Clark, Thomas D.** . . . . . '45 '72 C&L.1066 B.A., J.D. Asst. Port Atty. I, Port of Oakland
Clark, William S. . . . . . '34 '64 C.813 A.B. L.1065 LL.B. Dep. Atty. Gen.
**Clark-Riddell, Leila** . . . . . '65 '93 C.112 B.A. L.309 J.D. [Ⓐ Chilvers&T.]
Cleary, Christine L. . . . . . '— '88 L.284 J.D. 1440 Bway.
Cline, John P. . . . . . '44 '80 C.767 B.A. L.1026 J.D. 530 Water St.
Cline, Max, (BV) . . . . . '46 '70 C&L.94 A.B., J.D. 1300 Clay St.
Cline, Wilson E. . . . . '14 '40 C.623 A.B. L.1066 J.D. 3750 Harrison St., Suite 304‡
**Coan, Michael A.** . . . . . '51 '76 C.602 B.S. L.1066 J.D. [Aiken,K.&C.]
*PRACTICE AREAS: Estate Planning; Trusts; Probate; Nonprofit Corporations.
**Cobb, Charles A.** . . . . . '51 '78 C.629 B.B.A. L.1066 J.D. [Ⓐ Lempres&W.]
*PRACTICE AREAS: Real Estate Law; Corporate Law; Taxation Law.
Cody, Christopher T., (AV) . . . . . '51 '83 C.766 B.A. L.767 J.D. [Seltzer&C.]
Cohen, Barbara M. . . . . . '56 '84 C.174 B.A. L.112 J.D. [Gough&C.]
**Cohen, Jonathan M.** . . . . . '68 '93 C.910 B.A. L.1065 J.D. [Ⓐ Hardin,C.L.E.&B.]
*PRACTICE AREAS: Personal Injury; Products Liability; Insurance Defense.
Cohen, Mitchell S. Y. '63 '90
C.276 B.S.F.S. L.1065 J.D. Coun., Kaiser Found. Health Plan, Inc.
Cohen, Sidney J. . . . . . '41 '66 C.112 B.A. L.1066 J.D. [S.J.Cohen]
Cohen, Sidney J., Professional Corporation . . . . . 427 Grand Ave.
Cohn, Michael C. '46 '72
C.112 A.B. L.1065 J.D. Admin. Law J., Off. of Admin. Hearings
Cole, James O. . . . . '41 '71 C.824 B.A. L.309 J.D. V.P., Corp. Affs., The Clorax Company
Cole, William P., (BV) . . . . . '46 '80 [Krech&C.]
**Coles, Laura Jane** . . . . . '66 '93 C.861 B.A. L.1065 J.D. [Ⓐ Crosby,H.R.&M.]
**Collins, Carolyn** . . . . . '53 '78 C.112 B.A. L.767 J.D. [Berry&B.]
*LANGUAGES: Spanish.
Collins, Kendall D. . . . . . '42 '68 C.112 A.B. L.1065 J.D. [Collins&B.]
**Collins, Wayne M.**, (AV) . . . . . '45 '73 C.112 B.A. L.284 J.D. [McLemore,C.&T.]
*PRACTICE AREAS: Casualty Defense; General Civil Litigation; Construction Law.
Collins & Beeson, An Assn. incl. A Prof. Corp. . . . . . 1 Kaiser Plz.
**Colombo, John D.** . . . . . '60 '90 C.36 B.S. L.990 J.D. [Ⓐ Larson&B.]
**Colvig, Timothy A.** . . . . . '57 '84 C.112 B.S. L.1066 J.D. [Lempres&W.]
*REPORTED CASES: In re Foodsource, Inc., 130 B.R. 549 (N.D. Cal. 1991).
*PRACTICE AREAS: Environmental Law; Professional Liability Law; Insurance Coverage Law; Construction Law.
**Combs, Roy A.** . . . . . '59 '86 C.112 B.A. L.1066 J.D. [Kennedy,G.M.&C.]
**Conant, Matthew S.**, (AV) . . . . . '55 '80 C.112 B.A. L.1065 J.D. [Hardin,C.L.E.&B.]
*PRACTICE AREAS: Personal Injury Law; Products Liability Law; Insurance Defense Law.
Condie, R. Stevens, (BV) . . . . . '50 '74 C.112 A.B. L.1066 J.D. 11 Embarcadero, W.
Coney, Gail . . . . . '44 '72 C.170 B.A. L.1065 J.D. 370 Grand Ave.
**Conlon, Eamonn P.** . . . . . '61 '84 C&L.058 B.C.L., LL.M. [McInerney&D.]
*PRACTICE AREAS: Construction; Bankruptcy; Unfair Competition.
Cook, David C. . . . . . '61 '90 C.174 B.A. L.1065 J.D. Dep. Dist. Atty.
Cook, John L. . . . . . '34 '79 C&L.893 B.A. St. Atty.‡
Cook, Walter C. . . . . . '57 '83 C.112 B.S. L.284 J.D. 200 Webster St.
Coombs, Renate A. . . . . . '37 '81 C.966 Ph.D. L.776 J.D. 2 Windward Hill
Cooper, Colin R. . . . . . '64 '89 C.112 A.B. L.1066 J.D. Ste. N, 5900 Hollis St.

CAA425P

**Cooper, Gary C.** ....................................'55 '81 C.112 B.A. L.767 J.D. [Horton,W.&C.]
*PRACTICE AREAS: Customs; International Trade Law; Transportation Law.
Cooper, Lee C. .......................... '46 '72 C.597 B.A. L.1065 J.D. 45 Embarcadero Cove
**Cooper, Michael D.**, (AV) ..............'43 '69 C.766 B.A. L.767 J.D. [Wendel,R.B.&D.]
*PRACTICE AREAS: Bankruptcy Law; Reorganization Law; Business Workouts Law.
Cooper, Penelope M., (AV) ..............'38 '65 C.174 B.A. L.1066 J.D. [Cooper,A.&C.]
**Cooper, Thomas E.**, (BV) ..................'45 '70 C.112 A.B. L.1066 J.D. [Cooper,M.&B.]
*PRACTICE AREAS: Real Estate Law; Business Law.
Cooper, Arguedas & Cassman, (AV) ................ Ste. N, 5900 Hollis St. (Emeryville)

**Cooper, Margolin & Biatch, (BV)**
**1970 Broadway, Suite 940, 94612-2263**
**Telephone: 510-451-4114 Facsimile: 510-451-4115**
**Members of Firm: Thomas E. Cooper; Sanford H. Margolin; Joel A. Biatch. Of Counsel: Eric P. Gold; Frederick C. Hertz.**
**Real Estate Law and Lease Negotiations, Business Planning, Business Finance and Sales, Corporate and Partnership Law and Syndications, Architect and Construction Law, Estate and Tax Planning, Probate and Related Civil Litigation.**

***See Professional Biographies, OAKLAND, CALIFORNIA***

**Copeland, Bruce E.** ......................'61 '86 C.112 A.B. L.767 J.D. [Crosby,H.R.&M.]
*PRACTICE AREAS: Insurance and Environmental Coverage; Commercial Litigation.
**Coppinger, John J.** .......................'55 '81 C&L.770 B.S., J.D. [Donahue,G.W.&W.]
*PRACTICE AREAS: Complex Commercial Real Estate; Development and Land Use Law; Real Estate Finance.
Corbett, Laurence P., (AV) ........ '20 '50 C&L.309 A.B., J.D. 2000 Powell St. Ste. 1450

**Corbett & Kane, A Professional Corporation, (AV) BB**
**2000 Powell Street, Suite 1450 (Emeryville), 94608⊙**
**Telephone: 510-547-2434 Fax: 510-658-5014**
**Email: attorney@cklaw.com URL: http://www.cklaw.com**
**Judith Droz Keyes; Mary Maloney Roberts; Sharon J. Grodin; Tim J. Emert; Denise M. DeRose; Ian P. Fellerman;—Douglas N. Freifeld; Douglas J. Farmer; Philip Obbard; Joan Pugh Newman; Matthew H. Burrows; William L. Kasley.**
**Labor Relations, Employment Law and Litigation.**
**San Francisco, California Office: Citicorp Center, One Sansome Street, Suite 1900. Telephone: 415-956-4100.**

***See Professional Biographies, OAKLAND, CALIFORNIA***

Cornelius, Bruce A., (BV) .....'49 '75 C.112 B.A. L.1065 J.D. 2101 Webster St. Ste. 1590
Cornet, Stephen H., A Professional Corporation, (BV) '45 '71
C.112 A.B. L.1066 J.D. 3521 Grand Ave.
Cosgrove, Russel J. A., (BV) ...........'37 '69 C.768 B.A. L.1065 J.D. 3333 Grand Ave.
Costis, Athena R. ................................'64 '89 C&L.112 B.A., J.D. [🄰 Jewel&L.]
Cotter, Edward F., Jr. '51 '80
C.871 B.S. L.1065 J.D. Coun., Kaiser Found. Health Plan, Inc.
**Cottriel, Darren K.** ....................'69 '96 C.999 B.A. L.464 J.D. [🄰 Crosby,H.R.&M.]
Couenhoven, Paul .........................'54 '83 C.1144 B.A. L.912 J.D. Dep. Pub. Def.
Coulter-Peebles, Jacqueline, (CV) ..............................'— '80 L.1065 J.D. 180 Grand Ave.
Countryman, Ralph P., (BV) ............. '21 '73 C.112 B.S. L.1065 J.D. Dep. Dist. Atty.
Courts, Kathleen, (AV) ...................'46 '73 C.1036 B.A. L.1066 J.D. [White,C.M.&J.]
**Cowperthwaite, John G.**, (BV) ..........'53 '80 C.678 B.A. L.767 J.D. [Bennett,S.R.&A.]
*PRACTICE AREAS: Litigation; Surety Law; Construction Law.
Cox, Marjorie E., (AV) ........................'46 '78 C.289 B.A. L.767 J.D. Dep. Atty. Gen.
Crain, Nalda D. ......................................'54 '86 C.800 B.S. L.1065 J.D. 610 16th St.
**Cramer, Steven J.** ....................... '58 '83 C.770 B.S. L.1068 J.D. [Aiken,K.&C.]
*PRACTICE AREAS: Real Estate; Transactional Matters.
Creighton, John N., (BV) ................. '51 '84 C.112 B.A. L.767 J.D. Dep. Dist. Atty.

**Cresswell, Cake & Echeguren, A Professional Corporation, (AV)**
**270 Grand Avenue, 94610-0266**
**Mailing Address: P.O. Box 10266, Oakland, California 94610-0266**
**Telephone: 510-444-1735 Fax: 510-444-6923**
**Ronald D. Echeguren; G. Dennis Rodgers; Edward R. Karp; Andrew F. Noble; Greta L. Kaplan.**
**General Civil and Trial Practice. Casualty Insurance, Insurance Coverage and Professional Liability Law.**

***See Professional Biographies, OAKLAND, CALIFORNIA***

Crofton, Ralph L., (BV) ..........................'45 '75 C.912 B.B.A. L.477 J.D. Asst. Pub. Def.
**Cronen, Michael J.** ......................'58 '87 C.1097 B.A. L.1065 J.D. [🄰 H.Zimmerman]
*REPORTED CASES: Fraige v. American National Watermattress, 996 F.2d 295 (Fed.Cir. 1993).
*PRACTICE AREAS: Intellectual Property Litigation; Counseling.
**Crosby, Douglas A.** ............... '60 '87 C.813 B.A. L.770 J.D. [🄰 Donahue,G.W.&W.]
*PRACTICE AREAS: Real Estate; Commercial Leasing; Computer Law.

**Crosby, Heafey, Roach & May, Professional Corporation, (AV)**
**1999 Harrison Street, 94612-3573⊙**
**Telephone: 510-763-2000 FAX: 510-273-8832**
**Scott D. Baker; Kathy M. Banke (Certified Specialist, Appellate Law, The State Bar of California Board of Legal Specialization); Stephen G. Blitch; Douglas G. Boven; Timothy N. Brown; Richard A. Bruzzone; Mike C. Buckley; Boyd E. Burnison; Philip L. Bush; John E. Carne; Brad A. Chamberlain; Eun-Hee Chang; Hector J. Chinchilla; Bruce E. Copeland; Colleen T. Davies; Peter W. Davis (Certified Specialist, Appellate Law, The State Bar of California Board of Legal Specialization); Michael E. Delehunt; Charles W. Denny; John E. Dittoe; William A. Durgin; Bette B. Epstein; Paul D. Fogel (Certified Specialist, Appellate Law, The State Bar of California Board of Legal Specialization); Thomas M. Freeman; Joan M. Haratani; Edwin A. Heafey, Jr.; Ezra Hendon (Certified Specialist, Appellate Law, The State Bar of California Board of Legal Specialization); B. Clyde Hutchinson, III; Ned N. Isokawa; Howard A. Janssen; Jacqueline M. Jauregui; Gary A. Jeffrey; Craig S. J. Johns; Kenneth F. Johnson; John M. Kemp; John McD. Kern; Steven M. Kohn; F. Ronald Laupheimer; Michael J. Loeb; Joseph P. Mascovich; Louise M. McCabe; John L. McDonnell, Jr. (Certified Specialist, Probate, Estate Planning and Trust Law, The State Bar of California Board of Legal Specialization); Stephen A. McFeely (Managing Partner); Michele Ballard Miller; Randall D. Morrison; Ronald L. Murov; Jack R. Nelson; Lawrance W. Nile (1957-1994); Albert B. Norris, Jr.; Mary C. Oppedahl; Betty J. Orvell (Certified Specialist, Probate, Estate Planning and Trust Law, The State Bar of California Board of Legal Specialization); David V. Otterson; Kurt C. Peterson (Resident, Los Angeles Office); Thomas J. Quinlan; John A. Reding; Sean M. Rhatigan; Margaret R. Roisman (Certified Specialist, Probate, Estate Planning and Trust Law, The State Bar of California Board of Legal Specialization); Ronald V. Rosequist; Stephen H. Schadlich; William W. Schofield, Jr.; Gregory E. Schopf; Stephen G. Schrey; Charles H. Seaman; Kenneth M. Seeger; Ember L. Shinn; Boyd C. Sleeth; Walter E. Thomas; Morgan W. Tovey; Marshall Clark Wallace; Eric G. Wallis; William D. Wick; James T. Wilson; Malcolm B. Wittenberg; James M. Wood;—Jennifer Beckett; Susan P. Beneville; Marc R. Benson; Stephanie L. Berman; J. David Bickham; Steven J. Boranian; Anthony M. Bova; SusanBeth Bowden; Thomas E. Brinley; Duffy Carolan; Avalyn Y. Castillo; Kevin D. Caton; Laura Jane Coles; Darren K. Cottriel; Birgit A. Dachtera; David E. Durant; Barry N. Endick; W. Manning Evans; Alan S. Feiler; Gregg M. Ficks; Jennifer S. Fluet; Kerry McInerney Freeman; Todd Grant Gattoni; Stephanie A. Gleason; Jeffrey Goss; Samantha L. Hardaway; Terence N. Hawley; Helen S. Haynes; Lisa V. Heilbron; Carolyn E. Henel; Adaline Hilgard; John J. Horton; Tiffanie K. Kalmbach; Genevieve S. Katz; Jo Saxe Kerlinsky; Nathan P. Koenig; Jane Kow; Peter Laufenberg; Jacques B. LeBoeuf; Vera Marcus McEntee; Scott C. McKnight; Peter C. Meier; Tanda L. Neundorf; Robert A. Olson; Garth A. Osterman; William R. Overend; John P. Phillips; Toni A. Ragozzino; Shelagh K. Redding; James Daniel Riley, Jr.; Darren P. Roach; Jonathan C. Rolnick; Pamela G. H. Rupright; Robin J. Samuel; Pamela A. Schock; Jennifer A. Shy; John Lynn Smith; Randall J. Sperring; Walter M. Stella; Kristine De Serpa Stone; Adam H. Tachner; Robert A. Trodella, Jr.; Philip L. Tudor; Lindsey A. Urbina; Sonja S. Weissman; Leslie M. Yuki. Of Counsel: McKnight Brunn; Andre L. de Baubigny; James N. Dawe; Richard J. Heafey; Jay R. Martin; John D. Raskin (Certified Specialist, Estate Planning, Trust and Probate Law State Bar of California Board of Legal Specialization); Norman K. Tuttle II; Robert M. Winokur; Eugene K. Yamamoto.**
**General Civil Practice and Litigation in all State and Federal Courts. Litigation: Product Liability; Pharmaceutical and Medical Device; Insurance Coverage and Claims; Business Litigation; Labor and**

(This Listing Continued)



**Crosby, Heafey, Roach & May, Professional Corporation (Continued)**

**Employment; Intellectual Property; Environmental/Toxic Tort; Property, Land Use and Condemnation; Construction; Professional Liability; Antitrust; Appellate; Bankruptcy and Creditors' Rights; Media and First Amendment Rights; Health Care; Property Tax. Business: Real Estate; General Corporate and Partnership; Commercial Transactions; Mergers and Acquisitions, Trust and Estate Planning; Tax; Finance and Banking; Securities.**
**Representative Clients: Chrysler Corp.; Dean Witter Reynold, Inc.; Syntex Laboratories, Inc.; Union Pacific Railroad Co.; Westinghouse Electric Corp.**
**San Francisco, California Office: One Market Plaza Spear Street Tower, Suite 1800. Telephone: 415-543-8700. FAX: 415-391-8269.**
**Los Angeles, California Office: 700 South Flower Street, Suite 2200. Telephone: 213-896-8000. FAX: 213-896-8080.**
**Santa Rosa, California Office: 1330 N. Dutton. Telephone: 707-523-2433. FAX: 707-546-1360.**

***See Professional Biographies, OAKLAND, CALIFORNIA***

Crow, Margaret B. ... '58 '87 C.483 B.A. L.284 J.D. Staff Atty., Calif. Indian Legal Servs.
**Crow, Robert G.**, (BV) ...............'49 '74 C.112 B.A. L.1065 J.D. [Boornazian,J.&G.]
*PRACTICE AREAS: Toxic Tort; Environmental; Public Entity Litigation.
Cuellar, Armando G., Jr., (BV) ........... '51 '84 C.855 B.S. L.1153 J.D. Dep. Dist. Atty.

**Culley * Goodwin**
**(See Livermore)**

Culver, Taylor R., (BV) ......................... '44 '76 C.329 B.Arch. L.1066 J.D. [Culver]
Culver Law Firm, The, (BV) ................................................... P.O. Box 30393
Cumings, Anne Flower, (AV) ........................'42 '69 C.112 B.A. L.94 J.D. Pub. Def.
**Cummings, Fred V.**, (AV) ..................'28 '52 C&L.813 A.B., LL.B. [Aiken,K.&C.] ‡
Cunan, Jeffrey R. ........................... '61 '90 C.112 B.A. L.767 J.D. Off. of Dist. Atty.
**Curliano, Jason J.** ...................'64 '93 C.112 B.A. L.464 J.D. [🄰 Hardin,C.L.E.&B.]
*PRACTICE AREAS: Workplace Sexual Harassment and Discrimination; Personal Injury Torts Defense; Products Liability Defense.
Curnow, Rodger P. ...........'47 '82 C.645 B.A. L.464 J.D. 5856 College Ave., Suite 205
Curran, Donald W., (AV) ........'31 '59 C.112 A.B. L.1065 LL.B. 166 Santa Clara Ave.
**Curtis, Howard G., II** .......................'47 '77 C.870 B.S. L.1049 J.D. [🄰 Bell,R.&H.]
*PRACTICE AREAS: Government Contracts.
**Cutter, Edward A.**, (AV) '39 '65 C.813 B.A. L.309 J.D.
Sr. V.P., Gen. Coun. & Secy., The Clorox Co.
Cypher, James R., (AV) .............'30 '60 C.688 B.C.E. L.1066 J.D. 405 14th St. (Pat.)
Dabney-Smith, Candace ...................'64 '93 C.1077 B.A. L.36 J.D. 1951 Webster St.
**Dachtera, Birgit A.** ............... '63 '91 C.823 A.B. L.1065 J.D. [🄰 Crosby,H.R.&M.]
*LANGUAGES: German.

**Dailey, Garrett C., (AV) '47 '77 C.112 B.A. L.1067 J.D. BB**
**519 - 17th Street, 7th Floor, 94612**
**Telephone: 510-465-3920 Fax: 510-465-7348**
**Email: BriefCase@aol.com**
**(Certified Specialist, Family Law, The State Bar of California Board of Legal Specialization).**
**Practice Limited to Family Law.**
**Reference: Wells Fargo Bank (Oakland City Center Office).**

***See Professional Biographies, OAKLAND, CALIFORNIA***

Dal Porto, Steven David ......................'60 '89 C.770 B.A. L.767 J.D. Co. Dist. Atty.
**Daley, Michael J.** .............................'64 '90 C.112 A.B. L.280 J.D. [🄰 Ryan,A.&L.]
Daley, William P. ..................................'47 '72 C.154 A.B. L.1066 J.D. 1300 Clay St.
**Dalton, Michael J.** ....................'54 '84 C.112 A.B. L.1066 J.D. [Donahue,G.W.&W.]
*LANGUAGES: French, German and Italian.
*PRACTICE AREAS: Buying and Selling of Businesses; Corporate Law; Trademark Law.
**Dang, Douglas Y.**, (AV) ......................'42 '69 C.112 A.B. L.1065 J.D. [Dang&T.]
*PRACTICE AREAS: Municipal and Public Entity Defense; Environmental Law.

**Dang & Trachuk, (AV)**
**Suite 2360, Ordway Building, One Kaiser Plaza, 94612**
**Telephone: 510-832-8700 Fax: 510-836-2595**
**Members of Firm: Douglas Y. Dang; Thomas J. Trachuk.**
**General Civil Trial and Appellate Practice. Government, Business, Personal Injury, Real Property, Land Use, Products Liability, Insurance, Environmental and Construction Law.**

***See Professional Biographies, OAKLAND, CALIFORNIA***

Dangott, Morris A., (BV) .............................'31 '68 C.112 B.S. L.765 [Robbins&D.]
Danzig, Allison I. ..............................'60 '88 C.788 A.B. L.767 J.D. Dep. Dist. Atty.
**Darby, William L.** ............................'60 '88 C.118 B.A. L.494 J.D. [🄰 Lempres&W.]
*PRACTICE AREAS: Construction Litigation.
**Dardarian, Linda M.** ............'60 '87 C.147 B.A. L.1066 J.D. [🄰 Saperstein,G.D.&B.]
*PRACTICE AREAS: Litigation; Employment Law.
DaVega, Clayton W., (AV) ............... '31 '59 C.112 B.S. L.1065 J.D. Dep. Dist. Atty.
Davidson, Alan H., (A Professional Corporation), (BV) '31 '62
C.112 A.B. L.1026 J.D. Ref.
**Davies, Colleen T.** .......................'58 '83 C.112 B.A. L.770 J.D. [Crosby,H.R.&M.]
*PRACTICE AREAS: Product Liability; Pharmaceutical Liability; Commercial Litigation.
Davis, D. G. Jason .......................... '48 '74 C.112 A.B. L.1065 J.D. 405 14th St.
Davis, Frances M. ........................ '25 '54 C.112 B.A. L.1066 J.D. 3906 Laurel Ave.
**Davis, Kenneth A.** '51 '77 C.112 B.A. L.1065 J.D.
V.P. & Gen. Coun., American Protective Serv(s), Inc.
*RESPONSIBILITIES: General Corporate; Litigation; Employment Law.
Davis, Morris E. ....................'45 '70 C.548 B.S. L.352 J.D. 760 G Canyon Oaks Dr.
**Davis, Peter W.**, (AV) '42 '70
C.629 B.S. L.1065 J.D. [Crosby,H.R.&M.] (⊙San Francisco)
*PRACTICE AREAS: Appellate.
**Dawe, James N.**, (AV) ......................'43 '69 C&L.767 A.B., J.D. [🄲 Crosby,H.R.&M.]
Day, William K. ............................'26 '57 C.112 A.B. L.767 LL.B. 3792 Harrison St.‡
**Dean, Michael A.**, (AV) ..............'42 '67 C.768 B.A. L.1066 J.D. [Wendel,R.B.&D.]
*PRACTICE AREAS: Real Property Law; Business Law; Franchise Law.
**de Baubigny, Andre L.**, (AV) '32 '59
C&L.813 B.A., LL.B. [🄲 Crosby,H.R.&M.] (⊙San Fran.)
DeForce, Mark H., III ...................................................'43 '74 L.767 J.D. 1404 Franklin St.
**Delehunt, Michael E.**, (AV) ...........'48 '76 C.740 B.A. L.1065 J.D. [Crosby,H.R.&M.]
*PRACTICE AREAS: Commercial; Land Use; Environmental and Insurance Litigation.
Dell'Ario, A. Charles, (AV) ...............'47 '74 C.813 B.A. L.1065 J.D. [A.C.Dell'ario]
Dell'Ario, A. Charles, P.C., (AV) ........................................ 1999 Harrison St.
**Dell'Osso, Monica**, (AV) .........................'49 '82 C.739 B.A. L.1066 J.D. [Larson&B.]
DeLong, Robert D. ..............'59 '84 C.112 A.B. L.1066 J.D. 401 Grand Ave. Ste. 400
Delsman, Robert L. ......................'54 '89 C.285 B.A. L.1065 J.D. 1999 Harrison St.
Delucchi, Alfred A. ................................'31 '61 C.112 B.S. L.770 J.D. Super. Ct. J.
**De Martini, Vera C.** ............................'— '91 C.112 B.A. L.767 J.D. [🄰 Larson&B.]
*LANGUAGES: French.
**Demchak, Teresa** .....................'47 '76 C.161 B.A. L.1003 J.D. [Saperstein,G.D.&B.]
*PRACTICE AREAS: Litigation; Employment Law.
Denenberg, Barry A. '55 '80 C.546 B.S. L.770 J.D.
Coun., Kaiser Found. Health Plan, Inc.
**Denny, Charles W.**, (AV) .................'34 '59 C&L.502 A.B., LL.B. [Crosby,H.R.&M.]
*PRACTICE AREAS: Real Estate; Corporate; Domestic and International Transactions.
Denton, Charles M. ..................................'57 '82 C.112 B.A. L.1067 J.D. Asst. Pub. Def.
**De Pasquale, John A.** .................'62 '87 C.1044 B.A. L.884 J.D. [Hardin,C.L.E.&B.]
*PRACTICE AREAS: Products Liability Law; Toxic Substances Law; Civil Litigation.

**DeRose, Denise M.** .......................'51 '85 C&L.770 B.A., J.D. [Corbett&K.]⊙
*PRACTICE AREAS: Labor and Employment Law.
DeSantis, M. David .................'61 '86 C.94 B.S.B.A. L.228 J.D. 200 Webster St.
Desmond, Diane P. ...................'61 '89 C.1044 B.A. L.1065 J.D. 200 Webster St.
Devin, Michael D. ....................'53 '83 C.112 B.A. L.1065 J.D. 2101 Webster St.
**DeWalt, Eric R.** ........................'49 '88 C.838 B.A. L.767 J.D. [Kennedy,G.M.&C.]
Dewan, Bradford N. .....................'46 '72 C.309 A.B. L.966 J.D. 1999 Harrison
**DeWitt, Timothy A.** ....................'64 '90 C.112 B.S. L.1066 J.D. [Plageman&Assoc.]
Dias, Carol A. ...................................'60 '92 C.768 B.S. L.284 J.D. 200 Webster St.
Dibble, David ..............................'28 '63 C.112 A.B. L.1065 J.D. 2806 Bellaire Pl.
Dickerson, Dwight E. ......'52 '77 C.1036 B.A. L.477 J.D. Legal Aid Soc. of Alameda Co.
Dickie, Walter M., Jr., (BV) ...........'20 '50 C.112 B.A. L.1065 LL.B. 1624 Franklin St.
Dickman, Judith A. '52 '84 C.1140 B.A. L.1066 J.D.
Dept. of Health & Human Servs., Soc. Sec. Admn.
Dickson, Kathryn Burkett ...............'50 '76 C.813 B.A. L.1065 J.D. 1970 Broadway
Dickstein, Diane R. ...........................'51 '77 C.75 B.A. L.911 J.D. 1041 Hubert Rd.
Diem, Ann G. ...........................................'— '83 C.112 B.A. L.464 J.D. Dep. Dist. Atty.
**Digardi, Edward M., (AV)** ................'19 '47 C.112 A.B. L.1065 J.D. [Digardi&C.]
*PRACTICE AREAS: Admiralty; Aviation; Railroad; Products Liability; Work Related Accidents and Injuries.

**Digardi & Campbell, (AV)**
**Suite 600 Trans Pacific Centre, 1000 Broadway, 94607**
**Telephone: 510-832-5409; 832-5406**
**Members of Firm: Jesse Nichols (1899-1985); Edward M. Digardi; Joseph W. Campbell.**
**Civil Litigation including Personal Injury and Wrongful Death Claims in the Fields of Admiralty, Aviation, Motor Vehicle, Railroad, Premises, Government Tort, Products Liability and Work Related Accidents and Injuries. Professional Negligence.**
**Reference: First Interstate Bank.**
*See Professional Biographies, OAKLAND, CALIFORNIA*

Digiuseppe-Gillespie, Donna ....................'65 '92 C.112 B.A. L.767 J.D. 1330 Bway.
Dimas, Anthony .......................'49 '91 C.1201 B.S. L.1153 J.D. 2101 Webster St.
**Dini, Michael G.** ..........................'65 '92 C.112 B.A. L.770 J.D. [A Morton,L.&A.]
*SPECIAL AGENCIES: United States General Accounting Office.
*PRACTICE AREAS: Civil Trial; Insurance Defense.
**Dittoe, John E., (AV)** ....................'54 '79 C.112 B.S. L.1065 J.D. [Crosby,H.R.&M.]
*PRACTICE AREAS: Health Care; Insurance; Toxic Tort; Business Litigation.
**Dixon, Peter, (AV)** ...........................'41 '66 C.813 A.B. L.1065 LL.B. [Larson&B.]
Dolan, Michael C., (BV) .................'43 '78 C.112 B.A. L.1065 J.D. [B Boxer,E.&G.]
**Dolgoff, Susanne T.** ..............'64 '89 C.112 B.A. L.770 J.D. [A Donahue,G.W.&W.]
*PRACTICE AREAS: High Technology Law; Computer Law.
Dombrink, Stephen .................................'44 '69 C.770 B.A. L.1066 J.D. Mun. J.
Donahue, Anne K. ............................'60 '86 C.112 A.B. L.767 J.D. Dep. Dist. Atty.

**Donahue, Gallagher, Woods & Wood, (AV)**
**300 Lakeside Drive Suite 1900, 94612-3570⊙**
**Telephone: 510-451-0544 Facsimile: 510-832-1486**
**Members of Firm: William H. Donahue (1871-1948); James E. Gallagher (1911-1981); Bruce D. Gillies; Robert N. Wood; Wilfrid F. Roberge, Jr. (Certified Specialist, Estate Planning, Trust and Probate Law, The State Bar of California Board of Legal Specialization); Harrison S. Robinson; Andrew W. Lafrenz; George J. Barron; Lawrence K. Rockwell; Eric W. Doney; Thomas L. Hanavan; Gail Prebil Clark; John J. Coppinger; Michael J. Dalton; William R. Hill; Jonathan G. Wong. Associates: Douglas A. Crosby; A. Clifford Allen; Susanne T. Dolgoff; Gerald J. Karczewski; Jeanne M. Kluczник; David B. Sullivan; Robyn Renée Newcomb; Julie E. Hofer; Jonathan N. Osder; Paul J. Mori; Jason A. Geller; Barton L. Jacka; Carol B. O'Neill (Resident, Walnut Creek Office); Jonas W. Kant (Not admitted in CA); Stephen C. Gustafson; Leonid M. Zilberman. Of Counsel: Joseph A. Woods, Jr. Tax Counsel: Donald H. Read (Certified Specialist, Taxation Law, The State Bar of California Board of Legal Specialization).**
**General Civil and Trial Practice in all State and Federal Courts. Corporate, Real Property, Intellectual Property, Insurance, Immigration, Labor and Employment, Tax, Probate and Estate Planning Law.**
**Representative Clients: Adobe Systems, Inc.; American Stores Properties, Inc.; Autodesk, Inc.; Berkeley Farms; General American Life Insurance co.; Hancock Fabrics, Inc.; Jacuzzi, Inc.; Lucky Stores, Inc.; Mason-McDuffie Real Estate, Inc.**
**Mill Valley, California Office: Shelter Point, 591 Redwood Highway, Suite 1200. Telephone: 415-381-4161. Facsimile: 415-381-7515.**
**Walnut Creek, California Office: 1646 North California Boulevard, Suite 310. Telephone: 510-746-7770. Facsimile: 510-746-7776.**
*See Professional Biographies, OAKLAND, CALIFORNIA*

**Doney, Eric W.** ......'52 '77 C.112 B.A. L.1065 J.D. [Donahue,G.W.&W.] (⊙Mill Valley)
*PRACTICE AREAS: Computer Law; Computer Software; Copyright.
Dong, Donald D. ......................'39 '87 C.309 B.A. L.284 J.D. 801-A Franklin St.
Dorman, Kenneth J. .....................'55 '80 C.174 B.A. L.809 J.D. [Hanna,B.M.M.&J.]
Dorshkind, Michael I., (BV) ..............'48 '76 C.112 A.B. L.765 J.D. 1418 Lakeside Dr.
Doskow, Emily ...........................'62 '89 C.1169 B.A. L.1066 J.D. 2831 Telegraph Ave.
Dougherty, Michael R. ...........................'46 '75 C.112 A.B. L.1065 J.D. 1440 Bway.
Douglas, Anthony P., (BV) ...............'51 '85 C.112 B.S. L.1065 J.D. Dep. Dist. Atty..
Dovidio, Kathleen Ann ...................'55 '90 C.1078 B.A. L.1230 J.D. 3144 60th Ave.
Downey, Sheridan, III, (AV) .......'41 '67 C.813 B.A. L.1066 J.D. 4100-10 Redwood Rd.
**Downey, Thomas M.** ..............................'63 '89 C.608 B.A. L.851 J.D. [Larson&B.]
**Doyle, Gregory Michael, (AV)** ........'52 '80 C.112 B.A. L.767 J.D. [McLemore,C.&T.]
*PRACTICE AREAS: Insurance Defense; Litigation Defense; Construction Law (Defects).
Doyle, Philip J., (BV) ..............'18 '46 C.707 B.S. L.1066 LL.B. 4348 Montgomery St.
Draheim, David B., (AV) ...........'38 '65 C.112 B.A. L.1066 LL.B. [Hildebrand,M.&N.]
Drane, Robert W. ...........................'47 '86 C.184 B.A. L.1066 J.D. 1800 Harrison St.
Drexler, Charles ............................'46 '78 C.994 B.A. L.1065 J.D. 166 Santa Clara Ave.
**Dreyfuss, Kenneth A.** .................'52 '79 C.1036 B.A. L.767 J.D. [Knox R.] (⊙San Jose)
*PRACTICE AREAS: Civil Trial and Insurance Defense.
Droese, Karl E., Jr. ...........'36 '66 C.112 A.B. L.1065 J.D. Univ. Coun., Univ. of Calif.
Drown, Steven A. ...........'59 '85 C.112 A.B. L.629 J.D. Univ. Coun., Univ. of Calif.
**Drysdale, Philip E.** .....................'53 '90 C.309 A.B. L.861 J.D. [A Fitzgerald,A.&B.]
*PRACTICE AREAS: Labor and Employment Law; Litigation.
Dubner, Robin A. .............................'52 '84 C.221 B.F.A. L.284 J.D. 405 14th St.
Du Bois, Karen F. ..............'47 '79 C&L.813 B.A., J.D. Univ. Coun., Univ. of Calif.
Du Bois, William H. ............................'43 '70 C.629 B.A. L.1065 J.D. 1 Kaiser Plz.
**Dudley, Matthew G.** ..............................'69 '95 C.508 B.A. L.1065 J.D. [A Larson&B.]
Duggan, Deborah A. ...................'46 '84 C.1049 B.A. L.767 J.D. 6330 Telegraph Ave.
**Dunaway, Thiele R.** ...................'52 '87 C.57 A.B. L.1066 J.D. [A Wendel,R.B.&D.]
*PRACTICE AREAS: Environmental Law; Real Property Secured Transactions; Litigation.
**Dunlavey, James, (AV)** ...................'32 '57 C.187 A.B. L.1066 J.D. [Bell,R.&H.] ‡
Dunning, Scott T. .............'62 '87 C.112 B.A. L.284 J.D. [A.Laub] (⊙Walnut Creek)
**Durant, David E.** .......................'62 '90 C.705 B.A. L.145 J.D. [A Crosby,H.R.&M.]
Duren, Glen E., (BV) ............................'43 '70 C.112 A.B. L.284 J.D. Dep. Dist. Atty.
**Durgin, William A.** .....................'55 '84 C.321 A.B. L.770 J.D. [Crosby,H.R.&M.]
*PRACTICE AREAS: Real Estate.
Dusthimer, Jerry C., (P.C.), (AV) ......'34 '70 C.112 B.S. L.1026 J.D. [Hanna,B.M.M.&J.]
**Dutton, Sharon C.** '45 '87 C.112 B.S. L.464 J.D.
Coun., World Savings & Loan Assoc.
**Eassa, Robert D.** ......................'53 '83 C.766 B.A. L.1065 J.D. [Hardin,C.L.E.&B.]
*PRACTICE AREAS: Products Liability Law; Insurance Defense Law; Civil Litigation.
**Echeguren, Ronald D.** .....................'51 '77 C.112 A.B. L.1065 J.D. [Cresswell,C.&E.]
Edgar, William Robledo ..................'32 '59 C.112 A.B. L.1066 J.D. 4611 Malat St.

**Edises, Victoria, (BV)** ...................'51 '77 C.112 B.A. L.284 J.D. [Kazan,M.E.S.&A.]
*REPORTED CASES: General Foundry Service v. WCAB (Jackson), 42 Cal. 3d 331 (1986); Lustig v. Todd Shipyards Corp., 20 BRBS 207 (1988), aff'd 881 F.2d 593 (9th Cir. 1989); Bryant v. John's-Manville Corp., 137 Cal.App.3d 903 (1980); Berkebile v. Johns-Manville Corp. 144 Cal.App.3d 940 (1983); Steele v. Chevron, Inc., 219 Cal.App.3d 1265 (1990).
Edises, Higgins and Learn, (BV) ..................................................111 Broadway
Eger, Elena Marie '59 '89 C.112 A.B. L.1065 J.D.
Staff Coun., State Coastal Conservancy
Eggert, Paul H. '42 '68 C&L.966 B.A., J.D.
(adm. in WI; not adm. in CA) Reg. Atty., N.L.R.B.‡
**Eisner, Charles I., (BV)** ..............'49 '74 C.112 B.A. L.1065 J.D. [Boornazian,J.&G.]
*PRACTICE AREAS: Insurance Coverage; Wrongful Termination; Personal Injury Litigation.
Eldridge, Kathleen '48 '86 C&L.284 B.A., J.D.
Sr. Coun., Kaiser Found. Health Plan, Inc.
Elias, Erasmo E. ..........................'56 '81 C.425 B.A. L.1066 J.D. Co. Pub. Def.
Elias, Youseef ...........................'63 '91 C.296 B.S. L.1067 J.D. Off. of Pub. Def.
Elkind, Peter F., (AV) ......................'37 '63 C.604 A.B. L.813 LL.B. [Boxer,E.&G.]
Elkington, Sally J. .........................'48 '89 C.766 B.A. L.1230 J.D. 1440 Broadway
Ellis, Harold J. ..........................'40 '74 C&L.770 B.S., J.D. Dist. Atty's. Off.
**Emert, Tim J.** ..........................'49 '83 C.966 B.A. L.1065 J.D. [Corbett&K.]⊙
*PRACTICE AREAS: Labor and Employment Law.
Emeziem, Kelechi C. ....................'65 '92 C.061 B.Sc. L.494 J.D. 580 Grand Ave.
**Endick, Barry N.** ..........................'64 '89 C.145 B.A. L.569 J.D. [A Crosby,H.R.&M.]
**Engel, Barrie, (AV)** ..................'37 '63 C.112 A.B. L.1066 J.D. [Hardin,C.L.E.&B.]
*PRACTICE AREAS: Business Law; Corporate Law; Estate Planning Law.
**Engh, Elizabeth M.** ........................'52 '78 C.112 B.A. L.1066 J.D. [Aiken,K.&C.]
*PRACTICE AREAS: Estate Planning; Probate; Trust.
Ennix, Frank M., III ..................'35 '59 C.254 B.A. L.838 LL.B. 3300 Telegraph Ave.
**Epstein, Bette B., (AV)** ...............'44 '86 C.800 B.S. L.767 J.D. [Crosby,H.R.&M.]
*PRACTICE AREAS: Trust & Estate Litigation; Contested Conservatorships; Representation of Regional Centers.
Epstein, Keith A. ............................'57 '82 C.112 B.A. L.770 J.D. 155 Grand Ave.
**Epstein, Mark P.** ..........................'59 '90 C.882 B.A. L.273 J.D. [A Bjork,L.P.&K.]
*PRACTICE AREAS: Appellate Law; Automobile Law; Construction Defect Litigation; Defense of Legal and Medical Malpractice; Products Liability Law.
**Ercolini, Elaine** ....................'59 '87 C.112 A.B. L.1065 J.D. [A E.P.Schnurmacher]
*PRACTICE AREAS: Litigation.

**Ericksen, Arbuthnot, Kilduff, Day & Lindstrom, Inc., (AV)**
**530 Water Street Port Building, Suite 720, 94607-3746⊙**
**Telephone: 510-832-7770 Fax: 510-832-0102**
**Lois A. Lindstrom; William G. Hoback; Kendall A. Layne; Derek R. Longstaff; Pamela R. Peters; John V. Mejia; Gregory A. Mase.**
**General Civil, Trial and Appellate Practice in all State and Federal Courts. Insurance and Liability Defense, Environmental and Toxic Tort.**
**San Francisco, California Office: 260 California Street, Suite 1100. Telephone: 415-362-7126. Fax: 415-362-6401.**
**Sacramento, California Office: 100 Howe Avenue, Suite 240N. Telephone: 916-483-5181. Fax: 916-483-7558.**
**Fresno, California Office: 2440 West Shaw Avenue, Suite 101. Telephone: 209-449-2600. Fax: 209-449-2603.**
**San Jose, California Office: 152 North Third Street, Suite 700. Telephone: 408-286-0880. Fax: 408-286-0337.**
**Walnut Creek, California Office: 2700 Ygnacio Valley Road, Suite 280. Telephone: 510-947-1702. Fax: 510-947-4921.**
**Riverside, California Office: 1770 Iowa Avenue, Suite 210. Telephone: 909-682-3246. Fax: 909-682-4013.**
**Los Angeles, California Office: 835 Wilshire Boulevard, Suite 500. Telephone: 213-489-4411. Fax: 213-489-4332.**
*See Professional Biographies, OAKLAND, CALIFORNIA*

**Erickson, John H., (AV)** ...........'37 '69 C.976 B.A. L.1066 J.D. [Erickson,B.H.&W.]
Erickson, Robert J. ...........................'26 '55 C.629 A.B. L.309 LL.B. 1 Kaiser Plza.

**Erickson, Beasley, Hewitt & Wilson, (AV)**
**491 Ninth Street, 94607**
**Telephone: 510-839-3448 Fax: 510-839-1622**
**John H. Erickson; Alice M. Beasley; Henry S. Hewitt; Edwin J. Wilson, Jr.; Brenda Aguilar-Guerrero; Beatrice Liu; Margaret E. Moore; Sharon J. Persons.**
**Civil Litigation and Appellate Practice.**
*See Professional Biographies, OAKLAND, CALIFORNIA*

Ervin, Claire Irene ..........................'— '87 C.999 B.A. L.770 J.D. 300 Lakeside Dr.
Eshraghi, Sharmin Caroline ................'62 '89 C.605 A.B. L.276 J.D. Dep. Dist. Atty.
Eskanos, Irwin J., (BV) ........................'40 '66 C.174 L.767 J.D. [Eskanos&A.]
Eskanos & Adler, A Professional Corporation, (BV) .................. 5500 Redwood Rd.
Etheridge, Fred S. ..............'58 '86 C.112 B.A. L.878 J.D. East Bay Mun. Utility Dist.
Evans, Gloria G. '54 '78 C.43 B.A. L.836 J.D.
(adm. in TN; not adm. in CA) V.P. Human Resources, Coca-Cola Enterprises‡
Evans, Robert J. ..........................'45 '71 C.112 B.A. L.1066 J.D. 1440 Broadway
**Evans, W. Manning** ......................'61 '89 C.145 B.A. L.767 J.D. [A Crosby,H.R.&M.]
**Faber, Jollee C.** ................'65 '92 C.112 B.A. L.1068 J.D. [A Saperstein,G.D.&B.]
Fabian, Virginia R. .............................'17 '40 C&L.494 B.S.L., J.D. 82 Clarewood Ln.‡
Fairchild, Janet ............................'48 '75 C.976 B.A. L.1066 J.D. 3306 Harrison St.
Falche, Robert ..........................'46 '74 C.740 B.S. L.1065 J.D. 2 El Carmello Cir.
Falik, William A., (AV) ........................'46 '72 C.188 A.B. L.309 J.D. 1 Kaiser Plz.
Falt, Jeffrey L. ..............................'43 '71 C.112 B.A. L.1066 J.D. 314 Perkins
Famulener, Kathleen C. ...................'— '76 C.112 A.B. L.1065 J.D. Dep. Dist. Atty.
**Farley, Barbara Suzanne** ...............'49 '76 C.483 B.A. L.1065 J.D. [B Lempres&W.]
*PRACTICE AREAS: Business Litigation; Trust Law; Estates Law; Property Tax; Proposition 13.
**Farmer, Douglas J.** .......................'60 '89 C&L.309 A.B., J.D. [A Corbett&K.]⊙
**Farnsworth, Charles E., (AV)** ... '38 '69 C.378 B.S. L.813 LL.B. [B Van Blois,K.S.&B.]
*LANGUAGES: Spanish.
*PRACTICE AREAS: Employment Law; Personal Injury Law.

**Farrell, John J., (AV) '36 '74 C.1027 B.S. L.767 J.D.**
**414-13th Street, Sixth Floor, 94612**
**Telephone: 510-451-6732 Fax: 510-465-7023**
***PRACTICE AREAS: Civil Practice; Personal Injury Law; Products Liability Law; Federal Employers Liability Law.**
**General Practice.**

**Farrise, Simona A.** ...................'65 '94 C.209 B.S. L.284 J.D. [A Kazan,M.E.S.&A.]
*PRACTICE AREAS: Personal Injury; Toxic Torts.
**Fastiff Ellman, Pamela** ......................'64 '93 C.914 B.A. L.1065 J.D. [A Larson&B.]
*LANGUAGES: French.
Fasulis, Maxine ..............................'55 '87 C.766 B.A. L.767 J.D. Asst. Pub. Def.
**Feiler, Alan S.** ..............................'65 '91 C.30 B.A. L.597 J.D. [A Crosby,H.R.&M.]
Feinberg, Daniel M. ......................'61 '88 C.821 B.A. L.1066 J.D. [Sigman,L.&F.]
Felder, Frederick E., Jr. '43 '69 C&L.846 B.B.A., J.D.
(adm. in TX; not adm. in CA) 4124 Lincoln Ave.
Feldman, Linda S. ............................'47 '76 C.1036 L.1065 J.D. Dep. Pub. Def.
Feller, Susan .....................................'51 '80 C.1350 B.A. L.1066 J.D. 1970 Bway.
**Fellerman, Ian P.** ..........................'60 '85 C.112 B.A. L.1067 J.D. [Corbett&K.]⊙
*PRACTICE AREAS: Labor and Employment Law.

CALIFORNIA—OAKLAND MARTINDALE-HUBBELL LAW DIRECTORY 1997

Fenton, Nancy Elizabeth ............... '45 '76 C.881 A.B. L.1066 J.D. Off. of Co. Coun.
Ferguson, Richard L. ..................... '45 '78 C.309 A.B. L.813 J.D. 401 Grand Ave.
**Fergusson, Jennifer M.** .................. '68 '93 C.628 B.S. L.1065 J.D. [▣ Bell,R.&H.]
**Fernandez, Francis E.** ............ '48 '75 C.766 B.A. L.1066 J.D. [▣ Kazan,M.E.S.&A.]
*LANGUAGES: Spanish.
Ferreira, Michael Ann ..................... '47 '83 C.166 B.A. L.284 J.D. 2101 Webster St.
**Ferris, Peter H.** ........................... '50 '76 C.188 B.A. L.94 J.D. [Lempres&W.]
*PRACTICE AREAS: Insurance Coverage Law; Environmental Law; Professional Liability Law; Products Liability Law.
**Ficks, Gregg M.** ................... '65 '90 C.763 B.A. L.1067 J.D. [▣ Crosby,H.R.&M.]
Field, Douglas L., (AV) ..................... '48 '73 C.112 A.B. L.1067 J.D. [Taylor&F.]
Fierro, Rocio V. ............................ '61 '89 C.768 L.1065 J.D. Dep. City Atty.
Figman, Doris Michelle ..................... '49 '87 C.331 B.A. L.1153 J.D. 492 9th St.
Figueroa, Marta M. '50 '77 C.555 B.A. L.588 J.D.
(adm. in NJ; not adm. in CA) Nat. Labor Rel. Bd.
**Filice, Gennaro A., III**, (AV) ....... '49 '74 C.112 A.B. L.1065 J.D. [Hardin,C.L.E.&B.]
*PRACTICE AREAS: Products Liability Law; Toxic Substances Law; Environmental Law.
**Finberg, Charles E.** ............................. '51 '84 C.309 B.A. L.188 J.D. [Nevin&H.]
*PRACTICE AREAS: Accidents; Personal Injury; Insurance Defense; Litigation; Labor and Employment.
**Finch, Scott C.**, (BV) ........................ '53 '78 C.1074 B.A. L.464 J.D. [Larson&B.]
Fine, Naomi R. ........................ '— '81 C.1350 B.A. L.1067 J.D. Pres., Pro-Tec Data
**Finkle, Barbara** ..................... '53 '84 C.112 A.B. L.284 J.D. [▣ Wendel,R.B.&D.]
*PRACTICE AREAS: Corporate; General Business; Securities; Real Estate.
**Finn, Richard J.** ................................. '52 '81 C.569 B.A. L.767 J.D. [Larson&B.]
Finnegan, Michael D. .................. '46 '74 C.112 B.A. L.1067 J.D. Equitec Svgs. Bk.
**Firstman, Eric J.** ............................ '57 '83 C.112 B.A. L.1065 J.D. [Lempres&W.]
*PRACTICE AREAS: Construction Law; Real Property Litigation.
**Firtch, Susan E.** ................................ '55 '91 C.763 B.A. L.1067 [▣ Larson&B.]
**Fisher, Catherine M.** ........................ '55 '80 C.597 B.A. L.966 J.D. [Bell,R.&H.]
*PRACTICE AREAS: Business Law; Real Estate Law.
Fishleder, Marc G. .......................... '55 '82 C.477 B.A. L.1065 J.D. [King,K.&F.]

**Fitzgerald, Abbott & Beardsley LLP, (AV)** ▣▣
**A Partnership including Professional Corporations**
**1221 Broadway, 21st Floor, P.O. Box 12867, 94602-2867**
**Telephone: 510-451-3300 Telecopy: 510-451-1527**
**Members of Firm: Robert M. Fitzgerald (1858-1934); Carl H. Abbott (1867-1933); Charles A. Beardsley (1882-1963); James C. Soper (Inc.); Philip M. Jelley (Inc.) (Certified Specialist, Taxation Law, The State Bar of California Board of Legal Specialization); Gerald C. Smith; Lawrence R. Shepp; Richard T. White; Michael P. Walsh; J. Brittain Habegger; Virginia Palmer (Certified Specialist, Family Law, The State Bar of California Board of Legal Specialization); Timothy H. Smallsreed; Stephen M. Judson; Stephen M. Williams; Jonathan W. Redding; Beth E. Aspedon; Kristin A. Pace; Michael M.K. Sebree; Antonia L. More. Associates: Sarah Robertson McCuaig; Philip E. Drysdale; Kristen Thall Peters; Jay M. Goldman; Carlo C. Mormorunni; Michael S. Ward; Jean Buo-lin Chen Fung; Fatima Michon Brunson.**
**General Corporate, Business and Trial Practice. Banking, Taxation, Estate Planning, Probate, Trust and Estate Administration, Litigation, Securities Industry Litigation, Commercial Law, Real Estate Construction Law, Family and Elder law, Labor and Employment Law, Land Use Planning and Environmental Law.**
**Attorneys for: Peterson Tractor Co.; Sunset View Cemetery Assn.; Bigge Crane & Rigging Corp.; Gillig Corp.**
**Local Counsel for: Exxon Corp.**
*See Professional Biographies, OAKLAND, CALIFORNIA*

Fitzmaurice, Timothy Robert ......... '50 '94 C.112 B.S.C.E. L.1355 J.D. 2857 Hannah St.
**Fitzsimons, Dennis P.** ................ '52 '89 C.184 B.A. L.284 J.D. [▣ Boornazian,J.&G.]

**Flamm, Richard E. '53 '81 C.1169 B.A. L.705 J.D.**
**600 Grand Avenue, Suite 410, 94610**
**Telephone: 510-444-3075 Facsimile: 510-836-8927**
**Conflicts of Interest, Judicial Ethics, Disqualification, Motions and Appeals.**

Flanagan, John J. .................... '44 '69 C&L.215 A.B., J.D. Health & Human Servs.
Flashman, Stuart M. .................. '48 '90 C.103 A.B. L.1230 J.D. 5626 Ocean View Dr.

**Flehr, Hohbach, Test, Albritton & Herbert**
**(See San Francisco)**

Fletcher, James N. '52 '81 C.36 B.S. L.37 J.D.
(adm. in AZ; not adm. in CA) 7677 Oakport St.‡
**Fletcher, Laurel E.** ............... '63 '91 C.1036 B.A. L.309 J.D. [▣ Saperstein,G.D.&B.]
*PRACTICE AREAS: Litigation; Employment Law.
**Fletcher, Pamela C.** ......'50 '78 C.112 A.B. L.1065 J.D. Sr. Corp. Coun., The Clorox Co.
**Fluet, Jennifer S.** ....................... '68 '96 C.276 B.A. L.767 J.D. [▣ Crosby,H.R.&M.]
**Fogel, Paul D.** ........................ '49 '76 C.112 A.B. L.1068 J.D. [Crosby,H.R.&M.]
*LANGUAGES: French.
*PRACTICE AREAS: Appellate.
Fong, Marc A. ............................. '49 '78 C.1073 B.A. L.1026 J.D. [Fong&F.]
Fong, Marlene A. ............................ '55 '83 C.112 B.A. L.1153 J.D. [Fong&F.]
Fong, Richard, Jr., (P.C.) ...................... '51 '75 C.112 B.A. L.770 J.D. [Fong&F.]
Fong & Fong, A Law Corp. ...................................... 1 Kaiser Plaza, Ste. 785
Ford, Judith D. ................................ '35 '74 C.112 B.S. L.1066 J.D. Mun. Ct. J.
**Ford, Robert A.**, (AV) ..................... '43 '68 C.845 B.B.A. L.174 J.D. [Larson&B.]
Forte, Patrick L., (BV) ................. '51 '78 C.1073 B.A. L.1065 J.D. One Kaiser Plz.
**Fortes, R. Manuel** .......................... '58 '88 C&L.767 B.A., J.D. [▣ Mullen&F.]
Fowler, Teri, (Ms.) ..................... '29 '82 C.219 B.A. L.767 J.D. 300 Lakeside Dr.
Fox, A. Kathryn ................................................ '— '86 Community Law Ctr.
Fox, Anne K. (Katie) ................ '60 '86 C.219 B.A. L.767 J.D. Community Law Ctr.
Fox, Anthony Michael ........... '54 '88 C.766 B.A. L.770 J.D. 1900 Embarcadero Cove.
Fox, Pauline O., (AV) '51 '77 C.207 B.A. L.767 J.D.
Chf. Coun., Medical/Legal, Kaiser Found. Health Plan, Inc.
**Franciosa, Joel P.** ..................... '50 '93 C.740 B.A. L.1153 J.D. [McLemore,C.&T.]
*PRACTICE AREAS: Casualty Defense.
**Franklin, Theodore** ............................ '49 '93 L.1065 [▣ Van Bourg,W.R.&R.]
*PRACTICE AREAS: Labor.
Fraser, Brian ............................ '53 '89 C.112 B.A. L.1067 J.D. 6114 LaSalle Ave.
**Frassetto, Robert J.** ................... '56 '82 C.112 B.A. L.770 J.D. [Haims,J.M.&M.]
*PRACTICE AREAS: Insurance Defense Law; Products Liability Law; Fire Loss Litigation; Toxic Exposure; Alternative Dispute Resolution.
Frates, Robert A. '55 '81 C.112 A.B. L.1066 J.D.
Coun., Myron Zimmerman Investments
**Fraysse, Thomas E.**, (BV) ......... '56 '82 C.112 B.A. L.464 J.D. [Knox R.] (©San Jose)
*PRACTICE AREAS: Civil Trial; Insurance Defense and Asbestos Litigation.
Frediani, Lynette M. .................... '63 '88 C.1074 B.S. L.1065 J.D. One Kaiser Plaza
Fredrickson, David R. ................ '60 '87 C.112 A.B. L.276 J.D. 1999 Harrison St.
**Free, Douglas S.** ................................ '63 '91 C.93 B.A. L.770 J.D. [▣ Larson&B.]
**Freedman, Beth S.** ............................ '68 '93 C.112 B.A. L.770 J.D. [▣ Larson&B.]
Freedman, Robert B., (AV) .......... '43 '69 C.112 B.A. L.1066 J.D. Emeryville, Mun. J.
**Freeman, Kerry McInerney** ....... '68 '96 C.112 B.A. L.1066 J.D. [▣ Crosby,H.R.&M.]
**Freeman, Thomas M.** ................. '54 '83 C.112 A.B. L.1065 J.D. [Crosby,H.R.&M.]
*PRACTICE AREAS: Civil Litigation; Products Liability; Insurance Coverage.
**Freifeld, Douglas N.** ........................ '53 '84 C.813 A.B. L.178 J.D. [▣ Corbett&K.]©
Friborg, J. Robt. ........................... '11 '36 C.112 B.S. L.1066 LL.B. Ret. Mun. J.
Fried, Barbara D. ...................... '65 '93 C.918 B.A. L.1068 J.D. 1999 Harrison
Friedberg, Martha E. .......................... '47 '78 C.569 B.A. L.284 J.D. 1440 Broadway
Friedman, Alissa ................................. '61 '87 C.309 A.B. L.1066 J.D. [Friend&F.]
Friedman, Daniel P. ............ '47 '72 C.347 B.S. L.813 J.D. Partner, John Brooker & Co.
Friedman, Harold G., (BV) ............. '47 '72 C.112 A.B. L.1066 J.D. Chf. Asst. Pub. Def.

**Friedman, Jeremy L. '61 '88 C.103 A.B. L.145 J.D.**
**2801 Sylhowe Road, 94602**
**Telephone: 510-530-9060 Fax: 510-530-9087**
**Civil Trial and Appellate Practice. Civil Rights Litigation, Attorneys' Fees Litigation and Qui Tam False Claims Act Prosecutions.**
*See Professional Biographies, OAKLAND, CALIFORNIA*

Friend, Teresa Lynn .............................. '57 '84 C.145 B.A. L.1066 J.D. [Friend&F.]
Friend & Friedman ...................................................... 4054 Forest Hill Ave.
Fritz, Daniel R. ...... '51 '77 C.112 A.B. L.767 J.D. Coun., Kaiser Found. Health Plan, Inc.
Fry, Robert P., Jr. ................ '54 '79 C.800 A.B. L.1068 J.D. Dir., Mktg., Anselm, Inc.
Fuchs, Jan ..................................... '58 '84 C.1044 B.A. L.284 J.D. 155 Grand Ave.
Fung, Ralph .................................. '24 '61 C&L.284 B.B.A., LL.B. 4081 Oak Hill Rd.‡
Gaffey, Michael J., (BV) ................ '56 '84 C.426 B.A. L.1065 J.D. Dep. Dist. Atty.
**Galleano, Paula J.** ..................... '52 '80 C.112 B.A. L.128 J.D. [▣ Plageman&Assoc.]
*PRACTICE AREAS: Real Estate; Land Use; Corporate; Environmental; Municipal Finance.
Gannon, Michael J., (BV) .................. '43 '69 C.112 B.A. L.1065 J.D. 169 14th St.
Garcia, Yvonne R. ......................... '49 '75 C.112 A.B. L.1065 J.D. Off. of the Mayor
Gardner, Michael A., (BV) ............. '45 '73 C.107 B.A. L.1065 J.D. One Kaiser Plz.
**Garthe, David J.**, (AV) ................ '46 '72 C.112 B.A. L.1067 J.D. [Boornazian,J.&G.]
*PRACTICE AREAS: Insurance Coverage; Personal Injury; Products Litigation.
Gaskill, Jay B., (AV) ..................... '41 '67 C.336 B.A. L.1066 J.D. Chf. Pub. Def.

**Gassett, Perry & Frank, (AV)**
**One Kaiser Plaza, Suite 1330, 94612©**
**Telephone: 510-645-1487 Fax: 510-763-7284**
**Resident Members: Ronald Valencia; Thomas A. Wilberding; Robin Y. Trembath; Sean W. Morrisroe. Resident Associates: Dean A. Tompkins; Bruce A. Berman; Daniel J. Ban; Steven M. Leeb.**
**General Civil and Trial Practice in all State and Federal Courts. Insurance and Workers Compensation Law.**
**San Jose, California Office: 210 North Fourth Street, Suite 400. Telephone: 408-295-7034. Telecopier: 408-295-5799.**
**Santa Cruz, California Office: 55 River Street, Suite 200. Telephone: 408-425-5023. Fax: 408-427-3159.**
*See Professional Biographies, OAKLAND, CALIFORNIA*

Gates, Patricia M. '52 '77 C.241 B.S. L.767 J.D.
Admr., Painting & Drywall Work Preservation Fund
**Gatt, Frederick W.** ..................... '58 '87 C&L.767 B.A., J.D. [▣ Bennett,S.R.&A.]
*PRACTICE AREAS: Insurance Defense; Products Liability; Civil Litigation.
**Gattoni, Todd Grant** ..................'66 '91 C.477 B.A. L.209 J.D. [▣ Crosby,H.R.&M.]
Gaylord, Carl R. ....................... '28 '56 C&L.477 A.B., J.D. 492 Staten Ave.‡
Gee, Michelle M. ...................... '53 '79 C.914 B.A. L.284 J.D. 2626 Harrison St.
**Gelini, Thomas S.** ........................ '66 '91 C.1066 B.A. L.767 J.D. [▣ Bennett,S.R.&A.]
*PRACTICE AREAS: Litigation; Insurance Defense Law.
**Geller, Jason A.** ..................... '66 '93 C.112 B.A. L.285 J.D. [▣ Donahue,G.W.&W.]
*LANGUAGES: Spanish.

**General Counsel Services, A Professional Law Corporation, (AV)** ▣▣
**725 Washington Street, 2nd Floor, 94607©**
**Telephone: 510-891-0620 Fax: 510-836-3331**
**Email: dhicks@astsoft.com URL: http://www.genlaw.com**
**David Hicks. Associate Counsel: Daniel E. Behrendt, Esq. Of Counsel: Christopher P. Valle-Riestra, Esq.**
**Business, Labor, Governmental Regulation, Insurance, Unfair Competition, Trade Secrets, Negligence, First Amendment Litigation, Defamation, Food, Drug and Cosmetic Law. State and Federal Litigation Court.**
**Beverly Hills, California Office: 9606 Santa Monica Boulevard, Third Floor, 90210.**
*See Professional Biographies, OAKLAND, CALIFORNIA*

Gentry, H. Clarke ............................ '44 '73 C.197 A.B. L.575 J.D. 481 60th St.
Gerber, Mary A. .................... '43 '78 C.112 B.A. L.284 J.D. 4319 Piedmont Ave.
Gerson, Michael G., (AV) ..................... '48 '74 C.763 B.S. L.767 J.D. [Boxer,E.&G.]
Giachino, Michael L. ..................... '51 '79 C.112 A.B. L.765 J.D. [Hanna,B.M.M.&J.]
**Giacoletti, Paul A.** ..................... '63 '89 C.112 B.A. L.770 J.D. [▣ Boornazian,J.&G.]
Giambroni, Francis R., (AV) ........... '30 '55 C.602 A.B. L.1066 LL.B. [F.R.Giambroni]
Giambroni, Francis R., P.C., (AV) ........................................ P.O. Box 20129
Gianunzio, Victor J., (AV) ............. '33 '63 C.112 A.B. L.1065 200 Webster St.

**Gibbs, William D., (AV) '38 '64 C.766 B.A. L.1065 J.D.**
**169 14th Street, P.O. Box 1917, 94604-1917**
**Telephone: 510-893-2270**
**Practice Limited to Personal Injury, Negligence, Business Tort and Professional Negligence Actions.**
*See Professional Biographies, OAKLAND, CALIFORNIA*

Gibson, Daniel E. .................... '40 '66 C.1066 B.A. L.309 LL.B. 13778 Campus Dr.
Gibson, Marjory F. ............... '— '70 C.102 B.A. L.309 LL.B. 405 14th St. @ Franklin
Gifford, Jackson T. ............................................. '28 '59 L.1026 LL.B. Mun. J.
**Gilbert, Frank J.** ........................ '60 '87 C.477 B.A. L.767 J.D. [▣ Neal&Assoc.]
*PRACTICE AREAS: Litigation; Real Estate Law; Business Law.
**Gilbert, Peter R.**, (AV) ..................... '47 '74 C.549 B.A. L.284 J.D. [Berry&B.]
Giller, James, (AV) ........................ '28 '53 C&L.494 B.S.L., J.D. [Mintz,G.&M.]
**Gillies, Bruce D.**, (AV) ............. '35 '63 C.813 A.B. L.1066 J.D. [Donahue,G.W.&W.]
*PRACTICE AREAS: Business Law; Employee Benefit Law.

**Gillin, Jacobson, Ellis, Larsen & Doyle**
**(See Orinda)**

**Ginn, David W.** ........................ '59 '86 C.112 B.A. L.1065 J.D. [▣ Lempres&W.]
Ginsburg, Rachel D., (BV) ............. '51 '79 C.112 B.A. L.1067 J.D. 2030 Franklin St.
Girard, Dawn B. .............................. '32 '56 C&L.107 B.A., LL.B. Supr. Ct. J.
Giuntini, Russell J., (AV) ......... '50 '78 C.740 B.A. L.765 LL.B. Off. of Dep. Dist. Atty.

**Given, James T. '54 '79 C.347 A.B. L.1066 J.D.**
**5825 Margarido Drive, 94618**
**Telephone: 510-655-6749**
**Email: jtg@fwpa.com**
***PRACTICE AREAS: Intellectual Property (40%); Business Law (40%); Real Estate (20%). General Business.**
*See Professional Biographies, OAKLAND, CALIFORNIA*

**Glaessner, Peter O.** ................. '55 '80 C.112 B.A. L.1049 J.D. [Hardin,C.L.E.&B.]
*PRACTICE AREAS: Insurance Law and Litigation; Professional Liability.
Glavinovich, Gary P., (BV) .................. '37 '63 C&L.770 B.S., J.D. 1900 Embarcadero
**Gleason, Stephanie A.** ................ '67 '94 C.740 B.A. L.767 J.D. [▣ Crosby,H.R.&M.]
**Goddard, Wendell H.**, (AV) ............... '45 '75 C.976 B.A. L.1066 J.D. [Gordon&G.]
Goerl, Conrad H., (BV) ..................... '19 '52 C.112 B.A. L.765 LL.B. 405 14th St.
Goggin, Edw. A., (BV) ..................... '11 '37 C.112 A.B. L.1066 LL.B. City Atty.
**Gold, Eric P.** ............................ '45 '71 C.145 B.A. L.1066 J.D. [© Cooper,M.&B.]
Gold, Samuel L. ................... '06 '30 C.112 A.B. L.1066 J.D. 398 Adams St., Apt 305‡

**Goldberg, Stinnett, Meyers & Davis, A Professional Corporation**
**(See San Francisco)**

Goldblatt, Ellen S. .......... '48 '78 C.569 B.A. L.1066 J.D. Protection & Advocacy, Inc.

Golde, Stanley P. .................................. '28 '53 C.112 A.B. L.1066 LL.B. Supr. Ct. J.
**Goldman, David**, (BV) ............... '52 '77 C.475 B.A. L.1065 J.D. [Wendel,R.B.&D.]
*PRACTICE AREAS: Employment Litigation; Real Property Litigation; Business Litigation.
**Goldman, Jay M.** .................... '56 '93 C.766 B.A. L.310 J.D. [Ⓐ Fitzgerald,A.&B.]
*PRACTICE AREAS: Business and Commercial Litigation; Securities Litigation; Products Liability; Premises Liability.
Goldman, Ronald E. '55 '80
C.30 B.A. L.1049 J.D. Sr. Coun., Kaiser Found. Health Plan, Inc.
Goldsmith, William P. ......................... '45 '85 C.112 B.A. L.765 J.D. Asst. Pub. Def.
**Goldstein, Barry** ....................... '45 '71 C.309 B.A. L.178 J.D. [Saperstein,G.D.&B.]
*PRACTICE AREAS: Litigation; Employment Law.
Goldstein, Robert A., (BV) .................. '40 '66 C.659 B.S. L.1066 LL.B. [R.A.Goldstein]
Goldstein, Robert A., A Professional Corporation, (BV) ..................... 1430 Franklin St.
Gomberg, Joel ............................. '46 '71 C.597 B.A. L.145 J.D. Workers Comp. J.
Gomez, Marco '55 '82
C.139 B.A. L.1068 J.D. San Francisco Bay Area Rapid Transit Dist.
Gondak, Cristine E. ............................ '49 '75 C.813 A.B. L.1065 J.D. [Hanna,B.M.M.&J.]
**Gong, Raymond G.** ..................... '48 '73 C.813 B.A. L.1066 J.D. [Kennedy,G.M.&C.]
González, Eduardo A. ........................ '57 '86 C.800 B.S. L.1066 J.D. 519 17th St.
Goodale, Mark R. .................................. '67 '94 C.112 B.A. L.464 J.D. 200 Webster St.
Goodfellow, Jonathan J., (BV) ........ '51 '77 C.112 A.B. L.284 J.D. Sr. Dep. Dist. Atty.
Goodlaw, Deene ........................ '41 '66 C.813 B.A. L.309 LL.B. [⊡ Sigman,L.&F.]
Goodman, Larry J. ............................... '49 '74 C.813 A.B. L.767 J.D. Supr. Ct. J.
Goodman, Richard A., (AV) ............. '49 '74 C.112 B.A. L.1068 J.D. [Goodman&L.]
Goodman & Levine, (AV) ........................................................ 1 Kaiser Plz.
**Goodroe, H. Wayne**, (AV) .......................... '43 '75 C.871 B.S. L.61 J.D. [Larson&B.]
Gordon, Jules H. ................................ '26 '55 C.145 A.B. L.107 J.D. 631 Hillgirt Cir.
**Gordon, Paul M.**, (AV) ........................ '52 '77 C.112 A.B. L.1066 J.D. [Gordon&G.]

**Gordon & Goddard, L.L.P., (AV)**
**One Kaiser Plaza, Suite 2360, 94612**
**Telephone: 510-836-2400 Fax: 510-836-2595**
**Members of Firm: Paul M. Gordon; Wendell H. Goddard.**
**General Civil and Trial Practice, Business Litigation, Unfair Competition, Real Estate, Construction, Employment, Intellectual Property, Trademark, Product Liability, Insurance, Malpractice, Probate and Property Tax Litigation.**
*See Professional Biographies, OAKLAND, CALIFORNIA*

Gorman, Thomas R. ............. '48 '76 C.602 B.S. L.1067 J.D. 1736 Franklin St. 8th Fl.
Goss, Frederick L. ..................................... '44 '87 C.112 B.A. L.767 J.D. 1 Kaiser Plz.
**Goss, Jeffrey** ............................ '65 '95 C.825 B.S. L.893 J.D. [Ⓐ Crosby,H.R.&M.]
Gough, Judith D., (AV) ............ '38 '75 C.112 B.A. L.765 J.D. 3710 Grand Ave. 2nd Fl.
Gough, Kerry M., (AV) ........................ '37 '67 C.112 B.A. L.1066 J.D. [Gough&C.]
Gough & Cohen, (AV) ................................................................ 160 Franklin St.
**Gould, Glenn** .................................... '62 '89 C.910 B.A. L.978 J.D. [Ⓐ Ryan,A.&L.]
Graff, Thomas J. ....... '44 '68 C&L.309 B.A., J.D. Reg. Coun., Environmental Def. Fund
**Graham, Matthew F.** .................. '56 '80 C&L.767 B.A., J.D. [Aiken,K.&C.]
*PRACTICE AREAS: Litigation; Construction Law; Labor and Employment.
Grant, Jeffrey A., (AV) ................ '53 '80 C.112 B.A. L.1065 J.D. [Hanna,B.M.M.&J.]

**Graves & Allen, (AV)**
**2101 Webster Street, Suite 1746, 94612**
**Mailing Address: P.O. Box 30817, Oakland, CA 94604-6917**
**Telephone: 510-839-8777 Telecopier: 510-839-5192**
**Email: jallenlaw@aol.com**
**Jeffrey Allen.**
**Civil and Trial Practice. Real Estate and Business.**
*See Professional Biographies, OAKLAND, CALIFORNIA*

Gray, Robert B., (BV) ................................ '40 '72 C.1073 B.A. L.1066 J.D. 1970 Bdway.
**Gray, Steven J.** '55 '82 C.1044 B.S. L.1065 J.D.
Chf. Legal Coun., Mut. Fund. Org., World Savings & Loan Assoc.
**Green, Tracy** .................................. '57 '84 C.1169 B.A. L.767 J.D. [Ⓐ Wendel,R.B.&D.]
*REPORTED CASES: In re Seawinds, Ltd. v. Xtra, Inc., 91 B.R. 88 (Bankr. N.D. Cal. 1988).
*PRACTICE AREAS: Bankruptcy Law; Commercial Reorganization.
**Greene, Alison F.** .............................. '64 '90 C.112 B.A. L.1065 J.D. [Ⓐ Larson&B.]
*LANGUAGES: Hebrew.
Greene, Kevin K. .......................... '62 '90 C&L.464 B.A., J.D. 1999 Harrison St.
Greenfield, Gary, (AV) ....... '49 '75 C.813 A.B. L.1066 J.D. Litigation Cost Management
**Gritzer, Anne Cobbledick** ................. '51 '93 C.1273 B.A. L.744 J.D. [Ⓐ Larson&B.]
**Grodin, Sharon J.** ........................ '56 '83 C.103 B.A. L.831 J.D. [Corbett&K.]⊙
*PRACTICE AREAS: Labor and Employment Law.
Groen, Eugene G., (BV) ............... '34 '67 C.112 A.B. L.1066 J.D. 725 Washington St.
Gronowski, Katy M. ........... '60 '87 C.112 B.A. L.770 J.D. 1999 Harrison St. (⊙Orange)
Gross, Benton F., (BV) .................. '49 '74 C.112 A.B. L.1068 J.D. 1999 Harrison St.
Gross, Leonard A. ......................... '18 '61 C.112 B.S. L.284 J.D. [L.A.Gross]
**Gross, Terry** ............................ '49 '89 C.994 B.A. L.1097 J.D [Ⓐ Kazan,M.E.S.&A.]
Gross, Leonard A., A Professional Corporation ......................... 1999 Harrison St.
Grover, Margaret J. ............. '56 '84 C.446 B.S. L.930 J.D. 2000 Powell St. Ste. 1450
Grow, James R., (AV) '52 '78
C.112 A.B. L.1066 J.D. Staff Atty., Natl. Housing Law Proj.
Gruber, Burton A. ............ '38 '63 C.911 B.A. L.1066 LL.B. U.S. Dept. of Vets. Affairs
Grubman, Michael H. ................. '56 '84 C.112 B.A. L.1066 J.D. 1999 Harrison St.
**Gruen, Jan A.** ................................. '59 '87 C.112 B.A. L.1065 J.D. [Ⓐ Nevin&H.]
*LANGUAGES: Spanish.
*PRACTICE AREAS: Construction Defect Litigation; Personal Injury Litigation; Business Litigation.
Grunewald, Glen R., (AV) ........ '23 '55 C.46 B.S. L.209 J.D. 166 Santa Clara Ave. (Pat.)
Grupp, Michael C. ........................ '42 '70 C.112 A.B. L.1066 J.D. 500 Merritt Ave.
**Guberman-Garcia, Susan** ..................... '47 '75 L.1095 J.D. [Ⓐ Saperstein,G.D.&B.]
Guillory, Dorothy Davis ..................... '49 '84 C.766 B.A. L.1065 J.D. 1330 Broadway
Gurian-Sherman, Stacey, (AV) .............. '57 '84 C.860 B.A. L.770 J.D. Asst. Pub. Def.
**Gustafson, Stephen C.** ............... '66 '92 C&L.112 B.A., J.D. [Ⓐ Donahue,G.W.&W.]
**Gwilliam, J. Gary**, (AV) .......... '37 '63 C.668 B.A. L.1066 LL.B. [Gwilliam,I.C.C.&B.]
*PRACTICE AREAS: General Personal Injury; Products Liability; Medical and Legal Negligence; Wrongful Termination; Employment Discrimination.

**Gwilliam, Ivary, Chiosso, Cavalli & Brewer, A Professional Corporation, (AV)** BB
**1999 Harrison Street, Suite 1600, 94612-3528**
**Mailing Address: P.O. Box 2079, 94604-2079**
**Telephone: 510-832-5411 Fax: 510-832-1918**
**Email: Info@GICCB.com**
**J. Gary Gwilliam; Eric H. Ivary; James R. Chiosso; Steven R. Cavalli; Steven J. Brewer;—Marguerite E. Meade; Steven A. Reaves; Molly Harrington.**
**Practice Limited to Personal Injury, Products Liability, Negligence, Medical Malpractice, Legal Malpractice, Wrongful Termination, Employment Discrimination, Bad Faith and Insurance Litigation.**
**Reference: Civic Bank of Commerce, Oakland, California.**
*See Professional Biographies, OAKLAND, CALIFORNIA*

**Haapala, John E.**, (AV) .................. '39 '69 C.112 A.B. L.1065 J.D. [Strickland&H.]
*PRACTICE AREAS: Commercial Litigation; Personal Injury.
**Haas, Eric R.**, (AV) ........................... '51 '77 C.813 B.A. L.1065 J.D. [Larson&B.]
**Habegger, J. Brittain**, (AV) ......... '47 '73 C.629 B.A. L.1065 J.D. [Fitzgerald,A.&B.]
*PRACTICE AREAS: Business Law; Business Litigation; Estate and Probate Litigation.
Hachiya, Victor K., (BV) .................... '42 '71 C.112 A.B. L.1066 J.D. Dep. Pub. Def.
Hackenbracht, Mary E. ................. '50 '76 C.813 A.B. L.1065 J.D. Dep. Atty. Gen.
Haden, Anne S. ....................................... '43 '78 C.339 B.A. L.767 Asst. City Atty.
Hagberg, Peter N. '42 '67 C.668 B.A. L.178 LL.B.
Asst. Gen. Coun., Oakland Unified School Dist.
**Haims, Arnold B.**, (AV) ........................ '31 '60 C&L.813 A.B., J.D. [Haims,J.M.&M.]
*PRACTICE AREAS: Insurance Defense Law; Insurance Coverage; Civil Trial; Railway Law.

**Haims, Johnson, MacGowan & McInerney, (AV)** BB
**490 Grand Avenue, 94610**
**Telephone: 510-835-0500 Facsimile: 510-835-2833**
**Members of Firm: Arnold B. Haims; Gary R. Johnson; Clyde L. MacGowan; Thomas McInerney; Lawrence A. Baker; Randy M. Marmor; John K. Kirby; Robert J. Frassetto; Caroline N. Valentino; Dianne D. Peebles. Associates: Joseph Y. Ahn; Edward D. Baldwin; Marc P. Bouret; Anne M. Michaels; Michelle Diane Perry; Edward C. Schroeder, Jr.**
**General Civil and Trial Practice. Professional Liability, Products Liability, Aviation, Corporation, Casualty Insurance, Fire Insurance, Marine and Inland Marine Insurance, Life Insurance and Accident and Health Insurance Law.**
*See Professional Biographies, OAKLAND, CALIFORNIA*

Haley, J. Frederick, (AV) ................ '19 '49 C&L.767 B.S., J.D. 1633 San Pablo Ave.
Haley, Matthew D. ..................... '57 '82 C.112 B.A. L.767 J.D. 1633 San Pablo Ave.
**Hall, Gary A.** ................................................ '46 '75 L.273 J.D. [Nevin&H.]
*PRACTICE AREAS: Litigation; Labor and Employment; White Collar Crime Defense.
Hall, Howard C., (AV) .............. '37 '64 C.877 B.S. L.878 J.D. 286 Santa Clara Ave.
Hall, Julie L. ....... '57 '85 C.112 B.A. L.1292 J.D. Coun., Kaiser Found. Health Plan, Inc.
Hallifax, Peter ........................................ '51 '90 C.061 B.Mus. L.1065 J.D. Dep. City Atty.
**Halman, Susan Feldsted**, (BV) ............. '57 '83 C.228 B.S.N. L.770 J.D. [Larson&B.]
Halpin, William E., (AV) .................. '43 '67 C&L.734 B.A., J.D. 1 Kaiser Plz. Ste. 2360
Hamilton, Raymond W. ......................... '50 '74 C.112 B.A. L.1067 J.D. 436 14th St.
**Hamrick, Lillian F.** ............... '60 '89 C.976 B.A. L.1066 J.D. [Ⓐ Plageman&Assoc.]
*PRACTICE AREAS: Real Estate; Land Use; Corporate Law.
Hamrick, Patricia, (BV) ......................... '— '65 C.112 A.B. L.1026 LL.B. 100 Webster St.
**Hanavan, Thomas L.** ................ '52 '78 C.321 A.B. L.770 J.D. [Donahue,G.W.&W.]
*PRACTICE AREAS: Complex Commercial Real Estate; Environmental Law; Commercial Leasing.
**Hand, Margaret M.** ..................... '60 '93 C.112 B.A. L.1066 J.D. [Johnston,H.&R.]
*PRACTICE AREAS: Federal Tax Law; State Tax Law; Litigation; Probate; Estate Planning.
Handelman, Scott F. .......................... '48 '86 C.112 B.A. L.284 J.D. 1939 Harrison St.
Hanley, James M. '45 '73 C.588 B.S.M.E. L.904 J.D.
(adm. in VA; not adm. in CA; Pat.) U.S. Dept. of Energy
Hanna, Brophy, MacLean, McAleer & Jensen, (AV)
155 Grand Ave. (⊙San Fran., Fresno, Sacramento, Redding, Bakersfield, Santa Rosa, Salinas, Stockton & San Bernardino)
Hansen, Ann M. ............................... '53 '80 C.05 B.A. L.588 J.D. [Ⓐ Seltzer&C.]
**Hansen, Charles A.**, (AV) ............. '51 '77 C.112 B.A. L.1066 J.D. [Wendel,R.B.&D.]
*PRACTICE AREAS: Real Estate Litigation and Appeals; Commercial and Secured Transactions.
**Haratani, Joan M.** .................... '57 '85 C.1320 B.A. L.1067 J.D. [Crosby,H.R.&M.]
*PRACTICE AREAS: Pharmaceutical and Medical Device Litigation; Product Liability.
Harbin-Forte, Brenda F. ............................ '54 '79 C.112 B.A. L.1066 J.D. Mun. J.
**Hardaway, Samantha L.** ........... '71 '96 C.188 B.A. L.1068 J.D. [Ⓐ Crosby,H.R.&M.]

**Hardin, Cook, Loper, Engel & Bergez, (AV)** BB
**1999 Harrison Street, 18th Floor, 94612-3541**
**Telephone: 510-444-3131 Telecopier: 510-839-7940**
**Members of Firm: J. Marcus Hardin (1905-1993); L. S. Fletcher (1905-1964); Herman Cook (1914-1982); John C. Loper (Partner Emeritus); Barrie Engel; Raymond J. Bergez; George S. Peyton, Jr.; Ralph A. Lombardi; Sandra F. Wagner; Willard L. Alloway; Gennaro A. Filice, III; Stephen McKae; Bruce P. Loper; Bruce E. McLeod; Eugene Brown, Jr.; Linda C. Roodhouse (Certified Specialist, Estate Planning, Trust & Probate Law, The State Bar of California, Board of Legal Specialization); Matthew S. Conant; Chris P. Lavdiotis; Robert D. Eassa; Peter O. Glaessner; Nicholas D. Kayhan; John A. De Pasquale; Peter A. Strotz;—Amber L. Kelly; Elsa M. Baldwin; Marshall A. Johnson; Diane R. Stanton; Jennifer M. Walker; Margaret L. Kotzebue; Amee A. Mikacich; Timothy J. McCaffery; Stephen J. Valen; Troy D. McMahan; GayLynn Renee Kirn; Richard V. Normington III; Lisa M. Brown; Jason J. Curliano; Rachel L. Barack; Lynn S. Samuels; Gary S. Alexander; James S. Knopf; Jonathan M. Cohen. Of Counsel: Ronald A. Wagner (Certified Specialist, Family Law, The State Bar of California Board of Legal Specialization); Rachel K. Angress.**
**General Civil and Trial Practice. Insurance, Environmental, Toxic Torts, Estate Planning and Administration, Labor Relations, Corporation and Family Law.**
**Representative Clients: Firemans Fund Insurance Cos.; City of Piedmont; The Dow Chemical Co.; Nissan Motor Corp.; Subaru of America; Weyerhauser Co.; Bay Area Rapid Transit District; Diamond Shamrock; Home Indemnity Co.; Rhone-Poulenc.**
*See Professional Biographies, OAKLAND, CALIFORNIA*

Hardy, Emmett Grover, Jr. .............. '41 '75 C.766 B.A. L.1066 J.D. 12 Mandana Circle
Hardy, Gail Brewster, (AV) .......... '54 '80 C.767 B.A. L.1065 J.D. 10435 Greenview Dr.
**Hargleroad, Jewell J.** ................. '58 '87 C.1169 B.A. L.767 J.D. [McInerney&D.]
*LANGUAGES: Spanish.
*PRACTICE AREAS: Business; Construction and Commercial Litigation; Constitutional; Political and Election Law.
**Harkavy, John A.**, (AV) ..................... '43 '67 C.105 A.B. L.1066 J.D. [Aiken,K.&C.]
*REPORTED CASES: Beamer v. Franchise Tax Board, 19 Cal 3d 467, 138 Cal Rptr. 199, 563 P2d 238 (1977).
*PRACTICE AREAS: Transactional Matters; Business Acquisitions; Real Estate; Solid Waste; Municipal Solid Waste.
**Harnett, Christopher M., Jr.**, (BV) ....... '45 '74 C.112 B.A. L.767 J.D. [Strickland&H.]
*PRACTICE AREAS: Products Liability; Employer Liability; Public Entity Liability; Insurance Defense; Administrative Law.
**Harper, Jeffrey A.**, (AV) ......................... '47 '78 C.112 B.A. L.1065 J.D. [Knox R.]
*PRACTICE AREAS: Civil Trial and Insurance Defense.
Harper, Stephen S., (AV) ............... '43 '68 C.112 A.B. L.1065 J.D. 1999 Harrison St.
Harrigan, John M., (BV) ......................... '51 '77 C.867 B.A. L.284 J.D. [Boxer,E.&G.]
Harrington, Ann A. .................. '52 '77 C.112 B.A. L.1066 J.D. Legal Research Servs.
**Harrington, Molly** .................. '68 '96 C.276 B.A. L.800 J.D. [Ⓐ Gwilliam,I.C.C.&B.]
*LANGUAGES: Spanish.
*PRACTICE AREAS: Personal Injury; Employment Discrimination; Bad Faith.
**Harrington, Vincent A., Jr.** .......... '47 '74 C.93 B.A. L.188 J.D. [Van Bourg,W.R.&R.]
*PRACTICE AREAS: Labor Law.
Harris, Bridget McInerney ................. '54 '79 C.276 B.S.F.S. L.285 J.D. 1 Kaiser Plz.
Harris, Elihu M., (AV) ............................ '47 '73 C.1073 B.A. L.1067 J.D. Mayor
Harris, Kamala D. ....................... '64 '90 C.329 B.A. L.1065 J.D. Dep. Dist. Atty.
Harris, L. Randolph, (BV) ................................. '50 '79 L.285 J.D. 1 Kaiser Plaza
**Harris, Victor** .............. '46 '72 C.112 B.S. L.309 J.D. [Miller,S.&R.] (⊙Walnut Creek, CA)
*PRACTICE AREAS: Commercial Litigation; Commercial Transactions; Equipment Financing; Financial Institutions.
Harrison, John S. ........................................................................ '48 '75 [Harrison,T.&B.]
Harrison, Taylor & Bazile .............................................................. 449 15th St.
Hartford, David N. .................. '46 '79 C.665 B.S. L.659 J.D. 5955 Almaden Lane
Hartman, Robert J. ......................... '56 '82 C.93 B.A. L.767 J.D. Dep. Dist. Atty.
**Hassan, Ayesha Z.** ............................. '65 '90 C.145 B.A. L.1049 J.D. [Larson&B.]
*LANGUAGES: French and URDU.

CAA429P

**Hasse, Ann Fingarette**, (AV) '47 '73 C.112 B.A. L.1066 J.D.
V.P. & Gen. Coun., Amer. Pres. Lines Land Transit Servs., Inc.
*LANGUAGES: French.
*REPORTED CASES: Alliance Shippers Inc. v. Southern Pacific Trans. Co., 858 F2D 567, 1987.
*RESPONSIBILITIES: Transportation; Antitrust; Business.
Haswell, Harold R. .......... '16 '44 1021 Rose Ave.
Hatch, J. Michael .......... '43 '72 C.101 B.S. L.813 J.D. 3031 Totterdell
Hatcher, William W., Jr. .......... '66 '91 C.112 B.S. L.464 J.D. 300 Lakeside Dr., Ste. 1900
Haugner, Richd. A. .......... '28 '55 C.112 A.B. L.1066 LL.B. Supr. Ct. J.
**Hausrath, Les A.**, (BV) .......... '47 '73 C.112 B.A. L.1066 J.D. [Wendel,R.B.&D.]
*PRACTICE AREAS: Real Property Litigation; Land Use; Eminent Domain; Government Agency Law; Land Subsidence Litigation.
**Hawley, Terence N.** .......... '70 '95 C.112 B.A. L.1066 J.D. [A Crosby,H.R.&M.]
**Hayashida, Joel J.** '53 '80
C.1060 B.A. L.1065 J.D. Corp. Pat. Coun., The Clorox Co. (Pat.)
*LANGUAGES: German.
*RESPONSIBILITIES: Intellectual Property.
Hayes, Debra A. .......... '59 '84 C.483 B.A. L.284 J.D. [Hayes&M.]
Hayes, Robert S. .......... '39 '87 C.112 A.B. L.767 J.D. 1999 Harrison St.
Hayes & Mitchell .......... 1944 Embarcadero
**Haynes, Helen S.** .......... '63 '93 C.112 B.A. L.767 J.D. [A Crosby,H.R.&M.]
Head, James W. '52 '77 C&L.280 B.A., J.D.
(adm. in FL; not adm. in CA) National Econ. Develop. & Law Ctr.
**Headington, Rodney Ian** .......... '61 '88 C.169 B.A. L.800 J.D. [A Bennett,S.R.&A.]
*LANGUAGES: French.
*PRACTICE AREAS: Products Liability; Insurance Defense; Toxic Tort Litigation.
Headley, Laurel L. .......... '59 '91 C.766 B.A. L.767 J.D. Ste. N, 5900 Hollis St.
Headrick, Linda J. .......... '52 '78 C.967 B.A. L.284 J.D. 1330 Broadway
**Heafey, Edwin A., Jr.**, (AV) '30 '55
C.770 B.S. L.813 LL.B. [Crosby,H.R.&M.] (⊙San Francisco)
*PRACTICE AREAS: Civil Litigation.
**Heafey, Richard J.**, (AV) '35 '61
C.770 B.S. L.477 LL.B. [B Crosby,H.R.&M.] (⊙San Francisco)
*PRACTICE AREAS: Product Liability; Pharmaceutical and Medical Device Litigation.
**Hébert, Stanley P.** .......... '22 '50 C.966 Ph.B. L.436 LL.B. [B Wendel,R.B.&D.]
*PRACTICE AREAS: Public Finance; Transportation Law (ports and airports); International Trade Concerns; General Business.
**Hecht, Kenneth G., Jr.**, (AV) .......... '42 '69 C.169 B.A. L.146 J.D. [Knox R.]
*PRACTICE AREAS: Real Estate; Employee Relocation; Corporate and Insurance.
Heck, David A. .......... '47 '83 C.1097 B.A. L.809 J.D. 1800 Harrison St., Ste., 1616
**Heffes, Michele** .......... '— '92 C.112 B.S. L.767 J.D. Dep. Port Atty. II, Port of Oakland
**Hegen, Kathleen E.** .......... '46 '82 C.112 B.A. L.770 J.D. [Boornazian,J.&G.]
*PRACTICE AREAS: Insurance Coverage Litigation.
Heid, Janice M. .......... '47 '78 C.112 B.A. L.284 J.D. 6657 Gunn Dr.
Heil, Robert J., (AV) .......... '43 '70 C.976 B.A. L.1066 J.D. 2100 Bywood Dr.‡
**Heilbron, Lisa V.** .......... '65 '93 C.112 B.A. L.813 J.D. [A Crosby,H.R.&M.]
*LANGUAGES: Spanish.
*PRACTICE AREAS: Securities Litigation; Intellectual Property; Commercial Litigation; Environmental Litigation.
**Heilbron, Patricia B.**, (AV) '51 '77
C.813 A.B. L.976 J.D. Dep. Port Atty. IV, Port of Oakland
Helwick, Robert C. '48 '73
C.112 B.A. L.1065 J.D. Gen. Coun., East Bay Mun. Utility Dist.
Helzel, Leo B., (AV) .......... '17 '52 C.563 B.B.A. L.284 5550 Redwood Rd.‡
Henderson, Michael J., (AV) .......... '55 '81 C.309 A.B. L.1065 J.D. 5550 Redwood Rd.
**Hendon, Ezra**, (AV) .......... '36 '67 C&L.477 B.A., J.D. [Crosby,H.R.&M.]
*PRACTICE AREAS: Appellate.
**Henel, Carolyn E.** .......... '71 '96 C.976 B.A. L.893 J.D. [A Crosby,H.R.&M.]
Henze, Jeffrey L. .......... '50 '87 C.867 L.284 J.D. Nat. Labor Rel. Bd.
**Herold, Bruce G.**, (AV) .......... '38 '68 C.188 A.B. L.1065 J.D. [Aiken,K.&C.]
*PRACTICE AREAS: Litigation; Construction Law; Family Law.
Herrera-Solórzano, Rafaela .......... '57 '89 C.112 A.B. L.1065 J.D. 5050 Bway.
**Hershkowitz, Daniel A.** .......... '68 '94 C.1044 B.S. L.284 J.D. [A Liccardo,R.S.&M.]
*PRACTICE AREAS: Real Estate Litigation.
**Hertz, Frederick C.** .......... '52 '81 C.494 B.A. L.1066 J.D. [B Cooper,M.&B.]
*PRACTICE AREAS: Real Estate Transactions; Litigation; Land Use Administrative Proceedings.
Hess, Leah .......... '44 '86 C.763 A.B. L.1230 J.D. 1440 Broadway
Hetrick, Patrick H. .......... '42 '77 C.424 B.S. L.1179 J.D. 610 16th St.
**Hewitt, Henry S.**, (AV) .......... '43 '67 C.605 B.A. L.145 J.D. [Erickson,B.H.&W.]
Heywood, Robert G., (P.C.), (AV) .......... '49 '75 C.813 A.B. L.770 J.D. [Hanna,B.M.M.&J.]
Hickling, Douglas H. .......... '32 '60 C.188 B.S. L.309 LL.B. Asst. Co. Coun.
Hicks, Cheryl L. .......... '58 '83 C.112 A.B. L.1066 J.D. 1440 Bway.
**Hicks, David**, (AV) .......... '43 '72 C.768 A.B. L.1067 J.D. [General C.]⊙
Hicks, Joyce M. .......... '52 '77 C.668 A.B. L.1066 J.D. Asst. City Atty.
Higgins, Lynn E., (BV) .......... '31 '63 C.112 B.S. L.1066 J.D. [Edises,H.&L.]
Hightower, Anne .......... '47 '87 C.339 B.A. L.767 J.D. Legal Asst. for Seniors
Hildebrand, McLeod & Nelson, Inc., (AV) .......... 414 Thirteenth Street, Sixth Floor
**Hilgard, Adaline** .......... '65 '94 C.112 B.A. L.1067 J.D. [A Crosby,H.R.&M.]
Hill, John E., Law Offices of, (AV) '40 '70
C.339 A.B. L.145 J.D. 8105 Edgewater Dr. (⊙San Francisco)
**Hill, William R.** .......... '55 '84 C.112 B.A. L.1066 J.D. [Donahue,G.W.&W.]
*PRACTICE AREAS: Litigation; Intellectual Property Law; Employment Law.
Hillegas, Lisa L. .......... '63 '92 C.107 B.A. L.767 J.D. 1999 Harrison St.
Hillier, Margaret .......... '42 '74 C.768 B.A. L.1065 J.D. 653 11th St.
Hillman, James L. .......... '39 '65 C.477 B.A. L.597 J.D. 1 Kaiser Plaza
Himmelman, David A., (AV) .......... '29 '53 C&L.494 B.S.L., LL.B. 405 14th St.
Hing, Stuart .......... '56 '85 C.1060 B.S. L.464 J.D. Dep. Dist. Atty.
**Hinkle, Barry E.**, (BV) .......... '47 '76 C.112 B.A. L.1065 J.D. [Van Bourg,W.R.&R.]
*PRACTICE AREAS: Labor Law.
**Hoback, William G.**, (BV) .......... '44 '79 C.1060 L.1026 LL.B. [Ericksen,A.K.D.&L.]
*PRACTICE AREAS: Products Liability; Declaratory Relief; Errors and Omission; Discrimination; Wrongful Termination.
**Hodgkins, James F.** .......... '61 '89 C.112 B.A. L.464 J.D. [A Larson&B.]
Hoeppner-Freitas, Jacqueline Ann .......... '45 '88 C.188 A.B. L.1066 J.D. 5337 Coll. Ave.
**Hofer, Julie E.** .......... '55 '82 C.791 B.A. L.494 J.D. [A Donahue,G.W.&W.]
Hofstadter, Sarah K., (AV) .......... '52 '78 C.674 B.A. L.813 J.D. 485 Weldon Ave.
Hoh, Tony C. .......... '58 '83 C.112 A.B. L.1066 J.D. 200 Webster St.
**Hohnsbeen, Roger Blake** .......... '59 '85 C.112 B.A. L.273 J.D. [A Bennett,S.R.&A.]
Holland, Charlton G., III .......... '39 '65 C.112 A.B. L.1066 LL.B. 914 Longridge Rd.
Hollingshead, John, (BV) .......... '52 '82 C.767 B.A. L.464 J.D. 1999 Harrison St. (⊙Orange)
Holst, James E. .......... '38 '64 C.112 A.B. L.1066 LL.B. Gen. Coun., Univ. of Calif.
Homer, Stephen C., (AV) .......... '45 '72 C.112 B.S. L.1066 J.D. Asst. Pub. Def.
Hooker, Jay S., (AV) .......... '36 '69 C.188 B.A. L.477 J.D. Asst. Pub. Def.
Hooper, Randal W. .......... '52 '80 C.112 A.B. L.464 J.D. 1901 Harrison St.
**Hooten, Nancy E.** .......... '61 '89 C.1060 B.S. L.464 J.D. [A Larson&B.]
Hopper, Ralph E. .......... '24 '50 C.112 B.A. L.1065 LL.B. 1404 Franklin St.‡
Hormachea, Nancy '46 '74 C&L.326 B.B.A., J.D.
(adm. in TX; not adm. in CA) 405 14th St.

Horn, Barbara N. .......... '49 '83 C.846 B.A. L.1153 J.D. [Horn&J.]
Horn & Johnson .......... 505 17th St.
Horner, Jeffrey W. .......... '38 '64 C.112 A.B. L.1066 LL.D. Sup. Ct. J.
Horowitz, Daniel A., (BV) .......... '54 '80 C.999 B.A. L.809 J.D. 120 11th St., 2nd Fl.
**Horton, John J.** .......... '67 '93 C.112 B.A. L.767 J.D. [A Crosby,H.R.&M.]
**Horton, Michael J.**, (AV) .......... '41 '79 C.347 A.B. L.284 J.D. [Horton,W.&C.]
*PRACTICE AREAS: Customs Law; International Trade Law.
**Horton, Neil F.**, (AV) .......... '37 '62 C.293 B.A. L.309 LL.B. [Johnston,H.&R.]
*PRACTICE AREAS: Federal Tax Law; State Tax Law; Litigation; Probate; Estate Planning.

**Horton, Whiteley & Cooper, (AV)**
**An Association of Sole Practitioners**
**One Kaiser Plaza, Suite 455, 94612⊙**
**Telephone: 510-208-2955 Fax: 510-208-3321**
**Michael J. Horton; Robert Scott Whiteley; Gary C. Cooper; Craig A. Mitchell (Resident, Newport Beach Office).**
**Customs and International Trade Law.**
**Reference: Bank of Canton of California.**
**Newport Beach, California Office: 4590 MacArthur Boulevard, Suite 500. Telephone: 714-250-9066. Fax: 714-250-9076.**

**Horwich, William E.**, (AV) .......... '42 '69 C.674 A.B. L.976 LL.B. [Wendel,R.B.&D.]
*PRACTICE AREAS: Corporate; Securities.
Hosain, Tulasi '58 '89 C.518 B.A. L.184 J.D.
1999 Harrison St., Ste., 1300, Lake Merritt Plz.

**Hosemann, Constance M. '38 '90 C.610 B.S. L.284 J.D.**
**2101 Webster Street, Suite 1760, 94612**
**Telephone: 510-444-4941 Facsimile: 510-465-5985**
***PRACTICE AREAS: Estate Planning.**
**Estate Planning.**
*See Professional Biographies, OAKLAND, CALIFORNIA*

Houston, Gladys M. .......... '— '78 C.112 A.B. L.1026 J.D. Dep. Co. Coun.
**Hoyt, Ralph B.**, (AV) .......... '24 '55 C.112 B.S. L.1065 J.D. [Hoyt,M.&A.]⊙
*PRACTICE AREAS: Labor Relations Law; OSHA Law; Wrongful Termination Law.

**Hoyt, Miller & Angstadt, A Professional Corporation, (AV)**
**915 Financial Center Building, 405 Fourteenth Street, 94612⊙**
**Telephone: 510-893-0990 Fax: 510-930-7595**
**Ralph B. Hoyt; David Miller; Eric P. Angstadt.**
**Labor Relations and Employment Law. Employee Benefits, Equal Employment Opportunity, OSHA and Public Employment Relations. Unlawful Termination, Business and Corporation Law.**
**Walnut Creek, California Office: 1910 Olympic Boulevard, Suite 220. Telephone: 510-930-9255. Fax: 510-930-7595.**
*See Professional Biographies, OAKLAND, CALIFORNIA*

Hufford, Wade H. .......... '54 '80 C.112 B.A. L.1065 J.D. 5425 Shafter Ave.
**Hughes, Robert L.**, (AV) .......... '26 '58 C.112 B.A. L.1065 LL.B. [B Lempres&W.]
*PRACTICE AREAS: Bankruptcy Law; Insolvency Law; Creditors' Rights Law.
**Hughes, Roger M.**, (AV) .......... '46 '72 C.169 B.A. L.1065 J.D. [Bell,R.&H.]
*PRACTICE AREAS: Construction Law; Mediation and Arbitration.
Huneke, Nancy A. .......... '49 '84 C.549 B.S. L.273 J.D. 565 Kenmore Ave.
Hunt, James M. .......... '47 '77 C.67 B.A. L.950 J.D. 5315 College Ave.
**Hunter, Alvin D.** .......... '54 '94 C.112 B.A. L.1066 J.D. [McLemore,C.&T.]
*PRACTICE AREAS: Casualty Defense.
Hunter, Kim M. .......... '58 '86 C.112 B.A. L.1065 J.D. Dep. Dist. Atty.
**Huster, John S.** .......... '67 '94 C.112 B.A. L.767 J.D. [A Boornazian,J.&G.]
Hutchins, A. Mark, (BV) .......... '44 '77 C.768 B.S. L.464 J.D. Dep. Dist. Atty.
Hutchins, Robert B., (BV) .......... '34 '65 C.112 A.B. L.1065 LL.B. Dep. Dist. Atty.
**Hutchinson, B. Clyde, III**, (AV) .......... '41 '66 C.174 B.A. L.1066 J.D. [Crosby,H.R.&M.]
*PRACTICE AREAS: Transportation Law; Toxic Tort; Products Liability.
**Hysinger, David G.** .......... '65 '92 C.112 A.B. L.767 J.D. [A Veneruso&M.]
*LANGUAGES: French.
*PRACTICE AREAS: Professional Malpractice Defense; General Liability Insurance Defense.
Ingraham, Donald G., (AV) '37 '63
C.112 A.B. L.1066 LL.B. Asst. Dist. Atty.-High Tech Crime Team
Innes, Kenneth F., III '50 '84 C.766 B.A. L.765 J.D.
Reg. Inspec/Atty., U.S. Postal Serv.
Ioannou, Sheila Kirby .......... '66 '90 C.112 B.A. L.770 J.D. 5050 Broadway
Isenburg, Dennis L. '40 '65
C.605 B.A. L.1066 LL.B. Coun., The Permanente Medical Grp., Inc.
**Isenhour, Sharon A.** .......... '44 '92 L.765 J.D. [H.A.Trutner]
*PRACTICE AREAS: Probate; Trust Administration; Conservatorships; Estate Planning; Probate Litigation.
**Isokawa, Ned N.**, (AV) .......... '44 '75 C.112 B.S.E.E. L.1066 J.D. [Crosby,H.R.&M.]
*PRACTICE AREAS: Complex Litigation; Intellectual Property; Environmental; Toxic Tort.
**Ivary, Eric H.**, (AV) .......... '46 '72 C.740 B.A. L.770 J.D. [Gwilliam,I.C.C.&B.]
*PRACTICE AREAS: Negligence; Insurance Bad Faith; Products Liability.
**Jacka, Barton L.** .......... '65 '91 C.740 B.A. L.1066 J.D. [A Donahue,G.W.&W.]
*PRACTICE AREAS: Commercial Litigation; Employment Law; Intellectual Property.
Jackl, Ronni .......... '44 '72 C.112 B.A. L.1065 J.D. 491 Ninth St.
Jacobowitz, Ira Aaron, (BV) .......... '45 '80 C.318 L.999 1611 Telegraph Ave.
Jacobs, Mimi Johnson .......... '— '81 C.766 B.A. L.284 J.D. 155 Grand Ave.
**Jacobson, Andrew N.** .......... '60 '91 C.112 B.Arch. L.1066 J.D. [A Wendel,R.B.&D.]
*PRACTICE AREAS: Real Property Law; Land Use Law.
Jacobson, Thomas Hughes '46 '81
C.629 B.B.A. L.284 J.D. Hearing Offr., Dept. of Vet. Affs.
Jaffe, Harold M., (BV) .......... '47 '73 C.025 B.A. L.767 J.D. 3521 Grand Ave.
James, Frederick J. .......... '38 '74 C.266 B.A. L.1066 J.D. 1624 Franklin St.
James, Wayne Anthony .......... '54 '80 C.1073 B.A. L.1065 J.D. 1237 102nd Ave.
**Janssen, Howard A.**, (AV) .......... '43 '70 C.112 B.A. L.1065 J.D. [Crosby,H.R.&M.]
*PRACTICE AREAS: Litigation; Employment; Business; Insurance Coverage and Claims; Products Liability.
Januta, Donatas, (AV) .......... '41 '69 C.112 B.S. L.1066 LL.B. 5464 College Ave.
**Jardine, Julie** .......... '68 '95 C.112 B.A. L.1049 J.D. [A Larson&B.]
**Jauregui, Jacqueline M.**, (AV) .......... '52 '80 C.766 B.A. L.1065 J.D. [Crosby,H.R.&M.]
*PRACTICE AREAS: Complex Civil Litigation; Insurance Coverage; Employment.
Jay, John W., (BV) .......... '54 '79 C.154 B.A. L.464 J.D. Dep. Dist. Atty.
**Jeffrey, Gary A.** .......... '52 '86 C.424 B.S. L.767 J.D. [Crosby,H.R.&M.]
*PRACTICE AREAS: Business Litigation; Products Liability.
Jellen, Edward D. .......... '46 '72 C.112 A.B. L.1066 J.D. U.S. Bkrptcy J.
**Jelley, Philip M., (Inc.)**, (AV) .......... '32 '56 C.871 L.813 J.D. [Fitzgerald,A.&B.]
*PRACTICE AREAS: Business and Real Estate Law; Nonprofit and Charitable Organizations; Ranch and Water Law.
Jenkins, Deborah A. .......... '54 '91 C.945 B.A. L.893 J.D. 2030 Franklin St. 5th Fl.
Jenner, Fred T., (BV) .......... '27 '53 C.112 L.1065 J.D. 100 Webster St.
Jenner, Kenneth W. .......... '56 '81 C.147 B.A. L.464 J.D. 100 Webster St., PH Suite
Jensen, D. Lowell .......... '28 '52 C.112 A.B. L.1066 LL.B. U.S. Dist. J.
Jensen, Gilbert A., (BV) .......... '41 '68 C.589 A.B. L.1065 J.D. Sr. Dep. Dist. Atty.
**Jensen, Robert E.**, (AV) .......... '31 '71 C.112 B.A. L.284 J.D. [B Boornazian,J.&G.]
*PRACTICE AREAS: Personal Injury; Products Litigation; Medical Malpractice; Psychiatric Injury and Brain Damage.

Jensen, Thomas F. '63 '93 C.945 B.A. L.1029 J.D.
(adm. in CT; not adm. in CA) United Parcel Serv.
Jewel, Howard H., (AV) .................. '24 '50 C.112 A.B. L.1066 LL.B. [🄱 Jewel&L.]
Jewel & Leary, (BV) .................................. 1330 Bway.
Jiang, Earl L. ................................. '62 '88 C.767 B.S. L.770 J.D. 413 3rd St.
Joe, Gregory M. ........................ '49 '77 C.112 B.A. L.1065 J.D. 590 Merritt Ave.
Joffe, Abraham ................................ '34 '63 C.36 B.S. L.1065 449 15th St.
**Johns, Craig S. J.** .................. '61 '88 C.112 B.A. L.1067 J.D. [Crosby,H.R.&M.]
*PRACTICE AREAS: Environmental.
Johns, Margaret Z., (AV) .................. '48 '76 C.112 B.A. L.1067 J.D. [🄱 Seltzer&C.]
**Johnson, Bruce P.** ....................... '63 '88 C.228 B.A. L.1068 J.D. [Pezzola&R.]
*PRACTICE AREAS: Public and Private Securities Law; Corporate Law; Venture Capital Law; Mergers and Acquisitions.
Johnson, Clinton A., (BV) .............. '43 '73 C.674 B.S.E. L.813 J.D. 1939 Harrison St.
Johnson, Earl D. .................................. '52 '87 C.999 B.S. L.1153 J.D. [Horn&J.]
**Johnson, Gary R.**, (AV) ................ '43 '69 C.112 A.B. L.1065 J.D. [Haims,J.M.&M.]
*PRACTICE AREAS: Insurance Defense Law; Insurance Law; Litigation Defense; Tort Law; Bad Faith Law.
Johnson, Harry B., (BV) ................ '43 '72 C.101 B.A. L.1067 J.D. Sr. Dep. Dist. Atty.
**Johnson, Kenneth F.**, (AV) ........... '38 '70 C.112 B.S. L.1065 J.D. [Crosby,H.R.&M.]
*PRACTICE AREAS: Construction; Product Liability; Insurance; Business; Civil Litigation.
**Johnson, Marshall A.** .............. '54 '83 C.112 B.A. L.464 J.D. [🄰 Hardin,C.L.E.&B.]
*PRACTICE AREAS: Civil Trial Law; Insurance Defense Law; Toxic Substances Law.
**Johnson, Michael K.** ........................ '61 '87 C.813 B.A. L.1065 J.D. [Larson&B.]
**Johnson, Richard L.** ...... '49 '75 C.165 B.A. L.309 J.D. Sr. Corp. Coun., The Clorox Co.
*LANGUAGES: French, Spanish.
Johnson, Robert W., (BV) ............ '41 '74 C.1027 B.S. L.1026 J.D. [White,C.M.&J.]
Johnson, Stanley A., (BV) ............ '22 '50 C.112 B.S. L.1065 J.D. 150 Grand Ave.
Johnson, Tom G. '41 '72 C&L.623 B.B.A., J.D.
(adm. in OK; not adm. in CA) 460 Hegenberger Rd.
Johnson, William C. ....................... '50 '79 C.112 B.A. L.1153 J.D. 1901 Harrison
Johnston, Alexander .......................... '44 '73 C.154 B.A. L.284 J.D. 1 Kaizer Plz.
**Johnston, J. Richard**, (AV) ........... '15 '39 C.112 A.B. L.1066 J.D. [Johnston,H.&R.]
*PRACTICE AREAS: Federal Tax Law; State Tax Law; Litigation; Probate; Estate Planning.
Johnston, Richard E., (AV) ............. '32 '62 C.673 B.S. L.1065 J.D. 1970 Broadway

**Johnston, Horton & Roberts, (AV)**
**Suite 1500, 1901 Harrison Street, 94612**
**Telephone: 510-452-2133 Fax: 510-452-2280**
**Members of Firm: V. Judson Klein (1933-1976); J. Richard Johnston (Certified Specialist, Taxation Law, The State Bar of California Board of Legal Specialization); Neil F. Horton (Certified Specialist, Taxation Law and Probate, Estate Planning and Trust Law, The State Bar of California Board of Legal Specialization).; James G. Roberts. Associates: Margaret M. Hand.**
**Federal and State Tax Law. Litigation, Estate Planning, Probate, General Business and Corporate Law.**
***See Professional Biographies, OAKLAND, CALIFORNIA***

Jones, Betty J. ................. '60 '93 C.939 B.A. L.464 J.D. 300 Lakeside Dr., Ste. 1045
Jones, Darrel T. ....... '51 '79 C.770 B.S. L.1068 J.D. Alameda-Contra Costa Transit Dist.
Jones, Oliver A., (A Law Corp.) ........................... '48 '75 6334 Telegraph Ave.
Jones, Richard A., (BV) ............ '44 '71 C.1197 B.B.A. L.464 J.D. 286 Santa Clara Ave.
Jordan, Mark W. '41 '67
C.4 B.B.A. L.1066 LL.B. Sr. Coun., Kaiser Found. Health Plan, Inc.
Jordan, Virginia L. '43 '81 C.473 B.A. L.192 J.D.
(adm. in AL; not adm. in CA) NLRB
**Judson, Stephen M.**, (AV) ............ '60 '85 C.813 A.B. L.767 J.D. [Fitzgerald,A.&B.]
*PRACTICE AREAS: Business Law; Business Litigation; Commercial Law; Commercial Litigation; Bankruptcy Litigation.
Judson, Stewart A. '30 '65 C.604 A.B. L.284 LL.B.
Presiding Admin. Law J., Off. of Admin. Hearings
Kaitz, Spencer R. '48 '73 C.112 A.B. L.1066 J.D.
Pres. & Gen. Coun., Calif. Cable Television Assn.
**Kallgren, Charles E.** ......................... '64 '91 C.668 B.A. L.1065 J.D. [🄰 Ryan,A.&L.]
Kalm, Louise ..................................... '30 '86 L.1153 J.D. 2000 Embarcadero‡
**Kalmbach, Tiffanie K.** ............... '67 '93 C.112 B.A. L.464 J.D. [🄰 Crosby,H.R.&M.]
*PRACTICE AREAS: Litigation; Product Liability; Construction Law; Business Litigation.
Kaminer, Frances S. .......................... '55 '81 C.563 B.S. L.978 J.D. 405 14th St.
Kane, Daniel J. ............................. '59 '88 C.273 B.A. L.1065 J.D. 1999 Harrison St.
**Kant, Jonas W.** '65 '96 C.112 B.A. L.117 J.D.
(adm. in NY; not adm. in CA) [🄰 Donahue,G.W.&W.] (⊙Mill Valley)
**Kaplan, Greta L.** ........................ '61 '91 C.112 A.B. L.1068 J.D. [🄰 Cresswell,C.&E.]
*PRACTICE AREAS: Civil Litigation.

**Kaplan, Marjory A., (BV) '48 '74 C.643 B.A. L.1065 J.D.**
**The Ordway Building, One Kaiser Plaza, Suite 1725, 94612-3612**
**Telephone: 510-763-5611 Fax: 510-763-3430**
***PRACTICE AREAS: Family Law; Adoption/Guardianship Law.**
**Family Law. Adoption and Guardianship.**
***See Professional Biographies, OAKLAND, CALIFORNIA***

**Karczewski, Gerald J.** .......... '62 '89 C.740 B.S. L.1049 J.D. [🄰 Donahue,G.W.&W.]
*PRACTICE AREAS: Litigation; Intellectual Property.
Karelitz, Fonda '50 '77 C.112 A.B. L.1065 J.D.
Assoc. Reg. Coun., Kaiser Found. Health Plan, Inc.
Karesh, Jos. ................................. '09 '35 C.494 B.A. L.767 J.D. Supr. Ct. J.
Karlsson, Richard R. .................. '48 '76 C.1073 B.S. L.765 J.D. 2nd Dep. Co. Coun.
**Karp, Edward R.** ...................... '55 '83 C.966 B.A. L.284 J.D. [Cresswell,C.&E.]
Kasdin, Stephen L., (BV) .................. '43 '69 C.705 A.B. L.1292 J.D. 1440 Bway
**Kasley, William L.** ......................... '51 '76 C.98 B.S. L.339 J.D. [🄰 Corbett&K.]
Kass, Stephen M., (AV) ......................... '39 '66 C.103 A.B. L.94 J.D. [S.M.Kass]
Kass, Stephen M., P.C., (AV) ........................................ 1939 Harrison St.
Kassis, Richard L., (BV) '45 '73
C.112 B.A. L.464 LL.B. Alameda-Contra Costa Transit Dist.
Kastama, Marlin L. ......................... '27 '53 C&L.494 B.S.L., LL.B. 5607 Ascot Dr.
**Katano-Lee, Kathy M.** ............ '61 '88 C.312 B.A. L.1065 J.D. [🄰 Boornazian,J.&G.]
**Katz, Genevieve S.** .................. '68 '96 C.823 B.S. L.767 J.D. [🄰 Crosby,H.R.&M.]
Katz, Karen E., (BV) ................ '57 '87 C.1169 B.A. L.1065 J.D. Asst. Pub. Def.
Kaufman, Laurence O., (AV) .............. '34 '73 C.768 B.A. L.284 J.D. 1300 Clay St.
Kaufmann, William W. .......... '43 '72 C.1073 B.A. L.1065 J.D. 484 Lake Park Ave.
Kawaichi, Ken M. ....................... '41 '66 C.668 A.B. L.1066 J.D. Supr. Ct. J.

**Kay & Merkle**
**(See San Francisco)**

**Kayhan, Nicholas D.** .................. '57 '87 C.112 B.A. L.1065 J.D. [Hardin,C.L.E.&B.]
*PRACTICE AREAS: Products Liability Law; Civil Litigation; Toxic Substances Law.
**Kazan, Steven**, (AV) ................ '42 '67 C.1036 A.B. L.309 LL.B. [Kazan,M.E.S.&A.]
*TRANSACTIONS: Plaintiffs' Class Counsel: Ahearn v. Fibreboard. Creditors Committees for: H.K. Porter; Celotex and Amatex.

**Kazan, McClain, Edises, Simon & Abrams, A Professional Law Corporation, (AV)** 🄱🄱
**171 Twelfth Street, Suite 300, 94607**
**Telephone: 510-465-7728; 893-7211 TDD: (510) 763-8808 Fax: 510-835-4913**
**Email: postmaster@kmes.co**

(This Listing Continued)

**Kazan, McClain, Edises, Simon & Abrams, A Professional Law Corporation (Continued)**

**Steven Kazan; David M. McClain; Victoria Edises; Aaron H. Simon; Denise Abrams;—Francis E. Fernandez; Anne Michelle Burr; Dianna J. Lyons; Frances C. Schreiberg; Simona A. Farrise; Ronald J. Shingler; Susan S. Ochi; Terry Gross.**
**Environmental and Industrial Disease Law, Asbestos Litigation, Catastrophic Injuries, Plaintiffs' Class Action Litigation, Workers Compensation, Longshore and Harborworkers' Litigation, Medical Malpractice, Medical Products Liability, Personal Injury and Federal Tort Law. Trials in all State and Federal Courts.**
**Reference: Union Bank (Oakland Main Branch).**
***See Professional Biographies, OAKLAND, CALIFORNIA***

Keck, Martin W. .............................. '46 '79 C.33 B.A. L.765 J.D. Vet. Admn.
Keep, William A., (BV) ..................... '43 '69 C.628 B.S. L.1066 J.D. Asst. Pub. Def.
Kelleher, Robert F. ........................ '46 '85 C.831 B.S. L.284 J.D. Telecare Corp.
**Keller, Christopher J.** ............ '64 '95 C.747 B.A. L.494 J.D. [🄰 Saperstein,G.D.&B.]
*PRACTICE AREAS: Litigation; Employment Law; False Claims Act.
Keller, James E. ...... '48 '75 C.813 B.A. L.770 J.D. 8105 Edgewater Dr. (⊙San Francisco)
**Kelley, Mark W.** ......................... '55 '83 C.685 B.A. L.629 J.D. [🄰 Lempres&W.]
*PRACTICE AREAS: Construction Law; Commercial Litigation; Alternative Dispute Resolution.
Kelley, Richard C., (P.C.), (AV) '33 '74 C.262 B.S.S. L.1026 LL.B.
[Hanna,B.M.M.&J.]
**Kelly, Amber L.** .................. '59 '84 C.1073 B.A. L.767 J.D. [🄰 Hardin,C.L.E.&B.]
*PRACTICE AREAS: Civil Litigation; Toxic Torts; Governmental Liability.
**Kelly, Maureen A.** .................. '67 '92 C.112 B.A. L.1065 J.D. [Plageman&Assoc.]
*PRACTICE AREAS: Estate Planning.

**Kelson, John M., (AV) '44 '71 C.477 A.B. L.309 J.D.**
**Suite 1340, Ordway Building, One Kaiser Plaza, 94612**
**Telephone: 510-465-1326 Telecopier: 510-465-0871**
**General Civil Trial and Appellate Practice.**
**Reference: Civic Bank of Commerce.**
***See Professional Biographies, OAKLAND, CALIFORNIA***

Kelvin, David ........................... '52 '80 C.1169 B.A. L.1065 J.D. 2823 High St.
**Kemp, John M.**, (AV) ................... '45 '74 C.502 B.A. L.767 J.D. [Crosby,H.R.&M.]
*PRACTICE AREAS: Complex Tax Planning; Tax Exempt Entities; Mergers and Acquisitions; Corporate and Partnership Law; Tax Litigation.
Kendall, Lloyd W., Jr. ................... '46 '77 C.36 B.S. L.765 J.D. 180 Grand Ave.
Kenfield, Ann, (CV) ...................... '52 '78 C.112 A.B. L.464 J.D. Asst. Dist. Atty.
**Kennedy, Melvin L.**, (AV) ........ '40 '73 C.277 B.S.I.M. L.813 J.D. [Kennedy,G.M.&C.]
Kennedy, Stephen J., (BV) ........... '46 '70 C.767 A.B. L.1065 J.D. 1624 Franklin St.

**Kennedy, Gong, Mitchell & Combs, LLP, (AV)**
**1970 Broadway, 12th Floor, 94612**
**Telephone: 510-272-0433 Telecopier: 510-272-0579**
**Email: kgmc@hooked.net**
**Members of Firm: Melvin L. Kennedy; Raymond G. Gong; Wendall A. Mitchell; Roy A. Combs; Jo-Lynne Q. Lee; Eric R. DeWalt. Of Counsel: Joseph J. Brecher.**
**Real Estate, Land Use and Environmental Law, Construction, Financial Institutions, Bankruptcy, Public Finance, Redevelopment, Technology, Transfer, Business Trial and Appellate Practice.**
***See Professional Biographies, OAKLAND, CALIFORNIA***

Kennon, Amy R. ........................ '50 '73 C.808 B.A. L.861 J.D. 5723 Balboa Dr.‡

**Kent, Edward A., Jr.**
**(See Palo Alto)**

**Kenyon, Michelle Marchetta** ...... '57 '87 C.112 B.A. L.1067 J.D. [McDonough,H.&A.]
*PRACTICE AREAS: Public Law; Land Use; Litigation.
**Kepler, Karen Brown** ............ '60 '91 C.112 B.A. L.1068 J.D. [🄰 Wendel,R.B.&D.]
*PRACTICE AREAS: Litigation.
**Kerlinsky, Jo Saxe** ............ '64 '88 C.1036 B.A. L.309 J.D. [🄰 Crosby,H.R.&M.]
**Kern, John McD.**, (AV) '46 '74
C.190 B.A. L.273 J.D. [Crosby,H.R.&M.] (⊙San Francisco)
*PRACTICE AREAS: Civil Litigation.
Kershner, Gary R. ........................ '60 '86 C&L.770 B.S.C., J.D. 1970 Broadway
Kerss, Brian E. ........... '48 '79 C.112 B.A. L.284 J.D. 1432 Martin Luther King Jr. Way
Kessler, Albert H. ............. '10 '36 C.112 B.S. L.1066 LL.B. 12585 Brookpark Rd.‡
**Keyes, Judith Droz**, (AV) ............ '46 '75 C.645 B.S. L.1066 J.D. [Corbett&K.]⊙
*PRACTICE AREAS: Labor and Employment Law.
Kilkenny, Kelly Ann ..................... '60 '88 C.878 B.A. L.284 J.D. 200 Webster St.
**Kim, Julie Hwang** ........................ '67 '95 C.112 B.A. L.770 J.D. [🄰 Larson&B.]
**Kim, Terri Ann** .......................... '47 '84 C.112 B.A. L.284 J.D. [🄰 Lempres&W.]
*PRACTICE AREAS: Commercial Litigation; Construction Litigation.
Kimball, Jennifer L. .................. '50 '89 C.1264 B.A. L.1153 J.D. 200 Webster St.
Kimberlin, Robert T. ...................... '08 '35 C.210 A.B. L.309 J.D. 33 Linda Ave.‡
Kimura, Lily Mayumi, (BV) ............... '49 '76 C.112 A.B. L.1065 J.D. 405 14th St.
Kincaid, Donald H., (AV) ............... '27 '55 C.112 A.B. L.284 LL.B. 200 Webster St.
King, Daniel A. ................................ '60 '87 C.763 B.A. L.1065 J.D. [King,K.&F.]
King, George, (AV) ........................... '30 '59 C.112 B.S. L.1065 J.D. [King,K.&F.]
King, Shelby R., (BV) .................... '31 '60 C.112 B.A. L.1066 LL.B. 169 14th St.
King, King & Fishleder, P.C., (AV) ............................................ 1999 Harrison St.

**King, Shapiro, Mittelman & Buchman**
**(See Shapiro, Mittelman & Buchman, LLP, Walnut Creek)**

Kingsbury, Kenneth R. .......................... '39 '76 C.768 B.S. L.765 J.D. Supr. Ct. J.
Kinney, Charles G. ......................... '50 '75 C&L.112 B.S., J.D. 5826 Presley Way
**Kirby, John K.**, (BV) ..................... '47 '80 C.478 A.B. L.767 J.D. [Haims,J.M.&M.]
*PRACTICE AREAS: Litigation Defense; Environmental Insurance Litigation; Trial Practice; Insurance Coverage.
Kirkpatrick, David H. '43 '69
C.976 B.A. L.309 LL.B. National Econ. Develop. & Law Ctr.
**Kirn, GayLynn Renee** .............. '67 '92 C.112 B.A. L.464 J.D. [🄰 Hardin,C.L.E.&B.]
*PRACTICE AREAS: Products Liability; Civil Litigation; Insurance Law.
Kitchel, Woodrow W., (AV) ........... '13 '37 C.112 A.B. L.1066 LL.B. P.O. Box 2037‡
Kleeman, William M., (AV) ..................... '42 '69 C.112 L.767 J.D. Asst. Dist. Atty.
Klinge, Jill Vincent ........................ '62 '87 C.350 B.A. L.352 J.D. Dep. Dist. Atty.
Kliszewski, Mark A. ......... '49 '73 C.770 A.B. L.1065 J.D. Ref., Juv. Div., Co. Supr. Ct.
**Klotchman, Lisa S.** ..................... '64 '90 C.112 B.A. L.767 J.D. [🄰 Morton,L.&A.]
*LANGUAGES: French.
*PRACTICE AREAS: Civil Rights; Civil Trial; Insurance Defense; Personal Injury.
**Klucznik, Jeanne M.** ............. '65 '93 C.112 B.A. L.1066 J.D. [🄰 Donahue,G.W.&W.]
Knoll, Alfred P., (BV) ......................... '41 '68 C.763 B.A. L.1065 J.D. P.O. Box 30847
**Knopf, James S.** ....................... '67 '95 C.197 B.A. L.188 J.D. [🄰 Hardin,C.L.E.&B.]
*PRACTICE AREAS: Civil Litigation; Products Liability; Environmental Law.
**Knowles, Thomas C.**, (AV) ......... '42 '67 C.951 A.B. L.1065 J.D. [Van Blois,K.S.&B.]
*PRACTICE AREAS: Personal Injury Law; Products Liability Law; Medical Malpractice Law; Highway Design Law; Construction Accidents.

**Knox Ricksen, LLP, (AV)**
**Lake Merritt Plaza, Suite 1700, 1999 Harrison Street, 94612**⊙
**Telephone: 510-893-1000 Fax: 510-446-1946**
**Members of Firm: Wallace W. Knox (1905-1982); Marshall Ricksen (1908-1975); John C. Ricksen; Rupert H. Ricksen; William C. Robbins, III; Robert G. Allen; Thomas A. Palmer; Richard G. Logan,**

(This Listing Continued)

CAA431P

**Knox Ricksen, LLP (Continued)**

Jr.; Jeffrey A. Harper; Thomas E. Fraysse; Kenneth G. Hecht, Jr.; Mark L. Cederborg; Gregory D. Pike; Thomas V. Bret; Andrew J. Skaff; Kenneth A. Dreyfuss; Hubert Lenczowski; Kenneth J. McCarthy; R. Patrick Snook; Mark C. Skilling; John S. Boat. Associates: James T. Gotch (Resident, San Jose Office); Thomas H. LemMon; Timothy Cass McKenzie; Christine A. Carringer; Karen L. Peterson; Dennis Earl Raglin; Christopher P. Swenson; Nicole Brown Yuen; Jennifer L. Sipes.
General Civil and Trial Practice. Corporate, Real Estate, Land Use, Zoning and Urban Development and Environmental Law, Mergers and Acquisitions, Taxation, Probate, Trusts and Estate Planning, Conservatorships, Insurance and Medical Liability Defense, Energy Law, Public Utility and Regulatory Law.
Representative Clients: American Home Food Products Corp.; American Protective Services, Inc.; California State Automobile Assn., Inter Insurance Bureau; Citibank; Electric Clearinghouse, Inc.; Kaiser Foundation Hospitals; Markstein Beverage Co.; Natural Gas Clearinghouse; New York Mercantile Exchange; Safeco Insurance Co.
Fairfield, Solano County, California Office: Corporate Plaza, Suite 300, 1261 Travis Boulevard, 94533. Telephone: 707-426-3313 . Fax: 707-426-0426.
San Jose, Santa Clara County, California Office: 100 Park Center Plaza, Suite 560, 95113. Telephone: 408-295-2828. Fax: 408-295-6868.

*See Professional Biographies, OAKLAND, CALIFORNIA*

Knudsen, Philip H., (BV) .......... '48 '74 C.637 B.A. L.767 J.D. 1300 Clay St.
Koch, Richard P. .......... '47 '79 C.910 B.A. L.284 J.D. 1440 Bway.
**Koenig, Nathan P.** .......... '66 '93 C.309 B.A. L.1066 J.D. [Ⓐ Crosby,H.R.&M.]
**Kohn, Dorine Ruiz**, (AV) .......... '43 '75 C.766 B.A. L.767 J.D. [Bjork,L.P.&K.]
*LANGUAGES: Spanish and French.
*PRACTICE AREAS: Premises Liability; Medical and Professional Liability Defense; Employment; Products Liability; Construction Defects.
**Kohn, Steven M.**, (AV) .......... '42 '74 C.112 A.B. L.767 J.D. [Crosby,H.R.&M.]
*PRACTICE AREAS: Civil Litigation; Product Liability; Environmental; Insurance Coverage; Commercial Litigation.
Kolda, Ryan B. .......... '42 '68 C.767 A.B. L.1065 J.D. Dep. City Atty.

**Koller, Lynn Anderson, Law Offices of, (AV) '42 '69 C.768 A.B. L.1066 J.D.**
**Jack London Park Building, Suite 200 520 Third Street, 94607⊙**
Telephone: 510-893-5550 Fax: 510-893-5688
Bankruptcy and Reorganization. General Civil Trial and Appellate Practice in all State and Federal Courts. Real Estate and Commercial Business Law. Civil Litigation.
Tucson, Arizona Office: Number 35, 810 North Camino Santiago. 85745. Telephone: 520-884-9044. Fax: 520-623-3003.

*See Professional Biographies, OAKLAND, CALIFORNIA*

Komoroske, Kirsten .......... '66 '92 C.112 B.A. L.770 J.D. 1999 Harrison St.
Kong, Richter .......... '— '80 C.112 B.A. L.1065 J.D. [Kong&K.]
Kong-Brown, Barbara .......... '— '72 C.112 B.A. L.767 J.D. [Kong&K.]
Kong & Kong .......... 388 9th St.
Kornfeld, Alan D. .......... '49 '77 C.549 B.A. L.1065 J.D. 868 Threstle Glen Rd.
**Kornfield, Irving J.**, (AV) .......... '36 '63 C.112 B.S. L.1066 J.D. [Kornfield,P.&B.]
*PRACTICE AREAS: Bankruptcy Practice; Bankruptcy Law; Bankruptcy and Commercial Litigation.

**Kornfield, Paul & Bupp, A Professional Corporation, (AV)** BB
**Suite 800, Lake Merritt Plaza, 1999 Harrison Street, 94612**
Telephone: 510-763-1000 Fax: 510-273-8669
Irving J. Kornfield; Aaron Paul; C. Randall Bupp; Merridith A. Schneider; Eric A. Nyberg;—Charles D. Novack; Chris D. Kuhner; Gareth M. Chow.
Bankruptcy and Reorganization. General Civil Trial and Appellate Practice in all State and Federal Courts. Commercial, Business, Construction, Banking, Probate and Corporate Law.

*See Professional Biographies, OAKLAND, CALIFORNIA*

**Kotzebue, Margaret L.** .......... '63 '90 C.112 A.B. L.1065 J.D. [Ⓐ Hardin,C.L.E.&B.]
*PRACTICE AREAS: Insurance Law; Products Liability Law; Civil Litigation.
Kovsky, Robert .......... '46 '74 C.453 B.S.E.E. L.112 J.D. P.O. Box 240
**Kow, Jane** .......... '63 '94 C.188 B.S. L.569 J.D. [Ⓐ Crosby,H.R.&M.]
**Krakauer, Jolie** .......... '56 '84 C.1169 B.A. L.1065 J.D. [Ryan,A.&L.]
**Kramer, Bauer E.**, (AV) .......... '08 '35 C.112 B.A. L.309 LL.B. [Ⓒ Aiken,K.&C.] ‡
Kramer, Susan D. .......... '52 '84 C.966 B.A. L.767 J.D. 318 Harrison St.
Krashna, David .......... '49 '75 C.602 B.A. L.1066 J.D. Comr., Mun. Ct.
**Krebs, Robert E.** .......... '43 '69 C&L.174 B.S., J.D. [Pezzola&R.] (⊙Menlo Park)
Krech, Richard Joseph, (BV) .......... '46 '80 C.999 L.1230 LL.B [Krech&C.]
Krech & Cole, (BV) .......... 1611 Telegraph Ave.
Kresnak, Kathleen .......... '68 '93 C.477 B.A. L.989 J.D. 1901 Harrison St.
Kresse, J. Kendrick '43 '73 C.174 B.A. L.1065 J.D.
Legal Dir., Calif. Ctr. for Law & Deaf
Krohn, Kathy S., (BV) .......... '42 '68 C.659 A.B. L.94 J.D. 4208 Ridgemont Ct.
Kross, Jeffrey S. .......... '54 '89 C.1350 B.A. L.1066 J.D. P.O. Box 16224
kubota, Russell T. .......... '49 '74 C&L.112 B.A., J.D. 2101 Webster St.
Kuckuck, Jill A. .......... '66 '91 C.112 B.S. L.1067 J.D. Alameda Co., Dep. Dist. Atty.
Kuhn, David N. .......... '46 '74 C.381 B.A. L.178 J.D. 1433 Webster St.
**Kuhner, Chris D.** .......... '68 '95 C.112 B.A. L.767 J.D. [Ⓐ Kornfield,P.&B.]
*LANGUAGES: Spanish.
*PRACTICE AREAS: Bankruptcy; Commercial.
**Labadie, Craig** .......... '55 '81 C.112 B.S. L.1067 J.D. [McDonough,H.&A.]
*PRACTICE AREAS: Municipal Law; Land Use Law; Environmental Law.
Lacklen, John E. .......... '52 '81 C.112 A.B. L.273 J.D. 585 Mandana Blvd.
LaFollette, Gene P., (AV) .......... '43 '69 C.378 B.A. L.1065 J.D. 80 Grand Ave.
**Lafrenz, Andrew W.**, (AV) '47 '72
C.197 A.B. L.813 J.D. [Donahue,G.W.&W.] (⊙Walnut Creek)
*PRACTICE AREAS: Litigation; Insurance Defense; Real Estate; Environmental; Commercial Law.
**Lagasse, Peter Leo** .......... '67 '95 C.802 B.S. L.426 J.D. [Ⓐ Larson&B.]
Lagos, Panos .......... '48 '74 C.112 B.A. L.1065 J.D. 5032 Woodminster Lane

**Laidlaw, Sally J., (AV) '37 '70 C.1032 A.B. L.1066 J.D.**
**405-14th Street, Suite 710, 94612-2706**
Telephone: 510-891-3969 Fax: 510-891-3971
(Certified Specialist, Family Law, The State Bar of California Board of Legal Specialization).
*PRACTICE AREAS: Family Law.
Family Law.

*See Professional Biographies, OAKLAND, CALIFORNIA*

Lake, Ellen, (AV) .......... '44 '71 C.681 B.A. L.930 J.D. 4230 Lakeshore Ave.
Lakey, Theodore R. .......... '41 '71 C.112 B.A. L.1067 J.D. Asst. City Atty.

**Lampert, Wayne A. '56 '84 C&L.846 B.A., J.D.**
**180 Grant Avenue, Suite 1250, 94612**
Telephone: 510-834-0500 Fax: 810-835-1311
*PRACTICE AREAS: Business Representation; Real Property.
Business and Corporate Law.

*See Professional Biographies, OAKLAND, CALIFORNIA*

Landeros, Roberto R. .......... '58 '88 C.112 B.S. L.1066 J.D. Dep. Pub. Def.
Lane, Robert K., (BV) .......... '44 '70 C.112 A.B. L.426 J.D. [R.K.Lane]
Lane, R. Kingsbury, Corporation, (BV) .......... 1 Kaiser Plz.
Langer, John, (AV) .......... '07 '35 C.112 B.S. L.1065 J.D. 6564 Liggett Dr.
**Lanum, Steven G.** .......... '57 '84 C.112 A.B. L.767 J.D. [Ⓐ Boornazian,J.&G.]
**LaPietra, Lauren M.**, (AV) .......... '58 '83 C.112 A.B. L.1066 J.D. [Marshall,A.&L.]
*PRACTICE AREAS: Real Estate Law; Corporations; General Business Law.
Lapow, Bernice E. .......... '46 '74 C.329 B.A. L.1066 J.D. 491 Ninth St.

Larkin, Eileen .......... '60 '87 C.112 A.B. L.767 J.D. 1 Kaiser Plaza
Larkin, Jocelyn D. .......... '59 '83 C.112 B.A. L.1068 J.D. 1300 Clay St., 11th Fl.
**Larson, David O.**, (AV) .......... '35 '61 C&L.813 B.A., J.D. [Larson&B.]

**Larson & Burnham, A Professional Corporation, (AV)** BB
**1901 Harrison Street, 11th Floor, P.O. Box 119, 94604**
Telephone: 510-444-6800 Fax: 510-835-6666
A. Hubbard Moffitt, Jr. (1908-1969); Howard S. Rode (1907-1973); Arthur Jay Moore, Jr. (1918-1984); David O. Larson; Clark J. Burnham; Gregory D. Brown; George J. Ziser; Robert J. Lyman; Eric R. Haas; Scott C. Finch; Steven M. Marden; Ralph A. Zappala; Peter Dixon; Monica Dell'Osso (Certified Specialist, Probate, Estate Planning and Trust Law, The State Bar of California Board of Legal Specialization); Jeffrey G. Bairey; Susan Feldsted Halman; Patrick K. M. McCarthy; Gary R. Selvin; H. Wayne Goodroe; Robert A. Ford; David R. Pinelli; Michael R. Reynolds; James L. Wraith; Richard J. Finn; John J. Verber; Cathy L. Arias; Thomas M. Downey; Michael K. Johnson;—John P. Bevan; Tara D. Bodden; Caryn Bortnick; Paul D. Caleo; John D. Colombo; Vera C. De Martini; Matthew G. Dudley; Pamela Fastiff Ellman; Susan E. Firtch; Douglas S. Free; Beth S. Freedman; Alison F. Greene; Anne Cobbledick Gritzer; Ayesha Z. Hassan; James F. Hodgkins; Nancy E. Hooten; Julie Jardine; Julie Hwang Kim; Peter Leo Lagasse; Frank C. Liuzzi; Pelayo Antonio Llamas, Jr.; Joanna MacQueen; Randolph G. McCalla; Michael T. McKeeman; Steven A. Nielsen; Gustavo Peña; Noreen N. Quan; James J. Rosati; Stephen Q. Rowell; Walter C. Rundin, III; Bryan K. Stainfield; Anjali Talwar; Darrell T. Thompson; Shawn A. Toliver; Jedediah Wakefield; David H. Waters; David S. Webster; Bradley M. Zamczyk; Barry Zoller. Of Counsel: James H. Riggs (Certified Specialist, Probate, Estate Planning and Trust Law, The State Bar of California Board of Legal Specialization).
General Civil and Trial Practice. Construction, Environmental, Insurance, Professional Liability, Tax, Estate Planning and Probate.
Representative Clients: The Travelers Insurance Co.; Wholesale Building Supply Co.; U.S. Fidelity & Guaranty Co.; Home Insurance Co.; County of Alameda; City of Livermore; Shell Oil Co.; Exxon; Allied-Signal Inc.; Rohm and Haas Co.

*See Professional Biographies, OAKLAND, CALIFORNIA*

Lathan, Milton .......... '55 '87 C.906 B.A. L.767 J.D. 405 14th St.
Laub, Arnold, Law Offices of, A P.C., (BV)
2101 Webster St., 15th Flr. (⊙San Francisco, Sacramento, San Jose & Walnut Creek)
**Laufenberg, Peter** .......... '66 '94 C.112 B.A. L.1066 J.D. [Ⓐ Crosby,H.R.&M.]
**Laupheimer, F. Ronald**, (BV) .......... '45 '73 C.902 B.S. L.767 J.D. [Crosby,H.R.&M.]
*PRACTICE AREAS: Complex Civil Litigation; Toxic Tort Law; Environmental Law.
Lauren, Jason F. .......... '57 '84 C.705 B.A. L.61 J.D. Dep. Co. Coun.
**Lavdiotis, Chris P.**, (BV) .......... '52 '80 C.112 B.A. L.1065 J.D. [Hardin,C.L.E.&B.]
*PRACTICE AREAS: Products Liability Law; Civil Trials; Insurance Defense Law.
Law, Judy .......... '51 '83 C.358 B.A. L.767 J.D. 5315 College Ave.
Lawhorn, Victor R. .......... '53 '78 C.112 B.A. L.1137 J.D. 410 Merritt Ave.
**Lawrence, Robert K.**, (BV) .......... '53 '78 C&L.770 B.S., J.D. [Bjork,L.P.&K.]
*PRACTICE AREAS: Medical Malpractice Law; Hospital Law; Commercial Litigation; Employment Law; Insurance Defense.
Lawrence, Sarah L. .......... '— '82 C.312 B.S. L.1230 J.D. 2101 Webster St.
Lawson, Antonio M. .......... '62 '89 C.112 A.B. L.309 J.D. 835 Mandana Blvd.
**Layne, Kendall A.** .......... '53 '81 C.1169 A.B. L.813 J.D. [Ericksen,A.K.D.&L.]
*PRACTICE AREAS: Product Liability Defense; Professional Malpractice Defense; Wrongful Death Defense; Insurance Defense; Admiralty.
Lazear, Arthur William .......... '53 '78 C.112 A.B. L.1066 J.D. 180 Grand Ave.
Learn, Gerald M. .......... '40 '77 [Edises,H.&L.]
Leary, Brian O., (BV) .......... '41 '71 C.178 B.S. L.1066 J.D. [Jewel&L.]
**LeBoeuf, Jacques B.** .......... '65 '93 C.103 B.A. L.597 J.D. [Ⓐ Crosby,H.R.&M.]
**Lee, Albert** .......... '63 '92 C.112 B.A. L.1066 J.D. [Ⓐ Marion's I.]
*PRACTICE AREAS: Litigation.
Lee, Bradford H. .......... '52 '91 C.329 B.S. L.464 J.D. P.O. Box 2761★
Lee, David C. .......... '37 '70 C.846 B.A. L.284 J.D. Supr. Ct. J.
**Lee, Jack W.** .......... '51 '76 C.112 A.B. L.065 J.D. [Ⓐ Saperstein,G.D.&B.]
Lee, James M., (AV) .......... '46 '72 C&L.767 A.B., J.D. Off. of Dist. Atty.
**Lee, Jo-Lynne Q.** .......... '49 '74 C.102 B.A. L.178 LL.B. [Kennedy,G.M.&C.]
Lee, Lloyd C. '44 '69 C.311 B.A. L.188 J.D.
Univ. Coun., Regents of the Univ. of Calif.
Lee, Richard J. .......... '48 '74 C.813 A.B. L.1066 J.D. 11 Embarcadero, W.
Lee, Richard K. .......... '47 '75 C.112 B.S. L.169 J.D. 4456 Reinhardt Dr.
**Lee, Theodora R.** .......... '62 '87 C.811 B.A. L.846 J.D. [Littler,M.F.T.&M.]
**Leeb, Steven M.** .......... '69 '95 C&L.112 B.A., J.D. [Ⓐ Gassett,P.&F.]
*PRACTICE AREAS: Workers' Compensation Defense.
Leed, Claudia .......... '55 '85 C.454 B.A. L.588 J.D. City Attys. Off.
LeGates, Richard T. '43 '68 C.309 B.A. L.1066 J.D.
Prof., Urban Studies, San Francisco State Univ.
**LemMon, Thomas H.** .......... '57 '85 C.112 B.A. L.1137 J.D. [Ⓐ Knox R.]
*PRACTICE AREAS: Civil Trial and Insurance Defense.
**Lempres, Matthew D.**, (BV) .......... '57 '84 C.813 A.B. L.1065 J.D. [Lempres&W.]
*PRACTICE AREAS: Business Law; Corporate Law; Real Estate Law.

**Lempres & Wulfsberg, Professional Corporation, (AV)**
**Kaiser Center, 24th Floor, 300 Lakeside Drive, 94612⊙**
Telephone: 510-835-9100 Telecopier: 510-451-2170
Daniel N. Lempres (May 31, 1931 - March 19, 1987); H. James Wulfsberg; Charles W. Reese, Jr.; Peter H. Ferris; Jeffrey A. Sykes; Timothy A. Colvig; Eric J. Firstman; Gregory R. Aker; Matthew D. Lempres; Mark A. Stump; Molly J. Baier; David A. Rosenthal;—Charles A. Cobb; David W. Ginn; Mark W. Kelley; Terri Ann Kim; Paulette G. Andrews; Stephen L. Cali; Cameron C. Ward; William L. Darby; Gillian Small, G.M. Of Counsel: Robert L. Hughes; Barbara Suzanne Farley; Dianne K. Barry (Resident, San Francisco Office).
General Civil and Trial Practice. Construction, Environmental, Insurance Coverage, Products Liability, Professional Liability, Real Estate, Corporate, Merger and Acquisition, Taxation, Estate Planning and Probate, Bankruptcy, Insolvency and Creditor's Rights Law.
San Francisco, California Office: 1 Maritime Plaza, Suite 1600, 94111.

*See Professional Biographies, OAKLAND, CALIFORNIA*

Lenahan, George T., Jr., (BV) .......... '37 '67 C.112 A.B. L.1065 LL.B. 286 Santa Clara Ave.
Lenahan, Maureen Kay, (AV) .......... '42 '69 C.813 B.A. L.767 J.D. Asst. Dist. Atty.
**Lenczowski, Hubert** .......... '54 '81 C.309 A.B. L.1066 J.D. [Knox R.]
*LANGUAGES: French.
*PRACTICE AREAS: Corporate; Securities; Business; Commercial; Real Estate.
Lentz, William H. .......... '31 '66 C.397 B.S. L.284 LL.B. 385 Grand Ave.
**Leon, Deborah L.** .......... '57 '82 C&L.893 B.A., J.D. [Leon&L.]
*PRACTICE AREAS: Civil Litigation; Insurance.
**Leon, Jeffrey A.** .......... '56 '81 C&L.893 B.A., J.D. [Leon&L.]
*PRACTICE AREAS: Construction; Real Estate; Financial Institutions; Product Liability; Insurance.
Leon, Leonard '17 '41 C&L.190 LL.B.
(adm. in NE; not adm. in CA) 3815 Silverwood Ave.‡

**Leon & Leon**
**2101 Webster Street, Suite 1570, 94612**
Telephone: 510-208-6600 Facsimile: 510-451-1010
Email: jleon@a.crl.com
Jeffrey A. Leon; Deborah L. Leon. Of Counsel: John C. McCutchen.
General Litigation Practice.

*See Professional Biographies, OAKLAND, CALIFORNIA*

**Leonard, Cathye E.** .......... '56 '95 C.112 B.A. L.284 J.D. [Ⓐ McLemore,C.&T.]
*PRACTICE AREAS: Insurance Defense.
Leonard, Ellen J. .......... '53 '85 C&L.477 B.S., J.D. Coun., Kaiser Found. Health Plan, Inc.
**Leslie, Robert L.**, (AV) .......... '47 '74 C.870 B.S. L.1065 J.D. [McInerney&D.]

**Leung, Anthony S. '45 '87 C.774 B.S. L.1153 J.D.**
**436 14th Street, Suite 503, 94612**
**Telephone: 510-452-9111**
***LANGUAGES: Cantonese, Mandarin.**
**Real Property.**
***See Professional Biographies, OAKLAND, CALIFORNIA***

**Leung, Jacqueline Jordan** .......... '50 '91 C.506 B.S. L.494 J.D. [⊠ Boornazian,J.&G.]
Levine, B. Scott .......................... '58 '82 C.1036 B.A. L.767 J.D. [Goodman&L.]
Levinson, Edward S., (BV) .................. '48 '74 C.112 B.A. L.1065 J.D. 1330 Bway.
Levy, Deborah L. .............................. '54 '80 C.378 B.A. L.259 J.D. 580 Grand Ave
Levy, Leslie F. ..................... '55 '82 C.112 B.A. L.1065 J.D. 6536 Telegraph Ave.
Lew, Jonathan '54 '80 C.813 B.S. L.1065 J.D.
Admin. Law J., Calif. Off. Admin. Hearings

**Lewellyn, Thomas G. '51 '83 C.112 B.A. L.765 J.D.**
**2030 Franklin Street, 5th Floor, 94612**
**Telephone: 510-444-7530 Fax: 510-444-5027**
**Email: lewellyn@ccnet.com**
***PRACTICE AREAS: Personal Injury.**
**Personal Injury, Professional Negligence, Wrongful Termination, Legal Malpractice, Americans with Disabilities Act Law.**
***See Professional Biographies, OAKLAND, CALIFORNIA***

Lewis, Jeffrey G. ......................... '49 '75 C.976 B.A. L.1066 J.D. [Sigman,L.&F.]
Lewis, Valerie D. ........................ '57 '83 C&L.893 B.A., J.D. 1999 Harrison St.
LeWitter, Jody ............................... '56 '82 C.66 B.A. L.477 J.D. 1330 Bway.

**Liccardo, Rossi, Sturges & McNeil, A Professional Law Corporation, (AV)**
**1999 Harrison, Suite 1300, 94612⊙**
**Telephone: 510-273-8740 Fax: 510-832-4432**
**Martha Louise Caron (Resident);—Deborah T. Bjonerud (Resident); Daniel A. Hershkowitz (Resident).**
**General Trial and Appellate Practice. Personal Injury, Products Liability, Corporate, Real Property, Tort, Business, Condemnation, Tax, Estate Planning and Probate Law.**
**References: Pacific Western Bank; Plaza Bank.**
**San Jose, California Office: 1960 The Alameda, Suite 200. Telephone: 408-244-4570. Fax: 408-244-3294.**
***See Professional Biographies, OAKLAND, CALIFORNIA***

Lieberman, Edward G. ..................... '48 '82 C.112 B.A. L.767 J.D. 200 Webster St.
Lieberman, Elliott B. ..... '51 '84 C.273 B.S. EE L.767 J.D. 6009 Buenaventura Ave. (Pat.)
Lien, Herb G. ............................ '28 '70 C.112 B.A. L.767 J.D. 9163 Skyline Blvd.
**Lifter, Jill J.** ................................. '62 '85 C.112 B.A. L.800 J.D. [Ryan,A.&L.]
*PRACTICE AREAS: Civil Trial; Construction Defect Litigation; Insurance Coverage; Insurance Defense Law; Landslide and Subsidence Litigation.
**Lind, Howard W.**, (AV) ............. '53 '78 C.112 A.B. L.1065 J.D. [Wendel,R.B.&D.]
*PRACTICE AREAS: Real Property Law.
**Lindstrom, Lois A.** ................. '48 '83 C.966 B.A. L.284 J.D. [Ericksen,A.K.D.&L.]
*PRACTICE AREAS: Professional Liability; Product Liability Defense; Construction Defense; Discrimination; Harassment.
Lingelser, Richard J. '33 '67 C.685 B.A. L.1340 J.D.
(adm. in OH; not adm. in CA) The Clorox Co.
Lipkin, Jerome C. ............ '42 '69 C.846 A.B. L.1065 J.D. Ralph Baker Central Bldg.
Lippa, Rodger D. ............................. '35 '65 C.768 A.B. L.767 J.D. Wkrs. Comp. J.
Lippman, Gary E. ........................ '40 '79 C.112 Ph.D. L.767 J.D. 5589 Taft Ave.
Litke, Larry L. .......................... '35 '62 C.112 B.A. L.1065 J.D. Dep. Co. Coun.

**Littler, Mendelson, Fastiff, Tichy & Mathiason, A Professional Corporation, (AV)**
**1300 Clay Street, Suite 1020, 94612⊙**
**Telephone: 510-873-8650 Facsimile: 510-873-8656**
**URL: http://www.littler.com**
**Cynthia E. Maxwell; Theodora R. Lee;—Kevin A. Marks (Not admitted in CA).**
**Offices located in: California — Bakersfield, Fresno, Long Beach, Los Angeles, Menlo Park, Sacramento, San Diego, San Francisco, San Jose, Santa Maria, Santa Rosa and Stockton; Denver, Colorado; Washington, D.C.; Atlanta, Georgia; Baltimore, Maryland; Reno and Las Vegas, Nevada (a partnership with the Law Offices of Hicks & Walt); Morristown, New Jersey; New York, New York; and Dallas and Houston, Texas.**
***See Professional Biographies, OAKLAND, CALIFORNIA***

**Littwin, Barbara D., (BV) '47 '72 C.914 B.A. L.1065 J.D.**
**1999 Harrison Street, Suite 1300, 94612**
**Telephone: 510-893-9736**
**Email: BDLITTWIN@AOL.COM**
***PRACTICE AREAS: Family Law; Custody Law; Wills.**
**Family Law, Custody, Wills, General Practice.**
***See Professional Biographies, OAKLAND, CALIFORNIA***

**Liu, Beatrice** ......................... '65 '93 C&L.112 B.A., J.D. [⊠ Erickson,B.H.&W.]
**Liuzzi, Frank C.** ........................... '66 '92 C.770 B.S. L.767 J.D. [⊠ Larson&B.]
Livingston, Clarence ......................... '49 '79 C.766 B.A. L.767 J.D. 1 Kaiser Plaza
**Llamas, Pelayo Antonio, Jr.** ............. '63 '92 C.112 A.B. L.770 J.D. [⊠ Larson&B.]
Locke, Andrew C. .................. '58 '84 C.112 B.A. L.464 J.D. 80 Grand Ave., 6th Fl.
**Loeb, Michael J.**, (AV) .............. '47 '74 C.188 B.A. L.1065 J.D. [Crosby,H.R.&M.]
*PRACTICE AREAS: Labor; Employment; Employment Benefits; Alternative Dispute Resolution.
**Logan, Richard G., Jr.**, (AV) ................... '54 '79 C.112 A.B. L.1065 J.D. [Knox R.]
*PRACTICE AREAS: Business and Commercial Litigation.
**Lombardi, Ralph A.**, (AV) ......... '45 '71 C.112 A.B. L.1066 J.D. [Hardin,C.L.E.&B.]
*PRACTICE AREAS: Products Liability Law; Insurance Law; Civil Litigation.
Lomhoff, Peter G. ........................... '45 '74 C.685 B.A. L.1066 J.D. 1 Kaiser Plaza
**London, Michael E.** ..................... '51 '81 C&L.770 B.S.C.E., J.D. [McInerney&D.]
Long, George ............................. '23 '74 C&L.560 B.A., J.D. 1624 Franklin St.
**Longstaff, Derek R.** ............. '65 '90 C.36 B.S. L.464 J.D. [⊠ Ericksen,A.K.D.&L.]
Lonsdale, Fred D. ........................ '48 '76 C.813 B.A. L.1066 J.D. 5856 College Ave.
Loo, Minnie ............................... '57 '82 C.112 A.B. L.276 J.D. U.S. Dept. of Jus.
**Loper, Bruce P.**, (AV) .............. '50 '75 C.197 B.A. L.1067 J.D. [Hardin,C.L.E.&B.]
*PRACTICE AREAS: Civil Litigation; Insurance Law.
**Loper, John C.**, (AV) ............. '23 '50 C.112 A.B. L.1066 J.D. [Hardin,C.L.E.&B.] ‡
*PRACTICE AREAS: Estate Planning; Administration.

**Lord, Douglas E., Law Offices of, (AV) '36 '64 C.813 A.B. L.1066 LL.B.**
**1999 Harrison Street, Suite 2700, 94612**
**Telephone: 510-834-8210 Fax: 510-273-8632**
***PRACTICE AREAS: Plaintiffs Insurance Bad Faith; Insurance Coverage Litigation.**
**Plaintiff's Insurance Bad Faith, Insurance Coverage Litigation.**
***See Professional Biographies, OAKLAND, CALIFORNIA***

Lorig, Milton .............................. '52 '84 C.188 A.B. L.1066 J.D. 281 Cross Rd.
Lott, Willie, Jr. ............................ '47 '73 C.1073 B.A. L.1067 J.D. Dep. Co. Coun.
Loube, Irving ......................... '18 '52 C.112 A.B. L.1066 LL.B. 1433 Webster St.‡
Loveland, Darrcy ... '— '82 C.216 B.A. L.904 J.D. Coun., Kaiser Found. Health Plan, Inc.
Loving, Deborah June Pierre '53 '87 C.483 B.A. L.352 J.D.
(adm. in HI; not adm. in CA) 3911 Harrison
Low, Esther '52 '77 C.112 B.A. L.1067 J.D.
San Francisco Bay Area Rapid Transit Dist.
Lucey, Gerald R., (AV) ......... '44 '69 C&L.767 B.A., J.D. 2000 Powell St. Ste. 1450⊙

**Lucke, William P., Law Offices of, (AV) '42 '72 C.767 A.B. L.284 J.D.**
**3824 Grand Avenue, 94610-1004⊙**
**Telephone: 510-284-7881 Fax: 510-284-7886**
***PRACTICE AREAS: Civil and Business Litigation; Insurance and Environmental Law; Personal Injury; Product Liability and Professional Negligence; Employment Litigation.**
**Civil and Business Litigation, Insurance, Environmental Law, Product Liability and Professional Negligence.**
**Piedmont, California Office: 536 Magnolia Avenue, 94611. Telephone: 510-652-5185. Fax: 510-652-5175.**
***See Professional Biographies, OAKLAND, CALIFORNIA***

Luis, Rolando M. ........................ '47 '89 C.662 B.S.A. L.284 J.D. 1429 45th Ave.
**Lulofs, Larry E.**, (AV) ................. '49 '79 C.813 B.A. L.767 J.D. [Morton,L.&A.]
*PRACTICE AREAS: Civil Trial; Construction Law; Insurance Defense; Real Estate.
**Lund, Richard W.** .................. '60 '85 C.112 B.S. L.1065 J.D. [Plageman&Assoc.]
*PRACTICE AREAS: Real Estate and Construction Litigation; Environmental and Land Use Law.
Lundberg, John F. '44 '69 C.112 B.S. L.1066 J.D.
Dep. Gen. Coun., Off. of Regents, Univ. of Calif.
**Lyman, Robert J.**, (AV) ............................ '48 '74 C&L.36 B.A., J.D. [Larson&B.]
**Lymburn, Bruce** .................... '53 '82 C.112 A.B. L.1066 J.D. [Wendel,R.B.&D.]
*PRACTICE AREAS: Real Estate Transaction Law; Business Law.
Lynch, Patricia M. ... '51 '82 C.66 B.A. L.262 J.D. Coun., Kaiser Found. Health Plan, Inc.
**Lyon, Deanna Down**, (AV) .......... '47 '72 C.1109 B.A. L.1066 J.D. [Wendel,R.B.&D.]
*PRACTICE AREAS: Estate Planning Law; Probate Law; Trust Law.
Lyons, Alan D. ........'49 '77 C.569 B.A. L.365 J.D. 322 Hanover Ave. (⊙Oak Park, Ill.)
Lyons, Ann H. ................... '54 '85 C.685 B.A. L.629 J.D. 1736 Franklin St., 8th Fl.
**Lyons, Dianna J.** ................. '45 '77 C.1079 B.A. L.1067 J.D. [⊠ Kazan,M.E.S.&A.]
*LANGUAGES: Spanish.
Lyons, Gregory S. ..................... '54 '84 C.112 B.S. L.766 J.D. 405 14th St.
MacDonald, Celine M. '48 '86
C.454 B.A. L.1065 J.D. 1900 Kaiser Cntr., 300 Lakeside Dr.
MacDonald, Mary E. .......... '47 '76 C.112 A.B. L.767 J.D. Univ. Coun., Univ. of Calif.
**MacGowan, Clyde L.**, (AV) .......... '34 '64 C.112 A.B. L.1065 J.D. [Haims,J.M.&M.]
*PRACTICE AREAS: Automobile Negligence; Uninsured Motorist; Products Liability Law; Insurance Fraud; Insurance Defense Law.
Macmeeken, John P., (A Professional Corporation), (AV) '24 '48
C.112 L.309 J.D. Foundation for Books for China
MacMorris, John ..................... '47 '75 C.612 B.A. L.494 J.D. 1900 Embarcadero
**MacQueen, Joanna** ........................ '57 '92 C.999 B.A. L.1355 J.D. [⊠ Larson&B.]
Madajian, Michael, (BV) ...... '31 '65 C.966 B.B.A. L.1026 LL.B. 5160 Old Redwood Rd.
**Madsen, David S.** '46 '72 C.170 B.A. L.174 J.D.
(adm. in CO; not adm. in CA)
Sr. V.P. & Mgr., Loan Compl. Dept., World Savings & Loan Assoc.
Magaro, Gerald E. ................... '43 '67 C&L.930 B.A., J.D. 405 14th St., Ste. 915
**Maguire, Charles J., Jr.**, (BV) ........... '51 '81 C.282 B.A. L.765 J.D. [Strickland&H.]
*PRACTICE AREAS: Construction Defect; Toxic Claims; Environmental Claims; Intellectual Property.
Maier, Peter K., (AV) .................. '29 '53 C.154 B.A. L.1066 J.D. 1999 Harrison St.
**Maier, Thomas A.** ........................... '55 '79 C.801 B.A. L.1066 J.D. [Pezzola&R.]
**Main, Teresa Jenkins** ...................... '53 '85 C.813 B.A. L.770 J.D. [⊠ Bell,R.&H.]
*PRACTICE AREAS: Estate Planning; Probate; Litigation.
Malakoff, Joseph F. ........... '36 '62 C.33 B.A. L.309 LL.B. Adm. Law J., Soc. Sec. Admn.
Malamuth, Steven J., (BV) '44 '75
C.1169 B.A. L.770 J.D. The Temple of the Golden Rule
Mandel, Korey A. ........................ '46 '72 C.178 A.B. L.1066 J.D. Dep. Pub. Def.
Mandel, Mark W. ...................... '51 '80 C.178 B.A. L.1009 J.D. 488 Seventh St.
Mann, James C. ............................ '60 '88 C.1073 B.S. L.284 J.D. Dep. Pub. Def.
**Mann, Sara** ............................ '69 '95 C&L.112 B.A., J.D. [Plageman&Assoc.]
*PRACTICE AREAS: Real Estate; Land Use; Estate Planning.
Manuel, Joseph Warren .................. '46 '74 C.1073 B.A. L.284 J.D. 405 14th St.
Manuel, Raymond T., Jr. ............ '23 '51 C.112 A.B. L.1066 LL.B. 270 Wayne Ave.‡
Marchand, George L. '36 '62
C.112 A.B. L.1066 LL.B. Spec. Coun., Regents of Univ. of Calif.
Marcotte, Jo Ellen ........................... '51 '92 C.108 B.A. L.284 J.D. N.L.R.B.
**Marden, Steven M.** ........................... '52 '78 C.112 B.A. L.464 J.D. [Larson&B.]
**Margolin, Sanford H.** ................. '53 '79 C.112 A.B. L.1066 J.D. [Cooper,M.&B.]
*PRACTICE AREAS: Real Estate and Business Law; Probate and Related Civil Litigation.

**Marion's Inn, (AV)**
**A Law Partnership**
**1611 Telegraph Avenue, Suite 707, 94612**
**Telephone: 510-451-6770 Fax: 510-451-1711**
**Email: marions@marionsinn.com URL: www.marionsinn.com**
**Partners: Kennedy P. Richardson; Sam Walker; Mark A. Palley. Associates: Albert Lee; Yvonne M. Pierrou.**
**Appellate Advocacy, Products Liability, Unfair Competition, Insurance Coverage, Professional Liability Defense, Employment, Real Estate, Construction and General Business Litigation.**
***See Professional Biographies, OAKLAND, CALIFORNIA***

Mark, Valarie ............................ '61 '91 C.112 A.B. L.1066 J.D. 1999 Harrison St.
**Marks, Kevin A.** '67 '93 C.390 A.B. L.884 J.D.
(adm. in PA; not adm. in CA) [⊠ Littler,M.F.T.&M.]
**Marlin, Louis M.**, (AV) ...................... '47 '72 C.112 B.A. L.1065 J.D. [Marlin&S.]⊙
*LANGUAGES: French.
*REPORTED CASES: Christensen v. Superior Court, California Supreme Court 53 Cal 3rd 868.
*PRACTICE AREAS: Insurance Defense Law; Professional Malpractice Law; Construction Defect Law.

**Marlin & Saltzman, A Professional Law Corporation, (AV)**
**1999 Harrison Street, Suite 990, 94612⊙**
**Telephone: 510-208-9400 Fax: 510-208-9410**
**Louis M. Marlin; Stanley D. Saltzman.**
**Practice limited to Insurance Defense, Insurance Coverage and Bad Faith Litigation.**
**Woodland Hills, California Office: Westhills Plaza, 20700 Ventura Boulevard, Suite 227, 91364. Telephone: 818-702-0600. Fax: 818-702-6555.**
**Orange, California Office: 701 Parker Street, Suite 8800. Telephone: 714-541-1066. Fax: 714-542-4184.**
**San Diego, California Office: 750 "B" Street, Suite 1925. Telephone: 619-235-0600. Fax: 619-235-0675.**
***See Professional Biographies, OAKLAND, CALIFORNIA***

**Marmor, Randy M.**, (BV) ............ '48 '74 C.823 B.A. L.276 J.D. [Haims,J.M.&M.]
*PRACTICE AREAS: Insurance Coverage; Bad Faith Law; Construction Defect Litigation; Accident and Personal Injury; Landlord and Tenant.
Marsh, Joel E. ...................................... '38 '75 C.188 B.A. L.1065 J.D. [Marsh&P.]
Marsh, Judith Wilson ................... '44 '80 C.923 B.A. L.1065 J.D. 1941 Jackson St.
Marsh, Raymond L. ................................ '26 '52 C.112 L.1066 LL.B. Supr. Ct. J.
Marsh, Thomas, (AV) ....................... '23 '53 C.352 B.A. L.1065 J.D. 5351 Belgrave Pl.
Marsh & Perna, (BV) ............................................................... 1 Kaiser Plz.
**Marshall, Edward T.**, (AV) ............. '48 '76 C.477 B.A. L.1066 J.D. [Marshall,A.&L.]
*PRACTICE AREAS: Real Estate Law; Corporate and Business Law.
Marshall, Mariam S. .................... '64 '91 C.1073 B.S. L.767 J.D. 4797 Telegraph Ave.

**Marshall, Akawie & LaPietra, Professional Corporation, (AV)**
**One Kaiser Plaza, Suite 1340, 94612⊙**
**Telephone: 510-874-7200 Telecopier: 510-874-7219**
**Edward T. Marshall; Alice L. Akawie; Lauren M. LaPietra. Of Counsel: Bruce G. Peterson; Gregory S. Nerland (Resident, Walnut Creek Office).**

(This Listing Continued)

CALIFORNIA—OAKLAND MARTINDALE-HUBBELL LAW DIRECTORY 1997

**Marshall, Akawie & LaPietra, Professional Corporation (Continued)**

**Real Property, Corporate Law, General Business, Real Estate and Business Litigation, Financing, Partnerships, Securities, Taxation and Estate Planning.**
**Walnut Creek, California Office: 1981 North Broadway, Suite 330, 94596. Telephone: 510-947-4347. Telecopier: 510-947-6636.**

*See Professional Biographies, OAKLAND, CALIFORNIA*

**Martin, Amy D.** ................ '64 '90 C.767 B.A. L.464 J.D. [Ⓐ Van Bourg,W.R.&R.]
*PRACTICE AREAS: Labor Law; Employment Law.
Martin, Gerald P., Jr., (AV) ........... '31 '60 C.740 B.S. L.1066 LL.B. 300 Lakeside Dr.
Martin, Gregory L. '53 '91 C.150 B.S. L.1065 J.D.
(adm. in NJ; not adm. in CA) Coun., Mt. View Assoc.
**Martin, Jay R.**, (AV) '28 '53
C.112 B.S. L.1066 LL.B. [Ⓒ Crosby,H.R.&M.] (©San Fran.)
Martin, Myron A. .............................. '19 '49 C.112 A.B. L.1065 J.D. Ret. Supr. Ct. J.
Martinez, Christiansen B. ................ '48 '89 C.112 B.S. L.284 J.D. 1900 Embarcadero
**Martinez, Robert C.** .... '— '81 C&L.1066 A.B., J.D. Dep. Port Atty. II, Port of Oakland
Marx, Deborah J. ........................ '56 '81 C.696 B.A. L.1066 J.D. Community Law Ctr.
**Mascovich, Joseph P.** ................ '54 '80 C.112 A.B. L.1065 J.D. [Crosby,H.R.&M.]
*PRACTICE AREAS: Appellate.
**Mase, Gregory A.** ............... '63 '93 C.112 B.A. L.1065 J.D. [Ⓐ Ericksen,A.K.D.&L.]
*PRACTICE AREAS: Insurance Defense.
Masouredis, Linus S. ......................... '49 '77 C.112 A.B. L.309 J.D. Dep. Atty. Gen.
Mavromihalis, Vickie Kuvelis .......... '66 '90 C.112 B.A. L.1066 J.D. 1901 Harrison St.
**Maxwell, Cynthia E.** ................ '58 '84 C.103 A.B. L.1068 J.D. [Littler,M.F.T.&M.]
May, Lewis P. ................................ '19 '47 C.911 B.A. L.767 LL.B. Ret. Mun. Ct. J.
Mayeda, Mari ................................ '57 '83 C.112 B.A. L.309 J.D. 1300 Clay St.
**Mazza, Michael J.** ... '55 '83 C.112 B.S. L.770 J.D. Sr. Pat. Coun., The Clorox Co. (Pat.)
McAndrew, Eileen T. ..................... '60 '85 C.426 B.A. L.1065 J.D. Dep. Dist. Atty.
**McCabe, Louise M.** ........................ '57 '83 C.112 B.A. L.770 J.D. [Crosby,H.R.&M.]
*PRACTICE AREAS: Commercial Litigation; Professional Liability; Property Tax Litigation; Insurance and Environmental Coverage.
**McCaffery, Timothy J.** ..................... '66 '91 C.740 B.S. L.767 J.D. [Hardin,C.L.E.&B.]
*PRACTICE AREAS: Products Liability; Civil Litigation; Insurance Law.
**McCalla, Randolph G.** ..................... '67 '95 C&L.112 B.A., J.D. [Ⓐ Larson&B.]
**McCarthy, Kenneth J.** ..................... '57 '85 C.768 B.A. L.1026 J.D. [Knox R.]
*PRACTICE AREAS: Civil Trial; Insurance Defense; Asbestos Litigation; Products Liability.
McCarthy, Kevin M. ........................ '57 '85 C.112 B.A. L.1065 J.D. Asst. Pub. Def.
**McCarthy, Patrick K. M.** .................. '48 '83 C.112 B.A. L.765 J.D. [Larson&B.]
**McClain, David M.** ..................... '47 '72 C.112 B.A. L.1065 J.D. [Kazan,M.E.S.&A.]
McCoy, Ernest H., (AV) .............. '34 '63 C.477 B.S. L.1066 LL.B. [Bruce&M.] (Pat.)
**McCuaig, Sarah Robertson** .......... '65 '89 C.914 B.A. L.861 J.D. [Ⓐ Fitzgerald,A.&B.]
*PRACTICE AREAS: labor and Employment Law.
**McCutchen, John C.** ........................ '52 '77 C.861 B.A. L.128 J.D. [Ⓒ Leon&L.]
*PRACTICE AREAS: Construction Litigation; General Civil Litigation; Corporate Transactions.
McDonald, Jane A. ........................ '59 '86 C.1060 B.A. L.464 J.D. 200 Webster St.
**McDonnell, John L., Jr.**, (AV) ....... '37 '64 C.1256 A.B. L.767 J.D. [Crosby,H.R.&M.]
*PRACTICE AREAS: Estate Planning Law; Administration of Trust and Estates; Fiduciary Asset Management; Trust and Estate Litigation.

**McDonough, Holland & Allen, A Professional Corporation, (AV)**
**1999 Harrison Street, Suite 1300, 94612©**
**Telephone: 510-273-8780 Fax: 510-839-9104**
**Natalie E. West; Craig Labadie; Michelle Marchetta Kenyon;—Paul C. Anderson; Michelle Rudd.**
**General Civil, Trial and Appellate Litigation, Local Government, Redevelopment, Construction, Eminent Domain, Employment, Environmental, Land Use, Health Care, International, Water, Toxics.**
**Sacramento, California Office: 9th Floor, 555 Capitol Mall. Telephone: 916-444-3900. Fax: 916-444-8334.**
**Yuba City, California Office: 422 Century Park Drive, Suite A, P.O. Box 776. Telephone: 916-674-9761. Fax: 916-671-0990.**

*See Professional Biographies, OAKLAND, CALIFORNIA*

**McEntee, Vera Marcus** ........... '52 '90 C.674 B.A. L.1067 J.D. [Ⓐ Crosby,H.R.&M.]
**McFeely, Stephen A.**, (AV) '47 '72
C.740 B.S. L.1065 J.D. [Crosby,H.R.&M.] (©San Francisco)
*PRACTICE AREAS: Business Disputes; Insurance Bad Faith.
McGhee, Lynne P. ............. '65 '91 C.999 B.S. L.809 J.D. 1800 Harrison St., Ste. 1616
McGill, Terry D. '50 '77 C.312 B.A. L.1026 J.D.
Claims Mgr. & Contract Analyst, V.P., Dealey, Renton & Assoc. Ins. Brokers
**McGuiness, Robert D.**, (AV) .......... '51 '75 C.770 B.A. L.1068 J.D. [McGuiness&N.]
McGuiness, William R. ..................... '46 '72 C.770 B.A. L.767 J.D. Supr. Ct. J.

**McGuiness & Northridge, (AV)**
**1939 Harrison Street, 7th Floor, 94612**
**Telephone: 510-273-8870 Fax: 510-273-8830**
**Members of Firm: Robert D. McGuiness; Yolanda N. Northridge.**
**General Civil and Trial Practice. Family Law and Plaintiff Class Actions, Securities Litigation.**

*See Professional Biographies, OAKLAND, CALIFORNIA*

**McInerney, Thomas**, (AV) .......... '26 '56 C.770 B.S.C. L.1065 J.D. [Haims,J.M.&M.]
*PRACTICE AREAS: Insurance Defense Law; Civil Defense; Alternative Dispute Resolution.
**McInerney, Timothy L.** ................... '61 '86 C.770 B.S. L.464 J.D. [McInerney&D.]
**McInerney, William H.**, (AV) .......... '24 '51 C.770 B.S. L.1066 J.D. [McInerney&D.]
*PRACTICE AREAS: Construction Law.
**McInerney, William H., Jr.**, (AV) ........ '52 '80 C.770 B.S. L.464 J.D. [McInerney&D.]

**McInerney & Dillon, Professional Corporation, (AV)**
**18th Floor Ordway Building, One Kaiser Plaza, 94612-3610**
**Telephone: 510-465-7100 Facsimile: 510-465-8556**
**William H. McInerney; Timothy F. Winchester; Robert L. Leslie; William H. McInerney, Jr.; Michael E. London;—Franklin H. Yap; Timothy L. McInerney; Charles E. Toombs; Eamonn P. Conlon; William A. Barrett; Jewell J. Hargleroad; Carol Knight Watson; Quinlan S. Tom.**
**Construction Law, Government and Public Contract Law, Administrative Law (including practice before Boards of Contract Appeals). Civil Litigation, Environmental Law, Employment Law, Corporation, Real Property, Estate Planning and Probate Law. Business and Commercial Trial Practice. Tax Planning and Tax Litigation.**

*See Professional Biographies, OAKLAND, CALIFORNIA*

**McIntosh, Bruce A.** ..................... '59 '94 C.1239 B.A. L.1065 J.D. [Ⓐ Ryan,A.&L.]
**McIsaac, Donald A.**, (BV) ............ '53 '78 C.112 A.B. L.1066 J.D. [Wendel,R.B.&D.]
*PRACTICE AREAS: Construction Law; Real Property Law; Business Litigation.
**McKae, Stephen**, (AV) .............. '47 '75 C.813 B.A. L.1065 J.D. [Hardin,C.L.E.&B.]
*LANGUAGES: French.
*PRACTICE AREAS: Civil Litigation; Labor Law; Environmental Law.
McKee, Heather Anne ............. '60 '85 C.132 B.A. L.209 J.D. 4100-10 Redwood Rd.
**McKeeman, Michael T.** ..................... '68 '94 C.112 B.S. L.770 J.D. [Ⓐ Larson&B.]
**McKenzie, Timothy Cass** .................. '63 '92 C.623 B.A. L.767 J.D. [Ⓐ Knox R.]
*PRACTICE AREAS: Civil Trial Construction and Insurance Defense.
**McKnight, Scott C.** ........................ '60 '88 C.72 B.A. L.209 J.D. [Ⓐ Crosby,H.R.&M.]
McLaughlin, Dennis J., (AV) .................. '55 '80 C&L.770 B.S., J.D. Dep. Dist. Atty.
**McLemore, George D.**, (AV) ........ '50 '78 C.1169 A.B. L.284 J.D. [McLemore,C.&T.]
*PRACTICE AREAS: Casualty Defense.

**McLemore, Collins & Toschi, (AV)**
**200 Webster Street, Suite 200, 94607**
**Telephone: 510-835-3400 FAX: 510-835-7800**

(This Listing Continued)

**McLemore, Collins & Toschi (Continued)**

**George D. McLemore; Wayne M. Collins; Steven C. Toschi; Gregory Michael Doyle; Irene Takahashi;—Joel P. Franciosa; Alvin D. Hunter; Rebecca Weisman; Cathye E. Leonard.**
**General Civil Practice in all State and Federal Courts; Casualty Defense.**

*See Professional Biographies, OAKLAND, CALIFORNIA*

**McLeod, Bruce E.**, (AV) ........................ '49 '76 C&L.101 B.S., J.D. [Hardin,C.L.E.&B.]
*PRACTICE AREAS: Civil Trials; Products Liability Law; Toxic Substances Law.
McLeod, Chas. C. ..................... '10 '35 C.112 B.A. L.1066 [Hildebrand,M.&N.] ‡
McLeod, George M., (AV) ................. '15 '38 C&L.950 A.B., J.D. 1000 Broadway
**McMahan, Troy D.** ..................... '64 '90 C.336 B.S. L.878 J.D. [Ⓐ Hardin,C.L.E.&B.]
*PRACTICE AREAS: Asbestos Litigation; General Civil Litigation.
McMillan, Charles M., (AV) ............. '32 '62 C.434 A.B. L.1065 J.D. 155 Grand Ave.
McNair, Robert J. ........................................ '52 '90 L.765 J.D. 169 14th St.

**McNamara, Houston, Dodge, McClure & Ney**
**(See Walnut Creek)**

McRae, Margie ................................................ '— '87 L.284 J.D. P.O. Box 19244
McWilliams, James D., (AV) ...................... '43 '68 C&L.608 B.A., J.D. Pub. Def.
**Meade, Marguerite E.** ............. '57 '88 C.112 B.A. L.1065 J.D. [Gwilliam,I.C.C.&B.]
*PRACTICE AREAS: Personal Injury; Insurance Bad Faith; Employment Discrimination; Governmental Torts.

**Meadows, David J., (AV) '53 '79 C.860 B.A. L.1066 J.D.**
**679 Arimo Avenue, 94610**
**Telephone: 510-451-6410 Fax: 510-451-2651**
**Email: djmeadows@aol.com**
**Mediation & ADR Services.**

*See Professional Biographies, OAKLAND, CALIFORNIA*

Mears, Judith M. '46 '71 C.860 B.A. L.145 J.D.
V.P. & Asst. Gen. Coun., Kaiser Found. Health Plan, Inc.
Meehan, James Patrick, (BV) ............. '61 '86 C.112 B.A. L.767 J.D. Dep. Dist. Atty.
Meehan, John J. ........................................ '32 '60 C.767 B.S. L.765 J.D. Dist. Atty.
**Meier, Peter C.** ......................... '68 '95 C.178 B.A. L.1067 J.D. [Ⓐ Crosby,H.R.&M.]
Meier, Richard W., (BV) ............ '42 '67 C.112 B.A. L.1066 J.D. 11 Embarcadero W.
**Mejia, John V.** ........................ '66 '93 C.112 B.A. L.767 J.D. [Ⓐ Ericksen,A.K.D.&L.]
*LANGUAGES: Spanish.
Melisso, David L. ........................................ '55 '88 C&L.911 B.A., J.D. 200 Webster St.
Meloling, Albert W. ..................... '25 '52 C.763 L.809 LL.B. 1611 Telegraph Ave.‡
Mendel, Emily Schulman ................. '45 '77 C.569 B.A. L.1019 J.D. [E.S.Mendel]
Mendel, Emily Schulman, P.C. ...................................................... 1 Kaiser Plaza
Mendelson, Robert A. ......................... '09 '34 C&L.800 B.S., J.D. 3369 Crane Way‡
Mendelson, Steven E., (BV) ......... '48 '75 C.1169 A.B. L.284 J.D. 120 11th St., 2nd Fl.
Méndez, Armando ....................... '62 '88 C.309 A.B. L.1066 J.D. 291 Adams St.
Mendoza, Maria R. ........................................ '49 '75 C&L.378 B.A., J.D. Dep. City Atty.
**Meronek, Gregory D.** ..................... '56 '82 C.339 B.A. L.276 J.D. [Ⓐ Berry&B.]
Metcalf, Elizabeth Joan ................. '64 '90 C.112 B.A. L.770 J.D. 200 Webster St.
Metoyer, Carl B., (AV) ........................ '25 '53 C.112 L.1065 J.D. 6014 Market St.
Meyer, David M. ........................ '56 '87 C.154 B.A. L.770 J.D. 1999 Harrison St.
**Meyer, Laura K.** ..................... '60 '88 C.112 A.B. L.1065 J.D. [Ⓐ Wendel,R.B.&D.]
*PRACTICE AREAS: Litigation.
**Michaels, Anne M.** ................. '60 '88 C.783 B.A. L.284 J.D. [Ⓐ Haims,J.M.&M.]
*LANGUAGES: Spanish.
*PRACTICE AREAS: Insurance Defense Litigation; Landlord/Tenant Litigation; Construction Law.
Michaels, Richard S., (AV) .......... '46 '72 C.813 A.B. L.1065 J.D. Chf. Asst. Dist. Atty.
**Mickelson, Blythe** ................ '54 '80 C.813 B.A. L.1066 J.D. [Van Bourg,W.R.&R.]
*PRACTICE AREAS: Labor Law.
Mifsud, Kenneth ........................ '61 '89 C.112 B.A. L.770 J.D. Dep. Dist. Atty.
**Mikacich, Amee A.** ................. '62 '89 C.112 B.A. L.765 J.D. [Ⓐ Hardin,C.L.E.&B.]
*PRACTICE AREAS: Product Liability Law; Civil Litigation; Toxic Torts.
Mikkelson, Kathleen W., (AV) ............ '48 '73 C.668 B.A. L.976 J.D. Dep. Atty. Gen.
Miles, Patricia B., Law Office of .......... '57 '88 C.597 B.A. L.284 J.D. 1440 Broadway
Miller, Barbara J., (AV) ...................... '51 '78 C.383 B.A. L.767 J.D. Supr. Ct. Comm.
Miller, Chandra O'Brien .................... '50 '80 C.112 A.B. L.284 J.D. [Taylor&F.]
Miller, Christopher D. ...................... '57 '88 C.112 B.A. L.1065 J.D. [Ⓐ Jewel&L.]
**Miller, David**, (AV) ..................... '41 '70 C.563 B.A. L.1009 J.D. [Hoyt,M.&A.]©
*PRACTICE AREAS: Labor Relations Law; Wage and Hour Law; Employment Discrimination Law; Occupational Safety Law; Health Law.
**Miller, David M.** ........................ '66 '92 C.112 B.S. L.464 J.D. [Ⓐ Nevin&H.]
*PRACTICE AREAS: Construction Defect Litigation; Labor and Employment.
Miller, Harry D., (AV) ........................ '31 '58 C.112 B.A. L.1066 J.D. 1 Kaiser Plz.
Miller, John F. ........................ '38 '66 C.705 B.A. L.188 J.D. 6936 Armour Dr.
Miller, Kirk E. '51 '76 C.112 B.A. L.823 J.D.
Sr. V.P. & Gen. Coun., Kaiser Found. Health Plan, Inc.
**Miller, Michele Ballard** '54 '82
C.477 B.A. L.1065 J.D. [Crosby,H.R.&M.] (©San Francisco)
*PRACTICE AREAS: Labor and Employment Law; Litigation.
Miller, Thomas R. ........................ '38 '65 C.976 A.B. L.813 LL.B. [T.R.Miller]
Miller, William S. ........................ '47 '72 C&L.950 B.A., J.D. 1433 Webster St.

**Miller, Starr & Regalia, A Professional Law Corporation, (AV)**
**Suite 1575, Ordway Building, One Kaiser Plaza, 94612©**
**Telephone: 510-465-3800**
**Email: msr@msandr.com**
**Victor Harris; James A. Tiemstra; Lewis J. Soffer; John H. Wunsch;—Leslie E. Orr.**
**General Civil and Trial Practice. Real Estate, Zoning and Land Use, Environmental, Taxation, Securities, Commercial and Real Estate Finance, General Corporate, Bankruptcy, Reorganizations and Creditors Rights, Intellectual Property, Trusts, Title Insurance Practice.**
**Representative Clients: Bank of the West; Hewlett Packard; Prometheus Development; First American Title Insurance Co.; Weyerhaeuser Co.**
**Walnut Creek, California Office: 1331 North California Boulevard, Fifth Floor, P.O. Box 8177. Telephone: 510-935-9400.**
**Sacramento, California Office: 455 Capitol Mall, Suite 604. Telephone: 916-443-6700.**

*See Professional Biographies, OAKLAND, CALIFORNIA*

Miller, Thomas R., A Professional Law Corporation .......... 725 Washington St., 3rd Fl.
Mills, Cathy, (BV) ........................ '49 '81 C.427 B.A. L.300 J.D. 456 Eighth St.
**Minoletti, Paul G.** ................... '57 '85 C.767 B.A. L.284 J.D. [Ⓐ Boornazian,J.&G.]
**Mintz, Kevin R.** ................... '64 '94 C.112 B.A. L.1066 J.D. [Ⓐ Rankin,S.M.T.&R.]
Mintz, Lincoln N., (AV) ................. '42 '66 C.112 A.B. L.1066 J.D. [Mintz,G.&M.]
Mintz, Giller & Mintz, A Law Corporation, (AV)
405 Fourteenth St., Franklin at Fourteenth
Miranda, Carlos M. ............... '52 '82 C.454 B.A. L.1065 J.D. Research Atty., Supr. Ct.
**Mires, Geoffrey A.** ..................... '54 '81 C.112 B.A. L.284 J.D. [Rankin,S.M.T.&R.]
*PRACTICE AREAS: Medical Law; Legal Malpractice; General Insurance Defense; Products Liability Law; Commercial Litigation.
Mitchel, Kirk G. ........................ '55 '82 C.154 B.A. L.284 J.D. Asst. Pub. Def.
Mitchell, Arthur Kennedy ................ '48 '89 C.1073 B.A. L.1230 J.D. P.O. Box 201
Mitchell, Daniel L. ........................ '34 '63 C.767 B.S. L.1065 LL.B. [Hayes&M.]
Mitchell, Donald L. ........................ '41 '75 L.1026 LL.B. 1944 Embarcadero
Mitchell, John S. ........................ '15 '39 C&L.813 A.B., LL.B. 33 Lane Court‡

CAA434P

Mitchell, Kenneth E. ... '47 '72 C.502 B.S. L.767 J.D. [White,C.M.&J.]
**Mitchell, Wendall A.** ... '59 '85 C.1036 A.B. L.1066 J.D. [Kennedy,G.M.&C.]
Mitzman, Myra ... '62 '88 C.1040 B.B.A. L.262 J.D. 3824 Grand Ave.
**Miyake, Steven S.** ... '50 '84 C.1169 B.A. L.1065 J.D. [Ⓐ Neal&Assoc.]
Moffitt, Marilyn A. '43 '79 C.878 B.A. L.1206 J.D.
Coun., Kaiser Found. Health Plan, Inc.
Molesky, James E. ... '52 '80 C.112 B.A. L.284 J.D. [J.E.Molesky]
Molesky, James E., A Professional Corporation ... 80 Grand Ave.
Moll, Lawrence E., (BV) ... '43 '72 C.178 A.B. L.284 J.D. 5315 College Ave.
Molter, Timothy I., (BV) ... '48 '73 C.112 A.B. L.1066 J.D. 1 Kaiser Plz.
**Moncharsh, Leila H., (P.C.)**, (AV) ... '50 '77 C.1169 B.A. L.767 J.D. [Veneruso&M.]
*PRACTICE AREAS: Insurance Defense; Product Liability; Medical; Equine Law; Land Use.
Montgomery, Katherine A. ... '46 '81 C.668 B.A. L.1065 J.D. One Kaiser Plz.
Montgomery, Stephen K. ... '42 '66 C.36 B.S. L.893 LL.B. Vet. Admn.
Moore, Howard, Jr., (BV) ... '32 '61 C.511 B.A. L.94 LL.B. [Moore&M.]
Moore, Jane Bond ... '— '76 C.811 A.B. L.1066 J.D. [Moore&M.]
Moore, John A., Jr. ... '31 '56 C&L.912 A.B., J.D. 6780 Evergreen‡
**Moore, Margaret E.** ... '66 '72 C.575 B.A. L.767 J.D. [Ⓐ Erickson,B.H.&W.]
Moore, Richard P., Jr., (AV) ... '54 '81 C.475 B.A. L.362 J.D. Dist. Atty.
Moore, Vernon A. ... '28 '59 C.112 A.B. L.1065 J.D. Mun. J.
Moore & Moore, (BV) ... 445 Bellevue Ave., 3rd Floor
Moran, Rosa ... '60 '88 C.464 B.A. L.767 J.D. 600 21st Street
**More, Antonia L.** ... '59 '89 C.293 B.A. L.1065 J.D. [Fitzgerald,A.&B.]
*LANGUAGES: Russian and French.
*PRACTICE AREAS: Securities Litigation; NYSE and NASD Arbitration; Unfair Trade Practices; Noncompetition and Nonsolicitation Agreements; Trade secrets.
Moren, James R., (AV) ... '43 '69 C.674 B.S.E. L.1066 J.D. One Kaiser Plaza
Morgan, Melanie '— '74 C.813 B.A. L.1066 J.D.
Assoc. Gen. Coun., Metropolitan Transp. Comm.
**Morger, Steven M.** ... '59 '84 C.112 B.S. L.1066 J.D. [Wendel,R.B.&D.]
*PRACTICE AREAS: Real Estate and Secured Transactions Litigation.
**Mori, Paul J.** ... '66 '93 C.112 B.A. L.1355 J.D. [Ⓐ Donahue,G.W.&W.]
*LANGUAGES: Italian.
Morinelli, Elaine L. ... '49 '85 C.483 B.A. L.1230 J.D. 6009 Buena Ventura Ave.
Morley, John C. ... '63 '88 C&L.767 B.S., J.D. [Ⓐ Taylor&F.]
**Mormorunni, Carlo C.** ... '68 '94 C.893 B.A. L.767 J.D. [Ⓐ Fitzgerald,A.&B.]
*LANGUAGES: Italian.
*PRACTICE AREAS: Commercial Law; Corporate Law; Estate Planning; Business Litigation.
Morrell, Stephen P. ... '50 '77 C.112 B.A. L.770 J.D. Univ. Coun., Univ. of Calif.
Morris, Barry L. ... '47 '71 C.1036 B.A. L.178 J.D. 1 Kaiser Plz.
Morris, Carl W. ... '40 '72 C.766 B.A. L.284 J.D. Mun. J.
Morris, Katrina Kimberlyn, (AV) ... '56 '82 C&L.770 B.A., J.D. 456 Eighth St.
Morris, Wayne D. '53 '78
C.630 B.A. L.900 J.D. Sr. Coun., Kaiser Found. Health Plan, Inc.
Morrison, Gary ... '42 '69 C.174 B.A. L.813 LL.B. Dep. Gen. Coun., Univ. of Calif.
Morrison, Joanne E. ... '45 '83 C.454 B.S. L.1066 J.D. [White,C.M.&J.]
**Morrison, Randall D.** ... '46 '72 C.911 B.A. L.1066 J.D. [Crosby,H.R.&M.]
*PRACTICE AREAS: Commercial Litigation; Environmental Litigation.
**Morrisroe, Sean W.** ... '60 '83 C.1073 B.S. L.767 J.D. [Ⓐ Gassett,P.&F.]
*PRACTICE AREAS: General Civil Litigation; Trial Practice.
**Morrow, G. Trent** ... '66 '93 C.112 B.S. L.464 J.D. [Ⓐ Rankin,S.M.T.&R.]
**Morton, William R.**, (AV) ... '44 '69 C&L.336 B.S., J.D. [Morton,L.&A.]
*REPORTED CASES: Tarasoff v. Regents of U.C. (1976) 17 Cal. 3d 425.
*PRACTICE AREAS: Insurance Coverage; Products Liability; Bad Faith Litigation.

**Morton, Lulofs & Allen, A Professional Law Corporation, (AV)**
**Ordway Building, One Kaiser Plaza, Suite 801, 94612**
**Telephone: 510-444-5521 Fax: 510-444-8263**
**Email: rmorton@ix.netcom.com.**
**William R. Morton; Larry E. Lulofs; Roger F. Allen; G. Geoffrey Wood;—Tyler G. Olpin; Lisa S. Klotchman; Michael G. Dini.**
**Insurance Defense, Insurance Coverage and Bad Faith Litigation, Products Liability, Construction, Civil Trial, Real Estate.**
**Representative Clients: Hartford Insurance Group; Unigard Insurance Group; American International Cos.**
***See Professional Biographies, OAKLAND, CALIFORNIA***

Moscrip, Clark G. ... '45 '72 C.705 B.A. L.767 J.D. 500 12th St.
Mounts, Suzanne E. ... '45 '73 C.112 B.A. L.1066 J.D. 413 60th St.
Muellerleile, Mary Alice '— '77 C.713 B.A. L.1035 J.D.
(adm. in MN; not adm. in CA) 7000 Hemlock St.
Mugler, Frederick B. ... '51 '90 C.112 B.A. L.1065 J.D. One Kaiser Plaza
Mullally, Lawrence E., (AV) ... '13 '38 C.112 A.B. L.1066 J.D. [Mullally&C.]
Mullally and Cederborg, Inc., (AV) ... 436 14th St.

**Mullen & Filippi, (AV)**
**2101 Webster Street, Suite 1525, 94612⊙**
**Telephone: 510-444-1532**
**Members of Firm: Robert J. Cavallero; Warren A. Pulley; Carol L. Powell. Associate: R. Manuel Fortes.**
**Insurance Defense, Workers Compensation, Liability and Subrogation.**
**Other California Offices: San Francisco, San Jose, Sacramento, Fresno, Santa Rosa, Long Beach, Bakersfield, Salinas, Stockton, Woodland Hills and Redding.**
***See Professional Biographies, SAN FRANCISCO, CALIFORNIA***

**Mulvihill, William T.**, (BV) ... '50 '77 C.767 B.A. L.284 J.D. [Boornazian,J.&G.]
*PRACTICE AREAS: Personal Injury; Products; Psychological Injury; Medical Malpractice Litigation.
Munck, Benson & Skinner, (BV) ... 405 14th St.
Muraoka, William K., (BV) ... '47 '74 C.1042 A.B. L.770 J.D. Asst. Pub. Def.
**Murov, Ronald L.**, (AV) ... '46 '74 C.169 B.A. L.1068 LL.B. [Crosby,H.R.&M.]
*PRACTICE AREAS: Civil Litigation with emphasis on Business Torts; Finance Securities Litigation.
Murphy, Maureen ... '50 '91 C.28 B.A. L.770 J.D. Coun., Kaiser Found. Health Plan, Inc.
Murray, Kristina E. ... '64 '91 C.67 B.A. L.990 J.D. 1951 Webster St.
Murrell, Cheri C. ... '46 '80 C.112 B.S. L.464 J.D. 22 Moss Ave.

**Myers, Peter S. '60 '84 C.30 B.A. L.1065 J.D.**
**4100-10 Redwood Road #331, 94619**
**Telephone: 510-530-1593 Fax: 510-530-5272**
**Email: CBCG2@AOL.COM**
***PRACTICE AREAS: Civil Practice; Business Law; Real Estate; Corporations. Business Law.**
***See Professional Biographies, OAKLAND, CALIFORNIA***

Naish, John C. '45 '72 C.766 B.A. L.1066 J.D.
Assoc. Gen. Coun., San Francisco Bay Area Rapid Transit Dist.
Najpaver, Joseph C., (BV) ... '40 '65 C&L.912 LL.B. Asst. Pub. Def.
Nakao, Shirley '48 '78
C.112 A.B. L.1065 J.D. San Francisco Bay Area Rapid Transit Dist.
Napell, Bruce J. ... '59 '84 C.112 B.A. L.1065 J.D. 4250 Maybelle Ave.
Naphan, Alfred R., (AV) ... '19 '52 C.112 B.S. L.1065 J.D. 169 14th St.
Narby, Bonnie, (BV) ... '56 '84 C.685 B.A. L.1065 J.D. Dep. Pub. Def.
Nation, Fred D., Jr. '37 '63 C.586 B.B.A. L.846 LL.B.
(adm. in TX; not adm. in CA) Dir., Matthew Bender & Co., Inc.
Neagley, Clinton H. '47 '78 C.605 A.B. L.188 J.D.
Chf. Pat. Coun. & Dir., Lic., DNA Plant Tech. Corp. (Pat.)
**Neal, Howard D.**, (AV) ... '46 '74 C.813 A.B. L.1066 J.D. [Neal&Assoc.]
*LANGUAGES: German, Russian and Spanish.
*PRACTICE AREAS: Wills, Trusts and Estates; Real Estate Law; Bankruptcy Law; Computer Law.
Neal, Raymond P. ... '20 '63 C&L.764 B.S., LL.B. Veterans Admin. Reg. Off.

**Neal & Associates, (AV)**
**Montclair Village, 6200 Antioch Street, Suite 202, P.O. Box 13314, 500, 94661-0314**
**Telephone: 510-339-0233 FAX: 510-339-6672**
**URL: http://seamless.com/hdn/hdn.html**
**Howard D. Neal;—Frank J. Gilbert; Steven S. Miyake.**
**Computer Law, Start-up and Newly Acquired Companies, Wills, Trusts, Estates, Bankruptcy, Real Estate, Franchising, Copyrights, and Trademarks.**
***See Professional Biographies, OAKLAND, CALIFORNIA***

Nelson, Frederick L., (AV) ... '31 '60 C.813 B.A. L.309 LL.B. [Hildebrand,M.&N.]
**Nelson, Jack R.** ... '58 '83 C.494 B.S. L.1066 J.D. [Crosby,H.R.&M.]
*PRACTICE AREAS: Insurance and Commercial Litigation.
**Nelson, James C.**, (AV) ... '41 '67 C.597 B.A. L.1119 J.D. [Bell,R.&H.]
*PRACTICE AREAS: Business Law; Business and Real Estate Litigation.
Nelson, Lewis N. ... '44 '79 C.112 B.A. L.284 J.D. 3911 Harrison St.
Nelson, Luella E. ... '52 '76 C.429 B.S. L.309 J.D. P.O. Box 21268
Nelson, Maurice J., (BV) ... '31 '63 C&L.494 B.A., J.D. 3162 Burdeck Dr.
Nelson, Teresa L. '55 '81 C.112 B.A. L.818 J.D.
Supervising Atty., Protection & Advocacy, Inc.
**Neundorf, Tanda L.** ... '67 '95 C.112 B.A. L.813 J.D. [Ⓐ Crosby,H.R.&M.]
**Nevin, Jeffrey G.**, (AV) ... '53 '84 C.112 A.B. L.464 J.D. [Nevin&H.]⊙

**Nevin & Hall LLP, (AV)**
**180 Grand Avenue, Suite 950, 94612⊙**
**Telephone: 510-873-8600 Fax: 510-873-8601**
**Jeffrey G. Nevin; Gary A. Hall; Charles E. Finberg;—Jan A. Gruen; Jonathan C. Terry; David M. Miller.**
**Insurance Defense and Coverage, Construction, Railroad, Securities, Real Estate, Business and Commercial Litigation.**
**San Francisco, California Office: 507 Polk Street, Suite 300. Telephone: 415-834-1777. Fax: 415-834-1774.**
**Washington, D.C. Office: 2021 L Street N.W., Suite 300. Telephone: 202-887-0945. Fax: 202-887-0968.**
***See Professional Biographies, OAKLAND, CALIFORNIA***

Newacheck, David J. ... '53 '79 C.112 A.B. L.990 J.D. Matthew Bender & Co., Inc.
**Newcomb, Robyn Renée** '66 '93
C.112 B.A. L.767 J.D. [Ⓐ Donahue,G.W.&W.] (⊙Mill Valley)
**Newman, Joan Pugh** ... '59 '90 C.813 B.A. L.1068 J.D. [Ⓐ Corbett&K.]⊙
Newman, Richard L. ... '51 '81 C.33 B.S. L.1065 J.D. 1330 Broadway
Newsome, Randall J. ... '50 '75 C.94 B.A. L.150 J.D. U.S. Bkrptcy. J.
Newton, Frank W. ... '22 '62 L.1026 LL.B. 3535 Grand Ave.
Nichols, Patricia ... '42 '81 C.1313 B.A. L.05 LL.B. 2901 Fulton St.
**Nielsen, Steven A.** ... '62 '88 C.147 B.A. L.1066 J.D. [Ⓐ Larson&B.]
Nieuwenhuizen, Patricia B. '59 '85 C.846 B.A. L.1065 J.D.
Pres., Fast Track Litigation Support (⊙San Francisco)
**Nikles, Roland** ... '55 '83 C.911 B.A. L.678 J.D. [Bell,R.&H.]
*LANGUAGES: German.
*PRACTICE AREAS: Construction Law; Business and Real Estate Litigation.
Nile, Lawrance W. ... '57 '83 C.770 B.S. L.464 J.D. 1999 Harrison St.
**Noble, Andrew F.** ... '62 '88 C.347 B.A. L.1065 J.D. [Cresswell,C.&E.]
*PRACTICE AREAS: General Civil Litigation; Products Liability Law; Toxic Torts.
Nolan, David D. ... '37 '69 C.1066 A.B. L.284 J.D. 4432 Piedmont St.
Nolan, John E. ... '— '61 C&L.770 B.S., J.D. 530 Water St., 4th Fl.
Nolan, Patricia A. ... '46 '76 C&L.767 B.A., J.D. [Hanna,B.M.M.&J.]
Nolt, Robt. J. ... '21 '55 C.284 B.B.A. 1805 Harrison St.‡
**Noma, Christine K.** ... '57 '82 C.112 B.S. L.1065 J.D. [Wendel,R.B.&D.]
*PRACTICE AREAS: Environmental Law; Employment Law; Insurance Law.
Norman, William A. ... '12 '57 L.284 LL.B. National Econ. Develop. & Law Ctr.
**Normington, Richard V., III** ... '54 '83 C.668 B.A. L.1068 J.D. [Ⓐ Hardin,C.L.E.&B.]
*PRACTICE AREAS: Civil Litigation; Toxic Substance; Environmental Law.
**Norris, Albert B., Jr.**, (AV) ... '35 '64 C.800 B.S. L.1068 LL.B. [Crosby,H.R.&M.]
*PRACTICE AREAS: Toxic Tort; Environmental.
**Northridge, Yolanda N.**, (AV) ... '43 '79 C.166 B.A. L.1049 J.D. [McGuiness&N.]
Norton & Ross, P.C. ... 8 Emery Bay Drive (⊙San Francisco & San Ramon)
**Novack, Charles D.** ... '58 '84 C.705 B.A. L.1065 J.D. [Ⓐ Kornfield,P.&B.]
*PRACTICE AREAS: Bankruptcy Practice; Bankruptcy Litigation; Commercial Litigation.
**Nugent, Kelly T.** ... '68 '93 C&L.546 B.A., J.D. [Ⓐ Boornazian,J.&G.]
*LANGUAGES: Russian.
Nunley, Troy L. ... '64 '91 C.740 B.A. L.1065 J.D. Dep. Dist. Atty.
**Nussbaum, Jan L.** ... '57 '85 C.911 B.A. L.284 J.D. Corp. Coun., The Clorox Co.
*RESPONSIBILITIES: Advertising; Regulatory; Antitrust; Contracts; International.
**Nyberg, Eric A.**, (AV) ... '58 '87 C.740 L.765 J.D. [Ⓐ Kornfield,P.&B.]
*PRACTICE AREAS: Bankruptcy Practice; Bankruptcy and Commercial Litigation; Probate.
**Obbard, Philip** ... '60 '86 C.311 B.A. L.276 J.D. [Ⓐ Corbett&K.]⊙
Obeysekere, Indrajit '59 '85
C.112 A.B. L.1068 J.D. Coun., Kaiser Found. Health Plan, Inc.
**Ochi, Susan S.** ... '62 '91 C.112 A.B. L.766 J.D. [Ⓐ Kazan,M.E.S.&A.]
Ochoa, Victor R. ... '52 '77 C.813 B.A. L.1067 J.D. 1900 Fruitvale Ave.
O'Connell, Robert E. ... '44 '78 C.478 B.A. L.765 J.D. Vets. Admn.
O'Connor, Ana M. ... '51 '82 C.1073 B.A. L.767 J.D. Assoc. Dir., La Clinica de la Raza
O'Connor, Micheal T. ... '56 '86 C.112 A.B. L.1065 J.D. Dep. Dist. Atty.
**O'Dea, Brian M.**, (AV) ... '44 '70 C.740 B.A. L.767 J.D. [Randick&O.]
*REPORTED CASES: Gerdlund v. Electronic Dispensers International, 190 Cal. App. 3d 263.
*PRACTICE AREAS: Business Litigation; Petroleum Marketing Practices Law.
O'Dea, James L. ... '22 '48 L.309 J.D. 418 3rd St.
Odell, James Nellis ... '43 '71 C.477 B.A. L.1066 J.D. Univ. of Calif.
O'Dwyer, Thomas S. '49 '83 C.112 B.A. L.1202 J.D.
(adm. in ID; not adm. in CA; Pat.) Pat. Atty.
Offen, Frank ... '47 '74 C.112 A.B. L.1066 J.D. 1611 Telegraph Ave.
Offen-Brown, David F., (BV) ... '46 '75 C.309 B.A. L.1066 J.D. 1300 Clay St.
Ogren, Kenneth R., (BV) '42 '68 C.112 A.B. L.1068 J.D.
403 Martin Luther King Jr. Way
Olden, Michael A., (BV) ... '43 '71 C.112 A.B. L.1065 J.D. 1999 Harrison St.
Oleon, Glenn P., (BV) ... '52 '76 C.112 A.B. L.1066 J.D. 2101 Webster St.
Olivito, William P. '27 '64
C.112 A.B. L.284 LL.B. Sr. Spec. Coun., State Comp. Ins. Fund.
**Olmstead, Michael Eric** ... '60 '87 C.1085 B.S. L.878 J.D. [Ⓐ Wendel,R.B.&D.]
*PRACTICE AREAS: Litigation; Construction Law; Labor Law.
**Olpin, Tyler G.** ... '63 '91 C.112 A.B. L.1065 J.D. [Ⓐ Morton,L.&A.]
*PRACTICE AREAS: Insurance Coverage; Civil Trial; Commercial Litigation; Real Estate.
Olsen, Thomas J. ... '62 '89 C.546 B.S. L.823 J.D. [Sims&O.] (⊙Irvine)
**Olson, Robert A.** ... '64 '95 C.1358 B.A. L.1067 J.D. [Ⓐ Crosby,H.R.&M.]
O'Malley, Nancy E. ... '53 '83 C.1073 B.A. L.284 J.D. Off. of Dist. Atty.

**Omid, Lilly M.** ........................'66 '92 C.605 A.B. L.464 J.D. [Ⓐ Bjork,L.P.&K.]
*LANGUAGES: French.
*PRACTICE AREAS: Premises Liability; Lemon Law; Landlord and Tenant Law; Insurance Defense Law.
**Omsberg, Keith S.** '61 '88
C.800 B.A. L.1049 J.D. Sr. Coun., Amer. Protective Servs., Inc.
*LANGUAGES: German.
*RESPONSIBILITIES: Corporate Law; Litigation.
**O'Neal, Vivian D. Mack** '46 '78
C.766 B.A. L.1066 J.D. Dep. Port Atty. IV, Port of Oakland
O'Neil, William Patrick ........................'45 '72 C&L.36 B.A., J.D. 5890 Birch Ct.
Ong, George E., (BV) ........................'36 '71 C.813 B.A. L.284 J.D. 701 Franklin St.
**Ontiveros, Bertha A.** ............'53 '82 C.976 B.A. L.1066 J.D. [Ⓐ Wendel,R.B.&D.]
*LANGUAGES: Spanish.
*PRACTICE AREAS: Real Estate Law; Public Agency Law.
**Oppedahl, Mary C.** ....................'46 '83 C.166 B.A. L.767 J.D. [Crosby,H.R.&M.]
*PRACTICE AREAS: Professional Liability; Insurance Litigation; Products Liability Litigation.
Oppenheimer, Amy J. '52 '80
C&L.112 B.A., J.D. Admin. Law J., State Unemp. Ins. App. Bd.
Opton, Edward M., Jr. ........'36 '77 C.976 B.A. L.1066 J.D. Univ. Coun., Univ. of Calif.
Oreck, Eugene R. ........................'43 '75 C.1077 B.A. L.284 J.D. 1939 Harrison St.
Ormond, Carol Judith ....................'60 '87 C.112 B.A. L.767 J.D. 173 Samaria Lane
**Orr, Leslie E.** ........................'63 '90 C.228 B.A. L.813 J.D. [Ⓐ Miller,S.&R.]
*PRACTICE AREAS: Bankruptcy; Business Litigation.
Ortega, Richard ........................'60 '89 C&L.112 B.A., J.D. Asst. Pub. Def.
Ortiz, Celso D. .....'53 '80 C.813 A.B. L.1066 J.D. Coun., Kaiser Found. Health Plan, Inc.
**Orvell, Betty J.**, (BV) ...............'42 '86 C.860 B.A. L.1065 J.D. [Crosby,H.R.&M.]
*PRACTICE AREAS: Trusts and Estates; Estate Planning for Employee Benefits.
Osborn, Earl D., II ........................'48 '75 C.31 B.A. L.1065 J.D. Equitek Securities
**Osborne, Maribel Delgado** ........'69 '96 C.813 B.A. L.1066 J.D. [Ⓐ Rankin,S.M.T.&R.]
*LANGUAGES: Spanish.
**Osder, Jonathan N.** '67 '94
C.112 B.A. L.1355 J.D. [Ⓐ Donahue,G.W.&W.] (©Mill Valley)
*LANGUAGES: Spanish.
**Osterman, Garth A.** ...................'70 '96 C.911 B.A. L.767 J.D. [Ⓐ Crosby,H.R.&M.]
O'Toole, Thomas P., (BV) ....................'33 '68 C.999 A.B. L.724 J.D. Asst. Pub. Def.
**Otterson, David V.**, (AV) .............'53 '80 C.147 B.A. L.1065 J.D. [Crosby,H.R.&M.]
*PRACTICE AREAS: Corporate Finance; Mergers and Acquisitions; Domestic and International Product Distribution; Technology Licensing.
**Overend, William R.** ..............'68 '95 C.112 B.A. L.1066 J.D. [Ⓐ Crosby,H.R.&M.]
Owen, John A., (BV) ........................'34 '72 C.999 L.765 J.D. 1999 Harrison St.
**Ozak, Laura E.** ........................'58 '94 C.476 B.S.N. L.284 J.D. [Ryan,A.&L.]
**Pace, Kristin A.** ......................'63 '88 C.1075 B.A. L.767 J.D. [Fitzgerald,A.&B.]
*PRACTICE AREAS: Tax Law; Corporate Law; Estate Planning; Trust Administration; Elder Law.
Pachl, James P. ........................'45 '70 C.112 B.A. L.1066 J.D. 80 Grand Ave.
Padilla, Margarita ........................'55 '81 C.112 B.A. L.1066 J.D. Dep. Atty. Gen.
Padway, Laurence F. ........................'53 '78 C.112 B.A. L.1066 J.D. 1 Kaiser Plz.
**Palley, Mark A.** ........................'58 '86 C.1169 B.A. L.1068 J.D. [Marion's I.]
*LANGUAGES: Spanish.
*PRACTICE AREAS: Litigation; Alternative Dispute Resolution; Appellate Law; Health Law; Labor Law.
Palmer, Charles R., Jr. '59 '87 C.1049 B.B.A. L.1065 J.D.
Law Clk. to U.S. Bkrptcy. Ct.
Palmer, Elizabeth, (AV) ..........'10 '35 C.112 A.B. L.1066 LL.B. 13850 Skyline Blvd.‡
**Palmer, Thomas A.**, (AV) ...................'42 '66 C.112 B.A. L.1066 LL.B. [Knox R.]
*REPORTED CASES: Lowell v. Mothers Cake & Cookie Co. 79 Cal. App. 3d 13.
*PRACTICE AREAS: Corporate; Securities; Mergers and Acquisitions; Business; Commercial and Real Estate Law.
**Palmer, Virginia**, (BV) ................'50 '81 C.766 B.A. L.284 J.D. [Fitzgerald,A.&B.]
*PRACTICE AREAS: Family and Elder Law; Estate Planning; Probate; Conservatorships and Trust Related Litigation.
Pandell, James J., (BV) ....................'44 '70 C&L.813 A.B., J.D. Asst. Pub. Def.
Panzer, William G. ........................'55 '87 C.112 A.B. L.284 J.D. 370 Grand Ave.
Paoli, William D., (AV) ....................'48 '77 C.112 B.A. L.1065 J.D. [Paoli&B.]
Paoli & Bratter, (AV) ........................ 1939 Harrison Street, Suite 500
Paradis, Laurence W. ....................'59 '85 C.1169 B.A. L.309 J.D. 1 Kaiser Plz.
Parker, Shirley A. ........................'— '56 C.061 L.813 Pub. Def. Off.
Parks, Mary A. ............'49 '83 L.1026 J.D. Coun., Kaiser Found. Health Plan, Inc.
Parrish, William Shannon, (AV) ..........'16 '41 C.112 A.B. L.813 J.D. 80 Skyway Lane‡
Patton, Douglas K., (BV) ....................'34 '60 C.112 B.S. L.1066 J.D. 405 14th St.
Patton, Roger W., (AV) ...................'45 '72 C.628 B.S. L.1065 J.D. [Patton,W.&B.]
Patton, Scott D. ........................'61 '90 C.112 B.A. L.767 J.D. Dep. Dist. Atty.
Patton, Wolan & Boxer, (AV) ........................ 80 Grand Ave.
**Paul, Aaron**, (AV) ...................'34 '63 C.205 B.S. L.1065 J.D. [Kornfield,P.&B.]
*PRACTICE AREAS: Bankruptcy Practice; Commercial Litigation.
**Peebles, Dianne D.** ......................'60 '87 C.112 A.B. L.284 J.D. [Haims,J.M.&M.]
*PRACTICE AREAS: Insurance Defense Law; Automobile Negligence; Uninsured Motorist; Insurance Fraud; Construction Law.
Peeples, H. E. Christian ....................'47 '78 C.1169 B.A. L.1065 J.D. 4037 Howe St.
**Peña, Gustavo** ........................'66 '93 C.766 B.A. L.1065 J.D. [Ⓐ Larson&B.]
*LANGUAGES: Spanish.
Penick, Andrico Q. ....................'62 '88 C.273 B.A. L.537 J.D. 1901 Harrison St.
Perna, Michael W., (BV) ....................'44 '74 C.645 B.A. L.1065 J.D. [Marsh&P.]
**Perry, Michelle Diane** ..............'65 '93 C.767 B.S. L.1226 J.D. [Ⓐ Haims,J.M.&M.]
*PRACTICE AREAS: Insurance Defense; Insurance Coverage.
**Perry, Patricia H.** ......................'64 '89 C.705 B.A. L.273 J.D. [Ⓐ Bjork,L.P.&K.]
*PRACTICE AREAS: Arson and Insurance Fraud Defense Law; Hospital Law; Medical Malpractice Law; Products Liability Law; Professional Liability Law.
**Persons, Sharon J.** ..................'61 '96 C.178 B.A. L.813 J.D. [Ⓐ Erickson,B.H.&W.]
Pesonen, David E., (AV) ..............'34 '69 C.112 B.S. L.1066 J.D. 3015 Benvenue Ave.
**Peters, Kristen Thall** ..............'67 '92 C.112 B.A. L.770 J.D. [Ⓐ Fitzgerald,A.&B.]
*PRACTICE AREAS: Environmental Litigation; Regulatory Compliance; Land Use.
**Peters, Pamela R.** ....................'53 '92 C.473 B.S. L.284 J.D. [Ericksen,A.K.D.&L.]
*PRACTICE AREAS: Personal Injury; Asbestos; General Civil.
Petersen, Murray B. ........................'19 '65 C.112 A.B. L.765 J.D. 436 14th St.
**Peterson, Bruce G.**, (AV) .............'41 '77 C.112 B.S. L.284 J.D. [Ⓑ Marshall,A.&L.]
*PRACTICE AREAS: Taxation Law; Real Estate Law; General Business Law.
Peterson, Karen L. ....................'55 '88 C.112 A.B. L.767 J.D. 1999 Harrison St.
**Peterson, Karen L.** ....................'55 '88 C.112 A.B. L.767 J.D. [Ⓐ Knox R.]
*PRACTICE AREAS: Regulatory Law; Public Utility Law; Business Litigation.
Peterson, Kenneth B. ....................'49 '75 C.813 A.B. L.1065 J.D. Wkrs. Comp. J.
Petrick, W. W. '46 '71 C&L.659 B.S., J.D.
Gen. Coun., The Permanente Med. Grp., Inc.
Petzel, William J. ......................'43 '75 C.766 B.A. L.284 J.D. 1440 Broadway
**Peyton, George S., Jr.**, (AV) ........'38 '66 C.674 A.B. L.1066 J.D. [Hardin,C.L.E.&B.]
*PRACTICE AREAS: Estate Administration Law; Estate Planning Law; Municipal Law.
**Pezzola, Stephen P.**, (AV) ...............'56 '81 C.112 B.S. L.1066 J.D. [Pezzola&R.]©
*PRACTICE AREAS: Business Planning; Corporate Law; Venture Capital Law; Healthcare Law; Non-Profit Representation.

**Pezzola & Reinke, A Professional Corporation, (AV)** ⊞
**Suite 1300, Lake Merritt Plaza, 1999 Harrison Street, 94612**©
**Telephone: 510-273-8750 Telecopier: 510-834-7440**
**Stephen P. Pezzola; Donald C. Reinke; Thomas A. Maier (Certified Specialist, Taxation Law, The State Bar of California Board of Legal Specialization); Thomas C. Armstrong; Bruce D. Whitley; Bruce P. Johnson; Gizelle A. Barany; Jeremy E. Wenokur. Of Counsel: Robert E. Krebs.**
**Corporate, Partnership, Emerging Growth Companies, Health Care, Mergers and Acquisitions, State and Federal Securities Law, Computer Law, Venture Capital, Intellectual Property, Real Estate, Nonprofit Representation and State, Federal and International Taxation.**
**San Francisco, California Office: 650 California Street, 32nd Floor, 94111. Telephone: 415-989-9710.**
**Menlo Park, California Office: 3000 Sand Hill Road, Building 4, Suite 160, 94025. Telephone: 415-854-8797.**
***See Professional Biographies, OAKLAND, CALIFORNIA***

**Pfaffmann, Lori Lea** ..............'60 '86 C&L.477 A.B., J.D. Sr. Coun., The Clorox Co.
*RESPONSIBILITIES: Real Estate Law; Business Law; Secured Lending and Leasing Law; Software Licensing.
Pfeffer, Michael S. '49 '79 C.188 B.A. L.1066 J.D.
Exec. Dir., Calif. Indian Legal Servs.
Phelan, Jerry J. ........................'32 '56 C.668 A.B. L.1066 LL.B. 1 Kaiser Plza.
Philips, Susan Scarle ............'52 '91 C.714 B.A. L.284 J.D. 2831 Telegraph Ave.‡
Phillips, Alma F., (BV) ................'25 '79 C.112 B.A. L.765 J.D. P.O. Box 10004‡
**Phillips, John P.** ....................'65 '91 C.112 B.A. L.464 J.D. [Ⓐ Crosby,H.R.&M.]
Phillips, Walton M., (AV) ................'25 '53 C.112 L.1065 LL.B. [Caldecott&P.]
Picetti, Lawrence P., (BV) ....................'47 '72 C&L.767 B.S., J.D. 1212 Bway.
Pierce, John A. ............'37 '72 C.025 B.A. L.976 J.D. Health Planning Consultants
**Pierrou, Yvonne M.** ....................'68 '93 C.112 B.A. L.1066 J.D. [Ⓐ Marion's I.]
**Pike, Gregory D.** ........................'60 '86 C.112 B.S. L.950 J.D. [Knox R.]
*PRACTICE AREAS: Civil Trial and Insurance Defense.
Pineda, Victor H. ........................'38 '72 L.765 J.D. 1999 Harrison St.
**Pinelli, David R.** ........................'52 '85 C.767 B.S. L.765 J.D. [Larson&B.]
Pinkas, Debora L. ....................'56 '86 C.483 B.A. L.284 J.D. 1418 Lakeside Dr.
Pinkney, J. Dominique ....................'53 '85 C.112 B.S. L.1065 J.D. Asst. Pub. Def.
Pinney, Paul B. ........................'57 '90 C.378 B.A. L.721 J.D. Dep. Dist. Atty.
Piser, Steven B., (BV) ....................'49 '74 C.112 A.B. L.767 J.D. 1000 Bway.
Pitcock, Donald L. ........................'27 '70 C.494 B.A. L.284 J.D. 480 23rd St.
**Plageman, William H.**, (AV) ........'43 '69 C.112 B.A. L.1066 J.D. [Plageman&Assoc.]
*PRACTICE AREAS: Land Use; Real Estate; Estate Planning; Estate and Trust Administration.

**Plageman & Associates, (AV)**
**1999 Harrison, Suite 2700, 94612**
**Telephone: 510-273-8553 Fax: 510-273-8559**
**William H. Plageman; Richard W. Lund; Lillian F. Hamrick; Paula J. Galleano; Sara Mann; Timothy A. DeWitt; Maureen A. Kelly.**
**Real Estate, Land Use, Construction, General Litigation, General Corporate, Estate Planning and Estate Administration.**
***See Professional Biographies, OAKLAND, CALIFORNIA***

Plumhoff, Ray H. ........................'55 '83 C.33 B.A. L.1066 J.D. Asst. Pub. Def.
**Poeschl, Thomas F., Jr.** ....................'57 '86 C.740 B.A. L.767 J.D. [Bjork,L.P.&K.]
*PRACTICE AREAS: Insurance Defense Law; Landlord and Tenant Law; Lemon Law; Insurance Coverage; Automobile Design Liability.

**Poniatowski, Mark D., Law Offices of, (BV) '57 '86 C.477 B.B.A. L.770 J.D.**
**The Leimert-Old Building, 456 Eighth Street, 94607**©
**Telephone: 510-881-8700 Fax: 510-881-8702**
**Real Estate and Business Litigation; Real Estate and Business Transactions; Creditors Rights.**
**Castro Valley, California Office: 2811 Castro Valley Boulevard, Suite 208, 94546.**
***See Professional Biographies, OAKLAND, CALIFORNIA***

Poole-Khatib, Patricia A. ............'50 '88 C.112 B.S. L.767 J.D. 333 MacArthur Blvd.
**Poplawski, Kristine A.** ..........'50 '76 C.94 B.A. L.818 J.D. [Ⓐ Saperstein,G.D.&B.]
*LANGUAGES: Spanish.
Porter, Scipio, (BV) '34 '67
C.112 B.A. L.284 J.D. Adm. Law J., Calif. Unemp. Ins. App. Bd.
Portwood, Romulus B. ..............'35 '62 C.477 B.B.A. L.1066 LL.B. Univ. of Calif.‡
Pougiales, Mary E. ....................'49 '77 C.494 B.A. L.1066 J.D. Asst. U.S. Atty.
**Powell, Carol L.** ........................'60 '85 C.112 B.A. L.1065 J.D. [Mullen&F.]
Powell, Cole A. ........................'48 '74 C&L.976 B.A., J.D. Asst. Pub. Def.
Powell, Paul L., Jr. ....................'32 '75 C.98 L.999 LL.B. 5633 Hilton St.
Poy, Henry A. ........................'28 '56 C.154 B.A. L.1065 J.D. 1330 Bway.
Prada, Cynthia Beier ....................'— '88 C.112 A.B. L.767 J.D. 883 Island Dr.
Prager, Laurel J. ........................'60 '91 C.999 B.A. L.1230 J.D. Dep. Co. Coun.
**Preiss, David L.** ....................'55 '82 C.951 B.A. L.1067 J.D. [Wendel,R.B.&D.]
*PRACTICE AREAS: Land Use Law; Real Estate Law; Franchise Law.
Presher, Daniel A. ....................'60 '89 C.112 B.A. L.1065 J.D. 166 Santa Clara Ave.
**Price, John G.** ....................'59 '85 C.966 B.A. L.1065 J.D. [Ⓐ Wendel,R.B.&D.]
*PRACTICE AREAS: Business Law; Securities; Intellectual Property Law.
Price, Pamela Y. ........................'56 '83 C.976 B.A. L.1066 J.D. 1300 Clay St.
**Price, Suzanne I.** ........................'59 '85 C.483 B.A. L.767 J.D. [Wiley P.&R.]
*PRACTICE AREAS: Labor and Employment; Affirmative Action; Public Sector Labor Relations; Employment Discrimination; Age Discrimination in Employment.
Principato-Phipps, Elizabeth A. ..........'42 '83 C.959 B.S. L.1029 J.D. 2201 Broadway
Prutton, Douglas A. ........................'57 '82 C.475 B.S. L.339 J.D. 405 14th St.
**Przetak, Laura** ........................'57 '85 C.112 B.A. L.1065 J.D. [Ⓐ Berry&B.]
*PRACTICE AREAS: Insurance Defense.
**Pulley, Warren A.** ........................'64 '89 C.767 B.S. L.190 J.D. [Mullen&F.]
Purcell, John C. '46 '74
C.276 B.A. L.178 J.D. San Francisco Bay Area Rapid Transit Dist.
**Quan, Noreen N.** ........................'68 '94 C.112 B.A. L.770 J.D. [Ⓐ Larson&B.]
Quatman, John R., (BV) ..............'46 '72 C.112 B.A. L.1065 J.D. Sr. Dep. Dist. Atty.
Quesenberry, Stephen V. ........'45 '74 C.1097 B.A. L.426 J.D. Calif. Indian Legal Servs.
Quinby, William A., (AV) ..............'41 '67 C.309 A.B. L.1065 J.D. 1999 Harrison St.
**Quinlan, Thomas J.** '52 '85 C.770 B.S. L.767 J.D.
[Crosby,H.R.&M.] (©San Francisco)
*PRACTICE AREAS: Mergers and Acquisitions; Corporate Finance; Health; Intellectual Property.

**Quinn, Daniel F.**
**(See Stockton)**

Quittman, Peter F. ........................'46 '76 C.767 B.S. L.765 J.D. 125 12th St.
Radosevich, Ted C. '52 '78
C.112 B.A. L.309 J.D. Gen. Coun., East Bay Regional Pk. Dist.
**Radulovich, Monna R.** ....................'60 '85 C.112 B.A. L.1066 J.D. [Wiley P.&R.]
*PRACTICE AREAS: Labor and Employment; Employment Litigation; Personnel Policies; Wage and Hour Law; Employment Disability Discrimination.
Rafter, Phyllis N. ........................'62 '92 C.112 B.A. L.770 J.D. 1322 Webster St.
Raggio, A. Matthew ........................'28 '53 C.112 L.1065 J.D. Admin. Law J.
Ragland, Charles E. '34 '75
C.632 B.A. L.1026 J.D. Coun., Kaiser Found. Health Plan, Inc.
**Raglin, Dennis Earl** ........................'70 '95 C.112 B.A. L.1067 J.D. [Ⓐ Knox R.]
*PRACTICE AREAS: Insurance Defense.
**Ragozzino, Toni A.** ....................'64 '90 C.112 B.A. L.1065 J.D. [Ⓐ Crosby,H.R.&M.]
**Rahl, Richard H.**, (AV) ..........'34 '62 C.112 A.B. L.1066 LL.B. [Ⓑ Stark,W.R.S.&S.]

Raich, Robert A. .......................... '56 '85 C.309 A.B. L.846 J.D. 472 Cavour St.
**Raisner, Christian L.** .............. '40 '85 C.339 B.A. L.597 J.D. [Van Bourg,W.R.&R.]
*PRACTICE AREAS: Labor Law.
Ramsaur, James W. .......................... '46 '78 C.813 A.B. L.767 J.D. [Chapuis&R.]
Rand, Heidi .......................... '56 '92 C.705 B.A. L.1065 J.D. 1212 Bway.
**Randick, Robert A., Jr.**, (AV) .............. '43 '70 C.668 B.A. L.767 J.D. [Randick&O.]
*REPORTED CASES: Estate of Toy, 72 Cal. App. 3d 392; David K. Lindemuth Co. v. Shannon Financial Corp. 637 F Supp. 991; 660 F Supp. 261.
*PRACTICE AREAS: Antitrust Litigation; Franchise Litigation; Commercial Law; Real Estate Litigation; General Business Planning Law.

**Randick & O'Dea, (AV)**
**1800 Harrison Street, Suite 2350, 94612**
**Telephone: 510-836-3555 Telecopier: 510-834-4748**
**Members of Firm: Robert A. Randick, Jr.; Brian M. O'Dea; Bernard F. Rose. Associates: Julie Rose; William J. Trinkle. Of Counsel: Lisa Robinson Swanson.**
**General Civil and Trial Practice. Corporate, Antitrust, Commercial and Petroleum Marketing Practices, Environmental, Litigation and Franchise Law.**
***See Professional Biographies, OAKLAND, CALIFORNIA***

Rankin, Ann .......................... '50 '78 C.112 A.B. L.1066 J.D. 3911 Harrison St.

**Rankin, Sproat, Mires, Trapani & Reiser, A Professional Corporation, (AV)**
**Suite 1616, 1800 Harrison Street, 94612**
**Telephone: 510-465-3922 Fax: 510-452-3006**
**Email: rankin@best.com URL: http://www.rankinlaw.com**
**Joseph F. Rankin (-1977); Patrick T. Rankin (1943-1990); Ronald G. Sproat; Geoffrey A. Mires; Thomas A. Trapani; Michael J. Reiser;—David T. Shuey; G. Trent Morrow; Eugene G. Ashley; Kevin R. Mintz; Maribel Delgado Osborne.**
**General Civil and Trial Practice in all State and Federal Courts. Insurance Defense, Medical, Legal and other Professional Liability, Toxic Tort Litigation. Commercial, Business and Employment Law. Reference: Union Bank.**
***See Professional Biographies, OAKLAND, CALIFORNIA***

**Rapaport, Daniel**, (AV) .............. '50 '75 C.112 B.A. L.1067 J.D. [Wendel,R.B.&D.]
*PRACTICE AREAS: Business Litigation; Banking Law; Creditors Rights Law; Insurance Law.
Rapport, Ezra .......................... '53 '82 C.107 B.A. L.1065 J.D. 1 City Hall Plaza
**Raskin, John D.** .......................... '47 '73 C.813 B.A. L.309 J.D. [Crosby,H.R.&M.]
Rasmussen, Nancy L. '51 '76
C.112 A.B. L.1065 J.D. Admin. Law Judge, Off. of Admin. Hearings
Ratto, Anthony Gerald, (CV) .............. '56 '83 C.112 B.A. L.767 J.D. 385 Grand Ave.
Ravas, Andrea L. '51 '82
C.477 B.A. L.912 J.D. San Francisco Bay Area Rapid Transit Dist.
**Read, Donald H.**, (AV) '42 '69 C.112 B.A. L.178 J.D.
[Donahue,G.W.&W.] (⊙Berkeley & Palo Alto)
*PRACTICE AREAS: Taxation; Partnership Law; Business Law.
Ready, Daniel J., Jr., (AV) '44 '74 C.112 B.A. L.1065 J.D.
11 Embarcadero W., Suite 133
**Reaves, Steven A.** .......................... '51 '79 C.147 B.A. L.1026 J.D. [Gwilliam,I.C.C.&B.]
*PRACTICE AREAS: Personal Injury; Insurance Bad Faith; Wrongful Termination.
**Redding, Jonathan W.** .............. '54 '87 C.112 B.A. L.1065 J.D. [Fitzgerald,A.&B.]
*PRACTICE AREAS: Environmental Law; Land Use Planning; Hazardous Waste and Environmental Law.
**Redding, Shelagh K.** .............. '61 '90 C.112 B.A. L.93 J.D. [Crosby,H.R.&M.]
**Reding, John A.**, (AV) .............. '44 '70 C.112 A.B. L.1066 J.D. [Crosby,H.R.&M.]
*LANGUAGES: German.
*PRACTICE AREAS: Commercial Litigation; Environmental Litigation; Toxic Tort Litigation; Intellectual Property Litigation.
Reed, James E. .......................... '40 '70 C.112 A.B. L.1066 J.D. 2831 Telegraph Ave.
Reed, Rayford E. .......................... '61 '89 C.813 B.A. L.846 J.D. P.O. Box 31881
**Reese, Charles W., Jr.**, (AV) .............. '44 '70 C.902 B.A. L.1066 J.D. [Lempres&W.]
*PRACTICE AREAS: Environmental Law; Real Estate Law; Mergers and Acquisitions Law.
Reid, Warren G., (BV) .............. '21 '57 C.763 A.B. L.1066 LL.B. 169-14th St.
Rein, Paul L., (BV) .............. '44 '69 C.112 A.B. L.1066 J.D. 200 Lakeside Dr.
**Reinke, Donald C.**, (AV) '57 '83 C.668 B.A. L.1068 J.D.
[Pezzola&R.] (⊙San Francisco)
*PRACTICE AREAS: Corporate; Business Planning; Venture Capital Law; Mergers and Acquisitions; State and Federal Securities Law.
**Reiser, Michael J.** .......................... '61 '86 C&L.174 B.S., J.D. [Rankin,S.M.T.&R.]
*PRACTICE AREAS: Medical Law; Legal Malpractice; General Insurance Defense; Products Liability Law; Commercial Litigation.

**Resneck, William A., (AV) '45 '71 C.604 A.B. L.1119 J.D.**
**2201 Broadway, Suite 803, 94612**
**Telephone: 510-465-6505 Fax: 510-763-3674**
***PRACTICE AREAS: Civil Trial; Personal Injury; Legal Malpractice; Workers Compensation; Arbitration.**
**General Civil Litigation, Personal Injury, Legal Malpractice, Workers Compensation and Arbitration.**
***See Professional Biographies, OAKLAND, CALIFORNIA***

Resner, Amy J. .......................... '61 '89 C.788 B.A. L.1066 J.D. Dep. Dist. Atty.
**Reyes, Benjamin T., II** .............. '65 '93 C.112 B.A. L.765 J.D. [Boornazian,J.&G.]
**Reynolds, Michael R.**, (CV) .............. '54 '81 C.1078 B.A. L.765 J.D. [Larson&B.]
**Reynolds, Richard L.**, (BV) .............. '52 '77 C&L.767 B.A., J.D. [Bennett,S.R.&A.]
*PRACTICE AREAS: Litigation; Landslide Law; Subsidence Law; Public Entity Defense Law.
**Rhatigan, Sean M.**, (AV) .............. '54 '80 C.813 B.A. L.1066 J.D. [Crosby,H.R.&M.]
*PRACTICE AREAS: Income Tax; Corporate and Partnership; Mergers & Acquisitions.
Rhodes, Gene, (BV) .......................... '19 '40 C&L.45 A.B., LL.B. [Berkeley,R.&S.]
Rhynes, Gloria F. .......................... '53 '80 C.267 B.S. L.1065 J.D. 155 Grand Ave.
Riback, Linda, (BV) .............. '47 '72 C.112 A.B. L.1068 J.D. 1939 Harrison St.
Rice, Terry D. .......................... '40 '66 C.309 A.B. L.352 J.D. 6116 Merced Ave.
Rich, Emily Platt .............. '53 '93 C.112 B.A. L.1065 J.D. 450 Hegenberger Rd.
Richards, Keith M., (AV) .............. '22 '59 C.112 B.S.E. L.767 J.D. 405 14th St.
**Richardson, Kennedy P.**, (AV) .............. '49 '74 C.112 B.A. L.597 J.D. [Marion's I.]
Rickles, Rena .......................... '44 '77 C.112 B.A. L.1065 J.D. 1970 Broadway
**Ricksen, John C.**, (AV) .............. '31 '60 C.112 A.B. L.1065 J.D. [Knox R.]
*PRACTICE AREAS: Estate Planning; Probate, Trust and Tax Law.
**Ricksen, Rupert H.**, (AV) .............. '31 '60 C.112 A.B. L.1065 J.D. [Knox R.]
*PRACTICE AREAS: Civil Trial; Insurance; Medical Liability Defense; Asbestos Litigation; Mediation.
Riegg, Garrett F., (BV) .............. '45 '72 C.112 B.A. L.1066 J.D. 2100 Embarcadero St.

**Rifkind & Fuerch**
**(See Hayward)**

**Riggs, James H.**, (AV) .............. '24 '52 C.112 A.B. L.1066 LL.B. [Larson&B.]
**Riley, James Daniel, Jr.** .............. '70 '95 C.112 B.A. L.1067 J.D. [Crosby,H.R.&M.]
Rinaldi, Matthew J. .............. '47 '83 C.604 B.A. L.1065 J.D. [Boxer,E.&G.]
Rinehart, Gary R., (P.C.), (AV) .............. '35 '64 C.112 L.1066 J.D. [Rinehart&A.]
Rinehart & Amspoker, (AV) .......................... Suite 805, 2201 Broadway
**Roach, Darren P.** .............. '65 '92 C&L.188 B.S., J.D. [Crosby,H.R.&M.]
Roach, Edward G. .............. '38 '64 C.951 A.B. L.1066 LL.B. Pres., E R Develop.
Robbins, Paul, (BV) .............. '31 '59 C.112 A.B. L.1066 LL.B. [Robbins&D.]
**Robbins, William C., III**, (AV) .............. '41 '66 C.976 B.A. L.1066 LL.B. [Knox R.]⊙
*PRACTICE AREAS: Real Estate Law; Zoning, Land Use Planning and Estate Planning.
Robbins & Dangott, P.C., (BV) .......................... 1540 San Pablo Ave., 11th Fl.

**Roberge, Wilfrid F., Jr.**, (AV) '39 '65
C.112 A.B. L.813 J.D. [Donahue,G.W.&W.] (⊙Walnut Creek)
*PRACTICE AREAS: Estate Planning; Probate, Trust Law.
Roberts, David M. .............. '45 '75 C.228 B.A. L.1066 J.D. 5655 College Ave.‡
Roberts, Dennis, (AV) .............. '37 '64 C.705 B.A. L.1066 LL.B. [D.Roberts]
**Roberts, James G.** .............. '49 '79 C.103 A.B. L.1066 J.D. [Johnston,H.&R.]
*PRACTICE AREAS: Business Law; Corporate Law.
Roberts, Karen L. .............. '58 '87 C.1077 B.A. L.426 J.D. 200 Webster
**Roberts, Mary Maloney**, (AV) .............. '52 '81 C.312 B.Ed. L.1065 J.D. [Corbett&K.]⊙
*PRACTICE AREAS: Labor and Employment Law.
Roberts, Patti R. .............. '46 '71 C.102 B.A. L.1066 J.D. 407 North St.
Roberts, Dennis, A Professional Corporation, (AV) .............. 370 Grand Ave.
Robertson, Wayman M., Jr., (AV) .............. '33 '62 C.560 B.S. L.813 LL.B. Dep. Atty. Gen.
Robinson, Bari S. .............. '— '80 C.378 B.S. L.1066 J.D. [White,C.M.&J.]
**Robinson, Glenda** '41 '74
C.112 B.A. L.1065 J.D. Sr. Coun., World Savings & Loan Assoc.
**Robinson, Harrison S.**, (AV) .............. '42 '66 C.112 A.B. L.1065 J.D. [Donahue,G.W.&W.]
*PRACTICE AREAS: Complex Commercial Real Estate; Real Estate Finance; Business Law.
Robinson, Mary E. .............. '52 '79 C.1051 B.A. L.990 J.D. 236 Bonita Ave.
Robinson, Victoria .............. '44 '78 C.766 B.A. L.1065 J.D. 6114 Estates Dr.
Rochlin, Carole H., (BV) .............. '— '78 C.597 B.S. L.1197 J.D. 166 Santa Clara Ave.
**Rockwell, Gregory J.**, (AV) .............. '51 '75 C&L.767 B.A., J.D. [Boornazian,J.&G.]
*PRACTICE AREAS: Medical Malpractice; Personal Injury; Products and Public Entity Litigation.
**Rockwell, Lawrence K.** .............. '53 '76 C.112 A.B.B.S. L.1065 J.D. [Donahue,G.W.&W.]
*PRACTICE AREAS: Litigation; Complex Computer Law; Commercial Law.
**Rodgers, G. Dennis** .............. '52 '83 C.112 B.A. L.1065 J.D. [Cresswell,C.&E.]
**Rodman, Jordan A.** .............. '68 '94 C.112 B.A. L.284 J.D. [Boornazian,J.&G.]
*PRACTICE AREAS: Insurance Defense.

**Rodriguez, Anthony C., Law Office of '56 '85 C.112 B.A. L.1067 J.D.**
**1300 Clay Street, Suite 600, 94612-1427**
**Telephone: 510-464-8022 Fax: 510-464-8023**
***PRACTICE AREAS: Business Litigation; Real Estate Law; Administrative Law; Rent Control Law; Mobil Home Law.**

Roe, David .......................... '48 '74 C&L.976 B.A., J.D. Envir. Def. Fund
Roe, J. Ryan .......................... '55 '82 C.105 B.A. L.767 J.D. 1999 Harrison St.
Roemer, Michael James .............. '54 '81 C.1169 B.A. L.1065 J.D. 6652 Dana St.
**Roger, Michael B.**, (AV) .............. '41 '67 C.112 B.A. L.1065 J.D. [Van Bourg,W.R.&R.]
*PRACTICE AREAS: Labor Law.
Rogers, Elizabeth Fitzgerald .............. '54 '83 C.112 B.A. L.30 J.D. Asst. Pub. Def.
Rogers, Jim .......................... '55 '80 C.112 B.A. L.1067 J.D. 1941 Jackson St.
Rogers, Thomas C., (AV) .............. '51 '76 C.770 B.A. L.1049 J.D. Asst. Dist. Atty.
**Roisman, Margaret R.**, (AV) .............. '45 '82 C.604 B.A. L.1066 J.D. [Crosby,H.R.&M.]
*PRACTICE AREAS: Estate Planning; Probate and Trust Administration.
Roit, Joanne E. .......................... '57 '91 C.37 B.S. L.813 J.D. Co. Pub. Def. Off.
Rojek, Thaddeus .......................... '27 '57 L.145 J.D. 5025 Woodminster Ln.
**Rolnick, Jonathan C.** .............. '62 '90 C.170 B.A. L.1065 J.D. [Crosby,H.R.&M.]
*PRACTICE AREAS: Labor and Employment Law.
Rood, Steven .......................... '49 '76 C.112 B.A. L.770 J.D. 1999 Harrison St.
**Roodhouse, Linda C.**, (AV) .............. '43 '80 C.118 B.A. L.464 J.D. [Hardin,C.L.E.&B.]
*PRACTICE AREAS: Estate Planning Law; Estate Administration Law; Municipal Law.
Rooney, J. Kerwin, (AV) .............. '11 '36 C.112 A.B. L.1066 LL.B. 5403 Broadway Ter.‡
**Rosati, James J.** .............. '61 '89 C.112 B.A. L.1065 J.D. [Larson&B.]
**Rose, Bernard F.** .............. '43 '85 C.823 B.S. L.1153 J.D. [Randick&O.]
*PRACTICE AREAS: Environmental Law; Business Litigation; Petroleum Marketing Practices Law.
**Rose, Julie** .............. '52 '88 C.399 B.A. L.1153 J.D. [Randick&O.]
*PRACTICE AREAS: Environmental Law; Business Litigation; Petroleum Marketing Practices Law.
Rosen, Stephen, (BV) .............. '43 '72 C.112 A.B. L.1065 J.D. 1330 Bway.
Rosen, Victor D., (AV) .............. '28 '53 C.976 A.B. L.309 J.D. 1111 Bway., 24th Fl.‡
Rosenberg, Donald .............. '30 '56 C.966 B.S. L.813 J.D. 6961 Eluerton Dr.‡
**Rosenberg, Robert**, (AV) .............. '32 '57 C&L.813 A.B., LL.B. [Bell,R.&H.]
*PRACTICE AREAS: Estate Planning Law; Probate Law.
Rosenblum, Michael A. .............. '44 '87 C.260 B.A. L.1230 J.D. 1440 Bway.
Rosenfeld, Arthur B. '37 '66 C&L.665 B.B.A., J.D.
V.P. & Reg. Coun., Kaiser Found. Health Plan, Inc.
**Rosenfeld, David A.**, (AV) .............. '45 '73 C.103 B.A. L.1066 J.D. [Van Bourg,W.R.&R.]
*PRACTICE AREAS: Labor Law.
Rosenquist, James W. .............. '40 '66 C.112 B.A. L.1066 LL.B. Bay Area Rapid Transit Dist.
Rosenstein, Paul S. .............. '46 '72 C.1044 B.A. L.107 J.D. 405 14th St.
**Rosenthal, David A.** .............. '60 '85 C.813 A.B. L.1066 J.D. [Lempres&W.]
*PRACTICE AREAS: Corporate Law; Commercial Law; Real Estate Law; Estate Planning and Probate Law.
**Rosequist, Ronald V.**, (AV) '41 '70
C.605 A.B. L.1065 J.D. [Crosby,H.R.&M.] (⊙San Francisco)
*PRACTICE AREAS: Mergers & Acquisitions; Corporate.
Ross, Gerald Lynn .............. '38 '91 C.15 B.A. L.273 J.D. [Norton&R.] (⊙San Francisco)
**Ross, Gillian M.** .............. '46 '86 C.150 B.A. L.1065 J.D. [Wendel,R.B.&D.]
*PRACTICE AREAS: Commercial Law; Business Litigation; Employment Law.
Ross, Madie J. .............. '25 '63 C.331 A.B. L.809 LL.B. State Comp. Ins. Fund
Ross, Verna J. .............. '55 '93 C.597 B.A. L.1153 J.D. Amer. Cancer Soc., Inc.
Rossi, Daniel .............. '56 '89 C.197 A.B. L.1066 J.D. Dep. City Atty.
Roth, David L. .............. '53 '79 C.605 A.B. L.1065 J.D. 1 Kaiser Plaza
Roth, Robert Alex .............. '56 '84 C.339 B.A. L.209 J.D. 1300 Clay St.

**Rothhaar, Dennis K., (AV) '44 '72 C.813 A.B. L.309 J.D.**
**One Kaiser Plaza, Suite 1725, 94612-3612**
**Telephone: 510-763-5611 Fax: 510-763-3430**
**(Certified Specialist, Family Law, The State Bar of California Board of Legal Specialization). Family Law.**
***See Professional Biographies, OAKLAND, CALIFORNIA***

Rothman, Sherman '26 '53 C.178 B.S. L.1009 LL.B.
(adm. in NY; not adm. in CA) 483 Ninth St.‡
Rouder, Wendy P. .............. '42 '79 C.787 B.S. L.284 J.D. Asst. to the City Atty.
Rowand, Melanie A. P. .............. '59 '91 C.250 B.A. L.765 J.D. 7770 Pardee Ln.
**Rowe, Robert C.** '55 '82
C.813 B.A. L.770 J.D. Gen. Coun., World Savings & Loan Assoc.
**Rowell, Stephen Q.** .............. '54 '81 C.112 A.B. L.1065 J.D. [Larson&B.]
Roze, Amanda K. .............. '57 '88 C.597 B.S. L.1065 J.D. Sr. Resch. Atty., Supr. Ct.
**Rubin, Carl M.** .............. '54 '81 C.893 B.A. L.861 J.D. Sr. Coun., Amer. Pres. Lines, Ltd.
Rubin, Jeff H. .............. '58 '86 C.112 B.A. L.1066 J.D. Dep. Dist. Atty.
Rubinfeld, Gail N. '48 '76
C.783 B.A. L.477 J.D. Sr. Coun., Kaiser Found. Health Plan, Inc.
Rubinoff, David B. .............. '48 '79 C.112 B.A. L.284 J.D. 888 Rosemount Rd.‡
Rubke, Mark E. .............. '48 '75 C.766 B.A. L.284 J.D. 1970 Broadway
Ruby, Robert A., (AV) .............. '49 '75 C.477 B.A. L.912 J.D. [Schmit,M.B.&S.]
**Rudd, Michelle** .............. '63 '95 C.813 B.S.C.E. L.1066 J.D. [McDonough,H.&A.]
*PRACTICE AREAS: Municipal Law.
**Rudser, Mary M.**, (AV) .............. '48 '81 C.118 B.A. L.93 J.D. [Brody&S.]
*PRACTICE AREAS: Estate Planning; Probate; Tax; Business; Real Estate.

CAA437P

Rugh, Peter N., (BV) .....'33 '64 C.31 B.A. L.982 LL.B. 405 14th St.
**Rundin, Walter C., III** .....'49 '76 C.112 A.B. L.1065 J.D. [Larson&B.]
Rundstrom, William E. .....'43 '72 C.267 B.S. L.1066 J.D. Asst. Co. Coun.
**Rupright, Pamela G. H.** .....'66 '91 C&L.597 B.A., J.D. [Crosby,H.R.&M.]
Rusconi, Joseph C. .....'52 '77 C.112 B.A. L.464 J.D. Dep. Atty. Gen.
Russell, Joseph E., (BV) .....'41 '70 C.267 B.S. L.284 J.D. 484 Lake Park Ave.
Russell, Sara J. .....'51 '78 C&L.1067 B.A., J.D. Dep. Atty. Gen.
Russo, Frank D., (BV) .....'51 '76 C.976 B.A. L.1066 J.D. 492 Ninth St.
**Russo, John A.** .....'59 '85 C.976 B.A. L.569 J.D. [Bell,R.&H.]
*LANGUAGES: Spanish and Italian.
*PRACTICE AREAS: Construction Law; Commercial Real Estate; Professional Malpractice; Personal Injury.
**Rutkowski, James** .....'44 '71 C.712 B.A. L.36 J.D. [Van Bourg,W.R.&R.]
*PRACTICE AREAS: Labor Law.
**Ryan, Elizabeth K.** .....'59 '84 C.112 B.A. L.1065 J.D. [Bjork,L.P.&K.]
*PRACTICE AREAS: Drug and Medical Device Litigation; Fraud Law; Medical Malpractice Law; Medical Contract Staffing Law; Risk Management.
**Ryan, Joseph D., Jr.**, (AV) .....'46 '74 C.309 B.A. L.1065 J.D. [Ryan,A.&L.]
*PRACTICE AREAS: Civil Trial; Construction Defect Litigation; Insurance Coverage; Insurance Defense Law; Landslide and Subsidence Litigation.
Ryan, Kevin V., (BV) .....'57 '85 C.197 B.A. L.767 J.D. Dep. Dist. Atty.
Ryan, Nancie '48 '80 C.1073 B.A. L.284 J.D.
Asst. Gen. Coun., East Bay Mun. Utility Dist.

**Ryan, Andrada & Lifter, A Professional Corporation, (AV)**
**Tenth Floor, Kaiser Center Building, 300 Lakeside Drive, Suite 1045, 94612-3536**
**Telephone: 510-763-6510 Fax: 510-763-3921**
**Joseph D. Ryan, Jr.; J. Randall Andrada; Jill J. Lifter; Jolie Krakauer; Glenn Gould; Michael J. Daley; Charles E. Kallgren; Rhonda D. Shelton; Lora Vail French; Vikki L. Barron; Bruce A. McIntosh; Michael J. Thomas; Laura E. Ozak.**
**General Civil and Trial Practice. Insurance Defense and Coverage Law.**
**Representative Clients: Alameda Contra Costa County Transit District; CNA Insurance Companies; Truck Insurance Exchange; Liberty Mutual Insurance Group; Safeway Stores, Inc.**
***See Professional Biographies, OAKLAND, CALIFORNIA***

Sack, Dana .....'53 '80 C.309 A.B. L.1065 J.D. 1433 Webster St.
Safer, David M., (BV) .....'42 '66 C&L.966 B.S., J.D. Asst. Pub. Def.
Salazar, Jose Ramiro '56 '81
C.813 B.A. L.276 J.D. San Francisco Bay Area Rapid Transit Dist.
Salerno, Heidi T. .....'66 '91 C.112 B.A. L.1065 J.D. Dep. Atty. Gen.
Salniker, David J. .....'40 '66 C.597 B.A. L.1066 J.D. 6437 Regent St.‡
**Saltzman, Stanley D.**, (AV) .....'52 '79 C.12 D.C.S. L.800 J.D. [Marlin&S.]⊙
*LANGUAGES: French, Italian.
*REPORTED CASES: Christensen v. California Supreme Court 53 Cal 3d 868.
*PRACTICE AREAS: Insurance Defense Law; Professional Malpractice Law; Construction Defect Law.
Salvaty, Paul B. .....'67 '94 C.602 B.A. L.1065 J.D. 1221 Broadway, 21St Fl.
Salzman, Jaya .....'52 '84 C.72 B.A. L.284 J.D. 5511 Vincente Way‡
**Samuel, Robin J.** .....'68 '94 C.112 B.A. L.1065 J.D. [Crosby,H.R.&M.]
**Samuels, Lynn S.** .....'56 '81 C.228 B.A. L.846 J.D. [Hardin,C.L.E.&B.]
*PRACTICE AREAS: Insurance Litigation; Coverage Analysis and Litigation; Commercial Litigation.
**Samuelsen, David J.**, (AV) .....'50 '76 C.112 B.A. L.767 J.D. [Bennett,S.R.&A.]
*PRACTICE AREAS: Litigation; Insurance Defense Law; Insurance Law.
Santana, Jesse I. .....'63 '87 C.147 B.A. L.767 J.D. 1999 Harrison St.
**Saperstein, Guy T.**, (AV) .....'43 '69 C.112 A.B. L.1066 J.D. [Saperstein,G.D.&B.]
*PRACTICE AREAS: Litigation; Employment Law; False Claims Act.

**Saperstein, Goldstein, Demchak & Baller, A Professional Corporation, (AV)**
**1300 Clay Street, 11th Floor, 94612**
**Telephone: 510-763-9800**
**Email: info@saperstein.com**
**Barry Goldstein; Teresa Demchak; Morris J. Baller. Of Counsel: Guy T. Saperstein;—Michelle Alexander; David Borgen; Linda M. Dardarian; Jollee C. Faber; Laurel E. Fletcher; Susan Guberman-Garcia; Christopher J. Keller; Jack W. Lee; Kristine A. Poplawski; Michael A. Scarlett; Debra A. Smith; Roberta L. Steele (Not admitted in CA).**
**Civil Trial and Appellate Practice. Class Actions, Employment and Environmental Litigation, Attorneys' Fees Litigation; False Claims Act Prosecutions.**
***See Professional Biographies, OAKLAND, CALIFORNIA***

Sargent, Susan T. .....'58 '86 C.454 B.A. L.1065 J.D. Asst. Pub. Def.
Sarkisian, Philip V. .....'39 '65 C.813 A.B. L.1066 LL.B. Supr. Ct. J.
**Satz, Richard B.**, (AV) .....'45 '72 C.674 A.B. L.976 J.D. [Brody&S.]
*PRACTICE AREAS: Commercial Litigation; Real Property Litigation; Bankruptcy; Employer and Employee Representation.
Saunders, Ward B. .....'19 '48 C.112 B.S. L.813 J.D. 6123 Estates Dr.‡
**Sax, Shawn K.** '64 '89 C.276 B.S.F.S. L.1068 J.D.
Coun., World Savings & Loan Assoc.
Saylor, Susan M. .....'64 '91 C.477 B.A. L.767 J.D. Legal Aid Soc.
Scanlon, Joseph, (BV) .....'47 '73 C.425 B.A. L.284 J.D. 166 Santa Clara Ave.
**Scarlett, Michael A.** .....'54 '94 C.257 B.S. L.767 J.D. [Saperstein,G.D.&B.]
Scarr, Anthony E. .....'44 '70 C.112 A.B. L.1065 J.D. Dep. Co. Coun.
Schaaf, Libby B. .....'65 '93 C.699 B.A. L.426 J.D. 1999 Harrison St.
**Schadlich, Stephen H.**, (AV) .....'36 '64 C.112 B.S. L.1066 J.D. [Crosby,H.R.&M.]
*PRACTICE AREAS: Higher Education; Corporate; Business.
**Schaefer, Don Henry** .....'60 '89 C.284 B.S. L.767 J.D. [Bennett,S.R.&A.]
*PRACTICE AREAS: Insurance Defense.
Scharlach, Alan M., (BV) '48 '77 C.112 B.A. L.1026 J.D.
1540 San Pablo Ave., 11th Fl.
Schear, Stephen .....'50 '78 C.477 B.G.S. L.1066 J.D. 2831 Telegraph Ave.
Scheingart, Roy C., (BV) .....'52 '80 C.1073 B.S. L.765 J.D. Dist. Attys. Off.
**Schieffer, Joseph H.** .....'51 '76 C.767 B.A. L.1065 J.D. [Stark,W.R.S.&S.]
*PRACTICE AREAS: Real Estate Transactions; Real Estate Litigation; Business Transactions; Business Litigation.
Schimelfenig, Marianne '47 '81
C.452 B.A. L.596 J.D. Coun., Regents of the Univ., Univ. of Calif.
Schlachter, Ewald O. .....'26 '65 354 Vernon St.
Schmit, David J., (BV) .....'44 '73 C.112 B.A. L.276 J.D. [Schmit,M.B.&S.]
Schmit, Nancy Lawson .....'47 '73 C.347 A.B. L.273 J.D. 456 8th St.
Schmit, Morris, Bittner & Schmit, (AV) .....456 8th St.
**Schmitz, Anne** .....'61 '93 C.112 A.B. L.464 J.D. [Allswang,S.&W.]
Schneider, Eugene .....'30 '69 C.112 B.S.C.E. L.1065 J.D. 5050 Bway.
**Schneider, Merridith A.**, (AV) .....'52 '80 C.347 B.A. L.284 J.D. [Kornfield,P.&B.]
*LANGUAGES: French.
*PRACTICE AREAS: Bankruptcy Practice; Reorganization Law; Business Law; Commercial Mediation.
**Schnurmacher, Eric P.**, (AV) .....'29 '56 C.112 A.B. L.1066 J.D. [E.P.Schnurmacher]
*LANGUAGES: Spanish.
*PRACTICE AREAS: Civil Trial Practice; Business Law; Personal Injury; Family Law; Probate Litigation.

**Schnurmacher, Eric P., A Prof. Corp., Law Offices of, (AV)**
**Central Building, 436 Fourteenth Street, 94612**
**Telephone: 510-836-3534; 839-3990**
**Eric P. Schnurmacher;—Elaine Ercolini.**
**General Civil and Trial Practice. Business, Personal Injury, Family and Probate Law.**
***See Professional Biographies, OAKLAND, CALIFORNIA***

**Schock, Pamela A.** .....'60 '94 C.483 B.A. L.101 J.D. [Crosby,H.R.&M.]
Schock, Robert G., (BV) .....'41 '66 C.768 B.A. L.1065 J.D. 1970 Bway.
**Schofield, William W., Jr.**, (BV) .....'48 '74 C.112 B.A. L.1065 J.D. [Crosby,H.R.&M.]
*PRACTICE AREAS: General Litigation.
Scholtes, Michael E. .....'47 '79 C.1169 B.A. L.1065 J.D. [Fong&F.]
**Schopf, Gregory E.** .....'49 '86 C.670 B.A. L.1065 J.D. [Crosby,H.R.&M.]
*PRACTICE AREAS: General Civil Litigation; Insurance Coverage Disputes.
**Schreiberg, Frances C.** .....'46 '73 C.597 B.A. L.569 J.D. [Kazan,M.E.S.&A.]
*REPORTED CASES: In Re Garcia 41 C.A. 3d 997 116 Cal. Rptr. 503 (1974); Henning v Division of Occupational Safety & Health 219 CA 3d 747, 268 Cal Rptr. 476 (1990); Agricultural Labor Relations Bd. v. California Coastal Farms, Inc. 31 CAL. 3d 469 (1982).
*PRACTICE AREAS: Occupational Safety and Health; Construction Accidents; Litigation; Toxic Torts.
**Schrey, Stephen G.**, (AV) .....'48 '74 C.770 B.A. L.767 J.D. [Crosby,H.R.&M.]
*PRACTICE AREAS: Insurance Coverage and Claims Litigation.
**Schroeder, Edward C., Jr.** .....'58 '90 C.112 B.A. L.767 J.D. [Haims,J.M.&M.]
*PRACTICE AREAS: Insurance Defense.
Schulman, Joanne .....'52 '78 C.112 B.A. L.284 J.D. 1814 Franklin St.
Schwartz, Charles I., (BV) .....'44 '71 C.659 B.A. L.1065 J.D. [Berkeley,R.&S.]
Schwartz, Debbra Wood .....'— '84 C.999 M.M. L.1065 J.D. 4570 Sequoyah Road
**Schwartz, Ellen R.** .....'53 '80 C.1044 B.A. L.1153 J.D. [Van Blois,K.S.&B.]
*PRACTICE AREAS: Accident and Personal Injury; Medical Malpractice Law; Public Entity Law; Professional Malpractice Law; Class Actions.
Schwartz, Jennifer .....'59 '88 C.976 B.A. L.569 J.D. Asst. Dist. Atty.
Schwartz, Justin D. .....'63 '89 C.918 B.A. L.1065 J.D. 1305 Franklin
**Schwartz, Merrill J.**, (AV) .....'41 '66 C.589 A.B. L.597 J.D. [Stark,W.R.S.&S.]
*PRACTICE AREAS: Real Estate; Estate Planning; Probate; Commercial Transactions.
Schwarz, Frederick D., (AV) '38 '65 C.112 B.A. L.1066 J.D.
1999 Harrison St. Ste. 1700
Schweinberger, Berta Helbing .....'45 '84 C.112 B.A. L.1066 J.D. 200 Webster St.

**Schweitzer, Sandra L., (AV⊤) '52 '80 C.188 B.S.N. L.276 J.D.**
**5826 Fremont Street, 94608**
**Telephone: 510-652-8151 Fax: 510-547-1008**
***LANGUAGES: French.**
***PRACTICE AREAS: Family Law.**
**Family Law, including Divorce and Custody.**
***See Professional Biographies, OAKLAND, CALIFORNIA***

Scott, Eric R. .....'49 '79 C.112 B.S. L.284 J.D. Pacific Gas & Elec. Co.
Scott, James S. .....'41 '66 C.112 B.A. L.1066 LL.B. NLRB, Region 32
**Seaman, Charles H.**, (BV) .....'52 '78 C.112 A.B. L.1065 J.D. [Crosby,H.R.&M.]
*PRACTICE AREAS: Real Estate.
**Sebree, Michael M.K.** .....'64 '89 C.1074 B.A. L.911 J.D. [Fitzgerald,A.&B.]
*PRACTICE AREAS: Corporate; Real Estate; Commercial.
**Seeger, Kenneth M.** .....'55 '88 C.1044 B.A. L.831 J.D. [Crosby,H.R.&M.]
*PRACTICE AREAS: Insurance; Product Liability; Business Litigation.
Seltzer, Richard A., (AV) .....'44 '69 C.352 B.B.A. L.597 J.D. [Seltzer&C.]
Seltzer & Cody, (AV) .....180 Grand Ave., Ste 1300
**Selvin, Gary R.** .....'57 '83 C.605 A.B. L.1065 J.D. [Larson&B.]
**Sevekow, Frederick M., Jr.** '41 '66 C.262 B.S. L.569 LL.B.
(adm. in NY; not adm. in CA) V.P. & Gen. Coun., Amer. Pres. Lines, Ltd.
Seyranian, Leon G., (BV) .....'27 '55 C&L.767 B.S., J.D. 1404 Franklin St.
Shahoian, Kenneth J. .....'62 '92 C.36 B.S. L.284 J.D. 4110 Maynard Ave.
Shainholtz, Susan E. .....'62 '90 C.174 B.S. L.767 J.D. 1901 Harrison St.
Shapiro, Larry J., (AV) .....'50 '76 C.766 B.A. L.284 J.D. 6114 La Salle Ave.
Shapreau, Carla J. .....'52 '88 C.330 B.A. L.1065 J.D. 1999 Harrison St.
Shaw, Peter L. .....'49 '78 C.112 A.B. L.1066 J.D. 1999 Harrison St.
Shelton, Arthur M., Jr. .....'22 '51 C.188 A.B. L.815 J.D. 5910 Margarido Dr.
**Shelton, Rhonda D.** .....'62 '91 C.628 L.1065 J.D. [Ryan,A.&L.]
Shen, Simon .....'63 '92 C.1069 B.B.A. L.767 J.D. 1 Kaiser Plz., 16th Fl.
**Shepp, Lawrence R.**, (AV) .....'39 '65 C.813 A.B. L.1066 J.D. [Fitzgerald,A.&B.]
*PRACTICE AREAS: Estate Planning; Estate and Probate Litigation; Real Estate; Construction Law and Litigation.
Sher, Malcolm, (AV) .....'47 '76 C.061 L.054 LL.B. [Sher,B.]
Sher, Blumenfeld, Professional Corporation, (AV) .....1 Kaiser Plaza
Sherman, Ray W., Jr. .....'47 '72 C.1049 B.A. L.145 J.D. 1970 Broadway
Sherrer, Gary L. .....'56 '84 C.112 B.S. L.464 J.D. 166 Santa Clara Ave.
**Sherrill, Susan J.** .....'64 '89 C.1109 B.A. L.464 J.D. [Bjork,L.P.&K.]
*PRACTICE AREAS: Insurance Defense Law; Toxic Torts; Medical Malpractice Law.
Shers, Georges H. .....'47 '72 C.112 A.B. L.1066 J.D. Off. of City Atty.
Sherwood, Alan J. .....'54 '85 C.1044 B.A. L.770 J.D. 170 Santa Clara Ave.
Shields, Stanley E. .....'47 '89 C.284 B.A. L.765 J.D. [Boxer,E.&G.]
Shiffrin, Cynthia A. '55 '84
C.347 A.B. L.1119 J.D. Coun., Kaiser Found. Health Plan, Inc.
**Shingler, Ronald J.** .....'58 '89 C.1060 B.A. L.284 J.D. [Kazan,M.E.S.&A.]
*PRACTICE AREAS: Asbestos Litigation (100%, 25).
**Shinn, Ember L.** .....'50 '78 C.312 B.A. L.464 J.D. [Crosby,H.R.&M.]
*PRACTICE AREAS: Employment Litigation; Labor; Education.
Shipp, Joseph C., II .....'— '90 L.1067 J.D. P.O. Box 20347
Shipway, Robert, (BV) .....'54 '81 C.105 B.S.B.A. L.284 J.D. Asst. Pub. Def.
**Shuey, David T.** .....'66 '92 C.813 B.A. L.770 J.D. [Rankin,S.M.T.&R.]
Shuken, Robert S., (BV) .....'39 '66 C.112 B.A. L.1066 LL.B. 3710 Grand Ave., 2nd Fl.
Shulster, Stanley Anthony, (BV) .....'38 '65 C.319 A.B. L.1065 LL.B. 516 52nd St.
Shultz, Dana Howard .....'49 '77 C.477 A.B. L.1066 J.D. Princ., Dana Shultz & Assoc.
**Shy, Jennifer A.** .....'59 '87 C.112 B.A. L.1065 J.D. [Crosby,H.R.&M.]
Siegel, Jonathan H. .....'51 '77 C.1130 B.A. L.284 J.D. 1330 Bway.
Sigman, Alfred H. .....'44 '71 C.299 B.A. L.659 LL.B. [Sigman,L.&F.]
Sigman, Lewis & Feinberg .....405 14th St.
Siltanen, Robert S. .....'65 '90 C.197 A.B. L.1066 J.D. U.S. Dept. of Vet. Aff.
Silver, Franklin, (AV) .....'45 '74 C.813 B.A. L.1065 J.D. 385 Grand Ave.
Simmons, Joseph .....'23 '62 C.46 L.284 LL.B. Pres., Athena Credit & Collections, Inc.
Simmons, Ronald J. .....'44 '81 C.475 B.A. L.284 J.D. The Clorox Co.
Simmons, William E. .....'58 '85 C.112 B.A. L.770 J.D. 1800 Harrison St.
**Simon, Aaron H.**, (AV) .....'48 '75 C.150 B.A. L.1068 J.D. [Kazan,M.E.S.&A.]
Simpson, Anna L. .....'35 '76 C.611 B.A. L.1066 J.D. Asst. Pub. Def.
Sims, James A., Jr. .....'57 '83 C.282 B.A. L.809 J.D. [Sims&O.] (⊙Irvine)
Sims & Olsen .....1 Park Plaza, Suite 290 (⊙Irvine, CA.)
Sinclair, Andrew T. .....'43 '76 C.659 B.A. L.1067 LL.B. 492 9th St.
Singman, Thomas M. .....'45 '73 C.477 A.B. L.273 J.D. [Woodruff&S.]
**Sipes, Jennifer L.** .....'65 '92 C.112 B.A. L.464 J.D. [Knox R.]
*PRACTICE AREAS: Business; Real Estate; Civil Litigation.
Sipherd, Ronald K. .....'42 '75 C.976 B.A. L.1066 J.D. 5951 Chabolyn Terr.
**Sipos, Richard A.** .....'61 '86 C.112 B.A. L.770 J.D. [Aiken,K.&C.]
*PRACTICE AREAS: Business Law; Construction Law; Professional Malpractice; Insurance Litigation.
Sirbu, Gary M., (AV) .....'40 '66 C.112 A.B. L.1066 LL.B. 1999 Harrison St.
**Skaff, Andrew J.**, (AV) .....'45 '71 C.473 B.S. L.851 J.D. [Knox R.]
*PRACTICE AREAS: Energy Law; Regulatory Law; Public Utility Law; Business Litigation.
**Skilling, Mark C.** .....'60 '86 C.170 B.A. L.464 J.D. [Knox R.]
*REPORTED CASES: Rios v. Wagner, 4 Cal.App. 4th 608; Perez v. Smith 19 Cal.App. 4th 1595.
*PRACTICE AREAS: Civil Trial; Insurance Defense; Construction; Taxation and Appellate.
Skinner, Kathleen A. .....'47 '75 C.713 B.S. L.1065 J.D. 1 Kaiser Plaza (Pat.)

Skinner, Stephen C., (BV) .................'47 '74 C.112 B.S. L.284 J.D. [Munck,B.&S.]
**Sleeth, Boyd C.**, (AV) ............... '52 '82 C.342 B.A. L.1065 J.D. [Crosby,H.R.&M.]
*PRACTICE AREAS: Commercial and Insurance Litigation.
Slocumb, Thomas ..................... '43 '83 C.30 B.A. L.284 J.D. 1611 Telegraph Ave.
Slone, James J. ................................'65 '90 C.679 B.A. L.770 J.D. One Kaiser Plaza

**Sly, Peter W., (AV) '46 '75 C.813 A.B. L.976 J.D.**
**6138 Ocean View Drive, 94618-1841**
**Telephone: 510-653-7735 Telecopier: 510-654-7735**
***PRACTICE AREAS: Natural Resources; Water Quantity and Quality; Indian Law; Real Estate and Environmental Law; Legal Ethics.**
**Natural Resources, Water Quantity and Quality, Indian, Real Estate and Environmental Law; Legal Ethics.**

**Small, Gillian, G.M.** ....................'59 '92 C.8 B.A. L.1065 J.D. [Ⓐ Lempres&W.]
*LANGUAGES: Spanish.
*PRACTICE AREAS: Commercial Litigation; Insurance Coverage Litigation; Environmental Litigation.
Smallson, Fran '58 '87 C.112 A.B. L.276 J.D.
300 Lakeside Dr., Ste. 1900 (⊙Mill Valley)
**Smallsreed, Timothy H.**, (AV) ........ '46 '78 C.668 B.A. L.284 J.D. [Fitzgerald,A.&B.]
*PRACTICE AREAS: Corporate and Business Law; Estate Planning, Trust and Estate Administration; Probate Law.
Smith, C. R. E. ................................. '17 '56 C.112 A.B. 6281 Aspinwall Rd.‡
Smith, Caroline G. '62 '87
C.1074 B.S. L.1066 J.D. Coun., Kaiser Found. Health Plan, Inc.
**Smith, Debra A.** ...................'53 '81 C.518 B.A. L.588 J.D. [Ⓐ Saperstein,G.D.&B.]
*LANGUAGES: Spanish.
*PRACTICE AREAS: Litigation; Employment Law.
Smith, Elvera Wollitz .......................'06 '34 C.112 B.A. L.1066 J.D. 422 Lee St.‡
**Smith, Gerald C.**, (AV) ...................'40 '65 C.602 B.A. L.1066 J.D. [Fitzgerald,A.&B.]
*PRACTICE AREAS: Commercial Law; Corporate Law; Business Litigation.
Smith, Jared R. ..........................'60 '87 C.197 B.A. L.464 J.D. 1 Kaiser Plaza
Smith, Joan M. ........................'31 '63 C.1067 B.A. L.1066 LL.B. Co. Pub. Def.
Smith, John H. ...............................'40 '72 C.210 B.A. L.309 J.D. Asst. Pub. Def.
**Smith, John Lynn** ................'52 '91 C.112 B.A. L.1065 J.D. [Ⓐ Crosby,H.R.&M.]
Smith, Joseph E., (AV) ...............'13 '38 C.112 B.A. L.1066 LL.B. P.O. Box 29291‡
**Smith-Dabney, Candace** .............'64 '93 C.1077 B.A. L.36 J.D. [Ⓐ Bennett,S.R.&A.]
*PRACTICE AREAS: Civil Litigation; Insurance Defense.
Smoger, Gerson H. ..................'52 '78 C.1047 B.A. L.1066 J.D. [Smoger&Assoc.]
Smoger & Associates, P.C. ..........................3175 Monterey Blvd. (⊙Dallas, TX)
Sniderman, Harvey A. ....................'34 '62 C.665 B.A. L.809 LL.B. 833 Erie St.‡
**Snook, R. Patrick** .................................'58 '87 C.112 B.A. L.1065 J.D. [Knox R.]
*PRACTICE AREAS: Civil Trial; Insurance Defense; Insurance Coverage.
Soehnel, Sonja A. .......................'37 '73 C.813 A.B. L.767 J.D. 5356 Locksley
**Soffer, Lewis J.** ........................'49 '78 C.813 A.B. L.1066 J.D. [Miller,S.&R.]
*PRACTICE AREAS: Real Estate Litigation; Title Insurance; Secured Lending; Financial Institutions.
**Sokol, William A.**, (BV) .............'46 '76 C.966 B.A. L.1066 J.D. [Van Bourg,W.R.&R.]
*LANGUAGES: Spanish.
*PRACTICE AREAS: Labor Law.
Somit, Jed ...............................'51 '76 C.309 B.A. L.1066 J.D. 1440 Broadway
**Soper, James C., (Inc.)**, (AV) ............'29 '54 C&L.813 A.B., J.D. [Fitzgerald,A.&B.]
*PRACTICE AREAS: Corporate and Business Law; Estate Planning, Trust and Estate Administration.
Spain, William C., (BV) ...................'35 '66 C.112 B.S. L.1065 LL.B. 1330 Bway.
Spánier, Alan F., (BV) ....................'44 '71 C.659 B.S. L.1066 J.D. 385 Grand Ave.
**Spanos, Evanthia** ..........................'57 '83 C.112 B.A. L.1065 J.D. [Ⓐ Berry&B.]
Sparrow, John P. ...............................'15 '46 C&L.309 A.B., LL.B. Ret. Supr. Ct. J.
Spear, Charles S., (AV) ..................'36 '74 C.309 A.B. L.1066 J.D. Asst. Pub. Def.
Spear, Richd. J. ...........................'25 '50 C.112 A.B. L.1066 LL.B. 405 14th St.‡
Spease, Laura R. .................'40 '77 C.1073 B.S. L.1065 J.D. 7700 Edgewater Dr.
Spencer, Craig S., (AV) ........'52 '77 C.112 B.A. L.802 J.D. East Bay Mun. Utility Dist.
**Sperring, Randall J.** ................'63 '89 C.112 A.B. L.767 J.D. [Ⓐ Crosby,H.R.&M.]
Springs, Sandra J. .........................'45 '76 C.112 L.1026 LL.B. 1999 Harrison St.
**Sproat, Ronald G.**, (AV) ........ '34 '64 C.112 B.S. L.1066 LL.B. [Rankin,S.M.T.&R.]
*PRACTICE AREAS: Medical Law; Legal Malpractice; General Insurance Defense; Products Liability Law; Commercial Litigation.
Spurlark, Susan, (AV) '50 '75
C.118 B.A. L.813 J.D. Coun., Kaiser Foundation Health Plan, Inc.
**Stainfield, Bryan K.** ............................'60 '86 C.112 B.A. L.464 J.D. [Ⓐ Larson&B.]

**Staley, Jobson & Wetherell, A Professional Corporation**
**(See Pleasanton)**

Stang, Donald J. ..........................'43 '69 C&L.309 A.B., LL.B. 5571 Taft Ave.

**Stansbury, John O., (AV) '42 '69 C.112 B.A. L.1066 J.D.** BB
**5th Floor, 2030 Franklin Street, 94612**
**Telephone: 510-444-4022 Fax: 510-444-3667**
***PRACTICE AREAS: Commercial and Business Litigation.**
**General Civil and Trial Practice. Tort, Business, Real Estate, Partnership and Commercial Collection Law.**
***See Professional Biographies, OAKLAND, CALIFORNIA***

**Stanton, Diane R.** ...............'60 '89 C.112 B.A. L.1065 J.D. [Ⓐ Hardin,C.L.E.&B.]
*PRACTICE AREAS: Products Liability Law; Civil Litigation.
Stanwyck, Peter M., (BV) ...................'46 '72 C.112 A.B. L.1066 J.D. 1300 Clay St.
Starbuck, John ..............................'59 '85 C.197 B.A. L.1066 J.D. 1404 Franklin
Stark, Jeffrey P., (BV) .................'56 '82 C.1169 B.A. L.767 J.D. Off. of Dist. Atty.

**Stark, Wells, Rahl, Schwartz & Schieffer, (AV)**
**Lake Merritt Plaza, 1999 Harrison Street, Suite 1300, 94612**
**Telephone: 510-834-2200 Telecopier: 510-763-5121**
**Members of Firm: Herbert L. Breed (1878-1967); George F. Dunker, Jr. (1937-1986); Bestor Robinson (1898-1987); Franklin C. Stark (1915-1989); Merrill J. Schwartz; Joseph H. Schieffer; May Lee Tong. Of Counsel: John F. Wells; Richard H. Rahl (Certified Specialist, Estate Planning, Trust and Probate Law, California Board of Legal Specialization).**
**General Civil Trial and Appellate Practice. Business, Commercial, Real Estate, Estate Planning and Probate.**
**Reference: Wells Fargo Bank (Oakland City Center Branch).**
***See Professional Biographies, OAKLAND, CALIFORNIA***

Steane, Catherine M. '58 '84 C.93 A.B. L.976 J.D.
Sr. Atty., Environmental Defense Fund
Steel, Angela M. ...................'53 '91 C.147 B.A. L.1066 J.D. Community Law Ctr.
**Steele, Roberta L.** '54 '93 C.454 B.A. L.930 J.D.
(adm. in OH; not adm. in CA) [Ⓐ Saperstein,G.D.&B.]
*PRACTICE AREAS: Litigation.
Stein, Brian D. ..........................'58 '86 C.330 B.A. L.464 J.D. 5500 Redwood Rd.
**Stein, Harvey W.**, (AV) ............................'43 '69 C.112 B.A. L.1065 J.D. [H.W.Stein]
**Stein, Laura** ..................'61 '87 C.197 B.A. L.309 J.D. Corp. Coun., The Clorox Co.
*LANGUAGES: Chinese, Italian, Spanish & French.

**Stein, Harvey W., A Professional Corporation, (AV)** BB
**Suite 600 Transpacific Centre, 1000 Broadway, 94607**
**Telephone: 510-763-6233 Fax: 510-832-1717**
**Harvey W. Stein.**

(This Listing Continued)

**Stein, Harvey W., A Professional Corporation (Continued)**
**Civil and Trial Practice. Business, Corporate, Petroleum Marketing Practices, Real Estate, Estate Planning, Trust and Probate Law.**
***See Professional Biographies, OAKLAND, CALIFORNIA***

**Steinbock, Miriam, (AV) '41 '72 C.788 B.A. L.309 J.D.**
**1 Kaiser Plaza, Suite 1725, 94612-3612**
**Telephone: 510-763-5611 FAX: 510-763-3430**
**(Certified Specialist, Family Law, The State Bar of California Board of Legal Specialization).**
**Family Law.**
***See Professional Biographies, OAKLAND, CALIFORNIA***

**Stella, Walter M.** ..........................'65 '90 C.436 B.A. L.188 J.D. [Ⓐ Crosby,H.R.&M.]
Stewart, Donald W. ......................'25 '51 C.112 A.B. L.1066 LL.B. 34 Starview Dr.
Stokke, Sharon A. ....'— '87 C.494 L.1066 J.D. 180 Grand Ave., Ste. 1400 (⊙San Fran.)
Stokley, Janette E. ...... '52 '79 C&L.893 B.A., J.D. National Econ. Develop. & Law Ctr.
**Stone, Kristine De Serpa** ............'67 '94 C.112 B.A. L.426 J.D. [Ⓐ Crosby,H.R.&M.]
Stoneman, Ward Chalmers .................'31 '67 C.65 B.A. L.284 J.D. 3121 Jordan Rd.
Streicher, Deborah J. ..........................................'55 '84 L.1153 J.D. Dep. Dist. Atty.
Strellis, Spencer W., (AV) ............'34 '59 C.339 B.A. L.1066 LL.B. 1611 Telegraph Ave.
**Strickland, William R.**, (AV) ...........'42 '69 C.768 A.B. L.1065 J.D. [Strickland&H.]
*PRACTICE AREAS: Personal Injury; Construction Defect; Roof Industry Liability; Medical Negligence; Legal Negligence.

**Strickland & Haapala, (AV)** BB
**Suite 800, Park Plaza Building, 1939 Harrison Street, 94612**
**Telephone: 510-763-2324 Fax: 510-273-8534**
**Partners of Firm: William R. Strickland; John E. Haapala; Christopher M. Harnett, Jr.; Charles J. Maguire, Jr.; Clyde A. Thompson; Judith B. Altura.**
**General Civil and Trial Practice in all State and Federal Courts. Casualty Insurance Law.**
**Representative Clients: Allstate Insurance Co.; California State Automobile Assn.; County of Alameda; The Farmers Insurance Group of Companies; Sisters of Providence Hospital.**
***See Professional Biographies, OAKLAND, CALIFORNIA***

Strickman, Carol, (BV) .......................'50 '77 C.33 B.A. L.1066 J.D. 360 62nd St.
Strimling, Michael S. ...................'53 '80 C.1169 B.A. L.1066 166 Santa Clara Ave.
Stromme, Gary L. ................ '39 '73 C.1058 B.A. L.1065 J.D. 6106 Ocean View Dr.
**Strotz, Peter A.** ........................'60 '87 C.112 A.B. L.767 J.D. [Hardin,C.L.E.&B.]
*LANGUAGES: German and Swiss German.
*PRACTICE AREAS: Civil Defense Litigation; Toxic Torts; Product Liability Law.
**Stroud, Carter**, (BV) '37 '69
C.766 B.A. L.1065 J.D. Dep. Port Atty. IV., Port of Oakland
Stryker, Gary L. ..............................'39 '64 C.36 B.A. L.1066 LL.B. Int. Rev. Serv.
Stuckey, Felix, (BV) ..........................'32 '72 C.45 B.S. L.765 J.D. [Stuckey&P.]
Stuckey & Price, (BV) ..................................................1901 Harrison St.
**Stump, Mark A.**, (BV) ....................'56 '82 C.473 B.A. L.1066 J.D. [Lempres&W.]
*REPORTED CASES: Fireman's Fund Ins. Co. v Fibreboard Corp. (1986) 182 Cal. App. 3d 462: Guardino v. Santa Clara County Local Transportation Authority (1995) 11 Cal. 4th 462.
*PRACTICE AREAS: Insurance Coverage Law; Construction Litigation; Legal Malpractice.
Sullivan, Charles W., Jr. ......................'31 '70 C.309 B.A. L.767 J.D. Asst. Pub. Def.
**Sullivan, David B.** ..............'67 '92 C.767 B.A. L.1065 J.D. [Ⓐ Donahue,G.W.&W.]
Sullivan, Elizabeth Barbu ..............'61 '88 C.767 B.A. L.1065 J.D. 200 Webster St.

**Sullivan, Michael R. '50 '90 C.112 B.A. L.284 J.D.**
**2100 Emcarcadero, Suite 100, 94606**
**Telephone: 510-535-2580 Facsimile: 510-535-2579**
**Email: msulli5559@aol.com**
**Construction.**
***See Professional Biographies, OAKLAND, CALIFORNIA***

Sullivan, Patrick J. ............................'49 '75 C.112 A.B. L.770 J.D. 436 14th St.
**Supton, Paul D.** ...................... '40 '76 C.563 B.S. L.813 J.D. [Van Bourg,W.R.&R.]
*PRACTICE AREAS: Labor Law.
Sutter, John H. .....................................'28 '55 C.309 A.B. L.813 LL.B. Supr. Ct. J.
Swain, Kimberly Carol .......'55 '81 C.188 B.S. L.1067 J.D. Protection & Advocacy, Inc.
**Swanson, Lisa Robinson** ..................'58 '85 C&L.309 A.B., J.D. [Ⓒ Randick&O.]
*LANGUAGES: French.
*PRACTICE AREAS: Litigation; General Transactional.
Sweeney, Wilmont ...........................'25 '55 C.112 B.A. L.1065 J.D. Supr.Ct. J.
**Swenson, Christopher P.** .................'68 '94 C.112 B.A. L.990 J.D. [Ⓐ Knox R.]
*PRACTICE AREAS: Corporate Law; Business Transactions; Real Estate; Business Litigation.
**Swerdlow, Alan E.** ...................'61 '87 C.112 A.B. L.464 J.D. [Boornazian,J.&G.]
*PRACTICE AREAS: Personal Injury; Insurance Coverage.
Swisher, Richd. F., (BV) ...............'16 '42 C&L.602 B.S., LL.B. 80 Swan Way #340
Swisher, Scott A., (BV) ......................'58 '85 C.112 B.A. L.770 J.D. Dep. Dist. Atty.
**Syger, Elizabeth S.** ........................'59 '84 C.575 B.A. L.260 J.D. [Wiley P.&R.]
*PRACTICE AREAS: Labor and Employment; Sexual Harassment Law; Employment Litigation.
Sykes, Douglas G. .....................'43 '72 C.112 B.S. L.1066 J.D. 2101 Webster St.
**Sykes, Jeffrey A.**, (AV) .......................'52 '77 C.381 B.A. L.608 J.D. [Lempres&W.]
*PRACTICE AREAS: Construction Law; Real Estate Law; Insurance Law; Surety Litigation.
Taber, Carleton H. A., (BV) ..........'52 '78 C.1169 B.A. L.1065 J.D. [Schmit,M.B.&S.]
**Tachner, Adam H.** ........................'66 '94 C.112 B.A. L.629 J.D. [Ⓐ Crosby,H.R.&M.]
Taggi, Richard J. ........................'52 '77 C.867 B.S. L.1066 J.D. One Kaiser Plaza
Tagliarini, Thomas C. ...................'53 '82 C.1044 B.A. L.284 J.D. 1999 Harrison St.
**Takahashi, Irene**, (BV) ...............'49 '77 C.112 B.A. L.1067 J.D. [McLemore,C.&T.]
*PRACTICE AREAS: Litigation Defense.
Takemiya, Fred ... '49 '77 C.112 B.A. L.1066 J.D. Univ. Coun., Regents of Univ. of Calif.
**Talwar, Anjali** ..........................................'66 '90 C.112 B.A. L.770 J.D. [Ⓐ Larson&B.]
Tamaro, Therese Wynne ...................'36 '77 C.764 B.A. L.1065 J.D. [White,C.M.&J.]
Tamchin, Stephen M., (BV) ....... '46 '74 C.472 B.B.A. L.1065 J.D. 414-13th St., 5th Fl.
Tamura, Susan J. ....................'47 '72 C.668 B.A. L.1066 J.D. [Yonemura,Y.&B.]
Tan, Victor ..................................'40 '65 C.112 B.A. L.1065 LL.B. 586 Kenmore Ave.
**Tang, Judith Y.** ...........................'70 '95 C.112 B.S. L.1065 J.D. [Ⓐ Wendel,R.B.&D.]
*LANGUAGES: Cantonese.
*PRACTICE AREAS: Corporate and General Business Law.
Tarnoff, Shelley M. ...........................'50 '83 C.112 B.S. L.1065 J.D. 1036 Warfield Ave.
Tashjian, Nubar ................................'22 '52 C&L.477 A.B., J.D. 3655 Grand Ave.‡
Taylor, James C., Jr., (BV) ...........................'46 '73 C.112 B.A. L.1065 J.D. Pub. Def.
Taylor, Russell W., (AV) .......................'46 '72 C.112 B.A. L.1066 J.D. [Taylor&F.]
**Taylor, William "Zak"**, (AV) ..............'48 '76 C.976 B.A. L.309 J.D. [Chilvers&T.]
Taylor & Field, (AV) .................................................................1901 Harrison St.
Tchaikovsky, Leslie J. ....................'43 '76 C.1073 B.A. L.1066 J.D. U.S. Bkrptcy. J.
Teasdale, Harold W., (AV) ..................'40 '66 C.112 B.A. L.1066 LL.B. Dep. Atty. Gen.
Teel, Susan M. .......................'46 '81 C.112 B.A. L.765 J.D. 1800 Harrison St., Ste., 2350
Ter Beek, John E. ........................'52 '88 C.1265 B.S. L.767 J.D. 125 12th St.
Terrazas, Alfredo, (AV) ....................'52 '77 C.112 B.A. L.770 J.D. Dep. Atty. Gen.
**Terry, Jonathan C.** .............................'62 '93 C.101 B.A. L.1049 J.D. [Ⓐ Nevin&H.]
*LANGUAGES: Fijian.
*PRACTICE AREAS: Construction Defect Litigation; Real Estate Litigation; Tort Claims Defense; Business; Intellectual Property Litigation.
Thaler, Dena R., (BV) ...........................'41 '77 C.112 B.A. L.284 J.D. 125 12th St.
**Thayer, Ernest M.**, (AV) ......................'30 '61 C.210 A.B. L.309 LL.B. [E.M.Thayer]

CAA439P

CALIFORNIA—OAKLAND MARTINDALE-HUBBELL LAW DIRECTORY 1997

**Thayer, Ernest M., A Professional Corporation, (AV)**
**Lake Merritt Plaza, Suite 1300, 1999 Harrison Street, 94612**
**Telephone: 510-874-4122 Telecopier: 510-834-7440**
**Ernest M. Thayer.**
**Civil Trial and Appellate Practice. Insurance, Products Liability, Malpractice, Consumer and Business Litigation.**
*See Professional Biographies, OAKLAND, CALIFORNIA*

Theisen, Ronda M. ........ '51 '86 C.166 B.A. L.767 J.D. Dep. Dist. Atty.
Thews, Albert W., (BV) ........ '27 '68 C.628 B.A. L.1065 J.D. 286 Santa Clara Ave.
Thomas, K. Blair ........ '55 '84 C.112 B.A. L.464 J.D. Dist. Atty's Off.
**Thomas, Michael J.** ........ '66 '94 C.1074 B.S.M.E. L.112 J.D. [Ryan,A.&L.]
Thomas, Sheila Y. ........ '61 '88 C.976 B.A. L.276 J.D. 1300 Clay St. 11th Fl.
Thomas, Susan Marie '48 '77
C.684 A.B. L.1065 J.D. Univ. Coun., Regents of the Univ. of Calif.
**Thomas, Walter E.**, (BV) ........ '48 '72 C.309 A.B. L.813 J.D. [Crosby,H.R.&M.]
*PRACTICE AREAS: Business; Corporate.
Thomason, Douglas N. ........ '49 '88 C.112 B.S. L.770 J.D. 492 Ninth St.
**Thompson, Clyde A.** ........ '46 '76 C.766 B.A. L.410 J.D. [Strickland&H.]
*PRACTICE AREAS: Public Entity; Construction Injuries; Premises Liability; Business Torts; Contracts.
**Thompson, Darrell T.** ........ '64 '92 C.101 B.A. L.112 J.D. [Larson&B.]
*LANGUAGES: Spanish.
Thompson, Llewellyn E., II, (AV) ........ '42 '68 C&L.767 A.B., J.D. 1221 Bdwy., 21st Fl.
Thompson, Trina L. ........ '61 '87 C.112 A.B. L.1066 J.D. 1970 Broadway
Thomson, Katherine J. ........ '59 '85 C.112 B.A. L.1066 J.D. 1611 Telegraph Ave.
**Tiemstra, James A.** ........ '55 '80 C.399 B.A. L.284 J.D. [Miller,S.&R.]
*PRACTICE AREAS: Bankruptcy Law.
Tingle, William E., (BV) ........ '47 '77 C.112 B.A. L.1065 J.D. Dep. Dist. Atty.
Tocci, M.J., (AV) ........ '53 '81 C.184 B.A. L.767 J.D. Dep. Dist. Atty.
**Toliver, Shawn A.** ........ '61 '90 C.1288 B.S. L.464 J.D. [Larson&B.]
**Tom, Quinlan S.** ........ '63 '89 C.112 A.B. L.1065 J.D. [McInerney&D.]
Tomberlin, George E., Jr. '49 '76
C.674 A.B. L.1066 J.D. Sr. Coun., Kaiser Found. Health Plan, Inc.
Tomine, Eugene, (AV) ........ '46 '72 C.112 B.S. L.1066 J.D. 1 Kaiser Plaza
**Tompkins, Dean A.** ........ '66 '91 C.112 B.A. L.284 J.D. [Gassett,P.&F.]
*PRACTICE AREAS: Workers' Compensation Defense.
**Tong, May Lee** ........ '47 '83 C.668 B.A. L.284 J.D. [Stark,W.R.S.&S.]
*LANGUAGES: Chinese, Mandarin and Cantonese.
*PRACTICE AREAS: Civil Litigation; Estate Planning; Trust.
**Toombs, Charles E.** ........ '51 '84 C.112 B.A. L.767 J.D. [McInerney&D.]
*PRACTICE AREAS: Tax; Corporate Law; Real Estate.
Torbet, Hugo ........ '63 '90 C.112 B.A. L.629 J.D. 5332 College Ave.
**Toschi, Steven C.** ........ '61 '86 C.1169 B.A. L.464 J.D. [McLemore,C.&T.]
*PRACTICE AREAS: Casualty Defense.
**Tovey, Morgan W.** ........ '63 '88 C.112 A.B. L.1068 J.D. [Crosby,H.R.&M.]
*PRACTICE AREAS: Intellectual Property; Business Litigation.
**Trabish, Gail C.** ........ '55 '80 C.276 B.S.B.A. L.128 J.D. [Boornazian,J.&G.]
*PRACTICE AREAS: Personal Injury; Public Entity Litigation.
**Trachuk, Thomas J.** ........ '50 '79 C.1044 B.A. L.1026 J.D. [Dang&T.]
*PRACTICE AREAS: Insurance and Public Entity Tort Defense; Employment Discrimination; Civil Rights Law.
Trafford, Linda J. ........ '42 '85 C.1079 B.A. L.767 J.D. 6114 La Salle Ave.
**Trapani, Thomas A.** ........ '56 '81 C.112 B.A. L.1067 J.D. [Rankin,S.M.T.&R.]
*PRACTICE AREAS: Medical Law; Legal Malpractice; General Insurance Defense; Products Liability Law; Commercial Law.
Travis, Benjamin ........ '32 '61 C.766 L.1065 LL.B. Supr. Ct. J.
**Tremaine, Anne** ........ '38 '87 C.477 B.S. L.809 J.D. [E.L.Blum]
*LANGUAGES: French, German.
*PRACTICE AREAS: Real Estate; Civil Litigation.
**Trembath, Robin Y.**, (BV) ........ '60 '85 C.112 B.A. L.1065 J.D. [Gassett,P.&F.]
*PRACTICE AREAS: Personal Injury Defense; Legal Malpractice Defense.
Tremlett, Janet M. ........ '47 '78 C.112 A.B. L.1066 J.D. 1 Kaiser Plaza
**Treppa, Michael S.** ........ '64 '89 C.112 B.A. L.284 J.D. [Aiken,K.&C.]

**Triay, Charles A., Law Offices of, (BV) '50 '77 C.112 A.B. L.1049 J.D.**
**1 Kaiser Plaza, Suite 2360, 94612**
**Telephone: 510-832-8700 Fax: 510-836-2595**
**(Certified Specialist, Estate Planning, Trust and Probate Law, The State Bar of California Board of Legal Specialization).**
***PRACTICE AREAS: Probate Litigation; Probate and Trust Administration; Estate Planning.**
**Probate Litigation, Probate Administration and Estate Planning.**
*See Professional Biographies, OAKLAND, CALIFORNIA*

Triebel, Charles O., Jr. ........ '39 '70 C.61 A.B. L.1065 J.D. 405 14th Ave.
Trifon, Malcolm '43 '69 C.605 B.A. L.273 J.D.
Sr. Coun., Kaiser Found. Health Plan, Inc.
**Trigero, Jane L.**, (AV) ........ '52 '80 C.112 B.S. L.767 J.D. [Anthony&C.]
*PRACTICE AREAS: Labor and Employment; Civil Trial Practice.
**Trinkle, William J.** ........ '50 '81 C.767 B.A. L.464 J.D. [Randick&O.]
*PRACTICE AREAS: Business Law; Franchise Litigation; Commercial Litigation.
**Trodella, Robert A., Jr.** ........ '66 '96 C.112 B.A. L.767 J.D. [Crosby,H.R.&M.]
Trowbridge, Jeffery D. ........ '56 '81 C.174 B.A. L.1065 J.D. 2030 Franklin St., Fifth Fl.
**Trutner, Cynthia de Nevers** ........ '60 '89 C.112 B.A. L.1065 J.D. [H.A.Trutner]
*PRACTICE AREAS: Probate; Trust Administration; Conservatorships; Estate Planning.

**Trutner, Herman A., Law Offices of, (AV) '28 '65 C.112 B.S. L.765 LL.B.**
**Ordway Building, One Kaiser Plaza, Suite 1545, 94612**
**Telephone: 510-287-5222 FAX: 510-763-5010**
**(Certified Specialist, Estate Planning, Trust and Probate Law, The State Bar of California Board of Legal Specialization).**
***PRACTICE AREAS: Probate; Estate Planning; Trust Law; Trust Litigation; Conservatorships.**
**Sharon A. Isenhour. Associates: Cynthia de Nevers Trutner.**
**Business, Estate Planning, Trust, Probate and Related Litigation.**
*See Professional Biographies, OAKLAND, CALIFORNIA*

**Tudor, Philip L.** ........ '56 '90 C.766 B.A. L.1065 J.D. [Crosby,H.R.&M.]
Turner, Michael, (AV) ........ '40 '66 C&L.813 A.B., J.D. One Kaiser Plaza
Turner, Peter M., (AV) ........ '42 '67 C.112 B.A. L.569 J.D. 1033 Hubert Rd.
Turner, Robert W. ........ '19 '48 C.627 B.A. L.597 J.D. 15 Marr Ave.‡
**Turner, Walter R.**, (AV) ........ '51 '78 C.801 B.A. L.990 J.D. [Wendel,R.B.&D.]
*PRACTICE AREAS: Income Tax Law; Business Law.
**Tuttle, Norman K., II**, (AV) ........ '35 '64 C.112 A.B. L.1066 LL.B. [Crosby,H.R.&M.]
**Urbina, Lindsey A.** ........ '70 '95 C.112 B.A. L.813 J.D. [Crosby,H.R.&M.]

**Utrecht, Paul F., Law Offices of**
**(See San Francisco)**

**Vacchina, Leonardo J.** ........ '46 '74 C.767 B.A. L.1065 J.D. [Berry&B.]
Vail, Steven W. ........ '50 '85 C.112 B.S.M.E. L.284 J.D. 4163 Lyman Rd.
**Vail French, Lora** ........ '68 '93 C.112 B.A. L.767 J.D. [Ryan,A.&L.]
Vale, Michael D. ........ '56 '83 C.475 B.A. L.477 J.D. 1 Kaiser Plaza, 18th Fl.
**Valen, Stephen J.** ........ '62 '90 C.112 A.B. L.477 J.D. [Hardin,C.L.E.&B.]
*PRACTICE AREAS: Civil Litigation; Toxic Substances; Product Liability.

**Valencia, Ronald** ........ '57 '83 C.112 A.B. L.1065 J.D. [Gassett,P.&F.]
*PRACTICE AREAS: Workers' Compensation Defense; Employment Litigation.
**Valentino, Caroline N.** ........ '56 '85 C.1074 B.A. L.284 J.D. [Haims,J.M.&M.]
*LANGUAGES: German.
*PRACTICE AREAS: General Civil Litigation; Insurance Defense; Bad Faith Law; Health, Disability and Life Insurance Law and Coverage; Personal Injury Defense.
**Valle-Riestra, Christopher P., Esq.** ........ '56 '83 C.1169 B.A. L.1066 J.D. [General C.]
*PRACTICE AREAS: Commercial Collection; Business Litigation; General Practice; Bankruptcy Law; Probate.
**Van Blois, R. Lewis**, (AV) ........ '39 '66 C.273 B.A. L.1066 J.D. [Van Blois,K.S.&B.]
*PRACTICE AREAS: Personal Injury; Product Liability; Highway Design; Construction Accidents; Medical Malpractice.

**Van Blois, Knowles, Schwartz & Baskin, (AV)**
**Suite 2245 Ordway Building, One Kaiser Plaza, 94612**
**Telephone: 510-444-1906 Contra Costa County 510-947-1055 Fax: 510-444-1294**
**Members of Firm: R. Lewis Van Blois; Thomas C. Knowles; Ellen R. Schwartz; Richard J. Baskin. Of Counsel: Charles E. Farnsworth.**
**Plaintiffs Trial Practice in fields of Product Liability, Highway Design, Construction Accidents, Airplane Crash Litigation, Railroad Accidents, Medical Malpractice, Bad Faith, Employment, Negligence Law and Class Actions regarding Fraudulent Sales and Truth in Lending.**
*See Professional Biographies, OAKLAND, CALIFORNIA*

**Van Bourg, Victor J.**, (AV) ........ '31 '56 C.112 B.A. L.1066 LL.B. [Van Bourg,W.R.&R.]
*PRACTICE AREAS: Labor Law.

**Van Bourg, Weinberg, Roger & Rosenfeld, (AV)**
**180 Grand Avenue, Suite 1400, 94612-3741**
**Telephone: 510-839-6600 Fax: 510-891-0400**
**Stanford L. Gelbman (1932-1992); Victor J. Van Bourg; Stewart Weinberg; Michael B. Roger; David A. Rosenfeld; William A. Sokol; Vincent A. Harrington, Jr.; W. Daniel Boone; Paul D. Supton; Blythe Mickelson; Barry E. Hinkle; James Rutkowski; Sandra Rae Benson; James G. Varga; Christian L. Raisner; James J. Wesser; Amy D. Martin; Theodore Franklin.**
**Labor Relations and Workers Compensation Law.**
*See Professional Biographies, OAKLAND, CALIFORNIA*

Van Broek, Alexander G. ........ '41 '82 C.112 B.A. L.284 J.D. 405 14th St.
Van Houten, Leslie L. ........ '47 '81 C.101 B.A. L.1051 J.D. Coun., Univ. of Calif.
**Vankoll, Barbara L.** ........ '64 '93 C.740 B.S. L.767 J.D. [Anthony&C.]
*PRACTICE AREAS: Medical Malpractice; Personal Injury Law.
Van't Rood, Lydia T. ........ '64 '90 C.1077 B.A. L.101 J.D. 1999 Harrison St.
Van Wye, Harlan E. ........ '43 '68 C.930 B.B.A. L.477 J.D. Dep. Atty. Gen.
**Varga, James G.** ........ '49 '79 C.1044 B.A. L.1190 J.D. [Van Bourg,W.R.&R.]
Vaughan, William E. ........ '30 '60 C.112 A.B. L.1066 LL.D. 17 Embarcadero Cove
Vaughns, James Phillip ........ '59 '86 C.1073 B.S. L.464 J.D. Asst. Dist. Atty.
Vaught, Jon R. ........ '59 '84 C.112 A.B. L.1067 J.D. 80 Swan Way
**Veneruso, Donna M., (P.C.)**, (AV) ........ '44 '74 C.823 A.B. L.767 J.D. [Veneruso&M.]
*PRACTICE AREAS: Family; Insurance Defense; Sports Liability.

**Veneruso & Moncharsh, (AV)**
**A Partnership of Professional Corporations**
**440 Grand Avenue, Suite 360, 94610-5012**
**Telephone: 510-433-0390 Fax: 510-433-0389**
**Donna M. Veneruso (P.C.); Leila H. Moncharsh (P.C.);—David G. Hysinger.**
**Professional Malpractice Defense including Medical, Podiatric and Legal, Real Estate Litigation, Family, Sports Liability and Equine Law. General Liability Insurance Defense. Land Use.**
*See Professional Biographies, OAKLAND, CALIFORNIA*

**Verber, John J.** ........ '58 '89 C&L.767 B.S., J.D. [Larson&B.]
Veres, Richard Kimball ........ '63 '91 C.1073 B.A. L.765 J.D. 3871 Piedmont Ave.
Veres, Robt. L. ........ '11 '50 C.197 A.B. L.767 LL.B. 3871 Piedmont Ave.‡
Vergas, Richard D. ........ '47 '76 C&L.128 B.A., J.D. U. S. Dept. of Energy
Vickland, John R. ........ '45 '74 C.813 B.S. L.1065 J.D. 1000 Bway.
Vlazakis, George M., (BV) ........ '54 '79 C.112 B.S. L.1065 J.D. 225 Baush St.
Vogel, Virginia '46 '78 C.112 B.A. L.284 J.D.
Div. of Agric. & Nat. Res., Univ. of Calif.
Vohland, Lewis L. ........ '27 '57 C.112 B.S. L.1066 LL.B. 55 Santa Clara Ave.
Voisenat, Marc ........ '59 '94 C.1073 B.S. L.284 J.D. 383 4th St.
Volonte, Arthur C. ........ '21 '54 C.766 A.B. L.767 LL.B. 1091 BrookwoodRd.
von Geldern, Eric ........ '57 '83 C.112 A.B. L.477 J.D. Off. of Dist. Atty.
von Seeburg, Susan H. ........ '44 '83 C.477 B.A. L.284 J.D. Univ. of Calif.
von Ter Stegge, David ........ '41 '72 C.112 A.B. L.1065 J.D. 1418 Eighth St.
Wadhams, Cathleen A. ........ '57 '81 C.112 A.B. L.1065 J.D. 1999 Harrison St.
Wagner, Alfons G., (AV) ........ '38 '74 C.867 A.B. L.284 J.D. 1611 Telegraph Ave.
**Wagner, Ann** '— '75 C.112 B.A. L.1065 J.D.
Savings Legal, World Savings & Loan Assoc.
**Wagner, Ronald A.**, (AV) ........ '34 '60 C&L.813 A.B., LL.B. [Hardin,C.L.E.&B.]
**Wagner, Sandra F.**, (AV) ........ '43 '71 C.813 B.A. L.426 J.D. [Hardin,C.L.E.&B.]
*PRACTICE AREAS: Family Law.
Wahrhaftig, Jack, (AV) ........ '25 '53 C.112 L.1065 J.D. 1800 Harrison St.
Wahrhaftig, Marc ........ '60 '92 C.112 B.A. L.1065 J.D. 1800 Harrison St.
**Wakefield, Jedediah** ........ '69 '95 C.112 B.A. L.770 J.D. [Larson&B.]
Wakeman, Sherwood G. '46 '72 C.112 A.B. L.1066 J.D.
Gen. Coun., San Francisco Bay Area Rapid Transit Dist.
**Wald, Michael E.**, (AV) ........ '38 '64 C.174 B.A. L.1066 J.D. [Wald&B.]
*PRACTICE AREAS: Personal Injury; Family Law.

**Wald & Bendes, (AV)**
**1999 Harrison Street, Suite 1300, 94612**
**Telephone: 510-444-0560 Fax: 510-273-8707**
**Michael E. Wald; Charles N. Bendes.**
**General Civil and Trial Practice. Personal Injury, Real Property, Business, Family Law, Corporations.**
*See Professional Biographies, OAKLAND, CALIFORNIA*

**Walker, Jennifer M.** ........ '60 '85 C.112 B.A. L.1065 J.D. [Hardin,C.L.E.&B.]
*PRACTICE AREAS: Toxic Substances Law; Civil Litigation; Products Liability Law.
Walker, Morley ........ '23 '49 C&L.145 A.B., J.D. 2740 Las Aromas St.
Walker, Roland E., Jr. ........ '50 '76 C.197 A.B. L.1066 J.D. Asst. Pub. Def.
**Walker, Sam** ........ '53 '89 C.878 B.A. L.1065 J.D. [Marion's I.]
*PRACTICE AREAS: Appellate Law; Health Law; Business Litigation; Antitrust Law; Contract Law.
**Wallace, Marshall Clark** ........ '59 '87 C.674 B.S. L.1066 J.D. [Crosby,H.R.&M.]
*PRACTICE AREAS: Business and Insurance Litigation.
**Wallis, Eric G.**, (AV) ........ '50 '75 C.169 A.B. L.1065 J.D. [Crosby,H.R.&M.]
*PRACTICE AREAS: Commercial Litigation with emphasis in Securities; Products Liability.
Walsh, Joseph G. ........ '23 '54 C.602 Ph.D. L.262 J.D. 10732 Fallbrook Way (Pat.)
**Walsh, Michael P.**, (AV) ........ '49 '74 C.112 B.A. L.767 J.D. [Fitzgerald,A.&B.]
*PRACTICE AREAS: Litigation involving Securities, Real Estate, Contract and Employment Disputes.
Walsh, Susan A. ........ '52 '85 C.766 B.A. L.1065 J.D. Co. Pub. Def.
Walters, William, (AV) ........ '26 '53 C&L.767 B.A., J.D. 1970 Broadway
Walthall, Stacy L., (BV) ........ '36 '65 C.878 B.A. L.1066 Asst. Dist. Atty.
Waltner, Alan C. ........ '52 '79 C.112 A.B. L.1066 J.D. 1736 Franklin St., 8th Fl.
Wannenmacher, Felix M. ........ '60 '87 C.112 A.B. L.1065 J.D. 1941 Jackson St.
**Ward, Cameron C.** ........ '52 '76 C&L.02 B.A., LL.B. [Lempres&W.]
*PRACTICE AREAS: Construction Litigation; General Litigation.
Ward, Lawrence S., (BV) ........ '41 '72 C.555 B.A. L.770 J.D. 333 MacArthur Blvd.

Ward, Melissa Bauman '65 '92 C.976 B.A. L.1065 J.D. 1 Kaiser Plz.
**Ward, Michael S.** '67 '95 C.813 B.A. L.1066 J.D. [A Fitzgerald,A.&B.]
*PRACTICE AREAS: Employment and Labor Law; Litigation.
Ward, Robert L., (AV) '19 '44 C.112 B.S. L.1065 J.D. 610 16th St.
Ware, Dee A. '66 '91 C.823 A.B. L.1065 J.D. 1999 Harrison St.
Wasko, William A. '50 '77 C.608 B.S. L.1065 J.D. 2030 Franklin St.
**Wasserman, R. Zachary**, (BV) '47 '72 C.112 B.A. L.813 J.D. [Wendel,R.B.&D.]
*PRACTICE AREAS: Real Estate Law; Science and Technology Law.
**Waters, David H.**, (AV) '51 '77 C.112 A.B. L.1065 J.D. [Larson&B.]
Watkins, Susan '46 '73 C&L.813 B.A., J.D. 1453 Barrows Rd.
**Watson, Carol Knight** '48 '87 C.586 B.A. L.1065 J.D. [A McInerney&D.]
*PRACTICE AREAS: Construction and Real Estate Litigation; Commercial Litigation.
Watson, Stanley B., (AV) '47 '72
C.968 A.B. L.309 J.D. Coun., Kaiser Found. Health Plan, Inc.
Watts, Ronald J. '37 '65 C.112 A.B. L.284 LL.B. 6447 Hilegass Ave.
**Waxman, Richard P.** '52 '84 C.112 B.A. L.1065 J.D. [Wendel,R.B.&D.]
*PRACTICE AREAS: Business and Real Estate Law; Commercial Law; Franchise Law.
Weaver, Pauline Anne, (AV) '49 '79 C&L.836 B.A., J.D. Asst. Pub. Def.
Weber, Carl J., (AV) '28 '62 C.597 B.S. L.209 J.D. 155 Grand Ave.
**Webster, David S.** '65 '91 C.147 B.S. L.767 J.D. [A Larson&B.]
Webster, William H. '46 '76 C.569 B.A. L.1066 J.D. [Webster&A.]
Webster & Anderson 469 9th St.
Weil, Edward G. '54 '79 C.112 A.B. L.1066 J.D. Atty. Gen. Off.
Weil, Wendy T. '54 '82 C.174 B.A. L.229 J.D. Coun., Kaiser Found. Health Plan, Inc.
Weills, Anne Butterfield '42 '89 C.767 B.S. L.284 J.D. 1611 Telegraph Ave.
Weinberg, Steve G. '49 '74 C.1077 B.S. L.169 J.D. Dep. Pub. Def.
**Weinberg, Stewart**, (AV) '36 '61 C.112 A.B. L.1066 J.D. [Van Bourg,W.R.&R.]
*PRACTICE AREAS: Labor Law.
Weiner, Lauri L. '59 '90 C.401 B.A. L.1068 J.D. Dep. Dist. Atty.
Weinsoff, David Jonathan '58 '87
C.1044 B.A. L.1029 J.D. Calif. State Coastal Conservancy
Weinstein, Marlene Gay '51 '78 C.107 B.A. L.284 J.D.
1999 Harrison St., Ste., 800; Lake Merritt Plz.
**Weisman, Rebecca** '63 '94 C.1036 B.A. L.284 J.D. [A McLemore,C.&T.]
*PRACTICE AREAS: Insurance Defense.
Weiss, Joyce Ann '41 '90 C.1073 B.A. L.284 J.D. [A Boxer,E.&G.]
**Weissman, Sonja S.** '65 '91 C.112 B.A. L.1065 J.D. [A Crosby,H.R.&M.]
Welch, Michael R., (AV) '54 '80 C.112 B.A. L.990 J.D. [Caudle,W.P.&B.]©
Welker, Francia M. '43 '73 C.683 B.A. L.767 J.D. 405 14th St.
**Wells, John F.**, (AV) '26 '52 C.358 B.S. L.813 LL.B. [B Stark,W.R.S.&S.]
**Wendel, David I.**, (AV) '21 '49 C.112 A.B. L.309 J.D. [Wendel,R.B.&D.]
*PRACTICE AREAS: Business Law; Securities Law; Real Property Law.

**Wendel, Rosen, Black & Dean, LLP, (AV)**
**Twenty-Fourth Floor, 1111 Broadway, 94607**
**Telephone: 510-834-6600 Facsimile: 510-834-1928**
**Email: info@wendel.com**
**Members of Firm: C. Gregg Ankenman; Mark S. Bostick; Michael P. Carbone; Michael D. Cooper; Michael A. Dean; David Goldman; Charles A. Hansen; Les A. Hausrath; William E. Horwich; Howard W. Lind; Bruce Lymburn; Deanna Down Lyon (Certified Specialist, Estate Planning, Trust and Probate Law, The State Bar of California Board of Legal Specialization); Donald A. McIsaac; Steven M. Morger; Christine K. Noma; David L. Preiss; Daniel Rapaport; Gillian M. Ross; Walter R. Turner (Certified Specialist, Taxation Law, The State Bar of California Board of Legal Specialization); R. Zachary Wasserman; Richard P. Waxman; David I. Wendel; Timothy S. Williams; Richard E. Winnie; Jeffrey C. Wurms. Of Counsel: Stanley P. Hébert. Associates: Elizabeth Berke-Dreyfuss; Joan M. Cambray; Thiele R. Dunaway; Barbara Finkle; Tracy Green; Andrew N. Jacobson; Karen Brown Kepler; Laura K. Meyer; Michael Eric Olmstead; Bertha A. Ontiveros; John G. Price; Judith Y. Tang; Lucinda H. Young.**
**General Civil and Trial Practice. Real Property. Commercial. Taxation. Construction. Business. Securities. Corporate. Franchise. Pension and Profit Sharing. Bankruptcy. Estate Planning and Probate. Public Finance. Land Use and Environmental. Secured Transactions. Public Agency Law. Intellectual Property.**
**Representative Clients: Bramalea Pacific; Crescent Jewelers; East Bay Regional Park District; Hexcel Corp.; Kieburtz & Associates (Medical Office Building Development); Quik Stop Markets, Inc.**
***See Professional Biographies, OAKLAND, CALIFORNIA***

**Wenokur, Jeremy E.** '67 '92 C.878 B.S. L.477 J.D. [Pezzola&R.]
*PRACTICE AREAS: Federal Taxation.
Wenten, Robert P. '46 '74 C.282 B.A. L.184 J.D.
(adm. in CT; not adm. in CA) Admin. Law J., Soc. Sec. Admn.
Werner, Frances E., (AV) '44 '75
C.454 B.A. L.1066 J.D. National Econ. Develop. & Law Ctr.
**Wesser, James J.** '48 '89 C.112 B.A. L.284 J.D. [Van Bourg,W.R.&R.]
West, Arlene, (BV) '44 '70 C.112 A.B. L.767 J.D. 180 Grand Ave.
West, Joseph A. '36 '65 C.112 B.S. L.1066 LL.B. 5238 Claremont Ave.
**West, Natalie E.**, (AV) '47 '74 C.788 A.B. L.1066 J.D. [McDonough,H.&A.]
*PRACTICE AREAS: Public Agency Law; Land Use Law; Litigation.
**West, Ray W., Jr.** '53 '88
C.911 B.A. L.309 J.D. Corp. Coun., World Savings & Loan Assoc.
West, Valerie C. '45 '74 C.966 B.A. L.107 J.D. 1 Kaiser Plz.
**Westbrook, Stephen M.**, (AV) '40 '68 C.124 B.S. L.1065 J.D.
Assoc. Gen. Coun., Intell. Prop., The Clorox Co. (Pat.)
Wheaton, James R. '57 '84 C.103 B.A. L.1066 J.D.
Pres. & Exec. Dir., Environmental Law Found.
White, Bradley R. '63 '89 C.112 A.B. L.767 J.D. [A Taylor&F.]
White, James S. '30 '66 C.1073 L.767 LL.B. Mun. Ct. J.
White, Joseph T., Jr., (AV) '26 '55 C.768 A.B. L.1066 J.D. [White,C.M.&J.]
White, Ralph I. '25 '53 C.839 L.1065 J.D. 4385 Brodgeview Dr.
**White, Richard T.**, (AV) '47 '73 C.602 B.A. L.767 J.D. [Fitzgerald,A.&B.]
*PRACTICE AREAS: Business and Environmental Litigation; Employment Disputes; Antitrust and Competitive Business Practices.
White, Courts, Mitchell & Johnson, (AV) 2000 Embarcadero Ste 302
**Whiteley, Robert Scott**, (AV) '45 '77 C.769 B.A. L.284 J.D. [Horton,W.&C.]
*PRACTICE AREAS: Customs Law; International Trade Law.
**Whitley, Bruce D.** '60 '87 C.112 B.S. L.1065 J.D. [Pezzola&R.]
Whitman, David B., (BV) '46 '72 C.112 B.A. L.464 J.D. Dep. Dist. Atty.
**Wick, William D.** '49 '74 C.597 B.A. L.276 J.D. [Crosby,H.R.&M.]
*PRACTICE AREAS: Environmental.
**Wilberding, Thomas A.** '60 '85 C.112 A.B. L.464 J.D. [Gassett,P.&F.]
*PRACTICE AREAS: Workers' Compensation Defense; Employment Litigation.
Wilcox, Gregory, (AV) '46 '76 C.311 B.A. L.1066 J.D. 436 14th St.
**Wiley, Joseph E.**, (AV) '51 '78 C.475 B.A. L.770 J.D. [Wiley P.&R.]
*PRACTICE AREAS: Labor and Employment; Collective Bargaining; Public Sector Employment Law; Public Sector Labor Relations; Labor Arbitration.

**Wiley Price & Radulovich, (AV)**
**1300 Clay Street, Suite 600, 94612**
**Telephone: 510-466-6336 Fax: 510-466-6337**
**Email: wprlaw.com URL: http://www.wprlaw.com**
**Joseph E. Wiley; Suzanne I. Price; Monna R. Radulovich; Elizabeth S. Syger.**
**Labor and Employment Law and Litigation.**
***See Professional Biographies, OAKLAND, CALIFORNIA***

Wilken, Claudia '49 '75 C.813 B.A. L.1066 J.D. U.S. Dist. J.
Wilkinson, Steven Kent '52 '89 C.112 B.A. L.284 J.D.
4690 Tompkins Ave., Cottage #5
Williams, Barry J., (AV) '42 '67 C.112 A.B. L.1065 J.D. [A Boxer,E.&G.]
Williams, Eric E. '63 '90 C.766 B.A. L.464 J.D. [A Taylor&F.]
**Williams, Pamela J.** '62 '88 C.140 B.S. L.893 J.D. Sr. Coun., Clorox Co.
*RESPONSIBILITIES: Corporate Law; Employee Benefits; Labor and Employment.
**Williams, Stephen M.** '57 '85 C.506 B.A. L.767 J.D. [Fitzgerald,A.&B.]
*REPORTED CASES: Kennedy Cabot & Co. v. National Assn. of Securities Dealers, Inc. 41 Cal App. 4th 1167.
*PRACTICE AREAS: College and University Law; General Civil Litigation; Securities Litigation; Environmental Law; Labor and Employment Law.
**Williams, Timothy S.** '55 '80 C.813 B.A. L.1066 J.D. [Wendel,R.B.&D.]
*PRACTICE AREAS: Real Property Law; Construction Law.
Willman, Saundra R. '43 '80 C.911 B.A. L.310 J.D. 405 14th St.
**Wilson, Edwin J., Jr.**, (AV) '43 '71 C.112 A.B. L.1066 J.D. [Erickson,B.H.&W.]
**Wilson, James T.**, (BV) '46 '77 C.813 B.A. L.1066 J.D. [Crosby,H.R.&M.]
*PRACTICE AREAS: Environmental; Toxics Litigation; Insurance and Commercial Litigation.
Wilson, Marlene '48 '76 C.569 A.B. L.770 J.D. 601 Vernon Ave.
Wilson, Warren B. '21 '53 C.112 A.B. L.1065 J.D. 653 11th St.
**Winchester, Timothy F.**, (AV) '47 '72 C.112 A.B. L.1066 J.D. [McInerney&D.]
**Windle, Timothy J.** '48 '73 C.112 B.A. L.1068 J.D.
Asst. Gen. Coun. & Asst. Secy., American President Cos., Ltd.
**Winkelman, Bruce H.** '61 '86 C.112 A.B. L.1049 J.D. [Boornazian,J.&G.]
*PRACTICE AREAS: Toxic Tort; Environmental; Insurance Coverage Litigation.
**Winnie, Richard E.**, (BV) '47 '75 C.330 A.B. L.767 J.D. [Wendel,R.B.&D.]
*PRACTICE AREAS: Municipal Law; Public Finance; Land Use Law.
**Winokur, Robert M.**, (AV) '24 '49 C.563 B.S.S. L.178 J.D. [B Crosby,H.R.&M.]
Winslow, Priscilla S. '52 '77 C.1169 A.B. L.1067 J.D. 405 14th St.
Winter, Philip A. '19 '49 C.112 B.S. L.1066 J.D. 436 14th St.‡
Witser, Robert G. '30 '63 C.906 B.A. L.1355 LL.B. [R.G.Witser]
Witser, Robert G., A P.C., Law Offices of P.O. Box 13221
**Wittenberg, Malcolm B.** '46 '72 C.971 B.S. L.273 J.D.
[Crosby,H.R.&M.] (©Santa Rosa)
*PRACTICE AREAS: Patent, Trademark and Copyright Litigation; Prosecution and Counseling.
Wolan, Steven C., (BV) '46 '73 C.112 A.B. L.1065 J.D. [Patton,W.&B.]
Wolf, Paul Delano '52 '77 C.813 B.A. L.1066 J.D. 1212 Bway., 10th Fl.
Wong, Arthur L. '49 '75 C.37 B.A. L.1067 LL.B. P.O. Box 20406
**Wong, Jonathan G.** '59 '83 C.668 B.A. L.1067 J.D. [Donahue,G.W.&W.]
*LANGUAGES: French, German, Spanish and Mandarin Chinese.
*PRACTICE AREAS: Litigation; Immigration and Nationality Law; Employment Law.
Wong, Lawrence '50 '76 C.112 A.B. L.1065 J.D. 413 3rd St.
Wong, Nora Mein Locke '63 '89 C.112 A.B. L.1065 J.D. Co. Pub. Def.
**Wood, G. Geoffrey**, (BV) '52 '83 C.1075 B.A. L.770 J.D. [Morton,L.&A.]
*PRACTICE AREAS: Civil Trial; Construction Law; Insurance Defense; Personal Injury.
**Wood, James M.**, (AV) '48 '73 C.740 B.A. L.767 J.D. [Crosby,H.R.&M.]
*PRACTICE AREAS: Products Liability Law; Pharmaceutical and Medical Device Litigation.
**Wood, Robert N.**, (AV) '37 '63
C.597 B.S. L.1066 J.D. [Donahue,G.W.&W.] (©Walnut Creek)
*PRACTICE AREAS: Complex Litigation; Business Torts; Dealer and Distributor Terminations.
Woodruff, Dennis J. '46 '73 C.770 B.A. L.1065 J.D. [Woodruff&S.]
Woodruff & Singman 1999 Harrison St.
**Woods, Joseph A., Jr.**, (AV) '25 '50 C.112 A.B. L.1066 J.D. [B Donahue,G.W.&W.]
**Wraith, James L.** '58 '83 C.112 B.S. L.1065 J.D. [Larson&B.]
Wright, Dean W., (AV) '21 '52 C.112 B.S. L.1066 J.D. P.O. Box 29291
**Wulfsberg, H. James**, (AV) '44 '70 C.800 A.B. L.1066 J.D. [Lempres&W.]
*PRACTICE AREAS: Construction Law; Insurance Coverage Law; Professional Liability Law.
**Wunsch, John H.** '58 '83 C&L.911 B.A., J.D. [Miller,S.&R.]
*PRACTICE AREAS: Bankruptcy Law.
**Wurms, Jeffrey C.** '59 '84 C.276 B.A. L.1292 J.D. [Wendel,R.B.&D.]
*LANGUAGES: Dutch.
*REPORTED CASES: In re Pladson, 154 B.R. 305 (N.D.Cal. 1993); In re Bair Island Marina & Office Center, 116 B.R. 180 (Bankr. N.D. Cal. 1990).
*PRACTICE AREAS: Bankruptcy.
**Wyatt, Ellen Suzanne** '43 '79 C.1188 B.A. L.1065 J.D. [A Aiken,K.&C.]
Wynn, Marina Ramos '51 '89 C.112 B.A. L.1068 J.D. [A Boxer,E.&G.]
**Wynne, Joseph A.** '46 '83
C.112 B.A. L.1065 J.D. Sr. Coun., World Savings & Loan Assn.
Yamada, Ranko Carol '52 '78 C.1169 B.A. L.1065 J.D. [A Yonemura,Y.&B.]
**Yamamoto, Eugene K.**, (AV) '57 '83
C.426 B.A. L.1065 J.D. [B Crosby,H.R.&M.] (©San Francisco)
**Yap, Franklin H.** '55 '82 C.013 B.Engr. L.1065 J.D. [A McInerney&D.]
Ynostroza, Carlos G. '43 '69 C.112 B.A. L.1065 J.D. Mun. Ct. J.
Yocum, Carol K. '38 '76 C.112 A.B. L.1065 J.D. The Flecto Co., Inc.
Yonemura, Mas, (AV) '16 '47 C.112 A.B. L.1066 J.D. [Yonemura,Y.&B.]
Yonemura, Yasaki and Baizer, (AV) 405 14th St.
Young, Brian D. '54 '84 C.1073 B.A. L.765 J.D. 1212 Bway.
Young, Julius O., III, (BV) '49 '76 C.198 B.A. L.575 J.D. [A Boxer,E.&G.]
**Young, Lucinda H.** '56 '82 C&L.260 B.S., J.D. [A Wendel,R.B.&D.]
*PRACTICE AREAS: Estate Planning; Taxation; Probate.
Young, Michael H., (P.C.), (BV) '43 '69 C.112 A.B. L.1065 J.D. [Hanna,B.M.M.&J.]
Young, Wilson '28 '60 C.112 A.B. L.765 J.D. 1212 Broadway‡
Youngquist, Monica L. '61 '89 C.112 B.A. L.464 J.D. 200 Walnut St.
**Yuen, Nicole Brown** '71 '96 C.1075 B.A. L.767 J.D. [A Knox R.]
**Yuki, Leslie M.** '65 '91 C.767 B.A. L.1065 J.D. [A Crosby,H.R.&M.]
Zablen, Leslie M., (Mr.) '48 '81 C.112 B.A. L.1230 J.D. 3540 Grand Ave.
**Zackler, Allan I.** '— '72 C.339 B.A. L.597 J.D. [Zackler&Assoc.]
*PRACTICE AREAS: Marketing Law; Food, Drug and Cosmetic Law; Commercial Law; Advertising Law; Trade Regulations.

**Zackler & Associates**
**3824 Grand Avenue, Suite 100, 94610**
**Telephone: 510-834-4400 Fax: 510-834-9185**
**Allan I. Zackler. Associates: Georgia H. Burke.**
**Business Law (Domestic and International Transactions); Food & Drug Regulatory Matters (Federal and State Agencies); Consumer Products, Packaging and Labeling, Trademarks, Technology Licensing, Advertising Review and Customs Law.**
***See Professional Biographies, OAKLAND, CALIFORNIA***

**Zamczyk, Bradley M.** '63 '90 C.112 B.A. L.770 J.D. [A Larson&B.]
**Zappala, Ralph A.**, (BV) '54 '81 C.766 B.A. L.464 J.D. [Larson&B.]
Zatkin, Steven R. '46 '74 C.112 A.B. L.464 J.D.
Sr. V.P., Kaiser Found. Health Plan, Inc.
Zatkin, Victoria B. '53 '78
C.112 A.B. L.1065 J.D. Sr. Coun., Kaiser Found. Health Plan, Inc.
Zebrack, Joel, (AV) '36 '64 C.1097 B.A. L.809 J.D. 405-14th St.
Zeff, Tova L. '55 '88 C.112 B.A. L.284 J.D. 6062 Monroe Ave.
Zembsch, Kimberley C. '62 '88 C.112 B.A. L.767 J.D. 300 Lakeside Dr.
Zemelman, Mark S. '54 '83
C.1169 B.A. L.1065 J.D. Coun., Kaiser Found. Health Plan, Inc.

CAA441P

**CALIFORNIA—OAKLAND** **MARTINDALE-HUBBELL LAW DIRECTORY 1997**

**Zilberman, Leonid M.** ........... '68 '96 C.112 B.A. L.770 J.D. [⊠ Donahue,G.W.&W.]
*LANGUAGES: Russian.
*PRACTICE AREAS: Litigation.
Zimmer, Richard W., (AV) ...... '44 '70 C.475 B.S. L.477 J.D. [Andersen&Z.]

**Zimmerman, Harris, (AV) '19 '51 C.46 B.S. L.284 J.D.**
**Suite 710, 1330 Broadway, 94612**
**Telephone: 510-465-0828 Fax: 510-465-2041**
**Email: hzimerman@ix.netcom.com**
***PRACTICE AREAS: Intellectual Property Litigation; Counseling; Mediation; Arbitration; Patent Litigation.**
**Associates: Michael J. Cronen.**
**Patent, Trademark, Unfair Competition and Trade Secrets Law. Trials.**
*See Professional Biographies, OAKLAND, CALIFORNIA*

Zimmerman, Jamie W. ............'48 '77 C.381 B.S. L.1137 J.D. 1315 Trestle Glen Rd.
**Ziser, George J.**, (AV) ...................'47 '72 C.112 A.B. L.1066 J.D. [Larson&B.]
**Zoller, Barry** ........................... '66 '92 C.112 B.A. L.770 J.D. [⊠ Larson&B.]

## OAKLEY, —, *Contra Costa Co.*

Gurule, Agustin T. .................... '33 '71 C&L.560 B.A., J.D. 5243 Sandmound Blvd.
Koppel, Gary ...................... '52 '77 C.112 B.S. L.1065 J.D. 1530 Gamay Cir.

## OAK PARK, 2412, *Ventura Co.*

Drucker, Michael S. '50 '77
C.112 B.S. L.1065 J.D. 638 Lindero Canyon Rd. (⊙Los Angeles)

## OAK VIEW, 4,872, *Ventura Co.*

Coit, Rosanne J. ..........................'48 '77 C.112 A.B.Ec. L.276 J.D. 11044 Rodeo Dr.‡
McNally, James Michael ........................ '34 '61 C.707 L.793 J.D. P.O. Box 95‡
Moore, David Lee ........................'52 '85 C.208 B.S.B.A. 842 Santa Ana Blvd.
Thompson, Bruce A. ...................'25 '54 C.112 A.B. L.1066 J.D. Ret. Supr. Ct. J.‡

## OCCIDENTAL, —, *Sonoma Co.*

Kant, Harlan R. ...............................'48 '84 C.188 B.A. L.1065 J.D. 74 Main St.
Perry, Richard W. ........................'40 '66 C.112 B.A. L.1066 LL.B. 17267 Taylor Ln.

## OCEAN BEACH, —, *San Diego Co.*

Burns, Robert .............................'53 '80 C.608 A.A. L.1137 J.D. 4877 Voltaire St.

## OCEANSIDE, 128,398, *San Diego Co.*

Adelizzi, Joseph, (BV) .............. '58 '84 C.1192 B.B.A. L.1137 J.D. 3156 Vista Way
Austin, Dale ............................ '19 '47 C&L.336 B.A., LL.B. 3019 Mesa Dr.‡
Banche, Nicholas C., A Professional Corporation, (AV) '34 '64
C.734 B.S. L.1049 J.D. 810 Mission Ave., Suite 200
Barber, Frederick W. '15 '50 C&L.276 A.B., LL.B.
(adm. in DC; not adm. in CA) 1462 Puritan Dr.‡
Barnhart, William F. '41 '81 C.172 B.A. L.174 J.D.
(adm. in NE; not adm. in CA) Pres., The Barnhart Corp.
Blumen, Norman H. ............... '18 '48 C.563 B.S. L.1009 LL.B. 4921 Alicante Way
Bowers, Booth H. ........................ '12 '37 C&L.809 LL.B. 466 Parkside Dr.‡
**Brown, Jay J.** ......................'63 '90 C.112 B.A. L.1188 J.D. [Feist,V.K.&L.]
*PRACTICE AREAS: Homeowners Association; Collection; Real Estate.
Brzovic, Daniel P. ..................'54 '79 C.112 B.A. L.1066 J.D. 1629 Appaloosa Way
Bulman, Timothy Paul '66 '91 C.1044 B.A. L.602 J.D.
(adm. in MI; not adm. in CA) 4644 Brier Ridge Rd.★
**Burson, Alan H.**, (AV) .................... '46 '74 C.911 B.A. L.1049 J.D. [Feist,V.K.&L.]
*PRACTICE AREAS: Homeowners Association Law; Real Estate; Litigation; Collections.
Campbell, Victoria L. '57 '90 C.1169 B.A. L.1049 J.D.
Legal Aid Soc. of San Diego, Inc.
Conti, William L., (CV) .............'57 '84 C.1077 B.A. L.61 J.D. 2204 El Camino Real
Delaney, Bernard A., Jr. ................... '27 '50 C.588 L.94 J.D. 4714 Barcelona Way‡
Dietz, Kim H. ................... '55 '81 C.713 B.A. L.1035 J.D. 2204 S. El Camino Real
Doucette, Jodi Leazott ................... '62 '87 C.990 B.A. L.1049 J.D. Dep. City Atty.
**Feist, Raymond F., Jr.**, (AV) ............. '46 '75 C.112 B.A. L.61 J.D. [Feist,V.K.&L.]
*PRACTICE AREAS: Corporate Law; Business Law; Probate; Trust Law.

**Feist, Vetter, Knauf and Loy, A Professional Corporation, (AV)**
**Suite 300, 810 Mission Avenue, P.O. Box 240, 92049-0240**
**Telephone: 619-722-1914 Telecopier: 619-721-8943**
**Raymond F. Feist (1916-1988); Norman L. Vetter; Robert C. Knauf (1920-1979); John I. Loy (Retired); Raymond F. Feist, Jr.; Alan H. Burson; Henry R. Hague; Lisa Frazee Morgosh; Jay J. Brown.**
**General Civil Trial Practice. Corporate, Real Property, Personal Injury, Estate Planning and Probate Law, Condominium Law.**
**Reference: Bank of America National Trust & Savings Assn. (Oceanside Branch Office).**
*See Professional Biographies, OCEANSIDE, CALIFORNIA*

Galef, Janis Mitsue .....................'49 '77 C.112 A.B. L.426 J.D. 1772 Woodbine Pl.
Gardner, Michael R. .................. '58 '90 C.112 B.A. L.1049 J.D. 2206 Zabyn St.
Gore, Arthur E., (AV) ........... '19 '57 C.608 B.S. L.809 J.D. 3245 Avenida de Loyola‡

**Gore, Grosse, Greenman & Lacy, (AV)**
**A Partnership including a Professional Law Corporation**
**900 Pier View Way, P.O. Box 299, 92049-0299**
**Telephone: 619-722-1234 FAX: 619-722-5860**
**Kenneth L. Greenman, Jr., (A P.L.C.); Janet Bledsoe Lacy; Michael L. Klein; J. Delene St. John; Colleen C. O'Harra; Karen M. Heffron (Certified Specialist, Family Law, The State Bar of California Board of Legal Specialization).**
**Civil Litigation. Estate Planning, Probate, Business, Personal Injury, Real Estate, Corporation and Domestic Law.**
*See Professional Biographies, OCEANSIDE, CALIFORNIA*

**Greenman, Kenneth L., Jr., (A P.L.C.)**, (AV) '43 '72
C.800 B.S. L.1188 J.D. [Gore,G.G.&L.]
*PRACTICE AREAS: Civil Litigation; Commercial Law; Real Estate Law; Personal Injury Law; Probate Law.
Griswold, Craig R., (BV) .....................'44 '78 C.763 L.1137 LL.B. 3156 Vista Way
Grosz, G. Robert ........................ '30 '65 C.294 A.B. L.809 LL.B. 342 Saguaro Pl.
**Hague, Henry R.**, (AV) .................. '45 '73 C.951 B.A. L.1049 J.D. [Feist,V.K.&L.]
*PRACTICE AREAS: Business Law; Real Estate; Community Association Law.
Hallam, Linda ............................. '47 '77 C.763 B.A. L.1137 J.D. Dimension One
Halsey, William C., (CV) ...... '47 '76 C.112 B.A. L.1137 J.D. 3563 Evening Canyon Rd.
Hansen, John M. .......................'62 '89 C.174 B.S. L.1049 J.D. 810 Mission Ave.
Hansen, Milton C. '17 '53 C.966 B.S. L.424 J.D.
(adm. in IL; not adm. in CA) 4390 Dowitcher Way‡
**Heffron, Karen M.**, (BV) ............. '56 '84 C.494 B.S. L.1137 J.D. [⊠ Gore,G.G.&L.]
*PRACTICE AREAS: Family Law.
Holloway, Norman D., (AVⓉ) '18 '48 C&L.851 LL.B.
(adm. in OH; not adm. in CA) 4835 Marathon Way‡
Holz, Dennis E., (BV) '46 '72 C.112 B.A. L.1068 J.D.
Mgn. Atty., Legal Aid Soc. of San Diego, Inc.
Hooser, Eugene A., (BV) ..................................'48 '79 2204 S. El Camino Real

Ingram, Bernard E., (AV) ................ '18 '49 C.546 B.S. L.800 J.D. 4710 Athos Way‡
Jaekman, Michael N. .........'— '90 C.763 A.B. L.1049 J.D. Calif. Rural Legal Assistance
Karr, Philip R. ..........................'13 '76 C.128 Ph.D. L.1152 J.D. 1200 Harbor Dr. N.
King, Kenneth L., (AV) ................. '34 '69 C.870 B.S. L.893 LL.B. 2741 Vista Way
**Klein, Michael L.**, (BV) .................. '52 '78 C.112 A.B. L.426 J.D. [Gore,G.G.&L.]
*REPORTED CASES: Stecks v. Young, 38 Cal. App. 4th/365.
*PRACTICE AREAS: Civil Litigation; Bankruptcy Law; Business Law; Personal Injury Law.
**Lacy, Janet Bledsoe**, (AV) .................. '48 '74 C.763 B.A. L.61 J.D. [Gore,G.G.&L.]
*PRACTICE AREAS: Family Law.
Lightfoot, Stephen K., (AV) .........................'43 '73 L.1190 J.D. [Lightfoot&N.]⊙
Lightfoot & Northup, A Professional Corporation, (AV)
1351 Harbor Boulevard North, Suite B (⊙Pasadena, CA)
Lofgren, Robert J. '53 '84
C.999 B.A. L.976 J.D. Gen. Coun., Republic Security Corporation
**Loy, John I.**, (AV) ...................... '21 '51 C.112 A.B. L.273 J.D. [Feist,V.K.&L.] ‡
*PRACTICE AREAS: Real Estate; Trust Law; Probate Law.
Mangini, Maurizio A. ..................... '49 '91 C.188 B.S. L.362 J.D. 2424 Vista Way
McCarthy, Frank D. ................................. '24 '61 C&L.93 LL.B. 1496 Avocado‡
Menk, Wolfgang M. ...................... '48 '80 C.112 B.A. L.1137 J.D. 1729 Kurtz St.
Miller, David R., (BV) .....................'51 '77 C.645 B.S. L.1049 J.D. 3156 Vista Way
Mitzner, Floyd R. ................................ '22 '52 C&L.767 LL.B. 5168 El Secrito
**Morgosh, Lisa Frazee** .................. '61 '89 C.112 B.A. L.1049 J.D. [Feist,V.K.&L.]
*PRACTICE AREAS: Homeowners Association; Collections.
Nicolas, Samuel A., III ...............'60 '86 C.101 B.S. L.800 J.D. 4423 Composition Ct.
Oberle, Joseph F. ........................ '35 '80 C.475 B.A. L.1137 J.D. 2110 S. Hill St.
**O'Harra, Colleen C.**, (BV) ..........'37 '78 C.139 B.A. L.1137 J.D. [⊠ Gore,G.G.&L.]
*PRACTICE AREAS: Probate Law; Estate Planning Law.
Olsen, Harold L. .........................'46 '86 C.1078 B.A. L.128 J.D. 2424 Vista Way
O'Neal, James E., (BV) ...................'34 '66 C.763 A.B. L.1049 J.D. 2741 Vista Way
Orduno, Ramon R., (CV) ...................................... '46 '77 2170 El Camino Real

**Panther, James B., Law Offices of '42 '73 C.911 B.A. L.61 J.D.**
**2424 Vista Way, Third Floor, 92054**
**Telephone: 619-722-6895 Fax: 619-754-5132**
***PRACTICE AREAS: Real Estate; Finance; Business Law; Banking.**
**Business Law with an Emphasis in Real Estate, Mortgage Banking and Commercial Transactions and Consumer Credit Laws.**
*See Professional Biographies, OCEANSIDE, CALIFORNIA*

Rodman, Catherine A. ..... '57 '83 C.112 B.A. L.61 J. D. Legal Aid Soc. of San Diego, Inc.
Rosenfeld, Lorraine ...................................'57 '88 L.1241 J.D. 2131 El Camino Real
Sacks, Marcus B. '05 '31 C.659 L.831 LL.B.
(adm. in PA; not adm. in CA) 3621-50 Vista Campana S.‡
**St. John, J. Delene** ........................ '49 '87 C.1176 B.S. L.1137 J.D. [⊠ Gore,G.G.&L.]
*PRACTICE AREAS: Family Law and Mediation.
Scott, Robert L. ..........................'52 '81 C.763 B.A. L.1137 J.D. 2424 Vista Way
Stanton, John ............................................ '29 '56 C&L.665 B.S., LL.B. P.O. Box 384
Sullivan, Charles W. ........................... '27 '59 C&L.215 LL.B. 2149 Sorrento Dr.
Van de Water, John R. ................................ '17 '46 C&L.145 B.A., J.D. 603 1st St.
**Vetter, Norman L.**, (AV) ..................... '30 '58 C.763 A.B. L.1068 J.D. [Feist,V.K.&L.]
*PRACTICE AREAS: Personal Injury Law; Real Estate; Probate; Trust Law.
Walter, Robin T. .........................'50 '87 C.477 B.A. L.1339 J.D. 3579 Durham Cir.
Walwick, Robert S., (BV) ................... '27 '54 C.112 B.S. L.800 J.D. 322 N. Nevada
Weber, Daniel A., (AV) .......................'— '35 C.724 L.1009 LL.B. 4715 Agora Way‡
Wellman, James Harrison, (BV) ........... '48 '74 C.918 B.A. L.1049 J.D. Dep. Co. Coun.
White, Claron N. '13 '48 C.424 B.S.Ch. L.209 J.D.
(adm. in IL; not adm. in CA; Pat.) 3571 Papaya Way‡
Williams, Elizabeth Y. ...............'42 '72 C&L.426 B.A., J.D. 2049 Wedgewood Dr.‡
Wright, Marshal H ...........................'61 '88 C.1288 B.S. L.1339 J.D. 900 3rd St.
Yeomans, Peter L., (BV) ..................'45 '74 C.139 B.A. L.61 J.D. 2741 Vista Way

## OILDALE, 20,879, *Kern Co.*

Plummer, William T. '15 '46 C&L.546 J.D.
(adm. in NE; not adm. in CA) 1015 Glade St.‡

## OJAI, 7,613, *Ventura Co.*

Anderson, William T. ..................'22 '59 C.800 B.S. L.809 LL.B. 1676 Foothill Rd.‡
Antonelli, Alfred P. '29 '56 C.923 A.B. L.976 LL.B.
(adm. in PA; not adm. in CA) 1117 Del Nido Ct.‡
Atkinson, Ross E., (BV) ................... '54 '79 C.154 B.A. L.767 J.D. 603 W. Ojai Ave.
Bralley, Maurice W., Jr., (AV) '24 '53
C.112 B.A. L.1068 LL.B. 1211 Maricopa Hgwy (⊙Pasadena)
Danch, Christopher, (CV) ................ '54 '80 C.1074 B.S.B.A. L.61 J.D. [Danch&D.]
Danch, John R. ..................................'16 '42 C.347 B.S. L.1119 J.D. [Danch&D.]
Danch & Danch, (CV) ............................................................. 323 E. Matilija St.
Dougherty, Paul M. ...................... '33 '72 C.112 B.S. L.1026 J.D. P.O. Box 112‡
Frenkel, Marc ............................................ '30 '76 L.1136 J.D. P.O. Box 1043
Grimm, Daniel J. ........................'55 '79 C.999 B.A. L.464 J.D. 10882 Creek Rd.
Hames, David L., (CV) ......................... '58 '88 C&L.1186 A.S., J.D. 763 Country Dr.
Jacobs, Allan, (BV) ..........................'40 '68 C.112 B.S. L.1065 J.D. 603 W. Ojai Ave.
Jarrico, Bill ..................................'40 '78 C.685 B.A. L.426 J.D. 514 Del Norte Rd.
Johnson, Willoughby C. ........'36 '65 C.502 A.B. L.477 J.D. 402 W. Ojai Ave., Suite 103
Knicely, Clarke A. ...................................................... '17 '49 2276 Sumac Dr.‡
Lucking, William A., Jr., (AV) ...... '17 '50 C.197 A.B. L.477 J.D. 14845 Maricopa Hwy.
Malley, Thomas E., (BV) '44 '70 C.524 B.S. L.1065 J.D.
550 Del Oro Dr. (⊙Camarillo)
Molineaux, Jeanne E. ................... '45 '79 C.477 B.A. L.1137 J.D. 1406 La Paz Dr.
Osborne, Edwin M. ..............................'32 '60 C.910 A.B. L.1068 J.D. Ret. Supr. Ct. J.
Petersdorf, Rudolph ....................'30 '54 C.112 B.A. L.1066 LL.B. 930 N. Signal St.
Peyronnin, Edgar U. ............................ '15 '56 C.420 B.S. L.809 LL.B. 1907 Tiara‡
Recht, Orville F., (AV) .................. '34 '60 C.659 B.S.E. L.309 J.D. 323 E. Matilija‡
Schechter, Dorothy L., (AV) ............. '34 '65 C&L.800 B.S.L., LL.B. [T.L.Schechter]
Schechter, Thomas L., (BV) ............... '33 '60 C&L.800 B.A., LL.B. [T.L.Schechter] ‡
Schechter, Thomas L., A Prof. Corp., (AV) ..........................10432 Ojai Santa Paula Rd.
Shaw, Mary D. ......................... '30 '63 C.112 B.A. L.1065 J.D. 544 Gorham Rd.
Smithers, Brett .............................. '21 '49 C.867 L.174 LL.B. 1296 Foothill Rd.‡
Soares, Robert J. ..................... '31 '59 C.112 B.S. L.1066 LL.B. Ret. Supr. Ct. J.
Teegarden, Lewis C., (AV) ........................'05 '38 C.112 L.809 J.D. 701 N. Montgomery‡
Thatcher, Dickinson, (AV) ........................'19 '48 C.112 B.S. L.813 J.D. 211 Bristol Rd.‡
Verrastro, Gaetano J. .................'52 '79 C.665 B.A. L.809 J.D. 11617 Sulphur Mt. Rd.
Watnick, Brian D. ............................ '58 '88 C.112 L.1067 J.D. 603 W. Ojai Ave.

## OLEMA, —, *Marin Co.*

Dever, Charles H. '22 '63 C&L.477 B.B.A., J.D.
(adm. in MI; not adm. in CA) 9876 Sir Francis Drake‡

## OLYMPIC VALLEY, —, *Placer Co.*

Fenolio, Ronald L., (BV) .................. '43 '68 C.112 B.S. L.1065 J.D. P.O. Box 3725
Smith, Megan G. ........................... '60 '87 C.112 B.A. L.813 J.D. P.O. Box 3670

CAA442P

Wendt, Nancy R. ..........'44 '75 C.174 B.A. L.790 J.D. Coun., Squaw Valley Ski Corp.

## ONTARIO, 133,179, *San Bernardino Co.*

Allen, David B., (AV) .................. '31 '59 C.878 B.A. L.813 LL.B. [Ⓒ Allen,R.&S.]
**Allen, Tom M**, (BV) .................. '46 '77 C&L.1137 B.S.L., J.D. [Ⓐ Hemer,B.&C.]⊙
*PRACTICE AREAS: Medical Malpractice Defense.
Allen, Rhodes & Sobelsohn, LLP, (AV)
3281 Guasti Road, Suite 800 (⊙L.A., Santa Barbara, Santa Ana & Palm Desert)
**Anderson, Jette R.**, (BV) ................'44 '78 C.684 B.A. L.990 J.D. [Covington&C.]
*PRACTICE AREAS: Real Property Law; Management Employee Relations Law; General Business Law; Probate Law; Estate Planning Law.
Andrews, Jay B. Schiegg '41 '74 C.665 B.A. L.229 J.D.
(adm. in PA; not adm. in CA) 604 E. Hawthorne St.‡
Bailey-Jones, Bonnie B., (BV) ...'45 '83 C.028 B.A. L.398 J.D. 3602 Inland Empire Blvd.
**Barkus, Ramune E.** .....................'49 '79 C.991 B.A. L.809 J.D. [Hemer,B.&C.]⊙
*LANGUAGES: Lithuanian and French.
*PRACTICE AREAS: Medical Malpractice Defense.
**Barmack, Peter M.**, (BV) .................. '50 '81 C.112 A.B. L.398 J.D. [Best B.&K.]
*PRACTICE AREAS: Taxation Law.
Bentley, Gregory L. .... '64 '90 C.1109 B.S.L. L.1137 J.D. 3401 Centrelake Dr., Suite 650

**Best Best & Krieger LLP, (AV)**
**A California Limited Liability Partnership including Professional Corporations**
**800 North Haven, Suite 120, 91764⊙**
**Telephone: 909-989-8584 Fax: 909-944-1441**
**Resident Partners: Meredith A. Jury (P.C.); Wynne S. Furth; Stephen P. Deitsch; Peter M. Barmack; Dennis M. Cota. Resident Associates: Kevin K. Randolph; Richard T. Egger; Sonia Rubio Carvalho; Karen M. Lewis; Jeffrey T. Melching.**
**General Civil and Trial Practice. Corporation, Water Rights, Probate, Trusts and Estate Planning, Real Estate, Municipal, Bankruptcy Litigation, Environmental Law and Toxic Waste.**
**Riverside, California Office: 400 Mission Square, 3750 University Avenue, P.O. Box: 1028. Telephone: 909-686-1450. Fax: 909-686-3083; 909-682-4612.**
**Rancho Mirage, California Office: Hope Square Professional Centre, 39700 Bob Hope Drive, Suite 312, P.O. Box: 1555. Telephone: 619-568-2611. Fax: 619-340-6698; 619-341-7039.**
**San Diego, California Office: 402 West Broadway, 13th Floor. Telephone: 619-525-1300. Fax: 619-233-6118.**
**Victorville, California Office: High Desert Corporate Pointe Building, 14350 Civic Drive, Suite 270. Telephone: 619-245-4127. Fax: 619-245-6437.**
***See Professional Biographies, ONTARIO, CALIFORNIA***

Blackwell, Walter L., III .............'45 '70 C.684 B.A. L.1068 J.D. 427 N. Euclid Ave.
**Borenstein, Howard S.** ...............'59 '85 C.1077 B.S. L.809 J.D. [Ⓐ Covington&C.]
*PRACTICE AREAS: Taxation Law; Tax Controversy; Business Law.
Brantley, Teresa M. ........... '61 '92 C.1075 B.S. L.398 J.D. 3602 Inland Empire Blvd.
Burdman, Scott A., (A P.C.), (AV) '55 '81
C.610 B.B.A. L.61 J.D. [Silldorf,B.D.&E.] (⊙San Diego)
Callas, James C. ............................'51 '77 C.112 B.A. L.285 J.D. [Allen,R.&S.]
**Carvalho, Sonia Rubio** ..................'67 '92 C.112 B.A. L.1068 J.D. [Ⓐ Best B.&K.]
*PRACTICE AREAS: Municipal Law; Redevelopment Law; Land Use Law.
**Chesnut, Kristen L.** ....................'48 '90 C.740 B.A. L.284 J.D. [Ⓐ Hemer,B.&C.]⊙
*PRACTICE AREAS: Medical Malpractice Defense.
Cihigoyenetche, Jean, (BV) .......'57 '82 C.1074 B.S. L.990 J.D. [Cihigoyenetche,G.&C.]
Cihigoyenetche, Grossberg & Clouse, (BV) ................ 3602 Inland Empire Blvd.
**Clark, Bradley C.** ........................'55 '83 C.684 B.S. L.999 J.D. [Hemer,B.&C.]⊙
*PRACTICE AREAS: Medical Malpractice Defense.
Clouse, Richard R., (BV) ......... '57 '83 C.766 B.A. L.464 J.D. [Cihigoyenetche,G.&C.]
Coberly, E. Clark ..........'48 '78 C.1097 B.A. L.990 J.D. Corp. Coun., Calif. Pools, Inc.
Cohen, Stephen M. ..................... '60 '86 C.1042 B.S. L.940 J.D. 3350 Shelby St.
**Cota, Dennis M.** ...........................'58 '87 C.112 B.S. L.1067 J.D. [Best B.&K.]
Covington, Maurice G., (AV) ........... '09 '34 C.668 A.B. L.309 LL.B. 1131 W. 6th St.

**Covington & Crowe, (AV) BR**
**1131 West Sixth Street, P.O. Box 1515, 91762**
**Telephone: 909-983-9393 Fax: 909-391-6762**
**Email: covcrowe@ix.netcom.com**
**Members of Firm: Harold A. Bailin (1930-1988); Samuel P. Crowe (Certified Specialist, Taxation Law, The State Bar of California Board of Legal Specialization); George W. Porter (Certified Specialist, Criminal Law, The State Bar of California Board of Legal Specialization); Robert E. Dougherty; Donald G. Haslam (Certified Specialist, Family Law, The State Bar of California Board of Legal Specialization); Robert F. Schauer; Edward A. Hopson; Stephen R. Wade; Jette R. Anderson; Audrey A. Perri (Certified Specialist, Family Law, The State Bar of California Board of Legal Specialization); Tracy L. Tibbals; Melanie Fisch; Robert H. Reeder; R. Doug Donesky; Tammy S. Jager. Associates: Howard S. Borenstein; Denise Matthey; Katrina West; Richard R. Muir; Kimberly A. Rohn; J. Michael Kaler; Eric S. Vail.**
**General Civil and Trial Practice. Corporations, Municipal, Real Estate, Estate Planning, Trust, Probate, Family, Labor Law, Criminal Defense, Bankruptcy, Creditor's Rights and Water Rights Law.**
***See Professional Biographies, ONTARIO, CALIFORNIA***

**Crowe, Samuel P.**, (AV) ..................'35 '61 C.112 B.A. L.800 J.D. [Covington&C.]
*PRACTICE AREAS: Corporations Law; Partnerships Law; Estate Planning Law.
Davis, Monte R., Jr., (CV) .....'53 '81 C&L.398 B.A., J.D. 3401 Centrelake Dr., Suite 650
**Deitsch, Stephen P.** ..................... '48 '74 C.1036 B.A. L.659 J.D. [Best B.&K.]
Dennis, Louis Jay ..........................'— '92 C.112 B.A. L.770 J.D. 1131 W. 6th St.
Dinces, Jerard M. ......................'49 '78 C.415 B.A. L.1137 J.D. 615 N. Euclid Ave.
**Donesky, R. Doug** ..................... '60 '87 C.636 B.S. L.1067 J.D. [Covington&C.]
*PRACTICE AREAS: Civil Litigation; Real Estate Litigation.
Dong, Daniel Louis ................................'56 '82 C&L.800 B.S., J.D. 1047 W. 6th St.
**Dougherty, Robert E.**, (BV) ........... '37 '68 C.112 B.S. L.1068 J.D. [Covington&C.]
*PRACTICE AREAS: Municipal Law; General Civil Litigation; Water Rights Law.
**Egger, Richard T.** ........................ '67 '92 C.112 B.A. L.1067 J.D. [Ⓐ Best B.&K.]
*PRACTICE AREAS: Business Litigation; Public Law Litigation; Bankruptcy Litigation.
Evans, Richard J., (BV) ................... '27 '59 C.800 B.A. L.809 LL.B. 201 W. F St.
Eye, Charles T. ..........................................'34 '73 C.999 L.990 J.D. P.O. Box 1666‡
**Fisch, Melanie** ..........................'50 '85 C.112 B.A. L.770 J.D. [Covington&C.]
*PRACTICE AREAS: Civil Litigation.
Frost, Douglas C. ..........................'55 '83 C.813 A.B. L.1049 J.D. 1131 W.6th St.
**Furth, Wynne S.**, (AV) ......................... '47 '73 C.813 B.A. L.309 J.D. [Best B.&K.]
Garfunkel, Jeffrey A., (BV) ............'56 '82 C.93 B.A. L.1137 J.D. 800 N. Haven Ave.
**Gassner, Beverly J.**, (BV) ................. '31 '77 C.119 B.S. L.398 J.D. [Gassner&G.]
*PRACTICE AREAS: Family Law.
**Gassner, Lawrence M.**, (BV) .............. '32 '66 C.119 B.S. L.426 J.D. [Gassner&G.]
*PRACTICE AREAS: Family Law; Interstate Custody; Probate; Appeals.

**Gassner & Gassner, A Professional Corporation, (BV)**
**337 North Vineyard Avenue, Suite 205, 91764**
**Telephone: 909-983-1352 Fax: 909-391-0096**
**Lawrence M. Gassner (Certified Specialist, Family Law, The State Bar of California Board of Legal Specialization); Beverly J. Gassner (Certified Specialist, Family Law, The State Bar of California Board of Legal Specialization).**
**Family, Juvenile, Interstate Custody and Related Litigation. Appellate Practice.**
***See Professional Biographies, ONTARIO, CALIFORNIA***

Gillen, David M. ......................'64 '91 C.1068 B.A. L.426 J.D. P.O. Box 51464
Goldstein, David M. ........................................... '61 '85 [Maricic&G.]
**Gonzalez, Richard I.** ..................'67 '91 C.1110 B.A. L.990 J.D. [Ⓐ Hemer,B.&C.]⊙
*PRACTICE AREAS: Medical Malpractice Defense.
Grossberg, Scott J. ............... '58 '86 C.1075 B.A. L.398 J.D. [Cihigoyenetche,G.&C.]
**Haslam, Donald G.**, (AV) ..............'42 '70 C.112 A.B. L.1066 J.D. [Covington&C.]
Heise, W. Steven ............................'50 '85 C.999 B.A. L.398 J.D. [Allen,R.&S.]
**Hemer, Ralph S.**, (AV) ...................................'31 '62 [Hemer,B.&C.]⊙
*LANGUAGES: German.

**Hemer, Barkus & Clark, (AV) BR**
**3401 Centre Lake Drive, Suite 400, 91764⊙**
**Telephone: 909-467-0660 Fax: 909-390-3628**
**Ralph S. Hemer; Ramune E. Barkus; Bradley C. Clark. Associates: Kristen L. Chesnut; Tom M Allen; Richard I. Gonzalez.**
**Civil Trial and Appellate Practice. Medical and Legal Professional Liability, Products Liability, Negligence and Insurance Law.**
**Glendale, California Office: 550 N. Brand, Suite 1800, 91202-6002. Telephone: 818-241-8999. Fax: 818-241-2014.**
***See Professional Biographies, ONTARIO, CALIFORNIA***

**Henke, Robert E.** ..............'63 '90 C&L.608 B.A., J.D. [Ⓐ McClaugherty&Assoc.]⊙
*PRACTICE AREAS: Insurance Defense.
**Hopson, Edward A.**, (BV) ...............'47 '72 C.668 B.A. L.800 J.D. [Covington&C.]
*PRACTICE AREAS: Real Property Law; Real Estate Development Law; Real Estate Finance Law.
**Hoyt, Anastasia Swiatek** .... '64 '92 C.800 B.A. L.990 J.D. [Ⓐ McClaugherty&Assoc.]⊙
*PRACTICE AREAS: Insurance Defense.
Hudson, Thomas R., (BV) ................'37 '64 C.767 B.S. L.1065 LL.B. [T.R.Hudson]
Hudson, Thomas R., A Prof. Law Corp., Law Offices of, (BV)
3602 Inland Empire Blvd.
Izsak, Rory D. .........................'57 '85 C.30 B.S. L.861 J.D. 3045 S. Archibald Ave.
**Jager, Tammy S.** .......................'63 '89 C.1109 B.A. L.398 J.D. [Covington&C.]
*PRACTICE AREAS: Civil Litigation; Construction Law; Business Law.
**Jury, Meredith A., (P.C.)**, (BV) ........... '47 '76 C.174 B.A. L.1068 J.D. [Best B.&K.]
*PRACTICE AREAS: Business Litigation Law; Land Use and Natural Resources Law; Real Property Litigation; Bankruptcy Litigation Law.
**Kaler, J. Michael** .................... '59 '92 C.531 B.S. L.1049 J.D. [Ⓐ Covington&C.]
*PRACTICE AREAS: Business Litigation; Civil Litigation; Trial Practice; Municipal Law.
Kallins, Barbara A. ..................... '59 '86 C.800 B.A. L.426 J.D. 1131 W. 6th St.
Karikas, Peter G., (BV) ...................'46 '73 C.112 A.B. L.1065 J.D. [Allen,R.&S.]

**Kinkle, Rodiger and Spriggs, Professional Corporation**
**(See Riverside)**

Klinkert, James E. .......................'54 '84 C.1109 B.M. L.426 J.D. [Ritchie,K.&M.]
Kloepfer, Lynn W., (BV) ...........'13 '38 C.877 B.S. L.1066 J.D. 306 E. Hawthorne St.
Lance, Bruce J., Jr., (BV) ................ '30 '61 C.636 L.426 LL.B. 204 N. San Antonio
Lander, Daryl J. ......................... '58 '89 C.1109 B.S. L.1137 J.D. 1131 W. 6th St.
Langevin, Richard P. ..................... '56 '88 C.823 B.S. L.1137 J.D. 1063 W. 6th St.
Larson, Daniel N. '54 '81 C.221 B.A. L.976 J.D.
(adm. in CO; not adm. in CA) Pres., Kaiser Res., Inc.
**Lewis, Karen M.** ...........................'59 '95 C&L.1190 B.S., J.D. [Ⓐ Best B.&K.]
*PRACTICE AREAS: Litigation; Bankruptcy; Public Law.
Lindars, Arthur P., (BV) .............................'43 '75 L.398 LL.B. 3401 Centrelarke Dr.
Lopez, Eduardo, (AV) .....................'52 '79 C.976 B.A. L.800 J.D. [Ⓐ Allen,R.&S.]
Maricic, George, (CV) ............... '53 '83 C.1074 B.S.L. L.1137 J.D. [Maricic&G.]
Maricic & Goldstein, (CV) ........................................ 800 N. Haven Ave.
**Matthey, Denise** ................'45 '90 C.684 B.S.B.A. L.1049 J.D. [Ⓐ Covington&C.]
*PRACTICE AREAS: Family Law.
McCallion, James, (BV) ....................'51 '79 C.112 B.A. L.398 J.D. [Ritchie,K.&M.]
**McClaugherty, Jay S.**, (BV) '52 '81 C.1058 B.A. L.1049 J.D.
[McClaugherty&Assoc.]⊙
*LANGUAGES: Norwegian.
*REPORTED CASES: Valdez v. Smith (1985) 166 Cal. App. 3d 723; Holmes v. Roth (1992) 11 Cal. App. 4th 931.
*PRACTICE AREAS: High Exposure Personal Injury; Insurance Defense.

**McClaugherty & Associates, (BV)**
**3350 Shelby Street Suite 200, 91764⊙**
**Telephone: 909-944-2505**
**Jay S. McClaugherty. Associates: Robert E. Henke; Jeffrey B. Smith; Anastasia Swiatek Hoyt.**
**Insurance Defense, General Civil Trial in all State and Federal Court.**
**Pasadena, California Office: 301 North Lake Avenue, Suite 800, 91101. Telephone: 818-449-7522. FAX: 818-583-9187.**
***See Professional Biographies, ONTARIO, CALIFORNIA***

**Melching, Jeffrey T.** .................... '69 '95 C.112 B.A. L.1067 J.D. [Ⓐ Best B.&K.]
*PRACTICE AREAS: Litigation; Bankruptcy.
**Muir, Richard R.** ........................'58 '88 C.20 B.A. L.1049 J.D. [Ⓐ Covington&C.]
*PRACTICE AREAS: Business Law; Estate and Succession Planning; Taxation; ERISA; Qualified Domestic Relations Orders (QDRO's).
Murphy, Cheryl C. ..................... '62 '90 C.763 B.S. L.1137 J.D. 1063 W. 6th St,
Nickerson, Nancy E. ....... '45 '87 C.773 B.A. L.426 J.D. 3401 Centrelake Dr., Suite 650
Peach, Timothy W., (BV) ............... '53 '79 C&L.1137 B.S.L., J.D. [Peach&W.]⊙
Peach & Weathers, A Law Corporation, (BV)
337 N. Vineyard Ave., Suite 300 (⊙San Bernardino & Riverside)
**Perri, Audrey A.**, (BV) ..................'36 '76 C.684 B.A. L.398 J.D. [Covington&C.]
*PRACTICE AREAS: Family Law.
Polakovic, John M., (BV) ...............'36 '71 C&L.1127 LL.B. 3401 Centre Lake Dr.
**Porter, George W.**, (AV) ...............'30 '59 C.684 A.B. L.1066 J.D. [Covington&C.]
*REPORTED CASES: Progress Bulletin Pub Co. v. Superior Court 29 CA3 815, 105 Cal.Rptr. 873.
*PRACTICE AREAS: Criminal Defense Law; Business Litigation; Professional Disciplinary Hearings.
**Randolph, Kevin K.** ......................'58 '90 C.1075 B.S. L.426 J.D. [Ⓐ Best B.&K.]
*PRACTICE AREAS: Water Rights Law; Environmental Law; Litigation Law.
**Reeder, Robert H.** .......................'61 '86 C.112 B.A. L.800 J.D. [Covington&C.]
*PRACTICE AREAS: Business Law.
Reichert, Stanford E. ......................... '52 '78 C.878 B.A. L.178 J.D. 2143 E. D St.

**Reid & Hellyer, A Professional Corporation**
**(See Riverside)**

Ritchie, Thomas B., (BV) ................'47 '77 C.684 B.S. L.398 J.D. [Ritchie,K.&M.]
Ritchie, Klinkert & McCallion, (BV) ................................ 3281 Guasti Rd.
**Rohn, Kimberly A.** ...................'58 '91 C.909 B.A. L.398 J.D. [Ⓐ Covington&C.]
*PRACTICE AREAS: Business Law; Corporate Law; Municipal Law.
**Schauer, Robert F.**, (BV) ...............'45 '71 C.112 A.B. L.1067 J.D. [Covington&C.]
*PRACTICE AREAS: Construction and Commercial Litigation; Deferred Compensation Plans; General Corporate; Business.

**Schessler, John, (AV) '28 '49 C&L.790 A.B., J.D.**
**218 West E Street, 91762**
**Telephone: 909-986-2095 Fax: 909-391-0058**
**Corporation, Probate, Trust, Taxation and Real Estate Law.**
**Reference: First Interstate Bank (Ontario, California).**
***See Professional Biographies, ONTARIO, CALIFORNIA***

Schmidt, Raymond A. ........................ '40 '72 Coun., Lockheed Aircraft Serv. Co.
Sessa, Bruce Eugene ........... '37 '85 C.112 M.B.A. L.1198 J.D. 746 W. La Deney Dr.
Sharpless, Susan M. .................................'— '92 3602 Island Empire Blvd.

CAA443P

CALIFORNIA—ONTARIO MARTINDALE-HUBBELL LAW DIRECTORY 1997

Silldorf, Burdman, Duignan & Eisenberg, (AV)
3533 Inland Empire Blvd., Ste. 17 (⊙San Diego, Newport Beach)
Smith, Felix E., (AV) . . . . . . '39 '65 C.94 B.A. L.93 J.D. 800 N. Haven Ave.
Smith, H. Charles, (CV) . . . . . . '48 '79 L.1221 J.D. 615 N. Euclid Ave.
**Smith, Jeffrey B.** . . . . . . '65 '91 C.800 A.B. L.464 J.D. [Ⓐ McClaughery&Assoc.]⊙
*PRACTICE AREAS: Insurance Defense Litigation.
Smith, Judith A. . . . . . . '39 '79 C.1042 L.398 J.D. 1055 N. Euclid Ave.
Smith, Stephen R. . . . . . . '40 '73 C.353 B.A. L.981 LL.D. 337 N. Vineyard , 4th Fl.
Teunisse, Patricia A. . . . . . . '63 '88 C.800 B.A. L.464 J.D. 1131 W. 6th St.
**Tibbals, Tracy L., (BV)** . . . . . . '45 '74 C.112 B.A. L.61 J.D. [Covington&C.]
*LANGUAGES: German and Spanish.
*PRACTICE AREAS: Civil Litigation.
**Vail, Eric S.** . . . . . . '66 '92 C.1074 B.A. L.464 J.D. [Ⓐ Covington&C.]
*PRACTICE AREAS: Municipal Law; Civil Litigation.
Van Frank, Richard W. . . . . . '62 '90 C.1074 B.S. L.846 J.D. 3401 Centrelake Dr., Suite 650
**Wade, Stephen R., (BV)** . . . . . . '51 '78 C.112 B.A. L.1068 J.D. [Covington&C.]
*PRACTICE AREAS: Bankruptcy Law; Creditor's Rights Law.
Weathers, William W., (BV) . . . . . . '52 '77 C.112 B.A. L.1137 J.D. [Peach&W.]⊙
**West, Katrina** . . . . . . '63 '90 C.104 A.B. L.1068 J.D. [Ⓐ Covington&C.]
*PRACTICE AREAS: Family Law.

## ORANGE, 110,658, *Orange Co.*

Adams, John Q., (BV) . . . . . . '43 '74 L.990 J.D. 1421 N. Wanda Rd.
Adams, Robert B. . . . . . . '49 '75 C.112 A.B. L.464 J.D. 170 S. Main St.

**Agapay, Levyn & Halling, A Professional Corporation, (AV)**
**One City Boulevard West, Suite 835, 92668⊙**
**Telephone: 714-634-1744 Fax: 714-634-0417**
**—Glen R. Segal.**
**General Civil Practice. Real Estate, Construction, Corporation, Computer Law, Business, Banking, Unfair Competition, Taxation, Commercial Law and Related Litigation and Risk Management.**
**Los Angeles, California Office: Fourth Floor, 10801 National Boulevard, 90064. Telephone: 310-470-1700. Fax: 310-470-2602.**
***See Professional Biographies, ORANGE, CALIFORNIA***

**Agren, Carl F., (BV)** . . . . . . '44 '71 C.1042 B.S. L.426 J.D. [Agren&W.]
*PRACTICE AREAS: Business Litigation; Corporate Law; Insolvency; Taxation; Estate Planning.

**Agren & Werner LLP, (BV)**
**Suite 1210, 333 City Boulevard, West, 92868**
**Telephone: 714-634-8999 Fax: 714-634-2704**
**Members of Firm: Lee G. Werner; Carl F. Agren.**
**Business Litigation, Insolvency, Corporate Law, Real Estate, Taxation, Estate Planning and Probate.**
***See Professional Biographies, ORANGE, CALIFORNIA***

**Agrusa, Lisa M.** . . . . . . '64 '90 C.112 B.A. L.426 J.D. [Ⓐ Hillsinger&C.]
Aitken Irvin Lewin Berlin Vrooman & Cohn, LLP
500 North State College Boulevard Suite 1200 (⊙Washington, D.C.; Fulton, MD; White Plains, NY)
Aldrich, Theodore F. . . . . . . '53 '81 C.1060 B.A. L.464 J.D. [Ⓐ Mercer&Z.]
Allen, David E., Jr. . . . . . . '48 '77 C.806 B.A. L.61 J.D. [Ⓐ P.J.Gorelick]

**Alvarado, Smith, Villa & Sanchez, A Professional Corporation**
**(See Newport Beach)**

Anderson, John F., (BV) . . . . . . '42 '72 C&L.1137 B.S.L., J.D. 1745 W. Orangewood Ave.
**Andrus, Terry C.** . . . . . . '44 '73 C.477 A.B. L.426 J.D. [Woodruff,S.&S.]
*PRACTICE AREAS: Employment Law; Governmental Law.
**Anton, James A.** . . . . . . '62 '89 C.112 B.A. L.1137 J.D. [Walsworth,F.B.&M.]
*REPORTED CASES: City of San Diego v. U.S. Gypsum, 30 Cal. App. 4th 575, 35 Cal. rptr. 2d 876 (1994).
*PRACTICE AREAS: Business Litigation; Construction Litigation; Environmental Litigation.
Arroyo, Joseph A. '42 '69 C.426 B.A. L.1068 J.D.
(adm. in DC; not adm. in CA) 2120 E. Denise Ave.★
**Astor, John Kelly, (AV)** . . . . . . '57 '83 C.800 B.A. L.1137 J.D. [Astor&P.]
*PRACTICE AREAS: Solid and Hazardous Waste; Environmental Law; Governmental Affairs; Corporate Law; Family Law.
**Astor, Z. Harry, (AV)** . . . . . . '22 '49 C&L.800 A.B., J.D. [Ⓒ Astor&P.]
*PRACTICE AREAS: Corporate Law; Business Law; Probate Law; Governmental Affairs.

**Astor & Phillips, A Professional Law Corporation, (AV)**
**333 City Boulevard West, 17th Floor, 92668-2924⊙**
**Telephone: 714-634-8050 Facsimile: 714-634-8469**
**John Kelly Astor (Resident). Of Counsel: Z. Harry Astor (Resident);—Lya Kingsland-Canada (Resident).**
**Business, Real Estate, Corporate, Estate Planning, Probate, Taxation, Solid Waste Management/ Environmental Law. General Trial Practice in Business, Real Estate, Eminent Domain, Commercial Law, and Trust Litigation, Governmental Affairs, Family Law.**
**Los Angeles, California Office: 800 Wilshire Boulevard, Fifteenth Floor. Telephone: 213-680-9212.**
***See Professional Biographies, ORANGE, CALIFORNIA***

Atkinson, George E., III, (BV) . . . . . . '40 '66 C.112 B.A. L.1065 J.D. 500 N. State Coll.
Bailey, Julian W., Jr., (BV) . . . . . . '48 '74 C&L.112 B.A., J.D. [Bailey&B.]
Bailey & Brott, (BV) . . . . . . 333 City Blvd., W.
Baker, Bonnie Ann . . . . . '44 '76 C.1042 B.A. L.426 J.D. 333 City Blvd., W. (⊙Riverside)
Bakerink, Jeffrey S. . . . . . . '58 '89 C.800 B.S. L.1137 J.D. 721 S. Parker St.
Barson, Nora M. . . . . . . '58 '84 C.612 B.A. L.623 J.D. 1820 W. Orangewood Ave.
Barthrop, John A., Jr. . . . . . . '42 '69 C.911 B.A. L.1065 J.D. One City Blvd. W.
**Batchelor, James K., (AV)** . . . . . . '34 '60 C.1042 A.B. L.1065 J.D. [J.K.Batchelor]

**Batchelor, James K., A Professional Corporation, (AV) BB**
**765 South The City Drive Suite 270, 92668**
**Telephone: 714-750-8388; 714-542-2333 Fax: 714-750-8002**
**James K. Batchelor (Certified Specialist, Family Law, The State Bar of California Board of Legal Specialization).**
**Practice limited to Family Law.**
**Reference: Wells Fargo Bank**
***See Professional Biographies, ORANGE, CALIFORNIA***

**Bauer, Bruce T.** . . . . . . '64 '90 C.1042 B.S. L.426 J.D. [Ⓐ Fabozzi,T.&C.]
*LANGUAGES: Spanish.
*PRACTICE AREAS: Banking Litigation; Commercial Litigation; Business Law; Business Insurance; Bankruptcy.
**Bebb, David G.** . . . . . . '64 '89 C.112 B.A. L.1049 J.D. [Ⓐ Landau,O.&K.]
*PRACTICE AREAS: Professional Liability; Construction Defects; Directors and Officers Liability; Personal Injury.
**Bennett, Kelly A.** . . . . . . '65 '91 C&L.990 B.S., J.D. [Ⓒ W.P.Bennett]
*PRACTICE AREAS: Business Litigation; Construction Litigation; Corporations; Contracts.
**Bennett, William P., (AV)** . . . . . . '38 '64 C.1042 B.A. L.800 J.D. [W.P.Bennett]
*PRACTICE AREAS: Family Law; Real Property Law; General Civil Litigation.

**Bennett, William P., A P.L.C., (AV) BB**
**333 City Boulevard West, Suite 1810, 92668**
**Telephone: 714-978-3293 FAX: 714-634-3688**
**William P. Bennett. Of Counsel: Kelly A. Bennett.**
**Family Law, Real Estate and General Civil Litigation.**
***See Professional Biographies, ORANGE, CALIFORNIA***

Bergen, Robert C. . . . . . . '53 '78 C.112 A.B. L.464 J.D. 500 N. State Coll. Blvd.

**Bergstrom, Charles E., (BV) '42 '74 C&L.1137 B.S.L., J.D.**
**770 The City Drive Suite 8000, 92668-4956**
**Telephone: 714-750-0400 Fax: 714-740-1412**
**(Certified Specialist, Family Law, The State Bar of California Board of Legal Specialization).**
**Family Law and Juvenile Dependency. Abandonment.**
***See Professional Biographies, ORANGE, CALIFORNIA***

Bernard, Richard J. . . . . . . '55 '82 C.1042 B.A. L.1137 J.D. Lancer Claims Servs., Inc.

**Besser, Barry I., (BV) '52 '79 C.1077 B.S. L.1137 J.D.**
**333 City Boulevard West Suite 1700, 92668**
**Telephone: 714-978-1788 Fax: 714-938-3252**
***PRACTICE AREAS: Personal Injury Law; Family Law; Criminal Defense.**
**Family Law, Custody, Visitation Support, Criminal Law, Juvenile Criminal Law, Civil Litigation, Personal Injury, Auto, Slip and Fall.**
***See Professional Biographies, ORANGE, CALIFORNIA***

**Betley, William M.** . . . . . . '54 '84 C.690 B.A. L.809 J.D. [Ⓐ Morris,P.&P.]
Bevins, Ronald H., (AV) . . . . . . '33 '58 C&L.426 J.D. 333 City Blvd. W.
**Bevins, Ronald H., Jr., (BV)** . . . . . . '58 '83 C&L.426 B.A., J.D. [Walsworth,F.B.&M.]
Bhakta, Hitendra . . . . . . '59 '87 L.061 LL.B. 500 N. State College Blvd.
**Bialosky, David L., (AV) '58 '85 C.197 A.B. L.597 J.D.**
(adm. in OH; not adm. in CA) Sr. Coun., TRW Info. Systems & Servs. Grp.
Bilas, Jeffrey D. . . . . . . '61 '88 C.896 B.A. L.1148 J.D. 500 N. State Coll. Blvd.
**Binning, Mary E.** . . . . . . '59 '92 C.276 B.S. L.1049 J.D. [Ⓐ Woodruff,S.&S.]
*LANGUAGES: French, German.
*PRACTICE AREAS: Municipal Law.
Blackburn, Michael P. . . . . . . '45 '83 C.801 B.A. L.1137 J.D. [Mercer&Z.] (⊙Lafayette)

**Blaine, Dorothea C. R., P.C.**
**(See Santa Ana)**

Blanpied, Lloyd E., Jr. '23 '52
C.112 B.S. L.813 J.D. Jud. Arbitration & Mediation Servs. Inc.‡
Blaser, Arthur W. . . . . . . '53 '90 C.911 B.A. L.809 J.D. Assoc. Prof., Chapman Univ.
**Block, Elliott J.** . . . . . . '61 '90 C.188 B.S. L.46 J.D. [Ⓐ Hollins,S.&F.]
*PRACTICE AREAS: Litigation; Transactional; Business Law; Insurance Law.

**Bloom, David B., A Prof. Corp., Law Offices of**
**(See Los Angeles)**

Blum, Melanie R. . . . . . . '49 '81 C.1077 B.A. L.426 J.D. [Blum&R.]
Blum and Roseman, A Prof. Corp., (BV) . . . . . . 505 S. Main St.
**Bobak, M. Lois** . . . . . . '61 '87 C.112 B.A. L.464 J.D. [Woodruff,S.&S.]
*PRACTICE AREAS: Municipal Law; Writs and Appeals.
**Bonetati, Marilyn L.** . . . . . . '48 '85 C.800 B.S. L.1137 J.D. [Landau,O.&K.]
*PRACTICE AREAS: Professional E & O Defense; Products Liability Defense; Auto Defense; Construction.
**Boon, Alan H.** . . . . . . '54 '83 C.112 B.A. L.426 J.D. [Ⓐ Hagenbaugh&M.]
Booth, James C., (AV) . . . . . . '34 '61 C&L.477 B.B.A., J.D. [J.C.Booth]
**Booth, Laura M.** . . . . . . '70 '95 C.36 B.S. L.1049 J.D. [Ⓐ Hillsinger&C.]
Booth, James C., Inc., A Professional Corporation, (AV) . . . . 333 City Bvld. W., Ste. 1810
Boyer, Joel Steven . . . . . . '61 '87 C.112 B.A. L.800 J.D. 701 S. Parker St.

**Brasser, Teresita Fajilan '49 '84 C.502 B.A. L.629 J.D.**
**City Tower, 333 City Boulevard West, Suite 1700, 92868**
**Telephone: 714-938-3226 Fax: 714-938-3227**
***LANGUAGES: French, Tagalog and Spanish.**
***PRACTICE AREAS: Family Law; Business Law; Immigration and Naturalization; Corporate Law; Personal Injury.**

Braun, Marlys Kinnel, II . . . . . . '66 '92 C.800 B.S. L.464 J.D. 505 S. Main St.
Bright, Charles T. . . . . . . '16 '61 C.112 L.1001 LL.B. 777 S. Main St.‡
Brislin, Sandra K. . . . . . . '58 '82 C&L.1137 B.S., J.D. 770 The City Dr. S.
Brott, James W., (BV) . . . . . . '48 '72 C&L.112 B.A., J.D. [Bailey&B.]
Brownstein, Mark . . . . . . '52 '76 C.112 B.A. L.1065 J.D. 636 N. Eckhoff‡
Bryant, Michael E. '55 '82 C.161 B.A. L.989 J.D.
(adm. in OH; not adm. in CA) P.O. Box 1034‡
**Burnett, Betty C.** . . . . . . '59 '88 C.1110 B.A. L.426 J.D. [Woodruff,S.&S.]
*PRACTICE AREAS: Environmental Law; Hazardous Materials Law.
Burns, Alan R., (AV) . . . . . . '48 '76 C.1109 B.A. L.990 J.D. [Harper&B.]
**Bush, Bryan R.** . . . . . . '62 '88 C.323 A.B. L.990 J.D. [Ⓐ Hollins,S.&F.]
*PRACTICE AREAS: Civil Litigation; Products Liability; Subrogation.
Caiazza, Pasquale P. . . . . . . '50 '76 C.999 B.S.B.A. L.1095 J.D. 606 E. Chapman Ave.
**Calderon, David R.** . . . . . . '64 '92 C.1075 B.A. L.990 J.D. [Ⓐ Elliot,L.L.&S.]
*LANGUAGES: Spanish.
*PRACTICE AREAS: Insurance Defense; Medical Malpractice Defense.
**Caley, Rebecca A.** . . . . . . '62 '87 C.1109 B.A. L.426 J.D. [Fabozzi,T.&C.]
*PRACTICE AREAS: Banking Law; Bankruptcy Law; Business Litigation.
Camardi, Thomas C., Jr. . . . . . . '51 '90 C&L.1137 B.S., J.D. 770 The City Dr. S.
Cannon, Jonathan H. . . . . . . '47 '72 C.1042 L.809 J.D. Supr. Ct. J.
**Canter, David H., (AV)** . . . . . '37 '65 C.679 B.S. L.800 J.D. [Harrington,F.D.&C.] (⊙L.A.)
*PRACTICE AREAS: Products Liability Law; Toxic Torts Law; Medical Malpractice Law.
Cardinale, Frank C., Jr. . . . . . . '53 '79 C.1042 B.S. L.426 J.D. 500 N. State Coll. Blvd.
Carrasco, Sue N. . . . . . . '54 '88 C.1109 B.A. L.1137 J.D. 333 S. Anita Dr.
Carroll, Beverly A. . . . . . . '41 '79 C.1109 B.A. L.1137 J.D. 292 N. Main St.‡
**Carter, Kathy** . . . . . . '66 '92 C.708 B.A. L.1194 J.D. [Ⓐ Marlin&S.]
*PRACTICE AREAS: Insurance Law; General Insurance Defense; Copyright Law; Trademark Law.
Carter, Roger R. . . . . . . '62 '89 2534 N. Santiago Blvd.
Cate, Kathleen A. . . . . . . '50 '92 C.765 B.A. L.1137 J.D. 4341 E. Chapman Ave.
**Cavanaugh, John E.** . . . . . . '54 '86 C.800 B.A. L.809 J.D. [Woodruff,S.&S.]
*LANGUAGES: French and German.
*PRACTICE AREAS: Municipal Law; Redevelopment.
Cesena, James H., (BV) . . . . . . '46 '77 C.1109 B.A. L.1137 J.D. [Cesena&L.]
Cesena & Lee, (BV) . . . . . . 745 W. Chapman Ave.
Chadwick, Douglas A. . . . . . . '40 '66 C.178 A.B. L.569 LL.B. 4000 Metropolitan Dr.

**Chatterton, Robert D., (AV) '39 '69 C.112 B.A. L.426 J.D.**
**1400 Bank of America Tower, One City Boulevard West, 92668**
**Telephone: 714-547-8484 Facsimile: 714-634-2153**
**Criminal and Juvenile.**
***See Professional Biographies, ORANGE, CALIFORNIA***

**Chesebro, Susan C.** . . . . . . '56 '82 C.112 B.A. L.770 J.D. [Ⓒ Testa&Assoc.]⊙
*REPORTED CASES: Hastings v. Matlock (1985) 171 Cal. App. 3d 826, 217 Cal. Rept. 856.
Christianson, David P. . . . . . '41 '67 C.813 B.A. L.1065 J.D. 725 W. Town & Country Rd.
**Chute, David M.** . . . . . . '63 '88 C.112 B.A. L.426 J.D. [Ⓐ Hagenbaugh&M.]
**Cipiti, Nicholas A.** . . . . . . '55 '81 C&L.426 B.A., J.D. [Walsworth,F.B.&M.]
Clark, Glenn H. . . . . . . '53 '79 C.939 B.A. L.1137 J.D. [Ⓐ Schmid&V.]
Clements, Thomas V. . . . . . . '58 '83 C.1169 B.A. L.809 J.D. [Mercer&Z.] (⊙San Diego)
Clemmer, Robert W., (BV) . . . . . . '35 '60 C&L.813 A.B., J.D. [R.W.Clemmer]
Clemmer, Robert W., P.C., (BV) . . . . . . 1122 E. Lincoln Ave.
**Cohen, Deidre F.** . . . . . . '67 '93 C.813 B.A. L.945 J.D. [Walsworth,F.B.&M.]
Cohen, Stephen I. . . . . . . '44 '76 C.184 B.A. L.990 J.D. 309 N. Wrightwood St.
Collender, Richard A., (BV) . . . . . . '45 '78 C.1222 B.B.S. L.990 J.D. 505 S. Main St.

**Collins, Richard T.** .................... '66 '93 C.112 A.B. L.1148 J.D. [Ⓐ Hollins,S.&F.]
*PRACTICE AREAS: Insurance Bad Faith; Insurance Coverage; General Civil Litigation.
Collins, Thomas A. ........................ '59 '84 C.848 B.A. L.990 J.D. [Ⓐ G.W.Sanders] ‡
Compasso, Jeffrey A. ...................... '64 '91 C.112 B.A. L.990 J.D. [Ⓐ Mercer&Z.]
**Condas, Thomas M.** '57 '84 C.878 B.S. L.1137 J.D.
[Hollins,S.&F.] (⊙Moreno Valley)
*PRACTICE AREAS: Personal Injury Defense Law; Construction Law; Products Liability Law; Worker's Compensation; Subrogation.
Conlin, H. Robert '52 '91 C.1111 B.A. L.426 J.D.
Litig. Supvr., United Servs. Automobile Assoc.
**Connelly, Kay Ann** ........................ '66 '91 C&L.464 B.A., J.D. [Ⓐ Morris,P.&P.]
**Conner, Christy L.** ........................ '60 '87 C.112 B.A. L.990 J.D. [Ⓐ Marlin&S.]
*PRACTICE AREAS: Products Liability; Homeowner Association Disputes.

**Cook, Bert '41 '86 C.381 B.S. L.1137 J.D.**
**333 City Boulevard West Suite 1700, 92868**
**Telephone: 714-938-3239 Facsimile: 714-938-3249**
**Practice Exclusive to Real Estate Law, Residential, Transactional, Litigation, Financing, Contracts, Leases, Foreclosures, Escrow, Title Claims, Mediation and Arbitration.**
***See Professional Biographies, ORANGE, CALIFORNIA***

Cook, Bert J. ........................ '41 '86 C.381 B.S. L.1137 J.D. 333 City Blvd. W.
Corral, John ........................ '44 '80 C.1131 L.1137 J.D. Liberty Mutual Ins. Grp.
Cottle, Bertrand E. .............. '46 '77 C.1109 B.A. L.1137 J.D. 1035 E. Chapman Ave.
Coulter, J. Greg ............. '69 '94 C.623 B.A. L.615 J.D. 12th Fl. 505 S. Main St.
Cowdrey, Michael L., (BV) .................. '44 '75 C.999 B.S. L.990 J.D. [Mercer&Z.]
Cowhig, John S. ........................ '67 '93 C.1109 B.A. L.809 770 The City Dr.
**Crafts, Jeffrey L.** ........................ '52 '78 C&L.426 B.A., J.D. [Gilbert,K.C.&J.]
*PRACTICE AREAS: Insurance Defense; Construction Defect; Employment Law.
Crost, Paul E., (AV) ................ '43 '67 C.112 B.A. L.1066 J.D. [Reich,A.C.&C.]⊙
Curtin, Judi A., (AV) ........................ '51 '78 C.37 B.A. L.398 J.D. [J.A.Curtin]
Curtin, Judi A., A Professional Corporation, (AV) .................... 333 City Blvd. W.
Dall, Terrance S. ........................ '58 '90 C.959 B.B.A. L.1137 J.D. [Ⓐ Mercer&Z.]
**Damon, Jennifer M.** ........................ '59 '84 C.112 B.A. L.426 J.D. [Gilbert,K.C.&J.]
Daniels, Donald L., (BV) ........... '26 '61 C.800 B.A. L.1001 J.D. 1224 E. Katella Ave.
**Darrow-Means, Tanja** .............. '68 '94 C.1068 B.A. L.1148 J.D. [Ⓐ Hollins,S.&F.]
*PRACTICE AREAS: Business Litigation; Insurance Law.
Daurio, Jon R. ................ '61 '87 C.309 A.B. L.800 J.D. 1100 Town & Country Rd.
Davis, Lucille G. ........................ '— '83 L.1137 J.D. 4418 E. Chapman Ave.
De Berry, David ........................ '56 '89 C.763 B.A. L.1137 J.D. 701 S. Parker St.
**DeBiaso, J. Rodney**, (AV) ............. '49 '81 C.893 B.A. L.1137 J.D. [Ⓐ Landau,O.&K.]
**DeBuys, Edward A.**, (AV) ............. '25 '54 C&L.426 B.B.A., LL.B. [Ⓑ Hillsinger&C.]
Delatorre, Richard P. ................ '54 '83 C.668 B.A. L.426 J.D. 770 The City Dr. S.
DeLeon, Joan D. ........................ '— '90 C.1110 B.A. L.1137 J.D. 7930 S. Santa Cruz
Demerdjian, Elise ........................ '58 '93 C.113 B.A. L.809 J.D. One City Blvd., W.
Deming, Judith E. .................. '46 '83 C&L.1137 B.S.L., J.D. 5334 Chapman Ave.
**Demmerle, Kenneth T.** ................... '65 '92 C.112 B.A. L.426 J.D. [Ⓐ Minyard&M.]
*PRACTICE AREAS: Family Law.
**DeNichilo, Robert M.** ........................ '67 '93 C.112 B.A. L.426 J.D. [Ⓐ Hollins,S.&F.]
*LANGUAGES: Italian.
*PRACTICE AREAS: Insurance Bad Faith; Business Litigation; Insurance Coverage.
Devore, Mark S. ........................ '67 '92 C.113 B.A. L.426 J.D. Dep. Pub. Def.
**DiRocco, Albert P., Jr.** .................. '58 '84 C.112 B.A. L.426 J.D. [Gilbert,K.C.&J.]
**Do, Dao-Mary** ........................ '69 '96 C.112 B.A. L.809 J.D. [Ⓐ Hollins,S.&F.]
*LANGUAGES: Vietnamese.
*PRACTICE AREAS: Personal Injury Defense; Insurance; Business Law; Real Estate; Construction Defect.
**Donohue, Robert F.** .................. '51 '83 C.999 B.A. L.851 J.D. [Hagenbaugh&M.]
*PRACTICE AREAS: Civil Rights Defense; Serious Bicycle Accident; Accounting Malpractice; Partnership; Business Litigation.
**Donovan, Gary N.**, (AV) ................ '55 '82 C.262 B.A. L.809 J.D. [Donovan&D.]⊙
*PRACTICE AREAS: Products Liability; Construction Liability; Premises Liability; Automobile Law; Professional, Architect and Real Estate Agent Malpractice.

**Donovan & Draheim, A Professional Corporation, (AV)**
**500 North State College Boulevard, Suite 500, 92868⊙**
**Telephone: 714-938-0123 Fax: 714-938-0603**
**Gary N. Donovan; Jennifer E. Draheim.**
**Civil Trial Practice before all State and Federal Courts. Insurance Defense, Construction Defect, Products Liability, Premises Liability, Architect, Real Estate Agent and Engineering Malpractice, Automobile Liability and Insurance Coverage.**
**Representative Clients: Browning-Ferris Industries; Crawford and Co. Risk Management Services; Del Taco, Inc.; General Accident Insurance Co.; Pacific National Insurance; Taco Bell Corp.**
**San Diego, California Office: 402 W. Broadway, Suite 400. Telephone: 619-531-1919. Fax: 619-531-7911.**
***See Professional Biographies, ORANGE, CALIFORNIA***

Dowdall, Terry R., (BV) .................. '51 '78 C&L.800 A.B., J.D. 284 N. Glassell St.
Dracup, Jeffrey A. .................. '57 '83 C.112 B.S. L.426 J.D. Pres. [Dracup&P.]
Dracup & Patterson ................................................ 333 City Blvd., W.
**Draheim, Jennifer E.** .................. '61 '85 C.112 B.A. L.851 J.D. [Donovan&D.]⊙
*PRACTICE AREAS: Insurance Defense; Products Liability; Premises Liability; Construction Liability.
Druding, Michael J. ........................ '49 '86 C.424 B.A. L.999 J.D. [Ⓐ Mercer&Z.]
Drummond, Ralph M. .............. '18 '48 C&L.800 B.S., J.D. 500 N. State College Blvd.
Dudenhefer, Tina M. .............. '65 '92 C.999 B.S. L.1137 J.D. 5316 E. Chapman Ave.
**Duffy, Lawrence E., Jr.**, (BV) ........ '56 '82 C&L.426 B.A., J.D. [Walsworth,F.B.&M.]
**Duncan, John A.**, (AV) .................. '37 '64 C.911 B.A. L.1065 J.D. [J.A.Duncan]
*PRACTICE AREAS: Estate and Trust Litigation; Legal Malpractice Litigation and consulting in these fields.

**Duncan, John A., A Professional Corporation, (AV) BB**
**333 City Boulevard West, Suite 1420, 92668-2924**
**Telephone: 714-935-9800 FAX: 714-939-1485**
**John A. Duncan (Certified Specialist, Probate, Estate Planning and Trust Law, The State Bar of California Board of Legal Specialization).**
**Estate and Trust Litigation. Probate Litigation, Conservatorship Litigation, Estate Planning, Estate and Trust Law, Estate and Trust Professional Negligence Litigation, Legal Malpractice Litigation and Consulting in these fields.**
***See Professional Biographies, ORANGE, CALIFORNIA***

Eck, Paul S. .................. '59 '92 C.112 B.A. L.800 J.D. 500 N. State College Blvd.
Edelman, Jerome .................. '39 '68 C.831 B.A. L.284 LL.B. 303 W. Katella Ave.
Edgell, Elise M. .................. '41 '76 C.940 B.A. L.1137 J.D. 924 E. Chapman Ave.
Edwards, Jennifer D. .................. '64 '92 C&L.1137 B.A., J.D. 1224 E. Katella Ave.
**Eisenberg, Mark W.** .............. '65 '92 C.1044 B.A. L.61 J.D. [Ⓐ Harrington,F.D.&C.]
*PRACTICE AREAS: Civil Litigation.
**Elder, Brad M.** '67 '94 C.1109 B.A. L.1137 J.D.
[Ⓐ Harrington,F.D.&C.] (⊙Los Angeles)
*PRACTICE AREAS: Civil Defense Litigation.
Elias, Betty L. ................ '27 '53 C&L.546 B.S., J.D. 2855 Shady Glen Lane‡
**Elliot, D. Scott** .................. '52 '77 C.1077 B.A. L.809 J.D. [Elliot,L.L.&S.]⊙
*PRACTICE AREAS: Insurance Defense; Medical Malpractice Defense.

**Elliot, Lamb, Leibl & Snyder, (AV)**
**333 South Anita Street, Suite 660, 92668⊙**
**Telephone: 714-978-6255 Fax: 714-978-9087**

(This Listing Continued)

**Elliot, Lamb, Leibl & Snyder (Continued)**
**Michael V. Lamb; Michael R. Snyder; Loren S. Leibl; D. Scott Elliot; Rebecca J. Hogue;—David R. Calderon.**
**Civil Litigation. Insurance Defense and Medical Malpractice Defense.**
**Encino Office: 16501 Ventura Boulevard, Suite 301, 91436. Telephone: 818-380-0123; 310-553-5767. Facsimile: 818-380-0124.**
**Redlands, California Office: 101 East Redlands Boulevard, Suite 285, 92373. Telephone: 909-792-8861. Fax: 909-798-6997.**
***See Professional Biographies, ORANGE, CALIFORNIA***

**Elsberry, Michael J.** .............. '59 '86 C.221 B.S.B.A. L.1137 J.D. [Ⓐ Hillsinger&C.]
**Fabozzi, Dennis F.**, (AV) .................. '52 '77 C.36 B.S. L.426 J.D. [Fabozzi,T.&C.]
*PRACTICE AREAS: Banking Law; Bankruptcy Law; Business Litigation.

**Fabozzi, Thierbach & Caley, (AV) BB**
**3111 North Tustin Avenue, Suite 200, 92665**
**Telephone: 714-637-3385 FAX: 714-637-3489**
**Dennis F. Fabozzi; Marlene L. Thierbach; Rebecca A. Caley. Associates: Jima Ikegawa; Bruce T. Bauer.**
**Banking, Commercial, Bankruptcy, Real Estate, General Business and Civil Litigation in all State and Federal Courts.**
***See Professional Biographies, ORANGE, CALIFORNIA***

Fair, Catherine T. .................. '49 '75 C.1077 B.A. L.398 J.D. 4609-3 Via La Paloma
Farrell, Betty J. ........................ '22 '71 C.912 B.S. L.1137 J.D. Supr. Ct. Comr.
**Farrington, Craig G.** .................. '61 '86 C.112 B.A. L.990 J.D. [Woodruff,S.&S.]
*PRACTICE AREAS: Litigation.
Faust, Robert V., II, (BV) .................. '51 '78 C.1109 B.A. L.1137 J.D. [Faust&F.]⊙
Faust & Faust, (BV) ........................ 500 N. St. College Blvd. (⊙Mission Viejo)
**Feinstein, Marc J.**, (BV) '54 '81 C.659 B.S. L.464 J.D.
[Ⓑ Hollins,S.&F.] (⊙San Diego)
*PRACTICE AREAS: Insurance Law; Business Litigation; Professional Liability Law.
**Fergus, Donald E., Jr.**, (AV) .................. '51 '79 C.212 B.A. L.61 J.D. [Holden&F.]
Fessinger, Robert B. ........................ '64 '91 C.1077 B.A. L.464 J.D. [Ⓐ Schmid&V.]
**Fick, Rodell R.** ........................ '43 '87 C.1097 B.S. L.426 J.D. [Ⓐ Woodruff,S.&S.]
*SPECIAL AGENCIES: Appointed: California Peace Officer Standards and Training, Advisory Committee for Development of "Police Pursuit Guidelines," 1994.
*PRACTICE AREAS: Police Misconduct Liability Defense; Civil Rights; Municipal and Administrative Law; Litigation.
Filer, Norman A. ............ '53 '82 C.1042 B.A. L.1137 J.D. 500 N. State College Blvd.
**Filkins, Jodie P.** ........................ '68 '94 C.112 B.A. L.114 J.D. [Ⓐ Hollins,S.&F.]
*PRACTICE AREAS: Uninsured Motorist Law; Workers Compensation; Subrogation; Construction Defect; Civil Litigation.
Finley, Kirk H. ........................ '46 '75 C.112 B.S. L.426 J.D. 625 The City Dr. S., 4th Fl.
Finney, Janis L. ........................ '49 '82 C.8 B.A. L.1137 J.D. 701 S. Parker St.
Fisher, Barbara Elaine '54 '86
C.1110 B.S. L.831 J.D. Developmental Disabilities Ctr. of Orange
Fitzgerald, Gregory M. .................. '62 '91 C.1253 B.S. L.800 J.D. 140 S. Flower St.
Flynn, John L., Jr. .............. '26 '58 C.112 B.S. L.809 J.D. 500 N. State College Blvd.
**Forbath, Joseph W.** .................. '64 '90 C.112 B.A. L.426 J.D. [Ⓐ Woodruff,S.&S.]
*LANGUAGES: Spanish.
*PRACTICE AREAS: Personal Injury Defense; Business Litigation.
**Franklin, Ferdie F.**, (AV) .............. '47 '74 C.990 B.A. L.426 J.D. [Walsworth,F.B.&M.]
Franks, Robert O., (AV) ........................ '34 '68 C.846 B.S.E. L.1001 J.D. City Atty.
Frazee, Richard O., Sr. ........................ '38 '67 C.112 B.S. L.1065 J.D. Supr. Ct. J.
Fujita, Brian Y. ........................ '58 '85 C.940 B.A. L.1068 J.D. 2437 N. Santiago Blvd.
**Fullmer, William A.** '59 '84 C.385 B.A. L.608 J.D.
(adm. in OH; not adm. in CA) Sr. Coun., TRW Info. Systems & Servs. Grp.
Gaitan, Raymond .................. '55 '91 C.1097 B.A. L.1137 J.D. 1190 N. Lincoln St.
Garcia, L. Luis ........................ '59 '86 C.800 B.A. L.426 J.D. 701 S. Parker St.
Garrity, Charles W., (AV) .... '28 '61 C.383 A.B. L.426 LL.B. 625 The City Dr. S., 4th Fl.
**Gasparini, Thomas A.** '47 '72 C.659 B.S. L.800 J.D.
V.P. & Asst. Gen. Coun., TRW Info. Systems & Servs. Grp.
Gaughan, John S. ........................ '32 '62 C&L.209 B.S.C., J.D. 500 S. Main St.
Gergen, Paul J., (BV) ........................ '20 '61 C.1042 B.A. L.800 J.D. [P.J.Gergen]
Gergen, Paul J., A Law Corporation, (BV) ........................ 201 W. Collins Ave.
**Gertz, Kenneth E.** ........................ '58 '86 C.112 B.A. L.209 J.D. [Hollins,S.&F.]
*PRACTICE AREAS: Insurance Law; Personal Injury Defense Law; Products Liability Law; Governmental Entity Law; Business Litigation.
**Gibbons, Gregg M.** '52 '77 C.112 B.A. L.1068 J.D.
V.P., Corp. Affs., Gen. Coun. & Secy., Wynn's Intl., Inc.
**Gibson, William C.** ........................ '64 '90 C.1055 B.A. L.356 J.D. [Ⓐ Marlin&S.]
Gidekel, Carrin A. .............. '64 '90 C.112 B.A. L.1049 J.D. 1100 Town and Country Rd.

**Gilbert, Kelly, Crowley & Jennett, (AV)**
**Suite 310 Nexus Financial Center, 721 South Parker Street, 92668-4702⊙**
**Telephone: 714-541-5000 Fax: 714-541-0670**
**Resident Partners: Jeffrey L. Crafts; Stephen S. Grande; Albert P. DiRocco, Jr.; Jennifer M. Damon. Resident Associates: Geoffrey S. Morris; Mary Catherine Reid; Eric W. Thorson.**
**General Civil and Trial Practice in all State and Federal Courts. Appellate Practice. Corporation and Insurance Law.**
**Los Angeles, California Office: 1200 Wilshire Boulevard. Telephone: 213-580-7000. Fax: 213-580-7100.**
**Riverside County Office: 3801 University Avenue, Suite 700, Riverside, California. Telephone: 909-276-4000. Fax: 909-276-4100.**
**San Diego, California Office: 501 West Broadway, Suite 1260 Koll Center. Telephone: 619-687-3000. Fax: 619-687-3100.**
***See Professional Biographies, ORANGE, CALIFORNIA***

Gillette, Jeffrey R. ............ '59 '86 C.1109 B.A. L.426 J.D. 701 S. Parker St. Ste. 8800
Giuffre, Boo J., (Ms.), (BV) ........................ '45 '79 L.1137 J.D. One City Blvd. W.
Glovinsky, Eli H. '60 '85 C.112 B.A. L.1065 J.D.
Asst. V.P. & Corp. Coun., St. Joseph Health System
Goff, James R., (AV) ........................ '40 '66 C&L.800 B.A., LL.B. 275 S. Main St.
Goodman, Sheldon S., (A Professional Corporation), (BV) '37 '70
C.494 B.B.A. L.990 J.D. 505 S. Main St.
Gorczyca, Gary S. ........................ '51 '76 C.112 B.A. L.426 J.D. 333 City Blvd.
Gorelick, Peter J. ........................ '52 '79 C.112 B.A. L.1095 J.D. [P.J.Gorelick]
Gorelick, Peter J., P.C. ........................ 725 Town & Country Rd.
Gosselin, Craig E. '59 '84
C.426 B.B.A. L.809 J.D. V.P., Gen. Coun. & Corp. Secy., Varn, Inc.
Gould, F. Latimer ........................ '37 '72 C.321 B.S. L.602 J.D. Comr., Juv. Ct.
**Grande, Stephen S.** ........................ '56 '81 C.37 B.A. L.809 J.D. [Gilbert,K.C.&J.]
*PRACTICE AREAS: Insurance Defense; Business Litigation; Construction Defect; Employment Law.
Greenwald, Paul Evan, (AV) .... '44 '73 C.800 B.S. L.809 J.D. 500 N. State College Blvd.
**Gronowski, Katy M.** .............. '60 '87 C.112 B.A. L.770 J.D. [Ⓐ Marlin&S.] (⊙Oakland)
*PRACTICE AREAS: Governmental Tort; Liability Claims; Personal Injury; Construction Defect; General Liability.
Grosfeld, Robert ........................ '54 '80 C.112 B.A. L.809 J.D. [Ⓐ P.J.Gorelick]
Grubaugh, Bruce E., II, (BV) ............ '46 '77 C&L.1137 B.S.L., J.D. 1107 E. Chapman
**Guldimann, John L.** '56 '85
C.112 B.A. L.800 J.D. Sr. Coun., TRW Info. Systems & Servs. Grp.

**Gunny, Neil R.** ................................ '51 '77 C.112 B.A. L.770 J.D. [Hagenbaugh&M.]
*PRACTICE AREAS: Appraisal Malpractice; Homeowners Association Litigation; General Tort Litigation.
Guthrie, J. Barrett '22 '70 C&L.602 J.D.
(adm. in IN; not adm. in CA) Sr. Atty., Kemper Ins.
**Guziak, James J.**, (AV) ........................ '53 '78 C&L.966 B.A., J.D. [J.J.Guziak]

**Guziak, James J., A Professional Corporation, (AV)**
**333 City Boulevard West, Suite 1700, 92668**
**Telephone: 714-938-3282 Facsmile: 714-938-3284**
**James J. Guziak.**
**Civil Litigation with emphasis on Wrongful Termination and Employment Discrimination.**
*See Professional Biographies, ORANGE, CALIFORNIA*

**Hagenbaugh & Murphy, (AV)**
**A Partnership including Professional Corporations**
**701 South Parker Street, Suite 8200, 92668⊙**
**Telephone: 714-835-5406 Fax: 714-835-5949**
**Members of Firm: Neil R. Gunny; Daniel A. Leipold; Robert F. Donohue; Alan H. Boon;—David M. Chute; Cathy L. Shipe; Howard J. Hirsch.**
**General Civil and Trial Practice in all State and Federal Courts. Insurance, Casualty, Life, Health, Accident and Disability Insurance, Malpractice, Employment Law, Business Litigation (including Commercial and Advertising Disputes) and General Tort Litigation**
**Glendale, California Office: 700 North Central Avenue, Suite 500. Telephone: 818-240-2600. Fax: 818-240-1253. E-mail: hmurphy@interserv.com.**
**San Bernardino, California Office: 301 Vanderbilt Way, Suite 220. Telephone: 909-884-5331. FAX: 909-889-1250.**
*See Professional Biographies, ORANGE, CALIFORNIA*

Hagner, Faye E. ........................ '43 '76 C.303 B.A. L.1137 J.D. 770 The City Dr., S.
Hahn, Kenneth A. ........................ '37 '80 C.999 M.S. L.1137 J.D. 292 N. Main St.
Hales, Robert E. .................. '48 '80 C.101 B.S. L.809 J.D. 2200 W. Orangewood Ave.
Hall, Scott Middleton ............ '61 '88 C.763 B.A. L.1049 J.D. 112 N. McPherson Rd.
**Hamby, Bruce W.** ........................ '64 '91 C.502 B.S. L.339 J.D. [Kossler&H.]
*REPORTED CASES: Jennings v. Marralle (1994) 8 Cal. 4th 121.
*PRACTICE AREAS: Business Litigation (15%, 20); Commercial Litigation (15%, 20); Personal Injury (20%, 20); Civil Appeals (6%, 20); ERISA (5%, 20).
Hansen, Daryl D., (AV) ........ '41 '70 C.350 B.S.E.E. L.1065 J.D. 738 E. Chapman Ave.
Hanssler, Scott William ............ '56 '81 C.1109 B.A. L.990 J.D. 625 The City Dr., S.
**Harmata, John M.** .................. '62 '87 C.763 B.A. L.1049 J.D. [Ⓐ Testa&Assoc.]⊙
*PRACTICE AREAS: Real Estate; Employment Law; Insurance Law; Landlord and Tenant; Personal Injury.
Harper, John R., (AV) ........................ '47 '78 C.684 B.A. L.398 J.D. [Harper&B.]
Harper & Burns, (AV) .............................................. 453 S. Glassell St.
Harpst, Carlton L. ........................ '49 '75 C.112 B.A. L.990 J.D. [Ⓐ P.J.Gorelick]

**Harrington, Foxx, Dubrow & Canter, (AV)**
**Suite 1020, 1100 Town and Country Road, 92668⊙**
**Telephone: 714-973-4595 Facsimile: 714-973-7923**
**Members of Firm: David H. Canter; Edward R. Leonard. Associates: Peter A. Schneider; Mark W. Eisenberg; Brad M. Elder.**
**General Civil and Trial Practice in all State and Federal Courts and before Federal and State Administrative Agencies. Real Estate, Corporation, Business, Estate Planning, Trust, Probate, Medical, Products Liability, Health and Insurance Law.**
**Representative Clients: Farmers Insurance Group; Pet, Inc.; Royal Insurance Co.; Transport Indemnity Co.; Underwriters at Lloyd's, London.**
**Reference: Security Pacific National Bank (Los Angeles Main Office, Sixth and Spring Streets).**
**Los Angeles, California Office: Thirtieth Floor, 611 West Sixth. Telephone: 213-489-3222. Facsimile: 213-623-7929.**
**San Diego, California Office: Suite 1150, 401 West A Street. Telephone: 619-233-5553. Fax: 619-233-0005.**
**San Francisco, California Office: 444 Market Street, Suite, 3050. Telephone: 415-288-6600. Facsimile: 415-288-6618.**
*See Professional Biographies, ORANGE, CALIFORNIA*

Harris, Aurora D. ........................ '53 '80 C.1042 B.A. L.1137 J.D. 58 Plaza Sq.
Harris, Mark G. ................ '62 '87 C.112 B.A. L.464 J.D. 500 N. State College Blvd.
Harvey, Margot M., (BV) ................ '41 '84 C.1109 B.A. L.1137 J.D. [Ⓐ Mercer&Z.]
Hasty, Dennis K., (BV) ........ '40 '65 C.1042 B.S. L.1068 LL.B. 541 E. Chapman Ave.
Herrick, Robert D. ........................ '52 '81 C&L.101 B.A., J.D. Asst. City Atty.
Hewitt, Mark A. .................. '63 '92 C.628 B.S.L.A. L.1137 J.D. [Ⓐ Schwamb&S.]
Hickman, Gale P. .............................................. '42 '68 Juv. Ct. Ref.
Hilborne, Hawkin & Co. ... 2534 N. Santiago Blvd. (⊙Hong Kong, Bandar Seri Begawan)
**Hillsinger, George R.**, (AV) '26 '52 C.642 L.809 LL.B.
[Hillsinger&C.] (⊙Los Angeles)

**Hillsinger and Costanzo, Professional Corporation, (AV)**
**701 South Parker Street, Suite 6000, 92868-4741⊙**
**Telephone: 714-542-6241 Telecopier: 714-667-6806**
**George R. Hillsinger; Carol A. Salmacia (Resident);—Michael J. Elsberry (Resident); Lisa M. Agrusa (Resident); Laura M. Booth (Resident). Of Counsel: Edward A. DeBuys.**
**General Civil and Appellate Trial Practice in all State and Federal Courts. Insurance, Corporation, Commercial, Business, Medical and Professional Malpractice, Product Liability, Aviation, Asbestos, Toxic Tort, Bad Faith, Insurance Coverage, Declaratory Relief, Wrongful Termination, Vehicular, Property Damage, General Liability Cases.**
**Los Angeles, California Office: 12th Floor, 3055 Wilshire Boulevard. Telephone: 310-388-9441. Telecopier: 310-388-1592.**
**Rancho Cucamonga, California Office: 10737 Laurel Street, Suite 110 - Main Floor. Telephone: 909-483-6200. Telecopier: 909-483-6277.**
**Santa Barbara, California Office: 220 East Figueroa Street. Telephone: 805-966-3986. Telecopier: 805-965-3798.**
*See Professional Biographies, ORANGE, CALIFORNIA*

**Hirsch, Howard J.** ............... '64 '95 C.37 B.F.A. L.1137 J.D. [Ⓐ Hagenbaugh&M.]
**Hoffman, Gary L.** ........................ '59 '85 C.426 B.A. L.1049 J.D. [Morris,P.&P.]
Hogenson, Edward B. .................. '46 '73 C.966 B.A. L.945 J.D. Calif. Teachers Assn.
**Hogue, Rebecca J.** .................. '54 '84 C.112 B.A. L.1137 J.D. [Elliot,L.L.&S.]⊙
*PRACTICE AREAS: Insurance Defense; Medical Malpractice Defense.
**Holden, Daniel W.**, (AV) ........................ '34 '59 C.112 B.S. L.426 J.D. [Holden&F.]

**Holden & Fergus, (AV)**
**500 N. State College Boulevard Suite 780, 92868-1607**
**Telephone: 714-939-6776 Fax: 714-939-6840**
**Daniel W. Holden; Donald E. Fergus, Jr. (Certified Specialist, Estate Planning, Trust and Probate Law, The State Bar of California Board of Legal Specialization).**
**Corporate (Profit and Non-Profit), Estate Planning, Trust and Probate Law, Real Estate Transactions and Brokerage, Construction Law, Civil Litigation, Trials in all Courts.**
**Representative Clients: Tri-L Distributors; The Roman Catholic Bishop of Orange, a corporation sole; Catholic Charities of Orange County; Century 21-Able Realty; Excel Distributing, Inc.; Junckers Hardwood, Inc.; Centaur Products International, Inc.; B.T.L. Technologies, Inc.**
**Reference: Bank of America.**
*See Professional Biographies, ORANGE, CALIFORNIA*

**Hollingshead, John**, (BV) ....... '52 '82 C.767 B.A. L.464 J.D. [Ⓐ Marlin&S.] (⊙Oakland)
*PRACTICE AREAS: Insurance Defense.
**Hollins, Andrew S.**, (AV) '51 '78
C.838 B.S. L.1221 J.D. [Hollins,S.&F.] (⊙Palm Springs)
*PRACTICE AREAS: Insurance Law; Governmental Entity Law; Products Liability Law.

**Hollins, Schechter & Feinstein, A Professional Corporation, (AV)** BB
**12th Floor, 505 South Main Street, P.O. Box 11021, 92856⊙**
**Telephone: 714-558-9119 Fax: 714-558-9091**
**Andrew S. Hollins; Bruce Lee Schechter; Thomas M. Condas; Kenneth E. Gertz; Jack H. Snyder; Kenneth C. Jones; Thomas L. Hyatt;—Bryan R. Bush; Mary Ann Schiller; Joy L. Krikorian; Robert M. DeNichilo; Elliott J. Block; Wendy Aline Mitchell; Meka Moore; Eric M. Schiffer; Tanja Darrow-Means; Dao-Mary Do; Jodie P. Filkins; Richard T. Collins. Of Counsel: Marc J. Feinstein.**
**General, Civil and Trial Practice in all State and Federal Courts. Personal Injury Defense, Insurance Law, Construction Defect, Product Liability, Governmental Entity, Professional Liability, Director and Officers Liability, Workers Compensation, Wrongful Termination, Lender Liability, Employment Law, Real Estate Litigation and Business Litigation.**
**Representative Clients: Acceptance Risk Managers; Admiral Insurance Co.; American Drug Store, Inc.; American States Insurance Co.; Colonial Penn Insurance Co.; Commercial Union Insurance Cos.; Farmers Insurance Group; Home Base d.b.a. Waban; Hull & Co., Inc.; Investors Insurance Group.**
**San Diego, California Office: 12526 High Bluff Drive, Suite 300, 92130. Telephone: 619-792-3502.**
**Moreno Valley, California Office: 22690 Cactus Avenue, Suite 240, 92553. Telephone: 909-247-2903.**
**Palm Springs, California Office: 1111 Tahquitz Canyon Way, Suite 121, 92262. Telephone: 619-416-0288.**
*See Professional Biographies, ORANGE, CALIFORNIA*

**Holmes, Richard E. '47 '76 C.1102 B.A. L.1137 J.D.**
**One City Boulevard West Suite 410, 92868-3605**
**Telephone: 714-978-3311 Fax: 714-978-3425**
**Email: semlohr@aol.com**
***PRACTICE AREAS: Real Estate Law; Landlord and Tenant Law; Business; Credit; Probate.**
**Civil Practice including: Real Estate, Landlord/Tenant, Business, Credit, Probate and Collections.**
*See Professional Biographies, ORANGE, CALIFORNIA*

Hoolihan, Patrick J., (BV) ................ '30 '62 C.215 Ph.B. L.809 J.D. [P.J.Hoolihan]
Hoolihan, Patrick J., Law Corp., (BV) .............................. 275 S. Main St.
**Hughes, Cindy R.** ................ '57 '87 C.1042 B.S. L.800 J.D. [Walsworth,F.B.&M.]
Hughes, James D. '18 '48
C.860 A.B. L.309 LL.B. Adm. Law J., Off. of Hearings & Appeals
Hughes, Lisa M. ................ '59 '87 C.1044 B.A. L.809 J.D. 5316 E. Chapman Ave.
Hummel, Philip L., IV, (BV) ... '61 '86 C.1042 B.A. L.1137 J.D. 500 N. State Coll. Blvd.
Humphreys, Julie Payne ................ '54 '80 C.1042 B.A. L.809 J.D. [Hurwitz&H.]
Hurwitz, Lon F., (BV) ................ '54 '79 C.1042 B.S. L.809 J.D. [Hurwitz&H.]
Hurwitz, Mark E., (AV) ................ '36 '62 C.800 B.A. L.1068 LL.B. [Hurwitz&H.]
Hurwitz & Humphreys, A Prof. Law Corp., Law Offices of, (BV) ........ 333 S. Anita Dr.
Hurwitz & Hurwitz, (AV) ........................................ 100 W. Chapman Ave.
**Hyatt, Thomas L.** ................ '59 '91 C.549 B.S. L.809 J.D. [Hollins,S.&F.]
*PRACTICE AREAS: Personal Injury Defense; Products Liability; Construction Defect; Insurance Law.
**Ikegawa, Jima** ................ '67 '94 C.112 B.S. L.464 J.D. [Ⓐ Fabozzi,T.&C.]
Jackson, Glenn B. ................ '44 '80 C&L.1137 B.S.L., J.D. 450 N. Milford Rd.‡
Jaffe, Donna C. ................ '48 '91 C.1109 B.A. L.1137 J.D. 2592 N. Santiago Blvd.
Jamison, Frank L., Jr. ........ '36 '67 C.112 B.A. L.800 J.D. V.P. & Gen. Coun., IBS Corp.
Jaquith, Gary S. ................ '48 '84 C.1042 B.S. L.1137 J.D. 503 S. Glassell St.
Jeffery, Mona J. ................ '57 '87 C.112 B.A. L.1137 J.D. [Ⓐ P.J.Gorelick]
**Jeffrey, Lois E.**, (BV) ................ '43 '79 C.112 B.A. L.1137 J.D. [Woodruff,S.&S.]
*PRACTICE AREAS: Land Use Law; Water Law; Municipal Law.
Jimenez, Victor E. ................................................ '56 '83 [Ⓐ P.J.Gorelick]
**Johnson, Jennifer A.** '68 '93
C.205 B.S. L.420 J.D. [Walsworth,F.B.&M.] (⊙San Francisco)
Johnson, Vernon E., (BV) ............ '30 '70 C.626 L.990 J.D. 500 N. State Coll. Blvd.
**Jones, Kenneth C.** ................ '62 '87 C&L.940 B.A., J.D. [Hollins,S.&F.]
*REPORTED CASES: Baker v. Mid-Century Insurance Company (1993), 20 Cal. App. 4th, 921.
*PRACTICE AREAS: Business Litigation; Real Estate Litigation; Insurance Coverage Law; Community Association Law.
Judge, James F. ..... '25 '50 C.215 L.477 LL.B. Jud. Arbitration & Mediation Servs., Inc.
Judge, Robert P. ................ '62 '87 C.602 B.A. L.426 J.D. 275 S. Main St.
Kamanski, David D. ................ '57 '84 C.112 B.A. L.464 J.D. 765 The City Dr.
**Kayajanian & Brewsaugh**
**(See Irvine)**
Keenan, James J., Jr., (BV) ..... '46 '79 C.645 B.A. L.464 J.D. [Mercer&Z.] (⊙Lafayette)
**Kegel, Tobin & Truce, A Professional Corporation**
**(See Long Beach)**
**Kegel, Tobin & Truce, A Professional Corporation**
**(See Rancho Cucamonga)**
Kelly & Herlihy, (AV)
500 North State College Boulevard Suite 440 (⊙San Francisco & San Diego)
**Kennedy, Sandra G.** ................ '58 '83 C&L.426 B.A., J.D. [Walsworth,F.B.&M.]
Keough, Dennis J. ................ '49 '74 C.1042 B.A. L.500 J.D. Supr. Ct. Comr.
**Kern, Toni L.** ................ '54 '87 C.112 B.A. L.1179 J.D. [Ⓐ Marlin&S.]
*PRACTICE AREAS: Municipal Law; Law Enforcement Defense; Insurance Defense.
Kidwell, Carl J. ................ '31 '77 C.8 L.190 LL.B. Sr. Coun., Wynn's Intl., Inc.
Killeen, James Charles ..... '65 '94 C.112 B.A. L.426 J.D. 3111 N. Tustin Ave., Suite 200
**Kingsland-Canada, Lya** ................ '61 '88 C.1109 B.S. L.1137 J.D. [Ⓐ Astor&P.]
*PRACTICE AREAS: Family Law; Probate; Corporate Law.
Kneeland, Robert P. '16 '45
C.358 B.A. L.477 J.D. Jud. Arbitration & Mediation Servs., Inc.
Knight, H. Warren, III '29 '55 C&L.893 B.A., LL.B.
Chf. Jud. Offr., Jud. Arbitration & Mediation Servs., Inc.
Knight, James C. ................ '26 '82 C&L.1137 B.S.L., J.D. 438 E. Katella Ave.
**Koenig, Randall F.** ................ '54 '81 C.800 B.A. L.1049 J.D. [Morris,P.&P.]
Koester, David A. ................ '54 '79 C.388 B.A. L.502 J.D. 770 The City Dr.
Koper, Jacob ................ '59 '87 C.1109 B.A. L.1137 J.D. [Ⓐ Mercer&Z.]
**Kossler, Richard J., II** ................ '54 '81 C.1109 B.S. L.1137 J.D. [Kossler&H.]
*PRACTICE AREAS: Commercial Transactions (30%, 30); Transportation Law (30%, 30); Business Litigation (20%, 20); Personal Injury Litigation (20%, 20).

**Kossler & Hamby LLP**
**3111 North Tustin, Suite 235, 92665-1753**
**Telephone: 714-282-8050 Fax: 714-282-8867**
**Email: kosslerhamby@earthlink.net URL: http://www.kosslerhamby.com**
**Richard J. Kossler, II; Bruce W. Hamby.**
**Business, Transaction, Litigation, Personal Injury.**
*See Professional Biographies, ORANGE, CALIFORNIA*

**Krikorian, Joy L.** ................ '53 '84 C.267 B.A. L.464 J.D. [Ⓐ Hollins,S.&F.]
*PRACTICE AREAS: Workers' Compensation Defense; Insurance Defense.
**Kubis, Scott K.** ................ '62 '90 C.763 B.A. L.1049 J.D. [Ⓐ Landau,O.&K.]
*PRACTICE AREAS: Insurance Defense; Construction Defense; Medical Malpractice.
Kutinsky, Laurence ................ '49 '76 C.94 B.A. L.1009 J.D. 1 City Blvd., W.
**Lal, Rick C.** ................ '65 '91 C.1075 B.A. L.1067 J.D. [Ⓐ Minyard&M.]
*LANGUAGES: Hindi.
*PRACTICE AREAS: Family Law.
**Lamb, Michael V.** ................ '52 '79 C.477 B.A. L.990 J.D. [Elliot,L.L.&S.]⊙
*PRACTICE AREAS: Insurance Defense; Medical Malpractice Defense.

**Landau, Omahana & Kopka, Ltd.**
**500 North State College Boulevard Suite 1260, 92668-1638⊙**
**Telephone: 714-836-9630 Fax: 715-836-4401**

(This Listing Continued)

CAA446P

**Landau, Omahana & Kopka, Ltd. (Continued)**

**Marilyn L. Bonetati;—Dieter Zacher; Scott K. Kubis; Glenn L. Silverii; Daniel A. Reed; J. Rodney DeBiaso; David G. Bebb; Jacob M. Wiesel.**
**Chicago, Illinois Office: 222 North La Salle Street, Suite 200, 60601-1005. Telephone: 312-630-9630. Fax: 312-630-9001.**
**Lisle, Illinois Office: 1001 Warrenville Road, Suite 255, 60532-1393. Telephone: 708-434-9630. Fax: 708-434-9644.**
**Vernon Hills, Illinois Office: 850 North Milwaukee, Suite 880, 60061-1553. Telephone: 708-918-4700. Fax: 708-918-4719.**
**Belleville, Illinois Office: 23 South First Street, 62220-2029. Telephone: 618-746-9540. Fax: 618-746-9541.**
**St. Louis, Missouri Office: 7912 Bonhomme Avenue, Suite 400, 63105-1912. Telephone: 314-726-2310. Fax: 314-726-2360.**
**Merrillville, Indiana Office: 8585 Broadway Street, Suite 480, 46410-7001. Telephone: 219-769-9630.**
**Dallas, Texas Office: 5430 LBJ Freeway, Suite 980, 75240-6248. Telephone: 972-503-0100. Fax: 972-503-0110.**
**Carmel, Indiana Office: 11611 North Meridian Street, Suite 706, 46032-4542. Telephone: 317-846-6700. Fax: 317-846-6701.**
**South Bend, Indiana Office: 100 East Wayne Street, Suite 455, 46601-2353. Telephone: 219-288-3270. Fax: 219-288-3280.**
**Southfield, Michigan Office: 26877 Northwestern Highway, Suite 408, 48037-8418. Telephone: 810-208-8400. Fax: 810-208-8410.**

***See Professional Biographies, ORANGE, CALIFORNIA***

Langston, Joanne ... '49 '77 C.502 B.S. L.1137 J.D. 625 The City Dr., 4th Fl.
Lathen, Deborah A. '53 '78 C.188 A.B. L.309 J.D. (adm. in WI; not adm. in CA) 500 City Pkwy. W.‡
**Lazar, Alan S.** ... '57 '85 C.563 B.A. L.809 J.D. [🄰 Marlin&S.]
Lazarus, Peter M. ... '52 '86 C.24 B.A. L.1049 J.D. [🄰 Mercer&Z.]
Lee, Gregory A., (BV) ... '51 '77 C.790 B.A. L.1137 J.D. [Cesena&L.]
**Leibl, Loren S.**, (AV) ... '53 '83 C.1042 B.A. L.809 J.D. [Elliot,L.L.&S.] (⊙Encino)
*PRACTICE AREAS: Insurance Defense; Medical Malpractice Defense.
**Leipold, Daniel A.** ... '47 '77 C.736 B.A. L.1137 J.D. [Hagenbaugh&M.]
*PRACTICE AREAS: Serious Injury Cases; Malpractice Defense; First Amendment Defense; Elder Abuse Defense; Slapp Suit Defense.
**Leonard, Edward R.**, (AV) '53 '78 C.763 B.A. L.1049 J.D. [Harrington,F.D.&C.] (⊙L.A.)
*PRACTICE AREAS: Personal Injury Defense Law; Product Liability Law; Professional Negligence Law; Construction Defects Law.
Lether, Margaret ... '58 '88 [🄰 P.J.Gorelick]
Lippman, Lori S. ... '56 '84 C.112 B.A. L.426 J.D. [🄰 Schmid&V.]
**Lona-Wiant, Magdalena** ... '50 '82 C.1097 B.A. L.1137 J.D. [🄰 Woodruff,S.&S.]
*LANGUAGES: Spanish.
*PRACTICE AREAS: Litigation; Liability Defense.
Long, Michael J. ... '— '84 C.629 B.A. L.1049 J.D. [🄰 Mercer&Z.]
Longmead, Doris J. ... '38 '83 C.990 B.A. L.1137 J.D. 8236 E. Candleberry Cir.
Lounsbury, Donald A., (BV) ... '45 '72 C.1042 B.A. L.1137 J.D. 333 City Blvd. W.‡
Luetto, Helen M. ... '60 '85 C.1109 B.A. L.1137 J.D. 505 S. Main St.
Luetto, John A., (AV) ... '49 '76 C.1109 B.A. L.1137 J.D. 505 S. Main St.
**Lundquist, James W.**, (AV) ... '42 '72 C.1109 B.A. L.1068 J.D. [J.W.Lundquist]
*PRACTICE AREAS: Business Litigation; Real Estate Litigation; Landlord and Tenant Law; Contracts; Civil Litigation.

**Lundquist, James W., Inc., (AV)**
**850 East Chapman Avenue, Suite A, 92866**
**Telephone: 714-997-2394 Fax: 714-532-3996**
**James W. Lundquist. Of Counsel: Paula C. Matos (Certified Specialist, Probate, Estate Planning and Trust Law, The State Bar of California Board of Legal Specialization).**
**Business Litigation, Real Estate Litigation, Transactional.**

***See Professional Biographies, ORANGE, CALIFORNIA***

Lurya, Alan M. '49 '75 C.112 B.A. L.904 J.D. [Aitken I.L.B.V.&C.] (⊙Washington, DC)
MacDonald, Shirley J. ... '46 '86 C.62 B.A. L.1148 J.D. 1 City Blvd., W.
Madden, William H., Jr. '25 '51 C.597 B.S. L.276 J.D. (adm. in IL; not adm. in CA) 4000 Metropolitan Dr.
Malin, Robert L., (BV) ... '39 '74 C.174 B.S. L.1137 J.D. [Vander Molen&M.]
Manashil, Ned W. ... '38 '64 C.645 B.S. L.884 J.D. 505 City Pkwy. W.
Manley, John Francis '58 '88 C.381 B.A. L.930 J.D. (adm. in OH; not adm. in CA) Invest. Coun., Huntington Advisers
Mann, Pearl Gondrella, (AV) ... '38 '85 C.420 B.S. L.1137 J.D. 1122 E. Lincoln Ave.
Mardel, James L. ... '46 '80 [🄰 P.J.Gorelick]
**Marlin, Louis M.**, (AV) ... '47 '72 C.112 B.A. L.1065 J.D. [Marlin&S.]⊙
*LANGUAGES: French.
*REPORTED CASES: Christensen v. Superior Court, California Supreme Court 53 Cal 3rd 868.
*PRACTICE AREAS: Insurance Defense Law; Professional Malpractice Law; Construction Defect Law.

**Marlin & Saltzman, A Professional Law Corporation, (AV) BR**
**701 South Parker Street, Suite 8800, 92868-4720⊙**
**Telephone: 714-541-1066 Fax: 714-542-4184**
**Louis M. Marlin; Stanley D. Saltzman;—Kathy Carter; Christy L. Conner; Lynne A. Pearson; Toni L. Kern; Scott A. Marriott; William C. Gibson; Alan S. Lazar; Craig Pynes; Katy M. Gronowski; John Hollingshead; Jeffrey R. Vincent; Marilynn J. Winters; Daniel J. Yauger; Thomas F. Hozduk (Resident, Woodland Hills Office).**
**Practice limited to Insurance Defense, Insurance Coverage and Bad Faith Litigation.**
**Woodland Hills, California Office: Westhills Plaza, 20700 Ventura Boulevard, Suite 227, 91364. Telephone: 818-702-0600. Fax: 818-702-6555.**
**San Diego, California Office: 750 "B" Street Suite 1925. Telephone: 619-235-0600. Fax: 619-235-0675.**
**Oakland, California Office: 1999 Harrison Street, Suite 990. Telephone: 510-208-9400. Fax: 510-208-9410.**

***See Professional Biographies, ORANGE, CALIFORNIA***

**Marriott, Scott A.** ... '58 '87 C.112 B.A. L.990 J.D. [🄰 Marlin&S.]
*PRACTICE AREAS: Insurance Defense Law; Professional Malpractice Law; Construction Defect Law.
Marsh, D. Diane Hooks ... '67 '93 C.839 B.E.D. L.802 J.D. [Kelly&H.]
**Matos, Paula C.**, (AV) '43 '80 C.36 B.A. L.1137 J.D. [J.W.Lundquist] (⊙Laguna Hills)
*PRACTICE AREAS: Probate Law; Estate Planning Law; Trust Law.
Mayer, Marvin D., (AV) ... '33 '74 C.367 B.E. L.990 J.D. 1 City Blvd. W., Ste. 1400
Mayhew, Jeffrey C. '53 '79 C.800 A.B. L.1068 J.D. Coun. & Dir., Legal Affs., Bergen Brunswig Corp.
McBride, Frederick L., (BV) ... '43 '72 C.112 L.426 J.D. 1100 W. Town and Country Rd.
**McCall, Michael T.** ... '54 '83 C.800 B.A. L.61 J.D. [Walsworth,F.B.&M.]
McCarty, Kathryn E. '55 '89 C.629 B.A. L.1137 J.D. 500 N. State College Blvd., Ste. 1220
McClaskey, Wayne I. ... '29 '55 C&L.800 B.A., J.D. 850 E. Chapman Ave.
McClendon, John G. ... '53 '89 C.1239 B.A. L.800 J.D. 307 E. Chapman Ave.
McCormick, William E. ... '45 '71 C.770 B.A. L.426 J.D. 701 S. Parker St. Ste. 8800
McGill, John Graham, Jr. '47 '80 C.1042 B.S. L.1137 J.D. 625 The City of Orange Dr. S.
**McGreevy, Stephen J.** ... '69 '94 C.426 B.A. L.1049 J.D. [🄰 Morris,P.&P.]
McKeand, Jeri R., (AV) ... '45 '79 C.112 L.1137 J.D. One City Blvd., W.
McNamara, Eileen ... '53 '87 C.1259 B.A. L.1137 J.D. 595 The City Dr.S.
**McNamee, Daniel J.** ... '— '94 C&L.1049 B.A., J.D. [🄰 Morris,P.&P.]
Mercer, Thomas C., (AV) '40 '70 C.1077 B.A. L.426 J.D. [Mercer&Z.] (⊙Los Angeles)
Mercer and Zinder, A Professional Corporation, (AV) 321 North Rampart Street, First Floor (⊙Los Angeles, Walnut Creek, San Diego & Ventura)
Miles, John J. ... '33 '86 C.398 B.A. L.1186 J.D. [Mercer&Z.] (⊙Ventura)
**Miller, John P.**, (BV) ... '45 '71 C&L.426 B.A., J.D. [Morris,P.&P.]
**Miller, Steven C.** ... '56 '84 C.1042 B.A. L.426 J.D. [Morris,P.&P.]
Minshew, Gene R. ... '26 '70 C.800 A.B. L.990 J.D. 1830 E. Fairway Dr.
Minyard, Harold G., (BV) ... '29 '60 C.623 L.45 LL.B. 1 City Blvd.‡
**Minyard, Mark E.**, (AV) ... '51 '76 C.1109 B.A. L.426 J.D. [Minyard&M.]
*PRACTICE AREAS: Family Law.

**Minyard and Morris, (AV)**
**One City Boulevard West, 11th Floor, Suite 1100, 92868**
**Telephone: 714-937-1020 Facsimile: 714-978-6060**
**Mark E. Minyard (Certified Specialist, Family Law, The State Bar of California Board of Legal Specialization); Michael A. Morris (Certified Specialist, Family Law, The State Bar of California Board of Legal Specialization); Jacqueline A. Whisnant (Certified Specialist, Family Law, The State Bar of California Board of Legal Specialization); Lonnie K. Seide (Certified Specialist, Family Law, The State Bar of California Board of Legal Specialization); Rick C. Lal (Certified Specialist, Family Law, The State Bar of California Board of Legal Specialization); Kenneth T. Demmerle.**
**Practice Limited to Family Law.**

***See Professional Biographies, ORANGE, CALIFORNIA***

**Mitchell, Wendy Aline** ... '65 '92 C.800 B.A. L.1137 J.D. [🄰 Hollins,S.&F.]
*LANGUAGES: French and German.
*PRACTICE AREAS: Premises Liability; Insurance Defense; Construction Defect; Bad Faith; Medical Malpractice.
Monarch, Robert D. ... '33 '64 C.112 B.A. L.1068 LL.B. Supr. Ct. J.
Mongeon, Nichole ... '59 '92 C.1109 B.A. L.1137 J.D. 505 S. Main St.
**Montoya, Thierry R.** ... '60 '92 C.112 B.A. L.602 J.D. [🄰 Morris,P.&P.]
**Moore, Meka** ... '— '95 C.763 B.S. L.809 J.D. [🄰 Hollins,S.&F.]
*PRACTICE AREAS: Insurance Law; Personal Injury Defense.
**Morris, Geoffrey S.** ... '64 '91 C.800 A.B. L.464 J.D. [🄰 Gilbert,K.C.&J.]
*PRACTICE AREAS: Employment Law; Insurance Defense; Business Defense.
**Morris, Michael A.** ... '53 '82 C.112 B.A. L.1137 J.D. [Minyard&M.]
*PRACTICE AREAS: Family Law.

**Morris, Polich & Purdy, (AV)**
**500 North State College Boulevard, 11th Floor, 92666⊙**
**Telephone: 714-939-1100 Facsimile: 714-939-9261**
**Members of Firm: Gary L. Hoffman; Randall F. Koenig; John P. Miller; Steven C. Miller. Associates: William M. Betley; Kay Ann Connelly; Stephen J. McGreevy; Daniel J. McNamee; Thierry R. Montoya; Kristen Kay Nelson; Carlos A. Prietto, III; Paul S. Sienski.**
**General Civil Trial and Appellate Practice in all State and Federal Courts. Construction Law, Insurance Law Environmental Law, Products Liability Professional Liability, Architect and Engineer Liability, Government Tort Liability, Police Civil Liability, Pharmaceutical and Medical Device Liability, Toxic Tort Litigation and Commercial Litigation.**
**Los Angeles, California Office: 1055 West Seventh Street, Suite 2400. Telephone: 213-891-9100. Facsimile: 213-488-1178.**
**San Diego, California Office: 501 W. Broadway, Suite 500. Telephone: 619-557-0404. Facsimile: 619-557-0460.**

***See Professional Biographies, ORANGE, CALIFORNIA***

Morrison, Randy Sue, (BV) ... '50 '74 C.112 B.A. L.426 J.D. 1 City Blvd., W.
Moss, Roy O., Jr. ... '37 '74 C.112 A.B. L.809 J.D. 2560 N. Santiago Blvd.
Mostov, Charles H. ... '49 '77 C.475 B.A. L.910 J.D. [Schmid&V.]
Mueller, Gilbert N. ... '21 '48 C&L.930 A.B., J.D. Supr. Ct. Comr.
**Mulkerin, Mark J.** ... '65 '93 C.813 B.A. L.426 J.D. [🄰 Walsworth,F.B.&M.]
*LANGUAGES: Spanish and French.
*PRACTICE AREAS: Business Litigation; Construction Defects; Insurance Coverage.
Mulvaney, Kahan & Barry, A Professional Corporation, (AV) 500 N. State College Blvd. (⊙San Diego, Los Angeles, La Jolla)
Murphy, James Scott ... '59 '85 C.367 B.A. L.990 J.D. [Mercer&Z.]
Murphy, John F., (BV) ... '45 '73 C.768 B.S. L.990 J.D. 472 S. Glassell St.
**Murray, John S.** ... '56 '81 C.911 B.A. L.800 J.D. [🄰 Walsworth,F.B.&M.]
*PRACTICE AREAS: Business and Real Estate Litigation; Construction Law.
Murry, Julie Cloud ... '52 '78 C&L.1136 B.S., J.D. 3111 N. Tustin Ave.
Musgrave, Arvid L. ... '36 '75 C.988 B.S.M.E. L.1137 J.D. 431 E. Riverboat Way
Najman, Leon ... '47 '76 C.563 B.E.E. L.1137 J.D. P.O. Box 5424
Naresh, Suman ... '42 '71
Neill, Brian P. ... '— '92 C.112 B.A. L.1137 J.D. [🄰 Mercer&Z.]
Nelson, John S., (BV) ... '34 '73 C.1042 B.S. L.426 J.D. [Nelson&N.]
**Nelson, Kristen Kay** ... '68 '93 C.112 B.A. L.1068 J.D. [🄰 Morris,P.&P.]
Nelson, Pamela Miller ... '46 '75 C.112 B.A. L.426 J.D. [Nelson&N.]
Nelson & Nelson, (BV) ... 333 City Blvd. W.
Netty, Nicholas A. ... '50 '76 C.1109 B.A. L.678 J.D. 1835 W. Orangewood Ave.
Newport, John G. ... '44 '76 C.766 B.A. L.990 J.D. 770 The City Drive S.
Nguyen, Hong ... '59 '88 C&L.623 B.S., J.D. Dep. Pub. Def.
Nialis, Mark A. ... '52 '79 C.884 B.S. L.990 J.D. [Wildish&N.]
**Nichols, Stephen M.** ... '56 '81 C.770 B.S. L.426 J.D. [Walsworth,F.B.&M.]
*PRACTICE AREAS: Trial Law; Commercial Law; Banking Law; Personal Injury; Construction Defects.
Nielsen, Ken R. ... '61 '92 C.1042 B.S.W. L.1137 J.D. Sr. Soc. Worker, Co. of Orange
**Nishikawa, Wendy K. K.** '60 '85 C&L.312 B.B.A., J.D. Asst. Gen. Coun. & Asst. Secy., Wynn's Intl., Inc.
Nissen, David R., (AV) ... '32 '61 C.937 B.A. L.339 J.D. [D.R.Nissen]
Nissen, David R., A Professional Law Corporation, (AV) ... 333 City Blvd.
**Niven, Leslie L.** ... '64 '95 C.1137 B.S.L. L.1240 J.D. [L.M.Niven]
*PRACTICE AREAS: Personal Injury; General Civil Litigation; Sports/Entertainment Law; Family Law.
**Niven, Louis M.**, (BV) ... '33 '60 C.88 B.A. L.1068 J.D. [L.M.Niven]
*REPORTED CASES: Uva v. Evans, 83 CA 3d 356 (1978).
*PRACTICE AREAS: Family Law; Personal Injury; General Civil and Criminal Trial Practice; Business; Corporate.

**Niven, Louis M., A Professional Law Corporation, (BV)**
**333 City Boulevard West, Suite 1605, 92868-2924**
**Telephone: 714-978-7887 Fax: 714-978-7330**
**Email: louniv@earthlink.net**
**Louis M. Niven (Certified Specialist, Family Law, The State Bar of California Board of Legal Specialization); Leslie L. Niven.**
**Family Law, Personal Injury, General Civil and Criminal Trial Practice, Business, Corporate, Probate, Real Estate Law and Sports/Entertainment Law.**

***See Professional Biographies, ORANGE, CALIFORNIA***

**Nixon, Thomas F.** ... '54 '84 C.112 B.A. L.426 J.D. [Woodruff,S.&S.]
*PRACTICE AREAS: Environmental Law; Hazardous Materials Law; Litigation.
Nord, Arvid D., III ... '52 '81 C.608 B.A. L.809 J.D. 170 S. Main St.
Nordstrom, Steele, Nicolette and Jefferson, (AV) 770 The City Dr. S., Ste. 3000 (⊙Los Angeles, Calif. & Kenai, Alask.)
Nunez, Jay A. ... '59 '88 C.112 B.A. L.426 J.D. 1100 Town & Country Rd.
O'Dell, Stephen P. ... '59 '87 C.560 B.A. L.990 J.D. 505 S. Main St.
Odriozola, James S. ... '46 '80 C.999 L.1137 J.D. Juv. Ct. Ref.
Offner, Lawrence Steven ... '54 '85 C.112 B.A. L.809 J.D. 1700 W. Katella Ave.

Oliver, Jerrold S. '26 '57 C.628 B.S. L.800 J.D.
Jud. Arbitration & Mediation Servs., Inc.
Osajima, Glenn K., (AV) ... '46 '72 C.112 B.A. L.1068 J.D. 1 City Boulevard W.
Palladini, Marie E. ... '53 '86 C.651 B.A. L.809 J.D. 770 The City Dr., S.
Palmer, Michelle L. ... '50 '85 C.1164 B.A.Psych. L.436 J.D. Dep. Co. Coun.
Papica, Francis P. ... '68 '92 C.112 B.A. L.823 J.D. [⊠ Nordstrom,S.N.&J.]
Parish, Barbara S. ... '48 '91 C.835 B.S. L.1190 J.D. 500 N. State College Blvd.
Park, Kevin H., (AV) ... '54 '80 C.923 B.S. L.990 J.D. [Mercer&Z.]
Parke, James R., (BV) ... '52 '78 C.1109 B.A. L.990 J.D. 1 City Blvd. W., Suite 1400
Parker, James W., (BV) ... '55 '83 C.112 B.A. L.990 J.D. 701 S. Parker St.
Parker, John R., (AV) ... '34 '62 C.475 B.A. L.477 J.D. 1740 W. Katella Ave.
Parr-Peak, Winifred ... '47 '89 C.940 B.S.L. L.1137 J.D. 150 S. Waterwheel Way
Patterson, Martha Geisler ... '57 '83 C.1109 B.S. L.1137 J.D. 1740 W. Katella Ave.
Patterson, Pamela ... '57 '83 [Dracup&P.]
**Pearson, Lynne A.** ... '60 '86 C.477 B.B.A. L.61 J.D. [⊠ Marlin&S.]
Pederzani, Robert W. ... '52 '77 C.1075 B.A. L.990 J.D. 1 City Blvd., W.
**Pegan, Kevin** ... '56 '85 C.1042 B.A. L.770 J.D. [Walsworth,F.B.&M.]
Peterson, Claudia A. ... '54 '84 C.112 B.S. L.809 J.D. 5709 Bryce Ave.
Petty, Phillip A. ... '33 '70 C.339 B.A. L.1137 J.D. Ret. Supr. Ct. J.
Philipson, Stephen L. ... '47 '73 C.112 B.A. L.61 J.D. 950 E. Katella Ave

**Phillips, Gerald J., (AV) '40 '65 C.93 A.B. L.94 LL.B.**
**One City Boulevard West, Suite 1400, 92668**
**Telephone: 714-978-0325**
**(Certified Specialist, Family Law, The State Bar of California Board of Legal Specialization).**
**Family Law.**
***See Professional Biographies, ORANGE, CALIFORNIA***

Pierce, A. C. ... '32 '74 L.1137 LL.B. 1509 E. Chapman Ave.‡
Prescott, Tonya E. ... '47 '86 L.1137 J.D. 701 S. Parker
**Presley, Wilma E.**, (BV) ... '36 '77 C&L.1137 B.S., J.D. [W.E.Presley]

**Presley, Wilma E., A Professional Corporation, (BV)**
**333 City Boulevard West Suite 1420, 92868-2924**
**Telephone: 714-939-1420 Fax: 714-939-1485**
**Wilma E. Presley (Certified Specialist, Family Law, The State Bar of California Board of Legal Specialization).**
**Family Law Practice, including Child Custody, Child and Spousal Support, Community Property Evaluation and Division. Interstate Custody (U.C.C.J.A.), Post Dissolution Modifications, Juvenile Law and International Family Law.**
***See Professional Biographies, ORANGE, CALIFORNIA***

Price, David L., (AV) ... '43 '70 C.940 B.A. L.1066 J.D. 333 City Blvd., W.
**Prietto, Carlos A., III** ... '68 '93 C.426 B.A. L.770 J.D. [⊠ Morris,P.&P.]
Pursell, Michael D., Law Offices of, (AV) '36 '66
C.112 A.B. L.1065 J.D. 888 Town & Country Rd.
**Pynes, Craig** ... '64 '90 C.112 B.A. L.426 J.D. [⊠ Marlin&S.]
*LANGUAGES: Spanish.

**Quigley, Michael J., (AV) '30 '64 C.1027 B.S. L.564 LL.B.**
**1420 East Chapman Avenue, 92666**
**Telephone: 714-633-4921 Fax: 714-633-8014**
***PRACTICE AREAS: Business Law.**
**Civil and Insurance Litigation. Criminal, Probate, Business, Corporate and Family Law. Bankruptcy.**
***See Professional Biographies, ORANGE, CALIFORNIA***

Radensky, Madeleine ... '39 '75 C.112 B.A. L.1137 J.D. Off. of Hearing & Appeals
**Reed, Daniel A.** ... '61 '90 C.112 B.A. L.809 J.D. [⊠ Landau,O.&K.]
Rehaste, Rita A. ... '50 '91 C&L.1137 B.S.L., J.D. [⊠ G.W.Sanders]
Reich, Adell, Crost & Cvitan, (AV) ... 1918 W. Chapman Ave. (⊙Los Angeles)
**Reid, Mary Catherine** ... '60 '91 C.112 B.A. L.1049 J.D. [⊠ Gilbert,K.C.&J.]
*PRACTICE AREAS: Corporate Law; Employment Law; Estate Planning; Business Planning.
Reinhold, Marianne ... '55 '82 C.112 B.A. L.426 J.D. [Reich,A.C.&C.]
Renzi, Sharon M. ... '52 '91 C&L.1137 B.A., J.D. [⊠ P.J.Gorelick]
**Resnick, Jason E.** ... '70 '95 C.112 B.A. L.464 J.D. [⊠ Woodruff,S.&S.]
*PRACTICE AREAS: Litigation.
Resnick, John J. ... '18 '66 C.112 B.A. L.1001 J.D. 2720 E. Walnut Ave.
Rice, Saml. K. ... '24 '56 C.112 L.809 3229 Mandeville Pl.
Richmond, Scott D., (AV) ... '38 '65 C.813 A.B. L.1065 J.D. [Richmond&R.]⊙
Richmond & Richmond, (AV) ... 701 E. Chapman Ave. (⊙Laguna Hills)
Rients, David M. ... '67 '92 C&L.1137 B.S., J.D. 635 N. Main St.
**Ries, Deborah A.** ... '62 '87 C.105 B.A. L.802 J.D. [⊠ Testa&Assoc.]⊙
*PRACTICE AREAS: Business Disputes; Contract Drafting; Construction; Real Property; General Business.
Roberts, James F. ... '55 '80 C.112 B.A. L.464 J.D. 3111 N. Tustin St.
Robinson, Julee ... '48 '74 C.112 B.S. L.1066 J.D. Supr. Ct. Comr.
Rodgers, R. Neil ... '51 '79 C.112 B.A. L.1137 J.D. 550 E. Chapman Ave.
Rolle, Kristina ... '65 '89 C.800 B.S. L.37 J.D. 701 S. Parker St.
Roseman, Mark E., (BV) ... '49 '78 C.608 B.S. L.1137 J.D. [Blum&R.]
Rostan, Raymond J. ... '31 '70 C.1046 B.S. L.990 J.D. 3105 E. Ruth Pl.
Roston, Martin F. ... '25 '57 C.976 B.S. L.477 J.D. 11865 Prospect St.‡
Rovin, Justice L. ... '44 '73 C.112 B.A. L.1137 J.D. 595 The City Dr.
Rucker, James J. ... '48 '74 C.767 B.A. L.1068 J.D. 1745 W. Orangewood Ave.
**Ruggles, Allan W.** ... '52 '84 C.745 B.A. L.1194 J.D. [Walsworth,F.B.&M.]
*PRACTICE AREAS: Creditor Bankruptcy Representation; Civil Litigation.

**Rus, Miliband, Williams & Smith**
**(See Irvine)**

Russo, Vincent J. ... '45 '78 C.1042 B.A. L.1137 J.D. 606 E. Chapman Ave. Ste. 201
**Salmacia, Carol A.**, (AV) ... '45 '76 C.605 B.A. L.1190 J.D. [Hillsinger&C.]
**Saltzman, Stanley D.**, (AV) ... '52 '79 C.12 D.C.S. L.800 J.D. [Marlin&S.]⊙
*LANGUAGES: French, Italian.
*REPORTED CASES: Christensen v. California Supreme Court 53 Cal 3rd 868.
*PRACTICE AREAS: Insurance Defense Law; Professional Malpractice Law; Construction Defect Law.
Sanders, Gary W., (AV) ... '49 '77 C.1074 B.S. L.1137 J.D. [G.W.Sanders]
Sanders, Gary W., Law Offices of, (AV) ... 500 N. State College Blvd., Ste. 1220
Sauder, Phillip Paul ... '62 '95 C.999 B.S. L.1137 J.D. [⊠ Blum&R.]
**Sawdei, Milan A.** '46 '75 L.1137 J.D.
Exec. V.P., Chf. Legal Offr. & Secy., Bergen Brunswig Corp.

**Saylin, Brian G., (AV) '42 '68 C&L.800 B.S., J.D.**
**625 The City Drive South, Suite 355, 92668-4986**
**Telephone: 714-750-3200 Fax: 714-750-6250**
**(Certified Specialist, Family Law, The State Bar of California Board of Legal Specialization).**
**Appellate, Family and Matrimonial Law.**
***See Professional Biographies, ORANGE, CALIFORNIA***

**Schechter, Bruce Lee**, (BV) ... '56 '81 C.36 B.S. L.1188 J.D. [Hollins,S.&F.]
*PRACTICE AREAS: Personal Injury Defense Law; Products Liability Law; Construction Defect.
**Schiffer, Eric M.** ... '70 '95 C.112 B.A. L.809 J.D. [⊠ Hollins,S.&F.]
*LANGUAGES: Spanish.
*PRACTICE AREAS: General Practice; Civil Practice; Business Law; Insurance.

**Schiller, Mary Ann** ... '60 '87 C.112 B.A. L.770 J.D. [⊠ Hollins,S.&F.]
*PRACTICE AREAS: Uninsured Motorists Law; General Civil Litigation.
Schmid & Voiles, (AV) ... 333 City Blvd. W. (⊙L.A.)
Schmidt, Robert D. ... '55 '81 C.967 B.A. L.150 J.D. 1 City Blvd. W.
**Schneider, Peter A.** ... '59 '84 C.112 B.A. L.1049 J.D. [⊠ Harrington,F.D.&C.]
Schroer, Jeffrey S. ... '63 '89 C.37 B.A. L.1049 J.D. [⊠ Blum&R.]
Schwamb & Stabile, Inc., (AV) ... 333 City Blvd., W.
Seamans, R. Gary ... '49 '82 C&L.1137 B.S., J.D. 2951 28th St
Seastrom, Philip G., (AV) ... '47 '76 C&L.1137 B.S., J.D. 333 City Blvd W.
Secia, Rick M. ... '45 '74 C.1077 B.A. L.426 J.D. 3111 N. Tustin St.
**Segal, Glen R.** ... '61 '86 C.1109 B.A. L.800 J.D. [⊠ Agapay,L.&H.]
**Seide, Lonnie K.** ... '59 '86 C.588 B.S. L.724 J.D. [⊠ Minyard&M.]
*REPORTED CASES: Paulsen, et. al. v. County of Nassau, et. al., 925 F 2d 65 (2d Cir. 1991).
*PRACTICE AREAS: Family Law.
Setera, Gerald V. ... '35 '68 C.475 B.S.M.E. L.1095 LL.B. P.O. Box 3593
Shack, Richard M., (AV) ... '42 '72 C.800 A.B. L.1137 J.D. 1 City Blvd. W.
Shapiro, Cindy A. ... '66 '94 C.112 B.A.B.S. L.426 J.D. 333 S. Anita St., Ste. 660
**Shaw, John R.** ... '44 '71 C.112 B.A. L.1065 J.D. [Woodruff,S.&S.]
*PRACTICE AREAS: Municipal Law; Sanitation Law; Land Use Law.
Shaw, Stanford E., (BV) ... '34 '70 L.809 J.D. 1420 E. Chapman Ave.
Shea, Jerome J., Jr. ... '28 '56 C.745 B.A. L.276 LL.B. 811 N. Cambridge‡
Shelton, Cheryl L. ... '62 '89 C.1109 B.A. L.1137 J.D. Gen. Coun., Global Van Lines, Inc.
**Shelton, Demetrius D.** '65 '94
C&L.112 B.A., J.D. [Walsworth,F.B.&M.] (⊙San Francisco)
**Sherwood, Laurie E.** ... '57 '91 C.525 B.S. L.1065 J.D. [Walsworth,F.B.&M.]⊙
*PRACTICE AREAS: Litigation; Police Civil Liability Law.
**Shipe, Cathy L.** ... '60 '91 C.537 B.B.A. L.61 J.D. [⊠ Hagenbaugh&M.]
**Shorago, Alisa A.** ... '67 '93 C.1097 B.A. L.1065 J.D. [Walsworth,F.B.&M.]
**Sida, Arturo** ... '54 '80 C.813 B.A. L.1066 J.D. Coun., Bergen Brunswig Corp.
*LANGUAGES: Spanish.
*RESPONSIBILITIES: General Corporate Law; Finance and Securities Law; Real Estate Law; Business Transactions.
**Sienski, Paul S.** ... '58 '89 C.112 B.A. L.464 J.D. [⊠ Morris,P.&P.]
Sieveke, Patricia A. '60 '86 C.112 B.A. L.1049 J.D.
[⊠ Mulvaney,K.&B.] (⊙Los Angeles)
**Silverii, Glenn L.** ... '53 '79 C.1077 B.A. L.809 J.D. [⊠ Landau,O.&K.]
Simpson, Janella K. '52 '79
C.112 B.A. L.1137 J.D. Asst. Gen. Coun., Volt Info. Sciences, Inc.
**Smart, Kennard R., Jr.**, (AV) ... '44 '71 C.112 B.A. L.1065 J.D. [Woodruff,S.&S.]
*PRACTICE AREAS: Transportation Law.
Smilow, Edward L. ... '51 '77 C.188 B.S. L.1202 J.D. 505 City Pkwy. W.
**Snyder, Jack H.** ... '58 '83 C.112 B.A. L.1067 J.D. [Hollins,S.&F.] (⊙Moreno Valley)
*PRACTICE AREAS: Personal Injury Defense Law; Products Liability Law; Insurance Law; Uninsured Motorist/Underinsured Motorist Practice; Legal Malpractice Defense.
**Snyder, Michael R.** ... '58 '84 C.1042 B.A. L.1137 J.D. [Elliot,L.L.&S.]⊙
*PRACTICE AREAS: Insurance Defense; Medical Malpractice Defense.
Sowers, Donald G. ... '53 '86 C.999 A.S. L.809 J.D. [Takakjian&S.]⊙
**Spence, Danie I.** ... '57 '84 C&L.426 B.A., J.D. [⊠ Woodruff,S.&S.]
*PRACTICE AREAS: Banking Law; Real Estate Transactions.
**Spradlin, Daniel K.**, (AV) ... '53 '78 C.112 B.A. L.990 J.D. [Woodruff,S.&S.]
*PRACTICE AREAS: Litigation; Liability Defense Law; Environmental Law.
Stabile, Thomas P., (AV) ... '43 '71 C.190 B.A. L.1137 J.D. [Schwamb&S.]
Stagner, Robert D. ... '50 '77 C.642 B.A. L.1137 J.D. 630 N. Tustin St.
Stasnopolis, Dee H. ... '55 '83 C.36 B.S. L.809 J.D. [Mercer&Z.]
Stenger, Barron C. '43 '72 C.1042 B.S. L.426 J.D.
Centennial Community Developers, Inc.
Sterling, Patricia M. ... '45 '79 C&L.1190 B.S., LL.B. Lancer Claims Servs., Inc.
Stewart, Stephen C. ... '33 '66 C.549 B.A. L.813 770 The City Dr.
Stitz, Leonard W. ... '51 '85 L.999 J.D. 1122 E. Lincoln Ave., Ste. 203
Stone, Gene S. ... '— '92 C.1109 B.A. L.1139 J.D. [⊠ Mercer&Z.]
Stout, Stephanie L. ... '63 '89 C.645 B.S. L.665 J.D. Asst. V.P., St. Joseph Health Sys.
Strok, Lisa Bynum ... '62 '93 C.1185 B.S.N. L.807 J.D. [⊠ Schmid&V.]
Stroud, Greer H., (Mrs.) ... '39 '72 L.990 J.D. 500 N. St. College Blvd.‡

**Stutz, Gallagher, Artiano, Shinoff & Holtz, A Professional Corporation**
**(See San Diego)**

Swain, William Murphy ... '55 '82 C&L.1137 B.S.L., J.D. 1428 E. Chapman Ave.
Tait, Thomas F. ... '58 '85 C.972 B.S. L.880 J.D. Pres., Tait & Assocs., Inc.
Takakjian, Paul, (BV) '53 '79
C.112 B.A. L.426 J.D. [Takakjian&S.] (⊙Encino, L.A. & Oxnard)
Takakjian & Sowers, (BV)
333 City Blvd. W. (⊙Los Angeles, Encino, Oxnard, Pasadena & Long Beach)
Talley, Andrew A. ... '56 '81 C.1042 B.S. L.464 J.D. 500 N. State College Blvd.
Tavernier, Ernest M. ... '30 '62 C&L.878 B.A., LL.B. 16312 Fellows Dr.‡
**Testa, James A., (P.C.)**, (AV) ... '42 '75 C.112 B.A. L.1049 J.D. [Testa&Assoc.]⊙
*LANGUAGES: Spanish.
*REPORTED CASES: Lucas v. Pollock (1992) 7 Cal. App. 4th 668.

**Testa & Associates, (AV)**
**A Partnership including a Professional Corporation**
**765 The City Drive Suite 405, 92668⊙**
**Telephone: 714-748-8030 Facsimile: 714-748-1045**
**James A. Testa (P.C.). Associates: John M. Harmata; Deborah A. Ries. Of Counsel: Susan C. Chesebro.**
**General Civil and Trial Practice. Insurance, Medical Malpractice, Personal Injury, Construction, Business Disputes, Employment and Real Estate Law.**
**Reference: Grossmont Bank (Vista Branch).**
**Vista, California Office: Vista Corporate Center, 1800 Thibodo Road, Suite 300, P.O. Box 1720. Telephone: 619-599-9565. Facsimile: 619-599-9571.**
***See Professional Biographies, ORANGE, CALIFORNIA***

**Theologides, Stergios** ... '66 '92 C.674 A.B. L.178 J.D. Corp. Coun., Wynn's Int'l, Inc.
*LANGUAGES: Chinese and Greek.
**Thierbach, Marlene L.**, (AV) ... '51 '86 C.1109 B.A. L.426 J.D. [Fabozzi,T.&C.]
*PRACTICE AREAS: Banking Law; Bankruptcy Law; Business Litigation.
Thomason, Marlene, (BV) ... '51 '77 L.990 J.D. 472 Glassell
Thorne, Brian G. ... '56 '85 C.1097 B.S. L.809 J.D. [Kelly&H.]
Thornton, Hurd ... '21 '49 C.112 B.A. L.800 J.D. 7820 Broadmoor Trail
**Thorson, Eric W.** ... '63 '91 C.310 B.A. L.174 J.D. [⊠ Gilbert,K.C.&J.]
*PRACTICE AREAS: Insurance Defense.
Tornay, Peter C., (BV) ... '23 '59 C&L.800 A.B., LL.B. 625 The City Dr., S.
Twer, Daniel L. ... '43 '68 C.205 B.A. L.276 J.D. 4000 Metroplitan Dr.
Ufkes, Alvin J. ... '25 '51 C.98 B.S. L.910 J.D. 777 S. Main St.
Vander Molen, Milton J. ... '33 '74 C.477 B.S. L.1137 J.D. [Vander Molen&M.]
Vander Molen & Malin, (BV) ... 1509 E. Chapman Ave.

**Van Tatenhove, Dirk, (AV) '47 '75 C.1097 B.A. L.770 J.D.**
**Suite 355, 625 The City Drive South, 92668**
**Telephone: 714-750-3500 Fax: 714-750-6250**
***REPORTED CASES: Estate of Claffey (1989) 209 Cal. App. 3d254.**

(This Listing Continued)

**Van Tatenhove, Dirk (Continued)**

**Probate Administration, Will Contests, Probate and Trust Litigation, Conservatorship and Guardianship Law.**

*See Professional Biographies, ORANGE, CALIFORNIA*

Vedell, Robert L., (BV) ............'28 '72 C.339 B.S. L.990 J.D. 541 E. Chapman Ave.
Vian, Deborah Ann ..................... '64 '91 C.679 B.S. L.1187 J.D. 505 S. Main St.
Viens, Michele Marie ............... '54 '88 C.112 B.A. L.1065 J.D. 770 The City Dr. S.
**Vincent, Jeffrey R.** ..........................'56 '92 C.112 B.S. L.284 J.D. [Ⓐ Marlin&S.]
Vincent, Walter K. ...............'22 '75 C.800 B.S.E.E. L.1137 J.D. 11301 S. Colbow St
Wadsworth, Barbara ..............'47 '74 C.605 B.A. L.1049 J.D. 725 Town & Country
Wallace, Harry A. ........................ '58 '87 C.112 B.S. L.940 J.D. [Ⓐ Mercer&Z.]
Walls, William E. ........................ '51 '77 C.112 B.A. L.990 J.D. BDO Seidman
**Walsworth, Jeffrey P.**, (BV) ..... '53 '77 C&L.1137 B.S.L., J.D. [Walsworth,F.B.&M.]⊙

**Walsworth, Franklin, Bevins & McCall, (AV)**
**1 City Boulevard West, Suite 308, 92668⊙**
**Telephone: 714-634-2522 LAW-FAX: 714-634-0686**
**Jeffrey P. Walsworth; Ferdie F. Franklin; Ronald H. Bevins, Jr.; Michael T. McCall; Noel Edlin (Resident, San Francisco Office); Lawrence E. Duffy, Jr.; James A. Anton; Ingrid K. Campagne (Resident, San Francisco Office); Robert M. Channel (Resident, San Francisco Office); Nicholas A. Cipiti; Sharon L. Clisham (Resident, San Francisco Office); Richard M. Hills (Resident, San Francisco Office); Sandra G. Kennedy; Randall J. Lee (Resident, San Francisco Office); Kevin Pegan; Allan W. Ruggles; Laurie E. Sherwood; Cindy R. Hughes; Stephen M. Nichols; Cyrian B. Tabuena (Resident, San Francisco Office); Mary A. Watson; Alisa A. Shorago; Deidre F. Cohen; Demetrius D. Shelton; Jennifer A. Johnson; Mark J. Mulkerin; John S. Murray; Allyson B. Fox (Resident, Houston Office).**
**Business, Construction and Development, Real Estate, Corporate, Banking, Creditors Rights, Employment, Insurance Coverage, Products Liability, Environmental, General Appellate, Federal and State Trial Practice. Municipal Law.**
**San Francisco, California Office: 580 California Street, Suite 1335. Telephone: 415-781-7072. Fax: 415-391-6258.**
**Santa Barbara, California Office: 4520 Via Esperanza. Telephone: 805-569-3100 Fax: 805-569-1906.**
**Houston, Texas Office: 2425 West Loop South, Suite 200. Telephone: 713-787-9009. Fax: 713-787-9010.**

*See Professional Biographies, ORANGE, CALIFORNIA*

**Ward, Michael V.**, (BV) .....'56 '85 C.20 B.A. L.930 J.D. Coun., Bergen Brunswig Corp.
*RESPONSIBILITIES: Corporate Law; Securities Law; Real Estate Law; Litigation.
**Watson, Mary A.** ............................'65 '92 C.881 B.A. L.990 J.D. [Walsworth,F.B.&M.]
*LANGUAGES: Spanish.
**Watts, Alan R.**, (AV) ....................... '35 '61 C.768 B.A. L.1068 J.D. [Woodruff,S.&S.]
*PRACTICE AREAS: Public Utilities Law; Administrative Law; Municipal Law.
Weber, G. Donald, Jr., (AV) '34 '64 C.659 B.S.E.E. L.831 J.D.
333 City Blvd., W. (Pat.)
Weeks, Allan P. ............'40 '70 C.197 A.B. L.94 J.D. Gen. Coun., Systems Integrated

**Weiner, Bruce S. '52 '77 C.800 B.S. L.809 J.D.**
**333 City Boulevard West, Suite 1700, 92668**
**Telephone: 714-938-3216 FAX: 714-938-3217**
***PRACTICE AREAS: Real Estate Law; Bankruptcy; Civil Litigation; General Business.**
**Real Estate, Bankruptcy, Civil Litigation, General Business.**

*See Professional Biographies, ORANGE, CALIFORNIA*

**Werner, Lee G.** ...............................'53 '77 C.1151 B.A. L.424 J.D. [Agren&W.]
*PRACTICE AREAS: Real Estate; Business Litigation; Corporate Law.
Wesseln, Deborah Urell ....................'59 '86 C.112 B.A. L.464 J.D. 333 City Blvd. W.
West, Michelle, (AV) ..............'54 '83 C.1109 B.A. L.1137 J.D. 500 N. State College Blvd.
**Whisnant, Jacqueline A.** ..............'60 '87 C.1077 B.A. L.426 J.D. [Ⓐ Minyard&M.]
*PRACTICE AREAS: Family Law.
Whitaker, Fred M. '65 '90
C.112 B.A. L.426 J.D. V.P. & Gen. Coun., So. Counties Oil Co.
Whitcomb, Scott A. ............'61 '86 C.112 A.B. L.1137 J.D. 1100 Town & Country Rd.
**Wiesel, Jacob M.** .............................'50 '84 C.178 B.A. L.1009 J.D. [Ⓐ Landau,O.&K.]
*PRACTICE AREAS: Civil Tort Litigation.
Wilcoxson, John G. ........................'52 '81 C.112 B.A. L.1065 J.D. [Ⓐ P.J.Gorelick]
Wildish, Daniel R. ...............................'53 '81 C.477 B.A. L.990 J.D. [Wildish&N.]
Wildish & Nialis ................................................ 500 N. State College Blvd.
**Winters, Marilynn J.** .........................'42 '87 C.1247 B.S. L.1049 J.D. [Ⓐ Marlin&S.]
Winthers, Wayne W. ......................'58 '88 C.1044 B.A. L.1137 J.D. 701 S. Parker St.
Wittick, Michael J. ...........................'51 '80 C.1109 B.A. L.1137 J.D. [Ⓐ Mercer&Z.]
Wogee, Christine A. ..................'49 '79 C.1109 B.A. L.1137 J.D. 770 The City Dr., S.
Wollangk, Sandra J. '49 '84 C.1091 B.S. L.796 J.D.
(adm. in TX; not adm. in CA) St. Joseph Health Sys.
**Woodruff, Thomas L.**, (AV) ..........'39 '66 C.475 B.A. L.1065 J.D. [Woodruff,S.&S.]
*PRACTICE AREAS: Water Law; Sanitation Law; Environmental Law.

**Woodruff, Spradlin & Smart, A Professional Corporation, (AV)**
**Suite 7000, 701 South Parker Street, 92868-4720**
**Telephone: 714-558-7000 Facsimile: 714-835-7787**
**Thomas L. Woodruff; Daniel K. Spradlin; Kennard R. Smart, Jr.; Lois E. Jeffrey; Thomas F. Nixon; John R. Shaw; Craig G. Farrington; Terry C. Andrus; M. Lois Bobak; John E. Cavanaugh; Betty C. Burnett; Alan R. Watts;—Mary E. Binning; Rodell R. Fick; Joseph W. Forbath; Magdalena Lona-Wiant; Jason E. Resnick; Danie I. Spence.**
**General Civil and Trial Practice in State and Federal Courts. Administrative, Municipal, Water Rights, Public Utilities, Waste Water, Solid Waste, Environmental, Hazardous Waste, Transportation, School, Zoning, Real Estate Law and Liability Defense.**
**Representative Clients: City of Tustin; City of Laguna Hills; Orange County Transportation Authority; County Sanitation Districts of Orange County; Southern California Public Power Authority; Southern California Joint Powers Insurance Authority.**
**Reference: Union Bank.**

*See Professional Biographies, ORANGE, CALIFORNIA*

Wray, John M. '59 '84 C.347 A.B. L.1119 J.D.
Sr. V.P. & Gen. Coun., Affiliated Med. Enterprises
Yates, Sealy M., (AV) ........................'43 '69 C.69 B.B.A. L.1068 J.D. 505 S. Main St.
**Yauger, Daniel J.** ............'49 '79 C.165 B.A. L.245 J.D. [Ⓐ Marlin&S.] (⊙San Diego)
*PRACTICE AREAS: Insurance Defense Law; Professional Malpractice Law; Construction Defect Law.

**York, John K., (BV) '47 '72 C.112 B.A. L.1067 J.D.**
**Suite 1400, One City Boulevard West, 92668**
**Telephone: 714-547-8484 Facsimile: 714-634-2153**
**General Civil and Trial Practice. Family, Probate and Insurance Law.**

*See Professional Biographies, ORANGE, CALIFORNIA*

Younger, Keith A. ................................'46 '89 C.1181 B.S. L.1137 J.D. 2951 28th St
**Zacher, Dieter** .......................'65 '93 C.112 B.A. L.1137 J.D. [Ⓐ Landau,O.&K.]
*LANGUAGES: German.
*REPORTED CASES: Gernter v. VW Credit Cal. App. 4th.
*PRACTICE AREAS: Insurance; Torts; Medical Malpractice.
Zinder, Jeffrey E., (AV) .....................'53 '79 C.1097 B.S. L.426 J.D. [Mercer&Z.]

## NICARAGUAN LAWYERS RESIDENT IN ORANGE

**Minnella, Mendieta & Associates**
**202 West Lincoln Avenue, Suite H, 92865⊙**
**Telephone: (714) 998-4448 Facsimile: (714) 998-4026**
**John Lordsal Minnella Romano, Dr.; Uriel Mendieta Gutierrez (Not admitted in the United States).**

(This Listing Continued)

**Minnella, Mendieta & Associates (Continued)**

**Administrative, Appellate, Banking, Business, Civil Litigation/ Trial, Commercial, Confiscated Property Restitution, Contracts, Corporate, Constitutional Law, Criminal Matters, Customs, Divorce, Foreign (Jamaica, Panama, U.S.A.), Foreign Investment, Immigration and Nationality, Intellectual Property (Copyright, Patents and Trademark), International Business and Corporate Law, Labor, Letters and Powers, Personal Injury, Property Damage, Taxation (Nicaragua & U.S.A.), U.S.A. Laws, Wills, Trust and Probate.**
**Managua, Nicaragua Office: Apartado, 2448. Telephone: 42-22455. Facsimile: 41-22998.**

*See Professional Biographies, MANAGUA, NICARAGUA*

## ORANGEVALE, 16,493, *Sacramento Co.*

Binsch, Rudolf H. ..........................................'18 '57 L.464 LL.B. 8751 Potts Ct.
Bost, Burton T., (CV) ...................'29 '58 C.1060 A.B. L.464 LL.B. P.O. Box 168
Fowler, Roy W., Jr. ......................'35 '78 C.813 B.S. L.981 LL.B. 8855 Glori Dawn Dr.‡
Hughes, Ernest W. ............................'54 '82 C.770 B.S. L.464 J.D. 7453 Telegraph Ave.
Kinyon, Kendall E. '40 '72
C.508 B.A. L.464 J.D. Asst. Chf. Coun., Calif. Franchise Tax Bd.
Kneale, David H. ...................................'44 '78 L.1026 LL.B. Asst. Secy. of Senate
Perry, Emil B. .......................................'34 '82 C.383 B.S.E.E. L.981 P.O. Box 3
Sproul, Gene C. ..............................'24 '63 C.990 L.809 LL.B. 9330 Cherry Ave.
Trombley, Robert J., (CV) ...........'22 '57 C.215 L.809 LL.B. 9353 Village Green Way

## ORCUTT, —, *Santa Barbara Co.*

Namba, Jerry ........................................'57 '85 C.112 B.A. L.228 J.D. P.O. Box 2300

## ORINDA, 16,642, *Contra Costa Co.*

Adams, Robert G., (AV) ............'25 '49 C.112 A.B. L.1066 LL.B. 50 Brookside Rd.‡
Amerine, Roy R. ...........................'45 '79 C.112 B.S. L.809 J.D. 18 Orinda Way
Asher, Narra S., (Mrs.) '30 '53 C&L.900 A.B., LL.B.
Mason Mc Duffie Real Estate Inc.
Bain, Harold E., (BV) .......................'38 '72 C.112 B.S. L.284 J.D. 1 Las Aromas

**Balamuth, Barry, Law Offices of, (AV) '45 '72 C.112 B.S. L.1065 J.D.**
**3 Altarinda, Suite 210, 94563**
**Telephone: 510-254-1234 Fax: 510-254-0778**
**Email: info@balamuth.com URL: http://www.balamuth.com**
***PRACTICE AREAS: Professional Negligence (Legal, Medical and Accounting Law); Personal Injury Law.**
**—Kelly Balamuth.**
**Practice Limited to Personal Injury, Professional Malpractice (Legal, Medical and Accounting).**

*See Professional Biographies, ORINDA, CALIFORNIA*

**Balamuth, Kelly** ............................'68 '94 C.112 B.A. L.1067 J.D. [Ⓐ B.Balamuth]
*PRACTICE AREAS: Personal Injury; Attorney Negligence; Medical Negligence.
Berger, Sally ....................................'30 '79 C.823 B.A. L.1136 J.D. 522 Miner Rd.‡
Bingaman, Joseph P., (BV) ..........'34 '63 C.112 B.S. L.765 LL.B. 6001 Margarido Dr.
Blunden, Anthony A., (AV) ..........'42 '67 C.112 B.S. L.1065 J.D. 27 Watchwood Ct.‡
Brodsky, Dale L. ...............................'50 '77 C.813 B.A. L.767 J.D. 41 Estates Dr.
Brookes, Valentine, (AV) ..............'13 '37 C.112 A.B. L.1066 J.D. 7 Sycamore Rd.‡
Brown, Dyke ...................................'15 '41 C.051 M.A. L.976 LL.B. 196 Hall Dr.
Brown, Herbert L. ........................'44 '69 C&L.966 B.B.A., J.D. P.O. Box 2200
Camenisch, Shela C., (BV) ....................'48 '78 L.1153 J.D. 3 Altarinda Rd.
Carter, Christina M. .....................'58 '85 C.112 A.B. L.1065 J.D. 6 Monte Vista Rd.
Casey, Kathleen H., (AV⊙) ..............'37 '75 C.681 A.B. L.724 J.D. 120 Village Sq.
Cohn, Gerald A., (AV) ....................'37 '62 C.604 A.B. L.145 J.D. 140 Brookwood Rd.
Corbitt, R. Steven ........................'51 '76 C.208 B.S. L.169 J.D. 130 Amber Valley Dr.
Daffer, James H. .........................'29 '57 C.976 B.A. L.1066 LL.B. 129 Overhill Rd.
Daugherty, Kathleen H. .........................'56 '85 C.549 B.S. L.472 J.D. [Fleer&D.]
DeGirolamo, Joseph A. ......................'51 '76 C.150 B.B.A. L.930 J.D. 8 Irving Ct.
Den-Dulk, John D., (BV) ...............'14 '42 C.112 A.B. L.1066 LL.B. 3 Altarinda Road
Douglass, William D., (AV) .............'17 '46 C.112 A.B. L.1066 J.D. 3 Altarinda Rd.
**Doyle, Catherine T.** ....................'67 '93 C.436 B.A. L.767 J.D. [Ⓐ Gillin,J.E.L.&D.]
*LANGUAGES: French and Italian.
*PRACTICE AREAS: Trademark and Copyright Law.
**Doyle, Richard P., Jr.** ..................'58 '83 C.190 B.S. L.767 J.D. [Gillin,J.E.L.&D.]⊙
*PRACTICE AREAS: Intellectual Property; Litigation; Licensing and Protection; Prosecution.
Doyle, Susan M. ...............................'47 '81 C.112 A.B. L.1066 J.D. P.O. Box 1458
**Ellis, Luke**, (AV) ...........................'51 '76 C.33 B.A. L.1066 J.D. [Gillin,J.E.L.&D.]
*PRACTICE AREAS: Civil Trials; Intellectual Property Litigation; Commercial Torts; Plaintiff's Personal Injury.
Everett, Kenneth B. ..........................'46 '71 C.112 B.S. L.1065 J.D. P.O. Box 2015‡
Fivey, Daniel B. ...............................'55 '85 C.112 A.B. L.1065 J.D. 121 Ardith Dr.
Fledderman, H. L. ......................'26 '53 C.112 B.S. L.1066 J.D. 17 Vista del Mar‡
Fleer, John L., (AV) ...............................'51 '81 C.297 B.A. L.1066 J.D. [Fleer&D.]
Fleer & Daugherty, P.C., (AV) .................................................. 4 Orinda Way

**Foley, Christopher R. '62 '89 C.629 B.S. L.464 J.D.**
**89 Orinda Way, Suite 4, 94563**
**Telephone: 510-253-9970 Fax: 510-253-9973**
**Email: cfoley8971@aol.com**
***PRACTICE AREAS: Real Estate Law; Corporation Law; Estate Law.**
**General Civil Trial Practice and Real Estate Law.**

**Foley, Robert J., (AV) '22 '50 C.112 A.B. L.813 J.D.**
**89 Orinda Way, Suite 4, P.O. Box 1578, 94563**
**Telephone: 510-253-9970 Fax: 510-253-9973**
**General, Probate and Corporate Law.**
**Representative Clients: CAL West Periodicals; The Flecto Co.**

Friedman, Linda ...............'49 '73 C&L.813 B.S., J.D. Solomon Wilmington & Assoc.
Gelman, Robert S. ........................'45 '70 C.102 B.A. L.273 J.D. 39 Saint Stephens Dr.
Gerstler, Elaine ........................'46 '73 C.696 B.A. L.1009 J.D. 20 E. Altarinda Dr.‡
**Gillin, Andrew R.**, (AV) ...................'43 '70 C.112 A.B. L.145 J.D. [Gillin,J.E.L.&D.]
*PRACTICE AREAS: Civil Litigation; Trials and Appeals; Intellectual Property Litigation; Commercial Torts; Plaintiff's Personal Injury.

**Gillin, Jacobson, Ellis, Larsen & Doyle, (AV)**
**2 Theatre Square Suite 230, 94563⊙**
**Telephone: 510-258-0800 Fax: 510-848-0266**
**Email: lawfirm@gjeld.com**
**Andrew R. Gillin; Ralph L. Jacobson; Luke Ellis; James Paul Larsen; Richard P. Doyle, Jr.; Susan Hunt; Mitchell S. Rosenfeld; Catherine T. Doyle.**
**Civil Trial Practice including Intellectual Property Litigation, Commercial Torts, Products Liability, Personal Injury and Wrongful Death.**
**San Francisco Office: One Sutter Street, 10th Floor. Telephone: 415-986-4777.**

*See Professional Biographies, ORINDA, CALIFORNIA*

Glass, Gerard J. ..............................'36 '65 C.767 B.S. L.284 LL.B. 3 Altarinda Rd.
Glasser, Charles E., (BV) ....................'40 '71 C.207 B.A. L.1153 J.D. 62 Ardilla Rd.
Green, Shand L. ...............................'48 '75 C.911 B.A. L.276 J.D. 8 Sunnyside Ct.
Guidotti, Aldo P., (AV) ..................'20 '44 C.112 A.B. L.1066 LL.B. [Guidotti&L.]
Guidotti, Bernadine Bushman ...............................'21 '79 L.1153 J.D. 1 Bates Blvd.
Guidotti & Lee, (AV) ................................................................1 Bates Blvd.
Hagmann, David L. .............'15 '65 C.112 B.A. L.767 LL.B. 464 Camino Sobrante (Pat.)

CALIFORNIA—ORINDA MARTINDALE-HUBBELL LAW DIRECTORY 1997

Halperin, David J. '28 '58 C.46 B.S. L.146 J.D. 40 Robert Rd.
Harelson, Douglas E. '47 '80 C.1078 B.A. L.1153 J.D. 147 Meadow View Rd.
Harris, Norma '54 '84 C.587 B.S.B.A. L.813 J.D. 72 Camino Encinas
Hartog, John A., (AV) '52 '79 C.668 B.A. L.1065 J.D. [J.A.Hartog]
Hartog, Kathleen Irish '— '79 C.112 A.B. L.1065 J.D. [J.A.Hartog]
Hartog, John A., Inc., (AV) 4 Orinda Way
Hawkins, Daryl R., (AV) '32 '61 C.309 A.B. L.813 J.D. 4 Orinda Way, Ste. 270-D
Hegarty, Edward J., (AV) '36 '64 C.93 B.S. L.1065 LL.B. P.O. Box 699
Hetland, John R., (AV) '30 '56 C&L.494 B.S.L., J.D. [Hetland&K.]⊙
Hetland & Kneeland, A Professional Corporation, (AV) ... 20 Redcoach Lane (⊙Berkeley)
Higham, William R. '26 '55 C.628 B.S. L.1065 J.D. P.O. Box 327‡
Hoskins, William H. '32 '58 C&L.813 A.B., LL.B. 24 Calvin Dr.‡
Hudak, Jon A. '41 '66 C&L.508 B.A., J.D. 25 Orinda Way
**Hunt, Susan**, (BV) '63 '92 C&L.999 B.A., J.D. [Gillin,J.E.L.&D.]
*PRACTICE AREAS: Civil Litigation and Trials; Intellectual Property Litigation; Commercial Torts; Plaintiff's Personal Injury.
**Jacobson, Ralph L.**, (AV) '45 '70 C.910 B.A. L.813 J.D. [Gillin,J.E.L.&D.]
*PRACTICE AREAS: Civil Trials; Intellectual Property Litigation; Commercial Torts; Plaintiff's Personal Injury.
Jacobus, Jay M., (AV) '21 '53 C.112 B.S. L.1065 J.D. P.O. Box 666‡
Jovanovich, Stefan '45 '75 C.309 A.B. L.1066 J.D. 11 Sleepy Hollow Lane
Kimball, William H., (AV) '44 '70 C.684 B.A. L.1066 J.D. [W.H.Kimball]
Kimball, William H., Inc., (AV) 4 Orinda Way
Kneeland, Anne T. '36 '71 C.668 B.A. L.1066 J.D. 20 Redcoach Lane‡
**Lana, Edgar J.**, (AV) '42 '69 C.112 B.A. L.1065 J.D. [E.J.Lana]
*PRACTICE AREAS: Collection Law.

**Lana, Edgar J., A Professional Corporation, (AV)**
**18 Orinda Way, P.O. Box 2180, 94563**
**Telephone: 510-253-1010 Fax: 510-253-1742**
**Edgar J. Lana.**
**General Commercial and Civil Practice. Litigation. Creditors Rights, Bankruptcy, Corporate, Real Property, Landlord and Tenant, Real Estate, Wills, Trust and Probate.**
*See Professional Biographies, ORINDA, CALIFORNIA*

**Larsen, James Paul**, (AV) '59 '87 C.112 B.A. L.629 J.D. [Gillin,J.E.L.&D.]
*PRACTICE AREAS: Civil Litigation; Trials and Appeals; Plaintiff's Personal Injury; Intellectual Property Litigation; Commercial Torts.
Layton, H. F. '64 '91 C.101 B.A. L.426 J.D. 15 Altarinda Rd.
Leb, Michael H., (BV) '60 '86 C.976 B.A. L.477 J.D. 16 Robert Rd.
Lee, Charles A., (BV) '40 '66 C.668 B.A. L.1066 LL.B. [Guidotti&L.]
Loftis, Maureen H. '58 '91 C.112 B.A. L.284 J.D. [Fleer&D.]
Lynch, Richard C., (AV) '17 '41 C.112 B.S. L.1066 J.D. [Nichols,C.D.&R.]
Maimone, William G. '46 '76 C.112 B.S. L.1065 J.D. 55 Hillcrest Dr.‡
Markley, John K. '47 '75 C.263 L.1066 620 Greystone Ter.
McKinley, Gail G. '41 '87 C.174 B.A. L.767 J.D. 21 Santa Lucia
**McNabb, Sandra J.**, (AV) '52 '77 C.911 B.A. L.813 J.D. [Perez&M.]
*REPORTED CASES: Schmidt v. Foundation Health (1995) 35 Cal. App. 4th 1702; NCR ad. Hayes (9th Cir. 1995).
*PRACTICE AREAS: Business Litigation; Construction; Computer Law.
Medak, Walter H. '15 '51 C.112 M.A. L.309 LL.B. 173 Ardith Dr.
**Miller, Jeffrey A.** '50 '79 C.766 B.A. L.1066 J.D. [Perez&M.]
Minder, Gordon L. '13 '46 C.112 A.B. L.1066 LL.B. 420 Ridge Gate Rd.‡
Moore, Herbert P., Jr., (AV) '30 '55 C.112 B.S. L.1066 LL.B. 23 Orinda Way
Mouser, Paul W. '25 '49 C.942 A.B. L.813 J.D. 408 Ridge Gate Rd.‡
Nelson, Robt. T. '19 '51 C.147 B.E. L.146 J.D. 43 Camino Encinas‡
Nichols, Catterton, Downing & Reed, Inc., (AV) 3 Altarinda Rd.
O'Neil, Michael W. '41 '77 C.766 B.A. L.770 J.D. [M.W.O'Neil]
O'Neil, Michael W., A L.C. 120 Village Sq.
O'Neill, Gary M. '52 '79 C.668 B.A. L.770 J.D. N.Y. Life Ins. Co.
Orrell, Nancy I. '48 '73 C.112 A.B. L.767 J.D. 21 Valley View Rd.‡
Osofsky, Hilary M. '49 '77 C.112 A.B. L.426 J.D. 37 E. Altarinda Dr.
**Perez, Richard L.**, (AV) '46 '72 C.112 B.A. L.1066 J.D. [Perez&M.]
*REPORTED CASES: Consolidated Data Terminals v. Applied Digital Data Systems (9th Cir. 1983) 708 F. 2d 385; Glovatorium v. NCR Corporation (9th cir. 1992) 684 F2d 658.
*PRACTICE AREAS: Computer Law; Real Estate Law; Business Litigation.

**Perez & McNabb, A Professional Corporation, (AV)**
**140 Brookwood Road, 2nd Floor, 94563**
**Telephone: 510-254-6100 Fax: 510-254-0653**
**Richard L. Perez; Sandra J. McNabb; Jeffrey A. Miller; Marjorie A. Wallace; Richard G. Thomas (California Specialist, Taxation, California Board of Legal Specialization); Harold P. Selan.**
**Business and Real Estate Litigation in State and Federal Courts, Computer Disputes and Construction Claims. General Corporate, Real Estate and Commercial Law. Federal and State Income Taxation.**
*See Professional Biographies, ORINDA, CALIFORNIA*

Poggi, Thomas F., (BV) '24 '50 C&L.767 B.S., J.D. 4 Stanton Ct.
Prugh, George S. '20 '49 C.112 A.B. L.1065 J.D. 17 Cedar Ln.‡
Prugh, Virginia Patton '49 '81 C.1099 B.A. L.1065 J.D. 17 Cedar Lane★
Reed, Carol V. '52 '77 C.1073 B.A. L.765 J.D. [Nichols,C.D.&R.]
Reed, James E. '50 '76 C.112 B.S. L.765 J.D. [Nichols,C.D.&R.]
Reeve, Earl J. '38 '64 C.112 B.S. L.1065 J.D. 5 Idyll Ct.
Riley, Janet McCormick '58 '83 C.112 A.B. L.1065 J.D. 99 Van Ripper Ln.

**Robertson, Laurie J., Law Offices of '56 '84 C.112 A.B. L.767 J.D.**
**23 Altarinda Road, Suite 215, 94563**
**Telephone: 510-254-6721 Toll Free: 888-254-6721 Fax: 510-254-4787**
**Email: laurie@ljrlaw.com URL: http://www.ljrlaw.com**
**General Civil and Trial Practice, Business and Family Law.**
*See Professional Biographies, ORINDA, CALIFORNIA*

**Rosenfeld, Mitchell S.** '66 '92 C.228 B.S. L.273 J.D. [Gillin,J.E.L.&D.] (Pat.)⊙
*PRACTICE AREAS: Intellectual Property Litigation; Licensing and Prosecution.
Rothwell, Thomas H. '23 '52 C.112 B.S. L.1065 J.D. Ret. U.S. Mag.‡
Schimbor, Mark A. '45 '72 C.112 A.B. L.813 J.D. 25 Haciendas Rd.
**Selan, Harold P.** '56 '82 C.112 B.A. L.1065 J.D. [Perez&M.]
Shell, Diane E., (AV) '54 '79 C.1060 B.A. L.464 J.D. P.O. Box 704
Snook, W. Sayer, Jr., (AV) '25 '51 C.112 B.A. L.1066 LL.B. 34 St. Stephens Dr.‡
Stephens, Edw. H. '16 '41 C&L.878 B.S., LL.B.
(adm. in UT; not adm. in CA) 30 Tara Rd.‡
Swann, Eugene M., (BV) '34 '63 C.831 B.S. L.1066 LL.B. P.O. Box 1914
**Thomas, Richard G.** '48 '75 C.112 B.A. L.767 J.D. [Perez&M.]
*LANGUAGES: Russian.
*PRACTICE AREAS: Taxation; Real Estate; Corporate Law.
Tout, Robert E. '21 '55 C.169 A.B. L.1132 61 Avenida De Orinda
Van Hoesen, David M., (AV) '31 '59 C.31 B.A. L.813 LL.B. 2 Bel Air Dr.
Wakefield, William H., Jr. '13 '38 C.112 B.A. L.1066 LL.B. 85 Lombardy La.
**Wallace, Marjorie A.** '52 '76 C.112 B.A. L.1065 J.D. [Perez&M.]
*PRACTICE AREAS: Computer Law; Business Litigation; Technology Licensing.
Welch, Steven H., Jr. (P.C.), (BV) '21 '49 C.112 A.B. L.1065 J.D. 3 Warford Ter.‡
Willmarth, Francis G., (AV) '36 '62 C.112 A.B. L.1066 LL.B. P.O. Box 769
Wilson, Carol L. '43 '76 C.881 A.B. L.1065 J.D. 241 Glorietta Blvd.
Wilson, Clifford R., (BV) '46 '74 C.627 B.A. L.352 J.D. 184 Moraga Way
Wilson, W. Harney '22 '55 C.112 A.B. L.765 LL.B. 14 Hacienda Circle‡
Wolfe, Andrew P., (AV) '25 '61 C.112 A.B. L.767 LL.B. 11 Risa Ct.‡
Wolfe, Thomas F. '34 '61 C.116 B.S. L.107 LL.B. 112 Sleepy Hollow Lane
Wright, Orville I. '23 '55 C.112 B.S. L.767 LL.B. Adm. Law J., Pub. Utility Comm.
Ziegler, Alvin, (AV) '36 '60 C.1365 A.B. L.309 LL.B. 119 Camino don Miguel‡

## ORLAND, 5,052, *Glenn Co.*

Saint-Evans, Angus, (CV) '48 '79 C.147 B.A. L.1189 J.D. Jus. Ct. J.
Twede, Peter B., (CV) '47 '76 C.767 B.A. L.1026 J.D. 7 E. Walker St.

## ORLEANS, —, *Humboldt Co.*

Smith, Phillip W. '39 '77 C&L.1137 B.S.L., J.D. P.O. Box 157

## OROVILLE, * 11,960, *Butte Co.*

Albrecht, Kelly, (BV) '45 '75 C.112 A.B. L.770 J.D. 1440 Lincoln St.
Baber, William H., III, (BV) '46 '72 C&L.770 B.A., J.D. [Minasian,M.M.S.B.M.&S.]
Bach, Maxim N. '41 '68 C.112 B.A. L.1066 LL.B. 1950 Bird St.
Berglund, James B. '51 '76 [Hermansen,B.&W.]
Blackstock, Daniel V., (BV) '32 '56 C&L.861 B.A., LL.B. 1440 Lincoln
Bruce, Michael J. '40 '66 C.629 B.A. L.1049 J.D. 1550-C Myers St.
Deaver, Maurice A., Jr. '46 '77 C.1070 B.S. L.1067 J.D. 3778 Foothill Blvd.★
DeCastro, Michelle '69 '93 L.999 J.D. [Minasian,M.M.S.B.M.&S.]
Drossel, Robert J. '42 '77 C.1097 B.S. L.1231 J.D. Dep. Dist. Atty.
Fallman, James '44 '74 C.549 B.A. L.464 J.D. Dep. Dist. Atty.
Fishe, Tom E. '29 '78 C.597 L.1153 LL.B. Dep. Dist. Atty.
Galloway, Harry A., (CV) '24 '63 C.112 B.S. L.1065 LL.B. Dep. Dist. Atty.
Gilbert, Roger G. '47 '73 C.628 B.S. L.464 J.D. Supr. Ct. J.
Goldkind, Leonard D. '53 '78 C.766 B.A. L.765 J.D. Dep. Dist. Atty.
Goodwin, Norris M. '26 '52 C.112 L.1065 J.D. Jus. Ct. J.
Gray, John D. '20 '45 C&L.800 J.D. 216 Dun St.
Gunn, David E., (BV) '48 '76 C.112 A.B. L.1065 J.D. Butte Co. Ct. Comr.
Harberts, Helen, (BV) '52 '83 C.147 B.A. L.284 J.D. 25 County Ctr. Dr.
Heenan, Marianne '30 '60 C.112 A.B. L.767 LL.B. 1859 Bird St.‡
Heithecker, Philip H. '65 '92 [Hermansen,B.&W.]
**Hendren, Ed W.**, (AV) '38 '76 C.870 B.S. L.813 J.D. [Hendren]
*PRACTICE AREAS: Civil Trial and Appellate Practice; Aviation Law; Banking Litigation; Real Property; Business.

**Hendren Law Offices, (AV)** BB
**19 Nelson Avenue, P.O. Box 1822, 95965**
**Telephone: 916-533-0661 Fax: 916-533-3956**
**Ed W. Hendren.**
**Civil Trial and Appellate Practice, Aviation Law, Banking Litigation, Real Property, Business, Corporation and Partnership Law, Unfair Competition and Labor Law.**
**Reference: Butte Community Bank.**
*See Professional Biographies, OROVILLE, CALIFORNIA*

Hermansen, Gerald, (BV) '42 '71 C.112 A.B. L.1065 J.D. [Hermansen,B.&W.]
Hermansen, Berglund & Washington, (BV) 1639 Bird St.
Howell, M. Melanie '52 '78 C.122 B.A. L.770 J.D. 1639 Bird St.
Howell, Steven J. '52 '77 C.112 A.B. L.770 J.D. Supr. Ct. J.
Knippen, Gary R. '48 '79 C.112 A.B. L.1065 J.D. Supr. Ct.
LeClerc, Raoul J., (BV) '39 '66 C.285 B.A. L.1066 LL.B. [LeClerc&L.]
LeClerc & LeClerc, (BV) 1660 Lincoln St.

**Leonard & Lyde, (AV)**
**A Partnership including Professional Corporations**
**1453 Huntoon Street, 95965⊙**
**Telephone: 916-533-2662 Fax: 916-533-3843**
**Members of Firm: Sharon A. Stone (Resident).**
**General Civil and Trial Practice. Medical Law, Business, Probate, Insurance.**
**Chico, California Office: 1600 Humboldt Road, Suite 1. Telephone: 916-345-3494. Fax: 916-345-0460.**
*See Professional Biographies, OROVILLE, CALIFORNIA*

McCabe, Neil H., (BV) '40 '66 C.813 A.B. L.1066 J.D. Asst. Co. Coun.
McClain, David M. '49 '80 C.208 B.A. L.1049 J.D. Chief Dep. Co.
Meith, Jeffrey A., (CV) '47 '72 C.112 B.A. L.1067 J.D. [Minasian,M.M.S.B.M.&S.]
Miller, Doris F. '27 '90 C.112 B.A. L.999 J.D. 2112 5th Ave.
Minasian, David '19 '52 C.169 A.B. L.1065 3778 Foothill Blvd.‡
Minasian, Paul R., (AV) '42 '67 C.813 A.B. L.1066 J.D. [Minasian,M.M.S.B.M.&S.]
Minasian, Susan Roff '48 '76 C.1168 B.A. L.1026 J.D. Co. Coun.
Minasian, Minasian, Minasian, Spruance, Baber, Meith & Soares, (AV) 1681 Bird St.
Montgomery, Daniel G. '44 '75 C.767 L.765 J.D. Dep. Co. Coun.
Mueller, Robert M., (BV) '36 '61 C.475 B.S. L.800 J.D. Pub. Def.
Mulkey, Loyd H., Jr. '28 '54 C&L.813 B.A., LL.B. Supr. Ct. J.
Ogle, Gary M. '52 '78 C.169 B.A. L.950 J.D. Dep. Dist. Atty.
O'Laughlin, Tim '58 '84 C.112 B.A. L.770 J.D. [Minasian,M.M.S.B.M.&S.]
Paris, William C., III '68 '93 C.608 B.A. L.273 J.D. [Minasian,M.M.S.B.M.&S.]
Patrick, William R. '43 '74 C.147 B.A. L.464 J.D. Supr. Ct. J.

**Peters, Fuller, Rush, Farnsworth & Habib**
**(See Chico)**

**Price, Brown & Halsey**
**(See Chico)**

Ramsey, Michael L. '48 '77 C.112 B.A. L.464 J.D. Dist. Atty.
Robison, George C. '31 '73 C.911 L.426 J.D. 2112 5th Ave.‡
Rotar, Louis, Jr. '33 '71 C.999 L.1001 J.D. 2854-A Olive Hwy.
Sambol, Charles M. '47 '84 C.147 B.A. L.464 J.D. Dep. Dist. Atty.
Schroder, John C., Jr. '32 '66 C.999 L.765 LL.B. 2858 Olive Hway.
Sexton, Michael V. '45 '85 C.284 B.S. L.464 J.D. [Minasian,M.M.S.B.M.&S.]
Soares, M. Anthony '52 '77 C.147 B.A. L.464 J.D. [Minasian,M.M.S.B.M.&S.]
Spruance, William H., (AV) '40 '69 C.684 B.A. L.770 J.D. [Minasian,M.M.S.B.M.&S.]
Stapleton, Steven M. '52 '79 C.147 B.A. L.408 J.D. 1453 Huntoon St. (⊙Chico)
**Stone, Sharon A.** '56 '90 C.330 L.999 J.D. [Leonard&L.]
*PRACTICE AREAS: Business Law; Insurance Defense Law.
Trenholme, Steven '57 '86 C.154 B.A. L.464 J.D. 1650 Lincoln (⊙Paradise)
Washington, George E., (BV) '44 '70 C.112 B.A. L.1065 J.D. [Hermansen,B.&W.]
Watt, Reginald M. '12 '39 C.112 L.1065 J.D. Supr. Ct. J.
Wohlfeil, Herman D. '45 '76 C.636 B.S. L.61 J.D. [Wohlfeil&W.]
Wohlfeil, Melody A. '47 '76 C&L.1137 B.S.L., J.D. [Wohlfeil&W.]
Wohlfeil & Wohlfeil 13 Gleness Dr.

## OXNARD, 142,216, *Ventura Co.*

**Andersen, John M.** '63 '92 C.112 B.A. L.1065 J.D. [Nordman,C.H.&C.]⊙
*PRACTICE AREAS: Estate Planning; Taxation; Business Law; Civil Litigation.
**Arnold, Gary D.**, (BV) '51 '76 C&L.800 B.S., J.D. [Arnold,B.M.W.&Z.]⊙
*PRACTICE AREAS: Real Estate; Business Law; Banking and Finance; Creditor Rights; Appellate Law.

**Arnold, Back, Mathews, Wojkowski & Zirbel, (AV)**
**2901 North Ventura Road, Suite 240, 93030⊙**
**Telephone: 805-988-9886 Fax: 805-988-1937**

(This Listing Continued)

CAA450P

**Arnold, Back, Mathews, Wojkowski & Zirbel (Continued)**

Members of Firm: Gary D. Arnold; Brian J. Back; John M. Mathews; James Wojkowski; David R. Worley; Mark A. Zirbel; Wayne K. Baldwin. Associates: Denise B. Rothwell; Ellen S. Rosenberg (Not admitted in CA). Of Counsel: Kathleen J. Back.
Civil Litigation, Real Property, Corporations, Construction, Land Use, Estate Planning, Business, Commercial, Taxation, Mergers and Acquisitions, Administrative, Municipal and Governmental Law, Environmental, Solid and Liquid Waste, Water Rights, Probate and Trust, Homeowners' Associations.
Westlake Village, California Office: 100 North Westlake Boulevard, Suite 201, 91362. Telephone: 805-371-8800. Fax: 805-495-6212.
*See Professional Biographies, OXNARD, CALIFORNIA*

**Ash, Linda Kathryn** ............... '— '94 C.36 B.S. L.1049 J.D. [A England,W.S.&T.]
*PRACTICE AREAS: Business Law; Copyrights; Trademarks.
Atterbury, Kathryn M. ..................'60 '87 C.112 B.A. L.1065 J.D. 300 Esplanade Dr.
**Back, Brian J.**, (BV) ............... '50 '77 C.154 B.A. L.770 J.D. [Arnold,B.M.W.&Z.]⊙
*PRACTICE AREAS: General Civil Litigation; Landlord/Tenant Law; Construction Law and Disputes.
**Back, Kathleen J.** .................. '51 '79 C.773 B.A. L.770 J.D. [C Arnold,B.M.W.&Z.]
Baio, Rocky J., (BV) .................. '53 '79 C.112 B.A. L.1137 J.D. [Rosenmund,B.&M.]
**Baldwin, Wayne K.** .............. '60 '88 C.112 B.A. L.101 J.D. [Arnold,B.M.W.&Z.]⊙
*PRACTICE AREAS: Business; Construction and Real Estate Litigation; Broker Defense; Business and Commercial Transactions.
**Barney, Mark T.** ..................'63 '89 C.112 B.A. L.770 J.D. [A England,W.S.&T.]
*PRACTICE AREAS: Corporate Law; Business Law.
Barron, Dan D., (CV) ........................ '33 '79 C.378 B.S. L.1186 J.D. P.O. Box 1347
Beckwith, Michael V., (BV) ............'47 '77 C.1136 B.S. L.1221 J.D. 309 South A St.
Berenson, Jerome H. ....................'14 '38 C.112 A.B. L.1066 LL.B. Ret. Supr. Ct. J.
Berkowitz-Gilman, Barbara R. ............... '61 '89 C.769 B.A. L.1186 J.D. 405 S. B St.
Biety, Dennis M. '47 '76 C.339 B.A. L.896 J.D.
(adm. in ME; not adm. in CA) Coun., Aerospace Div. of Abex Corp.
**Bonham, Terrence J.**, (AV) ...............'38 '64 C.740 A.B. L.1065 J.D. [Lawler,B.&W.]
*PRACTICE AREAS: Products Liability Law; Administrative Law; Legal Malpractice; Arbitration.
Boratyn, Martin T. '49 '76 C.927 B.B. L.209 J.D.
(adm. in IL; not adm. in CA) Gen. Coun., Merchants Home Delivery Serv., Inc.
Bradish, J. Robert, (BV) .... '33 '63 C.800 B.E. L.426 J.D. 3844 W. Channel Islands Blvd.

**Brown, Edward R., (AV) '20 '64 C.112 A.B. L.426 J.D.**
**2521 Cabrillo Way, 93030-8405**
Telephone: 805-981-9645 Fax: 805-981-9655
Business and Real Estate Law. Civil Trial and Appellate Practice. Arbitration / Mediation.
Reference: Union Bank of California.
*See Professional Biographies, OXNARD, CALIFORNIA*

Brown, John ...................................'26 '53 C.878 B.S. L.810 J.D. 500 Esplanade Dr.
**Brown, Robert D.**, (BV) .................... '38 '64 C.112 B.S. L.1066 J.D. [Tiffany,H.&B.]
Burnham, Linda Norem ........................ '54 '81 C&L.508 B.S., J.D. 300 Esplanade Dr.
Callahan, David Patrick, (BV) .........'43 '69 C&L.426 B.A., J.D. 2252 E. Vineyard Ave.
**Campbell, Glenn J.**, (BV) ...... '52 '83 C.259 B.S. L.990 J.D. [Lowthorp,R.M.M.C.&T.]
*PRACTICE AREAS: Civil Trials.
Caron, Robert Troy, (A Professional Law Corporation) '57 '84
C.763 B.S. L.1336 J.D. 300 Esplanade Dr.
**Charney, Marc L.**, (AV) ...........'41 '68 C.112 A.B. L.1068 J.D. [Nordman,C.H.&C.]
*PRACTICE AREAS: Land Use Law; Environmental Regulation Law; Redevelopment Law; Real Estate Development Law.
**Christian, Madison M.** .................'63 '90 C.878 B.A. L.464 J.D. [England,W.S.&T.]
**Cohen, Melissa E.** .....................'62 '87 C.112 B.A. L.800 J.D. [A England,W.S.&T.]
*LANGUAGES: Spanish.
**Cohen, Randall A.**, (BV) ................'55 '86 C.112 B.S. L.990 J.D. [England&C.]
*PRACTICE AREAS: General Business; Civil Litigation; Real Property Use and Development.
**Cohen, Stanley E.**, (AV) .................'31 '58 C.339 B.A. L.1068 J.D. [C England&C.]
*PRACTICE AREAS: Real Property; Commercial; Land Use and Development.
**Comis, Stuart A.**, (BV) ............. '54 '78 C.112 B.S. L.1067 J.D. [England,W.S.&T.]⊙
*PRACTICE AREAS: Real Property Law; Business Law.
**Compton, Robert L.**, (AV) ........'31 '62 C.628 B.S. L.1066 LL.B. [Nordman,C.H.&C.]⊙
*PRACTICE AREAS: Civil Law; Business Litigation; Construction Law; Business Law; Oil and Gas Law.
**Conway, Charles J., Jr.**, (BV) '46 '73 C.770 B.A. L.1067 J.D.
[Lowthorp,R.M.M.C.&T.]
*PRACTICE AREAS: Real Estate Law; Probate Law; Estate Planning Law.
**Cormany, Ralph L.**, (AV) ....... '21 '50 C.177 B.A. L.502 LL.B. [C Nordman,C.H.&C.]
*PRACTICE AREAS: Real Estate Law; Oil and Gas Transactions.
**Cunningham, James L.**, (BV) '43 '71
C.932 B.S. L.1049 J.D. [Cunningham&L.] (⊙Simi Valley)

**Cunningham & Lansden, (BV)**
**500 Esplanade Drive, Suite 1000, 93030**⊙
Telephone: 805-485-6444 Fax: 805-485-5857
James L. Cunningham; Joe P. Lansden.
Plaintiffs Personal Injury, Family Law, Estate Planning and Probate, General Civil Litigation, Business, Real Estate, Bankruptcy and Debtor and Creditor Law.
Simi Valley, California Office: Suite 200, 2345 Erringer Road. Telephone: 805-583-1944.
Victorville, California Office: 14350 Civil Drive, Suite 200. Telephone: 619-241-2441. Fax: 619-241-0574.
Lancaster, California Office: 44404 16th Street West, #109. Telephone: 805-942-7588. Fax: 805-949-6290.
Marysville/Yuba City, California Office: 1445 Butte House Road, Suite K. Telephone: 916-671-9154 & 916-674-7405. Fax: 916-674-5653.
Modesto, California Office: 605 Standiford Avenue, #N. Telephone: 209-523-1771. Fax: 209-577-4474.

Dalton, Maryanne G. '61 '87
C.773 B.a. L.464 J.D. 6th Fl., Union Park Twr., 300 Esplanade Dr.
Diamond, Gary S. ...............................'47 '79 C.112 B.A. L.1095 J.D. 500 Esplanade Dr.
**Dickinson, Glenn J.** .................'59 '92 C.446 B.A. L.150 J.D. [A Nordman,C.H.&C.]
Dillon, Janet J. ....................'47 '81 C.178 B.A. L.1066 J.D. 300 E. Esplanade Dr., 9th Fl.
Disney, Mitchell F., (CV) ......................'62 '88 C&L.990 B.A., J.D. 1000 Town Ctr. Dr.
Douds, David B., & Associates, (BV) .... '49 '74 C.651 B.S. L.831 J.D. 300 Esplanade Dr.
Douds, Sally K. C. ...........................'50 '85 C.112 B.A. L.1049 J.D. 300 Esplanade Dr.

**Eade, Kenneth G. '57 '80 C.1077 B.A. L.809 J.D.**
**143 South B Street, 93030**
Telephone: 805-487-0403 Fax: 805-483-7634
*LANGUAGES: French.
Corporate, Securities Law and Public/Private Offerings.
*See Professional Biographies, OXNARD, CALIFORNIA*

**Ellis, Korman Dorsey**, (AV) ............'34 '65 C.1097 B.A. L.800 J.D. [Lawler,B.&W.]
*REPORTED CASES: Anderson v. Chancellor Western 53 CA.3d, 235; Lehto v. City of Oxnard 171 CA.3d, 285; Truhitte v. French Hospital 128 CA.3d, 332; Constantinescu v. Conejo Valley Unified School District 16 CA.4th, 1466; Joyce v. Simi Valley Unified School District 6 CA.4th, 80.
*PRACTICE AREAS: Civil Practice; Government Tort Liability Law; Insurance Law; Municipal Law; School Law.
**England, Robert B.**, (AV) .................... '43 '79 C.1077 B.S. L.262 J.D. [England&C.]
*PRACTICE AREAS: Taxation; Estate Planning; Probate and Trusts; Business and Real Estate Transactions.
**England, Theodore J.**, (AV) ....... '42 '67 C.112 B.A. L.1066 LL.B. [England,W.S.&T.]
*PRACTICE AREAS: Taxation Law; Real Property Law; Pension/Profit Sharing Law.

**England & Cohen, (AV)** BB
**300 Esplanade Drive Financial Plaza Tower, Suite 380, 93030**
Telephone: 805-983-8181; California Toll Free: 800-675-6166 FAX: 805-983-8813
Members of Firm: Robert B. England (Certified Specialist, Estate Planning, Trust and Probate Law, State Bar of California Board of Legal Specialization); Randall A. Cohen. Of Counsel: Stanley E. Cohen.
General Civil and Trial Practice, General Business, Commercial, Corporate, Real Property Transactions and Development, Tax, Probate, Trusts and Estate Planning.
*See Professional Biographies, OXNARD, CALIFORNIA*

**England, Whitfield, Schröeder & Tredway, L.L.P., (AV)** BB
**300 Esplanade Drive, 6th Floor, 93030**⊙
Telephone: 805-485-9627 Ventura: 647-8237 Southern California Toll Free: 800-255-3485 Fax: 805-983-0297
URL: http://www.tsurf.com/ewst/
Members of Firm: Theodore J. England (Certified Specialist, Taxation Law, The State Bar of California Board of Legal Specialization); Anson M. Whitfield; Robert W. Schröeder; David W. Tredway; Robert A. McSorley; Stuart A. Comis; Mitchel B. Kahn; Mark A. Nelson; Eric J. Kananen; Mary E. Schröeder; Oscar C. Gonzalez; Steven K. Perrin; Andrew S. Hughes; Madison M. Christian; Kurt Edward Kananen. Associates: William J. Kesatie; Melissa E. Cohen; Linda Kathryn Ash; Mark T. Barney.
Employment and Labor Law, Banking, Commercial, Corporate, Taxation, Land Use, Environmental, Real Property, Bankruptcy, Insolvency, Personal Injury, Construction, Trusts, Wills and Estate Planning Law. General Trial and Appellate Practice. Probate.
Representative Clients: Seneca Resources Corp. (oil & gas); Cal-Sun Produce Co.; Waste Management of California, Inc; Dah Chong Hong (Honda, Toyota, Mazda, Lexus, Acura, Saturn automobile dealerships); Willamette Industries; Oxnard Harbor Association of Realtors; Port of Hueneme; Conejo Valley Association of Realtors; Power-One, Inc.
Thousand Oaks, California Office: Rolling Oaks Office Center, 351 Rolling Oaks Drive. Telephone: Southern California Toll Free: 800-255-3485.
*See Professional Biographies, OXNARD, CALIFORNIA*

**Erickson, Philip** ............................ '59 '88 C.112 B.A. L.426 J.D. [A A.E.Wisotsky]
**Etchingham, Gerald M.** ..............'58 '86 C.57 B.A. L.1065 J.D. [Nordman,C.H.&C.]
*PRACTICE AREAS: Creditors Rights and Insolvency; Environmental Litigation; General Civil and Business Litigation; Non-Profit Organization Law.
Fehr, Lori Lee .............'60 '89 C.1110 B.A. L.990 J.D. 500 E. Esplanade Dr., 17th Fl.
Feuerborn, Carolyn Soprano ..................'57 '89 C.999 L.805 J.D. 300 Esplanade Dr.
Flick, John E. ........................................ '22 '48 C&L.597 LL.B. 2821 S. Harbor Blvd.
Francis, Richard L., (BV) ...........'48 '76 C.112 B.A. L.1065 J.D. 300 E. Esplanade Dr.
Frank, Deirdre Barkley ....................'53 '78 C.112 B.A. L.809 J.D. 500 Esplanade Dr.
Garcia, Robert R., (CV) ....................................... '49 '79 750 W. Gonzales Rd.
Garrett, Debra Frances '53 '81 C.112 B.A.B.S. L.767 J.D.
500 E. Esplanade Dr., 10th Fl.
**George, Randall H.**, (BV) ..........'53 '78 C.112 B.A. L.1067 J.D. [Nordman,C.H.&C.]
*PRACTICE AREAS: Corporate, General Business and Taxation Law; Banking Law.
Gerber, David A., (AV) .............. '44 '77 C.696 A.B. L.1068 J.D. 1000 Town Ctr. Dr.
Gherini, Francis, (BV) .............................. '14 '40 C.112 B.A. L.813 162 South A St.
**Gill, Ronald H.**, (AV) ..................'40 '66 C.112 A.B. L.1066 J.D. [Nordman,C.H.&C.]
*PRACTICE AREAS: Business and Real Estate Litigation; Commercial Law; Banking Law; Creditors Rights Law; Bankruptcy Law.
Gillig, Gary L., (BV) .............................. '46 '75 C.801 B.A. L.800 J.D. City Atty.
Gilman, Richard C., (BV) .............. '48 '75 C.112 B.A. L.1065 J.D. 405 S. B St.
Glass, Elliot H. '48 '87 C.477 B.A. L.1137 J.D.
500 Esplanade Dr., 10th Fl. (⊙Victorville)
**Gonzalez, Oscar C.** .................'59 '88 C.1077 B.A. L.1067 J.D. [England,W.S.&T.]
*PRACTICE AREAS: Civil Litigation; Real Property; Estate Planning; Probate.
Grant, David S. ................................'52 '77 C&L.477 A.B., J.D. 300 Esplande Dr.
Greenwood, Steven M. .......................'50 '79 C.112 B.A. L.1095 J.D. 135 S. G St.
Groom, Peter J. ................... '53 '79 C.111 B.S. L.1065 J.D. 300 Esplanade Dr. (Pat.)
Guerra, Robert ............................'48 '75 C.1077 B.A. L.426 J.D. 141 S. "A" St.
**Hair, William H.**, (AV) ..................'33 '60 C.1074 L.1065 J.D. [Nordman,C.H.&C.]
*PRACTICE AREAS: Land Use Law; Condemnation Litigation; Administrative Law.
Hansen, Stanley B. .....................................'24 '49 L.986 LL.B. 915 Dunes St.
Harary, Martin K. ........................'44 '71 C.112 B.S. L.1068 J.D. 820 Oarfish Ct.
Hatch and Parent, (AV) .....300 Esplanade Dr., 19th Fl. (⊙Santa Barbara; S. Lake Tahoe)
**Held, Jeffrey B.**, (BV) ......................'55 '82 C.112 B.A. L.426 J.D. [A A.E.Wisotsky]
Herman, J. Jeffrey, (CV) ...............'50 '77 C.1350 B.A. L.1049 J.D. 500 Esplanade Dr.
Herman, Robert J. ...........................'24 '52 C.776 L.705 LL.B. 500 Esplanade Dr.
**Hiepler, Mark O.** ..........................'61 '88 C.999 B.A. L.990 J.D. [Hiepler&H.]
*REPORTED CASES: Fox v. Health Net; deMeurers v. Health Net; Ching v. Gaines.
*PRACTICE AREAS: Bad Faith Insurance Practices; HMO and Healthcare Practices; Personal Injury; Construction; Defect Law.
**Hiepler, Michelle R.** ............................'63 '89 C.174 B.S. L.990 J.D. [Hiepler&H.]
*PRACTICE AREAS: General Civil Litigation; Employment Law.

**Hiepler & Hiepler, Law Offices of**
**A Professional Partnership**
**500 Esplanade Drive, Suite 1550, 93030**
Telephone: 805-988-5833 Facsimile: 805-988-5828
Members of Firm: Mark O. Hiepler; Michelle R. Hiepler. Associates: James D. McGinley; Darci D. Teobaldi.
General Civil Trial Practice. Bad Faith Insurance Practices, HMO and Healthcare, Personal Injury, Construction and Employment Law, Medical Malpractice.
*See Professional Biographies, OXNARD, CALIFORNIA*

**High, Kenneth M., Jr.**, (AV) ........'46 '71 C.112 A.B. L.1068 J.D. [Nordman,C.H.&C.]
*PRACTICE AREAS: Real Property Sales, Leasing, Financing and Development and Business Organization.
**Hines, Larry L.**, (AV) ..................'39 '70 C.330 B.A. L.950 J.D. [Nordman,C.H.&C.]
*PRACTICE AREAS: Complex Civil Business Litigation; Labor/Employment Law; Trust/Will Contests; Administrative Law.
Hiscocks, Patrick D. ...................... '56 '90 C.1077 B.A. L.809 J.D. 1000 Town Ctr. Dr.
Houska, Josef D., (BV) .... '57 '90 C.112 B.A. L.426 J.D. [A Hatch&P.] (⊙Santa Barbara)
**Houska, Maureen M.** ...............'65 '90 C.602 B.B.A. L.426 J.D. [A Lawler,B.&W.]
*PRACTICE AREAS: Civil Litigation; Premises Liability; Security Guard Law; Police Defense.
**Hughes, Andrew S.** ..................'65 '90 C.112 B.A. L.770 J.D. [England,W.S.&T.]
*PRACTICE AREAS: Business Litigation; Real Property Law.
Jennings, Jeffrey D., (BV) ..................... '43 '69 C.976 B.A. L.813 J.D. [Jennings&N.]
Jennings & Neuhaus, (BV) ...........................250 W. Citrus Grove Ln., Ste. 220
Johns, Ira ..................................'51 '79 C.339 B.S. L.809 J.D. 667 S. Ventura Rd.
Johnson, Susan Fay ....................'54 '90 C.112 B.A. L.1065 J.D. 300 Esplanade Dr.
Justl, David G. ............................................ '51 '79 C.112 B.A. L.426 J.D. I.R.S.
**Kahn, Mitchel B.**, (AV) .............. '46 '72 C.1077 B.S. L.426 J.D. [England,W.S.&T.]⊙
*PRACTICE AREAS: Land Use; Real Estate; Commercial Law; Business Law.
**Kananen, Eric J.** ..................'56 '83 C.1253 B.A. L.1067 J.D. [England,W.S.&T.]⊙
*PRACTICE AREAS: Civil Litigation; Construction Law; Environmental Law; Real Property Law.
**Kananen, Kurt Edward** ...............'59 '91 C.1049 B.A. L.426 J.D. [England,W.S.&T.]
*PRACTICE AREAS: Business Law; Business Litigation; Real Property Law.
**Karcis, E.P. Michael**, (BV) ......'61 '89 C.1129 B.A. L.94 J.D. [Lowthorp,R.M.M.C.&T.]
*PRACTICE AREAS: Civil Trials.
Katz, Michael I. .................'50 '76 C.800 B.S. L.1148 J.D. 300 Esplanade Dr., 9th Fl.
Katz, Robert D. .......................................'13 '37 C.137 L.146 5540 West 5th St.‡
**Keighron, Brian P.** ....................'50 '76 C.262 B.A. L.1049 J.D. [A A.E.Wisotsky]

**Kellegrew, Kent M.** ..............'53 '81 C.1077 B.A. L.809 J.D. [Nordman,C.H.&C.]⊙
*PRACTICE AREAS: Civil Litigation; Business Law.
Keller, W. Richard, (AV) ..................... '41 '67 C.378 B.S. L.477 J.D. P.O. Box 1269
Kerr, Robert, III ..................... '48 '80 C.705 B.A. L.1095 J.D. 750 W. Gonzales Rd.
**Kesatie, William J.** .................. '61 '87 C.1253 B.A. L.426 J.D. [[A] England,W.S.&T.]
*PRACTICE AREAS: General Business Law; Business Litigation; Bankruptcy; Debtor-Creditor Relations.
**Kitasaki, Chris K.** .................. '56 '83 C.112 B.S. L.767 J.D. [Nordman,C.H.&C.]
*PRACTICE AREAS: Corporate Securities Law; General Business Law.
Krause, Bernard S. '19 '75 C.867 A.B. L.262 J.D.
(adm. in NY; not adm. in CA) 1910 Holly Ave.‡
**Kurzeka, Paul W.**, (BV) ............. '52 '82 C.549 B.S. L.990 J.D. [Nordman,C.H.&C.]
*PRACTICE AREAS: General Business Law; Real Estate Transactions.
Lange, Mark Andrew '56 '83 C.907 B.A. L.950 J.D.
(adm. in WA; not adm. in CA) 500 Esplanade Dr.
**Lansden, Joe P.**, (BV) ........................ '38 '77 C.612 L.1186 J.D. [Cunningham&L.]
Larsen, Anne M. ......................... '64 '90 C.112 B.A. L.1067 J.D. 300 Esplanade Dr.
**Lawler, Byron J.**, (AV) ................. '36 '64 C.112 B.A. L.1068 J.D. [Lawler,B.&W.]
*PRACTICE AREAS: Civil Rights Law; Discrimination Law; Environmental Law; International Business Transactions Law.
Lawler, Gregory J. ........................ '64 '89 C.112 B.A. L.426 J.D. 300 Esplanade Dr.

**Lawler, Bonham & Walsh, (AV)** BB
**300 Esplanade Drive, Suite, 1900, P.O. Box 5527, 93031**
**Telephone: 805-485-8921 MCI Fax: 805-485-3766**
**Email: LBW@INTERNETMCI.COM**
**Members of Firm: Byron J. Lawler; Terrence J. Bonham; Henry J. Walsh; Carol A. Woo; Korman Dorsey Ellis. Associates: Richard A Shimmel; Maureen M. Houska.**
**General Civil Trial Practice in all State and Federal Courts. Municipal and School Representation. Personnel, Community Redevelopment, Land Use, Environmental and Toxic Tort Law. Products Liability, Casualty (Defense), General Insurance, Civil Rights, Security Law, Police Defense, Premises Liability and Commercial Transactions.**
***See Professional Biographies, OXNARD, CALIFORNIA***

Lax, Joseph .................................................... '— '71 315 W. 4th St.
**Lent, Robert J.** .................. '55 '85 C.30 B.A. L.1065 J.D. [Nordman,C.H.&C.]⊙
*PRACTICE AREAS: Business Litigation; Intellectual Property including Copyright; Trademark; Unfair Competition; Trade Secrets.
**Light, Jonathan Fraser**, (BV) ....... '57 '81 C.112 B.A. L.1068 J.D. [Nordman,C.H.&C.]
*PRACTICE AREAS: Employment; Employer Labor Litigation; Real Estate Litigation; Business Litigation.
**Loughman, Patrick T.**, (BV) ..... '56 '82 C&L.426 B.A., J.D. [Lowthorp,R.M.M.C.&T.]
*REPORTED CASES: Karrin v. Ocean-Aire Mobile Home Estates (1991) 1 Cal.App.4th, 1066; Hurst Concrete Products, Inc. v. Lane (In Re Lane) (Ninth Circuit 1992) 980 F2d 601.
*PRACTICE AREAS: Business Litigation; Bankruptcy Law; Real Property Law; Probate; Trusts.

**Lowthorp, Richards, McMillan, Miller, Conway & Templeman, A Professional Corporation, (AV)** BB
**300 Esplanade Drive, Suite 850, P.O. Box 5167, 93031**
**Telephone: 805-981-8555 FAX: 805-983-1967**
**Carl F. Lowthorp, Jr. (1933-1992); Richard A. Richards; Robert C. McMillan; Paul A. Miller; Charles J. Conway, Jr.; Alan R. Templeman; Patrick T. Loughman; Glenn J. Campbell; John Q. Masteller; E.P. Michael Karcis; Gregory J. Ramirez.**
**Real Estate, Agricultural, Taxation, Estate Planning, Probate, Zoning, Condemnation, Domestic, Insurance, Products Liability, Securities, Bankruptcy, Construction Law, Business and Personal Injury Law. General Civil Litigation.**
**Reference: Ventura County National Bank.**
***See Professional Biographies, OXNARD, CALIFORNIA***

Malmo, John ........................... '54 '87 C.112 B.A. L.1186 J.D. 500 Esplanade Dr.
Martin, Daryl G. ..................... '61 '87 C.585 B.B.A. L.1065 J.D. 300 Esplanade Dr.
Mason, Barbara E., (BV) ..................... '49 '89 C.112 B.A. L.1186 J.D. [Schwartz&M.]
**Masteller, John Q.**, (AV⊙) ..... '53 '82 C.620 B.A. L.734 J.D. [Lowthorp,R.M.M.C.&T.]
*PRACTICE AREAS: Business Law; Real Estate; Probate Law.
**Mathews, John M.**, (AV) .......... '48 '73 C.101 B.A. L.1068 J.D. [Arnold,B.M.W.&Z.]
*PRACTICE AREAS: Water Law; Public Agency Law; Land Use and Development; Liquid and Solid Waste; Environmental Law.
Maxwell, R. Blinn ........................ '19 '48 C.339 A.B. L.813 J.D. 326 So. A St.
May, Charles D. .............. '54 '85 C.426 B.A. L.809 J.D. [Tharpe&H.] (⊙Los Angeles)
**McAvoy, Laura K.**, (AV) ............. '47 '74 C.112 B.A. L.1068 J.D. [Nordman,C.H.&C.]
*PRACTICE AREAS: General Corporate Law; Business Law; Banking Law; Oil and Gas Law; Agricultural Law.
McDonald, Kenneth L. ..................... '48 '77 C.1077 B.S. L.464 J.D. 901 Oxford Dr.
**McGinley, James D.** .................. '59 '92 C.1042 B.A. L.990 J.D. [[A] Hiepler&H.]
*PRACTICE AREAS: General Civil Litigation.
**McLaughlin, Laurel A.** .............. '67 '92 C.770 B.S. L.990 J.D. [[A] Nordman,C.H.&C.]
*PRACTICE AREAS: Civil Litigation.
**McMillan, Robert C.**, (BV) ....... '40 '71 C.61 B.A. L.605 J.D. [Lowthorp,R.M.M.C.&T.]
*PRACTICE AREAS: Estate Planning Law; Probate Law; Real Estate Law; Agriculture Law.
McReynolds, Richard W. ................ '43 '73 C.763 B.S. L.61 J.D. 500 Esplanade Dr.‡
**McSorley, Robert A.**, (AV) ............ '45 '71 C.112 A.B. L.911 J.D. [England,W.S.&T.]
*PRACTICE AREAS: Business Law; Real Estate; Personal Injury Litigation; Labor and Employment; Government Employment.
Menard, Christian J. '50 '77
C.112 B.A. L.809 J.D. 3600 Harbor Blvd., Channel Island Harbor
Meyer-Morris, Deborah ..................... '64 '92 C.1077 B.A. L.426 J.D. [[A] Tharpe&H.]

**Miller, Irwin R. (Rob), (AV) '42 '69 C.1246 B.B.A. L.150 J.D.**
**300 Esplanade Drive, 19th Floor, 93030**
**Telephone: 805-485-2700 Fax: 805-485-2751**
***REPORTED CASES: Dibene v. Waste Management, Inc., Los Angeles Superior Court Case No. NWCO29341 (1993). Personal injury below knee amputation jury trial verdict $4,268,000 motorcycle v. truck accident.**
***PRACTICE AREAS: Personal Injury Law; Domestic Relations Law; Real Estate; Tort Law; Professional Liability Law.**
**General Civil and Trial Practice in State and Federal Courts. Real Estate, Family, Negligence and Malpractice Law.**
***See Professional Biographies, OXNARD, CALIFORNIA***

**Miller, Nancy** ........................ '45 '89 C.342 B.A. L.426 J.D. [[A] Nordman,C.H.&C.]
*PRACTICE AREAS: Education; Public Agency Law.
**Miller, Paul A.**, (AV) .......... '47 '74 C.426 B.S. L.1049 J.D. [Lowthorp,R.M.M.C.&T.]
*PRACTICE AREAS: Domestic Relations Law; Construction Law; Business Law.
Miyamoto, Ronald K. ........................ '55 '80 C.012 B.S. L.990 J.D. [West&M.]
Moomau, Richard L. .............. '38 '66 C.398 B.A. L.426 LL.B. 500 E. Esplanade Dr.
Mora, Herman P., (CV) ................................................ '46 '75 [Urias&M.]
Morrow, Michael A. ................. '52 '81 C.880 B.A. L.1137 J.D. [Rosenmund,B.&M.]
Najera, Carlos J., (CV) ..................... '48 '78 C.1077 B.A. L.285 J.D. 355 S. A St.
Nash, Robert L. .................... '32 '62 C.112 B.S. L.426 J.D. 1445 S. Harbor Blvd.‡
**Nelson, Mark A.**, (BV) ................ '54 '81 C.112 B.A. L.800 J.D. [England,W.S.&T.]
*PRACTICE AREAS: Business Litigation; Real Property Law; Family Law.
Neuhaus, Thomas E., (BV) ............. '51 '77 C.112 A.B. L.1065 J.D. [Jennings&N.]
**Noe, Robert G.** '46 '71 C.800 B.A. L.61 J.D.
V.P. & Reg. Coun., First Amer. Title Ins. Co.
*SPECIAL AGENCIES: First Exchange Corporation, 101 South California Street, Ventura, CA, 93001. Telephone: 800-613-2863.
*RESPONSIBILITIES: Real Estate; Taxation Law.

**Nordman, Cormany, Hair & Compton, (AV)** BB
**1000 Town Center Drive, Sixth Floor, P.O. Box 9100, 93031-9100⊙**
**Telephone: 805-485-1000 Ventura: 805-656-3304 Telecopier: 805-988-8387 805-988-7790**
**Ben E. Nordman, Founder (1913-1985). Members of Firm: William H. Hair; Robert L. Compton; Marc L. Charney; Ronald H. Gill; Larry L. Hines; Kenneth M. High, Jr.; Michael C. O'Brien; Laura K. McAvoy; Randall H. George; Janet Anne Reese; Paul W. Kurzeka; Anthony H. Trembley; Jonathan Fraser Light; Kent M. Kellegrew; William E. Winfield; Gerald M. Etchingham; Chris K. Kitasaki; Scott B. Samsky; Guy C. Parvex, Jr.; Robert J. Lent; Susan Westeen Novatt. Of Counsel: Ralph L. Cormany; John A. Slezak. Associates: Susan M. Seemiller; John M. Andersen; Laurel A. McLaughlin; Glenn J. Dickinson; Nancy Miller.**
**General Civil Litigation in all State and Federal Courts. Environmental and Hazardous Waste, Employment, Banking and Finance, Real Estate, Securities, Municipal and Special Districts, Creditors' Rights and Insolvency, Insurance Coverage, Commercial and Business, Corporation, Condemnation, Oil and Gas, Probate and Estate Planning, Taxation, Intellectual Property, Entertainment Litigation, Civil Service, Administrative Law, Education, State and Federal Appellate Practice.**
**Representative Clients: Berry Petroleum Co.; Real Estate Investment Trust of California; Amgen; Kmart Corp.; Saticoy Lemon Assn.; The Procter & Gamble Paper Products Co.; Halliburton Services; Schlumberger; The Prudential Insurance Company of America; Laguna Pacific Development.**
**Westlake Village, California Office: 920 Hampshire Road, Suite A-17, 91361. Telephone: 805-497-2795.**
***See Professional Biographies, OXNARD, CALIFORNIA***

Norris, Jeffrey B. ................... '50 '75 C.1077 B.A. L.1049 J.D. 500 Esplanade Dr.
**Novatt, Susan Westeen** ............... '58 '84 C.604 A.B. L.228 J.D. [Nordman,C.H.&C.]
*PRACTICE AREAS: Taxation.
**O'Brien, Michael C.**, (AV) .......... '47 '73 C.988 B.A. L.426 J.D. [Nordman,C.H.&C.]
*PRACTICE AREAS: General Civil Litigation with emphasis on real estate related matters.
O'Hearn, Leo A. ........................ '26 '71 C.966 B.S. L.1114 J.D. 3650 Ketch Ave.
O'Hearn, Michael J. ..................... '52 '75 C.112 B.A. L.1095 J.D. 3650 Ketch Ave.
O'Neill, Joseph D., (CV) ............ '51 '77 C.436 B.A. L.1095 J.D. 331 S. "C" St., Suite C
Ontiveras, Jose Marcelino ................. '44 '76 C.112 B.A. L.1068 J.D. 751 S. B St.
Ostrove, Robert Michael ..................... '54 '82 C.605 B.A. L.809 J.D. 1961 N. C St.
Owens, Robert A. ............................ '46 '79 C.112 A.B. L.1095 J.D. [Owens&O.]
Owens & Owens ........................................................ 426 N. "A" St.
Pachowicz, Mark R. ............... '62 '88 C.1077 B.A. L.1049 J.D. 1000 Town Ctr. Dr.
Parriott, James D., Jr. '23 '49 C&L.174 J.D.
(adm. in CO; not adm. in CA) 2825 S. Harbor Blvd.‡
**Parvex, Guy C., Jr.**, (CV) ............. '59 '89 C.112 B.A. L.1065 J.D. [Nordman,C.H.&C.]
*PRACTICE AREAS: Family Law; Civil Litigation.
Paulson, Hilary S. ........................ '64 '89 C.112 B.A. L.1065 J.D. 300 Esplanda Dr.
Peck, Eugene C., (CV) ........................ '22 '48 C.976 B.A. L.930 J.D. 426 N. A St.
Percy, Michael D. '52 '89 C&L.1186 A.B., J.D.
500 Esplanade Dr. (⊙Simi Valley & Lancaster)
**Perrin, Steven K.**, (CV) ............. '64 '89 C.105 B.A. L.464 J.D. [England,W.S.&T.]
*PRACTICE AREAS: Business Law; Civil Litigation; Personal Injury; Environmental Torts.
**Privett, Pamela J.** ........................... '57 '85 C.773 B.A. L.273 J.D. [P.J.Privett]
*PRACTICE AREAS: Real Estate; Secured Financing.

**Privett, Pamela J., A Professional Law Corporation**
**300 Esplanade Drive, Suite 1865, 93030**
**Telephone: 805-981-3611 Fax: 805-981-3616**
**Email: pjplaw@aol.com**
**Pamela J. Privett.**
**Real Estate, Real Estate Financing, Acquisitions/Dispositions.**
***See Professional Biographies, OXNARD, CALIFORNIA***

Quintana, David ........................... '61 '90 C.112 B.S. L.800 J.D. 3314 Ocean Dr.
**Ramirez, Gregory J.** .......... '59 '90 C.800 B.S. L.1068 J.D. [[A] Lowthorp,R.M.M.C.&T.]
*PRACTICE AREAS: Civil Trials; Products Liability; Employment Discrimination.
Ramirez, M. Carmen .......... '48 '74 C.1097 L.426 J.D. Channel Cos. Legal Servs. Assn.
Reaser, Cynthia Huang, (BV) '61 '85
C.1074 B.S. L.1068 J.D. 500 E. Esplanade Dr., 10th Fl.
**Reese, Janet Anne**, (AV) .......... '53 '78 C.940 B.A. L.426 J.D. [Nordman,C.H.&C.]⊙
*PRACTICE AREAS: Estate Planning; Probate; Trust Administration and Litigation.

**Regnier, Richard A., (AV) '31 '63 C.870 B.S. L.1066 LL.B.**
**301 North A Street, P.O. Box 5505, 93031**
**Telephone: 805-483-7040 Fax: 805-486-7393**
***REPORTED CASES: Adduddel vs Board of Administration, 8 Cal. App. 3d 243; Linvill vs Perello, 189 Cal. App. 3d 195.**
**Civil Trial Practice. Tort and Business Litigation. Trials in all Courts. Arbitrations, Administrative Law, Criminal Law.**
***See Professional Biographies, OXNARD, CALIFORNIA***

**Reiser, Glen M., Law Offices of, (AV) '53 '78 C.870 B.A. L.1068 J.D.**
**300 Esplanade Drive, Suite 2030, 93030**
**Telephone: 805-988-0826 Fax: 805-983-6146**
***REPORTED CASES: Lundquist v. Reusser, 7 Cal. 4th 1193; Burch v. George, 7 Cal. 4th 246; McKinney v. Board of Trustees, 31 Cal. 3d 79; Bradbury v. Superior Court, 49 Cal. App. 4th 1108; Ramos v. Estrada 8 Cal. App. 4th 1070.**
***PRACTICE AREAS: Environmental Litigation; Complex Real Property Litigation; Public Agency Litigation; Condemnation; Land Use.**
**Of Counsel: Carolyn Oh Taketa.**
**Environmental Matters including CCQA, Wetlands, Soil and Ground Water Issues, and Regulation, Real Property Litigation, Land Use, Public Agency Litigation, Business and Employment and Civil Appellate Litigation.**
***See Professional Biographies, OXNARD, CALIFORNIA***

Richards, Olive M .................. '51 '88 C.763 B.A. L.1137 J.D. 1825 N. Oxnard Blvd.
**Richards, Richard A.**, (BV) ... '34 '62 C.911 B.A. L.1068 J.D. [Lowthorp,R.M.M.C.&T.]
*PRACTICE AREAS: Real Estate Law; Business Law; Probate Law; Trust Law; Estate Planning.
Richards, Robert N. ............ '32 '70 C.870 B.S.M.E. L.800 J.D. 3411 Via Marina Ave.
Rose, Kevin L., (CV) ................. '60 '87 C.1049 B.A. L.273 J.D. 1000 Town Ctr. Dr.
**Rosenberg, Ellen S.** '56 '83 C.446 B.S. L.128 J.D.
(adm. in DC; not adm. in CA) [[A] Arnold,B.M.W.&Z.]⊙
Rosenfeld, Irving ........................ '27 '57 C.112 A.B. L.936 LL.B. [I.Rosenfeld]
Rosenfeld, Irving, A P.C. ................................ 500 Esplanade Dr. (⊙805-485-1902)
Rosenmund, Frederick, (BV) ......... '54 '79 C.112 B.A. L.464 J.D. [Rosenmund,B.&M.]
Rosenmund, H. F., (BV) ............. '16 '41 C&L.494 B.S.L., J.D. [Rosenmund,B.&M.]
Rosenmund, Baio & Morrow, (BV) ............................................ 162 S. "A" St.
**Rothwell, Denise B.** .............. '60 '86 C.170 B.A. L.990 J.D. [[A] Arnold,B.M.W.&Z.]
**Samsky, Scott B.** .................... '56 '81 C.494 B.S. L.1068 J.D. [Nordman,C.H.&C.]
*PRACTICE AREAS: Estate Planning; Taxation and Business Law.
Schmidt, Thomas D. ................ '37 '92 C.1097 B.S. L.990 J.D. 2252 E. Vineyard Ave.
**Schröeder, Mary E.**, (BV) .......... '48 '74 C.1042 B.A. L.426 J.D. [England,W.S.&T.]
*LANGUAGES: German.
*PRACTICE AREAS: Civil Litigation; Employment Law and Litigation; Probate.
**Schröeder, Robert W.**, (BV) ......... '46 '73 C.112 B.A. L.426 J.D. [England,W.S.&T.]⊙
*PRACTICE AREAS: Real Property Law; Commercial Law; Business Litigation; Automotive Franchises and Dealerships.
Schwartz, David P., (BV) ................... '42 '70 C.112 B.A. L.1065 J.D. [Schwartz&M.]
Schwartz, Michael .................. '47 '73 C.112 B.S. L.309 J.D. 3600 S. Harbor Blvd.
Schwartz and Mason, (BV) ............................ 2901 North Ventura Road, Suite 130
**Seemiller, Susan M.** ................ '59 '90 C.999 B.S. L.990 J.D. [[A] Nordman,C.H.&C.]
*PRACTICE AREAS: Civil Litigation and Appeals.

**Shain, David L.**, (AV) ................ '53 '78 C.1044 B.A. L.276 J.D. [Wennergren&S.]
*PRACTICE AREAS: Business Litigation; Personal Injury; Criminal Defense.
Sharaga, Gene B. .......................... '51 '87 C.994 B.A. L.912 J.D. [Tharpe&H.]
**Shea, David B.** .................................... '62 '90 L.1186 J.D. [Wennergren&S.]
*PRACTICE AREAS: Estate Planning; Real Estate Law; Business Law.
**Shimmel, Richard A** ................. '54 '88 C&L.1137 B.S.L., J.D. [Lawler,B.&W.]
*PRACTICE AREAS: Civil Litigation; Government Tort Liability; Construction Defect; Products Liability; Insurance Law.
**Slezak, John A.** ..................... '49 '74 C.154 B.A. L.880 J.D. [Nordman,C.H.&C.]
*PRACTICE AREAS: Civil Business Litigation; Environmental Law; Election Law.
Smith, Brenda C. '62 '90 C.330 B.A. L.990 J.D.
300 Esplanade Dr., #2050 (©Simi Valley & Lancaster)
Smith, Kathleen Janetatos ............ '58 '85 C.321 A.B. L.273 J.D. 1000 Town Ctr. Dr.
Sowers, Donald G. ........................ '53 '86 C.999 A.S. L.809 J.D. [Takakjian&S.]©
Stauffer, James E. ........................ '20 '53 C.264 A.B. L.273 LL.B. 4951 Coral Way
Takakjian, Paul, (BV) '53 '79
C.112 B.A. L.426 J.D. [Takakjian&S.] (©Encino, L.A. & Orange)
Takakjian & Sowers, (BV)
300 Esplanade Dr. (©Los Angeles, Encino, Orange, Pasadena & Long Beach)
**Taketa, Carolyn Oh** ..................... '67 '92 C.668 B.A. L.1066 J.D. [G.M.Reiser]
*LANGUAGES: Korean.
*PRACTICE AREAS: Business Litigation; Employment Law.
Tanchuck, Mark ... '52 '78 C.629 B.B.A. L.61 J.D. Sr. Staff Coun., State Comp. Ins. Fund
Tanksley, Bayard R. ......................... '21 '56 C.999 L.809 LL.B. 143 S. "B" St.
**Templeman, Alan R.**, (AV) ....'41 '72 C.610 B.A. L.1068 J.D. [Lowthorp,R.M.M.C.&T.]
*PRACTICE AREAS: Securities Litigation; Civil Trials; Personal Injury; Products Liability Litigation.
Tentler, Richard W. ...... '44 '75 C.112 B.A. L.426 J.D. 141 W. 2nd St. (©Santa Barbara)
**Teobaldi, Darci D.** ....................... '66 '92 C.763 B.S. L.990 J.D. [Hiepler&H.]
*PRACTICE AREAS: General Civil Litigation; Health Care Law; Dispute Resolution.
Tharpe & Howell, (AV)
300 Esplanda Dr. Suite 1820 (©Los Angeles, Santa Barbara, Newport Beach & Santa Maria)
Thompson, Richard D. ................. '19 '58 C.1246 B.B.A. L.809 4930 Marlin Way‡
**Tiffany, F. Gile, Jr.**, (BV) ............... '23 '51 C.813 A.B. L.426 J.D. [Tiffany,H.&B.]

**Tiffany, Hunt & Brown, A Professional Corporation, (BV)**
**300 Esplanade Drive, Suite 700, 93030-1248**
**Telephone: 805-981-4345 Fax: 805-981-4322**
**F. Gile Tiffany, Jr.; Robert D. Brown; Oswald A. Hunt (1912-1989).**
**Estate Planning and Probate Law, Wills, Trusts, Taxation, Real Estate, Business, Corporation, General Civil and Trial Practice.**
**Reference: Wells Fargo Bank (Ventura Trust Department).**

**Tredway, David W.**, (AV) ........ '49 '74 C.112 B.S.E.E. L.426 J.D. [England,W.S.&T.]
*PRACTICE AREAS: Civil Litigation; Construction Law; Land Use Law; Development Law.
**Trembley, Anthony H.**, (CV) .......'56 '83 C.112 B.A. L.1067 J.D. [Nordman,C.H.&C.]
*PRACTICE AREAS: Municipal Law; Administrative Law; Land Use Law; Environmental Regulation Law; Business Law.
Urias, Frank C. ............................ '36 '69 C.740 A.B. L.464 J.D. [Urias&M.]
Urias & Mora, (CV) ......................................................... 300 South C St.
**Walsh, Henry J.**, (AV) ..................'43 '71 C.813 B.A. L.426 J.D. [Lawler,B.&W.]
*PRACTICE AREAS: Automobile Law; Intentional Torts; General Civil Litigation; Arbitration.
Wasserman, Howard J. ..............'52 '77 C.1077 B.A. L.1095 J.D. 220 South "A" St.
Wedemeyer, Byron J., (CV) .................. '39 '69 C.426 B.A. L.276 J.D. 110 S. A St.
**Wennergren, Kenneth H.**, (AV) ....... '50 '79 C.112 B.A. L.1068 J.D. [Wennergren&S.]
*PRACTICE AREAS: Entertainment Law; Business and Estate Planning; Taxation.

**Wennergren & Shain, Professional Law Corporation, (AV)**
**300 Esplanade Drive, Suite 1180, 93030**
**Telephone: 805-983-2800; 988-0610 Telecopier: 805-988-1422**
**Email: WSPLC@AOL.COM**
**David L. Shain; Kenneth H. Wennergren. Of Counsel: David B. Shea.**
**Business and Entertainment Law, Personal Injury and Civil Litigation.**
*See Professional Biographies, OXNARD, CALIFORNIA*

West, Eugene F. .................................. '54 '81 C.1041 B.A. L.999 J.D. [West&M.]
West & Miyamoto ...................................................... 2001 N. Solar Dr.
**Whitfield, Anson M.**, (BV) ........ '31 '63 C.597 B.S. L.1066 LL.B. [England,W.S.&T.]
*PRACTICE AREAS: Real Property Leasing Law; Business Litigation; Bankruptcy Law; Business Law.
Wilson, Stephanie R. ....................... '68 '93 C.773 B.A. L.809 J.D. P.O. Box 9021
**Winfield, William E.**, (BV) .......... '58 '85 C.101 B.A. L.878 J.D. [Nordman,C.H.&C.]
*LANGUAGES: Dutch.
*PRACTICE AREAS: Bankruptcy Law; Creditors Rights Law; Commercial Law.

**Wisotsky, Alan E., Law Offices of, (AV) '48 '75 C.1097 B.S. L.809 J.D.**
**1000 Town Center Drive Suite 200, 93030**
**Telephone: 805-278-0920 Fax: 805-278-0289**
**Associates: Brian P. Keighron; Jeffrey B. Held; Philip Erickson.**
**Insurance and Self-Insured Defense and Civil Trial Practice. General, Automobile, Product, Public Entity and Police Misconduct Litigation.**
*See Professional Biographies, OXNARD, CALIFORNIA*

**Wojkowski, James**, (AV) ...........'48 '75 C.763 B.S. L.770 J.D. [Arnold,B.M.W.&Z.]
*PRACTICE AREAS: Taxation; Estate Planning; Probate and Trust Law; Real Estate and Business Law.
**Woo, Carol A.** .............................. '55 '86 C.112 B.A. L.990 J.D. [Lawler,B.&W.]
*REPORTED CASES: Cottle v. Superior Court, 1992, 30 A 4th 1367, 5 C.R. 2d 882.
*PRACTICE AREAS: Environmental Law; Municipal Law; School Law; Insurance Law; Commercial Transactions.
**Worley, David R.**, (BV) ........... '54 '81 C.1212 B.A. L.426 J.D. [Arnold,B.M.W.&Z.]
*PRACTICE AREAS: Business and Environmental Litigation; Oil and Gas Litigation; Probate and Trust Litigation; Construction Defects; Arbitration and Mediation.
Yee, Melodee A. ............... '68 '93 C.112 B.A. L.426 J.D. 300 Esplanada Dr. 6th Fl.
Zimmer, Steven D. ............ '47 '73 C.112 B.S. L.1065 LL.B. 721 S. "A" St., 2nd Fl.
**Zirbel, Mark A.**, (BV) ............. '50 '75 C.112 B.A. L.1051 J.D. [Arnold,B.M.W.&Z.]
*PRACTICE AREAS: Liquid and Solid Waste; Public Agency Law; Environmental Law; Land Use.

## PACIFICA, 37,670, *San Mateo Co.*

**Aimola, Nancy A., Law Offices of, (AV) '49 '75 C.112 A.B. L.1065 J.D.**
**515 Rockaway Beach Avenue, 94044-3228**
**Telephone: 415-355-4720 Fax: 415-355-8943**
**Civil Trial and Appellate Practice. Business Litigation, Bankruptcy Trusteeship, Receivership, Real Estate, Construction, Discrimination and Personal Injury Law.**
*See Professional Biographies, PACIFICA, CALIFORNIA*

Davies, Roy H. ................... '22 '52 C.112 B.S. L.767 J.D. 679 Parkview Ct. (Pat.)‡
Fox, Arthur L. ............................ '49 '74 C.156 B.A. L.767 J.D. 250 Paloma Ave.
Geary, Paul M. ......................... '26 '54 C.768 B.A. L.1066 J.D. 1109 Rainier Ave.

**George, Armen L. '59 '86 C.112 A.B. L.767 J.D.**
**80 Driftwood Circle, 94044**
**Telephone: 415-355-9314 Fax: 415-355-9315**
***REPORTED CASES: Dafonte v. Up-Right, Inc. (1992) 2 Cal. 4th 593; Hunter v. Up-Right, Inc. (1993) 6 Cal. 4th 1174.**
***PRACTICE AREAS: Civil; Business Litigation; Civil Appeals; Personal Injury; Real Property. Civil and Business Litigation, Civil Appeals, Real Property and Contract Law.**
*See Professional Biographies, PACIFICA, CALIFORNIA*

Gustavson, Stanley G., (BV) ............................ '48 '79 L.765 J.D. 4 Randolf Place
Hale, Richard L. ......................... '50 '89 C&L.767 B.S., J.D. 1042 Granada Dr.
Lorvan, Sidney, (CV) ........................ '33 '57 C.188 B.A. L.982 LL.B. 160 Milagra Dr.
Louden, Jeffrey Hadley ............'57 '83 C.112 B.A. L.1065 J.D. 146 Beachview Ave.
Lowney, Linda N. ......................... '50 '78 C.112 A.B. L.408 J.D. 1207 De Solo Dr.
Nelson, Walter R. ................ '43 '70 C.494 B.S. L.1035 J.D. 14 Kings Canyon Way
Northrop, Frederick J. ........... '53 '89 C.112 B.F.A. L.1065 J.D. 1277 Linda Mar Ctr.
Pelc Buyers, Celeste E. ..................... '55 '80 C.914 B.A. L.770 J.D. 23 Humboldt‡
Reynolds, David J., (AV) ................. '47 '75 C&L.767 B.A., J.D. 15 W. Manor Dr.
Schectman, Susan M., (BV) ..................... '50 '76 C.188 B.A. L.284 J.D. City Atty.
Soden, Jane B. ....................................... '45 '91 C.219 B.A. L.765 J.D. P.O. Box 583
Themelis, Nicholas M. .................... '50 '80 C.629 B.A. L.284 J.D. 628 Brighton Rd.
Torrigino, Mario M. ........................... '54 '80 C&L.767 B.A., J.D. 80 Eureka Square
Van Sciver, L. David ....................... '49 '89 C.112 B.S. L.765 J.D. 211 Marvilla Cir.

## PACIFIC GROVE, 16,117, *Monterey Co.*

Arellano, Anita C. ........................... '32 '81 C.768 B.A. L.770 J.D. P.O. Box 758
Benoit, Michael ........................ '— '90 C.767 B.S. L.1226 J.D. Legal Servs. for Seniors
Berlitz, Barbara Jean .......................... '50 '85 C.36 B.A. L.1226 J.D. P.O. Box 695
Bernstein, Edward G., (BV) ............'34 '61 C.659 A.B. L.569 LL.B. [E.G.Bernstein]
Bernstein, Edward G., P.C., (BV) ........................................ 721 Lighthouse Ave
Bileci, Joseph E., Jr. ......................... '51 '88 C.999 L.1226 J.D. P.O. Box 1029
Bowns, Carmela M. ............................. '47 '75 C&L.911 B.A., J.D. 606 Forest Ave.
Diehl, Sarah J. .................................'60 '85 C&L.813 B.A., J.D. 431 Spruce Ave.
Forbes, Timothy George ............................ '52 '86 L.1226 J.D. P.O. Box 51103
Gill, Brian F., (CV) ............................. '48 '73 C.154 B.A. L.284 J.D. [Gill]
Graves, Hideko I. ........................ '39 '71 L.1148 J.D. 196 Del Monte Blvd.
Hatcher, Robert T., (CV) ............................ '37 '74 L.1153 LL.B. 706 Forest Ave.
Hespe, Frank ..................... '— '88 C.705 B.A. L.1066 J.D. Legal Servs. for Seniors

**Jewett, Cynthia '46 '74 C.696 B.A. L.1065 J.D.**
**704 Forest Avenue, 93950**
**Telephone: 408-373-3300 Fax: 408-375-6418**
**(Certified Specialist, Criminal Law, The State Bar of California Board of Legal Specialization.).**
***PRACTICE AREAS: Criminal Law.**
**Criminal Law.**

Jorgensen, Henry I. ........................... '15 '57 C&L.813 A.B., LL.B. 317 Alder St.‡
Keough, James E. ................................. '44 '69 C.93 B.S. L.802 J.D. [J.E.Keough]
Keough, James E., Prof. Corp. .............................................. 519 Forest Ave.
Laredo, David C., (CV) ........................ '50 '75 C.112 A.B. L.809 J.D. 606 Forest Ave.
Manlin, Michael A. .................'45 '75 C.766 B.A. L.464 J.D. 1199 Forest Ave. #140
Moore, Charles L. ............................ '27 '52 C&L.813 A.B., LL.B. 1246 Buena Vista‡
Morris, Theodore G. ........................ '24 '51 C&L.477 A.B., LL.B. 1038 Balboa Ave.‡
Riddle, David A. '52 '78 C.312 B.A. L.1188 J.D.
(adm. in HI; not adm. in CA) 403 Gibson Ave.
Roberts, George S. ......................... '45 '75 C.1077 B.A. L.398 J.D. 610 Forest Ave.
Sabih, David S. ............................... '35 '73 C.563 B.S. L.1068 J.D. 405 Forest Ave.
Schmidt, Peggy A. .........................'48 '78 C.246 B.S.E. L.1065 J.D. [Stoner,W.&S.]
Seidel, John E. ........................... '28 '62 C.112 B.S. L.426 J.D. P.O. Box 52150‡
Slatkow, Steve A. ............................. '43 '69 C.800 B.A. L.1065 J.D. P.O. Box 37
Stoner, Katherine E., (BV) ............... '47 '78 C.1169 B.A. L.1226 J.D. [Stoner,W.&S.]
Stoner, Welsh and Schmidt, (BV) ................................................ 229 17th St.
Thacher, George C., (BV) ........................ '43 '69 C.813 B.A. L.1065 J.D. City Atty.
The Gill Law Offices, (CV) ..................................................... 164 Forest Ave.
Welsh, Michelle A., (BV) ................ '48 '78 C.651 B.A. L.1226 J.D. [Stoner,W.&S.]

## PACIFIC PALISADES, —, *Los Angeles Co.*

(Part of the incorporated City of Los Angeles)

Albert, Bernard L. '18 '46 C&L.569 B.S., LL.B.
(adm. in NJ; not adm. in CA) 1578 Michael Lane‡
Aldrich, Kenneth C., (AV) ........................ '38 '64 C&L.309 A.B., J.D. P.O. Box 827
Alexander, John R. .......................'18 '49 C.674 A.B. L.309 LL.B. 710 Chapala Dr.‡
Anderson, John Patrick, (AV) ..........'39 '67 C.546 B.A. L.976 LL.B. 1314 Goucher St.
Asimow, Nathan .......................... '18 '43 C.113 L.1001 J.D. 14601 Drummond St.‡
Avidan, Bernard M., (BV) ........... '29 '58 C.112 B.S. L.800 J.D. 15309 McKendree Ave.
Bauman, John A. '21 '47 C&L.494 B.S., LL.B.
(adm. in WI; not adm. in CA) Prof., Univ. of Calif. Sch. of Law‡
Bay, Don R. ............................. '34 '70 C.112 B.A. L.426 J.D. 15332 Antioch St.
Berggreen, Raymond G., (AV) ... '22 '66 C.118 A.B. L.767 LL.B. 16940 Dulce Ynez Ln.‡
Campbell, Frank A. ............................ '32 '76 C.112 A.B. L.1136 J.D. P.O. Box 25
Carroll, Susan L. ........................ '47 '73 C.881 B.A. L.659 J.D. 17041 Bollinger Dr.
Christol, Carl Q. ........................... '14 '48 C.793 A.B. L.976 LL.B. 1041 Anoka Pl.
Cohen, Leatrice L. ........................... '38 '80 C.1077 B.A. L.1136 J.D. P.O. Box 1707
Comras, Kelly ......................... '53 '92 C.112 B.A. L.426 J.D. 17721 Tramonto Dr.
Cook, Nevada Brooks ................. '51 '79 C.112 B.S. L.809 J.D. 13701 Sunset Blvd.‡
Cutler, Allan Harris ............................ '39 '80 C.800 B.A. L.1068 J.D. P.O. Box 160
Cutler, Helen Elmquist ........................ '38 '81 C.800 B.A. L.1068 J.D. P.O. Box 160
Damm, Lawrence H., (BV) ............... '52 '78 C.800 B.S. L.426 J.D. 15200 Sunset Blvd.
Damon, Max ................................... '06 '32 L.809 LL.B. 16800 Marquez Ave.‡
Davis, William F., (AV) ................. '39 '69 C.112 A.B. L.426 J.D. 881 Alma Real Dr.
Dean, Ronald ........................... '44 '70 C.33 B.A. L.966 J.D. 15135 Sunset Blvd.
DuBovy, N Jane, (BV) ............ '53 '81 C&L.990 B.A.M.A., J.D. 16712 Marquez Ave.
Edwards, LuEllen W. ..................... '48 '78 C.518 B.A. L.1190 J.D. 1331 Berea Pl.
Erpelding, John W. .................... '19 '49 C.477 A.B. L.597 J.D. 1061 Villa View Dr.‡
Fank, Carolyn Leigh, (Ms.) ........... '52 '82 C.1169 B.A. L.426 J.D. 15237 Sunset Blvd.
Feinerman, Robert ................ '26 '50 C.112 A.B. L.1066 LL.B. 1159 Lachman Lane
Flaherty, Isabelle C. '51 '79
(adm. in NY; not adm. in CA) 1308 Monument St.‡
Fried, Marilyn J. ............................ '50 '78 C.685 B.S. L.426 J.D. P.O. Box 1028
Genser, Stanley ............................ '42 '68 C.112 B.S. L.1068 J.D. Supr. Ct. Comr.
Greenfield, Ronald S. .................... '42 '69 C.112 B.A. L.426 J.D. 15415 Sunset Blvd.
Gutierrez, Thomas A. .................... '47 '73 C.112 B.A. L.1068 J.D. 726 Ocampo Dr.
Hoffenberg, Betty S. ................. '22 '87 C.821 B.A. L.1136 J.D. 1365 Marinete Rd.‡
Jones, Edgar A., Jr. '21 '48 C.918 B.A. L.893 LL.B.
(adm. in VA; not adm. in CA) Prof. of Law, Emeritus, Univ. of Calif.
Juliano, Mary F. ........................ '43 '78 C.800 B.S. L.426 J.D. 1064 Tellem Dr.
Kallberg, Kevin M. ........................ '53 '79 C&L.602 A.B., J.D. 916 Las Lomas Ave.

**Klopfenstein, John F. '53 '93 C.911 B.A. L.999 J.D.**
**1156 Embury Street, 90272**
**Telephone: 310-459-0447 Fax: 310-459-0053**
***PRACTICE AREAS: Civil Litigation; Criminal Litigation; Personal Injury; Bankruptcy. Civil and Criminal Litigation, Personal Injury and Bankruptcy.**

Knotts, Marcus M. ............................... '07 '30 C.999 L.900 LL.B. 23 Copra Lane‡
Kraus, Erwin H. ......................... '14 '48 C.339 B.S. L.910 J.D. 501 Palisades Dr.‡
Larsen, Shelby S., (Mrs.) .................. '45 '75 C.475 B.A. L.608 J.D. 1428 Floresta Pl.

CAA453P

CALIFORNIA—PACIFIC PALISADES MARTINDALE-HUBBELL LAW DIRECTORY 1997

Lennard, Melvin ... '15 '39 C&L.309 A.B., LL.B. 641 Jacon Way‡
Lerman, Jeffrey H. ... '56 '80 C.112 B.S. L.1068 J.D. [Lerman&L.]
Lerman, Michelle ... '58 '80 C.112 B.S. L.800 J.D. [Lerman&L.]
Lerman & Lerman ... 17366 Sunset Blvd.
Love, C. Stephen ... '47 '76 C.1077 B.A. L.1095 J.D. 14517 Sunset Blvd.
Magur, Louis ... '52 '80 C.1097 B.A. L.1068 J.D. 15327 Sunset Blvd.
Margolis, Benjamin Robert ... '45 '86 C.999 B.S. L.809 J.D. 1387 Monument St.
McNamar, Richard T. ... '39 '66 C.884 A.B. L.477 J.D. 1331 Goucher St.
Micken, Carol Ann ... '52 '78 C.763 B.A. L.1049 J.D. 13776 Sunset Blvd.
Moffat, Henry M., (AV) '25 '51 C&L.813 B.A., J.D.
Exec. Dir., National Assn. of Railroad Trial Coun.
Muhl, Lee ... '47 '74 C.112 B.A. L.1068 J.D. P.O. Box 1604
Nonberg, Randy E. ... '50 '75 C.597 A.B. L.276 J.D. 17383 Sunset Blvd.
Overland, Barbara C. ... '45 '72 C.112 A.B. L.426 J.D. 515 Chapala St.
**Pecsok, Marilyn S.**, (AV) ... '40 '83 C.930 B.B.A. L.1068 J.D. [Snyder&P.]
*PRACTICE AREAS: Family Law.
Posner, Margery S. ... '24 '86 C.477 B.A. L.1148 J.D. 15452 Albright St.
Postel, Elizabeth K. ... '20 '43 C&L.910 J.D. 16844 Bollinger Dr.
Ries, James N. ... '38 '65 C.112 B.A. L.1068 LL.B. 17383 W. Sunset Blvd.
Rosecrance, Barbara B. ... '— '87 C&L.188 B.A., J.D. 15237 Sunset Blvd.
Rothenberg, Leslie Steven, (AV) ... '41 '69 C.597 B.S. L.1068 J.D. [L.S.Rothenberg]
Rothenberg, Leslie Steven, A P.C., (AV) ... 16751 Edgar St.
Rubel, Suz ... '52 '81 C.112 B.A. L.426 J.D. 1349 Marinette Rd.
Rudof, Joel ... '23 '50 C.112 L.800 LL.B. Ret. Supr. Ct. J.

**Sampson, William A., II & Associates, (AV) '35 '61 C&L.813 B.A., J.D.**
**15332 Antioch Street, Suite 525, 90272**
**Telephone: 310-472-1839 Fax: 310-472-8670**
***LANGUAGES: Spanish (Written and Oral).**
***PRACTICE AREAS: Traumatic Injury; Bad Faith; Strict Liability; Professional Negligence; Criminal Law.**
**Civil Trial Practice in all State and Federal Courts. Personal Injury, Products Liability, Medical Malpractice, Aviation and Admiralty Law. Criminal Law.**

*See Professional Biographies, PACIFIC PALISADES, CALIFORNIA*

Sanborn, Carol Prenatt ... '53 '85 C.476 B.S. L.426 J.D. 1262 Villa Woods Dr.
Schwartz, Murray L. '20 '50 C.645 B.S. L.659 LL.B.
(adm. in PA; not adm. in CA) 1339 Marinette Rd.‡
Sevilla, Stanley, (AV) ... '20 '49 C.150 B.A. L.309 J.D. [S.Seville]
Seville, Stanley, A Prof. Law Corp., (AV) ... 16606 Merivale Ln.
Shirley, Heidi W. ... '37 '79 C.681 A.B. L.426 J.D. 740 Almafi Dr.
Siegel, Abraham ... '19 '50 C.563 B.S. L.273 J.D. 717 Toyopa Dr.
**Snyder, William Henri**, (AV) ... '31 '59 C.264 B.S. L.1068 J.D. [Snyder&P.]
*PRACTICE AREAS: Probate, Estate Planning and Trust Law; Residential Real Property.

**Snyder & Pecsok, (AV)**
**Suite 309, 881 Alma Real Drive, 90272-3773**
**Telephone: 310-454-1388 Telecopier: 310-459-9720**
**Email: WILLIAMHSNYDER76300.632@COMPUSERVE.COM**
**Members of Firm: William Henri Snyder (Certified Specialist, Estate Planning, Trust and Probate Law, The State Bar of California Board of Legal Specialization); Marilyn S. Pecsok.**
**Family Law, Probate, Estate Planning, Trusts, Real Estate.**
**References: Bank of America; Santa Monica Bank; Wells Fargo Bank.**

*See Professional Biographies, PACIFIC PALISADES, CALIFORNIA*

Solum-Middleton, Lorraine A. ... '61 '89 C.800 A.B. L.426 J.D. P.O. Box 952
Sweeters, Wilbur A. ... '17 '61 C.426 A.B. L.809 LL.B. 320 Swarthmore Ave.‡
Updegraff-Power, Teresa A. ... '62 '88 C.800 B.A. L.990 J.D. 633 Bienveneda Ave.
Victor, Mark A. '48 '74
(adm. in AZ; not adm. in CA) 707 Alma Real‡
Watman, Kenneth H. ... '48 '77 C.385 B.A. L.930 J.D. 16169 Sunset Blvd.‡
Webb, Eugene M., (AV) ... '32 '60 C&L.838 B.S., J.D. 15332 Antioch St.
Weitz, Ted C. ... '51 '77 C.800 B.A. L.107 J.D. 15332 Antioch St.
Welk, Thomas S. ... '61 '90 C.911 B.A. L.285 J.D. 853 Haverford Ave.
Werb, Neil N. ... '23 '48 C.112 B.S. L.800 J.D. 881 Alma Real
Wheeler, Lawrence D. ... '41 '75 C.36 B.S. L.1148 J.D. N.L.R.B.
Wulliger, Richard C. '32 '57 C.112 A.B. L.1068 J.D.
Admin. Law J. & Reg. Planning Comr. & Arbitrator
Zerfas, Daniel G., (AV) ... '39 '67 C.1077 B.A. L.1068 J.D. 14230 Sunset Blvd.
Ziering, Diane Delpit ... '56 '83 C.112 B.A. L.426 J.D. 516 Chapala Dr.‡

## PACOIMA, —, *Los Angeles Co.*

(Part of the incorporated City of Los Angeles)

Hollman, Lewis J. '46 '74 C.645 B.A. L.1066 J.D.
San Fernando Valley Neighborhood Legal Servs., Inc.
Mariajimenez, Yvonne Elizabeth '56 '85 C.800 B.S. L.426 J.D.
Sr. Atty., San Fernando Valley Neighborhood Legal Servs., Inc.
Sanders, Robin Lynn ... '51 '82 C.112 B.A. L.809 J.D. 13090 Louvre St.
Smith, James W., Jr. '43 '82 C.1077 B.A. L.426 J.D.
Coun., Archangel Co. Christian Legal Serv. Centers
Whisman, Tim '51 '80 C.112 B.A. L.426 J.D.
San Fernando Valley Neighborhood Legal Servs., Inc.

## PALMDALE, 68,842, *Los Angeles Co.*

Beaudet, Thomas J., (AV) ... '26 '52 C.988 B.A. L.426 LL.B. 41705 N. 10th St. W.‡
Borowski, Dannie R. ... '46 '77 C.911 B.A. L.426 J.D. 3166 E. Palmdale Blvd.
Cooper, Eugene H. ... '53 '81 C.563 B.A. L.809 J.D. 39317 Riverbend St.
Dachs, Louis D. '35 '78 C.1074 B.S. L.398 J.D.
Pat. Coun., Lockheed Advanced Develop. Co. (Pat.)
Ditzhazy, Shelly L. ... '54 '83 C.477 B.A. L.213 J.D. 39239 Gunsmoke Ct.‡
Epson, Michael W., (BV) ... '41 '67 C&L.1049 B.A., J.D. [Epson,M.&K.]
Epson, Milburn & Kahl, (BV) ... 1317 E. Palmdale Blvd.
Kahl, Kevin C., (BV) ... '54 '79 C.112 B.A. L.1095 J.D. [Epson,M.&K.]
Land, Alan E. '43 '67 C.605 B.A. L.1066 J.D.
Asst. Div. Coun., Lockheed Advanced Develop. Co.
Lawton, Stephen E., (BV) ... '24 '55 C.605 B.A. L.1068 J.D. 1113 W. Ave. M4
Long, A. Donald, (BV) ... '39 '72 C.1097 B.A. L.809 J.D. 1113 W. Ave. M4
**Milburn, Nolen P., Jr.**, (BV) ... '51 '78 [Epson,M.&K.]
Murray, William S. '16 '39 C&L.585 B.A., LL.B.
(adm. in ND; not adm. in CA) 38550 Frontier Ave.‡
Orr, Timothy L., (BV) ... '41 '67 C&L.426 LL.B. 41705 N. 10th St., W. (⊙San Fernando)
Pincher, Michael W. ... '50 '77 C.1044 B.A. L.1095 J.D. 38530 159th St., E.
Reichman, Dawn L. ... '51 '88 C.112 B.A. L.1148 J.D. 1305 E. Palmdale Blvd.
Rosen, Alan D., (AV) ... '41 '67 C.61 B.A. L.1049 J.D. 1317 E. Palmdale Blvd.
Seymour, Scott J. ... '50 '88 C.667 B.S.E.E. L.1137 J.D. 41564 Mission Dr. (Pat.)
Smith, Frederic P. ... '34 '63 Lockheed Aeronautical Systems Co. (Pat.)
Swindlehurst, Rodney Leon '49 '81 C&L.101 B.A., J.D.
Union Rel. Mgr., Lockheed Aeronautical Systems Co.

## PALM DESERT, 23,252, *Riverside Co.*

Adams, William J. ... '27 '55 C.768 A.B. L.1065 J.D. 44100 Monterey
Allen, Rhodes & Sobelsohn, LLP, (AV)
73-710 Fred Waring Drive, Suite 210 (⊙Los Angeles, Ontario, Santa Barbara & Santa Ana)
Anderholt, J. John, Jr. ... '43 '68 C.813 B.S. L.800 J.D. 42600 Cook St.
**Anderson, Gayle F.**, (AV) ... '33 '65 C.763 B.S. L.1049 J.D. [Hinchy,W.W.A.&H.]
*PRACTICE AREAS: Trusts; Wills; Probate; Estate Planning.
Armenta, Juan Manuel ... '63 '90 L.398 J.D. [English L.&A.]
Baran, Matthew J., (CV) ... '61 '86 C.645 B.S. L.1017 J.D. 43-645 Monterey Ave.
Beach, Marshall, (AV) '12 '36 C.502 B.A. L.477 J.D.
(adm. in MO; not adm. in CA) 905 Sandpiper Ave.‡
Bendon, Sandra L. ... '— '81 C.831 B.S. L.398 J.D. [Hanover&B.]
Bergmann, Donald L. '41 '69 C.165 B.A. L.309 J.D.
(adm. in NY; not adm. in CA) V.P., Gen. Coun. & Secy., U.S. Filter Corp.
**Berman, Martin M.**, (AV) ... '34 '63 C&L.800 B.Ch.E., LL.B. [Berman&W.]⊙
*PRACTICE AREAS: Medical Malpractice Law; Products Liability Law; Personal Injury Law; Aviation Law.

**Berman & Weiss, (AV)**
**73-710 Fred Waring Drive, Suite 100, 92260⊙**
**Telephone: 619-773-6677 Fax: 619-346-7779**
**Email: rw1224@aol.com URL: http://www.lawinfo.com/law/ca/berman.html**
**Members of Firm: Richard B. Weiss; Martin M. Berman.**
**Personal Injury, Products Liability, Medical and Legal Malpractice, Insurance and Bad Faith Law, Aviation Law, Construction Accidents.**
**Encino, California Office: 16055 Ventura Boulevard, Suite 900, 91436. Telephone: 818-986-8000. Facsimile: 818-986-3162.**
**Palm Springs, California Office: 1111 Tahquitz Canyon Way, Suite 203, 92262. Telephone: 619-327-1777. Fax: 619-346-7779.**

*See Professional Biographies, PALM DESERT, CALIFORNIA*

Blaisdell, Christopher M. ... '40 '71 C.112 B.A. L.1065 J.D. 73-200 El Paseo
Blakeney, James R. '13 '41 L.802 LL.B.
(adm. in OK; not adm. in CA) 38-303 Crocus Ln.‡
Blay, Robert D. ... '31 '86 C&L.1190 B.S.L., J.D. 41700 Corporate Way
**Bochnewich, Marie A.** ... '61 '93 C.763 B.S. L.61 J.D. [Ⓐ Criste,P.&G.]
*PRACTICE AREAS: Civil Litigation.

**Bolas, Donald M., (BV) '42 '67 C.152 B.A. L.1017 J.D.**
**44712 Monterey Avenue, 92260**
**Telephone: 619-568-0675**
***LANGUAGES: Czech.**
**Family Law, Workers Compensation, Personal Injury.**

*See Professional Biographies, PALM DESERT, CALIFORNIA*

Bolton, Robert A., (AV) ... '30 '63 C&L.770 B.S., LL.B. 72910 Somera Rd.
Bolton, Russell K., Jr., (AV) ... '21 '49 C&L.923 LL.B. 48 240 Adler Ln.‡
Childress, Hubert M. ... '21 '72 C.800 B.A. L.1068 J.D. 48988 Sunny Summit Ln.
Childs, Carol E. ... '31 '75 L.1190 74361 US Hwy. 111
Ciniello-Brislin, Marsha ... '44 '89 C.112 L.1198 J.D. 41865 Boardwalk
Clark, Walter T., (AV) ... '46 '72 C.112 B.A. L.1049 J.D. 74-075 El Paseo Ave.
Cleary, Henry V. ... '28 '53 C.112 A.B. L.1065 J.D. 73200 El Paseo
Cooper, James P. ... '36 '64 C.112 A.B. L.767 LL.B. Orandaco Inc.
Cosgrove, Michael J., (BV) ... '52 '77 C.112 B.A. L.426 J.D. [Cosgrove&C.]
Cosgrove, William N. ... '57 '82 C.813 A.B. L.1066 J.D. [Cosgrove&C.]
Cosgrove & Cosgrove, (BV) ... 45-120 San Pablo St.
Crandall, Lynn D., (AV) ... '35 '62 C.112 A.B. L.800 J.D. 43-645 Monterey Ave.
**Criste, Michael A.**, (AV) ... '43 '79 C.446 B.S.C.E. L.1017 J.D. [Criste,P.&G.]
*PRACTICE AREAS: Business Law; Real Estate.

**Criste, Virginia S., Law Offices of, (AV) '44 '69 C.518 B.A. L.273 J.D.**
**74-075 El Paseo, Suite A-14, 92260**
**Telephone: 619-776-1770 Fax: 619-776-1775**
***LANGUAGES: Spanish, French and German.**
***PRACTICE AREAS: Family Law; Bankruptcy Law.**
**Family Law and Bankruptcy Reorganization.**

*See Professional Biographies, PALM DESERT, CALIFORNIA*

**Criste, Pippin & Golds, (AV)**
**Suite 200, 73-550 Alessandro Drive, 92260**
**Telephone: 619-862-1111 Fax: 619-776-4197**
**Email: cpgca@aol.com**
**Members of Firm: Michael A. Criste; Robert L. Pippin; Irwin L. Golds. Associates: Marie A. Bochnewich.**
**Civil Litigation and Business Law Practice, including Real Estate and Business Transactions, Bankruptcy, Business Reorganizations, Real Property and Construction Litigation. Trial, Appellate and Extraordinary Writ Practice.**

*See Professional Biographies, PALM DESERT, CALIFORNIA*

Cropper, Mariann C. ... '35 '79 L.1026 LL.B. 208 Green Mountain Dr.

**Dedina, Steven J. '67 '93 C.139 B.S., B.A. L.767 J.D.**
**74-090 El Paseo, Second Floor, 92260**
**Telephone: 619-320-2500 Fax: 619-341-3635**
***PRACTICE AREAS: Real Estate; Business Law; Civil Litigation.**
**Real Estate, Business Law and General Civil Litigation.**

*See Professional Biographies, PALM DESERT, CALIFORNIA*

Deeb, Gary P. '44 '70 C.912 B.S. L.213 J.D.
(adm. in MI; not adm. in CA) 41250 Carlotta‡
DeLateur, Steven W. ... '51 '84 C.37 B.S.B.A. L.1209 J.D. 42600 Cook St.
Devin, Lisa L. ... '65 '91 C.259 B.S. L.990 J.D. 74361 Hwy.111
Donovan, Michael R. '18 '47 C&L.911 B.A., J.D.
(adm. in WA; not adm. in CA) 30 Maximo Way‡
Douglas, Alfred J. ... '47 '72 C.112 B.A. L.1049 J.D. 44-100 Monterey Ave., Apt. 203
Druten, Charles A., (AV) ... '30 '55 C.112 B.A. L.1068 LL.B. 370 Cypress Point Dr.
Eastman, Diane Wilkens ... '60 '90 C&L.1137 B.S.L., J.D. [Ⓐ Guralnick&Assoc.]
Eggebraaten, Toni ... '54 '93 C&L.1137 43-645 Monterey Ave.
Engel, Paul K. ... '46 '82 C.025 B.A.Sc. L.1134 J.D. Mng. Princ., Engel & Assocs.
English Lloyd & Armenta ... 73-710 Fred Waring Dr.
Erickson, Vincent N. ... '19 '49 C&L.800 A.B., LL.B. 124 Giralda Cir.‡

**Fiore, Walker, Racobs & Powers, A Professional Law Corporation, (AV)**
**74-361 Highway III, Suite 1, 92261-4250⊙**
**Telephone: 619-776-6511 Fax: 619-776-6517**
**Peter E. Racobs; Margaret G. Wangler.**
**Community Association, Real Property, Civil Litigation, Construction and Business.**
**Irvine, California Office: Koll Center Irvine. 18400 Von Karmen, Suite 600. 92612-1514. Telephone: 714-955-0560. Fax: 714-955-2894.**
**Riverside, California Office: 6670 Alessandro, Suite B. Telephone: 909-789-8100. Fax: 909-789-8105.**

*See Professional Biographies, PALM DESERT, CALIFORNIA*

**Franklin, David M., (BV) '40 '75 C&L.1137 B.S., J.D.**
**74-075 El Paseo, Suite A-6, 92261-3253**
**Telephone: 619-568-1585**
**(Certified Specialist, Family Law, The State Bar of California Board of Legal Specialization).**

(This Listing Continued)

CAA454P

**Franklin, David M. (Continued)**
**Practice limited to Family Law and Business Litigation.**
***See Professional Biographies, PALM DESERT, CALIFORNIA***

Friedman, Gilbert J. ............'24 '69 C&L.1095 B.A., LL.B. 48123 Monterra Circle W.‡

**Galton & Helm, (AV)**
**Suite 377, 73-290 El Paseo, 92260⊙**
**Telephone: 619-776-5600 Fax: 619-776-5602**
**Members of Firm: Daniel W. Maguire.**
**Civil Litigation Practice in State and Federal Courts. Insurance Defense. (Life, Accident and Health, Bad Faith Defense, Professional Negligence, Reinsurance Law and ERISA).**
**Los Angeles, California Office: 500 South Grand Avenue, Suite 1200. 213-629-8800. Fax: 213-629-0037.**
***See Professional Biographies, PALM DESERT, CALIFORNIA***

Garvin, Lisa A. ........................'56 '89 C&L.1137 B.S.L., J.D. 43-645 Monterey Ave.
Georgino, Damian C. '60 '86 C.216 B.S. L.245 J.D.
(adm. in PA; not adm. in CA) V.P. & Gen. Coun., U.S. Filter Corp.
Golan, Ronald T. ..................'30 '61 C&L.800 J.D. 73-725 El Pasco (⊙Santa Monica)
**Goldberg, Martin S.**, (AVⓉ) ..................'24 '52 C&L.608 B.S., J.D. [M.S.Goldberg]⊙

**Goldberg, Martin S., Co., L.P.A., (AVⓉ)**
**74-513 Old Prospector Lane, 92260⊙**
**Telephone: 619-773-4773**
**Martin S. Goldberg.**
**Personal Injury, Medical Malpractice, Products Liability. Trials in all State and Federal Courts.**
**References: Key Bank, Glendale Federal Bank.**
**Canfield, Ohio Office: Summit Professional Centre. 6600 Summit Drive. Telephone: 330-533-8300 Fax: 330-533-8303.**

**Golds, Irwin L.**, (BV) ......................'56 '81 C.112 B.A. L.1065 J.D. [Criste,P.&G.]
*PRACTICE AREAS: Real Estate Law; Business Law.
Gordon, Melvin ..........................'18 '49 C&L.339 B.S., LL.B. P.O. Box 1076
Gothard, John H., Jr. ....................'45 '92 C.1120 B.S. L.61 J.D. 74-075 El Paso
**Gribow, Dale S.**, (AV) ....................'43 '70 C.800 B.A. L.426 J.D. [D.S.Gribow]⊙
*LANGUAGES: Spanish.

**Gribow, Dale S., A Professional Corporation, (AV)**
**43-585 Monterey Avenue, 92260⊙**
**Telephone: 619-341-4411 Fax: 619-773-3636**
**Dale S. Gribow.**
**Civil and Criminal Litigation, General Business and Real Estate Law, Personal Injury, Medical and Legal Malpractice, Estate Planning and Airplane Accidents.**
**Los Angeles (Century City), California Office: 1925 Century Park East, Suite 2250. Telephone: 310-273-DALE. Fax: 310-203-0140.**
***See Professional Biographies, PALM DESERT, CALIFORNIA***

Guralnick, Wayne S., (BV) ............'53 '79 C.884 B.A. L.990 J.D. [Guralnick&Assoc.]
Guralnick & Associates, (BV) ..............................74-399 Highway 111 Suite M
Hanover, George M., (AV) ......................'41 '66 C.154 L.800 LL.B. [Hanover&B.]
Hanover & Bendon, (AV) ..................................73-710 Fred Waring, Suite 100
Hawkins, James S., (BV) ............'46 '74 C.1097 B.A. L.809 J.D. 74-075 El Paseo Ave.
**Healey, Dennis J.**, (CV) ......................'44 '69 C.846 B.A. L.744 J.D. [Healey&H.]
*PRACTICE AREAS: Probate and Estate Planning; Wills and Trusts; Elder Law; Real Estate; Personal Injury Law.
**Healey, James P.**, (BV) ......................'11 '36 C.112 B.S. L.1065 J.D. [Healey&H.]
*PRACTICE AREAS: Estate Planning; Probate; Wills and Trusts.

**Healey & Healey, (BV)**
**74075 El Paseo Avenue, Suite A-15, P.O. Box 3366, 92261-3366**
**Telephone: 619-341-8366 Fax: 619-341-4967**
**Email: LAWDJH@AOL.COM**
**Members of Firm: James P. Healey; Dennis J. Healey. Associates: Robert H. Stempler.**
**Estate Planning, Probate, Wills and Trusts, Elder Law, Real Estate, Personal Injury and General Business.**
***See Professional Biographies, PALM DESERT, CALIFORNIA***

Hilkey, Sigrid R. ......................................'43 '89 L.1137 J.D. [⊠ Regar&P.]

**Hinchy, Witte, Wood, Anderson & Hodges, A Law Corporation, (AV)**
**74-010 El Paseo, Suite 200, 92260⊙**
**Telephone: 619-779-8569 Fax: 619-568-6175**
**Gayle F. Anderson.**
**General Civil Litigation, General Commercial, including Corporations, Limited Liability Companies, Partnerships and Taxation; Real Estate, Estate Planning and Probate; Financial Institutions, Mortgage Banking, Collection, Bankruptcy, Family Law, Labor Relations and Employment Law and Related Litigation, Agricultural Labor Relations, Employee Stock Ownership Plans (ESOPs), ERISA, Pension and Profit Sharing, Employee Benefits Law and Litigation.**
**Reference: Scripps Bank.**
**Rancho Bernardo, California Office: 11440 West Bernardo Court, Suite 280. Telephone: 619-487-7948; 586-7696. FAX: 619-487-2177.**
**Irvine, California Office: 2030 Main Street, Suite 1300. Telephone: 714-260-4710. FAX: 714-260-4711.**
**San Diego, California Office: 525 B Street, Suite 1500. Telephone: 619-239-1901. FAX: 619-696-0555.**
***See Professional Biographies, PALM DESERT, CALIFORNIA***

**Hirschi, Jean Ann, (AV) '31 '58 C.112 B.A. L.1068 J.D.**
**74-075 El Paseo, Suite A-5, 92260**
**Telephone: 619-568-5661 Fax: 619-568-5668**
***PRACTICE AREAS: Estate Planning; Wills; Trusts; Probate; Conservatorship.**
**Estate Planning and Probate.**
***See Professional Biographies, PALM DESERT, CALIFORNIA***

Hoffen, Lillian P. ..........................................'21 '70 L.809 J.D. [Hoffen&H.]
Hoffen & Hoffen, A P.C. ............................................256 Castellana S.
Holbrook, Cris M. ..................'52 '79 C.1066 B.A. L.464 J.D. 73-710 Fred Waring Dr.
**Homme, Marc S.**, (BV) ......................'49 '74 C.174 B.S. L.426 J.D. [M.S.Homme]

**Homme, Marc S., A Professional Law Corporation, (BV)**
**74-361 Highway 111, Suite 1, 92260**
**Telephone: 760-568-5694 Facsimile: 760-568-1324**
**Marc S. Homme.**
**General Civil and Trial Practice. Business, Construction and Commercial Litigation. Banking, Real Estate, Estate Planning, Corporate and Partnership Law. Business and Commercial Litigation.**
***See Professional Biographies, PALM DESERT, CALIFORNIA***

**Hopp, Harold W.**, (BV) ..............'60 '86 C.636 B.S. L.800 J.D. [⊠ Quinn E.U.&O.]

**Houghton, Richard C., (BV) '47 '74 C&L.629 J.D.**
**74-075 El Paseo, Suite A14, 92260**
**Telephone: 619-773-4044 Fax: 619-776-1775**
**Email: houghtonr@earthlink.net**
**(Certified Specialist, Family Law, The State Bar of California Board of Legal Specialization).**
***LANGUAGES: Italian.**
***PRACTICE AREAS: Family Law; Civil Litigation.**
**Family Law.**
***See Professional Biographies, PALM DESERT, CALIFORNIA***

Hulme, Michael E., Jr. ....................'61 '86 C.112 A.B. L.800 J.D. U.S. Filter Corp.

Johns, Comet C. '29 '57 C.97 A.B. L.659 LL.B.
(adm. in PA; not adm. in CA) 73617 18th Fairway Lane‡
Katz, Richard M. '51 '79 C.1077 B.A. L.1148 J.D.
74-040 Highway III, Ste., L 204 (⊙Palm Springs)
Kent, Lewis ..........................................'27 '51 C.214 L.213 J.D. 38851 Lobelia Circle‡
Kogus, David I., (AV) ..........'39 '65 C.112 B.A. L.1068 LL.B. 43-585 Monterey Ave.
Lance, Brent Edward ......................'55 '80 C.763 B.S. L.426 J.D. 74-090 El Paseo
Landau, Jonathan S., (BV) ....................'52 '79 C.800 B.A. L.809 J.D. [J.S.Landau]
Landau, Jonathan S., A Professional Law Corporation, (BV) ...... 74090 El Paseo, 2nd Fl.
Langhauser, Eugene C. ..........'24 '55 C.98 B.S. L.1066 LL.B. 38-491 Devils Canyon‡
Larson, Patricia A., (BV) ..........'28 '90 C.112 B.S. L.1198 J.D. 43-645 Monterey Ave.
Leedy, Susan S. ......................'42 '79 C.845 L.1186 J.D. 754 Montana Vista Dr.
Leyval, Eugene R. ..................'36 '65 C.602 A.B. L.426 LL.B. 77789 St. Croix Dr.‡
Lloyd, Mary English ....................'54 '90 C.763 B.A. L.398 J.D. [English L.&A.]
Luhring, John W. ..........................................................'12 '36 Coll. of the Desert
Mack, L. Barry, (AV) ..........................'50 '76 C.378 B.A. L.900 J.D. [L.B.Mack]
Mack, L. Barry, A Professional Law Corporation, (AV)
Suite 105, 3001 East Tahquitz-Canyon Way
**Maguire, Daniel W.** ......................'60 '85 C.602 B.A. L.990 J.D. [Galton&H.]
*PRACTICE AREAS: Civil Litigation.
Marsh, Richard M. ......................'19 '47 C&L.477 B.S., J.D. 73266 Bursera Way‡
McCormack, Robert E., (BVⓉ) '39 '69 C&L.862 B.A., J.D.
(adm. in OK; not adm. in CA) 76783 Manor Lane‡
McIntosh, Cal, (BV) ......'32 '63 C.112 B.A. L.1066 J.D. 45-275 Prickly Pear Ln., Ste. 5

**McMillin, Joe B. '44 '68 C&L.623 B.A., J.D.**
**73-710 Fred Waring Drive #217, 92260**
**Telephone: 619-773-5886 Fax: 619-773-5814**
**Email: jmcmilli@aol.com**
***PRACTICE AREAS: Tort Defense; Governmental Liability; Business Litigation; Civil Litigation; Real Estate.**
**Tort Defense, Government Liability, Business Litigation, Civil Litigation and Real Estate Litigation.**
**Representative Clients: Palm Desert National Bank; Cities of Palm Desert, Cathedral City, Desert Hot Springs, Indian Wells, Coachella, Rancho Mirage, LaQuinta, Perris, San Jacinto, Blythe, Palm Springs, Calimesa; Sunline Transit Agency.**

Mehlman, Lester '23 '49 L.209 LL.B.
(adm. in IL; not adm. in CA) 201 Winterhaven Circle‡
Miller, Scott J. '55 '81 C.546 B.S. L.190 J.D.
(adm. in CO; not adm. in CA) 332 Vista Royale Dr.‡
Oleson, Kimberly G. ..........................'67 '93 C.1049 L.436 J.D. 43-645 Monterey Ave.
Olivier, Elizabeth, (BV) ..........'55 '80 C.112 B.S. L.1049 J.D. 43-645 Monterey Ave.
Ott, Raymond E. ......................'26 '50 C.346 L.800 J.D. 72990 Deer Grass Dr.‡
Parkinson, James W., (AV) ......................'49 '76 C&L.101 B.A., J.D. [Regar&P.]
Patterson, Andrew S., (AV) ..........................................................'36 '71 [Patterson&M.]
Patterson & Miller, (AV) ..........................................................42335 Washington St.
Paulson, Thomas A., (BV) ..................'11 '34 C.585 B.A. L.477 J.D. P.O. Box 1481
Pfaff, Samuel H., (BV) ......................'47 '73 C.112 B.A. L.802 J.D. 73-200 El Paseo
**Pippin, Robert L.**, (BV) ................'41 '67 C.763 B.A. L.1066 LL.B. [Criste,P.&G.]
*PRACTICE AREAS: Civil Litigation; Bankruptcy Law; Business Law; Construction Law.
**Plott, J. Alan** ..............................'52 '88 C.36 B.S. L.1179 J.D. [⊠ Thompson&C.]
*PRACTICE AREAS: Personal Injury Defense; Medical Malpractice Law; Products Liability.
Powell, Klysta J. ..............................'62 '88 C.483 B.A. L.1049 J.D. [⊠ J.S.Zundel]
**Quinn, John B.**, (AV) ..........................'51 '78 C.154 B.A. L.309 J.D. [Quinn E.U.&O.]⊙
*REPORTED CASES: Ficalora v. Lockheed Corp., 193 Cal. App. 3d 489 (1987); America's Cup Properties, Inc. v. America's Cup Club, Inc., 8 U.S.P.Q. 2d (BNA) 2025 (1988); Academy of Motion Picture Arts and Sciences v. Creative House Promotions, Inc., 944 F.2d 1446 (9th Cir. 1991) and 728 F. Supp. 1442 (C.D. Cal. 1989); Cinemateca Uruguaya v. Academy of Motion Picture Arts and Sciences, 826 F.Supp.323 (C.D. Cal. 1993).
*PRACTICE AREAS: Employment; Intellectual Property; Unfair Competition; Real Estate; General Commercial Litigation.

**Quinn, Nadine K. '37 '89 C.1109 B.A. L.1137 J.D.**
**74-361 Highway 111, Suite 1, 92260**
**Telephone: 619-346-0445 Fax: 619-341-7374**
***PRACTICE AREAS: Estate Planning; Probate; Probate Administration; Estate Administration; Family Trusts.**
**Estate Planning, Probate, Probate Administration, Estate Administration, Family Trusts and Contested Trusts and Estates.**
***See Professional Biographies, PALM DESERT, CALIFORNIA***

**Quinn Emanuel Urquhart & Oliver, LLP, (AV)**
**74-090 El Paseo, Suite 101, 92260⊙**
**Telephone: 619-340-2276 Telecopier: 619-346-1368**
**Members of Firm: John B. Quinn; David W. Quinto. Associates: Harold W. Hopp (Resident); Samuel Brooks Shepherd.**
**Business Litigation and Trial Practice, including Antitrust; Banking; Construction; Copyright, Trademark and Patent Litigation; Employment; ERISA; Government Contracts; Health Care; Intellectual Property; Product Liability; Real Estate; Securities; Unfair Competition; White Collar Crime.**
**Representative Clients: Academy of Motion Picture Arts and Sciences; American Medical International, Inc.; Bell & Howell; Dixie Savings and Loan Assn.; Jupiter Hospital Corp.; Landmark Land Company, Inc.; Lockheed Corp.; Mattel, Inc.; The Ralph M. Parsons Co.**
**Reference: First Interstate Bank of California, 707 Wilshire Boulevard, Los Angeles, 90017.**
**Los Angeles, California Office: 865 South Figueroa Street, 10th Floor. Telephone: 213-624-7707. Telecopier: 213-624-0643.**
***See Professional Biographies, PALM DESERT, CALIFORNIA***

**Quinto, David W.** ..........................'55 '82 C.31 B.A. L.309 J.D. [Quinn E.U.&O.]⊙
*LANGUAGES: Spanish.
*REPORTED CASES: Quinto v. Legal Times of Washington, Inc., 506 F. Supp. 554 and 511 F. Supp. 579 (1981); Ficalora v. Lockheed Corp., 193 Cal. App. 3d 489 (1987); America's Cup Properties, Inc. v. America's Cup Club, Inc., 8 U.S.P.Q. 2d (BNA) 2025 (1988); Academy of Motion Picture Arts and Sciences v. Creative House Promotions, Inc., 944 F.2d 1446 (9th Cir. 1991) and 728 F. Supp. 1442 (C.D. Cal. 1989); Cinemateca Uruguaya v. Academy of Motion Pictures Arts and Sciences, 826 F.Supp. 323 (C.D. Cal. 1993).
*PRACTICE AREAS: Copyright and Trademark; Real Property Litigation.
**Racobs, Peter E.** ..........................'57 '83 C.112 B.A. L.1067 J.D. [Fiore,W.R.&P.]⊙
Regar, Barry, (AV) ..........................'41 '66 C.112 A.B. L.1065 J.D. [Regar&P.]
Regar & Parkinson, (AV) ..........................................................77564 Country Club Dr.
Reinhardt, Benjamin M., (A Prof. Law Corp.) '17 '56 C.309 L.809 J.D.
73880 Grapevine
Reitz, James W., Jr. ..........................'39 '67 C.800 A.B. L.809 LL.B. P.O. Box 969
Rosenberg, Colleen M. ..................'49 '88 C.58 B.S. L.1137 J.D. 74075 El Paseo Ave.
Rosenberg, Nathan L., (BV) ............'51 '75 C.154 A.B. L.278 LL.B. 74-333 Hwy. 111
Samaha, Edward G. ..........................'58 '83 C.398 B.A. L.426 J.D. [⊠ Allen,R.&S.]
Segall, Matthew J. ..................................................'32 '68 L.398 J.D. [Segall&W.]
Segall & Wieder ..........................................................44-100 Monterey Ave.
Shamin, Rashid ..........................'— '87 C.766 B.S. L.1137 J.D. P.O. Box 3566
Sheldon, Christopher J. ..................'49 '74 C.1049 B.A. L.1068 J.D. Supr. Ct. J.
Shephard, John N. ..........................'12 '47 C.293 A.B. L.145 J.D. 77 315 Minesota Ave.‡
**Shepherd, Samuel Brooks** ............'66 '92 C.95 B.A. L.145 J.D. [⊠ Quinn E.U.&O.]⊙
**Shernoff, William M., (P.C.)**, (AV) '37 '62
C.472 B.B.A. L.966 J.D. [Shernoff,B.&D.] (⊙Claremont)

**Shernoff, Bidart & Darras, (AV)**
**A Partnership including Professional Corporations**
**73-111 El Paseo, Suite 208, 92260⊙**
**Telephone: 619-568-9944**
**Member of Firm: William M. Shernoff (P.C.).**
**Practice Limited to Plaintiff's Insurance Bad Faith, Automobile Insurance, Fire Insurance, Commercial Liability Insurance, Homeowners Insurance, Accident and Health Insurance, Catastrophic Personal Injury, Wrongful Death, Wrongful Termination, Lender's Liability and Consumer Law Litigation.**
**Claremont, California Office: 600 South Indian Hill Boulevard. Telephone: 909-621-4935. Fax: 909-625-6915.**
**Laguna Beach, California Office: 130 Cleo Street. Telephone: 714-494-6714. Fax: 714-497-0825.**
*See Professional Biographies, PALM DESERT, CALIFORNIA*

Singer, Gerald M., (AV) ........... '20 '69 L.426 J.D. 38-180 Del Webb Blvd., NPO 204‡
Smith, Donald E., (BV) ........................ '58 '84 C&L.770 B.S., J.D. [Ⓐ L.B.Mack]
Smith, Phillip K., Jr. ........................ '46 '71 C.112 B.A. L.800 J.D. Sunrise Co.
Soda, Rodney Lee, (AV) ........................ '50 '76 C.112 A.B. L.426 J.D. 74361 Hwy 111

**Stein, James H., (BV) '48 '74 C&L.502 B.S., J.D.**
**75-585 Dempsey Drive, 92211**
**Telephone: 619-346-7773 Fax: 619-346-9812**
**General Civil Litigation, Corporate, Real Estate, Probate and Estate Planning.**
*See Professional Biographies, PALM DESERT, CALIFORNIA*

**Stempler, Robert H.** ........................ '62 '92 C.154 B.A. L.464 J.D. [Ⓐ Healey&H.]
*PRACTICE AREAS: Estate Planning; Civil Litigation; Wrongful Termination.
Sternlieb, Charlotte R. ........................ '— '77 74-090 El Paseo Dr. Ste. 204
Stewart, Robert W., Jr., A Law Corporation, (BV) '46 '73
C.112 B.A. L.61 J.D. 73350 El Paseo
Stoddard, Patricia Ann ........................ '33 '58 C&L.477 A.B., J.D. 73-585 Encelia
Swajian, Dawn M., (CV) ........................ '59 '91 C.1049 B.A. L.999 J.D. [Swajian&S.]
Swajian, Gregory A., (BV) ........................ '48 '79 C.800 A.B. L.1137 J.D. [Swajian&S.]
Swajian & Swajian, (BV) ........................ 74-090 El Paseo
**Tegland, Leighton B.**, (AV) ........................ '47 '72 C.61 B.A. L.800 J.D. [Thompson&C.]
*PRACTICE AREAS: Personal Injury Defense; Medical Malpractice Law.

**Thompson & Colegate, (AV)**
**74-303 Highway III, Suite 2-B, 92260⊙**
**Telephone: 619-773-1998 Fax: 619-773-9078**
**Leighton B. Tegland;—J. Alan Plott.**
**General Civil and Trial Practice, Personal Injury Defense, Business Litigation, Construction, Medical Malpractice, Products Liability, Corporate, Estate Planning, Wills and Trusts, Probate, Insurance, Real Estate, Commercial, Education, Employment Law and Appellate Practice, Media-First Amendment Law and Bankruptcy.**
**Riverside, California Office: 3610 Fourteenth Street, P.O. Box 1299, 92502. Telephone, 909-682-5550. Fax: 909-781-4012.**
*See Professional Biographies, PALM DESERT, CALIFORNIA*

Van Buskirk, Robt., (AV) ........................ '17 '41 C&L.800 A.B., J.D. 169 Madrid Ave.‡
**Wangler, Margaret G.** ........................ '50 '86 C.352 B.A. L.1187 J.D. [Ⓐ Fiore,W.R.&P.]

**Weinberg, Steven J., Law Office of, (AV) '50 '75 C.112 B.A. L.990 J.D.**
**42-580 Caroline Court, Suite A, 92211**
**Telephone: 619-346-0227 Facsimile: 619-346-8573**
***LANGUAGES: Spanish.**
***PRACTICE AREAS: Medical Malpractice; Major Injury Tort Litigation.**
**Practice Limited to General Civil and Trial Practice in all State and Federal Courts. Aviation, Insurance, Medical Malpractice, Personal Injury, Products Liability, Negligence Law, Business Fraud.**
*See Professional Biographies, PALM DESERT, CALIFORNIA*

**Weiss, Richard B.**, (BV) ........................ '54 '82 C.201 B.A. L.1179 J.D. [Berman&W.]⊙
*PRACTICE AREAS: Construction Accident Law; Product Liability Law; Personal Injury Law; Medical Malpractice Law.
Wellins, Sheldon G., (BV) ........................ '44 '71 C.112 B.A. L.1065 J.D. 43-585 Monterey Ave.
White, Raymond W. ........................ '15 '40 L.765 LL.B. 70 Maximo Way‡
Wieder, Frederic S. ........................ '40 '69 C.608 B.S. L.426 J.D. [Segall&W.]
Wilcox, Mary E. ........................ '54 '80 C.112 B.A. L.1065 J.D. 76075 Palm Valley Dr.
Wilcox, Max, Jr. ........................ '20 '49 C.112 A.B. L.1066 LL.B. Supr. Ct. J.

**Williams and Ballas**
**(See Los Angeles)**

Wilms, Michael ........................ '30 '80 C.46 B.S. L.1190 J.D. 40-660 Golden Way
Wilson, Jeffrey M., (AV) ........................ '46 '72 C.112 B.A. L.426 J.D. [Allen,R.&S.]
Wraith, A. Parker, (AV) ........................ '14 '40 C&L.477 B.A., J.D. P.O. Box 1217‡
Wright, Robert B. ........................ '21 '50 C&L.800 LL.B. 243 Castellana N.‡
Zankich, Louis ........................ '26 '56 L.809 LL.B. 72 935 Deer Grass Dr.
Zundel, Craig E., (BV) ........................ '46 '82 C.878 B.A. L.61 J.D. 74-399 Hwy. 111
Zundel, J. Scott, (BV) ........................ '49 '74 C&L.878 B.A., J.D. [J.S.Zundel]
Zundel, J. Scott, A Prof. Law Corp., (BV) ........................ 73-255 El Paseo

## PALM SPRINGS, 40,181, *Riverside Co.*

Aaronson, Wayne ........................ '48 '72 C.112 A.B. L.1065 J.D. Dep. Pub. Def.
Anderson, Joseph B. '64 '90 C.813 A.B. L.276 J.D.
(adm. in CA; not adm. in CA) 777 E. Tahquitz Cnyn Way/ Marlar
Anderson, Marvin Keith '57 '87
C.813 B.A. L.276 J.D. 777 E. Tahquitz Cnyn Way / Marlar

**Anderson, Thomas T., P.C.**
**(See Indio)**

Arnold, Thurman, Jr. ....... '19 '49 C&L.976 B.A., J.D. 1111 E. Tahquitz McCallum Way‡
Arnold, Thurman W., III, Law Offices of, (CV) '56 '82
C.112 B.A. L.1051 J.D. 225 S. Civic Dr., Ste. 1-3
Avans, George L. ........................ '43 '72 C.623 L.809 J.D. 888 Calle De Mimosas
Baddour, Raymond J., (BV) .... '45 '72 C.1097 B.A. L.809 J.D. 1401 N. Palm Canyon Dr.
Baechtold, George H., (AV) ........................ '28 '60 C.238 B.S. L.800 J.D. 977 Rose Ave.‡
Baker, Elizabeth, (CV) ........................ '36 '79 C.1044 B.S. L.1186 J.D. 1321 E. Adobe Way
Banks, Don H. ........................ '15 '40 L.273 LL.B. 3472 Camino Rojos
**Baron, David L.**, (BV) ........................ '55 '82 C.112 B.A. L.1065 J.D. [Slovak&B.]
*PRACTICE AREAS: Business Law; Construction Defect; Litigation; Business Torts; Commercial.
Benjamini, Emily A. .......... '67 '92 C.477 B.A. L.1044 J.D. 1900 Tahquitz Canyon Wy.
**Berman, Martin M.**, (AV) ........................ '34 '63 C&L.800 B.Ch.E., LL.B. [Berman&W.]⊙
*PRACTICE AREAS: Medical Malpractice Law; Products Liability Law; Personal Injury Law; Aviation Law.

**Berman & Weiss, (AV)**
**1111 Tahquitz Canyon Way, Suite 203, 92262⊙**
**Telephone: 619-773-6677 Fax: 619-327-1646**
**Email: rw1224@aol.com URL: http://www.lawinfo.com//law/ca/berman.html**
**Members of Firm: Richard B. Weiss; Martin M. Berman.**
**Personal Injury, Products Liability, Medical and Legal Malpractice, Insurance and Bad Faith Law, Aviation Law, Construction Accidents.**
**Encino, California Office: 16055 Ventura Boulevard, Suite 900, 91436. Telephone: 818-986-8000. Facsimile: 818-986-3162.**
**Palm Desert, California Office: 74-040 Highway III, Suite L-204, 92260. Telephone: 619-773-6677. Facsimile: 619-346-7779.**
*See Professional Biographies, PALM SPRINGS, CALIFORNIA*

Bernheimer, Robert A. ......... '67 '94 C.112 B.A. L.464 J.D. 1900 Tahquitz Canyon Wy.
Binkow, Robert N. ........................ '38 '63 C&L.477 B.B.A., J.D. 777 Tahquitz
Blankenship, Mark I. ............ '60 '87 C.976 B.A. L.861 J.D. [Kritzer&B.] (⊙Redlands)
Block, Arthur S. ........................ '44 '72 C.475 B.A. L.1009 J.D. Supr. Ct. J.
**Bochnewich, Peter M.** ........................ '59 '92 C.829 B.S. L.1188 J.D. [Ⓐ Slovak&B.]
*PRACTICE AREAS: Civil Litigation; Business Litigation; Products Liability; Construction Defects; Medical Malpractice.

**Bock, Leonard A., (BV) '19 '51 C.112 A.B. L.569 J.D.**
**Suite C-3 1900 Tahquitz Canyon Way, 92262-7024**
**Telephone: 619-325-9686**
**General Civil Trial Practice. Business, Corporation, Real Estate, Probate, Family, Construction and Condominium Law.**
**Representative Clients: Radio Stations KCMJ and KPSL; Palm Springs Life Magazine; Whitewater Rock and Supply; Master Pools and Supplies; Frank Properties, Ltd; Palm Springs Opera Guild.**
*See Professional Biographies, PALM SPRINGS, CALIFORNIA*

**Bost, Stephen A.** ............ '55 '81 C.945 B.S. L.809 J.D. [Ives,K.&D.] (⊙Los Angeles)
Bourke, Brian J. ........................ '50 '77 L.1148 J.D. [Gilbert,G.&B.]
Boyd, F. Gillar, Jr., (BV) ........................ '28 '53 C&L.800 B.S., J.D. 225 S. Civic Dr.

**Bradak, Glen R., (AV) '37 '62 C.1120 L.878 J.D.**
**193 South Civic Drive, Suite 6, 92262**
**Telephone: 619-323-2648 Fax: 619-323-4755**
**Criminal Law, D.U.I., White Collar Crime, Assault and Battery, Felonies and Misdemeanors.**
*See Professional Biographies, PALM SPRINGS, CALIFORNIA*

Brakefield, Richard E. M. ........ '39 '77 C.768 B.A. L.809 J.D. 1000 S. Palm Canyon Dr.
**Brown, Raymond E.** ........................ '65 '93 C&L.36 B.A., J.D. [Ⓐ Tuverson&H.]
*LANGUAGES: German.
*PRACTICE AREAS: General Liability Defense; Legal Malpractice Defense.

**Caronna, Anthony C., P.C.**
**(See Rancho Mirage)**

Caruthers, D. Michael, (CV) .... '45 '77 C.1056 B.S. L.1026 J.D. 500 S. Palm Canyon Dr.
Casey, Clifford L. ........................ '53 '78 [Casey&M.]
Casey & Munn ........................ 202 N. Palm Canyon Dr., 2nd Fl.
Cassing, M. Craig .............. '49 '73 C.134 B.S. L.502 J.D. 1000 S. Palm Canyon Dr.
Chapin, Fleming & Winet, A Professional Corporation, (AV)
255 N. El Cielo Rd. Ste. 470 (⊙San Diego, Vista, Los Angeles)
Cole, Shirley H. ................ '25 '73 C&L.1136 B.S.L., J.D. 38-350 Maracaibo Cir. W‡
Cooper, Keith L. .............. '62 '95 C.112 B.A. L.1017 J.D. 125 Tahquitz Canyon Wy

**Cornelius, Byron G., Law Office of, (BV) '51 '83 L.1137 J.D.**
**225 South Civic Drive Suite 1-3, 92262**
**Telephone: 619-327-8119 Fax: 619-864-1285**
**General Civil and Trial Practice in all State and Federal Courts. Business Litigation, Personal Injury, Contract Law, and Probate.**
*See Professional Biographies, PALM SPRINGS, CALIFORNIA*

Cortez, Rodney A. ............ '65 '95 C&L.101 B.A., J.D. 1800 E. Tahquitz Canyon Way
Dally, Henry E. ........................ '18 '51 C.112 L.426 LL.B. 1334 Invierno Dr.‡
**Darrin, David** ........................ '63 '92 C&L.112 B.A., J.D. [Ⓐ Schlecht,S.&S.]
*PRACTICE AREAS: Civil Litigation; Real Estate Transactions; Probate; Business; Corporate.

**Davis, Russell L.**
**(See Indian Wells)**

**deBoer, Deborah**, (BV) ........................ '57 '83 C.1073 B.S. L.990 J.D. [Tuverson&H.]
**Deetman, Gregory E.** ........................ '67 '94 C.763 B.A. L.464 J.D. [Ⓐ Tuverson&H.]
*PRACTICE AREAS: Insurance Defense.
Del Pozzo, John ................ '47 '85 C.1071 B.S. L.464 J.D. 655 N. Palm Canyon Dr.
Devin, Andrew R., (CV) ................ '64 '91 C.174 B.A. L.990 J.D. 225 S. Civic Dr.

**De Vore, Daun Aline '— '81 C.112 B.A. L.1065 J.D.**
**P.O. Box 8987, 92262**
**Telephone: 619-773-2257 Fax: 619-325-2732**
**Public and Private International Law. Litigation. State and Federal Appeals.**
*See Professional Biographies, PALM SPRINGS, CALIFORNIA*

Downes, Bradley G. Bledsoe '69 '95 C.112 B.A. L.36 J.D.
1800 E. Tahquitz Canyon Way
**Dreier, Elizabeth A.** ........................ '61 '88 C.112 B.A. L.1067 J.D. [Ⓐ Schlecht,S.&S.]
*PRACTICE AREAS: Civil Litigation; Family.
Drexler, Robert J., Jr. ........................ '58 '83 C.608 B.S. L.930 J.D. 2900 Verona Rd.
Duellman, Clark J. ............ '66 '95 C.112 B.A. L.94 J.D. 600 E. Tahquitz Canyon Way
Eastman, Robert E. ........................ '23 '54 C.871 B.S. L.273 J.D. 225 S. Civic Dr.
Easton, Ronald R. ........................ '51 '82 C.1056 B.S. L.1051 J.D. 225 S. Civic Dr.
Ericksen, Craig G. ............ '47 '77 C&L.838 B.S., J.D. 2825 E. Tahquitz Canyon Wy.
European Business Law Firm, The, P.C.
1049 N. Palm Canyon Dr. (⊙Lisbon, Portugal, Paris, France, Rome, Italy & Warsaw, Poland)

**Farrell, C L**
**(See Redlands)**

Feenstra, MaryLou ......... '31 '86 C.112 B.A. L.1137 J.D. 1800 E. Tahquitz Canyon Way
Feingold, Richard M. ................ '22 '51 C.453 B.S. L.94 J.D. 260 N. Hermosa Dr.‡
Fenning, Morton C. '11 '37 C&L.309 A.B., LL.B.
(adm. in NY; not adm. in CA) 165 Desert Lakes Dr.‡
Ferguson, James Cato ......... '59 '93 C.37 B.A.S. L.464 J.D. 1900 Tahquitz Canyon Wy.
Fidler, Irving ................ '12 '50 C.563 B.S. L.809 LL.B. 2183 Via Mazatlan
**FitzGerald, John E., III**, (AV) ......... '45 '75 C.870 B.S. L.659 J.D. [Fitzgerald&Assoc.]
*PRACTICE AREAS: Employment and Discrimination Law; Wrongful Discharge; Litigation.

**FitzGerald & Associates, (AV) BB**
**3001 Tahquitz Canyon Way, Suite 105, 92262**
**Telephone: 619-325-5055 FAX: 619-327-9262**
**John E. FitzGerald, III;—Morton Gollin.**
**Employment Law, Wrongful Termination, Discrimination in all Courts.**
**Representative Clients: Armtec Defense Products; Desert Hospital; Association of California Hospital Districts; Eldorado Country Club; Palm Springs Savings Bank; Denny's; Desert Sun; Stratamerica, Inc.; Fantasy Springs Casino; KPSI; KWXY; KNWZ; KFRG; Smoke Tree Ranch; Keystone, Inc.**
**Reference: Palm Desert National Bank.**
*See Professional Biographies, PALM SPRINGS, CALIFORNIA*

**Fletcher & Patton**
**(See Carlsbad)**

Fromberg, Jeffrey E., (BV) ......... '47 '75 C&L.1186 J.D. 2825 E. Tahquitz Canyon Way

**Furness, Middlebrook, Kaiser & Higgins, A Professional Corporation, (AV)**
**3001 East Tahquitz Canyon Way, Suite 109, 92262⊙**
**Telephone: 619-322-0806 Fax: 619-322-8979**
**Michael R. Kaiser (Resident);—Jeffrey Mark Yoss (Resident); Sandra A. Shoupe-Gorga (Resident).**
**General Civil and Trial Practice. Personal Injury, Insurance and Government Law, Workers Compensation Subrogation, General Business and Construction Law.**
**San Bernardino, California Office: 1411 North "D" Street, P.O. Box 1319. Telephone: 909-888-5751. Fax: 909-888-7360.**
*See Professional Biographies, PALM SPRINGS, CALIFORNIA*

**Garcia-Colson, L. Joane**, (CV) .......... '60 '91 C.416 B.F.A. L.208 J.D. [A Slovak&B.]
*PRACTICE AREAS: Civil Litigation; Employment and Discrimination Litigation; Sexual Harassment Litigation; Family Law; Construction Defect Litigation.
**Gayer, Catherine A.** .......................... '61 '91 C.763 B.S. L.589 J.D. [Knapp,P.&C.]
Gergely, Alfred J., (BV) .......... '28 '53 C.923 B.A. L.276 J.D. 1335 S. San Joaquin Dr.

**Gershenson, Mark D. '53 '79 C.1006 B.A. L.245 J.D.**
**400 South Farrell Drive, Suite B-203, 92262**
**Telephone: 619-322-0555 Fax: 619-322-3395**
**Complex Business and Commercial Litigation in all States and Federal Courts; Family, Matrimonial Law and Marital Dissolutions.**
***See Professional Biographies, PALM SPRINGS, CALIFORNIA***

**Gibbs, Joseph A., (AV) '51 '78 C.1049 B.A. L.1137 J.D.**
**901 E. Tahquitz Canyon Way, Suite C-203, 92262⊙**
**Telephone: 619-320-9111 Fax: 619-320-6392**
***PRACTICE AREAS: Civil Litigation; Real Estate; Business; Commercial.**
**Associate: Gregory R. Oleson.**
**Civil Litigation, Real Estate, Business, Commercial, Corporate and Partnership Law.**
**Indian Wells, California Office: 74900 Highway 111, Suite 211. Telephone: 619-779-1790. Fax: 619-779-1780.**
***See Professional Biographies, PALM SPRINGS, CALIFORNIA***

Gibson, R. Sebastian ............'50 '77 C.112 B.A. L.1049 J.D. 125 Tahquitz Canyon Wy
Gilbert, M. .......................'18 '43 C.113 A.B. L.1001 LL.B. 225 S. Civic Dr.‡
Gilbert, Michael H. .................. '52 '78 C.112 B.A. L.1148 J.D. [Gilbert,G.&B.]
Gilbert, Gilbert & Bourke ........................................ 225 S. Civic Dr.
Giles, Susan ..........................'— '92 C.630 B.A. L.1145 J.D. 1800 Tahquitz Canyon Way
Goldman, Gary S. .......................... '37 '62 C.112 B.S. L.1068 2294 Toledo Ave.
**Gollin, Morton** ................................ '— '49 C&L.966 LL.B. [A Fitzgerald&Assoc.]
Gordon, Sidney L. ............................ '08 '32 C.563 L.732 LL.B. P.O. Box 2584‡
**Gorsage, JoAnna D.** ................... '69 '95 C.1110 B.A. L.464 J.D. [A Tuverson&H.]
Graphos, Antonia, (BV) ........'55 '80 C.591 B.S. L.61 J.D. 600 E. Tahquitz Canyon Way
Greene, Lance G. ...................'61 '93 C.36 B.S. L.494 J.D. 125 Tahquitz Canyon Wy
Guss, Bonnie Garland .............'53 '79 C.860 B.A. L.910 J.D. 400 S. Farrell Ste. B-203
Hansen, Robert L. ............'55 '87 C.101 B.A. L.809 J.D. 1800 E. Tahquitz Canyon Way
Harlow, Scott N. ............'56 '82 C.025 B.Sc. L.031 LL.B. 1900 Tahquitz Canyon Way
Hartman, Richard L., (BV) ...................... '33 '72 C.112 B.A. L.990 J.D. [Hartman&F.]⊙
Hartman and Francis, (BV) .............................. 530 W. Tahquitz Dr. (⊙Pasadena)
Helmuth, Karen S. .......... '61 '87 C.990 B.A. L.1148 J.D. 801 E. Tahquitz Canyon Way
Hennes, Matthew E. ..................... '25 '56 C.112 B.S. L.426 LL.B. 225 S. Civic Dr.
**Higgins, John J.** .......................... '59 '87 C.475 B.A. L.990 J.D. [Knapp,P.&C.]⊙
**Hill, Elaine E.**, (BV) .......................................... '44 '86 C.813 B.A. L.208 J.D. [Hill W.]
*PRACTICE AREAS: Estate Planning; Trust Planning; Probate; Corporate Law; Indian Land Law.

**Hill Walker, (BV)**
**1111 Tahquitz Canyon Way, Suite 117, 92262**
**Telephone: 619-864-9800 Fax: 619-864-9816**
**Elaine E. Hill (Certified Specialist, Estate Planning, Trust and Probate Law The State Bar of California Board of Legal Specialization); Sharyl Walker.**
**Business, Commercial, Corporate, Partnership, Estate Planning and Probate, Conservatorship and Guardianship, Real Estate, Environmental, Land Use and Zoning, Bankruptcy, Indian Law.**
**Representative Clients: Agua Caliente Band of Cahuilla Indians; Desert Adventures, Inc.; Eisenhower Medical Center; Kaiser Ventures Inc.; Mine Reclamation Corp.**
***See Professional Biographies, PALM SPRINGS, CALIFORNIA***

Hinsvark, Kenneth D. .......... '26 '51 C.112 A.B. L.1066 LL.B. 559 S. Palm Canyon Dr.
Hoffman, Irving .................................. '24 '62 C.999 L.810 LL.B. 858 Village Sq. N.‡
Hollins, Andrew S., (AV) ...... '51 '78 C.838 B.S. L.1221 J.D. [Hollins,S.&F.] (⊙Orange)
Hollins, Schechter & Feinstein, A Professional Corporation, (AV)
1111 Tahquitz Canyon Wy. Ste. 121 (⊙San Diego, Moreno Valley & Orange)
Horton, Lyle R. ............................ '52 '78 C.426 B.S. L.809 J.D. 1111 Tahquitz E.
**Howard, Jerry Wayne**, (BV) ............. '48 '83 C.267 B.S. L.809 J.D. [Tuverson&H.]
*PRACTICE AREAS: Premise Liability; Professional Malpractice; Product Liability; Construction Defect.

**Ives, Kirwan & Dibble, A Professional Corporation, (AV)**
**777 Tahquitz Way Suite 23, 92262⊙**
**Telephone: 619-778-2611 FAX: 619-778-2612**
**Stephen A. Bost; Steven B. Kotulak.**
**Major Insurance Company Clients: American Mutual Insurance Co.; Utica Mutual Insurance Co.**
**Los Angeles Office: The Biltmore Court, Fourth Floor, 520 South Grand Avenue. Telephone: 213-627-0113. FAX: 213-627-1547.**
**Ventura-Santa Barbara Office: 5210 Carpinteria Avenue, P.O. Box 360, Carpinteria, California. Telephone: 805-684-7641. FAX: 805-684-9649.**
**Orange-San Diego County Office: 101 Pacifica, Suite 250, Irvine, California. Telephone: 714-450-8900. FAX: 714-450-8908.**
**San Bernardino-Riverside Office: 777 Tahquitz Way, Suite 23, Palm Springs, California. Telephone: 619-778-2611. FAX: 619-778-2612.**
***See Professional Biographies, PALM SPRINGS, CALIFORNIA***

Jacobs, David Earl .................... '54 '88 C.755 B.A. L.1035 J.D. 1255 E. Ramon Rd.
Jamin, Noah Ned .................... '24 '50 C.563 B.S. in S.S. L.94 J.D. Ret. Supr. Ct. J.
Jaymes, William R. '46 '74 C.608 B.S. L.161 J.D.
(adm. in OH; not adm. in CA) 400 S. Farrell Dr.
Johnson, Bruce F. ..................... '34 '70 C.800 A.B. L.809 J.D. 1324 Primavera Dr.
**Johnson, Daniel T.**, (BV) ................... '54 '80 C.112 B.A. L.800 J.D. [Schlecht,S.&S.]
*PRACTICE AREAS: Real Estate Law; General Business Law.
**Johnson, Jennifer R.** ....................... '59 '92 C.061 B.S. L.37 J.D. [A Tuverson&H.]

**Johnson, Ronald W.**
**(See Indian Wells)**

**Kahn, Michael S., (BV) '46 '72 C.107 B.S. L.1065 J.D.**
**777 East Tahquitz Canyon Way, Suite 200, P.O. Box 2286, 92263-2286**
**Telephone: 619-320-5656 Fax: 619-320-5659**
**Probate, Estate Planning, Real Estate, Trust, Corporate and Business Law.**
***See Professional Biographies, PALM SPRINGS, CALIFORNIA***

**Kaiser, Michael R.**, (BV) ............'51 '77 C.1163 B.S. L.1049 J.D. [Furness,M.K.&H.]
*PRACTICE AREAS: Insurance Defense; Civil Trial; Business Litigation; Homeowners Association; Tort Litigation.
Kartzinel, Jacob M. ............................'11 '58 C.563 B.S. L.981 2112 S. Palm Canyon Dr.‡
Katz, Richard M. '51 '79 C.1077 B.A. L.1148 J.D.
1111 Tahquitz Canyon Way, Ste., 203 (⊙Palm Desert)
**Keane, Jeffrey G.**, (AV) ......................'49 '77 C.763 B.A. L.1137 J.D. [Tuverson&H.]

**Kinkle, Rodiger and Spriggs, Professional Corporation**
**(See Riverside)**

Kirkpatrick, Stephen M. ........... '52 '78 C.112 A.B. L.426 J.D. 559 S. Palm Canyon Dr.
Klatchko, Linda Stearns, (BV) .............. '49 '75 C.112 B.A. L.61 J.D. [Klatchko&K.]
Klatchko, Philip S., (BV) .................... '49 '74 C.800 B.A. L.61 J.D. [Klatchko&K.]
Klatchko & Klatchko, (BV) ........................................................ 177 S. Civic Dr.

**Knapp, Petersen & Clarke, A Professional Corporation, (AV)**
**960 East Tahquitz Canyon Way, Suite 101, 92262⊙**
**Telephone: 619-325-8500 Telecopier: 619-325-2454**
**Nancy Menzies Vaessen (Resident); John J. Higgins; William J. Rohr (Resident); Catherine A. Gayer (Resident); Debbie S. Harris Sherman (Resident).**

(This Listing Continued)

**Knapp, Petersen & Clarke, A Professional Corporation (Continued)**

**General Civil, Trial and Appellate Practice in all State and Federal Courts, Arbitration Tribunals and Administrative Agencies. General Insurance, Professional Liability, Product Liability, Environmental, Corporate and General Business, State, Federal and Local Taxation, Real Estate, Escrow Errors and Omissions Defense, Construction and Land Use, Construction Defect Litigation, Estate Planning, Probate, Labor and Employment, Administrative and Regulatory Insurance Law and Title Banking.**
**Glendale, California Office: 500 North Brand Boulevard, 20th Floor. Telephone: 818-547-5000; 213-245-9400. FAX: 818-547-5329.**
***See Professional Biographies, PALM SPRINGS, CALIFORNIA***

Knox, Barbara G. ................................................'46 '91 L.1198 J.D. 400 S. Farrell Dr.
Kochman, Howard C. ..................'21 '54 C.563 B.S. L.1009 LL.B. [H.C.Kochman]
Kochman, Howard C., A Law Corp. ........................................... 340 S. Farrell Dr.
Kossler, George F., (BV) ........................ '44 '73 C.1042 B.S. L.990 J.D. 610 S. Belardo
**Kotulak, Steven B.** ...... '59 '85 C.554 B.S. L.809 J.D. [Ives,K.&D.] (⊙Los Angeles, Ca.)
Kramer, Robert L., (BV) ......................... '44 '71 C.1097 B.A. L.809 J.D. 225 S. Civic Dr.
Kritzer, Lawrence, (BV) .................................. '34 '60 C.112 B.A. L.1068 J.D. [Kritzer&B.]⊙
Kritzer & Blankenship, (BV) ...... 777 E. Tahquitz Canyon Way (⊙Torrance & Redlands)
Lame, Allan ................ '17 '49 C.608 B.S.B.A. L.950 LL.B. 1729 E. Palm Canyon Dr.
Lande, Jack J. ........................................'11 '35 C&L.477 A.B., J.D. 2563 S. Camino Real
**LaPedis, Jack M.** ............................................. '67 '95 C.112 B.A. L.990 J.D. [A Tuverson&H.]
Lazar, Seymour M. ................'27 '52 C.112 A.B. L.800 LL.B. 334 Hermosa Place‡

**Ledger, William Steele, (BV) '39 '71 C.800 L.1117 J.D.**
**193 South Civic Drive, Suite 6, 92262**
**Telephone: 619-320-6691 Fax: 619-323-4755**
**Practice Limited to Criminal Defense, D.U.I., White Collar Crime, Drug Cases and Felonies.**
**Reference: Wells Fargo Bank.**
***See Professional Biographies, PALM SPRINGS, CALIFORNIA***

Lee, John A. ........................................... '46 '74 C.813 A.B. L.800 J.D. Canyon Hotel
Lopez, A. Amos, (BV) ............................... '49 '77 L.1137 J.D. 477 S. Palm Canyon Dr.
Lumbleau, Vincent E. ....................... '24 '54 C.426 B.S. L.276 J.D. 1345 Deepwell Blvd.‡

**Lyons, Kipp Ian, (BV) '56 '82 C.112 B.A. L.426 J.D.**
**400 South Farrell Drive, Suite B 200-2, 92262-7964**
**Telephone: 619-320-1213 Facsimile: 619-320-2466**
***PRACTICE AREAS: Real Estate; Business Law; Estate Planning; Probate; Corporate Law.**
**Real Estate, Business, Estate Planning, Probate and Corporate Law.**
***See Professional Biographies, PALM SPRINGS, CALIFORNIA***

**Manes, Christopher S.** ........................ '57 '93 C.112 B.A. L.1066 J.D. [A H.L.Sanger]
*PRACTICE AREAS: Business Litigation.

**Manning, Guy, Law Offices of**
**(See Rancho Mirage)**

**Martin, Douglas, A Law Corporation**
**(See Indian Wells)**

**Martinez, Alexander R.** ......................'70 '95 C.112 B.A. L.1065 J.D. [A Tuverson&H.]
*LANGUAGES: Spanish.
**Martz, Daniel P.** ..................................... '64 '90 C.37 B.A. L.1049 J.D. [A Tuverson&H.]
McGrath, Robert C. ...................'46 '74 C.754 B.S. L.229 J.D. 777 E. Tahquitz Canyon
McIntyre, Scott A., (CV) ......................'46 '74 C.112 B.S. L.1068 J.D. [A Rotkin,S.&M.]

**McMillin, Joe B.**
**(See Palm Desert)**

**McNelley, Donald B.** .............................'34 '70 C.16 B.A. L.800 J.D. [S Schlecht,S.&S.]
*PRACTICE AREAS: Corporate and Securities Law; Customer/Broker Dispute Resolution; Broker/Dealer Regulation Law; General Business Law; Estate Planning.
Meier, Karla Mykell ...........'66 '92 C&L.800 B.A., J.D. 1800 E. Tahquitz Canyon Way
Mies, Lorene Lynn ................................'47 '83 C&L.1137 B.S.L., J.D. 834 Rose Ave.
Millard, Rochelle ..................................'28 '71 L.1095 LL.B. 801 E. Tahquitz Way
Miller, Simon, (AV) .........................'10 '37 C.494 B.A. L.800 J.D. 2458 Paseo Del Rey‡
**Mohr, Lee R.**, (AV) ..................................'43 '70 C.112 B.A. L.1065 J.D. [L.R.Mohr]
*PRACTICE AREAS: Family Law.

**Mohr, Lee R., A Professional Law Corporation, (AV)**
**Suite 121, 1111 East Tahquitz Canyon Way, 92262**
**Telephone: 619-325-1711 Fax: 619-322-4171**
**Lee R. Mohr.**
**Family Law.**
***See Professional Biographies, PALM SPRINGS, CALIFORNIA***

Montapert, William D. ..................'30 '55 C&L.800 A.B., J.D. 1172 N. May Dr.
Moore, Franklin, (CV) .......................'61 '88 C.846 B.A. L.629 J.D. 225 S. Civic Dr.
Moran, J. K., (CV) ....... '44 '71 C.602 A.B. L.884 J.D. 777 Tahquitz Cyn Way, Suite 200
Munn, Ford Dent ..........................................'51 '79 C.112 B.A. L.990 J.D. [Casey&M.]
Naples, John J., (AV®) '14 '48 C.116 L.107 LL.B.
(adm. in NY; not adm. in CA) 1206 Antiqua Circle‡
Nissen, Louis A. ........................................'13 '37 C.597 B.S. L.436 LL.B. 459 Desert Lakes‡
Noia, Ernest G. .............................................'47 '79 L.1137 J.D. 429 E. Tahquitz Way
**Oleson, Gregory R.** .................................'67 '93 C.239 B.A. L.436 J.D. [A J.A.Gibbs]
*PRACTICE AREAS: Civil Litigation; Real Estate; Business Litigation.
Oswald, Bruce A. ...............................'54 '92 C.999 L.800 J.D. 1800 Tahquitz Canyon Way
Patterson, Douglas W. '30 '55 C.309 A.B. L.911 LL.B.
(adm. in WA; not adm. in CA) P.O. Box 2887‡
Pease, Jesse J. .......................'54 '88 L.1198 J.D. 777 E. Tahquitz Canyon Way, Ste., 200
**Perrier, Allen O.**, (BV) ..........................'29 '56 C.784 B.S. L.208 LL.B. [Schlecht,S.&S.] ‡
Pesin, Byron I. .......................'19 '72 C.563 B.S. L.809 J.D. 777 E. Tahquitz Canyon Way
Pollack, Bernard ...................................'13 '36 C.800 L.146 J.D. 1660 La Reina Wy.‡
**Popkoff, Burton R.**, (AV) ..............................'42 '71 C.112 B.S. L.809 J.D. [Popkoff&S.]⊙

**Popkoff & Stern, (AV)**
**225 South Civic Drive, Suite 212, 92262⊙**
**Telephone: 619-322-8041**
**Members of Firm: Burton R. Popkoff (Certified Specialist, Estate Planning, Trust and Probate Law, The State Bar of California Board of Legal Specialization); Gary N. Stern.**
**Estate Planning, Probate, Tax and Business Litigation. Personal Injury and Malpractice Law.**
**Los Angeles, California Office: 501 Shatto Place, Suite 100, 90020-1792. Telephone: 213-389-1358; 389-2174. Fax: 213-380-4154.**

**Quinn Emanuel Urquhart & Oliver, LLP**
**(See Palm Desert)**

**Reid & Hellyer, A Professional Corporation**
**(See Riverside)**

**Rohr, William J.**, (BV) ........................... '45 '76 C&L.1137 B.S., J.D. [Knapp,P.&C.]
Roman, Joseph A. ...................'57 '82 C.112 B.A. L.1049 J.D. 2825 E. Tahquitz Way
Rose, Robert Allen ...........................'29 '53 C.112 L.1065 LL.B. 400 S. Farrell Dr.
Rotkin, Schmerin & McIntyre ........................ 225 S. Civic Dr., Suite 212 (⊙Los Angeles)
Rotman, Arnold J. ...................'30 '54 C&L.94 A.B., LL.B. 200 E. Racquet Club Rd.‡
Rubel, Scott M. .........................'61 '89 C.589 B.S. L.1049 J.D. [A Gilbert,G.&B.]

**Ryder, Richard James, Law Offices of '45 '77 C.260 B.A. L.1137 J.D.**
**1111 East Tahquitz Canyon Way Suite 121, 92262**
**Telephone: 619-327-2999 Fax: 619-327-9838**
**(Certified Specialist, Family Law, California Board of Legal Specialization).**

(This Listing Continued)

CAA457P

CALIFORNIA—PALM SPRINGS MARTINDALE-HUBBELL LAW DIRECTORY 1997

**Ryder, Richard James, Law Offices of (Continued)**
Family Law.
*See Professional Biographies, PALM SPRINGS, CALIFORNIA*

**Salzman, Ira M.**
(See Pasadena)

**Sanger, Howard L., Law Offices of, (AV) '42 '68 C.112 B.A. L.1068 J.D.**
**Suite B-102, 400 South Farrell Drive, 92262**
Telephone: 619-320-7421 Fax: 619-320-0351
Email: @smlaw.ccmail.compuserve.com
(Certified Specialist, Taxation Law, The State Bar of California Board of Legal Specialization).
*PRACTICE AREAS: Taxation Law; Estate Planning Law; Probate Law.
Associates: Christopher S. Manes.
Corporate, Taxation, Planning and Tax Controversy, Probate, Estate Planning Real Property Law, Business Planning, Business Litigation in State and Federal Courts.
*See Professional Biographies, PALM SPRINGS, CALIFORNIA*

**Scherotter, Gary C.**, (AV) ..............'39 '65 C.208 B.A. L.1065 J.D. [G.C.Scherotter]
*LANGUAGES: Spanish.
*PRACTICE AREAS: Criminal Defense.

**Scherotter, Gary C., A Law Corporation, (AV)**
**Heritage Square, Suite C-203, 901 East Tahquitz Canyon Way, P.O. Box 2224, 92262**
Telephone: 619-320-7111 Fax: 619-320-6392
Email: GARSCH@AOL.COM
Gary C. Scherotter (Certified Specialist, Criminal Law, The State Bar of California Board of Legal Specialization).
Practice Limited to Criminal and Constitutional Law in all State Courts. Trials.
Reference: Palm Desert National Bank.
*See Professional Biographies, PALM SPRINGS, CALIFORNIA*

**Schlecht, James M.**, (AV) ...............'27 '55 C&L.800 B.S., LL.B. [Schlecht,S.&S.]
*PRACTICE AREAS: Real Estate Law; General Business Law.

**Schlecht, Shevlin & Shoenberger, A Law Corporation, (AV) [BB]**
**Suite 100, 801 East Tahquitz Canyon Way, P.O. Box 2744, 92263-2744**
Telephone: 619-320-7161 Facsimile: 619-323-1758; 619-325-4623
James M. Schlecht; John C. Shevlin (Certified Specialist, Estate Planning, Trust and Probate Law, The State Bar of California Board of Legal Specialization); Jon A. Shoenberger (Certified Specialist, Family Law, The State Bar of California Board of Legal Specialization); Daniel T. Johnson;—David Darrin; Elizabeth A. Dreier. Of Counsel: Donald B. McNelley; Allen O. Perrier (Retired).
Real Estate, Corporate and General Business Law, Estate Planning, Probate and Trust Administration, Probate Litigation, Family Law, General Trial Practice in all State and Federal Courts.
Representative Clients: Outdoor Resorts of America; The Escrow Connection; Wells Fargo Bank; Canyon Country Club; Waste Management Co.
*See Professional Biographies, PALM SPRINGS, CALIFORNIA*

**Schlesinger, Robert A.**, (AV) ...........'27 '53 C.112 B.S. L.800 J.D. [R.A.Schlesinger]
*PRACTICE AREAS: Estate Planning; Trusts; Probate; Related Litigation.

**Schlesinger, Robert A., A Law Corporation, (AV)**
**383 South Palm Canyon Drive, P.O. Box 2268, 92262-2268**
Telephone: 619-325-2076 FAX: 619-325-2070
Robert A. Schlesinger (Certified Specialist, Probate, Estate Planning and Trust Law, The State Bar of California Board of Legal Specialization).
Practice Limited to Estate Planning, Trust, Probate Law and Related Litigation.
Representative Clients: Irene W. & Guy L. Anderson Children's Foundation; Ednah Root Foundation; Frederick Loewe Foundation.
Reference: Bank of America (Palm Springs).
*See Professional Biographies, PALM SPRINGS, CALIFORNIA*

Schoettler, John H. ......................................'39 '70 1800 S. Sunrise Way‡
Schwartz, Elaine S. ............'40 '66 C.112 A.B. L.1068 LL.B. 994 Saint George Circle
Schwartz, Eugene M., (A Professional Corporation), (AV) '32 '61
C&L.800 B.S., LL.B. 500 S. Palm Canyon Dr.

**Scott, Richard L.**
(See San Bernardino)

**Sherman, Debbie S. Harris** ..............'61 '95 C.800 B.A. L.1137 J.D. [Knapp,P.&C.]
*LANGUAGES: Spanish.
**Shevlin, John C.**, (BV) .................'43 '69 C.197 B.A. L.813 LL.B. [Schlecht,S.&S.]
*PRACTICE AREAS: Estate Planning and Administration Law; Probate Litigation; General Business Law.
Shillito, Daniel G. '48 '73 C.201 B.S. L.607 J.D.
(adm. in OH; not adm. in CA) Field Solr., Dept. of the Interior
**Shoenberger, Jon A.**, (AV) ............'43 '67 C.112 B.A. L.1068 J.D. [Schlecht,S.&S.]
*PRACTICE AREAS: Civil Litigation; Family Law.
**Shoupe-Gorga, Sandra A.** .......'51 '95 C.999 B.F.A. L.1003 J.D. [[A] Furness,M.K.&H.]
*PRACTICE AREAS: Insurance Defense.

**Simon, William J, The Law Offices of**
(See Riverside)

Sklar, Scott W. .................'52 '82 C.112 B.A. L.1095 J.D. 777 E. Tahquitz Cyn Way
Slahor, Stephenie ..............'— '79 C.878 Ph.D. L.1137 J.D. 121 S. Palm Canyon Dr.
**Slovak, Thomas S.**, (AV) ...................'48 '74 C.1075 B.A. L.800 J.D. [Slovak&B.]
*PRACTICE AREAS: Business Law; Fraud; Business Torts; Real Estate; Construction Defect Litigation.

**Slovak & Baron, (AV)**
**1900 East Tahquitz Canyon Way, Suite B-1, 92262**
Telephone: 619-322-2275 Fax: 619-322-2107
Thomas S. Slovak; David L. Baron. Associates: L. Joane Garcia-Colson; Peter M. Bochnewich.
Civil Litigation with emphasis in the following areas: Business and Commercial Law, Real Estate, Fraud and Business Torts, Construction Defects, Public Law, Estate, Trusts & Conservatorships, Personal Injury, Products Liability and Bad Faith, Discrimination and Wrongful Termination. General Practice in Land Use, Zoning and Governmental Affairs, Agricultural Law, Labor Law. Trial Practice in all State and Federal Courts.
*See Professional Biographies, PALM SPRINGS, CALIFORNIA*

Smith, Chester R. ........................'29 '61 C.768 B.A. L.426 J.D. 909 Rose Ave.‡
Smith, Robert E. ..................'31 '58 C.790 B.S. L.446 LL.B. 1073 S. Palm Canyon Dr.
Stefanelli, Thomas M. ..........'56 '82 C&L.05 B.Sc., LL.B. 1800 Tahquitz Canyon Way

**Stein, Rick M., Law Offices of, (AV) '43 '68 C.893 B.A. L.846 LL.B. [BB]**
**400 South Farrell Drive Suite B-203, 92262**
Telephone: 619-325-5990 Facsimile: 619-325-6265
*REPORTED CASES: Phonetele, Inc. v. PUC, 11 Cal.3d 125, 113 Cal.Rptr. 16, 520 P.2d 400 (1974), en banc; DCD Programs, Ltd., et al. v. Leighton, 833 F2d 183 (9th Cir. 1987); Phonetele, Inc. v. AT&T, 664 F2d 716 (9th Cir. 1981); Phonetele, Inc. v. AT&T, 889 F2d 224 (9th Cir. 1981), cert. denied.; Hydrotech Systems v. Oasis Waterpark, 52 Cal.3d 988, 277 Cal.Rptr. 517, 803 P2.d 370 (1991), en banc.
General Civil Trial and Appellate Practice in all State and Federal Courts, Unfair Competition, Securities and Antitrust Litigation, Receivership and Real Property Law.
*See Professional Biographies, PALM SPRINGS, CALIFORNIA*

**Stern, Gary N.** ..........................'55 '80 C.112 B.A. L.809 J.D. [Popkoff&S.]⊙
Stevenson, Jerome E. ...............................'29 '65 L.1001 LL.B. 2982 Orella Cir.‡
Strongin, Jeffrey M. ..................'48 '74 C&L.1190 B.A., LL.B. 610 S. Belardo Rd.
Sullivan, Mark J. ....................'46 '74 C.454 B.A. L.904 J.D. 777 E. Tahquitz Way

Sussman, Mitchell R. .........'51 '77 C.273 B.B.A. L.990 J.D. 1053 S. Palm Canyon Dr.
**Swiller, Jennifer F.** ..........................'71 '95 C.112 B.A. L.464 J.D. [[A] Tuverson&H.]
Taylor, George E. .................'27 '59 C&L.813 B.A., J.D. 1388 Primavera Dr., W.‡
Taylor, Robert G. ...........................'51 '78 C.112 B.A. L.464 J.D. Supr. Ct. J.
Tortorelli, Maria C. ....................'54 '80 C.112 B.A. L.426 J.D. [[A] Hartman&F.]⊙
Trevino, John T. .............................'42 '67 C&L.800 B.S., J.D. 225 S. Civic Dr.

**Tuck, Ira N.**
(See Yucca Valley)

Turk, Frank J. ........................'21 '71 C.214 B.S. L.981 LL.B. 2991 Calle Loreto‡

**Tuverson & Hillyard, (AV)**
A Limited Liability Partnership, including Professional Corporations
**1800 Tahquitz Canyon Way, 92262⊙**
Telephone: 619-322-7855 Fax: 619-322-5121
Resident Members: Jeffrey G. Keane; Deborah deBoer; Jerry Wayne Howard. Resident Associates: Raymond E. Brown; Gregory E. Deetman; JoAnna D. Gorsage; Jennifer R. Johnson; Jack M. LaPedis; Alexander R. Martinez; Daniel P. Martz; Jennifer F. Swiller.
General Civil and Trial Practice in all State and Federal Courts. Medical and Legal Malpractice Defense, Public Entity and Insurance Defense.
Los Angeles, California Office: 12400 Wilshire Boulevard, Suite 900, Los Angeles, California 90025. Telephones: 310-826-7855; 625-1234. Fax: 310-826-8738.
Newport Beach, California Office: 4675 MacArthur Court, Suite 650, Newport Beach, California 82660. Telephone: 714-752-7855. Fax: 714-752-5437.
San Diego, California Office: 4365 Executive Drive, Suite 700, San Diego, California 92121. Telephone: 619-452-7855. Fax: 619-452-2153.
*See Professional Biographies, PALM SPRINGS, CALIFORNIA*

**Vaessen, Nancy Menzies**, (BV) ............'46 '75 C.908 B.A. L.426 J.D. [Knapp,P.&C.]

**Van Hulle & Prevost**
(See San Bernardino)

Vincent, Catherine A. ................'52 '78 C.139 B.A. L.1137 J.D. 1255 E. Ramon Rd.
Wahl, John E. ..........................'33 '66 C.112 A.B. L.1065 J.D. 3445 E. Paseo Barbara
**Walker, Sharyl** ................................'57 '83 C.165 B.A. L.188 J.D. [Hill W.]
*PRACTICE AREAS: Business Law; Corporate Law; Real Estate; Land Use; Environmental Law.
Walsh, James C., Jr., (BV) ...........'19 '46 C.767 A.B. L.765 LL.B. 975 E. Marion Way
Wasmund, Ronald L. .........'50 '79 C.813 B.A. L.061 LL.B. 1111 Tahquitz Canyon Way
Weaver, Jeffrey A. .....................'61 '87 C.112 B.A. L.1049 J.D. [[A] Chapin,F.&W.]
**Weiss, Richard B.**, (BV) ................'54 '82 C.201 B.A. L.1179 J.D. [Berman&W.]⊙
*PRACTICE AREAS: Construction Accident Law; Product Liability Law; Personal Injury Law; Medical Malpractice Law.

**Welebir & McCune, A Professional Law Corporation**
(See Redlands)

Wexler, Ben ...................................'12 '35 C&L.436 2160 E. Palm Canyon Dr.
Woodson, R. Donald '31 '84 C.378 B.A. L.851 J.D.
(adm. in OH; not adm. in CA) 555 E. Tachevah Dr.
**Yoss, Jeffrey Mark** ................'55 '92 C.61 B.Sc. L.426 J.D. [[A] Furness,M.K.&H.]
*LANGUAGES: Afrikaans.
*PRACTICE AREAS: Insurance Defense.

**Zitomer, Michael, (BV) '47 '72 C.477 B.A. L.800 J.D.**
**225 South Civic Drive, Suite 2-14, 92262-7201**
Telephone: 619-320-6443 Fax: 619-323-1699
*PRACTICE AREAS: Personal Injury Law; Civil Litigation; Real Estate Law.
Personal Injury, Civil Litigation, Real Estate Law.
*See Professional Biographies, PALM SPRINGS, CALIFORNIA*

## PALO ALTO, 55,900, *Santa Clara Co.*

Aaron, David A. ................'66 '93 C&L.770 B.S.C., B.S.C. 3350 W. Bayshore Blvd.
**Abel, Sally M.** ...............................'55 '84 C.112 B.A. L.1068 J.D. [Fenwick&W.]
*PRACTICE AREAS: Trademark.
Abend, Serge '38 '66 C.688 B.M.E. L.276 J.D.
(adm. in DC; not adm. in CA; Pat.) Xerox Corp.
**Abraham, Lois W.**, (AV) ..................'33 '73 C.813 B.A. L.36 J.D. [[B] Brown&B.]
*PRACTICE AREAS: Intellectual Property; Antitrust; General Litigation.
**Abramson, Richard H.** ...............'56 '81 C.154 B.A. L.1066 J.D. [Heller E.W.&M.]
*PRACTICE AREAS: Intellectual Property Counseling and Litigation.

**Ach, David Laurence, (AV) '47 '77 C.309 B.A. L.1067 J.D.**
**525 University Avenue, Suite 702, 94301**
Telephone: 415-321-4411 Fax: 415-326-0758
Email: achfamily@aol.com
*PRACTICE AREAS: Estate Planning Law; Estate Administration Law; Probate Litigation.
Estate Planning, Trusts and Wills, Probate, Estate Administration and Tax.
*See Professional Biographies, PALO ALTO, CALIFORNIA*

Ackerman, Michael J., (BV) .........'56 '82 C.112 B.A. L.770 J.D. 2666 E. Bayshore Rd.
**Adams, Marcia Howe** '48 '78 C.914 B.A. L.813 J.D.
Corp. Coun., Hewlett-Packard Co.
*RESPONSIBILITIES: General Corporate; Commercial Contracts; Intellectual Property/Compliance.
**Adeli, Mani** ..................'68 '95 C.112 B.S.E.E. L.1068 J.D. [[A] Morrison&F.] (Pat.)
Agiewich, Eve M., (BV) ................'44 '79 C.569 B.A. L.770 J.D. 2501 Park Blvd.
**Aji, Rajesh A.** ...............'62 '94 C.061 B.Tech. L.1066 J.D. [[A] McCutchen,D.B.&E.]
*LANGUAGES: Hindi, Urdu, Spanish.
*PRACTICE AREAS: Corporate; International Transactions; Licensing; Venture Capital Finance.
**Aka, Gary T.** ...........'46 '75 C.312 B.S. L.1065 J.D. [Townsend&T.&C.] (See Pat. Sect.)
*LANGUAGES: Japanese.
**Akerley, Stephen J.** ...............'67 '92 C.188 B.S. L.767 J.D. [[A] Townsend&T.&C.]
*PRACTICE AREAS: Intellectual Property Litigation; Commercial Litigation.
Alden, David M. .....................'55 '89 C.1206 B.S.B.A. L.472 J.D. 2431 Park Blvd.
**Alexander, Daniel** .....................'48 '79 C.112 B.A. L.767 J.D. [Alexander&H.]
*PRACTICE AREAS: Litigation; Civil Trial; Employment Law; Environmental Liability Law; Construction Defect Litigation.
Alexander, David M., (BV) .........'45 '71 C.813 B.A. L.1066 J.D. 2600 El Camino Real
Alexander, Janet Cooper '46 '78
C.821 B.A. L.1066 J.D. Assoc. Prof., Stanford Univ. Law Sch.
**Alexander, Paul**, (AV) ...............'46 '72 C.935 B.A. L.477 J.D. [Heller E.W.&M.]
*PRACTICE AREAS: Commercial Litigation.

**Alexander & Hanson**
**2600 El Camino Real, Suite 110, 94306**
Telephone: 415-812-8181
Daniel Alexander; Gordon N. Hanson.
General Business Practice. Civil Litigation and Appeals in all Federal and State Courts. Corporation, Securities, Employment, Real Estate, Environmental, Construction Defect, Trade Secret and Unfair Competition Law.
*See Professional Biographies, PALO ALTO, CALIFORNIA*

**Alkema, Susan M.** ...............................'66 '93 C&L.597 B.A., J.D. [[A] Fenwick&W.]
*PRACTICE AREAS: Corporate.
Allen, Betsy L. .................'53 '90 C.112 B.A. L.813 J.D. 5 Palo Alto Sq., Suite 400
**Allen, Cori M.** .....................'65 '93 C.674 A.B. L.188 J.D. [[A] Morrison&F.]
Allen, Ian G. ..........................................................'23 '62 460 California Ave.

CAA458P

**Allen, Karen Tietjen, (AV) '61 '88 C.770 B.S. L.1065 J.D.**
**285 Hamilton Avenue, Suite 400, 94301**
**Telephone: 415-327-7300 Fax: 415-327-7370**
**(Certified Specialist, Immigration and Nationality Law, The State Bar of California Board of Legal Specialization).**
***PRACTICE AREAS: Immigration and Naturalization.**
**Immigration and Nationality Law.**
***See Professional Biographies, PALO ALTO, CALIFORNIA***

**Allen, Kenneth R.**, (AV) '47 '75
C.101 B.S.E.E. L.588 J.D. [Townsend&T.&C.] (See Pat. Sect.)
*LANGUAGES: German.
**Allen, Michele Z.** '58 '95 C.768 B.A. L.770 J.D. [Graham&J.]
**Allison, Craig Y.** '55 '92 C.691 B.A. L.477 J.D. [Brobeck,P.&H.] (Pat.)
*LANGUAGES: French.
*PRACTICE AREAS: Intellectual Property Litigation.
**Alter, Aaron J.** '57 '85 C&L.309 A.B., J.D. [Wilson,S.G.&R.]
*LANGUAGES: Mandarin Chinese.
*PRACTICE AREAS: Corporate Law; Securities.
**Alton, Gregg H.** '66 '94 C.112 B.A. L.813 J.D. [Cooley G.]
**Alvarez, Edward M.**, (AV) '38 '66 C&L.770 B.S.C., LL.B. [Ferrari,O.O.&B.]⊙
*PRACTICE AREAS: State and Federal Taxation.
**Amantea, Denise M.**, (AV) '51 '80 C.112 B.A. L.770 J.D. [Wilson,S.G.&R.]
*PRACTICE AREAS: Litigation.
**Amaral, Edward M.**, (BV) '53 '80 C.1074 B.S. L.426 J.D. [Germino,R.A.J.C.&M.]⊙
*PRACTICE AREAS: Real Estate Law; Agricultural Law; Probate and Estate Planning; Elder Care Law; Business Law.
Ammons, Reginald K. S. '65 '91 C.1 B.A. L.990 J.D. Browne & Co.
**Ananian, R. Michael** '53 '92
C.477 B.S.E.E. L.770 J.D. [Flehr,H.T.A.&H.] (See Pat. Sect.)
*PRACTICE AREAS: Intellectual Property; Patents; Trademark; Copyright; Technology Licensing.
**Anawalt, Paul D.** '67 '96 C.112 B.A. L.1066 J.D. [Wilson,S.G.&R.]
*LANGUAGES: Russian.
*PRACTICE AREAS: Corporate; Securities.
Ancel, Nellie R. '58 '88 C.112 B.A. L.1067 J.D. 425 Sherman Ave.
Andersen, John G. '60 '85 C.800 B.A. L.169 J.D. 525 Univ. Ave.
**Anderson, James E.** '64 '89 C.813 B.A. L.1119 J.D. [Gray C.W.&F.]
*PRACTICE AREAS: Real Estate and Commercial Law.
**Anderson, William C.** '52 '77 C.957 B.A. L.494 J.D. [Brobeck,P.&H.]
*PRACTICE AREAS: Labor Law; Employment Law.
**Ansari, Kathleen S.** '65 '95 C.645 B.A. L.770 J.D. [Carr,D.&F.]
Ansnes, Terry '40 '66 C.976 B.A. L.1066 LL.B.
Assoc. Gen. Coun. & Dir., Litig. & Admin. Law, Syntex Corp.
**Anthony, William L., Jr.**, (AV) '39 '66 C.971 B.S. L.184 J.D. [Brobeck,P.&H.] (Pat.)
*PRACTICE AREAS: Patent Litigation.
Appelbaum, James B. '58 '91 C.966 B.A. L.188 J.D. 650 Page Mill Rd.
**Appelman, Daniel L.** '44 '81 C.766 B.A. L.1068 J.D. [Heller E.W.&M.]
*PRACTICE AREAS: Intellectual Property.
**Apple, R. Ted** '— '96 C.112 B.A. L.1066 J.D. [Townsend&T.&C.]
*PRACTICE AREAS: Biotechnology Patent Prosecution.
**Appleton, Jon M.** '63 '90 C&L.800 B.A., J.D. [Baker&M.]
*LANGUAGES: German.
Arbuckle, John H. '27 '57 C.477 A.B. L.665 LL.B.
(adm. in OH; not adm. in CA) 1275 Pitman Ave.‡
**Arima, Adrian** '50 '75 C.813 B.A.M.S. L.1066 J.D. [Gray C.W.&F.]
*PRACTICE AREAS: Licensing; Intellectual Property; Biotechnology.
**Armando, Lisa B.** '59 '84 C.112 B.S. L.770 J.D. [Wise&S.]
Armstrong, Jessica L. '67 '92 C.813 A.B. L.767 J.D. 650 Page Mill Rd.
**Armstrong, Michael W.**, (AV) '48 '79 C.813 B.A. L.597 J.D. [Nolan&A.]
*LANGUAGES: Italian.
*PRACTICE AREAS: Criminal Law; Felonies; Misdemeanors; Juvenile Law.
**Arner, Jessica F.**, (BV) '53 '77 C.976 B.A. L.1067 J.D. [Lakin S.]
*PRACTICE AREAS: Family Law.
**Arnold, Richard S., Jr.** '63 '94 C.870 B.S. L.228 J.D. [Wilson,S.G.&R.]
Aronstam, Brian C. '55 '87 C.813 A.B. L.1066 J.D. 5 Palo Alto Sq., Suite 400
**Arrieta, Aileen L.** '61 '87 C.112 A.B. L.178 J.D. [Wilson,S.G.&R.]
*PRACTICE AREAS: Litigation.
**Arrington, J. Michael** '70 '95 C.154 B.A. L.813 J.D. [Wilson,S.G.&R.]
*PRACTICE AREAS: Corporate Finance.
**Ashby, David C.** '63 '93 C.446 B.S.E.E. L.64 J.D.
[Flehr,H.T.A.&H.] (See Pat. Sect.)
*PRACTICE AREAS: Intellectual Property Law.
Ashby, Ned T., (BV) '44 '75 C.101 B.A. L.976 J.D. 852 Homer Ave.
**Ashley, Charles K., II** '63 '93 C.1097 B.A. L.1066 J.D. [Brobeck,P.&H.]
*PRACTICE AREAS: Corporations; Securities.
**Astiz, Peter M.** '58 '82 C.112 B.S. L.767 J.D. [Gray C.W.&F.]
*PRACTICE AREAS: Corporate and Partnership Law; Mergers and Acquisitions; Securities and Financial Products.
Athenour, Adele P. '60 '84 C&L.770 B.S., J.D. 5 Palo Alto Sq.
**Aufmuth, Lawrence A.**, (AV) '44 '70 C.103 A.B. L.813 J.D. [Aufmuth,F.W.&L.]
*PRACTICE AREAS: Taxation; Partnerships; Estate Planning.

**Aufmuth, Fox, Weed & LeBlanc, A Professional Corporation, (AV)**
**314 Lytton Avenue, Suite 200, 94301**
**Telephone: 415-322-7100 Fax: 415-322-6635**
**Lawrence A. Aufmuth (Certified Specialist, Taxation Law, The State Bar of California Board of Legal Specialization); Harry L. Fox; Michael H. Weed; Joan A. LeBlanc (Certified Specialist, Probate, Estate Planning and Trust Law, The State Bar of California Board of Legal Specialization).**
**Real Estate, Partnerships, Taxation and Estate Planning and Family Tax Law.**
***See Professional Biographies, PALO ALTO, CALIFORNIA***

**Austin, Alan K.**, (AV) '48 '75 C.309 B.A. L.813 J.D. [Wilson,S.G.&R.]
*PRACTICE AREAS: Corporate Law; Securities.
**Austin, James E.** '67 '93 C&L.012 B.S., LL.B. [Hickman,B.&W.] (See Pat. Sect.)
*PRACTICE AREAS: Patents.
**Austin, Kevin C.** '56 '93 C.988 B.A. L.813 J.D. [Cooley G.]
*PRACTICE AREAS: Corporate Law; Corporate Finance; Foreign Corrupt Practices Law.
**Axelrad, Jonathan** '62 '88 C.918 B.A. L.976 J.D. [Wilson,S.G.&R.]
*PRACTICE AREAS: Tax Law; Partnerships; Limited Liability Companies.
**Axford, Laurie A.** '57 '92 C.763 B.S. L.1137 J.D. [Morrison&F.] (Pat.)
Babcock, Barbara A. '38 '63 C.659 A.B. L.976 LL.B.
(adm. in MD; not adm. in CA) Prof. of Law, Stanford Law School
**Bachand, Edward N.** '54 '81
C.112 B.S.M.E. L.1066 J.D. [Flehr,H.T.A.&H.] (See Pat. Sect.)
*PRACTICE AREAS: Patents; Copyright; Trademark.
Bachman, Mervin N. '15 '39 C.690 B.S. L.309 LL.B.
(adm. in RI; not adm. in CA) 501 Forest Ave.
**Baeth, Judy Koong** '66 '93 C.813 A.B. L.1065 J.D. [Thoits,L.H.&M.]
*PRACTICE AREAS: Taxation; Corporate Law.
**Baker, Ronald A.** '56 '83 C.112 B.A. L.1068 J.D. [Wilson,S.G.&R.]
*LANGUAGES: Spanish and French.
*PRACTICE AREAS: Corporate; Securities; International.

**Baker & McKenzie, (AV)**
**660 Hansen Way, P.O. Box 60309, 94304-0309⊙**
**Telephone: (415) 856-2400 Int'l. Dialing: (1-415) 856-2400 Facsimile: (1-415) 856-9299**
**Members of Firm: Maurice S. Emmer; Tod L. Gamlen; John C. Klotsche (Not admitted in CA); Michael J. Madda; Susan H. Nycum; John M. Peterson, Jr.; J. Pat Powers; André M. Saltoun; Gary D. Sprague. Local Partner: Robin L. Filion. Associates: Jon M. Appleton; Michael Bumbaca; Robin A. Chesler; Brian Geoghegan; Stewart R. Lipeles (Not admitted in CA); Owen P. Martikan; Louise C. Ober; Taylor S. Reid (Not admitted in CA); James C. Ross; Michelle J. Wachs; Andrew D. Zeif (Not admitted in CA).**
**International and Domestic Practice. Administrative Taxation, Banking, Business and Civil Litigation and Arbitration, Commercial Transactions, Corporate and Securities, Customs Control, Employment Discrimination, Estate Planning, Immigration Law, Insurance, Legislative Practice, Mining and Natural Resources, Oil and Gas, Patent, Trademark and Copyright, Pension and Profit Sharing, Probate, Professional Liability, Publishing, Real Estate and Zoning Regulation, Taxation, Trade and Financing, Trade Regulation, Trust.**
**Associated Offices of Baker & McKenzie in: Almaty, Amsterdam, Bangkok, Barcelona, Beijing, Berlin, Bogotá, Brasília, Brussels, Budapest, Buenos Aires, Cairo, Caracas, Chicago, Dallas, Frankfurt, Geneva, Hanoi, Ho Chi Minh City, Hong Kong, Juárez, Kiev, Lausanne, London, Madrid, Manila, Melbourne, México City, Miami, Milan, Monterrey, Moscow, Münich, New York, Paris, Prague, Rio de Janeiro, Riyadh, Rome, St. Petersburg, San Diego, San Francisco, Santiago, São Paulo, Singapore, Stockholm, Sydney, Taipei, Tijuana, Tokyo, Toronto, Valencia, Warsaw, Washington, D.C. and Zürich.**
**Correspondent Law Firm: Hadiputranto, Hadinoto & Partners, Jakarta.**
***See Professional Biographies, PALO ALTO, CALIFORNIA***

**Bal, Colleen** '67 '93 C.228 B.S. L.309 J.D. [Wilson,S.G.&R.]
*PRACTICE AREAS: Litigation.
**Ball, Jeffrey D.** '68 '96 C.276 B.A. L.770 J.D. [Gray C.W.&F.]
**Ballon, Ian C.** '62 '86 C.860 B.A. L.273 J.D. [Brown&B.]
*PRACTICE AREAS: Intellectual Property; Internet related Litigation; Strategic Counseling.
Banas, John S., III '62 '91 C.860 B.A. L.597 J.D. 650 Page Mill Rd.
Bannerman, Julie Bomke '49 '77
C.813 B.A. L.1065 J.D. V.P. & Coun., Space Systems/Loral, Inc.
**Banquer, Andrew H.** '61 '86 C.197 B.A. L.893 J.D. Sr. Atty., Hewlett-Packard Co.
*RESPONSIBILITIES: Antitrust; Contracts; Software Licensing.
**Barclay, Michael**, (AV) '52 '79 C.112 B.A. L.1068 J.D. [Wilson,S.G.&R.] (Pat.)
*PRACTICE AREAS: Patent and Intellectual Property Litigation and Counseling.
Barkan, Randall I. '50 '75
C.309 A.B. L.1066 J.D. V.P. & Gen. Coun., Marcus & Millichap
Barker, Herbert E., Jr. '35 '64 C.112 A.B. L.1065 J.D. Pres. & CEO, Univ. ProNet
**Barlow, Annette** '68 '93 C.112 B.A. L.276 J.D. [Doty&S.]
*PRACTICE AREAS: Business and Corporate Law; Contracts.
**Barnett, James R.** '64 '90 C.685 B.A. L.770 J.D. [Thoits,L.H.&M.]
*PRACTICE AREAS: Corporate Law; Commercial Law; Intellectual Property and Licensing Law.
Barney, Philip C., Jr., (BV) '35 '65 C.976 B.S. L.813 LL.B. 2600 El Camino Real
**Barovsky, Kenneth** '52 '93 C.112 B.A. L.770 J.D. [Reed&R.] (See Pat. Sect.)
*PRACTICE AREAS: Patent Law; Patent Preparation and Prosecution; Chemistry; Biotechnology; Biomedical Engineering.
**Barr, Suzanne A.** '66 '92 C&L.309 A.B., J.D. [Cooley G.]
*PRACTICE AREAS: Securities Law; General Corporate Law.
**Barrett, Patrick J.** '44 '73 C.1167 B.S. L.813 J.D.
Asst. Gen. Coun., Intell. Prop. & Trademark Coun, Hewlett-Packard Co. (Pat.)
*RESPONSIBILITIES: Intellectual Property/Compliance; International.
**Barrish, Mark D.** '62 '94
C.112 B.S.M.E L.1065 J.D. [Townsend&T.&C.] (See Pat. Sect.)
*LANGUAGES: Spanish.
*PRACTICE AREAS: Medical Device, Mechanical and Electro - Mechanical Patent Prosecution.
**Barry, Henry V.** '49 '84 C.477 B.A. L.813 J.D. [Wilson,S.G.&R.]
**Bartholomay, John P.** '62 '90 C.846 B.B.A. L.94 J.D.
(adm. in MA; not adm. in CA) [Wilson,S.G.&R.]
**Barton, Daniel L.**, (AV) '61 '88 C.103 B.S. L.813 J.D. [Nolan&A.]
*LANGUAGES: Spanish and Catalan.
*PRACTICE AREAS: Criminal Law; Driving While Intoxicated (DWI); Felonies and Misdemeanors; Criminal Trial Practice.
**Barton, Thomas L.**, (AV) '42 '73 C.976 B.A. L.597 J.D. [Wise&S.]
*PRACTICE AREAS: Bio-Pharmaceutical Companies; Business Financing and Transactions.
**Baruh, Jeffrey A.**, (AV) '54 '79 C.112 B.A. L.767 J.D. [Bryant,C.O.M.&B.]
*PRACTICE AREAS: Real Estate Litigation; Business Litigation; Insurance Bad Faith; Construction Litigation; Lender Liability.
**Baskins, Ann O.** '55 '80 C.813 A.B. L.1068 J.D.
Asst. Secy. & Mng. Coun., Hewlett-Packard Co.
*RESPONSIBILITIES: General Corporate; Securities and Finance; Mergers and Acquisitions.
**Bassett, Barton W.S.** '— '96 C.112 B.A. L.1065 J.D. [Fenwick&W.]
*PRACTICE AREAS: Taxation.
**Bastian, Justin Lee** '60 '92 C&L.101 B.A., J.D. [Morrison&F.]
*LANGUAGES: Mandarin.
**Batchelder, James R.** '63 '88 C.264 B.A. L.1068 J.D. [Cooley G.]
*PRACTICE AREAS: Technology Litigation.
**Baudler, Mark B.** '68 '96 C.197 B.A. L.145 J.D. [Wilson,S.G.&R.]
*PRACTICE AREAS: Corporate Law; Securities Law.
Baum, Elizabeth M. '63 '91 C.112 B.A. L.770 J.D. 400 Hamilton Ave.
**Bauriedel, Marilyn U.**, (AV) '42 '80 C.518 A.B. L.770 J.D. [Wilson,S.G.&R.]
*PRACTICE AREAS: Intellectual Property.
**Bautista, Marilyn M.** '68 '93 C.112 B.A. L.93 J.D. [Gray C.W.&F.]
*PRACTICE AREAS: Bankruptcy; Commercial Lending; Commercial Litigation.
**Baw, Andrew** '69 '93 C.813 A.B. L.309 J.D. [Brobeck,P.&H.]
*LANGUAGES: Chinese (Mandarin).
*PRACTICE AREAS: Venture Capital Financing; Mergers and Acquisitions; General Corporate Practice.
**Beamer, Norman H.** '46 '79 C.401 B.S. L.477 J.D. [Fish&N.] (See Pat. Sect.)
*PRACTICE AREAS: Intellectual Property.
**Bebb, Richard S.**, (AV) '52 '77 C.813 A.B. L.1065 J.D. [Ferrari,O.O.&B.]⊙
*PRACTICE AREAS: Corporate Law; Business Law; Health Care; Estate Planning.
Becker, Lewis M. '47 '72 C.477 B.S.E. L.813 J.D. 2501 Park Blvd.
**Bedi, Ben H.** '65 '94 C.1067 B.S. L.146 J.D [Hickman,B.&W.] (See Pat. Sect.)
*PRACTICE AREAS: Semiconductor Technology; Electrochemical Systems; Alloy Compositions; Metallurgical Cladding; Patents.
**Bell, Cheri A.** '68 '93 C.112 B.A. L.464 J.D. [Flicker&K.]
*PRACTICE AREAS: Family Law.
**Bell, Julie Ann** '70 '96 C.608 B.A. L.880 J.D. [Wilson,S.G.&R.]
*PRACTICE AREAS: Corporate Law; Securities Law.
**Bell, Richard G.**, (AV) '47 '72
C.813 A.B. L.1065 J.D. V.P. & Gen. Coun., Watkins-Johnson Co.
**Bell, Suzanne Y.** '58 '88 C.478 B.A. L.813 J.D. [Wilson,S.G.&R.]
*PRACTICE AREAS: Intellectual Property.
**Benbrook, Bradley A.** '67 '95 C.813 A.B. L.1066 J.D. [Wilson,S.G.&R.]
*PRACTICE AREAS: Corporate; Securities; Mergers and Acquisitions.

**Benda, Stephen, (BV) '49 '87 C.813 M.S. L.999 J.D.**
**525 University Avenue, Suite 702, P.O. Box 479, 94302**
**Telephone: 415-323-6600 Facsimile: 415-323-6642**
***REPORTED CASES: Szabo v. Commissioner TC Memo 1992-255.**
***PRACTICE AREAS: Collections; Civil Litigation; Tax Litigation; Commercial Law; Bankruptcy. Collections and Enforcement of Judgments, Civil and Tax Litigation, Bankruptcy (Debtor, Creditor and Taxation).**

(This Listing Continued)

**Benda, Stephen (Continued)**
**Representative Clients: Hoyt Shepston, Inc.; Oncology Therapeutics Network LP; Barsac, Inc.; Prenatal Diagnostics, Inc.; Whitwham & Co.; Wines Ltd.; Brittania Building Society; First National Bank of Danville.**

Bender, Ann W., (BV) .... '41 '70 C.862 B.A. L.813 J.D. 2160 Newell Rd.
**Benerofe, Steven J.** .... '64 '96 C.103 S.B. L.309 J.D. [Ⓐ Wilson,S.G.&R.]
*PRACTICE AREAS: Intellectual Property; Patents; Licensing.
**Benes, Lois K.** .... '53 '87 C.309 A.B. L.1066 J.D. [Cooley G.]
*PRACTICE AREAS: Employment and Labor Law.
**Benn, Alex H.** .... '— '95 C.103 B.A. L.813 J.D. [Ⓐ Cooley G.]
*PRACTICE AREAS: Intellectual Property; Software Licensing; Emerging Growth Companies.
Bennett, Martin S. .... '16 '39 L.588 LL.B. 4130 Thain Way
**Benton, Lee F.**, (AV) .... '44 '70 C.604 A.B. L.145 J.D. [Cooley G.]
*PRACTICE AREAS: Mergers and Acquisitions; Business Law.
Beran, James T. .... '49 '77 C.1051 B.A. L.629 J.D. Sr. Coun., Xerox Corp.
**Berezin, Laura A.** .... '66 '92 C.112 B.A. L.659 J.D. [Ⓐ Cooley G.]
*PRACTICE AREAS: Mergers and Acquisitions; Securities.
**Berg, James L.** .... '53 '78 C&L.477 B.B.A., J.D. [Ⓒ Carr,D.&F.]
**Bergen, Seymour, (P.C.)**, (AV) .... '23 '74 C.563 B.B.A. L.770 J.D. [Bialson,B.&S.]
*PRACTICE AREAS: Business Law; Corporate Law.
Berger, Bruce .... '39 '64 C.659 B.S.E. L.309 J.D. Amer. Premium Property Grp.
**Berger, David J.** .... '59 '88 C&L.228 B.A., J.D. [Wilson,S.G.&R.]
*PRACTICE AREAS: Intellectual Property; Litigation.
Berger, Joseph S. .... '33 '59 C.102 B.A. L.1009 LL.B. 811 Chimalus Dr.
**Berghausen, Diana**, (AV) .... '48 '78 C.436 B.A. L.767 J.D. [Thoits,L.H.&M.]
*PRACTICE AREAS: Business Litigation; Employment Law; Insurance Bad Faith.
**Bergman, Peter H.** '69 '94 C.1365 B.A. L.569 J.D.
(adm. in NY; not adm. in CA) [Ⓐ Wilson,S.G.&R.]
*PRACTICE AREAS: Taxation.
**Bergreen, Timothy S.** .... '63 '95 C.881 B.A. L.813 J.D. [Ⓐ Brobeck,P.&H.]
*PRACTICE AREAS: Litigation.
**Berkman, Marcy** .... '65 '91 C.112 B.A. L.188 J.D. [Ⓐ Gray C.W.&F.]
*LANGUAGES: Spanish and French.
*PRACTICE AREAS: Civil Litigation; Environmental Litigation; Business Litigation; Aviation Law.
Berkowitz, Edward H. .... '38 '74 C.197 A.B. L.602 J.D. 3633 Ramona Cir. (Pat.)
**Bernal, Mark F.** .... '68 '94 C&L.770 B.A., J.D. [Ⓐ Hawkins,B.&F.]⊙
*PRACTICE AREAS: Personal Injury; Products Liability; Civil Litigation; Wrongful Termination.
**Bernard, Steven V.** .... '66 '91 C.893 B.A. L.569 J.D. [Ⓐ Wilson,S.G.&R.]
*PRACTICE AREAS: Corporate; Securities.
**Berney, Kurt J.** '61 '89 C.37 B.S. L.846 J.D.
(adm. in NY; not adm. in CA) [Ⓐ Wilson,S.G.&R.]
*PRACTICE AREAS: Mergers and Acquisitions; Securities; Banking; Corporate.
Berney-Key, Susan D. .... '58 '86 C.112 B.A. L.546 J.D. 1755 Embarcadero Rd., Suite 200
**Berry, Mary Elizabeth** .... '63 '92 C.813 B.A. L.770 J.D. [Ⓐ Gray C.W.&F.]
*PRACTICE AREAS: Litigation.
**Berson, Steven L.** .... '55 '82 C.575 B.A. L.880 J.D. [Wilson,S.G.&R.]
*PRACTICE AREAS: Corporate Law; Securities.
**Bertelsen, Mark A.**, (AV) .... '44 '70 C.112 B.A. L.1066 J.D. [Wilson,S.G.&R.]
*PRACTICE AREAS: Corporate Law; Securities.
Best, Laura V. .... '55 '80 C.813 B.A. L.770 J.D. 755 Page Mill Rd.
Beuche, William A., Jr. .... '43 '70 C&L.477 A.B., J.D. 300 Palo Alto Ave.‡
**Bevilacqua, Thomas A.** .... '56 '81 C.112 B.S. L.1065 J.D. [Brobeck,P.&H.]
*PRACTICE AREAS: Corporate Law.
**Beyer, Steve** .... '59 '86 C.37 B.S. L.273 J.D. [Hickman,B.&W.] (See Pat. Sect.)
*PRACTICE AREAS: Intellectual Property Law; Patents.
**Bhumralkar, Shailendra C.** .... '65 '93 C.813 B.S. L.276 J.D. [Ⓐ Townsend&T.&C.]
*LANGUAGES: German.
*PRACTICE AREAS: Patent Law; Intellectual Property.
**Bialson, Annette G., (Inc.)**, (AV) .... '46 '70 C.645 B.S. L.813 J.D. [Bialson,B.&S.]
*PRACTICE AREAS: Real Property Law; Business Law; Estate Planning Law.

**Bialson, Bergen & Schwab, (AV)**
**A Partnership of Professional Corporations**
**300 Stanford Financial Square, 2600 El Camino Real, 94306**
**Telephone: 415-857-9500 Fax: 415-494-2738**
**Email: bbs@bbslaw.com**
**Members of Firm: Annette G. Bialson (Inc.); Seymour Bergen (P.C.); Lawrence M. Schwab (Inc.);—Karen A. Koeppe; Kerry A. Kelly; Allison Walsh Hurley; Brian E. Doucette.**
**Business, Secured Transactions and Commercial Law, Real Property, Corporate, Creditor Representation, Estate Planning, Estate, Probate and Trust Administration, General Business Litigation and Trial Practice.**
***See Professional Biographies, PALO ALTO, CALIFORNIA***

**Biksa, Janis J. O.** '54 '87 C.112 B.S. L.770 J.D.
[Peters,V.J.&B.] (See Pat. Sect.) (⊙San Francisco)
*LANGUAGES: Latvian.
*PRACTICE AREAS: Patent, Trademark and Copyright Law.
**Biorn, Kristofer W.** .... '64 '92 C.228 A.B. L.1065 J.D. [Crist,G.S.&B.]
**Biorn, Robert A.**, (AV) .... '41 '69 C.174 A.B. L.1065 J.D. [Crist,G.S.&B.]
Bird, Rose E. .... '— '66 C.415 B.A. L.1066 LL.B. 2941 S. Court St.
**Birn, Jerome F., Jr.** .... '59 '84 C.103 B.A. L.309 J.D. [Wilson,S.G.&R.]
*PRACTICE AREAS: Litigation.
**Bishop, Gregory Scott** .... '62 '96 C&L.101 B.S.E.E., J.D. [Ⓐ Townsend&T.&C.]
*PRACTICE AREAS: Intellectual Property.
**Blackman, James W.**, (AV) .... '43 '69 C.112 A.B. L.1065 J.D. [J.W.Blackman]

**Blackman, James W., A Professional Corporation, (AV)**
**2370 Watson Court, Suite 200, 94304**
**Telephone: 415-843-1000**
**James W. Blackman (Certified Specialist, Criminal Law, The State Bar of California Board of Legal Specialization).**
**Criminal Law and Litigation. Civil Litigation.**
***See Professional Biographies, PALO ALTO, CALIFORNIA***

Blake, Harold N. .... '26 '52 C&L.813 A.B., LL.B. 841 Matadero Ave.

**Blakely, Sokoloff, Taylor & Zafman, LLP**
**(See Sunnyvale)**

**Blanch, Robert J., Jr.** '62 '94 C.321 B.A. L.94 J.D.
(adm. in IL; not adm. in CA; Pat.) [Ⓐ Brobeck,P.&H.]
*PRACTICE AREAS: Intellectual Property Litigation.
**Blanton, Timothy D.** .... '65 '93 C.1074 B.A. L.770 J.D. [Ⓐ Gibson,D.&C.]
*PRACTICE AREAS: Corporate Law; Intellectual Property.
**Blears, Norman J.**, (AV) .... '55 '80 C.207 B.A. L.813 J.D. [Heller E.W.&M.]
*PRACTICE AREAS: Securities Litigation.
Bleiberg, Victoria L. .... '53 '78 C.112 A.B. L.1065 J.D. 275 Southwood Dr.
**Blick, Stephen L.**, (AV) .... '44 '70 C.693 B.S. L.851 J.D. [Hawkins,B.&F.]⊙
*PRACTICE AREAS: Personal Injury; Products Liability; Insurance Bad Faith; Civil Litigation.
**Bloch, Kathleen Borrero** .... '56 '81 C.800 B.S. L.813 J.D. [Ⓒ Wilson,S.G.&R.]
*PRACTICE AREAS: Corporate Finance; Commercial Law.
**Bloom, Jeffrey M.** '66 '93 C.453 B.S. L.569 J.D.
(adm. in NY; not adm. in CA) [Ⓐ Wilson,S.G.&R.]
*PRACTICE AREAS: Taxation.

**Blumberg, Ira J.** .... '60 '93 C.659 B.A. L.893 J.D. [Ⓐ Wilson,S.G.&R.]
*PRACTICE AREAS: Technology Licensing.
**Blumenstein, Paul A.** .... '61 '88 C.696 B.A. L.477 J.D. [Gray C.W.&F.]
*PRACTICE AREAS: Corporate and Securities Law.
**Boadwee, Harry** .... '59 '88 C.813 A.B. L.178 J.D. [Ⓐ Fenwick&W.]
*PRACTICE AREAS: Corporate.
**Bochner, Steven E.** .... '55 '81 C.768 B.A. L.1066 J.D. [Wilson,S.G.&R.]
*PRACTICE AREAS: Corporate Law; Securities.
**Boes, Carol S.**, (AV) .... '45 '80 C.768 B.A. L.284 J.D. [Lakin S.]
*PRACTICE AREAS: Land Use; Transactional Real Estate; Business Transactions.
**Bohannon, Elizabeth K.** .... '62 '92 C.228 B.S.N. L.1355 J.D. [Ⓐ Fenwick&W.]
*PRACTICE AREAS: Litigation; Employment and Labor Law.
**Bohler, William J.** '57 '84 C.679 B.S.E.E. L.801 J.D.
[Townsend&T.&C.] (See Pat. Sect.)
*PRACTICE AREAS: Intellectual Property Litigation; Patents; Counseling.
Bohne, Russell L. .... '47 '75 C.112 B.S. L.767 J.D. 550 Hamilton Ave.
Bolanos, Raymond P. .... '61 '89 C.112 B.A. L.1065 J.D. 701 Welch Rd.
**Bomar, Kimberly A.** .... '65 '93 C.197 A.B. L.813 J.D. [Ⓐ Fenwick&W.]
*PRACTICE AREAS: Corporate.
**Bonfiglio, Gregory A.** .... '52 '83 C.475 B.A. L.477 J.D. [Morrison&F.]
*PRACTICE AREAS: Labor and Employment; Alternative Dispute Resolution.
**Bonham, Mark E.** .... '59 '88 C.101 B.A. L.309 J.D. [Wilson,S.G.&R.]
*PRACTICE AREAS: Corporate Law; Securities.
**Borns, Clarence**, (AVⓉ) '31 '56 C.477 A.B. L.597 LL.B.
(adm. in IN; not adm. in CA) [Ⓒ Packard,P.&J.] (⊙Merrillville, IN)
*PRACTICE AREAS: Personal Injury and Professional Malpractice.
**Boro, Lauren I.** .... '67 '92 C.112 B.A. L.569 J.D. [Ⓐ Wilson,S.G.&R.]
*LANGUAGES: Spanish.
*PRACTICE AREAS: Real Estate.
Bosch, Clement A. .... '38 '75 C.112 A.B. L.770 J.D. 4226 Ponce Dr.
Bosis, Daniel D., Jr. .... '61 '94 C.267 B.S. L.1068 J.D. 650 Page Mill Rd.
**Boskovich, Anthony M.**, (CV) .... '53 '85 C.951 B.A. L.770 J.D. [A.Boskovich]⊙
*REPORTED CASES: In re Mark Bettencourt, 20 Cal. Rptr. 2d 240; In re Babak S., 22 Cal. Rptr. 2d 893.
*PRACTICE AREAS: Litigation; Appellate Practice; Insurance Law; Civil Rights; Police Misconduct.

**Boskovich, Anthony, Law Offices of, (CV)**
**2155 Park Boulevard, 94306-1543⊙**
**Telephone: 415-323-0391 Fax: 415-323-0141**
**Email: 71750.2502@compuserve.com**
**Anthony M. Boskovich.**
**General Civil and Criminal Litigation, Civil and Criminal Appeals, Writs and Related Trial Court Matters, Civil Rights and Employment Law.**
**San Jose, California Office: 941 West Hedding Street. Telephone: 408-296-4345.**
***See Professional Biographies, PALO ALTO, CALIFORNIA***

Bostick, Carolyn F. .... '52 '90 C.103 B.A. L.813 J.D. 525 Univ. Ave.
**Bouchier, Robert L.**, (BV) .... '46 '70 C&L.813 A.B., J.D. [Ⓒ Lakin S.]
*PRACTICE AREAS: Real Estate and Business.
**Boudreau, Timothy P.** '65 '95 C&L.569 B.A., J.D.
(adm. in AZ; not adm. in CA) [Ⓐ Fenwick&W.]
*PRACTICE AREAS: Litigation.
Bourke, William C. .... '34 '66 C.976 B.A. L.767 J.D. 610 Coleridge Ave.
Bowden, Richard B. .... '25 '54 C.869 B.S. L.982 J.D. 255 N. California Ave.‡
**Bower, Susan** .... '66 '94 C.188 B.A. L.813 J.D. [Ⓐ Wilson,S.G.&R.]
*PRACTICE AREAS: Litigation.
**Boyd, Christopher F.** .... '66 '93 C.674 A.B. L.813 J.D. [Ⓐ Wilson,S.G.&R.]
*LANGUAGES: French.
*PRACTICE AREAS: Corporate; Securities.
**Bradfish, Larry J.** .... '52 '88 C.966 B.S. L.426 J.D. [Ⓐ Gray C.W.&F.]
*PRACTICE AREAS: Environmental Law.
**Bradley, Donald E.**, (AV) .... '43 '68 C.197 A.B. L.1065 J.D. [Wilson,S.G.&R.]
*PRACTICE AREAS: Tax.
**Brady, Jason M.** .... '68 '95 C.112 B.A. L.770 J.D. [Ⓐ Wilson,S.G.&R.]
*PRACTICE AREAS: Corporate; Securities.
**Braham, Tor** .... '57 '83 C.178 B.A. L.569 J.D. [Wilson,S.G.&R.]
*PRACTICE AREAS: Corporate Law; Securities.
**Brecher, Todd Samuel** .... '69 '94 C.976 B.A. L.1066 J.D. [Ⓐ Gray C.W.&F.]
*PRACTICE AREAS: Corporate/Securities.
**Bremond, Harry B.**, (AV) .... '34 '63 C.766 B.A. L.767 LL.B. [Wilson,S.G.&R.]
*PRACTICE AREAS: Litigation.
Brest, Paul '40 '67 C.821 A.B. L.309 LL.B.
(adm. in NY; not adm. in CA) Dean, Stanford Univ. Law Sch.

**Brewer, Janet L., (BV) '49 '75 C.965 B.A. L.208 J.D.**
**1755 Embarcadero Road, Suite 110, 94303**
**Telephone: 415-856-8286 Fax: 415-856-8296**
**Email: HiTekLawyr@aol.com**
***LANGUAGES: Russian and Spanish.**
***PRACTICE AREAS: Estate Planning; Probate and Trust Litigation; Corporate Law; Software Licensing.**
**Business and Corporate Law, Business Planning, Estate Planning, Probate and Probate Litigation, and High Technology Law.**
***See Professional Biographies, PALO ALTO, CALIFORNIA***

Brewer, Peter N. .... '49 '79 C.768 B.A. L.770 J.D. 401 Florence St.
**Bridges, Andrew P.** .... '54 '84 C.813 A.B. L.309 J.D. [Wilson,S.G.&R.]
*LANGUAGES: Modern Greek, French and Italian.
*PRACTICE AREAS: Trademark Law; Advertising Law; Consumer Protection and Unfair Competition; Litigation.
Briggs, Virginia P. .... '— '44 C.112 A.B. L.1066 LL.B. 55 Waverly Oaks
**Brigham, Robert J.** .... '61 '88 C.31 B.A. L.813 J.D. [Cooley G.]
*PRACTICE AREAS: Emerging Growth Companies; Corporate Law; Securities.
**Brigham, S. T. Jack, III**, (AV) '39 '67 C.1254 B.S. L.878 J.D.
V.P., Corp. Affs. & Gen. Coun., Hewlett-Packard Co.
*RESPONSIBILITIES: General Corporate.

**Brobeck, Phleger & Harrison LLP, (AV)** BB
**A Partnership including a Professional Corporation**
**Two Embarcadero Place, 2200 Geng Road, 94303⊙**
**Telephone: 415-424-0160 Facsimile: 415-496-2885**
**Managing Partner: Thomas W. Kellerman. Partners: William C. Anderson; William L. Anthony, Jr.; Thomas A. Bevilacqua; Michael J. Casey; Gari L. Cheever; Robert DeBerardine; S. James DiBernardo; J. Stephan Dolezalek; David M. Furbush; Noemi Espinosa Hayes; Karen N. Ikeda; Meredith Nelson Landy; John W. Larson; Warren T. Lazarow; Gregory S. Lemmer; Edward M. Leonard; Therese A. Mrozek; Luther Kent Orton; Ronald S. Wynn. Of Counsel: Thomas H. Carlson; Zaitun Poonja. Resident Associates: Craig Y. Allison; Charles K. Ashley II; Andrew Baw; Timothy S. Bergreen; Robert J. Blanch, Jr. (Not admitted in CA); Patricia G. Copeland; Jacqueline Cowden; Timothy R. Curry; Michael F. Cyran; Thomas P. Dennedy; Michael C. Doran; Amr A. El-Bayoumi; Helen G.F. Fields; Carol R. Freeman; Tamar Fruchtman; William P. Garvey; Hanna Casper George; Nora L. Gibson; Susan Giordano; Scot A. Griffin; Rodrigo M. Guidero; Ramesh Hamadani; Daniel R. Hansen; Kimberley Erin Henningsen; Jeffrey P. Higgins; Franklin P. Huang; H. Richard Hukari; Gregory C. Jackson; Andrew B. Koslow; James N. Kramer; Peter C. Ku; Sara M. Kurlich; Elaine Llewelyn; Taraneh Maghamé; Sharon E. Meieran; Margaret T. Miles; Patricia Montalvo; Benjamin P. Oelsner; Michael A. Plumleigh; Magan Ray; Christine L. Richardson; Melinda Collins Riechert; Christina Baker Robinson; Maura Roe; Anna A. Ruiz; Valerie L. Russell; Kevin A. Smith; Karen Y. Spencer; David W. Stevens; Andrew N. Thomases; Candace M. Tillman; Tomas C. Tovar; Peter**

(This Listing Continued)

**Brobeck, Phleger & Harrison LLP (Continued)**

**Vaughan; Craig R. Venable; Roburt J. Waldow (Not admitted in CA); Craig E. Walker; Stephen G. Wanderer; Sarah H. Whittle; Elizabeth A. R. Yee.**
**General Practice, including Business and Technology, Litigation, Securities Litigation, Technology Litigation, Environmental Litigation, Product Liability Litigation, Labor Law, Financial Services and Insolvency (including Bankruptcy and Loan Workout), Real Estate, and Tax/Estate Planning.**
**San Francisco, California Office: Spear Street Tower, One Market. Telephone: 415-442-0900. Facsimile: 415-442-0900.**
**Los Angeles, California Office: 550 South Hope Street. Telephone: 213-489-4060. Facsimile: 213-745-3345.**
**San Diego, California Office: 550 West C Street, Suite 1300. Telephone: 619-234-1966. Facsimile: 619-236-1403.**
**Orange County, California Office: 4675 MacArthur Court, Suite 1000, Newport Beach. Telephone: 714-752-7535. Facsimile: 714-752-7522.**
**Austin, Texas Office: Brobeck, Phleger & Harrison LLP, 301 Congress Avenue, Suite 1200. Telephone: 512-477-5495. Facsimile: 512-477-5813.**
**Denver, Colorado Office: Brobeck, Phleger & Harrison LLP, 1125 Seventeenth Street, 25th Floor. Telephone: 303-293-0760. Facsimile: 303-299-8819.**
**New York, N.Y. Office: Brobeck, Phleger & Harrison LLP, 1633 Broadway, 47th Floor. Telephone: 212-581-1600. Facsimile: 212-586-7878.**
**Brobeck Hale and Dorr International Office:**
**London, England Office: Veritas House, 125 Finsbury Pavement, London EC2A 1NQ. Telephone: 44 071 638 6688. Facsimile: 44 071 638 5888.**

***See Professional Biographies, PALO ALTO, CALIFORNIA***

**Broccole, Carmine J.** ................ '66 '92 C.188 B.A. L.813 J.D. [Ⓐ Wilson,S.G.&R.]
*PRACTICE AREAS: Corporate; Securities.
**Brockman, Ivan J.** ..................'69 '94 C.188 B.S. L.659 J.D. [Ⓐ Wilson,S.G.&R.]
Broderick, Timothy B. ............'51 '81 C.813 B.A. L.1068 J.D. 2600 El Camino Real
**Brooks, Lincoln A.**, (AV) .................'42 '75 C.473 B.S. L.770 J.D. [Brooks&R.]
*PRACTICE AREAS: Bankruptcy Law; Business Organization.

**Brooks & Raub, A.P.C., (AV)**
**721 Colorado Avenue, Suite 101, 94303-3913**
**Telephone: 415-321-1400 Facsimile: 415-321-1450**
**Lincoln A. Brooks; L. Donald Raub, Jr.; David S. Caplan.**
**Bankruptcy and Business Reorganization, Commercial Insolvency and Related Litigation.**

***See Professional Biographies, PALO ALTO, CALIFORNIA***

Brown, D. Gerald, (BV) ...................'35 '68 C.1085 L.770 J.D. 2600 El Camino Real
Brown, Henry A., III ....................'64 '89 C.10 B.A. L.767 J.D. 650 Page Mill Rd.
**Brown, Judith E.** ........................'57 '96 C.025 B.Sc. L.813 J.D. [Ⓐ Cooley G.]
*PRACTICE AREAS: Intellectual Property; Corporate.
**Brown, Theodore G., III** '52 '84
C.970 B.A. L.1066 J.D. [Townsend&T.&C.] (See Pat. Sect.)
*PRACTICE AREAS: Intellectual Property Litigation and Counseling.
**Brown, Thomas G.** ................ '67 '94 C.112 B.A. L.770 J.D. [Ⓐ Wilson,S.G.&R.]
*PRACTICE AREAS: Employee Benefits.

**Brown & Bain** [BR]
**1755 Embarcadero Road, Suite 200, 94306⊙**
**Telephone: 415-856-9411 Telecopier: 415-856-6061**
**Resident Personnel: Richard H. Harvey. Counsel: Lois W. Abraham; Ian C. Ballon; Douglas Clark Neilsson; Bernard Petrie.**
**Administrative, Antitrust, Appellate, Banking, Bankruptcy, Bond, Commercial, Corporate, Employment, Environmental, Estate Planning and Probate, Litigation, Government, Health, Immigration, Insurance Coverage, Intellectual Property, International, Land Use, Licensing, Media, Natural Resources, Patent, Product Liability, Public Utility, Real Estate, Securities, Tax, Trademark and Water.**
**Phoenix, Arizona Affiliated Office: Brown & Bain, A Professional Association, 2901 North Central Avenue, P.O. Box 400. Telephone: 602-351-8000. Telecopier: 602-351-8516.**
**Tucson, Arizona Affiliated Office: Brown & Bain, A Professional Association. One South Church Avenue, Nineteenth Floor, P.O. Box 2265. Telephone: 602-798-7900 Telecopier: 602-798-7945.**

***See Professional Biographies, PALO ALTO, CALIFORNIA***

**Brownell, Robert D.** ................ '61 '88 C.112 A.B. L.1068 J.D. [Wilson,S.G.&R.]
*PRACTICE AREAS: Corporate Law; Securities.
**Brownlee, Michelle** ................ '68 '96 C.197 A.B. L.178 J.D. [Ⓐ Wilson,S.G.&R.]
*LANGUAGES: French.
*PRACTICE AREAS: Trademarks; Copyright; Advertising and Promotion Law; Litigation.
**Bryant, William H.**, (AV) ........ '40 '65 C.112 B.S. L.813 LL.B. [Bryant,C.O.M.&B.]
*PRACTICE AREAS: Corporate; Securities (Private Placements); Real Estate; Mergers and Acquisitions.

**Bryant, Clohan, Ott, Maines & Baruh, (AV)**
**550 Hamilton Avenue, Suite 220, 94301**
**Telephone: 415-324-1606 Facsimile: 415-324-4613**
**Members of Firm: William H. Bryant; Frank E. Clohan; Robert L. Maines; Judith M. Ott; Jeffrey A. Baruh. Associates: Andrew L. Fagan; Meredith L. Fahn.**
**Corporation, Securities, Franchising, State and Federal Taxation, Sports and Real Estate Law. Estate Planning, Trusts and Probate. General Civil Trial Practice in all Courts. Administrative Law.**

***See Professional Biographies, PALO ALTO, CALIFORNIA***

**Bryski, Kathleen K.** ............... '64 '95 C.454 B.B.A. L.1066 J.D. [Ⓐ Gray C.W.&F.]
*PRACTICE AREAS: Commercial Law and Financial; Institutions Group.
**Bucha, Jason P.** ........................ '70 '95 C.813 A.B. L.228 J.D. [Ⓐ Wilson,S.G.&R.]
**Buchanan, Robert Kelly, Jr.** '64 '92
C.17 B.A. L.285 J.D. Tax Atty., Hewlett-Packard Co.
*RESPONSIBILITIES: International Tax Planning; Corporate Tax Planning; Mergers and Acquisitions.
**Bugdanowitz, Bradley A.** ........... '71 '96 C.1169 B.A. L.145 J.D. [Ⓐ Wilson,S.G.&R.]
*PRACTICE AREAS: Corporate; Securities.
Bull, Howard L. ....... '42 '73 C.210 A.B. L.893 LL.B. Corp. Coun., Varian Assocs., Inc.
**Bumbaca, Michael** ..............................'59 '90 C.035 L.018 LL.B. [Ⓐ Baker&M.]
*LANGUAGES: Italian.
*PRACTICE AREAS: Taxation.
**Burke, Pamela B.** ......................'67 '94 C.188 B.A. L.273 J.D. [Ⓐ Gray C.W.&F.]
Burnside, H. Steven ..................................................'50 '81 2211 Park Blvd.
Burnside, Howard S., (BV) ...............'18 '49 C.502 B.S. L.767 J.D. 2211 Park Blvd.‡
Burnside, Kirby J., (BV) ...............'53 '82 C.112 B.A. Hist. L.767 J.D. 2211 Park Blvd.
**Burnstein, Linda** ........'62 '88 C.477 B.A. L.1065 J.D. Tax Atty., Hewlett-Packard Co.
*RESPONSIBILITIES: Tax.
**Burr, Susan B.** ........................... '49 '82 C&L.846 B.A., J.D. [Ⓒ Gibson,D.&C.]
*PRACTICE AREAS: Labor and Employment Law.
Burress, Richard T. .........................'22 '48 C.627 A.B. L.302 J.D. Stanford Univ.‡
Burton, Clay C. .........................'46 '74 C.768 B.A. L.770 J.D. 725 Lincoln Ave.
Burton, Jane ....................'36 '84 C.812 A.B. L.1230 J.D. 2356 Palo Verde Ave.
**Busselle, James R.** .............. '46 '77 C.1070 B.S. L.1067 J.D. [Tomlinson Z.M.&M.]
*PRACTICE AREAS: Intellectual Property; Litigation.
**Byers, Brett D.** ......................'63 '95 C.188 B.S. L.976 J.D. [Ⓐ Wilson,S.G.&R.]
*PRACTICE AREAS: Corporate Law; Venture Capital Law; Securities Law; Mergers and Acquisitions.
**Byrd, Owen M.** ............................ '62 '91 C.170 B.A. L.145 J.D. [Ⓐ Mitchell&M.]
*PRACTICE AREAS: Land Use; Real Estate; Administrative Law; Environmental; Business Counseling.
**Cahill, Thomas J.**, (AV) ....................................'42 '67 C&L.767 B.A., J.D. [Lakin S.]
*PRACTICE AREAS: Civil Litigation.
**Caine, Gidon M.** '62 '88 C.659 B.A. L.569 J.D.
(adm. in NJ; not adm. in CA) [Ⓐ Wilson,S.G.&R.]
*LANGUAGES: Hebrew.
*PRACTICE AREAS: Litigation.

**Campbell, David M.** ................ '67 '96 C.668 B.A. L.569 J.D. [Ⓐ Wilson,S.G.&R.]
*PRACTICE AREAS: Corporate; Mergers and Acquisitions; Venture Capital.
**Campbell, Sam G., III** ..............'61 '96 C&L.260 B.S., J.D. [Ⓐ Townsend&T.&C.]
*PRACTICE AREAS: Patent Prosecution.
**Canady, Kelly Lynn** ....................'67 '94 C.188 B.A. L.352 J.D. [Ⓐ Gray C.W.&F.]
*PRACTICE AREAS: Corporate/Securities.
**Cannon, Alan W.** '56 '90 C.466 B.S. L.1184 J.D.
(adm. in VA; not adm. in CA; Pat.) [Ⓐ Morrison&F.]
**Caplan, David S.** ......................................'48 '77 C.766 A.B. L.767 J.D. [Brooks&R.]
*PRACTICE AREAS: Commercial Insolvency; Bankruptcy Reorganization.
**Caplan, Julian**, (AV) '14 '38
C.912 B.S.M.E. L.477 J.D. [Ⓒ Flehr,H.T.A.&H.] (See Pat. Sect.)
Carey, Robt. E. ................................'20 '49 C.112 A.B. L.767 LL.B. Ret. Supr. Ct. J.
**Carlen, Douglas A.** ............................'69 '94 C.800 B.A. L.1065 J.D. [Ⓐ Graham&J.]
*PRACTICE AREAS: Litigation; Insurance Coverage; Trade Secrets.
**Carlson, Cynthia Beth** ..................'59 '85 C.112 B.A. L.1067 J.D. [Gray C.W.&F.]
*PRACTICE AREAS: Employment Litigation and Counseling; Civil Business Litigation; Insurance Coverage and Bad Faith.
**Carlson, Michael M.**, (AV) ..............'55 '79 C.802 B.A. L.1066 J.D. [Morrison&F.]
*PRACTICE AREAS: Intellectual Property Litigation.
**Carlson, Thomas H.** ...................'58 '85 C.112 A.B. L.767 J.D. [Ⓒ Brobeck,P.&H.]
*PRACTICE AREAS: Civil Litigation.
Carlstrom, Theodore C., (AV) .......'33 '60 C.1058 A.B. L.950 J.D. 525 University Ave.
**Carnahan, Susan Bush** '48 '74
C.597 B.A. L.1068 J.D. Asst. Gen. Coun., Hewlett-Packard Co.
*RESPONSIBILITIES: General Corporate; Commercial Contracts; Antitrust; Software Licensing.
**Carpenter, Glenn C.** ............'55 '81 C.174 B.A. L.813 J.D. [Germino,R.A.J.C.&M.]⊙
*PRACTICE AREAS: Business Law; Real Property Law; Probate and Estate Planning; Trust Administration.
**Carr, Barry A.** ...............................'58 '83 C.112 B.A. L.178 J.D. [Carr,D.&F.]

**Carr, DeFilippo & Ferrell**
**2225 East Bayshore Road, Suite 200, 94303**
**Telephone: 415-812-3400 Fax: 415-812-3444**
**Members of Firm: Barry A. Carr; Stuart C. Clark; Gary A. DeFilippo; John S. Ferrell; Robert J. Yorio. Counsel: James L. Berg; Lisa A. Garono; Kevin A. Goodwin; J. Eppa Hite, III; Francis H. Lewis. Associates: Kathleen S. Ansari; Lloyd E. Dakin, Jr. (Not admitted in CA); Gregory J. Koerner; James W. Lucey; Leroy D. Maunu (Not admitted in CA); Marc A. Sokol.**
**Corporate and Securities, Employment Law, Intellectual Property (including Patent Prosecution and Litigation, Trademark, Copyright, Trade Secrets, and Unfair Competition), International Transactions, Licensing, Litigation (including Intellectual Property, Business Litigation and Insurance Coverage), Partnerships and Franchising, Real Estate, and Venture Financings and Placements.**

***See Professional Biographies, PALO ALTO, CALIFORNIA***

**Carroll, Megan J.** ................'59 '89 C.1169 B.A. L.1065 J.D. [Ⓐ Wilson,S.G.&R.]
*PRACTICE AREAS: Intellectual Property; Licensing.
**Carroll, Terrence J.** ........................ '60 '94 C.161 B.S. L.770 J.D. [Ⓐ Cooley G.]
*PRACTICE AREAS: Patent; Copyright.
**Cartun, Joyce M.** ..........................'59 '89 C.813 A.B. L.1065 J.D. [Heller E.W.&M.]
*PRACTICE AREAS: Securities and Corporate Governance Litigation; Complex Commercial Litigation.
**Cary, Charles C.** '48 '90 C.309 B.S. L.107 J.D.
(adm. in NY; not adm. in CA; Pat.) [Ⓐ Wilson,S.G.&R.]
*PRACTICE AREAS: Patent.
**Case, Hope A.** ............................ '66 '91 C&L.101 B.S., J.D. [Ⓐ Gray C.W.&F.]
*PRACTICE AREAS: Civil Litigation; Employment Law.
Case, Susan W. ...................................'44 '68 C&L.608 B.S., J.D. Sr. Asst. City Atty.
**Casebeer, Craig Hill** ...............................'47 '73 C.813 B.A. L.1066 J.D. [Cooley G.]
**Casente, Salvador A., Jr.** ....................'63 '89 C.893 B.S. L.309 J.D. [Ⓐ Cooley G.]
**Caserza, Steven F.** ........'55 '80 C&L.770 B.S., J.D. [Flehr,H.T.A.&H.] (See Pat. Sect.)
*PRACTICE AREAS: Patent; Trademark; Copyright.
**Casey, Michael J.** ...........................'62 '87 C.112 A.B. L.1068 J.D. [Brobeck,P.&H.]
*PRACTICE AREAS: Corporate Law.
**Cassedy, Sherrol L.**, (BV) ...................... '56 '83 C.813 A.B. L.276 J.D. [Lakin S.]
*PRACTICE AREAS: Family Law.
Casselman, James Kirk ... '45 '71 C.976 B.A. L.178 J.D. Mng. Dir., P.R. Taylor Grp., Inc.
**Cassidy, Bernard James** ........... '54 '89 C.425 B.A. L.309 J.D. [Ⓐ Wilson,S.G.&R.]
*PRACTICE AREAS: Litigation; Mergers and Acquisitions.
**Castillo, Amanda** ........................'72 '96 C.112 B.A. L.770 J.D. [Ⓐ Gray C.W.&F.]
*PRACTICE AREAS: Commercial Litigation; Technology/Intellectual Property Litigation; General Litigation.
Castleberry, Beth Detweiler ..........'57 '89 C.147 B.A. L.1067 J.D. 400 Hamilton Ave.
**Castro, Armando** ...................'62 '92 C.426 B.S. L.813 J.D. [Ⓐ Wilson,S.G.&R.]
*LANGUAGES: Spanish.
*PRACTICE AREAS: Corporate; Securities.
**Cattalini, Jeff** ........................... '70 '96 C.112 B.A. L.1066 J.D. [Ⓐ Wilson,S.G.&R.]
*LANGUAGES: Italian.
*PRACTICE AREAS: Corporate; Securities.
**Cattani, Kathleen** ........................'62 '93 C.101 B.S. L.1065 J.D. [Ⓐ Gray C.W.&F.]
Cauble, Debra L., (AV) ......................'53 '78 C.169 B.A. L.813 J.D. Sr. Asst. City Atty.
**Cervantes, Marta** ...................'63 '88 C.846 B.A. L.813 J.D. [Ⓐ Wilson,S.G.&R.]
*PRACTICE AREAS: Litigation.
**Chachkes, Alex** ........................'69 '96 C.453 S.B. L.178 J.D. [Ⓐ Wilson,S.G.&R.]
*LANGUAGES: Japanese and French.
*PRACTICE AREAS: Intellectual Property.
**Chambers, Daniel M.** .......... '63 '93 C.112 B.S. L.809 J.D. [Ⓐ Wilson,S.G.&R.] (Pat.)
*PRACTICE AREAS: Intellectual Property Law; Patent Law; Technology Licensing.
**Chan, H.C.** ...................... '50 '90 C.701 B.S.E.E. L.1065 J.D. [Ⓐ Wilson,S.G.&R.] (Pat.)
*LANGUAGES: Chinese.
*PRACTICE AREAS: Intellectual Property.
**Chan, Melvin D.** '65 '94
C.112 B.S.E.E.C.S. L.464 J.D. [Ⓐ Townsend&T.&C.] (See Pat. Sect.)
Chan, Vivian K. F. .............................................'66 '92 L.025 LL.B. 2200 Geng Rd.
**Chandra, Mona** ........................ '68 '95 C.454 B.S. L.893 J.D. [Ⓐ Fenwick&W.]
*PRACTICE AREAS: Corporate.
**Chang, Carmen I-Hua** .................. '48 '94 C.771 B.A. L.813 J.D. [Ⓐ Wilson,S.G.&R.]
*LANGUAGES: Chinese (Mandarin and Cantonese).
*PRACTICE AREAS: Corporate; International.
**Chang, Deborah M.** .........................'69 '94 C.813 B.A. L.477 J.D. [Ⓐ Graham&J.]
*LANGUAGES: Mandarin.
**Chang, Williana** ..................... '69 '95 C.112 B.A. L.800 J.D. [Ⓐ Wilson,S.G.&R.]
*PRACTICE AREAS: Employee Benefits.
**Chao, G. Chin** .................................. '— '96 C.339 B.S. L.813 J.D. [Ⓐ Fenwick&W.]
*PRACTICE AREAS: Corporate; Licensing Law.
**Chao, Warren** ...................... '68 '94 C.309 B.A. L.569 J.D. [Ⓐ Wilson,S.G.&R.]
*LANGUAGES: Chinese (Mandarin).
*PRACTICE AREAS: Corporate; Securities.
**Chaplick, Trevor J.** ........................ '63 '90 C&L.893 B.S., J.D. [Ⓐ Wilson,S.G.&R.]
*PRACTICE AREAS: Corporate; Securities.
Chapman, Michael A. ....................'59 '86 C.976 B.A. L.893 J.D. 650 Page Mill Rd.
**Char, C. Jeffrey** ........................'63 '93 C.061 B.S. L.1066 J.D. [Ⓐ Morrison&F.]
*LANGUAGES: Japanese.
**Char, Richard J.** .........................'59 '84 C.309 A.B. L.813 J.D. [Wilson,S.G.&R.]
*PRACTICE AREAS: Corporate Law; Securities.

**Chard, Leslie F., III** .................. '64 '92 C.918 B.A. L.150 J.D. [Ⓐ Fenwick&W.]
*PRACTICE AREAS: Intellectual Property Law; Licensing Law.
**Charlson, Michael L.** .................. '58 '85 C.813 B.S. L.1066 J.D. [Heller E.W.&M.]
*PRACTICE AREAS: Securities Litigation; Financial Institutions Litigation; Appellate Litigation.
**Charnas, Charles N.** ......'58 '85 C.813 B.A. L.1066 J.D. Sr. Atty., Hewlett-Packard Co.
*RESPONSIBILITIES: General Corporate; Securities and Finance; Mergers and Acquisitions.
**Cheever, Gari L.** .................. '57 '84 C.36 B.S.B.A. L.813 J.D. [Brobeck,P.&H.]
*PRACTICE AREAS: General Corporate and Securities Law; Venture Capital Law.
**Chen, Peter P.**, (AV) ............ '58 '83 C.813 B.S. L.1067 J.D. [Wilson,S.G.&R.] (Pat.)
*PRACTICE AREAS: Intellectual Property Litigation; Complex Commercial Litigation.
**Chen, Theodore A.** .................................. '69 '94 C&L.813 B.S., J.D. [Ⓐ Cooley G.]
*PRACTICE AREAS: Patent; Licensing.
**Chen, Theodore C.** '65 '92 C&L.659 B.S., J.D.
(adm. in NY; not adm. in CA) [Ⓐ Wilson,S.G.&R.]
*PRACTICE AREAS: Corporate; Securities.
Cherrington, Robert N. ......................'42 '67 C.8 B.A. L.813 J.D. 2211 Park Blvd.
Cherry, Desiree S. ....................'44 '81 C.768 B.A. L.1026 J.D. 2600 El Camino Real
Cherry, Jeffrey D. .................... '61 '90 C.1073 B.S. L.145 J.D. 400 Hamilton Ave.
**Chesler, Robin A.** .................... '64 '89 C.309 B.A. L.1066 J.D. [Ⓐ Baker&M.]
*PRACTICE AREAS: Taxation.
**Chew, Hanley** '70 '95 C.309 B.A. L.659 J.D.
(adm. in NY; not adm. in CA) [Ⓐ Wilson,S.G.&R.]
*LANGUAGES: Chinese.
**Chilton, Frederick R., Jr.** ................'45 '72 C.267 B.A. L.1065 J.D. [Fenwick&W.]
*PRACTICE AREAS: Domestic and International Corporate Taxation.
**Chin, Roger J.** ..................... '68 '96 C.188 A.B. L.976 J.D. [Ⓐ Wilson,S.G.&R.]
*PRACTICE AREAS: Intellectual Property Law; Litigation.
**Chisum, Donald**, (AVⓉ) ................'44 '70 C&L.813 A.B., LL.B. [Ⓒ Morrison&F.]
*PRACTICE AREAS: Patents; Intellectual Property.
Choi, George Y. ................ '62 '90 C.112 B.S. L.1068 J.D. 650 Page Mill Rd.
Chow, David ............................ '— '95 C.112 B.A. L.813 J.D. 600 Hansen Wy.
**Chow, Robert** .......................... '— '96 C.112 B.S. L.1066 J.D. [Ⓐ Fenwick&W.]
*PRACTICE AREAS: Corporate.
**Christmas, Troy F.** .......................'69 '95 C.112 B.A. L.813 J.D. [Ⓐ Cooley G.]
**Chua, Christine S.** '63 '89 C.188 A.B. L.1068 J.D.
Sr. Atty., Hewlett-Packard Company
*RESPONSIBILITIES: General Corporate; Securities; Mergers and Acquisitions.
**Chun, Kaui'ilani** ......................... '— '96 C.103 B.S. L.813 J.D. [Ⓐ Fenwick&W.]
*PRACTICE AREAS: Corporate.
Church, Shirley L. ...... '45 '84 C.792 B.S. Chem. L.426 J.D. Coun., Collagen Corp. (Pat.)
**Churchill, Paul** ............ '55 '86 C.112 B.S. L.1066 J.D. [Cooley G.] (©San Francisco)
**Chutorian, Sandra** .................. '55 '87 C.477 B.A. L.187 J.D. [Ⓐ Wilson,S.G.&R.]
*PRACTICE AREAS: Corporate Law; Securities.
**Cilley, James P.** ............................'66 '93 C.768 B.S. L.464 J.D. [Ⓐ Lakin S.]
*PRACTICE AREAS: Litigation.
**Ciotti, Thomas E.**, (AV) .......... '40 '65 C&L.477 B.S.Ch.E., J.D. [Morrison&F.] (Pat.)
*PRACTICE AREAS: Intellectual Property.
**Claassen, Robert** '66 '93 C&L.966 B.A., J.D.
(adm. in NY; not adm. in CA) [Ⓐ Wilson,S.G.&R.]
*PRACTICE AREAS: Corporate; Finance.
**Clark, Douglas J.** ........................ '63 '90 C.25 B.A. L.145 J.D. [Wilson,S.G.&R.]
*PRACTICE AREAS: Litigation.
**Clark, Kenneth A.** .................... '58 '85 C.880 B.A. L.846 J.D. [Wilson,S.G.&R.]
*PRACTICE AREAS: Technology Transactions; Intellectual Property; Corporate Law.
**Clark, Kenneth B.** ....................... '54 '79 C.684 B.A. L.569 J.D. [Fenwick&W.]
*PRACTICE AREAS: Litigation; Tax Litigation; Construction Law.
**Clark, Stuart C.** ........................ '46 '86 C&L.061 B.Comm., LL.B. [Carr,D.&F.]
Clarkson, Robert T. ...........................'53 '82 C.813 B.A. L.1068 J.D. 650 Page Mill Rd.
Clawson, Mark A. .......................'66 '94 C.101 B.A. L.228 J.D. 650 Page Mill Rd.
**Cleary, Todd** ........................ '70 '95 C.367 B.A. L.813 J.D. [Ⓐ Wilson,S.G.&R.]
*PRACTICE AREAS: Corporate; Securities.
**Climan, Richard E.** ...................................'53 '77 C&L.309 A.B., J.D. [Cooley G.]
Clinch, Nicholas B. ..............................'30 '59 C&L.813 A.B., LL.B. 2001 Bryant St.
**Clinton, Olabisi L.** .................... '66 '92 C.112 B.A. L.309 J.D. [Ⓐ Wilson,S.G.&R.]
*PRACTICE AREAS: Corporate Law; Corporate Governance; International Law.
**Clohan, Frank E.**, (AV) ............'38 '67 C.813 B.A. L.770 J.D. [Bryant,C.O.M.&B.]
*PRACTICE AREAS: Taxation; Estate Planning; Corporate; Real Estate; Mergers and Acquisitions.
**Clowes, Elisa** ................................'56 '82 C.1042 B.S. L.1066 J.D. [Ⓒ Cooley G.]
*PRACTICE AREAS: Employment Law.
**Clowes, John Howard** ..................'53 '83 C.112 B.A. L.1066 J.D. [Gray C.W.&F.]
**Cochrane, Julia L.** ...........................................'70 '95 L.770 J.D. [Gray C.W.&F.]
*PRACTICE AREAS: Products, Technology, Multimedia Licensing; Copyright.
**Cogan, Lawrence A.** ....................'51 '84 C.112 A.B. L.1067 J.D. [Gray C.W.&F.]
*PRACTICE AREAS: Environmental Law.
**Cohen, David**, (AV) .......................... '52 '78 C.103 B.A. L.477 J.D. [Cohen&O.]
*PRACTICE AREAS: Corporate; Tax Law.
Cohen, Nancy Mahoney .....'41 '75 C.242 A.B. L.813 J.D. Asst. Dir., Syntex (U.S.A.) Inc.
**Cohen, Steven G.** ........................'57 '83 C.112 B.A. L.1067 J.D. [Gray C.W.&F.]
*TRANSACTIONS: Multi-million dollar administrative mandamus action; California Environmental Quality Act (CEQA) litigation for various commercial and residential real estate developers; Construction defect litigation; Mechanic's lien counseling and litigation; Commercial unlawful detainer actions for both landlords and tenants.
*PRACTICE AREAS: Real Estate and Construction Defect Litigation; Land Use and CEQA Litigation; Commercial Lease Dispute Litigation; Mechanics' Lien Litigation.
Cohen, William .......... '33 '60 C.112 B.A. L.1068 LL.B. Prof. of Law, Stanford Univ.
Cohen, William I., (BV) ................'34 '59 C.178 A.B. L.813 J.D. 385 Sherman Ave.

**Cohen & Ostler, A Professional Corporation, (AV)**
**Suite 410, 525 University Avenue, 94301**
**Telephone: 415-321-3835 Telecopier: 415-321-0171**
**David Cohen; Mark R. Ostler; Andrew R. Kislik. Of Counsel: Hal E. Forbes; G. Kip Edwards. Special Counsel: Donald A. Slichter.**
**Corporate, Partnership, Securities, Finance, Venture Capital, Commercial, Federal, State, Local and International Taxation, Employee Benefits, Employment Law, Construction Law, Commercial and Civil Litigation, Antitrust, Trade Regulation and Unfair Competition, Estate Planning and Probate.**
***See Professional Biographies, PALO ALTO, CALIFORNIA***

**Cole, Rodger** .........................'69 '95 C.684 B.A. L.770 J.D. [Ⓐ Fenwick&W.]
*PRACTICE AREAS: Litigation.

**Cole, George S.**
**(See Menlo Park)**

**Colgin, William F., Jr.** '65 '92 C.972 B.A. L.208 J.D.
(adm. in VA; not adm. in CA) [Ⓐ Fenwick&W.]
*PRACTICE AREAS: Litigation; Tax Litigation.
**Collins, Paul J.** '66 '93 C.911 B.A. L.276 J.D.
(adm. in NY; not adm. in CA) [Ⓐ Gibson,D.&C.]
*PRACTICE AREAS: Securities Litigation; Mergers and Acquisitions; Business Litigation; First Amendment Litigation.
**Collom, Douglas H.** ................... '51 '78 C.813 B.A. L.1068 J.D. [Wilson,S.G.&R.]
*PRACTICE AREAS: Corporate Law; Securities.

**Colvin, Oliver P.** ...........................'62 '88 C.112 B.A. L.770 J.D. [Fthenakis&C.]
*PRACTICE AREAS: Business and Commercial Litigation; Intellectual Property; Securities; Construction; Real Property Disputes.
**Colwell, Robert C.** ..... '47 '73 C.378 B.S. L.813 J.D. [Townsend&T.&C.] (See Pat. Sect.)
**Compton, Charles T. C.** ................'43 '68 C.1070 B.S. L.569 J.D. [Wilson,S.G.&R.]
*PRACTICE AREAS: Antitrust; Litigation.
Comstock, Harry M. '18 '48 C&L.178 A.B., LL.B.
(adm. in NY; not adm. in CA) 3657 Louis Rd.‡
Cone, Anne D. ..................................................... '49 '79 [Di Maria&C.]
Cone, Steven J. ........................ '51 '78 C.1169 B.A. L.770 J.D. 425 Sherman Ave.
**Conner, Terrence P.**, (BV) ............. '54 '79 C&L.770 B.S.C., J.D. [Thoits,L.H.&M.]
*PRACTICE AREAS: Corporate Law; Commercial Law; Intellectual Property and Licensing.
Cook, Nicole Ernsberger ...............'64 '93 C.518 A.B. L.813 J.D. 650 Page Mill Rd.

**Cooley Godward LLP, (AV)** BB
**Five Palo Alto Square, 3000 El Camino Real, 94306**⊙
**Telephone: 415-843-5000 Telex: 380816 COOLEY PA Fax: 415-857-0663**
**Email: webmaster@cooley.com URL: http://www.cooley.com**
**Members of Firm: James R. Batchelder; Lois K. Benes; Lee F. Benton; Robert J. Brigham; Craig Hill Casebeer; Paul Churchill; Richard E. Climan; Janet L. Cullum; Brian C. Cunningham; Julia Loewy Davidson; Lloyd R. Day, Jr.; Stephen W. Fackler; William S. Freeman; John W. Girvin, Jr.; Willis E. Higgins; Michael R. Jacobson; Ronald L. Jacobson; Daniel Johnson, Jr.; Robert L. Jones; James C. Kitch; Barbara A. Kosacz; Martin L. Lagod; David M. Madrid; Andrei M. Manoliu; Deborah A. Marshall; Pamela J. Martinson; Herbert W. McGuire; Alan C. Mendelson; Webb B. Morrow, III (Certified Specialist, Taxation Law, The State Bar of California Board of Legal Specialization); Stephen C. Neal; Richard L. Neeley; Timothy G. Patterson; Anne Harris Peck; Mark B. Pitchford; Patrick A. Pohlen (Not admitted in CA); Anna B. Pope; Jeffrey G. Randall; Diane Wilkins Savage; Gregory C. Smith; Michael Stern; Daniel P. Westman; John F. Young. Special Counsel: Elisa Clowes; Ann Habernigg; James R. Jones; Tom M. Moran; Gary H. Ritchey; Deidre Lynn Sparks; Gretchen R. Stroud; Andrea H. Vachss; Christopher O. B. Wright. Associates: Gregg H. Alton; Kevin C. Austin; Suzanne A. Barr; Alex H. Benn; Laura A. Berezin; Judith E. Brown; Terrence J. Carroll; Salvador A. Casente Jr.; Theodore A. Chen; Troy F. Christmas; Patricia Louise Cox; Linda DeMelis; Scott D. Devereaux; Tracy Friedman Dobmeier; Chuck Ebertin; David T. Emerson; David J. Estrada; Melissa A. Finocchio; Jason D. Firth (Not admitted in CA); Keith A. Flaum; Molly Brown Forstall; Michelle Greer Galloway; Robert M. Galvin; Karen A. Gibbs; Michele K. Granaada; Bradley A. Handler; Judith A. Hasko; Lana K. Hawkins (Not admitted in CA); Matthew B. Hemington; Paula Holm Jensen; Suzanne Sawochka Hooper; Jeffrey N. Hyman; Viraj D. Jha (Not admitted in CA); Dan S. Johnston; Barclay J. Kamb; Anthony R. Klein; Judith Landis (Not admitted in CA); T. Gregory Lanier; Eleonora Leznik; David M. Lisi; Julie C. Lythcott-Haims; Matthew E. Marquis; Barbara J. McGeoch; Gerald T. McLaughlin; John D. Mendlein; Wm. Bradford Middlekauff; Jana R. Miller; Darren B. Mitchell; Shawn N. Molodow; Donald J. Morrissey, Jr.; Tahir J. Naim; Jackie N. Nakamura; Glenn Gerard Nash; Keith C. Nashawaty; Craig P. Opperman; Laura M. Owen; Stephanie J. Parr; Mehul T. Patel; Mary-Alice Pomputius; Kelvin P. Quan; Ruth Reitman; Matthew F. Roberts; Julie M. Robinson; Ricardo Rodriguez; Stephen N. Rosenfield; Gurjeev K. Sachdeva; Eric Schlachter; Joanne Marshall Shea; Myles B. Silton (Not admitted in CA); Matthew W. Sonsini; Seksom N. Suriyapa; Jonathan H. Takei; Barbara E. Tanzillo; Gregory C. Tenhoff; Vicki Ting; William S. Veatch; Julie A. Vehrenkamp; Erin M. Verneris; Laurie A. Webb; Michael L. Weiner; Brett D. White; Lara A. Williams; Kevin James Zimmer.**
**General Practice.**
**San Francisco, California Office: 20th Floor, One Maritime Plaza. Telephone: 415-693-2000. Telex: 380815 COOLEY SFO Fax: 415-951-3698 or 415-951-3699.**
**Menlo Park, California Office: 3000 Sand Hill Road, Building 3, Suite 230. Telephone: 415-843-5000. Telex: 380816 COOLEY PA. Fax: 415-854-2691.**
**San Diego, California Office: 4365 Executive Drive, Suite 1100. Telephone: 619-550-6000. Fax: 619-453-3555.**
**Boulder, Colorado Office: 2595 Canyon Boulevard, Suite 250. Telephone: 303-546-4000. Fax: 303-546-4099.**
**Denver, Colorado Office: One Tabor Center, 1200 17th Street, Suite 2100. Telephone: 303-606-4800. Fax: 303-606-4899.**
***See Professional Biographies, PALO ALTO, CALIFORNIA***

**Cooper, Byron W.** .......... '63 '93 C.879 B.S. L.1068 J.D. [Ⓐ Townsend&T.&C.] (Pat.)
*PRACTICE AREAS: Intellectual Property; Patents, Trademarks and Copyrights; Commercial Litigation.
**Cooper, David L., (P.C.)**, (AV) ............... '50 '79 C.94 B.A. L.770 J.D. [Irvine&C.]
*PRACTICE AREAS: Business Torts; Complex Litigation; Real Estate Litigation; Securities Litigation; Personal Injury Law.
**Copeland, Patricia G.** ................ '65 '90 C.112 B.S. L.1066 J.D. [Ⓐ Brobeck,P.&H.]
*PRACTICE AREAS: Employee Benefits.
**Corr, Jeanine M.** ........................'65 '93 C.1331 B.A. L.767 J.D. [Ⓐ Fenwick&W.]
*PRACTICE AREAS: Corporate.
**Costello, Patrick M.** ........................'58 '85 C.145 B.A. L.1065 J.D. [Murray&M.]
*PRACTICE AREAS: Business Workouts; Bankruptcy Reorganizations; Creditors Remedies.
**Covington, JoAnn Corti** ................'67 '93 C.156 B.A. L.309 J.D. [Ⓐ Fenwick&W.]
*PRACTICE AREAS: Litigation.
**Covington, Timothy A.** ..................'58 '86 C.112 B.A. L.1065 J.D. [Fenwick&W.]
*PRACTICE AREAS: Intellectual Property; Licensing Law.
**Cowden, Jacqueline** ................. '62 '92 C.1042 B.S. L.770 J.D. [Ⓐ Brobeck,P.&H.]
*PRACTICE AREAS: Corporate Law.
**Cox, Gregory T.** ........................'62 '88 C&L.813 A.B., J.D. [Ⓐ Wilson,S.G.&R.]
*PRACTICE AREAS: Corporate Law; Securities.
**Cox, Jonathan C. S.**, (AVⓉ) ............... '44 '71 C.813 B.A. L.208 J.D. [Cox B.P.&S.]
*PRACTICE AREAS: Commercial Litigation.
**Cox, Patricia Louise** ....................... '54 '88 C.767 B.S. L.813 J.D. [Ⓐ Cooley G.]
*LANGUAGES: Spanish.
*PRACTICE AREAS: General Corporate; Securities; Intellectual Property.

**Cox Buchanan Padmore & Shakarchy, (AVⓉ)**
**755 Page Mill Road, Suite A280, 94304**⊙
**Telephone: 415-424-0600 Telefax: 415-493-9408**
**Email: paoff@aol.com**
**Jonathan C. S. Cox (Resident); Vicki Marolt Buchanan (Resident, Newport Beach, California Office). Associates: Andrew F. Pierce.**
**Trial and Appellate Practice in State and Federal Courts. Corporation, Contracts and Business Law.**
**Denver, Colorado Office: 1775 Sherman Street, Suite 2500. Telephone: 303-839-9191. Fax: 303-839-9318.**
**Newport Beach, California Office: 840 Newport Center Drive, Suite 700. Telephone: 714-720-9100. Fax: 714-720-1508.**
**New York, New York Office: 630 Third Avenue. Telephone: 212-953-6633. Fax: 212-576-1614.**
***See Professional Biographies, PALO ALTO, CALIFORNIA***

**Cozzens, Tyler R.** ..........................'68 '95 C&L.813 B.S., J.D. [Ⓐ Fenwick&W.]
*PRACTICE AREAS: Corporate.
Cranfill, Raymond ................ '58 '88 C.383 B.S. L.1065 J.D. 401 Florence St. (Pat.)
Crawford, Susan B. ......................'51 '84 C.112 B.A. L.1065 J.D. 3030 Hansen Wy.
**Craycroft, Janet M.** ....................'61 '90 C.813 A.B. L.770 J.D. [Ⓐ Gray C.W.&F.]
*PRACTICE AREAS: Intellectual Property Litigation.
**Creighton, Susan A.** .............. '59 '86 C.309 A.B. L.813 J.D. [Wilson,S.G.&R.]
*PRACTICE AREAS: Litigation.
Cribbs, Ian M. ................................ '34 '73 C.813 A.B. L.770 J.D. 2450 Agnes Ct.
Crist, Frank Lee, Jr., (AV) .............'31 '58 C&L.813 B.A., LL.B. 550 Hamilton Ave.‡

**Crist, Griffiths, Schulz & Biorn, A Professional Corporation, (AV)** BB
**550 Hamilton Avenue, Suite 300, 94301**
**Telephone: 415-321-5000 Fax: 415-326-2404**
**Robert E. Schulz; Robert A. Biorn (Certified Specialist, Probate, Estate Planning and Trust Law, The State Bar of California Board of Legal Specialization); Kristofer W. Biorn; Mark R. Shepherd. Of Counsel: John R. Griffiths; Frank Lee Crist, Sr. (1898-1991).**
**General Civil & Trial Practice, Estate Planning, Real Estate, Tax Corporate.**
(This Listing Continued)

**Crist, Griffiths, Schulz & Biorn, A Professional Corporation (Continued)**
**Representative Clients: Peck & Hiller; Apple Computer, Inc.**
*See Professional Biographies, PALO ALTO, CALIFORNIA*

**Criswell, Brandyn** ........... '69 '96 C.813 B.A. L.597 J.D. [Ⓐ Wilson,S.G.&R.]
*PRACTICE AREAS: Corporate; Technology Transactions.
Croft, Christopher D. '46 '73 C.312 A.B. L.1065 J.D.
(adm. in HI; not adm. in CA) Pres., Christopher Croft, Inc.
**Croll, Timothy Rex** '57 '92 C.36 B.S.S.E. L.1065 J.D.
Atty., Hewlett-Packard Co. (Pat.)
*RESPONSIBILITIES: Patent; Trade Secret; Copyright.
**Cronan, Thomas L., III** .............. '59 '84 C.529 B.S. L.262 J.D. [Ⓑ Wilson,S.G.&R.]
*PRACTICE AREAS: Technology Transactions; Copyright; Antitrust.
Cross, Terrence H. '60 '86 C.813 A.B. L.1066 J.D.
Gen. Coun., Earth Systems Servs., Inc.
**Crossman, John K.** '62 '87 C.860 B.S. L.94 J.D.
(adm. in CT; not adm. in CA) [Zevnik H.G.&M.]⊙
**Crow, Paula S.** ..................... '53 '80 C.112 A.B. L.1066 J.D. [Ⓑ Ritchey F.W.&K.]
*PRACTICE AREAS: Technology and Real Estate Transactions.
**Cserr, Luann** ................. '53 '81 C.477 B.S. L.1065 J.D. 3000 El Camino Real (Pat.)
**Cullen, Gary S.** '51 '82 C.608 B.S. L.309 J.D.
Dep. Gen. Coun., Consolidated Freightways, Inc.
*RESPONSIBILITIES: General Corporate; Commercial Transactions.
Cullen, Michael J., (AV) .................... '23 '51 C.724 A.B. L.145 J.D. 525 Univ. Ave.
**Cullinane, Danielle C.** ...................... '65 '95 C&L.813 B.S., J.D. [Ⓐ Fenwick&W.]
*PRACTICE AREAS: Corporate.
**Cullum, Janet L.** ........................ '48 '82 C.1077 B.A. L.1065 J.D. [Cooley G.]
*PRACTICE AREAS: Intellectual Property Law; Litigation.
Culpepper, James A. ...................... '42 '69 C.309 B.A. L.813 LL.B. 2121 Amherst St.
Cunha, James R., (BV) ............... '21 '50 C.112 A.B. L.813 LL.B. 407 Sherman Ave.
**Cunningham, Brian C.** .......................... '43 '71 C&L.910 B.S., J.D. [Cooley G.]
*PRACTICE AREAS: Corporate and Securities Law; Life Sciences and Health Care Companies; Intellectual Property Law.
**Cuny, Linda M.** ................... '68 '96 C.770 B.S.C. L.1067 J.D. [Ⓐ Wilson,S.G.&R.]
*PRACTICE AREAS: Corporate; Securities.
Curlett, Jim C., (BV) .......... '46 '75 C.112 B.S. L.1066 J.D. 200 Page Mill Rd., 2nd Fl.
**Currie, Francis S.**, (AV) ................... '50 '75 C&L.309 B.A., J.D. [Wilson,S.G.&R.]
*PRACTICE AREAS: Corporate Law; Securities.
**Curry, Timothy R.** ................... '65 '90 C.112 B.A. L.1068 J.D. [Ⓐ Brobeck,P.&H.]
*PRACTICE AREAS: General Corporate and Securities Law.
**Curtis, Michael**, (AV) .................. '47 '72 C.999 B.S. L.1065 J.D. [Thoits,L.H.&M.]
*PRACTICE AREAS: Probate; Estate Planning; Trust Administration; Real Property; Business Law.
**Curtiss, Catherine L.** .................... '52 '89 C.967 B.A. L.276 J.D. [Ⓐ Fenwick&W.]
*PRACTICE AREAS: Taxation.
**Cyran, Michael F.** ....................... '70 '96 C.93 B.S. L.1065 J.D. [Ⓐ Brobeck,P.&H.]
*PRACTICE AREAS: Securities Litigation.
**Dahlby, Gary L.** ............................ '56 '94 C&L.112 B.S., J.D. [Ⓐ Gray C.W.&F.]
*PRACTICE AREAS: Intellectual Property; Technology Licensing.
**Dakin, Lloyd E., Jr.** '65 '94 C.645 B.S.E.E. L.846 J.D.
(adm. in TX; not adm. in CA) [Ⓐ Carr,D.&F.]
Danaher, James T., (AV) '29 '59 C.197 B.A. L.813 LL.B.
2600 El Camino Real, Ste. 506
**Danaher, Michael J.**, (AV) ............ '53 '80 C.976 B.A. L.813 J.D. [Wilson,S.G.&R.]
*PRACTICE AREAS: Corporate Law; Securities.
**Danella, Brian D.** '69 '95 C.674 A.B. L.823 J.D.
(adm. in NY; not adm. in CA) [Ⓐ Wilson,S.G.&R.]
*PRACTICE AREAS: Technology Licensing; Intellectual Property.
**Danforth, Gay Crosthwait** ............ '59 '85 C.914 B.A. L.178 J.D. [Ⓐ Fenwick&W.]
*PRACTICE AREAS: Litigation; Labor and Employment Law.
**Daniels, Jill** ...................... '70 '95 C.813 A.B. L.309 J.D. [Ⓐ Wilson,S.G.&R.]
*PRACTICE AREAS: Employment Law.
**Dare, Marilyn Tiki** ...................... '66 '93 C.197 B.A. L.228 J.D. [Ⓐ Fenwick&W.]
*PRACTICE AREAS: Intellectual Property; Copyright and Trademark.
**Dau, Paolo M. (Paul)** .................. '53 '94 C.012 B.A. L.1067 J.D. [Ⓐ Fenwick&W.]
*PRACTICE AREAS: Taxation.
**Daunt, Jacqueline A.**, (AV) .................. '53 '78 C&L.477 B.A., J.D. [Fenwick&W.]
*PRACTICE AREAS: Corporate.
**Davidson, Gordon K.**, (AV) .................. '48 '74 C&L.813 B.S., J.D. [Fenwick&W.]
*PRACTICE AREAS: Corporate.
**Davidson, Julia Loewy** ...................... '64 '88 C.112 B.A. L.309 J.D. [Cooley G.]
*PRACTICE AREAS: Mergers and Acquisitions; Securities.
**Davis, Donald R.**, (AV) ..................... '40 '66 C.597 B.A. L.178 LL.B. [Graham&J.]
*PRACTICE AREAS: International Business Law.
**Davis, Lisa A.** ......................... '62 '95 C.813 A.B. L.309 J.D. [Ⓐ Wilson,S.G.&R.]
*LANGUAGES: Spanish and French.
*PRACTICE AREAS: Securities Litigation; Intellectual Property.
**Davis, Paul** ........................ '51 '77 C.768 B.S. L.770 J.D. [Wilson,S.G.&R.] (Pat.)
*PRACTICE AREAS: Patents; Trademarks; Copyrights.
**Dawson, Valerie M.** ..................... '65 '93 C.945 B.A. L.477 J.D. [Ⓐ Fenwick&W.]
*PRACTICE AREAS: Litigation.
Dawson, William R., (BV) ............ '43 '72 C.215 B.S. L.904 J.D. 350 Tennyson Ave.
**Day, Lloyd R., Jr.** ........................ '52 '79 C.951 B.A. L.145 J.D. [Cooley G.]
*PRACTICE AREAS: Technology Litigation.
**Day, M. Elizabeth** ..................... '69 '95 C.197 B.A. L.1067 J.D. [Ⓐ Gray C.W.&F.]
*PRACTICE AREAS: Intellectual Property; Commercial Litigation.
**Day, Robert G.** ......................... '66 '93 C&L.813 A.B., J.D. [Ⓐ Wilson,S.G.&R.]
*PRACTICE AREAS: Corporate; Securities.
**Deanhardt, W. Clay** ...................... '66 '92 C.232 B.A. L.309 J.D. [Ⓐ Graham&J.]
*PRACTICE AREAS: Commercial Litigation; Intellectual Property Litigation; Securities Litigation.
**DeBerardine, Robert** ............ '58 '83 C.390 B.S. L.188 J.D. [Brobeck,P.&H.] (Pat.)
*PRACTICE AREAS: Patent, Trademark, Copyright, Trade Secrets and Related Litigation.
**DeBroeck, Dennis R.**, (AV) .............. '51 '76 C.174 B.S. L.1068 J.D. [Fenwick&W.]
*PRACTICE AREAS: Corporate.
DeBruine, Sean P. .......................... '60 '93 C.112 A.B. L.1066 J.D. 650 Page Mill Rd.
**DeFilippo, Gary A.** .......................... '57 '82 C.813 A.B. L.800 J.D. [Carr,D.&F.]
**DeFilipps, Thomas C.** ..................... '56 '81 C&L.813 A.B., J.D. [Wilson,S.G.&R.]
*PRACTICE AREAS: Corporate Law; Securities.
**DeFranco, Edward J.** ........... '60 '87 C.688 B.S. L.188 J.D. [Fish&N.] (See Pat. Sect.)
*PRACTICE AREAS: Intellectual Property.
DeFranco, Judith A. ..................... '46 '89 C.112 A.B. L.1065 J.D. 5 Palo Alto Sq.
DeGolia, Richard C. ..................... '50 '86 C.112 B.A. L.309 J.D. 650 Page Mill Rd.
**DeGraff, Harold R.** ................... '65 '96 C.870 B.S. L.477 J.D. [Ⓐ Wilson,S.G.&R.]
**Dehlinger, Peter J.** .... '44 '82 C.629 B.S. L.1051 J.D. [Dehlinger&Assoc.] (See Pat. Sect.)
*PRACTICE AREAS: Intellectual Property.

**Dehlinger & Associates**
**350 Cambridge Avenue, Suite 250, 94306-1546**
**Telephone: 415-324-0880 Telecopier: 415-324-0960**
**Peter J. Dehlinger. Associate: Carol Stratford.**
**Patent Law.**
*See Professional Biographies, PALO ALTO, CALIFORNIA*

DeLee, Garrison G. ..................................... '56 '84 C.112 B.S. L.800 J.D. First Data Corp.
deLemos, Donald R. ........................................................ '26 '50 C&L.813 4102 Verdosa Dr.‡
**de Leon, Cecilia M.** ................ '67 '93 C.112 B.A. L.1066 J.D. [Ⓐ Wilson,S.G.&R.]
**Dellenbach, Robert B.** ..................... '— '90 C.878 B.A. L.813 J.D. [Fenwick&W.]
*PRACTICE AREAS: Corporate.
Dellenbach, Winter S. .... '45 '83 L.1230 J.D. Dir., Midpeninsula Citizens for Fair Housing
**DeMarchi, Virginia K.** ................... '69 '93 C.813 B.S. L.309 J.D. [Ⓐ Fenwick&W.]
*PRACTICE AREAS: Litigation.
**DeMelis, Linda** ............................ '53 '94 C.681 B.A. L.1065 J.D. [Ⓐ Cooley G.]
*PRACTICE AREAS: Corporate Law; Securities Law.
**Dennedy, Thomas P.** ............... '66 '96 C.1070 B.S.E.E. L.813 J.D. [Ⓐ Brobeck,P.&H.]
*PRACTICE AREAS: Intellectual Property; Technology Licensing; Corporate Law.
**Dennis, Stephen A.** ...................... '57 '83 C.1049 B.A. L.770 J.D. [Thoits,L.H.&M.]
*PRACTICE AREAS: Taxation Law; Pensions Law; Corporate Law.
**de Petra, Laura Miller** ............. '70 '96 C.112 B.A. L.1066 J.D. [Ⓐ Wilson,S.G.&R.]
*PRACTICE AREAS: Corporate; Securities.
Desjardins, Cathleen M. ......... '56 '90 C.112 B.S. L.813 J.D. 5 Palo Alto Sq., Suite 400
**Desmarais, Michael G.**, (AV) ................ '48 '73 C.112 A.B. L.1065 J.D. [Lakin S.]
*PRACTICE AREAS: Estate Planning; Estate Administration and Estate Litigation.
**Devereaux, Scott D.** ........................ '63 '89 C.105 B.A. L.128 J.D. [Ⓐ Cooley G.]
*PRACTICE AREAS: Business Litigation; White Collar.
**Dew, Jennifer** ..................... '64 '92 C.773 B.A. L.1355 J.D. [Ⓐ Ritchey F.W.&K.]
*PRACTICE AREAS: Business Litigation; Labor and Employment.
**Dewees, Christopher S.** ............... '64 '89 C.197 A.B. L.597 J.D. [Ⓐ Morrison&F.]
**Dhawan, Sanjiv S.** ........................ '63 '90 C.112 B.S. L.1067 J.D. [Ⓐ Wise&S.]
*PRACTICE AREAS: Securities Law; Corporate Law.
**Dhuey, John A.** ................ '42 '76 C.966 B.S. L.424 J.D. [Ⓑ Heller E.W.&M.] (Pat.)
**DiBernardo, S. James** .................. '46 '73 C.321 A.B. L.178 J.D. [Brobeck,P.&H.]
*PRACTICE AREAS: Executive Compensation; Research and Development Financing.
**DiBoise, James A.**, (AV) ............... '52 '78 C.893 B.A. L.813 J.D. [Wilson,S.G.&R.]
*PRACTICE AREAS: Litigation.
**Dickey, Jonathan C.** ...................... '53 '79 C.309 A.B. L.477 J.D. [Gibson,D.&C.]
*PRACTICE AREAS: Securities Litigation; Intellectual Property Litigation; Accountants' Liability.
**Dickinson, Jon M.** '38 '64 C&L.188 B.E.E., LL.B.
(adm. in OR; not adm. in CA; See Pat. Sect.) [Kolisch H.D.M.&H.] (⊙Portland, OR.)
*PRACTICE AREAS: Patent, Trademark and Unfair Competition.
**Dickson, Richard L.** ............................ '— '94 C&L.813 B.A., J.D. [Ⓐ Fenwick&W.]
*PRACTICE AREAS: Corporate.
**Dienès, Martha L.** ................... '62 '94 C.112 B.A. L.813 J.D. [Ⓐ Wilson,S.G.&R.]
*PRACTICE AREAS: Technology Licensing; Intellectual Property.
DiGiovanni, Cynthia M. ................ '49 '84 C.483 B.S. L.770 J.D. 788 Palo Alto Ave.
**Dillon, Carol K.** '53 '82 C.813 B.A. L.1066 J.D.
[McCutchen,D.B.&E.] (⊙San Jose and San Francisco)
*PRACTICE AREAS: Real Estate Law; Environmental Compliance Law.
Dillon, Michael A. ......................... '58 '84 C.112 B.A. L.770 J.D. 3030 Hansen Way
**DiMarco, Bret M.** ........................ '68 '93 C.112 B.A. L.800 J.D. [Ⓐ Wilson,S.G.&R.]
*LANGUAGES: Swedish.
*PRACTICE AREAS: Corporate; Securities.
Di Maria, Jos. F. ............................. '12 '36 C&L.813 A.B., J.D. 701 Welch Rd.
Di Maria, Philip A., (BV) ................... '14 '39 C&L.813 A.B., LL.B. [Di Maria&C.]
Di Maria & Cone, (BV) ........................................................... 425 Sherman Ave.
**Dinkel, Polly A.** ...................... '55 '81 C.645 B.A. L.1065 J.D. [Tomlinson Z.M.&M.]
*PRACTICE AREAS: Intellectual Property; Business Transactions.
DiOrio, Rana B. ........................... '66 '92 C.228 A.B. L.880 J.D. 650 Page Mill Rd.
**Distler, Vivian B.** ................... '65 '94 C.94 B.S. L.1066 J.D. [Ⓐ Wilson,S.G.&R.]
*PRACTICE AREAS: Intellectual Property; Technology Licensing.
**Dobmeier, Tracy Friedman** .............. '68 '94 C.674 A.B. L.1066 J.D. [Ⓐ Cooley G.]
*PRACTICE AREAS: Intellectual Property; Biotechnology Licensing.
**Dolezalek, J. Stephan** ..................... '56 '82 C&L.893 B.A., J.D. [Brobeck,P.&H.]
*LANGUAGES: German.
*PRACTICE AREAS: General Corporate Law; Securities Law, Emerging Growth and Biotechnology Companies Law.
**Dolinko, Adam R.** .................. '68 '93 C.112 B.A. L.800 J.D. [Ⓐ Wilson,S.G.&R.]
*PRACTICE AREAS: Corporate; Securities.
**Dolkas, David Henry**, (AV) ............. '56 '83 C.426 B.A. L.1049 J.D. [Gray C.W.&F.]
*PRACTICE AREAS: Business Litigation (50%); Intellectual Property (25%); Personal Injury (25%).
Dolton, Gregory N. ...................... '57 '87 C.112 B.A. L.431 J.D. 755 Page Mill Rd.
**Donahey, M. Scott**, (AV) ........................ '45 '78 C.813 B.A. L.770 J.D. [Wise&S.]
*PRACTICE AREAS: Commercial Arbitration and Mediation (International and Domestic); Intellectual Property; Patent Litigation; General Commercial Litigation.
Donegan, John M., (AV) ............. '17 '49 C.37 B.S. L.813 J.D. 2600 El Camino Real
Donnelly, Brian V. ........................ '66 '92 C.128 B.A. L.1065 J.D. 2200 Geng Rd.
Donohue, John J., III '53 '77 C.299 B.A. L.309 J.D.
(adm. in CT; not adm. in CA) Prof. of Law, Stanford Univ.
**Donovan, Jeffery L.** ..................... '71 '95 C.1036 B.A. L.813 J.D. [Ⓐ Fenwick&W.]
*PRACTICE AREAS: Corporate Law; Securities.
**Donovan, Michael C.** .................. '52 '78 C.588 B.S. L.602 J.D. [Ⓐ Zevnik H.G.&M.]
*PRACTICE AREAS: Complex Civil and Criminal Environmental Litigation; Toxic Tort Litigation.
**Donovan, Stephen A.** ................ '67 '94 C.976 B.A. L.178 J.D. [Ⓐ Wilson,S.G.&R.]
*LANGUAGES: Spanish and French.
*PRACTICE AREAS: Corporate Finance.
**Doran, Michael C.** ..................... '59 '95 C.225 B.A. L.813 J.D. [Ⓐ Brobeck,P.&H.]
*PRACTICE AREAS: Securities; Venture Capital; Mergers and Acquisitions; Emerging Growth Companies; Corporate.
**Dorf, Eric H.** ......................... '63 '88 C.1044 B.A. L.273 J.D. [Ⓐ Gray C.W.&F.]
*PRACTICE AREAS: Commercial Litigation.
**Dorney, Maureen S.** .................. '57 '90 C.112 A.B. L.1066 J.D. [Ⓐ Gray C.W.&F.]
*PRACTICE AREAS: Technology Licensing; Intellectual Property Protection; Commercial Distribution.
**Doten, Stanley A.** ...................... '39 '65 C.309 A.B. L.813 LL.B. [Morrison&F.]
**Doto, Steven H.** '61 '86 C.264 B.A. L.1292 J.D.
(adm. in NJ; not adm. in CA) [Ⓐ Zevnik H.G.&M.]
*PRACTICE AREAS: Environmental; Complex Litigation; Commercial Litigation; Insurance Coverage Litigation.
**Doty, Stanley E.**, (AV) ......................... '52 '78 C.813 B.A. L.477 J.D. [Doty&S.]
*PRACTICE AREAS: Technology Contracts; Multimedia; Business Formation; Commercial Contracts; Business Planning.

**Doty & Sundheim, (AV)**
**420 Florence Street Suite 200, 94301**
**Telephone: 415-327-0100 Fax: 415-327-0101; Modem: 415-327-1123**
**Email: attorney@dotysund.com**
**Members of Firm: Stanley E. Doty; George M. Sundheim, III. Associates: Jared A. Slosberg; Annette Barlow; Reynaldo A. Durán.**
**Corporate, Real Estate, Intellectual Property, Technology Contracts, Financing, Securities, Trade Secrets, and Computer Law, Employment Law.**
*See Professional Biographies, PALO ALTO, CALIFORNIA*

**Doucette, Brian E.** ...................... '61 '94 C.454 B.A. L.284 J.D [Ⓐ Bialson,B.&S.]
*PRACTICE AREAS: Business Litigation; Business Law.
Dougherty, James F. '33 '76
C.352 B.S.C. L.1026 J.D. V.P. & Gen. Coun., Landbank Investments
**Dow, Karen B.** ........ '54 '79 C.97 B.S. L.345 J.D. [Townsend&T.&C.] (See Pat. Sect.)
*PRACTICE AREAS: Biotechnology and Chemistry Patent Prosecution; Related Technology Agreements.

CAA463P

CALIFORNIA—PALO ALTO MARTINDALE-HUBBELL LAW DIRECTORY 1997

**Downey, Patricia M.** ...................'67 '92 C.112 B.A. L.1065 J.D. [🄰 Fenwick&W.]
*PRACTICE AREAS: Intellectual Property Litigation; Commercial Litigation.
**Driggers, Stephen G.** ...................'50 '93 C.846 B.A. L.813 J.D. [🄰 Wilson,S.G.&R.]
*PRACTICE AREAS: Employee Benefits.
**Drummond, David C.** ...............'63 '89 C.770 B.A. L.813 J.D. [🄰 Wilson,S.G.&R.]
**Drumright, Donald A.** '48 '74 C&L.188 B.A., J.D.
Legal Coun., Intercontinental, Hewlett-Packard Co.
*RESPONSIBILITIES: General Corporate; International.
**Dubinsky, Kerre R.** ........................'64 '91 C.813 B.A. L.770 J.D. [🄰 J.E.Miller]
*PRACTICE AREAS: Family Law.
**DuBois, Lynn Howell** ...............'54 '94 C.788 A.B. L.813 J.D. [🄰 Thoits,L.H.&M.]
*PRACTICE AREAS: ERISA; Employee Benefits; Employment Counselling.
**Dubreuil, Francis W.**, (AVⓣ) '48 '74 C.93 B.A. L.309 J.D.
(adm. in MA; not adm. in CA) [🄲 Wilson,S.G.&R.]
*PRACTICE AREAS: Estate Planning; Business Planning.
Duff, David H., (P.C.), (BV) ..............'34 '63 C&L.813 B.A., LL.B. 420 Florence St.
Dumont, Mary T. ..........................'53 '85 C.112 B.S. L.1065 J.D. 2200 Geng Rd.
**Duncanson, Ella J.** ................................'69 '94 C.112 B.A. L.61 J.D. [🄰 Lakin S.]
*PRACTICE AREAS: Estate Planning.
Dunn, Raymond V. M. ......................'26 '77 C.93 M.A. L.767 J.D. 1010 Bryant
**Dunn, Susan A.** ...........................'57 '86 C.681 B.A. L.813 J.D. [🄲 Fenwick&W.]
*PRACTICE AREAS: Corporate.
Dunn, Tracy J. '62 '91 C&L.966 B.S., J.D.
(adm. in WI; not adm. in CA; Pat.) 379 Lytton Ave.
**Durán, Reynaldo A.** ........................'62 '91 C.605 A.B. L.1065 J.D. [🄰 Doty&S.]
*LANGUAGES: Spanish.
*PRACTICE AREAS: Business and Corporate; Commercial Litigation.
**Durant, Stephen C.** ..........'56 '83 C.602 B.S.E.E. L.188 J.D. [Wilson,S.G.&R.] (Pat.)
*PRACTICE AREAS: Intellectual Property.
Durham, Alan L. ..........................'63 '88 C.668 B.A. L.1066 J.D. 755 Page Mill Rd.
Dwiggins, Richard H. ...................'46 '72 C.605 B.A. L.1068 J.D. 425 Sherman Ave.
**Dy, Cynthia A.** ...............................'69 '94 C.575 B.A. L.813 J.D. [🄰 Wilson,S.G.&R.]
*PRACTICE AREAS: Litigation.
**Dyke, Charles M.** ..........................'60 '92 C.446 B.S. L.209 J.D. [🄰 Gray C.W.&F.]
*PRACTICE AREAS: Employee Benefits; Taxation; ERISA.
**Dylan, Tyler** ........................'61 '92 C.012 B.S. L.1066 J.D. [🄰 Morrison&F.] (Pat.)
**Eakin, James E.** ......'51 '76 C.112 B.S.E.E. L.1068 J.D. [Graham&J.] (Pat.) (⊙Belmont)
*PRACTICE AREAS: Intellectual Property; Licensing Law & Litigation.
**Easterbrook, John W.** ....................'50 '94 C.475 B.A. L.770 J.D. [🄰 Gray C.W.&F.]
*PRACTICE AREAS: Bankruptcy Litigation; Business Litigation; Commercial Loan Transaction.
Eaton, Margaret L. .......'48 '86 C.868 B.S. L.1065 J.D. Asst. Univ. Coun., Stanford Univ.
**Ebertin, Chuck** ..............................'67 '92 C.800 B.S. L.597 J.D. [🄰 Cooley G.]
*PRACTICE AREAS: Patent Litigation; Contract Litigation; General Litigation.
**Edvalson, Ian B.** ..................'66 '96 C.101 B.A./B.S. L.145 J.D. [🄰 Wilson,S.G.&R.]
*LANGUAGES: Korean.
*PRACTICE AREAS: Licensing.
**Edwards, G. Kip**, (AV) ........................'47 '72 C.911 B.A. L.1066 J.D. [🄲 Cohen&O.]
*PRACTICE AREAS: Antitrust, Distribution and Trade Regulation Law; Trademark Litigation.
Edwards, Randall W. ......'70 '95 C.976 B.A. L.597 J.D. 1755 Embarcadero Dr., Suite 200
Effland, Janet G. '48 '74 C&L.36 B.S., J.D.
(adm. in AZ; not adm. in CA) V.P., Patricof & Co. Ventures, Inc.
**Egger, Michael R.** ...'— '91 C.994 B.A. L.1065 J.D. [🄰 Fenwick&W.] (⊙San Francisco)
*PRACTICE AREAS: Intellectual Property; Licensing Law.
**Eggleton, Keith E.** ....................'65 '92 C.1075 B.S. L.597 J.D. [🄰 Wilson,S.G.&R.]
*PRACTICE AREAS: Litigation.
**Ehrman, Richard L.** ................'65 '91 C.112 B.A. L.1049 J.D. [🄰 Thoits,L.H.&M.]
*PRACTICE AREAS: Estate Planning; Trust Litigation; Probate Litigation.
**Elam, Nevan C.** ..........................'67 '93 C.329 B.A. L.309 J.D. [🄰 Wilson,S.G.&R.]
*PRACTICE AREAS: Corporate; Securities; Mergers and Acquisitions.
**El-Bayoumi, Amr A.** .............'65 '94 C.477 B.S.Ch.E. L.276 J.D. [🄰 Brobeck,P.&H.]
*LANGUAGES: Arabic and French.
*PRACTICE AREAS: Technology Law; Intellectual Property; Licensing; Foreign Trade; Middle East Law.
**Elkins, David S.** .........................'64 '90 C.112 A.B. L.1067 J.D. [🄰 Graham&J.]
*PRACTICE AREAS: Litigation.
**Eller, James J.** .............................'52 '77 C.112 B.A. L.770 J.D. [Ferrari,O.O.&B.]⊙
*LANGUAGES: French.
*PRACTICE AREAS: Real Estate Law; Environmental Law.
**Ellerbach, Connie L.** ...................'59 '90 C.350 B.A. L.893 J.D. [🄰 Fenwick&W.]
*PRACTICE AREAS: Intellectual Property; Copyright and Trademark.
**Ellingson, Patricia** ..........................................'40 '82 L.999 J.D. [Peters,P.&E.]
*PRACTICE AREAS: Family Law.
Elman, John L. ...........................'34 '81 C.252 B.A. L.999 J.D. 4150 Hubbart Dr.
**Elmer, Russell S.** .....................'64 '90 C.813 A.B. L.1066 J.D. [🄰 Gray C.W.&F.]
*PRACTICE AREAS: General Civil Litigation; Employment Litigation.
**Elson, Vera M.** ...................'— '91 C.112 B.S. L.800 J.D. [🄰 Wilson,S.G.&R.] (Pat.)
*LANGUAGES: German and Spanish.
*PRACTICE AREAS: Intellectual Property Litigation.
Ely, John Hart ...................'38 '65 C.674 A.B. L.976 LL.B. Dean, Stanford Law Sch.
Emami, Zahra ..............................'57 '92 C.476 B.A. L.770 J.D. 400 Hamilton Ave.
**Emerson, David T.** ........................'54 '93 C.97 B.S. L.1066 J.D. [🄰 Cooley G.]
*PRACTICE AREAS: Business Law; Securities Law.
Emmer, Jamie L. ..........................'49 '76 C.597 B.A. L.623 J.D. 517 Byron St.
**Emmer, Maurice S.** ..........................'47 '78 C.659 B.S. L.145 J.D. [Baker&M.]
*PRACTICE AREAS: Taxation.
**Eng, U. P. Peter** ......................'67 '93 C.860 B.S.E.E. L.990 J.D. [🄰 Graham&J.]

**Enterprise Law Group, Inc.**
**(See Menlo Park)**

**Epstein, Rebecca L.** ...................'68 '93 C&L.813 B.A., J.D. [🄰 Wilson,S.G.&R.]
*PRACTICE AREAS: Securities Litigation; General Commercial Litigation.
Epstein, Ronald S. ......................'64 '89 C.228 B.S. L.1066 J.D. 650 Page Mill Rd.
**Erasmus, Melanie E.** ...............................'58 '96 L.813 J.D. [🄰 Gray C.W.&F.]
**Erb, Brian C.** ............................'63 '90 C.629 B.S. L.950 J.D. [🄰 Wilson,S.G.&R.]
*PRACTICE AREAS: Corporate; Securities.
**Estrada, David J.** .............................'68 '93 C.112 B.A. L.1066 J.D. [🄰 Cooley G.]
*PRACTICE AREAS: Intellectual Property Law.

**Etnire, Geoffrey C.**
**(See Pleasanton)**

**Ezrati, Lester D.** ......'51 '77 C.696 B.A. L.93 J.D. Gen. Tax Coun., Hewlett-Packard Co.
*RESPONSIBILITIES: Tax.
Fabela, Robert ..........................'65 '90 C.112 B.A. L.1097 J.D. 650 Page Mill Rd.
**Fackler, Stephen W.** ..........................'57 '84 C.309 A.B. L.813 J.D. [Cooley G.]
*PRACTICE AREAS: Employee Benefits; Executive Compensation; Trade Associations; Public Charities and Private Foundations.
**Factor, Craig H.** ...........................'68 '94 C.228 A.B. L.309 J.D. [🄰 Wilson,S.G.&R.]
*PRACTICE AREAS: Corporate; Securities; Communications.
**Fagan, Andrew L.** .................'59 '85 C.911 B.A. L.1065 J.D. [🄰 Bryant,C.O.M.&B.]
*PRACTICE AREAS: Manufacturers Representative Litigation; Business Litigation; Real Estate Litigation.
**Fahn, Meredith L.** ....................'63 '91 C.659 B.A. L.831 J.D. [🄰 Bryant,C.O.M.&B.]
*PRACTICE AREAS: Litigation; Business Law; Estate Disputes; Trials and Appeals.
**Fall, Janice Leyrer** .....................'54 '84 C.112 B.A. L.1066 J.D. [🄰 Wilson,S.G.&R.]

Fallon, Shannon ......................'63 '90 C.846 B.B.A. L.1065 J.D. 400 Hamilton Ave.
**Fanning, David A.** '61 '88
C.101 B.S. L.1065 J.D. [Kolisch H.D.M.&H.] (See Pat. Sect.)⊙
*PRACTICE AREAS: Patent, Trademark and Unfair Competition.
**Faulkner, Kevin A.** .............................'61 '86 C.263 B.A. L.893 J.D. [🄰 Morrison&F.]
Feeley, Daniel M., (AV) ..................'14 '40 C&L.813 A.B., J.D. 1120 Hamilton Ave.‡
Feeley, Jerome W., (AV) .....................'21 '49 C.813 B.A. L.767 LL.B. 2555 Park Blvd.
Fehl, Kenneth P. .........................'52 '76 C.112 B.A. L.1065 J.D. 736 E. Meadow Dr.
**Feinberg, Ian N.**, (AV) ...........................'54 '79 C&L.813 A.B., J.D. [Gray C.W.&F.]
*PRACTICE AREAS: Intellectual Property Litigation; Antitrust Litigation; Distribution Litigation.
Feinberg, Sidney ...................'16 '41 C.112 B.A. L.1066 LL.B. 674 Wildwood Ln.
**Feldman, Boris**, (AV) ...........................'55 '80 C&L.976 B.A., J.D. [Wilson,S.G.&R.]
*PRACTICE AREAS: Litigation; Securities Law.
**Feldman, Robert P.** .......................'51 '76 C.1044 B.A. L.178 J.D. [Wilson,S.G.&R.]
*PRACTICE AREAS: Litigation.
**Feldstein, Steven R.**, (AV) ...........'48 '74 C.605 B.A. L.1066 J.D. [Heller E.W.&M.]
*PRACTICE AREAS: Labor and Employment.
**Fennell, Chris F.** ........................'61 '89 C.112 B.S. L.1068 J.D. [Wilson,S.G.&R.]
*PRACTICE AREAS: Corporate Law; Securities.
Fenner, Thomas W. ...........'51 '76 C&L.813 B.A., J.D. Sr. Univ. Coun., Stanford Univ.
**Fenwick, William A.**, (AV) ..............'38 '68 C.801 B.S. L.880 LL.B. [Fenwick&W.]
*PRACTICE AREAS: Litigation; Intellectual Property.

**Fenwick & West LLP, (AV)**
**Two Palo Alto Square, 94306⊙**
**Telephone: 415-494-0600 Fax: 415-494-1417**
**URL: http://www.fenwick.com**
**Members of Firm: Sally M. Abel; Roberta Cairney (Resident in San Francisco Office); Frederick R. Chilton, Jr.; Kenneth B. Clark; Timothy A. Covington; Jacqueline A. Daunt; Gordon K. Davidson; Dennis R. DeBroeck; Robert B. Dellenbach; William A. Fenwick; John C. Fox; Kathryn Jean Fritz (Palo Alto and San Francisco Offices); James P. Fuller; Jennifer L. Fuller; James C. Garahan; Roger M. Golden (Resident in Washington, D.C. Office); Fred M. Greguras; Garry S. Grossman (Resident in Washington, D.C. Office); David L. Hayes; David W. Healy; Bruce W. Jenett; Joel D. Kellman; C. Kevin Kelso; Patricia Nicely Kopf; Barry J. Kramer; Michael M. Landa (Resident in Washington, D.C. Office); Kenneth A. Linhares; Edwin N. Lowe; Patricia M. Lucas; Bruce F. Mackler (Resident in Washington, D.C. Office); Stuart P. Meyer; Charlene M. Morrow; Mark S. Ostrau; Michael J. Patrick; Edward J. Radlo; Walter T. Raineri; I. Joel Riff; Timothy K. Roake; Eileen Duffy Robinett; Paul H. Roskoph; Ronald B. Schrotenboer; Laird H. Simons, III; David W. Slaby; Albert C. Smith; Scott P. Spector; Blakeney Stafford; John J. Steele; Claude M. Stern; Mark C. Stevens (Palo Alto and San Francisco Offices); Greg T. Sueoka; Gail E. Suniga; Hirohisa Tachibana; John T. Westermeier, Jr. (Resident in Washington, D.C. Office); Mitchell Zimmerman. Of Counsel: Susan A. Dunn; Savery M. Gradoville (Resident in Washington, D.C. Office); John W. Kastelic; Valarie L. McInroy; David K. Michaels (Not admitted in CA); Katherine T. Tallman. Special Counsel: Craig A. Selness; James T. Given; John M. Mason (Not admitted in CA); William J. McCarren; Amir H. Raubvogel. Associates: Susan M. Alkema; Phyllis E. Andes (Resident in Washington, D.C. Office); Barton W.S. Bassett; Harry Boadwee; Elizabeth K. Bohannon; Kimberly A. Bomar; Timothy P. Boudreau (Not admitted in CA); Mona Chandra; G. Chin Chao; Leslie F. Chard III; Robert Chow; Kaui'ilani Chun; Rodger Cole; William F. Colgin, Jr. (Not admitted in CA); Jeanine M. Corr; JoAnn Corti Covington; Tyler R. Cozzens; Danielle C. Cullinane; Catherine L. Curtiss; Gay Crosthwait Danforth; Marilyn Tiki Dare; Paolo M. (Paul) Dau; Valerie M. Dawson; Virginia K. DeMarchi; Richard L. Dickson; Jeffery L. Donovan; Patricia M. Downey; Michael R. Egger (Palo Alto and San Francisco Offices); Connie L. Ellerbach; William P. Fitzpatrick (Palo Alto and San Francisco Office); David L. Forst; Virginia M. Fournier; Robert A. Freedman; Eric D. Frothingham; Gary E. Gamerman (Resident in Washington, D.C. Office); Rashmi Garde; James Gibbons-Shapiro; Rachel Hersey; Dorothy L. Hines; Christine Linh-Chau Hoang; Brian M. Hoffman (Not admitted in CA); Josephine T. Hucko; Todd A. Huge; Brian S. Kelly (Not admitted in CA); Christine L. Kopitzke; Jane Kranwinkle; Tim J. Lane; Mark A. Leahy; Michelle K. Lee; Tina M. Lessani; Andrew Luh; Carol L. Martin; Michael J. McAdam; Sandra Smith McCoy; David C. McIntyre; John T. McNelis; E. Porter Merriman (Palo Alto and San Francisco Offices); Kelly C. Mulholland (Not admitted in CA); Lisa D. Noble; James K. Okamoto; Carlton X. Osborne; Rajiv P. Patel; Tram Thi Phi; John F. Platz; Mark E. Porter; Patrick E. Premo; John G. Ryan; Robert R. Sachs; Michael A. Sands; Melissa H. Sayer; Jefferson F. Scher; Jason Scully; John J. Sullivan (Resident in San Francisco Office); Shawna M. Swanson; Mark C. Terrano; Christopher M. Tobin; Lynda M. Twomey; Edward M. Urschel; Jeffrey R. Vetter; Adam W. Wegner; Jeremy S. Woodburn; Mollee Sue Oxman Zoken.**
**General Practice. Corporate, Securities, International (Business, Trade and Customs, Trademark and Patent), Intellectual Property (Copyright, Trademark and Patent), Computer and High Technology Law, Biotechnology Law, Food and Drug Administration Law, Government Procurement, Litigation and Alternative Dispute Resolution, Antitrust and Trade Regulation, Tax, Estate Planning and Probate.**
**Washington, D.C. Office: Suite 650, 1920 N Street, N.W. Telephone: 202-463-6300. Fax: 202-463-6520, 202-887-5143.**
**San Francisco, California Office: 100 Embarcadero, 3rd Floor. Telephone: 415-281-1330. Fax: 415-281-1350.**

***See Professional Biographies, PALO ALTO, CALIFORNIA***

Ferguson, Richard A. .........'49 '76 C&L.813 B.S., J.D. 301 University Ave., Suite 480
**Fernandez, Dorothy L.** ..............'70 '96 C.813 A.B. L.309 J.D. [🄰 Wilson,S.G.&R.]
*PRACTICE AREAS: Litigation.
**Ferrari, Clarence J., Jr.**, (AV) ........'34 '60 C&L.813 A.B., LL.B. [Ferrari,O.O.&B.]⊙
*PRACTICE AREAS: Federal and State Taxation; Estate Planning; Trusts and Estates; Tax Litigation.

**Ferrari, Olsen, Ottoboni & Bebb, A Professional Corporation, (AV)**
**550 Hamilton Avenue, 94301⊙**
**Telephone: 415-327-3233**
**Clarence J. Ferrari, Jr. (Certified Specialist, Taxation Law, The State Bar of California Board of Legal Specialization); Kent E. Olsen (Certified Specialist, Taxation Law, The State Bar of California Board of Legal Specialization); John M. Ottoboni; Richard S. Bebb; James J. Eller. Of Counsel: Edward M. Alvarez (Certified Specialist, Taxation Law, The State Bar of California Board of Legal Specialization).**
**Corporation, Securities, Environmental and Health Law. State and Federal Taxation, Labor, Sports and Real Estate Law. Estate Planning, Trusts and Probate Law. General Civil Trial Practice in all Federal and State Courts. Administrative Law.**
**San Jose, California Office: 333 West Santa Clara Street, Suite 700. Telephone: 408-280-0535.**

***See Professional Biographies, PALO ALTO, CALIFORNIA***

Ferreira, Lisa ...........................'58 '84 C.813 A.B. L.309 J.D. 1401 Cowper St.
**Ferrell, John S.** ..........'57 '91 C.846 B.S.E.E. L.770 J.D. [Carr,D.&F.] (See Pat. Sect.)
**Ferruolo, Stephen C.** ..................'49 '92 C.918 B.A. L.813 J.D. [Heller E.W.&M.]
*PRACTICE AREAS: Corporate Securities.
Field, Bret ......................'67 '92 C.197 A.B. L.1065 J.D. 850 Hansen Way (Pat.)
**Fields, Helen G.F.** ..................'70 '96 C.104 B.A. L.813 J.D. [🄰 Brobeck,P.&H.]
*PRACTICE AREAS: General Corporate Practice.
Fike, Edward G. '66 '91 C.363 B.A. L.770 J.D.
V.P. & Gen. Coun., Hobee's Calif. Restaurants
**Filion, Robin L.** ..........................'51 '85 C.112 B.S. L.1065 J.D. [Baker&M.]
*PRACTICE AREAS: Securities and Financial Products; Intellectual Property Law; Computers and Technology; Commercial Litigation; Civil Litigation.
Filippi, John M. .......................'15 '46 C.770 B.S. L.284 J.D. 425 Sherman Ave.‡

**Finch, Montgomery & Wright, (AV) BR**
**350 Cambridge Avenue, Suite 175, 94306**
**Telephone: 415-327-0888 Fax: 415-327-5316**
**Members of Firm: Toby F. Montgomery; Barbara P. Wright; Nathan C. Finch (1909-1990).**
**Estate Planning and Probate, Trusts, Estate and Gift Tax and Nonprofit Organizations.**

***See Professional Biographies, PALO ALTO, CALIFORNIA***

**Finnan, Fleischut & Associates**
**3030 Hansen Way, Suite 120, 94304**
**Telephone: 415-493-5790 FAX: 415-493-2641**

(This Listing Continued)

CAA464P

**Finnan, Fleischut & Associates (Continued)**
**Members of Firm: Christopher J. Fleischut; Robert (Jack) Rix; Michael E. Gill.**
**Immigration and Nationality Law.**
*See Professional Biographies, PALO ALTO, CALIFORNIA*

**Finocchio, Melissa A.** ... '64 '90 C&L.770 B.A., J.D. [[A] Cooley G.]
*PRACTICE AREAS: Patent Litigation; Intellectual Property Litigation; Commercial Litigation; Employment Litigation.
**Finseth, Eric J.** ... '65 '94 C.309 B.A. L.178 J.D. [[A] Wilson,S.G.&R.]
*LANGUAGES: German and French.
*PRACTICE AREAS: Corporate; Securities; Partnerships; Limited Liability Companies.
**Firth, Jason D.** '66 '93 C.101 B.A. L.276 J.D.
(adm. in TX; not adm. in CA) [[A] Cooley G.]
*LANGUAGES: Portuguese.
*PRACTICE AREAS: Trademark; Copyright; Licensing.
**Fischer, Heike** ... '65 '96 L.061 [[A] Morrison&F.]
*LANGUAGES: German.
Fischl, Louis J. ... '23 '66 C.813 A.B. L.770 J.D. 405 Marlowe St.‡

**Fish & Neave, (AV⊤) [BR]**
**Fish, Richardson & Neave, New York (1916-1969)**
**525 University Avenue Suite 300, 94301⊙**
**Telephone: 415-617-4000 Telecopier: 415-617-4090**
**Resident Members: Edward F. Mullowney; Robert J. Goldman (Not admitted in CA); Norman H. Beamer; Mark D. Rowland; Edward J. DeFranco. Resident Associates: Vicki S. Veenker; Nicola A. Pisano; Gabrielle E. Higgins; Kevin P.B. Johnson; Petrina S. Hsi (Not admitted in CA); Derek Minihane (Not admitted in CA); Kurtis D. MacFerrin; Ann Marie Whitley (Not admitted in CA).**
**Intellectual Property including Patent, Trademark, Trade Secret, Copyright and Unfair Competition, Unfair Trade Practice and Antitrust Law. Trials and Appeals in all Federal and State Courts and Governmental Administrative Agencies.**
**New York, New York Office: 1251 Avenue of the Americas. Telephone: 212-596-9000. Telex: 14-8367. Cable Address: Fishneave. Telecopier: 212-596-9090.**
*See Professional Biographies, PALO ALTO, CALIFORNIA*

**Fish & Richardson P.C.**
**(See Menlo Park)**

Fisher, David B., (BV) ... '53 '79 C.112 A.B. L.770 J.D. 407 Sherman Ave.
**Fisher, George C.**, (AV) ... '43 '67 C.906 B.A. L.813 LL.B. [Ritchey F.W.&K.]
*PRACTICE AREAS: Business Litigation; Partnerships; Construction; Real Estate; Technology Litigation.
Fisher, Gerald M. '35 '69 C.223 B.S.E.E. L.273 J.D.
(adm. in MD; not adm. in CA) 1491 Greenwood Ave.
**Fitts, Renée A.** ... '52 '91 C.145 B.A. L.1066 J.D. [[C] Townsend&T.&C.] (See Pat. Sect.)
*PRACTICE AREAS: Patent Law.
**Fitzpatrick, Christine** ... '63 '88 C.770 B.S. L.1065 J.D. [[A] Morrison&F.]
**Fitzpatrick, Michael J.** ... '52 '84 C&L.1169 B.A., J.D. [Hawkins,B.&F.]⊙
*PRACTICE AREAS: Personal Injury Law; Product Liability Law; Civil Litigation; Insurance Bad Faith.
**Fitzpatrick, William P.** '66 '95
C.309 B.A. L.178 J.D. [[A] Fenwick&W.] (⊙San Francisco)
*PRACTICE AREAS: Intellectual Property; Licensing Law.
**Flanagan, Mark D.** ... '62 '87 C.112 B.A. L.1066 J.D. [Slenkovich&F.]
*PRACTICE AREAS: White Collar Criminal Defense; Business Litigation; Anti-Trust Litigation.
**Flanzraich, Neil W.**, (AV) ... '43 '69 C&L.309 A.B., J.D. [Heller E.W.&M.]
*PRACTICE AREAS: Life Sciences/Health Care includes: Corporate; Strategic Alliances; Transactional; Regulatory, Intellectual Property related to Pharmaceutical; Biotech; Medical Device Cos.; General Corporate and Transactional; Environmental.
**Flaum, Keith A.** ... '63 '89 C.112 B.A. L.1067 J.D. [[A] Cooley G.]
*PRACTICE AREAS: Mergers and Acquisitions; Corporate Securities.

**Flehr, Hohbach, Test, Albritton & Herbert, (AV)**
**Suite 200, 850 Hansen Way, 94304-1017⊙**
**Telephone: 415-494-8700 Telefax: 415-494-8771**
**Resident Attorneys: Harold C. Hohbach; Aldo J. Test; Thomas O. Herbert; Edward S. Wright; James A. Sheridan; Gary S. Williams; C. Michael Zimmerman; Steven F. Caserza; William S. Galliani. Associates: Janet Elizabeth Muller; Edward N. Bachand; R. Michael Ananian; David C. Ashby; Maria S. Swiatek. Of Counsel: Bertram I. Rowland; Julian Caplan.**
**Patent, Trademark, Copyright, Unfair Competition, Trade Secrets, Biotechnology and Computer Law. Trials.**
**San Francisco, California Office: Suite 3400, Four Embarcadero Center. Telephone: 415-781-1989.**
*See Professional Biographies, PALO ALTO, CALIFORNIA*

**Fleischut, Christopher J.** ... '55 '85 C.976 B.A. L.1065 J.D. [Finnan,F.&Assoc.]
*LANGUAGES: Russian, German.
*PRACTICE AREAS: Immigration and Nationality Law (100%).
Fletcher, Lee A. ... '57 '83 C.112 A.B. L.770 J.D. 31 Regent Pl.
**Flicker, Michael R.**, (AV) ... '40 '66 C.976 B.S. L.813 LL.B. [Flicker&K.]
*PRACTICE AREAS: Family Law.

**Flicker & Kerin, (AV) [BR]**
**Suite 460, 285 Hamilton, P.O. Box 840, 94302**
**Telephone: 415-321-0947 Fax: 415-326-9722**
**Members of Firm: Michael R. Flicker (Certified Specialist, Family Law, The State Bar of California Board of Legal Specialization); Anthony J. Kerin, III. Associates: Rhesa C. Rubin; Cheri A. Bell.**
**Civil and Trial Practice. Family, Personal Injury, Negligence, Business, Corporate and Real Estate Law.**
*See Professional Biographies, PALO ALTO, CALIFORNIA*

**Flint, Elizabeth R.** ... '60 '86 C.228 B.A. L.569 J.D. [Wilson,S.G.&R.]
*PRACTICE AREAS: Corporate Law; Securities.
Flocks, Franklin J., (BV) ... '48 '73 C.112 A.B. L.770 J.D. 260 Sheridan Ave.
**Fockler, Herbert P.**, (AV) ... '59 '84 C.674 A.B. L.309 J.D. [Wilson,S.G.&R.]
*PRACTICE AREAS: Corporate Law; Securities.
**Fogg, John M.** ... '68 '94 C.976 B.A. L.178 J.D. [[A] Gray C.W.&F.]
*PRACTICE AREAS: Corporate; Securities.
**Foley, David R.** ... '46 '74 C.309 A.B. L.178 J.D. [Wise&S.]
**Fong, Diane Jean** ... '54 '84 C.813 B.S. L.1068 J.D. [[A] Wilson,S.G.&R.]
*PRACTICE AREAS: Estate Planning.
**Forbes, Hal E.**, (BV) ... '39 '69 C.813 B.A. L.767 J.D. [[C] Cohen&O.]
*PRACTICE AREAS: Estate Planning; Probate; Trust Administration; Estate Tax.
**Fore, John A.** ... '56 '84 C.976 B.A. L.569 J.D. [Wilson,S.G.&R.]
*LANGUAGES: German.
*PRACTICE AREAS: Corporate Law; Securities.
**Forst, David L.** ... '67 '93 C.674 A.B. L.813 J.D. [[A] Fenwick&W.]
*PRACTICE AREAS: Taxation.
**Forstall, Molly Brown** ... '69 '94 C&L.813 A.B., J.D. [[A] Cooley G.]
*PRACTICE AREAS: General Litigation; Employment.
Foster, Winfield W. ... '36 '62 C.674 A.B. L.813 J.D. 425 Sherman Ave.
**Fournier, E. J.** ... '66 '92 C.145 B.A. L.659 J.D. [[A] Heller E.W.&M.] ‡
**Fournier, Virginia M.** ... '63 '93 C.173 B.A. L.770 J.D. [[A] Fenwick&W.]
*PRACTICE AREAS: Intellectual Property Law; Licensing Law.
**Fowler, Mark** ... '61 '86 C.112 A.B. L.813 J.D. [Gray C.W.&F.]
*PRACTICE AREAS: Commercial Litigation; Intellectual Property Litigation; ERISA Litigation; Real Estate Litigation.
**Fox, Deborah S.** ... '— '94 C.112 B.S. L.309 J.D. [[A] Wilson,S.G.&R.]
*PRACTICE AREAS: Corporate.
**Fox, Harry L.**, (AV) ... '56 '83 C.112 A.B. L.309 J.D. [Aufmuth,F.W.&L.]
*PRACTICE AREAS: Taxation; Real Estate; Partnerships.

**Fox, John C.** ... '52 '76 C.112 B.A. L.273 J.D. [Fenwick&W.]
*PRACTICE AREAS: Employment and Labor.
**Fox, Stephen P.** '41 '70 C.597 B.S.E.E. L.273 J.D.
Assoc. Gen. Coun. & Dir., Intell. Prop., Hewlett-Packard Co. (Pat.)
*RESPONSIBILITIES: Intellectual Property/Compliance; Manager/Director Patents.

**Fragomen, Del Rey & Bernsen, P.C., (AV)**
**525 University Avenue, Suite 1450, 94301⊙**
**Telephone: 415-323-7557 Facsimile: 415-323-5030**
**URL: http://www.fragomen.com**
**Peter H. Loewy;—Flora Houn Hoffman; Barbara C. Y. Laam; Jin Yi Park.**
**U.S. and Foreign Immigration and Nationality Law.**
**New York, New York Office: 515 Madison Avenue. Telephone: 212-688-8555. Facsimile: 212-319-5236; 212-758-7215.**
**Washington, D.C. Office: 1212 New York Avenue, N.W., Suite 850. Telephone: 202-223-5515. Facsimile: 202-371-2898.**
**Coral Gables, Florida Office: 890 South Dixie Highway. Telephone: 305-666-4655. Facsimile: 305-666-4467.**
**Chicago, Illinois Office: 300 South Wacker Drive, Suite 2900. Telephone: 312-263-6101. Facsimile: 312-431-0517.**
**Los Angeles, California Office: 11400 West Olympic Boulevard, Suite 1050. Telephone: 310-473-8700. Facsimile: 310-473-5383.**
**San Francisco, California Office: 88 Kearny Street, Suite 1300. Telephone: 415-986-1446. Facsimile: 415-986-7964.**
**Stamford Connecticut Office: Fragomen, Del Rey & Bernsen, 1177 High Ridge Road. Telephone: 203-321-1278. Facsimile: 203-321-1279.**
**Short Hills, New Jersey Office: Fragomen, Del Rey & Bernsen, 51 John F. Kennedy Parkway. Telephone: 201-564-5222. FAX: 201-564-5230.**
*See Professional Biographies, PALO ALTO, CALIFORNIA*

**Fram, Robert D.** ... '55 '86 C.674 A.B. L.309 J.D. [Heller E.W.&M.]
*PRACTICE AREAS: Intellectual Property and Antitrust Litigation.
**Frank, Brenda R.** ... '69 '95 C.1044 B.S. L.569 J.D. [[A] Wilson,S.G.&R.]
**Frankle, Diane Holt** ... '53 '79 C.970 B.A. L.276 J.D. [Gray C.W.&F.]
*PRACTICE AREAS: Corporate and Securities; Mergers and Acquisitions.
Franklin, Marc A. '32 '56 C&L.188 A.B., LL.B.
(adm. in NY; not adm. in CA) Prof. of Law, Stanford Univ.
**Franklin, Robert A.** ... '54 '80 C.770 B.S. L.809 J.D. [[A] Murray&M.]
*PRACTICE AREAS: Commercial Litigation; Business Workouts; Bankruptcy Reorganizations; Creditors Remedies.
**Fredericks, Karen P.** '71 '96 C.914 B.A. L.659 J.D.
(adm. in NJ; not adm. in CA) [[A] Wilson,S.G.&R.]
*PRACTICE AREAS: Corporate.
Freed, Marc-David ... '47 '74 C.112 B.A. L.1065 J.D. 2460 Agnes Way
**Freedman, Adele C.** ... '64 '90 C.188 B.A. L.262 J.D. [[A] Wilson,S.G.&R.]
*LANGUAGES: French.
*PRACTICE AREAS: Corporate; Securities.
**Freedman, Robert A.** ... '66 '93 C.95 A.B. L.813 J.D. [[A] Fenwick&W.]
*PRACTICE AREAS: Corporate.
**Freeman, Carol R.** ... '64 '93 C.178 B.A. L.767 J.D. [[A] Brobeck,P.&H.]
*PRACTICE AREAS: Labor; Tax.
**Freeman, William S.** ... '52 '78 C&L.309 A.B., J.D. [Cooley G.]
*PRACTICE AREAS: Securities Litigation; Accountant Liability.
**Freidenrich, John**, (AV) ... '37 '64 C&L.813 A.B., LL.B. [Gray C.W.&F.] ‡
**French, Thomas M.**, (AV) ... '41 '72 C.108 B.S. L.345 J.D. [Gray C.W.&F.]
**Freyberg, Derek P.** ... '48 '82 C.061 B.Sc. L.770 J.D. [[C] Heller E.W.&M.] (Pat.)
*LANGUAGES: Japanese.
Friedman, Jeff ... '69 '94 C.911 B.A. L.770 J.D. 650 Page Mill Rd.
Friedman, Jeffrey ... '46 '72 C.475 B.A. L.904 J.D. 650 Page Mill Rd.
Friedman, Lawrence M. '30 '51 C&L.145 A.B., J.D.
(adm. in IL; not adm. in CA) Prof. of Law, Stanford Univ.
**Friedman, Richard** ... '62 '87 C.696 B.A. L.145 J.D. [Heller E.W.&M.]
**Friedman, Susan J.** ... '— '92 C.788 B.A. L.276 J.D. [[A] Reed&R.] (See Pat. Sect.)
*PRACTICE AREAS: Patent Law; Patent Preparation and Prosecution; Chemistry; Biotechnology.
**Friedrich, Barbara** ... '65 '94 L.770 J.D. [[A] Gray C.W.&F.]
*PRACTICE AREAS: Corporate and Securities.
**Fritz, Kathryn Jean** ... '59 '86 C.112 B.A. L.276 J.D. [Fenwick&W.] (⊙San Francisco)
*PRACTICE AREAS: Intellectual Property Litigation; Trademark and Copyright Law; General Business Litigation.
**Frothingham, Eric D.** ... '— '95 C.882 B.A. L.813 J.D. [[A] Fenwick&W.]
*PRACTICE AREAS: Corporate.
**Fruchtman, Tamar** ... '66 '91 C.884 B.A. L.1065 J.D. [[A] Brobeck,P.&H.]
*PRACTICE AREAS: Corporate Law; Intellectual Property Law.
**Fthenakis, Basil P.**, (AV) ... '55 '79 C.112 A.B. L.770 J.D. [Fthenakis&C.]
*PRACTICE AREAS: Antitrust; Business and Commercial Litigation; Intellectual Property; Securities; Corporate Transactions.

**Fthenakis & Colvin, (AV) [BR]**
**540 University Avenue, Suite 300, 94301**
**Telephone: 415-326-1397 Telecopier: 415-326-3203**
**Members of Firm: Basil P. Fthenakis; Oliver P. Colvin.**
**General Civil and Trial Practice in all State and Federal Courts Including, Antitrust and Trade Regulation, Business Torts, Commercial Contracts, Construction and Real Property Disputes, Corporate Law, Director's and Officer's Liability, Distribution and Licensing, Environmental and Toxic Torts, Intellectual Property, Media Law, Product Distribution, Provisional Remedies, Real Estate Law, RICO, Sales and Leasing, Secured and Unsecured Lending, Securities Fraud, Securities Law, Suretyship, Trade Secrets, Corporate Transactions and Unfair Competition.**
*See Professional Biographies, PALO ALTO, CALIFORNIA*

Fuhrman, Fredk. E. ... '15 '38 C&L.966 Ph.B., LL.B.,J.D 4040 Amarante‡
**Fulkerson, Timothy R.** ... '63 '94 C.112 B.A. L.464 J.D. [[A] Wise&S.]
Fuller, Dale F., (AV) ... '35 '65 C&L.966 B.S., J.D. 862 San Antonio Ave.
**Fuller, James P.**, (AV) ... '42 '71 C.569 B.S. L.262 J.D. [Fenwick&W.]
*PRACTICE AREAS: Taxation.
**Fuller, Jennifer L.** ... '58 '87 C.940 B.A. L.426 J.D. [Fenwick&W.]
*PRACTICE AREAS: Taxation.
Fung, Richard C. '57 '83 C.767 B.A. L.911 J.D.
(adm. in MA; not adm. in CA) Sr. Contract Mgr., The Stanford Univ. Clinic
**Furbush, David M.**, (AV) ... '54 '78 C&L.309 B.A., J.D. [Brobeck,P.&H.]
*PRACTICE AREAS: Securities Litigation; Intellectual Property Litigation.
**Furlong, Thomas W.** ... '58 '87 C.145 A.B. L.597 J.D. [Gray C.W.&F.]
*PRACTICE AREAS: Securities; Intellectual Property.
**Furniss, Daniel J.**, (AV) ... '51 '76 C.813 A.B. L.1066 J.D. [Townsend&T.&C.]
**Fusich, Cecelia C.** ... '60 '89 C.112 B.A. L.1066 J.D. [[A] Zevnik H.G.&M.]
*PRACTICE AREAS: Environmental Law.
Gaal, Barbara S. ... '57 '83 C.118 B.A. L.813 J.D. Coun., Calif. Law Revision Comm.
**Gallardo, Gilbert** ... '65 '94 C.770 B.S. L.112 J.D. [[A] Gray C.W.&F.]
*PRACTICE AREAS: Corporate and Securities.
**Galliani, William S.** ... '62 '90 C.597 B.A. L.770 J.D. [Flehr,H.T.A.&H.] (See Pat. Sect.)
**Galligan, Kevin M.** ... '65 '95 C.174 B.S./B.A. L.1066 J.D. [[A] Wilson,S.G.&R.]
*PRACTICE AREAS: Corporate Law; Securities.

CAA465P

**Gallo, Gregory M.**, (AV) . . . . . . . . . . . . . . . .'41 '69 C.966 B.S. L.309 J.D. [Gray C.W.&F.]
*TRANSACTIONS: Synoptic Communications in merger with Wellfleet Communications to form Networks; General Magic Initial public offering; Network Peripherals and Microtech Research initial public offerings; Network General Corporation in acquisition of Progressive Computing, Inc.; Crystal Semicon debtor in acquisition of Pro Tools, Inc.
*PRACTICE AREAS: Corporate Securities; Mergers and Acquisitions; Venture Capital Financing; Technology Joint Ventures; Technology Licensing.
**Gallo, Penny Howe**, (AV) . . . . . . . . . . . . . . .'45 '70 C.112 B.A. L.309 J.D. [Gray C.W.&F.]
*LANGUAGES: French.
*TRANSACTIONS: Designed and implemented ESOP for national, privately held ESOP to buy out outside investors and retain employee ownership; Designed and qualified with IRS 401(k) plans for numerous public and private companies; Represented plan fiduciaries in ERISA litigation and governmental investigations.
*PRACTICE AREAS: ERISA; Employee Benefits; Executive Compensation.
**Galloway, Michelle Greer** . . . . . . . . . . . . . . . . . . . .'64 '89 C&L.813 B.A., J.D. [A Cooley G.]
*PRACTICE AREAS: Intellectual Property; Technology Litigation; General Litigation.
**Galvin, Robert M.** . . . . . . . . . . . . . . . . . . . .'68 '94 C.112 B.A. L.1068 J.D. [A Cooley G.]
*PRACTICE AREAS: Technology Litigation.
**Gamlen, Tod L.** . . . . . . . . . . . . . . . . . . . . . . .'51 '78 C.813 B.S.C.E. L.276 J.D. [Baker&M.]
*PRACTICE AREAS: Commercial Litigation; Computers and Technology; Intellectual Property Law.
**Garahan, James C.** . . . . . . . . . . . . . . . . . . . .'45 '80 C.311 B.A. L.1066 J.D. [Fenwick&W.]
*PRACTICE AREAS: Taxation.
**Garde, Rashmi** . . . . . . . . . . . . . . . . . . . . . .'— '95 C.112 B.A. L.1066 J.D. [A Fenwick&W.]
*PRACTICE AREAS: Corporate.
Garfinkel, Neil M. '66 '92 C.309 A.B. L.178 J.D.
(adm. in NY; not adm. in CA) Summit Partners
Garms, Margaret E. . . . . . . . . . . . . . . . . . . . .'51 '78 C.813 A.B. L.966 J.D. 2879 Louis Rd.‡
**Garono, Lisa A.** . . . . . . . . . . .'61 '87 C.363 B.S. L.608 J.D. [B Carr,D.&F.] (See Pat. Sect.)
**Garrett, W. H. Baird** . . . . . . . . . . . . . .'61 '96 C.645 B.A. L.893 J.D. [A Wilson,S.G.&R.]
*PRACTICE AREAS: Technology; Licensing.
**Garvey, William P.** . . . . . . . . . . . . . . . . . . . . . . .'65 '94 C.870 B.S. L.813 J.D. [A Brobeck,P.&H.]
Garvin, Dennis E. . . . . . . . . . . . . . . . . . . . . . . .'57 '82 C.378 B.A. L.813 J.D. 525 Univ. Ave.
Gates, Mark T., Jr., (AV) . . . . . . . . . . . . . . .'37 '63 C.197 B.A. L.813 LL.B. 700 Emerson St.
**Gelblum, Michael A.** . . . . . . . . . . . .'60 '94 C.674 B.S.E. L.025 LL.B. [A Townsend&T.&C.]
**Geoghegan, Brian** . . . . . . . . . . . . . . . . . . . .'55 '85 C.994 B.A. L.1066 J.D. [A Baker&M.]
*PRACTICE AREAS: Intellectual Property Law.
**George, Hanna Casper** . . . . . . . . . . . . . .'67 '93 C.976 B.A. L.893 J.D. [A Brobeck,P.&H.]
*LANGUAGES: German and French.
*PRACTICE AREAS: Labor and Employment Law; Litigation.
**George, Roger Edward** . . . . . . . . . . . . . . . .'66 '92 C&L.893 B.S., J.D. [A Wilson,S.G.&R.]
*PRACTICE AREAS: Corporate; Securities.
Georgopoulos & Pahlavan . . . . . . . . . . . 4151 Middlefield Road, Suite 110 (⊙San Francisco)
**Germino, Donald O.**, (BV) . . . .'39 '65 C.800 A.B. L.1066 J.D. [Germino,R.A.J.C.&M.]⊙
*PRACTICE AREAS: Transactional; Civil Litigation; Estate Planning; Probate.
**Germino, John O.**, (AV) . . . . . . . . .'36 '62 C&L.813 A.B., J.D. [Germino,R.A.J.C.&M.]⊙
*PRACTICE AREAS: Civil Litigation.

**Germino, Runte, Amaral, Jordan, Carpenter & MacKay, A Professional Law Corporation, (AV)**
**2500 El Camino Real, Suite 210, 94306⊙**
**Telephone: 415-857-9211 Fax: 415-852-9256**
**D. Oliver Germino (1903-1972); John O. Germino; John A. Runte (Certified Specialist, Taxation Law, The State Bar of California Board of Legal Specialization); Donald O. Germino.**
**Edward M. Amaral; J. Scott Jordan; Glenn C. Carpenter; Norman E. MacKay; Susan R. F. Solomon; Paul J. McDonald.**
**General Civil and Trial Practice in State and Federal Courts. Personal Injury, Probate, Water Rights, Corporation, Taxation, Agricultural, Condemnation, Family and Corporate Law.**
**Los Banos, California Office: 1120 West I Street, Suite B. Telephone: 209-826-5024. Fax: 209-826-3164.**
*See Professional Biographies, PALO ALTO, CALIFORNIA*

**Gerrish, Stephen C.**, (AV) . . . . . . . . . . . . . . . .'48 '74 C&L.950 B.A., J.D. [Thoits,L.H.&M.]
*PRACTICE AREAS: Business Litigation; Real Estate Litigation; Construction Litigation; Employment Law; Alternative Dispute Resolution.
**Ghiassi, Ali** . . . . . . . . . . . . . . . . . . . . . . .'67 '92 C.112 B.A. L.990 J.D. [A Heller E.W.&M.]
*LANGUAGES: Farsi.
Giamalis, Peter J., (BV) . . . . . . . . . . . . . .'32 '74 C.645 B.S.E.E. L.1065 J.D. 2501 Park Blvd.
Giamalis, Stacey A. . . . . . . . . . . . . . . . . . . . .'— '90 C.112 A.B. L.1066 J.D. 2501 Park Blvd.
**Gibbons-Shapiro, James** . . . . . . . . . . . . .'69 '94 C.976 B.A. L.1068 J.D. [A Fenwick&W.]
*PRACTICE AREAS: Litigation.
**Gibbs, Karen A.** . . . . . . . . . . . . . . . . . . . .'69 '95 C.112 B.A. L.1065 J.D. [A Cooley G.]
*PRACTICE AREAS: General Business Litigation; Employment Law; Trademark and Copyright Law.
**Gibson, Nora L.** . . . . . . . . . . . . . . . . . . . .'66 '91 C.112 B.A. L.767 J.D. [A Brobeck,P.&H.]
*PRACTICE AREAS: Business Law; Corporate Law; Securities Law.

**Gibson, Dunn & Crutcher LLP, (AV)**
**525 University Avenue, Suite 220, 94301⊙**
**Telephone: 415-463-7300 Telecopier: 415-463-7333**
**Partners: Bruce L. Gitelson (Palo Alto and San Francisco Offices); Denis R. Salmon; Christopher J. Martin (Palo Alto and San Francisco Offices); Jonathan C. Dickey. Of Counsel: Susan B. Burr. Associates: Riaz A. Karamali; H. Mark Lyon; Paul J. Collins (Not admitted in CA); Timothy D. Blanton; Laura C. Roche.**
**General Civil, Trial and Appellate Practice, State and Federal Courts. Antitrust Law, Specialized Criminal Defense. General Corporation, Securities, Administrative, Labor and Employment, Taxation, Estate Planning, Probate and Trust, International Business, Entertainment, Commercial, Insolvency, Bankruptcy and Reorganization, Natural Resources, Oil and Gas, Environmental Energy, Municipal and Public Utility Law.**
**Los Angeles, California Office: 333 South Grand Avenue. Telephone: 213-229-7000. Telex: 188171 GIBTRASK LSA (TRT), 674930 GIBTRASK LSA (WUT). Telecopier: 213-229-7520. Cable Address: GIBTRASK LOS ANGELES.**
*See Professional Biographies, PALO ALTO, CALIFORNIA*

Gilbert, Anthony C., (AV) . . . . . . .'37 '64 C.309 A.B. L.145 J.D. 5 Palo Alto Sq., Suite 400
Gilfix, Michael . . . . . . . . . . . . . . . . . . . . . . . .'47 '73 C&L.813 B.A., J.D. 4151 Middlefield Rd.
**Gill, Michael E.** . . . . . . . . . . . . . . . . . . . .'44 '77 C.884 B.A. L.1065 J.D. [A Finnan,F.&Assoc.]
*LANGUAGES: Spanish, Nepali.
*PRACTICE AREAS: Immigration and Nationality Law (100%).
**Gillette, Stephen E.** . . . . . . . . . . . . . . . . .'69 '96 C.659 B.A. L.1065 J.D. [A Wilson,S.G.&R.]
*LANGUAGES: Spanish.
*PRACTICE AREAS: Corporate; Securities; Mergers and Acquisitions.
**Gilson, Amy L.** . . . . . . . . . . . . . . . . . . . . . . . . .'60 '85 C.112 A.B. L.770 J.D. [Wise&S.]
**Giordano, Susan** . . . . . . . . . . . . . . . . . . .'69 '95 C.1074 B.A. L.767 J.D. [A Brobeck,P.&H.]
*PRACTICE AREAS: Corporate.
**Girvin, John W., Jr.** . . . . . . . . . . . . . . . .'38 '64 C.893 B.E.E. L.273 LL.B. [Cooley G.] (Pat.)
**Gitelson, Bruce L.** . . . . . . . . . . . .'41 '64 C&L.813 B.A., J.D. [Gibson,D.&C.] (⊙San Fran.)
*PRACTICE AREAS: Business and Financial Planning for Entrepreneurs; Business and Financial Planning for Closely Held Businesses, Particularly High Technology; Corporations; Securities Regulation; International Business Organization and Finance.
Glaubensklee, Marilyn '52 '90 C.1196 B.S. L.560 J.D.
(adm. in NM; not adm. in CA; Pat.) Pat. Coun., Varian Assocs., Inc.
**Glickman, Norman H.**, (AV) . . .'40 '66 C.174 B.A. L.1066 J.D. [N.H.Glickman&Assoc.]
*PRACTICE AREAS: Business Law; Domestic and International Estate and Tax Planning; Asset Protection; Probate; Trust Administration.

**Glickman, Norman H., & Associates, A Prof. Corp., (AV)**
**Suite A280, 755 Page Mill Road, 94304-9408**
**Telephone: 415-857-1300 Fax: 415-493-9408**

(This Listing Continued)



**Glickman, Norman H., & Associates, A Prof. Corp. (Continued)**
**Norman H. Glickman (Certified Specialist, Taxation Law, California Board of Specialization);— Robin P. Jamplis.**
**Practice limited to International and Domestic Tax, Estate and Business Matters.**
*See Professional Biographies, PALO ALTO, CALIFORNIA*

Glidden, Jonathan D. . . . . . . . . . . . . . . . . . . . .'46 '72 C.478 A.B. L.1067 J.D. 2898 Bryant St.
**Glover, R. Renee** . . . . . . . . . . . . . . . . . . .'61 '92 C&L.813 B.A., J.D. [A Heller E.W.&M.]
*LANGUAGES: Spanish.
**Goeckeler, Stephan** . . . . . . . . . . . . . . . . . . . . . . . . . . . . .'65 '96 C&L.061 [A Morrison&F.]
*LANGUAGES: German.
**Goff, Daniel R.** '65 '93 C&L.336 B.S., J.D.
(adm. in ID; not adm. in CA) Tax Atty., Hewlett-Packard Co.
*RESPONSIBILITIES: Corporate Taxation.
**Gold, Jana G.** . . . . . . . . . . . . . . . . . . . . . .'60 '91 C.112 B.A. L.1066 J.D. [A Morrison&F.]
**Goldberg, Selwyn B.** . . . . . . . . . . . . .'56 '87 C.705 M.S.E.E. L.564 J.D. [A Wilson,S.G.&R.]
*PRACTICE AREAS: Intellectual Property Licensing; Intellectual Property Counseling; Patent.
**Goldman, Beth M.** . . . . . . . . . . . . . . . . . .'52 '85 C.107 B.A. L.1066 J.D. [B Heller E.W.&M.]
**Goldman, Robert J.** '54 '78 C&L.178 B.S., J.D.
(adm. in NY; not adm. in CA) [Fish&N.]
*PRACTICE AREAS: Intellectual Property.
Goldscheider, Peter F., (BV) . . . . . . . . . . . . .'47 '72 C.696 A.B. L.813 J.D. 2501 Park Blvd.
Goldstein, Yonkel . . . . . . . . . . . . . . . . . . . . . .'49 '88 C.1044 B.A. L.813 J.D. 755 Page Mill Rd.
**Gonzales, Jon C.** '65 '92 C.846 B.B.A. L.813 J.D.
(adm. in MA; not adm. in CA) [A Wilson,S.G.&R.]
*PRACTICE AREAS: Corporate; Securities.
**Gonzalez, Vanessa R** . . . . . . . . . . . . . . . . . .'70 '95 C.973 B.A. L.112 J.D. [A Gray C.W.&F.]
*LANGUAGES: Tagalog.
*PRACTICE AREAS: Real Estate Transaction.
**Good, Sarah Ann** . . . . . . . . . . . . . . . .'64 '90 C.674 A.B. L.893 J.D. [A Wilson,S.G.&R.]
*PRACTICE AREAS: Litigation.
**Goodrich, John B.**, (AV) . . . . . . . . . . .'41 '67 C.813 B.A. L.800 J.D. [Wilson,S.G.&R.]
*PRACTICE AREAS: Corporate Law; Securities.
**Goodwin, Hugh, Jr.** . . . . . . . . . . . . . . . . . . . . . .'59 '86 C.112 B.S. L.1068 J.D. [Gray C.W.&F.]
**Goodwin, Kevin A.** . . . . . . . . . . . . . . . . . . . . .'55 '82 C.154 B.A. L.178 J.D. [Carr,D.&F.]
**Gordon, Judith V.** . . . . . . . . . . . . . . . . . . . . .'54 '78 C.260 B.A. L.276 J.D. [Grant&G.]
*PRACTICE AREAS: Probate; Estate Planning; Trust Administration; Taxation; Charitable Giving.
Gotlieb, Charles E. . . . . . . . . .'61 '93 C.813 B.S.E.E./I.E. L.1066 J.D. 2 Palo Alto Sq. (Pat.)
Gottfried, Harry J. . . . . . . . . . . . . . . . . . . . . .'65 '92 C.29 B.A. L.464 J.D. 3000 El Camino Real
**Gottschalk, Marc E.** . . . . . . . . . . . . . . . . .'61 '91 C.293 B.A. L.1065 J.D. [A Wilson,S.G.&R.]
*LANGUAGES: French.
*PRACTICE AREAS: Environmental Law.
**Goughan, Patricia L.** . . . . '49 '75 C.66 A.B. L.569 J.D. Corp. Coun., Hewlett-Packard Co.
*RESPONSIBILITIES: Environmental Law.
Gould, Laurie J. . . . . . . . . . . . . . . . . . . . . . . . . .'59 '85 C.813 A.B. L.1068 J.D. 525 Univ. Ave.
**Govaerts, Clifford M.**, (AV) . . . .'49 '77 C.1077 B.S. L.464 J.D. [A Tomlinson Z.M.&M.]
*PRACTICE AREAS: Tax; Trusts and Estates; Pension Law; ERISA.
**Graeser, Suzanne S.** . . . . . . . . . . . . . . . . . . .'61 '87 C.154 B.A. L.1067 J.D. [B Morrison&F.]
*PRACTICE AREAS: Corporate Law; Business Law.
**Graham, Chris Scott** . . . . . . . . . . . . . . . . . . . . . .'59 '84 C.147 B.A. L.464 J.D. [Graham&J.]
*PRACTICE AREAS: Litigation; Intellectual Property.
**Graham, David R.** . . . . . . . . . . . . . . . .'61 '91 C.277 B.M.E. L.188 J.D. [A Gray C.W.&F.]
*PRACTICE AREAS: Intellectual Property; Patents.

**Graham & James LLP, (AV) BB**
**600 Hansen Way, 94304⊙**
**Telephone: 415-856-6500 Telecopier: 415-856-3619**
**Email: dgross@gj.com URL: http://www.gj.com**
**Members of Firm: Donald R. Davis; James E. Eakin; Chris Scott Graham; Lawrence W. Granatelli; David F. Gross; Timothy T. Huber; Alan B. Kalin; Michael H. Kalkstein; Ronald S. Lemieux; Ralph M. Pais; Robert E. Patterson; Thomas R. Radcliffe; Joe C. Sorenson. Resident Associates: Michele Z. Allen; Douglas A. Carlen; Deborah M. Chang; W. Clay Deanhardt; David S. Elkins; U. P. Peter Eng; Jenny J. Kim; Brien B. Kirk; Jill F. Kopeikin; Laura A. Majerus; Thomas A. M'Guinness; Andrew Y. Piatnicia; Perpetua B. Tranlong; Harold T. Tsiang; Valerie M. Wagner.**
**General Practice, including Civil Litigation in State and Federal Courts, Corporation, Securities, Tax, Intellectual Property, Commercial, International Business, Bankruptcy.**
**Other offices located in: San Francisco, Los Angeles, Orange County, Sacramento and Fresno, California; Seattle, Washington; Washington, D.C.; New York, New York; Milan, Italy; Beijing, China; Tokyo, Japan; London, England; Dusseldorf, Germany.**
**Associated Offices: Deacons Graham & James, Hong Kong, Sydney, Melbourne, Brisbane, Perth and Canberra, Australia.**
**Affiliated Offices: Deacons Graham & James, Hanoi and Ho Chi Minh City, Vietnam; Taipei, Taiwan and Bangkok, Thailand; In association with Dewi Soeharto & Rekan, Jakarta, Indonesia; Graham & James in affiliation with Taylor Joynson Garrett, London, England, Bucharest, Romania and Brussels, Belgium; Mishare M. Al-Ghazali & Partners, Safat, Kuwait; Law Firm of Salah Al-Hejailan, Jeddah and Riyadh, Saudi Arabia.**
*See Professional Biographies, PALO ALTO, CALIFORNIA*

**Grais, Linda S.** . . . . . . . . . . . . . . . . . . . . .'56 '93 C.976 B.A. L.813 J.D. [A Wilson,S.G.&R.]
*LANGUAGES: French.
*PRACTICE AREAS: Corporate; Life Sciences.
**Granaada, Michele K.** . . . . . . . . . . . . . . . . . . . .'—'85 C.107 B.A. L.276 J.D. [A Cooley G.]
**Granatelli, Lawrence W.** . . . . . . . . . . . .'57 '84 C.1044 B.E. L.188 J.D. [Graham&J.] (Pat.)
*PRACTICE AREAS: Patent, Copyright and Trademark.
Grant, Gary . . . . . . . . . . . . . . . . . . . . . . . . . . . . .'41 '70 C.101 B.S. L.813 J.D. 11 Kirby Pl.
**Grant, Robert N.**, (AV) . . . . . . . . . . . . . . . . . . . .'45 '72 C.674 B.A. L.813 J.D. [Grant&G.]
*PRACTICE AREAS: Taxation; Estate Planning; Probate; Trust Administration; Charitable Giving.

**Grant & Gordon, (AV)**
**525 University Avenue, Suite 1325, 94301**
**Telephone: 415-614-3800 Fax: 415-614-3810**
**Members of Firm: Robert N. Grant; Judith V. Gordon (Certified Specialist, Probate, Estate Planning and Trust Law, The State Bar of California Board of Legal Specialization).**
**Taxation, Estate Planning, Probate, Trust Administration, Charitable Giving.**
*See Professional Biographies, PALO ALTO, CALIFORNIA*

**Gray Cary Ware & Freidenrich, A Professional Corporation, (AV) BB**
**Gray Cary Established in 1927**
**Ware & Freidenrich Established in 1969**
**400 Hamilton Avenue, 94301-1825⊙**
**Telephone: 415-328-6561 Telex: 348-372 Telecopier: 415-327-3699**
**Email: info@gcwf.com URL: http://www.gcwf.com**
**Peter M. Astiz; Cynthia Beth Carlson; John Howard Clowes; Lawrence A. Cogan; Steven G. Cohen; David Henry Dolkas; Ian N. Feinberg; Mark Fowler; Diane Holt Frankle; Thomas M. French; Thomas W. Furlong; Gregory M. Gallo; Penny Howe Gallo; Hugh Goodwin, Jr.; John B. Hale; William H. Hoffman; Rodrigo J. Howard; Joan S. Kato; Margaret H. Kavalaris; James M. Koshland; Eric J. Lapp; Mary LaVigne-Butler; Jeffrey J. Lederman; Patrick J. McGaraghan; Marvin Meisel; Mark F. Radcliffe; Jonathan E. Rattner; Arthur C. Rinsky (Certified Specialist, Taxation Law. California Board of Legal Specialization.); J. Martin Robertson; Bradley J. Rock; Robert T. Russell; Bruce E. Schaeffer; Daniel K. Seubert; John R. Shuman, Jr.; Stacy Snowman; Jay M. Spitzen; Lillian G. Stenfeldt; Dennis C. Sullivan; R. Allyn Taylor; Craig M. Tighe; Jeffrey A. Trant; Elizabeth H. Ward; Richard I. Yankwich; Barry N. Young (Not admitted in CA);—James E. Anderson; Jeffrey D. Ball; Marilyn M. Bautista; Marcy Berkman; Mary Elizabeth Berry; Paul A. Blumenstein; Larry J. Bradfish; Todd Samuel Brecher; Kathleen K. Bryski; Pamela B. Burke; Kelly Lynn Canady; Hope A. Case; Amanda Castillo; Kathleen Cattani; Julia L. Cochrane; Janet M. Craycroft; Gary L. Dahlby; M. Elizabeth Day; Eric H. Dorf; Maureen S. Dorney; Charles M. Dyke; John W. Easterbrook; Russell S. Elmer; Melanie E. Erasmus; John M. Fogg; Barbara Friedrich; Gilbert Gallardo; Vanessa R**

(This Listing Continued)

**Gray Cary Ware & Freidenrich, A Professional Corporation (Continued)**

**Gonzalez; David R. Graham; Christina Groll; Wilma (Woody) Growney; Michelle R. Harbottle; Daniel Ross Harris (Not admitted in CA); Sharon W. Hawkins; Linda M. Hayes; Cheryl K. House; David Alan Hubb; Mark Huppin; Christopher J. Hurley; Jeffrey R. Ii; Andrew M. Jacobson; Paul B. Johnson; Lawrence C. King; Victoria W-Y Lee; Ginger L. Levy (Not admitted in CA); Timothy W. Lohse; Charles M. Miller; Martin H. Myers; Nels Raymond Nelsen; Denise Woodson Ofria; L. Scott Oliver; Frank H. Pao; Pamela Pasti; Jamie C. Pawliczek; Darren J. Pittenger; David J. Plewa; Margaret M. Powers; Douglas J. Renert; William A. Rodoni; Dianne B. Salesin; Jason Schaumberg; Eileen Evans Schefsky; Jim A. Scheinman; William R. Schreiber; Mary E. Shallman; M. Andrew Sherman; Scott M. Stanton; Marilyn N. Taketa; Don Thornburgh; Andrew Paul Valentine; Karen K. Williams; Kirk Orlando Williams. Of Counsel: Adrian Arima; Albert F. Knorp; Marta L. Morando. Retired Partners: John Freidenrich; Leonard Ware.**
**General Civil and Trial Practice in all State and Federal Courts and Administrative Agencies. Admiralty, Agribusiness, Antitrust, Aviation, Banking, Bankruptcy and Insolvency, Business, Commercial, Computer Law, Compensation and Benefits, Condemnation, Construction, Copyright and Trademark, Corporation, Corporate Securities, Customs, Eminent Domain, Employment Counseling and Litigation, Environmental, Estate Planning, Family Law, Fidelity and Surety, Government Contracts, Hospital and Health Care, Immigration and Naturalization, Insurance, International Business and Litigation, Publishing, Labor, Land Use, Libel, Negligence, News Media, Pension and Profit Sharing, Privacy, Private Foundation, Probate, Products Liability, Professional Malpractice, Railroad, Real Property, Federal and State Securities, Taxation, Telecommunications, Trade Regulation, Unfair Competition, Wills and Trusts.**
**Representative Clients: Automobile Club of South California; Bank of America; Brooktree Corp.; C. A. Parr (Agencies), Ltd.; IMED; Pacific Bell; McMillin Development Co.; Scripps Clinic and Research Found.; SeaWorld, Inc.; Underwriters at Lloyds.**
**San Diego, California Office: 401 B Street, Suite 1700. Telephone: 619-699-2700.**
**San Diego/Golden Triangle, California Office: 4365 Executive Drive, Suite 1600, 92121. Telephone: 619-677-1400. Fax: 619-677-1477.**
**La Jolla, California Office: 1200 Prospect Street, Suite 575. Telephone: 619-454-9101.**
**El Centro, California Office: 1224 State Street, P.O. Box 2890. Telephone: 619-353-6140.**

*See Professional Biographies, PALO ALTO, CALIFORNIA*

Green, Lee D. ... '53 '80 C&L.101 B.A., J.D. 660 Hansen Wy.
Greenberg, Lawrence T. ... '63 '91 C.309 A.B. L.813 J.D. 650 Page Mill Rd.
**Greenberg, Monica L.** '68 '95 C.659 B.A. L.94 J.D.
(adm. in NY; not adm. in CA) [A Wilson,S.G.&R.]
*PRACTICE AREAS: Corporate; Securities; Life Sciences.
Gregg, Edward B., (AV) ... '09 '41 C.556 B.S. L.767 LL.B. 850 Hansen Way (Pat.)‡
Gregory, Waldron A. ... '18 '47 C.112 A.B. L.813 J.D. 261 Hamilton Ave.‡
**Greguras, Fred M.** ... '43 '76 C.627 B.A. L.546 J.D. [Fenwick&W.]
*PRACTICE AREAS: Corporate.
Grey, Thomas C. '41 '69 C.813 A.B. L.976 LL.B.
(adm. in DC; not adm. in CA) Prof. of Law, Stanford Univ.
**Griffin, Roland I.** '36 '66
C.101 B.S.E.E. L.813 LL.B. Asst. Gen. Coun., Hewlett-Packard Co. (Pat.)
*RESPONSIBILITIES: Intellectual Property/Compliance; International Patent.
**Griffin, Scot A.** ... '67 '93 C.453 B.S.E.E. L.1065 J.D. [A Brobeck,P.&H.] (Pat.)
*PRACTICE AREAS: Intellectual Property; Litigation; Counseling.
**Griffiths, John R.**, (AV) ... '34 '61 C&L.813 A.B., J.D. [Crist,G.S.&B.]
**Groll, Christina** ... '68 '94 C.197 B.A. L.813 J.D. [A Gray C.W.&F.]
**Gross, David F.**, (AV) ... '53 '78 C.722 B.A. L.309 J.D. [Graham&J.]
*PRACTICE AREAS: Intellectual Property; Commercial Litigation.
**Gross, Irwin R.** ... '69 '93 C.813 B.S. L.309 J.D. [A Wilson,S.G.&R.]
*PRACTICE AREAS: Intellectual Property Litigation.
Grossman, Herbert '25 '51 C.569 B.S. L.494 J.D.
(adm. in MN; not adm. in CA) 1121 Harriet St.‡
**Growney, Wilma (Woody)** ... '71 '96 C.198 B.A. L.309 J.D. [A Gray C.W.&F.]
*PRACTICE AREAS: Intellectual Property Litigation.
Gruber, Jordan S. ... '60 '88 C.1044 B.A. L.893 J.D. 5 Palo Alto S.
**Guibord, Barbara B.**, (AV(T)) '51 '77 C.183 B.A. L.262 J.D.
(adm. in NY; not adm. in CA) [Zevnik H.G.&M.]⊙
*LANGUAGES: French.
*PRACTICE AREAS: Environmental Law; Insurance Coverage.
**Guidero, Rodrigo M.** ... '70 '96 C.911 B.A. L.813 J.D. [A Brobeck,P.&H.]
*PRACTICE AREAS: Corporate Law; Securities.
Gullixson, Conrad F., (AV) ... '23 '52 C.605 A.B. L.813 LL.B. 2600 El Camino Real‡
Gunther, Gerald '27 '55 C.102 A.B. L.309 LL.B.
(adm. in NY; not adm. in CA) Prof. of Law, Stanford Univ.
Gurnani, Aarti C. ... '67 '93 C.813 B.S. L.1065 J.D. 2200 Geng Rd.
**Guse, Kyle** ... '63 '92 C.1060 B.S. L.770 J.D. [A Heller E.W.&M.]
Guslani, Lino M., (BV) ... '27 '52 C.112 A.B. L.1065 J.D. [L.M.Guslani]
Guslani, Lino M., A Prof. Corp., (BV) ... 425 Sherman Ave.
**Habernigg, Ann** ... '61 '87 C.674 A.B. L.1068 J.D. [C Cooley G.]
*PRACTICE AREAS: Equity Compensation; Employee Benefits.
Hachenburg, Erick ... '65 '90 C.339 B.S. L.309 J.D. 2 Palo Alto Sq.
Hackmann, John Morrow ... '47 '81 C.339 B.S. L.813 J.D. 300 Bryant
**Hagan, James** ... '— '64 C.623 B.A. L.813 J.D. [Hagan,S.&H.]⊙
*PRACTICE AREAS: Business Transactions; Corporations; Commercial Law; Real Estate Transactions; Securities Law.
Hagan, James R., (BV) ... '35 '65 C.623 B.A. L.813 J.D. 350 Cambridge Ave.
**Hagan, Jennifer J.** ... '— '91 [Hagan,S.&H.]
*PRACTICE AREAS: Business Transactions; Corporations; Commercial Law; Real Estate Transactions; Securities Law.

**Hagan, Saca & Hagan, Law Corporation, (AV)**
**350 Cambridge Avenue, Suite 150, 94306⊙**
**Telephone: 415-322-8498 Fax: 415-322-8499**
**James Hagan; Diana M. Saca; Jennifer J. Hagan; George M. Schisler, Jr.**
**Business Transactions, Commercial Law, Civil and Business Litigation, Securities, Intellectual Property, Employment, Real Estate and Construction.**
**San Francisco, California Office: 350 Cambridge Avenue, Suite 150, 94306. Telephone: 415-322-8498. Fax: 415-322-8499.**

*See Professional Biographies, PALO ALTO, CALIFORNIA*

Hagen, Stephen E. ... '50 '76 C.813 B.A. L.477 J.D. 1436 Hamilton Ave.
Haile, Elster S., (BV) ... '16 '41 C&L.813 A.B., J.D. 550 Calif. Ave.
**Hale, Geoffrey B.** ... '61 '93 C.478 B.A. L.893 J.D. [A Wilson,S.G.&R.]
*LANGUAGES: German and French.
*PRACTICE AREAS: Corporate; Securities.
**Hale, John B.** ... '57 '82 C.276 A.B. L.966 J.D. [Gray C.W.&F.]
**Hale, Timothy C.**, (AV) ... '50 '84 C.197 B.A. L.813 J.D. [Russo&H.]
*PRACTICE AREAS: Civil Litigation; Intellectual Property Litigation; Computer Law; Trade Secrets.
Hall, David L. '53 '80 C.813 B.A. L.1065 J.D.
Gen. Mgr., Fin. Develop., Electric Power Resch. Institute
**Hamadani, Ramesh** ... '71 '95 C.112 B.A. L.770 J.D. [A Brobeck,P.&H.]
*PRACTICE AREAS: Employment Law.
Hamilton, Marvin ... '25 '75 C.813 B.A. L.770 J.D. 3351 Alma St.
Hammerman, Jason A. ... '69 '94 C.659 B.S. L.309 J.D. 650 Page Mill Rd.
**Handler, Bradley A.** ... '67 '95 C.659 B.A. L.893 J.D. [A Cooley G.]
*PRACTICE AREAS: Corporate Finance; Intellectual Property.
**Hane, Laurie S.** ... '60 '84 C.388 B.A. L.597 J.D. [Morrison&F.]
*PRACTICE AREAS: Commercial Litigation; Intellectual Property Litigation; Alternative Dispute Resolution.

**Hann, James F.** '48 '77 C.886 B.S.M.E. L.1065 J.D.
[Townsend&T.&C.] (See Pat. Sect.)
**Hanna, John Paul**, (AV) ... '32 '60 C&L.813 B.A., J.D. [Hanna&V.]
*PRACTICE AREAS: Real Estate (Property) Law; Land Use and Development Law; Community Association Law; Common Interest Community Law; Continuing Care Communities.
**Hanna, Ramsey** ... '68 '94 C.061 B.A. L.813 J.D. [A Wilson,S.G.&R.]
*LANGUAGES: Arabic and German.

**Hanna & Van Atta, (AV) BB**
**A Partnership of Professional Corporations**
**525 University Avenue, Suite 705, 94301**
**Telephone: 415-321-5700 Fax: 415-321-5639**
**John Paul Hanna; David M. Van Atta.**
**Real Estate Law, Land Use and Development, Purchase, Sale and Leasing of Real Estate, Real Estate Financing, Joint Ventures and Partnerships, Residential and Commercial Condominiums, Planned Developments and Common Interest Developments, Continuing Care Retirement Communities, Community Association Law, Local and State Permits, Hearings Before State and Local Government Land Use Agencies, FNMA and FHLMC Opinion Letters, Environmental Law, Arbitration and Mediation: Real Estate Disputes.**

*See Professional Biographies, PALO ALTO, CALIFORNIA*

**Hansen, Daniel R.** ... '65 '92 C&L.878 B.S., J.D. [A Brobeck,P.&H.]
*PRACTICE AREAS: Intellectual Property.
**Hanson, Gordon N.** ... '50 '85 C.869 B.S. L.1066 J.D. [Alexander&H.]
*PRACTICE AREAS: Business Law; Corporate Law; Partnership Law; Real Estate; Estate Planning.
Harbin, Alisa A. '63 '92 C.893 B.A. L.276 J.D.
(adm. in NY; not adm. in CA; Pat.) Alza Corp.
**Harbottle, Michelle R.** ... '64 '91 C&L.112 B.A., J.D. [A Gray C.W.&F.]
*PRACTICE AREAS: Domestic and International Trademark Counseling and Prosecution.
**Hardcastle, Ian** ... '43 '89 C.061 B.A. L.1065 J.D. Hewlett-Packard Co. (Pat.)
*RESPONSIBILITIES: Patent Application Preparation; Patent Application Prosecution; Transactional.
**Harrington, Sara Duval** ... '64 '90 C.112 B.A. L.188 J.D. [A Wilson,S.G.&R.]
*PRACTICE AREAS: Litigation.
**Harris, Daniel Ross** '65 '92 C.1169 B.A. L.904 J.D.
(adm. in MA; not adm. in CA) [A Gray C.W.&F.]
*PRACTICE AREAS: Litigation; Intellectual Property.
**Harrison, Maureen Colligan** ... '63 '92 C&L.770 B.S., J.D. [A Murray&M.]
*PRACTICE AREAS: Business Workouts; Bankruptcy Reorganizations; Creditor Remedies.
**Hart, Richard J.** ... '64 '92 C.659 B.A. L.569 J.D. [A Wilson,S.G.&R.]
*LANGUAGES: Italian.
*PRACTICE AREAS: Corporate Law; Securities.
**Hartogs, Michael D.** ... '65 '92 C.37 B.S. L.273 J.D. [A McCutchen,D.B.&E.]
*PRACTICE AREAS: Patent; Intellectual Property.
Hartwick, Fred M., III ... '56 '81 C.813 A.B. L.1065 J.D. Stanford Univ.
Harvey, Dennis C. ... '49 '78 C.112 B.A. L.426 J.D. 400 Cambridge Ave.
**Harvey, Richard H.** ... '45 '75 C.1097 B.S. L.800 J.D. [Brown&B.]
*PRACTICE AREAS: Commercial; Corporate Securities; Mergers and Acquisitions; Intellectual Property; Licensing.
**Hasko, Judith A.** ... '64 '95 C.881 B.A. L.966 J.D. [A Cooley G.]
*PRACTICE AREAS: Intellectual Property Licensing; Business Transactions; Corporate.
**Haslam, Robert T.** ... '46 '76 C.453 B.S. L.1065 J.D. [Heller E.W.&M.]
*PRACTICE AREAS: Intellectual Property Litigation.
**Haughey, Paul C.** '54 '80
C.112 B.S.E.E. L.1065 J.D. [Townsend&T.&C.] (See Pat. Sect.)
*PRACTICE AREAS: Electronic Patent Prosecution, Counseling & Licensing.
**Haverstock, Thomas B.** '55 '85
C.679 B.S.E.E. L.770 J.D. [Haverstock&Assoc.] (See Pat. Sect.)
*PRACTICE AREAS: Maskworks; Software; Electrical and Computer Patents.

**Haverstock & Associates**
**260 Sheridan Avenue, Suite 420, 94306**
**Telephone: 415-833-0160 Facsimile: 415-833-0170**
**Email: tbh@crl.com**
**Thomas B. Haverstock;—Jonathan O. Owens; Derek J. Westberg.**
**Patent, Trademark and Copyright Law, Trade Secrets, Unfair Competition, Technology, Licensing and Evaluation and related Trial and Appellate Litigation in State and Federal Courts and Alternative Dispute Resolution.**

*See Professional Biographies, PALO ALTO, CALIFORNIA*

**Haviland, Dana** ... '45 '75 C.1059 A.B. L.245 J.D. [Wilson,S.G.&R.]
*LANGUAGES: French.
*PRACTICE AREAS: Litigation; Alternative Dispute Resolution; International Arbitration; Intellectual Property; Securities.
**Hawk, Robert B.** ... '58 '84 C.846 B.A. L.813 J.D. [Heller E.W.&M.]
*PRACTICE AREAS: Commercial, Antitrust and Trademark Litigation.
**Hawkins, Charles F.**, (AV) ... '43 '68 C.813 B.A. L.1068 J.D. [Hawkins,B.&F.]⊙
*PRACTICE AREAS: Personal Injury Law; Civil Litigation; Construction Site Litigation; Products Liability.
**Hawkins, Lana K.** '52 '88 C.1175 B.A. L.276 J.D.
(adm. in PA; not adm. in CA) [A Cooley G.]
**Hawkins, Sharon W.** ... '95 '95 C.659 B.A. L.112 J.D. [A Gray C.W.&F.]
*PRACTICE AREAS: Corporate/Securities.

**Hawkins, Blick & Fitzpatrick, (AV) BB**
**418 Florence Street, 94301⊙**
**Telephone: 415-321-5656 Fax: 415-326-9636**
**Charles F. Hawkins; Stephen L. Blick; Michael J. Fitzpatrick. Associates: Mark F. Bernal.**
**Personal Injury Trial Practice.**
**San Jose, California Office: 96 North Third Street, Suite 300. Telephone: 408-280-7111. Fax: 408-292-7868.**

*See Professional Biographies, PALO ALTO, CALIFORNIA*

**Hayes, David L.** ... '56 '86 C.691 B.S. L.309 J.D. [Fenwick&W.] (Pat.)
*PRACTICE AREAS: Intellectual Property.
**Hayes, Linda M.** ... '47 '76 C.112 A.B. L.770 J.D. [A Gray C.W.&F.]
*PRACTICE AREAS: Estate Planning; Probate.
**Hayes, Noemi Espinosa** ... '58 '84 C.768 B.S.Ch.E. L.1065 J.D. [Brobeck,P.&H.] (Pat.)
*PRACTICE AREAS: Patent, Trademark, Copyright, Tradesecrets and related Litigation.
**Haynes, Mark A.** ... '55 '81 C.846 B.S.E.E. L.813 J.D. [Wilson,S.G.&R.] (Pat.)
*PRACTICE AREAS: Patents; Trademarks; Copyrights.
**Hays, Gillian G.** ... '43 '69 L.051 [Ritchey F.W.&K.]
*PRACTICE AREAS: Estate Planning; Probate; Trust Law.
Hays, Walter V., (P.C.), (BV) ... '35 '62 C&L.813 B.A., LL.B. [Herrick&H.]
**Healy, David W.** ... '54 '79 C.112 B.A. L.1065 J.D. [Fenwick&W.]
*PRACTICE AREAS: Corporate.
**Heaney, Susan** ... '66 '94 C.112 B.A. L.1066 J.D. [A Wilson,S.G.&R.]
*PRACTICE AREAS: Litigation.
**Heck, Gaye Nell** ... '65 '90 C.1365 B.A. L.245 B.A. [A Murray&M.]
*PRACTICE AREAS: Commercial Litigation; Creditors Remedies; Bankruptcy.
**Heinecke, Peter S.** ... '65 '94 C.674 A.B. L.145 J.D. [A Wilson,S.G.&R.]
*PRACTICE AREAS: Corporate Law; Securities Law.

**Heller Ehrman White & McAuliffe, (AV)**
**A Partnership including Professional Corporations**
**525 University Avenue, Suite 1100, 94301-1908⊙**
**Telephone: 415-324-7000 Facsimile: 415-324-0638**
**URL: http://www.hewm.com**

(This Listing Continued)

CAA467P

**Heller Ehrman White & McAuliffe (Continued)**

**Members of Firm: Richard H. Abramson††; Paul Alexander††; Daniel L. Appelman††; Norman J. Blears††; Joyce M. Cartun††; Michael L. Charlson††; Steven R. Feldstein††; Stephen C. Ferruolo††; Neil W. Flanzraich††; Robert D. Fram††; Richard Friedman††; Robert T. Haslam††; Robert B. Hawk††; Cynthia L. Jackson††; Alan M. Krubiner††; Edward J. Lynch††; August J. Moretti††; Sarah A. O'Dowd††; Richard A. Peers††; Matthew P. Quilter††; Glenn A. Smith††; Kent A. Stormer††; Vanessa Wells††; Stanley Young††. Special Counsel: John A. Dhuey; Derek P. Freyberg; Beth M. Goldman; Charles M. Hungerford; Paula S. Kasler; Lisa N. Kaufman (Not admitted in CA); Julie Y. Mar-Spinola; William Schmonsees; Anne Williams. Of Counsel: Julian N. Stern. Associates: E. J. Fournier; Ali Ghiassi; R. Renee Glover; Kyle Guse; Linda G. Henry; Hope L. Hudson; William J. James; Jeffrey P. Jones; Thomas P. Maliska; Priscilla H. Mark; Sarah E. Mitchell (Not admitted in CA); Suzanne K. Roten; Randall B. Schai (Not admitted in United States); Jo-Anne Sinclair; Jonathan E. Singer (Not admitted in CA); Peter F. Stewart (Not admitted in CA); Nitin Subhedar; Peter N. Townshend; Michelle A. Travis; Christina L. Vail.**
**General Practice.**
**Los Angeles, California Office: 601 S. Figueroa Street. Telephone: 213-689-0200. Facsimile: 213-614-1868.**
**San Francisco, California Office: 333 Bush Street. Telephone: 415-772-6000. Facsimile: 415-772-6268. Cable Address: "Helpow". Telex: 340-895; 184-996.**
**Seattle, Washington Office: 6100 Columbia Center, 701 Fifth Avenue. Telephone: 206-447-0900. Facsimile: 206-447-0849.**
**Portland, Oregon Office: 200 S.W. Market Street, Suite 1750. Telephone: 503-227-7400. Facsimile: 503-241-0950.**
**Anchorage, Alaska Office: 1900 Bank of America Center, 550 West 7th Avenue. Telephone: 907-277-1900. Facsimile: 907-277-1920.**
**Tacoma, Washington Office: 1400 First Interstate Plaza, 1201 Pacific Avenue. Telephone: 206-572-6666. Facsimile: 206-572-6743.**
**Washington, D.C. Office: 815 Connecticut Avenue, N.W., Suite 200. Telephone: 202-785-4747. Facsimile: 202-785-8877.**
**Hong Kong Office: 1902A, 19/F, Peregrine Tower, Lippo Centre, 89 Queensway, Hong Kong. Telephone: (011) 852-2526-6381. Facsimile: (011) 852-2810-6242.**
**Singapore Office: 50 Raffles Place, 17-04 Shell Tower. Telephone: (011) 65 538-1756. Facsimile: (011) 65 538-1537.**
**††Lawyer who is a stockholder and an employee of a professional corporation which is a member of the firm**

***See Professional Biographies, PALO ALTO, CALIFORNIA***

Helms, Kenna J. ..... '46 '73 C.112 B.S. L.770 J.D. University Bk. & Tr. Co.
**Hemington, Matthew B.** ..... '63 '90 C.112 B.A. L.1068 J.D. [Ⓐ Cooley G.]
*PRACTICE AREAS: Emerging Companies; Intellectual Property Law; Venture Capital.
**Henningsen, Kimberley Erin** ..... '70 '95 C.112 B.A. L.188 J.D. [Ⓐ Brobeck,P.&H.]
*PRACTICE AREAS: Business and Technology.
**Henry, Linda G.** ..... '60 '91 C.937 B.A. L.813 J.D. [Ⓐ Heller E.W.&M.]
Hensley, Peter R. ..... '61 '90 C.112 B.A. L.310 J.D. 635 Bryant St.
**Herald, Susan** ..... '46 '81 C.112 B.A. L.1066 J.D. [Ⓒ McCutchen,D.B.&E.]
*PRACTICE AREAS: Business; Real Estate Transactions.
Herbert, George L. ..... '36 '64 C&L.309 A.B., LL.B. Varian Assocs., Inc.
**Herbert, Thomas O.**, (AV) '31 '61
C.128 B.E.E. L.273 J.D. [Flehr,H.T.A.&H.] (See Pat. Sect.)
**Herbst, David W.**, (AV) ..... '52 '77 C.668 B.A. L.813 J.D. [Wise&S.]
*PRACTICE AREAS: Income Taxation; Employee Benefits; Executive Compensation.
**Herbst, Jeffrey A.** ..... '64 '91 C.103 B.S. L.813 J.D. [Ⓐ Wilson,S.G.&R.]
*PRACTICE AREAS: Corporate Law; Securities Law; Technology Licensing; Intellectual Property.
**Herhold, Theodore T.** ..... '57 '86 C.813 A.B. L.1065 J.D. [Ⓐ Townsend&T.&C.]
*LANGUAGES: Spanish.
*PRACTICE AREAS: Commercial Litigation.
**Herman, Janet Stone** ..... '59 '84 C.112 B.S. L.1067 J.D. [Ⓒ Morrison&F.]
*PRACTICE AREAS: Corporate Law; Securities Law; Business Law.
Herman, Jayne F. ..... '52 '89 C.602 B.A. L.813 J.D. 5 Palo Alto Sq., Suite 400
**Hernandez, Joseph D.** ..... '— '92 C&L.770 B.A., J.D. [Wise&S.]
*PRACTICE AREAS: Corporate Transactions; Intellectual Property; Sports Representation.
Herrick, James J., (BV) ..... '30 '58 C.475 B.A. L.813 J.D. [Herrick&H.]
Herrick & Hays, An Assn. of Attys. incl. A P.C., (BV) ..... 2600 El Camino Real
**Hersey, Rachel** ..... '— '91 C.563 B.S. L.813 J.D. [Ⓐ Fenwick&W.]
*PRACTICE AREAS: Taxation.
**Hershberger, J. Ronald**, (AV) ..... '34 '61 C.629 B.A. L.950 J.D. [Thoits,L.H.&M.]
*PRACTICE AREAS: Probate; Estate Planning; Trust Law.
Herzog, Richard R., (AV) ..... '43 '70 C&L.813 B.A., J.D. [Mitchell&H.]
**Heslin, James M.** '50 '78
C.112 B.Sc.Ch.E. L.1066 J.D. [Townsend&T.&C.] (See Pat. Sect.)
**Hetherington, Michael** ..... '51 '82 C.813 B.A. L.767 J.D. [Ⓐ Wilson,S.G.&R.] (Pat.)
*LANGUAGES: German.
*PRACTICE AREAS: Intellectual Property.

**Hettig, David W. '42 '77 C.813 B.A. L.767 J.D.**
**1755 Embarcadero Road, Suite 110, 94303**
**Telephone: 415-856-2700 Fax: 415-856-2728**
**Email: DHETTIG@aol.com**
***PRACTICE AREAS: Estate Planning Law; Probate Law; Trusts Law; Real Estate Law; Tax Law.**
**Estate Planning, Trust, Wills, Small Business, Tax, and Real Estate.**

***See Professional Biographies, PALO ALTO, CALIFORNIA***

**Heuser, Peter E.**, (AV) '49 '76
C.1027 B.S. L.966 J.D. [Kolisch H.D.M.&H.] (See Pat. Sect.)⊙
*PRACTICE AREAS: Patent, Trademark and Unfair Competition.
**Hewett, Scott William** ..... '54 '96 C.112 B.S.E.E. L.1067 J.D. [Ⓐ Townsend&T.&C.]
*PRACTICE AREAS: Patent Law.
**Hickman, Paul L.** ..... '53 '84 C.813 A.B. L.770 J.D. [Hickman,B.&W.] (See Pat. Sect.)
*PRACTICE AREAS: Intellectual Property Law; Patents.

**Hickman, Beyer & Weaver, L.L.P.**
**620 Hansen Way, 94304**
**Telephone: 415-493-6400 Fax: 415-493-6484**
**Members of Firm: Paul L. Hickman; Steve Beyer; Jeffrey K. Weaver. Associates: David P. Lentini; Joseph A. Nguyen; C. Douglass Thomas; Jonathan Scott; Albert Penilla; Lee Van Pelt; Ben H. Bedi; James E. Austin.**
**Intellectual Property Law.**

***See Professional Biographies, PALO ALTO, CALIFORNIA***

**Higgins, Gabrielle E.** ..... '63 '89 C.321 B.A. L.262 J.D. [Ⓐ Fish&N.] (See Pat. Sect.)
*PRACTICE AREAS: Intellectual Property.
**Higgins, Jeffrey P.** ..... '65 '90 C.154 B.A. L.1065 J.D. [Ⓐ Brobeck,P.&H.]
*PRACTICE AREAS: Corporate Law.
**Higgins, Willis E.** ..... '40 '66 C.665 B.S.Ch.E. L.145 J.D. [Cooley G.] (Pat.)
*PRACTICE AREAS: Electronics and Software Patent Prosecution; Strategic Counseling; Patent Litigation Support.
Hillberg, Loren E. ..... '58 '85 C.813 B.A. L.1065 J.D. V.P. & Gen. Coun., Micro Focus
**Hines, Dorothy L.** ..... '52 '95 C.522 B.S. L.310 J.D. [Ⓐ Fenwick&W.]
*PRACTICE AREAS: Corporate.
**Hirsch, Andrew J.** ..... '60 '87 C.813 B.A. L.178 J.D. [Wilson,S.G.&R.]
*PRACTICE AREAS: Corporate; Commercial; Finance; Secured Lending.
Hirsch, Joseph I. '38 '66 C.679 B.S.Ch.E. L.273 J.D.
Assoc. Gen. Coun. & Dir., Syntex Corp. (Pat.)
**Hite, J. Eppa, III** ..... '51 '81 C.893 B.A. L.945 J.D. [Ⓒ Carr,D.&F.] (See Pat. Sect.)
**Hoang, Christine Linh-Chau** ..... '69 '93 C.276 B.S. L.1066 J.D. [Ⓐ Fenwick&W.]
*PRACTICE AREAS: Intellectual Property; Copyright and Trademark.

Hoerger, Robert G. ..... '44 '80 C.608 B.A. L.284 J.D. P.O. Box 3703
**Hoerger, Susan K.** ..... '44 '78 C.966 B.A. L.1065 J.D. [Ⓒ McCutchen,D.B.&E.]
*PRACTICE AREAS: Labor Law; Employment Law.
**Hoffman, Brian M.** '68 '94 C.178 B.S. L.146 J.D.
(adm. in IL; not adm. in CA; Pat.) [Ⓐ Fenwick&W.]
*PRACTICE AREAS: Intellectual Property; Patent Law.
**Hoffman, Flora Houn** ..... '65 '92 C.309 B.A. L.1066 J.D. [Ⓐ Fragomen,D.&B.]
**Hoffman, William H.** ..... '51 '89 C.966 B.A. L.1068 J.D. [Gray C.W.&F.]
*PRACTICE AREAS: Employee Benefits; Corporate Securities.
**Hoffmeister, David M.** ..... '58 '87 C.464 B.S. L.765 J.D. [Ⓒ Wilson,S.G.&R.]
*PRACTICE AREAS: Life Sciences; Food and Drug Law.
**Hohbach, Harold C.**, (AV) '21 '53
C.791 B.S. L.1066 LL.B. [Flehr,H.T.A.&H.] (See Pat. Sect.)
Hohnsbeen, George H., II ..... '54 '79 C.112 A.B. L.1068 J.D. 400 Hamilton Ave.
**Holland, Charles D.** ..... '53 '92 C.119 B.S. L.770 J.D. [Ⓐ Wilson,S.G.&R.] (Pat.)
*PRACTICE AREAS: Patents.
Holm, RoseAnn E. '48 '77 C.911 B.A. L.454 J.D.
V.P. & Gen. Coun., Lefcourt Golub Baer & Moneypenny, Inc.
**Holm Jensen, Paula** ..... '64 '94 C.918 B.A. L.770 J.D. [Ⓐ Cooley G.]
*PRACTICE AREAS: Corporate; Technology Licensing.
Holt, Peter Theodore ..... '62 '90 C.197 A.B. L.1065 J.D. 5 Palo Alto Sq., Suite 400
Holvick, Valerie A. ..... '49 '75 C.483 B.A. L.208 J.D. 2197 E. Bayshore Rd.
Holzschuher, Louisa ..... '58 '84 C.604 B.A. L.1066 J.D. Sr. Coun., Syntex (U.S.A.) Inc.
Homan, Arthur Wilbourn '59 '85
C.886 B.A. L.893 J.D. Sr. Corp. Coun., Varian Assocs., Inc.
**Homsy, Joseph G.** '45 '78 C.659 B.A. L.1202 J.D.
(adm. in NY; not adm. in CA) [Zevnik H.G.&M.]⊙
*PRACTICE AREAS: Environmental Law.
**Hooper, Suzanne Sawochka** ..... '65 '91 C.112 B.A. L.1066 J.D. [Ⓐ Cooley G.]
*PRACTICE AREAS: Corporate Securities; Mergers and Acquisitions.
**Hoover, Janette M.** ..... '51 '78 C.415 B.A. L.1066 J.D. [Ⓐ Tomlinson Z.M.&M.]
*PRACTICE AREAS: Intellectual Property; Construction Law.
**Hopenfeld, Bruce Robert** ..... '67 '93 C.112 B.S.E.E. L.145 J.D. [Ⓐ Wilson,S.G.&R.] (Pat.)
*PRACTICE AREAS: Intellectual Property; Technology Licensing.
**Hoppe, Frank I.** ..... '70 '96 C.893 B.A. L.1066 J.D. [Ⓐ Wilson,S.G.&R.]
*PRACTICE AREAS: Corporate; Securities.
Hopwood, Randal B., (BV) ..... '49 '78 C.813 A.B. L.1065 J.D. 407 Sherman Ave.
**Horan, John Mathias** ..... '53 '80 C.309 A.B. L.477 J.D. [Ⓐ Wilson,S.G.&R.]
*PRACTICE AREAS: Intellectual Property Litigation; Trade Secrets; Trademarks; Copyrights; Patents.
**Horning, Richard Allan**, (AV) ..... '44 '70 C.112 B.A. L.228 J.D. [Ⓒ Tomlinson Z.M.&M.]
*PRACTICE AREAS: Intellectual Property; Litigation; Arbitration.
**Horowitz, Kenneth H.** ..... '62 '88 C.112 B.A. L.284 J.D. [Ⓐ Thoits,L.H.&M.]
*PRACTICE AREAS: Probate; Estate Planning; Trust Administration; Real Property; Business Law.
**Horton, Michel Yves** ..... '51 '84 C.1090 B.S. L.945 J.D. [Zevnik H.G.&M.]⊙
*PRACTICE AREAS: Insurance Coverage; Commercial Litigation.
**House, Cheryl K.** ..... '66 '92 C.813 A.B. L.1065 J.D. [Ⓐ Gray C.W.&F.]
*PRACTICE AREAS: Corporate.
Howard, Christopher ..... '64 '91 C.112 A.B. L.813 J.D. 2 Palo Alto Sq.
**Howard, Rodrigo J.** ..... '55 '85 C.37 B.A. L.145 J.D. [Gray C.W.&F.]
*LANGUAGES: German.
*PRACTICE AREAS: Mergers and Acquisitions; General Corporate; Public Utilities.
**Hsi, Petrina S.** '68 '94 C.367 B.A. L.1066 J.D.
(adm. in NY; not adm. in CA; See Pat. Sect.) [Ⓐ Fish&N.]
*PRACTICE AREAS: Intellectual Property.
**Huang, Franklin P.** ..... '64 '92 C.188 B.A. L.1066 J.D. [Ⓐ Brobeck,P.&H.]
*PRACTICE AREAS: Corporate Law; Securities Law; Venture Capital Financing; Venture-Backed Companies.
**Hubb, David Alan** ..... '63 '91 C.170 B.A. L.1067 J.D. [Ⓐ Gray C.W.&F.]
**Huber, Marie Oh** ..... '61 '87 C.976 B.A. L.597 J.D. Sr. Atty., Hewlett-Packard Co.
*RESPONSIBILITIES: General Corporate; Securities/Finance; Mergers and Acquisitions.
**Huber, Timothy T.**, (BV) ..... '56 '81 C.838 B.S. L.228 J.D. [Graham&J.]
*PRACTICE AREAS: Business Litigation; Creditors' Rights; Bankruptcy Litigation.
**Hucko, Josephine T.** ..... '— '91 C.339 B.S. L.770 J.D. [Ⓐ Fenwick&W.]
*PRACTICE AREAS: Corporate.
Hudnall, Michael H. ..... '44 '68 C.674 A.B. L.813 LL.B. Dep. Gen. Coun., Stanford Univ.
**Hudson, Hope L.** ..... '65 '93 C.976 B.A. L.665 J.D. [Ⓐ Heller E.W.&M.]
**Huge, Todd A.** ..... '63 '95 C.813 B.S. L.1066 J.D. [Ⓐ Fenwick&W.]
*PRACTICE AREAS: Litigation; Employment and Labor Law.
**Hukari, H. Richard** ..... '67 '94 C.902 B.A. L.1068 J.D. [Ⓐ Brobeck,P.&H.]
*LANGUAGES: Spanish.
*PRACTICE AREAS: Business; Technology.
Hult, John K. ..... '49 '75 C.768 B.A. L.770 J.D. 550 Hamilton Ave.
**Humphreys, Ivan H.** ..... '57 '82 C.112 B.A. L.309 J.D. [Wilson,S.G.&R.]
*PRACTICE AREAS: Tax.
**Hungerford, Charles M.** ..... '50 '76 C.37 B.A. L.1049 J.D. [Ⓒ Heller E.W.&M.]
*LANGUAGES: French.
**Hunter, Shane Horan** ..... '67 '96 C.1229 B.S.E.E. L.1068 J.D. [Ⓐ Townsend&T.&C.]
*PRACTICE AREAS: Patent Law.
**Huppin, Mark** ..... '70 '96 C.112 B.A. L.813 J.D. [Ⓐ Gray C.W.&F.]
*PRACTICE AREAS: Corporate/Securities.
**Hurley, Allison Walsh** ..... '58 '86 C.112 B.A. L.767 J.D. [Ⓐ Bialson,B.&S.]
*PRACTICE AREAS: Business Law; Corporation Law.
**Hurley, Christopher J.** ..... '65 '93 C.550 B.A. L.93 J.D. [Ⓐ Gray C.W.&F.]
*PRACTICE AREAS: Corporate Law; Securities; Mergers and Acquisitions.
**Hursh, John G.** ..... '50 '82 C.629 B.S. L.508 J.D. [Ritchey F.W.&K.]
*PRACTICE AREAS: Real Estate; Construction Law; Employment Litigation.
Hurwitz, Edward M. ..... '63 '91 C.188 B.A. L.1066 J.D. 5 Palo Alto Sq.
**Husick, Gail Clayton** ..... '64 '89 C.691 B.A. L.309 J.D. [Wilson,S.G.&R.]
*PRACTICE AREAS: Corporate Law; Securities; Venture Capital.
Huynh, Francette H. ..... '62 '92 C.112 B.S. L.813 J.D. 955 Page Mill Rd.
**Hwang, Su W.** ..... '66 '94 C.918 B.A. L.813 J.D. [Ⓐ Morrison&F.]
**Hyman, Jeffrey N.** ..... '69 '94 C.1169 B.A. L.770 J.D. [Ⓐ Cooley G.]
*PRACTICE AREAS: Business Litigation; Securities Litigation; Real Estate Litigation.
**Ii, Jeffrey R.** ..... '63 '88 C.339 B.S. L.1066 J.D. [Gray C.W.&F.]
**Ikeda, Karen N.** ..... '59 '87 C.763 B.S. L.767 J.D. [Brobeck,P.&H.]
*PRACTICE AREAS: Technology and Intellectual Property.
**Irvine, Perry A., (P.C.)**, (AV) ..... '41 '66 C.823 B.A. L.276 J.D. [Irvine&C.]
*PRACTICE AREAS: Complex Litigation; Securities Litigation; Family Law; Personal Injury Law.

**Irvine & Cooper, (AV)**
**A Partnership of Professional Corporations**
**635 Bryant Street, 94301-2502**
**Telephone: 415-328-3001 Fax: 415-328-2934**
**Members of Firm: Perry A. Irvine (P.C.); David L. Cooper (P.C.).**
**Civil Trial Practice in all State and Federal Courts. Business Litigation, Personal Injury, Family Law, Securities, Insurance and Real Estate Litigation.**

***See Professional Biographies, PALO ALTO, CALIFORNIA***

Ito, Richard T. ..... '54 '84 C.112 B.A. L.809 J.D. Pat. Atty., Alza Corporation (Pat.)
**Itoi, Anna** ..... '69 '96 C.813 B.A. L.1066 J.D. [Ⓐ Wilson,S.G.&R.]
*PRACTICE AREAS: Corporate.
**Ives, Bruce S.** ..... '60 '86 C.309 B.A. L.1066 J.D. Atty., Hewlett-Packard Co.

**Izzo, Barbara A.** ....................... '69 '94 C.602 B.A. L.309 J.D. [[A] Wilson,S.G.&R.]
**Jack, Robert B.**, (AV) .................. '43 '69 C.674 B.A. L.813 J.D. [Wilson,S.G.&R.]
*PRACTICE AREAS: Corporate Law; Securities.
**Jackson, Cynthia L.**, (AV) ............. '54 '79 C.813 B.A. L.846 J.D. [Heller E.W.&M.]
*PRACTICE AREAS: Labor and Employment.
**Jackson, Gregory C.** .................... '58 '93 C.813 B.S. L.904 J.D. [[A] Brobeck,P.&H.]
**Jackson, Meredith S.** ................... '60 '88 C.674 A.B. L.1065 J.D. [Wilson,S.G.&R.]
*PRACTICE AREAS: Bank Financings; Public and Private Debt Securities; Structured Finance; Workouts and Debt Restructuring; Bankruptcy Planning.
**Jacob, Thomas B.** ....................... '51 '78 C.103 A.B. L.1065 J.D. [Thoits,L.H.&M.]
*PRACTICE AREAS: Real Estate Law.
**Jacobs, James L.** ....................... '63 '89 C.103 A.B. L.893 J.D. [[A] Wilson,S.G.&R.]
*PRACTICE AREAS: Litigation.
Jacobs, Justin M., Jr. .................... '33 '60 C.813 A.B. L.1066 LL.B. 555 Bryant St.‡
**Jacobson, Andrew M.** .................... '70 '96 C.668 B.A. L.94 J.D. [[A] Gray C.W.&F.]
*PRACTICE AREAS: Corporate/Securities.
**Jacobson, Michael R.** ................... '54 '81 C.309 A.B. L.813 J.D. [Cooley G.]
*PRACTICE AREAS: Securities; Mergers and Acquisitions.
**Jacobson, Ronald L.**, (AV) .............. '29 '55 C.112 B.S. L.1068 J.D. [Cooley G.]
*PRACTICE AREAS: Real Estate (Property) Law; Business Law.
Jacobstein, J. Myron '20 '53 C.912 B.A. L.146 LL.B.
(adm. in IL; not adm. in CA) Prof. of Law, Emeritus, Stanford Univ.
Jain, Peeyush .............................. '53 '91 C.145 B.A. L.813 J.D. 650 Page Mill Rd.
**James, William J.** ...................... '64 '94 C.871 B.S.M.E. L.813 J.D. [[A] Heller E.W.&M.]
**Jamplis, Robin P.** ...................... '52 '88 C.312 B.A. L.1065 J.D. [[A] N.H.Glickman&Assoc.]
*PRACTICE AREAS: Domestic and International Estate and Tax Planning; Asset Protection; Probate; Trust Administration.
Janah, Ashok K. ........... '60 '92 C.24 B.S. L.809 J.D. 125 California Ave., 2nd Fl. (Pat.)
Jang, Sudeok ............................... '49 '81 C.061 B.A. L.1068 J.D. 1844 Guinda St.
Jeffery, William D. ......... '49 '75 C.174 B.A. L.813 J.D. Asst. Dir., Syntex (U.S.A.) Inc.
**Jenett, Bruce W.** ........................ '46 '77 C.674 B.A. L.276 J.D. [Fenwick&W.]
*PRACTICE AREAS: Corporate.
**Jha, Viraj D.** '70 '95 C.1036 B.A. L.93 J.D.
(adm. in MA; not adm. in CA) [[A] Cooley G.]
*LANGUAGES: German.
*PRACTICE AREAS: Corporate; High Technology; Technology Licensing.
Johnson, Antje ............................. '62 '90 C.675 B.A. L.309 J.D. 2200 Geng Rd.
**Johnson, Craig H.** ...................... '52 '79 C.101 B.A. L.464 J.D. [Packard,P.&J.]⊙
*PRACTICE AREAS: Class Actions; False Claims Act; Complex Business Litigation.
**Johnson, Daniel, Jr.**, (AV) ............. '48 '73 C.112 A.B. L.976 J.D. [Cooley G.]
*PRACTICE AREAS: Commercial Litigation; Intellectual Property Litigation.
**Johnson, Kenneth L.** .......... '61 '95 C.277 M.S.E.E. L.276 J.D. [[A] Townsend&T.&C.]
*PRACTICE AREAS: Patent; Trademark; Antitrust.
**Johnson, Kevin P.B.** .... '66 '93 C.188 B.S.E.E. L.1019 J.D. [[A] Fish&N.] (See Pat. Sect.)
*PRACTICE AREAS: Intellectual Property.
**Johnson, Paul B.** ........................ '67 '96 C&L.101 B.S., J.D. [[A] Gray C.W.&F.]
Johnson, Rodney ........ '48 '73 C.1365 B.A. L.178 J.D. Sr. Univ. Coun., Stanford Univ.
**Johnson, Terry T.** ...................... '57 '81 C.813 A.B. L.1066 J.D. [Wilson,S.G.&R.]
*PRACTICE AREAS: Litigation.
**Johnston, Alan Cope**, (AV) ............... '46 '75 C.976 A.B. L.309 J.D. [Morrison&F.]
*PRACTICE AREAS: Intellectual Property Litigation; Securities Litigation; Alternative Dispute Resolution.
**Johnston, Dan S.** ....................... '63 '94 C.330 B.S. L.770 J.D. [[A] Cooley G.]
*PRACTICE AREAS: Intellectual Property Licensing; Corporate Partnering; Corporate Law.
**Jones, Allston L.** ...... '42 '77 C.223 B.S.E.E. L.770 J.D. [Peters,V.J.&B.] (See Pat. Sect.)
*PRACTICE AREAS: Patent, Trademark and Copyright Law.

**Jones, Bryan, (BV) '31 '57 C.674 A.B. L.813 LL.B.**
**Embarcadero Suites, 2465 East Bayshore Road, 94303⊙**
**Telephone: 415-856-2211 Fax: 415-726-9068**
**(Certified Specialist, Estate Planning, Trust and Probate Law, The State Bar of California Board of Legal Specialization).**
**Practice Limited to Estate Planning, Trust and Probate Law and Related Litigation, Real Estate Transactions.**
**Half Moon Bay, California Office: Shoreline Station, 225 S. Cabrillo Highway, Suite 111C, P.O. Box 967. Telephone: 415-726-7578. Fax: 415-726-9068.**

**Jones, James R.** ........................ '56 '82 C.309 B.A. L.813 J.D. [[C] Cooley G.]
*PRACTICE AREAS: Corporate Law; Mergers and Acquisitions.
**Jones, Jeffrey P.** ....................... '64 '93 C.112 B.A. L.464 J.D. [[A] Heller E.W.&M.]
**Jones, Robert L.** ........................ '54 '80 C.821 B.A. L.813 J.D. [Cooley G.]
*PRACTICE AREAS: Securities; Licensing; Intellectual Property Law.
Jordan, Althea Lee, (BV) ................... '49 '76 C.813 B.A. L.446 J.D. [Jordan&M.]
**Jordan, J. Scott** ................. '54 '79 C&L.770 B.S., J.D. [Germino,R.A.J.C.&M.]⊙
*PRACTICE AREAS: Family Law; Bankruptcy; Transactional; Litigation.
Jordan & Miller, (BV) ............................................ 385 Sherman Ave.
**Judge, Raju S.** ......................... '66 '93 C.112 B.A. L.1148 J.D. [[A] Wilson,S.G.&R.]
*LANGUAGES: Hindi, Panjabi, Urdu and French.
*PRACTICE AREAS: Corporate; Securities; Venture Capital.
**Judkins, Richard D.** .................... '47 '76 C.675 B.A. L.178 J.D. [Tomlinson Z.M.&M.]
*PRACTICE AREAS: Corporate Finance and Acquisitions; Securities.
Kahan, Ari ................................. '62 '90 C.1169 B.A. L.1068 J.D. 650 Page Mill Rd.
**Kahn, Sherman W.** ....................... '63 '93 C.112 B.A. L.1066 J.D. [[A] Morrison&F.]
**Kalin, Alan B.** .......................... '53 '78 C.339 B.S. L.1066 J.D. [Graham&J.]
*PRACTICE AREAS: Corporate and Securities Law; Mergers and Acquisitions.
**Kalkstein, Michael H.** .................. '42 '68 C.659 B.A. L.1066 J.D. [Graham&J.]
*PRACTICE AREAS: Intellectual Property Litigation; Complex Business Litigation; Securities Litigation.

**Kamangar, Robert B '66 '92 C.112 B.A. L.1049 J.D.**
**409 Sherman Avenue, Suite 212, 94306**
**Telephone: 415-327-2447 Facsimile: 415-327-2011**
***LANGUAGES: Farsi.**
***PRACTICE AREAS: Business Litigation; Real Estate Litigation; Wrongful Termination/Discrimination; Debt Collection; Family Law.**
**Business Litigation, Wrongful Termination/Discrimination Litigation (Employee and Employer Representation), Employment Law, Family Law, Collections and Personal Injury.**

*See Professional Biographies, PALO ALTO, CALIFORNIA*

**Kamb, Barclay J.** ....................... '58 '89 C.813 B.S. L.1066 J.D. [[A] Cooley G.]
*PRACTICE AREAS: Corporate Partnering; Intellectual Property Licensing; Business Law.
**Karamali, Riaz A.** ...................... '63 '88 C.691 B.A. L.178 J.D. [[A] Gibson,D.&C.]
*PRACTICE AREAS: Corporate and Securities; New Enterprise Formation.
**Kasler, Paula S.** ....................... '55 '83 C.188 B.A. L.1066 J.D. [[C] Heller E.W.&M.]
*LANGUAGES: French.
**Kastelic, John W.** ...................... '60 '85 C.910 B.S.B.A. L.276 J.D. [[C] Fenwick&W.]
*PRACTICE AREAS: Securities; Mergers and Acquisitions; General Corporate.
Kaster, Kevin R. '59 '88 C.880 B.S. L.347 J.D.
(adm. in IN; not adm. in CA; Pat.) Pat. Atty., Affymax
Katchman, Ross N. ......................... '61 '88 C.645 B.S. L.228 J.D. Hewlett-Packard Co.
**Kato, Joan S.** ........................... '45 '82 C.910 A.B. L.312 J.D. [Gray C.W.&F.]
*PRACTICE AREAS: Litigation.
Kaufman, Jeffrey A., (BV) ......... '44 '72 C.112 B.A. L.1065 J.D. 2600 El Camino Real
**Kaufman, Lisa N.** '53 '78 C.347 B.A. L.260 J.D.
(adm. in FL; not adm. in CA) [[C] Heller E.W.&M.]

**Kavalaris, Margaret H.**, (AV) ........... '55 '81 C.112 B.A. L.766 J.D. [Gray C.W.&F.]
*PRACTICE AREAS: Start-up Companies; Intellectual Property; Technology Transfer and Licensing; Business Transactions.
Kay, William F., (BV) ...................... '41 '71 C.976 B.A. L.273 J.D. [Kay&S.]
Kay & Stevens, (AV) .............................................. 101 University Ave.
**Kays, David A.** .......................... '57 '85 C.454 B.A. L.767 J.D. [Ritchey F.W.&K.]
*PRACTICE AREAS: Business Litigation; Environmental Litigation.
Kearney, Terrence J. P. ............... '59 '87 C.1049 B.A. L.276 J.D. 525 University Ave.
**Keating, E. Lyle** ........... '50 '75 C&L.767 B.A., J.D. Reg. Coun., Hewlett-Packard Co.
*RESPONSIBILITIES: Contracts; Litigation; General Corporate.
Keller, Irwin E. ........................... '60 '89 C.339 A.B. L.145 J.D. 679 Stanford Ave.
**Kellerman, Thomas W.** ............ '55 '80 C.927 B.Bus. L.1068 J.D. [Brobeck,P.&H.]
*PRACTICE AREAS: Emerging Growth Companies; Securities Law; Mergers and Acquisitions Law.
**Kelley, John A.D.** ...................... '55 '81 C.821 B.A. L.813 J.D. [Russo&H.]
*PRACTICE AREAS: Civil Litigation; Intellectual Property Litigation; Computer Law.
Kelley, W. Patrick, (BV) ............ '54 '82 C.1071 B.A. L.950 J.D. 525 University Ave.
**Kellman, Joel D.**, (AV) .................. '42 '67 C.1044 B.A. L.724 LL.B. [Fenwick&W.]
*PRACTICE AREAS: Corporate.
**Kelly, Brian S.** '68 '93 C.280 B.B.A. L.228 J.D.
(adm. in NC; not adm. in CA) [[A] Fenwick&W.]
*PRACTICE AREAS: Intellectual Property; Licensing Law.
**Kelly, John P.** .......................... '33 '63 C.477 A.B. L.93 J.D. [[C] Lakin S.]
*PRACTICE AREAS: Business Law.
**Kelly, Kerry A.** ......................... '59 '86 C.813 B.A. L.770 J.D. [[A] Bialson,B.&S.]
*LANGUAGES: German.
*PRACTICE AREAS: Litigation; Real Property; Bankruptcy Law.
**Kelly, Terence M.** ...................... '57 '84 C.813 A.B. L.1066 J.D. [Ritchey F.W.&K.]
*PRACTICE AREAS: Corporate Law; Business; Intellectual Property.
Kelman, Mark G. '51 '77 C&L.309 B.A., J.D.
(adm. in NY; not adm. in CA) Prof., Stanford Law School
**Kelso, C. Kevin** ........................ '54 '80 C.339 B.A. L.309 J.D. [Fenwick&W.]
*PRACTICE AREAS: Corporate Securities; Mergers and Acquisitions.
Kemp, James E. '55 '80
C.608 B.S. L.1065 J.D. Mid-Peninsula Bank Bldg., 430 Cowper St.,

**Kemp, Maurice, (BV) '32 '61 C.674 A.B. L.813 LL.B.**
**517 Byron Street, P.O. Box 1299, 94302⊙**
**Telephone: 415-321-5631 Fax: 415-326-0825**
***PRACTICE AREAS: Family Law; Personal Injury; Probate and Estate Planning; Trusts; Civil Trial.**
**Family, Personal Injury, Estate Planning, Trusts and Probate Law. General Civil Practice.**
**Middletown, California Office: 21208 Calistoga Road. 95461. Telephone: 707-987-9523.**

**Kendrick, Christine** .................... '68 '96 C.813 A.B. L.276 J.D. [[A] Wilson,S.G.&R.]
*PRACTICE AREAS: Litigation.
Kennedy, Bill '47 '86 C.813 A.B. L.588 J.D.
(adm. in MA; not adm. in CA; Pat.) 755 Page Mill Rd.
Kennedy, Donald J. ......................... '10 '46 C&L.813 A.B., LL.B. 4195 Willmar Dr.‡
Kennedy, Gregory S. ....................... '62 '88 C.339 B.A. L.276 J.D. 2200 Geng Rd.
**Kennelly, Anne Marie** ...... '49 '73 C.770 L.767 J.D. Corp. Coun., Hewlett-Packard Co.
*RESPONSIBILITIES: General Corporate; International; Sales Finance; Credit and Collections.
Kenny, Arthur ................................................ '54 '91 C.629 L.770 J.D. EPRI

**Kent, Edward A., Jr. '38 '66 C.103 A.B. L.813 LL.B.**
**2501 Park Boulevard, Suite 100, 94306**
**Telephone: 415-328-2089 Fax: 415-326-5430**
***REPORTED CASES: Matter of Fondiller 707 F2d 441 9th Cir; Irizarry v. Schmidt 171BR874 (9th Cir BAP).**
***PRACTICE AREAS: Bankruptcy; Insolvency.**
**Bankruptcy and Insolvency Law.**

*See Professional Biographies, PALO ALTO, CALIFORNIA*

Kent, Leslie P. '59 '87 C.112 B.A. L.101 J.D.
(adm. in UT; not adm. in CA) 5 Palo Alto Sq.

**Keogh, William T., Law Offices of, (AV) '— '52 C.375 B.S. L.813 LL.B.**
**Suite 460, 285 Hamilton Avenue, P.O. Box 840, 94302**
**Telephone: 415-321-0947 Fax: 415-326-9722**
**Civil and Criminal Trial Practice. Family, Juvenile, Personal Injury, Estate Planning and Probate Law.**

*See Professional Biographies, PALO ALTO, CALIFORNIA*

**Kerin, Anthony J., III**, (AV) ............ '51 '81 C.766 B.A. L.1065 J.D. [Flicker&K.]
*PRACTICE AREAS: Corporate Law; Business Law; Real Estate Law.
**Kern, Daniel H.** ......................... '58 '87 C.813 B.S.M.E. L.426 J.D. [[A] Wise&S.]
Kern, Sylvie Kulkin ....................... '51 '83 C.112 B.A. L.1065 J.D. 650 Page Mill Rd.
Kersten, Carol J. '56 '82 C.602 B.A. L.813 J.D.
Dir., Planned Giving, Stanford Univ. Medical Ctr.
Keyworth, Sharon M. ...................... '53 '82 C.112 B.S. L.767 J.D. 832 Homer Ave.
**Khorana, Adit M.** ....... '68 '94 C.679 B.S.C.E.E. L.813 J.D. [[A] Wilson,S.G.&R.] (Pat.)
*PRACTICE AREAS: Technology Transactions; Strategic Alliances; Licensing; Computer; Internet.
**Killam, David A.** ........................ '67 '93 C.94 B.A. L.976 J.D. [[A] Wilson,S.G.&R.]
**Kim, Jenny J.** ............................ '68 '93 C.112 B.A. L.464 J.D. [[A] Graham&J.]
*LANGUAGES: Korean and Spanish.
**Kim, Nan H.** '68 '93 C.188 B.S. L.276 J.D.
(adm. in PA; not adm. in CA) [[A] Wilson,S.G.&R.]
*PRACTICE AREAS: Corporate.
**Kim, Stephen E.** '69 '95 C.367 B.A. L.569 J.D.
(adm. in NY; not adm. in CA) [[A] Wilson,S.G.&R.]
*PRACTICE AREAS: Corporate.
Kimball, Walter N. ........................ '45 '78 C.813 A.B. L.770 J.D. 3517 Waverly
**Kinard, W. Brian** ....................... '64 '96 C.839 B.S.E.E. L.309 J.D. [[A] Wilson,S.G.&R.]
*PRACTICE AREAS: Corporate; Securities; Venture Capital; High Technology.

**King, A. Duncan, (AV) '37 '70 C.1254 B.S. L.1065 J.D. [BR]**
**Suite 501, 2471 East Bayshore Road, 94303**
**Telephone: 800-255-3636; 415-494-6000 FAX: 415-494-3012**
**Email: adking@ix.netcom.com**
***PRACTICE AREAS: Tax Deferred Exchanges (100%).**
**Tax Deferred Exchanges.**

*See Professional Biographies, PALO ALTO, CALIFORNIA*

**King, David R.** ......................... '68 '95 C.976 B.A. L.1066 J.D. [[A] Wilson,S.G.&R.]
*PRACTICE AREAS: Corporate; Securities.
**King, Lawrence C.** ...................... '62 '92 C.112 B.A. L.1065 J.D. [[A] Gray C.W.&F.]
*PRACTICE AREAS: Commercial Law; Financial Institutions.
**Kirk, Brien B.** ........................... '58 '87 C.112 B.A.S. L.1067 J.D. [[A] Graham&J.]
**Kirkman, Catherine S.** .................. '62 '90 C.309 A.B. L.813 J.D. [[A] Wilson,S.G.&R.]
*PRACTICE AREAS: Intellectual Property; Multimedia.
Kirkwood, Robert C., (AV) ......... '39 '66 C.668 B.A. L.309 LL.B. Hewlett-Packard Co.
Kish, Lori A. ............................... '53 '92 C.768 B.S. L.770 J.D. 400 Hamilton Ave.
**Kislik, Andrew R.** ....................... '54 '79 C&L.309 B.A., J.D. [Cohen&O.]
*PRACTICE AREAS: Civil Litigation; Commercial Litigation; Employment Law.
**Kitch, James C.**, (AV) ................... '47 '73 C.309 A.B. L.813 J.D. [Cooley G.]
*PRACTICE AREAS: Corporate Law; Securities; Emerging Growth Companies; Mergers and Acquisitions.
Kitchen, Gerald J. ........................ '40 '72 C.972 B.S. L.1065 J.D. 525 University Ave.

CALIFORNIA—PALO ALTO | MARTINDALE-HUBBELL LAW DIRECTORY 1997

Kjos, Andrew B., (AV) ................'34 '59 C&L.813 B.S., LL.B. 2600 El Camino Real
**Klein, Anthony R.** ........................'64 '90 C.309 A.B. L.1068 J.D. [▣ Cooley G.]
*PRACTICE AREAS: Information Technologies Licensing; Commercial Transactions.
**Klein, Lawrence A., (AV)** ..........'38 '64 C.188 B.A. L.309 LL.B. [Ritchey F.W.&K.]
*PRACTICE AREAS: Corporate Law; Business; Taxation.
Klein, Stuart L. ..............................'56 '84 C.103 A.B. L.813 J.D. P.O. Box 60760
**Klein, Thomas Christopher** ...........'62 '89 C.821 B.A. L.145 J.D. [Wilson,S.G.&R.]
*PRACTICE AREAS: Corporate Law; Securities.
Klinestiver, Beverly Glass ...........'52 '79 C.1042 B.A. L.809 J.D. 400 Miramonte Ave.
**Klotsche, John C.** '42 '67 C.37 B.S. L.966 J.D.
(adm. in WI; not adm. in CA) [Baker&M.]
Klynn, Michael, (BV) '37 '62 C.880 B.A. L.477 LL.B.
2600 El Camino Real, Suite 506‡
Knapp, Thomas A. ..........................'49 '77 C.813 A.B. L.477 J.D. [Knapp&V.]
Knapp & Vernon ..............................................................525 University Ave.
Knee, Martina W. ......................'54 '83 C.112 A.B. L.1066 J.D. 525 Univ. Ave.
Knell, Charles A., (BV) ......................'41 '66 C.120 B.A. L.508 J.D. [C.A.Knell]
Knell, Charles A., A Professional Corporation, (BV) ..................301 University Ave.
**Knorp, Albert F., (AV)** ..............'35 '61 C.813 B.A. L.770 LL.B. [▣ Gray C.W.&F.]
*PRACTICE AREAS: Corporate Law; Business Transactions; Real Property Law.
**Koa, Christopher M.** ..........................'66 '93 C.118 B.A. L.569 J.D. [▣ Wilson,S.G.&R.]
*LANGUAGES: Spanish.
*PRACTICE AREAS: Corporate Law; Securities.
**Kociol, Stephen M.** ...'— '76 C.861 B.S. L.813 J.D. V.P., Legal Affs., Roche Bioscience
*REPORTED CASES: Diaz v. San Jose Unified School District, 612 F.2d 411 (9 Cir. 1979), 518 F.Supp. 622 (N.D.Ca. 1981), 705 F.2d 1129 (9 Cir. 1982), 733 F.2d 660 (9 Cir. 1984) (en banc), cert. den. 471 U.S. 1065 (1985), 633 F.Supp. 808 (N.D.Ca. 1986).
*RESPONSIBILITIES: Labor and Employment Law.
Kocot, Nancy J. .........................'56 '82 C.518 A.B. L.276 J.D. 610 California Ave.
Koehler, Fritz K. ..................................'64 '90 C.813 B.A. L.112 J.D. 2 Palo Alto Sq.
**Koeppe, Karen A., (BV)** ..................'58 '83 C.768 B.A. L.770 J.D. [▣ Bialson,B.&S.]
*PRACTICE AREAS: Commercial Law; Probate; Trust Administration.
**Koerner, Gregory J.** ..........................'52 '95 C.219 B.A. L.61 J.D. [▣ Carr,D.&F.]
Kokores, Roger P., (AV) ....................'44 '69 C.768 B.S. L.1066 J.D. [R.P.Kokores]
Kokores, Roger P., A Professional Corporation, (AV) ..............2600 El Camino Real

**Kolisch Hartwell Dickinson McCormack & Heuser, A Professional Corporation, (AV)**
▣
**420 Florence Street, 94301**⊙
**Telephone: 415-325-8673 Facsimile: 415-325-5076**
**Email: concepts@concepts-law.com**
**Jon M. Dickinson (Not admitted in CA); John M. McCormack; Peter E. Heuser; David A. Fanning; Pierre C. Van Rysselberghe.**
**Patent, Trademark and Unfair Competition Law. Trials.**
**Portland, Oregon Office: 200 Pacific Building, 520 S.W. Yamhill Street. Telephone: 503-224-6655. Fax: 503-295-6679.**
**Boise, Idaho Office: 802 W. Bannock, Suite 403A. Telephone: 208-384-9166. Fax: 208-384-9169.**
***See Professional Biographies, PALO ALTO, CALIFORNIA***

**Konski, Antoinette F.** ..............'60 '89 C.205 B.S. L.262 J.D. [▣ Morrison&F.] (Pat.)
*PRACTICE AREAS: Intellectual Property; Patent Prosecution.
Kontrabecki, John T. ....................'51 '77 C&L.188 A.B., J.D. 3600 W. Bayshore Rd.
**Kopeikin, Jill F.** ..................................'66 '92 C.911 B.S. L.1066 J.D. [▣ Graham&J.]
**Kopel, Jared L.** ..............................'50 '79 C.178 B.A. L.569 J.D. [Wilson,S.G.&R.]
*PRACTICE AREAS: Litigation.
**Kopf, Patricia Nicely** ...........................'50 '75 C.914 A.B. L.309 J.D. [Fenwick&W.]
*PRACTICE AREAS: Litigation; Employment and Labor Law.
**Kopitzke, Christine L.** ......................'52 '88 C.668 B.A. L.1066 J.D. [▣ Fenwick&W.]
*PRACTICE AREAS: Litigation; Intellectual Property Law.
**Korman, Martin W.** .......................'63 '90 C.813 A.B. L.976 J.D. [Wilson,S.G.&R.]
*PRACTICE AREAS: Corporate Law; Mergers and Acquisitions; Securities.
**Kornegay, Robert F., Jr.** ...........'65 '93 C.276 A.B. L.1068 J.D. [▣ Wilson,S.G.&R.]
*LANGUAGES: French.
*PRACTICE AREAS: Corporate; Securities.
Korybut, Michael M. ........................'62 '90 C.154 B.A. L.813 J.D. 400 Hamilton Ave.
**Kosacz, Barbara A.** ............................'58 '88 C.813 B.A. L.1066 J.D. [Cooley G.]
*PRACTICE AREAS: Hi-tech Transactions; Emerging Growth Companies.
**Koshland, James M.** ........................'51 '78 C.311 B.A. L.813 J.D. [Gray C.W.&F.]
*PRACTICE AREAS: Venture Capital (Retail and High Technology Start Ups); Intellectual Property; Mergers and Acquisitions; General Commercial.
**Koslow, Andrew B.** ..........................'60 '87 C.367 B.A. L.569 J.D. [▣ Brobeck,P.&H.]
*PRACTICE AREAS: Corporate Law; Banking Law; Financial Services Law.
**Kostenbauder, Daniel** ....'50 '76 C.976 B.A. L.569 J.D. Tax Coun., Hewlett-Packard Co.
*RESPONSIBILITIES: Tax.
**Kramer, Barry J.** ..................................'58 '82 C.659 B.S. L.813 J.D. [Fenwick&W.]
*PRACTICE AREAS: Corporate.
**Kramer, David H.** ......................'68 '93 C.197 B.A. L.276 J.D. [▣ Wilson,S.G.&R.]
*PRACTICE AREAS: Intellectual Property.
**Kramer, James N.** ..........................'66 '91 C.446 B.S. L.846 J.D. [▣ Brobeck,P.&H.]
*PRACTICE AREAS: Securities; Commercial Litigation.
**Kramer, Karl J.** ..................................'60 '87 C.399 B.A. L.966 J.D. [Morrison&F.]
*PRACTICE AREAS: Commercial Litigation; Intellectual Property Litigation.
**Kranwinkle, Jane** ..........................'67 '94 C.813 B.A. L.477 J.D. [▣ Fenwick&W.]
*PRACTICE AREAS: Litigation.
**Krause, Susan P.** ..........................'71 '96 C.309 B.A. L.976 J.D. [▣ Wilson,S.G.&R.]
*PRACTICE AREAS: Corporate; Securities.
Kroff, Steven ....................................................................'38 '73 780 Welch Rd.
**Krohn, Douglas Keith** ..............'54 '79 C.813 A.B. L.1068 J.D. [▣ Wilson,S.G.&R.]
*PRACTICE AREAS: Real Estate; Commercial Law; International Law.
**Krubiner, Alan M.** ................'41 '75 C.994 B.S. L.776 J.D. [Heller E.W.&M.] (Pat.)
*PRACTICE AREAS: Patent Prosecution; Licensing; Intellectual Property Strategy.
Krueger, Jane L. ..........................'51 '73 C&L.477 B.A., J.D. 701 Welch Rd. #A3321
**Ku, Peter C.** ..................................'62 '92 C.691 B.S.E.E. L.273 J.D. [▣ Brobeck,P.&H.]
*PRACTICE AREAS: Corporate Transactions.
**Kumamoto, Andrew** ..............'58 '95 C.112 B.S. L.800 J.D. [▣ McCutchen,D.B.&E.]
*PRACTICE AREAS: Biotechnology Patent Law.
**Kumamoto, Don F.** ..........................'55 '87 C.112 B.S. L.1066 J.D. [Morrison&F.]
*PRACTICE AREAS: Intellectual Property; General Litigation.
**Kumin, Jane S.** '48 '74 C.309 B.A. L.1066 J.D.
Gen. Coun. & Corp. Secy., Elec. Power Resch. Instit., Inc.
*LANGUAGES: French.
*RESPONSIBILITIES: Tax Exempt Organizations Law; Antitrust Law; Contracts Law; Intellectual Property Law; Litigation Management.
Kuo, Janie T. ..................................'64 '89 C.339 B.A. L.597 J.D. 400 Hamilton Ave.
**Kurkowski, James F.** .........'62 '90 C.860 B.S. L.659 J.D. [▣ Townsend&T.&C.] (Pat.)
*PRACTICE AREAS: Patent Law.
**Kurlich, Sara M.** ..................................'— '95 C.94 B.S. L.1065 J.D. [▣ Brobeck,P.&H.]
*PRACTICE AREAS: Corporate and Securities.
**Kurr, Elizabeth M.** ..........................'64 '92 C.339 B.S. L.767 J.D. [▣ Wilson,S.G.&R.]
*PRACTICE AREAS: Corporate Law.
Kurtzman, Woof ..........................................'— '71 C.477 B.A. L.813 J.D. Theatreworks
**Kuwayti, Kenneth A.** ......................'64 '90 C.012 B.A. L.813 J.D. [▣ Morrison&F.]

**Laam, Barbara C. Y.** ..............'53 '92 C.347 B.A. L.284 J.D. [▣ Fragomen,D.&B.]
*LANGUAGES: Chinese (Cantonese and Mandarin).
**LaBoskey, Peter** ..........................'50 '76 C.605 B.A. L.770 J.D. [Wilson,S.G.&R.]
*PRACTICE AREAS: Estate Planning.
**Labrucherie, Gilbert M., Jr.** .........'71 '96 C.112 A.B. L.1066 J.D. [▣ Wilson,S.G.&R.]
*PRACTICE AREAS: Corporate; Securities; Mergers and Acquisitions.
**Ladra, Michael A., (AV)** ..........'49 '75 C.674 A.B. L.1065 J.D. [Wilson,S.G.&R.]
*PRACTICE AREAS: Intellectual Property.
**Lagod, Martin L.** ..................................'55 '81 C.575 B.A. L.880 J.D. [Cooley G.]
*PRACTICE AREAS: Patent, Copyrights, Trademark and General Intellectual Property Litigation and Counselling; Licensing; General Litigation; Securities Litigation.
**Laibson, Rebecca** ............................'69 '95 C.918 B.A. L.813 J.D. [▣ Nolan&A.]
*PRACTICE AREAS: Criminal Law; Driving While Intoxicated; Felonies; Misdemeanors.

**Lakin • Spears, (AV)**
**285 Hamilton Avenue, P.O. Box 240, 94301**
**Telephone: 415-328-7000**
**Egerton D. Lakin (1886-1968); Andrew M. Spears (1915-1988). Members of Firm: George H. Norton (Certified Specialist, Family Law, The State Bar of California Board of Legal Specialization); Frank A. Small; Thomas J. Cahill; Carol S. Boes; J. A. Tony Villanueva; Ronald A. VandenBerg (Certified Specialist, Estate Planning, Trust and Probate Law, California Legal Board of Specialization).; Michael G. Desmarais (Certified Specialist, Estate Planning, Trust and Probate Law, California Legal Board of Specialization); Jessica F. Arner (Certified Specialist, Family Law, The State Bar of California Board of Legal Specialization); Sherrol L. Cassedy (Certified Specialist, Family Law, The State Bar of California Board of Legal Specialization); Daniel R. Morris; Jennifer F. Wald; Laura L. Reynolds; James P. Cilley; Ella J. Duncanson. Of Counsel: Donald H. Read (Certified Specialist, Taxation Law, The State Bar of California Board of Legal Specialization); John P. Kelly; Robert L. Bouchier.**
**Civil Trial Practice in all State and Federal Courts. Civil Appeals, Insurance, Family, Estate Planning, Probate, Real Property, Finance and Development, Corporation, Federal and State Taxation, Arbitration and Mediation Law.**
***See Professional Biographies, PALO ALTO, CALIFORNIA***

Laliberte, Margaret G. ............................'42 '84 C.813 B.A. L.770 J.D. 2211 Park Blvd.
**Lambert, Joan E.** ..............................'65 '90 C.112 B.A. L.1068 J.D. [▣ Wilson,S.G.&R.]
*PRACTICE AREAS: Securities and Commercial Litigation; Alternative Dispute Resolution.
Lamblin, Kina ............................................'68 '92 C.112 B.A. L.145 J.D. 2200 Geng Rd.
Lancefield, Robert K. ................'36 '62 C.668 B.A. L.813 J.D. 189 Walter Hays Dr.‡
Landis, James P. ..........................'46 '77 C.1155 B.S. L.1066 J.D. 2115 Edgewood Dr.
**Landis, Judith** '— '94 C.112 A.B. L.178 J.D.
(adm. in NY; not adm. in CA) [▣ Cooley G.]
*PRACTICE AREAS: Tax Law.
**Landy, Meredith Nelson** ..............'60 '88 C.420 B.A. L.1066 J.D. [Brobeck,P.&H.]
*PRACTICE AREAS: SEC.
**Lane, Tim J.** ..........................................'— '95 C.846 B.S. L.352 J.D. [▣ Fenwick&W.]
*PRACTICE AREAS: Intellectual Property; Patent Law.
**Lang, Dan H.** ..........................'64 '93 C.930 B.S.E.E. L.1066 J.D. [▣ Townsend&T.&C.]
*PRACTICE AREAS: Patent Law; Intellectual Property.
**Langdon, Larry R.** '38 '61 C&L.608 B.Sc., J.D.
Dir., Tax, Lic. & Customs, Hewlett-Packard Co.
*RESPONSIBILITIES: Tax.
**Lanier, T. Gregory** ..............................'63 '88 C.770 B.A. L.1065 J.D. [▣ Cooley G.]
*PRACTICE AREAS: Securities; Mergers and Acquisitions; Business Litigation; Litigation.
La Poll, Francis A. ........................'58 '84 C.893 B.A. L.813 J.D. 4151 Middlefield Rd.
**Lapp, Eric J., (AV)** ..............................'48 '78 C.30 B.A. L.276 J.D. [Gray C.W.&F.]
**LaRosiliere, Marthe** ..................'64 '93 C.563 B.A. L.813 J.D. [▣ Wilson,S.G.&R.]
*LANGUAGES: French.
*PRACTICE AREAS: Litigation.
**Larson, David L.** ...........'56 '83 C.813 B.S.Ch.E. L.276 J.D. [Wilson,S.G.&R.] (Pat.)
*PRACTICE AREAS: Intellectual Property Litigation.
**Larson, John W., (AV)** ....................'35 '63 C&L.813 B.A., LL.B. [Brobeck,P.&H.]
*PRACTICE AREAS: Securities Law; Mergers and Acquisitions Law; General Corporate Law.
**Latta, Robert P., (AV)** ....................'54 '79 C&L.813 B.A., J.D. [Wilson,S.G.&R.]
*PRACTICE AREAS: Corporate Law; Securities.
**Lauher, Paul K.** ..............................'61 '95 C.499 B.S.B.A. L.770 J.D. [▣ Ritchey F.W.&K.]
*PRACTICE AREAS: Corporate Law.
**Laurice, Douglas M.** ......................'46 '72 C.597 B.S. L.1066 J.D. [Wilson,S.G.&R.]
*PRACTICE AREAS: Employee Benefits; Executive Compensation; Estate Planning.
**Laurie, Ronald S., (AV)** '42 '69 C.112 B.S.I.E. L.767 J.D.
[McCutchen,D.B.&E.] (⊙San Jose and San Francisco)
Lauritzen, Peter B. ..........................................'37 '65 C.813 A.B. L.1065 J.D. 701 Welch Rd.
**LaVigne-Butler, Mary** ..................'51 '85 C.610 B.G.S. L.705 J.D. [Gray C.W.&F.]
*PRACTICE AREAS: Employment; ERISA.
**Law, Kenneth T., (AV)** ..........................'53 '83 C&L.770 B.S., J.D. [Murray&M.]
*PRACTICE AREAS: Bankruptcy Litigation; Commercial Litigation; Creditors Remedies.
**LaWer, Thomas G.** ..........................'66 '96 C.659 B.S. L.145 J.D. [▣ Wilson,S.G.&R.]
*PRACTICE AREAS: Executive Compensation.
Lawlor, Mariellyn ..............................'63 '88 C.436 B.S. L.767 J.D. 3030 Hansen Way
**Lazarow, Warren T.** ......................'60 '88 C.674 A.B. L.1009 J.D. [Brobeck,P.&H.]
*LANGUAGES: French and Hebrew.
*PRACTICE AREAS: Corporate and Securities Law; Venture Capital Law; Emerging Growth Companies Law; Intellectual Property Law.
**Leahy, Mark A.** ..................................'61 '90 C.813 B.S. L.145 J.D. [▣ Fenwick&W.]
*PRACTICE AREAS: Corporate Law; Securities.
**LeBlanc, Joan A.** ..........................'53 '82 C.112 B.A. L.1065 J.D. [Aufmuth,F.W.&L.]
*PRACTICE AREAS: Estate Planning.
**Lederman, Jeffrey J.** ..........................'55 '82 C.112 B.S. L.1067 J.D. [Gray C.W.&F.]
*PRACTICE AREAS: Commercial Disputes; Real Estate and Construction Litigation; Insurance Coverage Disputes.
Lee, Ayleen Ito ..............................................'41 '81 C.768 B.A. L.813 J.D. 38 Erstwild Ct.
Lee, Catherine L. ..........................'28 '53 C.430 B.A. L.813 J.D. 2255 Dartmouth St.
Lee, Chilton H., (AV) ........................'43 '73 C.112 B.S. L.770 J.D. 2600 El Camino Real
**Lee, Michelle K.** ..............................'65 '92 C.453 B.S. L.813 J.D. [▣ Fenwick&W.]
*PRACTICE AREAS: Intellectual Property; Patent Law; Licensing Law.
Lee, Otto O. ......'67 '94 C.112 B.S.Ch.E. L.1065 J.D. 125 California Ave., 2nd Fl. (Pat.)
Lee, Patricia F. ..........................................'63 '89 C.813 B.A. L.1065 J.D. 101 University Ave.
Lee, Ralph S. ..................................'23 '71 C.112 B.S.E.E. L.284 LL.B. 459 Homer Ave.
Lee, Robert E., (BV) ......................'16 '52 C.112 B.S. L.284 LL.B. 355 Christopher Ct.
**Lee, Victoria W-Y** ..................................'68 '93 C&L.112 A.B., J.D. [▣ Gray C.W.&F.]
**Lehnhardt, Susan K.** ..........................'59 '93 C.205 B.A. L.262 J.D. [▣ Morrison&F.]
Leib, Charles B., (AV) ..................................'10 '36 C&L.813 A.B., J.D. 2349 Francisco St.‡
**Leibnitz, Andrew** ..............................'70 '96 C.951 B.A. L.569 J.D. [▣ Wilson,S.G.&R.]
*PRACTICE AREAS: Litigation.
Leitereg, Theodore J. ....................'41 '75 C.749 B.S. L.767 J.D. Syntex (U.S.A.) Inc.
**Lemieux, Ronald S.** ..............................'59 '85 C.813 A.B. L.1065 J.D. [Graham&J.]
*PRACTICE AREAS: Intellectual Property; Commercial Litigation.
**Lemmer, Gregory S.** ..........................'60 '89 C.475 B.A. L.966 J.D. [Brobeck,P.&H.]
*PRACTICE AREAS: Labor and Employment.
Lemos, Robert A. ..............................'41 '70 C.767 B.S. L.1065 J.D. CFO, Varian Assocs., Inc.
**Lenell, Jack Anderson** ... '— '92 C.112 B.S. L.1137 J.D. Pat. Atty., Hewlett-Packard Co.
*RESPONSIBILITIES: Intellectual Property/Compliance; Litigation; Patent.
**Lentini, David P.** ....'63 '93 C.145 B.S. L.1065 J.D. [▣ Hickman,B.&W.] (See Pat. Sect.)
*PRACTICE AREAS: Intellectual Property Law; Patents.

**Lentzner, Michelle E.** ....'66 '91 C.112 B.A. L.1065 J.D. [🄰 Wise&S.]
**Leonard, Edward M.**, (AV) ....'41 '72 C.976 B.A. L.813 J.D. [Brobeck,P.&H.]
*PRACTICE AREAS: Securities; Mergers and Acquisitions; Emerging Growth Companies; Venture Capital.
**Lessani, Tina M.** ....'— '95 C.691 E.E. L.477 J.D. [🄰 Fenwick&W.]
*PRACTICE AREAS: Intellectual Property; Patent Law.
**Lev, Abraham D.** '44 '73 C.112 B.S.C.E. L.1068 J.D.
Corp. Coun., Hewlett-Packard Co.
*RESPONSIBILITIES: General Corporate; Employee Benefits; Labor; Commercial Contracts.
Levens, Corey A. ....'56 '84 C.311 B.A. L.339 J.D. 7 Peter Coutts Circle
Levere, Steven D. ....'61 '87 C.918 B.A. L.813 J.D. Sr. Atty., The Staubach Co.
**Levin, David S.** ....'65 '91 C.597 B.A. L.145 J.D. [🄰 Murray&M.]
*PRACTICE AREAS: Commerical Litigation; Business Workouts; Creditors Remedies.
Levin, Edith S. ....'20 '44 C.788 B.A. L.178 LL.B. 1850 Willow Rd.‡
**Levin, Michael B.** ....'68 '94 C.309 A.B. L.1068 J.D. [🄰 Wilson,S.G.&R.]
*PRACTICE AREAS: Intellectual Property Litigation.
Levin, Phyllis S. ....'31 '62 C.813 A.B. L.1066 LL.B. 444 San Antonio Rd.
LeVine, Peter R. ....'49 '77 C.813 B.A. L.1067 J.D. Pres., Vencoa, Inc.
**Levine, Philip J.** ....'57 '82 C.367 B.A. L.569 J.D. [Morrison&F.]
*PRACTICE AREAS: Real Estate.
**Levy, Adam D.** ....'62 '94 C.311 B.A. L.276 J.D. [🄰 Wilson,S.G.&R.]
**Levy, Donald M., Jr.** ....'60 '88 C.966 B.A. L.273 J.D. [McCutchen,D.B.&E.]
*PRACTICE AREAS: Corporate; Intellectual Property.
**Levy, Ginger L.** '62 '91 C.659 B.A. L.976 J.D.
(adm. in PA; not adm. in CA) [🄰 Gray C.W.&F.]
*PRACTICE AREAS: Corporate and Securities.
**Levy, Michael J.** ....'66 '94 C.1074 B.S. L.1065 J.D. [🄰 Wilson,S.G.&R.]
*PRACTICE AREAS: Litigation.
**Lewis, Brian** ....'— '91 L.770 J.D. Dir., Intell. Prop., Roche Bioscience
**Lewis, Francis H.** ....'37 '74 C.816 M.E. L.767 J.D. [🄲 Carr,D.&F.]
**Lewis, John R.** ....'68 '95 C.94 B.S. L.145 J.D. [🄰 Wilson,S.G.&R.]
Lewis, William C., (AV) ....'52 '77 C.813 B.A. L.1065 J.D. 510 Waverly St.
**Leznik, Eleonora** ....'57 '95 C.326 B.B.A. L.813 J.D. [🄰 Cooley G.]
*LANGUAGES: Russian.
*PRACTICE AREAS: Intellectual Property; Corporate Law.
Lieberman, Marvin S. '33 '58 C&L.339 B.S., LL.B.
(adm. in IL; not adm. in CA) Elec. Power Research Institute
**Liebeschuetz, Joe** '59 '92 C.050 B.A. L.347 J.D.
[🄰 Townsend&T.&C.] (See Pat. Sect.)
*PRACTICE AREAS: Biotechnology Patents.
Lightner, Robin M. ....'64 '92 C.1169 B.A. L.1066 J.D. 3000 El Camino Real
**Lin, Joseph T.** ....'65 '93 C.188 B.S. L.1068 J.D. [🄰 Morrison&F.] (Pat.)
**Linhares, Kenneth A.**, (AV) ....'55 '80 C&L.770 B.A., J.D. [Fenwick&W.]
*PRACTICE AREAS: Corporate.
**Lion, Paul L., III**, (BV) ....'57 '82 C.112 B.A. L.770 J.D. [Morrison&F.]
*PRACTICE AREAS: Taxation Law; Estate Planning Law; Partnership Law; Business Law; Health Care Law.
**Lipeles, Stewart R.** '66 '92 C.691 B.A. L.145 J.D.
(adm. in IL; not adm. in CA) [🄰 Baker&M.]
*PRACTICE AREAS: Taxation.
**Lipp, Joshua A.** ....'67 '92 C.813 A.B. L.1066 J.D. [🄰 Wilson,S.G.&R.]
*LANGUAGES: Spanish.
*PRACTICE AREAS: Corporate Law; Securities Law.
**Lisi, David M.** ....'60 '91 C.976 B.A. L.188 J.D. [🄰 Cooley G.]
*PRACTICE AREAS: Securities Litigation; Technology Litigation.
**Liu, Francis Yan** ....'62 '87 C.453 S.B. L.178 J.D. Sr. Atty., Hewlett-Packard Co.
*RESPONSIBILITIES: Antitrust; Software Licensing; Commercial Contracts.
**Livornese, Deborah L.** ....'59 '84 C.659 B.A. L.1065 J.D. [🄰 Wise&S.]
*PRACTICE AREAS: Environmental.
**Llewelyn, Elaine** ....'63 '94 C.201 B.S. L.767 J.D. [🄰 Brobeck,P.&H.]
*PRACTICE AREAS: Corporate Law.
Lloyd, Dean ....'41 '82 C.793 B.S. L.999 J.D. 460 Calif. Ave.
Lo, Karl C. ....'50 '78 C.061 LL.B. L.1065 J.D. 1800 Trousdale Dr.
Lobdell, Teresa M. ....'53 '79 C&L.813 B.A., J.D. 1828 Byrant St.‡
**Locker, Nina** ....'58 '85 C.976 B.A. L.813 J.D. [Wilson,S.G.&R.]
*PRACTICE AREAS: Litigation.
**Loe, Cynthia M.** ....'55 '84 C.911 B.A. L.1065 J.D. [🄰 Tomlinson Z.M.&M.]
*PRACTICE AREAS: Corporate Securities and Acquisitions; Business Transactions.
**Loewy, Peter H.**, (AV) '55 '79
C.563 B.A. L.705 J.D. [Fragomen,D.&B.] (⊙L.A. & San Fran.)
*LANGUAGES: French.
**Logterman, Bridget** ....'64 '90 C.966 B.A. L.1065 J.D. [🄰 Wilson,S.G.&R.]
**Lohse, Timothy W.** ....'67 '95 C.860 B.S.E.E. L.284 J.D. [🄰 Gray C.W.&F.] (Pat.)
*PRACTICE AREAS: Patent.
Lomio, J. Paul '50 '79 C.712 B.A. L.911 LL.M.
(adm. in WA; not adm. in CA) Law Libr., Stanford Univ.
**Look, Laurie-Ann Mei Inn** ....'68 '94 C&L.770 B.S., J.D. [🄰 Wilson,S.G.&R.]
*PRACTICE AREAS: Estate Planning.
**Lopez, Cynthia L.** ....'69 '95 C.681 B.A. L.309 J.D. [🄰 Morrison&F.]
*LANGUAGES: Chinese and French.
**Lorr, Thomas J.** ....'66 '92 C.800 B.S. L.813 J.D. [🄰 Wilson,S.G.&R.]
*PRACTICE AREAS: Corporate.
**Lowe, Edwin N.**, (AV) ....'40 '67 C.813 B.A. L.1066 J.D. [Fenwick&W.]
*PRACTICE AREAS: Corporate.
Lowin, David A. ....'54 '80 C.319 B.A. L.1218 J.D. Pat. Atty., Syntex (U.S.A.) Inc. (Pat.)
Lowy, Michael J. ....'44 '80 C.112 Ph.D. L.813 J.D. 2600 El Camino Real
**Lucas, Patricia M.**, (AV) ....'54 '79 C.691 B.A. L.1066 J.D. [Fenwick&W.]
*PRACTICE AREAS: Litigation; Employment and Labor Law.
**Lucey, James W.** ....'65 '92 C&L.767 B.S., J.D. [🄰 Carr,D.&F.]
Ludewig, Deborah J. ....'58 '91 C.999 B.S. L.1066 J.D. 660 Hansen Wy.
**Luemers, Martha C.** ....'54 '82 C&L.813 A.B., J.D. [Ritchey F.W.&K.]
**Luh, Andrew** ....'— '96 C.893 B.A. L.813 J.D. [🄰 Fenwick&W.]
*PRACTICE AREAS: Corporate.
Lusher, Bradley A. ....'54 '90 C.97 B.S. L.275 J.D. 2 Palo Alto Sq.
**Lynch, Edward J.** ....'36 '68 C.768 B.S. L.767 J.D. [Heller E.W.&M.] (Pat.)
*PRACTICE AREAS: Intellectual Property.
**Lyon, H. Mark** ....'63 '92 C.475 B.S.E.E. L.770 J.D. [🄰 Gibson,D.&C.] (Pat.)
*PRACTICE AREAS: Intellectual Property; Patent Litigation.
**Lyon, Tiffany** ....'67 '92 C.112 B.S. L.770 J.D. [🄰 Wilson,S.G.&R.]
*PRACTICE AREAS: Civil Litigation.
Lyons, Matthew '67 '93 C&L.846 B.A., J.D.
(adm. in TX; not adm. in CA) 2200 Geng Rd.
**Lythcott-Haims, Julie C.** ....'67 '94 C.813 A.B. L.309 J.D. [🄰 Cooley G.]
*PRACTICE AREAS: Intellectual Property Litigation; Trademark Prosecution.
**MacAllister, William H.** '21 '56 C.216 A.B. L.1017 LL.B.
(adm. in DC; not adm. in CA; Pat.) Assoc. Gen. Coun., Litig., Hewlett-Packard Co.
*RESPONSIBILITIES: Intellectual Property/Compliance; Patent.
**Macey, Harry J.** ....'52 '88 C.861 B.A. L.904 J.D. [🄲 Morrison&F.] (Pat.)
**MacFerrin, Kurtis D.** ....'65 '95 C.605 A.B. L.309 J.D. [🄰 Fish&N.]
*PRACTICE AREAS: Patent.

**Macias, Jose F.** ....'66 '91 C.813 B.A. [🄰 Wilson,S.G.&R.]
*LANGUAGES: Spanish.
*PRACTICE AREAS: Corporate Law; Securities.
**MacKay, Norman E.**, (BV) ....'43 '75 C.813 B.A. L.770 J.D. [Germino,R.A.J.C.&M.]⊙
*PRACTICE AREAS: Business Litigation; Real Estate Transactions; Toxic or Hazardous Materials Litigation.
**MacKenzie, Matthew** ....'71 '96 C.112 B.A. L.1068 J.D. [🄰 Wilson,S.G.&R.]
*PRACTICE AREAS: Corporate; Securities.
**Madda, Michael J.** ....'45 '69 C.276 A.B. L.597 J.D. [Baker&M.]
*PRACTICE AREAS: Taxation.
Madison, Michael J. ....'61 '87 C.976 B.A. L.813 J.D. 400 Hamilton Ave.
**Madrid, David M.** ....'58 '84 C.976 B.A. L.813 J.D. [Cooley G.]
*PRACTICE AREAS: Intellectual Property Litigation.
**Maghamé, Taraneh** ....'61 '90 C.1077 B.A. L.276 J.D. [🄰 Brobeck,P.&H.]
*LANGUAGES: Farsi.
*PRACTICE AREAS: Intellectual Property Litigation; Immigration.
**Mailliard, Page** ....'60 '87 C.813 B.A. L.309 J.D. [Wilson,S.G.&R.]
*PRACTICE AREAS: Corporate Law; Securities.
**Maines, Robert L.**, (AV) ....'38 '67 C.473 B.S.B.A. L.813 J.D. [Bryant,C.O.M.&B.]
*PRACTICE AREAS: Business and Real Estate Litigation; Alternate Dispute Resolution.
**Majerus, Laura A.** ....'58 '87 C&L.352 B.S., J.D. [🄰 Graham&J.] (Pat.)
**Maker, Edward H., II** ....'41 '72 C.112 B.S. L.1065 J.D. Sr. Atty., Hewlett-Packard Co.
*RESPONSIBILITIES: Intellectual Property/Compliance; Patent; Patent Licensing.
**Maliska, Thomas P.** ....'60 '90 C&L.813 B.A., J.D. [🄰 Heller E.W.&M.]
Mallery, Craig T. ....'68 '94 C&L.813 A.B., J.D. 2200 Geng Rd.
Mandell, Edward L. ....'37 '68 C.563 B.Ch.E. L.904 J.D. Alza Corp. (Pat.)
Mann, J. Keith '24 '49 C.347 B.S. L.1119 LL.B.
(adm. in IN; not adm. in CA) Prof. of Law, Emeritus, Stanford Univ.
**Manoliu, Andrei M.** ....'51 '82 C.061 L.813 J.D. [Cooley G.]
*PRACTICE AREAS: Intellectual Property Law; Licensing; Securities.
Mansfield, Elinor W., (Mrs.) ....'36 '63 C&L.813 A.B., LL.B. 569 Lowell Ave.‡
**Mar-Spinola, Julie Y.** ....'56 '88 C.768 B.A.Ch. L.770 J.D. [🄲 Heller E.W.&M.] (Pat.)
**Marchant, Michael W.** ....'64 '95 C.431 B.S. L.767 J.D. [🄰 Tomlinson Z.M.&M.]
*PRACTICE AREAS: Corporate; Intellectual Property; Securities.
**Marchant, Michelle M.** '58 '85 C.112 A.B. L.94 J.D.
Sr. Reg. Atty., Hewlett-Packard Co.
*RESPONSIBILITIES: Contracts; General Corporate; Personal Injury; Labor; Employee Benefits.
Marer, Alan G. ....'34 '62 C.813 A.B. L.178 LL.B. 2521 Cowper St
Marer, Alison Cherry, (BV) ....'36 '78 C.813 B.A. L.770 J.D. 385 Sherman Ave.
Marinelli, Sarabeth A. '53 '83 C.994 B.A. L.1040 J.D.
(adm. in NY; not adm. in CA) 1564 Walnut Dr.‡
**Mark, Priscilla H.** ....'66 '96 C.454 B.S. L.1066 J.D. [🄰 Heller E.W.&M.]
**Marks, E. David** ....'62 '88 C.813 A.B. L.1065 J.D. [Mitchell&M.]
*PRACTICE AREAS: Real Estate; Homeowners Association Law; Construction Law; Labor and Employment; Business Litigation.
**Marquis, Matthew E.** ....'65 '91 C.112 B.A. L.904 J.D. [🄰 Cooley G.]
*LANGUAGES: German.
*PRACTICE AREAS: Information Technology; International Commercial.
**Marshall, Deborah A.** ....'54 '82 C.178 B.A. L.588 J.D. [Cooley G.]
*PRACTICE AREAS: Securities; Intellectual Property Law.
**Marshall, G. E., IV** ....'59 '85 C.112 A.B. L.1065 J.D. [Wilson M.&T.]
*PRACTICE AREAS: Corporate and Commercial Transactions; Corporate Law; Intellectual Property; Licensing; Real Property.
Marshall, Shauna I. '54 '79 C.910 B.A. L.1067 J.D.
Exec. Dir., E. Palo Alto Community Law Proj.
**Martikan, Owen P.** ....'65 '90 C.976 B.A. L.846 J.D. [🄰 Baker&M.]
*LANGUAGES: German and French.
*PRACTICE AREAS: Taxation.
**Martin, Carol L.** ....'66 '91 C.490 B.S. L.770 J.D. [🄰 Fenwick&W.]
*PRACTICE AREAS: Corporate; Healthcare; General Transactional Practice.
**Martin, Christopher J.** ....'51 '78 C.813 A.B. L.1068 J.D. [Gibson,D.&C.] (⊙San Fran.)
*PRACTICE AREAS: Labor and Employment Law.
**Martin, Thomas J.** ....'62 '90 C&L.813 B.A., J.D. [🄰 Wilson,S.G.&R.]
*PRACTICE AREAS: Securities; Commercial Litigation.
**Martindale, Nancy D.** ....'52 '83 C.768 B.S.B.A. L.1066 J.D. [🄰 Wilson,S.G.&R.]
*PRACTICE AREAS: Litigation.
**Martinson, Pamela J.** ....'59 '89 C.208 B.A. L.309 J.D. [Cooley G.]
*PRACTICE AREAS: Financial Institutions Law; Corporate Finance; Equipment Leasing.
**Maser, Thomas F.**, (BV) ....'42 '78 C.768 B.A. L.1066 J.D. [Tomlinson Z.M.&M.]
*PRACTICE AREAS: Real Estate Law; Construction Law; Construction Litigation.
**Mason, John M.** '— '74 C.976 B.A. L.902 J.D.
(adm. in DC; not adm. in CA) [🄲 Fenwick&W.]
*PRACTICE AREAS: Litigation; Employment and Labor Law.
**Massey, Henry P., Jr.**, (AV) ....'39 '69 C&L.188 A.B., J.D. [Wilson,S.G.&R.]
*PRACTICE AREAS: Corporate Law; Securities.
**Mattison, Tamara Gail** ....'59 '90 C.957 B.B.A. L.597 J.D. [🄰 Wilson,S.G.&R.]
**Maunu, Leroy D.** '63 '93 C.350 B.S. L.1035 J.D.
(adm. in MN; not adm. in CA; See Pat. Sect.) [Carr,D.&F.]
*PRACTICE AREAS: Patent Prosecution; Software Licensing; Procurement.
**Maurer, Stephen M.** ....'58 '82 C.976 B.A. L.309 J.D. [🄰 Ritchey F.W.&K.]
*PRACTICE AREAS: Business Litigation; Technology Litigation.
**McAdam, Michael J.** ....'67 '95 C.705 B.A. L.1068 J.D. [🄰 Fenwick&W.]
*PRACTICE AREAS: Corporate.
Mc Ausland, K. Iain '65 '92 C.050 B.A. L.93 J.D.
(adm. in MA; not adm. in CA; Pat.) 525 University Ave.‡
McBride, Thomas F. '29 '56
C.569 B.A. L.178 LL.B. Dir., Envir. Health & Safety, Stanford Univ.
**McCabe, James F.** ....'54 '82 C.674 A.B. L.1066 J.D. [Morrison&F.]
*PRACTICE AREAS: Litigation.
**McCarren, William J.**, (AVⓉ) '43 '67
C.749 B.A. L.813 LL.B. [🄲 Fenwick&W.] (⊙Denver, Colorado)
*PRACTICE AREAS: Litigation; Employment and Labor Law.
McCarthy, James Steven '— '85
C.766 M.A. L.765 J.D. 261 Hamilton Ave. (⊙San Francisco)
**McClory, Michael G.** ....'63 '89 C&L.602 B.A., J.D. [🄰 Wise&S.]
*PRACTICE AREAS: Labor and Employment Law; Business Litigation.
McCluskey, David ....'61 '90 C.813 B.A. L.770 J.D. P.O. Box 1303
**McCormack, John M.** '44 '75 C.628 B.S.M.E. L.30 J.D.
[Kolisch H.D.M.&H.] (See Pat. Sect.) (⊙Portland, OR.)
*LANGUAGES: Spanish.
*PRACTICE AREAS: Patent, Trademark and Unfair Competition.
**McCown, Jean K.**, (AV) ....'49 '77 C.477 B.A. L.1066 J.D. [Ritchey F.W.&K.]
**McCoy, Sandra Smith** ....'— '90 C.112 B.A. L.800 J.D. [🄰 Fenwick&W.]
*PRACTICE AREAS: Litigation.
**McCracken, Thomas P.G.** ....'62 '94 C.112 B.A. L.770 J.D. [🄰 Reed&R.] (See Pat. Sect.)
*PRACTICE AREAS: Patent Law; Patent Preparation and Prosecution; Biotechnology; Biomedical Engineering.
McCrary, John M., (BV) ....'47 '76 C.966 A.B. L.765 J.D. 301 University Ave.

CAA471P

CALIFORNIA—PALO ALTO

MARTINDALE-HUBBELL LAW DIRECTORY 1997

**McCutchen, Doyle, Brown & Enersen, (AV)**
**One Embarcadero Place, 2100 Geng Road, 94303-0913⊙**
**Telephone: 415-846-4000 Fax: 415-846-4086**
**Email: postmaster@mdbe.com URL: http://www.mccutchen.com**
**Members of Firm: Carol K. Dillon; Ronald S. Laurie; Donald M. Levy Jr.; Gary H. Moore; William J. Newell; Lynn H. Pasahow; Ulrico S. Rosales. Counsel: Susan Herald; Susan K. Hoerger. Associates: Rajesh A. Aji; Michael D. Hartogs; Andrew Kumamoto; Elan Q.G. Nguyen; Carissa M. Smith; Peter Tong; Joseph Yang, Dr.**
**General Practice.**
**San Francisco, California Office: Three Embarcadero Center, 94111-4066. Telephone: 415-393-2000. Facsimile: 415-393-2286 (G I, II, III) Telex: 340817 MACPAG SFO.**
**Los Angeles, California Office: 355 South Grand Avenue, Suite 4400, 90071-1560. Telephone: 213-680-6400. Facsimile: 213-680-6499.**
**San Jose, California Office: Market Post Tower, Suite 1500, 55 South Market Street, 95113-2327. Telephone: 408-947-8400. Facsimile: 408-947-4750. Telex: 910 250 2931 MACPAG SJ.**
**Walnut Creek, California Office: 1331 North California Boulevard, Post Office Box V, 94596-4502. Telephone: 510-937-8000. Facsimile: 510-975-5390.**
**Washington, D.C. Office: The Evening Star Building, Suite 800, 1101 Pennsylvania Avenue, N.W., 20004-2514. Telephone: 202-628-4900. Facsimile: 202-628-4912.**
**Taipei, Taiwan Republic of China Office: International Trade Building, Tenth Floor, 333 Keelung Road, Section 1, 110. Telephone: 886-2-723-5000. Facsimile: 886-2-757-6070.**
**Affiliated Offices In: Bangkok, Thailand; Beijing, China; Shanghai, China.**

*See Professional Biographies, PALO ALTO, CALIFORNIA*

**McDonald, Paul J.** ... '55 '89 C.959 B.S. L.765 J.D. [Germino,R.A.J.C.&M.]⊙
McDowall, Cotter, Dunn, Vale & Bracco, A Professional Corporation, (AV)
425 Sherman Ave., Suite 100 (⊙San Mateo)
McGannon, John L. ... '28 '63 C.734 B.S. L.986 LL.B. 4148 Donald Dr.‡
**McGaraghan, Patrick J.**, (AV) ... '44 '70 C.813 A.B. L.767 J.D. [Gray C.W.&F.]
*PRACTICE AREAS: Real Estate Development; Environmental Compliance.
**McGeoch, Barbara J.** ... '57 '92 C.472 B.A. L.276 J.D. [🄰 Cooley G.]
*PRACTICE AREAS: Employee Benefits; Equity Compensation.
**McGlynn, J. Casey**, (BV) ... '52 '78 C&L.770 B.S., J.D. [Wilson,S.G.&R.]
*PRACTICE AREAS: Corporate Law; Securities; Life Sciences.
**McGovern, Patrick Michael** '55 '86 L.061 LL.B.
(adm. in NY; not adm. in CA) [Zevnik H.G.&M.]⊙
*LANGUAGES: French.
*PRACTICE AREAS: International Law; Insurance Coverage; Commercial Litigation.
**McGuire, Herbert W.**, (BV) ... '40 '66 C.679 B.S. L.813 J.D. [Cooley G.]
**McInroy, Valarie L.** ... '53 '78 C.768 B.A. L.770 J.D. [🄲 Fenwick&W.]
*PRACTICE AREAS: Corporate.
**McIntyre, David C.** ... '62 '89 C.188 B.S. L.262 J.D. [🄰 Fenwick&W.] (Pat.)
*PRACTICE AREAS: Intellectual Property Litigation; General Civil Litigation.
McKee, Martha A. ... '52 '79 C.788 A.B. L.770 J.D. Stanford Univ.
**McKeever, Thomas E.** ... '67 '94 C.112 A.B. L.813 J.D. [🄰 Wilson,S.G.&R.]
*PRACTICE AREAS: Litigation.
**McLaughlin, Gerald T.** ... '63 '93 C.659 B.A. L.831 J.D. [🄰 Cooley G.]
*PRACTICE AREAS: Business; Intellectual Property.
**McLean, William J., III**, (AV) ... '37 '66 C.768 B.S. L.1065 J.D. [Thoits,L.H.&M.]
*PRACTICE AREAS: Business Litigation; Wrongful Termination Law and Legal Malpractice.
McLeod, Duncan A., Jr., (AV) ... '20 '49 C&L.813 A.B., LL.B. 595 W. Crescent Dr.
McMichael, J. Richard ... '43 '70 C.112 B.A. L.1066 J.D. JRM Properties
**McNamara, Bruce M.** ... '62 '90 C&L.112 A.B., J.D. [🄰 Wilson,S.G.&R.]
*PRACTICE AREAS: Corporate Law; Securities.
**McNees, Ruth Ann** ... '64 '91 C.877 B.A. L.770 J.D. [🄰 Wilson,S.G.&R.]
*PRACTICE AREAS: Securities Litigation.
**McNelis, John T.** ... '64 '92 C.602 B.S.E.E. L.945 J.D. [🄰 Fenwick&W.] (Pat.)
*PRACTICE AREAS: Intellectual Property; Patent Law.
McOmber, F. Bryant, Jr. '45 '73 C.101 B.A. L.878 J.D.
Gen. Coun., Cornish & Carey Residential, Inc.
**Meckfessel, Lisa G.** ... '67 '94 C.813 B.A. L.966 J.D. [🄰 Wilson,S.G.&R.]
*PRACTICE AREAS: Intellectual Property Litigation.
**Meeker, Heather** ... '59 '94 C.976 B.A. L.1066 J.D. [🄰 Wilson,S.G.&R.]
*PRACTICE AREAS: Intellectual Property; Technology Licensing.
**Meenaghan, James M.** ... '68 '93 C.94 B.A. L.276 J.D. [🄰 Morrison&F.]
*LANGUAGES: Spanish.
**Meieran, Sharon E.** ... '64 '89 C.112 B.A. L.1065 J.D. [🄰 Brobeck,P.&H.]
*PRACTICE AREAS: Trademarks.
Meisel, Lee B. ... '52 '92 C.867 B.S. L.813 J.D. 2200 Geng Rd.
**Meisel, Marvin**, (AV) ... '41 '79 C.112 B.A. L.813 J.D. [Gray C.W.&F.]
*SPECIAL AGENCIES: Internal Revenue Service; California Franchise Tax Board; California State Board of Equalization.
*PRACTICE AREAS: Taxation; Estate Planning.
Melchor, Gregory L. ... '48 '73 C.668 B.A. L.813 J.D. 635 Emerson St.
**Mellberg, Byron**, (AV) ... '46 '74 C.813 A.B. L.1065 J.D. [🄲 Ritchey F.W.&K.]
*PRACTICE AREAS: Real Estate; Business.
Menager, Valerie J. ... '53 '84 C.1169 A.B. L.426 J.D. 525 University Ave., 11th Fl.
**Mendelson, Alan C.**, (AV) ... '48 '73 C.112 B.A. L.309 J.D. [Cooley G.]
*PRACTICE AREAS: Corporate; Securities; Intellectual Property Law.
Mendez, Miguel A. ... '42 '68 C&L.273 A.B., J.D. Prof., Stanford Law School
**Mendlein, John D.** ... '59 '93 C.472 B.S. L.1065 J.D. [🄰 Cooley G.] (Pat.)
*PRACTICE AREAS: Intellectual Property Protection and Enforcement.
**Meroney, Millicent S.** ... '64 '90 C.228 A.B. L.846 J.D. [🄰 Wilson,S.G.&R.]
*PRACTICE AREAS: Labor and Employment Law; Litigation.
**Merriman, E. Porter** '65 '93 C.112 B.A. L.1355 J.D.
[🄰 Fenwick&W.] (⊙San Francisco)
*PRACTICE AREAS: Intellectual Property; Licensing Law.
**Mesel, Noah D.** ... '61 '89 C.154 B.A. L.893 J.D. [🄰 Wilson,S.G.&R.]
*PRACTICE AREAS: Litigation.

**Methven & Associates**
**(See Berkeley)**

**Metzler, Amy J.** ... '66 '92 C.976 B.A. L.178 J.D. Atty., Hewlett-Packard Co.
Meyer, Donald C. '42 '68 C.350 B.S. L.352 J.D.
(adm. in IA; not adm. in CA) Stanford Univ.
**Meyer, John C.** ... '60 '92 C.112 B.A. L.464 J.D. [🄰 Zevnik H.G.&M.]
*PRACTICE AREAS: Litigation; Complex Civil Environmental Litigation.
Meyer, Myrl A. ... '19 '54 C&L.813 A.B., J.D. 833 Sonoma Terr.‡
**Meyer, Stuart P.** ... '60 '88 C.119 B.S.E.E. L.976 J.D. [Fenwick&W.] (Pat.)
*PRACTICE AREAS: Intellectual Property.
Meyer, Susan K. ... '64 '90 C.945 B.A. L.309 J.D. 3030 Hansen Wy.
**M'Guinness, Thomas A.** ... '62 '92 C.112 B.S. L.1067 J.D. [🄰 Graham&J.]
*PRACTICE AREAS: Corporate Law; Business Transactions.
**Michaels, David K.** '61 '87 C.299 B.A. L.188 J.D.
(adm. in NY; not adm. in CA) [Fenwick&W.]
*PRACTICE AREAS: Securities; Mergers and Acquisitions; Venture Capital; General Corporate.
**Mickelson, Hal M.** ... '50 '74 C.813 A.B. L.309 J.D. Reg. Coun., Hewlett-Packard Co.
*RESPONSIBILITIES: Antitrust; General Corporate; Commercial Contracts; Personal Injury; Labor.
Middlehurst, Lori A. M. ... '60 '85 C.112 B.A. L.1067 J.D. 420 Florence St., Ste. 200
**Middlekauff, Wm. Bradford** ... '61 '94 C.103 A.B. L.976 J.D. [🄰 Cooley G.]
*PRACTICE AREAS: Securities Offerings; Corporate Law.
**Miles, Margaret T.** ... '— '96 C.802 B.S. L.1065 J.D. [🄰 Brobeck,P.&H.]
*PRACTICE AREAS: Corporate.

**Miller, Charles M.** ... '48 '90 C.907 B.A. L.767 J.D. [🄰 Gray C.W.&F.]
*PRACTICE AREAS: Environmental; Insurance; Native American.
**Miller, Jana R.** ... '59 '87 C.112 B.A. L.426 J.D. [🄰 Cooley G.]
*PRACTICE AREAS: Business - Technology Licensing.
Miller, Jane Brindle ... '47 '79 C.388 B.A. L.770 J.D. 407 Sherman Ave.
Miller, Jeffrey C., (BV) ... '51 '79 C.197 A.B. L.188 J.D. 401 Florence St.

**Miller, John E., (AV) '39 '65 C&L.813 B.A., LL.B.** BB
**250 Cambridge Avenue, Suite 102, 94306-1504**
**Telephone: 415-321-8886 Fax: 415-321-8998**
**(Certified Specialist, Family Law, The State Bar of California Board of Legal Specialization).**
***LANGUAGES: German.**
***REPORTED CASES: In Re Marriage of Cademartori 119 Cal App 3rd 970.**
***PRACTICE AREAS: Family Law; Wills and Probate.**
**Associates: Annalisa C Wood; Kerre R. Dubinsky.**
**Family Law, Estate Planning and Probate.**
**Reference: Bank of the West.**

*See Professional Biographies, PALO ALTO, CALIFORNIA*

Miller, Laurie A. ... '56 '87 C.375 B.S. L.770 J.D. 3030 Hansen Way
**Miller, Michael Patiky**, (AV) ... '44 '68 C.705 A.B. L.569 J.D. [Weinberg,Z.&M.]
*SPECIAL AGENCIES: Internal Revenue Service Appeals Division, California State Board of Equalization, Merit Systems Protection Board, California Unemployment Insurance Appeals Board.
*REPORTED CASES: Estate of Heggstad, 16 CA4th 943 (1993).
*PRACTICE AREAS: Tax Law; Estate Planning Law; Probate and Trust Litigation.
Miller, Robert H. ... '32 '60 C.112 B.A. L.1065 J.D. [Jordan&M.]
Miller, William C. ... '37 '61 C&L.902 B.A., LL.B. V.P. & Gen. Coun., Collagen Corp.
**Millie, Carol Webster** '45 '77
C.477 B.A. L.767 J.D. Assoc. Gen. Coun., Watkins-Johnson Co.
*RESPONSIBILITIES: International Transactions and Subsidiaries; General Contract and Business; Labor and Employment; Intellectual Property Protection; Chief Counsel to semiconductor equipment group.
**Milstein, Harold J.** ... '57 '84 C.415 B.S. L.1019 J.D. [🄰 Wilson,S.G.&R.] (Pat.)
Minger, Marilyn E. ... '51 '91 C.112 A.B. L.1065 J.D. 200 Page Mill Rd., 2nd Fl.
**Minihane, Derek** '69 '94 C.188 B.E.E. L.273 J.D.
(adm. in MA; not adm. in CA; See Pat. Sect.) [🄰 Fish&N.]
*PRACTICE AREAS: Intellectual Property.
Minkus, Mary Payton ... '33 '63 C.623 B.A. L.813 LL.B. 1600 Dana Ave.
**Mitchell, Christopher D.** ... '61 '86 C.311 B.A. L.494 J.D. [Wilson,S.G.&R.]
*PRACTICE AREAS: Corporate Law.
**Mitchell, Darren B.** ... '66 '95 C.112 B.S. L.813 J.D. [🄰 Cooley G.]
*PRACTICE AREAS: Patent Litigation.
Mitchell, Kent, (AV) ... '39 '65 C.813 B.S. L.1066 J.D. [Mitchell&H.]

**Mitchell, Lincoln A., (AV) '36 '64 C.197 A.B. L.813 J.D.** BB
**Suite 300, 550 Hamilton Avenue, 94301**
**Telephone: 415-321-5003 Fax: 415-326-2404**
**(Certified Specialist, Family Law, The State Bar of California Board of Legal Specialization).**
***PRACTICE AREAS: Family Law; Civil Trials.**
**Family Law. Civil and Trial Practice.**

*See Professional Biographies, PALO ALTO, CALIFORNIA*

**Mitchell, Mark T.** ... '63 '88 C.169 B.A. L.1065 J.D. [Mitchell&M.]
*REPORTED CASES: General American Life Insurance Co. v. Castonguay (9th Cir. 1993) 984 Fed.2d 1518.
*PRACTICE AREAS: Civil Practice; Appellate Practice; Administrative Courts; Alternative Dispute Resolution; Mediation.
**Mitchell, Sarah E.** '69 '96 C&L.309 A.B., J.D.
(adm. in MA; not adm. in CA) [🄰 Heller E.W.&M.]
Mitchell & Herzog, (AV) ... 550 Hamilton Ave.

**Mitchell & Marks, A Professional Corporation**
**525 University Avenue, Suite 1425, 94301-1903**
**Telephone: 415-833-0280 Facsimile: 415-833-0299**
**Mark T. Mitchell; E. David Marks;—Owen M. Byrd.**
**General Civil, Trial and Appellate Practice in Federal State and Administrative Courts. Alternative Dispute Resolution including Mediation and Arbitration. Business Law including Forming and Counseling Corporations, Partnerships and Limited Liability Companies. Litigation including Real Property, Construction, Agent and Broker, Disclosure, Employment and Insurance Law.**

*See Professional Biographies, PALO ALTO, CALIFORNIA*

**Mitchells, Rebecca A.** ... '63 '91 C.381 B.A. L.597 J.D. [🄰 Wilson,S.G.&R.]
*PRACTICE AREAS: Litigation; Unfair Trade Competition.
**Mitz, Daniel R.** ... '62 '89 C.477 A.B. L.569 J.D. [🄰 Wilson,S.G.&R.]
*PRACTICE AREAS: Corporate; Securities.
Moerdyke, Carl B. ... '53 '85 C.112 B.S. L.464 J.D. 540 University Ave., Suite 250
**Moll, Robert** ... '56 '88 C.768 B.S.Ch.E. L.800 J.D. [🄰 Wilson,S.G.&R.] (Pat.)
*PRACTICE AREAS: Intellectual Property Law.
**Molodow, Shawn N.** ... '65 '95 C.36 B.S. L.1066 J.D. [🄰 Cooley G.]
*PRACTICE AREAS: Intellectual Property Transactions; Corporate Law.
**Moltzen, Allan R., Jr.** ... '45 '74 C.768 B.A. L.1068 J.D. [Russell&M.]

**Monnet, Elizabeth R., (AV) '52 '78 L.061 LL.B.**
**701 Welch Road, Suite 3320, 94304**
**Telephone: 415-833-1885 Fax: 415-833-1888**
**Business and Corporate Law, Employment, Copyright, Trademark and International Law.**

*See Professional Biographies, PALO ALTO, CALIFORNIA*

**Monroy, Gladys H.** ... '37 '86 C.331 B.A. L.767 J.D. [Morrison&F.] (Pat.)
*PRACTICE AREAS: Intellectual Property.
Mont, Laurie ... '— '91 C.766 B.A. L.1066 J.D. 755 Page Mill Rd.
**Montalvo, Patricia** ... '71 '96 C.112 B.A. L.770 J.D. [🄰 Brobeck,P.&H.]
*LANGUAGES: Spanish.
*PRACTICE AREAS: Business; Technology.
**Montgomery, Toby F.**, (AV) ... '39 '78 C&L.813 B.A., J.D. [Finch,M.&W.]
*PRACTICE AREAS: Estate Planning; Gift and Estate Tax; Trusts and Wills; Probate, Estate and Trust Administration; Conservatorships.
Montgomery, Wayne W. ... '52 '90 C.112 B.A. L.770 J.D. Syntex (U.S.A.) Inc.
**Moore, Gary H.**, (AV) '43 '71
C.976 A.B. L.309 J.D. [McCutchen,D.B.&E.] (⊙San Francisco)
*PRACTICE AREAS: Intellectual Property Law; Litigation; Licensing.
**Moore, Thomas E., III** ... '57 '84 C.813 A.B. L.1066 J.D. [🄰 Tomlinson Z.M.&M.]
*PRACTICE AREAS: Breach of Fiduciary Duty; Corporations and Partnerships; Intellectual Property; Commercial Litigation.
Moore, Timothy J. ... '57 '85 C&L.813 B.A., J.D. 400 Hamilton Ave.
**Moran, Tom M.** ... '42 '73 C.72 B.S. L.284 J.D. [🄲 Cooley G.] ‡
*PRACTICE AREAS: Intellectual Property Law; Patent Law (Biopharmaceuticals).
**Morando, Marta L.**, (AV) ... '52 '75 C.112 A.B. L.1066 J.D. [🄲 Gray C.W.&F.]
**Morehead, Kelly Ames** ... '66 '94 C.112 B.A. L.1049 J.D. [🄰 Wilson,S.G.&R.]
*PRACTICE AREAS: Corporate Law; Securities Law.
**Moretti, August J.**, (AV) ... '50 '75 C.674 B.A. L.309 J.D. [Heller E.W.&M.]
*PRACTICE AREAS: Corporate; Securities; Mergers and Acquisitions.
**Morgan, Allen L.** ... '53 '81 C.197 A.B. L.893 J.D. [Wilson,S.G.&R.]
*LANGUAGES: Swedish.
*PRACTICE AREAS: Corporate Law; Securities.
Morin, Diane J. N. ... '50 '83 C.668 B.A. L.767 J.D. 2211 Park Blvd.
**Morosoli, Eugene B., Jr.**, (AV) ... '30 '55 C.112 B.A. L.1066 J.D. [Tomlinson Z.M.&M.]
*PRACTICE AREAS: Labor Law; Arbitration.

**Morris, Daniel R.** ............................ '58 '85 C.763 B.A. L.767 J.D. [Lakin S.]
*PRACTICE AREAS: General Civil Litigation; Personal Injury and Construction Litigation.
Morris, Edith L. ........................... '67 '93 C.893 B.A. L.813 J.D. 525 Univ. Ave.

**Morrison & Foerster LLP, (AV)**
**755 Page Mill Road, 94304-1018⊙**
**Telephone: 415-813-5600 Facsimile: 415-494-0792**
**URL: http://www.mofo.com**
**Members of Firm: Gregory A. Bonfiglio; Michael M. Carlson; Thomas E. Ciotti; Stanley A. Doten; Laurie S. Hane; Alan Cope Johnston; Karl J. Kramer; Don F. Kumamoto; Philip J. Levine; Paul L. Lion, III; James F. McCabe; Gladys H. Monroy; Michael C. Phillips; Stephen J. Schrader; William D. Sherman; Debra A. Shetka; Stephen M. Tennis; Raymond L. Wheeler; Peter E. Williams III; Bryan J. Wilson; David C. Wilson; Thomas Earl Wilson. Of Counsel: Donald Chisum; Suzanne S. Graeser; Janet Stone Herman; Antoinette F. Konski; Harry J. Macey; William L. Myers; E. Thomas Wheelock (Not admitted in CA). Associates: Mani Adeli; Cori M. Allen; Laurie A. Axford; Justin Lee Bastian; Hans J. Brasseler (Not admitted in the United States); Alan W. Cannon (Not admitted in CA); C. Jeffrey Char; Christopher S. Dewees; Tyler Dylan; Kevin A. Faulkner; Heike Fischer; Christine Fitzpatrick; Stephan Goeckeler; Jana G. Gold; Su W. Hwang; Sherman W. Kahn; Kenneth A. Kuwayti; Susan K. Lehnhardt; Joseph T. Lin; Cynthia L. Lopez; James M. Meenaghan; Freddie K. Park; Valerie R. Park; Dahna S. Pasternak; Marc J. Pernick; Sandra D. Peterson; Catherine M. Polizzi; Aki Y. Shoji; Eric A. Tate; Robert D. Thomas; Cynthia S. Weeks; Geoffrey A. Wexler; Anna Erickson White; Miriam Wugmeister.**
**Other offices located in: San Francisco, Los Angeles, New York, Washington, D.C., London, Brussels, Hong Kong, Tokyo, Sacramento, Walnut Creek, Orange County and Denver.**
*See Professional Biographies, PALO ALTO, CALIFORNIA*

**Morrissey, Donald J., Jr.** ..................... '66 '92 C.174 B.A. L.800 J.D. [Ⓐ Cooley G.]
*PRACTICE AREAS: Technology Licensing; Biotechnology; Emerging Growth Companies.
**Morrow, Charlene M.** .................... '62 '88 C.800 A.B. L.1066 J.D. [Fenwick&W.]
*PRACTICE AREAS: Litigation.
**Morrow, Diana M.** ................... '67 '92 C.112 B.A. L.880 J.D. [Ⓐ Wilson,S.G.&R.]
*PRACTICE AREAS: Real Estate; Environmental.
**Morrow, Webb B., III, (AV)** .................. '48 '74 C.813 B.A. L.1066 J.D. [Cooley G.]
*PRACTICE AREAS: Taxation; Partnerships.
**Moss, Caine T.** ..................... '71 '96 C.813 B.A. L.309 J.D. [Ⓐ Wilson,S.G.&R.]
*PRACTICE AREAS: Corporate; Securities.
**Mrozek, Therese A.** .................... '57 '85 C.112 B.S. L.597 J.D. [Brobeck,P.&H.]
*PRACTICE AREAS: Corporate Law; Emerging Companies and Venture Capital; Securities Law.
**Mucchetti, Monica** ................. '67 '93 C.976 B.A. L.1066 J.D. [Ⓐ Wilson,S.G.&R.]
*LANGUAGES: Spanish.
*PRACTICE AREAS: Intellectual Property Litigation.
Mudrich, Paul S. .... '56 '83 C.861 B.A. L.678 J.D. Asst. Gen. Coun., Marcus & Millichap
Muhlfelder, Dan ..................... '44 '74 C.1075 B.S. L.1026 J.D. 400 Cambridge Ave.
**Mulholland, Kelly C.** '67 '92 C.339 B.A. L.309 J.D.
(adm. in IL; not adm. in CA) [Ⓐ Fenwick&W.]
*PRACTICE AREAS: Taxation.
**Muller, Janet Elizabeth** '66 '91
C.112 B.S.M.E. L.770 J.D. [Ⓐ Flehr,H.T.A.&H.] (See Pat. Sect.)
*PRACTICE AREAS: Patents; Trademarks; Copyrights.
**Mullowney, Edward F., (AV⑦)** '43 '72
C.816 B.S.M.E. L.178 J.D. [Fish&N.] (See Pat. Sect.)
*PRACTICE AREAS: Intellectual Property.
**Munro, Bruce H., (AV)** .............. '38 '66 C.165 A.B. L.1065 J.D. [Thoits,L.H.&M.]
*PRACTICE AREAS: Business Litigation; Real Estate Litigation; Employment Law.
**Murphy, Matthew B.** .............. '65 '94 C.112 B.S. L.767 J.D. [Ⓐ Townsend&T.&C.]
*PRACTICE AREAS: Biotechnology, Patent Prosecution, Intellectual Property Licensing and Counseling.
**Murphy, Michael J.** ............... '67 '93 C&L.813 B.S., J.D. [Ⓐ Wilson,S.G.&R.] (Pat.)
*PRACTICE AREAS: Technology Licensing; Copyrights; Patents.
Murphy, Robert J., III '36 '66
C.103 A.B. L.813 LL.B. Staff Coun., Calif. Law Revision Comm.
**Murray, David S., (AV)** ........................ '43 '70 C&L.770 B.Sc., J.D. [Murray&M.]
*PRACTICE AREAS: Business Workouts; Bankruptcy Reorganizations; Creditors Remedies.
**Murray, Janice M., (AV)** .................... '49 '81 C.112 B.S. L.767 J.D. [Murray&M.]
*PRACTICE AREAS: Business Workouts; Bankruptcy Reorganizations; Creditors Remedies.
**Murray, John Walshe, (AV)** ................. '52 '77 C.112 B.A. L.284 J.D. [Murray&M.]
*REPORTED CASES: In re Swenor (N.D. Cal. 1978) 452 F.Supp. 673; In re Huang, (9th Cir. B.A.P. 1982) 23 B.R. 798.
*PRACTICE AREAS: Business Workouts; Bankruptcy Reorganizations; Creditors Remedies.

**Murray and Murray, A Professional Corporation, (AV) BB**
**Suite 200, 3030 Hansen Way, 94304**
**Telephone: 415-852-9000 Telecopier: 415-852-9244**
**David S. Murray; John Walshe Murray; Craig M. Prim; Janice M. Murray; Kenneth T. Law; Patrick M. Costello;—Stephen T. O'Neill; Robert A. Franklin; Maureen Colligan Harrison; David S. Levin; Gaye Nell Heck; Bradley N. Raderman.**
**Insolvency, Bankruptcy, Business Reorganization, Creditors Rights, Secured Transactions and Commercial Law. Trial Practice.**
*See Professional Biographies, PALO ALTO, CALIFORNIA*

**Myers, Martin H.** ......................'62 '87 C.473 B.A. L.477 J.D. [Ⓐ Gray C.W.&F.]
*PRACTICE AREAS: Insurance Litigation; Complex Commercial Litigation.
**Myers, William L.** ............ '58 '84 C.770 B.S.C. L.1065 J.D. [Ⓒ Morrison&F.]
*PRACTICE AREAS: Real Estate Law; Environmental Law.
Nadan, Michele Milnes ............'65 '91 C.112 B.S.E.E. L.1066 J.D. 400 Hamilton Ave.
Nag, Rupak ........................ '65 '95 C.178 B.S. L.262 J.D. 525 Univ. Ave. (Pat.)
**Naim, Tahir J.** .............................'61 '92 C.429 B.A. L.284 J.D. [Ⓐ Cooley G.]
*PRACTICE AREAS: Equity Compensation; ERISA/Qualified Plans; Federal Taxation.
**Nakamura, Jackie N.** ............... '62 '90 C.813 B.S. L.1066 J.D. [Ⓐ Cooley G.] (Pat.)
*PRACTICE AREAS: American Intellectual Property Law.
**Narayanan, Usha** ................ '65 '96 C.446 B.A., B.S. L.339 J.D. [Ⓐ Wilson,S.G.&R.]
*LANGUAGES: French and Tamil.
*PRACTICE AREAS: Intellectual Property Litigation.
**Nash, Glenn Gerard** ......................'64 '92 C.036 B.A. L.024 J.D. [Ⓐ Cooley G.]
*LANGUAGES: French.
*PRACTICE AREAS: Intellectual Property; International Law.
**Nashawaty, Keith C.** ........................'66 '91 C.813 A.B. L.145 J.D. [Ⓐ Cooley G.]
*PRACTICE AREAS: Securities; Mergers and Acquisitions.
**Nathanson, Neil** ..................'60 '92 C.477 B.S. L.813 J.D. [Ⓐ Wilson,S.G.&R.]
*PRACTICE AREAS: Intellectual Property Litigation; Antitrust.
Nau, Charles J., Jr. ................. '47 '75 C&L.602 B.A., J.D. Sr. Coun., Syntex (U.S.A.) Inc.
**Neal, Stephen C., (AV⑦)** ...................'49 '73 C.309 A.B. L.813 J.D. [Cooley G.]
*PRACTICE AREAS: Commercial Litigation; Civil; Criminal; Special Investigations; Contested Acquisitions.
Nearon, Arthur D. ................ '10 '42 C&L.284 LL.B. 953 Industrial Ave.
**Neeley, Richard L.** .......................'48 '85 C.198 B.S. L.273 J.D. [Cooley G.] (Pat.)
*PRACTICE AREAS: Patent Law.
Neely, David H. .... '54 '81 C.918 B.A. L.976 J.D. East Palo Alto Community Law Project
**Neilsson, Douglas Clark** ................ '47 '73 C.112 B.A. L.1068 J.D. [Ⓒ Brown&B.]
*PRACTICE AREAS: Commercial; Corporate; Securities; Mergers and Acquisitions; Equipment Leasing.
**Nelsen, Nels Raymond** ............... '62 '90 C&L.770 B.S.C., J.D. [Ⓐ Gray C.W.&F.]
*PRACTICE AREAS: Insolvency Law; Bankruptcy; Corporate Reorganization.
Nelson, Edward ........................'23 '57 C&L.813 A.B., LL.B. P.O. Box 705
Nelson, Laura ........................ '48 '89 C.645 B.A. L.893 J.D. 660 Hansen Wy.
**Newell, William J.** .............. '57 '83 C.197 A.B. L.477 J.D. [McCutchen,D.B.&E.]
*PRACTICE AREAS: Corporate Law; Securities Law; Public Utilities Law.

**Nguyen, Elan Q.G.** ............. '70 '95 C.813 B.A. L.1066 J.D. [Ⓐ McCutchen,D.B.&E.]
*PRACTICE AREAS: Corporate; Intellectual Property Transactions; Securities.
**Nguyen, Joseph A.** '65 '93
C.576 B.S.E.E. L.1066 J.D. [Ⓐ Hickman,B.&W.] (See Pat. Sect.)
*PRACTICE AREAS: Intellectual Property Law; Patents.
Nguyen, Phoenix T.P. ....................... '66 '91 C.910 B.S. L.188 J.D. 2200 Geng Rd.
Nichols, Alison M. ................... '54 '83 C.668 B.A. L.1066 J.D. 525 University Ave.
**Nichols, Marnia** .................. '64 '93 C.768 B.S. L.1065 J.D. [Ⓐ Wilson,S.G.&R.]
*PRACTICE AREAS: Corporate.
**Nicholson, Christopher G.** ........... '69 '95 C.112 B.A. L.1066 J.D. [Ⓐ Wilson,S.G.&R.]
**Nicolosi, Christina** ..................... '70 '95 C.112 B.A. L.477 J.D. [Ⓐ Wilson,S.G.&R.]
**Nishi, John C.** ......................... '55 '93 C.976 B.A. L.145 J.D. [Ⓐ Wilson,S.G.&R.]
*PRACTICE AREAS: Trademark; Advertising Practices.
**Noble, Lisa D.** ........................... '63 '94 C.691 B.S. L.813 J.D. [Ⓐ Fenwick&W.] (Pat.)
*PRACTICE AREAS: Intellectual Property Law; Licensing Law; Patent Law.
**Nolan, Thomas J., (AV)** .................... '45 '71 C.1060 B.A. L.1067 J.D. [Nolan&A.]
*PRACTICE AREAS: Criminal Law; Business Crimes Law; Capital Litigation; High Technology Law; White Collar Criminal Defense.

**Nolan & Armstrong, (AV) BB**
**600 University Avenue, 94301**
**Telephone: 415-326-2980 Fax: 415-326-9704**
**Members of Firm: Thomas J. Nolan (Certified Specialist, Criminal Law, The State Bar of California Board of Legal Specialization); Michael W. Armstrong (Certified Specialist, Criminal Law, The State Bar of California Board of Legal Specialization); Daniel L. Barton. Associate: Rebecca Laibson.**
**Criminal and Business Crimes Law. Trials and Appeals, Trade Secret and Juvenile Law.**
*See Professional Biographies, PALO ALTO, CALIFORNIA*

**Nordlund, D. Craig, (AV)** '49 '74 C.813 A.B. L.880 J.D.
Assoc. Gen. Coun., Secy. & Dir., Hewlett-Packard Co.
*RESPONSIBILITIES: General Corporate; Securities and Finance.
**Norman, Donna Katherine** ........... '66 '93 C.966 B.A. L.276 J.D. [Ⓐ Wilson,S.G.&R.]
*PRACTICE AREAS: Antitrust; Intellectual Property Litigation.
**Norris, Craig D.** ........................ '67 '94 C.813 A.B. L.1066 J.D. [Ⓐ Wilson,S.G.&R.]
*PRACTICE AREAS: Securities; Corporate.
**Norton, Burke F.** ...................... '66 '95 C.101 B.A. L.1066 J.D. [Ⓐ Wilson,S.G.&R.]
*PRACTICE AREAS: Corporate Law; Securities.
**Norton, George H., (AV)** ...................... '30 '57 C.103 A.B. L.813 J.D. [Lakin S.]
*PRACTICE AREAS: Family Law.
Norton, Stanley R., (BV) ................ '27 '54 C&L.813 B.A., LL.B. 407 Sherman Ave.‡
Norviel, Vernon A. .......................... '58 '85 C.174 B.S. L.767 J.D. 379 Lytton Ave. (Pat.)
Novotny, Janae H. ......................... '49 '81 C.267 B.A. L.276 J.D. 101 University Ave.
**Nuechterlein, Carole L.** '61 '86
C.879 B.A. L.477 J.D. Dir., Legal Affs., Roche Bioscience
*LANGUAGES: German.
*RESPONSIBILITIES: General Corporate Law; Securities Law; Real Estate Syndication Law.
**Nycum, Susan H., (AV)** ...................... '— '62 C.611 A.B. L.229 J.D. [Baker&M.]
*PRACTICE AREAS: Computers and Technology; Intellectual Property Law; Arbitration and Dispute Resolution.
Nygaard, Jon O. ........ '48 '78 C.976 B.A. L.770 J.D. Sr. Staff Atty., Syntex (U.S.A.) Inc.
**Ober, Louise C.** ........................... '59 '87 C.674 B.A. L.309 J.D. [Ⓐ Baker&M.]
*LANGUAGES: Spanish.
*PRACTICE AREAS: Taxation.
**O'Brien, Bradford C., (AV)** ........... '49 '74 C.674 A.B. L.1068 J.D. [Wilson,S.G.&R.]
*PRACTICE AREAS: Real Estate Law.
**O'Brien, David P.** '66 '92 C.309 B.A. L.188 J.D.
(adm. in MA; not adm. in CA) [Ⓐ Wilson,S.G.&R.]
*PRACTICE AREAS: Litigation.
**O'Brien, Judith Mayer, (AV)** .......... '50 '74 C.788 B.A. L.1068 J.D. [Wilson,S.G.&R.]
*PRACTICE AREAS: Corporate Law; Securities.
O'Byrne, Mary E. ............ '58 '85 C.339 B.A. L.1065 J.D. 200 Page Mill Rd., 2nd Fl.
**Occhiolini, Michael** ............... '60 '92 C.145 B.A. L.813 J.D. [Ⓐ Wilson,S.G.&R.]
*PRACTICE AREAS: Corporate Law.
**O'Connor, Robert G.** ................ '68 '93 C.112 B.A. L.426 J.D. [Ⓐ Wilson,S.G.&R.]
*PRACTICE AREAS: Corporate; Securities.
Odell, Robert S., Jr. .............................. '20 '56 C&L.813 A.B., J.D. 200 Lowell Ave.‡
**O'Donnell, Michael J.** ..................... '58 '83 C.105 B.A. L.309 J.D. [Wilson,S.G.&R.]
*PRACTICE AREAS: Corporate; Securities; Venture Capital.
**O'Dowd, Sarah A., (AV)** ............... '49 '78 C.341 A.B. L.813 J.D. [Heller E.W.&M.]
*PRACTICE AREAS: Corporate; Securities.
**Oelsner, Benjamin P.** .................. '63 '95 C.112 B.A. L.767 J.D. [Ⓐ Brobeck,P.&H.]
*PRACTICE AREAS: Intellectual Property.
**Ofria, Denise Woodson** .................... '46 '83 C.763 B.S. L.966 J.D. [Gray C.W.&F.]
*PRACTICE AREAS: Employee Benefits; Equity Compensation.
**Ogawa, Richard Takashi** ............ '62 '92 C.112 B.S. L.464 J.D. [Ⓐ Townsend&T.&C.]
*PRACTICE AREAS: Patent Prosecution and Licensing.
**Okada, Michael** ...................... '64 '89 C.178 A.B. L.800 J.D. [Ⓐ Wilson,S.G.&R.]
*LANGUAGES: German and Japanese.
**Okamoto, James K.** ...................... '— '96 C.111 B.S. L.813 J.D. [Ⓐ Fenwick&W.]
*PRACTICE AREAS: Intellectual Property; Patent Law.
**O'Leary, Timothy E.** ............... '60 '87 C.813 A.B. L.1068 J.D. Atty., Hewlett-Packard
*RESPONSIBILITIES: Antitrust; Software Licensing; Commercial Contracts.
**Oliver, L. Scott** ........................... '68 '94 C.309 A.B. L.1049 J.D. [Ⓐ Gray C.W.&F.]
*PRACTICE AREAS: Litigation.
**Olsen, Kent E., (AV)** .............. '43 '68 C.112 A.B. L.1065 J.D. [Ferrari,O.O.&B.]⊙
*PRACTICE AREAS: Corporate Law; Estate and Family Tax Planning; Employee Benefits.
**Olson, Erik J.** ....................... '68 '95 C.1239 B.A. L.813 J.D. [Ⓐ Ritchey F.W.&K.]
Olson, Lisa A. ................................ '62 '87 C&L.436 B.A., J.D. 2 Palo Alto Sq., 8th Fl.
Olson, Thomas H., (AV) ...... '28 '60 C.472 B.S.E.E. L.1068 LL.B. P.O. Box 60026 (Pat.)
O'Neill, Kevin ................................................................ '66 '93 400 Hamilton Ave.
**O'Neill, Stephen T.** ................... '57 '84 C.112 B.A. L.1065 J.D. [Ⓐ Murray&M.]
*PRACTICE AREAS: Business Workouts; Bankruptcy Reorganizations; Creditors Remedies.
**Opperman, Craig P.** ............. '62 '93 C&L.061 B.Sc., B.PROC. [Ⓐ Cooley G.] (Pat.)
*PRACTICE AREAS: Patents; Intellectual Property Strategies; Licensing; Trade Secret; International Intellectual Property.
**Orton, Luther Kent, (AV)** ........... '46 '72 C.597 B.S.I.E. L.813 J.D. [Brobeck,P.&H.]
*PRACTICE AREAS: Trade Secret, Patent and Unfair Competition Litigation; General Commercial Litigation.
**Osborne, Carlton X.** ..................... '69 '95 C.659 B.A. L.813 J.D. [Ⓐ Fenwick&W.]
*PRACTICE AREAS: Corporate.
**Osborne, Jonathan L., (BV⑦)** '61 '86 C.275 B.A. L.421 J.D.
(adm. in KY; not adm. in CA) [Zevnik H.G.&M.]
(⊙London, England, Los Angeles, CA., Wash., D.C., New York, NY.)
*PRACTICE AREAS: Insurance Coverage; Commercial Litigation.
Osman, Richard Aron .............. '62 '92 C.112 B.S. L.1065 J.D. 850 Hansen Way (Pat.)
Ostby, Bryn Roe ..................... '42 '70 C.747 B.A. L.273 J.D. Gen. Coun., Alten Corp.
**Ostler, Mark R.** ........................... '52 '79 C&L.101 B.A., J.D. [Cohen&O.]
*PRACTICE AREAS: Corporate Law.
**Ostrau, Mark S., (AV)** ................. '60 '85 C.976 B.A. L.813 J.D. [Fenwick&W.]
*PRACTICE AREAS: Corporate; Antitrust; Licensing Law.
**Ott, Judith M., (BV)** ................. '43 '78 C.629 B.A. L.770 J.D. [Bryant,C.O.M.&B.]
*PRACTICE AREAS: Franchising; Corporate Start-ups; Real Estate; Mergers and Acquisitions; Private Financing.

CAA473P

CALIFORNIA—PALO ALTO MARTINDALE-HUBBELL LAW DIRECTORY 1997

**Otteson, James C.** ....................'64 '92 C.101 B.S. L.976 J.D. [A Wilson,S.G.&R.]
*LANGUAGES: Swedish.
*PRACTICE AREAS: Intellectual Property Law; Litigation.
**Ottoboni, John M.**, (AV) ........... '47 '72 C.770 B.A. L.1066 J.D. [Ferrari,O.O.&B.]⊙
*PRACTICE AREAS: Business Litigation; Real Estate; Sports Law.
**Owen, Laura M.** ........................ '55 '94 C.766 B.S. L.770 J.D. [A Cooley G.]
*PRACTICE AREAS: Employment Claims; Labor Relations; Personnel Policies; Title VII Discrimination.
**Owens, Jonathan O.** '67 '93
C.508 B.S.E.E. L.770 J.D. [Haverstock&Assoc.] (See Pat. Sect.)
*PRACTICE AREAS: Electrical and Mechanical Patents.
**Owens, William B., Jr.** .............. '70 '95 C.902 B.A. L.802 J.D. [A Wilson,S.G.&R.]
*PRACTICE AREAS: Corporate; Securities.
**Oyenque, Esteban L.** '66 '93 C.197 A.B. L.477 J.D.
(adm. in NE; not adm. in CA) [A Zevnik H.G.&M.]
*LANGUAGES: Spanish.
*PRACTICE AREAS: Complex Environmental Litigation; Environmental Insurance Litigation.
**Ozburn, Christopher J.** ............. '64 '92 C.976 B.A. L.569 J.D. [A Wilson,S.G.&R.]
*PRACTICE AREAS: Corporate; Securities.
**Ozeroff, Myfanwy J.** ...'52 '80 C.112 B.S. L.765 J.D. Sr. Tax Atty., Hewlett-Packard Co.
*RESPONSIBILITIES: Corporate Taxation.
Packard, David R., (BV) ............... '42 '68 C.112 A.B. L.1066 J.D. 285 Hamilton Ave.
**Packard, Lon D.**, (AV) ............... '51 '77 C.813 B.A. L.101 J.D. [Packard,P.&J.]⊙
*LANGUAGES: Spanish and Russian.
*PRACTICE AREAS: Class Actions; False Claims Act; Complex Business Litigation.
**Packard, Ronald D.**, (AV) '48 '76
C.112 B.A. L.1165 J.D. [Packard,P.&J.] (⊙Salt City, UT)
*PRACTICE AREAS: Class Actions; False Claims Act; Complex Business Litigation.
**Packard, Von G.**, (BV) ................ '51 '77 C.813 B.A. L.101 J.D. [Packard,P.&J.]
*LANGUAGES: Spanish.
*PRACTICE AREAS: Class Actions; False Claims Act; Complex Business Litigation; Personal Injury.

**Packard, Packard & Johnson, A Professional Corporation, (AV)**
**260 Sheridan Avenue, Suite 208, 94306⊙**
**Telephone: 415-327-3000 Fax: 415-327-0695**
**Ronald D. Packard; Lon D. Packard; Von G. Packard; Craig H. Johnson. Of Counsel: Clarence Borns (Not admitted in CA).**
**False Claims Act Prosecution, Class Actions, Complex Business Litigation (including Fraud, Insurance Bad Faith and Securities) and Personal Injury.**
**Salt Lake City, Utah Office: 675 East 2100 South, Suite 350. Telephone: 801-485-6464. Fax: 801-485-3480.**
***See Professional Biographies, PALO ALTO, CALIFORNIA***

Pahlavan, Arman '64 '92 C.112 B.A. L.1065 J.D.
(adm. in NY; not adm. in CA) [Georgopoulos&P.]⊙
**Pais, Ralph M.** ...............................'48 '75 C.170 B.A. L.770 J.D. [Graham&J.]
*LANGUAGES: Dutch.
*PRACTICE AREAS: International Business Transactions; Corporate and Commercial Transactions; Technology Licensing; Intellectual Property.
**Pak, Agnes** '64 '89 C.112 B.A. L.1065 J.D.
(adm. in IL; not adm. in CA) [A Wilson,S.G.&R.]
*PRACTICE AREAS: Corporate.
Palter, Alan D. '61 '87 C.112 B.A. L.1065 J.D.
Assoc. Corp. Coun., Varian Assocs., Inc.
**Panepucci, Michael J.** ......... '65 '92 C&L.477 B.S.E.E., J.D. [A Wilson,S.G.&R.] (Pat.)
*PRACTICE AREAS: Intellectual Property Law; Patent, Copyright and Trade Secret Counseling.
**Pang, Stephen Y.F.** .............'63 '93 C.453 S.B.E.E. L.273 J.D. [A Townsend&T.&C.]
*PRACTICE AREAS: Electronics and Software Patent Prosecution.
**Pao, Frank H.** ........................'68 '94 C.112 B.S. L.1066 J.D. [A Gray C.W.&F.]
*LANGUAGES: Cantonese.
*PRACTICE AREAS: Technology Licensing (80%); Intellectual Property (20%).
Pappas, Stephen R. ........................'59 '84 C.813 B.A. L.1066 J.D. 2501 Park Blvd.
Paque, Anita M. .....'57 '82 C.959 B.S. L.464 J.D. Gen. Coun., The Wollongong Grp., Inc.
**Park, A. Richard** ....................'61 '96 C.112 B.S. L.1066 J.D. [A Wilson,S.G.&R.]
*PRACTICE AREAS: Intellectual Property Law; Patent Law.
**Park, Freddie K.** ..................'47 '90 C.845 B.S. L.1184 J.D. [A Morrison&F.] (Pat.)
*LANGUAGES: French.
**Park, Jin Yi** .......................... '69 '95 C.112 B.A. L.770 J.D. [A Fragomen,D.&B.]
*LANGUAGES: Korean.
Park, Theresa S. ...................'67 '92 C.1169 B.A. L.309 J.D. 5 Palo Alto Sq., Suite 400
**Park, Valerie R.** ............................'62 '91 C.112 A.B. L.813 J.D. [A Morrison&F.]
**Parnes, Mark** ......................'57 '82 C.112 B.A. L.1066 J.D. [Wilson,S.G.&R.]
*PRACTICE AREAS: Litigation.
**Parr, Stephanie J.** ......................'65 '90 C.112 B.A. L.1068 J.D. [A Cooley G.]
*PRACTICE AREAS: Securities; Emerging Growth Companies.
Parsons, Jon R. ..................................................'50 '79 2501 Park Blvd.
**Pasahow, Lynn H.**, (AV) '47 '72
C.813 B.A. L.1066 J.D. [McCutchen,D.B.&E.] (⊙San Francisco)
*PRACTICE AREAS: Intellectual Property Litigation; Technology Litigation.
**Pasternak, Dahna S.** ................ '66 '95 C.813 B.A.S. L.1066 J.D. [A Morrison&F.]
**Pasti, Pamela** ........................'54 '95 C.188 B.A. L.112 J.D. [A Gray C.W.&F.]
*LANGUAGES: Japanese.
*PRACTICE AREAS: Corporate and Securities; Intellectual Property.
**Patel, Mehul T.** ..........................'69 '95 C.103 A.B. L.893 J.D. [A Cooley G.]
*LANGUAGES: Gujarati.
*PRACTICE AREAS: Corporate; Securities.
**Patel, Rajiv P.** ..................'67 '95 C.705 B.S. L.1218 J.D. [A Fenwick&W.] (Pat.)
*PRACTICE AREAS: Intellectual Property; Patent Law.
**Patrick, Michael J.** ......................'59 '84 C.918 B.A. L.1068 J.D. [Fenwick&W.]
*PRACTICE AREAS: Corporate.
**Patterson, Robert E.**, (AV) ...............'42 '72 C.112 B.A. L.813 J.D. [Graham&J.]
*PRACTICE AREAS: Corporate Law; Venture Capital.
**Patterson, Timothy G.** ..................'54 '81 C.813 B.A. L.1065 J.D. [Cooley G.]
*PRACTICE AREAS: Employee Benefit Law; ERISA.
**Pawliczek, Jamie C.** .....................'69 '95 C.659 B.A. L.823 J.D. [A Gray C.W.&F.]
*PRACTICE AREAS: Multimedia Law; Intellectual Property Law.
**Pearce, John A.** .......................'69 '96 C.878 B.S. L.1066 J.D. [A Wilson,S.G.&R.]
*LANGUAGES: Spanish.
*PRACTICE AREAS: Litigation.
Pearson, Barclay Howard, (AV) ............ '51 '80 C.813 B.S. L.878 J.D. Stanford Univ.
Pearson, Lisa Madsen ........................'55 '79 C&L.878 B.A., J.D. Stanford Law Sch.
**Peck, Anne Harris** .....................'58 '86 C.276 B.S. L.1065 J.D. [Cooley G.]
*PRACTICE AREAS: Trademark, Copyright and Advertising.
**Pedraza, Francisco** .... '52 '80 C.674 A.B. L.184 J.D. Corp. Coun., Hewlett-Packard Co.
*RESPONSIBILITIES: General Corporate; Real Estate; Construction; Commercial Contracts.
**Peers, Richard A.** .......................'52 '79 C.813 B.A. L.309 J.D. [Heller E.W.&M.]
*PRACTICE AREAS: Corporate; Securities; Mergers and Acquisitions.
Pegg, Lori E. ........................... '61 '87 C.112 B.A. L.770 J.D. 101 University Ave.
Penick, Janet L. C. .............................. '51 '77 C&L.813 B.A., J.D. 2820 Bryant St.
**Penilla, Albert** .................'69 '95 C.112 B.S.E.E. L.36 J.D. [A Hickman,B.&W.]
*PRACTICE AREAS: Patents; Trademarks; Intellectual Property Licensing; Intellectual Property.

**Pennie & Edmonds LLP**
**(See Menlo Park)**

Peries, Rohan ....................... '54 '95 C.050 B.A. L.770 J.D. 379 Lytton Ave. (Pat.)

**Pernick, Marc J.** .......................'67 '92 C.186 B.S.E. L.569 J.D. [A Morrison&F.]
**Peschcke-Koedt, Lisa D. V.** '56 '83
C.813 B.A. L.188 J.D. Sr. Tax Atty., Intl., Hewlett-Packard Co.
*LANGUAGES: Danish.
*RESPONSIBILITIES: International Taxation Law.
**Peters, Colin**, (AV) ........................'19 '47 C.768 A.B. L.813 J.D. [Peters,P.&E.]
*PRACTICE AREAS: Family Law; Business Litigation; Personal Injury.
**Peters, Howard M.** ......... '40 '79 C.271 B.S. L.770 J.D. [Peters,V.J.&B.] (See Pat. Sect.)
*PRACTICE AREAS: Patent, Trademark and Copyright Law.
**Peters, Stephen M.**, (BV) .................'51 '76 C.309 B.A. L.813 J.D. [Peters,P.&E.]
*LANGUAGES: Spanish.
*PRACTICE AREAS: Personal Injury; Family Law; Construction Law; Wrongful Termination.

**Peters, Peters & Ellingson, A Professional Corporation, (AV)**
**550 Lytton Avenue, 3rd Floor, 94301**
**Telephone: 415-328-6770 Fax: 415-328-6776**
**Colin Peters; Stephen M. Peters; Patricia Ellingson.**
**General Civil and Trial Practice. Family Law, Personal Injury, Wrongful Discharge, Real Property and Business Litigation, Architects' and Engineers' Liability.**
***See Professional Biographies, PALO ALTO, CALIFORNIA***

**Peters, Verny, Jones & Biksa, L.L.P.**
**385 Sherman Avenue Suite 6, 94306-1840**
**Telephone: 415-324-1677 Fax: 415-324-1678**
**Email: pvjb@patentsfo.com**
**Members of Firm: Howard M. Peters; Hana Verny; Allston L. Jones; Janis J. O. Biksa.**
**Intellectual Property Law, including Patent, Trademark, Copyright, Trade Secret and Unfair Competition Law. Trials in all Local Courts, all Federal Courts, and before the U.S. Patent and Trademark Office.**
***See Professional Biographies, PALO ALTO, CALIFORNIA***

**Peterson, John M., Jr.** ..................... '51 '77 C.602 B.B.A. L.309 J.D. [Baker&M.]
*PRACTICE AREAS: Taxation.
**Peterson, Sandra D.** ................................'48 '92 C&L.813 B.A., J.D. [A Morrison&F.]
**Petkanics, Donna M.**, (BV) ............'58 '85 C.597 B.A. L.1066 J.D. [Wilson,S.G.&R.]
*LANGUAGES: German.
*PRACTICE AREAS: Corporate Law; Securities.
**Petruzzelli, Jerrold F.** ....................'52 '77 C.976 A.B. L.145 J.D. [Wise&S.]
*LANGUAGES: French and Italian.
**Petty, Keith**, (AV) ................................'20 '48 C.336 B.S. L.813 J.D. [K.Petty]

**Petty, Keith, A Professional Corporation, (AV)**
**1755 Embarcadero Road Suite 110, 94303**
**Telephone: 415-858-2000**
**Keith Petty.**
**Corporate, Estate Planning, Probate and Real Estate.**

Phair, Joseph B. '47 '73 C&L.767 B.A., J.D.
V.P., Gen. Coun. & Secy., Varian Assocs., Inc.
Phelps, J. Barton ...............................'17 '41 C.145 A.B. L.309 LL.B. Ret. Supr. Ct. J.
**Phi, Tram Thi** ...........................'70 '95 C.768 B.A. L.1066 J.D. [A Fenwick&W.]
*PRACTICE AREAS: Corporate.
**Phillips, Michael C.**, (AV) ...............'50 '76 C.813 B.A. L.1066 J.D. [Morrison&F.]
*PRACTICE AREAS: Corporate Finance; Multimedia.
**Piatnicia, Andrew Y.** .......................'60 '94 C.201 B.E.E. L.569 J.D. [A Graham&J.]
Pickering, Harold K. ...... '50 '77 C&L.150 B.A., J.D. Sr. Staff Atty., Syntex (U.S.A.) Inc.
Pickert, Paul C., (BV) .......................'27 '51 C.674 B.A. L.107 LL.B. 540 Univ. Ave.
Pier, William S. ............................'16 '42 C&L.309 A.B., LL.B. 1733 Webster St.‡
**Pierce, Andrew F.** ......................'56 '81 C.309 A.B. L.1066 J.D. [A Cox B.P.&S.]
Pinckert, Eric G. ..........................'67 '93 C.813 A.B. L.309 J.D. 650 Page Mill Rd.
Pirie, Sophie H. ...........................'61 '87 C.309 B.A. L.813 J.D. Stanford Law Sch.
**Pisano, Nicola A.** ............'59 '90 C&L.602 B.S.M.E., J.D. [A Fish&N.] (See Pat. Sect.)
*PRACTICE AREAS: Intellectual Property.
**Pitchford, Mark B.**, (AV) ......................'59 '84 C.813 A.B. L.770 J.D. [Cooley G.]
*PRACTICE AREAS: Commercial Litigation.
**Pittenger, Darren J.** .......................'67 '93 C.37 B.A. L.112 J.D. [A Gray C.W.&F.]
Place, John ............................................'— '91 C.768 B.S. L.813 J.D. 2200 Geng Rd.
**Platz, John F.** ...........................'60 '90 C&L.813 B.A., J.D. [A Fenwick&W.]
*PRACTICE AREAS: Corporate.

**Player, Stephen W., Law Offices, (AV) '41 '67 C.813 A.B. L.1065 LL.B.**
**2600 El Camino Real, Suite 410, 94306**
**Telephone: 415-494-9102 Fax: 415-856-8448**
**General Business and Real Estate Practice with an emphasis on Land Use, Zoning and Administrative Law.**
**Representative Clients: Peninsula Creamery; Channing House.**
***See Professional Biographies, PALO ALTO, CALIFORNIA***

**Plewa, David J.** ............................'61 '87 C&L.477 B.B.A., J.D. [A Gray C.W.&F.]
*PRACTICE AREAS: Tax.
**Plumleigh, Michael A.** ..................'59 '90 C&L.112 B.A., J.D. [A Brobeck,P.&H.]
*PRACTICE AREAS: Computer Law; Technology; Copyright; Corporate.
**Pohlen, Patrick A.** '59 '85 C.350 B.A. L.352 J.D.
(adm. in NY; not adm. in CA) [Cooley G.]
*LANGUAGES: Spanish, Japanese.
*PRACTICE AREAS: General Corporate; Securities; Financings; Mergers and Acquisitions.
**Polizzi, Catherine M.** ...............'54 '94 C.500 B.A. L.813 J.D. [A Morrison&F.] (Pat.)
*PRACTICE AREAS: Intellectual Property.
**Pomputius, Mary-Alice** ..................'65 '90 C.976 B.A. L.309 J.D. [A Cooley G.]
Pon, Lillian ..................................'50 '77 C.768 B.A. L.1065 J.D. Price Waterhouse
**Poonja, Zaitun** ..........................'53 '86 C.320 B.A. L.813 J.D. [A Brobeck,P.&H.]
*PRACTICE AREAS: Corporate Tax; International Tax; Executive Compensation.
**Pope, Anna B.** ............................'53 '84 C.112 B.A. L.1067 J.D. [Cooley G.]
*PRACTICE AREAS: Real Estate (Property) Law.
Popovich, Perry D. .............................. '44 '73 C&L.813 A.B., J.D. P.O. Box 51851
**Porter, Mark E.** .........................'59 '88 C.800 B.A. L.1065 J.D. [A Fenwick&W.]
*PRACTICE AREAS: Corporate; Securities; Bankruptcy.
Potter, Carol Ann .................. '43 '72 C.352 B.A. L.1066 J.D. Stanford Law School
Powell, Nancy V., (BV) ........................'49 '75 C.604 B.M. L.184 J.D. [N.V.Powell]
Powell, Nancy V., A Prof. Corp., (BV) ............................................. 399 Sherman Ave.
**Powers, J. Pat**, (AV) ......................'45 '74 C.112 B.A. L.1066 J.D. [Baker&M.]
*PRACTICE AREAS: Taxation.
**Powers, Margaret A.** .............'54 '94 C.339 B.S. L.1065 J.D. [A Townsend&T.&C.] (Pat.)
*PRACTICE AREAS: Intellectual Property; Litigation; Biotechnology.
**Powers, Margaret M.** .......................'60 '86 C.112 B.A. L.767 J.D. [Gray C.W.&F.]
*PRACTICE AREAS: Intellectual Property Law; Trademark Law.
Preas, Katherine A. ..........................'46 '82 C.69 B.S. L.846 J.D. 151 Cowper St.‡
**Preisler, Sarah** .......................'66 '94 C.112 A.B. L.813 J.D. [A Wilson,S.G.&R.]
*PRACTICE AREAS: Multimedia; Intellectual Property; Corporate.
**Premo, Patrick E.** ..........................'67 '96 C&L.770 B.S., J.D. [A Fenwick&W.]
*PRACTICE AREAS: Litigation.
Prendergast, Marlene H. '39 '79 C.228 B.A. L.770 J.D.
Exec. Dir. & Gen. Coun., Palo Alto Housing Corp.
**Prestidge, Myra J.** ...........................'56 '84 C.1169 B.A. L.770 J.D. [W.D.Ross]⊙
*REPORTED CASES: City of Redwood City V. Dalton Construction Company, 221 Cal.App.3d 1570 (1990).

**Price, Daniel R.**, (BV) ............... '47 '74 C.597 B.S.M.E. L.276 J.D. [Stanwood&P.]
*REPORTED CASES: Parr v. Superior Court (1983) 139 CA3d 440.
*PRACTICE AREAS: Labor and Employment Law; Business Litigation; General Civil Litigation; Personal Injury.
**Priebe, David** ............... '60 '90 C.1044 B.A. L.1066 J.D. [⊠ Wilson,S.G.&R.]
*PRACTICE AREAS: Litigation.
Priest, Gregory M. ............... '63 '90 C.674 A.B. L.813 J.D. 650 Page Mill Rd.
**Prim, Craig M.**, (AV) ............... '52 '77 C.770 B.S. L.1066 J.D. [Murray&M.]
*PRACTICE AREAS: Business Workouts; Bankruptcy Reorganizations; Creditors Remedies.
**Prochaska, Stacey G.** ............... '— '90 C.112 B.A. L.1066 J.D. [⊠ Wilson,S.G.&R.]
*PRACTICE AREAS: Technology Licensing.

**Prochnow, Kenneth H., (AV) '50 '78 C.178 B.A. L.569 J.D.**
**525 University Avenue, Suite 702, 94301-1906**
**Telephone: 415-327-0400 Fax: 415-326-0758**
**Email: prochlaw@aol.com**
***PRACTICE AREAS: Civil Litigation; Civil Appeals; Alternative Dispute Resolution.**
**Civil Trial Practice in State and Federal Courts. Arbitration/ADR, Referral Litigation (Compensated and Cooperative). Litigation in the following areas: Commercial, Business, Banking, Real Estate, Securities, Consumer and Investment Fraud, Employment, Professional Liability (Non-Medical), Trade Secret, Elder Law and Bankruptcy.**
*See Professional Biographies, PALO ALTO, CALIFORNIA*

**Quan, Kelvin P.** ............... '57 '93 C.112 B.A. L.1065 J.D. [⊠ Cooley G.]
*PRACTICE AREAS: Health Care Transactions.
**Quevedo, Edward L.** ............... '57 '90 C.112 B.A. L.1066 J.D. [⊠ Wise&S.]
**Quilter, Matthew P.** ............... '53 '82 C.674 B.A. L.659 J.D. [Heller E.W.&M.]
*PRACTICE AREAS: Corporate; Technology Licensing; Venture Capital.
Rabin, Robert L. '39 '63 C&L.597 B.S., J.D.
(adm. in IL; not adm. in CA) Prof., Stanford Law Sch.
**Rabson, Michael S.** ............... '53 '89 C.188 B.S. L.976 J.D. [Wilson,S.G.&R.]
*PRACTICE AREAS: Technology Licensing; Intellectual Property Counseling.
**Radcliffe, Mark F.** ............... '52 '82 C.477 B.S. L.309 J.D. [Gray C.W.&F.]
**Radcliffe, Thomas R.** ............... '53 '81 C.1051 B.A. L.629 J.D. [Graham&J.]
*LANGUAGES: Japanese.
*PRACTICE AREAS: Corporate Law; Technology Transfer.
**Raderman, Bradley N.** ............... '70 '96 C.174 B.A. L.767 J.D. [⊠ Murray&M.]
*PRACTICE AREAS: Bankruptcy Reorganizations.
**Radlo, Edward J.** ............... '46 '72 C.453 B.S. L.309 J.D. [Fenwick&W.] (Pat.)
*PRACTICE AREAS: Intellectual Property; Patent Law.
Radloff, John E. '10 '44 C&L.352 B.A., J.D.
(adm. in IA; not adm. in CA) 3514 S. Court St.‡
Rae-Venter, Barbara ............... '48 '86 C.112 B.A. L.846 J.D. 260 Sheridan Ave. (Pat.)
Raff, Spencer J. ............... '50 '78 C.112 A.B. L.284 J.D. Varian Assocs., Inc.
**Raffle, John Thomas** '68 '94
C.453 B.S. L.228 J.D. [⊠ Townsend&T.&C.] (See Pat. Sect.)
*PRACTICE AREAS: Aeronautical, Mechanical and Medical Device Patent Prosecution.
**Raider, Daniel F.** ....... '51 '77 C.809 B.A. L.813 J.D. Corp. Coun., Hewlett-Packard Co.
*RESPONSIBILITIES: Environmental Law.
**Raineri, Walter T.** ............... '59 '87 C.112 B.S. L.276 J.D. [Fenwick&W.]
*PRACTICE AREAS: Taxation.
Rand, Robert C., (BV) ............... '30 '73 C&L.813 A.B., J.D. 2211 Park Blvd.
**Randall, Jeffrey G.** ............... '62 '87 C.629 B.S. L.1065 J.D. [Cooley G.]
*PRACTICE AREAS: Intellectual Property Law.
Ranninger, Rebecca A. ............... '58 '84 C.309 B.A. L.813 J.D. 525 University Ave.
**Rashid, Soraya N.** ............... '68 '93 C.768 B.S. L.112 J.D. [⊠ Wilson,S.G.&R.]
*PRACTICE AREAS: Intellectual Property Transactions.
**Rasmussen, Mayre J.**, (AV) '44 '77
C.101 B.A. L.1066 J.D. Sr. Coun., Elec. Power Resch. Instit., Inc.
*RESPONSIBILITIES: Corporate; Contracts; Real Estate; International.
Rasmussen, MeMe Jacobs ............... '59 '89 C.882 B.S. L.818 J.D. 400 Hamilton Ave.
**Rattner, Jonathan E.** ............... '56 '82 C.880 B.A. L.178 J.D. [Gray C.W.&F.]
**Raub, L. Donald, Jr.** ............... '49 '83 C.659 B.A. L.1065 J.D. [Brooks&R.]
*PRACTICE AREAS: Bankruptcy Reorganization; Commercial Law; Bankruptcy; Insolvency; Workouts.
**Raubvogel, Amir H.** ............... '64 '91 C.025 B.A.Sc. L.976 J.D. [⊡ Fenwick&W.]
*PRACTICE AREAS: Intellectual Property; Patent Law.
**Rawnsley, Kathi A.** ............... '66 '95 C.882 B.A. L.770 J.D. [⊠ Tomlinson Z.M.&M.]
*PRACTICE AREAS: Corporate.
**Ray, Magan** ............... '63 '95 C.112 B.A. L.813 J.D. [⊠ Brobeck,P.&H.]
*PRACTICE AREAS: Employee Benefits; ERISA.
Ray, Maganendra Pritam ............... '63 '94 C.112 B.A. L.813 J.D. 2200 Geng Rd.
**Read, Donald H.**, (AV) '42 '69
C.112 B.A. L.178 J.D. [⊡ Lakin S.] (⊙Berkeley & Oakland)
*PRACTICE AREAS: Tax Law.
Ream, Anne K. ............... '43 '83 C.19 B.A. L.770 J.D. 1180 Forest Ave.

**Ream, Christopher, (AV) '42 '72 C.976 B.E. L.1066 J.D.**
**1717 Embarcadero Road, 94303**
**Telephone: 415-424-0821 Facsimile: 415-857-1288**
***PRACTICE AREAS: Business Law; Corporations; Securities Law; Civil Litigation.**
**Business, Corporation and Securities Law. General Business and Civil Litigation.**
*See Professional Biographies, PALO ALTO, CALIFORNIA*

**Reback, Gary L.**, (AV) ............... '49 '74 C.976 B.A. L.813 J.D. [Wilson,S.G.&R.]
*PRACTICE AREAS: Intellectual Property; Antitrust.
**Reed, Dianne E.** ............... '58 '84 C.453 S.B. L.1065 J.D. [Reed&R.] (See Pat. Sect.)
*PRACTICE AREAS: Patent Law; Strategic Counseling; Patent Preparation and Prosecution.

**Reed & Robins LLP**
**285 Hamilton Avenue, Suite 200, 94301**
**Telephone: 415-327-3400 Facsmile: 415-327-3231**
**Members of Firm: Dianne E. Reed; Roberta L. Robins. Associates: Kenneth Barovsky; Thomas P.G. McCracken; Susan J. Friedman.**
**Technology areas: Chemistry, Biotechnology and Biomedical Engineering, including Pharmaceuticals, Organic and Bio-Organic Chemistry, Polymer Science, Molecular Biology, Immunology and Genetics. Intellectual Property Law including Patent Preparation and Prosecution.**
*See Professional Biographies, PALO ALTO, CALIFORNIA*

**Rees, Amy E.** ............... '72 '96 C.813 B.A. L.228 J.D. [⊠ Wilson,S.G.&R.]
*PRACTICE AREAS: Corporate.

**Reese, Thomas D., (AV) '34 '61 C.605 B.A. L.813 J.D.**
**285 Hamilton Avenue, P.O. Box 240, 94301**
**Telephone: 415-328-7000 Fax: 415-329-8925**
**Email: thosreese@aol.com**
***PRACTICE AREAS: Dispute Resolution; Mediation; Arbitration; Special Master/Referee. Civil Litigation.**
*See Professional Biographies, PALO ALTO, CALIFORNIA*

**Reid, Taylor S.** '63 '93 C.112 B.A. L.597 J.D.
(adm. in IL; not adm. in CA) [⊠ Baker&M.]
*LANGUAGES: German.
*PRACTICE AREAS: Taxation.
**Reigel, Julia** ............... '65 '96 C.172 B.S. L.813 J.D. [⊠ Wilson,S.G.&R.]
*PRACTICE AREAS: Corporate; Securities.
**Reilly, Rosemary G.** '67 '95 C.918 B.A. L.178 J.D.
(adm. in NY; not adm. in CA) [⊠ Wilson,S.G.&R.]
*PRACTICE AREAS: Corporate; Securities.
**Reinstra, Mark L.** ............... '65 '92 C.966 B.S.I.E. L.813 J.D. [⊠ Wilson,S.G.&R.]
*PRACTICE AREAS: Corporate.
**Reinstra, Susan Pasquinelli** ............... '67 '92 C.602 B.A. L.813 J.D. [⊠ Wilson,S.G.&R.]
*PRACTICE AREAS: Real Estate.
**Reitman, Ruth** ............... '68 '94 C.112 B.A. L.770 J.D. [⊠ Cooley G.]
*PRACTICE AREAS: Civil Litigation; Business Securities.
**Renert, Douglas J.** ............... '67 '93 C.674 A.B. L.1066 J.D. [⊠ Gray C.W.&F.]
*LANGUAGES: Spanish.
*PRACTICE AREAS: General Corporate; International Corporate.
Ress, Sanford ............... '42 '67 C.659 B.Econ. L.813 LL.B. 253 Seale
**Reynolds, Laura L.** ............... '62 '91 C.103 A.B. L.767 J.D. [⊠ Lakin S.]
*LANGUAGES: Spanish.
*PRACTICE AREAS: Family Law.
**Rhough, Gene** ............... '71 '96 C.453 S.B.E.E. L.309 J.D. [⊠ Wilson,S.G.&R.]
*PRACTICE AREAS: Intellectual Property.
**Rice, Paul E.**, (AV) ............... '48 '74 C.477 B.A. L.1049 J.D. [Thoits,L.H.&M.]
*PRACTICE AREAS: Business Litigation; Real Estate Litigation; Bankruptcy Litigation.
**Richardson, Christine L.** ............... '65 '91 C.154 B.A. L.188 J.D. [⊠ Brobeck,P.&H.]
*PRACTICE AREAS: Employee Benefits Practice.
**Richardson, Kent R.** ............... '66 '93 C&L.02 B.S., LL.B. [⊠ Wilson,S.G.&R.] (Pat.)
**Riechert, Melinda Collins**, (AV) ..... '52 '75 C.054 LL.B. L.813 J.D. [⊠ Brobeck,P.&H.]
*PRACTICE AREAS: Civil Litigation; Contract Disputes; Landlord Tenant Disputes; Collection of Debts.
**Riegler, Erik F.** ............... '67 '95 C.112 B.A. L.1066 J.D. [⊠ Wilson,S.G.&R.]
*LANGUAGES: Spanish and German.
*PRACTICE AREAS: Corporate; Securities.
Rierson, Anne ............... '70 '95 C.112 B.A. L.1068 J.D. 2200 Geng Rd.
**Riff, I. Joel** ............... '51 '83 C.477 B.G.S. L.145 J.D. [Fenwick&W.]
*PRACTICE AREAS: Intellectual Property; Licensing Law.
**Rinsky, Arthur C.**, (AV) ............... '44 '69 C.150 A.B. L.477 J.D. [Gray C.W.&F.]
Riordan, Christine ............... '64 '92 C.813 B.A. L.178 J.D. 650 Page Mill Rd.
**Ritchey, Craig S.**, (AV) ............... '44 '70 C.813 A.B. L.1065 J.D. [Ritchey F.W.&K.]
**Ritchey, Gary H.** ............... '52 '88 C.770 B.S. L.1066 J.D. [⊡ Cooley G.]
*PRACTICE AREAS: Technology Litigation; Litigation.

**Ritchey Fisher Whitman & Klein, A Professional Corporation, (AV)**
**(Formerly Blase, Valentine & Klein)**
**1717 Embarcadero Road, P.O. Box 51050, 94303**
**Telephone: 415-857-1717 Telecopier: 415-857-1288**
**Email: rfwk@rfwklaw.com**
**George C. Fisher; Gillian G. Hays; John G. Hursh; David A. Kays; Terence M. Kelly; Lawrence A. Klein; Martha C. Luemers; Jean K. McCown; Craig S. Ritchey; Karen E. Wentzel; Peter A. Whitman;—Jennifer Dew; Paul K. Lauher; Stephen M. Maurer; Erik J. Olson; Patricia A. Welch. Of Counsel: Paula S. Crow; Byron Mellberg.**
**General Civil and Trial Practice, Alternative Dispute Resolution including Arbitration, Mediation, and Mini-Trials. Corporation, Emerging Growth Companies, Taxation, Tax Exempt Organizations, Trade Secret, Unfair Competition, Intellectual Property, Real Property, Probate, Estate Planning, Construction, Professional Liability, Product Distribution, Employment, Health Care and Environmental Law.**
*See Professional Biographies, PALO ALTO, CALIFORNIA*

Ritter, Jordan E. '56 '84 C.994 B.A. L.724 J.D.
V.P. & Gen. Coun., Essex Property Trust, Inc.
**Ritter, Michael J.** '65 '94 C&L.846 B.A.C.S., J.D.
[⊠ Townsend&T.&C.] (See Pat. Sect.)
*PRACTICE AREAS: Electronic and Software Patent Prosecution.
Ritzmann, Louise J. ............... '46 '77 C.914 B.A. L.770 J.D. 2111 Hanover St.
Rivera, Miriam ............... '64 '95 C&L.813 A.B., J.D. 2200 Geng Rd.
Rivette, Dorothy J. ............... '58 '85 C.378 B.A. L.770 J.D. 580 Newell Rd.
**Rix, Robert (Jack)** ............... '53 '86 C.623 B.A. L.284 J.D. [Finnan,F.&Assoc.]
*PRACTICE AREAS: Immigration and Nationality Law (100%).
**Roake, Timothy K.** ............... '52 '81 C.112 B.A. L.1067 J.D. [Fenwick&W.]
*PRACTICE AREAS: Business Litigation; including Securities and Trade Secret Litigation.
**Roberts, John W.** '29 '70 C.393 B.A. L.309 J.D.
(adm. in IL; not adm. in CA) [Zevnik H.G.&M.]⊙
*REPORTED CASES: Monsanto Company in Hines v. Vulcan, 658 F.Supp. 651 (N.D. Ill. 1988); Inland Steel Company in Inland Steel v. Koppers Company, 498 N.E.2d 1247 (Ind. App. 1986).
*PRACTICE AREAS: Commercial Litigation; Compensation and Liability; Environmental; Construction.
**Roberts, Matthew F.** ............... '70 '95 C.112 B.A. L.1066 J.D. [⊠ Cooley G.]
**Robertson, J. Martin** ............... '52 '78 C.473 A.B. L.150 J.D. [Gray C.W.&F.]
*PRACTICE AREAS: Environmental Litigation and Compliance.
**Robinett, Eileen Duffy** ............... '64 '89 C.770 B.S. L.1066 J.D. [Fenwick&W.]
*PRACTICE AREAS: Corporate.
**Robins, Roberta L.** ............... '53 '87 C.768 B.A. L.1065 J.D. [Reed&R.] (See Pat. Sect.)
*PRACTICE AREAS: Patent Law; Strategic Counseling; Patent Preparation and Prosecution.
**Robinson, Christina Baker** ............... '63 '91 C.112 B.S. L.813 J.D. [⊠ Brobeck,P.&H.]
*PRACTICE AREAS: Corporate.
**Robinson, Julie M.** ............... '56 '91 C.696 B.A. L.990 J.D. [⊠ Cooley G.]
*PRACTICE AREAS: Corporate Law; Corporate Finance; Securities.
Robinson, Kurt K., (CV) ............... '56 '83 C.602 B.A. L.770 499 Hamilton Ave.
Robinson, Susan C. ............... '67 '92 C.914 B.A. L.178 J.D. 525 Univ. Ave.
**Roche, Laura C.** ............... '65 '94 C&L.276 B.S.F.S., J.D. [⊠ Gibson,D.&C.]
**Rock, Bradley J.** ............... '57 '85 C.674 A.B. L.1066 J.D. [Gray C.W.&F.]
**Rodoni, William A.** ............... '70 '95 C&L.770 FNCE, J.D. [⊠ Gray C.W.&F.]
*PRACTICE AREAS: Securities Transactions; General Corporate Law.
**Rodriguez, Ricardo** ............... '69 '94 C.453 B.S. L.813 J.D. [⊠ Cooley G.]
*PRACTICE AREAS: Intellectual Property Litigation.
**Roe, Maura** ............... '64 '95 C.058 B.A. L.061 [⊠ Brobeck,P.&H.]
*PRACTICE AREAS: Executive Compensation; Securities Law Compliance.
Romines, Ron, (BV) ............... '43 '71 C.112 B.A. L.813 J.D. 480 California Ave.
**Roos, John V.**, (AV) ............... '55 '80 C&L.813 A.B., J.D. [Wilson,S.G.&R.]
*PRACTICE AREAS: Corporate Law; Securities.
**Rosales, Ulrico S.** ............... '58 '84 C&L.976 B.A., J.D. [McCutchen,D.B.&E.]
*LANGUAGES: Spanish.
*PRACTICE AREAS: Labor; Employment.
**Rosati, Mario M.**, (AV) ............... '46 '72 C.112 B.A. L.1066 J.D. [Wilson,S.G.&R.]
*PRACTICE AREAS: Corporate Law; Securities.
Rose, Mary Barton ............... '61 '87 C.813 B.A. L.893 J.D. Syntex (U.S.A.) Inc.
**Rose, Michele E.** ............... '65 '91 C.112 A.B. L.426 J.D. [⊠ Wilson,S.G.&R.]
*PRACTICE AREAS: Securities Litigation; Commercial Litigation; Antitrust.
Rosen, Anne-Marie ............... '67 '92 C.309 B.A. L.1066 J.D. 1510 Madrono
Rosen, Mitchell H. '35 '75 C.563 B.Mech.E. L.161 J.D.
(adm. in OH; not adm. in CA) 335 Diablo Ct.‡
**Rosen, Terri L.** '61 '89 C&L.494 B.S., J.D.
(adm. in GA; not adm. in CA) Reg. Atty., Hewlett-Packard Co.
*RESPONSIBILITIES: Labor Relations; Employment Law.
**Rosenfield, Stephen N.** ............... '49 '92 C.1019 B.S. L.588 J.D. [⊠ Cooley G.]
*PRACTICE AREAS: Corporate Finance; Emerging Growth Companies; General Corporate.
**Rosenzweig, Eric Jon** ............... '65 '96 C.309 B.A. L.1066 J.D. [⊠ Wilson,S.G.&R.]
*PRACTICE AREAS: Corporate; Securities.

CALIFORNIA—PALO ALTO MARTINDALE-HUBBELL LAW DIRECTORY 1997

**Roskoph, Paul H.**, (AV) ....................'38 '63 C&L.608 B.S., J.D. [Fenwick&W.]
*PRACTICE AREAS: Taxation; Estate Planning.
**Rosler, Debra B.** .................... '67 '94 C.976 B.A. L.813 J.D. [Wilson,S.G.&R.]
*PRACTICE AREAS: Corporate; Securities.
**Ross, James C.** .................... '58 '85 C&L.012 B.C.L., LL.B. [Baker&M.]
*PRACTICE AREAS: Taxation.
Ross, Linda S. .................... '53 '81 C.813 A.B. L.94 J.D. P.O. Box 60211
**Ross, William D.**, (AV) .................... '48 '75 C.813 B.A. L.770 J.D. [W.D.Ross]
*REPORTED CASES: William S. Hart Union High School Dist. v. Regional Planning Commission, 226 Cal.App.3d 1612 (1991); Long Beach Unified School District v. State of California, 225 Cal.App.3d 155 (1990), Petition for Review denied February 28, 1991; City of Sacramento v. State of California, 50 Cal.3d 51, 266 Cal.Rptr. 139 (1990); American River Fire Protection Dist. v. Board of Supervisors, 211 Cal.App.3d 1076, 259 Cal.Rptr. 858 (1989); Carmel Valley Fire Protection Dist. v. State of California, 190 Cal.App.3d 521, 234 Cal.Rptr. 795 (1987).
*PRACTICE AREAS: Land Use; Municipal; Zoning; Real Estate.

**Ross, William D., A Prof. Corp., Law Offices of, (AV)**
**425 Sherman Avenue, Suite 310, 94306**
**Telephone: 415-617-5678 Fax: 415-617-5680**
**William D. Ross; Myra J. Prestidge.**
**Civil Trial and Appellate Practice in State and Federal Courts. Business Litigation, Employment Rights, Land Use, Real Property, Environmental, Water Rights, Public Finance, State and Local Administrative Law.**
**Los Angeles, California Office: 520 South Grand Avenue, Suite 300. Telephone: 213-892-1592. Telecopier: 213-892-1519.**
*See Professional Biographies, PALO ALTO, CALIFORNIA*

**Rossen, Jeremy** .................... '71 '96 C&L.659 B.A., J.D. [Wilson,S.G.&R.]
*PRACTICE AREAS: Corporate.
**Rotandaro, RoseAnn Marie** '55 '96 C.649 B.A. L.813 J.D.
(adm. in AK; not adm. in CA) [Wilson,S.G.&R.]
*PRACTICE AREAS: Securities; Commercial Litigation; Intellectual Property.
**Roten, Suzanne K.** .................... '48 '90 C.112 B.A. L.1068 J.D. [Heller E.W.&M.]
**Roth, Ronald M.**, (AV) .................... '54 '79 C.401 B.S. L.813 J.D. [Wilson,S.G.&R.]
*PRACTICE AREAS: Tax Law.
Roth, Thomas J. .................... '33 '61 C.494 B.A. L.767 J.D. Elec. Power Research Institute
Rothkopf, Laura C. .................... '38 '65 C.668 A.B. L.94 LL.B. P.O. Box 8842
Rousseau, Norman P. '35 '62
C.674 B.S.E. L.309 LL.B. Dir., Trade Affairs Dept., Syntex Corp. (Pat.)
**Rowland, Bertram I.**, (AV) ...... '30 '62 C.112 B.S. L.273 LL.B. [Flehr,H.T.A.&H.] ‡
*PRACTICE AREAS: Patent Practice; Licensing; Company Formation.
**Rowland, Mark D.** .......... '61 '87 C.602 B.S.E.E. L.273 J.D. [Fish&N.] (See Pat. Sect.)
*PRACTICE AREAS: Intellectual Property.
**Rozynko, Alisande M.** .................... '59 '91 C.112 B.A. L.1065 J.D. [Wilson,S.G.&R.]
**Rubin, Rhesa C.** .................... '58 '90 C.112 B.A. L.1137 J.D. [Flicker&K.]
*PRACTICE AREAS: Family Law.
**Ruiz, Anna A.** .................... '70 '95 C.37 B.S. L.145 J.D. [Brobeck,P.&H.]
*LANGUAGES: Spanish.
*PRACTICE AREAS: Corporate Law.
Rundle, Catherine Hunt .................... '57 '83 C.112 A.B. L.1065 J.D. 650 Page Mill Rd.
**Runte, John A.**, (BV) .......... '38 '73 C.436 B.S. L.770 J.D. [Germino,R.A.J.C.&M.]
*PRACTICE AREAS: Real Property; Trusts; Commercial Transactions; Taxation; Probate.
**Ruskin, Rachel L.** .................... '67 '96 C.289 B.A. L.178 J.D. [Wilson,S.G.&R.]
*PRACTICE AREAS: Multimedia Law; Technology Licensing.
**Russell, Robert T.**, (AV) .................... '49 '75 C.477 B.A. L.1065 J.D. [Gray C.W.&F.]
*PRACTICE AREAS: Insurance Coverage and Bad Faith Litigation; Policyholders' Insurance Coverage; Real Estate Litigation; Construction Litigation; Environmental Litigation.
**Russell, Valerie L.** .................... '67 '94 C.112 B.S. L.477 J.D. [Brobeck,P.&H.]
*PRACTICE AREAS: Intellectual Property.
**Russell, William R.** .................... '47 '73 C.112 B.A. L.1065 J.D. [Russell&M.]

**Russell and Moltzen**
**2370 Watson Court, Suite 200, 94304**
**Telephone: 415-856-4800 FAX: 415-494-7006**
**Allan R. Moltzen, Jr.; William R. Russell (Certified Specialist, Family Law, The State Bar of California Board of Legal Specialization).**
**Civil Trial and Appellate Practice. Aviation, Business, Family, Insurance, Products Liability, Real Estate and Tort Law.**

**Russo, Jack**, (AV) .................... '54 '80 C.178 B.A. L.800 J.D. [Russo&H.]
*PRACTICE AREAS: Civil Litigation; Intellectual Property Litigation; Computer Law; Licensing.

**Russo & Hale, (AV)**
**401 Florence Street, 94301**
**Telephone: 415-327-9800 Fax: 415-327-3737**
**Email: info@computerlaw.com URL: http://www.computerlaw.com**
**Members of Firm: Jack Russo; Timothy C. Hale; John A.D. Kelley.**
**Computer Law, Intellectual Property, Patent, Copyright, Trademark and Licensing Litigation, Commercial Litigation and General Business Litigation.**
*See Professional Biographies, PALO ALTO, CALIFORNIA*

**Ryan, John G.** .................... '— '94 C.061 B.Sc. L.813 J.D. [Fenwick&W.]
*PRACTICE AREAS: Taxation.
**Ryan, Mark F.** .......... '50 '76 C.602 B.A. L.770 J.D. Sr. Atty., Hewlett-Packard Co.
*RESPONSIBILITIES: International Trade.
Saal, Frederick Neil .................... '58 '86 C.1169 B.A. L.564 J.D. 650 Page Mill Rd.
Sabatine, Paul L. '22 '64 C&L.273 B.S., LL.B.
(adm. in MD; not adm. in CA; Pat.) 455 Marlowe St.
**Saca, Diana M.** .................... '65 '91 C.763 B.A. L.770 J.D. [Hagan,S.&H.]
*PRACTICE AREAS: Corporate; Commercial; Real Estate Litigation and Transactions.
**Sachdeva, Gurjeev K.** .......... '65 '93 C.367 B.A. L.861 J.D. [Cooley G.] (Pat.)
*PRACTICE AREAS: Patent Prosecution.
**Sachs, Robert R.** .................... '65 '90 C.112 B.A. L.976 J.D. [Fenwick&W.]
*PRACTICE AREAS: Intellectual Property; Patent Law.
**Sadeghian, Christopher K.** .......... '66 '91 C.112 B.A. L.770 J.D. [Wilson,S.G.&R.]
*PRACTICE AREAS: Corporate Law; Securities.
**Salceda, Ignacio E.** .................... '67 '92 C.309 A.B. L.813 J.D. [Wilson,S.G.&R.]
*LANGUAGES: Spanish.
*PRACTICE AREAS: Litigation.
**Salesin, Dianne B.** .................... '63 '90 C&L.477 B.B.A., J.D. [Gray C.W.&F.]
*PRACTICE AREAS: General Corporate; Securities.
**Salmon, Denis R.**, (AV) .................... '51 '76 C.300 B.A. L.494 J.D. [Gibson,D.&C.]
*PRACTICE AREAS: Patent, Trademark and Copyright; Litigation; Trade Secrets; Computers and Software; Antitrust.
**Saltoun, André M.**, (AV) .................... '30 '60 C.575 B.A. L.966 J.D. [Baker&M.]
*PRACTICE AREAS: Taxation; Trade (International).
Saltzman, Eric T. .................... '62 '88 C.821 B.A. L.813 J.D. 5 Palo Alto Sq.
Salzman, Alan E. .................... '53 '78 C.025 B.A. L.813 J.D. 2200 Geng Rd.
Sanbrook, George A., (BV) .......... '38 '69 C.768 B.A. L.1026 J.D. 2600 El Camino Real
**Sanchez, Robert D.** .................... '65 '92 C.339 B.S. L.813 J.D. [Wilson,S.G.&R.]
*PRACTICE AREAS: Corporate Law; Securities Law.
**Sands, Michael A.** .................... '71 '95 C.861 B.A. L.770 J.D. [Fenwick&W.]
*PRACTICE AREAS: Litigation.
**Santos, Leslie S.** .......... '61 '93 C.976 B.A. L.309 J.D. [Wilson,S.G.&R.] (Pat.)
*PRACTICE AREAS: Corporate.
**Saper, Jeffrey D.**, (AV) .................... '48 '72 C&L.569 B.A., J.D. [Wilson,S.G.&R.]
*PRACTICE AREAS: Corporate Law; Securities.

**Sarrafian, Vahe H.** .................... '67 '93 C.112 B.A. L.1067 J.D. [Wilson,S.G.&R.]
*LANGUAGES: Armenian.
*PRACTICE AREAS: Corporate; Securities; Business Litigation; Employment; Communications Law.
**Saul, David J.** .................... '65 '91 C.112 B.A. L.145 J.D. [Wilson,S.G.&R.]
*LANGUAGES: German.
**Saunders, Elizabeth M.** .................... '62 '88 C&L.602 B.A., J.D. [Wilson,S.G.&R.]
*PRACTICE AREAS: Litigation.
Savage, David F. '17 '45 C&L.911
(adm. in WA; not adm. in CA) 746 De Sot Dr.‡
**Savage, Diane Wilkins**, (AV) .................... '50 '74 C.1365 B.A. L.276 J.D. [Cooley G.]
*PRACTICE AREAS: Computer Law; Technology Licensing; Product Distribution Agreements; Intellectual Property Protection.
**Savage, Thomas I.** '69 '95 C.309 B.A. L.145 J.D.
(adm. in IL; not adm. in CA) [Wilson,S.G.&R.]
*LANGUAGES: Japanese.
**Sayer, Melissa H.** .................... '66 '94 C.1236 B.A. L.770 J.D. [Fenwick&W.]
*PRACTICE AREAS: General Corporate; Securities.
**Schachtili, Richard J.** .......... '68 '92 C.112 B.A. L.1065 J.D. [Wilson,S.G.&R.]
*PRACTICE AREAS: Estate Planning.
**Schaeffer, Bruce E.** .................... '52 '77 C.178 B.A. L.309 J.D. [Gray C.W.&F.]
**Schatz, Steven M.**, (AV) .................... '48 '73 C.659 B.A. L.178 J.D. [Wilson,S.G.&R.]
*PRACTICE AREAS: Litigation.
**Schaumberg, Jason** .................... '67 '96 C.1078 B.A. L.112 J.D. [Gray C.W.&F.]
*PRACTICE AREAS: Commercial Law; Bankruptcy; Real Estate.
**Schefsky, Eileen Evans** .................... '— '96 C&L.112 B.A., J.D. [Gray C.W.&F.]
**Scheinman, Jim A.** .................... '66 '95 C.228 B.S. L.112 J.D. [Gray C.W.&F.]
*LANGUAGES: Hebrew.
*PRACTICE AREAS: Corporate Law; Securities.
**Scher, Jefferson F.** .................... '62 '91 C.112 A.B. L.813 J.D. [Fenwick&W.]
*PRACTICE AREAS: Intellectual Property; Trademark; Copyright.
Schiff, Susan E. .................... '44 '71 C.66 A.B. L.770 J.D. 550 Madison Way‡
**Schisler, George M., Jr.**, (AV) .......... '57 '82 C.659 B.S. L.477 J.D. [Hagan,S.&H.]
*PRACTICE AREAS: Civil Litigation in all State and Federal Courts; Patent Law.
**Schlachter, Eric** .................... '68 '94 C.112 B.A. L.1068 J.D. [Cooley G.]
*PRACTICE AREAS: Cyberspace Law; Intellectual Property; Emerging Growth Companies.
Schmidt, Ernest W., (BV) .................... '26 '53 C&L.813 B.A., LL.B. 407 Sherman St.
**Schmoller, Eberhard G. H.** '43 '69
C.813 B.S. L.1068 J.D. Gen. Coun., Consolidated Freightways, Inc.
**Schmonsees, William** .......... '47 '85 C.884 B.S. L.1338 J.D. [Heller E.W.&M.] (Pat.)
**Schneiderman, Arthur F.**, (AV) .......... '42 '67 C.72 B.A. L.966 J.D. [Wilson,S.G.&R.]
*PRACTICE AREAS: Corporate Law; Securities.
**Schrader, Stephen J.** .................... '56 '82 C.597 B.A. L.813 J.D. [Morrison&F.]
*PRACTICE AREAS: Corporate Finance; Intellectual Property.
**Schreiber, William R.** .................... '65 '93 C.112 B.S. L.1066 J.D. [Gray C.W.&F.]
*PRACTICE AREAS: Securities; General Corporate.
**Schrotenboer, Ronald B.** .................... '56 '80 C.114 B.A. L.477 J.D. [Fenwick&W.]
*PRACTICE AREAS: Domestic and International Corporate Taxation; California State Income and Sales Taxation.
Schuck, John F. .................... '51 '80 C&L.770 B.S., J.D. 2521 Cowper St
**Schultheis, Patrick J.** .................... '64 '89 C.813 A.B. L.145 J.D. [Wilson,S.G.&R.]
*LANGUAGES: French.
*PRACTICE AREAS: Corporate Law; Securities.
**Schulthies, Valerie** .................... '— '94 C.101 B.A. L.813 J.D. [Wilson,S.G.&R.]
*PRACTICE AREAS: Corporate; Securities.

**Schulz, Charles G., (AV) '32 '58 C.188 B.A. L.309 J.D.**
**517 Byron Street, P.O. Box 1299, 94302**
**Telephone: 415-326-8080 Fax: 415-326-0825**
***PRACTICE AREAS: Estate Planning; Trusts; Conservatorships; Probate Law; Civil Trial.**
**Estate Planning, Trust and Probate Law. General Civil Practice.**
**References: Wells Fargo Bank, Palo Alto; Bank of America National Trust & Savings Assn., Palo Alto, California.**
*See Professional Biographies, PALO ALTO, CALIFORNIA*

**Schulz, Robert E.**, (AV) .................... '39 '66 C&L.813 B.S.E.E., J.D. [Crist,G.S.&B.]
**Schulze, Herbert R.** '46 '71
C.453 S.B.E.E. L.145 J.D. Corp. Coun., Hewlett-Packard Co. (Pat.)
*RESPONSIBILITIES: Copyright; Intellectual Property/Compliance; Patent.
**Schuyler, Marc P.** .......... '64 '89 C.111 B.S. L.112 J.D. Hewlett-Packard Co. (Pat.)
*LANGUAGES: French.
*RESPONSIBILITIES: Patent; Copyrights; Trade Secrets; Trademarks.
Schwab, Brian J. .................... '64 '89 C.188 B.A. L.1068 J.D. 5 Palo Alto Sq., Suite 400
**Schwab, Lawrence M., (Inc.)**, (AV) ...... '53 '79 C.813 A.B. L.770 J.D. [Bialson,B.&S.]
*PRACTICE AREAS: Business Law; Commercial Law; Creditor's Representation Law.
**Schwab, Peter M.** .................... '57 '83 C.339 B.S. L.767 J.D. [Wilson,S.G.&R.]
*PRACTICE AREAS: Real Estate.
Schwartz, Richard H. .................... '51 '86 C.665 B.A. L.770 J.D. 525 Univ. Ave. Ste. 705
**Scott, Jonathan** '61 '95 C.112 B.S.E.E. L.765 J.D.
[Hickman,B.&W.] (See Pat. Sect.)
*PRACTICE AREAS: Patents; Trademarks; Copyrights; Trade Secrets; Intellectual Property.
Scott, Kenneth E. .................... '28 '57 C.945 A.B. L.813 LL.B. Prof., Stanford Law Sch.
**Scott, Timothy T.** .................... '59 '85 C.813 A.B. L.145 J.D. [Wilson,S.G.&R.]
*PRACTICE AREAS: Litigation.
Scoyen, Edward C. .................... '24 '51 C&L.813 A.B., LL.B. Mun. J.
**Scully, Jason** .................... '— '96 C.112 B.A. L.1065 J.D. [Fenwick&W.]
*PRACTICE AREAS: Litigation; Intellectual Property; Licensing Law.
**Scully, Joanne Renée** .................... '49 '92 C.112 B.A. L.309 J.D. [Wilson,S.G.&R.]
*PRACTICE AREAS: Litigation.
**Segre, David J.** .................... '59 '85 C.813 B.A. L.309 J.D. [Wilson,S.G.&R.]
*PRACTICE AREAS: Corporate Law; Securities.

**Selby, Earl Nicholas, (AV) '48 '77 C.813 B.A. L.309 J.D.**
**420 Florence Street, Suite 200, 94301**
**Telephone: 415-323-0990 Fax: 415-325-9041**
**Email: nselby@well.com**
**Public Utilities Law, Telecommunications, Cable Television, First Amendment and Administrative Law. General Civil and Trial Practice.**
**Representative Clients: Nextel Communications, Inc.; ICG Access Services, Inc (IntelCom Group U.S.A., Inc., Denver, CO); Bay Area Teleport; Linkatel of California, L.P. (San Diego, Calif.); Shared Telecommunication Systems, Inc. (Hayward, Calif.).**
*See Professional Biographies, PALO ALTO, CALIFORNIA*

**Selness, Craig A.** .................... '55 '85 C.494 B.A. L.1066 J.D. [Fenwick&W.]
*PRACTICE AREAS: Litigation; Employment and Labor Law.
Seltzer, David R. .................... '56 '80 C.1036 B.A. L.352 J.D. Hewlett-Packard Co.
**Seubert, Daniel K.** .................... '60 '89 C.629 B.A. L.846 J.D. [Gray C.W.&F.]
*LANGUAGES: Spanish and French.
*PRACTICE AREAS: Real Property; Commercial Law.
Sevely, Vincent C., (BV) .................... '29 '55 C&L.770 B.S., J.D. 230 California Ave.
Seymour, James H., (AV) .................... '43 '70 C.108 B.A. L.347 J.D. 706 Cowper St.‡
**Shaffer, William L.** '66 '92 C.880 E.E. L.802 J.D.
[Townsend&T.&C.] (See Pat. Sect.)
*PRACTICE AREAS: Electronic and Semiconductor Patent Prosecution.

CAA476P

**Shaffer, John C., Jr., A Prof. Law Corp., Law Offices of**
**(See Menlo Park)**

**Shakib, Kaivan M.** '67 '92 C.178 B.A. L.1068 J.D.
(adm. in NJ; not adm. in CA) [🄰 Wilson,S.G.&R.]
*PRACTICE AREAS: General Corporate; Securities; International Law.
**Shallman, Mary E.** .......................'58 '84 C.813 A.B. L.494 J.D. [🄰 Gray C.W.&F.]
*PRACTICE AREAS: Government Contracts.
**Shariati, Behrooz** .............'61 '94 C.576 B.S. L.1137 J.D. [🄰 Wilson,S.G.&R.] (Pat.)
*LANGUAGES: Farsi.
*PRACTICE AREAS: Intellectual Property; Patent Prosecution and Litigation.
**Sharron, Stephanie** ..................'64 '92 C.112 B.S. L.188 J.D. [🄰 Wilson,S.G.&R.]
*PRACTICE AREAS: Intellectual Property; Technology Licensing; Computer Law; Life Sciences.
**Shea, Joanne Marshall** ...........................'66 '91 C.602 B.A. L.276 J.D. [🄰 Cooley G.]
*PRACTICE AREAS: Corporate; Securities.
**Shelburne, Craig A.** ...............'68 '94 C.228 B.A. L.1068 J.D. [🄰 Wilson,S.G.&R.]
*PRACTICE AREAS: Mergers and Acquisitions; Venture Capital; Corporate Securities.
**Shelburne, Laura Lewis** ..........'67 '94 C.813 B.A. L.1068 J.D. [🄰 Wilson,S.G.&R.]
*PRACTICE AREAS: Corporate; Securities; Financial Services; Real Estate.
Shepherd, George B. ........................'60 '87 C.976 B.A. L.309 J.D. Stanford Univ.
**Shepherd, Mark R.** .........................'53 '82 C.766 B.A. L.284 J.D. [Crist,G.S.&B.]
*REPORTED CASES: Co-Counsel in Estate of Maria Cristofani, 97 TC 24 (1991, Acq. result only).
Sher, Byron D. '28 '52 C.910 B.S.B.A.
(adm. in MA; not adm. in CA) Prof. of Law, Stanford Univ.
**Sheridan, James A.** '41 '67 C.436 B.S.E.E. L.209 J.D.
[Flehr,H.T.A.&H.] (See Pat. Sect.)
**Sheridan, John T.** .......................'58 '86 C.770 B.S. L.1066 J.D. [Wilson,S.G.&R.]
*PRACTICE AREAS: Corporate Law; Securities.
**Sherman, M. Andrew** ......................'67 '92 C.800 B.S. L.464 J.D. [🄰 Gray C.W.&F.]
*LANGUAGES: Spanish and French.
*PRACTICE AREAS: Technology-related Commercial Litigation; Intellectual Property Litigation.
**Sherman, Martin P.** ..............'40 '65 C.112 A.B. L.145 J.D. [🄲 Tomlinson Z.M.&M.]
*PRACTICE AREAS: Intellectual Property; Antitrust; Commercial; International; Technology.
**Sherman, William D.**, (AV) ..............'42 '72 C.674 B.A. L.1066 J.D. [Morrison&F.]
*PRACTICE AREAS: Business; Corporate Finance; Securities.
**Shetka, Debra A.** ......................'58 '89 C.429 B.A. L.494 J.D. [Morrison&F.] (Pat.)
*PRACTICE AREAS: Business; Patent.
**Shim, Sungbo** ...........................'63 '94 C.918 B.A. L.813 J.D. [🄰 Wilson,S.G.&R.]
*LANGUAGES: Korean, Chinese and Japanese.
*PRACTICE AREAS: Business Law; International Law; Corporate Law.
Shimahara, Bonnie K. ..............'44 '78 C.1042 B.S. L.426 J.D. 450 San Antonio Rd.‡
**Shoji, Aki Y.** ..........................................'66 '94 C.999 B.A. L.813 J.D. [🄰 Morrison&F.]
*LANGUAGES: Japanese.
Shoub, Deborah S. ..........................'— '83 C.293 B.A. L.1066 J.D. 371 Whitclem Dr.‡
**Shulman, Ron E.** ..............................'55 '82 C.31 B.A. L.705 J.D. [Wilson,S.G.&R.]
*PRACTICE AREAS: Intellectual Property.
**Shuman, John R., Jr.**, (BV) ..............'56 '81 C.197 A.B. L.1065 J.D. [Gray C.W.&F.]
*PRACTICE AREAS: Employment Law; Litigation.
**Shupack, Richard A.** ..................'46 '71 C.97 B.A. L.273 J.D. [🄲 Wilson,S.G.&R.]
*PRACTICE AREAS: Drug and Device Regulatory Law.
**Siegel, Kenneth M.** ........................'58 '85 C.999 B.A. L.1065 J.D. [Wilson,S.G.&R.]
*PRACTICE AREAS: Corporate Law; Securities.
**Silton, Myles B.** '59 '91 C.188 B.A. L.659 J.D.
(adm. in NY; not adm. in CA) [🄰 Cooley G.]
*PRACTICE AREAS: Intellectual Property Licensing and Protection; General Corporate Counselling.

**Silver, Wayne A., Law Offices of, (BV) '53 '83 C.659 B.S. L.767 J.D.**
**409 Sherman Avenue Suite 212, 94306**
**Telephone: 415-323-7100 Fax: 415-323-4154**
**(Certified Specialist, Bankruptcy Law, State Bar of California Board of Legal Specialization).**
***PRACTICE AREAS: Bankruptcy; Bankruptcy Litigation.**
**Bankruptcy and Litigation.**
***See Professional Biographies, PALO ALTO, CALIFORNIA***

**Sim, Victor** ...........................'66 '95 C.276 B.S.F.S. L.245 J.D. [🄰 Wilson,S.G.&R.]
*PRACTICE AREAS: Corporate.
**Simons, Laird H., III** ..........................'49 '74 C.311 B.A. L.309 J.D. [Fenwick&W.]
*PRACTICE AREAS: Corporate.
**Sinclair, Jo-Anne** ..........................'61 '87 C.048 B.A. L.024 LL.B. [🄰 Heller E.W.&M.]
**Singer, Jonathan E.** '65 '93 C.197 A.B. L.145 J.D.
(adm. in IL; not adm. in CA) [🄰 Heller E.W.&M.]
**Singh, Tina M.** ..........................................'63 '88 C.12 B.A. L.1067 J.D. [🄰 Wise&S.]
Skaer, Susan Jul ................................'64 '90 C.575 B.A. L.893 J.D. 650 Page Mill Rd.
**Skiles, Jonathan M.** ..................'62 '95 C.1079 B.A. L.770 J.D. [🄰 Thoits,L.H.&M.]
*PRACTICE AREAS: Business Litigation.

**Skjerven, Morrill, MacPherson, Franklin & Friel LLP**
**(See San Jose)**

**Slaby, David W.** ...........................'47 '76 C.30 B.S.B.A. L.94 J.D. [Fenwick&W.]
*PRACTICE AREAS: Litigation.
**Slate, David L.**, (AV) '42 '74 C.766 B.A. L.1065 J.D.
Dep. Gen. Coun., Consolidated Freightways, Inc.
*RESPONSIBILITIES: Labor and Employment law; Litigation.
**Slenkovich, Keith** ..........................'61 '87 C.170 B.S. L.1066 J.D. [Slenkovich&F.]
*LANGUAGES: Spanish.
*PRACTICE AREAS: Real Estate; Construction; Intellectual Property; White Collar Criminal Defense; Commercial Litigation.

**Slenkovich & Flanagan**
**525 University Avenue, Suite 1420, 94301**
**Telephone: 415-688-6000 Facsimile: 415-688-6001**
**Email: info@SF-Law.com URL: http://www.sf-law.com**
**Keith Slenkovich; Mark D. Flanagan.**
**Civil Litigation, Real Property Transactions, Business Litigation, Commercial Leasing, Securities, Alternative Dispute Resolution, including Arbitration, Mediation and Administrative Law, White Collar Criminal Defense.**
***See Professional Biographies, PALO ALTO, CALIFORNIA***

**Slichter, Donald A.**, (AV) ..................'32 '62 C.674 A.B. L.477 J.D. [🄲 Cohen&O.]
*PRACTICE AREAS: Corporate Law.
**Slone, David N.** .......'46 '77 C.012 B.Sc. L.813 J.D. [Townsend&T.&C.] (See Pat. Sect.)
**Slosberg, Jared A.** ........................'69 '92 C.1036 B.A. L.1066 J.D. [🄰 Doty&S.]
*LANGUAGES: French.
*PRACTICE AREAS: Business Formation; Intellectual Property Licensing; Technology Contracts; Shareholder Agreements; Buying and Selling of Businesses.
**Small, Frank A.**, (AV) ............................'39 '65 C.197 B.A. L.813 LL.B. [Lakin S.]
*PRACTICE AREAS: Real Estate Development and Finance.
Small, Jonathan A. ...............................'59 '87 C.1074 B.S. L.770 J.D. Xerox Corp. (Pat.)
Smart, Francis A. ......................'10 '40 C.112 B.S. L.1065 LL.B. 4149 Willmar Dr.‡
**Smilan, Laurie B.** ...........................'59 '85 C.1044 B.A. L.1068 J.D. [Wilson,S.G.&R.]
*PRACTICE AREAS: Securities Litigation.
**Smith, Albert C.** ......................'37 '64 C.667 B.E.E. L.770 J.D. [Fenwick&W.] (Pat.)
*PRACTICE AREAS: Intellectual Property; Patent Law.
**Smith, Carissa M.** ..............'63 '93 C.893 B.A. L.1065 J.D. [🄰 McCutchen,D.B.&E.]
Smith, Carol L., (AV) ..............'52 '82 C.766 B.A. L.1065 J.D. 401 Florence St. (Pat.)

Smith, Eugene H. '27 '57 C&L.911 A.B., LL.B.
(adm. in WA; not adm. in CA) Lockheed Corp.
**Smith, Glenn A.**, (AV) '46 '72 C.668 B.A. L.1066 J.D.
[Heller E.W.&M.] (⊙San Fran.)
*PRACTICE AREAS: Federal Income Taxation; Tax Controversies.
**Smith, Gregory C.** ...........................................'63 '88 C.813 B.A. L.178 J.D. [Cooley G.]
*PRACTICE AREAS: Corporate Finance; Mergers and Acquisitions; Emerging Growth Companies.
**Smith, James M.** ...........................................'63 '88 C.112 B.A. L.1066 J.D. [🄰 Wise&S.]
*PRACTICE AREAS: Intellectual Property Litigation; General Commercial Litigation; Unfair Advertising Counselling.
**Smith, Kevin A.** ..........................'62 '94 C.951 B.A. L.930 J.D. [🄰 Brobeck,P.&H.]
*PRACTICE AREAS: Corporate.

**Smith, R. Patrick, (AV) '40 '69 C.174 B.S. L.1065 J.D.**
**2600 El Camino Real Suite 618, 94306**
**Telephone: 415-494-8977 Fax: 415-494-8979**
**Email: esq@batnet.com**
***PRACTICE AREAS: Real Estate; Corporate; General Business; Estate Planning; Mediation.**
**Real Estate, Corporate, Business, Contracts, Estate Planning, Mediation.**
***See Professional Biographies, PALO ALTO, CALIFORNIA***

**Smith, S. Dawn** ...................................'63 '96 C.871 B.S. L.813 J.D. [🄰 Wilson,S.G.&R.]
*PRACTICE AREAS: Corporate; Securities.
**Smith, William M.** '51 '79 C.112 B.S. L.800 J.D.
[Townsend&T.&C.] (See Pat. Sect.) (⊙Seattle, Wash.)
*PRACTICE AREAS: Biotechnology Patent Prosecution, Licensing & Enforcement; Molecular Immunology.
**Snowman, Stacy** .....................................'54 '86 C.473 B.S. L.1065 J.D. [Gray C.W.&F.]
*PRACTICE AREAS: Internet; Multimedia and Technology Licensing; Commercial Distribution (domestic and international); Intellectual Property Protection; Government Contracting.
**Snyder, Jeffrey A.** ..............................'62 '90 C.112 B.A. L.1049 J.D. [🄰 Thoits,L.H.&M.]
*PRACTICE AREAS: Business Litigation; Real Estate Litigation; Appeals and Writs; Employment Law.
Sobrato, Lisa Ann ...................................'66 '91 C.112 B.A. L.1066 J.D. 2200 Geng Rd.
Sofaer, Abraham D. '38 '65 C.978 B.A. L.569 LL.B.
(adm. in NY; not adm. in CA) George P. Schultz Sr. Fellow, The Hoover Institution
**Sokol, Marc A.** ...................................'67 '92 C.112 B.S.E.E. L.767 J.D. [🄰 Carr,D.&F.]
**Solomon, Susan R. F.**, (BV) ....'47 '80 C.659 B.A. L.770 J.D. [Germino,R.A.J.C.&M.]⊙
*PRACTICE AREAS: Real Property Law; Civil Litigation; Appellate Practice.
**Solomon-Gonzales, Ellen** '68 '93 C.659 B.A. L.309 J.D.
(adm. in MA; not adm. in CA) [🄰 Wilson,S.G.&R.]
*LANGUAGES: Spanish.
*PRACTICE AREAS: Litigation.
**Sonsini, Larry W.**, (AV) ...............'41 '66 C.112 A.B. L.1066 J.D. [Wilson,S.G.&R.]
*PRACTICE AREAS: Corporate Law; Securities; Mergers and Acquisitions.
**Sonsini, Matthew W.** ..........................'66 '92 C.197 B.A. L.1066 J.D. [🄰 Cooley G.]
*PRACTICE AREAS: Emerging Growth Companies; Corporate Finance; Mergers and Acquisitions.
Sorensen, Bonnie S. ...........................'47 '79 C.813 B.A. L.770 J.D. 2501 Park Blvd.
**Sorenson, Joe C.**, (AV) ...........................'47 '79 C.612 B.S. L.1066 J.D. [Graham&J.]
*PRACTICE AREAS: Corporate Law; Securities Law.
**Sparks, Deidre Lynn** ..........................'61 '87 C.267 B.S. L.1067 J.D. [🄲 Cooley G.]
*PRACTICE AREAS: Mergers and Acquisitions; Emerging Growth Companies.
**Sparks, Timothy J.** ....................'58 '83 C.112 B.S. L.1065 J.D. [Wilson,S.G.&R.]
*PRACTICE AREAS: Employee Benefits; Executive Compensation.
**Spector, Scott P.** .........................................'49 '75 C&L.861 B.A., J.D. [Fenwick&W.]
*PRACTICE AREAS: Corporate.
Spencer, David H. .......................'17 '74 C.350 B.S. L.770 J.D. 1403 Pitman Ave.‡
**Spencer, Karen Y.** .........................'64 '90 C.453 B.S. L.309 J.D. [🄰 Brobeck,P.&H.]
*PRACTICE AREAS: Intellectual Property Litigation.
**Spira, Noga Devecseri** .............................'69 '96 L.061 LL.B. [🄰 Wilson,S.G.&R.]
*LANGUAGES: Hebrew.
*PRACTICE AREAS: Corporate; Securities.
**Spitzen, Jay M.** .............................................'50 '88 C&L.309 A.B., J.D. [Gray C.W.&F.]
**Spong, Alison E.** ................................'65 '89 C.339 B.S. L.309 J.D. [🄰 Wise&S.]
*PRACTICE AREAS: Environmental Law.
**Sprague, Gary D.** ..........................................'55 '81 C.813 B.A. L.309 J.D. [Baker&M.]
*PRACTICE AREAS: Taxation; Executive Transfers.
**Stafford, Blakeney**, (BV) ................'42 '68 C.674 B.A. L.813 LL.B. [Fenwick&W.]
**Stanton, Scott M.** ...............................'66 '93 C.813 B.A. L.112 J.D. [🄰 Gray C.W.&F.]
*PRACTICE AREAS: Corporate.
**Stanwood, Thomas R.**, (AV) ............'48 '74 C.813 B.A. L.1065 J.D. [Stanwood&P.]
*PRACTICE AREAS: Corporations & Partnerships; Family Law; Real Estate; Estate Planning.

**Stanwood & Price, (AV)**
**Court House Plaza, Suite 300, 260 Sheridan Avenue, 94306**
**Telephone: 415-321-1440 Fax: 415-321-4746**
**Members of Firm: Daniel R. Price; Thomas R. Stanwood.**
**General Civil and Trial Practice. Employment, Business, Trade Secrets, Probate, Trust and Estate Planning, Family, Real Property, Personal Injury and Civil Litigation.**
***See Professional Biographies, PALO ALTO, CALIFORNIA***

**Stapleton, Susan L.** ..........................'65 '94 C.339 B.S. L.1065 J.D. [🄰 Wilson,S.G.&R.]
*PRACTICE AREAS: Corporate; Securities.
Steadman, Juliette M. .......'65 '90 C.976 B.A. L.813 J.D. Immigrant Legal Resource Ctr.
**Stebbins, Michael W.** ............'63 '88 C.813 A.B. L.770 J.D. [🄰 Tomlinson Z.M.&M.]
*LANGUAGES: French.
*PRACTICE AREAS: Intellectual Property Litigation; General Business Litigation; Employment Litigation.
**Steele, John J.** ........................................'60 '86 C.105 B.A. L.276 J.D. [Fenwick&W.]
*PRACTICE AREAS: Litigation.
**Steele, Richard G.** ......................'69 '96 C.112 B.A. L.1065 J.D. [🄰 Wilson,S.G.&R.]
*PRACTICE AREAS: Corporate; Securities.
Stein, Isaac .........................'46 '72 C.165 B.A. L.813 J.D. Pres., Waverley Assocs., Inc.

**Stein, Jotham S., Law Office of '62 '91 C.674 A.B. L.813 J.D.**
**400 Cambridge Avenue, 94306**
**Telephone: 415-327-1900 Fax: 415-327-2500**
**Email: jstein@jotham.com URL: http://www.jotham.com**
***LANGUAGES: Spanish.**
***PRACTICE AREAS: Litigation.**
**Concentrating on representing employees, mid-level managers and executives in employment-and-business-related matters, including stock option compensation disputes, corporate squeeze outs and power plays, controversies involving usurpation of key players' technology and sexual harassment, breach of contract and wrongful termination cases. General Civil Litigation Practice, including contract disputes, unfair trade practices, business torts, consumer rights and securities law.**
***See Professional Biographies, PALO ALTO, CALIFORNIA***

Stein, Pierce N., (AV) .....................'10 '41 C.112 A.B. L.800 LL.B. 1850 Willow Rd.‡
**Stenfeldt, Lillian G.** ...........................'55 '81 C.813 B.A. L.215 J.D. [Gray C.W.&F.]
*PRACTICE AREAS: General Business Law; Commercial Law; Bankruptcy Law.
**Stepanchenko, Vadim D.** ................'61 '93 C.061 B.A. L.178 J.D. [🄰 Wilson,S.G.&R.]
*LANGUAGES: Russian, Italian and Spanish.
*PRACTICE AREAS: Corporate; Securities.
**Stephens, Thomas N.** .....................'52 '95 C.1097 B.A. L.1066 J.D. [🄰 Wilson,S.G.&R.]
*PRACTICE AREAS: Corporate; Securities.
Sterling, Nathaniel '46 '70
C.112 B.A. L.1067 J.D. Exec. Secy., Calif. Law Revision Comm.

**Stern, Claude M.**, (AV) ....................'55 '80 C.112 B.A. L.1065 J.D. [Fenwick&W.]
*PRACTICE AREAS: Litigation; Intellectual Property Law.
Stern, Gerald D. ....................'33 '57 C&L.569 B.A., LL.B. 600 Hansen Way
**Stern, Julian N.**, (AV) ....................'24 '49 C.569 B.S. L.976 LL.B. [⊠ Heller E.W.&M.]
*PRACTICE AREAS: Corporate and Technology Licensing.
**Stern, Michael** ....................'48 '83 C.178 B.A. L.1066 J.D. [Cooley G.]
*PRACTICE AREAS: Intellectual Property Licensing and Protection; General Corporate Counselling.

**Stern, Peter S., Law Office of, (AV) '39 '81 C.207 B.A. L.813 J.D.**
**400 Cambridge Avenue, Suite A, 94306**
**Telephone: 415-326-2282 Fax: 415-326-1312**
**Email: pstern1939@aol.com**
***LANGUAGES: French.**
***PRACTICE AREAS: Estate Planning Law; Administration Law; Elder Law; Conservatorships; Incapacity Planning.**
**Estate Planning and Administration, Elder Law.**
***See Professional Biographies, PALO ALTO, CALIFORNIA***

**Stern, Roger D.** ....................'56 '89 C.112 A.B. L.145 J.D. [Wilson,S.G.&R.]
*PRACTICE AREAS: Employee Benefits Law; Executive Compensation.
**Steuer, David S.** ....................'57 '83 C.813 A.B. L.309 J.D. [Wilson,S.G.&R.]
*PRACTICE AREAS: Litigation.
**Stevens, David W.** ....................'65 '94 C.878 B.A. L.1068 J.D. [⊠ Brobeck,P.&H.]
*PRACTICE AREAS: Litigation.
Stevens, M. Carol, (AV) ....................'47 '78 C.300 B.A. L.1049 J.D. [Kay&S.]
**Stevens, Mark C.** ....................'59 '83 C.770 B.S. L.597 J.D. [Fenwick&W.] (⊙San Francisco)
*PRACTICE AREAS: Corporate; Licensing Law.
Stevens, Samuel S. ....................'43 '67 C&L.813 B.S.E.E. 101 Alma St.
**Stevens, Timothy J.** ....................'66 '91 C.629 B.S. L.1067 J.D. [⊠ Wilson,S.G.&R.]
*PRACTICE AREAS: Corporate Law; Securities.
Stevenson, Alan B. ....................'43 '77 C.401 B.A. L.284 J.D. 3401 Hillview Ave.
**Stewart, Blair W., Jr.**, (AV) ....................'45 '75 C.871 B.S. L.813 J.D. [Wilson,S.G.&R.]
*PRACTICE AREAS: Corporate Law; Securities.
Stewart, Jacqueline W., (BV) ....................'45 '76 C.174 B.A. L.813 J.D. 1580 Walnut Dr.
**Stewart, Peter F.** '69 '95 C.453 B.S. L.94 J.D.
(adm. in MA; not adm. in CA) [⊠ Heller E.W.&M.]
Stinchcomb, Patricia A. ....................'51 '78 C.813 B.A. L.1068 J.D. Syntex (U.S.A.) Inc.
Stone, Steven F. ....................'35 '61 C.688 B.Ch.E. L.273 J.D. Coun., Alza Corp. (Pat.)
Stoner, John, Jr. ....................'14 '52 C.691 B.S. L.276 J.D. 101 Alma St. (Pat.)
**Stormer, Kent A.** ....................'45 '70 C&L.813 B.A., J.D. [⊠ Heller E.W.&M.]
*LANGUAGES: Spanish.
*PRACTICE AREAS: Environmental; Life Sciences.
**Stratford, Carol** ....................'52 '95 C.813 B.S. L.770 J.D. [⊠ Dehlinger&Assoc.]
*PRACTICE AREAS: Intellectual Property.
**Strawbridge, James Neilson** ....................'61 '87 C.886 B.S. L.893 J.D. [Wilson,S.G.&R.]
*PRACTICE AREAS: Corporate Law; Securities.
**Strickland, Rodney G., Jr.** ....................'67 '92 C.602 B.A. L.770 J.D. [⊠ Wilson,S.G.&R.]
*PRACTICE AREAS: Litigation.

**Stringer, Nanette Schulze, (AV) '52 '78 C.681 B.A. L.813 J.D.** ⊠
**430 Cowper Street, 94301**
**Telephone: 415-617-4540 Fax: 415-617-4541**
**(Certified Specialist, Family Law, The State Bar of California Board of Legal Specialization).**
***LANGUAGES: French.**
***PRACTICE AREAS: Family Law.**
**Family Law and Family Law Mediation.**
***See Professional Biographies, PALO ALTO, CALIFORNIA***

**Stroud, Gretchen R.** ....................'61 '89 C.800 A.B. L.813 J.D. [⊠ Cooley G.]
*PRACTICE AREAS: Litigation.
**Struthers, James F.** '65 '93 C.691 B.S.M.E. L.846 J.D.
(adm. in TX; not adm. in CA; Pat.) Atty., Hewlett-Packard Co.
*RESPONSIBILITIES: Litigation; Intellectual Property; Patents; Trademarks.
**Subhedar, Nitin** ....................'68 '94 C&L.477 B.S.E., J.D. [⊠ Heller E.W.&M.]
**Sue, Betsey** ....................'67 '92 C.93 B.A. L.569 J.D. [⊠ Wilson,S.G.&R.]
*PRACTICE AREAS: Corporate.
**Sueoka, Greg T.** ....................'63 '89 C&L.878 B.S., J.D. [Fenwick&W.] (Pat.)
*PRACTICE AREAS: Intellectual Property; Patent Law.
**Suffoletta, J. Robert, Jr.** ....................'61 '90 C.347 B.S. L.602 J.D. [⊠ Wilson,S.G.&R.]
*PRACTICE AREAS: Corporate Law; Securities.
**Sullivan, Dennis C.**, (AV) ....................'46 '72 C.112 A.B. L.1066 J.D. [Gray C.W.&F.]
*PRACTICE AREAS: Corporate Law; Securities Law.
Sullivan, Kathleen M. '55 '82 C.188 B.A. L.309 J.D.
(adm. in NY; not adm. in CA) Prof. of Law, Stanford Univ.
Sullivan, Kevin B. '58 '91 C.679 B.S.E.E. L.1035 J.D.
(adm. in MN; not adm. in CA) Hewlett-Packard
**Summers, Debra S.** ....................'50 '81 C.921 B.S. L.767 J.D. [Wilson,S.G.&R.]
*PRACTICE AREAS: Real Estate; Environmental.
Sunde, Einar, (BV) ....................'42 '67 C.605 A.B. L.1066 J.D. 2600 El Camino Real
**Sundheim, George M., III**, (AV) ....................'52 '81 C.813 B.A. L.597 J.D. [Doty&S.]
*PRACTICE AREAS: Corporate Reorganization; Intellectual Property Licensing; Private Placements; Shareholder Agreements; Professional Sports Law.
**Suniga, Gail E.** ....................'45 '82 C.112 B.A. L.770 J.D. [Fenwick&W.]
*PRACTICE AREAS: Corporate.
**Suriyapa, Seksom N.** ....................'66 '95 C.951 B.A. L.813 J.D. [⊠ Cooley G.]
*LANGUAGES: Thai.
*PRACTICE AREAS: Securities Law (Mergers and Acquisitions); Securities Law (Finances); General Corporate Law.
**Sutis, Robert W.** ....................'48 '74 C.339 B.A. L.1065 J.D. Corp. Coun., Hewlett-Packard Co.
*RESPONSIBILITIES: Litigation; Commercial Contracts; Antitrust; Software Licensing.
**Swanson, Shawna M.** ....................'68 '93 C.335 B.A. L.309 J.D. [⊠ Fenwick&W.]
*PRACTICE AREAS: Litigation; Labor and Employment Law.
Swarth, George S. ....................'11 '37 C&L.813 A.B., J.D. 101 Alma St.‡
**Swartz, Matthew B.** ....................'68 '96 C.112 B.A. L.1065 J.D. [⊠ Wilson,S.G.&R.]
*PRACTICE AREAS: Securities; Corporate; Technology Licensing; Multimedia Licensing.
Swenson, Carol C. ....................'35 '76 C.494 B.A. L.813 J.D. Sr. Coun., Stanford Univ.
Swezey, C. Lawrence ....................'23 '49 C.188 A.B. L.813 LL.B. 212 Fulton St.‡
**Swiatek, Maria S.** '62 '92
C.1075 B.S.Ch.E. L.464 J.D. [⊠ Flehr,H.T.A.&H.] (See Pat. Sect.)
*PRACTICE AREAS: Patent; Licensing; Trademark; Copyright.
**Tachibana, Hirohisa** ....................'56 '82 C.976 B.S.M.S. L.1065 J.D. [Fenwick&W.]
*PRACTICE AREAS: Intellectual Property; Licensing Law.
**Taha, Ahmed E.** ....................'67 '96 C.659 B.A. L.813 J.D. [⊠ Wilson,S.G.&R.]
*PRACTICE AREAS: Litigation.
**Takei, Jonathan H.** ....................'67 '94 C.112 B.A. L.770 J.D. [⊠ Cooley G.] (Pat.)
*PRACTICE AREAS: Litigation.
**Taketa, Marilyn N.**, (BV) ....................'43 '70 C.424 B.S. L.813 J.D. [⊠ Gray C.W.&F.]
*PRACTICE AREAS: Securities; Equity Compensation Plans; Estate Planning; General Corporate.
**Taku, Yoichiro** ....................'68 '94 C.494 B.A. L.145 J.D. [⊠ Wilson,S.G.&R.]
*LANGUAGES: Japanese.
*PRACTICE AREAS: Corporate.
**Tal, Tomer** ....................'— '96 C.763 B.S. L.770 J.D. [⊠ Wilson,S.G.&R.]
*PRACTICE AREAS: Corporate Law; Securities Law.

**Tallman, Katherine T.**, (BV) ....................'47 '79 C.319 B.A. L.767 J.D. [⊠ Fenwick&W.]
*PRACTICE AREAS: Corporate.
Tallman, Richard J. ....................'60 '88 C.763 B.S. L.1065 J.D. 5 Palo Alto Sq.
**Tanke, Tony J.**, (AV) ....................'51 '75 C.958 B.A. L.494 J.D. [Tanke&W.]⊙
*PRACTICE AREAS: Litigation (60%); Appellate Practice (40%).

**Tanke & Willemsen, A Professional Association, (AV)**
**2501 Park Boulevard, 94306⊙**
**Telephone: 415-324-1468 Fax: 415-326-5430**
**Email: 75022.3105@compuserve.com**
**Tony J. Tanke; Michael A. Willemsen.**
**Appellate Law, Civil and Criminal, and Civil Litigation.**
**Belmont, California Office: 1523 Solana Drive, 94002. Telephone: 415-591-8627. Fax: 415-591-8635.**
***See Professional Biographies, PALO ALTO, CALIFORNIA***

**Tanzillo, Barbara E.** ....................'61 '93 C.1073 B.A. L.309 J.D. [⊠ Cooley G.]
*PRACTICE AREAS: Employment Law; Labor Law; Intellectual Property Law.
Tapolsky, Bruno A. ....................'59 '86 L.145 LL.M. 2200 Geng Rd.
**Tarkoff, Robert M.** ....................'68 '95 C.31 B.A. L.309 J.D. [⊠ Wilson,S.G.&R.]
*PRACTICE AREAS: Corporate Law; Securities Law.
**Tate, Eric A.** ....................'69 '95 C.112 B.A. L.1066 J.D. [⊠ Morrison&F.]
**Taubman, Romy S.** ....................'63 '93 C.813 B.A. L.1068 J.D. [⊠ Wilson,S.G.&R.]
*PRACTICE AREAS: Corporate; Securities.
**Taylor, Barry E.**, (AV) ....................'48 '75 C.216 B.A. L.893 J.D. [Wilson,S.G.&R.]
*PRACTICE AREAS: Corporate Law; Securities.
**Taylor, Kurt H.**, (BV) ....................'57 '86 C.112 B.A. L.770 J.D. [Wilson M.&T.]
*PRACTICE AREAS: Intellectual Property; Commercial and Technology Litigation; Corporate Law; Licensing.
**Taylor, R. Allyn** ....................'50 '77 C.813 B.A. L.178 J.D. [Gray C.W.&F.]
*PRACTICE AREAS: Intellectual Property; Trademark.
Teeters, Jack Eugene, (BV) ....'31 '60 C&L.813 A.B., J.D. [J.E.Teeters] (⊙San Francisco)
Teeters, Jack Eugene, P.C., (BV) .................... 2600 El Camino Real
**Telkamp, Bruce A.** ....................'67 '94 C.112 B.A. L.1065 J.D. [⊠ Wilson,S.G.&R.]
*PRACTICE AREAS: Litigation.
**Tenhoff, Gregory C.** ....................'62 '91 C.490 B.S. L.800 J.D. [⊠ Cooley G.]
**Tennis, Stephen M.**, (AV) ....................'42 '67 C&L.813 A.B., LL.B. [Morrison&F.]
*PRACTICE AREAS: Securities; Corporate Finance.
Tenuto, Mary Ann ....'36 '84 C.477 A.B. L.284 J.D. United Stanford Workers, Local 680
Tepper, Jeffrey A., (BV) '52 '80 C.112 B.A. L.765 J.D.
400 Cambridge Ave. (⊙San Jose)
Tepper, Rubin ....................'18 '52 C.112 B.A. L.1065 LL.B. 464 Ferne Ave.‡
**Terrano, Mark C.** ....................'67 '95 C.688 B.S. L.1218 J.D. [⊠ Fenwick&W.] (Pat.)
*PRACTICE AREAS: Intellectual Property; Patent Law.
**Test, Aldo J.**, (AV) ....'23 '52 C.112 B.S. L.1066 J.D. [Flehr,H.T.A.&H.] (See Pat. Sect.)
Theodorakis, D. John ....................'64 '90 C.112 A.B. L.188 J.D. 650 Page Mill Rd.
**Thoits, Warren R.**, (AV) ....................'22 '49 C&L.813 A.B., J.D. [Thoits,L.H.&M.]
*PRACTICE AREAS: Real Estate; Probate Law.

**Thoits, Love, Hershberger & McLean, A Professional Corporation, (AV)**
**245 Lytton Avenue, Suite 300, 94301-1426**
**Telephone: 415-327-4200 Telecopier: 415-325-5572**
**John E. Lehman (1919-1982); Diana Berghausen; Terrence P. Conner; Michael Curtis; Stephen A. Dennis; Stephen C. Gerrish; J. Ronald Hershberger (Certified Specialist, Estate Planning, Trust and Probate Law, The State Bar of California Board of Legal Specialization); Thomas B. Jacob; William J. McLean III; Bruce H. Munro; Paul E. Rice; Warren R. Thoits;—Judy Koong Baeth; James R. Barnett; Lynn Howell DuBois; Richard L. Ehrman; Kenneth H. Horowitz; Jonathan M. Skiles; Jeffrey A. Snyder.**
**General Civil Practice in State and Federal Courts, Trial and Appeals. Corporate, Partnership, Commercial, Securities, Real Estate, Environmental, Estate Planning, Probate, Taxation, Pension and Profit Sharing, Employee Benefits, Employment, Computer and High Technology Law.**
**Representative Clients: CPS Advanced Infusion Systems, Inc. (I.V. and Nutritional Supply Services); FMC Corp.; Guckenheimer Enterprises, Inc. (Food Services); Marriott Corp. (Entertainment); Mid-Peninsula Bank; Northern Telecom, Inc.; Pacific Western Systems, Inc. (Semi-conductor test equipment manufacturer); Spectra-Physics, Inc. (Lasers); Stellar Homes, Inc. (home builders).**
***See Professional Biographies, PALO ALTO, CALIFORNIA***

**Thomas, C. Douglass** '62 '88
C.645 B.S.E.E. L.1017 J.D. [⊠ Hickman,B.&W.] (See Pat. Sect.)
*PRACTICE AREAS: Intellectual Property Law; Patents.
Thomas, John M., (AV) ....................'37 '63 C&L.813 A.B., LL.B. 550 Hamilton Ave.
**Thomas, Robert D.** ....................'62 '93 C.112 B.A. L.1065 J.D. [⊠ Morrison&F.]
**Thomas, Susan Stuermer**, (BV) ....'42 '79 C.861 B.A. L.1065 J.D. [⊠ Wilson,S.G.&R.]
*PRACTICE AREAS: Real Estate Law.
**Thomases, Andrew N.** ....................'68 '94 C.31 B.A. L.145 J.D. [⊠ Brobeck,P.&H.]
*PRACTICE AREAS: Intellectual Property Litigation.
Thompson, Barry R. ....................'48 '74 C&L.770 B.S.C., J.D. 385 Sherman Ave., Suite 1
Thompson, Barton H., Jr. ....................'51 '76 C&L.813 A.B., J.D. Prof., Stanford Law School
Thompson, Lee A. ....................'49 '77 C.103 B.S. L.309 J.D. 301 University Ave., Ste. 480
**Thompson, Richard H.** '52 '95 C.813 A.B. L.1066 J.D.
(adm. in NY; not adm. in CA) [⊠ Wilson,S.G.&R.]
*PRACTICE AREAS: Corporate; Securities.
**Thornburgh, Don** ....................'69 '96 C.668 B.A. L.112 J.D. [⊠ Gray C.W.&F.]
*PRACTICE AREAS: Intellectual Property/Licensing.
**Tiedge, John H.** '— '84 C&L.201 B.S., J.D.
(adm. in OH; not adm. in CA) Sr. Trademark Atty., Hewlett-Packard Co.
*RESPONSIBILITIES: Trademarks.
**Tien, Susan** ....................'71 '96 C.681 A.B. L.659 J.D. [⊠ Wilson,S.G.&R.]
*PRACTICE AREAS: Litigation.
**Tighe, Craig M.** ....................'55 '81 C.918 B.A. L.813 J.D. [Gray C.W.&F.]
*PRACTICE AREAS: Lending; Workouts; Leasing; Corporate.
**Tillman, Candace M.** ....................'70 '95 C.112 B.A. L.1066 J.D. [⊠ Brobeck,P.&H.]
*PRACTICE AREAS: Corporate; Business; Technology.
**Ting, Vicki** ....................'— '95 C&L.813 A.B., J.D. [⊠ Cooley G.]
*LANGUAGES: Mandarin.
*PRACTICE AREAS: Corporate; Securities.
**Tobias, Paul R.** '64 '91 C&L.846 B.A.
(adm. in TX; not adm. in CA) [⊠ Wilson,S.G.&R.]
*PRACTICE AREAS: Corporate Law; Securities Law.
**Tobin, Christopher M.** ....................'64 '93 C&L.884 B.S.E.E., J.D. [Fenwick&W.]
*PRACTICE AREAS: Intellectual Property; Patent Law.
**Tomlinson, Timothy**, (AV) ....................'50 '76 C&L.813 B.A., J.D. [Tomlinson Z.M.&M.]
*PRACTICE AREAS: Corporate Finance and Acquisitions; Business Transactions.

**Tomlinson Zisko Morosoli & Maser LLP, (AV)**
**200 Page Mill Road, Second Floor, 94306**
**Telephone: 415-325-8666 Facsimile: 415-324-1808**
**Members of Firm: Timothy Tomlinson; William E. Zisko; Eugene B. Morosoli, Jr.; Thomas F. Maser; James R. Busselle; Polly A. Dinkel; Richard D. Judkins. Associates: Clifford M. Govaerts (Certified Specialist, Taxation Law, The State Bar of California Board of Legal Specialization); Janette M. Hoover; Thomas E. Moore, III; Oleg A. Vigdorchik; Cynthia M. Loe; Kathi A. Rawnsley; Michael W. Marchant; Michael W. Stebbins. Special Counsel: Martin P. Sherman; Richard Allan Horning.**
**General Business, Business Litigation, Construction, Corporate Finance, Environmental Litigation, Intellectual Property, Labor and Employment, Mergers and Acquisitions, Secured Lending, Securities, Taxation, Trusts and Estates.**
***See Professional Biographies, PALO ALTO, CALIFORNIA***

**Tong, Peter** ....................'56 '94 C.312 B.S.E.E. L.770 J.D. [[A] McCutchen,D.B.&E.]
*LANGUAGES: Cantonese, Mandarin.
*PRACTICE AREAS: Intellectual Property.
**Tosh, Tracy L.** ....................'71 '96 C.880 B.A. L.477 J.D. [[A] Wilson,S.G.&R.]
*PRACTICE AREAS: Litigation; Securities Litigation; Intellectual Property Litigation.
**Tovar, Tomas C.** ....................'69 '94 C.326 B.B.A. L.813 J.D. [[A] Brobeck,P.&H.]
*PRACTICE AREAS: Business; Technology; Corporate; Securities; Technology Licensing.

**Townsend and Townsend and Crew LLP, (AV)** [BB]
**A Limited Liability Partnership including a Professional Corporation**
**379 Lytton Avenue, 94301-1431**⊙
**Telephone: 415-326-2400 Telecopier: 415-326-2422**
**Email: inquire@townsend.com URL: http://www.townsend.com**
**Members of Firm: Kenneth R. Allen; Robert C. Colwell; Daniel J. Furniss; David N. Slone; James F. Hann; James M. Heslin; Gary T. Aka; William M. Smith; Paul C. Haughey; Theodore G. Brown, III; William J. Bohler; Karen B. Dow. Of Counsel: Henry K. Woodward; Renée A. Fitts. Associates: Joe Liebeschuetz; Joseph M. Villeneuve; William L. Shaffer; Richard Takashi Ogawa; Theodore T. Herhold; Shailendra C. Bhumralkar; Stephen Y.F. Pang; Dan H. Lang; Michael J. Ritter; John Thomas Raffle; Matthew B. Murphy; Mark D. Barrish; Melvin D. Chan; Margaret A. Powers; Kenneth L. Johnson; Stephen J. Akerley; Alice L. Wong; Michael A. Gelblum; Sam G. Campbell, III; Byron W. Cooper; Scott William Hewett; R. Ted Apple; Chiahua George Yu; Hao-Yuan Tung; Gregory Scott Bishop; Shane Horan Hunter; James F. Kurkowski.**
**Patent, Trademark, Copyright and Unfair Competition Law, Intellectual Property Law. Intellectual Property, Antitrust and Commercial Litigation.**
**San Francisco, California Office: Two Embarcadero Center, Eighth Floor. Telephone: 415-576-0200. Facsimile: 415-576-0300.**
**Denver, Colorado Office: 1200 17th Street, Suite 2700. Telephone: 303-571-4000. Fax: 303-571-4321.**
**Seattle, Washington Office: 601 Union Street, Suite 5400. Telephone: 206-467-9600. Telecopier: 206-623-6793.**
***See Professional Biographies, PALO ALTO, CALIFORNIA***

**Townshend, Peter N.** ....................'71 '96 C.976 B.A. L.1066 J.D. [[A] Heller E.W.&M.]
*LANGUAGES: Japanese, French, Spanish.
Train, Bruce, (AV) ....................'40 '70 C.813 A.B. L.309 J.D. 3305 Middlefield Rd.‡
**Tranlong, Perpetua B.** ....................'63 '89 C&L.309 B.A., J.D. [[A] Graham&J.]
*PRACTICE AREAS: Bankruptcy/Reorganization; Corporations.
**Trant, Jeffrey A., (BV)** ....................'51 '80 C.112 B.A. L.188 J.D. [Gray C.W.&F.]
**Travis, Michelle A.** ....................'69 '95 C.188 B.A. L.813 J.D. [[A] Heller E.W.&M.]
**True, Joi C.** ....................'69 '93 C.112 B.A. L.1066 J.D. [[A] Wise&S.]
Trumbull, Terry A. ....................'45 '71 C.112 B.A. L.276 J.D. [Trumbull]
Trumbull Law Firm, The .................... 1011 Lincoln Ave.
**Tsay, Jennifer** ....................'66 '92 C.813 B.A. L.309 J.D. [[A] Wilson,S.G.&R.]
*PRACTICE AREAS: General Corporate.
**Tsiang, Harold T.** .................... '65 '91 C.459 B.S.E.E. L.1065 J.D. [[A] Graham&J.] (Pat.)
*PRACTICE AREAS: Patent.
**Tung, Hao-Yuan** ....................'71 '96 C.453 B.S. L.813 J.D. [[A] Townsend&T.&C.]
**Turbow, Daniel W.** ....................'69 '94 C.813 A.B. L.276 J.D. [[A] Wilson,S.G.&R.]
*PRACTICE AREAS: Litigation.
Turbow, Ellen B. ....................'41 '76 C.813 B.A. L.770 J.D. 1870 Hamilton Ave.‡
Turner, Dewey E. ....................'19 '51 C&L.813 A.B., LL.B. 490 Loma Verde Ave.‡
**Turriff, Diane E.** ....................'63 '90 C.1074 B.S. L.1065 J.D. [[A] Wilson,S.G.&R.]
*PRACTICE AREAS: Trademarks; Advertising Practices; Litigation.
Tweedy, John B., Jr. ....................'60 '91 C.174 B.A. L.813 J.D. 755 Page Mill Rd.
**Twomey, Lynda M.** ....................'68 '93 L.058 LL.B. [[A] Fenwick&W.]
*PRACTICE AREAS: General Corporate; Securities.
Ulrich, Stan G. '47 '72 C.429 B.A. L.494 J.D.
Asst. Exec. Secy., Calif. Law Revision Comm.
**Urschel, Edward M.** ....................'63 '93 C.112 B.A. L.1065 J.D. [[A] Fenwick&W.]
*PRACTICE AREAS: Corporate Law; Securities.
**Urso, David M.** ....................'64 '96 C.685 B.A. L.309 J.D. [[A] Wilson,S.G.&R.]
*PRACTICE AREAS: Corporate Law; Intellectual Property.
**Vachss, Andrea H.** ....................'50 '85 C.184 B.A. L.262 J.D. [[B] Cooley G.]
*PRACTICE AREAS: Securities; Corporate; Business.
**Vail, Christina L.** ....................'69 '96 C.597 B.A. L.770 J.D. [[A] Heller E.W.&M.]
Vale, Robert D., (BV) ....................'53 '83 C.112 B.A. L.464 J.D. [McDowall,C.D.V.&B.]⊙
**Valentine, Andrew Paul** ....................'64 '92 C.95 B.A. L.770 J.D. [[A] Gray C.W.&F.]
*PRACTICE AREAS: Commercial Litigation; Intellectual Property Litigation.
Valentine, Paul C., (AV) .................... '32 '61 C.453 B.S. L.813 LL.B. 1717 Embarcadero Rd.
Van, Winnie ....................'63 '91 C&L.569 B.S., J.D. 2200 Geng Rd.
**Van Atta, David M., (AV)** ....................'44 '70 C.112 A.B. L.1065 J.D. [Hanna&V.]
*PRACTICE AREAS: Real Estate (Property) Law; Land Use Development Law; Real Estate Finance; Real Estate Arbitration; Real Estate Mediation.
**VandenBerg, Ronald A., (AV)** ....................'44 '73 C.763 L.1188 J.D. [Lakin S.]
*PRACTICE AREAS: Estate Planning; Estate and Trust Administration.
**van der Schee, Jan-Marc** ....................'68 '95 L.061 J.D. [[A] Wilson,S.G.&R.]
*LANGUAGES: Dutch, German, Italian and French.
**Van Pelt, Lee** ....................'65 '93 C.502 B.S. L.1066 J.D. [[A] Hickman,B.&W.] (See Pat. Sect.)
*PRACTICE AREAS: Patents.
**Van Rysselberghe, Pierre C.** '58 '90 C.668 B.A. L.284 J.D.
[Kolisch H.D.M.&H.] (See Pat. Sect.) (⊙Portland, OR.)
*PRACTICE AREAS: Patent, Trademark and Unfair Competition.
**Vanyo, Bruce G., (AV)** ....................'45 '74 C.473 B.S. L.178 J.D. [Wilson,S.G.&R.]
*PRACTICE AREAS: Securities Litigation; Intellectual Property Law.
Vartain, Michael J. ....................'51 '75 C&L.93 A.B., J.D. Sr. Univ. Coun., Stanford Univ.
**Vasquez, Alicia J.** ....................'62 '88 C.112 B.A. L.1065 J.D. [[A] Wilson,S.G.&R.]
*PRACTICE AREAS: Employment Law; Litigation.
**Vaughan, Peter** ....................'64 '90 C.207 B.A. L.262 J.D. [[A] Brobeck,P.&H.]
*PRACTICE AREAS: Securities Litigation.
**Vaughn, Daniel F.** '68 '95 C.906 B.A. L.893 J.D.
(adm. in TX; not adm. in CA) [[A] Wilson,S.G.&R.]
*PRACTICE AREAS: Corporate; Securities.
**Vaughn, Issac J.** ....................'62 '91 C.770 B.S. L.1065 J.D. [[A] Wilson,S.G.&R.]
*PRACTICE AREAS: Corporate.
**Veatch, William S.** ....................'61 '87 C.045 B.A. L.1065 J.D. [[A] Cooley G.]
*PRACTICE AREAS: Equipment Leasing; Asset-Based Finance; General Corporate.
**Veenker, Vicki S.** ....................'62 '88 C.347 B.S. L.276 J.D. [[A] Fish&N.] (See Pat. Sect.)
*PRACTICE AREAS: Intellectual Property.
**Vehrenkamp, Julie A.** ....................'59 '88 C.429 B.A. L.1065 J.D. [[A] Cooley G.]
*PRACTICE AREAS: Employee Benefit Law.
**Venable, Craig R.** ....................'62 '92 C.951 B.A. L.1066 J.D [[A] Brobeck,P.&H.]
**Verneris, Erin M.** ....................'66 '95 C.823 B.S. L.128 J.D. [[A] Cooley G.]
*PRACTICE AREAS: Employment Law; General Litigation.
Vernon, Stephen ....................'54 '78 C&L.813 A.B., J.D. [Knapp&V.]
**Verny, Hana** ....................'38 '82 C.999 PH.D L.184 J.D. [Peters,V.J.&B.] (See Pat. Sect.)
*LANGUAGES: Czech, Russian and German.
*PRACTICE AREAS: Patent, Trademark and Copyright Law.
**Vetter, Jeffrey R.** ....................'65 '90 C.112 B.A. L.1065 J.D. [[A] Fenwick&W.]
*PRACTICE AREAS: Corporate.
**Vigdorchik, Oleg A.** ....................'66 '93 C.768 B.S. L.284 J.D. [[A] Tomlinson Z.M.&M.]
*LANGUAGES: Russian.
*PRACTICE AREAS: Business Litigation; Corporate Tax.
**Villanueva, J. A. Tony, (AV)** ....................'56 '81 C.767 B.A. L.1065 J.D. [Lakin S.]
*PRACTICE AREAS: Transactional Real Estate; Corporate and Business Transactions.

**Villeneuve, Joseph M.** '63 '92 C.112 B.S.E.E. L.1065 J.D.
[[A] Townsend&T.&C.] (Pat.)
*PRACTICE AREAS: Electronic and Software Patents; Licensing.
Volk, John D. ....................'48 '75 C.154 B.A. L.228 J.D. 540 University Ave.
Volpe, Charles ....................'54 '80 C.705 B.A. L.262 J.D. 573 Ashton Ave.
**Wacha, Jason B.** ....................'63 '92 C.813 A.B. L.1067 J.D. [[A] Wilson,S.G.&R.]
*PRACTICE AREAS: Corporate; Securities.
**Wachs, Michelle J.** ....................'66 '93 C.103 B.A. L.309 J.D. [[A] Baker&M.]
*PRACTICE AREAS: Litigation (Intellectual Property, Securities).
Wachtel, Jeffrey H. ....................'56 '83 C.813 A.B. L.1065 J.D. Stanford Univ.
**Wade, Don M.** ....................'68 '94 C.188 B.A. L.1068 J.D. [[A] Wilson,S.G.&R.]
*PRACTICE AREAS: Intellectual Property; Technology Transactions; Corporate.
**Wagner, Valerie M.** ....................'65 '94 C.668 B.A. L.1065 J.D. [[A] Graham&J.]
*PRACTICE AREAS: Litigation.
**Wald, Jennifer F.** ....................'65 '91 C&L.813 B.A., J.D. [Lakin S.]
*PRACTICE AREAS: Family Law.
Waldow, Robert J. '69 '95 C.464 B.S. L.228 J.D.
(adm. in NY; not adm. in CA) 2 Embarcadero Pl.
**Waldow, Robert J.** '69 '94 C.169 B.S. L.228 J.D.
(adm. in NJ; not adm. in CA) [[A] Brobeck,P.&H.]
*PRACTICE AREAS: Taxation.
**Walker, Ann Yvonne, (AV)** ....................'54 '79 C&L.813 B.S., J.D. [Wilson,S.G.&R.]
*PRACTICE AREAS: Corporate Law; Securities.
**Walker, Craig E.** ....................'65 '95 C.112 B.A. L.1066 J.D. [[A] Brobeck,P.&H.]
*PRACTICE AREAS: Corporate; Securities.
**Walter, Victoria M.** '65 '96 C.178 B.A. L.188 J.D.
(adm. in NY; not adm. in CA) [[A] Wilson,S.G.&R.]
*PRACTICE AREAS: Litigation.
**Wanderer, Stephen G.** ....................'68 '95 C.911 B.S. L.1068 J.D. [[A] Brobeck,P.&H.]
*PRACTICE AREAS: Litigation.
**Wang, David C.** ....................'70 '96 C.112 B.S. L.188 J.D. [[A] Wilson,S.G.&R.]
*PRACTICE AREAS: Intellectual Property Litigation.
**Wanger, Christopher L.** ....................'64 '93 C.197 B.A. L.1065 J.D. [[A] Wise&S.]
Ward, Dawn M. ....................'63 '90 C.112 B.A. L.1066 J.D. 2370 Watson Ct.
**Ward, Elizabeth H.** ....................'58 '83 C.861 b.a. L.880 J.D. [Gray C.W.&F.]
*PRACTICE AREAS: Commercial Law; Financial Institutions.
**Ware, Leonard, (AV)** ....................'28 '53 C.911 L.823 LL.B. [Gray C.W.&F.] ‡
Washburn, Robert S. '31 '60 C.597 B.S. L.966 LL.B.
(adm. in WI; not adm. in CA) 455 Santa Rita‡
Washington, David Walter ....................'55 '90 C.705 B.A. L.284 J.D. 260 Sheridan Ave.
**Weaver, Jeffrey K.** ....................'60 '86 C.645 B.S. L.273 J.D. [Hickman,B.&W.] (See Pat. Sect.)
*PRACTICE AREAS: Intellectual Property Law; Patents.
**Webb, Laurie A.** ....................'65 '94 C.112 B.S. L.477 J.D. [[A] Cooley G.]
*PRACTICE AREAS: Corporate Law.
Weber, N. Terrill ....................'31 '72 C.36 B.S. L.37 J.D. 3632 Arbutus Ave.
Webster, Thomas M. '39 '67 C.679 B.S.E.E. L.276 J.D.
(adm. in IL; not adm. in CA; Pat.) Sr. Coun., Xerox Corp.
**Weed, Michael H., (AV)** ....................'54 '84 C.103 B.A. L.228 J.D. [Aufmuth,F.W.&L.]
*PRACTICE AREAS: Real Estate.
**Weeks, Cynthia S.** ....................'63 '89 C.112 B.A. L.770 J.D. [[A] Morrison&F.]
**Wegner, Adam W.** ....................'65 '91 C.659 B.A. L.276 J.D. [[A] Fenwick&W.]
*PRACTICE AREAS: General Corporate; Securities; Licensing.
**Wegner, Susan F.** ....................'66 '92 C.659 B.A. L.30 J.D. [[A] Wise&S.]
*PRACTICE AREAS: Environmental.
**Weinberg, David C., (BV)** ....................'40 '65 C&L.494 B.A., J.D. [Weinberg,Z.&M.]
*PRACTICE AREAS: Family Law; Tax Problems of Divorce Law; Custody Law.

**Weinberg, Ziff & Miller, (AV)**
**400 Cambridge Avenue, Suite A, 94306**
**Telephone: 415-329-0851 Fax: 415-324-2822**
**Email: taxlawyer@aol.com URL: http://www.taxlawyer.com**
**Members of Firm: David C. Weinberg (Certified Specialist, Family Law, The State Bar of California Board of Legal Specialization); Harvey L. Ziff; Michael Patiky Miller (Certified Specialist, Taxation Law, The State Bar of California Board of Legal Specialization).**
**General Civil and Trial Practice. Business, Corporate, Taxation, Family, Personal Injury, Collections, Estate Planning, Probate, Trust Litigation, Appeals and Administration. Criminal Trials.**
***See Professional Biographies, PALO ALTO, CALIFORNIA***

**Weiner, Michael L.** ....................'68 '94 C.659 B.S./B.A. L.1068 J.D. [[A] Cooley G.]
*PRACTICE AREAS: Corporate and Securities; Mergers and Acquisitions; Emerging Companies.
**Weitz, David J.** ....................'65 '92 C.453 B.S. L.112 J.D. [[A] Wilson,S.G.&R.]
Welch, M. Kip ....................'60 '90 C.846 B.A. L.107 J.D. 2200 Geng Rd.
**Welch, Patricia A.** ....................'59 '87 C.309 A.B. L.93 J.D. [[A] Ritchey F.W.&K.]
*PRACTICE AREAS: Business Litigation; Real Estate Litigation.
Weller, Alan H., (BV) ....................'45 '74 C.112 B.A. L.1065 J.D. 366 Calif. Ave.
**Wellington, Martin** ....................'63 '96 C.112 B.A. L.309 J.D. [[A] Wilson,S.G.&R.]
*PRACTICE AREAS: Corporate Law; Securities Law.
**Wells, Vanessa** ....................'59 '85 C.813 A.B. L.770 J.D. [Heller E.W.&M.]
*PRACTICE AREAS: Antitrust Litigation.
**Wentzel, Karen E.** ....................'55 '83 C.165 B.A. L.813 J.D. [Ritchey F.W.&K.]
*PRACTICE AREAS: Labor and Employment; Business Litigation.
West, Donald J. ....................'60 '90 C&L.477 B.B.A., J.D. 2 Palo Alto Sq.
West, Henry W., (AV) ....................'25 '55 C&L.813 B.A., J.D. 2 Palo Alto Sq.
West, Valerie K. ....................'48 '83 C.183 B.A. L.1029 J.D. 5 Palo Alto Sq.
**Westberg, Derek J.** ....................'67 '95 C.1074 B.S. L.284 J.D. [[A] Haverstock&Assoc.]
*PRACTICE AREAS: Electronic Patents; Mechanical Patents; Trademarks.
**Westman, Daniel P.** ....................'56 '82 C.813 A.B. L.145 J.D. [Cooley G.]
*PRACTICE AREAS: Labor and Employment.
**Wexler, Geoffrey A.** ....................'64 '93 C.813 B.A. L.178 J.D. [[A] Morrison&F.]
**Wheeler, Priscilla** ....................'45 '75 C.586 B.A. L.1065 J.D. [Wise&S.]
**Wheeler, Raymond L., (AV)** ....................'45 '72 C.846 B.A. L.309 J.D. [Morrison&F.]
*PRACTICE AREAS: Labor and Employment.
**Wheelock, E. Thomas** '47 '73 C.846 B.S. L.326 J.D.
(adm. in TX; not adm. in CA; Pat.) [[B] Morrison&F.]
*PRACTICE AREAS: Intellectual Property.
**Whisenant, Shannon D.** ....................'67 '93 C.878 B.A. L.101 J.D. [[A] Wilson,S.G.&R.]
*PRACTICE AREAS: Corporate; Securities; Venture Capital.
**White, Anna Erickson** ....................'63 '92 C.112 B.A. L.813 J.D. [[A] Morrison&F.]
**White, Brett D.** ....................'57 '91 C.112 A.B. L.309 J.D. [[A] Cooley G.]
*PRACTICE AREAS: Securities; Corporate.
**Whitley, Ann Marie** '70 '96 C.597 B.S.M.E. L.477 J.D.
(adm. in NY; not adm. in CA; See Pat. Sect.) [[A] Fish&N.]
**Whitman, Peter A., (AV)** ....................'43 '69 C&L.813 B.A., LL.B. [Ritchey F.W.&K.]
*PRACTICE AREAS: Corporation; Health Care.
Whitten, James A. ....................'61 '89 C.112 B.S. L.284 J.D. 3030 Hansen Way
**Whittle, Sarah H.** ....................'68 '96 C.103 B.A. L.188 J.D. [[A] Brobeck,P.&H.]
*PRACTICE AREAS: Labor and Employment Litigation.
Wickersham, Grover T. ....................'49 '77 C.309 M.B.A. L.1065 J.D. [G.T.Wickersham]
Wickersham, Grover T., Prof. Corp. .................... 430 Cambridge Ave.

CAA479P

**Widmann, Randall M., (AV) '49 '76 C.1060 B.A. L.770 J.D.**
**Suite 200, 2370 Watson Court, 94304**
**Telephone: 415-424-8400 Fax: 415-494-7006**
***LANGUAGES: Swedish.**
**Employment Law, Business and Real Estate Litigation.**

***See Professional Biographies, PALO ALTO, CALIFORNIA***

Wilkerson, R. Gerald .................. '30 '62 C.813 A.B. L.284 LL.B. 935 Ramona St.‡
**Willemsen, Michael A.** .................... '37 '63 C&L.813 B.A., LL.B. [Tanke&W.]⊙
*PRACTICE AREAS: Appellate Practice (85%, 15); Law and Motion Practice (15%, 2).
Willgohs, Eric H. .............. '65 '91 C.880 B.E. L.813 J.D. 379 Lytton Ave. (Pat.)
**Williams, Anne** ...................... '51 '76 C.30 B.A. L.273 J.D. [🄲 Heller E.W.&M.]
*LANGUAGES: French.
**Williams, Don S.** .................... '66 '93 C.813 A.B. L.309 J.D. [🄰 Wilson,S.G.&R.]
*LANGUAGES: Spanish.
*PRACTICE AREAS: Corporate.
**Williams, Gary S.** ...... '55 '82 C.976 B.S. L.309 J.D. [Flehr,H.T.A.&H.] (See Pat. Sect.)
Williams, Howard R. '15 '41 C.910 A.B. L.178 LL.B.
(adm. in NY; not adm. in CA) Prof. of Law, Emeritus, Stanford Univ.
Williams, James E. .................... '67 '93 C.103 B.A. L.145 J.D. 650 Page Mill Rd.
**Williams, Karen K.** .................. '54 '85 C.112 B.A. L.1065 J.D. [🄰 Gray C.W.&F.]
*PRACTICE AREAS: Intellectual Property Litigation; Licensing and Counselling; Copyright.
**Williams, Kirk Orlando** .............. '69 '94 C.813 B.A. L.569 J.D. [🄰 Gray C.W.&F.]
*PRACTICE AREAS: General Corporate (50%); Securities (50%).
**Williams, Lara A.** ..................... '68 '95 C.976 B.A. L.813 J.D. [🄰 Cooley G.]
**Williams, Neal M.** ..................... '47 '82 C.277 B.E.E. L.770 J.D. [🄲 Wise&S.]
**Williams, Peter E., III** ................ '61 '87 C.112 B.A. L.770 J.D. [Morrison&F.]
*PRACTICE AREAS: Corporate Finance; Intellectual Property.
**Williams, Susan A.** .... '49 '80 C.112 B.S. L.1068 J.D. Sr. Tax Atty., Hewlett-Packard Co.
*RESPONSIBILITIES: Executive Compensation; Employee Benefits; Real Estate Income Taxation; Foreign Service Employee; Payroll Tax.
**Willman, George A.** .................. '66 '96 C.813 B.S. L.276 J.D. [🄰 Wilson,S.G.&R.]
*LANGUAGES: German.
*PRACTICE AREAS: Intellectual Property; Patents; Technology Licensing.
**Wilson, Bryan J.** ...................... '61 '88 C.112 B.S. L.813 J.D. [Morrison&F.]
**Wilson, David C.** ..................... '54 '80 C.112 B.A. L.1065 J.D. [Morrison&F.]
*PRACTICE AREAS: Corporate; Securities; Intellectual Property.
Wilson, George David .................. '61 '86 C.112 B.A. L.276 J.D. 1180 Welch Rd.
Wilson, J. Ashley, Jr. .................. '13 '46 C.836 B.S. L.472 LL.B. P.O. Box 449‡
Wilson, John A., (AV) .............. '16 '41 C.674 A.B. L.976 LL.B. 650 Page Mill Rd.
Wilson, John P., (BV) .............. '14 '47 C.352 B.A. L.813 J.D. 2600 El Camino Real
**Wilson, Kenneth B.** ................ '62 '87 C.112 B.S. L.1066 J.D. [Wilson,S.G.&R.]
*PRACTICE AREAS: Intellectual Property; Business Litigation; Internet Law.
**Wilson, Philip J.** ...................... '53 '83 C.112 A.B. L.309 J.D. [Wilson M.&T.]
*LANGUAGES: German, Spanish and Swedish.
*PRACTICE AREAS: Corporate Law; Commercial Transactions; Intellectual Property; Securities; Mergers and Acquisitions.
**Wilson, Thomas Earl** ..................... '50 '76 C&L.813 B.A., J.D. [Morrison&F.]
*PRACTICE AREAS: Labor and Employment.

**Wilson Marshall & Taylor, (BV)**
**One Embarcadero Place, Suite 220, 2100 Geng Road, 94303-3317**
**Telephone: 415-424-9700 Fax: 415-424-9769**
**Email: wmt@wmtlaw.com**
**Members of Firm: Philip J. Wilson; G.E. Marshall IV; Kurt H. Taylor.**
**Corporate and Commercial Transactions, Intellectual Property, Securities, Mergers and Acquisitions, Real Property, International Business and Civil Litigation.**

***See Professional Biographies, PALO ALTO, CALIFORNIA***

**Wilson, Sonsini, Goodrich & Rosati, Professional Corporation, (AV) [BR]**
**650 Page Mill Road, 94304-1050**
**Telephone: 415-493-9300 Internet: postmaster@wsgr.com Telex: 345500 wilson pla Fax: 415-493-6811**
**Email: wsgr@wsgr.com URL: http://www.wsgr.com**
**Aaron J. Alter; Denise M. Amantea; Aileen L. Arrieta; Alan K. Austin; Jonathan Axelrad; Michael Barclay; Henry V. Barry; Suzanne Y. Bell; David J. Berger; Steven L. Berson; Mark A. Bertelsen; Jerome F. Birn, Jr.; Steven E. Bochner; Mark E. Bonham; Donald E. Bradley; Tor Braham; Harry B. Bremond; Andrew P. Bridges; Robert D. Brownell; Richard J. Char; Peter P. Chen; Douglas J. Clark; Kenneth A. Clark; Douglas H. Collom; Charles T. C. Compton; Susan A. Creighton; Francis S. Currie; Michael J. Danaher; Paul Davis; Thomas C. DeFilipps; James A. DiBoise; Stephen C. Durant; Boris Feldman; Robert P. Feldman; Chris F. Fennell; Elizabeth R. Flint; Herbert P. Fockler; John A. Fore; John B. Goodrich; Dana Haviland; Mark A. Haynes; Andrew J. Hirsch; Ivan H. Humphreys; Gail Clayton Husick; Robert B. Jack; Meredith S. Jackson; Terry T. Johnson; Thomas Christopher Klein; Jared L. Kopel; Martin W. Korman; Peter LaBoskey (Certified Specialist, Estate Planning, Trust and Probate Law, The State Bar of California Board of Legal Specialization); Michael A. Ladra; David L. Larson; Robert P. Latta; Douglas M. Laurice; Nina Locker; Page Mailliard; Henry P. Massey, Jr.; J. Casey McGlynn; Christopher D. Mitchell; Allen L. Morgan; Bradford C. O'Brien; Judith Mayer O'Brien; Michael J. O'Donnell; Mark Parnes; Donna M. Petkanics; Michael S. Rabson; Gary L. Reback; John V. Roos; Mario M. Rosati; Ronald M. Roth; Jeffrey D. Saper; Elizabeth M. Saunders; Steven M. Schatz; Arthur F. Schneiderman; Patrick J. Schultheis; Timothy T. Scott; David J. Segre; John T. Sheridan; Ron E. Shulman; Kenneth M. Siegel; Laurie B. Smilan; Larry W. Sonsini; Timothy J. Sparks; Roger D. Stern; David S. Steuer; Blair W. Stewart, Jr.; James Neilson Strawbridge; Debra S. Summers; Barry E. Taylor; Bruce G. Vanyo; Ann Yvonne Walker; Kenneth B. Wilson; Lloyd Winawer; Neil Jay Wolff; Howard S. Zeprun. Counsel: Douglas Keith Krohn; Thomas L. Cronan, III; Francis W. Dubreuil (Not admitted in CA); Kathleen Borrero Bloch; David M. Hoffmeister; Richard A. Shupack;—Paul D. Anawalt; Richard S. Arnold, Jr.; J. Michael Arrington; Ronald A. Baker; Colleen Bal; John P. Bartholomay (Not admitted in CA); Mark B. Baudler; Marilyn U. Bauriedel; Julie Ann Bell; Bradley A. Benbrook; Steven J. Benerofe; Peter H. Bergman (Not admitted in CA); Steven V. Bernard; Kurt J. Berney (Not admitted in CA); Jeffrey M. Bloom (Not admitted in CA); Ira J. Blumberg; Lauren I. Boro; Susan Bower; Christopher F. Boyd; Jason M. Brady; Carmine J. Broccole; Ivan J. Brockman; Thomas G. Brown; Michelle Brownlee; Jason P. Bucha; Bradley A. Bugdanowitz; Brett D. Byers; Gidon M. Caine (Not admitted in CA); David M. Campbell; Megan J. Carroll; Charles C. Cary (Not admitted in CA); Bernard James Cassidy; Armando Castro; Jeff Cattalini; Marta Cervantes; Alex Chachkes; Daniel M. Chambers; H.C. Chan; Carmen I-Hua Chang; Williana Chang; Warren Chao; Trevor J. Chaplick; Theodore C. Chen (Not admitted in CA); Hanley Chew (Not admitted in CA); Roger J. Chin; Sandra Chutorian; Robert Claassen (Not admitted in CA); Todd Cleary; Olabisi L. Clinton; Anton Theodore Commissaris (Not admitted in the United States); Gregory T. Cox; Brandyn Criswell; Linda M. Cuny; Brian D. Danella (Not admitted in CA); Jill Daniels; Lisa A. Davis; Robert G. Day; Harold R. DeGraff; Cecilia M. de Leon; Laura Miller de Petra; Martha L. Dienes; Bret M. DiMarco; Vivian B. Distler; Adam R. Dolinko; Stephen A. Donovan; Stephen G. Driggers; David C. Drummond; Cynthia A. Dy; Ian B. Edvalson; Keith E. Eggleton; Nevan C. Elam; Vera M. Elson; Rebecca L. Epstein; Brian C. Erb; Craig H. Factor; Janice Leyrer Fall; Dorothy L. Fernandez; Eric J. Finseth; Diane Jean Fong; Deborah S. Fox; Brenda R. Frank; Karen P. Fredericks (Not admitted in CA); Adele C. Freedman; Kevin M. Galligan; W. H. Baird Garrett; Roger Edward George; Stephen E. Gillette; Selwyn B. Goldberg; Jon C. Gonzales (Not admitted in CA); Sarah Ann Good; Marc E. Gottschalk; Linda S. Grais; Monica L. Greenberg (Not admitted in CA); Irwin R. Gross; Geoffrey B. Hale; Ramsey Hanna; Sara Duval Harrington; Richard J. Hart; Susan Heaney; Peter S. Heinecke; Jeffrey A. Herbst; Michael Hetherington; Charles D. Holland; Bruce Robert Hopenfeld; Frank I. Hoppe; John Mathias Horan; Anna Itoi; Barbara A. Izzo; James L. Jacobs; Raju S. Judge; Christine Kendrick; Adit M. Khorana; David A. Killam; Nan H. Kim (Not admitted in CA); Stephen E. Kim (Not admitted in CA); W. Brian Kinard; David R. King; Catherine S. Kirkman; Christopher M. Koa; Robert F. Kornegay, Jr.; David H. Kramer; Susan P. Krause; Elizabeth M. Kurr; Gilbert M. Labrucherie, Jr.; Joan E. Lambert; Marthe LaRosiliere; Thomas G. LaWer; Andrew Leibnitz; Michael B. Levin; Adam D. Levy; Michael J. Levy; John R. Lewis; Joshua A. Lipp; Bridget Logterman; Laurie-Ann Mei Inn Look; Thomas J. Lorr; Tiffany Lyon; Jose F. Macias; Matthew MacKenzie; Thomas J. Martin; Nancy D. Martindale; Tamara Gail Mattison; Thomas E. McKeever; Bruce M. McNamara; Ruth Ann McNees; Lisa G. Meckfessel; Heather Meeker; Millicent S. Meroney; Noah D. Mesel; Harold J. Milstein; Rebecca A. Mitchells; Daniel R. Mitz; Robert Moll; Kelly Ames Morehead; Diana M.**

(This Listing Continued)

**Wilson, Sonsini, Goodrich & Rosati, Professional Corporation (Continued)**

**Morrow; Caine T. Moss; Monica Mucchetti; Michael J. Murphy; Usha Narayanan; Neil Nathanson; Marnia Nichols; Christopher G. Nicholson; Christina Nicolosi; John C. Nishi; Donna Katherine Norman; Craig D. Norris; Burke F. Norton; David P. O'Brien (Not admitted in CA); Michael Occhiolini; Robert G. O'Connor; Michael Okada; James C. Otteson; William B. Owens, Jr.; Christopher J. Ozburn; Agnes Pak (Not admitted in CA); Michael J. Panepucci; A. Richard Park; John A. Pearce; Sarah Preisler; David Priebe; Stacey G. Prochaska; Soraya N. Rashid; Amy E. Rees; Julia Reigel; Rosemary G. Reilly (Not admitted in CA); Mark L. Reinstra; Susan Pasquinelli Reinstra; Gene Rhough; Kent R. Richardson; Erik F. Riegler; Michele E. Rose; Eric Jon Rosenzweig; Debra B. Rosler; Jeremy Rossen; RoseAnn Marie Rotandaro (Not admitted in CA); Alisande M. Rozynko; Rachel L. Ruskin; Christopher K. Sadeghian; Ignacio E. Salceda; Robert D. Sanchez; Leslie S. Santos; Vahe H. Sarrafian; David J. Saul; Thomas I. Savage (Not admitted in CA); Richard J. Schachtili; Valerie Schulthies; Peter M. Schwab; Joanne Renée Scully; Kaivan M. Shakib (Not admitted in CA); Behrooz Shariati; Stephanie Sharron; Craig A. Shelburne; Laura Lewis Shelburne; Sungbo Shim; Victor Sim; S. Dawn Smith; Ellen Solomon-Gonzales (Not admitted in CA); Noga Devecseri Spira; Susan L. Stapleton; Richard G. Steele; Vadim D. Stepanchenko; Thomas N. Stephens; Timothy J. Stevens; Rodney G. Strickland, Jr.; Betsey Sue; J. Robert Suffoletta, Jr.; Matthew B. Swartz; Ahmed E. Taha; Yoichiro Taku; Tomer Tal; Robert M. Tarkoff; Romy S. Taubman; Bruce A. Telkamp; Susan Stuermer Thomas; Richard H. Thompson (Not admitted in CA); Susan Tien; Paul R. Tobias (Not admitted in CA); Tracy L. Tosh; Jennifer Tsay; Daniel W. Turbow; Diane E. Turriff; David M. Urso; Jan-Marc van der Schee; Alicia J. Vasquez; Daniel F. Vaughn (Not admitted in CA); Issac J. Vaughn; Jason B. Wacha; Don M. Wade; Victoria M. Walter (Not admitted in CA); David C. Wang; David J. Weitz; Martin Wellington; Shannon D. Whisenant; Don S. Williams; George A. Willman; Richard L. Woodworth; Eric W. Wright; James C. Yoon; Christopher J. Younger; Stacey A. Zartler; Lior Zorea (Not admitted in CA).**
**General Civil and Trial Practice, Corporate, Securities, Mergers and Acquisitions, Antitrust, Domestic and International Taxation, Employee Benefits and Compensation, Estate Planning, Probate, Real Property and Intellectual Property Law.**

***See Professional Biographies, PALO ALTO, CALIFORNIA***

**Winawer, Lloyd** ..................... '63 '90 C.1036 B.A. L.569 J.D. [Wilson,S.G.&R.]
*PRACTICE AREAS: Litigation.

**Wise & Shepard, LLP, (AV) [BR]**
**3030 Hansen Way, Suite 100, 94304**
**Telephone: 415-856-1200 Telecopier: 415-856-1344**
**Partners: Lisa B. Armando; Thomas L. Barton; M. Scott Donahey; David R. Foley; Amy L. Gilson; David W. Herbst; Jerrold F. Petruzzelli; Edward L. Quevedo; James M. Smith; Priscilla Wheeler. Associates: Sanjiv S. Dhawan; Timothy R. Fulkerson; Joseph D. Hernandez; Michelle E. Lentzner; Daniel H. Kern; Michael G. McClory; Deborah L. Livornese; Tina M. Singh; Alison E. Spong; Joi C. True; Christopher L. Wanger; Susan F. Wegner. Counsel: Neal M. Williams.**
**Business and Litigation Law, representing Corporations and Individuals in Domestic and International Matters; including practice in Corporate Transactions, Financing/Securities, Taxation, Court Trials, Arbitration/Mediation, Environment, Employment/Labor, Employee Benefits, Real Estate, Technology Agreements/Intellectual Property, Mergers and Acquisitions/Strategic Alliances, Estate Planning and Domestic and European Community Competition Issues.**
**Representative Clients: City of San Jose; Insight Development Corp.; Pilkington Visioncare, Inc.; Sola Optical U.S.A.; Syntex Corp.; Wells Fargo Bank, N.A.; Varian Associates, Inc.; Videonics, Inc.**

***See Professional Biographies, PALO ALTO, CALIFORNIA***

Wolf, Marianne T. ........ '65 '91 C.770 B.S. L.767 J.D. 3000 El Camino Real, Suite 400
**Wolff, Neil Jay** ..................... '58 '85 C.260 B.A. L.1068 J.D. [Wilson,S.G.&R.]
*LANGUAGES: Japanese.
*PRACTICE AREAS: Corporate Law; Securities.
**Wong, Alice L.** '71 '95 C.8 B.S.E.E. L.1065 J.D.
[🄰 Townsend&T.&C.] (See Pat. Sect.)
*LANGUAGES: Mandarin, Cantonese, Malay.
*PRACTICE AREAS: Intellectual Property.
**Wong, Edward Y.** ...... '— '80 C.112 B.S. L.770 J.D. Mng. Coun., Hewlett-Packard Co.
*RESPONSIBILITIES: Intellectual Property/Compliance; Patent.
**Wood, Annalisa C** .................. '57 '87 C.813 A.B.A.M. L.770 J.D. [🄰 J.E.Miller]
*LANGUAGES: French and German.
*PRACTICE AREAS: Family Law.
**Woodburn, Jeremy S.** ................ '— '95 C.1036 B.A. L.309 J.D. [🄰 Fenwick&W.]
*PRACTICE AREAS: Intellectual Property; Licensing Law.
Woodson, William N., III, (BV) ...... '46 '76 C.813 B.A. L.284 J.D. 2479 E. Bayshore Rd.
**Woodward, Henry K.**, (AV) '38 '63
C&L.846 B.S.E.E., LL.B. [🄲 Townsend&T.&C.] (See Pat. Sect.)
*PRACTICE AREAS: Patent and Trade Secret Law; Technology Law; Electronics and Physics.
**Woodworth, Richard L.** ............. '67 '94 C.813 B.A. L.276 J.D. [🄰 Wilson,S.G.&R.]
*PRACTICE AREAS: Antitrust; Litigation; Intellectual Property.
**Wright, Barbara P.**, (AV) .............. '46 '83 C.813 B.A. L.426 J.D. [Finch,M.&W.]
*PRACTICE AREAS: Estate Planning; Nonprofit Organizations; Gift and Estate Tax; Trusts and Wills; Probate, Estate and Trust Administration.
**Wright, Christopher O. B.** ............... '59 '86 C.813 A.B. L.1066 J.D. [🄲 Cooley G.]
*PRACTICE AREAS: Antitrust Law; Intellectual Property.
**Wright, Edward S.** '41 '66 C&L.813 B.S.E.E., LL.B.
[Flehr,H.T.A.&H.] (See Pat. Sect.)
**Wright, Eric W.** ..................... '63 '90 C.813 A.B. L.569 J.D. [🄰 Wilson,S.G.&R.]
*PRACTICE AREAS: Corporate; Securities.
**Wu, Jack H.** '46 '78 C.453 B.S. L.464 J.D.
Sr. Intell. Prop. Atty., Hewlett-Packard Co. (Pat.)
*RESPONSIBILITIES: Copyright; Intellectual Property/Compliance; Patent.
Wu, Yi-Tze Seth .................... '50 '79 C.208 B.A. L.770 J.D. Varian Assocs., Inc.
**Wugmeister, Miriam** .................. '67 '92 C.1036 B.A. L.94 J.D. [🄰 Morrison&F.]

**Wunsch, Kathryn S., and Associated Counsel, (AV) '35 '77 C.347 A.B. L.345 J.D. [BR]**
**Law Chambers, 701 Welch Road, Suite 3320, 94304**
**Telephone: 415-833-1880 Fax: 415-833-1888**
**Corporate, Business and Real Property Transactions, Real Property Assessment Appeals, Contracts, Probate, Trusts and Estates.**

***See Professional Biographies, PALO ALTO, CALIFORNIA***

**Wynn, Ronald S.** ..................... '55 '82 C.112 B.A. L.1067 J.D. [Brobeck,P.&H.]
*PRACTICE AREAS: Intellectual Property and Antitrust Litigation.
Wyrod, Patricia M. ...................... '64 '91 C&L.477 B.A., J.D. 525 Univ. Ave.
Yakes, John C. .................... '46 '72 C&L.912 B.S., J.D. 320 Palo Alto Ave. (Pat.)
**Yang, Joseph** ................ '65 '96 C.111 Ph.D. L.813 J.D. [🄰 McCutchen,D.B.&E.]
*PRACTICE AREAS: Patent Law; Technology Licensing; Strategic Counseling.
Yankovsky, Kristine E. ................ '— '90 C.1196 B.A. L.770 J.D. 2370 Watson Ct.
**Yankwich, Richard I.** .................. '55 '79 C.813 A.B. L.228 J.D. [Gray C.W.&F.]
Yates, Christopher G. '59 '86 C.813 A.B. L.145 J.D.
Assoc. Dir. of Planned Giving, Stanford University
**Yee, Elizabeth A. R.** ................. '69 '96 C.112 B.A. L.770 J.D. [🄰 Brobeck,P.&H.]
*PRACTICE AREAS: Corporate.
**Yip, Philip S.** ........... '49 '92 C.429 B.A. L.352 J.D. Atty., Hewlett-Packard Co. (Pat.)
*LANGUAGES: Chinese.
*RESPONSIBILITIES: Patent Prosecution; Intellectual Property.
**Yoon, James C.** ...................... '67 '95 C.999 E.E. L.813 J.D. [🄰 Wilson,S.G.&R.]
**Yorio, Robert J.** ......................... '51 '78 C.823 B.A. L.276 J.D. [Carr,D.&F.]
**Young, Barry N.** '42 '75 C.420 B.S.E.E. L.64 J.D.
(adm. in MD; not adm. in CA; Pat.) [Gray C.W.&F.]
*REPORTED CASES: In re Lowry 32 F.3d 1570 (Fed. Cir. 1994).
*PRACTICE AREAS: Patents and Intellectual Property (75%); Licensing (15%); Litigation (10%).
**Young, John F.** ................ '43 '71 C&L.911 B.A., J.D. [Cooley G.] (⊙San Fran.)
*PRACTICE AREAS: Antitrust Law; Trade Secrets Law.

**Young, Stanley** ... '60 '85 C.813 A.B. L.309 J.D. [Heller E.W.&M.]
*PRACTICE AREAS: Commercial Litigation and Intellectual Property.
**Younger, Christopher J.** ... '66 '94 C.473 B.Phil. L.309 J.D. [🄰 Wilson,S.G.&R.]
*PRACTICE AREAS: Corporate.
**Yu, Chiahua George** ... '68 '96 C.453 B.S. L.178 J.D. [🄰 Townsend&T.&C.]
*LANGUAGES: Chinese (Mandarin).
*PRACTICE AREAS: Intellectual Property.
**Zartler, Stacey A.** ... '66 '92 C.813 B.A. L.770 J.D. [🄰 Wilson,S.G.&R.]
*PRACTICE AREAS: Labor and Employment Law.
**Zeif, Andrew D.** '62 '88 C.659 B.A. L.262 J.D.
(adm. in NY; not adm. in CA) [🄰 Baker&M.]
*PRACTICE AREAS: Corporate and Partnership Law.
**Zeprun, Howard S.** ... '58 '83 C.659 B.S. L.309 J.D. [Wilson,S.G.&R.]
*PRACTICE AREAS: Corporate Law; Securities; International Securities Offerings; Intellectual Property.
**Zevnik, Paul Anton**, (AVⓉ) ... '50 '77 C&L.309 A.B., J.D. [Zevnik H.G.&M.]⊙
*PRACTICE AREAS: Insurance Coverage; Environmental Law; Toxic Tort Litigation.

**Zevnik Horton Guibord & McGovern, P.C., (AVⓉ)**
**5 Palo Alto Square, 3000 El Camino Real, 94306⊙**
**Telephone: 415-842-5900 Facsimile: 415-855-9226**
**Paul Anton Zevnik; Michel Yves Horton; Barbara B. Guibord (Not admitted in CA); Patrick Michael McGovern (Not admitted in CA); Joseph G. Homsy (Not admitted in CA); John W. Roberts (Not admitted in CA); John K. Crossman (Not admitted in CA); Jonathan L. Osborne (Not admitted in CA);—Michael C. Donovan; Steven H. Doto (Not admitted in CA); Cecelia C. Fusich; John C. Meyer; Esteban L. Oyenque (Not admitted in CA).**
**Commercial Litigation, Environmental Law, Insurance Coverage, Toxic Tort Litigation, International Law, Practice before State and Federal Courts and Administrative Tribunals.**
**Washington, D.C. Office: Ninth Floor, 1299 Pennsylvania Avenue, N.W. Telephone: 202-824-0950. Fax: 202-824-0955.**
**Chicago, Illinois Office: Thirty Third Floor, 77 West Wacker Drive. Telephone: 312-977-2500. Telefax: 312-977-2560.**
**Los Angeles, California Office: 333 South Grand Avenue, Twenty First Floor. Telephone: 213-437-5200. Telefax: 213-437-5222.**
**New York, N.Y. Office: 745 Fifth Avenue, Twenty-Fifth Floor. Telephone: 212-935-2735. Telefax: 212-935-0614.**
**London, England Office: 4 Kings Bench Walk, Temple, London EC4Y 7DL. Telephone: 071-353-0478. Facsimile: 071-583-3549.**
**Norfolk, Virginia Office: Main Street Tower, 300 East Main Street, 13th Floor. Telephone: 757-624-3480. Fax: 757-624-3479.**

***See Professional Biographies, PALO ALTO, CALIFORNIA***

**Ziff, Harvey L.**, (BV) ... '42 '67 C.659 B.S. L.813 J.D. [Weinberg,Z.&M.]
*SPECIAL AGENCIES: Department of Motor Vehicles License Suspension Appeals.
*PRACTICE AREAS: Personal Injury; Commercial Law; Criminal Defense Law.
**Zimmer, Kevin James** ... '63 '91 C.1097 B.S.E.E. L.477 J.D. [🄰 Cooley G.] (Pat.)
*PRACTICE AREAS: Intellectual Property.
**Zimmerman, C. Michael**, (AV) '38 '66
C.506 B.S. L.765 LL.B. [Flehr,H.T.A.&H.] (See Pat. Sect.)
**Zimmerman, Mitchell**, (AV) ... '42 '79 C.563 B.A. L.813 J.D. [Fenwick&W.]
**Zisko, William E.**, (AV) ... '52 '78 C.763 B.S. L.1066 J.D. [Tomlinson Z.M.&M.]
*PRACTICE AREAS: Corporate Finance and Acquisitions; Business Transactions.
**Zoken, Mollee Sue Oxman** ... '62 '89 C.112 A.B. L.813 J.D. [🄰 Fenwick&W.]
*PRACTICE AREAS: Corporate.
**Zorea, Lior** '70 '96 C.976 B.A. L.477 J.D.
(adm. in NY; not adm. in CA) [🄰 Wilson,S.G.&R.]
*PRACTICE AREAS: Mergers and Acquisitions; Securities; General Corporate.
Zulch, Thelma Hogevoll ... '14 '36 C.813 L.1065 J.D. 3345 Saint Michael Ct.‡

## PALOS VERDES ESTATES, 13,512, *Los Angeles Co.*

Barth, Michael A. ... '45 '71 C.800 B.S. L.424 J.D. [M.A.Barth]
Barth, Michael A., A Prof. Corp. ... 31 Malaga Cove Plz.
**Birdt, Joan** ... '39 '75 C.112 B.A. L.1136 J.D. [🄰 Breon,O.M.B.&D.]

**Breon, O'Donnell, Miller, Brown & Dannis, (AV)**
**2550 Via Tejon Suite 3A, 90274⊙**
**Telephone: 310-373-6857 FAX: 310-373-6808**
**David G. Miller. Associates: Joan Birdt (Resident); Sue Ann Salmon Evans (Resident); Janet L. Mueller (Resident); Ivette Peña (Resident).**
**Labor, Employment Relations and Education Law and Related Litigation on Behalf of Public and Private Sector Employers, Business, Property, Construction Litigation.**
**San Francisco, California Office: 19th Floor, 71 Stevenson Street. Telephone: 415-543-4111. Fax: 415-543-4384.**
**Salinas, California Office: Suite H120, 17842 Moro Road, Suite F120, 93907. Telephone: 408-663-0470.**

***See Professional Biographies, PALOS VERDES ESTATES, CALIFORNIA***

Campbell, Katherine A., (P.C.) ... '54 '79 C.188 B.A. L.845 J.D. 12 Paseo De Pino
Carver, Edgar R., Jr. ... '17 '49 C.178 A.B. L.569 LL.B. 717 Paseo Del Mar
Chagi, Gary B. ... '46 '71 C.1077 B.A. L.800 J.D. 1909 Via Estudillo
Chevalier, John, Jr. ... '24 '64 C.151 B.S. L.30 LL.B. 928 Via Panorama
Coakley, Albert J., Jr. ... '25 '51 C.433 B.A. L.178 J.D. 2612 Via Rivera‡
Coyle, James J. ... '19 '48 C.988 L.273 LL.B. 30146 Via Victoria
Cozy, Jack A., (AV) ... '17 '56 C.809 B.C.S. L.1001 LL.B. 1803 Pedro Pl.‡
Davis, Ronald J. ... '51 '79 C.629 B.S. L.1198 J.D. 425 Via Corta
Dietrich, Val G. ... '53 '77 C&L.36 B.S., J.D. 1025 Via Zumaya

**Esensten, Jack I.**
**(See Rolling Hills Estates)**

**Evans, Sue Ann Salmon** ... '64 '90 C.112 B.A. L.426 J.D. [🄰 Breon,O.M.B.&D.]
Hartwick, R. Dean ... '36 '65 C.339 B.S. L.800 J.D. 2420 Palo Verdes Dr., W.
Haushalter, Jerry C. '38 '63 C.686 B.S. L.436 LL.B.
(adm. in WI; not adm. in CA) 1409 Via Cataluna Dr.‡
Heal, Noel F., (AV) ... '36 '72 C.061 B.E. L.1068 J.D. 2516 Via Tejon (Pat.)
Hourigan, Frank J., (AV) ... '18 '51 C.477 L.426 LL.B. 6961 Kings Harbor Dr.
Jaffe, Geraldine ... '49 '86 C.800 B.A. L.809 J.D. 2550 Via Tejon
Leeper, David M. ... '48 '77 C.800 B.S. L.990 J.D. 338 Tejon Pl.
Makin, Roy '37 '63 C.150 B.B.A. L.1340 J.D.
(adm. in OH; not adm. in CA) Lightcraft of Calif.
**Miller, David G.** ... '40 '68 C.33 B.A. L.61 J.D. [Breon,O.M.B.&D.]
*PRACTICE AREAS: Labor Law; Employment Law; Education Law.
Miller, Denise Hansen ... '50 '78 C.605 B.A. L.426 J.D. 2541 Via Sanchez
**Mueller, Janet L.** ... '63 '92 C.112 B.A. L.1067 J.D. [🄰 Breon,O.M.B.&D.]
O'Connor, James S. '31 '61 C&L.209 B.S.L., LL.B.
(adm. in IL; not adm. in CA) 2125 Paseo del Mar‡
Papazian, Gerald S. ... '55 '81 C.800 A.B. L.1068 J.D. 3701 Via Palomino
**Peña, Ivette** ... '65 '91 C.103 B.A. L.309 J.D. [🄰 Breon,O.M.B.&D.]
Raynes, Boris ... '20 '49 C.831 B.S. L.426 LL.B. 2532 Chelsea Rd.‡
Rouse, O. R. ... '30 '63 C.800 B.S. 418 Malaga Lane
Smiley, Carl T. ... '39 '80 C.208 B.S.B.A. L.1136 J.D. 516 Via Almar
Stolba, Norman E. ... '18 '59 C.112 A.B. L.426 LL.B. P.O. Box 788‡
Toftness, Cecil G., (BV) ... '20 '54 C.112 B.S. L.809 J.D. 2516 Via Tejon
Warren, Geoffrey M., (BV) ... '21 '70 C.800 L.1148 J.D. 609 Via Estrada
Willer, Michael D. ... '43 '88 C&L.1137 B.S.L., J.D. 2552 Via Anita

## PALOS VERDES PENINSULA, 38,918, *Los Angeles Co.*

Asano, Shirley S. ... '55 '84 C.112 B.A. L.800 J.D. P.O. Box 3975
Ceragioli, Raymond ... '32 '61 C.112 B.A. L.1068 LL.B. [R.Ceragioli]
Ceragioli, Raymond, A Professional Law Corporation ... P.O. Box 4140
Crehan, Thomas M. ... '35 '60 C&L.602 B.A., LL.B. U.S. Mag.
Curwen, Mary Jo ... '42 '72 C.966 B.S. L.1068 J.D. 26730 Eastvale Rd.
Honan, Maryanne E. ... '54 '80 C.66 B.A. L.569 J.D. 1637 Via Zurita
Hourigan, Francis J., III ... '42 '69 C.770 B.S. L.426 J.D. 6961 Kings Harbor Dr.
Kraus, Phillip ... '14 '41 C.112 A.B. L.800 J.D. 7088 Crest Rd.‡
MacKenzie, Albert H. ... '44 '71 C.1042 B.A. L.1190 J.D. Dep. Dist. Atty.

## PALO VERDE, —, *Imperial Co.*

Gross, Leonard ... '27 '60 C.563 L.809 J.D. 28441 Highridge Rd., Suite 501

## PANORAMA CITY, —, *Los Angeles Co.*

(Part of the incorporated City of Los Angeles)

Acosta, Mario L. ... '51 '88 C&L.398 B.S., J.D. 9130 Van Nuys Blvd.
Alison, Allison Merkle '62 '87 C.888 B.A. L.990 J.D.
Dependency Ct. Legal Servs., Inc.
Bailey, Joseph R. ... '26 '52 C&L.813 B.A., LL.B. [Bailey&B.]
Bailey & Block ... 8134 Van Nuys Blvd.
Block, Donald V. ... '26 '62 [Bailey&B.]
Boss, Donald J. ... '34 '62 C.112 B.S. L.1068 LL.B. 8134 Van Nuys Blvd.
Burns, Doris T. ... '36 '88 C.1042 B.V.E. L.1137 J.D. Dependency Ct. Legal Servs., Inc.
Burthe, Jack H., (BV) ... '33 '72 C.420 B.S. L.1127 J.D. 401 S. Main St. Suite 2018
Deems, Harry B. ... '21 '48 C.397 B.A. L.426 14307 Tupper St.
Diamond, Jerome ... '40 '66 C.112 B.S. L.1068 J.D. P.O. Box 9113‡
Duey-Stone, Barbara ... '61 '86 C.147 B.A. L.1067 J.D. Dependency Ct. Legal Servs., Inc.
Emmer, Fred H. ... '48 '72 C.352 B.A. L.446 J.D. 9608 Van Nuys Blvd.
Freedman, Leonard L., (AV) ... '26 '54 C.208 L.767 LL.B. 8155 Van Nuys Blvd.
Gepner, Philip N., (BV) ... '25 '52 C.112 B.S. L.809 J.D. 8134 Van Nuys Blvd.
Hawks, Joseph W. ... '20 '56 C.112 L.809 J.D. 7827 Cantaloupe‡
Kadin, David C. ... '52 '81 C.763 B.A. L.809 J.D. P.O. Box 4967
Laster, John W. ... '16 '51 C&L.809 LL.B. 8739 Katherine Ave.
Salkin, Valerie F. ... '66 '92 C.477 B.A. L.800 J.D. 14300 TYerra Bella St.

## PARADISE, 25,408, *Butte Co.*

Bagley, Ralph F., Jr. ... '27 '60 C.871 B.S. L.770 LL.B. 90 Harold Ln.
**Bakke, Randy L.**, (BV) ... '50 '77 C.330 B.A. L.464 J.D. [McKernan,L.B.B.&B.]⊙
Battle, Leo A., (BV) ... '46 '77 C.1042 B.S. L.1137 J.D. 5910 Clarke Rd.
**Benson, Stephen E.**, (BV) ... '46 '79 C.636 B.A. L.1137 J.D. [McKernan,L.B.B.&B.]⊙
*REPORTED CASES: Reed v. King (1983) 145C.A.3d 261, 193C.R.130.
**Bodney, John A.**, (BV) ... '48 '77 C.629 B.S. L.464 J.D. [McKernan,L.B.B.&B.]⊙
Brewer, Robert H. ... '42 '67 C.902 B.A. L.893 LL.B. 7052 Skyway
Casaus, Michael A. ... '52 '77 C.1143 B.A. L.208 J.D. 6451 Skyway
High, Jess F., (AV) ... '18 '44 C.112 A.B. L.1065 J.D. 408 Green Oaks Dr.‡
Horne, James R. ... '43 '74 C.813 B.A. L.1067 J.D. P.O. Box 1276
Johnson, James A., (CV) ... '38 '73 C.147 B.S. L.1065 J.D. 7448 Skyway
**Lanam, John D.**, (BV) ... '35 '64 C.147 A.B. L.1066 J.D. [McKernan,L.B.B.&B.]⊙
**McKernan, Roy**, (AV) '24 '53
C.147 A.B. L.1066 J.D. [McKernan,L.B.B.&B.] (⊙Chico)‡

**McKernan, Lanam, Bakke, Benson & Bodney, (BV)**
**732 Fir Street, P.O. Box 550, 95967⊙**
**Telephone: 916-877-4961 Fax: 916-877-8163**
**Email: mlbbbchico@aol.com**
**Members of Firm: Roy McKernan (Retired); John D. Lanam; Randy L. Bakke (Certified Specialist, Family Law, The State Bar of California Board of Legal Specialization); Stephen E. Benson; John A. Bodney.**
**General Civil Practice. Trusts, Probate, Real Estate, Estate Planning, Personal Injury, Professional Malpractice, Insurance and Corporate Law and Trials.**
**References: Bank of America; North State Bank.**
**Chico, California Office: 445 Normal Avenue, P.O. Box 3496. Telephone: 916-891-0247. Fax: 916-891-1704.**

***See Professional Biographies, PARADISE, CALIFORNIA***

Rank, John J. ... '64 '92 C.112 B.A. L.464 J.D. [Travers&R.]
Roberts, Barbara L. ... '55 '82 C.1077 B.A. L.464 J.D. [Schill&R.]
Rogers, David H. ... '29 '56 C&L.309 A.B., LL.B. 682 Edwards Lane‡
Ryker, Norman J., III, (BV) ... '54 '84 C.112 B.A. L.911 J.D. 529 Pearson Rd.
Schill, Frederick H. ... '54 '82 C.147 B.S. L.464 J.D. [Schill&R.]
Schill & Roberts ... 5951 Almond St.
Stanton, Donald F. ... '35 '73 C.546 B.S. L.1137 J.D. 6667 Evergreen Ln.
Sterle, Frank, (CV) ... '21 '53 L.809 5758 Almond St.
Travers, Donald R., (AV) ... '41 '75 C.1077 B.A. L.1095 J.D. [Travers&R.]
Travers & Rank, (AV) ... 529 Pearson Rd.
Trenholme, Steven ... '57 '86 C.154 B.A. L.464 J.D. P.O. Box 1836 (⊙Orville)
Willis, Donald C. ... '46 '75 C.147 B.A. L.464 J.D. Butte Co. Assessor

## PARAMOUNT, 47,669, *Los Angeles Co.*

Anderson, Theodore C. ... '46 '79 C.208 B.A. L.1241 J.D. Macco Contructors, Inc.
Atkinson, George E., Jr., (AV) '14 '37 C.112 B.A. L.1065 J.D.
16401 S. Paramount Blvd.
Hall, Howard H., (AV) ... '33 '60 C&L.823 A.B., J.D. [H.H.Hall]
Hall, Howard H., Inc., (AV) ... 15559 Paramount Blvd.
Kelton, Stanley M. ... '52 '78 C.800 B.A. L.426 J.D. 16437 S. Paramount Blvd.
Mindess, Robert G. ... '63 '92 C.174 B.A. L.1148 J.D. Paramount Pet. Corp.
O'Shea, Maurice F., (BV) ... '30 '61 C.112 B.S. L.1001 LL.B. City Atty.
Trice, David A. '48 '73 C.228 A.B. L.178 J.D.
(adm. in GA; not adm. in CA) 14700 Downey‡
Varner, Alan F. ... '52 '80 C.112 B.A. L.809 J.D. [🄰 H.H.Hall]
Waskul, Michael Alexander ... '56 '82 C.112 B.A. L.426 J.D. [🄰 H.H.Hall]

## PARLIER, 7,938, *Fresno Co.*

Loewen, Theodore W. ... '49 '79 C.83 B.A. L.1065 J.D. 17564 E. Clayton

## PASADENA, 131,591, *Los Angeles Co.*

Abels, Caroline R. ... '16 '72 C.108 B.A. L.1148 J.D. 255 S. Oak Knoll Ave.‡
Acuña, Richard M. '48 '75 C.740 B.S. L.1065 J.D.
First V.P. & Sr. Coun., Community Bk.
**Adamec, Justene M.** ... '61 '88 C.1044 B.A. L.809 J.D. [Pumilia&A.]
*PRACTICE AREAS: Litigation.

**Adams, Gerard G., (AV) '43 '72 C.1077 B.S. L.1095 J.D.**
**1122 East Green Street, 91106**
**Telephone: 818-795-4544 Fax: 818-796-2554**
***PRACTICE AREAS: Business Law; Estate Planning Law; Real Estate Law.**
**Business Transactional Law, with an emphasis on Real Estate and Taxation.**

***See Professional Biographies, PASADENA, CALIFORNIA***

**Adams, Roger** .......... '38 '70 C&L.800 A.B., J.D. [Adams&H.]
*PRACTICE AREAS: International and Domestic Business Transactions; Taxation; Corporate Law; Exempt Organizations; Pension and Profit Sharing Plans.
Adams & Alexander .......... 272 S. Los Robles (©Beverly Hills)

**Adams & Hawekotte**
**350 West Colorado Boulevard, Suite 310, 91105**
**Telephone: 818-583-8000; 213-684-0920 Facsimile: 818-449-1576**
**Roger Adams; Angela Hawekotte.**
**International and Domestic Business Transactions, Taxation, Business Organizations, Exempt Organizations, Pension and Profit Sharing, Estate Planning, Probate and Conservatorships.**
*See Professional Biographies, PASADENA, CALIFORNIA*

Adashek, David G. .......... '45 '79 C.1097 B.A. L.1148 J.D. 350 W. Colorado Blvd.
Adelman, Ben, (BV) .......... '30 '55 C.1016 B.S.C. L.365 LL.B. 836 S. Arroyo Pkwy.
Adham, Bita .......... '65 '90 C.112 B.A. L.1065 J.D. 3852 E. Colorado Blvd.
Adkins, Frank N. .......... '49 '74 C.112 B.A. L.809 J.D. 225 S. Lake Ave.
Agatstein, David J. .......... '44 '68 C.994 B.A. L.945 J.D. Admin. Law J.
Aghajanian, Alex P. .......... '56 '87 C.1075 B.A. L.1095 J.D. 225 S. Lake Ave.
Agnew, David E., (AV) .......... '18 '47 C&L.309 A.B., LL.B. 2256 Lambert Dr.‡
**Aguilera, Victor E.** .......... '45 '76 C.563 B.A. [Cooper,K.&S.]
*PRACTICE AREAS: Toxic Litigation; Products Liability Law; Municipal Entity Defense Law; Trial Practice; Appellate Litigation.
Akl, Maria Luisa .......... '54 '77 C&L.999 B.A., M.A. 440 W. Green St.
**Alavi, Ladan** .......... '67 '93 C.112 L.809 J.D. [K.W.Schoth&Assoc.]
*LANGUAGES: Farsi; Spanish.
*PRACTICE AREAS: Personal Injury Law; Medical Malpractice; Elder Abuse.
Alef, Arthur, (AV) .......... '26 '53 C.112 B.A. L.1068 LL.B. 35 Hugus Alley
Alexander, James E. .......... '34 '92 [Adams&A.]
Algorri, Ernest P., (BV) .......... '60 '87 C.112 B.A. L.426 J.D. 25 E. Union St.
Algorri, Mark S., (AV) .......... '52 '79 C.112 A.B. L.1095 J.D. 25 E. Union St.

**Alkana, Eugene S., (BV) '49 '74 C.800 B.S. L.1049 J.D.**
**Suite 310, 131 North El Molino Avenue, 91101**
**Telephone: 818-796-8170 Telecopier: 818-795-6138**
**General Civil Practice. Equine Law and Syndications. Litigation. Business, Commercial, Real Estate, Construction, Collections, Non-Profit Organizations.**
*See Professional Biographies, PASADENA, CALIFORNIA*

**Alschuler, Frederick Harold** .......... '49 '76 C.112 B.A. L.1068 J.D. [Cooper,K.&S.]
*PRACTICE AREAS: Civil Litigation; Criminal Appeals.
Amdur, Terry J., (AV) .......... '43 '70 C.33 B.A. L.1068 J.D. 1939 Rosa Villa St.
**Ammirato, Vincent A.**, (AV) .......... '42 '72 C.1042 B.A. L.1049 J.D. [Burns,A.P.M.&B.]©
*PRACTICE AREAS: Products Liability; Construction Accident; General Trial Work.
Amos, Daniel H. .......... '59 '85 C.112 B.A. L.426 J.D. [Vargas&V.]
Anderson, Clifford R., Jr., (AV) '28 '53 C.112 A.B. L.800 LL.B.
350 W. Colorado Blvd.‡
**Anderson, Denton L.** '46 '76
C.494 B.Ch.E. L.1152 J.D. [Sheldon&M.] (See Pat. Sect.) (©Upland)
Anderson, Greg I., (BV) .......... '52 '76 C.800 B.A. L.426 J.D. 225 S. Lake Ave., 9th Fl.
Anderson, Olivia Vasquez .......... '41 '78 C&L.800 B.A., J.D. 768 S. San Gabriel Blvd.
**Anderson, Robert W.**, (AV) .......... '25 '49 C&L.174 J.D. [Hahn&H.]
*PRACTICE AREAS: Estate Planning; Probate; Estate Planning; Taxation (Gift and Income).
Anderson, Steven L., (AV) .......... '39 '66 C.1060 B.A. L.464 LL.B. 155 N. Lake Ave.

**Anderson & Salisbury, A Professional Corporation, (AV)**
**Suite 310, 350 West Colorado Boulevard, 91105**
**Telephone: 818-449-4812; 213-684-0920 Telecopier: 818-449-1576**
**Lee W. Salisbury (Certified Specialist, Family Law, The State Bar of California Board of Legal Specialization);—Wesley Ann Hoge Hubanks.**
**Family Law.**
*See Professional Biographies, PASADENA, CALIFORNIA*

Andion, James L. .......... '50 '77 C.475 B.A. L.477 J.D. 155 El Molino Dr. (©Los Angeles)
Anglea, Berneice Alsweet, (AV) '22 '69
C.112 B.S. L.800 J.D. 199 S. Los Robles Ave. Ste. 711‡

**Anglea & Bannon, A Professional Corporation, (AV)**
**Suite 711, 199 South Los Robles Avenue, 91101-2460**
**Telephone: 818-584-8800 Fax: 818-584-8807**
**Robert D. Bannon (Certified Specialist, Probate, Estate Planning and Trust Law, The State Bar of California Board of Legal Specialization); Alexandra Laboutin Bannon (Certified Specialist, Estate Planning, Trust and Probate Law, The State Bar of California Board of Legal Specialization); Elizabeth T. Pierson (Certified Specialist, Probate, Estate Planning and Trust Law, State Bar of California Board of Legal Specialization); JoAnn Jackson Kalama. Of Counsel: Martha Burroughs Hogan.**
**Estate Planning, Probate and Trust Law, General Tax Matters, General Business Matters, Real Estate and Environmental Law; Fiduciary and Tax Litigation.**
*See Professional Biographies, PASADENA, CALIFORNIA*

**Anthony, Don Mike, (P.C.)**, (AV) .......... '38 '64 C.605 B.A. L.1068 LL.B. [Hahn&H.]
*PRACTICE AREAS: Civil Litigation.
Aquino, Paul .......... '41 '79 L.061 LL.B. 595 E. Colorado Blvd.
Aragon, Arthur O., (BV) .......... '22 '53 C&L.602 B.S., LL.B. Wausau Ins. Co.
Araiza, Francisca N. .......... '60 '89 C.1036 B.A. L.1068 J.D. [Potter,C.&S.]
Archer, Earl T. .......... '43 '79 C.877 B.S. L.809 J.D. Two N. Lake Ave.
Argento, Phillip J. .......... '45 '75 C.668 B.A. L.276 J.D. Mun. J.
Armour, George P., (AV) .......... '21 '50 C&L.831 B.A., J.D. 1621 Orlando Rd.‡
**Arnall, Alan C.** .......... '59 '85 C.112 B.A. L.602 J.D. [Cooper,K.&S.]
Arnerich, V. G., (AV) .......... '09 '32 C&L.426 B.A., LL.B. [Arnerich,d.&S.]
Arnerich, del Valle & Sinatra, (AV) .......... 424 N. Lake Ave.
Ashbran, Richard E. .......... '47 '74 C.940 A.B. L.426 J.D. 3280 E. Foothill Blvd.

**Ashley-Farrand, Margalo, (BV) '44 '81 C.569 B.A. L.809 J.D.**
**215 N. Marengo Avenue, Third Floor, 91101**
**Telephone: 818-792-4700 Facsimile: 818-356-7414**
**(Certified Specialist, Family Law, The State Bar of California Board of Legal Specialization).**
***PRACTICE AREAS: Family Law; Mediation; Family Trusts and Wills; Probate; Small Business.**
**Family Law, Mediation, Family Trusts and Wills, Probate, Small Business, Bankruptcy.**
*See Professional Biographies, PASADENA, CALIFORNIA*

Astle, Scott S. .......... '— '81 C&L.101 B.A., J.D. P.O. Box 7007
Atkin, Michael W. .......... '51 '76 C.800 B.S. L.809 J.D. 225 S.Lake Ave.
**Auer, Stephen G.** .......... '47 '77 C.201 B.S. L.1049 J.D. [J.D.Christensen&Assoc.]
**Avery, Douglas Stuart** '49 '76
C.1097 B.A. L.1095 J.D. Sr. Claims Coun., Chicago Title Co.
*RESPONSIBILITIES: Real Property; Title Insurance.
**Ayotte, Normand A.** .......... '57 '87 C.800 B.A. L.426 J.D. [Burns,A.P.M.&B.]
*PRACTICE AREAS: Premises Liability.
Baer, Cornelia G. .......... '37 '80 C.800 B.A. L.809 J.D. 221 E. Walnut St.
**Baffa, George R., (P.C.)**, (AV) .......... '37 '63 C&L.800 B.A., J.D. [Hahn&H.]
*PRACTICE AREAS: Corporations; Business.
Bahan, Della .......... '52 '79 C.1169 B.A. L.1066 J.D. [Rothner,S.&B.]
Bahan, Paul J. .......... '50 '87 L.426 J.D. 427 S. Marengo Ave.
**Baker, Brian Alan**, (BV) .......... '57 '84 C.1090 B.A. L.61 J.D. [Salz&S.]
*PRACTICE AREAS: Family Law; Civil Litigation; Real Estate; Business.

**Baker, Clifton A.** .......... '64 '94 C.760 B.F.A. L.809 J.D. [Gutierrez&P.]
*PRACTICE AREAS: Civil Rights Defense; Employer Liability; Local Government Liability.
Baker, Robert L., (AV) .......... '42 '67 C.1097 B.A. L.61 J.D. 1110 E. Green St.
**Balian, Nairie A.** .......... '63 '87 C.25 B.A. L.398 J.D. [Fairshter&Assoc.]
*LANGUAGES: Armenian, Arabic, French, Russian.
*PRACTICE AREAS: Family Law; Insurance Law.

**Balian, Nairie A. '63 '87 C.25 B.A. L.398 J.D.**
**225 South Lake Avenue, 9th Floor, 91101**
**Telephone: 818-564-2630 FAX: 818-564-2633 Modem: 818-564-2634**
**Email: nabalian@aol.com**
***LANGUAGES: Armenian, Arabic, French, Russian.**
**Civil Litigation, Insurance Coverage, Construction Defect, Business, Personal Injury with an emphasis on Vehicular, Products Liability and Premises Liability, Family Law including: Dissolutions, Spousal Support, Prenuptials, Custody and Cohabitation Agreements.**
*See Professional Biographies, PASADENA, CALIFORNIA*

Ball, Stephen C. .......... '54 '85 C.112 B.A. L.426 305 S. Hudson
Ballantyne, Enid G. .......... '43 '78 C.1097 B.A. L.1068 J.D. 125 N. Marengo
Bandy, Jack D. .......... '32 '72 C.388 B.A. L.1095 LL.B. 74 N. Pasadena Ave.
**Bannon, Alexandra Laboutin**, (AV) '49 '79 C.767 B.A.M.A. L.1066 J.D.
[Anglea&B.]
*LANGUAGES: Russian.
*PRACTICE AREAS: Probate Administration; Contested Trusts and Estates; Environmental Liability; Environmental Tax.
**Bannon, Robert D.**, (AV) .......... '26 '53 C.112 A.B. L.800 J.D. [Anglea&B.]
*PRACTICE AREAS: Estate Planning; Federal Estate and Gift Tax; Generation Skipping Tax; Family Wealth Transfer.
**Baraban, Jeffrey H.**, (BV) .......... '46 '78 C.836 B.A. L.1136 J.D. [Baraban&T.]
*REPORTED CASES: Brown v. Presley of Southern California, 213 Cal. App. 3d 612; 261 Cal. Rptr. 779; Hughes v. Southern California Rapid Transit Dist., 173 Cal. App. 3d 512; 219 Cal. Rptr. 82.
*PRACTICE AREAS: General Liability; Products Liability; Personal Injury; Insurance.

**Baraban & Teske, (BV)**
**Walnut Plaza, Suite 250, 215 North Marengo Avenue, 91101-1569**
**Telephone: 818-440-9882 Fax: 818-440-9393**
**Members of Firm: Jeffrey H. Baraban; Christopher S. Teske. Associates: Edward R. Neville; William C. Howison; Diane M. Corwin; Robin L. Haulman; James R. Kula; Kelli G. Hawley; David S. Schlueter.**
**Insurance Defense, Civil Litigation, General Liability, Product Liability, Personal Injury, Construction, Insurance Law.**
*See Professional Biographies, PASADENA, CALIFORNIA*

**Barbaro, Philip, Jr.** .......... '55 '80 C.112 B.S. L.1137 J.D. [Soldwedel,P.B.&C.]
*PRACTICE AREAS: Real Estate Property Law; Civil Practice; Litigation.
Baretta, Edward C., (BV) .......... '31 '61 C&L.800 B.S., J.D. 99 S. Lake Ave.
**Barker, Neil J.**, (AV) .......... '52 '77 C.112 B.A. L.1066 J.D. [Gronemeier&B.]
*PRACTICE AREAS: Banking Law; Real Estate; Unfair Competition Law; Business Litigation.

**Barker & Richardson**
**(See Richardson & Harman)**

**Barker & Romney, A Professional Corporation, (AV)**
**301 East Colorado Boulevard Suite 200, 91101-1977**
**Telephone: 818-578-1970; 213-617-3112 Facsimile: 818-578-0768**
**Lee Barker (1943-1996); David T. Romney; Timothy M. Howett; Blaine Jay Wanke; Cheryl A. Orr.**
**Construction, Construction Defect, Business, Real Estate, Land Use, Environmental Law, Eminent Domain, General Civil Litigation, Community Association Law, Insurance Law and Appellate Law.**
**Reference: City National Bank.**
*See Professional Biographies, PASADENA, CALIFORNIA*

**Barnum, Jerome D., (AV) '17 '44 C.37 A.B. L.813 LL.B.**
**430 Orange Grove Circle, Suite B, 91105**
**Telephone: 818-441-4807**
**Banking, Corporation, Estate Planning, Trust, Probate and Water Rights Law.**

**Baronian, Robert H.**, (AV) .......... '53 '78 C.1077 B.A. L.1148 J.D. [Burns,A.P.M.&B.]
*PRACTICE AREAS: Products Liability Law; Toxic Torts.
Barroll, J. Leeds, IV .......... '51 '77 C.309 B.A. L.790 J.D. Admin. Law J., Soc. Sec. Admn.
Barry, Lily, (AV) .......... '33 '66 L.809 J.D. 301 E. Colorado Blvd.
Bauer, Steven Frederick '56 '81
C.800 B.S. L.1065 J.D. V.P. & Coun., Continental Lawyers Title Co.
Beal, Bruce L. .......... '48 '75 C.1051 B.S. L.596 J.D. Sr. Coun., The Parsons Corp.
Beck, David A., (A Professional Corporation), (BV) '45 '76
C.1097 B.A. L.1190 J.D. 80 S. Lake Ave.
**Beck, Thomas P.**, (AV) .......... '51 '78 C&L.426 B.B.A., J.D. [Thon,B.V.P.&N.]
*PRACTICE AREAS: Personal Injury Law.
Beckett, Glenn Frank .......... '43 '82 C.1097 M.A. L.1137 J.D. 273 S. Euclid Ave.
**Beckstrom, Spencer S.**, (BV) .......... '35 '64 C&L.878 LL.B. [Throckmorton,B.O.&T.]
Belansky, Andrew John, (AV) '23 '56
C.976 B.E.Ch.E. L.326 J.D. 350 W. Colo. Blvd. (Pat.)
Bell, Daniel L. .......... '55 '80 C.827 A.B. L.1119 J.D. 2030 E. Foothill Blvd.
Bell, Garland O., Jr. .......... '46 '79 C.1097 B.S. L.809 J.D. 225 S. Lake Ave., 9th Fl.
Benjamin, Robert D. .......... '42 '74 C.1097 B.S. L.426 J.D. 1107 Fair Oaks Ave. #226

**Bennett, Joel R., (AV) '40 '64 C&L.37 B.A., J.D.**
**225 South Lake Avenue Ninth Floor, 91101**
**Telephone: 818-683-3031 Fax: 818-795-6321**
**Email: joel_bennett@earthlink.net**
***PRACTICE AREAS: Antitrust and Trade Regulation; Breach of Contract; Health Care; Intellectual Property; Unfair Competition.**
**Civil Litigation and Jury Trials in all State and Federal Courts, Antitrust, Unfair Competition, Trade Regulation, Trade Secrets, Breach of Contract, Unfair Trade Practices, Health Care Litigation, Telecommunications Antitrust, Intellectual Property, Trademark, Copyright, Patent.**
*See Professional Biographies, PASADENA, CALIFORNIA*

Bennett, Robert M. .......... '55 '79 C.112 B.A. L.990 J.D. 155 N. Lake Ave.
Bennett, Terrence J., (AV) .......... '47 '72 C.112 B.A. L.1068 J.D. 442 S. Marengo Ave.
**Bensinger, Kerry R.** .......... '60 '87 C.976 B.A. L.800 J.D. [Bensinger,G.&R.]
*LANGUAGES: Spanish.
*REPORTED CASES: United States v. Tabacca, 924 F 2d 906 (9th Cir. 1991).
*PRACTICE AREAS: Criminal and Civil Litigation.

**Bensinger, Grayson & Ritt**
**A Partnership**
**65 North Raymond Avenue, Suite 320, 91103**
**Telephone: 818-685-2550 Fax: 818-685-2562**
**Email: bgrdjr@aol.com**
**Kerry R. Bensinger; Pegine E. Grayson; D. Jay Ritt; Karen M. Gee. Of Counsel: Marilyn M. Smith; Carol A. Klauschie.**
**Criminal Defense in State and Federal Courts, General Civil and Appellate Practice in all State and Federal Courts, Business Litigation, Entertainment Law, Employment Discrimination, Sexual Harassment, and Mediation of Family, Divorce and Community Disputes.**
*See Professional Biographies, PASADENA, CALIFORNIA*

**Benson, Frederick B., (AV) '49 '75 C.264 B.A. L.1068 J.D.**
**200 South Los Robles Avenue, Suite 500, 91101**
**Telephone: 818-577-8808 Fax: 818-577-8887**
**(Certified Specialist, Immigration and Nationality Law, the State Bar of California Board of Legal Specialization).**

(This Listing Continued)

**Benson, Frederick B. (Continued)**
**Immigration and Naturalization, Probate and Estate Planning.**
***See Professional Biographies, PASADENA, CALIFORNIA***

**Berg, J. Harold, (Professional Corporation)**, (AV) '16 '40
C.112 A.B. L.1066 J.D. [Soldwedel,P.B.&C.]
*PRACTICE AREAS: Trust Administration Law; Corporate Law; Probate Law.
Bernal, J. Arthur ........................'57 '85 C.112 B.A. L.770 J.D. 225 S. Lake Ave.
**Betz, Gail M.** ................'51 '85 C.502 B.A. L.426 J.D. [J.D.Christensen&Assoc.]
*PRACTICE AREAS: Health Care Law; Medical Malpractice Litigation.
Bezaire, Maria ..........................'49 '76 C.112 B.A. L.1148 J.D. [Bezaire]
Bezaire, Neil S. ..........................................'29 '61 L.809 [Bezaire]
Bezaire, Stephen P. ..........................................'55 '81 [Bezaire]
Bezaire Law Offices ......................................444 N. Altadena Dr.
**Bigelow, Franklin T., Jr.**, (BV) .........'49 '78 C.668 B.A. L.426 J.D. [Bigelow,M.&T.]
*REPORTED CASES: White Dragon Productions v. Performance Guarantees, Inc., 196 Cal. App. 3d 163 (1987).
*PRACTICE AREAS: Corporate Law; Entertainment Law; Business Litigation; Real Estate Law; Appellate Practice.

**Bigelow, Moore & Tyre, (AV)**
**Easton House, 540 South Marengo Avenue, 91101**
**Telephone: 213-681-0174; 818-792-6806 Telecopier: 818-792-1402**
**Members of the Firm: Franklin T. Bigelow, Jr.; Joseph F. Moore (Certified Specialist in Taxation Law, The State Bar of California Board of Legal Specialization); James S. Tyre. Associates: Anne Reid Oppermann. Of Counsel: Timothy D. Hummel (Certified Specialist, Probate, Estate Planning and Trust Law, The State Bar of California Board of Legal Specialization).**
**Corporate, Tax, General and Business Litigation, Entertainment, Real Estate, Appellate Practice, Health Care, First Amendment, Administrative Law, Probate and Estate Planning.**
**Reference: Citizens Bank.**
***See Professional Biographies, PASADENA, CALIFORNIA***

Birnie, Elizabeth B. ....................'54 '83 C.940 B.A. L.1148 J.D. 325 Elmwood Dr.
Bishop, Lorraine Abell .......................'51 '81 C.605 B.A. L.809 J.D. [Bishop&B.]
Bishop, Randall Abell .....................'49 '85 C.694 A.B. L.809 J.D. [Bishop&B.]
Bishop & Bishop ..............................................161 Sequoia Dr.
**Bisno, Peter**, (AV) ............................'— '79 C.605 B.A. L.1148 J.D. [Bisno&S.]

**Bisno & Samberg, (AV)**
**201 South Lake Avenue, Suite 702, 91101-3015**
**Telephone: 818-585-8899 Fax: 818-585-1899**
**Members of Firm: John M. Samberg; Peter Bisno. Associate: Dennette A. Mulvaney. Of Counsel: Scott C. Tips.**
***See Professional Biographies, PASADENA, CALIFORNIA***

Bitters, Richard H. ........'48 '76 C.1097 B.A. L.1190 J.D. 3844 E. Foothill Blvd., 2nd Fl.
Blair, William Paul, (AV) ............'14 '40 C.691 A.B. L.846 LL.B. 711 E. Walnut St.‡
Blake, Rick A. ...........................'47 '78 C.1042 B.S. L.1137 J.D. 225 S. Lake Ave., 9th Fl.
Blankenhorn, John C. ..................'56 '88 C.219 B.A. L.990 J.D. 221 E. Walnut St.
**Blasco, Richard E.** ......................'55 '80 C.800 B.A. L.809 J.D. [Hunt,O.B.P.&R.]
*PRACTICE AREAS: Business Law; Transactions.
Blunt, Steven A., (BV) ...........'52 '78 C.800 B.A. L.1136 J.D. 131 N. El Molino Ave.
**Bobak, Martin C.** .......................'58 '83 C.112 B.S. L.464 J.D. [Rivkin,R.&K.]
*PRACTICE AREAS: General Civil Litigation; Commercial Litigation; Product Liability Litigation; Premises Liability; Real Estate Litigation.
Bogaard, William J., (AV) ..............'38 '66 C.426 B.S. L.477 J.D. 311 Congress Place
Bogdanchik, Mark David V. ............'62 '93 C.999 B.A. L.1190 J.D. 440 W. Green St.
**Bonilla, Christie Moon** '61 '88
C.911 B.A. L.990 J.D. Coun., Kaiser Found. Health Plan, Inc.
Boochever, Robert ..........................'17 '44 C&L.188 A.B., LL.B. U.S. Sr. Cir. J.
**Boutin, Ann Simmons** .......................'61 '87 C.112 B.S. L.464 J.D. [Boyle,O.&R.]
*PRACTICE AREAS: Estate Planning and Probate Law.
**Bow, Susan E.** '60 '85 C.20 A.B. L.93 J.D.
Sr. V.P. & Asst. Gen. Coun., Countrywide Funding Corp.
**Bowne, Robert R., II** ......................'68 '95 C.1097 B.A. L.990 J.D. [Reed&B.]
*PRACTICE AREAS: General Business; Corporate Law; Real Estate; Non-Profits/Tax; Estate Planning/Probate.

**Boxley, Norman F., Law Offices of '46 '75 C.766 B.A. L.1065 J.D.**
**1100 East Green Street, 91106-2513**
**Telephone: 818-395-7891 Facsimile: 818-395-7808**
***PRACTICE AREAS: Fraudulent Claims Defense; Product Liability; Construction Defect Claims; General Insurance Defense.**
**General Civil Trial and Appellate litigation representing Insurance Companies and their insureds, defense of fraud claims, defense of product manufacturers in product liability litigation, defense of building and homeowners, construction contractors, Design Professionals, Architects, Engineers and Land Surveyors in construction and construction defect matters involving property damage to structures, claims of delay and faulty construction management or defective construction and defective design as well as personal injury allegedly caused by claimed defects in construction or design.**
***See Professional Biographies, PASADENA, CALIFORNIA***

**Boyle, James B., Jr.**, (AV) ..................'30 '55 C&L.813 A.B., LL.B. [Boyle,O.&R.]
*PRACTICE AREAS: General Business Law; Family Law; Construction Law; Estate Planning.

**Boyle, Olson & Robinson, (AV)**
**170 South Euclid Avenue, 91101-2484**
**Telephone: 818-796-7181; 792-6191 Fax: 818-796-8652**
**Members of Firm: James B. Boyle, Jr.; A. William Olson; Edward O. Robinson; Stephen J. Miller; Ann Simmons Boutin; James B. Boyle (1927-1991); J. Kenneth Cameron (1975-1984); John R. Atwill, Jr. (1948-1985); J. Dean Barrick (1927-1978).**
**General Civil and Trial Practice in all State and Federal Courts. Corporation, Probate, Estate Planning, Family, Construction, State and Federal Tax Law.**
**Representative Clients: California Hydroforming Co.; Alhambra Foundry Co., Ltd.; Citizens Commercial Trust & Savings Bank of Pasadena; Neff Instrument Corp.; San Rafael Investment Corp.; Ben F. Smith, Inc. (Concrete Contractors); Trail Chemical Corp.**
**Reference: Sanwa Bank California (Pasadena Main Office).**
***See Professional Biographies, PASADENA, CALIFORNIA***

Bradley, Carole W. '44 '77 C.610 B.A. L.809 J.D.
Mgr. Subcontract Off., Caltech/Jet Propulsion Laboratory
**Bradley, John F.**, (AV) ..................'31 '57 C.800 B.S. L.813 J.D. [Lagerlof,S.B.&S.]
**Bradshaw, David S.**, (AV) ...............'45 '70 C.605 B.A. L.813 J.D. [Murray,B.&B.]
Brady, Owen J., (AV) ...................'19 '47 C.767 A.B. L.1065 J.D. 221 E. Walnut St.
**Branconier, Michael A.**, (AV) ...........'49 '74 C&L.426 B.A., J.D. [Cooper,K.&S.]
*PRACTICE AREAS: Civil Litigation.
**Brandt, Fred W.**, (AV) .............'33 '64 C.813 B.A. L.809 LL.B. [Freeburg,J.&N.]
Brennen, Richard P. ..................'61 '92 C.112 B.A L.1137 J.D. 547 S. Marengo Ave.
Brenner, Anita S., (AV) ...........................'49 '74 C.112 B.A. L.1068 J.D. [Torres&B.]
**Brewster, Donald P.** '57 '87 C.813 A.B. L.494 J.D.
1st V.P., Sr. Coun. & Asst. Secy., Countrywide Funding Corp.
Bridges, Allen K. ......................'42 '77 C.976 B.A. L.809 J.D. 380 S. Euclid Ave.
**Bright, Thomas C.** ......................'65 '93 C.880 B.A. L.990 J.D. [Rivkin,R.&K.]
*PRACTICE AREAS: Litigation; Entertainment Law; Employment Law; Insurance Litigation; Commercial Litigation.

**Brody, Kevin J.** .............................'59 '85 C.1169 B.A. L.188 J.D. [Hunt,O.B.P.&R.]
*LANGUAGES: French.
*PRACTICE AREAS: General Business Law; Real Estate Law.
**Brody, Robert S.** ........................'59 '84 C.705 B.A. L.1067 J.D. [Freeburg,J.&N.]
*PRACTICE AREAS: Premises Liability; Products Liability; Construction Defect Litigation; Personal Injury; Arbitration.

**Brooke, Darrell G. '57 '85 C.800 B.S. L.809 J.D.**
**30 North Raymond, Suite 713, 91103-3930**
**Telephone: 818-795-7400 Fax: 818-795-7496**
**(Also Of Counsel to Hart & Watters, Los Angeles).**
***PRACTICE AREAS: Estate Planning; Tax; Probate; Business Law.**
**Estate Planning, Tax, Probate and Business Law.**
***See Professional Biographies, PASADENA, CALIFORNIA***

Brosio, Frederick M., Jr., (AV) ...........'29 '57 C&L.813 A.B., LL.B. P.O. Box 93074‡
Brown, David C. '53 '80 C&L.420 B.A., J.D.
(adm. in LA; not adm. in CA) Soc. Sec. Admin.
**Brown, Edward A.** '59 '92 C.339 B.S.Met.E. L.30 J.D.
(adm. in PA; not adm. in CA; See Pat. Sect.) [Sheldon&M.]
**Brown, Eric** ...............................'68 '94 C.910 B.A. L.1066 J.D. [Hunt,O.B.P.&R.]
*PRACTICE AREAS: Construction Litigation; Real Estate Litigation.
Brown, Lorne J., (AV) ...............'37 '65 C.768 B.A. L.1065 LL.B. 600 S. LakeAve.
**Brown, Mark C.**, (AV) ....................'52 '77 C.112 B.A. L.426 J.D. [Reed&B.]
*PRACTICE AREAS: Estate Planning and Probate; Real Estate; General Corporate and Business Law.
**Brown, Michael R.**, (AV) ...................'51 '75 C.994 B.A. L.61 J.D. [Rivkin,R.&K.]
*PRACTICE AREAS: Commercial Litigation; Employment Litigation; Insurance Litigation; Fee Litigation; Entertainment Litigation.
Brown, Robert J. ...............'36 '78 C.1109 B.A. L.1190 J.D. 740 E. Colorado Blvd.
**Brumbach, Gabrielle Harner** ...........'67 '94 C.112 B.A. L.809 J.D. [Gutierrez&P.]
*LANGUAGES: German.
*PRACTICE AREAS: Civil Rights Defense; Local Government Liability; Employer Liability.
Brundige, Maurice L. '24 '55
C&L.208 B.A., LL.B. Asst. Staff Coun., Calif. Institute of Tech.
Bruning, Robert M. ...........................'52 '77 C.800 B.A. L.809 J.D. [R.M.Bruning]
Bruning, Robert M., Law Offices of ...............................225 S Lake Ave., 9th Fl.
Brunner, Sultra E. .................................'50 '83 C.112 B.A. 1541 N. Lake St.
**Brutocao, William J.**, (BV) ..............'50 '77 C.188 B.A. L.1065 J.D. [Sheldon&M.]
**Budzyn, Michael J.** .......................'50 '75 C.112 B.A. L.1068 J.D. [Murray,B.&B.]
*PRACTICE AREAS: Pension; Profit Sharing; ERISA; General Corporate.
**Bukata, Dianne H.**, (AV) ......................'45 '78 C.783 B.S. L.800 J.D. [Hahn&H.]
*PRACTICE AREAS: Estate Planning; Probate.
**Bull, Ingall W., Jr.**, (AV) ..................'27 '51 C&L.813 A.B., LL.B. [Freeburg,J.&N.]
*PRACTICE AREAS: Dental Malpractice; Products Liability; Insurance; Personal Injury Defense.
**Bunn, David G.**, (AV) ...........................'59 '85 C.1239 B.A. L.990 J.D. [Bunn&B.]
*PRACTICE AREAS: Estate Planning; Probate and Trust Administration and Litigation.
**Bunn, Thomas S., III**, (AV) ..........'55 '79 C.674 A.B. L.800 J.D. [Lagerlof,S.B.&S.]

**Bunn, Thomas S., Jr., (AV) '27 '50 C&L.800 A.B., J.D.**
**Suite 500 CenFed Building, 301 East Colorado Boulevard, 91101-1961**
**Telephone: 818-449-8804 Los Angeles: 213-684-2107**
**(Certified Specialist, Family Law, The State Bar of California Board of Legal Specialization).**
**Practice Limited to Family Law.**
**Reference: Tokai Bank of California (Pasadena Office).**

**Bunn, Wiley D.**, (AV) ..........................'29 '53 C&L.800 A.B., LL.B. [Bunn&B.]
*PRACTICE AREAS: Estate Planning; Trust; Probate Law.

**Bunn and Bunn, (AV)**
**410 Corporate Center Building, 225 South Lake Avenue, 91101**
**Telephone: 818-792-9421 Telecopier: 818-796-6839**
**Wiley D. Bunn (Certified Specialist, Estate Planning, Trust and Probate Law, The State Bar of California Board of Legal Specialization); David G. Bunn (Certified Specialist, Estate Planning, Trust and Probate Law, The State Bar of California Board of Legal Specialization).**
**Estate Planning, Trust and Probate Administration and Litigation.**
**Reference: Sanwa Bank, Pasadena, California.**
***See Professional Biographies, PASADENA, CALIFORNIA***

Burke, Robert E., (AV) .............'32 '61 C.112 B.A. L.976 LL.B. 1067 Pine Oak Lane

**Burkitt, William R., (AV) '41 '67 C&L.800 B.S., J.D.**
**716 Mutual Savings Building, 301 East Colorado Boulevard, 91101**
**Telephone: 818-304-0395 Telecopier: 818-304-0032**
**Family Law including Custody.**
***See Professional Biographies, PASADENA, CALIFORNIA***

**Burns, Michael A.**, (AV) .............'39 '70 C.728 B.S. L.809 J.D. [Burns,A.P.M.&B.]
*PRACTICE AREAS: Insurance Defense Law; Products Liability Law; Construction Law.

**Burns, Ammirato, Palumbo, Milam & Baronian, A Professional Law Corporation, (AV)**
**65 North Raymond Avenue, 2nd Floor, 91103-3919**
**Telephone: 818-796-5053; 213-258-8282 Fax: 818-792-3078**
**Michael A. Burns; Vincent A. Ammirato, Resident, Long Bch; Bruce Palumbo; Jeffrey L. Milam; Robert H. Baronian;—Normand A. Ayotte; Colleen Clark; Valerie Julien-Peto; Susan E. Luhring; Grace C. Mori, Resident, Long Bch; Michael P. Vicencia, Resident, LOng Bch; Michael E. Wenzel, Resident, Long Bch.**
**General Civil and Trial Practice in all Courts. Insurance Defense, Products Liability, Toxic Torts, Construction Litigation, Medical Malpractice, Personal Injury, Tort, Subrogation and Wrongful Termination.**
**Reference: First Los Angeles Bank.**
**Long Beach, California Office: One World Trade Center, Suite 1200. Telephone: 310-436-8338; 714-952-1047. Fax: 310-432-6049.**
***See Professional Biographies, PASADENA, CALIFORNIA***

Burt, George ...........................'63 '89 C.1077 B.S. L.990 J.D. 200 S. Los Robles
**Burton, John C.**, (AV) ......................'53 '79 C.112 B.A. L.1065 J.D. [Burton&N.]
*REPORTED CASES: Montiel v. City of Los Angeles, 2 F.3d 335 (9th Cir. 1993); Greenstreet v. County of San Bernardino, 41 F.3d 1306 (9th Cir. 1994).

**Burton & Norris, (AV)**
**35 South Raymond Avenue, Fourth Floor, 91105**
**Telephone: 818-449-8300 Fax: 818-449-4417**
**John C. Burton; Donald G. Norris; Victoria E. King.**
**Trial and Appellate Litigation in all State and Federal Courts including Civil Rights, Commercial, Securities, Intellectual Property, Professional Responsibility and Personal Injury. Medical Malpractice and Criminal Law.**
**Reference: Bank of America (Pasadena).**
***See Professional Biographies, PASADENA, CALIFORNIA***

Bussone, Ann Jennett ...................'56 '85 C.112 B.A. L.426 J.D. Calif. Inst. of Tech.

**Bussone, Joseph D. '54 '83 C.424 B.A. L.809 J.D.**
**225 South Lake Avenue, Ninth Floor, 91101-3021**
**Telephone: 818-583-9135 Fax: 818-583-9137**
**Email: bussone@msn.com URL: http://www.bussone.com**
**General Civil and Trial Practice in State and Federal Courts. Personal Injury, Professional Negligence, Construction, Employment, Business, Real Estate and Criminal Law.**
***See Professional Biographies, PASADENA, CALIFORNIA***

Butler, Debra K. ..............................'53 '89 C&L.1136 B.S., J.D. P.O. Box 2301

CAA483P

**Byam, Clark R., (P.C.),** (AV) ............... '43 '72 C.918 B.A. L.1065 J.D. [Hahn&H.]
*PRACTICE AREAS: Probate and Trust Litigation; Estate Planning; Employee Benefits.
**Cahill, Richard F.,** (AV) ............. '53 '78 C.712 B.A. L.602 J.D. [Hammond,Z.&C.]
*PRACTICE AREAS: Medical Malpractice.
**Cairns, John D.,** (AV) ............... '42 '72 C.800 B.A. L.1049 J.D. [Cairns,D.L.N.&S.]
*PRACTICE AREAS: Insurance Defense; General Civil Litigation; Malpractice; Toxic Torts.

**Cairns, Doyle, Lans, Nicholas & Soni, A Law Corporation, (AV)**
**Ninth Floor, 225 South Lake Avenue, 91101**
**Telephone: 818-683-3111 Telecopier: 818-683-4999**
**John D. Cairns; John C. Doyle; Stephen M. Lans; Francisco J. Nicholas; Rohini Soni (1956-1994).**
**General Civil and Trial Practice in all State and Federal Courts. Banking, Bankruptcy, Corporation, Business, Insurance, Negligence, Malpractice, Real Property, Construction, Motor Transport, Employment Law, Fraud and Toxic Torts.**
**Representative Clients: Allstate Insurance Companies; Burger King Corp.; California Insurance Guarantee Assn.; California United Bank; CIGNA Insurance Companies; City of Pasadena; Cumis Insurance Society, Inc.; Employer's Mutual Insurance Companies; State Farm Insurance Companies; Tokio Marine Insurance.**
*See Professional Biographies, PASADENA, CALIFORNIA*

**Calciano, Elizabeth Spedding, (AV) '39 '77 C.681 A.B. L.1066 J.D.**
**301 East Colorado Boulevard Suite 626, 91101**
**Telephone: 818-792-2173 Fax: Available Upon Request**
**Real Property, Business, Estate Planning and Probate Law.**
**Representative Clients: Crawford Stores, Inc.; Pacific Clinics.**
**Reference: Citizens Commercial Trust & Savings Bank.**
*See Professional Biographies, PASADENA, CALIFORNIA*

**Caldecott, E. J.,** (AV) ..................... '22 '49 C.112 A.B. L.800 LL.B. [Reed&B.]
*PRACTICE AREAS: Shopping Center Law.
Caldwell, John, (AV) ........................ '22 '44 C&L.623 LL.B. 225 S. Lake Ave.
Callahan, Richard M., Jr. ........... '52 '81 C.800 B.A. L.426 J.D. 2016 Queensberry Rd.
**Callister, John C.** .................. '53 '80 C.605 B.A. L.809 J.D. [Laughlin,F.L.&M.]
*PRACTICE AREAS: Workers' Compensation Defense.
Callister, Richard C. ..... '57 '86 C&L.878 B.S., J.D. Compensation Resources Group, Inc.

**Calvert, Melanie A., (AV) '54 '84 C.880 B.S. L.273 J.D.**
**Penthouse, 150 S. Los Robles Avenue, Suite 930, 91101-2437**
**Telephone: 818-585-3555 Fax: 818-577-5219**
***REPORTED CASES: Gooding v. Shearson Lehman (9th Cir.).**
**General Civil Litigation and Appellate Practice in State Courts, Employment Law and Business Litigation.**
**Reference: Coast Federal Bank, Pasadena.**

**Capeloto, J. Sheldon** ..................... '51 '79 C.112 A.B. L.284 J.D. [McKinley&C.]
*REPORTED CASES: In re Byron L. Kinney, Cite as 51 B.R. 840 (Bkrptcy. 1985); In re Delores Elizabeth Glasper, a/k/a Mrs. Wilford Glasper, Cite as 28 B.R. 6 (Bkrptcy. App. 1983); In re Kelley 199 B.R. 698 (9th Cir Bap 1996).
*PRACTICE AREAS: Bankruptcy; Creditor Rights; Financial Institutions; Real Estate.
Carlburg, Carolyn Hopkins ..... '46 '79 C.112 B.A. L.1068 J.D. 540 El Dorado St., 1st Fl.
Carlson, Maureen D. .................. '34 '81 C.687 B.A. L.426 J.D. 695 Prospect Blvd.
**Carlson, Scott W.,** (AV) .................. '57 '82 C.112 B.A. L.1068 J.D. [Carter,C.&E.]
*PRACTICE AREAS: Real Estate Law; Business Law; Litigation; Creditors' Rights Law.
Carmely, Klara ......................... '47 '85 C.1077 B.A. L.426 J.D. 393 E. Walnut St.
**Carney, Hayden A.,** (AV) '36 '64
C.999 B.S.N.A. L.800 LL.B. [Christie,P.&H.] (See Pat. Sect.)
*PRACTICE AREAS: Intellectual Property Licensing and Taxation; Domestic and International Patent and Trademark Prosecution; Mechanical and Physical Technologies.
**Carpenter, John D.** ....... '61 '89 C&L.800 B.S., J.D. [Christie,P.&H.] (See Pat. Sect.)
*PRACTICE AREAS: Patents; Trademarks; Copyrights.
**Carter, Robert E.,** (AV) ..................... '31 '60 C&L.800 A.B., J.D. [Carter,C.&E.]
*PRACTICE AREAS: Real Estate Law; Business Law.

**Carter, Carlson & Ellerman, LLP, (AV)**
**Suite 320, 301 East Colorado Boulevard, 91101**
**Telephone: 818-796-6161 Telecopier: 818-796-0593**
**Members of Firm: Robert E. Carter; Scott W. Carlson; Jana Ellerman. Of Counsel: Robert M. Peterson.**
**Real Estate and Business Law and Litigation.**
**Representative Clients: Boards of Realtors of Pasadena and San Marino-South Pasadena; Citizens Bank; Wells Fargo Bank; CenFed Bank.**
**Reference: Citizens Commercial Trust & Savings Bank, Pasadena.**
*See Professional Biographies, PASADENA, CALIFORNIA*

Carver, Mary V. ........................ '36 '79 C.813 B.A. L.1190 J.D. 221 E. Walnut St.
**Casares, Diana C.** ....'59 '92 C&L.426 B.A., J.D. Coun., Kaiser Found. Health Plan, Inc.

**Cashion, David C., (AV) '35 '62 C&L.800 A.B., J.D.**
**790 East Colorado Boulevard, Ninth Floor, 91101-2113**
**Telephone: 818-796-9606 Facsimile: 818-792-5035**
**Family, Personal Injury, Business, Probate and Commercial Law. General Civil and Trial Practice.**
*See Professional Biographies, PASADENA, CALIFORNIA*

Cassity, C. Fred .......................... '38 '66 C&L.477 B.S.E., J.D. [Cassity&M.]

**Cassity & Maseda**
**2 North Lake Avenue, Suite 860, 91101**
**Telephone: 818-585-3562 Fax: 818-585-3565**
**C. Fred Cassity; Stephen B. Maseda.**
**General Civil Practice, Brokerage, Commercial Leasing, Condominium and Homeowners Associations, Construction, Foreclosures, Land Use Development and Sales, Litigation.**

**Castle, Richard B.,** (AV) .......... '30 '56 C.112 A.B. L.1068 LL.B. [Freeburg,J.&N.]
*PRACTICE AREAS: Malpractice; Products Liability; Insurance; Personal Injury Defense.
Cato, Barbara L. ...................... '25 '78 C.112 B.A. L.1152 J.D. 1535 Kenmore Rd.‡
Cava, Dennis L. ........................ '44 '73 C.906 B.S. L.285 J.D. 115 W. California Blvd.
**Cavanagh, Daniel M.** ................. '65 '96 C.1167 B.S. L.800 J.D. [Christie,P.&H.]
*PRACTICE AREAS: Patent; Trademark; Copyright.
**Chaikovsky, Yar R.** ......'69 '94 C.800 B.S. L.112 J.D. [Christie,P.&H.] (See Pat. Sect.)
*PRACTICE AREAS: Patents; Trademarks; Copyrights.
**Chalison, Linda A.** ..................... '50 '75 C.112 B.A. L.809 J.D. [Cooper,K.&S.]
Chan, Sing ................................ '56 '89 C.061 B.A. L.966 J.D. 300 N. Lake Ave.
Chang, John S. ............................ '48 '75 C&L.813 B.A., J.D. 980 S. Arroyo Pkwy.
Chapman, Charles B., III '31 '79 C.871 B.S. L.589 J.D.
(adm. in IL; not adm. in CA) Jet Propulsion Lab.
Charboneau, Robert B., (BV) ............. '45 '74 C.1077 B.A. L.426 J.D. 35 S. Raymond
Chavez, E. Thomas .................. '54 '86 C.1097 B.A. L.809 J.D. 150 E. Colorado Blvd.
Chern, Cyril, (AV) ................ '44 '72 C.800 B.Arch. L.809 J.D. 234 E. Colorado Blvd.
**Chinen, Richard L.** ................... '58 '82 C.312 B.A. L.809 J.D. [Soldwedel,P.B.&C.]
*LANGUAGES: Japanese (verbal).
*PRACTICE AREAS: Family Law; Personal Injury; Estate Planning; Bankruptcy; Business Litigation.
**Christensen, Jay D., P.C.,** (AV) '46 '75 C.101 B.S. L.878 J.D.
[J.D.Christensen&Assoc.]

**Christensen, Jay D., and Associates, (AV)**
**225 South Lake, Ninth Floor, 91101**
**Telephone: 818-568-2900 Fax: 818-568-1566**
**Jay D. Christensen, P.C. Of Counsel: Stephen G. Auer; Gail M. Betz.**
**General Healthcare Law, Managed Health Care Arrangements, Peer Review Issues, Related Litigation.**
*See Professional Biographies, PASADENA, CALIFORNIA*

**Christie, Parker & Hale, LLP, (AV)**
**Fifth Floor, Wells Fargo Bank Building, 350 West Colorado Boulevard, P.O. Box 7068, 91109-7068**
**Telephone: 818-795-9900 Los Angeles: 213-681-1800 Cable Address: "Patlaw" Telex: ITT 4995129 (CPH PSD) Telecopier: 818-577-8800**
**Members of Firm: James B. Christie (1904-1959); Robert L. Parker (1920-1980); D. Bruce Prout; Hayden A. Carney; Richard J. Ward, Jr.; Russell R. Palmer, Jr.; LeRoy T. Rahn; Richard D. Seibel; Roderick G. Dorman; Walter G. Maxwell; John P. Grinnell; William P. Christie (Resident, Irvine Office); David A. Dillard; Thomas J. Daly; Vincent G. Gioia (Resident, Irvine Office); William J. O'Brien; Theodore A. Pianko; Edward R. Schwartz; John D. Carpenter. Associates: David A. Plumley; Wesley W. Monroe; Grant T. Langton; Syed A. Hasan; R. Dabney Eastham; Constantine Marantidis; John W. Eldredge (Resident, Irvine Office); Yar R. Chaikovsky; Marilyn R. Khorsandi; Craig A. Gelfound; Gregory S. Lampert; Jeffrey A. Fehervari; Steven P. Skabrat (Not admitted in CA); Daniel M. Cavanagh; Mark C. Scarsi; Kenyon S. Jenckes; Gary J. Nelson. Of Counsel: R. William Johnston; Paul W. Fish (Not admitted in CA); Marc Morris; Carl Kustin, Jr.; Jeffrey P. Wall.**
**Patent, Trademark and Copyright Law. Unfair Competition, Trade Secrets, Computer Law, Biotechnology, Licensing, Antitrust and Complex Business Litigation.**
**Reference: Wells Fargo Bank (Pasadena, California Main Offices).**
**Irvine, California Office: Suite 1440, 5 Park Plaza. Telephone: 714-476-0757.**
*See Professional Biographies, PASADENA, CALIFORNIA*

**Chuck, Stephen C.** ............................ '60 '85 C.267 B.S. L.1067 J.D. [Garrett&T.]
*PRACTICE AREAS: Business Litigation; Real Estate Litigation; Professional Liability.
Ciampa, James D. ..................'65 '92 C.1042 B.S. L.770 J.D. [Lagerlof,S.B.&S.]

**Clark, Charles Edward, (AV) '49 '77 C.800 B.A. L.276 J.D.**
**Suite 707, 301 East Colorado Boulevard, 91101**
**Telephone: 818-795-3640 FAX: 818-584-9206**
**Civil Practice. Personal Injury, Residential and Commercial Real Estate, Landlord and Tenant, Litigation, Business and Workers Compensation Law.**
**Reference: Bank of America (Pasadena Main Branch).**

**Clark, Colleen,** (BV) ................. '54 '81 C.330 B.A. L.809 J.D. [Burns,A.P.M.&B.]
*PRACTICE AREAS: Construction Defect; Corporate.

**Clark, James Dexter, (AV) '41 '71 C.976 B.A. L.800 J.D.**
**1 South Orange Grove Boulevard, Suite 11, 91105**
**Telephone: 818-583-4798 Fax: 818-583-4984**
***REPORTED CASES: Michelin Tire Corp. vs. Wages (1976) 423 U.S.276 (Amicus); Zee Toys vs. County of Los Angeles (1978) Cal.App. 3d 763, 149 Cal. Rptr. 750 Affirmed 449 U.S. 1119; Mandel vs. Hutchison (C.A. Cal. 1974) 494 F.2d 364; Craig Corp. vs. County of Los Angles (1975) 51 Cal.App. 3d 909, etc.**
***TRANSACTIONS: Plaza Las Fuentes Mix-Use Development, Pasadena, California; Museum of Contemporary Art, Los Angeles, California.**
***PRACTICE AREAS: Municipal Law; Economic Development; Redevelopment.**
**Municipal Law, Eminent Domain, Economic Development and Redevelopment.**
*See Professional Biographies, PASADENA, CALIFORNIA*

Clark, Robert G. ..........................'31 '80 C.976 B.A. L.178 J.D. 180 S. Lake Ave.
Clifford, Robert Scot ........................... '47 '74 C.112 B.A. L.809 J.D. [Jett&L.]
**Cochran, J. Michael** '49 '76
C.112 B.A. L.990 J.D. Assoc. Div. Coun., Chicago Title Ins. Co.
*RESPONSIBILITIES: Title Insurance; Real Estate.

**Cohen, Arlan A., Law Offices of '43 '90 C.178 B.A. L.309 J.D.**
**1100 East Green Street, 2nd Floor, 91106**
**Telephone: 818-449-0404 Fax: 818-449-1673**
***PRACTICE AREAS: Medical Malpractice, Wrongful Death; Litigation.**
**Medical Malpractice, Wrongful Death Litigation and Birth Injuries.**
*See Professional Biographies, PASADENA, CALIFORNIA*

Cohen, Benjamin S., (BV) '42 '69 C.831 B.S. L.446 J.D.
(adm. in MD; not adm. in CA) 400 E. California Blvd.
Cohen, Donna Frost ................ '35 '87 C.112 B.A. L.1190 J.D. [Cohen,R.S.&D.F.C.]
**Cohen, Jerilyn** ....................... '56 '80 C.112 B.A. L.809 J.D. [Laughlin,F.L.&M.]
*LANGUAGES: French, Spanish, Italian.
*PRACTICE AREAS: Workers' Compensation.
Cohen, Richard S., (AV) ......... '35 '61 C.477 B.B.A. L.813 LL.B. [Cohen,R.S.&D.F.C.]
Cohen, Thelma S., (AV) ...................... '50 '75 C.112 A.B. L.1065 J.D. [Potter,C.&S.]
Cohen, Richard S., & Donna Frost Cohen, Law Offices of, (AV) ... 301 E. Colorado Blvd.
Cole, Casey J. ........................ '62 '89 C.378 B.S.W. L.1148 J.D. 221 E. Walnut St.
Cole, Susan '39 '62 C.331 A.B. L.178 LL.B.
V.P. & Asst. Gen. Coun., The Parsons Corp.
**Collins, John J.,** (AV) ............. '36 '62 C.770 B.A. L.426 LL.B. [Collins,C.M.&T.]
*PRACTICE AREAS: General Trial Practice; Public Liability; Insurance Bad Faith; Products Liability; Construction Litigation.
Collins, Thomas M., (AV) ............'34 '62 C.770 B.S. L.813 LL.B. [McDermott&T.]

**Collins, Collins, Muir & Traver, (AV)**
**Successor to Collins & Collins**
**Suite 300, 265 North Euclid, 91101**
**Telephone: 818-793-1163 FAX: 818-793-5982**
**Members of Firm: James E. Collins (1910-1987); John J. Collins; Samuel J. Muir; Robert J. Traver; Frank J. D'Oro; Brian K. Stewart. Associates: Paul L. Rupard; Robert H. Stellwagen, Jr.; Tomas A. Guterres; Christine E. Drage; Peter L. Stacy; Stephen W. Olson.**
**Casualty, Products Liability, Construction, Malpractice Insurance, Employment Termination, Sexual Abuse, and Personal Injury Law. General Trial Practice.**
**Newport Beach, California Office: 333 Bayside Drive, 92660. Telephone: 714-723-6284. Fax: 714-723-7701.**
*See Professional Biographies, PASADENA, CALIFORNIA*

**Compeán, Efren A.** ......................... '59 '85 C.112 B.A. L.1068 J.D. [Garrett&T.]
*PRACTICE AREAS: Litigation; Business Law; Commercial Law; Professional Liability.
Condon, Daniel B., (AV) .................. '30 '59 C.262 B.S. L.1068 J.D. 225 S. Lake
**Conway, Kerry Brian** ......'71 '72 C.174 B.A. L.1066 J.D. Coun., Chicago Title Ins. Co.
Cooney, Edmond P. ............... '37 '76 C.1097 B.A. L.809 J.D. 350 W. Colorado Blvd.
**Cooper, Brand L.,** (AV) .......................'49 '75 C.800 B.S. L.426 J.D. [Cooper,K.&S.]
Cooper, Mary B. .......................'31 '83 C.112 B.A. L.1137 J.D. 1765 Rose Villa St.

**Cooper, Kardaras & Scharf L.L.P., (AV)**
**141 East Walnut Street, 91103**
**Telephone: 818-795-0814 Telefax: 818-795-3839**
**Partners: Brand L. Cooper; William P. Kardaras (Resident, New York Office); Jeffrey D. Scharf; Louise A. Kelleher (Resident, New York Office); Gerald G. Knapton; Paul H. Lusby; Linda A. Chalison; Bruce E. Nehlsen. Associates: Alan C. Arnall; Edward C. Wilde; Michael S. Overing; Lori S. Evenchick (Resident, New York Office); James B. Sanborn; Joseph P. Fogel; Mark M. Senior; Michael A. Branconier; Robert G. Ricco (Resident, New York Office); Edward E. Dollar; Michael T. Ohira; Victor E. Aguilera; Frederick Harold Alschuler; James C. Potepan; Keith A. Turner; Thomas V. O'Hagan; Thomas M. O'Leary. Of Counsel: Daniel C. David; Alison Kotlarz Katz; William Gwire.**
**Civil Litigation and Appellate Practice in all State and Federal Courts. Attorney Fee Dispute Resolution and Litigation Management, Insurance and Reinsurance Coverage, Insurance Bad Faith Litigation, Subrogation, Business, Commercial, Partnership, Personal Injury, Toxic Tort, Environmental, Products Liability, Professional, Marine and Property Litigation, General Business, Corporate and Commercial Law, Homeowner Association Law and Litigation, Construction Defect Litigation, Real Estate and Real Estate Finance, Federal and State Taxation and Tax Controversies, Estate Planning and Probate Law.**
**New York, N.Y. Office: 40 Wall Street, 32nd Floor. Telephone: 212-785-5050. Telefax: 212-785-5055.**
*See Professional Biographies, PASADENA, CALIFORNIA*

Copley, Jan ......................................... '55 '81 C.605 A.B. L.426 J.D. 25 Union St.

**Coppess, Michael J.** ......... '57 '84 C.426 B.A. L.1049 J.D. [Ⓐ Reed&B.]
*PRACTICE AREAS: Civil Litigation; Real Estate; General Corporate Law.
**Corwin, Diane M.** ......... '56 '83 C.112 B.A. L.990 J.D. [Ⓐ Baraban&T.]
*PRACTICE AREAS: Civil Litigation.
Coulter, George P. ......... '30 '58 C.112 A.B. L.273 J.D. 490 S. Fair Oaks Ave.‡
Coulter, Vernoff & Pearson, A Professional Corporation, (BV) ......490 S. Fair Oaks Ave.
**Cox, Sandra H.** '39 '63 C.329 B.A. L.608 J.D.
V.P. & Reg. Coun., Kaiser Found. Health Plan, Inc.
Creim, Marjorie R. ......... '14 '38 C.112 L.800 J.D. 3852 E. Colorado Blvd.‡
Crisologo, William B. ......... '54 '83 C.312 B.A. L.809 J.D. 301 E. Colorado Blvd.
**Crochet, Carla** ......... '63 '95 C.1131 B.S. L.1067 J.D. [Ⓐ Freeburg,J.&N.]
*PRACTICE AREAS: Toxic Exposure; Business Litigation; Premises Liability Litigation.
**Cumare, Rosa M. C.** ......... '49 '85 C&L.800 B.A., J.D. [Hamilton&C.]
*LANGUAGES: Dutch.
*PRACTICE AREAS: Employer Personnel Counseling; Employment Discrimination; Sexual Harassment; Wage and Hour Law; OSHA.
**Cushman, John C.**, (AV) ......... '33 '62 C.605 B.A. L.1066 LL.B. [Ⓒ Hammond,Z.&C.]
*PRACTICE AREAS: Probate Law; Estate Planning Law; Trust Law.
Cusker, John C. ......... '51 '90 C.178 A.B. L.1065 J.D. Soc. Sec. Admn.
Cutts, Karen D. ......... '41 '75 C.112 B.A. L.1095 J.D. 360 Rosita Ln.‡
**Cyr, Danielle D.** ......... '63 '96 C.860 B.A. L.809 J.D. [Ⓐ McKinley&C.]
*LANGUAGES: French.
*PRACTICE AREAS: Litigation; Bankruptcy.

**D'Alessandro & Ritchie, A Professional Corporation, (BV)**
**3521 East Yorkshire Road, Suite 1000, 91107-5432⊙**
**Telephone: 818-683-8800 Facsimile: 818-683-8900**
**David B. Ritchie. Of Counsel: Steven A. Swernofsky.**
**Patents, Trademarks, Copyrights, Intellectual Property.**
**San Jose, California Office: 1731 Technology Drive, Suite 710, 95110. Telephone: 408-441-1100. Fax: 408-441-8400.**

***See Professional Biographies, PASADENA, CALIFORNIA***

**Daly, Thomas J.**, (AV) '57 '85
C.339 B.S.Ch.E. L.426 J.D. [Christie,P.&H.] (See Pat. Sect.)
*PRACTICE AREAS: Patent, Trademark, Copyright and Unfair Competition Litigation.
**D'Angelo, Robert W., (P.C.)**, (AV) ......... '32 '60 C.426 B.B.A. L.1068 J.D. [Myers&D.]
*PRACTICE AREAS: Taxation; Real Estate; Estate Planning; Trust and Probate.
Darden, Larry W. ......... '46 '78 C.999 B.A. L.1190 J.D. 440 W. Green St.
DaRin, Edward J., (AV) ......... '25 '58 C.124 B.S.E.E. L.831 J.D. [E.J.DaRin] (Pat.)
DaRin, Edward J., Inc., A Law Corporation, (AV) ......... 301 E. Colorado Blvd. (Pat.)
**Darling, John D.** ......... '63 '91 C.560 B.A. L.464 J.D. [Ⓐ Hunt,O.B.P.&R.]
*PRACTICE AREAS: Construction Law; Real Estate Litigation.
Daroca, Sylvan P., III ......... '48 '80 C.1258 B.A. L.809 J.D. 301 E. Colorado Blvd.
**Darvey, Diane L.** ......... '47 '89 C.112 Pharm.D. L.426 J.D. [Ⓐ Kolts&N.]
*PRACTICE AREAS: Employment Discrimination and Wrongful Termination; Drug Products and Medical Device Litigation.
Dauber, Harriet S. ......... '32 '75 C.1077 B.A. L.809 J.D. 909 E. Green St.
**David, Daniel C.** ......... '55 '83 C.893 B.A. L.1066 J.D. [Ⓒ Cooper,K.&S.]
*PRACTICE AREAS: Estate Planning Law; Tax Law; Real Estate Law; Finance Law.
Davis, Richard L. ......... '15 '72 C.813 A.B. L.800 J.D. 301 E. Colorado Blvd.
Deacon, John, (AV) ......... '42 '68 C&L.800 B.A., J.D. 350 W. Colo. Blvd.
**Dear, Richard D.**, (AV) ......... '31 '62 C&L.800 B.S., J.D. [Dear&K.]
*PRACTICE AREAS: Corporate Formation; Partnership; Partnership Dissolutions; Limited Partnerships; Nonprofit Corporations.

**Dear & Kelley, (AV)**
**225 South Lake Avenue, Suite 510, 91101**
**Telephone: 818-568-2500 Fax: 818-405-0786**
**Members of Firm: Richard D. Dear; Thomas J. Kelley. Of Counsel: John L. Hunter.**
**Corporate, Commercial Gaming and Real Estate Transactions, Business Litigation and Bankruptcy.**

***See Professional Biographies, PASADENA, CALIFORNIA***

Dederick, Mary J. ......... '48 '78 C.1097 B.S. L.1190 J.D. 221 E. Walnut St.
Deiter, Paul D. ....'37 '73 C.674 A.B. L.981 LL.B. Southern Calif. Permanente Med. Grp.
**de los Reyes, Anthony**, (AV) ......... '42 '69 C.800 L.1148 J.D. [Ⓒ Thon,B.V.P.&N.]
*PRACTICE AREAS: Personal Injury Law; Products Liability; Medical Malpractice Law.
del Valle, Bernard J., (AV) ......... '08 '32 C&L.426 B.A., LL.B. [Arnerich,d.&S.]
De Marzo, Vincent F. ......... '53 '84 C.112 B.A. L.1136 J.D. 200 E. Del Mar Blvd.
DeSimone, James W. '32 '62 C.339 B.S.E.E. L.209 J.D.
(adm. in IL; not adm. in CA; Pat.) 1215 Parkview Ave.
Dewberry, Steven E., (AV) ......... '52 '80 C.940 L.809 J.D. [S.Dewberry]
Dewberry, Steven, Law Office of, A Professional Corporation, (AV) .....221 E. Walnut St.
Dickerson, Nancy B. .........'55 '84 C.188 B.S. L.596 J.D. Clk., U.S. Bkrptcy. App. Panel
Dickson, Christina E. ......... '50 '81 C.188 B.A. L.1065 J.D. 225 S. Lake Ave., 9th Fl.
Dickstein, Sallie L. ......... '61 '89 C.112 B.A. L.398 J.D. 117 E. Colorado Blvd.
**Dillard, David A.** ......... '52 '81 C.1075 B.S. L.1137 J.D. [Christie,P.&H.]
*PRACTICE AREAS: Patent, Trademark, Copyright and Unfair Competition Litigation.
Dodson, William D. ......... '47 '77 C.1258 B.A. L.426 J.D. Sr. Dep. City Atty.
**Dollar, Edward E.** ......... '43 '91 C.37 B.S. L.1186 J.D. [Ⓐ Cooper,K.&S.]
**Dorman, Roderick G.** ......... '50 '76 C.674 A.B. L.472 J.D. [Christie,P.&H.]
*PRACTICE AREAS: Antitrust Litigation; Business Law; Torts Litigation; Contracts Litigation; Patent, Trademark, Copyright and Unfair Competition Litigation.
**D'Oro, Frank J.** ......... '53 '78 C.323 B.A. L.990 J.D. [Collins,C.M.&T.]
*PRACTICE AREAS: General Liability; Public Liability; Premises Liability.

**Dosch, Lowell John, Law Office of, (AV) '45 '72 C&L.800 A.B., J.D.**
**301 N. Lake Avenue, 10th Floor, 91101-4107**
**Telephone: 818-577-1663 Fax: 818-793-5900**
**Civil Litigation in all State and Federal Courts, Insurance Defense, Construction Industry Law, Probate Litigation, Business Law, Commercial Litigation.**
**Representative Clients: Moffa Electrical Services, Inc.; Evilsizer Construction, Inc.; Marks Engineering and Grading Inc.; Absolut Construction; GTE.**

***See Professional Biographies, PASADENA, CALIFORNIA***

**Doshay, Steven** .... '53 '78 C.112 B.A. L.809 J.D. Coun., Kaiser Found. Health Plan, Inc.
Dourian, Robert, Law Offices of ......... '56 '84 C.112 B.A. L.398 J.D. 150 S. Los Robles
**Downer, Steven D.** ......... '52 '79 C.309 B.A. L.1065 J.D. [Fish,F.&D.]

**Downey, Thomas H. '47 '73 C.951 B.A. L.800 J.D.**
**Pasadena Corporate Center, Box 29, 225 South Lake Avenue, Suite 410, 91101-3005**
**Telephone: 818-577-9970 Fax: 818-796-6839**
**General Practice, Estate Planning including Wills and Trusts, Probate. Civil Litigation.**

***See Professional Biographies, PASADENA, CALIFORNIA***

**Doyle, John C.**, (AV) ......... '53 '78 C&L.770 B.A., J.D. [Cairns,D.L.N.&S.]
*PRACTICE AREAS: Insurance Law; Insurance Defense; Construction and General Civil Litigation.
**Doyle, Michael C.**, (AV) ......... '42 '69 C.150 B.B.A. L.1340 J.D. [Stone&D.]
*PRACTICE AREAS: Corporate; Tax Planning; Probate.
Doyle, Patricia Y. ......... '63 '94 C.103 A.B. L.426 J.D. 201 S. Lake Ave., 606
**Drage, Christine E.** ......... '68 '93 C.1049 B.A. L.101 J.D. [Ⓐ Collins,C.M.&T.]
*PRACTICE AREAS: Construction Defect; Architects and Engineers Professional Liability; Products Liability; Personal Injury Defense.
Draper, Marti Ann ......... '50 '76 C.112 B.A. L.426 J.D. 25 E. Union St.
Driscoll, Ellen F. ......... '54 '81 C.629 B.S. L.809 J.D. [Driscoll&D.]
Driscoll, William P. ......... '51 '78 C.800 B.S. L.809 J.D. [Driscoll&D.] (⊙Los Angeles)
Driscoll & Driscoll ......... 65 N. Raymond Ave., Ste. 340
**Drozin, Garth Matthew** ......... '53 '87 C.1044 B.A. L.809 J.D. [Ⓐ Franscell,S.R.&L.]⊙
*LANGUAGES: Portuguese, Spanish, German, Italian.
*PRACTICE AREAS: Governmental Entity Defense; Civil Litigation; Products Liability; Construction Defect; Fraud.
Drummond, Forrest S. '10 '34 C&L.550 Ph.B., J.D.
(adm. in IL; not adm. in CA) 2930 San Pasqual‡
Dryden, Wayne S., (BV) ......... '37 '69 C.605 B.A. L.800 J.D. 909 E. Green St.
Dubeau, Robert W. ......... '30 '53 C&L.94 LL.B. P.O. Box 5987
**Duckworth, Liza B.** ......... '56 '85 C.1077 B.A. L.426 J.D. [Ⓐ Larr&P.]
*PRACTICE AREAS: Commercial Litigation; Real Property Litigation; General Business Litigation; Insurance Law.
Dundas, John A., II, (AV) ......... '33 '58 C&L.813 A.B., J.D. 510 S. Marengo Ave.
Dunlap, James E. ......... '18 '48 C&L.477 A.B., LL.B. 3825 Edgeview Dr.‡
**Dzien, Kenneth E.** '43 '68 C&L.209 B.A., J.D.
(adm. in IL; not adm. in CA) V.P. & Div. Claims Coun., Chicago Title Ins. Co.
**Eastham, R. Dabney** ......... '54 '84 C.945 B.S. L.569 J.D. [Ⓐ Christie,P.&H.]
*PRACTICE AREAS: Intellectual Property Litigation; Patent Prosecution.

**Eckerman, Theodore C., (AV) '26 '54 C&L.800 B.S., J.D.**
**350 West Colorado Boulevard Suite 310, 91105**
**Telephone: 818-792-2144 Los Angeles: 213-681-2880 Fax: 818-795-6982**
**(Certified Specialist, Family Law, The State Bar of California Board of Legal Specialization).**
**Family, Business and Real Estate Law.**
**Reference: First Interstate Bank (Pasadena Main Office).**

***See Professional Biographies, PASADENA, CALIFORNIA***

**Edwards, Andrew R., (AV) '20 '52 C.502 B.S. L.809 LL.B.**
**Suite 530, 180 South Lake Avenue, 91101**
**Telephone: 818-792-1555; Los Angeles: 213-681-8819**
**(Certified Specialist, Criminal Law, The State Bar of California Board of Legal Specialization).**
**General and Trial Practice in all State and Federal Courts. Criminal Trial Practice. Negligence Law.**
**Reference: Bank of America National Trust & Savings Assn., Pasadena Main Office.**

**Edwards, Thomas H., (AV) '47 '75 C&L.846 B.A., J.D.**
**301 North Lake Avenue, Seventh Floor, 91101**
**Telephone: 818-440-5211 Fax: 818-577-8597**
**Email: THEDWA@ix.netcom.com**
**Business, Construction, Employment and Labor Litigation, Antitrust and Trade Regulation, Insurance Law, Trial Practice in all State and Federal Courts.**

***See Professional Biographies, PASADENA, CALIFORNIA***

Eells, Gwen J. ......... '50 '78 C.350 B.S. L.352 J.D. 155 N. Lake Ave.
Elam, Michael H. ......... '46 '91 C.1042 B.A. L.426 J.D. 265 N. Euclid
**Ellerman, Jana** ......... '57 '86 C.675 B.A. L.426 J.D. [Carter,C.&E.]
*PRACTICE AREAS: Real Estate Law; Business Law; Litigation.
Elliott, Kyle Lynn ......... '68 '93 C&L.378 B.S.M.E., J.D. 350 W. Colorado Blvd. (Pat.)
Epstein, Bruce Howard '52 '77 C.112 B.A. L.1065 J.D.
Coun. & Secy., Continental Lawyers Title Co.
**Epstein, Mark J.** ......... '55 '92 C.061 B.S. L.809 J.D. [Ⓐ Laughlin,F.L.&M.]
*PRACTICE AREAS: Workers' Compensation.
Eskijian, Nancy L. ......... '50 '75 C&L.800 B.A., J.D. Sr. Coun., The Parsons Corp.
Evans, Daniel M., (AV) ......... '37 '68 C.668 B.A. L.800 J.D. P.O. Box 93157
Evans, David R. ......... '46 '78 C.31 B.A. L.260 J.D. 35 S. Raymond
Evans, William D. ......... '29 '56 C.976 B.A. L.893 LL.B. 117 E. Colorado Blvd.
Ewert, James W. ......... '58 '94 C.1097 B.A. L.1190 J.D. 625 S. Fair Oaks Ave., Ste. 229
Ezor, A. Edward ......... '41 '72 C.800 B.S. L.1148 J.D. 201 S. Lake Ave.
Failer, David H. ......... '55 '81 C.597 B.A. L.910 J.D. 141 E. Walnut St.
**Fairshter, Matthew J.** ......... '61 '87 C.112 B.A. L.1049 J.D. [Fairshter&Assoc.]
*LANGUAGES: German, Spanish.
*PRACTICE AREAS: Business Law; Corporate Law.

**Fairshter & Associates**
**225 S. Lake Avenue, 9th Floor, 91101**
**Telephone: 818-568-1200 Fax: 818-568-8930**
**Matthew J. Fairshter. Of Counsel: Nairie A. Balian.**
**Corporate, Business, Bankruptcy, Entertainment, Media, International Transactions, Finance and Real Estate Law.**
**Representative Clients: Paul Davis Systems; Los Angeles New Service; Ventana Financial Services Group; Prico, Inc.; Chateau Mortgage Corp.; Newsreel Video Services; ABC Liovin Drilling; Inc.; Real Property Investment Services, Inc.; USCAN Free Trade Zones, Inc.**
**Reference: Wells Fargo Bank.**

***See Professional Biographies, PASADENA, CALIFORNIA***

**Falkenhainer, William C., (Professional Corporation)**, (AV) '34 '60
C&L.426 B.S., LL.B. [Fish,F.&D.]
Fallat, John L., Law Offices of '55 '84
C.112 B.A. L.61 J.D. 225 S. Lake Ave., Suite 300⊙
Falvey, Thomas W., (BV) ......... '46 '75 C.112 B.A. L.1068 J.D. 225 S. Lake Ave., 9th Fl.
**Farah, David** ......... '58 '93 C&L.477 B.S., J.D. [Ⓐ Sheldon&M.] (See Pat. Sect.)
*PRACTICE AREAS: Patent, Trademark and Copyright.
**Farber, Laura V.** ......... '65 '90 C.112 B.A. L.276 J.D. [Hahn&H.]
*LANGUAGES: Spanish.
*PRACTICE AREAS: Civil Litigation.
**Fehervari, Jeffrey A.** ......... '70 '95 C.976 B.S. L.893 J.D. [Ⓐ Christie,P.&H.]
**Feinberg, Richard I.**, (AV) ......... '38 '67 C.821 B.A. L.800 J.D. [R.I.Feinberg]

**Feinberg, Richard I., A Law Corporation, (AV)**
**301 East Colorado Boulevard, Suite 800, 91101**
**Telephone: 818-304-0805 FAX: 818-449-0946**
**Richard I. Feinberg.**
**Medical Malpractice and Personal Injury Law.**

***See Professional Biographies, PASADENA, CALIFORNIA***

Felice, Kathleen Dougherty ......... '52 '78 C.766 B.A. L.809 J.D. [Ⓒ Hogue&L.]
Fellman, Gerry L., (AV) ......... '32 '56 C&L.546 B.S., J.D.,LL.B 510 S. Marengo Ave.
Fergoda, Carolyn M. ......... '47 '83 C.112 A.B. L.770 J.D. 215 N. Marengo, 3rd Fl.
**Ferguson, Nohemi Gutierrez** ......... '60 '86 C.154 B.A. L.1068 J.D. [Gutierrez&P.]
*LANGUAGES: Spanish, French.
*PRACTICE AREAS: Civil Litigation; Police Liability Defense; Employer Liability; Local Government Liability; Civil Rights Defense.
Fernandez, Ferdinand F. ......... '37 '63 C&L.800 B.S.E.E., LL.B. U.S. Cir. J.
Fernandez, Javier F. ......... '46 '89 C.1097 B.A. L.940 J.D. 301 N. Lake Ave.
Ferns, Barry W., (AV) ......... '51 '77 C.1077 B.A. L.1095 J.D. [Ferns&F.]⊙
Ferns & Ferns, (AV) ......... 221 E. Walnut (⊙Concord)
Fertig, David R. ......... '56 '87 L.1238 J.D. 16 N. Marengo Ave.
Fields, Everett F. ......... '45 '77 C.426 B.A. L.1095 J.D. Pasadena Police Dept.
Fildew, Richard C. ......... '13 '38 L.809 LL.B. Ret. Supr. Ct. J.
Files, Gordon L., (AV) ......... '12 '37 C.112 A.B. L.976 LL.B. 154 S. Arroyo Blvd.‡

**Fine, Edward L. '34 '75 C.347 B.S. L.1148 J.D.**
**350 West Colorado Boulevard Suite 200, 91105**
**Telephone: 818-792-5177 Fax: 818-568-0930**
***PRACTICE AREAS: Bankruptcy.**
**Bankruptcy.**

***See Professional Biographies, PASADENA, CALIFORNIA***

CAA485P

Finn, Evelynn M., (AV) ................'24 '62 C&L.800 B.S., LL.B. 3665 Greenhill Rd.‡
**Finnell, Gary J.** '51 '77 C.560 B.A. L.1065 J.D.
(adm. in AK; not adm. in CA) Sr. Claims Coun., Chicago Title Ins. Co.
Fischer, John R. ........................'46 '76 C.1097 B.A. L.809 J.D. 35 S. Raymond
**Fischler, Marvin G.** ..................'57 '82 C.154 B.A. L.464 J.D. [Hosp,G.&Assoc.]
*PRACTICE AREAS: Tort Defense; Emphasizing Construction Defects and Soils Matters; Auto; Bankruptcy; Commercial and Banking Litigation.
**Fish, Paul W.** '33 '65 C.128 B.E.E. L.273 LL.B.
(adm. in DC; not adm. in CA; See Pat. Sect.) [🄲 Christie,P.&H.]
*PRACTICE AREAS: Patent, Trademark and Copyright Law; Computer Law; Lease Law; Corporate Law.
**Fish, Vincent, (Professional Corporation)**, (AV) '32 '63
C.1258 A.B. L.800 LL.B. [Fish,F.&D.]
*PRACTICE AREAS: Products Liability Litigation; Environmental Litigation; Construction Litigation.

**Fish, Falkenhainer & Downer, (AV)**
**An Association of Independent Counsel**
**301 East Colorado, Suite 200, 91101**
**Telephone: 213-626-8711**
**Members of Firm: Vincent Fish (Professional Corporation); William C. Falkenhainer (Professional Corporation); Steven D. Downer. Of Counsel: Clay Robbins, III.**
**General Civil.**

Fisher, James R., (BV) ............'50 '78 C.1188 B.A. L.61 J.D. 301 E. Colorado Blvd.
Fitzgerald, Ronald W. ..........'50 '78 C.112 B.A. L.1137 J.D. Topa Thrift & Loan Assn.
Fleming, Clarence E., Jr., (AV) '27 '54 C.813 B.A. L.800 J.D.
350 West Colorado Blvd.
Flores, David A. ........................'55 '82 C&L.800 A.B., J.D. Calif. Inst. of Tech.
**Flowers, John L.**, (AV) ......'41 '66 C&L.800 B.S.L., J.D. [J.L.Flowers] (⊙Los Angeles)
*REPORTED CASES: Springs Industries, Inc. v. Kris Knit, Inc. (9th Circuit 1989) 880 F.2d 1129.
*PRACTICE AREAS: Civil Litigation; Trust Planning; Business Planning; Estate Planning; Trust and Estate Litigation.

**Flowers, John L., P.C., Law Offices of, (AV)**
**225 South Lake Avenue, Third Floor, 91105**
**Telephone: 818-432-5494 Fax: 818-432-5401**
**John L. Flowers.**
**Civil Litigation, Trusts, Business and Estate Planning.**
***See Professional Biographies, PASADENA, CALIFORNIA***

**Fogel, Joseph P.** ......................'66 '91 C.145 B.A. L.1065 J.D. [🄰 Cooper,K.&S.]
*PRACTICE AREAS: Insurance Defense Law; Intellectual Property Law; Litigation.
Fogliani, Theodore J., (BV) .............'42 '75 C.813 A.B. L.809 J.D. 199 S. Los Robles
Folven, Fairy J. ....................'38 '62 C&L.629 B.S., LL.B. 1444 E. Mountain St.‡
**Foss, Howard W.** .........................'46 '73 C.309 A.B. L.1066 J.D. [🄲 Foss&R.]
**Foss, Linda Judd** ............................'49 '73 C.837 B.S. L.1066 J.D. [Foss&R.]
*PRACTICE AREAS: Financial Institutions; Creditor Rights; Bankruptcy; Real Estate.

**Foss & Roberts**
**Ninth Floor 225 South Lake Avenue, 91101**
**Telephone: 818-683-4925 Facsimile: 818-683-3986**
**Members of Firm: Linda Judd Foss; Patrick M. Roberts. Of Counsel: Howard W. Foss.**
**Financial Institutions, Creditor Rights, Bankruptcy, Real Estate, Workouts, Insolvency, Commercial Law.**
***See Professional Biographies, PASADENA, CALIFORNIA***

**Fossier, Michael P.** '54 '78
C.976 B.A. L.309 J.D. Sr. Coun., Kaiser Found. Health Plan, Inc.
Fountain, F. Rayford, (AV) ..........'37 '64 C.1060 B.A. L.1065 J.D. 1000 E. Walnut St.
**Francis, William R.**, (BV) ............'42 '71 C.940 B.A. L.426 J.D. [🄰 Freeburg,J.&N.]
*PRACTICE AREAS: Business Law; Commercial Law; Banking Litigation; Insurance; Personal Injury.
**Franscell, George J.**, (AV) .........'33 '59 C.426 B.A. L.1068 J.D. [Franscell,S.R.&L.]⊙
*PRACTICE AREAS: Police Misconduct Liability Defense; Civil Rights; Municipal and Administrative Law; Medical Malpractice Legal; General Civil.

**Franscell, Strickland, Roberts & Lawrence, A Professional Corporation, (AV)** ▣
**Penthouse, 225 South Lake Avenue, 91101-3005**⊙
**Telephone: 818-304-7830; 213-684-7830 Fax: 818-795-7460**
**George J. Franscell; Tracy Strickland (Resident, Santa Ana Office); Barbara E. Roberts (Resident, Riverside Office); David D. Lawrence; Carol Ann Rohr; Scott D. MacLatchie; S. Frank Harrell (Resident, Santa Ana Office); Donald C. McFarlane (Resident, Santa Ana Office); Libby Wong; Cindy S. Lee; Martin J. De Vries (Resident, Riverside Office); Ann Marie Sanders; Priscilla F. Slocum; Garth Matthew Drozin.**
**Police Misconduct Liability Defense, Civil Rights Defense, Employment Defense, Municipal and Administrative Law, Legal Malpractice, Medical Malpractice, General Civil and Criminal Trial and Appellate Practice and Litigation.**
**Santa Ana, California Office: Suite 800, 401 Civic Center Drive West. Telephone: 714-543-6511. Fax: 714-543-6711.**
**Riverside, California Office: Suite 670, 3801 University Avenue. Telephone: 909-686-1000. Fax: 909-686-2565.**
***See Professional Biographies, PASADENA, CALIFORNIA***

**Freeburg, Karen S.**, (AV) ...........'46 '72 C.1168 B.A. L.426 J.D. [🄰 Freeburg,J.&N.]
*PRACTICE AREAS: Products Liability; Personal Injury Defense.
**Freeburg, Steven J.**, (AV) ...............'44 '71 C.154 B.A. L.426 J.D. [Freeburg,J.&N.]
*PRACTICE AREAS: Products Liability; Insurance; Personal Injury Defense; Wrongful Termination; Employment Discrimination.

**Freeburg, Judy & Nettels, (AV)** ▣
**600 South Lake Avenue, 91106**⊙
**Telephone: 818-585-4150 FAX: 818-585-0718**
**Steven J. Freeburg; J. Lawrence Judy; Charles F. Nettels. Associates: Ingall W. Bull, Jr.; Richard B. Castle; Cynthia B. Schaldenbrand (Resident, Santa Ana Office); Robert S. Brody; Holly A. McNulty; Karen S. Freeburg; Jennifer D. Helsel; William R. Francis; Fred W. Brandt; Carla Crochet.**
**General Civil Trial and Appellate Practice. Casualty, Malpractice, Products Liability, Insurance and Environmental Law. Personal Defense.**
**Santa Ana, California Office: Xerox Centre. 1851 East First Street, Suite 120. 92705-4017. Telephone: 714-569-0950. Facsimile: 714-569-0955.**
***See Professional Biographies, PASADENA, CALIFORNIA***

**Freeman, Mary A.** '46 '78
C.494 B.A. L.1049 J.D. Asst. Gen. Coun., Avery Dennison Corp.
*RESPONSIBILITIES: Corporate Law; Employment Law; Environmental Law.
Frewing, H. Kent .......................'38 '68 C.111 B.S. L.770 J.D. Jet Propulsion Lab.
Friedman, Michael E. ...............'51 '76 C.112 B.A. L.1067 J.D. 215 N. Marengo Ave.
Funaro, Charles W., II .................'50 '78 C.1077 B.A. L.1095 J.D. 100 N. Hill Ave.

**Gallo, James A., (AV) '50 '77 C&L.426 B.A., J.D.**
**Suite One, The Bryan Court 427 South Marengo Avenue, 91101**
**Telephone: 818-304-0909 Facsimile: 818-304-0071**
**Civil Litigation in all State and Federal Courts. Real Estate, Criminal Defense and Business Litigation.**
***See Professional Biographies, PASADENA, CALIFORNIA***

Gancedo, Hector G. ....... '58 '87 C.1169 B.A. L.800 J.D. 625 S. Fair Oaks Ave., Ste. 229
**Garr, William S., (P.C.)** ...........................'59 '85 C&L.800 B.A., J.D. [Hahn&H.]
*LANGUAGES: Spanish.
*PRACTICE AREAS: Federal and State Court Civil Trial Litigation; Appellate Practice.
**Garrett, Robert**, (AV) .......................'50 '75 C.800 A.B. L.1068 J.D. [Garrett&T.]
*PRACTICE AREAS: Business Litigation; Real Estate Litigation; Professional Liability.

**Garrett & Tully, A Professional Corporation, (AV)**
**35 Hugus Alley, Suite 300, 91103**⊙
**Telephone: 818-577-9500 Telecopier: 818-577-0813**

(This Listing Continued)



**Garrett & Tully, A Professional Corporation (Continued)**
**Stephen J. Tully (Resident, Westlake Village Office); Robert Garrett; Stephen C. Chuck; Efren A. Compeán; Kevin S. Lacey; Peter B. Langbord; Kelli M. Wehn; Daniel David Kopman; Christopher G. Piety (Resident, Westlake Village Office). Of Counsel: James A. Moss.**
**Professional Liability, Legal Malpractice, Accountant Malpractice, Business and Real Estate Litigation in all State and Federal Courts.**
**Reference: 1st Business Bank, Los Angeles.**
**Westlake Village, California Office: 660 Hampshire Road, Suite 204. 91361. Telephone: 805-446-4141. Telecopier: 805-446-4135.**
***See Professional Biographies, PASADENA, CALIFORNIA***

**Gaston, Daniel K.**, (AV) ....................'51 '83 C.112 B.A. L.809 J.D. [Russell,H.&J.]
*PRACTICE AREAS: Administrative Law; Transportation Law; Commercial Law.
**Gee, Karen M.** ......................'60 '87 C.976 B.S. L.1066 J.D. [🄲 Bensinger,G.&R.]
*PRACTICE AREAS: Criminal and Civil Litigation; Entertainment Law.
Gelder, J. Thomas '49 '74 C.477 B.B.A. L.345 J.D.
(adm. in IN; not adm. in CA) Coun., Calif. Inst. of Tech.
**Gelfound, Craig A.** ............... '60 '95 C.763 B.S.E.E. L.809 J.D. [🄰 Christie,P.&H.]
*PRACTICE AREAS: Patents; Trademarks; Copyrights.
**Gibson, James L.**, (AV) .....................'40 '67 C.999 B.A. L.800 J.D. [Gibson&R.]
*PRACTICE AREAS: Employer-Employee Law; Personal Injury; Probate Litigation; Medical Malpractice.

**Gibson and Rivera, (AV)**
**55 South Lake Avenue, Suite 550, 91101**
**Telephone: 818-405-1122 Facsimile: 818-405-8966**
**Members of Firm: James L. Gibson; Clark W. Rivera.**
**General Business Litigation, including Real Estate, Unfair Business Practices, Employer-Employee Relations, Plaintiff and Defendant Personal Injury, Wrongful Death, Premises Liability Law and Probate Litigation.**
***See Professional Biographies, PASADENA, CALIFORNIA***

Giermann, Edward C., (AV) '47 '78
C.37 B.S. L.809 J.D. V.P. & Gen. Coun., J.G. Boswell Co.
Gilbert, James A., (BV) .............'16 '41 C.112 A.B. L.800 J.D. 16 N. Marengo Ave.‡
**Gilbert, Warren L.** ....................'51 '80 C.112 A.B. L.809 J.D. [Hosp,G.&Assoc.]
*REPORTED CASES: Hughes v. SCRTD (1985) 173 CA 3d 512, 219CR82.
*PRACTICE AREAS: Tort Defense Law; Products Liability; Premises Liability; Automotive Defects; Construction Defects.
Gille, Randolph K. ................'51 '85 C.1068 B.S. L.1136 J.D. 131 N. El Molino Ave.
Goldbach, Marc A. ..............................'57 '87 C.112 B.A. L.809 J.D. [🄰 Mills]
Goldberg, Larry '47 '74 C.112 B.A. L.426 J.D.
Corp. Coun., Gemstar Development Corporation (⊙Beverly Hills)
Golden, Stephen R. ....................'54 '93 C.1097 L.1190 J.D. 444 S. Pasadena Ave.

**Goldman, Martin B., (AV) '42 '70 C.4 B.A. L.1009 J.D.**
**CenFed Bank Building, 301 East Colorado Boulevard Suite 616, 91101**
**Telephone: 818-793-6774; 213-681-9160**
**(Certified Specialist, Probate, Estate Planning and Trust Law, The State Bar of California Board of Legal Specialization).**
**Probate, Estate Planning, Elder Law, Wills, Living Trusts, Trusts, Conservatorship and Guardianship.**
**References: Citizens Business Bank; Sanwa Bank; Northern Trust Co.; Senior Care Network; Huntington Hospital, Pasadena, Ca.**

Goldsmith, Claude O. '32 '56 C&L.608 B.S., J.D.
(adm. in OH; not adm. in CA) 1415 Lomita Dr.‡
**Goldstein, Sol L.** '25 '55 C.46 B.S.Ch.E. L.424 J.D.
(adm. in IL; not adm. in CA; See Pat. Sect.) [🄲 Sheldon&M.]
Gonzalez, Carmen R. ..................'63 '89 C.112 B.A. L.1068 J.D. Bandy & Koester

**Good, Ned, The Law Offices of, (AV) '28 '51 C&L.800 B.S., LL.B.**
**70 South Lake Avenue, 91101**
**Telephone: 818-440-0000 Telecopier: 818-449-0214**
***REPORTED CASES: Rodriguez v. McDonnell Douglas - damages; Newing v. Cheatham - aviation; Solis v. So. Cal. RTD - experts; Canavin v. PSA - prejudgment interests, taxes, jury verdicts; Nevels v. Yeager - bystander rule.**
***PRACTICE AREAS: Aviation; Personal Injury; Product Liability; Wrongful Death.**
**Associates: Mark West; Cary S. Macy; B. Eric Nelson.**
**Practice Restricted to Plaintiff Personal Injury, Aviation and Malpractice Law in all State and Federal Courts.**
**Reference: Union Bank, Pasadena, California.**
***See Professional Biographies, PASADENA, CALIFORNIA***

Goodin, Stephen J. '45 '75
C&L.502 B.A., J.D. Assoc. Coun., Continental Lawyers Title Co.
Goodwin, Alfred T. ............................ '23 '51 C&L.629 B.A., J.D. U.S. Sr. Cir. J.
Goodwine, J. William, Jr. '66 '91 C.602 B.S. L.309 J.D.
(adm. in IL; not adm. in CA) 385 S. Catalina Ave.‡
Gordon, Carolyn A. ......................'64 '90 C.838 B.S. L.809 J.D. 301 N. Lake Ave.
Gordon, Lance B. ...................... '55 '80 C.763 B.A. L.1065 J.D. 100 W. Walnut St.
Gorton, James A. ........................ '53 '82 C.623 B.A. L.1068 J.D. 221 E. Walnut St.
**Gosney, Timothy J.**, (AV) ..............'45 '74 C.112 B.A. L.61 J.D. [Lagerlof,S.B.&S.]

**Gotha, Frederick, (AV) '35 '67 C.679 B.S.A.E. L.767 J.D.** ▣
**Suite 823, 80 South Lake Avenue, 91101**
**Telephone: 818-796-1849 Telecopier: 818-405-0952**
**Patent, Trademark and Unfair Competition Law.**
***See Professional Biographies, PASADENA, CALIFORNIA***

Grace, Cecelia A. ............................ '60 '86 C.276 B.A. L.477 J.D. 1705 Homet Rd.
Graff, Cindy W., (AV) ....................... '54 '79 C.813 A.B. L.1068 J.D. [Shelley&G.]
Gragg, Walter L. ............................'29 '78 C.871 B.S. L.1224 J.D. [W.L.Gragg]
Gragg, Walter L., A Law Corporation ................................ 135 N. Marengo Ave.
**Gray, Lawrence S., Jr.**, (AV) ............. '28 '54 C.668 B.A. L.800 LL.B. [Gray&H.] ‡

**Gray & Hirrel, (AV)**
**Suite 600, 301 East Colorado Boulevard, 91101**
**Telephone: 818-795-3344 Los Angeles: 213-681-0665 Telecopier: 818-796-2683**
**Members of Firm: Lawrence S. Gray, Jr. (Retired); Richard J. Hirrel.**
**Probate and Estate Planning, Trusts and Taxation.**
**Reference: Citizens Commercial Trust & Savings Bank (Pasadena Main Office).**
***See Professional Biographies, PASADENA, CALIFORNIA***

**Grayson, Pegine E.** .................. '61 '87 C.478 B.A. L.800 J.D. [Bensinger,G.&R.]
*LANGUAGES: Spanish.
*PRACTICE AREAS: Employment Discrimination; Sexual Harassment; Family and Divorce Mediation.
**Greaves, Charles J., (P.C.)** ................... '55 '81 C.800 A.B. L.93 J.D. [Hahn&H.]
*PRACTICE AREAS: Civil Litigation.
Green, Barrett Kenneth ...........................'65 '89 C&L.012 LL.B. [🄰 Jones&M.]
Green, Patrick T. ....................... '51 '91 C.612 B.S. L.809 J.D. 1010 E. Union St.
**Gregg, Gene E., Jr. (P.C.)** .................... '52 '79 C.605 A.B. L.464 J.D. [Hahn&H.]
*PRACTICE AREAS: Corporations; Business; Employment Law.
Greifzu, Carl W. ........................... '43 '72 C.446 A.B. L.276 J.D. 300 S. Mentor
Griffin, Harry L. '14 '38 C.627 L.45 LL.B.
(adm. in AR; not adm. in CA) 1140 Riviera Dr.‡
Grimm, Rosemary .........................'44 '79 C.1097 L.426 J.D. P.O. Box 94153

**Grinnell, John P.**, (AV) '35 '68 C.367 B.E.S. L.262 J.D. [Christie,P.&H.] (See Pat. Sect.)
*PRACTICE AREAS: Patents; Trademarks; Copyrights.
Grogin, Jeffrey P. .......... '60 '87 C.260 B.S. L.426 J.D. [Samaha,G.&S.]
**Gronemeier, Dale L.**, (AV) .......... '39 '75 C.338 B.S. L.339 J.D. [Gronemeier&B.]
*PRACTICE AREAS: Employment Discrimination Law; Business Law; Civil Rights Law.

**Gronemeier & Barker, (AV)**
**55 South Lake Avenue, Suite 220, P.O. Box 90670, 91109-0670**
**Telephone: 818-568-4600 Los Angeles, California: 213-681-0702 Fax: 818-449-7560**
**Members of Firm: Dale L. Gronemeier; Neil J. Barker. Associates: Ellen R. Hurley.**
**Commercial, Business, Labor, Employment Discrimination, Real Estate, Land Use, Banking, Civil Rights and Public Law. Civil Litigation.**
***See Professional Biographies, PASADENA, CALIFORNIA***

Guerry, Connie .......... '38 '83 C.1097 B.S. L.809 J.D. 301 E. Colorado Blvd.
**Guterres, Tomas A.** .......... '65 '91 C.94 B.A. L.426 J.D. [▣ Collins,C.M.&T.]
*LANGUAGES: Spanish, Japanese, Portuguese.
*PRACTICE AREAS: Architects and Engineers Professional Liability; Construction Law; Products Liability; Premises Liability; Public Liability.

**Gutierrez & Preciado**
**200 South Los Robles Suite 210, 91105**
**Telephone: 818-449-2300 Facsimile: 818-449-2330**
**Email: apreciado@gutierrez-preciado.com URL: http://www.primenet.com/~crh4**
**Members of Firm: Arthur C. Preciado; Nohemi Gutierrez Ferguson; Calvin R. House. Associates: Gabrielle Harner Brumbach; Elisabeth F. Sheh; Brian P. Walter; Clifton A. Baker. Of Counsel: Linda L. Streeter.**
**Police Liability Defense, Civil Rights Defense, Employer Liability, Appellate Practice, Civil Litigation, Insurance Defense and Local Government Liability.**
***See Professional Biographies, PASADENA, CALIFORNIA***

**Gwire, William**, (AV) '46 '74
C.1193 B.A. L.284 J.D. [▣ Cooper,K.&S.] (⊙San Francisco)
Hadsell, Barbara E. .......... '45 '79 C.112 B.A. L.1068 J.D. [Hadsell&S.]
Hadsell & Stormer, (AV) .......... 128 N. Fair Oaks Ave.

**Haefliger, William W., (AV) '25 '56 C.111 B.S. L.426 LL.B.**
**Suite 512, 201 South Lake Avenue, 91101**
**Telephone: 818-449-0467 Los Angeles: 213-684-2707**
**Intellectual Property, Patent, Trademark, Copyright and Unfair Competition Law.**
**Reference: Union Bank (Pasadena Main Office).**
***See Professional Biographies, PASADENA, CALIFORNIA***

Hager, Ronald B., (AV) .......... '35 '60 C.267 B.A. L.800 LL.B. 180 S. Lake Ave.
**Hahn, Stanley L., (P.C.)**, (AV) .......... '10 '34 C.668 A.B. L.309 LL.B. [▣ Hahn&H.]
*PRACTICE AREAS: Estate Planning; Probate Law.

**Hahn & Hahn, (AV)** ▣
**A Partnership including Professional Corporations**
**Ninth Floor, 301 East Colorado Boulevard, 91101**
**Telephone: 818-796-9123 Los Angeles: 213-681-6948 Orange Co.: 714-971-5590 Cable Address: "Hahnlaw" Telecopier: 818-449-7357**
**Members of Firm: David K. Robinson (P.C.); Loren H. Russell (P.C.); Leonard M. Marangi (P.C.) (Certified Specialist, Family Law, The State Bar of California Board of Legal Specialization); William S. Johnstone, Jr., (P.C.) (Certified Specialist, Taxation Law, Probate, Estate Planning and Trust Law, The State Bar of California Board of Legal Specialization); George R. Baffa (P.C.); Don Mike Anthony (P.C.) (Certified Specialist, Family Law, The State Bar of California Board of Legal Specialization); Robert W. Anderson; William K. Henley (P.C.); Clark R. Byam (P.C.); Richard L. Hall (P.C.); Susan T. House (P.C.) (Certified Specialist, Estate Planning, Trust and Probate Law, The State Bar of California Board of Legal Specialization); Dianne H. Bukata; Gene E. Gregg, Jr. (P.C.); R. Scott Jenkins (P.C.); Charles J. Greaves (P.C.); Dale R. Pelch; William S. Garr (P.C.); Karl I. Swaidan; Sandra K. Murphy; Laura V. Farber; Tali Shaddow. Of Counsel: Stanley L. Hahn (P.C.); George E. Zillgitt; Emrys J. Ross.**
**General Civil and Trial and Appellate Practice in Federal and State Courts, Corporation, Real Estate, Estate Planning, Probate, Family, Federal and State Tax Law, Employment Law.**
**Representative Clients: Becton Dickinson & Co.; California Institute of Technology; City of Glendale; City of Pasadena, City of Long Beach; Flint Ink Corp.; Pasadena Tournament of Roses Assn.; Symes Cadillac, Inc.**
***See Professional Biographies, PASADENA, CALIFORNIA***

Haight, James T. .......... '24 '52 C&L.966 B.A., LL.B. 1390 Ridge Way
Hale, C. Russell, (AV) .......... '16 '50 C.813 A.B. L.262 J.D. 350 W. Colorado Blvd. (Pat.)
Hall, Alan L. .......... '44 '70 C&L.94 B.S.B.A., J.D. Raymar Book Corp.
Hall, Charlene S. .......... '25 '76 C.800 B.A. L.809 J.D. 422 S. Orange Grove Blvd.‡
Hall, Cynthia Holcomb .......... '29 '54 C&L.813 A.B., J.D. U.S. Cir. J.
**Hall, Richard L., (P.C.)**, (AV) .......... '38 '73 C.770 B.S.C. L.426 J.D. [Hahn&H.]
*PRACTICE AREAS: Real Property; Civil Litigation.
Hamidi, Marianne S. .... '60 '92 C.112 B.A. L.809 J.D. Pat. Atty., Calif. Institute of Tech.
**Hamilton, David J.** .......... '53 '80 C.1032 B.M.E. L.800 J.D. [Hamilton&C.]
*PRACTICE AREAS: Employment Representation; Management Labor Law; Airline Labor Law; Trade Secrets; Wrongful Termination Defense.

**Hamilton & Cumare**
**301 North Lake Avenue, Suite 320, 91101**
**Telephone: 818-585-2765 Fax: 818-585-2764**
**Rosa M. C. Cumare; David J. Hamilton.**
**Employment Discrimination, Trade Secrets, Traditional Labor Law and Client Counseling (Management), Age Discrimination, Civil Rights Defense, Americans with Disabilities Act, Wrongful Termination Defense, Sexual Harassment, Affirmative Action, Collective Bargaining, Employer Rights, Employment Contracts, Labor Relations, Personnel Policies, Title VII Discrimination, Wage and Hour Law and Whistleblower Litigation.**
***See Professional Biographies, PASADENA, CALIFORNIA***

**Hammond, P. Theodore**, (AV) .......... '47 '72 C&L.800 B.S., J.D. [▣ Hammond,Z.&C.]
*PRACTICE AREAS: Medical Malpractice; Personal Injury Law; Health Care Law.

**Hammond, Zuetel & Cahill, (AV)** ▣
**Suite 540, 180 South Lake Avenue, 91101**
**Telephone: 818-449-5144; 213-684-2898 FAX: 213-684-1275**
**Members of Firm: Kenneth R. Zuetel, Jr.; Richard F. Cahill. Associates: Cynthia L.K. Steele; Victoria K. Torigian. Of Counsel: John C. Cushman; P. Theodore Hammond.**
**General Civil and Trial Practice. Medical Malpractice, Personal Injury.**
***See Professional Biographies, PASADENA, CALIFORNIA***

**Hancock, Robert W.**, (AV) .......... '30 '63 C.597 B.S. L.800 LL.B. [Russell,H.&J.]
*REPORTED CASES: Liptak v. Diane Apartments, Inc., 109 Cal. App. 3d 762; 167 Cal. Rptr. 440 (1980).
*PRACTICE AREAS: Commercial Litigation; Land Subsidence Litigation; Probate.
**Harb, Noelle L.** '68 '95
C.800 B.A. L.990 J.D. Asst. Coun., Countrywide Home Loans, Inc.
Hardin, Terrence J. .......... '48 '82 C.1077 B.A. L.1095 J.D. 301 E. Colorado Blvd.

**Harding, Richard C. '47 '73 C.276 B.A. L.426 J.D.**
**35 S. Raymond Avenue Suite 400, 91105-1971**
**Telephone: 818-304-0320 Fax: 818-578-0768**
**General Civil Practice in State and Federal Courts. Appeals and Business Transactional Law, Personal Injury Law.**
***See Professional Biographies, PASADENA, CALIFORNIA***

Hardy, Lesley L. .......... '54 '80 C.112 B.A. L.426 J.D. 180 S. Lake Ave.‡
Hare, John P. .......... '24 '59 C.605 B.A. L.426 655 Euclid Ave.‡

**Harman, Steven G.** .......... '55 '83 C.112 B.A. L.800 J.D. [Richardson&H.]
*PRACTICE AREAS: Civil Litigation; General Business Law; Real Estate.
**Harpole, Myron E.**, (AV) .......... '27 '50 C.112 B.A. L.309 J.D. [Witter&H.]⊙
*PRACTICE AREAS: Federal and State Tax; Estate Planning; Tax Litigation; Trust and Probate Law; Arbitrator.
Harrell, Jack F. .......... '39 '71 L.990 J.D. Maryland Casualty Co.
Harris, George A., (AV) .......... '46 '72 C&L.800 B.S., J.D. 215 N. Marengo Ave., 3rd Fl.
**Harris, James D., (A Professional Corporation)**, (AV) '19 '48
C.378 B.S. L.813 LL.B. [▣ Witter&H.]
*PRACTICE AREAS: Federal and State Tax; Estate Planning; Tax Litigation; Trust and Probate Law.
Harris, William S., (AV) .......... '54 '79 C.668 B.A. L.800 J.D. [Stewart&H.]
Hart & Mieras, (BV) .......... 135 N. Los Robles Ave. Penthouse Ste 850
Hartman, Richard L., (BV) .......... '33 '72 C.112 B.A. L.990 J.D. [Hartman&F.]⊙
Hartman and Francis, (BV) .......... 1122 E. Green St., 2nd Fl. (⊙Palm Springs)
Hartson, David .......... '55 '85 C.112 B.A. L.809 J.D. 790 E. Colorado Blvd., Penthouse
Hartz, Edwin L., (AV) .......... '32 '63 C.174 B.S. L.776 LL.B. 350 W. Colo. Blvd. (Pat.)
**Hasan, Syed A.** .......... '68 '93 C.112 B.S.E.E. L.800 J.D. [▣ Christie,P.&H.]
*PRACTICE AREAS: Patents; Trademarks; Copyrights.
Hattersley, Patricia J. .......... '56 '83 C.112 B.A. L.426 J.D. 1000 E. Walnut St.
**Haulman, Robin L.** .......... '53 '92 C&L.1137 B.A., J.D. [▣ Baraban&T.]
*PRACTICE AREAS: Civil Litigation.
**Hawekotte, Angela** .......... '53 '80 C.525 B.A. L.426 J.D. [Adams&H.]
*LANGUAGES: French.
*PRACTICE AREAS: Tax Controversies; Tax Audits; International and Domestic Business Transactions; Taxation; Corporate Law.
Hawes, Eric Everett .......... '60 '88 C.1077 B.A. L.1186 J.D. 201 S. Lakw Ave., Ste. 606
Hawkins, H. Preston .......... '51 '78 C.800 B.S. L.990 J.D. 230 N. Lake Ave.
**Hawley, Kelli G.** .......... '60 '85 C.684 B.A. L.1049 J.D. [▣ Baraban&T.]
*PRACTICE AREAS: Civil Litigation; Construction Law.
Heckmann, Brian D., (BV) .......... '55 '82 C.477 B.S. L.809 J.D. 462 S. Marengo Ave.
Helge, Ralph K., & Associates, (AV) .......... '29 '54 C.597 L.209 J.D. 440 W. Green St.
**Helsel, Jennifer D.** .......... '57 '88 C.1077 B.A. L.809 J.D. [▣ Freeburg,J.&N.]
*PRACTICE AREAS: Malpractice; Employment; Personal Injury Defense.
**Henke, Robert E.** .......... '63 '90 C&L.608 B.A., J.D. [▣ McClaugherty&Assoc.]⊙
*PRACTICE AREAS: Insurance Defense.
**Henley, William K., (P.C.)**, (AV) .......... '44 '70 C.813 A.B. L.1065 J.D. [Hahn&H.]
*PRACTICE AREAS: Business Litigation; General Civil Litigation; Employment Litigation.
Henney, David D. .......... '56 '81 C.940 B.A. L.1148 J.D. 199 S. Los Robles
Henson, Larry D., (BV) .......... '42 '73 C.1097 B.S. L.800 J.D. [Henson&H.]⊙
Henson & Henson, (BV) .......... 338 S. Los Robles Ave. (⊙San Francisco)
Herlihy, Barry H., (AV) .......... '39 '64 C.37 B.S. L.800 J.D. 225 S. Lake Ave.
Hervey, Harcourt, III, (AV) .......... '46 '73 C.800 B.S. L.426 J.D. 815 N. Hill Ave.
**Hester, James C.**, (AV) .......... '45 '71 C.112 A.B. L.1065 J.D. [Laughlin,F.L.&M.]
*PRACTICE AREAS: Workers' Compensation.
**Hevia, Mariana A.** .......... '62 '89 C.112 B.A. L.61 J.D. [▣ Salz&S.]
*PRACTICE AREAS: Family Law.
Hill, Anthony J. .......... '44 '86 C.028 B.A. L.809 J.D. 260 S. Los Robles Ave.
Hill, Jonel C. '25 '51 C.490 L.748 LL.B.
(adm. in MN; not adm. in CA) 885 S. Orange Grove Blvd.‡
Hillman, Milton H. .......... '29 '90 C.472 B.S. L.1190 J.D. 1200 S. Oak Knoll Ave.
**Hirrel, Richard J.**, (AV) .......... '51 '80 C.800 B.A. L.1095 J.D. [Gray&H.]
*PRACTICE AREAS: Estate Planning; Probate Law; Trusts Law; Taxation Law.
Hodge, Brian Ray .......... '55 '79 C.813 B.A. L.1066 J.D. [Jett&L.]
Hoecker, Gary W., (AV) .......... '43 '69 C.112 A.B. L.767 J.D. 260 California Terr.
Hoegh, Richard B., (AV) .......... '21 '50 C.112 B.A.S. L.309 LL.B. 141 E. Walnut St.
**Hogan, Martha Burroughs**, (AV) .......... '29 '81 C.518 A.B. L.1068 J.D. [▣ Anglea&B.]
*PRACTICE AREAS: Estate Planning; Federal Estate and Gift Tax; Generation Skipping Tax; Family Wealth Transfer.
Hogue, Thomas D., (BV) .......... '50 '81 C.684 A.B. L.809 J.D. [Hogue&L.]
Hogue & Langhammer, (BV) .......... 180 S. Lake Ave.
Hollopeter, Charles, (AV) .......... '10 '35 C.642 L.1001 LL.B. Suite 823, 80 S. Lake Ave.
Hong, Frederick W. .......... '50 '77 C.112 B.A. L.426 J.D. 490 S. Fair Oaks Ave.
Hopkins, Albert E. .......... '28 '70 C.734 B.S. L.809 J.D. 1324 Wierfield Dr.
Hopkins, Ruth M. .......... '17 '49 C&L.912 LL.B. 925 E. Villa St.
Horn, Howard C. .......... '15 '52 L.809 1036 Cynthia Ave.
Horn, Sanford L., (AV) .......... '41 '67 C.112 B.A. L.800 J.D. 225 S. Lake Ave., 9th Fl.
**Hosp, F. Phillip**, (AV) .......... '44 '70 C.800 B.A. L.426 J.D. [Hosp,G.&Assoc.]
*PRACTICE AREAS: Banking; Commercial Transactions and Litigation; Tort Litigation Emphasizing Construction; Premises Liability, Products, Auto and Common Carriers.

**Hosp, Gilbert & Associates, A Law Corporation, (AV)**
**301 North Lake Avenue, Suite 720, 91101**
**Telephone: 818-792-2400 Telecopier: 818-356-9656**
**Email: 105323.2551@compuserve.com URL: http://websites.earthlink.net/~hosp-gilbert/**
**F. Phillip Hosp; Warren L. Gilbert; Marvin G. Fischler; Andrea E.L. Ross.**
**General Civil and Trial Practice in all State and Federal Courts. Banking, Commercial Creditors Rights and Bankruptcy Law, Corporation, Business, Insurance Defense, Automobile Liability, Bad Faith, Construction, Earth Movement, Environmental, ERISA Litigation, Equal Opportunity Law, Insurance Coverage, Insurance Fraud, Premises Liability, Product Liability, Professional Liability, Real Property, Landlord-Tenant Relations, Unlawful Detainer, Subrogation, Wrongful Termination.**
***See Professional Biographies, PASADENA, CALIFORNIA***

**House, Calvin R.** .......... '51 '77 C&L.178 B.A., J.D. [Gutierrez&P.]
*REPORTED CASES: Independent Investor Protective League v. Time, Inc., 66 A.D.2d 391, 412 N.Y.S.2d 898 (1979), rev'd, 50 N.Y. 2d 259, 406 N.E.2d 486, 428 N.Y.S.2d 671 (1980); Services Employees International Union v. Fair Political Practices Commission, 747 F.Supp. 580 (E.D. Cal. 1990), aff'd 955 F.2d 1312 (9th Cir.), cert. denied, 112 S. Ct. 3056, 3057 (1992); Shawmut Bank, N.A. v. Kress Associations, 33 F.3d 1477 (9th Cir. 1994); Tetra Pak, Inc. v. State Board of Equalization, 234 Cal. App. 3d 1751, 286 Cal. Rptr. 529 (1992); Union Bank v. Superior Court, 31 Cal. App. 4th 573, 37 Cal. Rptr. 2d 653 (1995).
*PRACTICE AREAS: Business Litigation; Appellate Practice; Employer Liability; Local Government Liability.
**House, Susan T., (P.C.)**, (AV) .......... '50 '75 C.914 A.B. L.1068 J.D. [Hahn&H.]
*PRACTICE AREAS: Estate Planning; Conservatorships; Probate; Trusts.
Howell, John R. .......... '49 '75 C.605 B.A. L.426 J.D. 510 S. Marengo Ave.
**Howett, Timothy M.** .......... '61 '89 C.154 B.A. L.426 J.D. [▣ Barker&R.]
*PRACTICE AREAS: Complex Civil Litigation; Construction; Community Association Law; Real Estate Law; Environmental Law.
**Howison, William C.** .......... '51 '78 C.1058 B.A. L.398 J.D. [▣ Baraban&T.]
*PRACTICE AREAS: Civil Litigation; Construction Law.
**Hoy, Edmund C.** .......... '42 '76 C.885 B.A. L.1136 J.D. [E.C.Hoy]
*LANGUAGES: Chinese, Mandarin; Cantonese.

**Hoy, Edmund C., A Prof Corp., Law Offices of**
**Suite 806, Union Bank Building, 201 South Lake Avenue, 91101**
**Telephone: 818-792-9945**
**Edmund C. Hoy.**
**Business Litigation, Bankruptcy, Probate, Estate Planning, Tax Planning, Landlord, Tenant Disputes, Civil Trial, Criminal Defense, Trademark, Family Law, Real Estate, Personal Injury.**
***See Professional Biographies, PASADENA, CALIFORNIA***

**Hoyt, Anastasia Swiatek** .... '64 '92 C.800 B.A. L.990 J.D. [▣ McClaugherty&Assoc.]⊙
*PRACTICE AREAS: Insurance Defense.

CAA487P

**Hsu, Lee** ............ '68 '94 C.112 B.S.E.E. L.809 J.D. [Sheldon&M.] (See Pat. Sect.)
*LANGUAGES: Chinese (Mandarin).
**Hubanks, Wesley Ann Hoge** ............ '40 '84 C.112 B.A. L.426 J.D. [Anderson&S.]
*PRACTICE AREAS: Family Law.
Hubbard, Ralph B., (AV) ........ '13 '39 C.112 A.B. L.309 LL.B. 2954 E. Del Mar Blvd.‡
**Hudson, Boyd D.**, (BV) ........................ '51 '79 C.154 B.A. L.1068 J.D. [Martin&H.]
*PRACTICE AREAS: Taxation; Civil Tax Litigation; Estate and Trust Planning; Corporation and Real Estate Law.
**Huffaker, David Alan** .............. '60 '85 C&L.101 B.S., J.D. [Throckmorton,B.O.&T.]
**Hummel, Timothy D.**, (AV) ............ '49 '79 C.668 B.A. L.1224 J.D. [Bigelow,M.&T.]
*PRACTICE AREAS: Estate Planning Law; Fiduciary Income Tax; Estate and Gift Tax; Probate and Trust; Conservatorship, Guardianship Administration.
**Hummer, John C.** '47 '76
C.260 B.S.B.A. L.809 J.D. Assoc. Div. Coun., Chicago Title Ins. Co.
Hunsucker, J. Thomas '46 '73 C.273 B.B.A. L.1068 J.D.
Mng. Atty., Prudential Insurance & Financial Servs. Co.
**Hunt, Gordon, (A Professional Corporation)**, (AV) '34 '60
C.1097 B.A. L.800 J.D. [Hunt,O.B.P.&R.]
*PRACTICE AREAS: Construction; Real Estate.

**Hunt, Ortmann, Blasco, Palffy & Rossell, Inc., A Prof. Law Corp., (AV)**
**301 North Lake Avenue, Suite 700, 91101**
**Telephone: 818-440-5200 Fax: 818-796-0107**
**Email: hunt-ortmann@hobpr.com URL: http://www.hobpr.com**
**Gordon Hunt (A Professional Corporation); Dale A. Ortmann; Richard E. Blasco; Thomas Palffy; Craig N. Rossell; Ronald E. White;—Laurence P. Lubka; Kevin J. Brody; Eric C. Smith; Omel A. Nieves; Jerome D. Meier; John D. Darling; Eric Brown. Of Counsel: F. Glenn Nichols.**
**Construction, Real Estate, Business and Commercial Litigation, Real Estate Finance, Estate Planning, Corporate, Environmental and Business Law.**
***See Professional Biographies, PASADENA, CALIFORNIA***

Hunter, Clark Mangum, (AV) ...... '23 '56 C.813 A.B. L.800 LL.B. 2975 Lombardy Rd.‡
**Hunter, John L.** ...................................... '59 '85 C.112 B.S. L.426 J.D. [Dear&K.]
**Hurley, Ellen R.** ........................ '54 '88 C.446 B.A. L.426 J.D. [Gronemeier&B.]
*PRACTICE AREAS: General Business Litigation.
Hurley, Marion M. ........................................ '13 '40 C&L.494 B.A., J.D. 530 S. Madre St.‡
Huryn, Natalia A. .............................. '57 '83 C.66 A.B. L.569 J.D. 58 N. San Rafael Ave.
Ingersoll, John Luis .................... '65 '90 C.112 B.A. L.1068 J.D. 155 N. Lake Ave.
Inouye, Patrick J.S. ................... '62 '94 C.312 B.S. L.629 J.D. 350 W. Colorado Blvd.
**Ipswitch, Candis Tyson, (Inc.)**, (AV) ......... '45 '76 C.668 B.A. L.800 J.D. [Tyson&I.]
*PRACTICE AREAS: Probate Litigation; Probate; Trusts; Conservatorship; Estate Planning.

**Irwin, Sandra McMahan, (AV) '46 '80 C.881 A.B. L.1049 J.D.**
**Penthouse Suite 930, 150 South Los Robles Avenue, 91101-2437**
**Telephone: 818-577-1065 Telecopier: 818-577-5219**
***REPORTED CASES: Hecht v. Superior Court (1993) 16 Cal.App 4th 836; Kane v. Superior Court (1995) 37 Cal. App. 4th 1577.**
**Corporate, General Business and Real Estate Law and related Litigation, Estate Planning, Probate including Surrogates Court Practice and Other Law of Reproduction.**
***See Professional Biographies, PASADENA, CALIFORNIA***

**Jacobs, Rex W., (AV) '48 '73 C.112 B.A. L.904 J.D.**
**350 West Colorado Boulevard, Suite 400, 91105-1894**
**Telephone: 818-440-1111 Fax: 818-440-9456**
***PRACTICE AREAS: Personal Injury; Construction Injuries.**
**Plaintiffs Personal Injury, Construction Accidents, Auto Accidents, Products Liability and Premises Liability.**
***See Professional Biographies, PASADENA, CALIFORNIA***

James, W. Ervin, II, (BV) ..................... '44 '73 C&L.846 B.A., J.D. 711 E. Walnut St.
Janosik, John T. ............................................. '56 '82 C&L.800 B.S., J.D. City Tres.
Janossy, Maria ...................................... '— '94 C.112 B.S. L.426 J.D. 750 Green St.
Jaso, Kim Lorraine ............................ '56 '88 C.999 B.A. L.809 J.D. Dep. City Pros.
Jeffries, H. Gary, (AV) ............ '36 '67 C.605 B.A. L.426 LL.B. 595 E. Colorado Blvd.
**Jeffries, Kathleen C.**, (AV) ............ '59 '83 C.1042 B.A. L.1068 J.D. [Russell,H.&J.]
*PRACTICE AREAS: Freight Claim Litigation; Interstate Commerce Commission Proceedings; Safety Related Criminal Defense.
**Jenckes, Kenyon S.** ........................ '70 '96 C.645 B.S. L.800 J.D. [Christie,P.&H.]
*PRACTICE AREAS: Patent; Trademark; Copyright.
**Jenkins, R. Scott, (P.C.)**, (AV) ................. '53 '79 C.112 A.B. L.800 J.D. [Hahn&H.]
*PRACTICE AREAS: Business; Corporations; Real Property.
Jenkins, William J., (AV) ............. '44 '72 C.94 A.B. L.426 J.D. 3280 E. Foothill Blvd.
Jett, Wayne, (AV) ............................................... '42 '67 C&L.623 B.S., J.D. [Jett&L.]
Jett & Laquer, (AV) ................................................. 225 S. Lake Ave. (©Bellevue, WA)
Johnson, Angelique Kathleen ......... '53 '80 C.112 B.A. L.809 J.D. 353 E. Orange Grove
**Johnson, Lynn M.** ........................................ '50 '88 C.112 B.A. L.426 J.D. [Kolts&N.]
*PRACTICE AREAS: Civil Litigation; Wrongful Termination.
Johnson, Steven K., (BV) '50 '76 C.800 B.A. L.809 J.D.
Legal Coun., Co. Employees Retirement Fund
Johnston, Patrick L. .................. '46 '75 C.1097 B.A. L.426 J.D. 30 N. Raymond Ave.
**Johnston, R. William**, (AV) '24 '53
C.691 B.S. L.796 LL.B. [Christie,P.&H.] (See Pat. Sect.)
*PRACTICE AREAS: Patents; Trademarks; Copyrights.
**Johnstone, William S., Jr., (P.C.)**, (AV) ......... '31 '58 C&L.800 A.B., J.D. [Hahn&H.]
*PRACTICE AREAS: Estate Planning; Probate; Estate and Gift Tax Litigation.
Jones, David B. ............................ '43 '71 C.197 A.B. L.800 J.D. InterVen Partners
Jones, Thomas H. ........................................ '28 '57 C.474 B.S. L.273 J.D. NASA (Pat.)
Jones, Urrea C., Jr. ................................ '44 '75 C.1232 B.A. L.800 J.D. [Jones&M.]
Jones & Matson .......................................................... 180 S. Lake Ave.
Joseph, Pius ..................................... '57 '87 L.061 LL.B. 199 S. Los Robles Ave.
Joslyn, Richard B., (AV) .............. '20 '49 C&L.800 B.S., J.D. 1 South Orange Grove‡
**Jouanicot, Maxwell L.** ................... '48 '80 C.1131 B.A. L.1148 J.D. [McKinley&C.]
*PRACTICE AREAS: Litigation; Regulatory; Transactional; Personnel; Credit Union.
**Joyce, Erin McKeown** ........................ '— '90 C.112 B.A. L.809 J.D. [Sheldon&M.]
Joyner, Robert C. '47 '72 C&L.260 B.S.B.A., J.D.
V.P. & Gen. Coun., Paracelsus Healthcare Corp.
**Judy, J. Lawrence**, (AV) ............... '45 '72 C.154 B.A. L.426 J.D. [Freeburg,J.&N.]
*PRACTICE AREAS: Products Liability; Insurance; Environmental and Toxic Torts; Personal Injury Defense.
**Julien-Peto, Valerie** ................ '61 '90 C.210 B.A. L.809 J.D. [Burns,A.P.M.&B.]
*LANGUAGES: Spanish.
*REPORTED CASES: Ramirez v. MacAdam (Cal. App. 2 Dist. 1993) 13 Cal. App. 4th 1638.
*PRACTICE AREAS: General Civil Litigation; Appellate Law.

**Kajan Mather and Barish, A Professional Corporation**
**(See Beverly Hills)**

**Kalama, JoAnn Jackson** ................... '47 '91 C.101 B.S. L.1068 J.D. [Anglea&B.]
*PRACTICE AREAS: Probate Administration; Trust Administration; Estate Planning; Estate Planning for the Elderly; Guardianship and Conservatorship.
Kaleta, Victor J., (AV) .......................... '38 '73 C.259 B.S. L.426 J.D. City Atty.
**Kalinski, Francis T., II** ......................... '58 '94 C.112 B.S. L.61 J.D. [Kolts&N.]
*PRACTICE AREAS: Medical Technology Litigation; Construction Defect Litigation.
Kalish, David T., (AV) .................. '54 '79 C.763 B.S. L.809 J.D. 225 S. Lake Ave.

**Kantrowitz, Stan** .............................. '50 '76 C.273 B.A. L.705 J.D. Coun., Fannie Mae
*RESPONSIBILITIES: Mortgage Purchase Contracts; Real Estate Finance; Real Estate; General Corporate and Administrative Law.
Karl, Frank J. ........................................ '44 '72 C.800 B.A. L.426 J.D. 3452 E. Foothill Blvd.
**Katz, Alison Kotlarz** ............................. '58 '85 C.393 B.A. L.809 J.D. [Cooper,K.&S.]
Katzenbach, G. R., Jr. '45 '70 C.216 B.A. L.378 J.D.
(adm. in KS; not adm. in CA) Bronco, Ltd.
Kaye, Walter M. ........................ '43 '70 C.800 B.S. L.1049 J.D. [McCarthy,G.&B.]

**Kearney, Gary W., (AV) '47 '76 C.1074 B.S.M.E. L.398 J.D.**
**Suite 410, 225 South Lake Avenue, 91101-3005**
**Telephone: 818-796-9621 Telecopier: 818-796-6839**
**(Certified Specialist, Family Law, The State Bar of California Board of Legal Specialization.).**
***PRACTICE AREAS: Family Law.**
**Associate: Ronald K. Ziff (Certified Specialist, Family Law, The State Bar of California Board of Legal Specialization).**
**Family Law, Dissolutions, Adoptions and Custody.**
***See Professional Biographies, PASADENA, CALIFORNIA***

Keller, Jeralyn B. ........................................ '44 '76 C.112 B.A. L.426 J.D. [Young&Y.]
**Kelley, Thomas J.**, (AV) ................................ '36 '66 C.770 B.S. L.426 J.D. [Dear&K.]
*PRACTICE AREAS: Bankruptcy; Civil Litigation; Business Litigation.
**Kellner, Richard L.** ............................. '61 '87 C.659 B.A. L.982 J.D. [Rivkin,R.&K.]
*PRACTICE AREAS: Commercial and Real Estate Litigation; Appellate Litigation; Employment Litigation.
Kelly, D. Mathias ...................................... '24 '72 C.112 B.A. L.809 J.D. 221 E. Walnut St.
**Kelsey, Susan E.** '47 '78 C.788 B.A. L.273 J.D.
Sr. V.P. & Asst. Gen. Coun., Countrywide Funding Corp.

**Kennedy, J. Steven '49 '78 C.846 B.A. L.1068 J.D.**
**225 South Lake Avenue, Suite 300, 91101-3005**
**Telephone: 818-432-5440 Fax: 818-432-5401**
***PRACTICE AREAS: Civil Litigation; General Business and Real Estate Law; Probate Law.**
**General Civil Trial Practice, Real Estate, Business, Probate and Estate, Personal Injury, Commercial Litigation and Family Law.**
***See Professional Biographies, PASADENA, CALIFORNIA***

Kerr, John G. ......................................... '31 '70 C.309 B.A. L.1068 J.D. 141 E. Walnut St.
**Khorsandi, Marilyn R.** .......................... '52 '94 C.1175 B.S. L.276 J.D. [Christie,P.&H.]
Kilts, Michael R. ............... '52 '77 C.1097 B.S. L.426 J.D. 215 N. Marengo, Suite 160
**King, Matthew J.** ........................... '52 '79 C.321 B.A. L.818 J.D. [Laughlin,F.L.&M.]
*PRACTICE AREAS: Workers' Compensation.
**King, Victoria E.** ......................................... '50 '92 C.262 B.A. L.112 J.D. [Burton&N.]

**Kirkpatrick, Alexander W. '46 '74 C.597 B.A. L.1068 J.D.**
**225 South Lake Avenue, 9th Floor, 91101**
**Telephone: 818-796-2965; 800-554-2965 Fax: 818-796-9039**
**General Civil Litigation in all State and Federal Courts, Business Litigation, Commercial Litigation, Real Estate, Healthcare and Appellate.**
***See Professional Biographies, PASADENA, CALIFORNIA***

**Kitagawa, Dawn T. '57 '83 C.112 B.A. L.1068 J.D.**
**201 South Lake Avenue, Suite 606, 91101**
**Telephone: 818-449-2391 Fax: 818-449-9484**
***PRACTICE AREAS: Employment Discrimination; Wrongful Termination; Sexual Harassment.**
**Labor: Employment, on behalf of Management.**

**Klarin, Richard M.** ......... '37 '65 C.800 B.S. L.809 LL.B. V.P., Chicago Title Ins. Co.
*RESPONSIBILITIES: Real Estate Law; Title Insurance.
**Klauschie, Carol A.** ......................... '57 '85 C.112 B.A. L.426 J.D. [Bensinger,G.&R.]
*PRACTICE AREAS: Criminal Defense; Civil Rights.
Klein, Jacqueline S. '32 '75 C.912 B.A. L.1137 J.D.
Supvr., Soc. Sec. Admn., Off. of Hearings & App.
Kliger, Lesley E. ....................................................................... '55 '88 [Wills&K.]
**Knapton, Gerald G.** ................... '40 '77 C.112 B.A. L.1068 J.D. [Cooper,K.&S.]
Kofford, Cree-L, (AV) '33 '62 C.878 B.S. L.800 J.D.
225 South Lake, Ste. 500 (©Irvine)
**Kolts, Kathlene Landgraf** ........................ '52 '86 C.932 B.S. L.770 J.D. [Kolts&N.]
*PRACTICE AREAS: Wrongful Termination; Medical Device Litigation.
**Kolts, Raymond G.**, (AV) ................................ '40 '67 C.1097 L.426 J.D. [Kolts&N.]
*PRACTICE AREAS: Products Liability Defense Law; Insurance Defense Law; General Civil Litigation; Wrongful Termination; Arbitration.

**Kolts and Nawa, (AV)**
**The Walnut Plaza, Suite 195, 215 North Marengo Avenue, 91101**
**Telephone: 818-584-6968 FAX: 818-584-5718**
**Members of Firm: Raymond G. Kolts; Gary C. Nawa. Associates: Lynn M. Johnson; Linda M. Toutant; Francis T. Kalinski, II; Diane L. Darvey; Michael A. J. Nangano. Of Counsel: Kathlene Landgraf Kolts.**
**Products Liability, Wrongful Termination, Medical Device Defense, Probate Law and Business Litigation, Construction Litigation, ERISA Litigation and General Civil Litigation.**
***See Professional Biographies, PASADENA, CALIFORNIA***

Kommerstad, Robert M. '27 '52 C.755 L.494 J.D.
(adm. in MN; not adm. in CA) Pres. & Chmn., Provident Invest. Coun.
**Kopman, Daniel David** ........................... '58 '92 C.112 B.S. L.426 J.D. [Garrett&T.]
*PRACTICE AREAS: Business Litigation; Real Estate Litigation; Professional Liability.
Kozinski, Alex ......................................... '50 '75 C.112 A.B. L.1068 J.D. U.S. Cir. J.
Kramer, Elaine F. ......................... '47 '77 C.1044 B.A. L.284 J.D. 255 Glensummer Rd.
Krappman, Andrew J., Jr. '32 '58 C&L.813 A.B., LL.B.
Exec. V.P. & Corp. Coun., O.K. Earl Corp., The
Kratz, Bryson M. ...... '31 '62 C.112 B.A. L.809 LL.B. 502 S. Rosemead Blvd. (©Bishop)
**Kruse, William F.**, (AV) ......................... '55 '79 C&L.800 B.S., J.D. [Lagerlof,S.B.&S.]
Kuenning, Brad .......... '56 '89 C.508 B.M.E. L.800 J.D. 215 N. Marengo Ave., 3rd Fl.
**Kula, James R.** ............................................. '46 '74 C.477 B.A. L.273 J.D. [Baraban&T.]
*PRACTICE AREAS: Civil Litigation; Construction Law.
Kusmiss, John H. ........................................ '38 '91 C.453 S.B. L.1136 J.D. Asst. Pat. Coun.
**Kustin, Carl, Jr.**, (AV) '36 '62 C.46 B.S. L.597 J.D.
[Christie,P.&H.] (See Pat. Sect.)
*PRACTICE AREAS: Patent, Trademark, Copyright and Unfair Competition Litigation.
Kutch, Edward N. .................. '52 '81 C.260 B.A. L.940 J.D. 322 W. Del Mar Blvd.
**LaBran, Ronald M.**, (BV) ................. '36 '65 C.659 B.S.Eco. L.273 J.D. [Zeutzius&L.]
*PRACTICE AREAS: Business Law; Commercial Law; Litigation; Family Law; Collections.
**Lacey, Kevin S.** ........................................ '56 '89 C.1077 B.A. L.809 J.D. [Garrett&T.]
*PRACTICE AREAS: Business Litigation; Real Estate Litigation; Professional Liability.
**Lagerlof, Stanley C.**, (AV) ........... '15 '39 C.494 A.B. L.800 J.D. [Lagerlof,S.B.&S.] ‡

**Lagerlof, Senecal, Bradley & Swift, LLP, (AV)**
**301 North Lake Avenue, 10th Floor, 91101-4108**
**Telephone: 818-793-9400 FAX: 818-793-5900**
**Members of Firm: Joseph J. Burris (1913-1980); Stanley C. Lagerlof (Retired); H. Melvin Swift, Jr.; H. Jess Senecal; Jack T. Swafford; John F. Bradley; Timothy J. Gosney; William F. Kruse; Thomas S. Bunn, III; Andrew D. Turner; Rebecca J. Thyne. Associates: James D. Ciampa; Robert W. Renken. General Civil, Trial and Appellate Practice in all State and Federal Courts and Administrative Agencies. Corporation, Antitrust, Labor, Tax, Real Estate, Probate, Trust, Estate Planning, Water, Natural Resources and Municipal Law.**

(This Listing Continued)

CAA488P

**Lagerlof, Senecal, Bradley & Swift, LLP (Continued)**

**Representative Clients: Anchor Glass Container Corp.; Bethlehem Steel Corp.; Orthopaedic Hospital; Palmdale Water District; Public Water Agencies Group; Ventura Port District; Walnut Valley Water District; Metric Construction Co., Inc.**

***See Professional Biographies, PASADENA, CALIFORNIA***

Laidig, Samuel L. ........................'18 '42 C&L.112 A.B., LL.B. Ret. Mun. Ct. J.
**Lally, David Brian** .......................'58 '89 C.1042 B.S. L.61 J.D. [⊠ McKinley&C.]
*LANGUAGES: French.
*PRACTICE AREAS: Creditors' Rights; Bankruptcy; Foreclosure.
Lamb, David W. ......................... '60 '86 C&L.838 B.S., J.D. 200 S. Los RoblesAve.
Lambert, Robert W., (AV) ........... '50 '76 C.154 B.A. L.1067 J.D. 35 North Lake Ave.
**Lampert, Gregory S.** ........ '64 '90 C.608 B.S.I.S.E. L.201 J.D. [⊠ Christie,P.&H.] (Pat.)
*PRACTICE AREAS: Intellectual Property.
**Langbord, Peter B.** ........................ '62 '89 C.1077 B.A. L.990 J.D. [Garrett&T.]
*PRACTICE AREAS: Litigation; Professional Liability.
Langhammer, Carl Edward, Jr., (BV) ............'55 '81 C&L.800 A.B., J.D. [Hogue&L.]
**Langton, Grant T.** '60 '92
C.1075 B.S.Ch.E. L.426 J.D. [⊠ Christie,P.&H.] (See Pat. Sect.)
*PRACTICE AREAS: Patents; Trademarks; Copyrights.
Lans, Sherman B., (AV) ............ '23 '50 C.424 B.S. L.597 J.D. 301 E. Colorado Blvd.
**Lans, Stephen M.** ....................'52 '78 C.668 B.A. L.178 J.D. [Cairns,D.L.N.&S.]
*LANGUAGES: Spanish.
*PRACTICE AREAS: General Commercial Litigation; Banking Law; Bankruptcy.
Lanzafame, Philip F. ................. '34 '59 C.823 B.A. L.1068 LL.B. 1010 E. Union St.
Lapekas, Ronald C. ........................ '44 '79 C.475 B.A. L.1065 J.D. 510 Marengo Ave.
Laquer, Christopher M. .......................... '49 '74 C.311 B.A. L.831 J.D. [Jett&L.]
**Larr, William Ray, (P.C.)** .........................'48 '74 C.112 A.B. L.174 J.D. [Larr&P.]
*REPORTED CASES: Kaufman v. Gross 23 Cal 3d 750 (1979); Allstate v. Lotito 116 CA 3d 998 (1981); Battle v. Kessler 149 CA 3d 853 (1983); Prichard v. Reitz 178 CA 3d 465 (1986); 1119 Delaware v. Continental Land Title Insurance Company 16 CA 4th 992 (1991).
*PRACTICE AREAS: Real Property Litigation; Insurance Coverage Litigation; Insurance Arbitration; Title Insurance Litigation; General Insurance Law.

**Larr & Poteet**
**A Partnership including a Professional Corporation**
**285 North Hill Avenue Suite 200, 91106**
**Telephone: 818-796-5588 Telecopier: 818-796-7635**
**Members of Firm: William Ray Larr (P.C.); Lawrence Jay Poteet. Associates: Liza B. Duckworth.**
**General Business, Litigation, Real Property Law, Commercial Law, Products Liability, FIRREA, Title Insurance Litigation, Title Insurance Claims, Insurance Law.**

***See Professional Biographies, PASADENA, CALIFORNIA***

Lasley, Linda M. ........................ '48 '78 C.684 A.B. L.1068 J.D. [McCarthy&L.]
Latts, Leatrice Lynne, (AV) .................. '— '69 C.1246 B.A. L.1068 J.D. [L.L.Latts]
Latts, Leatrice Lynne, A P.C., (AV) ........................... 1156 E. Green St., 2nd Fl.
Lauderdale, Robert V., (BV) .............. '25 '56 C.770 B.S. L.426 LL.B. 137 N. Marengo

**Laughlin, Falbo, Levy & Moresi LLP, (AV)**
**A Partnership including Professional Corporations**
**200 South Los Robles, Suite 500, 91101⊙**
**Telephone: 818-568-9700 Fax: 818-568-3905**
**Email: lflm@lflm.com URL: http://lflm.com**
**James C. Hester;—Jerilyn Cohen; Matthew J. King; Mark J. Epstein; Amy G. Rivera; John C. Callister.**
**General Civil and Trial Practice. Workers' Compensation Defense (State and Federal), Labor Relations and Employment Discrimination.**
**San Francisco, California Office: Two Embarcadero Center, Fifth Floor. Telephone: 415-781-6676. Fax: 415-781-6823.**
**Sacramento, California Office: 106 K Street - Second Floor. Telephone: 916-441-6045. Fax: 916-441-7067.**
**Redding, California Office: 930 Executive Way, Second Floor. Telephone: 916-222-0268. Fax: 916-222-5705.**
**Walnut Creek, California Office: 100 Pringle Avenue, Suite 630. Telephone: 510-210-0210. Fax: 510-210-0105.**
**Irvine, California Office: 3 Park Plaza, Suite 1400, P.O. Box 17659. Telephone: 714-251-0120. Fax: 714-251-0125.**
**San Jose, California Office: 1570 The Alameda, Suite 100. Telephone: 408-286-8801. Fax: 408-286-1935.**

***See Professional Biographies, PASADENA, CALIFORNIA***

Lawrance, H. Irvin, (AV) ............. '30 '57 C&L.477 A.B., LL.B. 16 N. Marengo Ave.
**Lawrence, David D.** .................. '54 '80 C.347 B.S. L.37 J.D. [Franscell,S.R.&L.]⊙
*PRACTICE AREAS: Police Misconduct Liability Defense; Civil Rights; Title VII Discrimination; Americans with Disabilities Act; Municipal and Administrative Law.
Lawrence, Sherry H. ............................'59 '90 C.174 B.A. L.770 J.D. 225 S. Lake Ave.
Lazarian, Stephen H., Jr., (BV) ......'48 '74 C.1239 B.A. L.61 J.D. CEO, City Works, Inc.
Le Beau, Charles J. ..................... '50 '79 C.763 B.A. L.1137 J.D. 301 N. Lake Ave.
**Lee, Cindy S.** ...............................'68 '93 C.112 B.A. L.426 J.D. [⊠ Franscell,S.R.&L.]
*LANGUAGES: Korean.
*PRACTICE AREAS: Municipal and Administrative Law; Civil Rights; Police Misconduct; Police Liability Defense; Appellate Practice.
Lee, Jeffrey C. ........................... '54 '82 C.800 L.770 J.D. 490 S. Fair Oaks Ave.
Leibl, Daniel, (BV) .........'25 '52 C.800 A.B. L.1065 J.D. 2234 E. Colorado St., 2nd Fl.
Leighton, Robert ............................................ '30 '71 L.1127 LL.B. 1 W. Calif.
Leishman, David M. '57 '89 C.101 B.S. L.878 J.D.
(adm. in UT; not adm. in CA) Corp. Coun.
**Lem, Theresa M.** '63 '88 C.112 B.A. L.426 J.D.
Coun., Kaiser Found. Health Plan, Inc.
Lembke, Michael J. ........................ '51 '78 C.679 B.A. L.809 J.D. 2 N. Lake Ave.
Lescoe, Richard J. ..................... '25 '71 C.665 B.S. L.1136 J.D. 986 Cornell Rd.
Lester, Charles P., (AV) ................'25 '49 C&L.800 B.S., J.D. 301 E. Colorado Blvd.
**Lewis, Edwin A.** .....................'57 '81 C.112 B.A. L.1068 J.D. [Overlander,L.&R.]
*PRACTICE AREAS: Personal Injury Law; Insurance Defense Law; Commercial Law; Torts; General Civil Trial Practice.
Lewis, Louise A. ................................ '42 '82 C.112 L.1190 101 E. Green St.
Liberio, Rocco Joseph ........................ '54 '81 C.800 B.S. L.426 J.D. 99 S. Lake Ave.
Lichtman, Peter D., (AV) ......... '52 '77 C.800 B.M. L.809 J.D. 225 S. Lake Ave., 9th Fl.
**Lightfoot, Stephen K., (AV)** .........................'43 '73 L.1190 J.D. [Lightfoot&N.]⊙
*PRACTICE AREAS: Corporate Law; Business Law; Probate Law; Estate Planning; Sales and Use Tax.

**Lightfoot & Northup, A Professional Corporation, (AV)**
**151 South El Molino Avenue, Suite 303, 91101-2510⊙**
**Telephone: 818-577-1382; 213-684-3066 Telecopier: 818-577-1459**
**Email: l-n@ix.netcom.com**
**Stephen K. Lightfoot; Robert W. Northup, Jr.**
**Business, Commercial, Corporate Law, Litigation, Sales and Use Tax Law, Real Estate, Probate and Estate Planning.**
**Oceanside, California Office: 1351 Harbor Boulevard North, Suite B, 92054. Telephone: 619-439-4647.**

***See Professional Biographies, PASADENA, CALIFORNIA***

Link, Diane B. .............................'46 '77 C.788 A.B. L.800 J.D. Dep. Pub. Def.

**Link, James S., (AV) '54 '80 C.767 B.A. L.809 J.D.**
**215 N. Marengo, 3rd Floor, 91101-1504**
**Telephone: 818-793-9570 Fax: 818-356-7414**
***REPORTED CASES: Alliance Insurance Co. v. Colella (9th Cir. 1993) 995 F.2d 944; Coleman v. Gulf Insurance Group (1986) 41 Cal.3d 782 (amicus counsel); Doctors Co. v. Superior Court (1989) 39**

(This Listing Continued)

**Link, James S. (Continued)**

**Cal.3d 39 (amicus counsel); Griffin v. State Farm Mutual Auto Insurance Co. (1991) 230 Cal.3d 59; Robinson v. Superior Court (1984) 158 Cal.App.3d 98.**
***PRACTICE AREAS: Appellate Practice (40%); Insurance Coverage (40%); Litigation (20%).**
**Appellate Practice in State and Federal Courts, Insurance Coverage and Litigation.**

***See Professional Biographies, PASADENA, CALIFORNIA***

Link, Norbert ................................................'53 '86 C&L.061 400 W. Green St.
Logan, J. Thomas, (AV) ....................'46 '75 C.813 B.A. L.800 J.D. 151 W. Calif. Blvd.
Logan, Lyndol M. .......................... '51 '75 C&L.800 B.A., J.D. 675 Busch Garden Dr.‡
Long, Robert P. ..........................................'44 '70 C.112 A.B. L.1068 J.D. 55 S. Lake Ave.
Losorelli, Luigi A. .....................................'54 '79 C.800 B.S. L.770 J.D. 1122 E. Green St.
Lowe, Eugene H., (BV) ............. '30 '77 C.800 B.S. L.999 LL.B. 3302 Villa Mesa Rd.
Lowell, J. Scott ...................................... '52 '84 C.885 B.A. L.809 J.D. 30 N. Raymond Ave.
Lowery, Jeffrey A. ...................................'59 '86 C.930 B.A. L.309 J.D. 440 W. Green St.
Loze, Donald ...........................................'32 '62 C.813 A.B. L.800 J.D. 39 S. El Molino Ave.
**Lubka, Laurence P.** ....................... '54 '80 C.178 B.A. L.273 J.D. [⊠ Hunt,O.B.P.&R.]
*PRACTICE AREAS: Government Contracts; Construction; Franchise.

**Lucas, Craig D., (AV) '46 '76 C.1097 B.A. L.1068 J.D.**
**Suite 407, 301 East Colorado Boulevard, 91101**
**Telephone: 818-796-7194 Telecopier: 818-449-6296**
**Estate Planning, Estate and Gift Taxation, Probate and Trust Administration.**
**Reference: Citizens Bank of Pasadena.**

**Luhring, Susan E.** ....................'60 '85 C.112 B.A. L.1049 J.D. [⊠ Burns,A.P.M.&B.]
*PRACTICE AREAS: General Civil Litigation.
**Lusby, Paul H.** ......................................... '55 '82 C&L.893 B.A., J.D. [Cooper,K.&S.]
Lyon, Roger '62 '90 C.112 B.A. L.990 J.D.
Assoc. Coun., Continental Lawyers Title Co.
Macchiagodena, Marina A., (BV) '55 '79
C.767 B.A. L.1065 J.D. 600 S. Lake Ave., 2nd Fl.

**MacFarlane, Edward D., (AV) '47 '73 C&L.426 B.B.A., J.D.**
**2 North Lake Avenue, Suite 860, 91101**
**Telephone: 818-585-3570 Fax: 818-585-3568**
**Real Estate and Business. General Civil Practice, Commercial Leasing, Condominium and Homeowners Association, Construction, Foreclosure, Litigation.**

***See Professional Biographies, PASADENA, CALIFORNIA***

**MacLatchie, Scott D.** ................... '57 '84 C.800 B.S. L.426 J.D. [Franscell,S.R.&L.]
*PRACTICE AREAS: Police Misconduct Liability Defense; Civil Rights; Municipal and Administrative Law; Medical Legal; General Civil.
Macneil, Hugh L., (AV) .....'18 '48 C.309 A.B. L.426 LL.B. 251 S. Orange Grove Blvd.‡
**Macy, Cary S.** ............................................ '61 '88 C.346 B.S. L.990 J.D. [⊠ N.Good]
*PRACTICE AREAS: Personal Injury; Wrongful Death.
Magaña, Martine ...................................'53 '83 C.813 B.A. L.800 J.D. [⊠ Jones&M.]
Mahaffey, Robert G. ..................... '19 '73 C.628 L.1008 LL.B. 1905 E. Mountain St.‡
**Mahrer, Lisa Diane** '54 '85
C.112 B.A. L.426 J.D. Coun., Kaiser Found. Health Plan, Inc.
**Mak, Danton K.** ...... '55 '84 C.911 B.S.Ch.E. L.1068 J.D. [Sheldon&M.] (See Pat. Sect.)
*LANGUAGES: Chinese, Mandarin and Cantonese.
Malham, Joseph P. ..........................'56 '84 C.1044 B.S. L.809 J.D. 25 E. Union St.
Mankovitz, Roy J. '41 '79 C.178 B.S.E.E. L.1095 J.D.
Corp. Coun. Intell. Prop., Gemstar Development Corporation (Pat.)
Manley, Wallace J., (BV) ...............'17 '49 C.982 B.S. L.800 LL.B. 2234 E. Colorado St.
Manning, Michael E. ........................ '61 '90 C.1288 B.S. L.999 J.D. 424 N. Lake Ave.
**Marangi, Leonard M., (P.C.), (AV)** .......... '29 '57 C.112 A.B. L.800 J.D. [Hahn&H.]
*PRACTICE AREAS: Civil Litigation; Family; Real Property; Business.
**Marantidis, Constantine** '60 '94
C.1333 B.S. L.426 J.D. [⊠ Christie,P.&H.] (See Pat. Sect.)
*PRACTICE AREAS: Patents; Trademarks; Copyrights.
**Marino, Antoinette M.** ...................'53 '84 C.1044 B.A. L.809 J.D. [⊠ J.E.Valdivia]
*PRACTICE AREAS: Insurance Law; Professional Liability; Health Management Care Contracting; Medical Malpractice.
Marino, Michael A. ........................ '56 '84 C.112 B.A. L.990 J.D. 225 S. Lake Ave.,
**Markley, William C., III** '45 '74
C.871 B.S. L.1065 J.D. V.P., Law, Jacobs Engg. Grp., Inc.
*RESPONSIBILITIES: Corporate and Business.
**Marquez, Robert B.**, (BV) ............... '59 '87 C.605 A.B. L.767 J.D. [Marquez&T.]
*LANGUAGES: Spanish.
*PRACTICE AREAS: Civil Litigation; Insurance; Employment and Labor Law.

**Marquez & Teperson, P.C., (BV)**
**301 North Lake Avenue, 8th Floor, 91101**
**Telephone: 818-793-0133 Fax: 818-793-1116**
**Robert B. Marquez; Jonathan B. Teperson.**
**General Civil Litigation and Appellate Practice in State and Federal Courts and Arbitration Tribunals, General Insurance, Casualty, Products Liability, Legal Malpractice and Labor and Employment.**

***See Professional Biographies, PASADENA, CALIFORNIA***

Marsh, Ann V. ..........................'53 '83 C.1044 B.A. L.426 J.D. 55 S. Lake Ave.
**Martin, Robert B., Jr.**, (AV) ................. '44 '70 C.381 A.B. L.800 J.D. [Martin&H.]
*PRACTICE AREAS: Taxation; Civil Tax Litigation; Estate and Trust Planning; Corporation and Real Estate Law.
Martin, Warren H. ...............................'64 '91 C.276 B.A. L.1067 J.D. [⊠ Jones&M.]

**Martin & Hudson, (AV) BB**
**350 West Colorado Boulevard, Suite 320, 91105**
**Telephone: 818-793-8500 Telecopier: 818-793-8779**
**Members of Firm: Robert B. Martin, Jr. (Certified Specialist, Taxation Law, The State Bar of California Board of Legal Specialization); Boyd D. Hudson.**
**Taxation, Civil Tax Litigation, Estate and Trust Planning, Corporation and Real Estate Law.**

***See Professional Biographies, PASADENA, CALIFORNIA***

**Maseda, Stephen B.** .............................'45 '71 C.378 B.S. L.426 J.D. [Cassity&M.]
Mason, Jan Stanley ...................... '37 '67 C.381 B.A. L.30 J.D. 490 S. Fair Oaks Ave.
**Mason, Sharon Lynn** ................. '51 '75 C.112 B.A. L.426 J.D. Coun., Fannie Mae
*RESPONSIBILITIES: Mortgage Finance; Real Estate; General Corporate.
Mathews, Charles Theodore ............'47 '73 C&L.426 B.S., J.D. 501 S. Marengo Ave.
Matson, Stephen K. ................................'42 '73 C.605 B.A. L.575 J.D. [Jones&M.]
**Maxwell, Walter G.** ........'39 '69 C.112 B.S. L.800 J.D. [Christie,P.&H.] (See Pat. Sect.)
*PRACTICE AREAS: Patents; Trademarks; Copyrights.

**Mayock, W. Michael, (AV) '44 '72 C.800 B.A. L.426 J.D. BB**
**The Braley Building, Fourth Floor, 35 South Raymond Avenue, 91105**
**Telephone: 818-405-1465; 310-552-1465 FAX: 818-578-0768**
**Criminal Trial and Appellate Practice in all State and Federal Courts.**
**Reference: Union Bank.**

***See Professional Biographies, PASADENA, CALIFORNIA***

McCarthy, Luke V. .............................'46 '74 C.1075 B.S. L.770 J.D. [McCarthy,G.&B.]
McCarthy, Gyemant & Babbits, A Professional Law Corporation
350 W. Colorado Blvd. (⊙San Francisco)
McCarthy & Lasley, P.C. ............................................................... 4 E. Holly St.

CAA489P

**McClaugherty, Jay S.**, (BV) '52 '81 C.1058 B.A. L.1049 J.D. [McClaugherty&Assoc.]⊙
*LANGUAGES: Norwegian.
*REPORTED CASES: Valdez v. Smith (1985) 166 Cal. App. 3d 723; Holmes v. Roth (1992) 11 Cal. App. 4th 931.
*PRACTICE AREAS: High Exposure Personal Injury; Insurance Defense.

**McClaugherty & Associates, (BV)**
**301 North Lake Avenue Suite 800, 91101⊙**
**Telephone: 818-449-7522 FAX: 818-583-9187**
**Jay S. McClaugherty. Associates: Robert E. Henke; Jeffrey B. Smith; Anastasia Swiatek Hoyt.**
**Insurance Defense, General Civil Trial in all State and Federal Court.**
**Ontario, California Office: 3350 Shelby Street, Suite 200, 91764. Telephone: 909-944-2505.**
*See Professional Biographies, PASADENA, CALIFORNIA*

McColgan, Hugh E., (AV) '29 '58 C.800 L.426 LL.B. [McColgan&V.]
McColgan and Vanni, (AV) 199 S. Los Robles
McCullough, Ray T., (BV) '51 '76 C.477 B.B.A. L.259 J.D. 215 N. Marengo Ave.3rd Fl.
McDermott & Trayner, Professional Law Corporation, (AV) 225 South Lake Avenue, Suite 410 (⊙Newport Beach)
McKay, Robert J., (AV) '44 '71 C.112 B.A. L.1068 J.D. One Colorado, 35 Hugus Alley
McKenna, John F., Jr., (AV) '21 '48 C.190 A.B. L.309 LL.B. 1185 Kinclair Dr.‡
**McKinley, Robert D.** '48 '79 C.1070 B.S. L.809 J.D. [McKinley&C.]
*PRACTICE AREAS: Creditor Rights; Commercial Litigation; Loan Workouts; Transaction Documentation; Elder Law.

**McKinley & Capeloto**
**201 South Lake Avenue, Suite 606, 91101**
**Telephone: 818-793-7788 Fax: 818-793-1013**
**Email: capeloto@aol.com**
**J. Sheldon Capeloto; Robert D. McKinley; James R. Selth. Associates: Maxwell L. Jouanicot; Danielle D. Cyr; David Brian Lally. Of Counsel: Cristopher Rahtz.**
**Financial Institutions, Creditor Rights, Bankruptcy, Real Estate, Workouts, Commercial Law, Civil Litigation, Elder Law, Construction Law.**
*See Professional Biographies, PASADENA, CALIFORNIA*

McLaren, Teresa Greco '54 '89 C.823 B.S. L.809 J.D. 411 S. Madison Ave.
McMillan, William N., III, (AV) '48 '79 C.988 B.A. L.1148 J.D. 350 W. Colorado Blvd.
McNatt, Marvin A. '31 '73 960 Ellington Lane
**McNulty, Holly A.** '64 '90 C.473 B.S. L.990 J.D. [A Freeburg,J.&N.]
*PRACTICE AREAS: Personal Injury Defense; Suspected Fraudulent Claims; Family Law; Subrogation.
Mead, Albert E., Jr., (BV) '50 '77 C.31 B.A. L.800 J.D. 192 Ramona Pl.

**Meenan, Kevin, (AV) '52 '78 C.184 B.A. L.1049 J.D. BB**
**790 East Colorado Boulevard Ninth Floor Penthouse, 91101-2105**
**Telephone: 818-398-0000 FAX: 818-585-0999**
**Email: 73313.1624@compuserve.com**
**Civil Trial Practice in all State and Federal Courts. Tort Litigation, Injury and Death, Negligence, Product Liability, Professional Negligence, Premises, Carriers and Insurance.**
*See Professional Biographies, PASADENA, CALIFORNIA*

**Meier, Jerome D.**, (AV) '39 '71 C.101 L.809 J.D. [A Hunt,O.B.P.&R.]
*PRACTICE AREAS: Construction; Real Estate; Torts.
Melton, Michael J. '46 '71 C.112 B.A. L.800 J.D. 150 S. Los Robles
Merchant, Margaret B. '17 '43 C.773 A.B. L.800 LL.B. 1085 Armada Dr.‡
Merritt, Amina R. '58 '92 C.31 B.A. L.800 J.D. 265 N. Euclid, Ste. 300
**Messner, Ernest L.** '46 '77 C.502 B.S. L.426 J.D. Coun., Fannie Mae
*RESPONSIBILITIES: Real Estate; Real Estate Finance; Mortgage Finance.
Metzger, Julia M. '49 '77 C.477 A.B. L.608 J.D. 215 N. Marengo Ave.
**Milam, Jeffrey L.** '50 '76 C.31 B.A. L.770 J.D. [Burns,A.P.M.&B.]
*PRACTICE AREAS: Products Liability Law.
**Miller, Craig J.** '63 '88 C.477 B.B.A. L.770 J.D. [Overlander,L.&R.]
*PRACTICE AREAS: Personal Injury Law; Insurance Defense Law; Commercial Law; Torts; General Civil Trial Practice.
Miller, James F. '49 '75 C.800 B.A. L.809 J.D. 45 S. Hudson, 9th Fl.
Miller, Nicolas H. '61 '89 C.1075 B.A. L.800 J.D. V.Pres. and Coun., Countrywide Home Loan
**Miller, Richard F.**, (AV) '37 '64 C&L.813 A.B., LL.B. [R.F.Miller]
**Miller, Stephen J.** '60 '86 C.112 B.A. L.800 J.D. [Boyle,O.&R.]
*PRACTICE AREAS: Business Litigation; Corporate Law; Real Property Law; Family Law; Partnership Law.

**Miller, Richard F., A Professional Corporation, (AV) BB**
**Suite 511, 199 South Los Robles Avenue, 91101**
**Telephone: 818-584-1400; 213-681-5400 Telecopier: 818-584-1447**
**Richard F. Miller (Certified Specialist, Estate Planning, Trust and Probate Law, The State Bar of California Board of Legal Specialization).**
**Probate, Estate Planning, Trust and Conservatorship Law.**
*See Professional Biographies, PASADENA, CALIFORNIA*

**Millikan, Catharine Karl** '56 '95 C.800 B.A. L.809 J.D. [A Millikan&T.]
*PRACTICE AREAS: Probate; Estate Planning; Business Law; Real Property Law.
**Millikan, Gregory F.**, (AV) '48 '77 C.605 B.A. L.1068 J.D. [Millikan&T.]
*PRACTICE AREAS: Real Property Law; Estate Planning Law; Business Law; Tax Law.

**Millikan and Thomas, (AV)**
**Second Floor, 704 Mira Monte Place, 91101**
**Telephone: 818-304-7065 Telecopier: 818-796-4738**
**C. E. Brad Millikan, Jr. (1925-1982); Lane J. Thomas; Gregory F. Millikan. Associates: Catharine Karl Millikan.**
**General Civil and Trial Practice in all State and Federal Courts. Corporate, Taxation, Construction, Government Contracts, Real Estate, Family, Estate Planning and Probate Law.**
**Reference: Wells Fargo Bank, Pasadena.**
*See Professional Biographies, PASADENA, CALIFORNIA*

Mills, Robert Parker, (AV) '45 '71 C&L.502 B.A., J.D. [Mills] (⊙West Covina)
Mills Law Corporation, (AV) 200 S. Los Robles Ave.
Mirecki, Philip '23 '50 C&L.793 A.B., J.D. 221 E. Walnut St.‡
Mirigian, Haig Joel '44 '84 C.112 B.S. L.809 J.D. Fin. Offr., L.A. Co. Housing
Misshore, Bryan C. '60 '86 C.880 B.A. L.276 J.D. 155 N. Lake Ave.

**Mitchell, Michael C. '47 '72 C&L.426 B.A., J.D.**
**Cen Fed Bank Building, Suite 616, 301 East Colorado Boulevard, 91101**
**Telephone: 818-683-9803 FAX: 818-356-0305**
***PRACTICE AREAS: General Business Law; Probate Law; Trust Administration Law; Estate Planning Law; Conservatorships Law.**
**General Business, Probate and Trust Administration, Estate Planning, Conservatorships and Tax Law.**
**Reference: Citizens Bank of Pasadena.**

**Mon, Donald D., (AV) '21 '51 C.111 B.S. L.813 J.D.**
**750 East Green Street, Suite 303 (See Pat. Sect.)**
Monkman, John G., Jr. '46 '72 C&L.800 B.S., J.D. [J.G.Monkman,Jr.]
Monkman, John G., Jr., Inc. 300 N. Lake Ave.
**Monroe, Wesley W.** '66 '90 C.112 B.S. L.426 J.D. [A Christie,P.&H.] (See Pat. Sect.)
*PRACTICE AREAS: Intellectual Property Law; Computer Law.

Monsma, Robbie Elizabeth '52 '79 C.1077 B.A. L.1068 J.D. Sr. V.P. & Corp. Coun., SOPAC Real Estate Grp.
**Montgomery, Cranston P.** '22 '51 C.112 A.B. L.1066 LL.B. [Montgomery&M.]
*PRACTICE AREAS: Government Contracts; Competition; Employee Relations.
**Montgomery, Edward R. P.**, (AV) '22 '51 C.112 A.B. L.1066 [Montgomery&M.]
*PRACTICE AREAS: Real Property; Estates and Trusts; Corporations; Civil Litigation.

**Montgomery and Montgomery, (AV)**
**Suite 303, 151 South El Molino Avenue, 91101**
**Telephone: 818-577-1387; 213-684-3065**
**Members of Firm: Edward R. P. Montgomery; Cranston P. Montgomery.**
**Real Property, Civil Litigation, Estates and Trusts, Corporations, Business Transactions and Competition.**
*See Professional Biographies, PASADENA, CALIFORNIA*

**Moore, Arthur B.** '52 '78 C&L.309 A.B., J.D. (adm. in MA; not adm. in CA) Chf. Pat. Coun., Avery Dennison Corp.
*RESPONSIBILITIES: Patent Law; Trademark Law; Copyright Law; Unfair Competition Law; Licensing Law.
**Moore, George E.**, (AV) '36 '65 C.800 B.S.C. L.426 J.D. [G.E.Moore]
*PRACTICE AREAS: Personal Injury; Medical Malpractice.
**Moore, Joseph F.**, (AV) '48 '75 C.668 B.A. L.818 J.D. [Bigelow,M.&T.]
*REPORTED CASES: Williams v. Commissioner, T.C. Memo 1989-439; 935 F.2d 1066 (9th Cir. 1991); Cole v. Commissioner, 863 F.2d 34 (9th Cir. 1988); Naftel v. Commissioner, 85 T.C. 527 (1985); Allen v. Crocker National Bank et al., 733 F.2d 642 (9th Cir. 1984).
*PRACTICE AREAS: Federal and State Taxation; Real Estate Law; Corporate Law.

**Moore, Paul F., (AV) '10 '36 C.276 A.B. L.986 LL.B.**
**The Walnut Plaza, Suite 310, 215 North Marengo Avenue, 91101-1503**
**Telephone: 818-405-0835 Fax: 818-356-7414**
**General Civil and Trial Practice in all State and Federal Courts. Corporation, Estate Planning, Trust and Probate Law.**
**References: Bank of America (California); Bank of America (Lake and Colorado Office, Pasadena).**

Moore, Richard W., Jr. '48 '75 C.228 A.B. L.208 J.D. Dir. of Taxes, Avery Dennison Corp.

**Moore, George E., A Professional Law Corporation, (AV) BB**
**Wells Fargo Building, 350 West Colorado Boulevard Suite 400, 91105-1894**
**Telephone: 818-440-1111 Fax: 818-440-9456**
**George E. Moore.**
**Plaintiff Personal Injury, Medical Negligence, Automobile, Products, Attorney Negligence, Premises Liability.**
*See Professional Biographies, PASADENA, CALIFORNIA*

Morales, Joseph M. '55 '79 C&L.426 B.S., J.D. 515 S. Madison #8
**Mori, Grace C.** '68 '93 C.112 B.S. L.809 J.D. [A Burns,A.P.M.&B.]⊙
*PRACTICE AREAS: General Civil Litigation.
Morris, Gary W., (BV) '45 '71 C.642 B.A. L.426 J.D. [Hart&M.]
Morris, Judson W., Jr. '42 '74 C.999 L.426 J.D. Mun. J.
**Morris, Marc**, (AV) '53 '79 C.72 B.S. L.1202 J.D. [C Christie,P.&H.]
*PRACTICE AREAS: Intellectual Property Litigation; Securities Litigation.
Morrow, George E. '21 '62 C.546 A.B. L.426 J.D. 221 E. Walnut St.‡
**Morseburg, Douglas H.** '50 '86 C.813 B.A. L.1065 J.D. [A Sheldon&M.]
Moscaret, Kenneth M. '54 '80 C.770 B.S. L.276 J.D. 215 N. Marengo Ave.
Moses, Alfred F. '43 '75 C.254 B.A. L.426 J.D. 193 E. Orange Grove Blvd., 2nd Fl.
Mosher, Sally E. '34 '82 C.706 B.Mus. L.800 J.D. Oakhill Enterprises
Mosley, Jerald L., (BV) '49 '82 C.927 B.A. L.1068 J.D. 301 E. Colorado Blvd. Ste. 320
**Moss, James A.** '52 '78 C.112 B.A. L.800 J.D. [C Garrett&T.]
*PRACTICE AREAS: Business Litigation; Real Estate Litigation; Professional Liability.
Moss, Richard A. '42 '68 C&L.800 B.A., J.D. 255 S. Marengo Ave.
Mrakich, Nick N. '29 '57 C.605 A.B. L.426 LL.B. 301 E. Colorado Blvd.
**Mueth, Joseph E.**, (AV) '35 '60 C.201 B.Ch.E. L.276 LL.B. [J.E.Mueth] (See Pat. Sect.)
*REPORTED CASES: Rex Chainbelt, Inc. v. Harco Products, Inc., U.S. Court of Appeals, 9th Cir. (1975); Herbert v. Diagnostic Products Corp., No. 85 Civ. 0856 (June 1986); Young Engineers, Inc. v. USITC; Hunting Hall of Fame Foundation v. Safari Club International, No. CIV 86-020 TUC ACM (May 1987); IMS Limited v. International Medical Systems, Inc, No. 84 CV 4126 (September 1986).
*PRACTICE AREAS: Patent, Trademark and Copyright Law; Trial Law; Appellate Practice; Food and Drugs.

**Mueth, Joseph E., A Law Corporation, (AV) BB**
**225 South Lake Avenue, Eighth Floor, 91101-1599**
**Telephone: 818-584-0396 Fax: 818-584-6862**
**Joseph E. Mueth.**
**Patent, Trademark and Copyright Law. Trials and Appellate Practice in all Courts.**
**Reference: Bank of America, 333 South Hope Street, Los Angeles, California.**
*See Professional Biographies, PASADENA, CALIFORNIA*

Muir, David L. '40 '74 C.1097 B.S. L.426 J.D. Chf. Coun.
**Muir, Samuel J.**, (AV) '54 '79 C.1232 B.A. L.426 J.D. [Collins,C.M.&T.]
*PRACTICE AREAS: Construction Law; Architects and Engineers Professional Liability; Trial Practice; Products Liability.
**Mulvaney, Dennette A.** '— '88 C&L.37 B.S., J.D. [A Bisno&S.]
Murdock, Carol A. '46 '84 C.347 B.S.N. L.1190 J.D. 1541 N. Lake Ave.
Murphy, Dennis M. '48 '75 C.112 B.A. L.426 J.D. First V.P. & Sr. Real Estate Coun., Community Bk.
**Murphy, Sandra K.** '51 '89 C&L.352 B.S.N., J.D. [Hahn&H.]
*PRACTICE AREAS: Estate Planning; Probate; Taxation.
**Murray, Vernon Edward**, (AV) '43 '69 C&L.800 B.A., J.D. [Murray,B.&B.]
*PRACTICE AREAS: Pension; Profit Sharing; ERISA; Business Litigation; General Corporate Transactions.

**Murray, Bradshaw & Budzyn, A Law Corporation, (AV)**
**The Walnut Plaza, 3rd Floor, 215 North Marengo Avenue, 91101**
**Telephone: 818-584-9860 FAX: 818-568-3967**
**Vernon Edward Murray; Michael J. Budzyn; David S. Bradshaw.**
**Pension, Profit Sharing, Employment, Labor and Corporate Tax Law, ERISA and Business Litigation.**
*See Professional Biographies, PASADENA, CALIFORNIA*

**Muschott, Alan E.** '62 '88 C.98 B.S. L.339 J.D. Coun., Kaiser Found. Health Plan, Inc.
Musich, Donald A. '36 '62 C.602 B.S. L.209 J.D. Dep. Dist. Atty.
**Myer, Phillip I.** '51 '76 C.966 B.A. L.426 J.D. [A M.J.Soodik]
*PRACTICE AREAS: Family Law; Bankruptcy; Personal Injury; Probate.
**Myers, R. Chandler, (P.C.)**, (AV) '33 '59 C&L.813 A.B., J.D. [Myers&D.]
*PRACTICE AREAS: Business Litigation; Estate Planning; Probate; Arbitration; Commercial.

**Myers & D'Angelo, (AV)**
**A Partnership of Professional Corporations**
**301 North Lake Avenue, Suite 800, 91101**
**Telephone: 818-792-0007; 213-380-2830 FAX: 818-792-0037**
**Members of Firm: R. Chandler Myers (P.C.); Robert W. D'Angelo (P.C.) (Certified Specialist, Taxation Law, The State Bar of California Board of Legal Specialization).**
**General Civil and Appellate Practice. Corporation, Taxation and Real Estate Law. Litigation. Estate Planning, Trust and Probate Law.**
*See Professional Biographies, PASADENA, CALIFORNIA*

Naideth, Stephen Sam '51 '77 C.112 B.A. L.809 J.D. 500 Mercedes Ave.
Nakahiro, Fumio R. '61 '87 C.800 B.S. L.426 J.D. 117 E. Colorado Blvd.

CAA490P

**Nangano, Michael A. J.** ... '60 '88 C.800 B.A. L.426 J.D. [🄰 Kolts&N.]
*LANGUAGES: Latin.
*PRACTICE AREAS: Products Liability; Premises; Construction Defect; Business Litigation; Medical Malpractice.
**Nawa, Gary C.** ... '47 '75 C.1097 B.A. L.809 J.D. [Kolts&N.]
*PRACTICE AREAS: Construction Litigation; ERISA Litigation; Arbitration.
**Nehlsen, Bruce E.** ... '47 '79 C.112 B.S. L.398 J.D. [Cooper,K.&S.]
**Nelson, B. Eric** ... '48 '80 C.112 B.A. L.809 J.D. [🄰 N.Good]
*REPORTED CASES: Rao v. Campo , 223 Cal.App.3d 1557, 285 Cal.Rptr. 691 (Cal.App. 2 Dist., Sept. 12, 1992) (NO. B053573); Wise v. Superior Court (Myers), 222 Cal. App. 3d 1008, 272 Cal.Rprtr. 222 (Cal.App. 2 Dist., Aug. 7, 1990) (NO. B046438); Paul v. Drost, 186 Cal. App.3d 1407, 231 Cal.Reptr. 361 (Cal.App. 2 Dist., Nov. 7, 1986) (NO. B016575); Freshman, Mulvaney, Comsky, Kahan & Deutsch v. Superior Court (Kreuger) 173 Cal.App.3d 223, 218 Cal.Rptr. 533 (Cal.App. 2 Dist., Sept. 26, 1985) (NO. CIV. B010554); Hollywood Refrigeration Sales Co., Inc. v. Superior Court (Von Lavrinoff) 164 Cal.App. 3d 754, 210 Cal.Rptr. 619 (Cal.App. 2 Dist., Feb. 15, 1985) (NO. CIV. B007351).
*PRACTICE AREAS: Personal Injury; Wrongful Death.
Nelson, Dorothy W. ... '28 '54 C.112 B.A. L.1068 LL.B. U.S. Sr. Cir. J.
**Nelson, Gary J.** ... '59 '96 C.1058 B.S. L.276 J.D. [🄰 Christie,P.&H.]
*PRACTICE AREAS: Patent; Trademark; Copyright.
Nelson, James E. ... '46 '82 C.112 B.S.C.E. L.809 J.D. 2500 E. Colorado Blvd.
Nelson, John H., (AV) ... '10 '35 C&L.37 LL.B. 1209 Afton St.‡
**Nettels, Charles F.** ... '56 '81 C.330 B.A. L.426 J.D. [Freeburg,J.&N.]
*PRACTICE AREAS: Insurance Fraud; Automobile; Products Liability; Premises Liability.

**Netter, George J., (AV) '24 '60 C&L.851 B.S., J.D.**
**260 South Los Robles Avenue Suite 216, 91101**
**Telephone: 818-578-0703 Fax: 818-578-1630**
**Email: gnetter@spotcom.com**
**Patents, Trademarks, Copyrights and Unfair Competition.**
**Reference: First Los Angeles Bank.**

**Neville, Edward R.** ... '51 '88 C.276 A.B. L.809 J.D. [🄰 Baraban&T.]
*PRACTICE AREAS: Civil Litigation.
**Newton, Richard B.**, (AV) ... '20 '45 C&L.800 A.B., LL.B. [R.B.Newton]

**Newton, Richard B., A Professional Corporation, (AV)**
**711 Mission Street, Suite A, 91030-3039**
**Telephone: 818-441-4549; 213-682-3339 Telecopier: 818-441-6075**
**Richard B. Newton.**
**General Civil and Trial Practice in all State and Federal Courts. Corporation, Probate Law. Trial Practice and Trust Administration.**
**Reference: Bank of America (Los Angeles Regional Head Office and South Pasadena Branch).**

**Nicholas, Francisco J.** ... '55 '83 C.112 B.S. L.426 J.D. [Cairns,D.L.N.&S.]
*PRACTICE AREAS: General Civil and Business Litigation; Employment Litigation; Insurance Defense.
**Nichols, F. Glenn** ... '48 '76 C.763 B.S. L.1049 J.D. [🄲 Hunt,O.B.P.&R.]
*PRACTICE AREAS: Construction; Real Estate; Municipal Law.
Nielsen, Carl D. ..... '56 '81 C.112 B.A. L.426 J.D. Coun., Continental Lawyers Title Co.
**Nieves, Omel A.** ... '61 '88 C.267 B.A. L.1067 J.D. [🄰 Hunt,O.B.P.&R.]
*LANGUAGES: Spanish.
Ninemire, W. Leigh ... '52 '86 C.502 B.A. L.616 J.D. 510 S. Marengo Ave.
Noble, David ... '42 '73 C.112 B.A. L.1148 J.D. 928 E. Elizabeth St.
Nobori, Dean ... '51 '76 C.112 B.A. L.809 J.D. 2715 Yorkshire Rd.
**Norris, Donald G.** ... '53 '79 C.112 B.A. L.813 J.D. [Burton&N.]
*LANGUAGES: Spanish.
**Northup, Robert W., Jr.** ... '58 '85 C.390 B.A. L.1049 J.D. [Lightfoot&N.]
*PRACTICE AREAS: Business Litigation; Construction Litigation.

**Nouskajian & Cranert**
**(See Pasadena)**

**Nutt, Brian C.**, (AV) ... '58 '83 C.800 B.A. L.426 J.D. [Thon,B.V.P.&N.]
*LANGUAGES: Spanish.
*PRACTICE AREAS: Personal Injury Law; Products Liability; Malpractice.
**Oakes, George A.** ... '37 '68 C.1097 B.S. L.800 J.D. [Throckmorton,B.O.&T.]
*LANGUAGES: Portuguese.
**O'Brien, William J.** ... '58 '81 C.112 A.B. L.1066 J.D. [Christie,P.&H.]
*PRACTICE AREAS: Intellectual Property Litigation; Business Law Litigation.

**O'Connor, Kathleen M. '47 '75 C.157 B.A. L.209 J.D.**
**301 North Lake Avenue, Suite 800, 91101-4108**
**Telephone: 818-304-2951; 304-2953 Fax: 818-583-9187**
***PRACTICE AREAS: Family Law.**
**Family Law including Dissolutions, establishment of Child and Spousal Support, Enforcement of Support, Child Custody, Visitation and Adoption.**
***See Professional Biographies, PASADENA, CALIFORNIA***

**O'Hagan, Thomas V.** ... '54 '80 C&L.209 B.A., J.D. [🄰 Cooper,K.&S.]
**O'Hanlon, Trischa J.** '47 '80
C.346 B.F.A. L.930 J.D. Sr. Coun., Kaiser Found Health Plan, Inc.
**Ohashi, John E.** ... '55 '81 C.112 B.A. L.1067 J.D. [Ohashi&P.]⊙
*REPORTED CASES: Reid vs. Moskovitz 208 Cal. App. 3d 29 (1989).
*PRACTICE AREAS: Business Law; Corporate Law; Real Estate; Employment Law; Federal and State Securities.

**Ohashi & Priver, (AV)**
**215 North Marengo Avenue Suite 225, 91101⊙**
**Telephone: 818-584-1107 Facsimile: 818-356-7414**
**Mark S. Priver; John E. Ohashi.**
**Business and Corporate Law. Real Estate, Federal and State Securities, Commercial and Tax Litigation.**
**El Segundo, California Office: 222 N. Sepulveda Boulevard. 20th Floor. 90245. Telephone: 310-364-5215. Fax: 310-364-5217.**
***See Professional Biographies, PASADENA, CALIFORNIA***

**Ohira, Michael T.** ... '57 '86 C.1042 B.S. L.426 J.D. [🄰 Cooper,K.&S.]
Okazaki, Brian K ... '61 '88 C.1042 B.S. L.464 J.D. [Okazaki]
Okazaki Law Offices, (AV) ... 1122 E. Green St. (⊙San Juan Capistrano)
Oldendorf, Margaret Lynn '58 '84 C.1109 B.A. L.426 J.D.
Staff Counsel, Los Angeles County Employees Retirement System
Olds, Ronald V., (AV) ... '14 '71 C.768 L.1148 LL.B. 885 S. Orange Blvd.‡
**O'Leary, Thomas M.** ... '58 '86 C.398 B.A. L.1049 J.D. [🄰 Cooper,K.&S.]
Oliver, Charles Douglas '45 '81 C.767 A.B. L.999 J.D.
(adm. in OR; not adm. in CA) Lawyers Title Ins. Corp.
Olsen, Dennis M. ... '42 '68 C.215 B.A.E. L.477 J.D. Gen. Coun., Cook Bros.
**Olson, A. William**, (AV) ... '22 '51 C.112 B.A. L.800 J.D. [Boyle,O.&R.]
*PRACTICE AREAS: Estate Planning; Probate and Trust Law; General Business Law.
Olson, Lester E. ... '27 '54 C&L.813 A.B., LL.B. Ret. Supr. Ct. J.
Olson, Robert M., Jr. ... '24 '51 C&L.800 B.A., J.D. Supr. Ct. J.
**Olson, Stephen W.** ... '56 '95 C.800 B.S. L.426 J.D. [🄰 Collins,C.M.&T.]
*PRACTICE AREAS: Architects and Engineers Liability; Construction Law.
Opel, Gordon A. ... '50 '76 C.112 B.A. L.464 J.D. 301 N. Lake Ave.
**Oppermann, Anne Reid** ... '58 '86 C.605 A.B. L.464 J.D. [🄰 Bigelow,M.&T.]
*LANGUAGES: Russian and French.
*PRACTICE AREAS: General Litigation; Business Litigation; Corporate Law; Non-Profit Organizations; Charitable Giving.

**Orendorff, James M., (AV) '38 '64 C.267 B.S. L.1066 J.D.** BR
**25 East Union Street, 91103**
**Telephone: 818-449-8200 FAX: 818-449-8370**

(This Listing Continued)

**Orendorff, James M. (Continued)**
**General Business and Transaction Practice. Business, Corporate, Real Property, Real Estate Development, Finance, Trusts and Wills.**
***See Professional Biographies, PASADENA, CALIFORNIA***

Ormes, Jack R., (AV) ... '25 '59 C.31 L.1001 LL.B. 301 N. Lake Ave.
**Orr, Cheryl A.** ... '62 '87 C.67 B.A. L.659 J.D. [🄰 Barker&R.]
*REPORTED CASES: National Union Fire Insurance v. Keating, 995 F.2d, 154 (9th Cir. 1993); Aetna Cas. & Insurance Co. v. Titan Corp., 22 Cal.App 4th 457 (1994); ACL Technologies v. Northbrook Property & Casualty Insurance, 17 Cal.App 4th 1773 (1994).
*PRACTICE AREAS: Construction Defect; General Business; Insurance Coverage; Appellate Litigation.
Orszag, Paul, III ... '51 '79 C.112 B.A. L.1077 J.D. 2 N. Lake Ave.
Ortell, Michael N. ... '43 '84 C.1097 B.A. L.999 J.D. 1489 E. Colorado Blvd.
**Ortmann, Dale A.** ... '55 '80 C.1075 B.A. L.426 J.D. [Hunt,O.B.P.&R.]
*PRACTICE AREAS: Construction; Real Estate.
Ortmeyer, Susan ... '63 '93 [🄰 Rothner,S.&B.]
**Overing, Michael S.** ... '61 '89 C.546 B.A. L.426 J.D. [🄰 Cooper,K.&S.]
**Overlander, Thomas F.**, (AV) ... '41 '73 C.563 B.A. L.809 J.D. [Overlander,L.&R.]
*PRACTICE AREAS: Personal Injury Law; Insurance Defense Law; Commercial Law; Torts; General Civil Trial Practice.

**Overlander, Lewis & Russell, (AV)** BR
**65 North Raymond Avenue, Suite 210, 91103**
**Telephone: 818-304-0500 Fax: 818-304-9750**
**Thomas F. Overlander; Edwin A. Lewis; Richard L. Russell, Jr.;—Craig J. Miller; Sherri Lynette Woods.**
**Business and Commercial Litigation. Personal Injury, Insurance Defense, Commercial and Tort Law, Civil Rights, Police Misconduct Defense, Public Entity Defense. General Civil Trial Practice.**
***See Professional Biographies, PASADENA, CALIFORNIA***

**Ownbey, Lloyd C., Jr., (AV) '32 '61 C&L.800 B.A., J.D.** BR
**180 South Lake Avenue, Suite 510, 91101-2683**
**Telephone: 818-440-5960 Fax: 818-585-9669**
**Labor and Employment Law, Public and Private Sectors.**
***See Professional Biographies, PASADENA, CALIFORNIA***

Packer, Robert B. ... '51 '76 C.112 B.A. L.464 J.D. 70 S. Lake Ave.
**Paik, Nam Sun** .... '59 '85 C.103 B.A. L.910 J.D. Coun., Kaiser Found. Health Plan, Inc.
**Palermo, Peter R., (Professional Corporation)**, (AV) '37 '64
C.605 A.B. L.1049 J.D. [Soldwedel,P.B.&C.]
*PRACTICE AREAS: Primary and Ancillary Probate Law; Trust Law; Estate Planning.
**Palffy, Thomas** ... '56 '82 C.800 B.A. L.809 J.D. [Hunt,O.B.P.&R.]
*PRACTICE AREAS: Construction; Real Estate.
Palmer, Jeffrey P., (BV) '44 '73 C.112 A.B. L.446 J.D.
Pres., Mediation Specialists, Inc.
**Palmer, Russell R., Jr.**, (AV) '27 '65
C.112 B.S. L.813 LL.B. [Christie,P.&H.] (See Pat. Sect.)
*PRACTICE AREAS: Patents; Trademarks; Copyrights.
**Palumbo, Bruce**, (AV) ... '47 '72 C.112 B.A. L.426 J.D. [Burns,A.P.M.&B.]
*REPORTED CASES: Imperial Cas. and Indem. Co. v. Sogomonian (Cal App. 2 Dist. 1988), 198 Cal App 3d 169.
*PRACTICE AREAS: Products Liability Law; Insurance Defense Law; Toxic Torts; Construction Defects; Construction Coverage.
Paparian, William M. ... '49 '79 C.1077 B.A. L.809 J.D. 16 N. Marengo Ave.
Parker, Daniel C. ... '59 '85 C&L.813 B.S., J.D. CalMat Co.
**Parker, Harvey M.**, (AV) ... '03 '27 C.112 A.B. L.1066 J.D. [Soldwedel,P.B.&C.] ‡
Patterson, Edward M. ... '15 '40 C.604 A.B. L.309 LL.B. 350 Elmwood Dr.‡
Patton, Sylvia K. ... '44 '74 300 E. Walnut
Payne, Lisa ... '65 '93 C.951 B.A. L.1068 J.D. [🄰 Rothner,S.&B.]
Paz, JoséR. ... '63 '91 C.112 B.A. L.809 J.D. 80 S. Lake Ave.
Peale, David Earl ... '47 '77 C.642 B.A. L.398 J.D. [Hart&M.]
Pearce, Charles W. ... '49 '76 C.813 B.A. L.770 J.D. 225 S. Lake Ave
Pearson, Darrell D. ... '49 '78 C.1109 B.A. L.426 J.D. [Coulter,V.&P.]
Peck, Ruth R. ... '37 '81 C.112 B.A. L.1148 J.D. 1188 Hillcrest Ave.

**Peck, John D.**
**(See San Marino)**

Peim, Joyce ... '59 '86 C.994 B.A. L.564 J.D. 393 E. Walnut
**Pelch, Dale R.**, (AV) ... '57 '83 C.112 B.A. L.426 J.D. [Hahn&H.]
*PRACTICE AREAS: Civil Litigation; Real Property; Environmental Law.

**Peters, Carol A., (AV) '41 '77 C.668 B.A. L.1148 J.D.**
**221 East Walnut Street, Suite 136, 91101-1554**
**Telephone: 818-793-9383 Fax: 818-793-3552**
***PRACTICE AREAS: Elder Law; Probate; Estate Planning, Wills, Trusts; Bioethics; Conservatorship and Related Litigation.**
**Probate, Estate Planning, Bio-Ethics, Conservatorship and Related Litigation.**
***See Professional Biographies, PASADENA, CALIFORNIA***

**Peters, Stephen F.**, (AV) ... '40 '67 C.668 B.A. L.1068 LL.B. [Taylor K.S.&R.]
*PRACTICE AREAS: Estate Planning; Estate Taxes; Probate; Estate Litigation; Trust Litigation.
**Peterson, Robert M.**, (AV) ... '34 '60 C.636 B.A. L.800 J.D. [🄲 Carter,C.&E.]
*PRACTICE AREAS: Business Law; Real Property Law.
**Petrey, Janet L.** ..... '52 '84 C.174 B.A. L.326 J.D. V.P., Countrywide Home Loans, Inc.
*RESPONSIBILITIES: Subprime Lending; HELOC; Regulatory.
Petrovich, Robert G. ... '54 '78 C.800 B.S. L.1049 J.D. 265 N. Gabriel Blvd.
Pfeiffer, Gordon W. ... '53 '89 C.112 B.A. L.809 J.D. 115 W. Calif. Blvd.
Phelps, Edward M., (AV) ... '50 '75 C.112 B.S. L.426 J.D. [Phelps,S.&P.]
Phelps, Ruth A. ... '51 '75 C.342 B.A. L.426 J.D. [Phelps,S.&P.]
Phelps, Schwarz & Phelps, A Professional Law Corporation, (AV)
527 S. Lake Ave. Ste. 106
Philipson, David J. ... '46 '73 C.112 B.A. L.1065 J.D. 87 N. Raymond Ave.
**Phillipi, Steven V.**, (AV) ... '58 '83 C.112 A.B. L.426 J.D. [Thon,B.V.P.&N.]
*PRACTICE AREAS: Personal Injury Law; Malpractice; Maritime Law.
Phillips, D. Gene ... '32 '74 C.339 B.S. L.1190 J.D. 234 E. Colo. Blvd.
**Phillips, David M.** ... '62 '90 C.605 B.A. L.426 J.D. [🄰 Thon,B.V.P.&N.]
*LANGUAGES: Spanish.
*PRACTICE AREAS: Personal Injury; Products Liability.
**Pianko, Theodore A.** ... '55 '78 C.1044 B.A. L.477 J.D. [Christie,P.&H.]
*PRACTICE AREAS: Litigation; Bankruptcy Litigation.
**Pierson, Elizabeth T.** ... '63 '88 C.228 A.B. L.800 J.D. [Anglea&B.]
*PRACTICE AREAS: Federal Estate and Gift Tax; Trust Administration; Probate Administration; Estate Planning.
**Pittman, Carla D.** '56 '82
C.597 B.A. L.329 J.D. Sr. Coun., Kaiser Found. Health Plan, Inc.
Pitzer, Gloria Scharre, (AV) ... '52 '78 C.1075 B.A. L.426 J.D. 301 E. Colorado Blvd.
Platt, Bob S., (AV) ... '47 '78 C.768 B.S. L.1136 J.D. 201 S. Lake Ave.
Plotkin, Leonard J., (BV) ... '46 '73 C.1097 B.A. L.426 J.D. 35 S. Raymond Ave.

**Plotkin, Michael E. '46 '77 C.588 B.A. L.1190 J.D.**
**150 South Los Robles Avenue Suite 910, 91101**
**Telephone: 818-568-8088 FAX: 818-793-9622**
**Business Litigation. Bankruptcy, Personal Injury and Criminal Law.**

(This Listing Continued)

CAA491P

# CALIFORNIA—PASADENA

**Plotkin, Michael E. (Continued)**
Representative Clients: Clarke & Lewis, Inc.; Butterfield Farms, Inc.; Synergy Construction Corp.; Omega Entertainment, Inc.; Mines Avenue Textile, Inc.; Westbrooke Enterprises, Inc.
*See Professional Biographies, PASADENA, CALIFORNIA*

**Plumley, David A.** ........ '60 '91 C.112 B.S. L.426 J.D. [A Christie,P.&H.] (See Pat. Sect.)
\*PRACTICE AREAS: Patents; Trademarks; Copyrights.
**Poe, Patricia I.** '55 '85 C.173 B.A. L.809 J.D.
    1st V.P., Sr. Coun. & Asst. Secy., Countrywide Funding Corp.
**Poole, Dorothy Braun** .................. '55 '80 C.813 B.A. L.800 J.D. 1613 Vista Ln.
**Poole, John H.**, (AV) ............... '12 '44 C.197 A.B. L.800 LL.B. 1030 S. El Milino‡
**Poole, John L.** ................ '56 '81 C.197 B.A. L.809 J.D. P.O. Box 60602
**Poteet, Lawrence Jay** ............ '53 '78 C.1042 B.S. L.112 J.D. [Larr&P.]
\*SPECIAL AGENCIES: FDIC.
\*REPORTED CASES: Harris v. Northwestern National Ins. Co. (1992); 6 CA 4th 1061; Stagen v. Stewart-West Coast Title Co. (1983) 149 CA 3d 114.
\*PRACTICE AREAS: Commercial and Real Property Litigation; Title Insurance Law and Litigation; FIRREA; General Insurance Law; General Business Litigation.
**Potepan, James C.** ............ '48 '82 C.112 B.A. L.426 J.D. [A Cooper,K.&S.]
\*PRACTICE AREAS: Insurance Coverage; General Civil Trial; Appellate Practice; Trademark Law; Copyright Law.
**Potter, Bertram L.**, (BV) ............. '17 '40 C.575 B.A. L.178 J.D. [Potter,C.&S.]
**Potter, Joshua W.**, (CV) ............ '53 '81 C.112 B.A. L.398 J.D. [Potter,C.&S.]
**Potter, Paul E.**, (AV) ................. '47 '80 L.1148 J.D. [Potter,C.&S.]
**Potter, Cohen & Samulon**, (AV) ............... 3852 E. Colorado Blvd.
**Pownall, H. E., Jr.** ............. '09 '34 C&L.800 B.S., LL.B. 707 S. Orange Grove Blvd.‡

**Pratt, Chad T-W** '63 '90 C.770 B.A. L.426 J.D.
221 East Walnut Street, Suite 245, 91101☉
Telephone: 818-441-CHAD Fax: 818-577-4561
Civil Trial and Appellate Practice in State and Federal Courts. Landlord and Tenant Law, Uninhabitability, Labor Law, Family Law, Personal Injury, Premises Liability and Torts Law.
Los Angeles, California Office: 4929 Wilshire Boulevard, Suite 300, 90010. Telephones: 213-936-9002. Fax: 213-938-6069.
*See Professional Biographies, PASADENA, CALIFORNIA*

**Pratte, Robert P.** ............ '27 '54 C.999 B.S. L.426 LL.B. 194 N. El Molino St.
**Preciado, Arthur C.** .............. '54 '83 C.1097 B.A. L.1065 J.D. [Gutierrez&P.]
\*LANGUAGES: Spanish.
\*PRACTICE AREAS: Civil Litigation; Police Liability Defense; Employer Liability; Local Government Liability; Civil Rights Defense.
**Priver, Mark S.**, (AV) ............ '55 '82 C.1169 B.A. L.1148 J.D. [Ohashi&P.]☉
\*PRACTICE AREAS: Business Litigation; Commercial Litigation; Tax Litigation.
**Prochazka, Jerry E.** '49 '89
    C.684 B.S./B.A. L.1136 J.D. Southern Calif. Permanente Med. Grp.
**Proctor, Robert C., Jr.**, (AV) ........ '36 '62 C.1042 B.S. L.1068 LL.B. [R.C.Proctor,Jr.]

**Proctor, Robert C., Jr., A Professional Corporation**, (AV)
553 South Marengo Avenue, 91101-3114
Telephone: 818-356-9720; 213-681-2601 FAX: 818-356-0351
Robert C. Proctor, Jr.
Personal Injury and Products Liability. Trial Practice in all State Courts. Third Party Cases, Medical Malpractice and Americans Disability Act.
*See Professional Biographies, PASADENA, CALIFORNIA*

**Prout, D. Bruce**, (AV) '34 '63 C&L.800 B.S.E.E., LL.B.
    [Christie,P.&H.] (See Pat. Sect.)
\*PRACTICE AREAS: Domestic and International Patents; Copyrights and Trademarks; Computer Technology.
**Pumilia, Richard B.**, (AV) ............. '58 '84 C.901 B.A. L.705 J.D. [Pumilia&A.]
\*PRACTICE AREAS: Corporate Law.

**Pumilia & Adamec**, (AV)
199 South Los Robles Avenue, Suite 711, 91101-2460
Telephone: 818-584-9600 Fax: 818-584-9699
Email: VSRR59B@PRODIGY.COM
Members of Firm: Richard B. Pumilia; Justene M. Adamec.
Business Transactions, Corporations, Partnerships, Contracts and Real Estate, Business and Commercial Litigation.
*See Professional Biographies, PASADENA, CALIFORNIA*

**Quade, Dennis H.** ............ '48 '76 C.950 B.A. L.285 J.D. Sr. Coun., The Parsons Corp.
**Quillin, Mary L.** ............ '49 '79 C.1097 B.A. L.1067 J.D. P.O. Box 50372
**Radel, Myra** ............ '38 '76 C.30 B.A. L.1095 J.D. Dep. Dist. Atty.
**Ragland, Karen A.** ............ '55 '82 C.813 B.A. L.809 J.D. [A Ferns&F.]
**Rahn, LeRoy T.**, (AV) '35 '63
    C.800 B.S.E.E. L.569 LL.B. [Christie,P.&H.] (See Pat. Sect.)
\*LANGUAGES: German.
\*PRACTICE AREAS: Intellectual Property Law.
**Rahtz, Cristopher** ............ '45 '74 C.165 B.A. L.1009 J.D. [G McKinley&C.]
\*PRACTICE AREAS: Commercial Litigation; Transaction Documentation; Creditor Rights'; Loan Workouts; Employment Law.
**Ramseyer, William M.** ............ — '74 C.293 B.A. L.1065 J.D. 272 S. Los Robles Ave.
**Randall, Richard P.** '47 '76 C&L.893 B.A., J.D.
    Asst. Gen. Coun. & Asst. Secy., Avery Dennison Corp.
\*RESPONSIBILITIES: General Corporate Law; International Law; Licensing Law.

**Reddingius, R. P.**, (BV) '20 '51 C.112 B.A. L.1065 J.D.
225 South Lake Avenue, Suite 1100, 91101☉
Telephone: 818-795-2117; 213-681-5043 FAX: 818-304-9652
Wills, Trusts, Probate, Estate Planning, Elder Law and Conservatorships.
Fallbrook, California Office: 566 East Alvarado Street, 92028. Telephone: 619-723-6604. Fax: 619-728-0210.

**Redmond, Margaret Ann**, (AV) '37 '76 C.707 B.A. L.1190 J.D.
Suite 726, 301 East Colorado Boulevard, 91101
Telephone: 818-584-9050 FAX: 818-584-6463
Email: 73411.230@compuserve.com
(Certified Specialist, Immigration and Nationality Law, The State Bar of California Board of Legal Specialization).
Immigration and Nationality Law, General Civil Practice.
*See Professional Biographies, PASADENA, CALIFORNIA*

**Redmond, Thomas M.** ............ '34 '72 C.36 L.809 J.D. Wkrs. Comp. J.
**Reed, Stephen W.**, (AV) ............ '44 '70 C.999 B.A. L.800 J.D. [Reed&B.]
\*PRACTICE AREAS: Commercial Real Estate; General Business and Corporate Law.

**Reed & Brown, A Law Corporation**, (AV)
35 North Lake Avenue, Suite 960, 91101
Telephone: 818-449-4521; 213-684-2202 Facsimile: 818-449-7453
Stephen W. Reed; Mark C. Brown;—Michael J. Coppess; Robert L. Toms, Jr.; Robert R. Bowne, II.
Of Counsel: E. J. Caldecott.
Real Estate; General Business and Corporate Law; Estate Planning and Probate Law; Civil Litigation.
*See Professional Biographies, PASADENA, CALIFORNIA*

**Reeves, Robert L.**, (A Prof. Corp.) ........ '42 '80 C.1139 B.A. L.990 J.D. 2 N. Lake Ave.
**Regalado, Amy J.** ............ '54 '88 C.112 B.A. L.426 J.D. 540 Orange Grove Pl.

CAA492P

# MARTINDALE-HUBBELL LAW DIRECTORY 1997

**Reinke, Jean M.** '62 '88
    C.112 B.A. L.426 J.D. V.P. & Coun., Countrywide Funding Corp.
**Renken, Robert W.** ............ '65 '92 C.464 B.S. L.426 J.D. [A Lagerlof,S.B.&S.]
**Reyes, Raul H.** ............ '49 '77 C.805 B.S. L.744 J.D. 440 W. Green St.

**Reyes, Richard R., Law Offices of**, (AV) '54 '82 C.800 B.A. L.1137 J.D.
1100 East Green Street, 91106
Telephone: 818-792-5672
\*LANGUAGES: Spanish.
Personal Injury, Products Liability, Wrongful Death, Contract Litigation. General Civil Litigation.
*See Professional Biographies, PASADENA, CALIFORNIA*

**Reynolds, Montie M., Law Office of** '42 '87 C.1097 B.S. L.809 J.D.
    30 N. Raymond Ave.
**Rezainia, Parvin** ............ '59 '91 C&L.878 M.S., J.D. 1143 Crowne Dr.
**Rhodes, Kenneth O.**, (AV) ............ '12 '37 C.813 A.B. L.309 LL.B. [Taylor K.S.&R.] ‡
**Richardson, Anne** ............ '62 '90 C.821 B.A. L.813 J.D. 128 N. Fair Oaks Ave.
**Richardson, Elise M.** ............ '44 '85 C.999 L.1190 J.D. 2 N. Lake Ave.
**Richardson, Kelly G.** ............ '58 '83 C.112 B.A. L.800 J.D. [Richardson&H.]
\*PRACTICE AREAS: Civil Litigation; General Business Law; Condominium Law; Construction Law.

**Richardson & Harman**
215 North Marengo Avenue, Third Floor, 91101
Telephone: 818-449-5577; 909-861-7244 Facsimile: 818-356-7414
Email: KGRESQ@AOL.COM
Members of Firm: Kelly G. Richardson; Steven G. Harman.
Civil Litigation, General Business Law, Condominium and Construction Law.
*See Professional Biographies, PASADENA, CALIFORNIA*

**Richey, Cassandra J.** ............ '58 '91 C.347 B.A. L.426 J.D. 201 S. Lake Ave., Ste. 606
**Rider, Ann Sherwood** ............ '56 '84 C.276 B.S.F.S. L.809 J.D. Sr. Dep. City Atty.
**Riela, Frank, Jr.** ............ '59 '92 C.276 B.S. L.1009 J.D. 50 North Arroyo Blvd.
**Rigdon, Michael D.**, (A Law Corp.) '45 '79
    C.1097 B.A. L.1190 J.D. 135 N. Marengo Ave.
**Riggall, Kneave**, (AV) ............ '52 '78 C.112 B.A. L.1068 J.D. 1917 Oxley St.
**Riley, John S.** ............ '48 '77 C.112 B.A. L.809 J.D. 199 S. Los Robles

**Risley, Robert L.**, (AV) '34 '64 C.605 B.A. L.1068 LL.B.
790 East Colorado Boulevard, 9th Floor, 91101
Telephone: 818-397-2745 Fax: 818-397-2746
Email: 102763.3005@compuserve.com
\*PRACTICE AREAS: Litigation; Real Estate Law; Medical Malpractice Defense Law. General Practice.
*See Professional Biographies, PASADENA, CALIFORNIA*

**Ritchie, David B.**, (BV) ............ '58 '83 C.111 B.S. L.800 J.D. [D'Alessandro&R.]☉
\*PRACTICE AREAS: Patents; Trademarks; Copyrights; Intellectual Property.
**Ritt, D. Jay** ............ '63 '88 C.112 B.A. L.1066 J.D. [Bensinger,G.&R.]
\*PRACTICE AREAS: Civil Litigation; Criminal Litigation; Employment Discrimination; Sexual Harassment.
**Rivera, Amy G.** ............ '58 '93 C.128 B.S.N. L.1148 J.D. [A Laughlin,F.L.&M.]
\*PRACTICE AREAS: Workers' Compensation.
**Rivera, Clark W.** ............ '52 '81 C.112 B.A. L.1068 J.D. [Gibson&R.]
\*PRACTICE AREAS: General Business Litigation; Employer-Employee Law; Wrongful Termination; Probate Litigation; Real Estate Litigation.

**Rivkin, Radler & Kremer**, (AV)
A Partnership including Professional Corporations
123 South Marengo Avenue, Suite 400, 91101☉
Telephone: 818-795-1800 Fax: 818-795-2255
URL: http://www.rivkinradler.com
Members of Firm: Michael R. Brown; George W. Williams, Jr. Associates: David Vendler; Thomas C. Bright; Martin C. Bobak; Richard L. Kellner.
General Civil Practice. Trials and Appeals in all Courts. Insurance Coverage Litigation, Toxic Torts, Professional Malpractice, Products Liability, RICO, Antitrust, Legislative and Administrative, Environmental, Corporate, Securities, Bankruptcy and Creditors Rights, Finance, Real Estate, Banking and Taxation, Trusts and Estates, Labor and Patent Infringement.
Uniondale, New York Office: EAB Plaza. Telephone: 516-357-3000. Cable Address: "Atlaw." Telex: 645-074. Telecopier: 516-357-3333.
Chicago, Illinois Office: Suite 4300, 30 North LaSalle Street. Telephone: 312-782-5680. Telecopier: 312-782-3112.
New York, New York Office: 275 Madison Avenue. Telephone: 212-455-9555. Telecopier: 212-687-9044.
Santa Rosa, California Office: 100 B Street, Suite 300, P.O. Box 14609. Telephone: 707-576-8033. Telecopier: 707-576-7955.
Newark, New Jersey Office: One Gateway Center, Suite 1226. Telephone: 201-622-0900. Fax: 201-622-7878.
*See Professional Biographies, PASADENA, CALIFORNIA*

**Robbins, Dean A.** ............ '50 '77 C.169 B.A. L.1068 J.D.
    Coun., Kaiser Found. Health Plan, Inc.
**Roberts, Barbara E.** ............ '48 '79 C.1097 B.S. L.426 J.D. [Franscell,S.R.&L.]☉
\*PRACTICE AREAS: Police Misconduct Liability Defense; Civil Rights; Municipal and Administrative Law; Medical Malpractice Legal; General Civil.

**Roberts, Larry M.** '57 '82 C.112 B.A. L.426 J.D.
292 South Vinedo Avenue, 91107☉
Telephone: 818-585-8683 Fax: 818-585-1774
\*LANGUAGES: French.
\*PRACTICE AREAS: Contract Law; International Law; Wrongful Discharge Law. Civil Rights, Labor Law, International Law and Business Law. General Civil Litigation.
Los Angeles, California Office: 3415 South Sepulveda Boulevard, Suite 1120. Telephone: 310-391-6800. Fax: 310-391-1725.
*See Professional Biographies, PASADENA, CALIFORNIA*

**Roberts, Patrick M.** ............ '57 '82 C.112 B.A. L.1065 J.D. [Foss&R.]
\*PRACTICE AREAS: Litigation (Financial Institutions); Workouts; Insolvency.
**Robertson, Jeffrey D.** '60 '88 C.679 B.S. L.339 J.D.
    (adm. in IL; not adm. in CA) Corp. Coun., N. Reg., Jacobs Engg. Grp., Inc.
\*RESPONSIBILITIES: Contracts/Business Practice; Litigation Management; Employment Law.
**Robin, Robert M.**, (AV) ............ '48 '76 C.1077 B.A. L.1221 J.D. 131 N. El Molino Ave.
**Robinson, David K.**, (P.C.), (AV) ............ '18 '47 C.674 A.B. L.813 J.D. [Hahn&H.]
\*PRACTICE AREAS: Civil Litigation; Savings and Loan; Condemnation; Redevelopment.
**Robinson, Edward O.** ............ '39 '64 C&L.800 B.S., J.D. [Boyle,O.&R.]
\*PRACTICE AREAS: Probate and Trust Law; Estate Planning.
**Robinson, Michael C.** ............ '54 '91 C.36 B.S. L.809 J.D. 350 W. Colorado Blvd.
**Robinson, Stephan B., Jr.**, (AV) ............ '18 '43 C.197 A.B. L.976 LL.B. 625 Old Mill Rd.‡
**Rodriguez, Maria C.** '53 '80
    C.813 B.A. L.1066 J.D. Coun., Kaiser Found. Health Plan, Inc.
**Rodriguez, Nicholas George** ............ '53 '77 C.188 B.A. L.1066 J.D. Asst. City Atty.
**Rogers, J. Richard**, (BV) ............ '39 '72 L.809 J.D. 155 N. Lake Ave.
**Rohr, Carol Ann** ............ '43 '79 C.800 B.A. L.1137 J.D. [Franscell,S.R.&L.]
\*PRACTICE AREAS: Police Misconduct Liability Defense; Civil Rights; Municipal and Administrative Law; Medical Malpractice Legal; General Civil.

**Romney, David T.**, (AV) .................... '44 '73 C.112 B.A. L.174 J.D. [Barker&R.]
*REPORTED CASES: Bowers v. San Buenaventura (1977, 2d Dist) 75 Ca3d 65; Kimura v. Roberts (1979, 3rd Dist) 89 Ca3d 871.
*PRACTICE AREAS: Business Litigation; Construction Defect Litigation; Community Association Law; Real Estate; Eminent Domain.
Ronay, Peter E., (BV) ..................'42 '70 C&L.426 B.A., J.D. 2234 E. Colorado St.
**Roper, Janine Nesbit** '54 '85 C.112 B.A. L.426 J.D.
Corp. Coun., W. Reg., Jacobs Engg. Grp. Inc.
*RESPONSIBILITIES: Contracts/Business Practice; Litigation Management; Real Estate; Employment Law.
**Rose, Robert J.**, (AV) ........................ '51 '75 C&L.37 B.S., J.D. [Sheldon&M.]
**Rosenstein, Irwin B.** ............ '36 '62 C.659 B.S.Econ. L.273 J.D. Coun., Fannie Mae
*RESPONSIBILITIES: Real Estate Finance; Real Estate.
**Ross, Andrea E.L.** ..................'69 '95 C.112 A.B. L.800 J.D. [Ⓐ Hosp,G.&Assoc.]
*PRACTICE AREAS: Tort Defense; Emphasizing Auto; Products Liability; Premises Liability; Construction Defects.
**Ross, Emrys J.**, (AV)......................... '12 '36 C&L.800 B.S., J.D. [Ⓒ Hahn&H.]
**Rossell, Craig N.** ......................... '51 '81 C.101 B.A. L.1137 J.D. [Hunt,O.B.P.&R.]
*LANGUAGES: French.
*PRACTICE AREAS: Construction; Real Estate.
Rotenberg, Frederick R., (BV) ............ '55 '82 C.112 B.A. L.398 J.D. [Rotenberg&R.]
Rotenberg, Lori Ilane G., (BV) ............ '56 '81 C.763 B.S. L.809 J.D. [Rotenberg&R.]
Rotenberg & Rotenberg, (BV) .......................................221 E. Walnut St.
Rothner, Glenn, (AV) .................'50 '75 C.112 A.B. L.1068 J.D. [Rothner,S.&B.]
Rothner, Segall and Bahan, (AV) ................................. 200 E. Del Mar Blvd.
Rothwell, George C. ......................'36 '72 C.1027 B.S. L.284 J.D. Wkrs. Comp. J.
Rowland, Rita .....................'48 '80 C.112 B.A. L.767 J.D. 1748 N. Sierra Bonita Ave.
Rubbert, Thomas E., (A Professional Corporation), (AV) '35 '61
C&L.800 B.S.L., J.D. PH 790 E. Colo. Blvd., 9th Fl.
**Rupard, Paul L.** .........................'35 '67 C.378 L.809 J.D. [Ⓐ Collins,C.M.&T.]
*PRACTICE AREAS: General Liability; Construction Law; Architects and Engineers Professional Liability.
Russell, David S., (BV) ............ '35 '67 C.668 B.A. L.809 J.D. 301 E. Colorado Blvd.
**Russell, John C.**, (AV) ................ '47 '78 C.1097 B.A. L.1188 J.D. [Russell,H.&J.]
*PRACTICE AREAS: Commercial Litigation; Transportation Law; Employment Law.
**Russell, Loren H., (P.C.)**, (AV) ............'25 '52 C.871 B.S. L.813 LL.B. [Hahn&H.]
*PRACTICE AREAS: Corporations; Business; Securities.
**Russell, Richard L., Jr.** ...............'56 '85 C.112 B.A. L.94 J.D.·[Overlander,L.&R.]
*PRACTICE AREAS: Business and Commercial Litigation; Real Property Litigation; Lender Liability; Wrongful Termination.
**Russell, Theodore W.**, (AV) .......... '10 '34 C.668 B.A. L.800 LL.B. [Russell,H.&J.] ‡

**Russell, Hancock & Jeffries, (AV)**
**200 South Los Robles, Suite 530, 91101**
**Telephone: 818-795-4700 FAX: 818-795-4790**
**Members of Firm: Theodore W. Russell (Retired); Robert W. Hancock; John C. Russell; Kathleen C. Jeffries; Daniel K. Gaston.**
**General Civil and Trial Practice in all State and Federal Courts. Employment, Public Utility, Transportation, Interstate Commerce and Corporation Law.**
**Reference: First Interstate Bank of California, Pasadena Main Office (Los Robles Ave. and Cordova).**
***See Professional Biographies, PASADENA, CALIFORNIA***

Ryan, James J. .................. '24 '52 C.112 B.S. L.893 LL.B. 770 S. Oak Knoll Ave.
Rymer, Pamela Ann ...............'41 '66 C.881 A.B. L.813 LL.B. U.S. Ct. of Appeals
Sai-Ngarm, Sukum ........................'48 '84 C.112 B.S. L.1065 J.D. [S.Sai-Ngarm]
Sai-Ngarm, Sukum, P.C. ................................................ 201 S. Lake Ave.
**St. John, Mary C.** '52 '86 C.112 B.S. L.426 J.D.
Coun., Kaiser Found. Health Plan, Inc.
**Salisbury, Lee W.**, (AV) ...................'51 '76 C.813 B.A. L.800 J.D. [Anderson&S.]
*PRACTICE AREAS: Family Law.
Salisian, Myron H., (AV) ............... '44 '70 C.800 B.A. L.1065 J.D. 100 N. Hill Ave.
Saltzer, Bruce '53 '78 C.668 B.A. L.800 J.D.
Exec. Dir. Assn. of Comm. Mental Health Agencies
Salumbides, Conrad A., Jr., Law Offices of '55 '87
C.1097 B.A. L.1136 J.D. 1122 E. Green St.
**Salz, Constance E.**, (AV) .......................'55 '83 C.1097 B.S. L.809 J.D. [Salz&S.]
*PRACTICE AREAS: Family Law; Criminal; Probate.
**Salz, Frank**, (AV) ......................................'36 '71 C.453 B.S. L.184 J.D. [Salz&S.]
*PRACTICE AREAS: Family Law; Personal Injury.

**Salz & Salz, (AV)**
**150 South Los Robles, Suite 910, 91101**
**Telephone: 818-793-2800 Facsimile: 818-793-9622**
**Members of Firm: Frank Salz (Certified Specialist, Family Law, The State Bar of California Board of Legal Specialization); Constance E. Salz;—Brian Alan Baker (Certified Specialist, Family Law, The State Bar of California Board of Legal Specialization); Mariana A. Hevia.**
**Family Law, Civil Litigation, Personal Injury and Criminal Law.**
***See Professional Biographies, PASADENA, CALIFORNIA***

**Salzman, Ira M. '52 '78 C.112 A.B. L.809 J.D.**
**600 South Lake Avenue, Suite 410, 91106**
**Telephone: 818-578-0043 Fax: 818-578-0503**
***PRACTICE AREAS: Criminal Defense; Public Entity Employee; Defense; Wrongful Termination.**
**General Civil Litigation in all State and Federal Courts with emphasis on the Defense of Professional Negligence, Personal Injury and Public Safety Employees, General Wrongful Termination, Criminal Defense in State and Federal Courts.**
***See Professional Biographies, PASADENA, CALIFORNIA***

Samaha, Thomas J. ......................'62 '87 C.477 B.A. L.426 J.D. [Samaha,G.&S.]
Samaha, Grogin & Stulberg, LLP ........................... 911 E. Colorado Blvd., 3rd Fl.
**Samberg, John M.**, (AV) ........................ '— '84 C.112 B.A. L.809 J.D. [Bisno&S.]
**Samuels, Sandor E.**, (AV) '52 '77 C.674 A.B. L.1068 J.D.
Mng. Dir., Legal, Gen. Coun. & Secy., Countrywide Funding Corp.
Samulon, Eliot R. ....................................'50 '75 C.112 B.A. L.426 J.D. [Potter,C.&S.]
**Sanborn, James B.** .......................'49 '78 C.112 B.A. L.809 J.D. [Ⓐ Cooper,K.&S.]
Sanchez, Ernest E., (AV) ................'30 '59 C&L.426 B.A., LL.B. 787 Lincoln Ave.
Sanchez, Terence M. ......................'47 '77 C.768 B.A. L.770 J.D. Coun., Community Bk.
**Sanders, Ann Marie** ......................'69 '95 C.477 B.A. L.809 J.D. [Franscell,S.R.&L.]
**Santos, Angel A.** .....'61 '86 C.112 B.S. L.464 J.D. Coun., Kaiser Found. Health Plan, Inc.
Santwier, Dennis Rickard, (AV) ..... '42 '70 C.767 B.A. L.1049 J.D. 35 S. Raymond Ave.

**Santwier, Rickard, (AV) '42 '70 C.767 B.A. L.763 J.D.**
**35 South Raymond Avenue Suite 301, 91105**
**Telephone: 818-449-6504; 213-681-4425 FAX: 213-681-4436**
**(Certified Specialist, Criminal Law, The State Bar of California Board of Legal Specialization).**
***REPORTED CASES: Joe Z. v. Superior Court, 3Cal 3rd 797, 1970; Carlos v. Superior Ct. 35 Cal 3rd 131, 1983.**
**Criminal and Juvenile Defense in all State and Federal Courts.**
***See Professional Biographies, PASADENA, CALIFORNIA***

Sassano, Matthew, (AV) ...................'54 '83 C.107 B.A. L.809 J.D. 200 S. Los Robles
**Scarsi, Mark C.** ............................'64 '96 C.823 B.S. L.276 J.D. [Ⓐ Christie,P.&H.]
*PRACTICE AREAS: Patent; Trademark; Copyright.
Schaefer, Howard G. ................... '45 '71 C.1097 B.S. L.800 J.D. Schaefer Bros. Ltd.
**Scharf, Jeffrey D.** ........................'55 '82 C.112 B.A. L.1049 J.D. [Cooper,K.&S.]⊙
Schlesinger, Lewis, (AV) ..........'46 '72 C&L.800 B.A., J.D. 527 S. Lake Ave. Ste. 106
**Schlueter, David S.** ...............................'57 '83 C.339 B.A. L.770 J.D. [Ⓐ Baraban&T.]
*REPORTED CASES: Richardson v. GAB Business Services, Inc., (1984) 161 Cal. App. 3d 519, 579 Cal. Rptr. 519.
*PRACTICE AREAS: Civil Litigation; Construction Law.

**Schneider, Steven A. '45 '78 C.605 B.A. L.800 J.D.**
**301 North Lake Avenue, Eighth Floor, 91101**
**Telephone: 818-886-4946 Fax: 818-583-9187**
**General Civil Trial and Appellate Practice in all State and Federal Courts, with emphasis in General Business and Commercial Litigation, including Construction Law and Insurance Law.**
***See Professional Biographies, PASADENA, CALIFORNIA***

**Schofield, Charles T. '49 '78 C.1097 B.A. L.1049 J.D.**
**200 S. Los Robles Avenue, Suite 500, 91101**
**Telephone: 818-578-0708 FAX: 818-578-0244**
**Trust, Wills, Probate, Estate Planning, Tax, Corporate Law, Business and Commercial.**
***See Professional Biographies, PASADENA, CALIFORNIA***

**Schoth, Karl W., & Associates, (AV) '55 '84 C.05 L.809 J.D.**
**1122 East Green Street, 91106**
**Telephone: 818-395-7514 Facsimile: 818-796-2554**
**Email: kschoth@earthlink.net**
***REPORTED CASES: Allstate v. Fibus, et al (9th Circ. 1988) 855 F.2d 660; Prieto v. State Farm (1991) 225 Cal.App. 3d 1188.**
***PRACTICE AREAS: Personal Injury Law; Medical Malpractice; Elder Abuse; Arbitrator; Mediator.**
**Associates: Ladan Alavi.**
**Personal Injury, Specializing in medical malpractice and elder abuse law.**
***See Professional Biographies, PASADENA, CALIFORNIA***

Schroeder, Roger M. ..................'56 '81 C&L.800 B.A., J.D. 215 No. Marengo Ave.
Schultz, Michael G. ....................'55 '87 C.101 B.A. L.178 J.D. 2570 E. Walnut St.
**Schwartz, Edward R.** .......................'47 '82 C.860 B.A. L.818 J.D. [Christie,P.&H.]
*PRACTICE AREAS: Patent; Trademark; Copyright and Unfair Competition; Litigation and Prosecution.
Schwarz, Deborah Ballins ..................'53 '78 C.940 B.A. L.426 J.D. [Phelps,S.&P.]
Schweger, Donald E. '26 '53 C.473 B.S. L.477 LL.B.
Sr. Coun., Fed. Natl. Mtge. Assn.‡
Schwimmer, Jerome, (AV) ............. '22 '49 C.112 A.B. L.800 J.D. 812 LaBellorita‡
Scolinos, Harry F., (BV) '44 '74 C.1075 B.S. L.1148 J.D.
350 West Colorado Blvd., #200
Scott, Andrea K. '52 '91 C.674 B.A. L.895 J.D.
(adm. in PA; not adm. in CA) 141 E. Walnut St.
Segall, Anthony R. .........................'55 '81 C.976 B.A. L.1066 J.D. [Rothner,S.&B.]
**Seibel, Richard D.**, (AV) '30 '61 C.813 B.S. L.208 J.D.
[Christie,P.&H.] (See Pat. Sect.)
*PRACTICE AREAS: Patent and Trademark Prosecution; Material Science.
Seifert, Melvin F. ..........................'52 '77 C.112 B.A. L.426 J.D. 155 North Lake Ave.
Seims, Alan G. ...........................'51 '83 C.800 B.A. L.426 J.D. 1605 N. Altadena Dr.
**Selth, James R.** ..........................'58 '86 C.112 B.A. L.1137 J.D. [McKinley&C.]
*PRACTICE AREAS: Banking Litigation; Bankruptcy; Receiverships; Foreclosure; Pre-Judgment Remedies.
Seminara, Philip C., Jr. '61 '90 C.107 B.A. L.1148 J.D.
(adm. in ND; not adm. in CA) 1252 N. Allen Ave.
**Senecal, H. Jess**, (AV) ............... '30 '56 C.684 A.B. L.1068 J.D. [Lagerlof,S.B.&S.]
**Senior, Mark M.** ...........................'47 '87 C.859 B.A. L.809 J.D. [Ⓐ Cooper,K.&S.]
Serio, Collette N. .....................'52 '78 C.112 B.A. L.1095 J.D. Comr., Mun. Ct.
Serra, Anthony J. .....................'31 '72 C.999 L.1190 LL.B. 234 E. Colorado Blvd.
**Shaddow, Tali** ...........................'65 '92 C.112 B.A. L.426 J.D. [Hahn&H.]
*LANGUAGES: Hebrew.
*REPORTED CASES: Western Union v. First Data, 20 Cal.App.4, 1530.
*PRACTICE AREAS: Civil Litigation.

**Shaller, Frederick C., Law Office of, (AV) '53 '79 C.800 B.A. L.426 J.D.**
**Walnut Plaza, 215 North Marengo Avenue, Second Floor, 91101**
**Telephone: 818-796-9669 Facsimile: 818-304-1399**
***PRACTICE AREAS: Personal Injury Law; Medical Malpractice Law; Torts.**
**Medical Malpractice, Products Liability, Personal Injury.**
***See Professional Biographies, PASADENA, CALIFORNIA***

Shaller, Kimberly W. ....................... '56 '80 C&L.800 J.D. 215 N. Marengo Ave.
Shannon, Michael Timothy, (AV) ... '44 '70 C.112 B.A. L.1068 J.D. 35 S. Raymond Ave.
Shardlow, Thomas E., (AV) ................ '50 '76 C.101 B.A. L.1068 J.D. [Shardlow&V.]
Shardlow & Vick, (AV) ........................................ 790 E. Colorado Blvd., 9th Fl.
**Sheh, Elisabeth F.** ......................'68 '94 C.112 B.A. L.426 J.D. [Ⓐ Gutierrez&P.]
*PRACTICE AREAS: Civil Rights Defense; Local Government Liability; Employer Liability.
**Sheldon, Jeffrey G.**, (AV) '47 '75
C.119 B.S. L.426 J.D. [Sheldon&M.] (See Pat. Sect.) (⊙Upland)

**Sheldon & Mak, (AV)**
**9th Floor, 225 South Lake Avenue, 91101-3005⊙**
**Telephone: 818-796-4000 Fax: 818-795-6321**
**URL: http://www.usip.com**
**Members of Firm: Jeffrey G. Sheldon; Danton K. Mak; Denton L. Anderson; Surjit P. Singh Soni; Robert J. Rose; William J. Brutocao. Of Counsel: Sol L. Goldstein (Not admitted in CA); Joseph E. Mueth. Associates: Erin McKeewn Joyce; Stephen R. Seccombe (Resident, San Bernadino Office); Douglas H. Morseburg; Anthony G. Vella (Not admitted in CA); Yingchao Xiao (Not admitted in CA); Edward A. Brown (Not admitted in CA); David Farah; Lee Hsu.**
**Patent, Trademark and Copyright Law. Antitrust and Unfair Competition, Trade Secrets, Customs Law and related causes in all State and Federal Courts.**
**Representative Clients: TRW; Raychem; Southern California Edison.**
**Reference: Citizens Bank (Pasadena, California).**
**San Bernardino, California Office: Suite 503, 290 North D Street, 92401. Telephone: 909-889-3649. Fax: 909-889-9865.**
**Upland, California Office: Suite 210, 222 North Mountain Avenue, 91786. Telephone: 909-946-3939.**
***See Professional Biographies, PASADENA, CALIFORNIA***

Shelley, Robert R., (AV) ..................'27 '54 C.112 B.A. L.1066 LL.B. [Shelley&G.]
Shelley & Graff, A Prof. Law Corp., (AV) .............................301 East Colorado Blvd.
Shenk, John W., (AV) ...................'15 '47 C.813 A.B. L.809 J.D. 1435 Parkview Ave.‡
Shoop, Robert E. ......................'56 '80 C.112 B.A. L.809 J.D. 74 N. Pasadena Ave.
Shore, Marcus S. ........................'57 '84 C.473 B.S. L.117 J.D. R.M. Parsons Co.
Shuai, Yee-Horn ..................'53 '82 C.061 LL.B. L.1065 J.D. 301 E. Colorado Blvd.
**Singh Soni, Surjit P.** ....... '54 '87 C.025 B.Sc. L.472 J.D. [Sheldon&M.] (See Pat. Sect.)
*LANGUAGES: Hindi and Punjabi.
**Skabrat, Steven P.** '62 '93 C.494 B.S.C.S. L.1035 J.D.
(adm. in MN; not adm. in CA; See Pat. Sect.) [Ⓐ Christie,P.&H.]
*PRACTICE AREAS: Patents; Copyrights; Computer Law.
Slate, William B. '66 '92 C.111 B.S. L.1068 J.D.
Assoc. Corp. Coun., Gemstar Development Corporation (Pat.)
Slater, Calvin A. ........................'56 '81 C.800 B.S. L.1068 J.D. 200 S. Los Robles

**Sloan, Michael L. '59 '87 C&L.426 B.A., J.D.**
**596 North Lake Avenue, Suite 204, 91101**
**Telephone: 818-584-9343 Fax: 818-584-9349**
***PRACTICE AREAS: Litigation (40%, 25); Labor and Employment (40%, 25); Workers Compensation (20%, 100).**

(This Listing Continued)

CAA493P

**Sloan, Michael L. (Continued)**
Employment Law including Sexual Harassment, Gender, Age & Race Discrimination, Workers Compensation, Civil Litigation, Business, Personal Injury.
*See Professional Biographies, PASADENA, CALIFORNIA*

Sloat, Robert Wm. '54 '78 C.774 B.A. L.309 J.D. 225 S. Lake Ave., 9th Fl.
**Slocum, Priscilla F.** '46 '92 C.112 B.S. L.426 J.D. [Franscell,S.R.&L.]
*PRACTICE AREAS: Civil Rights Defense; Appellate Practice.
Smith, Ann Lonergan '35 '80 C.112 B.A. L.1068 J.D. [Smith,C.&A.S.]
Smith, Chester Leo, (AV) '22 '49 C.145 B.A. L.309 J.D. [Smith,C.&A.S.]
**Smith, Eric C.** '60 '86 C.800 B.S. L.1137 J.D. [Hunt,O.B.P.&R.]
*PRACTICE AREAS: Construction; Real Estate.
Smith, Frederic M. '41 '76 C.674 A.B. L.800 J.D. 1100 E. Green St.
Smith, Helen Bunt '42 '72 C.112 B.S. L.809 J.D. 465 E. Union St.
**Smith, Jeffrey B.** '65 '91 C.800 A.B. L.464 J.D. [McClaugherty&Assoc.]⊙
*PRACTICE AREAS: Insurance Defense Litigation.
**Smith, Kristi J.** '59 '85 C.763 B.S. L.809 J.D.
Assoc. Div. Coun., Chicago Title Ins. Co.
*RESPONSIBILITIES: Real Property Law; Title Insurance Law.
**Smith, Marilyn M.** '51 '76 C.800 B.A. L.1068 J.D. [Bensinger,G.&R.]
*PRACTICE AREAS: Intellectual Property Law; Civil Litigation; Insurance.
Smith, Paul F. '41 '68 C.112 B.S. L.426 J.D. 424 N. Lake Ave.
Smith, R. William '45 '76 650 Sierra Madre Villa Ave.
Smith, Chester & Ann Smith, (AV) 636 East Walnut St.
Snider, Warren S. '51 '88 C.1097 B.S. L.426 J.D. [Jett&L.]
Snitzer, Alan B. '52 '78 C.107 B.A. L.809 J.D. [A.B.Snitzer]
Snitzer, Alan B., A Prof. Corp., Law Offices of 135 N. Los Robles Ave.
**Soderberg, Geraldine M.** '40 '84
C.112 A.B. L.426 J.D. Maj. Lend. Coun., Chicago Title Ins. Co.
*RESPONSIBILITIES: Real Property Title Insurance; Title Insurance Underwriting.
**Soldwedel, Fred W., (Professional Corporation),** (AV) '31 '58
C.597 B.S. L.813 LL.B. [Soldwedel,P.B.&C.]
*PRACTICE AREAS: Estate Planning Law; Primary and Ancillary Probate Law; Non-Profit Organizations Law.

**Soldwedel, Palermo, Barbaro & Chinen, (AV)**
A Partnership including Professional Corporations
Formerly Rinehart, Merriam, Parker & Berg
**Suite 700, 301 East Colorado Boulevard, 91101**
Telephone: 818-793-5196 Los Angeles: 213-681-7226 FAX: 818-793-3602
J. H. Merriam (1862-1934); Jay D. Rinehart (1891-1964); Ralph T. Merriam (1891-1968); Ronald D. Kincaid (1941-1980). Partners: Peter R. Palermo (Professional Corporation); Philip Barbaro, Jr.; Richard L. Chinen. Of Counsel: J. Harold Berg (Professional Corporation); Fred W. Soldwedel (Professional Corporation); Harvey M. Parker (Retired).
Probate, Estate Planning, General Civil and Trial Practice. Federal and State Tax Law. Corporation Law. Family Law. Real Property Law.
Representative Clients: Southern California Presbyterian Homes; Clearman's Restaurants; Monte Vista Grove Homes; Citizens Commercial Trust & Savings Bank of Pasadena; Northern Trust of California.
References: Bank of America National Trust & Savings Assn. (Pasadena Main Office); Sanwa Bank California (Pasadena Office); Northern Trust of California.
*See Professional Biographies, PASADENA, CALIFORNIA*

**Solis, Javier** '46 '74 C&L.426 B.S.M.E., J.D. Gen. Coun., Ameron Int'l Corp.
*LANGUAGES: Spanish.
*RESPONSIBILITIES: Transactions; Corporations; Securities; Litigation Management.
**Somberg, James S.** '37 '67
C.111 B.S. L.1068 LL.B. Asst. Gen. Coun., Ameron Int'l Corp.
*RESPONSIBILITIES: Transactional Agreements; Litigation Management.
Sommers, Stephen P. '49 '77 C.813 B.A. L.809 J.D. 350 W. Colorado Blvd.
**Soodik, Michael J., (BV) '50 '77 C.901 B.A. L.1190 J.D.**
**Suite 910, 150 South Los Robles, 91101**
Telephone: 818-793-3322 FAX: 818-793-9622
(Certified Specialist, Family Law, The State Bar of California Board of Legal Specialization).
*PRACTICE AREAS: Family Law; Personal Injury Law; Criminal Law.
Associates: Phillip I. Myer.
Family Law.
Sosna, Samuel L., Jr. '34 '59 C.813 A.B. L.1068 J.D. Pres. J., WCAB
Sosothikul, Janette H. '43 '80 C.1077 B.A. L.1095 J.D. 1122 E. Green St.
Sowers, Donald G. '53 '86 C.999 A.S. L.809 J.D. [Takakjian&S.]⊙
Speizer, Nancy Rosenblum '56 '80 C.339 A.B. L.1066 J.D. Norton Simon Museum
Spencer, Barbara A. '39 '83 C.439 B.A. L.1137 J.D. [McCarthy,G.&B.]
Sprague, Richard W., (AV) '13 '37 C.800 L.37 J.B. 909 E. Green St.
**Spraic, Mark A., (AV) '46 '72 C.800 B.A. L.1066 J.D.**
**150 East Colorado Boulevard, Suite 201, 91105**
Telephone: 818-792-9333 Facsimile: 818-449-6299
Civil Litigation, General Business including Mergers and Acquisitions, Partnerships, Creditors Rights, Corporate and Real Estate.
*See Professional Biographies, PASADENA, CALIFORNIA*
Stabile, Paul A. '48 '79 C.1097 B.A. L.398 J.D. 696 E. Colorado Blvd.
**Stacy, Peter L.** '70 '95 C.605 A.B. L.904 J.D. [Collins,C.M.&T.]
*PRACTICE AREAS: Public Entity Defense; General Liability; Construction Law.
Steck, Emil, Jr., (AV) '12 '35 C.800 A.B. L.309 J.D. 221 E. Walnut St.
**Steele, Cynthia L.K.** '63 '92 C.851 B.S.N. L.37 J.D. [Hammond,Z.&C.]
*PRACTICE AREAS: Professional Liability; Medical Malpractice Defense.
**Stellwagen, Robert H., Jr.** '64 '90 C.112 B.A. L.1065 J.D. [Collins,C.M.&T.]
*PRACTICE AREAS: Architects and Engineers Professional Liability; Premises Liability; Products Liability; Public Liability.
Stephens, Marie C. '46 '72 3501 San Pasqual St.
**Stewart, Brian K.** '61 '86 C.927 B.A. L.365 J.D. [Collins,C.M.&T.]
*PRACTICE AREAS: Architects and Engineers Professional Liability; Trial Practice; Public Entity Liability; Product Liability; Premises Liability.
Stewart, Garry D. '54 '79 C.668 B.A. L.800 J.D. [Stewart&H.]
Stewart, Harold W. '38 '68 C.800 B.S.P.Ad. L.809 J.D. 80 S. Lake Ave.
Stewart & Harris, (AV) 150 E. Colorado Blvd, Ste 216
Still, William E., (AV) '24 '51 C.112 B.A. L.1065 LL.B. 468 Allendale Rd.‡
Stoever, Thomas W. '36 '61 C.112 B.S. L.1065 J.D. Supr. Ct. J.
Stolzberg, Michael M., (AV) '14 '36 C.563 B.B.A. L.178 LL.B.
1540 Arroyo View Dr.‡
Stone, Gary L. '41 '72 C.112 B.A. L.309 J.D. Gen. Coun., The Parsons Corp.
Stone, Willard J., (AV) '13 '37 C&L.477 A.B., J.D. 700 S. Lake Ave.‡

**Stone & Doyle, (AV)**
**527 South Lake, Suite 103, 91101**
Telephone: 818-449-1196 Telecopier: 818-795-6402
Willard J. Stone (Retired); Michael C. Doyle; Paula G. Waluch.
Practice Limited to Estate Planning, Probate and Trust Administration, Corporation, Business and Tax Law, Business Litigation.
References: Wells Fargo Bank, N.A.; Sanwa Bank; Security Pacific National Bank (Trust Department); Citizens Commercial Trust & Savings Bank, Pasadena, California.
*See Professional Biographies, PASADENA, CALIFORNIA*

Stormer, Dan, (AV) '47 '74 C.895 B.A. L.569 J.D. [Hadsell&S.]

**Streeter, Linda L.** '57 '82 C.112 B.S. L.426 J.D. [Gutierrez&P.]
**Strickland, Tracy** '54 '79 C.602 B.A. L.990 J.D. [Franscell,S.R.&L.]⊙
*PRACTICE AREAS: Police Misconduct Liability Defense; Civil Rights; Municipal and Administrative Law; Medical Legal; General Civil.
**Stuart, Beverly A.** '— '77 C.329 B.A. L.800 J.D.
Coun., Kaiser Found. Health Plan, Inc.
Stulberg, Barry A. '61 '87 C.112 B.A. L.426 J.D. [Samaha,G.&S.]

**Stumreiter, John J., Law Offices of, (BV) '45 '73 C.976 B.A. L.309 J.D.**
**225 South Lake Avenue, Ninth Floor, 91101**
Telephone: 818-304-0300 Fax: 818-795-6321
General Practice with emphasis on Litigation and Bankruptcy.
*See Professional Biographies, PASADENA, CALIFORNIA*

Sugars, Steven L. '65 '91 C.112 B.A. L.990 J.D. 3579 E. Foothill Blvd.
**Summers, Robert C.,** (AV) '31 '59 C&L.800 B.S.L., J.D. [Taylor K.S.&R.]
*PRACTICE AREAS: Civil Trial; Estate Planning; Probate; General Practice.
Summers, Ronald L. '38 '78 C.912 L.809 J.D. 750 E. Green St.
Sutton, Christopher A. '53 '84 C.112 B.A. L.809 J.D. 35 E. Union St.
**Swafford, Jack T.,** (AV) '22 '53 C&L.800 B.S., J.D. [Lagerlof,S.B.&S.]
**Swaidan, Karl I.,** (AV) '58 '83 C&L.800 B.S., J.D. [Hahn&H.]
*PRACTICE AREAS: Estate Planning; Probate; Taxation.
Sweetman, Susan '56 '86 C.1042 B.A. L.398 J.D. 199 S. Los Robles
**Swernofsky, Steven A.** '56 '85 C.453 S.B. L.1068 J.D. [D'Alessandro&R.]⊙
*PRACTICE AREAS: Patents; Trademarks; Copyrights; Intellectual Property.
**Swift, H. Melvin, Jr.,** (AV) '24 '50 C&L.813 A.B., LL.B. [Lagerlof,S.B.&S.]
Takakjian & Sowers, (BV)
225 S. Lake Ave., 9th Fl. (⊙Los Angeles, Encino, Oxnard, Orange & Long Beach)

**Talt, Alan R., (AV) '29 '55 C.112 A.B. L.1065 J.D.**
**Suite 710, 790 East Colorado Boulevard, 91101**
Telephone: 818-356-0853 Telecopier: 818-356-0731
Estate Planning, Trust, Probate, Business and Real Property Law.
Reference: U.S. Trust Company California.
*See Professional Biographies, PASADENA, CALIFORNIA*

**Talton, David H.** '49 '74 C.1089 B.A. L.326 J.D.
(adm. in TX; not adm. in CA) Mgr., Legal Dept., Jacobs Engg. Grp., Inc.
*RESPONSIBILITIES: Contracts/Business Practice (Private Sector and Government); Litigation Management; Employment Law; Environmental Law; International Law.
Tan, Alwin S. M. '38 '73 C.897 B.A. L.352 J.D.
(adm. in IA; not adm. in CA) 1233 Encino Dr.‡

**Tarkanian, William V., Law Offices of '63 '89 C.154 B.A. L.36 J.D.**
**150 South Los Robles Avenue, Suite 860, 91101**
Telephone: 818-683-9373 Fax: 818-683-9787
General Civil Trial in all State and Federal Courts. Family Law, Bankruptcy including Creditors, Debtors, Chapter 7, Chapter 11, Personal Injury.
*See Professional Biographies, PASADENA, CALIFORNIA*

Tashima, A. Wallace '34 '62 C.112 A.B. L.309 LL.B. U.S. Cir. J.
**Taylor, Edwin W.,** (AV) '99 '30 C.659 B.S. L.800 J.D. [Taylor K.S.&R.] ‡
**Taylor, John D.,** (AV) '33 '60 C.112 B.S. L.1066 J.D. [Taylor K.S.&R.]
*PRACTICE AREAS: Estate Planning; Probate; Trusts; Taxation.
Taylor, Laurie J. '53 '87 C.967 B.A. L.112 J.D. Law Clk., U.S. Cir. J.

**Taylor Kupfer Summers & Rhodes, (AV)**
**301 East Colorado Boulevard, Suite 407, 91101-1911**
Telephone: 818-304-0953 Fax: 818-795-6375
Members of Firm: Stanley A. Barker (1920-1965); Owen E. Kupfer (1908-1991); Edwin W. Taylor (Retired); Kenneth O. Rhodes (Retired); John D. Taylor; Robert C. Summers; Stephen F. Peters (Certified Specialist, Estate Planning, Trust and Probate Law, The State Bar of California Board of Legal Specialization).
General Civil and Trial Practice in all State and Federal Courts. Estate Planning, Probate, Trust, Taxation, Business, Corporation, Securities and Real Estate Law.
Reference: CenFed Bank (Pasadena).
*See Professional Biographies, PASADENA, CALIFORNIA*

Teal, Mildred '28 '69 L.809 J.D. 441 E. California Blvd.
Telleria, Anthony F., (BV) '38 '64 C.426 L.809 LL.B. 675 S. Arroyo Pkwy.
**Teperson, Jonathan B.** '65 '91 C.112 B.A. L.1065 J.D. [Marquez&T.]
*PRACTICE AREAS: Civil Litigation; Casualty; Employment.
**Teragawa, Karen Y.** '53 '81
C.668 B.A. L.1068 J.D. Coun., Kaiser Found. Health Plan, Inc.
**Teske, Christopher S.** '54 '80 C.602 B.A. L.893 J.D. [Baraban&T.]
*REPORTED CASES: McDonald v. John P. Scripps Newspaper, 210 Cal. App. 3d 100; 257 Cal. Rptr. 473.
*PRACTICE AREAS: Civil Litigation; General Liability; Products Liability; Personal Injury; Construction Law.
Testa, Alfred '10 '33 L.809 LL.B. 1122 E. Green St.
**Thomas, Lane J.,** (BV) '51 '76 C.112 B.A. L.426 J.D. [Millikan&T.]
*PRACTICE AREAS: Business Litigation; Family Law; Real Property Law; Probate; Estate Planning.
**Thon, William M.,** (AV) '38 '69 C.642 L.1148 LL.B. [Thon,B.V.P.&N.]
*PRACTICE AREAS: Personal Injury Law; Malpractice; Maritime Law.

**Thon, Beck, Vanni, Phillipi & Nutt, A Professional Corporation, (AV)**
**1100 East Green Street, 91106-2506**
Telephone: 818-795-8333 Fax: 818-449-9933
William M. Thon; Thomas P. Beck; Gregory R. Vanni; Steven V. Phillipi; Brian C. Nutt;—David M. Phillips. Of Counsel: Anthony de los Reyes.
Civil Trial and Appellate Practice. Personal Injury, Products Liability, Medical Malpractice and Maritime Law.
*See Professional Biographies, PASADENA, CALIFORNIA*

Thorpe, Maura F. '62 '88 C.112 B.A. L.426 J.D. 2245 E. Colorado Blvd.‡
**Throckmorton, Robert S.** '67 '95 C&L.101 B.A., J.D. [Throckmorton,B.O.&T.]
*LANGUAGES: Spanish.
*PRACTICE AREAS: Civil Litigation; Construction Law; Partnership Law; Elder Law.

**Throckmorton, Beckstrom, Oakes & Tomassian LLP, (AV)**
**Corporate Center Pasadena, 225 South Lake Avenue, Suite 500, 91101-3005⊙**
Telephone: 818-568-2500; 213-681-2321 Fax: 818-405-0786
Members of Firm: A. Robert Throckmorton (Resident, Irvine Office); Spencer S. Beckstrom; George A. Oakes; Serge Tomassian (Resident, Irvine Office); David Alan Huffaker; Robert S. Throckmorton.
Construction (claims and defects), Real Estate, Insurance, Business, Commercial and Medical Legal Law. General Civil Litigation, Defense of Religious Institutions. All aspects of Trial and Appellate Work.
References Available Upon Request.
Irvine, California Office: Suite 350, 19800 MacArthur Boulevard 92715. Telephone: 714-955-2280. Fax: 714-467-8081.
*See Professional Biographies, PASADENA, CALIFORNIA*

**Thyne, Rebecca J.** '43 '86 C.112 B.A. L.426 J.D. [Lagerlof,S.B.&S.]
Tighe, M. Joan '19 '53 C.700 B.A. L.724 LL.B. 720 S. Orange Grove Blvd.
**Tips, Scott C.** '— '80 C.112 A.B. L.1066 J.D. [Bisno&S.]
Titus, Lewis R., Jr. '42 '73 C.800 B.A. L.426 J.D. 70 N. Catalina Ave.
Tkach, John A. '51 '80 L.1095 J.D. 462 S. Marengo
Tolkin, Jonathan A. '63 '92 C.112 B.A. L.426 J.D. Tolkin Grp.‡

**Toms, Robert L., Jr.** ...'58 '85 C.154 B.A. L.228 J.D. [A Reed&B.]
*PRACTICE AREAS: Business Litigation; Real Estate Transactions.
Tong, Adrianne ...'57 '82 C.112 B.A. L.1065 J.D. 323 S. Roosevelt
Toomer, Anne P., (AV) ...'30 '55 C.605 B.A. L.1068 LL.B. 99 S. Lake Ave.
Toomer, Bruce M., (BV) ...'57 '82 C.605 A.B. L.1148 J.D. 99 S. Lake Ave.
**Torigian, Victoria K.** ...'65 '93 C.990 B.S. L.809 J.D. [Hammond,Z.&C.]
*PRACTICE AREAS: Professional Liability; Medical Malpractice.
Torres, Leonard E., (AV) ...'43 '74 C.1097 B.A. L.1068 J.D. [Torres&B.]
Torres & Brenner, (AV) ...Ste. 614, 301 E. Colorado Blvd.
Tortorelli, Maria C. ...'54 '80 C.112 B.A. L.426 J.D. [A Hartman&F.]
Tosney, Daniel M. ...'41 '79 C.1097 M.A. L.809 J.D. 1978 Galbreth Dr.
**Toutant, Linda M.** ...'62 '88 C.112 B.A. L.602 J.D. [A Kolts&N.]
*PRACTICE AREAS: Construction; Wrongful Termination.
Towne, Raymond L. ...'51 '88 C.668 B.A. L.426 J.D. Research Atty. to Supr. Ct.
Townsend, Robert J. ...'37 '64 C.112 A.B. L.1065 J.D. 125 N. Allen Ave.
Traber, Theresa M. ...'56 '84 C.477 B.A. L.588 J.D. 772 E. Elizabeth St.
**Traver, Robert J.**, (AV) ...'48 '74 C&L.426 B.A., J.D. [Collins,C.M.&T.]
*PRACTICE AREAS: General Liability; Public Liability; Malpractice; Premises Liability; Construction Law.
Travis, Philip '14 '39 C.563 B.S. L.276 J.D.
(adm. in DC; not adm. in CA) NASA
Trayner, Ronald G., (AV) ...'42 '68 C.605 A.B. L.813 J.D. [McDermott&T.]
Tripodes, Peter L. ...'43 '69 C.112 A.B. L.1065 J.D. 117 E. Colo. Blvd.
Tronosco, Cedric ....'50 '79 C.1097 M.A. L.1137 J.D. Suite 209, 1214 E. Colorado Blvd.
Trowbridge, Glen M. W. '62 '87
C.999 B.A. L.469 J.D. V.P. & Coun., Lawyers Title Ins. Corp.
Tucker, Glen E. ...'44 '72 C.426 B.A. L.809 J.D. 155 S. El Molino Ave.
**Turner, Andrew D.** ...'54 '85 C.1169 B.A. L.800 J.D. [Lagerlof,S.B.&S.]
**Turner, Keith A.** ...'57 '85 C.1077 B.A. L.1066 J.D. [A Cooper,K.&S.]
*PRACTICE AREAS: Insurance Coverage; Bad Faith; Appellate Practice.

**Turner, Scott C., (AV) '48 '78 C.112 A.B. L.800 J.D. BB**
**301 North Lake Avenue Suite 700, 91101⊙**
**Telephone: 818-440-1822 FAX: 818-440-9409**
**Insurance Claims and Litigation regarding Insurance Coverage of Construction Disputes.**
**Carmel, California Office: P.O. Box 1671, 93921. Telephone: 408-626-5626. FAX: 408-626-5634.**
***See Professional Biographies, PASADENA, CALIFORNIA***

**Tyre, James S.**, (AV) ...'53 '78 C.197 A.B. L.426 J.D. [Bigelow,M.&T.]
*REPORTED CASES: Nahrstedt v. Lakeside Village Condominium Assn., 8 Cal. 4th 361 (1994) (briefed and argued as Amicus Curiae); Miller v. Nestande, 192 Cal. App. 3d 191 (1987); Day v. Rosenthal, 170 Cal. App. 3d 1125 (1985); Santa Clarita Water Co. v. Lyons, 161 Cal. App. 3d 450 (1984); Maple Properties v. Harris, 158 Cal. App. 3d 997 (1984).
*PRACTICE AREAS: Corporate Law; Business Litigation; Health Care Law; First Amendment; Real Estate Law.
Tyson, Kevin ...'59 '93 C.999 B.A. L.464 J.D. Ste., 300, 265 N. Euclid
**Tyson, Richard P. B., (Inc.)**, (AV) ...'19 '50 C.800 A.B. L.809 J.D. [Tyson&I.]
*PRACTICE AREAS: Criminal Defense.

**Tyson & Ipswitch, (AV)**
**A Partnership of Professional Corporations**
**Suite 526, 301 East Colorado Boulevard, 91101**
**Telephone: 818-792-1156; 213-681-6894 Telecopier: 818-792-9230**
**Richard P. B. Tyson (Inc.); Candis Tyson Ipswitch (Inc.) (Certified Specialist, Estate Planning, Trust and Probate Law, The California Board of Legal Specialization).**
**Criminal and Civil Trial Practice. Probate, Trusts and Conservatorships.**
**Reference: Citizens Commercial Trust & Savings Bank of Pasadena.**
***See Professional Biographies, PASADENA, CALIFORNIA***

Udovic, Michael J., (BV) ...'48 '76 C.1042 B.A. L.1190 J.D. 150 E. Colorado Blvd.
Unrot, David ...'37 '65 C.112 B.A. L.800 LL.B. 2234 E. Colorado Blvd.
Unruh, Carol G. ...'48 '82 L.1148 J.D. P.O. Box 94547
Urtuzuastegui, Charles ...'42 '67 C.642 B.A. L.37 J.D. [Hart&M.]
**Valdivia, Jeannette E.** ...'51 '80 C.112 B.A. L.426 J.D. [J.E.Valdivia]
*LANGUAGES: Spanish.
*PRACTICE AREAS: Warranty; Product Liability; Employer; Business and Insurance Litigation.

**Valdivia, Jeannette E., Law Offices of**
**301 East Colorado Boulevard Suite 200, 91101-1977**
**Telephone: 818-395-0395 Facsimile: 818-395-0396**
**Jeannette E. Valdivia. Of Counsel: Antoinette M. Marino.**
**Product Liability, Warranty, Insurance, Employer and Business Litigation. Health Management.**
***See Professional Biographies, PASADENA, CALIFORNIA***

Vanner, Bruce S. ...'44 '79 C.1109 B.A. L.809 J.D. Exec. V.P., Bierly & Assocs.
**Vanni, Gregory R.**, (AV) ...'53 '82 C.1075 B.A. L.426 J.D. [Thon,B.V.P.&N.]
*PRACTICE AREAS: Personal Injury Law; Medical Malpractice.
Vanni, Lawrence J., (AV) ...'28 '61 C.426 B.S. [McColgan&V.]
**van Schoonenberg, Robert G.** '46 '75 C.436 B.A. L.477 J.D.
Sr. V.P., Gen. Coun. & Secy., Avery Dennison Corp.
*RESPONSIBILITIES: Corporate Law; Mergers and Acquisitions Law; Securities Law; Antitrust Law; International Law.
Vargas, Ernest A., A Law Corporation, (AV) '38 '65 C.112 A.B. L.426 J.D.
[Vargas&V.]
Vargas, Robert A. ...'56 '88 C.426 B.A. L.398 J.D. [Vargas&V.]
Vargas & Vargas, (AV) ...350 W. Colorado Blvd., 4th Floor
**Vella, Anthony G.** '55 '91 C&L.589 B.S., J.D.
(adm. in IL; not adm. in CA) [A Sheldon&M.]
**Vendler, David** ...'60 '88 C.309 A.B. L.767 J.D. [A Rivkin,R.&K.]
*PRACTICE AREAS: Litigation.
Vernoff, Wallace R., (BV) ...'29 '55 C.563 B.S. L.1068 J.D. [Coulter,V.&P.]
**Vicencia, Michael P.** ...'64 '90 C.1109 B.A. L.169 J.D. [A Burns,A.P.M.&B.]⊙
*PRACTICE AREAS: Civil Defense.
Vick, Patricia G. ...'45 '84 C.800 B.A. L.426 J.D. [Shardlow&V.]
**Vignale, Susan Sherman** '55 '82
C.112 B.A. L.809 J.D. Assoc. Div. Coun., Chicago Title Ins. Co.
*RESPONSIBILITIES: Real Property; Title Insurance.
**Wade, James A., Jr.** ...'51 '77 C&L.575 B.A., J.D. Coun., Fannie Mae
*RESPONSIBILITIES: Mortgage Finance.
**Wall, Jeffrey P.** ...'60 '93 C.352 B.S. L.1068 J.D. [C Christie,P.&H.] (See Pat. Sect.)
*PRACTICE AREAS: Patents; Trademarks; Copyrights.
Walsh, John P. ...'47 '73 C&L.800 B.S., J.D. 848 S. Mentor Ave.
**Walter, Brian P.** ...'69 '94 C.112 B.A. L.426 J.D. [A Gutierrez&P.]
*PRACTICE AREAS: Civil Rights Defense; Local Government Liability; Employer Liability.
Walther, Muriel A. ...'21 '49 C.112 A.B. L.1066 LL.B. 2850 San Pasqual St.‡
**Waluch, Paula G.** ...'50 '75 C.112 B.A. L.284 J.D. [Stone&D.]
*PRACTICE AREAS: Corporate; Tax Planning; Probate.
**Wanke, Blaine Jay** ...'55 '91 C.1074 B.A. L.404 J.D. [A Barker&R.]
*PRACTICE AREAS: Construction Defect Litigation; Business Litigation; General Business; Community Association Law.
**Ward, Richard J., Jr.**, (AV) '36 '65
C.734 B.S.E.E. L.800 J.D. [Christie,P.&H.] (See Pat. Sect.)
*PRACTICE AREAS: Patent, Trademark and Copyright Litigation and Prosecution; Unfair Competition Litigation.

Ware, Paul H. ...'21 '76 C.511 B.S. L.809 J.D. Jet Propulsion Lab. (Pat.)
Warren, David P. ...'54 '78 C&L.1137 B.A., J.D. 650 Sierra Madre Villa Ave.
Warren, Leonard W., Jr. ...'38 '71 C.16 A.B. L.809 J.D. Workers Comp. J.
Weber, Anthony D. ...'47 '80 C.1097 B.S. L.809 J.D. P.O. Box 2200
Weber, Felix ...'46 '75 C.112 B.S. L.809 J.D. 689 E. Walnut St.
Wefald, Verna J. ...'52 '83 C.446 B.A. L.276 J.D. 1946 E. Villa St.
**Wehn, Kelli M.** ...'60 '90 C.112 B.A. L.809 J.D. [Garrett&T.]
*PRACTICE AREAS: Business Litigation; Real Estate Litigation; Professional Liability.
Weinberger, Steven E. ...'60 '87 C.1109 B.A. L.1137 J.D. 11755 Wilshire Blvd.
**Weingarten, M. Danielle** '49 '78 C.504 B.A. L.209 J.D.
(adm. in IL; not adm. in CA) Sr. Claims Coun., Chicago Title Ins. Co.
*RESPONSIBILITIES: Title Insurance; Real Estate.
**Weisbecker, William T.** '53 '78
C.546 B.A. L.190 J.D. Sr. Claims Coun., Chicago Title Ins. Co.
*RESPONSIBILITIES: Title Insurance; Real Property.
Weiss, Joseph A. ...'27 '71 C.339 B.S. L.809 J.D. 45 S. Hudson Ave.
Weissman, Alison B. ...'48 '74 C.112 B.A. L.1136 J.D. Dep. City Pros.

**Wells, Judith Jordan '43 '79 C.112 L.1095 J.D.**
**201 South Lake Avenue, Suite 606, 91101**
**Telephone: 818-304-9444 Fax: 818-304-9753**
**(Certified Specialist, Family Law, The State Bar of California Board of Legal Specialization).**
***PRACTICE AREAS: Family Law.**
**Family Law including Custody, Dissolution, Cohabitation Agreements, Paternity, Support and Adoption.**
***See Professional Biographies, PASADENA, CALIFORNIA***

**Wentz, Richard B.** '61 '85 C.951 B.A. L.1066 J.D.
Sr. V.P. & Asst. Gen. Coun., Countrywide Funding Corp.
**Wenzel, Michael E.** ...'45 '75 C.755 B.A. L.990 J.D. [Burns,A.P.M.&B.]⊙
*PRACTICE AREAS: General Trial; Premises; Malpractice; Construction; Insurance Defense.
**West, Mark** ...'60 '93 C.999 B.S. L.809 J.D. [A N.Good]
*PRACTICE AREAS: Personal Injury; Product Liability; Wrongful Death.

**Whatley, John H., (AV) '19 '41 C.800 LL.M L.16 J.D.**
**Suite 407 CenFed Building, 301 East Colorado Boulevard, 91101**
**Telephone: 818-796-7194 FAX: 818-449-6296**
**Estate Planning, Administration Trust and Probate Law.**
**References: Wells Fargo Bank; Citizens Business Bank.**

Wheatcroft, Gary D., (AV) ...'33 '59 C.112 B.A. L.1065 LL.B. 760 S. San Rafael Ave.
**White, Ronald E.** ...'56 '85 C&L.101 B.A., J.D. [Hunt,O.B.P.&R.]
*LANGUAGES: Japanese.
*PRACTICE AREAS: Construction; Real Estate.
**Wilde, Edward C.** ...'62 '89 C.112 B.A. L.1049 J.D. [A Cooper,K.&S.]
Williams, Clemont ...'61 '90 C.112 B.A. L.1065 J.D. Coun., The Davis Co.
**Williams, George W., Jr.** ...'40 '66 C&L.280 B.A., J.D. [Rivkin,R.&K.]
*PRACTICE AREAS: Commercial and Insurance Litigation; Employment Law; Business; Real Estate Transactions.

**Williams, Arnold F.**
**(See Los Angeles)**

Wills, Donald A., (AV) ...'46 '78 C.1074 B.S. L.1136 J.D. [Wills&K.]
Wills & Kliger, APLC, (AV) ...540 S. Marengo Ave.
**Willsey, Burke W.**, (AV) ...'33 '62 C.475 B.A. L.228 LL.B. [W.O.by]
*PRACTICE AREAS: Taxation; General Civil; Corporate; Natural Resources.
**Willsey, Daniel P., (A Prof. Corp.)** ...'60 '89 C.112 B.A. L.990 J.D. [A W.O.by]
*PRACTICE AREAS: Family Law; Bankruptcy; Real Estate.

**Willsey Law Offices, Owned by a Prof. Corp., (AV) BB**
**553 S. Marengo Avenue, 91101**
**Telephone: 818-577-1086 Fax: 818-304-2959**
**Burke W. Willsey; Daniel P. Willsey (A Professional Corporation).**
**General Civil Practice. Taxation Law, Family Law including Dissolutions, Paternity, Cohabitation, Spousal Support, Prenuptials and District Attorney Enforcement, Real Estate, Bankruptcy.**
**Reference: Sanwa Bank.**
***See Professional Biographies, PASADENA, CALIFORNIA***

Wilson, Emmet H., Jr. ...'12 '37 C.813 A.B. L.309 LL.B. 323 S. El Molino Ave.‡
Wilson, Robert J. ...'46 '87 C&L.1137 B.S., J.D. Dep. City Pros.
Winter, Joseph E., (AV) ...'43 '72 C.321 A.B. L.767 J.D. 225 South Lake Ave.
Winters, Patricia ...'57 '83 C.494 B.A. L.424 J.D. [C McCarthy&L.]
Wisner, Peter F., (A Law Corporation), (BV) '47 '74
C.589 B.S. L.809 J.D. 234 E. Colorado Blvd.
Withey, Pamela A., (BV) ...'50 '77 C.990 B.A. L.426 J.D. 1100 E. Green St.

**Witter and Harpole, (AV) BB**
**Wells Fargo Building, 350 W. Colorado Boulevard, Suite 400, 91105⊙**
**Telephone: 213-624-1311, 818-440-1111 FAX: 213-620-0430**
**Email: 102444.2117@compuserve.com**
**Members of Firm: Myron E. Harpole; George G. Witter (1895-1978); Eugene Harpole (1896-1987); Debra M. Olsen (Resident, Newport Beach Office). Of Counsel: James D. Harris (A Professional Corporation).**
**Federal and State Tax. Estate Planning, Tax Litigation, Trust and Probate Law.**
**Reference: Union Bank (Newport Beach, Calif.).**
**Newport Beach, California Office: Suite 1050, 610 Newport Center Drive. Telephone: 714-644-7600. Fax: 714-759-1014.**
***See Professional Biographies, PASADENA, CALIFORNIA***

Wohlner, Eugene L., (AV) ...'31 '57 C&L.546 B.S., J.D. 380 S. Orange Grove Blvd.‡
Wolloncicj, Thaddeus S. ...'43 '79 C.1097 B.S. L.426 J.D. Housing Res. Mgmt., Inc.
Wondries, Susan ...'51 '76 C.628 B.S. L.1049 J.D. Dep. Dist. Atty.
Wong, Jeffrey J. ...'64 '90 C.800 B.A. L.809 J.D. P.O. Box 60604
Woodard, Alan R., (AV) ...'27 '53 C.999 L.426 LL.B. [Woodard&W.]
Woodard, Daniel J. ...'57 '86 C.112 B.A. L.426 J.D. [Woodard&W.]
Woodard & Woodard, (AV) ...301 E. Colorado Blvd.
Woodburn, John M. ...'52 '79 C.1109 B.A. L.990 J.D. 272 S. Los Robles Ave.
Woods, Gary L. ...'43 '80 C.800 B.S. L.809 J.D. 740 N. Lake Ave.
**Woods, Sherri Lynette** ...'60 '86 C.766 B.A. L.1065 J.D. [A Overlander,L.&R.]
*PRACTICE AREAS: Personal Injury Law; Insurance Defense Law; Commercial Law; Torts; General Civil Trial Practice.
Woosley, Patrick G. '38 '68 C.586 B.B.A. L.802 J.D.
V.P. & Tax Mgr., The Parsons Corp.
Worrell, David L. ...'45 '72 C.188 B.S.M.E. L.813 J.D. 1469 Rose Villa St.
Wright, Geoffrey Willis ...'50 '81 C.112 A.B. L.809 J.D. 301 N. Lake Ave.
Wright, Robert K., (BV) ...'52 '76 C.112 B.A. L.800 J.D. 301 N. Lake Ave.
Wu, Alic S. H. ...'48 '80 L.607 J.D. 301 E. Colo. Blvd.
Xanthos, Christopherj ...'62 '90 C.1077 B.A. L.809 J.D. 301 N. Lake Ave.
**Xiao, Yingchao** '52 '93 C.061 B.A. L.188 J.D.
(adm. in PA; not adm. in CA) [A Sheldon&M.]
*LANGUAGES: Mandarin Chinese.
**Yamamoto, John M.** ...'63 '89 C.119 B.S. L.477 Coun., Kaiser Found. Health Plan, Inc.
Yohalem, Harry M., (AV) '43 '69
C.966 B.A. L.178 J.D. Gen. Coun., Calif. Institute of Tech.
Yong, Thomas T. ...'59 '89 C.1097 B.Sc. L.426 J.D. 1005 E. Colorado Blvd.

CAA495P

Young, George W. ........................ '50 '76 C.112 B.A. L.809 J.D. [Young&Y.]
Young & Young ........................ 790 E. Colorado Blvd., 9th Fl.
Yuen, Henry C. '48 '80 C.966 B.S. L.426 J.D.
Chf. Exec. Offr., Gemstar Development Corporation
**Zaragoza, Carlos** '46 '72
C.112 B.S. L.1066 J.D. Sr. Coun., Kaiser Found. Health Plan, Inc.
Zarett, Russell G. '46 '72 C.112 B.A. L.426 J.D.
Wkrs' Comp. J., Wkrs' Comp. Appls. Bd.
Zarrabian, F. Michael ...... '— '93 C.112 B.S. L.426 J.D. 225 S. Lake Ave., 9th Fl. (Pat.)
Zasa, Joseph S. '67 '92 C.16 B.A. L.902 J.D.
(adm. in VA; not adm. in CA) Corp. Coun., Premier Ambulatory Systems, Inc.
Zerg, Julie V. ........................ '61 '88 C.112 B.A. L.426 J.D. Sears, Roebuck & Co.
**Zeutzius, William J.**, (BV) ........................ '34 '61 C.426 B.S. L.809 J.D. [Zeutzius&L.]
*PRACTICE AREAS: Criminal Law; Torts; Probate Law.
**Zeutzius, William J., Jr.** ........................ '63 '91 C.1077 B.S. L.809 J.D. [A Zeutzius&L.]
*PRACTICE AREAS: Estate Planning; Business Transactions; Commercial Collections.

**Zeutzius & LaBran, (BV)**
**Suite 823, 80 South Lake Avenue, 91101**
**Telephone: 818-795-4276; 213-681-2426 FAX: 818-405-0952**
**Members of Firm: William J. Zeutzius; Ronald M. LaBran. Associates: William J. Zeutzius, Jr.**
**General Civil and Trial Practice in State and Federal Courts. Criminal, Personal Injury, Corporate, Real Property, Business, Commercial, Collections, Contract and Family Law. Trials and Appeals. Probate and Estate Planning.**
*See Professional Biographies, PASADENA, CALIFORNIA*

**Ziff, Ronald K.**, (BV) ........................ '53 '80 C&L.999 B.S., J.D. [A G.W.Kearney]
*LANGUAGES: Spanish.
*PRACTICE AREAS: Family Law; Domestic Relations.
Zigmund, Rudolph E. ........................ '40 '81 135 N. Marengo Ave.
**Zillgitt, George E.** ........................ '21 '49 C&L.813 B.A., LL.B. [Hahn&H.]
**Zimler, Jeffrey M.** '49 '75 C.165 A.B. L.930 J.D.
Coun., Kaiser Found. Health Plan, Inc.
Zimmerman, Steven M. ........................ '53 '87 C.112 A.B. L.426 J.D. 55 S. Lake Ave.
Zucker, Eric J. ........................ '59 '89 C.112 B.A. L.1019 J.D. Pub. Def.
**Zuetel, Kenneth R., Jr.**, (AV) ........ '54 '78 C.763 A.B. L.1049 J.D. [Hammond,Z.&C.]
*PRACTICE AREAS: Medical Malpractice; Business Litigation.
Zweig, Martin '29 '53 C.102 A.B. L.178 J.D.
V.P. & Coun., Loral Electro Optical Systems, Inc.

## PASO ROBLES, 6,677, *San Luis Obispo Co.*

Beaton, Gifford G. ........................ '53 '83 C.330 B.A. L.464 J.D. [Wheeler&B.]⊙
Dunaway, Kathryn ........................ '48 '81 L.1179 J.D. P.O. Box 130
Eschwig, W. W. ........................ '18 '50 C.766 A.B. L.1065 J.D. 246 12th St.‡
Fairbairn, Robin H., (BV) ........................ '34 '63 C.112 B.S. L.1068 J.D. 840 11th St.
**George, Gallo & Sullivan, A Law Corporation**
**(See San Luis Obispo)**
Green, Serenea H. ........................ '22 '49 C&L.352 B.A., J.D. P.O. Box 2179‡
Gustin, Dale I., (CV) ........................ '38 '77 L.1190 LL.B. 246 12th St.
Hansen, Marilyn E. S. ........................ '47 '72 C.475 B.A. L.61 J.D. [Hansen&H.]
Hansen, Robert F. ........................ '39 '72 C.323 A.B. L.61 J.D. [Hansen&H.]
Hansen & Hansen ........................ 809 13th St.
Iversen, Christian E. ........................ '48 '75 C.1074 B.S. L.734 J.D. 605 13th St.
Katz, Arthur Stanley, (AV) ........................ '23 '50 C.102 A.B. L.569 J.D. 4680 Jardine Rd.
**Knecht, James H.**, (AV) ........................ '25 '57 C.112 B.S. L.800 LL.B. [J.H.Knecht]

**Knecht, James H., A Professional Corporation, (AV)**
**1224 Spring Street, P.O. Box 2280, 93447**
**Telephone: 805-238-1224 Fax: 805-238-1302**
**James H. Knecht.**
**Federal and State Taxation, Estate Planning, Probate, Trust, Real Property and Corporation Law.**
**Reference: Bank of Santa Maria (Templeton).**
*See Professional Biographies, PASO ROBLES, CALIFORNIA*

Kocs, Frank E., (CV) ........................ '45 '77 C.990 B.S. L.1136 J.D. 605 13th St. (⊙Cambria)
Lemon, Boyd S., (AV) '40 '66 C&L.800 A.B., J.D.
1111 Riverside Ave. (⊙Los Angeles)
LeSage, Michael T., A Professional Corporation, (BV) '40 '65 C&L.426 J.D.
620 13th St.
Marlow, Tony, (CV) ........................ '50 '91 C.1077 B.A. L.999 J.D. 731 21st. St.
Munak, Pearl M. ........................ '41 '79 C.846 B.A. L.426 J.D. 3770 N. River Rd.
Peterson, Jay A. ........................ '50 '77 C.112 B.A. L.770 J.D. 935 Riverside
Phillips, Jack M., (BV) ........................ '46 '73 C.1074 B.S. L.1065 J.D. 1421 Park St.
Posner, Paul M., (AV) ........................ '29 '56 C.112 B.A. L.1068 LL.B. 1340 Beaver Creek‡
Roldan, Jonathan M. ........................ '57 '88 C.1077 B.A. L.426 J.D. 128 18th St.

**Sefton, Stephen B., (BV) '48 '78 C.1074 B.S. L.1189 J.D.**
**530 Tenth Street, P.O. Box 2962, 93447**
**Telephone: 805-238-7178 FAX: 805-238-7254**
**Email: asefton@tcsn.net**
***PRACTICE AREAS: Real Estate; General Corporation and Partnerships; Trusts and Estates; Probate; Wills.**
**Real Property, Corporate Law, Partnerships, Business Transactions, Probate and Trusts, Commercial Collections and Construction Law.**
*See Professional Biographies, PASO ROBLES, CALIFORNIA*

Shows, James W. ........................ '20 '75 C.112 B.S. L.1095 J.D. 1455 Spanish Camp Rd.
Stevens, Lyle E. ........................ '40 '74 C.1077 B.A. L.1136 J.D. [Woelfle&S.]
Stevens, Patricia A., (CV) ........................ '44 '78 C.112 B.A. L.1136 J.D. 1105 Vine St.
Stewart, Sylvia D., (CV) ........................ '32 '78 C.16 B.S. L.1189 J.D. 607 13th St.
von Felden, Ronald J., (BV) ........................ '43 '72 C.768 B.A. L.1065 J.D. 1421 Park St.
Watt, Theodore M. ........................ '31 '76 C.800 B.S. L.770 J.D. 675 Nacimiento Lake Dr.
Weir, Sam V. ........................ '36 '65 C.642 A.B. L.1068 J.D. 1935 Fieldstone Circle
Wheeler, Charles T. ........................ '46 '74 C.945 A.B. L.767 J.D. [Wheeler&B.]⊙
Wheeler & Beaton, P.C. ........................ 1421 Park St. (⊙San Luis Obispo and Santa Maria)
Woelfle & Stevens ........................ 1105 Vine St.

## PATTERSON, 8,626, *Stanislaus Co.*

Talia, Peter M., (BV) ........................ '46 '72 C&L.770 B.A., J.D. 10 S. Third St.

## PAUMA VALLEY, 550, *San Diego Co.*

Billips, Dale D., (AV) ........................ '30 '63 C&L.800 B.S., LL.B. 42 El Tac‡
**Lodge, Eric T., (P.C.)**, (AV) ........................ '43 '69 C.855 A.B. L.800 J.D. [Lodge&H.]⊙

**Lodge & Heller, (AV)**
**A Partnership including a Professional Corporation**
**The Pauma Building, Suite 403, 16160 Highway 76, P.O. Box 600, 92061⊙**
**Telephone: 619-749-3199**
**Eric T. Lodge (P.C.).**
**Commercial Litigation, Corporate, Real Estate, Estate Planning, Probate and Trust Law.**
**Carlsbad, California Office: 1901 Camino Vida Roble, Suite 110. Telephone: 619-931-9700. Fax: 619-931-1155.**
*See Professional Biographies, CARLSBAD, CALIFORNIA*

Stanley, Jack S., (BV) ........................ '26 '53 C.112 B.S. L.1065 J.D. P.O. Box 1513

## PEBBLE BEACH, —, *Monterey Co.*

Aulik, Gordon J., (BV) ........................ '20 '43 C&L.436 Ph.B., LL.B. P.O. Box 486
Christopher, Thomas ........................ '32 '64 C.994 B.A. L.1009 20 Spanish Bay Cir.‡
Devlin, Arthur V. ........................ '33 '59 C&L.813 A.B., LL.B. P.O. Box 35‡
Downey, Paula S. '42 '76 C.813 B.A. L.1066 J.D.
Assoc. Gen. Coun., Pebble Beach Co.
Freitas, Walter F. ........................ '11 '38 C.770 L.1065 J.D. 1002 Rodeo Rd.‡
Hawkinson, Richard S., (AV) ........ '27 '51 C.378 B.A. L.477 LL.B. 3029 Cormorant Rd.‡
Loftus, Donald J. '45 '73 C.352 B.A. L.190 J.D.
(adm. in NE; not adm. in CA) 89 Ocean Pines Ln.‡
Maller, John M., (AV) ........................ '32 '63 C.112 B.S. L.1068 J.D. 4051 Los Altos Dr.
Maxeiner, C. William, (AV) ........................ '14 '41 C.293 A.B. L.1066 J.D. 4071 Sunset Lane‡
Mills, Willard C., III '14 '40 C.112 A.B. L.276 LL.B.
(adm. in DC; not adm. in CA) 3020 Cormorant Rd.‡
Nichols, Heidi Gail LeMans ........................ '56 '80 C.631 B.A. L.464 J.D. P.O. Box 1261
Robinson, John M., (AV) ........................ '10 '36 C&L.309 A.B., LL.B. Oleada Rd.‡
Rohlff, Yale W., (AV) ........................ '31 '65 C.628 B.S. L.284 LL.B. [Rohlff,H.&F.]⊙
Rohlff, Howie & Frischholz, (AV) ........................ 1277 Lisbon Lane (⊙San Jose)
Stilwell, Mark E., (CV) '55 '81
C.976 B.A. L.273 J.D. V.P. & Gen. Coun., Pebble Beach Co.
Thompson, John A., (AV) ........................ '21 '48 C&L.838 B.S., J.D. P.O. Box 422‡
Truscott, Wesley L., Jr. ........................ '43 '69 C.198 B.S. L.420 J.D. Chf., Civil Law★

## PENNGROVE, —, *Sonoma Co.*

Borin, Aldo, (BV) ........................ '47 '73 C.401 B.S. L.276 J.D. P.O. Box 594‡
Swenson, Lawrence S. ........................ '33 '58 C&L.508 B.S., LL.B. 345 Highland Ave.‡

## PENN VALLEY, —, *Nevada Co.*

Benkert, Robt. R. ........................ '22 '55 C&L.809 17639 Chaparral Dr.‡
Hastert, Thomas J. ........................ '55 '89 C.1060 L.464 J.D. 13941 Lake Wildwood Dr.
Hopcroft, Ann Victoria ........................ '50 '78 C.475 B.A. L.215 J.D. P.O. Box 878‡
Ingram, Jeffrey C. ........................ '53 '79 C.818 B.S. L.1186 J.D. 11246 Pleasant Valley Rd.
Leach, Kenneth H., (BV) '25 '54
C.112 B.A. L.1066 LL.B. 11300 Pleasant Valley Rd., Suite 5
Lumbard, Michael B. ........................ '45 '72 C.1070 B.S. L.1065 J.D. 17582 Foxtail Dr.★
Snyder, Dorothy M. ........................ '40 '78 C.798 B.S.Ed. L.800 J.D. 13730 Strawberry Cir.‡
Wilkins, Paul Cooke, (BV) ........................ '33 '71 C.051 B.A. L.1065 J.D. 18598 Lake Forest Dr.

## PERRIS, 21,460, *Riverside Co.*

Camello, Marlowe O. ........................ '35 '79 C&L.061 B.S.C., LL.B. 1839 Havasu St.
Carter, Charles H., (BV) ........................ '17 '46 C&L.972 LL.B. 134 E. 4th St. (⊙Corona)
Constant, Dennis R. ........................ '53 '79 C.1042 B.A. L.1049 J.D. 19431 Gaines
Garcia, James Hunt, Jr. ........................ '31 '71 C.37 B.A. L.809 J.D. 17385 Penn Valley Dr.
Healy, Richard J., (BV) ........................ '46 '77 C.112 B.A. L.809 J.D. Supvr. Dep. Pub. Def.
Hough, Daniel L. ........................ '44 '80 L.1137 J.D. 26935 Patterson St.
Morgan, John B. ........................ '25 '54 C&L.813 A.B., LL.B. Mun. Ct. J.

## PETALUMA, 43,184, *Sonoma Co.*

Alfsen-Cleveland, W. L. ........................ '49 '78 C.766 B.A. L.1065 J.D. 1301 Redwood Way
Allen, Norman W. '49 '79 C&L.362 B.S., J.D.
(adm. in FL; not adm. in CA) V.P. & Gen. Coun., AEGON USA, Inc.
Anderson, Zeigler, Disharoon, Gallagher & Gray, Professional Corporation, (AV)
715 Southpoint Blvd. (⊙Santa Rosa)
**Behrens, Albert P., Jr., (P.C.)**, (AV) ........ '22 '49 C&L.813 A.B., LL.B. [Behrens,N.&K.]

**Behrens, Nelson & Knudson, (AV)**
**A Partnership of Professional Corporations**
**36 Fifth Street, P.O. Box 262, 94953**
**Telephone: 707-763-1911**
**Albert P. Behrens, Jr., (P.C.); Clyde A. Nelson, Jr., (P.C.) (Certified Specialist, Estate Planning, Trust and Probate Law, The State Bar of California Board of Legal Specialization); Warren T. Knudson (P.C.) (Certified Specialist, Estate Planning, Trust and Probate Law, The State Bar of California Board of Legal Specialization).**
**Probate, Estate Planning, Trusts, Real Property, Corporation and Business Law.**
**Reference: Bank of America.**

Braynard, Nathan C. ........................ '52 '79 C.1078 L.1227 J.D. 1040 Chapman Lane
Burger, Richard A. ........................ '56 '83 C.1078 B.A. L.1066 J.D. 17 Keller St.
Callahan, Cynthia Light ........................ '35 '75 C.188 B.S. L.1065 J.D. 9999 Valley Ford Rd.
Castagnola, George J., Jr. ........................ '50 '90 L.999 J.D. 802 Wine Ct.
Christy, Frank J., Jr. ........................ '59 '85 C.112 B.A. L.464 J.D. 4 Blue Hern Pl.
Cox, Desiree O. ........................ '58 '84 C.763 B.A. L.1065 J.D. 70 Balma Ln.
Crane, Charles E. ........................ '41 '86 C.260 B.S. L.284 J.D. 414 G St.
Denny, Karen M. '54 '81 C.1056 B.S. L.101 J.D.
(adm. in OR; not adm. in CA) 315 Olympic Ct.‡
Devine, Frank A. ........................ '46 '72 C.112 B.A. L.1067 J.D. PVO Internat. Inc.
Dombroski, James M., (BV) ........................ '44 '73 C.950 B.A. L.284 J.D. P.O. Box 751027
Elzi, Chris P. ........................ '52 '79 C&L.767 B.A., J.D. 40 Fourth St.
Fannin, William J. '40 '64 C&L.37 B.A., J.D.
(adm. in AZ; not adm. in CA) 519 Upham‡
Gaidos, Geoffrey Frank ........................ '42 '70 C&L.477 B.A., J.D. 751 Paula Lane
Healy, Michael T. ........................ '58 '88 C.813 A.B. L.767 J.D. 7 Fourth St.
Hirschfield, Frederic L., (BV) ........................ '35 '69 C.165 B.A. L.284 J.D. 205 Keller St.
Hoffman, Robert W. ........................ '50 '80 C.1044 B.A. L.426 J.D. 2710 Skillman Ln.
Hufstader, Richard W. ........................ '47 '87 C.1109 B.A. L.1051 J.D. 30 5th St.
Johnson, R. Charles ........................ '47 '78 L.1230 LL.B. P.O. Box 751138
Kahn, Mercia L. ........................ '10 '33 L.596 LL.B. 10 W. Napa Dr.‡
King, John J., Jr., (AV) ........................ '35 '62 C&L.767 B.S., LL.B. [Anderson,Z.D.G.&G.]⊙
**Knudson, Warren T., (P.C.)** ........................ '51 '85 C.602 B.A. L.1137 J.D. [Behrens,N.&K.]
*PRACTICE AREAS: Probate Law; Estate Planning Law; Corporation Law; Business Law.
Lawless, John H., Jr. '22 '48 C.611 L.94 LL.B.
(adm. in MA; not adm. in CA) 1555 Crown Rd.‡
**Lounibos, John B.**, (AV) ........................ '03 '28 C.721 A.B. L.767 LL.B. [Lounibos,L.&T.] ‡
**Lounibos, Leroy J., Jr.**, (AV) ........................ '40 '66 C&L.767 A.B., LL.B. [Lounibos,L.&T.]
**Lounibos, Robert G.**, (CV) ........................ '36 '65 C&L.767 B.S., LL.B. [Lounibos,L.&T.]

**Lounibos, Lounibos & Tinney, (AV)**
**Ten Fourth Street, P.O. Box 589, 94952**
**Telephone: 707-762-6631; 762-6632**
**Members of Firm: Robert G. Lounibos; Leroy J. Lounibos (1907-1979); Leroy J. Lounibos, Jr.; Joseph C. Tinney. Of Counsel: Joseph E. Tinney; John B. Lounibos (Retired).**
**General Civil and Trial Practice in all Courts. Probate, Corporation, Real Estate and Insurance Law.**
**Representative Clients: Sonoma Pacific Corp.; California Gold Dairy Products; Great American Indemnity Co.; General Insurance Company of America; Employers Group; Cotati Brand Eggs, Inc.; Sonoma Mission Inn.**
**Reference: Bank of America National Trust & Savings Assn. (Petaluma Branch).**

McPartland, Michael B. ........................ '54 '82 C.147 B.A. L.464 J.D. 1605 Sequoia Dr.
Mellor, Charles Jervis ........................ '56 '89 L.1137 J.D. 1628 Madeira Circle

Mickelsen, Max A., (BV) ... '44 '70 C.112 B.S. L.1067 J.D. [M.A.Mickelsen]
Mickelsen, Max A., P.C., (BV) ... P.O. Box 750487
Milward, Michael W. ... '54 '81 765 Baywood Dr.
Nebb, Veronica A. Franz ... '60 '89 C.219 B.A. L.284 J.D. 204 Stowring Rd.
**Nelson, Clyde A., Jr., (P.C.)**, (AV) ... '25 '52 C.112 A.B. L.1065 J.D. [Behrens,N.&K.]
Oliker, Robert P. ... '56 '84 C.112 B.S. L.426 J.D. 17 Keller St.
Parkinson, Barry D., (BV) ... '44 '72 C.147 B.A. L.464 J.D. P.O. Box 869
Piotrkowski, Irv ... '46 '75 C.1078 B.A. L.767 J.D. 35 Fifth St.
Polin, David L. ... '46 '76 C.112 A.B. L.284 J.D. Bancroft-Whitney Co.
Ram, Michael ... '14 '38 C&L.597 B.S.L., LL.B. 3775 Roblar Rd.
Sartori, Duane P. ... '51 '76 C&L.767 B.S., J.D. 17 Keller St.
Segal, Marilyn K. ... '52 '76 C.1044 B.A. L.273 J.D. 809 Schuman Lane
Sheeks, Joseph E., (BV) ... '17 '50 C&L.145 B.A., J.D. 765 Baywood Dr.
Thompson, Sue E. ... '46 '73 C.787 B.A. L.184 J.D. 1013 Palmetto Way‡
Thuesen, Victor C. ... '41 '80 C.1060 A.B. L.767 J.D. 7 4th St.
**Tinney, Joseph C.**, (BV) ... '42 '67 C.770 B.A. L.767 J.D. [Lounibos,L.&T.]
**Tinney, Joseph E.**, (AV) ... '10 '33 C&L.767 B.A., LL.B. [©Lounibos,L.&T.]
Traversi, David C., (AV) ... '34 '66 C&L.767 B.S., LL.B. 715 Southpoint Blvd.‡
Trott, John S. ... '46 '72 C&L.767 B.S., J.D. 227 Middle 2 Rock Rd.
Wisdom, Penelope S. ... '48 '80 C.763 B.S. L.1049 J.D. 149 "D" St.

## PHELAN, —, *San Bernardino Co.*

Conaway, Robert D. ... '52 '85 C.1109 B.A. L.1137 J.D. 8754 Hollister Rd.
Hardy, John F., (BV) ... '33 '68 C.990 B.S. L.800 J.D. 11275 Edgehill Rd.
Wertenberger, Marcia S. ... '61 '92 C.999 B.S. L.61 J.D. 4184 Phelan Rd.

## PHILO, —, *Mendocino Co.*

Follis, James G. ... '33 '61 C.674 A.B. L.309 LL.B. P.O. Box 345

**Kivel, Scott N., Law Offices of '50 '91 C.112 B.A. L.813 J.D.**
**P.O. Box 151, 95466**
**Telephone: 707-895-3278 Fax: 707-895-3360**
***REPORTED CASES: Doe v. Petaluma City School Dist., 830 F.Supp. 1560 (N.D. Cal. 1993); Doe by and through Doe v. Petaluma City School District, 54 F.3d 1447 (9th Circuit, 1995).**
**Governmental, Administrative and Environmental Law; Civil Litigation and Appeals.**

## PICO-RIVERA, 59,177, *Los Angeles Co.*

O'Donnell, William C., Jr. ... '24 '68 C.800 A.B. L.981 LL.B. 6823‡
Weiner, Stephen A. ... '46 '72 C.112 A.B. L.464 J.D. P.O. Box 878
Weintraub, Mark M. '48 '74
C.102 B.A. L.800 J.D. Sr. Staff Coun., Northrop Grumman Corp.

## PIEDMONT, 10,602, *Alameda Co.*

Abrams, Marilyn D. ... '56 '83 C.112 B.A. L.426 J.D. 39 York Dr.
Beilock, Ellen J., (AV) ... '44 '70 C.112 A.B. L.1066 J.D. 424 Pala Ave.
Bernstein, Arthur H. ... '25 '50 C.1016 A.B. L.145 J.D. 570 Scenic Ave.
Bostick, Robert L., (AV) ... '20 '50 C.112 B.A. L.1065 LL.B. 336 Mountain Ave.‡
Breault, Stephanie R. ... '49 '80 C.766 B.A. L.284 J.D. 101 Magnolia Ave.
Breeden, Linda L. ... '44 '70 C.813 A.B. L.1065 J.D. 92 Ramona Ave., N.W.
Chandler, Clive ... '36 '69 C.674 B.A. L.276 J.D. 1085 Winsor Ave.
Chen, Arthur S., Jr. ... '37 '77 C.112 B.S. L.284 J.D. 145 Caperton Ave.
Clark, Judith Swope ... '45 '76 C.112 B.A. L.284 J.D. 124 Olive Ave.‡
Cobb, Miles A., (AV) ... '30 '59 C.112 B.S.L. L.1066 LL.B. 126 Oracena Ave.‡
Deichler, Clark L. V., (AV) ... '36 '66 C.112 A.B. L.1065 J.D. 2058 Oakland Ave.
DeMonte, Robert J. ... '42 '84 C.1073 B.S. L.767 J.D. 2045 Oakland Ave.
Frankel, Nat, (BV) ... '18 '43 C.112 B.A. L.1066 J.D. 81 Calvert Ct.
Gates, Jan E. ... '46 '84 C.1259 B.A. L.767 J.D. 179 Estates Dr.‡
Gray, Robt. J. ... '13 '44 C.112 L.1065 146 Dale Ave.
Hendricks, Norman B. ... '34 '61 L.878 J.D. 934 Rose Ave.
Herbert, Charles E., (AV) ... '31 '67 C.475 B.S. L.765 LL.B. 100 Fairview Ave.
Howard, William H. F. ... '43 '75 C.1070 B.S.E. L.284 J.D. 928 Kingston Ave. (Pat.)
Jacobs, Jonnie ... '45 '82 C.112 B.A. L.1066 J.D. 36 Bonita
Johnson, Kenneth E., (AV) '39 '66 C.112 B.S. L.1066 J.D.
Pres., Johnson Investment Co.
Karren, Beth D. ... '41 '66 C.188 B.A. L.1066 LL.B. 79 Wildwood Gardens
Kress, Wendy L. ... '48 '85 C.477 B.A. L.209 J.D. 45 Jerome Ave.
Levenson, Carole S. ... '54 '79 C.112 B.A. L.1049 J.D. 111 Highland Ave.
Liss, Mark I. ... '48 '80 C.674 B.A. L.284 J.D. 958 Rose Ave.
Lucke, William P., (AV) '42 '72 C.767 A.B. L.284 J.D.
536 Magnolia Ave. (©Lafayette)
Matzger, John, (BV) ... '39 '65 C.659 B.A. L.1066 LL.B. 155 Woodland Way
McDonnell, Loretta W. ... '40 '90 C.764 B.A. L.284 J.D. 206 Mountain Ave.
Mead, Mary Sherrill '28 '80 C.813 B.A. L.174 J.D.
(adm. in CO; not adm. in CA) 5963 Wood Dr.‡
Odell, Kenneth A. ... '44 '69 C&L.309 A.B., J.D. 326 Pala Ave.
Pervere, Maude H., (AV) ... '48 '74 C.813 B.A. L.1066 J.D. 17 Mesa Ave.
Rafton, Michael G. ... '24 '51 C.216 A.B. L.1066 LL.B. 92 Seaview Ave.‡
Rapson, Ann G. ... '55 '84 C.604 B.A. L.767 J.D. 318 San Carlos Ave.
Rogers, John D., (AV) ... '20 '48 C&L.767 B.S., J.D. 125 Estates Dr.
Schneck, Stuart B. '42 '67 C.473 B.S. L.608 J.D.
V.P. & Gen. Coun., Columbia Falls Aluminum Co.
Schwartz, Howard L. ... '33 '60 C&L.813 B.A., LL.B. Ret. Supr. Ct. J.
Seligson, Robert A., (AV) ... '32 '57 C.103 A.B. L.1066 J.D. [R.A.Seligson]
Seligson, Robert A., Inc., (AV) ... 6 King Ave.
Simon, Lawrence S., (AV) ... '14 '38 C&L.800 B.S., LL.B. 1820 Trestle Glen Rd.‡
Stribling, Fred T. ... '21 '50 C.112 L.1065 J.D. 111 Waldo Ave.‡
Sutton, G. Zook ... '53 '78 C.112 B.S. L.1065 J.D. 100 La Salle Ave.‡
Sutton, Zook F. ... '22 '50 C&L.813 A.B., LL.B. Ret. Supr. Ct. J.
Wolfe, Cameron W. ... '10 '34 C.813 B.A. L.1066 LL.B. Ret. U.S. Bkrptcy. J.
Wyatt, John B. '26 '50 C&L.383 B.A., J.D.
(adm. in KY; not adm. in CA) 30 Blair Pl.‡
Yakutis, Alexander B. ... '25 '56 C.999 L.1065 J.D. 314 Sheridan Ave.‡

## PIEDRA, —, *Fresno Co.*

Swanson, Marla Lynn ... '44 '80 C.766 B.A. L.1189 J.D. P.O. Box 207

## PINEDALE, —, *Fresno Co.*

Campbell, Donald J. '40 '71 C.350 B.S. L.502 J.D.
(adm. in MO; not adm. in CA) The Vendo Co.
Gregory, Kathleen Burdic Goshgarian ... '43 '87 C.813 B.A. L.1189 J.D. P.O. Box 3145
Guymon, Paul D. ... '53 '82 C.877 B.A. L.1137 J.D. P.O. Box 14149

## PINE GROVE, 5,953, *Amador Co.*

Baldwin, Robt. D. ... '24 '55 C.107 B.A. L.1068 LL.B. 19211 Red Hill Mine Rd.

## PINOLE, 17,460, *Contra Costa Co.*

Adler, Richard W., (BV) ... '43 '70 C.766 L.284 J.D. 555 Sunnyview Dr.
Daughters, Turpen A. ... '43 '79 C.112 B.A. L.284 J.D. P.O. Box 529‡
Ruport, David O., Jr. ... '49 '89 C.1073 B.A. L.1153 J.D. 1131 Marionola Way
Schlintz, Gerald H. ... '53 '82 C.112 A.B. L.1065 J.D. 3241 Colusa St.

## PIONEER, —, *Amador Co.*

Anderson, Wm. E., Jr. ... '14 '47 L.813 25170 Sugar Pine Dr.‡

## PIONEERTOWN, —, *San Bernardino Co.*

McCracken, William J. ... '37 '69 L.809 J.D. P.O. Box 98

## PISMO BEACH, 7,669, *San Luis Obispo Co.*

Geihs, Paul A., (BV) ... '35 '66 C.627 B.S.B.A. L.1065 J.D. 354 Main St., Suite A
Gordon, Kirby K. ... '49 '74 C.112 B.A. L.1067 J.D. 405 Indio Dr.
Lanphear, Roger G. ... '36 '62 C.112 A.B. L.1066 LL.B. 194 Seacliff Dr.‡
Phillips, Paul M. ... '56 '82 C.1074 B.S. L.990 J.D. 981 Price St.
Stanley, Harry M., (CV) ... '22 '78 C.119 M.S. L.1136 J.D. P.O. Box 576
Stronge, David G. ... '39 '66 C.801 B.S. L.1068 LL.B. 575 Prince St.

## PITTSBURG, 47,564, *Contra Costa Co.*

Affinito, Alfred A., (BV) ... '28 '53 C&L.767 B.S., LL.B. [J.D.Morrison] ‡
Allen, John M. ... '40 '70 C.112 B.S. L.767 J.D. Mun. Ct. J.
Ashe, Anthony Guy ... '60 '89 C.112 B.A. L.464 J.D. 525 Marina Blvd.
Barsotti, Richard A., (BV) ... '45 '71 C&L.770 B.A., J.D. [Scott&B.]
Belleci, Gerald A. ... '36 '62 C.768 A.B. L.1065 J.D. Mun. Ct. J.
Binkowski, Donna F. ... '59 '85 C.912 B.A. L.215 J.D. The Dow Chem. Co.
Buchta, Alfred H., Jr., (CV) ... '45 '74 C.569 B.S. L.284 J.D. 72 William Way
Campbell, Patrick C. ... '53 '78 C.610 B.A. L.851 J.D. 900 Loveridge Rd.
Canciamilla, Joseph E. ... '55 '86 C.740 B.A. L.1153 J.D. 2211 Railroad Ave.
Charbonneau, Edward E. '42 '77 C.894 A.B. L.796 J.D.
(adm. in TX; not adm. in CA) U.S. Steel Corp.
Cloud, Dana J. ... '66 '92 C.37 B.A. L.766 J.D. 2980 Railroad Ave.
Coker, John Diaz ... '38 '67 C.763 A.B. L.284 J.D. 509 Railroad Ave.
**Conkling, Christopher Anderson** '52 '79
C.860 B.A. L.990 J.D. Gen. Coun., USS-POSCO Ind.
*RESPONSIBILITIES: Litigation; Regulatory Compliance; Employment; Transactional.
**Cox, James E.**, (AV) ... '20 '51 C&L.813 A.B., LL.B. [© Sanders,D.R.&C.]
*REPORTED CASES: Standard Oil Co. v. Oil, Chemical Etc. Intl. Union (1972) 23 Cal. App. 3d 585; People ex rel. Dept. Pub. Wks. v. Hunt (1969) 2 Cal. App. 3d 158; City of Pleasant Hill v. First Baptist Church (1969) 1 Cal. App. 3rd 384; County of Contra Costa v. Nulty (1965) 237 Cal. App. 2d 593; County of Alameda v. Meadowlark Dairy Corp. (1964) 227 Cal. App. 2d 80.
*PRACTICE AREAS: Condemnation Law; Eminent Domain; Inverse Condemnation; Real Estate Condemnation.
**Dodson, Stanley K.**, (BV) ... '34 '60 C.112 A.B. L.1066 J.D. [© Sanders,D.R.&C.]
*PRACTICE AREAS: Personal Injury.
**Garrett, Dan L., Jr.** ... '20 '49 C.208 L.1065 J.D. [© Sanders,D.R.&C.]
*REPORTED CASES: Pool v. City of Oakland (1986) 42 Cal. 3d 1051; Dimarco v. Dimarco (1963) 60 Cal. 2d 387; Keating v. Superior Court (1955) 45 Cal. 2d 440; Murray v. Superior Court (1955) 44 Cal. 2d 611; Carroll v. Superior Court (1954) 42 Cal. 2d 874.
*PRACTICE AREAS: Civil Appeals; Eminent Domain; Inverse Condemnation; Land Use Law.
Hawk, Richard E. ... '32 '57 C&L.813 A.B., J.D. 1901 Railroad Ave.
Herr, William H. ... '52 '80 C.477 A.B. L.215 J.D. End of Loveridge Rd.
**Jenny, Scott E.** ... '62 '93 C.766 B.S. L.464 J.D. [Ⓐ Sanders,D.R.&C.]
*PRACTICE AREAS: Eminent Domain; Inverse Condemnation; Real Estate Condemnation.
Klausman, David '53 '81 C.8 B.S.B.A. L.7 J.D.
(adm. in OH; not adm. in CA) U.S. Steel Corp.
**Littorno, Richard S.** ... '54 '84 C.740 B.A. L.1065 J.D. [Ⓐ Sanders,D.R.&C.]
*PRACTICE AREAS: Estate Planning; Probate; Taxation; General Business.
Morrison, James D., (BV) ... '52 '78 C.645 B.A. L.765 J.D. [J.D.Morrison]
Morrison, James D., Law Offices of, (BV) ... 2980 Railroad Ave.
Piantanida, Donald A. ... '38 '73 C.740 B.A. L.1153 J.D. Comr., Delta Jud. Dist.
**Rives, Ronald P.**, (BV) ... '48 '74 C.768 B.A. L.1067 J.D. [Sanders,D.R.&C.]
*PRACTICE AREAS: Personal Injury; Medical Malpractice; Products Liability.
Rose, Manuel Costa, Jr. ... '23 '51 C.112 A.B. L.1066 LL.B. Mun. Ct. J.
Rothenberg, Martin E. ... '18 '42 C.112 A.B. L.1066 LL.B. Ret. Supr. Ct. J.
**Sanders, Richard D.**, (AV) ... '26 '51 C&L.813 A.B., LL.B. [Sanders,D.R.&C.] ‡

**Sanders, Dodson, Rives & Cox, (BV)**
**2211 Railroad Avenue, 94565**
**Telephone: 510-432-3511; 228-7300 Fax: 510-432-3516**
**Members of Firm: Richard D. Sanders (Retired); Ronald P. Rives;—Scott E. Jenny; Richard S. Littorno. Of Counsel: James E. Cox; Stanley K. Dodson; Dan L. Garrett, Jr.**
**Personal Injury, Products Liability, Construction Defects, Eminent Domain, Wills, Probate, Tax, Estate Planning and Living Trusts.**

***See Professional Biographies, PITTSBURG, CALIFORNIA***

Scott, James E., (AV) ... '25 '59 C&L.950 B.S., LL.B. [Scott&B.]
Scott & Barsotti, (AV) ... 315 E. Leland Rd.
Stern, Jill T. ... '64 '90 C.1077 B.A. L.809 J.D. 3024 Railroad Ave.
Warshawsky, Robert Q. ... '59 '86 L.1153 J.D. 2211 Railroad Ave.
Webster, Diane ... '42 '87 C.1077 B.A. L.1153 J.D. [Webster&W.]
Webster, Fredric L., (BV) ... '43 '69 C.112 B.B.A. L.767 J.D. [Webster&W.]
Webster & Webster, (BV) ... 3743 Railroad Ave.
Williams, Allen ... '22 '64 C.800 L.765 LL.B. 1901 Railroad Ave.
Wilson-Rice, Rhonda K. ... '56 '90 C.112 B.A. L.273 J.D. 525 Marina Blvd.

## PLACENTIA, 41,259, *Orange Co.*

Anderson, Vicki ... '38 '77 L.1137 LL.B. 414 N. Placentia AVe.
Behle, Sheila M. ... '42 '78 C.1109 B.A. L.1137 J.D. 1057 E. Imperial Hwy.
Brown, Loren W. ... '44 '91 C.37 B.S. L.1137 J.D. 414 N. Placentia Ave.
Cain, Karen ... '54 '85 C.112 A.B. L.1065 J.D. 613 Mount Vernon Way
deBrucky, G. Keith, (AV) ... '49 '79 C.901 B.A. L.1218 J.D. 101 S. Kraemer Blvd. (Pat.)
Dholakia, Ullasini (Joy) ... '60 '88 L.061 LL.B. 413 Mass. Ln.
Downey, Jody L. ... '63 '92 C.1109 B.A. L.1137 J.D. 248 Rio Grande
Eaton, Gary Bruce, (BV) ... '32 '71 C.684 B.A. L.426 J.D. 101 S. Kraemer Blvd.
Evans, Winthrop S. ... '39 '80 C.1109 B.A. L.1137 J.D. P.O. Box 532
Francis, John W. ... '26 '61 C&L.112 B.A., LL.B. 761 W. Kimberly Ave.
Hindley, Charles T. ... '24 '73 C.112 A.B. L.297 J.D. 1224 E. Orangethorpe Ave.‡
Hiskey, David D. ... '54 '83 C.1109 B.A. L.426 J.D. 414 N. Placentia Ave.
Johnson, William E. ... '34 '79 C.645 B.S.A.E. L.1137 J.D. 101 S. Kraemer Blvd.
Kranseler, Robert S. ... '53 '79 C.112 B.A. L.426 J.D. 255 Backs Lane
Ottolia, Daniel A. ... '56 '83 C.112 B.A. L.276 J.D. 414 N. Placentia Ave.
Perotin, Gary A. ... '51 '76 C.139 B.A. L.1137 J.D. 151 N. Kraemer Blvd.
Soukup, Earle ... '40 '78 C.260 B.S.E.E. L.990 J.D. 319 El Camino Ln.
Sprang, Kermit N., (AV) ... '49 '74 C.112 B.A. L.1066 J.D. 414 N. Placentia Ave.
Stearman, Jeffrey D., (BV) ... '54 '82 C.1109 B.A. L.1137 J.D. 414 N. Placentia Ave.
Weiss, Leo '26 '54 C.569 L.477 J.D.
(adm. in NY; not adm. in CA) P.O. Box 1327
Whitmore, Robert N., (BV) ... '24 '72 C.999 L.1137 LL.B. 1220 Hacienda St.‡
Zavala, Riordan J. ... '56 '89 C.800 B.S. L.477 J.D. 700 Moonbeam

CALIFORNIA—PLACERVILLE MARTINDALE-HUBBELL LAW DIRECTORY 1997

## PLACERVILLE, * 8,355, *El Dorado Co.*

Adam, Walter J. ................'23 '57 C.112 B.S. L.809 J.D. 7220 Quartz Hill Rd. (Pat.)
**Adams, Stuart D.** ..............................'63 '89 C.902 B.A. L.1049 J.D. [Olson,G.&A.]
*PRACTICE AREAS: Labor and Employment; Criminal Defense; Civil Litigation.
Appelbaum, George D., (BV) '44 '75
C.178 B.A. L.1066 J.D. Directing Atty., Legal Ctr. for the Elderly
Bailey, Steven C. ...............'51 '90 C.1060 B.A. L.1026 J.D. 3980 Missouri Flat Rd.
Banning, Robert ..........................'51 '78 C.112 B.A. L.408 J.D. Dep. Pub. Def.
Belt, Frederick A., (CV) ...................'39 '77 C.1042 B.A. L.1137 J.D. 537 Main St.

**Berry, Phillip B., (AV) '39 '64 C.768 B.A. L.1066 J.D.**
**496 Main Street, 95667**
**Telephone: 916-622-2186 Fax: 916-622-2188**
**(Certified Specialist, Estate Planning, Trust and Probate Law, The State Bar of California Board of Legal Specialization).**
**Probate, Estate Planning, Taxation and Related Litigation.**
***See Professional Biographies, PLACERVILLE, CALIFORNIA***

**Brooks, Nelson Keith**, (CV) '48 '82
C.770 B.A. L.1065 J.D. [Laurie,M.&W.] (⊙Cameron Park)
Brown, Cherie J. .......................'57 '90 C.763 B.S. L.1137 J.D. Dep. Co. Coun. II
Caietti, William, (BV) ............'30 '63 C.1060 A.B. L.1065 J.D. 550 Main St., Ste. F-3
Clark, James S., (BV) .........................'52 '79 C.112 A.B. L.770 J.D. 465 Main St.
Cline, Jack A. ...........................'19 '66 C.112 B.S. L.1132 4710 Green Canyon Rd.‡
Cline, Roger F. .....................'46 '75 C.878 B.S. L.464 J.D. 3062 Cedar Ravine
**Combellack, David W.**, (BV) ..........'49 '75 C.112 B.A. L.464 J.D. [Combellack&D.]
*PRACTICE AREAS: Civil Trial; Real Property; Probate; Estate Planning; Business.

**Combellack & Driscoll, (BV)**
**263 Main Street, P.O. Box 1065, 95667**
**Telephone: 916-622-2992 Fax: 916-622-1506**
**David W. Combellack; John W. Driscoll. Associates: Andrew W. George.**
**General Civil, Criminal and Trial Practice. Real Property, Construction, Probate, Estate Planning, Business, Personal Injury, Family, Juvenile, Collection, Government, Personnel and Commercial Law.**
***See Professional Biographies, PLACERVILLE, CALIFORNIA***

Conti, Elizabeth Katherine ..............................'50 '85 L.1026 J.D. Dep. Dist. Atty.
Dezzani & Petersen, (BV) ...............................................Suite 1, 2828 Easy St.
Dosh, Ronald E., (BV) ....................'49 '77 C.717 B.A. L.1137 J.D. 3041 Forni Rd.
**Driscoll, John W.**, (BV) ...................'44 '70 C.112 A.B. L.1049 J.D. [Combellack&D.]
*PRACTICE AREAS: Trial; Real Property; Business; Government; Personnel.

**El Dorado Legal Clinic**
**319 Main Street, Suite 8, 95667**
**Telephone: 916-642-9182**
**Email: edlegal@pacbell.net**
**Kenric P. Torkelson.**
**Family Law including- Divorce, Child/Spousal Support, Alimony Domestic Relations, Wills, Probate, Landlord/Tenant, Civil Litigation.**

**George, Andrew W.**..................'63 '95 C.454 B.S. L.464 J.D. [A Combellack&D.]
**Goyette, Paul Q.** ...........................'60 '88 C.330 B.S. L.1049 J.D. [Olson,G.&A.]
*PRACTICE AREAS: Labor and Employment Law; Trials; Personal Injury; Criminal.
Haas, Gregory F. ...............................'49 '76 C.112 B.A. L.464 J.D. Mun. Ct. J.
Haffner, Robin B. .....................'62 '88 C.1036 B.A. L.273 J.D. Dep. Dist. Atty.
Hamilton, Lloyd B. .....................'28 '60 C.768 A.B. L.800 J.D. Ret. Supr. Ct. J.
Harasek, Craig ..........................'47 '88 C.877 B.S. L.464 J.D. 2937 Conrad St.
**Harrison, Elizabeth L.** ........................'57 '91 C.464 B.A. L.1110 J.D. [Tustin&H.]
*PRACTICE AREAS: Child Custody; Interstate Child Custody; Divorce; Divorce Mediation; Post Divorce.
Keller, Stephen B. R. ......................'41 '73 C.674 A.B. L.477 J.D. 465 Main St.
Kimzey, Bruce A. ......................'52 '82 C.112 A.B. L.1065 J.D. 360 Fair Ln.
Klotz, Jean S., (CV) ..............................................'32 '72 L.464 J.D. 2828 Easy St.
Knapp, Edward L., (AV) ..............'48 '76 C.94 B.A. L.284 J.D. Chf. Asst. Co. Coun.
Lacy, Gary L. ...........................'54 '83 C.589 B.S. L.1137 J.D. Dep. Dist. Atty.
Langner, William J. ................'17 '65 C.112 B.S. L.1066 LL.B. 6266 Sly Park Rd.‡
**Laurie, Robert A.**, (BV) '46 '75
C.112 B.A. L.464 J.D. [Laurie,M.&W.] (⊙Cameron Park)

**Laurie, Maloney & Wheatley, (AV)**
**345 Placerville Drive, 95667⊙**
**Telephone: 916-622-7769**
**Members of Firm: Robert A. Laurie; Brian E. Maloney; Nelson Keith Brooks. Associates: Richard D. Sopp.**
**Land Use, Business, Real Estate, Banking, Estate Planning, Municipal, Employment and Construction Law, Personal Injury and Civil Litigation.**
**Cameron Park (El Dorado County), California Office: 3420 Coach Lane, Suite 15. Telephone: 916-677-0245. Fax: 916-677-4802.**
**Folsom (Sacramento County), California Office: 1004 River Rock Drive, Suite 245. Telephone: 916-988-3857.**
***See Professional Biographies, PLACERVILLE, CALIFORNIA***

**Maloney, Brian E.**, (BV) '50 '76
C.112 A.B. L.464 J.D. [Laurie,M.&W.] (⊙Cameron Park)
McKinstry, Daryl J., (BV) ............'26 '59 C.112 B.A. L.284 LL.B. 309 Placerville Dr.
**Nielsen, J. Mark**, (BV) ......................'31 '75 C.597 B.S. L.464 J.D. [⊠ Tustin&H.]
*PRACTICE AREAS: General Civil Trial Practice; Real Property; Business; Water and Municipal Law.
**Olson, John R.**, (BV) ...........................'47 '77 C.352 B.A. L.464 J.D. [Olson,G.&A.]
*PRACTICE AREAS: Real Estate; Personal Injury; Probate and Estate Planning; Family Law; Civil Litigation.

**Olson, Goyette & Adams, (BV)**
**The Judge Thompson House, 3062 Cedar Ravine, 95667**
**Telephone: 916-622-6872 Fax: 916-622-4445**
**Members of Firm: John R. Olson; Paul Q. Goyette; Stuart D. Adams.**
**Civil and Trial Practice. Personal Injury, Probate, Real Property and Family Law, Labor and Employment and Criminal Law.**
***See Professional Biographies, PLACERVILLE, CALIFORNIA***

Petersen, Michael E., (A Professional Corporation), (BV) '38 '69
C.999 L.464 J.D. [Dezzani&P.]
Phillips, Carolyn Nivia Bell ...............'56 '83 C&L.608 B.A., J.D. Off. of Dist. Atty.
Pierce, Darrel E. ..............'27 '54 C&L.813 A.B., LL.B. Pres., Inter-County Title Co.‡
Raycraft, Laura A. ..............................'57 '92 C.112 B.A. L.464 J.D. Dist. Atty.
Riley, Patrick J. ..............................'30 '56 C.602 B.A. L.1066 J.D. Supr. Ct. J.
Roberts, John R., (BV) ...................'46 '77 C.1077 B.A. L.1095 J.D. [J.R.Roberts]
Roberts, John R., A Prof. Corp., (BV) ...........................................2744 Coloma St.
Sample, Ronald F., (CV) ...................'50 '77 C.801 B.A. L.910 J.D. 3041 Forni Rd.
Shampo, G. Christopher ........................'59 '87 C.54 B.A. L.94 J.D. 476 Main St.
**Sopp, Richard D.**, (CV) '58 '86 C&L.101 B.A., J.D.
[A Laurie,M.&W.] (⊙Cameron Park)
*LANGUAGES: French.
Sprunger, Noble ..................'34 '66 C.768 B.A. L.770 LL.B. 2828 Easy St., Suite 4
Sudman, John T., (BV) ......................'38 '67 C.678 B.A. L.1068 LL.B. Pub. Def.

**Tarlton, Michael A., (AV) '38 '66 C.763 B.S. L.1066 LL.B.**
**The Judge Thompson House, 3062 Cedar Ravine, P.O. Box 227, 95667**
**Telephone: 916-622-6870 FAX: 916-622-4445**
**(Certified Specialist, Criminal Law, The State Bar of California Board of Legal Specialization).**
***PRACTICE AREAS: Criminal Trial Litigation; Major Felonies and Misdemeanors.**
**Criminal, Personal Injury and Trial Practice.**
***See Professional Biographies, PLACERVILLE, CALIFORNIA***

**Torkelson, Kenric P.** ..........................................'52 '77 C.112 B.S. L.464 J.D. [El D.]
*PRACTICE AREAS: Divorce; Child/Spousal Support; Wills; Probate; Landlord/Tenant.
Turner, Pat Alan ......................................'53 '89 C.1060 B.S. L.464 J.D. 550 Main St.
**Tustin, Karen K.**, (BV) .........................'42 '70 C&L.813 A.B., LL.B. [Tustin&H.]
*PRACTICE AREAS: Estate Planning; Probate; Business; Real Property; Municipal.

**Tustin & Harrison, (BV)**
**The Judge Thompson House, 3062 Cedar Ravine, 95667**
**Telephone: 916-626-4300 Fax: 916-622-4445**
**Members of Firm: Karen K. Tustin; Elizabeth L. Harrison (Certified Specialist, Family Law, The State Bar of California Board of Legal Specialization). Of Counsel: J. Mark Nielsen.**
**General Civil and Trial Practice, Real Property, Estate Planning, Probate, Business, Municipal and Family Law.**
***See Professional Biographies, PLACERVILLE, CALIFORNIA***

Weber, Philip H., (CV) ...............'58 '83 C.770 B.A. L.596 J.D. 2828 Easy St., Ste.4
Weidman, John C. ...........................................'25 '55 L.1066 LL.B. 325 Main St.‡
White, Bertram C. ....................'33 '72 C.112 A.B. L.464 J.D. 3003 Bedford Ave.
Whittington, David E., (BV) .................'38 '66 C.1068 B.S. L.1065 J.D. County Coun.

## PLAYA DEL REY, —, *Los Angeles Co.*

(Part of the incorporated City of Los Angeles)

Bardin, Ian A. .......................'43 '69 C.112 B.S. L.1068 J.D. 8055 W. Manchester Ave.
Bloom, Morton J., (AV) .................'17 '41 C.112 A.B. L.1066 J.D. 201 Redlands St.‡
Flock, John A. ..........................'57 '83 C.178 B.A. L.569 J.D. 7538 W. 83rd St.
Garcia, Luis, Jr. ..................'34 '75 C.843 B.S.C.E. L.1136 J.D. 8515 Falmouth Ave.
Grossman, Max L. ...............................'10 '36 C&L.800 A.B., J.D. 7349 Trask Ave.‡
Hilton, Ariel C., (Miss), (AV) ..........'11 '35 C&L.800 B.F.S., LL.B. 241 Fowling St.‡
Jamieson, Stephen A. ..................'58 '84 C.112 B.A. L.426 J.D. [Solomon,S.&J.]
Jelmini, Dean A. ................'51 '77 C&L.426 B.A., J.D. 8055 W. Manchester Blvd.
Knudson, John F. ....................'42 '79 C.208 B.S.B.A. L.1136 J.D. 8601 Falmouth Ave.
Mayeron, Candace N. .......'50 '78 C.494 B.A. L.1148 J.D. Pres., Him & Her Productions
Moore, M. Berrien E., (BV) ...............'29 '59 C.673 B.A. L.1068 J.D. 7019 Trask Ave.
Moster, Todd N. ..................................'58 '82 C.260 B.A. L.1068 J.D. P.O. Box 5131
Reed, John F., (A P.C.) ........'17 '40 C.112 B.A. L.623 LL.B. 8055 W. Manchester Ave.
Ross, Barbara E. ......................'49 '77 C.112 A.B. L.809 J.D. 8055 W. Manchester Ave.
Saltsman, Jay R. ...................'42 '74 C.800 A.B. L.1148 J.D. 8055 W. Manchester Ave.
Saltsman, Ralph B., (BV) .......................'47 '74 C.800 A.B. L.426 J.D. [Solomon,S.&J.]
Snow, Lynn ..........................................'23 '68 C.112 A.B. L.61 J.D. 8650 Gulana Ave.‡
Solomon, Stephen Warren, (BV) ..........'39 '65 C&L.112 A.B., LL.B. [Solomon,S.&J.]
Solomon, Saltsman & Jamieson, (BV) ...................................................426 Culver Blvd.
Velasco, Valeria C. ..............'51 '86 C.1042 B.A. L.1136 J.D. 8055 W. Manchester Ave.
Weissman, Susan ...................'41 '77 C.112 B.A. L.1148 J.D. 6515 Ocean Front Walk
Wicks, Douglas C. ..................'61 '86 C.1109 B.A. L.809 J.D. 8328 Manitoba
Zahler, Eileen V. ..........................'51 '77 C.994 B.A. L.724 J.D. 7546 W. 81st St.
Zartman, Ned K. '20 '50 C&L.986 A.B., LL.B.
(adm. in MO; not adm. in CA) 6621 Vista Del Mar‡
Zoochie, William R. ...................'50 '91 C.843 B.S. L.678 J.D. 8515 Falmouth Ave.

## PLEASANT HILL, 31,585, *Contra Costa Co.*

Bailey, Robert P. ...............................'25 '80 C.169 B.A.Econ. L.1065 147 Chianti Pl.
Baldassari, Jack D. .....................'45 '70 C.267 B.A. L.1065 J.D. 206 Elaine Dr.
Barr, Edward E. ............................'29 '62 C.766 B.A. L.1065 J.D. 101 Gregory Lane
Bolinger, Kenneth W. ..........................'39 '73 C.636 B.S. L.1065 J.D. [K.W.Bolinger]
Bolinger, Kenneth W., Inc. ..................................................2300 Contra Costa Blvd
Bonnar, R. Paul, (BV) ............'48 '79 C.768 B.S. L.678 J.D. 2255 Contra Costa Blvd.
Bruno, Russell J., (BV) ..................'25 '59 C.188 B.A. L.1066 J.D. 200 Gregory Lane
Chapla, Valerie M. ..................................................................'50 '75 30 Collins Dr.
Colbath, Joe D. ...................................'43 '74 C.174 B.S. L.1065 J.D. 454 Turrin Dr.
Currie, Richard D. '48 '80 C.112 A.B. L.1153 J.D.
Asst. V.P. & Reg. Claims Mgr., Design Professionals Ins. Co.
Dent, Larry B., (BV) ...................'40 '66 C.629 B.S. L.1066 LL.B. 395 Taylor Blvd.
Dillon, Haradon M., (AV) ....................'21 '53 C.208 B.S. L.1065 J.D. 69 Spar Ct.‡
**Egger, Patrick R.**, (AV) '50 '79 C.602 B.B.A. L.809 J.D.
[Egger&H.] (⊙San Bernardino, Yorba Linda, City of Industry, Salinas)
*PRACTICE AREAS: Workers Compensation Defense.

**Egger & Hallett, Professional Law Corporation, (AV)**
**3478 Buskirk Avenue, Suite 1025, 94523⊙**
**Telephone: 510-746-7187 Fax: 510-937-1611**
**Patrick R. Egger; Michael G. McDonald (Resident).**
**Workers Compensation Defense and Wills and Probate Law.**
**San Bernardino, California Office: 325 West Hospitality Lane, Suite 300. P.O. Box 5009. Telephone: 908-890-0403. Fax: 908-890-0503.**
**Yorba Linda, California Office: 22800 Savi Ranch Parkway, Suite 218. Telephone: 714-974-6299. Fax: 714-974-7215.**
**San Diego, California Office: 600 B Street, Suite 2200. Telephone: 619-236-9377. Fax: 619-236-1329.**
**City of Industry, California Office: 13200 Crossroads Parkway North, Suite 400 Telephone: 310-695-4951. Fax: 310-695-9647.**
**Salinas, California Office: 158 Central Avenue, Suite 3. Telephone: 408-771-1414. Fax: 408-771-1408.**
***See Professional Biographies, SAN BERNARDINO, CALIFORNIA***

Girard, David W. ...........................'42 '70 C.912 M.B.A. L.477 J.D. [Girard&V.]
Girard & Vinson ...............................................................3478 Buskirk Ave.
Grimm, Beth A. ..........................................'48 '88 L.1153 J.D. 3478 Buskirk Ave.
Hancock, John B. ..........................'47 '76 C.813 B.A. L.145 J.D. 399 Taylor Blvd.
Hardisty, Geo. D., (AV) ............'24 '51 C.197 A.B. L.767 LL.B. 101 Gregory Lane
Hartinger, Ben F., (BV) .................'17 '56 C.112 A.B. L.767 LL.B. 200 Gregory Ln.
Heitman, George C., (BV) ..................'40 '76 C.766 B.A. L.1153 J.D. P.O. Box 23163
Huffman, Laura ..................................'60 '89 C.172 B.A. L.284 J.D. P.O. Box 23743
Kenady, Patrick M. ..........................'46 '72 C.112 B.A. L.1067 J.D. 25 Pillon Real
Kissel, Robert M. .............................'41 '76 C.767 L.1026 LL.B. 12 Fairway Pl.
Lukas, Thomas William '49 '82 C.363 B.A. L.589 J.D.
(adm. in IL; not adm. in CA) 20 Duffy Ct.
Maguire, James G., (BV) ....................'24 '61 C.755 L.765 J.D. 200 Gregory Lane‡
Margolis, Debra S. ..........................'58 '83 C.1060 B.A. L.1067 J.D. City Atty.
**McDonald, Michael G.** ..........................................'58 '86 C.436 B.A. L.61 J.D. [Egger&H.]
Milgate, John M., (AV) ................'51 '78 C.1259 B.A. L.284 J.D. 101 Gregory Ln.
Nalbandian, Roberta E. ......'54 '82 C.722 B.A. L.464 J.D. Sr. Atty., Amer. States Ins. Co.
Noffsinger, Henry O. .............................'28 '64 C.766 L.765 LL.B. 91 Gregory Ln.
Otis, Roy J., (BV) .............................'46 '80 C.813 B.A. L.284 J.D. P.O. Box 23588
Shambaugh, Cynthia '53 '86
C.104 B.A. L.1065 J.D. Mng. Atty. & Coun., Amer. States Ins. Co.

CAA498P

Siegel, Lesley Ann ........................'54 '88 C.1042 B.A. L.1065 J.D. 391 Taylor Blvd.
Sinnott, James A. ..............................'57 '91 C.147 B.S. L.1153 J.D. 3065 Vessing Rd.
Trujillo, Phillip A. ...........................'65 '91 C.674 A.B. L.813 J.D. 3478 Buskirk Ave.
Vierra-Boelk, Christine ............'49 '87 C.112 B.A. L.1065 J.D. 2800 Pleasant Hill Rd.
Villanueva, Orlando R. ................'24 '78 C.662 M.P.A. L.066 LL.B. 261 Apollo Way
Vinson, Allen R. ..........................'51 '78 C.1074 B.S. L.999 J.D. [Girard&V.]

**PLEASANTON, 50,553,** ***Alameda Co.***

Aloe, Robert C., Jr., (CV) ............'47 '82 C.475 B.S. L.765 J.D. 4869 Del Valle Pkwy.
Anaya, Robert J. ..................................................'59 '91 L.765 J.D. 275 Rose Ave.

**Atkinson, Andelson, Loya, Ruud & Romo, A Professional Corporation, (AV)**
**The Atrium, 5776 Stoneridge Mall Road Suite 200, 94588⊙**
**Telephone: 510-227-9200 Telecopier: 510-227-9202 Email: AALRR@KINCYB.COM**
**Email: Info@aalrr.com URL: http://aalrr.com**
**Paul M. Loya (Resident); Peter J. Lucey (Resident);—Patrick A. Gunn (Resident); Chesley D. Quaide (Resident); Todd A. Goluba (Resident); Elizabeth B. Hearey; Marleen Lee Sacks; Janice J. Hein; Angela K. Kreta; Felicia C. Curran; Christine D. Lovely.**
**Labor Relations representing Management. School and Construction Law. Civil Litigation.**
**Cerritos, California Office: 13304 East Alondra Boulevard. Telephone: 310-404-4444; 714-826-5480. Telecopier: 310-404-8905.**
**San Bernardino, California Office: 348 West Hospitality Lane, Suite 202. Telephone: 909-888-4165. Telecopier: 909-884-4118.**
***See Professional Biographies, PLEASANTON, CALIFORNIA***

**Baxter, Leslie A.** ....................'57 '90 C.112 B.A. L.1065 J.D. [▣ Hallgrimson M.M.]
*PRACTICE AREAS: Real Estate; Land Use; Environmental Law.
**Bean, Sandra Kay** ..............'52 '92 C.896 B.A.M.A. L.770 J.D. [Clapp,M.B.D.&V.]
*PRACTICE AREAS: Insurance Defense; General Civil Litigation.
**Beeman, Christopher J.** ..............'60 '85 C.602 B.A. L.770 J.D. [Clapp,M.B.D.&V.]
**Bellagamba, Robert A.,** (AV) ........'47 '73 C.112 B.A. L.765 J.D. [Clapp,M.B.D.&V.]⊙
Berch, Michael C. .... '56 '81 C.112 A.B. L.284 J.D. Information Science Consultants, Inc.
Blaha, Jerome A. ..........................'43 '73 C.112 B.A. L.1065 J.D. [Blaha&H.]⊙
Blaha & Hartford, A Professional Corporation
Suite 240, 4900 Hopyard Road (⊙Castro Valley)
Booth, Stephen H. ...........'43 '68 C.112 B.S. L.1065 J.D. Kaiser Alum. & Chem. Corp.
Booth, Thomas R. ....................'49 '84 C.1077 B.A. L.426 J.D. V.P., CAP Concrete
Bower, Bruce Duncan '61 '89 C.103 A.B. L.893 J.D.
Exec. V.P. & Gen. Coun., Yes! Entertainment
Boylan, Michael J. '52 '78 C.178 B.A. L.893 J.D.
V.P. & Asst. Gen. Coun., Safeway Inc.
Braff, Sharman ....................'53 '80 C.976 B.S. L.1066 J.D. Sr. Atty., Safeway Inc.
**Brown, Charles B.** '34 '58 C.350 B.S. L.904 J.D.
Asst. Gen. Coun., Kaiser Alum. & Chem. Corp.
Brown, J. Michael, (BV) ...........'41 '66 C.988 B.C.S. L.1065 J.D. 5674 Stoneridge Dr.
Burns, William F. ...........................'59 '85 C.1073 B.S. L.767 J.D. 5000 Hopyard Rd.
**Butler, E. Bruce** '39 '65 C.918 B.A. L.665 LL.B.
Asst. Gen. Coun., Int'l, Kaiser Alum. & Chem. Corp.
Cameron, H. Mal .........................'45 '78 C.768 B.A. L.284 J.D. 4460 Black Ave.
**Castleman, M. Lorin,** (AV) ...........'39 '68 C.112 B.A. L.823 J.D. [Castleman,M.&O.]
*REPORTED CASES: Ramirez v. Redevelopment Agency, 4 Cal. App. 3d 397 (1990).
*PRACTICE AREAS: Taxation Law; Corporate Law; Real Property Law; Business Litigation; Estate Planning.

**Castleman, McFalone & O'Blennis, (AV)**
**5870 Stoneridge Mall Road, Suite 207, 94588**
**Telephone: 510-463-2221 Fax: 510-463-0328**
**Email: castlelaw.com@counsel.com**
**Members of Firm: M. Lorin Castleman (Certified Specialist, Taxation Law, The State Bar of California Board of Legal Specialization); Raymond B. McFalone; M. Kathleen O'Blennis. Associates: Barbara Jane Savery; Terrence P. Murphey; Catherine A. Naumann.**
**General Civil and Trial Practice in State and Federal Courts. Insurance Defense Litigation, Personal Injury, Defense of Public Entities, Title Insurance, Construction Litigation, Business Litigation, Estate Planning and Estate Taxation, Probate, Corporate, Securities, Business, Real Property, Landslide and Subsidence, Administrative, Municipal and Taxation Law, Tax Litigation, Bankruptcy, Creditors, Defense of Employment Discrimination Cases.**
***See Professional Biographies, PLEASANTON, CALIFORNIA***

**Clapp, Moroney, Bellagamba, Davis and Vucinich, (AV)**
**6140 Stoneridge Mall Road Suite 545, 94588⊙**
**Telephone: 510-734-0990 Fax: 510-734-0888**
**Member of Firm: Robert A. Bellagamba; Christopher J. Beeman; Frank J. Perretta; Mark T. Guerra. Associates: Virginia L. Vasquez; Andrew S. Miller; John F. Doyle; Mark L. Dawson; James E. Hart, III; Sandra Kay Bean; Adrienne E. Dennis; James William Doran.**
**General Insurance Law and Civil Trial Practice. Casualty Insurance (Automobile and Fire), Aviation, Professional Liability, Medical and Legal Malpractice Law. Real Estate and Insurance Liability (Agent Errors and Omissions), Construction Litigation, Environmental and Toxic Tort, Products Liability Law, Employment Discrimination, Wrongful Termination, Discrimination Law (Sex and Housing) Insurance Coverage, Declaratory Relief and Bad Faith Litigation.**
**Menlo Park, California Office: 4400 Bohannon Drive, Suite 100. Telephone: 415-327-1300. Fax: 415-327-3707.**
**San Francisco, California Office: One Sansome Street, Suite 1900. Telephone: 415-398-6045. Fax: 425-327-3707**
***See Professional Biographies, PLEASANTON, CALIFORNIA***

Coelho, Clay A. ...............'66 '92 C.763 B.A. L.1148 J.D. 6140 Stoneridge Mall Rd.
Cooney, Jack R., Jr., A Prof. Law Corp., (BV) '44 '75 C.549 B.S. L.284 J.D.
234 Main St.
**Covington, H. Christopher** '49 '80
C.112 B.A. L.464 J.D. Sr. V.P., Gen. Coun. & Secy., Vanstar Corp.
**Crabb, Jennifer H.** '60 '85 C.228 B.A. L.446 J.D.
Asst. Gen. Coun., Dillingham Construction Corp.

**Critchfield, Burke M., (AV) '30 '61 C.429 B.A. L.793 J.D.**
**5510 Sunol Boulevard, Suite 5, 94566**
**Telephone: 510-484-3344 FAX: 510-484-3606**
**Real Estate, Business, Estate Planning and Probate Law.**
***See Professional Biographies, PLEASANTON, CALIFORNIA***

**Curran, Felicia C.** ............'55 '87 C.1168 B.A. L.1065 J.D. [▣ Atkinson,A.L.R.&R.]
*PRACTICE AREAS: Civil Litigation; Education Law and Litigation; Employment Law; Labor Law; Appellate Practice.
Cushing, Kay ..........................'21 '71 C.169 L.464 J.D. 5672 Stoneridge Dr.‡
**Dahlen, Daniel H.** '44 '74 C.768 A.B. L.770 J.D.
Sr. Corp. Coun., Kaiser Alum. & Chem. Corp.
**Dawson, Mark L.** ....................'66 '93 C.112 B.A. L.464 J.D. [Clapp,M.B.D.&V.]
*PRACTICE AREAS: Civil Litigation; Construction Defect; Errors & Omissions.
DeBuono, Laureen '57 '82 C.228 B.A. L.569 J.D.
V.P., Gen. Coun. & Secy., Nellcor, Inc.
DeDomenico, Dennis T. '46 '75
C.766 B.A. L.284 J.D. Gen. Coun., Golden Grain Macaroni Co.
**Dennis, Adrienne E.** ...............'67 '93 C.112 B.A. L.464 J.D. [▣ Clapp,M.B.D.&V.]
*PRACTICE AREAS: Construction Defect Litigation.
**Donnan, John M.** '61 '86 C.845 B.B.A. L.45 J.D.
(adm. in TX; not adm. in CA) Corp. Coun., Kaiser Alum. & Chem. Corp.

**Doran, James William** ................'59 '95 C&L.767 P.S., J.D. [▣ Clapp,M.B.D.&V.]
*PRACTICE AREAS: Construction Defect Litigation; Bodily Injury.
**Doyle, John F.** ..........................'64 '89 C.740 B.A. L.464 J.D. [▣ Clapp,M.B.D.&V.]
Dummer, William L. ..................'47 '78 C.767 B.A. L.284 J.D. 6304 Singletree Way
Eaton, Mark L. .....................................'38 '64 C.1036 A.B. L.813 J.D. Supr. Ct. J.
**Efremsky, Roger L.,** (BV) ................'56 '83 C.1254 B.S. L.770 J.D. [Efremsky&N.]
*PRACTICE AREAS: Civil Litigation; Creditor's Rights; Bankruptcy; Commercial Law.

**Efremsky & Nagel, (BV)**
**5776 Stoneridge Mall Road, Suite 360, 94588**
**Telephone: 510-463-0505 Fax: 510-463-8064**
**Roger L. Efremsky; Austin P. Nagel.**
**Civil Litigation, Creditor's Rights, Bankruptcy and Commercial Law.**
***See Professional Biographies, PLEASANTON, CALIFORNIA***

Elstead, John C., (BV) .........................'42 '74 C.112 B.A. L.1066 J.D. [Smith P.]
Emerson, Dian B. ...................'51 '79 C.112 B.A. L.1067 J.D. Sr. Atty., Safeway Inc.
**English, Richard D.** '48 '85 C.1120 B.A. L.990 J.D.
(adm. in NM; not adm. in CA) Corp. Coun., Vanstar Corp.
*RESPONSIBILITIES: General Corporate Law; Contracts; Leases; Disputes.
**Erickson, Ann B.** ...........'52 '90 C.390 A.B. L.1065 J.D. Corp. Coun., Vanstar Corp.
*RESPONSIBILITIES: Employment Law; General Litigation; Bankruptcy Matters; Disputes.

**Etnire, Geoffrey C., (AV) '48 '74 C.659 B.S. L.813 J.D. BB**
**4900 Hopyard Road, Suite 260, 94588**
**Telephone: 510-734-9950 Fax: 510-734-9170**
**Email: etnire@ricochet.net**
**Real Estate Transactions, Development and Land Use Issues.**
***See Professional Biographies, PLEASANTON, CALIFORNIA***

Farley-Rodgers, Jeanne A., (BV) '44 '83 C&L.770 B.A., J.D.
5674 Stoneridge Dr., Suite
Foland, Stephen F. ...............................'44 '75 C.347 B.A. L.284 J.D. Comr., Mun. Ct.
Garrison, William M. ................'39 '65 C.923 B.A. L.902 LL.B. 430 Hamilton Way
Garvin, John H., (BV) ..................'— '66 C.112 B.S. L.284 LL.B. 7901 Stoneridge Dr.
Giuffré, Barbara L. ......................'59 '87 C.188 A.B. L.893 J.D. [▣ Smith,M.&D.]
**Goluba, Todd A.** ..................'67 '92 C.112 B.A. L.1065 J.D. [▣ Atkinson,A.L.R.&R.]
*PRACTICE AREAS: Employment Law; School Law.
Gorman, Richard M. ................'20 '51 C.112 A.B. L.1065 J.D. 5049 Glenwood Ct.‡
Gouig, Steven J. ......................'47 '73 C.740 B.A. L.767 J.D. Sr. Atty., Safeway Inc.
Graham, Lawrence O. '61 '89 C.674 B.A. L.309 J.D.
(adm. in NY; not adm. in CA) [▣ Smith,M.&D.]
**Granger, Betsy S.** ......'53 '86 C.105 B.A. L.1065 J.D. Atty., Pacific Telesis Legal Group
Gray, Patricia A. '54 '82 C.188 B.A. L.276 J.D.
(adm. in NY; not adm. in CA) Assoc. Gen. Coun., The Cooper Cos., Inc.
Green, Heather M.D. ..........................'55 '86 C.605 B.A. L.284 J.D. [Green&N.]
Green & Neilsen, (BV) ..............................5820 Stoneridge Mall Road, Suite 102
Grossman, Alan, (BV) ................'44 '73 C.584 B.A. L.1065 J.D. 4460 Black Ave.
Guenther, Craig D. ..............'59 '89 C.112 B.A. L.770 J.D. 6140 Stoneridge Mall Rd.
Guerino, Jerrel L. ..............'41 '68 C.112 A.B. L.1065 J.D. Transamerica Title Ins. Co.
**Guerra, Mark T.** ......................'58 '83 C.112 B.A. L.767 J.D. [Clapp,M.B.D.&V.]
**Gulseth, James H.,** (AV) ...................................'— '74 C.112 A.B. L.1065 J.D. [JG]
*REPORTED CASES: PACKER TRANSPORATION CO. v. USA, 596 F. 2d 891.; PLATTS v. SACRAMENTO NORTHERN RAILWAY, 1988, Court of Appeal, First District, 253 Cal.Rptr 269; 205 Cal.App.3rd 1025.
*PRACTICE AREAS: Business Law; Corporations; Mergers and Acquisitions; Partnerships; Intellectual Property.
**Gunn, Patrick A.** ................'62 '88 C.1060 B.A. L.426 J.D. [▣ Atkinson,A.L.R.&R.]
*PRACTICE AREAS: Civil Litigation; Business Law; Construction Law; Real Property Development Disputes; Construction Defect Claims.
**Haist, Dennis P.** '49 '83 C.477 B.S.E. L.284 J.D.
V.P., Gen. Coun. & Secy., Dillingham Construction Corp.
**Hallgrimson, Steven L.,** (AV) .....'42 '68 C.154 B.A. L.1066 J.D. [Hallgrimson M.M.]⊙
*PRACTICE AREAS: Business and Real Estate Transactions.

**Hallgrimson McNichols McCann LLP, (AV)**
**5000 Hopyard Road, Suite 400, 94588⊙**
**Telephone: 510-460-3700 Fax: 510-460-0969**
**Members of Firm: Stephen L. R. McNichols, Jr.; Steven L. Hallgrimson; William D. McCann; Kevin W. Wheelwright; Nickolas P. Tooliatos, II (Certified Specialist, Estate Planning, Trust and Probate Law, The State Bar of California Board of Legal Specialization); Phillip G. Vermont; Michael E. Kyle; Phil Sasso. Associates: Shannon Waller; Leslie A. Baxter; James R. Moore.**
**Civil Trial Practice, Corporate and Business Law, Real Property, Land Use and Development, Environmental Law, Insurance Law, Tort Litigation, Construction Litigation, Employment Law, Estate Planning, Federal and State Taxation, Probate and Entertainment Law.**
**San Jose, California Office: 40 S. Market Street, Suite 700. Telephone: 408-275-6600. Facsimile: 408-275-0315. E-Mail: HMMSJ@aol.com**
***See Professional Biographies, PLEASANTON, CALIFORNIA***

Harding, John E., (CV) ........................'63 '89 C.740 B.A. L.284 J.D. [Harding&H.]
Harding, Merle L. ....................................'29 '65 C&L.1026 LL.B. [Harding&H.]
Harding & Harding, (CV) ........................................................... 78 Mission Dr.
Harmon, Megan Tootell ...............'52 '78 C.112 A.B. L.284 J.D. 7901 Stoneridge Dr.
**Hart, James E., III** ......................'65 '93 C.156 B.S. L.990 J.D. [Clapp,M.B.D.&V.]
*PRACTICE AREAS: Construction Defect.
Hartford, Vera K. ...................................'46 '79 C.112 B.A. L.1153 J.D. [Blaha&H.]
**Hassen, Joel** '44 '69 C.112 B.A. L.309 J.D.
Sr. Pension & Benefits Coun., Kaiser Alum. & Chem. Corp.
**Hearey, Elizabeth B.** ...........'47 '73 C.914 B.A. L.1065 J.D. [▣ Atkinson,A.L.R.&R.]
*PRACTICE AREAS: Education Law; Administrative Law; Labor Law; Employment Law.
Heasom, Cynthia, (BV) ..................'56 '83 C.112 L.1153 J.D. 480 Saint John St.
**Hein, Janice J.** ..............................'52 '83 C.136 B.S. L.477 J.D. [Atkinson,A.L.R.&R.]
*PRACTICE AREAS: Labor and Employment; Education.
Hinsley, Claude W. '46 '81
C.611 B.A. L.1065 J.D. Pres.& Gen. Coun., CWH Ventures, Inc.
Hirst, William A., (BV) ........................'40 '65 C.112 B.S. L.1065 J.D. 235 Main St.

**Hosterman, J. Michael, (BV) '51 '77 C.112 B.A. L.770 J.D.**
**555 Peters Avenue, Suite 115, 94566**
**Telephone: 510-426-8000 Fax: 510-426-8001**
**Personal Injury, Products Liability, Wrongful Death, Insurance and Civil Litigation.**
***See Professional Biographies, PLEASANTON, CALIFORNIA***

Husick, Gloria J. ....................................'48 '84 L.1153 J.D. 351 St. Marys St.
Hyde, D. Ronald .........................................'43 '70 C.740 B.S. L.284 J.D. Mun. Ct. J.
Inderbitzen, Martin W., (AV) ..............'51 '76 C.766 B.A. L.770 J.D. 62 W. Neal St.
Jackson, Carolyn C. ...................'48 '73 C.483 B.A. L.1066 J.D. 1376 Greenwood Rd.
Jacobs, Marisa F. '57 '82 C.216 B.A. L.178 J.D.
(adm. in NY; not adm. in CA) Assoc. Gen. Coun. & Secy., The Cooper Cos., Inc.
Jardin, Manuel C. ..........................'41 '66 C.740 B.A. L.1065 LL.B. 6 Deer Oaks Dr.
**Jenks, Rodney P., Jr.,** (BV) '50 '76 C.112 A.B. L.1065 J.D.
V.P. & Gen. Coun., Amer. & Asia Pacific Oper., Hexcel Corp.

CAA499P

CALIFORNIA—PLEASANTON MARTINDALE-HUBBELL LAW DIRECTORY 1997

**JG, P.C., Business & Corporate Law, (AV)**
**5000 Hopyard Road, Suite 400, 94588**
**Telephone: 510-463-9600 Facsimile: 510-463-9644**
**Email: GHTD08A@PRODIGY.COM**
**James H. Gulseth.**
**Business. Business Transactions and Formations. Corporations. Mergers and Acquisitions, Corporate, Partnership and Limited Liability Company Law. Business Contracts and Leases. Intellectual Property and Unfair Competition. Computers and Software.**
***See Professional Biographies, PLEASANTON, CALIFORNIA***

**Jobson, Bruce,** (AV) . . . . . . . . . . . . . . . . . . '46 '72 C.770 B.A. L.1066 J.D. [Staley,J.&W.]
*PRACTICE AREAS: Family Law; Litigation; Mediation; Private Judging.
Johnston, Marilyn K. . . . . '47 '75 C.309 A.B. L.597 J.D. Sr. Real Estate Atty., Safeway Inc.
Junta, Dale W. . . . . . . . . . . . . '37 '65 C.309 A.B. L.1065 J.D. V.P., Robert Dalton & Co.
Kaitz, Patricia M. '54 '79 C.112 B.S. L.1065 J.D.
Dir., Taxes & Tax Coun., Nellcor, Inc.
Karpf, Beth L. . . . . . . . . . . . . . . . . '54 '83 C.453 B.S. L.1066 J.D. Corp. Coun., Nellcor, Inc.
Kelly, Valarie L. . . . . . . . . . . . . . . . . . '60 '86 C.768 B.A. L.1066 J.D. 6402 Calle Esperanza
Kelly-Hollister, Lorene, (CV) . . . . . . . . . . . . . . . . '53 '81 C.589 B.S. L.208 J.D. P.O. Box 910
Kinley, David D. . . . . . . . . . '41 '68 C.675 B.A. L.309 LL.B. Sr. V.P., Viacom Cablevision
Kisner, Daniel R. . . . . . . . . . '46 '75 C.161 B.E.E. L.990 J.D. Div. Coun., Ponderosa Homes
Knight, Jeffrey W. . . . . . . . . . . . . . . . '49 '78 C.976 B.A. L.128 J.D. Computerland Corp.
Kovach, Dennis E. . . . . . . '53 '78 C.37 B.S. L.36 J.D. Dir., Intell. Prop., Nellcor, Inc. (Pat.)
**Kreta, Angela K.** . . . . . . . . . . . . . . '60 '85 C.605 B.A. L.36 J.D. [⊠ Atkinson,A.L.R.&R.]
*PRACTICE AREAS: School Law; Labor Law; Employment Law; Administrative Law.
**Kyle, Michael E.,** (BV) . . . . . . . . . . . '42 '71 C.112 B.A. L.1067 J.D. [Hallgrimson M.M.]
*PRACTICE AREAS: Civil Litigation; Construction Law; Business and Real Estate Transactions; Public Entities; Estate Planning.
**Langford, James R., III,** (BV) . . . . . . . . . '54 '81 C.813 B.A. L.1068 J.D. [⊠ J.G.Schwartz]
*PRACTICE AREAS: Commercial Real Estate; Civil Litigation; Landlord-Tenant Law; Commercial Leasing; Real Estate Brokers and Agents Liability.
Lonner, Matthew . . . . . . . . . . . '64 '93 C.766 B.A. L.767 J.D. 7901 Stoneridge Dr. Ste. 401
Lopez, Edward . . . . '60 '85 C.178 A.B. L.309 J.D. Corp. Coun. & Asst. Secy., Nellcor, Inc.
**Lovely, Christine D.** . . . . . . . . . . . . . . . '68 '96 C&L.112 A.B., J.D. [⊠ Atkinson,A.L.R.&R.]
*PRACTICE AREAS: Education; Labor; Employment.
**Loya, Paul M.,** (BV) . . . . . . . . . . . '46 '73 C.1073 B.S. L.1066 J.D. [Atkinson,A.L.R.&R.]
**Lucey, Peter J.** . . . . . . . . . . . . . . . '48 '75 C.112 B.A. L.1067 J.D. [Atkinson,A.L.R.&R.]
**Lyon, Ben H.** . . . . . . '53 '78 C.112 B.A. L.426 J.D. Sr. Coun., Pacific Telesis Legal Group
**MacAuley, Laury** . . . . . . . . . . . . '61 '87 C.112 B.A. L.767 J.D. Assoc. Coun., Hexcel Corp.
**MacDonald, Scott T.** '59 '90 C.691 B.A. L.846 J.D.
(adm. in TX; not adm. in CA) Lit. Coun., Kaiser Alum. & Chem. Corp.
Marshall, George D. . . . . . . . . . . . . . . . . . . '40 '66 C.31 B.A. L.1066 J.D. V.P., Safeway Inc.
**Matthews, K. Kyle** '62 '88 C&L.101 B.A., J.D.
Labor and Employ. Coun., Kaiser Alum. & Chem. Corp.
Mayes, Jonathan O. . . . . . . . . . . . . . . . '57 '87 C.999 B.S. L.950 J.D. Sr. Atty., Safeway Inc.
**McCann, William D.,** (BV) . . . '47 '72 C.112 A.B. L.1065 J.D. [Hallgrimson M.M.] (Pat.)
*LANGUAGES: Spanish and French.
*PRACTICE AREAS: Civil Litigation; Personal Injury; International Law.
McDaniel, Joe, Jr. '60 '88 C.259 B.S. L.893 J.D.
(adm. in NY; not adm. in CA) [Smith,M.&D.]
**McFalone, Raymond B.** . . . . . . . . . . . . '54 '82 C.768 B.A. L.1137 J.D. [Castleman,M.&O.]
*PRACTICE AREAS: Construction Law; Insurance Defense Law; Real Estate Law; Probate; Personal Injury.
McKeehan, James W., (AV) . . . . . . . . . . . '45 '72 C.684 B.A. L.1065 J.D. 6612 Owens Dr.
McKeown, Edwin S. . . . . . . . '22 '49 C.674 A.B. L.309 LL.B. Kaiser Alum. & Chem. Corp.
**McNichols, Stephen L. R., Jr.,** (AV) '43 '68 C.668 B.A. L.1066 J.D.
[Hallgrimson M.M.]
*PRACTICE AREAS: Business; Commercial; Real Estate; Tort Litigation; Dispute Resolution.
Meehan, Patrick M. . . . . . . . . . . . . . . . . . . . . . . . '50 '76 C&L.767 B.A., J.D. The Clorox Co.
Meidl, Christopher D. A. . . . . . . . '61 '89 C.112 B.A. L.770 J.D. 5000 Hopyard Rd. Ste. 400
Metz, Richard B. . . . . . . . . . . . . . . . . . . '48 '75 C.1254 B.S. L.813 J.D. 4237 Tamur Ct.
**Miller, Andrew S.** . . . . . . . . . . . . . . . . . '63 '89 C.147 B.A. L.767 J.D. [Clapp,M.B.D.&V.]
*PRACTICE AREAS: Construction; Personal Injury; Business; Commercial Litigation.
**Moore, James R.,** (AV⊙) . . . . . . . . '40 '69 C.1097 A.B. L.1066 J.D. [⊠ Hallgrimson M.M.]
*PRACTICE AREAS: Civil Litigation.
**Moore, Stanley J.** '46 '72 C.347 A.B. L.178 J.D.
Sr. Coun., Pacific Telesis Legal Group
**Mrozek, Ronald A.** . . . . . . '44 '69 C&L.339 A.B., J.D. Reg. Coun., GE Medcical Systems
**Murphey, Terrence P.** . . . . . . . . . . . '54 '91 C.475 B.S. L.1065 J.D. [⊠ Castleman,M.&O.]
*REPORTED CASES: Evans v. Paye, 32 Cal. App. 4th 265, 37 Cal. Rptr. 2d 915 (1995).
*PRACTICE AREAS: Civil Litigation; Business Law; Administrative Law; Personal Injury; Taxation Law.
Murphy, Jerry G., (BV) . . . . . . . . . . . . '20 '53 C.112 A.B. L.1066 LL.B. 4949 Hillcrest Way
**Nagel, Austin P.** . . . . . . . . . . . . . . . . . . . . . '57 '85 C.112 B.A. L.284 J.D. [Efremsky&N.]
*PRACTICE AREAS: Civil Litigation; Creditor's Rights; Bankruptcy; Commercial Law.
Nagel, Kenneth C., (AV) . . . . '22 '51 C.112 B.S. L.1066 LL.B. 5776 Stoneridge Mall Rd.‡
Nagle, Mark Carpenter . . . . . . . . . . . '66 '93 C.112 B.A. L.464 J.D. Sprint Telecom. Venture
**Naumann, Catherine A.** . . . . . . . . . . . . '64 '90 C.483 B.A. L.861 J.D. [⊠ Castleman,M.&O.]
*PRACTICE AREAS: Trademarks; Copyrights; Insurance; Business Transaction and Litigation; Tax Law.
Neilsen, R. Evan, Jr., (BV) . . . . . . . . . . . . . . . . . . . '51 '82 C.112 B.A. L.770 J.D. [Green&N.]
**Niemand, John Wm., II** '45 '70 C.112 B.S. L.1066 J.D.
Asst. Gen. Coun., Kaiser Alum. & Chem. Corp.
Noonan, John W., Prof. Corp., (AV) '33 '63 C.770 B.S. L.1026 J.D.
5674 Stoneridge Dr.
**O'Blennis, M. Kathleen** . . . . . . . . . . . . . . . . '51 '76 C&L.734 A.B., J.D. [Castleman,M.&O.]
*REPORTED CASES: Evans v. Paye, 32 Cal. App. 4th 265, 37 Cal. Rptr. 2d 915 (1995).
*PRACTICE AREAS: Estate Planning Law; Tax Law; Business Transaction and Business Litigation.
O'Flaherty, John F. . . . . . . . '44 '74 C.994 B.A. L.904 J.D. 5794 W. Las Positas Blvd. (Pat.)
Oliver, Bruce D. . . . . . . . . . . '28 '60 C.97 B.S.B.A. L.608 J.D. Kaiser Alum. & Chem. Corp.

**Opperwall, Stephen G., Law Offices of '53 '81 C.114 B.A. L.770 J.D.**
**4900 Hopyard Road, Suite 100, 94588**
**Telephone: 510-417-0300 Facsimile: 510-417-0301**
**Email: lawofcsgo@aol.com**
**Civil Litigation, Business Litigation, Commercial Litigation, Real Estate Litigation, Contract Litigation, Creditors' Remedies Law, Debt Collection.**

Parry, Meredith S. '60 '85 C.813 B.A. L.1068 J.D.
Sr. Atty. & Asst. Secy., Safeway Inc.
Paskevicius, Ruta '56 '87 C.1169 B.A. L.767 J.D.
Mgr., Legal Servs., Sun-Diamond Growers of Calif.
Patton, Laura W. . . . . . . . . '64 '90 C.861 B.A. L.1065 J.D. 5870 Stoneridge Mall Rd., #207
Paxson, Kirk M. '65 '91 C.813 B.A. L.678 J.D.
(adm. in WA; not adm. in CA) [⊠ Smith,M.&D.]
**Perretta, Frank J.** . . . . . . . . . . . . . . . . . . . '61 '86 C.112 B.A. L.770 J.D. [Clapp,M.B.D.&V.]
Petty, George O. . . . . . . . . . . . . . . '39 '65 C.112 A.B. L.1066 LL.B. 5568 Gibraltar Dr.
**Phillips, James J.,** (AV) . . . . . . . . . . . . . . . . . . . '54 '80 C.112 B.S. L.1065 J.D. [J.J.Phillips]⊙

**Phillips, James J., A Professional Corporation, (AV)** ⊞
**4900 Hopyard Road, Suite 260, 94588⊙**
**Telephone: 510-463-1980 Fax: 510-463-8656**
**James J. Phillips (Certified Specialist, Estate Planning, Trust and Probate Law, The State Bar of California Board of Legal Specialization).**
(This Listing Continued)

**Phillips, James J., A Professional Corporation (Continued)**
**Estate Planning, Trust and Probate Law.**
**Hayward, California Office: 1331 B Street, Suite 4. Telephone: 510-886-2120.**
***See Professional Biographies, PLEASANTON, CALIFORNIA***

**Pierno, Anthony R.,** (AV) '32 '60 C.940 A.B. L.813 J.D.
V.P. & Gen. Coun., Kaiser Alum. & Chem. Corp. (⊙Houston, Tx.)
Plessinger, James A. . . . . . . '29 '67 C.1027 B.S. L.184 J.D. 5870 Stoneridge Mall Rd., #207
Polson, Edward W., (BV) . . . . . . . . . . . . . . . . . . . '42 '74 C.347 B.S. L.1065 J.D. [Smith P.]
Poree, Victor J., (BV) . . . . . . . . . . . . . . . . . . '48 '78 C.112 A.B. L.1065 J.D. 4450 Black Ave.
**Quaide, Chesley D.** . . . . . . . . . . . . '59 '88 C.112 B.A. L.767 J.D. [⊠ Atkinson,A.L.R.&R.]
*PRACTICE AREAS: Labor Law; Employment Law; Education Law.

**Rifkind & Fuerch, A Professional Corporation**
**(See Hayward)**

**Ringwood, Stephen B.** '43 '70
C.966 B.S. L.339 J.D. Sr. Lit. Coun., Kaiser Alum. & Chem. Corp.
Robison, Elizabeth Jernigan '52 '80
C.790 B.A. L.1065 J.D. V.P. & Gen. Atty., Spreckels Sugar Co., Inc.
Rolefson, Jon R., (AV) . . . . . . . . . . . . . . '48 '73 C.112 A.B. L.1065 J.D. 5674 Stoneridge Dr.
Ross, Michael C., (AV) '48 '77
C&L.893 B.A., J.D. Sr. V.P., Secy. & Gen. Coun., Safeway Inc.
**Russell, Edward** . . . . . . . . . . . . . . . . . . . . . . . '59 '89 C.911 B.A. L.678 J.D. [⊠ J.G.Schwartz]
*PRACTICE AREAS: Creditor's Rights and Collection.
**Sacks, Marleen Lee** . . . . . . . . . . . '65 '92 C.112 B.A. L.1066 J.D. [⊠ Atkinson,A.L.R.&R.]
*PRACTICE AREAS: Employment Law; School Law.
Safreno, D. Casey . . . . . . . . . . . . . . . . . . . '59 '83 C.813 A.B. L.309 J.D. 1627 Vineyard Ave.
**Sasso, Phil** . . . . . . . . . . . . . . . . . . . . . . . . '56 '84 C&L.966 B.B.A., J.D. [Hallgrimson M.M.]⊙
*PRACTICE AREAS: Real Estate Acquisitions and Sales; Leasing; Development; Land Use.
**Savery, Barbara Jane** . . . . . . . . . . . . . . '46 '88 C.813 B.A. L.284 J.D. [⊠ Castleman,M.&O.]
*LANGUAGES: Portuguese and German.
*PRACTICE AREAS: Common Interest Community Law; Real Property Law.
Schlies, Christopher P. . . . . . . . . . . . . . . . '54 '79 C.1169 A.B. L.1067 J.D. 351 St. Mary St.
Schmalz, Robert L. '40 '65 C&L.494 B.S., LL.B.
V.P., Gen. Coun. & Secy., Spreckels Industries, Inc.

**Schwartz, James G., Law Offices of, (BV) '48 '76 C.768 B.S. L.464 J.D.**
**Suite 401, 7901 Stoneridge Drive, 94588**
**Telephone: 510-463-1073 Fax: 510-463-2937**
***PRACTICE AREAS: Creditor's Rights Law; Bankruptcy Law; Litigation; Collections; Business and Real Estate.**
**Associates: Edward Russell; James R. Langford, III.**
**Creditors Bankruptcy Rights, Business, Commercial Finance and Real Estate and Commercial Business Litigation. Estate Planning and Probate Law, Collections.**
***See Professional Biographies, PLEASANTON, CALIFORNIA***

Scott, G. Judson, Jr., (BV) . . . . . . . '45 '75 C.112 B.A. L.770 J.D. 6140 Stoneridge Mall Rd.
Shaw, Donald B. . . . . . . . . . . . '50 '76 C&L.477 B.G.S., J.D. V.P., Real Estate, Safeway Inc.

**Slater, Doris Hale, (BV) '46 '79 C.1073 B.A. L.770 J.D.**
**Suite 501, 7901 Stoneridge Drive, 94588**
**Telephone: 510-463-1818 Fax: 510-847-3079**
***LANGUAGES: German.**
**General Civil and Trial Practice. Family, Business, Real Estate, Bankruptcy, Personal Injury, Estate Planning and Probate Law.**
***See Professional Biographies, PLEASANTON, CALIFORNIA***

Smedley, Barbara, (CV) . . . . . . . . . . . . . . . . . . . . . . . '43 '86 L.1197 J.D. 5674 Stoneridge Dr.
Smith, G. Nelson, III '61 '86 C.329 B.A. L.893 J.D.
(adm. in VA; not adm. in CA) [Smith,M.&D.]
Smith, Lawrence G., (BV) . . . . . . . . . . . . . . . . . . . . '45 '78 C.112 B.A. L.767 J.D. [Smith P.]
Smith, McDaniel & Donahue . . . . . . . . . . . 4198 Peregrine Way (⊙Sacramento, Chicago, IL)
Smith • Polson, A Professional Law Corp., (BV) . . . . . . . . . . . . . . . . . . . . . . 500 Hopyard Rd.
**Staley, John F.,** (AV) . . . . . . . . . . . . . . . . . . . . '43 '72 C.267 B.A. L.1065 J.D. [Staley,J.&W.]
*REPORTED CASES: Prevailing counsel establishing copyright as community property (Irmo Worth, 195 Cal. App. 3d 768).
*PRACTICE AREAS: Family Law.

**Staley, Jobson & Wetherell, A Professional Corporation, (AV)** ⊞
**5776 Stoneridge Mall Road, Suite 310, 94588**
**Telephone: 510-463-0750 Fax: 510-463-0407**
**John F. Staley (Certified Specialist, Family Law, The State Bar of California Board of Legal Specialization); Bruce Jobson (Certified Specialist, Family Law, The State Bar of California Board of Legal Specialization); Joan M. Wetherell (Certified Specialist, Family Law, The State Bar of California Board of Legal Specialization).**
**Practice limited to Family Law and related areas.**
***See Professional Biographies, PLEASANTON, CALIFORNIA***

Storms, Stephanie Ann . . . . . . . . . . . . . . . . . . . '50 '75 C.813 B.A. L.846 J.D. Viacom Intl. Inc.
Straff, Donna E. . . . . . . . . . . . . '52 '80 C.273 B.A. L.128 J.D. Corp. Coun., Merisel FAB, Inc.
Tomcik, James R., (BV) . . . . . . . . . . . . . . . . . . '44 '74 C.608 B.Sc. L.284 J.D. 4450 Black Ave.
**Tooliatos, Nickolas P., II** . . . . . . . . . . . . . . '57 '83 C&L.770 B.S., J.D. [Hallgrimson M.M.]
*PRACTICE AREAS: Business Transactions; Tax; Probate; Estate Planning.
Tow, George Anna . . . . . . . . . . . . . . . . . '— '87 C.45 B.A. L.770 J.D. 1778 Beachwood Way
Traback, Harry J., Jr., (AV) . . . . . . . . . '44 '73 C.477 B.B.A. L.767 J.D. 5674 Stoneridge Dr.
**Tuthill, James P.** . . '47 '72 C.697 B.A. L.597 J.D. Sr. Coun., Pacific Telesis Legal Group
**Vasquez, Virginia L.** . . . . . . . . . . . . . '58 '88 C.1097 B.A. L.767 J.D. [⊠ Clapp,M.B.D.&V.]
*PRACTICE AREAS: Construction Defect Litigation; Personal Injury.
**Vermont, Phillip G.** . . . . . . '61 '87 C.112 B.A. L.770 J.D. [Hallgrimson M.M.] (⊙San Jose)
*LANGUAGES: French.
*PRACTICE AREAS: Products Liability; Personal Injury Litigation; Real Estate Litigation; Business Litigation; Insurance Bad Faith.
**Wade, Byron L.** '47 '74 C.1085 B.A. L.800 J.D.
V.P., Secy. & Dep. Gen. Coun., Kaiser Alum. & Chem. Corp. (⊙Houston, TX)
**Waller, Shannon** . . . . . . . . . . . . . . . . . . . '69 '94 C.112 B.A. L.1065 J.D. [Hallgrimson M.M.]
*PRACTICE AREAS: Corporate Law; Employment Law.
**Wallmann, James L.** . . . . . . . . . . '55 '90 C.101 B.A. L.276 J.D. Assoc. Coun., Hexcel Corp.
Walsh, Brenda J. M. '48 '86
C.588 B.A. L.1066 J.D. Corp. Coun. & Asst. Secy., Nellcor, Inc.
Welch, Mark J. . . . . . . . . . . . . . . . . '60 '89 C.454 B.A. L.1066 J.D. 5820 Stoneridge Mall Rd.
**Wetherell, Joan M.,** (BV) . . . . . . . . . . . . . . '46 '79 C.1073 B.A. L.284 J.D. [Staley,J.&W.]
*PRACTICE AREAS: Family Law; Deferred Compensation (Family Law).
**Wheelwright, Kevin W.** . . . . . . . . . . . '51 '76 C.1085 B.S. L.767 J.D. [Hallgrimson M.M.]
*PRACTICE AREAS: Employment and Real Estate Litigation; General Business.
**Williams, Robert I.** '50 '78
C.178 A.B. L.309 J.D. Reg. Coun. & Dir., Contracts, OHM Corp.
Wills, Lisa Dorian . . . . . . . . . . . . . . . '61 '87 C.112 B.A. L.464 J.D. 5820 Stoneridge Mall Rd.
Wilson, Joseph A. '52 '83 C.563 B.A. L.94 J.D.
(adm. in NY; not adm. in CA) [⊠ Smith,M.&D.]
Wilson, Richard A. . . . . . . . . . . . . . . '34 '60 C.797 A.B. L.1066 J.D. V.P., Tax, Safeway Inc.
Wondolowski, William W. . . . . . . . . . . '52 '77 C.112 B.S. L.1065 J.D. Treas., Hexcel Corp.
**Wong, Derek D.** '56 '85 C.1073 B.A.B.S. L.569 J.D.
Sr. Coun. & Asst. Secy., Dillingham Construction Corp.

CAA500P

## PLYMOUTH, 811, *Amador Co.*

Andreason, J. C. .......... '24 '59 C&L.813 A.B., LL.B. P.O. Box 39
Bartleson, Paul R. .......... '58 '85 C.112 B.A. L.464 J.D. P.O. Box 386
Cilenti, Steven .......... '47 '88 C.147 B.A. L.408 J.D. P.O. Box 370
D'Agostini, Mary Lou Flagg, (CV) .......... '35 '63 P.O. Box 775‡

## POINT REYES STATION, 300, *Marin Co.*

Baty, David R., (BV) .......... '27 '55 C&L.813 A.B., LL.B. P.O. Box 399
Burroughs, John D. .......... '34 '63 C.494 B.A. L.1065 J.D. [Burroughs&F.]
Burroughs & Froneberger .......... 145 A St.
Foote, Caleb '17 '56 C.309 A.B. L.659 LL.B.
(adm. in PA; not adm. in CA) Prof. of Law, Emeritus, Univ. of Calif. at Berkeley
Freitas, McCarthy, MacMahon & Keating, (AV) .......... Point Reyes Station (©San Rafael)
Froneberger, Henry D. .......... '46 '72 C.404 B.A. L.896 J.D. [Burroughs&F.]
Linford, James T. .......... '46 '82 C.31 B.A. L.284 J.D. P.O. Box 578
MacMahon, Jay Ross, (AV) .......... '30 '55 C.112 B.S. L.1066 J.D. [Freitas,M.M.&K.]©

**Powsner, Robert H., (AV) '29 '53 C&L.813 B.A., J.D.**
**11315 Shoreline, P.O. Box 1327, 94956**
**Telephone: 415-663-1035 Telefax: 415-663-1450**
***PRACTICE AREAS: General Business Representation; Litigation; Entertainment. General Business, Entertainment; Litigation.**

*See Professional Biographies, POINT REYES STATION, CALIFORNIA*

Saalfield, Janet H. .......... '43 '75 C.914 B.A. L.669 J.D. P.O. Box 807
Svirsky, Peter S. '34 '59 C.821 B.A. L.976 LL.B.
(adm. in CT; not adm. in CA) P.O. Box 637‡
Williams, Mary R. .......... '43 '81 C.33 B.A. L.1065 J.D. P.O. Box 1375

## POINT RICHMOND, —, *Contra Costa Co.*

Alexander, Richard J., (BV) .......... '48 '78 C.112 A.B. L.284 J.D. 137 Park Pl.
Bancroft, Richard A. .......... '18 '54 C&L.329 A.B., LL.B. Ret. Supr. Ct. J.
Burg, Kelley Ann .......... '44 '73 C.999 B.A. L.1066 J.D. 124A Washington Ave.
Hart, Patrick J. .......... '51 '80 C.112 B.S. L.284 J.D. 137 Park Pl.
Hollander, C. Jay .......... '21 '49 C.112 A.B. L.767 LL.B. 501 Cliffside Ct.
Kretzmer, William J. .......... '20 '47 C.112 A.B. L.1066 LL.B. 336 Washington Ave.‡

## POLLOCK PINES, —, *El Dorado Co.*

Barr, Linda S. .......... '48 '85 C.477 B.A. L.284 J.D. 6563 Onyx Trail
Barsamian, Armon .......... '36 '67 C.766 A.B. L.284 J.D. 5551 Shooting Star Rd.
Sules, Roy S. .......... '27 '63 C.1060 B.A. L.464 LL.B. 5797 Joni Ct.

## POMONA, 131,723, *Los Angeles Co.*

**Allard, Shelton & O'Connor**
**(See Claremont)**

Amendt, Christian J. .......... '51 '83 C.1042 B.A. L.1137 J.D. 363 S. Park Ave.
Bestard, Antonio J., (BV) .......... '51 '79 C.670 B.S. L.398 J.D. 315 W. Mission Blvd.
Bjelke, Donald K. '31 '56 C.668 B.A. L.1066 J.D.
Div. V.P. & Gen. Coun., General Dynamics Corp.
Borges, Joseph K., Jr., (BV) .......... '35 '66 435 W. Mission Blvd.
Bradofsky, Hyman J. .......... '06 '30 C.800 L.809 J.D. Spec. City Coun.
Burford, Albert L., Jr., (AV) .......... '14 '39 C.228 A.B. L.813 LL.B. 900 E. Harrison Ave.‡
Carroll, Leo R. .......... '23 '77 C.688 B.E.E. L.398 J.D. 1675 W. Mission Blvd. (Pat.)

**Covington & Crowe**
**(See Ontario)**

Curtis, Richard A. .......... '44 '70 C.813 A.B. L.1068 J.D. Supr. Ct. Comr.
Davis, Michael E. .......... '49 '76 C.1077 B.S. L.809 J.D. Dep. D.A.
de la Pena, Federico A., (AV) .......... '37 '71 C.605 B.A. L.809 J.D. 401 S. Main
Dolan, Joseph A., (BV) .......... '21 '71 C&L.309 B.A., LL.B. 105 E. Arrow Hwy.
Falls, Thomas C. .......... '60 '86 C&L.1137 B.S.L., J.D. Dep. Dist. Atty.
Faulkner, John E. .......... '30 '72 C.1042 B.S. L.990 J.D. State Workers Comp. J.
Ferris, Dennis E. .......... '43 '83 C&L.1137 B.S.L., J.D. Dep. Dist. Atty.
Fox, Daniel N., (BV) .......... '29 '58 C&L.145 B.A., J.D. 477 S. Main St.
Fuller, Ronald N. .......... '48 '74 C.608 B.S. L.8 J.D. 1675 W. Mission Blvd.

**Furness, Middlebrook, Kaiser & Higgins, A Professional Corporation**
**(See San Bernardino)**

Galperson, Herbert I., (AV) .......... '32 '55 C.102 B.A. L.569 J.D. [Rose,K.&M.]
Glass, James A. .......... '42 '70 C.800 B.A. L.809 J.D. Dep. Pub. Def.
**Gordon, Russell L.**, (AV) .......... '37 '71 C.1097 B.A. L.1148 J.D. [Parker&I.]
*PRACTICE AREAS: Workers Compensation.
Greenberg, Robert B. .......... '46 '82 C.1168 B.A. L.398 J.D. 399 W. Mission Blvd.
Gustaveson, Robert C. .......... '28 '59 C.877 B.S. L.878 J.D. Supr. Ct. J.
**Hannah, Randal P.** .......... '62 '88 C&L.770 B.S.C., J.D. [⊠ Young,H.H.&M.]
*PRACTICE AREAS: General Civil and Trial Practice; Business Law; Corporate Law; Real Estate; Personal Injury.
Heene, Fred L., Jr. .......... '46 '78 C.36 B.A. L.1137 J.D. Mun. J.
**Henrie, Homer H.**, (AV) .......... '09 '36 C.608 B.S. L.273 LL.B. [⊠ Young,H.H.&M.] ‡
Herrick, Lyle D. .......... '39 '65 C&L.426 B.B.A., LL.B. Dep. Pub. Def.
Hixson, Kenneth B. '09 '34 C&L.705 LL.B.
(adm. in NJ; not adm. in CA) 900 E. Harrison Ave.‡
Hofman, Harold W., Jr., (AV) .......... '39 '66 C.1063 B.S. L.1008 LL.B. Dep. Dist. Atty.
**Humphries, Bert W., Jr.**, (AV) .......... '40 '65 C.362 A.B. L.1068 J.D. [Young,H.H.&M.]
*PRACTICE AREAS: General Civil Practice; Business Law; Corporate Law; Estate Planning; Probate.
**Irwin, Ross C.**, (AV) .......... '33 '62 C.642 B.A. L.800 J.D. [Parker&I.]
*PRACTICE AREAS: Workers Compensation.
Jaffee, Arthur J., (AV) .......... '23 '49 C&L.813 A.B., J.D. 301 W. Mission Blvd.
Jakubowski, Donald S. .......... '53 '79 C.1078 B.A. L.990 J.D. Dep. Dist. Atty.

**Jones, Mahoney, Brayton & Soll**
**(See Claremont)**

Kandel, Carl S., (BV) .......... '38 '68 C.1043 B.A. L.809 LL.B. Pub. Def.
Kaufman, Stephen J .......... '56 '92 C.112 L.398 J.D. 1184 E. Mission Blvd.

**Kern, Robert L., (AV) '36 '62 C.684 A.B. L.813 J.D.**
**401 South Main Street, Suite 105, 91766**
**Telephone: 909-629-9314 Fax: 909-629-9314**
***REPORTED CASES: Southwest Concrete v. Gosh 51 Cal. 3rd 701 (1990).**
***PRACTICE AREAS: Probate; Civil Practice; Appellate Practice.**
**Litigation Trust and Estates, Probate and Estate Planning, Living Trusts, General Civil Litigation, Construction Litigation.**

**Kinkle, Rodiger and Spriggs, Professional Corporation**
**(See Riverside)**

Konigar, Adrienne D. '60 '87
C.197 B.A. L.1065 J.D. Gen. Coun., Pomona School Districts
Lacy, Theo .......... '34 '67 L.809 LL.B. 301 W. Mission Blvd.

**Lamb, Morris & Lobello, LLP**
**(See San Dimas)**

Lauper, Marc D. .......... '42 '71 C.101 A.B. L.1067 J.D. Mun. Ct. Comr.
Lemaster, L. Guy, Jr., (AV) .......... '23 '57 C.631 A.B. L.1068 LL.B. 250 S. Parcells St.
Lueck, John D., (CV) .......... '45 '76 C.112 B.A. L.398 J.D. 255 W. Mission
**Maietta, Richard J.** .......... '59 '84 C.112 A.B. L.809 J.D. [Parker&I.]
*PRACTICE AREAS: Workers Compensation.
Mandeville, Joseph S. .......... '46 '81 C.375 B.S. L.1137 J.D. Wkrs. Comp. J.
Mann, Leslie, Jr., (AV) .......... '18 '51 C.472 B.S.B.A. L.813 LL.B. 2040 N. Garey Ave.
**Mason, Barry S.**, (AV) .......... '40 '66 C.668 B.A. L.1068 J.D. [Young,H.H.&M.]
*PRACTICE AREAS: General Civil and Trial Practice; Business Law; Corporate Law; Estate Planning; Probate.
McCoy, Charles W., Jr. .......... '46 '75 C.679 B.S. L.846 J.D. Supr. Ct. J.
McDonough, Timothy A. .......... '62 '89 C&L.1137 B.S.L., J.D. 363 S. Park Ave.
McGreal, Thomas M. .......... '57 '84 C.112 B.A. L.312 J.D. 301 W. Mission Blvd.
McNevin, William J. .......... '24 '51 C&L.285 LL.B. Ref. Wkr's. Comp.
McVittie, William J. .......... '38 '65 C.339 B.S. L.800 J.D. Supr. Ct. J.
Meadows, Roger R., (BV) .......... '42 '70 C.112 L.1127 LL.B. 386 S. Gordon St.
**Morgan, Eric K.**, (BV) .......... '38 '72 C.112 B.A. L.800 J.D. [Parker&I.]
*PRACTICE AREAS: Workers Compensation.

**Nichols Stead Boileau & Kostoff, A Professional Corporation**
**(See Claremont)**

Olmo, Mark E. .......... '56 '92 C.839 B.S. L.1137 J.D. 522 W. Holt Ave.
Otero, Ramon, Jr. .......... '50 '75 C.112 B.A. L.1068 J.D. 522 W. Holt Ave.
Palmer, Robert A. '48 '77 C.665 B.A. L.273 J.D.
(adm. in VA; not adm. in CA) Prof., Calif. Polytechnic State Univ.

**Parker & Irwin, A Professional Corporation, (AV)**
**300 South Park Avenue, Ninth Floor, P.O. Box 2980, 91769-2980©**
**Telephone: 909-622-1357; 818-964-6488 Telecopier: 909-622-1618**
**Resident Personnel: Ross C. Irwin; Russell L. Gordon; Eric K. Morgan; Mary C. Scherb; Richard J. Maietta;—Joan E. Partritz; Geoffrey H. Spencer.**
**Workers Compensation and Casualty Insurance Law and Probate.**
**Representative Clients: The Travelers Insurance Co.; Industrial Indemnity Co.; Fireman's Fund American Insurance Cos.; Hartford Accident & Indemnity Co.; CIGNA; Continental Insurance Co.; Paula Insurance; Aetna; Constitution State Service Co.**
**Reference: Chino Valley Bank, Pomona Branch.**
**San Bernardino, California Office: 155 West Hospitality Lane, Suite 220. P.O. Box 11029. Telephone: 909-890-1800. Fax: 909-890-1801.**
**San Diego, California Office: 3131 Camino Del Rio North, Suite 900. Telephone: 619-283-7011. Fax: 619-293-7684.**

*See Professional Biographies, SAN BERNARDINO, CALIFORNIA*

**Partritz, Joan E.**, (AV) .......... '33 '77 C.63 A.B. L.426 J.D. [⊠ Parker&I.]
*PRACTICE AREAS: Workers Compensation.
Paule, Edward P., Jr., (BV) .......... '35 '83 C.684 B.A. L.398 J.D. 281 S. Thomas St., 3rd Fl.
Perry, Jerold L. .......... '36 '62 C.112 B.A. L.309 LL.B. 300 S. Park Ave.
Person, Victor H. .......... '46 '72 C.800 B.S. L.426 J.D. Supr. Ct. J.
Peterson, Thomas A. .......... '40 '66 C&L.602 A.B., LL.B. Mun. Ct. J.
Piatt, James H. .......... '33 '62 C.668 B.A. L.1068 J.D. Supr. Ct. J.
Piatt, Theodore D. .......... '37 '67 C.668 B.A. L.1065 J.D. Supr. Ct. J.
Polamero, Perry P., (BV) .......... '50 '75 C.800 B.S. L.809 J.D. 1192 N. White Ave.
Rose, Morgan E. .......... '65 '91 C.800 B.S. L.1065 J.D. Staff Atty., Legal Servs. Prog.
Rose, Klein & Marias, (AV)
281 S. Thomas St. (©L.A., Long Beach, San Bernardino, San Diego, Santa Ana & Ventura)
Russell, Grady M. .......... '44 '87 C.531 B.S. L.1136 J.D. Dep. Pub. Def.
Schaffer, Benson .......... '28 '70 C.999 B.A. L.809 J.D. Sup. Ct.Comr.
**Scherb, Mary C.** .......... '35 '60 C.525 B.A. L.426 J.D. [Parker&I.]
*PRACTICE AREAS: Workers Compensation.
Scyoc, David R. .......... '37 '63 C.711 B.A. L.602 LL.B. Dep. Pub. Def.
Selters, J. Benjamin, III, (BV) .......... '53 '78 C.668 B.A. L.1065 J.D. [Selters&S.]
Selters, John B., Jr., (BV) .......... '14 '47 C.668 A.B. L.800 [Selters&S.]
Selters & Selters, (BV) .......... 399 W. Mission Blvd.
Sherwin, Dennis J. .......... '46 '72 C.1077 B.A. L.426 J.D. [Rose,K.&M.]
Shirley, Marlin H. .......... '14 '39 C.911 B.A. L.1066 LL.B. 1906 Yorba Dr.‡
Shirley, Stephen M., (BV) .......... '41 '69 C.940 A.B. L.800 J.D. 435 W. Mission
Skaggs, Garvin W., (BV) .......... '33 '70 L.1095 J.D. Juv. Ref.
Smith, Evan L., (AV) .......... '51 '81 C.154 B.A. L.426 J.D. 8 A Village Loop Rd.
Smith, Gilbert F. '45 '72 C.684 A.B. L.426 J.D.
Sr. V.P. & Gen. Coun., Pomona First Fed. Svgs. & Loan Assn.
**Spencer, Geoffrey H.** .......... '64 '90 C.766 B.A. L.990 J.D. [⊠ Parker&I.]
*PRACTICE AREAS: Workers Compensation.
Suárez, Francisco A. .......... '55 '88 C.1097 B.A. L.398 J.D. 333 W. Mission Blvd.
Tarr, John S. .......... '22 '83 C.560 B.A. L.1137 J.D. 296 W. Second St.‡
Tessier, Victor G., (AV) .......... '27 '55 C.1042 A.B. L.426 LL.B. 296 Pomona Mall, W.
Uhalley, Charles J., (BV) .......... '44 '75 C.112 B.A. L.398 J.D. 300 S. Park Ave.
Uhler, Ingrid A., (BV) .......... '58 '82 C.36 B.A. L.37 J.D. Dep. Dist. Atty.

**Welebir & McCune, A Professional Law Corporation**
**(See Redlands)**

Wolfe, Thomas H. '58 '89
C.612 B.S. L.1065 J.D. Assoc. Coun., Calif. Credit Union League
Wooley, Richard D., (AV) .......... '52 '80 C.1109 B.A. L.1137 J.D. 363 S. Park Ave.
Wreisner, Robert C. .......... '20 '49 C.813 A.B. L.770 LL.B. Wkrs. Comp. J.
Wullschleger, Karen K. .......... '59 '87 C.112 B.A. L.809 J.D. Dep. Dist. Atty.
**Young, Richard T.**, (AV) .......... '11 '36 C&L.911 A.B., J.D. [⊠ Young,H.H.&M.] ‡

**Young, Henrie, Humphries & Mason, (AV)**
**Home Savings of America Building, 100 West Second Street, Suite 210, 91766**
**Telephone: 909-629-2521 Telecopier: 909-629-3108**
**Bert W. Humphries, Jr.; Barry S. Mason. Of Counsel: Richard T. Young (Retired); Homer H. Henrie (Retired). Associates: Randal P. Hannah.**
**General Civil and Trial Practice, Business and Corporate Law, Estate Planning, Probate, Trusts, Real Estate and Personal Injury.**

*See Professional Biographies, POMONA, CALIFORNIA*

## PORTERVILLE, 29,563, *Tulare Co.*

Barde, Knut W. .......... '52 '81 C.112 B.A. L.276 J.D. 33 E. Cleveland Ave.
Christenson, Don G., (BV) .......... '16 '49 C.101 A.B. L.1066 LL.B. 472 W. Putnam Ave.
Christenson, James A., (CV) .......... '55 '82 C.101 B.A. L.972 J.D. [Christenson&R.]
Christenson, Richard L., (BV) .......... '52 '79 C&L.101 B.A., J.D. [Christenson&R.]
Christenson, Robert D., (BV) .......... '50 '77 C&L.101 B.A., J.D. [Christenson&R.]
Christenson & Roper, (BV) .......... 472 W. Putnam Ave.
Heusdens, James, (CV) .......... '32 '72 L.1132 821 W. Morton Ave.
Hill, Christopher S. .......... '53 '85 C.172 B.S. L.1189 J.D. 341 N. 3rd St.
Hill, William A. .......... '25 '53 C.112 L.426 LL.B. 341 N. 3rd St.
Kralowec, Arthur C. .......... '35 '72 C.112 B.A. L.1067 J.D. City Atty.
Krase, Robert, (BV) .......... '47 '77 C.112 A.B. L.1065 J.D. [Spallina&K.]
Natzke, Robert C. .......... '28 '53 C.112 L.1065 J.D. 907 W. belleview Ave.
Porter, Don L. .......... '44 '81 C.112 A.B. L.1132 J.D. 1485 Forest Lane‡
Quirk, John F. .......... '27 '60 C.768 B.A. L.770 LL.B. Mun. Ct. J.
Roper, Glade F. .......... '53 '80 C&L.101 B.S., J.D. Mun. Ct. J.

CAA501P

Roper, Glena J. '54 '81 C&L.101 B.A., J.D. 472 W. Putnam Ave.
Spallina, Fred V., (BV) '48 '75 C.800 B.S. L.464 J.D. [Spallina&K.]
Spallina & Krase, (BV) 132 E. Morton Ave.
Vanderhorst, Robert E. '59 '84 C.790 B.A. L.809 J.D. 288 D. St.
Walsh, Robert (Robin) O., (CV) '38 '74 C.766 B.A. L.765 J.D. 141 E. Putnam Ave.

## PORT HUENEME, 20,319, *Ventura Co.*

Berman, Harry F. '47 '91 C.994 B.A. L.809 J.D. National Assn. of Govt. Employees
Dawson, Annette R. '59 '90 C.1253 B.S. L.1186 J.D. 360 N. Ventura Rd.
Dressler, Harold W. '23 '50 C&L.930 B.B.A., LL.B. 832 N. Ventura Rd.
Erich, M. Michelle '52 '79 C.314 B.S.Ed. L.1186 J.D. 1443 N. 5th St.
Gardner, Donald D., (CV) '48 '74 C.112 B.A. L.1049 J.D. 475 W. Channel Island
Houser, Herbert A. '10 '42 C.112 B.A. L.426 LL.B. 2552 Ukiah
Nagel, Stuart '53 '79 C.102 B.A. L.1095 J.D.
475 W. Channel Islands Blvd. (ⓒBeverly Hills)
Needham, Diana M. '45 '88 L.1186 J.D. P.O. Box 817
**Williams, Reed M., (AV)** '26 '54 C.1250 B.S. L.1065 LL.B. [Williams W.C.N.&R.]ⓒ
*REPORTED CASES: Orient Steam Navigation Co., Ltd. v. United States of America (Kearsarge-Orians), 231 F.Supp. 469, 1964 AMC 2163 (S.D. Cal. 1964); Chervy v. Peninsular & Oriental Steam Navigation Co., Ltd. (Arcadia), 364 F.2d 908, 1966 AMC 226 (9th Cir. 1966); Waterman Steamship Corp. v. Gay Cottons (Chickasaw) 414 F.2d 724, 1969 AMC 1682 (9th Cir. 1969); Japan Line, Ltd. v. County of Los Angeles, 441 U.S. 434, 99 S.Ct. 1813, 16 L.Ed.2d 336, 1979 AMC 881 (1979); Lubick v. Travel Service, Inc., 573 F.Supp. 904 (D.V.I. 1983).
*PRACTICE AREAS: Maritime Law; Environmental Law; Transportation and International Law; Commercial Transactions and Litigation; Personal Injury.

**Williams Woolley Cogswell Nakazawa & Russell, (AV)**
**237 E. Hueneme Road, Suite A, 93041**ⓒ
**Telephone: 805-488-8560 Fax: 805-488-7896**
**Email: wwlaw@msn.com**
**Reed M. Williams.**
**Commercial Transactions and Litigation, Maritime Law, Transportation and International Law, Environmental Law, Immigration Law, Personal Injury and Product Liability Litigation.**
**Long Beach, California Office: 111 West Ocean Boulevard, Suite 2000, 90802-4614. Telephone: 310-495-6000. Telecopier: 310-435-1359; 310-435-6812. Telex: ITT: 4933872; WU: 984929.**
**Rancho Santa Fe, California Office: P.O. Box 9120, 16236 San Dieguito Road, Building 3, Suite 3-15, 92067. Telephone: 619-497-0284. Fax: 619-759-9938.**
*See Professional Biographies, PORT HUENEME, CALIFORNIA*

## PORTOLA, 2,193, *Plumas Co.*

Hendrickson, Ted R., (AV) '41 '74 C.766 B.A. L.765 J.D. 217 commercialSt.

## PORTOLA VALLEY, 4,194, *San Mateo Co.*

Airola, Leslie J. '55 '82 C.112 A.B. L.284 J.D. 110 E. Floresta Way
Bageman, James C. '34 '66 C.813 B.S. L.800 J.D. 325 Willowbrook Dr.
Barrett, Robert C. '47 '72 C.813 A.B. L.1066 J.D. 191 Lucero Way
**Ellison, David H.** '37 '66 C&L.813 A.B., J.D. [D.H.Ellison]

**Ellison, David H., Professional Corporation**
**171 Durazno Way, 94028**
**Telephone: 415-325-5300 Fax: 415-323-7647**
**Email: dhellison@aol.com**
**David H. Ellison.**
**General Civil and Trial Practice in all Federal and State Courts. Corporation Securities, Unfair Competition, Trade Secrets and Technology and Computer Law.**
*See Professional Biographies, PORTOLA VALLEY, CALIFORNIA*

Ensign, Robert N. '19 '42 C&L.339 A.B., LL.B. 520 La Mesa Dr.‡
Flanigan, Donald F. '28 '56 C&L.813 A.B., LL.B. 90 Bear Gulch Dr.‡
Fleming, John P. '51 '76 C&L.770 B.S., J.D. 145 Meadowood Dr.
Ford, Thomas W. '21 '50 C.976 B.A. L.477 LL.B. 118 Solana Rd.‡
Hooper, John A. '17 '47 C.813 B.A. L.309 LL.B. 501 Portola Rd.‡
Hudson, Geoffrey R. '47 '72 C.112 A.B. L.1068 J.D. 35 Las Piedras
Lipman, James F. '34 '70 C.976 B.E. L.770 J.D. 25 Palmer Ln.‡
Mokelke, Susan K. '51 '78 C.800 B.S. L.426 J.D. 116 El Nido Rd.‡
Morshead, Merrill C., Jr. '27 '52 C&L.813 A.B., LL.B. 875 Portola Rd.
Nudelman, Michael V., (BV) '45 '74 C.112 B.A. L.1065 J.D. 170 Cherokee Way
Peterson, Dana C. '33 '60 C.309 A.B. L.813 LL.B. Captain U.S.N.R.
Pickholtz, Andrew '63 '89 C.309 A.B. L.893 J.D. 425 Golden Oak Dr.
Remke, Kathryn France '50 '74 C.97 B.A. L.607 J.D.
(adm. in OH; not adm. in CA) 303 Wyndham Dr.‡
Satterlee, Donald W. '39 '65 C.813 A.B. L.1066 LL.B. 20 Kiowa Ct.
Searles, Jasper L. '05 '32 C.112 B.S. L.1065 J.D. 70 Bear Gulch Dr.‡
Stetson, Robert C. '34 '59 C&L.813 A.B., J.D. 30 Pomponio Ct.‡
Webster, Robert O. '22 '58 C.608 B.M.E. L.273 LL.B.
(adm. in VA; not adm. in CA; Pat.) 1255 Westridge Dr.
White, Elaine Berlin, (BV) '53 '78 C.768 B.A. L.1065 J.D. 130 Mimosa‡
Wright, Gerald A., (AV) '40 '70 C.309 A.B. L.813 LL.B. 130 Andeta Way‡

## POWAY, 43,516, *San Diego Co.*

Allen, William E. '33 '79 C.763 B.A. L.1137 J.D. 12917 Evelyn Ct.
Butzen, Philip J. '45 '74 C.436 A.B. L.597 J.D. 13579 Del Poniente Rd.‡
Churchill, David B. '54 '92 C.35 B.S. L.1137 J.D. 12759 Poway Rd.
Culviner, William H. '31 '60 C.390 A.B. L.569 J.D.
(adm. in NY; not adm. in CA) 13036 Avenida La Valencia
Early, Michael J. '66 '92 C.763 B.A. L.61 J.D. 13420 Community Rd.
Ellison, Charles W., II, (BV) '55 '82 C.347 B.S. L.1148 J.D. 13553 Poway Rd.
Gillespie, William G. '56 '82 C.25 B.A. L.262 J.D. 14230 York Ave.
Goldsmith, Jan I., (BV) '51 '76 C.30 B.A. L.1049 J.D. P.O. Box 1410
Grossenbacher, Rebecca L. '51 '93 C.112 B.A. L.1049 J.D.
Coun., Diversified Hardwoods
Jeffries, E. James H., (BV) '42 '71 C.37 B.S.B.A. L.809 J.D. P.O. Box 1345
King, Donald K. '23 '49 C&L.273 B.A., J.D. 13750 Highlands Ter.‡
Mensor, Melvin E. '09 '34 L.765 LL.B. 13412 The Square‡
Nunn, Donald A. '47 '72 C.112 B.A. L.1049 J.D. 13426 Community Rd.
Smith, Clinton L. '50 '83 C.330 B.A. L.61 J.D. 16104 Del Norte
Smith, Sherri L. '68 '93 C&L.112 B.A., J.D. 13516 Starridge Rd.
Usell, Raymond J., Jr. '41 '75 C.150 B.S. L.213 J.D. 14341 Range Park Rd.
Vavra, Kenneth F. '41 '74 C&L.793 B.A., J.D.
(adm. in SD; not adm. in CA) 14250 Marianna Dr.‡

## PRINCETON, —, *Colusa Co.*

Garofalo, Vincenzo A. '46 '80 C.147 B.A. L.464 J.D. P.O. Box 15

## QUINCY, * 3,343, *Plumas Co.*

Adrian, David L. '39 '74 C.147 A.B. L.1132 J.D. 514 Jackson St.

**Craig and Shepherd**
**(See Chico)**

Crane, Michael A. '37 '85 C.1073 M.A. L.1137 J.D. Dist. Atty.
Hentschel, Peter C. '48 '74 C.112 A.B. L.464 J.D. 75 Court St.
Hilde, Janet A. '54 '85 C.645 B.A. L.300 J.D. 511 W. Main St.
Jamison, Michael Steven '56 '79 C.147 B.A. L.950 J.D. Dep. Dist. Atty.
Kaufman, Ira Robert '47 '72 C.1350 B.A. L.1188 J.D. 75 Court St.
**King, Alice M.** '34 '89 C.112 B.A. L.1068 J.D. [Zetterberg&K.]
*PRACTICE AREAS: Family Law; Estate Planning; Probate; Civil Litigation.
Leach, John F. '31 '59 C.546 B.S. L.800 LL.B. 1488 Butterfly Valley Rd.
Olney, Garrett W. '46 '75 C.602 B.A. L.1065 J.D. Jus. Ct. J.

**Peters, Fuller, Rush, Farnsworth & Habib**
**(See Chico)**

Reichle, James A. '44 '70 C.813 A.B. L.1067 J.D. Dist. Atty.
Settlemire, Roger M. '30 '61 C.112 B.A. L.1066 LL.B. Supr. Ct. J.
Shulman, Robert J. '— '77 L.1066 J.D. Co. Coun.
Thieler, Alan H. '16 '50 L.1065 J.D. Ret. Jus. Ct. J.
Young, Stanley C., Jr. '25 '53 C.768 A.B. L.1065 J.D. Ret. Supr. Ct. J.
Zernich, Robert J. '45 '71 C.645 B.A. L.1049 J.D. 477 W. Main St.

**Zetterberg & King, (AV)**
**P.O. Box 3926, 95971-3926**ⓒ
**Telephone: 916-283-0325 Fax: 916-283-5205**
**Alice M. King (Resident); Stephen I. Zetterberg (Claremont, California Office).**
**General Civil and Trial Practice in all State and Federal Courts. Wills, Probate, Trusts and Estate Planning Law, Civil Litigation, Family Law.**
**Claremont, California Office: 319 Harvard Avenue. Telephone: 909-621-2971. Fax: 909-625-5781.**
*See Professional Biographies, QUINCY, CALIFORNIA*

## RAMONA, 3,554, *San Diego Co.*

Agnew, Jeffrey A., (BV) '56 '82 C.763 A.B. L.1049 J.D. 1002 D St.
Bokovoy, Don E., (BV) '45 '78 C.763 B.S. L.1137 J.D. 15979 Gantry Way
Cole, Lewis N. '34 '71 C.477 B.B.A L.1049 J.D. P.O. Box 1214
Frazier, Sam J., III, (BV) '48 '78 C&L.1241 B.S.L., J.D. 406 16th St.
Halling, Byron P. '45 '78 C.101 B.S. L.1049 J.D. 16265 Arena Dr.
Has-Ellison, M.D., (BV) '34 '74 C.381 B.S. L.1137 J.D. 549 "D" St. (ⓒLa Mesa)
Johnson, Lester C. '31 '84 C.1060 B.A. L.1026 J.D. 23837 Green Haven Lane
Jordan, David F. '28 '53 C.674 A.B. L.569 LL.B.
(adm. in NY; not adm. in CA) 15732 Vista Vicente Dr.‡
Marshall, Gregory R. '49 '77 C.112 A.B. L.1068 J.D. P.O. Box 833
McAllister, Glenn Rowe '54 '85 C.809 A.A. L.1137 J.D. 2635 Sugar Plaum Wy.
Moody, John P., (BV) '28 '61 C.813 A.B. L.809 LL.B. 541 D St. (ⓒSan Diego)
Reid, Jeremiah F., (A P.C.), (BV) '49 '78 C.112 B.S. L.1137 J.D. 325 11th St.

## RANCHO BERNARDO, —, *San Diego Co.*

Blasband, Denise P. '64 '90 C&L.1049 B.A., J.D. [Hinchy,W.W.A.&H.]

**Bloomfield, Neil Jon, Law Office of**
**(See San Rafael)**

Caffarel, J. Douglas '62 '88 C.861 B.A. L.425 J.D. 11848 Bernardo Plz. Ct.‡
Hinchy, Witte, Wood, Anderson & Hodges, A Law Corporation, (AV)
11440 W. Bernardo Ct., Ste. 280 (ⓒSan Diego, Irving)
Kessler, Mark Steven, (BV) '49 '73 C.763 B.A. L.1049 J.D. [Kessler&L.]
Kessler & Larson, (AV) 11770 Bernardo Plaza Ct.
Larson, Evangeline J., (AV) '54 '85 C.172 B.S. L.972 J.D. [Kessler&L.]
Robinson, Roberta J., (AV) '52 '77 C.112 B.A. L.1049 J.D. 17055 Via Del Campo
Steinberg, Jim J. '52 '88 L.1137 J.D. 11828 Rancho Bernardo Rd. (ⓒSan Diego)
Woodring, James W. '55 '80 C.763 B.A. L.1137 J.D. 11848 Bernardo Plaza Ct.
Yocum, Lori M. '59 '90 C.763 B.A. L.1049 J.D. [Hinchy,W.W.A.&H.]

## RANCHO CALIFORNIA, —, *Riverside Co.*

(See Temecula)

## RANCHO CORDOVA, 30,451, *Sacramento Co.*

Allen, Hugh O., (BV) '41 '71 C.336 B.A. L.464 J.D. 11290 Point E. Dr.
**Alliston, Douglas R.** '61 '88 C.1315 B.A. L.464 J.D. [Farmer&M.]
Baldwin, Robert D. '24 '55 C.107 B.A. L.112 J.D. [Wyatt&B.]

**Berding & Weil, (AV)**
**2200 Sunrise Boulevard, Suite 220, 95670**ⓒ
**Telephone: 916-851-1910 FAX: 916-851-1914**
**Member of Firm: Deon R. Stein; Eugene P. Haydu. Associate: Evan D. Williams.**
**Construction Litigation and Community Association Law. Non-Profit Corporation Law. Appellate Practice.**
**Alamo, California Office: 3240 Stone Valley Road West, 94507. Telephone: 510-838-2090. Fax: 510-820-5592.**
**Santa Clara, California Office: 3600 Pruneridge Avenue, Suite 130. 95051. Telephone: 408-556-0220. Fax: 408-556-0224.**
**Fresno, California Office: 516 West Shaw Avenue, Suite 200. Telephone: 209-221-2556. Fax: 209-221-2558.**
*See Professional Biographies, RANCHO CORDOVA, CALIFORNIA*

**Bergtholdt, Hazel** '68 '93 C.05 B.A. L.285 [Ⓐ Herrig&V.]
*LANGUAGES: German.
Bevier, Robin Clark '58 '87 C.112 B.S. L.464 J.D. 2893 Sunrise Blvd.
Black, Travis '51 '92 C.101 B.S. L.1137 J.D.
Mgr., Spec. Investigation Unit, Progressive Ins. Co.
**Breunig, Mark R.** '57 '95 C.1042 B.S. L.1026 J.D. Corp. Coun., USCS Int'l., Inc.
*RESPONSIBILITIES: Corporate Law; Contracts; Intellectual Property; Telecommunications; Labor and Employment.
Bruscino, James E. '56 '91 L.464 J.D. [Ⓐ Wyatt&B.]
Burgess, Patricia A. '51 '76 C.906 B.A. L.767 J.D.
Corp. Coun., Foundation Health Corp.
Burke, Teresa M. '56 '83
C.767 B.S. L.464 J.D. Litig. Mgr., Progressive Insurance Company
Burns, Mitchell S., (BV) '53 '80 C.1077 B.A. L.426 J.D. [Wyatt&B.]
Carson, John P. '28 '56 C&L.174 B.S., LL.B. 11294 Coloma Rd.‡
Cass, Paul L. '62 '89 C.269 B.A. L.790 J.D. 2200 Sunrise Blvd.
**Chilgren, Delia M.** '48 '75 C.766 B.A. L.284 J.D. Coun., Allstate Ins. Co.
Coyne, Elizabeth A. '— '74 C.767 A.B. L.1065 J.D. [Wyatt&B.]
Dana, Louis, (BV) '31 '59 C.476 B.A. L.213 LL.B. 2890 Kilgore Rd.
Davis, Donald R. '39 '66 C.340 B.A. L.1066 J.D. 2724 Kilgore Rd.
Dorsey, Robert G. '28 '59 C&L.923 B.S., J.D. 2330 Vehicle Dr.
Drivon, James A. '47 '75 C.768 B.A. L.1132 J.D. [Wyatt&B.]
Duval, Nancy O. '46 '80 C.880 B.A. L.464 J.D. [Wyatt&B.]
Dyer, Christopher S. '57 '86 C.1060 B.A. L.464 J.D.
Supervising Clms. Atty., Progressive Insurance Company
Elie, Joseph M. '48 '74 C.426 B.B.A. L.809 J.D. 10860 Gold Center Dr. #350
Eriksson, Stephen J. '65 '92 C.112 A.B. L.846 J.D.
(adm. in TX; not adm. in CA) P.O. Box 2912‡
**Farmer, Craig E., (BV)** '48 '74 C.769 B.A. L.1065 J.D. [Farmer&M.]

**Farmer & Murphy, (AV)**
**2701 Prospect Park Drive, Suite 110, 95670**
**Mailing Address: P.O. Box 276226, Sacramento, CA 95287-6226**
**Telephone: 916-853-2420 Fax: 916-853-2424**
**Email: farmur@aol.com**
**Members of Firm: Craig E. Farmer; George E. Murphy; Douglas R. Alliston; Blane A. Smith. Associates: Frank J. Torrano; Gerald C. Hicks.**
**Civil Trial and Appellate Practice in all State and Federal Courts. Consultation and Litigation regarding Insurance Coverage, Claims Handling, Insurance "Bad Faith" and Environmental Coverage Issues; Business and Governmental Entity Self Insurance Law; Complex Litigation.**
***See Professional Biographies, RANCHO CORDOVA, CALIFORNIA***

Finch, Steven H. .................. '58 '93 L.999 J.D. [[A] Lanius&T.]
**Gannon, Cindy A.** .......... '62 '88 C.112 B.A. L.767 J.D. Atty., Southern Pacific Lines
Garcia, Lawrence B. '50 '75
C.112 A.B. L.1068 J.D. Corp. Coun., Catholic Healthcare West
Gerard, Carole A. '62 '87
C.602 B.B.A. L.990 J.D. Dir., Legal Servs., Sterling Software, Inc.
Gibbons, William M. '19 '47 C&L.424 Ph.B., J.D.
(adm. in IL; not adm. in CA) P.O. Box 2244‡
Halpern, Marvin J. '45 '72 C.911 B.A. L.112 J.D.
Sr. Tax Coun., State Franchise Tax Bd.
Haug, Terry I. .................. '43 '84 C.623 B.S. L.464 J.D. 2246 Baywater Ln.
**Haydu, Eugene P.** .......... '53 '88 C.911 B.A. L.284 J.D. [[A] Berding&W.] (⊙Alamo)
**Herrig, John R., (AVⓉ)** .................. '42 '78 C.277 B.S. L.990 J.D. [Herrig&V.]⊙
*PRACTICE AREAS: Construction; Contract Law.

**Herrig & Vogt, (AVⓉ)**
**2724 Kilgore Road, 95670⊙**
**Telephone: 916-631-7000 Telecopier: 916-631-7717**
**Members of Firm: John R. Herrig; George F. Vogt, Jr. (Resident). Associates: C. Patrick Stoll; Hazel Bergtholdt (Resident); Heidi Susan Hart (Resident, Los Angeles, California Office); David D. Hilton (Resident, Kennewick, Washington Office).**
**Civil and Trial Practice relating to Construction, Public Contract, Fidelity and Surety, Environmental Remediation, International Contracting, Corporate and General Civil Trial Matters.**
**Kennewick, Washington Office: 3104 West Kennewick Avenue, Suite D. Telephone: 509-943-6691. Fax: 509-783-8808.**
**Redmond, Washington Office: 7981 168th Avenue, N.E. Telephone: 206-3129. Fax: 206-556-0595.**
**Los Angeles, California Office: 100 Wilshire Boulevard, #950, Santa Monica. Telephone: 310-260-5088. Fax: 310-260-5089.**
***See Professional Biographies, RANCHO CORDOVA, CALIFORNIA***

**Hicks, Gerald C.** .................. '56 '90 C.1060 B.A. L.464 J.D. [[A] Farmer&M.]
**Johnson, Michael L.** .... '54 '79 C.426 B.A. L.464 J.D. Gen. Atty., Southern Pacific Lines
Johnson, Timothy R. '62 '91 C.575 B.S. L.228 J.D.
(adm. in MN; not adm. in CA) Blue Cross of Calif.
Jordan, Jeffrey C. .......... '55 '83 C.705 B.A. L.1068 J.D. V.P., Progressive Cas. Ins. Co.
**Jordan, Mary G.** '44 '80
C.112 B.A. L.464 J.D. V.P., Gen. Coun. & Secy., USCS Int'l., Inc.
*RESPONSIBILITIES: Computer Law; Intellectual Property; Labor & Employment; Telecommunications; Business Law.
**Kaufman, Terry** .......... '56 '82 C.118 B.A. L.1066 J.D. Corp. Coun., USCS Int'l., Inc.
*RESPONSIBILITIES: Corporate Law; Contracts; Intellectual Property; Labor and Employment; Leases and Leasing.
King, Franklin W. .................. '42 '74 C.16 B.A. L.228 J.D. 2893 Sunrise Blvd.
Klauschie, Jack A., Jr. .............. '52 '80 C.112 B.A. L.426 J.D. 10860 Gold Ctr. Dr.
Lanius, Patrick A., (BV) .................. '51 '76 C.98 B.A. L.846 J.D. [Lanius&T.]
Lanius & Tyler, (BV) .................. 10670 White Rock Rd., Suite 130
Lynch, Robert Berger .............. '31 '69 C.1027 B.S. L.464 J.D. 10615 Coloma Rd.‡
Mair, Steven E. '55 '85
C.339 B.S. L.464 J.D. Gen. Coun., McLaren Hart Envir. Eng. Corp.
Mathies, Lisa T. .................. '61 '86 C.763 B.A. L.990 J.D. 10969 Trade Center Dr.
McCarthy, John P. .................. '45 '76 C.1060 B.S. L.1026 J.D. [Wyatt&B.]
Mitchell, Richard J. ........ '53 '82 C&L.813 A.B., J.D. Gen. Atty., Southern Pacific Lines
Mohr, Kathleen E. .................. '57 '87 C.624 B.S.N. L.284 J.D. [[A] Wyatt&B.]
**Murphy, George E., (AV)** .................. '50 '80 C.112 B.A. L.284 J.D. [Farmer&M.]
Murphy, Kevin '60 '85 C.845 L.69 J.D.
(adm. in TX; not adm. in CA) 2165 Potomac River Ct.
O'Rourke, Christopher '58 '88 C.1044 B.A. L.1049 J.D.
Claims Atty., Progressive Insurance Company
Palmer, William W. .................. '62 '90 C.112 B.A. L.464 J.D. 2701 Prospect Pk Dr.
Post, Clifford L., Jr. .................. '52 '79 C.112 B.A. L.1065 J.D. 11290 Point East Dr.
Rahn, Michael T., (BV) .................. '47 '72 C.813 B.A. L.1066 J.D. [[A] Wyatt&B.]
Reese, Richard L., Jr., (BV) ........ '45 '72 C.1060 B.S. L.464 J.D. 10368 White Rock Rd.
Richmond, Janet M. '49 '91 C.549 L.309 J.D.
Assoc. Corp. Coun., Catholic Healthcare West
Sherrard-Alvarez, Barbara L. ........ '57 '87 C.1060 B.A. L.999 J.D. 10860 Gold Ctr. Dr.
Shookman, Loyd A. .................. '24 '51 C&L.273 B.A., LL.B. 2292 El Cejo Circle‡
Simmons, Frank C. ............ '36 '67 C.1060 A.B. L.1026 LL.B. 10933 Trade Ctr. Dr.‡
Skala, Michael J., Jr. .................. '65 '92 C.112 B.S. L.464 J.D. [[A] Wyatt&B.]
**Smith, Blane A., (BV)** .................. '55 '80 C.907 B.A. L.464 J.D. [Farmer&M.]
**Smith, Jo Ann** '45 '78 C.768 B.A. L.284 J.D.
V.P. & Dep. Gen. Coun., Beverly Enterprises, Inc.
**Stein, Deon R.** .................. '64 '88 C.112 B.A. L.1065 J.D. [Berding&W.]
*PRACTICE AREAS: Business; Real Estate; Nonprofit Corporation Law.
**Stoll, C. Patrick** .................. '48 '93 C.1070 B.S. L.464 J.D. [[A] Herrig&V.]
*PRACTICE AREAS: Construction Law; Business Litigation; Contract Law; Personal Injury; Domestic Relations.
Tallant, David A., (BV) .......... '40 '67 C.1163 B.A. L.800 J.D. 3035 Prospect Park Dr.
Tessier, G. Anthony, Jr., (BV) '47 '75
C.112 A.B. L.770 J.D. Sr. Tax Coun., Franchise Tax Bd.
**Torrano, Frank J.** .................. '63 '93 C.766 B.A. L.767 J.D. [[A] Farmer&M.]
Tyler, Robert F., (BV) .................. '47 '74 C.605 A.B. L.1068 J.D. [Lanius&T.]
Van Horne, Thomas S., (BV) ......... '47 '80 C.112 B.S. L.464 J.D. 2991 Gold Canal Dr.
**Vogt, George F., Jr.** .................. '56 '82 C&L.426 B.A., J.D. [[A] Herrig&V.]
*PRACTICE AREAS: Construction; Contract Law; Civil Law.
Walker, William L. .................. '60 '93 C.801 B.S. L.1067 J.D. [[A] Wyatt&B.]
Welch, James d'A. '44 '69 C.170 B.A. L.930 J.D.
Asst. Gen. Coun., Litig., CIGNA Corp.
Westerfeld, Barclay L. '44 '71 C.347 B.S. L.345 J.D.
(adm. in CO; not adm. in CA) Gen. Coun., Vision Service Plan
Whelan, Christopher H., (BV) ... '51 '78 C.112 B.A. L.1065 J.D. 11246 Gold Express Dr.
**Williams, Evan D.** .................. '64 '89 C.147 B.S. L.770 J.D. [[A] Berding&W.]
*PRACTICE AREAS: Personal Injury; Real Estate Litigation.
Winslow, Peter K., (BV) ............ '49 '79 C.813 B.A. L.770 J.D. 10600 White Rock Rd.
Wyatt, Raymond M., (AV) .................. '35 '76 C.999 B.A. L.770 J.D. [Wyatt&B.]
Wyatt & Burns, (AV) .................. 2920 Prospect Pk. Dr.

## RANCHO CUCAMONGA, 101,409, *San Bernardino Co.*

Albertine, Christine '— '89 C.763 B.A. L.1137 J.D.
Calif Correctional Peace Offrs. Assoc.

**Allard, Shelton & O'Connor**
**(See Claremont)**

Andrews, Robert D., (AV) .............. '37 '67 C&L.37 B.S., J.D. 10788 Civic Center Dr.
Banks, James, Jr., (BV) .......... '42 '68 C.813 B.A. L.112 J.D. 10788 Civic Center Dr.
Barrett, Patricia D., (CV) .............. '46 '80 C.1232 B.A. L.1137 J.D. 8280 Utica Ave.
Bartell, Tracy M., (CV) .................. '56 '81 C.1109 B.A. L.1067 J.D. Dep. Dist. Atty.
Bernstein, Naomi R. .................. '47 '81 C.112 B.A. L.1198 J.D. [Bernstein]
Bernstein Law Corporation .................. 10722 Arrow Rte.
Berry, Hugh W. .................. '65 '90 C.112 B.A. L.1068 J.D. Dep. Dist. Atty. III
Blaylock, Gary H., (CV) ............ '46 '80 C&L.1137 B.S.L., J.D. 8350 Archibald Ave.
Borba, Joan M. .................. '56 '85 C.112 B.A. L.990 J.D. Mun. Ct. J.
**Briguglio, Salvatore, (BV)** .............. '52 '79 C.705 B.A. L.1095 J.D. [Mannerino&B.]
*PRACTICE AREAS: Civil Litigation; Bankruptcy; Personal Injury Law; Criminal Defense.
Brodie, Ellen E. .................. '18 '74 C&L.398 LL.B. Ret. Mun. Ct. J.
Brown, Lee .................. '51 '79 C.101 B.S. L.809 J.D. [Moore&B.]
**Butler, Bruce M.** .................. '66 '91 C.1109 B.A. L.940 J.D. [[A] Genson,E.C.&W.]
Butler, John S. .................. '50 '78 C&L.280 B.A., J.D. 10763 Edison Ct.
Canty, Joseph D., Jr., (BV) '42 '66
C.112 A.B. L.1068 J.D. Off. Pub. Def., San Bernardino Co.
Carlisle, Alan, (CV) .................. '29 '84 C.171 B.S. L.1137 J.D. 10601 Civic Ctr. Dr.
Cole, Dennis G. .................. '41 '74 C.1042 A.B. L.398 J.D. Supr. Ct. J.
Cote, Craig G. .................. '51 '88 C.684 B.S. L.1137 J.D. P.O. Box 278

**Covington & Crowe**
**(See Ontario)**

Crafts, Alan L. .................. '45 '71 C.1075 B.S. L.1065 J.D. Adm. Law J.
Darlington, Michael, (CV) ............ '47 '83 C&L.1137 B.S.L., J.D. 10750 Civic Ctr.Dr.
Davidson, Richard A. ............ '31 '61 C.800 B.A. L.809 J.D. 8077 Calle Carabe Pl.‡
Davis, James S. .................. '53 '84 C.1179 B.S. L.398 J.D. 10470 Foothill Blvd.
Diamond, Patricia D., (BV) ............ '35 '76 C.645 B.A. L.1095 J.D. Dep. Pub. Def. IV
**Dobrin, Daniel A.** .................. '52 '76 C.1169 A.B. L.1068 J.D. [[A] Kegel,T.&T.]
DuPuis, Sharon B., (BV) .................. '44 '79 C&L.1198 B.S.L., J.D. Dep. Dist. Atty.
Edelbrock, Mark D., (CV) .............. '51 '78 C.112 B.A. L.1137 J.D. [Edelbrock&M.]
Edelbrock & Martin, (CV) .................. 7365 Carnelian
Emert, Laurence T. '49 '74
C.1044 B.A. L.1067 J.D. Adm. Law J., Unemploy. Ins. App. Bd.
Eppey, Richard J. .................. '43 '79 C.1075 B.S. L.1198 J.D. 10700 Civic Ctr. Dr.
Ferrante, Christina J. S., (CV) .............. '52 '78 C.398 B.A. L.1137 J.D. [Ferrante&F.]
Ferrante, Joseph M., (CV) .................. '48 '79 C.426 B.A. L.1137 J.D. [Ferrante&F.]
Ferrante & Ferrante, (CV) .................. 8350 Archibald St.
Fuller, Mary E., (AV) .................. '46 '72 C.112 B.A. L.1068 J.D. Dep. Dist. Atty.

**Furness, Middlebrook, Kaiser & Higgins, A Professional Corporation**
**(See San Bernardino)**

Garcia, Vincent B. .................. '54 '87 C.426 B.A. L.1137 J.D. 8316 Red Oak St.
Gebbie, William S., (BV) .......... '43 '70 C.426 B.A. L.1049 J.D. 8429 White Oak Ave.

**Genson, Even, Crandall & Wade, A Professional Corporation, (AV)**
**9483 Haven Avenue, Suite 102, 91730⊙**
**Telephone: 909-390-4811 FAX: 909-390-1907**
**Edmond D. Wade; William R. Lowe; Marc W. Hawkins; F. X. Sean O'Doherty; Robert J. O'Connor; Curtis L. Metzgar;—Bruce M. Butler; John A. Hauser; Lisa S. Morse.**
**Trial practice in State and Federal Courts: Employment Practices Liability, Third Party Violent Crime/Premises Security, Product Liability, Warranty Litigation, Insurance Coverage, Insurance Bad Faith, Insurance Fraud, HMO/Managed Care Defense, Medical Malpractice, Directors and Officers Liability, Professional Malpractice, Construction Defect, Government Liability, Premises Liability, Transportation Liability, Vehicle Liability, Environmental Liability, Recreational Sports and Leisure Activities Liability, Appellate Practice, Business Litigation (Class Action, Fraud, Misrepresentation, Breach of Contract, etc.).**
**Irvine, California Office: 7700 Irvine Center Drive, #700. Telephone: 714-753-1000. FAX: 714-753-1039.**
**Woodland Hills, California Office: 21031 Ventura Boulevard, Suite 801. Telephone: 818-999-4811. FAX: 818-999-1782.**
**San Diego, California Office: 9988 Hibert Street, Suite 300. Telephone: 619-635-6300. FAX: 619-635-6306.**
***See Professional Biographies, RANCHO CUCAMONGA, CALIFORNIA***

Gillan, Robert B. .................. '34 '58 C&L.508 B.A., LL.B. State Adm. Law J.
Goodrich, David R., (BV) .................. '51 '78 C.165 B.A. L.990 J.D. Dep. Dist. Atty.
Grajeda, Sandra .................. '48 '77 C.668 B.A. L.398 J.D. 10737 Laurel St.
Gunn, J. Mike, (BV) .................. '45 '76 C.1075 B.S. L.398 J.D. Mun. Ct. J.
**Hauser, John A.** .................. '56 '86 C.800 B.A. L.1137 J.D. [[A] Genson,E.C.&W.]
Havens, Charles S. .................. '35 '67 C.112 B.A. L.809 LL.B. Supr. Ct. J.
**Hawkins, Marc W.** .................. '52 '76 C.740 L.69 J.D. [Genson,E.C.&W.]
**Hengesbach, Daren E.** .......... '66 '93 C.154 B.A. L.464 J.D. [[A] Markman,A.H.C.&S.]
*PRACTICE AREAS: Municipal Litigation; Personal Injury Litigation.
Hildreth, Martin A. .................. '35 '67 C.1097 B.A. L.1068 J.D. Mun. J.

**Hillsinger and Costanzo, Professional Corporation, (AV)**
**10737 Laurel Street Suite 110 - Main Floor, 91730⊙**
**Telephone: 909-483-6200 Telecopier: 909-483-6277**
**Michael C. Kellar.**
**General Civil and Appellate Trial Practice in all State and Federal Courts. Insurance, Corporation, Commercial, Business, Medical and Professional Malpractice, Product Liability, Aviation, Asbestos, Toxic Tort, Bad Faith, Insurance Coverage, Declaratory Relief, Wrongful Termination, Vehicular, Property Damage, General Liability Cases.**
**Los Angeles, California Office: 12th Floor, 3055 Wilshire Boulevard. Telephone: 310-388-9441. Telecopier: 310-388-1592.**
**Orange, California Office: 701 South Parker Street, Suite 6000. Telephone: 714-542-6241. Telecopier: 714-667-6806.**
**Santa Barbara, California Office: 220 East Figueroa Street. Telephone: 805-966-3986. Telecopier: 805-965-3798.**
***See Professional Biographies, RANCHO CUCAMONGA, CALIFORNIA***

Jager, Jacob H. .................. '34 '71 C.999 L.981 LL.B. Mun. J.
Jensen, Carl Christian .............. '49 '77 C.912 B.A. L.213 J.D. 10601 Civic Cntr. Dr.
Johnson, Oscar E. .................. '34 '68 C.1246 B.B.A. L.809 LL.B. 8359 Edwin St.‡
Johnson, RiséJanette .................. '45 '84 C.628 B.S. L.809 J.D. 12517 Nasturtium Dr.
**Johnson, Stephan J.** .................. '54 '87 C.768 B.A. L.1137 J.D. [Reiss&J.]
*PRACTICE AREAS: Civil Litigation; Criminal Litigation.
Johnston, Joseph E. .................. '34 '68 C.911 B.A. L.809 J.D. Supr. Ct. J.
Jones, John M. .......... '27 '50 C&L.477 A.B., J.D. Admin. Law J., Unemp. Ins. App. Bd.
Kay, Barbara Metzger .......... '62 '92 C&L.426 B.A., J.D. 10535 Foothill Blvd. Ste. 410
Kayashima, Ben T. .................. '30 '59 C.112 B.A. L.1065 J.D. Supr. Ct. J.

**Kegel, Tobin & Truce, A Professional Corporation, (AV)**
**10737 Laurel Street, Suite 240, P.O. Box 3329, 91729-3329⊙**
**Telephone: 909-466-5555 Facsimile: 909-466-5562**
**Email: comp-law@ktt.com**
**John J. Tobin (Certified Specialist, Workers Compensation Law, The State Bar of California Board of Legal Specialization); Timothy D. Sanford-Wachtel;—Daniel A. Dobrin; Nancy J. Wallace (Certified Specialist, Workers' Compensation Law, The State Bar of California Board of Legal Specialization).**

(This Listing Continued)

CALIFORNIA—RANCHO CUCAMONGA MARTINDALE-HUBBELL LAW DIRECTORY 1997

**Kegel, Tobin & Truce, A Professional Corporation (Continued)**
Workers' Compensation, Longshore and Harborworkers, Public Employment, Retirement Law. Insurance Law, Third Party Subrogation.
Los Angeles, California Office: 3580 Wilshire Boulevard, 10th Floor, P.O. Box 76907. Telephone: 213-380-3880. FAX: 213-383-8346.
Ventura, California Office: 5450 Ralston Street, Suite 204, P.O. Box 7779. Telephone: 805-644-2216. Facsimile: 805-644-8625.
San Diego, California Office: 2535 Kettner Boulevard, Suite 2A1. Telephone: 619-696-0906.
Long Beach, California Office: 330 Golden Shore Drive, Suite 150. Telephone: 310-437-1108. Facsimile: 310-437-3742.
Van Nuys, California Office: 14545 Friar Street, Suite 104. Telephone: 818-947-0300. Facsimile: 818-947-0303.
*See Professional Biographies, RANCHO CUCAMONGA, CALIFORNIA*

**Kellar, Michael C.** '52 '78 C.1253 B.A. L.1068 J.D. [Hillsinger&C.] (©Los Angeles)
King, Jeffrey, (BV) '50 '76 C.684 B.A. L.464 J.D. 9113 Foothill Blvd.
**King, Pamela P.** '50 '77 C.684 B.A. L.464 J.D. [A Markman,A.H.C.&S.]
*PRACTICE AREAS: Municipal Litigation; Personal Injury Litigation.
Knell, Robert D. '44 '70 C.112 B.A. L.309 J.D. Admin. Law J., Unemp. Ins. App. Bd.
Kochis, John P., (BV) '49 '75 C.426 B.A. L.1049 J.D. Supervising Dep. Dist. Atty.
Kuhlman, Lawrence J., (CV) '57 '82 C.424 B.A. L.1049 J.D. 9267 Haven Ave.
Lai, Harold Gun, Jr., (BV) '48 '74 C.267 B.S. L.1132 J.D. 9587 Arrow Route
Leitao, Pamela Jean '56 '85 C&L.1137 B.S.L., J.D. Inland Cos. Legal Serv.
Lemkau, Robert J. '47 '72 C.112 A.B. L.846 J.D. Dep. Dist. Atty.
Libutti, Michael R. '61 '88 C.1109 B.A. L.1137 J.D. Dist. Atty.'s Ofc.
**Lowe, William R.** '43 '72 C.112 B.A. L.426 J.D. [Genson,E.C.&W.]
Maddux, John C., (CV) '46 '79
C.1097 B.S. L.1137 J.D. 10681 Foothill Blvd. (©Claremont)
Mandabach, Frederick A. '37 '72 C.284 B.B.A. L.426 J.D. Supr. Ct. J.
**Mannerino, John D.**, (BV) '49 '74 C.112 B.A. L.426 J.D. [Mannerino&B.]
*PRACTICE AREAS: Personal Injury Law; Business Litigation; Corporate Law.

**Mannerino & Briguglio, (BV)**
**9333 Baseline Road, Suite 110, 91730-1311**
Telephone: 909-980-1100 Telecopier: 909-941-8610
Members of Firm: John D. Mannerino; Salvatore Briguglio. Associates: Mitchell I Roth.
Practice Limited to Business Litigation, Personal Injury, Corporate, Real Estate, Bankruptcy, Probate, Family and Criminal Defense.
Representative Clients: Maclin Markets, Inc.; Testerion Inc.; Resin Technology Inc.
References: First Trust Bank, Upland Office; California State Bank, Ontario Office; Rancho Cucamonga Chamber of Commerce, Rancho Cucamonga, California.
*See Professional Biographies, RANCHO CUCAMONGA, CALIFORNIA*

**Markman, Arczynski, Hanson, Curley & Slough, A Professional Corporation, (AV)**
**9113 Foothill Boulevard, Suite 200, 91730©**
Telephone: 909-381-0218; 909-980-2742
Email: MARCZYNSKI@AOL.COM
Marsha G. Slough (Resident);—Pamela P. King (Resident); Daren E. Hengesbach (Resident).
Municipal, Redevelopment, Water Rights, Real Property, Condemnation, School and Corporation Law. Civil Litigation.
Brea, California Office: Second Floor, Number One Civic Center Circle, P.O. Box 1059. Telephone: 714-990-0901; 213-691-3811.
*See Professional Biographies, RANCHO CUCAMONGA, CALIFORNIA*

Martin, David W., (CV) '49 '79 C.668 B.A. L.398 J.D. [Edelbrock&M.]
**Metzgar, Curtis L.** '60 '86 C&L.426 B.B.A., J.D. [Genson,E.C.&W.]
*REPORTED CASES: Watamura v. State Farm (1988), 206 Cal. App. 3d 369; Commercial Life v. Superior Court (1988), 47 Cal. 3d 473.
Moga, Thomas W., (BV) '39 '66 C&L.585 B.S.B.A., LL.B.
10790 Civic Center Dr. #100
Moore, M. Douglas '48 '79 C.101 B.S. L.990 J.D. [Moore&B.]
Moore, Sully Wade '64 '90 C.112 B.A. L.1065 J.D. Dep. Dist. Atty.
Moore & Brown 7365 Carnelian St.
Morgan, Jennifer S. '65 '90 C.54 B.A. L.770 J.D. 11317 Mountain View Dr.
**Morse, Lisa S.** '53 '80 C.188 B.S. L.809 J.D. [A Genson,E.C.&W.]
Nadelman, Jeffrey Dale, (CV) '50 '85 C&L.398 B.A., J.D. 8316 Red Oak St.
Newman, Beverly '65 '91 C.464 B.A. L.809 J.D. 10737 Laurel St.
Niciforos, Maria G., (CV) '49 '82 C.1077 B.A. L.426 J.D. 10788 Civic Center Dr.
Novak, Louis C., (BV) '41 '69 C.112 B.A. L.1049 J.D. 10788 Civic Ctr. Dr.
Oberg, Howard C. '36 '78 C&L.1137 B.S.L., J.D. 10078A Artrow Rte. 95
**O'Connor, Robert J.** '51 '79 C.112 B.S. L.1148 J.D. [Genson,E.C.&W.]
**O'Doherty, F. X. Sean** '52 '79 C.745 B.A. L.1137 J.D. [Genson,E.C.&W.]
Paul, Charles H. '52 '77 C.381 B.B.A. L.1049 J.D. 10737 Laurel St.
Peelman, Danny L. '52 '92 C.1090 B.S. L.398 J.D. 10788 Civic Center Dr.
Poling, David M., (CV) '56 '82 C&L.398 B.A., J.D. Dep. Dist. Atty.
Pratt, Thomas V., (CV) '48 '80 C.1110 B.A. L.398 J.D. 8137 Malachite Ave.
Quinlan, Mary E. '42 '77 C.94 A.B. L.818 J.D. Adm. Law J., Unemp. App. Bd.
Rawlings, William R., (CV) '47 '80 C.1042 B.A. L.1137 J.D. 10681 Foothill Blvd.
**Reiss, James V.** '61 '87 C.426 B.A. L.678 J.D. [Reiss&J.]
*PRACTICE AREAS: Civil Litigation; Criminal Litigation.

**Reiss & Johnson**
**10535 Foothill Boulevard, Suite 410, 91730**
Telephone: 909-483-0515 Fax: 909-980-7945
James V. Reiss; Stephan J. Johnson.
General Civil and Trial Practice in all State and Federal Courts. Product Liability, Governmental Torts, Construction, Motor Carrier, Personal Injury, Criminal and Family Law.
*See Professional Biographies, RANCHO CUCAMONGA, CALIFORNIA*

Remes, Allen S., (CV) '32 '82 C.1097 B.A. L.398 J.D. 9330 Baseline Rd.
Remlinger, Roger R., (BV) '44 '79 C.1075 B.S. L.398 J.D. 10532 Acacia St.
Richter, Suzanne J. '39 '79 C.767 B.A. L.398 J.D. 10681 Foothill Blvd.
Rogers, Patrick J., (BV) '52 '77 C.560 B.A. L.398 J.D. 10681 Foothill Blvd.
Ross, Donald G. '36 '64
C.674 A.B. L.1066 LL.B. Admin. Law J., State Unemp. Ins. App. Bd.
Rosson, Robert R., Jr., (BV) '40 '70
C.112 A.B. L.1065 J.D. Admin. Law J., Unemp. Ins. App. Bd.
**Roth, Mitchell I** '61 '87 C&L.705 B.A., J.D. [A Mannerino&B.]
*LANGUAGES: English and Spanish.
*PRACTICE AREAS: Litigation; Family Law; Criminal; Bankruptcy.
Sabet, Shahla S. '46 '85 C.061 B.A. L.809 J.D. Mun. J.
**Sanford-Wachtel, Timothy D.** '48 '78
C.1109 B.S. L.1137 J.D. [Kegel,T.&T.] (©San Diego)
Sappenfield, Norma A. '53 '88 C.1109 B.S. L.1137 J.D. 10790 Civic Cntr. Dr.
Schiffman, Harve Jay '43 '72 C.112 B.A. L.426 J.D. 9140 Haven Ave.
Schmauss, Karen R. Ferrera '56 '84 C.1109 B.A. L.629 J.D. Dep. Dist. Atty.
Schneider, Charles E., (BV) '37 '71 C.999 L.809 J.D. 10788 Civic Ctr. Dr.
Shapiro, Diane S. '60 '90 C.766 B.A. L.426 J.D. Dep. Pub. Def.
**Slough, Marsha G.** '58 '87 C.630 B.A. L.1148 J.D. [Markman,A.H.C.&S.]
*PRACTICE AREAS: Municipal Litigation; Personal Injury Litigation.
Smith, Debra A. '55 '86 L.809 J.D. 10535 Foothill Blvd.
Snodgrass, Teresa Marie '53 '88 C.112 B.A. L.398 J.D. Dep. Pub. Def.
Spalding, Thomas L. '47 '84 C.1074 B.S. L.398 J.D. [Spalding,T.L.]

Spalding, Thomas L., Law Offices of 8280 Utica Ave.
Tenhagen, Barbara G. '47 '79 C.1042 B.A. L.1137 J.D. P.O. Box 3329
Thorne, D. Larry '29 '56 C.112 B.S. L.1066 LL.B. Ret. J.
Thorp, Larry L.J. '23 '89 C.494 B.Ch.E. L.1137 J.D. 10601 Civic Center Dr.‡
**Tobin, John J.**, (AV) '35 '69 C&L.1114 B.A., J.D. [Kegel,T.&T.] (©L.A.)
Valenzuela, Joel M. '38 '74 C.37 B.S. L.426 J.D. 11601 Candela Dr.
Van Stockum, Raymond P. '45 '79 C&L.1137 B.S.L., J.D. Mun. J.
Vollandt, Michael P., (CV) '42 '76 L.1127 J.D. 10535 Foothill Blvd.
**Wade, Edmond D.**, (AV) '41 '72 C.1077 B.A. L.426 J.D. [Genson,E.C.&W.]
**Wallace, Nancy J.** '58 '89 C.1075 B.S. L.1137 J.D. [A Kegel,T.&T.]
Welch, J. Michael '42 '68 C.426 B.A. L.1049 J.D. Supr. Ct. Comr.

**Welebir & McCune, A Professional Law Corporation**
(See Redlands)

Williams, Kent D. '60 '88 C.768 B.S. L.464 J.D. Dep. Dist. Atty.
Zartman, Therese M., (BV) '49 '84 C.112 B.A. L.398 J.D. 9140 Haven Ave.
Ziebarth, Kenneth G., Jr. '32 '59 C.723 B.A. L.1035 J.D. P.O. Box 546

## RANCHO LA COSTA, —, *San Diego Co.*

Griesbaum, Karl H., (BV) '39 '72 C.679 B.S. L.1049 J.D. 7720 B El Camino Real
Kardon, Bruce P. '48 '78 C.112 B.A. L.809 J.D. Transamerica Life Ins. Co.
Norris, Kathleen A. '43 '81 C&L.1137 B.S.L., J.D. 2327-4 Caringa Way‡

## RANCHO MIRAGE, 9,778, *Riverside Co.*

Allen, Kandy Lee '53 '84 C.1078 B.A. L.1065 J.D. 39700 Bob Hope Dr.
Altshuler, Michael D. '46 '72 C.112 B.A. L.188 J.D. 602 Desert West Dr.
**Andelson, Michael J., (P.C.)**, (BV) '47 '72 C.768 B.S. L.1065 J.D. [Best B.&K.]
Austin, Hayden D. '11 '53 C&L.902 J.D.
(adm. in WY; not adm. in CA) 62 Calle Solano‡
**Bailey, Jacqueline E.** '65 '93 C.1077 B.A. L.464 J.D. [A Best B.&K.]
*PRACTICE AREAS: Civil Litigation.
**Baron, Barbara R.** '52 '77 C.112 B.A. L.1065 J.D. [A Best B.&K.]
*PRACTICE AREAS: Business Litigation; Labor and Employment Litigation and Advice.

**Best Best & Krieger LLP, (AV)**
A California Limited Liability Partnership including Professional Corporations
**Hope Square Professional Centre, 39700 Bob Hope Drive, Suite 312, P.O. Box 1555, 92270©**
Telephone: 619-568-2611 Fax: 619-341-7039
Resident Partners: D. Martin Nethery (P.C.); David J. Erwin (P.C.); Michael J. Andelson (P.C.); Douglas S. Phillips (P.C.); Basil T. Chapman; Marc E. Empey; Brian M. Lewis; Matt H. Morris; Robert W. Hargreaves; Daniel E. Olivier; Michael D. Harris (P.C.); Martin A. Mueller; Jason D. Dabareiner. Resident Associates: Mary E. Gilstrap; Barbara R. Baron; Helene P. Dreyer; Jacqueline E. Bailey; Ana Maria Z. Fredgren; Jeffrey S. Flashman; Sandy A. Jacobson; G. Henry Welles.
General Civil and Trial Practice. Corporation, Water Rights, Probate, Trusts and Estate Planning. Labor, Real Estate and Municipal Law.
Representative Clients: Del Webb California Corp.; City of Palm Desert; City of Indio; City of Desert Hot Springs; County of Riverside; David Freedman & Co.; California Redi-Date; Westinghouse Desert Communities.
Riverside, California Office: 400 Mission Square, 3750 University Avenue, P.O. Box 1028. Telephone: 909-686-1450. Fax: 909-686-3083; 909-682-4612.
Ontario, California Office: 800 North Haven, Suite 120. Telephone: 909-989-8584. Fax: 909-944-1441.
San Diego, California Office: 402 West Broadway, 13th Floor. Telephone: 619-525-1300. Fax: 619-233-6118.
Victorville, California Office: High Desert Corporate Pointe Building, 14350 Civic Drive, Suite 270. Telephone: 619-245-4127. Fax: 619-245-6437.
*See Professional Biographies, RANCHO MIRAGE, CALIFORNIA*

**Blasdel, Diane C.**, (BV) '62 '91 C.1109 B.S. L.464 J.D. [Selzer,E.H.&B.]
*PRACTICE AREAS: Civil Litigation; Real Estate Litigation; Probate.
**Caronna, Anthony C.** (BV) '60 '88 C.800 B.S. L.1148 J.D. [A.C.Caronna]©

**Caronna, Anthony C., P.C., (BV)**
**71-650 Sahara Road, Suite 2, 92270©**
Telephone: 619-773-4849 Fax: 619-773-0849
Anthony C Caronna.
Practice limited to General Civil and Trial Practice in all State and Federal Courts. Aviation, Insurance, Malpractice, Personal Injury, Products Liability, Negligence, Workers' Compensation.
Coachella, California Office: 1623 6th Street, 92236. Telephone: 619-398-0001. Fax: 619-398-0281.
*See Professional Biographies, RANCHO MIRAGE, CALIFORNIA*

Casselman, Jeremiah, (BV) '31 '64 C.1043 B.A. L.809 LL.B. 74075 El Paso‡
**Chapman, Basil T.**, (BV) '47 '81 C.705 B.A. L.61 J.D. [Best B.&K.]
*PRACTICE AREAS: Litigation; Family Law.
Cheney, Marshall C. '24 '51 C.112 B.A. L.1065 LL.B.
(adm. in WY; not adm. in CA) 34820 Mission Hills Dr.‡
**Dabareiner, Jason D.** '63 '89 C.494 B.A. L.966 J.D. [Best B.&K.]
Demyanek, Walter, (BV) '32 '65 C.35 B.S. L.809 LL.B. 71 Lake Shore Dr.
Dolan, Jennifer Olson '67 '92 C.477 B.A. L.966 J.D. 39700 Bob Hope Dr.
Dorsey, William H., Jr. '23 '46 C.201 B.A. L.273 J.D. 7 Gleneagle Dr.
**Dreyer, Helene P.** '65 '92 C.477 B.A.Ed. L.846 J.D. [A Best B.&K.]
*PRACTICE AREAS: Litigation; Family Law.
**Ealy, W. Curt**, (AV) '44 '73 C.169 B.A. L.1067 J.D. [Selzer,E.H.&B.]
*PRACTICE AREAS: Real Estate Law.
**Empey, Marc E.** '57 '84 C.112 B.A. L.1065 J.D. [Best B.&K.]
**Erwin, David J., (P.C.)**, (AV) '34 '58 C&L.623 B.A., LL.B. [Best B.&K.]
**Flashman, Jeffrey S.** '65 '92 C.918 B.A. L.1066 J.D. [A Best B.&K.]
Ford, Gerald R. '13 '41 C.477 B.A. L.976 LL.B.
(adm. in MI; not adm. in CA) P.O. Box 927‡
**Fredgren, Ana Maria Z.** '68 '95 C.800 B.S. L.188 J.D. [A Best B.&K.]
*LANGUAGES: Spanish.
*PRACTICE AREAS: Corporate; Estate Planning.
Gerber, Harvey R., (AV) '34 '61 C.426 L.800 LL.B. 7 Johnar Blvd.‡
**Gilstrap, Mary E.** '61 '90 C.1042 B.A. L.494 J.D. [A Best B.&K.]
*PRACTICE AREAS: Real Estate; Construction Defect; Business Litigation.
Goldie, Ray R. '20 '57 C.999 L.800 J.D. 1 Hampton Ct.
Grant, Eric P. '29 '63 C.1043 B.A. L.809 LL.B. 42-730 Dunes View
Greenblott, Louis M. '19 '42 C&L.188 B.A., LL.B.
(adm. in NY; not adm. in CA) 630 Hospitality Dr.‡
Grossman, Thomas A., (BV) '45 '76 C.112 B.A. L.809 J.D. 69-730 Hwy. 111
**Hargreaves, Robert W.** '51 '88 C.112 B.A. L.1066 J.D. [Best B.&K.]
*LANGUAGES: Spanish.
*REPORTED CASES: Evans v. City of San Jose (1992) 3 Cal.App.4th 728; City of Needles v. Griswold, 6 Cal. App. 4th 1881.
*PRACTICE AREAS: Public Law; Land Use Law; Land Use Litigation.
**Harris, Michael D., (P.C.)**, (AV) '36 '73 C.576 B.S. L.575 J.D. [Best B.&K.]
**Hemphill, Emily P.** '54 '92 C.477 B.A. L.464 J.D. [Selzer,E.H.&B.]
*PRACTICE AREAS: Business; Real Estate; Estate Planning.
Hofstadter, David A. '58 '84 C.1077 A.B. L.978 J.D. 12152 Saint Andrews

**Housman, Simon A. '53 '81 C.705 B.A. L.809 J.D.**
**69730 Highway III, Suite 207, 92270**
Telephone: 619-328-7995 Fax: 619-324-8823
Civil Litigation, Real Estate and Creditors Remedies in Bankruptcy.
*See Professional Biographies, RANCHO MIRAGE, CALIFORNIA*

Irell, Eugene ................................'45 '77 C.112 B.A. L.1068 J.D. 43 Clansy Ln. S
**Jacobson, Sandy A.** ........................ '70 '95 C.112 B.A. L.426 J.D. [Ⓐ Best B.&K.]
*PRACTICE AREAS: Public Law.
Johnsen, Oluf J. '12 '36 C&L.911
(adm. in WA; not adm. in CA) 69850 U.S. Hwy. 111‡
Kahn, Sidney J., (AV) ....................... '12 '35 C&L.150 LL.B. 900 Island Dr.‡
King, Pamela '54 '83
C.605 B.A. Psych. L.990 J.D. Coun., Stephenson Financial Servs., Inc.
Kristal, Barbara E. ........................'45 '84 C.381 B.B.A. L.1049 J.D. [B.E.Kristal]
Kristal, Barbara E., A Prof. Law Corp. .................................. 69-730 Hwy. III
Kulber, Terry ........................ '41 '69 C.800 B.A. L.284 J.D. 30 San Sebastian Dr.
**Lewis, Brian M.** ..........................'57 '83 C.800 B.S. L.208 J.D. [Best B.&K.]
Litwack, Steven C. ..............................'43 '71 L.818 J.D. 532 Desert West Dr.‡
Mackell, Cheryl Hamer .................... '48 '84 C.178 B.S. L.1026 J.D. P.O. Box 279

**Manning, Guy, Law Offices of, (BV) '60 '88 C.549 B.S. L.398 J.D.**
**71-650 Sahara Road, Suite 2, 92270⊙**
**Telephone: 619-568-5474 Fax: 619-773-0849**
**Criminal Defense Trial Practice, Juvenile Criminal Defense, Personal Injury, Wrongful Death, Professional Liability Law.**
**Coachella, California Office: 1623 6th Street, 92236. Telephone: 619-398-0001. Fax: 619-773-0849.**
***See Professional Biographies, RANCHO MIRAGE, CALIFORNIA***

McClanahan, L. Scott, (BV) ........ '44 '73 C.1042 B.S.E. L.1137 J.D. 69-730 Hgwy 111
**Morris, Matt H.** ............................'60 '87 C&L.101 B.A., J.D. [Best B.&K.]
*LANGUAGES: Spanish.
**Mueller, Martin A.**, (BV) .................. '56 '84 C.112 B.A. L.1065 J.D. [Best B.&K.]
*PRACTICE AREAS: Business Litigation; Probate and Estate Litigation; Bankruptcy.
Nelson, Deane D. .........................'25 '52 C&L.494 B.B.A., J.D. 69-730 Hwy. 111
**Nethery, D. Martin, (P.C.)**, (AV) ........... '48 '75 C.112 A.B. L.800 J.D. [Best B.&K.]
**Olivier, Daniel E.** ......................... '58 '83 C.112 A.B. L.464 J.D. [Best B.&K.]
*PRACTICE AREAS: Real Estate Law; Redevelopment Law; Endangered Species.
Patterson, Jeffery S. R., (BV) ..........'45 '71 C.112 B.S. L.1065 J.D. 71-650 Sahara Rd.
**Phillips, Douglas S., (P.C.)**, (BV) .............'51 '77 C&L.823 B.A., J.D. [Best B.&K.]
*PRACTICE AREAS: Civil Litigation; Environmental; Land Use; Public Law; Litigation.
Pinkney, John .............................'65 '92 C&L.101 B.A., J.D. 39700 Bob Hope Dr.
Rudolph, Marshall S. ................ '65 '90 C.813 A.B. L.1065 J.D. 39700 Bob Hope Dr.
**Selzer, Paul T.**, (AV) ..................... '40 '66 C.436 A.B. L.813 J.D. [Selzer,E.H.&B.]
*PRACTICE AREAS: Real Estate Law; Governmental Affairs Law; Environmental Law.

**Selzer, Ealy, Hemphill & Blasdel, LLP, (AV)**
**69844 Highway 111 Suite K, 92270**
**Telephone: 619-202-1290 Fax: 619-202-1299**
**Members of Firm: Paul T. Selzer; W. Curt Ealy; Emily P. Hemphill; Diane C. Blasdel.**
**Real Estate, Business Transactions, Environmental Law, Homeowners Associations, Estate Planning, Trusts and Wills, Civil Litigation.**
***See Professional Biographies, RANCHO MIRAGE, CALIFORNIA***

Sherman, Peter ........................ '48 '74 C.112 B.A. L.1049 J.D. 752 Inverness Dr.
Shriver, Henry C. ..................................'17 '52 C.112 L.1001 LL.B. 131 Picadilly
Simon, Scott, (AV) ......................... '31 '60 C.112 B.S. L.800 J.D. P.O. Box 779‡
Sindoni, Stephen A. ..............'53 '78 C.1074 B.S. L.61 J.D. 71-650 Sahara Rd. Ste. 4
Watson, Nancy Belcher ..............'26 '59 C.813 B.A. L.1068 LL.B. Ret. Supr. Ct. J.‡
**Welles, G. Henry** ................... '63 '91 C.105 B.A. L.910 J.D. [Ⓐ Best B.&K.]
*PRACTICE AREAS: Business Litigation; Probate and Estate Litigation; Real Estate Litigation.
Wohlwend, Wells K., (AV) ...........'31 '57 C.112 B.S. L.1068 J.D. 42-700 Bob Hope Dr.

## RANCHO MURIETA, —, *Sacramento Co.*

Markley, Tom B. ........................'24 '50 C.112 B.A. L.1065 J.D. 6986 Carreta Lane
Scharlach, David A. ........................'47 '77 C&L.767 B.S., J.D. 6501 Puerto Dr.

## RANCHO PALOS VERDES, 41,659, *Los Angeles Co.*

Amador, Robert S. '54 '80 C.668 B.A. L.813 J.D.
Assoc. Gen. Coun. & V.P., Maxicare Health Plans, Inc.
Bodlander, Earl B. ............................'10 '36 C&L.800 B.A. 30920 Oceangrove Dr.
Brugman, William E. ................ '21 '73 C.911 B.S.M.E. L.426 J.D. 6312 Sattes Dr.‡
Camp, James S. ..............................'51 '76 C.800 B.S. L.770 J.D. 6460 Via Colinita
Cosgrove, Charles H. '55 '81 C.813 A.B. L.276 J.D.
(adm. in NY; not adm. in CA) 5987 Peacock Ridge Rd.
Davidson, Todd S. ............................'51 '77 C.1077 B.S. L.809 J.D. 5331 Waupaca
Flior, B. Edward ..........................'51 '79 C.1110 B.A. L.426 J.D. 29622 Stonecrest Rd.
Foster, Walter C. ...............................'23 '51 C&L.800 LL.B. 4246 Admirable Dr.‡
Gardner, Arthur ....................... '19 '51 C.210 A.B. L.800 J.D. 6429 Vista Colinta‡
Gist, Lawrence J., II '61 '90 C.166 B.A. L.285 J.D.
(adm. in MI; not adm. in CA) 4105 Exultant Dr.
Gordon, Sam ..........................................'18 '72 C.347 A.B. 6509 Nancy Rd.
Green, Raymond D. ........................'60 '86 C.112 A.B. L.464 J.D. 719 Yarmouth Rd.
Hastings, James H. ............................'17 '48 C&L.800 A.B., LL.B. 3455 Starline Dr.‡
Herro, Franklin W. .........................'16 '42 C.959 L.436 LL.B. 7137 Avenida Altisima
Hinz, Edward A., Jr. ..................'33 '62 C.112 A.B. L.1065 J.D. 29245 Firthridge Rd.‡
Hoff, Charles S. ...................'28 '79 C.112 A.B.,B.S. L.1179 J.D. 28205 Ambergate Dr.
Huizenga, Walter E. '49 '75 C&L.502 B.A., J.D.
(adm. in MO; not adm. in CA) 5557 Shoreview Dr.
Ingebretsen, James C., (AV) ..............'06 '33 C&L.813 A.B., J.D. 32859 Seagate Dr.‡
Jones, Russell D. .....................'33 '61 C&L.426 B.B.A., J.D. 4129 Admirable Dr.
Kato, James T. ......................... '34 '77 C.112 A.B. L.809 J.D. 6121 Queenridge Dr.
Knapp, Avery J. ........................'44 '79 C.1042 B.A. L.1136 J.D. 7435 Alida Pl.
Kunz, Earl G. '13 '38 C.878 B.S. L.145 J.D.
(adm. in IL; not adm. in CA) 28954 Crestridge Rd.‡
Margolis, Jane E. .......................'46 '71 C.477 B.A. L.597 J.D. 2938 Crownview Dr.
McNamara, Michael James ............'42 '89 C.112 B.A. L.426 J.D. 5402 Bayridge Road
Moewe, Parke W. ....................'20 '48 C.475 B.A. L.930 LL.B. 30097 Avenida Classica‡
Moore, John M. ........................'22 '51 C.112 B.A. L.861 LL.B. 26515 Mazur Dr.
Mountain, John J. .....................'33 '63 C.763 B.S. L.426 LL.B. 4105 Lorraine Rd.‡
Mustell, Landon G. ................'48 '76 C.1075 B.A. L.398 J.D. 6507 Ocean Crest Dr.
Patterson, Christine C. ....................'49 '74 C.112 B.A. L.800 J.D. 17 Diamonte Ln.
Perison, E. A. .................................................'27 '58 28736 Cedar Bluff Dr.‡
Picarelli, Joseph J. '32 '62 C.197 A.B. L.569 J.D.
(adm. in NY; not adm. in CA) 30311 Via Borica‡
Provenzano, John M., (AV) ..............'29 '59 C.299 B.A. L.1068 LL.B. 7240 Crest Rd.‡
Rawson, William C., Jr. ..................'49 '75 C.35 B.A. L.1068 J.D. 5048 Delacroix Rd.
Ross, Randy Ellen ...................'55 '79 C.1168 B.A. L.767 J.D. 32026 Sea Ridge Cir.‡
Ruderman, Horace A., (AV) ..................'23 '46 C&L.724 LL.B. 3274 Parkhurst Dr.‡
Sarjeant, John A. .............. '21 '54 C&L.93 A.B., J.D. 26832 Indian Peak Rd. (Pat.)‡
Schwartz, Barry '36 '62 C.143 B.S. L.150 LL.B.
(adm. in OH; not adm. in CA) 30081 Avenida Elegante‡
Smith, William George ..............'29 '81 C.472 B.S.M.E. L.1127 J.D. 3419 Deluna Dr.
Torres, William R., (BV) ....................'33 '70 C.800 B.S. L.809 J.D. P.O. Box 4813
Tower, Lee W. ......................'46 '80 C.112 M.S.E.E. L.426 J.D. 19 Saddle Rd. (Pat.)
Wagner, Donald R. ....................'21 '50 C&L.608 A.B., J.D. 3200 W. LaRotonda Dr.‡
Warren, Edwin B., (AV) ..........................'36 '65 C&L.800 B.A., J.D. [E.B.Warren]
Warren, Edwin B., Law Offices of, A Prof. Corp., (AV) ....................32550 Seahill Dr.
Westad, John W. '27 '62 C.208 B.S.B.A. L.564 LL.B.
(adm. in NY; not adm. in CA) 27602 Fawnskin Dr.‡
Winston, W. H., Jr. ...........................'26 '54 C&L.800 A.B., LL.B. Ret. Supr. Ct. J.
Wolfe, Christopher Sterling ...........'64 '92 C.800 B.A. L.1066 J.D. 4874 Elkridge Dr.

## RANCHO SANTA FE, —, *San Diego Co.*

Ackerly, Judith K. ........................'38 '67 C.483 B.A. L.767 J.D. P.O. Box 1883
Adams, Michael M. ......................'50 '88 C.112 D.D.S. L.1049 J.D. P.O. Box 8343
Arcaro, George C. '11 '37 C&L.262 B.A., LL.B.
(adm. in NY; not adm. in CA) P.O. Box 1574‡
Arms, Brewster L. .........................'25 '52 C&L.813 A.B., LL.B. P.O. Box 2484‡

**Blick, C. Samuel, (AV) '47 '71 C.912 B.A. L.1049 J.D.**
**P.O. Box 9477, 92067⊙**
**Telephone: 619-755-9794 Fax: 619-755-6335**
**Email: sblick@aol.com**
**Real Estate, Land Use and Government Law.**
**San Diego, California Office: 12625 High Bluff Drive, Suite 203, 92130. Telephone: 619-755-9794. E-Mail: sblick@aol.com**
***See Professional Biographies, RANCHO SANTA FE, CALIFORNIA***

Brockway, Robert C., (AV) ...............'18 '57 C.477 B.A. L.981 LL.B. P.O. Box 1394‡
Brown, Denny L. '36 '68 C.101 B.S. L.273 J.D.
(adm. in VA; not adm. in CA) P.O. Box 9695‡
**Burkhardt, Philip**, (BV) ...............'48 '75 C.1258 B.A. L.1049 J.D. [Burkhardt&L.]
*REPORTED CASES: Rancho Santa Fe Pharmacy, Inc. v. Seyfert, 219 Cal. App. 3d 875 (1990).
*PRACTICE AREAS: Real Estate Law; Business Litigation.

**Burkhardt & Larson, (BV)**
**A Partnership of Professional Corporations**
**6002 El Tordo, P.O. Box 1369, 92067**
**Telephone: 619-756-3743 Fax: 619-756-9805**
**Philip Burkhardt; Carl A. Larson.**
**General Civil Trial Practice. Real Estate, Real Property Development, Commercial Litigation, Eminent Domain, Taxation, Estate Planning and Probate Law.**
**References: Rancho Santa Fe National Bank; Union Bank.**
***See Professional Biographies, RANCHO SANTA FE, CALIFORNIA***

**Campitiello, Lawrence G.**, (AV) ..........'58 '83 C&L.426 B.A., J.D. [Ⓐ C.S.LiMandri]
*PRACTICE AREAS: Commercial Litigation; Real Property Law; Bankruptcy Litigation.
Carton, David S. ...........................'21 '49 C.563 B.A. L.309 LL.B. P.O. Box 3483‡
**Chidester, Steven J.** ..............................'57 '87 C&L.101 B.A., J.D. [Cowley&C.]
*PRACTICE AREAS: Estate Planning; Estate and Trust Administration; Charitable Giving; Nonprofit Organizations; Executive Compensation.
Coleman, Gerry Curtis, (BV) ...............'50 '76 C.597 B.A. L.61 J.D. P.O. Box 3827
**Coomber, Skip R., III** .........................'61 '90 C.112 B.A. L.426 J.D. [Coomber]⊙
*PRACTICE AREAS: Business Law.

**Coomber Law Firm**
**16909 Via de Santa Fe, Suite 200, P.O. Box 7299, 92067-7299⊙**
**Telephone: 619-759-3939 Facsimile: 619-759-3930**
**Email: scoomber@aol.com**
**Skip R. Coomber, III.**
**Business Transactions and Business Litigation.**
**Los Angeles, California Office: 601 S. Figueroa St., 41st Floor, 90017-5704. Telephone: 213-622-2200. Fax: 213-243-0000.**
***See Professional Biographies, RANCHO SANTA FE, CALIFORNIA***

Coultrap, James W. '10 '35 C.611 B.A. L.477 J.D.
(adm. in IL; not adm. in CA) P.O. Box 869‡
**Cowley, James M.**, (AV) ...................'40 '66 C.101 B.S. L.145 J.D. [Cowley&C.]
*PRACTICE AREAS: Estate Planning; Estate and Trust Administration; Charitable Giving; Nonprofit Organizations.

**Cowley & Chidester, (AV) BB**
**6050 El Tordo, P.O. Box 2329, 92067**
**Telephone: 619-756-4410 Fax: 619-756-4386**
**Members: James M. Cowley; Steven J. Chidester; Ellen L. van Hoften. Associates: Kristina A. Hancock; Nancy G. Henderson. Of Counsel: Lynn P. Hart.**
**Domestic and International Estate Planning; Trust, Will and Probate Law; Charitable Giving and Nonprofit Organizations.**
***See Professional Biographies, RANCHO SANTA FE, CALIFORNIA***

Criscuolo, Wendy L. ....................'49 '84 C.112 B.A. L.767 J.D. Ciros Investments
Dale, James M., (AV) ...................'32 '60 C.112 A.B. L.1068 J.D. P.O. Box 8960
Douglas, Clifford, (A Prof. Law Corp.) '42 '67 C.112 B.A. L.1068 LL.B.
P.O. Box 2729
Fairty, Richard K. ..........................'57 '82 C.112 B.A. L.1068 J.D. P.O. Box 3913
**Fitzpatrick, Barry C.**, (AV) .....................'46 '71 C.674 A.B. L.893 J.D. [Fitzpatrick&S.]

**Fitzpatrick & Showen, LLP, (AV)**
**5951 La Sendita, P.O. Box 428, 92067**
**Telephone: 619-756-1158 Fax: 619-756-3142**
**Barry C. Fitzpatrick; Richard E. Showen.**
**Practice Limited to Estate Planning, Trust, Will and Probate Law.**
**Reference: Union Bank of California, N.A. (La Jolla Trust Office and Trust Department, San Diego Main Office); Northern Trust Bank of California, N.A. (La Jolla Trust Office); Wells Fargo Bank, N.A. (La Jolla Trust Office).**

**Flynn, Sheridan & Tabb**
**6125 El Tordo, P.O. Box 690, 92067⊙**
**Telephone: 619-759-7000 Facsimile: 619-756-1575**
**Philip H. Stillman.**
**Civil Litigation, Commercial Litigation, Personal Injury, Products Liability, Medical Malpractice and Environmental Litigation.**
**Boston, Massachusetts Office: One Boston Place, 18th Floor. Telephone: 617-720-2700. Facsimile: 617-720-2709.**
***See Professional Biographies, RANCHO SANTA FE, CALIFORNIA***

**Freeberg, Eric O., (AV) '51 '79 C.112 A.B. L.1066 J.D.**
**P.O. Box Box 9440, 92067-4440**
**Telephone: 619-756-6632 Fax: 619-756-3506**
***PRACTICE AREAS: Business Mediation; Arbitration; Commercial Transactions; General Real Estate Law; Real Property Secured Transactions.**
**Commercial Transactions. General Real Estate, Real Property Secured Transactions, Business, Mediation and Arbitration.**
***See Professional Biographies, RANCHO SANTA FE, CALIFORNIA***

Goldberg, Theodore ..........................'40 '79 C.569 B.S. L.1137 J.D. P.O. Box 9545
Grant Cobb, Peggy '49 '75 C&L.378 B.A., J.D.
(adm. in KS; not adm. in CA) Pres., Venue Verde, Inc.
Green, Daniel K., (BV) ...........................'49 '75 C.147 B.S. L.1137 J.D. [Green&G.]
Green, Jana W. ........................................'51 '76 C&L.1137 B.S., J.D. [Green&G.]
Green and Green, (BV) ...................................................6050 El Tordo St.
Gullickson, Howard M. ..........................'11 '35 C&L.508 J.D. P.O. Box 1978

CAA505P

**Hancock, Kristina A.** ................... '53 '90 C.1163 A.S. L.1049 J.D. [Cowley&C.]
*PRACTICE AREAS: Nonprofit Organizations; Estate Planning; Estate and Trust Administration; Charitable Giving.
**Hart, Lynn P.**, (AV) ................... '54 '79 C.1239 B.A. L.1066 J.D. [Cowley&C.]
*PRACTICE AREAS: Estate Planning; Estate and Trust Administration; Charitable Giving.
Haskins, Nena Jo .................................— '86 C.1019 L.537 J.D. P.O. Box 1907
Heid, Harry W., (BV) .................... '28 '56 C.112 B.A. L.1065 J.D. P.O. Box 443
**Henderson, Nancy G.** ................. '60 '91 C.228 A.B. L.1066 J.D. [Cowley&C.]
*PRACTICE AREAS: Estate Planning; Charitable Giving; Taxation; Nonprofit Organizations.
Herrmann, Robert E., (AV) .................... '26 '54 C&L.215 LL.B. P.O. Box 1026‡
Johnson, Linda F. .......................'50 '77 C.813 B.A. L.276 J.D. P.O. Box 675203
Kahn, Ronald L. .......................... '30 '58 C.339 B.S. L.800 J.D. P.O. Box 8090
**Larson, Carl A.** ......................... '59 '88 C.112 B.A. L.1067 J.D. [Burkhardt&L.]
*REPORTED CASES: Heacock v. Ivorette-Texas, Inc. (1993), 20 Cal. App. 4th. 1665.
*PRACTICE AREAS: Taxation; Estate Planning; Civil Litigation.
Larson, Carl Anthony ...................'59 '88 C.112 B.A. L.1067 J.D. P.O. Box 1369
Leone, Michael F., Jr. ..................... '43 '69 C.112 A.B. L.800 J.D. P.O. Box 273
Lewi, Peter A., (AV) ...................... '37 '65 C.605 A.B. L.800 J.D. P.O. Box 8675‡
Liebermann, Jane ............'61 '87 C.788 A.B. L.1049 J.D. El Tordo & Linea Del Cielo

**LiMandri, Charles S., (AV) '55 '83 C.1049 B.A. L.276 J.D.**
**Building 3, 16236 San Dieguito Road, Suite 3-15, P.O. Box 9120, 92067**
**Telephone: 619-759-9930 Fax: 619-759-9938**
***PRACTICE AREAS: Admiralty Maritime Law; Business Law; Construction Law; Environmental Law; Insurance Defense.**
**Associates: Hugh K. Swift; Lawrence G. Campitiello.**
**Plaintiff's Personal Injury, Defense Maritime, Insurance, Construction and Business Litigation, Public Contracts, Claims and Disputes.**
**Representative Clients: The Standard Steamship Owners Protection and Indemnity Association, Ltd. (London); Caribbean Marine Service Co., Inc. (San Diego); Century National Insurance.**
**Reference: Wells Fargo Bank.**
*See Professional Biographies, RANCHO SANTA FE, CALIFORNIA*

Lynch, Donna J., (CV) ................................'40 '79 L.1137 J.D. P.O. Box 2207
Manasse, Herbert, (AV) ....................... '11 '36 C&L.966 B.A., J.D. Manasse Corp.
Millard, Gerald '13 '38 C&L.597 B.S., LL.B.
(adm. in IL; not adm. in CA) P.O. Box 9895‡
Monge, Joseph P. '12 '40 C.895 L.309 LL.B.
(adm. in NY; not adm. in CA) P.O. Box 1430‡
Moses, Maron, Jr. '39 '66 C.922 A.B. L.923 LL.B.
(adm. in WV; not adm. in CA) P.O. Box 2216‡
Myron, Robert E. ........................... '42 '69 C.436 B.S. L.209 J.D. P.O. Box 2515
Niebrugge, Chester W. ...................'17 '72 C&L.1095 B.A., J.D. 6119 La Granada
Perlman, Raymond L. '18 '41 C.145 B.A. L.309 LL.B.
(adm. in IL; not adm. in CA) P.O. Box 9821‡
Pike, Chan Poyner '48 '73 C&L.575 B.M.Ed., J.D.
(adm. in NC; not adm. in CA) P.O. Box 7166‡
Rensch, Joseph R. ........................'23 '55 C.813 B.S. L.284 LL.B. P.O. Box 9914‡
Scuba, Richard J., (BV) ...........'43 '80 C.871 B.S. L.61 J.D. 6106 La Flecha, Suite 201
Shapiro, Lee A. '56 '80 C.339 B.S. L.145 J.D.
(adm. in IL; not adm. in CA) Pres., SES Properties, Inc.
**Showen, Richard E.**, (AV) .................'57 '83 C.112 A.B. L.1065 J.D. [Fitzpatrick&S.]
*PRACTICE AREAS: Estate Planning Law; Probate Law; Trust Administration Law.
Sinning, Gordon R., II, (BV) .............. '47 '78 C.347 B.S. L.1198 J.D. P.O. Box 7062
Stanford, Dwight E., (AV) .................... '14 '36 C.763 A.B. L.61 J.D. P.O. Box 333‡
Stein, Lee H. ................................ '53 '78 C.823 B.S. L.884 J.D. P.O. Box 2771
**Stillman, Philip H.** ........................'58 '89 C.1036 B.A. L.94 J.D. [Flynn,S.&T.]
*PRACTICE AREAS: Securities; Commercial Law; Fraud Litigation; RICO Litigation.
**Swift, Hugh K.** .......................'59 '85 C.1049 B.B.A. L.61 J.D. [C.S.LiMandri]
Swirles, Frank M. ......................'18 '73 C.800 B.S. L.981 LL.B. P.O. Box 1490
**van Hoften, Ellen L.** ...................... '42 '83 C.813 A.B. L.1049 J.D. [Cowley&C.]
*PRACTICE AREAS: Estate Planning; Estate and Trust Administration; Charitable Giving.
Veltman, James M., (BV) .................'50 '75 C.763 B.A. L.426 J.D. P.O. Box 2043
Warner, Verne O. ................................'11 '46 C.375 B.S. L.61 J.D. P.O. Box 20‡
**Williams, Reed M.**, (AV) .... '26 '54 C.1250 B.S. L.1065 LL.B. [Williams W.C.N.&R.]
*REPORTED CASES: Orient Steam Navigation Co., Ltd. v. United States of America (Kearsarge-Orians), 231 F.Supp. 469, 1964 AMC 2163 (S.D. Cal. 1964); Chervy v. Peninsular & Oriental Steam Navigation Co., Ltd. (Arcadia), 364 F.2d 908, 1966 AMC 226 (9th Cir. 1966); Waterman Steamship Corp. v. Gay Cottons (Chickasaw) 414 F.2d 724, 1969 AMC 1682 (9th Cir. 1969); Japan Line, Ltd. v. County of Los Angeles, 441 U.S. 434, 99 S.Ct. 1813, 16 L.Ed.2d 336, 1979 AMC 881 (1979); Lubick v. Travel Service, Inc., 573 F.Supp. 904 (D.V.I. 1983).
*PRACTICE AREAS: Maritime Law; Environmental Law; Transportation and International Law; Commercial Transactions and Litigation; Personal Injury.

**Williams Woolley Cogswell Nakazawa & Russell, (AV)**
**16236 San Dieguito Road Building 3, Suite 3-15, 92067**
**Telephone: 619-497-0284 Fax: 619-759-9938**
**Email: wwlaw@msn.com**
**Reed M. Williams; Roger S. Woolley.**
**Commercial Transactions and Litigation, Maritime Law, Transportation and International Law, Environmental Law, Immigration Law, Personal Injury and Product Liability Litigation.**
**Long Beach, California Office: 111 West Ocean Boulevard, Suite 2000, 90802-4614. Telephone: 310-495-6000. Telecopier: 310-435-1359.**
**Port Hueneme, California Office: 237 E. Hueneme Road, Suite A, 93041. Telephone: 805-488-8560. Fax: 805-488-7896.**
*See Professional Biographies, RANCHO SANTA FE, CALIFORNIA*

Wood, Kenneth A., (BV) ................... '38 '67 C.112 B.S. L.1068 J.D. P.O. Box 2609
**Woolley, Roger S.**, (AV) .......... '24 '53 C.945 A.B. L.178 LL.B. [Williams W.C.N.&R.]
*PRACTICE AREAS: Probate; Real Property; Banking; Corporate Law.
Wright, William F. '42 '68 C.546 B.S. L.228 J.D.
(adm. in NE; not adm. in CA) Chmn. of the Bd. & CEO, Amcon Corporation

## RANCHO SANTA MARGARITA, —, *Orange Co.*

**Franchise Law Team, (AV)**
**30021 Tomas, Suite 260, 92688**
**Telephone: 714-459-7474 Fax: 714-459-7772**
**Email: 70702.725@compuserve.com**
**Robin Day Glenn.**
**Domestic and International Franchising, Licensing and Distribution Law.**
*See Professional Biographies, RANCHO SANTA MARGARITA, CALIFORNIA*

**Glenn, Robin Day**, (AV) ..................'47 '75 C.1275 B.A. L.1067 J.D. [Franchise L.T.]
*LANGUAGES: French.
Hebner, Robert J. '48 '80
C.1109 B.A. L.1137 J.D. 31441 Santa Margarita Pkwy. Ste. A278
Marshall, Peter J. ........................... '56 '81 C.309 B.A. L.477 J.D. 30021 Tomas St.
Nulle, Douglas E. ............................ '53 '89 C.1109 B.A. L.1137 J.D. 7 Carmesi
Westhafer, F. Eugene, (AV) ............... '42 '69 C.37 B.A. L.426 J.D. [F.E.Westhafer]
Westhafer, F. Eugene, A Law Corporation, (AV) ..........................30021 Tomas St.

## RED BLUFF, * 12,363, *Tehama Co.*

Albright, Dennis D., (BV) ................... '44 '73 C&L.336 B.S., J.D. 715 Madison St.
Allen, Edward J., (BV) ..................... '24 '55 C&L.770 B.S., J.D. 737 Washington St.
Buck, Nelson D., (CV) ................................ '37 '73 C.347 L.1137 LL.B. Co. Coun.
Coffman, Rawlins, (BV) ........................ '12 '38 C.228 A.B. L.276 J.D. 100 Rio St.

**Cowan, Dennis K.**
**(See Redding)**

Cragg, Walter Thorpe, Jr. ......................... '51 '78 C.273 B.A. L.990 J.D. 100 Rio St.

**Craig and Shepherd**
**(See Chico)**

Edwards, Diane, (CV) .......................................'57 '85 L.1137 J.D. 100 Rio St.
Guziel, Chester P. .................... '19 '50 C&L.339 B.S., J.D. 16075 Jellys Ferry Rd.‡
Hedlund, Earl F., (BV) ............................ '21 '51 C.684 L.1065 J.D. 100 Rio St.
Hilligan, Thomas J., (BV) .................... '35 '60 C.602 B.A. L.477 LL.B. Dist. Atty.
Hultgren, Richd. E. ........................ '25 '51 C.813 A.B. L.1065 J.D. Ret. Supr. Ct. J.
Irving, Daniel R., (CV) ................................'40 '85 L.1137 J.D. 550 Walnut St.
King, Edward J., III ..................................'50 '78 C.699 B.A. L.1137 J.D. Mun. J.
Lucas, Harold J., (BV) ........................ '34 '64 C.112 A.B. L.1066 J.D. City Atty.
Martin-Logan, Diane L., (CV) ..............'54 '81 C.658 B.A. L.1137 J.D. 407 Walnut St.
**McCarthy, Robert E.**, (AV) .............'20 '50 C.112 A.B. L.1066 J.D. [McCarthy&R.]
*PRACTICE AREAS: Fidelity and Surety; Construction Law.
**McCarthy, Steven B.**, (AV) ........... '48 '75 C.112 B.S.B.A. L.765 J.D. [McCarthy&R.]

**McCarthy & Rubright, LLP, (AV)**
**100 Rio Street, P.O. Box 190, 96080**
**Telephone: 916-527-0213 Fax: 916-527-7641**
**Members of Firm: Steven B. McCarthy; Scott E. Rubright; David J. Murray. Of Counsel: Robert E. McCarthy.**
**General Civil Trial and Appellate Practice in all Courts. Corporation, Partnership, Business and Commercial Law, Construction, Real Property, Land Use, Agricultural and Environmental, Insurance Law, Estate Planning, Probate and Trust Law.**
*See Professional Biographies, RED BLUFF, CALIFORNIA*

**McGlynn, Matthew C.**, (BV) ................ '61 '86 C&L.770 B.A., J.D. [McGlynn&M.]
**McGlynn, Thomas J.**, (P.C.), (AV) .........'38 '64 C&L.770 B.A., LL.B. [McGlynn&M.]

**McGlynn & McGlynn, (AV)**
**A Partnership including a Professional Corporation**
**737 Washington Street, P.O. Box 1110, 96080**
**Telephone: 916-527-1117 Fax: 916-527-1414**
**Members of Firm: Thomas J. McGlynn (P.C.); Matthew C. McGlynn.**
**General Civil and Trial Practice. Criminal, Negligence, Probate, Estate Planning, Corporation, Contract, Real Property and Family Law.**
**References: Bank of America National Trust & Savings Assn., Red Bluff, California; Tehama County Bank, Red Bluff, California.**
*See Professional Biographies, RED BLUFF, CALIFORNIA*

McIver, Ronald D., (BV) ............ '48 '77 C.267 B.A. L.1065 J.D. 334 Washington St.
**Murray, David J.** ............................. '55 '92 C.147 B.A. L.1137 J.D. [McCarthy&R.]
Murray, Dennis E. ..................................'50 '76 C.1042 B.S. L.398 J.D. Supr. Ct. J.
Papendick, Rolland L., (BV) ..................'45 '70 C.123 B.A. L.597 J.D. 905 Wash. St.

**Peters, Fuller, Rush, Farnsworth & Habib**
**(See Chico)**

Pugh, Richard S. ..........................'38 '66 C.147 A.B. L.1065 J.D. 737 Wash. St.‡
**Rubright, Scott E.** ........................... '59 '84 C.8 B.A. L.208 J.D. [McCarthy&R.]
*PRACTICE AREAS: Real Estate; Land Use; Construction Law; Business Law; Corporate Law.
Scheuler, Richard, (BV) ..................'44 '73 C.112 A.B. L.1065 J.D. P.O. Box 8548
Symons, Jeri Marie, (BV) ....................... '55 '80 C.628 B.A. L.629 J.D. 756 Rio St.
Thompson, Kathryn S., (CV) ..............'58 '87 C.1060 B.A. L.629 J.D. Dep. Dist. Atty.
Watkins, Noel ........................................ '32 '57 C.147 A.B. L.1066 LL.B. Supr. Ct. J.

**Webster, Donald B., (AV) '24 '50 C&L.813 A.B., J.D.**
**416 Pine Street, P.O. Box 870, 96080**
**Telephone: 916-527-0114**
**General Civil and Trial Practice in all State Courts. Probate, Real Property, Business and Family Law.**
**Reference: Bank of America National Trust & Savings Assn.**
*See Professional Biographies, RED BLUFF, CALIFORNIA*

## REDDING, * 66,462, *Shasta Co.*

Allen, Lawrence R., (CV) ............ '52 '80 C.950 B.S. L.1153 J.D. Sr. Dep. Dist. Atty.
**Altemus, Stewart C.** ............................ '53 '81 C.112 B.A. L.1065 J.D. [Moss&E.]
Anderson, Anthony A. .....................'48 '78 C.768 B.A. L.770 J.D. Asst. Dist. Atty.
Anderson, Donald R., (BV) ................. '53 '80 C.335 B.A. L.336 J.D. [D.R.Anderson]
Anderson, Donald R., A Law Corporation, (BV) .................. 443 Redcliff Dr., Suite 210
Arel, Gary G., (CV) ..................... '39 '67 C.1056 B.S. L.1066 LL.B. 1650 Oregon St.
Arlin, Carol H., (BV) ...................... '48 '77 C.112 A.B. L.1132 J.D. 1745 Yuba St.
**Arthofer, Kenneth B.**, (CV) .............'63 '89 C.1042 B.A. L.990 J.D. [Borton,P.&C.]
*PRACTICE AREAS: Real Estate; Business; Corporate Transactions; Insurance Defense; Civil Litigation.
**Ashby, Michael P.**, (BV) .................. '59 '84 C.169 B.A. L.800 J.D. [Carr,K.P.&F.]
*TRANSACTIONS: Knowl-Wood Restaurants, 1989; Tam's Stationers, 1990; Malcolm Smith Racing, 1990; Hansen Beverage Company, 1992; Encinitas Town Center, 1993.
*PRACTICE AREAS: Corporations; Partnerships; Real Estate; Taxation.
**Ayres, William D.**, (BV) .................. '55 '81 C.36 B.S. L.1049 J.D. [Halkides&M.]
**Baker, Stephen H.**, (BV) ................... '59 '87 C.629 B.S. L.464 J.D. [Carr,K.P.&F.]
*PRACTICE AREAS: Insurance Personal Injury; Tort Law; Real Estate Litigation; Construction Litigation.
Balavage, Michael S. ........................'52 '78 C.893 B.A. L.464 J.D. 443 Redcliff Dr.
**Balavage, Monica M.** ........................'52 '77 C.338 B.S. L.464 J.D. [Moss&E.]
Ball, Susan Cresto, (BV) .................. '54 '81 C.112 B.A. L.1065 J.D. Dep. Co. Coun.
Ballard, Stephen P. ......................'57 '87 C.1253 B.A. L.464 J.D. 930 Executive Way
**Bandell, Leonard J.**, (AV) ................... '49 '75 C.665 B.A. L.284 J.D. [Bandell S.]
*PRACTICE AREAS: Litigation; Real Estate; Land Use Planning; Corporation and Business Law.

**Bandell • Swanson, (AV)**
**1330 West Street, P.O. Drawer 994410, 96099-4410**
**Telephone: 916-243-8150 Fax: 916-243-1745**
**Members of Firm: Leonard J. Bandell; L. Alan Swanson.**
**Civil Trial Practice, Real Estate, Land Use Planning, Corporation, Education, Employer/Employee Relations, Administrative and General Business.**
*See Professional Biographies, REDDING, CALIFORNIA*

Barker, Lydia E. '50 '91 C.228 A.B. L.1059 J.D.
(adm. in GA; not adm. in CA) 2890 Donner Ct.‡
**Barr, Dugan**, (AV) ........................... '42 '68 C.685 B.A. L.145 J.D. [D.Barr&Assoc.]
*PRACTICE AREAS: Trials; Personal Injury; Professional Negligence; Products Liability; Highway Design and Maintenance.

**Barr, Dugan, & Associates, (AV)**
**1824 Court Street, P.O. Box 994390, 96099-1648**
**Telephone: 916-243-8008 Fax: 916-243-1648**
**URL: http://www.CA-Lawyer.com/**
**Dugan Barr. Associates: David L. Case; Douglas Mudford.**
**General Civil and Trial Practice, Business Litigation, Personal Injury, Negligence, Insurance, Aviation, Products Liability, Professional Liability, Elder Abuse and Public Entity Liability.**
**Representative Clients: City of Redding; Mid Valley Bank; Scott Valley Bank; 3M; Enloe Hospital.**
**References: Scott Valley Bank, Redding Branch; Mid Valley Bank, Redding Branch.**
*See Professional Biographies, REDDING, CALIFORNIA*

Bartholomew, Donald E. . . . . . . . . . . . . . . . . . . . . . '51 '83 C.608 B.A. L.851 J.D. 1738 Yuba St.★
Barulich, Marc C. . . . . . . . . . . . . . . . . . '54 '83 C.330 B.A. L.1137 J.D. 1135 Pine St., Ste. 015

**Bates, Richard N., (AV) '40 '69 C.101 B.S. L.1068 J.D.**
**Suite B, 1300 West Street, 96001**
**Telephone: 916-244-6442 Fax: 916-244-0216**
**General Civil Trial Practice. Corporation, Business, Real Estate, Estate Planning and Probate Law.**
***See Professional Biographies, REDDING, CALIFORNIA***

**Beasley, Patrick R.**, (BV) . . . . . . . . . . . . . . . . '43 '75 C.112 B.A. L.464 J.D. [Maire,M.&B.]
Bell, Paul M., (BV) . . . . . . . . . . . . . . . . . . . . . . . '37 '64 C.895 B.A. L.564 J.D. 1930 West St.
Belton, Bruce L., (BV) . . . . . . . . . . . . . . . . . . . '56 '84 C.1073 B.A. L.767 J.D. [McNeill&B.]
Benson, Rodney E., (CV) . . . . . . . . . . . . . . '54 '85 C.636 B.A. L.990 J.D. 1539 Chestnut St.
Bigelow, Molly A. . . . . . . . . . . . . . . . . '65 '91 C.112 B.A. L.770 J.D. Dep. Dist. Atty.
Blalock, Lorraine H. '35 '83 C.1056 B.S. L.950 J.D.
(adm. in WA; not adm. in CA) 2280 N. Bechelli Lane
Boeckman, Bradley L. . . . . . . . . . . . . . . . . . . . . '45 '71 C.766 B.A. L.1065 J.D. Supr. Ct. J.
Borchard, Gary C., (AV) . . . . . . . . . . . . . . . '40 '66 C.309 A.B. L.813 J.D. 448 Redcliff Dr.

**Borton, Petrini & Conron, (AV)**
**280 Hemsted Drive, Suite 100, 96002⊙**
**Telephone: 916-222-1530 Fax: 916-222-4498**
**Email: bpcred@bpclaw.com**
**Members of Firm: Randall L. Harr; Kenneth B. Arthofer. Associate: Alfred W. Mondorf.**
**Commercial/Real Estate Litigation, Insurance Law, General Civil Trial and Appellate Practice in State and Federal Courts, Personal Injury and Casualty Defense Litigation, Insurance Bad Faith and Coverage, Labor and Employment, Toxic Torts, Real Estate, Land Use Planning, Zoning, Municipal, Professional Errors and Omissions, Healthcare Provider Malpractice Defense, Products Liability, Oil and Gas, Water, Natural Resources, Environmental, Public Entity, Administrative, Agricultural, Banking, Contracts, Corporations, Partnerships, Taxation, Creditor's Remedies, Bankruptcy, Probate, Estate Planning, Family Law.**
**Bakersfield, California Office: The Borton, Petrini & Conron Building, 1600 Truxtun Avenue, P.O. Box 2026. Telephone: 805-322-3051. Fax: 805-322-4628. Email: bpcbak@bpclaw.com.**
**San Luis Obispo, California Office: 1114 Marsh Street. Telephone: 805-541-4340. Fax: 805-541-4558. Email: bpcslo@bpclaw.com.**
**Visalia, California Office: 206 South Mooney Boulevard, P.O. Box 1028. Telephone: 209-627-5600. Fax: 209-627-4309. Email: bpcvis@bpclaw.com.**
**Fresno, California Office: T. W. Patterson Building, 2014 Tulare Street, Suite 830. Telephone: 209-268-0117. Fax: 209-237-7995. Email: bpcfrs@bpclaw.com.**
**Sacramento, California Office: 2233 Watt Avenue, Suite 290. Telephone: 916-484-3555. Fax: 916-484-3550. Email: bpcsac@bpclaw.com.**
**Santa Barbara, California Office: 211 East Victoria Street, Suite D. Telephone: 805-564-2404. Fax: 805-564-2176. Email: bpcsb@bpclaw.com**
**Los Angeles, California Office: 707 Wilshire Boulevard, Suite 5100. Telephone: 213-624-2869. Fax: 213-489-3930. Email: bpcla@bpclaw.com.**
**San Diego, California Office: John Burnham Building, 610 West Ash Street, 9th Floor. Telephone: 619-232-2424. Fax: 619-531-0794. Email: bpcsd@bpclaw.com.**
**Newport Beach, California Office: 4675 MacArthur Court, Suite 1150. Telephone: 714-752-2333. Fax: 714-752-2854. Email: bpcnb@bpclaw.com.**
**Modesto, California Office: The Turner Building, 900 "H" Street, Suite D. Telephone: 209-576-1701. Fax: 209-527-9753. Email: bpcmod@bpclaw.com.**
**San Francisco, California Office: 111 Pine Street, Suite 730. Telephone: 415-981-4415. Fax: 415-391-5538. Email: bpcsf@bpclaw.com.**
**San Bernardino, California Office: 290 North "D" Street, Suite 500. Telephone: 909-381-0527. Fax: 909-381-0658. Email: bpcsbdo@bpclaw.com.**
**San Jose, California Office: 2 North Second Street. Telephone: 408-298-3997. Fax: 408-298-3365. Email: bpcsj@bpclaw.com.**
**Ventura, California Office: 1000 Hill Road, Suite 310. Telephone: 805-650-9994. Fax: 805-650-7125. Email: bpcvta@bpclaw.com.**
**Santa Rosa, California Office: 50 Santa Rosa Avenue, Suite 300. Telephone: 707-527-9477. Fax: 707-527-9488. Email: bpcsr@bpclaw.com.**
***See Professional Biographies, REDDING, CALIFORNIA***

Brady, David M., (BV) . . . . . . . . . . . . . . . . . . '46 '76 C&L.767 B.A., J.D. [Hanna,B.M.M.&J.]
Bramham, R. Michael . . . . . . . . . . . . . . . . . '51 '76 C.806 B.A. L.836 J.D. [Hanna,B.M.M.&J.]

**Breyer, Arnold David, (BV) '42 '67 C.339 B.A. L.426 J.D.**
**1721 Court Street, 96001⊙**
**Telephone: 916-244-3690 Fax: 916-244-0923**
**(Certified Specialist, Family Law, The State Bar of California Board of Legal Specialization).**
**Practice Limited to Personal Injury and Family Law.**
**Mount Shasta, California Office: 112 Siskiyou Avenue, P.O. Box 201. Telephone: 916-926-3134. Fax: 916-926-8607.**
***See Professional Biographies, REDDING, CALIFORNIA***

**Brickwood, Gary C.**, (BV) . . . . . . . . . . . . . . '52 '80 C.112 A.B. L.464 J.D. [Brickwood&K.]
*PRACTICE AREAS: Civil Litigation; Insurance; Business; Employment.

**Brickwood & Key, (BV)**
**1135 Pine Street, Suite 210, 96001**
**Telephone: 916-245-1877 Fax: 916-245-1879**
**Members of Firm: Gary C. Brickwood; Rodney J. Key.**
**Representative Clients: City of Redding, Shasta County; Pepsi of Northern California; State Farm Insurance; Farmers Insurance Exchange.**
***See Professional Biographies, REDDING, CALIFORNIA***

Briden, Mark W., (CV) . . . . . . . . . . . . . . . . . . '54 '80 C.1071 B.S. L.770 J.D. 691 Maraglia St.
Brophy, Walter R., Jr. . . . . . . . . . . . . . . . . . . . . '24 '55 C&L.1026 LL.B. Wrks. Comp. J.‡
Burns, Catherine, (CV) . . . . . . . . . . . . . . . . . . '51 '79 C.1060 B.A. L.1026 J.D. [Burns&B.]
Burns, Ronald F., (CV) . . . . . . . . . . . . . . . . . . . '38 '66 C.608 B.A. L.426 LL.B. [Burns&B.]
Burns & Burns, (CV) . . . . . . . . . . . . . . . . . . . . . . . . . . . . . . . . . . . . . . . 2201 Court St.
Calkins, Douglas H., (CV) . . . . . . . . . . . . '45 '83 C.112 B.A. L.464 J.D. Asst. City Atty.
Campbell, Robert, (BV) . . . . . . . . . . . . . . . '52 '80 C.112 B.A. L.1067 J.D. [Campbell&C.]
Campbell & Clark, A P.C., (BV) . . . . . . . . . . . . . . . . . . . . . . . . . . . . 1648 Riverside Dr.

**Carlton, Stephen S., (BV) '42 '69 C&L.770 B.S., J.D.**
**1716 Court Street, 96001**
**Telephone: 916-244-3778 Fax: 916-241-6167**
***PRACTICE AREAS: Criminal Law (100%).**
**Practice Limited to Criminal Defense in State and Federal Courts.**
***See Professional Biographies, REDDING, CALIFORNIA***

**Carpenter, Linda M.**, (BV) . . . . . . . . . . . '50 '79 C.112 B.A. L.1026 J.D. [[A] Maire,M.&B.]

**Carr, Kennedy, Peterson & Frost, A Law Corporation, (AV) [BB]**
**420 Redcliff Drive, P.O. Box 492396, 96049**
**Telephone: 916-222-2100 Fax: 916-222-0504**
**Francis Carr (1875-1944); Lawrence J. Kennedy, Sr. (1883-1975); Laurence J. Kennedy, Jr. (1918-1986); Laurence W. Carr (1912-1991); R. Russ Peterson; Daniel S. Frost; Robert M. Harding; Evan L. Delgado (Certified Specialist, Taxation Law and Estate Planning, Trust and Probate Law, The State Bar of California Board of Legal Specialization); Stephen H. Baker; Michael P. Ashby (Certified Specialist, Taxation Law, The State Bar of California Board of Legal Specialization); Randall C. Nelson; Robert A. West.**
**General Civil and Trial Practice in all State and Federal Courts. Real Estate, Taxation, Corporation, Commercial, Construction, Negligence, Products Liability, Water Rights, Estate Planning, Probate and Insurance Law.**
**Representative Clients: Chicago Title Insurance Co.; CH2M Hill California, Inc.; Fruit Growers Supply Co.; ITT Rayonier, Inc.; Louisiana-Pacific Corp.; Minnesota Mining & Manufacturing; Northbrook Insurance Co.; Roseburg Lumber Co.; Security Union Title Insurance Co.; Stewart Title Insurance Co.**
***See Professional Biographies, REDDING, CALIFORNIA***

Carter, J. Ross . . . . . . . . . . . . . . . . . . . . . . . . . . . . . '42 '70 C.112 A.B. L.464 U.S. Mag.
**Case, David L.**, (AV) . . . . . . . . . . . . . . '47 '73 C.905 B.A. L.1065 J.D. [[A] D.Barr&Assoc.]
*PRACTICE AREAS: Mediation; Trial.
**Challe, Cherry L.** . . . . . . . . . . . . . . . . '62 '91 C.112 B.A. L.61 J.D. [[A] R.L.Montarbo]
*LANGUAGES: Spanish.
*PRACTICE AREAS: Insurance Defense; Employer Liability; Subrogation.
Cibula, Franklin S., (BV) . . . . . . . . . . . . . . . '41 '66 C.674 A.B. L.1066 J.D. 1743 Tehama St.
Cibula, Mark Hanbury . . . . . . . . . . . . . . . . '66 '94 C.112 B.A. L.464 J.D. 1743 Tehama St.
Clark, Sandra J., (BV) . . . . . . . . . . . . . . . . '50 '81 C.763 B.S. L.1067 J.D. [Campbell&C.]

**Clement, Fredrick E. '60 '87 C.1239 B.A. L.1065 J.D.**
**280 Hemsted Drive, Suite C, 96002**
**Telephone: 916-224-7700 Fax: 916-224-2284**
**Business, Real Estate and General Civil Litigation; Corporations.**
***See Professional Biographies, REDDING, CALIFORNIA***

**Collins, Ralph T., III**, (CV) . . . . . . . . . . . . '61 '89 C.101 B.A. L.464 J.D. [Reese,S.W.&S.]
*PRACTICE AREAS: Civil Litigation; Appellate Practice.
**Cooper, Cynthia L.** . . . . . . . . . . . . . . . . . . '63 '93 C.839 B.S. L.1137 J.D. [[A] Maire,M.&B.]
Costello, Peter, (BV) . . . . . . . . . . . . . . . . . . '37 '65 C.112 B.A. L.770 J.D. 1738 Yuba St.

**Cowan, Dennis K., (AV) '40 '65 C.976 B.A. L.813 J.D. [BB]**
**280 Hemsted Drive, Suite B, P.O. Box 992090, 96099-2090**
**Telephone: 916-221-7300 Fax: 916-221-7389**
**Email: dennisk@snowcrest.net**
**Debtor and Creditor, Bankruptcy, Reorganizations, Collections and Commercial Law, Real Property, Business, and Corporation Law and Related Litigation in Federal Courts.**
***See Professional Biographies, REDDING, CALIFORNIA***

Cowling, Roger H., (BV) . . . . . . . . . . '39 '69 C.768 B.S. L.1065 J.D. 2301 Park Marina Dr.

**Craig and Shepherd**
**(See Chico)**

Curle, Wilson . . . . . . . . . . . . . . . . . . . . . . . . . '45 '72 C.477 B.A. L.273 J.D. Mun. Ct. J.
Dacquisto, Michael P., II . . . . . . . . . . . . . . '54 '78 C.813 B.A. L.800 J.D. 1901 Court St.
Dean, Stephen M., (BV) . . . . . . . . . . . . . . . . . '50 '76 C.112 B.A. L.1065 J.D. [S.M.Dean]
Dean, Stephen M., A Law Corporation, (BV) . . . . . . . . . . . . . . . . . . . 1300 West St., Suite 1
**Deems, Michael R.**, (BV) . . . . . . . . . . . . . . '53 '85 C.1253 B.A. L.767 J.D. [[A] Sinclair&H.]
*PRACTICE AREAS: Trials; Personal Injury Defense; Hospital and Professional Negligence; Products Liability; Insurance Coverage.
**Delgado, Evan L.**, (BV) . . . . . . . . . . . . . . . '59 '84 C.112 B.A. L.1067 J.D. [Carr,K.P.&F.]
*PRACTICE AREAS: Tax Law; Estate Planning and Administration; Business Transactions; Business Law.
DiBella, Nicolas M. W. '49 '75 C.383 B.A. L.421 J.D.
Staff Atty., State Comp. Ins. Fund
Dooley, James T., III, (BV) . . . . . . . . . . . . . '51 '77 C.112 A.B. L.464 J.D. 1549 Chestnut St.
Dukarich, Gary . . . . . . . . . . . . . . . . . . . . . . . '59 '88 C.453 S.B. L.36 J.D. 4881 Saratoga Dr.
Dunlap, John P., (BV) . . . . . . . . . . . . . . . . . '42 '69 C.112 A.B. L.1066 J.D. P.O. Box 994065
Durall, Richard M. . . . . . . . . . . . . . . . . . . . . . . . . '23 '51 C.112 L.809 LL.B. 2684 Ivy Hill Dr.‡
Eaton, R. B. . . . . . . . . . . . . . . . . . . . . . . . . . . . . '14 '38 C&L.813 B.A., J.D. Ret. Supr. Ct. J.‡
Eckhoff, Robert G. . . . . . . . . . . . . . . . . . . '28 '60 C.112 L.1065 LL.B. Wkrs. Comp. J.
Edwards, David L., (BV) . . . . . . . . . . . . . '46 '82 C.169 B.A. L.426 J.D. 434 Redcliff, Ste. B
**Enochian, Steven R.**, (AV) . . . . . . . . . . . . . . . '47 '74 C.112 B.S. L.284 J.D. [Moss&E.]
**Falbo, John S.** . . . . . . . . . . . . . . . . . . '65 '92 C.1060 B.A. L.464 J.D. [[A] Laughlin,F.L.&M.]
*PRACTICE AREAS: Workers' Compensation.
**Favor, J. Michael**, (BV) . . . . . . . . . . . . . . . '39 '79 C.871 B.S. L.1049 J.D. [[A] Sinclair&H.]
*LANGUAGES: German and French.
*PRACTICE AREAS: Personal Injury; Products Liability; Business Litigation.
Fisher, T. James, (BV) . . . . . . . . . . . . . . . . . . '47 '75 C.147 B.A. L.169 J.D. 1721 Court St.
Fitzpatrick, Michael C., (BV) . . . . . . . . . . . '44 '70 C.154 B.A. L.1066 J.D. 691 Maraglia St.
**Fleharty, Bartley S.**, (CV) . . . . . . . . . . . . . '55 '89 C.147 B.A. L.999 J.D. [Wells,S.S.&G.]
*PRACTICE AREAS: Real Estate Law; Environmental Law; Land Use Law; Contract Law.
Foruria, Theodore . . . . . . . . . . . . . . . . . . . . '33 '61 C.112 B.A. L.767 LL.B. P.O. Box 541
**Frost, Daniel S.**, (AV) . . . . . . . . . . . . . . . . '40 '67 C.768 B.A. L.1066 J.D. [Carr,K.P.&F.]
*PRACTICE AREAS: Commercial and Real Estate Litigation; Environmental Litigation; Personal Injury; Corporate Litigation; Natural Resources Litigation.
Garbutt, Lew A., (BV) . . . . . . . . . . . . . . . . '42 '68 C.112 B.A. L.1065 J.D. 2070 Shasta St.
Garcia, Manuel John, (BV) . . . . . . . . . . . '53 '82 C.112 B.A. L.1067 J.D. 1802 California St.
Gazzigli, Joseph A., (AV) . . . . . . . . . . . . . . . . . . '40 '70 C.112 L.1148 J.D. 1900 Gold St.
Gibson, Gary G., (BV) . . . . . . . . . . . . . . . . . . '56 '81 C.1060 B.A. L.285 J.D. [Manuel&G.]
Graff, James R., (BV) . . . . . . . . . . . . . . . . . . . . . . . . '45 '79 L.1026 J.D. 1300 W. St.
**Graham, Leo J.**, (AV) . . . . . . . . . . . . . . . . '50 '76 C.112 A.B. L.770 J.D. [Wells,S.S.&G.]
*PRACTICE AREAS: Business, Real Estate and Employment Litigation; Construction Law and Litigation; Banking Law; Creditor Bankruptcy.
**Grandaw, Monique** . . . . . . . . . . . . . . . . . . . '65 '92 C.112 B.S. L.809 J.D. [[A] Moss&E.]
Grogan, Richard G., (BV) . . . . . . . . . . . . . . '51 '78 C.112 B.S. L.464 J.D. 1721 Court St.
**Halkides, G. Dennis**, (AV) . . . . . . . . . . . . . '43 '69 C.330 B.A. L.950 J.D. [Halkides&M.]

**Halkides & Morgan, A Professional Corporation, (AV) [BB]**
**833 Mistletoe Lane, P.O. Drawer 492170, 96049-2170**
**Telephone: 916-221-8150 Fax: 916-221-7963**
**Email: gdh@halkides-morgan.com URL: http://www.halkides-morgan.com**
**G. Dennis Halkides; Arthur L. Morgan, Jr.; William D. Ayres; John P. Kelley; Mary Catherine Pearl.**
**General Civil and Trial Practice. Insurance, Products Liability, Medical and Legal Malpractice and Public Entity Defense Law.**
**Representative Clients: American Hardware Mutual Insurance Co.; Anheuser-Busch, Inc.; AVCO Financial Insurance Group; California State Automobile Assn.; Chubb-Pacific Insurance Group.**
**Reference: Bank of America.**
***See Professional Biographies, REDDING, CALIFORNIA***

Hamilton, Michael J., (BV) . . . . . . . . . . . . . . '50 '76 C.112 B.A. L.763 J.D. 1428 West St.
Hanna, Brophy, MacLean, McAleer & Jensen, (AV)
310 Hemsted Dr. (⊙San Fran., Fresno, Sacramento, Oakland, Bakersfield, Santa Rosa, Salinas, Stockton & San Bernardino)
**Harding, Robert M.**, (AV) . . . . . . . . . . . . . '55 '81 C.112 A.B. L.1049 J.D. [Carr,K.P.&F.]
*PRACTICE AREAS: Personal Injury; Commercial and Real Estate Litigation; Construction Litigation.
**Harr, Randall L.**, (BV) . . . . . . . . . . . . . . . . . '55 '82 C.112 B.A. L.464 J.D. [Borton,P.&C.]
*PRACTICE AREAS: Construction Defect; Crop Loss; Premises Liability; Real Estate Malpractice; Attorney Malpractice.
Haskins, Daniel R., (CV) . . . . . . . . . . . . . . . . '54 '82 C.169 B.A. L.1137 J.D. 1714 West St.
**Haslerud, Gary E.** . . . . . . . . . . . . . . . . . . . '68 '95 C.1058 B.B.A. L.744 J.D. [[A] Moss&E.]
Hernandez, Philip E., (CV) . . . . . . . . . . . '31 '70 C.768 B.A. L.1026 J.D. 20076 Vernita Dr.
Heuer, Ronald K. '52 '80 C.36 B.S. L.950 J.D.
(adm. in ID; not adm. in CA) 3764 Siskiyou St.★
**Hill, Larry L.**, (AV) . . . . . . . . . . . . . . . . . '41 '77 C.147 B.S. L.1026 J.D. [Sinclair&H.]
*PRACTICE AREAS: Trials; Personal Injury; Hospital and Professional Negligence; Business Litigation; Products Liability.
Hurley, Jere E., Jr. . . . . . . . . . . . . . . . . . . . '29 '55 C.112 A.B. L.1066 J.D. 1690 Calif St.
**Huscher, David V.**, (BV) . . . . . . . . . . . . '59 '85 C.112 B.S. L.464 J.D. [[A] Laughlin,F.L.&M.]
*LANGUAGES: Korean.
*PRACTICE AREAS: Workers' Compensation; Insurance Defense; Labor Relations; Subrogation.
Jackson, Raymond A. . . . . . . . . . . . . . . . . . . . . . . . . . . . . '36 '70 L.809 J.D. 1824 West St.
Jahr, Karen Keating, (BV) . . . . . . . . . . . . . . . '51 '78 C.1042 B.A. L.426 J.D. Co. Coun.
Jansen, Michael W., (BV) . . . . . . . . . . . . . . '52 '78 C.112 B.A. L.61 J.D. 300 Knollcrest Dr.
Jaqua, Preston, (CV) . . . . . . . . . . . . . . . . . '51 '79 C.1110 B.A. L.1137 J.D. 407 Lake Blvd.

Jens, Jeffrey L., (A Professional Corporation), (BV) '48 '74 C.112 B.A. L.1188 J.D. 1574 W. St.
**Johnson, Lawrence P.** '50 '75 C.112 A.B. L.284 J.D. [Mullen&F.]
**Johnson, Sandra L.**, (CV) '58 '88 C.226 B.A. L.285 J.D. [▣ Moss&E.]
Johnson, Verlin K., (BV) '46 '73 C.101 B.A. L.878 J.D. 1900 Gold St.
Johnstone, Bruce R. '52 '82 C.112 B.A. L.809 J.D. 1749 Mary Lake Dr.
**Jones, Brigham P.**, (BV) '43 '75 C.101 B.A. L.1132 J.D. [Laughlin,F.L.&M.]
*PRACTICE AREAS: Workers' Compensation; Insurance Defense; Subrogation.
Jones, Michael L. '48 '94 1416 W. St.
**Juchau, Todd Alan** '65 '94 C.1060 B.S. L.464 J.D. [▣ Sinclair&H.]
*PRACTICE AREAS: Personal Injury; Hospital and Professional Negligence; Business Litigation; Insurance Defense; Government Entity Litigation.
**Kelley, John P.** '68 '93 C&L.464 B.A., J.D. [▣ Halkides&M.]
Kenealy, Jack, (CV) '52 '77 C.813 B.A. L.1065 J.D. 1905 Pk Marina Dr.
**Kennedy, Daryl E.**, (CV) '57 '86 C.112 A.B. L.1065 J.D. [▣ Reiner&S.]
*PRACTICE AREAS: Product Liability; Medical Malpractice; Wrongful Death; Personal Injury; Negligence Actions.
Kennedy, Donald R. '26 '53 C.112 A.B. L.1065 J.D. Ret. Supr. Ct. J.
**Kenny, John S.**, (AV) '41 '66 C.767 B.A. L.1065 LL.B. [Moss&E.]
**Key, Rodney J.**, (BV) '58 '86 C.169 B.A. L.464 J.D. [Brickwood&K.]
*PRACTICE AREAS: Trials; Civil Litigation; Insurance Defense; Business and Commercial Litigation; Products Liability.
Kinghorn, Darwin '60 '89 C.101 B.A. L.1068 J.D. Dep. Co. Coun.
Kinney, Van O., (BV) '48 '77 C.464 L.1095 J.D. 1388 Court St.
Kucera, George R. '42 '70 C.112 A.B. L.1065 J.D. 15669 Ranchland Dr.
Kucera, John Michael, (CV) '54 '80 C.426 B.B.A. L.1095 J.D. 1416 West St.

**Laughlin, Falbo, Levy & Moresi LLP, (AV)**
**A Partnership including Professional Corporations**
**930 Executive Way, Second Floor, 96002⊙**
**Telephone: 916-222-0268 Fax: 916-222-5705**
**Email: lflm@lflm.com URL: http://lflm.com**
**Henry M. Slowik; Roy D. Woolfstead (Certified Specialist, Workers Compensation Law, The State Bar of California Board of Legal Specialization); Brigham P. Jones;—John S. Falbo; David V. Huscher.**
**General Civil and Trial Practice. Workers' Compensation Defense.**
**San Francisco, California Office: Two Embarcadero Center, Fifth Floor. Telephone: 415-781-6676. Fax: 415-781-6823.**
**Sacramento, California Office: 106 K Street - Second Floor. Telephone: 916-441-6045. Fax: 916-441-7067.**
**Pasadena, California Office: 200 South Los Robles, Suite 500. Telephone: 818-586-9700. Fax: 818-568-3905.**
**Walnut Creek, California Office: 100 Pringle Avenue, Suite 630. Telephone: 510-210-0210. Fax: 510-210-0105.**
**Irvine, California Office: 3 Park Plaza, Suite 1400, P.O. Box 17659. Telephone: 714-251-0120. Fax: 714-251-0125.**
**San Jose, California Office: 1570 The Alameda, Suite 100. Telephone: 408-286-8801. Fax: 408-286-1935.**
*See Professional Biographies, REDDING, CALIFORNIA*

**Leep, Ben**, (AV) '24 '51 C.766 L.767 LL.B. [Leep&T.]
*PRACTICE AREAS: Workers Compensation Law; Negligence Law.

**Leep & Tescher, Law Corporation, (AV)**
**1440 West Street, P.O. Box 2437, 96099**
**Telephone: 916-241-2211**
**Richard J. Asbill (1932-1991); Ben Leep; Maynard K. Tescher, Jr.**
**Workers Compensation, Negligence Law, Probate and Estate Planning.**
**Representative Clients: Lumber and Sawmill Workers Union Local 2608; Retail Clerks Union Local 1364; Machinist Union Local 1397; California State Council of Lumber and Sawmill Workers.**
**References: Bank of America National Trust & Savings Assn.; Bank of California; United California Bank.**

Leisz, Lauren E., (BV) '53 '87 C.766 B.A. L.1065 J.D. 1721 Court St.
Lewellen, George M. '41 '77 C.768 B.S. L.765 J.D. 1330 West St.‡
Lueders, Dean R. '63 '90 C.545 B.A.E. L.546 J.D. 300 Knollcrest Dr.
Lund, William R., Jr. '35 '64 C.813 B.A. L.1065 LL.B. Supr. Ct. J.
Lyerla, Ronald O. '40 '69 C.766 L.765 J.D. 1670 Market St.
Lyman, John C. '53 '88 C&L.1137 B.S.L., J.D. P.O. Box 492512
Lynch, Byron Lee, (BV) '44 '77 C.1131 B.S. L.1137 J.D. [B.L.Lynch]
Lynch, Byron Lee, A Professional Law Corporation, (BV) 6966 Danyeur
**Maire, Eric R.** '65 '95 C.147 B.A. L.1137 J.D. [▣ Maire,M.&B.]
**Maire, Wayne H.**, (AV) '53 '79 C.101 B.A. L.770 J.D. [Maire,M.&B.]

**Maire, Mansell & Beasley, A Law Corporation, (AV) BB**
**2851 Park Marina Drive Suite 300, P.O. Drawer 994607, 96099-4607**
**Telephone: 916-246-6050 Fax: 916-246-6060**
**Email: MAIREMB@AOL.COM**
**Wayne H. Maire; Patrick R. Beasley; Adam M. Pressman; Linda M. Carpenter; David S. Perrine; Cynthia L. Cooper; Eric R. Maire.**
**Insurance Defense and Civil Trial Practice, including Automobile, General and Products Liability, Casualty and Surety Law, Professional Errors and Omissions, Defense of Public Entities, Real Estate Litigation, Construction Litigation and General Litigation.**
*See Professional Biographies, REDDING, CALIFORNIA*

Malloy, William A., (CV) '52 '81 C.112 B.A. L.464 J.D. 1549 Chestnut St.
Mann, Ed, (BV) '49 '78 C.112 B.A. L.174 J.D. [Minoletti,J.&E.M.]
Manuel, Kirk M., (BV) '56 '84 C.112 A.B. L.1065 J.D. [Manuel&G.]
Manuel & Gibson, Law Offices of, (BV) 1616 West St.
**Martinez, Gustavo L.** '68 '94 C.147 B.A. L.770 J.D. [Moss&E.]
*LANGUAGES: Spanish.
Mauro, Donna N. '59 '85 C.112 B.A. L.285 J.D. 310 Hemsted Dr.
Maxion, Richard W., (BV) '49 '79 C.112 A.B. L.284 J.D. 1650 Oregon St.
Maxwell, Gene S. '31 '59 C.112 A.B. L.1065 J.D. 1650 Orgon St.
McAleer, Dennis P., (BV) '49 '78 C.112 B.A. L.1049 J.D. [Hanna,B.M.M.&J.]
**McCabe, Michael R.**, (BV) '60 '85 C.112 B.A. L.61 J.D. [Reese,S.W.&S.]
*PRACTICE AREAS: Civil Litigation; Business Litigation; Securities Consumer Litigation; Class Actions.
McNeill, Walter P., (BV) '54 '80 C.228 B.A. L.169 J.D. [McNeill&B.]
McNeill & Belton, (BV) 280 Hemsted Dr.
Meaney, Donald C. '31 '61 C.860 B.A. L.1065 J.D. Wkr's Comp. J.‡
Meek, William L. '44 '69 C.1163 B.S. L.912 J.D. [Meek&S.]
Meek and Swartz, A Law Corporation, (BV) 1824 West St.
Memeo, J. Randall '59 '84 C.147 B.A. L.464 J.D. Gen. Coun., Shasta Enterprises
Miller, M. Ann '52 '79 C.1044 B.A. L.477 J.D. Legal Servs. of Northern Calif.
Minoletti, John, (AV) '40 '66 C.813 A.B. L.1065 J.D. [Minoletti,J.&E.M.]
Minoletti, John, & Ed Mann, A Law Partnership, (AV) 1737 Yuba St.
**Mondorf, Alfred W.** '49 '86 C.684 B.A. L.1190 J.D. [▣ Borton,P.&C.]
*PRACTICE AREAS: Insurance Defense.

**Montarbo, Richard L., (BV) '60 '87 C.1060 B.S. L.464 J.D.**
**280 Hemsted Drive, Suite 110, 96002**
**Telephone: 916-221-6193 Fax: 916-221-6196**
**(Certified Specialist, Workers' Compensation, The State Bar of California Board of Legal Specialization).**
**Associate: Thomas E. Sundquist; Cherry L. Challe.**
**Workers Compensation. Insurance Defense. General Civil and Business Practice. Subrogation and Personal Injury.**
*See Professional Biographies, REDDING, CALIFORNIA*

Montgomery, Joseph R., Jr., (BV) '52 '78 C.1239 B.A. L.1049 J.D. [Hanna,B.M.M.&J.]
**Morgan, Arthur L., Jr.** '51 '77 C&L.1190 B.S., LL.B. [Halkides&M.]
Morrow, David L., (CV) '27 '65 C.208 B.S. L.1065 LL.B. 1736 Tehama St.
**Moss, Larry B.**, (AV) '45 '71 C.112 B.A. L.426 J.D. [Moss&E.]

**Moss & Enochian, A Law Corporation, (AV) BB**
**2701 Park Marina Drive, P.O. Drawer 994608, 96099-4608**
**Telephone: 916-225-8990 Fax: 916-241-5734**
**Steven R. Enochian; Larry B. Moss; Todd E. Slaughter; Stewart C. Altemus; John S. Kenny; Robert A. Spano;—Sandra L. Johnson; Mark D. Norcross; Eric A. Omstead; Darryl L. Wagner; Monica M. Balavage; Gustavo L. Martinez; Gary E. Haslerud; Monique Grandaw.**
**General Civil Trial Practice. Insurance, Products Liability, Professional Liability, Municipal, Real Estate and Accident and Health Insurance Law.**
**Reference: Tri Counties Bank.**
*See Professional Biographies, REDDING, CALIFORNIA*

**Mudford, Douglas**, (CV) '45 '91 C&L.999 B.A., J.D. [▣ D.Barr&Assoc.]
*PRACTICE AREAS: Personal Injury; Products Liability; Business Litigation; Labor Law; ADA.

**Mullen & Filippi, (AV)**
**1890 Park Marina Drive, Suite 200, 96001⊙**
**Telephone: 916-243-1133**
**Members of Firm: Lawrence P. Johnson (Certified Specialist, Workers Compensation Law, The State Bar of California Board of Legal Specialization); Jenna S. Rouse.**
**Insurance Defense, Workers Compensation, Liability and Subrogation.**
**Other California Offices: San Francisco, San Jose, Sacramento, Fresno, Santa Rosa, Long Beach, Bakersfield, Salinas, Stockton, Woodland Hills and Oakland.**
*See Professional Biographies, SAN FRANCISCO, CALIFORNIA*

Murphy, Earl D. '19 '47 C.605 A.B. L.309 LL.B. 4617 Underwood Dr.‡
**Nelson, Randall C.** '61 '88 C.112 B.A. L.770 J.D. [Carr,K.P.&F.]
*PRACTICE AREAS: Civil Litigation; Construction; Commercial; Personal Injury.

**Newlan, Douglas H., (AV) '31 '62 C.112 A.B. L.426 LL.B. BB**
**434 Redcliff Drive, Suite B, P.O. Box 491736, 96049-1736**
**Telephone: 916-221-0184 Fax: 916-221-8744**
**(Member of California Trial Lawyers Association, with recognized experience as a Trial Lawyer and recognized experience in the fields of Product Liability, Professional Negligence an General Personal Injury).**
**General Civil and Trial Practice, Insurance Defense and Business Litigation.**
*See Professional Biographies, REDDING, CALIFORNIA*

**Nickel, Robin L.** '69 '95 C.147 B.A. L.1188 J.D. [▣ Sinclair&H.]
*PRACTICE AREAS: Trials; Personal Injury Defense; Hospital and Professional Negligence; Products Liability.
**Nisson, Timothy J.**, (AV) '56 '82 C.112 A.B. L.767 J.D. [Nisson&P.]
*PRACTICE AREAS: Complex Civil Litigation.

**Nisson & Pincin, (AV)**
**1737 Yuba Street, P.O. Box 991966, 96099**
**Telephone: 916-246-4201 FAX: 916-246-1426**
**Members of Firm: Timothy J. Nisson; James W. Pincin.**
**Insurance Defense, Business Litigation, Personal Injury.**
*See Professional Biographies, REDDING, CALIFORNIA*

**Norcross, Mark D.** '56 '87 C.861 B.A. L.284 J.D. [▣ Moss&E.]
**O'Connor, Frank**, (BV) '44 '69 C.112 B.A. L.1065 J.D. [Tocher&O.]
*PRACTICE AREAS: Personal Injury; Criminal Law.
Olander, Jocelyn C. '60 '85 C.679 B.A. L.1067 J.D. 1690 Calif. St.
Olsen, Michael G., (CV) '50 '78 C&L.101 B.A., J.D. 1300 W. St.
**Omstead, Eric A.**, (BV) '56 '86 C.147 B.A. L.1065 J.D. [▣ Moss&E.]
Ostling, Eric E., (AV) '62 '87 C.112 A.B. L.464 J.D. 2930 Alfreda Way, Ste. 3 (⊙West Sacramento)
O'Toole-McNally, Erin K. '57 '85 C.429 B.A. L.1137 J.D. 1757 Yuba St.
Packard, David W., (BV) '29 '56 C.927 B.S. L.1065 J.D. [D.W.Packard]
Packard, David W., Inc., (BV) 1300 W. St., Ste. 3
Page, Tamra L., (CV) '58 '85 C.1073 B.A. L.1226 J.D. 1900 Gold St.
Pappas, James C '59 '87 C.112 B.A. L.1148 J.D. 1300 West St.
**Pearl, Mary Catherine** '45 '93 C.147 B.A. L.769 J.D. [▣ Halkides&M.]
**Perrine, David S.** '65 '92 C.112 B.A. L.284 J.D. [Maire,M.&B.]
*PRACTICE AREAS: Personal Injury; Wrongful Death; Negligence Actions; Products Liability; Professional Liability.
**Peterson, R. Russ**, (BV) '39 '66 C.112 B.S. L.1066 J.D. [Carr,K.P.&F.]
*PRACTICE AREAS: Commercial and Real Estate Litigation; Personal Injury; Construction Law; Business and Real Estate Transactions.
Phelps, William H. '21 '50 C.112 B.S. L.1065 J.D. Ret. Supr. Ct. J.
Pickering, Jerrald K. '30 '57 C.169 B.A. L.1065 J.D. [Pickering]
Pickering, Michael L. '58 '83 C.169 B.S. L.464 J.D. [Pickering]
Pickering Law Corporation 1915 Placer St.
**Pincin, James W.**, (BV) '61 '86 C.112 A.B. L.464 J.D. [Nisson&P.]
*PRACTICE AREAS: Complex Civil Litigation.
Porter, Dennis L. '48 '75 C.147 B.S.B.A. L.1026 J.D. 5165 Caterpillar
Prag, Kenneth S., (CV) '— '81 C.675 B.A. L.1137 J.D. 1388 Court St.
**Pressman, Adam M.**, (CV) '65 '91 C.685 B.A. L.464 J.D. [Maire,M.&B.]
Prouty, Gehring C., (BV) '47 '73 C.763 B.A. L.1049 J.D. 1755 E. St.
**Pugh, Archer F.**, (BV) '35 '63 C.112 B.A. L.1065 LL.B. [Pugh&V.]
*PRACTICE AREAS: Business Law (25%); Corporate Law (20%); Estate Planning (20%); Construction Law (15%); Real Estate (20%).

**Pugh & Van Voris, (BV)**
**1300 West Street, 96099**
**Telephone: 916-246-1430 Fax: 916-246-3816**
**Members of Firm: Brian J. Van Voris; Archer F. Pugh.**
**Estate Planning and Probate, Business, Corporate, Construction, Land Use, Real Estate and Taxation.**

Ralston, Michael A. '47 '77 C.628 B.S. L.1137 J.D. Asst. Co. Coun.
Redmon, Joseph H. '22 '52 C.912 A.B. L.477 LL.B. Ret. Supr. Ct. J.
**Reese, John W., Jr.**, (AV) '42 '69 C.101 A.B. L.1068 J.D. [Reese,S.W.&S.]
*PRACTICE AREAS: Real Estate Law; Estate Planning; Probate Law; General Business Law.

**Reese, Smalley, Wiseman & Schweitzer, (AV)**
**1265 Willis Street, P.O. Drawer 994647, 96099-4647**
**Telephone: 916-241-1611 Fax: 916-241-5106**
**John W. Reese, Jr.; Lawrence R. Smalley; Kent I. Wiseman; Howard L. Schweitzer; Victor R. Richardson; Ralph T. Collins, III; Michael R. McCabe.**
**General Business, Civil Litigation, Real Estate, Personal Injury, Land Development, Probate, Estate Planning and Taxation.**
*See Professional Biographies, REDDING, CALIFORNIA*

Rehberg, Robert A. '30 '61 C.906 B.S. L.1066 LL.B. 429 Redcliff Dr.
**Reiner, Russell**, (AV) '51 '78 C.37 B.A. L.1137 J.D. [Reiner&S.]
*PRACTICE AREAS: Personal Injury; Wrongful Death; Product Liability; Medical Malpractice.

**Reiner & Simpson, (AV)**
**2851 Park Marina Drive, Suite 200, 96001**
**Telephone: 916-241-1905 Fax: 916-241-0622**
**Russell Reiner; Robert G. Simpson. Associates: Daryl E. Kennedy.**
**Personal Injury, Products Liability, Medical Malpractice and Wrongful Death.**
*See Professional Biographies, REDDING, CALIFORNIA*

Reiser, Richard E., (BV) ... '53 '79 C.112 B.S. L.1065 J.D. Gifford Construction Company
**Richardson, Victor R.**, (BV) ... '51 '79 C.877 B.S. L.1137 J.D. [Reese,S.W.&S.]
*PRACTICE AREAS: Civil Litigation; Tort Law; Business Litigation.
Richins, Keith W., (BV) ... '46 '80 C.101 B.A. L.1026 J.D. [K.W.Richins]
Richins, Keith W., A Professional Corporation, (BV) ... 2124 Eureka Way
Rodriguez-Ivanhoe, Richard ... '51 '84 C.33 B.A. L.284 J.D. 215 Lake Blvd.
**Rouse, Jenna S.** ... '63 '89 C.294 B.A. L.770 J.D. [Mullen&F.]
Salter, Lee W., (AV) ... '42 '74 C.147 B.S. L.464 J.D. 420 Redcliff Dr.
Schmad, Wayne A. '34 '73 C.911 B.S. L.763 J.D.
(adm. in NE; not adm. in CA) P.O. Box 991478‡
Schmidt, Henry ... '20 '72 C.597 B.S. L.284 J.D. P.O. Box 4641
**Schweitzer, Howard L.**, (BV) ... '41 '67 C.575 B.S. L.472 J.D. [Reese,S.W.&S.]
*PRACTICE AREAS: Taxation; Real Estate Law; General Business Practice.
Scrivner, Chaland B., (CV) ... '— '79 C.1079 B.A. L.408 J.D. 2986 Bechelli Ln.
Sebat, Linda C. ... '48 '85 C.339 B.S. L.464 J.D. 1558 West St.
**Selke, Donald A., Jr.**, (BV) ... '47 '83 C.63 B.S. L.464 J.D. [Wells,S.S.&G.]
*PRACTICE AREAS: Civil Litigation; Employment Law; Real Estate Law; Commercial Landlord and Tenant Law.
Shadwell, Ira M. ... '09 '34 C.112 L.1065 J.D. 1265 Willis St.‡
Simons, Lowell J. ... '32 '64 C.792 B.S.Gen.Eng. L.426 LL.B. 454 Aquamarine Way‡
**Simpson, Robert G.**, (AV) ... '48 '75 C.112 A.B. L.1065 J.D. [Reiner&S.]
*PRACTICE AREAS: Personal Injury; Wrongful Death; Negligence Actions; Products Liability; Medical Malpractice.
**Sinclair, Craig A.**, (BV) ... '44 '73 C.112 B.S. L.464 J.D. [Sinclair&H.]
*PRACTICE AREAS: Trials; Hospital and Professional Negligence; Personal Injury; Business Litigation; Environmental Law.

**Sinclair & Hill, A Law Corporation, (AV)**
**100 East Cypress, Suite 200, 96002**
**Mailing Address: P.O. Box 992710, Redding, CA 96099-2710**
**Telephone: 916-226-9700 FAX: 916-226-9481**
**Craig A. Sinclair; Larry L. Hill;—Michael R. Deems; J. Michael Favor; Todd Alan Juchau; Robin L. Nickel.**
**General Civil and Trial Practice, Insurance, Medical Malpractice, Personal Injury, Business Litigation, Negligence.,**
***See Professional Biographies, REDDING, CALIFORNIA***

Skene, Annette R., (CV) ... '58 '91 C.1077 B.A. L.1068 J.D. 2444 N. Bechelli Lane
**Slaughter, Todd E.**, (BV) ... '53 '79 C.112 B.A. L.464 J.D. [Moss&E.]
**Slowik, Henry M.** ... '52 '85 C.67 B.A. L.1065 J.D. [Laughlin,F.L.&M.]
*PRACTICE AREAS: Workers' Compensation.
Small, Clyde, (AV) ... '24 '51 C&L.813 A.B., LL.B. 2301 Pk. Marina Dr.‡
**Small, Steven A.**, (BV) ... '48 '74 C.112 A.B. L.1065 J.D. [Wells,S.S.&G.]
*PRACTICE AREAS: Estate Planning; Estate Probate Law; Business Law.
**Smalley, Lawrence R.**, (BV) ... '51 '78 C.549 B.S. L.770 J.D. [Reese,S.W.&S.]
*PRACTICE AREAS: Taxation Law; Estate Planning Law; Probate Law; Trust Law; General Corporate Practice.
**Smith, Herbert Richard Harrison** ... '45 '71 C.112 A.B. L.05 LL.B. [H.Smith]⊙
*PRACTICE AREAS: Business Law; Government; Trusts and Estates; General Practice.

**Smith, Harrison, Law Offices of**
**1267 Willis Street, 96001⊙**
**Telephone: 916-246-1222; 241-3510; 241-6359 FAX: 916-246-1941**
**Email: hrharrisonsmith72123.2224@compuserve.com**
**Herbert Richard Harrison Smith; Herbert Stuart Harrison Smith (Resident, Shasta Office).**
**General, Civil, Trial and Appellate Practice. Corporation, Domestic Relations, Probate, Real Estate, Mining, Natural Resources, Water Rights and Private International Law. Commissioners for Affidavits for British Columbia.**
**Shasta, California Office: Shurtleff Alley, P.O. Box 367, 96087. Telephone: 916-241-3510; 241-6359. FAX: 916-246-1941.**
***See Professional Biographies, REDDING, CALIFORNIA***

**Spano, Robert A.**, (CV) ... '56 '81 C.1267 B.A. L.464 J.D. [Moss&E.]
Stotter, Jeffrey C. ... '60 '90 C.112 B.A. L.823 J.D. 434 Redcliff Dr.
**Sundquist, Thomas E.** ... '56 '94 C.147 B.S. L.464 J.D. [Ⓐ R.L.Montarbo]
*PRACTICE AREAS: Workers Compensation; Insurance Defense; Civil Practice; Business Law; Subrogation.
Suter, Jack, (BV) ... '45 '79 C.627 B.S. L.1137 J.D. 1548 West St.
Swanson, Jeffery J. ... '62 '91 C.260 B.A. L.1067 J.D. 280 Hemsted Dr.
**Swanson, L. Alan**, (AV) ... '51 '77 C.112 B.A. L.770 J.D. [Bandell S.]
*PRACTICE AREAS: Education; Employer/Employee Relations; Administrative Law.
Swanson, Robert K., (CV) ... '46 '84 C.957 B.S. L.1137 J.D. Dep. Dist. Atty.
Swartz, Russell J., (BV) ... '46 '73 C.243 B.A. L.912 J.D. [Meek&S.]
Sweeney, Marguerite, (BV) ... '— '78 C.112 B.A. L.1065 J.D. 1414 Gold St.
**Tescher, Maynard K., Jr.**, (AV) ... '43 '72 C.740 B.A. L.767 J.D. [Leep&T.]
*PRACTICE AREAS: Workers Compensation Law; Probate Law; Estate Planning Law.
Tillman, Patrick J., (BV) ... '41 '72 C.950 L.284 J.D. 3462 Bechelli Ln., Suite G
**Timmons, Duane H.**, (AV) ... '45 '72 C.309 A.B. L.813 J.D. [Wise,W.T.&W.]⊙
**Tocher, G. Neil**, (AV) ... '26 '52 C.999 L.1065 LL.B. [Tocher&O.]
*PRACTICE AREAS: Personal Injury; Wrongful Death; Negligence Actions.

**Tocher & O'Connor, (AV) BR**
**1901 Park Marina Drive, 96001**
**Telephone: 916-244-2525 Fax: 916-244-4941**
**Members of Firm: G. Neil Tocher; Frank O'Connor.**
**Personal Injury Law.**
***See Professional Biographies, REDDING, CALIFORNIA***

Trindade, Tamera C., (CV) ... '62 '88 C.1079 B.A. L.1189 J.D. 2124 Eureka Way
Underwood, C. Harold ... '23 '52 C.766 L.1065 J.D. 1869 Mary Lake Dr.‡
**Van Voris, Brian J.**, (BV) ... '48 '78 C.768 B.S. L.765 J.D. [Pugh&V.]
*PRACTICE AREAS: Estate Planning (50%); Probate (15%); Business Law (20%); Taxation (15%).
Vegh, Mark A. ... '59 '86 C.628 B.S. L.1051 J.D. Timber Operators Council
**Wagner, Darryl L.** ... '66 '92 C.112 B.A. L.464 J.D. [Ⓐ Moss&E.]
Wallace, Patrick E. ... '52 '91 C&L.112 A.B., J.D. 2905 Forest Hills Dr.
**Weil, Frederick J.** ... '58 '82 C.800 A.B. L.37 J.D. [Wells,S.S.&G.]
*PRACTICE AREAS: Tax Law; Business Law; Corporation Law; Health Care Law.
Welch, Howard L., (BV) ... '42 '69 C.768 B.A. L.1065 J.D. Dep. Pub. Def.
**Wells, J.M., Jr.**, (BV) ... '40 '66 C.813 B.A. L.1065 J.D. [Wells,S.S.&G.]
*PRACTICE AREAS: Business Law; Real Estate Law; Corporation Law; Estate Planning Law; Probate Law.

**Wells, Small, Selke & Graham, A Law Corporation, (AV)**
**292 Hemsted Drive, P.O. Box 991828, 96099-1828**
**Telephone: 916-223-1800 Fax: 916-223-1809**
**J.M. Wells, Jr.; Steven A. Small (Certified Specialist, Estate Planning, Trust and Probate Law, The State Bar of California Board of Legal Specialization); Leo J. Graham; Donald A. Selke, Jr.; Bartley S. Fleharty; Frederick J. Weil (Certified Specialist, Taxation Law, The State Bar of California Board of Legal Specialization).**
**Civil Litigation, Insurance and Employment Litigation, Corporation, Real Estate, Water, Business, Creditor Bankruptcy/Collection, Banking Law, Estate Planning and Probate, Environmental, Municipal and Land Use Law.**
***See Professional Biographies, REDDING, CALIFORNIA***

**West, Robert A.** ... '65 '92 C.36 B.S. L.990 J.D. [Ⓐ Carr,K.P.&F.]
*PRACTICE AREAS: Taxation; Estate Planning; Transactional.

White, James J. ... '38 '72 C.768 B.S. L.1065 J.D. Staff Coun., State Comp. Ins. Fund
White, Michael F., (BV) ... '52 '78 C.94 B.A. L.1049 J.D. [Hanna,B.M.M.&J.]
Whitfield, Lawrence M. ... '26 '66 C.628 B.S. L.1132 LL.B. 1650 Oregon St., Suite 209
Wilson, David A. ... '49 '87 1416 West St.
Wingate, W. Leonard, (AV) ... '38 '65 C.112 B.A. L.1065 LL.B. City Atty.

**Wise, Wiezorek, Timmons & Wise, A Professional Corporation, (AV)**
**443 Redcliff Drive, Suite 230⊙**
**Telephone: 916-221-7632 Fax: 916-221-8832**
**Duane H. Timmons.**
**General Civil and Trial Practice in State and Federal Courts. Corporation, International Business, Insurance, Real Property, Immigration, Estate Planning, Probate and Tax Law.**
**Long Beach, California Office: 3700 Santa Fe Avenue, Suite 300, P.O. Box 2190. Telephone: 213-834-5028. Fax: 213-834-8018.**
***See Professional Biographies, REDDING, CALIFORNIA***

**Wiseman, Kent I.**, (BV) ... '44 '79 C.101 B.A. L.1026 J.D. [Reese,S.W.&S.]
*PRACTICE AREAS: Civil Litigation; Collection Law; General Business Law.
**Woolfstead, Roy D.** ... '51 '76 C.35 B.S. L.1137 J.D. [Laughlin,F.L.&M.]
*PRACTICE AREAS: Workers' Compensation.
Wyatt, James A., (AV) ... '48 '78 C.880 B.A. L.37 J.D. 2130 Eureka Way
Youmans, Russell O. ... '51 '78 C.112 B.A. L.767 J.D. [Hanna,B.M.M.&J.]
Zamarian, Paul ... '41 '71 C.24 B.S. L.904 J.D. 1254 California St.
Zanotto, Fred A., (BV) ... '48 '76 C.112 B.A. L.767 J.D. 1690 Calif. St. (⊙Santa Rosa)

## REDLANDS, 60,394, *San Bernardino Co.*

**Akemon, Richard** ... '40 '72 C&L.1137 B.S., J.D. [Ⓐ Elliot,L.L.&S.] (⊙Redlands)
*PRACTICE AREAS: Insurance Defense; Medical Malpractice Defense.
Albrektson, Kathleen B. ... '49 '89 C.228 B.A. L.398 J.D. [Ⓒ R.E.Bawden]
Alvarez, Donald R., (BV) ... '52 '81 C.684 B.A. L.426 J.D. [Brunick,A.&B.]⊙
Arden, John ... '24 '51 C&L.818 LL.B. Ret. Mun. J.
Barr, Kenneth R. ... '50 '82 C&L.1137 B.S.L., J.D. Mun. J.
Battersby, Marguerite P. ... '49 '84 C.112 B.A. L.174 J.D. [Brunick,A.&B.]⊙
Bawden, Richard E., (BV) ... '46 '72 C.112 B.A. L.629 J.D. [R.E.Bawden]
Bawden, Richard E., A Prof. Law Corp., (BV) ... 300 E. State St.
Bevins, Kevin B. ... '57 '89 L.1198 J.D. [Ⓐ Tucker&R.]
Billington, Randall J. ... '51 '93 C.112 A.B. L.1067 J.D. 707 Brookside Ave.
Blanck, Eugene L. '21 '42 L.64 LL.B.
(adm. in MD; not adm. in CA) 130 Hillside Way‡
Blankenship, Mark I. ... '60 '87 C.976 B.A. L.861 J.D. [Kritzer&B.] (⊙Palm Springs)

**Branch, John W. '58 '90 C.684 B.S. L.1137 J.D.**
**2068 Orange Tree Lane, Suite 202, 92374**
**Telephone: 909-335-3533 Fax: 909-335-3530**
**Taxation, Business Law, Real Estate, Estate Planning and Probate.**

Brooks, Claudia M., (BV) ... '— '79 C.112 A.B. L.1065 J.D. 626 S. Buena Vista St.
Brunick, William J., (AV) ... '44 '70 C.768 A.B. L.1065 J.D. [Brunick,A.&B.]⊙
Brunick, Alvarez & Battersby, Professional Law Corporation, (AV)
215 Cajon St. (⊙San Bernardino)
Burkhart, Paul J. ... '56 '86 C.101 L.1198 J.D. [Tucker&R.]
Busi, V. Kumar ... '65 '94 C.035 B.A.S. L.809 J.D. 707 Brookside Avenue
Caporael, Francis T. ... '27 '75 C.339 L.1186 J.D. 1426 Pleasantview Dr.
**Carey-Wilson, Jacqueline** ... '64 '95 C.1109 B.A. L.809 J.D. [Ⓐ Welebir&M.]
*PRACTICE AREAS: Products Liability; Personal Injury.
Carlson, Daryl H., (AV) ... '51 '78 C&L.101 B.A., J.D. 104 E. Olive Ave.
Castle, Robert M. ... '23 '49 C.112 L.800 J.D. 280 La Colina Dr.
Cockrell, Christopher L., Sr., (AV) ... '55 '80 C.112 B.A. L.809 J.D. [Tucker&R.]
Coffin, James E., (BV) ... '51 '86 C.1163 B.S. L.1049 J.D. 222 E. Olive Ave.
**Cramer, Kathleen M.** ... '53 '82 C.1109 B.A. L.1137 J.D. [Ziprick,S.H.&C.]
Cranmer, Rex W. ... '18 '44 C&L.813 B.A., LL.B. 115 E. Sunset Dr. S.‡
Daniel, Deborah A., (BV) ... '54 '79 C.1110 B.A. L.800 J.D. 1916 Orange Tree Lane
**Dill, Fred H.**, (AV) ... '34 '59 C.112 L.800 LL.B. [Dill&S.]
*PRACTICE AREAS: Construction; Negligence; Real Estate; Corporate Law; Business Law.

**Dill & Showler, (AV)**
**411 Brookside Avenue, 92373**
**Telephone: 909-793-2377 Fax: 909-798-6557**
**Members of Firm: Fred H. Dill; Scott Showler.**
**General Civil and Trial Practice. Construction, Negligence, Insurance, Probate, Estate Planning, Real Estate, Corporate and Business Law.**
**Representative Clients: Alpha Corporation of Tennessee; Homestead Supplies, Inc.; Riverside County Lumber Co.; American Buildings Co.**
***See Professional Biographies, REDLANDS, CALIFORNIA***

Donahue, Bernard E., Jr. ... '44 '76 C.999 B.A. L.1202 J.D. 101 E. Redlands Blvd.
**Elliot, D. Scott** ... '52 '77 C.1077 B.A. L.809 J.D. [Elliot,L.L.&S.]⊙
*PRACTICE AREAS: Insurance Defense; Medical Malpractice Defense.

**Elliot, Lamb, Leibl & Snyder, (AV)**
**101 East Redlands Boulevard, Suite 285, 92373⊙**
**Telephone: 909-792-8861 Fax: 909-798-6997**
**Michael V. Lamb; Michael R. Snyder; Loren S. Leibl; D. Scott Elliot; Rebecca J. Hogue;—Bryan R. Reid; Richard Akemon; Douglas K. Mann; William R. Moffitt; Jeffrey Alan Walker.**
**Civil Litigation. Insurance Defense and Medical Malpractice Defense.**
**Encino, California Office: Suite 301, 16501 Ventura Boulevard, 91436. Telephone: 818-380-0123; 310-553-5767. Fax: 818-380-0124.**
**Orange County Office: 333 South Anita Drive, Suite 660, Orange, California, 92668. Telephone: 714-978-6255. Facsimile: 714-978-9087.**
***See Professional Biographies, REDLANDS, CALIFORNIA***

Ely, Northcutt, (P.C.) ... '03 '26 C&L.813 B.A., J.D. 300 E. State St.

**Farrell, C L, (CV) '55 '88 C.766 B.A. L.284 J.D.**
**P.O. Box 1470, 92373-1470**
**Telephone: 909-307-2677 Fax: 909-307-2680**
**Probate, Conservatorship, Guardianships, General Civil Trial Practice.**
***See Professional Biographies, REDLANDS, CALIFORNIA***

**Fergeson, Donald R.** ... '56 '93 C.1198 B.S.L. L.999 J.D. [Hartnell,H.&F.]⊙
*PRACTICE AREAS: Personal Injury; Civil Probate and Trust Litigation.
Fishell, Floyd F., (BV) ... '51 '85 C.846 B.S. L.1198 J.D. P.O. Box 6904
Forthun, Paula, (BV) ... '44 '80 C.1109 B.A. L.809 J.D. [Reynolds&F.]
**Fox, Jere L.** ... '51 '77 C.1163 B.A. L.990 J.D. [Ⓒ Hartnell,H.&F.] (⊙Yucaipa, Riverside)
*PRACTICE AREAS: Probate Litigation and Will Contests; Conservatorship Litigation; Trust Litigation; Real Property Law.
Francone, Bruce E. ... '43 '73 C.453 B.S. L.560 J.D. 435 Via Vista Dr.★
Gillespie, Kevin F., (BV) ... '65 '91 C.1077 B.A. L.426 J.D. 222 E. Olive Ave., Ste. 1
Glauser, Douglas K., (BV) ... '53 '81 C.1085 B.A. L.61 J.D. [Tucker&R.]
Graeber, Charles C., (BV) ... '21 '50 C&L.800 A.B., LL.B. 300 E. State St., Suite 450‡
Hales, Edwin B. ... '39 '70 C.684 B.A. L.1065 J.D. 826 Brookside Ave.‡
**Harper, James R.** ... '57 '86 C.101 B.S. L.464 J.D. [McPeters M.S.&H.]⊙
*LANGUAGES: Korean.
**Harter, Stanley A.**, (AV) ... '58 '87 C.101 B.S. L.61 J.D. [Mirau,E.C.H.&L.]⊙
*PRACTICE AREAS: Business; Tax; Estate Planning.

CAA509P

CALIFORNIA—REDLANDS
MARTINDALE-HUBBELL LAW DIRECTORY 1997

**Hartnell, Bryan C.**, (AV) ................'49 '75 C.636 B.A. L.464 J.D. [Hartnell,H.&F.]⊙
*PRACTICE AREAS: Probate; Conservatorships; Estate Planning.

**Hartnell, Horspool & Fox, A Professional Corporation, (AV)**
**25757 Redlands Boulevard, 92373-8453⊙**
**Telephone: 909-796-6881 Fax: 909-796-4196**
**Bryan C. Hartnell (Certified Specialist, Estate Planning, Trust and Probate Law, The State Bar of California Board of Legal Specialization); J. David Horspool (Certified Specialist, Estate Planning, Trust and Probate Law, The State Bar of California Board of Legal Specialization); Walter Moore; Donald R. Fergeson. Of Counsel: Jere L. Fox.**
**Probate, Estate Planning, Trust Administration, Conservatorships, Guardianships Personal Injury and Negligence Law, Real Property and Business Transaction, Corporate and Selected Civil Litigation.**
**Reference: Redlands Federal Bank (Loma Linda).**
**Yucaipa, California Office: 34544 Yucaipa Boulevard. Telephone: 909-790-6288. Fax: 909-790-6398.**

*See Professional Biographies, REDLANDS, CALIFORNIA*

**Hatt, Daniel T.**, (AV) ............'55 '80 C.637 B.A. L.1049 J.D. [McPeters M.S.&H.]⊙
Haun, Kymberly L. ........................ '64 '90 C.1075 B.S. L.61 J.D. [Tucker&R.]
Haynal, Andrew J., (BV) ................. '49 '78 C.32 L.1137 J.D. 25757 Redlands Blvd.
**Heinrich, Kerry L.** ................... '58 '83 C.897 B.A. L.629 J.D. [Ziprick,S.H.&C.]
**Hogue, Rebecca J.** .................. '54 '84 C.112 B.A. L.1137 J.D. [Elliot,L.L.&S.]⊙
*PRACTICE AREAS: Insurance Defense; Medical Malpractice Defense.
**Horspool, J. David**, (BV) ................. '50 '81 C&L.101 B.S., J.D. [Hartnell,H.&F.]⊙
*LANGUAGES: Portuguese.
*SPECIAL AGENCIES: Administrative Hearing Officer; County of San Bernardino Board of Supervisors.
*PRACTICE AREAS: Probate; Trust Administration; Conservatorships; Business Transactions; Real Property.
Hudspeth, Thomas S. ..........................................'49 '81 L.1198 J.D. Drawer 1770
Hultman, John R. ................................'51 '78 C&L.398 B.A., J.D. 1137 Via Antibes
Iwakoshi, Kenneth A. ........................ '61 '91 C.112 B.S. L.61 J.D. [Ⓐ Kritzer&B.]
Jones, William E. (Jack) ............'25 '68 C.999 L.45 LL.B. Coun., State Farm Ins. Cos.
Jordon, Carl F. ................................ '31 '59 C.363 B.A. L.1003 J.D. P.O. Box 8818
Jorgensen, Allen C., (CV) '52 '81 C.112 B.A. L.1049 J.D.
316 E. Olive Ave. (⊙Banning)
Jurkovich, John T. ...................... '44 '79 C.1075 B.S. L.1137 J.D. 104 E. State St.
Kean, David W. '54 '79 C.628 B.S. L.629 J.D.
(adm. in OR; not adm. in CA) 110 Bellvue Ave.‡
**Kelly, Arthur W., Jr.**, (AV) ......................... '21 '55 L.809 [▣ Welebir&M.] ‡
*PRACTICE AREAS: Personal Injury Litigation.
Keough, Barbara A. ..................................'55 '90 C.999 L.1198 J.D. [Tucker&R.]
Kritzer, Lawrence, (BV) .................. '34 '60 C.112 B.A. L.1068 J.D. [Kritzer&B.]⊙
Kritzer & Blankenship, (BV) ...............5 E. Citrus Ave. (⊙Torrance & Palm Springs)
**Lamb, Michael V.** .................... '52 '79 C.477 B.A. L.990 J.D. [Elliot,L.L.&S.]⊙
*PRACTICE AREAS: Insurance Defense; Medical Malpractice Defense.
**Leibl, Loren S.**, (AV) ................ '53 '83 C.1042 B.A. L.809 J.D. [Elliot,L.L.&S.]⊙
*PRACTICE AREAS: Insurance Defense; Medical Malpractice Defense.
MacDonald, Bryant C., (CV) ...... '51 '82 C.611 B.A. L.1049 J.D. 2048 Orange Tree Ln.
Mackin, Kevin ................................ '48 '75 C.112 B.S. L.1137 J.D. [Tucker&R.]
**Mann, Douglas K.** ...'65 '92 C.1075 B.S.I.E. L.1292 J.D. [Ⓐ Elliot,L.L.&S.] (⊙Redlands)
*PRACTICE AREAS: Insurance Defense; Medical Malpractice Defense.
**McAlearney, John D., Jr.**, (AV) '44 '70 C.602 B.A. L.1065 J.D.
[McPeters M.S.&H.]⊙
**McCune, Richard D., Jr.** ..................'59 '87 C.1163 B.S. L.800 J.D. [Welebir&M.]
*PRACTICE AREAS: Products Liability; Personal Injury.
**McPeters, Thomas H.**, (AV) ..... '37 '60 C.112 B.A. L.469 LL.B. [McPeters M.S.&H.]⊙

**McPeters McAlearney Shimoff & Hatt, A Professional Corporation, (AV)**
**615 Brookside Avenue, Suite B, P.O. Box 2084, 92373⊙**
**Telephone: 909-792-8919 Fax: 909-792-6234**
**Thomas H. McPeters (Certified Specialist, Taxation Law, The State Bar of California Board of Legal Specialization); John D. McAlearney, Jr.; Paul M. Shimoff (Certified Specialist, Taxation Law, The State Bar of California Board of Legal Specialization); Daniel T. Hatt (Certified Specialist, Estate Planning, Trust and Probate Law, The State Bar of California Board of Legal Specialization); James R. Harper.**
**Taxation, Business, Pension Plans, Estate Planning, Trusts and Probate Law.**
**San Bernardino, California Office: 330 North D Street, Suite 320, P.O. Box 6182. Telephone: 909-884-7747. Fax: 909-885-0848.**

*See Professional Biographies, REDLANDS, CALIFORNIA*

**Mirau, Edwards, Cannon, Harter & Lewin, A Professional Corporation, (AV)**
**222 East Olive Avenue, Suite 1, 92373⊙**
**Telephone: 909-793-0200 Fax: 909-792-2359**
**Stanley A. Harter (Certified Specialist, Taxation Law, The State Bar of California Board of Legal Specialization).**
**Business Law, Real Estate, Taxation, Partnerships, Corporations, Commercial Law, Wills and Trusts, and Health Care Law.**
**San Bernardino, California Office: 599 North "E" Street, Suite 205. Telephone 909-888-0200. Fax: 909-384-0203.**

*See Professional Biographies, REDLANDS, CALIFORNIA*

**Moffitt, William R.** ..................... '53 '95 C.112 B.A. L.809 J.D. [Elliot,L.L.&S.]
*PRACTICE AREAS: Insurance Defense; Medical Malpractice Defense.
**Moore, Walter** ................................ '57 '89 L.1137 J.D. [Hartnell,H.&F.]⊙
*PRACTICE AREAS: Probate; Conservatorships; Estate Planning; Family Law.
Mulligan, Richard A., (BV) ...........'29 '53 C&L.188 A.B., LL.B. 107 Garden Hill Dr.‡
Myers, Gary A., (CV) .................. '46 '78 C.1163 B.A. L.1137 J.D. 308 W. State St.
Nelms, E. Joan .............................. '43 '90 C.999 L.1137 J.D. 25757 Relands Blvd.
Palmer, Edward D. ...................... '30 '56 C.112 A.B. L.800 LL.B. 1310 Elizabeth St.
**Reid, Bryan R.** .................... '64 '91 C.1107 B.A. L.809 J.D. [Ⓐ Elliot,L.L.&S.]⊙
*PRACTICE AREAS: Insurance Defense; Medical Malpractice Defense.
Reider, D. Brian, (BV) '51 '76
C.1110 B.A. L.464 J.D. Sr. V.P. & Gen. Coun., Redlands Fed. Bk.
Reilly, Tara ...................................... '57 '89 C.112 B.A. L.990 J.D. Mun. Ct. J.
Reynolds, Robert L. ......................... '60 '90 C.684 B.S. L.1351 J.D. [Tucker&R.]
Reynolds & Forthun, (BV) ....................................300 E. State St., Ste 450
Ricks, Robert D., (BV) .....................'45 '73 C.1077 B.A. L.1095 J.D. [Tucker&R.]
Rookhuyzen, Lawrence S. ...................'49 '80 C.101 B.A. L.1137 J.D. [Tucker&R.]

**Roth, John E.**
**(See San Bernardino)**

Ryberg, Richard J. '47 '78 C.118 B.A. L.823 J.D.
(adm. in NY; not adm. in CA) 12688 Highview Ln.‡
**Schilt, E. Nathan**, (BV) ................. '48 '73 C.866 B.A. L.1068 J.D. [Ziprick,S.H.&C.]
**Shimoff, Paul M.**, (AV) ..........'47 '72 C.112 B.A. L.1065 J.D. [McPeters M.S.&H.]⊙
**Showler, Scott**, (BV) ..........................'46 '72 C.1110 B.A. L.1065 J.D. [Dill&S.]
*PRACTICE AREAS: Real Estate Law; Construction Litigation; Business Litigation; Probate.
Smith, James A., (AV) ...........'— '53 C.684 A.B. L.1065 J.D. 626 S. Buena Vista St.‡
**Snyder, Michael R.** .............. '58 '84 C.1042 B.A. L.1137 J.D. [Elliot,L.L.&S.]⊙
*PRACTICE AREAS: Insurance Defense; Medical Malpractice Defense.
Stanfield, Janet L. .................. '54 '88 C.645 B.S. L.1198 J.D. 229 Grand View Dr.
Stoker, Donald D. ............................ '19 '48 C&L.878 B.A., J.D. 719 Ester Way‡
**Theios, George S.**, (BV) ............... '48 '81 C.112 B.A. L.1137 J.D. [Ⓐ Welebir&M.]
*PRACTICE AREAS: Personal Injury Law; Products Liability.

Torchia, Michael J., (CV) .................'56 '81 C.800 B.A. L.1049 J.D. P.O. Box 8363
Torres, Abel ................................'56 '91 C.563 B.S. L.426 J.D. 1324 Arroyo Crest
Tucker, M. Wayne ............................'49 '81 C.999 A.A. L.1137 J.D. [Tucker&R.]
Tucker & Ricks, (AV) ............................................ 1615 Orange Tree Lane
Turner, Allen Charles ...................... '39 '89 C.774 B.S. L.336 J.D. P.O. Box 7704‡
Tyler, Stephen H. .............................'59 '85 C.101 B.S. L.990 J.D. 300 E. State St.
**Walker, Jeffrey Alan** ................ '70 '93 C.112 B.S. L.809 J.D. [Ⓐ Elliot,L.L.&S.]
*PRACTICE AREAS: Medical Malpractice; Insurance Defense.
**Welebir, Douglas F.**, (AV) .................'43 '66 C.999 A.B. L.800 J.D. [Welebir&M.]
*LANGUAGES: Spanish.
*PRACTICE AREAS: Products Liability Law; Personal Injury Law; Toxic Tort Litigation; Product Defect Class Action.

**Welebir & McCune, A Professional Law Corporation, (AV) BB**
**2068 Orange Tree Lane, Suite 215, 92374**
**Mailing Address: P.O. Box 10488, San Bernardino, California 92423**
**Telephone: 909-335-0444 Fax: 909-335-0452**
**Email: WM_Law@MSN.COM**
**Douglas F. Welebir; Richard D. McCune, Jr.;—George S. Theios; Jacqueline Carey-Wilson. Of Counsel: Arthur W. Kelly, Jr. (Retired).**
**Practice limited to Catastrophic Personal Injury and Wrongful Death, Products Liability, Aviation, Railroad and Toxic Torts. Class Actions related to Defective Products and Mass Torts.**

*See Professional Biographies, REDLANDS, CALIFORNIA*

**Whitley, Brian E.** ................ '66 '91 C.1163 B.B.A. L.800 J.D. [Ⓐ Ziprick,S.H.&C.]
Wieland, George A., Jr., (BV) .................. '46 '77 C.37 B.S. L.464 J.D. [Tucker&R.]

**Wilson, Guay P., (BV) '35 '61 C.012 B.A. L.1068 LL.B.**
**14 North Eighth Street, P.O. Box 166, 92373**
**Telephone: 909-793-2044 Fax: 909-793-9614**
***PRACTICE AREAS: Probate Law; Estate Planning Law; Real Estate Law.**
**Paul B. Wilson (1906-1974).**
**General Civil Practice. Probate, Estate Planning and Real Estate Law.**
**References: Bank of America National Trust & Savings Assn.; Redlands Federal Bank (Redlands Branch).**

*See Professional Biographies, REDLANDS, CALIFORNIA*

Wood, Thomas D. '14 '37 C.446 B.S. L.596 LL.B.
(adm. in OR; not adm. in CA) 658 La Mirada Dr.‡
Wuchenich, Danielle E. ...................'49 '77 C.243 B.A. L.94 J.D. 309 E. Fern Ave.
Young, Nancy J., (CV) ............ '33 '82 C.752 B.A. L.1163 J.D. 25757 Redlands Blvd.
**Ziprick, Robert H.**, (BV) ............'51 '76 C.1163 B.A. L.1049 J.D. [Ziprick,S.H.&C.]
**Ziprick, William F.**, (AV) ............ '56 '80 C.636 B.S. L.1068 J.D. [Ziprick,S.H.&C.]

**Ziprick, Schilt, Heinrich & Cramer, (AV)**
**707 Brookside Avenue, 92373-5101**
**Telephone: 909-824-4305 Telecopier: 909-478-4305**
**Members of Firm: Robert H. Ziprick; William F. Ziprick; E. Nathan Schilt; Kerry L. Heinrich; Kathleen M. Cramer. Associate: Brian E. Whitley.**
**Healthcare and Hospital Law, Corporate, Non-Profit Organizations, Medical Malpractice, University Law, Real Estate, Labor (Management).**

*See Professional Biographies, REDLANDS, CALIFORNIA*

## REDONDO BEACH, 60,167, *Los Angeles Co.*

Allen, Thomas P., III, (AV) ............... '51 '76 C.335 B.A. L.1128 J.D. [T.P.Allen,III]
Allen, Thomas P., III, A Prof. Corp., (AV) ........................120 Fisherman's Wharf
Anastasi, Scott J. .........................'63 '91 C.112 B.A. L.1137 J.D. 1200 Aviation Blvd.
Barrett, Joseph Martin ................'58 '89 C.454 B.A. L.809 J.D. 2204 Vail Ave. Blvd.
Belger, Laurie, (Mr.), (AV) .................'39 '66 C.990 B.S. L.1068 J.D. [Belger&N.] ‡
Belger & Norris, (BV) ..................................................120 Fishermen's Wharf
Berman-Barrett, Sara J. ........................'64 '89 C.112 B.A. L.1068 J.D. P.O. Box 959
Bethard, Williams S., (BV) ............. '43 '69 C.112 B.A. L.1066 J.D. 133 S. Bway. St.
Black, Douglas J. ...................... '49 '77 C.665 B.A. L.1095 J.D. 728 N. Juanita Ave.
Bloodgood, Leon E. ..................'16 '56 C.112 B.A. L.803 LL.B. 1611 Pacific Coast Hwy.
**Boxer, Jonathan A.** '50 '75 C.659 B.A. L.569 J.D.
(adm. in NY; not adm. in CA) Sr. Coun., Labor, TRW Inc.
**Braun, Michael S.** ........................... '62 '88 C&L.546 B.S., J.D. [Ⓐ J.J.Regan]
*PRACTICE AREAS: Personal Injury; Civil Litigation.
Broderick, John R., (AV) ............'31 '57 C.813 B.A. L.1068 J.D. 1840 S. Elena Ave.
Brown, David S. .................... '54 '79 C.112 A.B. L.1067 J.D. 1611 S. Catalina Ave.
Carlisle, Catherine M. ......................'56 '82 C.112 B.A. L.426 J.D. 102 Via Pasqual
**Chevillat, Terry** .......................... '45 '71 C&L.800 B.A., J.D. [▣ A.W.Francis,Jr.]
*PRACTICE AREAS: Insurance Defense; ERISA; Bad Faith; Life and Health Insurance; Disability Law.
Cisarik, Michael J. ..............................'45 '76 C.932 B.A. L.597 J.D. 1910 Slauson Ln.
Coffey, Daniel .......................... '55 '87 C.112 B.S.Ch.E. L.464 J.D. 1710 Esplanade
Cohen, Stanley D., (BV) ............. '28 '61 C.569 B.S. L.426 LL.B. 2522 Artesia Blvd.
Cohn, George L. ..........................'53 '80 C.1029 B.S. L.809 J.D. 2850 Artesia Blvd.
Conifrey, Regan .........................'66 '92 C.178 B.A. L.990 J.D. 707 Torrance Blvd.
Corbalis, Fred F., III ......................'62 '87 C.174 B.A. L.770 J.D. 707 Torrance Blvd.
Cordes, Richard J. ......................... '64 '91 C.800 B.S. L.93 J.D. 707 Torrance Blvd.
Courtney, Robert E., (AV) ........'35 '61 C&L.426 B.B.A., LL.B. 120 Fisherman's Wharf
Crowell, James N., (BV) ........................ '48 '75 C.637 B.S. L.464 J.D. 210 Ave. I
DeWitt, Benjamin ............ '24 '55 C.37 B.S.E.E. L.273 LL.B. One Space Park (Pat.)
**Doran, Michael David** ............ '52 '79 C.763 B.S. L.1188 J.D. [Ⓐ Keller,P.&M.]
*PRACTICE AREAS: Civil Litigation Defense.
Dutra, Sue ...................................... '47 '87 C.1042 B.A. L.809 J.D. 1707 Via El Prado
Ehrlich, Lisa S. ................... '62 '87 C.112 A.B. L.1066 J.D. Montoro Develop. Corp.
Epstein, Stanley O., (BV) .........'27 '62 C.472 B.B.A. L.800 LL.B. 2522 Artesia Blvd.
Finnen, Stephen V. .................... '59 '84 C.610 B.B.A. L.602 J.D. 1116 Ford Ave.
Fishbeck, J. C., Jr. '41 '66 C.586 B.A. L.802 LL.B.
(adm. in TX; not adm. in CA) F.B.I.
Fobke, Shirley A. ...........................'57 '90 C.112 B.A. L.1137 J.D. 1840 S. Elena
**Francis, Arthur W., Jr.**, (AV) ......... '41 '71 C.1097 B.S. L.800 J.D. [A.W.Francis,Jr.]
*PRACTICE AREAS: Insurance Defense; ERISA; Bad Faith; Life and Health Insurance; Disability Law.

**Francis, Arthur W., Jr., A Prof. Corp., Law Offices of, (AV) BB**
**2522 Artesia Boulevard, 90278**
**Telephone: 310-316-1988 Fax: 310-318-5894**
**Arthur W. Francis, Jr. Of Counsel: Terry Chevillat.**
**Insurance Defense, ERISA, Coverage and Bad Faith Matters; General Liability; Personal Injury; Casualty; Life, Disability, Health and Accident; Errors and Omissions; Construction Accident; and Workman's Compensation.**

*See Professional Biographies, REDONDO BEACH, CALIFORNIA*

Gale, Edward H. ................. '29 '75 C.061 B.S.M.E. L.1137 J.D. 1023 Camino Real
**Gallas, William E.** '47 '72 C.918 A.B. L.1068 J.D.
V.P. & Asst. Gen. Coun., TRW Space & Electronics Grp.
Gegenheimer, Patricia E. ...................'52 '80 C.1078 B.A. L.1049 J.D. 221 Ave. "I"
Goff, Roger B. ................. '56 '88 C.112 B.A. L.426 J.D. 700 N. Pacific Coast Hwy.
Goodman, Gerald, (BVⓉ) '35 '61 C&L.145 B.A., J.D.
(adm. in NM; not adm. in CA) 130 The Village‡
Greene, Donald B. ................... '58 '85 C.1077 B.A. L.990 J.D. 1525 Aviation Blvd.
Harrison, Sandra L. ........................ '49 '80 C.1183 B.A. L.209 J.D. [Harrison&N.]

CAA510P

Harrison and Naples .......... 816B N. Juanita Ave.
Hofer, Marianna .......... '24 '85 C.1131 B.A. L.426 J.D. 1611 S. Pacific Coast Hwy.
Howard, Richard D. .......... '25 '51 C&L.800 A.B., LL.B. 224 Via La Circula

**Hruska & Lesser**
**1 Pearl Street, 90277⊙**
**Telephone: 310-374-4808 Fax: 310-372-7715**
**URL: http:/www.divelaw.com**
**Members of Firm: Mark A. Hruska; Richard A. Lesser; William J. Turbeville, II; Jeana Sciarappa Schott; Hillary S. Meisels.**
**Civil Practice in State and Federal Courts specializing in the defense of Recreational and Commercial Diving Claims, Related Products Liability Actions, Insurance Litigation and Admiralty Law.**
**Boca Raton, Florida Office: 21 South East Fifth Street. Telephone: 407-338-2110. Fax: 407-338-0894.**
**Honolulu, Hawaii Office: 2400 PRI Tower, Grovesnor Center, 733 Bishop Street. Telephone: 808-526-2641. Fax: 808-531-8628.**
*See Professional Biographies, REDONDO BEACH, CALIFORNIA*

Isom, LaMonte H., (BV) .......... '41 '72 C.545 B.A. L.398 J.D. 423 S. Pacific Coast Hwy.
Jackson, Richard D. .......... '49 '75 C.112 B.A. L.1068 J.D. 120 Fishermans Wharf
Jarkow, Jeff H. '60 '88 C.260 B.S. L.188 J.D.
(adm. in NJ; not adm. in CA) 123 W. Torrance Blvd., Pier Plz.⊙
Karlin, Charles I. .......... '64 '90 C.668 B.A. L.809 J.D. 707 Torrance Blvd.
Kawa, Ada Kan .......... '63 '89 C&L.800 B.A., J.D. 1725 Spreckels Ln.
**Keller, Robert V., (P.C.), (AV)** .......... '36 '64 C.800 B.A. L.426 J.D. [Keller,P.&M.]
**Keller, Robert W.** '40 '68 C.46 B.S.E.E. L.209 J.D.
Sr. Coun., Pat. & Licensing, TRW Systems Integration Grp. (Pat.)

**Keller, Price & Moorhead, (AV)**
**An Association including a Professional Corporation**
**Second Floor, 229 Avenue I, 90277**
**Telephone: 310-540-1332 Fax: 310-540-8480**
**Robert V. Keller (P.C.); Leslie M. Price, Jr.; J. Phillip Moorhead;—Michael David Doran; James P. Thompson.**
**General Civil Trial and Appellate Practice, State and Federal Courts, Insurance Defense including Fire and Casualty Litigation, Premises Liability, Construction Litigation, Toxic and Environmental Torts and General Business Litigation.**
**Reference: Bay Cities National Bank (Redondo Beach).**

Kimose, Randall C., (BV) .......... '50 '75 C.763 A.B. L.464 J.D. 221 Ave. I
Kirby, Margaret L., (BV) .......... '50 '79 L.1136 J.D. [Kirby&K.]
Kirby, Steven C., (BV) .......... '49 '78 C.1077 B.A. L.1136 J.D. [Kirby&K.]
Kirby & Kirby, (BV) .......... 2614 Artesia Blvd.
Klein, Daniel L. .......... '68 '95 C.112 B.A. L.809 J.D. 2651 Manhattan Beach Blvd.
Lau, Stanford Y. K. .......... '55 '81 C.1077 B.A. L.1095 J.D. P.O. Box 7000
**Lesser, Richard A.** .......... '46 '74 C.1042 A.B. L.800 J.D. [Hruska&L.] (⊙Honolulu, HI)
*PRACTICE AREAS: Defense of Recreational Accidents.
**Lilly, Elisabeth Bates** .......... '58 '84 C.197 A.B. L.477 J.D. Sr. Coun., TRW Inc.
**Lindquist, Robert M.**, (AV) '51 '77
C.399 B.A. L.846 J.D. Coun., TRW Systems Integration Grp.
Litman, Arthur L. .......... '43 '79 L.1136 J.D. V.P., Twr. Grp. Intl., Inc.
Lundy, Johanna .......... '35 '75 C.1097 B.A. L.426 J.D. 1611 S. Pacific Coast Hwy.‡
Marcus, Ira .......... '46 '72 C.112 B.A. L.1068 J.D. 201 Via Buena Ventura
Masero, John F., (BV) .......... '38 '68 C.800 B.A. L.426 J.D. 2802 Pacific Coast Hwy.
Massey, Virginia L. .......... '41 '73 C.508 B.A. L.426 J.D. 1711 Via El Prado
Matyi, James E. .......... '12 '48 C.477 A.B. L.912 LL.B. 682 The Village‡
McDermott, Douglas W. .......... '46 '80 C.1042 B.S. L.1148 J.D. 835 Hopkins Way.
**Meisels, Hillary S.** .......... '64 '93 C.112 B.A. L.809 J.D. [A Hruska&L.]
*PRACTICE AREAS: Corporate Law; Defense of Recreational Accidents; Music Law.
Mercant, Jon .......... '50 '75 C.112 B.A. L.1068 J.D. 707 Torrance Blvd.
Michael, John A., (BV) .......... '19 '51 C&L.477 A.B., J.D. 1611 S. Pacific Coast Hwy.
**Millson, Jennifer E.**, (BV⊙) '60 '85
C.473 A.B. L.276 J.D. Sr. Coun., TRW Space & Electronics Grp.
Mirassou, Jean B., (AV) .......... '29 '58 C.426 B.S. L.800 LL.B. [Mirassou&W.]
Mirassou & Wegener, (AV) .......... 1840 S. Elena Ave.
Mix, Terence J., (AV) .......... '40 '67 C.800 B.S. L.1065 J.D. 1611 S. Catalina Ave.
Mohr, Nancy A. .......... '55 '81 C.602 B.A. L.426 J.D. 707 Torrance Blvd.
Moore, Tim, (AV) .......... '45 '79 C.800 B.S. L.809 J.D. 707 Torrance Blvd.
**Moorhead, J. Phillip**, (AV) .......... '56 '81 C.607 B.A. L.464 J.D. [Keller,P.&M.]
**Morgenstern, Richard L.** '58 '85 C.881 A.B. L.930 J.D.
(adm. in TX; not adm. in CA) Pres. & Chmn. of the Bd., Morgenstern Intl., Inc. (⊙Boca Raton FL)
Moriarty, Gerald F., (AV) .......... '28 '71 C.112 B.A. L.426 J.D. 618 Paseo De La Playa‡
Muehlenbeck, Robert S. .......... '48 '73 C.112 B.A. L.1065 J.D. 1650 S. Pacific Coast Hwy.
Muzik, Thelma J. .......... '47 '78 C.800 B.A. L.809 J.D. 1201 Ynez Ave.
Naples, Caesar J. .......... '38 '63 C.976 A.B. L.107 LL.B. [Harrison&N.]
Needle, Gerald M., (BV) .......... '36 '64 C.1068 A.B. L.1065 LL.B. P.O. Box 7000
Nelson, Byron G. .......... '37 '76 222 Avenida Del Norte
Norris, Michael, (BV) .......... '54 '79 C.112 B.A. L.1068 J.D. [Belger&N.]
**O'Connor, Colin** .......... '60 '91 L.1136 J.D. [O'Connor&O.]
*PRACTICE AREAS: Family Law; Probate.
**O'Connor, Erin** .......... '57 '96 L.1136 J.D. [A O'Connor&O.]
*PRACTICE AREAS: Family Law; Probate.
**O'Connor, Timothy M.**, (AV) .......... '35 '60 C&L.800 B.S.L., LL.B. [O'Connor&O.]
*PRACTICE AREAS: Family Law; Probate.

**O'Connor & O'Connor, (AV)**
**1840 South Elena Avenue, Suite 100, 90277**
**Telephone: 310-378-1242 Fax: 310-375-1967**
**Timothy M. O'Connor; Colin O'Connor. Associate: Erin O'Connor.**
**Family Law, Probate Law, Estate Planning, Trusts and Wills.**
**References: Bank of America; Wells Fargo Bank.**

Painter, Patricia A. .......... '55 '84 C.27 B.A. L.426 J.D. 1874 S. Pacific Coast Hwy.
Pantalena, David M., (AV) .......... '47 '74 C.93 A.B. L.128 J.D. 2504 Harriman Ln.
Pellino, Rose M. .......... '27 '82 C.1131 B.S. L.1068 J.D. 501 S. Gertruda Ave.
**Price, Leslie M., Jr.**, (BV) .......... '54 '82 C.112 B.A. L.426 J.D. [Keller,P.&M.]
*LANGUAGES: Spanish.

**Regan, James J., Law Offices of, (AV) '45 '78 C.1074 B.S.M.E. L.809 J.D.**
**2522 Artesia Boulevard, 90278-3258**
**Telephone: 310-372-1988; 316-1988 After Hours Answering Fax: 310-318-5894**
***PRACTICE AREAS: Civil Litigation; Personal Injury; Real Property; Corporate; Contracts.**
**Associates: Gene A. Wilker; Michele L. Wong; Michael S. Braun. Of Counsel: Arthur W. Francis, Jr. (A Professional Corporation); Frank Daniel Rorie; Frank A. Hillsinger (1927-1993).**
**Civil Litigation, Insurance Defense, Corporate, Real Estate, Family Law, Probate, Personal Injury Law, Immigration and Nationality, Alternate Dispute Resolution.**
**Representative Clients: Centennial Life Insurance Co.; Fremont Indemnity Co.; C&G Mercury Plastics; JSW Plastics Machinery; Gable Plastics; AEON Manufacturing; SE-GI Products Inc.**
*See Professional Biographies, REDONDO BEACH, CALIFORNIA*

Remelmeyer, Stanley E., (AV) .......... '18 '49 C.911 A.B. L.309 LL.B. 431 Calle de Castellana
Rice, Robert L. .......... '31 '72 C.800 B.S. L.426 J.D. 124 Via Monte D'oro‡
Rieder, Erwin, (BV) .......... '49 '77 C.426 B.B.A. L.464 J.D. 2615 190th St.
**Rorie, Frank Daniel** .......... '45 '80 C.45 B.S.I.E. L.809 J.D. [B J.J.Regan]
*PRACTICE AREAS: Criminal Defense.

Safford, Frederick B., Jr. .......... '53 '89 C.1051 B.A. L.1136 J.D. 1718 Esplanade
**Schott, Jeana Sciarappa** .......... '57 '92 C.588 B.S. L.1137 J.D. [A Hruska&L.]
**Shegog-Whitlock, Hermia** .......... '55 '80 C.597 B.S. L.145 J.D. Sr. Coun., TRW Inc.
Shidler, John A. .......... '11 '38 C.813 A.B. L.426 J.D. 317 Camino De La Colinas‡
Sneathern, Charles D., (AV) .......... '47 '73 C.1077 B.A. L.426 J.D. 1611 S. Catalina Ave.
**Sparks, Sheila L.** .......... '58 '83 C.309 A.B. L.893 J.D. Sr. Coun., TRW Inc.
Spierer, Steven F., (BV) .......... '53 '77 C.1131 B.A. L.809 J.D. [Spierer&W.]
Spierer, Woodward, Corbalis & Goldberg, A Professional Corporation, (BV)
707 Torrance Boulevard, Suite 200
**Thompson, James P.** .......... '56 '89 C.1042 B.A. L.426 J.D. [A Keller,P.&M.]
Tomaiko, Denise K. .......... '65 '93 C.36 B.S. L.426 J.D. P.O. Box 1447
Trowbridge, Douglas H., (BV) .......... '30 '57 C.112 B.A. L.813 LL.B. 1826 S. Elena Ave.
Vienna, Pattricia M. .......... '53 '86 L.1179 J.D. 220 Avenida del Norte
**Waschek, Pauline E.** '52 '85
C.766 B.S. L.1065 J.D. Coun., TRW Space & Electronics Grp.
Wegener, Stiles C., (BV) .......... '29 '59 C.911 B.A. L.800 J.D. [Mirassou&W.]
**Wilker, Gene A.** .......... '45 '80 C.800 B.S. L.426 J.D. [A J.J.Regan]
*PRACTICE AREAS: Civil Litigation.
Windsor, Laurence E. '47 '74 C.188 B.A. L.184 J.D.
(adm. in FL; not adm. in CA) Pres., Windsor Communications Corporation
Winters, Raymond L., (BV) '29 '57 C.112 B.S. L.1068 LL.B.
1611 S. Pacific Coast Hwy.
**Wong, Michele L.** .......... '68 '93 C.112 B.A. L.426 J.D. [A J.J.Regan]
*LANGUAGES: Cantonese, Spanish and French.
*PRACTICE AREAS: Immigration; Nationality.
**Wood, Kevin G.**, (BV) .......... '36 '75 C.1066 B.A. L.426 J.D. [K.G.Wood]
*LANGUAGES: French and German.
Wood, W. Mark .......... '16 '50 C&L.426 A.B., LL.B. Ret. Mun. Ct. J.

**Wood, Kevin G., A Professional Law Corporation, (BV)**
**229 Avenue I, 2nd Floor, 90277**
**Telephone: 310-540-4552 Fax: 310-540-8480**
**Kevin G. Wood.**
**General Civil Litigation, Personal Injury, Family Law including Dissolutions, Custody, Spousal Support, Cohabitation and Prenuptials, Real Estate, Business Law, Probate, Conservatorships, Commercial Litigation, Contracts.**
*See Professional Biographies, REDONDO BEACH, CALIFORNIA*

Woodward, John A., (BV) .......... '51 '77 C.172 B.S. L.809 J.D. [Spierer&W.]
Worth, Beverly .......... '48 '79 107 W. Torrance Blvd.
**Yatsko, Michael S.** '48 '74 C.105 B.S.E.E. L.229 J.D.
(adm. in PA; not adm. in CA; Pat.) Coun., TRW Space & Electronics Grp.
**Zeefe, Herrick A.** '58 '84 C.477 B.G.S. L.276 J.D.
(adm. in IL; not adm. in CA) Morgenstern, Intl., Inc. (⊙Boca Raton FL)

## REDWOOD CITY, * 66,072, *San Mateo Co.*

**Aaron, Riechert, Carpol & Riffle, A P.C., (AV)**
**Suite 400, 900 Veterans Boulevard, 94063**
**Telephone: 415-368-4662 Fax: 415-367-8531**
**Peter G. Riechert; Steven J. Carpol; Charles M. Riffle (Certified Specialist, Estate Planning, Trust and Probate Law, The State Bar of California Board of Legal Specialization); Scott C. Abrams.**
**General Civil and Trial Practice in all Courts. Real Property, Business, Corporate, Credit Unions, Probate, Conservatorship, Trust, Estate Planning, Family, Municipal and Personal Injury Law.**
**Reference: Wells Fargo Bank (Redwood City Office).**
*See Professional Biographies, REDWOOD CITY, CALIFORNIA*

**Abrams, Scott C.** .......... '67 '93 C.112 B.A. L.767 J.D. [Aaron,R.C.&R.]
**Acheson, Jennifer Elizabeth** .......... '55 '87 C.378 B.A. L.767 J.D. [Low,B.&L.]
*LANGUAGES: French, Spanish and Arabic.
Adams, Michael E. .......... '43 '70 C.112 B.A. L.1066 J.D. Suite 102, 399 Bradford St.
Aguiar, Lisa E. .......... '63 '89 C.770 B.S.B.A. L.464 J.D. 1775 Woodside Rd.
**Akdoruk, Jane S.** '66 '91 C.112 B.A. L.472 J.D.
(adm. in TX; not adm. in CA) Corp. Coun., Oracle Corp.
*LANGUAGES: French.
*RESPONSIBILITIES: Intellectual Property; Real Estate; Contracts.
**Alberti, Daniel E.**, (AV) .......... '49 '76 C.770 B.S.C. L.464 J.D. [Ropers,M.K.&B.]
*PRACTICE AREAS: Employment and Commercial Litigation; White Collar Criminal Defense; Complex Business Litigation including Intellectual Property Litigation.
Allen, James M. .......... '46 '72 C.605 A.B. L.1065 J.D. 700 Jefferson St.‡
Allhiser, Mary, (AV) .......... '49 '75 C&L.966 B.A., J.D. Dep. Dist. Atty.
Alsop, Douglas W., (BV) .......... '45 '74 C.101 B.S. L.284 J.D. 541 Jefferson Ave.
Alsop, Wayne I., (BV) .......... '18 '62 C.1246 B.B.A. L.765 J.D. 541 Jefferson Ave.
Amadeo, Louis L., Jr., (BV) .......... '46 '75 C&L.188 A.B., J.D. 10 Twin Dolphin Dr.
**Anastassiou, Terry** .......... '56 '92 C.474 B.A. L.770 J.D. [A Ropers,M.K.&B.]
*PRACTICE AREAS: Insurance Defense; Appellate Practice; Law and Motion; Alternative Dispute Resolution.
**Andris, Robert P., II** .......... '62 '87 C.768 B.A. L.770 J.D. [Ropers,M.K.&B.]
*PRACTICE AREAS: Insurance Coverage and Bad Faith Litigation; Civil Appellate Law.
Ash, Mary M., (BV) .......... '37 '72 C&L.813 A.B., J.D. Dep. Dist. Atty.
Baigent, Julia M., (BV) .......... '58 '82 C.112 B.A. L.1065 J.D. 13 Woodleaf Ave.
**Barulich, Paul J.**, (BV) .......... '57 '85 C.112 A.B. L.284 J.D. [P.J.Barulich]
*PRACTICE AREAS: Probate; Estate Planning; Trusts; Business Law; Corporate Law.

**Barulich, Paul J., A Professional Corporation, (BV)**
**Westshore Office Park, 250A Twin Dolphin Drive, 94065**
**Telephone: 415-595-0444 Fax: 415-595-3976**
**Email: barulich@pacbell.net**
**Paul J. Barulich (Certified Specialist, Estate Planning, Trust and Probate Law, The State Bar of California Board of Legal Specialization).**
**Estate Planning, Probate and Trust, Business, Corporate, Real Property and Taxation.**
*See Professional Biographies, REDWOOD CITY, CALIFORNIA*

Bass, Eugene L., (CV) .......... '37 '72 C.813 B.S. L.1026 J.D. 495 Seaport Ct.
Baumann, Helen B. .......... '46 '72 C.800 B.A. L.813 J.D. 495 Seaport Ct.
**Baumann, John R.** .......... '46 '93 C.309 A.B. L.813 J.D. [A Low,B.&L.]
Bell, John S. '42 '68 C&L.966 B.S., J.D.
(adm. in WI; not adm. in CA; Pat.) 401 Bway.
Belluomini, Sandra L., (BV) .......... '56 '83 C.112 B.A. L.770 J.D. Dep. Dist. Atty.
Belofsky, William A. .......... '46 '79 C.813 B.A. L.1202 J.D. 399 Bradford St.
Bennett, Deborah P., (BV) .......... '52 '76 C.112 A.B. L.284 J.D. Dep. Dist. Atty.
**Bennigson, Arnold I**, (AV) .......... '42 '72 C.336 B.S. L.1065 J.D. [B Coddington,H.&D.]
Benson, Robert H., (AV) '42 '82 C.260 B.S. L.326 J.D.
V.P. & Gen. Coun., Genelabs Technologies, Inc. (Pat.)
**Bentley, John M.**, (AV) .......... '29 '55 C&L.767 LL.B. [Ropers,M.K.&B.]
*PRACTICE AREAS: Professional Liability Law; Bad Faith Law; Environmental Coverage; General Trial Work.
**Bentley, Joshua M.** .......... '65 '91 C.112 B.A. L.770 J.D. [Smith&B.]
*PRACTICE AREAS: Criminal Law; Civil Litigation.
Berenson, Renee L. .......... '55 '81 C.112 B.A. L.767 J.D. 900 Veterans Blvd
Berke, Tricia M. .......... '49 '76 C&L.813 B.A., J.D. Legal Aid Soc.
Berlin, Sidney L., (AV) .......... '27 '53 C.267 A.B. L.770 J.D. 3742 Farm Hill‡
**Berliner, Shelly J.** .......... '64 '90 C.112 B.A. L.990 J.D. Sr. Atty., SEGA of America, Inc.

CAA511P

Bernardi, George F. .................... '41 '75 C.112 A.B. L.284 J.D. 318 Sea Cliff Lane
Bible, John J. .................................. '24 '60 C&L.767 B.S., LL.B. Supr. Ct. J.‡
Bishop, Thomas E., (BV) ............. '52 '77 C.878 B.S. L.464 J.D. [Goodman,Q.L.&F.]
Bjork, William E. ...........................'46 '76 C.589 B.S. L.966 J.D. 3140 Spring St.
Blackman, Clifford A. .....'49 '76 C.1019 B.A. L.765 J.D. 2000 Broadway (⊙Burlingame)
**Blake, Albert P., Jr.** .......................'63 '90 C.1074 B.S. L.770 J.D. [Ⓐ Owen&M.]
*LANGUAGES: Italian.
*PRACTICE AREAS: Construction Defect Litigation; Construction Law.
Blatt, Robert, Jr., (BV) ...................... '21 '52 C&L.813 A.B., J.D. P.O. Box 1269‡
**Blinn, David L.** ................................'61 '86 C.112 B.A. L.770 J.D. [Low,B.&L.]
**Blocker, Brad W.** .......................'60 '86 C.112 B.A. L.861 J.D. [Ropers,M.K.&B.]
*PRACTICE AREAS: Civil Trials and Arbitration; Commercial Litigation; Professional Liability; Environmental Litigation; Construction.
Blodgett, Lester W. .................................'31 '60 C.604 B.A. L.813 J.D. 401 Bway.‡
Blum, Jeffrey P., (BV) ............... '51 '78 C.705 B.A. L.284 J.D. 1771 Woodside Rd.
**Blumberg, Joan M.** '57 '82 C.597 B.S. L.472 J.D.
(adm. in MD; not adm. in CA) Sr. Corp. Coun., Oracle Corp.
**Boggs, John Phillip** ..........................'66 '94 C.101 B.A. L.464 J.D. [Ⓐ Fisher&P.]
*LANGUAGES: Spanish and Portuguese.

**Boland, Robert A. '60 '86 C&L.770 B.S., J.D.**
**702 Marshall Street, Suite 270, 94063**
**Telephone: 415-363-5799 Fax: 415-367-1086**
***PRACTICE AREAS: Business Law; Real Estate; Probate; Estate Planning.**
**Business Law, Real Estate, Probate and Estate Planning.**

***See Professional Biographies, REDWOOD CITY, CALIFORNIA***

Boles, Brian L. ............................. '51 '79 C.112 B.A. L.284 J.D. 600 Allerton St.
**Bolgard, Roger D.**, (BV) '39 '76
C.674 A.B. L.1026 J.D. [Ⓒ Jackson,M.M.&D.] (⊙Monterey)
*PRACTICE AREAS: Business Law; Construction Law; Partnership; Corporations Law; Business Litigation.
Bollhoffer, Allan J. ...............................'36 '61 C&L.813 A.B., LL.B. Supr. Ct. J.
Bolton, Daniel J. ...................... '60 '87 C.101 B.A. L.1068 J.D. [Ⓐ Bolton&B.]
Bolton, Shauna H. ......................... '60 '88 C&L.878 B.A., J.D. [Bolton&B.]
Bolton & Bolton .........................................................463 Brewster Ave.
**Bonino, Mark G.**, (AV) ...............'51 '76 C.112 A.B. L.770 J.D. [Ropers,M.K.&B.]
*PRACTICE AREAS: Appellate Law; Bad Faith Litigation; Insurance Coverage.
Bourquin, Dennis M., (BV) ............... '33 '62 C&L.770 B.S., LL.B. 2317 Broadway
**Brady, Michael J.**, (AV) .............'41 '67 C.813 B.A. L.309 LL.B. [Ropers,M.K.&B.]
*PRACTICE AREAS: Appellate Law; Insurance Coverage and Reinsurance; Bad Faith.
Brandfon, Martin ................... '49 '81 C.1349 B.A. L.564 J.D. 620 Jefferson Ave.
Branson, J. A. ......................'11 '36 C.770 B.S. L.1065 J.D. 1912 Cordilleras Rd.‡
**Branson, Thomas A.**, (AV) .......... '39 '64 C.770 B.A. L.1065 LL.B. [Branson,F.&H.]

**Branson, FitzGerald & Howard, A Professional Corporation, (AV)**
**Suite 400, 643 Bair Island Road, 94063**
**Telephone: 415-365-7710 Fax: 415-364-LAWS**
**Thomas A. Branson; Dermot J. FitzGerald; Joseph C. Howard, Jr.; Fred R. Brinkop; Henry D. Rome; Kristi L. Curtis; Glenn D. Martin; David L. Strong; Harry A. Griffith, III; Carol P. Smith; David S. Secrest; Judith Friederici; Shawn M. Ridley; John R. Campo; John H. Podesta; Sondra E. Kirwan; Elizabeth J. Von Emster. Of Counsel: Dwight S. Haldan.**
**Insurance, Professional Liability, Civil Litigation. Construction, Products Liability, Insurance Defense, Medical and Other Professional Liability, Landslide and Subsidence, Personal Injury, Wrongful Death, Real Estate, Probate and Business Law. General, Civil and Trial Practice.**
**Reference: Union Bank.**

***See Professional Biographies, REDWOOD CITY, CALIFORNIA***

Bresee, Patricia ........................... '36 '72 C.679 B.S. L.767 J.D. Supr. Ct. Comr.
Briggs, Patrick Timothy .................. '54 '86 C&L.767 B.A., J.D. Dep. Dist. Atty.
**Brighton, Nancy A.** ......................'55 '82 C.1307 B.A. L.767 J.D. [Ⓐ Litigation S.]
**Brinkop, Fred R.**, (AV) ..............'42 '67 C.910 A.B. L.813 LL.B. [Branson,F.&H.]
**Brown, Jeffrey O.**, (AV) .....................'42 '72 C.812 B.S. L.208 J.D. [Brown&B.]
*PRACTICE AREAS: Products Liability; Medical and Professional Liability; Construction Litigation; Alternate Dispute Resolution.
**Brown, Sheridan H.**, (BV) ................. '47 '72 C.169 B.A. L.208 J.D. [Brown&B.]
*PRACTICE AREAS: Construction Litigation; Health Care Providers and Licensing Law; Administrative Law; Personal Injury Law.

**Brown & Brown, (AV)**
**Bradford Professional Office Center, 399 Bradford Street, Suite 200, 94063**
**Telephone: 415-369-4499 Fax: 415-369-3753**
**Members of Firm: Jeffrey O. Brown; Sheridan H. Brown;—Claudia J. Gorham.**
**Civil Litigation and Administrative Law. Construction, Products Liability, Health Care and Licensing, Insurance Defense, Medical and Other Professional Liability, Landslide and Subsidence, Personal Injury, Wrongful Death, Wrongful Termination Law and Alternate Dispute Resolution.**

***See Professional Biographies, REDWOOD CITY, CALIFORNIA***

Browning, James L., Jr. ..................... '32 '60 C.267 A.B. L.1065 J.D. Supr. Ct. J.
Bryant, Donald C., Jr. '42 '70 C.813 B.S. L.1068 J.D.
Directing Atty., Legal Aid Soc. of San Mateo Co.
**Burns, Thomas J.** ......................... '57 '83 C&L.770 B.S., J.D. [Ⓐ Litigation S.]
Bush, David R. ........................ '66 '91 C.800 B.A. L.464 J.D. 1001 Marshall St.
**Campbell, Colin R.**, (BV) ............ '48 '76 C.112 B.S. L.770 J.D. [Ropers,M.K.&B.]
*PRACTICE AREAS: Environmental Litigation; Insurance Coverage; Construction Defect Litigation; Products Liability Litigation.
Campbell, Thomas J. '52 '76 C.145 B.A. L.309 J.D.
(adm. in DC; not adm. in CA) (M.C.)
**Campo, John R.** ...................... '66 '91 C&L.770 B.S., J.D. [Ⓐ Branson,F.&H.]
**Candy, Peter L.** .................'64 '90 C.464 B.A. L.770 J.D. [Ⓐ Coddington,H.&D.]
Carcione, Joseph W., Jr. ............... '47 '73 C.770 B.A. L.767 J.D. 601 Brewster Ave.
**Carpol, Steven J.**, (BV) ...............'50 '75 C.112 B.A. L.464 J.D. [Aaron,R.C.&R.]
*PRACTICE AREAS: Real Estate Law; Corporate Law; Tax Law; Estate Planning Law; Business Law.
Carr, Geoffrey T., (BV) ............... '51 '79 C.768 B.S. L.1065 J.D. [Rockhill,S.&C.]
Carr, John N. ......................'66 '92 C.896 B.S. L.770 J.D. 1775 Woodside Rd.

**Carr, McClellan, Ingersoll, Thompson & Horn, Professional Corporation**
**(See Burlingame)**

Casazza, Thomas ................... '45 '80 C.770 B.S.C. L.284 J.D. 10 Twin Dolphin
Casey, Thomas F., III, (AV) ....... '45 '71 C&L.767 B.S., J.D. Co. Coun., San Mateo Co.
**Casper, Mark** ...................... '67 '94 C&L.770 B.S., J.D. [Ⓐ Ropers,M.K.&B.]
*PRACTICE AREAS: Business Litigation; Transactional Work; Real Estate.
Castillo-Barraza, Monica ........... '63 '90 C.112 B.A. L.1065 J.D. 1775 Woodside Rd.
**Chan, Chi-Hung A.** ................'47 '82 C.723 B.A. L.770 J.D. [Ⓒ Ropers,M.K.&B.]
*LANGUAGES: Chinese (Mandarin, Cantonese, Taiwanese) and Japanese.
*PRACTICE AREAS: Contracts; International Matters; Real Estate; Immigration.
**Chan, Dorena J.** ............. '63 '89 C.813 B.A. L.1065 J.D. Corp. Coun., Oracle Corp.
**Cheng, Hubert H.** ............'64 '92 C.813 B.S. L.1066 J.D. Corp. Coun., Oracle Corp.
*LANGUAGES: Mandarin Chinese.
**Chou, Catherine L.** ............'69 '94 C.112 B.A. L.770 J.D. Corp. Coun., Oracle Corp.
*LANGUAGES: Mandarin Chinese.
Clapp, Dan C. ........................... '39 '69 C.768 B.A. L.112 J.D. 490 Winslow St.
**Clark, Alan W.** '58 '87 C.705 B.S. L.776 J.D.
(adm. in NJ; not adm. in CA) Sr. Corp. Coun., Oracle Corp.

**Clark, Katherine S.**, (BV) ...........'53 '80 C.112 A.B. L.1065 J.D. [Ropers,M.K.&B.]
*PRACTICE AREAS: Civil Litigation; Employment Law; Real Estate; Construction; Personal Injury.
**Clark, Lee W.** ................................'57 '94 C.670 B.A. L.770 J.D. [Ⓒ Smith&B.]
*PRACTICE AREAS: Criminal Law; Civil Litigation.
**Clarke, Thomas H., Jr.** ..............'45 '71 C.112 A.B. L.1066 J.D. [Ropers,M.K.&B.]
*PRACTICE AREAS: Environmental Law; Administrative Law; Toxic Torts; Real Estate; Civil Litigation.
Cline, Christina L. .................. '66 '93 C.597 B.A. L.284 J.D. 1775 Woodside Rd.
**Coates, Jennifer C.** ...............'68 '94 C.112 B.A. L.1065 J.D. [Ⓐ Ropers,M.K.&B.]
*PRACTICE AREAS: Litigation; Employment Law; Public Entity Defense.
**Coates, Raymond**, (AV) .................... '43 '67 C&L.767 B.A., LL.B. [Low,B.&L.]
**Coddington, Clinton H.**, (AV) ...... '39 '69 C.870 B.S. L.1066 J.D. [Coddington,H.&D.]

**Coddington, Hicks & Danforth, A Professional Corporation, (AV) BB**
**Suite 300, 555 Twin Dolphin Drive, Paragon Center, Redwood Shores, 94065**
**Telephone: 415-592-5400 Facsimile: 415-592-5027**
**Clinton H. Coddington; Randolph S. Hicks; Lee J. Danforth; David M. King; Richard G. Grotch;—Edward A. Heinlein; David W. Wessel; R. Wardell Loveland; Pamela Ann Smith; Peter L. Candy; David K. Levine. Of Counsel: William G. Tucker; Arnold I Bennigson.**
**Insurance, Aviation, Business, Tort and Products Liability Law. General Civil and Trial Practice in all State and Federal Courts.**

***See Professional Biographies, REDWOOD CITY, CALIFORNIA***

**Cogan, Pamela E.**, (CV) ..............'56 '82 C.454 B.A. L.464 J.D. [Ropers,M.K.&B.]
*LANGUAGES: French.
*PRACTICE AREAS: Insurance Law; Civil Litigation.
**Cole, Denise A.** ................. '70 '95 C.1044 B.A. L.1066 J.D. [Ⓐ Ropers,M.K.&B.]
*PRACTICE AREAS: Appellate Law; Insurance Defense Litigation.
Conklin, William R., (P.C.) ............. '36 '63 C.813 A.B. L.1065 J.D. 2317 Broadway
**Conlon, Robert C.** .................... '39 '71 C.749 B.S. L.262 J.D. Emery Worldwide
**Cope, Donald E.** .......................... '50 '93 C.862 B.S. L.464 J.D. [Ⓐ Fisher&P.]
**Creegan, Maurice J.** .................. '63 '93 C.112 B.S. L.770 J.D. [Ⓐ J.A.Thompson]
*LANGUAGES: Spanish.
*PRACTICE AREAS: General Practice (35%).
**Curry, Kathryn C.** ..................'65 '91 C.112 B.S. L.770 J.D. [Ⓐ Ropers,M.K.&B.]
*PRACTICE AREAS: Appeals; Insurance Litigation and Coverage.
**Curtis, Kristi L.** ...................... '55 '81 C.763 A.B. L.770 J.D. [Branson,F.&H.]
**Curtis, Shelley S.** .............'— '88 C&L.494 B.A., J.D. Sr. Corp. Coun., Oracle Corp.
Daba, Raymond J., (AV) ................. '16 '40 C&L.813 B.A., J.D. 50 Horgan Ave.‡
**Daley, Dorian E.** ...............'59 '87 C.813 B.A. L.770 J.D. Corp. Coun., Oracle Corp.
Daly, Thomas D., (AV) ................. '49 '74 C.112 A.B. L.1065 J.D. Asst. Co. Coun.
**Danforth, Lee J.**, (AV) ............'49 '76 C.1253 B.A. L.464 J.D. [Coddington,H.&D.]
**Darwish, Sayed M.** ...........'65 '91 C.339 B.S. L.767 J.D. Corp. Coun., Oracle Corp.
**Davis, Brian R.** .....................'62 '92 C.147 B.A. L.1026 J.D. [Ⓐ Ropers,M.K.&B.]
*PRACTICE AREAS: Insurance Contract, Bad Faith and Agency.
De Golia, James B. '49 '76 C.112 B.A. L.1065 J.D.
V.P. & Gen. Coun., Network Equipment Technologies, Inc.
Dell'Ergo, Robert J., (AV) ..................'18 '46 C.112 A.B. L.1066 LL.B. 1900 Bway.
Delucchi, William F. .......................'35 '61 C&L.770 B.A., LL.B. 51 Myrtle St.‡
Dematteis, L. B. ....................................................'11 '32 L.767 Ret. Supr. Ct. J.
Deremigio, Thomas E. ................ '54 '81 C.813 A.B. L.770 J.D. 702 Marshall St.
**Derner, Mary P.** ........................ '63 '89 C.112 B.A. L.1065 J.D. [Ⓐ Owen&M.]
*PRACTICE AREAS: Insurance Coverage; General Civil Litigation.
deRochemont, Sarah ...........................'57 '85 C.75 B.A. L.770 J.D. 702 Marshall St.
Dickson Fontaine, Kathryn, (BV) .....'49 '79 C.766 B.A. L.1197 J.D. [Goodman,Q.L.&F.]
Dimich, Milan C. ..................... '65 '92 C.112 B.A. L.1049 J.D. 1001 Marshall St.
Dinkelspiel, Steven E. ..................... '56 '86 C.976 B.A. L.813 J.D. Dep. Dist. Atty.
**Dobbrow, Allison Lindley** ............'60 '89 C&L.770 B.A., J.D. [Ⓐ Ropers,M.K.&B.]
Dodson, Michael J. ................'57 '84 C.588 B.S. L.896 J.D. 1775 Woodside Rd.
Donig, Reuben J. ......................'51 '75 C.112 B.A. L.464 J.D. [Goodman,Q.L.&F.]
**Donovan, Kimberly A.** ............ '61 '92 C.770 B.S. L.990 J.D. [Ⓐ Ropers,M.K.&B.]
DuBois, Richard H., (BV) ............ '50 '75 C.112 B.A. L.770 J.D. 702 Marshall St.
**Duchene, Dennis Alan** .......... '61 '95 C.339 A.A.E. L.1049 J.D. [Ⓐ Ropers,M.K.&B.]
*PRACTICE AREAS: Civil Litigation; Insurance Defense; Environmental.
**Dugoni, Lisa M., (P.C.)**, (BV) ....... '54 '80 C.550 B.A. L.1202 J.D. [Jackson,M.M.&D.]
*REPORTED CASES: In Re Marriage of Birnbaum, 211 Cal App 3d 1508 (1989).
*PRACTICE AREAS: Family Law; Business Law.
Durkin, Dennis John, (BV) .........'49 '75 C.147 B.A. L.464 J.D. 2400 Bway., Suite 203
**Dvorak, Linda J.**, (BV) ...............'42 '82 C.628 B.S. L.770 J.D. [Ⓐ Ropers,M.K.&B.]
*PRACTICE AREAS: Estate Planning Law; Probate Law; Trust Administration Law.
Easterbrook, Alexander B. ................. '51 '77 C.112 B.A. L.1068 J.D. 2395 Bway.
Eastman, Jean Y. .....................'40 '81 C.604 B.A. L.770 J.D. [Goodman,Q.L.&F.]
Eckenrod, Beth S., (BV) ...................'39 '80 C.174 B.A. L.767 J.D. Dep. Dist. Atty.
Eisenberg, Lawrence .................... '39 '88 C.994 B.A. L.178 J.D. 702 Marshall St.
**Ellingson, Stephen P.** ................'62 '88 C.112 B.A. L.1065 J.D. [Ropers,M.K.&B.]
*PRACTICE AREAS: Complex Litigation; Insurance Bad Faith Litigation; Intellectual Property Disputes Litigation.
Ellner, Kenneth B. ........................'48 '74 C&L.770 B.A., J.D. 3315 Oak Knoll Dr.

**Enkelis, Richard L., (AV) '43 '69 C.477 B.A. L.800 J.D.**
**1771 Woodside Road, 94061-3436**
**Telephone: 415-367-1771 Fax: 415-367-8711**
**Email: RENKELIS@DEBTCOLLECTOR.COM**
***PRACTICE AREAS: Commercial Collections; Retail Collections; Mechanics Liens.**
**Commercial and Retail Collections, Enforcement of Judgments and Mechanics Lien.**

***See Professional Biographies, REDWOOD CITY, CALIFORNIA***

**Enterprise Law Group, Inc.**
**(See Menlo Park)**

Eshoo, George P., (BV) ...............'37 '66 C.112 B.S. L.1065 LL.B. 702 Marshall St.
Etezadi, Susan, (BV) ..................'58 '83 C.112 B.A. L.1049 J.D. Dep. Dist. Atty. IV
Eufusia, Linda M. ...............'47 '87 C.766 B.A. L.284 J.D. Research Atty., Supr. Ct.
**Evans, Douglas B.** ..... '56 '83 C.945 B.A. L.597 J.D. Dir., Law, SEGA of America, Inc.
Fagan, James ..................................'26 '54 C&L.813 B.A., J.D. 255 Shoreline Dr.
Fama, Patricia M. ...................'62 '88 C.112 B.A. L.770 J.D. 1221 Edgewood Rd.
Fancher, Frederick M. ...................'24 '55 C&L.813 A.B., LL.B. 2045 Nassau Dr.‡
**Fenech, Joseph M.** ...............................'60 '90 C.112 B.A. L.770 J.D. [Ⓐ Low,B.&L.]
**Fields, Ron W.**, (AV) ..............'19 '52 C.409 B.A. L.765 LL.B. [Ⓒ Ropers,M.K.&B.]
Finch, Richard Bruce ................. '52 '81 C.112 A.B. L.1065 J.D. 702 Marshall St.
**Fine, Ned A.**, (AV) ................................'40 '71 C.860 B.A. L.1066 J.D. [Fisher&P.]
*PRACTICE AREAS: Labor (Management) Laws; Employment Law; Wrongful Discharge Law.
Finney, Charles E. ...................................'40 '65 C.112 B.S. L.426 LL.B. Dist. Atty.
**Fisher, Richard** .................... '64 '91 C.768 B.S. L.770 J.D. [Ⓐ Ropers,M.K.&B.]
*PRACTICE AREAS: Civil Litigation; Insurance Law; Environmental Law.

**Fisher & Phillips, (AV) BB**
**A Partnership including Professional Corporations and Associations**
**Suite 345, Three Lagoon Drive, 94065⊙**
**Telephone: 415-592-6160 Telecopier: 415-592-6385**
**Resident Members: Ned A. Fine; John D. McLachlan; Lynn D. Lieber. Resident Associates: Donald E. Cope; John Phillip Boggs; Martha V. Howton; C. Trevor Skarda.**
**Atlanta, Georgia Office: 1500 Resurgens Plaza, 945 East Paces Ferry Road, N.E., 30326. Telephone: 404-231-1400. Telecopier: 404-240-4249. Telex: 54-2331.**

(This Listing Continued)

CAA512P

**Fisher & Phillips (Continued)**

**Fort Lauderdale, Florida Office: Suite 2300 NationsBank Tower, One Financial Plaza, 33394. Telephone: 954-525-4800. Telecopier: 954-525-8739.**
**Newport Beach, California Office: 4675 MacArthur Court, Suite 550, 92660. Telephone: 714-851-2424. Telecopier: 714-851-0152.**
**New Orleans, Louisiana Office: 3710 Place St. Charles, 201 St. Charles Avenue, 70170. Telephone: 504-522-3303. Telecopier: 504-529-3850.**
***See Professional Biographies, REDWOOD CITY, CALIFORNIA***

**FitzGerald, Dermot J.**, (AV) ... '34 '67 C.058 B.A. L.061 [Branson,F.&H.]
**Fitzgerald, William F.** ... '57 '83 C.112 A.B. L.767 J.D. [Ⓐ Litigation S.]
Fleck, J. Byron ... '54 '92 C.665 B.A. L.464 J.D. 1001 Marshall St.
Flores, Carmen S., (Ms.) '51 '79 C.112 B.A. L.765 J.D.
Legal Aid Soc. of San Mateo Co.
Foiles, Robert D., (AV) ... '58 '84 C.112 B.A. L.767 J.D. Dep. Dist. Atty.
Foley, James W. ... '25 '63 C.670 A.B. L.767 LL.B. 227 Park St.‡
Forcum, Mark R. ... '54 '80 C&L.976 B.A., J.D. Sup. Ct. J.
Fox, James P., (AV) ... '44 '70 C&L.767 B.S., J.D. Dist. Atty.& Pub. Admr.
Franchi, Don R. ... '63 '93 C.1073 B.S. L.990 J.D. 805 Veterans Blvd.
**Franks, Kelly** ... '69 '93 C.846 B.B.A. L.1065 J.D. [Ⓐ Ropers,M.K.&B.]
*PRACTICE AREAS: Insurance and Bad Faith Litigation; General Commercial and Intellectual Property Litigation; Appellate Practice.
Frederick, Kevin D., (BV) ... '52 '78 C.813 B.A. L.1065 J.D. [Goodman,Q.L.&F.]
**Frederickson, Roger B.** ... '65 '92 C.112 B.A. L.990 J.D. [Ⓐ Ropers,M.K.&B.]
*PRACTICE AREAS: Civil Litigation.
**Friederici, Judith** ... '44 '86 C.208 B.F.A. L.767 J.D. [Ⓐ Branson,F.&H.]
*PRACTICE AREAS: General Litigation; Environmental/Toxic Tort Law; Insurance Coverage Law.
Gardella, Richard E., (BV) ... '31 '55 C.112 L.1065 LL.B. 333 Bradford St.
**Garrett, William R.** ... '59 '87 C.813 A.B. L.767 J.D. [Ropers,M.K.&B.]
*PRACTICE AREAS: Business Litigation; Construction Defect Litigation; Real Estate Litigation; Environmental Coverage Litigation; Personal Injury Matters.
Gatzert, Norman J., II ... '44 '68 C.112 A.B. L.1065 J.D. Comr. of Mun. Ct.
Gelbman, Kathryn ... '39 '69 C.703 B.S.N. L.284 J.D. 504 Keelso Circle
Gendotti, Diana Therese ... '61 '89 C.112 B.A. L.770 J.D. P.O. Box 250
Gibbs, Anthony W., (BV) ... '41 '70 C.112 B.S. L.1065 J.D. [Gibbs,Z.&Assoc.]
Gibbs, Zoucha & Associates, (BV) ... 600 Allerton St., 2nd Fl.
Giorgi, Dennis C., (BV) ... '44 '77 C.1060 B.A. L.1026 J.D. Dep. Dist. Atty.

**Givens, Richard D., (AV) '39 '66 C.813 A.B. L.1065 LL.B.**
**702 Marshall Street, 94063**
**Telephone: 415-365-6144**
***PRACTICE AREAS: Litigation; Real Estate; Environmental Law; Sports Law.**
**General Civil Trial Practice, Real Estate, Environmental Law and Sports Law.**
***See Professional Biographies, REDWOOD CITY, CALIFORNIA***

Goldstein, David M., (AV) ... '43 '76 C.112 B.A. L.767 J.D. 900 Veterans Blvd.
Goltz, Portor ... '51 '80 C.768 B.A. L.284 J.D. Dep. Co. Coun.
Gonella, Carol Samuelian, (BV) ... '37 '72 C.766 A.B. L.767 J.D. 702 Marshall St.
Goodman, I. R., (AV) ... '30 '57 C.1036 A.B. L.813 LL.B. [Goodman,Q.L.&F.]
Goodman, Quintero, Lubin & Frederick, An Assn. of Attys., (AV) ... 702 Marshall St.
**Gorham, Claudia J.** ... '62 '90 C.502 A.B. L.1065 J.D. [Ⓐ Brown&B.]
Gould, Gordon C. ... '20 '63 C&L.280 A.B., LL.B. 485 Woodside Rd.‡
**Grainger, Jeffry J.** '62 '91 C.813 B.S. L.911 J.D.
Sr. Pat. Coun., Intell. Prop., Heartport, Inc. (Pat.)
Grandsaert, John L., (AV) ... '52 '77 C.767 B.S. L.1065 J.D. Dep. Dist. Atty.
**Greene, Raymond A., III** ... '60 '87 C.112 B.A. L.767 J.D. [Ropers,M.K.&B.]
*PRACTICE AREAS: Personal Injury Law; Insurance Coverage Law; Intellectual Property Law; Construction Law; Products Liability Law.
**Griffith, Harry A., III**, (BV) ... '59 '84 C.768 B.A. L.767 J.D. [Branson,F.&H.]
*LANGUAGES: Spanish.
**Grotch, Richard G.** ... '61 '87 C.112 A.B. L.1065 J.D. [Coddington,H.&D.]
Gruber, Joseph N., (BV) ... '44 '70 C.331 B.A. L.284 J.D. 750 Middlefield Rd.
**Guerin, Cheryl** ... '67 '92 C.112 B.A. L.1065 J.D. Corp. Coun., Oracle Corp.
Guidotti, Karen Marzotto ... '58 '83 C.112 B.S. L.770 J.D. Dist. Atty.
Gunn, John F. ... '63 '89 C&L.770 B.S., J.D. P.O. Box 8030
**Guslani, Lawrence M.**, (BV) ... '57 '82 C.112 B.S. L.770 J.D. [Ropers,M.K.&B.]
*PRACTICE AREAS: Insurance Coverage Law; Bad Faith Litigation; Appellate Law.
Hahn, Dale A. ... '43 '73 C.112 A.B. L.1065 J.D. Supr. Ct. J.
**Haldan, Dwight S.**, (BV) ... '50 '76 C.112 B.A. L.1065 J.D. [Ⓑ Branson,F.&H.]
Hall, Stephen M., (BV) ... '54 '85 C.813 B.A. L.770 J.D. Dep. Dist. Atty.
**Handelman, Susan H.** ... '46 '89 C.906 B.A. L.284 J.D. [Ropers,M.K.&B.]
*LANGUAGES: Spanish.
*PRACTICE AREAS: Appellate Practice; Insurance Coverage Law.
Hannig, Frank L., (AV) ... '21 '49 C.631 A.B. L.813 J.D. 1001 Marshall St.‡
**Hannig, Ted J.**, (AV) ... '58 '83 C.1074 B.S. L.770 J.D. [Ropers,M.K.&B.]
*PRACTICE AREAS: Commercial Law; Corporate Law; Real Estate Law; Commercial Litigation.
Hansen, Julie M. ... '62 '90 C&L.813 B.A., J.D. 298 Fuller St.
**Hanss, Mary Beth** '61 '87 C.867 B.A. L.982 J.D.
(adm. in NY; not adm. in CA) Corp. Coun., Oracle Corp.
Harbert, David A. ... '26 '74 C.602 B.A. L.765 J.D. 234 Marshall St.
**Harllee, John William** '— '94 C.477 B.A. L.893 J.D.
(adm. in VA; not adm. in CA) Corp. Coun., Oracle Corp.
*RESPONSIBILITIES: Government Contracts; Commercial Contracts; Computer Law; Intellectual Property.
Harrington, Walter H., Jr. ... '26 '53 C.813 B.S. L.1065 J.D. Supr. Ct. J.
Hartford, John J. ... '44 '72 C&L.767 B.A., J.D. 2000 Bway.
**Hartnett, Jim**, (BV) ... '50 '76 C.061 B.A. L.770 J.D. [Smith&B.]
*PRACTICE AREAS: International Law; Business Law; Real Estate Law; Litigation.
Hawver, M. Stacey ... '61 '90 C.188 A.B. L.813 J.D. Legal Aid Soc. of San Mateo Coun.
**Hayes, Stephen M.**, (AV) ... '52 '78 C.112 B.A. L.1065 J.D. [Ropers,M.K.&B.]
*PRACTICE AREAS: Complex Commercial and Tort Litigation.
Heaps, Martin D. ... '64 '91 C.867 B.A. L.770 J.D. 702 Marshall St.
**Heinlein, Edward A.**, (BV) ... '39 '79 C.813 B.A. L.770 J.D. [Ⓐ Coddington,H.&D.]
**Helmer, Pamela J.**, (BV) ... '55 '84 C.763 B.A. L.912 J.D. [Owen&M.]⊙
*LANGUAGES: Spanish.
*PRACTICE AREAS: Construction Defect Litigation; Construction Law.
**Herr, Cynthia Greco** ... '59 '87 C.197 B.A. L.94 J.D. Sr. Corp. Coun., Oracle Corp.
**Hicks, Randolph S.**, (BV) ... '53 '78 C.112 A.B. L.770 J.D. [Coddington,H.&D.]
**Hoekendijk, Jens E.** '64 '92 C.112 B.S. L.767 J.D.
Pat. Coun., Intell. Prop., Heartport, Inc. (Pat.)
*RESPONSIBILITIES: Patent; Trademark; Licensing.

**Hogan, Thomas R., Law Offices of**
**(See San Jose)**

**Hoglund, Anthony Joseph** ... '67 '93 C.112 B.A. L.767 J.D. [Ⓐ Ropers,M.K.&B.]
*LANGUAGES: Spanish.
*PRACTICE AREAS: Civil Litigation; Construction Law; Employment Law; Personal Injury Litigation; Insurance Bad Faith.
Holm, Carl W. ... '44 '73 C.800 B.S. L.770 J.D. Mun. Ct. J.
**Holsinger, William H.**, (BV) ... '51 '78 C.1078 B.A. L.1065 J.D. [Low,B.&L.]
Houck, Annette Marie ... '65 '90 C.25 B.S. L.608 J.D. 3 Lagoon Dr.
**Howard, Joseph C., Jr.**, (AV) ... '43 '72 C.998 B.C.S. L.767 J.D. [Branson,F.&H.]
**Howton, Martha V.** ... '71 '95 C.976 B.A. L.1065 J.D. [Ⓐ Fisher&P.]
Hubbard, Julian J., (BV) ... '52 '82 C.976 B.A. L.770 J.D. 1775 Woodside Rd.
Hume, Edward D., (CV) ... '49 '75 C.1068 B.A. L.770 J.D. 379 Bradford St.
**Hunsaker, Kevin** ... '65 '94 C.112 B.A. L.284 J.D. [Ⓐ Ropers,M.K.&B.]
*PRACTICE AREAS: Appellate; Litigation and Insurance Coverage.
Hutcheson, Kevin S. ... '59 '89 C.766 B.A. L.1065 J.D. 1775 Woodside Rd.

**Inama, Christopher R., Law Office of, (BV) '52 '77 C.112 B.A. L.1065 J.D.**
**399 Bradford Street #102, 94063**
**Telephone: 415-365-7850 Fax: 415-365-4206**
**Email: crinama@ix.netcom.com**
***PRACTICE AREAS: Appellate Law (60%, 25); Criminal Law (10%, 10); Insurance Subrogation Law (10%, 5); Civil Trial (10%, 5); Family Law (10%, 5).**
**General Civil, Criminal and Appellate Practice. Civil Litigation, Insurance (Subrogation, Defense), Family Law, Administrative and Extraordinary-Writ Cases.**
***See Professional Biographies, REDWOOD CITY, CALIFORNIA***

**Ingolia, Diane E.** ... '58 '94 C.1099 B.S. L.770 J.D. [Ⓐ Medlen&C.]
*PRACTICE AREAS: Biotechnology; Molecular Biology; Biochemistry; Immunology; Biotechnology Patents.
**Ittig, Robert G.** ... '59 '86 C.112 B.A. L.767 J.D. [Ropers,M.K.&B.]
*PRACTICE AREAS: General Civil Law; Trial Practice.
**Ivanov, Bridget C. Hopkins** ... '68 '95 C.770 B.A. L.284 J.D. [Ⓐ Ropers,M.K.&B.]
*PRACTICE AREAS: Environmental Coverage Litigation.
**Jackson, Travis M.**, (AV) ... '30 '60 C.937 A.B. L.1066 J.D. [Jackson,M.M.&D.]
*PRACTICE AREAS: Estate Planning Law; Business Law.

**Jackson, Mittlesteadt, Miller & Dugoni, (AV)**
**An Association including a Professional Corporation**
**250 A Twin Dolphin Drive, 94065**
**Mailing Address: P.O. Box 1367, San Carlos, 94070-1367**
**Telephone: 415-595-0444 Fax: 415-595-3976**
**Travis M. Jackson; Carol L. Mittlesteadt; Cameron Miller; Lisa M. Dugoni (P.C.). Of Counsel: Roger D. Bolgard.**
**General Practice. Civil Litigation, Contract, Family, Corporation, Probate, Wills and Estate Planning, Personal Injury, Immigration, Business, Real Property, Commercial and Construction.**
***See Professional Biographies, REDWOOD CITY, CALIFORNIA***

Jacomb, Katherine A., (BV) ... '43 '73 C.813 B.A. L.1065 J.D. 142 Stambaugh St.
Jett, Regina H., (BV) ... '54 '80 C.1163 B.A. L.464 J.D. Dep. Dist. Atty.
Johnson, Dean E. ... '50 '81 C.976 B.A. L.569 J.D. Dept. Dist. Atty.
Johnson, Wilbur R. ... '28 '55 C&L.813 A.B., LL.B. Ret. Mun. Ct. J.
**Jordan, Anne S.** '51 '80
C.597 B.A. L.209 J.D. V.P. & Gen. Coun., SEGA of America, Inc.
Kamuchey, Cassandra T. '63 '91
C.112 B.A. L.276 J.D. 303 Twin Dolphin Dr., Redwood Shores
Kane, Philip M. ... '36 '95 C.186 B.E.E. L.765 J.D. 702 Marshall St.
Kaplan, Carolyn S. ... '62 '88 C.918 B.A. L.813 J.D. Dep. Dist. Atty.
Karesh, Jonathan E. ... '60 '85 C.112 B.A. L.1066 J.D. Dep. D.A.
**Kaul, Raja** '62 '88 C.012 B.Eng. L.188 J.D.
(adm. in NY; not adm. in CA) Corp. Coun., Oracle Corp.
**Keller, Heather L. Criss** '66 '91
C.228 B.A. L.880 J.D. Sr. Corp. Coun., Corp., Heartport, Inc.
Kelly, Kevin G., (AV) ... '46 '72 C.321 A.B. L.800 J.D. 702 Marshall St.
Kelly, Parker S., (AV) ... '34 '63 C.893 B.S. L.1065 J.D. Dep. Dist. Atty.⊙
Kelly, Parker S., (AV) ... '34 '63 C.893 B.S. L.1065 J.D. Dist. Atty. Ofc.⊙

**Kelly, Richard F., (AV) '44 '78 C.768 B.S. L.765 J.D.**
**First Interstate Bank Building, 702 Marshall Street, Suite 400, 94063-1829**
**Telephone: 415-365-3338 Fax: 415-368-7191**
***REPORTED CASES: California Casualty Indemnity Exchange vs. Pettis 193 Cal. App. 3d 1597, 239 Cal Rptr. 205; In Re the Requested Extradition of James Joseph Smyth, 863 F. Supp. 1137.**
***PRACTICE AREAS: Landlord-Tenant Law; Civil Trials; Personal Injury; Creditor's Rights.**
**General Civil and Trial Practice in all State and Federal Courts. Personal Injury, Insurance, Premises Liability, Landlord Tenant Law, Creditors Rights and Business Litigation, Estate Planning and Family Law.**
***See Professional Biographies, REDWOOD CITY, CALIFORNIA***

Kemp, Margaret J. ... '44 '72 C.339 B.S. L.1066 J.D. Supr. Ct. J.
Kennedy, Kerry E. ... '45 '91 C.768 B.A. L.284 J.D. 2000 Broadway
Kensil, Roger F., (CV) ... '37 '66 C.339 B.S. L.165 LL.B. 2395 Bway.
Kenward, Christopher F. ... '57 '86 C&L.260 B.S.B.A., J.D. P.O. Box 7034
Keyes, Richard K., (BV) ... '52 '76 C.112 B.A. L.1065 J.D. 620 Jefferson Ave.
**King, David M.**, (BV) ... '54 '80 C.112 B.A. L.770 J.D. [Coddington,H.&D.]
Kinney, Ansel D. ... '56 '85 C.112 B.A. L.284 J.D. 1775 Woodside Rd.
**Kirwan, Sondra E.** ... '64 '91 C.768 B.S. L.770 J.D. [Ⓐ Branson,F.&H.]
Klein, Ronald B. ... '50 '76 C.910 B.S.B.A. L.810 J.D. 255 Shoreline Dr., 3rd Fl.
Knight, Clarence B. ... '27 '51 C&L.813 A.B., J.D. Supr. Ct. J.
**Kohn, Walter C.**, (AV) ... '25 '54 C.597 B.S. L.1065 J.D. [Ⓒ Ropers,M.K.&B.]
*PRACTICE AREAS: Aircraft Litigation; Products Liability Law; Business Transaction Litigation.
**Kolakowski, Victoria S.** '61 '89 C.1275 B.A. L.420 J.D.
Pat. Atty., Ampex Corp. (Pat.)
*RESPONSIBILITIES: Patent; Trademark; Copyright; Unfair Competition; Related Litigation.
Kostmayer, Joseph D. ... '58 '90 C.768 B.A. L.770 J.D. 1775 Woodside Rd.
Krakow, Ellen R. ... '64 '89 C.846 B.A. L.273 J.D. 1001 Marshall St.
Kruse, Ann E. '49 '78 C.352 B.A. L.276 J.D.
(adm. in WA; not adm. in CA) 115 Orchard Ave.‡
Kubal, Patricia Tobin ... '54 '84 C&L.813 B.A., J.D. 400 Seaport Ct.
**Kulig, Janet** ... '54 '87 C.483 B.A. L.1065 J.D. [Low,B.&L.]
**Kurtz, Michael** ... '48 '73 C&L.597 B.A., J.D. V.P., Legal, Oracle Corp.
Kurtz, Sarah Elizabeth '53 '81 C.813 B.A. L.659 J.D.
Supervising Atty., Legal Aid Soc. of San Mateo Co.
Labson Freeman, Beth ... '53 '79 C.112 A.B. L.309 J.D. Dep. Co. Coun.
Lalle, Frank A. ... '55 '82 C.72 B.A. L.597 J.D. Staff Atty., Legal Aid Soc.
La Mar, Ben F., Jr., (BV) ... '35 '60 C.813 B.A. L.1065 LL.B. 2400 Bway
**Lampson, Elizabeth E.** ... '67 '93 C.112 B.A. L.809 J.D. [Ⓐ Litigation S.]
**Laugier, Francois G.** ... '63 '90 L.061 LL.M. [Ropers,M.K.&B.]
*LANGUAGES: French and Spanish.
*PRACTICE AREAS: French & EEC Law; Domestic and International Business Law.
Lauhon, Gregory T., (BV) ... '58 '84 C.813 B.A. L.770 J.D. 643 Bair Island Dr., Ste., 400
Lebsack, Chester W., (A Professional Corporation), (AV) '21 '48
C.378 B.S. L.813 LL.B. 525 Marshall St.
**Le Clerc, Desiree** ... '63 '90 C.112 B.S. L.1067 J.D. Corp. Coun., Oracle Corp.
*RESPONSIBILITIES: Commercial Litigation; Intellectual Property.
Lee, James V., (CV) ... '52 '77 C&L.770 B.S., J.D. 234 Marshall St.
Lelli, Ramon S. ... '32 '57 C&L.770 B.S., J.D. 702 Marshall St., Ste. 270
LemMon, Richard T., (BV) ... '29 '57 C.112 B.A. L.1066 LL.B. P.O. Box 2488
**Levine, David K.** ... '66 '92 C.813 B.A. L.94 J.D. [Ⓐ Coddington,H.&D.]
**Levy, David A.**, (BV) ... '52 '77 C.112 A.B. L.1065 J.D. [Ropers,M.K.&B.]
*PRACTICE AREAS: Healthcare and Professional Liability; General Civil Litigation.
Lew, Jocelyne J. K. ... '51 '77 C.02 B.A. L.011 LL.B. [J.J.K.Lew]

CAA513P

CALIFORNIA—REDWOOD CITY | MARTINDALE-HUBBELL LAW DIRECTORY 1997

Lew, Jocelyne J. Kim, A Prof. Law Corp., Law Offices of 2055 Woodside Road, Suite 150

Lewis, Robert J., (BV) ... '18 '54 C&L.813 A.B., LL.B. 499 Seaport Ct.

**Lieber, Lynn D.** ... '62 '87 C.169 B.A. L.770 J.D. [Fisher&P.]

**Liroff, H. Ann** ... '52 '78 C.914 B.A. L.884 J.D. [[A] Ropers,M.K.&B.]
*PRACTICE AREAS: General Commercial Litigation and Transactional Fields.

**Litigation Solutions Law Group LLP, (AV)**
**1775 Woodside Road, 94061**
**Telephone: 415-364-9110 Fax: 415-366-8995**
**Partners: John Skelton; Richard J. Romanski. Associates: Stephen H. Schmid; Jacqueline A. Willson; Anthony M. Santana; Thomas J. Burns; William F. Fitzgerald; Nancy A. Brighton; Joseph R. Polverari, Jr.; Elizabeth E. Lampson. Of Counsel: Joseph R. Polverari, Sr.**
*See Professional Biographies, REDWOOD CITY, CALIFORNIA*

**Louie, Michael L.** '61 '91 C.112 B.S.M.E. L.770 J.D. Pat. Coun., Intell. Prop., Heartport, Inc. (Pat.)
*RESPONSIBILITIES: Patent; Trademark; Licensing; Copyright.

**Loveland, R. Wardell** ... '59 '87 C.674 A.B. L.93 J.D. [[A] Coddington,H.&D.]

**Low, Ball & Lynch, A Professional Corporation, (AV)** BR
**10 Twin Dolphin, Suite B-500, 94065⊙**
**Telephone: 415-591-8822 Fax: 415-591-8884**
**Raymond Coates; Chester G. Moore, III; James D. Miller; William H. Holsinger; David L. Blinn; Janet Kulig; Thomas E. Mulvihill; Jennifer Elizabeth Acheson;—John R. Baumann; Joseph M. Fenech; Michael E. Sandgren.**
**General Civil and Trial Practice. Insurance, Environmental Law, Land Use, Real Estate, Corporate, Professional Malpractice, Products Liability, Securities, Commercial Litigation and Appellate Practice.**
**San Francisco, California Office: 601 California Street, Suite 2100, 94108. Telephone: 415-981-6630.**
**Monterey, California Office: 10 Ragsdale Drive, Suite 175, 93940. Telephone: 408-655-8822.**
*See Professional Biographies, REDWOOD CITY, CALIFORNIA*

Lubin, Robert M., (BV) ... '46 '73 C.1169 B.A. L.1067 J.D. [Goodman,Q.L.&F.]

Lynch, Peter O ... '63 '88 C.112 A.B. L.1067 J.D. Dist. Atty.'s Off.

**MacDonald, Perry A.** '47 '86 C.880 B.A. L.127 J.D. (adm. in MD; not adm. in CA) Corp. Coun., Oracle Corp.

**MacKay, Bruce M.** ... '52 '94 C.446 B.A. L.101 J.D. [[A] Ropers,M.K.&B.]
*LANGUAGES: Russian, German and Spanish.
*PRACTICE AREAS: Appellate; Bad Faith Insurance Defense; Environmental.

**MacKnight, Kamrin T.** ... '59 '93 C.101 B.S. L.770 J.D. [[A] Medlen&C.]
*LANGUAGES: Russian, French and German.
*PRACTICE AREAS: Biotechnology; Biochemistry; Microbiology; Immunology; Molecular Biology Patents.

**Majeski, Eugene J.,** (AV) ... '16 '40 C&L.209 B.S., J.D. [Ropers,M.K.&B.]
*PRACTICE AREAS: Civil Litigation.

Mandanis, Marjorie G. ... '31 '73 C.112 A.B. L.284 J.D. 900 Veterans Blvd.

**Mangiantini, Paul R.** ... '61 '88 C.112 B.A. L.770 J.D. [Owen&M.]⊙
*PRACTICE AREAS: Accident and Personal Injury; Airplane Crash Litigation; Insurance Defense Law; Products Liability.

Manso, Richard A. ... '57 '87 C.602 B.S. L.767 J.D. Three Lagoon Dr.

Marblestone, Ronald W., (BV) '52 '80 C.112 A.B. L.767 J.D. 702 Marshall St., Suite 270

Mares, Milton H., (AV) ... '37 '68 C.1060 B.A. L.1065 J.D. Dep. Co. Coun.

Margolis, Jonathan ... '56 '81 C.867 B.A. L.93 J.D. 10 Twin Dolphin

Marko, Sheila Cronin, (BV) ... '48 '77 C.770 B.A. L.767 J.D. 620 Jefferson Ave.

Martin, Gary A. '39 '66 C.813 B.S. L.309 LL.B. Pres. & Gen. Coun., Harvard Investment Co.

**Martin, Glenn D.,** (BV) ... '56 '81 C.1044 B.A. L.767 J.D. [Branson,F.&H.]

Mattioli, Gloria ... '48 '76 C.112 A.B. L.1066 J.D. 2400 Broadway

McAllister, Lucy S. ... '58 '87 C.1044 B.F.A. L.770 J.D. Suite 103, 399 Bradford St.

McBride, James J., (AV) '51 '79 C.112 B.A. L.1066 J.D. 499 Seaport Ct., 3rd Fl. (⊙San Francisco)

**McCurdy, Kevin G.** ... '58 '84 C.813 B.A. L.1066 J.D. [Ropers,M.K.&B.]
*PRACTICE AREAS: Insurance Coverage Litigation.

**McDonald, William F.** '34 '65 C.4 B.B.A. L.262 J.D. (adm. in NY; not adm. in CA) V.P., Corp. Coun. & Asst. Secy., Emery Worldwide

McGuire, John J. ... '40 '75 C.1256 B.A. L.767 J.D. Dep. Co. Coun.

McInerney, John K., (BV) '40 '66 C.767 A.B. L.284 J.D. Exec. Dir., San Mateo Co. Bar Assn.

**McKibben, James H.,** (AV) ... '38 '64 C&L.813 A.B., J.D. [[B] Ropers,M.K.&B.]
*PRACTICE AREAS: Construction Defect Litigation; Complex Litigation; Litigation.

**McLachlan, John D.** ... '43 '81 C.285 B.A. L.464 J.D. [Fisher&P.]
*PRACTICE AREAS: Labor (Management) Laws; Employment Law; Wrongful Discharge Law.

**McLaughlin, David M.** ... '61 '87 C.112 B.A. L.770 J.D. [Ropers,M.K.&B.]
*PRACTICE AREAS: Commercial Litigation; Employment Litigation; Personal Injury Litigation.

McLaughlin, Patrick E. '62 '87 C.112 B.A. L.767 J.D. Corp. Coun., First Amer. Title Ins. Co.

**McLay, Robert S.** ... '63 '95 C.1239 B.A. L.1186 J.D. [[A] Ropers,M.K.&B.]
*PRACTICE AREAS: Insurance Defense; Insurance Bad Faith.

**McNeal, Jacqueline A.** ... '— '92 C.309 B.A. L.1355 J.D. Corp. Coun., Oracle Corp.

**McPherson, Justice C.** ... '63 '89 C.112 B.A. L.1049 J.D. [[A] Ropers,M.K.&B.]
*PRACTICE AREAS: Insurance Bad Faith; Insurance Coverage; Appellate Practice; Insurance Agent Malpractice.

Mears, Edward I., (CV) ... '37 '72 C.871 B.S. L.1049 J.D. 702 Marshall St., Suite 306

Mears, Kay Carolyn, (CV) ... '38 '85 C.954 B.A. L.284 J.D. 702 Marshall St., Suite 306

**Medlen & Carroll, LLP, (AV)**
**702 Marshall Street, Suite 600, 94063⊙**
**Telephone: 415-299-8120 Facsimile: 415-299-8127**
**Associates: Kamrin T. MacKnight; Diane E. Ingolia; Christopher John Smith.**
**Patent, Trademark and Copyright Law, Trade Secrets, Unfair Competition, Technology Licensing and Evaluation and related Trial and Appellate Litigation in State and Federal Courts, and Alternative Dispute Resolution (ADR).**
**San Francisco, California Office: 220 Montgomery St., Suite 2200. Telephone:415-705-8410. Facsimile: 415-397-8338.**
**Cambridge, Massachusetts Office: Five Cambridge Center, Second Floor. Telephone: 617-354-5455. Facsimile: 617-354-8132.**
**Toledo, Ohio Office: One Seagate, Suite 960. Telephone: 419-247-1010. Facsimile: 419-247-1011.**
*See Professional Biographies, REDWOOD CITY, CALIFORNIA*

Medlin, Edwin B., (BV) ... '57 '85 C.112 B.A. L.770 J.D. 1001 Marshall St.

**Mei, Peter C.** ... '66 '94 C.705 B.S.E.E. L.276 J.D. Pat. Coun., Oracle Corp.
*LANGUAGES: Mandarin Chinese.

Meinhold, William T. ... '24 '53 C.112 B.S. L.1065 J.D. 707 Calif. Way‡

**Melbye, Richard B.,** (AV) ... '33 '59 C.112 A.B. L.1066 J.D. [Owen&M.]⊙
*PRACTICE AREAS: Accident and Personal Injury; Bad Faith Law; Defense of Legal and Medical Malpractice; Products Liability; Wrongful Discharge Law.

**Mesaros, John G.** '36 '64 C.119 B.S.E.E. L.665 J.D. Pat. Coun. & Asst. Secy., Ampex Corp. (Pat.)

**Meyers, Conor A.** ... '64 '92 C.112 A.B. L.602 J.D. [[A] Owen&M.]
*PRACTICE AREAS: Construction Defect Litigation.

**Miclean, David J.,** (BV) ... '59 '84 C.112 B.A. L.426 J.D. [Ropers,M.K.&B.]
*PRACTICE AREAS: Commercial Litigation; General Civil Litigation.

**Miller, Cameron,** (BV) ... '53 '78 C.112 B.A. L.1065 J.D. [Jackson,M.M.&D.]
*PRACTICE AREAS: Civil Litigation; Business Law; Real Estate.

**Miller, James D.,** (BV) ... '49 '75 C.188 A.B. L.276 J.D. [Low,B.&L.]

Miller, James O. ... '31 '60 C.112 A.B. L.1066 J.D. Ret. Supr. Ct. J.

Mitchell, Sally E., (BV) ... '52 '80 C.999 L.1231 LL.B. 399 Bradford St., Suite 102

**Mittlesteadt, Carol L.,** (BV) ... '53 '78 C.880 B.S. L.838 J.D. [Jackson,M.M.&D.]
*REPORTED CASES: Collins v. Smithson (1979) 585 S.W. 2d 598.
*PRACTICE AREAS: Business Litigation.

**Moncada, L. Patricia** '61 '87 C&L.813 A.B., J.D. Sr. Corp. Coun. & Asst. Secy., Oracle Corp.
*LANGUAGES: Spanish, French.

Moore, Adriana C. ... '64 '90 C.910 B.S. L.846 J.D. 1775 Woodside Rd.

**Moore, Chester G., III,** (BV) ... '42 '68 C.112 B.A. L.1065 J.D. [Low,B.&L.]

**Morehead, Michael David** ... '67 '94 C.112 B.A. L.1049 J.D. [[A] Ropers,M.K.&B.]
*PRACTICE AREAS: Insurance Coverage; Insurance Bad Faith Defense.

Morris, William R., (BV) ... '46 '73 C.112 B.A. L.1065 J.D. 1771 Woodside Rd.

**Moss, John J.** ... '62 '91 C.771 B.A. L.813 J.D. Corp. Coun., Oracle Corp.
*LANGUAGES: Spanish, Portuguese.

Mossino, Ralph L. ... '34 '70 C.1074 B.S. L.765 J.D. 401 Bway. (Pat.)‡

Motley, Christine E. ... '48 '76 C.696 B.A. L.284 J.D. Dep. Co. Coun.

**Mulvihill, Thomas E.** ... '58 '87 C.112 B.A. L.767 J.D. [Low,B.&L.]
*PRACTICE AREAS: Insurance Law; Civil Litigation.

Murphy, Michael P. ... '48 '78 C.870 B.S. L.1066 J.D. Dep. Co. Coun.

Murray, Martin T., (AV) ... '46 '77 C.766 A.B. L.284 J.D. Asst. Dist. Atty.

**Mushkin, Nicole L.** ... '66 '91 C.228 A.B. L.893 J.D. Corp. Coun., Oracle Corp.

Myers, Barbara A. ... '60 '92 C.645 B.A. L.1065 J.D. 1001 Marshall St.

**Navabpour, Neda** ... '67 '92 C&L.770 B.A., J.D. [[A] Ropers,M.K.&B.]

**Newhouse, Norman C. '42 '82 C.352 B.S. L.284 J.D.**
**795 Fourth Avenue, Suite 204, 94063**
**Telephone: 415-365-8534 Fax: 415-368-8910**
***PRACTICE AREAS: Civil Trial Practice; Personal Injury; Workers Compensation Law.**
**Civil Trial Practice. Personal Injury and Workers Compensation Law.**

**Ng, Matthew K.** ... '68 '91 C.112 B.S. L.1066 J.D. Corp. Coun., Oracle Corp.
*TRANSACTIONS: Datalogix International Inc.; Digital Video Systems, Inc.
*RESPONSIBILITIES: Corporate Law; Securities Law; Mergers and Acquisitions; Financings.

Nichols, Paul M., (BV) ... '55 '82 C.112 B.A. L.1065 J.D. Dep. Dist. Atty.

**Nolan & Armstrong**
**(See Palo Alto)**

Nowicki, Edmund M. ... '43 '73 C.999 B.S. L.1003 J.D. 10 Twin Dolphin Dr.

Oakes, John P., (BV) ... '35 '66 C.1042 A.B. L.1066 LL.B. Dep. Dist. Atty.

**Ocampo, Raymond L., Jr.,** (AV) '53 '76 C.112 A.B. L.1066 J.D. Sr. V.P., Gen. Coun. & Secy., Oracle Corp.

Ogle, H. Kelly, (BV) ... '32 '59 C&L.770 J.D. 702 Marshall St.

**Owen, William H.,** (AV) ... '31 '59 C.112 B.S. L.813 J.D. [Owen&M.]⊙
*PRACTICE AREAS: Airplane Crash Litigation; Insurance Defense; Products Liability.

**Owen & Melbye, A Professional Corporation, (AV)** BR
**700 Jefferson Street, 94063⊙**
**Telephone: 415-364-6500 Fax: 415-365-7036**
**William H. Owen; Richard B. Melbye; Norman J. Roger; Edmund M. Scott; Pamela J. Helmer; John S. Posthauer; Paul R. Mangiantini;—Albert P. Blake, Jr.; Dawn M. Patterson; Conor A. Meyers; Mary P. Derner.**
**General Civil and Trial Practice in all State and Federal Courts. Aviation, Products, Insurance Defense Law, and Insurance Coverage Analysis.**
**Representative Clients: Aetna Cravens Dargan Co.; Avco Lycoming; Beech Aircraft Corp.; California Casualty Indemnity Exchange; K & K Claims Service; Kemper Insurance Cos.; Mutual Service Insurance Co.; State Farm Mutual Insurance Cos.; Underwriters at Lloyds; United States Aviation Insurance Group.**
**Tahoe City, California Office: P.O. Box 1524. Telephone: 916-546-2473.**
*See Professional Biographies, REDWOOD CITY, CALIFORNIA*

**Pagliaro, Frank J., Jr.,** (AV) ... '40 '67 C.882 A.B. L.893 LL.B. [Ropers,M.K.&B.]
*PRACTICE AREAS: Construction Litigation; Products Liability Law; Fidelity and Surety Law.

**Palmer, James D., Jr., (BV) '35 '60 C&L.813 A.B., LL.B.**
**1771 Woodside Road, 94061**
**Telephone: 415-367-1771 FAX: 415-367-8711**
**Email: JDPalmerjr@aol.com**
***PRACTICE AREAS: Probate; Estate Planning; Special Needs Trusts; Trust Administration; Federal Taxation.**
**Estate Planning, Special Needs Trusts, Estate and Trust Administration, Federal and State Taxation, Probate, Charitable Organizations.**
*See Professional Biographies, REDWOOD CITY, CALIFORNIA*

**Parker, Mary C.** ... '62 '92 C.222 B.A. L.1066 J.D. Corp. Coun., Oracle Corp.

**Patterson, Dawn M.** ... '60 '87 C&L.424 B.A., J.D. [[A] Owen&M.]
*PRACTICE AREAS: Insurance Defense Law; Insurance Coverage Law; Construction Law.

Pereira, Philip A., (BV) ... '48 '78 C.112 B.A. L.770 J.D. 1775 Woodside Rd.

Pfeiffer, Rosemary Phipps ... '47 '77 C.766 B.A. L.767 J.D. Supr. Ct. J.

Phillips, Alan M. ... '44 '72 C.112 B.A. L.1065 J.D. 654 Bair Island Rd.

Piombo, Frank ... '24 '50 C.112 L.767 J.D. Supr. Ct. J.

**Pitts, Michael E.** ... '48 '82 C.112 B.A. L.284 J.D. [Ropers,M.K.&B.]

Pitts, R. Gary '45 '83 C.10 PH.D. L.705 J.D. (adm. in NJ; not adm. in CA) V.P., Oral B Labs., Inc.

Player, Judith Ann ... '56 '83 C.354 B.A. L.184 J.D. 800 Saginaw Dr.

**Podesta, John H.** ... '61 '91 C.112 A.B. L.767 J.D. [[A] Branson,F.&H.]
*PRACTICE AREAS: Insurance Coverage; Bad Faith.

Podrid, Paul A. ... '48 '76 C.994 B.A. L.1065 J.D. Technical Equities

**Polverari, Joseph R., Jr.** ... '67 '92 C&L.770 B.S., J.D. [[A] Litigation S.]

**Polverari, Joseph R., Sr.,** (BV) ... '43 '74 C.1078 B.A. L.770 J.D. [[B] Litigation S.]

Poole, L. Eric ... '46 '89 C.941 B.A. L.770 J.D. Gen. Coun., Sequoia Hosp. Dist.

**Poplack, Michael J.** ... '60 '85 C.309 L.472 J.D. Sr. Corp. Coun., Oracle Corp.

Port, L. L., (Mrs.) ... '— '52 C.563 L.1009 LL.B. Chf. Dep. Co. Coun.

**Posthauer, John S.,** (BV) ... '56 '84 C.813 B.A. L.1068 J.D. [Owen&M.]⊙
*PRACTICE AREAS: Accident and Personal Injury; Construction Accidents; Environmental Insurance Litigation; Insurance Defense Law; Products Liability Law.

Prothro, R. King, Jr. ... '51 '77 C.112 B.A. L.1066 J.D. 136 Duggan Ct.

Quintero, Salomon, (BV) ... '47 '73 C.112 A.B. L.1066 J.D. [Goodman,Q.L.&F.]

Rabin, Paul E., (BV) ... '41 '72 C.768 B.S. L.1065 J.D. 104 Vaquero Way

Raffaelli, Elizabeth L. ... '58 '89 C.1169 B.A. L.813 J.D. Dep. Dist. Atty.

Raftery, Mary K. ... '53 '83 C.112 B.A. L.1065 J.D. Dep. Co. Coun.

**Rapson, Roxanne R.** ... '57 '90 C.112 M.P.H. L.770 J.D. [[A] Ropers,M.K.&B.]
*PRACTICE AREAS: Environmental (Regulatory and Litigation).

Razo, Jose H. ... '51 '77 C.813 B.A. L.1049 J.D. 611 Veterans Blvd.

Rehanek, Edw. W. '21 '55 C.381 B.A. L.767 LL.B. Co. Dept. of Pub. Health & Welfare

**Reichel, JoAnna R.** ... '47 '86 C.767 B.S.B.A. L.284 J.D. [[A] Ropers,M.K.&B.]
*LANGUAGES: Spanish and Portuguese.

Reid, Peter H., (BV) ... '42 '69 C.813 A.B. L.569 J.D. Legal Aid Soc. of San Mateo Co.

**Reidenbach, Laura L.** ... '60 '92 C&L.770 B.S., J.D. [[A] Ropers,M.K.&B.]
*PRACTICE AREAS: Insurance Coverage and Appellate Matters.

Reiss, Mary Sheahan, (CV) ............... '42 '78 C.818 B.S. L.1065 J.D. 2395 Broadway
**Ridley, Shawn M.** ............... '63 '89 C.602 B.A. L.770 J.D. [Ⓐ Branson,F.&H.]
**Riechert, Peter G.**, (AV) ............... '50 '75 C.966 B.A. L.813 J.D. [Aaron,R.C.&R.]
*PRACTICE AREAS: Business Law; Corporate Law; Real Estate Law; Credit Unions and Related Litigation.
**Riffle, Charles M.**, (BV) ............... '47 '72 C&L.767 B.A., J.D. [Aaron,R.C.&R.]
*PRACTICE AREAS: Estate Planning and Probate; Family Law; Business Law.
Rigg, Charles G., (BV) ............... '43 '70 C.813 A.B. L.1068 J.D. 1001 Marshall St.
**Roberts, Todd A.** ............... '61 '87 C.629 B.S. L.1067 J.D. [Ropers,M.K.&B.]
*PRACTICE AREAS: Insurance Coverage Law; Litigation; Appellate Practice.
Robinson, Charles M., (BV) ............... '48 '73 C.112 A.B. L.767 J.D. 702 Marshall St.
**Robinson, Jill L.** ......... '61 '89 C.112 A.B. L.1066 J.D. Corp. Coun., Oracle Corp. (Pat.)
Rockhill, Gordon L., (AV) ............... '34 '63 C&L.911 B.A., J.D. [Rockhill,S.&C.]
Rockhill, Schaiman & Carr, A Professional Corporation, (AV)
399 Bradford St., Suite 102
**Roger, Norman J.**, (BV) ............... '49 '74 C.276 B.S.F.S. L.767 J.D. [Owen&M.]⊙
*LANGUAGES: French.
*PRACTICE AREAS: Insurance Coverage; Bad Faith Law; Insurance Defense.
Rogers, Sandra K. ............... '45 '71 C.112 B.A. L.1065 J.D. 1775 Woodside Rd.
**Romanski, Richard J.**, (AV) ............... '42 '66 C.1030 B.S. L.893 LL.B. [Litigation S.]⊙
**Rome, Henry D.**, (AV) ............... '45 '71 C.767 B.A. L.1065 J.D. [Branson,F.&H.]
Rooney, Daniel C. ............... '41 '71 C.999 B.A. L.597 J.D. 10 Twin Dolphin Dr.
**Ropers, Michael**, (AV) ............... '34 '62 C.813 A.B. L.1065 J.D. [Ropers,M.K.&B.]
*PRACTICE AREAS: Professional Liability; General Civil Litigation.

**Ropers, Majeski, Kohn & Bentley, A Professional Corporation, (AV)**
**1001 Marshall Street, 94063⊙**
**Telephone: 415-364-8200 Fax: 415-367-0997**
**Harold Ropers (1905-1966); John M. Rubens (1936-1993); Eugene J. Majeski; John M. Bentley; Michael J. Brady; Frank J. Pagliaro, Jr.; John S. Simonson; Stephen A. Scott; Daniel E. Alberti; Mark G. Bonino; Richard K. Wilson; Stephen M. Hayes; Katherine S. Clark; Lawrence M. Guslani; Ted J. Hannig; Theodore C. Zayner; David J. Miclean; Pamela E. Cogan; David A. Levy; Colin R. Campbell; Brad W. Blocker; Marc D. Rosati; Thomas H. Clarke, Jr.; Robert P. Andris, II; Todd A. Roberts; Michael Ropers (Resident); David M. McLaughlin; William R. Garrett; Raymond A. Greene III; Robert G. Ittig; V. Raymond Swope, III; Ralph Tortorella III; Francois G. Laugier; Susan H. Handelman; Kevin G. McCurdy; Stephen P. Ellingson. Of Counsel: Ron W. Fields; Walter C. Kohn; Chi-Hung A. Chan; James H. McKibben;—Michael E. Pitts; Linda J. Dvorak (Certified Specialist, Probate, Estate Planning and Trust Law, The State Bar of California Board of Legal Specialization); Peter C. Suhr; Allison Lindley Dobbrow; Justice C. McPherson; JoAnna R. Reichel; Kathryn C. Curry; Richard Fisher; Laura L. Reidenbach; Brian R. Davis; Kimberly A. Donovan; Robert P. Soran; Kelly Franks; Anthony Joseph Hoglund; Hans Stephen Steinhoffer; Kevin Hunsaker; Ida Samawi Skikos; Jennifer C. Coates; Bruce M. MacKay; Stacy Ann Smith (Resident); Michael David Morehead; Mark Casper; Bridget C. Hopkins Ivanov; Roxanne R. Rapson; Robert S. McLay; Terry Anastassiou; Dennis Alan Duchene; Roger B. Frederickson; Neda Navabpour; H. Ann Liroff; Tara Jane Walsh; Denise A. Cole; Michael R. Solomon.**
**Arbitration and Mediation, Appellate Services, Banking and Financial Institutions Services, Bankruptcy, Commercial Litigation, Construction Litigation, Employment Law, Environmental Compliance and Litigation, Estate Planning, Trusts Probate and Elder Law, Fidelity and Surety Law, Health Care Law, Insurance Coverage and Litigation, Insurance Regulatory and Reinsurance, Intellectual Property Protection and Litigation, Products Litigation, Professional Malpractice Litigation, Real Estate Law, Trials and Antitrust.**
**San Jose, California Office: 80 North 1st Street. Telephone: 408-287-6262. Fax: 408-297-6819.**
**San Francisco, California Office: 670 Howard Street. Telephone: 415-543-4800. Fax: 415-512-1574.**
**Santa Rosa, California Office: Fountaingrove Center, Suite 300, 3558 Round Barn Boulevard. Telephone: 707-524-4200. Fax: 707-523-4610.**
**Los Angeles, California Office: 550 South Hope Street, Suite 1900. Telephone: 213-312-2000. Fax: 213-312-2001.**
**Sacramento, California Office: 1000 G Street, Suite 400. Telephone: 916-556-3100. Fax: 916-442-7121.**
***See Professional Biographies, REDWOOD CITY, CALIFORNIA***

**Rosati, Marc D.** ............... '54 '86 C.112 B.A. L.464 J.D. [Ropers,M.K.&B.]
*PRACTICE AREAS: Business Law; Business Litigation; Real Property Law.
Rosen, Lawrence E. ............... '45 '94 C.197 B.A. L.770 J.D. 702 Marshall St.
**Rosenfeld, Jennifer W.** ............... '64 '90 C.976 B.A. L.569 J.D. Menlo Logistics, Inc.
Rossi, Marianne C., (CV) ............... '57 '84 C.112 B.A. L.770 J.D. 702 Marshall St.
Rouse, Dorothy B. ............... '25 '49 C.112 A.B. L.767 LL.B. 891 Edgewood Rd.‡
Ruggiero, Attillio P. ............... '17 '56 C.767 B.S. L.284 LL.B. 22 Woodstock Pl.
Rutgers, Gerritt A. ............... '63 '90 C.169 B.A. L.1065 J.D. 303 Bradford St.
Ryan, Jeffrey Michael, (BV) ............... '41 '80 C.611 B.A. L.607 J.D. 154 S. Palomar Dr.
**Sandgren, Michael E.** ............... '67 '95 C.1169 B.A. L.1355 J.D. [Ⓐ Low,B.&L.]
**Sandoval, Gabriel A.** ............... '66 '91 C.813 B.A. L.770 J.D. Corp. Coun., Oracle Corp.
*LANGUAGES: Spanish.
**Santana, Anthony M.** ............... '57 '85 C.767 B.A. L.284 J.D. [Ⓐ Litigation S.]
**Sawicki, George J.** '59 '95 C.881 A.B. L.326 J.D.
(adm. in TX; not adm. in CA) Corp. Coun., Oracle Corp.
Schaiman, Steven L., (BV) ............... '46 '72 C.174 B.A. L.1065 J.D. [Rockhill,S.&C.]
**Schmid, Stephen H.** ............... '51 '77 C.770 B.S. L.464 J.D. [Ⓐ Litigation S.]
Schneider, Gerald M., (BV) ............... '34 '65 C.267 B.A. L.1065 LL.B. 617 Veterans Blvd.
Schricker, David E., (BV) ..... '36 '65 C.976 B.A. L.1066 LL.B. City Atty. [D.E.Schricker]
Schricker, David E., Law Offices of, A Prof. Corp., (BV) ............... 702 Marshall St.
**Schurman, Juana M.** ...... '54 '85 C.1307 B.A. L.1065 J.D. Sr. Corp. Coun., Oracle Corp.
Schwartz, John G. ............... '43 '69 C.950 B.A. L.1066 J.D. Supr. Ct. J.

**Schwartzbach, M. Gerald, (AV) '44 '70 C.901 B.A. L.273 J.D.**
**601 Brewster Avenue, P.O. Box 3389, 94103**
**Telephone: 415-367-6811 Fax: 415-368-0367**
**Civil Trial, Criminal Trial and Appellate Practice in State and Federal Courts.**
***See Professional Biographies, REDWOOD CITY, CALIFORNIA***

Schwarz, Daniel R. ............... '61 '87 C.112 B.S. L.767 J.D. 1775 Woodside Rd.
**Scott, Edmund M.**, (AV) ............... '48 '81 C.767 B.A. L.284 J.D. [Owen&M.]⊙
*PRACTICE AREAS: Accident and Personal Injury; Defense of Legal and Medical Malpractice; Environmental Insurance Litigation; Insurance Defense Law; Products Liability Law.
Scott, Joseph C., (BV) ............... '50 '76 C.103 A.B. L.310 J.D. 702 Marshall St.
**Scott, Stephen A.**, (AV) ............... '50 '75 C.813 B.A. L.770 J.D. [Ropers,M.K.&B.]
*PRACTICE AREAS: Insurance Bad Faith Defense Law; Medical Malpractice; Products Liability Law.
**Secrest, David S.** ............... '55 '89 C.207 B.A. L.767 J.D. [Ⓐ Branson,F.&H.]
**Segal, Lauren Gage** ............... '63 '90 C.112 A.B. L.178 J.D. Corp. Coun., Oracle Corp.
Serrato, Albert A. ............... '60 '86 C.767 B.S. L.1066 J.D. Dep. Dist. Atty.
Serverian, Aram ............... '32 '67 C.1019 L.765 Supr. Ct. J.
Shadowens, Lamont W. ............... '22 '88 C.1333 B.P.A. L.1026 J.D. 898 Chestnut St.
**Shafer, Bradford J.** ... '60 '85 C.169 B.A. L.1065 J.D. Gen. Coun., Corp., Heartport, Inc.
Shea, Daniel C. ............... '22 '55 C.93 B.S. L.276 J.D. San Mateo Legal Aid. Soc.‡
Sigler, Sonya L. ............... '67 '93 C.112 B.A. L.770 J.D. 255 Shoreline Dr.
Simon, Sandra Rowell, (CV) ............... '40 '80 C.1085 L.1231 LL.B. 2000 Bway.
**Simonson, John S.**, (AV) ............... '47 '73 C.285 B.B.A. L.1065 J.D. [Ropers,M.K.&B.]
*PRACTICE AREAS: Professional Liability; Insurance Bad Faith; Governmental Entity Liability; Civil Litigation.
**Skarda, C. Trevor** ............... '69 '96 C.629 B.A. L.464 J.D. [Ⓐ Fisher&P.]
**Skelton, John**, (AV) ............... '48 '75 C.112 A.B. L.767 J.D. [Litigation S.]
**Skikos, Ida Samawi** ............... '64 '91 C.112 B.A. L.770 J.D. [Ⓐ Ropers,M.K.&B.]
*PRACTICE AREAS: Civil Litigation; Appellate; Insurance Coverage.
Sloan, David M., (BV) ............... '57 '84 C&L.770 B.S., J.D. 10 Twin Dolphin Dr.
Smith, Blair Rhodes ............... '51 '89 L.999 J.D. 600 Allerton St.
**Smith, Carol P.** ............... '62 '87 C.813 B.A. L.770 J.D. [Branson,F.&H.]
*LANGUAGES: French.
**Smith, Charles J.**, (AV) ............... '51 '76 C.401 B.A. L.770 J.D. [Smith&B.]
*PRACTICE AREAS: Criminal Law; Civil Litigation.
**Smith, Christopher John** '65 '94 C.112 B.S. L.1065 J.D.
[Ⓐ Medlen&C.] (See Pat. Sect.)
*PRACTICE AREAS: Chemical; Pharmaceutical; Biotechnology Patents; Intellectual Property Litigation; Medical Device.
Smith, Leila ............... '41 '72 C.104 A.B. L.1026 J.D. 620 Jefferson‡
**Smith, Pamela Ann** ............... '65 '90 C.112 A.B. L.770 J.D. [Ⓐ Coddington,H.&D.]
**Smith, Stacy Ann** ............... '64 '91 C.659 B.S. L.763 J.D. [Ⓐ Ropers,M.K.&B.]
*LANGUAGES: French, Danish.
Smith, Thomas McGinn ............... '37 '64 C&L.770 B.A., J.D. Supr. Ct. J.

**Smith & Bentley, (AV)**
**777 Marshall Street, 94063**
**Telephone: 415-568-2820 Fax: 415-568-2823**
**Members of Firm: Charles J. Smith; Joshua M. Bentley; Jim Hartnett. Of Counsel: Lee W. Clark.**
**General Civil and Trial Practice, Personal Injury Litigation, General Business Litigation and Criminal Defense Litigation.**
***See Professional Biographies, REDWOOD CITY, CALIFORNIA***

Solomon, Mark J. ............... '53 '78 C.813 A.B. L.800 J.D. 702 Marshall St.
**Solomon, Michael R.** ............... '59 '93 C.560 B.A. L.767 J.D. [Ⓐ Ropers,M.K.&B.]
*PRACTICE AREAS: Medical Malpractice; Public Entity; General Civil Litigation.
**Somorjai, John E.** ............... '66 '91 C.197 B.A. L.1066 J.D. Corp. Coun., Oracle Corp.
*LANGUAGES: French.
**Soran, Robert P.** ............... '66 '93 C.1079 B.A. L.770 J.D. [Ⓐ Ropers,M.K.&B.]
*PRACTICE AREAS: Civil Litigation; Environmental Law; Compliance and Litigation; Toxic Torts Litigation; Personal Injury Litigation.
Sorenson, Keith C., (AV) ............... '21 '47 C&L.878 B.S., LL.B. 3717 Farm Hill Blvd.‡
Sosnick, Randall D. ........ '59 '85 C.112 B.S. L.1066 J.D. COO, The Digital Foundry, Inc.
Staggs, Daniel T. ............... '56 '83 C.770 B.A. L.767 J.D. 611 Veterans Blvd.
**Stearns, Laurie** ............... '54 '93 C.399 B.A. L.1066 J.D. Corp. Coun., Oracle Corp.
**Steinhoffer, Hans Stephen** ............... '65 '94 C.813 B.A. L.276 J.D. [Ⓐ Ropers,M.K.&B.]
*PRACTICE AREAS: Appellate; Litigation.
Stevens, Lawrence T. ............... '42 '69 C.800 B.S. L.1065 J.D. Supr. Ct. J.
Stromberg, Jeffrey T. ............... '66 '93 C.1060 B.A. L.602 J.D. 1001 Marshall St.
**Strong, David L.** ............... '55 '82 C.112 B.A. L.770 J.D. [Branson,F.&H.]
**Suhr, Peter C.** ............... '57 '86 C.999 B.A. L.770 J.D. [Ⓐ Ropers,M.K.&B.]
*PRACTICE AREAS: First and Third Party Insurance Coverage and Coverage Litigation; Environmental and Business Litigation.
**Swope, V. Raymond, III** ............... '52 '88 C&L.221 B.A., J.D. [Ropers,M.K.&B.]
*PRACTICE AREAS: General Civil Litigation and Professional Liability; Environmental Law.
**Talcott, Joel D.** '42 '69 C.46 B.S. L.146 J.D.
V.P., Gen. Coun. & Secy., Ampex Corp. (Pat.)
Talcott, Leland H. ............... '65 '90 C.740 B.A. L.464 J.D. 1001 Marshall St.
Taylor, George G. ............... '19 '46 C.112 A.B. L.1065 J.D. 542 Lancaster‡
Taylor, George R. ............... '30 '54 C.679 B.S. L.1119 J.D. Supr. Ct. Comm.
**Theodores, Thomas** ............... '50 '78 C.209 B.A. L.1065 J.D. V.P., Legal, Oracle Corp.
Thomas, Eddie C., Jr. ............... '50 '75 C.813 B.A. L.352 J.D. Dep. Dist Atty.
Thomas, John P. ............... '46 '84 C.112 B.A. L.1066 J.D. 627 Poplar Ave.
Thomas, W. Bradley ............... '63 '91 C.112 B.A. L.990 J.D. 1001 Marshall St.

**Thompson, James A., Law Offices of, (BV) '43 '71 C.112 A.B. L.1065 J.D.**
**600 Allerton Street, Second Floor, 94063**
**Telephone: 415-365-7333 Fax: 415-365-7735**
***LANGUAGES: Spanish and French.**
***PRACTICE AREAS: Civil Litigation (25%, 30); Real Estate Law (20%, 5); Probate Law (25%, 15); Wills Law (25%, 30); Family Law (5%, 5).**
**Associate: Maurice J. Creegan.**
**General Civil and Trial Practice. Wills, Trusts, Probate and Personal Injury.**
***See Professional Biographies, REDWOOD CITY, CALIFORNIA***

**Thomson, James M.** '37 '65
C.336 B.S.E.E. L.273 J.D. Asst. Pat. Coun., Ampex Corp. (Pat.)
Tinsley, Carlos O., (AV) ............... '30 '61 C&L.37 J.D. 1900 Broadway, Ste. 200
Tipton, Elaine M., (AV) ............... '52 '79 C.112 A.B. L.1065 J.D. Asst. Dist. Atty.
Tong, Harry W. ............... '34 '72 C.1016 B.S.B.A. L.209 J.D. 490 Winslow
**Tortorella, Ralph, III** ............... '63 '89 C.867 B.A. L.770 J.D. [Ropers,M.K.&B.]
*PRACTICE AREAS: Insurance Coverage; Bad Faith Litigation; Appellate and Reinsurance.
**Trapani, Michelle C.** ............... '67 '92 C&L.339 A.B., J.D. Corp. Coun., Oracle Corp.
*RESPONSIBILITIES: Software Licensing; Trademarks; Copyrights; Contracts.
**Truong, Bobby K.** ......... '66 '92 C.326 B.S. L.1066 J.D. Pat. Coun., Oracle Corp. (Pat.)
**Tucker, William G.**, (AV) ............... '28 '57 C&L.426 B.S., J.D. [Ⓒ Coddington,H.&D.]
Tuerck, Timothy T. ............... '21 '51 C&L.911 B.A., LL.B. 2656 Eaton Ave.‡
Turner, Scott E. ............... '48 '75 C.112 B.A. L.1065 J.D. 2000 Bway.
Vanderveen, Sandra K., (BV) ............... '55 '83 C.1060 B.A. L.464 J.D. Dep. Dist. Atty.
Vannucci, John Fitzpatrick ............... '69 '94 C.770 B.A. L.767 J.D. 1001 Marshall St.
Veal, Harlan K. ............... '23 '52 C.112 B.S. L.813 J.D. Supr. Ct. J.
Viadro, Harriet Ann ............... '— '74 C.813 B.A. L.765 J.D. 2395 Bway.
Viera, Robert W., (CV) ............... '47 '85 C.112 B.A. L.284 J.D. 303 Bradford St.
Voisin, Eva B., (BV) ............... '45 '78 C.112 B.A. L.1231 J.D. 10 Twin Dolphin Dr.
**Von Emster, Elizabeth J.** ............... '67 '92 C.112 B.A. L.1065 J.D. [Ⓐ Branson,F.&H.]
Von Gustlin, Gretchen ............... '64 '91 C.518 A.B. L.813 J.D. Sugen, Inc.
**Wagner, Allen B.** ..... '43 '73 C.1044 B.S. L.1065 J.D. Sr. Pat. Coun., Oracle Corp. (Pat.)
**Wagstaffe, Dennis G.**, (AV) ............... '54 '78 C.800 A.B. L.1065 J.D. [Wagstaffe&W.]
*PRACTICE AREAS: Probate Law; Real Property Law; Business Law; Corporation Law; Hospital Law.
**Wagstaffe, Gerard**, (AV) ............... '17 '40 C&L.770 A.B., J.D. [Wagstaffe&W.]
*PRACTICE AREAS: Probate Law; Real Property Law; Business Law; Corporation Law; Hospital Law.
Wagstaffe, Stephen M., (AV) '52 '77
C.602 B.A. L.1065 J.D. Chf. Crim. Deputy Dist. Atty.

**Wagstaffe & Wagstaffe, (AV)**
**333 Bradford Street, P.O. Box 5009, 94063**
**Telephone: 415-366-9593**
**Members of Firm: Gerard Wagstaffe; Dennis G. Wagstaffe.**
**General Civil and Trial Practice. Probate, Real Property, Business, Corporation and Hospital Law.**
***See Professional Biographies, REDWOOD CITY, CALIFORNIA***

**Wall, Tyler E.** ............... '— '95 C.878 B.S. L.770 J.D. Corp. Coun., Oracle Corp.
*RESPONSIBILITIES: Intellectual Property; Contracts.
**Walsh, Tara Jane** ............... '69 '94 C.800 B.A. L.262 J.D. [Ⓐ Ropers,M.K.&B.]
*PRACTICE AREAS: Insurance Litigation.
Warsowe, Marc ............... '47 '74 C.178 A.B. L.813 J.D. Eco-Dent International, Inc.
Waste, Katherine M. ............... '59 '89 C.112 A.B. L.767 J.D. 900 Veterans Blvd.
**Watts, Pamela B.** '64 '95 C.945 B.A. L.1356 J.D.
(adm. in VA; not adm. in CA) Oracle Corp.
Way, G. Larison ............... '47 '76 C.347 A.B. L.284 LL.B. 10 Twin Dolphin
**Weinberg, Ziff & Miller**
**(See Palo Alto)**
Wentholt, H. Frank, (BV) ............... '41 '71 C.976 B.A. L.1065 J.D. 600 Allerton St.

CALIFORNIA—REDWOOD CITY MARTINDALE-HUBBELL LAW DIRECTORY 1997

**Wessel, David W.**, (BV) ..........'53 '84 C.960 B.A. L.966 J.D. [⊠ Coddington,H.&D.]
White, Jay C. ..........'25 '67 L.981 LL.B. P.O. Box 1148‡
Wilhelm, Robert O., (BV) ..........'18 '52 C.277 B.C.E. L.813 J.D. 600 Allerton St.
**Willson, Jacqueline A.**, (BV) ..........'51 '78 C.112 A.B. L.767 J.D. [⊠ Litigation S.]
**Wilmot, Robert D.** '51 '80 C.94 B.A. L.818 J.D.
(adm. in NJ; not adm. in CA) Sr. Corp. Coun., Oracle Corp.
Wilson, Donald A., (BV) ..........'43 '69 C.112 B.A. L.1065 J.D. [Wilson&W.]
Wilson, Elizabeth B., (BV) ..........'43 '82 [Wilson&W.]
Wilson, John E. ..........'54 '80 C&L.770 B.A., J.D. Dep. Dist. Atty.
**Wilson, Richard K.**, (BV) ..........'49 '76 C.112 B.S. L.1065 J.D. [Ropers,M.K.&B.]
*PRACTICE AREAS: Environmental Insurance Coverage; Reinsurance.
Wilson & Wilson, (BV) ..........928 Middlefield Rd.

**Winters, Krug & Delbon**
(See Burlingame)

**Woo, Terry K.** ..........'60 '87 C.112 A.B. L.188 J.D. Corp. Coun., Oracle Corp.
Woodman, Eric E., (BV) ..........'43 '70 C.768 B.S. L.770 J.D. [E.E.Woodman]
Woodman, Eric E., A P.C., (BV) ..........621 Middlefield
**Woodson, Brenda G.** '58 '83
C.713 B.A. L.309 J.D. V.P. & Assoc. Gen. Coun., Oracle Corp.
Woodward, Carol L. ..........'46 '78 C.477 B.A. L.767 J.D. Dep. Co. Coun.
Yamane, Niall G., (BV) ..........'59 '85 C.637 B.A. L.767 J.D. 539 Middlefield Rd.
Yeley, Vicki A., (BV) ..........'52 '79 C.112 B.A. L.1065 J.D. [Rockhill,S.&C.]
**Youssef, Ehab F.** ..........'66 '93 C.112 B.S. L.770 J.D. Corp. Coun., Oracle Corp.
**Zayner, Theodore C.**, (BV) ..........'56 '83 C.813 A.B. L.1065 J.D. [Ropers,M.K.&B.]
*PRACTICE AREAS: Environmental Coverage; Civil Litigation.
**Ziegenhorn, Angela** ..........'65 '89 C.549 B.A. L.1067 J.D. Corp. Coun., Oracle Corp.
Zirpoli, Cadio ..........'67 '95 C.12 B.A. L.767 J.D. 1001 Marshall St.
Zoucha, Joseph R., (BV) ..........'51 '77 C.602 B.A. L.767 J.D. [Gibbs,Z.&Assoc.]

## REDWOOD ESTATES, 1,300, *Santa Clara Co.*

Lew, Mark ..........'56 '80 C.112 B.S. L.770 J.D. P.O. Box 407

## REDWOOD VALLEY, —, *Mendocino Co.*

Kasler, Phyllis D. ..........'28 '63 C.472 L.765 LL.B. P.O. Box 720

## REEDLEY, 15,791, *Fresno Co.*

Bloyd, Wm. A. ..........'24 '51 L.408 LL.B. 1196 11th St.
Burgess, Myrtle M., (BV) ..........'21 '50 C.766 A.B. L.1065 J.D. 1107 G St.
Dupras, Fred J. ..........'39 '76 L.1132 J.D. Dist. J.
Edwards, Charles W., (BV) ..........'23 '57 C.267 A.B. L.1066 P.O. Box 243
Hamilton, Wm. A. ..........'17 '48 C.112 L.426 1625 G St.‡

## RESCUE, —, *El Dorado Co.*

Hester, Edward C. ..........'48 '80 C.1042 B.A. L.1127 J.D. P.O. Box 6
Lear, Adele ..........'25 '73 C.1073 B.A. L.1066 J.D. 3021 Pinchem Creek Dr.

## RESEDA, —, *Los Angeles Co.*

(Part of the incorporated City of Los Angeles)

Biafora, Joseph R., (AV) ..........'20 '47 C.923 A.B. L.800 LL.B. [Biafora,W.&L.]
Biafora, Weiner & Lampert, (AV) ..........7133 Etiwanda Ave.
Cocek, Carol ..........'54 '89 C.846 B.B.A. L.1068 J.D. 6167 Reseda Blvd.
Dickey, Darryl O. ..........'40 '72 C.906 B.A. L.1095 J.D. 19121 Enadia Way
Dlugatch, Harvey E. ..........'39 '82 C.999 D.D.S. L.1190 J.D. 18909 Sherman Way
Germann, Edward J. ..........'22 '50 C&L.426 B.S., LL.B. Staff Coun., Dept. of Ins.
Holland, Gregory L. ..........'60 '91 C.1342 B.S. L.1136 J.D. P.O. Box 473
Holland, Paul D., (AV) ..........'10 '34 C&L.800 B.A., J.D. 18337 Calvert St.
Keen, Roger A. ..........'50 '76 C&L.910 A.B., J.D. 19609 Sherman Way‡
Kepke, John R. ..........'17 '74 L.1095 J.D. 6720 Chimineas Ave.
Kushner, Larry ..........'46 '80 C.1077 B.A. L.1095 J.D. 8100 Zelzah Ave.
Lampert, Gary D. ..........'49 '75 C.112 B.A. L.1068 J.D. [Biafora,W.&L.]
Mast, Sandra ..........'55 '83 C.112 B.A. L.809 J.D. 8229 Wynne Ave.
Petterson, Jay R. ..........'47 '72 C.602 B.B.A. L.585 J.D. 18700 Sherman Way
Schlosser, J. Philip ..........'27 '75 C.800 A.B. L.1008 LL.B. 7133 Etiwanda Ave.
Telesca, Nicholas R., Jr. ..........'42 '74 C.1042 B.A. L.1095 J.D. 7420 Corbin
Weiner, Monroe B., (BV) ..........'33 '63 C.112 B.A. L.809 LL.B. [Biafora,W.&L.]

## RIALTO, 72,388, *San Bernardino Co.*

Carter, Earl F., (BV) ..........'47 '75 C.101 B.A. L.36 J.D. 333 N. Riverside Ave.
Mathews, Ward Os ..........'21 '49 C.886 B.S. L.813 LL.B. Ret. Mun. J.
Robinson, William L. ..........'50 '77 C.1077 B.A. L.809 J.D. Burlingame Industries Inc.
Sawyer, Marvin T. ..........'45 '83 C.1110 M.A. L.1198 J.D. 149 W. Rialto Ave.
Thornes, Frederick G. ..........'28 '78 C.174 B.S. L.1198 J.D. 5726 N. Sycamore Ave.‡

## RICHMOND, 87,425, *Contra Costa Co.*

Abelson, Howard P. ..........'44 '69 C.112 A.B. L.1065 J.D. 3150 Hilltop Mall Rd.
Ackerman, Joel G. ..........'41 '66 C.659 A.B. L.564 LL.B. Coun., Zeneca Inc. (Pat.)
Alderson, Michael L., (AV) ..........'45 '73 C.310 B.A. L.770 J.D. [Pelletreau,A.&C.]
Atkins, Jennifer A. '63 '89 C.311 B.A. L.1066 J.D.
Assoc. Dir., The Hawkins Ctr. of Law
Bancroft, Prentice K., (BV) ..........'29 '61 C.31 A.B. L.767 LL.B. P.O. Box 5376
**Barber, Gretchen B.** ..........'66 '95 C.914 B.A. L.1066 J.D. [⊠ Whiting&R.]
*PRACTICE AREAS: Family Law.
Barbieri, Karen R. ..........'55 '80 C.112 B.A. L.770 J.D. 3700 Barrett Ave.
Bartke, Richard H., (BV) ..........'36 '67 C.112 B.A. L.767 J.D. 3260 Blume Dr. Ave.
Berthenthal, Philip J. '46 '73 C.293 B.A. L.569 J.D.
Dir., Litig., Contra Costa Legal Servs. Found.
Bobrow, Oscar Jacob ..........'55 '86 C.112 B.A. L.904 J.D. Dep. Pub. Def.
Bonnell, William M., (BV) ..........'41 '66 C.197 B.A. L.623 J.D. Sr. Asst. City Atty.
Brewer, Robin A. ..........'62 '93 C.999 B.A. L.1065 J.D. 3260 Blume Dr.
Brorby, Robert P., (AV) ..........'25 '52 C.112 A.B. L.1066 LL.B. Station A
Brown, Diana B. ..........'51 '86 C.766 B.A. L.284 J.D. 3718 Macdonald Ave.
**Bunn, David D.** ..........'64 '89 C.112 A.B. L.178 J.D. [⊠ Whiting&R.]
*LANGUAGES: Spanish.
*REPORTED CASES: In Re Marriage of Moschetta, 25 Cal.App. 4th 1218 (1994).
*PRACTICE AREAS: Family Law; Civil Litigation.
Cabral, Alfred A. ..........'54 '80 C.112 B.A. L.767 J.D. [Pelletreau,A.&C.]
Cannon, Patrick G. ..........'58 '90 C.112 B.A. L.1065 J.D. Dep. Pub. Def.
Caploe, Fred, (AV) ..........'31 '60 C.309 A.B. L.813 J.D. [F.Caploe]
Caploe, Fred, A Professional Corporation, (AV) ..........P.O. Box 236-Station A
Carey, Mary P. ..........'57 '85 C.112 B.A. L.767 J.D. Dep. Pub. Def.
Carroll, George D. ..........'23 '50 C.102 B.A. L.1009 J.D. Ret. Mun. J.
**Caughman, Noël M.** ..........'66 '91 C.112 B.S. L.1065 J.D. [⊠ Norris&N.]
*LANGUAGES: German.
*PRACTICE AREAS: Employment Discrimination; Sexual Harassment.
Clark, William Michael ..........'55 '87 C.768 B.A. L.1153 J.D. Dep. Dist. Atty.

**Coffey, Colin J.** ..........'59 '83 C.112 B.A. L.1365 J.D. [Norris&N.]
*PRACTICE AREAS: Health Care Law; Government Approvals Law.
Coffey, Peggy R. ..........'26 '78 C.112 B.A. L.1065 J.D. 1201 Melville Sq.
Collins, James B. ..........'52 '77 C.768 B.A. L.1065 J.D. 69 Seagull Dr.
Corbin, Douglas T. ..........'28 '54 C.732 B.S. L.273 LL.B. 114 Crest Ave.‡
Covell, Henry E., Jr., (BV) ..........'35 '62 C.112 B.A. L.1065 J.D. 3260 Blume Dr.
Dean, Herbert W., Jr. ..........'44 '82 L.1153 J.D. 132 Curry St.
Del Simone, David R., (BV) ..........'53 '80 C.112 B.A. L.767 J.D. 137 Park Place
Dewey, H. Stanley, (BV) ..........'42 '82 C.112 B.A. L.1065 J.D. 3150 Hilltop Mall Rd.
Donaldson, Gene S. ..........'38 '71 C.906 L.765 J.D. 207 37th St.
Dreibelbis, Bessie P. ..........'27 '62 C.112 A.B. L.284 LL.B. Mun. J.‡
Dunn, Kelly ..........'57 '82 C.112 B.S. L.1066 J.D. Exec. Dir., The Hawkins Ctr. of Law
Engler, Gerald A. ..........'57 '82 C.112 A.B. L.1068 J.D. Dep. Dist. Atty.
**Epstein, Cy**, (AV) ..........'36 '77 C.112 B.A. L.1065 J.D. [Norris&N.]
*PRACTICE AREAS: Real Property Transactions; Litigation and Condemnation Law.
**Fallon, R. Ann** ..........'42 '84 C.262 B.A. L.1066 J.D. [⊠ Whiting&R.]
*PRACTICE AREAS: Family Law; Family Law Pensions.
Genser, Joshua G. ..........'58 '83 C.813 B.A. L.1065 J.D. 3150 Hilltop Mall Rd.
Gray, Thomas M. ..........'46 '75 C.112 B.S. L.1065 J.D. Dep. Pub. Def.
Grydyk, Stanley T., (BV) ..........'21 '53 C&L.767 B.S., J.D. [Grydyk&P.]
Grydyk & Pierce, (BV) ..........4006 Macdonald Ave.
**Hallikainen, David L.** ..........'55 '95 L.1153 J.D. [⊠ Watson,H.&H.]
*PRACTICE AREAS: Family Law; Civil Litigation.
**Harris, George A., III** ..........'63 '95 C.477 B.B.A. L.273 J.D. [⊠ Norris&N.]
**Hass, Peter A.**, (AV) ..........'60 '87 C.1169 B.A. L.767 J.D. [Watson,H.&H.]
*PRACTICE AREAS: Real Estate; Banking; Civil Litigation; Commercial Litigation; Construction Law.
**Hoffe, R. Bruce**, (AV) ..........'27 '54 C.112 A.B. L.1066 LL.B. [Watson,H.&H.]
*REPORTED CASES: Nelson v. Orosco (1981) 117 CA.3d 73; Trans Container Services v. Security Forwarders, Inc. (1985) 752 F2d 483; United States of America to the Use of Wayne Bailey dba Wayne Bailey Trucking v. Elmer J. Freethy, individually and dba Elmer J. Freethy Co. (1972) 469 F2d 1348.
*PRACTICE AREAS: Commercial Litigation; Real Property; Corporate; Construction Law.
**Iversen, Sharon Moody** ..........'41 '87 C.112 B.S. L.1153 J.D. [Norris&N.]
*PRACTICE AREAS: Health Care Law; General Business Law.
Jenkins, Everett W., Jr. ..........'53 '79 C.31 B.A. L.1066 J.D. Asst. City Atty.
**Johnsen, Jon A.**, (BV) ..........'46 '75 C.112 B.S. L.1065 J.D. [⊠ Whiting&R.]
*PRACTICE AREAS: Family Law.
Johnson, Alonzo M., (BV) ..........'51 '76 C.103 B.A.Ec. L.813 J.D. Dep. Dist. Atty.
Johnson, Myron A., (BV) ..........'21 '52 C.112 A.B. L.1066 LL.B. 549 S. 29th St.
Joscelyn, Miriam A. ..........'41 '87 C.589 B.S.Ed. L.765 J.D. State Dept. of Corrections

**Judge, Christopher E., (BV) '46 '72 C.112 B.A. L.1066 J.D.**
**3150 Hilltop Mall Road, Suite 48, 94806**
**Telephone: 510-970-7690 Fax: 510-970-7671**
**General Civil and Criminal Trial and Appellate Practice, including Negligence, Workers Compensation and Family Law.**

Law, Robert E., (BV) ..........'43 '74 C.490 B.S.B.A. L.767 J.D. Dep. Dist. Atty.
Lee, Jane M. ..........'63 '92 C.1068 B.A. L.767 J.D. 22 Deepwater Ct.
Levy, Leslie A., (BV) ..........'50 '77 C.112 B.A. L.770 J.D. 3260 Blume Dr.
Lundberg, Norman C., (BV) ..........'48 '72 C.112 B.A. L.1065 J.D. 3220 Blume Dr.
Madsen, Richard A., Jr. ..........'61 '90 C.1074 B.A. L.464 J.D. Dep. Dist. Atty.
Marcus, Karen D. ..........'55 '85 C.1183 B.A. L.146 J.D. 3220 Blume Dr.
Martin, Paul R. '35 '61 C.679 B.S. L.608 J.D.
(adm. in OH; not adm. in CA) Stauffer Chem. Co.
Martin, Sally E. ..........'53 '89 C.813 B.A. L.1065 J.D. Dep. Pub. Def.
McIntosh, Lesa Renee ..........'55 '89 C.112 B.S. L.1153 J.D. 2921 MacDonald Ave.
Mellen, James G. ..........'35 '85 C.766 B.A. L.1153 J.D. 3260 Blume Dr.
Micklas, M. Jeffrey, (BV) ..........'50 '77 C.121 B.S. L.464 J.D. 3260 Blume Dr.
Millspaugh, Phillip M. ..........'21 '50 C.112 A.B. L.1065 J.D. 3616 Macdonald Ave.
Morris, Andrew S., Jr. ..........'51 '76 C.112 A.B. L.284 J.D. Bartels Property Mgmt.
Morris, C. L., (AV) ..........'37 '68 C.623 B.F.A. L.767 J.D. Dep. Dist. Atty.
Mossina, Charles L. ..........'51 '80 C.740 B.A. L.767 J.D. 3700 Barrett Ave.
Nance, Karen F. ..........'58 '85 C.112 B.A. L.831 J.D. Dep. Pub. Def.
Nishioka, Wayne S. ..........'47 '72 C.766 B.A. L.1067 J.D. Asst. City Atty.
Norris, Allen L. ..........'24 '50 C.309 L.1065 J.D. Mun. Ct. J.
**Norris, Richard E.**, (BV) ..........'52 '77 C.112 B.A. L.1065 J.D. [Norris&N.]⊙
*PRACTICE AREAS: Business Transactions; Corporate Law; Discretionary Government Approvals; Environmental Law; Solid Waste Law.

**Norris & Norris, (AV)**
**3260 Blume Drive, Suite 400, 94806**⊙
**Telephone: 510-222-2100 Facsimile: 510-222-5992**
**Members of Firm: Richard E. Norris; Douglas C. Straus; Cy Epstein; Colin J. Coffey; Edward L. Shaffer; Sharon Moody Iversen. Associates: Leonard H. Watkins; Noël M. Caughman; George A. Harris, III; Michael A. Sweet.**
**Business, Commercial and Real Estate Litigation and Transactions, Class Action Defense and Complex Litigation, Government Approvals, Environmental, Solid Waste, Health Care Law, Cable Television, Property Taxation, Sales and Use Taxation, Employment, Discrimination, Wrongful Termination, Workplace Harassment, Land Use, Probate, Trust and Estate Planning.**
**Walnut Creek, California Office: 500 Ygnacio Valley Road, Suite 400, 94596. Telephone: 510-934-8181. Facsimile: 510-934-3665.**
***See Professional Biographies, RICHMOND, CALIFORNIA***

Patterson, Donald E., (BV) ..........'53 '85 C.112 A.B. L.767 J.D. [⊠ Pelletreau,A.&C.]
Pelletreau, Robert W., (A Professional Corporation), (AV) '19 '46
L.1065 LL.B. [⊠ Pelletreau,A.&C.]
Pelletreau, Alderson & Cabral, (AV) ..........3260 Blume Dr.
Pierce, John R., (BV) ..........'30 '62 C.766 A.B. L.767 J.D. [Grydyk&P.]
Reiss, Gary R. ..........'53 '77 C.112 B.S. L.813 J.D. Dep. Dist. Atty.
Robinson, Laura S. ..........'61 '88 C.339 B.Sc. L.1065 J.D. Dep. Pub. Def.
Rosenthal, David B., (BV) ..........'38 '63 C.477 B.A. L.1066 LL.B. 145 Park Pl.
**Ross, Andrew**, (AV) ..........'46 '72 C.732 B.A. L.1009 J.D. [⊠ Whiting&R.]
*PRACTICE AREAS: Family Law; Civil Litigation.
**Roth, Carol J.** ..........'54 '87 C.798 B.Sc. L.770 J.D. Pat. Coun., Berlex Biosciences (Pat.)
**Rubenstein, Ronald A.**, (BV) ..........'44 '70 C.112 B.A. L.1066 J.D. [Whiting&R.]
*REPORTED CASES: Bouquet v. Bouquet (1976) 16C3 583; In re Marriage of Van Sickle (1977) 68 CA3 728.
*PRACTICE AREAS: Civil Litigation; Commercial Law; Corporate Law; Business Law.
**Schulz, Jean M.** ..........'62 '91 C.436 B.A. L.990 J.D. [⊠ Watson,H.&H.]
*PRACTICE AREAS: Family Law; Civil Litigation.
**Shaffer, Edward L.** ..........'51 '86 C.94 B.A. L.1065 J.D. [Norris&N.]
*PRACTICE AREAS: Land Use and Environmental Regulation; Development Permitting; Local Government Law; Real Estate Law.
Sharp, William C. ..........'17 '52 C.112 B.A. L.767 LL.B. 4705 Upland Dr.‡
**Slootmaker, Leonard W.** '47 '72
C&L.705 B.A., J.D. Exec. Dir. & Gen. Coun., Berlex Biosciences
Smith, David S. ..........'53 '83 C.454 B.A. L.1066 J.D. 326.0 Blume Dr. Ste. 200
Solich, Gregory A. ..........'20 '50 C.112 L.1065 J.D. 126 Santa Fe Ave.‡
Solow, Linda J. ..........'62 '88 C.104 A.B. L.1065 J.D. Co. Pub. Def.
Spear, Ruth ..........'45 '71 C.112 A.B. L.1065 J.D. Dep. Pub. Def.
Stern, Brian S. ..........'47 '75 C.1044 B.A. L.284 J.D. 124 Washington Ave.
Straughn, Loren E., (BV) ..........'33 '63 C.112 L.1065 J.D. 3220 Blume Dr.

CAA516P

**Straus, Douglas C.** ....................'55 '80 C.597 B.S. L.1066 J.D. [Norris&N.]
*PRACTICE AREAS: Business; Real Estate and Contract Litigation.
**Sweet, Michael A.** .................... '69 '96 C.1036 B.A. L.112 J.D. [Ⓐ Norris&N.]
Thompson, Anthony C. .................... '60 '86 C.597 B.S. L.309 J.D. Dep. Pub. Def.
Thomson, Marian T. '58 '83 C.105 B.A. L.904 J.D.
(adm. in DC; not adm. in CA; Pat.) Mgr., Zeneca Inc.
Trice, Judith A. .................... '44 '74 Asst. City Atty.
Washington, Lemuel D. ....................'22 '61 C.112 L.1026 LL.B. 2716 Ctr. Ave.
**Watkins, Leonard H.** ....................'59 '87 C.1027 B.S. L.767 J.D. [Ⓐ Norris&N.]
*PRACTICE AREAS: Commercial Litigation; Lender Liability; Real Estate; Banking Law.
**Watson, Francis A., Jr.**, (AV) ........'29 '53 C.813 A.B. L.1066 LL.B. [Watson,H.&H.]
*REPORTED CASES: Estates of Propst (1990) 50 C.3d 448; Bouquet v. Bouquet (1976) 16 C.3d 583; In re Marriage of Van Sickle (1977) 68 C.A.3d 728; McMillan v. American General Finance Corp. (1976) 60 C.A. 3d 175; Estate of Barbikas (1959) 171 C.A.2d 452.
*PRACTICE AREAS: Family Law; Business; Commercial Litigation; Probate; Estate Planning.

**Watson, Hoffe & Hass, (AV)**
**3700 Barrett Avenue, P.O. Box 5001, 94805-2297**
**Telephone: 510-237-3700 Facsimile: 510-237-3714**
**Members of Firm: Francis A. Watson, Jr.; R. Bruce Hoffe; Peter A. Hass; Joseph E. B. Gaudet (1936-1983). Associates: Jean M. Schulz; David L. Hallikainen.**
**General, Civil and Trial Practice in all State and Federal Courts. Corporate, Banking, Family, Probate, Estate Planning, Real Estate, Construction, Environmental and Commercial Law.**
**Representative Clients: The Mechanics Bank of Richmond; Chevron U.S.A., Inc.; El Cerrito Mill & Lumber Co.; McNevin Cadillac.**

*See Professional Biographies, RICHMOND, CALIFORNIA*

Welden, Sondra E. .................... '55 '85 C.766 B.A. L.767 J.D. 623 Ventura St.
**Whiting, William F.**, (AV) ....................'40 '65 C.813 A.B. L.1066 J.D. [Whiting&R.]⊙
*REPORTED CASES: Valley Bank of Nevada v. Superior Court (1975) 15 Cal. 3d 652; Burger v. Superior Court (1984) 151 CA 3d 1013.
*PRACTICE AREAS: Family Law; Civil Litigation.

**Whiting & Rubenstein, (AV)**
**3260 Blume Drive, Suite 110, 94806⊙**
**Telephone: 510-222-6000 Fax: 510-222-6001**
**Members of Firm: William F. Whiting (Certified Specialist, Family Law, The State Bar of California Board of Legal Specialization); Ronald A. Rubenstein. Associates: Andrew Ross (Certified Specialist, Family Law, The State Bar of California Board of Legal Specialization); R. Ann Fallon; Jon A. Johnsen; David D. Bunn; Gretchen B. Barber.**
**General Civil and Trial Practice in all State and Federal Courts including Real Property, Family, Commercial, Corporate, and Business Law.**
**Walnut Creek, California Office: 1220 Oakland Boulevard, Suite 200. 94596.**

*See Professional Biographies, RICHMOND, CALIFORNIA*

Williams, Tracy L. ....................'63 '92 C.112 B.A. L.1065 J.D. 139 Woodstock Ct.
Younkin, Richard W. .................... '38 '65 C.426 B.A. L.1065 J.D. 132 Follett St.
Zavala, Nanette, (BV) ....................'56 '83 C.112 B.A. L.1066 J.D. 124 Washington Ave.

## RIDGECREST, 27,725, *Kern Co.*

Baker, Gerald F. .............. '15 '82 C.1051 M.Ed. L.999 J.D. 1960 S. Sunland St. (Pat.)
Burmeister, Michael T. .......... '59 '88 C.1109 B.A. L.1067 J.D. 601 W. Wildrose Ave.★
Haas, John B. .................... '51 '79 C.112 B.A. L.1190 J.D. 1960 S. Sunland St.
Hackney, Richard C. ....................'40 '81 C.267 B.A. L.1137 J.D. 608 Appaloosa St.
Pendleton, Robert L. .................... '37 '77 C.604 A.B. L.624 J.D. P.O. Box 129
Skeer, W. Thom .......... '31 '77 C.846 B.A. L.1137 J.D. 515 Weiman Ave. (Pat.)
Venola-Palmer, J. E., (Ms.) ........ '44 '75 C.766 B.A. L.1190 J.D. 321 N. Calvert Blvd.‡
West, Burke, (BV) .................... '21 '56 C&L.426 995 N. Norma St.

## RIO DELL, 2,687, *Humboldt Co.*

Briody, William F. .................... '24 '72 C.330 A.B. L.1026 J.D. 995 Riverside Dr.‡

## RIO NIDO, —, *Sonoma Co.*

Culver, Willis L. .................... '33 '60 C&L.813 A.B., J.D. P.O. Box 252‡

## RIO VISTA, 3,316, *Solano Co.*

Blegen, Jon A., (BV) .................... '47 '72 C.112 B.A. L.1067 J.D. City Atty.

## RIPON, 7,455, *San Joaquin Co.*

Beck, H. Thomas, (BV) .................... '47 '84 C.813 B.A. L.596 J.D. 1201 W. Main St.
Sharp, Kevin J., (CV) .................... '56 '86 L.1132 J.D. 204 W. Main St.
Williams, James E. .................... '30 '79 C.277 B.Ch.E. L.1132 J.D. 109 S. Stockton Ave.

## RIVERBANK, 8,547, *Stanislaus Co.*

Hedrick, J. W., Jr. .................... '24 '53 C.112 B.S. L.1065 LL.B. Ret. U.S. Bkrptcy. J.
Reid, Norman S. .................... '28 '57 C.267 B.A. L.1065 J.D. Ret. Supr. Ct. J.

## RIVERDALE, 1,722, *Fresno Co.*

Mendes, Anthony R. .................... '49 '75 C&L.770 B.S.C., J.D. 5544 24th Ave.

## RIVERSIDE, * 226,505, *Riverside Co.*

Aarvig, Maria K. .................... '63 '90 C&L.1137 B.S.L., J.D. 3993 Market St.
**Abbott, Steven B.** .................... '61 '86 C.112 B.A. L.1068 J.D. [Redwine&S.]
*PRACTICE AREAS: Water Law; Eminent Domain Law.
**Abel, Jeffrey W.** .................... '66 '96 C.1074 B.S. L.398 J.D. [Ⓐ Gilbert,K.C.&J.]
Adcock, Terry L. ....................'49 '87 C.112 B.A. L.398 J.D. 3900 Market St.
Aderton, Jane R. ....................'13 '68 C.800 B.S. L.809 J.D. 5190 Stonewood Dr.‡
Aguilar, Luis .................... '52 '91 C.911 B.A. L.494 J.D. 3610 14th St.
**Aklufi, Daniel R.** ....................'68 '94 C.112 B.A. L.61 J.D. [Ⓐ Aklufi&W.]
**Aklufi, Joseph S.**, (BV) ....................'47 '76 C.112 B.A. L.823 J.D. [Aklufi&W.]

**Aklufi and Wysocki, (AV)** BR
**3403 Tenth Street, Suite 610, 92501**
**Telephone: 909-682-5480 Telecopier: 909-682-2619**
**Members of Firm: Joseph S. Aklufi; David L. Wysocki. Associate: Daniel R. Aklufi.**
**General Civil, Trial and Appellate Practice in State and Federal Courts, Water Law, Municipal, Eminent Domain, Corporation, Real Property, Zoning, Public Agency, Business, Contract and Construction Law.**

*See Professional Biographies, RIVERSIDE, CALIFORNIA*

Aldrian, John Thomas .................... '46 '82 C.1097 B.A. L.1137 J.D. 5381 Velo Ct.
Aldrich, Frank C., III .................... '44 '73 C.112 B.A. L.1068 J.D. Off. of Co. Coun.
**Alhadeff, Samuel C.**, (AV) ........ '45 '71 C.154 B.A. L.1049 J.D. [Lorenz A.C.&R.]⊙
*PRACTICE AREAS: Real Estate; Mortgage Banking; Commercial Transactions.
**Allert, Thomas D.**, (BV) ....................'52 '78 C.112 B.A. L.1137 J.D. [Swarner&F.]
*PRACTICE AREAS: Marital Dissolutions.
**Alsop, Clark H.** .................... '47 '74 C.154 B.A. L.770 J.D. [Best B.&K.]
*PRACTICE AREAS: Municipal Law; Land Use and Environmental.
Altman, Joan ....................'49 '89 C.590 B.S. L.494 J.D. 5055 Canyon Crest Dr.
**Andersen, Robert T., Jr.**, (BV) ..........'50 '79 C.112 B.A. L.464 J.D. [Ⓐ Redwine&S.]
*PRACTICE AREAS: Business; Litigation; Probate; Public Law; Eminent Domain.
Anderson, Dorothy I. ....................'64 '91 C.112 B.A. L.464 J.D. 3750 University Ave.
**Anderson, Juliann** .................... '64 '90 C.813 A.B. L.309 J.D. [Ⓐ Best B.&K.]
*PRACTICE AREAS: Public Law; Public Law Litigation; Land Use.
Anderson, Pamela J. ....................'58 '76 C&L.769 B.A., J.D. Dep. Co. Coun.
**Anderson, Richard T., (P.C.)**, (AV) .......... '36 '63 C&L.972 B.S., LL.B. [Best B.&K.]
*PRACTICE AREAS: Municipal Finance Law; Natural Resources Law; Public Law.
Anderson, William A., Jr. ....................'50 '81 C.112 L.1137 J.D. P.O. Box 4246

**Anderson, McPharlin & Conners, (AV)**
**A Partnership including Professional Corporations**
**3750 University Avenue, Suite 225, 92501-3313⊙**
**Telephone: 909-787-1900 Telecopier: 908-787-6749**
**Brian S. Mizell (Resident). Associates: Stewart Dennis Reid (Resident); Arnold W. Holaday.**
**General Civil and Trial Practice in all State and Federal Courts. Fidelity and Surety, Environmental Litigation (Hazardous Waste, Toxic Torts), Products Liability, Property Insurance, Title Insurance, Maritime, Fire Insurance, Commercial and General Liability Insurance Defense, Insurance Coverage, Bad Faith Litigation, Business Torts, Architects' and Engineers' Errors and Omissions, Construction Litigation, Commercial·Litigation, Banking, Labor and Professional Malpractice Law.**
**Los Angeles, California Office: One Wilshire Building, Nineteenth Floor. 624 South Grand Avenue. Telephone: 213-688—0080. Telecopier: 213-622-7594.**

*See Professional Biographies, RIVERSIDE, CALIFORNIA*

Andrews, Douglas W. .......... '58 '85 C&L.101 B.A., J.D. [Breidenbach,B.H.H.&H.]⊙
Angell, Jas. H. .................... '20 '49 C&L.800 A.B., LL.B. P.O. Box 1182‡
Anger, Scott A. ....................'58 '89 C.705 B.A. L.629 J.D. 3880 Lemon St.
**Artiano, Ray J.**, (BV) .......... '53 '79 C.94 B.S. L.1049 J.D. [Stutz,G.A.S.&H.]⊙
*PRACTICE AREAS: Litigation; Personal Injury; Public Entity; Employment Discrimination Law.
Asberry, Irma D. Poole, (BV) .......... '54 '79 C.112 B.A. L.1049 J.D. 3877 12th St.
Ask, Ronald W. ....................'35 '81 C.1042 B.A. L.1137 J.D. 3243 Arlington Ave.
**Assael-Shafia, Michele** .......... '70 '95 C.1074 B.S. L.398 J.D. [Ⓐ Gilbert,K.C.&J.]
Astin, Wayne T. .......... '45 '75 C.940 A.B. L.1068 J.D. Supvr. Dep. Dist. Atty.
Bachtel, Warren L. .................... '39 '68 C&L.37 B.A., J.D. Dep. Dist. Atty.
Badger, LeMoyne S., (BV) .......... '24 '52 C.112 A.B. L.813 LL.B. 6117 Brockton Ave.
**Bailey, Jacqueline E.** .................... '65 '93 C.1077 B.A. L.464 J.D. [Ⓐ Best B.&K.]
*PRACTICE AREAS: Civil Litigation.
Bailey, John L. ....................'54 '82 C&L.1137 B.S.L., J.D. [Hall&B.]
Bailey, William R., Jr. ....................'38 '64 C&L.813 A.B., LL.B. Supr. Ct. J.
Baker, Bonnie Ann ....... '44 '76 C.1042 B.A. L.426 J.D. 3003 Orange St. (⊙Santa Ana)
**Baker, Donna M.** .................... '57 '89 C.426 B.S. L.1068 J.D. [Thomas,M.P.&K.]
*PRACTICE AREAS: Commercial Litigation.
Barksdale, Richard V., (CV) .......... '25 '55 C.668 B.A. L.800 LL.B. 4566 Jarvisn St.
Barnard, John H. .................... '29 '56 C.846 A.B. L.800 LL.B. Ret. Supr. Ct. J.
Barnes, Sharon L. .................... '59 '89 C.1109 B.A. L.1137 J.D. 4129 Main St.
Barnett, William N., (BV) ........'26 '76 C.112 B.S. L.1137 J.D. 5225 Canyon Crest Dr.
**Bates, Robert W.** .................... '61 '86 C.112 B.A. L.1068 J.D. [Ⓐ Bonne,B.M.O.&N.]
**Baum, Francis J., (P.C.)**, (AV) ....................'49 '78 C.112 B.S. L.1068 J.D. [Best B.&K.]
*PRACTICE AREAS: Public Finance Law.
Baydaline, Rod A. .................... '64 '93 C.112 B.A. L.464 J.D. 6670 Alessandro
Bayless, Thomas A. '43 '79
C.800 M.B.T. L.809 J.D. Dir. of Taxes, Fleetwood Enterprises, Inc.
**Bazzo, Michael L.** .................... '56 '96 C.112 B.A. L.1137 J.D. [Ⓐ Bonne,B.M.O.&N.]
*LANGUAGES: Spanish and Italian.
*PRACTICE AREAS: Medical Malpractice Defense.
Behlke, William M. ....................'61 '91 C.8 B.S.I.M. L.426 J.D. 3880 Lemon St.
Bell, Michael A., (AV) ....................'36 '64 C.549 L.426 LL.B. [Fidler,B.O.&W.]
Beloian, Glenn R. .................... '56 '81 C.112 B.A. L.398 J.D. 5053 La Mart Dr.
Belter, Michael R. ....................'54 '81 C.1266 B.A. L.1137 J.D. [Belter&C.]⊙
Belter & Cormicle, (BV) .................... 4060 Chestnut St. (⊙Santa Monica)
Belton, John H. ....................'52 '81 C.94 B.A. L.1077 J.D. 9315 Magnolia Ave.
Bentley, Richard A., (BV) ....................'47 '84 C.1097 B.A. L.1148 J.D. Dep. Dist. Atty.
Bermudez, Angel M. ....................'— '91 C.112 B.A. L.1049 J.D. Dep. Dist. Atty.

**Best Best & Krieger LLP, (AV)** BR
**A California Limited Liability Partnership including Professional Corporations**
**400 Mission Square, 3750 University Avenue, P.O. Box 1028, 92502⊙**
**Telephone: 909-686-1450 Fax: 909-686-3083; 909-682-4612**
**Members of Firm: Raymond Best (1868-1957); James H. Krieger (1913-1975); Eugene Best (1893-1981); Arthur L. Littleworth (P.C.); Glen E. Stephens (P.C.); William R. DeWolfe (P.C.); Christopher L. Carpenter (P.C.); Richard T. Anderson (P.C.); John D. Wahlin (P.C.); Michael D. Harris (P.C.) (Rancho Mirage Office); John E. Brown (P.C.); Michael T. Riddell (P.C.); Meredith A. Jury (P.C.) (Ontario Office); Michael Grant (P.C.); Francis J. Baum (P.C.); Anne T. Thomas (P.C.); D. Martin Nethery (P.C.) (Rancho Mirage Office); George M. Reyes; William W. Floyd, Jr.; Gregory L. Hardke; Kendall H. MacVey; Clark H. Alsop; David J. Erwin (P.C.) (Rancho Mirage Office); Michael J. Andelson (P.C.) (Rancho Mirage Office); Douglas S. Phillips (P.C.) (Rancho Mirage Office); Gregory K. Wilkinson; Wynne S. Furth (Ontario Office); Gene Tanaka; Basil T. Chapman (Rancho Mirage Office) (Certified Specialist, Family Law, The State Bar of California Board of Legal Specialization); Victor L. Wolf; Daniel E. Olivier (Rancho Mirage Office); Howard B. Golds; Stephen P. Deitsch (Ontario Office); Marc E. Empey (Rancho Mirage Office); John R. Rottschaefer; Martin A. Mueller (Rancho Mirage Office); J. Michael Summerour; Scott C. Smith (San Diego Office); Brian M. Lewis (Rancho Mirage Office); Jack B. Clarke, Jr.; Bradley E. Neufeld; Peter M. Barmack (Ontario Office); Matt H. Morris (Rancho Mirage Office); Jeffrey V. Dunn; Steven C. DeBaun; Eric L. Garner; Dennis M. Cota (Ontario Office); Patrick H.W.F. Pearce; Robert W. Hargreaves (Rancho Mirage Office); C. Michael Cowett (San Diego Office); Bruce W. Beach (San Diego Office); Arlene Prater (San Diego Office); Jason D. Dabareiner (Rancho Mirage Office); Mark A. Easter; Michelle Ouellette. Associates: William D. Dahling, Jr.; Kirk W. Smith; Kyle A. Snow; Bernie L. Williamson; Kevin K. Randolph (Ontario Office); Mary E. Gilstrap (Rancho Mirage Office); Cynthia M. Germano; Kim A. Byrens; James B. Gilpin (San Diego Office); G. Henry Welles (Rancho Mirage Office); Dina O. Harris; Barbara R. Baron (Rancho Mirage Office); Richard T. Egger (Ontario Office); Dean Derleth; Helene P. Dreyer (Rancho Mirage Office); Sonia Rubio Carvalho (Ontario Office); Patricia Byars Cisneros; Juliann Anderson; Susan Dumouchel Wilson; Jacqueline E. Bailey (Rancho Mirage Office); David Cabral (San Diego Office); David J. Hancock; Marc T. Rasich; Philip M. Savage, IV; Ana Maria Z. Fredgren (Rancho Mirage Office); Karen M. Lewis (Ontario Office); Hayley Elizabeth Peterson (San Diego Office); Michael J. Schaefer; Zachary R. Walton; Sandy A. Jacobson (Rancho Mirage Office); Jeffrey S. Flashman (Rancho Mirage Office); Jeffrey T. Melching (Ontario Office); Scott D. Howie; Marguerite S. Strand (San Diego Office); Roger K. Crawford; Keith L. Higgins (Victorville Office); John R. Perry; Shawn Hagerty (San Diego Office); Mitchell L. Norton; Pedro C. Dallarda; Kristi Lynn Gudoski; Caryn Leigh Craig (San Diego Office); Kevin Collins; James P. Morris; Dwight M. Montgomery. Of Counsel: John C. Tobin; Donald F. Zimmer; Henry R. Kraft (P.C.) (Victorville Office).**
**General Civil and Trial Practice. Corporation, Water Rights, Probate, Trusts and Estate Planning, Labor, Real Estate, Municipal, Public Finance, Health Care and Indian Land Law.**
**Rancho Mirage, California Office: Hope Square Professional Centre, 39700 Bob Hope Drive, Suite 312, P.O. Box 1555. Telephone: 619-568-2611. Fax: 619-340-6698; 619-341-7039.**
**Ontario, California Office: 800 North Haven, Suite 120. Telephone: 909-989-8584. Fax: 909-944-1441.**
**San Diego, California Office: 402 West Broadway, 13th Floor. Telephone: 619-525-1300. Fax: 619-233-6118.**
**Victorville, California Office: High Desert Corporate Pointe Building, 14350 Civic Drive, Suite 270. Telephone: 619-245-4127. Fax: 619-245-6437.**

*See Professional Biographies, RIVERSIDE, CALIFORNIA*

**Bianco, Elizabeth Ashley** .........'67 '92 C.878 B.A. L.990 J.D. [Ⓐ Gresham,V.S.N.&T.]
Billington, Craig R. ....................'55 '83 C.112 B.A. L.1136 J.D. 1770 Iowa Ave.
Bishop, John M. .................... '43 '72 C.112 B.A. L.1066 J.D. 18775 Bert Rd.
Blankenship, Gerald, Jr. .................... '38 '65 C&L.800 A.B., J.D. Dep. County Coun.
Blumenfeld, Richard ....................'56 '85 C.813 B.A. L.1065 J.D. 4200 Orange St.
Blumenthal, E. Martin, (BV) .................... '39 '64 C.696 B.A. L.982 J.D. 3890 10th St.
Blumenthal, Robert B., (BV) ....................'43 '70 C.696 A.B. L.982 J.D. [R.B.Blumenthal]
Blumenthal, Virginia M., (AV) ..........'48 '75 C.1077 B.A. L.1198 J.D. [Blumenthal&L.]
Blumenthal & Lomazow, A Professional Law Corporation, (AV) .......... 3993 Market St.
Blumenthal, Robert B., P.C., (BV) .................... P.O. Box 20559

CAA517P

CALIFORNIA—RIVERSIDE

MARTINDALE-HUBBELL LAW DIRECTORY 1997

**Bonne, Bridges, Mueller, O'Keefe & Nichols, Professional Corporation, (AV)**
**3403 Tenth Street, Suite 800, P.O. Box 747, 92501-0747⊙**
**Telephone: 909-788-1944 Fax: 909-782-4666**
**Michael D. Lubrani (Resident); Christopher B. Marshall (Resident);—Robert W. Bates (Resident); Douglas C. Smith (Resident); Henry Yekikian (Resident); Cynthia M. Herrera (Resident); Yoshiaki C. Kubota (Resident); Kimberly Netta (Resident); Holly H. McGregor (Resident); Michael L. Bazzo (Resident).**
**General Insurance Defense, Professional Malpractice, Products Liability Claims, Drug and Medical Device Claims, Environmental and Toxic Tort Claims, Insurance and Wrongful Termination, Professional Administrative Hearing Counsel.**
**Representative Clients: Kaiser Foundation Health Plan; Norcal Mutual Insurance Co.; County of San Bernardino; County of Riverside; National Chiropractic Mutual Insurance Co.**
**Los Angeles, California Office: 3699 Wilshire Boulevard, 10th Floor, 90010-2719. Telephone: 213-480-1900. Fax: 213-738-5888.**
**Santa Ana, California Office: 1750 East Fourth Street, Suite 450, P.O. Box 22018, 92702-2018. Telephone: 714-835-1157. Fax: 714-480-2585.**
**Santa Barbara, California Office: 801 Garden Street, Suite 300, 93101-5502. Telephone: 805-965-2992. Fax: 805-962-6509.**
**San Luis Obispo, California Office: 1060 Palm Street, 93401-3221. Telephone: 805-541-8350. Fax: 805-541-6817.**

*See Professional Biographies, RIVERSIDE, CALIFORNIA*

**Bowker, David B.**, (BV) .... '54 '77 C.112 B.A. L.1068 J.D. [Swarner&F.]
*PRACTICE AREAS: Probate; Conservatorship; Wills and Trusts; Estate Planning.
**Boyd, John A.**, (BV) .... '54 '79 C.763 B.S. L.990 J.D. [Thompson&C.]
*PRACTICE AREAS: Business Litigation; Construction Law; Real Estate; Bankruptcy.
Bradley, W. Charles .... '51 '88 C.172 B.A. L.464 J.D. 3801 University Ave.
Brand, Joel, (Miss) .... '17 '51 C.112 B.S. L.1065 J.D. 2872 Moorgate Pl.‡
**Brandt, Brendan W.** .... '64 '90 C.112 B.A. L.1049 J.D. [Ⓐ Gresham,V.S.N.&T.]
Breidenbach, Buckley, Huchting, Halm & Hamblet, A Law Corporation, (AV)
3403 Tenth Street (⊙Los Angeles, Santa Ana)
Bremer, Keith G. .... '64 '91 C.763 B.S. L.1137 J.D. [Kring&B.]
**Brewer, Diane S.**, (BV) .... '40 '78 C.1060 B.A. L.1049 J.D. [Reid&H.]
*PRACTICE AREAS: Probate Law; Estate Planning Law.

**Bridges, Terry, Law Offices of, (AV) '40 '66 C.770 B.A. L.800 LL.B. BB**
**Mission Square Plaza, 3750 University Avenue, Suite 240, 92501-3313**
**Telephone: 909-682-2760 Facsimile: 909-682-8626**
***PRACTICE AREAS: Civil Litigation.**
**Associate: Alan J. Leahy.**
**Civil Trial Practice.**

*See Professional Biographies, RIVERSIDE, CALIFORNIA*

**Bright, Michael T.**, (BV) .... '42 '68 C.330 A.B. L.61 J.D. [Butterwick,B.&O.]
*PRACTICE AREAS: Family Law; Estate Planning Law; Probate Law.
Briskin, Boyd E., (BV) .... '32 '55 C.112 L.1065 J.D. 3960 11th St.
**Brooks, Andrew D.**, (BV) .... '61 '86 C.112 A.B. L.800 J.D. [Thomas,M.P.&K.]
*PRACTICE AREAS: Business Law; Corporate Law; Municipal Finance; Securities; Tax Exempt Organizations.
Brooks, Tilden L. .... '13 '37 C.1059 B.C.S. L.969 J.D. 2353 Elsinore Rd.‡
Brown, Harry E. .... '35 '81 C.576 B.S.E.E. L.1137 J.D. 3763 Arlington St.
**Brown, John E., (P.C.)**, (AV) .... '49 '75 C.154 B.A. L.1066 J.D. [Best B.&K.]
*PRACTICE AREAS: School Law; Public Finance Law; Public Law; Redevelopment Law.
Brown, John H. .... '53 '92 C.112 B.S. L.1137 J.D. 1950 Market St.
**Bruyneel, Thomas E.** .... '42 '70 C.763 A.B. L.1065 J.D. [Redwine&S.]
*PRACTICE AREAS: Civil Trials; Appellate Practice (State and Federal) Law; Water Law; Business Law; Eminent Domain.
Brzytwa, James J. .... '45 '82 C.1110 B.A. L.1198 J.D. Dep. Co. Coun.
Buchanan, Dan E. .... '57 '86 C.112 B.A. L.1137 J.D. 5041 LaMart Dr.
Buchholz, Barbara A. .... '56 '91 C.1109 B.A. L.809 J.D. [Ⓐ Fidler,B.O.&W.]
**Bunker, William B.**, (AV) '51 '78 C.1075 B.S. L.101 J.D.
[Knobbe,M.O.&B.] (See Pat. Sect.) (⊙Newport Beach)
**Burke, Dennis M.** .... '67 '94 C&L.112 B.A., J.D. [Ⓐ Fiore,W.R.&P.]
Burkhart, Gordon R. .... '45 '72 C.101 B.A. L.61 J.D. Supr. Ct. J.
Burns, Michael F. .... '55 '83 C.1042 B.A. L.1148 J.D. 3403 Tenth St.
**Butterwick, J. D.**, (AV) .... '23 '48 C&L.585 Ph.B., J.D. [Butterwick,B.&O.]
*PRACTICE AREAS: Homeowners Association Law; Real Property Law; Corporate Law.

**Butterwick, Bright & O'Laughlin, Inc., A Professional Law Corporation, (AV) BB**
**4000 Tenth Street, P.O. Box 1229, 92502**
**Telephone: 909-686-3092 Telefax: 909-684-5743**
**J. D. Butterwick; Michael T. Bright; John F. O'Laughlin; Robert J. Mitchell.**
**Civil Litigation, Commercial Law, Collection, Financial Institutions Law, Debtor-Creditor Relations, Insolvency and Bankruptcy Law, Business, Torts, Probate, Estate Planning, Real Property, Family Law, Homeowner Association Law.**
**Reference: Riverside National Bank.**

*See Professional Biographies, RIVERSIDE, CALIFORNIA*

**Byrens, Kim A.** .... '65 '90 C.112 B.A. L.1049 J.D. [Ⓐ Best B.&K.]
*PRACTICE AREAS: Municipal Securities Law.
**Byrne, Andrew P.** .... '67 '94 C.1068 B.A. L.770 J.D. [Ⓐ Redwine&S.]
*PRACTICE AREAS: Water Law; Civil Litigation.
Cahraman, Thomas H., (CV) .... '51 '76 C.112 B.A. L.1066 J.D. 3649 9th St.

**Caldwell & Kennedy, A Professional Corporation**
**(See Victorville)**

Calof, Alvin .... '27 '56 C.112 B.S. L.1068 LL.B. Supr. Ct. Referee
Cantillon, R. Michael, (BV) .... '28 '57 C.112 B.A. L.809 LL.B. P.O. Box 424
**Carlos, Mary Jo**, (CV) .... '51 '83 C.1049 B.A. L.770 J.D. [Carlos]
*LANGUAGES: Spanish.
*PRACTICE AREAS: Workers Compensation Law; Personal Injury Defense.

**Carlos Law Firm, The, A Professional Corporation, (CV)**
**2000 Market Street, 92501**
**Telephone: 909-686-2310 Fax: 909-686-2640**
**Mary Jo Carlos; Wilfred J. Schneider, Jr.; Donald F. Cash; Marilee M. Reynolds.**
**General Practice.**

*See Professional Biographies, RIVERSIDE, CALIFORNIA*

**Carpenter, Christopher L., (P.C.)**, (AV) '40 '66 C.668 B.A. L.976 LL.B.
[Best B.&K.]
*PRACTICE AREAS: Estate Planning; Probate; Health Care.
**Cash, Donald F.** .... '51 '79 C.684 B.A. L.398 J.D. [Carlos]
*PRACTICE AREAS: Personal Injury; Insurance Defense.
**Chandler, Robert C., (P.L.C.)** .... '56 '88 C.818 B.S.B.A. L.426 J.D. [Chandler&Assoc.]
*PRACTICE AREAS: General Civil Litigation (Contracts) (60%, 140); Family Law (40%, 65).

**Chandler & Associates**
**3800 Orange Street, Suite 270, 92501**
**Telephone: 909-276-3022 Fax: 909-782-0230**
**Robert C. Chandler (P.L.C.); Steven M. Matulis; Mickey Walker.**
**General Civil Litigation, Family Law, Landlord and Tenant, Consumer Contracts, Lemon Law.**

*See Professional Biographies, RIVERSIDE, CALIFORNIA*

Chang, Arthur M. .... '62 '89 C.112 B.S. L.276 J.D. Dep. Dist. Atty.
Chant, George H., III .... '53 '86 C.112 B.A. L.1067 J.D. 5041 La Mart Dr.
Chavers, Herbert Lee .... '55 '89 C.999 B.S.B.A. L.1137 J.D. 7344 Magnolia Ave.
Chessell, John W., (BV) .... '43 '72 C.112 B.A. L.770 J.D. Dep. Dist. Atty.
**Cisneros, Patricia Byars** .... '64 '93 C.112 B.A. L.800 J.D. [Ⓐ Best B.&K.]
*PRACTICE AREAS: Public Law (Municipal).
**Clark, Conrad R.** .... '47 '90 C.684 B.S.B.A. L.1137 J.D. [Franscell,S.R.&L.]
*PRACTICE AREAS: Police Misconduct Liability Defense; Civil Rights; Municipal and Administrative Law; General Civil; Criminal Trial.
**Clarke, Jack B., Jr.**, (BV) .... '56 '85 C.112 B.S. L.464 J.D. [Best B.&K.]
*PRACTICE AREAS: Litigation.
Cleary, Richard M.J. .... '35 '61 C.454 B.B.A. L.93 J.D. Dep. Pub. Def.
Clepper, Michael H., (BV) .... '35 '61 C.813 A.B. L.1065 J.D. 4192 Brockton Ave.
**Collins, Kevin** .... '70 '96 C.684 B.A. L.464 J.D. [Ⓐ Best B.&K.]
*PRACTICE AREAS: Litigation.
Confer, Carolyn E. .... '42 '79 C.645 B.A. L.1198 J.D. Asst. City Atty.
Cope, Mark .... '58 '86 C&L.101 B.A., J.D. Mun. J.
Corison, James B., (P.C.), (AV) .... '27 '53 C.112 A.B. L.1065 J.D. 3750 University Ave.
Cote, Karen L. .... '60 '93 C.024 B.Sc. L.037 LL.B. [Ⓐ Olins,F.&H.]
**Craig, Caryn Leigh** .... '— '96 [Ⓐ Best B.&K.]
Craig, Larry A. .... '47 '87 C.1109 B.A. L.1137 J.D. 10370 Hemet St.
**Crawford, Roger K.** .... '65 '93 C.101 B.A. L.426 J.D. [Ⓐ Best B.&K.]
*LANGUAGES: Spanish.
*PRACTICE AREAS: Labor and Employment.
Croswell, Jeffrey N. .... '53 '80 C&L.61 B.A., J.D. 12980 Reindeer Ct.
Crowley, James E. '36 '61 L.190 LL.B.
(adm. in NE; not adm. in CA) Sr. Vet. Rep., Riverside Co. Vets. Serv. Off.
**Cruz, Sheri B.** .... '66 '94 C&L.1137 B.S., J.D. [Ⓐ Heiting&I.]
*PRACTICE AREAS: Business; Real Estate; Probate; Estate Planning; Guardianship/Conservatorship.

**Cummings & Kemp, A Professional Corporation, (AV)**
**3877 Twelfth Street, Suite 200, 92501⊙**
**Telephone: 909-781-1929 Fax: 909-788-9040**
**Clive J. Kemp;—Bruce E. Todd (Resident).**
**General Civil Trial and Appellate Practice in State and Federal Courts. Insurance, Corporation, Negligence, Malpractice, Construction, Products Liability and Public Entity Defense Law.**
**Santa Ana, California Office: 1851 East First Street, Suite 1000. Telephone: 714-835-8858. Fax: 714-835-1342.**

*See Professional Biographies, RIVERSIDE, CALIFORNIA*

**Cunningham, Arthur K.** .... '53 '81 C.112 B.S. L.1137 J.D. [Roberts&M.]
**Dahling, William D., Jr.** .... '56 '83 C.951 B.A. L.477 J.D. [Ⓐ Best B.&K.]
*PRACTICE AREAS: Estate Planning Law; Probate and Conservatorships.
Dahut, Henry .... '55 '86 C.112 B.A. L.284 J.D. 3900 Market St.
Dales, E. Scott .... '23 '51 C&L.800 LL.B. Ret. Supr. Ct. J.‡
**Dallarda, Pedro C.** .... '65 '92 C&L.276 B.S.F.S., J.D. [Ⓐ Best B.&K.]
*LANGUAGES: Spanish, Italian, French.
*PRACTICE AREAS: Business Litigation; Employment Law.
D'Arco, Thomas R. .... '41 '71 C.800 B.S.M.E. L.880 J.D. 6053 Enfield Pl.
Darling, Scott E., (A Professional Corporation) '49 '76
C.684 B.A. L.800 J.D. 7750 Limonite Ave.
Datig, Cregor G., (BV) .... '57 '82 C&L.426 B.A., J.D. Dep. Dist. Atty.
Davis, John M., (BV) .... '48 '84 C.112 B.A. L.809 J.D. Dep. Dist. Atty.
Davis, Kenneth '52 '79 C.755 B.A. L.1035 J.D.
(adm. in MN; not adm. in CA) Riverside Dental Grp.
Davis, Timothy J. .... '48 '76 C.1051 B.S. L.1065 J.D. Dep. Co. Coun.
**DeBaun, Steven C.** .... '62 '87 C.112 B.A. L.1068 J.D. [Best B.&K.]
*PRACTICE AREAS: Transportation Law; Municipal Law; Land Use/Environmental Law.
Deissler, Ronald T. .... '27 '57 C.911 A.B. L.1068 J.D. Supr. J.
Delany, Frank J., (BV) .... '46 '71 C.770 B.A. L.800 J.D. 3801 University Ave.
Delsman, Mary A. .... '24 '79 C.629 B.S. L.1137 J.D. Ret. Lt. Col. USAF‡
Dennis, William L. .... '45 '72 C.112 A.B. L.1068 J.D. 15765 Gila Way
**Derleth, Dean** .... '65 '92 C.112 B.A. L.464 J.D. [Ⓐ Best B.&K.]
*PRACTICE AREAS: Public Law; School Law; Environmental Law.
**DesJardins, Michael A.** .... '61 '86 C.494 B.A. L.436 J.D. [Ⓐ Thomas,M.P.&K.]
*LANGUAGES: Spanish.
**De Vries, Martin J.** '60 '90 C.1304 B.A. L.879 J.D.
[Ⓐ Franscell,S.R.&L.] (⊙Pasadena)
*PRACTICE AREAS: Police Misconduct Defense; Labor and Employment; Products Liability.
Dewey, Michael J. .... '55 '80 C.112 A.B. L.1068 J.D. Dep. Dir., Inland Cos. Legal Servs.
**DeWolfe, William R., (P.C.)**, (AV) .... '35 '62 C.112 B.A. L.1066 LL.B. [Best B.&K.]
*PRACTICE AREAS: Real Property Litigation; Business Litigation; Probate and Trust Litigation; Title Insurance Litigation.
Dexter, Scott J. .... '61 '90 C.1074 B.S. L.945 J.D. 400 N. Mountain Ave.
Dickerman, George F. .... '56 '85 C.112 B.A. L.1137 J.D. 3879 Brockton Ave.
**Dickman, John G.** .... '59 '86 C.112 B.A. L.464 J.D. [Dickman&H.]

**Dickman & Holt**
**3638 University Avenue Suite 212, 92501-3349**
**Telephone: 909-683-3693 Facsimile: 909-683-3670**
**Email: DICKHOLT@viasub.net**
**Members of Firm: John G. Dickman; Montessa D. Holt.**
**General Civil and Trial Practice in all State and Federal Courts. Construction Law, Landslide and Subsidence, Design Professionals, Product Liability, Premises Liability, Government Liability, Transportation Accidents, Errors and Omissions, Business and Commercial Litigation, Real Estate Litigation and Insurance.**

*See Professional Biographies, RIVERSIDE, CALIFORNIA*

Dilworth, James W., (AV) '29 '61
C.684 B.A. L.112 J.D. 5225 Canyon Crest Dr., Bldg. 400
**Disenhouse, Bruce E.**, (BV) .... '52 '77 C.165 B.A. L.464 J.D. [Kinkle,R.&S.]
**Diver, David M.** .... '51 '76 C.152 B.A. L.1049 J.D. [Reid&H.]
*PRACTICE AREAS: Labor Relations Law; Employment Law; Business Litigation.
**Dobler, Craig O.** .... '56 '81 C.911 B.A. L.285 J.D. [Gresham,V.S.N.&T.]
**Donner, Michael B.** .... '47 '83 C.1109 B.A. L.809 J.D. [Gilbert,K.C.&J.]
*PRACTICE AREAS: Construction Defect; Environmental Litigation; Products Liability Litigation.
Driscoll, David E., (BV) .... '54 '80 C&L.1137 B.S.L., J.D. [Foster,D.&R.]
**Dunn, Jeffrey V.** .... '57 '87 C&L.101 B.S., J.D. [Best B.&K.]
*LANGUAGES: Spanish.
*PRACTICE AREAS: Litigation.
Dutton, Patrick F. .... '55 '87 C.1074 B.H.S. L.398 J.D. Dep. Dist. Atty.
**Eagans, Gerald W.**, (BV) .... '54 '80 C.169 B.A. L.770 J.D. [Redwine&S.]
*PRACTICE AREAS: Federal and State Taxation Law; Contract Law; Real Property Law; Corporation Law.
**Easter, Mark A.** .... '64 '89 C.398 B.A. L.1067 J.D. [Best B.&K.]
*PRACTICE AREAS: Business Litigation; Real Estate Litigation; Eminent Domain Litigation.
**Elder, Toby J.**, (BV) .... '52 '78 C.1109 B.A. L.990 J.D. [Kinkle,R.&S.]
Ellis, Michael .... '39 '73 C.112 B.A. L.809 J.D. Dep. Co. Coun.
Elwell, Douglas M. .... '46 '77 C.154 B.A. L.426 J.D. [Waters&E.]

**Ericksen, Arbuthnot, Kilduff, Day & Lindstrom, Inc., (AV)**
**1770 Iowa Avenue, Suite 210, 92507-2403⊙**
**Telephone: 909-682-3246 Fax: 909-682-4013**
**E. Aurora Hughes; Anne Walker.**
**General Civil Practice in all State and Federal Courts. Medical Malpractice, Corporate, Probate and Insuranee Law.**
**Oakland, California Office: 530 Water Street, Port Building, Suite 720. Telephone: 510-832-7770. Fax: 510-832-0102.**

(This Listing Continued)

CAA518P

**Ericksen, Arbuthnot, Kilduff, Day & Lindstrom, Inc. (Continued)**
**San Francisco, California Office: 260 California Street, Suite 1100. Telephone: 415-362-7126. Fax: 415-362-6401.**
**Sacramento, California Office: 100 Howe Avenue, Suite 240N. Telephone: 916-483-5181. Fax: 916-483-7558.**
**Fresno, California Office: 2440 West Shaw Avenue, Suite 101. Telephone: 209-449-2600. Fax: 209-449-2603.**
**San Jose, California Office: 152 North Third Street, Suite 700. Telephone: 408-286-0880. Fax: 408-286-0337.**
**Walnut Creek, California Office: 2700 Ygnacio Valley Road, Suite 280. Telephone: 510-947-1702. Fax: 510-947-4921.**
**Los Angeles, California Office: 835 Wilshire Boulevard, Suite 500. Telephone: 213-489-4411. Fax: 213-489-4332.**

*See Professional Biographies, RIVERSIDE, CALIFORNIA*

**Erickson, Jeffery R.** ............. '61 '88 C.101 B.A. L.809 J.D. [Ⓐ La Follette,J.D.F.&A.]
*PRACTICE AREAS: Medical Malpractice.
Ermshar, Donald P., (BV) ..... '43 '74 C&L.1137 B.S.L., J.D. 5013 Arlington Ave. Ste. B
Espinosa, Arthur G. .................................'46 '76 C.112 B.A. L.800 J.D. 3600 Lime St.
Estell, Patricia .......................................'55 '84 C.112 B.A. L.809 J.D. Dep. Dist. Atty.
Estudillo, Francis M. ..............................'15 '43 C.605 A.B. L.809 LL.B. Ret. Supr. Ct. J.
**Ettinger, Joan F., (BV)** ..............'59 '86 C.36 B.S. L.1137 J.D. [Ⓐ Thompson&C.]
*PRACTICE AREAS: Personal Injury Defense; Medical Malpractice Law; Appellate Practice.
**Eubank, Bret W.** ....................'58 '83 C.112 B.A. L.1049 J.D. [Ⓐ Stutz,G.A.S.&H.]⊙
*PRACTICE AREAS: Litigation; Public Entity; Personal Injury; Construction Defect.
Ewart, Harold L. ..........................................'— '69 L.1148 J.D. Dep. Dist. Atty.
Fagan, Douglas F. .............................'60 '91 C.1232 B.A. L.546 J.D. 3333 14th St.
Fagin, Harold M., (CV) ......................'14 '40 C&L.724 LL.B. 5134 Stonewood Dr.
Falsetti, Allen A., (BV) ......................'37 '72 C&L.1137 B.S.L., J.D. [Falsetti&P.]
Falsetti & Pritchard, (BV) ...................................................7344 Magnolia Ave.
Farano, Jeffrey L. ............'56 '84 C&L.1137 B.S.L., J.D. 3638 Univ. Ave., Ste., 221⊙
Feiger, Mara W. ..........................'61 '89 C.1042 B.S. L.1137 J.D. Dep. Pub. Def.
**Fernandez, Edward A.** ...............'57 '83 C.112 B.A. L.1049 J.D. [Gilbert,K.C.&J.]
*PRACTICE AREAS: Construction Defect; Premises Liability Litigation.
**Ferre, Jeffry F.** ................................'63 '88 C.684 B.A. L.464 J.D. [Redwine&S.]
*PRACTICE AREAS: Public and Governmental Law; Contract Law; Real Property Law.
Fidler, Ronald W., (AV) ............'32 '63 C.133 B.A. L.1068 LL.B. [Fidler,B.O.&W.] ‡
Fidler, Bell, Orrock & Watase, (AV) ...................................... 2000 Market St.
Field, Charles D. ............................'36 '64 C.112 B.A. L.1068 LL.B. Supr. Ct. J.
Finley, Diane L. ...................'64 '89 C.636 B.B.A. L.1068 J.D. 3750 University Ave.
Finn, Dennis M., (BV) .....................'44 '70 C.676 B.A. L.800 J.D. 4060 Chestnut St.

**Fiore, Walker, Racobs & Powers, A Professional Law Corporation, (AV)**
**6670 Alessandro, Suite B, 92506⊙**
**Telephone: 909-789-8100 Fax: 909-789-8105**
**Peter E. Racobs;—Michael J. White; Erin A. Maloney; Dennis M. Burke.**
**Community Association, Real Property, Civil Litigation, Construction and Business.**
**Irvine, California Office: Koll Center Irvine. 18400 Von Karman, Suite 600. 92612-1514. Telephone: 714-955-0560. Fax: 714-955-2894.**
**Palm Desert, California Office: 74-361 Highway III, Suite 1. Telephone: 619-776-6511. Fax: 619-776-6517.**

*See Professional Biographies, RIVERSIDE, CALIFORNIA*

Fisher, Mac R., (BV) ......................'52 '80 C.112 B.S. L.1137 J.D. [Fisher,W.&G.]
Fisher, Weathers & Geeting, (BV) ...................................... 4261 N. Main St.
Flaherty, Thomas V., (BV) ............. '37 '66 C.37 B.S. L.1066 LL.B. 4545 Allstate Dr.
**Floyd, William W., Jr.** ..................'50 '79 C.763 B.A. L.464 J.D. [Best B.&K.]
*PRACTICE AREAS: Labor Law; Employment Law; Management Law.
Foltz, Gary A. ..................................'52 '77 C.879 B.A. L.1188 J.D. 4333 Orange St.
Ford, Robin J. .....................'57 '87 C&L.1137 B.S.L., J.D. 4129 Main St., Suite 205
Fortin, Ronald B. '47 '87 C.1248 B.A. L.1048 J.D.
(adm. in ME; not adm. in CA) 3932 Rosewood Pl.‡
Fortino, Micheal A., (CV) ...........'55 '90 C.112 B.A. L.1095 J.D. [Ⓐ Fidler,B.O.&W.]
Foster, Bryan F. ..................................'48 '74 C&L.767 B.S., J.D. [Foster,D.&R.]
Foster, Driscoll & Reynolds, (BV) ........................... 6960 Magnolia Ave., Suite 101
Fox, Daniel M. .............................'62 '90 C.446 B.A. L.273 J.D. Dep. Dist. Atty.
Fox, Jere L. '51 '77 C.1163 B.A. L.990 J.D.
3890 11th St., Ste. 101 (⊙Redlands, Yucaipa)
Fox, June Rene .....................'63 '94 C.999 B.S.N. L.1137 J.D. 3801 University Ave.
**Franscell, George J., (AV)** ..........'33 '59 C.426 B.A. L.1068 J.D. [Franscell,S.R.&L.]⊙
*PRACTICE AREAS: Police Misconduct Liability Defense; Civil Rights; Municipal and Administrative Law; General Civil; Criminal Trial.

**Franscell, Strickland, Roberts & Lawrence, A Professional Corporation, (AV)**
**Suite 670, 3801 University Avenue, P.O. Box 12008, 92502-2208⊙**
**Telephone: 909-686-1000 Fax: 909-686-2565**
**George J. Franscell; Tracy Strickland; Barbara E. Roberts; David D. Lawrence; Conrad R. Clark; Libby Wong (Resident); Martin J. De Vries; Kathleen A. Stosuy.**
**Police Misconduct Liability Defense, Civil Rights Defense, Employment Defense, Municipal and Administrative Law, General Civil and Criminal Trial and Appellate Practice, Administrative Law and Litigation.**
**Pasadena, California Office: Penthouse, 225 South Lake Avenue. Telephone: 818-304-7830. Fax: 818-795-7460.**
**Santa Ana, California Office: Suite 800, 401 Civic Center Drive West. Telephone: 714-543-6511. Fax: 714-543-6711.**

*See Professional Biographies, RIVERSIDE, CALIFORNIA*

Freeman, William M., (CV) '46 '79 C.1097 B.A. L.1148 J.D.
3801 University Ave. #550
Freer, Alina M. ..........................................'65 '90 C.112 B.A. L.37 J.D. Dep. Dist. Atty.

**Furness, Middlebrook, Kaiser & Higgins, A Professional Corporation**
**(See San Bernardino)**

Gables, Victor A., (BV) .................'27 '54 C.112 B.A. L.800 LL.B. 2900 Adams St.
Galante, Mary Ann F. .........................'52 '79 C&L.800 B.A., J.D. Dep. Pub. Def.
**Gallagher, Robert E., Jr., (AV)** .......'50 '75 C.1188 B.A. L.61 J.D. [Stutz,G.A.S.&H.]⊙
*PRACTICE AREAS: Construction Law; Litigation; Public Entity; Professional Liability; Municipal Law.
Gambera-Bentley, Elaina C., (CV) ..........'61 '88 C.169 B.S. L.464 J.D. Dep. Dist. Atty.
Gardner, Jeffrey B. '56 '84 C.745 B.S. L.61 J.D.
[Saxon,B.G.&K.] (⊙Newport Beach & San Dimas)
**Garner, Eric L.** ..................................'62 '87 C.231 A.B. L.477 J.D. [Best B.&K.]
*PRACTICE AREAS: Environmental Law; Water Law.
Garrett & Jensen, (AV) ...........................................3403 10th St., Suite 700 (⊙Santa Ana)
**Gary, Donald J., Jr.** ...........................'56 '92 C.64 B.S. L.809 J.D. [D.J.Gary,Jr.]

**Gary, Donald J., Jr., P.C.**
**3700 Sixth Street At Main, Second Floor, P.O. Box 664, 92502-0664⊙**
**Telephone: 909-786-0100 Facsimile: 909-683-8458**
**Harry M. Halstead (1918-1995); Donald J. Gary, Jr.**
**Federal and State Taxation, Probate and Estate Planning, General Business, Corporation, Partnerships, Limited Liability Company.**
**Los Angeles, California Office: 445 South Figueroa Street, Twenty Sixth Floor, 90017. Telephone: 213-439-5385.**

*See Professional Biographies, RIVERSIDE, CALIFORNIA*

Gaustad, John K. ...........................................'41 '69 C.112 B.A. L.426 J.D. Dep. Dist. Atty.
Gaut, Barton C., (P.C.), (AV) ......'35 '63 C.112 A.B. L.1066 LL.B. 3750 University Ave.
Gearhart, Carole Ann ..................................'54 '82 C&L.1137 B.S.L., J.D. 4371 Latham St.
**Geerlings, Gerald J., (AV)** ...........................'28 '55 C.112 B.S. L.1068 LL.B. [Ⓐ Reid&H.]
*PRACTICE AREAS: Land Use Law; Development Law; Government Law.
Geeting, Steven C., (BV) ..................'50 '80 C.1109 B.A. L.398 J.D. [Fisher,W.&G.]
**Germano, Cynthia M.** ...........................'65 '90 C.940 B.A. L.426 J.D. [Ⓐ Best B.&K.]
*PRACTICE AREAS: Civil Litigation Law.
**Gervais, Debra Bartle** ..........................'56 '84 C.112 B.A. L.770 J.D. [Reid&H.]
*LANGUAGES: Spanish.
*PRACTICE AREAS: Construction Law; Real Estate Litigation; Intellectual Property.
Gilbert, Howard M., (BV) ...........'38 '65 C.112 B.S. L.1066 LL.B. Dep. Pub. Def. Off.

**Gilbert, Kelly, Crowley & Jennett, (AV)**
**3801 University Avenue, Suite 700, 92501⊙**
**Telephone: 909-276-4000 Fax: 909-276-4100**
**Resident Partners: Michael B. Donner; Edward A. Fernandez; Andrew C. Hubert. Resident Associates: Jeffrey W. Abel; Michele Assael-Shafia; Kirk A. Lauby; James F. Lindsay; Peggy E. Markson; Rodger A. Maynes; Geraldine J. Putnam; Robert S. Roddick; Frank A. Romeu, Jr.; Stephanie J. Yamashita.**
**General Civil and Trial Practice in all State and Federal Courts. Appellate Practice. Corporation and Insurance Law.**
**Los Angeles, California Office: 1200 Wilshire Boulevard. Telephone: 213-580-7000. Fax: 213-580-7100.**
**Orange County Office: Suite 310 Nexus Financial Center, 721 South Parker Street, Orange, California. Telephone: 714-541-5000. Fax: 714-541-0670.**
**San Diego, California Office: 501 West Broadway, Suite 1260 Koll Center. Telephone: 619-687-3000. Fax: 619-687-3100.**

*See Professional Biographies, RIVERSIDE, CALIFORNIA*

**Gilligan, Michael J.** ..........................'48 '84 C.1110 B.A. L.1049 J.D. [Reid&H.]
*PRACTICE AREAS: Bankruptcy Title Law; Real Estate Law; General Civil Litigation.
Goggins, Renee M. ..................'65 '94 C.475 B.A. L.1187 J.D. 3801 University Ave.
Goldberg, Gary G. ........................'55 '81 C.112 B.A. L.809 J.D. 3673 Arlington Ave.
**Golds, Howard B., (BV)** ..................'58 '83 C.112 B.A. L.800 J.D. [Best B.&K.]
*PRACTICE AREAS: Public Resources; General Business; Litigation.
Goldstein, Lee J. .......................................'51 '78 C.112 B.A. L.1095 J.D. 4361 Latham
Gonzales, Kathleen M. ......................'52 '78 C.112 B.A. L.1067 J.D. Off. of City Atty.
Goodman, Melanie L. ..............'44 '93 C.228 B.S.N. L.285 J.D. 3801 University Ave.
**Granito, Gilbert J., (AV)** ...............'41 '74 C.1246 B.B.A. L.990 J.D. [Redwine&S.]⊙
*PRACTICE AREAS: Water Law; Water District Administration Law; State and Federal Tax Litigation; Administrative Appeals.
**Grant, Don G., (AV)** .........................'45 '72 C.112 B.A. L.61 J.D. [Thompson&C.]
*PRACTICE AREAS: Personal Injury Defense; Medical Malpractice Law.
**Grant, Michael, (P.C.), (BV)** ...............'45 '77 C.101 B.A. L.1065 J.D. [Best B.&K.]
*PRACTICE AREAS: Real Estate Law; Zoning and Subdivision Law; Real Estate Finance Law.

**Graves, Suzanne M.**
**(See Upland)**

Greene, Carol ........................................'64 '90 C.707 B.A. L.352 J.D. 3610 14th St.
Gregor, Garrett S., (AV) '47 '78
C.742 B.A. L.1137 J.D. 4129 Main St. (⊙Santa Ana Heights)
Gregory, David E. .......................................'60 '86 C&L.1137 B.S., J.D. [Jacobs&G.]

**Gresham, Varner, Savage, Nolan & Tilden, (AV)**
**3750 University Avenue, Suite 610 (92501), P.O. Box 1148, 92502⊙**
**Telephone: 909-274-7777 Fax: 909-274-7770**
**Email: info@gvsnt.com**
**Members: Bruce D. Varner; Stephan G. Saleson; Craig O. Dobler. Resident Associates: Michael O. Wolf; Brendan W. Brandt; Elizabeth Ashley Bianco.**
**General Civil and Trial Practice. Business Law, Corporate Law, Real Estate, Land Use, Administrative Law, Mining, Natural Resources, Environmental Law, Water Law, Probate, Estate Planning, Labor and Employment Law, Taxation, Natural Resources, Health Care and Hospital Law.**
**San Bernardino, California Office: 600 North Arrowhead Avenue, Suite 300. Telephone: 909-884-2171. Fax: 909-888-2120.**

*See Professional Biographies, RIVERSIDE, CALIFORNIA*

Grossman, Jay P., (BV) ......................'40 '67 C.112 B.A. L.1068 J.D. 3890 1th St.
**Gudoski, Kristi Lynn** ..........................'71 '96 C.165 B.A. L.800 J.D. [Ⓐ Best B.&K.]
*PRACTICE AREAS: Litigation.
Gurney, Richard L. ........................'50 '76 C.1163 B.A. L.678 J.D. 4324 Latham St.
Gurney, W. David, (BV) ..................'44 '71 C.1163 B.S. L.950 J.D. 4324 Latham St.
**Gwynn, Jeffrey T.** ...........................'66 '95 C.426 B.S. L.94 J.D. [Ⓐ Thompson&C.]
*PRACTICE AREAS: Insurance Defense.

**Haight, Brown & Bonesteel, (AV)**
**A Partnership including Professional Corporations**
**3750 University Avenue, Suite 650, 92501⊙**
**Telephone: 909-341-8300 FAX: 909-341-8309**
**Resident Members: Mark S. Lester. Resident Associates: Kevin M. Osterberg; Michael S. Kelly.**
**General Civil and Trial Practice in all State and Federal Courts. Municipality, Construction, Landowner/Operator and Products. Corporation. Commercial. Tax. Real Estate. Probate. Estate Planning, Business and Labor Law.**
**Santa Monica, California Office: 1620 26th Street, Suite 4000 North, P.O. Box 680. Telephone: 310-449-6000. Fax: 310-829-5117. Telex: 705837.**
**Santa Ana, California Office: Suite 900, 5 Hutton Centre Drive. Telephone: 714-754-1100. Telecopier: 714-754-0826.**
**San Francisco, California Office: 201 Sansome Street, Suite 300. Telephone: 415-986-7700. Fax: 415-986-6954.**

*See Professional Biographies, RIVERSIDE, CALIFORNIA*

Hall & Bailey, (AV) .......................................................6761 Brockton Ave. (⊙Irvine)
Hamilton, Thomas H. ......................'43 '77 C.1163 A.B. L.1137 J.D. 3877 12th St.
**Hancock, Aaron** ................................'— '92 C.112 B.A. L.1067 J.D. [Roberts&M.]
**Hancock, David J.** ..........................'66 '94 C&L.101 B.A., J.D. [Ⓐ Best B.&K.]
Hanks, J. Thompson .............................'44 '74 C.112 B.A. L.990 J.D. Supr. Ct. J.
Hanson, James A. ......................'55 '83 C&L.1137 B.S.L., J.D.L. 3610 14th St.
Hantman, Daniel .........................'42 '75 C.112 B.A. L.1095 J.D. 4072 Chestnut St
Harding, R. Michael, (BV) ..................'38 '73 C.1042 B.A. L.990 J.D. [R.M.Harding]
Harding, R. Michael, A Professional Law Corporation, (BV) ..........3891 Eleventh Street
**Hardke, Gregory L., (BV)** ..................'49 '76 C.475 B.A. L.1065 J.D. [Best B.&K.]
*PRACTICE AREAS: Real Estate Law.
Harer, Pamela K., (BV) ..............'33 '78 C.659 B.A. L.809 J.D. [Ⓐ Fidler,B.O.&W.]
Harman, Dodie A. ............................'56 '83 C.1136 B.A. L.809 J.D. Dep. Dist. Atty.

**Harmon, Steven L., (AV) '47 '72 C.112 B.A. L.426 J.D.**
**The Loring Building, 3685 Main Street, Suite 250, 92501**
**Telephone: 909-787-6800 Fax: 909-787-6700**
**Criminal Trial Practice.**

*See Professional Biographies, RIVERSIDE, CALIFORNIA*

**Harris, Dina O.** ..............................'67 '92 C&L.101 B.S., J.D. [Ⓐ Best B.&K.]
*PRACTICE AREAS: School Law; Public Law; Environmental Law.
Harrison, Charles A., (AV) ..........'16 '54 C.668 B.A. L.809 J.D. 4080 Pedley Rd., #61
Hattendorf, L. Steven .................'62 '91 C.1163 B.S. L.61 J.D. 3333 14th St.
Hays, Howard H., Jr. ..................'17 '46 C.813 B.A. L.309 LL.B. Press-Enterprise Co.
Hazelton, Gloria M. ........................'40 '84 C.1042 B.A. L.678 J.D. 3880 Lemon

CAA519P

Heaslet, Timothy J. ........ '44 '70 C.1246 B.A. L.1065 J.D. Mun. Ct. J.
**Heil, Scott Richard** ........ '63 '92 C.800 B.S. L.1065 J.D. [Ⓐ Redwine&S.]
*PRACTICE AREAS: General Civil Trial Law; Contract Law; Real Property Law.
**Heiting, James O.**, (BV) ........ '49 '76 C.112 B.S. L.1137 J.D. [Heiting&I.]
*REPORTED CASES: Fellers v. Fellers; Soto v. Royal Globe.
*PRACTICE AREAS: Medical Malpractice; Personal Injury Law; Legal Malpractice; Professional Negligence; Civil Litigation.

**Heiting & Irwin, (BV)**
**3845 Market Street, Third Floor, 92501**
**Telephone: 909-682-6400 Fax: 909-682-4072**
**James O. Heiting; Richard H. Irwin (Certified Specialist, Workers' Compensation Law, The State Bar of California Board of Legal Specialization). Associates: Rebecca S. Reed; Matthew G. Markham; Scot Thomas Moga; Sheri B. Cruz.**
**Civil Trial Practice, Personal Injury, Wrongful Death, Medical Malpractice, Professional Liability, Workers Compensation, Estate Planning and Probate, Business, Corporate, Family Law, Dispute Resolution.**
***See Professional Biographies, RIVERSIDE, CALIFORNIA***

Hekman, Ralph K., (BV) ........ '32 '62 C.768 A.B. L.1066 LL.B. 4060 Chestnut St.
Hensel, Donald J. ........ '56 '83 C.238 B.A. L.546 J.D. 5053 La Mart Dr.
Heredia, Barbara A. ........ '45 '88 L.1198 J.D. Dep. Dist. Atty.
**Hernandez, Fred C.** '67 '95
C.1074 B.S.A.E. L.112 J.D. [Knobbe,M.O.&B.] (See Pat. Sect.)
Hernandez, Helios J. ........ '44 '77 C.813 B.A. L.800 J.D. Dep. Dist. Atty.
**Herrera, Cynthia M.** ........ '63 '93 C.1109 B.A. L.1137 J.D. [Ⓐ Bonne,B.M.O.&N.]
Herring, Ann Elizabeth ........ '61 '89 C.112 B.A. L.169 J.D. Ernst & Young
Herring, Norman Y., (BV⊤) ........ '46 '76 C.836 B.S. L.1137 J.D. Chief Asst. City Atty.
Hesse, Michael V. ........ '53 '80 C.1109 B.A. L.1137 J.D. 4515 Tyler St.
Heumann, Ronald R. ........ '37 '66 C.1097 B.A. L.1065 J.D. Supr. Ct. J.
Hewatt, Clarence H. ........ '43 '76 C.112 B.A. L.1137 J.D. 4267 Quenton Dr.
Hicks, Randall B. ........ '56 '86 C.1109 B.A. L.990 J.D. 6690 Alessandro Blvd.
Hiegel, Mary Beth ........ '63 '90 C.763 B.A. L.1137 J.D. Dep. Pub. Def.
Higgins, Philip S. ........ '34 '79 C.932 B.A. L.1137 J.D. [R.J.Pickell]
Histen, Harry J. ........ '42 '76 C.1097 B.A. L.1137 J.D. 2000 Market St.
Hofeld, B. Curtis ........ '48 '76 C.112 B.A. L.1065 J.D. Dep. Dist. Atty.
**Holaday, Arnold W.** ........ '63 '93 C.112 B.A. L.767 J.D. [Ⓐ Anderson,M.&C.]
Hollenhorst, Thomas E. ........ '46 '72 C.768 B.A. L.1065 J.D. Supr. Ct. J.
Holmes, Dallas, (P.C.), (AV) ........ '40 '68 C.668 B.A. L.1066 J.D. 3750 University Ave.
**Holmes, J. E., III**, (AV) ........ '42 '68 C.154 A.B. L.1065 J.D. [Thompson&C.]
*PRACTICE AREAS: Products Liability; Personal Injury Defense; Public Entity Defense; Construction Law; General Litigation.
Holstein, Robert M., Jr., (AV) ........ '41 '72 C.285 B.A. L.1065 J.D. 4300 Latham St.
**Holt, Montessa D.** ........ '58 '87 C.1109 B.A. L.169 J.D. [Dickman&H.]
**Holtz, James F.**, (AV) ........ '52 '80 C.966 B.A. L.1049 J.D. [Stutz,G.A.S.&H.]⊙
*PRACTICE AREAS: Litigation; Insurance Coverage; Environmental Law.
Honn, Carver E. ........ '32 '66 C&L.900 B.A., J.D. Supr. Ct. Commr.
Honn, Dorothy L., (BV) ........ '44 '82 C.112 B.A. L.1198 J.D. 9939 Victoria Ave.
**Hopper, Geoffrey H.**, (BV) ........ '57 '82 C.112 B.A. L.61 J.D. [Thompson&C.]
*PRACTICE AREAS: Employment and Construction Law; Business Litigation.
Hosek, Nancy Lynn ........ '51 '85 C.1163 B.S. L.398 J.D. Riverside Co. Dept. of Health

**Howard, Moss, Loveder, Strickroth & Walker, (AV)**
**A Partnership including Professional Corporations**
**6700 Indiana Avenue, Suite 160, 92506-4200⊙**
**Telephone: 909-341-8353 Telecopier: 909-275-9637**
**Robert A. Walker. Associates: Mitchell L. Leverett.**
**General, Civil and Trial Practice in all State and Federal Courts. Personal Injury Defense, Business Litigation, Insurance Law, Construction Defect Litigation, Products Liability, Governmental Entity, Wrongful Termination, Appellate Practice.**
**Santa Ana, California Office: 2677 North Main Street, Suite 800. Telephone: 714-542-6300. Telecopier: 714-542-6987.**
***See Professional Biographies, RIVERSIDE, CALIFORNIA***

Howell, Eileen J. ........ '46 '77 C.766 B.A. L.1137 J.D. Dep. Dist. Atty.
**Howie, Scott D.** ........ '62 '95 C.668 B.A. L.1066 J.D. [Ⓐ Best B.&K.]
*PRACTICE AREAS: Business.
**Hubert, Andrew C.** ........ '59 '85 C.154 B.A. L.809 J.D. [Gilbert,K.C.&J.]
*LANGUAGES: French, Hungarian.
Huchting, Stephen H. ........ '48 '73 C&L.426 B.A., J.D. [Breidenbach,B.H.H.&H.]⊙
Huckabone, Joan M. ........ '69 '94 C.112 B.A. L.1065 J.D. 3750 University Ave.
Huff, Michael E. ........ '45 '78 C.622 B.A. L.61 J.D. 1770 Iowa Ave.
**Hughes, E. Aurora** ........ '54 '79 C.37 B.S. L.809 J.D. [Ericksen,A.K.D.&L.]
*PRACTICE AREAS: Class Action Defense; Complex Tort Litigation; Products Liability Defense; Malpractice Defense.
Hughes, John M., II ........ '41 '81 C.347 B.S. L.1198 J.D. 6567 Millbrea Dr.
Hummel, James E. ........ '38 '66 C&L.352 B.B.A., LL.B. [Ⓐ Fidler,B.O.&W.]
Hunt, Eileen M., (BV) ........ '55 '89 C.112 L.1137 J.D. Dep. Dist. Atty.
Huntley, Diane K. ........ '64 '89 C.112 B.A. L.809 J.D. 3403 10th St., Ste. 700
**Hurd, Marc S.** ........ '62 '87 C.112 B.A. L.1065 J.D. [Kinkle,R.&S.]
Imburg, Gary A. ........ '46 '77 C.17 B.S. L.1137 J.D. 3909 12th St.
Inskeep, Don R. ........ '41 '70 C.112 A.B. L.1066 J.D. Asst. Dist. Atty.
**Irwin, Richard H.** ........ '55 '80 C.112 B.A. L.809 J.D. [Heiting&I.]
*PRACTICE AREAS: Workers Compensation.

**Ives, Kirwan & Dibble, A Professional Corporation**
**(See Palm Springs)**

Jacobs, Kathleen Marie ........ '53 '85 C.1110 B.A. L.1137 J.D. [Jacobs&G.]
Jacobs & Gregory ........ 4001 11th St.
**Jacobsen, Lewis F., (A Professional Corporation)**, (AV) '26 '54
C.112 A.B. L.813 J.D. [Swarner&F.]
*PRACTICE AREAS: Real Property Law; Commercial; Corporate; Secured Transactions; Appellate Practice.
Jarvis, William A. ........ '60 '85 C.1109 B.A. L.1137 J.D. 7344 Magnolia Ave.
Jarvis, William M., (CV) ........ '25 '66 C.800 B.E. L.1008 LL.B. 7344 Magnolia Ave.
Jenkins, William P. ........ '53 '83 C.112 B.S. L.1137 J.D. 3501 Adams
Jensen, Boyd F., II, (AV) ........ '53 '79 C.878 B.A. L.990 J.D. [Garrett&J.]⊙
Johnson, Karen A. ........ '63 '90 C.1030 B.S. L.1049 J.D. Dep. Dist. Atty.
Johnson, Muriel L., (BV) ........ '42 '79 C.112 B.A. L.1198 J.D. 4072 Chestnut St.
Johnston, James W. ........ '53 '86 C.112 B.A. L.464 J.D. 3877 12th St.
Kahn, Samuel D. ........ '25 '62 L.809 LL.B. 4979 Via Campeche
Katzenstein, William C. ........ '46 '74 C.1109 B.A. L.1188 J.D. Co. Coun.
Keenan, Kelly P. ........ '60 '90 C.871 B.S. L.1049 J.D. Dep. Dist. Atty.
Keir, Loyal E. ........ '14 '38 C&L.352 B.A., J.D. 2671 Doubetree Dr.
Kellam, James L. ........ '24 '55 C.112 B.S. P.O. Box 1298
**Kelly, Michael S.** ........ '66 '91 C.112 B.A. L.602 J.D. [Ⓐ Haight,B.&B.] (⊙Santa Monica)
*PRACTICE AREAS: General Liability; Medical Malpractice; Products Liability.
**Kelly, Warren D.** ........ '62 '93 C.1074 B.S. L.1065 J.D. [Ⓐ Thomas,M.P.&K.]
**Kemp, Clive J.**, (AV) ........ '44 '73 C.1042 B.A. L.1137 J.D. [Cummings&K.]⊙
*PRACTICE AREAS: Construction Litigation; Insurance Defense.
Kenison, William D. ........ '48 '82 C.154 B.A. L.1198 J.D. Co. Coun.
Kennedy, William C. ........ '41 '77 C.800 B.S. L.990 J.D. 1525 3rd St.

**Kerbs, Michael G.** ........ '63 '87 C&L.1049 B.A., J.D. [Reid&H.]
*PRACTICE AREAS: Corporate Partnership Real Estate Law; Litigation.
Kincannon, Gary L. ........ '50 '80 C.1073 B.A. L.1049 J.D. [Saxon,B.G.&K.]⊙
King, Leah M. ........ '50 '85 C.690 B.A. L.931 J.D. [Miller&K.]

**Kinkle, Rodiger and Spriggs, Professional Corporation, (AV)**
**3333 14th Street, 92501⊙**
**Telephone: 909-683-2410; 800-235-2039 Fax: 909-683-7759**
**Everett L. Spriggs (Managing Attorney); Bruce E. Disenhouse; Claudia L. Reynolds; Scott B. Spriggs; Toby J. Elder; Thomas P. Schlax; Marc S. Hurd; Burton M. Selman; Michael D. Shafer.**
**General Trial Practice. Negligence, Malpractice, Products Liability, Construction and Insurance Law.**
**Los Angeles, California Office: 600 North Grand Avenue. Telephone: 213-629-1261. Fax: 213-629-8382.**
**Santa Ana, California Office: 837 North Ross Street. Telephone: 714-835-9011. Fax: 714-667-7806.**
**San Diego, California Office: Suite 900 Driver Insurance Center, 1620 Fifth Avenue, P.O. Box 127900. Telephone: 619-233-4566. Fax: 619-233-8554.**
**Santa Barbara, California Office: 125 East De La Guerra Street. Telephone: 805-966-4700. Fax: 805-966-4120.**
***See Professional Biographies, RIVERSIDE, CALIFORNIA***

Kipnis, Neal R. ........ '59 '85 C&L.112 B.A., J.D. Dep. Co. Coun.
**Kistler, Harlan B.** ........ '60 '89 C&L.352 B.A., J.D. [Kistler,M.&P.]
*PRACTICE AREAS: Tort; Personal Injury Litigation; Wrongful Death (Plaintiff and Defense); Construction Law; Commercial Collections.

**Kistler, McCarty & Pearcy**
**3890 Tenth Street, 3rd Floor, P.O. Box 1583, 92502-1583**
**Telephone: 909-686-1583 Fax: 909-686-1619**
**Harlan B. Kistler; Robert A. McCarty, Jr.; Brian C. Pearcy.**
**General Practice.**
***See Professional Biographies, RIVERSIDE, CALIFORNIA***

**Knobbe, Martens, Olson & Bear, LLP, (AV)**
**A Limited Liability Partnership including Professional Corporations**
**3801 University Avenue, Suite 710, 92501⊙**
**Telephone: 909-781-9231 Fax: 909-781-4507**
**William B. Bunker; William H. Nieman; Michael H. Trenholm; Fred C. Hernandez.**
**Intellectual Property Law including Patent, Trademark, Copyright, Unfair Competition, Trade Secret, Licensing, Computer Law, Antitrust Law, and related litigation.**
**Reference: Wells Fargo Bank.**
**Newport Beach, California Office: 620 Newport Center Drive, 16th Floor. Telephone: 714-760-0404. Fax: 714-760-9502.**
**San Diego, California Office: 501 West Broadway, Suite 1400. Telephone: 619-235-8550. Fax: 619-235-0176.**
***See Professional Biographies, RIVERSIDE, CALIFORNIA***

**Knudsen, Curtis E.** ........ '53 '78 C.590 B.S. L.793 J.D. [Thomas,M.P.&K.]
*PRACTICE AREAS: Real Estate; Lending; Lease Law.
Kotkin, Edward Z. ........ '66 '91 C.311 B.A. L.276 J.D. Dep. Dist. Atty.
**Kottmeier, Dennis**, (AV) ........ '44 '69 C.684 B.A. L.1065 J.D. [Reid&H.]
*PRACTICE AREAS: State and Local Government; Police Excessive Force Defense; Fair Political Practices; Environmental Crimes Defense; Zoning and Land Use Law.
Kowalski, Michael J. ........ '62 '91 C.1074 B.S. L.809 J.D. 3801 University Ave.
Kring & Brown ........ 5225 Canyon Crest Drive Bldg. 100, Ste. 166 (⊙Irvine & San Diego)
Kubacki, Robert W. ........ '47 '81 C.339 B.S. L.8 J.D. Corp. Secy. & Sr. Coun., Bourns, Inc.
**Kubota, Yoshiaki C.** ........ '64 '94 C.112 B.A. L.1137 J.D. [Ⓐ Bonne,B.M.O.&N.]
Kump, Kary R. ........ '52 '82 C.1109 B.A. L.1137 J.D. 6956 Indiana Ave.

**La Follette, Johnson, De Haas, Fesler & Ames, A Professional Corporation, (AV)**
**3403 Tenth Street, Suite 820, 92501⊙**
**Telephone: 909-275-9192 Fax: 909-275-9249**
**Steven R. Odell; Christopher L. Thomas; Robert K. Warford (Manager/Shareholder) (Resident); Mark S. Rader (Resident);—Jeffery R. Erickson (Resident); Eileen S. Lemmon (Resident); Larry E. White (Resident); Daniel D. Sorenson (Resident); Erin L. Muellenberg (Resident); Phyllis M. Winston (Resident).**
**Civil Litigation, Employment Law, Medical Malpractice, Professional Liability, Insurance Defense Coverage and Bad Faith, Construction Law and Product Liability.**
**A List of References will be furnished upon request.**
**Los Angeles, California Office: 865 South Figueroa Street, Suite 3100. Telephone: 213-426-3600. Fax: 213-426-3650.**
**San Francisco, California Office: 50 California Street, Suite 3350. Telephone: 415-433-7610. Telecopier: 415-392-7541.**
**Santa Ana, California Office: 2677 North Main Street, Suite 901. Telephone: 714-558-7008. Telecopier: 714-972-0379.**
***See Professional Biographies, RIVERSIDE, CALIFORNIA***

Langevin, Mary A. ........ '60 '90 C.959 B.A. L.1137 J.D. 115 Pine Ave. Ste 600
Lapica, Larry S. ........ '53 '79 C.112 B.A. L.1049 J.D. 4275 Lemon St.
Lapica, Ray ........ '15 '67 C.665 B.A. L.800 J.D. 4275 Lemon St.
**Larson, Ronald V.** ........ '68 '95 C.1109 B.A. L.1067 J.D. [Ⓐ Thompson&C.]
*PRACTICE AREAS: Labor and Employment; Business Litigation; Products Liability; Insurance Defense.
**Lauby, Kirk A.** ........ '49 '78 C.112 B.A. L.809 J.D. [Ⓐ Gilbert,K.C.&J.]
*PRACTICE AREAS: Products Liability; Construction Defect; Contract Litigation; Bad Faith; Energy Litigation.
**Lawrence, David D.** ........ '54 '80 C.347 B.S. L.37 J.D. [Franscell,S.R.&L.]⊙
*PRACTICE AREAS: Police Misconduct Liability Defense; Civil Rights; Title VII Discrimination; Americans with Disabilities Act; Municipal and Administrative Law.
**Leahy, Alan J.** ........ '67 '94 C.112 B.A. L.770 J.D. [T.Bridges]
*PRACTICE AREAS: Civil Litigation.
**Lear, William H.**, (BV) '39 '66 C.976 B.A. L.228 J.D.
V.P., Gen. Coun. & Secy., Fleetwood Enterprises, Inc.
*RESPONSIBILITIES: Corporate Law; Regulatory Law; Legislative Practice; Employment Law; International Law.
**Lee, Donald R.** ........ '60 '89 C.999 B.S. L.61 J.D. [Ⓐ Thompson&C.]
*PRACTICE AREAS: Products Liability; Lemon Law; Public Entity; General Civil.
**Lee, Steven G.** ........ '60 '88 C&L.101 B.A., J.D. [Reid&H.]
*PRACTICE AREAS: Business Law; Real Estate Law; Commercial Litigation.
Leer, Sandra G., (BV) ........ '40 '80 C.1042 B.A. L.1137 J.D. 4094 Chestnut St.
Leighton, Everett W. ........ '— '22 C.800 770 N. University Dr.
**Lemmon, Cyrus J.**, (BV) ........ '42 '70 C&L.174 B.A., J.D. [Roberts&M.]
**Lemmon, Eileen S.** ........ '41 '88 C.229 B.S. L.426 J.D. [Ⓐ La Follette,J.D.F.&A.]
*PRACTICE AREAS: Medical Malpractice.
**Lester, Mark S.** ........ '60 '85 C.112 B.A. L.1049 J.D. [Haight,B.&B.]
*PRACTICE AREAS: Land Owners Liability; Construction and Contractors Liability; Product Liability; Municipality Defense; Common Carrier and Transportation Claims.
**Leverett, Mitchell L.** ........ '66 '93 C.112 B.A. L.1137 J.D. [Ⓐ Howard,M.L.S.&W.]
Levine, Michele Donna, (BV) ........ '58 '83 C.112 B.A. L.426 J.D. Dep. Dist. Atty.
**Lightfeldt, John B.** ........ '58 '92 C&L.1137 B.S.L., J.D. [T.L.Miller]
*PRACTICE AREAS: Business Litigation; Real Estate Law.
Lind, Katherine A. ........ '58 '84 C.1042 B.A. L.426 J.D. Dep. Co. Coun.
**Lindsay, James F.** ........ '49 '89 C.436 B.S. L.809 J.D. [Ⓐ Gilbert,K.C.&J.]
*PRACTICE AREAS: Construction Defect Litigation.
**Littleworth, Arthur L., (P.C.)**, (AV) ........ '23 '51 C&L.976 B.A., LL.B. [Best B.&K.]
*PRACTICE AREAS: Water Law; Environmental.
Lloyd, Michael B., (A.P.C.) ........ '50 '76 C.1109 B.A. L.990 J.D. 4076 Brocton Ave.
Lomazow, Michael J., (AV) ........ '47 '74 C.1046 B.A. L.809 J.D. [Blumenthal&L.]
Lopez, Alexandra F. ........ '64 '94 C.112 B.A. L.1065 J.D. 3750 University Ave.

**Lorenz Alhadeff Cannon & Rose, (AV)**
**The Orleans Building, 3638 University Avenue, Suite 256, 92501⊙**
**Telephone: 909-369-3281 Facsimile: 909-683-4307**
**Samuel C. Alhadeff.**
**General Civil and Trial Practice in all State and Federal Courts, Administrative Law, Antitrust, Banking, Bankruptcy, Reorganization and Creditors Rights, Business, Construction, Corporations, Environmental, International Business and Litigation, Public Finance, Real Estate Litigation, Real Estate Transactions, Federal and State Securities and Trade Regulation, White Collar Crime, Estate Planning, Probate, Criminal.**
**San Diego, California Office: 550 West "C" Street, Nineteenth Floor, 92101-3540. Telephone: 619-231-8700. Facsimile: 619-231-8323.**
**Temecula, California Office: The Tower Plaza, 27555 Ynez Road, Suite 203 92591-4677. Telephone: 909-699-9088. Facsimile: 909-699-9878.**
**Lafayette, California Office: Lafayette Terrace, 3697 Mount Diablo Boulevard, Suite 100, 94549. Telephone: 510-283-1599. Facsimile: 510-283-5847.**
*See Professional Biographies, RIVERSIDE, CALIFORNIA*

Lowder, Juanda K. . . . '65 '91 C.1131 B.A. L.245 J.D. 3880 Lemon
Loya, Janice . . . '59 '89 1030 Bay Ridge Cir.
**Lubrani, Michael D.** . . . '59 '84 C.705 B.A. L.990 J.D. [Bonne,B.M.O.&N.]
Luchs, Elliott S., (BV) . . . '48 '73 C.112 B.A. L.990 J.D. [Luchs&M.]
Luchs & Mihelich, Inc., (BV) . . . 7344 Magnolia Ave.
Luebs, Roger A., (BV) . . . '52 '77 C.112 B.A. L.1068 J.D. Dept. Dist. Atty.
**Luke, Fiona G.** . . . '61 '89 C.1097 B.A. L.426 J.D. [Roberts&M.]
**Lundberg, Gerald R., The Law Offices of**
(See Victorville)
Lybbert, David M. . . . '42 '90 C.172 B.S. L.1137 J.D. 8726 Brunswick
Maas, Colleen Rutherford . . . '— '88 C.1042 B.A. L.1137 J.D. Dep. Dist. Atty.
Mace, Shirley Anne . . . '52 '92 C.1109 B.A. L.1137 J.D. 1650 Iowa Ave. Ste. 200
Macher, David J. . . . '53 '88 C.629 B.S. L.1137 J.D. 3685 Main St.
**Mackey, Edward L., (A Professional Corporation)**, (BV) '33 '59
C&L.813 B.A., LL.B. [Swarner&F.]
*PRACTICE AREAS: Corporations; Real Property; Trusts; Civil Litigation.
Macomber, Robert D. . . . '25 '65 C.1163 B.A. L.800 J.D. Supr. Ct. J.
Macomber, Thomas K. . . . '58 '85 C.1163 B.A. L.950 J.D. Dist. Atty.'s Off.
**MacVey, Kendall H.**, (BV) . . . '48 '73 C.605 B.A. L.1068 J.D. [Best B.&K.]
*PRACTICE AREAS: Litigation; Antitrust/Unfair Competition; Eminent Domain; Air Quality Law.
Madrid, Priscilla A. . . . '59 '92 C&L.1137 B.S.L., J.D. 1770 Iowa Ave.
Madsen, Tracey Y. '59 '92 C.501 B.A. L.260 J.D.
(adm. in FL; not adm. in CA) 21677 Auton Ave.★
Magno, JoAnn V. . . . '62 '90 C.112 B.A. L.802 J.D. 5700 Arlington Ave.
**Maloney, Erin A.** . . . '65 '91 C.112 B.A. L.426 J.D. [Ⓐ Fiore,W.R.&P.]
Maloney, Larry . . . '47 '77 C.1188 B.A. L.1137 J.D. 4780 Arlington Ave.
Mandel, Leonard H. . . . '40 '68 C.102 B.A. L.575 J.D. Dep. Dist. Atty.
Manis, Kathryn Irene . . . '54 '87 C.112 B.A. L.1137 J.D. Dep. Pub. Def.
**Manning, James J., Jr.**, (AV) . . . '49 '76 C.112 B.A. L.398 J.D. [Reid&H.]
*PRACTICE AREAS: Real Estate Law; Title Insurance Litigation; Construction Law; Newspaper Law.
**Markham, Matthew G.** . . . '50 '83 C.112 B.A. L.809 J.D. [Ⓐ Heiting&I.]
*REPORTED CASES: Brose v. Union Tribune 183 CA 3d. 1986; Thai v. Stang 214 CA 3d. 1989.
*PRACTICE AREAS: Civil Litigation; Family Law.
**Markson, Peggy E.** . . . '54 '86 C.1109 B.A. L.1137 J.D. [Ⓐ Gilbert,K.C.&J.]
*PRACTICE AREAS: Insurance Coverage.
**Marlatt, Michael J.**, (BV) . . . '57 '84 C.1075 B.A. L.990 J.D. [Thompson&C.]
*PRACTICE AREAS: Personal Injury Defense; Medical Malpractice Law; Public Entity Law.
Marmor, Barbara E. . . . '50 '81 C.813 B.A. L.284 J.D. Dep. Dist. Atty.
**Marnell, Matthew J.** . . . '55 '82 C&L.426 B.A., J.D. [Roberts&M.]
**Marshall, Christopher B.** . . . '51 '82 C.112 B.A. L.426 J.D. [Bonne,B.M.O.&N.] (⊙L.A.)
**Marshall, John W.**, (AV) . . . '46 '78 C.716 B.A. L.990 J.D. [Thompson&C.]
*PRACTICE AREAS: Personal Injury Defense; Construction Law; Commercial and Business Litigation; Insurance Coverage and Bad Faith Litigation; Public Entity Defense.
**Matulis, Steven M.** . . . '66 '94 C.1068 B.A. L.1065 J.D. [Chandler&Assoc.]
*PRACTICE AREAS: Civil Litigation (70%, 140); Business Litigation (20%, 20); Family Law.
**Maynes, Rodger A.** . . . '46 '85 C.1042 B.S. L.398 J.D. [Ⓐ Gilbert,K.C.&J.]
**McCarthy, Douglas**, (BV) . . . '46 '78 C.178 B.A. L.1068 J.D. [Roberts&M.]
**McCarthy, Justin M.**, (AV) . . . '26 '54 C&L.426 B.S., LL.B. [Redwine&S.]
*PRACTICE AREAS: Eminent Domain Law; Commercial Litigation; General Civil Trials.
**McCarty, Robert A.**, (BV) . . . '36 '64 C.112 B.A. L.1065 LL.B. [R.A.McCarty]
**McCarty, Robert A., Jr.** . . . '67 '93 C.1254 B.S. L.1148 J.D. [Kistler,M.&P.]
*PRACTICE AREAS: Family Law; D.A. Child Support Actions; Parental Kidnapping; Jurisdictional Issues; Adoptions.

**McCarty, Robert A., A Professional Corporation, (BV)**
**4545 Allstate Drive, 92501**
**Telephone: 909-781-2180 Fax: 909-781-6110**
**Robert A. McCarty.**
**Real Estate, Estate Planning, Probate, Business and Mediation.**
**Reference: Security Pacific National Bank.**
*See Professional Biographies, RIVERSIDE, CALIFORNIA*

McCollum, Duane L. . . . '60 '90 C.990 B.A. L.809 J.D. 3403 10th St., Ste. 700
McConaghy, Dennis A. . . . '41 '76 C.473 B.A. L.378 J.D. Mun. Ct. J.
**McCullough, Michael L.** '46 '77 C.800 B.S. L.990 J.D.
Asst. Gen. Coun., Fleetwood Enterprises, Inc.
*RESPONSIBILITIES: Litigation Management; Regulatory Law.
**McGregor, Holly H.** . . . '61 '95 C.1109 B.A. L.1137 J.D. [Ⓐ Bonne,B.M.O.&N.]
*PRACTICE AREAS: Medical Malpractice Defense.
McIntyre, Robert J. . . . '52 '77 C.36 B.S. L.426 J.D. Supr. Ct. J.
**McKinney, Dan G.**, (BV) . . . '56 '81 C.1209 B.A. L.464 J.D. [Reid&H.]
*PRACTICE AREAS: Real Estate Litigation; Land Use Law; Condemnation Law.
McKinstry, Charles L. '46 '77 C.1163 B.A. L.1049 J.D.
Southeastern Calif. Conf. of Seventh-day Adventists
McLaren, Linda J. . . . '49 '80 C.112 B.A. L.336 J.D. Depty. Dist. Atty.
Melton, Susan Evelyn . . . '62 '87 C.112 B.A. L.1049 J.D. Dep. Dist. Atty.
Meyer, Lee Ann . . . '57 '83 C.112 A.B. L.1068 J.D. 3750 University Ave.
Meyer, Raymond, Jr. . . . '62 '95 C.1044 B.S. L.1137 J.D. [Ⓐ Kring&B.]
Miceli, Victor L. . . . '28 '52 C.25 A.B. L.665 J.D. Supr. Ct. J.
Mihelich, Michael W., (BV) . . . '49 '81 C.763 B.A. L.1137 J.D. [Luchs&M.]
Miller, Dale C., (CV) . . . '24 '54 C.112 A.B. L.1066 LL.B. 3538 University Ave.
Miller, Geo. H. . . . '28 '53 C.112 L.1065 J.D. Ret. Mun. Ct. J.
Miller, Jaxon E. . . . '49 '80 C.112 B.A. L.1137 J.D. [Miller&K.]
**Miller, Thomas L.**, (BV) . . . '47 '78 C&L.1137 B.S.L., J.D. [T.L.Miller]
*PRACTICE AREAS: Real Estate Law; Construction Law; Business Law; Corporate Law.
Miller & King . . . 7750 Limonite Ave.
Miller-Meyer, Trista J. . . . '58 '87 C.999 L.1137 J.D. 3538 University Ave.

**Miller, Thomas L., A Professional Law Corporation, (BV)**
**3891 Eleventh Street, P.O. Box 949, 92502**
**Telephone: 909-683-7263 Fax: 909-683-3805**
**Thomas L. Miller; John B. Lightfeldt.**
**Real Estate, Construction, Business. Corporate, Transactional and Trial Practice in State and Federal Courts.**
*See Professional Biographies, RIVERSIDE, CALIFORNIA*

**Mitchell, Robert J.** . . . '52 '89 C.112 B.A. L.426 J.D. [Butterwick,B.&O.]
*PRACTICE AREAS: Business Litigation; Real Property Law; Personal Injury Law.
**Mizell, Brian S.** . . . '62 '88 C.768 B.A. L.990 J.D. [Anderson,M.&C.]
**Moga, Scot Thomas** . . . '— '96 [Ⓐ Heiting&I.]
*PRACTICE AREAS: Family Law; Workers' Compensation; Civil Litigation.
Monterosso, John M., (CV) . . . '65 '90 C&L.767 B.A., J.D. Dep. Dist. Atty.
**Montgomery, Dwight M.** . . . '58 '89 C&L.477 B.S., J.D. [Ⓐ Best B.&K.]
*LANGUAGES: German.
**Montgomery, Gary T.** . . . '67 '93 C.674 A.B. L.990 J.D. [Ⓐ Thompson&C.]
*PRACTICE AREAS: Personal Injury Defense; Insurance Defense.
**Moore, David G.**, (AV) . . . '38 '65 C.112 B.S. L.1065 LL.B. [Reid&H.]
*PRACTICE AREAS: Business and Real Estate Litigation; Tort Defense; Water Law; Legal and Medical Malpractice Defense; General Civil Litigation.
Moore, Robert H., (AV) . . . '30 '59 C&L.800 B.A., LL.B. 4046 Chestnut St.
Morales, Irene C. '48 '76 C.112 B.A. L.1068 J.D.
Exec. Dir., Inland Counties Legal Servs., Inc.
**Morgan, Bruce**, (AV) . . . '32 '65 C.36 B.S. L.809 J.D. [Roberts&M.]
Morgan, Joseph Michael . . . '45 '75 C.1042 B.A. L.1049 J.D. Wkrs. Comp. App. Bd. J.
Morgan, W. Charles . . . '47 '73 C.112 B.A. L.1188 J.D. Supr. Ct. J.
**Morisaki-Price, Maxine M.**, (BV) . . . '51 '88 C.1097 B.A. L.426 J.D. [Ⓐ Thompson&C.]
*PRACTICE AREAS: Personal Injury Defense; Medical Malpractice Law.
**Morris, James P.** . . . '68 '96 C.197 B.A. L.1068 J.D. [Ⓐ Best B.&K.]
*PRACTICE AREAS: Public Law; Environmental Law; Water Law; Land Use Law.
**Morris, Jeffery A.** . . . '63 '88 C.112 B.A. L.990 J.D. [Ⓐ Stutz,G.A.S.&H.]⊙
*PRACTICE AREAS: Litigation; Public Entity.
Morris, John L., (BV) . . . '31 '71 C.763 B.S. L.813 J.D. Dep. Pub. Def.
**Mort, Peter J.**, (AV) . . . '47 '78 C.112 B.A. L.184 J.D. [Thomas,M.P.&K.]
*PRACTICE AREAS: Business; Commercial; Real Estate; Construction Defect Litigation.
Mraz, Valerie, (BV) . . . '58 '87 C.1042 B.S. L.426 J.D. Dep. Dist. Atty.
**Muellenberg, Erin L.** . . . '54 '89 C&L.1137 B.S.L., J.D. [Ⓐ La Follette,J.D.F.&A.]
*PRACTICE AREAS: Medical Malpractice; Health Care; External Peer Review.
Mulligan, Raymond P. . . . '51 '84 C.724 B.A. L.426 J.D. 1950 Market St.
Murad, Leslie E., II . . . '52 '81 C.1075 B.A. L.1049 J.D. [Ⓐ Fidler,B.O.&W.]
Murakami, Judith Graumann . . . '— '93 C.112 B.A. L.1137 J.D. 3243 Arlington Ave.

**Myers, Joseph Peter, (BV) '40 '68 C.668 A.B. L.800 J.D.**
**4048 Tenth Street, 92501**
**Telephone: 909-684-4330 Fax: 909-686-6686**
**Email: myerslaw@aol.com**
**Civil and Criminal Trial Practice. Personal Injury, Workers Compensation and Medical Malpractice Law.**
*See Professional Biographies, RIVERSIDE, CALIFORNIA*

Nagby, Robert W., (BV) . . . '52 '84 C.139 B.A. L.426 J.D. [R.W.Nagby]
Nagby, Robert W., Law Office of, (BV) . . . 3540 Twelfth St.
Naruo, Richard T. '44 '74 C.813 B.S. L.966 J.D.
(adm. in WI; not adm. in CA) 17321 Sunset View Dr.‡
**Nash, D. Elizabeth** . . . '61 '88 C.1109 B.A. L.990 J.D. [Ⓐ O'Flaherty&B.]
Nassar, William M. . . . '58 '94 C.684 B.S.B.A. L.1137 J.D. Bourns, Inc.
Nauss, Susan C. . . . '58 '90 L.972 J.D. 3750 University Ave.
Neblett, John . . . '11 '35 C&L.800 A.B., LL.B. Ret. Supr. Ct. J.
**Netta, Kimberly** . . . '67 '95 C.1077 B.A. L.1137 J.D. [Ⓐ Bonne,B.M.O.&N.]
*PRACTICE AREAS: Medical Malpractice.
**Neufeld, Bradley E.** . . . '60 '86 C.112 B.S. L.1068 J.D. [Best B.&K.]
*PRACTICE AREAS: Labor and Employment (Management) Law.
**Nieman, William H.** '42 '80 C.910 B.S.E.E. L.1049 J.D.
[Knobbe,M.O.&B.] (See Pat. Sect.) (⊙Newport Beach)
Nixen, Liana DeB. . . . '30 '83 C.66 B.A. L.1137 J.D. 4333 Orange St.
Nixson, Gordon E. . . . '25 '52 C&L.352 B.A., LL.B. 6850 Brocton Ave.‡
Nolan, Vincent P., (AV) . . . '48 '79 C.560 B.A. L.464 J.D. 3877 12th St.
**Norton, Irena Leigh** . . . '69 '93 C.112 B.A. L.276 J.D. [Ⓐ Thomas,M.P.&K.]
**Norton, Mitchell L.** . . . '65 '93 C.112 B.A. L.276 J.D. [Ⓐ Best B.&K.]
*LANGUAGES: Spanish.
*PRACTICE AREAS: Litigation.
Oberstein, Alan C. . . . '41 '67 C&L.112 B.A., J.D. Pub. Def.
Oblachinski, Robert M. . . . '54 '85 C.1145 B.S. L.1148 J.D. Dep. Dist. Atty.
O'Brien, Desiree Anne . . . '64 '91 C.1075 B.S. L.285 J.D. 3403 10th St.
**Odell, Steven R.**, (BV) '51 '80
C.112 B.A. L.1137 J.D. [La Follette,J.D.F.&A.] (⊙Santa Ana)
*PRACTICE AREAS: General Liability; Medical Malpractice; Trucking and Products Liability; Construction Defects.

**O'Flaherty & Belgum, (AV)**
**3880 Lemon Street Suite 450, 92501-3301⊙**
**Telephone: 909-341-0049 Fax: 909-341-3919**
**Email: oandb@law.com URL: http://www.oandb-law/oandb**
**Members of Firm: Lee M. Thies. Associates: D. Elizabeth Nash.**
**General Civil, Trial and Appellate Practice in State and Federal Courts. Medical and Dental Malpractice, Products Liability, General Insurance Law, Insurance Coverage, Wrongful Termination, Workers' Compensation, Business and Environmental Litigation.**
**Glendale, California Office: 1000 North Central, Suite 300, 91202-2957. Telephone: 818-242-9229. Fax: 818-242-9114.**
**Long Beach, California Office: 100 Oceangate, Suite 500, 90802-4312. Telephone: 310-437-0090. Fax: 310-437-5550.**
**Orange County, California Office: 222 South Harbor Boulevard, Suite 600, Anaheim, CA 92805-3701. Telephone: 714-533-3373. Fax: 714-533-2607.**
**Ventura, California Office: 840 County Square Drive, Suite 200, 93003-5406. Telephone: 805-650-2600. Fax: 805-650-2658.**
*See Professional Biographies, RIVERSIDE, CALIFORNIA*

**O'Laughlin, John F.** . . . '53 '82 C.763 B.A. L.767 J.D. [Butterwick,B.&O.]
*PRACTICE AREAS: Civil Litigation; Construction Law; Commercial Law.
Olins, Foerster & Hayes, (AV) . . . 4361 Latham Street, Suite 240 (⊙San Diego, Santa Ana)
Olson, Daniel E., (BV) . . . '41 '76 C.774 B.A. L.990 J.D. 3974 Jurupa Ave.
Orr, Jay E. . . . '56 '85 C.112 B.A. L.1186 J.D. Supervising Dep. Dist. Atty.
Orrock, Stanley O., (AV) . . . '43 '77 C.112 B.A. L.398 J.D. [Fidler,B.O.&W.]
**Osterberg, Kevin M.** . . . '56 '88 C.1174 B.S. L.809 J.D. [Ⓐ Haight,B.&B.]
*PRACTICE AREAS: General Civil Liability; Premises Liability Law; Defense of Public Entities; Public Entity Liability.
**Ouellette, Michelle** . . . '58 '89 C.1169 B.A. L.800 J.D. [Best B.&K.]
*PRACTICE AREAS: Environmental Law; Water Law; Natural Resources Law; Litigation.
Owen, Dana M. . . . '68 '94 C.999 A.A. L.1137 J.D. [Ⓐ Fidler,B.O.&W.]
Pacheco, Rodric A., (AV) . . . '58 '83 C.112 B.A. L.1049 J.D. Sr. Dep. Dist. Atty.
**Packer, James C.**, (BV) . . . '51 '77 C.112 B.A. L.61 J.D. [Roberts&M.]
Padia, Robert M., (BV) . . . '50 '75 C.605 B.A. L.1066 J.D. [Ⓐ Fidler,B.O.&W.]
Palladino, John A., (BV) . . . '30 '58 C&L.309 B.A., LL.B. 4371 Latham St.
Palmer, Ralph B. . . . '45 '76 C.1070 B.S. L.309 J.D. 5055 Canyon Crest Dr.
Parrott, Angela . . . '63 '94 C.999 B.A. L.809 J.D. 3403 10th St.
Parsons, Randy D. '50 '81 C&L.900 B.A., J.D.
(adm. in KS; not adm. in CA) Supervisory Sr. Resident Agent, F.B.I.
Peach, Timothy W., (BV) . . . '53 '79 C&L.1137 B.S.L., J.D. [Peach&W.]⊙
Peach & Weathers, A Law Corporation, (BV)
3403 Tenth St., Suite 700 (⊙San Bernardino & Ontario)

**Pearce, Patrick H.W.F.** .......... '64 '88 L.061 LL.B. [Best B.&K.]
*PRACTICE AREAS: Employment Litigation; Insurance Coverage Analysis and Litigation; Commercial Transactions.
**Pearcy, Brian C.** .......... '61 '91 C.112 B.S. L.464 J.D. [Kistler,M.&P.]
*PRACTICE AREAS: Civil Litigation; Business and Commercial Litigation; Real Estate Law; Business Law; Trade Secrets.
Peasley, Frank S., (BV) .......... '41 '78 C.763 A.B. L.1198 J.D. 3877 12th St.
Pelikan, Ann Lawlor, (BV) .......... '34 '79 C.767 B.A. L.1198 J.D. 4072 Chestnut St.
**Pena, Dulce L.**, (CV) .......... '57 '90 C.1163 B.A. L.990 J.D. [Ⓐ Thompson&C.]
*PRACTICE AREAS: Civil and Employment Litigation.
Pepper, Letitia E. .......... '— '82 C.1074 B.S. L.1065 J.D. Resch. Atty., Fed. Dist. Ct.
Pepper, Robert M., Jr., (BV) '44 '76 C.1179 B.S.A.E. L.1137 J.D.
Princ. Dep. Co. Coun.
**Perry, John R.** .......... '66 '95 C&L.893 B.A., J.D. [Ⓐ Best B.&K.]
*PRACTICE AREAS: Business Transactions; Mergers and Acquisitions.
Peterson, Jeannette A. .......... '52 '85 C.1058 B.S.N. L.1066 J.D. 3750 University Ave.
Philips, David M., (BV) .......... '44 '69 C.112 B.A. L.1068 J.D. 3992 Brockton
Phippen, David P., Sr. .......... '53 '83 C.877 B.S.M.S. L.101 J.D. 3750 University Ave.
Pickell, Robert J., (BV) .......... '27 '56 C&L.208 A.B., J.D. [R.J.Pickell]⊙
Pickell, Robert J., A Law Corporation, (BV) ...... 7145 Magnolia Ave. (⊙Newport Beach)
Pittman, Guy Bradley .......... '61 '87 C.1060 B.A. L.37 J.D. Dep. Dist. Atty.
**Polis, Gerald D.**, (AV) .......... '41 '65 C.140 B.S. L.790 J.D. [G.D.Polis]

**Polis, Gerald D., A Professional Corporation, (AV)**
**The Loring Building, 3685 Main Street, Suite 250, 92501**
**Telephone: 909-684-0131 Fax: 909-684-2808**
**Gerald D. Polis (Certified Specialist, Criminal Law, The State Bar of California Board of Legal Specialization).**
**Practice Limited to Criminal Defense in all Courts.**
***See Professional Biographies, RIVERSIDE, CALIFORNIA***

Ponsor, Dennis J., (BV) '48 '74 C.112 B.A. L.1049 J.D.
[Steinman,N.&R.] (⊙Santa Ana)
**Porras, David J.** .......... '52 '88 C.426 B.A. L.1137 J.D. [Ⓐ Thompson&C.]
*PRACTICE AREAS: Personal Injury Defense; Medical Malpractice Law; Insurance Coverage; Product Liability Defense.
**Porter, John M.**, (AV) .......... '47 '74 C.763 B.A. L.1049 J.D. [Roberts&M.]
**Powell, Donald F.**, (AV) .......... '39 '66 C.112 A.B. L.1065 LL.B. [Reid&H.]
*PRACTICE AREAS: Business Litigation; Real Estate Litigation; Condemnation Law.
Pristojkovic, Teresa J. .......... '63 '87 C.112 B.A. L.426 J.D. 3801 Univ. Ave.
Pritchard, Ronald E., (BV) .......... '35 '72 C&L.1137 B.A., J.D. [Falsetti&P.]
**Prosser, Deborah C.**, (AV) .......... '50 '80 C.264 B.A. L.705 J.D. [Thomas,M.P.&K.]
*LANGUAGES: French.
*PRACTICE AREAS: Environmental; Civil Trial and Toxic Torts; Products Liability; Construction.
Purbaugh, Kim .......... '51 '76 C&L.101 B.S., J.D. Supr. Dep. Dist. Atty.
Purvis, Barbara A., (BV) .......... '40 '69 C.112 B.A. L.273 J.D. Asst. City Atty.
**Putnam, Geraldine J.** .......... '46 '88 C.1074 B.A. L.398 J.D. [Ⓐ Gilbert,K.C.&J.]
*PRACTICE AREAS: Personal Injury Defense.
Qualls, Dan E. .......... '54 '78 C&L.846 B.A., J.D. 6864 Indiana Ave.
Quesnel, Michael, (BV) .......... '52 '78 C.112 B.A. L.1068 J.D. Dist. Atty.'s Ofc.
**Racobs, Peter E.** .......... '57 '83 C.112 B.A. L.1067 J.D. [Fiore,W.R.&P.]⊙
**Rader, Mark S.**, (BV) .......... '44 '75 C.112 B.S. L.800 J.D. [La Follette,J.D.F.&A.]
*PRACTICE AREAS: Medical Malpractice Defense; Wrongful Termination Defense.
Raftery, Michael R., (BV) .......... '35 '62 C&L.813 B.A., LL.B. 3666 University Ave.
Ramos, Jose S. .......... '41 '79 C.973 B.S. L.398 J.D. Dep. Dist. Atty.
Ranard, Lori Huff .......... '58 '85 C.684 B.A. L.990 J.D. 3610 14th St.
Rank, Jody S., (Mr.) .......... '45 '84 C.1042 B.S. L.1198 J.D. Asst. Co. Coun.
Rash, Todd A., (BV) .......... '60 '89 C.847 B.S. L.809 J.D. 3900 Market St.
**Rasich, Marc T.** .......... '68 '94 C.1049 B.A. L.878 J.D. [Ⓐ Best B.&K.]
*PRACTICE AREAS: Litigation.
Redd, Charles H. .......... '31 '73 C.767 B.A. L.1137 J.D. 4000 Pierce St.‡
**Reddish, Gary E.**, (BV) .......... '35 '73 C.112 B.S. L.424 J.D. [Redwine&S.]
*PRACTICE AREAS: Federal and State Taxation Law; Corporate Law; Litigation.

**Redwine and Sherrill, (AV)**
**1950 Market Street, 92501**⊙
**Telephone: 909-684-2520 Facsimile: 909-684-9583**
**Earl Redwine (1894-1967). Of Counsel: Maurice C. Sherrill. Members of Firm: Justin M. McCarthy; Gerald D. Shoaf; Gary E. Reddish; Gerald W. Eagans; Gilbert J. Granito; Thomas E. Bruyneel; Steven B. Abbott; Jeffry F. Ferre. Associates: Robert T. Andersen, Jr.; Scott Richard Heil; Andrew P. Byrne; Seth C. Thompson.**
**General Civil, Trial and Appellate Practice in State and Federal Courts. Water Rights Law, Municipal, Eminent Domain, Corporation, Real Property, Business, Zoning, Probate Law, Contract, Intentional Tort and Defamation, Federal and State Taxation.**
**Representative Clients: Coachella Valley Water District; Eastern Municipal Water District; West San Bernardino County Water District; Twenty-nine Palms Water District; Beaumont-Cherry Valley Water Districts; Circle K Corp.**
**Santa Ana, California Office: 13611 Winthrope Street. 92705. Telephone: 714-832-2256. Fax: 714-832-1719.**
***See Professional Biographies, RIVERSIDE, CALIFORNIA***

**Reed, Rebecca S.** .......... '62 '92 L.112 J.D. [Ⓐ Heiting&I.]
*PRACTICE AREAS: Civil Litigation; Personal Injury; Medical Malpractice; Guardianships.
**Reid, Stewart Dennis** .......... '66 '95 C.112 B.A. L.398 J.D. [Ⓐ Anderson,M.&C.]
Reid, Wm. S. '18 '56 C.608 B.S. L.266 J.D.
(adm. in OH; not adm. in CA) 2651 Victoria Park Dr.‡

**Reid & Hellyer, A Professional Corporation, (AV)**
**3880 Lemon, 5th Floor, P.O. Box 1300, 92502-3834**
**Telephone: 909-682-1771 Telecopier: 909-686-2415**
**Email: rhlaw@rhlaw.com**
**Donald F. Powell; David G. Moore; James J. Manning, Jr.; Diane S. Brewer; Richard D. Roth; Dan G. McKinney; Charles T. Schultz; Michael J. Gilligan; Michael G. Kerbs; Debra Bartle Gervais; David M. Diver; Steven G. Lee; Dennis Kottmeier. Of Counsel: Gerald J. Geerlings.**
**General Civil and Trial Practice in all State and Federal Courts. Administrative, Bankruptcy, Commercial, Communications, Constitutional, Construction, Corporate, Environmental, Ethics and Professional Responsibility, Estate Planning, Eminent Domain and Water Rights Law, Government, High Technology, Insurance, Intellectual Property, Labor and Employment Law, Litigation, Malpractice, Military, Personal Injury, Probate, Real Property, Torts, Zoning and Municipal.**
**Representative Clients: Atchison, Topeka & Santa Fe Railway; Chicago Title Insurance Co.; Montgomery Ward & Co.; Rohr, Inc.**
***See Professional Biographies, RIVERSIDE, CALIFORNIA***

**Reisch, Kevin J.** .......... '70 '95 C.602 B.A. L.1065 J.D. [Ⓐ Thomas,M.P.&K.]
Renner, Richard R. .......... '44 '89 C.1042 B.S. L.1137 J.D. 3891 10th St.
Replogle, John .......... '49 '77 C.112 B.A. L.1068 J.D. Asst. Dist. Atty.
**Reyes, George M.**, (AV) .......... '53 '78 C.309 B.A. L.1067 J.D. [Best B.&K.]
*PRACTICE AREAS: Mergers and Acquisitions; Private Financing; General Business Law; Tax Law; Estate Planning Law.
**Reynolds, Claudia L.**, (BV) .......... '56 '82 C.112 A.B. L.809 J.D. [Kinkle,R.&S.]
Reynolds, Larry K. .......... '44 '70 C.112 B.A. L.950 J.D. 3233 Arlington Ave.
**Reynolds, Marilee M.** .......... '42 '86 C.1109 B.A. L.1137 J.D. [Carlos]
*PRACTICE AREAS: Personal Injury.
Reynolds, Paul B. .......... '56 '81 C.763 A.B. L.1049 J.D. [Foster,D.&R.]
Rich, Elwood M. .......... '20 '46 C.228 A.B. L.339 J.D. Ret. Supr. Ct. J.
Rich, Gloria T., (BV) .......... '29 '75 C.112 B.S. L.1137 J.D. 4780 Arlington Ave.
**Rich, Patricia L.** .......... '61 '89 C.1042 B.S. L.1137 J.D. [Ⓐ Thompson&C.]
*PRACTICE AREAS: Personal Injury Defense; Products Liability.
Richards, Don J .......... '59 '86 C.845 B.S. L.1137 J.D. 3993 Market St.
**Riddell, Michael T., (P.C.)** .......... '51 '76 C&L.602 B.A., J.D. [Best B.&K.]
*PRACTICE AREAS: Public Law; Water Law; Land Use; Contract Law.
Ritter, Tex .......... '57 '86 C.740 B.A. L.846 J.D. Dep. Dist. Atty.
**Roberts, Barbara E.** .......... '48 '79 C.1097 B.S. L.426 J.D. [Franscell,S.R.&L.]⊙
*PRACTICE AREAS: Police Misconduct Liability Defense; Civil Rights; Municipal and Administrative Law; General Civil; Criminal Trial.
Roberts, John L. .......... '11 '43 C.623 L.426 3550 Ramona Dr.‡

**Roberts & Morgan, (AV)**
**Citrus Park, 1650 Iowa Avenue, Suite 200, 92507**
**Telephone: 909-682-2881 FAX: 909-682-2928**
**Email: akcrjo@SoCa.com**
**Roger W. Roberts (1917-1986); Robert W. Engle (1923-1985); Bruce Morgan; John M. Porter; James C. Packer; Arthur K. Cunningham; Douglas McCarthy; Fiona G. Luke; Aaron Hancock; Cyril C. Stanfield, III; Matthew J. Marnell; Cyrus J. Lemmon.**
**General Civil and Trial Practice; Insurance Coverage Analysis and Litigation; Insurance Broker and Agent Litigation; Municipal Law; Police Misconduct Defense; Construction Defect Litigation; Subrogation; Products Liability Litigation; Uninsured Motorist Law; Medical and Legal Malpractice Defense; Appellate Practice.**
**Representative Clients: Farmers Insurance Group; Ohio Casualty Insurance Group; State Farm Mutual Automobile Insurance Co.; City of Riverside; County of Riverside; City of Corona; Automobile Club of Southern California; K-Mart Corporation; Aetna Casualty & Surety Co. (Personal & Commercial Lines); Liberty Mutual Insurance Co.**
***See Professional Biographies, RIVERSIDE, CALIFORNIA***

Rocha, Ricardo A. .......... '41 '71 C.37 B.S. L.809 J.D. 3579 University Ave.
**Roddick, Robert S.**, (BV) .......... '49 '77 C.112 B.A. L.426 J.D. [Ⓐ Gilbert,K.C.&J.]
*PRACTICE AREAS: Insurance Defense.
Rogers, Robyn A. .......... '43 '91 C.112 M.B.A. L.999 J.D. Dep. Co. Coun.
Rollins, Adam Lincoln .......... '57 '93 C.475 B.A. L.809 J.D. 3750 University Ave.
**Romeu, Frank A., Jr.** .......... '61 '87 C.1055 B.S. L.420 J.D. [Ⓐ Gilbert,K.C.&J.]
Ross, C. Ann .......... '28 '63 C.999 L.1026 LL.B. 3866 Main St.‡
Roth, Andrew I. .......... '46 '70 C.112 A.B. L.1065 J.D. 3750 University Ave.
**Roth, Richard D.**, (AV) .......... '50 '74 C.473 B.A. L.245 J.D. [Reid&H.]
*PRACTICE AREAS: Labor Relations Law; Employment Law; Business Litigation.
**Rottschaefer, John R.** .......... '50 '84 C.112 A.B. L.1066 J.D. [Best B.&K.]
*PRACTICE AREAS: Public Finance Law.
Ruddy, Kevin J. .......... '51 '77 C&L.1049 B.A., J.D. Dep. Dist. Atty.
Ruiz, John M. .......... '56 '81 C&L.426 B.A., J.D. Dep. Dist. Atty.
Ryneal, F. Steve, (BV) .......... '46 '72 C.112 B.A. L.426 J.D. [Ryneal&R.]
Ryneal, Fred H., (AV) .......... '18 '48 C.502 B.S. L.986 J.D. [Ryneal&R.]
Ryneal & Ryneal, A Law Corporation, (AV) .......... 4275 Lemon St.
Sager, Daniel D. .......... '55 '93 C.1042 B.A. L.1065 J.D. 3333 14th St.
**Saleson, Stephan G.**, (BV) .......... '49 '76 C.475 B.A. L.990 J.D. [Gresham,V.S.N.&T.]
*PRACTICE AREAS: State and Federal Civil Litigation; Labor and Employment Law; OSHA Law.
**Sampson, Patrick J.**, (AV) .......... '37 '63 C.112 B.A. L.1068 LL.B. [Singer&S.]
*PRACTICE AREAS: Municipal.
Sams, Robert A., (BV) .......... '47 '72 C.112 B.A. L.1066 J.D. Asst. City Atty.
Sandquist, Allan H., (BV) .......... '36 '74 3891 10th St.‡
**Savage, Philip M., IV** .......... '67 '94 C.813 B.A. L.426 J.D. [Ⓐ Best B.&K.]
*PRACTICE AREAS: Estate Planning; Trust Administration; Business Transactions; Healthcare.
Saxon, Barry, Gardner & Kincannon, A Professional Corporation, (AV)
3403 10th St. (⊙San Diego, Newport Beach & San Dimas)

**Scalisi, Peter W., (AV) '54 '79 C.154 B.A. L.809 J.D.**
**3890 Eleventh Street, Suite 115, 92501-3524**
**Telephone: 909-686-9914 Fax: 909-686-8401**
**(Certified Specialist, Criminal Law, The State Bar of California Board of Legal Specialization).**
***PRACTICE AREAS: Criminal Law.**
**Criminal Trial, Grand Jury, White Collar Crime and Appellate Practice in all State and Federal Courts.**
***See Professional Biographies, RIVERSIDE, CALIFORNIA***

Scarborough, Walter E., (BV) .......... '19 '52 C&L.426 LL.B. 4296 N. Orange St.
**Schaefer, Michael J.** .......... '70 '95 C.560 B.B.A. L.112 J.D. [Ⓐ Best B.&K.]
*PRACTICE AREAS: Litigation.
**Schell, Sherrie V.** '50 '81 C.112 A.B. L.284 J.D.
Asst. Gen. Coun., Fleetwood Enterprises, Inc.
*RESPONSIBILITIES: Litigation Management; Employment Law.

**Schell & Delamer, LLP**
**(See Los Angeles)**

**Schlax, Thomas P.** .......... '49 '94 C.871 B.S. L.1049 J.D. [Ⓐ Kinkle,R.&S.]
Schmaeling, Daniel T. '62 '89 C.330 B.A. L.464 J.D.
3801 University Ave. (⊙Santa Ana)
**Schneider, Wilfred J., Jr.**, (CV) .......... '51 '79 C.112 B.A. L.809 J.D. [Carlos]
Schulte, Gerald F. .......... '26 '54 C.813 L.1065 J.D. Ret. Supr. Ct. J.
**Schultz, Charles T.**, (BV) .......... '54 '83 C.112 B.A. L.464 J.D. [Reid&H.]
*PRACTICE AREAS: Land Use Law; Development Law; Government Law.
Schwartz, Bernard J. .......... '60 '87 C.02 B.A. L.464 J.D. 3877 12th St.
Seager, William .......... '42 '79 Sr. Probation Off.
Sears, Anthony Allison .......... '61 '87 C.1074 B.A. L.398 J.D. Dep. Co. Coun.
**Selman, Burton M.** .......... '42 '66 C.685 B.A. L.309 J.D. [Kinkle,R.&S.]
*LANGUAGES: Spanish.
Selvig, Victor E. .......... '28 '52 L.494 LL.B. 419 Prospect Ave.‡
Sepe, Robert J. .......... '52 '77 C.770 B.S.C. L.1066 J.D. 3750 University Ave.‡
**Shafer, Michael D.** .......... '58 '87 C.112 B.A. L.1137 J.D. [Kinkle,R.&S.]
Sherman, Vilia G., (CV) .......... '41 '83 C.061 B.A. L.1137 J.D. Sr. Dep. Dist. Atty.
**Sherrill, Maurice C.**, (AV) .......... '22 '50 C&L.800 B.S., J.D. [Ⓒ Redwine&S.]
*PRACTICE AREAS: Water Law; Water District Administration Law.
Shine, Alfred J., Jr. .......... '63 '89 C.1168 B.A. L.1066 J.D. 6700 Indiana Ave. Ste. 205
**Shinoff, Daniel R.**, (AV) .......... '55 '81 C.011 B.A. L.1137 J.D. [Stutz,G.A.S.&H.]⊙
**Shoaf, Gerald D.**, (AV) .......... '41 '67 C.763 B.A. L.1068 J.D. [Redwine&S.]
*PRACTICE AREAS: Water Law; Water District Administration Law; Inverse Condemnation Law.
Short, John W. .......... '53 '91 C.1110 B.A. L.426 J.D. 3333 14th St.
Silva, Dirk E. .......... '60 '88 C.846 B.B.A. L.326 J.D. [Ⓐ Kring&B.]
**Silvergleid, Naomi** .......... '43 '77 C.696 B.A. L.770 J.D. [Singer&S.]
*PRACTICE AREAS: Business and Real Estate Transactions; Estate Planning; Municipal.
Silverman, Michael .......... '66 '91 C.103 A.B. L.569 J.D. Dep. Dist. Atty.

**Simon, William J., The Law Offices of, (BV) '43 '76 C&L.1137 B.S.L., J.D.**
**4333 Orange Street, Suite 2, 92501**
**Telephone: 909-686-1561 Fax: 909-686-4859**
***PRACTICE AREAS: Bankruptcy Law; Insolvency Law.**
**Bankruptcy and Insolvency Law.**
***See Professional Biographies, RIVERSIDE, CALIFORNIA***

**Singer, M. Neal**, (BV) .......... '37 '63 C.174 B.S. L.208 J.D. [Singer&S.]
*PRACTICE AREAS: Municipal; Eminent Domain; Civil Litigation.

**Singer & Silvergleid, Inc., (AV)**
**3750 University Avenue, Suite 550, 92501**
**Telephone: 909-784-3800 Facsimile: 909-781-4083**
**M. Neal Singer; Naomi Silvergleid; Patrick J. Sampson.**
**Municipal Law, Civil Litigation. Eminent Domain, Real Estate, Probate and Business Law.**
*See Professional Biographies, RIVERSIDE, CALIFORNIA*

Sinkhorn, Karen A. .................. '52 '94 C.339 B.S. L.999 J.D. 3750 University Ave.
Skapik, Mark .................. '62 '93 C.1075 B.S.M.E. L.809 J.D. 3993 Market St.
Sklar, Wilford N. .......... '16 '60 C.665 B.S. L.809 LL.B. 4353 Main St., Suite 101-103
**Sleeth, Jack M., Jr.** .............. '45 '83 C.139 B.A. L.1188 J.D. [A] Stutz,G.A.S.&H.]⊙
Small, Warren J. .................. '52 '79 C.112 B.A. L.398 J.D. 4117 10th St.
Smith, David O. .................. '27 '79 C.1032 B.S. L.1198 J.D. 4610 Central Ave.
**Smith, Douglas C.** .................. '60 '86 C.385 B.A. L.117 J.D. [A] Bonne,B.M.O.&N.]
Smith, Jeffrey D., (BV) .................. '44 '69 C.154 B.A. L.770 J.D. 4129 Main St.
**Smith, Kirk W.** .................. '59 '86 C.154 B.A. L.276 J.D. [A] Best B.&K.]
*LANGUAGES: Swedish.
*PRACTICE AREAS: Real Estate Finance; Leasing; Redevelopment; Business Transactions; International Trade Law.
**Snow, Kyle A.** .................. '62 '89 C.1085 B.A. L.911 J.D. [A] Best B.&K.]
*LANGUAGES: Spanish.
*PRACTICE AREAS: Public Finance Law.
Sorbello, Joseph C. .............. '25 '75 C.906 B.S. L.1026 J.D. 17077 Singing Bird Ln.‡
**Sorenson, Daniel D.** .................. '63 '90 C&L.101 B.A., J.D. [A] La Follette,J.D.F.&A.]
*LANGUAGES: Portuguese.
*PRACTICE AREAS: Civil Litigation.
Spira, Robert A. .................. '51 '76 C.800 A.B. L.1068 J.D. Dep. Dist. Atty.
Spitzer, Robert G. .................. '49 '75 C.112 A.B. L.800 J.D. Mun. Ct. J.
**Spriggs, Everett L., (AV)** .................. '30 '60 C.36 B.S. L.37 J.D. [Kinkle,R.&S.]
**Spriggs, Scott B., (BV)** .................. '60 '85 C.800 B.S. L.809 J.D. [Kinkle,R.&S.]
**Stanfield, Cyril C., III, (BV)** .............. '48 '79 C.862 B.S. L.1198 J.D. [A] Roberts&M.]
*LANGUAGES: German.
Stein, Jay Scott .................. '— '89 C&L.589 B.A., J.D. 2900 Adams St.
Steinman, Ness & Robinson, The Law Offices of, (AV)
3801 University Ave., Suite 680 (⊙Santa Ana & San Diego)
**Stephens, Glen E., (P.C.), (AV)** .............. '27 '53 C.878 B.S. L.813 J.D. [Best B.&K.]
*PRACTICE AREAS: Public Finance and Securities Law.
Sterling, Frances W. .................. '44 '90 C.1078 M.A. L.537 J.D. 3428 6th St.
Steward, David G. .................. '66 '91 C.636 B.B.A. L.1049 J.D. Dep. Dist. Atty.
**Stosuy, Kathleen A.** .............. '59 '91 C.184 B.F.S. L.809 J.D. [A] Franscell,S.R.&L.]
*PRACTICE AREAS: Litigation.
Stream, Kenneth B., JR, (BV) .................. '44 '75 C.897 B.S. L.464 J.D. [Stream&S.]
Stream, Theodore Kelly, (BV) .................. '63 '88 C.897 B.A. L.950 J.D. [Stream&S.]
Stream & Stream, (BV) .................. 4201 Brockton Ave.
**Strickland, Tracy** .................. '54 '79 C.602 B.A. L.990 J.D. [Franscell,S.R.&L.]⊙
*PRACTICE AREAS: Police Misconduct Liability Defense; Civil Rights; Municipal and Administrative Law; General Civil; Criminal Trial.
**Strong, Eric M.** .................. '67 '95 C.284 B.S. L.870 J.D. [A] Thomas,M.P.&K.]
**Stutz, Sidney A.** .................. '32 '59 C.339 A.B. L.309 LL.B. [Stutz,G.A.S.&H.]⊙

**Stutz, Gallagher, Artiano, Shinoff & Holtz, A Professional Corporation, (AV)**
**43537 Ridge Park Drive, Suite 206, 92590⊙**
**Telephone: 909-699-1231 Fax: 909-699-1261**
**Sidney A. Stutz; Robert E. Gallagher, Jr.; Ray J. Artiano; Daniel R. Shinoff; James F. Holtz; Lesa Wilson; Robert R. Templeton, Jr.; Christopher J. Welsh; Robert B. Titus; Jack M. Sleeth, Jr.; Jeffery A. Morris; Bret W. Eubank.**
**General Civil Trial Practice with Special Emphasis in Product Liability, Employment, Environmental, Professional Liability, Construction Defect Litigation, Public Entity, Commercial Litigation, Insurance Coverage, Defense of the Hospitality Industry and Medical Providers.**
**San Diego, California Office: 15th Floor, First National Bank Building, 401 West "A" Street. Telephone: 619-232-3122. Fax: 619-232-3264.**
*See Professional Biographies, RIVERSIDE, CALIFORNIA*

Sullivan, Ray T., Jr., (AV) .................. '14 '39 C&L.813 A.B., J.D. 3780 12th St.‡
Sullivan, William H. .................. '28 '56 C&L.813 A.B., J.D. Supr. Ct. J.
**Summerour, J. Michael** .................. '56 '84 C.1169 B.A. L.426 J.D. [Best B.&K.]
*PRACTICE AREAS: Litigation.
Swanson, Mary A. S., (BV) .............. '53 '79 C&L.1137 B.S.L., J.D. 4094 Chestnut St.

**Swarner & Fitzgerald, (AV)**
**A Partnership including Professional Corporations**
**3403 Tenth Street, Suite 700, P.O. Box 827, 92502**
**Telephone: 909-683-4242 Telecopier: 909-683-4518**
**Email: attyonline@attorneys-on-line.com URL: http://www.attyonline@attorney_on_line.com**
**Members of Firm: Lewis F. Jacobsen (A Professional Corporation); Edward L. Mackey (A Professional Corporation); David B. Bowker; Thomas D. Allert (Certified Specialist, Family Law, The State Bar of California Board of Legal Specialization).**
**General Civil Trial and Appellate Practice, Business Litigation, Corporate, Estate Planning, Wills/Trusts, Probate, Family, Real Estate, Commercial, Negligence, Tort.**
*See Professional Biographies, RIVERSIDE, CALIFORNIA*

**Swortwood, Robert B., (BV)** .............. '46 '78 C.293 B.A. L.352 J.D. [Thompson&C.]
*PRACTICE AREAS: Estate Planning; Will Contests; Trust Litigation; Probate; Commercial Litigation.
Tagami, Randall K., (BV) .................. '— '75 C.112 B.A. L.770 J.D. Asst. Dist. Atty.
**Tanaka, Gene** .................. '56 '81 C&L.178 B.A., J.D. [Best B.&K.]
Taylor, Ronald L. .................. '42 '72 C.112 B.A. L.1067 J.D. Supr. Ct. J.
Teichert, Eileen Monaghan .................. '51 '93 C.629 B.S. L.398 J.D. 3333 14th St.
Teixeira, James C., (BV) .................. '50 '79 C.1109 B.A. L.1137 J.D. 3891 10th St.
**Templeton, Robert R., Jr.** .............. '57 '84 C.156 A.B. L.990 J.D. [Stutz,G.A.S.&H.]⊙
Thayer, Dennis A., (BV) .................. '46 '76 C.999 B.S. L.1198 J.D. 4094 Chestnut St.
**Theobald, Forrest D.** '42 '72 C.63 B.S. L.1137 J.D.
Assoc. Gen. Coun. & Dir., Real Estate, Fleetwood Enterprises, Inc.
*RESPONSIBILITIES: Corporate Law; Real Estate; Toxic Substances; Torts.
Thierbach, Christian F., III .................. '49 '76 C.112 B.A. L.1137 J.D. Supr. Ct. J.
**Thies, Lee M., (BV)** .................. '55 '87 C.1109 B.A. L.1137 J.D. [A] O'Flaherty&B.]
**Thomas, Anne T., (P.C.), (AV)** .......... '36 '78 C.228 B.A. L.1068 J.D. [Best B.&K.]
*PRACTICE AREAS: Water Rights Law; Environmental Land Use Law; Environmental Law; Hazardous Waste; Zoning Law.
**Thomas, Christopher L.** '54 '82
C.801 B.S. L.1137 J.D. [La Follette,J.D.F.&A.] (⊙Santa Ana)
*PRACTICE AREAS: Personal Injury Litigation; Insurance Litigation; Governmental Tort Litigation.
**Thomas, William E., (AV)** .............. '48 '73 C.112 B.A. L.1065 J.D. [Thomas,M.P.&K.]
*PRACTICE AREAS: Business Law; Health Care; Corporate Law; Municipal Finance; Real Estate.

**Thomas, Mort, Prosser & Knudsen, LLP, (AV)**
**3403 Tenth Street, Suite 300, P.O. Box 1609, 92502**
**Telephone: 909-788-0100 Facsimile: 909-788-5785**
**Members of Firm: William E. Thomas; Peter J. Mort; Deborah C. Prosser; Curtis E. Knudsen; Andrew D. Brooks; John W. Vineyard; Donna M. Baker. Associates: Michael A. DesJardins; Warren D. Kelly; Irena Leigh Norton; Kevin J. Reisch; Eric M. Strong.**
**Business, Corporate, Securities, Real Estate, Public Finance, Redevelopment, Environmental Law, Products Liability, Toxic Torts, Health Care, Land Use and Zoning. Appellate and Trial Practice in all State and Federal Courts.**
*See Professional Biographies, RIVERSIDE, CALIFORNIA*

Thompson, R. Dean .................. '22 '51 C&L.813 A.B., J.D. 4237 Mt. Vernon Ave.‡
**Thompson, Seth C.** .................. '66 '95 C.1068 B.A. L.1066 J.D. [A] Redwine&S.]
*LANGUAGES: Spanish.
*PRACTICE AREAS: Water Law; Civil Litigation.

**Thompson & Colegate, (AV)**
**3610 Fourteenth Street, P.O. Box 1299, 92502⊙**
**Telephone: 909-682-5550 Fax: 909-781-4012**
**H. L. Thompson (1885-1962); Roy W. Colegate (1906-1960); Leighton B. Tegland (Resident, Palm Desert Office); Don G. Grant; J. E. Holmes, III; Robert B. Swortwood; John W. Marshall; John A. Boyd; Geoffrey H. Hopper; Michael J. Marlatt;—Joan F. Ettinger; David J. Porras; J. Alan Plott (Resident, Palm Desert Office); Maxine M. Morisaki-Price; Lisa Victoria Todd; Patricia L. Rich; Diane M. Wiesmann; Dulce L. Pena; Donald R. Lee; Gary T. Montgomery; Jeffrey T. Gwynn; Ronald V. Larson; Kimberly Ann White.**
**General Civil and Trial Practice, Personal Injury Defense, Business Litigation, Construction, Medical Malpractice, Products Liability, Corporate, Estate Planning, Wills and Trusts, Probate, Insurance, Real Estate, Commercial, Education, Employment Law and Appellate Practice, Media-First Amendment Law and Bankruptcy.**
**Representative Clients: Farmers Insurance Group of Companies; Fireman's Fund; State Farm Insurance Company.**
**Palm Desert, California Office: 74-303 Highway III, Suite 2-B, 92260. Telephone: 619-773-1998. Fax: 619-773-9078.**
*See Professional Biographies, RIVERSIDE, CALIFORNIA*

Tickner, Kere K. .................. '62 '94 C.767 B.A. L.398 J.D. [A] Kring&B.]
Timlin, Robert J. .................. '32 '59 C&L.276 A.B., J.D. U.S. Dist. J.
Tindell, Verne H. .................. '36 '67 C.940 B.A. L.950 J.D. Off. of Co. Coun.
**Titus, Robert B., (BV)** .............. '57 '84 C.763 B.S. L.61 J.D. [A] Stutz,G.A.S.&H.]⊙
Tobey, Michal M. .................. '44 '79 C.1078 B.A. L.767 J.D. Dep. Dist. Atty.
**Tobin, John C.** .................. '52 '80 C.383 B.A. L.421 J.D. [A] Best B.&K.]
*PRACTICE AREAS: Bankruptcy; Financial Litigation.
Tobler, Kelton A. .................. '62 '91 C&L.101 B.S., J.D. Dep. Dist. Atty.
**Todd, Bruce E.** .................. '55 '81 C.763 B.A. L.1148 J.D. [A] Cummings&K.]⊙
*PRACTICE AREAS: Governmental Advocacy; Construction Litigation.
**Todd, Lisa Victoria, (CV)** .............. '62 '87 C.426 B.A. L.770 J.D. [A] Thompson&C.]
*PRACTICE AREAS: Personal Injury Defense; Medical Malpractice Law.
Torneo, Stephen C. .............. '53 '84 C.1074 B.A. L.1137 J.D. First Amer. Title Ins. Co.
Tranbarger, Gary B., (BV) .................. '52 '77 C.267 B.A. L.1066 J.D. Dep. Dist. Atty.
Trask, Grover C., II, (AV) .................. '47 '74 C&L.1049 B.A., J.D. Dist. Atty.
**Trenholm, Michael H.** '64 '92
C.112 B.S.E.E. L.464 J.D. [A] Knobbe,M.O.&B.] (See Pat. Sect.)
Tu-Willis, Nora, (BV) .................. '55 '86 C.628 B.A. L.1065 J.D. 3403 10th St.
Turner, Norman M. .................. '36 '79 C&L.1137 B.S.L., J.D. Mun. Ct. J.
Tuszynska, Danuta W. ........ '56 '81 C.494 B.A. L.1137 J.D. Dep. Supervising Dist. Atty.
Tweed, Roland D. .......... '48 '77 C.169 B.A. L.1068 J.D. 7177 Brockton Ave., Ste 444
Valadez, Leonard P., (BV) .............. '53 '79 C.112 B.A. L.1067 J.D. 4060 Chestnut St.
Van Daele, Patrick J. '60 '86 C.800 B.S. L.809 J.D.
COO & Exec. V.P., Van Daele Develop. Corp.

**Van Hulle & Prevost**
**(See San Bernardino)**

**Varner, Bruce D., (AV)** .......... '36 '63 C.112 B.A. L.1065 J.D. [Gresham,V.S.N.&T.]
*PRACTICE AREAS: Financing; Business Law; Corporate Law; Real Estate Law.
Vickers, Jay G., (BV) .................. '44 '71 C&L.800 A.B., J.D. Dep. Co. Coun.
Victor, Leon A. ............ '65 '90 C.112 B.A. L.1049 J.D. [A] Breidenbach,B.H.H.&H.]⊙
Victor, Marsha L. .................. '58 '85 C.1109 B.A. L.1049 J.D. Dep. Co. Coun.
**Vineyard, John W., (BV)** .............. '61 '89 C.1080 B.A. L.112 J.D. [Thomas,M.P.&K.]
*PRACTICE AREAS: Business; Real Estate; Toxic Tort Litigation.
Vinocour, Lee A. .................. '51 '81 C.276 B.S.F.S. L.1230 J.D. 35310th St.
**Wahlin, John D., (P.C.), (AV)** .................. '46 '71 C.57 A.B. L.966 J.D. [Best B.&K.]
*PRACTICE AREAS: Employee Benefits Law; Taxation Law.
**Walker, Anne** .................. '60 '89 C.890 B.A. L.990 J.D. [A] Ericksen,A.K.D.&L.]
*PRACTICE AREAS: Insurance Defense; Construction Defect; Employment Discrimination.
**Walker, Mickey** .................. '54 '95 C&L.999 A.S., J.D. [Chandler&Assoc.]
*PRACTICE AREAS: Contract Disputes (50%, 80); Warranty & Lemon Law (30%, 40); Real Property/Unlawful Detainer (10%, 15); Family Law (10%, 15).
**Walker, Robert A., (BV)** ........ '— '81 C.766 B.S.L. L.1137 J.D. [Howard,M.L.S.&W.]
Walsh, Jason R. .................. '67 '92 L.1137 J.D. [A] Jacobs&G.]
**Walton, Zachary R.** .................. '70 '95 C.112 B.A. L.880 J.D. [A] Best B.&K.]
*PRACTICE AREAS: Natural Resources; Water; Endangered Species; Public Law.
Ward, James D., (A Professional Corporation), (AV) '35 '60
C.793 B.A. L.767 J.D. 3610 14th St.
**Warford, Robert K.** .............. '46 '77 C.112 B.A. L.398 J.D. [La Follette,J.D.F.&A.]
*PRACTICE AREAS: Medical Malpractice.
Warren, James T. .................. '41 '67 C.112 B.A. L.1065 J.D. Presid. J., Juv. Ct.
Watase, Kenneth D. .................. '48 '77 C.112 B.A. L.426 J.D. [Fidler,B.O.&W.]
Waters, Sharon J., (AV) .................. '54 '81 C.1042 B.A. L.464 J.D. [Waters&E.]
Waters & Elwell, (AV) .................. 1950 Market St.
Watts-Bazan, Karin L. .................. '60 '86 C.1109 B.A. L.1137 J.D. Dep. Co. Coun.
Weathers, Douglas E., (BV) .................. '54 '80 C&L.1137 B.S.L., J.D. [Fisher,W.&G.]
Weathers, William W., (BV) .................. '52 '77 C.112 B.A. L.1137 J.D. [Peach&W.]⊙
Webb, Duncan Campbell .......... '35 '66 C.766 B.S. Econ. L.1065 LL.B. 2000 Market St.
Webster, Edward D. .................. '49 '74 C.112 B.A. L.1067 J.D. Supr. Ct. J.
Weinfurtner, Ellen, (BV) .................. '50 '77 C.112 A.B. L.1049 J.D. 3780 12th St.

**Welebir & McCune, A Professional Law Corporation**
**(See Redlands)**

**Welsh, Christopher J.** .............. '60 '85 C.112 B.A. L.1049 J.D. [Stutz,G.A.S.&H.]⊙
Werner, David D. .............. '60 '91 C.636 B.B.A. L.1148 J.D. 4201 Brockton Ave.
West, Richard A., (BV) .................. '55 '79 C.339 B.S. L.800 J.D. Dep. Dist. Atty.
**White, Kimberly Ann** .................. '68 '95 C.770 B.S. L.464 J.D. [A] Thompson&C.]
*PRACTICE AREAS: Public Entity; Civil Rights; Employment.
**White, Larry E., (BV)** .......... '56 '84 C.1109 B.A. L.398 J.D. [A] La Follette,J.D.F.&A.]
*PRACTICE AREAS: Personal Injury Defense Law; Medical Malpractice Law.
**White, Michael J.** .................. '57 '86 C.112 B.A. L.426 J.D. [A] Fiore,W.R.&P.]
Whitman, Douglas L. .................. '47 '76 C.339 B.S. L.209 J.D. 4085 Grimsby Lane
**Wiesmann, Diane M.** .................. '61 '86 C&L.37 B.A., J.D. [A] Thompson&C.]
*PRACTICE AREAS: Personal Injury Defense; Medical Malpractice Law.
**Wilkinson, Gregory K., (AV)** .............. '47 '72 C.154 B.A. L.1066 J.D. [Best B.&K.]
*PRACTICE AREAS: Water Rights Law; Water Quality Law; Endangered Species Law; Environmental Law.
Williams, David A. .................. '50 '79 C.800 B.S. L.1148 J.D. [A] Fidler,B.O.&W.]
Williams, Herbert H., III .............. '43 '91 C&L.1137 B.S.L., J.D. 7344 Magnolia Ave.
**Williamson, Bernie L.** .................. '58 '90 C.627 B.S. L.1068 J.D. [A] Best B.&K.]
*PRACTICE AREAS: Labor Law.
**Wilson, Lesa, (BV)** .................. '58 '83 C.352 B.A. L.61 J.D. [Stutz,G.A.S.&H.]⊙
Wilson, Lora Halcomb .................. '62 '93 C.225 B.A. L.378 J.D. 3750 University Ave.
**Wilson, Susan Dumouchel** .................. '66 '91 C.976 B.A. L.861 J.D. [A] Best B.&K.]
*PRACTICE AREAS: Litigation.
Wilson, Thomas H., Jr. .............. '60 '85 C.976 B.A. L.1066 J.D. 14170-A El Sobrante Rd.

**Wilson, Borror, Dunn & Davis**
**(See San Bernardino)**

Winder, Willard H., (BV) .................. '15 '42 C.813 B.A. L.1065 5414 Brittany Ave.

CALIFORNIA—RIVERSIDE | MARTINDALE-HUBBELL LAW DIRECTORY 1997

**Winston, Phyllis M.** ... '49 '87 C.716 B.S. L.724 J.D. [La Follette,J.D.F.&A.]
*PRACTICE AREAS: Medical Malpractice Defense.
Winters, Thomas B. ... '46 '85 C.112 A.B. L.426 J.D. 5033 Arlington Ave.
Wohl, David Evan ... '61 '89 C.763 B.A. L.61 J.D. 3403 Tenth St.
**Wolf, Michael O.** ... '42 '76 C.1042 B.S. L.990 J.D. [Gresham,V.S.N.&T.]
*PRACTICE AREAS: Tax and ERISA Law.
**Wolf, Victor L.** ... '58 '83 C.813 A.B. L.1065 J.D. [Best B.&K.]
*PRACTICE AREAS: General Business Litigation; Real Property Law; Title Insurance Litigation.
Wolfe, David B. ... '48 '77 C.829 B.A. L.1137 J.D. 6911 Magnolia Ave.
Womack, Ray O., Jr. A Law Corporation, (BV) '29 '63
C.846 B.B.A. L.208 LL.B. 4545 Allstate Dr.
**Wong, Libby** ... '68 '94 C.112 B.A. L.800 J.D. [Franscell,S.R.&L.]
*LANGUAGES: Mandarin Chinese.
*PRACTICE AREAS: Police Misconduct Liability Defense; Civil Rights; Municipal and Administrative Law; Sexual Harassment; Civil Practice.
Woodford, Wm. R., (CV) ... '30 '57 C.605 A.B. L.800 LL.B. 5304 Falkirk Ave.
Woodhead, John E., (BV) ... '27 '59 C.112 A.B. L.1065 J.D. City Atty.
Woolsey, Dean F., (BV) ... '46 '73 C.1075 B.S. L.1137 J.D. 7023 Gladys Rd.
Wortz, James M., (AV) ... '10 '34 C.112 A.B. L.1066 J.D. 3610 14th St.‡
**Wysocki, David L., (AV)** ... '52 '78 C.1042 B.A. L.809 J.D. [Aklufi&W.]
*REPORTED CASES: Wong v. Davidian, 206 Cal. App. 3d 264 (1988); Koehrer v. Superior Court, 181 Cal. App. 3d 1155 (1986); Guinn v. Dotson, 23 Cal. App. 4th 262 (1994); Schaefer Dixon Associates v. Santa Ana Watershed Project Authority, 48 Cal. App. 4th 524 (1996).
**Yamashita, Stephanie J.** ... '54 '87 C.800 B.S.Ch.E. L.809 J.D. [Gilbert,K.C.&J.]
*PRACTICE AREAS: Environmental Litigation; Products Liability Litigation.
Yee, Wayne P. ... '45 '78 C.846 B.S. L.1137 J.D. 4296 N. Orange St.
**Yekikian, Henry** ... '59 '86 C.1077 B.A. L.809 J.D. [Bonne,B.M.O.&N.]
*LANGUAGES: Armenian.
*REPORTED CASES: Casella v. Webb, 9th Cir., 1989, 883 F2d 805.
Zagorsky, Floyd A. ... '50 '77 C.150 B.A. L.990 J.D. Dep. Pub. Def.
Zellerbach, Paul E. ... '53 '78 C.112 B.A. L.61 J.D. Superv. Dep. Dist. Atty.
**Zimmer, Donald F., (AV)** ... '33 '63 C&L.800 B.S.L., J.D. [Best B.&K.]
*PRACTICE AREAS: General Civil Law; Trial Law; Appellate Practice; Real Estate Law; Municipal Law.
Zimmerman, Esther R. ... '47 '91 C.1169 L.395 J.D. 3880 Lemon

## ROBBINS, —, *Sutter Co.*

Butler, John Carleton ... '54 '80 C&L.426 J.D. P.O. Box 356

## ROCKLIN, 19,033, *Placer Co.*

Beaver, Jon P. ... '38 '70 C.1060 B.A. L.464 J.D. 5875 Pacific St.
Canar, Michael G. '40 '74 C&L.546 B.S., J.D.
(adm. in FL; not adm. in CA) 4020 Silver St.‡
Diamond, Gary M. ... '56 '91 C.766 B.A. L.1026 J.D. P.O. Box 371
Gallant, Leo K. ... '15 '53 C.999 L.464 LL.B. 5195 Topaz Ave.‡
Gilbert, Sabina D. ... '52 '78 C.605 B.A. L.1067 J.D. City Atty.
Lea, Nancy F. ... '43 '69 C.112 A.B. L.1065 J.D. 6100 Sierra College Blvd.‡
Meeker, David R. ... '41 '74 C.684 B.A. L.1137 J.D. P.O. Box 54
Miller, Marjorie '31 '86 C.914 A.B. L.1206 J.D.
(adm. in FL; not adm. in CA) 6010 Rustic Hills Dr.‡
Norris, Diane M. '54 '79 C.339 B.A. L.146 J.D.
(adm. in IL; not adm. in CA) 5316 Quane Ct.‡
Shumway, William Steven ... '53 '85 C.877 B.A. L.464 J.D. 5780 River Run Circle
Smith, Mary-Louise, (Mrs.) ... '31 '69 C.768 A.B. L.1132 J.D. 2711 Stream Ct.

## ROHNERT PARK, 36,326, *Sonoma Co.*

Broadbent, Cynthia A. ... '63 '89 C.219 B.A. L.284 J.D. 7471 Monique Pl.
Currie, Peggy R. ... '51 '81 C.112 B.S. L.398 2 Padre Pkwy.
Fisher, R. James, (CV) ... '46 '75 C.800 M.S. L.1095 J.D. P.O. Box 2025
Fredericks, Maurice H., (CV) ... '25 '52 C&L.770 J.D. 6950 Commerce Blvd.‡
King, William E. ... '51 '87 C.555 B.A. L.765 J.D. [Palladino&K.]
Kwasneski, Robert J. ... '42 '70 C.724 B.A. L.284 J.D. 101 Golf Course Dr.
Lansdowne, Patricia Joan ... '31 '87 C.1078 B.A. L.1227 LL.B. 2 Padre Pkwy.
Levin, Warren S. ... '36 '62 C.112 A.B. L.1066 LL.B. 475 Enterprise Dr.
Marczuk, Richard A. ... '46 '81 C.749 B.S. L.284 J.D. 2 Padre Pkwy.
Mills, Stephen H. ... '46 '76 C.154 B.A. L.464 J.D. 1500 E. Cotati Ave.‡
Palladino & King, Inc. ... 4491 Filbert Ct.
Palladino-King, Terri ... '48 '82 C.1044 B.A. L.765 J.D. [Palladino&K.]
Wicklow, S. W. ... '12 '38 C&L.767 A.B., LL.B. 112 Circulo Chapala‡

## ROLLING HILLS, 1,871, *Los Angeles Co.*

Adams, Janis E. ... '46 '75 C.813 B.A. L.1066 J.D. 21 Eastfield Rd.
**Babikian, Erin** ... '57 '83 C.823 B.S. L.990 J.D. [Owen&B.]
*PRACTICE AREAS: Litigation.
Balch, Bertram, Jr. ... '28 '56 C.659 B.S. L.831 J.D. 6 Hackamore Rd.‡
**Bernardino, Rafael, Jr.** ... '59 '84 C&L.800 A.B., J.D. [Owen&B.]
Ferris, Raymond W. ... '41 '67 C.112 A.B. L.1068 J.D. 50 Eastfield Dr.
Foye, Thomas P. ... '18 '51 C.602 A.B. L.426 LL.B. Ret. Mun. J.‡
Ginsberg, Gerry R. ... '40 '70 C.184 B.S. L.1065 J.D. 3 Morgan Lane
**Lloyd, Michael A.** ... '53 '92 C.813 A.B. L.999 J.D. [Owen&B.]
*PRACTICE AREAS: Civil Litigation.
**Owen, Timothy R.** ... '56 '82 C.165 B.A. L.1194 J.D. [Owen&B.]
*PRACTICE AREAS: Business Law; Litigation; Product Liability; Professional Liability; Insurance Coverage.

**Owen & Babikian, P.C.**
**550 Silver Spur Road, Suite 310, 90274**
**Telephone: 310-541-5655 Fax: 310-541-7643**
**Timothy R. Owen; Erin Babikian;—Michael A. Lloyd; Mary Pucelik. Of Counsel: Rafael Bernardino, Jr.**
**General Civil Litigation.**
***See Professional Biographies, ROLLING HILLS, CALIFORNIA***

**Pucelik, Mary** ... '64 '92 C.66 B.A. L.1051 J.D. [Owen&B.]
*PRACTICE AREAS: Civil Litigation.
Raydon, Gerald T. ... '30 '61 C.112 A.B. L.800 J.D. 2 Appaloosa Lane
Roberts, Thomas T. ... '23 '57 C&L.426 B.B.A., LL.B. 1 El Concho Lane
Rumbaugh, Charles E. ... '43 '72 C.112 B.S. L.61 J.D. P.O. Box 2636
Schnabel, Danl., (AV) ... '11 '38 C.813 A.B. L.800 J.D. 23 Caballeros Rd.‡
Siegal, Richard A. ... '29 '55 C.33 A.B. L.976 LL.B. 2 N. Quail Ridge‡
Simon, Perry M. '60 '85 C.311 B.A. L.884 J.D.
(adm. in NJ; not adm. in CA) 18 Eastfield Dr.‡
Tara, Christopher J. '54 '79 C.976 B.A. L.893 J.D.
(adm. in AZ; not adm. in CA) 6 Rawhide Ln.‡
Van Der Schyff, Rhodah ... '59 '88 C.800 B.S. L.809 J.D. 655 Deep Valley Dr. Ste. 125
Vawter, Richard H., (AV) ... '27 '55 C.112 A.B. L.1068 J.D. 27520 Hawthorne Blvd.
Welbourn, John L. ... '15 '46 C.1097 A.B. L.800 J.D. 25 Portuguese Bend Rd.‡

## ROLLING HILLS ESTATES, 7,789, *Los Angeles Co.*

Baffa, Frank ... '27 '54 C&L.800 B.A., LL.B. 4657 Rollando Dr.‡
Bauer, Laverne M. Sagmaster, (AV) ... '29 '53 C.112 B.A. L.1068 J.D. [Bauer&B.] ‡
Bauer, Stanley L. ... '26 '51 C.112 A.B. L.1065 J.D. [Bauer&B.]
Bauer & Bauer ... 27 Sycamore Ln.
Becker, Irvin ... '17 '39 C.502 L.910 J.D. 4030 Palos Verdes Dr. N.
**Boyle, Jeffrey L.** ... '59 '87 C.112 B.A. L.1137 J.D. [I.K.Stevenson]
Bradford, Mark D. ... '55 '81 C.929 B.S. L.383 J.D. 508 Peninsula Ctr. Dr.
Branson, David L. ... '35 '67 C&L.734 B.S., J.D. [D.L.Branson]
Branson, David L., A P.C. ... 777 Silver Spur Rd.
Elias, Charles A., (BV) ... '42 '70 C.453 B.S. L.659 LL.B. 4030 Palos Verdes Dr., N.

**Esensten, Jack I., (AV) '27 '55 C.800 B.S. L.809 J.D.**
**Suite 207, 4030 Palos Verdes Drive North, 90274-2584**
**Telephone: 310-377-5557 Telecopier: 310-544-5036**
**(Certified Specialist, Family Law, The State Bar of California Board of Legal Specialization).**
***PRACTICE AREAS: Domestic Relations; Personal Injury; General Practice.**
**Julie A. Milligan (Certified Specialist, Family Law, The State Bar of California Board of Legal Specialization).**
**Domestic Relations, Personal Injury and General Practice.**
***See Professional Biographies, ROLLING HILLS ESTATES, CALIFORNIA***

Feakins, Martha S. ... '45 '79 C.813 B.A. L.426 J.D. 4817 Browndeer Ln.
**Gee, Richard M.** ... '62 '88 C.112 B.A. L.426 J.D. [Gee&S.]
*LANGUAGES: Spanish, German and Irish.
*PRACTICE AREAS: Business; Entertainment; Real Estate; Estate Planning; International Law.

**Gee & Sunada**
**655 Deep Valley Drive, Suite 125, 90274**
**Telephone: 310-544-7161 Fax: 310-544-7162**
**Email: geesunada@aol.com**
**Members of Firm: Richard M. Gee; Craig S. Sunada.**
**Civil Practice emphasizing Business, Real Estate, Estate Planning, Entertainment and International Law and Litigation.**

Jason, Walter J. ... '14 '38 C&L.477 B.S.E., J.D. 49 Cypress Way‡
**Milligan, Julie A.** ... '61 '86 C.112 B.A. L.464 J.D. [J.I.Esensten]
*PRACTICE AREAS: Family Law; Personal Injury; General Litigation.
Nelson, Harry L., Jr., (AV) ... '28 '56 C.668 B.A. L.1066 LL.B. Pres. & CEO, Almar Ltd.

**Perkins, Ellen M. M. '52 '81 C.684 B.S. L.426 J.D.**
**Suite 207, 4030 Palos Verdes Drive North, 90274-2584**
**Telephone: 310-377-5557 Fax: 310-544-5036**
**Estate Planning, Probate, Wills and Trusts.**

Popoff, Kathy ... '50 '76 C.36 B.A. L.800 J.D. 50B Peninsula Ctr. Dr.
Ross, Ronald ... '33 '59 C.112 B.A. L.800 J.D. 904 Silver Spur Rd.‡
Sibbison, John H., III ... '49 '76 C.608 B.A. L.1003 J.D. 655 Deep Valley Dr.

**Stevenson, Ivan K., Law Offices of, (BV) '49 '74 C.112 B.A. L.809 J.D.**
**501 Deep Valley Drive, Suite 315, 90274©**
**Telephone: 310-541-9344**
**Jeffrey L. Boyle.**
**General Civil and Trial Practice in all State and Federal Courts. Personal Injury, Products Liability, Health Care, Professional Liability, Insurance, Military and Veterans Law, Governmental Entity Law.**
**Santa Ana, California Office: 1851 E. First Street, Suite 900, 92705. Telephone: 714-564-2522.**
***See Professional Biographies, ROLLING HILLS ESTATES, CALIFORNIA***

**Sunada, Craig S.** ... '63 '88 C.800 B.S. L.426 J.D. [Gee&S.]
*PRACTICE AREAS: Litigation; Insurance; Health Care; Personal Injury Law.
Ungar, Michael T. ... '49 '74 C.1077 B.A. L.809 J.D. 715 Silver Spur Rd.
Vogel, Brian I. ... '60 '87 C.1365 B.A. L.978 J.D. 670 Silver Spur Rd.

## ROSAMOND, 2,869, *Kern Co.*

Landsgaard, Olaf A. ... '60 '86 C.1051 B.S. L.336 J.D. 2718 Diamond
White, Cynthia L. ... '60 '91 C.790 B.A. L.464 J.D. 1431 Rosamond Blvd.

## ROSEMEAD, 51,638, *Los Angeles Co.*

Allen, Howard P. ... '25 '51 C.668 B.A. L.813 J.D. P.O. Box 800‡
**Bass, Leon, Jr.** ... '55 '86 C.188 A.B. L.1066 J.D. Atty., Southern Calif. Edison Co.
*RESPONSIBILITIES: Claims Litigation; Personal Injury; Property Damage; Commercial Litigation; Eminent Domain.
Beeny, Gerald B. '49 '75 C.134 B.S.B.A. L.502 J.D.
(adm. in MO; not adm. in CA) Ticor Title Ins. Co.
Belknap, Hobart D., Jr. ... '32 '61 C&L.421 B.S.L., J.D. P.O. Box 800‡
Block, Donna ... '22 '52 L.809 First City Bk.
Brody, Jerry A. ... '30 '60 C.910 B.S. L.1068 LL.B. P.O. Box 800‡
Bryson, John E. ... '43 '70 C.813 B.A. L.976 J.D. P.O. Box 800
Burkhardt, William J. ... '50 '88 C.112 B.A. L.809 J.D. Chicago Title Ins. Co.
**Cardoza, Brian A.** ... '60 '88 C.112 B.A. L.93 J.D. Southern Calif. Edison Co.
*RESPONSIBILITIES: Products Liability (50%, 50); General Civil Litigation (25%, 25); Personal Injury (15%, 15); Commercial Litigation (10%, 10).
Carter-SooHoo, Susan M. ... '62 '87 C&L.800 B.A., J.D. Chicago Title Ins. Co.
**Cohn, Ann Pauline** '53 '79
C.766 B.A. L.930 J.D. Asst. Gen. Coun., Southern Calif. Edison Co.
Conway, Kerry B. ... '41 '72 C.174 B.A. L.1066 J.D. Sr. Coun., Chicago Title Ins. Co.
**Cooley, Frank J.** ... '46 '79 C.605 B.A. L.809 J.D. Southern Calif. Edison Co.
**Cope, Larry R.** ... '47 '78 C.648 B.S. L.1137 J.D. Southern Calif. Edison Co.
*LANGUAGES: German.
*RESPONSIBILITIES: Real Property Law (50%); Environmental Law (25%); Indian Law (25%).
**Danner, Bryant C.**, (AV) '37 '64 C&L.309 A.B., LL.B.
Sr. V.P. & Gen. Coun., Southern Calif. Edison Co.
**Ditonto, Douglas P.** ... '49 '84 C.1042 B.A. L.426 J.D. Southern Calif. Edison Co.
**Durant, Richard K.** '40 '72 C.909 B.S.E.E. L.809 J.D.
Assoc. Gen. Coun., Southern Calif. Edison Co.
**Evans, John W.** ... '45 '73 C.629 B.S. L.770 J.D. Sr. Coun., Southern Calif. Edison Co.
Ferguson, Warren E. ... '35 '64 C&L.800 B.E., LL.B. P.O. Box 800
Fielder, John R. ... '45 '78 C.112 B.A. L.990 J.D. Southern Calif. Edison Co.
Frazee, Bryan W. ... '55 '80 C.154 B.A. L.1049 J.D. Southern Calif. Edison Co.
Frazee, Mark A. ... '53 '78 C.154 B.A. L.426 J.D. Southern Calif. Edison Co.
Gardner, Lynn M. ... '53 '83 C.112 B.A. L.990 J.D. P.O. Box 800
**Gaylord, Beth A.** ... '60 '89 C&L.276 B.S.B.A., J.D. Southern Calif. Edison Co.
*RESPONSIBILITIES: Real Estate Law.
Gilfoy, Tom P. ... '32 '60 C.800 B.S.L. L.809 LL.B. P.O. Box 800‡
**Gilliam, Annette** ... '47 '87 C.1097 B.S. L.426 J.D. Southern Calif. Edison Co.
Gober, Frederick ... '46 '80 C.1077 B.A. L.1136 J.D. Co. Coun., Chicago Title Ins. Co.
Gomez, Richard R. ... '56 '81 C.800 A.B. L.1066 J.D. 7634 Sunside Dr.
**Gonzales, Michael** ... '49 '84 C.426 B.B.A. L.809 J.D. Southern Calif. Edison Co.
**Guest, John F.** ... '57 '83 C.604 B.A. L.228 J.D. Sr. Atty., Southern Calif. Edison Co.
*RESPONSIBILITIES: Advice, Employment Law; Employment Litigation; Section Management.
Hamilton, Kathleen R. '57 '83 C.112 B.A. L.809 J.D.
V.P. & Underwriting Coun., Chicago Title Ins. Co.
Hellwig, Raymond G. ... '51 '79 C.502 B.A. L.260 J.D. Chicago Title Ins. Co.
**Henningson, Carol B.** ... '50 '76 C.36 B.S. L.878 J.D. Southern Calif. Edison Co.
**Hines, Kingsley B.** ... '44 '70 C.800 B.A. L.426 J.D. Southern Calif. Edison Co.
Hoag, John C. ... '44 '75 C.800 A.B. L.61 J.D. Asst. Reg. Coun., Chicago Title Ins. Co.

**Ing, Gloria M.** ... '62 '88 C.1075 B.A. L.426 J.D. Staff Coun., Southern Calif. Edison Co.
*RESPONSIBILITIES: Utility Law; Environmental Law.
**Kelinsky, Allen Edward** ...... '56 '88 C.273 B.B.A. L.30 J.D. Southern Calif. Edison Co.
Kendall, Robert W., Jr. .......'46 '77 C.339 B.S.E.E. L.809 J.D. Southern Calif. Edison Co.
Knebel, Henry A. ....................'47 '75 C.420 B.S.C.E. L.861 J.D. Chicago Title Ins. Co.
**Koch, Sumner J.** ...............'58 '84 C.976 B.A. L.188 J.D. Southern Calif. Edison Co.
Kuch, Norman G. .......................................'19 '61 C.800 L.809 LL.B. P.O. Box 800‡
**Larks, Laura A.** .............. '59 '85 C.674 B.A. L.569 J.D. Atty., Southern Calif. Edison Co.
*RESPONSIBILITIES: Litigation.
**Lehrer, James M.** ... '52 '79 C.112 B.A. L.809 J.D. Sr. Coun., Southern Calif. Edison Co.
Leung, Jeffrey S. .......... '63 '89 C.1042 B.A., B.S. L.426 J.D. 1717 Walnut Grove Ave.
Livingston, Mark V. '60 '87
C.1109 B.A. L.800 J.D. Asst. Claims Coun., Ticor Title Ins. Co.
**Lohmann, Janet Kay** .......... '51 '78 C.112 B.A. L.809 J.D. Southern Calif. Edison Co.
Lusetti, David M. ........ '51 '79 C.628 B.A. L.678 J.D. Asst. V.P., Chicago Title Ins. Co.
**Mackness, Michael D.** ........ '53 '85 C.1070 B.S. L.1068 J.D. Southern Calif. Edison Co.
MacMillan, John T. '50 '77
C.1097 B.A. L.1095 J.D. Asst. Reg. Coun., Chicago Title Ins. Co.
Maloney, Michael K. '60 '85
C.139 B.A. L.426 J.D. Asst. Claims Coun., Ticor Title Ins. Co.
Marsh, Richard M. '48 '77 C.112 A.B. L.809 J.D.
V.P. & Sr. Claims Coun., Chicago Title Ins. Co.
**Mascolo, Nino J.** ............. '57 '84 C.1077 B.S. L.426 J.D. Southern Calif. Edison Co.
**Mathews, Barbara E.** ....... '53 '81 C.170 B.A. L.128 J.D. Asst. Gen. Coun., Edison Int'l
*RESPONSIBILITIES: Transactions; Corporate Governance.
**Matthias, Elizabeth M.** ......... '59 '84 C.154 B.A. L.112 J.D. Southern Calif. Edison Co.
*LANGUAGES: Spanish.
**McDonald, Michael D.** ....... '48 '75 C.1097 B.S. L.426 J.D. Southern Calif. Edison Co.
**McNulty, Francis A.** .......... '48 '87 C.1097 B.A. L.426 J.D. Southern Calif. Edison Co.
**Melcher, Christopher J.** ........ '59 '88 C.118 B.A. L.976 J.D. Southern Calif. Edison Co.
*REPORTED CASES: U.S. v. Philip D. Winn; U.S. v. Benton Mortg. Co.; U.S. v. Queenan, Mahon, et al.
*RESPONSIBILITIES: Criminal Law; Administrative Law; Regulatory Law; Legislative Practice.
**Merryman, Dani Jo** '61 '87
C.112 B.A. L.1065 J.D. Antitrust Coun., Southern Calif. Edison Co.
*RESPONSIBILITIES: Antitrust; Trade Regulation; Unfair Competition.
Mikulka, Mark E. ................ '53 '78 C.112 B.A. L.426 J.D. Southern Calif. Edison Co.
**Miller, Julie A.** .......... '58 '86 C.339 B.S.Ch.E. L.1067 J.D. Southern Calif. Edison Co.
**Mines, Stacy Roberts** ....'67 '93 C.763 B.S. L.990 J.D. Atty., Southern Calif. Edison Co.
*RESPONSIBILITIES: Employment Litigation (60%); Union Matters (20%); Employment Law (20%).
**Montoya, Michael D.** ......... '61 '87 C.1075 B.S. L.1065 J.D. Southern Calif. Edison Co.
*RESPONSIBILITIES: Redevelopment Law; Land Use Litigation; Eminent Domain Law; Inverse Condemnation Law; Real Estate Acquisition and Disposition Law.
Moore, Miriam U. '60 '86
C.112 B.A. L.800 J.D. V.P. & Opers. Mgr., Chicago Title Ins. Co.
Moore-Hunley, Camille '61 '88
C&L.800 B.A., J.D. Asst. Claims Coun., Chicago Title Ins. Co.
Munoz-Silva, Carmen .......... '— '80 C.1046 B.A. L.426 J.D. Southern Calif. Edison Co.
Norris, J. Earle ....'44 '74 C.1120 B.S. L.1095 J.D. Sr. Title Coun., Chicago Title Ins. Co.
**Oubre, Tanya E.** ................. '64 '91 C&L.228 A.B., J.D. Southern Calif. Edison Co.
*RESPONSIBILITIES: Regulatory Law.
**Pearce, Beth J.** ......................'49 '86 C.46 B.S. L.800 J.D. Southern Calif. Edison Co.
**Pickett, Stephen E.** ........ '50 '81 C.1097 B.S.E.E. L.809 J.D. Southern Calif. Edison Co.
*RESPONSIBILITIES: Regulatory Law (Merger) (100%, 1); Regulatory Law (General Rate Cases 1991) (100%, 3).
Pignatelli, James S. ........................'43 '75 C.154 B.A. L.1049 J.D. P.O. Box 800
Popowitz, Rochelle ... '43 '83 C.102 B.A. L.426 J.D. Assoc. Coun., Chicago Title Ins. Co.
**Porter, Douglas K.** ................ '50 '77 C.813 B.A. L.1066 J.D. Southern Calif. Edison Co.
*RESPONSIBILITIES: Energy Law; Utilities Law; Administrative Law.
**Redd, Donald A.** ............... '50 '84 C.1075 B.S. L.809 J.D. Southern Calif. Edison Co.
**Reed, Bruce A.** ................ '52 '85 C.911 B.S. L.426 J.D. Southern Calif. Edison Co.
Rodrigues, Gene E. ............. '56 '89 C.35 B.S. L.1065 J.D. Southern Calif. Edison Co.
**Rogers, Timothy W.** ........... '60 '86 C.1097 B.A. L.426 J.D. Southern Calif. Edison Co.
*RESPONSIBILITIES: Corporate (40%); Contracts (30%); Employee Benefits (30%).
Sachar, Mark D. ....... '51 '81 C.112 B.A. L.426 J.D. Claims Coun., Chicago Title Ins. Co.
Sanchez, Elisa M. ..........................................'57 '82 C.813 B.A. L.1068 J.D. P.O. Box 800
**Schmid-Frazee, Carol** ........ '56 '81 C.112 B.S. L.1068 J.D. Southern Calif. Edison Co.
*RESPONSIBILITIES: Energy Law; Environmental Law.
**Schwartz, Victoria** ............ '59 '89 C.1049 B.S. L.426 J.D. Southern Calif. Edison Co.
**Scott, Tanya D.** .................. '63 '89 C.472 B.A. L.309 J.D. Southern Calif. Edison Co.
**Scott-Kakures, Megan** '59 '84
C.154 B.A. L.477 J.D. Sr. Atty., Southern Calif. Edison Co.
Serra, Stephen ......... '52 '77 C.276 B.A. L.426 J.D. Assoc. Coun., Chicago Title Ins. Co.
**Shotwell, James P. Scott** '64 '91
C.36 B.A. L.37 J.D. Corp. Atty., Southern Calif. Edison Co.
*RESPONSIBILITIES: Public Utility Law; Regulatory Law.
**Sommers, Margaret L.** ........ '57 '86 C.951 B.A. L.569 J.D. Southern Calif. Edison Co.
**Stewart, Kenneth S.** '51 '78
C&L.101 B.A., J.D. Asst. Gen. Coun., Southern Calif. Edison Co.
**Swartz, Russell C.** ............ '51 '77 C.800 A.B. L.1068 J.D. Southern Calif. Edison Co.
**Tinker, John S.** ................ '46 '74 C.800 B.S. L.1068 J.D. Southern Calif. Edison Co.
**Tom, Richard S.** ............... '61 '86 C.813 B.S. L.477 J.D. Southern Calif. Edison Co.
Tron, Lanny M. ...................... '60 '87 C.309 B.A. L.800 J.D. 3907 N. Rosemead Blvd.
Umeda, Glen S. .................. '59 '92 C.112 B.A. L.1137 J.D. 1096-B Walnut Grove Ave.
**Vallecorsa, Joseph A., Jr.** .... '44 '80 C.1075 B.S. L.809 J.D. Southern Calif. Edison Co.
**Van Iderstine, David E., Jr.** '54 '82
C.800 B.A. L.1068 J.D. Sr. Atty., Southern Calif. Edison Co.
*RESPONSIBILITIES: Labor and Employment.
Wagner, Eugene ................................ '38 '75 C.770 B.A. L.810 J.D. P.O. Box 800‡
Walters, Donald E. '20 '50 C&L.911 LL.B.
(adm. in WA; not adm. in CA) Sr. V.P. & Sr. Title Coun., Ticor Title Ins. Co.
**Watkins-Ivie, Janine M.** ........ '63 '90 C.674 A.B. L.309 J.D. Southern Calif. Edison Co.
**White, Paige W. R.** .............. '54 '79 C.790 B.S. L.893 J.D. Southern Calif. Edison Co.
*RESPONSIBILITIES: Corporate Law; Securities Law.
**Wilson, Dawn** .................. '61 '88 C.914 B.A. L.477 J.D. Southern Calif. Edison Co.
**Woodruff, James B.** ............ '56 '82 C.976 B.A. L.1068 J.D. Southern Calif. Edison Co.
**Ziol, Gwen Glenn** ............. '46 '80 C.800 B.S. L.426 J.D. Southern Calif. Edison Co.

## ROSEVILLE, 44,685, *Placer Co.*

Adams, Jerrold D. ........................'35 '82 C.1079 B.A. L.1026 J.D. 660 Commerce Dr.
Akin, John R. .................. '33 '72 C.768 L.981 LL.B. Coun., State Franchise Tax Bd.
Appelt, Gary N. ...............................'46 '72 C.763 B.A. L.61 J.D. 404 Sunbury Ct.
Ardizzone, C. Gary, (AV) .................. '39 '72 C.1163 L.1095 J.D. [C.G.Ardizzone]
Ardizzone, C. Gary, A Prof. Corp., (AV) .................................3017 Douglas Blvd.
**Baker, Bruce S.** ................................. '55 '86 C.1222 B.A. L.464 J.D. [▣ Liebman&R.]
Bartkiewicz, Byron M. ..........................................'52 '91 [Harrington&B.]
**Bedore, Jess C., III** ...................'49 '76 C.1060 B.A. L.1026 J.D. [Sinclair,W.&B.]
*REPORTED CASES: People v. Silverbrand (1990) 220 Cal. App. 3d 1621; People v. Moten (1989) 210 Cal. App. 3d 765; People v. Disandra (1987) 193 Cal. App. 3d 1354; People v. Dominquez (1989) 201 Cal. App. 3d 345; People v. Riffey (1985) 171 Cal. App. 3d 419.
*PRACTICE AREAS: Plaintiff's Personal Injury; Criminal Defense Law.
Brenner, Barbara A. ...................................'61 '89 C.1078 B.A. L.464 J.D. 609 Oak St.
Burford, Jack L., (BV) ....................'31 '59 C.112 A.B. L.1066 J.D. 218 Estate St.‡
Burk, John Rogers ...................................... '45 '73 C.112 A.B. L.1065 J.D. [J.R.Burk]
Burk, John Rogers, A Law Corporation ....................................2140 Professional Dr.
Carr, James R. ................ '52 '85 C.475 B.S. L.464 J.D. 3013 Douglas Blvd. Ste. 140
Carrier, John L. ................................. '51 '81 C&L.101 B.S., J.D. 1314 Daisy Ct.
Chaput, Anna M. ..........................'58 '83 C.112 B.A. L.1067 J.D. 735 Sunrise Ave.
Clark, Sharon L., (CV) ..................... '40 '82 C.1060 L.464 J.D. 218 Estates Dr.

**Cohen, Michael E. '47 '73 C.813 B.A. L.1097 J.D.**
**2140 Professional Drive, Suite 200, P.O. Box 2715, 95746-2715**
**Telephone: 916-789-0198**
**Email: metatron1@juno.com**
**Taxation Planning and Controversies, Estate Planning, Trusts and Probate, IRS Administrative Controversy and Federal Taxation.**

**Collier, Susan A. '53 '85 C.112 B.A. L.464 J.D.**
**419 Oak Street, 95678**
**Telephone: 916-784-2444 Fax: 916-784-3926**
**Personal Injury, Products Liability, Employment Law, Professional Malpractice.**
***See Professional Biographies, ROSEVILLE, CALIFORNIA***

Crawford, Howard G. ..................'20 '54 C.112 B.A. L.1065 LL.B. [▣ Eggleston&O.]
Day, W. Gregory ....................'54 '78 C.112 B.A. L.1068 J.D. 1210 Bunker Hill Dr.
Del Bino, Jon J. ..................................'44 '72 C&L.767 B.A.L., J.D. 100 Estates Dr.
Dewald, Linus J., Jr., (BV) ......... '32 '58 C.1042 A.B. L.1068 LL.B. 9190 Oakleaf Way
Dirks, Denise Lee ....................................'60 '89 C.629 B.A. L.464 J.D. 108 Main St.
**Dudugjian, Robert P.** ...................'47 '76 C.112 M.S. L.464 J.D. [Dudugjian&M.]
*REPORTED CASES: Hatch vs. Collins, 225 Ca3d 1104 (1980).
*PRACTICE AREAS: Business Dissolutions; Investor Fraud; Civil Litigation; Transactional Corporate; Tax.

**Dudugjian & Maxey, A Law Corporation**
**13 Sierragate Plaza, Building B, 95678**
**Telephone: 916-786-7272 Facsimile: 916-786-7306**
**Email: newerlaw@msn.com URL: http://pages.prodigy.com/newestlaw**
**Robert P. Dudugjian; John D. Maxey;—Edward A. Smith.**
**Corporate Law, Real Estate, Contract Law, Tax Law, Tax Planning, Bankruptcy, Franchise Law, Family Law, Estate Planning, Business Litigation and Litigation Support.**
***See Professional Biographies, ROSEVILLE, CALIFORNIA***

Dunbar, William L. ..................................................'45 '75 L.464 J.D. [Dunbar&V.]
Dunbar & Vodonick, A Law Corporation ......................................3013 Douglas Blvd.
Eggleston, Steven B., (BV) ............. '56 '82 C.446 B.A. L.1026 J.D. [Eggleston&O.]⊙
Eggleston & O'Brien, (BV) ................................... 100 Estates Dr. (⊙San Francisco)
Finley, Scott ..........................................'53 '79 C.112 B.S. L.1067 J.D. Dep. City Atty.
Fugazi, Robert A. ......................'20 '51 C.112 A.B. L.1065 J.D. 296 Castlewood Cir.‡
Gatfield, John L. ..........................................'46 '71 C&L.767 B.A., J.D. P.O. Box 578
Gibbons, Phillip E., (BV) ........................'42 '75 C.112 B.S. L.464 J.D. [P.E.Gibbons]
Gibbons, Phillip E., Inc., A Law Corporation, (BV) ................ 2330 Professional Dr.
**Gibson, Guy R., (AV)** ...........................'52 '77 C.112 B.A. L.464 J.D. [Gibson&G.]
*PRACTICE AREAS: Probate; Estate Planning and Trust Law; Real Property.

**Gibson & Gibson, Inc., A Law Corporation, (AV)**
**100 Estates Drive, P.O. Box 639, 95661-0639**
**Telephone: 916-782-4402 Fax: 916-782-4582**
**Howard G. Gibson (1921-1986); Guy R. Gibson (Certified Specialist, Probate, Estate Planning and Trust Law, The State Bar of California Board of Legal Specialization).**
**General Civil and Trial Practice. Business, Corporate, Real Property, Estate Planning, Probate Law and Elder Law.**
***See Professional Biographies, ROSEVILLE, CALIFORNIA***

Gieseler, F. Charles ....................................'49 '76 C.147 B.A. L.464 J.D. P.O. Box 519
Green, Marion R., (Mr.) .............. '52 '78 C.1060 B.A. L.464 J.D. 3017 Douglas Blvd.
Green, Stephen C. .......................'49 '76 C.1060 B.A. L.169 J.D. 2140 Professional Dr.
Green, Thomas E. ........................'50 '84 C.1060 B.A. L.464 J.D. 2140 Professional Dr.
Harrington, Afton L. .........................'55 '91 C.766 B.S. L.1026 J.D. [Harrington&B.]
Harrington & Bartkiewicz ........................................................... 735 Sunrise Ave.
Hoffman, Gary C. ...........................'43 '81 C.1070 B.S. L.464 J.D. 4120 Douglas Blvd.
Hue, Frank .................................................'27 '61 C.999 L.464 LL.B. 955 Keith Dr.‡
Jarrett, R. Douglas ............................................ '52 '93 L.999 J.D. [Eggleston&O.]
Jaszewski, Edward E. .................. '49 '87 C.112 B.A. L.464 J.D. 3300 Douglas Blvd.
**Jones, W. Ray** .............................................'40 '72 C.1060 B.A. L.169 [Jones&S.]
*PRACTICE AREAS: Personal Injury; Construction; Real Estate; Insurance.

**Jones & Stephens**
**2130 Professional Drive, Suite 250, 95661**
**Telephone: 916-786-0950; 800-304-5044 Fax: 916-786-6703**
**W. Ray Jones; Alisa J. Stephens. Associates: Michael D. Trainer; Thomas L. Walsh; Ralph W. Mann.**
**Workers' Compensation, Personal Injury, Construction, Real Estate, Insurance, Dissolution of Marriage, Probate, Wills and Trusts.**
***See Professional Biographies, ROSEVILLE, CALIFORNIA***

Lawson, Larry L. ..........................................'42 '71 C.999 L.464 2220 Douglas Blvd.

**Liebman & Reiner, A Professional Law Corporation, (AV)**
**3017 Douglas Boulevard, Suite 300, 95661⊙**
**Telephone: 916-852-0777 Fax: 916-852-8077**
**James M. O'Brien;—Bruce S. Baker.**
**General Liability, Defense, Products Liability, Workers Compensation Defense, Insurance and Subrogation Law, Insurance Coverage and Bad Faith, Professional Liability. Trial Practice. Appellate Practice. Environmental and Industrial Disease Law.**
**Los Angeles, California Office: 3255 Wilshire Boulevard, 12th Floor. Telephone: 213-387-0777. Fax: 213-383-6754.**
**San Francisco, California Office: 100 First Street, Suite 2250. Telephone: 415-227-0777. Fax: 415-227-0537.**
**San Diego, California Office: 225 Broadway, Suite 1500. Telephone: 619-232-0777. Fax: 619-238-5442.**
**San Jose, California Office: 95 South Market Street, Suite 300. Telephone: 408-993-0777. Fax: 408-993-0789.**
***See Professional Biographies, ROSEVILLE, CALIFORNIA***

**Livingston, J. Cleve, (BV)** ....................'47 '75 C.309 A.B. L.1162 J.D. [Robbins&L.]
Lo Duca, Marcus J., (BV) ............. '59 '86 C.1060 B.S. L.1066 J.D. 3017 Douglas Blvd.
Makol, Jennifer Hodges .................. '48 '80 C.94 B.S. L.464 J.D. 6485 Oak Hill Dr.
**Mann, Ralph W.** ....................................................... '66 '96 L.464 J.D. [▣ Jones&S.]
*PRACTICE AREAS: Workers Compensation; Personal Injury; General Civil; Criminal Law Defense.
**Maxey, John D.** ......................................'53 '85 C.147 B.S. L.464 J.D. [Dudugjian&M.]
*PRACTICE AREAS: Tax Litigation; Bankruptcy; Tax Work; Estate Planning.
McHugh, Denise Kay ................. '57 '86 C.112 B.A. L.464 J.D. 3300 Douglas Blvd.
Meyer, Thomas P. ...........................'44 '72 C.770 B.A. L.464 J.D. 730 Sunrise Ave.
O'Brien, Bernadette M. ..........................'56 '87 C.112 L.1026 J.D. [▣ Eggleston&O.]
O'Brien, David W. ........................... '28 '61 C.666 B.E. L.767 J.D. [▣ Eggleston&O.]

# CALIFORNIA—ROSEVILLE

**O'Brien, James M.** ..................... '52 '78 C.1077 B.S. L.809 J.D. [Liebman&R.]
  *PRACTICE AREAS: Personal Injury Defense Law; Insurance Law; Subrogation Law; Wrongful Discharge Law.
**O'Brien, Walter F.** ......................... '19 '51 C.454 L.818 J.D. 6022 Del Oro Rd.
**Ochrach, Jeffrey H.,** (BV) ............. '60 '87 C.1042 B.S. L.464 J.D. 3300 Douglas Blvd.
**Openshaw, James K.** .................. '53 '88 C.1165 B.S. L.464 J.D. 735 Sunrise Ave.
**Osman, James P.** ................... '51 '78 C.1042 B.A. L.809 J.D. 2220 Douglas Blvd.
**Paschon, Michael G.,** (CV) ................. '52 '78 C.98 B.S. L.801 J.D. 1101 Coral Dr.
**Pollock, Jo A.** ........................ '47 '87 C.1077 L.999 J.D. 1003 Madden Ln.
**Ring, Lawrence T.,** (BV) ................ '58 '84 C.112 B.A. L.1067 J.D. [A Sinclair,W.&B.]
  *PRACTICE AREAS: Real Estate; Personal Injury-Plaintiff; Business Transactional; Contract; Employment.
**Robbins, Stephen,** (AV) .................. '42 '73 C.112 A.B. L.976 J.D. [Robbins&L.]
  *LANGUAGES: Spanish, French.
  *REPORTED CASES: State of Koror v. Blanco et al 4 ROP Intrm. 310 (Sup. Ct. Palau).
  *TRANSACTIONS: North Central Roseville Specific Plan ($250,000,000 land use plan, master development agreement and related financing plan and assessment districts; Southeast Roseville Specific Plan ($200,000,000 land use plan, master development agreement and related financing plan and landscaping/lighting district); Northwest El Dorado Hills Specific Plan ($100,100,100 land use plan, master development agreement landscaping/lighting district).
  *PRACTICE AREAS: Zoning, Planning and Land Use; Environmental Law.

**Robbins & Livingston,** (AV) [BH]
  **3300 Douglas Boulevard, Suite 365, 95661**
  **Telephone:** 916-773-4700 **Facsimile:** 916-773-4747
  **Email:** plazolaw@aol.com
  **Members of Firm:** Stephen Robbins; J. Cleve Livingston.
  The Firm specializes in Land Use, Planning and Zoning matters, Environmental and Natural Resource issues, Energy and Utility matters and Real Estate.
  *See Professional Biographies, ROSEVILLE, CALIFORNIA*

**Rusk, Roberta L.** .................... '64 '90 C.1060 B.A. L.112 J.D. 2200 Professional Dr.
**Schostag, Alan D.** ....................... '58 '84 C.999 B.A. L.464 J.D. 720 Sunrise Ave.
**Simmons, Raymond J., Jr.** ............ '44 '84 C.1060 B.A. L.1026 J.D. 21 Professional Dr.
**Sinclair, F. Larry** .................... '14 '49 C.575 B.A. L.1066 J.D. [C Sinclair,W.&B.]
**Sinclair, John M.** ..................... '63 '90 C.112 B.A. L.1065 J.D. 1426 Tiffany Cir.

**Sinclair, Larry P.,** (BV) '47 '72 C.112 B.A. L.770 J.D.
  **2390 Professional Drive, 95661**
  **Telephone:** 916-783-3290 **Fax:** 916-783-5232
  (Certified Specialist, Family Law, The State Bar of California Board of Legal Specialization).
  *PRACTICE AREAS: Domestic and Family Law.
  Domestic and Family Law Trial and Appellate Practice. Premarital Transactional Planning. Child Custody. Child Support.
  *See Professional Biographies, ROSEVILLE, CALIFORNIA*

**Sinclair, Larry P.,** (BV) ................. '47 '72 C.112 B.A. L.770 J.D. [C Sinclair,W.&B.]
  *PRACTICE AREAS: Domestic and Family Law.
**Sinclair, Robert F.,** (BV) .............. '52 '77 C.112 B.S. L.770 J.D. [Sinclair,W.&B.]
  *PRACTICE AREAS: Real Estate Transactions and Litigation.

**Sinclair, Wilson & Bedore,** (BV)
  **2390 Professional Drive, 95661**
  **Telephone:** 916-783-5281 **Fax:** 916-783-5232
  Floyd H. Bowers (1896-1969); Robert F. Sinclair; Randall R. Wilson (Certified Specialist, Estate Planning, Trust and Probate Law, The State Bar of California Board of Legal Specialization); Jess C. Bedore, III (Certified Specialist, Criminal Law, The State Bar of California Board of Legal Specialization); Lawrence T. Ring. Of Counsel: Larry P. Sinclair (Certified Specialist, Family Law, The State Bar of California Board of Legal Specialization); F. Larry Sinclair.
  General Civil Trial and Appellate Practice, Personal Injury, Real Estate, Business, Estate Planning, Trust, Probate, Tax, Employment, Discrimination, Insurance and Criminal Defense.
  *See Professional Biographies, ROSEVILLE, CALIFORNIA*

**Smith, Edward A.** ................... '62 '89 C.112 B.A. L.464 J.D. [A Dudugjian&M.]
  *PRACTICE AREAS: Civil Litigation; Probate; Conservatorship; Elder Law.
**Stephens, Alisa J.** ..................... '52 '77 C.169 B.A. L.1067 J.D. [Jones&S.]
  *LANGUAGES: Spanish.
  *PRACTICE AREAS: Personal Injury Plaintiff; Dissolution of Marriage; Probate, Wills and Trusts.
**Struckmann, Donald K.** .................. '49 '74 C.1073 B.A. L.1065 J.D. 151 N. Sunrise
**Stuart, Holly L.** ........................ '67 '92 C.1074 B.S. L.464 J.D. 609 Oak St.

**Sweeney, William J.,** (AV) '46 '72 C&L.426 B.A., J.D.
  **100 Estates Drive, 95678-2310**
  **Telephone:** 916-786-2011 **Fax:** 916-782-4582
  **Email:** wsweeney@pacbell.net
  *PRACTICE AREAS: Construction Law; Personal Injury; Probate Law.
  (This Listing Continued)

**Sweeney, William J.** (Continued)
  Civil Practice, Construction, Engineering and Architectural Law Malpractice, Mechanics Liens, Personal Injury, Business, Corporation, Estate Planning, Trusts and Probate Law.
  *See Professional Biographies, ROSEVILLE, CALIFORNIA*

**Townley, J. Gordon** '41 '74 C.835 B.S. L.464 J.D.
  Gen. Coun., Gardemeyer Develop. Inc.
**Trainer, Michael D.** ..................... '54 '93 C.768 L.464 J.D. [A Jones&S.]
  *PRACTICE AREAS: Workers Compensation; Personal Injury; Criminal Defense; General Litigation.
**Travis, Mark** ...................... '46 '74 C.112 B.S. L.990 J.D. 3013 Douglas Blvd.
**Tronto, Karen Asplund** ............. '62 '89 C.285 B.A. L.464 J.D. 2200 Douglas Blvd.
**Vodonick, E. John** .................... '46 '74 C.1109 B.A. L.990 J.D. [Dunbar&V.]
**Walsh, Thomas L.,** (BV) ............... '36 '70 C.112 A.B. L.767 J.D. [A Jones&S.]
  *PRACTICE AREAS: Personal Injury; Commercial Torts; Environmental Law.
**Willoughby, W. Jackson** ..................... '35 '63 C.169 A.B. L.1066 J.D. Mun. J.
**Wilson, Randall R.,** (BV) ............. '56 '82 C.169 B.S. L.464 J.D. [Sinclair,W.&B.]
  *PRACTICE AREAS: Estate Planning Law; Taxation Law; Business Planning Law.
**Wylie, Wayne** ....................... '27 '55 C.999 L.1065 LL.B. 304 Inverness Ct.‡

## ROSS, 2,123, *Marin Co.*

**Bricca, Wm. C.** ................ '13 '40 C.112 A.B. L.1065 J.D. P.O. Box 159
**Chamberlain, J. Boatner** '08 '41 C.902 B.A. L.596 LL.B.
  (adm. in OR; not adm. in CA) P.O. Box 918‡
**Clarke, Diane D.** ................... '40 '78 C.724 B.A. L.1065 J.D. P.O. Box 414

**Curtiss, William H., Law Offices of** '48 '76 C.813 B.A. L.659 J.D.
  **7 Hillgirt Drive, P.O. Box 1743, 94957**
  **Telephone:** 415-454-0756 **Fax:** 415-454-0434
  **Email:** wcurtiss@msn.com
  General Civil Trial Practice, Business Litigation, Entertainment Law and Employment Law.
  *See Professional Biographies, ROSS, CALIFORNIA*

**d'Alessio, Jon W.** .................. '46 '74 C.112 B.S. L.813 J.D. Treas., McKesson Corp.
**Diamond, Ann L.,** (AV) .............. '12 '37 C&L.930 B.A., J.D. P.O. Box 999‡
**Dougherty, Linda Fairbanks** '48 '80 C.576 B.A. L.692 J.D.
  (adm. in VA; not adm. in CA) P.O. Box 635‡
**Elliott, Robert W.,** (AV) ................ '21 '49 C&L.813 A.B., J.D. P.O. Box 1365‡
**Garvey, Jack I.** ...................... '42 '69 C&L.309 A.B., J.D. P.O. Box 762
**Gately, Barbara L.** ................ '49 '77 C.788 B.A. L.1065 J.D. [Kemp&G.]
**Harbinson, Barbara N.** ............... '33 '61 C.112 A.B. L.1065 J.D. P.O. Box 456
**Herst, Samuel B.** ................... '11 '34 C.112 L.1065 J.D. P.O. Box 1308‡
**Kemp, Thomas W.,** (AV) ............ '35 '63 C.813 B.A. L.1066 LL.B. [Kemp&G.]⊙
**Kemp & Gately,** (AV) ................... 23 Ross Commons (⊙San Francisco)
**Lauter, Robert S.** ................. '28 '54 C.112 A.B. L.1065 J.D. P.O. Box 1022
**Sabini, Robert C.** ................. '50 '77 C.154 B.A. L.1186 J.D. P.O. Box 1491
**Sebastian, Raymond F.** '42 '67 C.350 B.S. L.813 LL.B.
  (adm. in WI; not adm. in CA) P.O. Box 1347‡
**Siegel, Henry M.** .......................... '35 '60 C&L.188 A.B., LL.B. 275
**Wynne, Edward J., Jr.,** (AV) .............. '38 '65 C.734 A.B. L.569 J.D. 91 Bridge Rd.

## ROSSMOOR, —, *Orange Co.*

**Brissenden, Robert J.** ............. '22 '61 C.112 B.A. L.809 J.D. 11501 Harrisburg Rd.‡

## ROUGH AND READY, —, *Nevada Co.*

**Van Note, David A.** ....................... '48 '76 C.363 A.B. L.765 J.D. P.O. Box 686

## ROWLAND HEIGHTS, 16,881, *Los Angeles Co.*

**Blackburn, John Marshall** ............ '33 '77 C.233 B.A. L.809 J.D. 2459 Recinto Ave.
**Frisby, Michael L.** .................... '48 '80 C.329 B.A. L.809 J.D. 17524 Colima Rd.
**Jauregui, Ron J.** ............... '63 '91 C.154 B.A. L.1068 J.D. U.S. Dept. of Energy
**Smith, Carroll J.** .................... '21 '78 C.312 L.1137 J.D. 18530 Dancy St.‡
**Yee, Daniel J.,** (P.C.) ............. '49 '78 C.112 B.S. L.464 J.D. 17800 Castleton St.

## RUNNING SPRINGS, —, *San Bernardino Co.*

**Carlisle, William O.** ............... '37 '68 C.112 B.A. L.1068 LL.B. 2642 Dade Dr.
**Duckworth, B. Christine** ................. '43 '72 C&L.800 A.B., J.D. P.O. Box 299‡
**Lachman, Branton G.** '52 '92
  C.1109 B.A. L.1137 J.D. Corp. Coun., The Guffey Companies, Inc.
**Ward, W. Stewart** ....................... '24 '67 L.981 LL.B. 2016 Poplar St.

# PATENT AND TRADEMARK PRACTICE PROFILES SECTION

## Legal Professionals Practicing

BEFORE THE

UNITED STATES PATENT AND TRADEMARK OFFICE

CALIFORNIA

A — R

The listings in this section are, according to information available to the publisher at press time, for those subscribers who are registered to practice Patent Law and for those who practice Trademark Law before the U.S. Patent and Trademark Office and who devote a considerable portion of their time or duties to Patent, Trademark and other related matters. It should be noted that registration is not necessary to practice Trademark Law before the U.S. Patent and Trademark Office.

Firms are not registered with the U.S. Patent and Trademark Office and the listings of such entities are limited to those whose practice includes Patent or Trademark and related matters.

The symbols shown have the same meaning as when used elsewhere in this directory. See inside front cover and facing page inside front cover for Explanatory Notes and Symbols.

## BEVERLY HILLS, 31,971, *Los Angeles Co.*

**Evanns, Joseph R.**, (AV) .................. '38 '69 C.800 B.S. L.1068 J.D. [Evanns&W.]
*REPORTED CASES: Mayview v. Rodstein, 620 F.2d 1347 (9th Cir. 1980), (Patent); Kamar International Inc. v. Russ Berrie & Co., Inc., 657 F.2d 1059 (9th Cir. 1981) (copyright); Hollingsworth Solderless Terminal Co. v. Turley, 622 F.2d 1324 (9th Cir. 1980) (Trade Secret).

**Evanns & Walsh, (AV)**
**Suite 206, 119 North San Vicente Boulevard, 90211**
**Telephone: 310-273-0938; 310-855-0872 Cable Address: "Jorev" Telecopier: 213-651-3027**
**Joseph R. Evanns; Edward C. Walsh (1912-1994).**
**Patent, Copyright, Trademark and Unfair Competition Law. Trials and Appeals in State and Federal Trial and Appellate Courts; proceedings before the United States Patent and Trademark Office and Copyright Office and before the International Trade Commission.**
*See Professional Biographies, BEVERLY HILLS, CALIFORNIA*

**Gross, J. Nicholas** ............................ '60 '88 C.111 B.S. L.426 J.D. [⊠ Trojan]
*LANGUAGES: Greek.
*PRACTICE AREAS: Intellectual Property; High Technology Litigation.

**Supnik, Paul D., (AV) '47 '72 C.112 B.S. L.1065 J.D.** ⊞
**Suite 1200 Wells Fargo Bank Building, 433 North Camden Drive, 90210**
**Telephone: 310-205-2050 Telex: 292416 Facsimile: 310-205-2011**
**Email: ps@supnik.com URL: http://www.supnik.com**
***REPORTED CASES: Brewer v. Hustler Magazine Inc., 749 F.2d 527 (9th Cir. 1984); Poe v. Missing Persons, 745 F. 2d 1238 (9th Cir. 1984).**
**Domestic and International Copyright and Trademark Law, Motion Picture, Television, Publishing, Media and General Entertainment Law, Multimedia and Internet Law. Licensing, Related Litigation.**
*See Professional Biographies, BEVERLY HILLS, CALIFORNIA*

**Trojan, R. Joseph** ............................ '61 '88 C.800 B.S. L.426 J.D. [Trojan]
*PRACTICE AREAS: Patent and Trademark Litigation and Prosecution; Intellectual Property Licensing; Copyright; Trade Secrets.

**Trojan Law Offices**
**Wells Fargo Bank Building, 433 North Camden Drive Fourth Floor, 90210**
**Telephone: 310-281-1662 Telecopier: 310-281-1664**
**Email: trojanlaw@aol.com**
**R. Joseph Trojan. Of Counsel: J. Nicholas Gross.**
**Patent and Trademark Litigation.**
*See Professional Biographies, BEVERLY HILLS, CALIFORNIA*

## COSTA MESA, 96,357, *Orange Co.*

**Blakely, Roger W., Jr.**, (AV) ........'35 '70 C.188 B.M.E. L.426 J.D. [Blakely,S.T.&Z.]

**Blakely, Sokoloff, Taylor & Zafman, (AV)**
**A Limited Liability Partnership**
**Suite 850, 611 Anton Boulevard, 92626⊙**
**Telephone: 714-557-3800 Facsimile: 714-557-3347**
**Email: BSTZ_mail@bstz.com URL: http://www.bstz.com**
**Members of Firm: Roger W. Blakely, Jr.†; Ben J. Yorks;—William W. Schaal; Kimberley G. Nobles; Kent M. Chen.**
**Intellectual Property Law including Patents, Trademarks, Copyrights, Related Prosecution and Litigation.**
**Los Angeles, California Office: 7th Floor, 12400 Wilshire Boulevard. Telephone: 310-207-3800. Facsimile: 310-820-5988.**
**Sunnyvale, California Office: 1279 Oakmead Parkway. Telephone: 408-720-8598. Facsimile: 408-720-9397.**
**Lake Oswego, Oregon Office: Suite 101, 5285 SW Meadows Road. Telephone: 503-684-6200. Facsimile: 503-684-3245.**
**†Indicates A Law Corporation.**
*See Professional Biographies, COSTA MESA, CALIFORNIA*

**Brogan, James P.** ........................... '65 '91 C.802 B.S.E.E. L.326 J.D. [⊠ Lyon&L.]
*PRACTICE AREAS: Patent, Trademark, Copyright, Unfair Competition; Intellectual Property.
**Chen, Kent M.** .................... '65 '94 C.494 B.E.E. L.569 J.D. [⊠ Blakely,S.T.&Z.]

**Fitzpatrick, Cella, Harper & Scinto**
**650 Town Center Drive, Suite 1800, 92626⊙**
**Telephone: 714-540-8700 Facsimile: 714-540-9823**
**Resident Partner: Michael K. O'Neill. Resident Associates: Mark J. Itri; Paul A. Pysher; Joseph G. Swan; Nandu A. Talwalkar.**
**Intellectual Property Practice. Patent, Trademark, Copyright, Trade Secret, Unfair Competition, Computer, Licensing, Antitrust and International Trade Law. Trials and Appeals in Federal and State Courts and Administrative Agencies.**
**New York, N.Y. Office: 277 Park Avenue. Telephone: 212-758-2400. International-Telex: FCHS 236262. Cable Address: "Fitzcel New York". Facsimile: 212-758-2982.**
**Washington, D.C. Office: 1001 Pennsylvania Avenue, N.W. Telephone: 202-347-8100. Facsimile: 202-347-8136.**
*See Professional Biographies, COSTA MESA, CALIFORNIA*

**Fowler, Charles Calvin** ..................'64 '94 C.112 B.S.B.E. L.1068 J.D. [⊠ Lyon&L.]
*PRACTICE AREAS: Patent, Trademark, Copyright; Intellectual Property.
**Freeman, Corrine M.** ........................ '64 '91 C.912 B.S. L.800 J.D. [⊠ Lyon&L.]
*PRACTICE AREAS: Intellectual Property.
**Geriak, James W., (A Professional Corporation)**, (AV) '34 '60
C.688 B.Ch.E. L.276 J.D. [Lyon&L.]
*PRACTICE AREAS: Patent, Trademark, Trade Regulation, Unfair Competition, Antitrust; Intellectual Property.
**Itri, Mark J.** .....................'63 '90 C.94 B.S.E.E. L.818 J.D. [⊠ Fitzpatrick,C.H.&S.]
**Jansen, Allan W.**, (AV) ....................... '48 '78 C.339 B.S. L.365 J.D. [Lyon&L.]
*PRACTICE AREAS: Patent, Trademark, Copyright, Unfair Competition.

**Lyon & Lyon LLP, (AV)**
**A Limited Liability Partnership Including Professional Corporations**
**Suite 1200, 3200 Park Center Drive, 92626⊙**
**Telephone: 714-751-6606 Fax: 714-751-8209**
**Email: lyon@lyonlyon.com URL: http://www.lyonlyon.com**
**Resident Partners: James W. Geriak (A Professional Corporation); Robert M. Taylor, Jr.; Samuel B. Stone (A Professional Corporation); Allan W. Jansen; David B. Murphy. Resident Associates: Kurt T. Mulville; James P. Brogan; Corrine M. Freeman; Kenneth S. Roberts; Charles Calvin Fowler.**
**Intellectual Property Law including Patent, Trademark, Copyright, Trade Regulation, Unfair Competition and Antitrust Law. Litigation.**
**Los Angeles, California Office: First Interstate World Center, 47th Floor, 633 West Fifth Street. Telephone: 213-489-1600.**
**San Jose, California Office: Suite 1150, 303 Almaden Boulevard. Telephone: 408-993-1555.**
**La Jolla, California Office: Suite 600, 4250 Executive Square. Telephone: 619-552-8400.**
*See Professional Biographies, COSTA MESA, CALIFORNIA*

**Mulville, Kurt T.** ........................................'62 '90 C.112 B.S. L.426 J.D. [⊠ Lyon&L.]
*PRACTICE AREAS: Intellectual Property.
**Murphy, David B.** ..........................'56 '82 C.112 B.A. L.1066 J.D. [Lyon&L.]
*SPECIAL AGENCIES: Section 337 Investigations in the International Trade Commission.
*PRACTICE AREAS: Patent, Software Protection; Intellectual Property.
**Nobles, Kimberley G.** .............'60 '92 C.608 B.S.E.E. L.800 J.D. [⊠ Blakely,S.T.&Z.]
**O'Neill, Michael K.** ...............'55 '86 C.816 B.S. L.564 J.D. [⊠ Fitzpatrick,C.H.&S.]
**Pysher, Paul A.** ..................'67 '94 C.688 B.S.E.E. L.94 J.D. [⊠ Fitzpatrick,C.H.&S.]
**Roberts, Kenneth S.** .............. '63 '93 C.886 B.S.M.E. L.1049 J.D. [⊠ Lyon&L.]
*PRACTICE AREAS: Patent, Trademark, Copyright; Trade Secret; Intellectual Property.
**Schaal, William W.** ..............'64 '92 C.112 B.S.E.E. L.426 J.D. [⊠ Blakely,S.T.&Z.]
**Stone, Samuel B., (A Professional Corporation)**, (AV) '34 '60
C.886 B.S.E.E. L.273 J.D. [Lyon&L.]
*PRACTICE AREAS: Patent, Trademark, Copyright; Intellectual Property.
**Swan, Joseph G.** ....................... '63 '93 C.107 B.S. L.178 J.D. [⊠ Fitzpatrick,C.H.&S.]
**Talwalkar, Nandu A.** .........'70 '96 C.339 B.S.E.E. L.800 J.D. [⊠ Fitzpatrick,C.H.&S.]
**Taylor, Robert M., Jr.**, (AV) ........... '34 '60 C.645 B.S.E.E. L.276 LL.B. [Lyon&L.]
*PRACTICE AREAS: Patent; Intellectual Property.
**Yorks, Ben J.** ............................ '59 '87 C.10 B.S.M.E. L.326 J.D. [Blakely,S.T.&Z.]

## CULVER CITY, 38,793, *Los Angeles Co.*

**Beehler & Pavitt, (AV)**
**Suite 330, 100 Corporate Pointe, 90230**
**Telephone: 310-215-3183 Facsimile: 310-215-3248 Groups 3, 2 & 1 Cable Address: "Interpat," Los Angeles**
**Email: BPLAWYER@AOL.COM**
**Members of Firm: William H. Pavitt, Jr.; Mario A. Martella. Associates: Natan Epstein; Robert Jacobs.**
**Patent, Trademark and Copyright Law. Unfair Competition Law. Trial Practice in the Federal Courts.**
**References: Alliance Bank.**
*See Professional Biographies, CULVER CITY, CALIFORNIA*

**Epstein, Natan** ......................... '47 '74 C.112 B.A. L.1068 J.D..[⊠ Beehler&P.]
*LANGUAGES: Spanish.
*PRACTICE AREAS: Intellectual Property Law; Federal Practice.
**Jacobs, Robert** ...................... '56 '81 C.454 B.B.A. L.472 J.D. [⊠ Beehler&P.]
*PRACTICE AREAS: Intellectual Property Law; Federal Practice.
**Martella, Mario A.**, (AV) ........... '31 '60 C.262 B.S.Chem. L.276 LL.B. [Beehler&P.]
*PRACTICE AREAS: Intellectual Property Law; Federal Practice.
**Pavitt, William H., Jr.**, (AV) ............... '16 '39 C&L.178 A.B., LL.B. [Beehler&P.]
*PRACTICE AREAS: Intellectual Property Law; Federal Practice.

## FRESNO, * 354,202, *Fresno Co.*

**Worrel, Rodney K.**, (AV) ................ '43 '72 C.267 B.A. L.1067 J.D. [Worrel&W.]

**Worrel & Worrel, (AV)** ⊞
**Suite 130, Civic Center Square, 2444 Main Street, 93721-1984**
**Telephone: 209-486-4526 Fax: 209-486-6948**
**Rodney K. Worrel.**
**Domestic and Foreign Patent, Trademark and Copyright and Related Intellectual Property Law. Trials in all Federal Courts.**
**Representative Clients: Bank of America; California State University, Fresno; California State University, Bakersfield; Duncan Enterprises; Fresno Pacific College; J. G. Boswell Co.; The Vendo Co.; City of Visalia.**
*See Professional Biographies, FRESNO, CALIFORNIA*

## GLENDALE, 180,038, *Los Angeles Co.*

**Smith, Robert C.** '26 '52 C.791 B.S. L.793 LL.B.
(adm. in SD; not adm. in CA) [⊠ Wagner&M.]
**Wagner, John E.**, (AV) ................'26 '51 C.350 B.S.G.E. L.352 J.D. [Wagner&M.]

**Wagner & Middlebrook, (AV)**
**3541 Ocean View Boulevard, 91208**
**Telephone: 818-957-3340 Fax: 818-957-8123**
**Members of Firm: John E. Wagner;—Robert C. Smith (Not admitted in CA).**
**Patent, Trademark and Copyright Law. Unfair Competition, Trade Secrets, Computer Law and related causes (transactional, administrative, prosecution and litigation in all state and federal courts).**
*See Professional Biographies, GLENDALE, CALIFORNIA*

## IRVINE, 110,330, *Orange Co.*

**Christie, Parker & Hale, LLP, (AV)**
**Suite 1440, 5 Park Plaza, 92714⊙**
**Telephone: 714-476-0757 Los Angeles: 213-681-1800 Cable Address: "Patlaw" Telex: ITT 4995129 (CP&H PSD) Telecopier: 714-476-8640**
**Members of Firm: Vincent G. Gioia. Associates: John W. Eldredge.**
**Patent, Trademark and Copyright Law. Unfair Competition, Trade Secrets, Computer Law, Biotechnology, Licensing, Antitrust and Complex Business Litigation.**
**References: Lloyds Bank California (Pasadena, Calif. Main Office); Wells Fargo Bank (Pasadena, California Main Offices).**
**Pasadena, California Office: Fifth Floor, Wells Fargo Bank Building, 350 West Colorado Boulevard. Telephone: 818-795-9900.**
*See Professional Biographies, IRVINE, CALIFORNIA*

**Eldredge, John W.** ................................'49 '92 C.67 B.S. L.1049 J.D. [⊠ Christie,P.&H.]
*PRACTICE AREAS: Patent; Trademark; Copyright; Unfair Competition.
**Gess, Albin H.**, (AV) ......................... '42 '72 C.215 B.E.E. L.904 J.D. [Price,G.&U.]
*REPORTED CASES: In re VE Holding v. Johnson Cos. Appliance, 917 F.2d 1574 (CAFC 1990). The U.S. Court of Appeals for the Federal Circuit cited Mr. Gess's writings in support of its decision; California Irrigation Services, Inc. v. Bartron Corp. 9 USPQ 2d 1859 (C.D. Cal. 1988).
*PRACTICE AREAS: Patent; Trademark; Copyright.
**Gioia, Vincent G.** .........................'35 '60 C.171 E.Met. L.273 J.D. [Christie,P.&H.]
*PRACTICE AREAS: Patents; Trademarks; Copyrights; Licensing; Plant Variety Protection Litigation.
**Kirchanski, Stefan J.** ......................'49 '92 C.1097 B.A. L.426 J.D. [⊠ Price,G.&U.]
*PRACTICE AREAS: Patent; Trademark; Copyright.
**Klein, Howard J.**, (AV) ..........................'50 '76 C.453 B.S. L.228 J.D. [Klein&S.]
*SPECIAL AGENCIES: Federal Election Commission.
*PRACTICE AREAS: Intellectual Property Law; Election Law.

**Klein & Szekeres, (AV)**
**4199 Campus Drive, Suite 700, 92715**
**Telephone: 714-854-5502 FAX: 714-854-4897**
**Email: hjklein@mail.calypso.com**
**Members of Firm: Howard J. Klein; Gabor L. Szekeres.**
**Patent, Trademark and Copyright Law. Unfair Competition Law. Election Law.**
**Reference: Sanwa Bank.**
*See Professional Biographies, IRVINE, CALIFORNIA*

**Lane, William G. '37 '69 C.112 B.A. L.284 J.D.**
**18400 Von Karman Avenue Suite 500, 92715**
**Telephone: 714-474-9961 Fax: 714-474-9973**
***PRACTICE AREAS: Patents; Trademark Litigation; Intellectual Property.**
**Intellectual Property Law.**
*See Professional Biographies, IRVINE, CALIFORNIA*

**Price, Joseph W., Jr.**, (AV) .............. '41 '68 C.884 B.M.E. L.276 J.D. [Price,G.&U.]
*REPORTED CASES: Angres v. Dioptics Medical Products, Inc., 2 USPQ 2d 1041 (C.D. Cal 1986).
*PRACTICE AREAS: Patent; Trademark; Copyright.

**Price, Gess & Ubell, P.C., (AV)**
**2100 S.E. Main Street, Suite 250, 92714**
**Telephone: 714-261-8433 Telecopier: 714-261-9072**
**Email: pgu@ix.netcom.com**
**Joseph W. Price, Jr.; Albin H. Gess; Franklin D. Ubell; Stefan J. Kirchanski.**
**Patent, Trademark, Copyright, Trade Secret and Antitrust Causes and Related Litigation and Counseling.**
*See Professional Biographies, IRVINE, CALIFORNIA*

CAA1T

**Szekeres, Gabor L.**, (AV) ................'44 '77 C.1044 Ph.D L.1137 J.D. [Klein&S.]
*LANGUAGES: Hungarian, German and Spanish.
*PRACTICE AREAS: Intellectual Property Law.
**Ubell, Franklin D.** ....................'49 '75 C.339 B.S.E.E. L.273 J.D. [Price,G.&U.]
*REPORTED CASES: Adray v. Adrayhart, Inc. 68 F.3d 362 (9th cir. 1995).
*PRACTICE AREAS: Patent; Trademark; Copyright.

## LAGUNA HILLS, 13,676, *Orange Co.*

**Brucker, William J.** ...................'64 '90 C.1062 B.E.E. L.930 J.D. [[A] Stetina B.&B.]
**Brunda, Bruce B.**, (AV) ...............'51 '78 C.570 B.S.E.E. L.1218 J.D. [Stetina B.&B.]
**Buyan, Robert Dean**, (AV) ...............'53 '85 C.1062 B.S. L.117 J.D. [Stetina B.&B.]
**Garred, Mark B.** ...................'64 '90 C.1062 B.M.E. L.161 J.D. [[A] Stetina B.&B.]
**Naber, Thomas C.** '41 '72 C&L.208 B.S., J.D.
(adm. in CO; not adm. in CA) [[A] Stetina B.&B.]
**Newboles, Matthew A.** ...............'65 '93 C.1074 B.S. L.770 J.D. [[A] Stetina B.&B.]
**Stetina, Kit M., (Mr.)**, (AV) ...............'52 '78 C.36 B.S. L.990 J.D. [Stetina B.&B.]
*REPORTED CASES: No Fear, Inc. v. Imagine Films, Inc., 38 U.S.P.Q.2d 1374; Big Ball Sports, Inc. v. No Fear, Inc., 38 U.S.P.Q. 2d 1383.
*PRACTICE AREAS: Patent, Trademark, Copyright, Unfair Competition; Antitrust; Commercial Litigation; Computer.

**Stetina Brunda & Buyan, A Professional Corporation, (AV)** BB
**Suite 401, 24221 Calle De La Louisa, 92653**
**Telephone: 714-855-1246 Telex: 704355 Facsimile: 714-855-6371**
**Email: 104052.1330@compuserve.com**
**Kit M. Stetina (Mr.); Bruce B. Brunda; Robert Dean Buyan;—Mark B. Garred; William J. Brucker; Matthew A. Newboles; Thomas C. Naber (Not admitted in CA).**
**Intellectual Property Law including Patent, Trademark, Copyright, Unfair Competition, Trade Secret, Licensing, Computer Law and Related Antitrust Law, Hands-On Computer Law.**
*See Professional Biographies, LAGUNA HILLS, CALIFORNIA*

**Weissenberger, Harry G.**, (AV) ....'28 '52 C.277 B.E.E. L.245 J.D. [H.G.Weissenberger]
*LANGUAGES: German, French.
*PRACTICE AREAS: Intellectual Property Law.

**Weissenberger, Harry G., Inc., Law Offices of, (AV)**
**Glendale Federal Building, Suite 309, 24221 Calle de la Louisa, 92653-7602**
**Telephone: 714-380-4046 Fax: 714-380-1179**
**Email: weisspat@aol.com**
**Harry G. Weissenberger.**
**Patent, Trademark, Copyright and Unfair Competition Law. Trials in Federal and State Courts.**
*See Professional Biographies, LAGUNA HILLS, CALIFORNIA*

## LA JOLLA, —, *San Diego Co.*

(Part of the City of San Diego)

**Benassi, John M.**, (AV) .....................'48 '75 C.339 B.S. L.273 J.D. [Lyon&L.]
*PRACTICE AREAS: Intellectual Property.
**Berkman, Charles S.** .........................'68 '93 C&L.846 B.S., J.D. [[A] Lyon&L.]
*PRACTICE AREAS: Patent, Unfair Competition, Antitrust; Intellectual Property.
**Biggs, Suzanne L.** ..........................'48 '78 C.668 B.A. L.800 J.D. [[C] Lyon&L.]
*LANGUAGES: (Reading) German, French.
*PRACTICE AREAS: Patent, Trademark, Copyright, Unfair Competition, Licensing; Intellectual Property.
**Consalvi, Mary S.** ..........................'58 '83 C.679 B.S. L.209 J.D. [Lyon&L.]
*LANGUAGES: Italian and French.
*PRACTICE AREAS: Patent, Trademark, Unfair Competition; Intellectual Property.
**Cordray, Monique L.** '64 '89 C.923 B.S. L.260 J.D.
(adm. in FL; not adm. in CA) [[A] Fish&R.]
*PRACTICE AREAS: Intellectual Property; International Trade Commission Practice.
**Duft, Bradford J.** ..........................'54 '80 C.174 B.A. L.61 J.D. [[C] Lyon&L.]
*PRACTICE AREAS: Intellectual Property.

**Fish & Richardson P.C., (AV)**
**4225 Executive Square, Suite 1400, 92037⊙**
**Telephone: 619-678-5070 Fax: 619-678-5099**
**Email: info@fr.com URL: http://www.fr.com**
**John F. Land; John R. Wetherell, Jr. (Not admitted in CA); Scott C. Harris (Not admitted in CA);—Monique L. Cordray (Not admitted in CA); Stacy L. Taylor; June Marie Learn; Lisa A. Haile; Christopher S. Marchese; Donald L. Wenskay.**
**Intellectual Property Law: Trials, Transactions, Patents, Trademarks, Copyrights, Trade Secrets, Entertainment Law, Telecommunications Law, Drug and Medical Device and Antitrust Law.**
**Boston, Massachusetts Office: 225 Franklin Street. Telephone: 617-542-5070. Fax: 617-542-8906.**
**Washington, D.C. Office: 601 13th Street, N.W. Telephone: 202-783-5070. Fax: 202-783-2331.**
**Houston, Texas Office: One Riverway, Suite 1200. Telephone: 713-629-5070. Fax: 713-629-7811.**
**Menlo Park, California Office: 2200 Sand Hill Road, Suite 100. Telephone: 415-322-5070. Fax: 415-854-0875.**
**Minneapolis, Minnesota Office: Fish & Richardson P.C., P.A., 60 South Sixth Street, Suite 3300. Telephone: 612-335-5070. Fax: 612-288-9696.**
**New York, N.Y. Office: 45 Rockefeller Plaza, Suite 2800. Telephone: 212-765-5070. Fax: 212-258-2291.**
*See Professional Biographies, LA JOLLA, CALIFORNIA*

**Guise, Jeffrey William** ...................'59 '93 C.352 B.S. L.763 J.D. [[A] Lyon&L.]
*PRACTICE AREAS: Patent, Trademark, Copyright; Intellectual Property.
**Haile, Lisa A.** ..............................'60 '92 C.699 B.A. L.61 J.D. [[A] Fish&R.]
*PRACTICE AREAS: Intellectual Property; Patents.
**Harris, Scott C.** '57 '87 C&L.273 B.S.E.E., J.D.
(adm. in PA; not adm. in CA) [Fish&R.]
*PRACTICE AREAS: Intellectual Property; Patents.
**Heber, Sheldon O.** .....................'60 '93 C.563 Ph.D. L.1188 J.D. [[A] Lyon&L.]
*PRACTICE AREAS: Patent; Intellectual Property.
**Hellenkamp, Amy Stark** .................'66 '96 C.645 B.S. L.1049 J.D. [[A] Lyon&L.]
*PRACTICE AREAS: Patent; Intellectual Property.
**Korniczky, Stephen S.** .................'63 '88 C.667 B.S.M.E. L.107 J.D. [[C] Lyon&L.]
*PRACTICE AREAS: Litigation; Patent; Trademark; Copyright; Unfair Competition.
**Land, John F.** ..........................'53 '78 C.111 B.S. L.800 J.D. [Fish&R.]
*PRACTICE AREAS: Intellectual Property; Copyrights; Patents; Trademarks; Trade Secrets.
**Laurenson, Robert C.** ....................'53 '87 C.453 S.B. L.273 J.D. [Lyon&L.]
*PRACTICE AREAS: Litigation; Patent, Trademark, Copyright; Intellectual Property.
**Learn, June Marie** .......................'37 '88 C.112 Ph.D. L.426 J.D. [[A] Fish&R.]
*PRACTICE AREAS: Intellectual Property; Patents.
**Lithgow, Timothy J.** ....................'62 '91 C.999 B.A. L.1066 J.D. [[A] Lyon&L.]
*PRACTICE AREAS: Patent Law; Trademark Law; Intellectual Property.

**Lyon & Lyon LLP, (AV)**
**A Limited Liability Partnership Including Professional Corporations**
**Suite 660, 4250 Executive Square, 92037⊙**
**Telephone: 619-552-8400 FAX: 619-552-0159**
**Email: lyon@lyonlyon.com URL: http://www.lyonlyon.com**
**Resident Partners: Douglas E. Olson (A Professional Corporation); John M. Benassi; Mary S. Consalvi; Robert C. Laurenson. Resident Associates: Richard Warburg; Jessica R. Wolff; Sheldon O. Heber; Jeffrey William Guise; Charles S. Berkman; Clarke W. Neumann, Jr.; Timothy J. Lithgow; Gary H. Silverstein; Amy Stark Hellenkamp; Howard N. Wisnia. Resident Of Counsel: Bradford J. Duft; Suzanne L. Biggs; F.T. Alexandra Mahaney; Stephen S. Korniczky.**
**Intellectual Property Law including Patent, Trademark, Copyright, Trade Regulation, Unfair Competition and Antitrust Law. Litigation.**
**Los Angeles, California Office: First Interstate World Center, 47th Floor, 633 West Fifth Street. Telephone: 213-489-1600.**
**Costa Mesa, California Office: Suite 1200, 3200 Park Center Drive. Telephone: 714-751-6606.**
**San Jose, California Office: Suite 1150, 303 Almaden Boulevard. Telephone: 408-993-1555.**
*See Professional Biographies, LA JOLLA, CALIFORNIA*

**Mahaney, F.T. Alexandra** .................'59 '86 C.103 B.S. L.1068 J.D. [[C] Lyon&L.]
*PRACTICE AREAS: Intellectual Property Litigation; Patent, Trademark, Copyright, Unfair Competition, Antitrust.
**Marchese, Christopher S.** ..................'64 '92 C.383 B.A. L.273 J.D. [[A] Fish&R.]
*PRACTICE AREAS: Intellectual Property; Patents; Copyrights; Trademarks; Trade Secrets.
**Neumann, Clarke W., Jr.** ..................'63 '93 C.645 B.S. L.426 J.D. [[A] Lyon&L.]
*PRACTICE AREAS: Intellectual Property.
**Olson, Douglas E., (A Professional Corporation)**, (AV) '37 '65
C.966 B.S.Ch.E. L.273 LL.B. [Lyon&L.]
*PRACTICE AREAS: Patent, Trademark, Unfair Competition; Intellectual Property.
**Silverstein, Gary H.** ......................'55 '96 C.165 A.B. L.1049 J.D. [[A] Lyon&L.]
*PRACTICE AREAS: Intellectual Property.
**Taylor, Stacy L.** ............................'59 '86 C.1074 B.S. L.61 J.D. [[A] Fish&R.]
*PRACTICE AREAS: Intellectual Property; Litigation; Trademarks; Copyrights.
**Warburg, Richard** ..........................'57 '90 C.061 B.Sc. L.818 J.D. [[A] Lyon&L.]
*PRACTICE AREAS: Patent, Trademark, Copyright; Intellectual Property.
**Wenskay, Donald L.** ........................'54 '88 C.477 B.S. L.912 J.D. [[A] Fish&R.]
*PRACTICE AREAS: Patent; Trademark; Intellectual Property.
**Wetherell, John R., Jr.** '48 '85 C.260 B.S.Chem. L.776 J.D.
(adm. in DC; not adm. in CA) [Fish&R.]
*PRACTICE AREAS: Intellectual Property; Patents; Trade Secrets; Unfair Trade Practices.
**Wisnia, Howard N.** ........................'69 '96 C&L.273 B.S.E.E., J.D. [[A] Lyon&L.]
*PRACTICE AREAS: Intellectual Property.
**Wolff, Jessica R.** ..........................'64 '92 C.104 A.B. L.1068 J.D. [[A] Lyon&L.]
*PRACTICE AREAS: Patent, Trademark, Copyright, Unfair Competition, Trade Secret; Intellectual Property.

## LONG BEACH, 429,433, *Los Angeles Co.*

**Anderson, Gary M.** ............'49 '81 C.112 B.S.M.E. L.809 J.D. [[A] Fulwider P.L.&U.]
*PRACTICE AREAS: Patent, Trademark, Copyright and Unfair Competition Law; Litigation.
**Casey, Sean M.** .................'62 '95 C.94 B.S.A.E. L.809 J.D. [[A] Fulwider P.L.&U.]
*PRACTICE AREAS: Patent; Copyright; Trademark Prosecution; Intellectual Property Litigation.

**Fulwider Patton Lee & Utecht, LLP, (AV)**
**200 Oceangate, Suite 1550, 90802-4351⊙**
**Telephone: 310-432-0453 Fax: 310-435-6014 Email: fulwidr@primenet.com**
**Email: fulwiderlb@aol.com**
**Member of Firm: Vern Schooley (Resident). Associates: Gunther D. Hanke (Resident); Gary M. Anderson (Resident); Russell C. Pangborn (Resident); Derrick W. Reed (Resident); JoAnne M. Ybaben (Resident); Sean M. Casey (Resident). Of Counsel: Francis A. Utecht (Resident).**
**Patent, Trademark, Copyright and Unfair Competition Law. Litigation.**
**Los Angeles, California Office: 10877 Wilshire Boulevard, 10th Floor. Telephone: 310-824-5555. Internet: fulwidr@primenet.com; fulwidr@aol.com. FAX: 310-824-9696.**
*See Professional Biographies, LONG BEACH, CALIFORNIA*

**Hanke, Gunther D.** ................'55 '86 C.800 B.S. L.809 J.D. [[A] Fulwider P.L.&U.]
*LANGUAGES: German.
*PRACTICE AREAS: Patent, Trademark, Copyright and Unfair Competition Law; Litigation.
**Pangborn, Russell C.** ............'66 '94 C.813 B.A. L.1065 J.D. [[A] Fulwider P.L.&U.]⊙
*PRACTICE AREAS: Trademark; Copyright; Patent Litigation; Trade Secret.
**Reed, Derrick W.** ..............'69 '95 C.112 B.S.E.E. L.426 J.D. [[A] Fulwider P.L.&U.]
*PRACTICE AREAS: Patent Prosecution; Patent Litigation; Trademark Law; Unfair Competition Law; Intellectual Property Law.
**Schooley, Vern**, (AV) ..........'37 '67 C.475 B.S.M.E. L.1049 J.D. [Fulwider P.L.&U.]
*PRACTICE AREAS: Patent, Trademark, Copyright and Unfair Competition Law; Litigation.
**Utecht, Francis A.**, (AV) .......'23 '52 C.800 B.S.M.E. L.809 J.D. [[C] Fulwider P.L.&U.]
*PRACTICE AREAS: Patent; Trademark Law; Copyright Law; Unfair Competition Law; Litigation.
**Ybaben, JoAnne M.** .................'66 '94 C.112 B.A. L.61 J.D. [[A] Fulwider P.L.&U.]
*PRACTICE AREAS: Patents and Trademark Prosecution and Litigation.

## LOS ANGELES, * 3,485,398, *Los Angeles Co.*

A number of communities in the Los Angeles area have individual identities, and therefore, in addition to the lawyers listed in the following Bar Roster, other lawyers and firms appear under the names of those towns and sections, some of which are part of the incorporated City of Los Angeles, while others are either unincorporated or separately incorporated. See list of towns and cities shown under the heading of Los Angeles County in index appearing on the first page of California Lawyers.

**Abrahams, Colin P.** ..........................'52 '82 C&L.061 B.Sc., LL.B. [Ladas&P.]
**Adriano, Sarah B.** '60 '90 C.1294 B.A. L.1049 J.D.
(adm. in NY; not adm. in CA) [[A] Merchant&G.]
**Anderson, Roy L.**, (AV) ......................'57 '82 C.340 B.A. L.273 J.D. [Lyon&L.]
*PRACTICE AREAS: Litigation; Patent, Trademark, Copyright, Unfair Competition, Antitrust; Intellectual Property.
**Arant, Gene W.**, (AV) ...............'20 '50 C.628 B.S.E.E. L.800 J.D. [Arant,K.L.&R.]
*PRACTICE AREAS: Counseling; Alternative Dispute Resolution; Licensing; Domestic and Foreign Patent and Trademark Prosecution.

**Arant, Kleinberg, Lerner & Ram, LLP, (AV)**
**Suite 1080, 2049 Century Park East (Century City), 90067-3112**
**Telephone: 310-557-1511 Telex: 5101012414 AKL LAX Cable Address: "PTCLAW" Facsimile: 310-557-1540**
**Members of Firm: Gene W. Arant; Marvin H. Kleinberg; Marshall A. Lerner; Michael J. Ram; Bradford E. Mattes.**
**Civil Trial and Appellate Practice in All State and Federal Courts Regarding Patents, Trademarks, Copyrights, Antitrust, Unfair Competition and Intellectual Property Law, Entertainment and Music Litigation and General Business Litigation. Transactional Matters For Corporate and Entertainment Law.**
**Reference: First Los Angeles Bank, Avenue of the Stars, Los Angeles, Calif.**
*See Professional Biographies, LOS ANGELES, CALIFORNIA*

**Ashen, Robert M.**, (AV) ............'34 '58 C.679 B.S.M.E. L.309 J.D. [Ashen,G.&L.]⊙

**Ashen, Golant & Lippman, (AV)** BB
**2029 Century Park East, Suite 2610, 90067⊙**
**Telephone: 310-203-0303 Fax: 310-203-8803**
**Members of Firm: Robert M. Ashen; Joseph H. Golant; Peter I. Lippman.**
**Patent, Trademark and Copyright Law. Intellectual Property Litigation and Licensing. Unfair Competition, Trade-Secret, Computer and High-Technology Law.**
**Reference: City National Bank (Beverly Hills Office).**
**Beverly Hills, California Office: 1737 Franklin Canyon Drive, 90210. Telephone: 310-274-8060. Fax: 310-858-1922.**
**Chicago, Illinois Office: 70 West Madison Street, 1700, 60602. Telephone: 312-422-0729. Fax: 312-422-0730.**
**Montrose, California Office: 4385 Ocean View Boulevard. Telephone: 818-249-5961. Fax: 818-249-8384.**
*See Professional Biographies, LOS ANGELES, CALIFORNIA*

**Babbitt, W. Thomas** ................'61 '93 C.112 B.S. L.464 J.D. [[A] Blakely,S.T.&Z.]
**Bailey, Craig B.** .....................'52 '78 C.105 B.A. L.273 J.D. [Fulwider P.L.&U.]
*PRACTICE AREAS: Patent, Trademark, Copyright and Unfair Competition Law; Litigation.
**Balgenorth, Charles R.** ..............'62 '92 C.912 B.S.E.E. L.477 J.D. [[A] Lyon&L.]
*PRACTICE AREAS: Intellectual Property.
**Bardin, Richard A.**, (AV) ..........'34 '65 C.112 B.S.E. L.800 J.D. [Fulwider P.L.&U.]
*PRACTICE AREAS: Patent, Trademark, Copyright and Unfair Competition Law; Litigation.
**Berg, Richard P.**, (AV) ..................'45 '76 C.800 B.S.E.E. L.1049 J.D. [Ladas&P.]
**Berliner, Robert**, (AV) ..................'35 '62 C.563 B.S. L.213 J.D. [Robbins,B.&C.]
*PRACTICE AREAS: Patents Law; Copyright Law; Trademark Law; Federal Litigation; Licensing Law.
**Berman, Charles** .......................'43 '78 C&L.999 B.S., LL.B. [Merchant&G.]

**Blakely, Sokoloff, Taylor & Zafman, (AV)**
**A Limited Liability Partnership**
**7th Floor, 12400 Wilshire Boulevard, 90025⊙**
**Telephone: 310-207-3800 Facsimile: 310-820-5988**
**Email: BSTZ_mail@bstz.com URL: http://www.bstz.com**
**Members of Firm: Roger W. Blakely, Jr.†; Stanley W. Sokoloff†; Edwin H. Taylor†; Norman Zafman†; Eric S. Hyman; George W Hoover II. Of Counsel: Stephen L. King; Ronald W. Reagin;—Thomas M. Coester; Eric Ho; W. Thomas Babbitt; Karen L. Feisthamel.**
**Intellectual Property Law, including Patents, Trademarks, Copyrights, Related Prosecution and Litigation.**
**Sunnyvale, California Office: 1279 Oakmead Parkway. Telephone: 408-720-8598. Facsimile: 408-720-9397.**
**Costa Mesa, California Office: Suite 850, 611 Anton Boulevard. Telephone: 714-557-3800. Facsimile: 714-557-3347.**
**Lake Oswego, Oregon Office: Suite 101, 5285 SW Meadows Road. Telephone: 503-684-6200. Facsimile: 503-684-3245.**
**†Indicates A Law Corporation.**

***See Professional Biographies, LOS ANGELES, CALIFORNIA***

**Bloomberg, Coe A., (A Professional Corporation),** (AV) '43 '72 C.277 B.M.E. L.426 J.D. [Lyon&L.]
*PRACTICE AREAS: Intellectual Property.
**Bogucki, Raymond A.,** (AV) .....'22 '52 C.602 B.S. in M.E. L.494 LL.B. [Merchant&G.]
**Bongini, Stephen** .................... '69 '95 C.472 B.S.E.E. L.1068 J.D. [A Loeb&L.]
*PRACTICE AREAS: Patent Law.
**Bright, Patrick F.,** (AV) ....................'43 '69 C.276 B.S. L.273 J.D. [Bright&L.]
*PRACTICE AREAS: Patent, Copyright, Trademark, Trade Secret and Antitrust including Litigation.

**Bright & Lorig, A Professional Corporation, (AV) BR**
**633 West Fifth Street, Suite 3330, 90071**
**Telephone: 213-627-7774 Telecopier: 213-627-8508**
**Patrick F. Bright;—Edward C. Schewe.**
**Patents, Trademarks, Copyright, Antitrust and Unfair Competition Law. Trials.**
**Reference: Manufacturers Bank (Headquarters Office).**

***See Professional Biographies, LOS ANGELES, CALIFORNIA***

**Brindisi, Thomas J.** ........................ '69 '95 C.119 B.S. L.64 J.D. [A Lyon&L.]
*PRACTICE AREAS: Intellectual Property.
**Brooks, James C.** ........................... '48 '79 C.911 B.S. L.276 J.D. [Lyon&L.]
*PRACTICE AREAS: Patent, Trademark, Copyright, Unfair Competition, Trade Secret; Intellectual Property.
**Carson, John,** (AV) ....................'42 '68 C.770 B.S. L.310 J.D. [Robbins,B.&C.]
*PRACTICE AREAS: Patent Law; Trademark Law; Copyright Law; Trade Secret Law; Unfair Competition Law.
**Cates, Richard B.** ..................'63 '93 C.174 B.S. L.1065 J.D. [A Fulwider P.L.&U.]
*PRACTICE AREAS: Patent; Trademark; Copyright; Litigation.
**Chapman, Bruce G.** .................... '60 '87 C.215 B.Mech. L.273 J.D. [A Lyon&L.]
*PRACTICE AREAS: Intellectual Property.
**Chen, Ying** .............................. '63 '95 C.061 B.S. L.596 J.D. [A Loeb&L.]
*LANGUAGES: Chinese.
**Codding, Richard J.** ...................... '44 '70 C.277 B.E.E. L.309 J.D. [Loeb&L.]
*PRACTICE AREAS: Patent; Trademark; Copyright; Litigation.
**Coester, Thomas M.** ..............'67 '94 C&L.352 B.S.E.E., J.D. [A Blakely,S.T.&Z.]
**Cohen, Lawrence S.**...................'39 '66 C.588 B.S.M.E. L.94 J.D. [Freilich,H.&R.]
*PRACTICE AREAS: Patent, Trademark and Copyright Law; Unfair Competition Law; Litigation; Licensing Law; Technology Transfer.
**Cooper, Victor G.** ...................'56 '94 C.1077 B.S.E. L.426 J.D. [A Merchant&G.]
*PRACTICE AREAS: Patent Law; Copyright Law; Trademark Law.
**Cox, Donald J., Jr.**..................'63 '92 C.705 B.S.E.E. L.464 J.D. [A Small L.&K.]
*PRACTICE AREAS: Patent, Copyright and Trademark; Computer Law.
**Craft, Jeffrey F.** ........................ '54 '81 C.477 B.S. L.912 J.D. [Pretty,S.&P.]
*PRACTICE AREAS: Patents; Trademarks; Copyrights; Unfair Competition; Litigation.
**Davidson, Ben M.** ................. '68 '95 C.867 B.S.E.E. L.273 J.D. [A Merchant&G.]
*LANGUAGES: French and Japanese.
*PRACTICE AREAS: Litigation; Patent Prosecution.
**Dickerson, Robert W.** ..................... '50 '79 C.112 B.S. L.809 J.D. [Lyon&L.]
*PRACTICE AREAS: Intellectual Property.
**Drucker, I. Morley, (A Professional Corporation),** (AV) '31 '59 C.453 B.Sc. L.809 J.D. [C Fulwider P.L.&U.]
*REPORTED CASES: Oromeccanica, Inc. v. Ottmar Botzenhardt GmbH & Co. KG, 226 USPQ 996 (USDC, D.C. Calif. 1985); MWS Wire Industries, Inc. v. California Fine Wire Industries, Inc., 230 USPQ 873 (Ct of Appeals, 9th Cir. 1986); Cento Group S.p.A. v. OroAmerica, Inc., 822 F. Supp 1058 (USDC, SDNY, 1993).
*PRACTICE AREAS: Patent Law; Trademark Law; Copyright Law; Unfair Competition Law.
**Elkind, Michael S.,** (AV) ................'48 '74 C.112 B.S. L.309 J.D. [Robbins,B.&C.]
*PRACTICE AREAS: Patent Law; Trademark Law; Copyright Law; Trade Secret Law; Unfair Competition Law.
**Erwin, Philippe O.** ....................... '66 '92 C.696 B.S. L.93 J.D. [A Loeb&L.]
**Farach, Horacio A.** ..................'55 '89 C.790 B.S. L.796 J.D. [A Robbins,B.&C.]
*LANGUAGES: Spanish.
*PRACTICE AREAS: Patent Law (Biotechnology); Trademark Law; Copyright Law; Federal Litigation.
**Farber, Michael B.** ................... '47 '87 C.111 B.S. L.809 J.D. [A Merchant&G.]
*PRACTICE AREAS: Patents; Trademarks.
**Feisthamel, Karen L.** ..............'65 '90 C.103 B.Sc. L.276 J.D. [A Blakely,S.T.&Z.]
**Feng, Paul Y.** ...............'60 '90 C.966 B.S.M.E. L.494 J.D. [A Fulwider P.L.&U.]
*LANGUAGES: Chinese (Mandarin).
*PRACTICE AREAS: Patent Prosecution; Intellectual Property; Trademark Law.
**Finkel, Evan** ............................'56 '81 C.1044 B.S. L.1065 J.D. [Loeb&L.]
*PRACTICE AREAS: Trademark; Patent; Copyright; Trade Secret and Unfair Competition; Computer and Multimedia Law.
**Fitzgerald, John K.** ...............'50 '93 C.209 B.S. L.1148 J.D. [A Fulwider P.L.&U.]
*PRACTICE AREAS: Patent; Trademark; Copyright.
**Freilich, Arthur,** (AV) .............. '35 '62 C.688 B.E.E. L.273 LL.B. [Freilich,H.&R.]
*PRACTICE AREAS: Patent Law; Trademark Law; Licensing Law; Litigation; Technology Business Startups.

**Freilich, Hornbaker & Rosen, P.C., (AV) BR**
**Suite 1434, 10960 Wilshire Boulevard, 90024**
**Telephone: 310-477-0578 Telex: 298725 Patl Ur Telecopy: 310-473-9277**
**Arthur Freilich; Robert D. Hornbaker; Leon D. Rosen; Timothy T. Tyson; Lawrence S. Cohen; Lee Jay Mandell.**
**Patent, Trademark, Copyright, Unfair Competition and Antitrust Law. Trials in State and Federal Courts.**
**Reference: Bank of America (Wilshire-Westwood Branch).**

***See Professional Biographies, LOS ANGELES, CALIFORNIA***

**Fulwider Patton Lee & Utecht, LLP, (AV) BR**
**10877 Wilshire Boulevard, 10th Floor, 90024⊙**
**Telephone: 310-824-5555 FAX: 310-824-9696 Email: fulwidr@primenet.com**
**Email: fulwidr@aol.com**
**Members of Firm: Richard A. Bardin; Gilbert G. Kovelman; Vern Schooley (Long Beach Resident Partner); James W. Paul; Craig B. Bailey; John S. Nagy; Stephen J. Strauss; Thomas H. Majcher; Thomas A. Runk. Associates: David G. Parkhurst; Paul M. Stull; Gunther D. Hanke (Long Beach Resident Associate); Gary M. Anderson (Long Beach Resident Associate); Ronald E. Perez; Robert L. Kovelman; Pamela G. Maher; John V. Hanley; Paul T. LaVoie; John K. Fitzgerald; James Juo (Not admitted in CA); Russell C. Pangborn (Long Beach Resident Associate); Richard B. Cates; Derrick W. Reed (Long Beach Resident Associate); Paul Y. Feng; JoAnne M. Ybaben (Long Beach Resident**

(This Listing Continued)

**Fulwider Patton Lee & Utecht, LLP (Continued)**

**Associate); Sean M. Casey (Long Beach Resident Associate); Muriel C. Haritchabalet. Of Counsel: Francis A. Utecht (Resident, Of Counsel, Long Beach Office); I. Morley Drucker (A Professional Corporation); Howard N. Sommers.**
**Patent, Trademark, Copyright and Unfair Competition Law. Litigation.**
**Long Beach, California Office: 200 Oceangate, Suite 1550. Telephone: 310-432-0453. Fax: 310-435-6014. Internet: fulwidrlb@aol.com.**

***See Professional Biographies, LOS ANGELES, CALIFORNIA***

**Gallenson, Mavis S.,** (AV) .......................'51 '79 C&L.878 B.S., J.D. [Ladas&P.]
**Garscia, Mark,** (AV) ..................... '55 '85 C.494 B.S. L.564 J.D. [Pretty,S.&P.]
*PRACTICE AREAS: Patents; Trademarks; Copyrights; Unfair Competition; Litigation.
**Gates, George Henry, III** ...........'57 '89 C.608 B.S.C.I.S. L.1035 J.D. [Merchant&G.]
**Golant, Joseph H.,** (AV) ........... '41 '66 C.399 B.S.M.E. L.145 J.D. [Ashen,G.&L.]⊙
**Gorowitz, Francie R.** ..................... '55 '81 C.1044 B.A. L.982 J.D. [Ladas&P.]
**Grace, David W.** ...........................'54 '82 C.1209 B.S. L.893 J.D. [Loeb&L.]
*PRACTICE AREAS: Trademark; Copyright; Intellectual Property Litigation.
**Gross, Clark D.** ..........................'52 '87 C.112 L.1148 J.D. [Robbins,B.&C.]
*PRACTICE AREAS: Patent, Trademark and Copyright Litigation.
**Hankin, Marc E.** ....................... '61 '94 C.94 B.A. L.659 J.D. [A Pretty,S.&P.]
*PRACTICE AREAS: Patent Litigation and Prosecution; Trademark Litigation and Registration; Copyright Litigation and Registration; Trade Secrets Litigation.
**Hanley, John V.** ...............'62 '92 C.112 B.S.M.E. L.767 J.D. [A Fulwider P.L.&U.]
*PRACTICE AREAS: Patent; Trademark; Copyright; Unfair Competition; Litigation.
**Haritchabalet, Muriel C.** ..........'68 '94 C.764 B.A. L.990 J.D. [A Fulwider P.L.&U.]
*LANGUAGES: French and Spanish.
*PRACTICE AREAS: Trademarks.
**Harriman, J. D., II,** (AV) .................. '57 '84 C.608 B.S.E. L.800 J.D. [Hecker&H.]
*PRACTICE AREAS: Patent and Trademark; Intellectual Property; Computer Law; Unfair Competition.
**Hecker, Gary A.,** (AV) .............. '55 '81 C.690 B.S.M.E. L.1049 J.D. [Hecker&H.]
*PRACTICE AREAS: Patent, Trademark and Copyright; Intellectual Property; Computer Law; Unfair Competition.

**Hecker & Harriman, (AV)**
**2029 Century Park East, 16th Floor, 90067**
**Telephone: 310-286-0377 Facsimile: 310-286-0488; 310-785-0016 Telex: 6503743401**
**Gary A. Hecker; J. D. Harriman II. Associates: Frank M. Weyer.**
**Intellectual Property Law including Patent, Trademark, Copyright, Computer Law, Unfair Competition, and Trade Secret. Technology Licensing and Litigation in Federal and State Courts and the International Trade Commission.**

***See Professional Biographies, LOS ANGELES, CALIFORNIA***

**Ho, Eric** ........................... '68 '94 C.112 B.S. L.800 J.D. [A Blakely,S.T.&Z.]
**Hokanson, Jon E.,** (AV) ..................... '48 '80 C.20 B.A. L.273 J.D. [Small L.&K.]
*PRACTICE AREAS: Patent, Trademark and Copyright.
**Hoover, George W, II** .................'46 '86 C.112 B.S. L.426 J.D. [Blakely,S.T.&Z.]
**Hornbaker, Robert D.,** (AV) ....... '26 '49 C.350 B.S.E.E. L.352 J.D. [Freilich,H.&R.]
*PRACTICE AREAS: Litigation; Patent Law; Trademark Law; Unfair Competition Law.

**Hurey, Michael '62 '88 C.1075 B.S. L.426 J.D.**
**11679 Montana Avenue, Suite 10, 90049**
**Telephone: 310-471-3273 Fax: 310-471-5898**
**Intellectual Property Law, Patent, Trademark, Copyright and related Litigation.**

***See Professional Biographies, LOS ANGELES, CALIFORNIA***

**Hyman, Eric S.** ..................'48 '79 C.800 B.S.E.E. L.1137 J.D. [Blakely,S.T.&Z.]

**Jones, Day, Reavis & Pogue, (AV) BR**
**555 West Fifth Street Suite 4600, 90013-1025⊙**
**Telephone: 213-489-3939 Telex: 181439 UD Telecopier: 213-243-2539**
**Members of the Firm in Los Angeles: Louis L. Touton; Kevin G. McBride. Associate: Allan Z. Litovsky.**
**Patent Trademark and Copyright Law.**
**In Irvine, California: 2603 Main Street, Suite 900. Telephone: 714-851-3939. Telex: 194911 Lawyers LSA. Telecopier: 714-553-7539.**
**In Atlanta, Georgia: 3500 One Peachtree Center, 303 Peachtree Street, N.E. Telephone: 404-521-3939. Cable Address: "Attorneys Atlanta". Telex: 54-2711. Telecopier: 404-581-8330.**
**In Brussels, Belgium: Avenue Louise 480, 7th Floor, B-1050 Brussels. Telephone: 32-2-645-14-11. Telecopier: 32-2-645-14-45.**
**In Chicago, Illinois: 77 West Wacker. Telephone: 312-782-3939. Telecopier: 312-782-8585.**
**In Cleveland, Ohio: North Point, 901 Lakeside Avenue. Telephone: 216-586-3939. Cable Address: "Attorneys Cleveland." Telex: 980389. Telecopier: 216-579-0212.**
**In Columbus, Ohio: 1900 Huntington Center. Telephone: 614-469-3939. Cable Address: "Attorneys Columbus." Telecopier: 614-461-4198.**
**In Dallas, Texas: 2300 Trammell Crow Center, 2001 Ross Avenue. Telephone: 214-220-3939. Cable Address: "Attorneys Dallas." Telex: 730852. Telecopier: 214-969-5100.**
**In Frankfurt, Germany: Triton Haus, Bockenheimer Landstrasse 42, 60323 Frankfurt am Main. Telephone: 49-69-9726-3939. Telecopier: 49-69-9726-3993.**
**In Geneva, Switzerland: 20, rue de Candolle. Telephone: 41-22-320-2339. Telecopier: 41-22-320-1232.**
**In Hong Kong: 29th Floor, Entertainment Building, 30 Queen's Road Central. Telephone: 852-2526-6895. Telecopier: 852-2868-5871.**
**In London England: Bucklersbury House, 3 Queen Victoria Street. Telephone: 44-171-236-3939. Telecopier: 44-171-236-1113.**
**In New Delhi, India: Pathak & Associates, 13th Floor, Dr. Gopal Das Bhaven, 28 Barakhamba Road. Telephone: 91-11-373-8793. Telecopier: 91-11-335-3761.**
**In New York, New York: 599 Lexington Avenue. Telephone: 212-326-3939. Cable Address: "JONESDAY NEWYORK." Telex: 237013 JDRP UR. Telecopier: 212-755-7306.**
**In Paris, France: 62, rue du Faubourg Saint-Honore. Telephone: 33-1-44-71-3939. Telex: 290156 Surgoe. Telecopier: 33-1-49-24-0471.**
**In Pittsburgh, Pennsylvania: 500 Grant Street, 31st Floor. Telephone: 412-391-3939. Cable Address: "Attorneys Pittsburgh". Telecopier: 412-394-7959.**
**In Riyadh, Saudi Arabia: The International Law Firm, Sulaymaniyah Center, Tahlia Street, P.O. Box 22166. Telephone: (966-1) 462-8866. Telecopier: (966-1) 462-9001.**
**In Taipei, Taiwan: 8th Floor, 2 Tun Hwa South Road, Section 2. Telephone: (886-2) 704-6808. Telecopier: (886-2) 704-6791.**
**In Tokyo, Japan: Toranomon MT Building, 4th Floor, 10-3, Toranomon 3-Chome, Minato-ku, Tokyo 105, Japan. Telephone: 81-3-3433-3939. Telecopier: 81-3-5401-2725.**
**In Washington, D.C.: Metropolitan Square, 1450 G Street, N.W. Telephone: 202-879-3939. Cable Address: "Attorneys Washington." Telex: 89-2410 ATTORNEYS WASH. Telecopier: 202-737-2832.**

***See Professional Biographies, LOS ANGELES, CALIFORNIA***

**Juo, James** '67 '93 C.158 B.S.E.E. L.273 J.D. (adm. in VA; not adm. in CA) [A Fulwider P.L.&U.]
*PRACTICE AREAS: Intellectual Property.
**Kang, Jonathan Y.** ....................... '61 '93 C.112 B.S. L.426 J.D. [A Loeb&L.]
*LANGUAGES: Korean.
*PRACTICE AREAS: Patent; Trademark; Copyright.
**King, Stephen L.,** (AV) ...........'31 '62 C.350 B.S.E.E. L.569 J.D. [C Blakely,S.T.&Z.]
**Klein, Henry,** (AV) ...................... '49 '75 C.1044 B.A. L.1049 J.D. [Ladas&P.]
**Kleinberg, Marvin H.,** (AV) ........... '27 '54 C.112 B.A. L.1066 J.D. [Arant,K.L.&R.]
*PRACTICE AREAS: Domestic and International Patent Prosecution; Intellectual Property; Patents; Trademarks; Intellectual Property Litigation.
**Konrad, William K.** .............................. '52 '77 C&L.339 B.S., J.D. [Loeb&L.]
*PRACTICE AREAS: Trademark; Patent; Copyright.
**Kovelman, Gilbert G.,** (AV) ........'36 '60 C.186 B.E.E. L.273 J.D. [Fulwider P.L.&U.]
*PRACTICE AREAS: Patent, Trademark, Copyright and Unfair Competition Law; Litigation.
**Kovelman, Paul H.** .................... '60 '92 C.1077 B.S.E.E. L.809 J.D. [A Loeb&L.]
*PRACTICE AREAS: Patent.

**Kovelman, Robert L.** ................'63 '91 C.112 B.A. L.809 J.D. [[A] Fulwider P.L.&U.]
*PRACTICE AREAS: Patent, Trademark, Copyright and Unfair Competition Law; Litigation.

**Kramsky, Elliott N., Law Offices of**
**(See Woodland Hills)**

**Kwasigroch, Lois M.** ..............................'— '87 C.766 B.A. L.426 J.D. [Lyon&L.]
*PRACTICE AREAS: Intellectual Property. A

**Ladas & Parry, (AV)**
**5670 Wilshire Boulevard, 90036⊙**
**Telephone: 213-934-2300 Telex: 240423 Cable Address: "LAWLAN LSA" Telecopier: 213-934-0202**
**URL: http://www.ladas.com**
**Members of Firm: Richard P. Berg; Henry Klein; Colin P. Abrahams; Mavis S. Gallenson; Francie R. Gorowitz. Associates: Iris Smith-Hess; France D. Lemoine; Richard J. Paciulan (Not admitted in CA); John Palmer. Of Counsel: Ira M. Siegel; Kam C. Louie. Patent Agent: Don A. Hollingsworth.**
**Patent, Trademark, Copyright, Unfair Competition, Licensing, Entertainment and Litigation.**
**New York, New York Office: 26 West 61st Street. Telephone: 212-708-1800. Telex: 233288. Telecopy: 212-246-8959. Cable Address: "Lawlan New York".**
**Chicago, Illinois Office: 224 South Michigan Avenue. Telephone: 312-427-1300. Telex: 203649. Telecopy: 312-427-6663; 312-427-6668. Cable Address: "Lawlan Chicago".**
**London, England Office: High Holborn House, 52-54 High Holborn, WC1V 6RR. Telephone: 44-71-242-5566. Telex: 262433 MONREF G. Telecopy: 44-71-405-1908 (Groups 2 & 3). Cable Address: "Lawlan London W.C.1".**
**Munich, Germany Office: Altheimer Eck 2, D-80331 Munich. Telephone: (089) 269077. Fax: (089) 269040. Cable Address: "Lawlan Munich".**

***See Professional Biographies, LOS ANGELES, CALIFORNIA***

**Lau, Ying-Kit** ........................'53 '86 C.966 B.S. L.178 J.D. [[A] Robbins,B.&C.]
*LANGUAGES: Chinese (Mandarin and Cantonese).
*PRACTICE AREAS: International Technology Transfers Law; Pharmaceutical and Chemical Technology Law; Business Planning Law; Litigation in the Peoples' Republic of China.

**LaVoie, Paul T.** ......................'65 '94 C&L.101 B.A., J.D. [[A] Fulwider P.L.&U.]
*PRACTICE AREAS: Patent; Trademark.

**Lerner, Marshall A.**, (AV) ..........'41 '66 C.570 B.S.E.E. L.273 J.D. [Arant,K.L.&R.]
*PRACTICE AREAS: Intellectual Property Litigation; Patent and Trademark Prosecution; Advertising Injury; Trade Secrets.

**Lippman, Peter I.**, (AV) ..................'39 '82 C.111 B.S. L.809 J.D. [Ashen,G.&L.]⊙

**Litovsky, Allan Z.** ......................'58 '96 C.061 B.S. L.36 J.D. [[A] Jones,D.R.&P.]

**Livornese, Don F.** ........................'60 '86 C.174 B.S.M.E. L.273 J.D. [Loeb&L.]
*PRACTICE AREAS: Patent; Trademark; Copyright; Intellectual Property Litigation; Antitrust.

**Loeb & Loeb LLP, (AV)** BB
**A Limited Liability Partnership including Professional Corporations**
**Suite 1800, 1000 Wilshire Boulevard, 90017-2475⊙**
**Telephone: 213-688-3400 Facsimile: 213-688-3460; 688-3461; 688-3462**
**Members of Firm: Alex Chartove (Washington, D.C. Office); Richard J. Codding (Century City Office); Evan Finkel (Century City Office); Jay M. Finkelstein (Washington, D.C. Office); David W. Grace; William K. Konrad (Century City Office); Don F. Livornese (Century City Office); Stuart Lubitz (Century City Office); Gary D. Mann (Century City Office); Stephen R. Mick; Victor A. Rodgers; David M. Simon (Century City Office); Roger R. Wise (Century City Office); Richard H. Zaitlen (Century City Office). Senior Counsel: Louis A. Mok (Century City Office); John P. Scherlacher (Century City Office). Associates: Stephen Bongini (Century City Office); Ying Chen (Century City Office); Philippe O. Erwin (Century City Office); Jonathan Y. Kang (Century City Office); Paul H. Kovelman (Century City Office); David L. Lubitz; David Alan Makman (Century City Office); Paul G. Nagy (Century City Office); Chris P. Perque (Century City Office); Ted Rittmaster (Century City Office); David W. Victor (Century City Office); Joseph F. von Sauers (Century City Office); Weining Yang (Century City Office); Wendy W. Yang (Century City Office).**
**General Civil Practice.**
**Century City, California Office: Suite 2200, 10100 Santa Monica Boulevard, Los Angeles, 90067-4164. Telephone: 310-282-2000. Facsimile: 310-282-2191; 282-2192.**
**New York, N.Y. Office: 345 Park Avenue, 10154-0037. Telephone: 212-407-4000. Facsimile: 212-407-4990.**
**Washington, D.C. Office: Suite 601, 2100 M Street N.W., 20037-1207. Telephone: 202-223-5700. Facsimile: 202-223-5704.**
**Nashville, Tennessee Office: 45 Music Square West, 37203-3205. Telephone: 615-749-8300; Facsimile: 615-749-8308.**
**Rome, Italy Office: Piazza Digione 1, 00197. Telephone: 011-396-808-8456. Facsimile: 011-396-808-8288.**

***See Professional Biographies, LOS ANGELES, CALIFORNIA***

**Losk, Jonathan T.** ..........................'58 '94 C.112 B.A. L.426 J.D. [[A] Lyon&L.]
*PRACTICE AREAS: Patent, Trademark, Contract and Unfair Competition; Intellectual Property.

**Louie, Kam C.** ............................'50 '79 C.112 B.A. L.1067 J.D. [[C] Ladas&P.]

**Lubitz, David L.** ..........................'66 '92 C.112 B.S. L.339 J.D. [[A] Loeb&L.]
*PRACTICE AREAS: Patent, Trademark and Copyright; International; Litigation.

**Lubitz, Stuart**, (AV) ......................'34 '61 C.260 B.E.E. L.273 LL.B. [Loeb&L.]
*PRACTICE AREAS: Trademark; Patent; Copyright.

**Lyon, Richard E., Jr., (A Professional Corporation)**, (AV) '43 '70
C.813 B.S. L.878 J.D. [Lyon&L.]
*PRACTICE AREAS: Patent, Trademark, Unfair Competition; Licensing of Intellectual Property; Intellectual Property.

**Lyon, Robert E., (A Professional Corporation)**, (AV) '36 '64
C&L.800 B.S., J.D. [Lyon&L.]
*PRACTICE AREAS: Patent, Trademark, Copyright, Unfair Competition; Intellectual Property.

**Lyon & Lyon LLP, (AV)** BB
**A Limited Liability Partnership including Professional Corporations**
**First Interstate World Center, 47th Floor, 633 West Fifth Street, 90071-2066⊙**
**Telephone: 213-489-1600 Fax: 213-955-0440**
**Email: lyon@lyonlyon.com URL: http://www.lyonlyon.com**
**Members of Firm: Roland N. Smoot; Conrad R. Solum, Jr.; James W. Geriak (A Professional Corporation) (Costa Mesa Office); Robert M. Taylor, Jr. (Costa Mesa Office); Samuel B. Stone (A Professional Corporation) (Costa Mesa Office); Douglas E. Olson (A Professional Corporation) (La Jolla Office); Robert E. Lyon (A Professional Corporation); Robert C. Weiss (A Professional Corporation); Richard E. Lyon, Jr., (A Professional Corporation); John D. McConaghy (A Professional Corporation); William C. Steffin (A Professional Corporation); Coe A. Bloomberg (A Professional Corporation); J. Donald McCarthy (A Professional Corporation); John M. Benassi (La Jolla Office); James H. Shalek; Allan W. Jansen (Costa Mesa Office); Robert W. Dickerson; Roy L. Anderson; David B. Murphy (Costa Mesa Office); James C. Brooks; Jeffrey M. Olson; Steven D. Hemminger (San Jose Office); Jerrold B. Reilly; Paul H. Meier; John A. Rafter, Jr.; Kenneth H. Ohriner; Mary S. Consalvi (La Jolla Office); Lois M. Kwasigroch; Robert C. Laurenson (La Jolla Office); Carol A. Schneider. Associates: Hope E. Melville; Michael J. Wise; Kurt T. Mulville (Costa Mesa Office); Theodore S. Maceiko; Richard Warburg (La Jolla Office); James P. Brogan (Costa Mesa Office); Jeffrey D. Tekanic; Corrine M. Freeman (Costa Mesa Office); David A. Randall; Christopher A. Vanderlaan; Bruce G. Chapman; David T. Burse (San Jose Office); Charles R. Balgenorth; Jeffrey A. Miller (San Jose Office); Jessica R. Wolff (La Jolla Office); Sheldon O. Heber (La Jolla Office); Jeffrey William Guise (La Jolla Office); David E. Wang; Kenneth S. Roberts (Costa Mesa Office); Brent D. Sokol; Clarke W. Neumann, Jr. (La Jolla Office); Thomas J. Brindisi; Jonathan T. Losk; Timothy J. Lithgow (La Jolla Office); Gary H. Silverstein (La Jolla Office); Amy Stark Hellenkamp (La Jolla Office); Howard N. Wisnia (La Jolla Office). Of Counsel: Bradford J. Duft (La Jolla Office); Suzanne L. Biggs (La Jolla Office); F.T. Alexandra Mahaney (La Jolla Office); Stephen S. Korniczky (La Jolla Office).**
**Intellectual Property Law including Patent, Trademark, Copyright, Trade Regulation, Unfair Competition and Antitrust Law. Litigation.**
**Costa Mesa, California Office: Suite 1200, 3200 Park Center Drive. Telephone: 714-751-6606. Fax: 714-751-8209.**
**San Jose, California Office: Suite 1150, 303 Almaden Boulevard. Telephone: 408-993-1555. Fax: 408-287-2664.**
**La Jolla, California Office: Suite 660, 4250 Executive Square. Telephone: 619-552-8400. Fax: 619-552-0159.**

***See Professional Biographies, LOS ANGELES, CALIFORNIA***

**MacDermott, Michael J.**, (AV) ............'50 '75 C.477 B.S. L.1068 J.D. [Pretty,S.&P.]
*PRACTICE AREAS: Patents; Trademarks; Copyrights; Unfair Competition.

**Maceiko, Theodore S.** ....................'62 '90 C.158 B.S.M.E. L.426 J.D. [[A] Lyon&L.]
*PRACTICE AREAS: Patent, Trademark, Unfair Competition, Antitrust; Intellectual Property.

**Maher, Pamela G.** ....................'59 '92 C.94 B.S. L.426 J.D. [[A] Fulwider P.L.&U.]
*PRACTICE AREAS: Intellectual Property Law.

**Majcher, Thomas H.** ..................'57 '83 C.816 B.E. L.809 J.D. [Fulwider P.L.&U.]
*PRACTICE AREAS: Patent, Trademark, Copyright and Unfair Competition Law; Litigation.

**Makman, David Alan** ......................'63 '95 C.604 A.B. L.228 J.D. [[A] Loeb&L.]
*LANGUAGES: Japanese.
*PRACTICE AREAS: Intellectual Property.

**Mallery, Daniel C. '60 '91 C.112 B.S. L.273 J.D.**
**1875 Century Park East, Suite 700, 90067**
**Telephone: 310-551-5252 Fax: 310-551-5251**
**Email: DCM100@concentric.net**
**Intellectual Property, Patent, Trademark, Copyright and Unfair Competition.**

***See Professional Biographies, LOS ANGELES, CALIFORNIA***

**Mandell, Lee Jay** ....................'48 '91 C.688 M.E.E.E. L.809 J.D. [Freilich,H.&R.]
*PRACTICE AREAS: Patent; Patent Applications.

**Mann, Gary D.** ..............................'50 '80 C.871 B.S. L.345 J.D. [Loeb&L.]
*PRACTICE AREAS: Patent; Trademark; Copyright; Litigation.

**Mattes, Bradford E.** ..............'56 '92 C.326 B.S.M.E. L.990 J.D. [[A] Arant,K.L.&R.]
*PRACTICE AREAS: Intellectual Property Litigation; Patent and Trademark Prosecution; Trade Secrets.

**May, John M.** ........................'41 '66 C.111 B.S. L.1068 LL.B. [Robbins,B.&C.]
*LANGUAGES: French, German, Russian (reading only).
*PRACTICE AREAS: Patents; Trademarks; Copyrights; Licensing.

**McBride, Kevin G.**, (AV⑦) '54 '85 C.602 B.S. L.597 J.D.
(adm. in IL; not adm. in CA) [Jones,D.R.&P.]

**McCarthy, J. Donald, (A Professional Corporation)**, (AV) '42 '68
C.188 B.M.E. L.309 J.D. [Lyon&L.]
*PRACTICE AREAS: Patent, Trademark, Copyright, Trade Regulation; Unfair Competition, Antitrust; Intellectual Property.

**McConaghy, John D., (A Professional Corporation)**, (AV) '43 '72
C.800 B.S.M.E. L.1068 J.D. [Lyon&L.]
*PRACTICE AREAS: Patent, Trademark; Intellectual Property.

**Meier, Paul H.** ..............................'57 '84 C.112 B.S. L.1066 J.D. [Lyon&L.]
*PRACTICE AREAS: Intellectual Property.

**Melville, Hope E.** ..........................'51 '89 C.957 B.S. L.800 J.D. [[A] Lyon&L.]
*PRACTICE AREAS: Patent, Trademark, Copyright, Unfair Competition; Intellectual Property.

**Merchant & Gould, (AV)**
**Suite 400, 11150 Santa Monica Boulevard, 90025⊙**
**Telephone: 310-445-1140 Facsimile: 310-445-9031**
**Email: info@merchant-gould.com URL: http://www.merchant-gould.com**
**Raymond A. Bogucki; Gregory B. Wood; George Henry Gates, III; Charles Berman;—Janice A. Sharp; Michael B. Farber; Sarah B. Adriano (Not admitted in CA); Victor G. Cooper; Ben M. Davidson.**
**Patent, Trademark and Copyright Law, Licensing, Trade Secrets, Unfair Competition, Computer Law and Related Litigation.**
**Representative Clients: AT&T Global Information Solutions; Airtouch Communications; Bristol Myers Squibb Co.; University of California.**
**Minneapolis, Minnesota Office: Merchant, Gould, Smith, Edell, Welter & Schmidt, Professional Association, 3100 Norwest Center, 90 South 7th Street. Telephone: 612-332-5300. Facsimile: 612-332-9081.**
**St. Paul, Minnesota Office: Merchant, Gould, Smith, Edell, Welter & Schmidt, Professional Association, One Thousand Norwest Center, 55 E. 5th Street. Telephone: 612-298-1055. Facsimile: 612-298-1160.**

***See Professional Biographies, LOS ANGELES, CALIFORNIA***

**Mick, Stephen R.** ..............................'63 '87 C.688 B.S. L.659 J.D. [Loeb&L.]
*PRACTICE AREAS: Intellectual Property; Litigation.

**Mok, Louis A.**, (AV) ......................'32 '63 C.688 B.M.E. L.800 J.D. [[C] Loeb&L.]
*PRACTICE AREAS: Patent; Trademark; Copyright.

**Nagy, John S.** ......................'51 '81 C.932 B.S.I.E. L.209 J.D. [Fulwider P.L.&U.]
*PRACTICE AREAS: Patent, Trademark, Copyright and Unfair Competition Law; Litigation.

**Nagy, Paul G.** ..........................'62 '94 C.112 B.S. L.426 J.D. [[A] Loeb&L.]
*PRACTICE AREAS: Patent Prosecution; Intellectual Property; Antitrust.

**Ohriner, Kenneth H.** ....................'56 '87 C.1044 B.E.M.E. L.724 J.D. [Lyon&L.]
*PRACTICE AREAS: Intellectual Property.

**Olson, Jeffrey M.**, (AV) ......................'55 '82 C.339 B.S. L.477 J.D. [Lyon&L.]
*PRACTICE AREAS: Intellectual Property.

**Paciulan, Richard J.** '47 '77 C.588 B.S.E.E. L.818 J.D.
(adm. in MA; not adm. in CA) [[A] Ladas&P.]

**Palmer, John** ..............................'— '90 C.976 B.A. L.893 J.D. [[A] Ladas&P.]

**Park, John K., & Associates '60 '94 C.1167 B.S.E. L.809 J.D.**
**445 South Figueroa, Twenty-Seventh Floor, 90071-1603**
**Telephone: 213-612-7730 Fax: 213-426-2171**
***LANGUAGES: Korean.**
***PRACTICE AREAS: Patent; Trademark; Copyright; Trade Secrets; Contracts.**
**Intellectual Property, Patent, Trademarks, Copyright, Contracts and Licensing.**

***See Professional Biographies, LOS ANGELES, CALIFORNIA***

**Parkhurst, David G.**, (BV) .........'47 '73 C.112 B.A. L.800 J.D. [[A] Fulwider P.L.&U.]
*PRACTICE AREAS: Patent, Trademark, Copyright and Unfair Competition Law; Litigation.

**Paul, James W.** ................'38 '79 C.608 B.S.M.E. L.1179 J.D. [Fulwider P.L.&U.]
*PRACTICE AREAS: Patent, Trademark, Copyright and Unfair Competition Law; Litigation.

**Perez, Ronald E.** ..................'56 '90 C.608 B.S. L.966 J.D. [[A] Fulwider P.L.&U.]
*PRACTICE AREAS: Patent, Trademark, Copyright and Unfair Competition Law; Litigation.

**Perque, Chris P.** ..............................'63 '91 C.420 B.S. L.861 J.D. [[A] Loeb&L.]

**Poplawski, Edward G.** ................'57 '84 C.223 B.S.M.E. L.884 J.D. [Pretty,S.&P.]
*PRACTICE AREAS: Patents; Trademarks; Copyrights; Trade Secrets; Unfair Competition.

**Pretty, Laurence H.**, (AV) ..................'36 '69 C.054 B.S. L.273 J.D. [Pretty,S.&P.]
*PRACTICE AREAS: Patents; Trademarks; Copyrights; Unfair Competition; Litigation.

**Pretty, Schroeder & Poplawski, A Professional Corporation, (AV)** BB
**Suite 2000, 444 South Flower Street, 90071**
**Telephone: 213-622-7700 Telecopier: 213-489-4210**
**Laurence H. Pretty; Robert A. Schroeder; Edward G. Poplawski; Mark Garscia; Jeffrey F. Craft; Michael J. MacDermott. Counsel: Richard A. Wallen. Of Counsel: Walton Eugene Tinsley;—Anne Wang; Marc E. Hankin.**
**Patents, Trademarks, Copyrights and Unfair Competition Law. Litigation.**

***See Professional Biographies, LOS ANGELES, CALIFORNIA***

**Rafter, John A., Jr.** ..........................'56 '86 C.602 B.S. L.426 J.D. [Lyon&L.]
*PRACTICE AREAS: Patent; Intellectual Property.

**Ram, Michael J.** ....................'40 '72 C.390 B.S.Ch.E. L.776 J.D. [Arant,K.L.&R.]
*PRACTICE AREAS: Domestic and International Patent Prosecution; Domestic and International Trademark Prosecution; Trade Secrets; Medical Patents and Technology; Licensing.

**Randall, David A.** ..............................'63 '91 C.37 B.S. L.36 J.D. [[A] Lyon&L.]
*PRACTICE AREAS: Patent, Trademark, Copyright, Unfair Competition; Intellectual Property.

**Reagin, Ronald W.**, (AV) ...........'36 '62 C.502 B.S. L.273 LL.B. [[C] Blakely,S.T.&Z.]

**Reilly, Jerrold B.** ..............................'47 '76 C.93 B.S. L.823 J.D. [Lyon&L.]
*PRACTICE AREAS: Intellectual Property.

**Rittmaster, Ted** ........................'61 '90 C.800 B.S.E.E. L.128 J.D. [[A] Loeb&L.]
*PRACTICE AREAS: Patent Prosecution.

**Robbins, Billy A.**, (AV) ...............'26 '58 C.45 B.S.E.E. L.800 J.D. [Robbins,B.&C.]
*PRACTICE AREAS: Patent Law; Trademark Law; Copyright Law; Trade Secret Law; Unfair Competition Law.

**Robbins, Berliner & Carson, (AV)**
**Fifth Floor, Figueroa Plaza, 201 North Figueroa Street, 90012-2628**
Telephone: 213-977-1001 Telecopier: 213-977-1003
Members of Firm: Billy A. Robbins; Robert Berliner; John Carson; Michael S. Elkind; John M. May; Clark D. Gross. Associates: Ying-Kit Lau; Horacio A. Farach; Sharon Wong; Pete A. Smits; Wean Khing Wong. Of Counsel: John P. Spitals.
Patent, Trademark, Copyright and Unfair Competition Law. Trial and Appellate Practice in all Federal and State Courts.
*See Professional Biographies, LOS ANGELES, CALIFORNIA*

**Rodgers, Victor A.** .........................'58 '81 C.800 B.S. L.1066 J.D. [Loeb&L.]
*PRACTICE AREAS: Trademark; Patent; Copyright.
**Rosen, Leon D.**, (AV) ..................'37 '62 C.145 B.A. L.178 LL.B. [Freilich,H.&R.]
*PRACTICE AREAS: Patent Law; Trademark Law; Patent Applications; Licensing Law.
**Runk, Thomas A.** ......................'48 '81 C.422 B.S. L.1137 J.D. [Fulwider P.L.&U.]
*PRACTICE AREAS: Patent, Trademark, Copyright and Unfair Competition Law; Litigation.
**Scherlacher, John P.**, (AV) ..........'38 '66 C.923 B.S.B.E. L.273 LL.B. [B Loeb&L.]
*PRACTICE AREAS: Patent; Trademark.
**Schewe, Edward C.** ......................'57 '89 C.36 B.S. L.990 J.D. [A Bright&L.]
*PRACTICE AREAS: Intellectual Property Law.
**Schneider, Carol A.** .......................'51 '88 C.112 B.A. L.800 J.D. [Lyon&L.]
*PRACTICE AREAS: Patent; Intellectual Property.
**Schroeder, Robert A.**, (AV) ...............'42 '69 C.158 B.S. L.188 J.D. [Pretty,S.&P.]
*PRACTICE AREAS: Patents; Trademarks; Copyrights; Unfair Competition; Litigation.
**Shalek, James H.** ..........................'53 '78 C.659 B.A. L.94 J.D. [Lyon&L.]
*PRACTICE AREAS: Patent, Trademark, Copyright; Intellectual Property.
**Sharp, Janice A.** ..........................'51 '90 C.061 B.Sc. L.1137 J.D. [A Merchant&G.]
*PRACTICE AREAS: Patent Law; Trademark Law; Copyright Law; Biotechnology Law.
**Siegel, Ira M.**, (AV) ......................'49 '77 C.563 B.E.E.E. L.472 J.D. [B Ladas&P.]
**Simon, David M.** ..........................'57 '82 C.453 S.B. L.276 J.D. [Loeb&L.]
*PRACTICE AREAS: Trademark; Patent; Copyright; Intellectual Property.
**Small, Thomas M.**, (AV) ...................'33 '57 C.679 B.S. L.1119 J.D. [Small L.&K.]
*PRACTICE AREAS: Trademark, Patent and Copyright; Arbitration; Mediation.

**Small Larkin & Kiddé, (AV)**
**10940 Wilshire Boulevard, Eighteenth Floor, 90024**
Telephone: 310-209-4400 Fax: 310-209-4450 Cable Address: SLK MARK Telex: 49616151
Email: SLK@SLKlaw.com URL: http://www.lainet.com/legal/
Members of Firm: Thomas M. Small; Jon E. Hokanson;—Donald J. Cox, Jr.
Domestic and International Intellectual Property Law, including Counseling, Due Diligence Investigations, Litigation and Licensing in Trademark, Patent, Copyright, Unfair Competition, Trade Secrets and related matters and Business and Commercial Litigation.
*See Professional Biographies, LOS ANGELES, CALIFORNIA*

**Smith-Hess, Iris** ...............................'— '82 L.1136 J.D. [A Ladas&P.]
**Smits, Pete A.** ......................'61 '90 C.475 B.S.E.E. L.846 J.D. [A Robbins,B.&C.]
*LANGUAGES: Latvian and Spanish.
*PRACTICE AREAS: Litigation; Trademark Law; Copyright Law; Patent Law; Intellectual Property.
**Smoot, Roland N.**, (AV) ...................'25 '55 C.111 B.S. L.276 J.D. [Lyon&L.]
*PRACTICE AREAS: Patent, Trademark, Trade Regulation, Unfair Competition; Intellectual Property.
**Sokol, Brent D.** ............................'64 '93 C.597 B.S. L.94 J.D. [A Lyon&L.]
*PRACTICE AREAS: Patent, Trademark, Copyright, Antitrust; Trade Secret, Unfair Competition; Intellectual Property.
**Sokoloff, Stanley W.**, (AV) .......'38 '66 C.971 B.S.Ch.E. L.818 J.D. [Blakely,S.T.&Z.]
**Solum, Conrad R., Jr.**, (AV) ...............'35 '60 C&L.800 B.E., LL.B. [Lyon&L.]
*PRACTICE AREAS: Patent, Trademark, Copyright, Unfair Competition; Intellectual Property.
**Sommers, Howard N.** ..........'42 '67 C.124 B.S.E.E. L.569 J.D. [B Fulwider P.L.&U.]
*REPORTED CASES: Raceway Components, Inc. v. Butler Mfg. Co., F.Supp. 856; 11 USPQ2d 1799 (USDC, SDWVa, 1989) MW; Cento Group, S.p.A. v. OroAmerica, Inc., 822 F.Supp 1058 (USDC, SDNY, 1993).
*PRACTICE AREAS: Patent Law; Trademark Law; Copyright Law; Unfair Competition Law.
**Spitals, John P.** ......................'53 '80 C.103 Sc.B. L.564 J.D. [B Robbins,B.&C.]
*LANGUAGES: French, German, Italian, Spanish.
*PRACTICE AREAS: Patent Prosecution Law (Biological and Chemical).
**Steffin, William C., (A Professional Corporation)**, (AV) '45 '72
C.966 B.S.Ch.E. L.1065 LL.B. [Lyon&L.]
*PRACTICE AREAS: Patent, Trademark, Copyright, Unfair Competition; Intellectual Property.
**Strauss, Stephen J.** ......................'56 '83 C.30 B.A. L.809 J.D. [Fulwider P.L.&U.]
*PRACTICE AREAS: Patent, Trademark, Copyright and Unfair Competition Law; Litigation.
**Stull, Paul M.** .......................'52 '77 C.967 B.A. L.477 J.D. [A Fulwider P.L.&U.]
*PRACTICE AREAS: Patent, Trademark, Copyright and Unfair Competition Law; Litigation.
**Tekanic, Jeffrey D.** .......................'66 '91 C.111 B.S. L.145 J.D. [A Lyon&L.]
*PRACTICE AREAS: Patent, Trademark, Trade Regulation, Unfair Competition, Antitrust; Intellectual Property.
**Tinsley, Walton Eugene**, (AV) ...........'21 '54 C.150 E.E. L.800 J.D. [B Pretty,S.&P.]
*PRACTICE AREAS: Patents; Trademarks; Unfair Competition.
**Touton, Louis L.** ......................'55 '82 C.453 S.B.E.E. L.178 J.D. [Jones,D.R.&P.]
**Tyson, Timothy T.** ......................'43 '77 C.880 B.A. L.809 J.D. [Freilich,H.&R.]
*PRACTICE AREAS: Patent, Trademark and Copyright Law; Trademark Law; Copyright Law; Litigation; Licensing Law.
**Vanderlaan, Christopher A.** ...............'65 '91 C.112 B.S. L.1065 J.D. [Lyon&L.]
*PRACTICE AREAS: Intellectual Property.
**Victor, David W.** ......................'65 '93 C.112 B.A. L.800 J.D. [A Loeb&L.]
**von Sauers, Joseph F.** ..................'59 '92 C.433 B.E.E.E. L.809 J.D. [A Loeb&L.]
*PRACTICE AREAS: Intellectual Property; Entertainment Law.
**Wallen, Richard A.**, (AV) ..................'37 '63 C.112 B.A. L.800 J.D. [Pretty,S.&P.]
*PRACTICE AREAS: Patents; Trademarks; Copyrights; Unfair Competition.
**Wang, Anne** .............................'62 '90 C.112 B.S. L.800 J.D. [A Pretty,S.&P.]
*LANGUAGES: Chinese (Mandarin).
*PRACTICE AREAS: Patent Law; Trademark Law.
**Wang, David E.** ......................'64 '93 C.800 B.S.E.E. L.1066 J.D. [A Lyon&L.]
*LANGUAGES: German and Chinese.
*PRACTICE AREAS: Patent, Trademark, Copyright, Unfair Competition, Antitrust; Intellectual Property.

**Weiss, David, (AV) '35 '65 C.112 B.S. L.1068 J.D.**
**2551 Colorado Boulevard, 90041**
Telephone: 213-254-5020 Telecopier: 213-254-4538
Technology, Patent, Trademark, and Copyright Law, Unfair Competition and Intellectual Property Law.
*See Professional Biographies, LOS ANGELES, CALIFORNIA*

**Weiss, Robert C., (A Professional Corporation)**, (AV) '40 '67
C.112 B.S.M.E. L.800 J.D. [Lyon&L.]
*PRACTICE AREAS: Patent, Trademark, Copyright, Trade Regulation; Unfair Competition, Antitrust, Litigation; Intellectual Property.
**Weyer, Frank M.** ......................'57 '87 C.999 B.E. L.1066 J.D. [A Hecker&H.]
**Wise, Michael J.** ......................'61 '89 C.112 B.S. L.426 J.D. [A Lyon&L.]
*PRACTICE AREAS: Patent, Trademark, Copyright, Unfair Competition; Antitrust; Intellectual Property.
**Wise, Roger R.** ......................'56 '84 C.339 B.S.E.E. L.365 J.D. [Loeb&L.]
*PRACTICE AREAS: Trademark; Patent; Copyright.
**Wong, Sharon** ......................'64 '92 C.112 B.S. L.426 J.D. [A Robbins,B.&C.]
*LANGUAGES: Chinese (Cantonese).
*PRACTICE AREAS: Patent Law; Trademark Law; Copyright Law; Unfair Competition Law.
**Wong, Wean Khing** ......................'60 '87 C.453 B.S. L.809 J.D. [A Robbins,B.&C.]
*LANGUAGES: Mandarin, Cantonese and Malay.
*PRACTICE AREAS: Patent Law; Trademark Law; Copyright Law.
**Wood, Gregory B.**, (AV) ...............'45 '75 C.112 B.S. L.1095 J.D. [Merchant&G.]
**Yang, Weining** ......................'63 '95 C.061 M.S. L.426 J.D. [A Loeb&L.]
*LANGUAGES: Chinese.
*PRACTICE AREAS: Patent Prosecution.
**Yang, Wendy W.** ......................'68 '95 C.112 B.A. L.94 J.D. [A Loeb&L.]
*LANGUAGES: Taiwanese and Mandarin.
*PRACTICE AREAS: Intellectual Property.
**Zafman, Norman**, (AV) ..............'34 '70 C.563 B.E.E. L.809 J.D. [Blakely,S.T.&Z.]
**Zaitlen, Richard H.**, (AV) ...............'46 '73 C.679 B.S.Ch.E. L.273 J.D. [Loeb&L.]
*PRACTICE AREAS: Trademark; Patent; Copyright.

## MENLO PARK, 28,040, *San Mateo Co.*

**Arnold, White & Durkee, A Professional Corporation, (AV)**
**155 Linfield Drive, 94025-3741**
Telephone: 415-614-4500 Facsimile: 415-614-4599
Email: info@awd.com URL: http://www.awd.com
Gerald P. Dodson; Glenn W. Rhodes; David L. Bilsker; James F. Valentine; Mark K. Dickson; Thomas C. Mavrakakis; Emily A. Evans; Karen J. Kramer (Not admitted in CA); John R. Moore (Not admitted in CA).
Intellectual Property including Patent, Trademark, Copyright, Trade Secret, Unfair Competition, Licensing and Related Government Agency Proceedings, Antitrust and International Trade Matters. Trials and Appeals in Federal and State Courts.
Houston, Texas Office: 750 Bering Drive, 77057-2198; P.O. Box 4433, 77210-4433. Telephone: 713-787-1400. Facsimile: 713-789-2679. Telex: 79-0924.
Austin, Texas Office: 1900 One American Center, 600 Congress Avenue, 78701-3248. Telephone: 512-418-3000. Facsimile: 512-474-7577.
Arlington, Virginia Office: 2001 Jefferson Davis Highway, Suite 401, 22202-3604. Telephone: 703-415-1720. Facsimile: 703-415-1728.
Chicago, Illinois Office: 800 Quaker Tower, 321 North Clark Street, 60610-4714. Telephone: 312-744-0090. Facsimile: 312-755-4489.
Minneapolis, Minnesota Office: 4850 First Bank Place, 601 Second Avenue South, 55402-4320. Telephone: 612-321-2800. Facsimile: 612-321-9600.
*See Professional Biographies, MENLO PARK, CALIFORNIA*

**Barr, Robert** ...........................'47 '74 C.453 S.B.E.E. L.94 J.D. [Weil,G.&M.]
*PRACTICE AREAS: Intellectual Property.
**Becker, Daniel M.** ......................'59 '95 C.309 B.A. L.813 J.D. [A Pennie&E.]
*PRACTICE AREAS: Intellectual Property; Patent Law.
**Benz, William H.**, (AV) ...............'42 '71 C.25 B.S.C. L.767 J.D. [Burns,D.S.&M.]
**Bilsker, David L.** ..................'62 '90 C.178 B.S.Ch.E. L.260 J.D. [Arnold,W.&D.]
**Borovoy, Roger S.**, (AV) ...............'35 '60 C.453 B.S. L.309 LL.B. [B Fish&R.]
*PRACTICE AREAS: Intellectual Property; Patent.
**Bozicevic, Karl**, (AV) ......................'52 '78 C.861 B.S. L.1206 J.D. [Fish&R.]
*PRACTICE AREAS: Medical Devices and Biotechnology; Cell and Molecular Biology; Biochemistry; Molecular Genetics; Biomedical Sciences.
**Bright, Earl A., II** ...............'65 '93 C&L.623 B.S.M.E., J.D. [A Burns,D.S.&M.]

**Burns, Doane, Swecker & Mathis, L.L.P., (AV)**
**Building 4, Suite 160, 3000 Sand Hill Road, 94025**
Telephone: 415-854-7400 Facsimile: 415-854-8275
Email: burnsdoane.com
Ralph L. Freeland, Jr.; James W. Peterson; Robert E. Krebs; T. Gene Dillahunty (Not admitted in CA); William H. Benz; Gerald F. Swiss. Associates: Michael J. Ure; Leslie A. Mooi; Earl A. Bright II; Charles H. Jew.
Patent, Trademark, Copyright, Trade, Unfair Competition and Related, Antitrust Law. Litigation. Practice before State and Federal Courts and U.S. International and Administrative Agencies.
Alexandria, Virginia Office: Suite 100, 699 Prince Street, 22314, P.O. Box 1404, 22313. Telephone: 703-836-6620. Facsimile: 703-836-2021; 836-7356; 836-3503; Group 4: 703-836-0028.
Research Triangle Park, North Carolina Office: P.O. Box 14846, Research Triangle Park, 27709-4846, 1009 Slatter Road, Suite 210, Durham, 27703. Telephone: 919-941-9240. Facsimile: 919-941-1515.
*See Professional Biographies, MENLO PARK, CALIFORNIA*

**Chao, Bernard H.** ..................'65 '90 C.679 B.S.E.E. L.228 J.D. [A Pennie&E.]
*PRACTICE AREAS: Intellectual Property; Litigation.
**Daiuto, Brian J.** ..................'64 '95 C.8 B.S.E.E. L.1066 J.D. [A Pennie&E.]
*PRACTICE AREAS: Intellectual Property; Patent Prosecution; Patent Litigation.
**De Stefano, Paul R.** ..................'50 '75 C.216 B.A. L.800 J.D. [Pennie&E.]
*LANGUAGES: German and French.
*PRACTICE AREAS: Intellectual Property; International Transactional Work related to the Biological Sciences.
**Dickson, Mark K.** ..................'55 '88 C.1196 B.S. L.326 J.D. [Arnold,W.&D.]
**Dillahunty, T. Gene** '42 '69 C.612 B.S.Ch.E. L.273 J.D.
(adm. in VA; not adm. in CA) [Burns,D.S.&M.]
**Dodson, Gerald P.**, (AV) ...........'47 '72 C.390 B.S.M.E. L.446 J.D. [Arnold,W.&D.]
**Egan, William J., III** ..................'47 '75 C.420 B.S.E.E. L.861 J.D. [Fish&R.]
*PRACTICE AREAS: Intellectual Property; Patents; Trademarks; Copyrights; Trade Secrets.

**Enterprise Law Group, Inc., (AV)**
**Menlo Oaks Corporate Center, 4400 Bohannon Drive, Suite 280, 94025-1041**
Telephone: 415-462-4700 Facsimile: 415-462-4747
Email: info@enterpriselaw.com
William B. Walker.
Business Transactional, Intellectual Property and Business Litigation, Practice Representing Domestic Technology Clients and Technology and Other Clients Headquartered Outside of the U.S.
*See Professional Biographies, MENLO PARK, CALIFORNIA*

**Evans, Emily A.** ..................'60 '92 C.178 B.S. L.262 J.D. [A Arnold,W.&D.]

**Fish & Richardson P.C., (AV)**
**2200 Sand Hill Road Suite 100, 94025**
Telephone: 415-322-5070 Fax: 415-854-0875
Email: info@fr.com URL: http://www.fr.com
Hans R. Troesch; John R. Schiffhauer; Karl Bozicevic; Jack L. Slobodin; William J. Egan, III; Reginald J. Suyat. Of Counsel: Mark A. Lemley; Roger S. Borovoy;—Wayne P. Sobon; David M. Shaw (Not admitted in CA); David J. Goren; Mark D. Kirkland; Audrey M. Sugimura.
Intellectual Property Law: Trials, Transactions, Patents, Trademarks, Copyrights, Trade Secrets, Entertainment Law, Telecommunications Law, Drug and Medical Device and Antitrust Law.
Washington, D.C. Office: 601 13th Street, N.W. Telephone: 202-783-5070. Fax: 202-783-2331.
Houston, Texas Office: One Riverway, Suite 1200. Telephone: 713-629-5070. Fax: 713-629-7811.
Boston, Massachusetts Office: 225 Franklin Street. Telephone: 617-542-5070. Fax: 617-542-8906. Telex: 200154.
Minneapolis, Minnesota Office: Fish & Richardson P.C., P.A., 60 South Sixth Street, Suite 3300. Telephone: 612-335-5070. Fax: 612-288-9696.
La Jolla, California Office: 4225 Executive Square, Suite 1400. Telephone: 619-678-5070. Fax: 619-678-5099.
New York, N.Y. Office: 45 Rockefeller Plaza, Suite 2800. Telephone: 212-765-5070. Fax: 212-258-2291.
*See Professional Biographies, MENLO PARK, CALIFORNIA*

**Fowler, Kathleen** ..................'60 '95 C.188 J.D. L.1065 J.D. [A Pennie&E.]
*PRACTICE AREAS: Patent Prosecution; Opinion Work; Intellectual Property; Biotechnology.
**Freeland, Ralph L., Jr.**, (AV) ...........'17 '47 C.813 B.A. L.273 J.D. [Burns,D.S.&M.]
**Goren, David J.** ..................'— '94 C.112 B.A. L.276 J.D. [A Fish&R.]
*PRACTICE AREAS: Intellectual Property; Patents; Trademarks.
**Greenwald, Bradley A.** ..................'62 '93 C.352 B.A. L.309 J.D. [A Pennie&E.]
*PRACTICE AREAS: Intellectual Property.

CAA5T

CALIFORNIA—MENLO PARK MARTINDALE-HUBBELL LAW DIRECTORY 1997

**Hadidi, Frederick F.** ........ '67 '92 C.188 B.S.E.E. L.813 J.D. [A Pennie&E.]
*PRACTICE AREAS: Intellectual Property; Patent Prosecution; Patent Litigation.
**Halluin, Albert P.** ........ '39 '70 C.420 B.A. L.64 J.D. [Pennie&E.]
*PRACTICE AREAS: Intellectual Property.
**Heit, Warren S.** ........ '65 '90 C.860 B.S.E.E. L.262 J.D. [A Pennie&E.]
*PRACTICE AREAS: Intellectual Property.
**Hoyng, Charles F.** ........ '50 '89 C.473 B.S. L.1066 J.D. [C Pennie&E.]
*PRACTICE AREAS: Licensing; Intellectual Property.
**Huntwork, Vicki L.** ........ '65 '91 C.472 B.S. L.575 J.D. [A Pennie&E.]
*PRACTICE AREAS: Intellectual Property; Corporate.
**Ishimoto, Lance K.** ........ '59 '94 C.112 B.A. L.813 J.D. [A Pennie&E.]
*PRACTICE AREAS: Intellectual Property.
**Jew, Charles H.** ........ '56 '85 C.178 B.A. L.569 J.D. [A Burns,D.S.&M.]
**Kirkland, Mark D.** ........ '62 '94 C.602 B.S.E.E. L.770 J.D. [A Fish&R.]
*PRACTICE AREAS: Patent; Technology Licensing; Trademark; Copyright.
**Kohler, Thomas D.** '61 '90 C.158 B.S.M.E. L.945 J.D.
(adm. in NY; not adm. in CA) [A Pennie&E.]
*PRACTICE AREAS: Intellectual Property; Medical and Mechanical Patents; Patent Litigation.
**Kramer, Karen J.** '64 '89 C.228 A.B. L.910 J.D.
(adm. in NY; not adm. in CA) [A Arnold,W.&D.]
**Krebs, Robert E.** ........ '43 '69 C&L.174 B.S., J.D. [Burns,D.S.&M.] & [C Pezzola&R.]
**Lee, Dennis Y.** ........ '64 '93 C.477 B.S.E.E. L.352 J.D. [A Weil,G.&M.]
**Lee, Victor K.** '58 '96 C.908 B.Sc. L.1009 J.D.
(adm. in NY; not adm. in CA) [A Pennie&E.]
*LANGUAGES: Chinese.
*PRACTICE AREAS: Biotechnology Patent Law; Intellectual Property.
**Lemley, Mark A.** ........ '66 '91 C.813 A.B. L.112 J.D. [C Fish&R.]
*PRACTICE AREAS: Intellectual Property; Antitrust.
**Lyons, Michael J.** '66 '93 C.645 B.S. L.276 J.D.
(adm. in NY; not adm. in CA) [A Pennie&E.]
*PRACTICE AREAS: Intellectual Property.
**Mandel, SaraLynn** ........ '56 '84 C.112 B.A. L.678 J.D. [C Pennie&E.]
*PRACTICE AREAS: Intellectual Property; Biotechnology.
**Mavrakakis, Thomas C.** ........ '64 '94 C.667 B.S.E.E. L.724 J.D. [A Arnold,W.&D.]
**Mooi, Leslie A.** ........ '59 '90 C&L.025 B.Sc., LL.B. [A Burns,D.S.&M.]
**Moore, John R.** '64 '92 C&L.953 B.S., J.D.
(adm. in NY; not adm. in CA) [Arnold,W.&D.]
**Pease, Ann M. Caviani** ........ '63 '95 C.966 B.S. L.813 J.D. [A Pennie&E.]
*PRACTICE AREAS: Intellectual Property.

**Pennie & Edmonds LLP**
**2730 Sand Hill Road, 94025⊙**
**Telephone: 415-854-3660 Fax: 415-854-3694**
**Email: pennie.com URL: http://www.pennie.com**
**Resident Partners: Jon R. Stark; Paul R. De Stefano; Albert P. Halluin. Resident Counsel: Charles F. Hoyng; SaraLynn Mandell. Resident Associates: Thomas D. Kohler (Not admitted in CA); Warren S. Heit; Michael J. Lyons (Not admitted in CA); Bernard H. Chao; Frederick F. Hadidi; Victor K. Lee (Not admitted in CA); Lance K. Ishimoto; Mark R. Scadina; William L. Wang; Daniel M. Becker; Brian J. Daiuto; Kathleen Fowler; Ann M. Caviani Pease; Vicki L. Huntwork; Bradley A. Greenwald.**
**Intellectual Property and Technology Litigation including Patent, Trademark, Trade Secrets, Copyright and Unfair Competition Causes, Computer and Communication Law and Related Government Agency Proceedings, Licensing, Arbitration and International Trade Matters. Trials and Appeals in all Federal and State Courts.**
**New York, N.Y. Office: 1155 Avenue of the Americas. Telephone: 212-790-9090. Telex: (WUI) 66141-Pennie. Cable Address: "Penangold." Facsimile: GII/GII/GIII (212) 869-9741; GIII (212) 869-8864.**
**Washington, D.C. Office: 1667 K Street, N.W., Suite 1000. Telephone: 202-496-4400. Facsimile: 202-496-4444.**

*See Professional Biographies, MENLO PARK, CALIFORNIA*

**Peterson, James W.**, (AV) ........ '44 '72 C.446 B.S. L.128 J.D. [Burns,D.S.&M.]
**Rader, Elizabeth H.** '65 '93 C.104 A.B. L.494 J.D.
(adm. in NY; not adm. in CA) [A Weil,G.&M.]
**Rhodes, Glenn W.** ........ '56 '85 C.947 B.A. L.326 J.D. [Arnold,W.&D.]
**Risberg, Robert L., Jr.** ........ '57 '90 C&L.966 B.S.E.E., J.D. [A Weil,G.&M.]
**Saraceni, Paul M.** ........ '64 '92 C.105 B.S. L.575 J.D. [A Weil,G.&M.]
**Scadina, Mark R.** ........ '69 '94 C.770 B.S.E.E. L.1066 J.D. [A Pennie&E.]
*PRACTICE AREAS: Intellectual Property, Patent Litigation and Prosecution.
**Schiffhauer, John R.** ........ '59 '85 C.453 S.B. L.982 J.D. [Fish&R.]
*PRACTICE AREAS: Intellectual Property; Litigation; Patents; Trademarks.
**Shaw, David M.** '66 '92 C.576 B.S.Ch.E. L.228 J.D.
(adm. in NY; not adm. in CA) [A Fish&R.]
*PRACTICE AREAS: Intellectual Property; Patents; Litigation.
**Slobodin, Jack L.**, (AV) ........ '35 '63 C.188 B.S. L.1066 LL.B. [Fish&R.]
*PRACTICE AREAS: Civil Litigation; Patent Law; Intellectual Property Law.
**Sobon, Wayne P.** ........ '62 '92 C.813 B.A.B.S. L.1066 J.D. [A Fish&R.]
*LANGUAGES: German.
*PRACTICE AREAS: Intellectual Property; Patents.
**Stark, Jon R.** ........ '51 '82 C.560 B.S. L.813 J.D. [Pennie&E.]
*PRACTICE AREAS: Intellectual Property; Litigation.
**Sugimura, Audrey M.** ........ '68 '94 C.112 B.A. L.276 J.D. [A Fish&R.]
*PRACTICE AREAS: Patent Prosecution.
**Suyat, Reginald J.** ........ '46 '76 C.911 B.S. L.276 J.D. [Fish&R.]
*PRACTICE AREAS: Intellectual Property.
**Swiss, Gerald F.** ........ '53 '81 C.602 B.S. L.776 J.D. [Burns,D.S.&M.]
**Troesch, Hans R.** ........ '49 '82 C.800 B.A. L.813 J.D. [Fish&R.]
*PRACTICE AREAS: Intellectual Property; Patents; Copyrights; Trade Secrets.
**Ure, Michael J.** ........ '60 '90 C.101 B.S.E.E. L.1184 J.D. [A Burns,D.S.&M.]
*LANGUAGES: Mandarin Chinese.
**Valentine, James F.** ........ '61 '90 C.608 B.S.E.E. L.424 J.D. [Arnold,W.&D.]
**Walker, William B.** ........ '35 '64 C.838 B.S.Ch.E. L.276 J.D. [Enterprise]
*PRACTICE AREAS: Patent Law; Trademark; Copyright; Unfair Competition; Licensing.
**Wang, William L.** ........ '65 '94 C.112 B.S.E.E. L.1066 J.D. [A Pennie&E.]
*PRACTICE AREAS: Intellectual Property; Patent Prosecution; Patent Litigation.

**Weil, Gotshal & Manges LLP**
**A Limited Liability Partnership including Professional Corporations**
**Silicon Valley Office**
**2882 Sand Hill Road, Suite 280, 94025-7022⊙**
**Telephone: 415-926-6200 FAX: 415-854-3713**
**Resident Partner: Robert Barr. Resident Associates: Dennis Y. Lee; Elizabeth H. Rader; Robert L. Risberg, Jr.; Paul M. Saraceni.**
**Patent, Trademark and Copyright Law.**
**New York, N.Y. Office: 767 Fifth Avenue. Telephone: 212-310-8000. Cable Address: "Wegoma". Telex: 424281; 423144. Telecopier: 212-310-8007.**
**Dallas, Texas Office: 100 Crescent Court, Suite 1300. Telephone: 214-746-7700. Fax: 214-746-7777.**
**Houston, Texas Office: 700 Louisiana Street, Suite 1600. Telephone: 713-546-5000. Telecopier: 713-224-9511.**
**Miami, Florida Office: 701 Brickell Avenue, Suite 2100. Telephone: 305-577-3100. Telecopier: 305-374-7159.**
**Washington, D.C. Office: 1615 L Street, N.W., Suite 700. Telephone: 202-682-7000. Telecopier: 202-857-0939; 857-0940. Telex: 440045.**
**Brussels, Belgium Office: 81 avenue Louise, Box 9-10, 1050 Brussels. Telephone: 011-32-2-543-7460. Telecopier: 011-32-2-543-7489.**
**Budapest, Hungary Office: Bank Center, Granite Tower, H-1944 Budapest. Telephone: 011 36 1 302-9100. Fax: 011 36 1 302-9110.**

(This Listing Continued)

CAA6T

**Weil, Gotshal & Manges LLP (Continued)**
**London, England Office: 99 Bishopsgate, London EC2M 3XD. Telephone: 44-171-426-1000. Telecopier: 44-171-426-0990.**
**Prague, Czechoslovakia Office: Charles Bridge Center, Krizovnicke nam. 1, 110 00 Prague 1, Czech Republic. Telephone: 011-42-2-24-09-73-00. Telecopier: 011-42-2-24-09-73-10.**
**Warsaw, Poland Office: ul. Zlota 44/46, 00-120 Warsaw. Telephone: 011-48-22-622-1300. Telecopier: 011-48-22-622-1301.**

*See Professional Biographies, MENLO PARK, CALIFORNIA*

## MORGAN HILL, 23,928, *Santa Clara Co.*

**Falk, Vestal & Fish, L.L.P.**
**16590 Oak View Circle, 95037⊙**
**Telephone: 408-778-3624 Fax: 408-776-0426 Pager: 408-683-1839 Cellular: 408-781-3145**
**Email: Rcfpatlaw@aol.com**
**Ronald C. Fish.**
**Matters of Intellectual Property and Trade Regulation. Patent, Trademark and Copyright Prosecution and Trial Practice. Trade Secret Protection. Related matters of Antitrust Law and Deceptive Trade Practices.**
**Reference: Provident Bank, Dallas, Texas.**
**Dallas, Texas Office: Plaza of the Americas, 700 North Pearl, Suite 970. Telephone: 214-954-4400.**

*See Professional Biographies, MORGAN HILL, CALIFORNIA*

**Fish, Ronald C.** ........ '47 '77 C.597 B.S.E.E. L.1065 J.D. [Falk,V.&F.]⊙
*PRACTICE AREAS: Intellectual Property Law.

## NEWPORT BEACH, 66,643, *Orange Co.*

**Altman, Daniel E.** ........ '58 '89 C.339 B.S. L.1066 J.D. [Knobbe,M.O.&B.]
**Anderson, Lowell** ........ '50 '82 C.546 B.S.M.E. L.1065 J.D. [Knobbe,M.O.&B.]
**Bear, James B.**, (AV) ........ '41 '69 C.112 B.S.E. L.1068 J.D. [Knobbe,M.O.&B.]
**Beuerle, Stephen C.** ........ '70 '96 C.477 B.S.M.E. L.997 J.D. [A Knobbe,M.O.&B.]
**Beutler, Ernest A., Jr.**, (AV) '33 '61 C.597 B.S.M.E. L.273 LL.B.
[A Knobbe,M.O.&B.]
**Bunker, William B.**, (AV) '51 '78
C.1075 B.S. L.101 J.D. [Knobbe,M.O.&B.] (⊙Riverside)
**Canuso, Vito A., III** ........ '58 '90 C.884 B.S. L.1049 J.D. [Knobbe,M.O.&B.]
**Friedland, Michael K.** ........ '66 '91 C.112 B.A. L.309 J.D. [Knobbe,M.O.&B.]
*LANGUAGES: Spanish and Russian.
**Jensen, Stephen C.** ........ '63 '90 C.101 B.S. L.112 J.D. [Knobbe,M.O.&B.]
*LANGUAGES: Dutch.
**Knobbe, Louis J., (P.C.)**, (AV) ........ '32 '60 C.350 B.S. L.426 J.D. [Knobbe,M.O.&B.]

**Knobbe, Martens, Olson & Bear, LLP, (AV) BR**
**A Limited Liability Partnership including Professional Corporations**
**620 Newport Center Drive, 16th Floor, 92660⊙**
**Telephone: 714-760-0404 Fax: 714-760-9502**
**Louis J. Knobbe (P.C.); Don W. Martens (P.C.); Gordon H. Olson (P.C.); James B. Bear; Darrell L. Olson (P.C.); William B. Bunker; William H. Nieman; Lowell Anderson; Arthur S. Rose; James F. Lesniak; Jerry T. Sewell; John B. Sganga, Jr.; Edward A. Schlatter; W. Gerard von Hoffmann, III; Joseph R. Re; Andrew H. Simpson; Daniel E. Altman; Ernest A. Beutler, Jr.; Stephen C. Jensen; Vito A. Canuso III; William H. Shreve; Steven J. Nataupsky; Craig S. Summers; Ronald J. Schoenbaum; Glenn R. Smith; R. Scott Weide; Michael K. Friedland; Stephen C. Beuerle.**
**Intellectual Property Law including Patent, Trademark, Copyright, Unfair Competition, Trade Secret, Licensing, Computer Law, Antitrust Law, and related litigation.**
**Representative Clients: AST Research Inc., Irvine; ASM America-Phoenix; NIH Washington, D.C.; Microsoft Corp.**
**San Diego, California Office: 501 West Broadway, Suite 1400. Telephone: 619-235-8550. Fax: 619-235-0176.**
**Riverside, California Office: 3801 University Avenue, Suite 710. Telephone: 909-781-9231. Fax: 909-781-4507.**

*See Professional Biographies, NEWPORT BEACH, CALIFORNIA*

**Lesniak, James F.** ........ '43 '69 C&L.477 B.S.E.E., J.D. [Knobbe,M.O.&B.]
**Martens, Don W., (P.C.)**, (AV) ... '34 '64 C.966 B.S.Eng. L.273 J.D. [Knobbe,M.O.&B.]
**Nataupsky, Steven J.** ........ '66 '91 C.860 B.S.E.S. L.569 J.D. [Knobbe,M.O.&B.]
**Nieman, William H.**, (BV) '42 '80
C.910 B.S.E.E. L.1049 J.D. [Knobbe,M.O.&B.] (⊙Riverside)
**Olson, Darrell L., (P.C.)**, (BV) ........ '52 '77 C.894 B.A. L.273 J.D. [Knobbe,M.O.&B.]
**Olson, Gordon H., (P.C.)**, (AV) ........ '33 '62 C.597 B.S. L.273 J.D. [Knobbe,M.O.&B.]
**Quiogue, Manuel**, (BV) ........ '49 '76 C.477 B.S.E. L.273 J.D. [Roberts&Q.]
*PRACTICE AREAS: Patent; Trademark; Intellectual Property.
**Re, Joseph R.** ........ '60 '86 C.705 B.S.C.E. L.724 J.D. [Knobbe,M.O.&B.]
**Roberts, Larry K.**, (AV) ........ '49 '76 C.339 B.S.E.E. L.426 J.D. [Roberts&Q.]
*PRACTICE AREAS: Patent; Trademark; Intellectual Property.

**Roberts and Quiogue, A Law Corporation, (AV)**
**660 Newport Center Drive, Suite 710, P.O. Box 8569, 92658**
**Telephone: 714-640-6200 Facsimile: 714-640-1206**
**Manuel Quiogue; Larry K. Roberts.**
**Intellectual Property Law, Patent, Trademark and Trade Secret and Related Matters.**

*See Professional Biographies, NEWPORT BEACH, CALIFORNIA*

**Rose, Arthur S.** ........ '51 '81 C.112 B.S. L.273 J.D. [Knobbe,M.O.&B.]
**Schlatter, Edward A.** ........ '59 '85 C.277 B.I.E. L.477 J.D. [Knobbe,M.O.&B.]
**Schoenbaum, Ronald J.** ........ '65 '93 C.861 B.S. L.260 J.D. [Knobbe,M.O.&B.]
**Sewell, Jerry T.** ........ '49 '80 C.502 B.S. L.494 J.D. [Knobbe,M.O.&B.]
**Sganga, John B., Jr.** ........ '60 '84 C.390 B.S. L.569 J.D. [Knobbe,M.O.&B.]
**Shreve, William H.** ........ '63 '90 C.112 B.S. L.273 J.D. [Knobbe,M.O.&B.]
**Simpson, Andrew H.** ........ '48 '91 C.61 B.S. L.426 J.D. [Knobbe,M.O.&B.]
**Smith, Glenn R.** ........ '51 '92 C.172 B.S.E.E. L.1068 J.D. [Knobbe,M.O.&B.]
**Summers, Craig S.**, (AV) ........ '56 '83 C.800 B.S. L.426 J.D. [Knobbe,M.O.&B.]
**von Hoffmann, W. Gerard, III** ........ '56 '84 C.605 A.B. L.1049 J.D. [Knobbe,M.O.&B.]
**Weide, R. Scott** ........ '65 '91 C.546 B.S. L.190 J.D. [Knobbe,M.O.&B.]

## OAKLAND, * 372,242, *Alameda Co.*

**Zimmerman, Harris, (AV) '19 '51 C.46 B.S. L.284 J.D.**
**Suite 710, 1330 Broadway, 94612**
**Telephone: 510-465-0828 Fax: 510-465-2041**
**Email: hzimerman@ix.netcom.com**
***PRACTICE AREAS: Intellectual Property Litigation; Counseling; Mediation; Arbitration; Patent Litigation.**
**Patent, Trademark, Unfair Competition and Trade Secrets Law. Trials.**

*See Professional Biographies, OAKLAND, CALIFORNIA*

## PALO ALTO, 55,900, *Santa Clara Co.*

**Aka, Gary T.** ........ '46 '75 C.312 B.S. L.1065 J.D. [Townsend&T.&C.]
*LANGUAGES: Japanese.
**Allen, Kenneth R.**, (AV) ........ '47 '75 C.101 B.S.E.E. L.588 J.D. [Townsend&T.&C.]
*LANGUAGES: German.
**Ananian, R. Michael** ........ '53 '92 C.477 B.S.E.E. L.770 J.D. [A Flehr,H.T.A.&H.]
*PRACTICE AREAS: Intellectual Property; Patents; Trademark; Copyright; Technology Licensing.
**Ashby, David C.** ........ '63 '93 C.446 B.S.E.E. L.64 J.D. [A Flehr,H.T.A.&H.]
*PRACTICE AREAS: Intellectual Property Law.
**Austin, James E.** ........ '67 '93 C&L.012 B.S., LL.B. [A Hickman,B.&W.]
*PRACTICE AREAS: Patents.

**Bachand, Edward N.** .......... '54 '81 C.112 B.S.M.E. L.1066 J.D. [🄰 Flehr,H.T.A.&H.]
*PRACTICE AREAS: Patents; Copyright; Trademark.
**Barovsky, Kenneth** ........................'52 '93 C.112 B.A. L.770 J.D. [🄰 Reed&R.]
*PRACTICE AREAS: Patent Law; Patent Preparation and Prosecution; Chemistry; Biotechnology; Biomedical Engineering.
**Barrish, Mark D.** .............'62 '94 C.112 B.S.M.E L.1065 J.D. [🄰 Townsend&T.&C.]
*LANGUAGES: Spanish.
*PRACTICE AREAS: Medical Device, Mechanical and Electro - Mechanical Patent Prosecution.
**Beamer, Norman H.** ..........................'46 '79 C.401 B.S. L.477 J.D. [Fish&N.]
*PRACTICE AREAS: Intellectual Property.
**Bedi, Ben H.** ........................'65 '94 C.1067 B.S. L.146 J.D [🄰 Hickman,B.&W.]
*PRACTICE AREAS: Semiconductor Technology; Electrochemical Systems; Alloy Compositions; Metallurgical Cladding; Patents.
**Beyer, Steve** ........................ '59 '86 C.37 B.S. L.273 J.D. [Hickman,B.&W.]
*PRACTICE AREAS: Intellectual Property Law; Patents.
**Biksa, Janis J. O.** ...... '54 '87 C.112 B.S. L.770 J.D. [Peters,V.J.&B.] (⊙San Francisco)
*LANGUAGES: Latvian.
*PRACTICE AREAS: Patent, Trademark and Copyright Law.
**Bohler, William J.** ...............'57 '84 C.679 B.S.E.E. L.801 J.D. [Townsend&T.&C.]
*PRACTICE AREAS: Intellectual Property Litigation; Patents; Counseling.
**Brown, Theodore G., III** ........... '52 '84 C.970 B.A. L.1066 J.D. [Townsend&T.&C.]
*PRACTICE AREAS: Intellectual Property Litigation and Counseling.
**Caplan, Julian**, (AV) ........... '14 '38 C.912 B.S.M.E. L.477 J.D. [🄲 Flehr,H.T.A.&H.]

**Carr, DeFilippo & Ferrell**
**2225 East Bayshore Road, Suite 200, 94303**
**Telephone: 415-812-3400 Fax: 415-812-3444**
**Members of Firm: John S. Ferrell. Counsel: Lisa A. Garono; J. Eppa Hite, III. Associates: Leroy D. Maunu (Not admitted in CA).**
**Corporate and Securities, Employment Law, Intellectual Property (including Patent Prosecution and Litigation, Trademark, Copyright, Trade Secrets, and Unfair Competition), International Transactions, Licensing, Litigation (including Intellectual Property, Business Litigation and Insurance Coverage), Partnerships and Franchising, Real Estate, and Venture Financings and Placements.**

***See Professional Biographies, PALO ALTO, CALIFORNIA***

**Caserza, Steven F.** ...................... '55 '80 C&L.770 B.S., J.D. [Flehr,H.T.A.&H.]
*PRACTICE AREAS: Patent; Trademark; Copyright.
**Chan, Melvin D.** ...........'65 '94 C.112 B.S.E.E.C.S. L.464 J.D. [🄰 Townsend&T.&C.]
**Colwell, Robert C.** ...................'47 '73 C.378 B.S. L.813 J.D. [Townsend&T.&C.]
**DeFranco, Edward J.** ..........................'60 '87 C.688 B.S. L.188 J.D. [Fish&N.]
*PRACTICE AREAS: Intellectual Property.
**Dehlinger, Peter J.** ...................'44 '82 C.629 B.S. L.1051 J.D. [Dehlinger&Assoc.]
*PRACTICE AREAS: Intellectual Property.

**Dehlinger & Associates**
**350 Cambridge Avenue, Suite 250, 94306-1546**
**Telephone: 415-324-0880 Telecopier: 415-324-0960**
**Peter J. Dehlinger.**
**Patent Law.**

***See Professional Biographies, PALO ALTO, CALIFORNIA***

**Dickinson, Jon M.** '38 '64 C&L.188 B.E.E., LL.B.
(adm. in OR; not adm. in CA) [Kolisch H.D.M.&H.] (⊙Portland, OR.)
*PRACTICE AREAS: Patent, Trademark and Unfair Competition.
**Dow, Karen B.** ........................'54 '79 C.97 B.S. L.345 J.D. [Townsend&T.&C.]
*PRACTICE AREAS: Biotechnology and Chemistry Patent Prosecution; Related Technology Agreements.
**Fanning, David A.** ..............'61 '88 C.101 B.S. L.1065 J.D. [Kolisch H.D.M.&H.]⊙
*PRACTICE AREAS: Patent, Trademark and Unfair Competition.
**Ferrell, John S.** ........................ '57 '91 C.846 B.S.E.E. L.770 J.D. [Carr,D.&F.]

**Fish & Neave, (AVⓉ) 🅱**
**Fish, Richardson & Neave, New York (1916-1969)**
**525 University Avenue Suite 300, 94301⊙**
**Telephone: 415-617-4000 Telecopier: 415-617-4090**
**Resident Members: Edward F. Mullowney; Norman H. Beamer; Mark D. Rowland; Edward J. DeFranco. Resident Associates: Vicki S. Veenker; Nicola A. Pisano; Gabrielle E. Higgins; Kevin P.B. Johnson; Petrina S. Hsi (Not admitted in CA); Derek Minihane (Not admitted in CA); Ann Marie Whitley (Not admitted in CA).**
**Intellectual Property including Patent, Trademark, Trade Secret, Copyright and Unfair Competition, Unfair Trade Practice and Antitrust Law. Trials and Appeals in all Federal and State Courts and Governmental Administrative Agencies.**
**New York, New York Office: 1251 Avenue of the Americas. Telephone: 212-596-9000. Telex: 14-8367. Cable Address: Fishneave. Telecopier: 212-596-9090.**

***See Professional Biographies, PALO ALTO, CALIFORNIA***

**Fitts, Renée A.** ...................... '52 '91 C.145 B.A. L.1066 J.D. [🄲 Townsend&T.&C.]
*PRACTICE AREAS: Patent Law.

**Flehr, Hohbach, Test, Albritton & Herbert, (AV)**
**Suite 200, 850 Hansen Way, 94304-1017⊙**
**Telephone: 415-494-8700 Telefax: 415-494-8771**
**Resident Attorneys: Harold C. Hohbach; Aldo J. Test; Thomas O. Herbert; Edward S. Wright; James A. Sheridan; Gary S. Williams; C. Michael Zimmerman; Steven F. Caserza; William S. Galliani. Associates: Janet Elizabeth Muller; Edward N. Bachand; R. Michael Ananian; David C. Ashby; Maria S. Swiatek. Of Counsel: Julian Caplan.**
**Patent, Trademark, Copyright, Unfair Competition, Trade Secrets, Biotechnology and Computer Law. Trials.**
**San Francisco, California Office: Suite 3400, Four Embarcadero Center. Telephone: 415-781-1989.**

***See Professional Biographies, PALO ALTO, CALIFORNIA***

**Friedman, Susan J.** ..........................'— '92 C.788 B.A. L.276 J.D. [🄰 Reed&R.]
*PRACTICE AREAS: Patent Law; Patent Preparation and Prosecution; Chemistry; Biotechnology.
**Galliani, William S.** ...................'62 '90 C.597 B.A. L.770 J.D. [Flehr,H.T.A.&H.]
**Garono, Lisa A.** ........................ '61 '87 C.363 B.S. L.608 J.D. [🄲 Carr,D.&F.]
**Hann, James F.** ................'48 '77 C.886 B.S.M.E. L.1065 J.D. [Townsend&T.&C.]
**Haughey, Paul C.** ...............'54 '80 C.112 B.S.E.E. L.1065 J.D. [Townsend&T.&C.]
*PRACTICE AREAS: Electronic Patent Prosecution, Counseling & Licensing.
**Haverstock, Thomas B.** .........'55 '85 C.679 B.S.E.E. L.770 J.D. [Haverstock&Assoc.]
*PRACTICE AREAS: Maskworks; Software; Electrical and Computer Patents.

**Haverstock & Associates**
**260 Sheridan Avenue, Suite 420, 94306**
**Telephone: 415-833-0160 Facsimile: 415-833-0170**
**Email: tbh@crl.com**
**Thomas B. Haverstock;—Jonathan O. Owens.**
**Patent, Trademark and Copyright Law, Trade Secrets, Unfair Competition, Technology, Licensing and Evaluation and related Trial and Appellate Litigation in State and Federal Courts and Alternative Dispute Resolution.**

***See Professional Biographies, PALO ALTO, CALIFORNIA***

**Herbert, Thomas O.**, (AV) ..........'31 '61 C.128 B.E.E. L.273 J.D. [Flehr,H.T.A.&H.]
**Heslin, James M.** ............ '50 '78 C.112 B.Sc.Ch.E. L.1066 J.D. [Townsend&T.&C.]
**Heuser, Peter E.**, (AV) ..........'49 '76 C.1027 B.S. L.966 J.D. [Kolisch H.D.M.&H.]⊙
*PRACTICE AREAS: Patent, Trademark and Unfair Competition.
**Hickman, Paul L.** .....................'53 '84 C.813 A.B. L.770 J.D. [Hickman,B.&W.]
*PRACTICE AREAS: Intellectual Property Law; Patents.

**Hickman, Beyer & Weaver, L.L.P.**
**620 Hansen Way, 94304**
**Telephone: 415-493-6400 Fax: 415-493-6484**

(This Listing Continued)

**Hickman, Beyer & Weaver, L.L.P. (Continued)**

**Members of Firm: Paul L. Hickman; Steve Beyer; Jeffrey K. Weaver. Associates: David P. Lentini; Joseph A. Nguyen; C. Douglass Thomas; Jonathan Scott; Lee Van Pelt; Ben H. Bedi; James E. Austin. Intellectual Property Law.**

***See Professional Biographies, PALO ALTO, CALIFORNIA***

**Higgins, Gabrielle E.** ........................ '63 '89 C.321 B.A. L.262 J.D. [🄰 Fish&N.]
*PRACTICE AREAS: Intellectual Property.
**Hite, J. Eppa, III** ...........................'51 '81 C.893 B.A. L.945 J.D. [🄲 Carr,D.&F.]
**Hohbach, Harold C.**, (AV) ......... '21 '53 C.791 B.S. L.1066 LL.B. [Flehr,H.T.A.&H.]
**Hsi, Petrina S.** '68 '94 C.367 B.A. L.1066 J.D.
(adm. in NY; not adm. in CA) [🄰 Fish&N.]
*PRACTICE AREAS: Intellectual Property.
**Johnson, Kevin P.B.** ....................'66 '93 C.188 B.S.E.E. L.1019 J.D. [🄰 Fish&N.]
*PRACTICE AREAS: Intellectual Property.
**Jones, Allston L.** ....................'42 '77 C.223 B.S.E.E. L.770 J.D. [Peters,V.J.&B.]
*PRACTICE AREAS: Patent, Trademark and Copyright Law.

**Kolisch Hartwell Dickinson McCormack & Heuser, A Professional Corporation, (AV) 🅱**
**420 Florence Street, 94301⊙**
**Telephone: 415-325-8673 Facsimile: 415-325-5076**
**Email: concepts@concepts-law.com**
**Jon M. Dickinson (Not admitted in CA); John M. McCormack; Peter E. Heuser; David A. Fanning; Pierre C. Van Rysselberghe.**
**Patent, Trademark and Unfair Competition Law. Trials.**
**Portland, Oregon Office: 200 Pacific Building, 520 S.W. Yamhill Street. Telephone: 503-224-6655. Fax: 503-295-6679.**
**Boise, Idaho Office: 802 W. Bannock, Suite 403A. Telephone: 208-384-9166. Fax: 208-384-9169.**

***See Professional Biographies, PALO ALTO, CALIFORNIA***

**Lentini, David P.** .................. '63 '93 C.145 B.S. L.1065 J.D. [🄰 Hickman,B.&W.]
*PRACTICE AREAS: Intellectual Property Law; Patents.
**Liebeschuetz, Joe** ................ '59 '92 C.050 B.A. L.347 J.D. [🄰 Townsend&T.&C.]
*PRACTICE AREAS: Biotechnology Patents.
**Maunu, Leroy D.** '63 '93 C.350 B.S. L.1035 J.D.
(adm. in MN; not adm. in CA) [Carr,D.&F.]
*PRACTICE AREAS: Patent Prosecution; Software Licensing; Procurement.
**McCormack, John M.** '44 '75
C.628 B.S.M.E. L.30 J.D. [Kolisch H.D.M.&H.] (⊙Portland, OR.)
*LANGUAGES: Spanish.
*PRACTICE AREAS: Patent, Trademark and Unfair Competition.
**McCracken, Thomas P.G.** ..................'62 '94 C.112 B.A. L.770 J.D. [🄰 Reed&R.]
*PRACTICE AREAS: Patent Law; Patent Preparation and Prosecution; Biotechnology; Biomedical Engineering.
**Minihane, Derek** '69 '94 C.188 B.E.E. L.273 J.D.
(adm. in MA; not adm. in CA) [🄰 Fish&N.]
*PRACTICE AREAS: Intellectual Property.
**Muller, Janet Elizabeth** ........ '66 '91 C.112 B.S.M.E. L.770 J.D. [🄰 Flehr,H.T.A.&H.]
*PRACTICE AREAS: Patents; Trademarks; Copyrights.
**Mullowney, Edward F.**, (AVⓉ) ........... '43 '72 C.816 B.S.M.E. L.178 J.D. [Fish&N.]
*PRACTICE AREAS: Intellectual Property.
**Nguyen, Joseph A.** ............. '65 '93 C.576 B.S.E.E. L.1066 J.D. [🄰 Hickman,B.&W.]
*PRACTICE AREAS: Intellectual Property Law; Patents.
**Owens, Jonathan O.** ............'67 '93 C.508 B.S.E.E. L.770 J.D. [Haverstock&Assoc.]
*PRACTICE AREAS: Electrical and Mechanical Patents.
**Peters, Howard M.** ..................... '40 '79 C.271 B.S. L.770 J.D. [Peters,V.J.&B.]
*PRACTICE AREAS: Patent, Trademark and Copyright Law.

**Peters, Verny, Jones & Biksa, L.L.P.**
**385 Sherman Avenue Suite 6, 94306-1840**
**Telephone: 415-324-1677 Fax: 415-324-1678**
**Email: pvjb@patentsfo.com**
**Members of Firm: Howard M. Peters; Hana Verny; Allston L. Jones; Janis J. O. Biksa.**
**Intellectual Property Law, including Patent, Trademark, Copyright, Trade Secret and Unfair Competition Law. Trials in all Local Courts, all Federal Courts, and before the U.S. Patent and Trademark Office.**

***See Professional Biographies, PALO ALTO, CALIFORNIA***

**Pisano, Nicola A.** ...................... '59 '90 C&L.602 B.S.M.E., J.D. [🄰 Fish&N.]
*PRACTICE AREAS: Intellectual Property.
**Raffle, John Thomas** ..............'68 '94 C.453 B.S. L.228 J.D. [🄰 Townsend&T.&C.]
*PRACTICE AREAS: Aeronautical, Mechanical and Medical Device Patent Prosecution.
**Reed, Dianne E.** .........................'58 '84 C.453 S.B. L.1065 J.D. [Reed&R.]
*PRACTICE AREAS: Patent Law; Strategic Counseling; Patent Preparation and Prosecution.

**Reed & Robins LLP**
**285 Hamilton Avenue, Suite 200, 94301**
**Telephone: 415-327-3400 Facsmilie: 415-327-3231**
**Members of Firm: Dianne E. Reed; Roberta L. Robins. Associates: Kenneth Barovsky; Thomas P.G. McCracken; Susan J. Friedman.**
**Technology areas: Chemistry, Biotechnology and Biomedical Engineering, including Pharmaceuticals, Organic and Bio-Organic Chemistry, Polymer Science, Molecular Biology, Immunology and Genetics. Intellectual Property Law including Patent Preparation and Prosecution.**

***See Professional Biographies, PALO ALTO, CALIFORNIA***

**Ritter, Michael J.** ...............'65 '94 C&L.846 B.A.C.S., J.D. [🄰 Townsend&T.&C.]
*PRACTICE AREAS: Electronic and Software Patent Prosecution.
**Robins, Roberta L.** ........................'53 '87 C.768 B.A. L.1065 J.D. [Reed&R.]
*PRACTICE AREAS: Patent Law; Strategic Counseling; Patent Preparation and Prosecution.
**Rowland, Mark D.** ......................'61 '87 C.602 B.S.E.E. L.273 J.D. [Fish&N.]
*PRACTICE AREAS: Intellectual Property.
**Scott, Jonathan** ............... '61 '95 C.112 B.S.E.E. L.765 J.D. [🄰 Hickman,B.&W.]
*PRACTICE AREAS: Patents; Trademarks; Copyrights; Trade Secrets; Intellectual Property.
**Shaffer, William L.** ...............'66 '92 C.880 E.E. L.802 J.D. [🄰 Townsend&T.&C.]
*PRACTICE AREAS: Electronic and Semiconductor Patent Prosecution.
**Sheridan, James A.** ............... '41 '67 C.436 B.S.E.E. L.209 J.D. [Flehr,H.T.A.&H.]
**Slone, David N.** ....................'46 '77 C.012 B.Sc. L.813 J.D. [Townsend&T.&C.]
**Smith, William M.** '51 '79 C.112 B.S. L.800 J.D.
[Townsend&T.&C.] (⊙Seattle, Wash.)
*PRACTICE AREAS: Biotechnology Patent Prosecution, Licensing & Enforcement; Molecular Immunology.
**Swiatek, Maria S.** .............'62 '92 C.1075 B.S.Ch.E. L.464 J.D. [🄰 Flehr,H.T.A.&H.]
*PRACTICE AREAS: Patent; Licensing; Trademark; Copyright.
**Test, Aldo J.**, (AV) ....................'23 '52 C.112 B.S. L.1066 J.D. [Flehr,H.T.A.&H.]
**Thomas, C. Douglass** ........... '62 '88 C.645 B.S.E.E. L.1017 J.D. [🄰 Hickman,B.&W.]
*PRACTICE AREAS: Intellectual Property Law; Patents.

**Townsend and Townsend and Crew LLP, (AV) 🅱**
**A Limited Liability Partnership including a Professional Corporation**
**379 Lytton Avenue, 94301-1431⊙**
**Telephone: 415-326-2400 Telecopier: 415-326-2422**
**Email: inquire@townsend.com URL: http://www.townsend.com**
**Members of Firm: Kenneth R. Allen; Robert C. Colwell; David N. Slone; James F. Hann; James M. Heslin; Gary T. Aka; William M. Smith; Paul C. Haughey; Theodore G. Brown, III; William J. Bohler; Karen B. Dow. Of Counsel: Henry K. Woodward; Renée A. Fitts. Associates: Joe Liebeschuetz; William L. Shaffer; Michael J. Ritter; John Thomas Raffle; Mark D. Barrish; Melvin D. Chan; Alice L. Wong.**

(This Listing Continued)

**Townsend and Townsend and Crew LLP (Continued)**

Patent, Trademark, Copyright and Unfair Competition Law, Intellectual Property Law. Intellectual Property, Antitrust and Commercial Litigation.
San Francisco, California Office: Two Embarcadero Center, Eighth Floor. Telephone: 415-576-0200. Facsimile: 415-576-0300.
Denver, Colorado Office: 1200 17th Street, Suite 2700. Telephone: 303-571-4000. Fax: 303-571-4321.
Seattle, Washington Office: 601 Union Street, Suite 5400. Telephone: 206-467-9600. Telecopier: 206-623-6793.

*See Professional Biographies, PALO ALTO, CALIFORNIA*

**Van Pelt, Lee** ........................ '65 '93 C.502 B.S. L.1066 J.D. [Ⓐ Hickman,B.&W.]
*PRACTICE AREAS: Patents.
**Van Rysselberghe, Pierre C.** '58 '90
C.668 B.A. L.284 J.D. [Kolisch H.D.M.&H.] (⊙Portland, OR.)
*PRACTICE AREAS: Patent, Trademark and Unfair Competition.
**Veenker, Vicki S.** ............................'62 '88 C.347 B.S. L.276 J.D. [Ⓐ Fish&N.]
*PRACTICE AREAS: Intellectual Property.
**Verny, Hana** .................................'38 '82 C.999 PH.D L.184 J.D. [Peters,V.J.&B.]
*LANGUAGES: Czech, Russian and German.
*PRACTICE AREAS: Patent, Trademark and Copyright Law.
**Weaver, Jeffrey K.** .................... '60 '86 C.645 B.S. L.273 J.D. [Hickman,B.&W.]
*PRACTICE AREAS: Intellectual Property Law; Patents.
**Whitley, Ann Marie** '70 '96 C.597 B.S.M.E. L.477 J.D.
(adm. in NY; not adm. in CA) [Ⓐ Fish&N.]
**Williams, Gary S.** ....................... '55 '82 C.976 B.S. L.309 J.D. [Flehr,H.T.A.&H.]
**Wong, Alice L.** ................. '71 '95 C.8 B.S.E.E. L.1065 J.D. [Ⓐ Townsend&T.&C.]
*LANGUAGES: Mandarin, Cantonese, Malay.
*PRACTICE AREAS: Intellectual Property.
**Woodward, Henry K.**, (AV) .... '38 '63 C&L.846 B.S.E.E., LL.B. [Ⓑ Townsend&T.&C.]
*PRACTICE AREAS: Patent and Trade Secret Law; Technology Law; Electronics and Physics.
**Wright, Edward S.** ........................'41 '66 C&L.813 B.S.E.E., LL.B. [Flehr,H.T.A.&H.]
**Zimmerman, C. Michael**, (AV) ...... '38 '66 C.506 B.S. L.765 LL.B. [Flehr,H.T.A.&H.]

## PASADENA, 131,591, *Los Angeles Co.*

**Anderson, Denton L.** ........'46 '76 C.494 B.Ch.E. L.1152 J.D. [Sheldon&M.] (⊙Upland)
**Brown, Edward A.** '59 '92 C.339 B.S.Met.E. L.30 J.D.
(adm. in PA; not adm. in CA) [Ⓐ Sheldon&M.]
**Carney, Hayden A.**, (AV) .........'36 '64 C.999 B.S.N.A. L.800 LL.B. [Christie,P.&H.]
*PRACTICE AREAS: Intellectual Property Licensing and Taxation; Domestic and International Patent and Trademark Prosecution; Mechanical and Physical Technologies.
**Carpenter, John D.** ....................'61 '89 C&L.800 B.S., J.D. [Ⓐ Christie,P.&H.]
*PRACTICE AREAS: Patents; Trademarks; Copyrights.
**Chaikovsky, Yar R.** ....................'69 '94 C.800 B.S. L.112 J.D. [Ⓐ Christie,P.&H.]
*PRACTICE AREAS: Patents; Trademarks; Copyrights.

**Christie, Parker & Hale, LLP, (AV)**
**Fifth Floor, Wells Fargo Bank Building, 350 West Colorado Boulevard, P.O. Box 7068, 91109-7068⊙**
Telephone: 818-795-9900 Los Angeles: 213-681-1800 Cable Address: "Patlaw" Telex: ITT 4995129 (CPH PSD) Telecopier: 818-577-8800
Members of Firm: D. Bruce Prout; Hayden A. Carney; Richard J. Ward, Jr.; Russell R. Palmer, Jr.; LeRoy T. Rahn; Richard D. Seibel; Walter G. Maxwell; John P. Grinnell; Thomas J. Daly; Vincent G. Gioia (Resident, Irvine Office); John D. Carpenter. Associates: David A. Plumley; Wesley W. Monroe; Grant T. Langton; Constantine Marantidis; John W. Eldredge (Resident, Irvine Office); Yar R. Chaikovsky; Steven P. Skabrat (Not admitted in CA). Of Counsel: R. William Johnston; Paul W. Fish (Not admitted in CA); Carl Kustin, Jr.; Jeffrey P. Wall.
Patent, Trademark and Copyright Law. Unfair Competition, Trade Secrets, Computer Law, Biotechnology, Licensing, Antitrust and Complex Business Litigation.
Reference: Wells Fargo Bank (Pasadena, California Main Offices).
Irvine, California Office: Suite 1440, 5 Park Plaza. Telephone: 714-476-0757.

*See Professional Biographies, PASADENA, CALIFORNIA*

**Daly, Thomas J.**, (AV) .............'57 '85 C.339 B.S.Ch.E. L.426 J.D. [Christie,P.&H.]
*PRACTICE AREAS: Patent, Trademark, Copyright and Unfair Competition Litigation.
**Farah, David** ...............................'58 '93 C&L.477 B.S., J.D. [Ⓐ Sheldon&M.]
*PRACTICE AREAS: Patent, Trademark and Copyright.
**Fish, Paul W.** '33 '65 C.128 B.E.E. L.273 LL.B.
(adm. in DC; not adm. in CA) [Ⓑ Christie,P.&H.]
*PRACTICE AREAS: Patent, Trademark and Copyright Law; Computer Law; Lease Law; Corporate Law.
**Goldstein, Sol L.** '25 '55 C.46 B.S.Ch.E. L.424 J.D.
(adm. in IL; not adm. in CA) [Ⓑ Sheldon&M.]

**Gotha, Frederick, (AV) '35 '67 C.679 B.S.A.E. L.767 J.D.** BB
**Suite 823, 80 South Lake Avenue, 91101**
Telephone: 818-796-1849 Telecopier: 818-405-0952
Patent, Trademark and Unfair Competition Law.

*See Professional Biographies, PASADENA, CALIFORNIA*

**Grinnell, John P.**, (AV) ...............'35 '68 C.367 B.E.S. L.262 J.D. [Christie,P.&H.]
*PRACTICE AREAS: Patents; Trademarks; Copyrights.

**Haefliger, William W., (AV) '25 '56 C.111 B.S. L.426 LL.B.**
**Suite 512, 201 South Lake Avenue, 91101**
Telephone: 818-449-0467 Los Angeles: 213-684-2707
Intellectual Property, Patent, Trademark, Copyright and Unfair Competition Law.
Reference: Union Bank (Pasadena Main Office).

*See Professional Biographies, PASADENA, CALIFORNIA*

**Hsu, Lee** ...................................'68 '94 C.112 B.S.E.E. L.809 J.D. [Ⓐ Sheldon&M.]
*LANGUAGES: Chinese (Mandarin).
**Johnston, R. William**, (AV) .........'24 '53 C.691 B.S. L.796 LL.B. [Ⓑ Christie,P.&H.]
*PRACTICE AREAS: Patents; Trademarks; Copyrights.
**Kustin, Carl, Jr.**, (AV) ....................'36 '62 C.46 B.S. L.597 J.D. [Ⓑ Christie,P.&H.]
*PRACTICE AREAS: Patent, Trademark, Copyright and Unfair Competition Litigation.
**Langton, Grant T.** ..............'60 '92 C.1075 B.S.Ch.E. L.426 J.D. [Ⓐ Christie,P.&H.]
*PRACTICE AREAS: Patents; Trademarks; Copyrights.
**Mak, Danton K.** .......................'55 '84 C.911 B.S.Ch.E. L.1068 J.D. [Sheldon&M.]
*LANGUAGES: Chinese, Mandarin and Cantonese.
**Marantidis, Constantine** ............'60 '94 C.1333 B.S. L.426 J.D. [Ⓐ Christie,P.&H.]
*PRACTICE AREAS: Patents; Trademarks; Copyrights.
**Maxwell, Walter G.** .....................'39 '69 C.112 B.S. L.800 J.D. [Christie,P.&H.]
*PRACTICE AREAS: Patents; Trademarks; Copyrights.

**Mon, Donald D., (AV) '21 '51 C.111 B.S. L.813 J.D.**
**750 East Green Street, Suite 303, 91101-2545**
Telephone: 818-793-9173 Telecopier: 818-793-9690
Patent and Trademark Law.

*See Professional Biographies, PASADENA, CALIFORNIA*

**Monroe, Wesley W.** ......................'66 '90 C.112 B.S. L.426 J.D. [Ⓐ Christie,P.&H.]
*PRACTICE AREAS: Intellectual Property Law; Computer Law.

**Mueth, Joseph E.**, (AV) .................'35 '60 C.201 B.Ch.E. L.276 LL.B. [J.E.Mueth]
*REPORTED CASES: Rex Chainbelt, Inc. v. Harco Products, Inc., U.S. Court of Appeals, 9th Cir. (1975); Herbert v. Diagnostic Products Corp., No. 85 Civ. 0856 (June 1986); Young Engineers, Inc. v. USITC; Hunting Hall of Fame Foundation v. Safari Club International, No. CIV 86-020 TUC ACM (May 1987); IMS Limited v. International Medical Systems, Inc, No. 84 CV 4126 (September 1986).
*PRACTICE AREAS: Patent, Trademark and Copyright Law; Trial Law; Appellate Practice; Food and Drugs.

**Mueth, Joseph E., A Law Corporation, (AV)** BB
**225 South Lake Avenue, Eighth Floor, 91101-1599**
Telephone: 818-584-0396 Fax: 818-584-6862
Joseph E. Mueth.
Patent, Trademark and Copyright Law. Trials and Appellate Practice in all Courts.
Reference: Bank of America, 333 South Hope Street, Los Angeles, California.

*See Professional Biographies, PASADENA, CALIFORNIA*

**Netter, George J., (AV) '24 '60 C&L.851 B.S., J.D.**
**260 South Los Robles Avenue Suite 216, 91101**
Telephone: 818-578-0703 Fax: 818-578-1630
Email: gnetter@spotcom.com
Patents, Trademarks, Copyrights and Unfair Competition.
Reference: First Los Angeles Bank.

**Palmer, Russell R., Jr.**, (AV) .......... '27 '65 C.112 B.S. L.813 LL.B. [Christie,P.&H.]
*PRACTICE AREAS: Patents; Trademarks; Copyrights.
**Plumley, David A.** ......................'60 '91 C.112 B.S. L.426 J.D. [Ⓐ Christie,P.&H.]
*PRACTICE AREAS: Patents; Trademarks; Copyrights.
**Prout, D. Bruce**, (AV) ...............'34 '63 C&L.800 B.S.E.E., LL.B. [Christie,P.&H.]
*PRACTICE AREAS: Domestic and International Patents; Copyrights and Trademarks; Computer Technology.
**Rahn, LeRoy T.**, (AV) .............'35 '63 C.800 B.S.E.E. L.569 LL.B. [Christie,P.&H.]
*LANGUAGES: German.
*PRACTICE AREAS: Intellectual Property Law.
**Seibel, Richard D.**, (AV) .................'30 '61 C.813 B.S. L.208 J.D. [Christie,P.&H.]
*PRACTICE AREAS: Patent and Trademark Prosecution; Material Science.
**Sheldon, Jeffrey G.**, (AV) ...... '47 '75 C.119 B.S. L.426 J.D. [Sheldon&M.] (⊙Upland)

**Sheldon & Mak, (AV)**
**9th Floor, 225 South Lake Avenue, 91101-3005⊙**
Telephone: 818-796-4000 Fax: 818-795-6321
URL: http://www.usip.com
Members of Firm: Jeffrey G. Sheldon; Danton K. Mak; Denton L. Anderson; Surjit P. Singh Soni. Of Counsel: Sol L. Goldstein (Not admitted in CA); Joseph E. Mueth. Associates: Stephen R. Seccombe (Resident, San Bernadino Office); Edward A. Brown (Not admitted in CA); David Farah; Lee Hsu.
Patent, Trademark and Copyright Law. Antitrust and Unfair Competition, Trade Secrets, Customs Law and related causes in all State and Federal Courts.
Representative Clients: TRW; Raychem; Southern California Edison.
Reference: Citizens Bank (Pasadena, California).
San Bernardino, California Office: Suite 503, 290 North D Street, 92401. Telephone: 909-889-3649. Fax: 909-889-9865.
Upland, California Office: Suite 210, 222 North Mountain Avenue, 91786. Telephone: 909-946-3939.

*See Professional Biographies, PASADENA, CALIFORNIA*

**Singh Soni, Surjit P.** ..........................'54 '87 C.025 B.Sc. L.472 J.D. [Sheldon&M.]
*LANGUAGES: Hindi and Punjabi.
**Skabrat, Steven P.** '62 '93 C.494 B.S.C.S. L.1035 J.D.
(adm. in MN; not adm. in CA) [Ⓐ Christie,P.&H.]
*PRACTICE AREAS: Patents; Copyrights; Computer Law.
**Wall, Jeffrey P.** ..........................'60 '93 C.352 B.S. L.1068 J.D. [Ⓑ Christie,P.&H.]
*PRACTICE AREAS: Patents; Trademarks; Copyrights.
**Ward, Richard J., Jr.**, (AV) ......... '36 '65 C.734 B.S.E.E. L.800 J.D. [Christie,P.&H.]
*PRACTICE AREAS: Patent, Trademark and Copyright Litigation and Prosecution; Unfair Competition Litigation.

## REDWOOD CITY, * 66,072, *San Mateo Co.*

**Medlen & Carroll, LLP, (AV)**
**702 Marshall Street, Suite 600, 94063⊙**
Telephone: 415-299-8120 Facsimile: 415-299-8127
Associates: Christopher John Smith.
Patent, Trademark and Copyright Law, Trade Secrets, Unfair Competition, Technology Licensing and Evaluation and related Trial and Appellate Litigation in State and Federal Courts, and Alternative Dispute Resolution (ADR).
San Francisco, California Office: 220 Montgomery St., Suite 2200. Telephone:415-705-8410. Facsimile: 415-397-8338.
Cambridge, Massachusetts Office: Five Cambridge Center, Second Floor. Telephone: 617-354-5455. Facsimile: 617-354-8132.
Toledo, Ohio Office: One Seagate, Suite 960. Telephone: 419-247-1010. Facsimile: 419-247-1011.

*See Professional Biographies, REDWOOD CITY, CALIFORNIA*

**Smith, Christopher John** ................'65 '94 C.112 B.S. L.1065 J.D. [Ⓐ Medlen&C.]
*PRACTICE AREAS: Chemical; Pharmaceutical; Biotechnology Patents; Intellectual Property Litigation; Medical Device.

## RIVERSIDE, * 226,505, *Riverside Co.*

**Bunker, William B.**, (AV) '51 '78
C.1075 B.S. L.101 J.D. [Knobbe,M.O.&B.] (⊙Newport Beach)
**Hernandez, Fred C.** .............'67 '95 C.1074 B.S.A.E. L.112 J.D. [Knobbe,M.O.&B.]

**Knobbe, Martens, Olson & Bear, LLP, (AV)**
A Limited Liability Partnership including Professional Corporations
**3801 University Avenue, Suite 710, 92501⊙**
Telephone: 909-781-9231 Fax: 909-781-4507
William B. Bunker; William H. Nieman; Michael H. Trenholm; Fred C. Hernandez.
Intellectual Property Law including Patent, Trademark, Copyright, Unfair Competition, Trade Secret, Licensing, Computer Law, Antitrust Law, and related litigation.
Reference: Wells Fargo Bank.
Newport Beach, California Office: 620 Newport Center Drive, 16th Floor. Telephone: 714-760-0404. Fax: 714-760-9502.
San Diego, California Office: 501 West Broadway, Suite 1400. Telephone: 619-235-8550. Fax: 619-235-0176.

*See Professional Biographies, RIVERSIDE, CALIFORNIA*

**Nieman, William H.** '42 '80
C.910 B.S.E.E. L.1049 J.D. [Knobbe,M.O.&B.] (⊙Newport Beach)
**Trenholm, Michael H.** .......... '64 '92 C.112 B.S.E.E. L.464 J.D. [Ⓐ Knobbe,M.O.&B.]

# PROFESSIONAL BIOGRAPHIES SECTION

---

CALIFORNIA
A — R

## KARNO, SCHWARTZ, FRIEDMAN, SHAFRON & WARREN

A Partnership including Professional Corporations

30497 CANWOOD STREET, SUITE 102
**AGOURA HILLS, CALIFORNIA 91301**
Telephone: 818-597-7977
Fax: 818-597-7970

*Encino, California Office:* Manufacturers Bank Building, Suite 1200, 16255 Ventura Boulevard. Telephone: 818-981-3400; 213-872-1800. Telecopier: 213-872-1278.

Real Estate, Tax, Corporate, Business, ERISA, Estate Planning and Probate Law. Litigation.

(For Biographical data on all Personnel, See Professional Biographies at Encino, California)

---

## KOSLOV & MEDLEN

**AGOURA HILLS, CALIFORNIA**

(See Los Angeles)

Insurance, Real Estate and Construction Law, Personal Injury, Products Liability, Insurance Brokerage. Trials.

---

## RICK A. SCHROEDER

638 LINDERO CANYON ROAD, SUITE 392
**AGOURA HILLS, CALIFORNIA 91301**
Telephone: 818-879-1943
Telecopier: 818-879-5443
Email: 73430.2763@compuserve.com

Bankruptcy, Insolvency, Creditors' Rights, Commercial and Business Litigation.

**RICK A. SCHROEDER**, born Edgerton, Wisconsin, June 10, 1961; admitted to bar, 1986, California and U.S. District Court, Central District of California; 1987, U.S. District Court, Eastern and Southern Districts of California; 1990, Minnesota and U.S. Court of Appeals, Ninth Circuit. *Education:* University of Wisconsin (B.B.A., 1983); University of California at Los Angeles (J.D., 1986). Beta Gamma Sigma. *Member:* Ventura County, San Fernando Valley and Minnesota State Bar Associations; State Bar of California. **PRACTICE AREAS:** Bankruptcy; Commercial Litigation; Business.

---

## MARY B. SCOTT

5699 KANAN ROAD, SUITE 339
**AGOURA HILLS, CALIFORNIA 91301**
Telephone: 818-889-9220
Fax: 818-889-9255

General Civil Practice, Business Matters including Intellectual Property, Trademark and Copyright, and Libel, Slander and Defamation.

**MARY B. SCOTT**, born Riverside, California, June 13, 1959; admitted to bar, 1991, California and U.S. District Court, Central and Southern Districts of California; U.S. Court of Appeals, Ninth Circuit. *Education:* Riverside Community College (A.A., 1979); San Diego State University (B.S., Microbiology, 1981); University of San Diego (J.D., 1991); University of California, Irvine (M.B.A., 1994). Member, Los Angeles Complex Litigation Inn of Court, 1992-1995. *Member:* Los Angeles County (Member, Intellectual Property, Entertainment and International Law Sections), Orange County and American Bar Associations; State Bar of California (Member, Intellectual Property Section, 1991—); California Women Lawyers Association.

---

## ANDREW ALEXANDER DÓSA

Established in 1989

2504 SANTA CLARA AVENUE
**ALAMEDA, CALIFORNIA 94501**
Telephone: 510-865-1600
FAX: 510-865-7245

Personal Injury, General, Civil and Business Litigation. Criminal Law.

**ANDREW ALEXANDER DÓSA**, born Aberdeen, Maryland, July 27, 1958; admitted to bar, 1984, California. *Education:* University of California at Berkeley (A.B., 1980); University of San Francisco (J.D., 1983). Phi Delta Phi. Adjunct Professor, United States History, National Hispanic University, Oakland, 1988-1989. Instructor, Paralegal Program, California State University at Hayward, 1988-1989. Judge Pro Tem, Fremont-Newark-Union City Judicial District, Alameda County Municipal Court, 1989-1995. Judge Pro Tem, Alameda Judicial District, Alameda County Municipal Court, 1993—. *Member:* Alameda County Bar Association; The State Bar of California; Christian Legal Society. **PRACTICE AREAS:** Personal Injury; General Civil Litigation; Litigation; Criminal Law.

---

## ELAINE F.B. LEADLOVE-PLANT

909 MARINA VILLAGE PARKWAY, SUITE 339
**ALAMEDA, CALIFORNIA 94501**
Telephone: 510-523-4586

Construction Law, Bankruptcy.

**ELAINE F.B. LEADLOVE-PLANT**, born Pt. Alice, Canada, January 9, 1949; admitted to bar, 1989, California. *Education:* San Francisco State University; John F. Kennedy University (J.D., 1989). *Member:* San Francisco County and Alameda County Bar Associations; State Bar of California. **PRACTICE AREAS:** Banking Litigation (70%); Business Law (10%); Bankruptcy (10%); Consumer Law (10%).

---

## MENDELSON & BROWN

A Partnership including Professional Corporations

Established in 1965

1040 MARINA VILLAGE PARKWAY, SUITE B
**ALAMEDA, CALIFORNIA 94501**
Telephone: 510-521-1211
FAX: 510-521-7879
Email: dm@mendelson-brown.com

General Civil and Trial Practice. Corporate, Commercial, Real Estate, Labor, Construction, Banking, Environmental, Securities, Technology, Trademark, and Energy.

*FIRM PROFILE: Mendelson & Brown is an established East Bay law firm committed to offering high quality, responsive legal services. Unlike most large law firms that are built on a pyramid structure, with numerous inexperienced associates working under a supervising partner, Mendelson & Brown relies on experienced attorneys performing the bulk of the work themselves. This "hands on" approach allows the client to have a close working relationship with the attorney in charge. The benefit is passed on to clients in the form of professional, responsive services at rates well below those of larger law firms.*

### MEMBERS OF FIRM

**MICHAEL S. BROWN, (P.C.)**, born Mount Kisco, New York, August 5, 1952; admitted to bar, 1978, California. *Education:* University of Denver (B.A., 1974); Loyola University of Los Angeles (J.D., 1978). *Member:* Alameda County and American Bar Associations. **PRACTICE AREAS:** Real Estate; Commercial; Insurance; Environmental. **Email:** MSB@mendelson-brown.com

**THOMAS P. SULLIVAN, (P.C.)**, born San Francisco, California, January 16, 1956; admitted to bar, 1981, California. *Education:* San Jose State University (B.S., with distinction, 1978); Hastings College of Law, University of California (J.D., 1981). Phi Kappa Phi; Beta Gamma Sigma. Note and Comment Editor, Hastings Law Journal, 1980-1981. Author: "Criminal Intent and The Sherman Act: The Label Per Se Can't Take Gypsum Away," 32 Hastings Law Journal, November, 1980. *Member:* Alameda County and American Bar Associations; The State Bar of California. **PRACTICE AREAS:** Commercial; Banking; Real Estate; Construction. **Email:** TPS@mendelson-brown.com

*(This Listing Continued)*

## MENDELSON & BROWN, Alameda—Continued

**GREGORY L. BEATTIE,** born Stockton, California, February 3, 1954; admitted to bar, 1980, California. *Education:* University of California at Davis and Stanford University (A.B., with distinction, 1976); Harvard University (J.D., cum laude, 1980). Phi Beta Kappa. Law Clerk to Justice Stanley Mosk, California Supreme Court, 1980-1981. *Member:* Alameda County Bar Association; State Bar of California. *PRACTICE AREAS:* Technology; Corporate; Securities; Commercial. *Email:* GLB@mendelson-brown.com

**RICHARD A. LYONS,** born Pasadena, California, July 28, 1949; admitted to bar, 1982, California. *Education:* University of California at Irvine (B.A., 1971); Boalt Hall School of Law, University of California (J.D., 1982). Recipient, Best Written Brief, Moot Court Award, 1980. Member, Moot Court Board, 1981-1982. Contributing Editor, Law and Finance, Independent Sources of Energy, 1983-1991. Member, Advisory Board, Senate Select Committee on Small Business Enterprises, 1986-1991. *Member:* Bar Association of San Francisco; State Bar of California (Member, Business Law and Intellectual Property Sections); American Bar Association (Member, Sections on: Corporation, Banking and Business Law; Science and Technology). *PRACTICE AREAS:* Corporate; Partnerships; Securities; Technology. *Email:* RAL@mendelson-brown.com

### ASSOCIATES

**BRUCE D. HOLLOWAY,** born Walnut Creek, California, November 30, 1955; admitted to bar, 1990, Washington and California. *Education:* University of California, Berkeley (A.B., with highest honors, 1978; M.A., 1982; Ph.D., 1985); Boalt Hall School of Law (J.D., 1989). Phi Beta Kappa. Regents Scholar. American-Scandinavian Foundation and University of California Fellow, 1983-1984. Visiting Scholar, University of Copenhagen, 1983-1984. Regents Fellow, University of California, Berkeley, 1980-1982. ITT International Scholarship, Norway, 1979-1980. Special Honors, University of California, Berkeley, College of Letters and Science Department of Scandinavian. *LANGUAGES:* Norwegian, German, Danish, Swedish, Dutch. *PRACTICE AREAS:* Trademark; Technology; Corporate; Commercial. *Email:* BDH@mendelson-brown.com

### OF COUNSEL

**RALPH N. MENDELSON, (P.C.),** born Oakland, California, July 13, 1930; admitted to bar, 1955, California. *Education:* University of Minnesota (B.A., summa cum laude, 1952); Yale University (LL.B., 1955); London School of Economics (LL.M., 1985). Phi Beta Kappa. Law Clerk to Albert Lee Stephens, Chief Judge, U.S. Court of Appeals for the 9th Circuit, 1957-1958. Member, Panel on Judicial Arbitration, Alameda County Superior Court, Business and Commercial Section, 1986—. Arbitrator, American Arbitration Association. General Counsel, California Bancshares, Inc., 1992. *Member:* Alameda County and American Bar Associations; The State Bar of California. *PRACTICE AREAS:* Commercial Law; Banking.

REPRESENTATIVE CLIENTS: Alameda First National Bank; Aval Communications, Inc.; Bank of San Ramon Valley; Bay Mirror, Inc.; Berkeley Systems, Inc.; California Bancshares, Inc.; Coastcom; Commercial Bank of Fremont; Farallon Computing, Inc.; Federal Deposit Insurance Corporation (FDIC); Ron Goode Toyota, Inc.; Grosvenor Securities; Howden Wind Parks, Inc.; Mountain Peoples's Warehouse, Inc.; Networking Technical Support Alliance, Inc.; The Saw Mill, Inc.; Sybase; UB Networks, Inc.

## OWEN & MELBYE

*A PROFESSIONAL CORPORATION*

**ALAMEDA, CALIFORNIA**

(See Redwood City)

*General Civil and Trial Practice in all State and Federal Courts. Aviation, Products, Insurance Defense Law, and Insurance Coverage Analysis.*

## WILLIAM ROBERT PEDDER

*A PROFESSIONAL CORPORATION*

Established in 1981

*2447 SANTA CLARA AVENUE, SUITE 201*
**ALAMEDA, CALIFORNIA 94501**
*Telephone: 510-523-9152*
*FAX: 510-523-9154*

*General Civil and Trial Practice. Real Estate, Personal Injury, Corporate Business, Estate Planning, Trust and Probate Law.*

(This Listing Continued)

**WILLIAM ROBERT PEDDER,** born Los Angeles, California, November 4, 1942; admitted to bar, 1968, California. *Education:* University of California at Riverside; Stanford University (A.B., with honors, 1964; J.D., 1967). Staff Attorney, Office of the General Counsel, U.S. Department of Agriculture, 1968-1969. *Member:* Alameda County and American Bar Associations; The State Bar of California.

## MARY H. WIDENOR

*2223 SANTA CLARA AVENUE SUITE B*
**ALAMEDA, CALIFORNIA 94501**
*Telephone: 510-865-2223; 1-800-40 Probate Ex. 135*
*FAX: 510-865-0375*

*Probate, Estate Planning, Estate and Trust Litigation, Real Property and Business Law.*

**MARY H. WIDENOR,** born Alamosa, Colorado, July 1, 1937; admitted to bar, 1977, California. *Education:* Pomona College (B.A., 1958); University of Munich, (Fulbright Fellowship, 1959); University of California (M.A., 1962); Boalt Hall School of Law, (J.D., 1977). Phi Beta Kappa. *Member:* Alameda County and American Bar Associations; State Bar of California. (Certified Specialist Estate Planning, Trust and Probate Law, State Bar of California Board of Legal Specialization).

## YOUNG & YOUNG LLP

*1826 CLEMENT STREET*
**ALAMEDA, CALIFORNIA 94501**
*Telephone: 510-865-2600*
*URL: http://www.samyoung@ihot.com*

San Francisco, California Office: Three Embarcadero Center, Suite 1160, 94111. Telephone: 415-438-3660. Fax: 415-291-9222.

*General Practice including Business Transactions, Major Loan Restructures, Hospital Law, Land Use and Development, Real Estate and Real Estate Syndication.*

(For Complete Biographical Data on all Personnel, see Biographies at San Francisco)

## BERDING & WEIL

*3240 STONE VALLEY ROAD WEST*
**ALAMO, CALIFORNIA 94507**
*Telephone: 510-838-2090*
*Facsimile: 510-820-5592*
*URL: http://www.berding-weil.com*

Rancho Cordova, California Office: 2200 Sunrise Boulevard, Suite 220. 95670 Telephone: 916-851-1910. Fax: 916-851-1914.

Santa Clara, California Office: 3600 Pruneridge Avenue, Suite 130. 95051 Telephone: 408-556-0220. Fax: 408-556-0224.

Fresno, California Office: 516 West Shaw Avenue, Suite 200, 93704. Telephone: 209-221-2556. Fax: 209-221-2558.

*Construction Litigation and Community Association Law. Non-Profit Corporation Law. Appellate Practice.*

*FIRM PROFILE: Berding & Weil was founded in 1988 by Tyler P. Berding and Steven S. Weil. The firm is experienced in Community Association, corporate and real property law and in construction defect litigation and serves the legal needs of clients throughout Northern California.*

*The firm represents community associations and other owners of large residential and commercial buildings in construction defect disputes, including soils failures and contamination and defective ABS plastic pipe. Members of the firm assist community association and other non-profit corporation clients in interpreting, enforcing and amending governing documents, aid in delinquent assessment collections and deal with insurance, title, real property and corporate matters. The firm provides practical advice to directors, officers and managers of common interest developments as well as to apartment building owners.*

*Berding & Weil is experienced in handling civil appeals and writs in state and federal courts.*

(This Listing Continued)

## PROFESSIONAL BIOGRAPHIES

### MEMBERS OF FIRM

**TYLER P. BERDING,** born Oakland, California, December 15, 1944; admitted to bar, 1974, California and U.S. District Courts, Eastern, Northern and Central Districts of California. *Education:* California State University at Hayward (B.A., 1966); Claremont Graduate School (M.A., 1969; Ph.D., 1971); University of California at Davis (J.D., 1974). Member, California Veterans Board, 1974-1975. Director, Executive Council of Homeowners (ECHO), 1990—; Chairman, ECHO Legislative Committee, 1990—; Member, ECHO Legal Resource Panel, 1988—. Member, California Department of Real Estate Task Force on Common Interest Developments, 1992-1993. Faculty Member, California Association of Community Managers (CACM), 1992—; Legal Advisory Committee, 1994—; Review Editor, CACM Law Journal, 1994. *Member:* Contra Costa County and American Bar Associations; State Bar of California (Member, Common Interest Development Subsection of the Real Property Section); Consumer Attorneys of California; Association of Business Trial Lawyers. [Major, USAFR] *Email:* t.berding@access2.com

**STEVEN S. WEIL,** born Brooklyn, New York, November 5, 1954; admitted to bar, 1980, California and U.S. District Court, Northern District of California. *Education:* State University of New York at Potsdam; State University of New York, Harpur College (B.A., 1976); University of San Francisco (J.D., 1980). Managing Director, Moot Court Board, 1979-1980. Director, Community Associations Institute (CAI), Bay Area Chapter, 1993—; President, 1994-1995. Instructor, San Francisco Law School, 1987-1995. Director, Council of Condominium Homeowner Associations (COCHA), 1992-1993. Legal Member, Executive Council of Homeowners (ECHO), 1990—; Faculty Member, California Association of Community Managers (CACM), 1995—. *Member:* Contra Costa County (Member, Fee Arbitration Panel, 1986) and American Bar Associations; State Bar of California (Member, Common Interest Development Subsection of the Real Property Section); Consumer Attorneys of California; Association of Business Trial Lawyers. LANGUAGES: French.

**JAMES O. DEVEREAUX,** born Pontiac, Michigan, December 23, 1940; admitted to bar, 1967, Michigan, U.S. Court of Appeals, Sixth Circuit and U.S. District Court, Eastern and Western Districts of Michigan; 1979, California, U.S. Court of Appeals, Ninth Circuit and U.S. District Court, Northern District of California; 1990, U.S. Supreme Court. *Education:* University of Detroit (A.B., 1963); University of Michigan Law School (J.D., 1966). Chief Assistant Clerk, Michigan Court of Appeals, Lansing, Michigan, 1969-1978. Instructor, Thomas M. Cooley Law School, Lansing, Michigan, 1979-1980. Faculty, National Appellate Judges Conference, 1973-1974. Legal Member, Executive Council of Homeowners (ECHO), 1991—; Legal Resource Panel, 1993—; North Bay Resource Panel, 1994—, Chairman, 1995—. *Member:* Bar Association of San Francisco; State Bar of California (Member, Common Interest Development Subsection of the Real Property Section); Consumer Attorneys of California; Association of Business Trial Lawyers. REPORTED CASES: Burnham v. Superior Court (1990) 495 U.S. 604, 109 L. Ed 2d 631, 110 S. Ct. 2105; Lauriedale Associates, Ltd. v. Wilson (1992) 7 Cal. App. 4th 1439, 9 Cal. Rptr. 2d 774; Nahrstedt v. Lakeside Village Condominium Association (1994) 8 Cal. 4th 361, 33 Cal. Rptr 2d 63, 878 P 2d 1275. *Email:* j.devereaux@access2.com

**JEFFREY B. CEREGHINO,** born Washington, D.C., October 6, 1953; admitted to bar, 1981, California and U.S. District Court, Northern District of California. *Education:* University of Maryland at College Park (B.A., 1977); Golden Gate University (J.D., 1981). Programs Chairman, Community Associations Institute (CAI), San Francisco Bay Chapter, 1991-1993. Legal Member, Executive Council of Homeowners (ECHO), 1990—, Legal Resource Panel, 1994—, Vice-Chairman, Santa Cruz/Monterey Resource Panel, 1996—. Member, Council of Condominium Homeowner Associations (COCHA), 1987. *Member:* Alameda County Bar Association; State Bar of California; Italian-American Bar Association; Consumer Attorneys of California. LANGUAGES: French.

**MICHAEL J. HUGHES,** born San Francisco, California, November 5, 1947; admitted to bar, 1974, California. *Education:* University of California at Santa Barbara (B.A., with honors, 1969); Hastings College of Law, University of California (J.D., 1972). *Member:* State Bar of California; Consumer Attorneys of California. [1st Lt., , U.S. Army, 1972-1974] *Email:* m.hughes@access2.com

**DEON R. STEIN,** born Pretoria, Republic of South Africa, March 5, 1964; admitted to bar, 1988, California. *Education:* University of California at San Diego (B.A., 1985); University of California, Hastings College of the Law (J.D., cum laude, 1988). Director, Community Associations Institute (CAI) California North Chapter, 1996—; Member, California Building Industry Association. *Member:* Sacramento County Bar Association; State Bar of California. (Resident at Rancho Cordova Office). *Email:* d.stein@access2.com

**EUGENE P. HAYDU,** born Longview, Washington, February 28, 1953; admitted to bar, 1988, California; 1993, Oregon. *Education:* St. Thomas College; University of Washington (B.A., 1976); Golden Gate University (J.D., 1987). *Member:* Sacramento County Bar Association; State Bar of California; Consumer Attorneys of California; Sacramento Consumer Attorneys of California. (Resident at Rancho Cordova Office).

**MARY WALKER FILSON,** born Rantoul, Illinois, June 17, 1950; admitted to bar, 1986, California; U. S. District Court, Northern District of California; U.S. Tax Court. *Education:* Southern Illinois University (B.A., with honors, 1972; M.A., 1973); Boalt Hall School of Law, University of California (J.D., 1985). Legal Member, Executive Council of Homeowners (ECHO). ECHO Wine Country Resource Panel. *Member:* Contra Costa County and American (Member, Business Law Section) Bar Associations; State Bar of California (Member, Real Property and Business Law Sections; Member, Non Profit Organizations Committee of the Business Law Section).

**DANIEL L. ROTTINGHAUS,** born Redwood City, California, December 20, 1961; admitted to bar, 1987, California and U.S. District Court, Northern District of California; 1988, U.S. Court of Military Review; 1989, U.S. Court of Military Appeals, U.S. Tax Court; 1991, U.S. Supreme Court; 1994, District of Columbia; U.S. Navy-Marine Corps Court of Military Review. *Education:* University of California at Los Angeles (B.S./B.S., 1984); University of Santa Clara School of Law (J.D., 1987); Georgetown University Law Center (LL.M., 1993). Legal Member, Executive Council of Homeowners (ECHO) 1995—. ECHO South Bay Resource Panel, 1995—. *Member:* Santa Clara County Bar Association; Consumer Attorneys of California. [U.S. Army Judge Advocate General Corps, 1988-1994, Capt.]. (Resident at Santa Clara Office). *Email:* d.rottinghaus@access2.com

### OF COUNSEL

**DAVID M. BIRKA-WHITE,** born Los Angeles, California, October 12, 1952; admitted to bar, 1979, California; U.S. District Court, Northern and Eastern Districts of California. *Education:* University of California at Berkeley (B.A., 1974); San Francisco Law School (J.D., 1978). Participant, University of California, Boalt Hall, Industrial Relations Law Review, 1975-1976. *Member:* The Bar Association of San Francisco; Alameda County and Contra Costa County Bar Associations; State Bar of California (Member: Litigation Section; Real Property Law Section); The Association of Trial Lawyers of America; Consumer Attorneys of California; Alameda-Contra Costa Trial Lawyers Association (Member, Board of Governors, 1992—). (Also practicing individually).

**RANDOLPH M. PAUL,** born Springfield, Ohio, June 11, 1947; admitted to bar, 1975, California and U.S. District Court, Northern and Central Districts of California. *Education:* Arizona State University (B.S.E., with distinction, 1969); University of Santa Clara (J.D., cum laude, 1974). Adjunct Professor, Santa Clara University School of Law, Evidence, 1984-1986. Judge Pro Tem, Santa Clara County Superior Court, 1989—. Member, Panel of Arbitrators, American Arbitration Association. Legal Member, Executive Council of Homeowners, 1995—. *Member:* Santa Clara County and American Bar Associations; State Bar of California; Consumer Attorneys of California. (Resident at Santa Clara Office). *Email:* r.paul@access2.com

### ASSOCIATES

**MICHAEL W. BARNES,** born Oakland, California, December 15, 1957; admitted to bar, 1991, California; 1992, U.S. District Court, Northern District of California. *Education:* University of California at Berkeley (A.B., 1987); Golden Gate University (J.D., 1991). Legal Member, Executive Council of Homeowners (ECHO), 1995—. *Member:* Consumer Attorneys of California. *Email:* m.barnes@access2.com

**SCOTT WILLIAM BARTON,** born Burlingame, California, March 3, 1963; admitted to bar, 1992, California; 1993, Pennsylvania, New Jersey, U.S. District Court, Eastern District of Pennsylvania, U.S. District Court, District of New Jersey and U.S. District Court, Northern District of California. *Education:* United States Merchant Marine Academy (B.S., with honors, 1985); Santa Clara University (J.D., magna cum laude, 1992). U.S.C.G. Master Oceans to 1600 tons, Second Mate Unlimited. *Member:* Contra Costa County Bar Association; Consumer Attorneys of California. [USNR, 1985—, Lieutenant Commander]

**JOSHUA SULTER BEREZIN,** born Boston, Massachusetts, September 22, 1969; admitted to bar, 1996, California. *Education:* The American University, Washington, D.C. (B.A., 1991); Widener University (J.D.,

*(This Listing Continued)*

## BERDING & WEIL, Alamo—Continued

1995). *Member:* Contra Costa County Bar Association; State Bar of California (Member, Business Law Section). **LANGUAGES:** Spanish. **Email:** j.berezin@access2.com

**DAVID DARROCH,** born San Francisco, California, October 19, 1952; admitted to bar, 1996, California and U.S. District Court, Northern District of California. *Education:* Mount Allison University (B.A., 1987); San Francisco Law School (J.D., with honors, 1996). *Member:* State Bar of California; California Young Trial Lawyers Association.

**JOHN P. GILL,** born Concord, California, September 5, 1964; admitted to bar, 1990, California; 1991, U.S. District Court, Northern District of California. *Education:* Santa Clara University (B.A., 1986); Hastings College of Law (J.D., 1989). *Member:* State Bar of California; Consumer Attorneys of California.

**CORI L. GOLDSTEIN,** born Bourne, Massachusetts, December 12, 1963; admitted to bar, 1992, California and U.S. District Court, Northern District of California. *Education:* San Jose State University (B.A., 1988); Santa Clara University (J.D., 1992). Legal Member, Executive Council of Homeowners (ECHO), 1995—, Charter Member, East Bay Resource Panel, 1995—. *Member:* Contra Costa Bar Association; State Bar of California; Consumer Attorneys of California. **Email:** c.goldstein@access2.com

**STEPHANIE J. HAYES,** born Newburgh, N.Y., June 11, 1954; admitted to bar, 1981, Illinois and U.S. District Court, Northern District of Illinois; 1994, California and U.S. District Court, Northern District of California. *Education:* University of Illinois, Chicago, (B.A., with honors, 1976); John Marshall Law School (J.D., with distinction, 1981). Deputy General Counsel and Assistant Secretary, Illinois Development Finance Authority, 1990-1993. *Member:* American Bar Association (Business Law, Real Property Law Sections); State Bar of California. **Email:** s.hayes@access2.com

**KIM I. HICKMAN,** born Soap Lake, Washington, May 24, 1955; admitted to bar, 1994, California. *Education:* John F. Kennedy University, Orinda (J.D., 1993). *Member:* State Bar of California; Contra Costa and American Bar Associations; Consumer Attorneys of California.

**DANA S. MARRON,** born New York City, N.Y., December 29, 1967; admitted to bar, 1993, California and U.S. District Court, Northern District of California; 1994, U.S. District Court, Central District of California; 1996, U.S. District Court, Southern and Eastern Districts of California. *Education:* Boston University (B.A., 1990); California Western School of Law (J.D., 1993). Director, Barristers Association of Contra Costa County. *Member:* Contra Costa County and American Bar Associations; State Bar of California; Consumer Attorneys of California. **LANGUAGES:** French. **Email:** d.marron@access2.com

**MARILYN J. STEWART,** born Berkeley, California, May, 4, 1949; admitted to bar, 1994, California. *Education:* University of California at Davis; St. Mary's College, Moraga; John F. Kennedy University (J.D., 1993). *Member:* State Bar of California.

**EVAN D. WILLIAMS,** born Eureka, California, August 11, 1964; admitted to bar, 1989, California and U.S. District Court, Northern District of California. *Education:* California State University at Chico (B.S., 1986); University of Santa Clara (J.D., 1989). *Member:* Sacramento County Bar Association; State Bar of California. (Resident at Rancho Cordova Office).

REPRESENTATIVE CLIENTS: 2200 Pacific Homeowners Assn; Alamo Stonegate Homeowners Assn; Alder Point Owners Assn (Johnson Ranch); Auburn Lake Trials Owners Assn; Blue Lake Springs Homeowners Assn; Casa de Redwood Foundation; Community of Harbor Bay Isle; Crosswoods Homeowners Assn; Crow Canyon County Club Estates Community Assn; Crown Colony Homeowners Assn; Country Club at Blackhawk Improvement Assn; El Dorado Hills Townhouse Assn; Greenstone Owners Assn; Islandia Homeowners Assn; Lake Wildwood Assn; Meridian Woods Assn; Muirwood Square Condominium Owners Assn; Ocean Beach Homeowners Assn; Olympian Hills Homeowners Assn; Opera Plaza Homeowners Assn; Orindawoods Assn; Pacific Park Plaza Homeowners Assn; Park Avenue By The Sea Homeowners Assn; Park Webster Homeowners Assn; Parkview Terrace Homeowners Assn; Pepperwood Hills Owners Assn; Placer County Stanford Village Homeowners Assn (Johnson Ranch); Pt. Tiburon Bayside and Lagoon Condominium Assns; Rancho Solano Master Assn; Regency Park Townhouse Assn; Ridge of San Rafael Owners Assn; Rinconada Hills Assn; Sanders Ranch Homeowners Assn; Second Walnut Creek Mutual (Rossmoor); Sierra Lakeside Village Property Owners Assn; Sonoma Greens Community Assn; Tahoe Keys Property Owners Assn; The Heritage of Fresno Homeowners Assn; The Residences of Spanish Bay Assn; The Keys Condominium Owners Assn; The Village Golf & Country Club; Timberlake Owners Assn; Tres Lagos North Homeowners Assn; Twin Creeks South Poolside Homeowners Assn; Village In The Park Homeowners Assn; Villa Marin Homeowners Assn; Villas of Almaden Homeowners Assn; Vineyard Homeowners Assn.

## LAW OFFICES OF
## DAVID M. BIRKA-WHITE

3240 STONE VALLEY ROAD WEST, SUITE 102

**ALAMO, CALIFORNIA 94507**

Telephone: 510-838-2090

Facsimile: 510-820-5592

*Construction Defects, ABS Plastic Pipe and General Products Liability, Insurance Coverage.*

**FIRM PROFILE:** David M. Birka-White has for the past 10 years specialized in litigation involving construction defects and ABS plastic pipe failures on behalf of plaintiffs throughout California. He further specializes in class actions involving product failures.

**DAVID M. BIRKA-WHITE,** born Los Angeles, California, October 12, 1952; admitted to bar, 1979, California; U.S. District Court, Northern and Eastern Districts of California. *Education:* University of California at Berkeley (B.A., 1974); San Francisco Law School (J.D., 1978). Participant, University of California, Boalt Hall, Industrial Relations Law Review, 1975-1976. *Member:* The Bar Association of San Francisco; Alameda County and Contra Costa County Bar Associations; State Bar of California (Member: Litigation Section; Real Property Law Section); The Association of Trial Lawyers of America; Consumer Attorneys of California; Alameda-Contra Costa Trial Lawyers Association (Member, Board of Governors, 1992—).

## FOLEY McINTOSH & FOLEY

PROFESSIONAL CORPORATION

**ALBANY, CALIFORNIA**

(See Lafayette)

*General Civil and Trial Practice in all Courts. Corporate, Business, Real Property, Tax and Probate Law.*

## TOMPKINS & PARRINGTON

Established in 1977

320 NORTH GARFIELD AVENUE

P.O. BOX 589

**ALHAMBRA, CALIFORNIA 91802**

Telephone: 818-289-3727; 213-283-3107

Telecopier: 818-289-0918

*Probate, Estate Planning, Taxation, Real Estate, Zoning and Business Law.*

### MEMBERS OF FIRM

**EMMETT A. TOMPKINS, JR.,** born Monterey Park, California, December 18, 1935; admitted to bar, 1961, California. *Education:* University of California at Los Angeles (B.A., 1957; LL.B., 1960). Phi Delta Phi. *Member:* San Gabriel Valley (President, 1973) and Los Angeles County (Member, Section on Probate and Trust Law) Bar Associations; State Bar of California; Estate Planning Council of San Gabriel Valley (President, 1975). **PRACTICE AREAS:** Probate and Trust; Estate Planning.

**THOMAS E. PARRINGTON,** born Pasadena, California, June 19, 1939; admitted to bar, 1965, California. *Education:* Stanford University (B.A., 1961); Boalt Hall School of Law, University of California (LL.B., 1964). Board Member, 1983-1989 and President, 1989, Legal Services Program for Pasadena and San Gabriel-Pomona Valley. *Member:* San Gabriel Valley President, 1983) and Los Angeles County (Member, Sections on: Government; Real Estate) Bar Associations; State Bar of California. **PRACTICE AREAS:** Real Estate; Redevelopment; Probate; Trust; Estate Planning.

REFERENCES: Bank of America, Alhambra Branch; California State Bank, Alhambra; Wells Fargo Bank Trust Department; Sanwa Bank Trust Department.

## WORDES, WILSHIN, GOREN & CONNER

*31 JOURNEY STREET, SUITE 120*
**ALISO VIEJO, CALIFORNIA 92656-3334**
*Telephone: 714-643-1000*
*Telecopier: 714-643-2000*
*Email: firm@wwgc.com*
*URL: http://www.wwgc.com*

*Real Estate and Business Law, Litigation.*

### MEMBERS OF FIRM

**RICHARD S. WORDES,** born 1950; admitted to bar, 1975, California. *Education:* University of California at Los Angeles (B.A.); Southwestern University (J.D.). *Member:* Los Angeles County and American Bar Associations; State Bar of California (Member: Real Property Section; Commercial and Industrial Subsection and Business Law Section); International Council of Shopping Centers; Building Owners and Managers Association; California Restaurant Association. **PRACTICE AREAS:** Real Estate; Business Law. *Email:* rswordes@wwgc.com

**DAVID B. WILSHIN,** born Baltimore, Maryland, March 11, 1942; admitted to bar, 1972, California. *Education:* United States Naval Academy (B.S., with honors, 1964); University of California at Los Angeles (J.D., 1971). Member, Moot Court Honors Program. Licensed Real Estate Broker, California, 1981. *Member:* Orange County Bar Association; State Bar of California (Member, Real Property, International Law and Business Sections); International Council of Shopping Centers; Building Owners and Managers Association; International Marketing Association; Global Network. [Capt., USMC, 1964-1968]. **PRACTICE AREAS:** Real Estate Law; Business Law; Litigation; International Trade Law. *Email:* dbwilshin@wwgc.com

**MICHAEL E. GOREN,** born 1950; admitted to bar, 1975, California. *Education:* University of California at Los Angeles (B.A.); University of California at Los Angeles (J.D.). Member: UCLA Law Review; Order of the Coif. *Member:* Los Angeles County Bar Association; State Bar of California (Member, Real Property Section); International Council of Shopping Centers. **PRACTICE AREAS:** Commercial Real Estate; Shopping Center Law. *Email:* megoren@wwgc.com

**FRANK A. CONNER,** born Victorville, California, February 28, 1953; admitted to bar, 1979, California; 1980, U.S. District Court, Central and Southern Districts of California. *Education:* Brigham Young University (B.S., 1976; J.D., cum laude, 1979). Senior Editor, Brigham Young University Journal of Legal Studies, 1978-1979. Author: "Chapter X, *Liens,"* Summary of Utah Real Property Law, Brigham Young University Journal of Legal Studies, 1978; "Basic Civil Litigation," California Supplement, MacMillan/McGraw-Hill, 1993; "Litigation Budgeting," Software, 1992. *Member:* Orange County Bar Association; State Bar of California; International Council of Shopping Centers. **PRACTICE AREAS:** Real Estate and Business Litigation. *Email:* faconner@ix.netcom.com

---

## CATANZARITE LAW CORPORATION

*Established in 1984*

*2331 WEST LINCOLN AVENUE*
**ANAHEIM, CALIFORNIA 92801**
*Telephone: 714-520-5544; 800- 326-5544*
*Fax: 714-520-0680*

*Business Transactions, Federal and State Taxation, Pensions, Employee Benefits, Real Estate, Securities, Estate Planning, Health Care, Labor, Corporate, Business Litigation, Professional Malpractice and Bankruptcy.*

FIRM PROFILE: *The firm is the successor of a practice established in Ohio in 1974. The firm of five attorneys also has a paralegal support staff which includes actuaries, forensic accountants and finance professionals.*

**KENNETH J. CATANZARITE,** born Lorain, Ohio, June 14, 1949; admitted to bar, 1974, Ohio; 1982, U.S. Tax Court; 1984, California; 1986, Kansas, 1988, Tennessee; 1990, New York; 1991, Texas and District of Columbia; 1993, Colorado and U.S. Claims Court; U.S. District Court, Central District of California; U.S. Supreme Court. *Education:* University of Akron (B.S.B.A., Accounting and Finance, 1971; J.D., 1973). Adjunct Professor of Law, Taxation, University of Akron, 1975-1978. Chartered Financial Analyst, Association for Investment Management & Research, 1986. Certified Public Accountant, Ohio, 1987. *Member:* Los Angeles County, California, Ohio, Kansas, Tennessee and New York State Bar Associations; State Bar of Texas; District of Columbia Bar; American Institute

*(This Listing Continued)*

---

of Certified Public Accountants. (Certified Specialist, Taxation Law and Personal and Small Business Bankruptcy, The State Bar of California Board of Legal Specialization). **PRACTICE AREAS:** Business Transactions and Litigation; Federal and State Taxation Law; Securities Law; Employee Benefits Law; Bankruptcy Law.

REPRESENTATIVE CLIENTS: Hegwer Industries, Inc.; ABC Products, Inc.; Benefit Resource Management, Inc.; East Tennessee Dialysis Centers; Vestax Properties, Inc.; Cal-West Marketing, Inc.; Square Tool & Machine Co., Inc.

---

## FARANO AND KIEVIET

*A PROFESSIONAL LAW CORPORATION*
*Established in 1977*

*2100 SOUTH STATE COLLEGE BOULEVARD*
**ANAHEIM, CALIFORNIA 92806**
*Telephone: 714-935-2400*
*Fax: 714-935-2410*

*General Civil Trial and Appellate Practice, State and Federal Courts. Transportation Law, Government Contract Law, Land Use, Zoning, Development and Real Estate Law, Municipal Law and Code Enforcement, Mobile Home Park Law, Corporate and Business Law, Creditors Rights, Probate and Estate Planning, Medical Malpractice, Insurance and Defense, Criminal Law, Labor Law.*

**FLOYD L. FARANO,** born Chicago, Illinois, September 2, 1927; admitted to bar, 1955, Illinois; 1963, California and U.S. District Court, Central District of California; 1984, U.S. Court of Appeals, Ninth Circuit; 1985, U.S. Supreme Court. *Education:* University of Illinois (B.A., 1951); John Marshall Law School (J.D., 1955). Delta Theta Phi. Member, 1966-1976 and Chairman, 1972 and 1975, Anaheim Planning Commission. Member, Orange County Planning Commission, 1976-1977. Judge Pro Tem, Orange County Superior Court, 1981-1991. Member: Orange County Fair Campaign Practices Commission, 1988-1991. Orange County Private Industry Council, 1988-1991. President, Anaheim Chamber of Commerce 1986-1987. Arbitrator, Orange County Superior Court. Member, Panel of Arbitrators, American Arbitration Association. Chief Counsel for U.S. Senator John Seymour, 1991-1992. *Member:* State Bar of Illinois; State Bar of California; Transportation Lawyers Association. [Sgt., U.S. Army, 1944-1946]. **PRACTICE AREAS:** Transportation Law; Land Use Law; Development Law; Zoning Law; Politics and Campaign Law.

**CHARLES M. FARANO,** born Chicago, Illinois, August 15, 1952; admitted to bar, 1979, California; 1980, U.S. District Court, Central District of California; 1984, U.S. Court of Appeals, Ninth Circuit; 1985, U.S. Supreme Court; 1986, U.S. Court of International Trade. *Education:* California State College, Stanislaus (B.A., 1974); Western State University (J.D., 1978). Author: "Limiting Damages in California," National Business Institute, 1993; "Basic Code Enforcement Methods," 1989 and "Code Enforcement, Policy and Procedure," 1992, Code Enforcement Institute. Lecturer/Instructor: National Business Institute, 1993; Code Enforcement Institute, 1990—. Judge Pro Tem: Orange County Superior Court, 1983—; Orange County Municipal Court, 1985—. Assistant Prosecutor, City of Orange, 1990-1992; City of Garden Grove, 1990-1991. *Member:* State Bar of California; The Association of Trial Lawyers of America. **REPORTED CASES:** Miller's National Insurance Company vs. Axel's Express (1988) 851 F2d 267; Global Van Lines vs. Superior Court (1983) 144 C.A. 3d 483; Suburban Motors vs. State Farm (1990) 218 C.A. 3d 1354. **PRACTICE AREAS:** Litigation; Trial Practice; Municipal Law; Code Enforcement.

**THOMAS G. KIEVIET,** born Grand Rapids, Michigan, September 10, 1954; admitted to bar, 1979, California; 1980, U.S. District Court, Central District of California; 1984, U.S. Court of Appeals, Ninth Circuit; 1985, U.S. Supreme Court. *Education:* Cypress College (A.A., 1974); California State University at Fullerton (B.A., 1976); Pepperdine University (J.D., cum laude, 1979). Phi Kappa Phi. Member, Pepperdine Law Review, 1978-1979. Author: "The Battered Wife Syndrome, A Potential Defense to a Homicide Charge," Pepperdine Law Review, Vol. 6, No. 1, 1978. *Member:* State Bar of California. **PRACTICE AREAS:** Corporate Law; Business Law; Real Estate Law; Estate Planning Law; Land use and Zoning.

**JEFFREY L. FARANO,** born Chicago, Illinois, August 4, 1956; admitted to bar, 1984, California and U.S. District Court, Central District of California; 1984, U.S. Court of Appeals, Ninth Circuit. *Education:* Western State University (B.S.L., 1982; J.D., 1983). *Member:* Orange County Bar Association; State Bar of California (Member, Real Property Section); Transportation Lawyers Association; California Trucking Association;

*(This Listing Continued)*

## FARANO AND KIEVIET, A PROFESSIONAL LAW CORPORATION, Anaheim—Continued

California Movers and Warehouseman Association. **PRACTICE AREAS:** Transportation Law; Land use and Zoning; Government Contract Law.

REPRESENTATIVE CLIENTS: Anaheim Chamber of Commerce; Denny's, Inc.; California Auto Dealers Exchange; Riverside Auto Action; Southern California Auto Auction; Manheim Auctions; Yellow Cab of North Orange County; Coast Yellow Cab; Boys and Girls Club of Anaheim; Firmenich Co.; M.C.P. Industrial Food Products; Photomation; Anaheim Memorial Hospital; Los Robles Mobile Home Estates; Cherokee Mobile Home Owners Assn.; Ramada Maingate of Anaheim; Jolly Roger Inn; The Lusk Co.; Southwest Motor Freight; U.S. Xpress; Crown Transport Systems; City of Bernardino; Catalina Express; The Eli Home; Crawford & Co.; Coregis Insurance Co.
REFERENCES: Corporate Bank, Anaheim, California; Landmark Bank, Anaheim, California.

---

## DON R. FORD

*A PROFESSIONAL CORPORATION*

Established in 1977

**8141 EAST KAISER BOULEVARD, SUITE 210**
**ANAHEIM, CALIFORNIA 92808-2214**
Telephone: 714-998-6214
Facsimile: 714-998-6551

*General Civil and Trial Practice. Personal Injury, Business, Probate, Estate Planning and Corporate.*

**DON R. FORD,** born Provo, Utah, December 23, 1945; admitted to bar, 1974, California and U.S. District Court, Central District of California. *Education:* California State University at Long Beach (B.S. in Accounting, 1971); Pepperdine University (J.D., 1974). *Member:* Orange County and American Bar Associations; State Bar of California; Orange County Trial Lawyers Association. [With U.S. Army, 1967-1969]

*LEGAL SUPPORT PERSONNEL*

**KATHY J. WRIGHT,** born Seattle, Washington. *Education:* University of Washington (B.A., 1974). *Member:* Orange County Paralegal Association. (Legal Assistant).

REPRESENTATIVE CLIENTS: Assured Advantage Mortgage Corp.; Atcheson's Express, Inc.; Marquez Fabrics, Inc.; Clark's Placentia Auto Wrecking; Dynalektrix; Industry Freight Forwarding, Inc.; Interactive Computer Corp.; Laycs Pacific, Inc.; Naylor Industries, Inc.; R. H. Fasteners, Inc.; The Write Shop; UniSearch Search & Recruiting, Inc.; Cal. Coast Repiping, Inc.; REFERENCE: Bank of America.

---

## KINKLE, RODIGER AND SPRIGGS

*PROFESSIONAL CORPORATION*

**ANAHEIM, CALIFORNIA**

(See Santa Ana)

*General Trial Practice. Negligence, Malpractice, Products Liability, Construction and Insurance Law.*

---

## RICHARD A. McFARLANE

**2323 WEST LINCOLN AVENUE**
**SUITE 127**
**P.O. BOX 1606**
**ANAHEIM, CALIFORNIA 92801**
Telephone: 714-991-9131
Fax: 714-991-6526
Email: richard.mcfarlane@counsel.com

Mailing Address: P.O. Box 1606, Orange, CA 92866

*Bankruptcy, Estate Planning, Corporate Transactions.*

**RICHARD A. MCFARLANE,** born Salt Lake City, Utah, July 6, 1962; admitted to bar, 1991, California, U.S. District Court, Central District of California and U.S. Court of Appeals, Ninth Circuit; 1992, Utah, District of Columbia and U.S. District Court, District of Utah. *Education:* California State University (B.A., 1987); Southwestern University (J.D., 1991). Member, Phi Alpha Theta History and Phi Alpha Delta Legal Honor Society. *Member:* Orange County, Utah State and American Bar Associations;

(This Listing Continued)

California State Bar; The District of Columbia. **LANGUAGES:** Afrikaans. **PRACTICE AREAS:** Bankruptcy; Estate Planning; Corporate Transactions.

---

## O'FLAHERTY & BELGUM

**222 SOUTH HARBOR BOULEVARD, SUITE 600**
**ANAHEIM, CALIFORNIA 92805-3701**
Telephone: 714-533-3373
Fax: 714-533-2607
Email: oandb&primenet.com
URL: http://www.oandb-law/oandb

*Glendale, California Office:* 1000 North Central, Suite 300, 91202-2957.
Telephone: 818-242-9229. Fax: 818-242-9114.
*Long Beach, California Office:* 100 Oceangate Suite 500, 90802-4312.
Telephone: 310-437-0090. Fax: 310-437-5550.
*Riverside, California Office:* 3880 Lemon Street, Suite 450, 92501-3301.
Telephone: 909-341-0049. Fax: 909-341-3919.
*Ventura, California Office:* 840 County Square Drive, Suite 200, 93003-5406.
Telephone: 805-650-2600. Fax: 805-650-2658.

*General Civil, Trial and Appellate Practice in State and Federal Courts. Medical and Dental Malpractice, Products Liability, General Insurance Law, Insurance Coverage, Wrongful Termination, Workers' Compensation and Business and Environmental Litigation.*

(For Complete Biographical Data on all Personnel, see Professional Biographies at Glendale).

---

## JOANNE S. ROCKS

**SUITE 207C ANAHEIM HILLS PROFESSIONAL CENTER**
**6200 EAST CANYON RIM ROAD**
**ANAHEIM, CALIFORNIA 92807**
Telephone: 714-974-2000
Fax: 714-974-2063

*General Practice. Business, Corporate, Partnership, State, Federal and International Taxation, Real Property and Real Estate Finance Law.*

**JOANNE S. ROCKS,** born Rockford, Illinois, June 22, 1942; admitted to bar, 1972, California. *Education:* University of Southern California (B.S., in Accounting, 1965; M.B.A., 1967); Loyola University of Los Angeles (J.D., 1970). Beta Gamma Sigma; Phi Delta Delta; Beta Alpha Psi. Member: St. Thomas More Law Honor Society; National Moot Court Team, 1969-1970. Member, Loyola University of Los Angeles Law Review, 1969-1970. Certified Public Accountant, California, 1967.

REFERENCE: Wells Fargo Bank, Anaheim Hills Branch.

---

## DENNIS J. KEHOE

*A LAW CORPORATION*

Established in 1964

**311 BONITA DRIVE**
**APTOS, CALIFORNIA 95003**
Telephone: 408-662-8444
Fax: 408-662-0227

*Eminent Domain, Land Use, Civil Litigation and Personal Injury Law.*

FIRM PROFILE: Dennis J. Kehoe, A Law Corporation is listed in the Bar Register of Preeminent Lawyers and Who's Who in American Law.

**DENNIS J. KEHOE,** born Culver City, California, November 12, 1937; admitted to bar, 1964, California; U.S. Supreme Court; U.S. Court of Appeals, Ninth Circuit and U.S. District Court, Northern District of California; 1989, U.S. District Court, Central District of California. *Education:* University of Santa Clara (B.S.C., 1960); Hastings College of the Law, University of California (J.D., 1963). Assistant County Counsel, Santa Cruz County, 1964-1966. Listed, Who's Who in American Law. *Member:* Santa Cruz County Bar Association; The State Bar of California; California Trial Lawyers Association; Santa Cruz County Trial Lawyers Association. **REPORTED CASES:** Aptos Seascape Corp. v. County of Santa Cruz (1982), 138 CA 3rd 484, 188 CR 191. **PRACTICE AREAS:** Eminent Domain; Land Use; Civil Litigation; Personal Injury.

(This Listing Continued)

REPRESENTATIVE CLIENTS: Aptos Seascape Corp.; Big Basin Water Co., Inc.; Ifland Engineers, Inc.; Blue Star Ready Mix; Olive Spring Quarry, Inc.; Duraflame, Inc.; Bontadelli Brothers Brussel Sprouts Grower; Plant Sciences, Inc.

## RUMMONDS, WALTZ & MAIR

*311 BONITA DRIVE*
*P.O. BOX 1870*
**APTOS, CALIFORNIA 95001**
*Telephone: 408-688-2911*

*Sacramento, California Office:* 6991 Garden Highway. 95837. Telephone: 916-927-4610.

*General Civil Litigation, Personal Injury, Professional Malpractice, Insurance Law, Wrongful Death, Wrongful Termination and Liability Defense.*

### MEMBERS OF FIRM

**JAMES S. RUMMONDS,** born Pomona, California, October 10, 1942; admitted to bar, 1974, California; 1985, U.S. District Court, Northern and Central Districts of California. *Education:* Stanford University (B.A., 1968; J.D., 1973). Author: "Environment and the Law," Pocket Books, 1971 David Sax ed.; "Fighting Crime," National Law Journal, May, 1982; "An Introduction to Insurance Crisis," CTL Forum, August, 1986. Contributing Editor, "West's California Legal Forms, Civil Trials and Evidence." Instructor and Lecturer: Hastings Institute for Trial and Appellate Advocacy, 1983—. Adjunct Faculty, Stanford School of Law, Trial Advocacy Workshop. Member, Presidential Commission on Population Growth and the American Future, 1970-1972. *Member:* State Bar of California; California Trial Lawyers Association; Association of Trial Lawyers of America; Diplomat on the American Board of Professional Liability Attorneys, 1992—. Certified as a Civil Trial Specialist by the National Board of Trial Advocacy. [With U.S. Navy, 1960-1963]. (Also Of Counsel, Mair, Camiel & Kovach, Seattle, Washington and Horn & Loomis, Los Angeles, California). *LANGUAGES:* Spanish. *PRACTICE AREAS:* Legal and Medical Malpractice; Personal Injury Law; Real Estate and Business Litigation.

**PATRICK J. WALTZ,** born Berkeley, California, April 29, 1948; admitted to bar, 1974, California and U.S. District Court, Northern and Eastern Districts of California. *Education:* University of California at Davis (B.A., 1970); McGeorge School of Law, University of the Pacific (J.D., 1974). Recipient, American Jurisprudence Award in Real Property. Faculty Member, Hastings College of Law, University of California, College of Advocacy, 1987—. *Member:* Sacramento County and American Bar Associations; State Bar of California. (Resident, Sacramento Office).

**PETER K. MAIR,** born Williamsport, Pennsylvania, March 8, 1945; admitted to bar, 1972, California, District of Columbia and U.S. Court of Appeals for the District of Columbia Circuit; 1975, Washington U.S. District Court Western District of Washington and U.S. Court of Appeals, Ninth Circuit; 1980, U.S. Supreme Court; 1982, U.S. Tax Court; 1984, U.S. District Court, Eastern District of Washington. *Education:* University of Michigan (B.A., 1967); Stanford University (J.D., 1971). Author: Chapter 7, "Immunity Proceedings: What Role for Counsel at this Stage?" Pre-Indictment Tactics in Criminal Cases, Hafetz Litigation and Administrative Practice Series, Criminal Law and Urban Problems, Series No. 121. Instructor and Lecturer at Hastings College of Advocacy, Hastings Law School, 1980—. Assistant U.S. Attorney: District of Columbia, 1972-1975; Seattle, 1975-1979. *Member:* State Bar of California; Washington State Bar Association; The Association of Trial Lawyers of America. (Also Member to Mair, Camiel & Kovac, Seattle, Washington). *PRACTICE AREAS:* Federal Criminal Law (50%, 15); State Criminal Law (20%, 16); Civil Litigation (20%, 10); Administration Law (10%, 3).

## HELMS, HANRAHAN & MYERS

*Established in 1973*

*SUITE 685 TOWNE CENTRE BUILDING*
*150 NORTH SANTA ANITA AVENUE*
**ARCADIA, CALIFORNIA 91006**
*Telephone: 818-445-1177*
*Email: helmsj@aol.com*

*General Civil and Trial Practice in all State and Federal Courts. Corporation, Estate Planning, Probate, Personal Injury, Negligence and Family Law.*

**JAMES R. HELMS, JR.,** born Chattanooga, Tennessee, September 24, 1925; admitted to bar, 1952, California. *Education:* University of the South (B.S., 1949); University of Southern California (J.D., 1952). Judge Pro Tem,

*(This Listing Continued)*

Superior Court, Law and Motion Probate, 1989—. President, Arcadia Community Chest, 1963-1964. Chairman, Foothill Area United Way, 1965-1967. Councilman, 1968-1976, Mayor Pro-Tem, 1970-1971 and Mayor, 1971-1972, City of Arcadia. Secretary, 1970-1973, Vice-President, 1973-1974 and President, 1974-1975, San Gabriel Valley Lawyers Referral Service. President, San Gabriel Valley Association of Cities, 1975-1976. Awarded Citizen of the Year, Arcadia, California, 1979. *Member:* Foothill (Secretary, 1964-1965; Treasurer, 1965-1966; Vice-President, 1966-1967; President, 1967-1968), Los Angeles County and American Bar Associations; The State Bar of California. [Maj. Inf., USA-Ret.]. (Certified Specialist, Probate, Estate Planning and Trust Law, The State Bar of California Board of Legal Specialization). *PRACTICE AREAS:* Estate Planning; Probate; Business; Real Property.

**JAMES J. HANRAHAN,** born Somerville, Massachusetts, June 30, 1934; admitted to bar, 1966, California. *Education:* Boston University (A.B., Sociology, 1959); Southwestern University (J.D., 1965). Member, Panel of Arbitrators, American Arbitration Association. Arbitrator, Los Angeles County Superior Court, 1978—. *Member:* Foothill (President, 1978-1979), Pasadena and Los Angeles County Bar Associations; The State Bar of California; Los Angeles Trial Lawyers Association; California Trial Lawyers Association. *PRACTICE AREAS:* Personal Injury; Worker's Compensation (Plaintiff's).

**STERLING E. MYERS,** born San Francisco, California, July 17, 1947; admitted to bar, 1972, California; 1973, U.S. Court of Military Appeals; 1974, U.S. Tax Court. *Education:* University of Southern California (B.A., cum laude, 1969; J.D., 1972). President, San Gabriel Valley Lawyers Referral Service, 1979-1980. *Member:* Foothill (President, 1982), Los Angeles County and American Bar Associations; State Bar of California; California Association of Certified Family Law Specialists (President, 1995). (Certified Specialist, Family Law, The State Bar of California Board of Legal Specialization). *PRACTICE AREAS:* Family Law.

### LEGAL SUPPORT PERSONNEL

### PARALEGALS

**Michelle L. Upp**         **Josephine Phillips**

REFERENCE: Bank of America National Trust & Savings Assn. (Arcadia Branch).

## SHINEY, FARGO & SALCEDO

*A LAW CORPORATION*

*301 EAST FOOTHILL BOULEVARD, SUITE 200*
**ARCADIA, CALIFORNIA 91006**
*Telephone: 818-359-8652*
*Fax: 818-357-8172*
*Email: cntymsclvr@aol.com*

*Sherman Oaks, California Office:* 13400 Ventura Boulevard, Second Floor. Telephone: 818-501-8100. Fax: 818-501-3824.

*Workers' Compensation Insurance Defense, Third Party Subrogation.*

FIRM PROFILE: Shiney, Fargo & Salcedo, a Professional Law Corporation, *is a firm that specializes in the defense of Worker's Compensation Claims and Civil Litigation involving claims of Subrogation and employment related claims under the Equal Employment Opportunity Commission and Americans with Disabilities Act. The firm as an established record for an aggressive and practical approach to the defense of workers compensation and employment related cases.*

**MICHAEL E. SHINEY,** born La Cross, Kansas, July 20, 1955; admitted to bar, 1980, California. *Education:* California State University at Los Angeles; University of La Verne (J.D., 1980). *Member:* State Bar of California. *PRACTICE AREAS:* Workers' Compensation Defense; Subrogation.

**MICHAEL D. FARGO,** born Ithaca, New York, May 31, 1954; admitted to bar, 1983, California. *Education:* Southern Connecticut State College (B.A., 1976); San Fernando Valley State College of Law (J.D., 1981). *Member:* State Bar of California. *PRACTICE AREAS:* Workers' Compensation Defense; Subrogation; Civil Litigation.

**PAUL J. SALCEDO,** born Los Angeles, California, January 25, 1945; admitted to bar, 1974, California and U.S. District Court, Central District of California. *Education:* California State University Los Angeles (B.A., 1970); Glendale University (J.D., 1974). Member, Mexican-American Legal Defense and Educational Fund. *Member:* Los Angeles County and Mexican American Bar Associations; State Bar of California; Los Angeles Trial Lawyers Association; California Trial Lawyers Association; Los Angeles

*(This Listing Continued)*

**SHINEY, FARGO & SALCEDO,** A LAW CORPORATION, Arcadia—Continued

Consumer Advocates Association. [Staff Sgt., USMC, 1962-1968]. *LANGUAGES:* Spanish. *PRACTICE AREAS:* Workers' Compensation Defense; Subrogation; Civil Litigation; Wrongful Termination.

---

**BRUCE H. ALBERT,** born New York, N.Y., April 22, 1964; admitted to bar, 1990, California and U.S. District Court, Central District of California. *Education:* State University of New York at Albany (B.A., 1986); Southwestern University School of Law (J.D., 1990). Recipient, Reiss Scholarship. *Member:* Beverly Hills, Los Angeles County and San Fernando Valley Bar Associations; State Bar of California. *LANGUAGES:* Swedish and German. *PRACTICE AREAS:* Workers' Compensation Defense; Subrogation; Civil Litigation.

**PETER NEIL MACKENZIE,** born Schenectady, New York, October 27, 1961; admitted to bar, 1991, California. *Education:* California State University Northridge (B.A., 1985); Southwestern University School of Law (J.D., 1990). *Member:* State Bar of California. *PRACTICE AREAS:* Workers' Compensation Defense; Subrogation.

**RICHARD VILLASENOR,** born Santa Monica, California, February 3, 1957; admitted to bar, 1989, California. *Education:* University of Sussex, England; Occidental College (B.A., 1979); University of California at Los Angeles (J.D., 1984). *Member:* Los Angeles County and American Bar Associations; State Bar of California. *PRACTICE AREAS:* Workers Compensation Law; Labor Law.

**GENARO LEGORRETA, JR.,** born Brawley, California, June 2, 1964; admitted to bar, 1991, California. *Education:* University of California Santa Barbara (B.A., history, 1987); Whittier College School of Law (J.D., 1991). Recipient: National Education Foundation Scholarship, 1988-1991; American Jurisprudence Award, Legal Writing. *Member:* State Bar of California; Mexican American Bar Association. [1st Lt., US Army Res., 1987— ]. *LANGUAGES:* Spanish. *PRACTICE AREAS:* Workers' Compensation Defense; Subrogation; Civil Litigation.

**EDWARD T. DE LA LOZA,** born Los Angeles, California, February 25, 1966; admitted to bar, 1991, California. *Education:* California State University Long Beach (B.A., 1988); University of Michigan (J.D., 1991). Moot Court Semi-Finalist and Best Brief, 1990. *Member:* State Bar of California; Mexican American Bar Association. *LANGUAGES:* Spanish. *PRACTICE AREAS:* Workers' Compensation Defense; Civil Litigation.

REPRESENTATIVE CLIENTS: Kemper Insurance Group; Argonaut Insurance Co.; American International Group; Golden Eagle Insurance Co.; Hertz Claim Management; Los Angeles Unified School District; CNA Risk Management Group; The Vons Companies; Sedwick Claims Management; LACMTA (Los Angeles County Metropolitan Transit Authority); MTA (Metropolitan Transit Authority); City of Los Angeles; American Stores.

---

## STOKES, STEEVES, ROWE & HAMER

A Partnership including a Professional Corporation

*381 BAYSIDE ROAD*
*P.O. BOX 1109*
**ARCATA, CALIFORNIA 95521-1109**
*Telephone: 707-822-1771*
*Fax: 707-822-1901*

*Real Estate, Construction, Business and General Civil Litigation, Probate and Estate Planning, Business, Real Estate, Taxation, Family, Criminal and Administrative Law.*

**DOROTHY L. STEEVES** (1926-1996).

**JOHN R. STOKES, (INC.),** born 1917; admitted to bar, 1948, California. *Education:* Santa Barbara State College; University of California at Berkeley (A.B., 1946); Boalt Hall, University of California at Berkeley (LL.B., 1948). City Attorney, Arcata, 1950-1973. *Member:* Humboldt County Bar Association (President, 1951); The State Bar of California (Member: Board of Governors, 1979-1982; Vice-President, 1981-1982; Committee of Bar Examiners, 1983-1987; Chairman, 1985-1986). [Capt., USAAF, 1942-1945]. *PRACTICE AREAS:* Business Law; Estate Planning and Probate Law; Real Property Law.

**THOMAS DEAN ROWE,** born Los Angeles, California, April 26, 1948; admitted to bar, 1985, California. *Education:* University of California at Santa Cruz (B.A., 1970); Humboldt State University; Hastings College of

*(This Listing Continued)*

---

the Law (J.D., 1985). Certified Public Accountant, California, 1977. Senior Tax Manager, CPA/Consulting Firm of Coopers & Lybrand, 1985-1990. *Member:* Humboldt County Bar Association; State Bar of California. *PRACTICE AREAS:* Taxation Law; Estate Planning and Probate Law; Business Law.

**JOHN R. STOKES, III,** born Berkeley, California, June 3, 1948; admitted to bar, 1975, California; 1985, U.S. District Court, Northern District of California. *Education:* University of California at Berkeley (A.B., 1971); University of the Pacific, McGeorge School of Law (J.D., 1975). Deputy District Attorney, County of Humboldt, 1982-1992. *REPORTED CASES:* Marriage of Henderson (1990) 225 Cal App 3d 531; County of Humboldt v. Harris (1988) 206 Cal App 3d 857. *PRACTICE AREAS:* Family Law; Criminal Law; General Litigation.

**CHRIS JOHNSON HAMER,** born Eureka, California, December 25, 1955; admitted to bar, 1982, California; 1983, U.S. District Court, Central District of California; 1986, U.S. District Court, Eastern District of California and U.S. Tax Court; 1994, U.S. District Court, Northern District of California. *Education:* University of California at Santa Barbara (B.A., with highest honors, 1978); Georgetown University (J.D., cum laude, 1982). Phi Alpha Delta. *Member:* Humboldt County Bar Association. *PRACTICE AREAS:* Real Estate; Business; Construction Litigation.

---

## LAW FIRM OF
## W. G. WATSON, JR.

**ARCATA, CALIFORNIA**

(See Eureka)

*General Civil and Criminal Trial Practice. Personal Injury, Negligence, Insurance, Real Estate, Estate Planning, Probate Law, Arbitration, Mediation.*

---

## GEORGE, GALLO & SULLIVAN

*A LAW CORPORATION*

**ARROYO GRANDE, CALIFORNIA**

(See San Luis Obispo)

*Probate, Estate Planning and Trust Administration, Business and Corporate Transactions, Taxation, Real Property and Construction, Civil Litigation.*

---

## GEORGE, GALLO & SULLIVAN

*A LAW CORPORATION*

**ATASCADERO, CALIFORNIA**

(See San Luis Obispo)

*Probate, Estate Planning and Trust Administration, Business and Corporate Transactions, Taxation, Real Property and Construction, Civil Litigation.*

---

## ROBERT M. JONES, JR.

*8655 MORRO ROAD, SUITE C*
**ATASCADERO, CALIFORNIA 93422**
*Telephone: 805-466-4422*
*Fax: 805-466-7267*

*General Civil Trial Practice, Corporate Litigation.*

**ROBERT M. JONES, JR.,** born 1949; admitted to bar, 1979, California. *Education:* University of California (B.A., 1975); McGeorge School of Law (J.D., 1978). *PRACTICE AREAS:* General Civil Trial Practice; Corporate Litigation.

*LEGAL SUPPORT PERSONNEL*

**CINDY HEMMING** (Paralegal).

---

## AUBURN LEGAL CLINIC

*152 MAPLE STREET, SUITE E*
**AUBURN, CALIFORNIA 95603-5042**
*Telephone: 916-888-1905*
*Fax: 916-888-1936*

*General Civil and Criminal Practice, Family Law, Estate Planning.*

*(This Listing Continued)*

**CHRISTOPHER R. COLLINS,** born Sacramento, California, April 9, 1958; admitted to bar, 1989, California. *Education:* St. Mary's of Moraga, California (B.A., 1980); Southwestern University School of Law (J.D., 1989). *Member:* El Dorado County and Placer County Bar Associations; State Bar of California. **PRACTICE AREAS:** Criminal; Family Law; General Civil Litigation; Trials; Estate Planning; Real Estate.

**MARY ANN COLLINS,** born Auburn, California, June 20, 1960; admitted to bar, 1989, California. *Education:* St. Mary's College of California (B.S., 1982); Southwestern University School of Law (J.D., 1989). *Member:* Placer County Bar Association; State Bar of California; Placer County Women Lawyers (Secretary, 1995). **PRACTICE AREAS:** Criminal Defense; Misdemeanors; Felonies; Juvenile; Family; Estate Planning.

---

## CHAMBERLAIN, CHAMBERLAIN & BALDO

*Established in 1888*

THE BANK OF CALIFORNIA BUILDING
P.O. BOX 32
**AUBURN, CALIFORNIA 95604**
Telephone: 916-885-4523
FAX: 916-885-5814

*General Civil Practice. Personal Injury, Probate, Estate Planning, Trusts, Real Estate, Corporation, Municipal, Public Utility and Special Districts Law.*

### MEMBERS OF FIRM

**L. L. CHAMBERLAIN** (1888-1913).

**T. L. CHAMBERLAIN** (1913-1975).

**T. L. CHAMBERLAIN, JR.** (1950-1984).

**PAUL H. CHAMBERLAIN,** born Sacramento, California, February 17, 1923; admitted to bar, 1951, California. *Education:* University of California at Berkeley (B.S., 1947); Hastings College of Law, University of California (LL.B., 1950). *Member:* Placer County and American Bar Associations; The State Bar of California; American Judicature Society. **PRACTICE AREAS:** Probate Law; Estate Planning Law; Municipal Law; Public Utility Law; Special Districts Law; Real Estate.

**RUSSELL P. BALDO,** born Auburn, California, April 13, 1946; admitted to bar, 1973, California. *Education:* University of California at Santa Barbara and University of California at Berkeley (A.B., 1968); McGeorge College of the Law (J.D., 1973). Phi Alpha Delta. Director, U.S. Bank of California. *Member:* Placer County and American Bar Associations; State Bar of California (Referee State Bar Court, 1982-1989; Member, Fee Arbitration Panel, 1990—). **PRACTICE AREAS:** Probate Law; Estate Planning Law; Trusts Law; Real Estate Law.

LOCAL COUNSEL FOR: The Bank of California N.A.; Tahoe City P.U.D.; North Tahoe Fire Protection District; Foresthill Public Utility District, Alpine Springs County Water District; Donner Summit P.U.D.; First American Title Insurance Co.
REFERENCES: The Bank of California N.A.; Bank of America; U.S. Bank of California.

---

## JOHN P. HENDERSON

251 AUBURN RAVINE ROAD, SUITE 105
**AUBURN, CALIFORNIA 95603**
Telephone: 916-889-0304
Fax: 916-885-7559

*Business, Real Estate, Personal Injury and Employment Litigation.*

**JOHN P. HENDERSON,** born Midland, Texas, November 24, 1959; admitted to bar, 1986, California; U.S. District Court, Eastern District of California. *Education:* University of California at Los Angeles (B.A., 1982); McGeorge School of Law (J.D., 1986). *Member:* Placer County and American Bar Associations; State Bar of California; Association of Northern California Insurance Defense Counsel. **PRACTICE AREAS:** Civil Litigation.

---

## JOHANSON, KOONS & CONSTANTINO

A Partnership including Professional Corporations

*Established in 1983*

SUITE 105, 251 AUBURN RAVINE ROAD
**AUBURN, CALIFORNIA 95603**
Telephone: 916-885-7538
Fax: 916-885-7559

*General Civil Practice. Real Estate, Corporation and Business Law. Title Insurance Defense, Estate Planning, Probate and Trust Law.*

### MEMBERS OF FIRM

**THEODORE L. JOHANSON, (P.C.),** born Oakland, California, August 8, 1933; admitted to bar, 1970, California. *Education:* University of California at Berkeley (B.S., 1955); McGeorge School of Law, University of the Pacific (J.D., 1969). Hearing Referee, State Bar Court, 1979-1989. Judge Pro Tem, Placer County Superior Court, 1983—. Member, Placer County Air Pollution Control Hearing Board, 1989—. *Member:* Placer County and American (Member, Section of Real Property, Probate and Trust Law) Bar Associations; The State Bar of California. (Certified Specialist, Probate, Estate Planning and Trust Law, The State Bar of California Board of Legal Specialization). **LANGUAGES:** German. **REPORTED CASES:** Tanko v. Dodds 117 Cal App 3d 588, 172 Cal Rptr 829; People v. Ryser 40 C.A. 3d 1, 114 Cal. Rptr 668. **PRACTICE AREAS:** Estate Planning; Trust; Probate; Title Insurance Law.

**EDWARD C. KOONS, (P.C.),** born Great Bend, Kansas, October 4, 1952; admitted to bar, 1978, California. *Education:* University of California at Berkeley (A.B., 1974); McGeorge School of Law, University of the Pacific (J.D., 1978). *Member:* Placer County Bar Association; The State Bar of California (Member, Real Property and Business Law Sections). **REPORTED CASES:** Vaughn Materials v. Security Pacific National Bank, 1985, 170 Cal App 3d 908. **PRACTICE AREAS:** Real Estate; Business Litigation.

**ALEXANDER L. CONSTANTINO,** born Stockton, California, September 6, 1956; admitted to bar, 1985, California; 1989, U.S. Supreme Court. *Education:* San Francisco State University (B.S., 1980); McGeorge School of Law (J.D., 1984). Deputy District Attorney, Placer County, 1986-1990. Judge Pro Tem, Placer County Municipal Court, 1991—. *Member:* Placer County Bar Association (Member, Board of Directors, 1993; Secretary Treasurer, 1994); The State Bar of California. **PRACTICE AREAS:** Real Estate; Business Litigation.

REPRESENTATIVE CLIENTS: Chicago Title Insurance Co.; Nevada County Board of Realtors, Inc.; Placer Credit Union; Valli Bank; TICOR Title Insurance Co.; U.S. Bank; Diamond Well Drilling; Sierra Nevada Memorial Hospital; Placer County Association of Realtors; Placer Savings Bank.
REFERENCE: Wells Fargo Bank, N.A.; Valli Bank.

---

## LEUPP & WACHOB

149 COURT STREET
**AUBURN, CALIFORNIA 95603**
Telephone: 916-888-1100
Fax: 916-888-1821

*General Civil and Trial Practice. Personal Injury, Family, Criminal, Insurance Defense.*

### MEMBERS OF FIRM

**THOMAS A. LEUPP,** born Berkeley, California, September 5, 1952; admitted to bar, 1978, California and U.S. District Court, Eastern District of California; 1988, U.S. District Court, District of Alaska. *Education:* Sierra College (A.A., 1971); University of California at Davis (B.A., 1973); McGeorge School of Law, University of the Pacific (J.D., 1977). *Member:* Placer County Bar Association (President, 1987); State Bar of California; California Attorneys for Criminal Justice (Member, Board of Governors, 1989-1993); California Public Defenders Association. (Certified Specialist, Family Law, The State Bar of California Board of Specialization). **PRACTICE AREAS:** Criminal Defense Law.

**CHARLES D. WACHOB,** born Oakland, California, September 22, 1952; admitted to bar, 1978, California, U.S. District Court, Eastern District of California and U.S. Court of Appeals, Ninth Circuit; 1983, U.S. Supreme Court. *Education:* University of California at Davis (A.B., with honors, 1974; J.D., 1977). City Attorney, City of Auburn, 1983—. Member, Auburn Planning Commission, 1982-1983. *Member:* Placer County

*(This Listing Continued)*

**LEUPP & WACHOB**, *Auburn—Continued*

Bar Association; State Bar of California; Association of Insurance Defense Counsel. **PRACTICE AREAS:** Personal Injury Law; Insurance Law.

*ASSOCIATE*

**TIMOTHY S. WOODALL,** born Escondido, California, November 22, 1956; admitted to bar, 1984, California; 1985, U.S. Court of Appeals, 9th Circuit. *Education:* Palomar Junior College; University of California at Santa Barbara (B.A., 1980); Hastings College of the Law, University of California (J.D., 1983). *Member:* Placer County Bar Association; Bar Association of San Francisco; State Bar of California. **PRACTICE AREAS:** Insurance Defense Law; Criminal Defense Law; Plaintiffs Personal Injury Law.

REPRESENTATIVE CLIENTS: City of Auburn; Auburn Urban Development Authority; Travelers Insurance; Grange Insurance Assn.; Rocky Mountain Fire and Casualty; Lexington Insurance; Northbrook Property and Casualty Insurance Co; American Bankers Insurance; Providence Washington Insurance Co.; Great West Casualty.

---

# ROBINSON, ROBINSON & LYON

A Partnership including a Professional Corporation

*Established in 1887*

ONE CALIFORNIA STREET
**AUBURN, CALIFORNIA 95603**
*Telephone: 916-885-8900*
*Fax: 916-885-0633*

*General Civil Practice. Real Estate, Litigation, Business, Personal Injury, Probate, Estate Planning, and Insurance Defense.*

*MEMBERS OF FIRM*

**D. R. ROBINSON, (P.C.),** born Auburn, California, April 19, 1917; admitted to bar, 1947, California, U.S. District Court, Eastern and Northern Districts of California and U.S. Tax Court. *Education:* University of California at Berkeley (A.B., 1939); Boalt Hall, University of California (J.D., 1947). Phi Alpha Delta. City Attorney, City of Auburn, 1947-1977. State President for Northern California, 1969-1972 and National Deputy Judge Advocate, 1975—, Navy League of the U.S. *Member:* Placer County (President, 1951-1952) and American (Member, Sections on: Real Property, Probate and Trust Law; Taxation) Bar Associations; State Bar of California. [USNR, 1939-1969, Capt. USNR, (Ret.)]. **PRACTICE AREAS:** Probate Law; Estate Planning.

**BRUCE A. LYON,** born Sacramento, California, September 24, 1951; admitted to bar, 1977, California and U.S. District Court, Eastern and Northern Districts of California. *Education:* University of the Pacific (A.B., 1974); Hastings College of Law, University of California (J.D., 1977). Order of the Coif. Member, Thurston Society. Managing Editor of COMM-/ENT, A Journal of Communication and Entertainment Law, 1976-1977. Professor, Sierra College, Business Law, 1982— and Real Property Law, 1984. Member, California League of Saving Institutions, Attorneys Committee, 1987—. Director, Auburn Community Foundation, 1996—. *Member:* Placer County and American Bar Associations; The State Bar of California; Consumer Attorneys of California. **PRACTICE AREAS:** Real Estate Law; Litigation; Business Law; Personal Injury; Probate and Estate Planning.

REPRESENTATIVE CLIENTS: Placer Savings Bank; Pacific Development Group; CBM Development Group; Central Square Co. Inc.; Best Properties. *Reference:* Bank of America, N.A.

---

# LAW OFFICES OF
# STUART LANSING SMITS

1515 LINCOLN WAY
**AUBURN, CALIFORNIA 95603**
*Telephone: 916-887-8585*
*Fax: 916-889-1711*

*Real Estate and Land Use Litigation, Mediation, Environmental Litigation, Select Business Litigation.*

**STUART LANSING SMITS,** born Watertown, New York, September 25, 1949; admitted to bar, 1975, California and U.S. District Court, Southern District of California; 1977, U.S. Court of Appeals, Fifth and Ninth Circuits; 1978, U.S. District Court, Central District of California; 1979,

*(This Listing Continued)*

---

U.S. Tax Court; 1986, U.S. District Court, Eastern District of California. *Education:* Menlo College (A.A., 1969); Tulane University (B.A., cum laude, 1971); California Western School of Law (J.D., 1975). Member: Moot Court Board; The Order of Barristers. Member, International Law Journal, 1974-1975. Recipient, Wall Street Journal Award. Author: Articles: "Development of the Superior Court Accelerated Civil Trial Project, The Litigator (March 1988); "Accelerated Civil Trial Program and Questionnaire," The Litigator (May 1989); "ACT Updates and Highlights: Recent Rulings on ACT Issues," The Litigator (July 1989). Pro Tem Judge, Sacramento Superior Court, 1988—; Pro Tem Judge, Placer County Superior Court, 1991—. Editor-in-Chief, The Litigator, a monthly publication, 1987-1989. Member, Select Committee on Industry Land Use Litigation, California Building Industry. *Member:* Sacramento County (Member, Bar/Bench Select Committee for Implementation of the Trial Court Delay Reduction Act) and Federal Bar Associations; State Bar of California (Member: Real Property Section; Subcommittee on Real Estate Litigation). **REPORTED CASES:** Kuhl v. Sullivan, California Court of Appeal, Third District, 1993 (13 Cal.App. 4th 1589); Lincoln Properties v. Higgins, U.S. District Court, Eastern District of California, 1993 (823 F. Supp. 1528); Hulsey v. Koehler, California Court of Appeal, Third District, 1990 (218 Cal.App.3d 1150); Jenkins v. Tuneup Masters, California Court of Appeal, Third District, 1987 (190 Cal.App.3d); United States v. Johnson, U.S. Court of Appeal, Ninth Circuit, 1981 (660 F.2d 749); United States v. Currency Totalling $48,318.08, U.S. Court of Appeal, Fifth Circuit, 1980 (609 F.2d 210); United States v. Haro-Espinosa, U.S. Court of Appeal, Ninth Circuit, 1979 (619 F.2d 689).

---

# ARRACHE, CLARK & POTTER

4800 EASTON DRIVE, SUITE 114
**BAKERSFIELD, CALIFORNIA 93309-9424**
*Telephone: 805-328-1800*

*General Civil Litigation. Business, Oil and Gas, Commercial, Taxation, Energy, Livestock, Agricultural Real Estate Law and Probate.*

*MEMBERS OF FIRM*

**JUAN E. ARRACHE, JR.** (1943-1990).

**THOMAS S. CLARK,** born Bakersfield, California, December 12, 1947; admitted to bar, 1973, California; 1978, U.S. District Court, Eastern District of California; 1979, U.S. Supreme Court; 1980, U.S. Tax Court; 1981, U.S. District Court, Southern District of California; 1982, U.S. District Court, Central District of California; 1983, U.S. District Court, Northern District of California. *Education:* University of Southern California (B.A., 1969; J.D., 1973). Phi Alpha Delta. Kern County Deputy District Attorney, 1975-1978. *Member:* Kern County Bar Association; State Bar of California. **PRACTICE AREAS:** Civil Litigation; Real Estate Development; Condemnation.

**DAVID B. POTTER,** born Paso Robles, California, December 15, 1952; admitted to bar, 1979, California and U.S. District Court, Central, Northern and Eastern Districts of California. *Education:* University of California at Los Angeles (B.A., 1975); University of Santa Clara (J.D., 1978). *Member:* Kern County Bar Association (Member, Board of Directors, 1988-1991); State Bar of California. **PRACTICE AREAS:** General Civil Litigation; Collection.

*LEGAL SUPPORT PERSONNEL*

*PARALEGAL*

**PEGGY J. POOR,** born Crescent City, California, February 28, 1951. *Education:* Loma Linda University; Bakersfield Jr. College; University of California, Santa Barbara (Legal Assistantship).

REPRESENTATIVE CLIENTS: J.I. Case Co.; Chicago Title; Common Wealth Title, Co.; Stewart Title Co.; Pacific Orthopedic Medical Group; Colbek Construction; J.L. Gray Development; Farm Pump & Irrigation Co., Inc.; Texaco Inc.; Waste Management of North America, Inc.; Martin-McIntosh Civil Engineers; Thomas O'Connor Civil Engineers; David Janes Company; Mike Mason Homes; Crider Construction, Inc.; Downs Equipment Rental.

---

# AZEMIKA & AZEMIKA

THE BANK OF AMERICA TOWER
1430 TRUXTUN AVENUE, SUITE 707
**BAKERSFIELD, CALIFORNIA 93301**
*Telephone: 805-322-8166*
*Fax: 805-322-8168*

*Family Law.*

*(This Listing Continued)*

**ANTHONY P. AZEMIKA,** born Tehran, Iran, January 26, 1967; admitted to bar, 1992, California. *Education:* California State University (B.S., 1988); University of California, Hastings College of Law (J.D., 1991). *Member:* Kern County (Board of Directors, Family Law Section) and Los Angeles County (Member, Family Law Section) Bar Associations; State Bar of California. *PRACTICE AREAS:* Family Law; Adoptions; Guardianships; Conservatorships.

**NICHOLAS P. AZEMIKA,** born Tehran, Iran, January 26, 1967; admitted to bar, 1992, California. *Education:* San Francisco State (B.S., 1988); University of California, Hastings College of Law (J.D., 1991). *Member:* Kern County (Member, Family Law Section) Los Angeles County and American Bar Associations; State Bar of California. *PRACTICE AREAS:* Family Law.

---

## *BAKER, MANOCK & JENSEN*

A PROFESSIONAL CORPORATION

**BAKERSFIELD, CALIFORNIA**

(See Fresno)

*General Civil and Trial Practice. Environmental, Agricultural, Bankruptcy, Cooperative, Corporation, Medical and Malpractice Legal, Taxation, Probate and Estate Planning, Real Estate, Water Rights, Family/Domestic Relations, Oil and Gas Law, Intellectual Property, and Employment Law.*

---

## *BIEL & BREHMER*

903 H STREET, SUITE 200
**BAKERSFIELD, CALIFORNIA 93304**
Telephone: 805-322-8113
Fax: 805-322-2575

*Personal Injury, Criminal Defense and Business Litigation. General Civil Trial Practice.*

*FIRM PROFILE: Le Atendemos en Español.*

**PHILLIP J. BIEL,** born Leoti, Kansas, June 12, 1967; admitted to bar, 1992, California. *Education:* Regis College (B.A., 1989); Pepperdine University (J.D., 1992). Phi Alpha Delta. Member, Kern County Hispanic Chamber of Commerce 1995—. Special Prosecutor, Kern County District Attorney, 1993. *Member:* Kern County, Los Angeles County and American Bar Associations; State Bar of California; California Consumer Lawyers Association. *PRACTICE AREAS:* Personal Injury and Criminal Defense; Traffic Violation; Commercial Litigation.

**CHARLES R. BREHMER,** born Cedar Rapids, Iowa, October 7, 1966; admitted to bar, 1992, California and Indiana; U.S. District Court, Southern District of Indiana; U.S. District Court, Eastern District of California. *Education:* Valparaiso University (B.A., 1989; J.D., 1992). San Joaquin Inns of Court. Member, Board of Directors, YMCA of Kern County, (1993—); Vice Chairman, (1995); Chairman, (1996). Member, Board of Directors, Project Clean Air, 1994-1995. Member, Kern County Hispanic Chamber of Commerce (1995—). *Member:* Kern County, Indiana State and American Bar Associations; State Bar of California (Member, Young Lawyers Division); The Association of Trial Lawyers of America. *PRACTICE AREAS:* Personal Injury; Business Litigation; Casualty Defense.

---

## *LAW OFFICES OF DAVID B. BLOOM*

A PROFESSIONAL CORPORATION

**BAKERSFIELD, CALIFORNIA**

(See Los Angeles)

*General Civil Practice, Litigation, Insurance, Personal Injury, Bankruptcy, Creditors Rights, Probate, Real Property, Banking and Entertainment Law.*

---

## *BORTON, PETRINI & CONRON*

THE BORTON, PETRINI & CONRON BUILDING
1600 TRUXTUN AVENUE
P.O. BOX 2026
**BAKERSFIELD, CALIFORNIA 93303**
Telephone: 805-322-3051
Voice Mail: 805-395-6700
Fax: 805-322-4628
Email: bpcbak@bpclaw.com

*San Luis Obispo, California Office:* 1114 Marsh Street. Telephone: 805-541-4340. Fax: 805-541-4558. Email: bpcslo@bpclaw.com.
*Visalia, California Office:* 206 South Mooney Boulevard, P.O. Box 1028. Telephone: 209-627-5600. Fax: 209-627-4309. Email: bpcvis@bpclaw.com.
*Fresno, California Office:* T. W. Patterson Building, 2014 Tulare Street, Suite 830. Telephone: 209-268-0117. Fax: 209-237-7995. Email: bpcfrs@bpclaw.com.
*Sacramento, California Office:* 2233 Watt Avenue, Suite 290. Telephone: 916-484-3555. Fax: 916-484-3550. Email: bpcsac@bpclaw.com.
*Santa Barbara, California Office:* 211 East Victoria Street, Suite D. Telephone: 805-564-2404. Fax: 805-564-2176. Email: bpcsb@bpclaw.com
*Los Angeles, California Office:* 707 Wilshire Boulevard, Suite 5100. Telephone: 213-624-2869. Fax: 213-489-3930. Email: bpcla@bpclaw.com.
*San Diego, California Office:* John Burnham Building, 610 West Ash Street, 9th Floor. Telephone: 619-232-2424. Fax: 619-531-0794. Email: bpcsd@bpclaw.com.
*Newport Beach, California Office:* 4675 MacArthur Court, Suite 1150. Telephone: 714-752-2333. Fax: 714-752-2854. Email: bpcnb@bpclaw.com.
*Modesto, California Office:* The Turner Building, 900 "H" Street, Suite D. Telephone: 209-576-1701. Fax: 209-527-9753. Email: bpcmod@bpclaw.com.
*San Francisco, California Office:* 111 Pine Street, Suite 730. Telephone: 415-981-4415. Fax: 415-391-5538. Email: bpcsf@bpclaw.com.
*Redding, California Office:* 280 Hemsted Drive, Suite 100. Telephone: 916-222-1530. Fax: 916-222-4498. Email: bpcred@bpclaw.com.
*San Bernardino, California Office:* 290 North "D" Street, Suite 500. Telephone: 909-381-0527. Fax: 909-381-0658. Email: bpcsbdo@bpclaw.com.
*San Jose, California Office:* 2 North Second Street. Telephone: 408-298-3997. Fax: 408-298-3365. Email: bpcsj@bpclaw.com.
*Ventura, California Office:* 1000 Hill Road, Suite 310. Telephone: 805-650-9994. Fax: 805-650-7125. Email: bpcvta@bpclaw.com.
*Santa Rosa, California Office:* 50 Santa Rosa Avenue, Suite 300. Telephone: 707-527-9477. Fax: 707-527-9488. Email: bpcsr@bpclaw.com.

*Commercial/Real Estate Litigation, Insurance Law, General Civil Trial and Appellate Practice in State and Federal Courts, Personal Injury and Casualty Defense Litigation, Insurance Bad Faith and Coverage, Labor and Employment, Toxic Torts, Real Estate, Land Use Planning, Zoning, Municipal, Professional Errors and Omissions, Healthcare Provider Malpractice Defense, Products Liability, Oil and Gas, Water, Natural Resources, Environmental, Public Entity, Administrative, Agricultural, Banking, Contracts, Corporations, Partnerships, Taxation, Creditor's Remedies, Bankruptcy, Probate, Estate Planning, Family Law.*

*FIRM PROFILE: Founded by Fred E. Borton in 1899, the firm offers high quality legal services in all of the practice areas described above through its California network of sixteen regional offices. Our mission is to handle each file as if we were the client. We are responsive to the clients' need for communication, cost effectiveness and prompt evaluation.*

### MEMBERS OF FIRM

**FRED E. BORTON** (1877-1948).

**JAMES PETRINI** (1897-1978).

**HARRY M. CONRON** (1907-1971).

**KENNETH D. PINSENT** (1953-1984).

**RICHARD E. HITCHCOCK,** born Bakersfield, California, April 16, 1925; admitted to bar, 1952, California. *Education:* University of California at Berkeley (B.A., 1948); Hastings College of the Law, University of California (J.D., 1951). Member, Editorial Board, California Defense Journal, 1988—. Deputy District Attorney, Kern County, California, 1958-1965. Member, 1976-1994, President, 1986-1993, Kern County Law Library.

*(This Listing Continued)*

**BORTON, PETRINI & CONRON,** Bakersfield—Continued

Member, Board of Trustees, Kern View Hospital, 1986-1993. *Member:* Kern County (President, 1968-1969) and American Bar Associations; The State Bar of California; Association of Defense Counsel, Northern California (Vice President, 1969-1970); Defense Research Institute. *PRACTICE AREAS:* Commercial/Real Estate Litigation; Personal Injury and Casualty Defense (including Malpractice); Insurance Litigation.

**JOHN F. PETRINI,** born Bakersfield, California, July 10, 1944; admitted to bar, 1971, California. *Education:* University of California at Davis (B.A., 1965; J.D., 1970). Editorial Board, California Defense Journal, 1988—. Assistant Dean, University of California at Davis, 1971. Deputy District Attorney: Yolo County, 1971-1973; Sacramento County, 1973-1978 (Supervising Deputy District Attorney, Major Crimes Division). *Member:* Kern County Bar Association (Member, Board of Directors, 1981-1983; Secretary-Treasurer, 1984; 2nd Vice President, 1985; 1st Vice President, 1986; President, 1987); The State Bar of California; Central California Bankruptcy Association; Defense Research Institute. *PRACTICE AREAS:* Commercial/Real Estate Litigation; Personal Injury and Casualty Defense; Professional E & O; Insurance Litigation; Banking.

**GEORGE F. MARTIN,** born Yuba City, California, July 7, 1944; admitted to bar, 1972, California. *Education:* Sacramento State College (B.A., 1968); University of California at Davis (J.D., 1971). Editor-in-Chief: Verdict Legal Journal, 1984-1985; California Defense Journal, 1988—. Dean of California Pacific School of Law. *Member:* Kern County and American Bar Associations; The State Bar of California; Association of Southern California Defense Counsel (Member, Board of Directors, 1978-1985; President, 1984); Association of Business Trial Lawyers; Greater Bakersfield Chamber of Commerce (Member, Board of Directors, 1988—; President, 1991); Central California Heart Institute (President, 1990-1992); Witkin Legal Institute (Member, Board of Directors, 1996); Bakersfield Memorial Hospital (Member, Board of Directors, 1987-1992); California State University at Bakersfield Foundation (Member, Board of Directors); Kern County Economic Development Corporation (Member, Board of Directors). *PRACTICE AREAS:* Commercial/Real Estate Litigation; Personal Injury and Casualty Defense (including Malpractice); Insurance Litigation.

**STEPHEN M. DAKE,** born Tonasket, Washington, March 13, 1954; admitted to bar, 1979, California; 1982, U.S. Tax Court. *Education:* California State University at San Luis Obispo (B.S., cum laude, 1976); Loyola University School of Law (J.D., 1979); University of Miami (LL.M. in Taxation, 1982). President, Bakersfield Museum of Art. *Member:* Kern County and American Bar Associations; The State Bar of California; Kern County Taxpayers Association; Downtown Business Association. *PRACTICE AREAS:* Taxation; Business Planning; Estate Planning; Corporations; Partnerships; Contract.

**PAUL LAFRANCHISE,** born Washington, D.C., March 30, 1950; admitted to bar, 1978, Georgia; 1980, District of Columbia; 1982, U.S. Supreme Court; 1986, California. *Education:* The Catholic University of America (B.A., 1974); University of Georgia (J.D., 1978); Georgetown University Law Center (LL.M., 1981). Author: "The Law of Wrongful Termination," California Defense Magazine, Spring, 1988. Member: U.S. Occupational Safety & Health Review Commission, 1978-1982; U.S. Social Security Administration, 1982-1984; California Agricultural Labor Relations Board, 1984-1986; Bakersfield Employers Advisory Council, State of California; Kern County Chapter, Society of Human Resource Management; California Industrial Safety Council; Golden Empire Safety Society; Bakersfield Rotary; Hispanic Chamber of Commerce of Kern County; Greater Bakersfield Chamber of Commerce (Co-chair Labor and Employment Law Committee). *Member:* Kern County Bar Association; The State Bar of California; The District of Columbia Bar; State Bar of Georgia; Association of Southern California Defense Counsel. [U.S. Naval Reserve, 1982-1986]. *LANGUAGES:* Spanish. *PRACTICE AREAS:* Labor and Employment (Management).

**STEVEN M. KARCHER,** born San Diego, California, October 25, 1956; admitted to bar, 1989, California. *Education:* California State University at Hayward (B.A., magna cum laude, 1984); Emory University Law School (J.D., 1988). Phi Alpha Delta. Member: East Bakersfield Rotary Club; Bakersfield City Schools Education Foundation Board. *Member:* Kern County Bar Association; State Bar of California. *PRACTICE AREAS:* Business Litigation; Alternative Dispute Resolution; Bankruptcy and Creditor's Rights; Professional Liability Defense.

**MARK ALAN JONES,** born Borger, Texas, December 2, 1954; admitted to bar, 1990, Texas; 1991, California. *Education:* University of Texas, Permian Basin (B.S., Geology, 1976); McGeorge School of Law (J.D., 1990). Order of Barristers. Primarily Law Review Editor, The Transnational Lawyer. Moot Court Finalist. Best Brief Finalist. National Moot Court Competition Team. Trial Advocacy Competition Team. Member: Board of Directors, Preferred Petroleum, Inc., 1981-1983; Freemark Corporation, 1984-1989. *Member:* Kern County Bar Association; Association of Defense Counsel; American Petroleum Institute, San Joaquin Valley Chapter; West Texas Geologic Society. *PRACTICE AREAS:* Business and Real Estate Litigation; Personal Injury and Casualty Defense Litigation; Medical Malpractice and Professional Negligence Defense Litigation; Oil, Gas and Mineral Law and Litigation; Environmental Law and Litigation.

**VICTORIA R. ALLARD,** born Oakland, California, April 30, 1963; admitted to bar, 1991, California. *Education:* University of California at San Diego (B.A., 1987); University of San Diego School of Law (J.D., 1991). Member, Board of Directors, 1993-1996, Project Clean Air. Board Member, Teen Alternative Court of Kern; Realizing Options for Student Excellence Program. *Member:* Kern County Bar Association; The State Bar of California; Kern County Women Lawyers Association (Board of Directors, 1996); Kern County Adjusters' Association (Vice President, 1995). *PRACTICE AREAS:* Personal Injury and Casualty Defense; Insurance Litigation.

*ASSOCIATES*

**CRAIG N. BEARDSLEY,** born Glendale, California, July 22, 1944; admitted to bar, 1973, California. *Education:* University of California at Santa Barbara (B.A., 1970); University of San Francisco (J.D., cum laude, 1973). *Member:* Los Angeles, San Bernardino, Kern County and American Bar Associations; The State Bar of California; Southern California Defense Council. *PRACTICE AREAS:* Personal Injury; Casualty Defense (including Malpractice); Product Liability; Insurance Litigation.

**RANDALL STEVEN JOYCE,** born Inglewood, California, November 8, 1950; admitted to bar, 1989, California. *Education:* Occidental College (B.A., 1972); University of California (M.A., 1976); Ventura College of Law (J.D., 1989). Delta Theta Phi. Member, Teen Alternative Court of Kern County. *Member:* Kern County and American Bar Associations; State Bar of California. *PRACTICE AREAS:* Medical Malpractice; Workers' Compensation; Labor/Employment Law; Personal Injury.

**WENDY E. COULSTON,** born Fullerton, California, July 26, 1966; admitted to bar, 1992, California; 1994, U.S. District Court, Central District of California. *Education:* California State University Fullerton (B.A., 1988); Western State University (J.D., cum laude, 1992). Member, Rotary Club of Bakersfield (President). *Member:* Kern County Bar Association (Chairperson, Mandatory Continuing Legal Education Committee); State Bar of California; Kern County Women Lawyer's Association; Rotaract Club of Bakersfield (President); Orange County Barristers Association; Kern County Adjuster's Association. *PRACTICE AREAS:* Insurance Defense; Medical Malpractice; Civil Litigation.

**GREG L. FERRARI,** born Long Beach, California, February 6, 1952; admitted to bar, 1993, California. *Education:* Long Beach State University (B.A., 1995); Western State University (J.D., 1993). Board Member, Kern County Tax Organization. *Member:* Kern County and American Bar Associations; State Bar of California. *PRACTICE AREAS:* Municipal Law; Estate Planning; Probate; Corporate Law.

**BRIAN E. BISOL,** born Santa Barbara, California, March 26, 1968; admitted to bar, 1995, California. *Education:* University of California, Los Angeles (B.A., 1991); University of Arizona (J.D., 1995). *Member:* Kern County Bar Association. *PRACTICE AREAS:* Insurance Defense.

**TOBIAS A. DORSEY,** born Concord, Massachusetts, May 10, 1967; admitted to bar, 1993, Massachusetts and Maine; 1996, California. *Education:* Cornell University (B.A., 1989); University of California School of Law (J.D., 1993). *Member:* Maine State, Massachusetts and American Bar Associations. *PRACTICE AREAS:* Business Litigation; Constitutional Law; Insurance Defense.

**RICHARD E. MORTON,** born Buhl, Idaho, December 12, 1940; admitted to bar, 1972, California; 1987, U.S. District Court, Central District of California and U.S. Court of Appeals, Ninth Circuit. *Education:* Mason City College (A.A., 1962); California State University at Fullerton (B.A., 1965); Pepperdine University (J.D., 1972). *Member:* Orange County and American (Member: Section of Tort and Insurance Practice; Toxic and

*(This Listing Continued)*

Hazardous Substances and Environmental Law Committee) Bar Associations; State Bar of California; Defense Research Institute; Association of Southern California Defense Counsel. *PRACTICE AREAS:* Insurance Defense; Business Litigation; Construction Defects; Real Property; Environmental Law.

*ANDREW C. THOMSON,* born Santa Barbara, California, July 11, 1956; admitted to bar, 1990, California; 1992, U.S. District Court, Northern, Eastern, Central and Southern Districts of California. *Education:* California State University at Bakersfield (B.A., 1981); California Pacific School of Law (J.D., 1990). *Member:* Kern County Bar Association; State Bar of California; Southern California Defense Association; Defense Research Institute. *PRACTICE AREAS:* Insurance Defense; Public Entity Representation and Defense; Business Litigation.

*JOE W. WHITTINGTON,* born Bakersfield, California, December 20, 1951; admitted to bar, 1996, California. *Education:* California Pacific School of Law (J.D., 1994). *Member:* State Bar of California. *PRACTICE AREAS:* Employment Law; Construction Law; Civil Litigation.

*ELIZABETH M. GIESICK,* born Joliet, Illinois, September 15, 1966; admitted to bar, 1996, California. *Education:* Arizona State University (B.S., 1988); Western State University College of Law (J.D., 1994). *Member:* Kern County Bar Association; The State Bar of California; Kern County Womens Lawyer Association.

*TIMOTHY C. HALE,* born Santa Barbara, California, November 21, 1967; admitted to bar, 1996, California. *Education:* California State University, Sacramento (B.A., 1992); University of Utah College of Law (J.D., 1996). *Member:* The State Bar of California.

*J. DAVID BOURNAZIAN,* born Westfield, New Jersey, July 30, 1969; admitted to bar, 1996, California. *Education:* Rutgers University (B.S., 1991); University of San Diego (J.D., 1996). *Member:* The State Bar of California.

*LINDA M. MARSCHANG,* born Joliet, Illinois, January 5, 1959; admitted to bar, 1996, California. *Education:* Southeast Missouri State University (B.S., 1981); University of Denver (J.D., 1995). Certified Public Accountant, 1982. *Member:* Kern County Bar Association; The State Bar of California; Kern County Women Lawyers Association; California Society of CPAs.

*WILLIAM H. CANTRELL* (Resident Member, Newport Beach Office).

*J. DAVID PETRIE* (Resident Member, Fresno Office).

*DANIEL L. FERGUSON* (Resident Member, San Bernardino Office).

*ROCKY K. COPLEY* (Resident Member, San Diego Office).

*CRAIG R. MCCOLLUM* (Resident Member, San Luis Obispo Office).

*MARK S. NEWMAN* (Resident Member, Sacramento Office).

*JAMES M. MCKANNA* (Resident Member, San Luis Obispo, Office).

*RICHARD M. MACIAS* (Resident Member, Los Angeles Office).

*DALE M. DORFMEIER* (Resident Member, Fresno Office).

*PHILLIP B. GREER* (Resident Member, Newport Beach Office).

*ROBERT H. GROVE* (Resident Member, Ventura Office).

*STEVEN M. SHEWRY* (Resident Member, San Diego Office).

*ROBERT J. GUNDERT* (Resident Member, San Luis Obispo Office).

*RANDALL L. HARR* (Resident Member, Redding Office).

*GEORGE J. HERNANDEZ, JR.* (Resident Member, Los Angeles Office).

*ROBERT N. RIDENOUR* (Resident Member, Los Angeles Office).

*RICK D. HARDIN* (Resident Member, Santa Barbara Office).

*PAUL KISSEL* (Resident Member, San Diego Office).

*CARLA J. HARTLEY* (Resident Member, San Francisco Office).

*SHARON G. PRATT* (Resident Member, San Jose Office).

*BRADLEY A. POST* (Resident Member, Modesto Office).

*MICHAEL J. MACKO* (Resident Member, Modesto Office).

*TRACY W. GOLDBERG* (Resident Member, San Bernardino Office).

*SAMUEL L. PHILLIPS* (Resident Member, Modesto Office).

*CALVIN R. STEAD* (Resident Member, Santa Rosa Office).

*(This Listing Continued)*

*GARY C. HARVEY* (Resident Member, Fresno Office).

*MICHAEL F. LONG* (Resident Member, Newport Beach Office).

*THOMAS A. GIFFORD* (Resident Member, Sacramento Office).

*THOMAS J. STODDARD* (Resident Member, San Diego Office).

*KENNETH B. ARTHOFER* (Resident Member, Redding Office).

*DARLENE M. BALL* (Resident Member, Visalia Office).

*STEVEN G. GATLEY* (Resident Member, Los Angeles Office).

*ROSEMARIE SUAZO LEWIS* (Resident Member, Los Angeles Office).

*DENNIS D. RESH* (Resident Associate, Los Angeles Office).

*R. STEPHEN KINNAIRD* (Resident Associate, Santa Barbara Office).

*THOMAS F. BROOKS* (Resident Member, Ventura Office).

*RICHARD E. KORB* (Resident Associate, San Francisco Office).

*NELSON H. CHAN* (Resident Associate, Sacramento Office).

*J. ALBERT BOADA* (Resident Associate, San Luis Obispo Office).

*TUVANA B. JEFFREY* (Resident Associate, San Francisco Office).

*GARY A. BIXLER* (Resident Associate, San Luis Obispo Office).

*MICHAEL V. PEROS* (Resident Associate, San Bernardino Office).

*CHRISTOPHER DER MANUELIAN, JR.* (Resident Associate, San Jose Office).

*LYNNE L. BENTLEY* (Resident Member, San Jose Office).

*BARTON C. MERRILL* (Resident Member, Santa Barbara Office).

*MARC C. GESSFORD* (Resident Associate, Sacramento Office).

*PAIGE M. HIBBERT* (Resident Member, Sacramento Office).

*DONALD A. DIEBOLD* (Resident Associate, Newport Beach Office).

*WILLIAM F. KLAUSNER* (Resident Member, San Bernardino Office).

*ARCANGELO CLARIZIO* (Resident Associate, Ventura Office).

*PAUL T. MCBRIDE* (Resident Associate, Newport Beach Office).

*MARK T. COFFIN* (Resident Associate, Santa Barbara Office).

*MICHELLE L. VAN DYKE* (Resident Associate, San Diego Office).

*STEVEN P. OWEN* (Resident Associate, Los Angeles Office).

*PAUL C. CLAUSS* (Resident Associate, Santa Rosa Office).

*MICHAEL J. BOYAJIAN* (Resident Associate, Fresno Office).

*DANIEL J. TEKUNOFF* (Resident Associate, Fresno Office).

*GUY CHIRINIAN* (Resident Associate, Los Angeles Office).

*SHARON P. MCALEENAN* (Resident Associate, Los Angeles Office).

*ALFRED W. MONDORF* (Resident Associate, Redding Office).

*ROBERT D. REED* (Resident Associate, San Luis Obispo Office).

*CAROL D. JANSSEN* (Resident Associate, San Luis Obispo Office).

*ERIC J. LARSON* (Resident Associate, San Diego Office).

*CARI S. BAUM* (Resident Associate, Newport Beach Office).

*CAROLYN M. KERN* (Resident Associate, Newport Beach Office).

*JOYCE M. STOVALL* (Resident Associate, San Bernardino Office).

*KARI L. RUTHERFORD* (Resident Associate, San Bernardino Office).

*BARTON F. HOEY* (Resident Associate, San Luis Obispo Office).

*JANICE K. LACHMAN* (Resident Associate, Sacramento Office).

*GREG RUBINOFF* (Resident Associate, Sacramento Office).

*OF COUNSEL*

*ROY J. GARGANO,* born Seattle, Washington, July 8, 1917; admitted to bar, 1946, California. *Education:* St. Mary's College (J.B.A., 1937); University of Southern California (LL.B., 1946). Phi Kappa Phi; Order of the Coif. County Counsel of Kern County, 1951-1963. Superior Court Judge of Kern County, 1963-1966. Associate Justice, California Court of Appeals, Fifth Appellate District, 1966-1977. *Member:* Kern County and American Bar Associations; The State Bar of California; Association of Southern Cali-

*(This Listing Continued)*

## BORTON, PETRINI & CONRON, Bakersfield—Continued

fornia Defense Counsel; Association of Business Trial Lawyers; California Conference of Judges; California Judicial Counsel.

**JERE N. SULLIVAN, SR.,** born Cortland, New York, September 18, 1920; admitted to bar, 1949, New York; 1950, California; 1960, U.S. Supreme Court. *Education:* Amherst College (A.B., 1944); Harvard University (J.D., 1948). Deputy District Attorney, 1951. President, Bakersfield East, Rotary International, 1966-1967. Judge Pro Tem, Kern County Superior Court, Family Law, 1983—. *Member:* Kern County Bar Association (President, 1957-1958; Chairman, Legal Aid and Lawyer Reference Plan, 1952-1956); State Bar of California (Member, Executive Committee, Conference of Junior Bar Members, 1951-1952). [U.S. Army, 45th Infantry, 1943-1945; Recipient, P.O.W. Medal and bronze Star]

REPRESENTATIVE CLIENTS: Wells Fargo Bank; First Interstate Bank of California; Community First Bank; Sierra National Bank; Valley Farm Credit Bank; Southern Pacific Transportation Company; Atchison, Topeka and Santa Fe Railroad; Mobil Oil Co.; Shell Western Exploration & Production, Inc.; Cessna Aircraft; Firestone Tire and Rubber Company; Goodyear Tire and Rubber Company; CNA Insurance Group; State Farm Insurance Companies; Farmers Insurance Group; Allstate Insurance; Home Insurance Company; International Harvester; Deere and Company; Pacific Gas & Electric; Pacific Lighting Company; Nabors Industries, Inc.; Pride Petroleum Services, Inc.; Halliburton Services; Carnation Company; Castle & Cooke Development Company; Karpe Real Estate Co.; Century 21 Realty; McDonald's Corp.; Yellow Freight Systems, Inc.; Freymiller Trucking, Inc.; Pacific Trucking Motor Company; Albertson's Inc.; Food-4-Less Supermarkets; Granite Construction Co.; CBR Cement Corp.; Mesa Marin Raceway; Tejon Ranch; Golden Cat Corporation; Laidlaw Environmental Services, Inc.; M.P. Environmental Services; Gibson Environmental; North of the River Sanitation District; Commonwealth Title Company; Building Industry Association of Kern County; Developer's Financial Group; Greater Bakersfield Chamber of Commerce; Kern Economic Development Corporation; Kern County Water Agency; Kern Radiology Medical Group, Inc.; Pacific Health Care, Inc.

---

## JOHN J. BURKE, JR.

1600 TRUXTUN AVENUE, THIRD FLOOR
**BAKERSFIELD, CALIFORNIA 93301**
*Telephone: 805-324-7627*

*Estate Planning, Probate and Elder Law.*

**JOHN J. BURKE, JR.,** born Washington, D.C., 1951; admitted to bar, 1985, California and U.S. District Court, Central and Eastern Districts of California; 1987, U.S. Tax Court. *Education:* University of California at Los Angeles (B.A., 1973); Southwestern University (J.D., 1985). *Member:* State Bar of California (Member, Estate Planning, Trust and Probate Law Section).

---

## DONALD F. BUTZ

*Established in 1988*
1402 26TH STREET
**BAKERSFIELD, CALIFORNIA 93301**
*Telephone: 805-327-2367*

*Family Law.*

**DONALD F. BUTZ,** born Evanston, Illinois, April 24, 1947; admitted to bar, 1979, California. *Education:* Stanislaus State College (B.A., 1973); California State University, Humboldt; University of San Francisco (J.D., 1979). *Member:* Kern County Bar Association (Member, Family Law Section; Past President, 1989); The State Bar of California. (Certified Specialist, Family Law, The State Bar of California Board of Legal Specialization). *PRACTICE AREAS:* Family Law.

---

## BYRUM, HOLLAND, BRUMFIELD & DIETRICH

5201 CALIFORNIA AVENUE, SUITE 450
**BAKERSFIELD, CALIFORNIA 93309**
*Telephone: 805-861-6191*
*Facsimile: 805-861-6190*

*General Civil and Trial Practice in all State and Federal Courts. Administrative Agencies, Business and Tax Planning, Estates Planning, Trusts and Probate, Insolvency, Real Property, Real Property Taxation, Title Insurance, Banking, Construction, Natural Resources, Environmental, Public Health and Personal Injury.*

*(This Listing Continued)*

---

**KENNETH M. BYRUM,** born San Bernardino, California, September 19, 1939; admitted to bar, 1966, California and U.S. District Court, Eastern District of California; 1969, U.S. Supreme Court; 1988, U.S. Tax Court. *Education:* Bakersfield College (A.A., 1960); University of California at Los Angeles (B.S., 1962; J.D., 1965). Director, Bakersfield College Foundation, 1975—. *Member:* Kern County (Director, 1977-1980) and American Bar Associations; State Bar of California; American Judicature Society. *PRACTICE AREAS:* Real Estate Law; Business and Construction Litigation; Natural Resources Law.

**KENNETH A. HOLLAND,** born Milwaukee, Wisconsin, May 16, 1947; admitted to bar, 1973, California; 1981, U.S. Supreme Court. *Education:* Glendale College (A.A., 1967); University of California at Los Angeles (A.B., cum laude, 1969); Graduate School of Education, University of California at Los Angeles (Cert. of Completion, 1970); University of Notre Dame (J.D., 1973). Member, National Moot Court Team, 1972-1973. Champion, Notre Dame Law School Moot Court Final Argument, 1973. Recipient, Dean's Award, 1973. Law Clerk to Hon. John F. Kilkenny, Senior Circuit Judge, U.S. Court of Appeals, Ninth Circuit, 1973-1974. Instructor, "Terminating Litigation Without Trial," California Continuing Education of the Bar, 1979. Lecturer, Lawyer's Mutual Minimum Continuing Legal Education Seminar, "Preventing Legal Malpractice in the Specialties," Bakersfield, California, 1991. Honors Attorney, U.S. Department of Justice, Criminal Division, Appellate Section, Washington, D.C., 1974-1976. *Member:* Kern County Bar Association; State Bar of California. *REPORTED CASES:* United States vs. Turcotte, 515 F.2d 145, (CA 2 1975); States vs. DiMuro, 540 F.2d 503 (CA 1 1976); J. Paul Getty Museum vs. County of Los Angeles, 248 Cal. App. 3d 600 (1980); Rancho La Costa vs. County of San Diego, 111 Cal.App.3d 54, (1980); Pope vs. State Board of Equalization, 146 Cal.App.3d 1132 (1983); Alpha Therapeutic Corporation vs. County of Los Angeles, 179 Cal.App.3d, 265 (1986); Moore vs. Kayport Package Express, Inc., 885 F.2d 531 (CA9 1990). *PRACTICE AREAS:* General Civil Litigation; Real Property; Title Insurance Defense; Professional Negligence Defense; Administrative Agencies.

**ROBERT H. BRUMFIELD, III,** born New Orleans, Louisiana, July 18, 1958; admitted to bar, 1984, California, U.S. District Court, Eastern, Central, Southern and Northern Districts of California and U.S. Tax Court. *Education:* California Polytechnic State University, San Luis Obispo (B.A., 1980); McGeorge School of Law, University of the Pacific (J.D., 1983; LL.M., in Taxation, 1985). Phi Alpha Delta. *Member:* Kern County Bar Association (Director, 1990—; President, 1996; First Vice President, 1995; Second Vice President, 1994; Secretary-Chief Financial Officer, 1993); State Bar of California (Member, State Bar Committee on Mandatory Fee Arbitration); Commercial Law League of America; Central California Bankruptcy Association. *PRACTICE AREAS:* Bankruptcy; Corporation Law; Partnership Law; General Civil Litigation; Construction Law.

**CHRISTOPHER M. DIETRICH,** born Berkeley, California, July 20, 1959; admitted to bar, 1985, California; 1986, U.S. District Court, Northern District of California; 1990, U.S. Tax Court. *Education:* University of California at Santa Barbara (B.A., 1981); McGeorge School of Law (J.D., 1985). Member, Executive Committee, Board of Trustees, Bakersfield Memorial Health Foundation. *Member:* Kern County Bar Association (Past President, Probate and Estate Planning Section); State Bar of California. *REPORTED CASES:* Estate of Robert Daniels, Deceased, (1991) 228 Cal. .App.3d 486. *PRACTICE AREAS:* Estate Planning; Probate; Business Transactions.

### ASSOCIATES

**ALAN B. HARRIS,** born Altus, Oklahoma, August 31, 1955; admitted to bar, 1982, California. *Education:* University of California at Santa Barbara (B.A., 1978); California Western School of Law (J.D., 1982). Recipient, American Jurisprudence Award in Civil Procedure. Staff Writer and Notes & Comments Editor, California Western Law Review, 1981-1982. Author: "Kubrick vs. United States: Accrual of Medical Malpractice Claim Under the Federal Tort Claims Act," 18 Cal. W. L. Rev, 1982. *Member:* State Bar of California. [Captain, U.S. Marine Corp (Reserve)]. *PRACTICE AREAS:* Civil Litigation; Title Insurance Defense; Real Property Law.

**BRIAN M. LEDGER,** born Trenton, New Jersey, October 28, 1960; admitted to bar, 1991, California; 1994, U.S. District Court, Eastern District of California. *Education:* East Stroudsburg University (B.S., magna cum laude, 1983); University of California at Los Angeles (Masters of Public Health, Environmental and Occupational Health Science, 1987); University of Michigan (J.D., 1991). Recipient: Award for outstanding academic achievement. Extern, California Attorney General's Office Dept. of Natural Resources, 1989; U.S. Dept. of Labor-OSHA, Compliance Officer, 1987-

*(This Listing Continued)*

1988. *Member:* State Bar of California; American Bar Association. Environmental Law Society; American Industrial Hygiene Association. *PRACTICE AREAS:* Environmental Litigation and Regulatory Compliance; Real Property Litigation; Business Litigation.

REPRESENTATIVE CLIENTS: A-C Electric Company; Baker Performance Chemicals, Inc.; Bakersfield Pipe & Supply; Bakersfield Tank Company; Baker Hughes, Inc. (Houston, Texas); Bank of America N.T.S.A.; Chelsea Investment Company; Chicago Title Company; Chicago Title Insurance Company; Cliff Mock Co. Inc. (Houston, Texas); Delano Rock Company; Dunn-Edwards Company; Eimco Process Equipment Company; Gibson Irrigation Systems; Golden Empire Transit District; Kern Rock Company; Laidlaw Environmental; McCarthy Steel, Inc.; Mercy Hospital; Pameco Corporation; Pick Your Part Auto Wrecking, Inc.; Quail Valley Water District; S.A. Camp Companies; Sears, Roebuck & Company; Southern California Edison Company; Ticor Title Insurance Company; Wedel Farms; Weidenbach Brothers Farms; Wells Fargo Bank; Wheeler Ridge-Maricopa Water Storage District.

## CLIFFORD & BROWN
*A PROFESSIONAL CORPORATION*
SUITE 900
*1430 TRUXTUN AVENUE*
**BAKERSFIELD, CALIFORNIA 93301**
Telephone: 805-322-6023
Fax: 805-322-3508
Email: cblaw@lightspeed.net

*General Civil Practice in all State and Federal Courts. Civil and Business Litigation, Negligence, Products Liability, Matters of Professional Negligence, Creditor's Rights, Insurance, Estate Planning and Probate, Tax Planning, Land Use, Agriculture, Real Estate, Corporation, Employment, Oil and Gas and Environmental Law.*

**STEPHEN T. CLIFFORD,** born Bakersfield, California, November 27, 1940; admitted to bar, 1966, California and U.S. District Court, Eastern District of California. *Education:* University of California at Davis (B.S., 1963); Hastings College of the Law, University of California (LL.B., 1966). Phi Delta Phi. *Member:* Kern County Bar Association; State Bar of California; American Board of Trial Advocates; Association of Defense Counsel of Northern California (Member, Board of Directors, 1980); Defense Research Institute; National Association of Railroad Trial Counsel; International Association of Insurance Counsel. Fellow, American College of Trial Lawyers. *PRACTICE AREAS:* Civil Litigation.

**JAMES E. BROWN,** born Grand Forks, North Dakota, November 23, 1940; admitted to bar, 1966, California. *Education:* University of North Dakota (B.S., 1963); Hastings College of the Law, University of California (LL.B., 1966). *Member:* Kern County Bar Association; State Bar of California; American Board of Trial Advocates; Association of Defense Counsel of Northern California. Fellow, American College of Trial Lawyers. [With U.S. Army, 1966-1968]. *PRACTICE AREAS:* Civil Litigation.

**ROBERT D. HARDING,** born Pasadena, California, January 24, 1949; admitted to bar, 1974, California. *Education:* University of California (B.A., 1970); Hastings College of the Law, University of California (J.D., 1974). *Member:* Kern County Bar Association; State Bar of California; American Board of Trial Advocates; Association of Defense Counsel of Northern California; Defense Research Institute; Association of Southern California Defense Counsel (Member, Board of Directors, 1987-1991). *PRACTICE AREAS:* Civil Litigation.

**ARNOLD ANCHORDOQUY,** born Bakersfield, California, August 16, 1948; admitted to bar, 1973, California. *Education:* St. Mary's College (B.A., 1970); University of the Pacific, McGeorge School of Law (J.D., 1973). Phi Alpha Delta. Member, Moot Court Honors Board, 1972-1973. *Member:* Kern County Bar Association; State Bar of California; American Board of Trial Advocates; Association of Defense Counsel of Northern California. *PRACTICE AREAS:* Civil Litigation.

**ANTHONY L. LEGGIO,** born Bakersfield, California, September 12, 1952; admitted to bar, 1977, California. *Education:* University of the Pacific (B.A., summa cum laude, 1974); University of the Pacific, McGeorge School of Law (J.D., with distinction, 1977). Phi Delta Phi. Member, Traynor Society. Member, Moot Court Honors Board. *Member:* Kern County and American Bar Associations; State Bar of California; Association of Defense Counsel of Southern California. *PRACTICE AREAS:* General Business Planning Law; Litigation.

**PATRICK J. OSBORN,** born Bakersfield, California, July 28, 1951; admitted to bar, 1977, California. *Education:* University of California at Riverside (A.B., 1975); University of the Pacific, McGeorge School of Law

*(This Listing Continued)*

(J.D., 1977). *Member:* Kern County Bar Association; State Bar of California; Association of Defense Counsel of Northern California; Defense Research Institute; American Board of Trial Advocates; Trial Attorneys of America. *PRACTICE AREAS:* Civil Litigation.

**MICHAEL L. O'DELL,** born Pasadena, California, March 7, 1955; admitted to bar, 1980, California. *Education:* San Diego State University (A.B., 1977); Hastings College of the Law, University of California (J.D., 1980). *Member:* Kern County and American Bar Associations; State Bar of California; Association of Defense Counsel of Southern California. *PRACTICE AREAS:* Civil Litigation; Employment Law.

**GROVER H. WALDON,** born Bakersfield, California, October 7, 1958; admitted to bar, 1983, California and U.S. District Court, Eastern District of California; 1984, U.S. District Court, Central District of California and U.S. Court of Appeals, Ninth Circuit. *Education:* California State University at Sacramento (B.S., 1980); University of the Pacific, McGeorge School of Law (J.D., with distinction, 1983). Member: Traynor Society; Trial Advocacy Competition Team; Community Legal Services Honor Board. Recipient, Best Combined Brief and Oralist, International Moot Court. *Member:* Kern County Bar Association; State Bar of California; American Arbitration Association (Panelist). *PRACTICE AREAS:* Civil Litigation; Business.

**JOHN R. SZEWCZYK,** born Inglewood, California, February 5, 1957; admitted to bar, 1983, California; 1984, U.S. District Court, Eastern District of California. *Education:* University of California at San Diego (B.A., History, 1980); Loyola University of Los Angeles (J.D., cum laude, 1983). Phi Alpha Delta. Member, Sir Thomas Moore Law Honor Society. *Member:* Kern County and American (Member, Sections on: Litigation; Employment Law) Bar Associations; State Bar of California (Member, Employment Law Section). *PRACTICE AREAS:* Civil Litigation; Employment Law; Landlord/Tenant Appellate Law.

**STEPHEN H. BOYLE,** born San Tomé, Venezuela, May 12, 1953; admitted to bar, 1978, California and U.S. District Court, Southern District of California; 1986, U.S. Tax Court. *Education:* University of California at Santa Barbara (B.A., in Political Science, 1975); California Western School of Law (J.D., cum laude, 1978); University of San Diego (LL.M., 1984). Member, Philip C. Jessup International Law Moot Court Team. Member and Lead Articles Editor, California Western International Law Journal, 1983-1984. Recipient, American Jurisprudence Award in Civil Procedure. *Member:* Kern County Bar Association; State Bar of California (Member, Section on Taxation); Christian Legal Society. *PRACTICE AREAS:* Estate Planning/Probate Law; Taxation Law; Corporation Law.

**JAMES B. WIENS,** born Porterville, California, April 7, 1949; admitted to bar, 1978, California; 1982, U.S. District Court, Eastern and Southern Districts of California. *Education:* University of Oregon; University of California at Berkeley (B.A., Psychology, 1971); California Western School of Law (J.D., 1977). Deputy District Attorney, District Attorney's Office, Tulare County, 1979-1982. Member and President, 1995-1996, Estate Planning Council of Bakersfield. *Member:* Kern County Bar Association; State Bar of California. *PRACTICE AREAS:* Estate Planning/Probate Law; General Business; Agricultural Law.

**RICHARD G. ZIMMER,** born Vestal, New York, May 19, 1956; admitted to bar, 1982, California; 1983, North Carolina and U.S. District Court, Western District of North Carolina. *Education:* Rochester Institute of Technology (B.S., with highest honors, 1979); California Western School of Law (J.D., 1982). Member, Cal Western Law Review, 1980-1982. National Moot Court Team Leader, Advocacy Honors Board, National Order of The Barristers. Publication: "Anonymous Political Literature: California's Compulsory Identification Statute Held Unconstitutional in Fourth District," 18 California Western Law Review 363, 1982. *Member:* Kern County Bar Association; The State Bar of California; North Carolina State Bar; National Order of Barristers. *PRACTICE AREAS:* Civil Litigation; Business Litigation.

**CHARLES D. MELTON,** born Bakersfield, California, April 29, 1962; admitted to bar, 1987, California, U.S. Court of Appeals, Ninth Circuit and U.S. District Court, Eastern, Northern and Southern Districts of California. *Education:* University of the Pacific (B.S., cum laude, 1984); Hastings College of the Law, University of California (J.D., 1987). Judicial Extern for Judge William R. Channel, California Court of Appeals, First District, 1986. *Member:* Kern County Bar Association (Chairman, Law library Book Committee); State Bar of California. *PRACTICE AREAS:* Commercial Law; Constitutional Law; Creditors' Rights; General Business; Landlord-Tenant; Sales.

*(This Listing Continued)*

**CLIFFORD & BROWN**, A PROFESSIONAL CORPORATION, Bakersfield—Continued

---

**TERI A. BJORN,** born Burlington, Iowa, April 12, 1953; admitted to bar, 1979, California; 1995, Oregon. *Education:* University of Iowa (B.A., summa cum laude, 1974; M.A., 1976); George Washington University (J.D., with honors, 1979). Phi Beta Kappa. Member, 1977-1978 and Managing Editor, 1978-1979, George Washington Law Review. Author: "The Discriminatory Effect Standard Under the Fair Housing Act," 46 George Washington Law Review 615, May 1978. Associate Professor, California State University Bakersfield, 1986—. Professor, California Pacific School of Law, 1990—. Planning Commissioner, 1987-1992 and Chairman, 1989-1990, City of Bakersfield. *Member:* Kern County (Member, Board of Directors, 1986-1989) and American (Member, Section on Real Property, Probate and Trust Law) Bar Associations; The State Bar of California; Oregon State Bar; Kern County Women Lawyers Association (President, 1986-1987; Member, Board of Directors, 1988-1991). *LANGUAGES:* French. *PRACTICE AREAS:* Real Estate Law.

**GREGORY J. KOHLER,** born Glendora, California, September 8, 1960; admitted to bar, 1989, California and U.S. Court of Appeals, Ninth Circuit; 1990, U.S. District Court, Central District of California. *Education:* University of California at Santa Barbara (B.A., 1985); Pepperdine University (J.D., 1989). *Member:* Kern County Bar Association; State Bar of California. *LANGUAGES:* Spanish. *PRACTICE AREAS:* Civil Litigation; Insurance Coverage; Insurance Litigation.

**STEPHEN P. WAINER,** born Oroville, California, May 2, 1966; admitted to bar, 1991, California; 1992, U.S. District Court, Eastern District of California. *Education:* University of California at Berkeley (A.B., 1988); University of San Diego, (J.D., 1991). Alpha Kappa Delta; Phi Alpha Delta. American Jurisprudence Award in Property. Appellate Moot Court Board; National Moot Court Team. *Member:* Kern County Bar Association; State Bar of California. *PRACTICE AREAS:* Civil Litigation.

**SCOTT L. HARPER,** born Lodi, California, February 8, 1961; admitted to bar, 1991, California. *Education:* McGeorge School of Law (J.D., 1991). Moot Court Orals Finalist, Moot Court Honor Board, Trial Advocacy Competition Team. *Member:* Kern County Bar Association; State Bar of California. *PRACTICE AREAS:* Civil Litigation.

**BILL J. KUENZINGER,** born Modesto, California, August 3, 1965; admitted to bar, 1992, California and U.S. District Court, Eastern District of California; 1996, U.S. District Court, Central District of California. *Education:* California State University, Stanislaus (B.A., 1988); Thomas M. Cooley Law School (J.D., cum laude, 1991). Recipient, American Jurisprudence Award in Advocacy. *Member:* Kern County and American Bar Associations; State Bar of California. *PRACTICE AREAS:* General Business Planning Law; Litigation.

**BETH A. VAN VOORHIS,** born Bakersfield, California, November 30, 1965; admitted to bar, 1992, California; 1993, U.S. District Court, Eastern District of California. *Education:* Central College (B.A., summa cum laude, 1987); University of Edinburgh (Diploma, 1988); University of California, Hastings College of the Law (J.D., 1992). Member, Hastings International and Comparative Law Journal (1990-1992). *Member:* Kern County and American Bar Associations; State Bar of California. *PRACTICE AREAS:* General Business; Real Estate.

**WINIFRED THOMSON HOSS,** born Bakersfield, California, November 19, 1951; admitted to bar, 1981, California. *Education:* University of California at Berkeley; University of California at Davis (B.S., with honors, 1976; J.D., 1981). Lecturer, Real Property Law, California State College at Bakersfield, 1985 and 1987. District Board Member, Kern County Air Pollution Control, 1986. *Member:* Kern County Bar Association; The State Bar of California; Kern County Women Lawyers Association (President, 1985). *PRACTICE AREAS:* Business Transactions; Agricultural Law; Business Formation; Real Estate; Estate Planning.

**PETER S. THORNE,** born San Francisco, California, September 28, 1968; admitted to bar, 1996, California. *Education:* San Francisco State University (B.A., magna cum laude, 1992); California School of Law, Los Angeles (J.D., 1996).

**MARK E. PAFFORD,** born San Jose, California, June 25, 1971; admitted to bar, 1996, California. *Education:* Pepperdine University (B.A., 1993); McGeorge School of Law (J.D., with great distinction, 1996). Member: Order of the Coif; National Moot Court Honor Board.

*(This Listing Continued)*

---

*OF COUNSEL*

**CURTIS DARLING,** born Mt. Solo, Washington, December 13, 1918; admitted to bar, 1949, California. *Education:* Pasadena Junior College and University of California at Berkeley (B.S., 1940); Stanford Law School (J.D., 1948). Author: California Closely Held Corporations - Chapter 15, "Planning for Distributions to Shareholders," Matthew Bender, 1987; 37th Institute on Federal Taxation, New York University, Published 1979. Lecturer: New York University Tax Institute, 1971; 1974; 1976; 1978; 1985; New York University Institute on Taxation-Estate Planning, Chicago General Chairman, 1983. Member, Board of Visitors, Stanford Law School, 1969-1972. *Member:* Kern County (President, 1957; Member, Board of Directors, 1959) and American (Member, Taxation Section) Bar Associations; The State Bar of California (Member: Taxation Committee, 1965-1968; Taxation Section); American Institute of Certified Public Accountants. Fellow, American Bar Foundation. (Certified Specialist, Taxation Law, The State Bar of California Board of Legal Specialization). *PRACTICE AREAS:* Real Estate Law; Business Law; Tax Planning Law; Corporate Law; Estate Planning.

**THOMAS M. STANTON,** born Bakersfield, California, June 8, 1942; admitted to bar, 1967, California and U.S. District Court, Northern District of California; 1970, U.S. District Court, Eastern District of California. *Education:* University of California at Berkeley (A.B., 1964); Stanford University (LL.B., 1967). *Member:* Kern County Bar Association; State Bar of California; Northern California Association of Defense Counsel. (Also practicing individually in Bakersfield, California). *PRACTICE AREAS:* Civil Litigation; Insurance Defense.

GENERAL COUNSEL FOR: General Production Service of California, Inc.; Jim Burke Ford; Bill Wright Toyota; Three Way Chevrolet; Wm. Bolthouse Farms, Inc.; Kern Ridge Growers, Inc.; Gary Drilling.
REPRESENTATIVE CLIENTS: *Corporate:* ARB, Inc.; Deere and Co.; General Motors Acceptance Corporation; K-Mart; Catholic Health Care West; Mercy Healthcare Bakersfield; Monsanto Agricultural Products Co.; Pacific Telephone; Pacific Gas and Electric Co.; Service Corporation International; U.S. Home (Bakersfield); Valley Plaza Shopping Center; Wilbur-Ellis Co.; Bank of Stockdale; CalResources LLC; First Interstate Bank; McDonald's Corp.; Target Stores; The May Company; Vons Companies; Wells Fargo Bank; Enron Oil & Gas Co. *Insurance:* Aetna Casualty & Surety Co.; Allstate Insurance Co.; Aviation Adjustment Bureau; CIGNA; COREGIS (Crum and Forster Managers Group); Design Professionals Insurance Co.; The Maryland; Zurich Insurance Co.; Farmers Insurance Group; Hartford Insurance; The Home Insurance Co.; Northbrook Insurance Co.; Safeco Insurance Co.; St. Paul Insurance Companies; State Farm Insurance Companies; Travelers Insurance Companies; Reliance Insurance Companies; Southern California Physicians Insurance Exchange; American National Property & Casualty; California Insurance Group; Constitution State Insurance; Great West Casualty; Insurance Company of the West; Kemper Group Insurance; Liberty Mutual Insurance Co.; Nationwide Insurance Co.; Progressive Casualty Insurance Co.; Prudential Property and Casualty Insurance Co.; Transamerica Insurance Co.; Truck Insurance Exchange; financial Pacific Insurance Co. . *Transportation:* The Atchison, Topeka and Santa Fe Railway Co.; H.F. Cox Trucking, Inc.

---

## DANIELS, BARATTA & FINE

A Partnership including a Professional Corporation

*Established in 1982*

SUITE 400

5201 CALIFORNIA AVENUE

**BAKERSFIELD, CALIFORNIA 93309**

*Telephone:* 805-335-7788
*Telecopier:* 805-324-3660

*Los Angeles, California Office:* 1801 Century Park East, 9th. Floor. Telephone: 310-556-7900. Telecopier: 310-556-2807.

*General Civil Trial and Appellate Practice in all State and Federal Courts. Insurance, Products Liability, Tort, Wrongful Termination and Employment Discrimination, Business, Entertainment, Real Estate and Construction Law, Environmental and Toxic Torts*

*FIRM PROFILE:* Daniels, Baratta & Fine was founded in 1982. The firm specializes in civil trial practice in all State and Federal Courts, with emphasis in the areas of Insurance (including defense, coverage and bad faith), business litigation, real estate and construction law (including litigation, commercial leasing and transactional matters), entertainment (including litigation and transactional matters), environmental and toxic torts.

(For complete biographical information on all personnel, see Professional Biographies at Los Angeles)

## DI GIORGIO, DAVIS, KLEIN, WEGIS, DUGGAN & FRIEDMAN
**BAKERSFIELD, CALIFORNIA**
(See Klein, Wegis, DeNatale, Goldner & Muir)

---

## LINDA ETIENNE
*4140 TRUXTUN AVENUE, SUITE 200*
**BAKERSFIELD, CALIFORNIA 93309**
*Telephone: 805-633-2341*
*Fax: 805-321-9016*

*General Business, Real Estate, Civil Litigation and Appellate Practice in all State and Federal Courts.*

**LINDA ETIENNE,** born Washington, D.C., November 4, 1954; admitted to bar, 1978, Louisiana; 1979, U.S. District Court, Western District of Louisiana; 1980, U.S. District Court, Eastern and Middle Districts of Louisiana and U.S. Court of Appeals, Fifth Circuit; 1990, California; U.S. District Court, Eastern and Central Districts of California; 1993, U.S. Court of Appeals, Ninth Circuit. *Education:* Louisiana State University (J.D., 1978). Assistant Parish Attorney, Lafayette Parish, Louisiana, 1984-1987. *Member:* Kern County and American Bar Associations; State Bar of California. **PRACTICE AREAS:** General Business Litigation.

---

## GANONG & KLEIER
*924 TRUXTUN AVENUE*
**BAKERSFIELD, CALIFORNIA 93301**
*Telephone: 805-327-3337*
*Fax: 805-327-3395*

*General Civil Trial Practice, Oil & Gas, Personal Injury, Labor and Business Litigation, Medical and Legal Malpractice.*

### MEMBERS OF FIRM

**PHILIP W. GANONG,** born Bakersfield, California, August 8, 1953; admitted to bar, 1979, California. *Education:* California State College, Bakersfield, Maximilians University, Munich, West Germany and University of California, Berkeley (A.B., cum laude, 1976); Hastings College of Law, University of California (J.D., 1979). Member, Hastings Constitutional Law Quarterly, 1977-1978. *Member:* Kern County Bar Association (Vice President); State Bar of California; The Association of Trial Lawyers of America; California Trial Lawyers Association; California Independent Producers Association; Kern County Trial Lawyers Association (President, 1977-1978). **LANGUAGES:** German. **PRACTICE AREAS:** Business Litigation; Personal Injury; Oil and Gas Litigation; Wrongful Termination.

**TIMOTHY L. KLEIER,** born Fresno, California, June 24, 1957; admitted to bar, 1984, California; U.S. District Court, Southern and Eastern Districts of California. *Education:* University of San Diego (B.A., Philosophy, 1981; J.D., 1984). SCRFU (Vice President, 1991-1992. KCAA (Founding Board of Directors, 1988). ADA, Kern County Chapter (Founding Board of Directors, 1988). *Member:* Kern County Bar Association (Board of Directors, 1994—; Fee Arbitration Panel, 1987—); Kern County District Attorney's Association (Vice President, 1986-1987). **PRACTICE AREAS:** Business Litigation; Business and Real Estate Transactions; Construction; Agri Business; Environmental.

REPRESENTATIVE CLIENTS: Pyramid Oil Company; Armored Transport of California; Con-Glass, Inc.; U.P.F.; Ridgeline Oil Company.

---

## STEVEN G. GIBBS
*ARCO TOWER*
*4550 CALIFORNIA AVENUE*
*SUITE 150*
**BAKERSFIELD, CALIFORNIA 93309**
*Telephone: 805-633-1144*
*Fax: 805-636-0703*
*Email: gibbs@lightspeed.net*

*Real Estate, Construction, Partnerships, Corporations, General Business Litigation, Personal Injury Litigation, Labor and Employment Law.*
(This Listing Continued)

---

**STEVEN G. GIBBS,** born Mt. Pleasant, Iowa, January 14, 1960; admitted to bar, 1987, California and U.S. District Court Eastern, Southern and Northern Districts of California; 1988, U.S. District Court, Central District of California. *Education:* Oakland University (B.A., 1982); McGeorge School of Law, University of the Pacific (J.D., 1986). *Member:* Kern County and American Bar Associations; State Bar of California (Member, Sections on: Real Property, Litigation and Employment Law). **PRACTICE AREAS:** Real Estate; Employment; Partnerships; Corporations; General Business Litigation; Personal Injury Litigation.

REPRESENTATIVE CLIENTS: Old River Brewing Company; Calpi, Inc.; Bucks Owen Production Co., Inc.; S.A. Camp Pump Co.; Chemex, Inc.; TEMO, Inc.; Admiral Inc.; Hernstedt Farms; Accelerated Technologies, Inc.; Philadelphia Life Insurance Co.; Van Wyk's of Bakersfield, Inc.; Bryant Tank Co., Inc.

---

## GOLDBERG & FISHER
(An Association of Attorneys, Not a Partnership)
*COMMONWEALTH BUILDING*
*3300 TRUXTUN AVENUE, SUITE 390*
**BAKERSFIELD, CALIFORNIA 93301-3145**
*Telephone: 805-327-2231*
*Fax: 805-327-2397*

*General Civil Practice in all State and Federal Courts. Personal Injury, Corporation, Probate, Real Property, Commercial, Bankruptcy.*

**DAVID F. GOLDBERG,** born Ukraine, July 21, 1918; admitted to bar, 1946, California. *Education:* University of Southern California (A.B., 1939); Boalt Hall School of Law, University of California (LL.B., 1942). Chief Trial Deputy, Kern County District Attorneys Office, 1946-1951. *Member:* Kern County (President, 1951) and American Bar Associations; State Bar of California (Member, Administrative Committee, 1960); The Association of Trial Lawyers of America; American Judicature Society. [Lt. Col., USAR]. **PRACTICE AREAS:** Business Law; Probate Law.

**ARTHUR F. FISHER, (A PROFESSIONAL CORPORATION),** born Huron, South Dakota, November 17, 1929; admitted to bar, 1955, Wyoming; 1965, California. *Education:* University of South Dakota (B.S., 1951); University of Wyoming (J.D., 1955). Assistant Attorney General, State of Wyoming, 1955-1957. Deputy District Attorney, Kern County, 1965-1966. *Member:* Kern County Bar Association (Member, Board of Directors, 1978-1979); Wyoming State Bar; State Bar of California. **PRACTICE AREAS:** Personal Injury Law; Workers Compensation Law; Business Law.

REPRESENTATIVE CLIENTS: First Trust Bank; Mazzie Trust; Oil Well Service Co.; Great Western Builders, Inc.; Casa Moore Entities; Alumax Fabricated Products, Inc.; Bender Oil Operations; K.A. Shelton, Inc.; Lead Producer's, Inc.; Water Treatment Equipment; Goebel Trust; Western Irrigation; Reed Truck Industrial; San Joaquin Tractor Co.; Pipeline Trucking Co.; Cowan Farms. Bank; Dynamic Properties of Calif.
REFERENCES: First Interstate Bank; Bank of America.

---

## LAW OFFICES OF JOHN C. HALL
*SUITE 114*
*1200 TRUXTUN AVENUE*
**BAKERSFIELD, CALIFORNIA 93301**
*Telephone: 805-328-1200*
*Telecopier: 805-328-1281*

*General Trial Practice. Personal Injury, Products Liability, Medical Malpractice, Toxic Tort Litigation, Environmental Law, Business Litigation, Employment Law and Insurance Law.*

**JOHN C. HALL,** born Bakersfield, California, June 29, 1954; admitted to bar, 1981, California. *Education:* University of California at Davis (B.S., 1976); McGeorge School of Law, University of the Pacific (J.D., 1981). *Member:* Kern County Bar Association; State Bar of California. **PRACTICE AREAS:** Medical/Pharmaceutical Malpractice Litigation; Product Liability Litigation; Personal Injury Negligence Litigation; Insurance Law.

## JACK B. HISLOP

Established in 1988

SUITE 420, 5201 CALIFORNIA AVENUE
**BAKERSFIELD, CALIFORNIA 93309**
Telephone: 805-321-9900
FAX: 805-327-0137

*Insurance Defense, Personal Injury, Real Property, Probate, Civil Litigation, Products Liability and Insurance Law.*

**JACK B. HISLOP,** born Bakersfield, California, July 15, 1926; admitted to bar, 1954, California. *Education:* Stanford University (B.A., 1950; LL.B., 1953). Phi Alpha Delta. *Member:* Kern County (President, 1971) and American Bar Associations; The State Bar of California; International Association of Insurance Counsel; Association of Defense Counsel of Northern California (Past Director); Association of Southern California Defense Counsel (Past Director). **PRACTICE AREAS:** Insurance Defense; Personal Injury; Probate; Products Liability; Insurance Law.

### ASSOCIATES

**LORNA HISLOP BRUMFIELD,** born Bakersfield, California, March 29, 1957; admitted to bar, 1983, California; U.S. District Court, Eastern District of California. *Education:* California State Polytechnic University (B.S., 1981); McGeorge School of Law (J.D., 1983). Assistant Editor, Pacific Law Journal, 1982-1983. Author: "Judicial Recovery for the Post-Service Tort: A Veteran's Last Battle," Pacific Law Journal, Vol. 14, No. 2, Jan. 1983. Member and Past President Victim/Witness Auxiliary, 1986—. *Member:* The State Bar of California; Kern County Bar Association; Kern County Women Lawyers; California Women Lawyers Association; Association of Southern California Defense Counsel. **PRACTICE AREAS:** Insurance Defense; Personal Injury; Civil Litigation; Products Liability; Insurance Law.

REPRESENTATIVE CLIENTS: State Farm Fire and Casualty Co.; John Deere Co.; Greyhound Lines, Inc.; Deere & Company; Deans & Homer; Blue Bird Body Co.; California Planting Cotton Seed Distributors; Risk Administrators, Inc.; National Automobile and Casualty Insurance Co.
REFERENCES: Available Upon Request.

---

## ELDON R. HUGIE

841 MOHAWK STREET, SUITE 140
**BAKERSFIELD, CALIFORNIA 93309**
Telephone: 805-328-0200
Fax: 805-328-0204

*State and Federal Taxation, Probate, Estate Planning, Business, Partnership, Trust, Corporate, Agriculture and Real Estate Laws.*

**ELDON R. HUGIE,** born Logan, Utah, July 17, 1932; admitted to bar, 1960, Utah; 1961, California; 1984, Oregon. *Education:* Utah State University (B.A., cum laude, 1954); University of California at Berkeley (J.D., 1960). Phi Kappa Phi. Certified Public Accountant, California, 1964. *Member:* Kern County (Vice President, 1968) and American (Member, Taxation Section) Bar Associations; State Bar of California; Utah State Bar; Oregon State Bar; American Institute of Certified Public Accountants; California Society of Certified Public Accountants. [Capt. U.S. Air Force, 1954-1957]

REPRESENTATIVE CLIENTS: Tri-Fanucchi Farms, Inc.; Kern College Land Co.; Swanston Properties; Cal-Fruit International, Inc.; Lake Boulevard Shopping Center.
REFERENCES: Valliwide Bank (Bakersfield Main Branch).

---

## JACOBSON, HANSEN, NAJARIAN & FLEWALLEN

A PROFESSIONAL CORPORATION
**BAKERSFIELD, CALIFORNIA**
(See Fresno)

*Civil Litigation emphasizing Insurance Defense.*

---

## JENKINS, BARNES & BRADY

1675 CHESTER AVENUE, SUITE 300
**BAKERSFIELD, CALIFORNIA 93301**
Telephone: 805-631-2196
Facsimile: 805-631-2199

*General Civil Practice in all State and Federal Courts, with emphasis in Health Care Law, Professional Liability Defense, Oil and Gas Law, Personal Injury Defense, Public Entity Defense, Civil and Business Litigation, Negligence, Products Liability and Insurance Law.*

### MEMBERS OF THE FIRM

**J. CRAIG JENKINS,** born Santa Ana, California, December 27, 1941; admitted to bar, 1966, California; 1967, U.S. District Court, Eastern District of California; 1985, U.S. Supreme Court. *Education:* Bakersfield College; Southwestern University (LL.B., 1965). Deputy District Attorney, Kern County, 1966. Judge Pro Tem, West Kern Municipal Court, 1981. Trustee, Kern High School District Board of Trustees, 1973-1982. Member, Panel of Arbitrators, American Arbitration Association. *Member:* Kern County Bar Association; State Bar of California; Association of Southern California Defense Counsel; Defense Research Institute. **Email:** litig8r@jenkinslaw.com

**KAREN S. BARNES,** born Oakland, California, July 2, 1953; admitted to bar, 1991, California; 1993, U.S. District Court, Eastern District of California. *Education:* Bakersfield College; California State College, Bakersfield (A.A., Nursing, 1978); California Pacific School of Law (J.D., 1991). Registered Nurse, California, 1978—. Risk Manager, Mercy Hospital, Bakersfield, California, 1984-1992. *Member:* Kern County Bar Association; State Bar of California; National Health Lawyers Association. **Email:** litig8r@jenkinslaw.com

**MATHEW M. BRADY,** born Ridgecrest, California, June 19, 1960; admitted to bar, 1988, California and U.S. District Court, Eastern District of California. *Education:* California State College, Bakersfield (B.A., 1982); University of the Pacific, McGeorge School of Law (J.D., 1988). Commissioner, City of Bakersfield Planning Commission, 1994—. *Member:* Kern County Bar Association; State Bar of California (Member, Litigation Section); National Health Lawyers Association. **Email:** litig8r@jenkinslaw.com

### ASSOCIATE

**JENNIFER A. MCGILL,** born Bethesda, Maryland, May 20, 1971; admitted to bar, 1996, California and U.S. District Court, Eastern District of California. *Education:* University of California, Riverside (B.S., 1993); University of the Pacific, McGeorge School of Law (J.D., with distinction, 1996). *Member:* Kern County Bar Association; State Bar of California. **Email:** litig8r@jenkinslaw.com

REPRESENTATIVE CLIENTS: Corporate: Chevron U.S.A. Inc.; Chevron Pipe Line Company; Mobile Oil Corporation; Baker Performance Chemicals Incorporated; Baker Hughes Incorporated; Unocal; Mercy Healthcare Bakersfield; San Joaquin Community Hospital; Adventist Health System/West; Mervyn's. Insurance: Fremont Indemnity Company; The Doctors' Company; Fireman's Fund Insurance Company; State Farm Mutual Automobile Insurance Company; The Travelers Insurance Company; Americas Insurance Company; Truck Insurance Exchange.

---

## LAW OFFICES OF PATRICK KAVANAGH

1331 "L" STREET
**BAKERSFIELD, CALIFORNIA 93301**
Telephone: 805-322-5553
Fax: 805-322-5779

*Practice Limited to Bankruptcy Law Including Representation of Debtors, Creditors, Trustees and Creditors Committees.*

**PATRICK KAVANAGH,** born Greenpoint, Brooklyn, New York, 1953; admitted to bar, 1981, California. *Education:* Syracuse University (B.S., 1977); University of San Francisco (J.D., 1981). *Member:* State Bar of California; American Bankruptcy Institute; National Association of Bankruptcy Trustees. **PRACTICE AREAS:** Bankruptcy; Debtors/Creditors; Trustee Law; Creditors Committees Law.

*(This Listing Continued)*

### ASSOCIATES

**PAUL A. GALE,** born Oakland, California, September 6, 1967; admitted to bar, 1994, California. *Education:* California State University Fresno (B.A., 1990); McGeorge School of Law (J.D., 1994). Law Clerk to the Honorable Joseph W. Hedrick, Jr., U.S. Bankruptcy Court, 1993. *Member:* State Bar of California. *PRACTICE AREAS:* Bankruptcy.

REFERENCE: California Republic Bank.

---

## KIMBLE, MacMICHAEL & UPTON

### A PROFESSIONAL CORPORATION

### BAKERSFIELD, CALIFORNIA

(See Fresno)

*Civil, Trial and Appellate Practice in all Courts with Emphasis in Business, Construction and Environmental Litigation, Real Estate, Bank Securities, Lender and Creditors Rights, Bankruptcy, Secured Lending, Banking, Federal and State Income, Gift and Estate Tax, Securities, Antitrust, Corporation and Probate and Estate Planning, Patent, Trademark and Copyright, Water Rights, Environmental Law, Employee Benefits Law, Products Liability Defense, ERISA Litigation, Employment Defense, Administrative and Health Care Law.*

---

## KLEIN, WEGIS, DeNATALE, GOLDNER & MUIR, LLP

A Partnership including Professional Corporations

(Formerly Di Giorgio, Davis, Klein, Wegis, Duggan & Friedman)

ARCO TOWER
4550 CALIFORNIA AVENUE, SECOND FLOOR
P.O. BOX 11172
**BAKERSFIELD, CALIFORNIA 93389-1172**
Telephone: 805-395-1000
Telecopier: 805-326-0418
Email: kwdgm@kwdgm.com

*General Civil Trial and Appellate Practice. Federal Trial Practice, Commercial, Litigation, Bankruptcy, Construction, Eminent Domain, Agriculture, Real Estate, Employment Law, Environmental, ERISA Litigation, Estate Planning, Negligence, Oil and Gas, Pension and Profit Sharing, Probate, Products Liability, Tax.*

FIRM PROFILE: *Founded in 1953. Committed to providing clients the highest caliber of legal services available. First law firm in the State of California to be accepted into the International Society of Primerus Law Firms: a group with very high standards for intellect, experience and integrity. The firm offers a full range of services that have been utilized by clients throughout the nation as well as abroad.*

**THOMAS R. DAVIS** (1920-1990).

### MEMBERS OF FIRM

**ANTHONY J. KLEIN, (INC.),** born Bakersfield, California, December 20, 1938; admitted to bar, 1964, California. *Education:* Stanford University (A.B., 1960); Boalt Hall, University of California at Berkeley (LL.B., 1963). Phi Delta Phi. Deputy District Attorney, Kern County, 1964-1966. Member, Board of Directors, Secretary and General Counsel, 1971-1994, Nahama & Weagant Energy Co. President, 1971-1981, Bakersfield Public Education Facilities Corporation, 1986—. Member, Kern County Air Pollution Control District, 1972-1973. Member, Board of Directors, Secretary and General Counsel, 1988-1995, Freymiller Trucking Company. *Member:* Kern County Bar Association (Member, Board of Directors, 1974-1976); State Bar of California (Member, Litigation Section); California Trial Lawyers Association; The Association of Trial Lawyers of America. *REPORTED CASES:* B.P. Alaska Exploration Nahama Weagant Energy Co. (1988) 199 Cal.App. 3d 1240. *PRACTICE AREAS:* Complex Litigation; Products Liability Litigation; Environmental Litigation; Oil and Gas Litigation; Business Litigation.

**RALPH B. WEGIS, (INC.),** born Taft, California, September 6, 1944; admitted to bar, 1975, California. *Education:* California Polytechnic State University (B.S., 1971); University of San Fernando Valley (J.D., 1975). *Member:* Kern County Bar Association; The State Bar of California; California Trial Lawyers Association; American Board of Trial Advocates.

*(This Listing Continued)*

*PRACTICE AREAS:* Products Liability Litigation; Personal Injury Negligence Litigation; Civil Litigation.

**THOMAS V. DENATALE, JR.,** born Los Angeles, California, February 21, 1949; admitted to bar, 1975, California. *Education:* University of California at Los Angeles (B.A., 1971); University of San Fernando Valley (J.D., 1975). Member, Kern County Juvenile Justice Commission, 1989—. *Member:* Los Angeles County, Kern County and American Bar Associations; The State Bar of California (Member, Litigation, Business and Real Property Section); California Trial Lawyers Association. *PRACTICE AREAS:* Business/Commercial Litigation; Real Property Litigation; Eminent Domain Litigation. *Email:* tdenatal@kwdgm.com

**GREGORY A. MUIR,** born Wasco, California, February 25, 1950; admitted to bar, 1982, California. *Education:* University of California at Los Angeles (B.A., 1972); University of San Francisco (J.D., 1980). *Member:* Kern County, Los Angeles County and Orange County Bar Associations; The State Bar of California; California Trial Lawyers Association; The Association of Trial Lawyers of America. *PRACTICE AREAS:* Products Liability Litigation; Personal Injury Negligence Litigation; Psychotherapy Law Litigation.

**BARRY L. GOLDNER,** born North Hollywood, California, May 10, 1957; admitted to bar, 1982, California; U.S. District Court, Northern, Eastern, and Central Districts of California. *Education:* Claremont Men's College (Claremont McKenna College) (B.A., cum laude, 1979); University of California at Los Angeles (J.D., 1982). Member, 1980-1982 and Comment Editor, 1981-1982, UCLA Law Review. Author: "The Torrens System of Title Registration: A New Proposal for Effective Implementation," 29 UCLA Law Review 661, 1982. Legal Research and Writing Teaching Assistant, UCLA School of Law, 1980. Deputy District Attorney, Contra Costa County, 1983-1984. Extern for Justice Mathew O. Tobriner, California Supreme Court, 1981. Member, Board of Trustees, Kern County Law Library. *Member:* Kern County (Member, Board of Directors; Chair, Judicial Evaluations Committee) and American (Member: Committee on Trial Practice; Sections on: Litigation; Real Estate; Construction Law) Bar Associations; State Bar of California (Member: Joint Advisory Committee, Continuing Education of the Bar, 1993-1994; Board of Governors, 1994-1995). *REPORTED CASES:* American National Bank v. Stanfill (1988) 205 Cal. App. 3d 1089. *PRACTICE AREAS:* Business/Commercial Litigation; Agriculture Litigation; Real Estate Litigation; Construction Litigation.

**JAY L. ROSENLIEB,** born Bakersfield, California, January 7, 1958; admitted to bar, 1983, California. *Education:* University of California at Los Angeles; Claremont Men's College (Claremont McKenna College) (B.A., cum laude, 1980); Hastings College of the Law, University of California (J.D., 1983). *Member:* Kern County (Member, Fee Arbitration Panel) and American (Member, Labor and Employment Law Management Section) Bar Associations; State Bar of California (Member, Labor and Employment Law Management Section). *REPORTED CASES:* BP Alaska Exploration v. Nahama Weagant Energy Company (1988) 199 Cal. App. 3d 1240. *PRACTICE AREAS:* Employment Litigation; Oil and Gas Litigation. *Email:* jrosenli@kwdgm.com

**DAVID J. COOPER,** born Bethesda, Maryland, May 2, 1945; admitted to bar, 1971, California; U.S. District Court, Northern and Eastern Districts of California. *Education:* University of California at Berkeley (B.A., 1967); Boalt Hall School of Law, University of California (LL.B., 1970). Order of the Coif. Member, University of California Law Review, 1969-1970. *Member:* Kern County Bar Association (Member, Fee Arbitration Panel); State Bar of California (Member: Litigation, Environmental Law, and Legal Services Section). *PRACTICE AREAS:* Business/Commercial Litigation; Appellate Law; Environmental Law.

**CLAUDE P. KIMBALL,** born Los Angeles, California, October 13, 1939; admitted to bar, 1966, California; 1971, U.S. Tax Court. *Education:* University of Santa Clara (B.A., 1962); University of California at Los Angeles (LL.B., 1965); New York University (LL.M., in Taxation, 1970). Phi Alpha Delta. Instructor, "How to Draft Wills," Continuing Education of the Bar, 1982-1985. Lecturer, Family Investment Partnerships Income and Estate Tax Savings, California Society of CPA's. Member, Board of Directors, Bakersfield Rotary Waterman Foundation. *Member:* Kern County and American Bar Associations. *PRACTICE AREAS:* Taxation Law; Business Planning; Acquisitions, Divestitures and Mergers; Estate Planning; Partnership Taxation; Partnership Law; Real Estate Law.

**WILLIAM A. BRUCE,** born Grand Junction, Colorado, September 2, 1953; admitted to bar, 1980, California and U.S. District Court, Eastern District of California. *Education:* University of California at Davis (B.A., 1976); Pepperdine University (J.D., 1979). *Member:* Kern County and American Bar Associations; State Bar of California; American Board of

*(This Listing Continued)*

### KLEIN, WEGIS, DeNATALE, GOLDNER & MUIR, LLP,
Bakersfield—Continued

Trial Advocates; Association of Southern California Defense Counsel (Director, 1991-1994). *PRACTICE AREAS:* Civil Litigation; Agri-Business; Product Liability Litigation; Environmental Litigation.

#### ASSOCIATES

**DENISE MARTIN,** born Chicago, Illinois, May 26, 1960; admitted to bar, 1989, California. *Education:* University of California at Santa Barbara (B.A., with honors, 1982); Hastings College of Law, University of California (J.D., 1988). *Member:* Kern County and American Bar Associations; State Bar of California; Consumer Advocates of California; The Association of Trial Lawyers of America. *PRACTICE AREAS:* Products Liability Law; Negligence Litigation; Personal Injury Law.

**DAVID L. SAINE,** born Atlanta, Georgia, October 13, 1949; admitted to bar, 1982, Colorado; 1989, California and U.S. Supreme Court. *Education:* University of Colorado (B.A., 1971); University of Wisconsin (M.A., 1972); Colorado State University (M.A., cum laude, 1978); University of Denver (J.D., 1982). Phi Beta Kappa. Law Clerk to Honorable David W. Enoch, Chief Judge, Colorado Court of Appeals, 1982-1983. Adjunct Professor, California Pacific Law School, Appellate Advocacy; Negotiations and Mediations. Adjunct Lecturer, California State University, Bakersfield, Legal Reasoning, 1991—. *Member:* Kern County (Chair, ADR Committee, 1993—) and American Bar Associations; State Bar of California; Southern California Mediation Association. *PRACTICE AREAS:* Appeals; Appellate Law.

**LAURENCE C. HALL,** born Santa Monica, California, April 11, 1947; admitted to bar, 1972, California. *Education:* University of Southern California (B.A., 1969); Southwestern University School of Law (J.D., 1972). Speaker: "What If Warnings Worked?", The Association of Trial Lawyers of America, 1992 Annual Convention; "Can David Still Win Against Goliath", 1993 California Trial Lawyers Association Seminar on Complex Litigation for the Small Practitioner, Kern County Chapter; "Premises Liability: Preparation and Trial of Difficult Case in California", 1994 NBI, Anaheim, California. Arbitrator, Los Angeles Superior and Municipal Courts; "Vior Dire Strategy for the 90's, Kern County Bar Association, 1996. Judge Pro Tem, Los Angeles Municipal Court, 1979—. Chairman, State Bar Committee on Jury Instructions, 1979-1985. *Member:* Los Angeles County Bar Association; State Bar of California; Los Angeles Trial Lawyers Association; Orange County Trial Lawyers Association; The Association of Trial Lawyers of America; American Board of Trial Advocates; California Trial Lawyers Association (Recognized experience in the fields of Trial Lawyer and Products Liability). *PRACTICE AREAS:* Products Liability Law; Premises Liability Law; Insurance Law.

**WILLIAM H. SLOCUMB,** born Oakland, California, February 18, 1951; admitted to bar, 1981, California; 1985, U.S. Supreme Court. *Education:* University of California at Davis (B.A., 1973); Western State University (J.D., 1980). Vice Chairman, Minimum Continuing Legal Education, State Bar of California. *Member:* Kern County Bar Association; State Bar of California. *PRACTICE AREAS:* Real Property Law; Land Use and Planning; Products Liability Law; Civil Trial; Defense Litigation; Oil and Gas Law. *Email:* bslocumb@kwdgm.com

**NED E. DUNPHY,** born New York, N.Y., February 11, 1958; admitted to bar, 1987, California. *Education:* University of Toronto; Honorary J.D. received through Law Office Study, 1986. *Member:* The State Bar of California; American Bar Association; California Trial Lawyers Association. *LANGUAGES:* Spanish. *PRACTICE AREAS:* Personal Injury; Negligence Litigation; Product Liability.

**BARRY E. ROSENBERG,** born Brooklyn, New York, September 4, 1959; admitted to bar, 1986, New York; 1989, District of Columbia; 1991, California. *Education:* Brooklyn College of the City University of New York (B.A., magna cum laude, 1981); Albany Law School, Union University (J.D., cum laude, 1985). Associate Editor, Albany Law Review. Author: Comment, Leg-ups And Lock-ups: An Analysis For Manipulation Under Section 14(e) Of The Williams Act, 49 Albany Law Review 479 (1985). *Member:* The State Bar of California; District of Columbia and American Bar Associations. *REPORTED CASES:* Hayter Trucking, Inc. v. Shell Western E&P, Inc., (1993) 18 Cal. App. 1; Marques v. Telles Ranch, Inc. (N.D. CA 1995) 11 IER Cases 36. *PRACTICE AREAS:* Labor and Employment Law; Business/Commercial Litigation; Appellate Law; ERISA Litigation. *Email:* brosenbe@kwdgm.com

**KIRK S. TRACEY,** born Los Angeles, California, December 24, 1959; admitted to bar, 1989, California and U.S. District Court, Eastern District of California. *Education:* California State University at Dominguez Hills (B.A., 1985); Southwestern University (J.D., 1989). Recipient, American Jurisprudence in Legislation. *Member:* Kern County Bar Association; State Bar of California. *PRACTICE AREAS:* Business/Commercial Litigation.

**CHRISTOPHER P. BURGER,** born Woodland, California, May 28, 1952; admitted to bar, 1992, California. *Education:* University of California at Davis (B.S., 1975); California State University, Fresno (M.S., 1977); California Pacific (J.D., 1991). Registered Environmental Health Specialist. *Member:* California Environmental Health Association; National Environmental Health Association. *Member:* Kern County Bar Association; State Bar of California (Member, Environmental Section)). *PRACTICE AREAS:* Environmental Law; Administrative Law; Business/Commercial Litigation.

**KEVIN C. FINDLEY,** born Denver, Colorado, February 20, 1953; admitted to bar, 1979, California. *Education:* University of Missouri (B.A., 1976); Pepperdine University School of Law (J.D., 1979); Washington University School of Law (LL.M. in Taxation, 1983). *Member:* Kern County and American Bar Associations; State Bar of California. *PRACTICE AREAS:* Estate Planning; Probate Law; Trust Law; Pension and Profit Sharing Law; ERISA; Taxation Law; Partnership Taxation; Corporate Tax Planning; Tax Exempt Organizations.

**CAROL J. GROGAN,** born Columbus, Ohio, June 24, 1949; admitted to bar, 1992, California. *Education:* Ohio State University (B.S.Ed., 1971); Xavier University (M.H.A., 1980); University of San Diego (J.D., 1992). Recipient, Foster G. McGaw Scholarship Award. *Member,* Journal of Contemporary Legal Issues, 1988-1990. *Member:* Kern County and American Bar Associations; State Bar of California; California Trial Lawyers Association; California Women Lawyers; Kern County Women Lawyers Association. *PRACTICE AREAS:* Business Litigation; Health Care Law.

**JOSE BENAVIDES,** born Reedley, California, December 4, 1956; admitted to bar, 1982, California; 1983, U.S. District Court, Central District of California; 1988, U.S. Court of Appeals, Ninth Circuit; 1993, U.S. District Court, Eastern District of California. *Education:* University of California at Los Angeles (B.A., 1979; J.D., 1982). Editor-in-Chief, UCLA Chicano Law Review. Member, Moot Court Honors Program. Law Clerk to the Honorable David V. Kenyon, U.S. District Court Judge, Central District of California, 1982-1984. *Member:* Kern County Bar Association; The State Bar of California; Los Angeles Trial Lawyers Association; California Trial Lawyers Association. *LANGUAGES:* Spanish. *PRACTICE AREAS:* Products Liability; Employment Law; Major Tort Litigation; Insurance Bad Faith.

**MICHAEL S. ABRIL,** born Bakersfield, California, March 12, 1960; admitted to bar, 1986, California and U.S. District Court, Central District of California; 1987, U.S. District Court, Northern, Southern and Eastern Districts of California and U.S. Court of Appeals, Ninth Circuit. *Education:* University of California at Davis (A.B., 1982); University of Southern California (M.B.A., 1986; J.D., 1986). Licensed Real Estate Broker, California, 1991. Moderator/Author: "Pre-Bankruptcy Planning", Eighth Annual Central California Bankruptcy Institute, 1994. Speaker, Fundamentals of Bankruptcy Law, Central California Bankruptcy Association, 1994. Member: Government Review Council, Greater Bakersfield Chamber of Commerce, 1994—; Government Affairs Committee, Los Angeles Junior Chamber of Commerce. 1991-1992; Prevailing Wage Task Force, City of Bakersfield, 1994; Bankruptcy and Commercial Law Sections, Los Angeles County Bar Association, 1987-1992; Los Angeles Bankruptcy Forum, 1987-1992. *Member:* Beverly Hills, Kern County and American (Member: Business Law and Economics of Law Practice Sections) Bar Associations; State Bar of California (Member: Business Law Section; Agri Business Committee, 1994—); Central California Bankruptcy Association; Financial Lawyers Conference; American Bankruptcy Institute; San Joanquin Agricultural Lenders Society; National Association of Bankruptcy Trustees. Certified Specialist, Business Bankruptcy Law, American Bankruptcy Board Of Certification). (Certified Specialist, Business Bankruptcy Law, The State Bar of California Board of Legal Specialization). *TRANSACTIONS:* Attorney for Bank One, Columbus, N.A. (Indenture Trustee), *in Chapter 11 Reorganization of Leisure Technology, Inc.* . *PRACTICE AREAS:* Bankruptcy; Corporate Reorganizations; Creditors Rights; Corporate and Business Transactions; Real Estate Law.

**MELVIN L. EHRLICH,** born Russell, Kansas, January 30, 1945; admitted to bar, 1974, Kansas and Texas; 1978, California. *Education:* University of Kansas (B.S., 1967; J.D., 1974). Recipient, American Jurisprudence Awards for: Criminal Procedure; Estate Planning. Lecturer, California State University, Bakersfield, California, Petroleum Land Studies - Oil and Gas Contracts and Senior Seminar for Petroleum Land Studies

*(This Listing Continued)*

Degree, 1985-1987. *Member:* Kern County and American Bar Associations; State Bar of California; State Bar of Texas. [First Lt., U.S. Army, 1968-1974]. *PRACTICE AREAS:* Oil and Gas Law; Environmental Law; Real Estate Law.

**KRYSTYNA L. JAMIESON,** born Pasadena, California, March 30, 1964; admitted to bar, 1990, California. *Education:* University of Colorado (B.A., 1986); Kent State University-Genevé, Switzerland; Catholic University (J.D., 1990). Recipient, American Jurisprudence Awards in: Wills and Trusts; Administrative Law. Member, Moot Court. Member, The Journal of Contemporary Health Policy. *Member:* Kern County Bar Association; State Bar of California; Orange County Barristers; Kern County Women Lawyer's Association; California Trial Lawyers Association.

**STACY HENRY BOWMAN,** born Glendale, California, October 21, 1959; admitted to bar, 1993, California. *Education:* Georgetown University (B.S., 1981); Southwestern University (J.D., 1993). Member, Law Review Southwestern University, 1993. Certified Public Accountant, California, 1985. *Member:* Kern County Bar Association; State Bar of California; Kern County Women Lawyer's Association.

**THOMAS J. JAMIESON, JR.,** born Fresno, California, December 10, 1963; admitted to bar, 1993, California; 1994, U.S. District Court, Central and Eastern Districts of California. *Education:* University of California, Berkeley (B.A., 1987); McGeorge School of Law (J.D., 1993). *Member:* Kern County Bar Association; State Bar of California. *PRACTICE AREAS:* Business Litigation; Personal Injury. *Email:* jjamieso@kwdgm.com

**JEFFREY W. NOE,** born Whittier, California, December 19, 1967; admitted to bar, 1993, California. *Education:* Georgetown University (A.B., magna cum laude, 1990); University of California, Boalt Hall School of Law (J.D., 1993). Phi Beta Kappa. Editor in Chief, Berkeley Journal of Employment and Labor Law, 1992-1993. *Member:* Kern County Bar Association; State Bar of California. *PRACTICE AREAS:* Labor and Employment Law; Business/Commercial Litigation.

*OF COUNSEL*

**BRUCE F. BUNKER,** born Porterville, California, December 10, 1924; admitted to bar, 1951, California; 1956, U.S. District Court, Southern and Eastern Districts of California; 1958, U.S. Tax Court; 1967, U.S. district Court, Eastern District of California; 1994, U.S. Court of Appeals, Ninth Circuit. *Education:* Porterville Junior College (A.A., 1946); University of Southern California (J.D., 1950). Phi Alpha Delta. Member, Editorial Board, The California Lawyer, 1981-1982. *Member:* Kern County (President, 1961) and American (Senior Lawyers Division, Regional Vice Chair of Organization of Senior Lawyers Groups Committee, 1992-1996 and Affiliated Outreach Committee, 1996—) Bar Associations; The State Bar of California (Conference of Delegates, Resolutions Committee, 1961, Vice-Chair, 1962; Chair, 1964, 1965, Executive Committee, 1965-1969; State Disciplinary Board, 1969-1972, Chair, 1972; Client Security Fund, 1972-1975, Chair, 1975; Member and Chair of Standing Committee on Courts, 1983-1985; Organizing Committee of Senior Lawyer's Section, 1996—); American Judicature Society; National Academy of Elder Law Attorneys; Fellow, American 43500oundation. *PRACTICE AREAS:* Business Litigation; Business Planning; Estate Planning; Trusts and Probate; Real Property; Oil and Gas Law.

REPRESENTATIVE CLIENTS: Bank of America; Security Pacific National Bank; Great Western Bank; Mojave Pipeline Co.; Transamerica Title Insurance Co.; World Title Co.; Dean Witter Reynolds, Inc.; California Federal Bank; California Republic Bank; San Joaquin Bank; Halliburton Services; Nahama & Weagant Energy Co.; Freymiller Trucking, Inc.; Mechanics National Bank; County of Kern; Kern Faculty Medical Group; The Travelers Realty Investment Co.; The Prudential America West; San Joaquin Refining; Westinghouse Electric Co.; Eastman Christensen; Controlco, Inc.; Wheeler Development Corporation; Gibson Irrigation Systems; Wellhead, Inc.; Paramount Farming Company; Kern County Water Agency; Kern High School District; Mike Yurosek and Son; Stephen Pavich and Sons; Kern County Hay Growers Association, Inc.; Sandrini Brothers.

## LAW OFFICES OF
## HAL M. KOONTZ

*Established in 1992*

*2821 "H" STREET*
***BAKERSFIELD, CALIFORNIA 93301***
*Telephone: 805-634-1141*
*Fax: 805-327-1923*

*Estate Planning, Estate Administration, Taxation Law, and Business Transactions.*

**HAL M. KOONTZ,** born Whittier, California, June 11, 1949; admitted to bar, 1974, California; 1976, U.S. District Court, Eastern District of California; 1979, U.S. Tax Court. *Education:* University of Southern California (B.A., cum laude, 1971); Loyola University of Los Angeles (J.D., cum laude, 1974); New York University (LL.M. in Taxation, 1979). Member, Saint Thomas More Law Honor Society. Staff Member, Loyola of Los Angeles Law Review, 1972-1973. *Member:* Kern County and American Bar Associations; State Bar of California. (Certified Specialist, Taxation Law, The State Bar of California Board of Legal Specialization).

## KUHS, PARKER & STANTON

*SUITE 200, 1200 TRUXTUN AVENUE*
*P.O. BOX 2205*
***BAKERSFIELD, CALIFORNIA 93303***
*Telephone: 805-322-4004*
*FAX: 805-322-2906*
*Email: kpslaw@maillightspeed//.net*

*General Civil, Trial and Appellate Practice. Administrative, Construction, Environmental, Municipal, Oil and Gas, Real Property and Water Law.*

**WILLIAM C. KUHS,** born Bakersfield, California, December 12, 1937; admitted to bar, 1966, District of Columbia and California. *Education:* University of California at Berkeley (B.S., Civil Engineering, 1959; M.S., Civil Engineering, 1960); Georgetown University (J.D., 1966). Associate Editor, The Georgetown Law Journal, 1965-1966. *Member:* Kern County (President, 1979-1980) and American (Member, Sections on: Local Government Law; Natural Resources Law) Bar Associations; The State Bar of California.

**JAMES R. PARKER, JR.,** born Burbank, California, March 19, 1947; admitted to bar, 1974, California. *Education:* Yale University (B.A., cum laude, 1968); University of California at Davis (J.D., 1974). *Member:* Kern County and American (Member, Construction Industry Section) Bar Associations; The State Bar of California.

**DAVID B. STANTON,** born Chicago, Illinois, August 7, 1941; admitted to bar, 1965, California. *Education:* University of California, Santa Barbara; University of Southern California (B.S.L., 1962; LL.B., 1964). Member, Southern California Law Review, 1962-1964. Author: "Taft-Hartley §301, An Encroachment on the National Labor Relations Board," 36 Southern California Law Review 606. Instructor: Corporations Law, Contracts, Business Law, California State University, Bakersfield, 1985—; Corporation Law, University of California, Santa Barbara Extension, 1983-1985. Member: California Superintendent of Schools AIDS Advisory Board, 1987—; Board of Trustees, Kern High School District, 1983—; Agricultural Task Force, California Senate Select Committee on Long Range Policy Planning, 1985. *Member:* Kern County (Member, Board of Trustees, 1973-1976) and American Bar Associations; State Bar of California.

---

**ROBERT G. KUHS,** born Washington, D.C., July 3, 1965; admitted to bar, 1992, California. *Education:* University of California, Santa Barbara (B.A., 1988); Southwestern University School of Law (J.D., 1992). Recipient, American Jurisprudence Award in Commercial Paper. Member, Executive Committee, Teen Alternative Court of Kern. *Member:* Kern County and American (Member, Litigation Section) Bar Associations; The State Bar of California.

**JOSEPH D. HUGHES,** born 1968; admitted to bar, 1993, California; U.S. District Court, Eastern and Northern Districts of California. *Education:* University of California at Santa Barbara (B.A., 1990); University of Santa Clara (J.D., 1993). *Member:* Kern County and American Bar Associations; State Bar of California.

*(This Listing Continued)*

**KUHS, PARKER & STANTON,** Bakersfield—Continued

REPRESENTATIVE CLIENTS: Belridge Water Storage District; Environmental Protection Corp.; Granite Construction Company; Kern-Tulane Water District; Lost Hills Water District; Mendiburu Land & Livestock; Pioneer Nursery; Tehachapi-Cummings County Water District; Tumblin Company; Tenneco West, Inc.; Zaloom Brothers Co., Inc.
REFERENCE: Home Savings of America (Bakersfield Main Office).

## LeBEAU, THELEN, LAMPE, McINTOSH & CREAR

5001 EAST COMMERCE DRIVE
SUITE 300
BAKERSFIELD, CALIFORNIA 93309-1667
Telephone: 805-325-8962
FAX: 805-325-1127

*Civil Trial Practice in all State and Federal Courts. Insurance, Employment Litigation, Business, Real Estate, Corporate, Partnership, Taxation, Probate, Estate Planning, Commercial, Agricultural, Administrative and Oil and Gas Law.*

### MEMBERS OF FIRM

**DAVID R. LAMPE,** born Oakland, California, January 8, 1952; admitted to bar, 1977, California and U.S. District Court, Eastern District of California; 1982, U.S. District Court, Central District of California; 1985, U.S. District Court, Northern District of California. *Education:* California State College at Bakersfield (B.A., cum laude, 1973); University of Santa Clara (J.D., magna cum laude, 1977). *Member:* Kern County (Director, 1980-1982) and American (Member, Section on Litigation) Bar Associations; The State Bar of California; Association of Southern California Defense Counsel; Association of Business Trial Lawyers.

**DENNIS R. THELEN,** born Washington, D.C., March 1, 1953; admitted to bar, 1978, California. *Education:* University of Santa Clara (B.A., cum laude, 1975; J.D., magna cum laude, 1978). *Member:* Kern County and American Bar Associations; The State Bar of California; Association of Southern California Defense Counsel (Member, Board of Directors, 1993—); American Board of Trial Advocates.

**BERNARD G. LEBEAU, JR.,** born Phoenix, Arizona, October 9, 1953; admitted to bar, 1978, California. *Education:* University of Santa Clara (B.S.C., cum laude, 1975; J.D., summa cum laude, 1978); New York University (LL.M. in Taxation, 1979). Beta Gamma Sigma. *Member:* Kern County Bar Association; The State Bar of California.

**THOMAS S. McINTOSH,** born Cincinnati, Ohio, March 11, 1952; admitted to bar, 1977, California and U.S. District Court, Northern District of California; 1983, U.S. District Court, Central District of California; 1986, U.S. District Court, Eastern District of California. *Education:* Washington State University (B.A., cum laude, 1974); University of San Diego (J.D, 1977). *Member:* Kern County Bar Association; The State Bar of California.

**THOMAS A. CREAR,** born Redlands, California, April 13, 1951; admitted to bar, 1977, California; 1980, U.S. District Court, Northern District of California, U.S. Court of Appeals, Ninth Circuit and U.S. Tax Court. *Education:* University of California (B.A., with high honors, 1973); University of Santa Clara (J.D., magna cum laude, 1976); New York University (LL.M. in Taxation, 1977). Trial Attorney, Tax Division, U.S. Department of Justice, 1977-1978. Assistant U.S. Attorney, Tax Section, U.S. Department of Justice, Northern District of California, 1978-1980. *Member:* Kern County and American (Member, Taxation Section) Bar Associations; The State Bar of California (Member, Taxation Section).

**J. NILE KINNEY,** born Tacoma, Washington, July 25, 1953; admitted to bar, 1983, California and U.S. District Court, Central District of California. *Education:* University of Southern California (B.A., magna cum laude, 1975; J.D., 1982); University of California, Santa Barbara (M.A., 1979). *Member:* Kern County Bar Association; The State Bar of California.

**BOB H. JOYCE,** born Dennison, Texas, October 11, 1947; admitted to bar, 1978, California. *Education:* University of California at Berkeley (B.A., 1975); University of the Pacific, McGeorge College of the Law (J.D., 1978). *Member:* Kern County and Ventura County Bar Associations; The State Bar of California; Association of Business Trial Lawyers.

*(This Listing Continued)*

**W. STEVEN SHAYER,** born Providence, Rhode Island, February 19, 1960; admitted to bar, 1985, California. *Education:* University of California at Irvine (B.A., 1982); Pepperdine University (J.D., 1985). *Member:* Kern County and Los Angeles County Bar Associations; The State Bar of California.

**THOMAS P. FEHER,** born Milwaukee, Wisconsin, May 2, 1963; admitted to bar, 1990, California. *Education:* University of California at San Diego; San Diego State University (B.A., 1986); University of San Diego (J.D., 1990). Member, National Trial Team, University of San Diego. Associate Editor, Journal of Contemporary Legal Issues, 1989-1990. *Member:* Kern County Bar Association; State Bar of California. *LANGUAGES:* Hungarian.

**KERRY L. LOCKHART,** born Indianapolis, Indiana, September 3, 1962; admitted to bar, 1996, California. *Education:* Indiana University (B.A., 1986; J.D., 1995). [U.S. Army, 1982-1984, 1987-1990; Indiana National Guard, 1990-1995; Captain, California Army National Guard, 1995—]

REPRESENTATIVE CLIENTS: Corporate: Arco Oil and Gas Co.; San Joaquin Bank; Giumarra Vineyards; King Pak Farms; Federal Land Bank and Production Credit Assn.; Greater Bakersfield Memorial Hospital; Houchin Bros., Inc.; Varner Bros., Inc.; Clark Pest Control, Inc.; West Mark Group; First American Title Insurance Co.; San Dimas Medical Group, Inc.; Municipalities: County of Kern; City of Bakersfield; Kern County Water Agency; Insurance: Crawford and Co.; Ohio Casualty; Farmers Insurance Group; Golden Eagle Ins.; Atlantic Insurance Co.; Southern California Physicians Insurance Exchange; California Casualty; Transamerica Insurance Co.; State Farm Fire and Casualty Co.; St. Paul Insurance Co.; Cooperative of American Physicians; State Farm Automobile Insurance Co.; Physicians & Surgeons/Fremont Indemnity Co.

## LYNCH AND LYNCH

4800 EASTERN DRIVE, SUITE 114
BAKERSFIELD, CALIFORNIA 93309
Telephone: 805-322-8396
Fax: 805-328-0380

*San Fernando, California Office:* 501 South Brand Boulevard, Suite 5. Telephone: 818-361-3838. Fax: 818-361-1126.

*Civil Litigation, Personal Injury, Negligence and Business Law.*

(For Complete Biographical Data on all Personnel, see Professional Biographies at San Fernando, California)

## McCARTNEY & MERCADO

Established in 1981

3434 TRUXTUN AVENUE, SUITE 280
BAKERSFIELD, CALIFORNIA 93301-3044
Telephone: 805-327-4147
Telecopier: 805-325-9309

*Business, Civil Trial and Appellate Practice, Business, Insurance, Personal Injury, Real Estate and Commercial Litigation.*

**N. THOMAS MCCARTNEY,** born Los Angeles, California, May 22, 1950; admitted to bar, 1975, California; 1976, U.S. District Court, Eastern and Central Districts of California. *Education:* St. Mary's College of California (B.A., magna cum laude, 1972); University of San Francisco (J.D., cum laude, 1975). Recipient, American Jurisprudence Award in Property. Member, McAuliffe Honor Society. Member, University of San Francisco Law Review, 1974-1975. *Member:* Kern County Bar Association; State Bar of California. *LANGUAGES:* Spanish. *REPORTED CASES:* Clark Equipment Company v. Mastellotto, 87 Cal. App. 3d 88 (1978); American National Bank v. Stanfill, 205 Cal. App. 3d 1089 (1988). *PRACTICE AREAS:* Business Litigation; Environmental Litigation; Civil Litigation; Personal Injury.

**JESS A. MERCADO,** born Antioch, California, May 7, 1961; admitted to bar, 1986, California; 1987, U.S. District Court, Central, Eastern, Northern and Southern Districts of California. *Education:* DePaul University (B.A., 1983); Pepperdine University (J.D., 1986). Pi Gamma Mu; Pi Sigma Alpha; Phi Delta Phi. Member, Blue Key. Recipient, American Jurisprudence Award for Property Law. *Member:* Kern County Bar Association; State Bar of California. *LANGUAGES:* Spanish and Portuguese. *PRACTICE AREAS:* Insurance; Business; Civil Litigation.

*(This Listing Continued)*

REPRESENTATIVE CLIENTS: State Farm Fire and Casualty; Coleman Construction, Inc.; Mid State Development Company; Security Pacific National Bank; Reliance United Pacific Surety Managers; Underwriters Settlement Services; Match Construction.

## PATTERSON, RITNER, LOCKWOOD, GARTNER & JURICH

A Partnership including Professional Corporations

SUITE 522, 1415 EIGHTEENTH STREET
**BAKERSFIELD, CALIFORNIA 93301-5216**
Telephone: 805-327-4387
FAX: 805-327-9041

*Los Angeles, California Office:* Suite 900, 3580 Wilshire Boulevard. Telephone: 213-487-6240.

*Ventura, California Office:* Suite 231, 260 Maple Court. Telephone: 805-644-1061.

*San Bernardino, California Office:* 325 Hospitality Lane, Suite 204. Telephone: 909-885-6063.

*Insurance, Personal Injury, Products Liability, Casualty and Medical Malpractice Law. Trials. Legal Malpractice.*

**JOHN A. JURICH,** born Minneapolis, Minnesota, January 13, 1945; admitted to bar, 1978, California. *Education:* California State University at Northridge (B.A., cum laude, 1973); Loyola University of Los Angeles (J.D., 1978). *Member:* State Bar of California.

**MARISA S. VIDAURRETA,** born Bakersfield, California, March 31, 1965; admitted to bar, 1990, California. *Education:* Occidental College (B.A., 1987); George Washington University (J.D., 1990). Member, Executive Board, Teen Alternative Court of Kern. *Member:* Kern County Bar Association; The State Bar of California; California Women Lawyers; Kern County Women Lawyer's Association; California Trial Lawyers Association.

(For Biographical Data on all Partners, see Professional Biographies at Los Angeles, California).

## LAW OFFICES OF BRETT L. PRICE

Established in 1983

GREYSTONE PLAZA BUILDING
841 MOHAWK STREET, SUITE 200
**BAKERSFIELD, CALIFORNIA 93309**
Telephone: 805-323-3400
Fax: 805-323-3957
Email: bkfldlaw@aol.com

*Business and Commercial Law, Litigation, Property Taxation, Bankruptcy, Farm and Ranch Law, Real Estate, Construction Law, Oil and Gas Law.*

**BRETT L. PRICE,** born Los Angeles, California, May 2, 1950; admitted to bar, 1975, California; 1976, U.S. District Court, Central District of California and U.S. Tax Court; 1978, U.S. District Court, Eastern District of California; 1981, U.S. Supreme Court, U.S. Court of Appeals, Ninth Circuit and U.S. District Court, Northern District of California; 1985, U.S. District Court, Southern District of California. *Education:* University of California at Los Angeles (B.A., cum laude, 1972); University of California at Davis (J.D., 1975). *Member:* Kern County (Director, 1979) and American Bar Associations; State Bar of California (Member: Business and Real Estate Sections; Standing Committee on Lawyer Reference Services, 1983-1985); American Bankruptcy Institute; Central California Bankruptcy Association; Kern County Bankruptcy Forum.

### ASSOCIATE

**SAM MCDERMOTT,** born Los Angeles, California, January 24, 1967; admitted to bar, 1995, California; 1996, U.S. District Court, Central and Eastern Districts of California and U.S. Court of Appeals, Ninth Circuit. *Education:* University of San Diego; University of Southern California (J.D., 1995). Topic Editor, Hale Moot Court Program, University of Southern California, 1994-1995. Member, Hale Moot Court Program, 1993-1995. Member: Federalist Society; Christian Legal Society. *Member:* Kern county Bar Association.

*(This Listing Continued)*

### LEGAL SUPPORT PERSONNEL

**NICOLE M. MISNER,** born Torrance, California, June 25, 1970. *Education:* Texas A & M University (B.S., 1993); Drake University Law School (J.D., 1996). *Member:* American Agricultural Law Association. (Law Clerk).

REPRESENTATIVE CLIENTS: Kern County; Indepent Pipe and Tubing, Inc.; Century 21 Stroope Realty; Lambourne Travel, Inc.; San Joaquin County; Inyo County; Ellis Electric; Trico Mechanical, Inc.; Kern Tulare Safe Federal Credit Union; Santa Fe Federal Credit Union; Grapevine Oil Co.; The Highland Cafe; Subway; Chicago Title Insurance Co.; Yosemite Escrow Services; Sonoma County; Santa Barbara County; Tuolumne County; Cordell Construction; Martins Pharmacy; Action Sports; Humboldt County.

## ROBINSON, PALMER & LOGAN

SUITE 150, 3434 TRUXTUN AVENUE
**BAKERSFIELD, CALIFORNIA 93301**
Telephone: 805-323-8277
Fax: 805-323-4205

*General Civil and Trial Practice. Insurance Defense, Water Rights, Public, Land Use and Business Law.*

### MEMBERS OF FIRM

**OLIVER U. ROBINSON,** born Fresno, California, July 27, 1939; admitted to bar, 1966, California. *Education:* University of California at Berkeley (B.A., 1961); Hastings College of Law, University of California (LL.B., 1965). Deputy County Counsel, 1966-1967. Deputy District Attorney, 1967-1971. *Member:* Kern County Bar Association; State Bar of California; Southern California Association of Defense Counsel. [U.S. Army Reserve, active duty, 1963-1969]. *PRACTICE AREAS:* Civil Litigation.

**WILLIAM D. PALMER,** born Bakersfield, California, April 20, 1943; admitted to bar, 1969, California and U.S. District Court, Southern District of California; 1970, U.S. Court of Military Appeals; 1972, U.S. District Court, Eastern District of California. *Education:* University of Nevada (B.S., 1965); University of San Diego (J.D., cum laude, 1968). Phi Delta Phi. Notes and Comments Editor, San Diego Law Review, 1967-1968. *Member:* Kern County Bar Association; State Bar of California; Northern Association of Defense Counsel; Defense Research Institute. [Lt. Col., USMCR]. *PRACTICE AREAS:* Civil Litigation; Water Law; Business Law; Public Entity.

**GARY L. LOGAN,** born Berkeley, California, April 19, 1953; admitted to bar, 1979, California; 1981, U.S. District Court, Eastern District of California; U.S. Court of Appeals, 9th Circuit. *Education:* California State University at Chico (B.A., 1975); University of San Diego (J.D., 1979). *Member:* Kern County Bar Association; State Bar of California; Northern California Association of Defense Counsel. *PRACTICE AREAS:* Civil Litigation.

### ASSOCIATES

**LUKE A. FOSTER,** born Fairfield, California, July 12, 1966; admitted to bar, 1993, California. *Education:* University of California, Davis (B.S., Physiology, 1989); McGeorge School of Law (J.D., 1993). Writer Pacific Law Journal Legislative Review Staff, 1990-1991. Primary Editor, Pacific Law Journal, 1991-1992. Traynor Honor Society. *Member:* Kern County Bar Association; State Bar of California. *PRACTICE AREAS:* Civil Litigation.

**MARSHALL S. FONTES,** born Santa Maria, California, September 28, 1961; admitted to bar, 1989, California and U.S. District Court, Eastern District of California. *Education:* Miami University (B.S., 1984); Case Western Reserve University (J.D., 1987). *Member:* Kern County and American Bar Associations. *PRACTICE AREAS:* Civil Litigation.

REPRESENTATIVE CLIENTS: State Farm Insurance Co.; Allstate Insurance Co.; United States Fidelity & Guaranty Co.; Firemans Fund Insurance Co.; Commercial Union Assurance; Foremost Insurance Co.; United Pacific-Reliance; The Hartford; Travelers Insurance Co.; Armco Insurance Group; GAB Business Services Inc.; Self Insurance Administrators; Kemper Insurance Cos.; Unigard Insurance Group; Foremost Insurance Co.; Underwriters Adjusting Co.; Automobile Club of Southern California; California State Automobile Assn.; Liberty Mutual Insurance Co.; Rosedale-Rio Bravo Water Storage District; East Niles Community Service District; Lamont Public Utility District; County of Kern; SISC; Mojave Public Utility District; Plainview Public Utility District; Arvin Community Service District.
REFERENCES: Bank of America National Trust & Savings Association.

## THOMAS M. STANTON

1430 TRUXTUN AVENUE, SUITE 900
BAKERSFIELD, CALIFORNIA 93301
Telephone: 805-861-8655
Fax: 805-322-3508

*General Civil Practice, Insurance Defense.*

**THOMAS M. STANTON,** born Bakersfield, California, June 8, 1942; admitted to bar, 1967, California and U.S. District Court, Northern District of California; 1970, U.S. District Court, Eastern District of California. *Education:* University of California at Berkeley (A.B., 1964); Stanford University (LL.B., 1967). *Member:* Kern County Bar Association; State Bar of California; Northern California Association of Defense Counsel. (Also of Counsel to Clifford and Brown, Bakersfield, California). **PRACTICE AREAS:** Civil Litigation; Insurance Defense.

REPRESENTATIVE CLIENTS: The Travelers; Firemans Fund; San Joaquin Valley Risk Management Authority; Laporte Inc.; The Boeing Company; Rio Colorado Seeds, Inc.

## THE LAW OFFICES OF PATRICK J. STEELE

1401 19TH STREET, SUITE 200
BAKERSFIELD, CALIFORNIA 93301
Telephone: 805-334-1145

*Commercial Litigation, Real Estate Litigation, Construction Litigation, Environmental Litigation, Trusts and Estates and Wills.*

**PATRICK J. STEELE,** born Bakersfield, California, January 18, 1957; admitted to bar, 1982, California and U.S. District Court, Central District of California; 1987, U.S. District Court, Eastern and Northern Districts of California. *Education:* University of California, Berkeley (B.A., 1979); Boalt Hall School of Law, University of California (J.D., 1982). Phi Beta Kappa. Associate Editor, Ecology Law Quarterly, 1981-1982. Deputy County Counsel, Kern County, California, 1986-1989. *Member:* State Bar of California. **PRACTICE AREAS:** Commercial Litigation; Real Estate Litigation; Construction Litigation; Environmental Litigation; Trusts and Estates; Wills.

## EDWARD J. THOMAS

A PROFESSIONAL CORPORATION

Established in 1981

SUITE 400, 5201 CALIFORNIA AVENUE
BAKERSFIELD, CALIFORNIA 93309
Telephone: 805-322-1777
Fax: 805-324-3660
Email: thomaslaw@lightspeed.net

*Practice Limited to Family Law and Estate Planning.*

**EDWARD J. THOMAS,** born Sioux City, Iowa, April 11, 1946; admitted to bar, 1971, California. *Education:* University of Minnesota at Duluth (B.A., 1967); University of Minnesota at Minneapolis (J.D., 1970). Member, Minnesota Law Review, 1968-1970. Certified Family Law Specialist, California, 1980—. *Member:* Kern County and American Bar Associations; The State Bar of California. Fellow, American Academy of Matrimonial Lawyers. **PRACTICE AREAS:** Family Law.

**MICHAEL ANDREW CARLOVSKY,** born San Luis Obispo, California, December 30, 1965; admitted to bar, 1992, California. *Education:* California Polytechnic University (B.A., 1992); California Western School of Law (J.D., 1992). Recipient, American Jurisprudence Award, California Civil Procedure, 1992. *Member:* Kern County Bar Association; State Bar of California. **PRACTICE AREAS:** Family Law.

**HEATHER JUNE CHRISTIANSEN,** born San Jose, California, August 26, 1971; admitted to bar, 1996, California. *Education:* University of California, Santa Cruz (B.A., 1993); McGeorge School of Law (J.D., 1996). Phi Delta Phi. *Member:* Kern County Bar Association; State Bar of California. **PRACTICE AREAS:** Family Law.

## LEONARD K. WELSH

MING OFFICE PARK
5500 MING AVENUE, SUITE 350
BAKERSFIELD, CALIFORNIA 93309
Telephone: 805-835-1122
Fax: 805-835-8918

*Insolvency, Bankruptcy, Business and Farm Reorganization, Debtor and Creditor Rights and Business Law.*

**LEONARD K. WELSH,** born Fort Worth, Texas, April 14, 1954; admitted to bar, 1981, California; U.S. District Court, Eastern, Central, Northern and Southern Districts of California and U.S. Tax Court. *Education:* Brigham Young University (B.A., magna cum laude, 1977); Washington & Lee University (J.D., 1980). Phi Kappa Phi; Phi Alpha Theta. Member, Moot Court Honor Board. Recipient, American Jurisprudence Award in Criminal Law. Member, Central California Bankruptcy Association and Kern County Bankruptcy Forum. Adjunct Professor of Law at California State University, Bakersfield. Attorney, Delegate Conference for the United States District Court for the Eastern District of California (8 times). *Member:* Kern County and American Bar Associations; State Bar of California.

## MICHAEL T. WHITTINGTON

COMMONWEALTH PLAZA
3300 TRUXTUN AVENUE, SUITE 390
BAKERSFIELD, CALIFORNIA 93301
Telephone: 805-327-2294
Fax: 805-323-8731

Newport Beach, California Office: 4590 MacArthur, Suite 550, 92660.
Telephone: 714-833-2370. Fax: 714-833-0949.
Los Gatos, California Office: 15425 Los Gatos Boulevard, Suite 120, 95032.
Telephone: 408-369-9655. Fax: 408-369-0355.

*Real Estate, Business, General Civil Litigation and Trials.*

**MICHAEL T. WHITTINGTON,** born Whittier, California, December 22, 1958; admitted to bar, 1984, California and U.S. District Court, Northern District of California; U.S. District Court, Eastern District of California. *Education:* University of Santa Clara (B.S., 1981; J.D., 1984). *Member:* Kern County Bar Association; State Bar of California.

## LAW OFFICES OF YOUNG WOOLDRIDGE

Established in 1927

1800 30TH STREET, FOURTH FLOOR
BAKERSFIELD, CALIFORNIA 93301
Telephone: 805-327-9661
Facsimile: 805-327-1087

*General Civil and Trial Practice. Corporation. Condemnation, Oil and Gas, Water Rights, Probate and Estate Planning Law. Agricultural, Bankruptcy, Business, Domestic Relations, Personal Injury and Workers' Compensation.*

**FIRM PROFILE:** Founded in 1927, Young Wooldridge is a full service firm divided into seven departments: Business, Special Districts, Complex Litigation, Environmental, Litigation, Probate and Domestic Relations. Its partners and associates pride themselves in their ability to provide high quality, personalized service to their clients. They have distinguished themselves both in practice and in their respective specialties as the attached biographies indicate.

### MEMBERS OF FIRM

**JOSEPH WOOLDRIDGE,** born Holtville, California, July 11, 1913; admitted to bar, 1939, California. *Education:* El Centro Junior College; Loyola University (J.D., 1938). Phi Delta Phi. Assistant District Attorney, 1943-1946. District Attorney, Kern County, 1952-1956. *Member:* Kern County Bar Association; The State Bar of California (Member, Legislative Committee, 1960-1966); The Association of Trial Lawyers of America. **PRACTICE AREAS:** Personal Injury; Litigation.

**A. CAMERON PAULDEN** (1927-1984).

**ROBERT J. SELF,** born Bakersfield, California, May 25, 1932; admitted to bar, 1961, California. *Education:* Bakersfield College (A.A., 1952); University of California at Los Angeles (B.S., 1954); University of California at Berkeley, Boalt Hall (J.D., 1960). Member, Board of Building Code Appeals, 1964-1966. Member, Board of Directors, Bakersfield College

*(This Listing Continued)*

Foundation. *Member:* Kern County Bar Association (President, 1976); The State Bar of California. [Legal Officer, U.S.S. Wasp, 1955-1956]. *REPORTED CASES: People v. Brock,* 57 Cal2d 644 (1962); *Keen v. Harling,* 61 Cal2d 318 (1964); *Runyan v. Pacific Air Industries,* 2 Cal3d 304 (1970). *PRACTICE AREAS:* Business Law; Real Property Law; Commercial Litigation.

**G. NEIL FARR,** born Los Angeles, California, January 9, 1932; admitted to bar, 1961, California; 1977, U.S. Supreme Court. *Education:* University of California (A.B., 1957); Hastings College of Law, University of California (J.D., 1960). Phi Delta Phi. Deputy District Attorney; Solano County, 1961-1966; Kern County, 1966-1969. Recreation Commissioner, City of Fairfield, 1964-1966. Chairman, Kern County Juvenile Justice Commission, 1988—. *Member:* Kern County Bar Association (President, 1984); The State Bar of California; California Trial Lawyers Association. [U.S. Navy, 1950-1952]. (Certified Specialist, Family Law, California Board of Specialization). *PRACTICE AREAS:* Domestic Relations; Litigation.

**MICHAEL R. YOUNG,** born Santa Monica, California, December 19, 1940; admitted to bar, 1966, California. *Education:* University of California at Los Angeles (A.B., 1962); Hastings College of Law, University of California (J.D., 1966). Member, Thurston Honor Society. *Member:* Kern County Bar Association; The State Bar of California; California Trial Lawyers Association. *PRACTICE AREAS:* Personal Injury; Probate; Litigation.

**ERNEST A. CONANT,** born Marysville, California, May 3, 1953; admitted to bar, 1979, California. *Education:* California Polytechnic State University (B.S., with honors, 1975); Pepperdine University (J.D., 1979). Phi Kappa Phi; Phi Alpha Delta. *Member:* Kern County and American Bar Associations; The State Bar of California. *PRACTICE AREAS:* Administrative Law.

**STEVE W. NICHOLS,** born Payson, Utah, March 7, 1953; admitted to bar, 1980, California. *Education:* Utah State University (B.A., 1975); Pepperdine University (J.D., 1979). Judicial Law Clerk, Superior Court, County of Ventura, 1978-1979. Judge Pro Tem, 1985-1986. *Member:* Kern County and American (Member, Sections on: Corporation, Banking and Business Law; Litigation) Bar Associations; The State Bar of California; California Trial Lawyers Association; Kern County Trial Lawyers Association. *PRACTICE AREAS:* Business Litigation; Commercial Litigation; Personal Injury Litigation.

**LARRY R. COX,** born Charleston, South Carolina, September 3, 1950; admitted to bar, 1979, South Carolina and California. *Education:* University of Arizona (B.S., with distinction, 1972); University of South Carolina (J.D., 1978). Beta Gamma Sigma; Kappa Kappa Psi. Law Clerk to Chief Justice J. Woodrow Lewis, Supreme Court of South Carolina, 1979-1981. *Member:* Kern County Bar Association (President, Probate and Estate Planning Section, 1985-1986); The State Bar of California. [Capt., USAF, 1972-1976]. *PRACTICE AREAS:* Probate Law; Estate Planning; Litigation.

**SCOTT K. KUNEY,** born Tulare, California, August 14, 1956; admitted to bar, 1983, California. *Education:* University of California at Santa Barbara (B.A., with high honors, 1979); University of Birmingham, England; McGeorge School of Law, University of the Pacific (J.D., 1983). Member, National Moot Court Honors Board. *Member:* Kern County and American Bar Associations; The State Bar of California. *PRACTICE AREAS:* Water Rights Law; Eminent Domain.

**MICHAEL A. KAIA,** born Fresno, California, May 28, 1953; admitted to bar, 1986, California. *Education:* California State University, Fresno (B.S.B.A.; M.B.A.); San Joaquin College of Law (J.D., 1984). Delta Theta Phi; Sigma Iota Epsilon. *Member:* Kern County and American Bar Associations; The State Bar of California; California Trial Lawyers Association; The Association of Trial Lawyers of America. *PRACTICE AREAS:* Real Property Litigation; Contract Litigation.

## ASSOCIATES

**RUSSELL B. HICKS,** born Evanston, Illinois, August 14, 1949; admitted to bar, 1976, California; 1986, Utah. *Education:* Brigham Young University (B.A., 1973; M.Ed., 1985); University of Southern California (J.D., 1976). *Member:* Salt Lake City and Kern County Bar Associations; State Bar of California; Utah State Bar. *LANGUAGES:* Spanish. *REPORTED CASES: Dwyer v. Crocker National Bank,* 194 Cal. App. 3d 1418 (2nd Dist. 1987). *PRACTICE AREAS:* Business Law; Business Litigation; Personal Injury Litigation.

**VICKIE Y. SONGER,** born Bakersfield, California, December 6, 1948; admitted to bar, 1992, California. *Education:* Bakersfield College (A.A., 1970); University of California, Santa Barbara Extension; California Pacific School of Law (J.D., with honors, 1991). *Member:* Kern County Bar Association; State Bar of California. *PRACTICE AREAS:* Workers' Compensation Law.

**STEVEN M. TORIGIANI,** born Bakersfield, California, March 21, 1967; admitted to bar, 1993, California. *Education:* California Polytechnic State University (B.S., 1990); McGeorge University (J.D., 1993). Real Estate License, California, 1990. *Member:* State Bar of California. *PRACTICE AREAS:* Water Law; Business Law; Litigation.

**SCOTT D. HOWRY,** born Santa Monica, California, August 13, 1968; admitted to bar, 1993, California; 1994, U.S. District Court, Central District of California. *Education:* Claremont McKenna College (B.A., cum laude, 1990); Santa Clara University (J.D., 1993). *Member:* Kern County and American (Member, Business Law Section) Bar Associations; The State Bar of California. *PRACTICE AREAS:* Business Litigation; Commercial Litigation; Real Estate Litigation; Construction Litigation.

**DAVID F. LEON,** born Tulare, California, September 4, 1967; admitted to bar, 1994, California. *Education:* University of California at Berkeley (B.S., 1989); University of California at Los Angeles (J.D., 1994). *PRACTICE AREAS:* Business Law.

**TODD A. GALL,** born Milton, Florida, September 13, 1968; admitted to bar, 1995, California. *Education:* California Polytechnic State University (B.A., 1991); Notre Dame Law School, London, England; California Western University (J.D., 1995). Phi Alpha Delta. *Member:* Kern County Bar Association; State Bar of California. *PRACTICE AREAS:* Personal Injury Litigation; Business Litigation; Commercial Litigation.

## OF COUNSEL

**JOHN B. YOUNG,** born Bakersfield, California, August 10, 1913; admitted to bar, 1937, California. *Education:* University of California at Los Angeles (A.B., 1934); Boalt Hall School of Law, University of California (J.D., 1937). Deputy County Counsel, Kern County, 1940-1942. Chief Rationing Attorney, Fresno District Office, OPA, 1942. Member, Judge Advocate General's Department, 1944-1946. *Member:* Kern County Bar Association (President, 1949); The State Bar of California. *PRACTICE AREAS:* Probate Law; Estate Planning.

**EDWARD M. CARPENTER,** born Lodi, California, October 5, 1930; admitted to bar, 1964, California. *Education:* Stanford University (A.B., 1952); Stanford Graduate School of Business (M.B.A., 1953); LaSalle Extension University (LL.B., 1964). *Member:* State Bar of California; American Bar Association. [Officer, U.S. Navy, 1953-1955]. *PRACTICE AREAS:* Banking Litigation; Commercial Litigation.

**JAMES E. MILLAR,** born Arcata, California, May 18, 1950; admitted to bar, 1980, California. *Education:* University of California at Santa Barbara (B.A., with high honors, 1976); Hastings College of Law, University of California (J.D., 1979). Phi Beta Kappa. Member, Hastings College of Law, University of California Law Review, 1978-1979. *Member:* Kern County Bar Association; The State Bar of California. [Sergeant, U.S. Marine Corps, 1968-1972]. *PRACTICE AREAS:* Personal Injury Law; Labor Law; Workers' Compensation Law; Employment Law Management; Civil Litigation Business.

REPRESENTATIVE CLIENTS: Arvin-Edison Water Storage District; Bank of America; The Barrentine Co.; Buttes Gas and Oil Company; Buttonwillow Ginning Company; John Hancock Mutual Life Insurance Co.; Heritage Title Company; Hewlett-Packard; Homestead Savings and Loan Assn.; Junior League of Bakersfield, Inc.; Kern Steel Fabrication; Motor City Truck Sales and Service; North Kern Water Storage District; Pacific Gas and Electric Co.; Police Officers Research Association of California-Legal Defense Fund; Pyramid Oil Co., Inc.; Rag Gulch Water Storage District; Semitropic Water Storage District; Shafter-Wasco Irrigation District; Southern San Joaquin Municipal Utility District; Superior Oil Co.; Tenneco West, Inc.; Toyo Cotton Co.; Transamerica Title Insurance Co.; US Sprint Communications Corp.; Vaughn Water Co., Inc.; Wells Fargo Bank; Wheeler Ridge-Maricopa Water Storage District; Bakersfield Sandstone Brick Company; Kern Electric Distributors; Lawyers Title Insurance Corporation; National Hot Rod Association; San Joaquin Capitol Corp.; Sun World International, Inc.; Tejon Agricultural Partners; Valley National Bank of Arizona; Watson Realty Co.; Golden State Metals; Schlumberger Technology Corporation; Consolidated Fiberglass Corporation; Greater Bakersfield Convention & Visitor Bureau; Bakersfield Police Officers Benefit Association.

*(This Listing Continued)*

## CALDWELL & KENNEDY
### A PROFESSIONAL CORPORATION
**BARSTOW, CALIFORNIA**
(See Victorville)

*Corporate, Real Property, Business, Commercial Transactions, Construction Disputes, Civil Litigation, Family Law, Estate Planning, Wills and Trusts, Personal Injury Law. Criminal Law and Special Appearances in Local, State and Federal Courts.*

---

## HAYTON LAW CORPORATION
**BARSTOW, CALIFORNIA**
(See Victorville)

*Practice Limited to Trial Practice of Personal Injury, Wrongful Death, General Negligence, Products Liability, Medical Malpractice, Wrongful Termination and Workers Compensation Law in all State Courts.*

---

## THE LAW OFFICES OF
## GERALD R. LUNDBERG
**BARSTOW, CALIFORNIA**
(See Victorville)

*State and Federal Litigation, Real Estate, Estate Planning, Probate, Trust Administration, Corporate Law, Creditor and Debtor Bankruptcy, Business Law, Collection, Construction Law, Family Law, Subpoenas, Unlawful Detainer, Employment and Labor Law.*

---

## WELEBIR & McCUNE
### A PROFESSIONAL LAW CORPORATION
**BARSTOW, CALIFORNIA**
(See Redlands)

*Practice limited to Catastrophic Personal Injury and Wrongful Death, Products Liability, Aviation, Railroad and Toxic Torts. Class Actions related to Defective Products and Mass Torts.*

---

## LYNN E. ZUMBRUNN
### A LAW CORPORATION
**BARSTOW, CALIFORNIA**
(See Victorville)

*General Civil and Trial Practice. Family, Personal Injury, Corporations, Real Estate, Construction and Probate Law.*

---

## GEORGE C. MARTINEZ
*Established in 1960*

**1610 TIBURON BOULEVARD**
**BELVEDERE-TIBURON, CALIFORNIA 94920**
Telephone: 415-789-5086
FAX: 415-789-5088
Email: GCMartinez@aol.com

*Complex White Collar Criminal and Civil Litigation including Real Estate, Business, Transactional and Personal Injury Litigation.*

**GEORGE C. MARTINEZ,** born San Francisco, California, July 27, 1934; admitted to bar, 1960, California. *Education:* San Francisco State University (A.B., 1956); University of San Francisco (J.D., 1959). Phi Delta Phi. Author: "The Rodrigues Review and the Adult Authority," California Trial Lawyers Association Syllabus, April, 1976; "Physicians Protect Thyselves—Prescribing Controlled Substances" and "Suppression of Identification Evidence," published in California Trial Lawyers Journal 15th Annual Convention Syllabus Education. Member of Faculty, Hastings College of Trial and Appellate Advocacy, 1977-1992. Lecturer: Tort Law, Dominican College of San Rafael, 1982; "Presidents Pardoning Power," The Association of Trial Lawyers of America, Summer, 1989. Member: Board of Directors, Marin Opera Company, 1978—; President's Advisory Board, San Francisco State University 1987—. Member, Board of Trustees, San Francisco State University Foundation, 1994-1996. *Member:* The Bar Association of San Francisco; State Bar of California; American Bar Association (Member, Sections on: Criminal Justice; Litigation); Lawyers Club of San Francisco; California Trial Lawyers Association (Chairman: Criminal Law Section of Northern California, 1976-1977; Amicus Criminal Committee, 1977-1979); The Association of Trial Lawyers of America. **REPORTED CASES:** Silverthorne v. United States, 400 F. 2d 627 (1968). US v. Hearst 638 F.2d 1190 (1979).

---

## LAW OFFICES OF
## RANDAL M. BARNUM
*Established in 1993*

**PARKWAY EXECUTIVE CENTER**
**2044 COLUMBUS PARKWAY**
**BENICIA, CALIFORNIA 94510**
Telephone: 707-745-3747
Fax: 707-745-4580
Email: RMBLAW@community.net

*Walnut Creek, California Office:* 319 Lennon Lane, 94598. Telephone: 510-943-2313.

*Wrongful Termination, Employment Litigation, Insurance Coverage, Insurance Defense, Personal Injury Law, Alternative Dispute Resolution Services.*

**RANDAL M. BARNUM,** born New York, N.Y., April 30, 1958; admitted to bar, 1983, California. *Education:* Stanford University (B.A., with honors, 1980); Hastings College of the Law, University of California (J.D., 1983). Phi Alpha Delta. Note and Comment Editor, Hastings Constitutional Law Quarterly, 1982-1983. Author: "Winning the Battle and the War: Defending Against Motions for Attorney's Fees Under Section 1988 of Title 42," 52 Insurance Counsel Journal 320, April, 1985; "Sexual Harassment: Prevention and Remedies," The Business Journal, Vol. 7, No. 23 (1994). Partner: Bowles and Verna, 1989-1993. Judge Pro Tem, Contra Costa County Superior Court, 1990-1996. Arbitrator, Contra Costa County Superior Court Arbitration Panel, 1990-1996. President, Benicia Chamber of Commerce, 1995. Benicia Civil Service Commission, 1995—. *Member:* Contra Costa County (Member, Alternative Dispute Resolution Panel), Solano County and American (Member, Sections on: Tort and Insurance Practice Law; Litigation) Bar Associations; State Bar of California (Member, Labor and Employment and Litigation Sections); Northern California Mediation Association; The Society of Professionals in Dispute Resolution.

---

## NANCY M. NOLTE
**159 EAST D STREET, SUITE G**
**BENICIA, CALIFORNIA 94510**
Telephone: 707-745-8999

*Fairfield, California Office:* 710, Missouri Street, Suite 3. Telephone: 717-425-1058. Fax: 707-425-1059.

*Family Law, Family Mediation.*

(For Complete Biographical data on all Personnel, see Professional Biographies at Fairfield)

---

## BRADY & BERLINER
*Established in 1985*

**2560 NINTH STREET, SUITE 316**
**BERKELEY, CALIFORNIA 94710-2567**
Telephone: 510-549-6926
Telecopier: 510-649-9793

*Washington, D.C. Office:* 1225 Nineteenth Street N.W., Suite 800. Telephone: 202-955-6067. Telecopy: 202-822-0109.
*Los Angeles, California Office:* 1875 Century Park East, Suite 700. Telephone: 310-282-6848. Telecopy: 310-282-6841.
*Sacramento, California Office:* 1121 L Street, Suite 606. Telephone: 916-448-7819. Telecopy: 916-448-1140.

*(This Listing Continued)*

Electricity Restructuring, Administrative Law, Commercial Litigation, Appellate Advocacy, Intergovernmental Affairs, Legislative Practice, Health Policy, International Trade, North American Energy Transactions, Oil and Gas Law and Public Utility Law.

(For Complete Biographical data on all personnel, see Professional Biographies at Washington, D.C.)

## BURESH, KAPLAN, JANG, FELLER & AUSTIN

Established in 1982

2298 DURANT AVENUE
**BERKELEY, CALIFORNIA 94704**
Telephone: 510-548-7474
Fax: 510-548-7488

*General Civil Appellate and Trial Practice. Insurance Defense, Personal Injury, Business Litigation, Landlord-Tenant, Real Property, Construction and Products Liability.*

**SCOTT BURESH,** born San Rafael, California, July 5, 1951; admitted to bar, 1976, California. *Education:* University of Oregon (B.S., 1973); McGeorge School of Law, University of the Pacific (J.D., 1976). Member, Moot Court Honors Board. *Member:* Bar Association of San Francisco; State Bar of California. **PRACTICE AREAS:** Insurance Defense.

**ANN S. KAPLAN,** born San Francisco, California, December 26, 1951; admitted to bar, 1977, California; 1979, District of Columbia. *Education:* Stanford University (B.A., 1973); University of San Francisco (J.D., 1977). *Member:* Bar Association of San Francisco; Berkeley-Albany, Alameda County and American Bar Associations; State Bar of California; Association of Defense Counsel. **PRACTICE AREAS:** Insurance Defense.

**ALAN J. JANG,** born Stockton, California, April 1, 1953; admitted to bar, 1978, California. *Education:* University of California at Berkeley (B.A., 1975); Golden Gate University (J.D., 1978). *Member:* Alameda County, American and Asian American Bar Associations; State Bar of California; Association of Defense Counsel. **PRACTICE AREAS:** Insurance Defense.

**FRED M. FELLER,** born Washington, D.C., February 13, 1949; admitted to bar, 1976, California. *Education:* Pomona College (B.A., 1971); Georgetown University (J.D., 1975). Member, Executive Board, Georgetown University Law Journal, 1974-1975. Editor, Landlord-Tenant Practice Manual, Bar Association of San Francisco, 1986. Teaching Fellow, Stanford University Law School, 1975-1976. Member, Berkeley Police Review Commission, 1983-1984. *Member:* Bar Association of San Francisco; Berkeley-Albany and Alameda County Bar Associations; State Bar of California. **PRACTICE AREAS:** Insurance Defense; Landlord Tenant.

**STEVEN K. AUSTIN,** born Sumter, South Carolina, October 14, 1956; admitted to bar, 1981, California. *Education:* University of California at Los Angeles (B.A., 1978); Hastings College of Law, University of California (J.D., 1981). Member, Moot Court Board. *Member:* Bar Association of San Francisco; Alameda County Bar Association; State Bar of California; Association of Defense Counsel. **PRACTICE AREAS:** Insurance Defense.

**GINA DASHMAN BOER,** born New York, N.Y., June 11, 1959; admitted to bar, 1986, California. *Education:* University of California at Berkeley (B.A., with honors, 1982); George Washington University National Law Center (J.D., with honors, 1986). Associate Editor, George Washington Journal of International Law and Economics, 1985-1986. Author: "United States Corporate Disinvestment from South Africa: The Financial Rand and Exchange Control," South African Yearbook of International Law, Vol. 11, 1985-1986. *Member:* Bar Association of San Francisco; Berkeley-Albany and Alameda County Bar Associations; State Bar of California; Association of Defense Counsel. **PRACTICE AREAS:** Insurance Defense.

**PEGGY CHANG,** born San Francisco, California, September 29, 1964; admitted to bar, 1989, California. *Education:* San Francisco State University (B.A., 1986); University of California at Berkeley (J.D., 1989). *Member:* Bar Association of San Francisco; Alameda County Bar Association; State Bar of California. **LANGUAGES:** Mandarin. **PRACTICE AREAS:** Insurance Defense.

**DANIEL L. COOK** (1965-1996).

**NOËL SIDNEY PLUMMER,** born New York, New York, April 9, 1966; admitted to bar, 1992, California. *Education:* Yale University (B.A., 1988); University of Texas (J.D., 1991). *Member:* Bar Association of San

*(This Listing Continued)*

Francisco; State Bar of California; American Bar Association; California Women Lawyers; San Francisco Women Lawyers Alliance; Defense Research Institute; Association of Defense Counsel; Charles Houston Bar Association. **PRACTICE AREAS:** Insurance Defense.

REPRESENTATIVE CLIENTS: State Farm Fire & Casualty Insurance Co.; State Farm Mutual Automobile Insurance Co.; Grubb & Ellis Co.; USAA Property and Casualty Co.; Safeway Stores, Inc.; Continental Heller/S.A.E.; A.R.G. Enterprises, Inc. dba Stuart Anderson's Black Angus Restaurants; Crawford & Company; Fire Insurance Exchange; Truck Insurance Exchange; Hanover Insurance Co.

## BURNSTEIN & TRIMBUR

1816 FIFTH STREET
**BERKELEY, CALIFORNIA 94710**
Telephone: 510-548-5075
FAX: 510-548-5074

*Civil Litigation in State and Federal Courts. Employment, Family, Custody, Probate and Entertainment Law. Appellate Practice.*

### MEMBERS OF FIRM

**MALCOLM S. BURNSTEIN,** born Detroit, Michigan, December 2, 1933; admitted to bar, 1960, California, U.S. Court of Appeals, Ninth Circuit and U.S. District Court, Northern District of California; 1971, U.S. Supreme Court. *Education:* Wayne University; University of California at Los Angeles (A.B., 1955); Boalt Hall School of Law, University of California (LL.B., 1958); Institute des Haute Etudes International, University of Paris, 1958-1959. Order of the Coif. Instructor, International Law, 1965-1970, Criminal Law and Investigation and Trial Preparation, Para-Legal Program, 1973-1976, San Francisco State University. Judge Pro Tem, San Francisco Superior Court, 1989—. Arbitrator, San Francisco Bar Association. Attorney Fee Disputes Committee, 1991—. State Bar Special Master, 1988—. *Member:* Bar Association of San Francisco; State Bar of California (Member, Litigation Section); San Francisco Trial Lawyers Association.

**CATHERINE TRIMBUR,** born San Francisco, California, April 30, 1947; admitted to bar, 1982, California; 1983, U.S. District Court, Northern District of California and U.S. Court of Appeals, Ninth Circuit; 1990, U.S. Supreme Court. *Education:* University of California at Berkeley (B.A., 1970); University of San Francisco (J.D., magna cum laude, 1982). Member, McAuliffe Honor Society. *Member:* Bar Association of San Francisco; State Bar of California (Member, Family Law Section); San Francisco Trial Lawyers Association.

## JEFFREY A. DENNIS-STRATHMEYER

2300 SHATTUCK AVENUE, ROOM 308
P.O. BOX 533
**BERKELEY, CALIFORNIA 94701**
Telephone: 510-642-8317
Email: STRATHJ@CEB.UCOP.EDU

*Estate Planning, Probate, Trust and Related Tax Law.*

**JEFFREY A. DENNIS-STRATHMEYER,** born Philadelphia, Pennsylvania, October 9, 1945; admitted to bar, 1973, California. *Education:* Stanford University (A.B., 1967); University of California at Davis (J.D., 1973). Presentations at Annual UCLA-CEB Estate Planning Institute in Los Angeles: May 1992, 1993, 1994, 1996, 1996. Book Chapter: "The Generation Skipping Transfer Tax" 2 CEB Estate Planning Practice, Chapter 16 (1995). Articles: "The IRC Section 2032A Cropshare Lease," Probate and Property, May-June 1988; "The IRS Requires Cotenants to Consent to Section 2032A Special Use Valuation Elections: Overreaching or Confusion?" Taxes, Aug., 1984; "Minors Custodianships Come of Age," California Lawyer, April, 1985; "More on Spousal Purchases of Split Interests: A Rebuttal," Tax Notes, October 5, 1987; Articles in CEB Estate Planning and California Law Reporter: "The Not-So-Final GST Tax Regulations: Good, Bad, and Ugly", February, 1996; "View From The Rafters: Perspective for Learning the GST Tax", August 1994; "Self-Canceling Estate Plans: Critique of a Flawed Strategy," April 1993; "Whither Probate? 1991 California Legislation," December 1991; "Melting the Freeze: Déjà Vu All Over Again," December, 1990; "Taxes on Excess Pension Benefits: It May Be Better To Pay The Piper," June, 1990; California Probate Code Reform," December, 1987; "California Disclaimers: A Warning and a Primer," April, 1986; "The New California Estate Tax Return: Illegal Taxation of Multistate Estates?" June, 1983; "Simple Probate-Avoidance Trusts: Higher Stakes and Old Problems," February, 1983. Qualified expert witness for estate planning malpractice, Superior Court of California, County of Alameda. *Member:* American

*(This Listing Continued)*

**JEFFREY A. DENNIS-STRATHMEYER,** Berkeley—
Continued

Bar Association (Member, Real Property, Probate and Trust Law Section). (Certified Specialist, Estate Planning, Trust and Probate Law, The State Bar of California Board of Legal Specialization).

## GILLIN, JACOBSON, ELLIS, LARSEN & DOYLE

BERKELEY, CALIFORNIA

(See Orinda)

*Civil Trial Practice including Intellectual Property Litigation, Commercial Torts, Products Liability, Personal Injury and Wrongful Death.*

## GROSSMAN & GIBBS

1510 FOURTH STREET
BERKELEY, CALIFORNIA 94710-1707
Telephone: 510-524-4141

*Criminal Law.*

### MEMBERS OF FIRM

**ELIZABETH R. GROSSMAN,** born Los Angeles, California, November 5, 1956; admitted to bar, 1982, California and U.S. Court of Appeals, Ninth Circuit. *Education:* University of California at Berkeley (B.A., 1978); Hastings College of the Law, University of California (J.D., 1982). Phi Beta Kappa. Attorney: Solano County Public Defender's Office, 1983-1984; Alameda County Public Defender's Office, 1984-1987; Cooper, Arguedas & Cassman, 1987-1992. *Member:* Alameda County Bar Association; State Bar of California; Bay Area Lawyers for Individual Freedom; National Lawyers Guild; National Association of Criminal Defense Lawyers; California Women Lawyers; California Attorneys for Criminal Justice (Member, Board of Governors); California Public Defender's Association; Women Defenders (Chair). **PRACTICE AREAS:** Criminal Trials; Juvenile and Professional Disciplinary Hearings.

**LAWRENCE A. GIBBS,** born San Francisco, California, January 15, 1952; admitted to bar, 1980, California and U.S. Court of Appeals, Ninth Circuit. *Education:* Stanford University (B.A., 1974); University of Chicago (M.A., 1975); Boalt Hall School of Law, University of California (J.D., 1980). Law Clerk to the Honorable John F. Grady, U.S. District Court, Northern District of Illinois, 1981-1982. Editor, Forum Magazine of the California Attorneys for Criminal Justice. Attorney: Friedman, Ross and Hersh, 1982-1986; Law Office of Lawrence A. Gibbs, 1986-1992. *Member:* California Attorneys for Criminal Justice; California Appellate Defense Counsel. **PRACTICE AREAS:** Criminal and Civil Appeals and Writs.

## MARK HIMELSTEIN

2030 ADDISON STREET, SEVENTH FLOOR
BERKELEY, CALIFORNIA 94704-1104
Telephone: 510-548-2301
Facsimile: 510-848-0266

*Representation of Business Entities, Nonprofit Organizations and Educational Institutions. Civil Trial Practice, Commercial Transactions, Real Estate, Trusts and Probate.*

**MARK HIMELSTEIN,** born Ft. Wayne, Indiana, September 19, 1939; admitted to bar, 1968, District of Columbia; 1969, California; 1972, U.S. Supreme Court. *Education:* Indiana University (A.B., 1962); George Washington University (LL.B., 1967). *Member:* Alameda County Bar Association; State Bar of California; District of Columbia Bar. [With Peace Corps, Ethiopia, 1962-1964]. **REPORTED CASES:** Smith v. Regents, 4 Cal.4th 843, 844 P.2d 500, 16 Cal.Rptr. 2d 181 (1993); Mann v. Alameda County, 85 CA3d 505, 149 Cal.Rptr. 552 (1978); Zumwalt v. Trustees, 33 CA3d 665, 109 Cal.Rptr. 344 (1973); Mabey v. Reagan, 376 F.Supp. 216 (1974) 537 F.2d 1036 (1976); Toney v. Reagan, 326 F.Supp. 1093, 467 F.2d 953, cert. denied, 409 U.S. 1130 (1972); People v. Colbert, 24 CA3d 497, 101 Cal.Rptr. 283 (1972).

## PAUL W. HOLMES

2171 SHATTUCK AVENUE
BERKELEY, CALIFORNIA 94704
Telephone: 510-843-5800
Facsimile: 510-843-3999

*Estate Planning, Probate and Trust Administration.*

**PAUL W. HOLMES,** born Berkeley, California, September 1, 1954; admitted to bar, 1981, California; 1982, U.S. Tax Court. *Education:* Brigham Young University (B.S., 1978; J.D., 1981). *Member:* Alameda County Bar Association (Member, Estate Planning, Trust and Probate Section); State Bar of California (Member, Estate Planning, Trust and Probate Section).

## SUSAN B. JORDAN

P.O. BOX 5805
BERKELEY, CALIFORNIA 94705-0805
Telephone: 510-849-1143
FAX: 510-849-4843

Ukiah, California Office: 515 S. School Street. Telephone: 707-462-2151. FAX: 707-462-2194.

*Criminal and Civil Trial and Appellate Practice.*

**SUSAN B. JORDAN,** born Chicago, Illinois, June 21, 1941; admitted to bar, 1970, Illinois; 1971, California. *Education:* University of Michigan at Ann Arbor (B.A., 1963); Yeshiva University (M.S., 1965); Northwestern University (J.D., 1970). Author: "Representation of Women in Self-Defense Crimes," Rutgers University Law Review, 1979; Trial tactics articles in *Women Trial Lawyers,* Prentice-Hall, Inc., 1987; *Trial Masters,* Prentice Hall, 1985. Instructor, New College of California Law School, 1976-1980. *Member:* Illinois State Bar Association (inactive); State Bar of California.

## KATZOFF & RIGGS

Established in 1991
3088 CLAREMONT AVENUE
BERKELEY, CALIFORNIA 94705
Telephone: 510-597-1990
FAX: 510-597-0295

Cobb, California Office: Meadow Springs Shopping Center, P.O. Box 1250. Telephone: 707-928-4600. Fax: 707-928-5075.

*Civil and Criminal Trial Practice, Juvenile Dependency and Appeals. Real Estate and Real Estate Transactions, Construction, Insurance Defense and Insurance Coverage Law, Computer Software Licensing Law.*

### MEMBERS OF FIRM

**ROBERT R. RIGGS,** born Baltimore, Maryland, June 11, 1958; admitted to bar, 1983, California; 1984, District of Columbia. *Education:* Johns Hopkins University (B.A., 1979); Stanford University (J.D., 1982). Order of the Coif. First Year Honor, 1980. Best Team, Best Brief, Kirkwood Moot Court Competition, 1981. Law Clerk to: Hon. Betty B. Fletcher, U.S. Court of Appeals for the Ninth Circuit, 1982-1983; Hon. Stanley A. Weigel, U.S. District Court, Northern District of California, 1983-1984. Special Master, United States District Court for the Northern District of California in: Toussaint v. McCarthy, No. C 73-1422 SAW, 1984—; Thompson v. Enomoto, No. C 79-1630 SAW, 1985—. *Member:* Alameda County and Lake County Bar Associations; The District of Columbia Bar. **LANGUAGES:** French and Italian. **PRACTICE AREAS:** Civil Litigation; Construction Law; Computer Software Licensing Law; Real Estate Law; Criminal Law; Appeals and Writs. **Email:** Robriggs@aol.com

**KENNETH S. KATZOFF,** born New York, N.Y., January 30, 1956; admitted to bar, 1982, California. *Education:* Tulane University (B.A., cum laude, 1978); University of San Francisco (J.D., 1981). Law Clerk for the U.S. Department of Justice, San Francisco U.S. Attorneys Office. Judge Pro Tempore, Berkeley-Albany Municipal Court. *Member:* Bar Association of San Francisco; Alameda County and American Bar Associations; The State Bar of California; California Trial Lawyers Association. **PRACTICE AREAS:** Civil Litigation; Real Estate Law; Insurance Defense; Insurance Coverage Law; Juvenile Dependency Law. **Email:** Kskvs99@aol.com

*(This Listing Continued)*

### ASSOCIATES

**JESSE D. PALMER,** born Kansas City, Kansas, May 12, 1968; admitted to bar, 1995, California. *Education:* University of California at Berkeley (B.S., 1990); Hastings College of Law (J.D., 1995). Recipient, Best Brief Award, First Year Moot Court.

---

## LAW OFFICE OF
## MALCOLM LEADER-PICONE

P.O. BOX 7598
**BERKELEY, CALIFORNIA 94707-0598**
*Telephone: 510-528-2975*
*Fax: 510-528-2954*
*Email: mlp@leader-picone.com*
*URL: http://www.leader-picone.com*

*Commercial Litigation, Bankruptcy, Environmental Law, Employment Discrimination, Real Estate.*

**MALCOLM LEADER-PICONE,** born London, England, January 15, 1954; admitted to bar, 1982, California, U.S. District Courts, Northern and Eastern Districts of California, U.S. Court of Appeals, Ninth Circuit and U.S. Supreme Court. *Education:* University of California at Santa Cruz (A.B., with honors, 1975); University of California, Boalt Hall School of Law (J.D., 1982). Extern for Justice Frank Newman, California Supreme Court. *Member:* Bar Association of San Francisco (Member, Commercial Law and Bankruptcy and Litigation Sections); American Bar Association; State Bar of California (Member, Law and Technology Committee; Member, Sections on: Litigation, Commercial Law and Bankruptcy). *LANGUAGES:* Spanish. *REPORTED CASES:* In re Roxford Foods Litigation (E.D.Cal. 1991) 790 F.Supp. 987; Civic Center Square, Inc. v. James Ford (In re Roxford Foods, Inc.) (9th Cir. 1993) 12 F.3d 875; F.D.I.C. v. Jackson-Shaw Partners No. 46, Ltd. (N.D.Cal. 1994) 790 F.Supp. 987. *PRACTICE AREAS:* Commercial Litigation; Bankruptcy; Environmental Law; Employment Discrimination; Real Estate.

---

## DAVID A. LERMAN

2030 ADDISON STREET, 7TH FLOOR
**BERKELEY, CALIFORNIA 94704**
*Telephone: 510-841-6124*
*Fax: 510-848-0266*

*Labor and Employment Law, Whistleblower Litigation, Wrongful Termination (Plaintiff), Personal Injury, Federal False Claims.*

**DAVID A. LERMAN,** born Detroit, Michigan, May 19, 1963; admitted to bar, 1991, California; 1992, U.S. District Court, Northern District of California. *Education:* University of Michigan (A.B., 1985); Southwestern University School of Law (J.D., 1990). *Member:* Bar Association of San Francisco; State Bar of California (Member, Labor & Employment Section); Barrister's Club; Consumer Attorneys of California. *PRACTICE AREAS:* Employment; Whistleblower Litigation; Wrongful Termination; Personal Injury; Federal False Claims.

---

## LAW OFFICE OF
## STANLEY B. LUBMAN

In Association with Allen & Overy

1422 ARCH STREET
**BERKELEY, CALIFORNIA 94708**
*Telephone: 510-843-8881*
*Fax: 510-843-8882*
*Email: slubman@well.com*

*Associated Hong Kong Office:* Allen & Overy, 9/F, Three Exchange Square, 8 Connaught Place. Telephone: 852.2840.1282. Fax: 852.2840.0515.

*Associated Beijing Office:* Allen & Overy, Jing Guang Centre, Suite 3204, Hu Jia Lou, Chao Yang District, 100020, PRC. Telephone: 86-10-65014681. Fax: 86-10-65014682.

*Associated London Office:* Allen & Overy, One New Change, EC4M 9QQ. Telephone: 44-171-330-3000. Fax: 44-171-330-9999.

*General Business Law, International Law, Trade Law and Investment involving the People's Republic of China.*

*(This Listing Continued)*

---

**STANLEY B. LUBMAN,** born New York, N.Y., March 29, 1934; admitted to bar, 1959, New York; 1971, California; 1974, District of Columbia. *Education:* Columbia University (A.B., 1955; LL.B., 1958; LL.M., 1959; J.S.D., 1969); Institut de Droit Compare, University of Paris (1959-1960); Study of Chinese and research on China under grants from the Rockefeller Foundation, Foreign Area Fellowship Program and Columbia University (1963-1967). Phi Beta Kappa. Law Clerk to Hon. Wilfred Feinberg, U.S. District Court, Southern District of New York, 1961-1962. Visiting Professor: University of Heidelberg, Spring 1993; Stanford University Law School, Spring 1990, 1992; Hart Visiting Lecturer, School of Oriental and African Studies, University of London, Spring 1991; Harvard Law School, Fall 1982, Winter 1984, Spring 1988, 1989. Acting Associate Professor, University of California at Berkeley, 1968-1972. Co-Chair, Committee on the People's Republic of China, American Bar Association, 1977-1984, 1986-1988. Member, Council on Foreign Relations, 1982—. Board Member, National Committee on U.S.-China Relations, 1984-1993. Member, Committee on Legal Educational Exchanges with China, 1982—. *LANGUAGES:* Modern Chinese; French. *PRACTICE AREAS:* Trade and investment matters involving the People's Republic of China.

---

## LAW OFFICES OF
## SUSAN BURNETT LUTEN

Established in 1986

SUITE 401
2140 SHATTUCK AVENUE
**BERKELEY, CALIFORNIA 94704**
*Telephone: 510-548-5500*
*Fax: 510-548-6363*

*Litigation, Rent Control Law and Appeals.*

**SUSAN BURNETT LUTEN,** born Champaign-Urbana, Illinois, January 8, 1950; admitted to bar, 1980, California and U.S. District Court, Northern District of California; 1990, U.S. District Court, Central District of California. *Education:* University of California (B.A., with honors, 1976); University of California, Hastings College of Law (J.D., 1980). Author: "Give Me A Home Where No Salesmen Phone: Telephone Solicitation and the First Amendment," 7 Hastings Constitutional Law Quarterly; California Civil Litigation, West, 1988; California Civil Litigation, Second Edition, West 1993; "Landlord's Forum", Intercity Express, 1992—; "Legal Forum", Apartment Owners' News, 1992—. *Member:* San Francisco, Berkeley-Albany and Alameda County (Board Member, Real Estate Section) Bar Associations; State Bar of California. *REPORTED CASES:* Marani v. Jackson (1986) 183 Cal App. 3d 695; Davis v. City of Berkeley (1990) 51 Cal. 3d 227; City of Berkeley v. City of Berkeley Rent Stabilization Bd. (1994) 27 Cal.App. 4th 951. *PRACTICE AREAS:* Civil Litigation; Rent Control Law; Appellate Law; Real Estate Law; Expert Witness: Landlord-Tenant; Rent Control.

REPRESENTATIVE CLIENTS: Berkeley Property Owners' Association; Civic Bank of Commerce; Sandel Realty; Caspian Associates, Inc.

---

## METHVEN & ASSOCIATES

2232 SIXTH STREET
**BERKELEY, CALIFORNIA 94710**
*Telephone: 510-649-4019*
*Fax: 510-649-4024*
*Email: bmethven@aol.com*
*URL: http://members.aol.com/bmethven*

*Computer, Multimedia and Telecommunications Law, Business Advising, Litigation and Arbitration, Copyright, Trademark and Trade Secret Law, Corporate, Partnership and Limited Liability Company Work, Business Leases.*

FIRM PROFILE: *Methven & Associates was founded by Bruce E. Methven, a graduate of Boalt Hall (U.C. Berkeley's law school). The firm provides a wide range of legal services to businesses. A considerable amount of the work is related to the software, publishing and multimedia industries. Our practice involves drafting, reviewing and negotiating contracts and licenses; securing and litigating copyrights, trade secrets and trademarks; corporate work, partnerships and limited liability companies; business litigation and arbitration; business leases and business advice.*

**BRUCE E. METHVEN,** born Santa Barbara, California, June 5, 1952; admitted to bar, 1980, California and U.S. District Court, Northern and

*(This Listing Continued)*

## METHVEN & ASSOCIATES, Berkeley—Continued

Eastern Districts of California; 1985, U.S. Court of Appeals, Ninth Circuit; 1986, U.S. District Court, Central District of California. *Education:* Massachusetts Institute of Technology; University of California at Berkeley (A.B., 1974); Boalt Hall School of Law, University of California (J.D., 1980). Phi Beta Kappa. Associate Editor, California Law Review, 1978-1980. Author: "First Amendment Standards for Subsequent Punishment of Dissemination of Confidential Information," California Law Review, January 1980, Vol. 68, No. 1; "Copyright Protection for Computer Programs," Silicon Valley Magazine, October, 1983; "Trade Secret Protection for Computer Programs," Silicon Valley Magazine, January, 1984; "Patent Protection for Computer Programs," Silicon Valley Magazine, March/April, 1984; "Creating and Maintaining Trade Secret Protection," VAR Magazine, July and November, 1985; "How to Benefit From Copyright Protection," VAR Magazine, January and February, 1986; "Legal Protection for Trademarks," VAR Magazine, March and April, 1986; "Reorganizing the Financially Distressed Company," VAR Magazine, October, 1986; "Securing the Right to Rents and Profits After Commercial Real Estate Loan Defaults," Lending for the Commercial Banker, Spring, 1987. Member and President, 1988-1991, The High Technology Entrepreneurial Council. Board Member, Junior Achievement of the Bay Area. Chair, Broad Alliance for Multimedia Applications and Technology (Intellectual Property Workgroup). Member, Multimedia Development Group (Capital and Business Solutions). *Member:* Bar Association of San Francisco (Member, Sections on: Computer Law; Commercial Law and Bankruptcy; Corporate Law Department; Intellectual Property); Los Angeles County, Alameda County (Chair, Intellectual Property and Computer Law Committee) and American (Member, Sections on: Business Law; Science and Technology; Patent, Trademark and Copyright Law) Bar Associations; State Bar of California. *PRACTICE AREAS:* Computer/Multimedia Law; Business Litigation. *Email:* bmethven@aol.com

### OF COUNSEL

**FRANK J. GILBERT,** born Chicago, Illinois, December 14, 1960; admitted to bar, 1987, California, U.S. District Court, Northern District of California and U.S. Court of Appeals, 9th Circuit. *Education:* University of Michigan (B.A., 1983); University of San Francisco (J.D., cum laude, 1987). Member, McAuliffe Honor Society. Recipient, American Jurisprudence Award in Civil Procedure. Staff Member, University of San Francisco Law Review, 1985-1987. Teaching Assistant, University of San Francisco Legal Writing Program, 1986. Judicial Extern, Chief Justice Malcolm M. Lucas and Associate Justice, Marcus M. Kaufman, California Supreme Court, 1987. *Member:* Bar Association of San Francisco; State Bar of California; American Bar Association. (Also Associate, Neal & Associates, Oakland, California). *PRACTICE AREAS:* Litigation; Real Estate Law; Business Law.

**LIZABETH SARA CONNOLLY,** born New York, New York, January 18, 1962; admitted to bar, 1987, Connecticut, New York; 1994, California. *Education:* Southern Connecticut State University (B.S., cum laude, in Political Science, 1984); Fordham University School of Law (J.D., 1987); Golden Gate University (LL.M., in Taxation, 1994). *Member:* Bar Association of San Francisco (Member, Estate Planning and Taxation Sections); New York State Bar Association; State Bar of California; TAX AID. *PRACTICE AREAS:* Commercial Litigation; Estate Planning; Taxation.

REPRESENTATIVE CLIENTS: Infotainment World (publisher of Gamepro Magazine and PC Games); National Refractories & Minerals Corporation (Formerly a division of Kaiser Aluminum); Live Oak Multimedia; Southland Associates (software); Knowledge Point (software); Bankers Mutual (loan brokers); Axean Group (network infrastructure); Xinet (Unix/Macintosh connectivity).

## YORK & SMITH
2560 9TH STREET, SUITE 218
**BERKELEY, CALIFORNIA 94710**
Telephone: 510-841-1171
Fax: 510-841-1666

General Civil Appellate and Trial Practice. Insurance, Personal Injury, Business Litigation, Landlord Tenant, Real Property, Construction and Product Liability.

### MEMBERS OF FIRM

**JON H. YORK,** born Washington, D.C., May 21, 1945; admitted to bar, 1971, California. *Education:* Pomona College (A.B., 1967); Boalt Hall School of Law, University of California (J.D., 1970). *Member:* State Bar of California; Association of Defense Counsel of Northern California; Na-
*(This Listing Continued)*

CAA30B

---

tional Lawyers Guild. Diplomate, American Board of Trial Advocacy. (Certified as a Civil Trial Advocate by the National Board of Trial Advocacy.)

**KEVIN M. SMITH,** born Denver, Colorado, March 9, 1954; admitted to bar, 1979, California. *Education:* University of California at Los Angeles (B.A., magna cum laude, 1975); Loyola Marymount University (J.D., cum laude, 1979). *Member:* State Bar of California; Association of Defense Counsel of Northern California. *PRACTICE AREAS:* General Negligence; Professional Negligence (Medical and Legal); Bad Faith Defense.

### ASSOCIATES

**LAURA FISHER PARÉ,** born Lexington, Kentucky, June 30, 1959; admitted to bar, 1990, California, U.S. District Court, Northern District of California and U.S. Court of Appeals, Ninth Circuit. *Education:* Transylvania University (B.A., magna cum laude, 1987); University of San Francisco (J.D., 1990). President and Founder, Employment and Labor Law Society, University of San Francisco. Judicial Extern, Justice Allen Broussard, Supreme Court, California. 1989. *Member:* Alameda County and American Bar Associations; State Bar of California; Association of Defense Counsel of Northern California.

**MARGARET J. ALLEN,** born Englewood, New Jersey, July 28, 1952; admitted to bar, 1984, California and U.S. District Court, Northern, Eastern and Central Districts of California. *Education:* Smith College (B.A., 1974); Golden Gate University (J.D., cum laude, 1984). Editor, Golden Gate University Law Review, 1983-1984. *Member:* Bar Association of San Francisco; American Bar Association. *PRACTICE AREAS:* Bankruptcy; Civil Litigation.

**JAMES P. MOLINELLI, JR.,** born San Francisco, California, August 14, 1963; admitted to bar, 1990, California. *Education:* University of Santa Clara (B.S., 1985); University of San Francisco (J.D., 1990). Research Attorney, San Francisco Superior Court, Law and Motion Department, 1990-1991. *Member:* Bar Association of San Francisco; State Bar of California; Association of Defense Counsel of Northern California.

**JOSÉ A. TABUENA,** born Philippines, June 4, 1962; admitted to bar, 1988, California. *Education:* University of California at San Diego (B.A., cum laude, 1984; M.A., 1985); University of California, Berkeley (J.D., 1988). *Member:* State Bar of California; Association of Defense Counsel of Northern California.

REPRESENTATIVE CLIENTS: State Farm Mutual Automobile Insurance Company; State Farm Fire and Casualty Company; Fire Insurance Exchange; Farmers Insurance Exchange; Truck Insurance Exchange; Homestead Insurance; California State Automobile Association.

## ROBERT A. ADELMAN,
*A LAW CORPORATION*
Established in 1975
**9454 WILSHIRE BOULEVARD
SUITE PH-29
BEVERLY HILLS, CALIFORNIA 90212-2937**
Telephone: 310-858-1201
Fax: 310-858-6558

*Family Law.*

**ROBERT A. ADELMAN,** born Los Angeles, California, March 17, 1950; admitted to bar, 1975, California; 1976, U.S. District Court, Central District of California and U.S. Court of Appeals, Ninth Circuit; 1978, U.S. District Court, Southern District of California; 1979, U.S. Supreme Court. *Education:* University of California at Los Angeles (B.A., cum laude, 1972); Loyola University School of Law (J.D., cum laude, 1975). Senior Adjunct Professor of Evidence Law, University of La Verne School of Law, 1988—. Judge Pro Tem, Family Law Court, 1992—. Arbitrator and Mediator, Family Law Court, 1985—. *Member:* Beverly Hills (Member, Family Law Section), Los Angeles County (Member, Family Law Section) and American (Member, Family Law Section) Bar Associations; State Bar of California (Member, Family Law Section). (Certified Specialist, Family Law, The State Bar of California Board of Legal Specialization). *PRACTICE AREAS:* Family Law; Dissolution of Marriage; Spousal and Child Support; Child Custody; Valuation of Marital Assets; Pre and Post-Nuptial Agreements; Paternity Cases.

REFERENCE: City National Bank.

## HONEY KESSLER AMADO

261 SOUTH WETHERLY DRIVE
**BEVERLY HILLS, CALIFORNIA 90211**
Telephone: 310-550-8214
Fax: 310-274-7384

*Civil Appeals with Emphasis in Family Law.*

**FIRM PROFILE:** Ms. Amado Lectures and Authors extensively on topics of Appellate Practice and Family Law.

**HONEY KESSLER AMADO,** born Brooklyn, New York, July 20, 1949; admitted to bar, 1977, California; 1981, U.S. Court of Appeals, Ninth Circuit; 1994, U.S. Supreme Court. *Education:* California State University, Long Beach (B.A., 1971); Western State University (J.D., 1976). Los Angeles County Bar Association (Member, Family Law Section 1982—, Appellate Courts Committee, 1987—, Appellate Judicial Evaluations Committee, 1992—; Editorial Board, Los Angeles Lawyer Magazine, 1996—); California State Bar (Family Law Section, Executive Committee 1988-1991; California Women Lawyers. **REPORTED CASES:** In re Marriage of Stephenson (1984) 162 Cal.App.3d 1057. In re Marriage of Gavron (1988) 203 Cal.App.3d 705. Posey v. Leavitt (1991) 229 Cal.App. 1236, 280; People v. DeLeon (1994) 22 Cal. Rep. 4th 1265. In re Marriage of Battenburg (1994) 28 Cal.App.4th 1336. In re Marriage of Hargrave (1995) 36 Cal.App.4th 1313. **PRACTICE AREAS:** Civil Appeals.

## LAW OFFICE OF
## EMMA H. BALLESTEROS

Established in 1992

433 NORTH CAMDEN DRIVE, SUITE 600
**BEVERLY HILLS, CALIFORNIA 90210**
Telephone: 310-288-1829
Fax: 310-273-6329

*General, Civil and Trial Practice.*

**FIRM PROFILE:** Founded in 1992, Serves L.A., Orange and Riverside Counties. Firm is very active in professional association activities and civic affairs.

**EMMA H. BALLESTEROS,** born Philippines, August 30; admitted to bar, 1992, California and U.S. District Court, Central District of California. *Education:* California State Polytechnic University (M.B.A., 1984); Western State University (J.D., 1991); University of Santo Tomas, Philippines (Chem. Engineering). *Member:* Beverly Hills, Los Angeles County, Orange County and San Gabriel Valley Bar Associations; State Bar of California. **LANGUAGES:** Tagalog. **PRACTICE AREAS:** Estate Planning; Family Law; Civil Litigation; Immigration; Personal Injury; Negligence Litigation; Bankruptcy.

## BEIGEL LASKY RIFKIND FERTIK GELBER & WHITE

A Partnership including a Professional Corporation

Established in 1984

9952 SANTA MONICA BOULEVARD
**BEVERLY HILLS, CALIFORNIA 90212**
Telephone: 310-843-9300
Facsimile: 310-843-0303

*Chicago, Illinois Office:* 250 South Wacker Drive, Suite 1500. Telephone: 312-466-9444. Fax: 312-466-0347.

*New York, N.Y. Office:* 750 Lexington Avenue, 30th Floor. Telephone: 212-705-5300. Fax: 212-826-1580.

*Business and Securities Litigation, Toxic Tort, Product Liability and Tax Litigation, Criminal Defense, Corporate and Transactional Matters, Bankruptcy, Estate Planning and International Law, Environmental Law, Contract Litigation and Entertainment Contract Negotiation.*

(For Complete Biographical Data on all Personnel, see New York, N.Y. Professional Biographies)

## JONATHAN W. BIDDLE

SUITE 750 THE WILSHIRE SAN VICENTE PLAZA
8383 WILSHIRE BOULEVARD
**BEVERLY HILLS, CALIFORNIA 90211**
Telephone: 213-653-4713
Telefax: 213-852-1310

*General Civil Practice before State and Federal Courts. Labor and Employment Law.*

**JONATHAN W. BIDDLE,** born Bryn Mawr, Pennsylvania, February 17, 1946; admitted to bar, 1975, California. *Education:* University of Colorado (B.A., 1969); Southwestern University School of Law (J.D., 1975). Author: "Litigating Wrongful Discharge Charge Claims," Employment and Labor Law Institute, University of California and University of Houston Law Foundation, 1992. Co-author: *Employment Discrimination Handbook,* Matthew Bender, 1992; "Public Policy Wrongful Termination Action," Los Angeles Lawyer Magazine, October, 1992; *The Immigration Reform & Control Act Handbook* Parker & Sons, 1992, 2d. Ed., 1990; California Continuing Education of the Bar Publications, 1984—. Labor and Commercial Arbitration Panel, American Arbitration Association. *Member:* Los Angeles County (Labor and Employment Law Section, Executive Committee) and American (Labor and Employment Law Section) Bar Associations; State Bar of California (Labor and Employment Section, Executive Committee). **PRACTICE AREAS:** General Civil Practice before State and Federal Courts; Labor Law; Employment Law.

REFERENCE: Bank of America.

## BLOOM, HERGOTT, COOK, DIEMER & KLEIN, LLP

150 SOUTH RODEO DRIVE
THIRD FLOOR
**BEVERLY HILLS, CALIFORNIA 90212**
Telephone: 310-859-6800
Omnifax: 310-859-2788

*Entertainment Law, General Business, Corporate.*

### MEMBERS OF FIRM

**JACOB A. BLOOM,** born Brooklyn, New York, April 10, 1942; admitted to bar, 1968, California. *Education:* Columbia University (B.A., 1963); Cornell University (LL.B., 1966). Moot Court Champion. *Member:* State Bar of California.

**ALAN S. HERGOTT,** born Chicago, Illinois, January 19, 1950; admitted to bar, 1975, Illinois; 1976, California. *Education:* The University of Michigan (A.B., with high distinction, 1972); Northwestern University (J.D., 1975). Senior Editor, Journal of Criminal Law and Criminology, 1974-1975. Author: "Supreme Court Review: Obscenity," 65 Journal of Criminal Law and Criminology 499, 1974. *Member:* Beverly Hills and Illinois State Bar Associations; State Bar of California.

**LAWRENCE H. GREAVES,** born Dallas, Texas, November 26, 1951; admitted to bar, 1977, California. *Education:* Harvard University (A.B., cum laude, 1974); University of Munich, Germany; University of Texas (J.D., 1977). Research Editor, Texas Law Review, 1976-1977. *Member:* Los Angeles County and American Bar Associations; State Bar of California.

**CANDICE S. HANSON,** born Calgary, Alberta, 1953; admitted to bar, 1978, California and Ontario, Canada. *Education:* University of British Columbia, Canada; University of Toronto, Canada; Osgoode Hall, Toronto, Canada (LL.B., 1976). *Member:* State Bar of California; American Bar Association (Member, Forum Committee on Entertainment and Sports Industries, Patent, Trademark and Copyright Law Section, 1978-1982); Canadian-American Bar Association (Director, 1985).

**MELANIE K. COOK,** born Salt Lake City, Utah, June 3, 1953; admitted to bar, 1979, California. *Education:* University of California at Los Angeles (B.S., magna cum laude, 1974; J.D., 1978). Phi Beta Kappa; Order of the Coif. Member, 1976-1977 and Book Review Editor, Board of Editors, 1977-1978, University of California at Los Angeles Law Review. Author: "Moving to a New Beat: Copyright Protection for Choreographic Works," 24 UCLA Law Review 1287, 1977. Winner, University of California at Los Angeles, Nathan Burkan Memorial Copyright Competition, 1977. *Member:* Beverly Hills, Los Angeles County and American Bar Associations; State Bar of California.

*(This Listing Continued)*

## BLOOM, HERGOTT, COOK, DIEMER & KLEIN, LLP, Beverly Hills—Continued

**TINA J. KAHN,** born Los Angeles, California, January 4, 1954; admitted to bar, 1982, California. *Education:* University of California (B.A., summa cum laude, 1975); University of Chicago (M.A., 1977); Northwestern University (J.D.,1981). Pi Gamma Mu; Phi Beta Kappa. Symposium Editor, Northwestern Journal of International Law of Business, 1980-1981. *Member:* Los Angeles County and American Bar Associations; State Bar of California.

**THOMAS F. HUNTER, JR.,** born Painesville, Ohio, December 10, 1951; admitted to bar, 1982, California; 1983, U.S. District Court, Central District of California and U.S. Court of Appeals, Ninth Circuit. *Education:* Hiram College; University of Houston (B.A., summa cum laude, 1979); University of Texas (J.D., with honors, 1982). *Member:* Beverly Hills (Member, Entertainment Law Section) and Los Angeles County (Member, Intellectual Property Section) Bar Associations; The State Bar of California (Member, Patent, Trademark and Copyright Section).

**JOHN D. DIEMER,** born Los Angeles, California, November 20, 1953; admitted to bar, 1980, California. *Education:* University of California at Santa Cruz; University of California at Los Angeles (B.A., magna cum laude, 1976); University of California at Los Angeles School of Law (J.D., 1980). Member, University of California at Los Angeles Law Review, 1978-1979. *Member:* Beverly Hills and Los Angeles County Bar Associations; State Bar of California.

**STEPHEN D. BARNES,** born Los Angeles, California, May 29, 1953; admitted to bar, 1981, District of Columbia; 1987, California. *Education:* University of Southern California (B.A., English, 1978); Harvard University (J.D., 1981). Senior Developments Editor, Harvard Journal of International Law, 1981. Author: "Panama Canals; Implementing Legislation - The Panama Canal Act of 1979," 21 Harvard International Law Journal 283 (1980). *Member:* The District of Columbia Bar; State Bar of California.

**STUART M. ROSENTHAL,** born River Edge, New Jersey, August 16, 1957; admitted to bar, 1985, California. *Education:* University of California at Berkeley (A.B., 1979); University of California at Los Angeles (J.D./M.B.A., 1984). *Member:* Beverly Hills, Los Angeles County and American Bar Associations; State Bar of California.

**LEIGH C. BRECHEEN,** born Phoenix, Arizona, February 4, 1955; admitted to bar, 1979, Arizona and U.S. District Court, District of Arizona; 1981, California; 1986, New York. *Education:* University of Arizona; Mills College (B.A., 1976); Arizona State University (J.D., cum laude, 1978). Topics Editor, Arizona State University Law Journal, 1977-1978. Author: "Advertiser Produced Programming: An Old Idea Whose Time Has Come," Television Syndication: A Practical Guide to Business and Legal Issues, 1987 LA Bar Association. Co-Author: "Arizona Probate Code Practice Manual," 1980; "The Client: Income and Estate; Tax Aspects of Moving To Or From a Community Property State," Taxation for Accountants Magazine, 1980. Member: UCLA Entertainment Symposium Steering Committee, 1990; Women in Film; Hollywood Radio and Television Society. *Member:* New York State and American Bar Associations; State Bar of Arizona; State Bar of California.

**STEPHEN F. BREIMER,** born New York, N.Y., December 6, 1950; admitted to bar, 1985, California. *Education:* Stanford University (B.A., with honors, 1972); University of California at Los Angeles (J.D., 1985). Phi Delta Phi. Member, U.C.L.A. Moot Court Honors Program, 1984-1985. Member, Federal Communications Law Journal, 1983-1985. Comments Editor, University of California, 1984-1985. Author: "The Financial Interest and Syndication Rules: An Analysis of the FCC's Controversial Proposal for Repeal," Entertainment, Publishing and the Arts Handbook, 1984; "Copyrighting Literary and Visual Characters: A Picture is Worth a Thousand Words," Entertainment, Publishing and the Arts Handbook, 1986. *Member:* Beverly Hills, Los Angeles County and American Bar Associations; State Bar of California.

**DEBORAH L. KLEIN,** born May 7, 1960; admitted to bar, 1985, California. *Education:* University of California, Berkeley (B.S., 1982); University of Southern California (J.D., 1985). Phi Beta Kappa; Beta Gamma Sigma. Member, Moot Court Honors Program. *Member:* Beverly Hills, Los Angeles County and American Bar Associations; State Bar of California.

**STEVEN L. BROOKMAN,** born Passaic, New Jersey, May 2, 1959; admitted to bar, 1985, California. *Education:* Colgate University (B.A., cum laude, 1981); University of California at Berkeley (J.D., 1984). *Member:* State Bar of California.

*(This Listing Continued)*

**JOHN S. LAVIOLETTE,** born New Haven, Connecticut, July 10, 1957; admitted to bar, 1986, California. *Education:* Yale University (B.A., 1979); University of Southern California (J.D., 1986). *Member:* State Bar of California.

**ROBYN L. ROTH,** born Los Angeles, California, March 12, 1964; admitted to bar, 1989, California. *Education:* University of California at Los Angeles (B.A., summa cum laude, 1985); Harvard Law School (J.D., 1988). Phi Beta Kappa; Chancellor's Scholar. *Member:* Beverly Hills (Member, Executive Committee, Entertainment Law Section) and Los Angeles (Member, Executive Committee, Intellectual Property and Entertainment Law Section) Bar Associations; State Bar of California.

**RICHARD D. THOMPSON,** born Lexington, Kentucky, August 14, 1955; admitted to bar, 1980, California. *Education:* Harvard University (A.B., summa cum laude, 1977); Stanford University (J.D., 1980). Phi Beta Kappa; Order of the Coif. *Member:* Los Angeles County Bar Association; State Bar of California; Los Angeles Copyright Society (Trustee and Treasurer).

**JONATHAN K. BLAUFARB,** born Alexandria, Virginia, March 20, 1957; admitted to bar, 1984, California. *Education:* University of California at Berkeley (B.A., with distinction, 1979); Hastings College of Law, University of California (J.D., 1984). Staff Member, 1982-1983 and Associate Research Editor, 1983-1984, Comm/Ent- Hastings Journal of Communications and Entertainment Law. Author: Note, "The Seven-Year Itch: California Labor Code Section 2855," Comm/Ent-Hastings Journal of Communications and Entertainment Law, Vol. 6, No. 3, Spring, 1984; "Legislative Developments Affecting the Mid-Term Renegotiation of Recording Contracts Under California Labor Code Section 2855," 1986 Entertainment Publishing and the Arts Handbook, Clark-Boardman. Assistant Editor, "The Musician's Manual—Practical Career Guide," Beverly Hills Bar Association Barristers Committee for the Arts, rev. ed., 1986. *Member:* Beverly Hills and Los Angeles County Bar Associations; State Bar of California; California Copyright Conference.

**DAVID B. FELDMAN,** born Los Angeles, California, August 16, 1959; admitted to bar, 1990, California and U.S. District Court, Central District of California. *Education:* University of California at Berkeley (B.S., cum laude, 1981); Boalt Hall School of Law, University of California (J.D., 1990). Associate Editor, California Law Review, 1989-1990. Author: Note, "Finding a Home For Fictional Characters: A Proposal For Change in Copyright Protection," California Law Review, May, 1990. *Member:* Beverly Hills Bar Association; State Bar of California.

### ASSOCIATES

**ROGER L. PATTON, JR.,** born Elizabeth, New Jersey, September 2, 1963; admitted to bar, 1988, Maryland and New Jersey; 1989, District of Columbia; 1990, U.S. Court of Appeals, 11th Circuit; 1991, California. *Education:* Yale University (B.A., 1985); Harvard University (J.D., 1988). Notes Editor, Harvard Law Review, 1986-1988. Author: Case Comment, "McClesky v. Kemp," 101 Harvard Law Review 451, 1989. *Member:* State Bar of California.

**ROBERT OFFER,** born Los Angeles, California, November 21, 1964; admitted to bar, 1992, California. *Education:* Tufts University (B.S., magna cum laude, 1986); University of California, Los Angeles (J.D., 1992). Order of the Coif. *Member:* State Bar of California.

**THOMAS B. COLLIER,** born Elizabeth City, North Carolina, January 31, 1966; admitted to bar, 1993, California. *Education:* University of North Carolina at Chapel Hill (B.A., with highest distinction, 1988); University of Chicago Law School (J.D., with highest honors, 1991). Phi Beta Kappa; Order of the Coif. Member, 1989-1990 and Associate Comment Editor, 1990-1991, University of Chicago Law Review. Law Clerk, Honorable Frank H. Easterbrook, United States Court of Appeals for the Seventh Circuit, 1991-1992. *Member:* State Bar of California.

**DAVID E. WEBER,** born Los Angeles, California, July 27, 1960; admitted to bar, 1986, California. *Education:* Stanford University (A.B., 1982); University of Southern California (J.D., 1986). *Member:* Century City, Beverly Hills and Los Angeles County Bar Associations; State Bar of California.

**ERIC M. BROOKS,** born Philadelphia, Pennsylvania, June 14, 1963; admitted to bar, 1991, California and U.S. District Court, Central District of California. *Education:* Yale University (A.B., cum laude, 1984); Boalt Hall School of Law, University of California (J.D., 1990). Member and Editor, California Law Review, 1988-1990. Author: Comment, "Site-Specific Art and Moral Rights," 77 California Law Review 1431, 1989.

*(This Listing Continued)*

*Member:* Los Angeles County, Beverly Hills and American Bar Association; State Bar of California. *PRACTICE AREAS:* Entertainment Law.

**MICHAEL L. SCHENKMAN,** born Los Angeles, California, July 24, 1965; admitted to bar, 1990, California. *Education:* Stanford University (B.A., Phi Beta Kappa, 1987; M.A., 1987); Boalt Hall School of Law (J.D., 1990). *Member:* Beverly Hills, Beverly Hills and American Bar Associations; State Bar of California. *PRACTICE AREAS:* Entertainment Law.

## ELI BLUMENFELD LAW CORPORATION

*Established in 1976*

**433 NORTH CAMDEN DRIVE, SUITE 900**
**BEVERLY HILLS, CALIFORNIA 90210**
*Telephone: 310-205-0800*
*FAX: 310-888-1120*

*Tax Litigation (Civil and Criminal), Tax and Estate Planning.*

**ELI BLUMENFELD,** born New York, N.Y., May 17, 1933; admitted to bar, 1964, California, U.S. Tax Court, U.S. District Court, Eastern and Central Districts of California and U.S. Court of Appeals, Ninth Circuit; 1976, U.S. Supreme Court. *Education:* University of California at Los Angeles (B.S., with honors, 1958; J.D., 1963). Phi Alpha Delta. Certified Public Accountant, California, 1960. Former Trial Attorney, Internal Revenue Service and by Special Appointment, Department of Justice. *Member:* Beverly Hills (Member, Section on Taxation), Los Angeles County (Member, Section on Taxation) and Federal Bar Associations; State Bar of California (Member, Section on Taxation). (Certified Specialist, Taxation Law, The State Bar of California Board of Legal Specialization).

REFERENCE: Union Bank (Century City Office).

## LAW OFFICE OF
## MARK E. BOWERS

**9777 WILSHIRE BOULEVARD, SUITE 512**
**BEVERLY HILLS, CALIFORNIA 90212-1905**
*Telephone: 310-275-3591*
*Fax: 310-275-4690*
*Email: markebowers@earthlink.com*

*Tax, Real Estate, Business, Corporate and Securities Law, International Business Transactions.*

*FIRM PROFILE: Mark E. Bowers is a seasoned attorney with tax, international law and employee benefits experience gained through practice as corporate counsel, law firm partner and sole practitioner, capable of handling complex legal matters alone or as a team player. Mr. Bowers has written and lectured extensively on the topics of tax and business law.*

**MARK E. BOWERS,** born Abilene, Texas, July 29, 1948; admitted to bar, 1973, Texas; 1976, California. *Education:* Southern Methodist University (B.B.A., 1969); University of Texas (J.D., 1972). *Member:* Beverly Hills, Los Angeles and American (Member, Sections on: Real Estate; Tax) Bar Associations; State Bar of Texas; State Bar of California.

REPRESENTATIVE CLIENTS: Century Pacific Holdings, LLC; Wire One, LLC.

## PHYLLIS R. BROURMAN

**315 S. BEVERLY DRIVE, SUITE 315**
**BEVERLY HILLS, CALIFORNIA 90212-4390**
*Telephone: 310-557-9911; 277-2323*
*Fax: 310-556-2308*

*Family Law.*

**PHYLLIS R. BROURMAN,** born Pittsburgh, Pennsylvania; admitted to bar, 1984, California. *Education:* University of Pittsburgh (B.S., magna cum laude, 1951); Loyola University of Los Angeles (J.D., 1983). *Member:* Beverly Hills, Los Angeles County and American Bar Associations; State Bar of California (Member, Family Law Section). (Certified Specialist, Family Law, The State Bar of California Board of Legal Specialization). *LANGUAGES:* Spanish.

## BROWNE & WOODS LLP

**450 NORTH ROXBURY DRIVE, 7TH FLOOR**
**BEVERLY HILLS, CALIFORNIA 90210**
*Telephone: 310-274-7100*
*Telecopier: 310-275-5697*

*General Civil Trial and Appellate Practice in all State and Federal Courts with emphasis on Competitive Business Practices, Unfair Competition, Trade Secrets, Business Torts, Defamation, Entertainment Litigation and Insurance Litigation.*

### MEMBERS OF FIRM

**ALLAN BROWNE,** born Los Angeles, California, May 29, 1938; admitted to bar, 1964, California; 1972, U.S. Supreme Court. *Education:* University of California at Los Angeles (B.A., 1960); University of Southern California (LL.B., 1963). Phi Alpha Delta; Order of the Coif; Phi Kappa Phi. Member, Board of Editors, 1961-1962 and Editor in Chief, 1962-1963, Southern California Law Review. Author: "The 'Right' to an Attorney's Fee and Other Sanctions in Discovery Proceedings," 1 Journal of the Beverly Hills Bar Association (No. 1) 15; "Proving Up 'Good Cause' in Discovery Proceedings," 1 Journal of the Beverly Hills Bar Association (No. 4) 7; "The Bill of Particulars-A Neglected Discovery Aid," 3 Journal of the Beverly Hills Bar Association (No. 8) 11; "Compelling Discovery and Obtaining Sanctions," California Continuing Education of the Bar, 1973; "Advising Clients Regarding Liability For Unfair Competition," 48 California State Bar Journal No. 5, 542; "Effective Use of Covenants Not to Compete," 3 University of San Fernando Law Review, No. 2, 33; "Unfair Competition: Preventive Planning and Litigation," 1975, California Continuing Education of the Bar; "Compelling Discovery and Obtaining Sanctions," (Chapter 3), "Bill of Particulars," (Chapter 12) and "California Civil Discovery Practice," 1975, California Continuing Education of the Bar; "Guarding Against Unfair Competition and Business Piracy through Preventive Law," 51 Los Angeles Bar Journal, No. 4, 153; "Discovery Procedures in Federal Civil Practice," 1976, California Continuing Education of the Bar; "Trade Secrets and Unfair Competition," 1977, California Continuing Education of the Bar; "Actionable Unfair Competition: Prevention and Litigation," 12 Beverly Hills Bar Association Journal, 169; "Trade Secrets and Unfair Competition" (Supplement), California Continuing Education of the Bar, 1978; "Unfair Competition and Trade Secrets-Problems and Remedies," California Continuing Education of the Bar, 1979; "How to Win an Unfair Competition Lawsuit," 2 Los Angeles Lawyer 44, 1979. Assistant Editor, Beverly Hills Bar Association Journal, 1969-1971. Editor: Attorney's Guide to the Law of Competitive Business Practices; California Continuing Education of the Bar, 1981; Supplement to Attorney's Guide to the Law of Competitive Business Practices, California Continuing Education of the Bar, 1982-1995; "Bad Faith After Moradi-Shalal," Vol. 11, No. 11, Los Angeles Lawyer 32, February, 1989; "Do's and Don'ts in Jury Selection," Vol. 11, No. 11, Los Angeles Lawyer 17, February, 1989. "The Delicate Art of Cross Examination," California Lawyer No. 4, April 1985. Planner, Editor and Contributing Author: Competitive Business Practices (Second Edition), Calif. Cont. Educ. of the Bar, 1991; "Direct and Cross-Examination of Celebrity Witnesses," Vol. 16, No. 7, Los Angeles Lawyer, Oct. 1993; "Are Business Torts an Endangered Species?" Los Angeles Lawyer, Vol. 32, No. 4, 1996. Judge Pro Tem, Beverly Hills Municipal Court, 1972-1976. President, 1973-1974 and Ex-Officio Member Board of Governors, 1975-1995, Association of Business Trial Lawyers. Arbitrator, per California Judicial Arbitration Statute, Chapter 743, 1978-1995. Delegate to State Bar Convention, Beverly Hills Bar Association, 1974-1979. Arbitrator, Los Angeles Superior Court, 1979-1980. Member, Trial Practice Committee, California Continuing Education of the Bar, 1974-1976. Member, California Council on Criminal Justice, California State Senate Subcommittee, 1981. Chairperson and Member of Los Angeles County Bar Committee to Study the Commission on Judicial Performance, 1981-1982. Director and Member of Planning Committee for Continuing Education of the Bar Institute on Competitive Business Practices, 1981-1982. Member, Telephonic Law and Motion Committee, ad hoc, Superior Court Judges and Bar Members Committee, 1982. Chairman, Institute for Competitive Business Practices, California Continuing Education of the Bar, 1982. Referee, Los Angeles Superior Court, 1982. California Senate Appointees to the Simon Wiesenthal Center Museum Advisory Committee, 1988. Arbitrator, Los Angeles County Superior Court 1994-1996). *Member:* Beverly Hills (Resolutions Committee; Chairman: Judiciary, Practice and Procedure Committee; TV Related Committee; Program Committee; Member, Board of Governors, 1977-1979); Los Angeles County (Member, Board of Trustees) and American (Member, Litigation Section) Bar Associations; State Bar of California. *PRACTICE AREAS:* General Civil; Trial; Appellate Practice; Unfair Competitive Business Practices.

*(This Listing Continued)*

## BROWNE & WOODS LLP, Beverly Hills—Continued

**EDWARD A. WOODS,** born Los Angeles, California, October 4, 1946; admitted to bar, 1972, California and U.S. District Court, Central District of California; U.S. Supreme Court; U.S. Court of Appeals, Ninth Circuit; U.S. District Court, Northern District of California. *Education:* University of California at Berkeley and University of California at Los Angeles (B.A., 1968); University of California at Los Angeles (J.D., 1972). Order of the Coif. Member, University of California at Los Angeles Law Review, 1970-1971. Co-Author: "Antitrust," Competitive Business Practices, California Continuing Education of the Bar, 1981. *Member:* State Bar of California; American Bar Association (Member, Litigation Section); Association of Business Trial Lawyers.

**MARCY RAILSBACK,** born New York, N.Y., November 14, 1952; admitted to bar, 1978, California, U.S. District Court, Central District of California and U.S. Court of Appeals, Ninth Circuit. *Education:* San Diego State University (B.A., with high honors, 1974) Phi Kappa Phi; Hastings College of Law, University of California (J.D., 1978). Member: Thurston Society; Order of the Coif. Associate Research Editor, Hastings Law Journal, 1977-1978. Co-Author: "Availability of Preliminary Relief," Chapter 2, Competitive Business Practices, California Continuing Education of the Bar, 2nd Edition. *Member:* Beverly Hills, Los Angeles County and American (Member, Litigation Section) Bar Associations; State Bar of California; Association of Business Trial Lawyers.

**BENJAMIN D. SCHEIBE,** born Washington, D.C., June 27, 1956; admitted to bar, 1981, California; 1982, U.S. District Court, Northern, Central and Eastern Districts of California. *Education:* University of California at Berkeley (A.B., 1978) Psi Chi; University of California at Los Angeles (J.D., 1981). Order of the Coif. Member, UCLA Law Review, 1980-1981. Co-Author: "Trade Secrets," Chapter 4, Competitive Business Practices, California Continuing Education of the Bar, 2d ed., 1991. Author: "Sworn to Secrecy", Vol. 18, No. 3, Los Angeles Lawyer 40, 1995; "The Constitutional Defense of Opinion", Vol. 14, No. 2, Los Angeles Lawyer 36, 1992. *Member:* Beverly Hills, Los Angeles County and American (Chairman, Committee on Intellectual Property, Tort and Insurance Practice Section, 1989-1990; Vice-Chairman, Committee on Intellectual Property, Tort and Insurance Section, 1988-1989, 1991-1992) Bar Associations; State Bar of California; Association of Business Trial Lawyers.

**ALLEN B. GRODSKY,** born Los Angeles, California, April 25, 1959; admitted to bar, 1983, California; 1984, U.S. Court of Appeals, Fifth and Ninth Circuits and U.S. District Court, Central and Northern Districts of California. *Education:* University of California at Santa Barbara (B.A., 1980); Leningrad State University, Leningrad, USSR (1979-1980); University of California at Berkeley (J.D., 1983). Author: "Recent Developments in Intellectual Property Law," 27 Tort and Insurance Law Journal 310; "Intellectual Property Law: New Developments," 25 Tort and Insurance Law Journal 329. Co-Author: "Antitrust," Chapter 5, Competitive Business Practices, California Continuing Education of the Bar, 1991. Law Clerk to the Hon. Thomas G. Gee, U.S. Court of Appeals for the Fifth Circuit. *Member:* Los Angeles County, Beverly Hills and American (Vice Chairman, Committee on Intellectual Property, Tort and Insurance Section, 1989-1990) Bar Associations; State Bar of California.

**PETER W. ROSS,** born New York, N.Y., May 13, 1958; admitted to bar, 1983, California and U.S. District Court, Central District of California. *Education:* Carleton College (B.A., magna cum laude, 1980); Stanford University (J.D., 1983). Phi Beta Kappa. Co-Author: "Trade Secrets," Chapter 4, *Attorney's Guide to the Law of Competitive Business Practices,* California Continuing Education of the Bar, (2d Ed.) 1991. *Member:* Los Angeles County Bar Association; State Bar of California.

**ROBERT B. BROADBELT,** born Fontana, California, November 11, 1959; admitted to bar, 1984, California, U.S. Court of Appeals, Ninth Circuit and U.S. District Court, Northern, Eastern and Central Districts of California; U.S. Supreme Court. *Education:* University of California at Berkeley (A.B., with honors, 1981); University of Southern California Law Center (J.D., 1984). Co-Author: "Competitive Business Practices," California Continuing Education of the Bar, 1991. *Member:* State Bar of California.

**JON M. LEADER,** born Holyoke, Massachusetts, June 30, 1961; admitted to bar, 1987, Colorado, U.S. District Court, District of Colorado and U.S. Court of Appeals, Tenth Circuit; 1990, California and U.S. District Court, Central District of California; U.S. Court of Appeals, Ninth Circuit. *Education:* Tulane University (B.A., 1983); George Washington University (J.D., 1986). Co-Author: Attorney's Guide To The Law of Competitive Business Practices, California Continuing Education Of The Bar. *Member:* Colorado and American Bar Associations; State Bar of California; Association of Business Trial Lawyers.

**MICHAEL J. OLECKI,** born Garfield Heights, Ohio, February 25, 1959; admitted to bar, 1988, California, U.S. District Court, Central, Northern, Southern and Eastern Districts of California and U.S. Court of Appeals, Ninth Circuit. *Education:* Haverford College (B.A., 1981); University of Virginia (J.D., 1986). Order of the Coif. Member, 1984-1985, and Notes Editor, 1985-1986, University of Virginia Law Review. Law Clerk to Hon. Edward N. Cahn, U.S. District Court, Eastern District of Pennsylvania, 1986-1987. Co-Author: Attorney's Guide To The Law of Competitive Practices, California Continuing Education Of The Bar. Arbitrator, Los Angeles Superior Court Arbitration Panel. *Member:* Beverly Hills, Los Angeles County and American Bar Associations; State Bar of California; Association of Business Trial Lawyers.

### ASSOCIATES

**JAMES D. KOZMOR,** born Bayonne, New Jersey, October 3, 1968; admitted to bar, 1993, California, U.S. District Court, Central District of California and U.S. Court of Appeals, Ninth Circuit; 1996, U.S. District Court, Northern District of California. *Education:* Columbia University (A.B., 1990); U.C.L.A. School of Law (J.D., 1993). Member, 1991-1992 and Editor, 1992-1993, U.C.L.A. Law Review. Co-Author: "Attorney's Guide to the Law of Competitive Business Practice," Continuing Education of the Bar. *Member:* State Bar of California.

**MILES J. FELDMAN,** born Danville, New Jersey, December 24, 1965; admitted to bar, 1994, California, U.S. District Court, Southern District of California and U.S. Court of Appeals, Ninth Circuit. *Education:* University of California, Berkeley (B.A., with honors); Boalt Hall School of Law, University of California (J.D., 1994). Moot Court Board. Editor, High Technology Law Journal. Extern to the Hon. D. Lowell Jensen, U.S. District Court, San Francisco, Northern District of California (Fall 1993). Author: "Towards a Clearer Standard of Protectable Information: Trade Secrets and Employment Relationship" 9:1 High Technology Law Journal 151, 1994, 27 Intellectual Property Law Review 477, 1995. Co-Author: "Attorney's Guide to the Law of Competitive Business Practices," Continuing Education of the Bar. *Member:* Los Angeles and American Bar Associations; State Bar of California.

**ELLA MARIE MARTINSEN,** born Manhattan Beach, California, February 19, 1969; admitted to bar, 1994, California. *Education:* University of California at Los Angeles (A.B., cum laude, 1991; J.D., 1994). Moot Court Honor Roll. Member, Moot Court Advisory Board. *Member:* State Bar of California. *PRACTICE AREAS:* Civil Litigation.

---

## CHALEFF & ENGLISH
### BEVERLY HILLS, CALIFORNIA
(See Santa Monica)

*Criminal and Juvenile Law Practice.*

---

## LAW OFFICES OF
## CHARLES P. CHARLTON

**9454 WILSHIRE BOULEVARD, SUITE 500**
**BEVERLY HILLS, CALIFORNIA 90212-2908**
Telephone: 310-471-5365
Fax: 310-471-5374
Email: cpclaw@aol.com

*Personal Injury, Wrongful Death, Products Liability, Civil Trial Practice, Medical Malpractice and Appellate Practice.*

**CHARLES P. CHARLTON,** born Chicago, Illinois, June 1, 1948; admitted to bar, 1986, California; U.S. District Court, Northern, Central and Southern Districts of California. *Education:* University of California at Los Angeles (B.A., 1974); Western State University at Fullerton (J.D., 1978). Phi Alpha Delta. Editorial Board Member, Western State University Law Review, 1977-1978. Author: "Civil Discovery and Self-Incrimination," Advocate, March, 1995. *Member:* Los Angeles County Bar Association; State

*(This Listing Continued)*

Bar of California (Member, Litigation Section); Consumer Attorneys of Los Angeles (Member, Education Section); Consumer Attorneys Association of California; The Association of Trial Lawyers of America. [With U.S. Army, 1967-1970]

## DINA B. CHERNICK

SUITE 150, 369 SOUTH DOHENY DRIVE
**BEVERLY HILLS, CALIFORNIA 90211**
*Telephone: 310-275-3520*

*General Business Transactions, Estate Planning, Probate and Trust Administration.*

**DINA B. CHERNICK,** born Los Angeles, California, December 18, 1957; admitted to bar, 1983, California and U.S. District Court, Central District of California. *Education:* University of Pennsylvania (A.B., cum laude, 1979); University of California, Hastings College of Law (J.D., 1983). Member, Hastings College of the Law Constitutional Law Quarterly, 1981-1982. *Member:* Los Angeles County (Member, Probate and Trust Section) and American (Member, Sections on: Business Law; Real Property, Probate and Trust Law) Bar Associations; State Bar of California.

## L. DAVID COLE

A LAW CORPORATION
Established in 1989

433 NORTH CAMDEN DRIVE, 12TH FLOOR
**BEVERLY HILLS, CALIFORNIA 90210**
*Telephone: 310-205-2080*
*FAX: 310-275-5409*

*Real Property Law, General Business and Corporate Law.*

**L. DAVID COLE,** born Louisville, Kentucky, September 3, 1937; admitted to bar, 1962, New York; 1968, California. *Education:* Swarthmore College (B.A., with high honors, 1959); Columbia University (LL.B., 1962). Trial Attorney, Antitrust Division, U.S. Department of Justice, 1962-1967. *Member:* Los Angeles County and American (Member, Sections on: Antitrust Law; Business Law; Real Estate) Bar Associations; State Bar of California (Member, Real Estate Section).

## DAPEER, ROSENBLIT & LITVAK, LLP

9460 WILSHIRE BOULEVARD, FIFTH FLOOR
**BEVERLY HILLS, CALIFORNIA 90212**
*Telephone: 310-203-8200; 310-777-6676*
*Fax: 310-203-8213; 310-777-6675*

Metropolitan Cities Office: 2770 East Slauson Avenue, P.O. Box 2067, Huntington Park, 90255. Telephone: 213-587-5221. Fax: 213-587-4190.

*Business and Real Estate Litigation, Commercial and Corporate Law, including Creditors Rights Law and Commercial Collections, Professional Liability Litigation, Municipal Law and Land Use Law, Civil Trial Practice.*

*FIRM PROFILE: William Litvak is highly trained and broadly experienced in complex litigation. He has extensive experience in resolving professional liability issues related to complex litigation and underlying real estate, corporate and legal issues. His creative approach to strategy analysis of each case and his unique ability in communicating his clients' positions have been demonstrated by consistent results for his clients, both at settlement and in trial.*

**WILLIAM LITVAK,** born Ukraine, USSR., September 15, 1955; admitted to bar, 1979, California. *Education:* University of California (B.A., 1976); California Western School of Law (J.D., 1979). Phi Delta Phi. Featured Speaker, California Contract Cities Association, 1995. Lecturer, California Association of Code Enforcement Officials, 1992-1993; Featured Speaker, Real Estate/Land Use Litigation. Member, National Institute of Trial Advocacy, 1992. Arbitrator and Settlement Officer, Los Angeles Superior Court and Los Angeles County Court. Judge Pro Tem, Los Angeles Municipal Court. *Member:* San Diego County, Los Angeles County (Member, Sections on: Real Estate; Trial Lawyers) and American Bar Associations; State Bar of California (Member, Litigation, Business and Real Estate Sections, 1983—). Founding Member and Chairman, Lawyers Professional Liability Bar Association, 1993—. (Also Of Counsel to Dapeer & Rosenblit). **PRACTICE AREAS:** Business and Real Estate Litigation;

*(This Listing Continued)*

Commercial and Corporate Litigation; Professional Liability--Legal Malpractice; Accounting Malpractice; Insurance Malpractice.

**STEVEN H. ROSENBLIT,** born Montreal, Canada, May 21, 1951; admitted to bar, 1976, California. *Education:* University of California at Los Angeles (B.S., 1973); University of San Fernando (J.D., 1976). Lecturer: California Association of Code Enforcement Officers; Code Enforcement Workshops; Southern California Association of Code Enforcement Officials. *Member:* State Bar of California.

**KENNETH B. DAPEER,** born Los Angeles, California, June 11, 1950; admitted to bar, 1976, California. *Education:* California State University, Northridge (B.S., 1973); University of San Fernando Valley (J.D., 1976). Lecturer: California Association of Code Enforcement Officers; Code Enforcement Workshops; Southern California Association of Code Enforcement; Los Angeles Fire Department, Fire Prevention. Judge Pro Tem, Los Angeles Municipal Court. *Member:* State Bar of California; National Institute of Trial Advocacy.

REPRESENTATIVE CLIENTS: Bank of America; Caesar's Palace; MGM Desert Inn; MGM Sands; Bally's Grand Resorts, Inc.; Associated Foreign Exchange; Munchkin Bottling, Inc.; Markowugh Nevada, Inc.; Fund For Higher Education; American Rock & Asphalt, Inc.; Extrel Corporation.

## DAVIDOFF & DAVIDOFF

Established in 1983

SUITE 888, 433 NORTH CAMDEN DRIVE
**BEVERLY HILLS, CALIFORNIA 90210**
*Telephone: 310-274-2883*
*Telecopier: 310-274-2761*

*General, Civil Trial and Appellate Practice in all State and Federal Courts. Business, Commercial, Estate and Probate Litigation.*

### MEMBERS OF FIRM

**RICHARD C. DAVIDOFF,** born W. Lafayette, Indiana, February 8, 1948; admitted to bar, 1978, California. *Education:* University of Wisconsin-Madison (B.A., with distinction, 1970); Hastings College of Law, University of California (J.D., 1978). Member, Faculty, CEB, 1986—. *Member:* Beverly Hills, Los Angeles County (Chair, Litigation Section, 1988-1989; Executive Committee, Litigation Section, 1982-1993; Chair, Delegation to State Bar Conference of Delegates, 1989-1991; State Courts Committee, 1989—; Chair, 1989-1991; Probate Section; Prejudgment Remedies Section), and American (Member, Litigation Section) Bar Associations; The State Bar of California (Executive Committee, State Bar Conference of Delegates, 1990-1993; Member, Litigation Section); Association of Business Trial Lawyers.

**SUSAN K. DAVIDOFF,** born Green Bay, Wisconsin, January 7, 1950; admitted to bar, 1979, California. *Education:* University of Wisconsin-Madison (B.A., with distinction, 1971); Hastings College of Law, University of California (J.D., 1979). Member, COM/MENT, Communications and Entertainment Law Journal, 1978-1979. Staff Attorney, Anti-Defamation League of B'nai B'rith, 1980-1983. *Member:* Los Angeles County Bar Association; The State Bar of California; California Women Lawyers Association.

## JUDITH A. ENRIGHT

9100 WILSHIRE BOULEVARD
SEVENTH FLOOR - WEST TOWER
**BEVERLY HILLS, CALIFORNIA 90212**
*Telephone: 310-274-1830*
*Facsimile: 310-274-2330*

*General Civil Litigation in all Federal and State Courts and Administrative Tribunals.*

*FIRM PROFILE: Our attorneys and professional staff bring large-firm experience into a small-firm environment that allows for a more personal relationship with our clients. We endeavor to minimize fees and costs while providing the highest quality legal representation.*

**JUDITH A. ENRIGHT,** born Seattle, Washington, December 11, 1946; admitted to bar, 1977, California and U.S. District Court, Northern and Central Districts of California. *Education:* University of California at Los Angeles (B.A., 1969); Southwestern University SCALE Program (J.D., 1977). *Member:* Los Angeles County Bar Association; State Bar of California (Sections on: Legal Services; Litigation). **REPORTED CASES:** Estate of Trynin (1989) 49 Cal.3d 868. **PRACTICE AREAS:** Non-Profit Corpora-

*(This Listing Continued)*

## JUDITH A. ENRIGHT, Beverly Hills—Continued

tion Law; Conservatorship; Elder Abuse; Mental Health Law; Employment Law.

### ASSOCIATE

**JULIE A. OCHELTREE,** born Fullerton, California, November 30, 1961; admitted to bar, 1995, California and U.S. District Court, Central District of California. *Education:* California State University, Fullerton (B.A., 1986); Southwestern University School of Law (J.D., cum laude, 1995). Member, Southwestern Law Review, 1993-1995. Recipient: American Jurisprudence Award, Property II; Highest Achievement Award, Immigration. *Member:* Beverly Hills, Los Angeles County Bar Association; State Bar of California.

---

# ERVIN, COHEN & JESSUP LLP

A Limited Liability Partnership including Professional Corporations

*Established in 1953*

9401 WILSHIRE BOULEVARD
**BEVERLY HILLS, CALIFORNIA 90212-2974**
Telephone: 310-273-6333
Facsimile: 310-859-2325
Email: ErvinCohenJessup@counsel.com

Federal and State Taxation, Business, Corporation, Securities and Real Estate Law. General Business and Commercial Litigation in all State and Federal Trial and Appellate Courts with emphasis on Unfair Competition, Business Torts, Intellectual Property, Trademarks, Trade Secrets and Insurance Coverage and Litigation. Environmental Law, Probate, Estate Planning and Trusts, Insolvency and Creditors' Rights Law, Health Care and Entertainment Law.

*FIRM PROFILE:* Ervin, Cohen & Jessup (ECJ) was founded in 1953. The Firm has an extensive and diversified client base and practice. ECJ clients are involved in a wide variety of business pursuits, including real estate, banking and finance, venture capital, computers and data processing, health care, retailing, manufacturing and distribution, professional services, insurance, defense contracting, and scientific research and development. The Firm encourages continuing professional development by all partners and associates, including their participation in continuing legal education seminars, professional association activities and civic affairs.

### MEMBERS OF FIRM

**JOHN W. ERVIN** (1917-1982).

**W. EDGAR JESSUP, JR.,** born Los Angeles, California, September 9, 1922; admitted to bar, 1950, California. *Education:* Brown University (B.S., magna cum laude, 1943); University of Southern California (J.D., 1949). Tau Beta Pi; Phi Kappa Phi; Order of the Coif; Phi Alpha Delta. Member, Editorial Board, *Southern California Law Review*, 1947-1949. Lecturer in Law, University of Southern California Law Center, 1957, 1959-1972, 1977-1978. Lecturer, Engineering Law, University of Southern California, 1950-1953. Co-author: "Law and Specifications for Engineers and Scientists," Prentice-Hall, 1963. Member, National Panel of Arbitrators, American Arbitration Association, 1964—. *Member:* Beverly Hills, Los Angeles County and American Bar Associations; American Judicature Society. *PRACTICE AREAS:* Corporate; Taxation; Business Law.

**MELVIN S. SPEARS,** born San Bernardino, California, April 10, 1927; admitted to bar, 1952, California and U.S. Tax Court. *Education:* University of California at Los Angeles (A.A., 1948); University of Southern California (J.D., 1951). Nu Beta Epsilon; Order of the Coif. Member, Editorial Board, *Southern California Law Review*, 1949-1951. Author: "Disposition of Non Marital Deduction Assets: Tax and Family Protection Considerations," 1975, New York University Institute on Federal Taxation 231. Co-Author: "Tax-Free Exchanges of Real and Business Property," J.K. Lasser's *Income Tax Techniques*, 1965; "Problems Relating to Administration of Trust Assets," Chapter 9, "Inter Vivos Trusts," Shepards Citations, Inc., 1975 and Chapter 12, "Drafting California Irrevocable Inter Vivos Trusts," California Continuing Education of the Bar, 1973. Member, Faculty, University of Southern California Law Center, 1961-1968. Member, Planning Committee, University of Southern California Tax Institute, 1976-1993. *Member:* Beverly Hills, Los Angeles County and American Bar Associations. *PRACTICE AREAS:* Taxation Law; Estate Planning Law; Probate Law.

**BERTRAM K. MASSING,** born Cleveland, Ohio, July 13, 1933; admitted to bar, 1961, California; 1962, U.S. Tax Court. *Education:* University of California at Los Angeles (B.S., 1955); University of Southern California (J.D., 1960). Nu Beta Epsilon; Order of the Coif. Member, Board of Editors, *University of Southern California Law Review*, 1959-1960. Lecturer, University of Southern California Law Center, 1965-1966, 1975-1976. Vice President of Community Alumni Relations, 1974-1976, Member, Board of Directors, 1974-1976; 1980-1982 and General Counsel, 1980-1982, UCLA Alumni Association. *Member:* Beverly Hills, Los Angeles County and American Bar Associations. *PRACTICE AREAS:* Corporate Law; Securities Law; Mergers and Acquisitions Law.

**MARVIN H. LEWIS,** born Portland, Oregon, November 1, 1929; admitted to bar, 1962, California; 1962, U.S. Tax Court. *Education:* University of California at Berkeley (B.S., 1951; M.B.A., 1953); University of San Francisco (J.D., 1961); University of Southern California (LL.M. in Taxation, 1966). Phi Delta Phi; Beta Gamma Sigma. Member, McAuliffe Law Honor Society. Lifetime Honorary Member, *University of San Francisco Law Review*. Author: "Loans to Participants from Corporate Retirement Plans," *California Business Law Reporter*, July, 1982; "Tax Planning for Compensation and Retirement," Chapter 3, Personal Tax Planning for Professionals and Owners of Small Businesses, California Continuing Education of the Bar, 1983; "Self-Cancelling Installments Notes and the Private Annuity," UCLA-CEB Estate Planning Institute 377, 1983. Lecturer, University of Southern California Law Center Advanced Professional Program, 1973-1978. Member, Board of Counselors, University of San Francisco School of Law, 1981-1995; *Member:* Beverly Hills, Los Angeles County and American Bar Associations; Beverly Hills Estate Planning Council (President, 1987-1988). *PRACTICE AREAS:* Taxation Law; Estate Planning Law; Trust and Probate Law.

**DAVID P. KASSOY,** born New York, N.Y., December 6, 1935; admitted to bar, 1964, California; 1967, U.S. Tax Court. *Education:* Columbia University (A.B., 1957); Harvard University (LL.B., 1963). Author: "Court Says Landlord Can't Stop Sublets," *Shopping Centers Today*, International Council of Shopping Centers, May, 1986; "Landlords Can Nix Sublets that Reduce Percentage Rent," *Shopping Center Legal Update*, Spring, 1987; "Assigning and Subletting Commercial Leases," *Los Angeles Lawyer*, January, 1988; "New Law Affects Assignment of Commercial Leases in California," *Shopping Center Legal Update*, Fall, 1990; "More Landlord/Tenant Legislation," *Shopping Center Legal Update*, Winter, 1991. Lecturer: Drafting Real Property Leases, California Continuing Education of the Bar, 1981, 1984 and 1986; Advanced Seminar on Drafting and Negotiating Commercial Leases and Seminar on Office Building Leasing, Northwest Center for Professional Education, 1982-1988; Commercial Leasing, California State Bar Convention, 1986; Real Estate Law, University of Southern California Graduate School of Urban and Regional Planning, 1987—; CLE International Seminar on Tenant Improvement Agreements, 1995. Co-Chair, Benjamin Crocker Symposium, 1988 and Chair, 1990. Member: Executive Committee, Real Estate Section, Los Angeles County Bar Association, 1986-1993; California Attorney General's Commission on Racial, Ethnic, Religious and Minority Violence, 1984-1986. *Member:* Los Angeles County, Beverly Hills and American Bar Associations. [Lt. Cmdr., USNR, 1957-1960]. *PRACTICE AREAS:* Commercial Real Property Development Law.

**GARY J. FREEDMAN, (P.C.),** born Bloomington, Illinois, October 1, 1942; admitted to bar, 1968, California. *Education:* University of Illinois (A.B., 1964); University of California, Hastings College of the Law (J.D., 1967). Deputy Attorney General, State of California, 1967-1969. *Member:* Beverly Hills and Los Angeles County Bar Associations. *PRACTICE AREAS:* Corporate Securities Law; Real Property Law; International Law.

**LEE I. SILVER,** born Indianapolis, Indiana, December 4, 1943; admitted to bar, 1969, California. *Education:* University of California at Berkeley and University of California at Los Angeles (A.B., 1965); University of California at Los Angeles (J.D., 1968). Order of the Coif. Chairman, Beverly Hills Chamber of Commerce Economic Development Council, 1993—. *PRACTICE AREAS:* Real Property Law.

**ROGER J. HOLT,** born Los Angeles, California, September 8, 1946; admitted to bar, 1972, California. *Education:* University of California at Los Angeles (B.A., cum laude, 1968); Harvard Law School (J.D., 1971). Phi Beta Kappa. Chairman, California State Heritage Task Force, June, 1982-November, 1984. Author: Subchapter on "Air Toxics Hot Spots Act," California Environmental Law and Law Use Practice, Matthew-Bender, 1993; "Fundamentals of Environmental Law," *California Real Estate Reporter*, Matthew-Bender, October, 1993. Member, Committee on Environment, State Bar of California, 1980-1983. *PRACTICE AREAS:* Environmental Law.

*(This Listing Continued)*

**ELIOT G. DISNER,** born Detroit, Michigan, April 19, 1947; admitted to bar, 1972, Michigan; 1976, District of Columbia and California; 1980, U.S. Court of Appeals, Ninth Circuit and U.S. Supreme Court. *Education:* University of Michigan (B.A., with high distinction, 1969); Harvard University (J.D., 1972). Phi Beta Kappa. Member, Harvard legal Aid Bureau, 1970-1971. Author: "Barrier Analysis in Antitrust Law," 58 *Cornell Law Review* 862, 1973; "Overpayments in Supplier Promotional Programs," 19 *Villanova Law Review* 397, 1974; "Federal Trade Commission Regulation of Patent and Trademark Abuses," 11-2 *Beverly Hills Bar Journal* 34, 1977; "The Rule of Reason: Fudge Factor in Antitrust Law," *Los Angeles Daily Journal Report* No. 79-13, 4, 1979; "Market Definition," chapter in *Antitrust: New Developments*, published by California Continuing Education of the Bar, August, 1982; "The Availability of Divestiture Relief to Private Litigants Under Section 7 of the Clayton Act," 1 *Allegheny County Bar Association Antitrust and Class Action Journal* 29, Fall-Winter, 1982; "Antitrust for Business: Questions and Answers," 1989; "Is There Antitrust After 'Syufy': Recent Ninth Circuit Cases Create Barriers to Enforcement," *California Lawyer* 1991; *California Antitrust Law Jury Instructions*, State Bar of California (1996), General Editor and Co-Author. Trial Attorney, Bureau of Competition and Assistant to Commissioner, Federal Trade Commission, 1972-1975. Member, Bureau of National Affairs Advisory Board on Antitrust and Trade Regulation, 1983-1989. Arbitrator, Los Angeles Superior Court, 1993—; American Arbitration Association, 1995—. *Member:* Los Angeles County (Member, 1977— and Chairman, Executive Committee, Antitrust Section, 1982-1983) and American (Member: Private Antitrust Litigation Committee, 1978—; Litigation and Antitrust Law Sections) Bar Associations; State Bar of California (Member, Executive Committee, Antitrust and Trade Regulation Law Section, 1987-1992; Chairman, 1991-1992; Advisor, 1992—). *PRACTICE AREAS:* Antitrust and Trade Regulation; Complex Business Litigation.

**ALLAN B. COOPER,** born Los Angeles, California, July 26, 1949; admitted to bar, 1974, California; 1978, U.S. Court of Appeals, Ninth and Fifth Circuits and U.S. Supreme Court. *Education:* University of California at Los Angeles (A.B., magna cum laude, 1971; J.D., 1974). Phi Beta Kappa; Order of the Coif. Associate Editor, 1972-1973 and Comment Editor, 1973-1974, *UCLA Law Review.* Author: "The Prosecutor's Role in California Sentencing: Advocate or Informant?" 1973, 20 *UCLA Law Review 1379.* Contributing Author: "Use and Abuse of Interrogatories," California Continuing Education of the Bar, 1982; "Terminating Actions Without Trial," California Continuing Education of the Bar, 1983, 1986. Consultant: "Handling a Real Property Foreclosure," California Continuing Education of the Bar, 1992. Clinical Lecturer in Law, University of Southern California, 1980-1981. Planning Commissioner, City of Calabasas, 1992-1994. *Member:* Beverly Hills and American Bar Associations; Association of Business Trial Lawyers. *REPORTED CASES:* Han v. U.S., 944 F.2d 526; Worldwide Church of God, Inc. v. State of California, 623 F.2d 613; Wright v. Schock, 571 F.Supp. 642; Lambert v. Commonwealth Land Title Ins. Co., 53 Cal.3d 1072; Isaac v. A&B Loan Company, Inc., 201 Cal.App.3d 307; Elysian Heights Residents Ass'n, Inc. v. City of Los Angeles, 182 Cal..App.3d 21. *PRACTICE AREAS:* Real Property Litigation; Title and Land Use Litigation; Competitive Business Practices; Legal Malpractice.

**JOHN A. MEYERS,** born Los Angeles, California, August 1, 1946; admitted to bar, 1974, California. *Education:* University of California at Berkeley (A.B., 1969); University of California School of Law at Los Angeles (LL.B., 1974). *Member:* State Bar of California. *PRACTICE AREAS:* Healthcare; Business; Real Estate.

**DAVID R. EANDI,** born San Francisco, California, June 19, 1949; admitted to bar, 1975, California. *Education:* University of California at Berkeley (B.A., 1971); University of California at Los Angeles (J.D., 1975). Order of the Coif. *PRACTICE AREAS:* Corporate Law; Securities Law; Mergers and Acquisitions Law; General Business Law.

**GARY Q. MICHEL, (A P.C.),** born Chicago, Illinois, June 1, 1951; admitted to bar, 1975, California; 1976, U.S. Tax Court. *Education:* University of California at Los Angeles (B.A., cum laude, 1972; J.D., 1975). Member: Order of the Coif; Board of Editors, *UCLA Law Review*, 1974-1975. Recipient, Elijah Watt Sells Honor Award, C.P.A. Exam, May, 1972. *Member:* Beverly Hills and Los Angeles County Bar Associations. *PRACTICE AREAS:* Health Care; Corporate; Taxation; Real Property Law.

**JOAN B. VELAZQUEZ,** born New York, N.Y., January 31, 1950; admitted to bar, 1978, California. *Education:* University of Bridgeport (B.S. magna cum laude, 1972); University of Southern California (J.D., 1978). Member, Board of Directors: Big Sisters of Los Angeles; California Women Lawyers. *Member:* Los Angeles County Bar Association (Member, Taxation and Real Estate Sections). *PRACTICE AREAS:* Finance Taxation

*(This Listing Continued)*

Law; Real Property Law; Environmental Law; Business and Securities Law.

**E. A. (STACEY) OLLIFF III,** born Tampa, Florida, September 16, 1955; admitted to bar, 1978, California. *Education:* University of Central Florida (B.A., summa cum laude, 1974); Harvard Law School (J.D., cum laude, 1978). Member, Board of Editors, 1976-1977, and Research Editor, 1977-1978, *Harvard Journal on Legislation.* Author: "Aspen Enterprises, Inc. v. Bodge: Mixed Collateral Goes Flat," UCC Bulletin 1, Nov 1995; "The Remedies Opinion: Precautions and Pitfalls for Business Lawyers," 24 *Beverly Hills Bar Association Journal* 43, 1990; "New California Legislation Affecting Corporations: Taming *White Dragon* and Facilitating Mergers," 12 *California Business Law Reporter* 67, 1990; *Member:* Los Angeles County (Member, Board of Trustees, 1992-1995; Chair, 1994-1995 and Member, Executive Committee, Business and Corporations Law Section, 1989-1995) and American (Member, Special "Silverado" Committee on Legal Opinions, 1989-1993) Bar Associations; State Bar of California; Financial Lawyers Conference; Los Angeles County Bar Foundation (Trustee, 1994-1995). *PRACTICE AREAS:* Corporate Law; Commercial Law; Real Property Law.

**THOMAS F. R. GARVIN,** born Miami, Florida, December 3, 1955; admitted to bar, 1979, California, U.S. District Court, Central and Northern Districts of California and U.S. Court of Appeals, Ninth Circuit; 1982, U.S. Tax Court. *Education:* Loyola Marymount University, Los Angeles (B.A., magna cum laude, 1976); University of California, Hastings College of the Law (J.D., 1979). Phi Delta Phi; Alpha Sigma Nu; Pi Gamma Mu. Recipient, Outstanding Appellate Advocacy Award, University of California, Hastings College of the Law. Editor, University of California, *Hastings Law News*, 1977-1978. Member, *Hastings Communications & Entertainment Law Journal*, 1977-1978. Associate Editor, 1978-1979, *Hastings Law Journal.* Law Clerk: Hon. John T. Racanelli, Presiding Justice, California Court of Appeals, District 1, Division 1, 1978; Hon. Cecil F. Poole, U.S. District Court, Northern District of California, 1978-1979. Chairman, International Tax Committee, State Bar of California. *Member:* Los Angeles County, American, Inter-Pacific and International Bar Associations; State Bar of California (Member, Executive Committee, Taxation Section); International Fiscal Association; Association Internationale Des Jeunes Avocats. *PRACTICE AREAS:* Taxation Law; Entertainment Law; International Business Law; International Trust and Estate Planning.

**ROBERT M. WAXMAN,** born Los Angeles, California, December 11, 1953; admitted to bar, 1979, California. *Education:* University of Southern California (B.A., cum laude, 1976); University of California School of Law, Los Angeles (J.D., 1979). Order of the Coif. Member, Editor-in-Chief, *UCLA-Alaska Law Review*, 1978-1979. Author: "Unfinished Business and Law Firm Dissolutions: Allocation of Revenues Earned and Expenses Incurred During the Winding-Up Process," 13 *Los Angeles Lawyer* 19, 1990. *Member:* Los Angeles County Bar Association. *PRACTICE AREAS:* Partnership Problems and Dissolutions; Real Property Law; Unfair Competition; Business Tort Litigation.

**REEVE E. CHUDD,** born Los Angeles, California, August 10, 1951; admitted to bar, 1980, California, U.S. District Court, Central District of California and U.S. Court of Appeals, Ninth Circuit; 1982, U.S. Tax Court; 1984, U.S. Supreme Court. *Education:* University of Pennsylvania (B.A., B.S., 1973; M.S., 1974); University of Southern California (J.D., 1980). Order of the Coif. Certified Public Accountant, California, 1976. Co-Author: "Self-Cancelling Installment Notes and the Private Annuity," UCLA-CEB Estate Planning Institute 377, 1983. Lecturer, University of Southern California Institute on Federal Taxation, "Marital Deduction: Developments and Problems," 1986; "The Unlimited Marital Deduction: To Use or Not to Use," 1993. *Member:* Beverly Hills and Los Angeles County Bar Associations. *PRACTICE AREAS:* Taxation Law; Estate Planning Law.

**KENNETH A. LUER,** born Columbus, Ohio, November 2, 1950; admitted to bar, 1980, California; 1981, U.S. District Court, Central District of California. *Education:* University of Richmond (B.A., 1975); University of Virginia (J.D., 1980). Author: "The Silverado Report and the California Response," 27 *Beverly Hills Bar Association Journal* 61, 1993. Contributing Author: "Guide to Organizing a California Corporation," Business Law Section, State of California, 1992. *Member:* Los Angeles County and American Bar Associations. *PRACTICE AREAS:* Corporate Law; Securities Law; General Business Law.

**PHILIP STARR,** born New York, N.Y., October 6, 1949; admitted to bar, 1982, California; 1984, U.S. District Court, Central District of California and U.S. Court of Appeals, Ninth Circuit; 1985, U.S. Tax Court. *Education:* State University of New York at Binghamton (B.A., 1971); University of California School of Law at Los Angeles (J.D., 1982). Order of the

*(This Listing Continued)*

## ERVIN, COHEN & JESSUP LLP, Beverly Hills—Continued

Coif. Author: "Guidelines for the Termination of the Accrual of Interest on Federal Tax Deficiencies," Spring, 1983 Tax Section News, State Bar of California Tax Section; "New Transitional Provisions Enacted for OID and Imputed Interest Rules," *California Business Law Reporter*, January, 1985. Co-Author: "Tax Reform Act of 1984: Pitfalls and Opportunities for the Business Lawyer," *California Business Law Reporter*, October, 1984; "Personal Tax Planning for Professionals and Owners of Small Businesses," April, 1985, June, 1986, June, 1987, September, 1988, September, 1989, and February, 1991 Supplements, California Continuing Education of the Bar. *Member:* Los Angeles County and Beverly Hills (Chair, Taxation Section, 1988-1989) Bar Associations.

**BARRY J. MACNAUGHTON,** born International Falls, Minnesota, October 9, 1957; admitted to bar, 1982, California; 1983, U.S. District Court, Central, Southern and Northern Districts of California and U.S. Court of Appeals, Ninth Circuit. *Education:* Trinity University (B.A., magna cum laude, 1979); University of Texas at Austin (J.D., with honors, 1982). Phi Beta Kappa; Alpha Lamda Delta; Alpha Chi Epsilon. Contributing Author: "Attorney's Guide to Law of Competitive Business Practices," (1985 Supp.) - Antitrust (Chapter 5). *Member:* Los Angeles County Bar Association; Defense Research Institute. *PRACTICE AREAS:* Business and Commercial Litigation; Real Property Litigation with an emphasis on Environmental and Construction Matters; Insurance Coverage Disputes; Antitrust; Trade Secrets; Unfair Competition; Real Property Law.

**JACOB D. LEE,** born August 10, 1959; admitted to bar, 1986, California. *Education:* University of California at Los Angeles (B.A., 1982, Dean's Scholar); University of California, Hastings College of the Law (J.D., 1985). Finalist, Annual Moot Court Competition, 1983-1984. Author: Publication, "Discovery of Dishonesty Under a Fidelity Bond," Monograph, Defense Research Institute in conjunction with American Bar Association, 1989. Panelist, Seminar, "Doing Business in the Pacific Rim," Los Angeles County Bar Association, 1993. *Member:* Los Angeles County and American Bar Associations; Los Angeles Surety and Fidelity Claims Association; California Banker's Association; Korean-American Bar Association. *LANGUAGES:* Korean. *PRACTICE AREAS:* Banking; General Business Litigation; Insurance Coverage; Surety and Fidelity Litigation; Bank Loans and Foreclosures.

**KELLY O. SCOTT,** born La Jolla, California, November 7, 1961; admitted to bar, 1987, California and U.S. District Court, Central District of California. *Education:* University of California at Los Angeles (B.A., 1984); University of Southern California (J.D., 1987). Phi Delta Phi. Member, California Lawyers for the Arts. *Member:* American Bar Association. *PRACTICE AREAS:* Commercial Litigation; Entertainment Law; Employment Law.

### ASSOCIATES

**SYLVIA D. LAUTSCH,** born Santiago, Chile, May 12, 1957; admitted to bar, 1982, California. *Education:* Stanford University (A.B., 1978); University of California, Berkeley (M.C.P., 1982); Boalt Hall School of Law, University of California (J.D., 1982). *PRACTICE AREAS:* Commercial Real Property Development Law.

**HOWARD Z. BERMAN,** born Santa Monica, California, February 16, 1962; admitted to bar, 1986, California, U.S. District Court, Central District of California and U.S. Court of Appeals, Ninth Circuit. *Education:* University of Southern California (B.S., magna cum laude, 1983; J.D., 1986). Order of the Coif. Recipient, American Jurisprudence Awards in Commercial Law, Torts II, Agency Reading and Estate Planning. *Member:* Los Angeles County Bar Association. *PRACTICE AREAS:* Corporate Law; Securities Law; Commercial Law; General Business Law.

**LAYTON L. PACE,** born Lebanon, Oregon, October 28, 1957; admitted to bar, 1987, Oregon (inactive); 1988, Washington; 1989, California. *Education:* University of Washington (B.A., in Bus. Adm., 1980); University of Oregon; University of California, Hastings College of the Law (J.D., cum laude, 1987). Phi Beta Kappa. Associate Managing Editor, *Hastings International and Comparative Law Review.* Author: "Earth, Wind, and Fire," 1995, 17 *Los Angeles Lawyer*, 22. Contributing Editor, State Bar of California's *The Tax Reporter.* Federal Tax Editor for the *California Tax Lawyer.* *Member:* Los Angeles County Bar Association. *PRACTICE AREAS:* Taxation Law; Corporate Law.

**MARK T. KAWA,** born Los Angeles, California, July 13, 1962; admitted to bar, 1988, California and U.S. Court of Appeals, Ninth Circuit; U.S. District Court, Central District of California. *Education:* University of California at Berkeley (A.B., with honors, 1984); University of Southern California (J.D., 1988). Managing Editor: Major Tax Planning, 1987-1988; *Computer Law Journal,* 1987-1988. Author: "Cable Television Exclusive Franchise Agreements: Has State Action Immunity Gone Too Far?" 1988, 8 *Computer Law Journal* 311. *Member:* National Association of Chinese American Bankers. *PRACTICE AREAS:* Intellectual Property; Real Property Litigation; Banking Law.

**DARCY L. SIMON,** born Brooklyn, New York, November 24, 1963; admitted to bar, 1990, California. *Education:* Brown University (A.B., 1985); University of California School of Law at Los Angeles (J.D., 1990; M.B.A., 1990). *Member:* Los Angeles County Bar Association. *PRACTICE AREAS:* Corporate and Securities Law.

**BARI J. COOPER,** born Glen Ridge, New Jersey, October 17, 1964; admitted to bar, 1990, California; 1993, District of Columbia. *Education:* American College in Paris (1985); George Washington University (B.B.A., 1986; J.D., 1990). Book Review/Book Notes Editor, *George Washington Journal of International Law and Economics,* 1989-1990. *Member:* Beverly Hills and American Bar Associations. *PRACTICE AREAS:* Real Property Law; Entertainment Law.

**CHUNG JAY WON,** born Seoul, Korea, July 23, 1964; admitted to bar, 1990, California and U.S. District Court, Central District of California. *Education:* University of Michigan at Ann Arbor (B.A., 1987); University of California School of Law at Los Angeles (J.D., 1990). *Member:* Korean American Bar Association. *LANGUAGES:* Korean. *PRACTICE AREAS:* Banking Law; General Business Law.

**ELLEN S. KORNBLUM,** born Los Angeles, California, April 14, 1957; admitted to bar, 1992, California; U.S. Court of Appeals, Ninth Circuit and U.S. District Court, Central and Eastern Districts of California. *Education:* University of California at Berkeley (B.S., 1978); Loyola Law School (J.D., 1992). Order of the Coif. Editor, *Loyola of Los Angeles Law Review.* Recipient, Judge Barry Russell Award for Outstanding Achievement Federal Courts and Practice Course. *Member:* Beverly Hills and Los Angeles Bar Associations; Los Angeles Bankruptcy Forum. *PRACTICE AREAS:* General Business Litigation; Bankruptcy Law.

**KEVIN K. HAAH,** born Taegu, Republic of Korea, April 23, 1965; admitted to bar, 1992, California and U.S. District Court, Central District of California. *Education:* University of California at Davis (B.A., 1988); Cornell Law School (J.D., 1992). Phi Sigma Alpha; Golden Key Honor Society. Recipient: Ken Levy Memorial Scholarship; University Alumni Scholarship. Member, Cornell Law Review, 1990-1991. President, Associated Students of University of California at Davis, 1987-1988. Executive Council Member, Associated Students of University of California at Davis, 1985-1986. Co-Chair, Korean American National Organizing Committee, 1992-1994. Vice President of Development, Korean American Coalition, 1995—. *Member:* Los Angeles County (Member, Committee on Pacific Rim; Committee on Access to Justice Section on Bankruptcy) and Federal Bar Associations; State Bar of California (Member, Sections on: Litigation; Bankruptcy, 1992—); Korean American Bar Association of Southern California (Co-Chair, Bench and Bar/Judicial Appointments Committee, 1993—); Christian Legal Society; International Legal Society. *LANGUAGES:* Korean. *PRACTICE AREAS:* Bankruptcy; Creditors' Rights; Business Reorganization. *Email:* khaah@sidley.com

**JOELLE M. DRUCKER,** born Washington, D.C., December 17, 1967; admitted to bar, 1994, California. *Education:* University of California, Irvine (B.A., 1990); University of San Francisco School of Law (J.D., cum laude, 1993); New York University School of Law (LL.M., Taxation, 1994). Member, University of San Francisco Law Review. Recipient, American Jurisprudence Award in Wills and Trusts, Bankruptcy and Remedies. *Member:* Los Angeles County Bar Association. *PRACTICE AREAS:* Estate Planning; Probate; ERISA.

**ELIZABETH E. WEBB,** born Indianapolis, Indiana, October 20, 1955; admitted to bar, 1992, California. *Education:* Indiana University (A.B., 1976); Webster University (M.A., 1986); University of Southern California (J.D., 1991). Administrative Vice Chair, Hale Moot Court Honors Program, 1990-1991. Quarterfinalist, Hale Moot Court Honors Program, 1990. *Member:* Los Angeles County Bar Association; State Bar of California. [Major, U.S. Air Force Reserve, 1976—]. *PRACTICE AREAS:* Business Litigation.

**MICHELLE LEE FLORES,** born Castro Valley, California, April 25, 1968; admitted to bar, 1993, California. *Education:* Arizona State University (B.A., magna cum laude, 1990); University of California School of Law at Los Angeles (J.D., 1993). Phi Beta Kappa; Psi Chi; Alpha Lambda Delta; Golden Key National Honor Society. Arizona Regents Scholarship Recipient. Arizona State Legislature Senate Intern. UCLA Moot Court

*(This Listing Continued)*

Participant. El Centro Legal Student Director. University Law School Fellowship. Business Editor *Federal Communications Law Journal. Member:* State Bar of California (Member, Labor and Employment Law Section); American Bar Association (Member, Labor and Employment Law Section); Association of Southern California Defense Counsel. ***PRACTICE AREAS:*** Business Litigation; Labor and Employment Law.

**KAREN LYN DYMANT,** born Plainview, New York, January 8, 1969; admitted to bar, 1994, California. *Education:* University of Pennsylvania (B.A., 1991); University of Michigan (J.D., 1994). *Member:* State Bar of California. ***LANGUAGES:*** French, Italian, Spanish. ***PRACTICE AREAS:*** Business and Securities Law.

All Members and Associates of the Firm are Members of the State Bar of California.

REFERENCE: Bank of California, N.A. (Beverly Hills).

---

## EVANNS & WALSH

*Established in 1983*

**SUITE 206, 119 NORTH SAN VICENTE BOULEVARD**
**BEVERLY HILLS, CALIFORNIA 90211**
*Telephone: 310-273-0938; 310-855-0872*
*Cable Address: "Jorev"*
*Telecopier: 213-651-3027*

*Patent, Copyright, Trademark and Unfair Competition Law. Trials and Appeals in State and Federal Trial and Appellate Courts; proceedings before the United States Patent and Trademark Office and Copyright Office and before the International Trade Commission.*

**JOSEPH R. EVANNS,** born New York, N.Y., March 18, 1938; admitted to bar, 1969, California and U.S. District Court, Central District of California; 1973, U.S. Court of Appeals, Ninth Circuit; 1980, U.S. District Court, Northern District of Texas; 1990, U.S. Court of Appeals for the Federal Circuit; registered to practice before U.S. Patent and Trademark Office, 1970. *Education:* University of Southern California (B.S. in Physics, cum laude, 1959); University of California at Los Angeles (M.A. in Physics, 1961); Loyola University of Los Angeles and University of California at Los Angeles (J.D., 1968). *Member:* Los Angeles County Bar Association; State Bar of California (Member, Intellectual Property Law Section); Los Angeles Association of Business Trial Lawyers. ***REPORTED CASES:*** Mayview v. Rodstein, 620 F.2d 1347 (9th Cir. 1980), (Patent); Kamar International Inc. v. Russ Berrie & Co., Inc., 657 F.2d 1059 (9th Cir. 1981) (copyright); Hollingsworth Solderless Terminal Co. v. Turley, 622 F.2d 1324 (9th Cir. 1980) (Trade Secret).

**EDWARD C. WALSH** (1912-1994).

---

## HARRY M. FAIN

**121 SOUTH BEVERLY DRIVE**
**BEVERLY HILLS, CALIFORNIA 90212**
*Telephone: 310-275-5132; 213-272-7807*
*Fax: 310-271-5269*

*Practice Limited to Family Law.*

**HARRY M. FAIN,** born Canora, Canada, December 30, 1918; admitted to bar, 1946, California; 1947, U.S. District Court, Southern District of California and U.S. Court of Appeals, Ninth Circuit; 1974, U.S. Supreme Court. *Education:* University of Manitoba and University of California at Los Angeles (A.B., 1939); University of Southern California (J.D., 1946). Nu Beta Epsilon. Member, Board of Editors, University of Southern California Law Review, 1940-1941. Member: Citizens Advisory Committee, California Assembly Judiciary Committee To Review Marriage and Divorce Laws, 1964-1969; Governors Commission on the Family, 1966. President, American Academy Matrimonial Lawyers, 1979-1981. Lecturer: Family Law Program, Continuing Education of the Bar, 1978-1983; Pre-Nuptial and Post-Nuptial Agreements in an Uncertain Marital Climate, American Bar Association, March and April, 1983. Panelist, Negotiating to Settlement in Divorce, Sponsored by Harcourt Brace Jovanovich, Publishers, 1985—. Mediator, Family Law Mediation Program, Los Angeles County, 1984-1992. Listed in The Best Lawyers in America, Harvard publication, 1989-1994. *Member:* Los Angeles County (Executive Member, Los Angeles County State Bar Committee, 1967-1968, 1984) and American (Section Chairman, 1968-1969 and Chairman, Custody Committee, 1963-1968; Family Law Section) Bar Associations; The State Bar of California (Member, Family Law Committee, 1968-1969). Fellow, American Bar

*(This Listing Continued)*

---

Foundation. [Capt., USAF, Military Intelligence, 1942-1945]. ***REPORTED CASES:*** "Marriage of Frick 181 CA3 997 226CR 766," Linsk vs. Linsk, 70 Cal. 2d 272,449 pac. 2d 760.

REFERENCE: City National Bank (Beverly Hills Main Office).

---

## MICHAEL S. FIELDS

*Established in 1981*

**VILLAGE ON CAÑON**
**PROMENADE SUITE 220, 301 NORTH CAÑON DRIVE**
**BEVERLY HILLS, CALIFORNIA 90210**
*Telephone: 310-273-1209*
*Fax: 310-273-8229*

*Cerritos, California Office:* 11554 South Street, Suite 2. Telephone: 310-860-6601.

*Practice limited to Personal Injury Litigation, Professional Malpractice, Product Liability, Vehicular Accidents, Construction Accidents and Insurance Company Bad Faith Actions.*

**MICHAEL S. FIELDS,** born Chicago, Illinois, September 17, 1939; admitted to bar, 1969, California and U.S. District Court, Central District of California; 1982, U.S. District Court, Southern District of California. *Education:* California State University at San Jose (B.S., 1962); Southwestern University (LL.B., 1968). Editor and Author: California Practice Handbook, Tort Damages, Matthew Bender, 1992; California Forms of Pleading and Practice, Negligence, Matthew Bender, 1995; California Forms of Pleadings and Practice, Contractual Arbitrations and other ADR procedures. Author: "Recovering Punitive Damages," Los Angeles Lawyer Magazine, September 1992; California Points and Authorities, Negligence, Matthew Bender, 1995. Adjunct Professor, Torts, Western States University School of Law, 1972-1978. Member, Board of Governors, Consumer Attorneys Association of Los Angeles. President, Trial Practice Inn of Court. *Member:* Los Angeles County Bar Association (Trustee; Chair-Elect, Executive Committee Litigation Section; Executive Committee Lawyer Referral Service); California Trial Lawyers Association; The Association of Trial Lawyers of America; Business Trial Lawyers Association. ***PRACTICE AREAS:*** Torts and Litigation.

REFERENCE: Wells Fargo Bank.

---

## JACK D. FINE

**424 SOUTH BEVERLY DRIVE**
**BEVERLY HILLS, CALIFORNIA 90212**
*Telephone: 310-553-8533*
*FAX: 310-203-9853*

*General Civil Practice, Civil litigation, Contracts, Business Litigation and Commercial Litigation, Probate, Trust, and Estate Planning, Landlord-Tenant, Personal Injury, Arbitration and Mediation.*

**JACK D. FINE,** born Los Angeles, California, April 3, 1933; admitted to bar, 1958, California and U.S. Supreme Court. *Education:* Stanford University (A.B., 1954; J.D., 1956). Phi Alpha Delta. Member, Board of Directors, 1966— and Past President, Sunair Home for Asthmatic Children. Instructor, Real Property, University of West Los Angeles School of Law, 1969-1971. Member, Board of Trustees, Center for Early Education, 1975-1986. Member: Board of Directors, Liason Citizens, 1986—; Vice-President, American Jewish Committee; Executive Board, Community Relations Commission, Los Angeles Jewish Federation Council, 1986—. Member, National Panel of Arbitrators, American Arbitration Association. Member, Los Angeles City Landlord-Tenant Mediation Board, 1978-1983. *Member:* Los Angeles County Bar Association; The State Bar of California; Los Angeles Consumer Attorneys Association. ***PRACTICE AREAS:*** Civil Litigation; General Practice.

REFERENCES: Bank of America (Wilshire & San Vicente); Wells Fargo Bank (Cedars-Sinai Branch).

## CHARLES M. FINKEL

SUITE 919, 8383 WILSHIRE BOULEVARD
**BEVERLY HILLS, CALIFORNIA 90211**
Telephone: 213-655-9989
FAX: 213-655-7865
Email: CharlesMFinkel@msn.com

*Aviation Law, Personal Injury and Wrongful Death.*

**CHARLES M. FINKEL,** born New York, N.Y., November 11, 1950; admitted to bar, 1981, California. *Education:* University of Miami (B.A., 1971); Whittier College (J.D., 1981). Member, Moot Court Honors Board. Legal Editor: Air Progress Magazine, 1984—; Flying Careers Magazine, 1995—. Author: "The Necessity for Causal Connection In Aviation Public Liability Policies", LPBA Journal, Spring 1986; "What Every Civil Air Patrol Volunteer Should Know About Insurance and the Liability of the Civil Air Patrol", LPBA Journal, Fall 1986; "Governmental Contractor Liability under Boyle v. United Technologies Corporation", CTLA Forum, September 1988; "Liability of the Federal Aviation Administration for Negligent Inspection and Certification of Aircraft", LATLA Advocate, February 1989 and CTLA Forum, March 1989; "What you See is What You Get," LPBA Journal, Summer 1996. Speaker, Lawyer Pilots Bar Association, Summer 1996. Teacher, Aviation Law, California State University, Los Angeles, 1986-1994. Judge Pro Tem Los Angeles County Superior Court. Arbitrator Los Angeles County Bar Association Dispute Resolution Services. *Member:* State Bar of California; Los Angeles County Bar Association; Lawyer-Pilots Bar Association; American Trial Lawyers Association; Aircraft Owners and Pilots Association; Consumer Lawyers of Los Angeles; Consumer Attorneys of California.

---

## LAW OFFICES OF GARY FISHBEIN

9454 WILSHIRE BOULEVARD, SUITE 203
**BEVERLY HILLS, CALIFORNIA 90212**
Telephone: 310-887-6190
Fax: 310-887-6193

*Family Law.*

**GARY FISHBEIN,** born Los Angeles, California, October 26, 1949; admitted to bar, 1980, California; 1985, U.S. District Court, Central District of California. *Education:* California State University at Northridge (B.A., 1972); University of West Los Angeles (J.D., 1980). Judge Pro Tem, Family Law and Small Claims. Mediator, Family Law. *Member:* Los Angeles County Bar Association (Member, Family Law Section); State Bar of California (Member, Family Law Section). **PRACTICE AREAS:** Family Law.

### ASSOCIATE

**CHERI L. WOOD,** born Santa Monica, California, October 4, 1960; admitted to bar, 1995, California and U.S. District Court, Central District of California. *Education:* University of California, Los Angeles (B.A., magna cum laude, 1992); Loyola Marymount University (J.D., 1995). President, 1994-1995 and Member, 1993-1994, St. Thomas More Law Honor Society. Recipient: Department of Political Science High Honors, University of California, Los Angeles, 1991; American Jurisprudence Award, Constitutional Law, Loyola Law School, 1993. Articles Editor, 1994-1995 and Staff Member, 1993-1994, Loyola of Los Angeles Law Review. Author: "Childless Mothers?--The New Catch-22: You Can't Have Your Kids and Work For Them Too," Loyola of Los Angeles Law Review, Volume 29, Issue 1, November 1995; "The Parental Alienation Syndrome: A Dangerous Aura of Reliability," Loyola of Los Angeles Law Review, Volume 27, Issue 4, June 1994. Teaching Assistant, Loyola Law School, Constitutional Law I, 1993-1994. *Member:* Beverly Hills and American Bar Associations; State Bar of California. **PRACTICE AREAS:** Family Law.

---

## FRANDZEL & SHARE

*A LAW CORPORATION*
**BEVERLY HILLS, CALIFORNIA**
(See Los Angeles)

*Banking, Commercial Creditors Rights and Bankruptcy Law. General Civil, Trial Practice and Real Estate Law.*

---

## FRESHMAN, MARANTZ, ORLANSKI, COOPER & KLEIN

*A LAW CORPORATION*
Established in 1959

EIGHTH FLOOR, EAST TOWER
9100 WILSHIRE BOULEVARD
**BEVERLY HILLS, CALIFORNIA 90212**
Telephone: 310-273-1870
Telecopier: 310-274-8293

*General Civil Trial and Appellate Practice. Banking, Corporate, Securities, Commercial, Employment, Real Estate, Real Estate Lending, Sports Law and Creditors Rights.*

**FIRM PROFILE:** Organized in 1959, Freshman, Marantz, Orlanski, Cooper & Klein is an established general business practice law firm. The firm is composed of experienced and dynamic attorneys representing clients in emerging as well as established industries (see Representative Client List) and is well-known in the legal community for high-quality and cost-effective work on complex matters. The firm's litigation department focuses on such areas as securities, real estate, employment and other commercial disputes, in both state and federal courts. The firm's securities practice includes representation of emerging and established corporations, venture capital partnerships and investment banking firms in public and private equity and debt financing. The firm also has a broad range of experience in the real estate area including purchases, sales and exchanges, construction and lending, receiverships and foreclosures.

**PHILIP F. MARANTZ,** born Los Angeles, California, February 15, 1934; admitted to bar, 1958, California; 1963, U.S. Supreme Court. *Education:* University of Southern California (B.S.L., 1957; LL.B., 1957). Author: "Consumerism Reaches the Sacrosanct Trust Deed," California State Bar Journal, 1977. Lecturer: University of Southern California Law School, 1983-1986; Southwestern School of Law, 1982-1983. Mediator, Los Angeles Superior Court. *Member:* State Bar of California; Western League of Savings Institutions. **PRACTICE AREAS:** Business Law; Commercial Law; Real Estate Finance; Secured Lending; Sports Law.

**LEIB ORLANSKI,** born Siberia, Russia, February 15, 1942; admitted to bar, 1968, California. *Education:* University of California at Los Angeles (B.A., 1964); University of Southern California (J.D., 1967). Order of the Coif. Notes and Comments Editor, Southern California Law Review, 1966-1967. Author: "Stock for Assets Acquisitions," 45 Los Angeles Bar Bulletin 361, 1970; "Going Public through the Back Door and the Shell Game," 58 Virginia Law Review 1451, 1972; "The Resale of Securities in Reorganization and the Bankruptcy Reform Act of 1978," 53 American Bank Law Journal 327, 1979; "The California Private Offering Prospectus," Business Law News, State Bar of California, Spring, 1980; "SEC Comments on the Offering Prospectus," 17 Review of Securities Regulation, 887, 1984; "Positioning for the Public Offering," 3 Bio/Technology 882, 1985; "Going Public," 8 Medical Device and Diagnostic Industry 67, 1986; "High Technology Leveraged Buyouts," The Journal of Buyouts and Acquisitions, August, 1985. Member: Corporations Committee, State Bar of California, 1982; American Electronics Association; CAL Tech/MIT Enterprise Forum. Lecturer: Los Angeles County Bar Association Annual Update on Developments in Securities Law, 1982; Lecturer and Chairman, UCLA Extension Courses on "Off-Balance Sheet Financing and Positioning for the Public Offering," 1983. *Member:* State Bar of California. **PRACTICE AREAS:** Securities; Leveraged Buyouts; Technology Business Startups; Venture Capital.

**RICHARD H. COOPER,** born Los Angeles, California, February 26, 1942; admitted to bar, 1966, California; 1976, U.S. Supreme Court. *Education:* University of California at Los Angeles (B.A., 1963; J.D., 1966); University of California at Berkeley. Phi Alpha Delta. Member, U.C.L.A. Law Review, 1964-1965. Author: "FSLIC as Adjudicator of Claims Against Failed Savings & Loan Associations," Volume 11, No. 7, Los Angeles Lawyer, October (1988); "Coit Independence Joint Venture v. FSLIC: The Supreme Court Speaks on Creditor Claims Against Failed Savings Institutions," Volume 12, No. 5, Los Angeles Lawyer, July-August (1989); "Resolving Real Estate Disciplinary Matters Prior to Hearing," 47 California State Bar Journal 330 (1972). Instructor in Litigation, UCLA Extension, 1988—. Judge Pro Tem, Los Angeles Municipal Court, 1991. Deputy Attorney General, 1966-1969. *Member:* State Bar of California. **PRACTICE AREAS:** Complex Litigation; Creditors' Rights; Securities Litigation; Alternative Dispute Resolution; Administrative Hearings and Appeals.

*(This Listing Continued)*

# PROFESSIONAL BIOGRAPHIES

## CALIFORNIA—BEVERLY HILLS

**MARK ALEXANDER KLEIN,** born Los Angeles, California, January 14, 1947; admitted to bar, 1972, California; 1976, U.S. Supreme Court. *Education:* University of California at Los Angeles (B.A., 1968); Hastings College of Law, University of California (J.D., 1971). Order of the Coif. Member, Thurston Scholastic Honor Society. Recipient, Sheffield Sanborn Scholarship and American Jurisprudence Awards for Agency and Civil Practice. Note and Comment Editor, Hastings Law Journal, 1970-1971. Author: "Statutory Construction Problems," 21 Hastings Law Journal 1303, 1970; "The Non-Signatory Party and his Rights to Attorneys' Fees," 13 Beverly Hills Bar Association Journal 229, 1979;; "Employee Stock Option Forfeiture Provisions," 12 Los Angeles Lawyer, No. 7, p. 41, October 1989. Panelist: "How to Prepare an Initial Public Offering," Sponsored by the Practising Law Institute, 1989. *Member:* State Bar of California. **PRACTICE AREAS:** Securities; Corporate Law; Mergers and Acquisitions. Email: makleinesq@aol.com

**PAUL W. SWEENEY, JR.,** born Atlanta, Georgia, December 11, 1950; admitted to bar, 1975, District of Columbia; 1984, California. *Education:* University of Southern California (B.S., cum laude, 1972); Columbia University (J.D., 1975). White House Fellow. Member, White House Staff, 1979-1980. Author: "How to Cut Litigation Costs," California Lawyer (1991). *Member:* State Bar of California; The District of Columbia Bar. **PRACTICE AREAS:** Commercial Litigation; Real Estate Litigation; Banking Litigation; Creditor's Rights; Employment Litigation.

**WILLIAM J. BERNFELD,** born Los Angeles, California, October 19, 1953; admitted to bar, 1979, California. *Education:* University of California at Los Angeles (B.A., 1975); Southwestern University (J.D., 1978). Phi Delta Phi. Author: "The Aftermath of Creative Financing," The California Lawyer, June 1983; "New Seller Financing Disclosure Legislation," Financing Real Property Transactions, Program Materials, June 1984 (CEB); "Creditors' Rights and §1121(d) Exclusivity Extensions—A Cry in the Forest?" California Bankruptcy Journal, Winter, 1990. Editor, Bankruptcy Study Group Bulletin, 1981-1982. *Member:* Beverly Hills Bar Association (Member, Legislative Committee); State Bar of California; Financial Lawyers Conference; Los Angeles Bankruptcy Forum. **PRACTICE AREAS:** Real Estate; Real Estate Finance; Creditor's Rights; Business Law; Commercial Law.

**THOMAS J. POLETTI,** born Omaha, Nebraska, June 19, 1957; admitted to bar, 1982, California. *Education:* Georgetown University (B.S.F.S., 1979); University of Santa Clara (J.D., magna cum laude, 1982). Recipient, American Jurisprudence Award in Criminal Law and Conflicts of Law. Lecturer: UCLA/MIT Venture Forum, 1986; USC School of Business Administration, 1987. *Member:* State Bar of California. **PRACTICE AREAS:** Corporate Securities; Intellectual Property.

---

**ROBERT E. FEYDER,** born Rochester, New York, May 13, 1961; admitted to bar, 1987, California. *Education:* Stanford University (A.B., with distinction, 1983); University of California at Los Angeles (J.D., 1987). Phi Alpha Delta. Member, Moot Court Honors Program. *Member:* State Bar of California. [Capt., JAGC, California Army National Guard, 1983-1992]

**MARK J. KELSON,** born Los Angeles, California, September 19, 1959; admitted to bar, 1991, California. *Education:* California State University at Northridge (B.S., 1985); Loyola Law School of Los Angeles (J.D., 1991). Order of the Coif. Staff Member, 1989-1990 and Executive Editor, 1990-1991, Loyola of Los Angeles Law Review. **PRACTICE AREAS:** Corporate; Corporate Securities.

**PATRICIA TASK CRAIGIE,** born Los Angeles, California, October 6, 1966; admitted to bar, 1993, California and U.S. District Court, Central District of California. *Education:* University of California, Irvine; California State University, Northridge (B.A., 1990); Loyola Law School (J.D., 1993). Chief Justice, Scott Moot Court Honors Board, 1992-1993. **PRACTICE AREAS:** Business Litigation; Employment Law; Bankruptcy.

**SUSAN B. KALMAN,** born Boston, Massachusetts, September 13, 1962; admitted to bar, 1993, California. *Education:* Tufts University (B.A., cum laude, 1984); Suffolk University (J.D., cum laude, 1992). Fulbright Scholar, West Berlin, Germany, 1984-1985. *Member:* Los Angeles County Bar Association (Member, Commercial Law and Bankruptcy Section, 1993—). (Resident). **LANGUAGES:** German, Spanish. **PRACTICE AREAS:** Corporate; Corporate Securities.

**CHRISTOPHER J. KONDON,** born Cleveland, Ohio, August 28, 1966; admitted to bar, 1994, California. *Education:* University of Colorado at Boulder (B.A., 1989); Loyola Law School (J.D., 1994). Staff Member, Loyola of Los Angeles, Law Review, 1993-1994. **PRACTICE AREAS:** Business Litigation; Bankruptcy.

*(This Listing Continued)*

**KATHERINE J. BLAIR,** born Fullerton, California, September 29, 1969; admitted to bar, 1994, California. *Education:* University of California, San Diego (B.A., 1991); Pepperdine University School of Law (J.D., 1994). **PRACTICE AREAS:** Securities; Corporate; Mergers and Acquisitions.

**JAMES K. LEE,** born Republic of Korea, October 31, 1963; admitted to bar, 1992, California and U.S. District Court, Central District of California. *Education:* University of Michigan (B.A., 1986); University of Minnesota Law School (J.D., 1992). Name and Comment Editor, Minnesota Journal of Global Trade, 1991-1992. Member: National Moot Court Team, 1990-1991; International Law Society, 1989-1990. Recipient, Stone Scholarship. Commissioner, Michigan Governor's Advisory Commission on Asian American Affairs, 1985-1986. *Member:* Los Angeles County and American Bar Associations; State Bar of California; Korean American Bar Association; Barristers Club. **LANGUAGES:** Korean. **PRACTICE AREAS:** Commercial Litigation; Real Estate Litigation; Securities Litigation.

**DARREN O. BIGBY,** born Los Angeles, California, August 28, 1969; admitted to bar, 1994, California. *Education:* University of Southern California (B.S., Finance, 1991; J.D., 1994). *Member:* State Bar of California. **PRACTICE AREAS:** Business Litigation.

**DEBORAH M. STURMAN,** born Los Angeles, California; admitted to bar, 1995, California, U.S. District Court, Central District of California and U.S. Court of Appeals, Ninth Circuit. *Education:* Royal Brussels Conservatory (Prix d'Excellence, 1992); University of California School of Law (J.D., 1995). **PRACTICE AREAS:** Securities.

REPRESENTATIVE CLIENTS: Benihana of Tokyo, Inc.; Brentwood Associates; Broadway Federal Bank; California Federal Bank; Cruttenden Roth Incorporated; Commonwealth Associates; Deswell Industries, Inc.; Downey Savings Bank; Eastman Kodak Company, Inc.; Family Federal Savings Bank; Federal Deposit Insurance Corporation; First Nationwide Bank; Great Western Bank; Heller Financial, Inc.; Highland Federal Bank; H.J. Meyers & Co., Inc.; Imperial Bank; Imperial Credit Industries, Inc.; Joseph Charles & Associates, Inc.; Lomas Mortgage USA; MRV Communications; Mustang Software, Inc.; Nam Tai Electronics, Inc.; Philip Morris Companies, Inc.; PNC Mortgage Mortgage; PriMerit Bank; Prudential Securities, Inc.; R.J. Reynolds Tobacco Co.; Rexhall Industries, Inc.; Robertson, Stephens & Company; Seda Specialty Packaging Corp.; Southern California Savings; Sutro & Co., Inc.; Utah Jazz Basketball Club; Western Financial Savings Bank; Wheat First Securities, Inc.; Wilshire State Bank.

---

## ROBERT J. FRIEDMAN

8648 WILSHIRE BOULEVARD
**BEVERLY HILLS, CALIFORNIA 90211**
*Telephone: 310-659-5757; 213-655-8861*
*Fax: 310-659-7773*

*Family Law.*

**ROBERT J. FRIEDMAN,** born Rockford, Illinois, December 18, 1946; admitted to bar, 1972, California. *Education:* University of California at Los Angeles (B.A., 1968); University of Southern California (J.D., 1971). *Member:* Beverly Hills (Member: 1980 —, Family Law Section and Member, Executive Committee, Family Law Section, 1988—; Chairperson, 1994) and Los Angeles County (Member, 1980—, Family Law Section and Member, Executive Committee, Family Law Section, 1982-1984) Bar Associations; State Bar of California (Member, 1980—, Family Law Section and Member: Executive Law Committee, Family Law Section, 1984-1987; Custody and Visitation Committee, 1980—; Property Committee, 1987—). (Certified Specialist, Family Law, The State Bar of California Board of Legal Specialization). **PRACTICE AREAS:** Family Law; Dissolution of Marriage Law; Prenuptial Agreements.

---

## FRIEDMAN & FRIEDMAN

*Established in 1975*

9454 WILSHIRE BOULEVARD, SUITE 313
**BEVERLY HILLS, CALIFORNIA 90212-2904**
*Telephone: 310-273-2800*
*Fax: 310-273-3642*

*General Civil and Trial Practice. Family Law.*

**IRA M. FRIEDMAN,** born Brooklyn, New York, March 22, 1946; admitted to bar, 1975, California and U.S. District Court, Central District of California; 1976, U.S. Tax Court; 1978, U.S. Court of Appeals, Ninth Circuit; 1980, U.S. Supreme Court. *Education:* Arizona State University (B.S., 1967); Lincoln University (J.D., 1974). Judge Pro Tempore: Beverly Hills Municipal Court, 1980-1994; Los Angeles Municipal Court, 1980—; Los

*(This Listing Continued)*

## FRIEDMAN & FRIEDMAN, Beverly Hills—Continued

Angeles Superior Court, 1980—. Mediator, Family Law, Los Angeles Superior Court, 1983—. Speaker: "Enforcement of Judgments in Family Law By Means Other Than Wage Assignment," Los Angeles County Bar Association, October, 1996; "Representing Clients in Child and Spousal Support Proceedings," Continuing Education of the Bar, 1985; 1987 Los Angeles County Bar Association "Recent Developments In Family Law;" 1987, Family Court Services-Conciliation Court Divorce Seminar; 1987 Beverly Hills Bar Association Family Law Symposium on, Post Trial Rights Remedies in Family Law. Barrister Workshop Panelist, "Child and Spousal Support: Consideration and Enforcement," 1988; "Discovery in Low & Medium Asset Cases," Beverly Hills Bar Association, 1991; "Drafting Marital Settlement Agreement", Continuing Education of the Bar, 1989. Panelist, Family Law Symposium, Beverly Hill Bar Association, 1984. Panelist, Family Law Section, American Bar Association Meeting, 1995. Featured Subject: "Lawyers Find Profits in Overdue Fees," California Law Business, September 28, 1992 and Two Join Forces To Help Firms Get Paid," California Law Business, January 25, 1993. Author: "Interspousal Torts, What Family Law Attorneys Should Know," Los Angeles Lawyer, May, 1992. "Dischargeability of Counsel Fees and Third Party Payments, in Bankruptcy, ", American Bar Association, Section of Family Law, Spring, 1995; "Non-Paying Clients: How to Spot Them and How to Deal With Them", Family Law News and Review, Los Angeles County Bar Association, Spring 1995; "Attorney-Client Fee Arbitration," Los Angeles Lawyer, October 1996. *Member:* Beverly Hills (Member, Board of Governors, 1981-1983; Treasurer, 1978-1979 and Chairman, 1980-1981, Family Law Committee), Los Angeles County (Member, Family Law Executive Committee, 1989-1992) and American (Member, Family Law Section; Vice Chair, Bankruptcy Committee, 1994, Chair, 1995) Bar Associations; State Bar of California. (Certified Specialist, Family Law, The State Bar of California Board of Legal Specialization). *REPORTED CASES:* In Re the Marriage of Allison (1979) 99 Cal. App. 3d 993, 168 Cal Rptr 160; In Re the Marriage of Gavron (1988) 203 Cal. App. 3d 705, 250 Cal Rptr 148. *PRACTICE AREAS:* Family Law; Civil and Commercial Litigation.

**ABBY B. FRIEDMAN,** born Uniontown, Pennsylvania, September 14, 1946; admitted to bar, 1990, California; 1991 U.S. District Court, Central District of California; 1992, U.S. District Court, Northern, Southern and Eastern Districts of California and U.S. Court of Appeals, Ninth Circuit; 1995, U.S. Supreme Court. *Education:* Arizona State University (B.A., 1967; M.A., 1968); University of West Los Angeles (J.D., 1990). Editor in Chief, 1990 and Assistant Editor 1989, University of West Los Angeles, Law Review. Judge Pro Tempore, Beverly Hills Municipal Court, 1996—; Los Angeles Municipal Court, 1996—. Author; "Personal Jurisdiction: The Evolution of the Minimum Contacts Analysis as Advanced Through Asahi Metal Industry Co. vs Superior Court and Federal Deposit Insurance Corp. vs British American Insurance Co.," University of West Los Angeles Law Review, Volume 20; "Interspousal Torts, What Family Law Attorneys Should Know," Los Angeles Lawyer, May 1992; "Dischargeability of Counsel Fees and Third Party Payments In Bankruptcy", American Bar Association, Section of Family Law, Spring, 1995; "Non-Paying Clients: How to Spot Them and How to Deal With Them", Family Law News and Review, Los Angeles County Bar Association, Spring, 1995; "Attorney-Client Fee Arbitration," Los Angeles Lawyer, October 1996. Listed in, Who's Who Among Students in American Universities & Colleges, Volume XXXIII. *Member:* Beverly Hills, Los Angeles County and American Bar Associations; State Bar of California. *PRACTICE AREAS:* Civil and Commercial Litigation; Family Law.

## FRYDRYCH & WEBSTER, INC.

Established in 1978

9777 WILSHIRE BOULEVARD, SUITE 1018
**BEVERLY HILLS, CALIFORNIA 90212**
Telephone: 310-274-0643
Telecopier: 310-274-5485

*Business Planning involving Corporations, Partnerships and Taxation, Civil Litigation, Family Law, Estate Planning, Commercial Law, Real Estate, Transactional Matters and Labor Relations.*

**JACK A. FRYDRYCH,** born Munich, Germany, August 15, 1948; admitted to bar, 1973, California and U.S. District Court, Central District of California; U.S. Supreme Court. *Education:* California State University, Northridge (B.A., 1970); Washington University (J.D., 1973); University of San Diego (LL.M. in Taxation, 1986). Who's Who in California. *Member:*

*(This Listing Continued)*

Los Angeles, Beverly Hills and American Bar Associations; State Bar of California. *PRACTICE AREAS:* Business Planning; Employment Law; Intellectual Property.

**J. MICHAEL WEBSTER,** born Los Angeles, California, July 28, 1947; admitted to bar, 1974, California and U.S. District Court, Central District of California. *Education:* California State University, Northridge (B.A. in History and Political Science, cum laude, 1970); Loyola Marymount University (J.D., with honors, 1974). Blue Key; Pi Sigma Alpha; Phi Alpha Theta. Candidate, Woodrow Wilson Fellowship (Masters Program). *Member:* Los Angeles, Beverly Hills and American Bar Associations; State Bar of California; California Trial Lawyers Association; Federation of Insurance and Corporate Counsel; Defense Research Institute; Association of Southern California Defense Counsel. [California Air National Guard, 1970-1976]. *PRACTICE AREAS:* Products Liability Law; Business Litigation; Family Law.

---

**RICHARD L. SPRUNGER,** born Los Angeles, California, January 5, 1949; admitted to bar, 1976, California; 1982, U.S. Tax Court. *Education:* University of Southern California (A.B., cum laude, 1971; J.D., 1975). Certified Public Accountant, California, 1982. Treasurer, City of San Marino, California, 1981-1983. *Member:* Los Angeles County and American Bar Associations; State Bar of California (Member, Sections on: Taxation; Real Property Law). [Captain, California Army National Guard, 1971-1980]. *PRACTICE AREAS:* General Corporate; Partnerships; Real Estate Law; Real Estate Finance; Land Use; Federal, State and Local Taxation; Estate Planning.

**GARY R. LINDER,** born Boston, Massachusetts, August 13, 1954; admitted to bar, 1986, Illinois and U.S. District Court, Northern District of Illinois (Not admitted in California). *Education:* Hebrew University, Jerusalem, Israel; Yeshiva University (B.A., summa cum laude, 1977); Northwestern University (J.D., 1986). Recipient, Frankel Award. *Member:* Chicago, Illinois State and American Bar Associations; Decalogue Society of Lawyers. *LANGUAGES:* Hebrew. *PRACTICE AREAS:* Corporate Law; Real Estate Law; Environmental Law.

**STEPHANIE H. IZEN,** born Regina, Saskatchewan, Canada, June 30, 1967; admitted to bar, 1993, California. *Education:* University of California, Los Angeles (B.A., 1989); Loyola Marymount University (J.D., 1993). Articles Editor, Entertainment Law Journal, 1991-1993. *Member:* Beverly Hills and American Bar Associations; State Bar of California; Los Angeles Women's Law Association.

## FUNSTEN & FRANZEN

An Association of Law Corporations

9595 WILSHIRE BOULEVARD, SUITE 305
**BEVERLY HILLS, CALIFORNIA 90212-2500**
Telephone: 310-273-3221 and 310-785-1710
Fax: 310-273-3229 and 310-785-1720

*Business, Entertainment and Tax Law. Civil Litigation (State and Federal).*

**PETER L. FUNSTEN,** born San Francisco, California, May 20, 1951; admitted to bar, 1978, California. *Education:* University of California, Berkeley (A.B., 1973); Hastings College of Law, University of California (J.D., 1977). Author: "TRA '86 Minimum Participation Rules" Pension Perspective 1, 1989; "California Loan Out Corporations," ALI-ABA Qualified Plans, PCs and Welfare Benefits 1023, 1989. Editor, "Professional Service Corporation Newsletter," 1987-1991. Lecturer, "Qualified Plans, PCs and Welfare Benefits," 1988, 1989; ALI-ABA, "Loan Out Corporation After The Tax Reform Act of 1986," Beverly Hills-Hollywood C.P.A. Society, 1988. *Member:* Los Angeles County and American Bar Associations; State Bar of California. *LANGUAGES:* Italian. *PRACTICE AREAS:* Taxation; Business; Entertainment Law.

**DON ERIK FRANZEN,** born Whittier, California, December 8, 1949; admitted to bar, 1975, California; 1976, U.S. District Court, Central District of California and U.S. Court of Appeals, Ninth Circuit; 1978, U.S. District Court, Eastern and Southern Districts of California, U.S. Court of Appeals, District of Columbia Circuit and U.S. Court of Appeals, Fifth Circuit; 1979, U.S. Supreme Court. *Education:* University of Southern California (B.A. in Philosophy, summa cum laude, 1972; J.D., 1975). Member, Southern California Law Review, 1973-1975. Author: Note, "The Development of the Sherman Act Section 2," 49 Southern California Law Review 154, 1975; "Enforcing A Cartel: A Study of the ICC," 11 Southwestern University Law Review 597, 1980; "Santa Monica Rent Control on its Tenth

*(This Listing Continued)*

Anniversary", 44, Oklahoma City University Qrtly. Rpt. 237, 1990. Lecturer, MBA Program, "Law and Regulatory Environment," Golden Gate University, 1982. *Member:* Los Angeles County and American Bar Associations. *LANGUAGES:* Spanish and Italian. *REPORTED CASES:* (Partial): Nourafchan v. Miner, 169 Cal.App.3d 746, 215 Cal.Rptr. 450 (1985); Tamarind Lithography Workshop, Inc. v. Sanders, 143 Cal.App.3d 571, 168 Cal.Rptr. 409 (1983); Cain v. Air Cargo, Inc., 599 F.2d 316 (9th Cir. 1979). *PRACTICE AREAS:* Entertainment Law; Business Law; Civil Litigation.

### OF COUNSEL

**JAMES H. LEHR,** born Omaha, Nebraska, August 17, 1953; admitted to bar, 1979, California; 1980, U.S. District Court, Central District of California and U.S. Court of Appeals, Ninth Circuit; 1981, U.S. District Court, Southern District of California. *Education:* Princeton University (A.B., 1975); Southwestern University (J.D., 1979). Member: Board of Governors; Moot Court Honors Program. Recipient, Schweizer Memorial Award for Best Brief. Associate Editor, Southwestern University Law Review, 1978-1979. Panelist, Seminar on Real Estate Broker Liability, Judicial Arbitration and Mediation Service, 1994. *Member:* Los Angeles County and American Bar Associations; State Bar of California. *REPORTED CASES:* Shell Oil Co. v. Nelson Oil Co., Inc., 627 F.2d 228 (T.E.C.A. 1980), cert. den. 449 U.S. 1022; Mobil Oil Corporation v. Rossi (1982), 138 Cal.App. 3d 256, 187 Cal. Rptr. 845; Schroeder v. TWA, Inc., 702 F.2d 189 (9th Cir. 1983); Davis v. Gulf Oil Corp., 572 F.Supp. 1393 (C.D. Cal. 1983); Prestin v. Mobil Oil Corp., 741 F.2d 268 (9th Cir. 1984); A.L.L. Roofing & Bldg. Materials Corp. v. Community Bank (1986), 182 Cal.App. 3d 356, 227 Cal. Rptr. 308. *PRACTICE AREAS:* Business Litigation and Appeals; Banking Law; Unfair Competition Law.

## GANG, TYRE, RAMER & BROWN, INC.

Established in 1931

132 SOUTH RODEO DRIVE
**BEVERLY HILLS, CALIFORNIA 90212-2403**
Telephone: 310-777-4800
Fax: 310-777-4801

*Entertainment and Communications Industries Law and Related Services.*

*FIRM PROFILE: Gang, Tyre, Ramer & Brown, Inc. focuses on general transactional representation in the entertainment and communications industries and also furnishes counselling and representation in connection with intellectual property, personal business matters, wealth transfers and real estate.*

**NORMAN R. TYRE,** born Boston, Massachusetts, August 28, 1910; admitted to bar, 1933, California. *Education:* University of California at Berkeley; Stanford University (B.A., great distinction, 1930); Harvard University (LL.B., 1933). Phi Beta Kappa. Author, "Structuring of the Entertainment Project," presented before Entertainment Industry Conference of California Certified Public Accountants Foundation, 1972. Vice President and Director, Motion Picture and Television Tax Institute, 1975—. Member, Foreign Policy Association, 1972-1986. *Member:* Los Angeles County and American Bar Associations; State Bar of California; Los Angeles Copyright Society. *PRACTICE AREAS:* Entertainment Law; Real Estate; General Business.

**HERMIONE K. BROWN,** born Syracuse, New York, September 29, 1915; admitted to bar, 1947, California; 1970, U.S. Supreme Court. *Education:* Wellesley College (B.A., 1934); University of Paris, Sorbonne, Paris, France; University of California at Berkeley; University of Southern California (LL.B., 1947). Phi Beta Kappa; Order of the Coif. Editor-in-Chief, University of Southern California Law Review, 1946-1947. Author: "Copyright, Death and Taxes—Some Observations on Administering Estates with Literary Property Assets," The 21st Annual Tax and Probate Forum sponsored by Title Insurance and Trust Company, 1969; "Human Aspects of Estate Representation," Notre Dame Estate Planning Institute, 1976 Proceedings. Lecturer, Entertainment Law, University of Southern California Law School, 1973-1977. *Member:* Los Angeles County and American Bar Associations; State Bar of California (Member, Executive Committee/Estate Planning, Trust and Probate Law Section, 1983-1990); Los Angeles Copyright Society (Member, Board of Trustees, 1976-1981; President, 1979-1980). *PRACTICE AREAS:* Estate Planning and Administration; Intellectual Property; Real Estate; General Business.

**PAYSON WOLFF** (1921-1995).

**BRUCE M. RAMER,** born Teaneck, New Jersey, August 2, 1933; admitted to bar, 1959, New Jersey; 1963, California; 1971, U.S. Supreme Court. *Education:* Princeton University (A.B., 1955); Harvard University

*(This Listing Continued)*

(LL.B., 1958). Executive Director, Entertainment Law Institute, University of Southern California Law Center, 1972—. Member: Board of Councilors, University of Southern California Law Center, 1985-1986; Board of Trustees, Loyola Marymount University; Board of Directors, KCET; Board of Directors, California Community Foundation. Chairman, Board of Governors, American Jewish Committee. *Member:* Los Angeles County (Member, Section on Intellectual Property), Beverly Hills (Member, Entertainment Law Committee, 1971—) and American (Member, Sections on: Patent, Trademark and Copyright Law; Taxation) Bar Associations; State Bar of California; Los Angeles Copyright Society (President, 1974-1975); California Copyright Conference (President, 1973-1974). *PRACTICE AREAS:* Entertainment Law.

**CHARLES A. SCOTT,** born Vienna, Austria, May 9, 1932; admitted to bar, 1957, California; 1960, U.S. Supreme Court. *Education:* University of California at Los Angeles (A.B., 1954); Harvard University (LL.B., 1957). Phi Beta Kappa. *Member:* State Bar of California; Los Angeles Copyright Society. *PRACTICE AREAS:* Entertainment Law.

**DONALD S. PASSMAN,** born Dallas, Texas, November 3, 1945; admitted to bar, 1971, California. *Education:* University of Texas (B.A., 1967); Harvard University (J.D., 1970). Phi Beta Kappa. Member: Harvard Law School Board of Student Advisors, 1969-1970; Harvard Law School Legal Aid Society, 1968-1969. Instructor, University of Southern California Law Center Advanced Professional Program, Business and Legal Aspects of the Music Business, 1978—; Business and Legal Aspects of Home Video and Pay Television, 1982. President and Chairman, Music Industry Division of City of Hope, 1986-1990. Author: "All You Need to Know About The Music Business" (Simon & Schuster), 1994. *Member:* Los Angeles County and Beverly Hills (Member, Entertainment Law Committee, 1971—) Bar Associations; State Bar of California; Los Angeles Copyright Society. *PRACTICE AREAS:* Entertainment Law.

**HAROLD A. BROWN,** born Los Angeles, California, January 27, 1952; admitted to bar, 1976, California. *Education:* Occidental College (B.A., 1973); Boalt Hall School of Law, University of California (J.D., 1976). Order of the Coif. Member, California Law Review, 1975-1976. Co-Author: "Disqualification of the Testifying Advocate—A Firm Rule," The North Carolina Law Review, Vol. 57, pg. 597; "What Counsels the Counselor? The Code of Professional Responsibility's Ethical Considerations— A Preventive Law Analysis," Valparaiso University Law Review Vol. 10, Page 453. Instructor, The Television Industry: Practical and Business Aspects, University of Southern California Law Center Advanced Professional Program, 1980, 1983. Director, 1984-1994 and Executive Director, 1994—, Entertainment Law Institute, University of Southern California. Member: Board of Directors, Geffen Playhouse, 1995— (Chairman, Finance and Audit Committee, 1996—; Board of Directors, Activision, Inc., 1996—. *Member:* Beverly Hills (Member, 1977— and Co-Chairman, 1984-1986, Entertainment Law Committee) and Los Angeles County Bar Associations; Los Angeles Copyright Society. *PRACTICE AREAS:* Entertainment Law.

**TOM R. CAMP,** born Lincoln, Nebraska, September 6, 1954; admitted to bar, 1979, California; 1980, Nebraska. *Education:* University of Nebraska (B.S., 1975); Stanford University (J.D., 1979). Beta Gamma Sigma; Omicron Delta Epsilon; Phi Eta Sigma; Order of the Coif. Member, Stanford Law Review, 1979. *Member:* State Bar of California; Nebraska State and American Bar Associations. *PRACTICE AREAS:* General Business; Corporate; Entertainment Law; Real Estate.

**LAWRENCE D. ROSE,** born Los Angeles, California, October 12, 1955; admitted to bar, 1984, California, U.S. District Court, Central District of California and U.S. Court of Appeals, Ninth Circuit. *Education:* University of California at Los Angeles (B.A., 1980); University of Southern California (J.D., 1984). Order of the Coif (Southern California Chapter). Recipient: Law Alumni Award for Highest Scholastic Average, Class of 1984; American Jurisprudence Awards for Excellence in Evidence, Criminal Law and Torts. Member, Southern California Law Review, 1983-1984. *Member:* Beverly Hills, Los Angeles County and American Bar Associations; State Bar of California. *PRACTICE AREAS:* Entertainment Law.

**JEFFREY M. MANDELL,** born New York, N.Y., October 27, 1952; admitted to bar, 1978, New York and U.S. District Court, Southern and Eastern Districts of New York; 1986, California. *Education:* University of Wisconsin (B.A., cum laude, 1974); University of Michigan (J.D., 1977). Note and Comment Editor, University of Michigan Journal of Law Reform, 1976-1977. General Counsel, National Endowment for the Arts, 1982-1985. Judge Pro Tem, Los Angeles County Municipal Court. *Member:* American Film Marketing Association (Arbitrator). *PRACTICE AREAS:* Entertainment Law.

*(This Listing Continued)*

CALIFORNIA—BEVERLY HILLS

**GANG, TYRE, RAMER & BROWN, INC., Beverly Hills—** Continued

**KEVIN S. MARKS,** born Santa Monica, California, January 5, 1957; admitted to bar, 1982, California; 1983, District of Columbia. *Education:* Stanford University (A.B., with distinction, 1979); Boalt Hall School of Law, University of California (J.D., 1982). Phi Beta Kappa. Projects Editor, California Law Review, 1981-1982. Recipient, First National Prize, Nathan Burkan Memorial Copyright Competition, 1982. **PRACTICE AREAS:** Entertainment Law; Intellectual Property.

**GREGG HARRISON,** born Los Angeles, California, December 21, 1946; admitted to bar, 1971, California. *Education:* University of California at Berkeley (A.B., 1967); Harvard University (J.D., 1970). Phi Beta Kappa. *Member:* State Bar of California. **PRACTICE AREAS:** Entertainment Law.

**FRED D. TOCZEK,** born Long Beach, California, November 5, 1964; admitted to bar, 1989, California. *Education:* University of California at Los Angeles (B.A., 1986); University of Southern California (J.D., 1989). Recipient, Merit Scholar Award, 1986-1989. Member, Southern California Law Review, 1988-1989. Co-author: "Protecting Artistic Vision: A Transactional Approach", Syllabus, 1991 Entertainment Law Institute, University of Southern California. Member; Planning Committee, Entertainment Law Institute, University of Southern California, 1992—. *Member:* Los Angeles County Bar Association; State Bar of California. **PRACTICE AREAS:** Entertainment Law.

**NANCY L. BOXWELL,** born Encino, California, June 24, 1963; admitted to bar, 1991, California, U.S. District Court, Central District of California and U.S. Court of Appeals, Ninth Circuit. *Education:* University of Southern California (B.S., summa cum laude, 1985); University of California, Los Angeles School of Law (J.D., 1990). Order of the Coif. Recipient, American Jurisprudence Award for Excellence in Real Property and Commercial Law. Articles Editor, Environmental Law Journal, 1989-1990. Clerk to Honorable Arthur L. Alarcon, U.S. Court of Appeals for the Ninth Circuit, 1990-1991. **PRACTICE AREAS:** General Business; Corporate; Real Estate.

**STEVEN G. KRONE,** born Winter Park, Florida, February 21, 1964; admitted to bar, 1994, California. *Education:* University of Southern California School of Cinema-Television (A.B., 1988); University of Chicago Law School (J.D., 1992). Law Clerk to: the Honorable Abner J. Mikva, Chief Judge, U.S. Court of Appeals for the District of Columbia Circuit, 1992-1993; the Honorable William J. Brennan, Jr. and the Honorable David H. Souter, Justices of the U.S. Supreme Court, 1993-1994. *Member:* Beverly Hills, Los Angeles County and American Bar Associations; State Bar of California. **PRACTICE AREAS:** Entertainment Law.

**BARBARA SILBERBUSCH,** born Rotterdam, The Netherlands, December 27, 1966; admitted to bar, 1995, New York and U.S. District Court, Southern and Eastern Districts of New York; 1996, California, U.S. District Court, Central District of California and U.S. Court of Appeals, Ninth Circuit. *Education:* University of Amsterdam, School of Law (J.D., 1991); University of California, Los Angeles School of Law (LL.M., 1992). *Member:* American Bar Association; State Bar of California; State Bar of New York. **LANGUAGES:** Dutch, German. **PRACTICE AREAS:** Entertainment Law; Estate Planning.

*OF COUNSEL*

**MARTIN GANG** (Retired, 1995).

**ARNOLD D. BURK** (Retired, 1995).

REFERENCES: Bank of America (Los Angeles Main Office, also Hollywood Main Office); City National Bank (Beverly Hills Main Office).

---

## *LAW OFFICE OF EMMETT J. GANTZ*

SUITE 208, 280 SOUTH BEVERLY DRIVE
**BEVERLY HILLS, CALIFORNIA 90212**
Telephone: 213-879-7866; 310-276-3800
Fax: 310-275-5087

*Professional Liability, Products Liability, Medical Malpractice, Insurance Bad Faith, Complex Civil Litigation and Personal Injury. Civil Trial and Appellate Practice.*

**EMMETT J. GANTZ,** born Chicago, Illinois, February 15, 1943; admitted to bar, 1973, California; 1974, U.S. District Court, Central District of *(This Listing Continued)*

CAA44B

MARTINDALE-HUBBELL LAW DIRECTORY 1997

California; 1984, U.S. District Court, Northern District of California. *Education:* University of Illinois Medical Center, Chicago, Illinois (B.S., 1967); Loyola Law School (J.D., 1973). *Member:* State Bar of California; American Bar Association (Member, Section of Litigation); California Trial Lawyers Association; Los Angeles Trial Lawyers Association; Association of Trial Lawyers of America; American Society of Pharmacy Law. **PRACTICE AREAS:** Professional Liability Law; Products Liability Law; Medical Malpractice; Insurance Bad Faith Law; Personal Injury Law.

---

**BARRY P. KAYE,** born Bronx, New York, October 24, 1960; admitted to bar, 1986, California and U.S. District Court, Central District of California; U.S. District Court, Southern District of California. *Education:* University of California at Los Angeles (B.A., 1982); Loyola Marymount University (J.D., 1985). *Member:* Los Angeles County and American Bar Associations; State Bar of California; Los Angeles Trial Lawyers Association; California Trial Lawyers Association. **PRACTICE AREAS:** Products Liability; Premises Liability; Personal Injury; General Civil Litigation.

REFERENCE: City National Bank, Beverly Hills, California.

---

## *GERNSBACHER & McGARRIGLE*

9100 WILSHIRE BOULEVARD
EAST TOWER, SUITE 710
**BEVERLY HILLS, CALIFORNIA 90212**
Telephone: 310-281-0100
Telecopier: 310-281-0755

*Real Estate Transactions; Financing, Management and Litigation; Business Litigation; Corporate and General Civil Litigation; Entertainment Litigation; Federal and State Court Appeals.*

*MEMBERS OF FIRM*

**DAVID L. GERNSBACHER,** born Fort Worth, Texas, August 21, 1953; admitted to bar, 1979, California. *Education:* University of California at Los Angeles (B.A., magna cum laude, 1976); University of Southern California (J.D., 1979). Judge Pro Tem, Los Angeles Municipal Court, 1986—.

**PATRICK C. McGARRIGLE,** born Saratoga Springs, New York, March 12, 1965; admitted to bar, 1990, California. *Education:* Columbia University (B.A., 1986); Southwestern University School of Law (J.D., 1990).

**PAUL B. BEACH,** born Pasadena, California, November 14, 1967; admitted to bar, 1993, California, U.S. District Court, Central District of California and U.S. Court of Appeals, Ninth Circuit. *Education:* University of California at Los Angeles (B.A., 1989); Loyola Law School (J.D., 1993). Phi Delta Phi (Secretary, 1992; President, 1993). Recipient: American Jurisprudence Award in Criminal Procedure; Property II: Future Interests. 43rd Annual National Moot Court Competition: Western United States Region, First Place and Best Brief. Scott Moot Court Competition: Finalist, Best Oralist and Best Brief; Third Place, Overall Competition. Member, Moot Court Team. Extern to the Honorable Alex Kozinski, U.S. Court of Appeals, Ninth Circuit, 1991-1992. Member, Scott Moot Court Honors Board, National Team, 1992-1993. *Member:* Beverly Hills, Los Angeles County, California Bar Associations; Bar Association of the District of Columbia; District of Columbia Bar.

---

## *GLASSMAN, BROWNING & SALTSMAN, INC.*

Established in 1968

SUITE 204, 360 NORTH BEDFORD DRIVE
**BEVERLY HILLS, CALIFORNIA 90210**
Telephone: 310-278-5100
Fax: 310-271-6041

*Civil and Criminal Litigation in all State and Federal Trial and Appellate Courts. Defamation and Invasion of Privacy, Family Law, Estate, Trust and Income Tax Planning, Probate, Corporate, Entertainment, Personal Injury, Malpractice Litigation, Real Estate and General Business Law.*

**ROGER A. BROWNING,** born Long Beach, California, June 22, 1940; admitted to bar, 1966, California, U.S. District Court, Central and Northern Districts of California and U.S. Court of Appeals, Ninth Circuit; 1973, U.S. Supreme Court. *Education:* University of California at Berkeley (B.S., 1962); Boalt Hall School of Law, University of California (J.D., 1965). Phi *(This Listing Continued)*

Delta Phi. Assistant U.S. Attorney, Central District of California, 1966-1968. Special Assistant to Department of Justice, 1969. *Member:* Beverly Hills and Los Angeles County Bar Associations; State Bar of California; American Judicature Society. *PRACTICE AREAS:* Business Transactional Matters; Civil and Criminal Tax Matters; Corporate and Partnership Planning; Real Estate; Income Taxation.

**ANTHONY M. GLASSMAN,** born Los Angeles, California, December 18, 1939; admitted to bar, 1966, California; U.S. District Court, Central and Northern Districts of California; U.S. Court of Appeals, Fifth, Ninth and Eleventh Circuits; U.S. Supreme Court. *Education:* University of Southern California (B.A., 1962); Boalt Hall School of Law, University of California (J.D., 1965). Assistant U.S. Attorney, Central District of California, 1966-1968. Special Assistant to the Department of Justice, 1968. *Member:* Beverly Hills and Los Angeles County Bar Associations; State Bar of California. *REPORTED CASES:* Ward v. News Group, 733 F.Supp. 83 USDC 1990); Tamarind Lithography Workshop, Inc. v. Sanders, 143 Cal. App.3d 571, 193 Cal.Rptr. 409 (1983); Koch v. Goldway, 817 F.2d 507 (9th Cir. 1987). *PRACTICE AREAS:* Defamation; Invasion of Privacy; Misappropriation; Copyright; Entertainment Litigation; Constitutional Civil Litigation; White Collar Criminal Defense.

**JANE D. SALTSMAN,** born Los Angeles, California, June 13, 1950; admitted to bar, 1974, California and U.S. District Court, Central and Northern Districts of California. *Education:* University of California at Berkeley (B.A., 1971); Boalt Hall School of Law, University of California (J.D., 1974). Phi Beta Kappa. *Member:* Beverly Hills and Los Angeles County Bar Associations; State Bar of California. *PRACTICE AREAS:* Family Law; General Civil Litigation.

**AMY OSRAN JACOBS,** born Highland Park, Illinois, October 21, 1958; admitted to bar, 1983, California; 1984, U.S. Tax Court and U.S. District Court, Central District of California. *Education:* Iowa State University (B.S., 1980); University of Illinois (J.D., 1983). Phi Alpha Delta. *Member:* Beverly Hills and American Bar Associations; State Bar of California. *PRACTICE AREAS:* Estate Planning; Taxation Law; Corporate Planning; General Business.

**BARBARA TARLOW,** born Boston, Massachusetts, April 23, 1944; admitted to bar, 1986, California and U.S. District Court, Central District of California. *Education:* Boston University (B.A., 1966; M.A., 1971); Loyola Law School of Los Angeles (J.D., cum laude, 1986). Member, Loyola Law Review, 1985-1986. *Member:* Los Angeles and Century City Bar Associations; State Bar of California. *PRACTICE AREAS:* Defamation and Invasion of Privacy; Defense of Media Torts; Civil Litigation.

---

**LORI A. NIELSEN,** born Logan, Utah, August 16, 1963; admitted to bar, 1988, Utah; 1992, California. *Education:* Utah State University (B.S., 1985); University of Utah (J.D., 1988). William H. Leary Scholar. Staff Member, 1986-1988 and Associate Editor, 1987-1988, Utah Law Review. Judicial Clerk, Honorable Chief Justice Gordon R. Hall, Utah Supreme Court, 1991-1992. *Member:* Utah State Bar. *PRACTICE AREAS:* Civil Litigation; Appellate Practice.

**DAVID A. CARMAN,** born Newport News, Virginia, August 23, 1962; admitted to bar, 1990, California. *Education:* Kenyon College (B.A., summa cum laude, 1984); Syracuse University (J.D., summa cum laude, 1990). Phi Beta Kappa; Phi Alpha Delta; Order of the Coif. Member, Syracuse University Law Review, 1989-1990; Moot Court Board. *Member:* Century City, Beverly Hills and Los Angeles County Bar Associations; State Bar of California. *PRACTICE AREAS:* Civil Litigation; General Litigation.

**STEVEN BERKOWITZ,** born Detroit, Michigan, December 13, 1958; admitted to bar, 1985, Massachusetts; 1986, California. *Education:* University of Michigan (B.A., 1981); Boston University (J.D., 1984). Joseph Tauro Scholar. School Team Coach for ATLA National Student Trial Competition, 1984-1986. *Member:* San Diego County and American Bar Associations; State Bar of California (Member, Civil Litigation Section). *PRACTICE AREAS:* Civil Litigation; General Litigation; Family Law.

**KATHRYN L. TURPIN,** born Corpus Christi, Texas, September 22, 1955; admitted to bar, 1980, California. *Education:* University of Texas (B.A., with high honors, 1977; J.D., 1980). Phi Kappa Phi; Phi Beta Kappa; Beta Alpha Psi. Author: "Taxation— Control of Foreign Corporations," Texas International Law Journal, Vol. 14, No. 3, 1979. Instructor, Legal Research and Writing/Oral Advocacy, University of Texas School of Law, 1979-1980. *Member:* Los Angeles County (Member, Business Law Section) and American Bar Associations; State Bar of California. *PRACTICE*

*(This Listing Continued)*

*AREAS:* Business Transactional; Corporate Planning; Taxation Law; General Business; Partnership Planning.

*OF COUNSEL*

**BARBARA IRSHAY ZIPPERMAN,** born Cleveland, Ohio, February 27, 1951; admitted to bar, 1978, California. *Education:* California State University at Northridge (B.A., 1973); San Fernando Valley College of Law (J.D., 1978). *Member:* Beverly Hills, San Fernando Valley (Member, Executive Committee, Family Law Section, 1981-1984) and Los Angeles County Bar Associations; State Bar of California. *PRACTICE AREAS:* Family Law; Probate Law.

REPRESENTATIVE CLIENTS: Playboy Enterprises, Inc.; Hugh M. Hefner; Globe International, Inc.; The Magnin Company, Inc.; Pittard Design, Inc.; Gold Mountain Entertainment; Flying U Rodeo; ARNCO, Inc.; Automotive Dealers' Marketing, Inc.; The Carsey-Werner Company; California Publishing Liquidating Corporation; Marco Mfg., Inc.; Jerry Magnin; Bill Medley; Del West Engineering.

---

## GLICKFELD, FIELDS & JAFFE

*A PROFESSIONAL CORPORATION*

**9460 WILSHIRE BOULEVARD, FIFTH FLOOR**
**BEVERLY HILLS, CALIFORNIA 90212-2711**
Telephone: 310-550-7222
Fax: 310-550-6222

*Civil Trial and Appellate Practice in State and Federal Courts, with emphasis on Business, Entertainment and Intellectual Property, Real Estate and Construction, Antitrust, Banking, Bankruptcy, Probate and Securities Litigation.*

*FIRM PROFILE: Glickfeld, Fields and Jaffe represents both individuals and businesses in a broad range of sophisticated business litigation. The firm's lawyers and staff are dedicated to providing the highest quality service on a personal, timely and cost-effective basis.*

**MICHAEL L. GLICKFELD,** born New York, N.Y., July 1, 1944; admitted to bar, 1970, California, U.S. District Court, Central, Northern and Southern Districts of California and U.S. Court of Appeals, Ninth Circuit. *Education:* University of California at Los Angeles (B.A., 1966; J.D., 1969). Arbitrator, Business Law Panel, Los Angeles Superior Court, 1979-1990. *Member:* Beverly Hills (Member, Entertainment Law Committee, 1982-1990), Los Angeles County (Member, State Courts Executive Committee, 1988-1994) and American (Member, Sections on: Antitrust Law; Litigation) Bar Associations; The State Bar of California; Association of Business Trial Lawyers.

**CRAIG M. FIELDS,** born Los Angeles, California, July 29, 1956; admitted to bar, 1982, California. *Education:* University of California at Berkeley (A.B., 1978); University of California at Los Angeles (J.D., 1982). Phi Beta Kappa. Member, UCLA Law Review, 1981-1982. *Member:* Los Angeles County Bar Association; State Bar of California; Association of Business Trial Lawyers.

**JUDIANNE JAFFE,** born Washington, D.C., May 29, 1951; admitted to bar, 1976, California. *Education:* University of California at Los Angeles (A.B., summa cum laude, 1972); University of Southern California (J.D., 1976). Phi Beta Kappa; Phi Alpha Delta; Order of the Coif. Associate Editor, Beverly Hills Bar Journal, 1977-1980. Author: "License to Kill-Strengthening the Attorney's Privilege to Advise Clients Not to Perform Contracts," 4 Entertainment and Sports Lawyer, 1985. *Member:* Beverly Hills (Chairman, Litigation Section, 1980-1981; 1994-1996); Los Angeles County (Member, Committee on the Status of Women in the Legal Profession, 1989) and American (Member, Sections on: Antitrust Law; Litigation) Bar Associations; The State Bar of California (Chairman, Committee on Administration of Justice, 1990-1991).

*OF COUNSEL*

**LAWRENCE M. JACOBSON,** born Los Angeles, California, June 4, 1956; admitted to bar, 1981, California and U.S. District Court, Central District of California; 1982, U.S. Court of Appeals, Ninth Circuit; 1983, U.S. District Court, Northern and Southern Districts of California; 1986, U.S. District Court, Eastern District of California. *Education:* University of California at Berkeley (A.B., 1978); University of California at Los Angeles (J.D., 1981). Member, Moot Court Honors Program. *Member:* Los Angeles County and American Bar Associations; State Bar of California. (Also of counsel to, Baker and Jacobson, A Professional Corporation).

REFERENCE: First Los Angeles Bank (Century City Main Branch).

## CYRUS V. GODFREY

360 NORTH BEDFORD DRIVE, SUITE 204
**BEVERLY HILLS, CALIFORNIA 90210**
Telephone: 310-278-8871
Fax: 310-271-6041

*Entertainment Litigation.*

**CYRUS V. GODFREY,** born Pittsburgh, Pennsylvania, August 30, 1949; admitted to bar, 1975, California; 1985, New York. *Education:* University of California at Santa Barbara (B.A., with honors, 1971); University of California at Davis (J.D., 1975). Member, University of California at Davis Law Review, 1973-1975. Author: "Emergency Care: Physicians Should be Placed Under an Affirmative Duty to Render Essential Medical Care to Emergency Situations," 7 University of California at Davis Law Review 246, 1974. *Member:* Los Angeles County, Federal and American Bar Associations; The State Bar of California (Member: Committee on Administration of Justice, 1987-1990; Litigation Section).

## EUGENE GOLDEN

9595 WILSHIRE BOULEVARD, SUITE 900
**BEVERLY HILLS, CALIFORNIA 90212-2509**
Telephone: 310-275-9040
Fax: 310-271-4062

*General Civil Practice, Litigation, Corporation, Business, Real Property, Trust, Probate, Will Contests and Personal Injury.*

**EUGENE GOLDEN,** born Norristown, Pennsylvania, January 16, 1929; admitted to bar, 1953, Texas; 1954, California. *Education:* University of Texas (B.B.A., 1950; LL.B., 1953). Beta Gamma Sigma; Order of the Coif; Phi Delta Phi; The Chancellors. Texas Law Review. *Member:* Beverly Hills, Los Angeles County and American Bar Associations; State Bar of California; State Bar of Texas; American Symphony Orchestra League; Chamber Music America; Association of Mexican Symphony Orchestras.

## SUSAN T. GOLDSTEIN

9401 WILSHIRE BOULEVARD, SUITE 1100
**BEVERLY HILLS, CALIFORNIA 90212**
Telephone: 310-724-5380
Fax: 310-274-8351

*Practice limited to Family Law.*

**SUSAN T. GOLDSTEIN,** born New York, N.Y., January 6, 1954; admitted to bar, 1978, Ohio; 1979, California. *Education:* University of Connecticut (B.A., magna cum laude, 1975); University of Toledo (J.D., 1977). *Member:* Beverly Hills (California) Bar Associations (Member, Family Law Section).

## GREBOW, MARUYAMA, PRINSTER & YEE

131 SOUTH RODEO DRIVE, SUITE 250
**BEVERLY HILLS, CALIFORNIA 90212**
Telephone: 310-247-7550
Fax: 310-247-7552

*Corporate and Real Estate Transactions, Commercial and Tort Litigation, Mobilehome Park Law, Premises Liability and Insurance Defense Litigation.*

**ARTHUR GREBOW,** born New York, New York, November 17, 1942; admitted to bar, 1968, California, U.S. District Court, Central and Southern Districts of California; 1977, U.S. Court of Appeals, Ninth Circuit. *Education:* Columbia University (B.A., 1964); Cornell University (J.D., 1967). Law Clerk to Presiding Justice, Lester Wm. Roth, California Court of Appeals, 1967-1968. Judge Pro-Tem, Los Angeles Municipal Court, 1977—. Judge Pro Tem, Beverly Hills Municipal Court, 1980—. Principal Hearing Referee, State Bar Court, 1980—. Arbitrator, Los Angeles Superior Court, 1980—. Disciplinary Officer, Beverly Hills Bar Association; Arbitration Officer, Beverly Hills Bar Association; Arbitration Officer, State Bar of California. Lecturer, Continuing Education of the Bar, Evaluating and Proving Damages, 1977. Lecturer and Author: Mobilehome Housing Litigation, Western Mobilehome Parkowners Association WMA Reporter, 1991—. Senior Editor, Beverly Hills Bar Association Journal, 1975. Co-Author, with Paul R. Lees-Haley, PH.D., CPCU Journal, Fear of Future Illness, March, 1994. *Member:* Beverly Hills (Board of Governors, 1976-1978; Board of Governors, Barrister, 1972-1978), Los Angeles County and American (Member, Litigation Section) Bar Associations; California Trial Lawyers Association; Association of Business Trial Lawyers. **REPORTED CASES:** Rubin v. Green (1993) 4 Cal.4th 1187; Westbrook v. Fairchild (1992) 7 Cal.App.4th 889; Estate of Zucker (1990) 218 Cal.App.3d 1198; John F. Mutall and Associates, Inc. v. Cloutier (1987) 194 Cal.App.3d 1049; Westbrook v. Superior Court (1986) 176 Cal.App.3d 703; Appalachin Insurance Company v. Superior Court (1984) 162 Cal.App.3d 427; Freeman v. Jacques Orthopedic and Joint Implant Surg. 721 F.2d 654 (9th Cir. 1983); Columbus Line, Inc. v. Gray Line Sight-seeing Companies Associated, Inc. (1981) 120 Cal.App.3d 622; Hummell v. S.E. Rykoff (1980) 634 F.2d 446; Lindros v. Torrance School Board (1973) 9 Cal.3d 524. **PRACTICE AREAS:** Business Litigation; Probate Litigation; Insurance Defense Litigation; Mobilehome Park Defense Litigation.

**WILLIAM K. MARUYAMA,** born Culver City, California, April 4, 1962; admitted to bar, 1988, California; 1991, U.S. District Court, Central District of California; 1995, U.S. District Court, Northern District of California. *Education:* University of California at Los Angeles (B.A., 1985); McGeorge School of Law, University of the Pacific (J.D., 1988). Phi Alpha Theta; Phi Delta Phi. "Ethical Stands", California Law Business Journal, Feb. 8, 1996. Asian Professional Exchange (APEX), 1996—. Japanese American Citizen's League, Legal Advisor, National Youth Counsel, 1988-1991. Member, Japanese American Republicans, Vice President, Legislative Affairs, 1996—. *Member:* Los Angeles County and American Bar Associations; National Asian Pacific American Bar Association (Chair, Legislation Committee, 1994—); Japanese American Bar Association (Board of Directorship, Treasurer, 1995-1996); Asian Pacific American Law Students Association (McGeorge Chapter, Vice President (1986-1988). **LANGUAGES:** Japanese. **PRACTICE AREAS:** Commercial/Corporate Litigation; Tort Insurance Defense Litigation; Product Liability; Probate Litigation; Bankruptcy Litigation.

**PATRICK K. PRINSTER,** born Grand Junction, Colorado, November 28, 1952; admitted to bar, 1979, California. *Education:* Brigham Young University (B.A., 1976); McGeorge School of Law, University of the Pacific (J.D., 1979). Phi Kappa Phi. International Moot Court Champion. Commissioner, Los Angeles County Real Estate Commission, 1996—. Member, City of West Hollywood. Fine Arts Advisory Board, 1996—. Adjunct Professor, Business Law, National University, Los Angeles, California, 1993—. Adjunct Professor, Business Law, American Management-Tech University, Los Angeles, California, 1994—. California Licensed Real Estate Broker, 1980—. *Member:* Los Angeles County and Beverly Hills Bar Associations; International Council of Shopping Centers; Building Owners and Managers Association. **LANGUAGES:** Spanish. **PRACTICE AREAS:** Real Estate Transactions; Corporate Transactions; General Business; Securities.

**WILLIAM S. YEE,** born Hong Kong, November 15, 1964; admitted to bar, 1989, California; 1990, U.S. District Court, Central and Southern Districts of California; 1996, U.S. Court of Appeals, Ninth Circuit. *Education:* Occidental College (A.B., 1986); McGeorge School of Law, University of the Pacific (J.D., 1989). Staff Writer, Pacific Law Journal Legislative Review, 1987-1988. Author: Perspectives, Vol. 111 No. 3 Spring, 1985, "U.S. Covert Action: An Overview". *Member:* State Bar of California; Southern California Chinese Lawyers Association; Asian Business Association. **LANGUAGES:** Chinese. **PRACTICE AREAS:** Business and Tort Litigation.

### ASSOCIATE

**JULIE H. RUBIN,** born November 19, 1964; admitted to bar, 1990, California; 1991, U.S. District Court, Central District of California. *Education:* University of California at Los Angeles (B.A., 1986); Loyola Law School (J.D., 1989). *Member:* Los Angeles County, Beverly Hills and American Bar Associations. **PRACTICE AREAS:** Real Estate Litigation; Business Litigation; Probate Litigation; Mobilehome Park Defense Litigation.

## RANDALL E. GREER

9430 OLYMPIC BOULEVARD, SUITE 400
**BEVERLY HILLS, CALIFORNIA 90212-4552**
Telephone: 310-551-1232
Fax: 310-551-4926

*General Civil Trial, Business, Commercial, and Real Estate Law.*

**RANDALL E. GREER,** born Inglewood, California, March 15, 1949; admitted to bar, 1974, California, U.S. District Court, Central, Eastern, Northern and Southern Districts of California and U.S. Court of Appeals, Ninth Circuit. *Education:* University of Southern California (B.S., cum

*(This Listing Continued)*

laude, 1971); Loyola University of Los Angeles (J.D., 1974). Phi Eta Sigma; Sigma Gamma Epsilon. Former Senior Vice President and Assistant General Counsel, CB Commercial Real Estate Group, Inc. Dean's Circle, Southwestern University, School of Law. *Member:* Beverly Hills and Los Angeles County Bar Associations; The State Bar of California. *PRACTICE AREAS:* Civil Trial; Business; Commercial; Real Estate Law.

---

## *GREINES, MARTIN, STEIN & RICHLAND*
### SUITE 544, 9601 WILSHIRE BOULEVARD
### BEVERLY HILLS, CALIFORNIA 90210
*Telephone: 310-859-7811*
*Telecopier: 310-276-5261*

*Appellate, Law and Motion and Related Practice in State and Federal Courts.*

FIRM PROFILE: *Greines, Martin, Stein & Richland established in 1983, specializes in appellate practice. The firm has briefed and argued appeals in the United States Supreme Court, in every state and federal appellate court in California, and in the Supreme Courts of California, Alaska and Nevada. In addition to appeals, the firm has prepared and filed numerous petitions for review, for certiorari and for extraordinary writs and has argued these matters in the reviewing courts. The firm's attorneys appear as counsel of record or as amicus counsel on scores of published and hundreds of unpublished appellate decisions.*

*Although the firm's practice is concentrated in the appellate courts, it is not limited to appeals and writs. The same skills and discipline needed to craft a legal argument that will withstand close appellate scrutiny are available to provide a broad range of services to the firm's clients. For example, clients also call upon the firm for advice and assistance in briefing and arguing post-trial motions in anticipation of an appeal. In addition, a substantial portion of the firm's practice consists of consultation regarding complex legal issues, including those dealing with matters of insurance coverage and bad faith.*

*The firm has represented both plaintiffs and defendants in a wide variety of matters, including constitutional law, civil rights, torts, title insurance, insurance coverage and bad faith, copyright, unfair competition, antitrust, RICO, real estate law, securities, environmental law, wrongful termination, and family law.*

*Representative cases in the United States Supreme Court, California Supreme Court, Ninth Circuit Court of Appeals, and California Courts of Appeals: County of Riverside v. McLaughlin (1991) 111 S.Ct. 1661; Central Pathology Service Medical Clinic, Inc. v. Superior Court (1992) 3 Cal.4th 181; Bank of the West v. Superior Court (1992) 2 Cal.4th 1254; Lubetzky v. State Bar (1991) 54 Cal.3d 308; Adams v. Murakami (1991) 54 Cal.3d 105; Schneider v. State Bar (1987) 43 Cal.3d 784; Coleman v. Gulf Ins. Group (1986) 41 Cal.3d 782; Gutierrez v. Mofid (1985) 39 Cal.3d 892; Empire Blue Cross v. Janet Greeson's A Place For Us (9th Cir. 1993) 985 F.2d 459; Thomas v. County of Los Angeles (9th Cir. 1993) 978 F.2d 504; Westlands Water Dist. v. Amoco Chemical Co. (9th Cir. 1991) 953 F.2d 1109; Shaw v. Lindheim (9th Cir. 1990) 919 F.2d 1353; Washington v. United States (9th Cir. 1989) 868 F.2d 332; Animal Lovers Volunteer Ass'n., Inc. v. Carlucci (9th Cir. 1989) 867 F.2d 1224; Fjelstad v. American Honda Motor Co., Inc. (9th Cir. 1985) 762 F.2d 1334; Aguilar v. Los Angeles County (9th Cir. 1985) 751 F.2d 1089; Main Line Pictures, Inc. v. Basinger (Sept. 22, 1994) BO77509 (nonpub. opn.); Lewis v. Superior Court (1994) 30 Cal.App. 4th 1850; Roddenberry v. Roddenberry (Apr. 16, 1996) 96 Daily journal D.A.R. 4411; BMW of North America, Inc. v. Gore (1996) 116 S.Ct. 1589.*

### *MEMBERS OF FIRM*

**ALAN G. MARTIN** (1948-1990).

**IRVING H. GREINES,** born Los Angeles, California, July 26, 1941; admitted to bar, 1967, California and U.S. District Court, Central District of California; 1970, U.S. Court of Appeals, Ninth Circuit; 1972, U.S. District Court, Northern District of California; 1984, U.S. Supreme Court. *Education:* University of California at Los Angeles (B.S., with highest honors, 1963; J.D., 1966). *Honorary Societies:* Phi Beta Kappa; Beta Gamma Sigma; Phi Eta Sigma. *Clerkships:* Research Attorney to Presiding Justice Otto M. Kaus, California Court of Appeal, Second Appellate District, 1966-1967 and Presiding Justice John J. Ford, California Court of Appeal, Second Appellate District, 1967-1968, 1973-1975. Lecturer, Los Angeles County Bar Association. *Member:* Beverly Hills, Los Angeles County (Member, Appellate Courts Committee, 1980—; Litigation Committee, 1984—) and American (Member, Litigation Section, Appellate Practice Committee, 1983—) Bar Associations; State Bar of California; California Academy of Appellate Lawyers (President, 1991-1992); Design Team, Appellate Delay Reduction Committee, California Court of Appeal, Second

*(This Listing Continued)*

Appellate District; Executive Legislative Action Network Committee (ELAN), California Court of Appeal, Second Appellate District; Attorney Settlement Officer, Appellate Settlement Program, California Court of Appeal, Second Appellate District; Panel of Arbitrators, American Arbitration Association. *PRACTICE AREAS:* Appellate practice, including related trial court practice.

**MARTIN STEIN,** born Los Angeles, California, May 21, 1940; admitted to bar, 1966, California and U.S. District Court, Central District of California; 1967, U.S. Court of Military Appeals; 1969, U.S. Supreme Court and U.S. Army Court of Military Review; 1981, U.S. Court of Appeals, Ninth Circuit; 1988, U.S. District Court, Eastern District of California; 1989, U.S. District Court, Southern District of California. *Education:* University of California at Los Angeles (A.B., 1962; J.D., 1965). Phi Alpha Delta. Member, Moot Court Honors Program. Deputy Public Defender, Los Angeles County Public Defenders Office, 1970-1976. Deputy State Public Defender, California, 1976-1979. Chief Assistant State Public Defender, California, 1979-1980. *Member:* Beverly Hills, Los Angeles County and American Bar Associations; State Bar of California. [Capt., JAGC, U.S. Army, 1966-1970]. *PRACTICE AREAS:* Appellate Law.

**KENT L. RICHLAND,** born Cleveland, Ohio, November 28, 1946; admitted to bar, 1972, California, U.S. District Court, Central District of California and U.S. Court of Appeals, Ninth Circuit; 1975, U.S. Supreme Court. *Education:* University of California at Berkeley (A.B., 1968); University of California at Los Angeles (J.D., 1971). Member, Moot Court Honors Program. Author: "Taming The Odds: Increasing The Chances of Getting Relief From The Supreme Court," California Litigation, Volume 5, No. 2., Winter 1992; "Depublication," Los Angeles Lawyer, Volume 13, No. 6, Aug. & Sept., 1990. Lecturer: "Step By Step: The Appellate Process," CEB, June, 1983; "The Court of Appeal Speaks," CEB, April, 1987; "Extraordinary Writ Practice," CEB, December, 1987; Appellate Practice Seminar, ABA, March, 1988; "Learning From The Appellate Experts," 1994; "Ninth Circuit Practice," 17th Annual Federal Practice Institute, 1994. Co-Chair, ABA National Institute on Medical Malpractice, 1989, 1990; "Developments in Civil Procedure," CEB, 1989, 1990, 1991, 1992, 1993, 1994, 1995, 1996; "Handling Civil Writs In The Court of Appeal," CEB, 1991; 1996 California Appellate Courts Institute, "Views From The Other Side of The Bench", CJER. Deputy Attorney General, California (Supervising Attorney), 1972-1976. Examiner, California Commission on Judicial Qualifications, 1975. Deputy State Public Defender (Supervising Attorney), 1976-1978. Senior Staff Attorney to Presiding Justice Otto M. Kaus, California Court of Appeal, Second Appellate District, 1978-1980. Member, Board of Advisors, Hastings Constitutional Law Quarterly, 1978-1988. Adjunct Professor of Law, Southwestern University School of Law, 1986-1987. *Member:* Beverly Hills, Los Angeles County Bar Association (Member, Editorial Board, Los Angeles Bar Journal, 1973-1978; Managing Editor and Articles Editor, Los Angeles Bar Journal, 1977-1978; Member, Board of Editors, Los Angeles Lawyer, 1978-1982. Member, Committee on Delivery of Legal Services, 1977-1978; Member, Judicial Evaluation Committee, 1984-1996; Member, California Judicial Systems Committee, 1986-1988; Chair, 1988-1989; Appellate Courts Committee, 1978—; Co-Vice Chair, 1983-1985; Chair, 1985-1988; Member, Ad Hoc Committee on State Appellate Judicial Appointments, 1988-1989; State Appellate Judicial Evaluation Committee, 1989—; Vice-Chair, 1990-1992; Chair, 1992-1994) and American (Vice-Chair, Appellate Advocacy Committee, Torts and Insurance Practice Section, 1989-1990; Chair-Elect, 1990-1991) Bar Associations; State Bar of California (Conference of Delegates, State Bar Convention, 1980); California Academy of Appellate Lawyers (Secretary-Treasurer, 1992-1993; Second Vice President, 1993-1994; First Vice President, 1994-1995; President, 1995-1996). *PRACTICE AREAS:* Appellate Law.

**MARC J. POSTER,** born Glendale, California, April 4, 1945; admitted to bar, 1971, California, U.S. District Court, Central District of California and U.S. Court of Appeals, Ninth Circuit; 1978, U.S. Supreme Court. *Education:* Stanford University (B.A., 1967); University of California at Los Angeles (J.D., 1970). Senior Research Attorney for Associate Justice Macklin Fleming, California Court of Appeal, 1970-1977. Author: "Limits To The Contempt Power in California Courts," 49 Los Angeles Bar Journal 98; "The Proposed Panel To Resolve Intercircuit Conflicts: A Brief View From The Litigator's Perspective," 11 Hastings Constitutional Law Quarterly 371 (with E.J. Horowitz). Consultant, Bancroft-Whitney, California Civil Practice, "Record on Appeal". Lecturer: L.A. County Bar Association, "Taking An Appeal: Civil". Settlement Officer, California Court of Appeals. *Member:* Los Angeles County (Chair, Appellate Courts Committee, 1984-1985; Member, State Appellate Judicial Evaluation Committee) and American (Member: Torts and Insurance Practice Section; Appellate Practice Com-

*(This Listing Continued)*

## GREINES, MARTIN, STEIN & RICHLAND, Beverly Hills—Continued

mittee) Bar Associations; California Academy of Appellate Lawyers (President, 1989-1990). *PRACTICE AREAS:* Appellate Law.

**ROBIN MEADOW,** born Los Angeles, California, January 24, 1947; admitted to bar, 1972, California. *Education:* University of California at Berkeley (A.B., 1968); Boalt Hall School of Law, University of California (J.D., 1971). Phi Beta Kappa; Order of the Coif. Associate Editor, California Law Review, 1970-1971. Author: "Sanctions for Frivolous Appeals," Los Angeles Lawyer, September 1985. Co-editor, Los Angeles Lawyer Special Issue on Appellate Practice, August-September 1990. Author: "Protecting the Record on Appeal," Los Angeles Lawyer, August-September 1990; "Summary Judgment Motions, Los Angeles Lawyer, May 1991; "Appealability of Trial Court Orders," Los Angeles Lawyer, May 1992; "Taking Control of the Record on Appeal," Los Angeles Lawyer, March 1993; "Heirs Unapparent," Los Angeles Lawyer, June 1994. Co-Author: Is It Too Late To Settle? Problems With Settlement After Adjudication, ABTL Report, February 1996. Settlement Officer, Division Seven of the Court of Appeal for the Second District. *Member:* Los Angeles County (Trustee, 1984-1987; Member, Judicial Evaluation Committee, 1979-1981 and 1983-1985, Chair, 1983-1985; Appellate Courts Committee, 1982—; State Appellate Judicial Evaluation Committee, 1989—; Vice-Chair, 1992-1993) and American (Member, Litigation Section and Appellate Practice Committee) Bar Associations; The State Bar of California; Association of Business Trial Lawyers; California Academy of Appellate Lawyers. *PRACTICE AREAS:* Appellate Law.

**TIMOTHY T. COATES,** born Glendale, California, February 14, 1957; admitted to bar, 1983, California; 1984, U.S. Court of Appeals, Ninth Circuit; 1986, U.S. District Court, Central District of California; 1988, U.S. District Court, Eastern District of California; 1989, U.S. District Court, Northern and Southern Districts of California; 1990, U.S. Supreme Court; 1992, U.S. Court of Appeals, Eleventh Circuit. *Education:* University of Southern California (B.A., summa cum laude, 1979), Phi Beta Kappa; University of California at Los Angeles (J.D., 1983). Primary Editor, UCLA-Alaska Law Review, 1981-1983. Lecturer: Appellate Practice For Public Entities, County Counsel Association of California Annual Meeting, Fall, 1994; Civil Writs In The California Court of Appeal, California State Bar Convention, September, 1995. *Member:* Los Angeles County Bar Association (Member: Superior Courts Committee, 1987-1988; Appellate Courts Committee, 1988—; Barristers Bench and Bar Relations Committee, 1987-1989); Federal (Member, Appellate Practice Section, Los Angeles Section) and American (Member, Sections on: State and Local Government Law, 1988; Governmental Liability, Subcommittee on Liability of Individual Governmental Officials) Bar Associations; State Bar of California. *PRACTICE AREAS:* Appellate Law.

**FERIS M. GREENBERGER, (MS.),** born Bronx, New York, July 15, 1956; admitted to bar, 1980, California and U.S. District Court, Central District of California; 1985, U.S. Court of Appeals, Ninth Circuit; 1987, U.S. Supreme Court. *Education:* University of Southern California (A.B., magna cum laude, 1977); University of California at Los Angeles (J.D., 1980). Phi Beta Kappa. Comment Editor, UCLA Law Review, 1979-1980. Research Attorney to Presiding Justice Otto M. Kaus, California Court of Appeal, Second Appellate District, 1980-1981. Adjunct Assistant Professor of Law, University of Southern California Law Center, 1981-1984. Temporary Judge, Los Angeles Municipal Court since 1989. *Member:* Los Angeles County and American Bar Associations; State Bar of California; Women Lawyers of Los Angeles. *PRACTICE AREAS:* Appellate Law.

**BARBARA W. RAVITZ,** born Milwaukee, Wisconsin, June 10, 1945; admitted to bar, 1979, California and U.S. District Court, Central District of California; 1988, U.S. Court of Appeals, Ninth Circuit; 1989, U.S. Supreme Court. *Education:* University of California at Los Angeles (B.A., with highest honors, 1966; J.D., 1978). Phi Beta Kappa. Lecturer in Law, University of California at Los Angeles School of Law, 1981-1985. Consultant in Legal Writing, Bar Review Center of America, 1983 and "Bar '84," 1984. Creator and Lecturer, Legal Writing Seminar for Attorneys, 1984—. *Member:* Beverly Hills, Los Angeles County and American Bar Associations; State Bar of California (Member, Appellate Courts Committee, 1990-1993); Women Lawyers Association of Los Angeles; California Women Lawyers; California Academy of Appellate Lawyers. *PRACTICE AREAS:* Appellate Law.

**ROBERT A. OLSON,** born Bethesda, Maryland, June 28, 1957; admitted to bar, 1983, California; 1984, U.S. Court of Appeals, Ninth Circuit; 1985, U.S. District Court, Central District of California; 1990, U.S. Supreme Court; 1991, U.S. District Court, Eastern, Northern and Southern Districts of California. *Education:* Rice University; Stanford University (A.B., with honors, 1979; J.D. 1983). Order of the Coif; Phi Beta Kappa. Law Clerk, Hon. Anthony M. Kennedy, U.S. Court of Appeals, Ninth Circuit, 1983-1984. Co-Author: Is It To Late To Settle? Problems with Settlement after Adjudication, ABTL Report, February, 1996. Attorney, Settlement Officer, California Court of Appeals. Instructor and Lecturer: Association of Southern California Defense Counsel, 1995 in Review: A Summary of Recent Cases, January, 1996. *Member:* Los Angeles County, American (Member, Litigation and Torts and Insurance Practice Sections) and Federal (Member, Los Angeles Chapter, Appellate Committee) Bar Associations; State Bar of California (Member, Litigation Section). *PRACTICE AREAS:* Appellate Law; Insurance Coverage.

### ASSOCIATES

**CAROLYN OILL,** born Glen Cove, New York, February 18, 1957; admitted to bar, 1987, California and U.S. District Court, Central District of California; 1991, U.S. Court of Appeals, Eleventh Circuit. *Education:* Northwestern University (B.A., 1978); Southwestern University School of Law (J.D., 1987). *Member:* Beverly Hills Bar Association; Los Angeles County and American Bar Associations; State Bar of California. *PRACTICE AREAS:* Appellate Law.

**SHEILA S. KATO,** born Kaneohe, Hawaii, November 30, 1947; admitted to bar, 1973, California; 1974, U.S. District Court, Central District of California; 1976, U.S. District Court, Southern District of California; 1980, U.S. District Court, Northern District of California; 1983, U.S. Court of Appeals, Ninth Circuit. *Education:* University of Hawaii (A.B., with high honors, 1969); University of California at Berkeley (J.D., 1973). Phi Beta Kappa; Phi Kappa Phi; Alpha Lambda Delta. Member, University of California Law Review, 1970-1971. Associate Editor, Ecology Law Quarterly, 1971-1972. Research Attorney, Justice Marcus M. Kaufman, Court of Appeal, Fourth District, Division Two (Later Associate Justice, California Supreme Court), 1973-1974. *Member:* Los Angeles County and American Bar Associations; State Bar of California (Member, Litigation Section). *PRACTICE AREAS:* Appellate Law.

**ALISON M. TURNER,** born New York, N.Y., September 11, 1940; admitted to bar, 1984, California and U.S. District Court, Central District of California; 1985, U.S. District Court, Northern, Southern and Eastern Districts of California and U.S. Court of Appeals, Ninth Circuit. *Education:* Radcliffe College, Harvard University (A.B., cum laude, 1962); University of California at Los Angeles (J.D., 1984). *Member:* Beverly Hills, Los Angeles County and American Bar Associations; State Bar of California; Women Lawyers Association of Los Angeles. *PRACTICE AREAS:* Appellate Law.

**RANDEL L. LEDESMA,** born Inglewood, California, November 26, 1959; admitted to bar, 1984, California. *Education:* Pomona College (B.A., 1981); University of Southern California (J.D., 1984). Order of the Coif. Executive Articles Editor, Southern California Law Review, 1983-1984. *Member:* American Bar Association; State Bar of California. *PRACTICE AREAS:* Appellate Law.

**BARRY M. WOLF,** born Queens, New York, October 18, 1950; admitted to bar, 1977, California; 1980, Virginia; 1983, District of Columbia. *Education:* State University of New York at Binghamton (B.A., 1972); Georgetown University (J.D., 1976). *Member:* State Bar of California; Virginia State Bar; District of Columbia Bar. *PRACTICE AREAS:* Appellate Law.

**BRIAN J. WRIGHT,** born Pittsburgh, Pennsylvania, March 24, 1961; admitted to bar, 1993, California. *Education:* Harvard University (B.A., 1983); University of California at Los Angeles (J.D., 1993). Harvard College Scholar. Moot Court: Briefwriter, National Team; Distinguished Advocate; Member, Advisory Board. *LANGUAGES:* Spanish. *PRACTICE AREAS:* Appellate Law.

**JENNIFER L. KING,** born Pomona, California, March 26, 1962; admitted to bar, 1988, California and U.S. District Court, Central District of California; 1989, U.S. District Court, Southern District of California; 1995, U.S. Court of Appeals, Ninth Circuit. *Education:* Stanford University (B.A., with distinction, 1984; J.D., 1987). Law Clerk, Honorable Alicemarie H. Stotler, U.S. District Judge, Central District of California, 1987-1988. Extern, Honorable Allen E. Broussard, Associate Justice, California Supreme Court, 1986. *Member:* Los Angeles County Bar Association; State Bar of California. *PRACTICE AREAS:* Appellate.

**EDWARD LAUCKS XANDERS,** born Baltimore, Maryland, May 8, 1963; admitted to bar, 1990, California; 1991, District of Columbia. *Education:* Duke University (B.A., magna cum laude, 1985); University of Vir-

*(This Listing Continued)*

ginia (J.D., 1989). Finalist, William Minor Lile Moot Court. Recipient, Johnson & Swanson Award. Notes Editor, Journal of Law and Politics, 1988-1989. Author: "A Handyman's Guide to Fixing National Security Leak: An Analytical Framework for Evaluating Proposals to Curb Unauthorized Publication of Classified Information," 5 Journal of Law and Politics 759 (1989). *Member:* State Bar of California; The District of Columbia Bar. *PRACTICE AREAS:* Appellate Practice.

### OF COUNSEL

**BARBARA S. PERRY,** born New York, January 27, 1938; admitted to bar, 1968, California and U.S. District Court, Central District of California. *Education:* University of California at Los Angeles (B.A., with highest honors, 1959); Loyola Marymount University (J.D., magna cum laude, 1967). Phi Beta Kappa. Lecturer, University of Southern California School of Engineering, 1976-1977. Consultant, California Civil Writ Practice, California Continuing Education of the Bar, 1987. Research Attorney, Presiding Justice Otto M. Kaus, California Court of Appeal, Second District, Division 5, 1967-1970. Senior Attorney, Criminal Law Specialist, California Court of Appeal, Second District, Division 5, 1970-1975. Writs Attorney, California Court of Appeal, Second District, Division 5, 1975-1984. Senior Research Attorney to Presiding Justice Robert Feinerman, California Court of Appeal, Second District, Division 5, 1984-1988. *Member:* State Bar of California. (Also practicing individually at same address). *PRACTICE AREAS:* Appellate Law.

REFERENCE: City National Bank (Beverly Hills Branch).

---

## BRIAN GUNSHOR INC.
### A CALIFORNIA LAW CORPORATION
POST OFFICE BOX 7429
**BEVERLY HILLS, CALIFORNIA 90212-7429**
Telephone: 310-273-2704; 818-906-0050
Telefacsimile: 310-273-2706; 818-906-0067
Email: bgunshor@IX.netcom.com
URL: http://www.gunshorlaw.com

*Complex Civil Litigation and Trial, Arbitration and Alternative Dispute Resolution Practice in all State and Federal Courts and Administrative Agencies involving Contract Disputes, Business Torts, Unfair Competition, Trade Secrets, Intra-Corporate and Partnership Disputes, Probate Contests, Securities, Real Estate, and Commercial Fraud, Insurance Coverage and Interpleader, and Conservatorships. Negotiation and Drafting of Contractual and Related Documents for Business Transactions, including Corporate, Partnership and Sole Proprietorship Business Planning, Formation, Operations, Venture Capital Finance, Acquisitions and Dispositions and Personal Affairs; Investment Risk Counselling and Preventive Law. Serving as Neutral Arbitrator, Mediator or Case Evaluator in Complex Business and Commercial Disputes.*

FIRM PROFILE: *The firm has represented small business, entrepreneurs and professionals in dispute resolution since 1981.*

**BRIAN GUNSHOR,** born New York, New York, July 28, 1949; admitted to bar, 1974, New York and U.S. District Court, Eastern and Southern Districts of New York; 1979, California and U.S. District Court, Central District of California; 1992, U.S. District Court, Southern District of California. *Education:* University of Pennsylvania, Wharton School of Finance and Commerce (B.S. in Economics, 1971); New York University School of Law (J.D., 1974). Member: Panel of Receivers, Los Angeles County Superior Court Writs and Receivers Department; Probate Volunteer Panel, Los Angeles County Superior Court Probate Department. Judge Pro Tem: Los Angeles Municipal Courts; Los Angeles County Superior Court Small Claims Appeals and Santa Monica Small Claims Court. Member, Panel of Commercial Arbitrators, American Arbitration Association and Los Angeles County Superior Court Civil Arbitration Panel. *Member:* Beverly Hills, Santa Monica, Los Angeles County and New York State Bar Associations; State Bar of California.

---

## HAMBURG, HANOVER, EDWARDS & MARTIN
**BEVERLY HILLS, CALIFORNIA**
(See Los Angeles)

*General Civil Practice in all State and Federal Courts. General Real Estate Corporate, Employment, Business. Construction, Entertainment, Taxation, Immigration, Environmental, Zoning, Insurance and Insurance Defense, Ad-*
*(This Listing Continued)*

*ministrative, Tradenames and Trademarks Infringement, and Copyright Enforcement.*

---

## HANSEN, JACOBSON, TELLER & HOBERMAN
450 NORTH ROXBURY
8TH FLOOR
**BEVERLY HILLS, CALIFORNIA 90210**
Telephone: 310-271-8777
Telecopier: 310-276-8310
Email: la@hjth.com

*Entertainment, Motion Picture, Television, Music and Copyright Law.*

**WALTER S. TELLER,** born Doylestown, Pennsylvania, February 19, 1945; admitted to bar, 1978, California and U.S. District Court, Central District of California. *Education:* Cornell University (A.B., 1966); Columbia University (M.A., 1968); Boalt Hall School of Law, University of California at Berkeley (J.D., 1978). *Member:* Beverly Hills and Los Angeles County Bar Associations; State Bar of California. *PRACTICE AREAS:* Entertainment Law; Motion Picture Law; Television Law; Copyright Law. *Email:* tellerwa@hjth.com

**CRAIG A. JACOBSON,** born Kansas City, Missouri, July 3, 1952; admitted to bar, 1979, California; 1980, U.S. District Court, Central District of California. *Education:* Brown University (B.A., 1974); George Washington University (J.D., 1979). Phi Beta Kappa. Co-author, "The Enforceability of Construction Industry Pre-Hire Agreements After Higdon," University of California at Berkeley Industrial Relations Law Journal, Fall 1979. *Member:* State Bar of California. *PRACTICE AREAS:* Entertainment Law; Motion Picture Law; Television Law; Copyright Law. *Email:* jacobscr@hjth.com

**THOMAS M. HANSEN,** born Los Angeles, California, October 24, 1949; admitted to bar, 1978, California. *Education:* University of California at Santa Barbara (B.A., 1975); University of Southern California (J.D., 1978). Order of the Coif. Member, Board of Editors, Southern California Law Review, 1977-1978. Adjunct Professor, Copyright, Southwestern University Law School, 1980. *Member:* State Bar of California. *PRACTICE AREAS:* Entertainment Law; Motion Picture Law; Television Law; Copyright Law.

**THOMAS H. HOBERMAN,** born Detroit, Michigan, November 11, 1950; admitted to bar, 1975, California. *Education:* University of California at Santa Barbara (B.A., 1972); University of California at Santa Cruz; University of California at Los Angeles; Southwestern University School of Law (J.D., 1975); Georgetown University Law Center. Recipient: American Jurisprudence Book Award—Evidence Conflict of Laws Estates. *Member:* Beverly Hills and American Bar Associations; State Bar of California; Federal Communications Bar Association; Los Angeles Copyright Society. *PRACTICE AREAS:* Entertainment Law. *Email:* hobermth@hjth.com

**STEPHEN P. WARREN,** born Rochester, New York, September 3, 1960; admitted to bar, 1985, California. *Education:* Dartmouth College (B.A., 1982); Harvard University (J.D., 1985). *Member:* Beverly Hills and Los Angeles County Bar Associations; State Bar of California. *PRACTICE AREAS:* Entertainment Law; Motion Picture Law; Television Law; Copyright Law.

**JEANNE M. NEWMAN,** born Cleveland, Ohio, September 12, 1954; admitted to bar, 1980, California. *Education:* Connecticut College (B.A., with honors, 1977); University of Southern California (J.D., 1980). Recipient, Holbrook Award for Greatest Contribution to Southern California Law Review. Editor and Staff Member, Southern California Law Review, 1979-1980. *Member:* Beverly Hills, Santa Monica and Los Angeles County Bar Associations; The State Bar of California. *PRACTICE AREAS:* Entertainment Law; Motion Picture Law; Television Law; Copyright Law. *Email:* newmanje@hjth.com

**THOMAS B. MCGUIRE, JR.,** born San Francisco, California, June 17, 1953; admitted to bar, 1983, California. *Education:* University of California at Berkeley; University of California at Los Angeles (B.A., magna cum laude, 1975); Boalt Hall School of Law, University of California at Berkeley (J.D., 1983). *Member:* The State Bar of California (Member, Intellectual Property Law Section); American Bar Association. *PRACTICE AREAS:* Entertainment Law; Motion Picture Law; Television Law; Copyright Law. *Email:* mcguirth@hjth.com

*(This Listing Continued)*

**HANSEN, JACOBSON, TELLER & HOBERMAN,** Beverly Hills—Continued

**FRED E. GOLDRING,** born Philadelphia, Pennsylvania, June 4, 1957; admitted to bar, 1983, New York and California. *Education:* Duke University (A.B., 1979); University of Miami School of Law (J.D., cum laude, 1982). Recipient: First Prize, ASCAP Nathan Burkan Memorial Copyright Competition, 1981; American Bar Association Award for Most Outstanding Law School Project in the Nation, 1981. Author: Lindley on Entertainment, Publishing and the Arts, "Music Video" Section, 1989. Co-Author: 1984 Entertainment, Publishing and the Arts Handbook, Clark Boardman. Clerk: Martin E. Silfen, P.C., New York, N.Y., Summer 1980; Weiss, Meibach & Bomser, New York, N.Y., Summer 1981. Articles Editor, Journal of Copyright, Entertainment and Sports Law of the Tennessee Bar Association, 1983-1984. Co-Founder and Co-Chairman, Entertainment Law Circle, 1982-1986. *Member:* New York State Bar Association; State Bar of California; Copyright Society of the U.S.A. *PRACTICE AREAS:* Entertainment Law; Music Recording Law; Copyright Law.

**KENNETH B. HERTZ,** born Washington, D.C., September 9, 1959; admitted to bar, 1984, California and U.S. District Court, Central District of California. *Education:* University of California at Berkeley (B.S., 1981); University of California at Los Angeles (J.D., 1984). Alumni Scholar. Member, Executive Board, Moot Court Honors Program. Member, University of California Law Review, 1983-1984. *Member:* Los Angeles County (Member, Executive Committee, Intellectual Property and Unfair Competition Section) and American (Member: Patent, Trademark and Copyright Law Section; Forum Committee on Entertainment and Sports Industries) Bar Associations; The State Bar of California. *PRACTICE AREAS:* Entertainment Law; Music Recording Law; Copyright Law. *Email:* hertzke@hjth.com

**JASON C. SLOANE,** born Los Angeles, California, June 10, 1963; admitted to bar, 1988, California; 1989, U.S. District Court, Central District of California. *Education:* University of California at Berkeley (B.S., 1985); University of California at Los Angeles (J.D., 1988). Order of the Coif. Distinguished Advocate, Moot Court Honors Program. Member, Executive Board of Judges, Moot Court Honors Program. *Member:* Beverly Hills Bar Association; State Bar of California. *PRACTICE AREAS:* Entertainment Law; Motion Picture Law; Television Law; Copyright Law. *Email:* sloaneja@hjth.com

**KENNETH C. CHRISTMAS, JR.,** born San Jose, California, February 23, 1963; admitted to bar, 1991, California. *Education:* Stanford University (B.A., Psych., 1985; B.A., Econ., with distinction, 1985); Yale University (J.D., 1991). *Member:* Beverly Hills Bar Association; State Bar of California. *PRACTICE AREAS:* Entertainment Law; Motion Picture Law; Music Law; Television Law. *Email:* christke@hjth.com

**KENNETH M. RICHMAN,** born Brooklyn, New York, March 14, 1968; admitted to bar, 1993, California. *Education:* Harvard College (A.B., summa cum laude, 1990); Harvard University (J.D., magna cum laude, 1993). Phi Beta Kappa. *Member:* State Bar of California. *PRACTICE AREAS:* Entertainment Law; Motion Picture Law; Television Law; Copyright Law.

**DONALD W. STEELE,** born St. Louis, Missouri, July 21, 1960; admitted to bar, 1986, California; 1987, U.S. District Court, Central District of California. *Education:* University of Texas at Austin (B.S., with high honors, 1982; J.D., with high honors, 1986). Order of the Coif. Associate Editor, Texas Law Review, 1985-1986. *Member:* The State Bar of California. *PRACTICE AREAS:* Motion Picture/Television Law; Copyright Law; Intellectual Property Law. *Email:* steeledo@hjth.com

**JONATHAN D. HAFT,** born Bronxville, New York, December 6, 1956; admitted to bar, 1982, California; 1986, New York. *Education:* Columbia University (B.A., magna cum laude, 1978; J.D., 1982). Phi Beta Kappa. Harlan Fiske Stone Scholar. *PRACTICE AREAS:* Entertainment Industry Law. *Email:* haftjo@hjth.com

**SETH LICHTENSTEIN,** born Washington, D.C., March 24, 1951; admitted to bar, 1986, California. *Education:* Antioch College (B.A., 1973); Howard University (J.D., magna cum laude, 1984). Associate Editor, Howard Law Journal, 1983-1984. Law Clerk to: Honorable Henry F. Greene, District of Columbia, 1983; Honorable James M. Sprouse, U.S. Court of Appeals, Fourth Circuit, 1984-1985. *Member:* State Bar of California. *Email:* lichtese@hjth.com

**DANIEL L. FISHKIN,** born New York, New York, March 27, 1953; admitted to bar, 1988, California; 1996, U.S. Supreme Court. *Education:* Brooklyn College (B.A., 1975; M.F.A., 1978); Brooklyn Law School (J.D., cum laude, 1988). Moot Court Honors Program. Co-Chair, Syllabus Committee, Entertainment Law Institute, University of Southern California Law Center, 1996. Co-Chair, Financial Institutions Section, Century City Bar Association, 1993. *Member:* Beverly Hills and Los Angeles County Bar Associations; State Bar of California. *PRACTICE AREAS:* Entertainment Law; Television Law; Copyrights.

## HEENAN BLAIKIE
### A CALIFORNIA PROFESSIONAL CORPORATION
SUITE 1100, 9401 WILSHIRE BOULEVARD
**BEVERLY HILLS, CALIFORNIA 90212-2924**
Telephone: 310-275-3600
Telecopier: 310-724-8340

*Affiliated With:* Heenan Blaikie of Canada.

U.S. and International Entertainment, Corporate, General Business, Commercial, Litigation, Intellectual Property, Securities, Banking and Finance, Tax, Estate Planning and Real Estate.

**JEFFREY BERKOWITZ,** born Bronx, New York, February 18, 1954; admitted to bar, 1980, California; 1983, U.S. Claims Court; 1984, U.S. Tax Court. *Education:* State University of New York at Buffalo (B.S., 1974); Boston University (J.D., 1979). Certified Public Accountant, Massachusetts, 1979. Co-Speaker and Co-Author: "Tax Aspects of Real Estate Development," Thirty-Eighth Annual USC Tax Institute, 1986. Co-Author: "Chapter 6, Federal Tax Practice of California," Continuing Education of Bar Publication, 1984. *Member:* Los Angeles County, Beverly Hills and American Bar Associations; The State Bar of California; American Institute of Certified Public Accountants. *PRACTICE AREAS:* U.S. and International Taxation; Estate Planning; General Business; Corporate; Entertainment.

**DANIEL H. BLACK,** born New York, N.Y., October 30, 1951; admitted to bar, 1977, New York; 1987, California. *Education:* New York University (B.A., cum laude, 1973); University of Copenhagen; George Washington University (J.D., 1976). Phi Beta Kappa. *Member:* Los Angeles County, New York State and American Bar Associations; The State Bar of California. *PRACTICE AREAS:* Entertainment; General Business; Corporate.

**FRED A. FENSTER,** born Hartford, Connecticut, October 8, 1946; admitted to bar, 1972, California. *Education:* University of Southern California (B.A., 1968; J.D., 1971). Phi Beta Kappa; Phi Kappa Phi; Order of the Coif; Phi Eta Sigma; Pi Sigma Alpha; Blue Key. Member, Board of Editors, University of Southern California Moot Court, 1970-1971. Adjunct Professor of Law, University of Southern California, 1977—. *Member:* Los Angeles County Bar Association; The State Bar of California. *PRACTICE AREAS:* Civil Litigation; General Business.

**DANIEL B. LEON,** born Encino, California, August 17, 1959; admitted to bar, 1986, California. *Education:* University of Southern California (B.S., with honors, 1981), Beta Gamma Sigma; Northwestern University (J.D., 1985). *Member:* Los Angeles County Bar Association; The State Bar of California. *PRACTICE AREAS:* Real Estate; General Business; Corporate; Commercial.

**JODY SIMON,** born New York, N.Y., October 16, 1953; admitted to bar, 1983, New York; 1991, California. *Education:* Sarah Lawrence College (B.A., 1975); Columbia University, School of Law (J.D., 1982). Kent Scholar, 1981; Stone Scholar, 1980, 1982. Editor, Columbia Law Review, 1981-1982. Notes Editor, Columbia-VLA Journal of Law and Arts. Author: "The Collapse of Consensus: Effects of the Deregulation of Cable Television," 81 Colum. L. Rev. 612. *Member:* The State Bar of California; Academy of Television Arts and Sciences (Member: Board of Governors, Executive Committee, Members at Large; Activities Advisory Committee). *PRACTICE AREAS:* Entertainment; Intellectual Property.

**DEBORAH F. SIRIAS,** born Los Angeles, California, November 25, 1956; admitted to bar, 1982, California; 1985, U.S. District Court, Central and Southern Districts of California and U.S. Court of Appeals, Ninth Circuit. *Education:* University of Southern California (A.B., summa cum laude, 1978); Graduate Institute of International Studies, Geneva, Switzerland (Certificate, 1977); Southwestern University School of Law (J.D., 1982). Phi Beta Kappa. Teaching Assistant, International Law and Constitutional Law, University of Southern California, 1977-1978. Judge Pro Tem, Beverly Hills Municipal Court. *Member:* Beverly Hills, Los Angeles County and American Bar Associations; The State Bar of California; The Association of

*(This Listing Continued)*

Trial Lawyers of America; California Women Lawyers. **LANGUAGES:** Spanish, French and Italian. **PRACTICE AREAS:** Civil Litigation.

**B.J. YANKOWITZ,** born Los Angeles, California, May 24, 1955; admitted to bar, 1981, California; 1989, New York. *Education:* Johns Hopkins University and University of California at Berkeley (B.A., 1977); University of Southern California (J.D., 1980); Cambridge University, Cambridge, England (LL.M., First Class Honours, 1981). Evan Lewis-Thomas Scholar, Sidney Sussex College, Cambridge, England, 1980-1981. Note Editor, Southern California Law Review, 1979-1980. Author: "Acceptance by Performance When the Offeror Demands a Promise," 52 Southern California Law Review 1917, 1980. *Member:* The State Bar of California; New York State Bar Association. **PRACTICE AREAS:** Corporate Law; Securities; Banking and Financial Transactions.

**SCOTT B. ZOLKE,** born Chicago, Illinois, February 21, 1954; admitted to bar, 1980, Illinois; 1984, Georgia; 1988, California. *Education:* Georgia Institute of Technology (B.S., with high honors, 1976); University of Miami School of Law (J.D., 1979). Contributing Editor, University of Miami Law Review, 1978-1979. Co-Author: "Copyright and The First Amendment," 33 University of Miami Law Review 207, 1978. Author: "Non-Competition Clauses in Contracts Between Stations and On-Air Talent," Entertainment Law and Finance, Vol. III, No. 3, June 1987. Co-Author: "Employment Privacy: Legal and Research Developments and Implications for Personnel Administration," Sloan Management Review, Winter 1985, vol. 26, no. 2. *Member:* Beverly Hills (Member, Entertainment Law Section, Vice-Chairman, 1992-1994), Los Angeles County, Illinois State and American (Member, Intellectual Property Law Section; Chairman, Subcommittee on Artists Rights in Sound Recordings, 1990-1991) Bar Associations; The State Bar of California; The State Bar of Georgia. **PRACTICE AREAS:** Entertainment; Intellectual Property; Civil Litigation.

---

## HELLER & EDWARDS

*9454 WILSHIRE BOULEVARD, SUITE 500*
**BEVERLY HILLS, CALIFORNIA 90212-2982**
*Telephone: 310-550-8833*
*Fax: 310-858-6637*

*General Civil Trial and Appellate Practice in all State and Federal Courts.*

### MEMBERS OF FIRM

**LAWRENCE E. HELLER,** born New York, N.Y., October 9, 1948; admitted to bar, 1976, California, Illinois, U.S. District Court, Central District of California and U.S. Court of Appeals, Seventh and Ninth Circuits. *Education:* Colorado State University (B.S., 1972); John Marshall Law School (J.D., 1975). Judge Pro Tem, Los Angeles County Municipal Court, 1983—. Arbitrator, American Arbitration Association, 1981—. Member, Panel of Arbitrators, American Arbitration Association. *Member:* Beverly Hills, Chicago, Los Angeles County and Illinois State Bar Associations; The State Bar of California; California Trial Lawyers Association; Los Angeles Trial Lawyers Association. **PRACTICE AREAS:** Complex Business Litigation; Real Estate; Constitutional and Employment Law.

**MARK L. EDWARDS,** born Chicago, Illinois, January 14, 1959; admitted to bar, 1985, California, U.S. District Court, Central District of California and U.S. Court of Appeals, Ninth Circuit. *Education:* Indiana University (B.S., 1981); Loyola University of Los Angeles (J.D., 1984). Phi Alpha Delta. Instructor, University of California at Los Angeles, Paralegal Program, 1987—. *Member:* Beverly Hills and Los Angeles County Bar Associations; State Bar of California. **PRACTICE AREAS:** Complex Business Litigation; Real Estate; Insurance and Corporate Law.

---

## NEAL R. HERSH

*9150 WILSHIRE BOULEVARD, SUITE 209*
**BEVERLY HILLS, CALIFORNIA 90212**
*Telephone: 310-786-1910*
*Fax: 310-786-1917*

*Family and Divorce Law. Mediation Practice.*

**NEAL R. HERSH,** born Los Angeles, California, July 12, 1951; admitted to bar, 1976, California; 1977, U.S. District Court, Central District of California; 1982, U.S. Supreme Court. *Education:* University of California at Los Angeles (B.A., 1973); Southwestern University (J.D., 1976). Author: "In Re Marriage of Brennan and In Re Marriage of Wichander." Lecturer, Family Law Symposium, Vocational Rehabilitation Counselors, Beverly Hills Bar Association, 1982. Principal, American Association for Mediated Divorce, 1993—. *Member:* Beverly Hills (Member, Family Law Section; *(This Listing Continued)*

Member, Family Mediation Panel; Past Member, Family Law Section Executive Committee), Los Angeles County (Member, Family Law Section) and American (Member, Family Law Section) Bar Associations; State Bar of California (Member, Family Law Section). **PRACTICE AREAS:** Family Law.

---

## HERZOG, FISHER & GRAYSON

*A LAW CORPORATION*
*9460 WILSHIRE BOULEVARD*
*FIFTH FLOOR*
**BEVERLY HILLS, CALIFORNIA 90212**
*Telephone: 310-278-4300*
*Fax: 310-278-5430*

*Business and Corporate Law, Business and Commercial Litigation, Administrative Law, Health Care Law, Civil Appeals, Real Estate and Entertainment Law.*

**JAMES P. HERZOG,** born Los Angeles, California, November 11, 1942; admitted to bar, 1968, California and U.S. District Court, Central District of California; 1976, U.S. District Court, Southern District of California; 1982, U.S. District Court, Northern District of California. *Education:* University of California at Los Angeles (A.B., 1964; J.D., 1967). Co-Author: "Antitrust Immunity for Peer Review under the Health Care Quality Improvement Act," The Medical Staff Counselor, Spring, 1993. *Member:* Beverly Hills, Los Angeles County (Member: Health Care; Family Law; Human Rights; Chairman, Administrative Law and Litigation Committee, 1980) and American Bar Associations; State Bar of California.

**DAVID R. FISHER,** born New York, N.Y., January 3, 1960; admitted to bar, 1985, California; U.S. District Court, Central and Eastern Districts of California and U.S. Court of Appeals, Ninth Circuit. *Education:* State University of New York at Buffalo (B.A., magna cum laude, 1982); Georgetown University (J.D., 1985). Phi Beta Kappa. Articles and Notes Editor, American Criminal Law Review, 1984-1985. Author: "Securities Fraud in the Survey of White-Collar Crime," 22 Am. Crim. L. Rev. 271, 1985. Co-Author: "Antitrust Immunity for Peer Review under the Health Care Quality Improvement Act," 7 The Medical Staff Counselor, Spring, 1993. *Member:* State Bar of California.

**MICHAEL A. GRAYSON,** born Detroit, Michigan, March 18, 1943; admitted to bar, 1968, California and U.S. District Court, Central District of California. *Education:* University of Michigan, California State University at Northridge and University of California at Los Angeles (B.S., 1964); University of California at Los Angeles (J.D., 1967). Phi Delta Phi. Co-Author: "The World According to Garn: Congress Writes the Last Act in the Due-On-Sale Saga," 17 Beverly Hills Bar Association Journal 2; "The Tax-Free Exchange of Real Estate Partnership Interests," V California Business Law Reporter 1, July, 1983: "The Window Period Exception to the Enforcement of Due-On-Sale Clauses Under the Garn Act," 17 Beverly Hills Bar Association Journal 3, Summer, 1983: "New Federal Legislation Preempts State Law Permitting Assumption of Real Property Loans," Real Estate Review, Fall, 1983: 49 Journal of the State Bar of Nevada, January/-February, 1984: "New State Disclosure Requirements in Seller Financed Residential Property Sales," 18 Beverly Hills Bar Association Journal 1, Winter, 1983-1984: "When Buyers Can Assume Low Rate Loans," 13 Real Estate Review 4, 1984; "Real Estate Aspects of the Tax Reform Act of 1984," 73 Illinois Bar Journal, March, 1985. Member: Los Angeles County and American Bar Associations; State Bar of California (Member, Real Property Law Section). **PRACTICE AREAS:** Corporate; Finance; Real Estate Law; Hospitality, Leisure; Entertainment; Publishing.

---

**PAMELA M. ROSENTHAL,** born Los Angeles, California, December 13, 1964; admitted to bar, 1991, California and U.S. District Court, Central District of California. *Education:* University of Pennsylvania (B.A., 1987); University of Southern California (J.D., 1991). International Relations Honors Society, 1986-1987; Hale Moot Court Honors Program, 1989-1990. Member, National Moot Court Team, 1990-1991. Recipient, American Jurisprudence Award in Business Organizations. *Member:* Beverly Hills Bar Association; State Bar of California.

**ERIC M. ROSIN,** born Detroit, Michigan, July 6, 1967; admitted to bar, 1994, California. *Education:* Yale University (B.A., 1989); University of Southern California (J.D.; M.A., 1994). Recipient, Edward and Elanor Shattuck Award. *Member:* Beverly Hills Bar Association; State Bar of California.

*(This Listing Continued)*

**HERZOG, FISHER & GRAYSON,** A LAW CORPORATION,
Beverly Hills—Continued

*OF COUNSEL*

**TODD I. GRAYSON,** born Encino, California, January 31, 1969; admitted to bar, 1993, California and U.S. District Court, Central District of California. *Education:* University of Southern California (B.S., 1990); Southwestern University Law School (J.D., 1993). *Member:* Los Angeles County Bar Association; State Bar of California. **PRACTICE AREAS:** Corporate Law; Real Estate; Commercial Litigation.

REPRESENTATIVE CLIENTS: Truck Insurance Exchange; Cedars-Sinai Medical Center; Pacific Health Corporation; Anaheim General Hospital; Santa Teresita Hospital; Childrens Hospital of Los Angeles; The Cheesecake Factory; Leon Max, Inc.; Grill Concepts, Inc.; Terry York Motor Cars Ltd.; Budget Rent A Car, Beverly Hills; Motors Holding, Division of General Motors Corp.

## ROBERT W. HIRSH & ASSOCIATES

9100 WILSHIRE BOULEVARD, SEVENTH FLOOR, WEST
**BEVERLY HILLS, CALIFORNIA 90212**
Telephone: 310-275-7800; Fax: 310-274-2330

*Business, Real Estate, Banking, Bankruptcy, Corporate, Entertainment, Apparel Industry and Health Care Law.*

*FIRM PROFILE: Our goal oriented firm litigates each case aggressively, yet, intelligently and economically.*

**ROBERT W. HIRSH,** born Bronx, N.Y., September 13, 1956; admitted to bar, 1982, California and U.S. District Court, Central District of California; 1983, U.S. Court of Appeals, Ninth Circuit; 1984, U.S. District Court, Northern, Southern and Eastern Districts of California; 1985, New York and Massachusetts. *Education:* State University of New York at Albany (B.A., magna cum laude, 1978); Boston University (J.D., 1981). Lecturer, Foreclosure of Cross Collateralized and/or Mixed Security Under the One Form of Action Rule, Real Estate Section, Beverly Hills Bar Association, 1991. Lecturer, Lender Liability, Orange County Bar Association, 1987. *Member:* Beverly Hills, Los Angeles County, Orange County and American (Member, Litigation Section) Bar Associations; State Bar of California; Association of Business Trial Lawyers.

*OF COUNSEL*

**ELIE J. GINDI,** born 1950; admitted to bar, 1978, California. *Education:* University of Colorado at Boulder (B.A., 1972); Southwestern University School of Law (J.D., 1977).

*ASSOCIATE*

**SHALOM RUBANOWITZ**

## HOCHMAN, SALKIN AND DeROY

A PROFESSIONAL CORPORATION
Established in 1969
9150 WILSHIRE BOULEVARD
SUITE 300
**BEVERLY HILLS, CALIFORNIA 90212-3414**
Telephone: 310-281-3200; 273-1181
Fax: 310-859-1430

*Federal and State Taxation and Corporation Law. Civil and Criminal Tax Litigation and Tax Controversies, Business and Real Estate Transactions, Probate, Civil Forfeitures.*

*FIRM PROFILE: Hochman Salkin and DeRoy is a tax oriented firm serving clients throughout the Western United States in federal and state tax controversy and tax litigation matters, tax, estate and business planning matters, and in business and corporate transactions. The firm has a particular specialty in federal and state criminal tax matters. The firm provides tax and planning services for corporations, partnerships, individuals and nonprofit organizations.*

**BRUCE I. HOCHMAN,** born Toronto, Canada, January 15, 1929; admitted to bar, 1952, California; 1960, U.S. Supreme Court. *Education:* University of Toronto and University of California at Los Angeles (B.A., 1949); University of California at Los Angeles (J.D., 1952); University of Southern California; Graduate Certificate in Taxation. Nu Beta Epsilon. Author: "Income Tax Evasion and other Fraud Problems-The Administrative Process," part I, 1972 and part II, 1972, The Tax Adviser; "The Accountant as a Defendant," Professional Development Course, California Certified Public Accountants Foundation, 1972. Co-Author: "Attorney-Client Privilege in Criminal Tax Cases," March, 1965; "Jeopardy Assessments—A System in Jeopardy," Taxes, June, 1967, The Tax Magazine; "Current Issues in Civil and Criminal Tax Fraud," State Bar SEI, December 1995; "Tax Fraud," State Bar SEI, November 1995. "Criminal Tax Disputes, A Systems Approach," UCLA Tax Disputes Institute, 1985. Assistant U.S. Attorney, Central District, 1953-1956. Hearing Officer, Department of Justice, 1958-1968. Chief Editor, "Tax Crimes-Bureau of National Affairs (Tax Management), 1993. Lecturer, Taxation of Litigation Damage Awards, 1996. *Member:* Los Angeles County and American Bar Associations; The State Bar of California. Fellow, American College of Trial Lawyers. (Certified Specialist, Criminal and Taxation Law, The State Bar of California Board of Legal Specialization). **PRACTICE AREAS:** Criminal and Civil Tax Controversy and Tax Litigation (Federal and State).

**AVRAM SALKIN,** born Los Angeles, California, July 23, 1935; admitted to bar, 1960, California; 1974, U.S. Supreme Court. *Education:* University of California at Los Angeles (B.S., 1956); University of California at Berkeley (LL.B., 1959). Author: "Recent Tax Developments in Real Estate Financing," California Continuing Education of the Bar, 1986. Co-Author: "Tax Aspects of California Partnerships," Chapters 9 and 10, California Continuing Education of the Bar, 1983; "Deductions and Allocations For Real Estate Investment Partnerships, Under TRA 1984," Major Tax Planning, USC Tax Institute, 1985; "Administrative Tax Appeals," May 1995; "Independent Contractor Versus Employee Status," Major Tax Planning, U.S.C. Institute on Federal Taxation, 1993. Lecturer, Taxation of Litigation Damage Awards, 1996. *Member:* Beverly Hills (Chairman, Tax Committee, 1969), Los Angeles County (Member, Tax Section) and American Bar Associations; The State Bar of California. (Certified Specialist, Taxation Law, The State Bar of California Board of Legal Specialization). **PRACTICE AREAS:** Civil and Criminal Tax Controversy; Individual Business and Corporate Tax Planning; Business and Real Estate Transactions; Tax, Business and Estate Planning; Probate.

**CHARLES P. RETTIG,** born Los Angeles, California, November 18, 1956; admitted to bar, 1981, California and Arizona; 1982, U.S. Tax Court, U.S. District Court, Central and Southern Districts of California and U.S. Court of Appeals, Fifth and Ninth Circuits; U.S. District Court, District of Arizona; U.S. District Court, District of Hawaii. *Education:* University of California at Los Angeles (B.A., 1978); Pepperdine University (J.D., cum laude, 1981); New York University (LL.M. in Taxation, 1982). Author: "Financial Status Audits: The Internal Revenue Service Returns to Basic Investigative Techniques," The Federal Lawyer, August 1996; "Financial Status Audits," Lawyer's World, December 1996; "Financial Status Audits: A Return to Basic Investigative Techniques," The Attorney-CPA, November 1996; "IRS and EDD Implement New Approach to Worker Classification," The Tax Reporter, August 1996; "The EDD Implements its New Tax-Settlement Authority," Los Angeles Lawyer, May 1996; "Economic Reality and the Internal Revenue Service," California Tax Lawyer, November, 1995; Deductibility of Client Costs by a Law Firm," The Tax Reporter, July 1995; "Privileged Communications," The Tax Reporter, October, 1995. Co-Author: "Tax Crimes," Bureau of National Affairs (Tax Management), Publication 636, 1993. Lecturer: "The CPA's Role in Tax Litigation and Controversy," 1996; "Preparing for Financial Status Audits, 1996; "IRS Project Esquire - Latest Developments of IRS Audits of Your Attorney Clients," 1996; "Taxation of Litigation Damage Awards, 1996; "Nuts and Bolts of State Tax Procedure," 1996; "IRS Financial Status Audits - Avoiding Accountant Malpractice," 1996; "California Tax Settlements," 1996; "California Residency Issues," 1996; "Bringing a Crime Sensitive Taxpayer in From the Cold," 1996; "Family Law and the IRS - A Collision of Issues," 1996; "Current Developments in Federal and State Tax Procedure," 1996; "Tax Crimes in Family Law Cases," 1995; "Recent Developments in Tax Procedure and Litigation," 1994-1996; "Sales and Use Tax Procedure Before the State Board of Equalization," 1993; "Selected Topics in Civil and Criminal Tax Practice," 1991-1992. Instructor, University of California at Los Angeles, Extension - Attorney Assistant Training Program, 1988—. Adjunct Professor, Golden Gate University, School of Taxation, 1996—. *Member:* Beverly Hills, Los Angeles County (Member and Chair, Committee on Tax Procedure and Litigation; Member: Entertainment Tax Committee and Committee on State and Local Tax) and American (Member: Section on Taxation; Committee on Civil and Criminal Tax Penalties) Bar Associations; The State Bar of California (Member: Taxation Section Executive Committee, 1995—; Tax Procedure and Litigation Committee; State and Local Tax Committee); State Bar of Arizona. (Certified Specialist, Taxation Law, The State Bar of California Board of Legal Specialization). **PRACTICE AREAS:** Civil and Criminal Tax Litigation; Tax Controversies; Federal Tax Controversies; Tax Planning; Business Planning; Estate Planning; Probate; Civil Forfeiture.

*(This Listing Continued)*

**DENNIS PEREZ,** born San Diego, California, May 8, 1956; admitted to bar, 1982, California, U.S. Tax Court and U.S. District Court, Central, Eastern and Southern Districts of California; U.S. Court of Appeals, Ninth Circuit. *Education:* San Diego State University (A.B. in English, cum laude, 1978); University of California at Los Angeles (J.D., 1982). Trial Attorney, District Counsel, Internal Revenue Service, 1982-1986. Lecturer: "Current Issues in Civil and Criminal Tax Fraud," December 1995; "Administrative Tax Appeals," May 1995; "Tax Litigation: Civil and Criminal," May 1995. "Recent Developments in Tax Procedure and Litigation", May 1994; "What Civil Tax Lawyers Should Know About State Criminal Tax Prosecutions," June 1993; "Selected Topics in Civil and Criminal Tax Practice," January 1991. Author, "U.S. Tax Court Settlement Judge Proposal," State Bar Taxation Section, May 1996. Co-Author: "Tax Crimes," Bureau of National Affairs (Tax Management) 1993. *Member:* Beverly Hills, Los Angeles County (Member: Committee on Tax Procedure and Litigation) and American Bar Associations; The State Bar of California (Vice-Chair, Taxation Section, Executive Committee, 1994-1995; Member, Tax Procedure and Litigation Subcommittee). *PRACTICE AREAS:* Civil and Criminal Tax Litigation and Tax Controversy Law (Federal and State).

**STEVEN R. TOSCHER,** born New York, N.Y., November 9, 1953; admitted to bar, 1979, California; 1981, U.S. District Court, Central District of California, U.S. Court of Appeals, Ninth Circuit and U.S. Tax Court. *Education:* University of Nevada (B.S.B.A., with distinction, 1975); University of San Diego (J.D., summa cum laude, 1979) (First in Class). Trial Attorney, Tax Division, U.S. Department of Justice, 1979-1983; United States Department of Justice Outstanding Attorney Award (1982); California Law Business, "Up and Coming Tax Litigator Under 40" (1992). Adjunct Professor: Criminal and Civil Tax Procedure, University of San Diego Graduate Tax Program, 1987-1989; Tax Procedure, University of Southern California School of Accounting, 1995. Moderator, California Tax Discussion Group, Lexis Counsel Connect, 1995. Lecturer: "Employment Development Department Tax Procedure," 1993; "Taxpayer Bill of Rights - More Procedural Fairness in Tax Administration," November 1988; "Civil Tax Penalty Reform - Some Sanity Brought to an Insane Situation," June 1990; "Selected Topics Concerning Sales and Exchanges of Real Property: Like Kind Exchanges" and "Sales of Principal Residence," October 1990; Program Coordinator - "Recent Developments in Tax Procedure and Administration" CEB January-March, 1991; "Selected Topics Concerning TEFRA Partnership Proceedings - 'Judicial Stages' and 'California Rules,'" May 1991; "Dealing with Potential IRS and EDD Reclassification of Independent Contractors" 1991-1993; "Recent Developments in Tax Procedure and Litigation" June 1992; "Non-Tax Tax Disputes" September 1992; "Contesting California Employment Development Department Assessments," September 1993; "EDD offers in Compromise," January 1994; "Lawyer Beware! The Tax Man Cometh," November 1994; "Administrative Tax Appeals," May 1995. Co-Author: Employment Tax, "Advising California Partnerships and Sole Proprietorships" Matthew Bender, 1992; "Tax Crimes," Bureau of National Affairs (Tax Management), 1993. Author: "Federal Sentencing Guidelines for Tax Crimes," Nevada Lawyer, May 1994. "Do the Right Thing," Lawyer Non-compliance with the Internal Revenue Code, L.A. Lawyer, June 1994; "The new EDD Offer-in-Compromise Legislation," L.A. Lawyer, February 1994; "Buying Time From the Collector - - Negotiating Installment Agreements with the Internal Revenue Service," Beverly Hills Bar Journal, 1991; "proposed Amendments to the U.S. Sentencing Commission Guidelines for Tax Crimes: A More Accurate Determination of Tax Loss; Longer Periods of Incarceration for Tax Offenders," Tax Management Weekly Report, June 1993; "Government Turns Up Heat on Criminal Tax Enforcement," Tax Management Weekly. February 11, 1994; "Materiality in False Tax Return Cases- Who Decides, Judge or Jury?" Tax Management Weekly, October 10, 1994; "The EDD Tax Amnesty Program," L.A. Lawyer, May 1995; "Materiality in False Tax Return Cases- The Supreme Courts Decision in Gaudin," Tax Management Weekly, August 7, 1995. *Member:* Beverly Hills, Los Angeles County (Past-Chair, Committee on Tax Procedure and Litigation) and American Bar Associations; State Bar of California; State Bar of Nevada. *PRACTICE AREAS:* Civil and Criminal Tax Litigation and Tax Controversy (Federal and State).

*OF COUNSEL*

**GEORGE DEROY,** born Pittsburgh, Pennsylvania, May 30, 1926; admitted to bar, 1951, California; 1974, U.S. Supreme Court. *Education:* University of California at Berkeley (B.A., 1945); University of California at Los Angeles (M.B.A., 1948); University of Southern California (LL.B., 1951). Order of the Coif; Beta Gamma Sigma. *Member:* Los Angeles County and American Bar Associations; The State Bar of California.

*(This Listing Continued)*

*PRACTICE AREAS:* Corporate and Business Litigation; Accounting and Legal Malpractice Defense.

**STUART A. SIMON,** born Glendale, California, December 30, 1954; admitted to bar, 1978, California. *Education:* California State University at Northridge (B.S., 1975); University of Southern California (M.B.T., 1982); Loyola University of Los Angeles, School of Law (J.D., 1978); New York University (LL.M. in Taxation, 1985). Phi Alpha Delta. Certified Public Accountant, California, 1981. *Member:* Los Angeles County Bar Association; State Bar of California; California Society of Certified Public Accountants.

**MICHAEL W. POPOFF,** born Los Angeles, California, January 20, 1953; admitted to bar, 1980, California; 1992, U.S. District Court, Central District of California and U.S. Tax Court. *Education:* University of Southern California (B.A., 1975); Boalt Hall School of Law, University of California (J.D., 1980). Co-Author: "Tax Crimes" Bureau of National Affairs (Tax Management), 1992; "Independent Contractor v. Employee Status," Major Tax Planning (U.S.C.), 1993. *PRACTICE AREAS:* Civil and Criminal Tax Controversy (Federal and State).

**FREDERIC J. ADAM,** born Los Angeles, California, January 13, 1964; admitted to bar, 1993, New York and U.S. Tax Court; 1994, District of Columbia; 1995, California. *Education:* University of California at Berkeley (B.A., 1986); University of Denver (J.D., with honors, 1992); New York University (LL.M., Taxation, 1993). Order of St. Ives. Attorney-Advisor, to the Honorable William M. Fay, United States Tax Court, 1993-1995. Lecturer, "Taxation of Litigation Damage Awards," 1996. *Member:* Beverly Hills, Los Angeles County (Chair, Young Tax Lawyers, Westside) and American Bar Association. *LANGUAGES:* Swedish, French, German. *PRACTICE AREAS:* Civil and Criminal Tax Litigation; Tax Controversies; Tax; Business; Estate Planning; Corporate; Partnership and Individual Taxation.

REFERENCE: Bank of California.

---

## *LAW OFFICES OF*
## *LEONARD HORWIN*

*Established in 1936*

*121 SOUTH BEVERLY DRIVE*
**BEVERLY HILLS, CALIFORNIA 90212**
*Telephone: 310-275-5132*
*Los Angeles: 213-272-7807*
*Fax: 310-275-7216*

*General Civil and Trial Practice. Business, Family, Estate Planning, Trust, Real Property and International Law.*

**LEONARD HORWIN,** born Chicago, Illinois, January 2, 1913; admitted to bar, 1936, California and U.S. District Court, Southern District of California; 1939, U.S. Circuit Court of Appeals, Ninth Circuit; 1942, U.S. Supreme Court. *Education:* University of California at Los Angeles (B.A., 1933); Yale University (LL.B., cum laude, 1936). Order of the Coif. Comments in Yale Law Journal: "Protection of Reputation of States Products," July, 1934; "Railroad Retirement Act," December, 1934; "Writing Down Fixed Assets and Stated Capital," April, 1935; "Public Interest in Labor Disputes," 1941 State Bar Journal. Leading Article in 1942 California Law Review, "Los Angeles Labor Relations Court," Partner and Teacher, Witkin-Horwin Review Course on California Law, 1939-1941. Author: "Plain Talk", 1931—; "Insight and Foresight (14 Vols.) December 1, 1990, Dawn Publications, Ltd., Quebec, Canada, U.S. Library of Congress No. 91-158974. Lecturer on Labor Law, University of Southern California Law School, 1941. Judge Pro-Tem, Los Angeles Superior Court, 1941. Counsel for Board of Economic Warfare, 1942-1943 and concurrently Member of Program Adjustment Committee and Alternate Member of Requirements Committee, War Production Board. Attaché, U.S. Embassy, Madrid, Spain, 1943-1947 and concurrently American Member of Representatives in Spain of Allied Control Council for Germany, 1945-1947. Chairman, Court Reorganization Committee League of California Cities, 1963-1965. Member, City Council, City of Beverly Hills, 1962-1966; Mayor, 1964-1965. Chairman, Committee on Transportation, Los Angeles Goals Council, 1968-1972. Board Member, Southern California Rapid Transit District, 1964-1966. Chairman, City of Beverly Hills Rent Control Committee, 1980. *Member:* Beverly Hills (Chairman, Newlyweds Law Counselling Committee, 1977-1979), International and American Bar Associations; State Bar of

*(This Listing Continued)*

## LAW OFFICES OF LEONARD HORWIN, Beverly Hills—Continued

California. Fellow, American Academy of Matrimonial Lawyers. **LANGUAGES:** Spanish, German.

REPRESENTATIVE CLIENTS: Horwin-Gordon Properties; Horwin 1983 Trust.
REFERENCES: Bank of America National Trust & Savings Assn. (Beverly Wilshire Branch, Beverly Hills, Calif.); Merrill Lynch (Beverly Hills, Office).

---

## SAMUEL D. INGHAM, III

Established in 1975

SUITE 830, 8383 WILSHIRE BOULEVARD
**BEVERLY HILLS, CALIFORNIA 90211-2407**
Telephone: 213-651-5980
FAX: 213-651-5725
Email: sdiesq@aol.com

*Estate Planning, Trusts, Probate, Guardianship and Conservatorship, Oil and Gas and Real Estate Law.*

**SAMUEL D. INGHAM, III,** born Los Angeles, California, February 19, 1952; admitted to bar, 1975, California; 1979, U.S. Tax Court. *Education:* University of California at Irvine (B.A., summa cum laude, 1972); University of California at Los Angeles (J.D., 1975). *Member:* Los Angeles County Bar Association (Member: Executive Committee, National Resources Law Section, 1979-1982; Sections on: Taxation; Real Property; Corporations; Probate and Trust Law); State Bar of California. (Certified Specialist, Probate, Estate Planning and Trust Law).

REPRESENTATIVE CLIENTS: Wells Fargo Bank; Bank of America; Union Bank; Northern Trust of California; Long Beach-Signal Hill Oil Producers Assn.; Signal Hill Petroleum, Inc.; U.S. Trust Company of California.

---

## INMAN, STEINBERG, NYE & STONE, APC

Established in 1985

(Formally Inman, Weisz & Steinberg, APC)

9720 WILSHIRE BOULEVARD, PENTHOUSE
**BEVERLY HILLS, CALIFORNIA 90212**
Telephone: 310-274-7111
Fax: 310-274-8889

*General Business Law with an emphasis on Business, Real Estate, Intellectual Property, Employment, and Insurance Litigation in Federal and State Courts, Immigration Law, Estate Planning, Trust Administration, Probate and Corporate Law.*

FIRM PROFILE: *The philosophy of the firm is simple. The firm strives to provide the highest quality legal services while giving the utmost personal attention to each and every client.*

*The firm is recognized worldwide for its representation of investors who invest in the United States and seek U.S. immigration benefits. The firm's staff is fluent in more than ten foreign languages.*

*The firm's lawyers handle complex, multi-million dollar business litigation cases as well as the small individual cases, giving each case the special personal attention that it deserves. The firm welcomes the opportunity to serve each of its client's particular needs.*

**MATTHEW S. STEINBERG,** born Los Angeles, California, October 20, 1953; admitted to bar, 1978, California and U.S. District Court, Central District of California; 1981, U.S. District Court, Northern and Southern Districts of California; 1986, U.S. Court of Appeals, Ninth Circuit; 1990, U.S. Supreme Court. *Education:* University of California at Los Angeles; University of California at Berkeley (B.A., 1975); University of San Diego (J.D., cum laude, 1978). Author: "How to Win a Malicious Prosecution Case," Los Angeles Lawyer (April 1994). Member, Million Dollar Advocates Forum. *Member:* State Bar of California. **REPORTED CASES:** Atari Corporation v. Ernst & Whinney, 970 F.2d 641 (9th Cir. 1992). Air Sea Forwarders v. Air Asia Company, Ltd., 880 F.2d 176 (9th Cir. 1989). Coopers & Lybrand v. Superior Court, 212 Cal.App.3d 524, 260 Cal.Rptr. 713 (1989). **PRACTICE AREAS:** Civil Litigation; Trial and Appeals in State and Federal Courts.

**MAURICE C. INMAN, JR.,** born Portland, Oregon, November 21, 1931; admitted to bar, 1957, California and U.S. District Court, Central District of California; 1964, U.S. Court of Appeals, Ninth Circuit; 1967, U.S. Supreme Court; 1983, District of Columbia. *Education:* University of California at Los Angeles (B.S., summa cum laude, 1953); Harvard University (J.D., LL.B., 1956). Phi Beta Kappa; Beta Gamma Sigma; Phi Kappa Psi; Gold Key. General Counsel, Immigration and Naturalization Service, Department of Justice, Washington, D.C., 1981-1986. Member: Commission of the California's Delegate, Appointed, 1979; Federal Immigration Law Reporter Advisory Council, 1984—; Board of Trustees, West Coast University, 1986—; United States Olympic Fund Raising Committee, 1986—; Harvard Law School Association of Southern California. Member, National Panel of Arbitrators, American Arbitration Association. *Member:* Beverly Hills, Los Angeles County (Attorney Client Relations Committee), Federal and American Bar Associations; The State Bar of California (Alternate Delegate and Delegate to Conference of Delegates, 1965-1972); The District of Columbia Bar; Association of Business Trial Lawyers (Founding Member); American Judicature Society.

**GARY A. NYE,** born Dallas, Texas, November 25, 1961; admitted to bar, 1986, California; 1988, U.S. Court of Appeals, Ninth Circuit and U.S. District Court, Central, Southern and Northern Districts of California. *Education:* University of California at Santa Barbara (B.A., cum laude, 1983); Loyola Law School (J.D., 1986). Member: Scott Moot Court Honors Program; Los Angeles Superior Court, Panel of Judicial Arbitrators. Author: "The Customer List as a Trade Secret" Intellectual Law Journal (1994). *Member:* Beverly Hills, Los Angeles County and American Bar Associations; State Bar of California. **PRACTICE AREAS:** Commercial Litigation; Employment Law; Intellectual Property; Insurance.

**LINCOLN STONE,** born Inglewood, California, November 29, 1960; admitted to bar, 1986, Illinois; 1990, California; 1993, U.S. Court of International Trade. *Education:* Loyola Marymount University (B.A., 1983); University of Notre Dame (J.D., 1986). Law Clerk to U.S. Judge Robert A. Grant, Northern District of Indiana, 1986-1987. Trial Attorney, U.S. Immigration & Naturalization Service, 1987-1988.

---

**VERONICA MAYA JEFFERS,** born Los Angeles, California; admitted to bar, 1988, Arizona; 1989, Illinois and U.S. District Court, District of Arizona; 1990, U.S. District Court, Northern District of Illinois (Not admitted in California). *Education:* Wellesley College (B.A., 1983); Harvard University (J.D., 1986). Author: "Labor Certification for Alien/Beneficiary Shareholders," Manual on Labor Certification Practice and Procedure (AILA), 1990; "Obtaining H-3 Classification," Immigration and Nationality Law Handbook (AILA), 1992. Member, Board of Directors, Community Law Project, Inc., 1992-1995. Law Clerk to Judge Bambi E. Meil, Fifth Circuit, State of Hawaii, 1994-1995. *Member:* Illinois State Bar Association; State Bar of Arizona; American Bar Association; American Immigration Lawyers Association (Chair, Midwest Regional Conference Committee, 1993-1994; Member, National Conference Planning Committee, 1991-1992).

**PATRICK S. RODRIGUEZ,** born New York, N.Y.; admitted to bar, 1990, California; U.S. District Court, Central District of California. *Education:* University of Southern California (B.S., 1983); Loyola Law School (J.D., 1989). Order of the Coif; St. Thomas More Law Honor Society. Executive Editor, Loyola of Los Angeles Law Review, 1988-1989. Certified Public Accountant, California, 1989. *Member:* American Bar Association; Hispanic National Bar Association; American Institute of Certified Public Accountants; California Society of Certified Public Accountants.

**REGINA O. REYES,** born Manila, Philippines; admitted to bar, 1995, California and U.S. District Court, Central District of California; U.S. Court of Veteran Appeals. *Education:* Georgetown University (B.S.F.S., 1978); Ateneo de Manila University (L.L.B., 1982). Board of Editors, Ateneo Law Journal, 1978-1982. Trial Attorney, Office of The Solicitor General, 1983-1987. Judge, Office of the Solicitor General, 1987-1993. *Member:* Glendale and Los Angeles County Bar Associations; American Immigration Lawyers Association; Integrated Bar of the Philippines; Filipino American Bar Association.

**MELANIE K. LOWERY,** born Clovis, California, September 12, 1969; admitted to bar, 1994, California; U.S. District Court, Central District of California; U.S. Court of Appeals, Ninth Circuit. *Education:* University of California at Santa Barbara (B.A., honors, 1991); University of Southern California (J.D., 1994). Extern, U.S. Bankruptcy Court (1992), and U.S. District Court, Central District of California (1993). President, Native American Law Student Association, 1993-1994. *Member:* Beverly Hills, Century City, Los Angeles County and American Bar Associations; State Bar of California. **PRACTICE AREAS:** Business Litigation; Entertainment and Business Transactions; Intellectual Property.

*(This Listing Continued)*

## PROFESSIONAL BIOGRAPHIES

**CALIFORNIA—BEVERLY HILLS**

**ASHKHEN A. GAMBOURIAN,** born Yerevan, Armenia, April 10, 1966; admitted to bar, 1991, California. *Education:* University of California, Los Angeles (B.S., 1988); Whittier College School of Law (J.D., 1991). Moot Court Honors Board. Recipient, American Jurisprudence Award, Legal Research and Writing, 1989. Panel Member, "Immigration Issues Now Necessary for all Practitioners, Including Employer Sanctions, Anti-Discrimination, Deportation Defense, Adjustment of Status and Document Fraud," Federal Bar Association Seminar, Los Angeles, California, February 17, 1996. Trial Attorney, 1991-1996 and Asylum Prescreening Officer, 1992-1996, U.S. Department of Justice Immigration and Naturalization Service. *Member:* State Bar of California. **LANGUAGES:** Armenian, French, Russian and Turkish. **PRACTICE AREAS:** Immigration.

**GARY W. PARK,** born Seoul, Korea, June 23, 1966; admitted to bar, 1994, California and U.S. District Court, Central District of California. *Education:* University of California, Los Angeles (B.A., 1988); Loyola Law School (J.D., 1994). Law Clerk to Judge Vincent P. Zurzulo, U.S. Bankruptcy Court, Central District of California, 1995. *Member:* State Bar of California; Korean American Bar Association; Southern California Chinese Lawyers; Japanese American Bar Association. **PRACTICE AREAS:** Business Litigation; Franchise Litigation; Consumer Finance; Creditors' Rights; Bankruptcy; Immigration.

### OF COUNSEL

**ANDREW J. WEISZ,** born New York, N.Y., November, 1925; admitted to bar, 1952, California. *Education:* City College of New York (B.S., 1948); University of Southern California (J.D., 1952). Order of the Coif; Phi Kappa Phi. Editor and Member, USC Law Review, 1951-1952. Law Clerk to Justice Roger Traynor, California Supreme Court, 1952-1953. Assistant U.S. Attorney, Los Angeles, California, 1953-1956. Commissioner, Superior Court, 1962-1964. Judge, Beverly Hills Judicial District, 1965-1986. *Member:* Beverly Hills (Member, Board of Governors, 1977-1978, 1985-1992; Co-Chair, Committee on Legal Competency, Ethics and Discipline, 1985—), Los Angeles County and Federal Bar Associations; California Judge's Association; Municipal Court Judge's Association of Los Angeles; Southern California Medico-Legal Society. [Lt. Col. JAGC (active duty, 1943-1946)]

**THOMAS C. FERGUSON,** admitted to bar, 1959, Illinois; 1961, Kentucky (Not admitted in California). *Education:* Vanderbilt University (B.A., 1955; J.D., 1959); Hague Academy of International Law. Harvard University, Kennedy School of Government, 1985. Listed in, Who's Who in America, 1987. Member, U.S. Army Chemical Corps., 1963. Deputy Commissioner, U.S. Immigration and Naturalization Service, 1984-1987. United States Ambassador to Brunei, 1987-1989. *Member:* American Bar Association.

**JEFFREY D. LEWIS,** born Los Angeles, California, May 11, 1949; admitted to bar, 1974, California and U.S. District Court, Central District of California. *Education:* University of Southern California (B.A., magna cum laude, 1971); Cambridge University, Cambridge, England (Certificate in Economics, 1971); University of California, Boalt Hall School of Law (J.D., 1974). Phi Beta Kappa; Phi Kappa Phi. Lecturer, Business Law, California State University at Northridge, 1976-1987. Author: "Professional Corporations in California" in California Business Law Forum. *Member:* Los Angeles County Bar Association; State Bar of California (Member, Sections on Business Law, Estate Planning, and Trusts and Probate); Beverly Hills Estate Planning Council. **PRACTICE AREAS:** Estate Planning; Trust Administration; Corporation Law; Business Transactions; Real Estate; Probate.

REFERENCE: Wells Fargo Bank, Barrington Place Branch, Los Angeles, CA.

---

## ISAACMAN, KAUFMAN & PAINTER
*8484 WILSHIRE BOULEVARD, SUITE 850*
**BEVERLY HILLS, CALIFORNIA 90211**
Telephone: 213-782-7700
Fax: 213-782-7744

*Civil Litigation, Entertainment, Tax, Employment and Business Litigation. Business and Real Estate Transactions. Intellectual Property Matters.*

**ALAN L. ISAACMAN,** born Harrisburg, Pennsylvania, July 12, 1942; admitted to bar, 1968, California, U.S. Supreme Court and U.S. Courts of Appeals, 1st, 2nd, 4th, 9th and 10th Circuits. *Education:* Pennsylvania State University (B.S., 1964); Harvard University (J.D., 1967). Law Clerk to U.S. District Judge Harry Pregerson, Central District, California, 1969-1970. Lecturer: "Defamation and Invasion of Privacy," Practicing Law Institute, Los Angeles, California, 1992 and New York, New York, 1988; University

*(This Listing Continued)*

of California Los Angeles, 1989; Hastings College of Law, 1989; Georgia Bar Association, 1988; Richmond, Virginia Bar Association, 1989; Orange County, California Bar Association, 1988; Libel Defense Resource Center, New York, New York, 1988; American Newspaper Publishers Association and National Association of Broadcasters, Denver, Colorado, 1987; Dauphin County, Pennsylvania Bar Association, 1988; "Law of Copyright", Los Angeles Copyright Society, 1989; "Negotiating Motion Picture Contracts and Profit Disputes," Miami, Florida Bar Association, 1990; Tampa, Florida Bar Association, 1990. Special Master, Federal Court, Copyright. Fellow, American College of Trial Lawyers. The Best Lawyers in America. **PRACTICE AREAS:** Civil Litigation; Defamation; Copyright; Entertainment; Employment; General Business Litigation.

**BRIAN KAUFMAN,** born Los Angeles, California, July 11, 1945; admitted to bar, 1971, California; 1978, U.S. Customs Court; 1981, U.S. Court of International Trade. *Education:* University of California at Los Angeles (B.S., 1967); University of Southern California (J.D., 1970). Phi Delta Phi. Member, University of Southern California Law Review, 1969-1970. Author: "Investment Companies and Restricted Securities: Pearls or Perils?" 43 Southern California Law Review 516, 1970. Winner, James G. Holbrook Award for Outstanding Publication in Law Review, on vote of faculty, 1970. *Member:* Los Angeles County Bar Association; State Bar of California. **PRACTICE AREAS:** Civil Litigation; Business Law; Real Estate; Litigation.

**MICHAEL A. PAINTER,** born Philadelphia, Pennsylvania, March 5, 1939; admitted to bar, 1969, California; 1979, U.S. Court of Appeals, Ninth and Federal Circuits; registered to practice before U.S. Patent and Trademark Office; 1991, U.S. Court of International Trade. *Education:* University of California at Los Angeles (B.S., 1961; M.S., 1964); Loyola University of Los Angeles (J.D., 1968). Phi Alpha Delta. Author: "Proprietary Rights in Video Tape," Journal of the Beverly Hills Bar Association, May, 1973. *Member:* Beverly Hills and Los Angeles County Bar Associations; State Bar of California. **PRACTICE AREAS:** Customs Matters; Domestic and Foreign Patents, Trademark and Copyright Prosecution and Litigation; Related Unfair Competition Matters.

**STEVEN H. BLACKMAN,** born Chicago, Illinois, December 6, 1955; admitted to bar, 1980, California. *Education:* University of California at Los Angeles (B.A., 1977); Harvard University (J.D., 1980). *Member:* Los Angeles County Bar Association; State Bar of California. **PRACTICE AREAS:** Employment Law; Entertainment; First Amendment and Business Litigation.

**WILLIAM S. COHEN,** born Jersey City, New Jersey, December 22, 1928; admitted to bar, 1953, New York; 1969, California; 1972, U.S. Tax Court. *Education:* New York University (B.S., cum laude, 1949; LL.M., in Taxation, 1961); Brooklyn Law School (LL.B., 1953). Beta Gamma Sigma. Certified Public Accountant, New York, 1958 and California, 1967. Co-Author: "Tax Considerations of Copyrights," Century City Bar Association Journal, Spring, 1984. Adjunct Professor, Graduate School of Taxation, Golden Gate University, Los Angeles, 1976-1985. *Member:* Beverly Hills, Los Angeles County (Member, Section on Taxation) and American (Member, Section on Taxation) Bar Associations; State Bar of California; New York County Lawyers Association; American Institute of Certified Public Accountants. [1st Lt., JAG, USAF, 1953-1956]. (Certified Specialist, Taxation Law, The State Bar of California Board of Legal Specialization). **PRACTICE AREAS:** Taxation Law; Estate Planning Law; Probate Administration; Corporate Law.

**NEIL B. FISCHER,** born Chicago, Illinois, April 18, 1936; admitted to bar, 1961, Illinois; 1972, California. *Education:* University of Wisconsin (B.B.A., 1957); Northwestern University (J.D., 1961). Tau Epsilon Rho. *Member:* Beverly Hills, Los Angeles County and American (Member, Forum Committee on The Entertainment and Sports Industries, Corporation, Banking and Business Law Section, 1983—) Bar Associations; State Bar of California. **PRACTICE AREAS:** Entertainment; Corporate; Securities; Financing.

**ROBERT S. FREIMUTH,** born Sheboygan, Wisconsin, December 27, 1959; admitted to bar, 1987, California and U.S. District Court, Central and Northern Districts of California. *Education:* University of Wisconsin (B.A., summa cum laude, 1982; M.A., 1983); Harvard Law School (J.D., 1987). Phi Beta Kappa. *Member:* Los Angeles County Bar Association; State Bar of California. **LANGUAGES:** French. **PRACTICE AREAS:** First Amendment; Copyright.

## JACOBSON, SANDERS & BORDY, LLP

A Partnership including a Professional Corporation
9777 WILSHIRE BOULEVARD, SUITE 718
**BEVERLY HILLS, CALIFORNIA 90212-1907**
Telephone: 310-777-7488

*Business Litigation and Transactions, Real Estate, Probate and Trust Litigation, Tax and Estate Planning.*

FIRM PROFILE: Jacobson, Sanders & Bordy, LLP was established in response to the Partners' belief that there existed a need for a small, cost-efficient law firm that could provide quality legal services to publicly traded and closely held businesses. With over fifty (50) years of collective experience, the attorneys of Jacobson, Sanders & Bordy, LLP are prepared to render a wide range of legal services to publicly traded and closely held businesses and their families. Clients of Jacobson, Sanders & Bordy, LLP cover a wide range of international and domestic industries, including real estate development, commercial leasing, mortgage banking, garment manufacturing, textile manufacturing, chemical manufacturing, biotechnical research, rare earth magnet sales, insurance services, soft and hard goods manufacturers, appraisers and entertainment. The firm strives to combine its depth of expertise with cost-efficient legal services. In many cases, the firm acts as general counsel for its clients, handling virtually every legal problem presented. Although the firm's client base is predominately located in Southern California, clients are located throughout the United States as well as in Europe and Japan.

Attorneys for the firm regularly lecture in and write for, continuing education programs, the National Business Institute, as well as for numerous industry groups on topics including creditor's rights, secured transactions, real, estate and litigation. In addition, attorneys with the firm have taught and are presently teaching, legal courses in various universities and law schools.

### MEMBERS OF FIRM

**LAWRENCE H. JACOBSON, (A P.C.),** born Los Angeles, California, February 9, 1943; admitted to bar, 1968, California; 1977, U.S. Supreme Court. *Education:* University of California at Los Angeles (A.B., 1964; J.D., 1967). Order of the Coif. Senior Editor, U.C.L.A. Law Review, 1966-1967. Author: "Inverse Condemnation, Foreseeability Abandoned in California," 13 U.C.L.A. Law Review 871, 1966; "Lessor's Bankruptcy," 1 Real Estate Law Journal 152, 1972; "State Regulation of Stock Cooperatives," 7 Beverly Hills Bar Journal 12, 1973; "The California Lottery Law," 48 California State Bar Journal 58, 1973; "Independent Motion Picture Productions," 9 Beverly Hills Bar Journal 33, 1975; "Broker's Liability for Sale of Defective Homes," 52 Los Angeles Bar Journal 346, 1977; "Resolving Real Estate Disputes Through Arbitration," 27 Am. Jur. Trials 621, 1980; "Appraiser's Liability for False or Negligently Prepared Appraisal," 12 Appraisal Review and Mortgage Underwriting Journal 20, 1990; "Acquisition of Mortgage Banking Assets," 36 San Fernando Valley Bar Bulletin (4-9) 10, 1993. Adjunct Professor of Law, University of San Fernando Valley College of Law, 1982-1983. Vice President Legal Affairs, California Association of Realtors, 1975-1976. Judge, Pro Tem, Beverly Hills and Los Angeles Municipal Court, 1977-1987. Arbitrator, Los Angeles Superior Court. Lecturer, California Continuing Education of the Bar. *Member:* Beverly Hills, Los Angeles County and American Bar Associations; State Bar of California; Association of Real Estate Attorneys (President, 1978-1979). **PRACTICE AREAS:** General Business; Real Estate Transactions; Finance Law; Estate Planning. **Email:** 1hjac@aol.com

**MICHAEL J. BORDY,** born Kansas City, Missouri, July 24, 1952; admitted to bar, 1986, California. *Education:* Hamilton College (B.A., 1974); University of Kansas (Ph.D., 1980); Johns Hopkins University School of Hygiene and Public Health (Post-Ph.D., 1980-1983); University of Southern California (J.D., 1986). Phi Alpha Delta. NIH Pre-Doctoral Scholarship. Mellon Foundation Post-Doctoral Fellow. Member, University of Southern California Journal of Law and Environment, 1985-1986. Vice-Chair, National Jewish Law Students Association, 1985-1986. *Member:* State Bar of California. **PRACTICE AREAS:** General Business and Real Estate Transactions; Environmental Law.

**MICHAEL R. E. SANDERS,** born San Diego, California, April 13, 1946; admitted to bar, 1987, California, U.S. Court of Appeals, Ninth Circuit, U.S. District Court, Northern, Central, Eastern and Southern Districts of California, U.S. Tax Court and U.S. Court of International Trade; 1991, Washington; 1992, U.S. District Court, Western District of Washington; 1993, Oregon. *Education:* University of Utah (B.A., 1981); University of Illinois (J.D., 1985); University of Washington (LL.M., 1986); University of Southern California (Master of Business Taxation, 1992). Delta Theta Phi. U.S./Japan Friendship Commission Fellowship (Asian and Comparative Law), 1985-1986. President, Utah Chapter, Real Estate Securities and Syndication Institute, 1980-1982. *Member:* National Home Builders Association, 1977-1982; National Association of Realtors, 1976-1982; Associated General Contractors of America, 1979-1982. National Association of Securities Dealers, Inc., registered financial, options and operations Principal, 1982-1986. Judge, Pro Tem, Los Angeles Municipal Court, 1993-1994. Arbitrator, Los Angeles Superior Court, 1994. *Member:* Los Angeles County, Washington State and American (Member, Taxation Section, Foreign Activities of U.S. Taxpayers Committee, 1989-1991) Bar Associations; State Bar of California; Oregon State Bar; South Bay Bar Association. [U.S.M.C.R., 1970]. **LANGUAGES:** Japanese. **PRACTICE AREAS:** Taxation (International, Federal and State); Transactional Business Planning; Antitrust; Antitrust.

### OF COUNSEL

**DAVID S. WHITE,** born Brookline, Massachusetts, January 16, 1950; admitted to bar, 1977, California. *Education:* Clark University (A.B., 1971); University of California at Davis (J.D., 1977). Phi Kappa Phi National Honor Society. First Place, U.C. Davis Environmental Law Moot Court Competition, 1976. *Member:* National Moot Court Team, 1976; Moot Court Honors Board, 1977. Recipient, State Bar Pro Bono Commendation, 1983-1984. Author: "Business Tort Remedies," "Consumer Protection Remedies," Association of Business Trial Lawyers (Seventh Annual Seminar), "Remedies in Business Litigation," 1980; "Demeanor in the Courtroom," Association of Business Trial Lawyers (Eighth Annual Seminar); "Techniques of Persuasion," 1981. Member, Panel of Arbitrators, Commercial Panel, American Arbitration Association. *Member:* Beverly Hills (Arbitrator, Mandatory Fee Arbitration Program, 1982—), Los Angeles County (Member: Ethics Committee, 1984-1985; Superior Courts Committee, 1984-1985; Arbitrator, Mandatory Fee Arbitration Program, 1982—) and American Bar Associations; State Bar of California; Association of Business Trial Lawyers (Member, Board of Governors, 1982-1984; Chairperson, Ninth Annual Seminar on "Business Torts", 1982). (Practicing individually, Los Angeles). **PRACTICE AREAS:** Real Estate; Business and Entertainment Litigation; Alternate Dispute Resolution; Arbitration.

**PATRICIA B. KOLBER,** born Great Neck, New York, November 23, 1961; admitted to bar, 1986, California; U.S. District Court, Central District of California. *Education:* University of California at Davis (B.A., 1983); McGeorge School of Law, University of the Pacific (J.D., 1986). Best Brief, McGeorge Moot Court Competition. Legal Writing Instructor, McGeorge School of Law, 1985-1986. *Member:* Beverly Hills, Los Angeles County and American Bar Associations; State Bar of California; National Order of the Barristers. **LANGUAGES:** French and Spanish.

---

## JACOBY & CAPOGROSSO

9100 WILSHIRE BOULEVARD
7TH FLOOR-WEST TOWER
**BEVERLY HILLS, CALIFORNIA 90212**
Telephone: 310-274-8301
Fax: 310-274-9910

*Busines Litigation, Labor and Employment Law.*

### MEMBERS OF FIRM

**AARON H. JACOBY,** born San Francisco, California, December 11, 1960; admitted to bar, 1988, California; 1989, U.S. District Court, Central District of California. *Education:* University of Paris, Sorbonne, Paris, France; University of California at Santa Cruz (B.A., 1983); University of San Francisco (J.D., 1988). *Member:* Los Angeles County and American Bar Associations; State Bar of California. **LANGUAGES:** French, Italian. **SPECIAL AGENCIES:** California Public Utilities Commission; Federal Energy Regulatory Commission; California New Motor Vehicle Board. **PRACTICE AREAS:** Business Litigation; Administrative Law and Litigation; Crude Oil Regulatory Matters; Environmental Compliance Litigation; Land Use. **Email:** AARON@JCLAW.COM

**ERIC G. CAPOGROSSO,** born New York, N.Y., May 17, 1950; admitted to bar, 1979, California and U.S. District Court, Central District of California. *Education:* Fordham University; Hartwick College (B.A., 1975); Whittier College (J.D., 1979). Member, Whittier Law Review, 1977. Author and Managing Editor: *The Labor Guide. Member:* Los Angeles County (Member, Labor Law Section) and American (Member, Sports and Entertainment Forum, Labor Law Section) Bar Associations; State Bar of California. **PRACTICE AREAS:** Labor and Employment Law. **Email:** ERIC@JCLAW.COM

*(This Listing Continued)*

## ASSOCIATE

**KRISTIN GAMBLE,** born Pittsburgh, Pennsylvania, September 7, 1971; admitted to bar, 1996, California. *Education:* University of California, Los Angeles (B.S., 1993); University of California School of Law, Los Angeles (J.D., 1996). Phi Alpha Delta. Recipient, American Jurisprudence Award, Legal Research and Writing.

---

# *JAFFE & CLEMENS*

A Partnership including Professional Corporations

**SUITE 1000, 433 NORTH CAMDEN DRIVE
BEVERLY HILLS, CALIFORNIA 90210**

*Telephone: 310-550-7477
Telecopier: 310-271-8313*

*Practice Limited to Family Law.*

**DANIEL J. JAFFE, (A PROFESSIONAL CORPORATION),** born Cleveland, Ohio, August 6, 1937; admitted to bar, 1962, California. *Education:* University of Michigan (B.B.A., 1959); University of California at Los Angeles (J.D., 1962). Phi Alpha Delta. Listed in The Best Lawyers in America. Author: Chapter on "Attorney's Fees," California Continuing Education of Bar Books, July 1975; "Evidentiary Problems II," American College of Family Trial Lawyers, April 1996. Co-Author: "Practical Tax Considerations in Marriage Dissolutions," Practical Law Courses, Inc., 1977 and 1978; "Division and Taxation of Retirement Benefits in Dissolution Proceedings," California Continuing Education of the Bar, 1979, revised editions, 1982, 1984, 1986 and 1989; "Drafting and Litigating Prenuptial, Cohabitation and Marital Settlement Agreements," with Bruce A. Clemens, California Continuing Education of the Bar, 1981; "Employee Retirement and Deferred Compensation Plans on Dissolution of Marriage," Continuing Education of the Bar, July 1995. Lecturer: "Current Case Law Update from Community Property States and Related Tax Issues," American Institute of Certified Public Accountants National Conference on Divorce, June, 1993; "Divorce Taxation: Strategies and Traps," California Continuing Education of the Bar, October 1993; "Dissecting the Corporate and Partnership Tax Returns," South Carolina Trial Lawyers Association, August, 1993; "Children and the Law," Los Angeles County Bar Association, November 1993; "Employee Retirement and Deferred Compensation Plans on Dissolution of Marriage," Continuing Education of the Bar, July 1995; "Keeping Client Out of Jail," American Bar Association, August 1995; "Professional Goodwill and Alimony," American Bar Association, September 1995; "Negotiating and Drafting Tax Clauses in Marital Settlement Agreements," American Bar Association, April 1996; "Evidentiary Problems II," American College of Family Trial Lawyers, April 1996; "Keeping the Client (and Yourself) Out of Jail II," American Bar Association, August 1996; "Planning and Drafting for Business Buyouts in Divorce Cases," American Bar Association, August 1996. Lecturer and Moderator: "Divorce Tax Hot Tips," American Bar Association, August 1994. Diplomate, The American College of Family Trial Lawyers. *Member:* Beverly Hills (Chairman, Family Law Section, 1974-1975), Los Angeles County (Chairman, Executive Committee, Family Law Section, 1976-1977) and American (Member, Family Law Section Council, Taxation Committee) Bar Associations; State Bar of California (Member, Executive Committee, Family Law Section, 1986-1989). Fellow: American Academy of Matrimonial Lawyers (Counsel, 1991-1992); International Academy of Matrimonial Lawyers; Association of Certified Family Law Specialist. (Certified Specialist, Family Law, The State Bar of California Board of Legal Specialization). **PRACTICE AREAS:** Family Law. **Email:** MrDisso@AOL.COM

**BRUCE A. CLEMENS, (A PROFESSIONAL CORPORATION),** born San Francisco, California, September 23, 1946; admitted to bar, 1974, California. *Education:* Michigan State University (A.B., high honors, 1967); Stanford University (M.S., 1971); University of California at Los Angeles (J.D., 1974). Pi Mu Epsilon. Recipient: Wilson Scholarship; Distinguished Advocate Award, Moot Court. Listed in The Best Lawyers in America. Member, Moot Court Honors Program. Judicial Clerkship, Chief Justice, High Court of the Trust Territory of the Pacific Islands, 1973-1974. Co-Author: "Division and Taxation of Retirement Benefits in Dissolution Proceedings," California Continuing Education of the Bar, 1979, revised editions, 1982, 1984, 1986 and 1989; "Drafting and Litigating Prenuptial, Cohabitation and Marital Settlement Agreements," with Daniel J. Jaffe, California Continuing Education of the Bar, 1981; "Marital Dissolution," California Certified Public Accountants Foundation for Education and Research, 1981; "The Business Divorce," California Continuing Education of the Bar, 1987; "Employee Retirement & Deferred Compensation Plans on Dissolution of Marriage," California Continuing Education of the Bar,

*(This Listing Continued)*

1995. Co-Author and Lecturer: "Tax Planning for Marital Termination Settlement," California Continuing Education of the Bar, October, 1987. Lecturer: "Divorce Taxation: Property Division," American Bar Association, 1993; "Tax Traps in Divorce," State Bar of Nevada, 1994; "Avoiding the 10% Penalty for Early Distributions from Retirement Plans," Beverly Hills Bar Association, 1994; "Employee Retirement & Deferred Compensation Plans on Dissolution of Marriage," California Continuing Education of the Bar, 1995; "Bridging the Gap," Lawyers Club of Los Angeles County, 1995 and 1996; "Executive and Celebrity Goodwill in Family Law," 1990 Family Law Symposium; "Use of Demonstrative Exhibits and Evidence," American Bar Association, May 1, 1993; "Divorce Taxation, Strategies and Traps," Continuing Education of the Bar, October, 1993. Master's Panel Lecturer: "Cash Client, Controlling Experts, Fifth Amendment, Etc.," Beverly Hills Bar Association, 1996. Panelist: United States Commission on Interstate Child Support, 1991; "Master Strategies for Modifying and Terminating Support," Beverly Hills Bar Association Family Law Symposium, November 7, 1992. Instructor, Family Law: University of Southern California Law Center Advanced Program, 1981-1982; University of California at Los Angeles, 1988. *Member:* Beverly Hills (Member, Executive Committee, Family Law Section, 1986-1987), Los Angeles County (Member, Executive Committee, Family Law Section, 1987-1988) and American (Member, Section of Family Law) Bar Associations; State Bar of California. Fellow, American Academy of Matrimonial Lawyers; Association of Certified Family Law Specialists. (Certified Specialist, Family Law, The State Bar of California Board of Legal Specialization). **PRACTICE AREAS:** Family Law.

**WILLIAM S. RYDEN,** born San Bernardino, California, January 23, 1952; admitted to bar, 1980, California. *Education:* Claremont Mens' College (B.A., 1974); Southwestern University (J.D., cum laude, 1980). Phi Alpha Delta. Recipient, American Jurisprudence Book Award for Business Organizations. Instructor, Family Law, Southern California Paralegal Institute, 1987-1988. *Member:* Beverly Hills and Los Angeles County Bar Associations; State Bar of California (Member, Family Law Mediation Panel, 1987—). (Certified Specialist, Family Law, The State Bar of California Board of Legal Specialization). **PRACTICE AREAS:** Family Law.

## ASSOCIATES

**JUDY BOGEN,** born Los Angeles, California, March 6, 1955; admitted to bar, 1981, California; 1982, U.S. Court of Appeals, Ninth Circuit. *Education:* University of California at Los Angeles (B.A., 1976); Southwestern University School of Law (J.D., 1980). *Member:* Beverly Hills and Los Angeles County Bar Associations; State Bar of California (Member, Family Law Advisory Commission). (Certified Specialist, Family Law, California Board of Legal Specialization). **PRACTICE AREAS:** Family Law.

**DAVID M. LUBOFF,** born Santa Monica, California, August 5, 1954; admitted to bar, 1979, California; 1980, U.S. District Court, Central District of California; 1987, U.S. Court of Appeals, Ninth Circuit. *Education:* University of California at Los Angeles (B.A., summa cum laude, 1976; J.D., 1979). Phi Beta Kappa; Pi Gamma Mu. Member, Executive Board of Justices, Moot Court Honors Program, 1978-1979. Extern law clerk for William J. Lasarow, Presiding Bankruptcy Judge, Central District, California, 1978. Judge Pro Tem, Los Angeles Municipal Court, 1984-1988. Co-Author: "Responding to Demands for Inspection of Documents," Family Law News and Review, 1991; Chapter on "Domestic Torts," Family Law Reference Book, Los Angeles County Bar Association Family Law Section-Los Angeles Superior Court, 1991, revised editions, 1992, 1993. "Attorney Certifications to Prenuptial and Marital Settlement Agreements May Waive the Attorney-Client and Work Product Privileges," American Bar Association, Section on Family Law, 1991 Annual Meeting Compendium; Chapter on "Recomputation of Alimony Payments," California Continuing Education of the Bar, 1991. *Member:* Beverly Hills (Member, Family Law Section), Los Angeles County (Member, Family Law Section) and American Bar Associations; The State Bar of California. (Certified Specialist, Family Law, The State Bar of California Board of Legal Specialization). **REPORTED CASES:** Trimble v. Steinfeldt (1986) 178 Cal.App.3d 646, 224 Cal. Rptr. 195; Yates v. Pollock (1987) 194 Cal.App.3d 195, 239 Cal.Rptr. 383. **PRACTICE AREAS:** Family Law; Appellate Litigation.

**MARK L. LEVINSON,** born Los Angeles, California, November 14, 1946; admitted to bar, 1971, California. *Education:* San Fernando Valley State College (B.A., 1968); University of Southern California (J.D., 1971). *Member:* State Bar of California; American Bar Association. **PRACTICE AREAS:** Family Law.

**GRETCHEN WELLMAN TAYLOR,** born Los Angeles, California, November 10, 1945; admitted to bar, 1979, California. *Education:* Marymount Palos Verdes College (B.A., with honors, 1966); University of Cali-

*(This Listing Continued)*

## JAFFE & CLEMENS, Beverly Hills—Continued

fornia at Los Angeles; Southwestern University (J.D., 1979). Member, Panel of Attorneys for Child Dependency, Los Angeles County Juvenile Court. *Member:* Los Angeles County (Member, Family Law Section) and American Bar Associations; State Bar of California. (Certified Specialist, Family Law, The State Bar of California Board of Legal Specialization). LANGUAGES: Spanish, French. *PRACTICE AREAS:* Family Law.

**RICHARD MACKAY,** born Jersey City, New Jersey, September 28, 1942; admitted to bar, 1972, New Jersey; 1977, U.S. Supreme Court; 1981, New York (Not admitted in California). *Education:* Brown University (A.B., 1965); University of Jerusalem, Israel (M.B.A., 1971); Rutgers University (J.D., 1969). Assistant Prosecutor, Hudson County Prosecutor's Office, 1972-1977. *Member:* Essex County, New Jersey State (Chairman, Family Law Subcommittee on Ethics, 1979-1980) and American Bar Associations. *PRACTICE AREAS:* Family Law.

**CYNTHIA S. MONACO,** born Los Angeles, California, November 9, 1950; admitted to bar, 1976, California, U.S. District Court, Central District of California and U.S. Court of Appeals, Ninth Circuit. *Education:* California State University at Northridge (B.A., magna cum laude, 1972); Southwestern University (J.D., 1975). Instructor, Family Law, Southern California Paralegal Institute, 1987-1988. Member, Editorial Committee and Index, Hon. Billy G. Mills Family Law Deskbook, State Bar of California, 1981. Member, Family Law Mediation Panel, 1979-1984, 1988-1990. *Member:* Beverly Hills (Member, Executive Committee, Family Law Section, 1978-1983) and Los Angeles County (Member, Family Law Section) Bar Associations; State Bar of California (Member, Family Law Section); Italian-American Lawyers Association (Member, Board of Governors, 1982-1989). (On Leave). *PRACTICE AREAS:* Family Law.

---

## RONALD M. KABRINS

SUITE 1250, 9401 WILSHIRE BOULEVARD
**BEVERLY HILLS, CALIFORNIA 90212**
Telephone: 310-550-8076
Fax: 310-859-3949

*Taxation, Estate Planning, Trust and Estate Administration.*

**RONALD M. KABRINS,** born Los Angeles, California, March 24, 1938; admitted to bar, 1964, California. *Education:* University of California at Los Angeles (B.S., with highest honors, 1960; LL.B., 1963). Order of the Coif; Phi Alpha Delta; Beta Gamma Sigma. Member, U.C.L.A. Law Review, 1961-1963. Certified Public Accountant, California, 1961. Author: "The Baptism of Section 2039—A New Look at Estate Taxation of Employee Death Benefits Under Nonqualified Plans," 10 U.C.L.A. Law Review 619, 1963; "Using Life Insurance to Fund Buy-Sell Agreements," Prentice-Hall *Tax Ideas*, 1985. Lecturer, Seventh Annual Conference on Estate Planning, New York University Institute on Federal Taxation, 1986. Member, Board of Directors, Jewish Federation Council, Greater Los Angeles, 1988—. Member, Board of Trustees, Jewish Community Foundation of JFC of GLA, 1994—. *Member:* Beverly Hills (Chairman, Probate and Trusts Committee, 1970-1971) and Los Angeles County Bar Associations; State Bar of California. (Certified Specialist, Taxation Law, The State Bar of California Board of Legal Specialization).

---

## STEPHEN R. KAHN

9150 WILSHIRE BOULEVARD, SUITE 209
**BEVERLY HILLS, CALIFORNIA 90212-3429**
Telephone: 310-246-9227
Fax: 310-246-9656

*Civil and Criminal Litigation, Family Law and Employment Law.*

**STEPHEN R. KAHN,** born New York, N.Y., November 14, 1947; admitted to bar, 1973, California and U.S. District Court, Central District of California; 1974, U.S. Court of Appeals for the Ninth Circuit. *Education:* University of California (B.A., 1969); Loyola Marymount University (J.D., 1972). *Member:* Los Angeles County (Member, Family Law Section) and American Bar Associations; State Bar of California; Los Angeles Trial Lawyers Association; California Trial Lawyers Association; Los Angeles Criminal Courts Bar Association.

---

## KAJAN MATHER AND BARISH

A PROFESSIONAL CORPORATION
SUITE 805, 9777 WILSHIRE BOULEVARD
**BEVERLY HILLS, CALIFORNIA 90212**
Telephone: 310-278-6080
Fax: 310-278-4805
Email: EHKKOTAX@PACBELL.NET

*Civil and Criminal Tax Controversy and Tax Litigation.*

**ELLIOTT H. KAJAN,** born Cleveland, Ohio, June 26, 1938; admitted to bar, 1965, Ohio; 1967, U.S. Tax Court; 1968, U.S. Supreme Court and U.S. Claims Court; 1969, District of Columbia; 1972, California and U.S. District Court, Central District of California; 1975, U.S. Court of Appeals, Ninth Circuit. *Education:* The Ohio State University (B.S. in Business Administration, 1960); Cleveland State University (J.D., magna cum laude, 1965). Beta Gamma Sigma; Beta Alpha Psi. Member, Board of Editors, Cleveland-Marshall Law Review, 1963-1965. Certified Public Accountant, Ohio, 1965. Author: "The Pour-Over Trust," 13 Cleveland-Marshall Law Review 544, 1964; "Some Problems in Liquidating Personal Holding Companies," 14 Cleveland-Marshall Law Review 391, 1965; "The Accumulated Earnings Tax—Still a Need for Concern?" The Los Angeles Bar Bulletin, Vol. 50, No. 8, pp. 320-331, June, 1975; The Practices and Procedures of Federal Tax Collection, "Federal Tax Practice and Procedure: Practicing Before The Internal Revenue Service," Practicing Law Institute, Tax Law and Practice, Course Handbook Series, No. 103, p. 35, 1976; "The New Single Level of Appeal—New Directions for IRS Audits, Disputes and Appeals," New York Law Journal, Course Handbook #417, 1979; "I.R.S. Compliance and Tax Shelter Audits," New Tactics for Real Estate Syndication Under the 1984 Tax Act, Law & Business, Inc., Harcourt Brace Jovanovich, Publishers, pp. 294-321, 1984. Co-author: "Responsible Officer (100 percent) Penalty Cases— Where Are They Headed?" Journal of the Beverly Hills Bar Association, Vol. 8, No. 5, pp. 52-27, November-December, 1974. Lecturer: California Continuing Education of the Bar, IRS Controversies, 1982, 1987; Advance Income Tax Seminar, California State University, Northridge; California Society of Certified Public Accountants; ALI-ABA Committee on Continuing Professional Education, Tax Shelters Under Attack, 1984; UCLA Extension, Business & Management, Tax Disputes Institute, 1984, 1985, 1987, 1995, 1996; University of Southern California Institute on Federal Taxation, 1986, 1990; Los Angeles Practitioners Forum, 1990—; California Certified Public Accountants Education Foundation, "Tax Controversies, How To Represent Your Client Before Tax Authorities", 1995, 1996, Georgetown University Law Center Continuing Legal Education Division, 1995. Attorney: U.S. Department of Justice, Tax Division, Refund Trial Sections, Washington, D.C., 1966-1971; Office of the United States Attorney, Tax Division, Los Angeles, California, 1971-1974. *Member:* Beverly Hills (Member, Tax Section), Los Angeles County (Member, Tax Section) and American (Member, Section on Taxation) Bar Associations; State Bar of California (Member, Tax Section); California Society of Certified Public Accountants (Member, Los Angeles Tax Committee); American Association of Attorney-Certified Public Accountants. *PRACTICE AREAS:* Tax Controversy Law; Tax Litigation.

**STEVEN R. MATHER,** born Sac City, Iowa, April 30, 1957; admitted to bar, 1982, Iowa; 1983, California and U.S. Tax Court; 1987, U.S. District Court, Central District of California; 1989, U.S. District Court, Northern District of California; 1994, U.S. Court of Appeals, Ninth Circuit. *Education:* University of Iowa (B.B.A., with highest distinction, 1978; J.D., with distinction, 1982). Phi Eta Sigma; Beta Gamma Sigma; Beta Alpha Psi. Certified Public Accountant, Iowa, 1979. Topics Editor, The Journal of Corporation Law, Vol. 7, 1982. Author: "Audit Procedures for Pass-Through Entities," 467-2d B.N.A. Tax Management Portfolio (1991); "Federal Tax Collection Procedure," 404-2d B.N.A. Tax Management Portfolio (1990); "Whipsaw Revisited," 43 The Tax Lawyer 343 (1990); "The Elusive Definition of a Tender Offer," 7 The Journal of Corporation Law 171, (1981); "TSN Liquidating Corporation, Inc. v. United States—Negotiation Focus in Substance-Over-Form," 7 The Journal of Corporation Law 171 (1981). Lecturer, Federal Tax Procedure, Golden Gate University, Masters in Taxation Program, 1989—. Attorney, Office of Chief Counsel, Internal Revenue Service, 1983-1987. *Member:* Beverly Hills (Chair, Tax Section, 1996-1997) and Los Angeles County (Member, Taxation Section; Co-Director, Tax Court Pro Se Program, 1989—; Chair, Tax Procedure and Litigation Committee, 1991-1992; Chair, Pro Bono Committee, 1993—) Bar Associations; State Bar of California (Member, Tax Section). *PRACTICE AREAS:* Tax Controversy; Tax Litigation.

*(This Listing Continued)*

**KENNETH M. BARISH,** born Brookline, Massachusetts, August 31, 1945; admitted to bar, 1973, California, U.S. District Court, Central District of California and U.S. Court of Appeals, Ninth Circuit; 1979, District of Columbia and U.S. Tax Court; U.S. Court of Appeals, Tenth Circuit; U.S. Supreme Court. *Education:* Southwestern University (J.D., 1973); New York University (LL.M. in Taxation, 1975). Adjunct Professor of Law, University of San Diego School of Law, Graduate Tax Program, 1982—. Trial Attorney, U.S. Department of Justice, Tax Division, Criminal Section, 1975-1979. Assistant U.S. Attorney, Central District of California, Tax Division, 1979-1981. Author: "Criminal Tax Investigations" portion of Tax Practice in California Book; "The Innocent Spouse Provision" American Bar Association Journal, Jan, 1995, quoted: "Leaving A Trial Of Paper" California Law Business (Oct. 25, 1993). Lecturer: State Bar of California, "Attorneys as IRS Targets," (1995, 1996); Orange County CPA Society, "Avoiding Civil and Criminal Penalties from Foreign Transactions," (1996); University of California at Los Angeles Tax Disputes Institute (1987- "Discovery in the United States Tax Court, 1989- "TEFRA Tax Audits", 1995—"Criminal Tax Administrative Investigations and Grand Jury Proceedings" ), California State University at Los Angeles, (1992—"An Overview of Tax Litigation Issues"), ESOP Association (1991- "Valuation Issues and ESOP Litigation") Orange County CPA Society, 1993- "Criminal and Civil Tax Issues in Use of Asset Protection Trusts and Foreign Bank Accounts"): International Association of Financial Planning, (1993- "Pitfalls Of Leaving Trusts and Family United Partnerships and Use of Foreign Trusts). *Member:* Los Angeles County (Member, Tax Section), Beverly Hills (Member, Tax Section) and American (Member Section of Taxation) Bar Associations; State Bar of California. **PRACTICE AREAS:** Tax Controversy; Tax Litigation.

## KALISCH, COTUGNO & RUST

Established in 1982

PENTHOUSE SUITE, 9606 SANTA MONICA BOULEVARD
**BEVERLY HILLS, CALIFORNIA 90210**
Telephone: 310-274-6683
Telecopier: 310-859-7743

*General Civil Trial and Appellate Practice in State and Federal Courts, including Business, Real Property, Banking, Insurance, Title Insurance, Entertainment, Commercial, Corporate, Transactional and Personal Injury Litigation.*

**MARK KALISCH,** born New York, N.Y., July 12, 1952; admitted to bar, 1977, England and Wales; 1978, California; 1980, U.S. District Court, Central District of California. *Education:* University of Keele, Staffordshire, England (B.A., Law and Psychology, with honors, 1975); Inns of Court School of Law, London, England (Barrister-at-Law, with honors, 1976). Settlement Officer/Judge Pro Tem, Beverly Hills Municipal Court, 1993—. *Member:* Beverly Hills, Los Angeles County and American Bar Associations; State Bar of California; Honourable Society of Gray's Inn, London, England; Association of Business Trial Lawyers (Member, Arbitration Committee, 1993—). **LANGUAGES:** German and French.

**LEE W. COTUGNO,** born Chicago, Illinois, August 8, 1951; admitted to bar, 1977, California; 1978, U.S. District Court, Central District of California; 1980, U.S. District Court, Southern and Northern Districts of California and U.S. Court of Appeals, Ninth Circuit; 1982, U.S. District Court, Eastern District of California. *Education:* University of Minnesota (B.A., summa cum laude, 1973); Boalt Hall School of Law, University of California (J.D., 1977). Member, Moot Court Board, 1975-1977. *Member:* Los Angeles County (Member, Sections on: Litigation; Business Law) and American (Member, Sections on: Litigation; Business Law; Insurance) Bar Associations; State Bar of California (Member, Sections on: Litigation; Business Law).

**RICHARD N. RUST,** born Spokane, Washington, May 12, 1952; admitted to bar, 1977, California; 1978, U.S. District Court, Central District of California; 1979, U.S. Court of Appeals, Ninth Circuit; 1982, U.S. District Court, Northern District of California; 1986, U.S. District Court, Southern District of California. *Education:* Stanford University (B.A., 1974); University of California at Los Angeles (J.D., 1977). Member, Moot Court Honors Program, 1975-1976. Recipient, Distinguished Advocate Award. Judge Pro Tem, Los Angeles Municipal Court, 1988—. *Member:* Los Angeles County and American (Member, Litigation Section) Bar Associations; State Bar of California; Association of Business Trial Lawyers.

*(This Listing Continued)*

*OF COUNSEL*

**JAMES S. ROUNTREE,** born Bakersfield, California, April 9, 1948; admitted to bar, 1982, California and U.S. District Court, Central District of California. *Education:* University of California at Santa Barbara (A.B., 1972); University of California at Los Angeles (J.D., 1982). Member, 1980-1981 and Managing Editor, 1981-1982, UCLA Law Review. *Member:* Los Angeles County Bar Association; State Bar of California.

**KATHLEEN G. SMITH,** born Gainesville, Florida, August 4, 1947; admitted to bar, 1981, California and U.S. District Court, Northern and Central Districts of California. *Education:* Hollins College (B.A., with honors, 1968); University of Southern California (J.D., 1981). Order of the Coif; Phi Alpha Delta. Quarter-finalist, 1979-1980 and Topic Editor, 1980-1981, Hale Moot Court Competition *Member:* Beverly Hills, Los Angeles County and American Bar Associations; The State Bar of California. **PRACTICE AREAS:** Litigation.

## GAIL D. KASS

228 SOUTH BEVERLY DRIVE
**BEVERLY HILLS, CALIFORNIA 90212-3880**
Telephone: 310-273-0393
Fax: 310-273-2663

*Estate Planning, Probate, Trust Law and Taxation Law.*

**GAIL D. KASS,** born San Francisco, California, July 4, 1950; admitted to bar, 1975, California; 1976, U.S. District Court, Central District of California. *Education:* University of California at Berkeley (A.B., magna cum laude, 1972); University of California at Los Angeles (J.D., 1975). Phi Beta Kappa. Moot Court Honors Program. Lecturer, UCLA School of Law, 1978-1979. Adjunct Associate Professor, Southwestern University School of Law, 1980. Lecturer, Mathematics of Estate Planning, Probate Administration, Recent Developments in Estate Planning and Administration, California Continuing Education of the Bar, 1983, 1985, 1986, 1992. *Member:* Beverly Hills and Los Angeles County Bar Associations; State Bar of California; Lawyer-Pilots Bar Association.

## KAUFMAN & YOUNG

A PROFESSIONAL CORPORATION

Established in 1989

121 SOUTH BEVERLY DRIVE
**BEVERLY HILLS, CALIFORNIA 90212-3002**
Telephone: 310-275-5132
Los Angeles: 213-272-7807
Fax: 310-275-2919

*Family Law and Trial Practice in all State and Federal Courts.*

**ROBERT S. KAUFMAN,** born New York, N.Y., July 15, 1937; admitted to bar, 1964, California; 1975, U.S. Court of Appeals, Ninth Circuit. *Education:* University of California at Los Angeles (B.A., 1959); Southwestern University (J.D., 1963). Adjunct Professor of Law, Pepperdine University School of Law, 1988-1996, Advanced Family Law. Lecturer: Family Law Program, Continuing Education of the Bar, University of California, 1980; University of California at Los Angeles Extension Seminar, Family Law Concerns of Individuals in the Entertainment Industry, 1983. Guest Speaker and Lecturer Alaska State Bar Association: "Premarital Agreements, Preparation and Enforceability from the Office to the Court Room," June, 1986. Referee, State Bar Courts, 1969-1986. Member, Family Law Mediation Program, Los Angeles Superior Court, 1981—. Panelist: Negotiating to Settlement in Divorce Sponsored by Harcourt Brace, Jovanovich, Publishers, 1985; An Evening with the Masters, Beverly Hills Bar Association, 1996. Speaker: California Society of CPA'S Litigation Consulting Conference Subject: Executive and Celebrity Goodwill, 1990; California Society of CPA's, Celebrity Goodwill, 1993-1996; City Bar Association, "Family Law Aspects of The Music Business, 1994"; Entertainment Law Conference; California CPA Education Foundation, 1996 Entertainment Industry Conference. Co-Author: "Valuing a Law Practice in Divorce," Los Angeles Lawyer, March, 1995; Co-Authored with Marcy Kenerson "New Mate Income," State Bar Family News, Volume 17, No 4 (Winter), 1995; *Member:* Beverly Hills, Los Angeles County (Member: Executive Committee, Family Law Section, 1992-1993; Judicial Liaison Committee, 1992-1993) and American (Member, Professionalism Committee of the Family Law Section, 1993; Family Law and Litigation Sections, 1965—) Bar Asso-

*(This Listing Continued)*

**KAUFMAN & YOUNG,** A PROFESSIONAL CORPORATION,
Beverly Hills—Continued

ciations; State Bar of California. The Association of Trial Lawyers of America. *PRACTICE AREAS:* Family Law; Trial Practice.

**KENNETH M. YOUNG,** born Los Angeles, California, August 1, 1938; admitted to bar, 1965, California and U.S. Tax Court. *Education:* University of California at Los Angeles (B.S., 1960; LL.B., 1964). Phi Delta Phi. Certified Public Accountant, California, 1965, (inactive). Lecturer: Recent Legislation in Family Law, Los Angeles County Family Law Symposium, 1985; Annual Family Law Workshop, The Rutter Group, 1985. Mediator: Family Law Mediation Program, 1980-1996; Family Law Program, Continuing Education of the Bar, University of California, Recent Developments in Family Law, 1983 and 1984. Panelist: Beverly Hills Family Law Symposium on Taxation, 1981. *Member:* Beverly Hills and Los Angeles County Bar Associations; The State Bar of California. *PRACTICE AREAS:* Family Law; Trial Practice.

**MARCY L. KENERSON,** born Greenbrae, California, August 28, 1964; admitted to bar, 1993, California. *Education:* University of California, Los Angeles (B.A., 1986); Loyola University (J.D., 1991). Co-Author with Robert S. Kaufman, "New Mate Income" State Bar Family News, Volume 17, No. 4, Winter, 1995. *Member:* Beverly Hills and Los Angeles County Bar Associations; State Bar of California. *PRACTICE AREAS:* Family Law; Trial Practice. *Email:* MLKKAUF@aol.com

**SCOTT K. ROBINSON,** born Santa Monica, California, September 16, 1962; admitted to bar, 1988, California. *Education:* University of California at Berkeley (B.A., 1984); Arizona State University College of Law (J.D., 1987). Externship: Judge Mildred Lillie, California Court of Appeal, District 2, Division 7, 1985; Honorable Stephen Reinhardt, Ninth Circuit Court of Appeals, 1986. *PRACTICE AREAS:* Family Law; Civil Litigation; Business; Corporate Law; Secured Transactions. *Email:* SKRKAUF@aol.com

*OF COUNSEL*

**LANCE S. SPIEGEL,** born Los Angeles, California, October 5, 1945; admitted to bar, 1972, California; 1975, U.S. Court of Appeals, Ninth Circuit. *Education:* University of Southern California (B.A., 1968; J.D., 1971). Member, University of Southern California Law Review, 1970-1971. Author: "First Amendment Rights of Television Viewers," University of Southern California Law Review, 1971; "Status of Expert Witnesses," Continuing Education of the Bar, 1980; "Attorneys Fees in Marital Dissolution Proceedings," California Marital Dissolution Practice, Continuing Education of the Bar, 1983; "Duration of Spousal Support: Bridge Burning or Enough is Enough," Vol. 24 Beverly Hills Bar Journal, Sept., 1990. Lecturer: Panel Attorney Fees, 1976, 1979 and 1981; Civil Procedure, 1980-1986, Negotiating and Drafting Marital Agreements, 1985, Continuing Education of the Bar; Family Law Symposium, Los Angeles County Bar Association, 1991. Advanced Professional Program, University of Southern California Law School, 1982. Adjunct Professor, Community Property, Southwestern University School of Law, 1982. *Member:* Beverley Hills, Los Angeles County and American Bar Associations; The State Bar of California. (Also Of Counsel to Harry M. Fain). *PRACTICE AREAS:* Family Law; Trial Practice.

REFERENCE: City National Bank (Beverly Hills Main Office).

## MILES L. KAVALLER

A PROFESSIONAL LAW CORPORATION

SUITE 315, 315 SOUTH BEVERLY DRIVE
**BEVERLY HILLS, CALIFORNIA 90212**
Telephone: 310-277-2323
Fax: 310-556-2308
Email: MKavaller@themall.net
URL: http://www.LA-Freight.com/Kavaller.htm

*General Civil and Trial Practice in all Courts. Transporation Law.*

**MILES L. KAVALLER,** born New York, N.Y., February 17, 1947; admitted to bar, 1972, New York; 1977, California, U.S. District Court, Northern, Eastern, Southern and Central Districts of California, U.S. District Court, District of Arizona, U.S. Courts of Appeals, Ninth, Tenth and District of Columbia Circuits and U.S. Tax Court; 1988, U.S. Supreme Court. *Education:* State University of New York at Buffalo (B.A., with distinction, 1968); State University of New York at Buffalo (J.D., 1972). Phi Alpha Delta (President, 1970-1971). Member, Buffalo Law Review, 1972.

*(This Listing Continued)*

Trial Attorney, Washington, D.C., 1972 and Chicago, 1972-1975, Interstate Commerce Commission. Assistant Regional Counsel, Los Angeles, California, 1975-1977. *Member:* Los Angeles County and American (Member, Litigation Section) Bar Associations; State Bar of California; Transportation Lawyers Association; Association For Transportation Law, Logistics and Policy.

REFERENCE: City National Bank (6th & Olive Branch).

## LAW OFFICE OF
## DENA A. KLEEMAN

499 NORTH CANON DRIVE, SUITE 200
**BEVERLY HILLS, CALIFORNIA 90210-4248**
Telephone: 310-247-0727
Fax: 310-273-3030

*Family Law.*

**DENA A. KLEEMAN,** born New Haven, Connecticut, October 25, 1954; admitted to bar, 1983, California and U.S. District Court, Northern District of California. *Education:* Wesleyan University (B.A., summa cum laude, with honors in Anthropology, 1977; M.A., 1977); Stanford Law School (J.D., 1983). Phi Beta Kappa. *Member:* Century City (Member, Family Law Section) and Los Angeles County (Member: Family Law Section; Executive Committee, Management Section) Bar Associations. (Certified Specialist, Family Law, The State Bar of California Board of Legal Specialization). *PRACTICE AREAS:* Family Law; Estate Planning; Guardianship.

*OF COUNSEL*

**RUTH S. KREMEN,** born Long Beach, California, September 16, 1954; admitted to bar, 1982, California; 1983, Massachusetts and U.S. District Court, District of Massachusetts; 1985, U.S. District Court, Northern District of California. *Education:* Amherst College (B.A., 1976); Occidental College (M.A., 1980); Georgetown University Law Center (J.D., 1982). Law Clerk to Judge William B. Bryant, U.S. District Court for the District of Columbia, 1982-1983. *Member:* Los Angeles County Bar Association (Member, Family Law Section). *PRACTICE AREAS:* Civil Litigation; Business Law; Family Law.

## GARY P. KOHN

9601 WILSHIRE BOULEVARD, SUITE 828
**BEVERLY HILLS, CALIFORNIA 90210**
Telephone: 310-205-0870
Fax: 310-205-0187
Email: GPKOHN@aol.com

*Entertainment, Sports, Music and Corporate Law.*

**GARY P. KOHN,** born Champaign, Illinois, February 12, 1958; admitted to bar, 1984, New York; 1985, California; 1987, U.S. District Court, Southern District of New York; 1989, U.S. District Court, Central District of California. *Education:* State University of New York at Binghamton (B.A., with highest honors, 1980); Emory University (J.D., with distinction, 1983). Member: Order of the Coif; Phi Beta Kappa; National Trial Advocacy Team. Editor-in-Chief, Emory Law Journal, 1982-1983. Author: "Sports Agents Representing Professional Athletes-Being Certified Means Never Having to Say You're Qualified," in 6 The Entertainment and Sports Lawyer Number 3, Winter 1988. "A Fresh Look: Lowering the Mortality Rate of Covenants Not to Compete Ancillary to Employment Contracts and to Sale of Business Contracts in Georgia," 31 Emory Law Journal 635, 1982. Assistant Editor, American Bar Association Entertainment and Sports Lawyer, 1989-1992. *Member:* Beverly Hills, Los Angeles County (Co-Chair, Artists and the Law Committee, 1988-1989), New York State and American Bar Associations; State Bar of California; National Academy of Recording Arts & Sciences.

## KOLODNY & ANTEAU

Established in 1995
9100 WILSHIRE BOULEVARD
SUITE 900
**BEVERLY HILLS, CALIFORNIA 90212**
Telephone: 310-271-5533
FAX: 310-271-3918

*Practice Limited to Family Law, Domestic Torts, Juvenile Dependency; Paternity; Palimony.*

### MEMBERS OF FIRM

**STEPHEN A. KOLODNY,** born Monticello, New York, June 25, 1940; admitted to bar, 1966, California. *Education:* Boston University (B.A., 1963; LL.B., 1965). Author: *Divorce Practice Handbook;* 1994; "Family Law Contempt," Los Angeles Bar Association, Los Angeles Superior Court Symposium Book, Annual Publication; LL.B. Book; Creator: West's California Family Law Forums, Annually. Contributing Author: *Judge Mills Family Law Benchbook,* Los Angeles County Bar Symposium Book, 1981. Co-Author: Family Law Judicial Council Forms, 1992; Author: Family Law Practice Forms; "Tort Recovery Against Aiders and Abettors in Child Stealing Cases," Family Advocate, ABA Family Law Section, 1981; "Evidence And Direct Examination," Family Advocate, ABA Family Law Section, 1996. Panelist and Presenter: American Academy of Matrimonial Lawyer - Advanced Motion Practice, Southern California Regional Institute, Los Angeles Superior Court Family Law Supervision, 1993, 1994 and 1997; Panelist: Complex Motions in Family Law, Beverly Hills Bar Association Symposium, 1996; Panelist: Southwestern Regional Conference, Executive and Celebrity Goodwill, 1992; Presentation: Bifurcation of Judgements and Use of Computers in a Family Law Office, Certified Family Law Specialists, San Diego County; Panel Presenter: How to Try Family Law Cases, California Judges College, 1981; Presenter: Family Law and Trial Tactics, Procedures, Contempt, Evidence and Family Law Torts; Panelist: How to Try a Complex Family Law Case, Beverly Hills Bar Association Special Symposium, 1981—; Lecturer: Marital Torts, Bifurcation of Marital Status, 1989, 1990-1991; Family Symposium, Los Angeles County Bar Association, 1978—; American Academy of Matrimonial Lawyers, 1981; International Academy of Matrimonial Lawyers, 1988—; California Continuing Education of the Bar, 1982-1985; California Society of Certified Public Accountants, 1985-1988. State Bar of California, Disciplinary Hearing Officer; Los Angeles Superior Court, Family Law Judge Pro Tem Program. *Member:* Beverly Hills, Los Angeles County (Chair: Executive Committee, 1987-1988) and American Bar Associations; State Bar of California; International Bar Association (Member, Board of Managers, 1989-1993; USA Chapter, Board of Governors; President-Elect, 1994-1995; President, 1996-1997); American Academy of Matrimonial Lawyers (Vice President, 1987-1993 and 1996-1997; Southern California Chapter, 1993-1994; National: Board of Governors, 1990-1995); American Association of Family Conciliation Courts; Women's Lawyers Association (Los Angeles, 1986—). (Certified Specialist, Family Law, The State Bar of California Board of Legal Specialization).

**RONALD W. ANTEAU,** born Detroit, Michigan, July 26, 1940; admitted to bar, 1966, California; 1969, U.S. Supreme Court. *Education:* University of California at Los Angeles (B.A., 1962; J.D., 1965). Author: Death and Dissolution," Los Angeles County Bar Association, Family Law Symposium Reference Book, May, 1992, updated and republished May, 1993, May, 1994 and May 1996; Editor, State Bar of California Family Law News, 1994-1995; Desk Editor, State Bar of California Family Law News, 1995-1997; "A New Source of Available Income," Los Angeles County Bar Association, Family Law Symposium Reference Book-Practice Pointer, May, 1994; "Moore/Marsden Enters the 21st Century," Mandatory Continuing Legal Education Test, State Bar of California, May, 1994; "New Wrinkles in Our Suit - Cutting Edge," The State Bar of California, Section Education Institute, Syllabus, November, 1992; "New Wrinkles in Our Suit - Interspousal Liability," The State Bar of California, Annual Meeting Syllabus, October, 1992; "Can You Take it With You? - Severance of Joint Tenancy," Los Angeles County Bar Association, Family Law Symposium Reference Book - Practice Pointer, May, 1992; Coordinator and co-author, *Family Law Litigation Guide,* Matthew Bender, 1991; "Moore/Marsden/-Neal - Increasing Your Separate Property Position," Los Angeles County Bar, *Family Law News and Review,* March, 1986; Article on Expert Witnesses for Beverly Hills Bar Association, Family Law Symposium, November, 1987; "Custody and Visitation Handbook - Family Law Colloquium," 1982-1983; "The Five P's of Pension Practice," Orange County Trial Lawyers Association, May, 1982; "Mediation Policy and Procedure in Southern California Counties," Los Angeles County Bar Association, Family Law Section, December, 1982; Panelist: "The Ethics of Presenting Evidence in Family Law Cases: What are the Bounds of Advocacy?" Los Angeles County Bar Association/University of Southern California, 4th Annual Family Law Institute, Los Angeles, California, December 7, 1996; Direct and Cross Examination of an Expert Witness," American Academy of Matrimonial Lawyers, The American Academy Trial Advocacy Institute, Los Angeles, California, January, 13-15, 1996; Moderator, Children of Divorce Symposium, Center for the Family in Transition, Santa Monica, California, April 1, 1995; "Everything You've Always Wanted to Know About Psychiatric Evaluations' - An Insider's View," American Academy of Matrimonial Lawyers, Southern California Chapter Meeting, Anaheim, California, December 10, 1994; Moderator and Panelist: "Death and Dissolution," Los Angeles County Bar Association, 26th Annual Family Law Symposium, May, 1994; "How to Present a Complex Case Involving Tracing and Van Camp/Pereira," American Academy of Matrimonial Lawyers, Institute of Trial Advocacy, January, 1994; "New Wrinkles in Our Suit - Domestic Torts," Certified Family Law Specialists Section of the Northern San Diego County Bar Association, September 1993; "How to Prosecute and Defend a Contempt," Association of Certified Family Law Specialists and Century City Bar Association Family Law Section, June, 1993; "Hot Tips," The State Bar of California, Family Law Section, Family Law Institute, May, 1993; "Domestic Torts," Beverly Hills Bar Association, Family Law Section Dinner Meeting, March, 1993; "New Wrinkles in Our Suit - Cutting Edge," The State Bar of California, Section Education Institute, November, 1992; "New Wrinkles in the Suit - Interspousal Liability," The State Bar of California 1992 Annual Meeting, October, 1992; "Direct and Cross Examination of Expert Witnesses," Los Angeles County Bar Association, Family Law Symposium, May, 1992; "Real Estate Appraisal Problems," Beverly Hills Bar Association, Family Law Section Dinner Meeting, January, 1992; "Executive and Celebrity Goodwill," American Academy of Matrimonial Lawyers, Southwest Regional Conference, January, 1992; "Recent Developments in Family Law," Beverly Hills Bar Association, Family Law Symposium, October, 1990; "New Spouse/Cohabitor Income in Modification of Support Matters," Beverly Hills Bar Association, Family Law Symposium 1989; "Malpractice, Avoidance or Cover Your Assets," Coordinator of Panel, Beverly Hills Bar Association, Family Law Section, Family Law Symposium, November, 1988; "Law and Motion Practice Panel," Beverly Hills Bar Association, May, 1988; "Post Trial to Entry of Judgment," Beverly Hills Bar Association, Family Law Section, Family Law Symposium, November, 1987; "The Mental Health Practitioner in the Courtroom," Children's Institute National, Three-Day Conference, May, 1987; "Law and Motion Practice: Discovery Under the New Act," Los Angeles County Bar Association, Family Law Symposium, April, 1987; "Use of Accountants in Family Law Proceedings," The State Bar of California, Family Law Section, January, 1987; "Trial Presentation-OSC for Support and OSC re Contempt," Los Angeles County Bar, Family Law Symposium, April 1986; "Attorneys Fees and Costs," Beverly Hills Bar Association, Family Law Symposium, November, 1985; "Testimony of Expert Witnesses," Beverly Hills Bar Association, Family Law Symposium, November, 1985; Participant, Los Angeles Superior Court, California Chapter of Association of Family Conciliation Courts, and Los Angeles County Bar Association, Family Law Section, Eighth Family Law Colloquium, October, 1984; "Trial Techniques for Short Cause Hearings," Seminar Participant, Los Angeles County and Beverly Hills Bar Association, 1984; "Marital Settlement Agreements," The Rutter Group, Family Law Workshop, 1984; "Preparing For and Taking Depositions," Member of Faculty and Planning Committee and Panelist, Beverly Hills Bar Association 10th Annual Family Law Symposium, 1984; "Discovery and Expert Witnesses," Beverly Hills Bar Association, Family Law Symposium, 1984; "UCCJA," Los Angeles County Bar Association, Family Law Colloquium, 1982. Speaker: "Bifurcation and Family Law Code §1100 (formerly CC §5125)," Beverly Hills Bar Association, Family Law Section, April, 1994; "Expand Your Mind Through Microbiology - The Impact of Genetic Engineering on Family Law," Delegate and Speaker, First World Congress on Family Law and Children's Rights, Sydney, Australia, July, 1993; "Family yaw Practice: Initial Interview to Hearing in Thirty Days," Los Angeles Paralegal Association, Thirteenth Annual October Seminar, 1989; "Initiating Family Law Action," Los Angeles Trial Lawyers Association; Invited Guest Lecturer, University of Southern California Law Center, Advanced Professional Program, 1986; "By the Master: Deferred Compensation - Trial Tips and Practical Consideration," Orange County Trial Lawyers Association, 8th Annual Family Law Seminar, 1982. Member, Planning Committee, California Certified Public Accountants Education Foundation, 1996 Family Law Conference, Los Angeles, California, December 11, 1996/San Francisco, California, December 12, 1996. Fellow of the American Academy of Matrimonial Lawyers (National Membership and Public Relations Committees; Chair, National Chapter Advertising Committee, 1995-1996; Southern California Chapter President-Elect,

*(This Listing Continued)*

**KOLODNY & ANTEAU, Beverly Hills—Continued**

1995-1996; Southern California Chapter Past Vice President-Membership, Past Chair-Programs, Past Chair-Board of Examiners, Southern California Chapter Membership and Marketing/Public Relations Committee Southern California Chapter Board of Examiners). Fellow of the International Academy of Matrimonial Lawyers. Diplomate, American College of Family Trial Lawyers. Family Law Pro Tem Program, Department 2, 1980, 1981. Los Angeles County Superior Court, Central District, Department 2, 1980, 1981. Family Law Mediation Panel, October (inception) 1981—. *Member:* Beverly Hills (Member: Family Law Executive Committee, Family Law Section and Member and Participant in various standing committees, including but not limited to, Symposium Program, Resolutions, Law Revision Commission and Surrogate Parenting, 1983—), Los Angeles County (Member, Family Law Section, Family Law Executive Committee and Member and Participant, standing committees, including but not limited to, Public Relations and Mediation, 1984—), American and International Bar Associations; State Bar of California (Member, Disciplinary Proceedings/Peer Review Committee for Family Matters, 1993 (inception), Family Law Section; Family Law Executive Committee); Association of Certified Family Law Specialists. [USNR, 1966-1972, Lt. Commander, (Ret.) JAG.]. (Certified Specialist, Family Law, The State Bar of California Board of Legal Specialization). **PRACTICE AREAS:** Family Law. **Email:** ANTEAU@KOLODNY-ANTEAU.COM

**HARLEE M. GASMER,** born Los Angeles, California, September 18, 1960; admitted to bar, 1985, California and U.S. District Court, Central and Northern Districts of California; 1987, U.S. Court of Appeals, Ninth Circuit. *Education:* University of California at Los Angeles (B.A., cum laude, 1982); Loyola Marymount University (J.D., 1985). Member, Scott Moot Court National Team. *Member:* Beverly Hills and Los Angeles County Bar Associations; The State Bar of California. **PRACTICE AREAS:** Family Law.

**WILLIAM P. GLAVIN IV,** born Lafayette, Indiana, June 26, 1965; admitted to bar, 1988, California. *Education:* North Central College (B.A., cum laude, 1985); Pepperdine University (J.D., 1988). Publicity Director, Pepperdine University Entertainment Law Society, 1985-1987. Mediator, Los Angeles County Bar Association, Family Law Section, 1992-1995. Featured Speaker: British Broadcasting Company's National Radio Program, "Celebrity Rock Wives," September 1996. *Member:* Beverly Hills (Member, Family Law Section), Los Angeles (Member, Family Law Section; Children's Rights Committee; Domestic Violence Project Committee) and American Bar Associations; State Bar of California. **REPORTED CASES:** McGinley v. Herman, 1996 Daily Journal, D.A.R. 13509. **PRACTICE AREAS:** Family Law; Juvenile Dependency; Trial Practice.

**WILLIAM J. GLUCKSMAN,** born Philadelphia, Pennsylvania, March 19, 1951; admitted to bar, 1976, California; 1977, U.S. District Court, Central District of California and U.S. Court of Appeals, Ninth Circuit. *Education:* University of California at Los Angeles (B.A., 1973); Southwestern University (J.D., 1976). Director, Southwestern University School of Law Clinical Program, 1975-1976. Author: "Equal Protection For Unmarried Cohabitors: An Insider's Look at Marvin vs. Marvin," Pepperdine Law Review, Vol. 5, 1978; "Palimony: Divorce Sans Marriage," Trial Magazine, June, 1980. Judge Pro Tem, Los Angeles Superior Court, 1990-1992. Member, Family Law Mediation Panel, Los Angeles Superior Court. Pro Haec Vice Admission in Nevada, Colorado, Michigan, Ohio, New Jersey, Pennsylvania and Florida on selected complex Family Law Litigation. *Member:* Los Angeles County and American Bar Associations; State Bar of California. (Certified Specialist, Family Law The State Bar of California Board of Legal Specialization). **REPORTED CASES:** Kroopf vs. Guffey, 183 L.A. 3d. 1351, 228 C.R. 807, 1986.

**LAUREN S. PETKIN,** born Santa Monica, California, March 1, 1958; admitted to bar, 1987, California. *Education:* University of California at Berkeley (B.S., 1980); University of Southern California (J.D., 1985). Author: "The Dilemma of Practicing Safe Waivers of Qualified Retirement Benefits in a Prenuptial Agreement," Journal of Asset Protection, 1996. *Member:* Beverly Hills and Los Angeles County (Member, Family Law Section) Bar Associations; State Bar of California; Women Lawyers Association of Los Angeles; Hamet Buhai Center (Pro Bono Committee; Barristers Annual Rights Committee). **PRACTICE AREAS:** Family Law.

**PETER T. HERMES,** born Pasadena, California, June 14, 1948; admitted to bar, 1974, California and U.S. District Court, Central District of California. *Education:* Loyola Marymount University (B.S., 1970); Southwestern University (J.D., 1973). Mediator, Los Angeles Superior Court

*(This Listing Continued)*

Family Law Mediator Panel, 1980—. *Member:* Los Angeles County Bar Association; State Bar of California. **PRACTICE AREAS:** Family Law.

**TERRY LEVICH ROSS,** born Cleveland, Ohio, February 16, 1964; admitted to bar, 1990, California. *Education:* University of California at Berkeley (B.A., 1986); University of California, Hastings College of the Law (J.D., 1990). Phillip C. Jessup International Law Moot Court Competition, 1989. Recipient, American Jurisprudence Award, 1989. Author: "Over the River and Through the Court to Grandmother's House They Go," Family Law News 1996. Volunteer: Harriet Buhai Center for Family Law and Public Counsel (Children's Rights Committee). *Member:* Beverly Hills and Los Angeles County (Member, Section of Family Law) Bar Associations; State Bar of California; Public Counsel Children's Rights Committee. **PRACTICE AREAS:** Family Law Practice.

**ERIN L. GREY,** born Los Angeles, California, January 25, 1970; admitted to bar, 1994, California. *Education:* University of West Los Angeles (B.A., 1991); Southwestern University School of Law (J.D., 1994). **PRACTICE AREAS:** Family Law.

REFERENCE: Wells Fargo Bank, Los Angeles, CA.

---

## STEVEN M. KRAMER & ASSOCIATES
9606 SANTA MONICA BOULEVARD
SECOND FLOOR
**BEVERLY HILLS, CALIFORNIA 90210**
Telephone: 310-519-5708
Telecopier: 310-550-8982

*New York, New York Office:* City Spire, 150 West 56th Street, 65th Floor, 10019. Telephone: 212-586-0707. Telecopier: 212-586-0104.
*Wayne, New Jersey Office:* Gateway 80 Office Park, 30 Galesi Drive, Suite 201, 07470. Telephone: 201-785-0143. Telecopier: 201-785-3380.

*Complex Business Litigation, Antitrust, Securities, Entertainment.*

(For Complete Biographical Data on all Personnel, see Professional Biographies at New York, New York)

---

## JAMES M. KRZYMINSKI
345 NORTH MAPLE DRIVE, SUITE 294
**BEVERLY HILLS, CALIFORNIA 90210**
Telephone: 310-777-7481
FAX: 310-777-8754
Email: jimkrzymin@aol.com

*Business, Corporation, Real Estate, Federal and State Taxation, Estate Planning, Trust and Probate Law.*

**JAMES M. KRZYMINSKI,** born Fort Wayne, Indiana, May 12, 1954; admitted to bar, 1979, California. *Education:* Indiana University (B.S., summa cum laude, 1976); Stanford University (J.D., 1979). Beta Gamma Sigma; Beta Alpha Psi. *Member:* Los Angeles County Bar Association; The State Bar of California.

REFERENCE: City National Bank, Olympic Plaza Office.

---

## JAMES H. LEHR
9595 WILSHIRE BOULEVARD, SUITE 305
**BEVERLY HILLS, CALIFORNIA 90212**
Telephone: 310-553-8080
Fax: 310-550-7244

*Business Litigation, Banking Law.*

**JAMES H. LEHR,** born Omaha, Nebraska, August 17, 1953; admitted to bar, 1979, California; 1980, U.S. District Court, Central District of California and U.S. Court of Appeals, Ninth Circuit; 1981, U.S. District Court, Southern District of California. *Education:* Princeton University (A.B., 1975); Southwestern University (J.D., 1979). Member, Board of Governors, Moot Court Honors Program. Recipient, Schweizer Memorial Award for Best Brief. Associate Editor, Southwestern University Law Review, 1978-1979. *Member:* Los Angeles County and American Bar Associations; State Bar of California. (Also Of Counsel to Funsten & Franzen). **REPORTED CASES:** Shell Oil Co. v. Nelson Oil Co., Inc., 627 F.2d 228 (T.E.C.A. 1980), cert. den. 449 U.S. 1022; Mobile Oil Corporation v. Rissi (1982) 138 Cal.App. 3d 256, 187 Cal. Rptr. 845; Schroeder v. TWA, Inc., 702 F.2d 189 (9th Cir. 1983); Davis v. Gilf Oil Corp., 572 F. Supp. 1393 (C.D. Cal. 1983);

*(This Listing Continued)*

Prestin v. Mobile Oil Corp., 741 F.2d 268 (9th Cir. 1984); A.L.L. Roofing & Bldg. Materials Corp. v. Community Bank (1986) 182 Cal. App. 3d 356, 227 Cal. Rptr. 308. *PRACTICE AREAS:* Litigation; Banking Law; Unfair Competition Law.

## LEONARD, DICKER & SCHREIBER

A Partnership including Professional Corporations

Established in 1987

SUITE 400
9430 OLYMPIC BOULEVARD
**BEVERLY HILLS, CALIFORNIA 90212**
Telephone: 310-551-1987
FAX: 310-277-8050

*Business and Real Estate Litigation, Entertainment and Copyright Litigation, Estate and Trust Litigation Bankruptcy Litigation and Appellate Practice in State and Federal Courts, Business, Real Estate, Entertainment, Commercial and Corporate Law, Estate Planning, Family Law.*

**JAMES P. SCHREIBER, (A PROFESSIONAL CORPORATION),** born Cleveland, Ohio, January 7, 1942; admitted to bar, 1966, California. *Education:* University of California at Los Angeles (B.A., cum laude, 1963); Boalt Hall, University of California (LL.B., 1966). *Member:* Beverly Hills and Los Angeles County Bar Associations. *PRACTICE AREAS:* Entertainment and Copyright Law; Business Transactions and Entertainment, Copyright and Business Litigation; Family Law.

**LEE T. DICKER,** born New York, N.Y., June 28, 1945; admitted to bar, 1971, California, District of Columbia and U.S. Court of Appeals, District of Columbia; 1972, U.S. District Court, Central District of California; 1974, U.S. District Court, Southern District of California and U.S. Court of Appeals, Ninth Circuit; 1978, U.S. Supreme Court; 1981, U.S. District Court, Northern and Eastern District of California. *Education:* University of Iowa (B.A., with honors, 1967); Boalt Hall School of Law, University of California (J.D., 1970). Phi Eta Sigma. Recipient, American Jurisprudence Award in Trial Practice. Judge Pro Tem, Los Angeles Municipal Court, 1977-1996. Family Law Mediator, Los Angeles Superior Court, 1981-1991. Member, Brentwood School Trustees, 1984-1986. *Member:* Los Angeles County (Arbitrator, 1988-1996), Beverly Hills and American Bar Associations; The District of Columbia Bar. *PRACTICE AREAS:* Business and Real Estate Transactions and Litigation; Probate Litigation.

**RICHARD C. LEONARD, (A PROFESSIONAL CORPORATION),** born New York, N.Y., March 21, 1946; admitted to bar, 1971, California and U.S. District Court, Central District of California; 1974, U.S. District Court, Southern District of California and U.S. Court of Appeals, Ninth and Tenth Circuits; 1975, U.S. Supreme Court; 1976, U.S. Court of Appeals, District of Columbia. *Education:* University of California at Los Angeles (B.A., 1967); Boalt Hall School of Law, University of California (J.D., 1970). Major Walter J. Dinkelspeil Scholarship. Judge Pro Tem, Los Angeles Municipal Court, 1977-1979. Arbitrator, Los Angeles Superior Court Business Arbitration Division, 1977-1996. Member, Panel of Arbitrators, American Arbitration Association, 1975-1996. *Member:* Los Angeles County Bar Association; Association of Business Trial Lawyers. *PRACTICE AREAS:* Business, Real Estate, Entertainment and Copyright Litigation.

**DAVID S. GUBMAN, (A PROFESSIONAL CORPORATION),** born Los Angeles, California, June 6, 1950; admitted to bar, 1975, California. *Education:* California Institute of Technology and Stanford University (B.A., with distinction, 1972); Harvard University (J.D., cum laude, 1975). *Member:* Los Angeles County and Beverly Hills Bar Associations; The State Bar of California. *PRACTICE AREAS:* Commercial, Real Estate and Bankruptcy Court Litigation.

### ASSOCIATES

**MICHAEL R. ROGERS,** born Los Angeles, California, June 16, 1943; admitted to bar, 1969, California; U.S. District Court, Southern District of California; 1970, U.S. District Court, Central District of California and U.S. Court of Appeals, Ninth Circuit; 1975, U.S. Supreme Court. *Education:* Loyola University of Los Angeles (B.A., 1965); University of San Diego (J.D., 1968). Phi Delta Phi; Pi Gamma Mu. Judge Pro Tem, Los Angeles Municipal Court, 1989-1996. Author, Note: "Securities Regulation," 212 and "Process," 347, 4 San Diego Law Review, 1967. Notes and Comments Editor, San Diego Law Review, 1967-1968. *Member:* American Bar Association. *PRACTICE AREAS:* Business and Real Estate Transactions and Litigation.

*(This Listing Continued)*

**DAVID N. SCHULTZ,** born Jackson Heights, New York, November 10, 1958; admitted to bar, 1986, California and U.S. District Court, Central District of California. *Education:* Princeton University (A.B., summa cum laude, 1980); Harvard Law School (J.D. magna cum laude, 1984). Executive Editor, Harvard Civil Rights-Civil Liberties Law Review, 1983-1984. Law Clerk to Hon. Robert E. Keeton, U.S. District Court, District of Massachusetts, 1984-1985. *Member:* Los Angeles County and American Bar Associations. *LANGUAGES:* Hebrew. *PRACTICE AREAS:* Business and Entertainment Litigation.

**STEVEN A. SCHUMAN,** born Los Angeles, California, July 18, 1962; admitted to bar, 1989, California. *Education:* St. Andrews University; University of California at Berkeley (B.A., 1984); University of California at Los Angeles (J.D., 1989). Order of the Coif. *Member:* Los Angeles County Bar Association. *PRACTICE AREAS:* Business and Real Estate Litigation.

**JACK M. SNYDER,** born Cleveland, Ohio, December 6, 1967; admitted to bar, 1993, California. *Education:* University of California, Santa Barbara (B.A., with high honors, 1990); University of California, Los Angeles (J.D., 1993). Staff Member, Women's Law Journal, 1991-1993. *Member:* Los Angeles County and American Bar Associations. *PRACTICE AREAS:* Business; Real Estate Litigation.

**KEVIN S. DICKER,** born Los Angeles, California, October 23, 1969; admitted to bar, 1995, California and U.S. District Court, Central District of California. *Education:* Tufts University (B.A., 1991); University of Southern California (J.D., 1995). *Member:* Los Angeles County and Amercian Bar Associations,. *PRACTICE AREAS:* Business Litigation; Entertainment Law.

### OF COUNSEL

**GUNTHER H. SCHIFF, (P.C.),** born Cologne, Germany, 1927; admitted to bar, 1953, California; 1952, District of Columbia. *Education:* Georgetown University (B.S.F.S., 1949; J.D., 1952). *Member:* Beverly Hills, Los Angeles County and American Bar Associations; Los Angeles Copyright Society. (Also practicing individually). *LANGUAGES:* German. *PRACTICE AREAS:* Real Estate; Entertainment Law; Copyright Law.

**D. STEVE CAMERON,** born Los Angeles, California, June 8, 1949; admitted to bar, 1974, California; 1975, U.S. District Court, Central District of California; 1976, U.S. Distriet Court, Eastern and Southern Districts of California and U.S. Court of Appeals, Ninth Circuit. *Education:* University of Southern California (B.A., cum laude, 1971; J.D., 1974). Member, University of Southern California Law Review, 1973-1974. *Member:* Los Angeles County and Federal Bar Associations. (Also Practicing Individually). *PRACTICE AREAS:* Business and Real Estate Litigation.

**DAVID J. LEONARD,** born New York, N.Y., July 6, 1940; admitted to bar, 1964, Arizona and California; 1988, U.S. Supreme Court. *Education:* University of Arizona (B.A., 1962; LL.B., 1964). Phi Beta Kappa. Trial Attorney, Trial Section, Antitrust Division, U.S. Department of Justice, Washington, D.C., 1964-1966. Judge Pro Tempore, Arizona Superior Court, 1986-1994. Adjunct Professor of Law, University of Arizona College of Law, 1986. *Member:* Pima County (Member, Civil Practice and Procedure Committee, 1984—) and American (Member, Litigation Section) Bar Associations; State Bar of Arizona (Chairman, Civil Rules for Federal District Courts Committee, 1977-1987; Member of Council, Antitrust Section, 1977-1988; Vice Chairman, 1977-1978, 1984-1987; Member: Committee on Civil Practice and Procedure, 1974-1984; Standing Committee for Liaison with U.S. District Court, 1974). (Also Member of Leonard, Felker, Altfeld & Battaile, P.C. Tucson, Arizona). *PRACTICE AREAS:* Commercial Litigation; Insurance Bad Faith Litigation; Real Estate Transactions.

## LEVINE & UNGER

9454 WILSHIRE BOULEVARD-PENTHOUSE
**BEVERLY HILLS, CALIFORNIA 90212-2937**
Telephone: 310-273-3555
Fax: 310-278-5002
Email: lenunger@earthlink.net

*General Civil and Trial Practice. Corporation, Real Estate, Estate Planning, Probate and Taxation.*

### MEMBERS OF FIRM

**LEONARD UNGER,** born Germany, February 20, 1947; admitted to bar, 1971, California and New York; 1981, U.S. Supreme Court. *Education:* University of California at Los Angeles (B.A., 1967); Boalt Hall School of Law, University of California (J.D., 1970). Phi Beta Kappa; Phi Eta Sigma;

*(This Listing Continued)*

# CALIFORNIA—BEVERLY HILLS

**LEVINE & UNGER**, Beverly Hills—Continued

Pi Gamma Mu; Pi Sigma Alpha; Blue Key. *Member:* Beverly Hills, Los Angeles County and American Bar Associations; State Bar of California. **PRACTICE AREAS:** Civil Trial; Corporate; Real Estate; Estate Planning; Probate.

**SID B. LEVINE** (1912-1995).

REFERENCE: City National Bank (Beverly Hills Main Office)

---

## *LEVINSON, LIEBERMAN & MAAS*

*A PROFESSIONAL CORPORATION*

Established in 1973

SUITE 1250, 9401 WILSHIRE BOULEVARD
**BEVERLY HILLS, CALIFORNIA 90212**
Telephone: 310-550-0500
Telecopier: 310-859-3949

*General Real Estate and Commercial Practice. Civil Litigation.*

FIRM PROFILE: *Levinson, Lieberman & Maas is a mid-sized law firm specializing in sophisticated litigation and commercial transactions. The firm, which was founded over twenty years ago, handles all phases of litigation from investigation through appeals involving such issues as antitrust, securities fraud, insurance coverage, environmental claims, class actions, insurance bad faith defense and other issues involving financial institutions, real estate and defense of liability claims.*

*The firm's lead trial attorneys have extensive experience in Federal and State Courts throughout the country, trying complex antitrust, insurance coverage, real estate, title insurance and business matters before juries and courts.*

*Transactional matters involve a similar scope of representation. The firm services the business needs of numerous contractors, land developers, escrow companies, title companies, title insurers, real estate brokers and owners of real estate and other businesses.*

*The firm's client base consists of banks, savings and loans, the FDIC, title insurance and related companies, developers, contractors, escrow companies and individuals with substantial real estate and other business holdings.*

**BURTON S. LEVINSON,** born New York, N.Y., June 8, 1931; admitted to bar, 1962, California and U.S. District Court, Central District of California; 1963, U.S. Court of Appeals, Ninth Circuit; 1976, U.S. Supreme Court; 1981, U.S. District Court, Eastern District of California and U.S. Tax Court; 1982, U.S. District Court, Northern District of California; 1986, U.S. Court of Appeals, Third Circuit. *Education:* Los Angeles State College; University of California at Los Angeles; Southwestern University (J.D., magna cum laude, 1962). Co-Author: "Ownership Transfer," *The Real Estate Handbook,* Chapter 3, Dow Jones-Irwin, 1980. Faculty Member, University of San Fernando College of Law, 1961-1969. Lecturer: Real Property and Conveyancing Matters: Continuing Education of the Bar, State Bar of California, 1985—; Escrow and Escrow Litigation, 1985-1989; Practising Law Institute, 1982-1990; Title Insurance, California Judges Conference, Coronado, 1992; Hastings College of Advocacy, 1982. *Member:* Beverly Hills, Los Angeles County and American Bar Associations; State Bar of California; American College of Real Estate Lawyers; American Land Title Association (Associate Member); California Land Title Association (Associate Member). **PRACTICE AREAS:** Title Insurance Law; Real Property Law; Commercial Transactions.

**LAWRENCE R. LIEBERMAN,** born Nashville, Tennessee, October 15, 1945; admitted to bar, 1972, California; 1973, U.S. District Court, Central District of California and U.S. Court of Appeals, Ninth Circuit; 1976, U.S. Supreme Court; 1977, U.S. District Court, District of Massachusetts; 1981, U.S. District Court, Eastern District of California; 1983, U.S. District Court, Northern District of California and U.S. District Court of Guam (pro hac vice); 1985, U.S. District Court, District of Colorado; 1988, U.S. District Court, District of Nevada (pro hac vice). *Education:* University of California at Los Angeles (B.S., 1968; J.D., 1971). Lecturer, Hastings College of Advocacy, 1981. C.E.B. Panelist on Real Property Matters, 1985-1986, 1989, 1993. Judge Pro Tem, Los Angeles Superior Court, 1985, 1987, 1988, 1994. *Member:* Los Angeles County Bar Association (Member, Real Property Section); State Bar of California. **LANGUAGES:** German and Greek. **REPORTED CASES:** Whiteside v. United States of America, 833 F.2d 820 (9th Cir. 1987); Cortese v. United States of America, 782 F.2d 845 (9th Cir. 1986); Republic Bank v. Nelson, 761 F.2d 1320 (9th Cir. 1985); Share v. Air Properties G., Inc., 536 F.2d 279 (9th Cir. 1976); Wright v. Schock, 571 F.Supp. 642 (N.D. Cal. 1983); Cornelison v. Kornbluth, 15

*(This Listing Continued)*

---

# MARTINDALE-HUBBELL LAW DIRECTORY 1997

Cal.3d 590 (1975); Far West Savings & Loan v. Mclaughlin, 201 Cal.App.3d 67 (1988); Orr v. Byers, 198 Cal.App.3d 666 (1988); Transamerica Title Insurance Co. v. Superior Court (Bank of the West), 188 Cal.App.3d 1047 (1987); R.W. Blois Company v. Imperial Bank, 151 Cal.App.3d 1163 (1984); Coldwell Banker & Company v. Department of Insurance, 102 Cal.App.3d 381 (1980); First American Title Insurance Company v. Casper, 157 Cal.Rptr. 798 (1979). **PRACTICE AREAS:** Real Property Litigation; Commercial Litigation; Defense of Bad Faith Insurance Claims; Securities Litigation; Anti-Trust Litigation; Liability Claims Defense; Construction Litigation; Environmental Litigation.

**FRANCIS S. MAAS,** born Los Angeles, California, April 27, 1944; admitted to bar, 1970, California and U.S. District Court, Central District of California. *Education:* University of California at Berkeley (B.A., 1966); University of Southern California (J.D., 1969). Phi Delta Phi. Chairman of the Board, University of Judaism, 1993—. *Member:* Los Angeles County, Beverly Hills and American Bar Associations; State Bar of California. **LANGUAGES:** German. **PRACTICE AREAS:** Real Property Law; Business Law.

**NANCY E. MARCUS,** born New York, December 25, 1962; admitted to bar, 1987, California. *Education:* Texas Tech University (B.A., 1984); University of Texas at Austin (J.D., 1987). Member, Honor Tribunal, 1985-1986 and Teaching Quizmaster, 1986-1987, University of Texas School of Law. *Member:* Beverly Hills, Los Angeles County and American Bar Associations; State Bar of California. **PRACTICE AREAS:** Title Insurance Defense Litigation; Real Estate Law.

**PETER M. HEBERT,** born Seattle, Washington, April 16, 1960; admitted to bar, 1985, Washington and U.S. Court of Appeals, Ninth Circuit; 1986, U.S. District Court, Western District of Washington; 1991, California; 1992, Arizona. *Education:* University of Washington (B.A., 1982); University of Notre Dame (J.D., 1985). Phi Alpha Delta. Judicial Clerk to Judge John F. Kilkenny, U.S. Court of Appeals, Ninth Circuit, 1985-1986. *Member:* Beverly Hills, Los Angeles County and Washington State Bar Associations; State Bar of Arizona. **PRACTICE AREAS:** Real Estate; Commercial Litigation; Banking.

**BRIAN KENT BROOKEY,** born Oxnard, California, May 18, 1965; admitted to bar, 1990, California; 1991, U.S. District Court, Central District of California and U.S. Court of Appeals, Ninth Circuit. *Education:* Pepperdine University (B.A., magna cum laude, 1987); University of California at Los Angeles Law School (J.D., 1990). Member, Executive Board of Judges, UCLA Moot Court Honors Program. Teaching Assistant, Legal Research and Writing and Constitutional Law, University of California, 1989-1990. Volunteer Attorney, AIDS Legal Services Project, 1991—. *Member:* State Bar of California. **LANGUAGES:** German. **PRACTICE AREAS:** Real Estate Litigation; Title Insurance Litigation.

APPROVED ATTORNEYS FOR: First American Title Insurance Co.; Ticor Title Insurance Co.; Title Insurance Company of Minnesota; Safeco Title Insurance Co.; Transamerica Title Insurance Co.; Chicago Title Insurance Co.; St. Paul Title Insurance Co.; Commonwealth Land Title Insurance Co.; Lawyers Title Insurance Corp.; First American Title Company of Los Angeles; Investors Title Co.; Founders Title Group; Continental Land Title Co.; California Trustee's Association.
REFERENCE: City National Bank (Beverly Hills Office).

---

## *LIPOFSKY & RUBEN*

*A Partnership including a Professional Corporation*

Established in 1986

SUITE 708, 8383 WILSHIRE BOULEVARD
**BEVERLY HILLS, CALIFORNIA 90211-2408**
Telephone: 213-653-2004
Telecopier: 213-653-6228

*General Civil and Trial Practice. Real Estate and Business Litigation, Land Security Transactions, Real Estate Development and Commercial Law.*

### MEMBERS OF FIRM

**LOUIS A. LIPOFSKY, (A PROFESSIONAL CORPORATION),** born New York, N.Y., May 30, 1938; admitted to bar, 1963, California. *Education:* University of California at Los Angeles (B.S., with honors, 1959); University of California, Boalt Hall School of Law (LL.B., 1962). Member, Moot Court. Lecturer for California Continuing Education of the Bar on Real Estate Matters, 1976, 1980, 1983, 1986, 1988, 1990, 1992 and 1994. *Member:* Beverly Hills and Los Angeles County Bar Associations; State Bar of California. **PRACTICE AREAS:** Real Estate; Business Litigation; Land Security Transactions; Real Estate Development; Commercial Law.

*(This Listing Continued)*

**JOEL D. RUBEN,** born Los Angeles, California, May 21, 1949; admitted to bar, 1977, California. *Education:* University of California at Los Angeles (B.A., summa cum laude, 1971); University of California at Davis (J.D., 1977). Phi Beta Kappa; Order of the Coif. President's Scholar; Regent's Scholar. *Member:* Los Angeles County Bar Association; The State Bar of California. *PRACTICE AREAS:* Real Estate and Business Litigation; Commercial Law; Competitive Business Practices; Environmental Law.

### ASSOCIATES

**MARK L. SHARE,** born Los Angeles, California, April 4, 1964; admitted to bar, 1990, California. *Education:* Reed College (B.A., 1986); Northwestern School of Law of Lewis and Clark College (J.D., cum laude, 1990). Moot Court Honor Board, 1989-1990. Member, 1988-1989 and Editor, 1989-1990, Environmental Law Journal, Northwestern School of Law. Extern Law Clerk to Judge Otto R. Skopil, Jr., United State Court of Appeals, Ninth Circuit, 1989. Author: "Don't Fence Me Out," Los Angeles Lawyer, January 1977. Judge Pro Tem, Los Angeles Municipal Court, 1997. *Member:* Los Angeles County Bar Association. State Bar of California. *PRACTICE AREAS:* Real Estate; Business Litigation.

---

## LOCKE, LOCKE, RUDMAN & ABERLE

332 SOUTH BEVERLY DRIVE
**BEVERLY HILLS, CALIFORNIA 90212**
Telephone: 310-553-0602
Los Angeles: 213-879-3973

*General Civil and Trial Practice in all State and Federal Courts and Securities Law.*

### MEMBERS OF FIRM

**MARTIN S. LOCKE** (1929-1988).

**BERRY D. LOCKE,** born Los Angeles, California, October 14, 1927; admitted to bar, 1954, California. *Education:* University of Southern California (B.A., 1950; LL.B., 1953). Author: "The Use and Abuse of Demonstrative Evidence," Personal Injury Annual, 1977. Member, Board of Immigration Appeals, U.S. Department of Justice, 1957. Arbitrator, Los Angeles Superior Court, 1973—. Member, National Panel of Arbitrators, American Arbitration Association. *Member:* Beverly Hills Bar Association; The State Bar of California; Los Angeles County Trial Lawyers Association; California Trial Lawyers Association; The Association of Trial Lawyers of America.

**BARRY M. RUDMAN,** born Chicago, Illinois, February 6, 1945; admitted to bar, 1971, California. *Education:* University of California at Los Angeles (B.A., 1967); Loyola University at Los Angeles (J.D., 1970). Phi Alpha Delta. Arbitrator, Los Angeles Superior Court, 1980—. *Member:* Beverly Hills Bar Association; The State Bar of California.

**DOUGLAS S. ABERLE,** born Los Angeles, California, September 24, 1958; admitted to bar, 1984, California. *Education:* University of California at Berkeley (B.A., 1980); Golden Gate University (J.D., 1983). Arbitrator, Los Angeles Superior Court, 1988—. *Member:* Los Angeles County Bar Association; State Bar of California; Los Angeles County Trial Lawyers Association.

REFERENCE: First Charter Bank, Beverly Hills, CA.

---

## LUND & LUND

Established in 1972

9595 WILSHIRE BOULEVARD
**BEVERLY HILLS, CALIFORNIA 90212**
Telephone: 310-273-2555
FAX: 310-271-4062

*International Law. Engineering, Construction, Business, Commercial, Real Estate and Corporation Law. Civil Trial and Appellate Practice.*

**JAMES L. LUND,** born Long Beach, California, October 4, 1926; admitted to bar, 1955, California U.S. Court of Appeals, Ninth Circuit and U.S. Tax Court; 1964, U.S. Supreme Court. *Education:* Stanford University; University of Southern California (B.A., 1946); Southwestern University School of Law (J.D., 1955). Phi Alpha Delta. *Member:* State Bar of California; American Bar Association; Inter-American Bar Association. [Lt., Cmdr., USNR]. *LANGUAGES:* French. *PRACTICE AREAS:* International Law; Engineering; Construction Law.

*(This Listing Continued)*

**ERIC JAMES LUND,** born Los Angeles, California, March 30, 1959; admitted to bar, 1983, California; 1984, U.S. District Court, Central District of California, U.S. Court of Appeals, Ninth Circuit and U.S. Supreme Court. *Education:* Stanford University (B.A., 1979); University of Southern California (J.D., 1983; M.B.A., 1983). Author: "Estate Planning for the Non-Professional," Beverly Hills Adult School, 1990; "Substance Abuse Among Attorneys and Their Clients," Southern California Tax and Estate Planning Forum, September 1995 and September 1996. Co-Author: with Gerald E. Lunn, Jr., "Income, Estate and Gift Tax Consequences of Transfers Between Unmarried Partners," Century City Family Law Council, 1994. Director, Spinal Cord Injury Network International, 1988—. Director, Advisory Board, 1991-1995 and Member, Chairman's Council, 1994—, Betty Ford Center at Eisenhower. Member, Alumni Board, Buckley Schools, 1996. Member, Development Committee, Neighborhood Youth Association, 1996. *Member:* Los Angeles County Bar Association; State Bar of California. (Also Member Lund Law Corporation at Los Angeles). *LANGUAGES:* French and Farsi. *PRACTICE AREAS:* Estate Planning; Trust and Probate Law.

REFERENCES: Bank of America (Beverly Wilshire Branch); First Los Angeles Bank (Beverly Hills Branch).

---

## LURIE & ZEPEDA

A PROFESSIONAL CORPORATION

Established in 1983

SUITE 800, 9107 WILSHIRE BOULEVARD
**BEVERLY HILLS, CALIFORNIA 90210**
Telephone: 310-274-8700
Fax: 310-274-2798
Email: luriezep@ix.netcom.com

*Business Litigation, Construction and Real Estate Litigation. Corporate and Securities Litigation, Banking Litigation, Creditors Rights, Landlord and Tenant, Corporate, Partnership, Antitrust, Intellectual Property, Professional Malpractice, State and Federal Civil Trial and Appellate Practice, Entertainment and Aviation. Diplomatic and Foreign Sovereign Immunity. International Child Custody Litigation.*

**BRUCE J. LURIE,** born St. Louis, Missouri, November 8, 1945; admitted to bar, 1970, Missouri; 1972, California. *Education:* University of Illinois (B.S., 1967); New York University (J.D., 1970). Root-Tilden Scholar. Certified Public Accountant, Illinois, 1967.

**ANDREW W. ZEPEDA,** born Olympia, Washington, April 14, 1957; admitted to bar, 1982, California. *Education:* Thomas Aquinas College (B.A., 1979); University of Notre Dame (J.D., 1982). Justice William J. Brennan Scholar. Member, Board of Governors, Thomas Aquinas College.

**KURT L. SCHMALZ,** born Mansfield, Ohio, May 10, 1956; admitted to bar, 1983, California. *Education:* Vanderbilt University (B.A., cum laude, 1978; J.D., 1983). Senior Articles Editor, Vanderbilt Law Review, 1982-1983. Editorial Board, Los Angeles Lawyer. Member, Planning Commission, City of Redondo Beach.

**ROBERT W. DENTON,** born Lamar, Missouri, January 27, 1951; admitted to bar, 1984, California. *Education:* Southeast Missouri State University (B.A., magna cum laude, 1973); University of Minnesota (J.D., magna cum laude, 1983). Order of the Coif. Member, 1981-1982 and Article Editor, 1982-1983, Minnesota Law Review. Law Clerk to the Honorable William C. Canby Jr., U.S. Court of Appeals, Ninth Circuit, 1983-1984.

---

**STEVEN L. HOGAN,** born Los Angeles, California August 31, 1953; admitted to bar, 1978, California. *Education:* University of California at Los Angeles (B.A., magna cum laude, 1975); University of Southern California (J.D., 1978). Order of the Coif.

**OLE R. SANDBERG,** born New York, N.Y., August 29, 1943; admitted to bar, 1977, Norway; 1984, California. *Education:* Hamar Katedralskole Hamar, Norway (Baccalaureate, 1962); University of Oslo, Oslo, Norway (J.D., 1968). Professor of Law, University of Oslo, Norway, 1968-1975. *LANGUAGES:* Norwegian, French, German, Swedish and Danish.

*(This Listing Continued)*

**LURIE & ZEPEDA,** *A PROFESSIONAL CORPORATION, Beverly Hills—Continued*

**L. KIMBERLY PEPPER,** born Anniston, Alabama, September 25, 1964; admitted to bar, 1989, California. *Education:* Auburn University (B.F.A., 1986); Southwestern University (J.D., 1989). Recipient, Paul W. Wildman Merit Scholarship. Note and Comment Editor, Southwestern University Law Review, 1989. Member, Moot Court Honors Program.

**BRENDAN F. MACAULAY,** born Long Beach, California, June 23, 1967; admitted to bar, 1992, California and U.S. District Court, Central District of California; 1994, U.S. District Court, Southern District of California. *Education:* Whittier College (B.A., 1989); Duke University (J.D., 1992). **LANGUAGES:** Spanish.

**MICHAEL J. CONWAY,** born Santa Monica, California, July 7, 1970; admitted to bar, 1995, California and U.S. District Court, Central District of California. *Education:* University of California at Los Angeles (B.A., cum laude, 1992); Loyola Law School (J.D., 1995). Order of the Coif. Chief Justice, Scott Moot Court Honors Board. Extern, United States Attorney's Office, Civil Fraud Division.

**DONNA M. DEAN,** born Covina, California, April 11, 1965; admitted to bar, 1996, California. *Education:* University of California, Irvine (B.A., 1988); University of California School of Law, Los Angeles (J.D., 1996). Chief Articles Editor, 1995-1996, Managing Editor, 1994-1995, Member, 1992-1996, Journal of Environmental Law & Policy, UCLA.

# STEPHEN C. MARPET

9454 WILSHIRE BOULEVARD
SUITE 313
BEVERLY HILLS, CALIFORNIA 90212
Telephone: 310-274-6971
Fax: 310-273-3642
Email: SCMRUN@aol.com

*General Civil and Trial Practice in all State and Federal Courts. Corporate, Business, Entertainment, Products Liability. Malpractice and Personal Injury Law. Employment.*

**STEPHEN C. MARPET,** born Washington, D.C., May 8, 1941; admitted to bar, 1967, California. *Education:* University of California at Berkeley (B.S., 1963); Hastings College of Law, University of California (LL.B., 1966). Member: Los Angeles Consumer Lawyers Association; California Consumer Lawyers Association. *Member:* Beverly Hills and Los Angeles Bar Associations; The State Bar of California; California Consumer Lawyers Association; Criminal Courts Bar Association.

# LEWIS B. MERRIFIELD, III

270 NORTH CANON DRIVE SUITE 1281
BEVERLY HILLS, CALIFORNIA 90210-5323
Telephone: 310-274-0693

Securities Law.

**LEWIS B. MERRIFIELD, III,** born Philadelphia, Pennsylvania, October 22, 1939; admitted to bar, 1968, California. *Education:* Yale University; University of California at Los Angeles (A.B., 1962); University of Southern California (J.D., 1966). Law Alumni Award Scholar, Highest Scholastic Average. Order of the Coif; Phi Delta Phi. Associate Editor, University of Southern California Law Review, 1965-1966. Author: "Making Markets in Shells," 3 Review of Securities Regulation 872, 9/21/70; "NASD Guidelines," 3 Review of Securities Regulation 946, 4/3/70; "Registration Covenants," 3 Review of Securities Regulation 968, 2/18/70; "Revised NASD Guidelines," 4 Review of Securities Regulation 963, 3/4/71; "Private Placement Exemption," 4 Review of Securities Regulation 940, 4/22/71; "Underwriting Compensation," The Business Lawyer, April, 1971; "Projections in SEC Filings," New York Law Journal, December, 1974; "Investigations by The Securities and Exchange Commission," The Business Lawyer, July, 1977. Law Clerk to Associate Justice William O. Douglas, Supreme Court of the United States, 1966-1967. Assistant Professor, University of Southern California Law School, 1967-1968. *Member:* Los Angeles County (Member, Executive Committee, Business and Corporations Law Section, 1971-1976), American (Co-Chairman, Securities Law Committee, Administrative Law Section, 1970-1972; Member, Committee on Federal Regula-

*(This Listing Continued)*

tion of Securities, Corporation, Banking and Business Law Section, 1972—; Chairman, Annual Review of Securities Regulation Subcommittee, 1983-1987) and International (Member, Committee on Securities Issues and Trading, 1971—) Bar Associations; State Bar of California; American Judicature Society.

REFERENCE: City National Bank (Pershing Square Office, Los Angeles).

# MITCHELL R. MILLER

315 SOUTH BEVERLY DRIVE, SUITE 501
BEVERLY HILLS, CALIFORNIA 90212
Telephone: 310-277-1848
Fax: 310-551-1929
Email: MitchMllr@aol.com

*Taxation Law, Administrative Law and Estate Planning Law.*

**MITCHELL R. MILLER,** born 1946; admitted to bar, 1977, Pennsylvania; 1979, U.S. Tax Court; 1981, California. *Education:* Michigan State University (B.A., 1968; M.A., 1969); Temple University (J.D., 1977). Certified Public Accountant, Pennsylvania, 1979. Author: "Independent Contractor vs. Employee," 48 U.S.C. Tax Institute 1,000; Updated, "Personal Tax Planning for Professionals and Owners of Small Businesses," Cal. Continuing Education at the Bar, 1996; "The IRS and the Entertainment Industry," L.A. Lawyer, May 1994. Instructor, "Tax Considerations for the Film and Television Industry," Extension, Entertainment Studies Program, UCLA, 1994—. Member, Motion Picture and Television Tax Institute. *Member:* Beverly Hills, Los Angeles County (Chair, Entertainment Tax Committee) and American Bar Associations; State Bar of California; American Association of Attorney-CPA's. **REPORTED CASES:** Boykin v. Cobin, 30 Cal. Rptr. 428, (1994) appeal dismissed 41 Cal. Rptr. 2d. 219 (1995); Lomma Linda Community Hospital v. Shalala, 907 F. Supp. 1399 (U.S.D.C. Cent. Dist. Ca. 1995). **PRACTICE AREAS:** Taxation; Estate Planning; Administrative Law.

# MOSTEN & TUFFIAS

BEVERLY HILLS, CALIFORNIA
(See Los Angeles)

*Practice Limited to Family Law and Family Law Mediation.*

# LAW OFFICES OF GEORGE I. NAGLER

9777 WILSHIRE BOULEVARD, SUITE 1009
BEVERLY HILLS, CALIFORNIA 90212-1901
Telephone: 310-278-0034
Telecopier: 310-859-7890

*Business Law, Real Estate & Probate.*

**GEORGE I. NAGLER,** born Calgary, Canada, December 11, 1936; admitted to bar, 1970, California. *Education:* University of British Columbia (B.Com., 1958); Harvard University (J.D., cum laude, 1969). Lecturer, Representing Parties to Real Property Sales, 1976 and 1978 and Introduction to Secured Real Property Transactions, 1980, 1983, 1985 and 1990, Continuing Education of the Bar. Consultant, California Real Property Sales Transactions, Continuing Education of the Bar, 1981 and 1983. *Member:* Beverly Hills, Los Angeles County (Member, Real Estate, Corporations and Taxation Sections; Chairman, Taxation Subcommittee, Real Property Section, 1976-1977) and American (Member, Sections on: Corporation, Banking and Business Law; Taxation) Bar Associations; The State Bar of California. **PRACTICE AREAS:** Real Estate; Business Law; Corporate Law; Estate Planning; Wills.

## NAGLER & ASSOCIATES
*Established in 1991*
**9595 WILSHIRE BOULEVARD, SUITE 510**
**BEVERLY HILLS, CALIFORNIA 90212-2505**
*Telephone: 310-273-2666*
*Facsimile: 310-550-7956*
*Email: info@nagler.com*

*Complex Multi-Party Litigation Practice in State and Federal Courts.*

**FIRM PROFILE:** *The firm specializes in complex multi-party litigation, state and federal courts, trial and appellate levels. Current cases include major subrogation and contribution claims, large, multi-party securities matters, RICO claims, defense against guarantee agreements and other bank claims, breach of contract, fraud, partnership disputes, professional errors and omissions, fiduciary duty, defense of serious tort claims, business torts, and related appellate proceedings.*

**LAWRENCE H. NAGLER,** born Queens, New York, July 1, 1940; admitted to bar, 1966, California and U.S. District Court, Central and Southern Districts of California; U.S. Court of Appeals, Ninth Circuit and Federal Circuit; U.S. Supreme Court. *Education:* University of California at Los Angeles (B.A., 1962; J.D., 1965). Member: Moot Court Honor Program; National Moot Court Team. Judge Pro Tem, Beverly Hills Municipal Court and Los Angeles Municipal Court, 1976-1978. *Member:* Beverly Hills, (Member, Litigation Section) Los Angeles County (Member, Litigation Section) and American (Member, Litigation Section) Bar Associations; State Bar of California (Member, Litigation Section). **REPORTED CASES:** Aragon Haas v. Family Security Insurance Services, 231 Cal. App. 3d 232, 282 Cal. Rptr. 233 (1991); Mirkin v. Wasserman, et al. 227 Cal.App. 3d 1537, 278 Cal. Rptr. 729 (1991); Mirkin v. Wasserman, et al., 5 Cal. 4th 1082, 23 Cal.Rptr. 2d 101 (California Supreme Court 1993); Employers Insurance of Wausau and Federal Insurance Co. v. Musick, Peeler & Garrett, Peat, Marwick, Main & Co. 954 F.2d 575 (9th Cir. 1992); Musick, Peeler & Garrett, et al., v. Employers Insurance of Wausau, et al., 113 S.Ct. 2085, 124 L.Ed.2d 194, 61 U.S.L.W. 4520 (United States Supreme Court, 1993); Employers Insurance of Wausau and Federal Insurance Co. v. Musick, Peeler & Garrett et al., 871 F.Supp. 381 (1994). **PRACTICE AREAS:** Business Litigation.

**ROBERT MICHAEL ZABB,** born Brooklyn, New York, September 3, 1953; admitted to bar, 1980, New York and Massachusetts; 1983, California; 1986, U.S. District Court, Central, Northern, Eastern and Southern Districts of California. *Education:* Yale University (B.A., cum laude, 1976); Columbia University (J.D., 1979); New York University (LL.M. in Taxation, 1983); University of Southern California (M.B.A., Accounting and Finance, 1987). Stone Scholar. Certified Public Accountant, California, 1987. Member: Los Angeles County Bar Association; State Bar of California. **REPORTED CASES:** Employers Insurance of Wausau and Federal Insurance Co. v. Musick, Peeler & Garrett, Peat, Marwick, Main & Co. 954 F.2d 575 (9th Cir. 1992); Musick, Peeler & Garrett, et al., v. Employers Insurance of Wausau, et al., 113 S.Ct. 2085, 124 L.Ed. 194, 61 U.S.L.W. 4520 (United States Supreme Court 1993); Employers Insurance of Wausau and Federal Insurance Co. v. Musick, Peeler & Garrett et al., 871 F.Supp. 381 (1994). **PRACTICE AREAS:** Business Litigation. **Email:** RZabb@nagler.com

**JAMES F. BOYLE,** born Orange, New Jersey, June 25, 1946; admitted to bar, 1982, California, U.S. District Court, Central and Southern Districts of California and U.S. Court of Appeals, Ninth Circuit. *Education:* Loyola Marymount University (B.A., 1968; J.D., cum laude, 1981); California State University at Northridge (M.A., 1972). Member: St. Thomas More Law Honor Society; Chancery Club, 1991. Author: "Labor Law in the Ninth Circuit: Recent Developments - The Representation Process and Union Recognition," 13 Loyola Law Review 411, 1980. Law Student Representative, ABA Special Committee on Alternative Means of Dispute Resolution. *Member:* Los Angeles County (Member: Litigation Section; Legislative Review Committee) and American (Member, Sections on: Tort and Insurance Practice; Litigation) Bar Associations; State Bar of California (Member, Conference of Delegates, 1995, 1996); Chancery Club-Los Angeles. **REPORTED CASES:** Bowie v. Home Insurance Co., 923 F.2d. 705 (9th Cir. 1991). **PRACTICE AREAS:** Business Litigation. **Email:** JBoyle@nagler.com

**SUSAN D. PRASKIN,** born Bronx, N.Y., October 24, 1957; admitted to bar, 1985, California; U.S. District Court, Central District of California. *Education:* State University of New York at Albany (B.A., 1979); South-

*(This Listing Continued)*

western University School of Law (J.D., 1985). Author: "Pelletier v. Eisenberg: Gallery Liability for Loss or Damage to Consigned Works of Art," The Visual Artists Manual, A Practical Guide to Your Career, 1987 Supplement, Beverly Hills Bar Association Barristers, 1987. Instructor, Paralegal Certificate Program, Introduction to Litigation, California Lutheran University, Spring 1990. Lecturer, California State University at Long Beach, Public Art Symposium, Fall, 1990; Lecturer, University of Southern California, Public Art Symposium, Spring, 1991. *Member:* Beverly Hills and Los Angeles County Bar Associations; State Bar of California; Women Lawyers Association of Los Angeles; International Society for Intercultural Education, Training and Research (Secretary, Southern California Chapter, 1994-1996). **LANGUAGES:** French. **PRACTICE AREAS:** Business Litigation.

**JOAN E. LEWIS-HEARD,** born Boston, Massachusetts, September 25, 1961; admitted to bar, 1986, California and U.S. District Court, Central District of California. *Education:* Tufts University (B.S., cum laude, 1983); University of California, Los Angeles (J.D., 1986). Member, Moot Court. *Member:* State Bar of California. **REPORTED CASES:** Royal Neckwear Co., Inc. v. Century City, Inc., 205 Cal.App.3d 1146 (1988). **PRACTICE AREAS:** Business Litigation.

**THOMAS H. CASE,** born Buffalo, New York, September 10, 1957; admitted to bar, 1984, California, U.S. District Court, Central, Northern and Eastern Districts of California. *Education:* Yale University (B.A., 1980); University of Southern California (J.D., 1984). Order of the Coif. Articles Editor, Southern California Law Review. Member, Los Angeles County Bar's Trial Attorney Project. Volunteer, Los Angeles City Attorney's Office. *Member:* The State Bar of California.

**DAVID F. BERRY,** born Neptune, New Jersey, February 27, 1956; admitted to bar, 1983, California, U.S. Court of Appeals, Ninth Circuit and U.S. District Court, Central District of California; 1985, U.S. District Court, Southern District of California; 1992, U.S. District Court, Northern District of California. *Education:* Rutgers University (B.A., 1979); University of Georgia; University of Southern California (J.D., 1983). Staff Member, Southern California Law Review, 1981-1983. Recipient, Judge Barry Russell Award for Highest Honors in Federal Courts and Practice. Author: Note, "The First Amendment and Law Enforcement Infiltration of Political Groups," 56 Southern California Law Review 207, November, 1982. *Member:* State Bar of California. **REPORTED CASES:** Kerins v. Hartley, 27 Cal. App. 4th 1062 (1994); A-Mark Financial v. CIGNA, 34 Cal. App. 4th 1179 (1995). **PRACTICE AREAS:** Appellate Practice; Civil Litigation. **Email:** DBerry@nagler.com

**J. STACIE JOHNSON,** born Pittsburgh, Pennsylvania, August 1, 1959; admitted to bar, 1984, California; 1986, U.S. District Court, Central, Southern, Eastern and Northern Districts of California. *Education:* University of California at Los Angeles (A.B., magna cum laude, 1981); University of California School of Law, Los Angeles (J.D., 1984). Phi Beta Kappa. Chair, Administrative Executive Board, 1983-1984, Participant, Moot Court, 1982-1983. Member, Probate Volunteer Panel, Los Angeles County Superior Court. *Member:* Los Angeles County Bar Association (Member, Sections on: Litigation; Estate Planning); State Bar of California (Member, Litigation Section). **PRACTICE AREAS:** Business Litigation; Real Estate. **Email:** SJohnson@nagler.com

## LOUISE NEMSCHOFF
**433 NORTH CAMDEN DRIVE, SUITE 1200**
**BEVERLY HILLS, CALIFORNIA 90210**
*Telephone: 310-274-4627*
*FAX: 310-274-5039*

*Entertainment, Copyright and Trademark Law. International Law.*

**LOUISE NEMSCHOFF,** born San Francisco, California, September 12, 1950; admitted to bar, 1975, California;. *Education:* Harvard University (B.A., magna cum laude, 1972); Yale University (J.D., 1975). Phi Beta Kappa. Author: "A Rose by Any Other Name: The U.S. and Moral Rights," 1995; "Intellectual Property," Women's Legal Desk Reference, 1994; "Registration of Copyrights in Textile Designs," Visual Artists Manual, 1994; "Authorship and Employment: Life in the Entertainment Industry after CCNV v. Reid," 4 Ent. L. Rev. (UK) 80, 1993; "Border Skirmishes at the Fair Use Outpost: The Boundary Between Copyright and the First Amendment," Creative Restraints on the Entertainment Industry, 1991. Co-Author: "Back to the Future: Exploiting Vintage Films in the Public Domain," Los Angeles Lawyer, Vol. 10, No. 3, May, 1987. Arbitrator, American Film Marketing Association, 1992—. *Member:* Beverly Hills, Los Angeles County (Member: Board of Trustees, 1994—; Chair, Intellec-

*(This Listing Continued)*

## LOUISE NEMSCHOFF, Beverly Hills—Continued

tual Property and Entertainment Law Section, 1993-1994); International Association of Entertainment Lawyers (Executive Committee, 1993—) and International Bar Associations; State Bar of California; Los Angeles Copyright Society.

---

## FREDERICK M. NICHOLAS

SECOND FLOOR, 9300 WILSHIRE BOULEVARD
**BEVERLY HILLS, CALIFORNIA 90212**
Telephone: 310-273-3077; 271-5176
Fax: 310-276-5632

*Business and Real Estate Law.*

**FREDERICK M. NICHOLAS,** born New York, N.Y., May 30, 1920; admitted to bar, 1952, California. *Education:* University of Southern California (A.B., 1947); University of Chicago and University of Southern California (J.D., 1952). Author: "Setting Up a Shopping Center," *California Land Security and Development,* California Continuing Education of the Bar, 1960. Co-Author: "Commercial Real Property Lease Practice," California Continuing Education of the Bar, 1976. Founder, 1970, President, 1970-1973, Director 1970-1978, Public Counsel. Recipient: Citizen of the Year, Beverly Hills Board of Realtors, 1978; Citizen of the Year, Beverly Hills Chamber of Commerce, 1983; Coro Foundation Award for Public Service, 1988; Founders Award from Public Counsel, 1990; Outstanding Founder in Philanthropy Award from National Philanthropy Day Committee, 1990; The Medici Award from Los Angeles Chamber of Commerce, 1990; Trustees Award, California Institute of the Arts, 1993; City of Angels Award, Los Angeles Central Business Association, 1994. General Counsel, Beverly Hills Board of Realtors, 1971-1979. Chairman: Museum of Contemporary Art, 1988-1993; Chairman, Walt Disney Concert Hall Committee, 1987-1994. Trustee: The Music Center of Los Angeles County, 1987-1995; Museum of Contemporary Art, 1982-1996; Los Angeles Philharmonic Association, 1993-1995. Trustee: American Arts Alliance, 1988-1991; American Federation, 1989-1991. *Member:* Beverly Hills (Member, 1966-1986 and Chairman, 1968-1970, Committee on Real Property Law; Public Relations, 1967-1968. Member, Board of Governors, 1970-1972; 1975-1978; Distinguished Service Award, 1974 and 1981; Exceptional Service Award, 1986); Los Angeles County (Member: Executive Committee, Real Property Law Section, 1962-1985; Committee on California Judicial System, 1983-1985) and American Bar Associations; The State Bar of California; Lawyers Committee for Civil Rights Under Law (Member: Executive Committee, 1972—; Board of Trustees, 1972—).

REFERENCE: Union Bank (Beverly Hills, California Regional Main Office).

---

## GREGORY NICOLAYSEN

A PROFESSIONAL CORPORATION
*Established in 1983*

8530 WILSHIRE BOULEVARD, SUITE 404
**BEVERLY HILLS, CALIFORNIA 90211**
Telephone: 310-397-0737
Fax: 310-397-1001
Email: greg@ac.net
URL: http://www.afda.org

*Federal Criminal Defense, White Collar Defense.*

**FIRM PROFILE:** *Since 1989, Mr. Nicolaysen has specialized exclusively in federal criminal defense. He represents both individual and business clients in a broad range of federal criminal matters covering all stages including pre-indictment grand jury appearances, government investigations, trials and appeals. Mr. Nicolaysen regularly serves as a consultant to attorneys nationwide on federal criminal matters and is a frequent lecturer at seminars. He is the founder of the Association of Federal Defense Attorneys and publishes the on-line newsletter located at http://www.afda.org*

**GREGORY NICOLAYSEN,** born New York, N.Y., June 21, 1956; admitted to bar, 1981, California. *Education:* Dartmouth College (B.A., in Government, with distinction, 1977); Benjamin Cardozo School of Law, Yeshiva University (J.D., magna cum laude, 1980). Law Clerk, Judge H. Curtis Meanor, Federal District Court, District of New Jersey, 1979. Member, Cardozo Law Review. Author: "The Complete Manual of Federal Criminal Discovery," 1994. Publisher of online newsletter on Federal Criminal Law: http://www.afda.org. Editor, Corporate Criminal Liability Reporter, 1985-1990; Program Chair and Course Book Editor, "Protecting The Corporation And Management From Criminal Prosecution," Federal Litigators Group, 1987 (San Francisco, New York); Program Chair, "The New Federal Sentencing Guidelines," Federal Litigators Group, 1988-1989 (Los Angeles, San Francisco, New York); Program Chair, "Key Developments In Federal Criminal Defense," Federal Litigators Group, 1992 (Los Angeles). Assistant Regional Director, Federal Trade Commission, Los Angeles, 1988-1989; Federal Indigent Defense Panel, Central District of California, 1989—. Founder and Director, Association of Federal Defense Attorneys (AFDA). Program Chair, "The New Federal Crime Bill," Association of Federal Defense Attorneys, 1994 (Los Angeles). Program Chair, "Federal Sentencing Updates and Strategies," Association of Federal Defense Attorneys, 1994, 1995, 1996 (Los Angeles); Program Chair, "What Every Defense Lawyer Should Know About the Federal Bureau of Prisons," Association of Federal Defense Attorneys, 1995 (Los Angeles). Appointed by the State Bar of California, Criminal Law Advisory Commission, 1996—. *Member:* State Bar of California; American Bar Association (Criminal Justice Section); National Association of Criminal Defense Lawyers; California Attorneys for Criminal Justice. **REPORTED CASES:** United States v. Javier Vasquez-Valasco, 15 F.3d 833 (9th Cir. 1994); United States v. Richard Miller, 984 F.2d 1028 (9th Cir 1993); Federal Trade Commission v. Figgie International, 1990 WL507421; RRX Industries vs. Lab. Con, Inc., 772 F.2d 543 (9th Cir. 1985). **PRACTICE AREAS:** Federal Criminal Trial and Appellate Practice; Criminal Law; White Collar Defense. *Email:* greg@ac.net

*(This Listing Continued)*

---

## NORMINTON & WIITA

A Partnership of Professional Corporations

433 NORTH CAMDEN DRIVE
TWELFTH FLOOR
**BEVERLY HILLS, CALIFORNIA 90210**
Telephone: 310-288-5900
Facsimile: 310-288-5901
Email: norminton@aol.com

*Civil, Trial and Appellate.*

**THOMAS M. NORMINTON, (P.C.),** born Los Angeles, California, September 21, 1948; admitted to bar, 1973, California; 1981, U.S. Supreme Court. *Education:* University of California at Los Angeles (A.B., magna cum laude, 1970); Boalt Hall School of Law, University of California (J.D., 1973). Phi Beta Kappa. Recipient, American Jurisprudence Award in Contract Law. Vice President, UCLA Alumni Association, 1974-1977. Trustee, UCLA Foundation, 1971-1980. *Member:* Beverly Hills and Los Angeles County Bar Associations; State Bar of California.

**DOUGLAS P. WIITA, (P.C.),** born Whittier, California, June 24, 1946; admitted to bar, 1977, California and U.S. District Court, Central, Southern, Eastern and Northern Districts of California. *Education:* University of New Mexico (B.A., 1968); McGeorge College of the Law, University of the Pacific (J.D., 1977). Member, Traynor Society. Editor-in-Chief, Pacific Law Journal, 1976-1977. Author: Comment, "California's New General Corporation Law: Directors' Liability to Corporations," 7 Pacific Law Journal 613, 1976; "Review of Selected 1976 California Legislation, Criminal Procedure," 7 Pacific Law Journal 376, 1976. *Member:* Los Angeles County and American Bar Associations; State Bar of California. [Capt., USMC, 1968-1974]

**KATHLEEN DORITY FUSTER, (P.C.).,** born New York, N.Y., August 18, 1960; admitted to bar, 1985, California. *Education:* Rutgers College (B.A., summa cum laude, 1982); University of Pennsylvania (J.D., cum laude, 1985). Phi Beta Kappa; Phi Sigma Iota; Order of the Coif. *Member:* Los Angeles County Bar Association; State Bar of California.

**A. RICK ATWOOD, JR.,** born Nashville, Tennessee, June 4, 1965; admitted to bar, 1991, California. *Education:* University of Tennessee (B.A., 1987); Katholieke Universiteit Leuven, Belgium (B.A., 1988); Vanderbilt University (J.D., 1991). *Member:* State Bar of California.

PROFESSIONAL BIOGRAPHIES                                   CALIFORNIA—BEVERLY HILLS

## BARRY NOVACK

SUITE 830, 8383 WILSHIRE BOULEVARD
**BEVERLY HILLS, CALIFORNIA 90211**
Telephone: 213-852-1030
Fax: 213-655-9655

*Personal Injury, Wrongful Death Matters, Tort Actions.*

**BARRY NOVACK,** born Brooklyn, New York, August 14, 1943; admitted to bar, 1973, California. *Education:* University of Southern California (B.S., magna cum laude, 1964; Ph.D., 1971); Princeton University (M.S., 1968); Loyola University of Los Angeles (J.D., cum laude, 1973). Phi Kappa Phi; Tau Beta Pi; Pi Tau Sigma; Sigma Xi. Member, St. Thomas More Law Honor Society. Member, Loyola University of Los Angeles Law Review, 1972-1973. Author: "Informed Consent and the Patient's Right to 'No'," 6 Loyola University of Los Angeles Law Review 384, 1973; Proceedings of the Second International Conference on Numerical Methods in Fluid Dynamics, Vol. 8; Lecture Notes in Physics, 395-400, Ed. by M. Holt (Springer-Verlag), 1971; "Investigation and Discovery in Products Liability Case," Los Angeles Trial Lawyers Association Las Vegas Seminar, October, 1985; "Motorcycle Rider Leg Protection: An Overview," California Trial Lawyers Association Lake Tahoe Seminar, March, 1985; Moderator: "Motorcycles on Trial: Taking on the Big Five," California Trial Lawyers Association Lake Tahoe Seminar, March, 1985. Fellow, National Aeronautics and Space Administration (Princeton). Legal Advisor, System Safety Society, 1979-1981. Coordinator, UCLA Extension, Tort Litigation for Legal Secretaries, Paralegals and Legal Assistants, 1986—. *Member:* Los Angeles County (Member, Superior Courts Committee, 1987—) and American Bar Associations; State Bar of California; Los Angeles Trial Lawyers Association (Member, Board of Governors, 1985-1992; Chairman, "Discovery '87," June, 1987, "Los Angeles Tort Law," June, 1988; Recipient, Presidential Award, 1987, 1988) California Trial Lawyers Association; The Association of Trial Lawyers of America; American Association for the Advancement of Science; American Society of Mechanical Engineers; American Institute of Aeronautics and Astronautics; System Safety Society.

REFERENCE: City National Bank, Beverly Hills, California.

## DEBRA A. OPRI

A PROFESSIONAL CORPORATION
8383 WILSHIRE BOULEVARD
SUITE 830
**BEVERLY HILLS, CALIFORNIA 90211**
Telephone: 213-658-6774
Facsimile: 213-658-5160

*Civil Litigation. Business and Commercial Law. Entertainment Law. Personal Injury Law.*

**DEBRA A. OPRI,** born Paterson, New Jersey, June 10, 1960; admitted to bar, 1989, California; 1991, New Jersey and District of Columbia. *Education:* New York University (B.F.A., 1982); Whittier College School of Law (J.D., 1987). Author: "Video Rentals and the First Sale Doctrine: The Deficiency of Proposed Legislation" Whittier School of Law Law Review, 1986. *Member:* State Bar of California; Los Angeles Trial Lawyers Association; California Trial Lawyers Association; The Association of Trial Lawyers of America.

## VICTOR E. PORTANOVA

A LAW CORPORATION
601 NORTH FOOTHILL ROAD
P.O. BOX 17419
**BEVERLY HILLS, CALIFORNIA 90209-3419**
Telephone: 310-273-5691
Fax: 310-285-0895
Email: vportano@counsel.com

*Taxation, Corporation, Pension and Estate Planning Law.*

**VICTOR E. PORTANOVA,** born Rye, New York, February 10, 1944; admitted to bar, 1972, New York and California. *Education:* Dartmouth College (A.B., 1969); Fordham University (J.D., 1971); New York University (LL.M., 1972). Author: "Using an IRA and Related Rollover Provisions," Prentice-Hall, 1975; "A Guide to Setting Up a Group Term Life Insurance Program," Prentice-Hall, 1976; "How to Live & Die with California

*(This Listing Continued)*

Probate," Gulf Publishing, Houston, 1990. Professional Lecturer, Golden Gate Univ., M.B.A. Tax Program, Los Angeles, Courses Given: Tax Research and Decision Making, 1989; Executive Compensation Planning, 1980; Estate Planning, 1980; Financial Planning, 1985. *Member:* State Bar of California (Member, Independent Inquiry and Review Panel, Program for Certifying Legal Specialists). (Certified Specialist, Taxation Law, California Board of Legal Specialization).

## HOWARD L. RASCH

9454 WILSHIRE BOULEVARD
PENTHOUSE SUITE
**BEVERLY HILLS, CALIFORNIA 90212-2937**
Telephone: 310-247-2298
Fax: 310-247-8214

*Family Law, Adoptions, Domestic Violence, Cohabitation Agreements, Pre-Nuptial Agreements, Child Custody, Spousal Support, International Family Law, General Civil Litigation and Business Litigation.*

**HOWARD L. RASCH,** born New York, N.Y., April 22, 1941; admitted to bar, 1971, California and U.S. Court of Appeals, Ninth Circuit. *Education:* University of California (A.B., 1963); Southwestern University School of Law (J.D., cum laude, 1970). *Member:* Los Angeles County and American Bar Associations; State Bar of California (Member, Family Law Section). **PRACTICE AREAS:** Family Law; Business Litigation; General Civil Litigation.

## REUBEN & NOVICOFF

(An Association including Timothy D. Reuben, Inc., A Professional Corporation)
9601 WILSHIRE BOULEVARD, SUITE 644
**BEVERLY HILLS, CALIFORNIA 90210-5270**
Telephone: 310-777-1990
Fax: 310-777-1989
Email: Attorney initials @rnlaw.com

*Business Litigation, including Real Estate, Entertainment, International Commercial Disputes, Intellectual Property, Securities, Complex Civil Matters, Bankruptcy, Insurance, Environmental.*

**TIMOTHY D. REUBEN,** born Chicago, Illinois, April 28, 1955; admitted to bar, 1980, California and Supreme Court of California; 1981, U.S. District Court, Northern, Southern and Eastern Districts of California and U.S. Court of Appeals, Ninth Circuit; 1984, U.S. Supreme Court. *Education:* Harvard University (B.A., magna cum laude, 1977; J.D., 1980). Author: "Use of the California Correction Statute in Defense of Media and Entertainment Clients: Pitfalls and Problems," Beverly Hills Bar Association Journal, Volume 19, No. 3, 1985; "All This About a Breach of Contract," Intellectual Property Newsletter, TIPS, ABA, Winter 1990; "Abend v. MCA: An Author's Copyright Dream," Intellectual Property Newsletter, TIPS, ABA, Spring 1991; "Binding Arbitration: A System Fraught with Injustice," ADR Newsletter Volume 6, Issue 11, October 1996. Member, Pro Tem Judge Panel in West Los Angeles Small Claims Court. *Member:* Beverly Hills, Century City, Los Angeles County (Member, Litigation Section; Judicial Evaluation Committee) and American (Past Chair, Intellectual Property Committee, Section of Tort and Insurance Practice, 1990-1991) Bar Associations; The State Bar of California (Member, Sections on Litigation and Intellectual Property); Los Angeles Copyright Society; Los Angeles Complex Litigation Inn of Court. **PRACTICE AREAS:** Business; Real Estate; Entertainment Litigation; Intellectual Property; Unfair Competition; Employment; Antitrust; Trial and Appeals; Complex Matters. **Email:** tdr@rnlaw.com

**MICHAEL L. NOVICOFF,** born Whittier, California, August 23, 1960; admitted to bar, 1985, California, U.S. District Court, Central District of California and U.S. Court of Appeals, Ninth Circuit; 1986, U.S. District Court, Northern, Southern and Eastern Districts of California; 1988, U.S. Supreme Court; 1989, U.S. District Court, District of Arizona and U.S. Claims Court. *Education:* University of California at Los Angeles (B.A., cum laude, 1982); Harvard University (J.D., cum laude, 1985). Author: "Blocking and Clawing Back in the Name of Public Policy: The United Kingdom's Protection of Private Economic Interests Against Adverse Foreign Adjudications," 7 NW. J. Int'l. Law and Bus, 12, 1985; "Recent Developments in International Entertainment Law: The Application of American Law Abroad," 17 Whittier L. Rev. 191, 1995. Judge Pro Tempore, Los Angeles County Municipal Court, 1993—. Adjunct Professor of Law, Whittier

*(This Listing Continued)*

## REUBEN & NOVICOFF, Beverly Hills—Continued

College School of Law, 1994—. *Member:* Beverly Hills, Los Angeles County and American Bar Associations; State Bar of California. *PRACTICE AREAS:* Business; Real Estate; Entertainment Litigation; International Commercial Disputes; Intellectual Property; Unfair Competition; Employment; Securities; Antitrust; Construction; Trial and Appeals; Complex Matters. *Email:* mln@rnlaw.com

**STEPHEN L. RAUCHER,** born Los Angeles, California, November 4, 1967; admitted to bar, 1992, California, U.S. District Court, Central, Northern, Southern and Eastern Districts of California and U.S. Court of Appeals, Ninth Circuit. *Education:* University of California, Los Angeles (B.A., summa cum laude, 1989); Boalt Hall School of Law, University of California (J.D., 1992). Phi Beta Kappa. Author: "Raising The Stakes For Environmental Polluters: The Exxon Valdez Criminal Prosecution," 19 Ecology L.Q. 147, 1992. Environmental Certificate. Member, Board of Governors, Beverly Hills Bar Association, Barristers. *Member:* Beverly Hills and Los Angeles County Bar Associations; State Bar of California. *PRACTICE AREAS:* Commercial Litigation; Environmental Litigation; Entertainment Litigation. *Email:* slr@rnlaw.com

**RANLYN TILLEY HILL,** born Los Angeles, California, March 28, 1965; admitted to bar, 1991, California. *Education:* University of California at Los Angeles (B.A., History, 1987); Loyola University of Los Angeles (J.D., 1991). Member, Trial Advocacy Team, 1990-1991. Finalist, Byrne Trial Advocacy Competition, 1990. *Member:* Beverly Hills and Los Angeles Bar Associations; State Bar of California. *PRACTICE AREAS:* Employment; Construction; Administrative Law; Non Profit Entities; Intellectual Property Litigation. *Email:* rth@rnlaw.com

**DAVID Z. RIBAKOFF,** born Los Angeles, California, January 26, 1966; admitted to bar, 1992, California and U.S. District Court, Central, Southern and Northern Districts of California. *Education:* California State University, Northridge (B.A., magna cum laude, 1988); Hastings College of the Law, University of California (J.D., 1992). Member, Moot Court Board. Contributing Author: Chapter 8, "Multiple Insurers," *California Practice Guide:* Insurance Litigation, (Rutter Group, 1995). *Member:* State Bar of California; American Bar Association (Member, Tort and Insurance Practice Section). *LANGUAGES:* Hebrew. *PRACTICE AREAS:* Employment; Insurance; Entertainment Litigation; Intellectual Property. *Email:* dzr@rnlaw.com

**TRAVIS PAUL PIERSON,** born Los Angeles, California, October 16, 1969; admitted to bar, 1995, California, U.S. District Court, Central District of California and U.S. Court of Appeals, Ninth Circuit. *Education:* Williams College (B.A., with honors, cum laude, 1991); University of California at Los Angeles (J.D., 1995). Recipient, American Jurisprudence Award in Professional Responsibility. *Member:* Beverly Hills (Member, Entertainment Law Section Executive Committee) and Los Angeles County Bar Associations; State Bar of California. *PRACTICE AREAS:* Entertainment Law; Employment Law; Civil Litigation. *Email:* tpp@rnlaw.com

---

## RICHMAN, LAWRENCE, MANN, GREENE, CHIZEVER, FRIEDMAN & PHILLIPS

*A PROFESSIONAL CORPORATION*

PENTHOUSE
9601 WILSHIRE BOULEVARD
**BEVERLY HILLS, CALIFORNIA 90210-5270**
Telephone: 310-274-8300
Telecopier: 310-274-2831

*Marin County Office:* Suite 250, 300 Drakes Landing Road, Greenbrae, California 94904. Telephone: 415-925-0700. Telecopier: 415-925-1293.

*Transactional Business, Securities, Labor, Entertainment, Real Estate and Environmental Law. Litigation in all Courts.*

*FIRM PROFILE: Founded in 1971, Richman, Lawrence, Mann, Greene, Chizever, Friedman & Phillips is a full service business law, entertainment and civil litigation firm serving local, national and international clients. Its lawyers are specialists in commercial and corporate matters, securities regulations, real estate, estate planning, taxation, entertainment, labor and employment matters and all types of civil litigation. The firm prides itself on its ability to provide high quality, personalized service to its clients.*

(This Listing Continued)

**FREDRIC N. RICHMAN,** born Chicago, Illinois, February 17, 1937; admitted to bar, 1960, Illinois and U.S. District Court, Northern District of Illinois; 1963, U.S. Court of Appeals, Seventh Circuit; 1964, U.S. Court of Appeals, Ninth Circuit; 1971, California and U.S. District Court, Central District of California. *Education:* University of Illinois (B.A., 1957); De Paul University (LL.B., 1960). Associate Editor, DePaul Law Review, 1958-1960. Labor Arbitrator: Los Angeles County, 1975-1980; City Public Employee Relations Board, 1975-1980. Member, Los Angeles County Employee Relations Boards, 1980-1983. Member, Arbitration Panels, American Arbitration Association and Federal Mediation and Conciliation Service. *Member:* Beverly Hills (Chairman, Labor Law Section, 1976-1978), Los Angeles, Chicago, Illinois State and American (Member, Section on Labor Relations Law) Bar Associations; State Bar of California.

**JOHN A. LAWRENCE,** born West Covina, California, June 12, 1951; admitted to bar, 1976, California; 1977, U.S. District Court, Central District of California; 1978, U.S. District Court, Eastern District of California and U.S. Court of Appeals, Ninth Circuit; 1980, U.S. District Court, Southern District of California, U.S. Claims Court and U.S. Supreme Court; 1982, U.S. Court of Appeals, Federal Circuit; 1990, U.S. District Court, Northern District of California; 1992, U.S. Court of Appeals, Seventh Circuit. *Education:* Occidental College (B.A., cum laude, 1973); University of California at Los Angeles (J.D., 1976). Co-Author: "Using Arbitration to Handle Discrimination Grievances," Personnel Journal, November, 1978. Author: "Issues Facing Employers on Sale or Transfer of a Business," Town Hall Reporter, December, 1985. Member, Board of Trustees, The Buckley School, Sherman Oaks, California, 1986—. *Member:* Los Angeles County Bar Association; State Bar of California. *PRACTICE AREAS:* Labor Law; Litigation.

**RICHARD L. MANN,** born Chicago, Illinois, September 7, 1944; admitted to bar, 1975, California; 1976, U.S. District Court, Central District of California; 1980, U.S. District Court, Northern District of California and U.S. Court of Appeals, Ninth Circuit. *Education:* Stanford University (B.A., 1966); Loyola University of Los Angeles (J.D., cum laude, 1975). Member, Loyola University Law Review, 1973-1975. *Member:* Los Angeles County Bar Association; State Bar of California. *PRACTICE AREAS:* Labor Relations Law; Employment Law.

**BRUCE R. GREENE,** born New York, N.Y., February 22, 1952; admitted to bar, 1976, California and U.S. District Court, Central District of California; 1980, U.S. Supreme Court. *Education:* University of Pennsylvania, Wharton School of Finance and Commerce (B.S., magna cum laude, 1973); University of California at Los Angeles (J.D., 1976). Beta Gamma Sigma. *Member:* Beverly Hills, Santa Monica, Los Angeles County and American Bar Associations; State Bar of California.

**GERALD M. CHIZEVER,** born Brooklyn, New York, November 19, 1943; admitted to bar, 1968, California and U.S. Court of Appeals, Ninth Circuit; 1970, U.S. Supreme Court. *Education:* George Washington University (B.B.A., 1964; J.D., 1967). *Member:* Beverly Hills, Los Angeles County and American Bar Associations; State Bar of California. *PRACTICE AREAS:* Corporate Law; Business Law; Partnership Law.

**BARRY A. FRIEDMAN,** born Chicago, Illinois, August 2, 1941; admitted to bar, 1966, Illinois; 1969, California. *Education:* University of Illinois (B.S., cum laude, 1963); Northwestern University (J.D., 1966). Member, Board of Editors, Northwestern University Law Review, 1965-1966. Beta Gamma Sigma; Phi Kappa Phi. Certified Public Accountant, Illinois, 1963. Attorney, Atomic Energy Commission, 1966-1968. *Member:* Beverly Hills, Los Angeles County, Illinois State and American Bar Associations; State Bar of California. *PRACTICE AREAS:* Business Planning; Securities Law; Real Estate Law; Entertainment Law.

**JERRY S. PHILLIPS,** born Los Angeles, California, May 15, 1940; admitted to bar, 1966, California; 1967, U.S. District Court, Northern District of California; 1971, U.S. District Court, Central District of California; 1975, U.S. Court of Appeals, Ninth Circuit; 1969, U.S. Tax Court; 1975, U.S. Customs Court; 1984, U.S. Court of International Trade. *Education:* University of California at Los Angeles (B.A., 1962; J.D., 1965). *Member:* Los Angeles County Bar Association; State Bar of California. *PRACTICE AREAS:* Business; Commercial; Probate; Real Estate; Securities; Insurance; Personal Injury Litigation.

**ALLAN B. DUBOFF,** born Los Angeles, California, November 10, 1958; admitted to bar, 1984, California. *Education:* University of California at Los Angeles (B.A., magna cum laude, 1980); Wharton School, University of Pennsylvania (M.B.A., 1984); University of Pennsylvania (J.D., cum laude, 1984). Pi Gamma Mu; Phi Delta Phi. Member, University of Pennsylvania, Law Review, 1981-1983. Teaching Assistant, Accounting Department, Wharton School, University of Pennsylvania, 1981-1984. Co-Author:

(This Listing Continued)

"Merging California Limited Partnerships," California Business Law Reporter, Vol. X, No. 3, 1988. Consultant, Drafting Agreements for the Sale of Business, Second Ed., Continuing Education of the Bar, 1988. *Member:* Los Angeles County (Member, Business Law Section) and American (Member: Business Law Section; Ad Hoc Committee on Bulk Transfers; Partnership and Unincorporated Business Organizations Committee) Bar Associations; State Bar of California (Member, Business Law Section).

**PAUL M. ENRIQUEZ,** born Los Angeles, California, October 17, 1947; admitted to bar, 1973, California; 1974, U.S. District Court, Central and Southern Districts of California. *Education:* University of Southern California (B.S., cum laude, 1969); University of California at Los Angeles (J.D., 1972). *Member:* Westwood (Board of Governors and Secretary/Treasurer, 1992) and American Bar Associations; State Bar of California. *PRACTICE AREAS:* Real Estate Law; Business Planning; Securities Law; Environmental and Land Use Law.

**CYNTHIA E. FRUCHTMAN,** born Chicago, Illinois, August 16, 1958; admitted to bar, 1986, California. *Education:* Northwestern University (B.A., 1979); IIT Chicago-Kent College of Law (J.D., 1986). Guest Lecturer, University of California at Los Angeles Law School, 1987-1990. Clerk: Honorable N. Fred Woods, Superior Court for the County of Los Angeles, Central District of California; Honorable Prentice H. Marshall, U.S. District Court, Northern District of Illinois, 1985. *Member:* Los Angeles County (Member, Bioethics Committee) and American Bar Associations; State Bar of California; Women Lawyers Association of Los Angeles.

**MADGE S. BELETSKY**

**WILLIAM JOSEPH BRIGGS, II**

**BRIAN M. COLLIGAN**

**CRAIG D. HARDWICK**

**KYLE P. KELLEY**

**HOWARD J. KERN**

**JENS B. KOEPKE**

**BARBARA S. LEMERMAN**

OF COUNSEL

**RONALD D. GARBER**

**RAYMOND S. KAPLAN** (Also practicing individually at Los Angeles, California).

**GARY P. KOHN** (Also practicing individually at same address).

**DAVID H. MENDELSOHN, LTD.** (Not admitted in California).

**RICHARD B. SKOLNICK** (Also practicing individually at same address) (Certified Specialist, Taxation Law, The State Bar of California Board of Legal Specialization).

MARIN COUNTY OFFICE

**KENNETH C. GREENE**

## RONDEAU & HOMAMPOUR
A PROFESSIONAL LAW CORPORATION
8383 WILSHIRE BOULEVARD, SUITE 830
BEVERLY HILLS, CALIFORNIA 90211-2407
Telephone: 213-658-8077
Fax: 213-658-8477

*Federal and State Litigation, Taxation, Bankruptcy, Entertainment Law.*

**CHARLES R. RONDEAU,** born New Orleans, Louisiana, October 14, 1966; admitted to bar, 1993, California, New York, New Jersey, U.S. Court of Appeals, Third Circuit, U.S. District Court, Southern and Eastern Districts of New York and U.S. District Court, District of New Jersey; 1994, U.S. Tax Court; 1995, U.S, District Court, Central and Eastern Districts of California. *Education:* Columbia College (A.B., 1988); Southwestern University School of Law (J.D., 1992); University of the Pacific, McGeorge School of Law (Degree in Advanced International Legal Studies, 1993). Research Editor, Southwestern University Law Journal. Visiting Jurist, Cabinet Berlioz et Compagnie, Paris, 1992. Story Consultant, Grant Vision Productions. *Member:* Beverly Hills and Los Angeles County Bar Associations. *LANGUAGES:* French, German and Russian.

**ARASH HOMAMPOUR,** born Chicago, Illinois, December 8, 1967; admitted to bar, 1993, California and U.S. District Court, Central and Eastern Districts of California. *Education:* University of Southern California (B.S., 1989); Southwestern University School of Law (J.D., 1992). Recipient, American Jurisprudence Award in Criminal Law. Member, Beverly Hills Chamber of Commerce. *Member:* Beverly Hills and Los Angeles Bar Associations.

**HEDIEH MISKINYAR,** born Evanston, Illinois, December 13, 1969; admitted to bar, 1995, California. *Education:* University of California (B.A., 1991); University of Southern California (J.D., 1995). *Member:* California State Bar. *LANGUAGES:* Farsi.

## ROSENFELD, MEYER & SUSMAN, LLP
Established in 1957
FOURTH FLOOR, FIRST INTERSTATE BANK BUILDING
9601 WILSHIRE BOULEVARD
BEVERLY HILLS, CALIFORNIA 90210-5288
Telephone: 310-858-7700
Telecopier: 310-271-6430

*General Civil, Trial and Appellate Practice in all State and Federal Courts. Banking and Savings and Loan Law, Copyright, Corporate, Employee Benefits, Entertainment (Motion Picture, Television and Music) Transactions, Errors and Omission Clearance, Estate Planning, Family Law, Insurance Coverage and Defense Litigation, International Business Law, Labor and Employment Law, Motion Picture Financing, New Media Technologies, Real Estate, Real Property, Securities, Succession Planning, Taxation (Federal, State and International), Trademark, Trusts and Probate, Unfair Competition, Intellectual Property and Media Finance.*

*FIRM PROFILE: The firm was founded in 1957 to represent clients in the entertainment industry and that practice is still significant. Over the years we have grown into a full service firm and our firm's areas of expertise are centered around the following major departments: Litigation, Business/Corporate, Entertainment, Insurance Coverage and Defense, Labor and Employment Law, Estate Planning, Trusts and Probate, Taxation, Family Law and Employee Benefits Law. We also have groups specializing in Interactive Multimedia, Intellectual Property, Media Finance and Trademark, Merchandising and Licensing.*

MEMBERS OF FIRM

**DONALD T. ROSENFELD** (1917-1986).

**MARVIN B. MEYER,** born New York, N.Y., May 19, 1924; admitted to bar, 1949, California. *Education:* University of Southern California and Pomona College; Harvard Law School (J.D., cum laude, 1948). Adjunct Professor, University of Southern California, Peter Stark Graduate Film School. *Member:* Beverly Hills and American Bar Associations; The State Bar of California. *PRACTICE AREAS:* Entertainment Law. *Email:* mmeyer@rmslaw.com

**ALLEN E. SUSMAN,** born Chelsea, Massachusetts, February 12, 1919; admitted to bar, 1947, California. *Education:* Harvard University (A.B., 1940; J.D., 1946). Adjunct Professor of Law, Southwestern University, 1947-1951. *Member:* Beverly Hills, Los Angeles County and American Bar Associations; The State Bar of California. Fellow, American Bar Foundation. *PRACTICE AREAS:* Litigation; Antitrust Law; Entertainment Law. *Email:* asusman@rmslaw.com

**JEFFREY L. NAGIN,** born Los Angeles, California, February 12, 1933; admitted to bar, 1960, California. *Education:* University of California at Los Angeles (B.A., 1954); Harvard University (LL.B., 1959). Phi Beta Kappa. Member, Board of Editors, Harvard Law Review, 1957-1959. Law Clerk to Mr. Justice William J. Brennan, Jr., U.S. Supreme Court, 1959-1960. Lecturer: in Constitutional Law, University of California at Los Angeles, 1963-1966; "Litigation Copyright & Unfair Competition Cases," Practicing Law Institute, 1983-1990. *Member:* Beverly Hills, Los Angeles County and American Bar Associations; The State Bar of California; Los Angeles Copyright Society (President, 1980-1981). *PRACTICE AREAS:* Real Estate Law; General Business Law; Copyright Law. *Email:* jnagin@rmslaw.com

**LAWRENCE S. KARTIGANER,** born New York, N.Y., April 8, 1934; admitted to bar, 1959, New York; 1964, California. *Education:* Harvard University (A.B., 1955); New York University (LL.B., 1958; LL.M., Taxation, 1959). Trial Attorney (Tax Court), Regional Counsel's Office, Internal Revenue Service, Los Angeles, 1960-1964. *Member:* Beverly Hills, Los Angeles County and American Bar Associations; The State Bar of California.

*(This Listing Continued)*

**ROSENFELD, MEYER & SUSMAN, LLP, Beverly Hills—**
*Continued*

**PRACTICE AREAS:** Entertainment Law; Music Law; Tax Law. **Email:** lkartiga@rmslaw.com

**DAVID D. WEXLER,** born Milwaukee, Wisconsin, July 27, 1939; admitted to bar, 1963, Wisconsin; 1966, California. *Education:* University of Wisconsin at Milwaukee (B.S., 1961); University of Wisconsin (LL.B., 1963). Order of the Coif; Tau Epsilon Rho. Member, Board of Editors, 1961-1962 and Note Editor, 1962-1963, Wisconsin Law Review. Law Clerk to Justice Thomas E. Fairchild, Wisconsin Supreme Court, 1963-1965. Chair, Board of Directors, AIDS Project Los Angeles, 1989-1992; Member, Board of Directors, 1992—; AIDS Action Council, Washington, D.C., AIDs Action Counsel, Washington, D.C., 1994—, Chair, 1996. Trustee, Midway Hospital, 1994—. *Member:* Beverly Hills, Los Angeles and American Bar Associations; The State Bar of California; State Bar of Wisconsin (Inactive). **PRACTICE AREAS:** Corporate Law; Securities Law; Health Law; General Business Law. **Email:** dwexler@rmslaw.com

**ROBERT H. THAU,** born New York, N.Y., March 8, 1939; admitted to bar, 1965, California. *Education:* University of California at Los Angeles (B.A., 1961); Harvard University (LL.B., 1964). Lecturer, "Bringing a Case to Trial," 1982 and "Preparing and Examining Witnesses," 1984, California Continuing Education of the Bar; "Protecting Confidential Information Protective Orders," LA Business Trial Lawyers Association. *Member:* Beverly Hills, Los Angeles County and American Bar Associations; The State Bar of California. **PRACTICE AREAS:** Commercial Law; Entertainment Litigation; Family Law. **Email:** rthau@rmslaw.com

**MEL ZIONTZ,** born Boston, Massachusetts, May 4, 1942; admitted to bar, 1968, California. *Education:* University of California at Berkeley and University of California at Los Angeles (A.B., 1964); University of California at Los Angeles (J.D., 1967). Order of the Coif. *Member:* Beverly Hills, Los Angeles County and American Bar Associations; The State Bar of California. **PRACTICE AREAS:** Business Law; Corporate Law; Mergers and Acquisitions Law; Securities Law; Corporate Financings. **Email:** mziontz@rmslaw.com

**STEVEN E. FAYNE,** born Brooklyn, New York, April 24, 1944; admitted to bar, 1971, California. *Education:* Rensselaer Polytechnic Institute and Kent State University (B.A., 1967); Columbia University (J.D., cum laude, 1970). Pi Sigma Alpha; Phi Alpha Theta. Member, Board of Editors, Columbia Law Review, 1969-1970. Lecturer: UCLA Film School, 1996. *Member:* Beverly Hills (Chairman, Entertainment Law Committee, 1983-1984) and Los Angeles County Bar Associations; The State Bar of California; Los Angeles Copyright Society (Member, Board of Trustees, 1982-1984). **PRACTICE AREAS:** Entertainment Law; Media Finance. **Email:** sfayne@rmslaw.com

**MAREN J. CHRISTENSEN,** born Santa Monica, California, December 22, 1943; admitted to bar, 1976, California. *Education:* University of California at Los Angeles (B.A., 1965); University of Southern California (J.D., 1976). Member, Southern California Law Review, 1974-1976. Member, Board of Trustees, Los Angeles Copyright Society, 1986-1995. President, Los Angeles Copyright Society, 1994-1995. Seminars: Copyright Litigation, USC School of Law; Fair Use Copyright, Intellectual Property Section of State bar of California; Idea Submission, USC Annual Entertainment Lawyers Seminar and LA County Bar Entertainment Section. Co-Author: "Whose Idea Is It Anyway? Written Submission Agreements Can Benefit Writers and Producers," *Los Angeles Lawyer* (April 1995). *Member:* Beverly Hills and Los Angeles County Bar Associations; The State Bar of California; Association of Business Trial Lawyers. **PRACTICE AREAS:** Intellectual Property and General Entertainment Litigation; Copyright Law; Trademark Law; General Entertainment Law. **Email:** mchriste@rmslaw.com

**DONALD E. KARL,** born Warren, Ohio, August 20, 1949; admitted to bar, 1976, California. *Education:* University of Michigan (B.S., 1971); Harvard University (M.P.P., 1976); Harvard University (J.D., cum laude, 1976). Tau Beta Pi. Author: "Multimedia Joint Ventures: The Business of Combining Art and Technology," *Los Angeles Lawyer* (April 1993); "Islands and the Delimitation of the Continental Shelf: A Framework for Analysis," 71 *American Journal of International Law* 642. Honor: Selected for inclusion in "Who's Who in High Technology," *Los Angeles Business Journal,* April 1996 and *New Media,* May 1996. Law Clerk to Hon. William J. Holloway, Jr., U.S. Court of Appeals, Tenth Circuit. *Member:* Beverly Hills, Los Angeles County and American Bar Associations; The State Bar of California; International Bar Association; American Society of International Law. **PRACTICE AREAS:** Corporate Law; Mergers and Acquisitions Law; New Media Technologies; International Law. **Email:** dkarl@rmslaw.com

**OVVIE MILLER,** born July 14, 1935; admitted to bar, 1962, California. *Education:* University of California at Los Angeles (B.A., 1956); Harvard University (J.D., 1961). Phi Beta Kappa; Pi Sigma Alpha. Author: "Appreciation in Value of A Husband's Business-Separate or Community Property?" 4 *Journal of the Beverly Hills Bar Association* No. 7, Sept. 1970; "The Return of Common Law Marriage to California," 8 *Journal of the Beverly Hills Bar Association* No. 2, March-April, 1974; "Valuing the Goodwill of a Professional Practice," 50 *California State Bar Journal,* No. 2, March-April, 1975; "Where Are We Now On Spousal Support?" 53 *California State Bar Journal,* No. 5, September-October, 1978; "The Offer of Proof: A Trial Lawyers Trial," 55 *California State Bar Journal,* No. 12, Dec. 1980; "The Doctrine of Alter Ego," 4 *Los Angeles Lawyer* No. 6, September, 1981; "Divorce In The Entertainment Industry - Some Special Problems," 5 *Comm/Ent Law Journal* No. l, Fall, 1982; Supplement, *California Marital Dissolution Practice,* Vol. l, January, 1983; "Recent Federal Non-Tax Laws Affecting Family Law Practice," *Family Law News and Review,* Vol. VI, No. 3, Spring, 1985; "Protecting Community Personal Property Before Getting Into Court," *Family Law News and Review,* No. 4, Fall, 1983; "Update, Custody and Visitation, Los Angeles Superior Court Family Law Symposium, 1987, 1989 and 1990; "The Name Game," 17 *Los Angeles Lawyer,* No. 11, February, 1995; "End Papers: Enforceable Spousal Support Termination Clauses," *Los Angeles Daily Journal,* Sept. 11, 1995; "California Divorce Reform After 25 Years," 28 *Journal of the Beverly Hills Bar Association,* No. 4, Fall 1994 (published Nov. 1995). Co-Author: "Practical Considerations in Entertainment Litigation," Tenth Annual Program on Legal Aspects of the Entertainment Industry, 1964; Supplement, *California Marital Dissolution Practice,* Vol. 1, September, 1984 and May, 1986; Changes in California Marital Dissolution Practice Under the Tax Reform Act of 1984; Special Supplement to 1 California Marital Dissolution Practice, California Marital Termination Settlements and Tax Aspects of Marital Dissolution; "Partnership Litigation," *Advising California Partnerships,* (2nd Edition) by California C.E.B., 1988; "Should I Make A Will?" How to Live-and Die with California Probate (3d Ed. 1992). Law Clerk to Judge William M. Byrne, U.S. District Court, Southern District of California, 1961-1962. Mediator, Los Angeles Superior Court (Family Law); Arbitrator, Los Angeles Superior Court. *Member:* Beverly Hills (Member, Board of Governors, 1970-1973; Chairman, Family Law Section, 1975-1976 and 1984-1985), Los Angeles County and American Bar Associations; The State Bar of California; American Academy of Matrimonial Lawyers. **PRACTICE AREAS:** Family Law; Divorce Law; Civil Trials; Child Custody; Pre-Nuptials. **Email:** omiller@rmslaw.com

**WILLIAM M. ROSS,** born Los Angeles, California, March 28, 1957; admitted to bar, 1981, California. *Education:* University of California at Berkeley (A.B., with great distinction, 1978); Harvard University (J.D., cum laude, 1981). Phi Beta Kappa. Author: "Who Can Wield The LLP Shield," *Daily Journal* (March 1996). *Member:* Los Angeles County and American Bar Associations; The State Bar of California. **PRACTICE AREAS:** Business Law; Securities Law; Mergers and Acquisitions. **Email:** wross@rmslaw.com

**KIRK M. HALLAM,** born Los Angeles, California, June 19, 1956; admitted to bar, 1982, California. *Education:* University of California at Los Angeles (B.A., summa cum laude, 1978); Harvard University (J.D., 1981). Phi Beta Kappa. Counsel to: Estate of Audrey Hepburn, Bella Godiva Music (Jimi Hendrix Publishing Company), Lisa Frank, Inc. *Member:* Beverly Hills and American Bar Associations; The State Bar of California. **PRACTICE AREAS:** Entertainment Law; Copyright and Trademark; Unfair Competition. **Email:** khallam@rmslaw.com

**JAMES L. SEAL,** born Dayton, Ohio, July 29, 1945; admitted to bar, 1971, California; 1974, U.S. Supreme Court. *Education:* University of Cincinnati (B.B.A., 1967); Harvard University (J.D., 1970). Phi Eta Sigma; Beta Gamma Sigma; Tau Kappa Alpha; Delta Sigma Rho. Member, Board of Directors, 1973-1976 and Vice President, 1974-1976, California Barristers Association. Judge Pro Tem, Los Angeles County Municipal Court, 1984-1986. Author: "Market Definition in Antitrust Litigation in the Sports and Entertainment Industries," 61 *Antitrust Law Journal* 737 (1993). *Member:* Los Angeles County (Member, Antitrust Section) and American (Member, Sections on: Antitrust; Litigation; Patent, Trademark & Copyright Law) Bar Associations; The State Bar of California. **PRACTICE AREAS:** General Business Litigation; Antitrust and Trade Regulation; Insurance Coverage and Defense Litigation. **Email:** jseal@rmslaw.com

**KATHRYN A. YOUNG,** born Inglewood, California, May 18, 1952; admitted to bar, 1980, California. *Education:* University of California at

*(This Listing Continued)*

Los Angeles (B.A., magna cum laude, 1977); Boalt Hall School of Law, University of California (J.D., 1980). Member and Production Manager, California Law Review, 1978-1980. Co-Author: "Political Association under the Burger Court: Fading Protection," 15 *U.C. Davis Law Review* 53, 1981. *Member:* Los Angeles County and American Bar Associations; The State Bar of California. **PRACTICE AREAS:** Business Litigation; Entertainment Litigation; Criminal Defense Litigation. **Email:** kyoung@rmslaw.com

**RONALD R. ROBINSON,** born Richland, Center, Wisconsin, September 16, 1942; admitted to bar, 1972, California; 1980, U.S. Supreme Court. *Education:* California State University at Los Angeles (B.A., 1968); Northwestern University (J.D., 1971). Chief of Branch Operations, Criminal Trials, Los Angeles City Attorney's Office, 1977-1980. Assistant City Attorney-In-Charge of Organized Crime Prosecutions and Sound Piracy Task Force, 1975-1977. Author: "A New Strategy for Cost-Effective Coverage Litigation Management," *Defense Research Institute,* 1993; "Single Carrier Settlements in Multi-Carrier Coverage Actions - How to Bar Further Claims," *Defense Research Institute,* 1992; "The Best of Intentions: Drafting the 1966 Occurrence and 1973 Pollution Exclusion Policy Language," *Environmental Claims Journal,* Vol. 4, No. 3, Spring 1992; "Underwriting Exposure Claims: The Drafting of Comprehensive General Liability Policies, 1939-1973," *Defense Research Institute,* 1991; "Drafting History: The Scope and Limits of Underwriting Intent Arguments," *Executive Enterprises,* 1991; "Good Faith-A Field Guide for Troops In the Trenches," *Defense Research Institute,* 1994; "Allocation of Coverage: The Drafting History, Evolution and Current State of the Law Concerning Multiple Policy Indemnity and Defense Obligations," *Defense Research Institute,* 1995. Co-Author: "Insurance Coverage for Environmental Claims Under the Comprehensive General Liability Policy," ALI-ABA, 1991. Chair, 1992-1993, Chair: Defense Research Institute's Insurance Law Committee, 1992-1993, Chair, Emeritus, 1993-1994. Editor-in-Chief, "Covered Events," Defense Research Institute Insurance Committee Newsletter, 1991-1992. Guest Lecturer: Northwestern University School of Law. Seminar Speaker: ALI-ABA; Defense Research Institute; Executive Enterprises; Practice Law Institute. *Member:* Los Angeles County and American Bar Associations; State Bar of California; Defense Research Institute. **PRACTICE AREAS:** Insurance Coverage Law; Environmental Law; Asbestos and Toxic Tort Claim Coverage Law; Litigation; Insurance Defense Litigation. **Email:** rrobinso@rmslaw.com

**MICHAEL A. ROBBINS,** born Philadelphia, Pennsylvania, 1952; admitted to bar, 1978, California. *Education:* San Diego State University (A.B., with highest honors, Phi Beta Kappa, 1975); University of California at Los Angeles (J.D., 1978). Member, Moot Court. Honor: Selected for mention in "Who's Who in Law," *L.A. Business Journal,* 1995. Author: "State Wrongful Termination Law: Are Unionized Employees Covered?" *Employee Relations Law Journal,* Summer 1986; "Restrictions on the Wrongful Discharge Mother Lode - Foley v. Interactive Data Corp.," *Civil Litigation Reporter,* Feb., 1989. Contributing Editor: The Developing Labor Law, Bureau of National Affairs, Second Edition, 1983; Third Edition, 1990; Contributing Author, Workers Compensation Abuse, 1993. Field Attorney, National Labor Relations Board, 1978-1979. Instructor: Loyola Marymount University, Center for Industrial Relations, 1987-1989. Speaker: "Elimination of Bias In the Legal Profession," California and LA Trial Lawyers Associations, Beverly Hills Barristers, Westwood Santa Barbara, South Bay, Orange County and Inglewood Bar Associations; "Prevention of Sexual Harassment" speaker for various clients; Employment Law Practice, Recent Developments Program presented for the Continuing Education of the Bar, 1992-1996. **LANGUAGES:** Spanish. **PRACTICE AREAS:** Labor Litigation and Labor and Employment Law. **Email:** mrobbins@rmslaw.com

**WILLIAM J. SKRZYNIARZ,** born Tachikawa, Japan, September 18, 1956; admitted to bar, 1986, California. *Education:* Harvard University (A.B., 1979); Stanford University (J.D., 1984). Law Clerk to Hon. Wm. Matthew Byrne, Jr., U.S. District Court, Central District of California, 1984-1985. *Member:* Beverly Hills and Los Angeles County Bar Associations; State Bar of California. **PRACTICE AREAS:** Entertainment Transactions; Motion Picture; New Media Technologies; Theme Parks, Special Effects, Television and Music. **Email:** bskye@@rmslaw.com

**TODD W. BONDER,** born Glen Cove, New York, December 28, 1958; admitted to bar, 1984, California. *Education:* The Wharton School of Finance and Commerce, University of Pennsylvania (B.S., cum laude, 1980); University of California at Los Angeles (J.D., 1984). Comments Editor, Federal Communications Law Journal, 1983-1984. Author: "A Better Marketplace Approach to Broadcast Regulation," *Federal Communications Law Journal,* Vol. 36, Part 1. *Member:* Beverly Hills, Los Angeles County and American Bar Associations; The State Bar of California; The Association of Trial Lawyers of America; Federal Communications Bar Association. **PRACTICE AREAS:** Entertainment Litigation; Intellectual Property Law; Constitutional Law Litigation; General Business Litigation; Construction Litigation; Real Property Litigation. **Email:** tbonder@rmslaw.com

**STACEY M. BYRNES,** born Pottstown, Pennsylvania, July 21, 1958; admitted to bar, 1985, California. *Education:* College of William & Mary (B.A., 1980); University of California, Berkeley (J.D., 1984). *Member:* The State Bar of California. **PRACTICE AREAS:** Entertainment Litigation. **Email:** sbyrnes@rmslaw.com

**DAVID C. ULICH,** born California, 1959; admitted to bar, 1984, California. *Education:* Haverford College (B.A., 1981); University of Heidelberg, Germany; University of California at Los Angeles (J.D., 1984); New York University (LL.M., Taxation, 1985). Member, UCLA Law Review, 1983-1984. Lecturer: Taxation of Corporations and Shareholders at U.S.C. Graduate Tax Program. *Member:* American Bar Association (Adjunct Member, Tax Section Subcommittee on Corporate Taxation; Member, Tax Section Subcommittee on Partnership Taxation). **LANGUAGES:** German and French. **PRACTICE AREAS:** Taxation Law; Corporate Law; Tax-Exempt Organizations; Charitable Trusts and Foundations; Amateur Sports Law. **Email:** dulich@rmslaw.com

**JEFFREY L. SHUMWAY,** born Whittier, California, August 20, 1957; admitted to bar, 1987, California; 1988, U.S. District Court, Central and Eastern Districts of California. *Education:* University of California at Irvine (B.A., 1980); University of Southern California (J.D., 1984). Phi Delta Phi. *Member:* Beverly Hills (Member, Entertainment Section) and Los Angeles County (Member, Intellectual Property Section) Bar Associations; State Bar of California. **PRACTICE AREAS:** Entertainment Law. **Email:** jshumway@rmslaw.com

**HARRIS J. KANE,** born Los Angeles, California, April 1, 1962; admitted to bar, 1986, California. *Education:* University of California at Los Angeles (B.A., magna cum laude, 1983; J.D., 1986). Phi Beta Kappa. *Member:* Beverly Hills and Los Angeles County Bar Associations; State Bar of California. **PRACTICE AREAS:** Entertainment Litigation; Business Litigation. **Email:** hkane@rmslaw.com

**DAVID F. GRABER,** born London, England, January 8, 1962; admitted to bar, 1987, California and U.S. District Court, Central and Southern Districts of California. *Education:* University of California at Los Angeles (B.A., magna cum laude, 1984); Harvard University (J.D., cum laude, 1987). Phi Beta Kappa. *Member:* Beverly Hills and Los Angeles County Bar Associations. **LANGUAGES:** French and German. **PRACTICE AREAS:** Entertainment Litigation; Business Litigation. **Email:** dgraber@rmslaw.com

**BURT LEVITCH,** born St. Louis, Missouri, December 22, 1953; admitted to bar, 1980, California, U.S. District Court, Central, Eastern, Northern and Southern Districts of California and U.S. Tax Court; 1984, U.S. Claims Court. *Education:* Harvard College (A.B., 1976); New York University School of Law (J.D., 1979). Speaker on Estate Planning Topics to various professional organizations and companies. Vice President and Chair, Schools Committee, Harvard-Radcliffe Club of Southern California, 1990-1993. Member, Schools and Scholarship Committee, Harvard Alumni Association, 1992—; Member, National Advisory Council, Harvard AIDs Institute, 1995—. *Member:* Beverly Hills and Los Angeles County Bar Associations; State Bar of California. **PRACTICE AREAS:** Trusts and Estates; Estate Administration; Estate Planning; Trust Administration; Charitable Trusts and Foundations. **Email:** blevitch@rmslaw.com

**GREG S. BERNSTEIN,** born Los Angeles, California, May 10, 1958; admitted to bar, 1982, California and U.S. District Court, Central District of California; 1983, U.S. Tax Court and U.S. Court of Appeals, Ninth Circuit. *Education:* University of California at Los Angeles (B.A., magna cum laude, 1979; J.D., 1982). Phi Beta Kappa; Pi Gamma Mu; Phi Eta Sigma. Recipient, American Jurisprudence Award in Debtor-Creditor Law, 1982. Author: "SEC Giving Syndicators a Break," *The Real Estate Syndicator,* December 1987; "Digest of Current Developments," *The Real Estate Syndicator,* August 1988; "Indies Must Look Beyond H'wood," *Daily Variety,* March, 1992; "American & Europe - A Partnership Made in Hollywood," *Business of Film,* May, 1994; "Producers Become Easy Mark," *Daily Variety,* February, 1994; "Content Wins Over Commerce," *Daily Variety,* February 1995; "Globalization of a Film's Production Leads to Financing," *Business of Film,* May 1995; "Pre-Selling Co-Productions---With a Twist," *Business of Film,* May 1996. Honor: Century City Chamber of Commerce, "Next Generation" Award, October 1995. Lecturer: UCLA: Independent Film Project Financing and Distribution; Motion Picture Distribution and Finance; Independent Motion Picture Financing Through Public/Private Syndication; Financing Feature Film Production; Independent Feature Film Distribu-

*(This Listing Continued)*

**ROSENFELD, MEYER & SUSMAN, LLP,** Beverly Hills—
*Continued*

tion and Finance; Tennessee Film Commission, August, 1994; Drafting Partnership Agreements in the 90's, Beverly Hills Bar Association, 1993; Motion Picture Distribution and Finance, Puerto Rico Film Commission, 1992; Motion Picture Investing - Challenges and Opportunities, The National Association of Investment Companies, 1992. Board Member, Century City Chamber of Commerce; Chairman, Entertainment Industries Committee of the Century City Chamber of Commerce. *Member:* Century City, Los Angeles County and American Bar Associations; State Bar of California. **PRACTICE AREAS:** Motion Picture Finance/Distribution Law; Entertainment Syndication Law; Business Acquisition Law; General Business Law. *Email:* gbernste@rmslaw.com

**MITCHELL D. KAMARCK,** born New York, 1960; admitted to bar, 1987, Massachusetts, U.S. Court of Appeals, First Circuit and U.S. District Court, District of Massachusetts; 1990, California; 1991, U.S. District Court, Central District of California. *Education:* Colgate University (B.A., 1982); Cornell University (J.D., magna cum laude, 1987). Phi Kappa Phi; Order of the Coif. Lecturer, Cornell School of Hotel Management, 1986-1987. Author, "The First Sale Doctrine and Evolving Technologies," *The Multimedia Law Report,* May 1996. *Member:* Beverly Hills, Los Angeles and Massachusetts Bar Associations; State Bar of California. **PRACTICE AREAS:** New Media Technologies; Copyright, Trademark and Trade Secrets Litigation; General Business Litigation; Products Liability Litigation. *Email:* mkamarck@rmslaw.com

**BRUCE TELLES,** born New Bedford, Massachusetts, October 30, 1954; admitted to bar, 1987, Massachusetts; 1988, U.S. District Court, Southern, Northern and Central Districts of California and Massachusetts and U.S. Court of Appeals, Ninth and First Circuits; 1991, California. *Education:* Boston University (B.A., 1981); Boston College (J.D., magna cum laude, 1987). Phi Beta Kappa. Editor, Boston College International and Comparative Law Review, 1986-1987. Author: "Von Dardel v. U.S.S.R: Overcoming the Defense of Foreign Sovereign Immunity in Cases Under the Alien Tort Claims Act," 10 *Boston College International and Comparative Law Review* 343, 1987. Author: "Full Investigation: Insurer's Discovery Rights Are Intact," *Daily Journal* (July 1995). Co-Author: "SAD Situation: When Does the Potential for Coverage Arise?" *Los Angeles Daily Journal* (March 1995). Author: "Full Investigation: Insurer's Discover Right Are Infact," *Los Angeles Daily Journal* (July 1995). Chairperson, Los Angeles Junior Chamber of Commerce LA/Watts Summer Games Music and Arts Competition, 1992—. *Member:* Los Angeles County and Beverly Hills Bar Associations; State Bar of California; Los Angeles County Barristers (Education Committee). **LANGUAGES:** Portuguese. **PRACTICE AREAS:** Civil Litigation; Insurance Coverage Law; Environmental Law; Intellectual Property. *Email:* btelles@rmslaw.com

**LISA MARIE JACOBSEN,** born Brooklyn, New York, December 12, 1962; admitted to bar, 1989, California. *Education:* University of California at Davis (B.A., with high honors, 1985); University of California at Los Angeles, (J.D., 1989). Phi Beta Kappa; Distinguished Advocate, 1988 UCLA Moot Court Competition. *Member:* Beverly Hills and American Bar Associations. **PRACTICE AREAS:** Labor Litigation; Labor, Employment Law and Litigation. *Email:* ljacobse@rmslaw.com

**PETER SPELMAN,** born New York, N.Y., August 29, 1946; admitted to bar, 1987, California; 1988, U.S. District Court, Central District of California. *Education:* University of Wisconsin; Loyola Law School, Los Angeles (J.D., cum laude, 1987). Member, St. Thomas More Law Honor Society. Recipient, American Jurisprudence Awards for Excellent Achievement in the Study of Constitutional Law and Labor Law. Completed Family Mediation Institute of American Bar Association. Former Member, American Federation of Musicians. *Member:* Los Angeles County Bar Association (Member, Family Law Section); State Bar of California. **PRACTICE AREAS:** Family Law: Litigation and Mediation of Family Law Disputes; Civil Litigation. *Email:* pspelman@rmslaw.com

**PAUL S. WHITE,** born Salt Lake City, Utah, July 11, 1962; admitted to bar, 1990, California; 1991, U.S. District Court, Central, Northern and Southern Districts of California. *Education:* Brigham Young University (B.A., 1985); University of Utah (J.D., 1989). Phi Delta Phi; American Inns of Court Foundation; National Moot Court Team. Judicial Extern-Honorable David Sam, U.S. District Court, District of Utah, 1989. Honorary Member, Board of Trustees, University of Utah College of Law, 1988-1989. President, University of Utah Student Bar Association, 1988-1989. Seminars: "Construction Defect Coverage," *Defense Research Institute,* Insurance Coverage and Practice Symposium, June 1996; "Hottest Issues In Environmental Insurance Coverage: Latest Developments in Pollution Exclusion Decisions," *Executive Enterprises,* May 1995; "Environmental Awareness and Property Ownership: Do the Skeletons In Your Closet Glow?" *Southern California Chapter of the Appraisal Institute,* November 1994. Author: "Recent Developments in Pollution Exclusion Decisions," *Environmental Claims Journal* (Fall 1995). Co-Author: "Good Faith-A Field Guide for Troops In The Trenches," Defense Research Institute (1994). *Member:* Beverly Hills, Los Angeles County and American Bar Associations; State Bar of California; Defense Research Institute (Publications Board, 1993-1995); Los Angeles County Barristers (Education Committee, 1991-1992). **PRACTICE AREAS:** Insurance Coverage Law; Insurance Defense Law; Civil Litigation; Environmental Law; Intellectual Property Law. *Email:* pwhite@rmslaw.com

*ASSOCIATES*

**SCOTT I. BARER,** born Los Angeles, California, June 12, 1957; admitted to bar, 1990, California, U.S. Court of Appeals, Ninth Circuit, U.S. District Court, Central, Southern, Eastern and Northern Districts of California; 1992, District of Columbia. *Education:* University of California at Los Angeles (B.A., 1979); Loyola Marymount University (J.D., 1989). *Member:* San Fernando Valley, Los Angeles (Member, Labor Law Section) and American (Member, Section on Labor and Employment Law) Bar Associations; State Bar of California (Member, Section on Labor and Employment Law); District of Columbia Bar. **PRACTICE AREAS:** Labor and Employment Law; Labor Litigation. *Email:* sbarer@rmslaw.com

**RAY TAMADDON,** born August 26, 1963; admitted to bar, 1989, California; 1990, U.S. Court of Appeals, Ninth Circuit and U.S. District Court, Central, Northern, Southern and Eastern Districts of California. *Education:* Bowdoin College (A.B., 1986); University of Michigan; Boston University (J.D., 1989). Recipient, American Jurisprudence Award. Co-Author, "SAD Situation: When Does the Potential For Coverage Arise?" *Los Angeles Daily Journal* (March 1955). *Member:* Beverly Hills, Los Angeles County and American Bar Associations; State Bar of California. **LANGUAGES:** Farsi. **PRACTICE AREAS:** Insurance Law; General Business; Appellate Practice; Environmental Law. *Email:* rtamaddo@rmslaw.com

**SUSAN E. HOLLEY,** born Pasadena, California, August 7, 1961; admitted to bar, 1991, California. *Education:* University of California, Los Angeles (B.A., summa cum laude, 1988); Stanford University (J.D., 1991). Phi Beta Kappa. Author: "Alternatives to Legal Interventions: Educational Reforms for Social Change," *Stanford Journal of Gender and the Law,* 1992; "Global Warming: Construction and Enforcement of an International Accord," *Stanford Environmental Law Journal,* 1992; "Smoke Screen: The Statewide Workplace Smoking Standards," *Daily Journal,* (June 1995). *Member:* State Bar of California; Screen Actors Guild. **PRACTICE AREAS:** Labor and Employment Law; Labor Litigation; Trade Secrets; Trademark; Copyright Litigation. *Email:* sholley@rmslaw.com

**RENEE A. GALKA,** born Evanston, Illinois, March 2, 1968; admitted to bar, 1992, California; 1994, Colorado. *Education:* Princeton University (A.B., 1989); University of California at Los Angeles (J.D., 1992). **PRACTICE AREAS:** Entertainment; Entertainment Industry Transactions; Film Productions; Television Productions; Motion Picture Law. *Email:* rgalka@rmslaw.com

**STACY J. BARANCIK,** born Santa Monica, California, September 10, 1967; admitted to bar, 1992, California. *Education:* University of California at Berkeley (B.A., 1989); University of California at Los Angeles (J.D., 1992). Phi Beta Kappa; Phi Alpha Delta. Recipient, Golden Key Honor Society, Scholastic Achievement Award. *Member:* Beverly Hills, Los Angeles County and American Bar Associations; State Bar of California. **PRACTICE AREAS:** Transactional Entertainment; Film and Television Production. *Email:* sbaranci@rmslaw.com

**D. THOMAS TRIGGS,** born Whittier, California, June 16, 1967; admitted to bar, 1993, California. *Education:* Pepperdine University (B.A., 1989; J.D., cum laude, 1993); Cambridge University, England. Phi Delta Phi. Editor, Pepperdine Law Review. Instructor, Legal Writing, Pepperdine University, 1991-1993. Author: "Lechmere Decision Reshapes Union Access to Company Property For Purposes of Organization," 27 Beverly Hills Bar Journal 10 (Winter, 1993); Note, Term Limits: "Legislature v. Eu," 20 Pepperdine Law Review 353 (1992); "California Supreme Court Survey," 20 Pepperdine Law Review 270 (1992). Law Clerk Armand Arabian, California Supreme Court, 1992-1993. Contributor, "California Real Estate Law and Practice," Matthew Bender (1993). **LANGUAGES:** Spanish. **PRACTICE AREAS:** Corporate; Securities; Intellectual Property; Entertainment. *Email:* ttriggs@rmslaw.com

*(This Listing Continued)*

**BRIAN H. MCPHERSON,** born Upland, California, December 15, 1964; admitted to bar, 1992, California. *Education:* Claremont McKenna College (B.A., Government, 1987); Loyola Law School (J.D., 1991). *Member:* Los Angeles and Beverly Hills Bar Associations. **PRACTICE AREAS:** Music; Film; Multimedia. *Email:* bmcphers@rmslaw.com

**SUZANNE H. KESSLER,** born Baltimore, Maryland, March 19, 1964; admitted to bar, 1994, California. *Education:* Brown University (A.B. with honors, magna cum laude, awarded Harvey A. Baker Fellowship for graduate study, 1986); Stanford University (M.A. in Communication and Film, awarded Frank Burt Fellowship for script writing, 1989; J.D., 1994). Phi Beta Kappa; First-Place, ASCAP Nathan Burkan Memorial Competition in copyright law, Stanford Law School; Hilmer Oehlmann, Jr. Award for legal research and writing; Editor-in-Chief, *Stanford Environmental Law Journal;* Chair, Entertainment Law Society. *Member:* Los Angeles County and Beverly Hills Bar Associations. **PRACTICE AREAS:** Entertainment; Intellectual Property. *Email:* skessler@rmslaw.com

**DARREN M. TRATTNER,** born Los Angeles, California, November 18, 1968; admitted to bar, 1994, California. *Education:* University of California at Berkeley (B.A., with highest distinction, 1990); Hertford College, Oxford University, England (1990-1991); Boalt Hall School of Law, University of California (J.D., 1994). Phi Beta Kappa, History Honor's Society, Moot Court Board Member; Certificate of Merit for Outstanding Academic Achievement, 1988, 1989; Moot Court Commendation for oral and written excellence. *Member:* Los Angeles County and Beverly Hills Bar Associations; Entertainment Law Society; Golden Key Honor Society. **LANGUAGES:** French. *Email:* trattner@rmslaw.com

**ORRIN M. FELDMAN,** born New York, N.Y., July 27, 1954; admitted to bar, 1979, New York; 1981, District of Columbia; 1990, California. *Education:* New York University (A.B. 1975; M.P.A., 1975; J.D., 1978); Georgetown Law School (Master in Taxation, 1984). **PRACTICE AREAS:** Employee Benefits; Taxation; Pension. *Email:* ofeldman@rmslaw.com

**MOLLY C. HANSEN,** born San Diego, California, November 14, 1959; admitted to bar, 1990, California, U.S. District Court, Central District of California and U.S. Court of Appeals, Ninth Circuit. *Education:* California State University at Los Angeles (B.A., cum laude, 1986); University of Southern California (J.D., 1990). Executive Editor, Major Tax Planning, 1989-1990 and Executive Editor, 1989-1990, Computer Law Journal. Recipient, Norma Zarky Memorial Award for Academic Excellence in Entertainment Law. **PRACTICE AREAS:** Estate Planning; Trust and Probate Administration; Charitable Organizations. *Email:* mhansen@rmslaw.com

**TRAVIS MANN,** born New Orleans, Louisiana, November 11, 1967; admitted to bar, 1993, California. *Education:* Southern Methodist University (B.B.A., magna cum laude, 1990); University of California at Los Angeles (J.D., 1993). Beta Gamma Sigma. Editor, UCLA Law Review. Co-Author, "Fraud in the Health Care Industry," Matthew Bender, 1994. **PRACTICE AREAS:** Entertainment. *Email:* tmann@rmslaw.com

**LOIS R. FISHMAN,** born New York, N.Y., October 16, 1950; admitted to bar, 1994, California. *Education:* Swarthmore College; Yale University (B.A., magna cum laude, Psychology, 1972); Georgetown University (J.D., 1993). Phi Beta Kappa. Author: "Tips for Artists, Writers and Entertainment Applicants," *Trademark World,* November, 1992; "Multimedia Works," *Corporate Counsellor,* September, 1995; "Restoring Copyright in Public Domain Works," *Corporate Counsellor,* November 1995. Member, Women in Film, 1996. *Member:* Beverly Hills, Los Angeles County and American (Member, Forum on Entertainment and Sports Law, 1992—) Bar Associations; Women Lawyers Association of Los Angeles; Copyright Society of the United States. **LANGUAGES:** Spanish and French. **PRACTICE AREAS:** Copyright; Trademark; Litigation; Intellectual Property; Entertainment. *Email:* lfishman@rmslaw.com

**SAUL D. BRENNER,** born Los Angeles, California, October 13, 1962; admitted to bar, 1987, California. *Education:* University of California at Berkeley (B.A., 1983); Harvard University (J.D., 1987). Notes Editor, Harvard Law Review, 1986-1987. Assistant U.S. Attorney, U.S. Attorney's Office, Central District of California, Criminal Division, 1991-1996. *Member:* Beverly Hills, Los Angeles County and American Bar Associations; State Bar of California. **LANGUAGES:** Hebrew, Arabic and Spanish. **PRACTICE AREAS:** Intellectual Property; Entertainment Litigation; General Commercial Litigation; White Collar. *Email:* sbrenner@rmslaw.com

**JENNIFER L. CAMPBELL,** born Encino, California, September 9, 1962; admitted to bar, 1991, California. *Education:* Pasadena City College (A.A., 1983); Whittier College (B.A., 1985); University of California, Hastings College of the Law (J.D., cum laude, 1991). Order of the Coif. Member, Thurston Society. Recipient, American Jurisprudence Award in Legal Writing. Judicial Extern, Judge Stanley A. Weigel, U.S. District Court, Northern District of California, 1991. **PRACTICE AREAS:** Estate Planning and Administration. *Email:* jcampbel@rmslaw.com

**MARISSA J. ROMÁN,** born Washington, D.C., November 30, 1968; admitted to bar, 1993, California; 1994, District of Columbia. *Education:* Princeton University (A.B., 1990); Stanford University (J.D., 1993). Co-Author, 1995 Supplement to Chapter 18 ("Securities Activities of Thrifts") of M. Fien, *Securities Activities of Banks* (Aspen Law & Business, 1995). *Member:* Los Angeles County (Member, Business and Corporations Law Section, 1994—) and Beverly Hills Bar Associations. **PRACTICE AREAS:** Financial Institutions; Corporate; Securities; Real Estate; Media Finance. *Email:* mroman@rmslaw.com

**CAMERON JONES,** born Casper, Wyoming, June 13, 1967; admitted to bar, 1992, California. *Education:* Cornell University (A.B., Comparative Literature, summa cum laude, 1989) Phi Beta Kappa; Harvard University (J.D., cum laude, 1992). Member, National Moot Court Team. National Champion Impromptu Speaking, 1988-1990. Teaching Assistant, Federal Civil Litigation. Co-Author: "Do Ground Leases Solve the Problems of Partnership?" The ACREL Papers, Volume II: Real Estate Partnerships; Selected Problems and Solutions, The American Bar Association Press (1991). *Member:* State Bar of California. **PRACTICE AREAS:** Entertainment Law; New Media Technologies; Intellectual Property. *Email:* cjones@rmslaw.com

**NINA L. PAN,** born Taipei, Taiwan, March 27, 1969; admitted to bar, 1994, California and U.S. District Court, Central District of California. *Education:* University of California at Los Angeles (B.A., magna cum laude, 1991); George Washington University (J.D., 1994). Phi Beta Kappa. *Member:* State Bar of California; Los Angeles and Beverly Hills Bar Associations; Southern California Chinese Lawyers Association. **PRACTICE AREAS:** Labor and Employment; Litigation. *Email:* npan@rmslaw.com

**KEVIN S. FIUR,** born New York, N.Y., December 4, 1966; admitted to bar, 1991, Texas (Not admitted in California). *Education:* University of Texas (B.A., 1988; J.D., with honors, 1991). Order of the Coif. Member, Texas International Law Journal. Law Clerk to the Hon. James R. Nowlin, U.S. District Court, Western District of Texas, 1991-1992. *Member:* State Bar of Texas. **PRACTICE AREAS:** Litigation; Entertainment Litigation. *Email:* kfiur@rmslaw.com

*OF COUNSEL*

**MICHAEL ROSENFELD,** born Washington, D.C., March 15, 1942; admitted to bar, 1968, California. *Education:* University of California at Los Angeles (A.B., 1964; J.D., 1967). Order of the Coif. Senior Editor, University of California at Los Angeles Law Review, 1966-1967. Author: "The Fourth and Fifth Amendments—Dimensions of an Intimate Relationship," 13 University of California at Los Angeles Law Review 857, 1963. *Member:* Beverly Hills Bar Association; State Bar of California. **PRACTICE AREAS:** Entertainment Law. *Email:* mrosenfe@rmslaw.com

**JAMES M. A. MURPHY,** born Brooklyn, New York, October 9, 1945; admitted to bar, 1975, New York; 1977, U.S. Tax Court; 1978, California; U.S. Court of Appeals, Fifth and Ninth Circuits; U.S. District Court, Central District of California. *Education:* Harvard University (A.B., magna cum laude, 1968; J.D., 1973). *Member:* Beverly Hills, Los Angeles County, New York State and American Bar Associations; The State Bar of California. **PRACTICE AREAS:** Employee Benefits; Tax; Estate Planning. *Email:* jmurphy@rmslaw.com

**BERNARD A. GREENBERG,** born Los Angeles, California, January 15, 1931; admitted to bar, 1959, California; 1960, U.S. Tax Court; 1962, U.S. District Court, Central District of California. *Education:* University of California, Los Angeles (B.S., with highest honors, 1953; LL.B., 1958). Phi Beta Kappa; Beta Gamma Sigma; Order of the Coif. Member, 1956-1957 and Editor-in-Chief, 1957-1958, University of California, Los Angeles Law Review. Teaching Fellow, Harvard Law School, 1958-1959; Adjunct Professor of Law, University of California, Los Angeles, 1976-1980. Member, Advisory Board, UCLA-CEB Estate Planning Institute, 1978-1992. *Member:* Beverly Hills, Los Angeles County and American Bar Associations; State Bar of California; Los Angeles Music Center Opera Association (Chair); Los Angeles Music Center (Member, Board of Directors). **PRACTICE AREAS:** Estate Planning Law; Tax Planning; Business Aspects of Entertainment Law. *Email:* bgreenbe@rmslaw.com

**RONALD M. GREENBERG,** born Detroit, Michigan, August 21, 1939; admitted to bar, 1965, California and U.S. District Court, Central District of California; 1966, U.S. District Court, Southern District of California; 1971, U.S. Supreme Court; 1979, U.S. Claims Court. *Education:* University

*(This Listing Continued)*

## ROSENFELD, MEYER & SUSMAN, LLP, Beverly Hills—Continued

of Michigan (A.B., 1961); Stanford University (LL.B., 1964). Phi Delta Phi. Author: "Electronic Surveillance of Public Telephone Booths," 41 *Los Angeles Bar Bulletin* 490, September, 1966; "Secondary Activity and the Labor Antitrust Exception: An Historical Presentation," 47 *Antitrust Law Journal* 1301, Summer, 1979; "The Use of Arbitration by Companies Doing Business in Developing Countries to Resolve Multinational Employee Disputes," *The World Peace Through Law Center,* July, 1985; "The Los Angeles Center for International Commercial Arbitration - A New Alternative," *The World Peace Through Law Center,* September, 1987; "Proposal for World Jurist Association Model Arbitration," *The World Jurist Association,* October 1991; "ADR-Considerations for Use in International Commercial Dispute Resolution," *World Jurist Association,* October 1993; "ADR Disclosure Legislation in California-Impact on Confidentiality, Disqualification and Finality," *World Jurist Association,* August 1995. Supplement Author for 1976, 1977, 1979 and 1981 "California Civil Appellate Practice" and for 1977, 1978, 1979 and 1981 "California Civil Discovery Practice," CEB. Revision Editor, 1970-1978 for Organized Labor Portion of Supplement to "Antitrust Developments 1955-1968," the American Bar Association. Consulting Attorney for California Civil Appellate Practice 2nd Ed., CEB, 1985 and Author of Chapters on "Standing to Appeal," and "Costs, Attorney's Fees and Sanctions". Consulting Attorney for Bancroft-Whitney, "California Civil Practice" (1993). Law Clerk to the Honorable Jesse W. Curtis, U.S. District Court, Los Angeles, 1964-1965. Honor: World Jurist Association's World Lawyer Award, 1995. *Member:* Los Angeles County (Member, Federal Practice and Procedure Committee, 1969—), Federal and American (Member: Sections on Litigation and General Practice; Forum Committee on the Entertainment Industry) Bar Associations; American Judicature Society; Association of Business Trial Lawyers; World Association of Lawyers; World Jurist Association of the World Peace Through Law Center. (Also Litigation Counsel, Whittaker, Simi Valley, California). **PRACTICE AREAS:** Civil Litigation; Arbitration; Appellate Practice; Products Liability; Alternative Dispute. *Email:* rgreenbe@rmslaw.com

**P. JOHN BURKE,** born Toronto, Ontario, Canada, January 27, 1952; admitted to bar, 1978, California; 1979, U.S. Tax Court and U.S. District Court, Central District of California. *Education:* University of Southern California (B.A., 1973); Southwestern University (J.D., 1976); New York University (LL.M., Taxation, 1977). Recipient, Gerald Wallace Scholarship. *Member:* Beverly Hills (Member: Business Law, Entertainment Law and Real Estate Law Sections) and Los Angeles County (Member: Business and Corporations Law, Commercial Law and Bankruptcy, International Law, Intellectual Property and Entertainment and Real Property Law Sections) Bar Associations; State Bar of California (Member: Business, International, Intellectual Property and Real Property Law Sections). **PRACTICE AREAS:** Media Finance; Commercial Transactions; Real Estate Law; International Law. *Email:* jburke@rmslaw.com

**MARYBETH JACOBSEN,** born Evergreen Park, Illinois, May 19, 1955; admitted to bar, 1982, Illinois; 1990, California. *Education:* University of Illinois (B.A., magna cum laude with high distinction, 1977; J.D., 1982). Author: "Drafting Process Evidence: Trial Evidentiary Objections and Arguments," Defense Research Institute, 1990. Co-Author, Compendium of Bad Faith Law, 1992; *Compendium of Bad Faith Law Supplement* 1995; "Good Faith A Field Guide for Troops in the Trenches," Defense Research Institute, 1994. *Member:* Illinois State and American Bar Associations; State Bar of California. **LANGUAGES:** Spanish. **REPORTED CASES:** W.R. Grace and Co. vs. Continental Casualty Co. et. al., and Carey Canada, Inc. vs. California Union Insurance Co. et. al. **PRACTICE AREAS:** Insurance Coverage and Defense Law. *Email:* mjacobse@rmslaw.com

**JOSEPH M. GABRIEL,** born Toronto, Canada, April 12, 1960; admitted to bar, 1985, California; 1986, U.S. District Court, Central District of California and U.S. Court of Appeals, Ninth Circuit. *Education:* University of Illinois (B.A., 1982); Loyola University of Chicago (J.D., 1985). Phi Alpha Delta. Member, National Moot Court Team. *Member:* Los Angeles County Bar Association; The State Bar of California. **PRACTICE AREAS:** Entertainment Litigation; Intellectual Property; Defamation; First Amendment; Business Litigation. *Email:* jgabriel@rmslaw.com

## RUBIN & EAGAN, P.C.
SUITE 801, 9665 WILSHIRE BOULEVARD
**BEVERLY HILLS, CALIFORNIA 90212**
*Telephone: 310-785-1700*
*Telecopier: 310-785-1701*

San Francisco, California Office: Suite 1900, 601 California Street. Telephone: 415-434-4946. Telecopier: 415-362-1179.

*Civil Practice. State and Federal Litigation. Controversies and Disputes involving Insurance, Real Property, and Commercial Matters. Insurance Controversies including Insurance Bad Faith, Title Insurance, Property Insurance, Professional Liability Insurance, Directors and Officers Insurance, Suretyship, Subrogation, Mortgage Guaranty Insurance and Reinsurance. Real Property Controversies including Financing, Title, Foreclosure, Construction, Lien, Easement, Legal Description, Specific Performance and Escrow.*

*FIRM PROFILE: Rubin & Eagan is a nationally recognized firm that provides exemplary legal services in its areas of specialization. Rubin & Eagan has recognized expertise in insurance, real estate, and business litigation and disputes. The firm's expertise enables it to take a unique approach in resolving its clients legal needs in these areas.*

*Because of Rubin & Eagan's extraordinary combination of skills, the firm uses an interdisciplinary approach to complex legal matters that permits the achievement of extraordinary results. The firm's nationally acknowledged capability in specialized areas of law brings diverse and unique resources to handle various legal issues within its practice.*

*Rubin & Eagan has developed a national reputation through its representation of companies in matters throughout the United States. The quality of the firm's practice is reflected in both its clientele and work product.*

**JOHN J. EAGAN** (1913-1982).

**SHELDON RUBIN,** born Chicago, Illinois, March 30, 1936; admitted to bar, 1960, Illinois; 1972, California. *Education:* University of Illinois (B.S., 1957; J.D., 1960). Phi Alpha Delta. Member of Faculty, Practicing Law Institute: Title Insurance—Beyond Basics, 1981; Title Insurance in Current Transactions, 1983. Contributing Author: "The American Law of Real Property," Matthew Bender, 1991. Member, Panel of Arbitrators, American Arbitration Association. *Member:* Beverly Hills, Chicago, Los Angeles County, Illinois State, American (Chairman, Title Insurance Committee, Real Property, Probate and Trust Section, 1985-1989; General Practice Section: Committee on Real Property Transactions, 1978-1979; Model Conveyancing Subcommittee of Real Property Committee, 1980; Chairman, Condominium Conversion Subcommittee of the Real Property Litigation Committee, 1982-1983; Vice-Chair, Title Insurance Committee, Tort and Insurance Practice Section, 1993-1994); Inter-Pacific and International Bar Associations; International Real Estate Institute (RIM); Turnaround Management Association; American Land Title Association (Associate Member and Member of Lenders' Counsel Group, 1979—); American College of Real Estate Lawyers. **PRACTICE AREAS:** Real Estate Law; Insurance Law; Title Insurance Law.

**ROBERT RYAN,** born Providence, Rhode Island, October 4, 1956; admitted to bar, 1983, California and U.S. District Court, Central District of California; 1986, U.S. Court of Appeals, Ninth Circuit; 1987, U.S. District Court, Southern District of California; 1990, U.S. District Court, Eastern District of California; 1991, U.S. District Court, Northern District of California. *Education:* Hampshire College (B.A., 1978); Washington College of Law, The American University (J.D., 1981). *Member:* Los Angeles County and American (Member, Sections on: Tort and Insurance Practice, Insurance Coverage Litigation Subsection; Litigation) Bar Associations; State Bar of California (Member, Sections on: Business Law; Litigation). **PRACTICE AREAS:** Insurance Coverage Litigation; Real Estate Law; Title Insurance; Business Litigation.

**MICHAEL C. FLYNN,** born Rochester, New York, December 6, 1955; admitted to bar, 1981, California; 1982, U.S. District Court, Central District of California; 1984, U.S. District Court, Eastern District of California; 1986, U.S. Court of Appeals, Ninth Circuit. *Education:* Indiana University (B.A., with distinction, 1978); Duke University (J.D., 1981). Phi Beta Kappa; Phi Eta Sigma. Arthur R. Metz Scholar; William Neal Reynolds Scholar. *Member:* Los Angeles County (Member, Title Insurance Subsection) and American Bar Associations; State Bar of California (Vice-Chairman, Title Insurance Claims Committee, A.B.A. Torts and Insurance Practice Section, 1956-1996; Editor, A.B.A. Title Insurance Claims Committee Regulatory and Legislative Affairs Newsletter, 1999-1996). **PRACTICE AREAS:** Business and Commercial Litigation; Real Estate Litigation; Insurance and Insurance Coverage Litigation.

*(This Listing Continued)*

**KEITH J. TURNER,** born Chicago, Illinois, April 6, 1964; admitted to bar, 1991, California and U.S. Court of Appeals, Ninth Circuit; U.S. District Court, Southern, Central and Northern Districts of California. *Education:* University of Wisconsin (B.A., Philosophy, 1986); Illinois Institute of Technology, Chicago Kent College of Law (J.D., 1990). Recipient, Webster Burke Merit Scholarship. *Member:* Beverly Hills and Los Angeles County Bar Associations; State Bar of California (Member, Litigation and Real Property Sections). **PRACTICE AREAS:** Business Litigation; Title Insurance Law; Real Property; Insurance Coverage.

**PATRICK R. BROADWAY,** born Kinston, North Carolina, August 6, 1965; admitted to bar, 1990, California and U.S. District Court, Central District of California. *Education:* University of North Carolina at Chapel Hill (B.S., Administration of Criminal Justice, 1987; B.A., Psychology, 1987; J.D., 1990). Recipient, Phi Delta Phi Block Improvement Award. James M. Johnston Scholar, Order of the Old Well. *Member:* Los Angeles County and American Bar Associations; State Bar of California. **PRACTICE AREAS:** Insurance Litigation.

---

## SCHNEIDER, GOLDBERG & YUEN

A LAW CORPORATION

9100 WILSHIRE BOULEVARD
SEVENTH FLOOR-WEST TOWER
**BEVERLY HILLS, CALIFORNIA 90212**
Telephone: 310-274-8201
FAX: 310-274-2330

*General, Civil and Trial Practice in State and Federal Courts. Corporation, Partnership, Business, Real Property, Securities, Business Reorganization, Creditor's Rights, Bankruptcy, Sports and Entertainment, Trademark, Copyright, Estate Planning, Probate and Trust Law.*

**STEPHEN A. SCHNEIDER,** born Los Angeles, California, April 16, 1940; admitted to bar, 1966, California and U.S. District Court, Central District of California; 1983, U.S. Tax Court; 1992, U.S. District Court, Eastern District of California; U.S. Court of Appeals, Ninth Circuit. *Education:* University of California at Los Angeles (B.A., 1962; LL.B., 1965). Phi Alpha Delta. Chief Justice, University of California, Los Angeles, School of Law Moot Court Honors Program, 1964-1965. Author and Lecturer: "Forming and Terminating Partnerships," Practical Law Courses, Inc., 1981; "Representing Professional Athletes and Teams," Practising Law Institute, 1986. Law Clerk to Justice Gordon L. Files, Presiding Justice, Division Four, Second Appellate District, California Court of Appeal, 1965-1966. *Member:* Beverly Hills (Member, Business Law, Entertainment Law and Litigation Sections; Mandatory Fee Arbitration Panel) and Los Angeles County (Member, Business Law Section) Bar Associations; State Bar of California.

**KENNETH W. KOSSOFF,** born Los Angeles, California, July 19, 1958; admitted to bar, 1983, California; 1984, U.S. District Court, Central District of California; 1985, U.S. Court of Appeals, Ninth Circuit. *Education:* University of California at Berkeley (A.B., with great distinction, 1979); Duke University (J.D., with honors, 1983). Phi Beta Kappa. Member, Duke Law Journal, 1981-1982; Editorial Board, Duke Law Journal, 1982-1983. Author: Note, "Director Independence and Derivative Suit Settlements," 1983 Duke Law Journal 645. Judge Pro Tem: Los Angeles Municipal Court, 1990—; Los Angeles Superior Court, 1992—. *Member:* Los Angeles County and American Bar Associations; The State Bar of California; National Network of Estate Planning Attorneys; American Bankruptcy Institute.

---

**STACY NORENE SCHNAID,** born Los Angeles, California, June 23, 1966; admitted to bar, 1992, California; 1993, U.S. District Court, Central and Eastern Districts of California. *Education:* University of California at Berkeley (B.A., with high distinction, 1988); Universite de Montpellier, France (1986-1987); Loyola Law School of Los Angeles (J.D., 1992). *Member:* Beverly Hills and Los Angeles County Bar Associations; State Bar of California. **LANGUAGES:** French.

**MITCHELL I. BURGER,** born Orange, New Jersey, March 13, 1961; admitted to bar, 1989, California; 1992, U.S. District Court, Central District of California. *Education:* Wharton School, University of Pennsylvania (B.S., Economics, 1983); Fordham University School of Law (J.D., 1989). Staff, Fordham Law Review, 1986-1987. Certified Public Accountant, New York, 1986. *Member:* Los Angeles County Bar Association; State Bar of California.

*(This Listing Continued)*

---

OF COUNSEL

**LARRY GOLDBERG,** born Prague, Czechoslovakia, June 29, 1947; admitted to bar, 1974, California; 1981, U.S. District Court, Central and Southern Districts of California. *Education:* University of California at Los Angeles (B.A., cum laude, 1969); Loyola University of Los Angeles (J.D., cum laude, 1974). Phi Beta Kappa. *Member:* Los Angeles County Bar Association; State Bar of California. (Also Corporate Counsel for Gemstar Development Corporation, Pasadena, California).

**ESTHER G. BOYNTON,** born Flint, Michigan, December 17, 1946; admitted to bar, 1978, Michigan; 1983, Illinois; 1986, California. *Education:* University of Michigan (A.B., with distinction, 1967); Syracuse University (M.S., 1972); Wayne State University Law School (J.D., cum laude, 1978). Trial Attorney, Commercial Litigation and Torts Branches, Civil Division, U.S. Department of Justice, 1978-1980. *Member:* Los Angeles County and Illinois State Bar Associations; State Bar of California.

REPRESENTATIVE CLIENTS: General Electric Company; Alcoa; Dollar Systems, Inc.; Gemstar Development Corporation; Clifford Electronics, Inc.; Helionetics, Inc.; Boss Film Studio, Inc.; Fireman's Fund Insurance Co.; Truck Insurance Exchange.

---

## J. BRIN SCHULMAN

**BEVERLY HILLS, CALIFORNIA**

(See Los Angeles)

*General Civil, Criminal, Trial and Appellate Practice in all State and Federal Courts. Business, Commercial, Entertainment, Real Estate, conservatorship, Trust and Probate Litigation. White Collar Criminal Defense, Organ Transplantation and Family Law.*

---

## SCHWARTZ, WISOT & WILSON, LLP

SUITE 315, 315 SOUTH BEVERLY DRIVE
**BEVERLY HILLS, CALIFORNIA 90212**
Telephone: 310-277-2323
Fax: 310-556-2308

*General Civil and Trial Practice in all State and Federal Courts. Business Corporate, Civil Litigation, Real Property Transactions, Litigation and Title Insurance, Probate Litigation, Construction Litigation.*

FIRM PROFILE: *Schwartz, Wisot & Wilson, LLP was founded in 1991 when Valerie Wisot and Valentina Rodov joined the existing firm of Bruce E. Schwartz, A Professional Law Corporation, founded in 1984, expanding the existing Business and Commercial Law Practice to include the areas of Transactional Real Property Law secured real property transactions and title insurance. The firm was joined in 1996 by John D. Wilson and Kathleen A. Calaway and continues its' active practice in Business, Corporate, Real Property and Insurance Litigation, Title Insurance, Real Property Transactions and Probate Litigation.*

**BRUCE EDWARD SCHWARTZ,** born Bridgeport, Connecticut, March 31, 1947; admitted to bar, 1974, California; 1977, U.S. District Court, Central District of California; 1979, U.S. Court of Appeals, Ninth Circuit and U.S. Supreme Court; 1982, U.S. Tax Court. *Education:* Los Angeles City College (A.A., 1967); California State University at Northridge (B.A., 1970); University of San Diego (J.D., 1973); University of Southern California. Author: "A Psychiatrist On Trial For Medical Malpractice," University of West Los Angeles Law Review, 1985. Adjunct Professor of Evidence Law, University of West Los Angeles, 1978—. Los Angeles County Superior Court Settlement Hearing Officer, 1986—. Judge Pro Tem, Los Angeles County Municipal Court, 1983—. Arbitrator: Beverly Hills Bar Association, 1984—; Los Angeles County Bar Association, 1987—. *Member:* Beverly Hills (Member, Sections on: Business Law; Probate), Los Angeles County (Member: Business and Corporate Law Sections; Lawyer-Client Relations Committee, 1982—) and American (Member, Litigation Section) Bar Associations; State Bar of California (Member, Tax Section; Investigator, Office of Trial Counsel, 1986). **PRACTICE AREAS:** Business; Corporate; Civil Litigation; Insurance Litigation; Probate Litigation.

**VALERIE WISOT,** born Long Beach, California, February 4, 1947; admitted to bar, 1983, California. *Education:* University of California at Berkeley (B.A., 1968); University of California at Los Angeles; University of West Los Angeles (J.D., cum laude, 1983). Guest Lecturer, ABA General Meeting 1988: "Significant Changes in 1987 ALTA Owners Policy," Practicing Law Institute Faculty Member, 1989. Faculty, ABA National Institute, "Attorneys' Role in Title Insurance," 1990. Co Author: "Title In-

*(This Listing Continued)*

## SCHWARTZ, WISOT & WILSON, LLP, Beverly Hills—Continued

surance," the American Law of Real Property, Matthew Bender, 1991. *Member:* Beverly Hills (Member, Real Property Section; Business Law Section), Los Angeles County (Member: Real Property Section; Business Law Section) and American (Member: Real Property Section Standing Committee Membership; Residential Task Force, Business Law Section, Title Insurance Section; Committee Chair, Homeowners and Community Association Committee, 1988-1991) Bar Associations; State Bar of California; Business Property Council; Association of Real Estate Attorneys; Community Associations Institute; American Land Title Association. *PRACTICE AREAS:* Real Property Transactions; Commercial; Business Law.

**JOHN D. WILSON,** born Los Angeles, California, April 30, 1953; admitted to bar, 1980, California; 1981, U.S. District Court, Central District of California. *Education:* University of Wisconsin-Madison (B.S., cum laude, 1976); University of West Los Angeles (J.D., with honors, 1980). Judge Pro Tem, Los Angeles Small Claims Court, 1986-1987. Arbitrator, Los Angeles County Bar, 1990—. Guest Lecturer, Escrow Institute of California, 1994: "Mock Trial For Escrow Offices", California Escrow Association, 1995; "The Role Of The Expert Witness In Escrow Litigation". *Member:* Beverly Hills (Member, Sections on: Business Law and Real Property) and Los Angeles County (Member, Sections on: Business Law, Construction Law and Real Property Law) Bar Associations; State Bar of California. *PRACTICE AREAS:* Real Property Litigation; Business Litigation; Escrow and Title Insurance Litigation; Construction Litigation.

**KATHLEEN A. CALAWAY,** born Fresno, California, March 26, 1952; admitted to bar, 1986, California and U.S. District Court, Central District of California. *Education:* University of West Los Angeles School of Law (J.D., 1985). *Member:* Los Angeles County and American Bar Associations; State Bar of California. *PRACTICE AREAS:* Civil and Business Litigation.

### OF COUNSEL

**PAULA REDDISH ZINNEMANN,** born Newark, New Jersey, August 12, 1936; admitted to bar, 1983, California. *Education:* Marjorie Webster Junior College (A.A., 1955); University of West Los Angeles School of Law (J.D., 1983). Recipient, American Jurisprudence Awards in Real Property and Civil Procedure. Real Estate Salesperson, California, 1965—. Real Estate Broker, California, 1969—. Author: "Alternatives to Litigation," California Real Estate, July/August, 1990. Member, 1973-1992 and President, 1984, Beverly Hills Board of Realtors. Member, California Association of Realtors, 1976—. President: Real Estate Mediation and Arbitration, 1987—; Westside Exchange Accommodators, Inc., 1987—. Settlement Officer, Los Angeles Municipal Court, 1984-1993. Member: California Department of Real Estate, Task Force on Broker Supervision, 1987-1988; Department of Fair Employment and Housing, Southern California Roundtable Steering Committee, 1984-1988. *Member:* Los Angeles County Bar Association (Chairperson, Real Estate Brokerage and Escrow Subsection, 1989-1992, Executive Committee, Real Property Section, 1992-1994); State Bar of California. *PRACTICE AREAS:* Real Property Law.

REFERENCE: Great Western Bank (Century City Office, Los Angeles, California)

## BURTON MARK SENKFOR

9100 WILSHIRE BOULEVARD
SEVENTH FLOOR - WEST TOWER
BEVERLY HILLS, CALIFORNIA 90212
Telephone: 310-274-8771

*Complex Business Litigation and Arbitration in all State and Federal Courts, involving Securities, Intra-Corporate and Partnership Disputes, Corporate Control and Proxies, Lender Liability and Banking, Unfair Competition, Insurance Bad Faith, Real Estate, Construction, Entertainment, Copyright, Contracts and General Business and Corporate Practice.*

**BURTON MARK SENKFOR,** born Cleveland, Ohio, March 14, 1949; admitted to bar, 1974, California and U.S. District Court, Central District of California; 1977, U.S. Court of Appeals, Ninth Circuit. *Education:* University of California at Riverside (B.A., in Economics, 1971); University of California at Los Angeles (J.D., 1974). Past Arbitrator: National Association of Securities Dealers, Inc.; Pacific Stock Exchange. *Member:* State Bar of California. *REPORTED CASES:* Spencer v. Older, 133 Cal.App.3d 95 (1982) (corporate control); Mara v. Farmers Group, Inc., 271 Cal.Rptr. 620 (1990) (insurance coverage); First City National Bank and Trust Company v. Zellner, 782 F.Supp. 232 (S.D.N.Y. 1992); Joint Venture Asset Acquisition v. Zellner, 808 F.Supp. 289 (S.D.N.Y. 1992) (banking).

## WILLIAM A. SHAW

425 SOUTH BEVERLY DRIVE
BEVERLY HILLS, CALIFORNIA 90212
Telephone: 310-556-2155

*Civil Trial Practice in State and Federal Courts. Personal Injury, Real Estate Syndication and Entertainment Law.*

**WILLIAM A. SHAW,** admitted to bar, 1969, Iowa; 1971, California; 1981, District of Columbia; 1987, New York. *Education:* Drake University (B.S., in Pharmacy, 1966); University of Iowa (J.D., 1969). Deputy District Attorney, Los Angeles, 1971-1974. U.S. Attorney, Southern District of California, 1974-1976. Staff Member, White House Conference, 1975-1976. Listed in Who's Who in American Law, 1987—.

REFERENCE: Trans World Bank.

## SHERMAN, DAN & PORTUGAL

A PROFESSIONAL CORPORATION
SUITE 550, 9454 WILSHIRE BOULEVARD
BEVERLY HILLS, CALIFORNIA 90212
Telephone: 310-275-5077
Fax: 310-276-5871

*Practice Limited to Personal Injury, Products Liability, Malpractice, Environment, and Aviation Law, Mass Tort Litigation.*

**ARTHUR SHERMAN,** born Los Angeles, California, March 8, 1931; admitted to bar, 1953, California and U.S. Court of Appeals, Ninth Circuit; 1962, Missouri; 1974, U.S. Court of Appeals, Fifth Circuit; 1975 Texas and Colorado; 1979, Tennessee; 1981, Washington. *Education:* Los Angeles State College (A.A., 1950); Loyola University of Los Angeles (J.D., 1953). Author: "Preparing Your Client for Settlement: Limiting Their Unrealistic Expectations," Insurance Settlements Journal, 1990. Lecturer: Judicial Council, 1972-1973; Continuing Education of the Bar, State of California, 1975 and 1981-1982 (Trial Related Topics); L-Tryptophan Related Topics, Association of Trial Lawyers of America Conference, 1992-1994). Breast Implant Related Topics (Association of Trial Lawyers of America Conference, 1994). Gammagard Related Topics (Association of Trial Lawyers of America Conference, 1995). Designated Arbitrator, Voluntary Settlement Conference Panel, Los Angeles Superior Courts. Liaison Counsel and Plaintiffs' Steering Committee Member, L-Tryptophan, Los Angeles, San Francisco, MDL (National-State Discovery Committee). Member, Plaintiffs' Steering Committee, State of California, Breast Implant Litigation. Claims Advisory Committee In Re Silicone Gel Breast Implant Product Liability Litigation; Member, Steering Committee and Chairman of the Audit Committee In Re Norplant Litigation Liason Counsel and Member of the Executive Committee; In Re Gammagard Litigation: Member, Plaintiff Steering Committee and Co-Class Counsel In Re Felbatol Litigation. Member, Plaintiff Steering Committee: In Re Telectronics Litigation. *Member:* State Bar of California; American Bar Association; Los Angeles Trial Lawyers Association; California Trial Lawyers Association; The Association of Trial Lawyers of America; Lawyers for Public Justice. [U.S. Army Artillery, 1953-1955]. *REPORTED CASES:* Darling v. Caterpillar Tractor, 1959, California Supreme Court; Miller v. U.S.; Gelbardt v. U.S., United States Supreme Court; Paris Air Crash; PSA Air Crash; Sioux City Air Crash; Complex Litigation, including L-Tryptophan Felbatol, Gammagard Telectronics and Breast Implant; Gammagard, Norplant, Felbatol and Telectronics. *PRACTICE AREAS:* Plaintiff's Personal Injury; Product Liability Law; Complex and MDL Litigation; Pharmaceutical; Medical Device.

**MICHAEL A. K. DAN,** born Los Angeles, California, September 15, 1944; admitted to bar, 1970, California. *Education:* University of California at Santa Barbara (B.A., Political Science, with honors, 1966); University of California at Los Angeles (J.D., 1969); Kings College, University of London, England (LL.M., International Law, 1970). Phi Delta Phi. Associate Editor Advocate. President, Senior Class, Kings College. Author: Monthly Column, "From the Courthouse," Advocate. Lecturer, Continuing Education of the Bar, Los Angeles Trial Lawyers, Association of Trial Lawyers of America, U.C.L.A. Law Alumni Class Representative, Program Coordinator and Chairperson, UCLA Tort Litigation for Legal Secretaries. Designated Arbitrator, Superior Court, Los Angeles County, California. Voluntary Settlement Conference Panel for Los Angeles Superior Court(s);

*(This Listing Continued)*

Volunteer Arbitrator. Mass Tort Litigation Responsibilities: Plaintiffs Committee, Karachi Hijacking, 1986; Plaintiffs Committee, L-Tryptophan, Los Angeles and San Francisco, MDL (National State Liaison, Discovery Committee); Felbatol (Steering Committee and Class Action Counsel); MDL Sioux City Air Crash (Class Action Committee); Breast Implant (Discovery Committee); MGL and Complex Litigation: Pago Pago Air Crash, Tahiti Air Crash, Paris Air Crash; Bali Air Crash, Sioux City Air Crash, P.S.A. Air Crash, Tenerife Air Crash, Duarte Mid Air, SAS Crash (Santa Monica Bay), Bendectin, L-Tryptophan, Breast Implant, Norplant, Gammagard, Felbatol, D.E.S., Dalkon Shield, Birth Control Pills, Compazine, Thalidomide, Tigan, Tofranil, Telectronics, SOS Toxic Claims. *Member:* Beverly Hills, Malibu and Los Angeles County (Member, Committees on: Superior Courts; Court Improvements; Joint Liaison Committee/Los Angeles County Medical Association) and American (Member, Committees on: Medicine and Law; Aviation Subcommittee) Bar Association; Los Angeles Trial Lawyers Association (Member, Board of Governors); California Trial Lawyers Association; The Association of Trial Lawyers of America (Treasurer, Tobacco Section); Trial Lawyers for Public Justice. *REPORTED CASES:* Doering v. SAS; Harris v. Irish Truck Lines. *PRACTICE AREAS:* Plaintiff Personal Injury; Product Liability; Medical Malpractice; Obstetrical/Neonatal Malpractice; Pharmaceutical; Medical Device; Federal and State Complex/Mass Tort Litigation.

**ALAN M. SALKOW, (A PROFESSIONAL CORPORATION),** born Los Angeles, California, December 8, 1941; admitted to bar, 1968, California. *Education:* University of California at Los Angeles (B.S., 1963); Southwestern University (LL.B., 1967). *Member:* Los Angeles County and American Bar Associations; State Bar of California; Los Angeles Trial Lawyers Association; California Trial Lawyers Association.

**NATT PORTUGAL,** born Brooklyn, New York, June 18, 1952; admitted to bar, 1979, California. *Education:* University of California at Berkeley (B.A., 1974); Southwestern University (J.D., 1979). *Member:* State Bar of California; Los Angeles Trial Lawyers Association; California Trial Lawyers Association; The Association of Trial Lawyers of America.

---

**JONATHAN S. WEBER,** born Long Island, New York, January 22, 1957; admitted to bar, 1983, California and U.S. District Court, Central District of California. *Education:* State University of New York at Stony Brook (B.A., 1979); Whittier College (J.D., 1982). Regents Scholar. Recipient, American Jurisprudence Award in Criminal Procedure. *Member:* Los Angeles County and American Bar Associations; State Bar of California; Los Angeles Trial Lawyers Association; The Association of Trial Lawyers os America.

**MARCUS A. PETOYAN,** born Los Angeles, California, January 10, 1956; admitted to bar, 1983, California. *Education:* Pepperdine University; California State University; University of California at Los Angeles (B.A., 1978); Southwestern University (J.D., 1982). *Member:* Los Angeles County Bar Association; State Bar of California.

*OF COUNSEL*

**JOHN W. HORNBECK,** born Pittsburgh, Pennsylvania, January 23, 1940; admitted to bar, 1967, California; 1975, Colorado. *Education:* Dartmouth College (B.A., 1963); University of Michigan (LL.B., 1966). Assistant United States Attorney, 1968-1972. Chief Deputy, Federal Public Defender, 1972-1975, Los Angeles, California. General Chief, Criminal Division, Attorney General, State of Colorado, 1975-1978. Senior Counsel, Select Committee on Assassinations, 1978-1979. L-Tryptophan Related Topics (Association Of Trial Lawyers of America Conference, 1992-1994), L-Tryptophan and Felbatol Litigations. *Member:* Boulder and Colorado Bar Associations; Colorado Trial Lawyers Association; The Association of Trial Lawyers of America. (Also Of Counsel to Bragg & Baker, Denver, Colorado). *PRACTICE AREAS:* Complex & MDL Litigation; Pharmaceutical and Medical Device Cases.

**JULIANNE BLOOMER,** born Montclair, New Jersey, July 20, 1949; admitted to bar, 1980, California. *Education:* Bucknell University (B.S. in Education, 1971); Loyola University of Los Angeles (J.D., cum laude, 1980). Member, St. Thomas More Law Honor Society. Author: "Bankruptcy —To File or Not to File, For the General Partner, That Is The Question!" The Real Estate Syndicator, Vol. 3, No. 2, March, 1987; "How Partnerships Can Buy Time With Bankruptcy," The Real Estate Syndicator, Vol. 3, No. 6, July, 1987. Mass Tort Litigation Responsibilities: Discovery and Law Committees In Re Norplant Litigation; In Re Silicone Gel Breast Implant Product Liability Litigation; Plaintiffs Steering Committee, Co-Class Counsel, Discovery and Law Committees; In Re Felbatol Litigation; In Re L-Tryptophan Litigation (Los Angeles, San Francisco, MDL); In Re

*(This Listing Continued)*

Gammagard Litigation (MDL); In Re Telectronics Products Liability litigation (MDL). *Member:* State Bar of California; Association of Trial Lawyers of America. *PRACTICE AREAS:* Products Liability; Federal and State Complex & Multi District Litigation; Class Actions.

**LOUIS I. BELL, (A PROFESSIONAL CORPORATION)**
REFERENCE: Mitsui Manufacturers Bank.

---

## SHERMAN, NATHANSON & MILLER

*A PROFESSIONAL CORPORATION*
9454 WILSHIRE BOULEVARD, SUITE 820
**BEVERLY HILLS, CALIFORNIA 90212**
Telephone: 310-246-0321
Facsimile: 310-246-0305

*Commercial Litigation, Corporate and Partnership Law, Real Estate, Commercial and Financial Transactions, Contracts, Wrongful Termination, Sexual Harassment, Landlord-Tenant, Personal Injury, Intellectual Disputes and Alternative Dispute Resolution.*

**RICHARD LLOYD SHERMAN,** born Freeport, New York, March 16, 1957; admitted to bar, 1982, California; U.S. Court of Appeals, Ninth Circuit and U.S. District Court, Central, Northern, Southern and Eastern Districts of California; 1992, Commonwealth of Northern Mariana Islands. *Education:* University of Southern California (B.A., summa cum laude, 1979); University of California at Los Angeles (J.D., 1982). Phi Beta Kappa; Phi Kappa Phi. Member: UCLA-Alaska Law Review, 1981-1982; UCLA Moot Court Honors Program. *Member:* Los Angeles County Bar Association; State Bar of California. *PRACTICE AREAS:* Contracts; Wrongful Termination; Commercial Landlord-Tenant Disputes; Real Estate; International Trading; Personal Injury; Business Torts.

**KEN NATHANSON,** born Los Angeles, California, July 31, 1951; admitted to bar, 1977, California; 1978, U.S. District Court, Central and Northern Districts of California and U.S. Court of Appeals, Ninth Circuit. *Education:* Claremont Men's College (B.A., 1973); Whittier College School of Law (J.D., 1977). *Member:* Beverly Hills and Los Angeles County Bar Associations; State Bar of California. *PRACTICE AREAS:* Real Estate Law; Commercial Acquisition; Contracts.

**MICHAEL B. MILLER,** born Cincinnati, Ohio, March 21, 1960; admitted to bar, 1988, New York; 1990, California. *Education:* London School of Economics, London, England (1981); Rutgers College (B.A., 1982); New York University School of Law (J.D., 1987). Economics Honor Society. *Member:* Beverly Hills and New York State Bar Associations; State Bar of California. *PRACTICE AREAS:* Corporate Transactions; Contracts; Partnerships and Joint Ventures; Labor and Franchising.

---

## PAUL S. SIGELMAN

Established in 1970
9595 WILSHIRE BOULEVARD, SUITE 900
**BEVERLY HILLS, CALIFORNIA 90212**
Telephone: 310-278-8011
Fax: 310-278-2254
Email: PSLF@jovanet.com

*Civil Trial, Business, Real Estate and Injury Practice.*

**PAUL S. SIGELMAN,** born Fergus Falls, Minnesota, February 24, 1942; admitted to bar, 1967, Minnesota and District of Columbia; 1970, California. *Education:* Carnegie-Mellon and University of Minnesota (B.A., 1964); University of Minnesota (J.D., 1967). *Member:* State Bar of California; District of Columbia Bar; Minnesota State Bar Association.

---

## SINCLAIR TENENBAUM OLESIUK & EMANUEL

*THE ICE HOUSE*
9348 CIVIC CENTER DRIVE, SUITE 200
**BEVERLY HILLS, CALIFORNIA 90210**
Telephone: 310-777-7777
Fax: 310-777-7778

*Entertainment, Domestic and International Business, Corporate and Finance.*

*(This Listing Continued)*

**SINCLAIR TENENBAUM OLESIUK & EMANUEL,**
*Beverly Hills—Continued*

**LEAH K. ANTONIO,** born Hartford, Connecticut, July 23, 1961; admitted to bar, 1987, Massachusetts; 1988, California and District of Columbia. *Education:* London School of Economics, London, England; Tufts University (B.A., 1983); Suffolk University Law School (J.D., 1987). First Prize, 1986 ASCAP Nathan Burkan Memorial Competition, Suffolk University Law School. Book Review Editor, Suffolk University Law School Transnational Law Journal, 1986-1987. Author: "The International Art Trade," 10 Suffolk University Transnational Law Journal, 1986. Chairperson, Barristers' Artists and the Law Committee, Los Angeles County Bar Association, 1990-1992. Member, Executive Committee, Entertainment Law Section, Beverly Hills Bar Association. *Member:* Massachusetts Bar Association; State Bar of California; District of Columbia Bar. **PRACTICE AREAS:** Entertainment Law; Intellectual Property Law.

**CRAIG A. EMANUEL,** born Melbourne, Australia, June 19, 1959; admitted to bar, 1982, Victoria, Australia and Australian Federal and High Courts; 1986, California. *Education:* Monash University, Melbourne, Australia (Bachelor of Juris Prudence, 1979; Bachelor of Law, 1981). *Member:* Los Angeles County Bar Association (Member, International Section); State Bar of California.

**WALTER W. J. OLESIUK,** born Louth, Lincolnshire, England, May 21, 1950; admitted to bar, 1977, England; 1984, California. *Education:* Oxford University, England (B.A., 1972; M.A., 1976); College of Law England (Solicitor of the Supreme Court, 1977). *Member:* Los Angeles County and American Bar Associations; State Bar of California; Law Society of England and Wales.

**NIGEL G. PEARSON,** born Royal Leamington Spa, England, October 12, 1950; admitted to bar, 1973, England; 1985, New York; 1988, California. *Education:* Warwick School, England (Advanced Level Certificates); College of Law, London, England (Solicitor of the Supreme Court, 1973). *Member:* Los Angeles County and New York State Bar Associations; State Bar of California.

**NIGEL SINCLAIR,** born Corbridge, England, March 31, 1948; admitted to bar, 1974, England; 1981, California. *Education:* Cambridge University, England (M.A., 1969); Columbia University (LL.M., 1980). *Member:* Los Angeles County Bar Association; State Bar of California; Law Society of England and Wales.

**IRWIN J. TENENBAUM,** born Philadelphia, Pennsylvania, March 22, 1939; admitted to bar, 1964, Pennsylvania; 1965, New York and U.S. District Court, Southern District of New York; 1975, New Jersey and U.S. District Court, District of New Jersey; 1981, California. *Education:* University of Pennsylvania Wharton School (B.S.E., 1961); University of Pennsylvania (LL.B., 1964). *Member:* Century City, Los Angeles County and New York State Bar Associations; State Bar of California.

---

**JANET L. STOTT,** born Mt. Kisco, New York, July 16, 1948; admitted to bar, 1976, New York; 1987, California; 1991, Utah. *Education:* Harvard University (B.A., 1970); Boston College (J.D., 1975). **PRACTICE AREAS:** Entertainment Law.

**ROBERTA MARLENE WOLFF,** born Los Angeles, California, April 18, 1959; admitted to bar, 1988, California and U.S. District Court, Central District of California and U.S. Court of Appeals, Ninth Circuit. *Education:* Yale University (B.A., with distinction, 1981); Benjamin N. Cardozo School of Law; University of Southern California (J.D., 1988). Order of the Coif. Recipient, American Jurisprudence Award in Torts. *Member:* Beverly Hills, Los Angeles County and American Bar Associations; State Bar of California (Member, Sections on: Business Law; Intellectual Property). **PRACTICE AREAS:** Corporate; Intellectual Property.

*OF COUNSEL*

**KEITH G. FLEER,** born Great Neck, New York, February 28, 1943; admitted to bar, 1967, District of Columbia; 1968, New York; 1976, California. *Education:* American University (B.A., 1964; J.D., 1967). Phi Delta Phi. Business Editor, Law Review, 1967 and Member, National Moot Court Team, 1967, American University. Recipient, Alumni Award, Outstanding Senior, 1967. Author: "Williams v. Walker-Thomas Furniture Company," Case Note, American University Law Review, February 1, 1966. Co-Editor: *Back to the Future* (TM), Prognostications on the Motion Picture and Television Industries, Syllabus for 10th Annual UCLA Entertainment Symposium, 1985; *Following the Dollars from Retail to Net Profits,* An Examination of Creating and Using Revenues from Motion Pictures

*(This Listing Continued)*

and Television Programs, Syllabus for 11th Annual UCLA Entertainment Symposium, 1986. Legislative Counsel, New York State Assemblyman Vincent R. Balletta, 1968-1970. Co-Chairman, UCLA Entertainment Symposium Advisory Committee, 1985-1986. *Member:* State Bar of California; American Bar Association (Member, Section on Patent, Trademark and Copyright); Los Angeles Copyright Society (Secretary, 1985; Vice President, 1986; President-Elect, 1987; President, 1988).

**KENNETH H. MEYER,** born Chattanooga, Tennessee, September 15, 1943; admitted to bar, 1970, California. *Education:* University of California at Los Angeles (B.S., 1966; J.D., 1969). Order of the Coif. Senior Editor, University of California at Los Angeles Law Review, 1968-1969. *Member:* State Bar of California.

---

## SMITH & SMITH

*121 SOUTH BEVERLY DRIVE*
**BEVERLY HILLS, CALIFORNIA 90212**
Telephone: 310-275-5132
Los Angeles: 213-272-7807

*Civil and Trial Practice in all State and Federal Courts. Corporation, Partnership, Real Property, Construction, Administrative, Estate Planning, Trust, Probate, Entertainment, Family and Personal Injury Law.*

**DAVID S. SMITH,** born March 25, 1917; admitted to bar, 1943, California. *Education:* University of California at Los Angeles (A.B., 1939); Loyola University School of Law (J.D., 1942). *Member:* Los Angeles County (Chairman, Committee on Substantive Law, 1960-1961), Beverly Hills (Chairman, Committee on Public Relations, 1963-1964), Federal and American Bar Associations; The State Bar of California (Member, Conference of State Bar Delegates, 1947-1961; Chairman, Conference Conditional Sales Contracts Committee, 1948; Chairman, Southern Section, Committee on Unauthorized Practice of Law, 1959-1962; Member, State Bar Committee on Legislation, 1959-1962; Executive Committee, 1961-1965; Advisory Committee to Executive Committee, Conference of State Bar Delegates, 1965-1967); Lawyers' Club of Los Angeles County (President, 1954); American Judicature Society.

**LEE S. SMITH,** born Los Angeles, California, July 24, 1956; admitted to bar, 1981, California. *Education:* University of California at Santa Barbara (B.A., 1978); Loyola Marymount University (J.D., 1981). *Member:* Los Angeles County (Member, Barristers Legislation-Conference of Delegates Committee, 1983-1984) and American Bar Associations; The State Bar of California.

REPRESENTATIVE CLIENTS: A. Morgan Maree, Jr. and Associates; All Auto Parts; Bristol House; California League of Senior Citizens; Diamond Mattress; Drago Enterprises; Electronic Expediters; Graphic Media; Nationwide Business Resources; Patrick Terrail; Plum Productions; Senior Citizens Village; Sheffield Furniture Corp.; Snak King.
REFERENCE: Union Bank, Beverly Hills Main Office.

---

## STEPHEN E. SOLOMON

**BEVERLY HILLS, CALIFORNIA**

(See Los Angeles)

*Federal and state income tax planning and controversy matters.*

---

## KENT A. SPIELLER

*8383 WILSHIRE BOULEVARD, SUITE 549*
**BEVERLY HILLS, CALIFORNIA 90211**
Telephone: 310-859-8080; 213-655-7505
Fax: 213-651-5742

*Government Relations, Technology Transfer, Health Care Law, Land Use Regulation, Waste/Energy.*

**KENT A. SPIELLER,** born San Francisco, California, September 21, 1951; admitted to bar, 1980, California. *Education:* University of California at Davis (B.A., 1976); Hastings College of Law, University of California (J.D., 1979). *Member:* Los Angeles County, Beverly Hills and American Bar Associations. **LANGUAGES:** Spanish, French and German.

## STERN & GOLDBERG
9150 WILSHIRE BOULEVARD, SUITE 100
**BEVERLY HILLS, CALIFORNIA 90212**
Telephone: 213-272-2711; 310-278-8686
Fax: 310-278-5248

*General Business Law with emphasis in Business Litigation, Real Estate, Corporate, Taxation, Probate and Estate Planning.*

**ELLIS R. STERN,** born Brooklyn, New York, September 23, 1946; admitted to bar, 1974, Florida; 1975, California; 1976, U.S. District Court, Central District of California; 1978, U.S. Tax Court. *Education:* Fairleigh Dickinson University (B.A., 1968); Tulane University (J.D., 1974); New York University (LL.M., in Taxation, 1975). Tulane Moot Court. Adjunct Professor of Law, Federal Estate and Gift Taxation: University of San Diego School of Law, 1983; University of San Fernando Valley School of Law, 1982. *Member:* Los Angeles County Bar Association; The Florida Bar; State Bar of California. [Special Agent, US Army Military Intelligence, 1968-1971]. (Certified Specialist: Taxation Law; Probate, Estate Planning and Trust Law, California Board of Legal Specialization). **PRACTICE AREAS:** Taxation Law; Trusts Law; Estates Law; Business Transactions; Real Property Transactions.

**ALAN N. GOLDBERG,** born Brooklyn, New York, March 7, 1958; admitted to bar, 1983, California; 1984, U.S. District Court, Central District of California and U.S. Tax Court; 1985, U.S. Court of Appeals, Ninth Circuit. *Education:* Arizona State University (B.S., in accounting, 1980); Pepperdine University (J.D., cum laude, 1983); University of Florida (LL.M., in Taxation, 1984). Phi Delta Phi. Recipient: American Jurisprudence Award, Remedies. *Member:* Los Angeles County Bar Association; State Bar of California. (Certified Specialist, Taxation Law, The State Bar of California Board of Legal Specialization). **PRACTICE AREAS:** Business and Civil Litigation.

**RUSSELL T. GINISE,** born Woodland, California, March 17, 1963; admitted to bar, 1989, California; 1990, U.S. District Court, Central District of California. *Education:* University of California at Los Angeles (B.A., 1986); Pepperdine University (J.D., 1989). *Member:* Los Angeles County (Member: Barristers Executive Committee, 1992-1995, Vice-President 1995-1996; Barristers Homeless Shelter Committee) and American (Member, Business Law Section) Bar Associations; State Bar of California (Member, Labor and Employment Law Section). **PRACTICE AREAS:** Business Litigation; Employment Law.

### ASSOCIATE

**JUSTIN J. LANSBERG,** born Sylmar, California, March 9, 1964; admitted to bar, 1989, California and U.S. District Court, Central District of California. *Education:* Stanford University (B.A., 1986); University of Southern California at Los Angeles (J.D., 1989). Editor, Hale Moot Court Honors Program. *Member:* Los Angeles County Bar Association; State Bar of California. **PRACTICE AREAS:** Business and Real Estate Litigation; Personal Injury Law.

### OF COUNSEL

**LAWRENCE W. HAIT,** born Oakland, California, May 23, 1942; admitted to bar, 1970, California; 1971, U.S. District Court, Central District of California. *Education:* University of California at Los Angeles (B.A., 1967); University of California at Los Angeles School of Law (J.D., 1970). Recipient: American Jurisprudence Award, Torts. *Member:* Los Angeles County Bar Association; State Bar of California. **PRACTICE AREAS:** Business Litigation; Personal Injury Law; Family Law; General Corporate Law.

---

## STONE & HILES
9440 SANTA MONICA BOULEVARD, PENTHOUSE
**BEVERLY HILLS, CALIFORNIA 90210**
Telephone: 310-274-8749
Telecopier: 310-550-0483
Email: stonehil@he.net
URL: http://www.he.net/~stonehil

*General Civil Practice in State and Federal Courts. Civil, Business, Probate, and Corporate Litigation, Tort, Real Estate, Insurance, Personal Injury and Toxic Tort Law.*

**FIRM PROFILE:** Stone & Hiles was founded in 1988 by Richard A. Stone and Russel D. Hiles. Commencing with a practice primarily located in Southern California, the firm now serves the State of California, maintaining offices in Beverly Hills and Oakland, and offers a wide range of legal services to corporations, businesses, and individuals.

### MEMBERS OF FIRM

**RICHARD A. STONE,** born New York, N.Y., April 3, 1927; admitted to bar, 1955, California and U.S. District Court, Central District of California; 1960, U.S. Supreme Court. *Education:* University of California at Los Angeles (B.S., 1950); Loyola University (J.D., 1954). Certified Public Accountant, California, 1952. Councilman, City of Beverly Hills, 1968-1980. Mayor, City of Beverly Hills, 1972-1973; 1977-1978. President, Board of Education, Beverly Hills Unified School District, 1992-1993. Member, Board of Education, Beverly Hills Unified School District, 1992—. *Member:* Beverly Hills and Los Angeles County Bar Associations; State Bar of California. **PRACTICE AREAS:** Real Estate Law; Business Law; Complex Litigation.

**RUSSEL D. HILES,** born Pittsburgh, Pennsylvania, August 21, 1942; admitted to bar, 1974, California; U.S. District Court, Central District of California; U.S. District Court, Southern District of California; U.S. Court of Appeals, Ninth Circuit. *Education:* California State Polytechnic University (B.S., 1969); California Western School of Law (J.D., 1973). Phi Delta Phi; Pi Gamma Nu. Deputy District Attorney, 1973-1976. *Member:* Los Angeles County and American Bar Associations; State Bar of California; Association of Defense Counsel of Southern California; Conference of Insurance Counsel, Beverly Hills. **PRACTICE AREAS:** Tort Defense Law.

**BENJAMIN S. CARDOZO,** born Brooklyn, New York, November 9, 1942; admitted to bar, 1979, California and U.S. District Court, Central District of California; 1982, U.S. Court of Appeals, Ninth Circuit; 1983, U.S. District Court, Southern District of California; 1985, U.S. District Court, Eastern District of California. *Education:* University of California at Riverside (B.A., with honors, 1964); University of Southern California (J.D., 1979). Judge Pro Tem, Los Angeles Municipal Court, 1988—. Settlement Officer, Los Angeles Superior Court, 1988—. Arbitrator, Los Angeles Superior Court. *Member:* Los Angeles County (Member, Law and Technology Section), Santa Monica, and American (Member, Tort and Insurance Coverage Sections) Bar Associations; State Bar of California. **REPORTED CASES:** Mercury Insurance vs. Checkerboard Pizza 15 Cal. Rptr 657 (1993). **PRACTICE AREAS:** Insurance Bad Faith; Insurance coverage; Business Litigation; Tort Litigation.

### ASSOCIATES

**MARC A. LEGGET,** born Los Angeles, California, August 13, 1961; admitted to bar, 1987, California and U.S. District Court, Central District of California. *Education:* California State University at Northridge (B.A., cum laude, 1984); Hastings College of Law, University of California (J.D., 1987). Phi Delta Phi. *Member:* Beverly Hills, Los Angeles County and American Bar Associations; State Bar of California.

**DOREEN M. MERCADO,** born Los Angeles, California, June 18, 1958; admitted to bar, 1991, California. *Education:* Rio Hondo College (A.A., 1981); University of California at Los Angeles (B.A., 1986); Loyola Marymount University (J.D., 1990). Phi Alpha Delta.

**MARGARET MONOS,** born Los Angeles, California, August 31, 1964; admitted to bar, 1990, California. *Education:* University of California (B.A., 1986); University of Southern California (J.D., 1989). *Member:* State Bar of California.

**ANGELA D. ROBLEDO,** born San Jose, California, October 14, 1963; admitted to bar, 1989, California. *Education:* California Polytechnic University (B.S., 1985); University of California at Davis (J.D., 1988). Member, Moot Court Board. *Member:* Los Angeles County and Beverly Hills Bar Associations; State Bar of California.

**DAVID L. SCHAFFER,** admitted to bar, 1975, Florida; 1976, California; 1990, U.S. District Court, Central District of California. *Education:* University of California at Berkeley; University of California at Los Angeles (B.A., 1972); University of Miami (J.D., 1975); Loyola Marymount University (M.B.A., 1986). Author: "Paying for Proposition 103: Constitutional and Other Legal Infirmities in the Insurance Commissioner and the State Board of Equalization Billing Insurers," (with Joseph Hegedas) in Calif. Ins. Law and Regulation, April 1990. *Member:* The Florida Bar; State Bar of California; California District Attorneys Association. **PRACTICE AREAS:** Insurance Coverage and Bad Faith; Tort Prosecution and Defense.

**HEATHER L. WEAKLEY,** born Buffalo, New York, November 25, 1968; admitted to bar, 1995, California. *Education:* San Diego State University (B.A., 1990); Southwestern University, School of Law (J.D., 1995).

*(This Listing Continued)*

STONE & HILES, Beverly Hills—Continued

**ROBERT D. STUBBLEFIELD,** born Wheat Ridge, Colorado, December 18, 1968; admitted to bar, 1996, California. *Education:* University of California, Los Angeles (B.A., 1992); University of Denver (J.D., 1996). Phi Delta Phi. General Editor, University of Denver Law Review. Recipient, Award for Scholastic Excellence: Basic Tax, Spring, 1995; Family Law, Spring, 1996. Listed in, Who's Who in American Law Schools, 1994-1996.

REPRESENTATIVE CLIENTS: Alpha Beta Co.; Hughes Markets, Inc.; Great American Insurance Co.; United Artists Communications, Inc.; Warner Brothers; The Burbank Studios; Thrifty-Payless, Inc.

## PAUL D. SUPNIK

SUITE 1200 WELLS FARGO BANK BUILDING
433 NORTH CAMDEN DRIVE
**BEVERLY HILLS, CALIFORNIA 90210**
Telephone: 310-205-2050
Telex: 292416
Facsimile: 310-205-2011
Email: ps@supnik.com
URL: http://www.supnik.com

*Domestic and International Copyright and Trademark Law, Motion Picture, Television, Publishing, Media and General Entertainment Law, Multimedia and Internet Law. Licensing, Related Litigation.*

**PAUL D. SUPNIK,** born San Diego, California, September 9, 1947; admitted to bar, 1972, California and U.S. District Court, Central District of California; 1980, U.S. District Court, Southern and Northern Districts of California; 1981, U.S. Court of Appeals, Ninth Circuit; 1985, U.S. Court of Appeals, Federal Circuit. *Education:* University of California at Los Angeles (B.S., 1968); Hastings College of Law, University of California (J.D., 1971). *Member:* Editorial Board, Los Angeles Lawyer, 1988—. Co-Editor: "Idea Submissions," Seminar Syllabus, 1979; "Trademarks—Expanding Areas for the 80's," Seminar Syllabus, 1980; "Copyright: Selected Practical Approaches to Protection and Enforcement," Seminar Syllabus, 1984. Author: "The Bell and Howell: Mamiya Case- Where Now Parallel Imports," 74 The Trademark Reporter 1, January-February, 1984; "Diluting the Counterfeiters: New Trademark Rights and Remedies in Dealing with Entertainment and Merchandising Properties," The Entertainment and Sports Lawyer, Fall, 1985; "Designations of Source-Are They Necessary to Support Entertainment Industry Merchandising Rights?," Cardozo Arts and Entertainment Law Journal, 1986; "Lawyers Using Computers/Making the Most of the New Technology," Los Angeles Lawyer, June, 1987. Editor, "Enforcement of Copyright and Related Rights Affecting the Music Industry", International Association of Entertainment Lawyers, MIDEM, Cannes, 1993. Author, "Copyright" in *Proof in Competitive Business Litigation,* California Continuing Education of the Bar, 1993. Arbitrator, American Film Marketing Association International Arbitration Tribunal, 1984—. President, Hastings Alumni Association, Los Angeles Chapter, 1984-1985. *Member:* Beverly Hills (Member, Barristers Committee for the Arts, 1978-1982, Co-Editor, "The Actors Manual," 1978), Los Angeles County (Chairperson: Intellectual Property and Entertainment Law Section, 1979-1980; Seminar, "Merchandising: Legal and Business Aspects," 1978; Chair, Lawyers Using Computers Committee, 1986-1988; Member, Barrister Executive Committee, 1977-1978 and Member, 1975, 1976, 1978, 1980, State Bar Conference Delegation), American (Member, Sections on: Patent, Trademark and Copyright Law; Litigation; International Law; Member: Forum Committee on the Entertainment and Sports Industries, 1979—) and International Bar Associations; State Bar of California (Member, Section of Intellectual Property Law); International Trademark Association; Association Internationale des Jeunes Avocats (Honorary Vice-President, 1993—; National Vice President for United States, 1990-1992; Seminar: Motion Picture Production and Distribution, London, 1991); Union Internationale des Avocats (Seminar: "Multimedia Production Agreements and Rights Clearances," Marrakech, Morocco 1994); Association of Business Trial Lawyers; Los Angeles Copyright Society. **REPORTED CASES:** Brewer v. Hustler Magazine Inc., 749 F.2d 527 (9th Cir. 1984); Poe v. Missing Persons, 745 F. 2d 1238 (9th Cir. 1984).

## SWERDLOW, FLORENCE & SANCHEZ

A LAW CORPORATION
SUITE 828, 9401 WILSHIRE BOULEVARD
**BEVERLY HILLS, CALIFORNIA 90212**
Telephone: 310-201-4700
Fax: 310-273-8680
Email: lucihamilton@compuserve.com

*Management, Labor and Employment Law.*

FIRM PROFILE: Swerdlow, Florence & Sanchez, exclusively practicing management labor and employment law, was founded in 1984 with a total commitment to provide outstanding service to its small business to multi-billion dollar international corporate clientele.

We offer comprehensive counselling, planning and litigation services with emphasis on education and prevention.

**SEYMOUR SWERDLOW,** born New York, N.Y., June 17, 1938; admitted to bar, 1963, New York; 1967, California, U.S. District Court, Northern, Southern and Central Districts of California and U.S. Court of Appeals, 2nd and 9th Circuits; 1971, U.S. Supreme Court. *Education:* Cooper Union (B.C.E., 1960); New York University (LL.B., 1963). Associate Editor, New York University Law Review, 1962-1963. *Member:* Beverly Hills (Chairperson, Labor Law Committee, 1980-1982), Los Angeles County (Member, Executive Committee, Labor Law Section, 1981-1984, 1986-1988) and American (Member: Section on Labor and Employment Law; Committee on Employee Rights and Responsibilities, 1982—) Bar Associations; State Bar of California (Member, Section on Labor and Employment Law). *PRACTICE AREAS:* Management, Labor and Employment Law.

**KENNETH J. FLORENCE,** born Hanford, California, July 31, 1943; admitted to bar, 1974, California and U.S. District Court, Central District of California; 1975, U.S. Court of Appeals, 9th Circuit; 1976, U.S. District Court, Northern, Southern and Eastern Districts of California; 1984, U.S. Supreme Court. *Education:* Whittier College (B.A., cum laude, 1965); Hastings College of Law, University of California (J.D., 1974). Pi Sigma Alpha; Phi Alpha Theta. *Member:* Beverly Hills, Los Angeles County (Member, Sections on: Labor Law; Trial Lawyers) and American (Member: Labor and Employment Law Section; Management Chairman, Committee on State Labor Law Developments, 1988-1991) Bar Associations; State Bar of California (Member, Section on Labor and Employment Law). [Lt., USNR, 1966-1969]. *PRACTICE AREAS:* Management, Labor and Employment Law.

**MILLICENT N. SANCHEZ,** born Honolulu, Hawaii, September 5, 1954; admitted to bar, 1981, Hawaii, U.S. District Court, District of Hawaii and U.S. Court of Appeals, Ninth Circuit; 1983, California; 1985, U.S. District Court, Central District of California; 1987, U.S. District Court, Eastern and Southern Districts of California; 1988, U.S. District Court, Northern District of California. *Education:* University of Hawaii (B.A., 1977); University of California at Los Angeles (J.D., 1980). *Member,* UCLA Law Review, 1978-1979. Executive Editor, UCLA-Alaska Law Review, 1979-1980. *Member:* Beverly Hills, Los Angeles County (Member: Labor Law Section; Executive Committee, 1990—); Hawaii State and American (Member, Labor and Employment Law Section) Bar Associations; State Bar of California (Member, Ethic Minority Relations Committee, Chairperson, 1992-1993; Section on Labor and Employment Law); Philippine American Bar Association of Los Angeles (Board of Directors, President-Elect, 1993). *PRACTICE AREAS:* Management, Labor and Employment Law.

**SANDY K. RATHBUN,** born Ellsworth, Kansas, December 28, 1959; admitted to bar, 1988, Missouri, California and U.S. District Court, Western District of Missouri; 1990, U.S. District Court, Northern, Southern, Central and Eastern Districts of California and U.S. Court of Appeals, 9th Circuit. *Education:* Kansas State University (B.S., 1984); Northwestern University (J.D., 1987). Phi Kappa Phi. *Member:* Beverly Hills, Los Angeles County (Member, Labor Law Section) and American Bar Associations; State Bar of California; The Missouri Bar; Women Lawyers Association of Los Angeles. *PRACTICE AREAS:* Management, Labor and Employment Law.

**ROSARIO M. TOBIAS,** born Philippine Islands, May 2, 1956; admitted to bar, 1988, California. *Education:* University of California at Berkeley (A.B., 1978); University of California at Los Angeles (J.D., 1985). *Member:* State Bar of California (Member, Labor Law Section); California Women Lawyers Association. *LANGUAGES:* Spanish.

*(This Listing Continued)*

## PROFESSIONAL BIOGRAPHIES

**AMY R. PLEATMAN,** born Cincinnati, Ohio, May 30, 1958; admitted to bar, 1986, California. *Education:* University of California at San Diego (B.A., 1980); Whittier College School of Law (J.D., 1985). Recipient, Outstanding Young Woman of America Award, 1982. *Member:* State Bar of California.

### LAW OFFICES OF
### DAVID C. TARDIFF

8888 OLYMPIC BOULEVARD
**BEVERLY HILLS, CALIFORNIA 90211**
Telephone: 310-247-8237
Facsimile: 310-271-8196
Email: 76020.1167@COMPUSERVE.COM

*Personal Injury and Criminal Law.*

**DAVID C. TARDIFF,** born 1934; admitted to bar, 1963, California. *Education:* University of California (B.A., 1959) California School of Law, University of Los Angeles (J.D., 1962). *PRACTICE AREAS:* Civil RICO; Criminal Law; Personal Injury; Products Liability; Medical Malpractice.

### EVE TRIFFO

9300 WILSHIRE BOULEVARD, SUITE 200
**BEVERLY HILLS, CALIFORNIA 90212**
Telephone: 310-278-7556
Fax: 310-276-5632

*Bankruptcy, Business Litigation, Health, Civil Law, Appellate Law.*

**EVE TRIFFO,** admitted to bar, 1974, California. *Education:* State University of New York at Buffalo (B.A., magna cum laude, 1969); University of California at Santa Barbara (M.A., 1971); University of California at Los Angeles (J.D., 1974). Author: "Sense from Nonsense: Justice Powell, The Burger Court, and the Religion Clauses of the First Amendment," 15 Southwestern Univ. Law Rev. 637, 1985. Associate Professor, Southwestern University School of Law, 1983-1985. *PRACTICE AREAS:* Bankruptcy; Business Litigation; Health Care Litigation; Appellate.

### TROJAN LAW OFFICES

WELLS FARGO BANK BUILDING
433 NORTH CAMDEN DRIVE
FOURTH FLOOR
**BEVERLY HILLS, CALIFORNIA 90210**
Telephone: 310-281-1662
Telecopier: 310-281-1664
Email: trojanlaw@aol.com

*Patent and Trademark Litigation.*

FIRM PROFILE: *The firm practices in the Pacific Rim, with full time native Japanese speaking staff, in the following areas of law: patents, trademarks, copyrights, trade secrets, unfair competition, false advertising and related antitrust issues.*

**R. JOSEPH TROJAN,** born Winston-Salem, North Carolina, April 12, 1961; admitted to bar, 1988, California, U.S. District Court, Central District of California, U.S. Court of Appeals, Ninth and Federal Circuit; 1994, U.S. District Court, District of Arizona; 1990, registered to practice before U.S. Patent and Trademark Office. *Education:* University of Southern California (B.S., 1985); Loyola Law School (J.D., 1988). Recipient, American Jurisprudence Award in Patent Law. Member, Jessup International Moot Court Competition. *Member:* State Bar of California; Federal and American Bar Associations; American Intellectual Property Law Association. *PRACTICE AREAS:* Patent and Trademark Litigation and Prosecution; Intellectual Property Licensing; Copyright; Trade Secrets.

#### ASSOCIATE

**ERIC J. AAGAARD,** born Madison, Wisconsin, April 22, 1965; admitted to bar, 1995, California and U.S. District Court, Central District of California. *Education:* Arizona State University (B.S.M.E., 1987); Pepperdine University (J.D., 1995). Pi Tau Sigma. *Member:* State Bar of California. *PRACTICE AREAS:* Patents; Trademarks; Copyrights; Trade Secrets; Intellectual Property Litigation. *Email:* trojanlaw@aol.com

*(This Listing Continued)*

## CALIFORNIA—BEVERLY HILLS

#### OF COUNSEL

**J. NICHOLAS GROSS,** born Bangor, Maine, May 31, 1960; admitted to bar, 1988, California; 1990, registered to practice before U.S. Patent and Trademark Office. *Education:* California Institute of Technology (B.S., 1983); Loyola Law School (J.D., cum laude, 1988). *Member:* Los Angeles County and Beverly Hills Bar Associations; State Bar of California. *LANGUAGES:* Greek. *PRACTICE AREAS:* Intellectual Property; High Technology Litigation.

**L. RAE CONNET,** born San Luis Obispo, August 25, 1957; admitted to bar, 1991, California; 1992, U.S. District Court, Central District of California. *Education:* University of California at Los Angeles (B.S., 1983); Loyola Law School (J.D., 1991). *Member:* Los Angeles County and American Bar Associations. *PRACTICE AREAS:* Complex Intellectual Property Litigation; Trademarks; Patents; Trade Secrets; Related Business Torts; Corporate Law; Employment Law.

REPRESENTATIVE CLIENTS: United Chemical Corporation; Kotobuki Corporation; California Museum of Science and Industry; California Museum Foundation; Sengoku Works, Ltd.; American Unimax; Health and Body Fitness.

### TUCKER & BAUM

228 SOUTH BEVERLY DRIVE
**BEVERLY HILLS, CALIFORNIA 90212**
Telephone: 310-246-6600
Telecopier: 310-246-6622

*General Commercial and Business Practice. Civil Litigation, Commercial, Arbitration, Real Estate, Corporate, Copyright and Family Law.*

**KAYE E. TUCKER,** born Des Moines, Iowa, September 28, 1951; admitted to bar, 1976, California; 1977, U.S. District Court, Central District of California; 1981, U.S. Court of Appeals, Ninth Circuit. *Education:* University of California of Los Angeles (B.A., cum laude, 1973); Loyola University of Los Angeles (J.D., cum laude, 1976). Member, St. Thomas More Society. *Member:* State Bar of California; Los Angeles County Bar Association (Member, Executive Committee, Pre and Post Judgement Remedies Section); Association of Business Trial Lawyers.

**MICHAEL C. BAUM,** born San Francisco, California, December 4, 1951; admitted to bar, 1975, California; 1976, U.S. District Court, Central District of California; 1980, U.S. Court of Appeals, Ninth Circuit. *Education:* University of California at Berkeley (B.A., with distinction, 1972); University of California at Los Angeles (J.D., 1975). *Member:* Los Angeles County (Executive Committee Pre and Post Judgement Remedies Section, 1988-1990) and American (Member, Sections on: Business Law; Litigation) Bar Associations; State Bar of California; Association of Business Trial Lawyers.

#### ASSOCIATES

**GARY J. LORCH,** born Hempstead, New York, September 8, 1960; admitted to bar, 1985, California; 1986, U.S. District Court, Central District of California and U.S. Court of Appeals, Ninth Circuit; 1989, U.S. District Court, Northern and Southern Districts of California; 1994, U.S. Court of Appeals, District of Columbia Circuit. *Education:* University of California at Los Angeles (B.A., 1982); Washington and Lee University School of Law; Hastings College of the Law, University of California (J.D., 1985). Phi Alpha Delta. *Member:* Los Angeles County and American Bar Associations; State Bar of California.

### TURNER, GERSTENFELD, WILK, AUBERT & YOUNG, LLP

Established in 1979

Formerly Turner, Gerstenfeld, Wilk & Tigerman

SUITE 510, 8383 WILSHIRE BOULEVARD
**BEVERLY HILLS, CALIFORNIA 90211**
Telephone: 213-653-3900
Facsimile: 213-653-3021

*General Civil Practice. Civil Litigation. Real Estate, Construction, Probate, Tax, Estate Planning and Family, Franchise, Entertainment, Intellectual Property, Cellular Communication, International, Corporation and Business Law.*

*(This Listing Continued)*

## TURNER, GERSTENFELD, WILK, AUBERT & YOUNG, LLP, Beverly Hills—Continued

### MEMBERS OF FIRM

**RUBIN M. TURNER,** born Sofia, Bulgaria, June 23, 1937; admitted to bar, 1961, California and U.S. District Court, Southern District of California; 1965, U.S. District Court, Northern District of California; 1971, U.S. Supreme Court; 1982, U.S. Tax Court. *Education:* University of California at Los Angeles (B.A., 1958; J.D., 1961). Author: "Selected Aspects of Real Estate Syndication," Forum of the Real Estate Syndication Syllabus by Gooden & Dickey, Realty Seminar Institute, 1980. Professor of Law, Real Estate Law and Trusts, University of San Fernando Valley College of Law, 1962-1970. *Member:* Los Angeles County Bar Association; State Bar of California. **PRACTICE AREAS:** Real Estate Law; Construction Law; Corporate Law; International Law; Business Law; Intellectual Property Law.

**GERALD F. GERSTENFELD,** born Chicago, Illinois, May 11, 1931; admitted to bar, 1953, Illinois; 1957, California and U.S. District Court, Southern District of California. *Education:* North Park College and Northwestern University (B.S.L., 1952); Northwestern University (J.D., 1953); University of Southern California (LL.M., in Taxation, 1965). Phi Alpha Delta. Member, Board of Editors, Northwestern University Law Review, 1952-1953. Author: "The 'Due-On-Sale' Clause—Time for a Change," Journal of the Beverly Hills Bar Association, November, 1970; "The QOT: New Solution for a New Problem," California Continuing Education of the Bar Estate Planning of California Probate Reporter, April, 1989. Part-time Professor, Real Property Law, University of San Fernando Valley College of Law, 1972-1975. *Member:* Beverly Hills (Member: Board of Governors, Barristers, 1966; Board of Governors, 1978-1980; Foundation Board of Directors, 1983—; Sections on Real Estate and Probate, Trust and Estate Planning, Alternative Dispute Resolution); Los Angeles County (Member, Sections on Real Estate and Probate and Trust) Bar Associations; State Bar of California (Member, Sections on: Real Estate; Business Law and Probate and Trust); Estate Counselors Forum. **PRACTICE AREAS:** Estate Planning Law; Probate Law; Trust Law; Real Estate Law; Business Law; Mediation; Arbitration.

**BARRY R. WILK,** born Chicago, Illinois, August 16, 1930; admitted to bar, 1955, Illinois; 1957, California and U.S. District Court, Southern District of California. *Education:* University of Illinois (B.S., 1951); Northwestern University (J.D., 1954). Phi Alpha Delta. Part-time Professor of Real Property Law, University of San Fernando Valley, 1972-1980. Judge Pro Tem, Los Angeles and Beverly Hills Municipal Courts, 1979-1985. *Member:* Beverly Hills Bar Association (Member, Real Estate and Family Law Sections); State Bar of California. **PRACTICE AREAS:** Real Estate Law; Business Law; Family Law.

**RONALD D. AUBERT,** born 1936; admitted to bar, 1966, California. *Education:* University of California; University of Hastings College of the Law. *Member:* State Bar of California.

**STEVEN E. YOUNG,** born Los Angeles, California, March 6, 1948; admitted to bar, 1974, California, U.S. Court of Appeals, Ninth Circuit and U.S. District Court, Southern, Central and Northern Districts of California. *Education:* University of California at Los Angeles (B.A., 1970); University of Southern California (J.D., 1973). Member, University of Southern California Law Review, 1971-1972. Member, Executive Board, Hale Moot Court Honors Program, 1972-1973. Author: "The California Experience," 1976 Committee Reports, Agricultural Labor Law Sub-committee of the Committee on State Labor Law of the American Bar Association Section of Labor Relations Law. Judge Protem, Beverly Hills and Los Angeles Municipal Courts, 1980—. *Member:* Beverly Hills, Los Angeles County (Member, Ad Hoc Committee to Study the California Discovery Act, 1986—) and American (Member, Sections on: Antitrust Law; Litigation; Member, Committees on: State Labor Law, 1976-1978; Antitrust and Labor Relations Law, 1978-1980; Private Antitrust Litigation, 1981-1982) Bar Associations; State Bar of California; Association of Business Trial Lawyers. **PRACTICE AREAS:** Business Litigation; Entertainment Law; Real Estate Law.

**EDWARD FRIEDMAN,** born Cleveland, Ohio, May 9, 1949; admitted to bar, 1975, California, U.S. District Court, Central District of California and U.S. Court of Appeals, Ninth Circuit. *Education:* Pomona College (B.A., 1971); Loyola University of Los Angeles (J.D., 1975). Judge Pro Tem, Los Angeles and Beverly Hills Municipal Courts, 1983-1990. *Member:* Beverly Hills and Los Angeles County (Member, Sections on Real Property, Trial Lawyers, Business and Corporations Law) Bar Associations; State Bar of California. **PRACTICE AREAS:** Business Litigation; Real Estate Law; Mediation; Arbitration.

*(This Listing Continued)*

**MICHAEL J. HANNA,** born 1944; admitted to bar, 1974, California. *Education:* California State University, Long Beach; McGeorge School of Law. *Member:* State Bar of California.

**LINDA WIGHT MAZUR,** born Tampa, Florida, May 22, 1959; admitted to bar, 1984, California, U.S. District Court, Central District of California and U.S. Tax Court. *Education:* University of Florida; Pomona College (B.A., 1981); University of California at Los Angeles (J.D., 1984); University of San Diego (Diploma in Taxation, 1985). Member: Moot Court Honors Program; UCLA-Alaska Law Review, 1983-1984. *Member:* Beverly Hills (First Vice President, 1996-1997; Second Vice President, 1995-1996; Secretary/Treasurer, 1994-1995; Member, Board of Governors, 1991-1994; Chair, Resolutions Committee, 1990-1991; California State Bar Conference of Delegates, 1986-1992; Chair, Probate, Trust and Estate Planning Section, 1993-1994), Los Angeles County (Member: Board of Trustees, 1995-1996; Trusts and Estates Section) and American Bar Associations; State Bar of California (Member, Calendar Coordinating Committee, 1993-1997). **PRACTICE AREAS:** Probate; Estate Planning; Trust Law; Intellectual Property; Entertainment Law; Mediation.

### ASSOCIATES

**DORTHA LARENE PYLES,** born Yuma, Arizona, November 19, 1949; admitted to bar, 1976, California. *Education:* Los Angeles City College (A.A., 1970); Santa Monica City College; Whittier College (J.D., 1976). *Member:* Beverly Hills and Los Angeles County Bar Associations; State Bar of California.

**STEVEN A. MORRIS,** born Calcutta, India, October 29, 1960; admitted to bar, 1986, California; 1988, U.S. District Court, Central District of California. *Education:* California State University at Northridge (B.S., with honors, 1983); Southwestern University (J.D., 1986). *Member:* Los Angeles County Bar Association; State Bar of California. **PRACTICE AREAS:** Business Law; Real Estate Litigation; Construction Litigation.

**DIANE H. PAPPAS,** born San Diego, California, September 25, 1955; admitted to bar, 1982, California. *Education:* University of California, Los Angeles; Southwestern University School of Law (J.D., 1980). *Member:* State Bar of California. **LANGUAGES:** Spanish, Portuguese and Greek. **PRACTICE AREAS:** Real Estate; Business Law.

**VICKI L. CRESAP,** born Burlington, Iowa, January 28, 1950; admitted to bar, 1990, California. *Education:* University of California, Santa Barbara (B.A., 1975); Loyola Law School, Los Angeles (J.D., 1989). Member, St. Thomas More Honor Society. *Member:* State Bar of California. **PRACTICE AREAS:** Business Litigation.

### OF COUNSEL

**BERT Z. TIGERMAN,** born Chicago, Illinois, September 13, 1929; admitted to bar, 1954, Illinois; 1957, California and U.S. Tax Court; 1978, U.S. Supreme Court. *Education:* University of Illinois and Northwestern University (B.S., 1951); Northwestern University (J.D., 1954); University of Southern California. **PRACTICE AREAS:** Probate Law; Real Property Law; Business Litigation.

REPRESENTATIVE CLIENTS: Al & Ed's Autosound; ALDA Properties; Aries Prepared Beef Co.; Beverly Hills Country Club; Booda Products; Botanicals International; Craig Breedlove; Brilliant Lighting; Business Title Escrow Co.; Certified Technology; Consumer Mortgage, Inc.; Continental Land Title Co.; Deer Creek Farms; William Devane; Deist Safety, Ltd.; Dorsett & Jackson, Inc.; The Drain Surgeon, Inc.; FAB Enterprises; First American Title Company of Los Angeles; Fu/Lyons Associates; Furniture Guild; General Mobile Electronics; Guildcraft Manufacturing Co.; Hudson Land & Dev. Co.; Intex Services, Inc.; Jan Development Co.; Jerry's Famous Deli Inc.; Kenney Manufacturing Co., Inc.; Libbey-Owens Ford Co.; Long Beach Bank; Lyons & Lyons Properties; Medical Digital Technologies, Inc.; Mobile Fidelity Sound Labs; Mr. Tax of America, Ltd.; Original Master Recordings; Power To Create, Inc.; Showbiz Enterprises, Inc.; Triple Check Income Tax Service, Inc.; Turf Construction, Inc.

## VORZIMER, GARBER, MASSERMAN & ECOFF

*A PROFESSIONAL CORPORATION*
**8383 WILSHIRE BOULEVARD
SUITE 750
BEVERLY HILLS, CALIFORNIA 90211**
Telephone: 213-782-1400
Facsimile: 213-782-1850
Email: vgm8383@earthlink.net
URL: http://members.aol.com/vgm8383/vgmhome.htm

General Civil, Trial and Appellate Practice in all State and Federal Courts and Administrative Agencies. Business Litigation, Corporate, Real Estate, Criminal Defense, Insurance Coverage, Entertainment, Wrongful Termination and Discrimination, Unfair Competition, Constitutional and Civil Rights Litigation.

FIRM PROFILE: Vorzimer, Garber, Masserman & Ecoff is a boutique litigation firm whose founders developed their trial skills at major Los Angeles law firms, but believed that they could best serve the interest of their clients in the atmosphere of a small firm. Members of the firm have frequently been quoted in the national press and have appeared on national television news shows. Quality, creativity, integrity, efficiency, and an uncompromising accessibility to clients are the backbone of Vorzimer, Garber, Masserman & Ecoff's approach. The Firm is determined to work with its clients to offer the highest quality, aggressive legal representation in the areas of civil and criminal litigation. The Firm is also experienced in commercial and business transactions, business entity formation and reorganization, business and partnership dissolutions, appellate practice and family law.

**ANDREW W. VORZIMER,** born New York, N.Y., October 21, 1963; admitted to bar, 1988, California, U.S. District Court, Central, Eastern, Southern and Northern Districts of California and U.S. Court of Appeals, Ninth Circuit. *Education:* Harvard University; University of Miami (B.B.A., 1985); Whittier College School of Law (J.D., magna cum laude, 1988). Member, Moot Court Honors Board. Recipient: American Jurisprudence Awards in Torts, Criminal Law, Legal Process, Constitutional Law, Unfair Trade Practices and Remedies; Corpus Juris Secundum Award. Externalized Member, Whittier Moot Court, 1986. Executive Editor, *Whittier Law Review,* 1987-1988. Contributing Author: *Insurance Handbook for Business Litigators,* 1989; "CEB Civil Procedure Before Trial," 1990 and the *Insurance Handbook for Litigators,* 1991. Author: "Workplace Environment: Sexual Harassment," *CC&F Legal Update,* Winter 1992; "Business & Professions Code Section 17200: California's Unfair Competition Law - Parts I & II," *C&C Legal Update,* Summer and Fall, 1992. Co-Author: "Sexual Harassment: Increase in Claims Strikes Fear in Employers," *C & C Legal Update,* Summer 1993. Author: "Hostile Work Environment Claims Have Employers on the Defensive," *C&C Legal Update,* Fall 1993. *Member:* Beverly Hills (Member, Entertainment Section), Los Angeles County and American Bar Associations; State Bar of California; Association of Business Trial Lawyers. **REPORTED CASES:** North River Insurance Co. v American Home Assurance Co., 210 Cal. App. 3d 108 (1989). **PRACTICE AREAS:** Complex Business Litigation; General Civil Litigation; Appeals; Entertainment.

**STEVEN M. GARBER,** born Encino, California, December 12, 1965; admitted to bar, 1991, California, U.S. District Court, Central, Southern, Eastern and Northern Districts of California and U.S. Court of Appeals, Ninth Circuit. *Education:* California State University at Northridge (B.A., 1988); Whittier College School of Law (J.D., 1991). Phi Alpha Delta; Pi Kappa Alpha. Member, Moot Court. Recipient, American Jurisprudence Award in Legal Analysis. Author: "Walking the Tightrope: Contesting Coverage During the Underlying Case," ABA Torts and Insurance Practice Section Publication; "The ABC's of ERISA," program materials for the USC Institute for Corporate Counsel, March 1992, also published in *Employee Benefits Counselor,* January 1994. *Member:* Los Angeles County and American Bar Associations; State Bar of California; Association of Business Trial Lawyers. **PRACTICE AREAS:** Complex Business Litigation; Real Estate; Corporations and Partnerships; Insurance Coverage; General Civil Practice.

**DEAN MASSERMAN,** born Los Angeles, California, October 13, 1963; admitted to bar, 1988, California; U.S. District Court, Central, Eastern, Northern and Southern Districts of California; U.S. Court of Appeals, Ninth Circuit. *Education:* University of California at San Diego (B.A., 1985); University of Colorado at Boulder; Southwestern University (J.D., 1988). Author: "No More Double Dipping For Injured Employees," *C&C*

*(This Listing Continued)*

*Legal Update,* Winter 1994. Attorney Volunteer, Los Angeles Superior Court Domestic Violence Program. *Member:* Los Angeles County (Member, Sections on: Litigation and Criminal Defense) and Federal Bar Associations; State Bar of California; California Trial Lawyers Association; San Fernando Valley Criminal Bar Association; California Attorneys for Criminal Justice. **LANGUAGES:** Spanish. **PRACTICE AREAS:** Premises Liability Defense; Criminal Defense Litigation; Civil Litigation.

**LAWRENCE C. ECOFF,** born Granada Hills, California, May 17, 1964; admitted to bar, 1989, California and U.S. District Court, Central District of California; 1990, Arizona and U.S. District Court, Southern District of California. *Education:* University of California at Irvine (B.A., cum laude, 1986); Loyola Law School (J.D., 1989). *Member:* Beverly Hills and American Bar Associations; State Bar of California. **REPORTED CASES:** People vs. Kevin Merritt, 19 Cal. App. 4th 1573 (1993). **PRACTICE AREAS:** White Collar; Criminal Defense; Complex Business Litigation; Appeals.

---

**DATEV K. SHENIAN,** born Beirut, Lebanon, March 12, 1967; admitted to bar, 1993, California; U.S. District Court, Central District of California; U.S. Court of Appeals, Ninth Circuit. *Education:* University of California at Los Angeles (B.A., cum laude, 1990; J.D., 1993). Phi Delta Phi. Assistant Editor, Pacific Basin Law Journal, 1992-1993. *Member:* Los Angeles County and American Bar Associations; State Bar of California. **LANGUAGES:** Armenian. **PRACTICE AREAS:** General Civil Litigation; Real Estate; Appeals.

**DENISE D. ULLOA,** born Saskatoon, Saskatchewan, Canada, March 9, 1960; admitted to bar, 1996, California. *Education:* University of Saskatchewan (B.Ed. , 1983); Whittier College School of Law (J.D., 1996). Recipient: American Jurisprudence Award, Legal Research and Writing. Author: Advanced Televisions Systems: A Reexamination of Broadcasters' Use of the Spectrum From a Twenty-First Century Perspective," 16 Whittier L. Rev. 1155, 1996. *Member:* State Bar of California. **LANGUAGES:** French. **PRACTICE AREAS:** Entertainment Law; Civil Litigation.

**LYNN R. LEVITAN,** born Washington, D.C., March 22, 1968; admitted to bar, 1993, Maryland; 1995, California and U.S. District Court, Central District of California. *Education:* University of Maryland (B.A., 1990); University of Baltimore (J.D., 1993). **LANGUAGES:** Spanish and Sign Language. **PRACTICE AREAS:** Civil Litigation; Real Estate; Entertainment Litigation.

*OF COUNSEL*

**WILLIAM W. HANDEL,** born Brazil, August 25, 1951; admitted to bar, 1979, California; U.S. District Court, Central District of California; U.S. Court of Appeals, Ninth Circuit. *Education:* California State University at Northridge (B.A., 1976); Whittier College School of Law (J.D., 1979). Professor, Whittier College School of Law. Radio Talk Show Host, KFI Radio. Host, "Judge For Yourself," nationally syndicated television talk show. *Member:* State Bar of California. **LANGUAGES:** Spanish. **PRACTICE AREAS:** Surrogacy Law; Civil Litigation.

**JOHN K. CICCARELLI,** born Pittsburgh, Pennsylvania, June 28, 1958; admitted to bar, 1988, California; U.S. District Court, Central District of California; U.S. Court of Appeals, Ninth Circuit. *Education:* Florida State University; Whittier College School of Law (J.D., summa cum laude, 1988). *Member:* State Bar of California. **PRACTICE AREAS:** Insurance Coverage; Civil Litigation.

**THOMAS J. RYU,** born Seoul, Korea, January 29, 1965; admitted to bar, 1991, California; U.S. District Court, Central District of California; U.S. Court of Appeals, Ninth Circuit. *Education:* University of California at Los Angeles (B.A., 1988); Whittier College School of Law (J.D., 1991). *Member:* State Bar of California. **LANGUAGES:** Korean. **PRACTICE AREAS:** Construction; Professional Malpractice; Premises Liability.

---

## LAW OFFICES OF CHARLES K. WAKE

**8484 WILSHIRE BOULEVARD, SUITE 850
BEVERLY HILLS, CALIFORNIA 90211-3227**
Telephone: 213-782-7730
Fax: 213-782-0177

*Entertainment Law, Business Litigation, Employment Law.*

**CHARLES K. WAKE,** born Oakland, California, August 29, 1951; admitted to bar, 1978, California, U.S. District Court, Northern, Central and

*(This Listing Continued)*

**LAW OFFICES OF CHARLES K. WAKE**, Beverly Hills—
*Continued*

Southern Districts of California and U.S. Court of Appeals, Ninth Circuit. *Education:* University of California at Santa Cruz (B.A., with honors, 1974); University of California at Berkeley (J.D., 1978). *Member:* State Bar of California; Los Angeles County (Member: Ethics Committee, 1983-1989; Barristers Executive Committee, 1983-1984) and American Bar Associations. *REPORTED CASES:* Arista Films v. Gilford Securities.

---

## WEINSTEIN AND HART

A Partnership including a Professional Corporation

*Established in 1984*

IMPERIAL BANK BUILDING
9777 WILSHIRE BOULEVARD, SUITE 1009
**BEVERLY HILLS, CALIFORNIA 90212-1901**
Telephone: 310-274-7157
Fax: 310-274-1437
Email: joehartlaw@aol.com

*General Civil and Trial Practice in all State and Federal Courts. Entertainment, Copyright, Corporate and Commercial Law.*

### MEMBERS OF FIRM

**JEROME E. WEINSTEIN, (P.C.),** born Boston, Massachusetts, August 9, 1935; admitted to bar, 1960, Massachusetts; 1966, New York; 1970, California. *Education:* Boston University (A.B., magna cum laude, 1956); Trinity Hall, University of Cambridge, England (B.A., and M.A., 1958); Harvard University (LL.B., cum laude, 1960). Phi Beta Kappa; Pi Gamma Mu. Author: "Some Problems in the Field of State Securities Regulation," Boston College Law Review, Spring 1962; "Commercial Appropriation of Name or Likeness: Section 3344 and the Common Law," Los Angeles Bar Journal, March, 1977; "Commercial Appropriation of Name or Likeness Revisited," Beverly Hills Bar Journal, Summer, 1988; "What Do Robots, James Dean and Doritos Corn Chips Have in Common?," Beverly Hills Bar Journal, Fall 1994. Chairman, Board of Public Welfare, Town of Needham, Massachusetts, 1963-1965. Member, Board of Governors, Beverly Hills Municipal League, 1975-1977. Member, Executive Committee and Director, National Association of Better Broadcasting, 1971-1993; Lawyers Advisory Committee on Legal Matters (appointed by the Beverly Hills Board of Education), 1975-1976; Member, 1977-1985 and President, 1979-1980, 1984, Board of Education, Beverly Hills School District; Chairman, Affirmative Action Committee, Beverly Hills Board of Education, 1975-1977. Member: Beverly Hills Rent Stabilization Committee, 1978-1979; Advisory Commission, State of California Motion Picture Council, 1982-1987; Beverly Hills Cable TV Advisory Committee, 1985-1987. Director and President, Beverly Hills Community Access Corporation (appointed by Beverly Hills City Council), 1988-1989. *Member:* The Association of the Bar of the City of New York; Boston, Beverly Hills, Los Angeles County and Massachusetts Bar Associations; State Bar of California. *PRACTICE AREAS:* Entertainment Law; Copyright; Corporate Law.

**JOSEPH F. HART,** born Bethesda, Maryland, October 23, 1952; admitted to bar, 1978, California; 1988, U.S. Supreme Court. *Education:* University of California at Berkeley (A.B., 1974); University of California at Los Angeles (J.D., 1978). Staff Member, University of California at Los Angeles Law Review, 1977-1978. Law Clerk to Judge Robert J. Kelleher, U.S. District Court, Central District of California, 1978-1979. Co-Author: "Less Than Zero," Los Angeles Lawyer, April 1996. Judge Pro Tem, Los Angeles Municipal Courts, 1984—. Arbitrator, Better Business Bureau, 1984-1986. President, Down Syndrome Association of Los Angeles, 1992-1994. Commissioner, Westside Basketball Association, 1984. *Member:* Beverly Hills and Los Angeles County (Vice-Chair, Attorney Client Relations Committee, 1990—) Bar Associations; State Bar of California. *PRACTICE AREAS:* Litigation; Entertainment Law.

---

## WEISSMANN, WOLFF, BERGMAN, COLEMAN & SILVERMAN

A Law Partnership including Professional Corporations

9665 WILSHIRE BOULEVARD, SUITE 900
**BEVERLY HILLS, CALIFORNIA 90212-2316**
Telephone: 310-858-7888
Facsimile: 310-550-7191
Email: WWBCS@EARTHLINK.NET

*General Civil, Trial and Appellate Practice in all Courts. Entertainment, Motion Picture, Television, Cable, Copyright, Real Estate, Corporate and Securities Law, Taxation, Estate Planning and Probate.*

### MEMBERS OF FIRM

**MICHAEL BERGMAN,** born New York, N.Y., February 9, 1939; admitted to bar, 1963, New York; 1966, California. *Education:* Syracuse University (B.A., 1960); New York University (LL.B., 1963). Order of the Coif. Author: "The Corporate Joint Venture Under the Antitrust Laws," 37 N.Y.U. Law Review 712, 1962. Staff Member, 1962 and Editor, 1963, N.Y.U. Law Review. Law Clerk to Chief Judge Joseph C. Zavatt, U.S. District Court, Eastern District of New York, 1963-1965. *Member:* Beverly Hills and Los Angeles County Bar Associations; The State Bar of California. *PRACTICE AREAS:* Litigation; Litigation, Intellectual Property and Entertainment.

**STEWART S. BROOKMAN,** born Passaic, New Jersey, May 2, 1959; admitted to bar, 1984, California. *Education:* Colgate University (B.A., cum laude, 1981); Boalt Hall School of Law, University of California at Berkeley (J.D., 1984). *Member:* Los Angeles County Bar Association; State Bar of California. *PRACTICE AREAS:* Entertainment.

**STAN COLEMAN,** born Brooklyn, New York, October 31, 1944; admitted to bar, 1970, California. *Education:* Cornell University (A.B., cum laude, 1966); Columbia University (J.D., cum laude, 1969). Harlan Fiske Stone Scholar. Barney Jaffin Scholar. *Member:* Beverly Hills, Los Angeles County and American Bar Associations; The State Bar of California. *PRACTICE AREAS:* Entertainment Law; New Technologies; Media.

**MICHAEL LEE EIDEL,** born Hempstead, N.Y., January 28, 1960; admitted to bar, 1985, California. *Education:* Cornell University (B.S., 1982; J.D., 1985). California Municipal Court Settlement Officer. *Member:* Los Angeles County and American (Section, Litigation) Bar Associations; State Bar of California. *LANGUAGES:* French. *PRACTICE AREAS:* General Civil Litigation; Contracts; Entertainment; Sports Law; Real Estate; Employment; Intellectual Property.

**MITCHELL EVALL,** born New York, N.Y., May 10, 1956; admitted to bar, 1980, California. *Education:* Brandeis University (A.B., magna cum laude, 1977); Columbia University (J.D., 1980). *Member:* Beverly Hills and Los Angeles County Bar Associations; The State Bar of California. *PRACTICE AREAS:* Real Property Law.

**ALAN L. GRODIN,** born Pittsburgh, Pennsylvania, January 29, 1943; admitted to bar, 1967, New York; 1974, California. *Education:* Pennsylvania State University (B.S., 1964); New York University (LL.B., 1967). Law Clerk to Judge Orrin G. Judd, U.S. District Court, Eastern District of New York, 1970. *Member:* Beverly Hills, Los Angeles County and New York State Bar Associations; State Bar of California; State Bar of New York. *PRACTICE AREAS:* Entertainment.

**DAVID J. GULLEN, (P.C.),** born Rochester, New York, April 1, 1942; admitted to bar, 1968, New York, U.S. Tax Court and U.S. Claims Court; 1973, California. *Education:* Boston College (A.B., cum laude, 1964); Georgetown University (J.D., 1968); New York University (LL.M., 1973). Member, Georgetown Law Journal, 1972-1973. Trial Attorney, U.S. Department of Justice, 1968-1973. Chairman, UCLA Entertainment Tax Institute, 1986. *Member:* Beverly Hills, Los Angeles County and American (Member, Taxation Section) Bar Associations; State Bar of California. *PRACTICE AREAS:* Federal & State Income Tax; Federal Estate Tax; State Inheritance Tax; Business Transactions; Trademark Licensing.

**HENRY W. HOLMES,** born Malden, Massachusetts, April 1, 1943; admitted to bar, 1970, California; 1971, U.S. District Court, Central and Southern Districts of California and U.S. Court of Appeals, Ninth Circuit; 1972, American Samoa. *Education:* San Diego State University; University of California at Berkeley (B.A., 1966); Boalt Hall School of Law, University of California (J.D., 1969). Recipient, Ford Foundation Professional Fellowship, New Delhi, India. Co-Author: "Rules of Practice Before High Court of American Samoa," published by the High Court of American Samoa, 1972.

*(This Listing Continued)*

Lecturer: "Plaintiff's Copyright Litigation," Los Angeles Copyright Society, 1981; "Motion Picture Copyright Issues," State Bar of Wisconsin, 1986. Contributor and Lecturer, 1981 Symposium on "Copyrights a Look into the 80's" and Contributor to Syllabus, 1979 Symposium "Ideas Submission," sponsored by the Intellectual Property and Unfair Competition Section of the Los Angeles County Bar Association. Law Clerk to the Honorable William J. McKnight, 1972-1973. Judge Pro Tem, Beverly Hills Municipal Court, 1980—. Consultant to California Attorney General's Office on Copyright and Fair Use, 1981. Trustee, Women's Sports Foundation, 1982-1993. General Counsel, Science Fiction Writers of America, 1983-1992. Certified Player Agent, National Basketball Players Association. *Member:* Beverly Hills and Los Angeles County Bar Associations; State Bar of California. *PRACTICE AREAS:* Entertainment; Sports Law.

**LINDA A. KALM,** born Santa Monica, California, February 9, 1963; admitted to bar, 1988, California; 1989, U.S. District Court, Northern District of California; U.S. District Court, Central District of California. *Education:* Stanford University (B.A., 1984); New York University (J.D., 1988). Note and Comment Editor, New York University Law Review, 1987-1988. Author: "The Burden of Proving Truth or Falsity in Defamation: Setting a Standard for Cases Involving Nonmedia Defendants," 62 N.Y.U. L. Rev. 812, 1987. *PRACTICE AREAS:* Corporate Law; Real Estate Law.

**STEVEN KATLEMAN,** born Los Angeles, California, July 11, 1954; admitted to bar, 1980, California; 1981, U.S. District Court, Central District of California; 1983, U.S. Court of Appeals, Ninth Circuit. *Education:* University of California at Los Angeles (A.B., magna cum laude, 1977); Hastings College of Law, University of California (J.D., 1980). *Member:* Los Angeles County and American Bar Associations; State Bar of California. *PRACTICE AREAS:* Entertainment Law.

**ALAN G. KIRIOS, (LAW CORPORATION),** born Lynn, Massachusetts, September 26, 1945; admitted to bar, 1973, Massachusetts; 1974, California; 1980, U.S. District Court, Central District of California and U.S. Tax Court. *Education:* Tufts University (B.A., 1967); Boston University (J.D., 1973); New York University (LL.M., 1977). Instructor, University of Southern California Law Center Advanced Professional Program, 1978-1980. Author: "Territoriality and International Copyright Infringement Actions," 22 ASCAP Copyright Law Symposium 53, 1977. Lecturer: Practicing Law Institute Annual Immigration and Naturalization Institutes, 1979, 1982 and 1984; UCLA Entertainment Tax Institute, 1986 and 1989. *Member:* Los Angeles County Bar Association; State Bar of California. *PRACTICE AREAS:* Taxation; Estate Planning; Foreign Investment in U.S..

**ANJANI MANDAVIA,** born Kampala, Uganda, August 9, 1956; admitted to bar, 1980, California; 1981, U.S. Court of Appeals, Ninth Circuit. *Education:* Stanford University (A.B., with distinction, 1977); Boalt Hall School of Law, University of California (J.D., 1980). Member, Moot Court Board, 1979-1980. *Member:* Beverly Hills and Los Angeles County Bar Associations; The State Bar of California. *PRACTICE AREAS:* Civil Litigation.

**RONALD J. SILVERMAN, (P.C.),** born New York, N.Y., August 29, 1946; admitted to bar, 1973, District of Columbia; 1978, California. *Education:* Pennsylvania State University (B.A., with honors, 1967); George Washington University (J.D., 1972). Member, George Washington Law Review, 1971-1972. Special Assistant United States Attorney, Washington, D.C., 1973. Trial Attorney, Antitrust Division, U.S. Department of Justice, 1972-1977. Member, Legal Committee, Progress L.A., 1994—. *Member:* District of Columbia Bar; Los Angeles County and American Bar Associations; The State Bar of California. *PRACTICE AREAS:* Civil Litigation.

**TODD M. STERN,** born Chicago, Illinois, November 12, 1963; admitted to bar, 1988, California. *Education:* University of Illinois (B.S., with highest honors, 1985); University of California at Los Angeles (J.D., 1988). Comments Editor, Federal Communications Law Journal, 1987-1988. Recipient, American Jurisprudence Award in Corporations. *Member:* Beverly Hills Bar Association; State Bar of California. *PRACTICE AREAS:* Entertainment Law.

**ERIC WEISSMANN, (P.C.),** born Zurich, Switzerland, May 31, 1930; admitted to bar, 1955, California. *Education:* University of California at Los Angeles (A.A., 1950; B.A., 1951; LL.B., 1954). Phi Beta Kappa. First Recipient, Independent Feature Project West INDIE Award; Recipient, 1996, Anti-Defamation League "Distinguished Entertainment Leadership Award. Lecturer: "Legal Aspects of Film", Sherwood Oaks Experimental College, 1976-1979; "Business Aspects of Entertainment Law", Northwest Media Project, Portland, Oregon, 1980, Australian Film Symposiums, Sydney, Australia, 1980-1989 and Soviet State Committee for the Motion Picture Industry, April 1989. Member, Advisory Board, Independent Feature

*(This Listing Continued)*

Project, 1985. Listed in Best Lawyers in America, 1993-1994. Named Among Best Entertainment Lawyers in America, Town & Country Magazine, 1985. Listed among "The Ten Best Entertainment Lawyers" on the Internet. *Member:* Los Angeles County Bar Association; The State Bar of California; The Los Angeles Copyright Society (President, 1968-1969). *LANGUAGES:* French, German and Spanish. *PRACTICE AREAS:* Entertainment Law (Representing Directors); International Transactions.

**DANIEL H. WOLFF,** born St. Louis, Missouri, November 24, 1937; admitted to bar, 1965, Missouri; 1969, California. *Education:* Washington University (B.A., 1959); Columbia University (M.B.A., 1961); Harvard University (LL.B., 1965). Phi Beta Kappa; Beta Gamma Sigma. *Member:* Beverly Hills, Los Angeles County and American Bar Associations; The State Bar of California; The Missouri Bar. *PRACTICE AREAS:* Corporate Law.

## ASSOCIATES

**LUCY NOBLE INMAN,** born Indianapolis, Indiana, May 7, 1961; admitted to bar, 1990, North Carolina and U.S. District Court, Eastern District of North Carolina; 1992, California; 1993, U.S. District Court, Central District of California. *Education:* North Carolina State University (B.A., with highest honors, 1984); University of North Carolina School of Law at Chapel Hill (J.D., with honors, 1990). Phi Kappa Phi. Member, The James E. and Carolyn B. Davis Society, University of North Carolina School of Law at Chapel Hill, 1990. Articles Editor, North Carolina Law Review, 1989-1990. Law Clerk to the Honorable James G. Exum, Jr., Chief Justice, North Carolina Supreme Court, 1990-1992. Author: "An Appeal for Clear Litigation Writing," The North Carolina Bar Quarterly, Spring 1991; "Hall v. Post: North Carolina Rejects Claim of Invasion of Privacy by Truthful Publication of Embarrassing Facts," 67 North Carolina Law Review 1474, 1989; "Mental Impairment and Mens Rea: North Carolina Recognizes the Diminished Capacity Defense in State v. Shank and State v. Ross," 67 North Carolina Law Review 1293, 1989. *Member:* Beverly Hills Bar Association; North Carolina State Bar; State Bar of California. *PRACTICE AREAS:* Litigation.

**MELANIE GRANT JONES,** born St. Louis, Missouri, October 24, 1965; admitted to bar, 1992, California. *Education:* Spelman College (B.A., cum laude, 1987); Columbia University School of International and Public Affairs; Columbia Law School (J.D., 1991). Co-Author: Sedition Redux: The Abuse of Libel Law in U.S. Courts, Oxford U. Press, 1991. *LANGUAGES:* French.

**DAVID B. MIERCORT,** born New Orleans, Louisiana, December 15, 1967; admitted to bar, 1994, California. *Education:* Brown University (B.A., magna cum laude, 1990); Columbia University (J.D., 1994). Phi Beta Kappa. Stone Scholar. *Member:* State Bar of California. *PRACTICE AREAS:* Motion Picture and Television Law; Entertainment Contracts; Copyright Law.

**KATHARINE SABICH-ROBISON,** born Placerville, California, November 2, 1968; admitted to bar, 1996, California, U.S. District Court, Central District of California and U.S. Court of Appeals, Ninth Circuit. *Education:* Stanford University (B.A., 1991); University of California at Davis (J.D., 1995). Justice Frances Newell Carr Scholar. Law Clerk to the Honorable George H. King, U.S. District Court, Central District of California, 1995-1996. *Member:* Beverly Hills, Los Angeles County and Federal Bar Associations; State Bar of California; Women Lawyers Association of Los Angeles. *LANGUAGES:* French, Spanish and Latin. *PRACTICE AREAS:* Litigation.

**ANDREW J. SCHMERZLER,** born Plainview, New York, November 6, 1964; admitted to bar, 1989, California. *Education:* University of Pennsylvania (B.A., 1986); University of California at Los Angeles (J.D., 1989). *Member:* Beverly Hills and American Bar Associations; State Bar of California. *PRACTICE AREAS:* Corporate Law; Real Estate.

**ROBERT M. SZYMANSKI,** born Warsaw, Poland, June 19, 1968; admitted to bar, 1995, California. *Education:* University of California, Berkeley (A.B., Highest Honors and High Distinction in General Scholarship, 1991); Harvard University (J.D., cum laude, 1995). Phi Beta Kappa. First Place, Nathan Burkham Memorial Competition (1995). Author: "Audio Pastiche: Digital Sampling, Intermediate copying, Fair Use," Vol. 3 Issue 2 pg 271 (Spring, 1996). *Member:* Los Angels and Beverly Hills Bar Associations; State Bar of California. *PRACTICE AREAS:* Entertainment Law; Media Law.

**JULIE B. WALDMAN,** born Los Angeles, California, September 14, 1967; admitted to bar, 1992, California. *Education:* Brown University (B.A., 1989); University of Southern California (J.D., 1992). Order of the

*(This Listing Continued)*

**WEISSMANN, WOLFF, BERGMAN, COLEMAN & SILVERMAN,** Beverly Hills—Continued

Coif. *Member:* Los Angeles and Beverly Hills Bar Associations; State Bar of California. **PRACTICE AREAS:** Entertainment; Business Litigation.

OF COUNSEL

**IRA S. EPSTEIN,** born Omaha, Nebraska, April 23, 1932; admitted to bar, 1956, Nebraska; 1959, California. *Education:* University of Nebraska at Lincoln (B.S., 1956; J.D., 1956). Phi Delta Phi. Editor, Nebraska Law Review, 1955-1956. *Member:* Beverly Hills and Los Angeles County Bar Associations; Nebraska Bar Association; State Bar of California. [Capt., Judge Advocate Corps, U.S. Air Force, 1957-1959]

**LAWRENCE B. STEINBERG,** born Brooklyn, New York, February 17, 1957; admitted to bar, 1981, California; 1982, U.S. District Court, Central, Northern, Eastern and Southern Districts of California and U.S. Court of Appeals, Ninth Circuit. *Education:* Yale University (B.A., magna cum laude with distinction in political science, 1978); Harvard University (J.D., 1981). Editor, Harvard Civil Rights - Civil Liberties Law Review, 1980-1981. Member, Board of Directors, 1984-1991, Treasurer, 1987-1988, Secretary, 1988-1989, Vice President, 1989-1990 and President, 1990-1991, Public Counsel. Member, Board of Directors, Inner City Law Center, 1991-1993. Judge Pro Tem, Los Angeles and Beverly Hills Municipal Courts, 1986—. Judicial Arbitrator, Los Angeles Superior Court, 1993-1994. *Member:* Beverly Hills (Member, Board of Governors, 1991-1995), Los Angeles County (Member, Litigation Section) and American (Member: Litigation Section) Bar Associations; State Bar of California (Member: Committee on Fair Trial and Free Press, 1983-1984; Delegate, Conference of Delegates, 1985-1990. **REPORTED CASES:** Levin v. Knight, 780 F.2d 786 (9th Cir. 1986); Rosenthal v. Fonda, 862 F.2d 1398 (9th Cir. 1988); Christensen v. United States District Court, 844 F.2d 694 (9th Cir. 1988); In re Tia Carrere, 64 B.R. 156 (Bankr. C.D. Cal. 1986). **PRACTICE AREAS:** Commercial, Real Estate and Entertainment Litigation.

---

## ARNOLD F. WILLIAMS
### BEVERLY HILLS, CALIFORNIA
(See Los Angeles)

*Wills, Trusts and Estate Planning, Probate, Charitable Tax Planning and Elder Law.*

---

## WILNER, KLEIN & SIEGEL
A PROFESSIONAL CORPORATION
SUITE 700, 9601 WILSHIRE BOULEVARD
**BEVERLY HILLS, CALIFORNIA 90210**
Telephone: 213-272-8631; 310-550-4595
Facsimile: 213-272-4339

*Brea, California Office:* 3230 East Imperial Highway, Suite 309. Telephone: 714-579-2600. Facsimile: 714-579-2549.

*General Civil and Trial Practice in all State and Federal Courts. Admiralty and General Maritime Law. Real Property, Corporate, Community Association Law, Insurance, Federal Employers Liability Act and Professional Liability Law.*

**WALTER KLEIN,** born Los Angeles, California, June 22, 1937; admitted to bar, 1963, California and U.S. District Court, Central District of California; 1964, U.S. District Court, Northern District of California; 1979, U.S. District Court, Southern District of California. *Education:* University of California at Los Angeles (B.S., 1959); Loyola University of Los Angeles (LL.B., 1962); University of Southern California. Phi Alpha Delta. Judge Pro Tem, Beverly Hills Municipal Court. Member, Panel of Arbitrators, American Arbitration Association. *Member:* Los Angeles County and American (Member, Section on Litigation) Bar Associations; State Bar of California; Maritime Law Association of the United States; Southern California Applicant's Attorneys Association; National Association of Railroad Trial Counsel.

**SAMUEL WILNER,** born Munich, Germany, October 11, 1948; admitted to bar, 1974, California and U.S. Court of Appeals, Ninth Circuit. *Education:* University of California at Santa Barbara (B.A., cum laude, 1970); Loyola Marymount University. Member, Loyola Law Review, 1973-1974.

*(This Listing Continued)*

Author: "Due On Sale and Due On Encumbrance Clauses in California," 7 Loyola Law Review 306, 1974. *Member:* Los Angeles County and American Bar Associations; State Bar of California; Maritime Law Association of the United States.

**LEONARD SIEGEL,** born Inglewood, California, April 12, 1950; admitted to bar, 1974, California, U.S. District Court, Central District of California and U.S. Court of Appeals, Ninth Circuit. *Education:* University of California at Los Angeles (B.A., 1971); Netherlands School of Business, Breukelen, The Netherlands; Loyola University of Los Angeles (J.D., 1974). Member, St. Thomas More Law Honor Society. Member of Staff, 1973 and Note Editor 1974, Loyola Law Review. President, 1981-1982 and Member, Board of Directors, 1980-1984, Community Associations Institute. *Member:* The State Bar of California (Member, Sub-committee on Condominiums, 1981, 1982 and 1983).

**LAURA J. SNOKE,** born Durham, North Carolina, September 25, 1949; admitted to bar, 1981, California. *Education:* California State University at Northridge (B.A., 1973); California State University at Los Angeles; Loyola University of Los Angeles (J.D., 1981). Phi Alpha Theta. *Member:* Los Angeles County and American (Member, Litigation Section) Bar Associations; The State Bar of California; Women Lawyers Association.

**WENDY A. GOLDBERG,** born Sacramento, California, August 3, 1946; admitted to bar, 1980, California; 1981, U.S. District Court, Central, Southern and Northern Districts of California and U.S. Court of Appeals, Ninth Circuit. *Education:* San Francisco State College (B.A., 1969; M.A., 1970); Loyola University of Los Angeles (LL.B., 1980). *Member:* Los Angeles County and American Bar Associations; State Bar of California.

**JODI ZUCKER TAKSAR,** born Los Angeles, California, September 14, 1958; admitted to bar, 1985, California; 1987, U.S. District Court, Central District of California. *Education:* University of California at Santa Barbara (B.A., 1980); Southwestern University (J.D., cum laude, 1984); New York University (LL.M., Taxation, 1985). Recipient, American Jurisprudence Award in Corporations. *Member:* State Bar of California.

**EDWARD E. WALLACE,** born Sumner, Washington, June 17, 1953; admitted to bar, 1979, California and U.S. Court of Appeals, Ninth Circuit. *Education:* California State University at Chico (B.A., cum laude, 1976); Hastings College of Law, University of California (J.D., 1979). *Member:* Bar Association of San Francisco; Los Angeles County Bar Association; State Bar of California.

**ALAN GOLDBERG,** born Detroit, Michigan, February 14, 1955; admitted to bar, 1980, California; 1981, U.S. District Court, Central District of California; 1984, U.S. District Court, Southern, Northern and Eastern Districts of California. *Education:* University of Michigan; University of California at Los Angeles (B.A., 1977); Loyola Law School of Los Angeles (J.D., 1980). *Member:* San Fernando Valley and Los Angeles County Bar Associations; State Bar of California; Association of Business Trial Lawyers.

**JOSEPH R. SERPICO,** born Los Angeles, California, September 23, 1951; admitted to bar, 1977, California and U.S. District Court, Central District of California; 1978, U.S. Court of Appeals, Ninth Circuit. *Education:* California State University at Northridge (B.S., cum laude, 1973); Southwestern University (J.D., 1976). *Member:* Los Angeles County and American Bar Associations; State Bar of California; Association of Southern California Defense Counsel.

---

**GARY S. KESSLER,** born Los Angeles, California, November 12, 1955; admitted to bar, 1980, California; 1981, U.S. District Court, Central District of California and U.S. Court of Appeals, Ninth Circuit; 1984, U.S. District Court, Southern District of California. *Education:* University of California at Berkeley (A.B., summa cum laude, 1977); Loyola University of Los Angeles (J.D., 1980). Phi Beta Kappa. Advocates Scholarship For Excellence in Study of Law, Loyola University of Los Angeles, 1979. Board of Editors, Ninth Circuit Loyola Law Review, 1979-1980. Member, St. Thomas More Law Honor Society. Author: "Developments in Criminal Law on Procedure in the Ninth Circuit, 1978, Warrantless Searches," 12 Loyola Law Review, 505, 533, 1979. *Member:* Century City and Los Angeles County Bar Associations; State Bar of California; Los Angeles Trial Lawyers Association; California Trial Lawyers Association.

**MARC H. GOLDSMITH,** born Hammond, Indiana, June 1, 1953; admitted to bar, 1983, Illinois; 1985, California. *Education:* University of California, Santa Cruz (A.B., 1975); University of Minnesota (M.A., with honors, 1979; J.D., cum laude, 1983). Adjunct Professor, Southwestern University School of Law, 1990. *Member:* Bar Association of San Francisco

*(This Listing Continued)*

(Member, Business Law Section); Los Angeles County Bar Association (Member, Business Law Section, 1985-1986); State Bar of California.

**FLOYD W. CRANMORE,** born Ardmore, Oklahoma, June 25, 1958; admitted to bar, 1986, California; 1989, U.S. District Court, Central, Northern and Eastern Districts of California and U.S. Court of Appeals, Ninth Circuit. *Education:* University of Oklahoma (B.S., magna cum laude, 1982); The Ohio State University (J.D., 1985); Exeter University. Law Clerk to: Honorable Judge Jack B. Streepy, U.S. Magistrate, U.S. District Court, Northern District of Ohio, 1986-1988; Presiding U.S. Magistrate Judge Ralph Geffen, U.S. District Court, Central District of California, 1988-1989. *Member:* State Bar of California. **REPORTED CASES:** Hood vs. City of Los Angeles, 804 F.Supp. 65 (C.D. Cal. 1992).

**TERI E. LAWSON,** born Little Rock, Arkansas, September 7, 1960; admitted to bar, 1987, California and U.S. District Court, Central District of California. *Education:* Pitzer College (B.A., 1982); Harvard University (J.D., 1986). *Member:* Los Angeles County Bar Association; State Bar of California; John M. Langston Bar Association; Black Women Lawyers Association of Los Angeles.

**EDWIN J. HOWARD,** born Tel Aviv, Israel, August 5, 1955; admitted to bar, 1988, California; 1990, U.S. District Court, Central District of California. *Education:* University of California at Los Angeles (B.A., 1978); Whittier College School of Law (J.D., 1987). *Member:* Los Angeles County Bar Association; State Bar of California.

**THOMAS M. WARE, II,** born Glendale, California, September 17, 1964; admitted to bar, 1989, California, U.S. Court of Appeals, Ninth Circuit and U.S. District Court, Central District of California; 1991, Nevada. *Education:* University of Nevada at Las Vegas (B.A., with high distinction, 1986); Loyola University of Los Angeles (J.D., cum laude, 1989). Order of the Coif. Member, St. Thomas More Honor Society. *Member:* Beverly Hills, Clark County, Los Angeles County and American Bar Associations; State Bar of California; State Bar of Nevada.

**JOSHUA B. BERENY,** born Los Angeles, California, September 8, 1964; admitted to bar, 1991, California and U.S. District Court, Central District of California; 1993, District of Columbia; 1994, U.S. District Court, Southern District of California; 1996, U.S. Court of Appeals, Ninth Circuit. *Education:* University of California at Santa Barbara (B.A., 1987); Southwestern University School of Law (J.D., 1991). Order of Barristers. Member and Board of Governors, Moot Court Honors Program. Judicial Extern for the Hon. Ronald S. W. Lew, Central District of California. U.S. Merchant Marine, Master, 100 G.T., 1988. *Member:* Maritime Law Association of the United States.

**JAMES P. DEXHEIMER,** born Los Angeles, California, August 19, 1950; admitted to bar, 1983, California, U.S. District Court, Central District of California and U.S. Court of Appeals, Ninth Circuit. *Education:* University of West Los Angeles (B.A., 1983; J.D., 1983). Recipient, American Jurisprudence Book Award in Constitutional Law and Criminal Law. Adjunct Professor, Commercial Code, University of West Los Angeles, 1984-1987. Appointed to Judicial Arbitration Panel, Los Angeles , Superior Court, 1989. *Member:* Los Angeles County (Member, Arbitrator, Fee Dispute Panel, 1989—) and American Bar Association; The State Bar of California. [Sgt., U.S.M.C., 1967-1991]. **PRACTICE AREAS:** Civil Practice; Insurance Defense.

**ERIC S. BLUM,** born Hollywood, California; admitted to bar, 1992, California, U.S. District Court, Central District of California and U.S. Court of Appeals, Ninth Circuit. *Education:* University of Pennsylvania (B.A., cum laude, 1989); University of Southern California (J.D., 1992). Member, Honors Program and Vice Chair, Hale Moot Court. Member, Orange County Legion Lex Inn of Court. *Member:* Orange County Bar Association (Member, Business Litigation Section); State Bar of California (Member, Litigation Section). (Resident, Brea Office).

**PATRICK M. MALONE,** born Fontana, California, April 26, 1964; admitted to bar, 1993, California and U.S. District Court, Central District of California. *Education:* University of California (B.S., 1987); Loyola Law School (J.D., 1993). Staff, 1991-1992, Articles Editor, 1992-1993, Loyola of Los Angeles Law Review. Author, Notes, "Adams v. Murakami--New Judicially Made Rules Affecting Punitive Damages in California," 25 Loyola of Los Angeles Law Review 1441 , June 1992. *Member:* Los Angeles County and American Bar Associations; State Bar of California.

**NORA J. HITE,** born Pico Rivera, California, January 11, 1958; admitted to bar, 1995, California, U.S. Court of Appeals, Ninth Circuit and U.S. District Court Central, Southern, Northern and Eastern Districts of California. *Education:* Cerritos College (A.A., 1986); Pepperdine University (B.A., 1988); Western State University (J.D., 1994). Recipient, American

*(This Listing Continued)*

Jurisprudence Awards, Property I, Contracts II and Remedies I and II. Author, "Its Time to Declare a Truce in the War on Drugs," Western State University, Fall, 1994.

**MITCHELL S. BRACHMAN,** born Hempstead, New York, January 21, 1961; admitted to bar, 1987, California; 1988, U.S. District Court, Central District of California; 1990, District of Columbia. *Education:* University of Michigan (A.B., 1983); Washington College of Law, The American University (J.D., 1986). Phi Alpha Delta. *Member:* Los Angeles and American Bar Associations; The State Bar of California; District of Columbia Bar; California Trial Lawyers Association. **PRACTICE AREAS:** Real Estate; Construction Defect.

**STEPHEN COOPERSMITH,** born Chicago, Illinois, April 21, 1941; admitted to bar, 1970, California. *Education:* University of California at Los Angeles (B.A., 1963); University of La Verne College of Law (LL.B., 1969). *Member:* Los Angeles County and San Fernando Valley Bar Associations; State Bar of California. **PRACTICE AREAS:** Insurance Defense; Construction Law; Civil Litigation.

**NEIL M. POPOWITZ,** born Brooklyn, New York, November 29, 1963; admitted to bar, 1989, California and U.S. District Court, Central District of California; 1991, U.S. District Court, Eastern District of California and U.S. Court of Appeals, Ninth Circuit; 1993, U.S. District Court, Southern District of California. *Education:* University of California at Berkeley (B.A., 1985); Loyola Marymount University (J.D., 1988). Phi Alpha Delta. Author: "Compromising Positions, The Good Faith Requirement of Section 998 Offers to Compromise is Judged Case by Case", Los Angeles Lawyer, December, 1995 Vol. 18 No. 9. *Member:* Los Angeles County, Federal and American Bar Associations (Tort and Insurance Practice Section; Litigation Section); State Bar of California (Member, Litigation Section). **PRACTICE AREAS:** Litigation.

**JEFFREY W. DEANE,** born Los Angeles, California, January 3, 1961; admitted to bar, 1987, California and U.S. District Court, Northern and Southern Districts of California. *Education:* University of California at Los Angeles (B.A., Psychology, 1984; B.A., Economics, 1984); Golden Gate University (J.D., 1987). *Member:* Los Angeles County and American Bar Associations. **PRACTICE AREAS:** Litigation; Product Liability; Attorney Malpractice; Premises Liability.

**STEVEN J. PARKER,** born Pasadena, California, March 20, 1964; admitted to bar, 1989, California and U.S. District Court, Central District of California. *Education:* University of California at Davis (B.A., 1985); University of San Diego (J.D., 1989). *Member:* Orange County and American Bar Associations; State Bar of California. (Resident, Brea Office). **PRACTICE AREAS:** Insurance Defense; Personal Injury; Professional Liability Defense.

**HEIDI H. ELLYN,** born Berkeley, California, December 9, 1963; admitted to bar, 1993, California. *Education:* University of California (B.A., 1987); Pepperdine University (J.D., 1991). Phi Alpha Delta. *Member:* State Bar of California.

**DARRELL J. MARIZ,** born Portland, Oregon, April 8, 1967; admitted to bar, 1993, California. *Education:* University of California at Davis (B.A., with highest honors, 1990); Tulane Law School (J.D., 1993).

### OF COUNSEL

**ALLAN E. WILION, INC.,** born Paris, France, January 29, 1950; admitted to bar, 1974, California and U.S. District Court, Central District of California. *Education:* University of California at Los Angeles (B.A., 1971); Loyola University of Los Angeles (J.D., 1974). St. Thomas More. Executive Editor, Loyola Law Review, 1973-1974. Law Clerk to the Honorable Clarke Stephens, Associate Justice, California Court of Appeals, 1975. Adjunct Professor of Law, Loyola Law School, 1978-1981. *Member:* Los Angeles County Bar Association; State Bar of California.

**RICHARD B. KOTT,** born Lynwood, California, October 3, 1957; admitted to bar, 1984, California, U.S. District Court, Central District of California and U.S. Court of Appeals, Ninth Circuit; 1988, U.S. Supreme Court. *Education:* University of Redlands (B.S., with distinction, 1979); Western State College of Law (J.D., 1983). Sigma Gamma Epsilon; Phi Alpha Delta (President, 1982). Recipient, American Jurisprudence Award, Professional Responsibility. Judge Pro Tem, Orange County Municipal Court, North, 1993—. *Member:* Orange County and American Bar Associations; State Bar of California; American Trial Lawyers Association. (Resident, Brea Office). **PRACTICE AREAS:** Casualty Insurance Defense; Professional Liability Insurance Defense.

**MICHAEL J. GROBATY,** born Long Beach, California, September 14, 1961; admitted to bar, 1986, California; 1987, U.S. District Court, Central

*(This Listing Continued)*

## WILNER, KLEIN & SIEGEL, A PROFESSIONAL CORPORATION, Beverly Hills—Continued

and Southern Districts of California. *Education:* Loyola Marymount University (B.A., 1983; J.D., 1986). Staff Member, Loyola Entertainment Law Journal, 1985-1986. Author: "Miami Ordinance Regulating Cable Television Transmission of 'Indecent' Material: The First Amendment to the Rescue," 5 Loyola of Los Angeles Entertainment Law Journal 198, 1985. *Member:* Whittier, Orange County, Los Angeles County and American Bar Associations; State Bar of California; California Trial Lawyers Association; Defense Research Institute (Member, Liaison to Lawyers Professional Responsibility and Liability Committee). (Resident, Brea Office). **REPORTED CASES:** Barber v. Rancho Mortgage and Investments, 16 Cal. App. 4th 1819, 1994. **PRACTICE AREAS:** Professional Liability; Product Liability; Insurance Defense.

REPRESENTATIVE CLIENTS: UNOCAL; Crowley Maritime Corp.; Home Insurance Company; Chubb Group of Insurance Companies; Fluor Corp.; CIGNA; Stevedoring Services of America; The Rowan Companies; Commercial Union Insurance Company; St. Paul Fire & Marine Insurance Co.; State Farm Insurance Co.; Talbot, Bird & Co.; Farmers Insurance Truck Exchange; American International Group; Assuranceforenigen Skuld; Continental Insurance Company; Union Pacific Railroad; Helmerich & Payne.
REFERENCES: Mitsui Manufacturers Bank; City National Bank.

## ALLEN BARRY WITZ

505 SOUTH BEVERLY DRIVE, SUITE 1066
**BEVERLY HILLS, CALIFORNIA**
Telephone: 310-581-4030
Fax: 310-275-3187

*Securities and Finance.*

**ALLEN BARRY WITZ,** admitted to bar, 1967, Illinois; 1972, New York (Not admitted in California). *Education:* University of Illinois; Roosevelt University (B.S.B.A., 1962); Loyola University (J.D., 1966). Author: "The New York Stock Exchange and the Security Analyst," 42 Wall Street Transcript 35, 069, November, 1973. Chairman, Edgewood Films, Inc., 1983. Chairman, Golden State Broadcasting Co., 1982. Director, Lindy's Food Products Co., Inc., 1986—. Director and Secretary, The Music Shop, Inc., 1986—. *Member:* Federal (Member: Corporation, Banking and Business Law; Taxation; Litigation) and American Bar Associations.

## BRIAN D. WITZER

301 NORTH CANON DRIVE, SUITE 210
**BEVERLY HILLS, CALIFORNIA 90210-4704**
Telephone: 310-777-5999
Fax: 310-777-5988

*Personal Injury, Premises Liability, Insurance Bad Faith, Professional Negligence with emphasis on Medical Malpractice, Wrongful Termination, Entertainment/Copyright Infringement and Criminal Law.*

**BRIAN D. WITZER,** born Philadelphia, Pennsylvania, June 26, 1953; admitted to bar, 1977, Pennsylvania; 1986, California. *Education:* Temple University (B.S., magna cum laude, 1974; J.D., 1977). Phi Beta Kappa. Assistant Attorney General, Department of Justice, State of Pennsylvania, 1977-1979. Assistant District Attorney, City of Philadelphia, 1979-1985. *Member:* Beverly Hills, Los Angeles County and American Bar Associations; State Bar of California; California Trial Lawyers Association; The Association of Trial Lawyers of America; Consumer Attorneys Association of Los Angeles.

### ASSOCIATES

**ANDREW J. SPIELBERGER,** born Goose Bay Labrador, Canada, October 7, 1959; admitted to bar, 1985, California and U.S. District Court, Central District of California. *Education:* Tulane University (B.A., 1981); McGeorge School of Law (J.D., 1985). Associate Editor, International Law Journal. Recipient, American Jurisprudence Award in Administrative Law. *Member:* Los Angeles County Bar Association; State Bar of California. **LANGUAGES:** French. **PRACTICE AREAS:** Personal Injury; Construction Defect; Entertainment; Business Litigation.

## LAW OFFICES OF GREGORY A. YATES

A PROFESSIONAL CORPORATION
GLENDALE FEDERAL BUILDING, SUITE 850
9454 WILSHIRE BOULEVARD
**BEVERLY HILLS, CALIFORNIA 90212**
Telephone: 310-858-6944
Fax: 310-858-7586

*Personal Injury and Products Liability, Civil Litigation.*

**GREGORY A. YATES,** born Glendale, California, July 2, 1947; admitted to bar, 1972, South Dakota; 1974, California; U.S. Federal District Court, Central District of California. *Education:* University of Wyoming; University of South Dakota (B.A., 1969; J.D., 1972). Member, Moot Court Board and Law Review Staff, University of South Dakota. Judge Pro Tem, Los Angeles County. *Member:* Beverly Hills, Los Angeles County and American Bar Associations; State Bar of California; Consumer Attorneys Association of Los Angeles; California Trial Lawyers Association; Million Dollar Advocates Forum. (Member of California Trial Lawyers Association, with recognized experience in the fields of Product Liability, Trial Lawyer and General Personal Injury). **PRACTICE AREAS:** Product Liability; Tort; Public Entity; Civil Litigation; Trial Practice.

**MICHAEL S. DAVENPORT,** born Stuttgart, Germany, June 1, 1965; admitted to bar, 1991, California. *Education:* University of Wisconsin (B.S., 1987); Southwestern University School of Law (J.D., 1991). Member, Barristers Sports Project, 1993. *Member:* Los Angeles County and American Bar Associations; State Bar of California; Los Angeles Trial Lawyers Association. **PRACTICE AREAS:** Products Liability; Tort; Police Misconduct; Premises Liability; Civil Litigation; General Personal Injury; Trial Practice.

## ZUKOR & NELSON

A PROFESSIONAL LAW CORPORATION
9665 WILSHIRE BOULEVARD, SUITE 505
**BEVERLY HILLS, CALIFORNIA 90212**
Telephone: 310-274-0846
Fax: 310-278-4862

*Personal Injury Litigation.*

**ABRAM C. ZUKOR,** born Los Angeles, California, March 2, 1946; admitted to bar, 1974, California, U.S. District Court, Central District of California and U.S. Court of Appeals, Ninth Circuit; 1978, U.S. Supreme Court. *Education:* University of Arizona (B.S., 1969); Southwestern University (J.D., 1973). *Member:* Beverly Hills Bar Association; State Bar of California; California Trial Lawyers Association; The Association of Trial Lawyers of America; Million Dollar Advocates Forum; Consumer Attorneys Association of Los Angeles. **PRACTICE AREAS:** Personal Injury Litigation.

**MARILYN H. NELSON,** born Wilmington, Delaware, December 29, 1945; admitted to bar, 1988, California and U.S. District Court, Central District of California. *Education:* University of California at Los Angeles (B.A., 1985); Southwestern University (J.D., 1988). Recipient, American Jurisprudence Awards: Property I; Forensic Evidence. *Member:* State Bar of California; Womens Lawyers Association of Los Angeles (Board of Governors, 1995—); Consumer Attorneys Association of Los Angeles. **PRACTICE AREAS:** Personal Injury Litigation.

## CALDWELL & KENNEDY

A PROFESSIONAL CORPORATION

**BIG BEAR CITY, CALIFORNIA**

(See Victorville)

*Corporate, Real Property, Business, Commercial Transactions, Construction Disputes, Civil Litigation, Family Law, Estate Planning, Wills and Trusts, Personal Injury Law. Criminal Law and Special Appearances in Local, State and Federal Courts.*

## ANNE SCANLON ZIMMERMAN
895 NEEDLES LANE
P.O. BOX 2458
**BIG BEAR CITY, CALIFORNIA 92314**
Telephone: 909-585-6485
Fax: 909-585-6485
Email: 74051.432@compuserve.com

*Business, Family Law, Real Estate, Bankruptcy and Civil Litigation.*

**ANNE SCANLON ZIMMERMAN,** born San Jose, California, April 13, 1956; admitted to bar, 1980, California; 1984, U.S. District Court, Central District of California. *Education:* University of Southern California (B.A., 1977); Loyola University at Los Angeles (J.D., 1980). Project Editor, Sum & Substance of Law Series, Josephson's Bar Review, 1979, 1980. Contractor, California, License Class C20-C10, 1989—. **PRACTICE AREAS:** Real Estate; Construction; Family Law; Debtor Collections; Appellate; Criminal Defense.

REPRESENTATIVE CLIENTS: Pacific Mortgage Exchange; Country Heart Homes; Coldwell Banker; Qranc USA, Inc.

## McINTIRE LAW CORPORATION
41191 BIG BEAR BOULEVARD
P.O. BOX 1647
**BIG BEAR LAKE, CALIFORNIA 92315**
Telephone: 909-866-7697/866-8772
Fax: 909-866-8307

*General Civil Litigation (trial and appeal), emphasizing Real Property, Eminent Domain and Inverse Condemnation, Business and Commercial (contract and tort), Personal Injury (plaintiff and defense), Insurance Coverage and Bad Faith, Products Liability.*

**MICHAEL V. McINTIRE,** born Zanesville, Ohio, September 10, 1935; admitted to bar, 1964, California, U.S. District Court, Northern and Southern Districts of California and U.S. Court of Appeals, Ninth Circuit; 1965, U.S. District Court, Central District of California; 1974, Indiana; 1988, U.S. Supreme Court. *Education:* University of Notre Dame (B.S.C.E., 1957); University of Wisconsin-Madison (J.D., 1963). Phi Alpha Delta; Order of the Coif. National Moot Court Team. Member, University of Wisconsin Law Review, 1962-1963. Author: "Urban Reconstruction Could Be As Close As The Statehouse", 60 American Bar Association Journal 578, May, 1974; "'Necessity' In Condemnation Cases - Who Speaks For The People?", 22 Hastings Law Journal 561, 1971; "I Wonder Where The Water Went' The Disparity Between State Water Rights Records and Actual Water Use Patterns", 5 Land and Water Law Review 23, 1970; "Are Court Rules Made To Be Broken? Eminent Domain Trial Preparation And The Swarzman Case", 43 California State Bar Journal 556, July-August, 1968; Report, "Effective Control of Industrial Waste Discharge Into Sewerage Systems", for U.S. Environmental Protection Agency, October, 1973; Report, "Legal Study of The Federal Competitive And Non-Competitive Oil and Gas Leasing Systems", 3 Vol., (co-author and editor), for the Public Land Law Review Commission under contract with Rocky Mountain Mineral Law Foundation; "The Environment Movement: A Governmental Renewal Project", 1 Journal of the Insurance, Negligence and Compensation Law Section, New York State Bar Association 4, 1971; "Bringing Polluters to Justice", *Ecology Today,* March, 1971, p. 48. Associate Professor of Law: Land Planning Law, Torts, Products Liability, Natural Resources Law, Environmental Law, State and Local Governmental Law and Legal Research, University of Notre Dame, 1970-1974. Visiting Assistant Professor of Law: Water Pollution Law, Law of Federal Court Jurisdiction and Real Property Law, Syracuse University, 1969-1970. Assistant Professor of Law: Water Law, Natural Resources Law and Oil and Gas Income Taxation, University of Wyoming, College of Law, 1967-1969. Assistant City Attorney, Morro Bay, California, 1964-1967. Member, American Society of Civil Engineers, 1954-1957; 1972-1974. *Member:* State Bar of California. [Capt., USAF, 1957-1961]. **SPECIAL AGENCIES:** Consultant, U.S. Environmental Protection Agency, 1973-1975. Consultant, U.S. Land Law Review Commission under contract with Rocky Mountain Mineral Law Foundation, 1968-1970. **REPORTED CASES:** People ex rel Dept. of Transportation v. Jenkins (1996) 44 Cal. App.4th 306; Markley v. Superior Court (1992) 5 Cal.App.4th 738; Hartenstine v. Superior Court (1987) 196 Cal.App.3d 206; Graydon v. Pasadena Redevelopment Agency (1980) 104 Cal.App.3d 631 (trial attorney); Hawthorne Redevelopment Agency v. Friedman (1977) 76 Cal.App.3d 188; Marina Plaza v. California Coastal Zone Conservation Commission (1977) 73 Cal.App.3d 311; Bakman v. Superior Court (1976) 63 Cal.App.3d 306; People v. Garner (1965) 234 Cal..App.2d 212. **PRACTICE AREAS:** Real Property Litigation; Eminent Domain; Inverse Condemnation; Business Litigation; Governmental Tort Litigation; Insurance Bad Faith.

**CHRISTOPHER D. McINTIRE,** born Newfoundland, Canada, November 11, 1959; admitted to bar, 1985, California and U.S. District Court, Southern District of California and U.S. Court of Appeals, Ninth Circuit; 1993, U.S. District Court, Central District of California. *Education:* Loyola Marymount University (B.A., 1981; J.D., 1985); University of San Diego School on International and Comparative Law. Phi Alpha Theta; Recipient: American Jurisprudence Award, Corporations, Community Property. Associate Editor, Loyola Entertainment Law Journal, 1984-1985. Author: Case Note, "RICO, Reporter's Privilege and The Boston College Point Shaving Scandal," 5 Loyola Entertainment Law Journal 269, 1985. *Member:* State Bar of California; American Bar Association; The Association of Trial Lawyers of America; California Trial Lawyers Association. **REPORTED CASES:** People ex rel Dept of Transportation v. Jenkins (1996) 44 Cal. App.4th 306; Pacific Scene, Inc. v. Penasquitos, Inc. (1988) 46 Cal.3d 407; Yamaha Motor Co. v. Paseman (1989) 210 Cal.App.3d 958; Markley v. Superior Court (1992) 5 Cal.App.4th 738; People v. Jackson (1991) 1 Cal.App.4th 697; People v. Perez (1989) 216 Cal.App.3d 1346; People v. Provencio (1989) 210 Cal.App.3d 290. **PRACTICE AREAS:** Real Property Litigation; Personal Injury (Plaintiff and Defendant); Business and Government Tort; Insurance; Products Liability.

REPRESENTATIVE CLIENTS: Bear Valley Voice; Mountain Broadcasting Corporation; Summit Urgent Care, Inc.; Lutheran Social Services of Southern California; A.F. Services Enterprises, Inc.; Plaza Freeway, Ltd.; Cerro Gordo Mines; Eagles' Knoll Community Association; Honey Bear Lodge; Bavarian Lodge; North Pole Fudge Company; Belotti's Bakery and Pizzeria; Baldwin Lake Stables; Blauer Ski Rentals, Inc.; Fast Lane Ski Rentals; Robertson Properties.
REFERENCES: Desert Community Bank, Victorville, California.

## LYNN E. ZUMBRUNN
A LAW CORPORATION

**BIG BEAR LAKE, CALIFORNIA**

(See Victorville)

*General Civil and Trial Practice. Family, Personal Injury, Corporations, Real Estate, Construction and Probate Law.*

## DOUGLAS BUCHANAN
Established in 1977
459 WEST LINE STREET
P.O. BOX 846
**BISHOP, CALIFORNIA 93515**
Telephone: 619-873-4211
Fax: 619-873-4637

*General and Trial Practice. Criminal and Civil Litigation, Probate and Commercial Law, Bankruptcy.*

**DOUGLAS BUCHANAN,** born Modesto, California, August 7, 1941; admitted to bar, 1975, California; U.S. District Court, Eastern and Northern Districts of California; U.S. Court of Appeals, Ninth Circuit. *Education:* University of Nevada (B.A., 1963); University of the Pacific, McGeorge School of Law (J.D., cum laude, 1975). Phi Delta Phi. Deputy District Attorney, 1976; Public Defender, 1977-1978, Inyo County, California. *Member:* Inyo County Bar Association (President, 1980); The State Bar of California. [1st Lt., U.S. Army, 1963-1965]. **REPORTED CASES:** Jacobson v. Glidden, 84 Cal. App. 3d 748 (1978). **PRACTICE AREAS:** Criminal; Probate; Estate Planning; Civil Litigation; Probate Law; Commercial Law.

### ASSOCIATES

**MARK A. RADOFF,** born Culver City, California, November 23, 1959; admitted to bar, 1985, California and U.S. District Court, Eastern District of California; 1987, New Mexico; 1992, Washington and U.S. District Court, Western District of Washington. *Education:* University of California at Santa Barbara (B.A., 1981); McGeorge School of Law, University of the Pacific (J.D., 1985). Adjunct Professor, Business Law, Navajo Community College, Crownpoint, New Mexico, 1988. Member, New Mexico Medical Review Commission, 1987-1988. Vice-Chair, Snohomish County Community Housing Resource Board, 1992-1993. Board Member, Inyo Mono Advocates for Community Action, 1994-1996. Board Chairman, Inyo-Mono

*(This Listing Continued)*

## DOUGLAS BUCHANAN, Bishop—Continued

Advocates for Community Action, 1996. Hearings Board Officer, Great Basin Unified Air Pollution Control District, 1994-1996. *Member:* Inyo County (President, 1994) and Washington State (Inactive) Bar Associations; State Bar of California; State Bar of New Mexico (Inactive).

### OF COUNSEL

**DOROTHY ALTHER,** born Martin, South Dakota, May 14, 1957; admitted to bar, 1985, New Mexico; 1986, Navajo Nation and U.S. District Court, District of New Mexico; 1989, California and U.S. District Court, Eastern District of California; 1990, U.S. Court of Appeals, Ninth District; 1992, Washington, U.S. District Court, Western District of Washington and Suquamish Tribal Court. *Education:* University of South Dakota (B.A., 1978); Northeastern University (J.D., 1985). *Member:* State Bar of California; State Bar of New Mexico (Inactive); Washington State Bar Association (Inactive).

REPRESENTATIVE CLIENTS: City of Los Angeles Department of Water and Power; Northern Inyo Hospital; Amargosa Opera House; Eastern Sierra Motors, Inc.; Eureka Fuel Co.; Tiger Tote, Inc.; Chalfant Press, Inc.; L. M. Williams Corp.; Shoshone Development Co.; Copeland Lumber Yards, Inc.; Mission Power Engineering; M & L Financial XXIV, a Partnership; Pestmaster Services, Inc.; Erick Schat's Bokkeri; Inyo-Mono Association for the Handicapped; Lady Bug Art Gallery; Inyo-Mono Title Company; Pioneer Home Health, Inc.; ABCOM; Atlantic Richfield Company; Great Country Broadcasting, Inc.; Inyo-Mono Advocates for Community Action; National Farmers Union Insurance.
REFERENCES: Dean Witter Reynolds, Bishop; Union Bank, Bishop

---

## THOMAS L. HARDY

*Established in 1993*

645 WEST LINE STREET
P.O. BOX 547
**BISHOP, CALIFORNIA 93515**
*Telephone: 619-873-8010*
*Fax: 619-873-8011*
*Email: 74663.731@compuserve.com*

*Litigation and Criminal Defense.*

**THOMAS L. HARDY,** born Pana, Illinois, October 21, 1961; admitted to bar, 1987, California. *Education:* Claremont McKenna College (B.A., magna cum laude, 1983); University of California, Los Angeles (J.D., 1987). Order of the Coif. Teaching Assistant, UCLA School of Law Legal Research and Writing Program, 1986. Inyo County Juvenile Public Defender, 1989—. *Member:* Inyo County (President, 1991) and American Bar Associations; The State Bar of California; California Attorneys for Criminal Justice; National Association of Criminal Defense Lawyers. **REPORTED CASES:** In Re Cicely L. (1994) 28 Cal App. 4th 1697. **PRACTICE AREAS:** Civil Litigation; Appeals; Criminal and Juvenile Law; Business; Real Estate.

REPRESENTATIVE CLIENTS: U.S. Tungsten Corp.; Meadowcreek II Homeowners Assoc.; Inyo Recovery, Inc.; Ponderosa Properties; Inyo Home Care Registry; Eldridge Electric, Inc.; DKR Automotive; The Root Seller.
REFERENCES: Monument National Bank; Union Bank, Bishop Branch; County of Inyo.

---

## ARTHUR J. MAILLET, JR.

106 SOUTH MAIN STREET, SUITE 200
P.O. BOX 485
**BISHOP, CALIFORNIA 93515**
*Telephone: 619-872-1101*
*Fax: 619-872-2781*

*General Civil and Criminal Practice Litigation with emphasis on Criminal, Family, Bankruptcy, Probate, Mining, Personal Injury, Real Estate and Indian Law.*

**ARTHUR J. MAILLET, JR.,** born Schurz, Nevada, May 30, 1946; admitted to bar, 1978, California and U.S. District Court, Northern and Eastern Districts of California; 1981, U.S. District Court, Central District of California and U.S. Court of Appeals, Ninth Circuit; 1983, U.S. Supreme Court. *Education:* Pasadena College (B.A., 1968); Pennsylvania State University (M.Ed., 1973); Golden Gate University (J.D., 1977). Kappa Phi Kappa. Teaching Assistant, University of California at Berkeley, 1973-1976. Instructor, Federal Indian Law, American Indian Lawyer Training Program, 1976—. Member, Governor's Task Force on Civil Rights, 1981-1982. Consultant, Legal Services Corporation, 1984-1986. Inyo County Public Defender Pro Tem, 1985—. Member, Board of Trustees, California Indian Legal Services, 1988—. *Member:* Inyo-Mono Counties Bar Association (Vice President, 1981; President, 1982); State Bar of California. [1st Lt., U.S. Army, 1969-1971]

REPRESENTATIVE CLIENTS: Owens Valley Indian Housing Authority; Lone Pine Construction; Bishop Creek Water Association; Indian Creek Water Association; Lone Pine Indian Reservation.
REFERENCES: Bank of America and Monument National Banks, Bishop, California.

---

## LAW OFFICE OF PETER E. TRACY

*Established in 1977*

THE BANK BUILDING
106 SOUTH MAIN STREET, SUITE 200
P.O. BOX 485
**BISHOP, CALIFORNIA 93514**
*Telephone: 619-872-1101*
*Fax: 619-872-2781*

*General Civil and Criminal Practice. Litigation, Personal Injury, Real Estate, Business, Bankruptcy, Probate, Mining and Indian Affairs Law.*

**PETER E. TRACY,** born Schenectady, New York, January 12, 1946. Admitted to bar, 1976, New York and U.S. District Court, Northern and Western Districts of New York; 1977, California; 1978, U.S. District Court, Eastern District of California, U.S. District Court, Southern District of California and U.S. Court of Appeals, Ninth Circuit; 1979, Idaho, U.S. District Court, District of Idaho and U.S. Supreme Court; 1980, U.S. Tax Court; 1983, U.S. Court of Appeals, Second Circuit, U.S. Court of Appeals, District of Columbia Circuit and U.S. Claims Court; 1985, Nevada; 1986, U.S. District Court, District of Nevada and U.S. District Court, Northern District of California. *Education:* Dartmouth College (A.B., 1968); Stanford University (A.M., 1969); Albany Law School of Union University (J.D., 1975). City Attorney, City of Bishop, California, 1981—. Town Attorney, Town of Mammoth Lakes, 1987—. Special Deputy District Attorney, Mono County, California, 1992-1995. *Member:* Inyo County (Chairman, Fee Arbitration Program, 1981—) and New York State Bar Associations; State Bar of California; Idaho State Bar; State Bar of Nevada. **REPORTED CASES:** McClatchy Newspapers vs. Superior Court (1983-1984 Grand Jury for Fresno County) (1988) 44 C3d 1162, 245 C.R.; People v. Mason (1981) 124 CA 3d 346, 177 C.R. 284.

REPRESENTATIVE CLIENTS: City of Bishop; Cal-Tron Corp.; Nikolaus & Nikolaus, Inc.; Llo-Gas, Inc.; Bishop Fire Dept.; Luther Motors, Inc.; Bank of America, N.T. & S.A.; Bishop Glass, Inc.; Bishop Waste, Inc.; Town of Mammoth Lakes; Chicago Title Insurance Co.; Bishop Country Club, Inc.; Perry Motors, Inc.; Nikolaus Transportation, Inc.; Bishop Chamber of Commerce; Bishop Mule Days Celebration; Rose Valley Properties, Inc.; Lloyd Petroleum, Inc.; White Mountain Ranch; Rock Creek Pack Station, Inc.; Barnato Distributing; Dean's Plumbing, Inc.; Motor Cargo; Sunwest Bank; CalEnergy Company, Inc.; Mono Rock LLC.
REFERENCES: City of Bishop; Town of Mammoth Lakes; Bank of America, Bishop Branch.

---

## DOLAN LAW OFFICES

*Established in 1978*

THREE POINTE DRIVE
SUITE 302
**BREA, CALIFORNIA 92821**
*Telephone: 714-257-3400*
*Fax: 714-257-3424*

*Criminal Law.*

FIRM PROFILE: *Two attorney firm established in 1978 emphasizing trial practice in both State and Federal Courts. The firm has a practice involving criminal defense, and estate planning.*

**JOHN PATRICK DOLAN,** born Orange, California, March 25, 1949; admitted to bar, 1977, California; 1978, U.S. District Court, Central District of California; 1981, U.S. District Court, Southern District of California; 1982, U.S. District Court, Eastern District of California and U.S. Supreme Court. *Education:* California State University, Fullerton (B.A., 1971); Western State University (J.D., 1977). *Member:* Orange County Bar Association; State Bar of California; National Speakers Association. **PRACTICE AREAS:** Criminal Defense Law.

*(This Listing Continued)*

## ASSOCIATES

**STEPHANIE M. GOETZE-KUHNS,** born San Jose, California, January 28, 1964; admitted to bar, 1991, California; 1994, U.S. District Court, Central and Eastern Districts of California. *Education:* University of California, Santa Barbara (B.A., 1986); Southwestern University School of Law (J.D., 1990). *Member:* Orange County Bar Association; State Bar of California. **PRACTICE AREAS:** Criminal Defense Law; Estate Planning.

---

## MARKMAN, ARCZYNSKI, HANSON, CURLEY & SLOUGH

*A PROFESSIONAL CORPORATION*

Established in 1978

SECOND FLOOR
NUMBER ONE CIVIC CENTER CIRCLE
P.O. BOX 1059
**BREA, CALIFORNIA 92822-1059**
Telephone: 714-990-0901; 310-691-3811
Email: MARCZYNSKI@AOL.COM

Rancho Cucamonga, California Office: 9113 Foothill Boulevard, Suite 200. Telephone: 909-381-0218; 909-980-2742.

*Municipal, Redevelopment, Water Rights, Real Property, Condemnation, School and Corporation Law. Civil Litigation.*

**JAMES L. MARKMAN,** born Los Angeles, California, May 7, 1943; admitted to bar, 1969, California, U.S. District Court, Central District and U.S. Court of Appeals, Ninth Circuit; 1970, U.S. District Court, Northern District of California; 1990, U.S. Supreme Court. *Education:* Dartmouth College (A.B., 1965); Cornell University (J.D., 1968). Member, Cornell Moot Court Board, 1967-1968. California Deputy Attorney General, 1969-1970. Member, 1975-1978; President, 1977-1978, Board of Education, East Whittier School District. City Attorney: Brea, California, 1978—; La Mirada, California, 1980—; Buena Park, California, 1983—; Rancho Cucamonga, California, 1985—; Hesperia, California, 1988—; Upland, California, 1993. *Member:* Los Angeles County and American Bar Associations; The State Bar of California; Los Angeles City Attorneys Association. **PRACTICE AREAS:** Municipal; Redevelopment; Water Law.

**ANDREW V. ARCZYNSKI,** born Maracaibo, Venezuela, May 17, 1948; admitted to bar, 1978, California; 1980, U.S. District Court, Central District of California; 1981, U.S. Court of Appeals, Ninth Circuit and U.S. District Court, Northern District of California; 1990, U.S. Supreme Court. *Education:* Fullerton College and California State University at Fullerton (B.A., 1974); Western State University (J.D., 1978). Phi Alpha Delta. City Attorney: Diamond Bar, California, 1989-1993; Irwindale, 1992—. Assistant City Attorney: Brea, California, 1978—; La Mirada, California, 1980—; Buena Park, California, 1983—; Rancho Cucamonga, California, 1985—; Hesperia, California, 1988—; Upland, California, 1993. *Member:* Orange County Bar Association; The State Bar of California; Orange County City Attorneys Association; Association of Southern California Defense Counsel. **PRACTICE AREAS:** Municipal; Redevelopment; Housing Law; Municipal Litigation; Public Works; Construction Law.

**RALPH D. HANSON,** born Portland, Oregon, May 16, 1952; admitted to bar, 1980, California; 1986, U.S. District Court, Central District of California and U.S. Court of Appeals, Ninth Circuit. *Education:* California State University at Fullerton (B.A., 1974); California Western School of Law (J.D., 1978). *Member:* Orange County Bar Association; The State Bar of California. **PRACTICE AREAS:** Municipal; Redevelopment; Land Use Law; Municipal Litigation.

**WILLIAM P. CURLEY, III,** born Grand Rapids, Michigan, February 19, 1957; admitted to bar, 1986, California; 1990, U.S. District Court, Central District of California. *Education:* California State Polytechnic University, Pomona (B.S., 1980); Western State University, Fullerton (J.D., 1986). *Member:* The State Bar of California. **PRACTICE AREAS:** Municipal; Housing; Redevelopment Law; Fairs and Exposition Law.

**MARSHA G. SLOUGH,** born Plainview, Texas, 1958; admitted to bar, 1987, California and U.S. District Court, Central District of California. *Education:* Ottawa University (B.A., 1980); Whittier College School of Law (J.D., 1986). *Member:* San Bernardino County and American Bar Associations; State Bar of California; Association of Southern California Defense Counsel. (Resident, Rancho Cucamonga Office). **PRACTICE AREAS:** Municipal Litigation; Personal Injury Litigation.

*(This Listing Continued)*

---

**D. CRAIG FOX,** born Terre Haute, Indiana, October 30, 1952; admitted to bar, 1981, California; 1986, U.S. District Court, Central District of California and U.S. Court of Appeals, Ninth Circuit. *Education:* California State University at Fullerton (B.A., 1975); Western State University (J.D., 1979). *Member:* Orange County Bar Association; The State Bar of California. **PRACTICE AREAS:** Municipal Law and Litigation.

**PAMELA P. KING,** born Arcata, California, June 8, 1950; admitted to bar, 1977, California; 1990, U.S. District Court, Central District of California. *Education:* University of Redlands (B.A., 1972); McGeorge School of Law, University of the Pacific (J.D., 1977). *Member:* San Bernardino Bar Association; The State Bar of California. (Resident, Rancho Cucamonga Office). **PRACTICE AREAS:** Municipal Litigation; Personal Injury Litigation.

**DAREN E. HENGESBACH,** born Thousand Oaks, California, April 8, 1966; admitted to bar, 1993, California and U.S. District Court, Central District of California. *Education:* Claremont McKenna College (B.A., 1988); McGeorge School of Law, University of the Pacific (J.D., 1993). *Member:* State Bar of California. (Resident, Rancho Cucamonga Office). **PRACTICE AREAS:** Municipal Litigation.

**BOYD L. HILL,** born Provo, Utah, July 23, 1960; admitted to bar, 1989, California; 1991, U.S. District Court, Central District of California. *Education:* Brigham Young University (B.S., 1985); University of Virginia (J.D., 1988). Intern, U.S. Supreme Court, 1983. *Member:* The State Bar of California. **LANGUAGES:** Italian. **PRACTICE AREAS:** Water; Environmental; Real Estate; Construction; Commercial; Municipal Law.

REPRESENTATIVE CLIENTS: City of Brea; City of Buena Park; City of Hesperia; City of Irwindale; City of La Mirada; City of Rancho Cucamonga; City of Upland; Los Angeles County Fair Association; Hesperia Water District.
GENERAL COUNSEL FOR: Brea Redevelopment Agency; Buena Park Redevelopment Agency; Hesperia Redevelopment Agency; Irwindale Community Redevelopment Agency; Irwindale Housing Authority; La Mirada Redevelopment Agency; Rancho Cucamonga Redevelopment Agency; Stanton Redevelopment Agency; Upland Redevelopment Agency.
REFERENCE: Southern California Bank (Brea Branch).

---

## ROBERT B. AMIDON

*A LAW CORPORATION*

3900 WEST ALAMEDA AVENUE, SUITE 1700
**BURBANK, CALIFORNIA 91505-4316**
Telephone: 818-972-1800

*Civil and Criminal Litigation, Commercial Law, Business Law, Employment Law, White Collar Criminal Defense Law.*

**ROBERT B. AMIDON,** born Washington, D.C., December 14, 1946; admitted to bar, 1977, Virginia and District of Columbia; 1980, U.S. Supreme Court; 1982, California; 1987, New York. *Education:* United States Naval Academy (B.S., 1968); Catholic University of America (M.S., 1972); Georgetown University (J.D., 1976). Licensed Commercial Pilot, 1969. Instructor, Attorney General's Advocacy Institute, U.S. Department of Justice, 1979. Lecturer, Criminal Law and Ethics, Georgetown University Law Center, 1980. Assistant U.S. Attorney, U.S. Department of Justice, 1977-1981. *Member:* State Bar of California; Federal (National Delegate, Roanoke Chapter, 1977-1979), American (Vice-Chairman, RICO Cases Committee, 1980—) and International Bar Associations; Lawyer Pilots Bar Association; Association of Business Trial Lawyers (Los Angeles); The Association of Trial Lawyers of America; National Lawyers Club. [U.S. Navy Midshipman, 1964-1968; U.S. Navy, 1968-1976; U.S. Naval Reserves, 1976-1990; Commander U.S. Naval Reserves (Retired)]. **LANGUAGES:** French. **REPORTED CASES:** In Re: Investigation Before Feb., 1977, Lynchburg Grand Jury 1977, United States Court of Appeals, Virginia 563 F.2d 652; In Re: U.S. 1978, United States Court of Appeals, Virginia 588 F. 2d 56; U.S. v. Whitehead 1980, United States Court of Appeals, Virginia 5 Fed. R. Evid Serv. 1046.

---

## JOHN R. BLANCHARD

290 EAST VERDUGO AVENUE, SUITE 20
**BURBANK, CALIFORNIA 91502-1346**
Telephone: 818-295-6955
Fax: 818-295-6955

*General Civil Litigation, Business Litigation and Transactions, Personal Injury, Criminal Defense and Family Law.*

*(This Listing Continued)*

JOHN R. BLANCHARD, Burbank—Continued

JOHN R. BLANCHARD, born August 24, 1962; admitted to bar, 1996, California. *Education:* Loma Linda University - Riverside (B.A., 1990); Southwestern University School of Law (J.D., 1995). Los Angeles County District Attorney's Office (Central Trials, Major Crimes), 1993-1995. *Member:* Los Angeles County Bar Association (Member, Death and Dying Subcommittee, Bioethics Committee, 1993—; Member, Guns and Violence Committee, 1996—); Los Angeles Trial Lawyers Association.

## CAROL D. KELLOGG

290 EAST VERDUGO AVENUE, SUITE 209
BURBANK, CALIFORNIA 91502-1340
Telephone: 818-843-6890
Fax: 818-559-5575

San Clemente, California Office: 118 Avenida Victoria, Suite C. Telephone: 818-843-6890.

*Personal Injury Law. General Civil Practice.*

CAROL D. KELLOGG, born Los Angeles, California, November 8, 1962; admitted to bar, 1988, California; 1992, U.S. District Court, Central District of California. *Education:* University of La Verne (B.A., 1984; J.D., 1987). Delta Theta Phi; Phi Alpha Delta. Instructor: Paralegal Program, Los Angeles Mission College, 1987-1991. Director, Legal Assisting Program, Pasadena City College, 1990 —. *Member:* Glendale, Pasadena, Los Angeles County and American Bar Associations; Consumer Attorneys Association of Los Angeles; The Association of Trial Lawyers of America; Consumer Attorneys of California. (Also Of Counsel to L. Edmund Kellogg.)

REFERENCE: Sterling Bank, Burbank.

## ALVIN N. LOSKAMP

A LAW CORPORATION
290 EAST VERDUGO AVENUE, SUITE 103
BURBANK, CALIFORNIA 91502
Telephone: 818-846-9000
Fax: 818-843-1441

*Estate Planning, Revocable Living Trusts, Wills, Probate, Asset Protection, Business Entities, Business Trusts and Corporate Law.*

ALVIN N. LOSKAMP, born Midland, Texas, December 26, 1934; admitted to bar, 1969, California. *Education:* Stanford University (B.S., 1958); University of Alaska (M.S., 1964); Loyola University of Los Angeles (J.D., 1968). Alpha Sigma Nu; Phi Alpha Delta (Justice, 1967-1968; Justice, Los Angeles Alumni, 1975-1976). Member, 1972-1974 and Chairman, 1973-1974, Burbank Planning Board. President, Loyola University of Los Angeles Alumni Association, 1973-1975. Judge Pro Tem, Burbank Municipal Court, 1974—. President, Burbank Y.M.C.A. Board, 1979-1980. President, Burbank Chamber of Commerce, 1980. *Member:* Burbank (President, 1974-1975), Los Angeles County; State Bar of California. [Capt., U.S. Army, 1958-1963]

REFERENCES: Wells Fargo Bank, Glenoaks Branch, Burbank; Highland Savings & Loan, Burbank.

## MARRONE ROBINSON FREDERICK & FOSTER

PROFESSIONAL CORPORATION
111 NORTH FIRST STREET, SUITE 300
BURBANK, CALIFORNIA 91502-1851
Telephone: 818-841-1144
Fax: 818-841-0746

*General Civil and Trial Practice in all State and Federal Courts. Corporation, Business, Insurance and Probate Law.*

FIRM PROFILE: *Marrone, Robinson, Frederick & Foster is a law firm situated in the heart of Los Angeles County. The firms attorneys are experienced trial lawyers specializing in all aspects of civil litigation as well as insurance defense. Marrone, Robinson, Frederick & Foster handles matters throughout California.*

(This Listing Continued)

PHILLIP R. MARRONE, born Amsterdam, New York, August 11, 1943; admitted to bar, 1970, California. *Education:* California State University at Los Angeles (B.A., 1965); Loyola University of Los Angeles (J.D., 1969). Phi Alpha Delta. Member, Pasadena Tournament of Roses Association, 1970—. Member, Panel of Arbitrators, American Arbitration Association. Arbitrator, Los Angeles Superior Court, 1979—. *Member:* Los Angeles County and American Bar Associations; The State Bar of California; California Defense Counsel (Member, Board of Directors, 1986, 1987); Association of Southern California Defense Counsel (President, 1987-1988); Defense Research and Trial Lawyers Association; International Association of Defense Counsel. **REPORTED CASES:** Him v. Superior Court, (1986) 228 Cal. Rptr. 839, 184 Cal. App. 3d 35; Olson v. Arnett, (1989) 169 Cal. Rptr. 629, 113 Cal. App. 3d 59; Waite v. Godfrey, (1980) 163 Cal. Rptr. 106 Cal. App. 760; Transit Casualty Co. v. Giffin (1974) 116 Cal. Rptr. 110, Cal. App. 3d 489. **PRACTICE AREAS:** Insurance Defense; Product Liability; Business Litigation; Personal Injury; Construction.

JAY ROBINSON, born Los Angeles, California, September 10, 1946; admitted to bar, 1972, California. *Education:* Orange Coast College (A.A., 1966); California State College at Fullerton (B.A., 1968); University of California at Los Angeles (J.D., 1971). *Member:* Los Angeles County Bar Association; State Bar of California; Association of Southern California Defense Counsel; Defense Research Institute. **PRACTICE AREAS:** Products Liability; Professional Liability; Insurance Defense; Personal Injury; Construction; Coverage; Bad Faith.

J. ALAN FREDERICK, born Tacoma, Washington, March 5, 1949; admitted to bar, 1974, California. *Education:* University of California at Santa Barbara (B.A., 1971); University of California at Los Angeles (J.D., 1974). Member, Moot Court Honors Program. Arbitrator, Los Angeles Superior Court, 1979-1985. Settlement Officer, JASOP Program, Los Angeles Superior Court. *Member:* Beverly Hills and Burbank Bar Associations; State Bar of California (Member, Litigation Section); Association of Southern California Defense Counsel. **REPORTED CASES:** Wechsler v. Home Savings & Loan Association (1976) 57 Cal. App. 3d 563; Aetna Casualty & Surety Co. v. Superior Court (1980) 114 Cal. App. 3d 49; Wynn v. Monterey Club (1980) 111 Cal. App. 3d 789; Alameda Tank Co. v. Starkist Foods, Inc.; C.I. Engineers & Constructors Inc. v. Johnson & Turner Painting Co. (1983) 140 Cal. App. 3d 1011; Traveler's Insurance Co. v. Hyster Co. (1994) Daily Journal DAR 13442. **PRACTICE AREAS:** Products Liability; Professional Liability; Insurance Defense; Personal Injury; Construction; Coverage; Bad Faith.

THOMAS A. FOSTER, born Los Angeles, California, December 6, 1947; admitted to bar, 1973, California. *Education:* Whittier College (B.A., 1969); University of California at Los Angeles (J.D., 1972). Pi Sigma Alpha. Judge Pro Tem: Municipal Court, 1981—; Los Angeles Superior Court, 1993. Judicial Settlement Officer Program, Los Angeles Central, Long Beach and Pasadena. *Member:* Los Angeles County Bar Association; State Bar of California; Association of Southern California Defense Counsel. **PRACTICE AREAS:** Products Liability; Professional Liability; Insurance Defense; Personal Injury; Construction; Coverage.

ROBERT BOON, born Los Angeles, California, July 2, 1954; admitted to bar, 1979, California. *Education:* University of California at Berkeley and University of California at Los Angeles (B.A., 1976); Loyola University of Los Angeles (J.D., 1979). *Member:* Los Angeles County Bar Association; State Bar of California; Association of Southern California Defense Counsel. **PRACTICE AREAS:** Products Liability; Professional Liability; Insurance Defense; Personal Injury; Construction; Coverage.

---

DENNIS P. DE FRANZO, born Van Nuys, March 17, 1952; admitted to bar, 1976, California; 1985, U.S. District Court, Central and Southern Districts of California. *Education:* University of California at Los Angeles (B.A., magna cum laude, 1973; J.D., 1976). Phi Beta Kappa. *Member:* State Bar of California; Association of Southern California Defense Counsel.

GARY D. ELLINGTON, born Wichita, Kansas, March 12, 1952; admitted to bar, 1990, California and U.S. District Court, Central and Southern Districts of California. *Education:* George Mason University (B.A. in English, 1978); Southwestern University School of Law (J.D., cum laude, 1990). Member, Law Review, 1989-1990. Who's Who Among American Law Students, 1990. *Member:* State Bar of California; American Bar Association; Association of Southern California Defense Counsel.

SCOT G. SANDOVAL, born Brighton, Colorado, July 24, 1967; admitted to bar, 1993, California and U.S. District Court, Central and Southern Districts of California. *Education:* University of Colorado (B.S., 1989); California Western School of Law (J.D., 1992). Phi Delta Phi. Recipient,

(This Listing Continued)

American Jurisprudence Award, Criminal Law. *Member:* American Bar Association; State Bar of California; Southern California Defense Counsel.

**KATHRYN M. LOOCK,** born Peoria, Illinois, July 9, 1958; admitted to bar, 1993, California and U.S. District Court, Central and Southern Districts of California. *Education:* University of Southern California (B.A., cum laude, 1980); Los Angeles County Medical Center School of Nursing (Nursing Diploma, 1982); Southwestern University School of Law (J.D., 1993). Philathian Honor Society. Who's Who Among American Law Students, 1993. Registered Nurse, California, 1982—. Member, American Association of Critical Care Nurses, 1984-1990. *Member:* Los Angeles County and American Bar Associations; State Bar of California; California Young Lawyers Association.

**PETER Y. LEE,** born Seoul, Korea, March 12, 1966; admitted to bar, 1993, California; 1995, U.S. District Court, Central and Southern Districts of California. *Education:* University of California at Berkley, (B.A., honors, 1989; J.D., 1992). *Member:* State Bar of California; Association of California Defense Counsel. **LANGUAGES:** Korean. **PRACTICE AREAS:** Civil Litigation.

**JAMES FITZGERALD ROBINSON,** born Santa Monica, California, December 11, 1966; admitted to bar, 1994, California; U.S. District Court, Central and Southern Districts of California. *Education:* University of California at Irvine; University of California at Los Angeles (B.A., 1989); McGeorge School of Law (J.D., 1994). Moot Court. Top Oralist Finalist. Trial Advocacy Honors. Recipient, Emil Gunpert Award, 2nd Honors for Trial Advocacy. *Member:* Southern California Defense Counsel.

**JOHN F. SCHILLING,** born New Hampton, Iowa, September 25, 1940; admitted to bar, 1973, California. *Education:* Iowa State University (B.S.A.E., 1963); University of Southern California (M.S.A.E., 1969); Loyola University (J.D., 1973). American Association of Automotive Medicine. International Society of Air Safety Investigators. Judge Pro-Tem, 1991-1993. *Member:* Los Angeles County and American Bar Associations; State Bar of California; American Bar Association.

**KATHERINE P. SHANNON,** born Los Angeles, California, February 16, 1969; admitted to bar, 1995, California. *Education:* University of California at Los Angeles (B.A., 1971); McGeorge School of Law (J.D., 1995). National Moot Court Honors Board, McGeorge School of Law, 1994-1995. Community Legal Services, Governing Board, 1994-1995.

**KAREN B. GOLDBERG,** born Los Angeles, California, November 16, 1968; admitted to bar, 1995, California. *Education:* University of California at Los Angeles (B.S., 1991); Southwestern University (J.D., 1995). **LANGUAGES:** Spanish.

**DONALD M. STONE,** born Los Angeles, California, April 14, 1943; admitted to bar, 1972, California and U.S. District Court, Southern and Northern Districts of California. *Education:* University of Paris, France (Diploma, 1964); University of California at Los Angeles (B.A., 1966; M.A., 1967); Loyola University of Los Angeles (J.D., 1971). *Member:* Los Angeles County Bar Association; State Bar of California. **LANGUAGES:** French. **PRACTICE AREAS:** Tort Litigation; Real Estate Litigation; Real Estate Transactional.

**DOUGLAS FEE,** born Los Angeles, California, December 31, 1950; admitted to bar, 1984, California; 1985, U.S. Court of Appeals, Ninth Circuit and U.S. District Court Central District of California; 1989, U.S. District Court, Southern District of California. *Education:* California State University (B.A., 1979); University of Arkansas (J.D., 1983; LL.M., 1988). Member, Arkansas Law Review, 1982-1983. Author: "Frivolous Appeals," Los Angeles Lawyer Magazine, Aug. - Sept. 1990. Co-Author: "Potential Liability of Directors of Agricultural Cooperatives," 37 Arkansas Law Review 60, 1984. Lecturer, Appellate Advocacy, University of Arkansas School of Law, 1983. Instructor, Hospitality Industry Law, Central Texas College, 1984. Adjunct Professor, Water Resources Management, California State Polytechnic University, 1985. Associate Professor, Law for Business Administrators, University of Redlands, 1992. Editor, Verdict magazine. *Member:* Los Angeles County Bar Association (Bench-Bar Committee); State Bar of California; Association of Southern California Defense Counsel; Irish American Bar (President, 1995). [U.S. Army Medical Corps, 1971-1973]. REPORTED CASES: Brigante v. Hung, 20 Cal.App.4th 1569, 25 Cal.Rptr.2d 354 (Cal.App. 2 Dist., Dec 14, 1993) (NO. BO48731); Andrea N. v. Laurelwood Hosp., 16 Cal.Rptr.2d 894, Previously published at 13 Cal.App.4th 1492; 18 Cal.App.4th 1698, (See Rules 976, 977, 979 Cal. Rules of Ct.), (Cal.App. 2 Dist., Mar 03, 1993 (NO. BO47221); Stallman v. Bell, 235 Cal.App.3d 740, 286 Cal.Rptr. 755 (Cal.App. 2 Dist., Oct 28, 1991) (NO BO5O327); American Star Ins. Co. v. Insurance Co. of The West, 232 Cal.App.3d 1320, 284 Cal.Rptr. 45 (Cal

*(This Listing Continued)*

.App. 4 Dist., Jul 30, 1991) (NO. GOO9430); Woods v. Young, 53 Cal.3d 315, 807 P.2d 455, 279 Cal.Rptr. 613 (Cal., Apr 04, 1991) (NO. SOO5969); Moore v. May Dept. Store Co., 222 Cal.App.3d 836, 271 Cal.Rptr. 841, 122 Lab.Cas. P 56, 967, 5 IER Cases 956 (Cal.App. 2 Dist., July 31, 1990) (NO. BO43481); Preis v. American Idem. Co., 220 Cal.App.3d 752, 269 Cal.Rptr. 617 (Cal.App. 2 Dist., May 21, 1990) (NO. BO40196); County of Los Angeles v. Guerrero, 209 Cal.App.3d 1149, 257 Cal.Rptr. 787 (Cal.App. 2 Dist., Apr 24, 1989) (NO. CIV BO32900); Liu v. Interinsurance Exchange of Auto. Club of Southern California, 252 Cal.Rptr. 767 Ordered Not Published, Previously published at 205 Cal.App.3d. 968 (See Rules 976, 977, 979 Cal. Rules of Ct.), (Cal.App. 2 Dist., Nov 03, 1988) (NO. CIV. BO23217); Anderson v. Northrop Corp., Cal.App.3d 772, 250 Cal.Rptr. 189 (Cal.App. 2 Dist., Aug 10, 1988) (NO. CIV BO2338); Maheu v. CBS, Inc., 201 Cal.App.3d 662, 247 Cal.Rptr. 304, 1988 Corp.L.Dec. P 26, 306 7 U.S.P.Q.2d 1238, 15 Media L. Rep. 1548 (Cal.App. 2 Dist., May 24, 1988) (NO. BO26485); Woods v. Young, 246 Cal.Rptr. 768, Previously published at 225 Cal.App.3d 1434, (See Rules 976, 977, 979 Cal. Rules of Ct.), (Cal.App. 2 Dist., Apr 28, 1988) (NO. BO2633); Coates v. Newhall Land & Farming, Inc., 191 Cal.App.3d 1, Corp. (C) West 1996 No claim to orig. U.S. govt. works 236 Cal.Rptr. 181 (Cal.App. 2 Dist., Apr 14, 1987); McDonald v. Superior Court (Flintkote Co.), 180 Cal.App.3d 297, 225 Cal.Rptr. 394 (Cal.App. 2 Dist., Apr 24, 1986) (NO.BO16776). **PRACTICE AREAS:** Appeals; Insurance; Complex Litigation.

REPRESENTATIVE CLIENTS: Admiral Insurance Co.; The Aetna Casualty and Surety Co.; Argonaut Insurance Company; The Bethlehem Corporation; Carlise Ins. Co.; Collier-Keyworth Co.; Columbia Pictures Industries, Inc.; Dillingham construction N.A., Inc.; Fireman's Insurance of Washington, D.C.; General Star Management Co.; Holiday Inns, Inc.; Home Insurance Company & The Home Indemnity Company; Hyster Co.; Investor's Insurance Company; Lancer Claim Management; MCI Inc.; Murphy and Beane, Inc.; NACCO Materials Handling Group, Inc.; National Continental Insurance Co.; National Farmers Union Property Co.; Northland Insurance Co.; Norton Company; Paramount Pictures Corp.; Progressive Casualty Insurance Co.; Reliance Insurance Co.; Simcoe & Erie General Insurance Co.; Sony Music, Inc.; Sony Pictures Entertainment, Inc.; Sony Picture Studios, Inc.; Southern Insurance Co.; The Standard Fire Insurance Co.; Textron, Inc.; Tokio Marine and Fire Insurance Co.; Transport Insurance Co.; Tristar Pictures; U.S. Liability Insurance Co.; United Pacific Insurance Co.; United States Forgecraft Corporation; Universal City Studios, Inc.; Wickes Companies, Inc.; Yale Materials Handling Company.

REFERENCES: Union Bank, Los Angeles, California (Main Office).

## ARNOLD F. WILLIAMS

BURBANK, CALIFORNIA

(See Los Angeles)

*Wills, Trusts and Estate Planning, Probate, Charitable Tax Planning and Elder Law.*

## CARR, McCLELLAN, INGERSOLL, THOMPSON & HORN

PROFESSIONAL CORPORATION

216 PARK ROAD
P.O. BOX 513
BURLINGAME, CALIFORNIA 94011-0513
Telephone: 415-342-9600
Telecopier: 415-342-7685
Email: cmith@cmithlaw.com

San Francisco, California Office: Suite 1120, Four Embarcadero Center.
Telephone: 415-362-1400. Telecopier: 415-362-5149.

*General Civil and Trial Practice. Corporation, Hospital and Health Care, Labor and Employment, Bankruptcy, Creditors Rights, Commercial, International Business, Tax, Real Estate, Estate Planning and Probate Law.*

**E. H. COSGRIFF** (1880-1947).

**J. ED MCCLELLAN** (1895-1985).

**ROBERT R. THOMPSON** (1921-1995).

**NORMAN I. BOOK, JR.,** born Buffalo, New York, November 5, 1939; admitted to bar, 1965, California. *Education:* Haverford College and Pomona College (B.A., 1961); Stanford University (J.D., 1964). Phi Beta Kappa. City Attorney, Hillsborough, California, 1996—. Chairman, San Mateo County Economic Development Association, 1993-1995. **PRAC-**

*(This Listing Continued)*

## CARR, McCLELLAN, INGERSOLL, THOMPSON & HORN, PROFESSIONAL CORPORATION, Burlingame—Continued

TICE AREAS: General Corporate Law; Real Estate Law; Tax Law. Email: nib@cmithlaw.com

**ROBERT A. NEBRIG,** born Missoula, Montana, February 4, 1938; admitted to bar, 1966, California. *Education:* University of Kansas (B.A., 1960); Stanford University (J.D., 1965). Counsel on Foreign Law, Tokyo, Japan, 1965-1967. Deputy District Attorney, San Mateo County, 1968-1970. *Member:* California Trial Lawyers Association (Member, Board of Governors, 1982); San Mateo County Trial Lawyers Association (President, 1982). *PRACTICE AREAS:* Civil Litigation; International Transactions. *Email:* ran@cmithlaw.com

**MARION L. BROWN,** born Memphis, Tennessee, May 6, 1938; admitted to bar, 1967, California. *Education:* University of Notre Dame (B.B.A., 1960); Stanford University (J.D., 1967). (Certified Specialist, Taxation Law and Probate, Estate Planning and Trust Law, The State Bar of California Board of Legal Specialization). *PRACTICE AREAS:* Estate Planning Law; Trust Law; Probate Law; Business Law. *Email:* mlb@cmithlaw.com

**L. MICHAEL TELLEEN,** born Davenport, Iowa, January 30, 1947; admitted to bar, 1973, California. *Education:* Carleton College (B.A., 1969); Stanford University (J.D., 1973). Phi Beta Kappa. *PRACTICE AREAS:* General Corporate Law; Business Law. *Email:* lmt@cmithlaw.com

**LAGE E. ANDERSEN,** born Chicago, Illinois, November 22, 1950; admitted to bar, 1977, California. *Education:* Northwestern University (B.S., 1972); University of Wisconsin-Madison (M.A., 1974); Stanford University (J.D., 1977). (Certified Specialist, Taxation Law, The State Bar of California Board of Legal Specialization). *PRACTICE AREAS:* Taxation Law. *Email:* lea@cmithlaw.com

**KEITH P. BARTEL,** born Jaffa, Israel, June 3, 1950; admitted to bar, 1978, California. *Education:* University of California at Berkeley (B.A., 1972); M.A., 1973); University of San Francisco (J.D., 1978). *PRACTICE AREAS:* Probate Litigation; Health Care Litigation. *Email:* kpb@cmithlaw.com

**MARK A. CASSANEGO,** born San Francisco, California, December 19, 1953; admitted to bar, 1979, California. *Education:* Santa Clara University (B.S., 1976); Boalt Hall School of Law, University of California (J.D., 1979). *PRACTICE AREAS:* General Corporate Law; Business Law; Securities Law. *Email:* mac@cmithlaw.com

**LAURENCE M. MAY,** born San Francisco, California, May 7, 1951; admitted to bar, 1976, California. *Education:* University of California at Berkeley (A.B., 1973); University of Santa Clara (J.D., 1976). Deputy Attorney General, State of California, 1976-1979. *PRACTICE AREAS:* Real Estate Transactions; Financing Law. *Email:* lmm@cmithlaw.com

**MICHAEL J. McQUAID,** born San Francisco, California, August 28, 1954; admitted to bar, 1980, California. *Education:* University of California at Berkeley (A.B., 1977); University of Santa Clara (J.D., 1980). *PRACTICE AREAS:* Bankruptcy Law; Insolvency Law. *Email:* mjm@cmithlaw.com

**PENELOPE CREASEY GREENBERG,** born Bakersfield, California, April 3, 1943; admitted to bar, 1980, California. *Education:* Stanford University (B.A., 1965); Boalt Hall School of Law, University of California (J.D., 1980). Assistant City Attorney, Hillsborough, California, 1986—. *Member:* American Academy of Hospital Attorneys; National Health Lawyers Association; California Society for Healthcare Attorneys. *PRACTICE AREAS:* Hospital Law; Health Care Law; Municipal Law. *Email:* pcg@cmithlaw.com

**JAMES R. CODY,** born San Francisco, California, December 20, 1955; admitted to bar, 1982, California. *Education:* Yale University (B.A., 1978); University of California at Berkeley (MBA, 1982); Hastings College of the Law, University of California (J.D., 1982). Member, Executive Committee, Estate Planning, Trust and Probate Law Section, The State Bar of California, 1993—. Fellow, American College of Trust and Estate Counsel. (Certified Specialist, Estate Planning, Trust and Probate Law, The State Bar of California Board of Legal Specialization). *PRACTICE AREAS:* Probate Law; Trust Law; Estate Planning Law; Tax Planning Law. *Email:* jrc@cmithlaw.com

**EDWARD J. WILLIG, III,** born San Francisco, California, August 21, 1959; admitted to bar, 1984, California. *Education:* Stanford University (A.B., 1981); Boalt Hall School of Law, University of California (J.D., 1984). *PRACTICE AREAS:* Corporate and General Business Law; Healthcare Law. *Email:* ejw@cmithlaw.com

**SARAH J. DiBOISE,** born Tucson, Arizona, November 28, 1956; admitted to bar, 1982, California. *Education:* Stanford University (B.A., 1978); Boalt Hall School of Law, University of California (J.D., 1982). Order of the Coif. *Member:* American Academy of Hospital Attorneys; National Health Lawyers Association. *PRACTICE AREAS:* Hospital & Health Care Law. *Email:* sjd@cmithlaw.com

**W. GEORGE WAILES,** born Corona, California, April 4, 1954; admitted to bar, 1981, California. *Education:* University of California at Santa Barbara (B.A., 1977); University of California at Davis (J.D., 1981). Co-chair and faculty member, Hastings College of Advocacy, 1990—. *PRACTICE AREAS:* Civil Litigation; ERISA Litigation; Bankruptcy Litigation. *Email:* wgw@cmithlaw.com

**CAROL B. SCHWARTZ,** born Eugene, Oregon, December 24, 1945; admitted to bar, 1982, California. *Education:* Mills College (B.A., 1967); Hastings College of Law, University of California (J.D., 1982). *PRACTICE AREAS:* Real Estate Law. *Email:* cbs@cmithlaw.com

**LORI A. LUTZKER,** born Brooklyn, New York, May 14, 1961; admitted to bar, 1986, California. *Education:* Pennsylvania State University (B.A., 1983); Stanford University (J.D., 1986). Phi Beta Kappa. *PRACTICE AREAS:* Civil Litigation. *Email:* lal@cmithlaw.com

**MOIRA C. WALSH,** born San Francisco, California, August 15, 1962; admitted to bar, 1987, California. *Education:* University of California at Santa Barbara (B.A., 1984); George Washington University (J.D., 1987). *PRACTICE AREAS:* Bankruptcy Law; Insolvency Law. *Email:* mcw@cmithlaw.com

**JEREMY W. KATZ,** born New York, N.Y., August 20, 1952; admitted to bar, 1985, California. *Education:* University of California at Berkeley (B.A., 1975); University of Michigan, Ann Arbor (M.A., 1977); Hastings College of the Law, University of California (J.D., 1985). *PRACTICE AREAS:* Bankruptcy Law; Insolvency Law. *Email:* jwk@cmithlaw.com

**LISA HAYHURST STALTERI,** born Inglewood, California, May 3, 1963; admitted to bar, 1987, California. *Education:* Claremont McKenna College (B.A., 1984); Hastings College of the Law, University of California (J.D., 1987). *PRACTICE AREAS:* Real Estate Law; Environmental Law. *Email:* lhs@cmithlaw.com

**ELIZABETH A. FRANKLIN,** born New York, N.Y., December 19, 1961; admitted to bar, 1988, California. *Education:* University of California at Berkeley (B.A., 1984); Hastings College of the Law, University of California (J.D., 1987). *PRACTICE AREAS:* Labor Law; Employment Law. *Email:* eaf@cmithlaw.com

**STEVEN D. ANDERSON,** born Oklahoma City, Oklahoma, November 21, 1960; admitted to bar, 1988, California. *Education:* University of California at Berkeley (A.B., 1983); Boalt Hall School of Law, University of California (J.D., 1988). Phi Beta Kappa. (Certified Specialist, Estate Planning, Trust and Probate Law, The State Bar of California Board of Legal Specialization). *PRACTICE AREAS:* Probate Law; Trust Law; Estate Planning Law; Tax Planning Law. *Email:* sda@cmithlaw.com

**JAMES F. BLOOD,** born Ft. Collins, Colorado, January 20, 1959; admitted to bar, 1988, California. *Education:* Brigham Young University (B.A., 1983); George Washington University (M.A., 1987; J.D., 1987). *PRACTICE AREAS:* General Corporate Law; Business Law. *Email:* jfb@cmithlaw.com

### SENIOR COUNSEL

**DENNY S. ROJA,** born Quezon City, Philippines, March 26, 1946; admitted to bar, 1989, California. *Education:* University of Santo Tomas, Manila, Philippines (B.S., 1966); University of Washington (M.S., 1969); Stanford University (M.B.A., 1971); Fordham University (J.D., 1986). *PRACTICE AREAS:* Corporate and General Business Law; Mergers and Acquisitions; Securities Law. *Email:* dsr@cmithlaw.com

---

**TODD L. BURLINGAME,** born Chicago, Illinois, December 14, 1958; admitted to bar, 1986, California; 1987, District of Columbia. *Education:* University of California at Berkeley (B.A., 1981); Hastings College of Law, University of California (J.D., 1986). *Email:* tlb@cmithlaw.com

**MICHELE G. DULSKY,** born Oakland, California, October 7, 1960; admitted to bar, 1992, California; 1993, Florida. *Education:* University of California at San Diego (B.A., 1989); University of San Diego School of Law (J.D., 1992). *Email:* mgd@cmithlaw.com

*(This Listing Continued)*

**PROFESSIONAL BIOGRAPHIES**                                    CALIFORNIA—BURLINGAME

**MICHAEL D. LIBERTY,** born San Francisco, California, February 17, 1957; admitted to bar, 1988, California. *Education:* University of California at Berkeley (A.B., 1985); McGeorge School of Law, University of the Pacific (J.D., 1988). *Email:* mdl@cmithlaw.com

**WENDY L. MACILWAINE,** born Dayton, Ohio, May 13, 1967; admitted to bar, 1993, California. *Education:* Northwestern University (B.A., 1989); George Washington University (J.D., 1993). *Email:* wlm@cmithlaw.com

**TERESE M. RADDIE,** born San Francisco, California, October 15, 1958; admitted to bar, 1984, California. *Education:* Willamette University (B.A., 1980); Golden Gate University (J.D., 1983). Psi Chi. *Email:* tmr@cmithlaw.com

*CHAIRMAN EMERITUS*

**ALBERT J. HORN,** born Cologne, Germany, July 1, 1926; admitted to bar, 1952, California. *Education:* Stanford University (A.B., 1948; J.D., 1951). President, Stanford Alumni Association, 1981-1982. Chairman, Committee on Taxation, State Bar of California, 1972-1973. Fellow, American College of Trust and Estate Counsel. *PRACTICE AREAS:* Probate Law; Trust Law; Estate Planning Law; Tax Planning Law. *Email:* ajh@cmithlaw.com

*OF COUNSEL*

**LUTHER M. CARR,** born Kewanee, Illinois, 1906; admitted to bar, 1929, Iowa; 1945, California. *Education:* Drake University (A.B., 1927; J.D., 1929). *Member:* The State Bar of California (Member, Board of Governors, 1966-1969). (Retired).

**FRANK B. INGERSOLL, JR.,** born Manila, P.I., 1912; admitted to bar, 1939, California. *Education:* Stanford University (A.B., 1935; J.D., 1938). City Attorney, Hillsborough, California, 1953-1982. (Retired).

**CYRUS J. MCMILLAN,** born Richfield, Utah, March 28, 1921; admitted to bar, 1947, California. *Education:* University of Santa Clara (A.B., 1942; J.D., 1947). Professor of Law, University of Santa Clara Law School, 1947. (Retired).

**DAVID C. CARR,** born Forest City, Iowa, October 9, 1931; admitted to bar, 1961, California. *Education:* Stanford University (A.B., 1954; J.D., 1960). Phi Delta Phi. Trustee, Burlingame Elementary School District, 1963-1974. (Retired).

All Attorneys are Members of the San Mateo County and/or Bar Association of San Francisco and The State Bar of California.

---

## THE CORPORATE LAW GROUP
*WATERFRONT PLAZA, SUITE 120*
*500 AIRPORT BOULEVARD*
**BURLINGAME, CALIFORNIA 94010-1914**
Telephone: 415-349-8000
Fax: 415-349-8099
Email: mail@tclg.com
URL: http://www.tclg.com

Corporate, Finance, Securities, Mergers and Acquisitions, Business Transactions, Licensing and Technology Law. Partnerships and Limited Liability Companies, International Law, Trademarks and Copyrights.

**PAUL DAVID MAROTTA,** born Washington, D.C., October 20, 1957; admitted to bar, 1983, California and U.S. District Court, Northern District of California; 1986, U.S. Court of Appeals, Ninth Circuit. *Education:* University of Southern California (B.A., 1980); Pepperdine University School of Law (J.D., cum laude, 1983). Phi Delta Phi. Recipient, American Jurisprudence Award for Conflicts of Law. Author: "Rejection of Executory Contracts in the Context of Software License Agreements: The Problem and Some Suggested Solutions," Vol. 10, No. 1, The Business Law News, 1987; "The Injunction Bond in High Technology Litigation: The Need for Reform," 4 S.C. Comp. and High Technology Law Journal, 1988. Member, Editorial Board, The Business Law News, 1987-1990. *Member:* American Bar Association; The State Bar of California. *Email:* pmarotta@counsel.com

**MATTHEW I. BERGER,** born Los Angeles, California, September 5, 1950; admitted to bar, 1979, California and U.S. District Court, Central District of California; 1982, U.S. District Court, Southern District of California and U.S. Court of Appeals, Ninth Circuit; 1983, U.S. District Court, Northern District of California; 1991, U.S. District Court, Eastern District of California. *Education:* University of California at Santa Barbara (B.A., *(This Listing Continued)*

with honors, 1972); University of Oregon (J.D., 1979). Associate Editor, Oregon Law Review, 1978-1979. Recipient, American Jurisprudence Award, Trusts and Estates. Author: "Liquified Natural Gas Facility Siting On The Oregon Coast," Oregon Coastal Management Commission, 1979. Staff Attorney, "Felix S. Cohen's Handbook of Federal Indian Law," 1982 edition, Michie Bobbs-Merrill. *Member:* State Bar of California (Member: Law Office Management Committee, 1979—; Business Law Committee, 1980—). *Email:* achoota@aol.com

**KRISTEN ROELLIG,** born Bellevue, Washington, May 23, 1965; admitted to bar, 1994, California. *Education:* University of California at Santa Barbara (B.A., 1987); Golden Gate University (J.D., 1993). *Member:* State Bar of California; American Bar Association. *Email:* kroellig@counsel.com

**WILLIAM J. MORAN,** born New York, N.Y., July 2, 1941; admitted to bar, 1966, New York; 1970, California. *Education:* Fordham University (B.A., 1963); Yale University (J.D., 1966). Phi Beta Kappa. *Email:* wmoran@counsel.com

---

## COTCHETT & PITRE
*SAN FRANCISCO AIRPORT OFFICE CENTER*
*SUITE 200, 840 MALCOLM ROAD*
**BURLINGAME, CALIFORNIA 94010**
Telephone: 415-697-6000
Email: CandPLegal@aol.com

*Los Angeles, California Office:* Suite 1100, 12100 Wilshire Boulevard. Telephone: 310-826-4211.

*Affiliated Office:* Friedlander & Friedlander, P.C., 2018 Clarendon Boulevard, Arlington, Virginia 22201. Telephone: 703-525-6750.

Practice limited to Tort Law, Environmental, Products Liability, Securities, Antitrust and Commercial Litigation. General Trial and Appellate Practice.

*MEMBERS OF FIRM*

**JOSEPH W. COTCHETT,** born Chicago, Illinois, January 6, 1939; admitted to bar, 1965, California; 1972, U.S. Supreme Court; 1980, District of Columbia. *Education:* California State Polytechnic College (B.S., Engineering, 1960); Hastings College of Law, University of California (LL.B., 1964). Author: "Discovery of Experts Work," California Trial Lawyers Association Journal, Spring, 1967; "Experimental Evidence in Products Liability," California State Bar Journal, November, 1969; "The Class Action-The Coming Tool," American Trial Lawyers Association, February, 1971; "Judicial Salaries: Inflation vs. Justice," Trial Magazine, July, 1980; "Shield or Sword: The Fifth Amendment Privilege In Commercial Cases," Trial Magazine, May, 1982; "Lawyer and Accountant Liability in Business Litigation," CTLA Forum, 1985; "Liability of Accountants and Lawyers," Trial Magazine, April, 1987; "Punitive Damages: They Belong to the Public," International Society of Barristers Quarterly, Vol. 28, No. 4 (1994). Co-author: *California Products Liability Actions,* Matthew-Bender, 1970; *California Courtroom Evidence,* Parker & Son, 1972; *Federal Courtroom Evidence,* Parker & Son, 1976; The Ethics Gap, Parker & Son, 1991. *California Courtroom Evidence Foundations,* Parker Publications, 1993. *Persuasive Opening Statements and Closing Arguments,* California Continuing Education of the Bar, 1988; "Effective Opening Statements," *California Litigation,* Journal of the Litigation Section, State Bar of California, 1991; "Jury Trial Tips: Witnesses," *California Litigation,* Journal of the Litigation Section, California State Bar, 1991; "Winning Through A More Effective Direct Examination," *California Litigation,* Journal of the Litigation Section, California State Bar, 1991; "Jury Trial Tips: High Tech Tools," *California Litigation,* Journal of the Litigation Section, California State Bar, 1992; "Arguing Punitive Damages," *Civil Litigation Reporter,* California Continuing Education of the Bar, 1990. Contributing Author: *Class Action Primer,* Law Journal Press, 1973; *Objections to Evidence and Preserving the Record,* California Civil Procedure During Trial, CEB, 1982; Winning Strategies and Techniques For Civil Litigators, Practising Law Institute, 1992. Lecturer: Antitrust Actions, The National College of Advocacy, Harvard Law School, 1974; Class Actions; University of Southern California, 1975; Multidistrict Procedure, 1977 and Federal Evidence, 1979, University of Nevada; Securities Litigation, Georgetown University, 1978; Trial Practice, Hastings Center for Advocacy, 1985; CEB, Federal Practice Institute, 1985-1996; CEB Annual Federal Trial Practice Institute, 1985-1996. Special Counsel to Governor Edmund G. Brown, Jr., 1975. Co-Chairman, Governor's Task Force On Agricultural Labor Relations Law, 1976. Member, Judicial Council of the State of California, 1977-1978. Member, Judicial Council Commission on the Future of The Courts, 1991-1993. Member: Select Committee on Judicial Retirement, 1993—, Appointed by Chief Justice Malcom Lucas. Special Assistant Attorney General, State of South Dakota, 1978-1984. Member, California Commis- *(This Listing Continued)*

## COTCHETT & PITRE, Burlingame—Continued

sion on Judicial Performance, 1985-1989. Member, Board of Directors, Hastings College of the Law, University of California, 1981-1993. Member, Board of Directors, Disability Rights Advocates, 1995—. Member, Board of Directors, Witkin Legal Institute, 1996—. Member, National Panel of Arbitrators, American Arbitration Association. Member, Board of Directors, Bay Meadows Foundation (1995—); Member, Board of Directors, Public Citizen Foundation (1996—). *Member:* San Mateo County (Member, Board of Directors, 1970) and American (Member, Antitrust Section; Vice-Chair, Committee on Commercial Torts, Section of Tort and Insurance Practice, 1989-1990) Bar Associations; The State Bar of California (Member, Board of Governors, 1972-1975; Vice President, 1974-1975); San Francisco Lawyers Club; San Mateo County Trial Lawyers Association (President, 1969); California Trial Lawyers Association (Member, Board of Governors, 1969-1972; Vice President, 1972); Association of Business Trial Lawyers; The Association of Trial Lawyers of America (Secretary, Commercial Tort Litigation Section, 1971; Chairman: Consumer Protection Committee, 1971; Chairman, Federal Courts Committee, 1978-1982; Member, Board of Governors, 1983-1986); Trial Lawyers for Public Justice (President, 1986-1987; Member, Board of Governors, 1982—); American Board of Trial Advocates (Advocate, 1981—); Founder, Roscoe Pound-American Trial Lawyers Foundation. Fellow: American College of Trial Lawyers; American Bar Foundation; International Academy of Law and Science; International Academy of Trial Lawyers; International Society of Barristers. [Col., JAGC, USAR, 1960-1990, active duty, 1960-1961]. (Certified as a Civil Trial Advocate, National Board of Trial Advocacy).

**FRANK M. PITRE,** born San Francisco, California, January 17, 1955; admitted to bar, 1981, California; 1985, U.S. Supreme Court. *Education:* University of San Francisco (B.S., cum laude, 1977; J.D., 1981). Legal Externship, California Supreme Court, 1980. Law Clerk, San Mateo County Superior Court, 1981. Author: "Abuse of Process," *California Tort Damages,* California Continuing Education of the Bar, 1988; "Tort Trends," The Docket, San Mateo County Bar Association, 1989-1994. Co-Author: "Jury Instructions: A Practical Approach to their Use," Civil Litigation Reporter, March, 1984; "Arguing Punitive Damages," *Civil Litigation Reporter,* California Continuing Education of the Bar, 1991; "Effective Opening Statements," *California Litigation,* Journal of the Litigation Section, California State Bar, 1991; "Jury Trial Tips: Witnesses," *California Litigation,* Journal of the Litigation Section, California State Bar, 1991; "Winning Through A More Effective Direct Examination," *California Litigation,* Journal Of The Litigation Section, California State Bar, 1991; "Jury Trial Tips: High Tech Tools," *California Litigation,* Journal of the Litigation Section, California State Bar, 1992. Consultant, "California Civil Practice," Bancroft-Whitney, 1992. Panelist: "Fundamentals of Civil Litigation Before Trial," California Continuing Education of the Bar, 1988 and 1990; "Jury Instructions," California Continuing Education of the Bar, 1986; "Proving Injuries To The Body And Mind," San Diego Trial Lawyers Association, 1989; "Tort Damages: How To Identify And Prove Them," California Continuing Education of the Bar, 1989; "Jury Voir Dire Skills Workshop," California Continuing Education of the Bar, 1989; "Trial Preparation: The War To End All Wars," Association of Defense Counsel of Northern California, 1991; "Evaluation & Settlement," San Mateo County Trial Lawyers Association, 1991; "Trial Video: Litigation In The Televisual Age," California Continuing Education of the Bar, 1991; "Premises Liability Seminar," San Mateo Trial Lawyers Association, 1994; "Deposition Fundamentals," Lorman Business Center, 1995; "Preparing For Trial The Last 100 Days," California Continuing Education of the Bar, 1994 and 1996. Lecturer: "Trial Preparation," Hastings College of Advocacy, 1992; Closing Arguments, Hastings College of Advocacy, 1989; Overlooked Torts in Business Litigation, California Trial Lawyers Association, 1987; Working With Experts, Hastings College of Advocacy, 1987. Faculty: Hastings College of Advocacy, 1988—; University of San Francisco, "Trial Skills Workshop," 1992 and 1995; "Creative Opening Statements," California Trial Lawyers Association, 1994; "Creative Use Of Video Evidence," Consumer Attorneys of California, 1995; "Evaluation Of A Case," Santa Clara University, 1996. Judge Pro Tem, San Mateo County Superior Court, 1993—. Certified Civil Trial Advocate, National Board of Trial Advocacy. *Member:* Bar Association of San Francisco; San Mateo County (Member, Board of Directors, 1990-1992) and American Bar Associations; The State Bar of California; San Mateo County Barristers (Member, Board of Directors, 1984-1986); California Trial Lawyers Association; Consumer Attorneys of San Mateo County (Member, Board of Directors, 1996—); Association of Business Trial Lawyers (Member, Board of Directors, 1996—); Association of Trial Lawyers of America.

**BRUCE L. SIMON,** born San Francisco, California, November 19, 1953; admitted to bar, 1980, California; 1985, U.S. Supreme Court. *Education:* University of California at Berkeley (A.B., with high honors, 1977); Hastings College of Law, University of California (J.D., 1980). Contributor, Communication and Entertainment Law Journal of the Hastings College of Law, 1979-1980. Co-Author: "Plaintiff's Perspective on Jury Strategies" and "Creative Use of Deposition Testimony at Trial," Accountants' Liability, 1990: Trial Strategies, Practicing Law Institute and California Continuing Education of the Bar. Co-Author: "Accountants' Liability: Calculation of Damages," Accountants' Liability 1991, Practicing Law Institute. Practice Consultant, "Malicious Prosecution and Abuse of Process," Bancroft Whitney's California Civil Practice, Torts, Chap. 19. Guest Lecturer, "Accountants' Liability," San Jose State University Business School, 1990-1992. Speaker, "Current Issues in Accountant Liability," Santa Clara County Bar Business Litigation Section, 1990. Author and Speaker: "Coming to Grips With the Complex Commercial Case," California Trial Lawyer Association Annual Tahoe Seminar, 1992; Practice Consultant Bancroft-Whitney's California Civil Practice, Torts, Chapter 19 "Malicious Prosecution and Abuse of Process," 1992. Faculty Member, National Institute for Trial Advocacy, Western Deposition Program, 1992-1993. Panelist, The Litigation Section of the Bar Association of San Francisco and the San Francisco Chapter of the California Society of CPA's, "The Accounting Profession on Trial--Bily and Beyond," 1993. Panelist, American Inns of Court, "The Leadership Challenge: Practical Applications for the Trial Lawyer", 1993. Speaker, Continuing Education of the Bar 13th Annual Development Program, February 1996. Speaker: "The Use of Video Depositions," CSPA SF Chapter CPE Extravaganza, May 1996; "Products Liability," ALI-ABA Course, July 1996. Consumer Attorneys of California, Speaker, "Legal Technology You Must Know to Practice Law In the 21st Century," 1996. Pro Tem Judge and Court Commissioner, San Mateo County Municipal Court, 1985-1992. Pro Bono Member, San Mateo County Bar Ad Hoc Committee assisting the Municipal Court in drafting Local Rules on Delay Reduction, 1990. Volunteer Investigative Attorney, California State Bar, 1985-1986. Volunteer, San Mateo County Legal Aid Society. *Member:* San Mateo County (Member, Bench, Bar, Media, Community Affairs Committees and Membership Committee; San Mateo County Legal Technology Section) and American Bar Associations; The State Bar of California; California Trial Lawyers Association; San Mateo County Trial Lawyers Association; The Association of Trial Lawyers of America; Association of Business Trial Lawyers, Northern California. Edward J. McFetridge American Inn of Court, Barrister.

**MARIE SETH WEINER,** born Milwaukee, Wisconsin, February 7, 1959; admitted to bar, 1983, California; 1989, U.S. Supreme Court. *Education:* University of San Francisco (B.S., cum laude, 1980); Hastings College of Law, University of California (J.D., 1983). Phi Alpha Delta (Vice Justice, 1982-1983). Co-Author, "Pensions, Life Insurance and Annuities-Future Litigation," CLTA Forum, August 1991. Faculty, University of Santa Clara, Civil Trial Skills Workshop, 1993-1994. Panelist: "Anatomy of An Insurance Policy," The Rutter Group, October 1991; "1992 Insurance Litigation Update," The Rutter Group, February/March 1992; Women Lawyers Section, San Mateo County Bar, "Rain-making," October, 1992; "1993 Insurance Litigation Update," The Rutter Group, January/February, 1993; "1994 Insurance Litigation Update", January/March 1994; "1995 Update Insurance Litigation," The Rutter Group, January, 1995; "Making a Difference: Commercial Tort Cases," CTLA 1994 Annual Convention, November 1994; California Judges Association, "Insurance Litigation 1994", January, 1994; California Women Lawyers, April 1996 "So You Want To Be A Judge." Speaker: "Accountant's Liability to Third Parties," San Jose and San Francisco Bank Attorneys Associations, 1990; "Investment Schemes," San Francisco Financial Women's Association, June, 1992; Peninsula Financial Women's Association, September, 1992; San Francisco Women Lawyers Alliance, October, 1992. *Member:* San Mateo County (Secretary, 1997; Board of Directors, 1993-1997; Conference of Delegates, Delegate, 1991, 1994, 1996,1997; Vice Chair of Delegates, 1992; Chair of Delegates, 1993; Women Lawyers Section, Chair, 1996-1997; Executive Committee, 1992-1997; Chair, Arrangements Committee, 1995) and American (Co-Chair, Directors and Officers Sub-Committee of Insurance Coverage Litigation Committee of Litigation Section, 1994-1997; Member, Litigation Section, Section of Tort and Insurance Practice) Bar Associations; State Bar of California (Commissioner, Commission on Judicial Nominees Evaluation, 1993-1994); California Women Lawyers Association; Consumer Attorneys of California; San Mateo County Trial Lawyers Association; The Association of Trial Lawyers of America; Association of Business Trial Lawyers; Financial Women's Association (Secretary, Peninsula Chapter, 1997).

**NANCY LEAVITT FINEMAN,** born San Francisco, California, April 29, 1960; admitted to bar, 1986, California. *Education:* University of California, Berkeley (A.B., 1981); Hastings College of the Law; Boalt Hall School of Law (J.D., 1986). Member, Thurston Society. Recipient, Ameri-

*(This Listing Continued)*

can Jurisprudence Award in Evidence. Contributing Author: Chapter on Partition and Distribution in Texas Probate, Estate and Trust Administration, Matthew Bender, 1993. Panelist: San Mateo County Women Lawyers Section on Law and Motion Practice, 1993. Commissioner, Commission on Judicial Nominees Evaluation, 1996—. Judge Pro Tem, San Mateo County Superior Court, 1996—. *Member:* San Mateo County and American Bar Associations; State Bar of California.

### ASSOCIATES

**VIRGINIA ELLEN HEWITT,** born Greenville, North Carolina, March 24, 1969; admitted to bar, 1994, North Carolina; 1995, California and U.S. District Court, Northern District of California. *Education:* University of North Carolina (B.A., 1991); Columbia University (J.D., 1994). Executive Editor, Columbia Journal of Law and Social Problems, 1993-1994. Law Clerk to the Honorable John Webb, Associate Justice, North Carolina Supreme Court, 1994-1995. *Member:* San Mateo COunty Bar Association; State Bar of California.

**JACK P. HUG,** born Lewistown, Montana, July 1, 1938; admitted to bar, 1966, California; 1967, U.S. Court of Military Appeals; 1970, U.S. Supreme Court. *Education:* United States Military Academy (B.S., 1960); Boalt Hall School of Law, University of California (J.D., 1966); National Judicial College, Reno (1983). Author: "Presumptions and Inferences in Criminal Law," 56 Mil. L. Rev. 81,(1972). Chief Circuit Judge, Trial Judiciary, U.S. Army Europe, 1987. Staff Judge Advocate, Sixth U.S. Army, Presidio of San Francisco, 1987-1990. *Member:* San Mateo and American Bar Associations; State Bar of California; San Mateo County Trial Lawyers Association; Association of Business Trial Lawyers. [U.S. Army, Col., JAGC, USA, active duty, 1960-1990]

**STEVEN C. KELLER,** born Detroit, Michigan, June 7, 1955; admitted to bar, 1980, California. *Education:* University of Southern California (B.A., 1977); Columbia University (J.D., 1980). *Member:* San Francisco and San Mateo County Bar Associations; State Bar of California; San Francisco Trial Lawyers Association; Association of Business Trial Lawyers; California Lawyers for the Arts.

**GREGG M. MACMILLAN,** born Portland, Oregon, January 4, 1970; admitted to bar, 1995, California; 1996, Hawaii and U.S. District Court, Northern District of California. *Education:* University of California (B.A., 1992); Santa Clara University (J.D., 1995). Judicial Extern to the Hon. James Ware, U.S. District Court, Northern District of California, 1994. *Member:* San Mateo County, Hawaii State and American Bar Associations; State Bar of California.

**NIALL P. MCCARTHY,** born San Francisco, California, May 6, 1967; admitted to bar, 1992, California. *Education:* University of California at Davis (B.A., 1989); Santa Clara University (J.D., 1992). Guest Speaker, Legal Currents in "Health Insurance," 1994. Guest Speaker, Your Legal Right, "Reverse Mortgages," 1995. *Member:* San Mateo County and American Bar Associations; State Bar of California; San Mateo County Barristers, San Mateo County (President, 1997; Director, 1993—); San Mateo Trial Lawyers Association; Association of Business Trial Lawyers; University of San Francisco American Inn of Court (Barrister).

**MARK C. MOLUMPHY,** born San Mateo, California, September 28, 1966; admitted to bar, 1993, California. *Education:* University of California at Berkeley (B.A., 1989); Edinburgh University; University of San Francisco (J.D., 1993). Law Clerk, San Francisco County Superior Court, 1992. *Member:* San Mateo County (Member, Business and Litigation Section, 1995; Executive Committee, 1995-1996; Chair, 1996) and American Bar Associations; State Bar of California; San Mateo County Barristers, San Mateo County (Director, 1993-1996; Treasurer, 1996).

**MARILYNN THAM,** born Singapore, October 27, 1965; admitted to bar, 1995, California. *Education:* Ohio University (B.B.A., summa cum laude, 1987); University of San Francisco (J.D., 1994). Phi Kappa Phi; Beta Gamma Signa. Co-Author: "When The Client Harasses The Attorney--Recognizing Third-Party Sexual Harassment in The Legal Profession," 28 U.S.F.L. Rev. 715 (1994). *Member:* San Mateo County and American Bar Associations; Association of Business Trial Lawyers; State Bar of California.

*(This Listing Continued)*

*OF COUNSEL*

**ALFRED V. CONTARINO** (Resident, Los Angeles Office; Also practicing individually).

**MARK P. FRIEDLANDER, JR.** (Also Member, Friedlander & Friedlander, P.C., 2018 Clarendon Boulevard, Arlington, VA 22201).

REFERENCE: Peninsula Bank of Commerce, Millbrae.

## BARBARA ANN CRAY

Established in 1991

800 AIRPORT BOULEVARD, SUITE 504
**BURLINGAME, CALIFORNIA 94010**
Telephone: 415-375-1220
Fax: 415-375-1410

*Financial Institutions, Lender Liability, Bankruptcy, Creditors Remedies, Real Property, Unfair Business Practices, Commercial Code and Commercial Litigation.*

**BARBARA ANN CRAY,** born Palo Alto, California, 1954; admitted to bar, 1979, California and U.S. District Court, Northern, Eastern and Central Districts of California. *Education:* Wellesley College (B.A., 1976); Hastings College of Law, University of California (J.D., 1979). Issues Editor, COMM/ENT, Journal of Communications and Entertainment Law, 1978-1979. Participant, Hastings Constitutional Law Quarterly, 1977-1978. Author: "Due Process Considerations in Hospital Staff Privileges Cases," 7 Hastings Constitutional Law Quarterly 217-262, reprinted in Health Care Law, B.N.A., 1981. Chief Law Clerk to the Hon. Robert P. Aguilar, U.S. District Judge for the Northern District of California, 1980-1983. Instructor, Legal Writing and Research, Hastings College of Law, 1982-1983. Research Attorney, Superior Court of Santa Clara County, 1979-1980. Extern to the Hon. Winslow Christian, California Court of Appeal, 1st District, 1979. *Member:* Bar Association of San Francisco; Santa Clara County and San Mateo County Bar Associations; State Bar of California. *PRACTICE AREAS:* Lender Liability; Bankruptcy; Creditors Remedies; Real Property; Commercial Code Litigation.

### ASSOCIATE

**ELEANOR T. MIRANDA,** born Los Angeles, California, November 10, 1954; admitted to bar, 1988, California and U.S. District Court, Northern and Central Districts of California. *Education:* University of Southern California (B.A., magna cum laude, 1976; M.S.W., 1977); University of California at Los Angeles (J.D., 1987). *Member:* Santa Clara County and San Mateo County Bar Associations. *PRACTICE AREAS:* Creditors Remedies; Bankruptcy.

## LAW OFFICES OF
## HERMAN H. FITZGERALD

*A PROFESSIONAL CORPORATION*

Established in 1968

SUITE 302, 345 LORTON AVENUE
**BURLINGAME, CALIFORNIA 94010**
Telephone: 415-348-5195
Fax: 415-348-3518

*Eminent Domain Litigation, General Redevelopment and Housing Authority Counseling.*

**HERMAN H. FITZGERALD,** born Toledo, Ohio, September 28, 1932; admitted to bar, 1962, California; 1974, U.S. Claims Court. *Education:* University of Toledo (B.B.A., 1954; J.D., 1961). Trustee, 1971 and President, 1973-1974, Burlingame Elementary School Board. Moderator, Continuing Education of the Bar, New Eminent Domain Law, 1976. *Member:* Bar Association of San Francisco; San Mateo County and American Bar Associations; State Bar of California (Member, 1985-1989, Chairman, 1988-1989, Vice-Chairman, 1987-1988 and Secretary, 1986-1987, Condemnation Committee). [With U.S. Army, active duty, 1954-1956]. *PRACTICE AREAS:* Eminent Domain Litigation; General Redevelopment Counseling.

**CHRISTINE C. FITZGERALD,** born San Francisco, California, February 1, 1962; admitted to bar, 1987, California and U.S. District Court, Northern District of California. *Education:* Santa Clara University (B .A., 1984); University of London, London, England (1982-1983); McGeorge

*(This Listing Continued)*

## LAW OFFICES OF HERMAN H. FITZGERALD A PROFESSIONAL CORPORATION, Burlingame—Continued

School of Law, University of the Pacific (J.D., 1987). Legal Intern: County Counsel, County of San Mateo, 1984; Justice John W. Holmdahl, California Court of Appeal, First Appellate District, 1985; Judge Milton L. Schwartz, Federal District Court, Eastern District of California, 1986-1987. *Member:* San Mateo County Bar Association; State Bar of California; International Right of Way Association. **PRACTICE AREAS:** Eminent Domain Litigation; General Redevelopment; Housing Authority Counseling.

REPRESENTATIVE CLIENTS: Genesco/S.H. Kress; National Dollar Stores, Ltd.; Southern Pacific Transportation Co.; Spieker Associates; McCuen/Steele Development Co.; Catellus Development Corporation; Travelodge International Motels, Inc.; City of Santa Maria; Redevelopment Agency of the City of Santa Maria; Redevelopment Agency of the City of Pittsburg; Redevelopment Agency of the City of Richmond; Redevelopment Agency of the City of Tulare; City of Tulare; County of Del Norte; City of Richmond; Dean Distributors, Inc.; Antonelli Brothers, Inc.; City of South San Francisco; Redevelopment Agency of the City of Belmont; City of San Mateo; City of Sacramento; Almaden Plaza Shopping Center; Bressie Associates; Richmond Sanitary Service; Redwood City Port Authority; Delta Diablo Sanitation District; South Bayside System Authority; Housing Authority of the City of Pittsburgh; Redevelopment Agency of the City of Emeryville.
REFERENCE: Bank of America.

## McCRACKEN & BYERS
### 840 MALCOLM ROAD, SUITE 100
### BURLINGAME, CALIFORNIA 94010
Telephone: 415-259-5979
Fax: 415-259-5975

*Civil Litigation and Trial Practice. Land Use, Land Development, Zoning, Real Estate, Environmental, Condemnation, Public Utility, Property Tax and Administrative Law.*

### MEMBERS OF FIRM

**MICHAEL D. MCCRACKEN,** born Scotts Bluff, Nebraska, October 25, 1945; admitted to bar, 1972, California; 1981, U.S. District Court, Northern District of California and U.S. Court of Appeals, Ninth Circuit. *Education:* University of Nebraska (B.A., cum laude, 1968); Stanford University (J.D., 1971). Phi Beta Kappa. Deputy District Attorney, Civil Division, County of San Mateo, 1975-1980. Chairman, Growth Policy Council, San Mateo County Development Association, 1986-1987. *Member:* San Mateo County Bar Association; State Bar of California. **PRACTICE AREAS:** Land Use; Real Estate; Administrative Law; Real Estate Litigation; Broker Liability.

**DAVID J. BYERS,** born Beloit, Wisconsin, October 4, 1951; admitted to bar, 1978, California and U.S. District Court, Northern District of California. *Education:* University of Illinois (B.A. in Economics with high honors, 1973); Boalt Hall School of Law, University of California (J.D., 1978). Member, Moot Court Board. Associate Editor, 1976-1977 and Articles Editor, 1977-1978, California Law Review. Deputy District Attorney, Civil Division, County of San Mateo, 1980-1984. *Member:* San Mateo County Bar Association; State Bar of California. **PRACTICE AREAS:** Public Utility; Condemnation; Land Use; Real Estate; Real Estate Litigation.

**THOMAS A. ENSLOW,** born Milwaukee, Wisconsin, December 7, 1967; admitted to bar, 1996, California. *Education:* University of Wisconsin at Madison (B.S., 1991); Boalt Hall School of Law, University of California (J.D., 1995). Articles Editor, Ecology Law Quarterly. President, Committee on Race, Poverty and Environmental Justice, 1993-1994.

## LAW OFFICE OF
## RUSSELL H. MILLER
### 20 PARK ROAD, SUITE E
### BURLINGAME, CALIFORNIA 94010-4443
Telephone: 415-401-8735
Fax: 415-401-8739
Email: MILLPESS@WORLDNET.ATT.NET

*Campaign and Election Law Enforcement Campaign, Lobby and Ethics Law Compliance, Estate Planning for Unmarried Individuals and Couples, Real Estate Transactions.*

**RUSSELL H. MILLER,** born San Francisco, California, March 6, 1952; admitted to bar, 1983, California and U.S. District Court, Northern District of California. *Education:* University of California at Berkeley (B.A.,

*(This Listing Continued)*

---

with highest honors, 1974); Hastings College of Law, University of California (J.D., 1983); Stanford University (Ph.D. in Sociology of Law, 1984). Phi Beta Kappa. Revision Author: *"McLaughlin on Weinstein's Evidence,"* Matthew Bender & Co., 1996. Contributing Author: *"California Forms of Pleading and Practice,"* Matthew Bender & Co., 1995-1996; *"California Real Estate Law and Practice,"* Matthew Bender & Co., 1995-1996; *"California Legal Forms,"* Matthew Bender & Co., 1995-1996. *Member:* Los Angeles County Bar Association; State Bar of California; California Political Attorneys Association. **SPECIAL AGENCIES:** California Fair Political Practices Commission.

### LEGAL SUPPORT PERSONNEL

**KIRK ALAN PESSNER,** born Oakland, California, December 26, 1952. *Education:* Georgetown University; University of California at Berkeley (B.A., in Political Science, 1977). Member, Marin County Civil and Criminal Grand Jury, 1978-1979. (Paralegal/Administrator). **PRACTICE AREAS:** Election, Campaign, Lobby and Ethics Law Compliance.

REPRESENTATIVE CLIENTS: The Flanigan Law Firm; Printing Industries of St. Louis; Cooperative of American Physicians/Mutual Protection Trust; Bay 101; L. John Doerr, III; Public Affairs Associates, LLC.; Matthew Bender & Co.

## CHARLES E. VOLTZ
### 1290 HOWARD AVENUE, SUITE 333
### BURLINGAME, CALIFORNIA 94010
Telephone: 415-342-4491
FAX: 415-342-4441
Email: law@voltz.com
URL: http://www.voltz.com

*Labor and Employment Law for Employers, Alternative Dispute Resolution, Mediations and Arbitrations.*

**CHARLES E. VOLTZ,** born Chicago, Illinois, March 24, 1934; admitted to bar, 1963, California. *Education:* Northwestern University (B.S., 1955); University of Michigan (J.D., 1962).

REPRESENTATIVE CLIENTS: Sunset Publishing Corporation; Time Publishing Ventures; Del Monte Foods; Beck Stuffer Vinyards; Saga of America.

## WINTERS, KRUG & DELBON
### 345 LORTON AVENUE, SUITE 204
### BURLINGAME, CALIFORNIA 94010-4116
Telephone: 415-579-1422
Fax: 415-579-1852

*General Civil and Trial Practice, including Insurance Law, General and Product Liability, Aviation Law, Construction Law, Environmental and Toxic Tort Claims.*

### MEMBERS OF FIRM

**WILLIAM L. NAGLE,** born San Mateo, California, December 24, 1948; admitted to bar, 1974, California, U.S. District Court, Northern and Eastern Districts of California and U.S. Court of Appeals, Ninth Circuit. *Education:* University of California at Davis; Stanford University (A.B., 1971); University of San Francisco (J.D., 1974). Phi Alpha Delta. Member, University of San Francisco Law Review, 1973-1974. Arbitrator: San Mateo County, 1977—; Santa Clara County, 1979—. Judge Pro Tem, San Mateo County, 1981—. Special Master, San Mateo, Santa Clara, San Francisco, Alameda and Contra Costa Counties, 1987—. *Member:* San Mateo County (Member, Board of Directors, 1987—; President, 1993), Santa Clara County and American Bar Associations; The State Bar of California; Northern California Association of Defense Counsel; Defense Research Institute; International Association of Defense Counsel.

**JOHN S. KRUG,** born Los Angeles, California, June 6, 1950; admitted to bar, 1976, California, U.S. District Court, Northern District of California. *Education:* Stanford University (B.S., 1972); Golden Gate University (J.D., 1975). Arbitrator: San Mateo County, 1984—; Santa Clara County, 1985—. Judge Pro Tem, San Mateo County, 1985—. *Member:* San Mateo County, Santa Clara County and American Bar Associations; The State Bar of California; Northern California Association of Defense Counsel; Defense Research Institute.

**DANIEL W. WINTERS,** born Cambridge, Massachusetts, April 10, 1947; admitted to bar, 1972, California and U.S. District Court, Northern District of California. *Education:* DePauw University (B.A., cum laude, 1969); University of Illinois (J.D., magna cum laude, 1972). Order of the Coif. Member, University of Illinois Law Review, 1971-1972. Arbitrator,

*(This Listing Continued)*

San Mateo County, 1979—. Judge Pro Tem, San Mateo County, 1983—. *Member:* San Mateo County and American Bar Associations; State Bar of California; Northern California Association of Defense Counsel; International Society of Air Safety Investigators.

**DAVID A. DELBON,** born San Francisco, California, May 23, 1962; admitted to bar, 1988, California and U.S. District Court, Northern District of California. *Education:* Menlo College (A.A., 1982); University of California, Davis (B.A., 1984); University of San Francisco (J.D., 1987). *Member:* San Mateo County Bar Association; The State Bar of California; Northern California Association of Defense Counsel.

**CHERYL A. NOLL,** born Pasadena, California, November 17, 1962; admitted to bar, 1988, California, U.S. District Court, Northern District of California, and U.S. Court of Appeals, Ninth Circuit. *Education:* California State Polytechnic University (B.A., 1985); University of San Diego School of Law (J.D., 1988). *Member:* San Mateo County and San Francisco County Bar Associations; The State Bar of California; Northern California Association of Defense Counsel. **PRACTICE AREAS:** Insurance Defense; General Practice.

**JERRY E. NASTARI,** born San Francisco, California, September 29, 1959; admitted to bar, 1990, California and U.S. District Court, Northern District of California. *Education:* California State University at Sacramento (B.A., 1981); California State University at Hayward (M.A., 1985); University of Santa Clara (J.D., 1990). Member, San Mateo County Probation Department, 1982-1985. Master Calendar Coordinator, San Mateo County Superior Court, 1985-1991. *Member:* San Mateo County Bar Association; State Bar of California; Northern California Association of California.

**DAVID F. ZUCCA,** born San Francisco, California, August 13, 1965; admitted to bar, 1991, California and U.S. District Court, Northern District of California. *Education:* California State University, Sacramento (B.A., 1987); University of California, Davis (J.D., 1991). *Member:* San Mateo County Bar Association; The State Bar of California; Northern California Association of California.

REPRESENTATIVE CLIENTS: State Farm Mutual Automobile Insurance Co.; State Farm Fire & Casualty Co.; Fireman's Fund Insurance Cos.; California State Automobile Assn.; Tokio Marine Management Co.; Chubb Group of Insurance Cos.; Argonaut Insurance Co.; Aviation Office of America; City of Burlingame; City of Half Moon Bay; City of South San Francisco; City of San Carlos; Towns of: Hillsborough and Woodside; Miyata Bicycle of America; USAA Insurance.

## BERG AND BERG

Established in 1976

P.O. BOX 8817

**CALABASAS, CALIFORNIA 91372-8817**

Telephone: 818-883-9905
Facsimile: 818-883-9913
Email: RSBERGLA@AOL.COM

*General Transactional Law, Mergers and Acquisitions, Real Estate and Business Litigation and Entertainment Law.*

**RONALD S. BERG,** born Los Angeles, California, April 1, 1952; admitted to bar, 1976, California; 1977, U.S. District Court, Central District of California, U.S. Court of Appeals, Ninth Circuit and U.S. Supreme Court. *Education:* University of California at Los Angeles (B.A., 1973); Southwestern University (J.D., 1976). *Member:* Los Angeles County Bar Association; State Bar of California. **PRACTICE AREAS:** Real Property Transactions; Business/Corporate Transactions; Litigation-Business/Corporate/Real Property; Entertainment. *Email:* RSBERGLA@AOL.COM

REFERENCE: Western Bank, Santa Monica, California.

## JEFFREY D. DIAMOND

A PROFESSIONAL CORPORATION

Established in 1987

5010 NORTH PARKWAY CALABASAS, SUITE 200
**CALABASAS, CALIFORNIA 91302-1483**
Telephone: 818-225-5035
Fax: 818-225-5032

*Insurance Coverage, Civil Litigation.*

**JEFFREY D. DIAMOND,** born Los Angeles, California, March 28, 1953; admitted to bar, 1978, California; 1979, U.S. District Court, Central
*(This Listing Continued)*

District of California; 1984, U.S. District Court, Southern District of California; 1990, U.S. Court of Appeals, Ninth Circuit. *Education:* University of California at Santa Barbara (B.A., with high honors, 1975); Loyola University of Los Angeles (J.D., 1978). Sigma Chi. Phi Alpha Delta. Adjunct Professor, Insurance Law, University of La Verne College of Law, 1995, 1996. Registered Life Insurance Agent, State of California, 1994. Registered Representative, National Association of Securities Dealers (Series 6 and 63), 1995. Lecturer: "Claim Representative and Litigation Responsibilities," Allstate Insurance Company, Marina District Claims Office, August, 1983; "Concurrent Causation," United Pacific/Reliance Insurance Companies, Santa Ana Regional Claims Office, May, 1984; "Concurrent Causation: An Update," Albatross Association of Los Angeles, Feb., 1987; "Don't Let Your Real Property Claims Slide: An Update on Concurrent Causation," Independent Insurance Agents and Brokers of Los Angeles, Sept., 1987; "Managing Agent Liability" Ventura County Association of Health Underwriters, May, 1992. Guest Speaker, "Earthquake Claims Seminar": February, 1995, Sponsored by Rubin, Palache & Associates, Public Adjusters and James R. Gary, Realtors; April, 1995, Sponsored by Farmers Insurance Group Policy Holders. Author: "Managing Agent Liability," California Broker Magazine, October, 1991. Moot Court Judge, Loyola Law School, Semi-Finals Moot Court Competition, 1994, 1995. *Member:* Los Angeles County, San Frenando Velley and American (Member, Tort and Litigation Practice Section; Committees on Property Insurance Law and Insurance Coverage Litigation) Bar Associations; State Bar of California. **REPORTED CASES:** Preis v. American Indemnity Company (1990) 220 Cal.App.3d 752. **PRACTICE AREAS:** Insurance Coverage; Insurance Litigation; Civil Litigation; Appellate.

REPRESENTATIVE CLIENTS: Available Upon Request.
REFERENCE: Charter Pacific Bank.

## GARY M. GITLIN

A PROFESSIONAL LAW CORPORATION

SUITE 110, 23945 CALABASAS ROAD
**CALABASAS, CALIFORNIA 91302**
Telephone: 818-591-3757
Telefax: 818-591-2779

*General Civil Practice. Real Estate, Business, Civil Litigation and related causes.*

**GARY M. GITLIN,** born September, 17, 1951; admitted to bar, 1976, California. *Education:* University of California (B.A., 1973); Whittier College School of Law (J.D., 1976). *Member:* Beverly Hills, Santa Monica and Los Angeles County (Member, Sections On: Intellectual Property, Real Property, Litigation, Present and Past Judgement, Taxation, Trusts and Estates, Business and Corporation, Family Law, Commercial Law, Bankruptcy, Labor and Employment Law) Bar Associations; State Bar of California (Member, Sections on: Business Law, Estate Planning, Trust and Probate, Litigation, Real Property and Taxation); San Fernando Valley Bar Association. **PRACTICE AREAS:** Real Estate and Business Law and Litigation; Corporate Law.

## SABO & GREEN

A PROFESSIONAL CORPORATION

Established in 1980

23801 CALABASAS ROAD, SUITE 1015
**CALABASAS, CALIFORNIA 91302-1547**
Telephone: 818-704-0195
Fax: 818-704-4729

*San Bernardino, California Office:* 201 North "E" Street, Suite 206. 92401-1507. Telephone: 909-383-9373. Fax: 909-383-9378.
*Cathedral City, California Office:* 35-325 Date Palm Drive, Suite 150, 92234. Telephone: 619-770-0873. Fax: 619-770-1724.

*Municipal Law, Public Finance, Real Estate, Redevelopment, Condemnation, Litigation and Military Base Closures.*

*FIRM PROFILE:* The firm was founded in 1980 as Law Offices of Timothy J. Sabo, specializing in public finance and redevelopment law, and assumed its present configuration in 1990. The firm represents clients throughout the state in the areas of public finance, municipal law, redevelopment, real estate, condemnation, and litigation and has served as counsel in numerous out-of-state public finance transactions. Members of the firm are active in conducting semi-
*(This Listing Continued)*

**SABO & GREEN,** A PROFESSIONAL CORPORATION.
Calabasas—Continued

nars and conferences and are frequent guest lecturers on public finance and redevelopment law issues.

**TIMOTHY J. SABO,** born Youngstown, Ohio, May 17, 1947; admitted to bar, 1977, California. *Education:* Youngstown State University (B.M.E., magna cum laude, 1969); Colorado State University (M.M., 1970); University of Colorado; University of Denver (J.D., 1977). *Member:* Los Angeles County and American (Member, Section of Urban, State and Local Government Law) Bar Associations; State Bar of California; National Association of Bond Lawyers. **PRACTICE AREAS:** Redevelopment Law; Public Finance Law.

**CHARLES R. GREEN,** born Del Rio, Texas, April 8, 1950; admitted to bar, 1976, California and U.S. District Court, Central District of California. *Education:* University of California at Los Angeles (B.A., 1972; J.D., 1975). Judge Pro Tem, Los Angeles Superior Court, 1989—. Member: State Bar Panel of Special Masters, 1991; Panel of Voluntary Settlement Conference Referees, Los Angeles Superior Court (Van Nuys), 1990. *Member:* Los Angeles County Bar Association; State Bar of California (Member, Sections on: Real Estate and Litigation). **PRACTICE AREAS:** Redevelopment; Eminent Domain; Environmental Law; Inverse Condemnation; Litigation; Municipal Law; Municipal Solid Waste Resource Recovery; Public Agency; Real Estate Condemnation; Solid and Hazardous Waste; Trial Practice; Military Base Closures.

**ANDREAS G. DE BORTNOWSKY,** born Wellington, New Zealand, September 25, 1957; admitted to bar, 1985, California and U.S. District Court, Central District of California. *Education:* University of California at Los Angeles (B.A., 1980); Southwestern University School of Law (J.D., 1985). *Member:* Los Angeles County and American Bar Associations; State Bar of California. **PRACTICE AREAS:** Real Estate Law; Redevelopment Law; Municipal Law; Military Base Closures.

**ALEXIS G. CRUMP,** born National City, California, September 6, 1962; admitted to bar, 1988, California and U.S. District Court, Northern District of California; 1989, U.S. District Court, Central District of California. *Education:* University of California at Berkeley (A.B., 1984); Georgetown University Law Center (J.D., 1987). Phi Delta Phi. *Member:* Los Angeles County Bar Association; State Bar of California; Black Woman Lawyers Association. **PRACTICE AREAS:** Public Finance Law; Redevelopment Law; Real Estate Law; Civil Litigation.

**JOEL T. BOEHM,** born Wausau, Wisconsin, October 14, 1946; admitted to bar, 1972, New York and Nebraska (Not admitted in California). *Education:* Creighton University (B.S.B.A., 1968; J.D., 1971). *Member:* New York State, Nebraska State and American Bar Associations. **PRACTICE AREAS:** Municipal Law; Public Finance.

---

**EDWARD W. PILOT,** born Los Angeles, California, November 3, 1963; admitted to bar, 1988, California and U.S. District Court, Central District of California. *Education:* Tulane University, New Orleans, Louisiana, (B.S.M., 1985); Loyola Law School, Los Angeles (J.D., 1988). Member, Los Angeles County Superior Court of Voluntary Arbitrators, (Northwest District) 1994. *Member:* Los Angeles County and American (Member, Sections on: Public Law; Real Estate Law and Environmental Law); State Bar of California. **PRACTICE AREAS:** Civil Litigation; Municipal Law; Redevelopment Law; Real Estate Law; Environmental Law.

**LINDA CHAHINE,** born Youngstown, Ohio, March 9, 1961; admitted to bar, 1991, Ohio; 1992, California; 1993, District of Columbia. *Education:* Youngstown State University (B.S., 1988); Cleveland State University (J.D., 1990). *Member:* Ohio State and American Bar Associations; State Bar of California; District of Columbia Bar. **PRACTICE AREAS:** Redevelopment; Municipal Law; Real Estate; Litigation.

**GALE SCHLESINGER,** born New York, N.Y., October 9, 1958; admitted to bar, 1989, California. *Education:* University of California at Santa Barbara (B.A., with honors, 1980); University of Los Angeles (M.A., 1982); University of Denver (J.D., 1988). Author: "Airport Noise: The Proprietor's Dilemma," Transportation Law Journal, Volume XVI, No. 2; "Nuisance Control in Colorado Municipalities," Published by The Colorado Municipal League; "The Male-Female Transportation Gap", Published by The Transportation Research Forum. *Member:* The State Bar of California. **PRACTICE AREAS:** Municipal Law; Redevelopment Law.

(This Listing Continued)

**STEVEN B. QUINTANILLA,** born Honolulu, Hawaii, September 5, 1958; admitted to bar, 1992, California. *Education:* University of California, Los Angeles (B.A., magna cum laude, 1986; J.D., 1991); University of California, Los Angeles Graduate School of Architecture and Urban Planning (M.A., 1992). University of California at Los Angeles, Journal of Environmental Policy, 1990-1991. Lecturer, Land Use Law, People's College of Law, Spring 1993. *Member:* Los Angeles County and American Bar Associations; State Bar of California; American Planning Association; Association of Environmental Professionals. **PRACTICE AREAS:** Eminent Domain; Inverse Condemnation; Civil Litigation.

**ROBERT L. PATTERSON,** born Los Angeles, California, December 30, 1961; admitted to bar, 1989, California. *Education:* University of California at Los Angeles (B.A., cum laude, 1985); Loyola Marymount University (J.D., 1989). *Member:* Ventura County Bar Association; State Bar of California. **PRACTICE AREAS:** Business Law; Municipal Law; Homeowner Association Law.

---

## DORON M. TISSER

Established in 1989

23622 CALABASAS ROAD, SUITE 121
**CALABASAS, CALIFORNIA 91302-1553**
Telephone: 818-222-9085
Fax: 818-222-9087
Email: dmtisser@pacificnet.net

*Estate Planning, Probate and Trust Law, Trust Administration, Estate and Gift Tax Planning, Business Secession Planning, Taxation, Business Law, Corporations and Partnerships.*

**DORON M. TISSER,** born Tel-Aviv, Israel, March 3, 1955; admitted to bar, 1981, California; 1982, U.S. District Court, Central District of California; U.S. Court of Appeals, Ninth Circuit and U.S. Tax Court. *Education:* University of California at Los Angeles (B.A., 1978); Southwestern University (J.D., cum laude, 1981); New York University (LL.M., in Taxation, 1982). Phi Alpha Delta. Author: "The Omnibus Budget Reconciliation Act of 1993," Parts I & II, 15 C.E.B. Cal. Bus. L. Rep. 91, 131 (1993); Chapter 3, "Corporate Buy-Sell Agreements," Business Buy-Sell Agreements, California C.E.B., (1991); Chapter 4, "Partnership Buy-Sell Agreements," Business Buy-Sell Agreements, California C.E.B., (1991); Chapter 4, "Dividends and Distributions," Counseling California Corporations, California C.E.B., (1990); "Choosing the Corporate Entity: S Corporations and Other Options after Tax Reform," California C.E.B., 1987. Co-Author: "Covenants Not To Compete," 3 C.E.B. Cal. Bus. L. Prac. 81 (Spring 1988); "Practitioner's Understanding of Attribution Rules is Key to Tax-Deferral Eligibility," 11 Estate Planning 150, 1984. Contributing Editor, Taxation, California Business Law Reporter, 1986-1994. Lecturer: "Fundamental's of Estate Planning", California C.E.B., 1996; Estate Planning for Executives and the Highly Compensated, California State Bar, Taxation Section, November, 1989; "Choice of Entity," Corporate Tax Planning Workshop, California State Bar, Taxation Section, May 1989; "Tax Planning for Choosing the Corporate Entity: S Corporations and Other Options After Tax Reform," California C.E.B., 1987; "Doing Business After the 1986 Tax Reform Act," C.E.B., 1986; "Recent Developments in Business Law Practice," C.E.B.,1986, 1988, 1989, 1990, 1991, 1992, 1993. *Member:* Los Angeles County, San Fernando Valley and American Bar Associations; State Bar of California. (Certified Specialist, Probate, Estate Planning and Trust Law, Taxation Law, The State Bar of California Board of Legal Specialization).

---

## BURKE, WILLIAMS & SORENSEN

A Partnership including a Professional Corporation

SUITE 1, 2310 PONDEROSA DRIVE
**CAMARILLO, CALIFORNIA 93010**
Telephone: 805-987-3468
Email: bws@bwslaw.com
URL: http://www.bwslaw.com

*Los Angeles, California Office:* 611 West Sixth Street, 25th Floor. Telephone: 213-236-0600.

*Orange County Office:* 3200 Park Center Drive, Suite 750, Costa Mesa, California. Telephone: 714-545-5559.

*General Civil and Trial Practice in all State and Federal Courts. Securities, Corporate, Taxation, Insurance and Commercial Law. Municipal and Public Agency Representation. Local Government Financing, Taxation and Assessments. Community Redevelopment, Eminent Domain, Environmental and*

(This Listing Continued)

Land Use Law. Employee Benefit Plans, Probate and Estate Planning. Health Care, Medical Research, College and University and Non-Profit Organization Law, Employment and Personnel Law. Tort, Workers Compensation and Insurance Defense.

### RESIDENT ATTORNEYS

J. Robert Flandrick        Cheryl J. Kane
Brian A. Pierik            Don G. Kircher
           Mary Redus Gayle

REFERENCE: First Interstate Bank, Los Angeles Main Office.

(For Complete Biographical Data on all Personnel, see Professional Biographies at Los Angeles).

## H. ROY JEPPSON

*A PROFESSIONAL CORPORATION*

Established in 1964

1100 PASEO CAMARILLO
**CAMARILLO, CALIFORNIA 93010**
Telephone: 805-482-3322
FAX: 805-482-6672
Email: roy@vcol.net

Business Litigation in State and Federal Courts. Corporate, Tax, Real Estate, Government Contracts, Labor and Employment, and Estate Planning.

FIRM PROFILE: Firm is listed in the Bar Register of Preeminent Lawyers.

**H. ROY JEPPSON,** born Salt Lake City, Utah, May 16, 1938; admitted to bar, 1964, California; U.S. District Court, Central District of California; U.S. Tax Court; U.S. Court of Claims; U.S. Supreme Court. *Education:* Pasadena City College; University of California at Los Angeles (B.S., 1960); University of California at Los Angeles (J.D., 1963); University of Southern California (LL.M., in Taxation, 1968). Phi Alpha Delta. *Member:* Beverly Hills, Los Angeles County and American Bar Associations; The State Bar of California.

---

**ROBYN F. STALK,** born New York, N.Y., May 23, 1956; admitted to bar, 1987, California; 1988, U.S. District Court, Central District of California. *Education:* California State University (B.A., magna cum laude, 1980); Southwestern University (J.D., 1986). Psi Chi. *Member:* Beverly Hills and Los Angeles County Bar Associations; State Bar of California.

REPRESENTATIVE CLIENTS: Mountaingate, A Lockheed Martin Company; Hill Industries, Inc.; Lo-Car, Inc.; Geronimo Service Co.; International Resort Operators; Southwest Veco, Inc.;
REFERENCE: Ventura County National Bank.

## THOMAS E. MALLEY

1200 PASEO CAMARILLO, SUITE 295
**CAMARILLO, CALIFORNIA 93010**
Telephone: 805-482-2199

Civil Trial Practice in State Courts. Real Property, Corporations, Estate Planning, Probate, Wrongful Termination.

**THOMAS E. MALLEY,** born Yuma, Arizona, May 18, 1944; admitted to bar, 1970, California. *Education:* Mt. St. Mary's College (B.S., cum laude, 1966); Loyola University, Rome, Italy; Hastings College of Law, University of California (J.D., 1969). Ventura County Planning Commission, 1981-1985. *Member:* Ventura County Bar Association (Member, Board of Directors, 1990); State Bar of California (Member, Sections on: Real Property Law; Estate Planning Trust and Probate).

REFERENCE: Camarillo Community Bank.

## WOOD & ASSOCIATES, L.L.P.

751 DAILY DRIVE, SUITE 250
**CAMARILLO, CALIFORNIA 93010**
Telephone: 805-484-3940
Fax: 805-484-2319
Email: dew@wood-associates.com
URL: http://www.wood-associates.com

*Insurance and Business Litigation.*

(This Listing Continued)

**DAVID E. WOOD,** born Baltimore, Maryland, January 29, 1957; admitted to bar, 1985, California and U.S. District Court, Northern District of California; 1986, U.S. District Court, Eastern District of California and U.S. Court of Appeals, Ninth Circuit. *Education:* Williams College (B.A., in English, cum laude, 1979); University of California, Hastings College of Law (J.D., 1985). *Member:* Ventura County and American (Member: Tort and Insurance Practice Section; Fidelity and Surety Committee, 1986—) Bar Associations. **PRACTICE AREAS:** Insurance; Business Litigation. **Email:** dew@wood-associates.com

**ELIZABETH M. RICE,** born New York, N.Y. January 11, 1952; admitted to bar, 1985, California and U.S. District Court, Northern District of California. *Education:* Boston University (B.S., summa cum laude, 1973); University of California, Hastings College of Law (J.D., magna cum laude, 1985). **PRACTICE AREAS:** Business. **Email:** sfrdad@aol.com

**PAUL B. TYLER,** born Kilgore, Texas, October 19, 1966; admitted to bar, 1996, California and U.S. District Court, Central District of California. *Education:* Pepperdine University (B.A., in English and Religion, 1988; J.D., 1996). *Member:* Ventura County Bar Association. **PRACTICE AREAS:** Insurance; Business Litigation. **Email:** pault@wood-associates.com

**JOHN C. BARKER,** born Boston, Massachusetts, July 29, 1956; admitted to bar, 1992, California and U.S. District Court, Northern District of California; 1993, U.S. District Court, Eastern and Central Districts of California. *Education:* Williams College (B.A., in Religion, cum laude, 1978); University of California, Hastings College of Law (J.D., 1992). *Member:* San Francisco County and Alameda County Bar Associations. **PRACTICE AREAS:** Insurance; Business Litigation.

## BECKER & RUNKLE

3161 CAMERON PARK DRIVE, SUITE 225
**CAMERON PARK, CALIFORNIA 95682**
Telephone: 916-676-6464
Fax: 916-676-5805

Personal Injury, Real Estate, Business, Corporate, Commercial, Family and Civil Litigation.

### MEMBERS OF FIRM

**DAVID C. BECKER,** born Torrance, California, December 13, 1957; admitted to bar, 1983, California. *Education:* California State University at Los Angeles (B.A., 1980); University of the Pacific (J.D., 1983). Member, Moot Court Honors Board. Recipient, American Jurisprudence in Estates and Trusts. Certified Trial Counsel in Military Courts, 1984. Instructor, Criminal Law, Central Texas College, 1987-1988. Member, International Legal Society, Tokyo, Japan, 1986. *Member:* El Dorado County, Sacramento County and American Bar Associations; State Bar of California. [Lieut., U.S. Navy, 1983-1988; Staff Judge Advocate, Japan, U.S. Navy, 1986-1988]. **PRACTICE AREAS:** Personal Injury (50%, 100); Real Estate (30%, 100); Business Law (20%, 50).

**ROGER A. RUNKLE,** born Sacramento, California, January 2, 1961; admitted to bar, 1986, California. *Education:* University of California at Davis (B.A., 1983); University of the Pacific, McGeorge School of Law (J.D., 1986). *Member:* El Dorado and American Bar Associations; The State Bar of California. **PRACTICE AREAS:** Family Law (65%, 200); Personal Injury (35%, 30).

**RICK MAYER,** born Dominican Republic, May 8, 1956; admitted to bar, 1993, California. *Education:* California State University, Sacramento (B.S., 1989); Lorenzo Patino School of Law (J.D., 1992). *Member:* El Dorado County and Sacramento County Bar Associations. **PRACTICE AREAS:** Personal Injury; Real Estate; Business Law.

REPRESENTATIVE CLIENTS: KFRD Investments; Stancil's Toyota; Jim Broman Properties; Western Sierra National Bank; American Institute of Business Managers; Allan H. Lindsey Realty; Pride Realty.

## LAURIE, MALONEY & WHEATLEY

Established in 1988

3420 COACH LANE, SUITE 15
**CAMERON PARK, CALIFORNIA 95682**
Telephone: 916-677-0245
Fax: 916-677-4802

Placerville (El Dorado County), California Office: 345 Placerville Drive. Telephone: 916-622-7769.

(This Listing Continued)

## LAURIE, MALONEY & WHEATLEY, Cameron Park—Continued

*Folsom (Sacramento County), California Office:* 1004 River Rock Drive, Suite 245. Telephone: 916-988-3857.

*Land Use, Business, Real Estate, Banking, Estate Planning, Municipal, Employment and Construction Law, Civil and Personal Injury Litigation, Franchising.*

### MEMBERS OF FIRM

**ROBERT A. LAURIE,** born Los Angeles, California, June 5, 1946; admitted to bar, 1975, California and U.S. District Court, Southern District of California; 1977, U.S. District Court, Eastern District of California. *Education:* Los Angeles City College (A.A., 1966); University of California at Irvine (B.A., 1972); McGeorge School of Law, University of the Pacific (J.D., 1975). Phi Alpha Delta. Member, Moot Court Honors Board. Instructor, Business Law, American River College, 1981-1990. President, El Dorado County Bar Association, 1981. Chairman, Land Use Committee of Public Law Section, State Bar of California, 1984. President, El Dorado County Chamber of Commerce, 1985, 1988; El Dorado County Board of Education, 1988-1994; 1996—. Member, 1992—; Chairman, 1994, Contractors State License Board, State of California. **PRACTICE AREAS:** Government Land Use; Business; Real Estate.

**BRIAN E. MALONEY,** born Pomona, California, March 11, 1950; admitted to bar, 1976, California; 1980, U.S. District Court, Eastern District of California. *Education:* University of California at Davis (A.B., 1972); McGeorge School of Law, University of the Pacific (J.D., 1976). Instructor, Real Estate Law, Cosumnes River College, Placerville Campus, 1984—. Panel Member, El Dorado County Superior Court Arbitration Panel, 1983—. *Member:* El Dorado County Bar Association (Secretary/Treasurer, 1981). **PRACTICE AREAS:** Real Estate; Business Law; Estate Planning.

**ROBERT M. WHEATLEY,** born San Mateo, California, April 2, 1943; admitted to bar, 1969, California; 1971, U.S. Tax Court; U.S. District Court, Northern and Eastern Districts of California; U.S. Supreme Court. *Education:* Stanford University (A.B., 1965); Hastings College of the Law, University of California (J.D., 1968). Superior Court Settlement Judge Pro Tem, 1988—. Municipal Court Judge Pro Tem, 1974—. Member, Sacramento County Superior Court Judicial Arbitration Panel, 1976—. *Member:* Sacramento County (President, Young Lawyers Association, 1972-1973; Member: Bar Council, 1972-1974; Fee Arbitration Committee, 1982—) and American (Member, Economics of Law Practice Section) Bar Associations; The State Bar of California; El Dorado County Round Table on Human Rights. (Resident Partner, Sacramento County (Folsom) Office). **REPORTED CASES:** Lodestar v. Mono County, 639 F.Supp 1439 (1986); Lilly v. USAA, 217 CA 3d 1396 (1990). **PRACTICE AREAS:** Probate; Commercial Litigation; Business; Real Estate.

**NELSON KEITH BROOKS,** born Columbus, Ohio, January 10, 1948; admitted to bar, 1982, California and U.S. District Court, Eastern District of California. *Education:* University of Santa Clara (B.A., 1973); Hastings College of the Law, University of California (J.D., 1982). Member: Oscar LaVant Society; American Inn of Court. *Member:* El Dorado County (President, 1993) and National Bar Associations; State Bar of California. **REPORTED CASES:** Lonestar v. Mono County (1986) 639 F. Supp. 1439; Lilly v. USAA (1990) 217 Caed 1396. **PRACTICE AREAS:** Business; Real Estate; Personal Injury Litigation; Employment; Civil Rights Litigation.

**RICHARD D. SOPP,** born Pasadena, California, July 20, 1958; admitted to bar, 1986, California and U.S. District Court, Eastern and Northern Districts of California; 1987, U.S. Court of Appeals, Ninth Circuit. *Education:* Brigham Young University (B.A., 1982; J.D., 1986). Kappa Tau Alpha; Stewart Grow Scholar. Member: Board of Advocates; American Inns of Court. *Member:* El Dorado County and American (Forum on Franchising, 1989-1992) Bar Associations; State Bar of California. **PRACTICE AREAS:** Franchising; Business; Real Estate; Litigation.

REPRESENTATIVE CLIENTS: Precision Contacts, Inc.; Cameron Park Airport District; City of Plymouth; Cameron Park Community Services District; Coker-Ewing Development Co.; Coldwell Banker Exceptional Properties, Inc.; Dolan's Lumber; El Dorado County Association of Realtors, Inc.; Lasher Porsche; Lewis Homes; McCuen Properties; McDonald's Corp.; Niello Lincoln Mercury; Reynen, Bardis & Winn; Roseville BMW; Smith & Gabbert, Inc.; Western Sierra National Bank; Winncrest Homes; Thomas Pontiac GMC; Thompson Jeep-Eagle Pontiac GMC; Founders Title Company of Sacramento, Inc.; Old Republic Title Company; Employers Reinsurance Co.; Willow Creek Homeowner's Association, Inc.; Hacienda de Estrellas Homeowners Association, Inc; FTM Plastics, Inc.; Synergy Consulting, Inc.; Folsom Lake Ford/Toyota; Folsom Chevrolet.

## JACKSON H. MASON, JR.
POINT LOMA CENTER
3161 CAMERON PARK DRIVE, SUITE 209
**CAMERON PARK, CALIFORNIA 95682**
Telephone: 916-677-6877
FAX: 916-677-2824

*Campbell, California Office:* Pruneyard Towers II, 1999 South Bascom Avenue, Suite 700. Telephone: 408-371-1011.

*Estate Planning, Wills and Trusts, Probate, Business, Corporate and Commercial Law Practice.*

**JACKSON H. MASON, JR.,** born Lewes, Delaware, February 19, 1944; admitted to bar, 1969, California and U.S. District Court, Central District of California. *Education:* University of California at Los Angeles (A.B., 1965; J.D., 1968). Member, UCLA Law Review, 1966-1968; Senior Editor, 1967-1968. *Member:* El Dorado, Sacramento and Santa Clara County Bar Associations (Chair, 1994—, El Dorado County, Estate Planning, Probate and Trust Section).

REPRESENTATIVE CLIENTS: Armstrong Technologies, Inc.; Carbon Copy, Inc.; Cason Engineering, Inc.; Glastronics; Intricast Company; Micro-Comp Industries, Inc.; Silicon Packaging Express, Inc.

## ADLESON, HESS & KELLY
577 SALMAR AVENUE, SECOND FLOOR
**CAMPBELL, CALIFORNIA 95008**
Telephone: 408-341-0234
Telecopier: 408-341-0250
Email: pjkelly1@ix.netcom.com

*Real Estate and Foreclosure Matters, Creditor Bankruptcy Representation, Insurance Coverage for Policy Holders.*

**PHILLIP M. ADLESON,** born Inglewood, California, November 4, 1949; admitted to bar, 1976, California; 1992, U.S. Supreme Court; 1993, U.S. Court of Appeals, Ninth Circuit. *Education:* California State University at Northridge (B.A., with honors); University of Santa Clara (J.D., cum laude). Contributor, California Trustee's Association Newsletter, 1983—. Instructor: De Anza College, Real Estate and Business Law, 1978-1985; San Jose State University, Real Estate Law, 1978-1985. President, 1986-1988, Corporate Counsel and Director, California Trustees Association. Director, California Trustees Association, Bay Area Chapter. Chairman, Northern California Legislative Committee, 1984-1985, 1988. *Member:* Santa Clara County Bar Association; State Bar of California. **REPORTED CASES:** I. E. Associates v. Safeco Title Ins. Co. (1985) 39 Cal.3d 281, 216 Cal.Rptr. 438; Anderson v. Heart Fed. Sav. & Loan (1989) 208 Cal.App.3d 202, 256 Cal.Rptr. 180; In Re BFP (1994) 114 S.Ct. 1757, 62 U.S.L.W. 4359. **PRACTICE AREAS:** Lending/Mortgage Brokering; Real/Personal Property Foreclosures; Real Estate Lending/Civil Litigation; Real Property Sales/Exchanges. *Email:* Adleson@ix.netcom.com

**RANDY M. HESS,** born Chicago, Illinois, April 21, 1955; admitted to bar, 1979, California and U.S. District Court, Northern District; 1983, U.S. Court of Appeals, Ninth District; 1986, U.S. Supreme Court; 1990, U.S. District Court, Central, Southern and Eastern Districts of California. *Education:* Arizona State University (B.S., cum laude, 1976); Santa Clara University (J.D., 1979). Author: "Malicious Prosecution Coverage Issues/Personal Injury Coverage Issues," Bad Faith Blockbusters, Annual Monterey Bad Faith Seminar, August 1996; "Run for Cover (Employer's Insurance Coverage for Claims Made by Employees)," California Trustee's Association Legal Newsletter, Summer 1995; "Obtaining Insurance Coverage for Employers in Wrongful Termination, Constructive Termination and Sexual Harassment Claims," California Lawyer Magazine, February 1992; "Beware of Attacks on the Liability Insurance Notice-Prejudice Rule," Continuing Legal Education. Co-Author: "Recent Developments in Insurance Law, Lorman Education Services, April 1994-1996; "Foreclosure and Insurance Issues," Mortgage Association of California, January 26, 1996; "The Workplace in Transition/Labor and Employment Law Supplement," Los Angels Daily Journal and San Francisco Daily Journal, July 27, 1995; "Antitrust Laws and Insurers," California Trial Lawyers Association Forum, December 1993; *Member:* Santa Clara County Bar Association (Member, Insurance Law Executive Committee, 1993—). **REPORTED CASES:** Wong v. State Compensation Ins. Fund (1993) 12 Cal.App.4th 686; La Jolla Beach & Tennis Club v. Industrial Indemnity Co. (1994) 9 Cal.4th 27; Apte v. Japra, Inc., —F.3d—, 96 Daily Journal D.A.R. 11960 (9th Cir. 1996); Lesser v. State Farm Ins. Co., 1996 WL 339854 (C.D.Cal. 1996); Gillespie v. Hartford Inc. Co. Midwest, 1996 WL 61155 (N.D.Cal. 1996); I. E. As-

*(This Listing Continued)*

sociates v. Safeco Title Ins. Co. (1985) 39 Cal.3d 281. *PRACTICE AREAS:* Insurance Coverage/Bad Faith (90%, 100); Personal Injury (10%, 25). *Email:* Adleson@ix.netcom.com

**PATRIC J. KELLY,** born Salt Lake City, Utah, January 15, 1951; admitted to bar, 1976, California; 1992, U.S. Supreme Court and U.S. Court of Appeals, Ninth Circuit. *Education:* California State University, Hayward (B.A., summa cum laude, 1973); University of Santa Clara (J.D., summa cum laude, 1976). Contributor, California Trustee's Association Newsletter, 1983—. Instructor: De Anza College, Real Estate and Business Law, 1978-1985; San Jose State University, Real Estate Law, 1978-1985. California Real Estate Broker, 1980—. *Member:* Santa Clara County Bar Association; State Bar of California. *REPORTED CASES:* Abdallah v. United Savings Bank 43 Cal.App.4th 1101 (1996); I. E. Associates v. Safeco Title Ins. Co. (1985) 216 Cal.Rptr. 438, 39 Cal.3d 281-amicus; In re Apte, 180 B.R. 223 (9th Cir.BAP (Cal.) 1995); In re McFadyen, 145 B.R. 657 (E.D.-Cal. 1992); In re BFP, 114 S.Ct. 1757, (U.S., Supreme Court 1994)-amicus. *PRACTICE AREAS:* Creditor Bankruptcy Law (75%); Real Estate Litigation (20%); Civil and Commercial Litigation (5%).

**DUANE W. SHEWAGA,** born Toronto, Ontario, Canada, September 23, 1958; admitted to bar, 1984, California; 1985, U.S. District Court, Northern District of California; 1990, U.S. District Court, Eastern District of California; 1992, U.S. Supreme Court and U.S. Court of Appeals, Ninth Circuit. *Education:* San Jose State University (B.A., 1981); University of Santa Clara (J.D., summa cum laude, 1984). Author: "Obtaining Insurance Coverage In Wrongful Termination Claims," CTLA Forum, December 1993. Judge Pro Tem, Santa Clara Municipal Court, 1996. Special Master, State Bar, 1993-1996. Executive Committee Member, Insurance Law Section, Santa Clara County Bar Association, 1993-1996. *Member:* State Bar of California. *REPORTED CASES:* Abdallah v. United Savings Bank (1995) 943 Cal.App.4th 1101; Wong v. State Compensation Insurance Fund (1993) 12 Cal.App.4th 686; In re Nelson (1988) 91 BRW 904; In re Apte, (1996) WL551443 (9th Cir. 1996); In re BFP, (1994) 114 S.Ct. 1757. *PRACTICE AREAS:* Real Property Secured Transactions (35%); Insurance Coverage (50%); Bankruptcy (15%).

**STEVEN B. HALEY,** born Chicago, Illinois, August 17, 1950; admitted to bar, 1976, California and U.S. District Court, Northern and Eastern Districts of California. *Education:* San Jose State University (B.A.; 1972); University of Santa Clara (J.D.; 1976). Member, California Trustee's Association, 1991—. State Director, 1995—and Member, 1993-1996, State Legislative Committee. Member, State Federal Legislative and Regulation Committee, 1996—. President, Bay Area Chapter California Trustee's Association, 1995—. Contributor, California Trustee's Association Newsletter, 1992—. Panelist, Appraisal Institute, South Bay and Monterey Chapter, 1989-1995; California Trustee's Association, 1992-1996; California Trust Deed Broker's Association, 1996. Settlement Pro Tem, Family Court, Superior Court, Santa Clara County, June 1988-December 1990. *Member:* Santa Clara County Bar Association; State Bar of California. *REPORTED CASES:* Trustors Security Service v. Title Recon Tracking et al. (1996) 56 Cal.Rptr.2d 793. *PRACTICE AREAS:* Real Property Litigation (65%); Bankruptcy Law and Secured Creditors (25%); Real Property Transactions (5%); General Civil (5%).

**DAVID M. TRAPANI,** born San Jose, California, April 6, 1962; admitted to bar, 1987, California and U.S. District Court, Northern District of California; 1990, U.S. District Court, Southern, Eastern and Central Districts of California. *Education:* Santa Clara University (B.S., 1984; J.D., 1987). *Member:* Santa Clara County and American Bar Associations; State Bar of California. *PRACTICE AREAS:* Plaintiffs Personal Injury (60%, 35); Insurance Coverage (25%, 10); General Civil Litigation (15%, 5).

**QUENTIN F. MOMMAERTS,** born Durham, North Carolina, July 15, 1953; admitted to bar, 1979, California and U.S. District Court, Northern and Central Districts of California. *Education:* University of California at Santa Cruz (B.S., 1976); University of Santa Clara (J.D., 1979). Arbitrator: Insurance Coverage; Personal Injury; Medical Malpractice. *Member:* Santa Clara and American Bar Associations; State Bar of California. *PRACTICE AREAS:* Insurance Coverage (90%); Personal Injury Litigation (5%); General Civil Litigation (5%).

REPRESENTATIVE CLIENTS: Aames Home Loan; Aames Financial Corporation; Acc-U-Tune & Brake; Benham Management Group; Golden Gate University; Redwood Mortgage; Residential Services and Validated Publications; Standard Trust Deed Service; Sunboro Development Corporation.

## HOMER & PHILLIPS
*A LAW CORPORATION*

SUITE 1010 THE PRUNEYARD TOWERS II
1999 SOUTH BASCOM AVENUE
**CAMPBELL, CALIFORNIA 95008**
Telephone: 408-377-3901
Fax: 408-377-2971

*Estate Planning, Probate, Taxation and Trust Law.*

**LLOYD W. HOMER** (Retired).

**GEOFFREY W. PHILLIPS,** born Alameda, California, February 8, 1959; admitted to bar, 1987, California and U.S. District Court, Northern District of California. *Education:* Santa Clara University (B.S.C., 1981; J.D., cum laude, 1987). Certified Public Accountant, California, 1985. *Member:* Santa Clara County Bar Association (Member, Executive Committee, Section on Estate Planning, Trust and Probate Law, 1989—, Chair, 1992; Member, Section on Taxation); State Bar of California (Member, Section on Estate Planning, Trust and Probate Law); California Society of Certified Public Accountants. (Certified Specialist, Probate, Estate Planning and Trust Law, The State Bar of California Board of Legal Specialization). *PRACTICE AREAS:* Estate Planning; Probate; Taxation and Trust Law.

## DE SIMONE & ASSOCIATES

6928 OWENSMOUTH AVENUE
SECOND FLOOR
P.O. BOX 352
**CANOGA PARK, CALIFORNIA 91305**
Telephone: 818-715-7171
Facsimile: 818-715-9843

*Litigation, Premises Liability, Products Liability, Personal Injury, Torts, Insurance, Insurance Defense, Medical Malpractice, Labor and Employment, Alternative Dispute Resolution.*

**GERALD DE SIMONE,** born Englewood, New Jersey, March 20, 1959; admitted to bar, 1984, California and U.S. District Court, Central District of California; 1986, District of Columbia. *Education:* Hofstra University (B.A., 1980); Pepperdine University (J.D., 1983). Phi Alpha Delta. Recipient, Outstanding Advocate, LACBA Trial Advocacy Program, 1987. *Member:* Los Angeles County and American Bar Associations; California Trial Lawyers Association; The Association of Trial Lawyers of America. *REPORTED CASES:* Southland v. Superior Court; Jurado v. Toys "R" Us, Inc.; Thomas v. Intermedics Orthopedics, Inc.

**JAMES J. CASEY, JR.,** born Irvington, New Jersey, January 8, 1966; admitted to bar, 1993, California and U.S. District Court, Central District of California. *Education:* Trenton State College (B.A., 1990); Whittier College School of Law (J.D., 1993). *Member:* State Bar of California.

OF COUNSEL

**DANIEL J. SALOMON,** born New York, N.Y., April 15, 1950; admitted to bar, 1975, California and U.S. District Court, Central District of California. *Education:* University of Southern California (B.A., 1972); University of California at Los Angeles (J.D., 1975). *Member:* State Bar of California.

REPRESENTATIVE CLIENTS: Familian Corporation; Toys "R" Us, Inc.; La Petite Academy Preshools; GATX Corporation; CALNEX Pipe Line Company; BTR Corporation; GAP, Inc.; Cigna Property and Casualty; ESIS, Inc.; The Travelers Insurance Company; Constitution State Service Company.

## MARTIN P. ERAMO

34700 COAST HIGHWAY, SUITE 205
**CAPISTRANO BEACH, CALIFORNIA 92624**
Telephone: 714-240-4425
Fax: 714-240-7881

*Business, Construction, Real Estate, Landlord, Tenant and Collections.*

**MARTIN P. ERAMO,** born Pittsfield, Massachusetts, June 24, 1952; admitted to bar, 1978, California. *Education:* University of Massachusetts (B.A., 1974); Western State University (J.D., 1977). *Member:* State Bar of California.

## JOHN PATRICK McGOVERN

Established in 1989

2533 SOUTH HIGHWAY 101, SUITE 280
**CARDIFF-BY-THE-SEA, CALIFORNIA 92007**
Telephone: 619-944-9941
Facsimile: 619-943-0494
Email: JPMcGESQ@AOL.COM

*Business, Corporate and Real Estate, Intellectual Property, Commercial Litigation, Construction Law and Mechanics Liens, Employment Litigation and Personal Injury.*

**JOHN PATRICK MCGOVERN,** born Jersey City, New Jersey, December 26, 1957; admitted to bar, 1984, California and U.S. District Court, Southern and Central Districts of California. *Education:* University of California at San Diego (B.A., 1981); University of California at Davis (J.D., 1984). Judge Pro Tempore, Small Claims Division, San Diego County Municipal Court, 1994—. Member: Greater Del Mar Chamber of Commerce; Cardiff by the Sea Chamber of Commerce. *Member:* San Diego County and Northern San Diego County Bar Associations; State Bar of California; San Diego Trial Lawyers Association; Consumer Attorneys of San Diego County; Barristers Club of San Diego (Director, 1988-1989, President 1989); San Diego County Superior Court Arbitration Panel.

## MILBERG & DePHILLIPS

PROFESSIONAL CORPORATION

Established in 1981

2163 NEWCASTLE AVENUE, SUITE 200
**CARDIFF-BY-THE-SEA, CALIFORNIA 92007**
Telephone: 619-943-7103
Telecopier: 619-943-6750

*General Civil Practice. Business, Corporation, Real Property, Bankruptcy, Commercial, Personal Injury, Products Liability, Workers Compensation and Securities Law. Trials and Appeals.*

**FREDERIC J. MILBERG,** born New York, N.Y., July 14, 1949; admitted to bar, 1976, California and U.S. District Court, Central District of California; 1977, U.S. District Court, Southern and Northern Districts of California; 1980, U.S. Court of Appeals, Ninth Circuit. *Education:* Syracuse University (B.A., 1971); Golden Gate University (J.D., 1976). *Member:* San Diego County and American (Member, Section of Corporation, Banking and Business Law) Bar Associations; State Bar of California; California Trial Lawyers Association; San Diego Trial Lawyers Association. **LANGUAGES:** Spanish. **PRACTICE AREAS:** Personal Injury; Products Liability; Workers Compensation; Securities Law.

**RUSSELL M. DePHILLIPS,** born Chicago, Illinois, June 20, 1949; admitted to bar, 1980, California and U.S. District Court, Southern District of California; 1985, U.S. Court of Appeals, Ninth Circuit; U.S. District Court, Northern District of California; 1986, U.S. District Court, Central District of California. *Education:* Northern Illinois University (B.S., 1974); California Western School of Law (J.D., 1980). Member, Bankruptcy Mediation Panel, U.S. Bankruptcy Court, Southern District of California. Member, San Diego Bankruptcy Forum. *Member:* San Diego County and American (Member, Section of Corporation, Banking and Business Law) Bar Associations; Bar Association of Northern San Diego County; State Bar of California; San Diego Trial Lawyers Association; American Bankruptcy Institute. **REPORTED CASES:** In re Dix, 140 B.R. 997 (Bankr. S.D. Cal. 1992). **PRACTICE AREAS:** Bankruptcy; Corporate Reorganization; Creditors Rights; Business and Real Property Matters; Commercial Litigation.

**WILLIAM A. SKOOG, JR.,** born Santa Monica, California, December 9, 1954; admitted to bar, 1984, California and U.S. District Court, Southern District of California; 1985, U.S. Court of Appeals, Ninth Circuit. *Education:* California State University at San Diego (B.A., with honors, 1978); California Western School of Law (J.D., 1982). *Member:* San Diego County Bar Association; State Bar of California; California Trial Lawyers Association; San Diego Trial Lawyers Association. **LANGUAGES:** Spanish. **PRACTICE AREAS:** Personal Injury; Products Liability; Workers Compensation; General Civil Litigation; Maritime Law; Insurance Bad Faith.

**ROY L. CARLSON, JR.,** born Morris, Illinois, November 13, 1958; admitted to bar, 1986, California and U.S. District Court, Southern District of California; 1992, U.S. District Court, Central District of California; 1995, U.S. District Court, District of Arizona; U.S. Court of Appeals, Ninth Circuit and U.S. Supreme Court. *Education:* University of California at San Diego (B.A., with honors, 1980); Western State University (J.D., with scholastic meritt, 1985). Recipient, American Jurisprudence Award in Criminal Law. Member, Criminal Justice Journal, 1985. Law Clerk, Hon. John J. Hargrove, Judge, U.S. Bankruptcy Court, Southern District of California, 1988-1991. Member, Attorney Advisory Committee to the Clerk of the U.S. Bankruptcy Court for the Southern District of California. Member, San Diego Bankruptcy Forum. *Member:* San Diego County (Chair, Local Bankruptcy Rules Revision Committee, 1994-1996; Member, Bankruptcy Section) and American (Member: Lawyers Conference Committee of Judicial Performance and Conduct Committee) Bar Associations; State Bar of California; American Bankruptcy Institute; U.S. Bankruptcy Court (Member, Electronic Filing Committee). **REPORTED CASES:** In re Consolidated Pioneer Mortgage, 178 B.R. 222 (9th Cir. BAP 1995); In re Casey, 193 B.R. 942, 1996 WL 137293 (Bkrptcy. S.D., Cal. 1996). **PRACTICE AREAS:** Bankruptcy; Corporate Reorganization; Creditors Rights; Business Litigation.

**TIMOTHY G. MCNULTY,** born Los Angeles, California, March 10, 1966; admitted to bar, 1992, California, Arizona and U.S. District Court, Southern District of California; U.S. District Court, Central District of California; U.S. District Court, District of Arizona. *Education:* University of California, Santa Barbara (B.A., 1988); California Western School of Law (J.D., 1991). Recipient, American Jurisprudence Award in Appellate Advocacy at California Western, Fall 1990. Law Clerk to the Honorable Gilbert Nares, California Court of Appeal, Fourth Appellate District, Division One, 1990. *Member:* San Diego County Bar Association; State Bar of California. State Bar of Arizona. **LANGUAGES:** Spanish. **PRACTICE AREAS:** Civil Litigation; Personal Injury; Maritime Law; Products Liability; Insurance Law; Criminal Law; Appellate Practice.

**SEAN C. COUGHLIN,** born Annapolis, Maryland, December 30, 1966; admitted to bar, 1993, California and U.S. District Court, Southern District of California; 1994, U.S. District Court, Central District of California. *Education:* University of San Diego (B.A., 1989); California Western School of Law (J.D., 1993). Judicial Extern to the Honorable Louise DeCarl Adler, Chief Judge, U.S. Bankruptcy Court, Southern District of California, 1992. *Member:* San Diego County and American Bar Associations; State Bar of California (Member, Business Law Section); San Diego Bankruptcy Forum. **PRACTICE AREAS:** Creditor's Rights; Bankruptcy; Business and Real Estate Litigation; Commercial Litigation.

**KENT L. SHARP,** born Fontana, California, October 5, 1967; admitted to bar, 1995, California, and U.S. District Court, Southern District of California. *Education:* San Diego State University (B.A., 1991); California Western School of Law (J.D., 1995). *Member:* San Diego County and American Bar Associations; State Bar of California. **PRACTICE AREAS:** Business; Litigation; Creditor's Rights; Bankruptcy; Personal Injury; Maritime Law; Insurance Law.

REPRESENTATIVE CLIENTS: Capitol Thrift & Loan Association; Draper & Kramer, Inc.; Omni USA, Inc.; Consulate General of Mexico; Glenwood Management.

## BRAHMS & DUXBURY

800 GRAND AVENUE, SUITE C-14
**CARLSBAD, CALIFORNIA 92008**
Telephone: 619-434-4433
Fax: 619-434-1223

*General Civil and Criminal Trial Practice in all Courts. Military Law, Bankruptcy, Personal Injury, Criminal and Divorce Law.*

**MARC A. DUXBURY,** born Santa Barbara, California; April 17, 1962; admitted to bar, 1989, California. *Education:* California Polytechnic State University (B.A., 1985); California Western School of Law (J.D., 1988). *Member:* North San Diego County Bar Association; San Diego County Bar Association. **PRACTICE AREAS:** Civil; Criminal; Bankruptcy; Personal Injury; Divorce Law.

**DAVID MICHAEL BRAHMS,** born New York, N.Y., January 31, 1938; admitted to bar, 1963, Massachusetts; 1967, U.S. Court of Military Appeals; 1978, U.S. Court of Claims; 1990, California. *Education:* Harvard University (A.B., cum laude, 1959; LL.B., 1962); George Washington University (LL.M., psychology and criminology, highest honors, 1977). *Member:* San Diego County, North San Diego County and American Bar Asso-

*(This Listing Continued)*

ciations; State Bar of California. [USMC, Brig. Gen., (ret.).]. *PRACTICE AREAS:* Military Law; Criminal Law; Personal Injury; Employment Law; Federal Law; Civil Service Law.

REFERENCE: Bank of America.

## THE LAW OFFICES OF
## SHARON A. BROUGHTON

*Established in 1995*

**2755 JEFFERSON STREET, SUITE 203**
**CARLSBAD, CALIFORNIA 92008**
Telephone: 619-720-9780
Fax: 619-434-6832
Email: 105137.26@compuserve.com

*Business and Civil Litigation with emphasis on Breach of Contract and Insurance Bad Faith. Representation of Corporations, Small Businesses, Partnerships and Limited Liability Companies. Bankruptcy, Preparation of Wills and Trusts.*

**SHARON A. BROUGHTON,** born Evansville, Indiana, November 29, 1945; admitted to bar, 1989, California, U.S. District Court, Central District of California and U.S. Court of Appeals, Ninth Circuit; 1990, U.S. District Court, Northern, Eastern and Southern Districts of California. *Education:* Purdue University; Indiana University (A.B., 1969; M.L.S, 1970); University of Southern California (J.D., 1989). Beta Phi Mu. Managing Editor, Journal of Law and the Environment, 1988-1989. *Member:* San Diego County and American Bar Associations; State Bar of California.

## BROWN AND PEARSON, P.C.

**5963 LA PLACE COURT, SUITE 114**
**CARLSBAD, CALIFORNIA 92008**
Telephone: 619-438-5998
Facsimile: 619-438-7587

*Civil Litigation in all Courts with special emphasis in Securities and Construction Litigation, Insurance Law, Plaintiff Issues, Representation of Bonding Companies and Governmental Agencies.*

**FLOYD R. BROWN,** born 1935; admitted to bar, 1962, California. *Education:* Brigham Young University (B.S., 1958); University of California at Los Angeles School of Law (J.D., 1961). *PRACTICE AREAS:* Business Law (25%); Securities Litigation (25%); Cable T.V. (20%); Corporate Law (20%); Insurance Law (10%).

**CHRISSA N. CORDAY,** born Las Vegas, Nevada, December 24, 1960; admitted to bar, 1986, California and U.S. District Court, Southern District of California; U.S. District Court, Eastern District of California; U.S. District Court, Northern District of California. *Education:* Arizona State University (B.S., 1983); University of San Diego (J.D., 1986). Instructor of Law, Property, First Year Instructional Program, University of San Diego School of Law, 1984-1985. *Member:* San Diego County Bar Association (Member: Real Property Section; Construction Law Sections); State Bar of California; Lawyers Club of San Diego. *REPORTED CASES:* Campbel v. Superior Court, 44 Cal.App. 4th 1308. *PRACTICE AREAS:* Civil Litigation; Mechanics Lien Remedies; Surety and Fidelity Bond Law.

## FLETCHER & PATTON

*A Partnership of Professional Corporations*

*Established in 1978*

**2777 JEFFERSON STREET, SUITE 200**
**P.O. BOX 4598**
**CARLSBAD, CALIFORNIA 92018-4598**
Telephone: 619-434-4130
Facsimile: 619-434-0288
Email: pattonlaw@aol.com

*Criminal Defense Litigation in all State and Federal Courts, Felonies and Misdemeanors, Drug Crimes, Violent Crimes, Theft, Sex Crimes, D.U.I. and Administrative Hearings.*

**WILLIAM R. FLETCHER, (A P.C.),** born Lynwood, California, October 9, 1949; admitted to bar, 1975, California; 1976, U.S. District Court, Southern District of California. *Education:* California State University at San Diego (B.A., 1972); University of San Diego (J.D., 1975). Recipient:

*(This Listing Continued)*

Criminal Defense Attorney of the Year, Criminal Defense Bar Association, 1988. Author: "Due Process in School Discipline," 12 San Diego Law Review 912, 1975. Attorney, Defenders Inc., 1975-1977. Associate, Rhoades & Hollywood 1977-1978. Partner, Fletcher & Patton, 1978—. Judge Pro Tempore, North County Municipal Court, 1989—. Member, Board of Directors, 1983-1991 and President, 1989-1990, Defenders Program of San Diego, Inc. *Member:* San Diego County Bar Association (Member: Advisory Committee; Chairperson, Private Conflicts Counsel, 1996); The State Bar of California; California Attorneys for Criminal Justice; National Association for Criminal Lawyers; Criminal Defense Lawyers Club. (Certified Specialist, Criminal Law, The State Bar of California Board of Legal Specialization). *REPORTED CASES:* People v. Nixon (1982) 131 Cal.App.3d 687; Johnson v. Superior Court (1984) 163 Cal.App.3d 85; Copley Press, Inc. v. Superior Court (1991) 228 Cal.App.3d 77. *PRACTICE AREAS:* Criminal Law.

**C. BRADLEY PATTON, (A P.C.),** born Torrance, California, October 7, 1949; admitted to bar, 1975, California. *Education:* University of Southern California (B.S., 1972); California Western University (J.D., 1975). Recipient: Criminal Defense Attorney of the Year, Criminal Defense Lawyers, 1988; Lawyer of The Year Award, North San Diego County Bar Association, 1988. Research Attorney, San Diego Superior Court, 1975-1976. Attorney, Defenders Inc., 1976-1978. Partner, Fletcher & Patton, 1978—. Lecturer: "Hot Tips from the Experts: Opening Statements/Closing Arguments," Northern San Diego County Bar Association, February 1995; "Ethics for the Real World," San Diego County Bar Association, November 1994; "Ethics-The New Rules of Professional Conduct," Northern San Diego County Bar Association, January 1993; "Second Annual DUI Mock Trial," Century City Bar Association, September 1995; "Bar and the Press," San Diego Legion Lex, March 1996. Author: "Child Abuse Accommodation Syndrome," FORUM, January-February 1988; "How Law Office Staff Can Impact an Attorney's Ethical Obligation," The Legal Secretary, November 1992. Co-Author: Chapter 5, "Right to Counsel," and Chapter 18, "Professional Responsibilities," California Criminal Law Procedure and Practice, Second and Third Edition. *Member:* Northern San Diego County (Board of Directors, 1985-1987 and 1993-1995) and North County (Board of Directors, 1982-1984; Member, Lawyer Referral Service) Bar Associations; State Bar of California (Member, Committee on Professional Responsibilities and Conduct, 1989-1992); California Attorneys for Criminal Justice; Criminal Defense Lawyers Bar Association (Board of Directors, 1982-1984); Criminal Defense Association (Board of Directors, 1981); San Diego Legion Lex American Inns of Court, 1994—. (Certified Specialist, Criminal Law, The State Bar of California Board of Legal Specialization). *PRACTICE AREAS:* Criminal Law.

## GATZKE, MISPAGEL & DILLON

*A Partnership including a Professional Law Corporation*

**SUITE 200, 1921 PALOMAR OAKS WAY**
**P.O. BOX 1636**
**CARLSBAD, CALIFORNIA 92009**
Telephone: 619-431-9501
Fax: 619-431-9512

*Litigation in all State and Federal Courts. General Civil Litigation, Aviation, Governmental, Environmental, Zoning, Planning and Land Use, Administrative, Construction and Real Estate Law.*

### MEMBERS OF FIRM

**MICHAEL SCOTT GATZKE,** born Pasadena, California, August 2, 1945; admitted to bar, 1973, California and U.S. District Court, Southern District of California; 1977, U.S. Supreme Court; 1978, U.S. Court of Appeals, Ninth Circuit; 1980, U.S. Court of Appeals for the District of Columbia Circuit; 1981, U.S. District Court, Central District of California; 1985, U.S. District Court, Eastern District of California; 1986, U.S. District Court, Northern District of California; 1988, U.S. Court of Appeals, Sixth Circuit. *Education:* University of California at Santa Barbara (B.A., 1970); University of California at Los Angeles (J.D., 1973). *Member:* San Diego County and American Bar Associations; State Bar of California.

**MARK F. MISPAGEL,** born Inglewood, California, January 4, 1942; admitted to bar, 1975, California; 1978, U.S. District Court, Central District of California; 1979, U.S. Court of Appeals, Ninth Circuit; 1980, U.S. Supreme Court; 1985, U.S. District Court, Eastern District of California; 1986, U.S. District Court, Northern District of California. *Education:* Loyola University (B.A., 1964); McGeorge School of Law, University of the Pacific (J.D., 1974). Phi Delta Phi. Chief, Division of Aeronautics, California Department of Transportation, 1980-1984. Vice President, National

*(This Listing Continued)*

**GATZKE, MISPAGEL & DILLON, Carlsbad—Continued**

Association of State Aviation Officials, 1982-1984. Member: U.S. Congressional Airport Access Task Force, 1982-1983; California Department of Transportation, Legal Division, 1975-1980. Delegate, Commission of the California's, 1981-1982. Appointee, California Aviation Task Force, 1981-1982. Director, The Aero Club of Northern California, 1988—. President, Aerial Firefighting Industry Association, 1988-1990. Member: State of California Technical Advisory Committee on Aeronautics, 1989—; Congressional Advisory Panel on Drug Interdiction Technology, 1985-1987. Member: San Diego County and Sonoma County Bar Associations; State Bar of California.

**MARK J. DILLON,** born Chicago, Illinois, November 26, 1955; admitted to bar, 1983, California and U.S. District Court, Southern District of California; 1986, U.S. District Court, Eastern and Northern Districts of California and U.S. Court of Appeals, Ninth Circuit; 1992, U.S. District Court, Central District of California. *Education:* California State University at Fullerton (B.A., with honors, 1979); California Western School of Law (J.D., 1982). Co-Author, "CEQA - Judicial Review," Longtin's California Land Use (2nd Ed.), 1992 Supplement. Co-Author: "California Environmental Quality Act" and "Other Environmental Controls", Longtin's California Land Use (2nd Ed.) 1993, 1994 and 1995 Supplements. *Member:* San Diego County Bar Association; State Bar of California; American Inns of Court; Association of Environmental Professionals.

**LORI D. BALLANCE,** born Los Alamos, New Mexico, December 16, 1960; admitted to bar, 1988, California and U.S. District Court, Central District of California. *Education:* University of San Diego (B.A., 1982); Hastings College of the Law, University of California (J.D., 1987). Recipient, American Jurisprudence Award. Co-Author: "Hazardous Waste Controls", Longtin's California Land Use (2nd Ed.), 1991 and 1992 Supplements; "CEQA - Judicial Review," Longtin's California Land Use (2nd Ed.), 1992 Supplement; "California Environmental Quality Act" and "Other Environmental Controls", Longtin's California Land Use (2nd Ed.) 1993, 1994 and 1995 Supplements. Member, Board of Governors, Hastings College of the Law, 1990—. *Member:* San Diego County Bar Association; State Bar of California; Association of Environmental Professionals.

ASSOCIATES

**DAVID P. HUBBARD,** born Oceanside, California, November 22, 1962; admitted to bar, 1990, California and U.S. District Court, Northern District of California; 1992, U.S. District Court, Central and Southern Districts of California. *Education:* University of California at Santa Cruz (B.A., with honors, 1985); University of Chicago (M.A., 1987); Boalt Hall School of Law, University of California (J.D., 1990). *Member:* San Diego County Bar Association; State Bar of California.

**KRISTIN BETH WHITE,** born Newport Beach, California, February 24, 1965; admitted to bar, 1992, California and U.S. District Court, Southern District of California. *Education:* University of California Berkeley (B.S., 1987); University of California Hastings (J.D., 1992). *Member:* North San Diego County Bar Association; State Bar of California.

**STEPHEN F. TEE,** born Oceanside, California, January 14, 1969; admitted to bar, 1994, California and U.S. District Court, Southern District of California. *Education:* University of California San Diego (B.A., with distinction, 1991); University of San Diego (J.D., 1994). *Member:* San Diego County Bar Association; State Bar of California.

**TOM DEAK,** born Pasadena, California, January 30, 1967; admitted to bar, 1996, California. *Education:* University of Washington (B.A., 1989); University of Oregon (J.D., 1995). Member, Oregon Law Review. *Member:* San Diego County Bar Association; State Bar of California.

---

## PATRICIA D. HOFFMANN

2131 PALOMAR AIRPORT ROAD, SUITE 300
**CARLSBAD, CALIFORNIA 92009**
Telephone: 619-729-1234
Fax: 619-431-1223

*Wills, Trusts, Durable Powers of Attorney, Probate and Probate Litigation, Corporations (Set-Up, Dissolution and Maintenance), Contracts and Business Law.*

**PATRICIA D. HOFFMANN,** born Pompton Plains, New Jersey, April 24, 1963; admitted to bar, 1990, California. *Education:* County College of Morris (A.A.S., 1983); New Jersey Institute of Technology (B.S., 1986);

*(This Listing Continued)*

---

California Western School of Law (J.D., 1990). *Member:* San Diego and American Bar Associations; State Bar of California. **PRACTICE AREAS:** General Practice.

---

## HOLLIS & MAUERMAN

7720 B EL CAMINO REAL, SUITE 174
**CARLSBAD, CALIFORNIA 92009**
Telephone: 619-942-9404
Facsimile: 619-942-9403
Email: mtmlpm@IX.netcom.com

Santa Ana, California Office: 2677 North Main Street, Suite 930. Telephone: 714-835-4100. Facsimile: 714-972-4926.

*Civil Litigation in all State and Federal Courts. Securities, Corporate and Business Transactions, Taxation.*

(For Complete Biographical data on all personnel, see Professional Biographies at Santa Ana, California)

---

## LAW OFFICE OF
## RICHARD V. HYATT

Established in 1976

SUITE 130, 7220 AVENIDA ENCINAS
**CARLSBAD, CALIFORNIA 92009**
Telephone: 619-438-3088
Telecopier: 619-438-1443
Email: rvhesq@aol.com

*Practice limited to Dissolution of Marriage and related proceedings.*

**RICHARD V. HYATT,** born San Diego, California, August 31, 1946; admitted to bar, 1976, California and U.S. District Court, Southern District of California. *Education:* San Diego State University (B.A., 1969); Western State University (J.D., 1975). Pi Sigma Alpha. Judge Pro Tempore, Family Law, Superior Court, 1989—. *Member:* Northern San Diego County (Chairman, Family Law Section, 1993-1994) and San Diego County Bar Associations; State Bar of California. (Certified Family Law Specialist, California Board of Legal Specialization, 1991).

REPRESENTATIVE CLIENTS: San Dieguito Boys & Girls Club.

---

## LODGE & HELLER

A Partnership including a Professional Corporation

Established in 1987

1901 CAMINO VIDA ROBLE, SUITE 110
**CARLSBAD, CALIFORNIA 92008**
Telephone: 619-931-9700
Fax: 619-931-1155

Pauma Valley, California Office: The Pauma Building, Suite 403, 16160 Highway 76, P.O. Box 600. Telephone: 619-749-3199.

*General Civil and Commercial Trial Practice. Corporate, Real Estate, Construction, Estate Planning, Probate, Trust and Governmental and Land Use Law.*

MEMBERS OF FIRM

**ERIC T. LODGE, (P.C.),** born Orange, California, June 16, 1943; admitted to bar, 1969, California. *Education:* Trinity College (A.B., 1965); University of Southern California (J.D., 1968). Southern California Law Review, 1966-1968; Note and Comment Editor, 1967-1968. Lecturer, California Continuing Education of the Bar on Estate Planning Subjects. Consulting Editor: C.E.B., "Drafting California Living Trusts" (2d Ed. 1984); "California Will Drafting" (3d Ed. 1992). *Member:* San Diego County (Board of Directors, 1993—; President, 1997), Northern San Diego County (Chair, Probate Section, 1992) and American (Member, Real Property, Probate and Trust Law Section) Bar Associations. (Certified Specialist, Probate, Estate Planning and Trust Law, The State Bar of California Board of Legal Specialization). **PRACTICE AREAS:** Estate Planning; Probate and Trust Law; Corporate Law. **Email:** 76200.3310@compuserve.com

**RICHARD A. HELLER,** born Sacramento, California, September 21, 1949; admitted to bar, 1975, California; 1980, District of Columbia. *Education:* University of California at Berkeley (A.B., 1971); University of San Diego (J.D., 1975). Staff Writer, San Diego Law Review, 1974-1975. Lecturer: California Continuing Education of the Bar, Estate & Trust Litiga-

*(This Listing Continued)*

tion, 1991-1996. *Member:* San Diego and Northern San Diego County (President, 1995; Member, Board of Directors, 1992-1995; Chair, Civil Litigation Section, 1990-1992) Bar Associations; State Bar of California. *PRACTICE AREAS:* Business Litigation; Estate Litigation.

**DOROTHY T. LODGE** (Retired).

---

**MARY V.J. CATALDO,** born Oklahoma City, Oklahoma, February 4, 1953; admitted to bar, 1994, California. *Education:* University of Arizona (B.A., 1975); Western State University San Diego (J.D., 1994). *Member:* San Diego County Bar Association; Bar Association of Northern San Diego County; State Bar of California. *PRACTICE AREAS:* Civil Litigation.

**HARRIET AVNER WAANDERS,** born Brooklyn, New York, May 2, 1947; admitted to bar, 1982, California. *Education:* Queens College of the City University of New York (B.A., 1968); Michigan State University (M.A., 1969); University of San Diego (J.D., 1982). Adjunct Faculty Member, California Western School of Law, 1993-1994. Lecturer, California Continuing Education of the Bar on Estate Planning Subjects. *Member:* San Diego County and Northern San Diego County (Chair, Probate Section, 1993) Bar Associations; State Bar of California; Lawyer's Club Bar Association (Member, Board of Directors, 1986-1989). (Certified Specialist, Estate Planning, Trust and Probate Law, The State Bar of California Board of Legal Specialization). *PRACTICE AREAS:* Estate Planning Law; Probate and Trust Law.

## GEORGE P. MILLS
2755 JEFFERSON STREET, SUITE 205
**CARLSBAD, CALIFORNIA 92008**
Telephone: 619-434-8688
Fax: 619-434-6832

*Practice limited primarily to Family Law. Practice also includes Family Mediation, Bankruptcy and Guardianships.*

**GEORGE P. MILLS,** born Oceanside, California, May 4, 1945; admitted to bar, 1978, California and U.S District Court, Southern District of California. *Education:* Pomona College (B.A., in Economics, 1967); Syracuse University (M.P.A., 1968); Brooklyn Law School (J.D., 1976). Licensed Real Estate Broker, California. Author: "The Illinois Structural Work Act," The St. Louis Law Journal, 1979. Judge Pro Tem for Family Law, Superior Court of San Diego County. Member, Family Law Mediation Panel, Superior and Municipal Court Civil Cases. *Member:* Bar Association of North San Diego County; San Diego County Bar Association. (Certified Specialist, Family Law, The State Bar of California Board of Legal Specialization). *PRACTICE AREAS:* Family Law; Mediation; Bankruptcy Law; Guardianships.

## RUSHALL & McGEEVER
A PROFESSIONAL LAW CORPORATION
Established in 1980
SUITE 200, GRAHAM INTERNATIONAL PLAZA
2111 PALOMAR AIRPORT ROAD
**CARLSBAD, CALIFORNIA 92009**
Telephone: 619-438-6855
Fax: 619-438-3026

*Securities, Corporation, Real Property, Employment and Commercial Litigation. Trial and Appellate Practice.*

**FIRM PROFILE:** *Founded in 1980, the firm limits its practice to transactional law and civil litigation. It emphasizes securities, corporate and real estate representation and litigation, employment law and appellate practice. We believe that a small firm of experienced practitioners can effectively provide integrated, sophisticated and cost-effective services to businesses and individuals.*

**BRUCE J. RUSHALL,** born La Jolla, California, April 14, 1946; admitted to bar, 1974, California; U.S. District Court, Central, Southern and Northern Districts of California. *Education:* University of California at Santa Barbara (B.S., 1970); University of California at Los Angeles (J.D., 1974). Arbitrator, National Association of Securities Dealers, Inc., 1982—. *Member:* San Diego County and American Bar Associations; State Bar of California. *PRACTICE AREAS:* Securities Law; Corporation Law; Real Property Law.

*(This Listing Continued)*

**EILEEN L. McGEEVER,** born Pittsburgh, Pennsylvania, December 13, 1948; admitted to bar, 1974, California; U.S. District Court, Central, Southern and Northern Districts of California. *Education:* University of California at Los Angeles (B.A., 1971; J.D., 1974). Phi Beta Kappa; Alpha Lambda Delta. *Member:* San Diego County and American Bar Associations; State Bar of California. *PRACTICE AREAS:* Securities; Commercial Litigation; Employment Litigation.

**GRETCHEN COWEN,** born Cedar City, Utah, November 9, 1968; admitted to bar, 1993, California and U.S. District Court, Southern District of California. *Education:* Southern Utah University (B.S., 1990); California Western School of Law (J.D., 1993). Author: The Recognition and Enforcement of Foreign Judgments, Transnational Lawyer Vol. 5, 1992. *Member:* State Bar of California. *PRACTICE AREAS:* Securities/Transactional and Employment Law.

REPRESENTATIVE CLIENTS: Farmers Insurance Group of Cos.; The Excel Companies; The Centurion Companies; The Aquapro Companies; Torrey Pines Securities, Inc.; Superior National Insurance Company.

## WEIL & WRIGHT
Established in 1992
1921 PALOMAR OAKS WAY, SUITE 301
**CARLSBAD, CALIFORNIA 92008**
Telephone: 619-438-1214
Telefax: 619-438-2666

*General Civil, Trial and Appellate Practice. Banking, Corporate, Commercial, Real Estate, Creditor Rights and Property Taxation.*

**PAUL M. WEIL,** born Pittsburgh, Pennsylvania, June 14, 1927; admitted to bar, 1959, California; 1964, U.S. Supreme Court. *Education:* Stanford University; University of California at Los Angeles; Southwestern University (J.D., cum laude, 1958). Member, 1967-1975 and President, 1970-1972; 1974-1975, East Whittier City School District Board of Trustees. *Member:* Whittier, Northern San Diego and San Diego County Bar Associations; State Bar of California; Association of Business Trial Lawyers. *PRACTICE AREAS:* Real Estate; Business; Commercial; Banking; Civil Litigation.

**ARCHIE T. WRIGHT III,** born Orangeburg, South Carolina, February 23, 1946; admitted to bar, 1974, California and U.S. District Court, Southern District of California; 1976, U.S. Court of Appeals, Ninth Circuit. *Education:* Duke University (B.A., 1968); Cornell University (J.D., 1974). Editor, Cornell Law Review, 1972-1974. Author: "Awarding Attorney & Expert Witness Fees in Environmental Litigation," 58 Cornell Law Review 1222 (1973). Panelist, Seventh Annual Real Property Practice Institute, (C.E.B., 1990). *Member:* San Diego County Bar Association; State Bar of California; International Council of Shopping Centers. **REPORTED CASES:** Main & VonKarman Assoc. v. County of Orange (1994) 23 Cal. App. 4th 337 Property Taxes. *PRACTICE AREAS:* Real Estate and Business Transactions; Property Taxation.

**DAVID A. EBERSOLE,** born Port Jefferson, New York, April 20, 1956; admitted to bar, 1985, New York; 1987, California. *Education:* Northeastern University (B.S., Acctg., 1979); California Western School of Law (J.D., 1984). *Member:* Northern San Diego and San Diego County Bar Associations; State Bar of California. **REPORTED CASES:** Flojo Int'l v. Cassleben (1992) 4 Cal. App. 4th 713 Commercial Contract. *PRACTICE AREAS:* Business; Commercial; Landlord and Tenant; Real Estate; Civil Litigation; Banking.

**JOHN F. HILBERT,** born Los Angeles, California, March 5, 1957; admitted to bar, 1982, California. *Education:* University of California at Santa Barbara (B.A., with honors, 1979); University of San Diego (J.D., cum laude, 1982). Member, San Diego Law Review, 1980-1982. Author: "A Criticism of the Gertz Public Figure: Private Figure Test in the Context of the Corporate Defamation Plaintiff," 18 San Diego Law Review 721 (1981). *Member:* San Diego County and American Bar Associations; State Bar of California.

REPRESENTATIVE CLIENTS: First National Bank of North County; Aetna Life Insurance Co.; Wells Fargo Bank; Great West Life Insurance Co.; Pacific Western National Bank; Hermosa Construction, Inc.; Capital Bank of North County; Bank of the West; Blue Haven Pools; Golden State Industries; Sun 'n Sea Escrow; All Star Fire Equipment; Donohue Schriber; Nationwide Home Loans, Inc.; Approved Contract Provider, Resolution Trust Corp.; Federal Deposit Insurance Corp.

## KELLEY GUEST

26435 CARMEL RANCHO BOULEVARD
P.O. BOX 221578
**CARMEL, CALIFORNIA 93922**
Telephone: 408-624-6800
Facsimile: 408-624-6731

*Intellectual Property, Business Law, Computer Law and Technology Transactions.*

**KELLEY GUEST,** born Clarksville, Texas, June 29, 1948; admitted to bar, 1973, California; 1984, Texas. *Education:* University of Texas (B.B.A., with honors, 1970); University of California (J.D., 1973). Member, Board of Editors, California Law Review, 1972-1973. Extern Law Clerk to Chief Justice Donald R. Wright, California Supreme Court, 1973. *Member:* State Bar of California; State Bar of Texas; American Bar Association. **PRACTICE AREAS:** Business; Computer Law and Technology Transactions.

## THOMAS HART HAWLEY

SAN CARLOS BETWEEN 7TH & 8TH
P.O. BOX 805
**CARMEL, CALIFORNIA 93921**
Telephone: 408-624-5339
Fax: 408-624-5839

*Estate Planning, Probate and Trust.*

**THOMAS HART HAWLEY,** born June 19, 1944; admitted to bar, 1970, California. *Education:* Stanford University (B.A., 1966; LL.B., 1969). Instructor, Real Property Law, Monterey College of Law, 1976. Member: Carmel-by-the-Sea Planning Commission, 1976. Treasurer, Mozart Society of California, 1988. Board Member, Carmel Public Library Foundation. Board Member, The Carmel Foundation, 1995—. Author: "The Artful Dodgers Guide to Planning Your Estate," Linthicum Press, 1996. *Member:* Monterey County Bar Association; State Bar of California. (Certified Specialist, Estate Planning, Trust and Probate Law, The State Bar of California Board of Legal Specialization).

## HEISINGER, BUCK, MORRIS & ROSE

A PROFESSIONAL CORPORATION
DOLORES AND SIXTH STREETS
P.O. BOX 5427
**CARMEL, CALIFORNIA 93921**
Telephone: 408-624-3891
Fax: 408-625-0145
Email: hbmandr@aol.com

*General Civil and Trial Practice. Corporations and Partnerships. Real Estate. Estate Planning, Probate, Trusts and Estates.*

**JAMES G. HEISINGER, JR.,** born Carmel, California, August 17, 1952; admitted to bar, 1979, California and U.S. District Court, Northern District of California; 1985, U.S. Supreme Court. *Education:* University of California at Santa Cruz (B.A., 1974); Lewis and Clark College (J.D., 1979). Instructor, Environmental Law, Monterey College of Law, 1983 and 1985. City Attorney, City of Sand City. *Member:* Monterey County and American (Member, Urban, State and Local Government Law Section) Bar Associations; State Bar of California. **PRACTICE AREAS:** Administrative Agency; Trial Practice involving Environmental and Land Use Matters; Real Estate Transactions; Trusts; Estates; Charitable Foundations.

**ROBERT B. BUCK,** born Berkeley, California, July 4, 1945; admitted to bar, 1971, California; U.S. District Court, Northern and Eastern Districts of California. *Education:* Dartmouth College (B.A., cum laude, 1967); Hastings College of Law, University of California (J.D., 1970). Associate Member, Urban Land Institute, 1991. President, Frank H. & Eva B. Buck Foundation, 1996. Member, Board of Directors, Robinson Jeffers Tor House Foundation, Inc., 1980—. *Member:* Monterey County and American (Member, Sections on: Natural Resources, Energy and Environmental Law; Real Property, Probate and Trust Law) Bar Associations; State Bar of California. **PRACTICE AREAS:** Real Estate Development and Transactions; General Business; Trusts; Estates; Charitable Foundations.

**SIDNEY M. MORRIS,** born Nashville, Tennessee, December 22, 1944; admitted to bar, 1970, Kentucky; 1974, California; 1975, U.S. Tax Court. *Education:* University of Louisville (B.A., 1967); University of Kentucky (J.D., 1970). Order of the Coif. Notes Editor, Kentucky Law Journal, 1969-

*(This Listing Continued)*

1970. Instructor, Wills and Trusts, Monterey College of Law, 1982-1996. *Member:* Monterey County and Kentucky Bar Associations; The State Bar of California. [Lt. JAGC, USNR, 1970-1974]. (Certified Specialist, Estate Planning, Trust and Probate Law, The State Bar of California Board of Legal Specialization). **PRACTICE AREAS:** Trust Law; Probate; Estate Planning.

**GERARD A. ROSE,** born Melbourne, Australia, June 13, 1946; admitted to bar, 1973, California and U.S. District Court, Eastern District of California; 1974, U.S. Court of Appeals, Ninth Circuit and U.S. District Court, Northern District of California; 1975, U.S. District Court, Central District of California; 1987, U.S. Supreme Court and U.S. District Court, Southern District of California; 1988, U.S. Court of Appeals for the Federal Circuit. *Education:* University of Santa Clara (B.A., 1968; J.D., 1973); Loyola University, Rome, Italy. *Member:* Monterey County and American Bar Associations; State Bar of California. [Officer, U.S. Navy, active duty, 1968-1970]. **PRACTICE AREAS:** Trial and Appellate Practice involving General Business; Real Estate; Insurance; Construction Disputes; Oil and Gas Law.

---

**CHRISTOPHER CAMPBELL,** born Hyannisport, Massachusetts, June 12, 1948; admitted to bar, 1973, California. *Education:* University of California at Riverside (B.A., magna cum laude, 1970); Boalt Hall School of Law, University of California (J.D., 1973). Phi Beta Kappa. *Member:* The State Bar of California.

**KEVIN W. FISHER,** born Pryor, Oklahoma, December 2, 1962; admitted to bar, 1988, Texas; 1992, California; 1996, Oklahoma. *Education:* University of Oklahoma (B.A., with special distinction, 1985); Harvard University (J.D., cum laude, 1988). Phi Beta Kappa. Trustee, Monterey Museum of Art. *Member:* State Bar of Texas; State Bar of California.

REPRESENTATIVE CLIENTS: Bank of America; Northern California Congregational Retirement Homes, Inc. (Carmel Valley Manor); Pacific Grove-Asilomar Operating Corp.; Wells Fargo Bank.
REFERENCES: First National Bank of Monterey County; Household Bank; Wells Fargo Bank.

## Horan, Lloyd, Karachale, Dyer, Schwartz, Law & Cook

*Incorporated*

**CARMEL, CALIFORNIA**

(See Monterey)

*General Civil and Trial Practice. Corporation, Taxation, Employee Benefit, Real Estate, Personal Injury, Professional Negligence, Wrongful Termination, Condemnation, Land Use, Environmental, Commercial, Trusts, Estate Planning, Probate, Trust and Estate Litigation.*

## IAN D. McPHAIL

A PROFESSIONAL CORPORATION
VILLA CARMEL, SUITE 4
MISSION AT FOURTH
P.O. BOX 2734
**CARMEL, CALIFORNIA 93921**
Telephone: 408-625-4135
Telecopier: 408-625-4155

Santa Cruz, California Office: 331 Soquel Avenue, 95062. Telephone: 408-427-2363. Telecopier: 408-427-0511.

*Estate Planning, Living Trusts, Trust and Probate Law. Gift and Estate Taxation.*

**IAN D. McPHAIL,** born England, March 8, 1934; admitted to bar, 1963, California. *Education:* Cambridge University (B.A., honors, 1956; M.A., 1960); University of California at Berkeley (LL.B., 1962). President, 1983-1984, Board Member Emeritus, 1989—, Greater Santa Cruz County Community Foundation. *Member:* Santa Cruz Bar (President, 1976) and Monterey County Bar Associations; The State Bar of California (Member, Section on Estate Planning, Trust and Probate Law). **PRACTICE AREAS:** Estate Planning; Estate Settlement including Probate.

REFERENCES: Comerica Bank; Home Savings; Coast Commercial Bank.

## OLDFIELD & CREELY
26619 CARMEL CENTER PLACE, SUITE 202
**CARMEL, CALIFORNIA 93923**
Telephone: 408-625-3900
Fax: 408-625-6043

*Business Litigation, Securities Litigation and Arbitration. Real Estate, Partnership, Corporation, Trust Law and Estate Planning.*

**DOUGLAS W. OLDFIELD,** born San Francisco, California, October 8, 1955; admitted to bar, 1981, California; 1983, U.S. District Court, Northern District of California; 1993, U.S. Court of Appeals, Ninth Circuit. *Education:* University of Southern California (A.B., magna cum laude, 1978); Hastings College of Law, University of California (J.D., 1981). Editorial Associate, COMM/ENT Law Journal, 1980-1981. Law Clerk Extern to California Supreme Court, Central Staff, 1980-1981. Arbitrator, National Association of Securities Dealers, 1989—; Member, Monterey County Pro Bono Panel, 1989—. *Member:* Monterey County (Member, Executive Committee) and American Bar Associations; The State Bar of California. **PRACTICE AREAS:** Business Litigation; Securities Litigation and Arbitration; Real Estate; Trust Law; Partnerships and Corporations.

**ANDREW E. CREELY,** born Denver, Colorado, June 17, 1957; admitted to bar, 1985, California and U.S. District Court, Northern District of California; 1990, U.S. Tax Court. *Education:* University of California at Davis (B.A., 1981); Hastings College of the Law, University of California (J.D., cum laude, 1985). Order of the Coif. Member, Thurston Society. Judicial Extern to Justice Alan Broussard, California Supreme Court, 1985. *Member:* Monterey County Bar Association; State Bar of California; Monterey County Bar Barristers (President, 1992). **PRACTICE AREAS:** Corporations; Taxation; Estate Planning; Real Estate and Business Transactions.

REFERENCE: Bank of America.

## PERRY AND FREEMAN
SAN CARLOS BETWEEN 7TH & 8TH
P.O. BOX 805
**CARMEL, CALIFORNIA 93921**
Telephone: 408-624-5339
Fax: 408-624-5839
Email: cityatty@ix.netcom.com

*Civil and Trial Practice. Estate Planning, Probate, Real Property, Business, Environmental, Land Use and Planning, Municipal.*

**THOMAS K. PERRY** (1904-1971).

**DONALD G. FREEMAN,** born Portsmouth, Virginia, April 29, 1942; admitted to bar, 1971, California and U.S. District Court, Southern and Northern Districts of California; 1976, U.S. Supreme Court. *Education:* California State University at San Diego (B.A., 1965); University of San Fernando Valley (J.D., 1968). Instructor, Golden Gate University, 1973-1981. Elected Monterey Peninsula College Board of Trustees, 1977—. Chairman, Monterey Peninsula College Board of Trustees, 1991-1994. Appointed California State Bar Court Referee, 1982-1989. Member, Pacific Grove Planning Commission, 1988-1990. Carmel-by-the-Sea, City Attorney, 1984—. *Member:* Monterey County and American Bar Associations; State Bar of California. **REPORTED CASES:** Ewing v. City of Carmel-by-the-Sea 234 Cal. App. 3d 1579 (1992).

REPRESENTATIVE CLIENT: City of Carmel-by-the-Sea.

## STEWART, GREEN & McGOWAN
26415 CARMEL RANCHO BOULEVARD
**CARMEL, CALIFORNIA 93923**
Telephone: 408-624-6473
Fax: 408-624-6639

*Probate, Estate Planning, Taxation, Real Estate, Family and Civil Trial Litigation.*

### MEMBERS OF FIRM

**WILLIAM KIRK STEWART,** born Los Angeles, California, June 26, 1917; admitted to bar, 1943, California; 1947, U.S. Court of Appeals, Ninth Circuit; 1977, U.S. District Court, Northern District of California. *Education:* University of California at Berkeley (A.B., cum laude, 1939); Harvard University (LL.B., 1942); Monterey Institute of International Studies (M.A., 1979). Author, "Trial of the Seven Bishops," California State Bar Journal, Jan. 1980. *Member:* Monterey County Bar Association; State Bar of California. [Cmdr., U.S. Navy, 1942-1946, Ret., awarded Silver Star; Purple Heart]. **PRACTICE AREAS:** Real Estate; Estate Planning; Probate. *Email:* ngreen1897@aol.com

*(This Listing Continued)*

**NANCY W. GREEN,** born Pilot Mound, Manitoba, Canada, December 5, 1931; admitted to bar, 1979, California and U.S. District Court, Northern District of California. *Education:* California Polytechnic State University (B.S., 1965); University of California (M.A., 1967) University of California, Hastings College of the Law (J.D., 1979); Golden Gate University (LL.M., 1991). *Member:* Monterey County Bar Association (Member, Pro Bono Panel, 1983—); State Bar of California (Member, Ethics Committee, Estate Planning, Trust and Probate Law Section). (Certified Specialist, Probate, Estate Planning and Trust Law, California Board of Legal Specialization). **PRACTICE AREAS:** Probate and Estate Planning; Trusts; Will Contests; Family Law; Taxation; Real Estate. *Email:* ngreen1897@aol.com

**ANNE D. McGOWAN,** born Allentown, Pennsylvania, April 3, 1938; admitted to bar, 1979, California; 1986, U.S. Court of Appeals, Ninth Circuit; U.S. District Court, Northern District of California. *Education:* Carlow College (B.S., cum laude, 1960); Pepperdine University (J.D., 1979). Recipient: Outstanding Woman, Monterey County, California, 1992. Author: "Monterey County Legal Considerations," Big Sur Local Coastal Program, July 1980; "Why the ABA Should Adopt a Pro-Choice Policy," CWL News, August 1992. Lecturer, Law Professor in Ethics, Monterey College of Law, 1987-1992. Director, Mid-Carmel Valley Fire Protection District, 1985—. *Member:* Monterey County Bar Association; State Bar of California (California State Bar Committee on Professional Responsibility and Conduct, 1991-1994); American Bar Association; California Women Lawyers (President, 1991-1992; Life Member); Monterey County Women Lawyers. **SPECIAL AGENCIES:** District Counsel, Monterey Peninsula Regional Park District. **REPORTED CASES:** Sobeck v. B & R Investments (1989) 215 Cal.App. 861, 264 Cal.RPTR.156. **PRACTICE AREAS:** Estates Planning; Environmental Law; Government; Real Property; Small Business; Trusts and Probate.

## SCOTT C. TURNER
P.O. BOX 1671
**CARMEL, CALIFORNIA 93921**
Telephone: 408-626-5626
FAX: 408-626-5634

*Pasadena, California Office:* 301 North Lake Avenue, Suite 700. Telephone: 818-440-1822 FAX: 818-440-9409.

*Insurance Claims and Litigation regarding Insurance Coverage of Construction Disputes.*

(For Complete Biographical Data on all Personnel, see Professional Biographies at Pasadena, California)

## DONALD W. ULLRICH, JR.
8037 FAIR OAKS BOULEVARD, SUITE 113
**CARMICHAEL, CALIFORNIA 95608**
Telephone: 916-944-8184
Fax: 916-944-8186
Email: dwulaw@cwnet.com

*Bankruptcy, Business, Commercial, Corporations, Finance, Intellectual Property, Investments, International Transactions, Real Estate, Securities, Taxation, Trusts and Estates Law.*

**DONALD W. ULLRICH, JR.,** born Pasadena, California, September 26, 1952; admitted to bar, 1985, California and U.S. District Court, Northern, Eastern, Central and Southern Districts of California. *Education:* University of California, Santa Barbara (B.A., Political Science, 1974); McGeorge School of Law (J.D., 1984; LL.M., Business and Tax Law, 1989). Recipient: AUS ROTC Scholarship; U.S. Marine Corps Law Scholarship; Merit Scholarship; LL.M. Fellowship. Listed in Who's Who in American Law. Real Estate Broker, California, 1990. *Member:* Federalist Society, 1989—; California Association of Realtors. *Member:* Sacramento County (Member, Sections on: Business Law; International Law; Tax Law) and American (Member, Sections on: Business Law; Tax Law) Bar Associations; State Bar of California (Member, Sections on: Business Law; International Law; Tax Law). [Judge Advocate, USMC, 1984-1988; active duty, USMC, 1977-1988; Major, USMCR, 1988—]

## IVES, KIRWAN & DIBBLE

A PROFESSIONAL CORPORATION

Established in 1939

5210 CARPINTERIA AVENUE
P.O. BOX 360
**CARPINTERIA, CALIFORNIA 93013**
Telephone: 805-684-7641
FAX: 805-684-9649

*Los Angeles, California Office:* The Biltmore Court, Fourth Floor, 520 South Grand Avenue. Telephone: 213-627-0113. FAX: 213-627-1547.
*Orange-San Diego County Office:* 101 Pacifica, Suite 250, Irvine, California, 92718. Telephone: 714-450-8900. FAX: 714-450-8908.
*San Bernardino-Riverside Office:* 777 Tahquitz Way, Suite 23, Palm Springs, California. Telephone: 619-778-2611. FAX: 619-778-2612.

FIRM PROFILE: Ives, Kirwan & Dibble specializes in general civil litigation in both State and Federal Courts. For many years we have practiced in the traditional area of general liability defense, including but not limited to products liability, premises liability, professional liability, auto liability, truckers liability, cargo loss and damage, fire loss and damage, construction defect litigation, general negligence, international torts, insurance coverage (primary, excess, and reinsurance), and workers' compensation. In more recent years, our practice has grown in several developing areas such as business torts, directors and officers errors and omissions, trademark and copyright infringement, business transactional work and litigation, wrongful termination, legal malpractice, child abuse, insurance bad faith, toxic torts, environmental pollution litigation, Americans with Disabilities Act claims, and municipal liability and Federal civil rights litigation.

**THOMAS P. MINEHAN,** born Los Angeles, California, December 12, 1944; admitted to bar, 1975, California and U.S. District Court, Central District of California. *Education:* University of Santa Clara (B.A., 1966); Southwestern University (J.D., 1975). *Member:* Santa Barbara County, Los Angeles County and American Bar Associations; The State Bar of California; Association of Southern California Defense Counsel.

**JAMES M. MCFAUL,** born Los Angeles, California, August 5, 1951; admitted to bar, 1978, California; U.S. District Court, Central District of California and U.S. Supreme Court. *Education:* University of California at Los Angeles (B.A., 1973); Loyola University of Los Angeles (J.D., 1978). *Member:* Santa Barbara County Bar Association; The State Bar of California; Association of Southern California Defense Counsel.

**JERRY E. MCLINN,** born 1939; admitted to bar, 1977, California; U.S. District Court, Central District of California. *Education:* The Ohio State University (B.S.E.E., 1961); University of California at Santa Barbara (M.S.E.E., 1968); California Western School of Law (J.D., 1977). Member, Santa Barbara Barrister Club. *Member:* Santa Barbara Bar Association; State Bar of California; Association of Southern California Defense Counsel.

MAJOR INSURANCE COMPANY CLIENTS: Acceptance Insurance Companies; Allianz Insurance Company; Allianz Underwriters Insurance Company; American International Group, Inc.; American Mutual Insurance Company; American States Insurance Company; Amica Mutual Insurance Company; The Canadian Insurance Company of California; Citation Insurance Group; The Chubb Group of Insurance Companies; California Insurance Guaranty Association; First State Insurance Company; Government Employees Insurance Company; Harbor Insurance Company; The Hartford Specialty Company; Home & Automobile Insurance Company; Houston General Insurance Company; Industrial Fire & Casualty; Industrial Indemnity Company; Industrial Underwriters, Inc.; Jefferson Insurance Group; Monticello Insurance Co.; National Indemnity Company; National Union Fire Insurance Company; Planet Insurance Company; Preferred Risk Mutual Insurance Company; Prudential-LMI Mutual Insurance Company; Reliance Insurance Company; Safeco Insurance Company; Stonewall Insurance Company; Tokio Marine & Fire Insurance Company; Transport Insurance Company; Union Bankers Insurance Company; Utica Mutual Insurance Company; Westchester Specialty Group.

(For Complete Biographical Data on all Personnel, see Los Angeles, California Professional Biographies.)

## PETER S. MEYERHOFF

20235 REDWOOD ROAD
**CASTRO VALLEY, CALIFORNIA 94546**
Telephone: 510-538-1116
Fax: 510-538-1208

*Personal Injury, Family Law, Divorce, Criminal.*

**PETER S. MEYERHOFF,** born San Francisco, California, April 8, 1948; admitted to bar, 1974, California, U.S. District Court, Northern and Eastern Districts of California. *Education:* University of California at Berkeley (B.A., cum laude, 1970); University of California at Davis (J.D., 1973). Instructor: Criminal Justice Administration, San Francisco State University, 1979-1980. *Member:* San Francisco and Alameda County Bar Associations. **REPORTED CASES:** Gerhardt v. Olsen (San Mateo, California, 1979). **PRACTICE AREAS:** Personal Injury (35%, 75); Family Law (25%, 75); Divorce (25%, 100); Criminal (15%, 50).

## SABO & GREEN

A PROFESSIONAL CORPORATION

Established in 1980

35-325 DATE PALM DRIVE, SUITE 150
**CATHEDRAL CITY, CALIFORNIA 92234**
Telephone: 619-770-0873
Fax: 619-770-1724

*San Bernardino, California Office:* 201 North "E" Street, Suite 206, 92401-1507. Telephone: 909-383-9373. Fax: 909-383-9378.
*Calabasas, California Office:* 23801 Calabasas Road, Suite 1015, 91302-1547. Telephone: 818-704-0195. Fax: 818-704-4729.

*Municipal Law, Public Finance, Real Estate, Redevelopment, Condemnation, Litigation and Military Base Closures.*

FIRM PROFILE: The firm was founded in 1980 as Law Offices of Timothy J. Sabo, specializing in public finance and redevelopment law, and assumed its present configuration in 1990. The firm represents clients throughout the state in the areas of public finance, municipal law, redevelopment, real estate, condemnation, and litigation and has served as counsel in numerous out-of-state public finance transactions. Members of the firm are active in conducting seminars and conferences and are frequent guest lecturers on public finance and redevelopment law issues.

**STEVEN B. QUINTANILLA,** born Honolulu, Hawaii, September 5, 1958; admitted to bar, 1992, California. *Education:* University of California, Los Angeles (B.A., magna cum laude, 1986; J.D., 1991); University of California, Los Angeles Graduate School of Architecture and Urban Planning (M.A., 1992). University of California at Los Angeles, Journal of Environmental Policy, 1990-1991. Lecturer, Land Use Law, People's College of Law, Spring 1993. *Member:* Los Angeles County and American Bar Associations; State Bar of California; American Planning Association; Association of Environmental Professionals. **PRACTICE AREAS:** Eminent Domain; Inverse Condemnation; Civil Litigation.

## ATKINSON, ANDELSON, LOYA, RUUD & ROMO

A PROFESSIONAL CORPORATION

13304 EAST ALONDRA BOULEVARD
**CERRITOS, CALIFORNIA 90703-2263**
Telephone: 310-404-4444; 714-826-5480
Telecopier: 310-404-8905
Email: AALRR@KINCYB.COM
Email: Info@aalrr.com
URL: http://www.aalrr.com

*Pleasanton, California Office:* The Atrium. 5776 Stoneridge Mall Road, Suite 200. 94588. Telephone: 510-227-9200. Telecopier: 510-227-9202.
*San Bernardino, California Office:* 348 West Hospitality Lane, Suite 202. 92408. Telephone: 909-888-4165. Telecopier: 909-884-4118.

*Labor Relations representing Management. School Law. Construction and Real Estate Law. Civil Litigation. Corporate, Securities and Tax Law. Estate Planning Law.*

*(This Listing Continued)*

# PROFESSIONAL BIOGRAPHIES

## CALIFORNIA—CERRITOS

**FIRM PROFILE:** Atkinson, Andelson, Loya, Ruud & Romo is a dynamic, growing full-service law firm which represents public and private sector clients throughout California and other states.

The firm's attorneys and paralegals have the experience and education to represent businesses, public entities and individuals in legal matters ranging from labor relations, business formation and operation, and public school law, to estate and financial planning.

Atkinson, Andelson, Loya, Ruud & Romo represents a variety of school districts and other public agencies, including cities, counties, and special districts. The firm has developed a statewide reputation for public sector representations and has served as lead counsel in several precedent setting cases.

**STEVEN D. ATKINSON,** born Rockford, Illinois, March 12, 1947; admitted to bar, 1972, Florida; 1974, California; 1976, U.S. Court of Appeals, Ninth Circuit; 1983, U.S. Supreme Court. *Education:* University of Florida (B.A., 1969; J.D., 1972). *Member:* Orange County (Member, Labor Law Section) and Los Angeles County Bar Associations; The Florida Bar (Member, Labor Law Section); State Bar of California (Member, Labor Law Section). [1st Lt., U.S. Army, 1972]. *PRACTICE AREAS:* Employment Law; Construction Law.

**STEVEN J. ANDELSON,** born Los Angeles, California, August 23, 1944; admitted to bar, 1971, California; 1973, U.S. Court of Appeals, Ninth Circuit and U.S. District Court, Central District of California. *Education:* University of California at Los Angeles (B.A., 1966); University of California at Davis (J.D., 1970). Author: "California Public Employee Relations," National Labor Relations Board Procedures with Reference to S.B. 160, 1977; "FRISK Documentation Model," a manual on employee documentation. *Member:* Los Angeles County and American (Member, Labor and Employment Law Section) Bar Associations; State Bar of California (Member, Labor and Employment Law Section). *PRACTICE AREAS:* School Law; Labor Law; Employment Law; Employment Discrimination Law.

**PAUL M. LOYA,** born Oakland, California, September 25, 1946; admitted to bar, 1973, California, U.S. Supreme Court, U.S. Court of Appeals, Ninth Circuit and U.S. District Court, Northern District of California; 1983, U.S. District Court, Eastern District of California. *Education:* University of California at Berkeley; California State University at Hayward (B.S., 1970); Boalt Hall School of Law, University of California (J.D., 1973). Member, California Law Review, 1971-1972. Contributing Author: "California Public Sector Labor Relations," Matthew Bender, 1989. Director, 1983-1984, and President, 1985, San Ramon Valley Education Foundation. Director, University of California Alumni Association, 1988-1991. Director, Boalt Hall Alumni Association, 1991-1996; Vice President, 1995-1996. *Member:* State Bar of California; American Bar Association (Member, Section of Labor and Employment Law). (Resident, Pleasanton Office). *PRACTICE AREAS:* School Law; Labor Law; Employment Law; Administrative Law.

**RONALD C. RUUD,** born Minneapolis, Minnesota, October 20, 1940; admitted to bar, 1968, Minnesota; 1978, California; 1980, U.S. District Court, Central District of California; 1983, U.S. Court of Appeals, Ninth Circuit. *Education:* University of Minnesota (B.A., 1963); William Mitchell College of Law (J.D., cum laude, 1968). Co-Author: *Supervisors Guide to Documentation and File Building for Employee Discipline,* Advisory Publishing Company, 1981. Member: San Bernardino County, Los Angeles County (Member, Labor Law Section) and Minnesota State Bar Associations; State Bar of California. (Resident, San Bernardino Office). *PRACTICE AREAS:* Education Law; Labor and Personnel Law.

**JAMES C. ROMO,** born Burbank, California, November 27, 1951; admitted to bar, 1976, California; 1979, U.S. District Court, Central District of California; 1992, U.S. Supreme Court. *Education:* San Fernando Valley State College; San Diego State University (A.B., cum laude, 1973); University of California at Los Angeles (J.D., 1976). Member, Moot Court Honors Program. Author: "Negotiating Teacher Salary Wage Freezes," California Public Employer Reporter, 1978; Labor Articles, "Labor Relations Support Services," Quarterly Publication, 1977-1980. Editor School Law Update, 1980—, Guest Lecturer, Employment Relations Matters: University of California at Los Angeles, 1978; University of California, Davis, 1978 and 1982; University of California, Riverside, 1982; California State University, Dominguez Hills, 1980; Personnel and Industrial Relations Association, 1987 and 1989. *Member:* Los Angeles County and American Bar Associations; State Bar of California (Member, Labor Section; Vice Chair, Public Sector, 1987). *PRACTICE AREAS:* Labor Law (Public and Private Sector); School Law; Employment Law, Public and Private (Representing Management).

*(This Listing Continued)*

**EUGENE F. MCMENAMIN,** born New York, N.Y., May 31, 1949; admitted to bar, 1976, New Jersey; 1979, California; 1980, District of Columbia; 1982, U.S. Court of Appeals, Ninth Circuit. *Education:* Fordham University (B.A., cum laude, 1971; J.D., 1976); Georgetown Law Center (LL.M., 1978). *Member:* State Bar of California (Member, Labor and Employment Law Section); American Bar Association (Member, Section of Labor and Employment Law). [1st Lt., U.S. Army, Military Police Corps, 1971-1973]. *PRACTICE AREAS:* Civil Litigation; Labor Relations Law; Management Law; Construction Default; Delay Claims.

**THOMAS W. KOVACICH,** born Anaconda, Montana, October 22, 1953; admitted to bar, 1980, California; 1981, U.S. District Court, Central and Southern Districts of California and U.S. Court of Appeals, Ninth Circuit; 1989, U.S. District Court, Northern and Eastern Districts of California. *Education:* University of California at Los Angeles; University of California at Irvine (B.A., 1977); Loyola Marymount University (J.D., 1980). *Member:* Orange County (Member, Labor and Employment Law Section), Los Angeles County and American (Member, Section of Labor and Employment Law) Bar Associations; State Bar of California. *PRACTICE AREAS:* Management Labor Relations; Public Works; Construction Law.

**PETER J. LUCEY,** born Martinez, California, January 2, 1948; admitted to bar, 1975, California; 1980, U.S. District Court, Northern District of California; 1984, U.S. Court of Appeals, Ninth Circuit; 1986, U.S. Supreme Court. *Education:* University of California at Berkeley (B.A., 1970); University of California at Davis (J.D., 1975). Phi Delta Phi. President, County Counsels School Association Northern Division, Contra Costa County Bar Association, 1983—. Deputy County Counsel, Contra Costa County, 1976-1985. *Member:* Contra Costa County Bar Association; State Bar of California. (Resident, Pleasanton Office). *PRACTICE AREAS:* Education Law; Labor Law; Employment Law; Municipal Law.

**DAVIS D. THOMPSON,** born Los Angeles, California, April 19, 1949; admitted to bar, 1976, California and U.S. District Court, Central District of California. *Education:* University of Santa Clara (B.A., magna cum laude, 1971); Yale University (M.A., 1973; M.Phil., 1974); University of California at Los Angeles (J.D., 1976); University of Southern California (M.B.T., 1991). Alpha Sigma Nu. Author: Chapter 8 and 9, *Windfalls for Wipeouts:* The Quiet Undoing of Land-Use Controls, American Society Planning Officials, Donald G. Hagman, Editor, 1976. Author: "Land-Use Allocation," 6 Environmental Law 231, 1975. Co-Author: "Planning for the R & D Tax Shelter: An Analysis of the Essential Tax Elements," 53 Journal of Taxation 215, October, 1980. Member, Board of Realtors: Los Angeles, 1981-1987; Pasadena, 1981-1987. Member, American Economic Association. Limited Registration Principal, 1980-1988, National Association of Security Dealers. Member, Tax and Business and Corporate Sections, Los Angeles County Bar Associations. *Member:* State Bar of California. *PRACTICE AREAS:* Corporate and Commercial Law; Corporate and Public Finance; Tax and Estate Planning; Real Estate Law.

**JAMES H. PALMER,** born Elizabeth, New Jersey, November 5, 1948; admitted to bar, 1979, California; U.S. District Court, Central District of California and U.S. Court of Appeals, Ninth Circuit. *Education:* Michigan State University (B.A., 1970); Pepperdine University (J.D., 1979). *Member:* Orange County and Los Angeles County Bar Associations; State Bar of California. *PRACTICE AREAS:* Civil Law; Business Litigation.

**KAREN E. GILYARD,** born Orlando, Florida, February 1, 1958; admitted to bar, 1983, California and U.S. District Court, Central District of California; 1986, U.S. Court of Appeals, Ninth Circuit. *Education:* University of California at Los Angeles (B.A., 1980); University of California at Los Angeles (J.D., 1983). *Member:* Los Angeles County and American Bar Associations; State Bar of California. *PRACTICE AREAS:* School Law; Labor Law; Employment Law; Employment Discrimination Law; Eminent Domain; Student Discipline; Special Education.

**JAMES BACA,** born Santa Fe, New Mexico, August 30, 1957; admitted to bar, 1984, California; 1987, U.S. District Court, Central District of California and U.S. Court of Appeals, Ninth Circuit. *Education:* Whittier College (B.A., with honors, 1979); University of California at Los Angeles (J.D., 1983). Haynes Scholar. *Member:* Los Angeles County and American Bar Associations; State Bar of California. *PRACTICE AREAS:* School Law; Labor Law; Employment Law; Employment Discrimination Law.

**ROBERT L. WENZEL,** admitted to bar, 1981, California and U.S. District Court, Central District of California. *Education:* Carthage College (B.A., 1966); University of California at Los Angeles; Western State University (J.D., 1980). President, Personnel and Industrial Relations Association, 1981. *Member:* State Bar of California. [U.S. Army, 1967-1969]. *PRACTICE AREAS:* Employment Law; Management Law.

*(This Listing Continued)*

**ATKINSON, ANDELSON, LOYA, RUUD & ROMO,** A PROFESSIONAL CORPORATION, Cerritos—Continued

**MARILOU F. MIRKOVICH,** born Palo Alto, California, January 17, 1958; admitted to bar, 1985, California; 1986, U.S. District Court, Central District of California. *Education:* University of Redlands (B.S., 1979); Loyola Law School (J.D., 1985). *Member:* Los Angeles County (Member, Labor Law Section) and American Bar Associations. *PRACTICE AREAS:* Labor Relations Law; Employment Law.

**ROY R. NEWMAN,** born Los Angeles, California, September 25, 1962; admitted to bar, 1986, California; 1987, U.S. District Court, Central District of California. *Education:* University of Redlands (B.A., 1983); Loyola Law School (J.D., 1986). *Member:* Los Angeles County and American Bar Associations; State Bar of California. *PRACTICE AREAS:* Business Litigation; Construction Law; Employment Law; School Law.

**WARREN S. KINSLER,** born Los Angeles, California, October 10, 1955; admitted to bar, 1982, California and U.S. District Court, Eastern District of California; 1983, U.S. District Court, Central and Southern Districts of California and U.S. Court of Appeals, Ninth Circuit; 1990, U.S. Supreme Court. *Education:* University of California, Berkeley (A.B., 1978); Loyola Marymount University (J.D., 1981). Member, Loyola Entertainment Law Journal, 1980-1981. General Counsel, Los Angeles Community College District, 1987-1990. *Member:* Los Angeles County (Member, Labor Law Section) and American (Member, Sections on: Labor and Employment Law; Urban, State and Local Government Law Sections) Bar Associations; State Bar of California. *PRACTICE AREAS:* Education Law; Labor Law.

**SHERRY G. GORDON,** born Long Beach, California, March 17, 1946; admitted to bar, 1985, California; 1986, U.S District Court, Central District of California and U.S. Court of Appeals, Ninth Circuit. *Education:* California State University at Long Beach (B.A., 1968); University of Redlands (M.A., 1977); Southwestern School of Law (J.D., 1985). Alpha Lambda. Recipient: Exceptional Achievement Award in Employment Discrimination, Southwestern School of Law, 1984; American Jurisprudence Award in Property. *Member:* Los Angeles County and American Bar Associations. (Resident, San Bernardino Office). *PRACTICE AREAS:* School Law; Employment Law; Employment Discrimination Law.

---

**WINLOCK W. MILLER,** born Tulsa, Oklahoma, February 16, 1927; admitted to bar, 1955, California and U.S. District Court, Southern District of California; 1970, U.S. Court of Appeals, Ninth Circuit; 1979, U.S. Supreme Court. *Education:* University of Southern California (A.B., cum laude, 1951; J.D., 1954). Delta Theta Phi. *Member:* State Bar of California. (Resident, San Bernardino Office). *PRACTICE AREAS:* School Law; Personnel Law; Municipal Law.

**ELIZABETH B. HEAREY,** born East Orange, New Jersey, March 3, 1947; admitted to bar, 1974, California and U.S. District Court, Northern District of California; 1985, U.S. Court of Appeals, Ninth Circuit. *Education:* Wellesley College (B.A., 1969); Yale University; Hastings College of the Law, University of California, San Francisco (J.D., 1974). Phi Beta Kappa; Wellesley Scholar. *Member:* State Bar of California. (Resident, Pleasanton Office). *PRACTICE AREAS:* Education Law; Administrative Law; Labor Law; Employment Law.

**HECTOR E. SALITRERO,** born Chihuahua, Mexico, March 10, 1951; admitted to bar, 1977, Wisconsin; 1978, California and U.S. District Court, Southern District of California; 1979, U.S. Court of Appeals, Ninth Circuit. *Education:* Loyola University of Los Angeles (B.A., 1973); University of California at Los Angeles (J.D., 1976). U.S. Attorney's Office, San Diego, 1978-1984. Member: Lewis D'Amato Brisbois & Bisgaard, 1984-1987; Littler Mendelson Fastiff & Tichy, 1987-1990. *Member:* Riverside County, San Bernardino County (Member, Employment Law Section) and San Diego County (Member, Employment Law Section) Bar Associations; State Bar of California (Member, Employment Law Section). *LANGUAGES:* Spanish. *PRACTICE AREAS:* Employment Law; Litigation.

**HELEN RYAN FRAZER,** born New York, N.Y., February 12, 1955; admitted to bar, 1980, California, U.S. Court of Appeals, Ninth Circuit and U.S. District Court, Central and Southern Districts of California. *Education:* University of Southern California (B.A., 1976); Southwestern University (J.D., 1979). Judicial Clerkship with the Honorable Richard Mednick, U.S. Bankruptcy Judge, Central District of California. Counsel under FSLIC Management Consignment Program to Butterfield Savings & Loan Association, 1985-1987. Author: "Collection of Undercharged Freight Tariffs-A Windfall for Trustees or Highway Robbery?" 21 Cal. Bankr. J. No. 1 (1993). *Member:* Los Angeles County (Member, Commercial Law and Bankruptcy Section), Federal (Member, Subcommittee on Bankruptcy Rules, 1984-1985) and American Bar Associations; State Bar of California; Financial Lawyers Conference of Southern California; Los Angeles County and Orange County Bankruptcy Forum (Director, L.A., 1985-1986; Director, Orange County, 1989-1990). (Certified Specialist, Personal and Small Business Bankruptcy Law, The State Bar of California Board of Legal Specialization). *PRACTICE AREAS:* Bankruptcy Law; Banking Law; Commercial Law.

**ASA E. REAVES,** born Carlisle, Arkansas; admitted to bar, 1980, California. *Education:* California State University, Los Angeles (B.A.; M.A., 1965); University of West Los Angeles (J.D., 1979). *Member:* State Bar of California. *PRACTICE AREAS:* Administrative Law; Labor Law.

**JANICE J. HEIN,** born Flint, Michigan, February 28, 1952; admitted to bar, 1983, California. *Education:* Central Michigan University (B.S., cum laude, 1974; M.A., summa cum laude, 1980); University of Michigan (J.D., 1983). *Member:* State Bar of California (Labor Law Section, 1994—). (Resident, Pleasanton Office). *PRACTICE AREAS:* Labor and Employment; Education.

**ANGELA K. KRETA,** born July 14, 1960; admitted to bar, 1985, California and U.S. District Court, Northern District of California; 1989, U.S. Court of Appeals, Ninth Circuit and U.S. District Court, Eastern District of California. *Education:* Occidental College (B.A., 1981); Arizona State University College of Law (J.D., 1984). *Member:* Los Angeles County and American Bar Associations; State Bar of California. (Resident, Pleasanton Office). *PRACTICE AREAS:* School Law; Labor Law; Employment Law; Administrative Law.

**TINA L. KANNARR,** born Peoria, Illinois, September 26, 1961; admitted to bar, 1986, California; 1994, U.S. District Court, Central District of California and U.S. Court of Appeals, Ninth Circuit. *Education:* University of Southern California (B.A., cum laude, 1983); College of William & Mary (J.D., 1986). Phi Alpha Delta. *Member:* Los Angeles County and American Bar Associations; State Bar of California. *PRACTICE AREAS:* Public School Employment and Labor Law; Public Education Law; Employment Discrimination Law; Litigation.

**BARBARA S. VAN LIGTEN,** born Philadelphia, Pennsylvania, August 10, 1961; admitted to bar, 1987, California. *Education:* University of California at Santa Barbara (B.A., 1983); Loyola Marymount University (J.D., 1987). *Member:* Los Angeles County Bar Association; State Bar of California; St. Thomas More Honor Society. *PRACTICE AREAS:* Labor Law; Business Litigation.

**FELICIA C. CURRAN,** born Cambridge, Massachusetts, February 3, 1955; admitted to bar, 1987, California and U.S. District Court, Northern District of California; 1989, U.S. Court of Appeals, Ninth Circuit. *Education:* Pitzer College (B.A., 1977); University of California at Berkeley (Department of Philosophy, 1984); Hastings College of the Law, University of California (J.D., 1987). Member, Hastings College Moot Court Board, 1986-1987. Teaching Assistant in Philosophy and Logic, University of California, Berkeley, 1978-1981 , 1982-1983. *Member:* Bar Association of San Francisco; State Bar of California; American Bar Association. (Resident, Pleasanton Office). *PRACTICE AREAS:* Civil Litigation; Education Law and Litigation; Employment Law; Labor Law; Appellate Practice.

**PATRICK A. GUNN,** born San Francisco, California, August 8, 1962; admitted to bar, 1988, California and U.S. District Court, Northern, Southern, Eastern and Central Districts; U.S. Court of Appeals, Ninth Circuit; U.S. Supreme Court. *Education:* California State University at Sacramento (B.A., 1984); Loyola Law School of Los Angeles (J.D., 1988). Staff Writer, 1986-1987 and Managing Editor, 1987-1988, Entertainment Law Journal. Scott Moot Court Honors Competitor. *Member:* Alameda County, Contra Costa County and American Bar Associations; State Bar of California. (Resident, Pleasanton Office). *PRACTICE AREAS:* Civil Litigation; Business; Construction; Real Property Development; Construction Defect Claims.

**CHESLEY D. QUAIDE,** born Berkeley, California, July 6, 1959; admitted to bar, 1988, California and U.S. District Court, Northern District of California; 1990, U.S. District Court, Eastern and Central Districts of California. *Education:* University of California at Berkeley (B.A., 1982); University of San Francisco (J.D., 1988). (Resident, Pleasanton Office). *PRACTICE AREAS:* Labor Law; Employment Law; Education Law.

**THOMAS A. LENZ,** born Moline, Illinois, October 1, 1963; admitted to bar, 1988, Illinois; 1991, California and U.S. District Court, Central District of California; 1992, U.S. District Court, Northern, Southern and Eastern Districts of California and U.S. Court of Appeals, Ninth Circuit; 1994,

*(This Listing Continued)*

U.S. Supreme Court. *Education:* Universidad Complutense de Madrid; Marquette University (B.A., 1985); Universite d'Aix-en-Provence; Louisiana State University (J.D., 1988). Spanish Honor Society. Recipient, American Jurisprudence Award in Employment Discrimination Law. President: Marquette University Alumni Association for Los Angeles County, 1993—. Co-Author: "Le Mariage en Droit Louisianais: Etude Juridique et Sociologique," Law In Mixed Jurisdictions (CNRS, 1989); Case Note: "Thornburgh v. American College of Obstetricians and Gynecologists," The Pocket Constitutionalist, LSU Press, 1988. Officer, Associated Builders and Contractors Los Angeles-Ventura Chapter, 1994—. *Member:* Illinois State and American Bar Associations; State Bar of California. *PRACTICE AREAS:* Labor Relations and Employment Law for Management.

**KENNETH S. LEVY,** born Newport Beach, California, June 21, 1963; admitted to bar, 1990, California and U.S. District Court, Central District of California. *Education:* University of California at Berkeley (B.A., 1986); Boston University (J.D., 1989). *PRACTICE AREAS:* School Law; Public Works; Land Use; Construction Litigation; Environmental Law.

**ROBERT L. SAMMIS,** born Los Angeles, California, September 22, 1959; admitted to bar, 1990, California; 1991, U.S. District Court, Central District of California and U.S. Court of Appeals, Ninth Circuit. *Education:* California State University (B.S., 1981); Glendale University (B.S.L., 1988; J.D., 1990). President/Editor-in-Chief, Glendale Law Review, Volume 9. Nos. 1-2. Author: "Permissible Use of Agency Shop Fees Under the California Educational Employment Relations Act: Cumero v. Public Employment Relations Board," Glendale Law Review, Volume 9, Nos. 1-2, 1990. Instructor, Collective Bargaining in Schools, California State University, Long Beach, Educational Administration, 1990, 1991. *PRACTICE AREAS:* Labor Law; Employment Law; Education Law.

**ANN K. SMITH,** born Hollywood, California, November 29, 1964; admitted to bar, 1990, California and U.S. District Court, Central, Northern and Southern Districts of California. *Education:* Sussex University; University of California at Irvine (B.A., 1986); University of Notre Dame (J.D., cum laude, 1990). Member, 1988-1990 and Note Editor, 1989-1990, Notre Dame Law Review. *Member:* American Bar Association; State Bar of California. *PRACTICE AREAS:* Civil Litigation; Labor Law.

**TERRY T. TAO,** born Los Angeles, California, September 24, 1964; admitted to bar, 1991, California and U.S. District Court, Central District of California. *Education:* University of California at Berkeley (A.B., Architecture, 1986); Loyola University of Los Angeles (J.D., 1991). Registered Architect, California, 1994. *Member:* Los Angeles County, Orange County and American Bar Associations; State Bar of California; American Institute of Architects. *PRACTICE AREAS:* Construction Litigation; Land Use; Environmental Law; Public Contracts; Procurement Law. *Email:* tttao@aol.com

**KAREN T. MEYERS,** born Detroit, Michigan, October 19, 1966; admitted to bar, 1991, California. *Education:* University of Michigan (B.A., with distinction, 1988); Georgetown University (J.D., cum laude, 1991). *PRACTICE AREAS:* School Law; Municipal Law; Labor and Employment Law.

**DAVINA F. HARDEN,** born Whittier, California, May 1, 1966; admitted to bar, 1991, California and U.S. District Court, Central District of California. *Education:* University of Redlands (B.A., cum laude, 1988); University of California, Hastings College of Law (J.D., magna cum laude, 1991). Phi Beta Kappa; Order of the Coif. Member, Thurston Society. Recipient, American Jurisprudence Awards in Civil Procedure and Criminal Law. *Member:* Orange County and American Bar Associations; State Bar of California. *PRACTICE AREAS:* School Law; Public Sector; Government Law; Labor and Employment Law; Redevelopment.

**B. KIMBERLY ADAMS,** born Albuquerque, New Mexico, April 24, 1964; admitted to bar, 1992, California; 1993, U.S. District Court, Central District of California and U.S. Court of Appeals, Ninth Circuit. *Education:* Hamilton College (B.A., 1985); Loyola Law School (J.D., 1992). Staff-writer, 1990-1991 and Articles Editor, 1991-1992, Loyola of Los Angeles Entertainment Law Journal. Author: "Andy Rooney Gets the Laugh, but Rubs Rain-X the Wrong Way," Loyola of Los Angeles Entertainment Law Journal, Volume II, 1991, Number 2. *Member:* Orange County (Member, Insurance Law Section Executive Committee, 1994), Los Angeles County and Federal Bar Associations; State Bar of California. *PRACTICE AREAS:* Business Litigation.

**TODD A. GOLUBA,** born Madison, Wisconsin, August 21, 1967; admitted to bar, 1992, California, U.S. District Court, Northern District of California and U.S. Court of Appeals, Ninth Circuit. *Education:* University of California, Berkeley (B.A., 1989); University of California, Hastings College of the Law (J.D., 1992). *Member:* State Bar of California. (Resident, Pleasanton Office). *PRACTICE AREAS:* Employment Law; School Law.

**MARLEEN LEE SACKS,** born Berkeley, California, March 18, 1965; admitted to bar, 1992, California, U.S. District Court, Northern District of California and U.S. Court of Appeals, Ninth Circuit. *Education:* University of California at Davis (B.A., summa cum laude, 1987); Boalt Hall School of Law, University of California at Berkeley (J.D., 1992). Phi Beta Kappa. *Member:* State Bar of California. (Resident, Pleasanton Office). *PRACTICE AREAS:* Employment Law; School Law.

**DONALD S. FIELD,** born Los Angeles, California, June 7, 1967; admitted to bar, 1993, California. *Education:* University of California, Irvine (B.A., 1990); Southwestern University School of Law (J.D., magna cum laude, 1993); New York University (LL.M., Taxation, 1994). Recipient: Exceptional Achievement Award in Corporate Tax; American Jurisprudence Awards in Wills & Trusts and Remedies. *PRACTICE AREAS:* Taxation; Corporate; Business; Real Estate; Estate Planning.

**HOWARD J. FULFROST,** born Brooklyn, New York, January 13, 1966; admitted to bar, 1995, California. *Education:* University of California at Los Angeles (B.A., 1987); Columbia University (M.A., 1990); University of San Francisco (J.D., 1993). Recipient, American Jurisprudence Award for Legal Research and Writing I and II, 1990-1991. *Member:* State Bar of California (Employment and Labor Law Section). (Resident, San Bernardino Office). *PRACTICE AREAS:* School Law; Labor and Employment Law; Employment Litigation.

**ROBERT R. ROGINSON,** born Pasadena, California, February 25, 1967; admitted to bar, 1996, California. *Education:* Georgetown University (B.A., 1989); Loyola Law School (J.D., 1996). *Member:* State Bar of California. *PRACTICE AREAS:* Labor and Employment Law; Employment Litigation.

**CHRISTINE D. LOVELY,** born Santa Clara, California, December 25, 1968; admitted to bar, 1996, California. *Education:* University of California, Berkeley (A.B., 1991); University of California, Davis (J.D., 1996). (Resident, Pleasanton Office). *PRACTICE AREAS:* Education; Labor; Employment.

**AARON V. O'DONNELL,** born Turner's Falls, Massachusetts, September 6, 1971; (admission pending). *Education:* Brown University (B.A., 1993); University of California, Los Angeles (J.D., 1996). *PRACTICE AREAS:* Public Sector Labor; Employment Relations; General School Law.

*OF COUNSEL*

**JAMES T. WINKLER,** born South Bend, Indiana, April 22, 1946; admitted to bar, 1971, California; 1977, U.S. District Court, Central District of California; 1980, U.S. District Court, Eastern District of California; 1982, U.S. Supreme Court; 1992, U.S. Court of Appeals, Ninth Circuit and U.S. Court of Appeals, District of Columbia Circuit. *Education:* University of Arizona (B.S., 1968); Hastings College of Law, University of California (J.D., 1971). Member and Note and Comment Editor, Hastings College of the Law, Law Review, 1970-1971. Member, Thurston Society. Deputy Regional Attorney, 1979-1980, National Labor Relations Board, Region 31, Los Angeles, 1971-1993. Mayor, Lake Elsinore, California, 1988-1990. *Member:* Los Angeles County Bar Association; State Bar of California. *PRACTICE AREAS:* Labor Relations Law; Management Law.

**NANCY LONG COLE,** born Leon, Iowa, April 26, 1952; admitted to bar, 1976, California. *Education:* University of California at Riverside (B.A., 1973); University of San Diego (J.D., 1976). Adjunct Professor of Law, Legal Writing, Loyola Law School, L.A., 1995. *Member:* State Bar of California. *PRACTICE AREAS:* Civil Litigation.

REPRESENTATIVE CLIENTS: Associated Builders & Contractors; Southern California Contractors Assn.; California Landscape and Irrigation Council; California Rental Assn.; Shapell Industries, Inc.; Donald L. Bren Co.; J.C. Penney Co.; Carl Karcher Enterprises; W.R. Grace and Co.; Huntington National Bank; Over 200 State of California School Districts.

---

# GARY K. CHAN

*10945 SOUTH STREET, SUITE 106A*
**CERRITOS, CALIFORNIA 90703**
*Telephone: 562-402-7338*
*Fax: 562-402-8958*
*Email: gkchan@earthlink.net*

*Probate, Conservatorship, Trusts and Trusts Administration, Estate Planning, U.S. and International Taxation, Business Planning and Formation and Immigration Law.*

*(This Listing Continued)*

## GARY K. CHAN, Cerritos—Continued

**GARY K. CHAN,** born Casa Grande, Arizona, March 9, 1957; admitted to bar, 1993, California; 1994, U.S. District Court, Central District of California; 1995, U.S. Tax Court. *Education:* California State University, Los Angeles (B.S., with honors, 1979); Loyola Marymount University (J.D., 1985). Beta Gamma Sigma. Teacher, California State University, Los Angeles, Tax and Accounting, Fall 1996. Certified Public Accountant, California, 1982. Member: American Institute of Certified Public Accountants; California Society of Certified Public Accountants; Chinese-American Certified Public Accountants. Member, Alhambra Rotary Club. *Member:* Los Angeles County (Member, Sections on: Trust and Estates; Taxation) and American (Member, Sections on: Business Law; Real Property, Probate and Trust Law; Taxation) Bar Associations; State Bar of California (Member, Sections on: Estate Planning, Trust and Probate Law; Taxation); Southern California Chinese Lawyers Association; National Academy of Elder Law Attorneys. **PRACTICE AREAS:** Estate Planning; Trusts; Trust Administration; Probate; U.S. and International Taxation; Business Formation and Planning; Conservatorships and Guardianships; Elder Law; Immigration.

## WILLIAM F. POWERS, JR.
DEVONSHIRE PROFESSIONAL BUILDING
20933 DEVONSHIRE STREET, SUITE 102
**CHATSWORTH, CALIFORNIA 91311**
Telephone: 818-773-9800
Fax: 818-773-1130

*Real Estate, Business Litigation, Commercial Law, Commercial Landlord-Tenant, Construction Law, Transactional and Litigation Focus.*

FIRM PROFILE: *Experiential background as Title Insurance Counsel, Manager of Bank Legal Department, Senior Partner of mid-sized law firm and boutique private practice.*

**WILLIAM F. POWERS, JR.,** born Youngstown, Ohio, September 28, 1945; admitted to bar, 1971, California and U.S. District Court, Central District of California; 1985, U.S. Supreme Court. *Education:* University of California, Santa Barbara, (B.A., 1967); Loyola University (J.D., St. Thomas More Honor Society, 1970). Phi Alpha Delta. Author: "Negligence & The Holder In Due Course Doctrine," BHBJ Fall 1982; "Negotiable Instruments and Negligence Liability," LA Lawyer 1982-1983. Instructor: California State University Northridge, Real Estate Law, Fall 1977. Los Angeles Superior Court Arbitrator 1980-1983; Los Angeles Superior Court Referee and Settlement Office, 1989—; Judge Pro Tem, Los Angeles Municipal and Superior Courts, 1982—. Life Member, Two-Term President, Chatsworth Chamber of Commerce; San Fernando Valley Bar Network Committee, 1996—. Los Angeles County Homeless Commissioner. *Member:* San Fernando Valley and Los Angeles County Bar Associations; Valley Industry Commerce Assn.; United Chambers of Commerce; Building Industry Association; Northridge Kiwanis Club; Cal. State Northridge Athletic Advisory Board; Twelfth Councilmanic District Earthquake Advisory Board; Chatsworth Business Improvement, District Steering Committee. **LANGUAGES:** French; Spanish.

## JOHN JEFFERY CARTER
LAW OFFICE
426 BROADWAY, SUITE 308
P.O. BOX 3606
**CHICO, CALIFORNIA 95927-3606**
Telephone: 916-342-6196
Fax: 916-342-6195
Email: JJZephyr@aol.com

*Business Transactions and Litigation, Contracts, Corporation, Local Government Law, Employment Law, Partnerships, Real Estate, Land Use and Water Law.*

**JOHN JEFFERY CARTER,** born Lapeer, Michigan, February 11, 1951; admitted to bar, 1978, California. *Education:* Boston University and Georgetown University (B.S., Dean's Citation Graduate, 1973); University of Santa Clara (J.D., cum laude, 1977). Member and Vice-Chairman, City of Chico Planning Commission, 1996—. *Member:* Butte County Bar Association (President, 1996—; Secretary and Treasurer, 1994); The State Bar of California. **PRACTICE AREAS:** Business; Corporation; Partnership Law; Real Property; Local Government; Water Law.

REPRESENTATIVE CLIENTS: Associated Students of California State University, Chico; Chemtec Ag Chemicals, Inc.; Chico Area Recreation & Park District; Drainage District # 100 of Butte County; Sierra Nevada Brewing Co.; Thermalito Irrigation District; University Butte School Employees Credit Union.

## CHRISTENSEN & SCHWARZ
45 MAIN STREET
P.O. BOX 676
**CHICO, CALIFORNIA 95927**
Telephone: 916-343-5875
Fax: 916-343-6454

*General Civil and Trial Practice. Probate, Corporation, Real Estate, Insurance, Title Insurance, Escrow and Business Law.*

### MEMBERS OF FIRM

**NELS A. CHRISTENSEN,** born Chico, California, July 16, 1940; admitted to bar, 1966, California. *Education:* Stanford University (A.B., 1962; J.D., 1965). President, Butte County Barristers, 1970-1972. Hearing Officer: California State University and Colleges, 1971—. *Member:* Butte County Bar Association; State Bar of California.

**JOHN D. SCHWARZ, JR.,** born Seattle, Washington, July 22, 1956; admitted to bar, 1984, California. *Education:* California State University at Chico (B.A., 1980; M.A., 1984); University of California; Hastings College of the Law, University of California (J.D., 1984). *Member:* Butte County Bar Association; State Bar of California.

## CRAIG AND SHEPHERD
Established in 1988
SUITE 1, 1367 EAST LASSEN AVENUE
P.O. BOX 658
**CHICO, CALIFORNIA 95927-0658**
Telephone: 916-893-3700
Fax: 916-893-1579

*Civil and Trial Practice including Business, Insurance Defense, Employment Discrimination and Wrongful Termination, Probate, Professional Liability, Corporate and Criminal Law.*

FIRM PROFILE: *The firm combines the experience of four trial litigators in matters as diverse as defending professionals, employers, and contractors to business and personal injury cases throughout the Sacramento Valley area. Selected business, probate, and criminal representations are also undertaken. As general counsel for one of the largest air tanker providers in the United States the firm demonstrates its capabilities in dealing with complex business concerns. The firm also handles litigation defense for counties and other governmental bodies. Recently, several environmental law and land use cases have also been successfully concluded. In addition, public service in the form of direct participation or the enhancement of the administration of justice is encouraged.*

### MEMBERS OF FIRM

**MAYNARD C. CRAIG,** born Kirtland, Ohio, May 18, 1932; admitted to bar, 1960, California; 1977, U.S. Supreme Court. *Education:* University of California at Berkeley (A.B., 1954); Hastings College of Law, University of California (J.D., 1959). Deputy District Attorney, Butte County, California, 1960-1961. President, Butte County Barristers, 1963. Hearing Officer, California State University, Chico, 1971-1976. *Member:* Butte County (President, 1968-1970) and American Bar Associations; The State Bar of California (Chairman, Local Administrative Committee, 1968-1971); Association of Defense Counsel of Northern California (Member, Board of Directors, 1975-1977); American Board of Trial Advocates. **PRACTICE AREAS:** Insurance Defense; Business Litigation; corporate.

**MICHAEL T. SHEPHERD,** born Stockton, California, November 1, 1946; admitted to bar, 1974, California; 1981, U.S. Court of Appeals, Ninth Circuit; 1983, U.S. District Court, Northern and Eastern Districts of California; 1990, U.S. Supreme Court. *Education:* University of California at Santa Barbara (B.A., 1968); Hastings College of Law, University of California (J.D., 1973). Arbitrator, American Arbitration Association. Director: Chico Area Recreation Department, 1988—; and President, Board of Mediation Center of the North Valley, 1992—; Board of Aero Union Corporation, 1997. *Member:* Butte County Bar Association; State Bar of California;

*(This Listing Continued)*

# PROFESSIONAL BIOGRAPHIES

Association of Defense Counsel of Northern California. **PRACTICE AREAS:** Insurance Defense; Business Litigation.

### ASSOCIATES

**BRUCE S. ALPERT,** born Brockton, Massachusetts, April 27, 1951; admitted to bar, 1977, California; 1978, U.S. District Court, Central District of California; 1982, U.S. District Court, Southern District of California; 1986, U.S. Court of Appeals, Ninth Circuit. *Education:* University of California at Los Angeles (B.A., 1973); Southwestern University School of Law (J.D., 1977). Judge Pro Tem, Los Angeles Superior Court, 1993-1994. *Member:* Los Angeles County, Butte County and San Fernando Valley Bar Associations; State Bar of California (Member, Litigation Section, 1985-1994); Association of Defense Counsel of Northern California. **PRACTICE AREAS:** Insurance Defense; Business Litigation; General Business; Real Estate.

**RICHARD L. CRABTREE,** born Iowa, July 2, 1959; admitted to bar, 1990, California, U.S. District Court, Northern and Eastern Districts of California and U.S. Court of Appeals, Ninth Circuit. *Education:* University of California at Davis (B.A., 1987); University of California School of Law, Davis (J.D., 1990). Contributing Author: "Understanding Development Regulations," Solano Press Books. Mayor, 1982-1983 and Council Member, 1981-1984, Town of Paradise, California. *Member:* Butte County Bar Association; State Bar of California (Member: Environmental Law Section; Executive Committee; California Environmental Quality Act (CEQA) Review Committee; California State Senate Housing and Urban Affairs Committee, CEQA Task Force); Association of Defense Counsel of Northern California. **PRACTICE AREAS:** Litigation; Employment Law; Environmental.

A List of Representative Clients will be Furnished Upon Request.

---

## LEONARD & LYDE

A Partnership including Professional Corporations

*Established in 1963*

1600 HUMBOLDT ROAD, SUITE 1
**CHICO, CALIFORNIA 95927**
Telephone: 916-345-3494
Fax: 916-345-0460

*Oroville, California Office:* 1453 Huntoon Street. Telephone: 916-533-2662. Fax: 916-533-3843.

*General Civil and Trial Practice. Medical Law, Business, Probate, Insurance.*

**FIRM PROFILE:** Leonard & Lyde was established in 1963 by Raymond A. Leonard and C. Keith Lyde, both past district attorneys of Butte County. Leonard & Lyde maintains fully-staffed offices in both Oroville and Chico, through which it provides a wide range of legal services, emphasizing civil litigation, throughout rural Northern California. Leonard & Lyde also routinely presents seminars to the local medical communities regarding various aspects of medical law and professional medical liability.

**RAYMOND A. LEONARD** (1961-1981).

**C. KEITH LYDE, (INC.),** born Evansville, Indiana, March 11, 1921; admitted to bar, 1950, California; 1961, U.S. Supreme Court; 1966, Florida. *Education:* Palm Beach Junior College; Hastings College of Law, University of California (J.D., 1949). District Attorney, Butte County, California, 1955-1963. City Attorney, City of Oroville, 1963-1979. *Member:* State Bar of California; The Florida Bar; The Association of Trial Lawyers of America; National Institute of Municipal Law Officers; International Association of Trial Lawyers; American Board of Trial Advocates.

**DORSETT MARC LYDE,** born Oakland, California, May 19, 1954; admitted to bar, 1988, California. *Education:* Occidental College (B.A., 1976); University of San Diego (J.D., cum laude, 1987). Mobile Intensive Care Paramedic, Santa Barbara County, California, 1981-1993. Author: "Wickline V. State: The Emerging Liability of Third Party Health Care Payors," 24.4 San Diego Law Review, 1987. *Member:* Butte County Bar Associations; State Bar of California. **PRACTICE AREAS:** Professional Liability Defense; Insurance Defense Liability; Business Law; Health Care Law; Personal Injury; Medical Product Liability Defense.

### ASSOCIATES

**SHARON A. STONE,** born Arcata, California, October 29, 1956; admitted to bar, 1990, California. *Education:* Shasta Junior College (A.A., 1985); California Northern School of Law (J.D., 1989). Professor of Law, Cal-Northern School of Law, Business Associations, 1990—. *Member:* Butte County Bar Association; State Bar of California; California Health

*(This Listing Continued)*

Lawyers Association; Women Lawyers and Judges Association. **PRACTICE AREAS:** Business Law; Insurance Defense Law.

**MARIA LATHROP WINTER,** born Chico, California, October 1, 1967; admitted to bar, 1994, California and U.S. District Court, Eastern District of California. *Education:* University of California, Los Angeles (B.A., 1990) The American University, Washington College of Law (J.D., cum laude, 1994). Recipient, Equal Justice Foundation Public Interest Fellowships 1992, 1993. *Member:* State Bar of California; Butte County Women Lawyers and Judges Association. **PRACTICE AREAS:** Medical Malpractice; Employment Law.

**LARRY S. BUCKLEY,** born Burbank, California, October 21, 1959; admitted to bar, 1996, California. *Education:* California State University at Chico (B.A., in Physical Science, 1988); Gonzaga University (J.D., 1995). Recipient, American Jurisprudence Award in Legal Research & Writing IV, Gonzaga University, 1995. Law Clerk (extern) to Honorable Robert H. Whaley, Spokane Superior Court, 1995. *Member:* State Bar of California. **PRACTICE AREAS:** Medical Malpractice; Employment Law; Contract Law.

### LEGAL SUPPORT PERSONNEL

**DIANA C. BEREXA,** born Chico, California, January 13, 1968. *Education:* California State University (B.S., 1994; Paralegal Certificate, 1995); California Northern School of Law. (Certified Paralegal). **PRACTICE AREAS:** Deposition; Summaries; Settlement; Demands; Discovery Motions. **Email:** DB1Paralgl@AOL.Com

REPRESENTATIVE CLIENTS:
MEDICAL AND DENTAL PROFESSIONAL LIABILITY INSURANCE: Norcal Mutual Insurance Co.; Cooperative of American Physicians Mutual Protection Trust; Safeco Insurance.
GENERAL LIABILITY INSURANCE: Golden Eagle Insurance Company; P.V. Ranch & Home Stores; 20th Century Insurance Co.; Cal-Farm Insurance Co.; K-Mart Corporation; Fireman's Fund; GAB Business Services, Inc.; Federated Insurance Company; Sears Roebuck & Company; Equity Insurance company; Shand Morahan & Co.; Dayco Corporation; Universal Underwriters Insurance Co.; Weslo, Inc.; California Insurance Guarantee Association; Crawford & Co.; American Family Insurance Co.; Utica Insurance Co.; General Star Management Company.
BUSINESS: Chico Sports Club; Chico Medical Group; Butte County Title Co.; Butte Glenn Medical Society.
PUBLIC ENTITIES: County of Butte.

---

## RICHARD S. MATSON

THE SILBERSTEIN BUILDING
426 BROADWAY, SUITE 305
P.O. BOX 4141
**CHICO, CALIFORNIA 95927-4141**
Telephone: 916-342-5396
Fax: 916-342-5395
*Email:* rsmatson@maxinet.com

*Corporate, Partnership, Business, Contracts, Acquisitions, Real Property, Probate, Wills, Trusts, Estate Planning, Trademarks and Franchise Law.*

**RICHARD S. MATSON,** born Chico, California, March 30, 1951; admitted to bar, 1977, California; 1982, U.S. Tax Court. *Education:* California State University, Chico and University of California, Santa Barbara (B.A., 1973); McGeorge School of Law, University of the Pacific (J.D., 1977); University of Miami (LL.M. in Taxation, 1978). Phi Delta Phi. Lecturer in Income Taxation, Golden Gate University, Sacramento, 1980. Director, Chico Economic Planning Corporation, 1984—. Director, 1988-1991 and Member, Finance Committee, 1991, Sierra Cascade Girl Scout Council. Member, Loan Administration Board—Tri-County Economic Development Corporation, 1988—. Associate, Stockman & Martorana, Sacramento, California, 1979-1982. Partner, Marshall, Burghardt, Matson & Kelleher, Chico, California, 1982-1988. General Counsel, Option Care, Inc., 1988-1994. *Member:* State Bar of California; American Bar Association (Member: Section on Business Law; Forum Committees on Franchising and Health Law). **PRACTICE AREAS:** Contracts; Acquisitions; Corporations; Partnerships; Real Property; Franchising; Trademarks; Wills and Trusts.

## DANIEL J. McCAMPBELL
2607 THE ESPLANADE
**CHICO, CALIFORNIA 95926**
*Telephone: 916-893-1141*
*Fax: Available Upon Request*

Bankruptcy (Debtor and Creditor), Business and Agricultural Reorganization and Business Law.

**DANIEL J. McCAMPBELL,** born Chico, California, October 4, 1958; admitted to bar, 1984, California. *Education:* California State University, Chico (B.A., 1981); McGeorge School of Law, University of the Pacific (J.D., 1984). Phi Alpha Delta. *Member:* Butte County Bar Association; State Bar of California (Member, Board of Legal Specialization Personal and Small Business Bankruptcy Advisory Committee).

REPRESENTATIVE CLIENTS: Yuba County Tax Collectors.

---

## McKERNAN, LANAM, BAKKE, BENSON & BODNEY
Established in 1947
445 NORMAL AVENUE
P.O. BOX 3496
**CHICO, CALIFORNIA 95927**
*Telephone: 916-891-0247*
*Fax: 916-891-1704*
*Email: mlbbbchico@aol.com*

Paradise, California Office: 732 Fir Street, P.O. Box 550. Telephone: 916-877-4961. Fax: 916-877-8163

General Civil Practice. Trusts, Probate, Real Estate, Estate Planning, Personal Injury, Medical Malpractice, Legal Malpractice and Bad Faith Law, Corporate Law and Trials.

### MEMBERS

**ROY McKERNAN** (Retired).

**JOHN D. LANAM,** born Los Angeles, California, February 10, 1935; admitted to bar, 1964, California. *Education:* Chico State College (A.B., 1960); University of California at Berkeley (J.D., 1963). Phi Alpha Delta. President, 1977-1978, 1982-1983, 1986-1987 and 1991-1992; Board Member, 1976—, Paradise Unified School District. *Member:* Butte County Bar Association; State Bar of California.

**RANDY L. BAKKE,** born Bemidji, Minnesota, June 8, 1950; admitted to bar, 1977, California. *Education:* California State University, Humboldt (B.A., 1973); McGeorge School of Law, University of the Pacific (J.D., 1977). *Member:* Butte County Bar Association; State Bar of California. (Certified Specialist, Family Law, The State Bar of California Board of Legal Specialization).

**STEPHEN E. BENSON,** born San Francisco, California, August 15, 1946; admitted to bar, 1979, California. *Education:* Pacific Union College (B.A., 1968; M.A., 1971); Western State University (J.D., 1978). Phi Alpha Delta. *Member:* Butte County Bar Association; State Bar of California. **REPORTED CASES:** Reed v. King (1983) 145C.A.3d 261, 193C.R.130.

**JOHN A. BODNEY,** born Boise, Idaho, November 4, 1948; admitted to bar, 1977, California; 1988, Arizona; U.S. District Court, Northern, Central and Eastern Districts of California; U.S. District Court, Southern District of New York. *Education:* University of Oregon (B.S., 1970); University of Iowa (M.S., 1972); McGeorge School of Law, University of the Pacific (J.D., 1977). Editor-in-Chief, Owens, California Forms and Procedure, 1975-1977. Author: "Debt Collection Practice in Sacramento County," De Minimus, 1974; "Minimizing Environmental Liability in Real Estate Transactions," May 5, 1990; "Experts & Consultants in Litigation," July 25, 1991, University of California, Santa Barbara; "Insurance Bad Faith Litigation in California," February 12, 1993, National Business Institute, Sacramento, Ca.; "Insurance Litigation in California - 1994," January 21, 1994; "Recent Developments in Insurance Litigation - 1995," January 20, 1995, Lorhman Business Center, Sacramento, Ca. Judge Pro Tem, Sacramento Superior Court. Associate Mediator, North Valley Mediation Center. *Member:* Sacramento County, Butte County and American (Member, Section of Tort and Insurance Practice) Bar Associations; State Bar of California; State Bar of Arizona.

CAA118B

---

## PETERS, FULLER, RUSH, FARNSWORTH & HABIB
Established in 1896
414 SALEM STREET
P.O. BOX 3509
**CHICO, CALIFORNIA 95928**
*Telephone: 916-342-3593*
*FAX: 916-342-4272*

General Civil and Trial Practice in all State and Federal Courts. Insurance Defense, Real Property, Estate Planning and Administration, Business and Commercial Law, Workers Compensation.

FIRM PROFILE: *The firm traces its origin back to General Bidwell, who developed the Chico area through a land grant in the 1800's. Areas of practice have now been expanded to all of Northern California. Emphasis is placed on litigation, probate and estate planning and business. The firm encourages active community involvement by its members in civic and professional activities.*

### MEMBERS OF FIRM

**JEROME D. PETERS, JR.,** born Chico, California, November 26, 1914; admitted to bar, 1939, California; 1972, U.S. Supreme Court. *Education:* Stanford University (A.B., 1936; LL.B., 1939). Phi Delta Phi. *Member:* Butte County and American Bar Associations; The State Bar of California; International Society of Barristers. Fellow, American College of Trust and Estate Counsel. **PRACTICE AREAS:** Estate Planning; Probate; Business Law; Water Law; Real Estate Law.

**DAVID H. RUSH,** born Independence, Kansas, August 24, 1938; admitted to bar, 1966, California; 1972, U.S. Supreme Court. *Education:* Rice University (B.A., cum laude, 1959); Boalt Hall School of Law, University of California (J.D., 1966). Phi Alpha Delta. *Member:* Butte County Bar Association; The State Bar of California; Association of Defense Counsel (Director, 1995—); American Board of Trial Advocates; Defense Research Institute; Association of Defense Trial Lawyers. **PRACTICE AREAS:** Insurance Defense; Personal Injury Law; Property Damage Law; Real Estate Law; Products Liability Law; Public Entity Liability Law; Civil Trial.

**JAMES C. FARNSWORTH,** born Santa Monica, California, July 12, 1957; admitted to bar, 1983, California; 1989, U.S. Supreme Court. *Education:* University of California at Berkeley (A.B., 1979); McGeorge School of Law, University of the Pacific (J.D., 1983). *Member:* Butte County Bar Association; The State Bar of California; Butte County Barristers Association; Association of Defense Counsel. **PRACTICE AREAS:** Insurance Defense; Personal Injury Law; Property Damage Law; Workers Compensation Law; Products Liability Law; Public Entity Liability Law; Aviation Law.

**MARK A. HABIB,** born Detroit, Michigan, June 4, 1952; admitted to bar, 1990, California. *Education:* California State University (B.A., 1976); Pepperdine University (J.D., 1990). Dean's Merit Scholarship. Business: Export Management, Consulting and Sales of American made products overseas, 1980-1986. *Member:* Butte County and American Bar Associations; State Bar of California. **PRACTICE AREAS:** Insurance Defense; Personal Injury Law; Property Damage Law; Real Property Law; Civil Litigation.

### ASSOCIATES

**JAMES P. MCKENNA,** born Sonoma, California, July 9, 1963; admitted to bar, 1989, California. *Education:* California State University at Chico (B.A., 1986); University of San Francisco (J.D., 1989). Oder of the Barristers. Judicial Extern, Supreme Court, State of California. Managing Director, Moot Court Board. *Member:* Butte County Bar Association; State Bar of California. **PRACTICE AREAS:** Premises Liability Law; Personal Injury Law; Civil Litigation; Property Damage.

**HARLEY A. MERRITT,** born Los Angeles, California, June 21, 1943; admitted to bar, 1972, California; 1973, U.S. Court of Appeals, Ninth Circuit. *Education:* University of California at Berkeley; San Jose City College; Lincoln University (LL.B., 1972). Member, Lincoln University Law Review, 1970-1971. Lecturer, Criminal Law, Butte College, 1977-1981. *Member:* Butte County Bar Association (Chairman, Fee Dispute Arbitration, 1983-1985); State Bar of California. **PRACTICE AREAS:** Workers Compensation; Personal Injury; Defense.

GENERAL COUNSEL: University School Employees Credit Union; North State National Bank; Ranchero Flight Center, Inc.; Air Carriages, Inc.; Drainage District #2 of Butte County; County of Plumas.
LOCAL COUNSEL: Pacific Gas & Electric Co.; Southern Pacific Co.; California Water Service Co.; Helena Chemical Co.

*(This Listing Continued)*

INSURANCE COMPANIES: Allied Insurance Co.; Allianz Insurance Co.; American Bankers Insurance Group; American Hardware Mutual; American International Insurance Group; Associated Aviation Underwriters; Claims Management, Inc.; CIGNA; Colonial Penn Insurance Co.; Corroon & Black Management, Inc.; Crawford & Co.; Cumis Insurance Society, Inc.; Fireman's Fund Insurance Cos.; Frank B. Hall & Co.; Fremont Indemnity Co.; George Hills Co., Inc.; Great American Insurance Co.; Gregory Bragg & Associates; Grange Insurance Assoc.; Bragg & Morse; Industrial Indemnity; Interstate Insurance Group; Landmark Insurance Co.; Michigan Millers; M. J. Hall & Co.; National Automobile & Casualty Insurance Co.; Nationwide Insurance Co.; Northwestern National Insurance Group; Ohio Casualty Insurance Group; Progressive Insurance Co.; Recovery Services Int'l; St. Paul Fire and Marine; United Pacific/Reliance; Utica Mutual Insurance Co.; U.S.F. & G.; Zurich American Insurance Co.

## PRICE, BROWN & HALSEY

Established in 1899

466 VALLOMBROSA AVENUE
P.O. BOX 1420
**CHICO, CALIFORNIA 95927**
Telephone: 916-343-4412
Fax: 916-343-7251

*General Civil and Trial Practice. Business, Insurance and Public Entity Defense, Real Property and Probate Law.*

**GRAYSON PRICE** (1902-1988).

**PHILIP B. PRICE,** born Chico, California, May 10, 1935; admitted to bar, 1962, California. *Education:* University of Santa Clara (B.S., 1958; J.D., 1961). Assistant City Attorney, 1963-1975. *Member:* Butte County and American Bar Associations; The State Bar of California; Northern California Association of Defense Counsel. *PRACTICE AREAS:* Civil Litigation; Insurance Defense; Public Entity Defense.

**W. Z. JEFFERSON BROWN,** born Baltimore, Maryland, January 9, 1942; admitted to bar, 1966, California. *Education:* Pomona College (B.A., cum laude, 1963); Harvard University (J.D., cum laude, 1966). Phi Beta Kappa. *Member:* Butte County Bar Association; The State Bar of California. *PRACTICE AREAS:* Business Law; Real Estate and Agricultural Law; Estate Planning Law; Construction Law.

**F. DENNIS HALSEY,** born Corning, California, September 16, 1944; admitted to bar, 1975, California. *Education:* Chico State College (B.A., magna cum laude, 1971); Hastings College of Law, University of California (J.D., 1975). Phi Kappa Phi. *Member:* Butte County Bar Association; The State Bar of California; Northern California Association of Defense Counsel. *PRACTICE AREAS:* Civil Litigation; Insurance Defense; Public Entity Defense.

### ASSOCIATES

**LINDA M. SCHULKEN,** born Seattle, Washington, May 1, 1957; admitted to bar, 1995, California. *Education:* California State University, Chico (B.S., 1980); Cal Northern School of Law (J.D., 1995). *Member:* State Bar of California.

REPRESENTATIVE CLIENTS: Cities of Chico, Marysville, Oroville and Willows (Self Insured); County of Butte (Self Insured); County of Siskiyou (Self Insured); Allstate Insurance Co.; Baldwin Contracting Co. Inc.; Chubb/Pacific Indemnity Co.; Continental Insurance Group; Cravens, Dargen & Co.; Deans and Homer; Security Insurance Co.; Auto. Club Southern California (Inter-Insurance Exchange); St. Paul Fire & Marine; Lassen Land Co.; Canadian Indemnity Co.; Aetna Casualty and Surety Co.; Maryland Casualty Co.; Bidwell Title & Escrow Co.; Mercury Casualty Co.; Teachers Insurance Co.; Progressive Casualty Insurance Co.; K Mart Corp.; Marsh & McClennan Associates; Pacific Telesis; Baldwin-Minkler Farms; Donrey Media Group; Sunseri Construction, Inc.

## RICH, FUIDGE, MORRIS & IVERSON, INC.

**CHICO, CALIFORNIA**

(See Marysville)

*General Civil and Trial Practice. Corporation, Water Rights, Insurance, Real Estate, Crop Damage, Estate Planning, Family and Probate Law, Medical and Legal Malpractice, Personal Injury, Employment Law, Criminal Law, Alternative Dispute Resolution.*

## STEWART, HUMPHERYS, BURCHETT, SANDELMAN & MOLIN

Established in 1979

SUITE 6, 3120 COHASSET ROAD
P.O. BOX 720
**CHICO, CALIFORNIA 95927**
Telephone: 916-891-6111
Telecopier: 916-894-2103
Email: shbsm@sunset.net

*General Civil and Trial Practice, Probate, Estate Planning, Corporation, Real Estate, Personal Injury, Business Law, Construction, Education Law, Public Entity, Employment Law, Insurance Law, Municipal Law, Public Entity Defense, Wrongful Termination Defense.*

FIRM PROFILE: STEWART, HUMPHERYS, BURCHETT, SANDELMAN & MOLIN was established in 1979 by Chico area lawyers with many years of legal experience. The firm founders have been residents of Butte County and active in its growth for as long as fifty years. The law firm was formed with a plan for meeting a broad spectrum of clientele and legal needs.

### MEMBERS OF FIRM

**RONALD E. STEWART,** born Chico, California, 1939; admitted to bar, 1968, California; 1973, U.S. Supreme Court. *Education:* Chico State College (B.A., 1964); Boalt Hall School of Law, University of California (J.D., 1967). Mayor of Chico, 1975-1977. Referee, State Bar Disciplinary Committee, 1977-1988. *Member:* Butte County Bar Association; State Bar of California; Consumer Attorneys of California; The Association of Trial Lawyers of America; American Board of Trial Advocates. *PRACTICE AREAS:* Personal Injury Law; Medical Malpractice; Business Litigation; Trial Practice; Public Entity Defense.

**KEITH S. HUMPHERYS,** born Thayne, Wyoming, 1929; admitted to bar, 1961, California; 1973, U.S. Supreme Court. *Education:* Brigham Young University (B.S., 1955); George Washington University (J.D., 1959). Hearing Officer, California State University, Chico, 1977-1981. *Member:* Butte County Bar Association; State Bar of California; Consumer Attorneys of California. *PRACTICE AREAS:* Personal Injury Law; Probate Law; Business Law.

**ALAN E. BURCHETT,** born Chico, California, May 18, 1943; admitted to bar, 1969, California. *Education:* University of California at Berkeley (B.S., 1965); Hastings College of Law, University of California (J.D., 1968). Member, Thurston Society, Deputy County Counsel, Butte County, California, 1971-1973. Attorney for the City of Paradise, 1979-1982. *Member:* Butte County and American Bar Associations; State Bar of California. *PRACTICE AREAS:* Business Law; Real Estate Law; Probate Law.

**RAYMOND L. SANDELMAN,** born Los Angeles, California, January 14, 1953; admitted to bar, 1977, California and U.S. District Court, Northern, Eastern, Central and Southern Districts of California. *Education:* University of California, Davis (A.B., Economics, with high honors, 1974); University of Santa Clara (J.D., summa cum laude, 1977). Butte County, Bench-Bar Lecturer. *Member:* Butte County Bar Association; State Bar of California. *PRACTICE AREAS:* Commercial Litigation; Real Estate Litigation; Probate Litigation.

**RICHARD J. MOLIN,** born Oakland, California, January 10, 1946; admitted to bar, 1975, California, U.S. District Court, Eastern District of California; U.S. Court of Appeals, Ninth Circuit; U.S. Supreme Court. *Education:* San Francisco State University (B.A., 1968); McGeorge School of Law, University of the Pacific (J.D., 1975). Recipient, American Jurisprudence Award in Contracts. Author: "Contingency Fee Contracts," Butte County Bar Journal, Contributor to Owens Forms of Pleading & Practice, 1983. Lecturer, Butte County Child Abuse Council, 1976 and 1986. Butte County Delegate to California State Bar Convention, 1986 and 1987. *Member:* Butte County Bar Association; State Bar of California; Association of Defense Counsel; Defense Research Institute, Inc. *PRACTICE AREAS:* Personal Injury Litigation; Public Entity Defense; Wrongful Termination Defense.

**CAROL J. TENER,** born Los Angeles, California, May 17, 1943; admitted to bar, 1977, California; 1991, U.S. District Court, Northern and Eastern Districts of California. *Education:* California State University, Chico (B.A., 1966; M.A., 1990); Western State University (J.D., 1977). Recipient, American Jurisprudence Awards in Contracts and Real Property. Associate Editor, Western State University Law Review, 1976-1977. Instructor, Business Law, California State University at Chico, 1982-1987. *Member:* Butte County Bar Association; State Bar of California; Butte County Women

*(This Listing Continued)*

**STEWART, HUMPHERYS, BURCHETT, SANDELMAN & MOLIN,** Chico—*Continued*

Lawyers and Judges (Founder, 1984-1989); Legal Services of Northern California (Board of Directors, 1992—). *PRACTICE AREAS:* Education Law; Employment Law.

**STEPHEN P. TROVER,** born Concord, California, January 18, 1954; admitted to bar, 1989, California and U.S. District Court, Eastern District of California. *Education:* California State University at Chico (B.A., 1983); McGeorge School of Law, University of the Pacific (J.D., 1989). *Member:* Butte County and American Bar Associations; State Bar of California. *PRACTICE AREAS:* Commercial Litigation; Construction Litigation; Real Estate Law.

REPRESENTATIVE CLIENTS: Business: North State National Bank; Northern California Federal Land Bank; Northern California Production Credit Assn.; Drake Homes; Avag, Inc.; Ray Morgan Company, Inc.; Cal. Oak Products, Inc.; Chico Physical Rehab, Inc.; Epick, Inc.; APS, Inc.; Land's End Real Estate; Hignell & Hignell Investments; Wentz, Inc.; Johnson Family Shoe Stores; FMC Corp.; Prison Health Services, Inc.; Beverly Manor Convalescent Hospitals; Beacon Oil Co.; Lassen Tractor Co., Inc.; March 1, Inc.; Tri-County Economic Development Corp.; Sunseri Construction; Sunseri & Associates; Frost Oil Company; North Valley Oil Works; Western Foods; Chico Produce; Fox Electric; Jessee Heating and Air Conditioning; Meeks Building Center; Judicial Arbitration & Mediation Service (JAMS/Endispute); Sacramento County Deputy Sheriffs Association.
PUBLIC ENTITY: County of Butte; City of Oroville Special Labor Counsel; Butte County Superintendent of Schools; Shasta-Trinity Regional Occupational Center; Chico Unified School District; Paradise Unified School District; Palermo School District; Thermalito School District; Gateway Unified School District; Gridley High School District; Gridley Elementary School District; Manzenita School District; Pioneer Union School District; Bangor School District; Feather Falls School District; Red Puff Union High School District; Hamilton High School District; North Crow Creek Elementary School District; Butte Community College District; Lassen Community College District; Lassen View Union Elementary School District; Reeds Creek School District; Golden Feather Union Elementary School District; Lassen County Office of Education; Los Molinos Unified School District.
INSURANCE: Special District Risk Management Authority; North Valley Schools Insurance Group; Butte County School Self-Funded Medical Benefits Joint Powers Authority; Shasta Health Joint Powers Authority; Northern California Community College Joint Venture Authority; Harbor Insurance Co.; Carolina Corp.; Hurst-Holme Insurance Co.; Zurich-American Insurance Co.

---

## WILLIAM S. VOLPE

466 VALLOMBROSA AVENUE
CHICO, CALIFORNIA 95926
*Telephone: 916-343-4414*
*Facsimile: 916-343-7251*

*Business, Commercial, Corporation, Real Estate, Construction, Debtor/Creditor, Probate, Wills, Trusts and Estates.*

**WILLIAM S. VOLPE,** born San Francisco, California, June 12, 1949; admitted to bar, 1974, California and U.S. District Court, Eastern District of California. *Education:* University of California at Davis (A.B., with honors, 1971; J.D., 1974). Lecturer, Business Law, California State University at Chico, 1977-1984. *Member:* Butte County Bar Association; State Bar of California (Member, Sections on: Real Property; Business Law); North Valley Estate Planning Council. *REPORTED CASES:* Ely v. Gray (1990) 224 Cal. App. 3rd 1257; Filmore v. Irvine (1983) 146 Cal. App. 3d 649.

REPRESENTATIVE CLIENTS: A List of Representative Clients will be furnished upon request.

---

## WILLIAM A. WARD

A PROFESSIONAL CORPORATION
9 WILLIAMSBURG LANE
STONEBRIDGE PROFESSIONAL VILLAGE
CHICO, CALIFORNIA 95926
*Telephone: 916-342-2225*
*Fax: 916-342-7920*

*General Civil and Trial Practice, Real Estate, Business, Probate, Corporation, Personal Injury.*

**WILLIAM A. WARD,** born Arnold, Nebraska, July 9, 1938; admitted to bar, 1965, California. *Education:* University of California at Los Angeles
*(This Listing Continued)*

---

(B.A., 1960); University of California School of Law (J.D., 1964). *Member:* Butte County Bar Association (President, 1986-1987); State Bar of California; Northern California Association of Defense Counsel.

List of Representative Clients will be furnished on request.

---

## ZELLMER LAW GROUP

1660 HUMBOLDT ROAD, SUITE 6
CHICO, CALIFORNIA 95928
*Telephone: 916-345-6789*
*Fax: 916-345-6836*
*Email: zellmo@aol.com*

*Real Estate, Business Law, Litigation, Zoning, Planning and Land Use, Commercial Law.*

**JOSEPH F. ZELLMER, III,** born San Diego, California, May 4, 1957; admitted to bar, 1983, California. *Education:* University of San Diego; University of California at Santa Barbara (B.A., 1980); Hastings College of Law, University of California (J.D., 1983). Member and Executive Note and Comment Editor, Hastings International and Comparative Law Review, 1981-1983. *Member:* State Bar of California. *PRACTICE AREAS:* Real Estate; Business Law; Litigation; Zoning, Planning and Land Use; Commercial Law.

---

## LEACH, McGREEVY & BAUTISTA

13643 FIFTH STREET
CHINO, CALIFORNIA 91710
*Telephone: 909-590-2224*

*San Francisco, California Office:* 1735 Pacific Avenue. Telephone: 415-775-4455. Telefax: 415-775-7435.

*Insurance Defense and Civil Litigation, Wrongful Termination and Maritime Law, Construction Defects, Medical Malpractice, Workers Compensation, Environmental Law.*

**DAVID G. LEACH,** born Detroit, Michigan, August 25, 1936; admitted to bar, 1960, Michigan; 1963, California. *Education:* Wayne University (A.B., 1957); Detroit College of Law (LL.B., 1960). Delta Theta Phi. *Member:* Bar Association of San Francisco; State Bar of California; State Bar of Michigan; American Bar Association; Association of Defense Counsel; Defense Research Institute; California Trial Lawyers Association; The Association of Trial Lawyers of America. (Also at San Francisco Office). *PRACTICE AREAS:* Insurance Defense; Civil Litigation; Construction Defects; Medical Malpractice; Workers Compensation; Environmental Law.

**RICHARD E. McGREEVY,** born Tacoma, Washington, July 18, 1946; admitted to bar, 1976, California. *Education:* San Francisco State University (B.S., 1971); University of San Francisco (J.D., cum laude, 1976). *Member:* Bar Association of San Francisco; State Bar of California; Defense Research Institute; Association of Southern California Defense Counsel; California Trial Lawyers Association. (Also at San Francisco Office). *PRACTICE AREAS:* Insurance Defense; Civil Litigation; Construction Defects; Medical Malpractice; Workers Compensation; Environmental Law.

**A. MARQUEZ BAUTISTA,** born Manila, Philippines, March 13, 1934; admitted to bar, 1956, California, U.S. District Court, Northern District of California and U.S. Court of Appeals, Ninth Circuit. *Education:* University of San Francisco (J.D., 1955). Phi Alpha Delta (Treasurer, 1954-1955). *Member:* State Bar of California; Lawyers Club of San Francisco (Member, Board of Directors, 1967-1969). *LANGUAGES:* Spanish and Filipino. *PRACTICE AREAS:* Products Liability; Business Litigation; Real Estate Litigation; Environmental Law.

---

**JOHN C. CONNOLLY,** born June 18, 1942; admitted to bar, 1977, California. *Education:* St. John's University (B.A., 1964); Western State University (J.D., 1977). *Member:* State Bar of California.

REPRESENTATIVE CLIENTS: Allianz Insurance Co.; Allstate Insurance Co.; Arkansas Best Corp.; Auto Insurance Services (Interstate); Baldwin & Lyons, Inc.; Black & Decker; Brinks; Chubb Group; General Accident Insurance Co.; Home Insurance Co.; Orion Security Group; Protective Insurance Co.; Republic Indemnity; Rollins Leasing Corp.; Sutter Insurance Co.; United States Fidelity & Guaranty Co.

## LAW OFFICES OF
## ELLEN VAN WAGNER
12490 CENTRAL AVENUE, SUITE 104
**CHINO, CALIFORNIA 91710**
Telephone: 909-902-1210
Fax: 909-902-1215

*Workers Compensation Law.*

**ELLEN VAN WAGNER,** born Chicago, Illinois, December 10, 1942; admitted to bar, 1984, California; 1985, U.S. District Court, Central District of California and U.S. Court of Appeals, Ninth Circuit. *Education:* University of Arizona (B.A., 1964); California State University at Los Angeles (M.A., 1971); University of La Verne (J.D., 1984). Writer and Editor-in-Chief, Journal of Juvenile Law, 1982-1984. Associate Professor of Law, University of La Verne College of Law, 1987—. Instructor, Continuing Education of the California Bar, 1989—. Certified Teacher and Administrator, State of California. Commissioner, Citizens Advisory Commission on Youth Activities for the City of Baldwin Park, California, 1974-1979. *Member:* Los Angeles and East Valley Bar Associations; State Bar of California (Executive Committee, Workers Compensation Section, 1986—); California Applicant's Attorneys Association. (Certified Specialist, Workers Compensation Law, The State Bar of California Board of Legal Specialization). *REPORTED CASES:* Barrett Mobil Home Transport v. Bittle; Duroy v. Glass Door; Serrano V. Butler Paper. **PRACTICE AREAS:** Worker's Compensation Law.

---

## ATHERTON & ALLEN
*Established in 1925*
210 TOWNE CENTRE PROFESSIONAL BUILDING
345 "F" STREET
**CHULA VISTA, CALIFORNIA 91910**
Telephone: 619-420-6869

*General Civil Practice. Estate Planning, Probate, Corporate and Real Estate Law.*

### MEMBERS OF FIRM

**HARVEY H. ATHERTON** (1881-1972).

**KEITH ATHERTON** (Retired).

**DAVID R. ALLEN,** born Oak Park, Illinois, July 30, 1942; admitted to bar, 1969, California. *Education:* Stanford University (A.B., 1964); University of Southern California (J.D., 1968). Phi Delta Phi. President, Rotary Club of Chula Vista, 1976-1977. Governor, Rotary District 5340, 1989-1990. *Member:* South Bay and San Diego County (Chairman, Estate Planning, Trust and Probate Law Section, 1986) Bar Associations; The State Bar of California; American Inn of Court (Legion Lex Chapter). [Lt. U.S.N.R., 1964-1965]. (Certified Specialist, Estate Planning, Trust and Probate Law, The State Bar of California Board of Legal Specialization). **PRACTICE AREAS:** Estate Planning; Trust and Probate Law; Corporate Law; Real Estate Law.

REPRESENTATIVE CLIENTS: Encinitas Ford; Western Surety Co.; H.D. West Builders, Inc.; Fernandez Construction Company, Inc.; Dick Kau Land Co.; Jon Miller Realty, Inc.; Prochem Specialty Products, Inc.; AR Stables, Inc.; Lake Morena RV Park; R & R/Advance, Inc.

---

## GEERDES & GEERDES
210 TOWNE CENTRE PROFESSIONAL BUILDING
345 "F" STREET
**CHULA VISTA, CALIFORNIA 91910**
Telephone: 619-420-6560

*Civil Litigation, Securities Investor Litigation, Surety Law, Real Estate, Environmental Waste and Corporate Maintenance.*

### MEMBERS OF FIRM

**FRANKLIN GEERDES,** born Woodstock, Minnesota, June 21, 1932; admitted to bar, 1966, California; 1971, U.S. Supreme Court. *Education:* San Diego City College; La Salle Extension University (LL.B., 1965). Naval Criminal Investigator, 1953-1955. Police Officer, 1957-1966. President, South Bay Bar Association, San Diego County, 1975. President, Rotary Club of Chula Vista, 1985-1986. Arbitrator, NASD. *Member:* South Bay and San Diego County Bar Associations; The State Bar of California; American Inn of Court (Legion Lex Chapter); Association of Business Trial

*(This Listing Continued)*

Lawyers. **PRACTICE AREAS:** Civil Litigation; Securities Investor Litigation; Surety Law; Real Estate Law; Environmental Waste Law.

**MARY ELIZABETH GEERDES,** born Albuquerque, New Mexico, November 6, 1947; admitted to bar, 1994, California. *Education:* University of New Mexico (B.S.N., 1969; MAEd., 1971); Thomas Jefferson School of Law (J.D., 1994). Listed in: Who's Who in the West, Medicine & Healthcare, American Nursing, American Women. Registered Nurse, 1969—. Member, South Bay Salvation Army Advisory Board. *Member:* South Bay Bar Association; State Bar of California; Navy Nurse Corps Association; Emergency Nursing Association. [Lieut Commander, U.S. Navy, 1971-1991; Risk Management Coordinator Balboa Naval Hospital Regional Medical Center, San Diego, 1988-1991]

REPRESENTATIVE CLIENTS: G & G; Encinitas Ford; Western Surety Co.; Dick Kau Land Co.; Jon Miller Realty; The Ruff Company Realty; Chazan & Rosenthal Food Company, Inc.; Adler Investment Co.

---

## JOHN H. SERRANO
SUITE 311
4045 BONITA ROAD
**CHULA VISTA, CALIFORNIA 91902**
Telephone: 619-267-7300
Email: jserr13006@aol.com

*Yuma Arizona Office:* 221 West Second Street, 85364. Telephone: 520-329-7185.

*Civil and Criminal Trial Practice. Criminal Law, Personal Injury, Negligence, and Civil Rights.*

**JOHN H. SERRANO,** born San Diego, California, September 12, 1950; admitted to bar, 1977, Arizona and U.S. District Court, Southern District of Arizona; 1979, California and U.S. District Court, Central and Southern Districts of California; 1984, U.S. Supreme Court; 1992, U.S. Court of Appeals, Ninth Circuit. *Education:* University of California at San Diego (B.A., Anthropology, 1974); University of Southern California (J.D., 1977). 1st place oral argument-1st year Moot Court. Participant, Hale Moot Court Competition. Director, El Centro Chicano Legal Aid. Co-chair, Chicano Law Students Association. Instructor: Los Angeles Police Academy, 1980-1982; San Diego Police Reserve Academy, 1985-1988; Palomar College, 1986-1988; San Diego County Police Chief's Association Traumatic Incident Seminar, 1987. Reginald Heber Smith Fellowship, 1977. Arizona Attorney General's Office, 1978-1979; Los Angeles City Attorney's Office, 1979-1984; Escondido City Attorney's Office, 1984-1990. Instructor, Wrongful Death in Police Misconduct Litigation, 1992. State Bar of California Committee on Rules and Procedures of Court, 1992-1995. *Member:* State Bar of Arizona; State Bar of California; Hispanic National Bar Association; La Raza Lawyers Association; Mexican and American Business and Professional Association; Chicano Federation (Board of Directors). **LANGUAGES:** Spanish and French.

---

## CRAWFORD & BANGS
**CITY OF INDUSTRY, CALIFORNIA**
(See West Covina)
*Construction and Business Law.*

---

## ALLARD, SHELTON & O'CONNOR
*Established in 1946*
319 HARVARD AVENUE
**CLAREMONT, CALIFORNIA 91711-4746**
Telephone: 909-626-1041
Facsimile: 909-625-5781

*General Civil and Trial Practice in all State and Federal Courts. Corporation, Non-Profit Organizations, Municipal, Real Estate, Taxation, Family Law, Estate Planning, Trust and Probate Law.*

**FIRM PROFILE:** Situated near the boundaries of Los Angeles, San Bernardino and Orange Counties, the firm emphasizes a general civil practice, including estate planning and probate, real estate, business and tax planning, and civil litigation. A majority of the firm's clients are individuals and small businesses. However, the firm also has a substantial municipal law practice (currently representing the City of Placentia), and represents colleges and other

*(This Listing Continued)*

## ALLARD, SHELTON & O'CONNOR, Claremont—Continued

*non-profit organizations. Members of the firm have been active in the State and local bar associations, and several former members have become judges.*

### MEMBERS OF FIRM

**JOSEPH A. ALLARD, JR.** (1887-1968).

**MAURICE O'CONNOR** (1911-1987).

**LEONARD A. SHELTON** (1911-1994).

**KEITH A. JOHNSON,** born Los Angeles, California, January 30, 1950; admitted to bar, 1974, Virginia; 1975, California. *Education:* Loma Linda University (B.S., with honors and with honors in physics, 1971); University of Virginia (J.D., 1974). *PRACTICE AREAS:* Taxation Law; Business and Non-Profit Organization Law; Real Estate Law.

**KEITH S. WALKER,** born Los Angeles, California, February 9, 1952; admitted to bar, 1976, California. *Education:* California State University at Fullerton (B.A., 1973); Hastings College of Law, University of California (J.D., 1976). Director, Greater Pomona Housing Development Corp., 1987-1993. Trustee, 1989-1993. Treasurer, 1989-1990, Chaffey Community Art Association. *Member:* Los Angeles County and American Bar Associations; Eastern Bar Association of Los Angeles County; The State Bar of California. *PRACTICE AREAS:* Estate Planning Law; Probate Law; Trusts Law.

**GARY C. WUNDERLIN,** born Kalamazoo, Michigan, October 13, 1947; admitted to bar, 1976, California. *Education:* Western Michigan University (A.B., 1969); University of Tennessee at Knoxville (J.D., 1975). Phi Eta Sigma. *PRACTICE AREAS:* Civil Litigation; Family Law.

**CAROL B. TANENBAUM,** born Zurich, Switzerland, June 15, 1935; admitted to bar, 1976, California. *Education:* Brown University (B.A., magna cum laude, 1956); Case Western Reserve University (J.D., 1975). Associate Editor, Case Western Reserve Law Review, 1973-1974. Deputy City Attorney: Claremont, 1981-1986; La Verne, 1981-1986. Special Counsel, City of Azusa, 1988-1993. City Attorney, City of Placentia, 1987—. Special Counsel, City of La Verne, 1987—. Member, Legislative Committee, City Attorney's Department, League of California Cities,. 1992-1995. Special Counsel, Placantie Library District, 1990—. *Member:* Los Angeles County Bar Association; Eastern Bar Association of Los Angeles County (Trustee, 1977-1983; Secretary, 1983-1984; Vice President, 1984-1985; President, 1985-1986); State Bar of California; Orange County City Attorneys Association. *PRACTICE AREAS:* Civil Litigation; Municipal Law; Probate Law.

### OF COUNSEL

**DONALD K. BYRNE,** born St. Louis, Missouri, April 10, 1924; admitted to bar, 1957, California; 1983, U.S. Supreme Court. *Education:* University of Missouri (B.A., 1948); Southwestern University (LL.B., 1956). Author: "California Civil Writs," Ch. 4, Prohibition, 1970. Deputy County Counsel, 1958-1968. Chief, Trials Division, County Counsel, 1968-1973. Los Angeles Chief Deputy County Counsel, 1973-1985. *Member:* Los Angeles County (Chair, Governmental Law Section, 1978) Bar Association; The State Bar of California (Delegate, State Bar Conference, 1977-1978); Eastern Bar Association of Los Angeles County. [With U.S. Army, 95th Infantry Division, 1943-1945]. *PRACTICE AREAS:* Civil Litigation; Municipal Law.

REPRESENTATIVE CLIENTS: Pomona College; Claremont Graduate School; Western University of Health Services; Humane Society of Pomona Valley; City of Placentia.

---

## BUXBAUM & CHAKMAK

*A LAW CORPORATION*

Established in 1971

**414 YALE AVENUE**
**CLAREMONT, CALIFORNIA 91711**
Telephone: 909-621-4707
Fax: 909-621-7112

*Newport Beach, California Office:* 5160 Campus Drive. Telephone: 714-833-3107. Fax: 714-833-2466.

Business, Commercial, Banking, Insurance Coverage (Coverage & Defense) Corporate, Real Estate, Bankruptcy (Creditors' Rights), Estate Planning, Administrative Law and Family Law, Trials in all State and Federal Courts.

*(This Listing Continued)*

CAA122B

---

**DAVID A. BUXBAUM,** born Long Beach, California; admitted to bar, 1970, California and U.S. District Court, Central District of California; 1976, U.S. Supreme Court. *Education:* Occidental College (B.A., 1966); University of California at Los Angeles (J.D., 1969). Licensed Real Estate Broker, California, 1982. *Member:* Los Angeles County and American Bar Associations; State Bar of California. *PRACTICE AREAS:* Business Banking; Estate Planning; Commercial; Real Estate.

**JOHN CHAKMAK,** born Fresno, California, August 17, 1945; admitted to bar, 1971, California and U.S. District Court, Central District of California; 1977, U.S. Court of Appeals, Ninth Circuit; 1988, U.S. District Court, Southern District of California; 1990, U.S. District Court, Eastern District of California. *Education:* Stanford University (B.A., 1967); University of California at Los Angeles (J.D., 1970). Member, Moot Court. Licensed Real Estate Broker, California, 1982. Judge Pro Tem, 1984— and Court Appointed Arbitrator, 1980-1986, Orange County Superior Court. *Member:* Orange County Bar Association (Member, Client Relations Committee, 1976-1981); State Bar of California (Member, Litigation Section). *PRACTICE AREAS:* Civil Litigation; Insurance; Commercial; Banking.

**CHARLES L. ZETTERBERG,** born Pomona, California, October 15, 1943; admitted to bar, 1971, California and U.S. District Court, Central District of California; 1976, U.S. Court of Appeals, Ninth Circuit; 1988, U.S. District Court, Southern District of California. *Education:* Wesleyan University (B.A., with honors, 1965); Columbia University (LL.B., 1968). Law Clerk to Hon. Leonard P. Moore, United States Circuit Judge, 2nd Circuit, 1968-1969. *Member:* Los Angeles County Bar Association; State Bar of California. *PRACTICE AREAS:* Civil Litigation; Insurance; Real Estate; Business.

**BETTY O. YAMASHIRO,** born Honolulu, Hawaii; admitted to bar, 1985, California; 1986, U.S. District Court, Central District of California and U.S. Court of Appeals, Ninth Circuit. *Education:* University of Hawaii, (B.Ed.); University of Illinois (M.A.); Western State University College of Law (J.D., cum laude, 1985). Recipient, American Jurisprudence Awards in Torts, Evidence, Real Property, Remedies and Professional Responsibility. Member and Planning Editor, Western State University Law Review, 1982-1983. President, 1992-1993, Orange County Japanese-American Lawyers' Association. *Member:* Orange County (Assistant Co-Chairman, Minority Issues Committee, 1993-1994; Member, Long Range Planning Committee, 1993-1994 and Commercial Law and Bankruptcy Sections) and Los Angeles County Bar Associations; State Bar of California; Orange County Bankruptcy Forum. *PRACTICE AREAS:* Banking; Bankruptcy; Creditors Rights; Civil Litigation.

---

**JOHN P. HOWLAND,** born New York, N.Y., June 23, 1941; admitted to bar, 1967, New York; 1989, California; 1991, U.S. District Court, Central District of California. *Education:* Dartmouth College (B.A., 1963); University of Pennsylvania (LL.B., 1966). Member, Moot Court Finals. Small Claims Court Arbitrator, New York City, 1970-1974. Member, Law Committee, National Consumer Finance Association, 1984-1986. *Member:* Los Angeles County and American Bar Associations; State Bar of California. *PRACTICE AREAS:* Estate Planning; Corporate; Business; Bankruptcy (Creditors Rights).

**JOAN PENFIL,** born Cleveland, Ohio, July 13, 1938; admitted to bar, 1985, California; 1986, U.S. District Court, Central District of California and U.S. Court of Appeals, Ninth Circuit. *Education:* University of Michigan (B.A., cum laude, 1960); Wayne State University (M.A., 1964); Western State University (J.D., cum laude, 1984). Recipient: Corpus Juris Secundum Award; American Jurisprudence Award; Foundation Press Award. Editor, Western State University Law Review, 1984-1985. *Member:* Orange County Bar Association; State Bar of California. *PRACTICE AREAS:* Family Law.

---

## DRYDEN, MARGOLES, SCHIMANECK, KELLY & WAIT

*A LAW CORPORATION*

**341 WEST FIRST STREET**
**CLAREMONT, CALIFORNIA 91711**
Telephone: 909-621-5672
Fax: 909-399-0645

*San Francisco, California Office:* Suite 2600, One California Street. Telephone: 415-362-6715.

*(This Listing Continued)*

*General Civil and Trial Practice. Medical Legal, Product Liability, Insurance, Aviation and Environmental Law.*

**THOMAS B. WAIT,** born Cleveland, Ohio, September 26, 1950; admitted to bar, 1978, California and U.S. District Court, Northern District of California. *Education:* Denison University (B.A., 1973); University of San Francisco (J.D., 1977). Pi Sigma Alpha. *Member:* State Bar of California; American Bar Association; Association of Defense Counsel of Southern California; Defense Research Institute; Trucking Industry Defense Association. (Managing Partner). **PRACTICE AREAS:** Products Liability; Construction Defect; Negligence; Professional Liability; Bad Faith; Wrongful Termination; Sexual Harassment; Insurance Coverage.

**MARY CHILDS,** born Orlando, Florida, April 2, 1960; admitted to bar, 1988, California; U.S. District Court, Central District of California. *Education:* California State University at Northridge (B.S., 1983); University of West Los Angeles (J.D., 1988). Recipient: American Jurisprudence Awards in Contracts, Remedies, Real Property and Community Property; Justice Jefferson Award. *Member:* Pasadena Bar Association; State Bar of California; Pasadena Young Lawyers Association (Past-President); Southern California Defense Council. **PRACTICE AREAS:** Construction Defect; Products Liability; Professional Liability; General Negligence; Premises Liability.

---

**AARON RAY BOYD,** born Durham, North Carolina, August 9, 1957; admitted to bar, 1990, California and U.S. District Court, Central District of California. *Education:* California State Polytechnic University (B.A., 1980); University of La Verne (J.D., 1988). *Member:* State Bar of California; American Bar Association; Los Angeles County Bar Association. **PRACTICE AREAS:** Civil Litigation-Emphasizing Defense of Trucking Companies; ERISA; Products Liability; Premises Liability; Construction Defect; General Negligence.

**STEVEN J. BROWN,** born Covina, California, October 12, 1960; admitted to bar, 1995, California and U.S. District Court, Central District of California. *Education:* California State Polytechnic University, Pomona (B.S., 1984); University of La Verne College of Law (J.D., 1988). Recipient, American Jurisprudence Award U.C.C. *Member:* State Bar of California; American Bar Association. **PRACTICE AREAS:** Products Liability; Premises Liability; Construction Defect; General Negligence.

**SHAWN E. MCMENOMY,** born Alhambra, California, June 15, 1959; admitted to bar, 1990, California. *Education:* California State University at Los Angeles (B.S., 1982); Howard University (J.D., 1989). **PRACTICE AREAS:** Products Liability; Premises Liability; Construction Defect; General Negligence.

**A. KERRY STACK,** born Los Angeles, California, November 24, 1956; admitted to bar, 1987, California; 1990, U.S. District Court, Central District of California; 1993, U.S. District Court, Southern District of California. *Education:* University of California at Riverside (B.A., cum laude, 1978); Western State University (J.D., cum laude, 1986). Member, Western State University Law Review, 1984-1986. *Member:* Los Angeles County Bar Association; State Bar of California; Southern California Defense Counsel. **PRACTICE AREAS:** Products Liability; Premises Liability; Tort Litigation; Construction Defect; Negligence; Professional Liability; Bad Faith; Wrongful Termination; Sexual Harassment; Insurance Coverage; Personal Injury; Contract.

(For complete Biographical Data on all personnel see Professional Biographies at San Francisco, California)

---

## CARL F. HERBOLD
*Established in 1991*
**201 WEST FOURTH STREET**
**CLAREMONT, CALIFORNIA 91711**
Telephone: 909-625-6305
FAX: 909-625-3870

*General Civil Litigation, General Commercial Law, Business Law, Corporate Law, Non Profit Organizations, Employment Law including, Sexual Harassment, Wrongful Termination, Discrimination and Tax Law.*

**CARL F. HERBOLD,** born Lima, Ohio, March 29, 1940; admitted to bar, 1968, Connecticut; 1981, California. *Education:* Dartmouth College (A.B., cum laude, 1962); Yale Graduate School (M.Phil., 1969; Ph.D., 1973); Yale University (LL.B., 1968). President, Corbey Court, 1963-1964. Lecturer in Comparative Law, Facultad de Derecho, Pontificia Universidad Católica del Perú, 1970. Author, California Transactions Forms, 1st edition, 23rd chapter, Bancroft Whitney, 1996. *Member:* Los Angeles County and American (Member, Exempt Organizations Committee of Tax Section, 1989—) Bar Associations; State Bar of California (Member and Former Chair, 1987-1988, Committee on Nonprofit Organizations of Business Law Section; Member, Employment Law Section). **LANGUAGES:** Spanish, Portuguese and French. **PRACTICE AREAS:** General Business; Non-Profit Corporations; Health Care; Employment.

---

## JONES, MAHONEY, BRAYTON & SOLL
*Established in 1980*
**150 WEST FIRST STREET, SUITE 280**
**CLAREMONT, CALIFORNIA 91711**
Telephone: 909-399-9977
Fax: 909-399-5959

*General Civil and Trial Practice in State and Federal Courts. Business, Construction, Corporation, Insurance, Civil Litigation, Estate Planning, Probate, Taxation, Real Property and Family Law.*

FIRM PROFILE: *Highly experienced lawyers who have served the needs of the area for over 25 years. In addition to specialties listed as to each attorney, firm has substantial appellate practice.*

### MEMBERS OF FIRM

**STEPHEN C. JONES,** born Pomona, California, January 31, 1944; admitted to bar, 1969, California. *Education:* Loyola University of Los Angeles (B.B.A., 1965); University of California at Los Angeles (J.D., 1968). Alpha Sigma Nu. Assistant Dean, University of La Verne Law Center, 1971-1977. Treasurer, Eastern Bar Association, 1996—. *Member:* Los Angeles County Bar Association; State Bar of California; Eastern Bar Association (Treasurer, 1996—). **PRACTICE AREAS:** Corporate Law; Business Law; Probate Law; Estate Planning Law; Taxation Law; Litigation.

**THOMAS C. BRAYTON,** born Toronto, Ohio, November 13, 1941; admitted to bar, 1968, California. *Education:* California State University at Los Angeles (A.B., 1963); University of California at Los Angeles (J.D., 1967). Phi Alpha Delta. Author: Chapter, "Jurisdiction, Venue and Service of Process," California Marital Dissolution Practice, California Continuing Education of the Bar, Vol. I, Chapter 11. Research Attorney, Appellate Department, Superior Court, Los Angeles County, 1967-1968. Member, California Judicial Council, Advisory Committee on Legal Forms, 1975-1977. Lecturer, Recent Developments in Family Law, Continuing Education of the Bar, Annual Lectures, 1983-1996. *Member:* Los Angeles County (Member, Executive Committee, Family Law Section, 1983-1987) and American Bar Associations; Eastern Bar Association of Los Angeles County; State Bar of California (Member, 1973-1979 and Chairman, 1976-1978, Executive Committee, Family Law Section). (Certified Specialist, Family Law, The State Bar of California Board of Legal Specialization). **PRACTICE AREAS:** Family Law.

**PAUL M. MAHONEY,** born Los Angeles, California, September 30, 1942; admitted to bar, 1969, California. *Education:* University of California at Los Angeles (A.B., 1965; J.D., 1968). Moot Court Honors Program. Member, National and State Moot Court Teams. Trustee, 1973— and Treasurer, 1977—, Pomona Valley Bar Association. *Member:* Pomona (Chairman, Education of Youth in Law Committee, 1974-1977), Los Angeles County (Member: Barrister's Jail O.R. Committee, 1977-1978; Judicial Evaluation Committee, 1980-1981; Court Improvement Committee, 1980-1981; Vice Chairman, Speakers Bureau Committee, 1979-1981; Trustee, 1986-1987, 1988; Distinguished Judge Committee, 1986; Judicial Evaluation Committee, 1988, 1992, 1996) and American (Member: Pretrial Release Committee, Criminal Justice Section, 1977-1978; Committee on CT Problems in High Publicity Cases, 1979-1981) Bar Associations; Eastern Bar Association of Los Angeles County (Treasurer, 1978; Secretary, 1979; Vice President, 1980; President, 1981-1982); State Bar of California (Member, Criminal Law and Procedure Committee, 1973-1976); American Inns of Court (1994-1996, Executive Committee 1994-1995). **REPORTED CASES:** Southwest Concrete Products v. Gosh Construction Corp., 51 Cal.3d 701 (1990); American International Group, Inc. v. Superior Court, 234 Cal.App.3d 749 (1991); Horeczko v. State Board of Registration, 232 Cal.App.3d 1352 (1991); Sutake v. Orange County Federal Credit Union, 186 Cal.App.3d 140 (1986); Deckert v. County of Riverdale, 115 Cal.App.3d 85 (1981); Span Inc. v. Associated International Insurance Co., 227 Cal.App.3d 463 (1991); Martinez-Ferrer v. Richardson Merrell, Inc., 105 Cal.App.3d 316 (1980); Cornish v. Superior Court, 209 Cal.App.3d (1989); Milo Equipment Corp. v. Elsinore Valley Municipal Water District, 205 Cal.App.3d 1282 (1988). **PRACTICE AREAS:** Civil Litigation; Per-

*(This Listing Continued)*

**JONES, MAHONEY, BRAYTON & SOLL**, Claremont—
*Continued*

sonal Injury Law; Government Contract Construction Litigation; Bad Faith Law; Medical Malpractice; Employment Law; Surety Law; Commercial Law; Appellate Practice.

**RICHARD A. SOLL,** born Los Angeles, California, July 25, 1949; admitted to bar, 1975, California. *Education:* University of California at Los Angeles (A.B., 1971; J.D., 1975). Phi Beta Kappa; Pi Gamma Mu. Staff Member, University of California at Los Angeles Law Review, 1974-1975. Judge Pro Tem, Los Angeles Municipal Court, 1982-1984. Judge, Vincent S. Dalsimer Moot Court Competition, 1983-1984. Guest Lecturer, Contract Disputes, Mechanics' Liens, Stop Notices and Bond Claims in the Construction Industry, California Polytechnic State University, Pomona, 1987-1995. *Member:* Los Angeles County Bar Association (Member, Real Estate Section); Eastern Bar Association of Los Angeles County; State Bar of California. **PRACTICE AREAS:** Civil Litigation; Construction Law; Corporate Law; Real Estate Litigation; Appellate Practice.

REFERENCE: Bank of American National Trust and Savings Assn; Cumis Insurance Society, Inc.; Safeco Insurance Company of America; General Insurance Company of America.

## JOHN C. McCARTHY

*401 HARVARD AVENUE*
**CLAREMONT, CALIFORNIA 91711**
Telephone: 909-621-4984
Telecopier: 909-621-5757

*Practice limited to Punitive Damage, Labor, Employment law including Wrongful Discharge, Discrimination, Insurance and Commercial Bad Faith Cases (Plaintiff Only).*

**JOHN C. McCARTHY,** born Chicago, Illinois, November 14, 1923; admitted to bar, 1953, California; 1964, U.S. Supreme Court. *Education:* Miami University, Oxford, Ohio; University of Southern California (B.S., 1947); University of California at Los Angeles (J.D., 1952). Author: "Recovery of Damages for Bad Faith," 1st Ed. 1976, 5th Ed. 1029pp., 1990, Lawpress; "Recovery of Damages for Wrongful Discharge Cases," 2nd Ed. 656 pp. 1990, Lawpress; Chapter, "A view of Plaintiff's Counsel," in "Critical Issues in Labor and Employment Law," Commerce Clearing House, 342 pp. 1990; "Punitive Damages' Chapter of 'California Torts' Treatise," Matthew Bender, 1986; Chapter, "How to Win an Insurance Bad Faith Case," *Masters of Trial Practice,* Wiley Law Pub., 1988. Director, Peace Corps, Thailand, 1963-1966. Selected Alumnus of The Year for 1973, UCLA Law School. "Trial Lawyer of the Year," California Employment Lawyers Association, 1989. Listed in The Best Lawyers in America (Employment, Insurance). Special Trial Counsel, City of Beverly Hills, 1974-1980. *Member:* The State Bar of California; American Board of Trial Advocates (Diplomate); Consumer Attorneys of California (Member, Board of Governors, 1970-1974; President, Inland Chapter, 1969-1970); The Association of Trial Lawyers of America (Vice-Chairman, 1971-1972; National Chairman, 1972-1974, Environmental Law Section). [LTJG, USNR, 1943-1946]. (Also Member, Morrisons, McCarthy & Moore, in Whitefish, Montana).

REFERENCE: Bank of America, Claremont Branch.

## MELANIE JULIAN MUCKLE

*146 WEST BUTLER COURT*
**CLAREMONT, CALIFORNIA 91711**
Telephone: 909-625-8432
Fax: 909-625-2771

*Environmental Law, Litigation.*

**MELANIE JULIAN MUCKLE,** born State College, Pennsylvania, 1959; admitted to bar, 1987, California; 1990, Minnesota; 1994, District of Columbia. *Education:* Stanford University (B.A., with distinction, 1982); University of Michigan (J.D., cum laude, 1986). Order of the Coif. Deputy Attorney General, State of California, 1987-1989.

## SHERNOFF, BIDART & DARRAS

A Partnership including Professional Corporations
*600 SOUTH INDIAN HILL BOULEVARD*
**CLAREMONT, CALIFORNIA 91711-5498**
Telephone: 909-621-4935
Fax: 909-625-6915

*Laguna Beach, California Office:* 130 Cleo Street. Phone: 714-494-6714. Fax: 714-497-0825.
*Palm Desert, California Office:* 73-111 El Paseo, Suite 208. Telephone: 619-568-9944.

*Practice Limited to Plaintiff's Insurance Bad Faith, Automobile Insurance, Fire Insurance, Commercial Liability Insurance, Homeowners Insurance, Accident and Health Insurance, Catastrophic Personal Injury, Wrongful Death, Wrongful Termination, Lender's Liability and Consumer Law Litigation.*

### MEMBERS OF FIRM

**WILLIAM M. SHERNOFF, (P.C.),** born Chicago, Illinois, October 26, 1937; admitted to bar, 1962, Wisconsin; 1966, California. *Education:* University of Miami (B.B.A., 1959); University of Wisconsin (J.D., 1962). Co-Author: Legal Treatise, "Insurance Bad Faith Litigation," published by Matthew Bender, 1984; "How to Make Insurance Companies Pay Your Claims and What to do if They Don't," Hastings House, 1990. Author: "Payment Refused," published by Richardson & Steirman, 1986. *Member:* State Bar of California; Los Angeles Trial Lawyers Association (Trial Lawyer of the Year, 1975); California Trial Lawyers Association (President, 1981); The Association of Trial Lawyers of America. (Also practicing individually at Newport Beach, California). **PRACTICE AREAS:** Insurance Bad Faith.

**MICHAEL J. BIDART, (P.C.),** born Chino, California, September 15, 1950; admitted to bar, 1974, California; 1980, U.S. District Court, Eastern, Central and Southern Districts of California; 1980, U.S. Supreme Court. *Education:* California State Polytechnic University (B.S., 1971); Pepperdine University (J.D., 1974). Phi Alpha Delta. Author: CTLA Article, "The Appropriate Use of Assignments in Insurance Bad Faith Actions: Do's and Don't's". Rutter Group Lecturer, Insurance Bad Faith, 1989. Lecturer/Panelist: CTLA Continuing Legal Education, Insurance Bad Faith, 1989; First Party Bad Faith Cases, Rutter Group, 1993. *Member:* Western San Bernardino County and San Bernardino County Bar Associations; State Bar of California; California Trial Lawyers Association; The Association of Trial Lawyers of America; Trial Lawyers for Public Justice; Los Angeles Trial Lawyers Association. **LANGUAGES:** Basque. **PRACTICE AREAS:** Insurance Bad Faith.

**FRANK N. DARRAS,** born Chicago, Illinois, April 15, 1954; admitted to bar, 1987, California; U.S. District Court, Eastern, Central, Northern and Southern Districts of California. *Education:* Oakton Community Junior College; Emory University (1977); Western State University (J.D., 1986). Certified Paramedic, Illinois, 1973. Trial Attorney Project, Hastings College of Advocacy, 1987. Lecturer/Panelist: "Discovery in Bad Faith Law Suit," ATLA National Convention, 1989; "A Discovery Checklist for Bad Faith Litigation," ATLA, National Convention, 1990; "Medical Life & Disability Fraud," ATLA Convention, 1991; "First Party Bad Faith Cases," Rutter Group, 1993. *Member:* Los Angeles County, San Bernardino County and American Bar Associations; State Bar of California; Los Angeles Trial Lawyers Association; California Trial Lawyers Association (Board Member, PAC Drive); The Association of Trial Lawyers of America (Member, Insurance Section Executive Board, 1991—); Trial Lawyers for Public Justice. **LANGUAGES:** Greek. **PRACTICE AREAS:** Insurance Bad Faith.

### ASSOCIATES

**SHARON J. ARKIN,** born Long Beach, California, August 14, 1952; admitted to bar, 1991, California; 1992, U.S. District Court, Central District of California and U.S. Court of Appeals, Ninth Circuit. *Education:* University of California at Riverside (B.S., 1974); Western State University School of Law (J.D., summa cum laude, 1991). Panelist/Lecturer: "First Party Bad Faith Cases," Rutter Group, 1993. *Member:* Los Angeles and American Bar Associations; California Trial Lawyers Association; Los Angeles Trial Lawyers Association; American Trial Lawyers Association. **PRACTICE AREAS:** Insurance Bad Faith.

**THERESA J. BARTA,** born Minneapolis, Minnesota, June 12, 1963; admitted to bar, 1990, California and U.S. District Court, Central District of California; 1991, U.S. District Court, Northern District of California; 1992, U.S. District Court, Southern and Eastern Districts of California.

*(This Listing Continued)*

*Education:* California State University (B.A., 1987); Loyola Law School (J.D., cum laude, 1990). Order of the Coif. *Member:* Los Angeles County and Orange County Bar Associations; State Bar of California. **PRACTICE AREAS:** Insurance Bad Faith.

**TIMOTHY P. DILLON,** born Buffalo, New York, June 4, 1956; admitted to bar, 1982, New York and U.S. District Court, Southern District of New York; 1986, California and U.S. District Court, Central District of California. *Education:* State University of New York at Albany (B.S., summa cum laude, 1978); College of William & Mary (J.D., 1981). Executive Editor for Professional Articles, William & Mary Law Review, 1980-1981. Author: "Title I of PURPA: The Effect of Federal Intrusion into Regulation of Public Utilities," 21 William & Mary Law Review 491, 1979. Panelist/Lecturer: "First Party Bad Faith Cases," Rutter Group, 1993. **PRACTICE AREAS:** Insurance Bad Faith.

**RICARDO ECHEVERRIA,** born Chino, California, March 29, 1968; admitted to bar, 1993, California and U.S. District Court, Central and Northern Districts of California. *Education:* California Polytechnic State University (B.S., magna cum laude, 1990); Santa Clara University (J.D., 1993). Phi Alpha Delta. *Member:* State Bar of California. **LANGUAGES:** Basque. **PRACTICE AREAS:** Insurance Bad Faith.

**REBECCA G. RUGGERO,** born Davenport, Iowa, March 30, 1964; admitted to bar, 1993, California and U.S. District Court, Central District of California. *Education:* University of Iowa (B.A., 1987); University of LaVerne (J.D., 1993). *Member:* State Bar of California; Los Angeles Trial Lawyers Association. **PRACTICE AREAS:** Insurance Bad Faith.

**EVANGELINE L. FISHER,** born Pasadena, California, May 3, 1967; admitted to bar, 1995, California. *Education:* Occidental College (B.A., honors in History, 1989); Santa Clara University (J.D., 1994). *Member:* Los Angeles County Bar Association; State Bar of California; Consumer Attorneys Association of Los Angeles. **PRACTICE AREAS:** Insurance Bad Faith.

**MARK E. BENSON,** born Santa Monica, California, March 23, 1952; admitted to bar, 1986, California and U.S. District Court, Central District of California. *Education:* Pierce College (A.A., 1977); California State University at Northridge (B.A., with honors, 1979); Loyola University of Los Angeles (J.D., with honors, 1984). Settlement Officer and Arbitrator of the Los Angeles Superior Court. *Member:* Los Angeles County Bar Association; State Bar of California. **PRACTICE AREAS:** Insurance Bad Faith; Insurance Coverage; Appellate Practice.

---

## JOHN W. TULAC

*Established in 1981*

**401 HARVARD AVENUE
CLAREMONT, CALIFORNIA 91711**

Telephone: 909-445-1100
Fax: 909-445-1104
Email: jwtulac@ix.netcom.com

*International Business Law, International Trade Law, General Business and Corporate Law, Foreign Investment in the United States, International Arbitration, Mediation and Litigation, Business Litigation. Professional Mediator and Arbitrator.*

FIRM PROFILE: *John W. Tulac established his firm in 1981. The Firm's practice evolved from almost exclusively litigation to international business transactions (import, export, licensing, distribution, joint ventures, direct investment) and general corporate practice. Mr Tulac's philosophy of practice is based on concepts of proactive and preventive law.*

**JOHN W. TULAC,** born Los Angeles, California, August 9, 1952; admitted to bar, 1977, California. *Education:* California State Polytechnic University, Pomona (B.S., with honors, 1974); Loyola University (J.D., 1977). Phi Kappa Phi (President, Cal Poly Chapter, 1978-1979). Staff Member, Loyola University Law Review, 1976-1977. Lecturer: International Business Transactions, Entrepreneurial Law, Contract Law and Corporate Law, California State Polytechnic University, Pomona, 1979—; California State University, Fullerton, Business Law, 1981; America College of Law, Legal Writing, 1992; Small Business Certificate Program, Chaffey College, 1992—. Adjunct Professor, International Business Transactions and Corporations, University of La Verne Law School, 1996—. Dean, Irvine University College of Law, 1992-1995. Judge Pro Tem, Los Angeles Municipal Court, 1984—; Los Angeles Superior Court, 1989—. Volunteer Settlement Officer and Mediator, 1995—. Arbitrator, Orange County Bar Association Attorney-Client Fee Dispute Panel, 1984—; Los Angeles County Panel, 1995—. *Member:* Orange County (Delegate to State Bar Convention, 1985,

*(This Listing Continued)*

---

1990), Los Angeles County (Member, International Law Section, Executive Committee, 1996-1997) and American (Member, Small Business Committee, 1989-1990) Bar Associations; State Bar of California; California Venture Forum.

REPRESENTATIVE CLIENTS: Miralite Communications, Inc., Freight Train Trucking, Inc.; International Structural Engineers, Inc.; Cal-Chem Corp.; R.F. Electronics Corp.; Cal Poly Pomona Alumni Assn.; Pacific Infotech Corporation; Trans Pacific Information Systems Corporation; Don Bosco Technical Institute; St. Mary's Syrian Orthodox Church; Darach International; Ergo Sum, Inc.; St George Energy Corporation; World-Wide Freight Corp.; 10-4 Transport, Inc.; Dick Huizenga Trucking, Inc.; Netel Educational Systems; Commercial Carriers Insurance Agency; Dytronic, Inc.; Emblematics, Inc.; Safe-to-Smile; Union Investment Interactions.
REFERENCES: Marine National Bank, Irvine, California; Vineyard National Bank, Diamond Bar, California.

---

## RONALD T. VERA

**FOOTHILL INDEPENDENT BANK BUILDING
223 WEST FOOTHILL BOULEVARD, 2ND FLOOR
CLAREMONT, CALIFORNIA 91711**

Telephone: 909-624-2941
Fax: 909-398-1000

*General Civil Trial Practice in all State and Federal Courts. Public Agency, Education, Environmental Law and Municipal Law.*

**RONALD T. VERA,** born Pomona, California, October 16, 1946; admitted to bar, 1974, California. *Education:* Michigan State University (B.S., 1970); University of California at Los Angeles (J.D., 1973). Author: "The Legal Obligation to Secure Access for Minority Students in Higher Education," Key Issues in Minority Education, (Wanda E. Ward and Mary M. Cross, Eds.), University of Oklahoma, 1989; "Protecting Access in Higher Education: Minimizing Unfairness Through Legislative Protection," Measures in the College Admission Process, New York, The College Board, 1986; "The Politics of Inequality," Journal of Higher Education, Vol. 58, No. 3, 1987. Visiting Professor of Law, 1992-1993 and Adjunct Professor of Law, 1993—, Loyola Law School (Los Angeles). Deputy Director, California Rural Legal Assistance, San Francisco, California, 1977-1979. Staff Counsel, Mexican American Legal Defense and Educational Fund, 1979-1985. Senior Resident Scholar, Tomas Rivera Center for Policy Studies, The Claremont Graduate School, 1985-1995. Judge Pro-Tem, Bay Municipal Court District, Contra Costa County, California, 1985-1986. Vice-Chair, Contra Costa County Personnel Merit Review Board, 1985-1987. Member, Board of Directors, Pomona Valley Hospital Medical Center, 1992—. *Member:* Los Angeles County (Member, Committee on Professional Responsibility and Ethics, 1989-1992) and American (Member, Committee on Rights of Children, 1990-1993) Bar Associations; The State Bar of California (Member, Commission to Evaluate Judicial Nominees, 1979-1980; Vice-Chair and Member, Client Security Fund Commission, 1993—). **PRACTICE AREAS:** Municipal Law; Education Law; Environmental Law; Litigation.

---

## WILKINSON & WILKINSON

**341 WEST FIRST STREET
CLAREMONT, CALIFORNIA 91711**

Telephone: 909-482-1555
Fax: 909-482-1557

*Estate Planning, Trusts, Probate and Elder Care Law.*

**PATRICIA JO WILKINSON,** born Monterey Park, California, July 29, 1940; admitted to bar, 1974, California. *Education:* University of California at Los Angeles (A.B., 1970); Loyola University of Los Angeles (J.D., 1973). Author: "The Use of the IRA's in QTIP and Bypass Trust Planning," NAELA News, March 1995. Assistant U.S. Attorney, Central District of California, 1974-1980. Partner, Rubin, Eagan and Feder, 1980-1985. Talk Show Hostess, "Estate Planning Made Easy," KIEV Radio, 1993—. *Member:* Los Angeles County Bar Association; State Bar of California; National Academy of Elder Law Attorneys. (Certified Specialist, Elder Care Law, National Academy of Elder Law Attorneys).

**CONRAD M. WILKINSON,** born Burbank, California, August 10, 1937; admitted to bar, 1977, California. *Education:* University of California at Los Angeles (B.A., 1960); The American Graduate School of International Management (B.F.T., 1962); Mid Valley College of Law (J.D., 1976); Golden Gate University (M.S., Taxation, 1981). Recipient, American Jurisprudence Award. Administrative Coordinator, Justice System Advisory Group, Los Angeles County, California. Certified Business Arbitrator,

*(This Listing Continued)*

**WILKINSON & WILKINSON, Claremont—Continued**

American Arbitration Association. *Member:* Los Angeles County Bar Association; State Bar of California; Panel Member, National Association of Elder Law Attorneys. (Certified Specialist, Estate Planning, Trust and Probate Law, The State Bar of California Board of Legal Specialization).

## ZETTERBERG & KING

*Established in 1963*

**319 HARVARD AVENUE**
**CLAREMONT, CALIFORNIA 91711**
Telephone: 909-621-2971
Fax: 909-625-5781

*Quincy, California Office:* P.O. Box 3926. Telephone: 916-283-0325. Fax: 916-283-5205.

*General Civil and Trial Practice in all State and Federal Courts. Wills, Probate, Trusts and Estate Planning Law, Civil Litigation.*

**STEPHEN I. ZETTERBERG,** born Galesburg, Illinois, August 2, 1916; admitted to bar, 1942, Indiana; 1946, U.S. Supreme Court; 1947, California. *Education:* Pomona College (A.B., with honors, 1938); Yale Law School (LL.B., 1942). Member, National Institute of Public Affairs, Washington, D.C., 1938-1939. Mediation Officer, National War Labor Board, 1942. Legislative Assistant, U.S. Senate, 1946. Member, California State Board of Public Health, 1958-1967. Member, Board of Directors, Trial Lawyers for Public Justice Foundation, 1987—. *Member:* Los Angeles County and American Bar Associations; State Bar of California; Consumer Attorneys of California (Member, Amicus Curiae Committee, 1973-1985); The Association of Trial Lawyers of America. [Lieut., U.S. Coast Guard Reserve, 1942-1945]. **PRACTICE AREAS:** Trusts; Wills; Estate Planning; Civil Litigation.

**ALICE M. KING** (Quincy, California Office).

## BOLEN, FRANSEN & BOOSTROM LLP

**414 POLLASKY AVENUE**
**CLOVIS, CALIFORNIA 93612**
Telephone: 209-226-8177
Fax: 209-322-6778

*Fresno, California Office:* Suite 430, East Tower, Guarantee Financial Center, 1322 East Shaw Avenue. Telephone: 209-266-8177. Fax: 209-227-4971.

*General Business, Banking, Creditor's Rights, Corporate, Real Estate and Taxation Law, Agricultural and Water Rights Law, Estate Planning and Probate Law.*

(For Complete Biographical data on all personnel, see Professional Biographies at Fresno)

## KATZOFF & RIGGS

*Established in 1991*

**MEADOW SPRINGS SHOPPING CENTER**
**P.O. BOX 1250**
**COBB, CALIFORNIA 95426**
Telephone: 707-928-4600
Fax: 707-928-5075

*Berkeley California Office:* 3088 Claremont Avenue. Telephone: 510-597-1990. Fax: 510-597-0295.

*Civil and Criminal Trial Practice, Juvenile Dependency and Appeals. Real Estate and Real Estate Transactions, Construction, Insurance Defense and Insurance Coverage Law, Computer Software Licensing Law.*

(For Complete Biographical data on all Personnel, see Professional Biographies at Berkley, California)

## TEDD A. MEHR

**249 5TH STREET**
**P.O. BOX 1286**
**COLUSA, CALIFORNIA 95932**
Telephone: 916-458-5481
Fax: 916-458-5482

*General Civil and Trial Practice in all Courts. Business, Real Property, Governmental Law, Criminal Law and Family Law.*

**TEDD A. MEHR,** born New Brunswick, New Jersey, September 2, 1960; admitted to bar, 1988, California; 1989, U.S. District Court, Central District of California; 1994, U.S. District Court, Eastern District of California. *Education:* California State University at Chico (B.S., 1982); Western State University College of Law (J.D., 1988). Contract City Attorney, City of Colusa, 1995—. *Member:* Colusa County Bar Association; State Bar of California. **PRACTICE AREAS:** General Civil and Criminal Litigation; Business; Real Property; Governmental Law; Family Law.

## RICH, FUIDGE, MORRIS & IVERSON, INC.

**COLUSA, CALIFORNIA**

(See Marysville)

*General Civil and Trial Practice. Corporation, Water Rights, Insurance, Real Estate, Crop Damage, Estate Planning, Family and Probate Law. Medical and Legal Malpractice, Personal Injury, Employment Law, Criminal Law, Alternative Dispute Resolution.*

## ANDERSEN & BONNIFIELD

**1355 WILLOW WAY, SUITE 255**
**P.O. BOX 5926**
**CONCORD, CALIFORNIA 94520**
Telephone: 510-602-1400
Fax: 510-825-0143
Email: AandB@AandB.com

*General Civil and Trial Practice in State and Federal Courts. Construction, Financial Institutions, Commercial, Negligence, Real Estate, Corporation, Toxic Torts and Insurance Defense.*

### MEMBERS OF FIRM

**CRAIG F. ANDERSEN,** born San Francisco, California, March 24, 1949; admitted to bar, 1974, California. *Education:* University of Washington (B.A., 1971); McGeorge College of the Law, University of the Pacific (J.D., 1974). General Engineering License, California, 1988. Temporary Court Commissioner, Contra Costa County, California. Arbitrator, American Arbitration Association. *Member:* Contra Costa County and American Bar Associations; State Bar of California; Associated General Contractors. **PRACTICE AREAS:** Construction Law; Land Use.

**ROBERT M. BONNIFIELD,** born Vallejo, California, June 25, 1947; admitted to bar, 1974, California. *Education:* California State University, San Jose (B.S., 1969); University of the Pacific, McGeorge College of the Law (J.D., 1974). *Member:* Contra Costa County Bar Association; State Bar of California. **PRACTICE AREAS:** Toxic Tort; Construction Defense.

### ASSOCIATES

**MADELINE L. BUTY,** born Oakland, California, July 23, 1967; admitted to bar, 1991, California and U.S. District Court, Northern District of California. *Education:* University of California, Berkeley; California State University (B.A., 1988); Santa Clara University (J.D., 1991). *Member:* Contra Costa County and American Bar Associations; State Bar of California. **PRACTICE AREAS:** Toxic Tort Litigation; Products Liability Defense; Construction Litigation Defense.

**SEAN A. COTTLE,** born Wichita Falls, Texas, January 2, 1964; admitted to bar, 1990, California, U.S. District Court, Northern, Eastern, Central and Southern Districts of California and U.S. Court of Appeals, Ninth Circuit. *Education:* Kenyon College (B.A., 1986); Tulane University of Louisiana (J.D., 1989). Omicron Delta Kappa. *Member:* Bar Association of San Francisco (Chair, Barristers' Litigation Committee, 1993); State Bar of California; American Bar Association (Member, Sections on: Torts and Insurance Practice and Litigation Sections). **PRACTICE AREAS:** Construction Law; Tort Litigation Defense.

**J. KEIKO KOBAYASHI,** born Concord, California, February 14, 1967; admitted to bar, 1995, California; U.S. Court of Appeals, Ninth Circuit.

*(This Listing Continued)*

## PROFESSIONAL BIOGRAPHIES

*Education:* University of California, Davis (B.A., 1989); Whittier Law School (J.D., 1995). *Member:* State Bar of California. **PRACTICE AREAS:** Tort Litigation Defense.

**KENNETH H. LEE,** born Reno, Nevada, July 1, 1966; admitted to bar, 1994, California, U.S. District Court, Northern District of California and U.S. Court of Appeals, Ninth Circuit; 1995, Minnesota, Colorado and District of Columbia. *Education:* University of California, Davis (B.A., 1988); Syracuse University (J.D., 1993). Omicron Delta Epsilon. Recipient, O.S.-C.A. (Outstanding College Students of America), 1989. Legislative Research Bureau Editor, Syracuse Law Journal, 1992-1993. *Member:* Contra Costa County and American Bar Associations; State Bar of California. **PRACTICE AREAS:** Insurance Defense; Construction Law.

REPRESENTATIVE CLIENTS: Aspen Construction; Bank of Pleasanton; Budget Rent-A-Car; City of Brentwood; City of Concord; Concord Commercial Bank; Corey-Delta Construction; Costco Wholesale; Doric Construction; Golf Resources, Inc.; Petro Power Construction; Reynolds and Brown; Trans-Pacific Golf, Inc.; Marriott Hotels; Wood Valley Development.
REPRESENTATIVE INSURANCE CLIENTS: Available Upon Request.
REFERENCES: Concord Commercial Bank, Concord, California.

---

### WILLIAM B. BOBETSKY
2204 CONCORD BOULEVARD
**CONCORD, CALIFORNIA 94520**
*Telephone: 510-685-2440*

*Family Law.*

**WILLIAM B. BOBETSKY,** born Rego Park, New York, October 23, 1952; admitted to bar, 1978, California. *Education:* State University College of New York at Brockport (B.S., 1973); Western State University (J.D., 1977). Member, Western State University Law Review, 1977. *Member:* Contra Costa County Bar Association; The State Bar of California; Alameda-Contra Costa Trial Lawyers Association. **PRACTICE AREAS:** Family Law; Personal Injury Law; Probate Law; Wills.

---

### CAUDLE, WELCH, POLITEO & BOVÉE, LLP
1390 WILLOW PASS ROAD, SUITE 200
**CONCORD, CALIFORNIA 94520**
*Telephone: 510-688-8800*
*Fax: 510-688-8801*
*Email: CWPB@aol.comm*

Oakland, California Office: 383 Fourth Street, Suite 201. Telephone: 510-433-9300. Fax: 510-433-9301.

*Automobile/Bodily Injury, Construction Defect Litigation, Discrimination Defense, General Business Litigation, Governmental Entity Defense, Insurance Bad Faith Defense, Appellate Work, Mediations, Arbitrations, Homeowners Liability, Landlord/Tenant, Insurance Coverage, Premises Liability, Products Liability, Professional Malpractice Defense, Toxic Substances Litigation, Wrongful Termination and Legal Opinions.*

FIRM PROFILE: *The firm was created from a core group of partners including the senior partner, John P. Caudle, who worked together for many years at the law offices of Kincaid, Gianunzio, Caudle & Hubert. Caudle, Welch, Politeo & Bovee has attorneys with broad areas of expertise and experience. The four named partners have over 73 years experience in handling insurance defense. The firm engages primarily in insurance defense, coverage and damage litigation. With offices centrally located in Oakland and Concord, the firm handles cases primarily in the nine Bay Area Counties of Alameda, Contra Costa, Solano, Napa, Sonoma, Marin, San Francisco, San Mateo and Santa Clara. Members of the firm reside in several different counties and consequently have easy access to all courts. Upon special request of clients, the firm will handle cases throughout Northern California and elsewhere.*

**JOHN P. CAUDLE,** born Richmond, California, March 22, 1943; admitted to bar, 1969, California. *Education:* University of California at Berkeley (A.B., 1965); Boalt Hall School of Law, University of California (J.D., 1968). Phi Alpha Delta. Lawyers Club of Almeda County Lawyer of the Year, 1991. Arbitrator: Contra Costa County and Alameda County. Board of Trustees, Contra Costa Legal Services Foundation. Judge Pro-Tem, Contra Costa County. *Member:* Alameda County, Contra Costa County and American Bar Associations; The State Bar of California; Association of Defense Counsel - Northern California; Defense Research and Trial Lawyers Association; American Board of Trial Advocates; Defense Research Institute; Federal Court Trial Lawyers Association. [With U.S. Air Force, 1961-1968]. **PRACTICE AREAS:** Insurance Defense; Defense

*(This Listing Continued)*

---

Litigation; Medical Malpractice Defense; Products Liability; Insurance Bad Faith; Insurance Coverage.

**MICHAEL R. WELCH,** born Berkeley, California, January 9, 1954; admitted to bar, 1980, California. *Education:* University of California at Berkeley (B.A., 1976); Pepperdine University (J.D., 1979). Arbitrator, Contra Costa County. *Member:* Contra Costa County and Alameda County Bar Associations; The State Bar of California; Association of Defense Counsel - Northern California. **PRACTICE AREAS:** Insurance Defense; Defense Litigation; Products Liability.

**DEANNE B. POLITEO,** born Vallejo, California, February 11, 1958; admitted to bar, 1984, California. *Education:* University of California at Berkeley (B.A., 1980); Hastings College of Law, University of California (J.D., 1984). *Member:* Alameda County Bar Association; The State Bar of California; Association of Defense Counsel - Northern California. **PRACTICE AREAS:** Insurance Defense; Defense Litigation; Environmental Law; Toxic Substances; Construction Defects.

**SCOTT A. BOVÉE,** born Hollywood, California, November 13, 1955; admitted to bar, 1986, Virginia; 1987, U.S. District Court, Eastern District of Virginia; 1988, California. *Education:* University of California at Berkeley (B.A., in History, 1979); Willamette University (J.D., 1984). Member, Jessup International Moot Court Team Competition. *Member:* State Bar of California; Virginia State Bar; American Bar Association; Virginia State Bar; Legal Aid Society. **PRACTICE AREAS:** Insurance Defense; Defense Litigation; Environmental Law; Hazardous Waste; Toxic Substances; Insurance Coverage; Insurance Bad Faith; Construction Law; Construction Defects.

---

### COKE & COKE
Established in 1977
1485 ENEA COURT, SUITE G-1450
**CONCORD, CALIFORNIA 94520**
*Telephone: 510-825-4600*
*Fax: 510-688-0325*

*Personal Injury.*

**MICHAEL E. COKE,** born London, England, March 2, 1938; admitted to bar, 1969, California. *Education:* University of Toronto (B.A., 1959); Golden Gate University (J.D., 1968). *Member:* Contra Costa County; Bar Association; Alameda Contra Costa Bar Association; State Bar of California; The Association of Trial Lawyers of America; California Trial Lawyers Association. **PRACTICE AREAS:** Personal Injury.

**LAUREL D. COKE,** born Kansas City, Missouri, August 20, 1939; admitted to bar, 1976, California. *Education:* College of William & Mary (B.A., 1961); Golden Gate University (J.D., 1976). *Member:* State Bar of California. **PRACTICE AREAS:** Personal Injury.

---

### LAW OFFICE OF DONALD J. LIDDLE
1985 BONIFACIO STREET, SUITE 102
**CONCORD, CALIFORNIA 94520**
*Telephone: 510-685-9000*
*Fax: 510-685-6722*

*Family Law.*

**DONALD J. LIDDLE,** born Detroit, Michigan, February 17, 1937; admitted to bar, 1973, Utah and U.S. District Court, District of Utah; 1975, California and U.S. District Court, Northern District of California. *Education:* Trinity University (B.S., 1960); University of San Diego; University of Utah (J.D., 1972). Editor, Bancroft Whitney, 1974-1975. Deputy District Attorney, Contra Costa County, 1975-1979. *Member:* Contra Costa County Bar Association (Board Member, Family Law Section) Utah State Bar; The State Bar of California (Member, Sections on: Family Law; Wills, Probate and Estate Planning). [Capt., U.S. Navy; U.S. Naval Reserve, Retired, 1960-1990]. (Certified Specialist, Family Law, The State Bar of California Board of Legal Specialization). **PRACTICE AREAS:** Family Law; Probate.

## MICHAEL McCABE
903 RIDGE DRIVE
**CONCORD, CALIFORNIA 94518**
Telephone: 510-687-3450
Fax: 510-687-3450
Email: mccabe@tpi.net

*San Francisco, California Office:* 50 California Street, Suite 1500. Telephone: 415-392-3450.

Mediation.

**MICHAEL McCABE,** born Eureka, California, July 12, 1939; admitted to bar, 1964, California. *Education:* University of San Francisco (A.B., 1961; J.D., 1963). Member, McAuliffe Honor Society (President, 1962-1963). Graduate, Theological Union, Berkeley (C.T.S., 1994). Deputy District Attorney, Alameda County, 1964-1965. Instructor of Law, John F. Kennedy University, 1969-1971. Lecturer: Medi/Legal Institute, 1988; "Advanced Evidence Seminar," Hastings College of the Law, 1991. Superior Court Judge Pro-Tem, Contra Costa County. California Department of Insurance Earthquake Damage Mediator. *Member:* San Francisco; Alameda County Contra Costa County and American Bar Associations; American Arbitration Association; Society of Professionals in Dispute Resolution. **PRACTICE AREAS:** Mediator.

## CLAYSON, MANN & YAEGER
A PROFESSIONAL LAW CORPORATION
Established in 1910
CLAYSON LAW BUILDING
601 SOUTH MAIN STREET
P.O. BOX 1447
**CORONA, CALIFORNIA 91718-1447**
Telephone: 909-737-1910
Riverside: 909-689-7241
Fax: 909-737-4384

*General Civil and Trial Practice. Appellate Practice. Probate, Estate Planning, Taxation, Corporation, Real Estate, Employment, Municipal and Water Law, Family Law.*

*FIRM PROFILE: Clayson, Mann & Yaeger was founded in 1910 and is the principal firm in the Corona-Norco area. The firm has a general, business and civil practice and offers a wide range of legal services in business formation and transactions, litigation, real property, estate planning, probate and family law.*

**WALTER S. CLAYSON** (1887-1972).

**E. SPURGEON ROTHROCK** (1918-1979).

**ROY H. MANN,** born Illinois, March 31, 1923; admitted to bar, 1951, California; 1962, U.S. Supreme Court. *Education:* California Institute of Technology and University of California at Los Angeles (A.B., 1948); University of Southern California (J.D., 1951). Delta Theta Phi; Order of Coif. Student Editor In-Chief, Southern California Law Review, 1951. *Member:* Riverside County and American Bar Associations; The State Bar of California. **PRACTICE AREAS:** Business Transactions; Water Rights.

**DERRILL E. YAEGER,** born Lincoln, Nebraska, April 2, 1927; admitted to bar, 1964, California; 1969, U.S. Supreme Court. *Education:* La Sierra College (B.A., 1950); University of Southern California (J.D., 1963). *Member:* Riverside County Bar Association; The State Bar of California. **PRACTICE AREAS:** Real Property Development Law; Land Use Law.

**GARY K. ROSENZWEIG,** born Brooklyn, New York, April 11, 1951; admitted to bar, 1977, California; 1978, U.S. District Court, Central District of California; 1990, New Jersey, Pennsylvania, U.S. District Court, District of New Jersey and Pennsylvania; 1991, New York. *Education:* University of Virginia (B.A., with distinction, 1973); University of Colorado (J.D., 1976). Phi Beta Kappa. Member, National Moot Court, Regionals, 10th Circuit. *Member:* Riverside County Bar Association (Member, Probate, Trust, Estate Planning and Taxation Section; Chairman, 1985-1986; Member, Taxation Section; Riverside Estate Planning Council); The State Bar of California (Member, Estate Planning, Trust and Probate Section). (Certified Specialist, Estate Planning, Trust and Probate Law, The State Bar of California Board of Legal Specialization). **PRACTICE AREAS:** Probate Law; Trust Administration Law; Estate Planning Law.

**ELISABETH SICHEL,** born Clifton Springs, New York, January 16, 1954; admitted to bar, 1979, California and U.S. District Court, Central District of California; 1981, U.S. Court of Appeals, Ninth Circuit; 1983, *(This Listing Continued)*

U.S. District Court, Southern District of California. *Education:* University of Edinburgh, Scotland and University of California at Riverside (B.A., with high honors, 1976); University of California at Los Angeles (J.D., 1979). Phi Beta Kappa. *Member:* Riverside County Bar Association (Member, Family Law Section); The State Bar of California. (Certified Specialist, Family Law, The State Bar of California, Board of Legal Specialization). **PRACTICE AREAS:** Family Law.

**KENT A. HANSEN,** born Watsonville, California, September 2, 1953; admitted to bar, 1979, California; 1981, U.S. District Court, Central District of California; 1983, U.S. Court of Appeals, Ninth Circuit. *Education:* Loma Linda University (B.A., with honors, 1975); Willamette University (J.D., 1979). Casenote Editor, Willamette Law Review, 1978-1979. Assistant Professor of Political Science, Loma Linda University, 1981—. Member, Board of Directors, Riverside Community College Foundation, 1987-1992. *Member:* Riverside County and American (Member, Sections on: Business, Labor Law and Employment Law) Bar Associations; The State Bar of California; National Association of College and University Attorneys; California Society of Health Care Attorneys; American Academy of Hospital Attorneys. **PRACTICE AREAS:** Employment Law; Corporate Law; Business Law.

**ROLAND C. BAINER,** born Glendale, California, September 13, 1945; admitted to bar, 1974, California and U.S. District Court, Central District of California. *Education:* Loma Linda University (B.A., 1967); Andrews University (B.D., cum laude, 1969); California Western School of Law (J.D., 1974). Phi Alpha Delta. Lead Articles Editor, California Western Law Review, 1973-1974. Author: "Nestle v. City of Santa Monica: An Inadequate Remedy For Aircraft Noise," California Western Law Review, 1973. *Member:* Riverside County and American (Member, Section of Litigation) Bar Associations; The State Bar of California; Riverside Barristers Association (President, 1977-1978); American Inns of Court; The Association of Trial Lawyers of America; California Trial Lawyers Association. **PRACTICE AREAS:** Civil Trial Practice; Personal Injury Law; Business Litigation.

**DAVID R. SAUNDERS,** born Bellflower, California, December 29, 1955; admitted to bar, 1983, California; 1984, U.S. District Court, Southern and Central Districts of California. *Education:* University of Redlands (B.A., with distinction, 1980); University of Santa Clara (J.D., 1983). Phi Beta Kappa. Member, Order of Barristers. Chairman, University of Santa Clara Honors Moot Court Board, 1982-1983. *Member:* Riverside County and American Bar Associations; The State Bar of California. **PRACTICE AREAS:** Real Property Development Law; Land Use Law; Administrative Law.

**SALLIE BARNETT,** born Tachikawa Air Force Base, Japan, November 14, 1959; admitted to bar, 1985, California. *Education:* Southern Illinois University (B.S., 1982; J.D., magna cum laude, 1985). Phi Kappa Phi; Alpha Lambda Delta; Alpha Epsilon Rho. *Member:* Riverside County, Los Angeles County and American Bar Associations; State Bar of California; The Association of Trial Lawyers of America; Association of Business Trial Lawyers. **PRACTICE AREAS:** Corporate Law; Business Law; Civil Litigation.

---

**SCOTT CARLETON BRENNER,** born Anaheim, California, September 3, 1961; admitted to bar, 1993, California. *Education:* Liberty Baptist College (B.S., 1984); Whittier College School of Law (J.D., cum laude, 1992). Editor in Chief, Whittier Law Review 1991-1992. Member, Moot Court Honors Board, 1990-1992. Author: "Judicial Taxation as a Means of Remedying Public School Segregation Under Missouri v. Jenkins: Bolding Going Where No Federal Court Has Gone Before," 12 Whittier Law Review 551, 1991. *Member:* State Bar of California.

COUNSEL FOR: Adventist Health Systems/Loma Linda Risk Management; Loma Linda University; Palo Verde Irrigation District; Citizens Business Bank; D.B.S. Management, Inc.; Riverside Community College District Development Corp.; Fleetwood Aluminum, Inc.; House of Imports, Inc. (Mercedes Benz); Price Mfg.; Gencon Plastics, Inc; Sierra Aluminum; Lee Lake Municipal Water District; Kawasaki of Riverside; Hemet Community Medical Group; La Sierra University; Columbia Union College; Anatomic Concepts, Inc.; American National Manufacturing, Inc.; Ditch Witch of Southern California; KEC Engineering, Inc.
LOCAL COUNSEL FOR: Minnesota Mining & Mfg. Co.; Silvercrest Industries, Inc.; Western Waste Industries; Innoserv Technologies, Inc.; MMI Medical, Inc.
REFERENCE: Citizens Business Bank (Corona, Calif. and Riverside, Calif. Main Offices).

## GERALD M. SHAW
*A PROFESSIONAL CORPORATION*
1111 BAYSIDE DRIVE, SUITE 270
**CORONA DEL MAR, CALIFORNIA 92625**
Telephone: 714-759-5600
Telefax: 714-759-5656

*General Civil Litigation in all State and Federal Courts, Insurance Law, General Tort Litigation, Personal Injury.*

**GERALD M. SHAW,** born Los Angeles, California, April 16, 1948; admitted to bar, 1974, California and U.S. District Court, Central and Southern Districts of California; 1976, U.S. Tax Court. *Education:* University of Southern California (B.S., 1970); University of San Diego and University of Southern California (J.D., 1973). President and Trustee, Orange County Board of Education, 1978-1982. Judge Pro Tem, Orange County Superior Court, 1987 and 1989, 1990. Panelist, "Basic Training - Civil Procedure Before Trials," The Rutter Group, 1983-1995. Lecturer, "Preparing a Case for Trial - The Last 100 Days," 1984 and "Law and Motion Workshop," State Bar of California Continuing Education of Bar, 1988, 1990. *Member:* Orange County and American Bar Associations; State Bar of California; California Trial Lawyers Association.

REPRESENTATIVE CLIENTS: Western Financial Savings Bank; The Hammond Co.; Centurion Capital Group; Meghraj & Sons Bank; State Farm Insurance Co.; McMahon Oliphant Development.
REFERENCES: Marine National Bank, Irvine; Western Financial Savings Bank, Orange.

## SHARON LYNN SHERMAN
*A PROFESSIONAL CORPORATION*
*Established in 1980*
1109 EIGHTH STREET
**CORONADO, CALIFORNIA 92118-2217**
Telephone: 619-435-2282
Fax: 619-435-6417

*General Civil Practice. Business Law, Probate, Estate Planning and Family Law.*

**SHARON LYNN SHERMAN,** born Annapolis, Maryland, October 7, 1951; admitted to bar, 1977, California; 1981, U.S. Tax Court and U.S. District Court, Southern District of California; 1987, U.S. Supreme Court; 1992, U.S. Court of Appeals, Ninth Circuit. *Education:* University of California at Santa Barbara (B.A., 1973); University of San Diego (J.D., 1977). Founder and Director, 1975-1976 and Member, Board of Directors, 1975-1987, Women's Legal Center of San Diego. Delegate, U.S./China Joint Economic Summit, Beijing, 1987. Delegate, U.S./Soviet Union Joint Exchange on Trade, Moscow, 1991. *Member:* San Diego County Bar Association; State Bar of California (Referee, State Bar Court, 1985-1987).

REPRESENTATIVE CLIENTS: Cal Coast Mortgage Corp.; Vannox Diversified Entertainment, Incorporated; Euro American Pictures Inc.; EDP; Ausatech.
REFERENCE: Bank of Coronado.

## F. CONGER FAWCETT
240 TAMAL VISTA BOULEVARD, SUITE 163
**CORTE MADERA, CALIFORNIA 94925**
Telephone: 415-945-0995
Facsimile: 415-945-0996

*General Practice, with emphasis on Corporate, Business and Securities, Alcoholic Beverage and Maritime Regulatory Law.*

**F. CONGER FAWCETT,** born Newton, Massachusetts, 1934; admitted to bar, 1963, California; 1966, U.S. Supreme Court, U.S. Court of Appeals; Ninth Circuit and District of Columbia Circuit. *Education:* Harvard University (A.B., cum laude, 1956; LL.B., 1962). Co-Author: "U.S. Ocean Shipping: The History, Development & Decline of the Conference Antitrust Exemption," 1 Northwestern Journal of International Law and Business, 1979. *Member:* Bar Association of San Francisco; Marin County and American (Member, Section of Business Law) Bar Associations; Maritime Law Association of the United States. (Also Of Counsel, Graham & James, San Francisco). **SPECIAL AGENCIES:** Federal Maritime Commission; Bureau of Alcohol, Tobacco and Firearms. **REPORTED CASES:** Miranda v. Arizona, 384 U.S. 436 (1966). **PRACTICE AREAS:** Business; Securities; Alcoholic Beverage; Maritime Regulation.

REFERENCE: Bank of America.

## ROBERT E. GORDON
SUITE 840, 5725 PARADISE DRIVE
**CORTE MADERA, CALIFORNIA 94925**
Telephone: 415-924-1112
Fax: 415-924-7013

*Copyright, Entertainment, Music and Recording, Motion Picture, Video, Television, Publishing and Unfair Competition Law.*

**ROBERT E. GORDON,** born Los Angeles, California, September 20, 1932; admitted to bar, 1960, California. *Education:* University of California at Los Angeles (A.B., 1954); Middlebury College; Boalt Hall School of Law, University of California (J.D., 1959); University of Hamburg, Germany, 1959-1960. Lecturer on Insurance Law, International Faculty of Comparative Law, Luxembourg, 1960. Member, 1967— and Trustee, 1968-1970, Los Angeles Copyright Society. Adjunct Professor: Entertainment Law, Hastings College of the Law, 1990-1991; Boalt Hall School of Law, 1992. *Member:* Bar Association of San Francisco; State Bar of California (Member, Intellectual Property Section); American Bar Association (Member: Patent, Trademark and Copyright Law Section; Personal Appearances Division of the Forum Committee of the Entertainment and Sports Industries, 1978—).

## THOMAS E. NIEDERREUTHER
5633 PARADISE DRIVE
**CORTE MADERA, CALIFORNIA 94925**
Telephone: 415-927-4535
Fax: 415-927-7672

*Civil Litigation Practice including Personal Injury, Business, Contracts, Real Estate, Lender Liability, Insurance Coverage and Bad Faith, Fraud and R.I.C.O.*

**THOMAS E. NIEDERREUTHER,** born San Francisco, California, September 30, 1961; admitted to bar, 1987, California; 1990, U.S. District Court, Northern District of California. *Education:* College of Marin (A.A., 1983); San Francisco Law School (J.D., 1987). Member, Moot Court Board. *Member:* Bar Association of San Francisco (Member, Section on Litigation); Marin County and American Bar Associations; State Bar of California (Member, Section on Litigation); The Association of Trial Lawyers of America (Member, Sections on Commercial Litigation and Insurance). **LANGUAGES:** German.

## CHARLES J. PHILIPPS
300 TAMAL PLAZA DRIVE
SUITE 250
**CORTE MADERA, CALIFORNIA 94925**
Telephone: 415-927-9449
Fax: 415-927-0660

*Fidelity and Surety, Construction Litigation and Contract Law. General Civil and Trial Practice.*

**CHARLES J. PHILIPPS,** born Los Angeles, California, October 2, 1943; admitted to bar, 1969, California. *Education:* University of California at Los Angeles (B.A., 1965); Loyola University of Los Angeles (J.D., 1968). *Member:* State Bar of California; American Bar Association (Member: Forum Committee on Construction Industry, 1979—; Fidelity and Surety Committee, Section of Torts and Insurance Practice, 1976—); Northern California Surety Claims Association (President, 1991-1992); International Association Defense Counsel.

*ASSOCIATES*

**TERESA L. POLK,** born Akron, Ohio, May 1, 1954; admitted to bar, 1983, California; 1991, New York and U.S. Claims Court. *Education:* University of California at Berkeley (B.A., 1976); Hastings College of the Law, University of California (J.D., 1983). *Member:* San Francisco and American Bar Associations; State Bar of California; New York State Bar Association.

*(This Listing Continued)*

**CHARLES J. PHILIPPS, Corte Madera—Continued**

REPRESENTATIVE CLIENTS: INSCO Insurance; Indemnity Company of California; Carlisle Insurance Co.; AmWest Surety Insurance Co.; Transamerica Insurance Co.; Cigna Property and Casualty Insurance Co.; Developers Insurance Co.; Fairmont Insurance Co.; American Bonding Co; National American Insurance Co.; Indiana Lumbermans Mutual Insurance Co.; Security Insurance Company of Hartford; Automotive Insurance Co.; Allied Mutual Insurance Co.

## ALBERT, WEILAND & GOLDEN
CENTER TOWER
650 TOWN CENTER DRIVE, SUITE 1350
**COSTA MESA, CALIFORNIA 92626**
Telephone: 714-966-10000
FAX: 714-966-1002
Email: awglawyers@aol.com

*Bankruptcy Matters Including the Representation of Creditors, Debtors and Trustees, and Real Estate Including Subdivision Development, Commercial Leasing, Financing, Loan Workouts, Receiverships and Foreclosures.*

FIRM PROFILE: *The Albert, Weiland & Golden firm is listed in the PIE Law Directory. The law firm being one of the largest Bankruptcy Group in Orange County that is diversified in all aspects of Bankruptcy Law. The firm also has Real Estate Transaction Support.*

**THEODOR C. ALBERT,** born Fort Sill, Oklahoma, April 2, 1953; admitted to bar, 1978, California and U.S. District Court, Central District of California; 1982, U.S. District Court, Southern District of California. *Education:* Stanford University (B.A., 1975); University of California, Los Angeles (J.D., 1978). *Member:* Orange County Bar Association (Member and Chair, 1987, Commercial Law and Bankruptcy Section; Member, Civil Litigation Section); State Bar of California (Member, Business Law Section); Orange County Bankruptcy Forum (Director, 1988-1992; Vice-President, 1989-1990; President, 1990-1991). **PRACTICE AREAS:** Bankruptcy; Commercial Litigation.

**MICHAEL J. WEILAND,** born Grand Rapids, Michigan, June 26, 1952; admitted to bar, 1980, California. *Education:* University of California at Los Angeles (B.A., 1974); Loyola University of Los Angeles (J.D., with honors, 1980). Member, Loyola International and Comparative Law Review, 1979-1980. Adjunct Professor, Paralegal Program, University of Southern California Law School, 1984-1985. *Member:* Orange County and American (Member, Section on Real Property, Probate and Trust Law) Bar Associations; State Bar of California (Member, Sections on Business Law and Real Property Law).

**JEFFREY I. GOLDEN,** born Milwaukee, Wisconsin, August 27, 1962; admitted to bar, 1987, California. *Education:* University of California at San Diego (B.A., 1984); University of Southern California (J.D., cum laude, 1987). *Member:* Orange County Bar Association (Member, Bankruptcy Forum Special Projects Committee and Commercial Law and Bankruptcy Section). **PRACTICE AREAS:** Insolvency and Litigation.

**JENNIFER ANN GOLISON,** born Santa Monica, California, March 25, 1964; admitted to bar, 1989, California, U.S. District Court, Central, Northern, Eastern and Southern Districts of California and U.S. Court of Appeals, Ninth Circuit. *Education:* Loyola Marymount University (B.A., History, cum laude, 1986; B.B.A., cum laude, 1986); University of Notre Dame (J.D., 1989). *Member:* Long Beach, Orange County and American Bar Associations; State Bar of California; Orange County Bankruptcy Forum. **LANGUAGES:** French. **PRACTICE AREAS:** Insolvency; Trustee Representation; General Business Litigation.

**EVAN D. SMILEY,** born Los Angeles, California, November 5, 1966; admitted to bar, 1992, California and U.S. District Court, Central District of California; 1993, U.S. District Court, Southern and Eastern Districts of California. *Education:* California State University, Northridge (B.S., 1989); McGeorge School of Law (J.D., 1992). Traynor Honor Society. Recipient, American Jurisprudence Award in Commercial Law, 1992. Associate Legislation Editor, Board of Editors, Pacific Law Journal, 1991-1992. Law Clerk, Hon. John E. Ryan, U.S. Bankruptcy Judge. Extern, Hon. James N. Barr, U.S. Bankruptcy Judge, Central District of California. Author, "Review of Selected 1990 California Legislation," 22 Pac. L.J. 323, 1991. *member:* Orange County Bar Association; Orange County Bankruptcy Forum. **PRACTICE AREAS:** Bankruptcy; Insolvency; Litigation.

**LEI LEI WANG EKVALL,** born Taipei, Taiwan, December 19, 1965; admitted to bar, 1992, California, U.S. District Court, Central District of California and U.S. Court of Appeals, Ninth Circuit. *Education:* University of California, Irvine (B.S., 1988); University of Southern California (J.D., *(This Listing Continued)*

1992). Law Clerk, Honorable Kathleen P. March, U.S. Bankruptcy Judge, Central District of California. Relief Law Clerk, Honorable Alan M. Ahart, William L. Lasarow, Kathleen T. Lax, Vincent P. Zurzolo, U.S. Bankruptcy Judges, Central District of California. *Member:* Orange County Bar Association; Orange County Bankruptcy Forum; Orange County Asian American Bar Association; Southern California Chinese Lawyer's Association. **LANGUAGES:** Chinese. **PRACTICE AREAS:** Bankruptcy; Litigation.

**PHILIP E. STROK,** admitted to bar, 1993, California. *Education:* California State Polytechnic University (B.S., in Business Administration, magna cum laude, 1986); Southwestern University (J.D., magna cum laude, 1993). Moot Court Honors Program. Finalist, Moot Court Appellate Brief Competition. Recipient: American Jurisprudence Awards in Bankruptcy and Legal Research Writing; Exceptional Award in Civil Procedure II. Research Editor, Southwestern Law Review, 1992-1993. Law Clerk to the Honorable Robert W. Alberts; Thomas B. Donovan; Arthur M. Greenwald; Kathleen T. Lax; Geraldine Mund; Erithe A. Smith, U.S. Bankruptcy Judges, Central District of California, 1993-1996. Extern, Honorable Arthur M. Greenwald, U.S. Bankruptcy Judge, Central District of California. Author: "Hi, My Name is Bob. I'll Be Your Robber," Southwestern University Law Review, Vol. 22, No. 2, 1993. *Member:* State Bar of California.

## THOMAS P. APLIN
535 ANTON BOULEVARD, SUITE 800
**COSTA MESA, CALIFORNIA 92626**
Telephone: 714-546-4608
Facsimile: 714-546-4614

*Civil Litigation, Emphasizing Landlord/Tenant, Real Property, Construction and Business.*

**THOMAS P. APLIN,** born Oakland, California, October 10, 1960; admitted to bar, 1985, California; 1986, U.S. District Court, Central District of California and U.S. Court of Appeals, Ninth Circuit; 1987, U.S. District Court, Eastern District of California; 1992, U.S. District Court, Southern District of California. *Education:* University of Redlands (B.A., 1982); McGeorge School of Law, University of the Pacific (J.D., 1985). Lecturer, National Business Institute Legal Seminar entitled "Residential and Commercial Evictions", Anaheim, California, December 1994; March, 1996. *Member:* Orange County Bar Association; State Bar of California; International Council of Shopping Centers.

REPRESENTATIVE CLIENTS: The Taubman Company; Pacific Development Group; Econo Lube N' Tune, Inc.; Optima Asset Management Services, Inc.; Robert H. Grant; Crestmark Real Estate & Investments, Inc.; ITT Hartford; Transtronix Corporation; Christian Okoye; Panacea Investment Corp.; Anthony Lugo; Canbridge Properties, Inc.; Custom Laminators, Inc.

## BALFOUR MacDONALD MIJUSKOVIC & OLMSTED
A PROFESSIONAL CORPORATION
SUITE 1110
3200 PARK CENTER DRIVE
**COSTA MESA, CALIFORNIA 92626**
Telephone: 714-546-2400
Fax: 714-546-5008

*Corporate and Business Practice. Estates and Trust Planning and Administration. Litigation in all Federal and State Courts. Mergers and Acquisitions. Real Property.*

FIRM PROFILE: *We serve growing Southern California businesses, their owners, including manufacturing, service, high-tech, medical and natural resource. Our litigation includes all business matters, business torts, wrongful terminations and regulatory issues. Our estate and trust practice includes tax planning, trustee and beneficiary rights and duties, and employee benefits. Our real property practice includes real property transactions and real estate finance.*

**RALPH E. BALFOUR,** born Indianapolis, Indiana, February 29, 1944; admitted to bar, 1969, California. *Education:* University of Southern California (A.B., 1965; J.D., 1968). Corporate Counsel, Amcord, Inc. (NYSE), 1972-1975. General Counsel and Corporate Secretary, Amcord, Inc., 1975-1980. *Member:* State Bar of California. **PRACTICE AREAS:** Corporate Law; Business Law; Transactional Law; Mergers and Acquisitions; Real Property.

*(This Listing Continued)*

**JAMES B. MACDONALD,** born Los Angeles, California, February 14, 1942; admitted to bar, 1967, California; 1968, U.S. District Court, Central District of California; 1979, U.S. Supreme Court. *Education:* University of California at Santa Barbara (A.B., 1964); Boalt Hall School of Law, University of California, Berkeley (J.D., 1967). Author: "Coping with the Economic Recovery Tax Act of 1981: What Do You Tell Your Clients? How Do You Do It?", Vol. 121 No. 9 Trusts & Estates, pg. 35. General Counsel, First American Trust Company, 1983. *Member:* Orange County and American Bar Associations; State Bar of California; Orange Coast Estate Planning Council. (Certified Specialist, Estate Planning, Trust and Probate Law, The State Bar of California Board of Legal Specialization). *REPORTED CASES:* Kistler v. Vasi, 71 C. 2d 261; Ryman v. American National Insurance Co., 5C. 3d 620. *PRACTICE AREAS:* Estate and Trust Planning and Administration.

**RUTH MIJUSKOVIC,** born Grand Rapids, Michigan, July 17, 1943; admitted to bar, 1977, California. *Education:* Calvin College (B.A., 1965); Yale University; Southern Illinois University (J.D., summa cum laude, 1977). Articles Editor, Southern Illinois University Law Review, 1976-1977. Law Clerk to Judge Harlington Wood, Jr., U.S. Court of Appeals, Seventh Circuit, 1977-1978. Partner: Luce, Forward, Hamilton & Scripps, San Diego, 1978-1986. General Counsel, Chief Operating Officer, Access Research Corporation, San Diego, 1986-1991. *Member:* State Bar of California. *PRACTICE AREAS:* Corporate Law; Securities; Business Law; Transactional Law; Real Property.

**R. WAYNE OLMSTED,** born Brainerd, Minnesota, April 3, 1939; admitted to bar, 1983, California; 1984, U.S. District Court, Central and Southern Districts of California; 1985, U.S. District Court, Northern District of California. *Education:* University of Minnesota (B.A., magna cum laude, 1961; B.S., with distinction, 1961); Andover Newton Theological School (B.D., 1965); University of California at Los Angeles (J.D., 1983). Phi Beta Kappa; Phi Alpha Delta. Member, Governor's Commission on Agricultural Labor, State of Minnesota, 1974-1976. Executive Vice President, Owatonna Canning Company, Owatonna, Minnesota, 1976-1980. Registered Lobbyist, State of Minnesota, 1972-1980. *Member:* State Bar of California. *PRACTICE AREAS:* Business Law; Employment Law; Litigation; Landlord and Tenant Law; Mechanics Lien Law.

---

## BLAKELY, SOKOLOFF, TAYLOR & ZAFMAN

A Limited Liability Partnership
*Established in 1975*
SUITE 850, 611 ANTON BOULEVARD
**COSTA MESA, CALIFORNIA 92626**
Telephone: 714-557-3800
Facsimile: 714-557-3347
Email: BSTZ__mail@bstz.com
URL: http://www.bstz.com

*Los Angeles, California Office:* 7th Floor, 12400 Wilshire Boulevard. Telephone: 310-207-3800. Facsimile: 310-820-5988.
*Sunnyvale, California Office:* 1279 Oakmead Parkway. Telephone: 408-720-8598. Facsimile: 408-720-9397.
*Lake Oswego, Oregon Office:* Suite 101, 5285 SW Meadows Road. Telephone: 503-684-6200. Facsimile: 503-684-3245.

*Intellectual Property Law including Patents, Trademarks, Copyrights, Related Prosecution and Litigation.*

### MEMBERS OF FIRM

**ROGER W. BLAKELY, JR.,** born Pulaski, New York, August 9, 1935; admitted to bar, 1970, California; registered to practice before U.S. Patent and Trademark Office. *Education:* Cornell University (B.M.E., 1958); University of Southern California (M.S.E.E., 1965); Loyola University of Los Angeles (J.D., 1969). †(Resident).

**BEN J. YORKS,** born Saginaw, Michigan, October 9, 1959; admitted to bar, 1987, Texas; 1988, California; registered to practice before U.S. Patent and Trademark Office. *Education:* Auburn University (B.S.M.E., 1981); University of Houston (J.D., 1987). Pi Tau Sigma; Tau Beta Pi.

**WILLIAM W. SCHAAL,** born Inglewood, California, December 9, 1964; admitted to bar, 1992, California; registered to practice before U.S. Patent and Trademark Office. *Education:* University of California at San Diego (B.S.E.E., 1988; B.A. in Management Science, 1988); Loyola Law

*(This Listing Continued)*

School (J.D., 1992). *Member:* Orange County Bar Association (Officer, Technology Law Section); Orange County Patent Law Association.

**SUNNY TAMAOKI,** born Tokyo, Japan, December 9, 1965; admitted to bar, 1993, California. *Education:* University of California at Irvine (B.S.I.C.S., 1988); Loyola Law School (J.D., 1992). Phi Alpha Delta. *Member:* State Bar of California; Japanese American Bar Association (Member, Intellectual Property Section); Orange County Patent Law Association; Japan America Society.

**KIMBERLEY G. NOBLES,** born Singapore; admitted to bar, 1992, California; registered to practice before U.S. Patent and Trademark Office. *Education:* Ohio University (B.S.E.E., 1984; M.S.E.E., 1985); University of Southern California (J.D., 1992). Order of the Coif; Tau Beta Pi (President); Eta Kappa Nu; Phi Kappa Phi. Who's Who in American Universities and Colleges. Editor, Southern California Law Review. Author, "Birthright or Life Sentence: Controlling the Threat of Genetic Testing," Southern California Law Review, Volume 65, Number 4. *Member:* American Bar Association; Orange County Asian-American Bar Association (Member, Board of Governors); Institute of Electrical and Electronic Engineers; Southern California Chinese Lawyers' Association; Orange County Patent Law Association (Co-Vice Chairperson, Technology Law Section).

**KENT M. CHEN,** born Tallahassee, Florida, December 14, 1965; admitted to bar, 1994, California; registered to practice before U.S. Patent and Trademark Office. *Education:* University of Minnesota (B.S.E.E., 1987); University of Southern California (M.S.E.E., 1989); New York University (J.D., 1994). Eta Kappa Nu. Rockwell-USC Graduate Fellowship. Staff Editor, NYU Environmental Law Journal, 1992-1994. *Member:* Institute of Electrical and Electronic Engineers.

**THINH V. NGUYEN,** born Haiphong, Vietnam, June 5, 1954; admitted to bar, 1996, California. *Education:* University of California, Irvine (B.S.E.E., 1976; Ph.D., 1986); University of Southern California (M.S.E.E., 1979); Southwestern University School of Law (J.D., 1995). *Member:* Institute of Electrical and Electronic Engineers.

**BABAK REDJAIAN,** born Tehran, Iran, January 31, 1967; admitted to bar, 1996, California. *Education:* California State University, Long Beach (B.S.E.E., 1990); Southwestern University School of Law (J.D., magna cum laude, 1996). Lead Articles Editor, Southwestern University Law Review, 1995-1996.

†Indicates A Law Corporation.

REPRESENTATIVE CLIENTS: Allfast Fastening Systems; Applied Materials, Inc.; Apple Computer, Inc.; Auto-Shade, Inc.; Bay Networks; California Institute of Technology; Cirrus Logic; Citicorp; Computer Motion, Inc.; Cymer Laser Technologies; Cypress Semiconductor; Dep Corporation; Echelon Corporation; Fred Hayman Beverly Hills, Inc.; Freeman Cosmetic Corporation; Imperial Toy Corporation; Information Storage Devices; Intel Corporation; Landmark Entertainment Group; LTX Corporation; Maxim Integrated Products; McDonnell Douglas Corporation; Mentor Corporation; Mentor Graphics Corporation; Netscape Communications; On Trak Systems, Inc.; Oracle Corporation; Pacific Communication Sciences, Inc.; Pharmavite Corporation; Rambus, Inc.; Ricoh Corporation; Silicon Graphics; Sony Corporation of America; Sterling Software; Stratacom, Inc.; Sun Microsystems, Inc.; Systemix; Tekelec; Thermal Equipment Corporation; Time Warner Cable; Weider Health & Fitness; Xilinx.

(For complete biographical data on personnel at Los Angeles and Sunnyvale, California and Lake Oswego, Oregon, see Professional Biographies at those locations)

---

## BOOTH, MITCHEL & STRANGE

3080 BRISTOL STREET, SUITE 550
P.O. BOX 5046
**COSTA MESA, CALIFORNIA 92628-5046**
Telephone: 714-641-0217
Fax: 714-957-0411

*Los Angeles, California Office:* 3435 Wilshire Boulevard, 30th Floor. Telephone: 213-738-0100. Fax: 213-380-3308.
*San Diego, California Office:* 550 West "C" Street. Suite 1560. Telephone: 619-238-7620. Fax: 619-238-7625.

*General Civil and Commercial Trial Practice in all State and Federal Courts. Construction, Professional Liability, Environmental, Corporation, Real Property, Savings and Loan, Tax, Insurance, Surety, Estate Planning, Trust and Probate Law.*

*(This Listing Continued)*

## BOOTH, MITCHEL & STRANGE, Costa Mesa—Continued

### MEMBERS OF FIRM

**MICHAEL T. LOWE,** born Salt Lake City, Utah, May 8, 1943; admitted to bar, 1970, Utah; 1971, California. *Education:* University of Utah (B.S., 1967; J.D., 1970). Member, Moot Court Board, 1968-1970. *Member:* Los Angeles County, Orange County and American (Member, Sections of: Litigation; Insurance, Negligence and Compensation Law) Bar Associations; State Bar of California; Utah State Bar; Association of Southern California Defense Counsel; Defense Research Institute. (Resident).

**WALTER B. HILL, JR.,** born Long Beach, California, June 16, 1943; admitted to bar, 1977, California and U.S. District Court, Central District of California; 1983, U.S. District Court, Southern District of California. *Education:* Occidental College (B.A., 1965); Southwestern University (J.D., 1976). Recipient, American Jurisprudence Award on Civil Procedure. *Member:* Los Angeles County, Orange County and American Bar Associations; State Bar of California; Association of Southern California Defense Counsel. (Resident).

**ROBERT H. BRIGGS,** born San Francisco, California, June 1, 1949; admitted to bar, 1977, California; 1978, U.S. District Court, Central District of California. *Education:* Brigham Young University (B.A., 1974); Pepperdine University (J.D., 1977). *Member:* Orange County (Member, Sections on: Litigation; Environmental Law), Los Angeles County and American (Member, Sections on: Litigation; Tort and Insurance Practice) Bar Associations; State Bar of California. (Resident).

**DAVID R. KIPPER,** born Denver, Colorado, January 2, 1952; admitted to bar, 1982, California; 1983, U.S. District Court, Southern, Northern and Central Districts of California. *Education:* University of California at San Diego (B.A., 1974); University of San Diego (J.D., cum laude, 1982). Member, San Diego Law Review, 1980-1982. *Member:* Orange County and American (Member, Section on Tort and Insurance Practice) Bar Associations; State Bar of California; Defense Research Institute. (Also at Los Angeles Office).

**MARLA LAMEDMAN KELLEY,** born Bethpage, New York, January 27, 1958; admitted to bar, 1983, California and U.S. District Court, Central District of California. *Education:* University of California at Irvine (B.A., with honors, 1980); Loyola Law School (J.D., 1983). Member, Moot Court. Staff Editor, Entertainment Law Journal, 1982-1983. *Member:* Orange County and American Bar Associations; Association of Southern California Defense Counsel. (Resident).

**PAUL R. HOWELL,** born Salt Lake City, Utah, December 22, 1948; admitted to bar, 1977, Washington; 1978, Utah; 1988, California, U.S. District Court, District of Arizona, U.S. Court of Appeals, Ninth, Tenth and the Federal Circuits, U.S. Court of Federal Claims and U.S. Supreme Court. *Education:* University of Utah (B.S., 1972; M.B.A., 1973); University of Puget Sound School of Law (J.D., 1976). Panel Member, American Arbitration Association. *Member:* American Bar Associations (Member, Sections on: Litigation; Tort and Insurance Practice; Government Contracts; Member, Forum on the Construction Industry). [with U.S. Army Reserve, 1967-1973]. (Also at San Diego Office).

**CRAIG E. GUENTHER,** born Anaheim, California, August 12, 1960; admitted to bar, 1986, California. *Education:* California State University at Fullerton (B.A., 1983); Loyola University of Los Angeles (J.D., 1986). *Member:* Orange County, Los Angeles County and American (Member, Fidelity and Surety Law Committee, Tort and Insurance Practice Section) Bar Associations; State Bar of California. (Resident).

**DAVID L. HUGHES,** born Spokane, Washington, January 8, 1949; admitted to bar, 1986, Utah; 1987, California. *Education:* Brigham Young University (B.S., 1973); McGeorge School of Law, University of the Pacific (J.D., 1985). Recipient, American Jurisprudence Award for Community Property, 1983. Registered Medical Technology, 1973-1976. *Member:* Utah State and American (Member: Tort and Insurance Practice Section, 1986—; Forum Committee on the Construction Industry, 1985—) Bar Associations; State Bar of California. [With U.S. Army, 1967-1969]. (Resident).

**JAMES G. STANLEY,** born Lakewood, California, March 11, 1962; admitted to bar, 1988, California; 1992, U.S. District Court, Central District of California. *Education:* California State University at Long Beach (B.S.C.E., 1985); McGeorge School of Law, University of the Pacific (J.D., 1988). *Member:* Orange County Bar Association; State Bar of California. (Resident).

*(This Listing Continued)*

### ASSOCIATES

**ELIZABETH CURRIN BONN,** born Flagstaff, Arizona, June 25, 1956; admitted to bar, 1984, California; 1985, U.S. District Court, Central and Southern Districts of California. *Education:* University of Arizona (B.S., with distinction, 1978); Pepperdine University (J.D., cum laude, 1984). Member, Los Angeles County Bar Association, 1985-1988. *Member:* Orange County and American Bar Associations; State Bar of California. (Resident).

**STACIE L. BRANDT,** born Steubenville, Ohio, August 8, 1957; admitted to bar, 1993, California; 1994, U.S. District Court, Central and Southern Districts of California. *Education:* Cornell University (B.S., 1979); University of San Diego (J.D., 1993). Member, San Diego Law Review, 1992-1993. Member: Society of Women Engineers, 1975-1979; Society of Plastic Engineer, 1979-1990. *Member:* State Bar of California. (Resident).

**DAVID F. MCPHERSON,** born Pomona, California, April 4, 1969; admitted to bar, 1994, California. *Education:* University of Southern California (B.S., 1991); Southwestern University School of Law (J.D., 1994). *Member:* State Bar of California. (Resident).

**SCOTT S. MIZEN,** born Buffalo, New York, December 31, 1964; admitted to bar, 1990, California. *Education:* University of Illinois at Champaign/Urbana (B.S., 1987); Pepperdine University (J.D., 1990). Phi Alpha Delta. *Member:* Beverly Hills and Orange County Bar Associations; State Bar of California; Southern California Defense Counsel. (Resident).

**SEAN T. OSBORN,** born Highland Park, Illinois, May 8, 1958; admitted to bar, 1984, California; 1985, U.S. District Court, Central District of California; 1987, U.S. District Court, Northern, Southern and Eastern Districts of California and U.S. Court of Appeals, 9th Circuit; 1988, U.S. Tax Court; 1990, U.S. Supreme Court. *Education:* University of Southern California (B.S., 1980); McGeorge School of the Law, University of the Pacific (J.D., 1984). Member, Moot Court Honors Board, 1983-1984. *Member:* The State Bar of California; American Bar Association; Association of Southern California Defense Counsel. (Resident).

**LAILA MORCOS SANTANA,** born Hollywood, California, March 27, 1965; admitted to bar, 1991, California; 1994, U.S. District Court, Central District of California. *Education:* Pepperdine University, Seaver College (B.A., 1987); Pepperdine University School of Law (J.D., 1991). Phi Alpha Delta. Orange County Barristers. Member, Arab-American Law Society, 1990-1991. *Member:* Kern County, Orange County and American (Member, Litigation Section) Bar Associations; State Bar of California; California Women Lawyers Association. (Resident).

REPRESENTATIVE CLIENTS: See listing at Los Angeles, California.

(For Complete Personnel and Biographical Data, see Professional Biographies at Los Angeles, California Office)

---

## BUCKNER, ALANI & YOUNG

*3146 REDHILL AVENUE, SUITE 200*
**COSTA MESA, CALIFORNIA 92626**
*Telephone: 714-432-0990*
*Fax: 714-432-0352*
*Commercial Real Estate.*

**WILLIAM D. BUCKNER,** born Los Angeles, California, January 31, 1956; admitted to bar, 1982, California. *Education:* University of California at Santa Barbara; University of Southern California (A.B., 1978); Loyola University of Los Angeles (J.D., 1981). Business Editor, Loyola Entertainment Law Journal, 1981-1981. *Member:* Beverly Hills (Member, Committees on: Barristers for Urban Environment, 1983; Artists and the Law, 1983), South Bay and Los Angeles County Bar Associations; State Bar of California. **PRACTICE AREAS:** Real Estate Law; Real Estate Finance; Mortgage Based Financing.

**DOUGLAS D. ALANI,** born Sacramento, California, February 26, 1953; admitted to bar, 1987, California and U.S. District Court, Central District of California. *Education:* University of California (B.A., Pol. Science, 1976); Southwestern University School of Law (J.D., 1987). Member, Southwestern University Law Review, 1985-1986. Recipient: Dean's Merit Scholarship, 1985-1986; American Jurisprudence Award in Contracts and Criminal Law Theory. *Member:* Orange County and Los Angeles County Bar Associations; State Bar of California. **PRACTICE AREAS:** Commercial Lease Litigation.

**MATTHEW S. DUNCAN,** born Pasadena, California, October 29, 1953; admitted to bar, 1984, California; 1986, U.S. District Court, South-

*(This Listing Continued)*

ern, Northern, Eastern and Central Districts of California. *Education:* University of California at Santa Barbara (B.A., 1979); Southwestern University School of Law (J.D., 1984). Phi Alpha Delta. Staff Member, Southwestern University Law Review, 1983. Recipient, Thomas Bradley Award, 1983. Deputy District Attorney, 1988-1988. *Member:* Los Angeles County Bar Association; State Bar of California; Southern California Association of Defense Counsel.

**BRETT L. HAYES,** born Oakland, California, October 13, 1969; admitted to bar, 1996, California and U.S. District Court, Central District of California. *Education:* Vanderbilt University (B.S., 1991); Loyola Marymount University (J.D., 1995). **PRACTICE AREAS:** Corporate Law; Real Estate Law; Litigation.

*OF COUNSEL*

**MICHAEL J. MIRKOVICH,** born Carmel, California, December 3, 1951; admitted to bar, 1983, California. *Education:* University of California at Santa Barbara (B.A., 1973); California State University at Dominguez Hills (M.S., 1976); Western State University at Fullerton (J.D., 1982). *Member:* American Bar Association. **PRACTICE AREAS:** Commercial Real Estate Law; Real Estate Law.

## BURKE, WILLIAMS & SORENSEN

A Partnership including a Professional Corporation

3200 PARK CENTER DRIVE, SUITE 750
**COSTA MESA, CALIFORNIA 92626**
Telephone: 714-545-5559
Email: bws@bwslaw.com
URL: http://www.bwslaw.com

*Los Angeles, California Office:* 611 West Sixth Street, 25th Floor. Telephone: 213-236-0600.

*Ventura County Office:* 2310 Ponderosa Drive, Suite 1, Camarillo, California. Telephone: 805-987-3468.

General Civil and Trial Practice in all State and Federal Courts. Securities, Corporate, Taxation, Insurance and Commercial Law. Municipal and Public Agency Representation. Local Government Financing, Taxation and Assessments. Community Redevelopment, Eminent Domain, Environmental and Land Use Law. Employee Benefit Plans, Probate and Estate Planning. Health Care, Medical Research, College and University and Non-Profit Organization Law, Employment and Personnel Law. Tort, Workers Compensation and Insurance Defense.

*RESIDENT ATTORNEYS*

| J. Robert Flandrick | Thomas C. Wood |
| Leland C. Dolley | Thomas W. Allen |
| Jerry M. Patterson | Gregory G. Diaz |
| | Bryan Cameron LeRoy |

REFERENCE: First Interstate Bank, Los Angeles Main Office.

(For Complete Biographical Data on all Personnel, see Professional Biographies at Los Angeles).

## CAPPEL LAW OFFICES

Established in 1988

CENTER TOWER * SUITE 1950
650 TOWN CENTER DRIVE
**COSTA MESA, CALIFORNIA 92626-1925**
Telephone: 714-850-1900
Facsimile: 714-850-1902

General Civil, Trial and Appellate Practice in all State and Federal Courts. Commercial, Corporation and Corporate Financing, Real Estate, and Technology Law.

FIRM PROFILE: Timothy R. Cappel practiced law with Rogers & Wells in New York, New York, and with Bryan Cave in St. Louis, Missouri and Los Angeles, California, for 13 years. Mr. Cappel formed his own firm in Orange County, California, in 1988 to provide sophisticated legal services to clients with personalized care and concern and without compromising excellence or timeliness. Mr. Cappel practices preventative law by constantly seeking to anticipate and avoid legal problems in advance and to manage each legal matter in a manner which avoids unnecessary costs and hardships.

**TIMOTHY R. CAPPEL,** born St. Louis, Missouri, January 18, 1949; admitted to bar, 1976, New York; 1978, Missouri; 1979, California and

*(This Listing Continued)*

U.S. Supreme Court. *Education:* University of Missouri (B.S., magna cum laude, 1971); Duke University (M.A., with highest honors, Public Policy Sciences, 1975; J.D., with distinction, 1974). Recipient, First Joint Degree in Law and Public Policy Sciences, Duke University. Instructor, OCBA College of Trial Advocacy, 1992—. Lecturer, "Conflicts and Exposure in Client Relationships", "Frivolous Lawsuits and Abusive Lawyers", "Fiduciary Duties in Closely Held Businesses" and "Surviving An Audit of Your Legal Bills", OCBA Continuing Education of the Bar, 1991—. Intern, Foreign Service Officer, National Security Council Task Force on the Law of the Sea, 1974. Chairman, Board of Trustees, Cornelia Connelly School of the Holy Child Jesus , 1992-1995. *Member:* Orange County, Los Angeles County, Federal and American Bar Associations; Association of Business Trial Lawyers. **REPORTED CASES:** British Airways Board vs. The Port Authority of New York, 564 F.2d 1002 (2nd Cir. 1977); Browne vs. McDonnell Douglas Corporation, 504 F.Supp. 514 (N.D. Cal. 1980); Eldridge vs. Tymshare, Inc., 186 Cal.App.3d 767 (6th App Dist. 1986).

REPRESENTATIVE CLIENTS: Orange Bancorp; The Bank of Orange County; Bank of Anaheim; Creative Business Concepts, Inc.; KPMG Peat Marwick; Systemhouse, Inc.; Bowermaster & Associates Insurance Agency, Inc.; Makim Business Systems, Inc.; On-Call Communications, Inc.

## CASE & ASSOCIATES

THE CENTER TOWER
650 TOWN CENTER DRIVE, SUITE 550
**COSTA MESA, CALIFORNIA 92626**
Telephone: 714-540-3636
Fax: 714-540-3680

Construction and Business Litigation, Real Property Law, Surety and Insurance Law.

FIRM PROFILE: Case & Associates ("C & A") is a litigation and trial firm specializing in Construction Law with emphasis in both private and public works. C & A maintains a "smaller-firm" atmosphere emphasizing prompt, efficient and personal service for its clients, while also providing service for a wide array of clients involving large complex cases. The firm is based in Costa Mesa, California; however, C & A has clients throughout most of the state from Northern California throughout Southern California, as well as in surrounding states.

**BRIAN S. CASE,** born Torrance, California, October 26, 1958; admitted to bar, 1984, California, U.S. Supreme Court, U.S. Court of Appeals, Ninth Circuit, U.S. District Court, Northern, Eastern, Central and Southern Districts of California and U.S. Court of Federal Claims. *Education:* University of California at Los Angeles (B.A., 1980); Pepperdine University, Malibu (J.D., 1984). Delta Theta Phi. Author/Lecturer: "Construction Managers-Rights, Liabilities, etc." for the Legal Advisory Committee to the Associated General Contractors of California ("AGCC"), 1991; "California Construction Law-What To Do When" for the National Business Institute (Anaheim), 1992. Lecturer: "Construction Contracts Workshop" for Triaxial Management Services, Los Angeles, Orange and San Diego, 1987-1996; "Bonding and How to Profit in the 90's, (AGCC), 1992; "Contract Clauses That Make You Money and Those That Don't," Women Construction Owners and Executives, USA, May, 1992; "Contracts Workshop" for The County of Los Angeles Department of Airports, July, 1991; "Construction Delays, Impact Claims, Change Orders and Acceleration Claims for CAL-SMACNA and Co-Author of the CAL-SMACNA Legal Manual". "C0-Author of the CAL-SMACNA Legal Manual. *Member:* Orange County and American (Member, Forum Committee on the Construction Industry) Bar Associations; State Bar of California (Member, Section on: Real Property and Construction); American Subcontractors Association; Associated General Contractors (Member, Legal Advisory Committee); Sheet Metal, Air Conditioning, Heating Contractors Association. **REPORTED CASES:** Wright v. USPS, 29 Fed 3rd. 1426, 1994 (Subcontractor's right to pursue federal agency for equitable lien right to payment where prime contractor and surety are insolvent). **PRACTICE AREAS:** Construction Litigation; Business Litigation and Transactions; Real Property Law; Surety and Insurance Law.

*ASSOCIATES*

**F. ALBERT IBRAHIM,** born Alexandria, Egypt, January 20, 1961; admitted to bar, 1988, California; 1989, U.S. District Court, Central, Southern and Northern Districts of California. *Education:* Bowling Green State University (B.A., 1984); Pepperdine University School of Law (J.D., 1987). *Member:* Orange County, and Los Angeles County Bar Associations; State Bar of California; The American Subcontractors Association; The Sheet Metal and Air Conditioning National Association, Inc., (Orange

*(This Listing Continued)*

## CASE & ASSOCIATES, Costa Mesa—Continued

County/Long Beach Chapter); Orange County Business Council (Member, Legislative and Small Business Committees). *LANGUAGES:* French and Arabic. *PRACTICE AREAS:* Civil Trial Practice; Construction Defects/Claims; Business General Litigation; Real Estate Litigation.

**D. MICHAEL CLAUSS,** born Buffalo, New York, December 24, 1957; admitted to bar, 1989, California and U.S. District Court, Northern, Southern and Central Districts of California. *Education:* St. Bonaventure University (B.S., Economics, 1980); Western State University (J.D., 1986). *Member:* Orange County, Los Angeles, and American Bar Associations; State Bar of California; Past Member, Orange County Barristers; Past Member, The Association of Trial Lawyers of America. *PRACTICE AREAS:* Business; Construction Law; Mechanics Lien Law; Real Estate; Commercial; Collections; Civil Litigation; Wrist of Attachment.

**PHILLIP ANDREW CASE,** born Fullerton, California, June 7, 1965; admitted to bar, 1996, California. *Education:* Chapman College (B.A., 1989); Western State University (J.D., 1995).

## CASEY & RICHARDS
3200 PARK CENTER DRIVE, TENTH FLOOR
COSTA MESA, CALIFORNIA 92626
Telephone: 714-850-4575
Facsimilie: 714-850-4577

*Estate Planning, Charitable Giving, Probate, Wills and Trust Law and Administration.*

### MEMBERS OF FIRM

**WAYNE J. CASEY,** born Brooklyn, New York, January 22, 1955; admitted to bar, 1981, California; 1982, U.S. Tax Court. *Education:* Manhattan College (B.A., summa cum laude, 1977); University of Southern California (J.D., 1981). Phi Beta Kappa. *Member:* Orange County Bar Association (Member, Estate Planning Council); State Bar of California. *PRACTICE AREAS:* Estate Planning; Charitable Giving; Probate; Wills and Trust Law; Administration.

**MARC H. RICHARDS,** born Lewiston, Idaho, November 18, 1960; admitted to bar, 1985, California. *Education:* Claremont Men's College (B.A., cum laude, 1983); Columbia University (J.D., 1985); Accelerated Interdisciplinary Legal Education Program. Phi Beta Kappa; Omicron Delta Epsilon. *Member:* Orange County Bar Association; State Bar of California. *PRACTICE AREAS:* Estate Planning; Charitable Giving; Probate; Wills and Trust Law; Administration.

## CHAPMAN & GLUCKSMAN
A PROFESSIONAL CORPORATION
COSTA MESA, CALIFORNIA
(See Los Angeles)

*General Civil Practice in all State and Federal Trial and Appellate Courts. Commercial and Business Litigation and General Insurance Practice, including Products Liability, Professional Liability, Coverage, Construction Litigation, Complex and Multi-District Litigation, Commercial, Wrongful Termination, Corporation, Director and Officer Liability, Association Liability, Toxic and Hazardous Substance, Real Estate and Estate Planning, Excess and Surplus Insurance.*

## LAW OFFICES OF MARTIN M. COHEN
Established in 1967
3200 PARK CENTER DRIVE, SUITE 610
COSTA MESA, CALIFORNIA 92626-1908
Telephone: 714-549-1499
Fax: 714-549-8970

*Corporate, Partnership, Business Law, Litigation, Wills and Trusts, Probate, Federal Tax, State and Local Tax and International Law.*

**MARTIN M. COHEN,** born Brooklyn, New York, October 23, 1940; admitted to bar, 1965, Tennessee; 1966, California; 1968, U.S. Tax Court. *Education:* Temple University (B.S., 1962); Vanderbilt University (J.D.,

*(This Listing Continued)*

1965). Certified Public Accountant, California, 1966. *Member:* Orange County and American Bar Associations; State Bar of California; California Institute of Certified Public Accountants.

## COOKSEY, HOWARD, MARTIN & TOOLEN
A PROFESSIONAL CORPORATION
Established in 1967
535 ANTON BOULEVARD, 10TH FLOOR
COSTA MESA, CALIFORNIA 92626-1947
Telephone: 714-431-1100
Telecopier: 714-431-1119

*General Civil and Trial Practice in all Courts. Personal Injury, General Liability Insurance, Defense Litigation, Commercial Law, Business Litigation, Creditor-Bankruptcy Law, Corporate, Insurance, Probate, Estate Planning, Real Estate, Antitrust Law and Employment Law.*

FIRM PROFILE: *Cooksey, Howard, Martin & Toolen was founded in 1967. The firm began as a four attorney office with a general practice, including insurance defense, business litigation, Business and real estate transactions. In the last 29 years, the firm has grown to 32 attorneys and serves the entire Western United States, offering a wide range of services.*

**MARVEN E. HOWARD,** born Reno, Nevada, February 6, 1932; admitted to bar, 1964, California; 1973, U.S. Supreme Court. *Education:* University of California at Los Angeles (B.S., 1956); Southwestern University (J.D., 1963). Chairman of the Board, United Western Medical Centers, 1986. *Member:* Orange County Bar Association (Member, Estate Planning, Probate and Trust Section); State Bar of California. *PRACTICE AREAS:* Probate; Trusts; Estate Planning Law.

**JAMES M. MARTIN,** born Montebello, California, December 20, 1944; admitted to bar, 1971, California; 1974, U.S. Supreme Court. *Education:* University of Southern California (B.S., 1967); Duke University (J.D., 1970). Phi Alpha Delta. Recipient: American Jurisprudence Award in Estate Planning; Orange County Board of Supervisors Certificate of Merit, 1980. Licensed Real Estate Broker, California, 1993. Judge Pro Tem, Orange County Superior Court, 1983—. *Member:* Orange County and American Bar Associations; State Bar of California. *REPORTED CASES:* Humphries Investments, Inc. v. Walsh, (1988) 202 Cal.App.3d 766. *PRACTICE AREAS:* Real Estate; Business; Corporate Law.

**DAVID R. COOKSEY,** born Des Moines, Iowa, October 1, 1946; admitted to bar, 1972, California; 1976, U.S. Supreme Court. *Education:* University of California, Irvine (B.A., 1969); Hastings College of the Law, University of California (J.D., 1972). Judge Pro Tem, Orange County Superior Court, 1980—. *Member:* Orange County and American Bar Associations; State Bar of California; Association of Southern California Defense Counsel. *PRACTICE AREAS:* Litigation; Personal Injury; Insurance Defense Law.

**ROBERT L. TOOLEN,** born Lynwood, California, June 15, 1948; admitted to bar, 1974, California; 1978, U.S. Supreme Court. *Education:* University of California at Los Angeles (B.A., 1970); Southwestern University (J.D., 1974). Administrative Editor, Southwestern University Law Review, 1973-1974. Author: "Nestle v. City of Santa Monica: A Test Case for General Immunity Statute," Southwestern University Law Review, Vol. 5 No. 1, 1973. *Member:* Orange County Bar Association; State Bar of California; Association of Southern California Defense Counsel. *REPORTED CASES:* Jeffrey E. v. Central Baptist Church, (1988) 197 Cal.App.3d 718. *PRACTICE AREAS:* Litigation; Insurance Law; Insurance Defense Litigation.

**KIM P. GAGE,** born Los Angeles, California, January 21, 1953; admitted to bar, 1978, California; 1979, U.S. District Court, Central, Southern and Eastern Districts of California. *Education:* University of California at Los Angeles (B.A., 1975); California Western School of Law (J.D., 1978). *Member:* Orange County and American Bar Associations; State Bar of California; Orange County Bankruptcy Forum; California Trial Lawyers Association. *PRACTICE AREAS:* Business and Commercial Litigation; Creditor Bankruptcy Litigation.

**PATRICK J. DUFFY,** born Havre, Montana, August 19, 1938; admitted to bar, 1966, California. *Education:* Arizona State University (B.S., 1963); University of Arizona (LL.B., 1965). Judge Pro Tem, Orange County Superior Court, 1979-1987. *Member:* State Bar of California; American Board of Trial Advocates. *PRACTICE AREAS:* Litigation; Personal Injury; Insurance Defense Law; Employment Litigation.

*(This Listing Continued)*

# PROFESSIONAL BIOGRAPHIES

**PHILIP M. WOOG,** born Merced, California, August 3, 1957; admitted to bar, 1988, California. *Education:* University of Nebraska; California State University at Fullerton (B.A., 1984); Western State University (J.D., 1987). Recipient: American Jurisprudence Awards in Contracts, Civil Procedure and Appellate Brief Writing, 1986-1987. *Member:* Orange County Bar Association; State of California; Association of Southern California Defense Counsel. *PRACTICE AREAS:* Litigation; Personal Injury; Insurance Defense Law; Construction Litigation; Insurance Coverage.

---

**JON A. HAMMERBECK,** born Pasadena, California, January 15, 1955; admitted to bar, 1981, California; 1986, U.S. Supreme Court. *Education:* University of California at San Diego (B.A., magna cum laude, 1977); University of Southern California (J.D., 1981). Recipient, American Board of Trial Advocates Award, University of Southern California, 1981. *Member:* Orange County and American Bar Associations; State Bar of California. *PRACTICE AREAS:* Litigation; Personal Injury; Insurance Defense Law.

**LEROY EINSPAHR,** born Alta, Iowa, October 14, 1946; admitted to bar, 1985, California; 1986, U.S. District Court, Central and Southern Districts of California; 1988, U.S. Supreme Court. *Education:* University of California at Berkeley (B.S., 1968); Iowa State University; Western State University College of Law (J.D., 1984). *Member:* Orange County Bar Association; State Bar of California; American Society of Safety Engineers (Certified Safety Professional, 1978—); Association of Southern California Defense Counsel. *PRACTICE AREAS:* Litigation; Personal Injury; Insurance Defense; Domestic Relations Law.

**BYRON J. BAHR,** born Novato, California, July 3, 1962; admitted to bar, 1987, California ; 1988, U.S. District Court, Central District of California; 1989, U.S. District Court, Southern District of California; 1991, U.S. Court of Appeals, Ninth Circuit; 1992, U.S. District Court, Northern District of California. *Education:* California State University at Chico (B.S., cum laude, 1984); University of California at Davis (J.D., 1987). Recipient, American Jurisprudence Award in Constitutional Law. *Member:* Orange County Bar Association (Member, Sections on: Business Litigation; Commercial Law and Bankruptcy); State Bar of California. *PRACTICE AREAS:* Business and Commercial Litigation; Creditor Bankruptcy Litigation.

**BARBARA L. BOLLERO,** born Afragola, Italy, March 25, 1953; admitted to bar, 1981, Texas; 1982, Maryland; 1983, Illinois; 1988, California; 1989, U.S. Supreme Court; 1992, U.S. Court of Appeals, Ninth Circuit. *Education:* University of Illinois (B.A., 1975) James Scholar; University of Texas (J.D., 1981). Recipient, American Jurisprudence Award. Representative, Honor Council, University of Texas School of Law, 1978-1979. *Member:* Orange County Bar Association; State Bar of California; Orange County Women Lawyer's Association; California Women Lawyers. *PRACTICE AREAS:* Litigation; Personal Injury; Insurance Defense Law.

**LAWRENCE E. LANNON,** born Providence, Rhode Island, June 2, 1943; admitted to bar, 1988, California. *Education:* Brown University (B.S., 1965); Penn State University (M.S., 1967); Loyola Marymount University (J.D., 1980). Professional Mechanical Engineer, 1975—. *Member:* Orange County Bar Association; State Bar of California. *PRACTICE AREAS:* Litigation; Personal Injury; Insurance Defense Law.

**CHRISTOPHER J. HENDERSON,** born Denver, Colorado, August 10, 1963; admitted to bar, 1988, California; 1989, U.S. District Court, Central and Southern Districts of California. *Education:* Arizona State University (B.A., 1985); University of San Diego (J.D., 1988). Who's Who in American Law Students, 1986. *Member:* State Bar of California. *PRACTICE AREAS:* Business Litigation; Personal Injury; Insurance Defense Law.

**LAWRENCE H. MILLER,** born Chicago, Illinois, March 21, 1951; admitted to bar, 1989, California and U.S. District Court, Central and Southern Districts of California; 1991, U.S. District Court, Eastern District of California and U.S. Court of Appeals, Ninth Circuit. *Education:* Chapman University (B.A., 1974); University of Denver (M.B.A., 1977); Western State University (J.D., magna cum laude, 1989). Recipient, Ten American Jurisprudence Awards. Member, Western State University Law Review. President's Scholar. Member, California and Orange County Bankruptcy Forum, 1987—. *LANGUAGES:* German. *PRACTICE AREAS:* Business and Commercial Litigation; Creditor Bankruptcy Litigation.

**MARIA DE LUNA,** born Durango, Mexico; admitted to bar, 1991, California. *Education:* University of Southern California (B.S., 1983); University of California at Los Angeles, (J.D., 1990). Certified Public Accountant, California, 1986. Member, Hispanic Chamber of Commerce. *Member:* Hispanic Bar Association. *LANGUAGES:* Spanish. *PRACTICE AREAS:* Business; Corporate Law; Real Estate; NAFTA.

**MOINA C. SHIV,** born Bombay, India, March 29, 1958; admitted to bar, 1987, New York; 1989, California. *Education:* University of Bombay (B.S., 1979; LL.B., 1982); Cornell Law School (LL.M., 1983). Recipient, Merit Scholarship from Government of India, 1981-1982. *Member:* State Bar of California; Orange County Women Lawyer's Association. *LANGUAGES:* Spanish and Hindi. *PRACTICE AREAS:* Personal Injury; Insurance Defense Law; Litigation; Coverage Law.

**JOSEPH M. PARKER,** born Ridgewood, New Jersey, March 12, 1966; admitted to bar, 1992, California and U.S. District Court, Central District of California. *Education:* California State University, Long Beach (B.A., cum laude, 1989); University of San Diego School of Law (J.D., 1992). *Member:* State Bar of California. *PRACTICE AREAS:* Litigation; Insurance Defense Law; Personal Injury; Employment Litigation.

**STEVEN R. BANGERTER,** born Salt Lake City, Utah, July 29, 1961; admitted to bar, 1993, California, U.S. District Court, Central and Southern Districts of California, U.S. Court of Appeals, Ninth Circuit. *Education:* University of Utah (R.T.T., 1986); Arizona State University (B.A., magna cum laude, 1989); Western State University (J.D., 1993). Licensed Radiation Therapist by the California and American Registries of Radiation Therapy. Adjunct Professor, Legal Environment of Business, California State University at Fullerton, 1993—. Member: American Registry of Radiation Therapist, 1986—; California Registry of Radiation Therapists, 1986—. *Member:* Los Angeles County, Orange County and American (Member, Tort and Insurance Practice Section) Bar Associations; State Bar of California. *PRACTICE AREAS:* Litigation; Insurance Defense Law.

**RANDALL P. MROCZYNSKI,** born Sacramento, California, June 16, 1963; admitted to bar, 1991, California and U.S. District Court, Eastern District of California; 1992, U.S. District Court, Central District of California; 1994, U.S. District Court, Southern District of California. *Education:* Santa Clara University (B.A., 1985); University of the Pacific, McGeorge School of Law (J.D., 1991). Member, Orange County Bankruptcy Forum, 1992—. *Member:* State Bar of California. *PRACTICE AREAS:* Business and Commercial Litigation; Creditor Bankruptcy Litigation.

**THOMAS F. ZIMMERMAN,** born Kansas City, Missouri, February 19, 1967; admitted to bar, 1993, California, U.S. District Court, Central District of California, U.S. Court of Appeals, Ninth Circuit. *Education:* University of California at Santa Barbara (B.A., with highest honors in History, 1989); Whittier Law School (J.D., summa cum laude, 1993). Lead Articles Editor, Whittier Law Review, 1992-1993. Recipient: American Jurisprudence Awards: Torts II, Commercial Transactions I, Legal Skills II, Professional Responsibility, Real Property I. *Member:* Orange County Bar Association. *PRACTICE AREAS:* Litigation; Construction Defect; Personal Injury; Insurance Defense.

**GREGORY R. WARNAGIERIS,** born Ridgecrest, California, October 11, 1957; admitted to bar, 1992, California and U.S. District Court, Central District of California. *Education:* University of California at Riverside (B.S., 1979; California State University (M.A., 1985) Kappa Tau Alpha; Loyola Marymount University (J.D., 1991). Member, Loyola International Law Journal, 1989-1990. Recipient, American Jurisprudence Award in Ethics and Negotiation. *Member:* Orange County Bar Association; State Bar of California. *PRACTICE AREAS:* Litigation; Insurance Defense Law; Personal Injury.

**CHRISTOFER R. CHAPMAN,** born Zaragoza, Spain, February 29, 1960; admitted to bar, 1991, California, U.S. District Court, Central District of California. *Education:* Pacific Union College (B.A., 1982); Loma Linda University (M.A., 1984); Southwestern University (J.D., 1990). *Member:* San Bernadino, Riverside and American Bar Associations; State Bar of California; Southern California Defense Counsel Association; Inns of Courts. *LANGUAGES:* Spanish. *PRACTICE AREAS:* Litigation; Personal Injury; Insurance Defense Law.

**BRADLEY T. DAVIS,** born Hemet, California, April 21, 1966; admitted to bar, 1993, California; U.S. District Court Central District of California; U.S. Court of Appeals, Ninth Circuit. *Education:* Western State University (B.A., 1992; J.D., 1993). *Member:* Orange County and Riverside County Bar Associations; State Bar of California. *LANGUAGES:* Korean. *PRACTICE AREAS:* Litigation; Insurance Defense Law.

**JOHN A. MARLO, III,** born Santa Cruz, California, June 12, 1966; admitted to bar, 1994, California and U.S. Court of Appeals, Ninth Circuit. *Education:* University of Southern California (B.S., 1988); Western State University (J.D., 1993). Recipient, American Jurisprudence Award, Secured Land Transactions. *Member:* Orange County Bar Association.

*(This Listing Continued)*

**COOKSEY, HOWARD, MARTIN & TOOLEN, A PROFESSIONAL CORPORATION**, Costa Mesa—Continued

**PRACTICE AREAS:** Litigation; Insurance Defense; Construction Defect Litigation.

**BRIAN R. VAN MARTER,** born Syracuse, New York, October 10, 1966; admitted to bar, 1993, California, U.S. District Court, Central District of California and U.S. Court of Appeals, Ninth Circuit. *Education:* California State University at Fullerton (B.A., 1990); Whittier College School of Law (J.D., cum laude, 1993). Member, 1991-1993 and Executive Editor, 1992-1993, *Whittier Law Review. Member:* Orange County Bar Association; State Bar of California. **PRACTICE AREAS:** Litigation; Construction Defect; Insurance Defense Law.

**RICHARD E. BUCK,** born Chillicothe, Missouri, September 27, 1955; admitted to bar, 1985, California and U.S. District Court, Central District of California; 1995 Missouri. *Education:* University of California at Los Angeles (B.A. in Political Science/International Relations, 1977); Washburn University of Topeka (J.D., 1984). Blue Key. Member, Washburn Law Journal, 1983-1984. Author: Comments, "Malicious Prosecution," Washburn Law Journal, 1983. *Member:* Orange County and Desert Bar Associations; State Bar of California. **PRACTICE AREAS:** Litigation; Insurance Law; Insurance Defense.

**MICHAEL J. MACIE,** born Wichita, Kansas, February 28, 1966; admitted to bar, 1992, California. *Education:* University of San Diego (B.A., 1988); University of Santa Clara (J.D., 1992). *Member:* State Bar of California. **PRACTICE AREAS:** Construction Defect Litigation; Construction Injury; Products Liability.

**THERESA H. LAZORISAK,** born San Francisco, California, February 8, 1965; admitted to bar, 1989, California. *Education:* University of South Carolina (B.S., cum laude, 1986); Hastings College of the Law, University of California (J.D., 1989). Snodgrass Moot Court Competition. Recipient, American Jurisprudence Award. Associate Technical Editor, Comment, Hastings Law Journal, 1988-1989. Who's Who Among American Law Students. *Member:* Los Angeles County and American (Member, Law Student Division, 1986-1988) Bar Associations; State Bar of California.

**C. BRAD JOHNSON,** born Rexburg, Idaho, August 8, 1958; admitted to bar, 1988, California; 1989, U.S. District Court, Central District of California; 1991; Utah and U.S. District Court, District Court of Utah; 1995, U.S. District Court, Northern, Southern and Eastern Districts of California and U.S. Court of Appeals, Ninth Circuit. *Education:* Brigham Young University (B.S., 1983); University of Utah (J.D., 1988). *Member:* Los Angeles County Bar Association; State Bar of California (Member, Sections on: Business Law; Real Property Law). **PRACTICE AREAS:** Real Estate; Corporate; Business Litigation.

**DAVID W. SEAL,** born Culver City, California, May 22, 1964; admitted to bar, 1995, California and U.S. District Court, Central District of California. *Education:* California State University at Long Beach (B.A., Economics, 1989); Western State University (J.D., 1994). Delta Theta Phi. Recipient, American Jurisprudence Awards in Contracts and Moot Court Competition. Listed in Who's Who in American Universities and Colleges. 1993 Winner, Warren Ferguson Moot Court Competition. Associated with Program Analyst Office of Regional Commissioner, U.S. Immigration & Naturalization Service, 1989-1990. *Member:* State Bar of California; California Young Lawyers Association. **PRACTICE AREAS:** Construction Defect; Insurance Defense; Litigation.

**GRIFFITH H. HAYES,** born San Diego, California, December 19, 1957; admitted to bar, 1985, California; 1986, U.S. District Court, Southern District of California. *Education:* University of California at San Diego (B.A., 1981); California Western School of Law (J.D., 1984). Phi Alpha Delta. Lead Articles Editor, California Western International Law Journal, 1983-1984. Instructor, Legal Research and Writing, California Western School of Law, 1982-1983. *Member:* San Diego County and American Bar Associations; State Bar of California. **PRACTICE AREAS:** Construction Defect Litigation; Personal Injury Litigation.

REPRESENTATIVE CLIENTS: AETNA Casualty & Surety Co.; American Display Co.; American States Insurance Cos.; Chrysler Credit Corp.; Chrysler Financial Corp.; Chrysler First Business Credit Corporation; Chrysler Insurance Company; Citizens Insurance Co.; Del Industries; Deutsche Credit; Eldorado Bank; Employers Mutual Companies; Fluor Corp.; Fluor Daniel, Inc.; Grange Insurance Assn.; Hartford Insurance Co.; Jackson National Life Insurance; Main Credit Corp.; Midwest Mutual Insurance Co.; Mutual of Enumclaw; National Casualty Co.; Nautilus Insurance Co.; Norwest Financial, Inc.; Norwest Financial California, Inc.; Norwest Financial Leasing, Inc.; Porsche Credit Corp.; Preferred Risk Mutual Insurance Co.; Scottsdale Insurance Co.; Stanley-Bostitch, Inc.; Toyota Motor Credit Corp.; USF&G; VW Credit, Inc.

---

# HENRY J. COOPERSMITH

Established in 1974

611 ANTON BOULEVARD, SUITE 1110
**COSTA MESA, CALIFORNIA 92626**
Telephone: 714-433-7340
Fax: 714-436-6109

*Probate Law, Tax, Estate Planning, Wills and Trusts, Real Estate and Corporate Law and Limited Liability Companies.*

**HENRY J. COOPERSMITH,** born Oakland, California, 1943; admitted to bar, 1969, California; 1977, U.S. Tax Court. *Education:* Oakland City College (A.A., 1963); California State University (B.S., 1965); University of California at Berkeley (J.D., 1968); New York University (LL.M., Taxation, 1969). *Member:* Orange County (Past Chairman, Tax Section; Member: Probate and Estate Planning Section; Tax Section; Real Estate Section) and American Bar Associations; State Bar of California. (Certified Specialist, Taxation Law and Estate Planning, Trust and Probate Law, State Bar of California Board of Legal Specialization).

---

# COULOMBE & KOTTKE

A PROFESSIONAL CORPORATION

Established in 1985

COMERICA BANK TOWER
611 ANTON BOULEVARD, SUITE 1260
**COSTA MESA, CALIFORNIA 92626**
Telephone: 714-540-1234
Fax: 714-754-0808; 714-754-0707
Email: c-k@coulombe.com

*Civil Litigation in all State and Federal Courts. Bankruptcy Litigation, Appeals, Business, Insurance Coverage and Bad Faith, Real Estate, Title Insurance, Securities, Construction, Commercial, Collections, Landlord-Tenant.*

FIRM PROFILE: *Coulombe & Kottke is a specialized civil litigation practice. The firm represents national and local corporations and financial institutions, county governments, title insurance companies, real estate development companies, manufacturers and service organizations and closely held corporations, as well as individuals. While the firm handles matters of statewide and national scope, its primary focus is to service the needs of its clients in Southern California. The firm is small by design to allow the attorneys to work directly with their clients, and to control litigation costs. Coulombe & Kottke is listed in the Martindale-Hubbell Bar Register of Preeminent Lawyers.*

**RONALD B. COULOMBE,** born Los Angeles, California, June 20, 1950; admitted to bar, 1979, California; 1981, U.S. District Court, Central District of California; 1985, U.S. District Court, Northern District of California; 1987, U.S. District Court, Southern District of California; 1993, U.S. Supreme Court. *Education:* California State University, Long Beach (B.A., 1972; M.A., 1973); Loyola University School of Law (J.D., with honorable mention, 1979). Phi Kappa Phi. Member, Joseph Scott Moot Court, 1978. Member, Loyola of Los Angeles International and Comparative Law Annual, 1978-1979. *Member:* Los Angeles County, Orange County and American Bar Associations; State Bar of California. **REPORTED CASES:** Margaret Van Luven v. Rooney Pace, Inc,, 195 Cal.App.3d 1201 (1987); BFP v. Resolution Trust Corporation, 114 S.Ct. 1757 (1994). **PRACTICE AREAS:** Civil Trial; Business; Real Estate; Title Insurance; Securities; Construction; Commercial; Collections; Insurance Coverage and Bad Faith; Landlord/Tenant; Bankruptcy; Federal Court Litigation; Complex Litigation. **Email:** c-k@coulombe.com

**JON S. KOTTKE,** born Los Angeles, California, July 10, 1955; admitted to bar, 1981, California and U.S. District Court, Central District of California; 1989, U.S. District Court, Northern and Southern Districts of California. *Education:* University of California, Los Angeles (B.A., 1977); Loyola University School of Law (J.D., 1981). Joseph Scott Moot Court Honors Program, 1979. Panelist: Orange County Bar Association, Insurance Law Section, Anatomy of a Bad Faith Case; National Business Institute, Residential and Comerical Evictions in California. *Member:* Orange County Bar Association (Member, Sections on: Creditor's Rights; Business Litigation; Real Estate Law; Insurance Law); State Bar of California. **PRACTICE AREAS:** Collections; Enforcement of Judgments; Prejudgment Attachment Proceedings; Commercial; Civil Trial; Business; Real Estate; Title Insurance; Construction; Landlord/Tenant; Business Insurance; Insurance Coverage and Bad Faith; Federal Court Litigation.

*(This Listing Continued)*

## PROFESSIONAL BIOGRAPHIES

### CALIFORNIA—COSTA MESA

#### COUNSEL

**ROY B. WOOLSEY,** born Pasadena, California, July 23, 1917; admitted to bar, 1942, California, U.S. District Court, Northern District of California and U.S. Court of Appeals, Ninth Circuit; 1967, U.S. Supreme Court; 1968, U.S. District Court, Central and Southern Districts of California. *Education:* University of California, Los Angeles (B.A., 1937); University of Southern California (J.D., 1942). Associate Editor in Chief, U.S.C. Law Review, 1941-1942. *Member:* Orange County Bar Association; State Bar of California. **REPORTED CASES:** BFP v. Resolution Trust Corporation, 114 S.Ct. 1757 (1994).

#### LEGAL SUPPORT PERSONNEL

##### PARALEGALS

**VICKY M. PEARSON,** born Yokosuka, Japan, April 13, 1969. *Education:* University of California, Irvine (B.S., Biological Sciences, 1993; Certificate of Legal Assistantship, 1994). (Senior Paralegal).

**ABEER F. RIDER,** born Amman, Jordan, September 8, 1964. *Education:* Jordan University (B.A., English Literature, 1985); University of California, Irvine (Certificate of Legal Assistantship, with honors, 1996). **LANGUAGES:** Arabic.

#### LEGAL ADMINISTRATOR

**YVONNE MENDOZA,** born Whittier, California, April 2, 1960. *Education:* Cypress College (A.A., Business, 1988); University of California, Irvine.

---

## DAEHNKE & CRUZ
### GREAT WESTERN BANK TOWER
### 3200 PARK CENTER DRIVE
### SUITE 800
### COSTA MESA, CALIFORNIA 92626
Telephone: 714-557-8255
Fax: 714-557-9344

Environmental Law, Corporate Law, Real Estate Law, Commercial Law, Labor Law, Civil Litigation.

FIRM PROFILE: The Daehnke & Cruz firm is committed to provide the highest legal service, integrity and unfailing dependability. The law firm is listed in the International and Canadian sections of The Martindale Hubbell opening their arms to the world. Several languages are spoken throughout the firm allowing the firm to better serve and communicate throughout the world.

### MEMBERS OF FIRM

**KEVIN J. DAEHNKE,** born Omaha, Nebraska, April 19, 1958; admitted to bar, 1984, California, U.S. District Court, Central District of California and U.S. Court of Appeals, Ninth Circuit. *Education:* Arizona State University (B.A., cum laude, with honors, 1980); University of Southern California (J.D., 1983). Hale Moot Court Honors Program. Editor-in-Chief, USC Journal of Law and the Environment, 1982-1983. Co-Author: "Hazardous Waste Management Handbook: Guidelines for Compliance," California Chamber of Commerce, May, 1987. Chairman, University of Southern California Environmental Law Advisory Board, 1989-1990. Member: Orange County (Section on Environment and Toxics) and American (Member, Natural Resources Section) Bar Associations; Environmental Law and Real Property Sections, Los Angeles County Bar Association. **PRACTICE AREAS:** Environmental Law.

**JOHN G. CRUZ,** born New York, N.Y., May 4, 1951; admitted to bar, 1979, California. *Education:* California State University, Fullerton (B.A., 1975); University of California at Los Angeles; University of Michigan (J.D., 1979). Beta Alpha Psi. *Member:* Orange County (Member, Real Property and Taxation Sections) and American (Member, Sections on: Real Property, Probate and Trust Law; Corporation, Banking and Business Law; Taxation) Bar Associations; State Bar of California (Member, Sections on: Taxation; Corporate and Business; Real Property); Hispanic Bar Association of Orange County (Member, Board of Trustees). **PRACTICE AREAS:** Business; Corporate; Real Estate Law; Transactional Law & Lenders.

**WILLIAM J. MORAN,** born Brooklyn, New York, July 10, 1953; admitted to bar, 1978, Texas and U.S. District Court, Southern District of Texas; 1979, New Jersey and U.S. District Court, District of New Jersey; 1980, Pennsylvania; 1988, California and U.S. District Court, Central District of California; 1990, U.S. Court of Appeals, Ninth Circuit; U.S. District Court, Easter n, Northern and Southern Districts of California; 1992, U.S. Supreme Court; 1994, U.S. Court of Appeals, Fourth Circuit. *Education:*

*(This Listing Continued)*

---

Fordham University (B.A., summa cum laude, 1974); Yale University (J.D.,1977). Phi Beta Kappa; Alpha Mu Gamma. Instructor, University of California Extension, Certificate Program in Legal Assistantship, University of California, Irvine, 1988-1992. Adjunct Professor, Western State University College of Law, 1993—. Associate General Counsel, Subaru of America, Inc., 1982-1987. General Counsel, Daihatsu America, Inc., 1987-1988. *Member:* Orange County, New Jersey State, Pennsylvania and American Bar Associations; State Bar of Texas; State Bar of California. **LANGUAGES:** French. **PRACTICE AREAS:** employment Law; Environmental Litigation; Business Litigation; Appeals.

#### ASSOCIATES

**MAUREEN R. GRAVES,** born Duncan, Oklahoma, October 22, 1957; admitted to bar, 1990, California; 1991, New York. *Education:* Cornell University (B.A., 1979); Yale University (M.A., 1982; M.Phil., 1983); New York University (J.D., 1987). Order of the Coif. Fullbright Scholar, 1979-1980; Hays Civil Liberties Fellowship; Frank H. Sommer Memorial Award; Alumnae Club Key Pin; Goldstein Prize (labor law); Recipient: Anne Litchfield Prize, Cornell University. Articles Editor, New York University Law Review, 1984-1987. Author: "From 'Definition'to Exploration: 'Social Groups' & Political Asylum Eligibility," 26 San Diego Law Review 739. 1989. Adjunct Professor, Loyola Law School, 1989-1990. *Member:* State Bar of California. **LANGUAGES:** Spanish and Mandarin Chinese. **PRACTICE AREAS:** Litigation; Special Education Law.

**GILLIAN STEIN,** born Pretoria, South Africa, July 19, 1954; admitted to bar, 1978, South Africa; 1984, California; 1989, U.S. District Court, Central District of California. *Education:* University of Witwatersrand (B. Proc, 1978). President, Law Student Council. *Member:* State Bar of California. **PRACTICE AREAS:** Special Education; Environmental.

#### OF COUNSEL

**STEVEN W. KEREKES,** born New Brunswick, New Jersey, November 20, 1958; admitted to bar, 1983, California, U.S. District Court, Central District of California and U.S. Court of Appeals, Ninth Circuit. *Education:* Duke University (A.B., magna cum laude, 1980); University of Southern California (J.D., 1983). Phi Alpha Delta. Staff Member, Major Tax Planning, 1981-1982. Judicial Extern to the Hon. Jack B. Weinstein, Eastern District of New York, Spring, 1983. Candidate for Masters of Business Taxation, University of Southern California. *Member:* Beverly Hills Bar Association (Member, Section on: Litigation and Real Estate); State Bar of California (Member, Sections on: Litigation, Real Estate and Business Law). **LANGUAGES:** French. **PRACTICE AREAS:** Commercial Litigation; Real Estate Law.

**RUSSELL J. THOMAS, JR.,** born Cambridge, Massachusetts, December 19, 1942; admitted to bar, 1967, Massachusetts; 1970, U.S. Court of Appeals, 4th, 6th and 9th Circuits; 1972, Michigan, District of Columbia and U.S. District Court, Eastern District of Michigan; 1977, U.S. Supreme Court; 1979, California and U. S. District Court, Central District of California; 1981, U.S. District Court, Northern District of California; 1984, U.S. District Court, District of Massachusetts and Western District of Michigan; 1985, U.S. District Court, Eastern District of California and U.S. Court of Appeals, 5th Circuit; 1987, U.S. Court of Appeals, 7th Circuit; 1988, U.S. District Court, Eastern District of Wis. *Education:* Harvard University (A.B., cum laude, 1964; LL.B., 1967). *Member:* State Bar of Michigan; State Bar of California. **PRACTICE AREAS:** Litigation; Employment Law.

---

## STEVEN L. DICKINSON
### SUITE 1920
### 650 TOWN CENTER DRIVE
### COSTA MESA, CALIFORNIA 92626
Telephone: 714-662-1600
Fax: 714-754-0444
Email: dassoc@chelsea.ios.com

Insurance Coverage, General Corporate, Intellectual Property Litigation and General Civil and Appellate Litigation in all State and Federal Courts.

FIRM PROFILE: The Dickinson Law firm a full service law firm catering to small and large companies that are in the process of forming new business. The firms philosophy is, cancel the client before he gets into trouble. Mr. Dickinson believes that his clients are his friends. A telephone call doesn't bring dollar signs to his eyes. What works best for the clients and how can the firm help them.

*(This Listing Continued)*

CAA137B

## STEVEN L. DICKINSON, Costa Mesa—Continued

**STEVEN L. DICKINSON,** born Chicago, Illinois, May 27, 1958; admitted to bar, 1981, Ohio; 1982, U.S. District Court, Southern District of Ohio; 1983, California; 1984, U.S. District Court, Central District of California. *Education:* University of California at Los Angeles (B.A., cum laude, 1978; J.D., 1981). Member, National Moot Court Team, 1981. *Member:* Columbus, Ohio State and American Bar Associations; State Bar of California. **PRACTICE AREAS:** Commercial Litigation; Intellectual Property Law; Insurance Policy Holders Law; Coverage Litigation.

REPRESENTATIVE CLIENTS: CitiBank International; CitiBank N.A.; CitiBank F.I.B.; Cascade Systems, Inc.; Nitinol Devices & Components; Advanced Metal Components Inc.

---

# DORSEY & WHITNEY LLP

CENTER TOWER
650 TOWN CENTER DRIVE, SUITE 1850
P.O. BOX 5066
**COSTA MESA, CALIFORNIA 92626**
Telephone: 714-662-7300

*Minneapolis, Minnesota Office:* 220 South 6th Street, 55402. Telephone: 612-340-2600. Cable Address: "Dorow" Telex: 290605. Answer-back "Dorsey Law MPS".

*Rochester, Minnesota Office:* 201 First Avenue, S.W., Suite 340, 55902. Telephone: 507-288-3156.

*Des Moines, Iowa Office:* 801 Grand, Suite 3900, 50309. Telephone: 515-283-1000.

*New York, New York Office:* 250 Park Avenue, 10177. Telephone: 212-415-9200.

*Washington, D.C. Office:* Suite 200, 1330 Connecticut Avenue, N.W., 20036. Telephone: 202-452-6900.

*Brussels, Belgium Office:* 35 Square De Meeûs 1000. Telephone: 011-32-2-504-4611.

*London, England Office:* 3 Gracechurch Street, EC3V OAT. Telephone: 011-44-171-929-3334.

*Billings, Montana Office:* 1200 First Interstate Center, 401 North 31st Street, P.O. Box 7188, 59103. Telephone: 406-252-3800.

*Great Falls, Montana Office:* 507 Davidson Building, 8 Third Street North, P.O. Box 1566, 59401. Telephone: 406-727-3632.

*Missoula, Montana Office:* 127 East Front Street, Suite 310, 59802. Telephone: 406-721-6025.

*Denver, Colorado Office:* 370 Seventeenth Street, Republic Plaza Building, Suite 4400, 80202-5644. Telephone: 303-629-3400.

*Salt Lake City, Utah Office:* First Interstate Plaza, 170 South Main Street, Suite 925, 84101. Telephone: 801-350-3581.

*Fargo, North Dakota Office:* Dakota Center, 51 North Broadway, Suite 402, P.O. Box 1344, 58107-1344. Telephone: 701-235-6000.

*Seattle, Washington Office:* Second and Seneca Building, 1191 Second Avenue, Suite 1440, 98101. Telephone: 206-654-5400.

*Hong Kong Office:* Suite 4003, Two Exchange Square, 8 Connaught Place, Central Hong Kong. Telephone: 011-852-252-65000. Fax: 011-852-252-43000.

*Banking and Commercial, Corporate Finance, Employee Benefits, Environmental, Estate Planning and Administration, Foreign Trade, Health Law, Government and Regulatory Affairs, Intellectual Property, International, Labor and Employment Law, Litigation, Real Estate, Tax, and Municipal and Public Authority Financing.*

### MEMBER OF FIRM

**DONALD A. KAUL,** born 1935; admitted to bar, 1962, District of Columbia; 1980, New York; registered to practice before U.S. Patent and Trademark Office (Not admitted in California). *Education:* Lehigh University and Ohio State University (B.M.E., 1958); George Washington University (J.D., 1962). **PRACTICE AREAS:** Trademark; Copyright; Litigation. *Email:* kaul.donald@dorseylaw.com

**JEFFREY L SIKKEMA,** born 1955; admitted to bar, 1983, Minnesota; 1993, California. *Education:* University of Michigan (B.A., 1978); Harvard University (J.D., 1982). **PRACTICE AREAS:** Litigation. *Email:* sikkema.jeff@dorseylaw.com

**DENNIS WONG,** born 1952; admitted to bar, 1978, California. *Education:* University of California, Los Angeles (B.A., 1975); University of San Francisco (J.D., 1978). **PRACTICE AREAS:** Public Finance; Banking. *Email:* wong.dennis@dorseylaw.com

*(This Listing Continued)*

### ASSOCIATES

**JUAN C. BASOMBRIO,** born 1964; admitted to bar, 1989, Minnesota; 1991, California; 1992, U.S. Supreme Court. *Education:* University of Houston (B.A., 1986); Indiana University (J.D., 1989). **LANGUAGES:** Spanish. **PRACTICE AREAS:** Business Litigation; Corporate Law; International Law. *Email:* basombrio.juan@dorseylaw.com

**NANCY B. SMITH,** born 1959; admitted to bar, 1990, Minnesota; 1992, Colorado (Not admitted in California). *Education:* University of Colorado (B.A., 1981); William Mitchell College of Law (J.D., 1990). **PRACTICE AREAS:** Litigation. *Email:* smith.nancy@dorseylaw.com

**PAUL NATHAN TAUGER,** born 1953; admitted to bar, 1992, California. *Education:* University of Massachusetts at Amherst (B.A., 1974); University of North Carolina at Greensboro (M.F.A., 19767); Loyola of Los Angeles (J.D., 1992). **PRACTICE AREAS:** Intellectual Property Litigation; Business Litigation. *Email:* paul.tauger@dorseylaw.com

FIRM IS COUNSEL FOR: 3M; ADC Telecommunications, Inc.; Aetna Life & Casualty; Air & Water Technologies, Inc.; Alliant Techsystems, Inc.; American Academy of Ophthalmology; American Express Financial Advisors, Inc.; Apogee Enterprises, Inc.; Armco Inc.; Board of Investments of the State of Montana; Boise Cascade Corporation; Byerly's Inc.; Cargill, Incorporated; City of Edina; CNA Insurance Companies; The Cretex Companies, Inc.; Curative Technologies, Inc.; D.A. Davidson, Inc.; Dain Bosworth, Incorporated; Equitable Real Estate; Erickson Petroleum Corporation; Fairview Hospital & Healthcare; Fingerhut Companies, Inc.; First Bank National Association; First Bank System, Inc.; Fortis Funds; George A. Hormel & Co.; Goldman, Sachs & Co.; Goodyear Tire & Rubber Co.; Graco Inc.; Green Tree Financial Corporation; Grupo Sidek, S.A. de C.V.; HealthSystem Minnesota; ITT Financial; Imation; Inter-Regional Financial Group; Interactive Technologies, Inc.; Iowa Finance Authority; Johnson Brothers Corporation; Kraus-Anderson, Incorporated; Mayo Clinic; Minneapolis Employees' Retirement Fund; National Computer Systems Inc.; Northwest Airlines, Inc.; Otter Tail Power Company; Piper Jaffray; Porsche Cars North America, Inc.; Ryan Construction Company of MN; Southern Minnesota Municipal Power Agency; SUPERVALU INC.; United Healthcare Corporation; University of Minnesota; Voyageur Funds Group; Waldorf Corporation; ZEOS International, Ltd.

---

# DRAPER & WALSH

3420 BRISTOL STREET, #225
**COSTA MESA, CALIFORNIA 92626**
Telephone: 714-557-9874
Fax: 714-557-9908

*Litigation, General Business Litigation.*

**PAUL D. DRAPER,** born Portland, Oregon, November 21, 1947; admitted to bar, 1990, California and U.S. District Court, Central District of California; 1992, U.S. District Court, Southern District of California. *Education:* San Jose State University (B.A., with great distinction, 1978); University of British Columbia, Vancouver (M.A., 1985); University of California, Hastings College of the Law (J.D., 1990). Recipient, American Jurisprudence Award in Trial Advocacy. *Member:* Orange County Bar Association; State Bar of California. [Sgt., U.S. Army, 1965-1968]. **LANGUAGES:** Mandarin. **PRACTICE AREAS:** Business Litigation; Property Tax Appeals; Employers Rights; Employees Rights; Real Estate Litigation. *Email:* dwllp@earthlink.net

**MICHAEL J. WALSH,** born Norwalk, California, March 20, 1967; admitted to bar, 1991, California, U.S. District Court, Central, Southern, Northern and Eastern Districts of California and U.S. Court of Appeals, 9th Circuit. *Education:* California State University at Fullerton (B.A., 1988); University of Southern California (J.D., 1991). Phi Alpha Delta. *Member:* Orange County Bar Association; State Bar of California. **PRACTICE AREAS:** Mechanics Liens; Construction Litigation; Business Litigation; Real Estate Litigation; Commercial Collections. *Email:* dwllp@earthlink.net

---

# DRUMMY KING WHITE & GIRE

A PROFESSIONAL CORPORATION

Established in 1991

3200 PARK CENTER DRIVE, SUITE 1000
**COSTA MESA, CALIFORNIA 92626**
Telephone: 714-850-1800
Fax: 714-850-4500

*General Civil Practice, Litigation in all State and Federal Courts. Trial and Appellate Practice, Business, Real Estate, Public and Private Works Construction Law, Financial Institution Liability, Labor Law Matters, Commercial*

*(This Listing Continued)*

Litigation, Corporate Mergers and Acquisitions, Partnerships, Joint Ventures, Licensing, Securities Offerings, Sale and Leasings of Real Property.

FIRM PROFILE: The senior members of Drummy King White and Gire have practiced law in Orange County for three decades and have achieved high levels of expertise in civil litigation, with an emphasis on commercial and real estate litigation, financial institution litigation, labor related matters, and corporate/real estate transactions. The firm handles litigation in all state and federal courts throughout California, and provides advice on corporate and real estate matters for individuals, privately held companies, and public corporations. The members and associates of Drummy King White and Gire are committed to providing top quality legal services for their clients.

**STEPHEN C. DRUMMY,** born Santa Monica, California, March 20, 1938; admitted to bar, 1966, California. *Education:* University of California at Los Angeles (B.S., 1962; J.D., 1965). Panelist, Continuing Education of the Bar Courses: Short Nonjury Trial, 1976 and 1982; Courtroom Conduct-Tactics and Ethics, 1982; Handling the Short Nonjury Civil Trial, 1986. Member, American Arbitration Association Large Complex Case Panel. *Member:* Orange County (Member, Board of Directors, 1979-1981) and American Bar Associations; The State Bar of California (Member, Ethics Committee, 1976-1978); The Association of Trial Lawyers of America. *PRACTICE AREAS:* Commercial and Real Estate Litigation.

**JOHN P. KING, JR.,** born Huntington Park, California, May 8, 1944; admitted to bar, 1969, California. *Education:* Occidental College (A.B., 1965); University of California at Berkeley (J.D., 1968). *Member:* Orange County and American Bar Associations; The State Bar of California. *PRACTICE AREAS:* Corporate Law; Corporate Acquisitions Law; Securities Law.

**ALAN I. WHITE,** born Boston, Massachusetts, November 29, 1945; admitted to bar, 1971, California. *Education:* University of Massachusetts (A.B., 1967); Georgetown University (J.D., 1971). Editor, Georgetown University Law Journal, 1970-1971. *Member:* Orange County and American Bar Associations; The State Bar of California. *PRACTICE AREAS:* Civil litigation with emphasis on General Business Law; Real Estate Law; Commercial Litigation; Bankruptcy Litigation.

**CHARLES W. PARRET,** born Santa Monica, California, August 9, 1950; admitted to bar, 1977, California. *Education:* University of California at Los Angeles (B.S., 1972); University of Southern California (J.D., 1977). *Member:* Orange County Bar Association; The State Bar of California. *PRACTICE AREAS:* Civil Litigation with emphasis on Business and Real Estate Law.

**LEROY M. GIRE,** born Los Angeles, California, October 17, 1938; admitted to bar, 1964, California. *Education:* University of California at Los Angeles (B.S., 1960; LL.B., 1963). Order of the Coif. Member, U.C.L.A. Law Review, 1961 and 1962. Member, Associated General Contractors. Arbitrator, State Panel, Public Construction Disputes and American Arbitration Association Panel Complex Construction Disputes. *Member:* Los Angeles County and American (Member, Section of Public Contract Law) Bar Associations; State Bar of California. *PRACTICE AREAS:* Public and Private Works Construction; Bid Disputes; Contract Formation and Interpretation; Preparing and Defending against Claims arising during construction; Litigation and ADR Procedures.

**MICHAEL G. JOERGER,** born Whittier, California, January 13, 1954; admitted to bar, 1981, California. *Education:* California State University at Fullerton (B.A., 1977); Loyola Law School, Los Angeles (J.D., cum laude, 1981). Recipient, American Board of Trial Advocates Award, 1981. Member, Loyola International and Comparative Law Annual, 1979-1980. Member, St. Thomas More Law Honor Society. *Member:* Orange County Bar Association; The State Bar of California. *PRACTICE AREAS:* Civil Litigation with emphasis on Labor, Business and Construction Law.

**GEOFFREY S. PAYNE,** born St. Louis, Missouri, August 25, 1957; admitted to bar, 1987, California, U.S. District Court, Central and Southern Districts of California, U.S. Tax Court and U.S. Court of International Trade. *Education:* Whittier College; California State University at Fullerton (B.A. in Finance, 1979); Loyola Law School, Los Angeles (J.D., 1985). Member, Hughes Aircraft Company, Finance, 1980-1986. *Member:* Long Beach and Los Angeles Bar Associations; State Bar of California (Member, Long Beach Legislative Committee; Delegate, State Bar Annual Meetings, 1993-1994). *PRACTICE AREAS:* Commercial Real Property; Corporate Finance; Leases; Lending and Secured Transactions.

**JEFFREY M. RICHARD,** born Tucson, Arizona, May 13, 1957; admitted to bar, 1982, California. *Education:* University of California at Riverside (A.B., with honors, 1979); Boalt Hall School of Law, University of

*(This Listing Continued)*

California at Berkeley (J.D., 1982). Regents' Scholar. Judicial Externship, California State Court of Appeal, First District, 1981. *Member:* Orange County Bar Association; The State Bar of California. *PRACTICE AREAS:* Civil Litigation with emphasis on Business and Real Estate Law.

**LISA A. STEPANSKI,** born Terre Haute, Indiana, December 19, 1959; admitted to bar, 1986, California. *Education:* Pepperdine University (B.S., 1981); Georgetown University (J.D., 1985). *Member:* Orange County Bar Association; State Bar of California. *PRACTICE AREAS:* Civil Litigation with emphasis on Business Law.

**KENNETH W. CURTIS,** born Orange, California, October 5, 1963; admitted to bar, 1988, California. *Education:* California State University at Long Beach (B.S., 1985); Loyola Law School, Los Angeles (J.D., 1988). Recipient, American Jurisprudence Award, Trial Advocacy. Staff Member, 1986-1987 and Senior Note and Comment Editor, 1987-1988, Loyola of Los Angeles Law Review. Author: Comment, "The Fiduciary Controversy: Injection of Fiduciary Principles into The Bank-Depositor and Bank-Borrower Relationships," 20 Loyola of Los Angeles Law Review 795, 1987. *Member:* Orange County Bar Association; State Bar of California. *PRACTICE AREAS:* Civil Litigation with emphasis on Business and Real Estate Law; Lender Liability; Public and Private Works Construction.

**ALAN A. GREENBERG,** born Brooklyn, New York, April 7, 1964; admitted to bar, 1989, New York; 1990, California, U.S. District Court, Central and Southern Districts of California; 1991, U.S. District Court, Northern and Eastern Districts of California; 1993, U.S. Court of Appeals, Ninth Circuit. *Education:* Cornell University (A.B., 1985); Boston University (J.D., cum laude, 1988). G. Joseph Tauro Scholar; Paul J. Liacos Scholar. Recipient, American Jurisprudence Award in Commercial Paper. *Member:* Orange County Bar Association; State Bar of California. *PRACTICE AREAS:* Civil Litigation with emphasis on General Business Law; Real Estate Law; Commercial Litigation; Bankruptcy Litigation.

---

**MARK R. BECKINGTON,** born Los Angeles, California, September 17, 1957; admitted to bar, 1986, California. *Education:* University of California, Davis (B.A., 1979); Hastings College of the Law (J.D., 1986). *Member:* Orange County Bar Association; State Bar of California. *PRACTICE AREAS:* Litigation.

**LAWRENCE M. BUREK,** born Detroit, Michigan, November 9, 1950; admitted to bar, 1987, California, U.S. District Court, Northern, Eastern, Central and Southern Districts of California and U.S. Court of Appeals, Ninth Circuit. *Education:* Grace College (B.A., 1977); Biola University (M. Div., 1982); Pepperdine University (J.D., 1987). Kappa Tau Epsilon. Author: "Right to Restrain v. Right to Refrain," 13 Pepperdine Law Review 691, 1986; "Clergy Malpractice: Making Clergy Accountable to a Lower Power," 14 Pepperdine Law Review 137, 1986. *Member:* Orange County Bar Association; State Bar of California; Association of Business Trial Lawyers; California Trial Lawyers Association. *PRACTICE AREAS:* Civil Litigation; General Business; Real Estate Law; Commercial Litigation.

**KAREN SMITH FRENCH,** born Somers Point, New Jersey, July 3, 1965; admitted to bar, 1991, Delaware; 1992, Florida; 1996, California. *Education:* Georgetown University (B.S.B.A., cum laude, 1987); University of Pittsburgh (J.D., cum laude, 1990). Author: Note - Tort and Contract: "Pennsylvania Denies a Products Liability Claim for Economic Loss Resulting From a Product Damaged as a Result of Its Own Defect," 9 Journal of Law and Commerce 99, 1989. Head Notes and Comments Editor, The Journal of Law and Commerce, 1989-1990. *Member:* Orange County, Delaware and American Bar Associations; The Florida Bar; State Bar of California. *PRACTICE AREAS:* Business and Corporate Law.

**JOHN D. OTT,** born Long Beach, California, July 26, 1964; admitted to bar, 1992, California; 1993, U.S. District Court, Central District of California; 1995, U.S. District Court, Eastern District of California. *Education:* California State University, Fullerton (B.A., 1986); Loyola Law School; University of Richmond (J.D., 1992). Phi Alpha Delta. *Member:* Los Angeles County and Federal Bar Associations. *PRACTICE AREAS:* Construction Litigation; Products Liability; Real Estate Litigation; Financial Institutions Representation; Employment; Insurance Coverage.

**LEIGH OTSUKA,** born Garden Grove, California, December 13, 1968; admitted to bar, 1994, California. *Education:* University of Southern California (B.A., 1990); Loyola Law School, Los Angeles (J.D., 1994). St. Thomas More Law Honor Society. Member, Loyola of Los Angeles Law Review, 1993-1994. *PRACTICE AREAS:* Litigation.

A List of Representative Clients will be furnished upon request and after Client Approval.

## LAW OFFICES OF
## W. DOUGLAS EASTON

*Established in 1991*

3200 PARK CENTER DRIVE, SUITE 1000
**COSTA MESA, CALIFORNIA 92626**
Telephone: 714-850-4590
Fax: 714-850-4500

*Civil Litigation in Personal Injury, Medical Malpractice, Products Liability and Legal Malpractice.*

FIRM PROFILE: *Standing between the individual and the abuse of power by the government, corporations and other individuals, the Easton firm is committed to providing quality legal representation in the personal injury and medical malpractice arenas to those individuals seriously injured by such abuse. This commitment to excellence is enhanced by the familial nature of the firm, and all share the same vision of assisting those who have been seriously injured in obtaining fair and adequate compensation for the harm done them.*

*The firm takes pride in its listing in the Bar Register of Preeminent Lawyers.*

**W. DOUGLAS EASTON,** born Los Angeles, California, September 21, 1942; admitted to bar, 1971, California. *Education:* Brigham Young University (A.B., cum laude, 1967); University of California at Berkeley (J.D., 1970). *Member:* Orange County and American Bar Associations; The State Bar of California; California Trial Lawyers Association; The Association of Trial Lawyers of America; Orange County Trial Lawyers Association. **LANGUAGES:** Finnish. **PRACTICE AREAS:** Personal Injury Law; Medical Malpractice Law; Legal Malpractice Law; Products Liability Law; Insurance Bad Faith.

---

**ANDERSON L. WASHBURN,** born Whittier, California, November 18, 1956; admitted to bar, 1988, California. *Education:* Brigham Young University (B.A., 1982; J.D., cum laude, 1987). *Member:* Orange County Bar Association; State Bar of California. **LANGUAGES:** Spanish.

**RUSSEL W. JONES,** born Hawthorne, California, August 17, 1966; admitted to bar, 1994, California. *Education:* Brigham Young University (B.A., 1990); Western State University (J.D., 1994). *Member:* State Bar of California. **LANGUAGES:** Spanish. **PRACTICE AREAS:** Personal Injury; Medical Malpractice; Business Litigation.

**BRIAN W. EASTON,** born Oakland, California, December 30, 1968; admitted to bar, 1995, California. *Education:* Brigham Young University (B.S., magna cum laude, 1992; J.D., cum laude, 1995). Journal Dispute Resolution, Missouri School of Law, 1996. *Member:* American Bar Association; The State Bar of California. **PRACTICE AREAS:** Torts; Personal Injury; Litigation; Medical Malpractice.

---

## ELY, FRITZ & HOGAN

*Established in 1988*

3100 BRISTOL STREET #200
**COSTA MESA, CALIFORNIA 92626**
Telephone: 714-556-1480
Telecopier: 714-556-2863

*General Civil Practice in all State and Federal Courts. Products Liability, Construction, Insurance and General Negligence, Toxic Tort Defense, Aviation Law, Insurance Fraud.*

FIRM PROFILE: *Ely, Fritz & Hogan was formed in 1988.*

*The firm maintains standards of excellence in all areas of litigation practice. Its corporate and insurance industry clients expect and receive an innovative and aggressive approach to their litigation matters.*

*Although located in Orange County, the firm's practice is not so geographically limited. The firm's attorneys regularly appear in courts throughout Southern California, including Ventura, Los Angeles, San Diego, Riverside and San Bernardino Counties.*

### MEMBERS OF FIRM

**THOMAS W. ELY,** born Los Angeles, California, January 16, 1942; admitted to bar, 1973, California. *Education:* University of California at Los Angeles and California State University at Northridge (B.A., 1966); Pepperdine University (J.D., 1973). *Member:* Pepperdine University Law Review, 1971-1972. *Member:* Orange County Bar Association; The State Bar of California; American Board of Trial Advocates. **PRACTICE AREAS:** Products Liability Law; Negligence Law.

**JAMES H. FRITZ,** born LaSalle, Illinois, April 7, 1945; admitted to bar, 1974, California; 1975, Illinois; U.S. District Court, Central, Southern, Northern and Eastern Districts of California; U.S. Court of Appeals, Ninth Circuit; U.S. Supreme Court. *Education:* University of Illinois (B.S.E.E., 1967; M.S.E.E., 1968); Loyola University of Los Angeles (J.D., 1974). Tau Beta Pi; Eta Kappa Nu. Research Assistant, University of Illinois, 1967-1968. Registered Professional Engineer. *Member:* Los Angeles County, Orange County, Illinois State and American Bar Associations; The State Bar of California; Institute of Electrical and Electronics Engineers; Society of Automotive Engineers; Association of Southern California Defense Counsel; Lawyer-Pilots Bar Association. **PRACTICE AREAS:** Aviation Law; Products Liability Law; Construction Law; Negligence Law; Patent Litigation; General Litigation; Business Litigation.

**MICHAEL G. HOGAN,** born Indianapolis, Indiana, November 16, 1946; admitted to bar, 1976, Iowa; 1978, Michigan; 1980, California; U.S. District Court, Central, Southern, Eastern and Northern Districts of California; U.S. Court of Appeals, Ninth Circuit; U.S. Supreme Court. *Education:* Purdue University (B.S., 1972); Indiana University (J.D., magna cum laude, 1976); Wayne State University. Delta Theta Phi. Instructor, Trial Advocacy and Legal Research, Detroit College of Law, 1978-1980. *Member:* Orange County and American Bar Associations; Iowa State Bar Association; State Bar of Michigan; State Bar of California; Lawyer-Pilots Bar Association (Member, Product Liability Advisory Council). [With USMC, 1966-1967]. **PRACTICE AREAS:** Products Liability Law; Negligence Law.

**JEROME D. RYBARCZYK,** born Hazleton, Pennsylvania, September 26, 1954; admitted to bar, 1982, California; U.S. District Court, Central, Southern, Eastern and Northern Districts of California; U.S. Court of Appeals, Ninth Circuit. *Education:* Villanova University (B.A., magna cum laude, 1976; J.D., 1981). Pi Sigma Alpha. *Member:* Orange County and American Bar Associations; The State Bar of California. **PRACTICE AREAS:** Products Liability Law; Insurance Defense; Business Litigation; General Civil Litigation.

---

**CHARLES A. CORREIA,** born San Diego, California, April 9, 1952; admitted to bar, 1979, California; 1981, U.S. District Court, Central District of California. *Education:* University of California at Berkeley (A.B., 1974); University of Southern California (J.D., 1978). Recipient: Departmental Citation and Certificate of Merit, University of California at Berkeley. Member, Los Angeles Defense Lawyers, 1988-1991. *Member:* Orange County Bar Association; The State Bar of California; Association of Southern California Defense Counsel. **LANGUAGES:** French. **PRACTICE AREAS:** Insurance Defense; Insurance Fraud.

**RONALD F. TEMPLER,** born Whittier, California, August 10, 1963; admitted to bar, 1989, California and U.S. Court of Appeals, Ninth Circuit; 1990, U.S. District Court, Central District of California. *Education:* University of Southern California (B.S., 1985); Pepperdine University (J.D., 1989). *Member:* Orange County Bar Association; State Bar of California; Association of Southern California Defense Counsel; Defense Research Institute. **PRACTICE AREAS:** Products Liability; Insurance Defense; Insurance Fraud; Business Litigation; General Civil Litigation.

**ALLEN D. MACNEIL,** born Bitburg, Germany, September 26, 1963; admitted to bar, 1994, California and U.S. District Court, Central District of California. *Education:* University of California at Davis (B.A., 1985); Loyola University of Los Angeles (J.D. 1994). Phi Alpha Delta. *Member:* Orange County and American Bar Associations; State Bar of California. **PRACTICE AREAS:** General Civil Defense; Insurance Fraud.

### OF COUNSEL

**GERALD W. MOUZIS,** born Burbank, California, May 23, 1953; admitted to bar, 1980, California; 1981, U.S. District Court, Central District of California. *Education:* University of Southern California (B.A., 1975; M.A., 1976); Southwestern University (J.D., 1979). *Member:* Orange County Bar Association; The State Bar of California. **PRACTICE AREAS:** Civil Litigation; Products Liability; Construction Defect/Land Subsidence; Real Estate Litigation; Business Litigation and Transactional Matters.

REPRESENTATIVE CLIENTS: Xerox Corp.; Nissan North America, Inc.; United States Elevator Corp.; Kawasaki Motors Corp., U.S.A; American Isuzu Motors, Inc.; Associated Aviation Underwriters of America; Subaru of America, Inc.; Nissan Motor Co., Ltd.; Kawasaki Heavy Industries, Ltd.; Corning Glass Works; Tokio Marine and Fire Insurance Company, Ltd.; Isuzu Motors, Ltd.; Mercury Casualty Co.; Federal Pacific Electric Co.; Reliance Electric; State

*(This Listing Continued)*

Farm Fire and Casualty Co.; Kemper Insurance Co.; Pro Mark Products; Argonaut Insurance Co.; McKesson Corp.; State Farm Automobile Insurance Co.; TRW, Inc.; Snap-On Tools Corp.; Progressive Insurance Co.; Gallo Wine. REFERENCE: Sunwest Bank, Tustin.

## LAW OFFICES OF
## ROBERT J. FELDHAKE
PLAZA TOWER, SUITE 1730
600 ANTON BOULEVARD
COSTA MESA, CALIFORNIA 92626-7124
Telephone: 714-438-3885
Fax: 714-438-3888

*San Diego, California Office:* 501 West Broadway, Suite 1600, Koll Center, 92101. Telephone: 619-235-9443. Facsimile: 619-235-9449.

Litigation. General Business-Corporate Law.

**ROBERT J. FELDHAKE,** born Trenton, New Jersey, December 13, 1954; admitted to bar, 1979, Illinois and U.S. District Court, Northern District of Illinois; 1982, California, U.S. Court of Appeals, Seventh Circuit and U.S. District Court Central District of California; 1984, U.S. District Court, Northern District of California; 1985, U.S. Court of Appeals, Ninth Circuit; 1987, U.S. District Court, Southern District of California; 1988, U.S. Supreme Court; 1990, U.S. Tax Court. *Education:* Augustana College (B.A., cum laude, 1976); DePaul University (J.D., with highest honors, 1979). Phi Alpha Delta; Phi Beta Kappa. National Debate Tournament: 1974, 1975, 1976; First Speaker, 1976; Second Speaker, 1976; Second Place Team, 1974; Third Place Team, 1976. Recipient: American Jurisprudence Awards in Constitutional Law; Administrative Law, Unfair Trade Practice and Antitrust; Bureau of National Affairs and DePaul University Award for Scholastic Achievement. Co-Chairperson, Moot Court, Board, 1978-1979. Member, National Moot Court Team. Regional Director, American Bar Association/YLD National Law Explorer Moot Court Competition, 1985, 1986. Lecturer: Pre-Law Society, California State University, Fullerton, 1989-1995; Communication and the Law, University of Southern California, 1987; Communication and the Legal Arena, California State University, Fullerton, 1987-1995. Author: "Undergraduate Curriculum and Law School Performance, Western Communication Association Convention, Albuquerque, New Mexico, 1983; "Research and Strategy Needs in Selection of Juries," Journal of Argumentation Conference, 1984; "Jury Selection and Communication Variables", National Conference on Communication and the Legal Arena, Communication Skills and the Practice of Lawyering, Crawford and Matlon, 1984; "Evaluation of Communication Theory and Applicability to the Practice of Law", Speech Communication Association's Commission on Communication and the Law, Chicago, Illinois, 1984; "Evaluation of Current Behavioral Research in Legal Communication," Critic on Communication and Law Consortium Panel on Current Behavioral Research, Speech Communication Association, 1984; "Forensics Education as Preparation for Legal Education," Western Communication Conference, 1983; "A Critique of Communications, Sociology and Psychology Research", Speech Communication Association Convention, Denver, Colorado, 1985; "Communications Research: Evaluations of Needs and Functional Utility in the Practice of Civil Litigation," Speech Communications Association National Convention, Denver, 1985; "Requisites for Law School and Preparation as a Legal Consultant," Western Communication Association, Sacramento, California, 1990; "Analysis of Hindsight Bias in Jury Trials," American Trial Consultants Convention, New Orleans, Louisiana, 1993; "Liability Analysis of Co-Curricular and Extra-Curricular Programs," 1996, Speech Communications Association, National Convention. Board of Directors, Pacific National Bank, 9 Alarm 1 Security Corporation, Talicor, Inc. and E-Funds Corporation. *Member:* Orange County, Chicago, Los Angeles County, Illinois State and American Bar Associations; State Bar of California; Business Trial Lawyers Association; National School Board Association; National Council of School Attorneys. **PRACTICE AREAS:** Litigation; General Business Law.

### ASSOCIATES

**GARY W. DOLINSKI,** admitted to bar, 1983, California and Ontario, Canada. *Education:* California State University at Fullerton (B.A., 1976); Osgoode Hall Law School (LL.B., 1979); University of Sheffield at England (M.A., Law, with distinction, 1980). National Debate Tournament, California State University, 1973, 1975, 1976. *Member:* San Diego County and North San Diego County Bar Associations; State Bar of California; Law Society of Upper Canada (Province of Ontario); American Trial Lawyers Association; California Trial Lawyers Association; San Diego Trial Law-

*(This Listing Continued)*

yers Association. (Resident, San Diego Office). **PRACTICE AREAS:** Litigation (100%).

**LORINDA B. HARRIS,** born Walnut Creek, California, September 21, 1968; admitted to bar, 1995, California. *Education:* University of California at Irvine (B.A., in History, 1991); University of San Diego (J.D., 1994). Phi Alpha Delta. Order of Omega. *Member:* Ocean County, San Diego and American Bar Associations; State Bar of California. **LANGUAGES:** German. **PRACTICE AREAS:** Business Litigation.

## FITZPATRICK, CELLA, HARPER & SCINTO
650 TOWN CENTER DRIVE, SUITE 1800
COSTA MESA, CALIFORNIA 92626
Telephone: 714-540-8700
Facsimile: 714-540-9823

*New York, N.Y. Office:* 277 Park Avenue. Telephone: 212-758-2400. International-Telex: FCHS 236262. Cable Address: "Fitzcel New York". Facsimile: 212-758-2982.
*Washington, D.C. Office:* 1001 Pennsylvania Avenue, N.W. Telephone: 202-347-8100. Facsimile: 202-347-8136.

*Intellectual Property Practice. Patent, Trademark, Copyright, Trade Secret, Unfair Competition, Computer, Licensing, Antitrust and International Trade Law. Trials and Appeals in Federal and State Courts and Administrative Agencies.*

FIRM PROFILE: Founded in 1971, Fitzpatrick, Cella, Harper & Scinto has grown to over 100 attorneys specializing in intellectual property law. The firm has offices in New York, Washington, D.C., and Orange County, California. Each of our lawyers practices exclusively in the intellectual property field, and most have extensive experience in various fields of technology including electronics, chemistry, physics, biotechnology, pharmaceuticals, software, and computers. The firm's clients include some of the world's largest multinational corporations as well as smaller corporations and universities in the United States, Asia, Europe, Australia and South America. Counseling of clients includes advice for both domestic and global intellectual property strategies. The firm is involved in all aspects of litigation with respect to patents, trademarks, counterfeiting, trade secrets, unfair competition, international trade, and copyrights, including trials and appeals, and proceedings before the International Trade Commission. The firm has an extensive practice in the prosecution of patent and trademark applications in the United States and abroad, and handles patent interferences, trademark oppositions and cancellations, due diligence studies, patent and trademark opinions, technology transfers and licensing.

### RESIDENT PARTNER

**MICHAEL K. O'NEILL,** born New York, N.Y., December 25, 1955; admitted to bar, 1986, New Jersey; 1987, New York; 1991, California. *Education:* Stevens Institute of Technology (B.S. Math., magna cum laude, 1977; M.E. Elec. Eng., magna cum laude, 1980); New York Law School (J.D., magna cum laude, 1986). Research Editor, New York Law School Law Review. *Member:* New York State Bar Association; Orange County Patent Law Association; Licensing Executives Society; New York Intellectual Property Law Association.

### RESIDENT ASSOCIATES

**MARK J. ITRI,** born Boston, Massachusetts, February 14, 1963; admitted to bar, 1990, California. *Education:* Boston University (B.S.E.E., 1985); Suffolk University Law School (J.D., 1990). *Member:* Orange County and American Bar Associations; Orange County Patent Law Association; American and Los Angeles Intellectual Property Law Associations; Licensing Executive Society.

**PAUL A. PYSHER,** born Catskill, New York, February 19, 1967; admitted to bar, 1994, California. *Education:* Rensselaer Polytechnic Institute (B.S.E.E., 1989) Eta Kappa Nu; Boston University School of Law (J.D., 1994). Intellectual Property Concentration with honors. *Member:* Orange County Bar Association.

**JOSEPH G. SWAN,** born Kenmore, New York, February 19, 1963; admitted to bar, 1993, California and U.S. District Court, Central District of California. *Education:* State University of New York at Buffalo (B.S., Electrical Engineering, 1984); University of Southern California (M.S., Electrical Engineering, 1987); Columbia University (J.D., 1992). Harlan Fiske Stone Scholar. Business Law Review. *Member:* State Bar of California.

**NANDU A. TALWALKAR,** born Bradford, Pennsylvania, June 1, 1970; admitted to bar, 1996, California. *Education:* University of Illinois

*(This Listing Continued)*

**FITZPATRICK, CELLA, HARPER & SCINTO,** Costa Mesa—Continued

(B.S.E.E., 1992); University of Southern California Law Center (J.D., 1995). *Member:* Orange County and American Bar Associations; American Intellectual Property Law Association.

(For complete biographical data on all personnel, see Professional Biographies at New York, New York)

## LAW OFFICES OF
## CHARLES H. GIAMPOLO
*A PROFESSIONAL CORPORATION*
*Established in 1982*
IMPERIAL BANK TOWER
695 TOWN CENTER DRIVE
SUITE 1450, FOURTEENTH FLOOR
**COSTA MESA, CALIFORNIA 92626**
Telephone: 714-979-9044
Fax: 714-979-9047

*Corporate Law; Sales and Secured Commercial Transactions; Contract Law; Business Law; Enforcement of Judgments; Collections.*

*FIRM PROFILE: Charles Giampolo's extensive background in Sales and Marketing has been an invaluable asset to the law firm's corporate clients and has complimented the law firm's representation of Fortune 1000 industrial manufacturers and distributors. The Firm is able to deliver a large-firm senior attorney without large-firm overhead. Since the firm's associates are licensed in various states across the country, it is able to offer a cost effective national legal network to large corporations who choose to retain the smaller firm which is sophisticated in delivering cost-efficient quality services in an efficient manner.*

**CHARLES H. GIAMPOLO,** born Orange, New Jersey, December 3, 1956; admitted to bar, 1982, California; 1983, New Jersey, U.S. District Court, Central District of New Jersey and U.S. Court of Appeals, Ninth Circuit; 1989, New York. *Education:* Montclair State College (B.A., 1978); Southwestern University School of Law (J.D., 1982). *Member:* Orange County, New York State, New Jersey State and American Bar Associations; State Bar of California. *PRACTICE AREAS:* Sales and Secured Commercial Transactions; Contract Law; Enforcement of Judgement Law; Collection Law.

*LEGAL SUPPORT PERSONNEL*

**STACY J. HILL** (Certified Legal Assistant).

Languages: French and Italian

REPRESENTATIVE CLIENTS: Wyle Laboratories; Roland Digital America; Escod Industries; XECOM Communications.

## GINSBURG, STEPHAN, ORINGHER & RICHMAN, P.C.
535 ANTON BOULEVARD
SUITE 800
**COSTA MESA, CALIFORNIA 92626-1902**
Telephone: 714-241-0420
Fax: 714-241-0622

*Los Angeles, California Office:* 10100 Santa Monica Boulevard, Eighth Floor, 90067-4012. Telephone: 310-557-2009. Fax: 310-551-0283.

*General Civil Practice, General Business Litigation, Health Care Law, Corporate and Business Transactions, Professional Liability Defense, Employment Litigation, Coverage Litigation, Intellectual Property Litigation, White Collar Criminal Defense, Real Estate Litigation, Product Liability, Securities Fraud and RICO Defense, Consumer Credit Litigation, Copyright, Trademark, Antitrust and Unfair Competition Law.*

*OF COUNSEL*

**STEVEN BROWER,** born Los Angeles, California, February 28, 1954; admitted to bar, 1980, California and U.S. District Court, Central, Southern, Eastern and Northern Districts of California; U.S. Court of Appeals, Ninth Circuit. *Education:* University of California at Los Angeles (A.B., cum laude, 1976; J.D., 1980). Phi Alpha Delta. Author: "Function Design Document: Toward Documentation for Data Processing Contracts," Association of Computing Machinery, Proceedings of the International Conference on Systems Documentation, January, 1982; "Title VII: Early Investigation and Analysis of Exposure Provides the Opportunity to Limit Liability," Los Angeles Daily Journal Report, May 6, 1983; "Software Malpractice: Headline of the Future," Software in Healthcare, February/March, 1984; "Insurance Issues for the Computer Industry," Bos Bar Journal, Sept/Oct. 1989. Judge Pro Tempore, Los Angeles Municipal Court, 1985-1988; Orange County Superior Court, 1990—. *Member:* Orange County, Los Angeles County (Vice-Chair, Attorney-Client Relations Committee, 1981-1985) and American (Member, Sections on: Science and Technology; Litigation; Tort and Insurance Practice) Bar Associations; State Bar of California; Computer Law Association.

**GARY S. MOBLEY,** born San Francisco, California, September 14, 1949; admitted to bar, 1976, California. *Education:* University of California at Los Angeles (B.A., cum laude, 1971); University of San Francisco (J.D., cum laude, 1976). McAuliffe Society. Member, University of San Francisco Law Review, 1975-1976. Author: Comment "Bans on Interviews of Prisoners: Prisoner and Press Rights After Pell and Saxbe," 9 University of San Francisco Law Review 718, 1975. *Member:* Orange County and American Bar Associations; The State Bar of California. *PRACTICE AREAS:* Civil Trial.

**STERLING A. SMITH,** born Sacramento, California, April 12, 1950; admitted to bar, 1978, California and U.S. District Court, Eastern District of California; 1982, U.S. District Court, Central District of California. *Education:* California State University at Sacramento (B.A., 1974); McGeorge School of Law, University of the Pacific (J.D., 1978). Permanent Member, Traynor Honor Society. Managing Editor, Owens Forms and Procedure for California Practice, 1978. Contributing Author: "Motions for Summary Judgment, Joinder of Parties, Dismissals, Judgment on the Pleadings," Owens Forms and Procedure for California Practice, 1976-1978. *Member:* Sacramento County and Orange County Bar Associations; The State Bar of California. *PRACTICE AREAS:* Civil Trial; Real Estate; Taxation.

---

**TRACY L. ANIELSKI,** born Pasadena, California, December 27, 1958; admitted to bar, 1989, California and U.S. District Court, Central and Southern Districts of California. *Education:* Western State University (J.D., summa cum laude, 1988). Extern to the Honorable Warren J. Ferguson, U.S. Court of Appeals, Ninth Circuit, 1988. *Member:* Orange County and American Bar Associations; State Bar of California (Member, Litigation Section).

**JOEL DAVID COVELMAN,** born Philadelphia, Pennsylvania, January 9, 1956; admitted to bar, 1981, California; 1982, U.S. District Court, Central, Southern and Northern Districts of California; 1984, U.S. Court of Appeals, Ninth Circuit; 1986, U.S. Supreme Court. *Education:* Claremont McKenna College (B.A., 1977); Vanderbilt University School of Law (J.D., 1980). Problem Editor, Vanderbilt Moot Court Program, 1979-1980. *Member:* American Bar Association (Member, Sections on: Litigation; Tort and Insurance Practice Law).

**KEYVAN SAMINI,** born Tehran, Iran, September 19, 1966; admitted to bar, 1993, California; 1994, U.S. District Court, Central and Northern Districts of California. *Education:* University of Wisconsin-Madison (B.S., 1989); The Ohio State University (J.D., 1993). Member, Ohio State Law Journal, 1992. Law Clerk, Supreme Court of Ohio, 1993. *Member:* Orange County Bar Association (Member, Taxation Section); State Bar of California.

(For Biographical Data on Personnel at Los Angeles, see Professional Biographies at Los Angeles, California)

## GRAHAM & JAMES LLP
650 TOWN CENTER DRIVE, 6TH FLOOR
**COSTA MESA, CALIFORNIA 92626**
Telephone: 714-751-8800
Cable Address: "Chalgray Newport Beach"
Telex: 4722041
Telecopier: 714-751-8808
Email: jscott@gj.com
URL: http://www.gj.com

*Other offices located in:* San Francisco, Los Angeles, Palo Alto, Sacramento and Fresno, California; Washington, D.C.; Seattle, Washington; New York, New York; Milan, Italy; Beijing, China; Tokyo, Japan; London, England; Dusseldorf, Germany.

*(This Listing Continued)*

*Associated Offices:* Deacons Graham & James, Hong Kong, Sydney, Melbourne, Brisbane, Perth and Canberra, Australia.

*Affiliated Offices:* Deacons Graham & James, Hanoi and Ho Chi Minh City, Vietnam; Taipei, Taiwan and Bangkok, Thailand; In association with Dewi Soeharto & Rekan, Jakarta, Indonesia; Graham & James in affiliation with Taylor Joynson Garrett, London, England, Bucharest, Romania and Brussels, Belgium; Mishare M. Al-Ghazali & Partners, Safat, Kuwait; Law Firm of Salah Al-Hejailan, Jeddah and Riyadh, Saudi Arabia.

General Practice including Litigation in State and Federal Courts. Corporation, Commercial, Intellectual Property, International Business, Labor, Real Estate, Tax, Environmental, Bankruptcy.

### RESIDENT PARTNERS

**EDWARD B. DJANG,** born Zhejiang, China, 1937; admitted to bar, 1976, California, U.S. District Court, Central District of California and U.S. Tax Court; 1980, U.S. Supreme Court; 1984, U.S. District Court, Northern District of California; U.S. District Court, Southern District of California. *Education:* Columbia Union College (B.A., 1962); American University (J.D., 1964). Recipient: American Jurisprudence Awards in Law and Society. Delegate, 1961 White House Conference on Youth. Guest Lecturer, Zhongshan University, Guangzhou, China, Summer, 1985. Director, Counsel to Los Angeles-Jakarta Sister City Association. *Member:* American Bar Association. **LANGUAGES:** Mandarin Chinese. **PRACTICE AREAS:** International Commercial Transactions; Real Estate; Intrastructure; Project Finance. *Email:* edjang@gj.com

**JAMES A. MCQUEEN,** born Milwaukee, Wisconsin, 1952; admitted to bar, 1984, California. *Education:* University of Southern California (B.S., cum laude, 1975; J.D., 1984). Author: Note, "Tax Litigation and Attorneys' Fees: Still a Win-Lose Dichotomy," 57 Southern California Law Review 471, 1984. Student Editor-in-Chief, Major Tax Planning, 1983-1984. Editor-in-Chief, Computer/Law Journal, 1983-1984. Law Clerk to Senior Presiding Justice Margaret J. Morris, California Court of Appeals, Fourth District, 1984-1985. *Member:* Orange County and American Bar Associations. **PRACTICE AREAS:** Business Litigation; Eminent Domain Law. *Email:* jmcqueen@gj.com

**W. JAMES SCOTT, JR.,** born Brooklyn, New York, 1946; admitted to bar, 1972, California. *Education:* Dartmouth College (B.A., 1969); University of Southern California (J.D., 1972). Order of the Coif. Member, University of Southern California Law Review, 1971-1972. *Member:* Orange County and International Bar Associations. **PRACTICE AREAS:** Corporate Law; Business Law. *Email:* jscott@gj.com

**KEVIN K. TAKEUCHI,** born Stockton, California, 1955; admitted to bar, 1982, California and U.S. District Court, Central District of California; 1983, U.S. District Court, Northern, Eastern and Southern Districts of California and U.S. Court of Appeals, Ninth Circuit. *Education:* University of California at Berkeley (B.A., with honors, 1977); Tokyo University, Tokyo, Japan, 1977-1979; Hastings College of Law, University of California (J.D., 1982). Editor-in-Chief, Hastings International and Comparative Law Review, 1981-1982. Member, Litigation Section, State Bar of California, Chairman, Orange County Chapter, 1993-1995. Member, Japan America Society of Southern California, 1983—. Member: Business Advisory Committee, University of California, Irvine Extension International, 1994—; Board of Directors, Irvine Sister Cities Foundation, 1992—. *Member:* Orange County, Los Angeles County (Member, Litigation Section) and American (Member, Litigation Section) Bar Associations; Orange County Japanese-American Lawyers Association (Member, Board of Directors, 1989—); Orange County Asian Bar Association (Member, Board of Directors, 1995—). **LANGUAGES:** Japanese. **PRACTICE AREAS:** Litigation; Corporate Law; Japanese Business. *Email:* ktakeuchi@gj.com

**RICHARD K. ZEPFEL,** born Fullerton, California, 1960; admitted to bar, 1985, California. *Education:* University of California at Irvine; University of California at Los Angeles (B.A., cum laude, 1981); University of Southern California (J.D., 1985). Notes Editor, 1984-1985 and Staff Member, 1983-1984, Southern California Law Review. Licensed Real Estate Broker, California, 1989. Author: "Stopping a Gruesome Parade of Horribles: Criminal Sanctions to Deter Corporate Misuse of Recombinant DNA Technology," 59 Southern California Law Review, 1986; "U.S. Law Could Ground Sales from Portfolios," Venture Capital Journal, Aug. 1990. Legal Writing Instructor, University of Southern California Law Center, 1984-1985. Instructor, University of California at Irvine Extension Legal Assistantship Program, 1986-1991. Trustee, Art Institute of Southern California. Member, Sections on Labor Law and Business Law, State Bar of California. *Member:* Orange County Bar Association (Chair, Business and Corporate Law Section). **PRACTICE AREAS:** Employment Law; Business Law. *Email:* rzepfel@gj.com

**MARK A. ZIEMBA,** born Long Beach, California, 1958; admitted to bar, 1983, California; 1984, U.S. District Court, Southern District of California; 1985, U.S. Tax Court. *Education:* University of California at Irvine (B.A., cum laude, 1980); McGeorge School of Law, University of the Pacific (J.D., with great distinction, 1983); New York University (LL.M. in Taxation, 1984). Order of the Coif; Phi Alpha Delta. Member, Traynor Honor Society. Recipient: Prentice Hall Tax Award; American Jurisprudence Awards in Civil Procedure and Negotiable Instruments. *Member:* The State Bar of California; American Bar Association (Member, Section of Taxation). **PRACTICE AREAS:** State and Federal Taxation Law; Corporate Law; Mergers and Acquisitions Law; Tax Litigation; Estate Planning Law. *Email:* mziemba@gj.com

### OF COUNSEL

**DANIEL L. DAWES,** born Bremerton, Washington, 1946; admitted to bar, 1974, California; 1982, U.S. Court of Appeals for the Federal Circuit; U.S. Court of Appeals, Ninth Circuit; U.S. District Court, Central, Southern and Northern Districts of California; registered to practice before U.S. Patent and Trademark Office. *Education:* University of California at Los Angeles (B.S. in Physics, 1967; J.D., 1974); University of Oregon (M.S. in Physics, 1968). President and Founder of UCLA Attorney and Physics Alumni, 1992—. Member, Board of Directors, Orange County Multimedia Users Group, 1996. *Member:* Los Angeles County Bar Association (Member, Fee Dispute Resolution Committee); Orange County Patent Lawyers Association (Chairman, Patent Practice Committee, 1990-1992). [U.S. Navy Reserve, JAGG, 1978-1986]. **PRACTICE AREAS:** Patent; Trademark; Copyright. *Email:* ddawes@gj.com

**GREGG P. MARTINO,** born New Brunswick, New Jersey, 1952; admitted to bar, 1978, California. *Education:* University of California at Los Angeles and University of California at Berkeley (B.A., cum laude, 1974); University of California at Los Angeles (J.D., 1978). Order of the Coif. *Member:* Orange County Bar Association (Member, Section of Real Estate Law). **PRACTICE AREAS:** Litigation; Real Estate (Property) Law. *Email:* gmartino@gj.com

### SPECIAL COUNSEL

**PHILLIP ASHMAN,** born Salinas, California, 1962; admitted to bar, 1989, California and U.S. District Court, Central District of California; 1990, U.S. District Court, Southern, Northern and Eastern Districts of California and U.S. Court of Appeals, Ninth Circuit; 1991, District of Columbia; 1992, U.S. Tax Court. *Education:* University of California, Berkeley (B.A., with honors, 1986); Southern Methodist University (J.D., 1989). Phi Delta Phi. Recipient, American Jurisprudence Award in Administrative Law. Law Clerk to the Honorable John E. Ryan, U.S. Bankruptcy Judge, 1989-1990. *Member:* Orange County Bar Association (Member: Commercial Law and Bankruptcy Section and Business Litigation Section); Orange County Bankruptcy Forum (Former Member, Special Projects Committee); California Bankruptcy Forum. **PRACTICE AREAS:** Creditors' Rights; Bankruptcy; Business Litigation. *Email:* pashman@gj.com

### RESIDENT ASSOCIATES

*Laura A. Homan; Kenneth B. Julian; Brian A. Kumamoto; Sandra Lau; Karl Sandoval.*

All Members and Associates are Members of the State Bar of California.

## HARTLEY & MAZAREI

PLAZA TOWER
600 ANTON BOULEVARD, SUITE 1250
**COSTA MESA, CALIFORNIA 92626**
*Telephone:* 714-444-0777
*Facsimile:* 714-444-1229

*Workers Compensation, Family Law, Immigration and Transactional Business Law, Corporate Law.*

### MEMBERS OF FIRM

**TERESA M. HARTLEY,** born Pasadena, California, September 20, 1953; admitted to bar, 1991, California and U.S. District Court, Central District of California; 1994, U.S. District Court, Northern District of California. *Education:* Arizona State University (B.A., 1977); Western State University (J.D., magna cum laude, 1991). Executive Editor, Western State University Law Review. *Member:* Orange County Bar Association; State

*(This Listing Continued)*

HARTLEY & MAZAREI, Costa Mesa—Continued

Bar of California. **PRACTICE AREAS:** Workers Compensation; Family Law.

**RAYEHE MAZAREI,** born Shiraz, Iran, July 23, 1966; admitted to bar, 1991, California and U.S. District Court, Central District of California; 1993, U.S. District Court, Northern District of California. *Education:* University of California at Irvine (B.A., cum laude, 1988); Wester State University College of Law (J.D., 1991). *Member:* Orange County (Chair, Immigration Section) and American Bar Associations; State Bar of California; American Immigration Lawyers Association. **LANGUAGES:** Farsi. **PRACTICE AREAS:** Immigration Law; Transactional Business Law; Corporate Law.

## JEFFRIES ADVOCATES LAW OFFICES

485 EAST 17TH STREET, SUITE 390
COSTA MESA, CALIFORNIA 92627
Telephone: 714-722-0055
Fax: 714-722-8416
Email: JeffAdvLaw@aol.com

*Enforcement of Judgments, Commercial Litigation, Collections, Subrogation.*

**COUNTESS PEASE JEFFRIES,** born Washington, D.C., November 24, 1945; admitted to bar, 1977, California and U.S. District Court, Central District of California. *Education:* Howard University (B.S.E.E., 1969); New York University Graduate School of Business (M.B.A., 1974); Harvard University (J.D., 1977). Member, Harvard International Law Society, 1974-1977. Author: "Regulation of Transfer of Technology: An Evaluation of the UNCTAD Code of Conduct," 18 Harvard International Law Journal 309-342, Spring 1977. Assistant Professor, International Business, Department of International Business, California State University of Los Angeles, Spring, 1980. Director: Museum of African American Art, January, 1980—; Free Arts for Abused Children, Charter 100, 1994-1996. HUD Foreclosure Commissioner. Private Collection Counsel, U.S. Dept. of Justice. Arbitrator and Receiver, Orange County Courts. *Member:* Orange County (Chair, Creditor's Rights Section, 1996) and American Bar Associations; State Bar of California; CLLA; AOPA. **LANGUAGES:** Spanish and Farsi. **PRACTICE AREAS:** Commercial Litigation; Collections; Subrogation. *Email:* JeffAdvLaw@aol.com

## LARSEN & ASSOCIATES

3200 PARK CENTER DRIVE, SUITE 720
COSTA MESA, CALIFORNIA 92626
Telephone: 714-540-1770
Fax: 714-540-1020

*Federal and State Taxations, Probate, Estate Planning, Corporations, Mergers and Acquisitions, Real Estate Property, Tax and Commercial Litigation.*

**GERALD L. LARSEN,** born Van Nuys, California, February 27, 1949; admitted to bar, 1982, Texas; 1990, Florida; 1991, U.S. Tax Court; 1992, California. *Education:* California State University-Northridge (B.S., 1975); University of San Diego, Institute on International and Comparative Law; Stetson University College of Law (J.D., 1989); University of Florida College of Law (LL.M., in Taxation, 1990). Certified Public Accountant, California, 1977, Texas, 1982 and Florida, 1987. Certified Financial Planner, 1989. Member, International Board of Standards and Practices for Certified Financial Planners. Planned Giving Advisor to University of California, Irvine. Member: International Board of Standards and Practices for Certified Financial Planners; Planned Giving Roundtable of Orange County; Professional Advisory Council of Irvine Valley College Foundation; Endowment Fund Council of Orange County Performing Arts Center; Planned Giving Council; Orange County Boy Scouts of America. *Member:* Orange County and American Bar Association; State Bar of California; The Florida Bar; American Association of Attorneys Certified Public Accountants; Orange Coast Estate Planning Council. **PRACTICE AREAS:** Federal and State Taxation; Probate; Estate Planning; Partnerships; Corporate Law.

### ASSOCIATES

**DAVID S. BEARD,** born San Diego, California, March 31, 1966; admitted to bar, 1996, California. *Education:* San Diego State University (B.S., 1989); Arizona State University (J.D., cum laude, 1995); New York University School of Law (LL.M., Taxation, 1996). Certified Public Accountant,

*(This Listing Continued)*

California, 1992. *Member:* Orange County and American Bar Associations. **PRACTICE AREAS:** Corporations; Real Property; Federal and State Taxation.

**WAYNE ROBERT JOHNSON,** born Grafton, North Dakota, March 18, 1964; admitted to bar, 1996, California. *Education:* North Dakota State University (B.S., 1989); University of North Dakota (J.D., with distinction, 1994); New York University School of Law (LL.M., Taxation, 1995). Member, North Dakota Law Review. Member, North Dakota Moot Court Association. Recipient: Order of Barristers; Distinguished Oralist Award, 1994 Tulane National Sports Law Moot Court Competition. Adjunct Professor, Golden Gate University School of Law, 1996—. Author: "North Dakota's New Contempt Law: Will it Mean Order in the Court?," 70 N.D. Law Review 1027, 1994. Adjunct Professor, Western State University College of Law, 1996—. Treasurer, North Dakota Student Bar Association, 1993-1994. *Member:* Orange County (Member, Sections on: Tax; Business Law), Federal and American Bar Associations; State Bar of California (Member: Tax Section; Business Law Section; Young Tax Lawyers Committee). **PRACTICE AREAS:** Corporations; Mergers and Acquisitions; State and Federal Taxation; Litigation; Commercial.

**DANNY R. BOON,** born Dallas, Texas, August 11, 1966; admitted to bar, 1995, Texas; 1996, California. *Education:* Texas A & M University (B.B.A., 1989); South Texas College of Law (J.D., 1995); University of Florida College of Law (LL.M., in Taxation, 1996). *Member:* American Bar Association (Member, Tax Section). **PRACTICE AREAS:** Estate Planning; Probate; Federal and State Taxation.

## LASKIN & GRAHAM

COSTA MESA, CALIFORNIA

(See Glendale)

*General Civil and Trial Practice in all State and Federal Courts, Eminent Domain, Municipal Law, Environmental Law, Real Property Damage, Employment Law, Construction Law, Land Use, Insurance Law, Professional Liability, Banking, Leasing, Bankruptcy, Financial Institutions Law, Commercial Documentation, Business Law and Litigation.*

## LATHAM & WATKINS

SUITE 2000, 650 TOWN CENTER DRIVE
COSTA MESA, CALIFORNIA 92626-1918
Telephone: 714-540-1235
Telecopier: 714-755-8290
URL: http://www.lw.com

*Los Angeles, California Office:* 633 West Fifth Street, Suite 4000. Telephone: 213-485-1234.

*San Diego, California Office:* Suite 2100, 701 B Street. Telephone: 619-236-1234.

*San Francisco, California Office:* 505 Montgomery Street, Suite 1900. Telephone: 415-391-0600.

*Washington, D.C. Office:* Suite 1300, 1001 Pennsylvania Avenue, N.W. Telephone: 202-637-2200.

*Chicago, Illinois Office:* Suite 5800 Sears Tower. Telephone: 312-876-7700.

*Newark, New Jersey Office:* One Newark Center. Telephone: 201-639-1234. Fax: 201-639-7298.

*New York, N.Y. Office:* Suite 1000, 885 Third Avenue. Telephone: 212-906-1200.

*London, England Office:* One Angel Court, EC2R 7HJ. Telephone: +-44-171-374 4444. Telecopier: +-44-171-374 4460.

*Moscow, Russia Office:* Suite C200, 113/1 Leninsky Prospeckt, 117198. Telephone: +-7 503 956-5555. Fax: +-7 503 956-5556.

*Hong Kong Office:* 11th Floor Central Building, Number One Pedder Street, Central Hong Kong. Telephone: 011-852-2841-7779. Fax: 011-852-2841-7749.

*Tokyo, Japan Office:* Infini Akasaka, 8-7-15 Akasaka, Minato-Ku, Tokyo 107, Japan. Telephone: 011 81 3 3423-3970. Fax: 011 81 3 3423 3971.

*General Practice.*

### RESIDENT PARTNERS

**JOSEPH A. WHEELOCK JR.,** born Wilmington, Delaware, July 2, 1939; admitted to bar, 1965, District of Columbia; 1966, California. *Education:* Williams College (A.B., magna cum laude, 1960); Harvard University (LL.B., cum laude, 1964). Phi Beta Kappa.

*(This Listing Continued)*

**ROBERT E. CURRIE,** born Jackson, Tennessee, October 10, 1937; admitted to bar, 1967, California. *Education:* United States Naval Academy (B.S., with distinction, 1959); Harvard University (LL.B., cum laude, 1967). Fellow, American College of Trial Lawyers.

**ALAN W. PETTIS,** born May 17, 1940; admitted to bar, 1967, Texas; 1969, California. *Education:* University of Texas (B.A., 1965; LL.B., 1967). Associate Editor, Texas Law Review, 1966-1967. Trial Attorney, Antitrust Division, U.S. Department of Justice, 1967-1969. Special Assistant U.S. Attorney, 1968-1969.

**JOSEPH I. BENTLEY,** born Safford, Arizona, August 6, 1940; admitted to bar, 1969, California. *Education:* Brigham Young University (A.B., 1965); University of Chicago (J.D., with honors, 1968), National Honor Scholarship. Order of the Coif. Executive Editor, University of Chicago Law Review, 1967-1968.

**JAMES W. DANIELS,** born Chicago, Illinois, October 13, 1945; admitted to bar, 1971, California; U.S. Supreme Court. *Education:* Brown University (A.B., cum laude and with honors, 1967); University of Chicago (J.D., with honors, 1970).

**MORRIS A. THURSTON,** born Logan, Utah, May 25, 1943; admitted to bar, 1971, California; 1978, U.S. Supreme Court. *Education:* Brigham Young University (B.A., with high honors, 1967); Harvard University (J.D., 1970).

**JEFFREY T. PERO,** born Utica, New York, August 16, 1946; admitted to bar, 1972, California. *Education:* University of Notre Dame (B.A., cum laude, 1968); New York University (J.D., 1971). Root-Tilden Scholar, 1968-1971. Articles Editor, Annual Survey of American Law, 1970-1971.

**BRUCE A. TESTER,** born September 28, 1941; admitted to bar, 1972, California. *Education:* Iowa State University (B.S., 1963); Stanford University (M.B.A., 1972; J.D., 1972).

**ROBERT K. BREAK,** born Redlands, California, February 12, 1948; admitted to bar, 1975, California. *Education:* Claremont Men's College (B.A., 1970); Columbia University (J.D., 1975). Harlan Fiske Stone Scholar. Casenote and Comments Editor, Columbia Journal of Transnational Law, 1974-1975.

**JON D. ANDERSON,** born Wichita, Kansas, October 29, 1952; admitted to bar, 1977, California. *Education:* University of Washington (B.A., cum laude, 1974); Brigham Young University (J.D., magna cum laude, 1977). Editor-in-Chief, 1976-1977, Brigham Young University Law Review. J. Reuben Clark Scholar.

**PATRICK T. SEAVER,** born Los Angeles, California, March 28, 1950; admitted to bar, 1978, California. *Education:* Yale University (B.A., cum laude, 1972); Stanford University (M.B.A., 1977; J.D., 1977).

**GREGORY P. LINDSTROM,** born Hollywood, California, August 4, 1953; admitted to bar, 1978, California. *Education:* University of California at Los Angeles (A.B., summa cum laude, 1975); University of Chicago (J.D., 1978). Phi Beta Kappa.

**BRUCE P. HOWARD,** born Washington, D.C., May 8, 1953; admitted to bar, 1984, California. *Education:* Yale University (B.A., 1974); Harvard University (J.D., magna cum laude, 1978).

**MARY K. WESTBROOK,** born Billings, Montana, September 16, 1955; admitted to bar, 1980, California. *Education:* Gonzaga University (B.S., 1977); Stanford University (J.D., 1980).

**KENNETH A. WOLFSON,** born September 24, 1957; admitted to bar, 1982, California. *Education:* University of Cincinnati (B.B.A., summa cum laude, 1979; University of Texas at Austin (J.D., 1982). Order of the Coif.

**CARY K. HYDEN,** born December 4, 1957; admitted to bar, 1984, California. *Education:* University of Dallas (B.A., with highest distinction, 1980); University of Texas (J.D., with highest honors, 1983). Order of the Coif.

**DAVID W. BARBY,** born Philadelphia, Pennsylvania, August 1, 1956; admitted to bar, 1984, California. *Education:* Wharton School of Business (B.S., 1978; M.B.A., 1984); University of Pennsylvania (J.D., 1984).

**GLENDA SANDERS,** born Durban, South Africa, January 21, 1956; admitted to bar, 1981 (as Barrister), Durban, South Africa; 1986, California. *Education:* University of Natal, Durban, South Africa (B.A., with distinction, 1976; LL.B., with distinction, 1979); University of Cambridge, England (LL.M., 1980).

**PETER J. WILSON,** born Butterworth, South Africa, April 10, 1953; admitted to bar, 1977, South Africa; 1986, California. *Education:* Rhodes
*(This Listing Continued)*

University (B. Comm., 1974; LL.B., 1976); Edinburgh University, Scotland (Diploma in Criminology, 1978).

**JOSEPH B. FARRELL,** born Wilkes-Barre, Pennsylvania, June 6, 1963; admitted to bar, 1988, California; U.S. District Court, Northern, Central and Southern District of California; U.S. Court of Appeals, Ninth Circuit. *Education:* Pennsylvania State University (B.A., 1985); Villanova University School of Law (J.D., magna cum laude, 1988). Order of the Coif. **PRACTICE AREAS:** Employment Law; Public Accommodations; Housing Discrimination; Litigation.

**WILLIAM J. CERNIUS,** born Washington, D.C., September 29, 1960; admitted to bar, 1985, California. *Education:* University of Southern California (B.A., 1982); University of California, Hastings College of the Law (J.D., 1985). Phi Delta Phi. Editor, Hastings Law Journal, 1984-1985.

**LINDA SCHILLING,** born Philadelphia, Pennsylvania, June 12, 1960; admitted to bar, 1988, California. *Education:* University of California (B.A., 1981); University of California School of Law, Davis (J.D., 1987).

### RESIDENT OF COUNSEL

**JOHN R. STAHR,** born Fort Dodge, Iowa, October 29, 1932; admitted to bar, 1961, California. *Education:* Stanford University (A.B., with great distinction, 1954); Harvard University (LL.B., 1960). Phi Beta Kappa.

**JEAN M. DONNELLY,** born Inglewood, California, June 15, 1955; admitted to bar, 1981, District of Columbia; 1983, California. *Education:* College of the Holy Cross (A.B., summa cum laude, 1977); Georgetown University (J.D., cum laude, 1981). Editor, Law and Policy in International Business, Georgetown University, 1980-1981.

**REGINA M. SCHLATTER,** born Detroit, Michigan, May 13, 1957; admitted to bar, 1987, California. *Education:* Harper Hospital School of Nursing, Detroit, Michigan (Diploma, 1977); University of Michigan (B.A., with high honors in Philosophy, 1983; J.D., cum laude, 1987).

**ANDREA L. MERSEL,** born New York, N.Y., March 11, 1963; admitted to bar, 1987, California. *Education:* Wharton School of Business, University of Pennsylvania (B.S., magna cum laude, 1984); University of California, Boalt Hall School of Law (J.D., 1987).

**DEAN G. DUNLAVEY,** born San Pedro, California, March 2, 1958; admitted to bar, 1984, California. *Education:* Harvard University (A.B., 1980); University of California at Berkeley (J.D., 1984).

### RESIDENT ASSOCIATES

**ADELE K. CARDOZA,** born July 20, 1959; admitted to bar, 1987, California. *Education:* University of California at Los Angeles (B.S., summa cum laude, 1981); Graduate School of Business Administration, University of California at Berkeley (M.B.A., 1987); University of California, Boalt Hall School of Law (J.D., 1987). Phi Beta Kappa. Associate Articles Editor, Industrial Relations Law Journal, 1986.

**DAVID C. MECKLER,** born Long Beach, California, November 24, 1963; admitted to bar, 1989, California. *Education:* University of California at Los Angeles (B.A., cum laude, 1986); University of Southern California (J.D., 1989). Order of the Coif.

**DAVID C. FLATTUM,** born Libertyville, Illinois, August 27, 1964; admitted to bar, 1990, California. *Education:* University of Southern California (B.A., B.S., 1987); Yale University (J.D., 1990). Phi Beta Kappa.

**R. BRIAN TIMMONS,** born Ashton, Idaho, February 11, 1963; admitted to bar, 1991, California. *Education:* Duke University (A.B., summa cum laude, 1988); London School of Economics (M.Sc., 1988); Harvard Law School (J.D., cum laude, 1991). Managing Editor, Harv. J. of Law.

**SCOTT B. GARNER,** born Harrison, New York, February 25, 1966; admitted to bar, 1991, California. *Education:* Stanford University (A.B., with distinction, 1988); Harvard University (J.D., cum laude, 1991).

**CHARLES W. COX, II,** born Oakland, California, July 19, 1962; admitted to bar, 1992, California. *Education:* United States Naval Academy (B.S., with distinction, 1984); Georgetown University (M.A., 1985); University of Michigan (J.D., cum laude, 1992). Associate Editor, Michigan Journal of International Law, 1990-1991.

**CHARLES K. RUCK,** born Mount Pleasant, Michigan, August 26, 1967; admitted to bar, 1993, California. *Education:* University of California (B.A, 1989); University of Michigan (J.D., 1992). Phi Beta Kappa. Associate Editor, Michigan Law Review, 1990-1992.

**PAUL N. SINGARELLA,** born Boston, Massachusetts, December 1, 1958; admitted to bar, 1991, California. *Education:* Wesleyan University
*(This Listing Continued)*

## LATHAM & WATKINS, Costa Mesa—Continued

(B.A., 1980); Massachusetts Institute of Technology (M.S., 1982); University of Southern California (J.D., 1991). Order of the Coif.

**ANDREA S. MATIAUDA,** born Corona, California, December 18, 1966; admitted to bar, 1993, California. *Education:* Duke University (B.A., 1988); University of California at Los Angeles (J.D., 1993).

**DANIEL A. THOMSON,** born Sierra Madre, California, September 14, 1964; admitted to bar, 1993, California. *Education:* Brigham Young University (B.S., cum laude, 1988; J.D., cum laude, 1993). Senior Editor, BYU Law Review. Certified Public Accountant, California, 1994.

**DAVID L. KUIPER,** born Niagara Falls, New York, September 21, 1960; admitted to bar, 1993, California. *Education:* Syracuse University (B.S., magna cum laude, 1982); Troy State University (M.S., 1986); University of Southern California (J.D., 1993). Beta Gamma Sigma.

**DANIEL W. BURKE,** born Burbank, California, September 7, 1967; admitted to bar, 1994, California. *Education:* University of California at Los Angeles (B.A., summa cum laude, 1990); Stanford University (J.D., 1993). Phi Beta Kappa. Associate Editor, Stanford Law Review, 1992-1993.

**LAURA I. BUSHNELL,** born Palo Alto, California, July 4, 1967; admitted to bar, 1994, California. *Education:* Stanford University (A.B., 1989); Georgetown University (J.D., 1994).

**R. SCOTT SHEAN,** born Inglewood, California, March 18, 1969; admitted to bar, 1994, California. *Education:* Williams College (B.A., cum laude, 1991); University of California at Los Angeles (J.D., 1994).

**MARK A. FINKELSTEIN,** born Stanford, California, May 16, 1968; admitted to bar, 1994, California. *Education:* University of California at Los Angeles (B.A., magna cum laude, 1990); University of Southern California (J.D., 1994). Order of the Coif.

**MARY A. DONOVAN,** born San Francisco, California, October 28, 1968; admitted to bar, 1994, California. *Education:* University of California at Berkeley (B.A., 1990); University of California at Los Angeles (J.D., 1994). Phi Beta Kappa.

**DAVID PITMAN,** born South Africa, April 15, 1953; admitted to bar, 1994, California. *Education:* University of Cape Town, South Africa (B.S., 1975); Oxford University (M.A., 1979); University of Witwatersrand, South Africa (LL.B., 1986). Rhodes Scholar.

**SCOTT B. COOPER,** born Lakenheath, England, April 12, 1969; admitted to bar, 1994, California. *Education:* University of California at Berkeley (B.A., with highest distinction, 1991); University of Chicago (J.D., with honors, 1994). Phi Beta Kappa.

**JAMIE L. WINE,** born Boston, Massachusetts, June 10, 1970; admitted to bar, 1995, California. *Education:* Lehigh University (B.A., 1992); Harvard University (J.D., 1995). Phi Beta Kappa.

**RONIT D. EARLEY,** born Los Angeles, California, May 31, 1971; admitted to bar, 1995, California. *Education:* University of California, Los Angeles (B.A., 1992); Columbia University (J.D., 1995). Harlan Fiske Stone Scholar.

**JOSEPH M. YAFFE,** born Concord, California, April 16, 1969; admitted to bar, 1994, California. *Education:* Columbia University (A.B., 1990); University of California at Davis (J.D., 1994).

**MARK W. SENECA,** born Salt Lake City, Utah, June 3, 1967; admitted to bar, 1996, California. *Education:* Brigham Young University (B.S., 1990); Stanford Graduate School of Business (M.B.A., 1995); Stanford University (J.D., 1995).

**DAVID B. ALLEN,** born Orange, California, January 15, 1970; admitted to bar, 1996, California. *Education:* Yale University (B.A., magna cum laude, 1992); Yale University Law School (J.D., 1996).

**JONN R. BEESON,** born Cincinnati, Ohio, March 11, 1969; admitted to bar, 1996, California. *Education:* University of California (B.S., Mech. Eng., 1991); University of Pennsylvania (J.D., 1996). Pi Tau Sigma; Order of the Coif. Editor, University of Pennsylvania Law Review.

**JULIE VIGIL KING,** born Santa Monica, California, February 7, 1971; admitted to bar, 1996, California. *Education:* University of California at Santa Barbara (B.A., 1993); Pepperdine University School of Law (J.D., 1996).

**STEPHANIE H. KNUTSON,** born Logan, Utah, July 10, 1971; admitted to bar, 1996, California. *Education:* University of California at Los Angeles (B.A., cum laude, 1992); University of California, Hastings College of the Law (J.D., magna cum laude, 1996). Order of the Coif; Thurston Society.

**GREGORY M. SAYLIN,** born Torrance, California, September 16, 1968; admitted to bar, 1996, California. *Education:* Sarah Lawrence College (B.A., 1992); Vanderbilt University School of Law (J.D., 1996). Order of the Coif. Recipient, American Jurisprudence Awards. Editor-in-Chief, Vanderbilt Journal of Transnational Law.

**CLAY SHEVLIN,** born Pasadena, California, February 11, 1961; admitted to bar, 1996, California. *Education:* University of the Pacific (B.S., Econ., 1983); University of California, Boalt Hall School of Law (J.D., 1996).

**STEPHEN J. VENUTO,** born New York, N.Y., August 26, 1971; admitted to bar, 1996, California. *Education:* University of California at Los Angeles (B.A., 1993); Cornell University Law School (J.D., cum laude, 1996).

Unless otherwise indicated all Members and Associates of the Firm are Members of the State Bar of California.

(For biographical data on Los Angeles, California, San Diego, California, San Francisco, California, Washington, D.C., Chicago, Illinois, Newark, New Jersey, New York, New York, London, England, Moscow, Russia, Hong Kong and Tokyo, Japan personnel, see Professional Biographies at each of those cities)

## LEWIS, D'AMATO, BRISBOIS & BISGAARD

A Partnership including Professional Corporations

**650 TOWN CENTER DRIVE, SUITE 1400**
**COSTA MESA, CALIFORNIA 92626**
Telephone: 714-545-9200

*Los Angeles, California Office:* Suite 1200, 221 North Figueroa Street. Telephone: 213-250-1800. Fax: 213-250-7900.

*San Diego, California Office:* 550 West "C" Street, Suite 800. Telephone: 619-233-1006. Fax: 619-434-0882.

*San Francisco, California Office:* 601 California Street, Suite 1900. Telephone: 415-362-2580. Fax: 415-434-0882.

*San Bernardino, California Office:* 650 E. Hospitality Lane, Suite 600. Telephone: 714-387-1130. Fax: 714-387-1138.

*Sacramento, California Office:* 2500 Venture Oaks, 95833. Telephone: 916-564-5400. Fax: 916-564-5444.

*Affiliated Offices:*

*Jakarta, Indonesia Affiliated Office:* Mulya Lubis and Partners, Wisma Bank Dharmala, 16th Floor, Jendral, Sudirman, Kav. 28, Jakarta 12920, Indonesia. Telephone: (62)(21) 521-1931/521-1932. Facsimile: (62)(21) 521-1930.

*Bangkok, Thailand Affiliated Office:* Kanung & Partners Law Offices, Raintree Office Garden, 272 Japanese School Lane, Rama IX Road, Bangkok 10310, Thailand. Telephone: (662) 319-7571/319-7574. Facsimile: (662) 319-6372.

*General Practice.*

FIRM PROFILE: *Founded in 1979, the Firm has over 220 lawyers specializing in the following areas: Antitrust and Trade Regulation; Compensation and Benefits; Corporate, Corporate Finance and Securities, Domestic Private Finance, Financial Institutions, International Private Finance, and Mergers and Acquisitions; Environmental; Individual Clients, Trusts, Estates, and Probate; General Insurance, Professional Liability, Products Liability and Securities Class Actions; International Trade, Government Relations and Business Law; Oil and Gas; Real Estate; Litigation, including Complex Business Litigation; Employment and Labor Law; State and Federal Tax; Intellectual Property; Public Entity Defense; Community Redevelopment Law, and Aircraft and Equipment Leasing.*

### PARTNERS

**ROBERT F. LEWIS, (P.C.)**

**DONALD A. RUSTON,** born Globe, Arizona, November 28, 1929; admitted to bar, 1955, California. *Education:* George Pepperdine College (B.A., 1951); University of California at Los Angeles (J.D., 1954). Phi Alpha Delta. Member, National Panel of Arbitrators, American Arbitration Association. *Member:* Orange County (Member, Board of Directors, 1965-1974) and American Bar Associations; Association of Southern California Defense Counsel (President, 1971-1972). Fellow. American College of Trial

*(This Listing Continued)*

Lawyers. Diplomate, American Board of Trial Advocates (President, Orange County, 1970; National President, 1981; Trial Lawyer of the Year, 1982); International Academy of Trial Lawyers; International Society of Barristers.

**KEITH D. TAYLOR,** born Los Angeles, California, June 5, 1952; admitted to bar, 1980, California. *Education:* California State University at Fullerton (B.A., 1977); University of San Diego (J.D., 1980). *Member:* Orange County and American Bar Associations.

**GARY M. LAPE,** born Fountain Hill, Pennsylvania, January 24, 1953; admitted to bar, 1978, California; 1979, Texas. *Education:* Georgetown University (A.B., 1975); University of California at Davis (J.D., 1978). Phi Beta Kappa. *Member:* State Bar of Texas.

**NANCY E. ZELTZER,** born Los Angeles, California, October 12, 1951; admitted to bar, 1978, California. *Education:* California State University at Fullerton; Western State University (B.S., 1975; J.D., 1977). *Member:* Orange County Bar Association.

**LEE A. WOOD,** born Sapulpa, Oklahoma, September 10, 1944; admitted to bar, 1973, California and U.S. District Court, Northern, Southern and Central Districts of California; U.S. Supreme Court. *Education:* University of Maryland; Pierce College (A.A., 1969); Southwestern University School of Law (J.D., 1973). Member, Arbitration Panel, Orange County Court, 1982—. Member, Panel of Arbitrators, American Arbitration Association. *Member:* San Fernando, Los Angeles County, Orange County and American (Member: Negligence Committee, 1977—; Torts and Insurance Panel, 1976—; Negligence and Insurance Panel, 1976—) Bar Associations; State Bar of California; Lawyers-Pilots Bar Association.

**THOMAS E. FRANCIS,** born Sacramento, California, May 7, 1962; admitted to bar, 1987, California; 1988, U.S. District Court, Central, Southern, Northern and Eastern Districts of California and U.S. Court of Appeals, Ninth Circuit. *Education:* University of California at Irvine (B.A., 1984); McGeorge School of Law, University of the Pacific (J.D., 1987).

**H. GILBERT JONES,** born Fargo, North Dakota, November 2, 1927; admitted to bar, 1957, California. *Education:* Yale University (B.E., 1947); University of Michigan and University of California at Los Angeles (J.D., 1956). Phi Delta Phi; Tau Beta Pi. *Member:* Orange County, Los Angeles County (Chairman, Medical Legal Relations Committee, 1975) and American Bar Associations; The State Bar of California; Association of Southern Defense Counsel; American Board of Trial Advocates (Diplomate; President, Los Angeles Chapter, 1980; Member, National Board of Directors, 1977—; National President, 1988-1989). Fellow: American College of Trial Lawyers; International Academy of Trial Lawyers.

**MICHAEL W. CONNALLY,** born Long Beach, California, July 8, 1957; admitted to bar, 1981, California and U.S. District Court, Central District of California; 1982, U.S. Court of Appeals, Ninth Circuit and U.S. District Court, Northern, Eastern and Southern Districts of California; 1990, U.S. Supreme Court. *Education:* Loyola Marymount University (B.A., magna cum laude, 1978) Alpha Sigma Nu; Pi Gamma Mu; Phi Alpha Theta; Loyola University Law School (J.D., 1981). Champion, Scott Moot Court Honors Program. Finalist, National Moot Court Competition. First Place, Trial Advocacy Competition, Fall, 1980. Member, National Trial Advocacy Competition Team, 1980-1981. Recipient: Daughters of the Founders and Patriots Award, Loyola Marymount University; International Academy of Trial Lawyers Award; West Publishing Award. *Member:* Century City and Los Angeles County Bar Associations; State Bar of California.

**ANNIE VERDRIES,** born Rotterdam, Holland, January 29, 1949; admitted to bar, 1979, California; 1980, U.S. District Court, Central District of California; 1985, U.S. District Court, Northern District of California; 1986, U.S. District Court, Eastern and Southern Districts of California. *Education:* Pedagogische Acadamie, Rotterdam, Holland; University of La Verne (B.A., Social Science, 1976; J.D., cum laude, 1979). Law Clerk to the Honorable Francis J. Garvey, Superior Court of Los Angeles, Pomona, California, 1977. Member, Orange County and Los Angeles County Bankruptcy Forum. *Member:* Orange County Bar Association; The State Bar of California. **LANGUAGES:** Dutch.

**JAMES G. BOHM,** born Glendale, California, February 18, 1962; admitted to bar, 1987, California. *Education:* University of California at Los Angeles (B.A., 1984); Pepperdine University (J.D., magna cum laude, 1987). Pi Sigma Alpha. Recipient, American Jurisprudence Awards for Contracts, Criminal Procedure, Remedies, Constitutional Law and Creditors Rights and Bankruptcy. Survey Editor, Pepperdine Law Review, 1986-1987. Co-Author: Comment, "California Supreme Court Survey," 13 Pepperdine Law Review 861, 1101, 1986.

*(This Listing Continued)*

**SCOTT W. MONSON,** born Seattle, Washington, November 15, 1956; admitted to bar, 1983, California. *Education:* University of Southern California (B.A., 1979); Loyola Marymount University (J.D., 1982). *Member:* Orange County and American Bar Associations; State Bar of California; Association of Southern California Defense Counsel.

**MICHAEL C. OLSON,** born Detroit, Michigan, September 21, 1954; admitted to bar, 1980, Michigan; 1986, U.S. District Court, Eastern District of Michigan and U.S. Court of Appeals, Sixth Circuit; 1987, California; 1988, U.S. District Court, Central District of California. *Education:* Michigan State University (B.S., cum laude, 1976); Wayne State University (J.D., 1980). Recipient, American Jurisprudence Award in Evidence. *Member:* State Bar of Michigan. **PRACTICE AREAS:** Insurance Defense Law; Professional Malpractice Law; Construction Defect Law.

**DAVID E. ISENBERG,** born Los Angeles, California, June 21, 1960; admitted to bar, 1986, California and U.S. District Court, Central District of California; 1987, U.S. Court of Appeals, Ninth Circuit. *Education:* University of California at Los Angeles (B.A., magna cum laude, 1983; J.D., 1986). Recent Developments Editor, UCLA Pacific Basin Law Journal, 1985-1986. *Member:* American Bar Association (Member: Business Bankruptcy Committee; Creditor's Rights Committee).

**BRAD D. KRASNOFF,** born Mobile, Alabama, March 24, 1960; admitted to bar, 1986, California. *Education:* University of California, Los Angeles (B.A., magna cum laude, 1982; J.D., 1986). Phi Beta Kappa. Advocacy Chairman, Moot Court Honor Program. Member, Order of the Barrister. *Member:* Century City, Beverly Hills and Los Angeles County Bar Associations; State Bar of California; Financial Lawyers Conference. **REPORTED CASES:** In re Kruger, 77 Bankr. 785 (Bk. C.D. Cal. 1987).

**MICHAEL J. LANCASTER,** born Berkeley, California, April 18, 1952; admitted to bar, 1980, California and U.S. Court of Appeals, Ninth Circuit; 1985, U.S. District Court, Central District of California and U.S. Supreme Court. *Education:* Western State University College of Law (J.D., 1979). Author: California Real Estate Broker Duties, Continuing Education of the Bar (CEB). CEB Speaker: Real Estate Broker Practice; Insurance Counsel Trial Academy Workshops, 1984; Medi-Legal Institute, 1985; Harvard Law School, Professional Mediation and ADR System Design Workshop, 1992; DRS Mediator Trained in Advanced Negotiation, Settlement and Mediation Techniques Sponsored by the Los Angeles County Bar Association, 1991; Advanced Negotiation and Settlement Strategy for Experienced Lawyers, Sponsored by CEB, Institute for Dispute Resolution and Pepperdine School of Law, 1991. Judge Pro Tem - Orange County Superior Court. *Member:* Orange County (Member, Real Estate and Litigation Section Committees) and American (Member, Litigation Section Committee) Bar Associations; State Bar of California (Member, Litigation, Real Estate and Business Section Committees); Orange County Trial Lawyers Association; Association of Southern California Defense Counsel; Defense Research Institute and Trial Lawyers of America (Member, Real Estate Section Committee).

**ROGER L. BELLOWS,** born Omaha, Nebraska, June 17, 1955; admitted to bar, 1980, California; 1986, Maryland and District of Columbia. *Education:* University of Nebraska at Omaha (B.A., 1977); Creighton University (J.D., 1980). Author: Comment, "Developing Parameters for Municipal Liability After Monell v. Department of Social Services," Creighton Law Review, 1979. *Member:* State Bar of California. **PRACTICE AREAS:** Litigation-Business and Personal Injury.

### RESIDENT ASSOCIATES

**LESLIE S. BOWEN,** born Auburn, Nebraska, May 5, 1966; admitted to bar, 1995, California. *Education:* Arizona State University (B.S., 1988); Western State University (J.D., 1995). Member, Western State University Law Review. Recipient, American Jurisprudence Award. Listed in Who's Who Among American Law Students.

**LORI CREASEY,** born North Hollywood, California, December 24, 1957; admitted to bar, 1984, California; 1985, U.S. District Court, Central District of California and U.S. Court of Appeals, Ninth Circuit. *Education:* University of California at Los Angeles (B.A., 1980); Southwestern University (J.D., 1984). *Member:* Orange County and American Bar Associations; The State Bar of California; Association of Southern California Defense Counsel; American Academy of Hospital Attorneys.

**TROY A. EDWARDS,** born San Diego, California, September 8, 1962; admitted to bar, 1990, California. *Education:* San Diego State University (B.S., 1985); University of San Diego School of Law (J.D., 1990).

**KELLY M. FLANAGAN,** born Laguna Beach, California, August 21, 1964; admitted to bar, 1989, California; 1990, U.S. Court of Appeals, Ninth

*(This Listing Continued)*

CAA147B

## LEWIS, D'AMATO, BRISBOIS & BISGAARD, Costa Mesa—Continued

Circuit and U.S. District Court, Central District of California. *Education:* University of California at Irvine (B.A., cum laude, 1985); Loyola Marymount Law School (J.D., cum laude, 1989). Order of the Coif; St. Thomas More Law Honor Society. Editor, Loyola of Los Angeles, 1988-1989. Author: "Away From Justice and Fairness: The Foreign Country Exception to the Federal Tort Claims Act," 22 Loyola of Los Angeles Law Review 603, 1989.

**ALLISON A. GREENE,** born Pomona, California, November 12, 1968; admitted to bar, 1995, California. *Education:* Yale University (B.A., 1990); Harvard Law School (J.D., 1994). *Member:* Orange County, Los Angeles County and American Bar Associations.

**JAY D. HARKER,** born Long Beach, California, July 13, 1966; admitted to bar, 1993, California. *Education:* Brigham Young University (B.S., magna cum laude, 1990); Boalt Hall School of Law, University of California (J.D., 1993). Member, Moot Court Board. Member, Boalt Hall Law Review.

**HEATHER ANNE HENDERSON,** born Pasadena, California, July 4, 1961; admitted to bar, 1992, California. *Education:* Saddleback Community College (A.A./R.N., 1984); California State University at Fullerton (B.S., 1988); Whittier College (J.D., 1991). Phi Delta Phi. Registered Nurse, Pennsylvania, 1984. Health Law Symposium Editor, Whittier College Law Review, 1990-1991. *Member:* Sate Bar of California. (Resident).

**PAULA F. HENRY,** born Sharon, Pennsylvania, May 1, 1951; admitted to bar, 1988, California. *Education:* Quinay City Hospital School of Nursing (R.N., 1972); Northeastern University (B.S.N., 1976); Peter Bent Brighan Hospital, Harvard University Adult Nurse Practitioner Program (N.P., 1977); ANA Board Certified Nurse Practitioner (ANPC, 1979); Southwestern University School of Law (J.D., 1987). Medical-Legal Editor, Nurse Practitioner Forum. Licensed Registered Nurse, California, 1978 and Massachusetts, 1972. Board Certified Adult Nurse Practitioner, A.N.A., 1980. *Member:* American Association of Nurse Attorneys; California Coalition of Nurse Practitioners.

**HELEN E. HESSE,** born El Centro, California, May 4, 1947; admitted to bar, 1988, California. *Education:* University of California at Riverside (B.A., 1969); Western State University College of Law (J.D., 1987). Recipient, American Jurisprudence Award. Author: Comment, "Steinberg v. Amplica, Inc., Appraisal is the Dissenting Shareholder's Remedy in a Merger," 1986. *Member:* Orange County Bar Association; State Bar of California; American Judicature Society.

**MADONNA L. HULTMAN,** born Kenmore, New York, August 28, 1967; admitted to bar, 1992, California. *Education:* State University of New York, Geneseo (B.A., summa cum laude, 1989); State University of New York at Buffalo (J.D., cum laude, 1992).

**CHARLES J. HYLAND,** born Naperville, Illinois, September 1, 1961; admitted to bar, 1988, California and U.S. District Court, Southern District of California; 1989, U.S. District Court, Central District of California. *Education:* University of California at Los Angeles (B.A., 1984); University of San Diego (J.D., 1988). *Member:* Orange County and American Bar Associations; State Bar of California; Orange County Insurance Defense Association.

**CATHERINE J. KIM,** born Seoul, Korea, January 24, 1970; admitted to bar, 1995, California. *Education:* Claremont McKenna College (B.A., 1992); University of Paris, Sorbonne; University of San Diego (J.D., 1995); Oxford University, England.

**HARRY T. KOZAK,** born Uniontown, Pennsylvania, May 5, 1940; admitted to bar, 1990, California. *Education:* California State University at Los Angeles (B.A., cum laude, 1970); University of Southern California (M.P.A., 1972); Southwestern University School of Law (J.D., 1990). Extern, Judge Steven Lachs, Los Angeles Superior Court. Retired Captain, Los Angeles Police Department. *Member:* State Bar of California (Member, Litigation Section); The Association of Trial Lawyers of America.

(For Complete Biographical Data on Personnel in Los Angeles, San Bernardino, San Diego, San Francisco and Sacramento, California Offices, see Professional Biographies at those Cities)

## LYON & LYON LLP

A Limited Liability Partnership Including Professional Corporations

*Established in 1911*

SUITE 1200, 3200 PARK CENTER DRIVE
**COSTA MESA, CALIFORNIA 92626**
*Telephone: 714-751-6606*
*Fax: 714-751-8209*
*Email: lyon@lyonlyon.com*
*URL: http://www.lyonlyon.com*

*Los Angeles, California Office:* First Interstate World Center, 47th Floor, 633 West Fifth Street. Telephone: 213-489-1600.

*San Jose, California Office:* Suite 1150, 303 Almaden Boulevard. Telephone: 408-993-1555.

*La Jolla, California Office:* Suite 600, 4250 Executive Square. Telephone: 619-552-8400.

*Intellectual Property Law including Patent, Trademark, Copyright, Trade Regulation, Unfair Competition and Antitrust Law. Litigation.*

### RESIDENT PARTNERS

**JAMES W. GERIAK, (A PROFESSIONAL CORPORATION),** born Brooklyn, New York, September 16, 1934; admitted to bar, 1960, Virginia; 1961-1982, U.S. Court of Customs and Patent Appeals; 1962, California and U.S. District Court, Central District of California; 1965, U.S. Court of Appeals, Ninth Circuit; 1982, U.S. Court of Appeals for the Federal Circuit; registered to practice before the U.S. Patent and Trademark Office. *Education:* Rensselaer Polytechnic Institute (B.Ch.E., 1956); Georgetown University (LL.B., 1960). Member, 1958-1960 and Editorial Staff Member, 1959-1960, Georgetown Law Journal. *Member:* Los Angeles County and American (Member, Section on Patent, Trademark and Copyright Law; Member of Council, 1974-1978; Chairman, Committee on Intellectual Properties, 1977-1980, Litigation Section) Bar Associations; Virginia State Bar; American Intellectual Property Law Association (Member, Board of Directors, 1978-1982). **PRACTICE AREAS:** Patent, Trademark, Trade Regulation, Unfair Competition, Antitrust; Intellectual Property.

**ROBERT M. TAYLOR, JR.,** born Drexel Hill, Pennsylvania, May 25, 1934; admitted to bar, 1960, Virginia; 1962, California; registered to practice before the U.S. Patent and Trademark Office. *Education:* Pennsylvania State University (B.S. in E.E., 1956); Georgetown University (LL.B., 1960). *Member:* Orange County Bar Association; Virginia State Bar; American Intellectual Property Law Association; Los Angeles Intellectual Property Law Association; Orange County Patent Law Association. **PRACTICE AREAS:** Patent; Intellectual Property.

**SAMUEL B. STONE, (A PROFESSIONAL CORPORATION),** born Martinsville, Virginia, February 4, 1934; admitted to bar, 1960, Maryland; 1961, District of Columbia; 1963, California; registered to practice before the U.S. Patent and Trademark Office. *Education:* Virginia Polytechnic Institute and State University (B.S., E.E., 1955); George Washington University (J.D., 1960). Member, Panel of Arbitrators, American Arbitration Association (IP Panelist). . Member, Executive Committee, Intellectual Property Section, The State Bar of California, 1987-1990. *Member:* Los Angeles County, Orange County (Member, Board of Directors, 1988-1991) and American Bar Associations; American Intellectual Property Law Association; Los Angeles Intellectual Property Law Association; Orange County Patent Law Association (President, 1986); American Electronics Association (Co-Chair, Lawyers Committee, 1996-1997; Member, Software Forum). **PRACTICE AREAS:** Patent, Trademark, Copyright; Intellectual Property.

**ALLAN W. JANSEN,** born Oak Park, Illinois, July 22, 1948; admitted to bar, 1978, California, U.S. District Court, Central District of California and U.S. Court of Appeals, Ninth Circuit; registered to practice before the U.S. Patent and Trademark Office. *Education:* University of Illinois (B.S. in Aerospace Eng., 1971); John Marshall Law School (J.D., 1978). Phi Delta Phi. Member, John Marshall Journal of Practice and Procedure 1977-1978. *Member:* Los Angeles County and American Bar Associations; State Bar of California; American Intellectual Property Law Association; Los Angeles Intellectual Property Law Association. **PRACTICE AREAS:** Patent, Trademark, Copyright, Unfair Competition.

**DAVID B. MURPHY,** born Covina, California, November 25, 1956; admitted to bar, 1982, California; U.S. District Court, Central, Northern and Southern Districts of California and U.S. Court of Appeals for the Federal Circuit; registered to practice before the U.S. Patent and Trademark Office. *Education:* University of California, Irvine (B.A., summa cum laude,

*(This Listing Continued)*

# PROFESSIONAL BIOGRAPHIES

### CALIFORNIA—COSTA MESA

1978); University of California at Berkeley (M.A., Physics, 1981); Boalt Hall School of Law, University of California (J.D., 1982). Phi Beta Kappa. First Prize, Ascap Nathan Burkan Memorial Competition, in Copyright Law, "The Case for Copyrightability of Microelectronics," 1981. *Member:* Orange County and American Bar Associations; American Intellectual Property Law Association; Orange County Patent Law Association. **SPECIAL AGENCIES:** Section 337 Investigations in the International Trade Commission. **PRACTICE AREAS:** Patent, Software Protection; Intellectual Property.

### RESIDENT ASSOCIATES

**KURT T. MULVILLE,** born Los Angeles County, California, July 3, 1962; admitted to bar, 1990, California; 1991, U.S. District Court, Central, Southern and Northern Districts of California; U.S. Court of Appeals for the Federal Circuit; registered to practice before the U.S. Patent and Trademark Office. *Education:* University of California at Irvine (B.S., 1985); Loyola Marymount University (J.D., 1990). Recipient, Society of American Writers on Legal Subjects Award. Editor-in-Chief, Loyola Marymount Law Review, 1989-1990. *Member:* American Bar Association; Orange County Patent Law Association. **PRACTICE AREAS:** Intellectual Property.

**JAMES P. BROGAN,** born Ann Arbor, Michigan, January 12, 1965; admitted to bar, 1991, California; registered to practice before the U.S. Patent and Trademark Office. *Education:* Southern Methodist University (B.S.E.E., 1988); University of Houston Law Center (J.D., 1991). Order of Barons. Associate Editor, University of Houston Law Review, 1990-1991. Co-Author: "Damages for Patent Infringement," State Bar of Texas Professional Development Program. *Member:* Orange County (Co-Chair, Crystal Casino Fundraiser Committee, 1995 and 1996) and American Bar Associations; Orange County Barristers (Director, 1992—; Treasurer, 1994-1996; President Elect, 1997); American Intellectual Property Law Association. **PRACTICE AREAS:** Patent, Trademark, Copyright, Unfair Competition; Intellectual Property.

**CORRINE M. FREEMAN,** born Compton, California, September 30, 1964; admitted to bar, 1991, California; registered to practice before the U.S. Patent and Trademark office. *Education:* Wayne State University (B.S. Chemistry, 1986); University of Southern California (J.D., 1991). Executive Editor: *Major Tax Planning and Computer/Law Journal,* University of Southern California; University of Southern California. Legion Lex. *Member:* Orange County Bar Association; Orange County Patent Law Association (Member, Board of Directors); American Intellectual Property Law Association. **PRACTICE AREAS:** Intellectual Property.

**MARK J. CARLOZZI,** born Greenport, New York, May 17, 1963; admitted to bar, 1993, California, U.S. Court of Appeals, Ninth Circuit and U.S. District Court, Central and Northern Districts of California. *Education:* Duke University (B.S.E.E., 1985); Loyola Law School (J.D., 1992). Order of the Coif. Recipient: American Jurisprudence Award in Criminal Law. **PRACTICE AREAS:** Patent, Trademark, Copyright; Unfair Competition, Trade Secret; Intellectual Property.

**KENNETH S. ROBERTS,** born Kendall Park, New Jersey, January 21, 1963; admitted to bar, 1993, California; registered to practice before the U.S. Patent and Trademark Office. *Education:* Virginia Polytechnic Institute and State University (B.S.M.E., 1985); University of San Diego (J.D., cum laude, 1993). Phi Alpha Delta. Member, San Diego Law Review, 1991-1993; Merit Scholarship, 1991-1992. Author: "Curing the Ake of An Incompetent Expert: A Separate Reviewable Issue?" 29 San Diego Law Review 799 (Fall, 1992). *Member:* Orange County and American Bar Associations; American Intellectual Property Law Association; Orange County Patent Law Association. **PRACTICE AREAS:** Patent, Trademark, Copyright; Trade Secret; Intellectual Property.

**JOHN C. KAPPOS,** born Anaheim, California, November 22, 1963; admitted to bar, 1994, California, U.S. Court of Appeals, Ninth and Federal Circuits and U.S. District Court, Eastern, Western, Northern and Southern Districts of California; registered to practice before the U.S. Patent and Trademark Office. *Education:* University of California at Irvine (B.S., cum laude, 1986); Harvard University (Ph.D., 1991); University of California at Los Angeles (J.D., 1994). Phi Beta Kappa, Phi Lambda Upsilon. Sigma Xi. Fannie and John Hertz Predoctoral Fellowship. Recipient: Don Bunker Award for Undergraduate Chemistry Research, (1986); Melville B. Nimmer Award in Intellectual Property Law (1993). *Member:* Orange County and American Bar Associations; Federal Circuit Bar Association; American Intellectual Property Law Association; Los Angeles Intellectual Property Law Association; Orange County Patent Law Association; American Chemical Society. **PRACTICE AREAS:** Patent, Trademark, Copyright; Intellectual Property.

*(This Listing Continued)*

**CHARLES CALVIN FOWLER,** born Pomona, California, February 10, 1964; admitted to bar, 1994, California; registered to practice before the U.S. Patent and Trademark Office. *Education:* University of California at Davis (B.S.Ch.E., 1986); University of California at Los Angeles (J.D., 1994). Tau Beta Pi. Editor, UCLA, Law Review, 1993-1994. *Member:* American Bar Association. **PRACTICE AREAS:** Patent, Trademark, Copyright; Intellectual Property.

**JAMES K. SAKAGUCHI,** born Bournes, Massachusetts, February 18, 1964; admitted to bar, 1995, California. *Education:* University of California, Irvine (B.S.E., cum laude, 1986); University of California, Los Angeles (J.D., 1995). Tau Beta Pi. *Member:* American Bar Association; Orange County Patent Law Association. **PRACTICE AREAS:** Intellectual Property.

**NEAL MATTHEW COHEN,** born Westwood, New Jersey, November 18, 1964; admitted to bar, 1996, California. *Education:* University of California at Los Angeles (C.S.E., 1987); Loyola University of Los Angeles (J.D., 1996). Order of the Coif. **PRACTICE AREAS:** Patent.

(For Complete Biographical Data on all Personnel, see Professional Biographies at Los Angeles)

---

## McCAULEY & ASSOCIATES, LLP

Established in 1990

611 ANTON BOULEVARD, SUITE 1260

**COSTA MESA, CALIFORNIA 92626**

Telephone: 714-438-9108

Fax: 714-957-3718

*Trial and Appellate Practice in all State and Federal Courts and Arbitration Tribunals, with emphasis on Complex Business Disputes.*

**FIRM PROFILE:** *McCauley & Associates are a well established law firm who takes pride in their clients relations. The law firm is listed in the Bar Register of Preeminent Law Directory.*

### MEMBERS OF FIRM

**JOHN J. MCCAULEY,** born Washington, D.C., May 4, 1949; admitted to bar, 1980, California. *Education:* University of California at Irvine (B.A., 1971); University of Pennsylvania (M.A., 1973); Harvard University (J.D., cum laude, 1980). *Member:* Orange County and American Bar Associations; State Bar of California. **REPORTED CASES:** Jenkins v. Tuneup Masters, 190 Cal. App. 3d 1, 235 Cal. Rptr. 214 (Cal. App. 3d Dist., 1987) *review denied* (June 17, 1987); US Aluminum Corporation/Texas v. Alumax, Inc., 831 F. 2d 878 (9th Cir. 1987), *cert. denied,* 488 U.S. 822, 109 S. Ct 68, 102 L. Ed. 2d 45 (1988); Lund v. Albrecht, 936 F. 2d 459 (9th Cir. 1991). **PRACTICE AREAS:** Trial and Appellate.

---

**MARK S. FLYNN,** born Santa Monica, California, October 3, 1953; admitted to bar, 1984, California; 1985, U.S. Court of Appeals, Ninth Circuit; U.S. District Court, Northern, Central and Southern Districts of California. *Education:* University of California at Los Angeles (B.A., 1978; J.D., 1984). Co-Author: "Can Science be Inopportune?—Constitutional Validity of Governmental Restrictions on Race-IQ Research," University of California at Los Angeles Law Review, Vol. 31, October, 1983. *Member:* Orange County (Member, Business Litigation Section) and Federal Bar Associations; State Bar of California; Public Investor Arbitration Bar Association; Association of Business Trial Lawyers. **REPORTED CASES:** National Solar Equipment Owners' Assn. v. Grumman Corp., 235 Cal.App.3d 1273 (1991); Three Valleys Municipal Water District v. E. F. Hutton & Co., Inc., 925 F.2d 1136 (9th Cir. 1991); Knapp v. Gomez, (1991 Transfer Binder) Fed. Sec.L.Rep. (CCH) paragraphs 96, 166, at 90, 918 (S.D.Cal. June 25, 1991). **PRACTICE AREAS:** Securities Litigation.

## McCORMICK, KIDMAN & BEHRENS, LLP

A Partnership of Professional Corporations

*IMPERIAL BANK BUILDING
695 TOWN CENTER DRIVE
SUITE 1400
COSTA MESA, CALIFORNIA 92626-1924*
Telephone: 714-755-3100
Fax: 714-755-3110; 1-800-755-3125
Email: mkb1@ix.netcom.com

*General Civil Practice and Litigation in all State and Federal Courts. Environmental Law, Water Law, Special Districts, Municipal Law, Real Property, Real Estate Transactions and Real Estate Finance, Estate Planning and Probate, Land Use, (including CEQA Compliance), Natural Resources (including Oil and Gas Matters), Property Tax Matters, and Condemnation Actions.*

FIRM PROFILE: *The partners and associates of McCormick, Kidman & Behrens have specialized in representing municipalities, special districts, business entities and individuals state-wide in matters of public law, eminent domain, water rights, environmental and land use issues. The firm's extensive experience in representing public entities enables it to provide a unique expertise to public entities as well as private companies and individual clients in these areas. The firm also provides representation and advise in the area of probate and estate planning, business transactions and litigation with considerable expertise. It is the philosophy of the firm to provide clients with attentive and efficient legal services.*

### MEMBERS OF FIRM

**HOMER L. (MIKE) McCORMICK, JR., (P.C.)**, born Frederick, Maryland, November 11, 1928; admitted to bar, 1961, California, U.S. District Court, Central District of California, U.S. District Court, Northern District of California and U.S. Court of Appeals, Ninth Circuit; 1976, U.S. District Court, Southern District of California; 1977, U.S. Tax Court, U.S. Claims Court and U.S. Supreme Court. *Education:* George Washington University and San Jose State College (A.B., 1951); Hastings College of the Law, University of California (J.D., 1961). Delta Theta Phi; Order of the Coif; Thurston Society. Member, 1959-1961 and Associate Editor, 1961, Hastings Law Review. Lecturer, Real Property Remedies, 1976-1977, 1979-1980, 1982, 1988 and Proposition 13 and Property Tax Matters, 1980-1981, 1987, California Continuing Education for the Bar. Author: "Recovery in Deceit Actions in California," 11 Hastings Law Journal 183. Contributing Author: "Real Property Remedies," California Continuing Education for the Bar Book, 1982. Speaker Alternative Dispute Resolution State Bar Convention, 1988—; Member, Board of Governors, 1966— and President, 1973, Hastings Alumni Association. President, Board of Trustees, Hastings 1066 Legal Foundation, 1975-1977; Selected Hastings Alumnus of the Year, 1992. Judge Pro Tem, Orange County Superior Court, 1975, 1981, 1984. Member, Panel of Arbitrators, American Arbitration Association. *Member:* The Bar Association of San Francisco; Orange County (Member, Judiciary Committee, 1982-1985. Administration of Justice Committee, 1990—; (Chairman, 1991-1992). Lawyers Reference Service 1993; Liaison to State Commission of Future of The State Bar and Legal Profession, 1993-1994. Delegate State Bar, 1985-1993), Federal and American (Member: Condemnation and Condemnation Procedure Committee, Section on Local Government Law, 1963—; Committee on Legal Education, 1975—; Committee on Natural Resources, 1973—) Bar Associations; The State Bar of California (Member: Condemnation Law and Procedure Committee, 1965-1968; Public Law Section; Litigation Section); The Association of Trial Lawyers of America; American Board of Trial Advocates (President, Orange County Chapter, 1973); American Judicature Society; Orange County City Attorneys Association (President, 1972); California Condemnation Lawyers Group; National Health Lawyers Association; Consumer Attorneys of California. *PRACTICE AREAS:* Real Estate Law; Property Tax Law; Civil Litigation; Condemnation Law.

**ARTHUR G. KIDMAN, (P.C.)**, born Bremerton, Washington, June 14, 1946; admitted to bar, 1974, California and U.S. District Court, Southern, Central and Eastern Districts of California. *Education:* Washington State University (B.A., with high honors, 1968); University of Chicago (J.D., 1974). Phi Beta Kappa; Phi Kappa Phi; Omicron Delta Kappa; Phi Eta Sigma. Co-Author: "The Relationship of Just Compensation to the Land Use Regulatory Power: An Analysis and Proposal," Symposium-Land Use Planning and Control, Pepperdine Law Review, Vol 2, 1974. Author; "San Gabriel Valley Groundwater Contamination as Cause of Water Scarcity," Proceedings, 17th Biennial Conference on Groundwater. University of California Water Resources Center, California Department of Water Resources and State Water Resources Control Board, Report No. 72, May 1990; "Pros and Cons of Groundwater Management or Look Out For Some Extremely Bogus Thinking," Proceedings, 18th Biennial Conference on Groundwater, University of California Water Resources Center, California Department of Water Resources and State Water Resources Control Board, September 1991. Extension Instructor in Water Law, University of California, Irvine. General Counsel, San Gabriel Basin Water Quality Authority, 1993—; Rancho California Water District, 1980-1992; Yorba Linda Water District 1979—; Santiago County Water District, 1983—; Three Valleys Municipal Water District 1983-1988; Upper San Gabriel Valley Municipal Water District 1985-1991; Mesa Consolidated Water District, 1978-1981. *Member:* Orange County Bar Association; The State Bar of California (Member, Sections on: Public Law; Real Property Law); Association of California Water Agencies (Member: Legislative Committee and Legal Affairs Committee; Chairman, Attorneys Conference, 1976-1980). [1st Lt., U.S. Army, 1968-1971]. *PRACTICE AREAS:* Public Law; Water Law; Environmental Law.

**RUSSELL G. BEHRENS, (P.C.)**, born Los Angeles, California, May 19, 1936; admitted to bar, 1961, California. *Education:* Santa Ana College (A.A., 1956); University of Southern California (J.D., 1960). Phi Delta Phi. Co-Author: "Domestic Uses of Water: A Battleground Over a Short Supply," Public Law, a publication of the State Bar of California Public Law Section, Summer, 1992. Deputy District Attorney, 1961-1963. General Counsel, Municipal Water District of Orange County, 1978—; San Gorgonio Pass Water Agency, 1989—; Hemet/San Jacinto Groundwater Association, 1994—. Special Counsel to cities and special districts on water rights and public law matters. *Member:* Orange County (Member, Client Relations Committee, 1972-1990; Real Estate Section; Secretary, Orange County Barristers, 1964-1965) and American (Member: Natural Resources Section; Economics of Law Practice Section; Real Property, Probate and Trust Law Section) Bar Associations; The State Bar of California (Member, Public Law Section Executive Committee; Vice-Chairman, 1991-1992; Real Property Law Section); Association of California Water Agencies (Member, Legal Affairs Committee and Legislative Committee, 1975-1991; Chairman: Attorneys Conference, 1986—; Continuing Legal Education Committee, 1994—); American Inns of Court (Member, Executive Committee, Board of Directors, Legion Lex Inn, Orange County). *PRACTICE AREAS:* Public Law; Water Law; Real Property; Construction Law; Environmental Law.

**SUZANNE M. TAGUE, (P.C.)**, born Huntington Park, California, June 30, 1952; admitted to bar, 1977, California. *Education:* University of California at Irvine (B.A., 1974); Pepperdine University (J.D., 1977). Phi Alpha Delta. Lecturer, California Continuing Education for the Bar. *Member:* Orange County (Member: Estate Planning, Probate and Trust Section, 1978—; Committee on Probate Policy Memorandum, 1981; Probate Fees-Ordinary and Extraordinary Fees, 1983; Executive Committee, 1995; Law Office Management Section, 1994—) and American (Member, Sections on: Taxation; Real Property, Probate and Trust Law) Bar Associations; The State Bar of California (Member, Section on Estate Planning, Trust and Probate; Lecturer for CEB, NBI and Various Educational Institutions in the Area of Estate Planning and Probate). *PRACTICE AREAS:* Probate Law; Estate Planning Law; Administration of Class Actions; Adjunct Public Agency Representation.

**JANET R. MORNINGSTAR, (P.C.)**, born Orange, California, August 2, 1956; admitted to bar, 1981, California, U.S. District Court, Central District of California and U.S. Court of Appeals, Ninth Circuit. *Education:* Pomona College (B.A., 1978); University of Southern California (J.D., 1981). General Counsel, Rowland Water District, 1989—. *Member:* Orange County (Member, Real Property Section) and American Bar Associations; The State Bar of California; American Inns of Court (Member, Board of Directors, Legion Lex, Orange County, 1992-1993); Association of California Water Agencies. *REPORTED CASES:* Biddle v. Superior Court (1985) 170 CalApp3d 135; Brydon v. East Bay Mun. Utility Dist. (1994) 24 CalApp4th 178 (as amicus curiae). *PRACTICE AREAS:* Public Law; Water Law; Real Property Law.

**KEITH E. McCULLOUGH, (P.C.)**, born Orange, California, October 31, 1962; admitted to bar, 1989, California and Wisconsin; 1990, U.S. District Court, Central District of California; 1993, U.S. District Court, Eastern District of California. *Education:* Brigham Young University (B.A., Political Science, 1986); University of Wisconsin (J.D., 1989). Member, Federalist Society (Secretary, Madison, Wisconsin Chapter, 1987-1988). *Member:* Orange County (Member, Business Litigation Section) and Riverside County (Board of Directors, 1992-1993) Bar Associations; State Bar of California; State Bar of Wisconsin; Riverside County Barristers-California (President, 1992-1993). *LANGUAGES:* German. *PRACTICE AREAS:* Business Litigation; Water Law; Real Property Law; Condemnation.

*(This Listing Continued)*

## PROFESSIONAL BIOGRAPHIES

### ASSOCIATES

**DAVID D. BOYER,** born Peoria, Illinois, October 6, 1960; admitted to bar, 1985, Alabama; 1986, U.S. District Court, Middle District of Alabama and U.S. Court of Appeals, Eleventh Circuit; 1989, California; 1990, U.S. District Court, Central District of California and U.S. Court of Appeals, Ninth Circuit; 1994, U.S. District Court, Southern District of California. *Education:* Bowling Green State University (B.S., 1982); University of Alabama (J.D., 1985). Recipient, American Jurisprudence Award in Damages. Frazier Reams Fellowship. Harold Anderson Scholarship. *Member:* American and Federal Bar Associations; State Bar of California. **PRACTICE AREAS:** Litigation in the areas of Public Law, Real Property and Land Use Planning; Water Law; Business; Commercial Practices and Transactions; Insurance Coverage.

**ROBERT A. JOHNSON,** born Elkader, Iowa, August 14, 1966; admitted to bar, 1991, California; 1995, U.S. District Court, Central District of California. *Education:* University of Iowa (B.B.A., with distinction, 1988; J.D., with high distinction, 1991). Phi Eta Sigma; Beta Gamma Sigma. Order of the Coif. Articles Editor, The Journal of Corporation Law, 1990-1991. Author: Comment, In re Moore: Moore Confusion on Excluding ERISA Pension Plans From the Bankruptcy Estate Under Code Section, 541(c)(2), 16 Journal of Corporation Law 575 (1991). Listed in Who's Who in American Law, 1995-1996; International, 1995-1996. *Member:* Orange County and American Bar Associations; State Bar of California. **PRACTICE AREAS:** Business Litigation; Civil Litigation; Water Law; Real Property Law; Condemnation; Environmental Law.

**JOHN O. CLUNE,** born Philadelphia, Pennsylvania, December 9, 1968; admitted to bar, 1995, California. *Education:* University of San Diego (B.A., magna cum laude, 1991); Hastings College of Law, University of California, San Francisco (J.D., 1994). Pi Sigma Alpha. Honors Program: U.S.D. Universidad de Valencia, Valencia, Spain, 1989; Fundación José Ortega y Gasset, Toledo, Spain, 1989; Spanish-American Institute, Seville, Spain, 1990. Recipient: Presidential Scholarship; Department Award for Outstanding Political Science Student; American Jurisprudence Award in Moot Court. Member and Production Editor, Hastings Constitutional Law Quarterly, 1992-1994. Extern, San Francisco Superior Court, Law and Motions Department, 1993. Member, Third-Year Council, 1994. University of San Diego Institute of International and Comparative Law, Guanajuato, Mexico, Summer, 1992. Member, Inland Boatman's Union, 1988-1990. *Member:* The State Bar of California; American Inns of Court (Member, Legion Lex Inn, Orange County). **LANGUAGES:** Spanish.

**BRADLEY D. PIERCE,** born Downey, California, June 5, 1965; admitted to bar, 1994, California and U.S. District Court, Central District of California. *Education:* Chapman University (B.S., 1987); Loyola Marymount University (J.D., 1994). St. Thomas More Society. *Member:* Los Angeles County and Orange County (Member, Environmental Law Section) Bar Associations; State Bar of California; Los Angeles County Barristers (Member, Committee on the State Bar); American Inns of Court (Member, Legion Lex Inn). **PRACTICE AREAS:** Business Litigation; Real Property and Environmental Law; Condemnation.

REPRESENTATIVE CLIENTS: Yorba Linda County Water District; Santiago County Water District; Municipal Water District of Orange County; Rowland Water District; San Gorgonio Pass Water Agency; Foothill Properties; Sweetwater Authority, City of Barstow; City of Colton; Calleguas Municipal Water District; BKK; Metropolitan Water District of Southern California.
REFERENCE: First Los Angeles Bank.

---

## McINNIS, FITZGERALD, REES & SHARKEY

A PROFESSIONAL CORPORATION

Established in 1941

650 TOWN CENTER DRIVE, SUITE 1240
**COSTA MESA, CALIFORNIA 92626**
Telephone: 714-513-2209
Fax: 714-513-2210

San Diego, California Office: 1230 Columbia Street, Suite 800. Telephone: 619-236-1711. Fax: 619-236-0387.

Professional Liability, Including Medical, Dental, Legal, Accounting, Architectural and Engineering, Business Litigation, Products Liability, Construction and Soils Erosion Litigation, Hospital Liability, Automobile, Aviation and Public Carrier Liability and Insurance Litigation, Including Bad Faith Liability, Employment Law, Environmental Law, Financial Institutions, Banking and Asset Management Litigation, Transactional and Real Estate.

(For complete biographical data on all personnel, see Professional Biographies at San Diego, California)

---

## McINTYRE BORGES & BURNS LLP

3070 BRISTOL STREET, SUITE 450
**COSTA MESA, CALIFORNIA 92626**
Telephone: 714-545-7835
Fax: 714-545-7524
Email: wtgay@ix.netcom.com
URL: http://www.mcilaw.com

Corporate, Corporate Finance, Securities, Real Estate, General Business and Energy. Civil Litigation in all Federal and State Courts.

### MEMBERS OF FIRM

**JOEL F. McINTYRE,** born Fairbury, Nebraska, September 19, 1938; admitted to bar, 1963, California. *Education:* Stanford University (A.B., 1960); University of California at Los Angeles (J.D., 1963). Order of the Coif. Articles Editor, UCLA Law Review, 1962-1963. **PRACTICE AREAS:** Corporate Law; Real Estate; Securities; Business Law.

**EVAN C. BORGES,** born San Juan, Puerto Rico, September 5, 1960; admitted to bar, 1987, California. *Education:* University of California at Berkeley (B.A., 1982); Yale University (J.D., 1985). Phi Beta Kappa. Law Clerk to Judge Juan R. Torruella, U.S. Court of Appeals, First Circuit, 1985-1986. **PRACTICE AREAS:** Litigation.

**GEORGE S. BURNS,** born Ferndale, Michigan, 1960; admitted to bar, 1986, California and U.S. District Court, Central District of California; 1988, U.S. District Court, Northern and Southern Districts of California. *Education:* University of Southern California (B.A., magna cum laude, 1982); Loyola Law School (J.D., 1986). Author: "Litigating Computer Trade Secrets in California," USC Computer Law Journal, Vol. VI No. 3, 1986; "Work Product Issues for Corporate Counsel," 1988 ALI-ABA Symposium Course Book. **REPORTED CASES:** MDFC Loan Corp. v. Greenbrier, et al, 21 Cal.App. 4th 1045 (1994). **PRACTICE AREAS:** Litigation.

**WILLIAM T. GAY,** born Washington, 1957; admitted to bar, 1983, Washington; 1989, California. *Education:* University of Washington (B.A., Economics, Japanese Studies, 1978; J.D., 1982; M.B.A., Finance, Business Economics and International Business, 1983; LL.M., Japanese Law, 1984). **LANGUAGES:** Japanese. **PRACTICE AREAS:** Corporate; Finance; Real Estate; High Technology; International Transactions; Securities. **Email:** wtgay@ix.netcom.com

**VICTORIA E. MOSS,** born Upland, California, April 28, 1964; admitted to bar, 1990, Texas; 1994, California. *Education:* San Diego State University (B.S., 1987); University of San Diego (J.D., 1990). Phi Delta Phi. Recipient: American Jurisprudence Award, Constitutional Law; Moore Hall Public Interest Award. **PRACTICE AREAS:** Litigation.

**STEFANIE L. MILLER,** born Lafayette, Indiana, January 15, 1967; admitted to bar, 1995, California. *Education:* University of North Carolina (B.A., 1988); Santa Clara University (J.D., 1995). Recipient, American Jurisprudence Award in Legal Research and Writing. **LANGUAGES:** French. **PRACTICE AREAS:** Litigation.

---

## MURTAUGH, MILLER, MEYER & NELSON

A Partnership including Professional Corporations

Established in 1979

3200 PARK CENTER DRIVE, 9TH FLOOR
P.O. BOX 5023
**COSTA MESA, CALIFORNIA 92628-5023**
Telephone: 714-513-6800
Facsimile: 714-513-6899

General Civil and Trial Practice in all State and Federal Courts. Insurance, Personal Injury, Employment, Professional Liability, Environmental, Business, Franchising, Construction and Commercial Law.

FIRM PROFILE: Murtaugh, Miller, Meyer & Nelson was founded in 1979 by Mike Murtaugh and Brad Miller, both graduates of the UCLA School of Law. Its members have extensive experience in handling a wide variety of litigation including construction defect, products liability, professional liability, labor and employment, personal injury, toxic tort and environmental, insurance coverage/bad faith. It also provides a full range of counseling and business transaction services including franchising. The firm services primarily Los Angeles, Orange, San Bernardino, Riverside and San Diego Counties, and practices in state and federal trial and appellate courts, as well as before various administrative agencies. As responsible members of the legal community,

(This Listing Continued)

**MURTAUGH, MILLER, MEYER & NELSON,** Costa Mesa—Continued

firm members serve in such positions as judges pro tem for the Orange County Superior Court and as panelist for the continuing legal education programs of the Orange County Bar Association, the Association of Southern California Defense Counsel and the C.E.B. All firm members are required to participate in professional development programs, and firm members are actively involved in various community and professional associations.

**MICHAEL J. MURTAUGH, (A PROFESSIONAL CORPORATION),** born Dayton, Ohio, November 10, 1947; admitted to bar, 1973, California. *Education:* University of Cincinnati (B.A., with highest honors, 1970); University of California at Los Angeles (J.D., 1973). Member, Order of the Barristers. *Member:* Los Angeles County, Orange County and American Bar Associations; State Bar of California; Defense Research Institute; Association of Southern California Defense Counsel (Member, Board of Directors, 1982-1984). *PRACTICE AREAS:* Construction Litigation; Employment Law; Insurance Law; General Civil Trial.

**BRADFORD H. MILLER, (A PROFESSIONAL CORPORATION),** born Kalamazoo, Michigan, August 11, 1950; admitted to bar, 1975, California. *Education:* University of California at Los Angeles (B.A., 1972; J.D., 1975). *Member:* Orange County and American (Member, Section on Torts and Insurance Practice) Bar Associations; State Bar of California; Association of Southern California Defense Counsel (Director, 1987-1988); Defense Research Institute. *PRACTICE AREAS:* Insurance Coverage/Bad Faith Law; Professional Errors and Omissions Law; Personal Injury Litigation.

**MICHAEL J. NELSON,** born Lynwood, California, May 24, 1953; admitted to bar, 1979, California. *Education:* Santa Ana College and University of Southern California (B.S., cum laude, 1976); Pepperdine University (J.D., 1979). *Member:* Orange County Bar Association; State Bar of California; Orange County Trial Lawyers Association. *PRACTICE AREAS:* Construction Litigation and related claims; General Civil Trial.

**ROBERT T. LEMEN,** born Los Angeles, California, September 8, 1955; admitted to bar, 1980, California and U.S. District Court, Central and Southern Districts of California. *Education:* University of California at Irvine (B.A., magna cum laude, 1977); University of California at Los Angeles (J.D., 1980). Phi Beta Kappa. *Member:* Orange County Bar Association (Member, Environmental Law Section); State Bar of California; Association of Southern California Defense Counsel. *PRACTICE AREAS:* Tort Litigation; Business Litigation; Environmental Litigation; General Civil Trial.

**MARK S. HIMMELSTEIN,** born Lake Charles, Louisiana, October 2, 1957; admitted to bar, 1982, California and U.S. District Court, Central and Southern Districts of California. *Education:* Duke University (B.A., 1979); McGeorge School of Law, University of the Pacific (J.D., 1982). Member, Traynor Honor Society. Recipient, American Jurisprudence Awards in Torts and Criminal Law. *Member:* State Bar of California; Association of Southern California Defense Counsel. *PRACTICE AREAS:* Construction Litigation; Professional Malpractice; General Civil Trial.

**HARRY A. HALKOWICH,** born Newark, New Jersey, April 12, 1945; admitted to bar, 1975, California; 1977, U.S. District Court, Central District of California. *Education:* Rutgers University (B.S. and B.A., 1968); Pepperdine University (J.D., 1975). Member, Pepperdine University Law Review, 1974-1975. *Member:* Orange County Bar Association; State Bar of California (Member, Business Section); American Arbitration Association. [With U.S. Coast Guard, 1969-1972]. *PRACTICE AREAS:* Business Law; Franchising; Real Estate; Commercial Litigation.

**MADELYN A. ENRIGHT,** born Los Angeles, California, March 15, 1955; admitted to bar, 1983, California. *Education:* California State University at San Diego (B.A., high honors, 1977); Loyola Marymount University (J.D., 1983). Adjunct Professor, UCI Extension Program. *Member:* Orange County Bar Association (Member, Insurance and Construction Sections); State Bar of California. *PRACTICE AREAS:* Construction Litigation; Personal Injury Law; Insurance Defense Law; General Civil Trial.

**JAMES A. MURPHY, IV,** born Seattle, Washington, March 20, 1944; admitted to bar, 1978, California. *Education:* University of California at Los Angeles (B.A., 1967); California State University at Long Beach (M.B.A., 1969); Western State College of Law (J.D., cum laude, 1978). Editor, Western State College of Law Review, 1977-1978. Judge Pro Tempore, Orange County Superior Court. *Member:* Los Angeles County (Member, Corporate and Employment Sections), Orange County (Member, Labor and Employment Sections) and American (Member Section on Labor and Employment Litigation) Bar Associations; State Bar of California (Member Sections on Labor and Employment). *PRACTICE AREAS:* Labor and Employment Counseling and Litigation.

**LAWRENCE A. TREGLIA, JR.,** born Mount Vernon, New York, December 10, 1960; admitted to bar, 1986, California; 1993, U.S. Supreme Court. *Education:* San Diego State University (B.A., 1982); McGeorge School of Law (J.D., 1986). *Member:* Orange County and American Bar Associations; State Bar of California. *PRACTICE AREAS:* Construction Litigation.

---

**DEBRA L. BRAASCH,** born Lynnwood, California, February 11, 1959; admitted to bar, 1983, California, U.S. District Court, Central District of California and U.S. Court of Appeals, Ninth Circuit. *Education:* University of California at Irvine (B.A., cum laude, 1980); University of Southern California (J.D., 1983). Phi Alpha Delta. *Member:* Orange County Bar Association (Member, Construction Law Section); State Bar of California; Association of Southern California Defense Counsel.

**THOMAS J. SKANE,** born Bridgeport, Connecticut, June 22, 1959; admitted to bar, 1984, California. *Education:* University of California at Irvine (B.A., 1981); Loyola Law School (J.D., 1984). *Member:* Orange County and American Bar Associations; State Bar of California. *PRACTICE AREAS:* Construction; Personal Injury Litigation; Insurance Coverage/Bad Faith.

**DAVID C. HOLT,** born Fontana, California, December 13, 1961; admitted to bar, 1988, California and U.S. District Court, Central and Southern Districts of California. *Education:* San Bernardino Valley College (A.A., 1982); University of California at Riverside (B.S., 1984); University of San Diego (J.D., 1988). Recipient, American Jurisprudence Award, Property. Comments Editor, San Diego Law Review, 1987-1988. *Member:* Orange County Bar Association; State Bar of California.

**LAWRENCE J. DiPINTO,** born Diamond Bar, California, July 5, 1964; admitted to bar, 1990, California. *Education:* Occidental College (A.B., cum laude, 1986); Loyola Law School (J.D., 1989). *Member:* Orange County Bar Association; State Bar of California.

**DEBRA L. REILLY,** born San Diego, California, August 25, 1962; admitted to bar, 1990, California and U.S. District Court, Central District of California. *Education:* Brigham Young University (B.S., 1984); Yavapai College; University of San Diego (J.D., 1989). Phi Alpha Delta. Comments Editor, San Diego Law Review, 1989-1990. Judicial Extern to the Honorable David R. Thompson, U.S. Court of Appeals, Ninth Circuit, 1990. Author: "Reversal of a RICO Predicate Offense on Appeal: Should the RICO Court Be Vacated?" San Diego Law Review, Vol. 27, No. 1, 1990. *Member:* Orange County and American (Member, Labor and Employment Sections) Bar Associations; State Bar of California; Association of Southern California Defense Counsel.

**SUSAN WESTOVER,** born Jersey City, New Jersey, July 3, 1962; admitted to bar, 1990, California and U.S. District Court, Central District of California. *Education:* Boston College (B.A., 1984); University of San Diego School of Law (J.D., 1990). Member, San Diego Law Review, 1988-1990. Author: "NCAA v. Tarkanian: If NCAA Action Is Not State Action, Can Its Members Meaningfully Air Their Dissatisfaction?" 26 San Diego Law Review 953 (1990). *Member:* Orange County and American Bar Associations; State Bar of California; Association of Southern California Defense Counsel; Orange County Barristers. *PRACTICE AREAS:* Labor and Employment Law; Business Litigation; Civil Appeals.

**GREGORY M. HEUSER,** born Chicago, Illinois, September 29, 1946; admitted to bar, 1990, California and U.S. District Court, Central District of California. *Education:* University of Santa Clara (B.S., 1968); University of Connecticut (M.B.A., 1981); Western State University (J.D., with honors, 1990).

**CARRIE E. PHELAN,** born Fullerton, California, January 13, 1965; admitted to bar, 1990, California; 1991, U.S. District Court, Central District of California. *Education:* Loyola Marymount University (B.S. in Civil Engineering, cum laude, 1987); Loyola Law School (J.D., 1990). Tau Beta Pi; Alpha Sigma Nu; Phi Delta Phi; Order of the Coif; St. Thomas More Honor Society. Production Editor, 1989-1990, Loyola of Los Angeles International and Comparative Law Journal. *Member:* Orange County Bar Association; The State Bar of California; American Society of Civil Engineers.

**MARYLS K. BRAUN,** born Dallas, Texas, 1966; admitted to bar, 1992, California. *Education:* University of Southern California (B.S., 1987);

*(This Listing Continued)*

McGeorge School of Law (J.D., 1991). *Member:* Orange County Bar Association; State Bar of California; Orange County Barristers.

**JOHN R. BROWNING,** born Pasadena, California, January 1, 1966; admitted to bar, 1992, California. *Education:* University of California, Irvine (B.A., 1989); University of the Pacific, McGeorge School of Law (J.D., 1992). Phi Delta Phi; Sigma Chi. *Member:* Orange County Bar Association; State Bar of California; Association of Southern California Defense Counsel.

**ERIC J. DUBIN,** born Detroit, Michigan, May 5, 1966; admitted to bar, 1992, California. *Education:* University of Arizona (B.S., 1988); California Western School of Law (J.D., cum laude, 1992). Lead Articles Editor, California Western Law Review, 1991-1992. Recipient, American Jurisprudence Award in Torts, 1990, 1991-1992. Judicial Extern to the Honorable Howard B. Wiener, California Court of Appeal, Fourth District, Division One, 1992. *Member:* State Bar of California; American Bar Association.

**GEOFFREY A. GRAVES,** born Huntington Beach, California, August 19, 1969; admitted to bar, 1994, California. *Education:* University of Southern California (B.A., 1991); University of San Diego (J.D., 1994). *Member:* Orange County Bar Association (Member, Construction Section); State Bar of California.

**TAMARA DADD SMITH,** born Mississauga, Ontario, Canada, October 24, 1968; admitted to bar, 1994, California. *Education:* University of Alabama (B.A., 1990); Pepperdine University (J.D., 1994). *Member:* Orange County Bar Association. **LANGUAGES:** French.

**JOHN KIRK DONNELLY,** born Honolulu, Hawaii, December 27, 1967; admitted to bar, 1995, California and U.S. District Court, Southern District of California; 1996, U.S. District Court, Central District of California. *Education:* College of William & Mary (B.A., 1989); University of San Diego (J.D., 1995). Order of the Barristers; Recipient: American Bankruptcy Law Journal Prize; Amercian Jurisprudence Award, Bankruptcy. Appellate Moot Court Board; Appellate Moot Court National Team.

**RICHARD PAUL HIDALGO,** born Miami, Florida, June 19, 1967; admitted to bar, 1995, California. *Education:* University of Texas (B.A., 1989); University of San Diego (J.D., 1995). Associate Editor, Journal of Contemporary Legal Issues, 1994-1995. *Member:* Orange County (Member, Business Litigation Section).

### OF COUNSEL

**SUSAN W. MENKES,** born Shelbyville, Kentucky, February 18, 1952; admitted to bar, 1979, California. *Education:* Transylvania University (B.A., 1974); Loyola Law School (J.D., 1979). *Member:* Orange County and American Bar Associations; State Bar of California.

**JAY D. FULLMAN,** born Annapolis, Maryland, February 4, 1956; admitted to bar, 1980, California, U.S. District Court, Central District of California and U.S. Court of Appeals, Ninth Circuit. *Education:* Pepperdine University (B.A., summa cum laude, 1977); University of Southern California (J.D., 1980). Member, Executive Board, Hale Moot Court, 1979-1980. *Member:* Orange County (Member, Business Litigation Section) and American (Member, Litigation Section) Bar Associations; State Bar of California; Christian Legal Society. **PRACTICE AREAS:** Real Property Law; Construction Litigation; Franchise Law.

**RICHARD E. MEYER,** born Los Angeles, California, May 10, 1937; admitted to bar, 1963, California; 1968, U.S. Supreme Court. *Education:* University of Southern California (B.A., 1959; J.D., 1962). Phi Alpha Delta (Secretary, 1960-1961). Member, Panel of Arbitrators, American Arbitration Association. *Member:* Los Angeles County, Orange County and American Bar Associations; State Bar of California; Association of Southern California Defense Counsel; Defense Research Institute. **PRACTICE AREAS:** Products Liability Law; Catastrophic Personal Injury Law; Premises Liability Law; Governmental Entity Defense Law; Insurance Bad Faith Law; General Civil Trial.

REPRESENTATIVE CLIENTS: American International Adjustment Co., Inc.; Automobile Club of Southern California; Citation Insurance Group; CNA Risk Management Group; Continental Insurance Cos. (Continental Loss Adjusting Services); Design Professionals Insurance Co.; Fireman's Fund Insurance Co.; Golden Eagle Insurance Co.; New Hampshire Insurance Co.; Home Club; Ralph's Grocery Company; Sears, Roebuck & Co.; Ward - THK.
DESIGN PROFESSIONAL CLIENTS: Architects Orange; Brion S. Jeannette & Assoc.; Delawie/Bretton/Wilkes; Dike/Runa; Dougherty & Dougherty; Florian Martinez Assoc.; HRP LanDesign; Knowles and La Bonte Architects; STB Structural Engineers, Inc.; Stockton/Hidey Assoc.; Tsuchiyama & Kaino; W. Ted Tyler & Assoc.; Warkentin & Wraight; Williamson & Schmid; Van Dell & Assoc.

# PAUL, HASTINGS, JANOFSKY & WALKER LLP

A Limited Liability Partnership including Professional Corporations
Firm Established in 1951; Office in 1974
SEVENTEENTH FLOOR, 695 TOWN CENTER DRIVE
**COSTA MESA, CALIFORNIA 92626-1924**
Telephone: 714-668-6200
Fax: 714-979-1921
Email: info@PHJW.com
URL: http://www.phjw.com

*Los Angeles, California Office:* Twenty-Third Floor, 555 South Flower Street. Telephone: 213-683-6000.
*Washington, D.C. Office:* Tenth Floor, 1299 Pennsylvania Avenue, N.W. Telephone: 202-508-9500.
*Atlanta, Georgia Office:* 24th Floor, 600 Peachtree Street, N.E. Telephone: 404-815-2400.
*Santa Monica, California Office:* Fifth Floor, 1299 Ocean Avenue. Telephone: 310-319-3300.
*Stamford, Connecticut Office:* Ninth Floor, 1055 Washington Boulevard. Telephone: 203-961-7400.
*New York, New York Office:* 31st Floor, 399 Park Avenue. Telephone: 212-318-6000.
*Tokyo, Japan Office:* Ark Mori Building, 30th Floor, 12-32 Akasaka, P.O. Box 577, 1-Chome, Minato-Ku. Telephone: (03) 3586-4711.

*General Practice.*

### COUNSEL

**OLIVER F. GREEN,** born Cambridge, Massachusetts, August 17, 1924; admitted to bar, 1951, Massachusetts; 1953, California; 1987, New York. *Education:* Harvard College (A.B., 1946); University of Pennsylvania (LL.B., 1951). Fellow, American College of Trial Lawyers. **Email:** OFGreen@PHJW.com

**LEE G. PAUL,** born Denver, Colorado, July 27, 1907; admitted to bar, 1933, California. *Education:* Bowdoin College (A.B., 1929; LL.D., 1978); Harvard University (J.D., 1932). **Email:** LGPaul@PHJW.com

### MEMBERS OF FIRM

**STEPHEN D. COOKE,** born Bakersfield, California, June 20, 1958; admitted to bar, 1985, California. *Education:* University of California at Davis (A.B., with honors, 1980); University of California at Los Angeles (M.B.A., 1985; J.D., 1985). Member, Pacific Basin Law Journal, 1983. **Email:** SDCooke@PHJW.com

**GLENN D. DASSOFF,** born Santa Monica, California, February 20, 1954; admitted to bar, 1980, California. *Education:* University of Southern California (B.S., magna cum laude, 1976); University of California, Boalt Hall (J.D., 1980). **Email:** GDDassoff@PHJW.com

**JANET TOLL DAVIDSON,** born Los Angeles, California, July 25, 1939; admitted to bar, 1978, California. *Education:* Cornell University; George Washington University; Loyola Law School, Los Angeles (J.D., cum laude, 1977). St. Thomas More Law Honor Society. Alpha Sigma Nu. Ninth Circuit Editor, Loyola of Los Angeles Law Review, 1976-1977. Member, Board of Visitors, Loyola Law School. Member, Board of Directors: Legal Aid Foundation of Los Angeles, 1986-1990; United Way of Orange County, 1988-1994. **Email:** JTDavidson@PHJW.com

**JOHN F. DELLA GROTTA,** born New York, New York, July 17, 1953; admitted to bar, 1978, California; 1984, District of Columbia. *Education:* University of Southern California (B.A., cum laude, 1975); Pepperdine University (J.D., 1978); Georgetown University (M.L.T., 1980). Attorney, U.S. Securities and Exchange Commission, Washington, D.C., 1978-1981. **Email:** JFDellaGrot@phjw.com

**HOWARD C. HAY,** born Portland, Maine, April 16, 1944; admitted to bar, 1970, California. *Education:* Duke University (B.A., with distinction, 1966); University of Michigan (J.D., magna cum laude, 1969). Order of the Coif. Note and Comment Editor, University of Michigan Law Review, 1968-1969. Law Clerk to Hon. Frank W. Coffin, Chief Judge, United States Court of Appeals, First Circuit, 1969-1970. Attorney, Appellate Court Division, National Labor Relations Board, 1970-1971. Co-Author: "Advising California Employers," 1981 and "Wrongful Employment Termination Practice," 1987, California Continuing Education of the Bar. **Email:** HCHay@PHJW.com

*(This Listing Continued)*

**PAUL, HASTINGS, JANOFSKY & WALKER LLP,** Costa Mesa—Continued

**MATTHEW A. HODEL,** born Whittier, California, August 22, 1955; admitted to bar, 1980, California. *Education:* California Polytechnic State University, San Luis Obispo (B.A., with high honors, 1977); University of California, Hastings (J.D., 1980). Member, 1978-1979 and Note and Comment Editor, 1979-1980, Hastings Law Journal. Member, Board of Directors, Orange County Constitutional Rights Foundation, 1986-1988. Chairman, 1991 and Member, 1988-1990, Judiciary Committee, Orange County Bar Association. **Email:** MAHodel@PHJW.com

**MICHAEL A. HOOD,** born Santa Ana, California, November 24, 1949; admitted to bar, 1976, California. *Education:* University of Southern California (A.B., magna cum laude, 1971); University of California at Los Angeles (J.D., 1976). Order of the Coif; Phi Beta Kappa. Member, Board of Editors, UCLA Law Review, 1974-1975. Chairman, Board of Directors, YMCA of Orange County, 1988-1990. Trustee, South Coast Repertory Theater, 1994—. **Email:** MAHood@PHJW.com

**DONALD L. MORROW,** born Inglewood, California, April 14, 1951; admitted to bar, 1975, California. *Education:* University of Southern California (B.A., cum laude, 1972; J.D., 1975). Member, Southern California Law Review, 1974-1975. Director, Orange County Bar Association, 1991-1993. Lawyer Representative, Ninth Circuit Judicial Conference, 1989, 1991-1992. Master Bencher, Robert A. Banyard American Inn of Court, 1987—. President, 1993 and Director, 1990—, Orange County Bar Foundation. Director, Pacific Symphony Orchestra, 1990-1991. Fellow, American College of Trial Lawyers. **Email:** DLMorrow@PHJW.com

**DOUGLAS A. SCHAAF,** born Green Bay, Wisconsin, November 18, 1955; admitted to bar, 1981, Illinois; 1987, California. *Education:* St. Norbert College (B.B.A., magna cum laude, 1978); University of Notre Dame (J.D., 1981). Note Editor, Notre Dame Law Review, 1980-1981. Chair, Corporate Tax Committee, Tax Section, Los Angeles County Bar Association, 1991-1992. Chair, Tax Section, Orange County Bar Association, 1995-1996. Member, Board of Directors, Alzheimer's Association of Orange County, 1995-1996. **Email:** DASchaaf@PHJW.com

**WILLIAM J. SIMPSON,** born Los Angeles, California, April 20, 1954; admitted to bar, 1979, California. *Education:* University of Virginia (B.A., with high honors, 1976; J.D., 1979). Chairman, Business and Corporate Law Section, Orange County Bar Association, 1987. **Email:** WJSimpson@PHJW.com

**PETER J. TENNYSON,** born Winona, Minnesota, March 18, 1946; admitted to bar, 1975, California. *Education:* Purdue University (B.A., with highest distinction, 1968); University of Virginia (J.D., 1975). Order of the Coif. Member, 1973-1974, Executive Editor, 1974-1975, University of Virginia Law Review. Member, 1975—, California Commission on the Future of the State Bar. **Email:** PJTennyson@PHJW.com

**JOHN E. TRINNAMAN,** born Salt Lake City, Utah, August 17, 1942; admitted to bar, 1970, California. *Education:* Columbia University (B.A., 1964; M.B.A., 1966); University of Virginia (J.D., 1969). Order of the Coif. Treasurer, Managing Board of Editors, Virginia Law Review, 1968-1969. (Certified Specialist in Estate Planning, Trust and Probate Law, The State Bar of California Board of Legal Specialization). **Email:** JETrinnaman@PHJW.com

*SENIOR COUNSEL*

**ROBERT R. BURGE,** born Jacksonville, Florida, January 1, 1935; admitted to bar, 1961, California. *Education:* McPherson College (B.S., 1956); University of California, Boalt Hall (J.D., 1959). Member, Board of Editors, California Law Review, 1958-1959. **Email:** RRBurge@PHJW.com

**JAMES W. HAMILTON,** born Omaha, Nebraska, September 6, 1932; admitted to bar, 1960, California. *Education:* Stanford University (A.B., 1954; LL.B., 1959). Member, Board of Editors, Stanford Law Review, 1958-1959. Member, Board of Visitors, Stanford Law School, 1975-1978, 1987-1989; 1996—. Chairman, Business and Corporations Law Section, Los Angeles County Bar Association, 1973-1974. Chairman, Board of Trustees, Art Institute of Southern California, 1992-1993. Vice-Chair, Board of Directors, Opportunity International, Inc., 1994—. **Email:** JWHamilton@PHJW.com

*(This Listing Continued)*

*OF COUNSEL*

**MARY L. CORNWELL,** born Chicago, Illinois, January 20, 1962; admitted to bar, 1987, California. *Education:* University of Southern California (B.S., magna cum laude 1983; J.D., 1986). **Email:** MLCornwell@PHJW.com

**JASON O. ENGEL,** born Royal Oak, Michigan, August 17, 1962; admitted to bar, 1987, California. *Education:* University of Kansas (B.S., with distinction, 1984); University of Michigan (J.D., 1987).

**SCOTT N. LESLIE,** born Oakland, California, July 1, 1960; admitted to bar, 1986, California. *Education:* California State University, Fullerton (B.A., with honors, 1982); University of Southern California (J.D., 1986). Staff Member and Articles Editor, Computer Law Journal and Major Tax Planning. Member, Board of Directors, United Way of Orange County, 1995—. **Email:** SNLeslie@PHJW.com

**SEAN A. O'BRIEN,** born Brooklyn, New York, January 8, 1961; admitted to bar, 1988, California. *Education:* University of California at Los Angeles (B.A., magna cum laude, 1983); University of California at Berkeley (M.B.A., 1986); University of California, Boalt Hall (J.D., 1987). Phi Beta Kappa. **Email:** SAOBrien@PHJW.com

**DARLA L. YANCEY,** born Biloxi, Mississippi, March 31, 1960; admitted to bar, 1987, California. *Education:* University of Denver; California State University at Long Beach (B.S., with great distinction, 1982); University of Southern California (J.D., 1987). Certified Public Accountant, California, 1984. Publication Editor, Major Tax Planning and Computer Law Journal, 1986-1987. **Email:** DLYancey@PHJW.com

*ASSOCIATES*

**TERRY JON ALLEN,** born Tucson, Arizona, September 9, 1946; admitted to bar, 1991, California. *Education:* United States Naval Academy (B.S., 1968); Naval Postgraduate School (M.S., 1969); University of West Florida (M.S., 1970); University of California at Los Angeles (J.D., 1991). Order of the Coif. [U.S. Navy, 1968-1979, 1986-1987; USNR, 1980-1986, 1987-1992, Captain (ret.)] **Email:** TJAllen@PHJW.com

**STEVEN D. ALLISON,** born Lancaster, Pennsylvania, July 18, 1968; admitted to bar, 1994, California. *Education:* Messiah College (B.A., magna cum laude, 1990); Georgetown University (J.D., 1994). Order of the Coif. Member and Notes and Comments Editor, Georgetown Law Journal. **Email:** SDAllison@PHJW.com

**BRENT R. BOHN,** born Inglewood, California, August 20, 1966; admitted to bar, 1991, California. *Education:* University of California at Berkeley (B.A., 1988); Loyola Law School, Los Angeles (J.D., 1991). Order of the Coif. St. Thomas More Law Honor Society. Member, Loyola of Los Angeles Law Review, 1989-1990. **Email:** BRBohn@PHJW.com

**GLENN L. BRIGGS,** born Sacramento, California, March 28, 1968; admitted to bar, 1994, California. *Education:* University of California at Los Angeles (B.A., 1990); University of California, Boalt Hall (J.D., 1994). **Email:** GLBriggs@PHJW.com

**ROBERT P. BRYANT,** born Burbank, California, January 28, 1968; admitted to bar, 1993, California. *Education:* Loyola Marymount University (B.A., cum laude, 1990); University of California, Boalt Hall (J.D., 1993). **Email:** RPBryant@PHJW.com

**BARBARA R. DANZ,** born New York, New York, April 18, 1946; admitted to bar, 1992, California. *Education:* Vassar College (B.A., cum laude, 1966); University of Southern California (J.D., 1992). **Email:** BRDanz@PHJW.com

**JESSICA S. DORMAN-DAVIS,** born Starkville, Mississippi, June 23, 1948; admitted to bar, 1986, California. *Education:* California State University, Long Beach (B.A., 1971); University of Southern California (M.B.A., 1977; J.D., 1986). Order of the Coif. Extern, Hon. Harry L. Hupp, U.S. District Court, Central District of California, 1986. **Email:** JDormanDavis@PHJW.com

**MALINDA A. FABER,** born Panorama City, California, July 27, 1968; admitted to bar, 1993, California. *Education:* University of California, Berkeley (B.A., 1990); University of Southern California (J.D., 1993). Member, Moot Court Board, 1992-1993. **Email:** MAFaber@PHJW.com

**VIOLET F. FIACCO,** born San Diego, California, May 21, 1949; admitted to bar, 1988, California. *Education:* California State University, Long Beach (B.S., 1971); California State University, Dominguez Hills (M.S.M.T., 1981); Loyola Law School, Los Angeles (J.D., 1988). St Thomas More Law Honor Society. Member, Loyola of Los Angeles Law Review, 1987-1988. **Email:** VFFiacco@PHJW.com

*(This Listing Continued)*

## PROFESSIONAL BIOGRAPHIES

**CALIFORNIA—COSTA MESA**

**LAURA A. FORBES,** born Newport Beach, California, December 17, 1963; admitted to bar, 1990, California. *Education:* University of California at Los Angeles (B.A., magna cum laude, 1985); University of Southern California (J.D., 1990). Phi Beta Kappa. **Email:** LAForbes@PHJW.com

**ANDREW P. HANSON,** born Newport Beach, California, July 20, 1968; admitted to bar, 1995, California. *Education:* Brigham Young University (B.A., 1992); Duke University (J.D., with honors, 1995). Member, Duke University Law and Contemporary Problems, 1994-1995. **Email:** APHanson@PHJW.com

**JARRET L. JOHNSON,** born Kansas City, Missouri, July 22, 1967; admitted to bar, 1993, California. *Education:* Oklahoma State University (B.S., 1990); Loyola Law School, Los Angeles (J.D., cum laude, 1993). Order of the Coif. Editor, Entertainment Law Journal. **Email:** JLJohnson@PHJW.com

**LISA M. LAFOURCADE,** born Harbor City, California, July 6, 1965; admitted to bar, 1992, California. *Education:* University of Redlands (B.S., magna cum laude, 1987); University of Southern California (J.D., 1992). Phi Beta Kappa. Member, Moot Court Board. **Email:** LMLaFourcade@PHJW.com

**VINCENT D. LOWDER,** born Van Nuys, California, May 20, 1966; admitted to bar, 1994, California. *Education:* University of California at Los Angeles (B.A., 1988); Loyola Law School, Los Angeles (J.D., 1994). Certified Public Accountant, California, 1990. **Email:** VDLowder@PHJW.com

**SCOTT R. MILLER,** born Bethesda, Maryland, June 25, 1964; admitted to bar, 1995, California. *Education:* University of California at Irvine (B.A., 1987); Loyola Law School (J.D., cum laude, 1995). Order of the Coif. **Email:** SRMiller@PHJW.com

**JOHN B. STEPHENS,** born Pasadena, California, January 14, 1963; admitted to bar, 1989, California. *Education:* California Polytechnic, Pomona (B.S., magna cum laude, 1986); University of California at Davis (J.D., 1989). Order of the Coif. Member, University of California at Davis Law Review, 1988-1989. Member, Trial Practice Honors Board, 1989. **Email:** JBStephens@PHJW.com

---

## PILLSBURY MADISON & SUTRO LLP

PLAZA TOWER, 600 ANTON BOULEVARD
SUITE 1100
**COSTA MESA, CALIFORNIA 92626**
Telephone: 714-436-6800
Fax: 714-662-6999

*Los Angeles, California Office:* Citicorp Plaza, 725 South Figueroa Street, Suite 1200, 90017. Telephone: 213-488-7100. Fax: 213-629-1033.

*Silicon Valley Office:* 2700 San Hill Road, Menlo Park, 94025. Telephone: 415-233-4500. Fax: 415-233-4545.

*New York, New York Office:* 520 Madison Avenue, 40th Floor, 10022. Telephone: 212-328-4810. Fax: 212-328-4824.

*Sacramento, California Office:* 400 Capitol Mall, Suite 1700, 95814. Telephone: 916-329-4700. Fax: 916-441-3583.

*San Diego, California Office:* 101 West Broadway, Suite 1800, 92101. Telephone: 619-234-5000. Fax: 619-236-1995.

*San Francisco, California Office:* 235 Montgomery Street, 94104. Telephone: 415-983-1000. Fax: 415-983-1200.

*Washington, D.C. Office:* 1100 New York Avenue, N.W., Ninth Floor, 20005. Telephone: 202-861-3000. Fax: 202-822-0944.

*Hong Kong Office:* 6/7 Asia Pacific Finance Tower, Citibank Plaza, 3 Garden Road, Central. Telephone: 011-852-2509-7100. Fax: 011-852-2509-7188.

*Tokyo, Japan Office:* Pillsbury Madison & Sutro, Gaikokuho Jimu Bengoshi Jimusho, 5th Floor, Samon Eleven Building, 3-1, Samon-cho, Shinjuku-ku, Tokyo 160 Japan. Telephone: 800-729-9830; 011-813-3354-3531. Fax: 011-813-3354-3534.

General Civil Practice and Litigation in all State and Federal Courts. Business: Banking and Corporate Finance; Commercial Transactions/Energy; Corporate, Securities and Technologies; Creditors' Rights and Bankruptcy; Employee Benefits; Employment and Labor Relations; Environment, Health & Safety; Estate Planning; Finance and Commercial Transactions; Food and Beverage Regulation; Health Care; Political Law; Real Estate; Tax (domestic and international); and Telecommunications. Litigation: Alternative Dispute Resolution; Antitrust/Trade Regulation; Appellate; Banking/Financial Institutions; Commercial Disputes; Construction/Real Estate; Creditors' Rights; Bankruptcy and Insurance Insolvency; Energy Matters; Employment/Equal

*(This Listing Continued)*

Opportunity; Environmental/Land Use; ERISA; Insurance; Intellectual Property; Maritime/Admiralty; Media/Entertainment/Sports; Securities; Tort/Product Liability; and White Collar Defense. Intellectual Property: Aesthetic Design & Trade Dress Protection; Biotechnology; Computer Law; Copyright Law; Intellectual Property Audits and Strategic Planning; International Trade Commission; Licensing and Technology Transfer; Procurement of Property Rights; Patent Prosecution; Trade Secrets and Unfair Competition; Trademark Law; Interference Practice; Mechanical/Biomed/Aeronautical; and Physics/Optics.

FIRM PROFILE: Founded in 1874, Pillsbury Madison & Sutro LLP has grown to become one of the largest law firms in the United States, with more than 560 attorneys and expertise in virtually every area of the law. With offices in seven California cities, New York, Washington, D.C., and two offices in Asia, Hong Kong and Tokyo, the firm combines a strong domestic practice with a dynamic presence in the rapidly changing international markets. The firm's corporate expertise encompasses all aspects of business law and covers the full range of legal needs. Our litigation practice is conducted by trial lawyers who have handled landmark cases in the federal and state courts. Our intellectual property practices focuses on litigation, patent and trademark prosecution, licensing and copyright protection. Pillsbury attorneys also work in other legal areas where technology interacts with law, including international trade, environmental protection and food and drug regulation. The firm's clients range from large national and international corporations to start-up companies, the U.S. and foreign governments to universities to individuals. The Cushman Darby & Cushman Intellectual Property Group of Pillsbury Madison & Sutro LLP has practiced intellectual property law since 1892, concentrating on United States and international patent, trademark, copyright and unfair competition law, other technology-associated matters, and related litigation in all courts and administrative agencies. Our patent attorneys have degrees in technical disciplines, and a number hold advanced degrees. Many have practical experience as engineers, microbiologists, physicists, computer experts and chemists.

### MEMBERS OF FIRM

**MARVIN I. BARTEL,** born Dayton, Ohio, July 10, 1952; admitted to bar, 1982, California. *Education:* University of Colorado at Boulder (B.A., 1974); Oregon State University (M.A., 1976); Southwestern University (J.D., 1982). **Email:** bartel__mi@pillsburylaw.com

**THOMAS L. BECKET,** born Los Angeles, California, August 14, 1951; admitted to bar, 1976, California. *Education:* University of Southern California (B.S., 1973); University of California, Hastings College of the Law (J.D., 1976). **Email:** becket__tl@pillsburylaw.com

**ALAN J. DROSTE,** born Mt. Olive, Illinois, August 24, 1956; admitted to bar, 1982, California. *Education:* University of Illinois (B.S., 1978); Boalt Hall School of Law, University of California (J.D., 1982). **Email:** droste__aj@pillsburylaw.com

**JOHN C. GARRETT,** born Los Angeles, California, December 17, 1939; admitted to bar, 1966, California. *Education:* Stanford University (B.A., 1961); University of California, Hastings College of Law (J.D., 1966). **Email:** garrett__jc@pillsburylaw.com

**DONALD P. HICKMAN,** born San Rafael, California, August 12, 1946; admitted to bar, 1974, California. *Education:* University of Wisconsin (B.S., 1968); University of California Hastings College of Law (J.D., 1974); New York University (LL.M in Taxation, 1976). **Email:** hickman__dp@pillsburylaw.com

**ROBERT L. KLOTZ,** born Kearney, Nebraska, July 6, 1944; admitted to bar, 1977, California. *Education:* Stanford University (B.A., 1971); University of Washington (J.D., 1974). **Email:** klotz__rl@pillsburylaw.com

**RICHARD S. RUBEN,** born Brooklyn, New York, January 21, 1950; admitted to bar, 1975, California. *Education:* University of Southern California (B.S., 1972); University of California at Los Angeles School of Law (J.D., 1975). **Email:** ruben__rs@pillsburylaw.com

**HENRY R. STIEPEL,** born Jersey City, New Jersey, April 11, 1956; admitted to bar, 1981, California. *Education:* University of California at Irvine (B.A., 1978); University of Southern California (J.D., 1981). **Email:** stiepel__hr@pillsburylaw.com

### SENIOR COUNSEL

**MARCELLO F. DE FRENZA,** born Upland, California, January 29, 1963; admitted to bar, 1988, California. *Education:* University of California at Santa Barbara; University of California at Los Angeles (B.S., 1985); University of Southern California (J.D., 1988). **Email:** defrenza__mf@pillsburylaw.com

*(This Listing Continued)*

CALIFORNIA—COSTA MESA

**PILLSBURY MADISON & SUTRO LLP,** Costa Mesa—Continued

**ROBERT J. GERARD, JR.,** born September 26, 1955; admitted to bar, 1987, California. *Education:* Monmouth College (B.A., 1978); University of San Diego (J.D., 1987). *Email:* gerard_rj@pillsburylaw.com

ASSOCIATES

Jennifer Penoyer Ashley
Craig A. Barbarosh
Carolyn C. Burger
Andrew C. Callari
Peter W. Martinez
Marci Lerner Miller
William N. Scarff, Jr.
Christopher J. Seiber

(For biographical data on San Diego, Los Angeles, Sacramento, San Francisco, San Jose and Menlo Park, CA, Washington, DC, Tokyo, Japan, New York, NY and Hong Kong personnel, see Professional Biographies at each of those cities.)

## RICKS & ANDERSON

A LAW CORPORATION

3200 PARK CENTER DRIVE, SUITE 1155
**COSTA MESA, CALIFORNIA 92626-4413**
Telephone: 714-966-9190

*General Civil Litigation and Appellate Practice. Wrongful Termination, Employment and Discrimination Law.*

**CECIL E. RICKS, JR.,** born Bell, California, October 4, 1939; admitted to bar, 1964, California; U.S. District Court, Central District of California; U.S. Court of Appeals, Ninth Circuit; U.S. Supreme Court. *Education:* University of California at Los Angeles (B.A., 1960; J.D., 1963). Phi Delta Phi (Magister, 1963). Member, U.C.L.A. Law Review, 1961-1963. Special Counsel, Project Area Committee, City of Anaheim Redevelopment Agency, 1977-1986. Member, Orange County Arbitration Panel, 1978-1986. *Member:* Orange County and American Bar Associations; State Bar of California (Member: Executive Council, Conference of Barristers, 1969-1972; Disciplinary Referee Pro Tem, 1970-1978); Orange County Trial Lawyers Association (Member of Board, 1983-1985); Consumer Attorneys of California; The Association of Trial Lawyers of America; California Employment Lawyers Association (Member, Advisory Board, 1987—). *PRACTICE AREAS:* Civil Litigation; Wrongful Termination; Employment and Discrimination Law.

**ANNETTE L. ANDERSON,** born Los Angeles, California, May 24, 1957; admitted to bar, 1981, California; U.S. District Court, Central District of California; U.S. Court of Appeals, Ninth Circuit; U.S. Supreme Court. *Education:* University of California at Irvine; Western State University (B.S.L., 1979; J.D., 1980). Phi Alpha Delta. Member, Western State University Law Review, 1979-1980. Author: "Zenith Radio Corporation v. Matsushita Electric Industrial Company: Jury Trials in Complex Civil Litigation," Western State University Law Review, Vol. 7 No. 2, Spring, 1980. *Member:* Orange County Bar Association; State Bar of California; Consumer Attorneys of California; The Association of Trial Lawyers of America; Orange County Trial Lawyers Association; Orange County Women Lawyers Association; California Employment Lawyers Association. *PRACTICE AREAS:* Civil Litigation; Wrongful Termination; Employment and Discrimination Law.

## RIORDAN & McKINZIE

A PROFESSIONAL LAW CORPORATION

Established in 1987

695 TOWN CENTER DRIVE, SUITE 1500
**COSTA MESA, CALIFORNIA 92626**
Telephone: 714-433-2900
FAX: 714-549-3244

*Los Angeles, California Office:* California Plaza, 29th Floor, 300 South Grand Avenue. Telephone: 213-629-4824. FAX: 213-229-8550.
*Westlake Village, California Office:* 5743 Corsa Avenue, Suite 116. Telephones: 818-706-1800; 805-496-4688. FAX: 818-706-2956.

*General Civil and Trial Practice in all State and Federal Courts. Corporation, Corporate Securities, Real Estate, Antitrust, Patent, Trademark, Copyright and Unfair Competition Law. Taxation, Estate Planning, Trust and Probate Law.*

*(This Listing Continued)*

CAA156B

MARTINDALE-HUBBELL LAW DIRECTORY 1997

**MARTIN J. THOMPSON,** born Seattle, Washington, November 11, 1948; admitted to bar, 1973, California; 1981, District of Columbia. *Education:* University of the Pacific; University of California at Davis (A.B., 1970); University of California at Berkeley (J.D., 1973). Phi Beta Kappa; Order of the Coif. Associate Editor, California Law Review, 1972-1973. Author: "Antitrust and the Health Care Provider," Aspen Systems, 1979; "Health Planning and Antitrust Exemptions," 2 Whittier Law Review 649, 1980; "Antitrust Considerations and Defenses in Reorganizing for Multi-Institutional Activities," 26 St. Louis Law Journal 465. Co-Author: CH. 13, ABA Antitrust Law Section, State Antitrust Practice and Statutes (1990). *Member:* Los Angeles County and American (Member, Antitrust Law Section) Bar Associations; State Bar of California; District of Columbia Bar; National Health Lawyers Association (Member, Board of Directors, 1981-1987). *Email:* mjt@riordan.com

**KIRK F. MALDONADO,** born Omaha, Nebraska, March 7, 1950; admitted to bar, 1978, Nebraska; 1982, California. *Education:* Cornell College; University of Nebraska at Omaha (B.A., 1975); Creighton University (J.D., 1978) Georgetown University (M.L.T., 1981). Staff Editor, Creighton Law Review, 1977-1978. Member, Editorial Advisory Board, Benefits Law Journal, 1993—. Member, Committee on Continuing Professional Education, ALI-ABA, 1995—. Author of more than forty articles dealing with executive compensation and executive compensation matters, including forthcoming Tax Management Portfolio 362, *Securities Laws Aspects of Employee Benefit Plans.* Attorney, Employee Plans and Exempt Organizations Division, Office of Chief Counsel, Internal Revenue Service, 1978-1981. Member: Employee Benefits Committee, Section of Taxation, State Bar of California; Employee Benefits Committee, Section of Taxation, American Bar Association; Western Pension and Benefits Conference. *Email:* kfm@riordan.com

**JAMES W. LOSS,** born Kenosha, Wisconsin, April 2, 1953; admitted to bar, 1980, Wisconsin; 1983, California. *Education:* Princeton University (A.B., cum laude, 1976); Yale Law School (J.D., 1980). Law Clerk to the Honorable Malcolm M. Lucas, U.S. District Judge for the Central District of California, 1981-1983. *Member:* State Bar of California. *Email:* jwl@riordan.com

**MICHAEL P. WHALEN,** born Detroit, Michigan, December 3, 1954; admitted to bar, 1981, California. *Education:* Princeton University (A.B., cum laude, 1977); University of California at Berkeley (M.A. in Mathematics, 1978); Harvard University (J.D., cum laude, 1981). Author: "Causation and Reliance in Private Actions Under SEC Rule 10b-5," 14 Pacific Law Journal 101, 1982. *Member:* State Bar of California; State Bar of Wisconsin. *LANGUAGES:* German. *Email:* mpw@riordan.com

**ELAINE R. LEVIN,** born Chicago, Illinois, June 9, 1957; admitted to bar, 1986, New York; 1992, California. *Education:* Stanford University (A.B., 1979); IIT Chicago-Kent College of Law (J.D., with high honors, 1985). Note and Comment Editor, 1984-1985 and Member, 1983-1985, Chicago-Kent Law Review. Co-Author: "Legislative Intervention: The Assembly's 'Anti-Referral' Bill," Northern California Medicine, 1992; "Self Referral Laws: Understanding the Limits on Health Care Professionals," California Business Law Reporter, 1994. *Member:* Los Angeles County (Member, Healthcare Law Section) and American (Member, Business Law Section) Bar Associations; State Bar of California (Member, Business Law Section). *Email:* erl@riordan.com

---

**JAMES H. SHNELL,** born Los Angeles, California, August 19, 1950; admitted to bar, 1981, California. *Education:* Stanford University (A.B., 1972); Harvard Business School (M.B.A., 1978); University of California at Berkeley (J.D., 1981). Associate Editor, California Law Review, 1980-1981. *PRACTICE AREAS:* Corporate; Mergers and Acquisitions; Financings. *Email:* jhs@riordan.com

**BART GREENBERG,** born Garden Grove, California, January 14, 1963; admitted to bar, 1989, California. *Education:* University of California at Los Angeles (B.A., magna cum laude, 1986); University of California, Boalt Hall School of Law (J.D., 1989). Phi Beta Kappa. President and Director, Arroyo Maintenance Corporation, 1990—. *Member:* Orange County (Member, Business Law Section) and American (Member, Business Law Section) Bar Associations; State Bar of California (Member, Business Law Section). *PRACTICE AREAS:* Business and Finance. *Email:* bg@riordan.com

**KAREN C. GOODIN,** born Los Angeles, California, February 27, 1963; admitted to bar, 1991, California. *Education:* University of Southern California (A.B., summa cum laude, 1985); University of Pennsylvania (M.A., 1987); University of California, Boalt Hall School of Law (J.D., 1991). Phi

*(This Listing Continued)*

Beta Kappa. Associate Editor, International Tax & Business Lawyer, 1989-1990. *Member:* State Bar of California. **PRACTICE AREAS:** General Corporate; Securities. *Email:* kcg@riordan.com

**MICHAEL G. McKINNON,** born Newport Beach, California, May 27, 1968; admitted to bar, 1994, California. *Education:* Cornell University (B.S., 1990); Pepperdine University (J.D., cum laude, 1994). *Member:* State Bar of California; National Health Lawyers Association. **LANGUAGES:** Spanish. **PRACTICE AREAS:** Corporate; Securities. *Email:* mgmck@riordan.com

**JEANNE MILLER-ROMERO,** born San Luis Obispo, California, June 7, 1965; admitted to bar, 1995, California. *Education:* University of California at Los Angeles (B.A., magna cum laude, 1987); University of California School of Law, Davis (J.D., 1995). Phi Beta Kappa; Phi Delta Phi; Order of the Coif. Recipient, American Jurisprudence Award, Legal Writing, Labor Law. *Member:* Orange County Bar Association; State Bar of California. **PRACTICE AREAS:** Corporate Securities. *Email:* jm-r@riordan.com

REFERENCE: Citibank, 333 S. Grand Ave., Los Angeles, Calif.

(For complete biographical data on all personnel, see Professional Biographies at Los Angeles, California)

## RISLEY & ASSOCIATES
*Established in 1986*

**SUITE 225, 3420 BRISTOL STREET**
**COSTA MESA, CALIFORNIA 92626**
Telephone: 714-557-9712
Fax: 714-557-9908
Email: Harviell@aol.com

*Taxation, Estate Planning, Probate, Real Estate Law, Asset Protection and General Business.*

*FIRM PROFILE:* Mr. Risley was a partner of Rutan and Tucker, 1962-1983. He left to establish his own firm to work more closely with his clients from beginning to end. Mr. Risley's desire was to be involved with the client and contribute to the client attaining their goal. Mr. Risley takes pride in the accomplishments for his clients. He is listed in Who's Who Directory, The Men of Achievement and The Bar Register Preeminent Law Directory under Tax Law.

**ROBERT L. RISLEY,** born Poplar Bluff, Missouri, October 25, 1930; admitted to bar, 1957, Kansas; 1962, California; 1982, U.S. Tax Court; 1983, U.S. Supreme Court; 1984, District of Columbia. *Education:* University of Missouri (B.S., 1952); University of Kansas (LL.B., 1957; J.D., 1968); University of Southern California Graduate Law School (Taxation). Delta Theta Phi. Member, Kansas University Law Review, 1955-1956. Delegate, Commission of the California's, 1981-1982. Grand Bailiff, Chief Legal Officer, Sovereign Order of the Oak, 1989. *Member:* Orange County, Kansas and American (Member, Section on Real Estate and Probate Law) Bar Associations; The State Bar of California (Member: Continuing Education Committee, 1966-1976; Public Relations Committee, 1969-1973); Bar Association of the District of Columbia; The District of Columbia Bar; International Academy of Estate and Trust Law (Academician); Orange Coast Estate Planning Council (President, 1968). Fellow, American College Trust and Estate Counsel. (Certified Specialist, Taxation Law, The State Bar of California Board of Legal Specialization).

### LEGAL SUPPORT PERSONNEL

**PAMELA D. DAGURO** (Paralegal).

**GISELLE E. KAVNER** (Paralegal).

REFERENCES: Sanwa Bank, South Coast Office, Santa Ana; First American Trust Co., Newport Beach.

## ROBINS, KAPLAN, MILLER & CIRESI
*Established in 1938*

**600 ANTON BOULEVARD, SUITE 1600**
**COSTA MESA, CALIFORNIA 92626-7147**
Telephone: 714-540-6200
Fax: 714-545-6915

*Atlanta, Georgia Office:* 2600 One Atlanta Plaza, 950 East Paces Ferry Road NE. Telephone: 404-233-1114. Fax: 404-233-1267.

*Boston, Massachusetts Office:* Suite 2200, 222 Berkeley Street. Telephone: 617-267-2300. Fax: 617-267-8288.

*(This Listing Continued)*

*Chicago, Illinois Office:* Suite 1400, 55 West Wacker Drive. Telephone: 312-782-9200. Fax: 312-782-7756.

*Los Angeles, California Office:* 2049 Century Park East, Suite 3700. Telephone: 310-552-0130. Fax: 310-229-5800.

*Minneapolis, Minnesota Office:* 2800 LaSalle Plaza, 800 LaSalle Avenue. Telephone: 612-349-8500. Fax: 612-339-4181.

*San Francisco, California Office:* Suite 2700, 444 Market Street. Telephone: 415-399-1800. Fax: 415-391-1968.

*Washington, D.C. Office:* Suite 1200, 1801 K Street, N.W. Telephone: 202-775-0725. Fax: 202-223-8604.

*Trials and Appeals in all Federal and State Courts. Administrative, Antitrust, Appellate, Banking, Bankruptcy and Reorganization, Construction, Communications, Corporate, Employment and Employee Benefits, Environmental, Estate Planning and Probate, Franchising, Finance, Health, Insurance Law, Intellectual Property, International Litigation and Trade, Medical Malpractice, Personal Injury, Products Liability, Real Estate, Securities, Tax, Transportation.*

*FIRM PROFILE:* The California offices (Costa Mesa, Los Angeles and San Francisco) focus on insurance, business, and personal injury/mass tort litigation. The insurance practice includes property and liability coverage disputes, subrogation, bad faith claims, environmental claims, crime and fidelity disputes, excess and reinsurance issues. The business litigation practice involves complex disputes in areas of antitrust and trade regulation, intellectual property, employment law, communications litigation, finance and other commercial matters. The personal injury/mass tort practice involves representation of plaintiffs in mass torts and large-scale personal injury cases.

### MEMBERS OF FIRM

**GEOFFREY T. GLASS,** born Washington, D.C., June 17, 1954; admitted to bar, 1980, Minnesota; 1981, U.S. District Court, District of Minnesota; 1982, California; 1983, U.S. District Court, Central District of California; 1984, U.S. District Court, Northern and Eastern Districts of California; 1985, U.S. District Court, Southern District of California and U.S. Court of Appeals, Ninth Circuit. *Education:* Amherst College (B.A., cum laude, 1976); University of Virginia (J.D., 1980). *Member:* Orange County (Secretary, Insurance Law Section), Minnesota State and American (Member: Section on Tort and Insurance Practice; Fidelity and Surety Law Committee, Section on Litigation) Bar Associations; State Bar of California; The Association of Trial Lawyers of America; California Trial Lawyers Association; Orange County Trial Lawyers Association. **PRACTICE AREAS:** Insurance Litigation; Commercial Litigation.

**SCOTT G. JOHNSON,** born Albert Lea, Minnesota, November 23, 1959; admitted to bar, 1986, Minnesota and U.S. District Court, District of Minnesota; 1987, U.S. Court of Appeals, Eighth Circuit; 1991, California and U.S. District Court, Central and Southern Districts of California. *Education:* Winona State University (B.S., magna cum laude, 1982); William Mitchell College of Law (J.D., magna cum laude, 1986). Member, William Mitchell Law Review, 1985-1986. *Member:* Orange County, Hennepin County, Minnesota State and American Bar Associations. **PRACTICE AREAS:** Insurance Litigation; Commercial Litigation; General Litigation.

**ALAN M. JONES,** born Oregon City, Oregon, November 19, 1947; admitted to bar, 1980, California, Michigan and U.S. District Court, Northern District of California; 1981, U.S. District Court, Eastern District of Michigan; 1987, U.S. District Court, Eastern District of California; 1988, U.S. District Court, Central District of California; 1991, U.S. Court of Appeals, Ninth Circuit. *Education:* Metropolitan State College (B.S., 1973); Golden Gate University (J.D., 1979). **PRACTICE AREAS:** Personal Injury Law; Insurance Litigation; Construction Litigation.

**WILLIAM P. LINHOFF, JR.,** born Stillwater, Minnesota, December 4, 1946; admitted to bar, 1974, Minnesota and U.S. District Court, District of Minnesota; 1983, California; 1992, U.S. Court of Appeals, Eighth Circuit, U.S. District Court, Central, Eastern, Southern and Northern Districts of California and District of Arizona. *Education:* University of Minnesota (B.A., 1968); University of Colorado (J.D., 1973). *Member:* Hennepin County, Orange County (Member, Insurance Law Section) and American Bar Associations; State Bar of California. **PRACTICE AREAS:** Insurance Litigation; General Litigation.

**THOMAS A. MILLER,** born Adrian, Michigan, March 25, 1952; admitted to bar, 1978, Michigan; 1986, California; 1987, U.S. District Court, Central, Northern and Eastern Districts of California. *Education:* Siena Heights College (B.A., cum laude, 1974); University of Michigan (J.D., 1978). *Member:* Orange County (Member, Sections on: Business Litigation; Labor and Employment), American (Member, Litigation Section) and Fed-

*(This Listing Continued)*

### ROBINS, KAPLAN, MILLER & CIRESI, Costa Mesa—Continued

eral Communications Bar Associations. *PRACTICE AREAS:* Business Litigation; Cable Television Law; Employment Law.

**ERNEST I. REVEAL, III,** born Chicago, Illinois, October 19, 1948; admitted to bar, 1973, Minnesota and U.S. District Court, District of Minnesota; 1974, U.S. Court of Appeals, 8th Circuit; 1976, U.S. District Court, District of South Dakota and U.S. Claims Court; 1984, U.S. Court of Appeals, 7th Circuit; 1991, California, U.S. District Court, Central District of California, U.S. Court of Appeals, Ninth Circuit and U.S. Supreme Court. *Education:* Cornell University (B.A., 1970); University of Michigan (J.D., cum laude, 1973). *Member:* Orange County, Minnesota State and American Bar Associations; State Bar of California; The Association of Trial Lawyers of America. *PRACTICE AREAS:* Business Litigation.

**PATRICK E. SHIPSTEAD,** born Bremen, Germany, October 20, 1948; admitted to bar, 1976, Minnesota and U.S. District Court, District of Minnesota; 1979, California; 1980, U.S. District Court, Central and Eastern Districts of California; 1987, U.S. District Court, Northern and Southern Districts of California. *Education:* Harvard University (A.B., 1971); Princeton University (M.P.A., 1973); University of Michigan (J.D., 1976). *Member:* Orange County (Member, Insurance Law Section) and American Bar Associations. *PRACTICE AREAS:* Insurance Litigation; Personal Injury Law; Mass Tort; Commercial Litigation.

#### ASSOCIATES

**ALEXANDRA M. DAY,** born Paris, France, August 8, 1952; admitted to bar, 1990, California. *Education:* Mills College; Stanford University (B.A., 1974); University of Southern California (J.D., 1990). Phi Alpha Delta; Legion Lex. Recipient, Judge Barry Russell Federal Bar Association Award for Excellence in the Field of Federal Practice in Law School. *Member:* California Women Lawyers Association. *LANGUAGES:* French. *PRACTICE AREAS:* Product Liability Law; Tort and Personal Injury; General Civil Litigation.

**TOD R. DUBOW,** born Boston, Massachusetts, July 27, 1964; admitted to bar, 1991, California and U.S. District Court, Central District of California. *Education:* University of California at Riverside (B.A., 1988); Pepperdine University (J.D., 1990). Member, Pepperdine Law Review, 1989-1991. Extern to the Honorable Stephen Reinhardt, U.S. Court of Appeals, Ninth Circuit. Co-Author: "Recent Development in Franchise Overbuilds and Other First Amendment Litigation," PLI, Feb. 1992. *PRACTICE AREAS:* Commercial Litigation; Products Liability.

**MICHAEL S. HENDERSON,** born Seattle, Washington, January 12, 1970; admitted to bar, 1995, California and U.S. District Court, Central District of California. *Education:* Pacific Union College (B.S., 1991); McGeorge School of the Law, University of the Pacific (J.D., 1994). *PRACTICE AREAS:* Insurance; Litigation.

**JENNY LEE,** born Xi'an, People's Republic of China, July 22, 1967; admitted to bar, 1991, California and U.S. District Court, Central District of California; 1992, U.S. District Court, Southern and Eastern Districts of California. *Education:* University of California at Irvine (B.S., 1988); University of California at Los Angeles (J.D., 1991). Member, UCLA Moot Court, 1989-1990. Executive Board of Justices, 1990-1991, Board of Editors, 1989-1990, Business Manager, 1990-1991, Pacific Basin Law Journal. *Member:* Orange County and American Bar Associations; State Bar of California. *LANGUAGES:* Mandarin, Cantonese. *PRACTICE AREAS:* Litigation; Professional Liability; Real Estate; Casualty.

**SUSAN LOPE,** born 1966; admitted to bar, 1995, California. *Education:* California State University at Long Beach (B.A., Pol. Sc., cum laude, 1990); Southwestern University Law School (J.D., cum laude, 1994). Recipient, Paul Wildman Academic Scholarship. Southwestern Law Moot Court Honors Program, 1992-1993, Oralist Roger Traynor Competition. Articles Editor, Editorial Board, Southwestern University Law Review. Author: "Indian Giver: The Illusion of Effective Legal Redress for Native American Land Claims," 23 SW. U.L. Rev. 331 (1994). *PRACTICE AREAS:* General Civil Litigation; Business; Employment Law.

**STAN A. MORTENSEN,** born June 19, 1967; admitted to bar, 1994, California. *Education:* Brigham Young University (B.A., Pol. Sc., 1991; J.D., cum laude, 1994). Lead Note and Comment Editor, Brigham Young University Law Review, 1992-1994. *LANGUAGES:* Spanish. *PRACTICE AREAS:* Insurance Law; Litigation; General Civil Practice; Product Liability Law.

*(This Listing Continued)*

**ROBERT J. TERRY,** born Chicago, Illinois, 1966; admitted to bar, 1996, California. *Education:* University of Illinois (B.S., 1988); University of Minnesota (J.D., 1996). *PRACTICE AREAS:* Litigation.

**HOLLY A. H. WILLIAMS,** born Minneapolis, Minnesota, July 30, 1966; admitted to bar, 1991, California, U.S. District Court, Northern, Central, Eastern and Southern Districts of California and U.S. Court of Appeals, Ninth Circuit. *Education:* Loyola Marymount University (B.A., 1988); Boalt Hall School of Law, University of California; University of Minnesota at Minneapolis (J.D., 1991). Alpha Sigma Nu; Pi Gamma Mu; Pi Alpha Theta. Associate Member, California Law Review, 1990-1991. *Member:* Orange County and American Bar Associations; Orange County Women Lawyers Association; California Women Lawyers Association. *LANGUAGES:* Spanish. *PRACTICE AREAS:* Litigation; General Civil Business.

**SHATARA R. WRIGHT,** born Washington, D.C., 1970; admitted to bar, 1996, California. *Education:* Howard University (B.A., 1992); Northwestern Law School (J.D., 1996). *PRACTICE AREAS:* Litigation.

(For other biographical data, see Professional Biographies at all other offices)

---

## JEFFREY W. ROSE

CENTER TOWER
650 TOWN CENTER DRIVE, SUITE 1930
**COSTA MESA, CALIFORNIA 92626**
Telephone: 714-751-9215
FAX: 714-754-0444
Email: jrose000@counsel.com

*Intellectual Property, Copyrights, Trademarks, Trade Secrets, Multimedia Licensing, Litigation and General Business.*

**JEFFREY W. ROSE,** born Michigan City, Indiana, August 24, 1962; admitted to bar, 1987, California; 1988, U.S. District Court, Central and Southern Districts of California. *Education:* Duke University (A.B., magna cum laude, 1984); University of California at Los Angeles School of Law (J.D., 1987). *Member:* Orange County (Chairman, Technology Law Section, 1995-1996) and American (Vice Chair, Intellectual Property Law Committee for Tort and Insurance Practice Section, 1996) Bar Associations; State Bar of California; Computer Law Association. *PRACTICE AREAS:* Intellectual Property; Business Litigation; High Technology Law; Insurance Coverage Law.

---

## THE RUDOLPH LAW GROUP

A PROFESSIONAL CORPORATION
3200 PARK CENTER DRIVE, SUITE 1370
**COSTA MESA, CALIFORNIA 92626**
Telephone: 714-545-7272; 714-757-7272
Fax: 714-545-7273

*General Trial and Appellate Practice in State and Federal Courts, including General Business and Commercial Litigation, Real Estate Litigation, Product Liability, Intellectual Property, Trade Secrets and Unfair Competition, Environmental, Employment and Partnership, Corporate and Trust Disputes.*

**GEORGE C. RUDOLPH,** born Butte, Montana, June 29, 1951; admitted to bar, 1976, California; 1977, U.S. District Court, Central and Northern Districts of California and U.S. Court of Appeals, Ninth Circuit; 1983, U.S. District Court, Southern District of California; 1985, U.S. Supreme Court. *Education:* University of Southern California (B.A., Psychology, magna cum laude, 1973); Hastings College of the Law, University of California (J.D., 1976). Lecturer: Fundamentals of Civil Procedure Before Trial Trial, California Continuing Education of the Bar, 1993; Fundamentals of Civil Trial Practice, California Continuing Education of the Bar, 1985, 1986, 1989; Preparing and Examining Expert Witnesses, California Continuing Education of the Bar, 1992; Fundamentals of Civil Procedure During Trial, California Continuing Education of the Bar, 1991, 1994; How to Win Post Trial Motions and Enforce Judgments, California Continuing Education of the Bar, 1987; Litigation Paralegal, University of California, Irvine, 1989; Litigation Support Systems, University of California at Irvine, San Diego, Santa Barbara and Los Angeles, 1985-1991; Pleadings for Paralegals, University of California at Irvine, Riverside and Los Angeles,

*(This Listing Continued)*

1986-1993. *Member:* Beverly Hills, Los Angeles County, Orange County and American Bar Associations; State Bar of California; The Association of Trial Lawyers of America.

## RUTAN & TUCKER, LLP

A Partnership including Professional Corporations
611 ANTON BOULEVARD, SUITE 1400
P.O. BOX 1950
COSTA MESA, CALIFORNIA 92626
Telephone: 714-641-5100; 213-625-7586
Telecopier: 714-546-9035
Email: rutan&tucker@mcimail.com
URL: http://www.rutan.com

General Civil and Trial Practice in all State and Federal Courts. Municipal Law, Real Estate, Corporate, Securities, Employment and Labor Relations (Management and Public Sector), Taxation, Estate Planning, Trust and Probate, Environmental and Land Use Law, Municipal Finance, Water Rights, Education Law, Bankruptcy and Creditors Rights.

FIRM PROFILE: Firm founder, Alexander Rutan, began practicing law in Orange County in 1906. In 1936 he formed the firm of Rutan & Tucker with former Utah Superior Court Judge James B. Tucker. Today, with more than 100 attorneys, Rutan & Tucker is the largest Orange County, California based law firm. The Firm's practice extends throughout the United States and includes both the representation of foreign companies doing business in the United States and domestic companies engaged in activities abroad.

### MEMBERS OF FIRM

**JAMES R. MOORE, (P.C.),** born Highland Park, Michigan, February 17, 1927; admitted to bar, 1957, California. *Education:* University of Michigan (A.B., 1953); Stanford University (LL.B., 1956). Delta Theta Phi. Stanford Moot Court Board, President, 1955-1956. Co-Author: "California Real Estate Sales Transactions," CEB Book, 1967. *Member:* Orange County (President, 1968) and American Bar Associations; The State Bar of California (Member, Real Estate Sub-Committee of CEB Joint Advisory Committee, 1976-1981). *PRACTICE AREAS:* Real Estate.

**PAUL FREDERIC MARX,** born Los Angeles, California, August 9, 1931; admitted to bar, 1957, California. *Education:* University of California at Berkeley and University of Southern California (B.A., cum laude, 1953); Harvard University (LL.B., cum laude, 1956). Member, Board of Student Advisors, Harvard Law School, 1954-1956. *Member:* Orange County and American Bar Associations; The State Bar of California. (Certified Specialist, Taxation Law, The State Bar of California Board of Legal Specialization). *PRACTICE AREAS:* Probate and Estate Planning; Tax Law.

**WILLIAM R. BIEL,** born Chicago, Illinois, June 3, 1932; admitted to bar, 1961, California. *Education:* University of California at Los Angeles (B.S., 1954; LL.B., 1960). Order of the Coif; Phi Delta Phi. Member, U.C.-L.A. Law Review, 1958-1960. *Member:* The State Bar of California; Orange County and American Bar Associations. *PRACTICE AREAS:* Commercial; Real Estate.

**RICHARD A. CURNUTT,** born Santa Ana, California, October 4, 1939; admitted to bar, 1965, California; U.S. District Court, Central and Southern Districts of California; U.S. Court of Appeals, Ninth Circuit. *Education:* Pomona College (B.A., 1961); University of California at Los Angeles (LL.B., 1964). Phi Delta Phi; Order of the Coif. Member, University of California at Los Angeles Law Review, 1963-1964. *Member:* Orange County Bar Association; The State Bar of California. *PRACTICE AREAS:* Real Estate. *Email:* dcurnutt@mcimail.com

**LEONARD A. HAMPEL, JR.,** born St. Louis, Missouri, July 7, 1939; admitted to bar, 1965, California; U.S. District Court, Central, Southern and Eastern Districts of California; U.S. Court of Appeals, Ninth Circuit; U.S. Supreme Court. *Education:* University of California at Los Angeles (B.A., with highest honors, 1961; LL.B., 1964). Phi Beta Kappa; Order of the Coif. Associate Editor, University of California at Los Angeles Law Review, 1963-1964. Author: "Agency Shop Lawful Form of Union Security Under National Labor Relations Act," 11 University of California at Los Angeles Law Review 143, 1963; League of California Cities Paper, "What Are a City's Legal Responsibilities to Provide for Housing Needs," Spring, 1979; "Affordable Housing - 1981 Style," Spring, 1981; "Housing in the 80's and 90's, The City's Perspective," Annual Conference, 1988; "Update on Housing - Spring - 1992," Spring, 1992. City Attorney: City of Yorba Linda, 1972—; City of Villa Park, 1978—. *Member:* Orange County Bar Association; The State Bar of California; Orange County City Attorneys'

*(This Listing Continued)*

Association; The Association of Trial Lawyers of America; American College of Trial Lawyers. *PRACTICE AREAS:* Civil Trial; Land Use Law; Environmental.

**JOHN B. HURLBUT, JR.,** born Palo Alto, California, June 14, 1939; admitted to bar, 1965, California and U.S. District Court, Central and Southern Districts of California; U.S. Court of Appeals, Ninth Circuit. *Education:* Stanford University (B.A., 1961; J.D., 1964). Pi Sigma Alpha. *Member:* Orange County Bar Association; State Bar of California; American Bar Association (Member, Sections on: Litigation; Economics of Law Practice). *PRACTICE AREAS:* Real Estate Litigation; Civil Trial.

**MICHAEL W. IMMELL,** born Cherokee, Oklahoma, August 20, 1938; admitted to bar, 1965, California. *Education:* Stanford University (B.A., 1960); University of California at Los Angeles (J.D., 1964). Phi Delta Phi. Member, University of California at Los Angeles Law Review, 1963-1964. *Member:* Orange County (Member, Real Estate Section) and American (Member, Real Property, Probate and Trust Law Section) Bar Associations; The State Bar of California (Member, Real Property Law Section). *PRACTICE AREAS:* Real Estate.

**MILFORD W. DAHL, JR.,** born San Francisco, California, June 10, 1940; admitted to bar, 1965, California; U.S. District Court, Central and Southern Districts of California; U.S. Court of Appeals, Ninth Circuit. *Education:* University of California at Los Angeles (B.S., 1962; J.D., 1965). Phi Delta Phi; Order of the Coif. Member, U.C.L.A. Law Review, 1963-1965. Lecturer, Unlawful Detainer, 1971, Bad Faith, 1977 and What Business Lawyers Need to Know About the Law of Evidence, 1977 and 1982, California Continuing Education for the Bar. Author: Note, "Rule Against Perpetuities: Application of Rule to Commercial Lease to Commence 'Upon Completion' of Building," 12 U.C.L.A. Law Review, 246, 1964. *Member:* Orange County and Federal Bar Associations; The State Bar of California. Fellow, American College of Trial Lawyers. *PRACTICE AREAS:* Civil Trial.

**THEODORE I. WALLACE, JR., (P.C.),** born Opelika, Alabama, April 15, 1937; admitted to bar, 1962, Illinois and U.S. District Court, Northern District of Illinois; 1969, California; 1974, U.S. District Court, Central District of California; 1977, U.S. Court of Appeals, Ninth Circuit; 1980, U.S. Supreme Court. *Education:* Harvard University (B.A., magna cum laude, 1959; J.D., 1962). Phi Beta Kappa. *Member:* Orange County Bar Association; The State Bar of California. *PRACTICE AREAS:* Civil Trial.

**RICHARD P. SIMS,** born Pasadena, California, November 11, 1941; admitted to bar, 1969, California. *Education:* San Diego State College (B.S., 1965); Columbia University (LL.B., cum laude, 1968). Phi Alpha Delta. Co-Author: "California Real Property Sales Transactions," California Continuing Education for the Bar Book, 1981. *Member:* The State Bar of California. *PRACTICE AREAS:* Real Estate.

**ROBERT C. BRAUN,** born San Luis Obispo, California, May 4, 1945; admitted to bar, 1971, California; U.S. District Court, Central and Southern Districts of California; U.S. Supreme Court. *Education:* University of Southern California (B.A., with honors, 1967); Boalt Hall School of Law, University of California (J.D., 1970). Blue Key; Skull and Dagger. Member: Boalt Hall National Moot Court Team (winner of regional championship); Boalt Hall Moot Court Board, 1969-1970 . Recipient: Outstanding Oral Argument in Boalt Hall Moot Court Competition; Outstanding Oral Argument in National Moot Court Regional Championship, Final Round. Lecturer: CEB, Evidence in Civil Trials, 1978 and 1980; Evidence at California Judges Conference, 1978. *Member:* Orange County (Member, Business Litigation Section; Construction Litigation Section; Judiciary Committee, 1979-1981) and American Bar Associations; State Bar of California. *PRACTICE AREAS:* Civil Trial.

**EDWARD D. SYBESMA, JR., (P.C.),** born Anderson, Indiana, October 11, 1947; admitted to bar, 1972, California. *Education:* Indiana University (B.S., 1968); University of Michigan (J.D., 1971). Order of the Coif. *Member:* Orange County (Member, Business Litigation Section) and American (Member, Litigation Section, Committees on Intellectual Properties Litigation, Business Torts & Litigation Management and Law Practice Management Sections) Bar Associations; The State Bar of California (Member, Sections on: Intellectual Property and Litigation). *PRACTICE AREAS:* Antitrust; Business; Civil Trial; Trademark, Copyright, Unfair Competition; Computer; Tax Litigation. *Email:* esybesma@mcimail.com

**THOMAS S. SALINGER, (P.C.),** born Los Angeles, July 28, 1945; admitted to bar, 1972, California; U.S. District Court, Central and Southern Districts of California; U.S. Court of Appeals, Ninth Circuit. *Education:* Cornell University (B.A., 1967); Boalt Hall School of Law, University of California (J.D., 1971). Member, Moot Court Board, 1969-1970. Law Clerk

*(This Listing Continued)*

## RUTAN & TUCKER, LLP, Costa Mesa—Continued

to the Hon. Richard H. Chambers, Chief Judge, U.S. Court of Appeals, Ninth Circuit, 1971-1972. *Member:* Orange County (Member, Sections on: Business Litigation and Construction) and American (Member, Sections on: Litigation and Construction) Bar Associations; The State Bar of California. *PRACTICE AREAS:* Construction; Real Estate; Title Insurance; Financial Institutions.

**DAVID C. LARSEN, (P.C.),** born Salt Lake City, Utah, November 24, 1946; admitted to bar, 1973, California; U.S. District Court, Central and Southern Districts of California; U.S. Court of Appeals, Ninth Circuit; U.S. Supreme Court. *Education:* Johns Hopkins University; Brigham Young University; University of Utah (J.D., 1973). Staff Member, 1971-1972; Managing Editor, 1972-1973, Utah Law Review. Order of the Coif. Author: "Confining and Structuring Administration Discretion," Utah Law Review 388, 1971; "Regulation of Judicial Ethics in Utah: Adoption and Enforcement of Code of Judicial Conduct," Utah Law Review 29, 1973. *Member:* Orange County Bar Association; The State Bar of California. *PRACTICE AREAS:* Employment Benefits; Workers' Compensation; Labor and Employment; Construction; Civil Rights; Appellate Practice.

**CLIFFORD E. FRIEDEN,** born Los Angeles, California, March 8, 1949; admitted to bar, 1974, California. *Education:* University of California at Los Angeles (B.A., summa cum laude, 1971); Boalt Hall School of Law, University of California (J.D., 1974). Phi Beta Kappa; Order of the Coif. Recipient, American Jurisprudence Award for Property, 1972. *Member:* Orange County Bar Association (Chairman, Judiciary Committee, 1986-1987; Member, Board of Directors, 1989-1991; Delegate to State Bar Conference of Delegates); The State Bar of California. *PRACTICE AREAS:* Civil Trial; Commercial.

**MICHAEL D. RUBIN,** born Cleveland, Ohio, May 19, 1948; admitted to bar, 1974, California; 1975, U.S. District Court, Central District of California and U.S. Claims Court; 1983, U.S. Supreme Court. *Education:* Lehigh University and University of Michigan (B.A., 1970); University of Michigan (J.D., magna cum laude, 1974). James B. Angell Scholar. Member, Order of the Coif. Associate Editor, Michigan Law Review, 1973-1974. Author: "A Sixth Amendment Right to Counsel Under Article 15 of the Uniform Code of Military Justice," 72 Michigan Law Review 1431, 1974. *Member:* Orange County (Member, Education Committee, Sections on: Business Litigation; Environmental Law) and American (Member, Sections on: Litigation; Natural Resources, Energy and Environmental Law; Urban, State and Local Government Law) Bar Associations; The State Bar of California. *PRACTICE AREAS:* Civil Trial; Real Estate; Municipal and Zoning; Land Use Law; Environmental; Construction. *Email:* miked@mcimail.com

**IRA G. RIVIN, (P.C.),** born Los Angeles, California, September 21, 1948; admitted to bar, 1974, California; U.S. Court of Appeals, Ninth Circuit; U.S. District Court, Central and Southern Districts of California. *Education:* University of California at Los Angeles (A.B., 1970); Boalt Hall School of Law, University of California (J.D., 1974). Phi Beta Kappa. *Member:* Orange County and American Bar Associations; The State Bar of California. *PRACTICE AREAS:* Real Estate; Commercial; Civil Trial. *Email:* irivin@mcimail.com

**JEFFREY M. ODERMAN, (P.C.),** born Orange, New Jersey, October 30, 1949; admitted to bar, 1975, California; U.S. Supreme Court; U.S. Court of Appeals, Ninth Circuit; U.S. District Court, Central and Northern Districts of California. *Education:* University of California at Los Angeles (B.A., summa cum laude, 1971); Stanford University (J.D., 1974). Phi Beta Kappa; Order of the Coif. *Member:* The State Bar of California. *PRACTICE AREAS:* Land Use Law; Real Estate; Municipal and Zoning.

**JOSEPH D. CARRUTH,** born Oakland, California, September 11, 1942; admitted to bar, 1968, California. *Education:* Stanford University (B.A., 1964); University of California at Berkeley (J.D., 1967); George Washington University (LL.M. in Taxation with highest honors, 1973). *Member:* The State Bar of California (Member, Sections on: Business Law and Taxation); American Bar Association (Member, Sections on: Taxation; Business; Natural Resources Law). *PRACTICE AREAS:* Business; Tax Law.

**STAN WOLCOTT, (P.C.),** born Riverside, California, December 9, 1946; admitted to bar, 1973, California; U.S. District Court, Northern and Central Districts of California; U.S. Court of Appeals, Ninth Circuit. *Education:* University of Northern Colorado (B.A., summa cum laude, 1970); Boalt Hall School of Law, University of California, Berkeley (J.D., 1973). Associate Editor, Ecology Law Quarterly, 1972-1973. Author: "Parker v. United States; The Forest Service Role in Wilderness Preservation," 3 Ecology Law Quarterly 145. *Member:* Orange County Bar Association; The State Bar of California; Orange County City Attorneys Association; National Association of Bond Lawyers; California Association of Bond Lawyers (President, Board of Directors, 1991-1995). *PRACTICE AREAS:* Municipal Finance; Bond and Underwriter Counsel.

**ROBERT S. BOWER,** born Cleveland, Ohio, June 22, 1947; admitted to bar, 1976, California; U.S. Supreme Court; U.S. Court of Appeals, Ninth Circuit; U.S. District Court, Central and Southern Districts of California. *Education:* Williams College (B.A., cum laude, honors in history, 1969); University of California, Hastings College of Law (J.D., 1976). Order of the Coif. Member, 1974-1975 and Associate Articles Editor, 1975-1976, Hastings Law Journal. Lecturer: Urban Planning and Zoning, University of California at Irvine Extension, 1979-1980; California Continuing Education of the Bar, Appellate Review Before Judgement, 1982. City Attorney, City of San Fernando, 1982-1993; City of Indian Wells, 1989-1992, and City of Baldwin Park, 1990—. *Member:* Orange County Bar Association; The State Bar of California. [Lt.(j.g.), USNR, 1970-1972]. *PRACTICE AREAS:* Civil Rights; Environmental; Municipal and Zoning; Civil Trial.

**DAVID J. ALESHIRE,** born Palo Alto, California, September 1, 1950; admitted to bar, 1975, California; 1976, U.S. District Court, Central District of California; 1977, U.S. Court of Appeals, Ninth Circuit. *Education:* Stanford University (B.A., cum laude, 1972); University of California at Los Angeles (M.A., 1976; J.D., 1975). Phi Beta Kappa. Adjunct Professor, Southwestern University School of Law, 1980-1983. City Attorney: Lawndale, 1983-1994; Signal Hill, 1985—; Palm Springs, 1991—. General Counsel: Lawndale Housing Authority, 1984-1994; Signal Hill Redevelopment Agency, 1985—; Palm Springs Redevelopment Agency and Housing Authority, 1991; Joint Powers Employee Benefit Authority, 1988; Rossmoor Community Services District, 1987-1991. *Member:* Los Angeles County and American (Member, Section of Local Government) Bar Associations; The State Bar of California (Member, Local Government Section); American Planning Association. *PRACTICE AREAS:* Labor and Employment; Environmental; Construction; Municipal and Zoning; Land Use Law.

**MARCIA A. FORSYTH,** born Dayton, Ohio, May 24, 1951; admitted to bar, 1977, California. *Education:* University of California at Berkeley (B.A., 1974); University of California at Los Angeles (J.D., 1977). Member, Order of the Barristers. *Member:* Orange County Bar Association (Member, Real Estate Section); The State Bar of California (Member, Real Estate Section). *PRACTICE AREAS:* Commercial; Business; Real Estate; Construction. *Email:* mforsyth@mcimail.com

**WILLIAM M. MARTICORENA,** born Montebello, California, May 15, 1952; admitted to bar, 1977, California; 1981, U.S. District Court, Northern District of California and U.S. Court of Appeals, Ninth Circuit. *Education:* Loyola University of Los Angeles (B.A., cum laude, 1974); Harvard University (J.D., cum laude, 1977). Alpha Sigma Nu. Recipient: First Place, Ames Moot Court Competition, 1975; Hornbook Award for Legal Writing, 1975. Author: "One Step Beyond the Right to Treatment-The 'Right to Nontreatment' for the Juvenile Status Offender in California," 5 Orange County Bar Journal, No. 2, Summer, 1978; "Take My Child, Please —A Plea for Radical Nonintervention," 6 Pepperdine Law Review, No. 3, Summer, 1979; "Recent Developments in Regulating Cable Television," 6 Orange County Bar Journal, No. 2, Summer, 1979; "Municipal Cable Television Regulation - Is There Life after Boulder?" 9 Western State University Law Review, No. 2, Spring, 1983; "State Preemption of Cable Television Regulations - Whatever Happened to the Sanctity of Contract", 10 Pepperdine Law Review, No. 4, May 1983. Assistant Professor, Media Law, Entertainment Law, Civil Procedure, Corporations, Trust Law and Legal Research, Western State University College of Law, 1978-1985. Instructor, California State University at Fullerton, 1980-1981. Lecturer, Administrative and Zoning Law, University of California at Irvine, 1979-1980. *Member:* Orange County Bar Association (Member, Board of Directors, 1987). [Capt., U.S.A.F.R.]. *PRACTICE AREAS:* Civil Trial; Communications; Municipal Bond.

**JAMES L. MORRIS,** born Clinton, Indiana, November 11, 1952; admitted to bar, 1978, Texas; 1979, U.S. Court of Appeals, Third Circuit and U.S. District Court, Northern District of Texas; 1980, U.S. Court of Appeals, Fifth Circuit and U.S. District Court, Eastern District of Texas; 1983, California, U.S. District Court, Central and Eastern Districts of California and U.S. Court of Appeals, Ninth Circuit; 1984, U.S. District Court, Southern District of California; 1987, U.S. District Court, Northern District of California. *Education:* Duke University (B.A., magna cum laude, 1974); Georgetown University Law Center (J.D., 1977). Staff Member,

*(This Listing Continued)*

1976 and Editor, 1977, *American Criminal Law Review.* Author: "Civil Rights Litigation Under 42 U.S.C. §1983," *Texas Practice Guide,* 2d ed. 1985. *Member:* Orange County (Member, Labor Law Section; Section Chairperson, 1992-1993) and American (Member, Sections on: Labor and Employment Law; Litigation) Bar Associations; The State Bar of California; State Bar of Texas. **PRACTICE AREAS:** Labor and Employment Law (Management). **Email:** jlmorris@mcimail.com

**ANNE NELSON LANPHAR,** born Sacramento, California, May 8, 1952; admitted to bar, 1977, California. *Education:* California State University at Fullerton (B.A., 1974); Hastings College of Law, University of California (J.D., 1977). Beta Alpha Psi; Accounting Honor Society. Lecturer: "Fundamentals of Real Property," and "Real Property Residential and Commercial Leases, Development and Construction," Continuing Education of the Bar, 1982-1990. *Member:* Orange County and American Bar Associations; The State Bar of California. **PRACTICE AREAS:** Municipal and Zoning; Real Estate. **Email:** alanphar@mcimail.com

**WILLIAM J. CAPLAN,** born Brooklyn, New York, September 7, 1953; admitted to bar, 1978, California; U.S. District Court, Central and Eastern Districts of California. *Education:* University of California at Los Angeles (B.A., 1975; J.D., cum laude, 1978). Contributing Education Panelist: "Landlord-Tenant Litigation," The Rutter Group, Ltd., 1983, 1985, 1988 and 1993. *Member:* Orange County Bar Association; The State Bar of California. **PRACTICE AREAS:** Real Estate Litigation; Commercial Landlord-Tenant Litigation; Earth Movement Litigation; Civil Trial.

**MICHAEL T. HORNAK,** born Inglewood, California, October 1, 1953; admitted to bar, 1978, California; 1979, U.S. District Court, Central District of California; 1984, U.S. District Court, Southern District of California; 1995, U.S. Court of Appeals, Ninth Circuit. *Education:* Yale University (B.A., cum laude, 1975); University of California School of Law at Los Angeles (J.D., 1978). Panelist and Contributing Author: "Litigation Concepts for the Business Lawyer," Orange County Bar Association, 1991; "Ending Bad Cases Early: Effective Use of the Summary Judgment Motion," Orange County Bar Association, 1992. Trustee, Orange County Bar Foundation. Director, Yale Club of Orange County. *Member:* Orange County and American (Member, Litigation Section) Bar Associations; The State Bar of California. Master, Peter M. Elliott Inn of Court. **PRACTICE AREAS:** Officers, Directors, Fiduciary Litigation and Counseling; Computer and Proprietary Rights Litigation and Licensing; Unfair Competition; Business Litigation; Trademark; Securities; Antitrust; Civil Trial. **Email:** mhornak@mcimail.com

**PHILIP D. KOHN,** born Downey, California, January 19, 1953; admitted to bar, 1979, California and U.S. District Court, Central District of California; 1982, U.S. District Court, Northern District of California and U.S. Court of Appeals, Ninth Circuit; 1984, U.S. District Court, Eastern District of California; 1986, U.S. Supreme Court. *Education:* California State University at Fullerton (B.A., 1974); University of Birmingham, England (M. Soc.Sc., 1976); Hastings College of Law, University of California (J.D., 1979). Marshall Scholar (United Kingdom). Phi Kappa Phi. City Attorney, Laguna Beach, 1982—. *Member:* Orange County, Federal and American Bar Associations; The State Bar of California. **PRACTICE AREAS:** Constitutional Law; Environmental; Land Use Law; Municipal and Zoning.

**JOEL D. KUPERBERG,** born Sacramento, California, March 18, 1954; admitted to bar, 1979, California, U.S. District Court, Central District of California and U.S. Court of Appeals, Ninth Circuit; 1987, U.S. Supreme Court. *Education:* Pomona College (B.A., cum laude, 1976); University of California School of Law at Los Angeles (J.D., 1979). Member, Order of Barristers. Author: "Handbook of Appellate Advocacy," West Publishing Co., 1980. *Member:* Orange County and Federal Bar Associations; The State Bar of California. **PRACTICE AREAS:** Environmental; Municipal and Zoning; Civil Trial; Land Use Law.

**STEVEN A. NICHOLS,** born Inglewood, California, December 23, 1952; admitted to bar, 1980, California; U.S. District Court, Northern, Central and Southern Districts of California; U.S. Court of Appeals, Ninth Circuit; U.S. Court of Federal Claims. *Education:* California State University (B.A., cum laude, 1977); University of Southern California (J.D., 1980). *Member:* Orange County (Member, Construction Law Section) and American (Member, Forum Committee on Construction Industry) Bar Associations; The State Bar of California (Member, Real Property Law Section); American Arbitration Association (Member, Construction and Commercial Law Panel of Arbitrators). **PRACTICE AREAS:** Business Litigation.

**THOMAS G. BROCKINGTON,** born Torrance, California, November 26, 1955; admitted to bar, 1980, California and U.S. District Court, Central District of California. *Education:* Stanford University (A.B., with distinc-

*(This Listing Continued)*

tion, 1977); University of California at Berkeley (J.D., 1980). Books and Research Editor, Ecology Law Quarterly, 1979-1980. *Member:* Orange County Bar Association; The State Bar of California (Member, Business Law Section). **PRACTICE AREAS:** Business; Securities.

**WILLIAM W. WYNDER,** born Cardston, Alberta, Canada, October 30, 1948; admitted to bar, 1978, California; 1994, U.S. Supreme Court, U.S. Courts of Appeals, Sixth and Ninth Circuits; U.S. District Court, Northern, Eastern and Central Districts of California; 1979, U.S. Tax Court. *Education:* University of Utah (B.S., magna cum laude, 1975); Pepperdine University (J.D., cum laude, 1978). Member, 1976-1977 and Editor-in-Chief, 1977-1978, Pepperdine Law Review. Member, Moot Court Board, 1977-1978. Author: "Beyond Weighing and Sifting: Narrowed Judicial Focus as an Alternative to Burton v. Wilmington Parking Authority," 5 Pepperdine Law Review 95, 1977. Law Clerk to Judge Harry Phillips, Chief Judge, U.S. Court of Appeals, Sixth Circuit, 1978-1979. *Member:* Orange County (Member, Sections on: Litigation; Municipal; Labor and Employment Law) and American (Member, Sections on: Litigation; Municipal; Labor and Employment Law) Bar Associations; The State Bar of California. **PRACTICE AREAS:** Appellate Practice; Civil Trial; Municipal and Zoning; Civil Rights; Labor and Employment.

**EVRIDIKI (VICKI) DALLAS,** born Miami, Florida, April 20, 1952; admitted to bar, 1979, California; 1981, U.S. Tax Court. *Education:* Florida International University (B.A., with highest honors, 1974); University of Florida (J.D., 1976; LL.M. in Taxation, 1977). Author: "Transferring a Partnership Interest in Exchange For Services," Tax Ideas, 1991. Consulting Editor, California Practice Guide Corporations (The Rutter Group); Senior Adjunct Professor, Corporate Tax, Corporate Acquisitions and Reorganizations, Taxation of High Technology, Federal Income Taxation of Individuals, Golden Gate University, Masters of Taxation, 1980—. *Member:* Orange County Bar Association (Chairman, Business and Corporate Law Section, 1986, Member, Corporate Law Section); The State Bar of California. **PRACTICE AREAS:** Business; Securities; Tax Law.

**RANDALL M. BABBUSH,** born Long Beach, California, March 5, 1956; admitted to bar, 1981, California and U.S. Court of Appeals, Ninth Circuit. *Education:* University of California at Santa Barbara; University of California at Irvine (B.A., 1978); Hastings College of Law, University of California (J.D., 1981). Member, Thurston Society. Member, 1979-1981 and Article Editor, 1980-1981, Hastings Law Journal. *Member:* The State Bar of California. **PRACTICE AREAS:** Real Estate.

**MARY M. GREEN,** born Seattle, Washington, September 8, 1955; admitted to bar, 1980, California, U.S. District Court, Central District of California and U.S. Court of Appeals, Ninth Circuit. *Education:* University of Southern California (B.A., magna cum laude, 1977; J.D., 1980). President, Mortar Board, 1976-1977. Vice President, Hale Moot Court Honors Program, 1979-1980. *Member:* Orange County (Member, Real Estate Section) and American (Member, Real Estate Section) Bar Associations; The State Bar of California. **PRACTICE AREAS:** Real Estate; Environmental.

**THOMAS J. CRANE,** born Bayshore, New York, January 5, 1957; admitted to bar, 1982, California, U.S. District Court, Central and Southern Districts of California and U.S. Court of Appeals, Ninth Circuit. *Education:* Dartmouth College (A.B., cum laude, 1979); Georgetown University (J.D., cum laude, 1982). Editor, American Criminal Law Review, 1981-1982. Co-Author: "Securities Fraud," Vol. 19, American Criminal Law Review, 1982. Trustee, Dartmouth Alumni Association of Orange County, 1984-1986. *Member:* Orange County Bar Association; The State Bar of California. **PRACTICE AREAS:** Business; Computer; Commercial; Securities. **Email:** tjcranelaw@mcimail.com

**MARK B. FRAZIER,** born Long Beach, California. July 10, 1956; admitted to bar, 1982, California, U.S. District Court, Central District of California and U.S. Court of Appeals, Ninth Circuit. *Education:* Occidental College (A.B., with honors, 1979); University of Southern California (J.D., 1982). Topic Editor, University of Southern California Hale Moot Court Honors Program, 1981-1982. *Member:* Orange County Bar Association (Member, Legislative Committee, 1994-1994); The State Bar of California; American Inns of Court, Legion Lex Chapter. **PRACTICE AREAS:** Environmental Counseling and Litigation (Liability for Contamination and Cost Recovery); Business Litigation; Unfair Competition; Trade Secrets; Real Property Litigation (Secured Transactions and Seismic Liability); Environmental.

**M. KATHERINE JENSON,** born Lorain, Ohio, March 4, 1958; admitted to bar, 1983, California; 1984, U.S. District Court, Central District of California and U.S. Court of Appeals, Ninth Circuit; 1991, U.S. Supreme Court. *Education:* Cleveland State University (B.A., summa cum laude, 1980); Ohio State University (J.D., summa cum laude, 1983). Order of the

*(This Listing Continued)*

## RUTAN & TUCKER, LLP, Costa Mesa—Continued

Coif. Recipient: American Jurisprudence Award for Evidence and Torts; Corpus Juris Secundum Award for Significant Legal Scholarship; John E. Hallen Memorial Award; Donald C. Power Fund; John Rosenbrough Memorial Scholarship. Staff Member, 1981-1982 and Issue Planning Editor, 1982-1983, Ohio State Law Journal. Author: "State v. Thomas: The Final Blow to Battered Women?" 43 Ohio State Law Journal 491, 1982; "Free Legal Services: A Matter of Choice?" South Coast Metro, 1984; "A Plaintiff With Standing - Every Lawsuit Needs One," Los Angeles Daily Journal, Practitioner, 1993; San Francisco Daily Journal, Practitioner, 1993; "Nonresident Plaintiffs Lack Standing to Challenge Amendment to Redevelopment Plan," Redevelopment Journal, 1995. American Planning Association-State Conference 1990, "The Right of Access to Information Held by Public Agencies;" 1991 Continuing Education Seminar for Municipal Attorneys, Emerging Trends in 1983 Liability "Avoiding Section 1983 Liability for Regulation of First Amendment Rights..." American Planning Association Orange County Nuts and Bolts Conference, "Recent Developments Regarding the California Environmental Quality Act." Deputy City Attorney for City of Yorba Linda, City of Palm Springs and City of San Clemente. *Member:* Orange County (Director, Harbor Division, 1995; Appellate Law Section, Vice Chair, 1992, Chair, 1993) and Federal Bar Associations; The State Bar of California (Member, Sections on: Litigation and Public Law). Robert A. Banyard American Inns of Court (pupil, charter year 1987-1988; Barrister, 1993—). *PRACTICE AREAS:* Civil Rights; Municipal and Zoning; Land Use Law; Appellate Practice.

**DUKE WAHLQUIST,** born Ogden, Utah, December 5, 1956; admitted to bar, 1982, Utah; 1985, California. *Education:* University of Utah (B.S., magna cum laude, 1977; M.S., 1979); University of California at Los Angeles (J.D., 1982). Phi Beta Kappa; Phi Kappa Phi. *Member:* Orange County and American Bar Associations; Utah State Bar; The State Bar of California. *PRACTICE AREAS:* Appellate Practice; Civil Trial. *Email:* dwahlquist@mcimail.com

**RICHARD MONTEVIDEO,** born Warren, Ohio, September 19,1959; admitted to bar, 1984, California; 1985, U.S. District Court, Central District of California; U.S. Court of Appeals, Ninth Circuit; 1995, U.S. Supreme Court. *Education:* The Ohio State University (B.S., summa cum laude, 1981; J.D., 1984). Author: "Hypnosis - Should the Courts Snap Out of It? A Closer Look at the Critical Issues," 44:4 Ohio State Law Journal, 1983. *Member:* Orange County (Member, Environmental Law Section) and American Bar Associations; The State Bar of California. *PRACTICE AREAS:* Environmental Law; Cost Recovery; Toxic Tort Litigation; Municipal and Zoning.

**LORI SARNER SMITH,** born New York, N.Y., June 6, 1956; admitted to bar, 1984, California. *Education:* University of Delaware; Portland State University (B.S., cum laude, 1980); University of California at Davis (J.D., 1984). Order of the Coif. Recipient: American Jurisprudence Award in Family Law; Corpus Juris Secundum Award; Wall Street Journal Award. Note and Comment Editor, University of California at Davis Law Review, 1983-1984. Author: "An Examination of VEBA's and Deductions: Current or Deferred Compensation?" 17 University of California at Davis Law Review, 1984. *Member:* Orange County Bar Association (Member, Section on: Real Estate, Commercial Law and Bankruptcy and Financial Institutions); Bankruptcy Law Forum; The State Bar of California. *PRACTICE AREAS:* Real Estate; Bankruptcy.

**ERNEST W. KLATTE III,** born San Rafael, California, March 8, 1956; admitted to bar, 1984, California and U.S. District Court, Northern, Central, Southern and Eastern Districts of California. *Education:* University of California at Santa Cruz (B.A., with highest honors, 1981); University of California at Davis (J.D., 1984). Member: Moot Court Board; Semi-Finalist Team, Wagner National Labor Law Moot Court Competition; Finalist, Neumiller Moot Court Competition. Recipient, American Jurisprudence Awards in Criminal Law and Corporations. Co-recipient, 1991 California State Bar, President's Pro Bono Service Award. *Member:* Orange County (Member, Labor and Employment Section; Judiciary Committee; Pro Bono Services Committee), Federal and American (Member, Labor and Employment Sections) Bar Associations; The State Bar of California. *LANGUAGES:* French. *PRACTICE AREAS:* Labor Law; Employment Law. *Email:* eklatte@mcimail.com

**ELIZABETH L. MARTYN,** born San Diego, California, January 22, 1951; admitted to bar, 1981, California. *Education:* University of California at Riverside (B.A., summa cum laude, 1978); University of California at Los Angeles (J.D., 1981). Phi Beta Kappa. Member, Order of the Barristers. Lecturer, Senior Seminar, Law and Society Program, University of California, Riverside, 1985-1986. City Attorney, Twentynine Palms, 1987—. Assistant City Attorney, West Covina, 1988-1990. City Attorney, 1990—. City Attorney, Canyon Lake, 1991—. *Member:* The State Bar of California. *LANGUAGES:* Spanish and French. *PRACTICE AREAS:* Municipal Law; Solid Waste; Land Use Law; Environmental.

**KIM D. THOMPSON,** born Owatonna, Minnesota, January 8, 1960; admitted to bar, 1985, California, U.S. District Court, Central District of California and U.S. Court of Appeals, Ninth Circuit. *Education:* Northern Arizona University (B.S., summa cum laude, 1982); University of Southern California (J.D., 1985). Phi Kappa Phi; Beta Gamma Sigma; Phi Delta Phi. Staff Member, Major Tax Planning and Computer Law Journal, 1984-1985. *Member:* Orange County and American Bar Associations; State Bar of California. *PRACTICE AREAS:* Real Estate Transactions; Tax-deferred Exchanges; Environmental Law; Commercial Leasing; Americans with Disabilities Act. *Email:* kdthompson@mcimail.com

**JAYNE TAYLOR KACER,** born Dayton, Ohio, October 2, 1951; admitted to bar, 1985, California; 1986, U.S. District Court, Central District of California and U.S. Court of Appeals, Ninth Circuit; 1987, U.S. District Court, Eastern District of California; 1991, U.S. District Court, Southern District of California. *Education:* California State University at San Jose (B.A., 1974); Loyola University of Los Angeles (J.D., cum laude, 1985). Member, St. Thomas More Law Honor Society. Member, Loyola Law School Trial Advocacy Team, 1985. Member, 1983-1984 and Chief Note and Comment Editor, 1984-1985, Loyola of Los Angeles Law Review. Co-Author: "Criminal Law in the Ninth Circuit: Recent Developments," 18: 1 & 2 Loyola of Los Angeles Law Review, 1984-1985. *Member:* Orange County (Business Litigation Section) and American Bar Associations; State Bar of California. Barrister, Robert A. Banyard Inn of American Inns of Court. *PRACTICE AREAS:* Complex Litigation; Title Insurance Litigation; Product Liability; Civil Trial. *Email:* jkacer@mcimail.com

**DAVID B. COSGROVE,** born Valparaiso, Indiana, August 13, 1959; admitted to bar, 1984, California; 1985, U.S. Court of Appeals, Ninth Circuit and U.S. District Court, Central District of California. *Education:* Xavier University (H.A.B., summa cum laude, 1981; Alpha Sigma Nu; Phi Alpha Theta); The Ohio State University (J.D., 1984). Recipient: American Jurisprudence Book Award in Property; Judge Joseph M. Harter Memorial Award. *Member:* Orange County Bar Association (Member, Appellate Law Section); The State Bar of California (Member, Public Law Section); Association of California Water Agencies; International Right of Way Association. *PRACTICE AREAS:* Eminent Domain; Water; Municipal Law.

**HANS VAN LIGTEN,** born Amsterdam, Netherlands, July 29, 1959; admitted to bar, 1985, California; 1986, U.S. District Court, Central District of California; U.S. Court of Appeals, Ninth Circuit U.S. Supreme Court. *Education:* California State University at Northridge; University of California at Santa Barbara (B.A., cum laude, 1981); Loyola Law School (J.D., cum laude, 1985). Member, St. Thomas Moore Honor Society. Recipient, American Jurisprudence Award in Criminal Law. Staff Member, 1983-1984 and Managing Editor, 1984-1985, Loyola of Los Angeles International and Comparative Law Journal. *Member:* Orange County and Federal Bar Associations; State Bar of California. *PRACTICE AREAS:* Municipal and Zoning; Environmental; Land Use Law; Civil Rights. *Email:* hvanligten@mcimail.com

**STEPHEN A. ELLIS,** born Monterey, California, February 18, 1957; admitted to bar, 1985, California; U.S. District Court, Central, Eastern, Norther and Southern Districts of California; U.S. Court of Appeals, Ninth Circuit. *Education:* California State University at Long Beach (B.A., summa cum lade, 1980); University of California at Los Angeles (J.D., 1985). Phi Alpha Delta. *Member:* Orange County Bar Association; The State Bar of California; American Inns of Court. *PRACTICE AREAS:* Real Estate; Construction; Civil Trial.

**MATTHEW K. ROSS,** born Orange, California, August 10, 1959; admitted to bar, 1985, California; U.S. District Court, Eastern, Northern, Southern and Central Districts of California; U.S. Court of Appeals, Ninth Circuit. *Education:* University of California at Irvine (B.A., summa cum laude, 1980); University of California, Boalt Hall (J.D., 1985). Phi Beta Kappa. Law Clerk to Hon. Robert E. Coyle, U.S. District Court, Eastern District of California, 1985-1986. *Member:* State Bar of California; Orange County Bar Association (Member, Business Litigation Section and Appellate Law Section); Federal Bar Association. *PRACTICE AREAS:* Civil Trial; Appellate Practice.

**JEFFREY WERTHEIMER,** born Cleveland, Ohio, December 10, 1957; admitted to bar, 1985, California, U.S. District Court, Central and Northern Districts of California, U.S. Court of Appeals, Ninth Circuit and U.S. Supreme Court. *Education:* Northwestern University (B.A., 1980); Case

*(This Listing Continued)*

Western Reserve University Law School (J.D., 1985). Order of the Coif. Member, Case Western Reserve University Law Review, 1983-1984. *Member:* Orange County and Federal Bar Associations; State Bar of California. **PRACTICE AREAS:** Civil Rights; Labor and Employment; General Practice.

**ROBERT OWEN,** born Chicago, Illinois, March 25, 1961; admitted to bar, 1986, California and U.S. District Court, Central District of California. *Education:* Pomona College (B.A., 1983); Loyola Law School (J.D., cum laude, 1986). Member, St. Thomas More Honor Society. Recipient, American Jurisprudence Award in Evidence. Member, Loyola Law School International and Comparative Law Journal, 1985-1986. *Member:* Orange County Bar Association; State Bar of California. **PRACTICE AREAS:** Municipal and Zoning; General Practice; Construction; Land Use Law.

**ADAM N. VOLKERT,** born Sacramento, California, March 18, 1961; admitted to bar, 1986, California and U.S. District Court, Central District of California. *Education:* Stanford University (A.B., with distinction, 1983); Northwestern University (J.D., 1986). Executive Editor, Northwestern University Journal of Criminal Law and Criminology, 1985-1986. Author: "Fifth Amendment-Double Jeopardy: Two-Tier Trial Systems and the Continuing Jeopardy Principle," 75 Journal of Criminal Law and Criminology 653, 1984. *Member:* Orange County Bar Association (Member, Real Estate Section); State Bar of California. **PRACTICE AREAS:** Real Estate Transactions; Commercial and Industrial Leasing; Environmental; Construction.

**JEFFREY A. GOLDFARB,** born Heidelberg, Germany, April 5, 1960; admitted to bar, 1986, California. *Education:* University of California (A.B., with high honors, 1983); Hastings College of Law (J.D., cum laude, 1986). Phi Beta Kappa. Staff Member, 1984-1985 and Note Editor, 1985-1986, Hastings Law Journal. Judicial Extern for Justice Allen A. Broussard, California Supreme Court, 1986. Assistant City Attorney, San Clemente and Irvine, California. *Member:* State Bar of California; American Bar Association (Member, Urban, State and Local Government Section). **PRACTICE AREAS:** Land Use Law; Municipal and Zoning; Civil Rights. *Email:* jfarb@mcimail.com

**F. KEVIN BRAZIL,** born Washington, D.C., October 9, 1961; admitted to bar, 1987, California and U.S. District Court, Central District of California. *Education:* California State University at Long Beach (B.S. with distinction 1984); University of California at Davis (J.D., 1987). Order of the Coif. Recipient: School of Law Medal for graduating first in class; American Jurisprudence Awards in Constitutional Law II; Trusts, Wills and Decedents' Estates; Criminal Procedure. *Member:* Orange County Bar Association; State Bar of California. **PRACTICE AREAS:** Real Estate; Environmental; Land Use Law; Construction.

**LAYNE H. MELZER,** born Los Angeles, California, November 8, 1961; admitted to bar, 1987, California; 1988, U.S. District Court, Central District of California. *Education:* California State University at Northridge (B.A., 1984); University of California at Davis (J.D., 1987). Phi Kappa Phi; Beta Gamma Sigma; Order of the Coif. Member, Moot Court Board. Recipient, American Jurisprudence Award in Evidence. Certificate of Completion, Trial Skills Program, NITA, 1991. Assistant City Attorney, City of Palm Springs, 1990—. *Member:* Orange County and American Bar Associations. Barrister: Peter M. Elliot Inn; American Inns of Court. **PRACTICE AREAS:** Municipal and Zoning; Environmental; Civil Trial; Land Use Law.

**LIEN SKI HARRISON,** born Chanute, Kansas, September 11, 1945; admitted to bar, 1987, California; 1988, U.S. District Court, Central District of California. *Education:* University of California at Santa Barbara (B.A., 1967); California State University at Fullerton (M.S., 1972); Western State University (J.D., 1987). Deputy City Attorney, Irvine, Signal Hill. *Member:* Orange County Bar Association; State Bar of California. **PRACTICE AREAS:** Education Law; Public Sector; Labor Law; Municipal; Administrative; Environmental. *Email:* skiharrison@mcimail.com

## ASSOCIATES

**MICHAEL K. SLATTERY,** born Los Angeles, California, June 8, 1955; admitted to bar, 1982, California and U.S. District Court, Central District of California; 1993, U.S. District Court, Northern and Southern Districts of California. *Education:* University of Southern California; Princeton University (B.A., 1978); University of Southern California (J.D., 1982). Member, Southern California Law Review. Author, *FIRREA Receivership and Conservatorship Law,* Clark Boardman Callaghan, 1992, 2d ed, 1994, 3rd ed, 1995; "The Allowability and Priority of Tax Claims in Bankruptcy Cases," 1992 Annual Survey of Bankruptcy Law 153; "Breakdown of the Bargain," California Continuing Education of the Bar *Sales & Leases in California Commercial Law Practice, Chapter 12.* Co-author: with Thomas Kelch, *(This Listing Continued)*

"Real Property Issues in Bankruptcy," Clark Boardman Callaghan, 1995; with Mary Santandrea, "Conflicts Between the Special Rights and Powers of the Banking Regulators and the Bankruptcy Trustee," published in B. Dunaway and D. Dunaway, *FIRREA: Law and Practice,* Clark Boardman Callaghan 1992; with Ronald Martinetti, "The Rights of 'Owners' of Lost or Stolen Instruments Under Uniform Commercial Code§3-804; Can They be Holders In Due Course?" *98 Commercial Law Journal 328* No. 3, Fall, 1993. Adjunct Professor, Western State University College of Law, Bankruptcy Law, Commercial Law, Contracts, Civil Procedure, 1987-1990. Panelist; 1992 State Bar Convention, Real Property Section, "Caesar Giveth, Caesar Taketh Away," Governmental involvement in Real Estate Transactions, Los Angeles County Bar Association, Commerical Land and Bankruptcy Section. "Conflicts Between the Special Signs and Powers of the Bankruptcy Trustee and The Banking Regulators," August 1993; CEB 1994 Real Property Symposium, February 1994. **LANGUAGES:** French, Italian, Spanish, Swedish. **PRACTICE AREAS:** Bankruptcy; Financial Institution Insolvency; Commercial.

**DEBRA DUNN STEEL,** born Newport Beach, California, August 17, 1955; admitted to bar, 1980, California; 1981, U.S. District Court, Central District of California. *Education:* University of California at Irvine (B.A., summa cum laude, 1977); University of California School of Law at Los Angeles (J.D., 1980). Phi Beta Kappa; Order of the Coif. **PRACTICE AREAS:** Real Estate Litigation; Lease Litigation; Financial Institution Litigation.

**DAVID H. HOCHNER,** born New York, N.Y., January 10, 1948; admitted to bar, 1982, California, U.S. District Court, Central District of California and U.S. Court of Appeals, Ninth Circuit. *Education:* Pace University (B.A., 1970); State University of New York (M.A., 1972; M.A.T., 1974); University of California at Davis (J.D., 1982). Order of the Coif. Recipient, American Jurisprudence Award in Contracts. *Member:* Orange County Bar Association; The State Bar of California. **PRACTICE AREAS:** General Practice; Civil Trial; Business; Construction; Real Estate.

**ELISE K. TRAYNUM,** born Toledo, Ohio, October 21, 1949; admitted to bar, 1987, California. *Education:* California State University at San Bernardino (B.A., 1983); Hastings College of the Law, University of California (J.D., 1986). *Member:* San Bernardino and Riverside County Bar Associations; The State Bar of California. **PRACTICE AREAS:** Educational Law; Land Use Law; Public Law.

**DAN SLATER,** born Los Angeles, California, July 6, 1949; admitted to bar, 1988, California and U.S. District Court, Central District of California. *Education:* University of the Pacific (B.A., 1971); University of Southern California (M.P.A., 1973); University of Oregon (Ph.D., 1977); University of California at Berkeley, Boalt Hall (J.D., 1988). Recipient: Prosser Prize in Criminal Procedure; Moot Court Board Award. Co-Author: "Lay Definitions of Legal Insanity," 7 International Journal of Law and Psychiatry 105, 1984; "Public Opinion of Forensic Psychiatry," 141 American Journal of Psychiatry 675, 1984; "Cameras in the Courts," 2(2) Delaware Lawyer 56, 1983. Assistant City Attorney: City of Indian Wells, 1989-1992; City of Yorba Linda, 1992—; City of Villa Park, 1992—; City of Palm Springs, 1992—. *Member:* Orange County and American Bar Associations; State Bar of California. **PRACTICE AREAS:** Land Use Law; Redevelopment Law; Municipal and Zoning. *Email:* dslat@mcimail.com

**JAMES S. WEISZ,** born Fresno, California, May 18, 1961; admitted to bar, 1988, District of Columbia and U.S. Court of Appeals, Sixth Circuit; 1989, California and U.S. District Court, Central District of California and U.S. Court of Appeals, Ninth Circuit; 1992, Kentucky and U.S. District Court, Western District of Kentucky. *Education:* University of Texas at Austin (B.B.A., 1982); University of Virginia (J.D., 1988). Beta Gamma Sigma. Licensed Real Estate Broker, California, 1982. Certified Public Accountant, California, 1985. *Member:* Kentucky and American Bar Associations; The District of Columbia Bar. **PRACTICE AREAS:** Individual and Corporate Taxation; Business Law; Securities Law; Estate Planning and Administration; Trademark, Copyright and Unfair Competition.

**CAROL LANDIS DEMMLER,** born Pittsburgh, Pennsylvania, December 24, 1963; admitted to bar, 1989, California; 1990, U.S. District Court, Central District of California; 1992, U.S. District Court, Eastern and Southern Districts of California. *Education:* Capital University (B.A., summa cum laude, 1985); The Ohio State University (J.D., 1989). Member: National Moot Court Team; Order of Barristers. Recipient, Donald Becker Moot Court Award. *Member:* Orange County Bar Association (Member, Labor Law and Employment Section); State Bar of California. **PRACTICE AREAS:** Management, Labor and Employment Law.

**PATRICK D. MCCALLA,** born Santa Ana, California, October 21, 1963; admitted to bar, 1989, California. *Education:* Arizona State Univer-
*(This Listing Continued)*

CALIFORNIA—COSTA MESA                                                       MARTINDALE-HUBBELL LAW DIRECTORY 1997

*RUTAN & TUCKER, LLP, Costa Mesa—Continued*

sity (B.S., 1986); University of Southern California (J.D., 1989). Order of the Coif. Staff Member, Southern California Law Review, 1988-1989. Author: "Judicial Disciplining of Federal Judges is Constitutional," 62 Southern California Law Review 1263. *Member:* Orange County Bar Association (Member, Sections on: Real Estate and Environmental); State Bar of California (Member, Real Property Law Section). **PRACTICE AREAS:** Banking; Environmental; Construction; Real Estate. *Email:* pmccalla@mcimail.com

**RICHARD K. HOWELL,** born San Francisco, California, November 8, 1964; admitted to bar, 1989, California, U.S. District Court, Central District of California. *Education:* University of California at Santa Barbara (B.A., 1986); Boalt Hall School of Law, University of California (J.D., 1989). *Member:* State Bar of California. **PRACTICE AREAS:** General Practice; Civil Trial; Sports and Entertainment.

**A. PATRICK MUÑOZ,** born New Rochelle, New York, October 14, 1964; admitted to bar, 1989, California, U.S. District Court, Central District of California, U.S. Court of Appeal, Ninth Circuit. *Education:* University of California at Irvine (B.A., 1986); Loyola Marymount University (J.D., magna cum laude, 1989). Alpha Sigma Nu; Order of the Coif. Member, Loyola Law Review, 1988-1989. Member, National Moot Court Team; St. Thomas More Law Honor Society. Recipient: American Jurisprudence Awards in Torts, Criminal Law, Constitutional Law and Ethics; West Publishing Company Award for Superior Proficiency in the Study of Law. *Member:* State Bar of California. **PRACTICE AREAS:** Land Use Law; Municipal and Zoning; Civil Trial.

**PAUL J. SIEVERS,** born St. Louis, Missouri, June 15, 1961; admitted to bar, 1991, California and U.S. District Court, Southern, Central and Eastern Districts of California. *Education:* University of California, Irvine (B.A., 1983); University of Southern California (M.P.A., 1986); Loyola University of Los Angeles (J.D., 1991). Order of the Coif; St. Thomas More Honor Society. Author, "Punitive Damages in Products Liability Actions: A Comparative Critique of the Puerto Rican and Californian Traditions," 13 Loyola International and Comparative Law Journal, 695, 1991. *Member:* Orange County Bar Association; State Bar of California; Orange County Bankruptcy Forum. **PRACTICE AREAS:** Bankruptcy; Commercial; Real Estate; Civil Trial.

**S. DANIEL HARBOTTLE,** born Shelbyville, Indiana, January 20, 1957; admitted to bar, 1991, California and U.S. District Court, Central and Northern Districts of California; U.S. Court of Appeals, Ninth Circuit. *Education:* Purdue University (B.A., 1981; M.A., 1984); Indiana University (J.D., summa cum laude, 1991); University of Michigan (Ph.D., 1995). Phi Beta Kappa; Jump Fellowship. Recipient, George O. Dix Legal Writing Award. Board of Editors, Indiana Law Review, 1990-1991. Author, "The Proper Scope of Claimant Coverage Under the Indiana Medical Malpractice Act," Indiana Law Review, Vol. 23, No. 4. *Member:* Orange County and American Bar Associations; State Bar of California. **PRACTICE AREAS:** General Practice; Land Use Law; Environmental; Civil Trial.

**JOSEPH LOUIS MAGA III,** born Anaheim, California, April 4, 1966; admitted to bar, 1992, California. *Education:* University of California at Los Angeles (B.A., cum laude, 1988); University of Southern California (J.D., 1992). *Member:* Orange County Bar Association; State Bar of California. **PRACTICE AREAS:** Real Estate. *Email:* jmaga@mcimail.com

**KRAIG C. KILGER,** born Los Angeles, California, July 17, 1966; admitted to bar, 1992, California and U.S. District Court, Central District of California. *Education:* University of California at Los Angeles (B.A., 1988); University of California at Davis (J.D., 1992). Phi Delta Phi; Order of the Coif; Order of the Barristers. Winner, Roger Traynor Moot Court Competition. *Member:* Orange County Bar Association; State Bar of California. **PRACTICE AREAS:** Real Estate; Business; Banking.

**SCOTT R. SANTAGATA,** born Rochester, New York, June 8, 1967; admitted to bar, 1992, California. *Education:* San Diego State University (B.S., summa cum laude, Business, 1989); Boalt Hall, University of California (J.D., 1992). Phi Eta Sigma; Golden Key National Honor Society; Moot Court Board. *Member:* Orange County Bar Association; State Bar of California. **PRACTICE AREAS:** Business; Securities.

**SANDRA J. YOUNG,** born San Francisco, California, October 26, 1966; admitted to bar, 1993, California. *Education:* Mount Holyoke College (A.B., cum laude, 1988); University of California School of Law, Los Angeles (J.D., 1993). Phi Beta Kappa; Sigma Xi. Recipient, American Jurisprudence Award in Bankruptcy. *Member:* Orange County Bar Association; State Bar of California. **PRACTICE AREAS:** Labor and Employment.

*(This Listing Continued)*

**ALLEN C. OSTERGAR III,** born Provo, Utah, May 18, 1966; admitted to bar, 1993, California; U.S. District Court, Central District of California; U.S. Court of Appeals, 9th Circuit. *Education:* Brigham Young University (B.A., 1990); McGeorge School of Law (J.D., 1993). Order of the Coif; Order of Barristers. Recipient, American Jurisprudence Award in Decedents' Estates and Trusts. *Member:* Orange County Bar Association; State Bar of California. **LANGUAGES:** Portuguese. **PRACTICE AREAS:** Civil Trial.

**JULIA L. BOND,** born Long Beach, California, December 15, 1967; admitted to bar, 1993, California. *Education:* Smith College (B.A., cum laude, 1990); University of California School of Law, Los Angeles (J.D., 1993). Phi Beta Kappa. *Member:* State Bar of California. **PRACTICE AREAS:** Municipal and Zoning; Personal Injury; Land Use Law.

**JENNIFER WHITE-SPERLING,** born Stratford, Ontario, Canada, January 27, 1959; admitted to bar, 1993, California. *Education:* University of California, Irvine (B.A., 1981); California Polytechnic University (M.U.P., 1988); Hastings College of the Law, University of California, San Francisco (J.D., cum laude, 1993). Order of the Coif. Member, Thurston Honor Society. *Member:* Orange County Bar Association; State Bar of California. **PRACTICE AREAS:** Civil Trial; Land Use Law; Labor and Employment; Municipal and Zoning.

**ROBERT ELLIOT ADEL II,** born Atlanta, Georgia, February 7, 1962; admitted to bar, 1993, California. *Education:* University of California, Santa Barbara (B.A., summa cum laude, 1984); University of California, Berkeley, Boalt Hall (J.D., 1993). Member, Moot Court Board, 1992-1993. Technical Editor, International Tax and Business Lawyer, 1991-1993. Instructor, Legal Research and Writing, Boalt Hall, 1992. *Member:* Orange County Bar Association; State Bar of California. **PRACTICE AREAS:** Securities Litigation; Real Estate Litigation; Business Litigation; Civil Trial; Construction. *Email:* radel@mcimail.com

**ANWARD LI,** born Taipei, Taiwan, May 24, 1967; admitted to bar, 1993, California and U.S. District Court, Central District of California. *Education:* University of California, Riverside (B.S., 1989); Loyola University of Los Angeles Law School (J.D., 1992). *Member:* Orange County Bar Association; State Bar of California. **LANGUAGES:** Mandarin Chinese. **PRACTICE AREAS:** Public Law; Land Use; Litigation.

**STEVEN M. COLEMAN,** born Detroit, Michigan, August 22, 1968; admitted to bar, 1994, California. *Education:* University of California, Santa Barbara (B.A., Political Science, 1990); Hastings College of the Law, University of California, San Francisco (J.D., magna cum laude, 1994). Order of the Coif. Member, Thurston Honor Society. *Member:* Orange County Bar Association; State Bar of California. **PRACTICE AREAS:** Municipal Law; Litigation; Land Use Law.

**STEVEN JOHN GOON,** born Santa Monica, California, March 10, 1968; admitted to bar, 1994, California. *Education:* University of California, Los Angeles (B.A., Economics, 1990); Hastings College of the Law, University of California, San Francisco (J.D., 1994). *Member:* Orange County Bar Association; State Bar of California. **PRACTICE AREAS:** Construction; Civil Trial; Business Litigation.

**DOUGLAS J. DENNINGTON,** born Riverside, California, May 3, 1967; admitted to bar, 1994, California; 1995, U.S. District Court, Central District of California. *Education:* California Polytechnic State University (B.S., cum laude, Civil Engineering, 1990); Pepperdine University (J.D., magna cum laude, 1994). Tau Beta Pi; Chi Epsilon; Golden Key Honor Societies. Recipient: American Jurisprudence Award for Contracts II. Member, Pepperdine Law Review, 1992-1994. Author: California Supreme Court Survey, Pepperdine Law Review, 1993-1994. *Member:* State Bar of California. **PRACTICE AREAS:** Public Law.

**KARA S. CARLSON,** born Los Angeles, California, November 24, 1970; admitted to bar, 1995, California. *Education:* California State University, Northridge (B.A., 1992); Hastings College of the Law, University of California, San Francisco (J.D., 1995). Associate Managing Editor, Hastings Constitutional Law Quarterly, 1993-1994. *Member:* Orange County Bar Association; State Bar of California. **PRACTICE AREAS:** Public Law.

**SUE LEE COLLINS,** born Washington, D.C., September 6, 1968; admitted to bar, 1995, California, U.S. District Court, Central District of California and U.S. Court of Appeals, Ninth Circuit. *Education:* University of California, Berkeley (B.A., 1990); Anderson Graduate School of Management at University of California, Los Angeles (M.B.A., 1995); University of California School of Law, Los Angeles (J.D., 1995). Beta Gamma Sigma. *Member:* Orange County Bar Association; State Bar of California. **PRACTICE AREAS:** Business. *Email:* slcollins@mcimail.com

*(This Listing Continued)*

CAA164B

## PROFESSIONAL BIOGRAPHIES

CALIFORNIA—COSTA MESA

**ERIC L. DUNN,** born Los Angeles, California, June 12, 1962; admitted to bar, 1995, California. *Education:* Southern Illinois University (B.S., magna cum laude, 1989); Western State University (J.D., magna cum laude, 1994). *Member:* Riverside County Bar Association; State Bar of California (Member, Public Law Section). **PRACTICE AREAS:** Public Law.

**TODD OWEN LITFIN,** born Tracy, Minnesota, November 3, 1965; admitted to bar, 1995, California, U.S. District Court, Central District of California and U.S. Court of Appeals, Ninth Circuit. *Education:* Harvard University (A.B., 1988); University of California School of Law, Los Angeles (J.D., 1995). Order of the Coif. Member, Moot Court. *Member:* Orange County Bar Association; State Bar of California. **PRACTICE AREAS:** Public Law; Civil Litigation.

**STEVEN M. MULDOWNEY,** born Providence, Rhode Island, October 21, 1963; admitted to bar, 1995, California. *Education:* Brown University (B.A., 1985); University of California School of Law, Davis (J.D., 1995). *Member:* Orange County Bar Association; State Bar of California. **PRACTICE AREAS:** Civil Trial.

**DEBORAH J. CHUANG,** born Buffalo, New York, March 1, 1971; admitted to bar, 1995, California and U.S. Court of Appeals, Ninth Circuit. *Education:* Duke University (B.A., cum laude, 1992); Boalt Hall School of Law (J.D., 1995). Law Clerk, Hon. Melvin Brunetti, U.S. Court of Appeals, Ninth Circuit, 1995-1996.

**NATALIE SIBBALD DUNDAS,** born Welland, Ontario, Canada, December 10, 1971; admitted to bar, 1996, California. *Education:* University of Western Ontario (B.A., 1993); Georgetown University (J.D., 1996). Administrative Editor, American Criminal Law Review.

**SEAN P. FARRELL,** born San Bernardino, California, December 27, 1967; admitted to bar, 1996, California. *Education:* University of California, Santa Barbara (B.A., magna cum laude, 1989); Hastings College of the Law, University of California, San Francisco (J.D., 1996). Senior Note and Development Editor, Hastings Communications & Entertainment Law Journal. Author, "Telecommunications in the United Kingdom: A Prototype for Deregulation," Hastings Communications & Entertainment Law Journal, Vol. 18:2. **LANGUAGES:** Spanish, French and Portuguese. **PRACTICE AREAS:** Civil Litigation.

**FRED A. JENKINS,** born Long Beach, California, December 20, 1969; admitted to bar, 1996, California. *Education:* Harvard University (B.A., 1992); Hastings College of the Law, University of California, San Francisco (J.D., 1996). Order of the Coif. Member, Thurston Society. Member, Hastings Law Journal.

**MARLENE POSE,** born Hollywood, California, July 29, 1971; admitted to bar, 1996, California. *Education:* University of California, Los Angeles (B.A., 1993); Hastings College of the Law, University of California, San Francisco (J.D., 1996). **LANGUAGES:** Spanish.

**APRIL LEE WALTER,** born Montebello, California, April 26, 1971; admitted to bar, 1996, California. *Education:* California State University, Long Beach (B.S., 1993); Loyola Marymount University (J.D., magna cum laude, 1996). Order of the Coif; Alpha Sigma Nu. Fritz B. Burns Scholar. Staff Member, Loyola of Los Angeles Law Review, 1994-1995. Recipient: American Jurisprudence Award in Civil Procedure, Constitutional Law, Torts, Family Law, Administration of Criminal Justice and Criminal Procedure; J. Rex Dibble Honor Award; William Tell Aggeler Award. **Email:** awaltertarti%rutan__&__tucker@mcimail.com

**KAREN E. WALTER,** born Fullerton, California, July 8, 1971; admitted to bar, 1996, California. *Education:* Stanford University (B.A., 1993; J.D., 1996). Phi Beta Kappa. Member, Christian Legal Society, 1993-1996. *Member:* American Bar Association. **LANGUAGES:** Spanish and French. **PRACTICE AREAS:** Public Law. **Email:** kewalter@mcimail.com

### OF COUNSEL

**GARVIN F. SHALLENBERGER,** born Beloit, Wisconsin, January 7, 1921; admitted to bar, 1949, California and U.S. District Court, Southern District of California; 1957, U.S. Court of Appeals, Ninth Circuit; 1961, U.S. Supreme Court. *Education:* University of Montana (B.A., 1942); University of California at Berkeley (J.D., 1949). Founder and First Secretary, American Board of Trial Advocates, 1959. Chair, State Bar Commission on Judicial Nominee Evaluation, 1980. *Member:* Orange County Bar Association (Secretary, 1969; Vice President, 1970; President, 1972). Recipient, Franklin West Award for Service to the Profession, 1978; Member, Business Litigation Section); The State Bar of California (Member, Board of Governors, 1975-1977; President, 1977-1978). Fellow, American College of Trial Lawyers. [Capt., U.S. Army, 1943-1947]

*(This Listing Continued)*

**DAVID J. GARIBALDI III,** born Los Angeles, California, September 19, 1953; admitted to bar, 1978, California. *Education:* University of California at Irvine (B.A., summa cum laude, 1975); University of California at Los Angeles (J.D., 1978). Phi Beta Kappa; Order of the Coif. *Member:* Orange County Bar Association; State Bar of California. (Certified Specialist, Probate, Estate Planning and Trust Law, The State Bar of California Board of Legal Specialization). **PRACTICE AREAS:** Probate and Estate Planning.

## SCHULMAN & McMILLAN

INCORPORATED

Established in 1984

3200 PARK CENTER DRIVE, SUITE 600
**COSTA MESA, CALIFORNIA 92626-7148**
Telephone: 714-434-9596
Telecopier: 714-434-1823

*Criminal Trial Practice in all State and Federal Courts.*

FIRM PROFILE: Mr. Schulman is a well known established criminal lawyer. He was the prosecutor on the famous Onion Field Case. Mr. Schulman maintains his client relations through dedicated hard work and perseverance.

**MARSHALL M. SCHULMAN,** born Los Angeles, California, February 14, 1927; admitted to bar, 1953, California. *Education:* University of California at Los Angeles; Loyola University of Los Angeles (J.D., 1952). Deputy District Attorney, Los Angeles County, 1956-1965. Faculty Member, College of Trial Advocacy, Pepperdine University School of Law, 1976-1980, Hastings College of Trial and Appellate Advocacy, 1983— and Orange County College of Trial Advocacy, 1976—. Instructor on Criminal Law and Procedure, Western State University School of Law, 1976. Lecturer, California Continuing Education of the Bar, State Bar/University of California Extension on Criminal Law and Procedure, 1972. President, Orange County Criminal Courts Bar Association, Inc., 1967. Chairman, Orange County Criminal Defense Advocates, 1970-1978. *Member:* Orange County (Director, 1973-1978; 1983-1987; Chairman, Delegation to State Bar Conference, 1976-1977; Chairman, Criminal Law Section, 1991—) and American (Member, Criminal Law Section) Bar Associations; The State Bar of California (Member: Criminal Law and Procedure Committee, 1972-1975; Committee on Criminal Justice, 1976-1977; Chairman, 1981-1985 and Member, 1977-1985, Advisory Commission to the State Board of Legal Specialization, Criminal Law Section; Member, Board of Legal Specialization, Criminal Law Section; Member Executive Committee, Criminal Law Section, 1992—); California Trial Lawyers Association; American Board of Trial Advocates (President, Orange County Chapter, 1977-1978; Member, National Executive Committee, 1978-1979); California Attorneys for Criminal Justice (Charter Member, Board of Directors, 1975—). Fellow: American Board of Criminal Lawyers; American College of Trial Lawyers; American Inns of Court (Master Bencher, 1988—). (Certified Specialist, Criminal Law, The State Bar of California Board of Legal Specialization). **PRACTICE AREAS:** Criminal Law.

## SHEPPARD, MULLIN, RICHTER & HAMPTON LLP

A Limited Liability Partnership including Professional Corporations

650 TOWN CENTER DRIVE, 4TH FLOOR
**COSTA MESA, CALIFORNIA 92626**
Telephone: 714-513-5100
Telecopier: 714-513-5130
Email: info@smrh.com
URL: http://www.smrh.com

*Los Angeles, California Office:* Forty-Eighth Floor, 333 South Hope Street. Telephone: 213-620-1780. Telecopier: 213-620-1398. Cable Address: "Sheplaw". Home Page Address: http://www.smrh.com.
*San Francisco, California Office:* Seventeenth Floor, Four Embarcadero Center. Telephone: 415-434-9100. Telecopier: 415-434-3947. Telex: 19-4424. Home Page Address: http://www.smrh.com.
*San Diego, California Office:* Nineteenth Floor, 501 West Broadway. Telephone: 619-338-6500. Telecopier: 619-234-3815. Telex: 19-4424. Home Page Address: http://www.smrh.com.

*General Civil Trial and Appellate Practice in all State and Federal Courts; Financial Institutions Law; Commercial Law; Banking; Bankruptcy and Reorganization; Corporate; Securities; Antitrust; Intellectual Property; Unfair*

*(This Listing Continued)*

## SHEPPARD, MULLIN, RICHTER & HAMPTON LLP, Costa Mesa—Continued

Competition; Labor and Employment; Pension and Employee Benefits; Federal, State and Local Taxation; Real Estate; Land Use; Environmental; White Collar Criminal Defense; International Business; Administrative; Probate; Trust; and Estate Planning.

### MEMBERS OF FIRM

**ROBERT S. BEALL,** admitted to bar, 1987, California. *Education:* University of Southern California (J.D., 1987). Executive Editor of Articles, Major Tax Planning, 1986-1987. Executive Editor of Articles, Computer Law Journal, 1986-1987. **PRACTICE AREAS:** Financial Institutions Litigation, Shareholders and Partnership Dispute Litigation. **Email:** rbeall@smrh.com

**DAVID M. BOSKO,** born Denver, Colorado, September 17, 1940; admitted to bar, 1965, California. *Education:* Stanford University (B.S., 1962; J.D., 1965). Member, Moot Court Board, 1965. **PRACTICE AREAS:** Corporate Law; Mergers and Acquisitions; Securities Law. **Email:** dbosko@smrh.com

**STEVEN W. CARDOZA,** born Walnut Creek, California, October 6, 1961; admitted to bar, 1987, California. *Education:* University of California, Berkeley (J.D., 1987; M.B.A., 1987). *Member:* Orange County and American Bar Associations; Financial Lawyers Conference. **PRACTICE AREAS:** Finance and Banking Law; Commercial Law; Problem Loan Workouts. **Email:** scardoza@smrh.com

**DEAN A. DEMETRE,** born Pasadena, California, March 6, 1955; admitted to bar, 1980, California. *Education:* University of California at Irvine (B.A., 1977); University of California at Los Angeles (J.D., 1980). Phi Beta Kappa. Member, University of California at Los Angeles Law Review, 1979-1980. *Member:* Orange County and American Bar Associations; State Bar of California. **PRACTICE AREAS:** Finance and Banking Law; Commercial Law; Problem Loan Workouts. **Email:** ddemetre@smrh.com

**JOHN J. GIOVANNONE,** born Culver City, California, April 8, 1950; admitted to bar, 1975, California. *Education:* Princeton University (A.B., 1972); Hastings College of Law, University of California (J.D., 1975). Attorney, Office of Chief Counsel, Division of Trading and Markets, Commodity Futures Trading Commission, 1975-1977. Arbitrator: National Association of Securities Dealers; National Futures Association. **PRACTICE AREAS:** Commodities Law; Securities Law; Life Sciences. **Email:** jgiovannone@smrh.com

**RANDOLPH B. GODSHALL,** born Phoenixville, Pennsylvania, March 10, 1952; admitted to bar, 1979, California. *Education:* Yale University (B.A., magna cum laude, 1974); University of California at Berkeley (J.D., 1979). Order of the Coif. Fellow, ACTEC; Adjunct Professor, USD Law School. **PRACTICE AREAS:** Litigation; Estate Planning; Probate Law; Trust Law. **Email:** rgodshall@smrh.com

**ANDREW J. GUILFORD,** born Santa Monica, California, November 28, 1950; admitted to bar, 1975, California; 1979, U.S. Supreme Court. *Education:* University of California at Los Angeles (A.B., summa cum laude, 1972; J.D., 1975). Phi Beta Kappa. Member, 1973-1974 and Associate Editor, 1974-1975, UCLA Law Review. Judge Pro Tem, Orange County Superior Court, 1984—. **PRACTICE AREAS:** Business Trial Law, Appellate Practice, Arbitration Law. **Email:** aguilford@smrh.com

**BRENT R. LILJESTROM,** born Pasadena, California, March 24, 1956; admitted to bar, 1981, California. *Education:* University of California at Los Angeles (B.A., 1977; J.D., 1981). *Member:* Orange County and American Bar Associations; The State Bar of California. **PRACTICE AREAS:** Real Estate Law; Real Estate Finance Law; Tax Exempt Bond Financing. **Email:** bliljestrom@smrh.com

**ALAN H. MARTIN,** admitted to bar, 1987, California. *Education:* University of Virginia (J.D., 1987). Member, Ninth Circuit Bankruptcy Judge Screening Committee of the Central District of California, 1991-1993. *Member:* Orange County and American Bar Associations; Orange County Bankruptcy Forum; The American Bankruptcy Institute. **PRACTICE AREAS:** Bankruptcy Law, Banking Law, Finance Law. **Email:** amartin@smrh.com

**RYAN D. MCCORTNEY,** admitted to bar, 1987, California. *Education:* Occidental College (B.A., magna cum laude, 1984); University of Southern California (J.D., 1987). Phi Beta Kappa. Labor and Employment Section, Los Angeles County Bar Association. *Member:* American Bar Association

*(This Listing Continued)*

(Labor and Employment and Litigation Sections). **PRACTICE AREAS:** Labor and Employment Law. **Email:** rmccortney@smrh.com

†**JOHN R. SIMON,** born Los Angeles, California, September 16, 1939; admitted to bar, 1965, California. *Education:* University of Michigan and University of California at Berkeley (B.S., 1961); Boalt Hall School of Law, University of California (LL.B., 1964). Phi Beta Kappa; Beta Gamma Sigma; Order of the Coif. *Member:* Orange County and American Bar Associations; State Bar of California. **PRACTICE AREAS:** Real Property Law; Partnership Law; Real Estate Development Law. **Email:** jsimon@smrh.com

**R. MARSHALL TANNER,** born Santa Monica, California, December 4, 1946; admitted to bar, 1977, California. *Education:* Brigham Young University (B.A., magna cum laude, 1970); University of California at Los Angeles (J.D., 1977). Phi Kappa Phi. Comment Editor, UCLA Law Review, 1976-1977. *Member:* Orange County Bar Association; State Bar of California (Real Estate and Business Law Section). [Lt., USNR, 1970-1974] **Email:** rmtanner@smrh.com

†**FINLEY L. TAYLOR,** born Florence, Alabama, August 31, 1945; admitted to bar, 1971, California. *Education:* University of California at Santa Barbara (B.A., 1967); Vanderbilt University (J.D., 1970). Order of the Coif. Articles Editor, Vanderbilt Law Review, 1969-1970. *Member:* Orange County and American Bar Associations; The State Bar of California. **PRACTICE AREAS:** Business Litigation. **Email:** ftaylor@smrh.com

**PERRY JOSEPH VISCOUNTY,** born Orange, California, September 29, 1962; admitted to bar, 1987, California; U.S. District Court, Central, Southern, Northern and Eastern Districts of California, U.S. Court of Appeals, Ninth Circuit and U.S. Supreme Court. *Education:* University of Southern California (B.S., Business Administration and Finance, 1984; J.D., 1987). **PRACTICE AREAS:** Litigation; Intellectual Property Law. **Email:** pviscounty@smrh.com

### SPECIAL COUNSEL

**FREDRIC I. ALBERT,** born Philadelphia, Pennsylvania, August 1, 1961; admitted to bar, 1987, Pennsylvania; 1988, California, U.S. District Court, Central, Southern, Northern and Eastern Districts of California; U.S. Court of Appeals, Ninth Circuit; U.S. Supreme Court. *Education:* Pennsylvania State University (B.A., 1983); University of Toledo (J.D., 1987); University of Notre Dame London Law Centre, 1985. Member, The National Order of the Barristers. The U.S. Department of Justice Attorney General's Honor Law Program. *Member:* Orange County, Los Angeles County and American Bar Associations; State Bar of California (Litigation and Criminal Justice Sections). **PRACTICE AREAS:** Civil and Business Litigation; White Collar Criminal Defense. **Email:** falbert@smrh.com

**STEVEN C. NOCK,** admitted to bar, 1980, California. *Education:* Harvard University (J.D., 1980). **Email:** snock@smrh.com

**PAUL F. RAFFERTY,** born Austin, Texas, June 6, 1959; admitted to bar, 1987, California and U.S. District Court, Southern, Central, Eastern and Northern Districts of California. *Education:* LaSalle University (B.S., 1981); Rutgers University Law School (J.D., 1986). Judge Pro Tempore, Orange County Superior Court. *Member:* Orange County Bar Association; State Bar of California; California Trial Lawyers Association. **PRACTICE AREAS:** Corporate and Real Estate Litigation. **Email:** prafferty@smrh.com

### ASSOCIATES

| | |
|---|---|
| Cindy Thomas Archer | Greg S. Labate |
| Justine Mary Casey | Aaron J. Malo |
| Gene R. Clark | Susan S. Matsui |
| Brian M. Daucher | Lara A. Saunders |
| Beverly A. Johnson | Michael D. Stewart |
| Tawnya R. Wojciechowski | |

†Professional Corporation

All Orange County Attorneys are Members of the State Bar of California and Orange County Bar Associations.

(For complete biographical data on all personnel, see Professional Biographies at Los Angeles, California)

## PAUL C. SLAYBACK
950 SOUTH COAST DRIVE, SUITE 130
**COSTA MESA, CALIFORNIA 92626**
Telephone: 714-761-1516
Fax: 714-751-1044

*Personal Injury.*

**PAUL C. SLAYBACK,** born Finland, Minnesota, October 16, 1937; admitted to bar, 1973, California. *Education:* Michigan State University (B.S., 1963); Western State University (J.D., 1973). *Member:* Orange County Bar Association; State Bar of California; Orange County Trial Lawyers. **PRACTICE AREAS:** Personal Injury.

## STERN, NEUBAUER, GREENWALD & PAULY
*A PROFESSIONAL CORPORATION*
**COSTA MESA, CALIFORNIA**
(See Santa Monica)

*General Civil and Trial Practice in all State and Federal Courts, Corporate, Partnership, Real Estate, Insolvency, Insurance, Secured Transactions, Municipal and Commercial Law.*

## ALAN V. THALER
*Established in 1981*
CENTER TOWER, SUITE 1900
650 TOWN CENTER DRIVE
**COSTA MESA, CALIFORNIA 92626-1925**
Telephone: 714-545-3485
Facsimile: 714-755-8290
Email: thalerlaw@juno.com

*General Civil Litigation. Creditor's Rights and Bankruptcy Litigation. Arts and Entertainment.*

**ALAN V. THALER,** born Miami, Florida, November 26, 1955; admitted to bar, 1981, California; 1983, U.S. Court of Appeals, Eleventh Circuit; 1984, Georgia and U.S. Court of Appeals, Ninth Circuit; 1985, U.S. Court of Appeals, Tenth Circuit; U.S. District Court, Central, Eastern, Northern and Southern Districts of California. *Education:* University of California at Berkeley (A.B., 1976); Pepperdine University (M.B.A., 1978); Loyola University (J.D., 1981). Member, Loyola Law Review. Editor-in-Chief, Entertainment Law Journal. Recipient, Lawyer of the Year Award, Constitutional Rights Foundation of Orange County, 1992. Certified Mediator. Listed in the National List Directory of Bonded Collection and Creditors' Rights Attorneys. *Member:* Orange County and American Bar Associations; State Bar of California; State Bar of Georgia; Bankruptcy Forum and Financial Lawyers Conference. **LANGUAGES:** French and German.

## LAW OFFICES OF
## PATRICK E. WHALEN
3090 BRISTOL STREET, SUITE 650
**COSTA MESA, CALIFORNIA 92626**
Telephone: 714-435-6600
Fax: 714-435-6690

*Products Liability, Professional Liability, Premises Liability, Workers' Compensation and Auto.*

STAFF COUNSEL
AMERICAN INTERNATIONAL COMPANIES
MANAGING ATTORNEY

**PATRICK E. WHALEN,** born Los Angeles, California, February 18, 1945; admitted to bar, 1973, California and U.S. District Court, Central District of California. *Education:* University of Santa Clara (B.A., 1967; J.D., 1973). *Member:* Orange County Bar Association; State Bar of California; Association of Southern California Defense Counsel; Defense Research Institute.

*(This Listing Continued)*

*SENIOR TRIAL ATTORNEYS*

**JAMES B. DOWLING,** born Greensboro, North Carolina, September 17, 1947; admitted to bar, 1978, California and U.S. District Court, Southern District of California; 1979, Texas, U.S. Court of Military Appeals, U.S. District Court, Western District of Texas and U.S. Supreme Court. *Education:* University of Wisconsin (B.A., 1969); Pepperdine University (J.D., 1977). *Member:* State Bar of California; State Bar of Texas.

**JAMES M. FRASER,** born British Columbia, Canada, November 16, 1954; admitted to bar, 1981, California; 1985, U.S. Supreme Court; 1989, District of Columbia. *Education:* University of California, Los Angeles (B.A., 1976); Western State University (J.D., 1980). *Member:* Orange County Bar Association; State Bar of California; Orange County Trial Lawyers Association.

**TAMMY HORTON LUND,** born San Francisco, California, October 22, 1962; admitted to bar, 1986, California. *Education:* University of California, Los Angeles (B.A., 1983); Loyola Law School (J.D., 1986). *Member:* Orange County and Los Angeles County Bar Associations; State Bar of California.

**ALAN L. SKELLY,** born Orange, California, December 19, 1955; admitted to bar, 1987, California and U.S. District Court, Central District of California; 1988, U.S. District Court, Southern, Northern and Eastern Districts of California. *Education:* California State University, Fullerton (B.A., 1979); Western State University (J.D., 1985). *Member:* Orange County Bar Association; State Bar of California.

## ROBERT A. CHRISMAN
SUITE 200, 908 SOUTH VILLAGE OAKS DRIVE
**COVINA, CALIFORNIA 91724-3605**
Telephone: 818-967-0526
Fax: 818-967-5904

*Family Law.*

**ROBERT A. CHRISMAN,** born Los Angeles, California, August 17, 1931; admitted to bar, 1962, California. *Education:* California State Polytechnic College (B.S., 1953); University of Texas (J.D., 1960). Delta Theta Phi. Judge Pro Tempore, Los Angeles County Superior Court, 1980—. Adjunct Professor of Law, University of La Verne. *Member:* Los Angeles County Bar Association (Member, Board of Trustees, 1981-1983; Member, Executive Committee, Family Law Section, 1987-1988); Eastern Bar Association of Los Angeles County (President, 1978-1979); The State Bar of California (Subcommittee on Disciplinary Matters, 1975-1977; Chairman, Subcommittee of Bar Examiners, 1976-1979; Referee State Bar Court, 1979-1983; Member, Family Law Executive Committee, 1991-1994); East-West Family Law Council (President, 1988; 1993). Fellow: American Academy of Matrimonial Lawyers; American Academy of Family Mediators. (Certified Specialist, Family Law, The State Bar of California Board of Legal Specialization).

## LAW OFFICES OF
## ALLAN DOLLISON
917 SOUTH VILLAGE OAKS DRIVE, 2ND FLOOR
**COVINA, CALIFORNIA 91724**
Telephone: 818-339-8947
Fax: 818-339-8678
Email: bcorg1979@aol.com

*General Civil Litigation, Business, LandLord-Tenant, Real Estate, Criminal, Personal Injury, Family Law.*

**ALLAN L. DOLLISON,** born Los Angeles, California, May 22, 1966; admitted to bar, 1995, California and U.S. District Court, Central District of California. *Education:* California State University (B.A., 1991); Western State University (J.D., 1994). Delta Theta Phi. Recipient, American Jurisprudence Award, Tort Law. Democratic Candidate, California State Legislature D-72, 1994. *Member:* Los Angeles County, Beverly Hills, Eastern and American Bar Associations. [Commissioned Officer, Field Artillery, California National Guard; Capt., U.S. Army Reserves, 1991—.]. **LANGUAGES:** German. **PRACTICE AREAS:** Civil Litigation; Personal Injury; Landlord/Tenant; Real Estate; Criminal Defense. **Email:** bcorg1979@aol.com

REPRESENTATIVE CLIENTS: 4MN Television Productions ; Vision Builders Development, Inc.

## LAW OFFICES OF
## DANIEL J. DOONAN, INC.

*A PROFESSIONAL CORPORATION*

Established in 1993

**935 WEST BADILLO STREET**
**SUITE 200**
**COVINA, CALIFORNIA 91722-4110**
*Telephone: 818-332-5090*
*Telecopier: 818-332-5190*
*Email: DDOONAN@WOW.COM*

*Personal Injury, Products Liability, Negligence, Business, Real Estate, Creditors' Rights and Collections. Wills, Trusts and Estate Planning, Malicious Prosecution.*

*FIRM PROFILE: Original practice in Covina, California in 1974. Present office structure and location commencing in 1993. The firm offers a full range of legal services with emphasis on real property, business, personal injury, creditors rights, asset protection, wills and trust, and litigation associated therewith.*

**DANIEL J. DOONAN,** born Stoneham, Massachusetts, 1938; admitted to bar, 1974, California and U.S. Supreme Court. *Education:* California State Polytechnic University (B.S., 1971); Loyola University of Los Angeles (J.D., 1974). Former Real Estate Broker, California. *Member:* Eastern and Federal Bar Association; State Bar of California; Consumer Attorneys of California. [With U.S. Air Force, 1956-1960]. **PRACTICE AREAS:** Civil and Business Litigation; Real Estate; Products Liability; Personal Injury; Negligence; Collections; Creditors Rights; Wills and Trusts.

**SUZANNE K. NALLEY,** born Saginaw, Michigan, 1950; admitted to bar, 1992, California. *Education:* Western State University of Law, Fullerton, California (B.S., 2991; J.D. 1992). **PRACTICE AREAS:** Real Estate; Creditors Rights; Products Liability; Personal Injury; Negligence.

REPRESENTATIVE CLIENTS: California State Bank; Chick's Sporting Goods, Inc.

## JOHN J. GUZMAN

Established in 1989

**917 SOUTH VILLAGE OAKS DRIVE**
**SECOND FLOOR**
**COVINA, CALIFORNIA 91724**
*Telephone: 818-339-8947*
*Fax: 818-339-8678*

*Family Law including Dissolutions, Paternity, Adoptions, Child Custody Modifications, Child Support Modifications, Spousal Support, Grandparents Visitation Rights, Personal Injury, Criminal and Civil Law in all California State Courts.*

**JOHN J. GUZMAN,** born Montebello, California, April 30, 1957; admitted to bar, 1989, California and U.S. District Court, Ninth Circuit. *Education:* University of California at Irvine; Western State University, Fullerton (B.S.L., 1986; J.D., 1988). Board of Directors, Legal Services Corporation, 1993-1996. House of Ruth (Advisory Counsel) Los Angeles Superior Court. Family Law Mediator, 1992—. *Member:* Los Angeles County, Eastern, American and Mexican-American Bar Associations; State Bar of California; The Association of Trial Lawyers of America; Consumer Association of Attorneys (Los Angeles Section, Family Law).

## LAW OFFICES OF
## M. SUE KRAFFT

Established in 1985

**342 WEST BADILLO**
**COVINA, CALIFORNIA 91723**
*Telephone: 818-331-7241*
*Telecopier: 818-967-6456*
*Email: mskrafft@earthlink.net*
*URL: http://www.krafft.com/legal*

*Probate Law, Conservatorship/Guardianship Law, Estate Planning, Real Estate Law, Corporate Law.*

*(This Listing Continued)*

**M. SUE KRAFFT,** born Hackett, Arkansas, December 29, 1938; admitted to bar, 1985, California. *Education:* San Francisco State University; San Mateo College; Mt. San Antonio College; Citrus College (A.S., 1982); Western State University (B.L., 1984; J.D., 1985). Licensed Real Estate Broker, California, 1974. *Member:* Los Angeles and American Bar Associations; State Bar of California (Member, Sections on: Law Practice Management; Estate Planning and Administration; Real Estate; Land Use); Eastern Bar Association of Los Angeles; California Association of Realtors; National Association of Realtors; East San Gabriel Valley Board of Realtors. **PRACTICE AREAS:** Estate Planning; Probate Law; Real Property; Corporate Law.

## McALPIN & NORTHWOOD

*A PROFESSIONAL CORPORATION*

**211 SOUTH CITRUS AVENUE**
**COVINA, CALIFORNIA 91723**
*Telephone: 818-331-6376*
*Fax: 818-339-2450*

*General Civil and Trial Practice. Probate, Living Trusts, Negligence, Family, Workers Compensation, Corporation, Real Estate, Criminal and Personal Injury Law.*

**V. J. MCALPIN,** born Marion, Illinois, October 17, 1925; admitted to bar, 1960, California; 1972, U.S. Supreme Court. *Education:* Southern Illinois University; Washington University; St. Louis University; Southwestern University (LL.B., 1957). *Member:* Eastern Bar Association (President, 1985); Los Angeles County Bar Association; State Bar of California; California Trial Lawyers Association; Los Angeles Trial Lawyers Association. **PRACTICE AREAS:** Workers Compensation (50%); Personal Injury (40%); Probate (10%).

**INEZ NORTHWOOD,** born Peoria, Illinois; admitted to bar, 1977, California. *Education:* California State Polytechnic University (B.A., 1974); LaVerne College Law Center (J.D., cum laude, 1977). *Member:* Eastern and Los Angeles County Bar Associations; State Bar of California; East West Family Law Council. **PRACTICE AREAS:** Family Law (90%); Real Estate (5%); Probate (5%).

## DANIEL G. McMEEKIN

**OLD COVINA BANK BUILDING**
**101 NORTH CITRUS, SUITE 3A**
**COVINA, CALIFORNIA 91723**
*Telephone: 818-331-0458*
*Fax: 818-331-4618*

*General Civil and Criminal Litigation in all State and Federal Courts, Family Law, Real Estate.*

**DANIEL G. MCMEEKIN,** born Glendale, California, September 24, 1953; admitted to bar, 1980, California; 1981, U.S. District Court, Central District of California. *Education:* California State University at Los Angeles (B.A., 1976); La Verne College Law Center (J.D., 1980). *Member:* Eastern and Los Angeles County Bar Associations; State Bar of California. **PRACTICE AREAS:** Family Law; Real Estate; Personal Injury; Probate; Criminal Law.

*LEGAL SUPPORT PERSONNEL*

**JEANNE E. MOHNEY,** born Oklahoma City, Oklahoma, December 31, 1956. *Education:* Mount San Antonio College (A.S., 1996). (Legal Assistant).

## HEBER S. MEEKS

**P.O. BOX 2505**
**COVINA, CALIFORNIA 91722-8505**
*Telephone: 818-332-3754*

*Bankruptcy, Family Law, Personal Injury, Construction Litigation, Civil Trial.*

**HEBER S. MEEKS,** born Jacksonville, Florida, February 7, 1952; admitted to bar, 1986, California, U.S. District Court, Central and Southern Districts of California and U.S. Court of Appeals, Ninth Circuit. *Education:* Brigham Young University; University of Utah (B.A., 1980); California Western School of Law (J.D., 1985). *Member:* Los Angeles County

*(This Listing Continued)*

(Member, Sections on: Family Law; Real Property) and Eastern Bar Associations; State Bar of California. LANGUAGES: Japanese. PRACTICE AREAS: Personal Injury Law (30%, 20); Domestic Relations Law (30%, 20); Real Estate (20%, 5); Bankruptcy Law (20%, 20).

## LAW OFFICES OF
## THOMAS J. MILLER

Established in 1983

412 NORTH BARRANCA AVENUE
**COVINA, CALIFORNIA 91723**
Telephone: 818-974-8111
Fax: 818-974-8114

*General Civil Litigation, Medical Malpractice, Personal Injury and Criminal Law.*

**THOMAS J. MILLER,** born Butte, Montana, October 15, 1942; admitted to bar, 1979, California and U.S. District Court, Central District of California; 1982, U.S. District Court, Eastern District of California; 1983, U.S. District Court, Southern District of California. *Education:* California State University, Stanislaus (B.A., 1972); Claremont Graduate School; Loyola University of Los Angeles (J.D., 1978). *Member:* Eastern, Los Angeles County Bar Association; State Bar of California. [With U.S. Air Force, 1960-1965]. **PRACTICE AREAS:** Medical Malpractice; Personal Injury; Wrongful Death; Criminal Law.

## ALBERT PEREZ, JR.

917 SOUTH VILLAGE OAKS DRIVE, SECOND FLOOR
**COVINA, CALIFORNIA 91724**
Telephone: 818-339-9484
Fax: 818-915-3301

*Civil and Criminal Litigation.*

**ALBERT PEREZ, JR.,** born West Los Angeles, October 7, 1961; admitted to bar, 1990, California. *Education:* University of California at Los Angeles (B.S., 1985); Western State University (J.D., 1989). Judge Pro Tem, Citrus Municipal Court, Covina, California, 1993—. Administration Housing Officer at California Polytechnic University, Pomona, California, 1992—. Teacher of the Mock Trial for The Rowland Unified School District, 1996—. *Member:* State Bar of California; American Bar Association; California Trial Lawyers Association. **PRACTICE AREAS:** Criminal; Civil Litigation; Trial Work.

## ROBERT E. WEISS

INCORPORATED

Established in 1973

920 VILLAGE OAKS DRIVE
**COVINA, CALIFORNIA 91724**
Telephone: 818-967-4302
Telecopier: 818-967-9216

*Real Estate, Corporation and Mortgage Law.*

**ROBERT E. WEISS,** born Los Angeles, California, September 14, 1928; admitted to bar, 1959, California. *Education:* Southwestern University (LL.B., 1958). Trustee, Los Angeles County Law Library, 1986-1989. *Member:* Los Angeles County, Pomona Valley (Trustee, 1968-1975; First Vice-President, 1973-1974; President, 1974-1975), Eastern Bar Association of Los Angeles County; American Bar Association; State Bar of California. **PRACTICE AREAS:** Real Estate; Corporation and Mortgage Law.

**CRIS A. KLINGERMAN,** born Covina, California, November 14, 1952; admitted to bar, 1978, California. *Education:* California State University at Los Angeles (B.S., 1975); LaVerne College (J.D., cum laude, 1978). Nu Beta Epsilon. *Member:* Los Angeles County Bar Association; State Bar of California; Los Angeles Trial Lawyers Association. **PRACTICE AREAS:** Real Estate; Corporation and Mortgage Law.

**EDWARD A. TREDER,** born Libertyville, Illinois, November 3, 1959; admitted to bar, 1984, California. *Education:* California State Polytechnic University (B.S., 1981); Pepperdine University School of Law (J.D., 1984). Delta Mu Delta. Recipient, American Jurisprudence Award in Commercial Law. *Member:* Los Angeles County (Member, Real Property Law Section) and American Bar Associations; State Bar of California (Member, Sections

*(This Listing Continued)*

on: Business Law; Real Property); Eastern Bar Association of Los Angeles. **PRACTICE AREAS:** Real Estate; Corporation and Mortgage Law.

**STEPHEN E. ENSBERG,** born Freeport, New York, December 3, 1952; admitted to bar, 1981, California. *Education:* University of California, Los Angeles (B.A. 1977); University of Southern California (J.D., 1981). Phi Alpha Delta; Order of the Coif. Member: UCLA College of Letters and Science Honors Program; UCLA Political Science Honor Society. *Member:* Los Angeles County and American Bar Associations; Association of Business Trial Lawyers. **PRACTICE AREAS:** Business, Commercial and Real Estate Litigation.

**JAMES T. LEE,** born South Haven, Michigan, February 4, 1956; admitted to bar, 1983, California. *Education:* Michigan State University (B.A., with honors, 1978); Pepperdine Law School (J.D., 1981). *Member:* Los Angeles County Bar Association; State Bar of California; The Association of Business Trial Lawyers; Bankruptcy Study Group. **PRACTICE AREAS:** Bankruptcy Law; Real Estate Law; Commercial Law.

REPRESENTATIVE CLIENTS: Federal National Mortgage Assn. (FNMA) (Field Counsel); Government National Mortgage Assn. (GNMA) (Field Counsel); GMAC Mortgage Service Co.; Citibank; CityFed Mortgage Co.; Citicorp Homeowners, Inc.; Margaretten & Co., Inc.; Lomas Mortgage USA, Inc.; Fireman's Fund Mortgage Corp.; Metmor Financial Co.; Manufacturers Hanover Mortgage Corp.
REFERENCE: Sanwa Bank.

## JANSSEN, MALLOY, MARCHI, NEEDHAM & MORRISON

**CRESCENT CITY, CALIFORNIA**

(See Eureka)

*General Civil and Business Litigation. Products Liability, Negligence and Professional Liability. Insurance, Bankruptcy (Creditor). Medical Malpractice Defense. Insurance Coverage Litigation. General Personal Injury Litigation. Real Estate Litigation.*

## MITCHELL, BRISSO, DELANEY & VRIEZE

**CRESCENT CITY, CALIFORNIA**

(See Eureka)

*General Civil and Trial Practice in all Courts. Probate, Insurance, Corporation, Real Property, Timber and Logging Law.*

## BEEHLER & PAVITT

SUITE 330
100 CORPORATE POINTE
**CULVER CITY, CALIFORNIA 90230**
Telephone: 310-215-3183
Facsimile: 310-215-3248 Groups 3, 2 & 1
Cable Address: "Interpat," Los Angeles
Email: BPLAWYER@AOL.COM

*Patent, Trademark and Copyright Law. Unfair Competition Law. Trial Practice in the Federal Courts.*

FIRM PROFILE: *Beehler & Pavitt is the successor to one of the oldest patent firms in Los Angeles, and continues to offer a spectrum of full intellectual property law services, including matters in patent, trademark, copyright, trade secret, unfair competition laws and related matters in the United States and through a network of foreign associates throughout the world. The firm has experience and background in a wide diversity of technical fields, including the mechanical, electrical, and chemical arts with particular emphasis in digital electronics, semiconductor processing, medical devices, aeronautical devices, consumer products, petroleum tools and materials, and industrial chemical processes. Substantial experience and assistance is available to clients in the litigation of intellectual property rights, in the procurement of patent, trademark and copyrights, and in the licensing and transfer of technology rights.*

### MEMBERS OF FIRM

**VERNON D. BEEHLER** (1904-1989).

**WILLIAM H. PAVITT, JR.,** born Brooklyn, New York, December 9, 1916; admitted to bar, 1939, New York; 1946, Maryland; 1947, District of

*(This Listing Continued)*

**BEEHLER & PAVITT,** Culver City—Continued

Columbia; 1949, U.S. Claims Court; 1955, Ohio; 1956, U.S. Supreme Court; 1958, California; registered to practice before U.S. Patent and Trademark Office. *Education:* Columbia College (A.B., 1937); Columbia Law School (LL.B., 1939); National University School of Law. Author: "Patents Under Code Section 1235," The Tax Magazine, April, 1955. President, Los Angeles Patent Law Association, 1969-1970. *Member:* The State Bar of California (Chairman, Patent, Trademark and Copyright Conference, 1972-1973; Director, Patent, Trademark and Copyright Section, 1976-1978); Los Angeles Intellectual Property Law Association; Federal Bar Association. *PRACTICE AREAS:* Intellectual Property Law; Federal Practice.

**MARIO A. MARTELLA,** born New York, N.Y., March 6, 1931; admitted to bar, 1960, Virginia and Ohio; 1971, U.S. Supreme Court; 1973, California; registered to practice before U.S. Patent and Trademark Office. *Education:* Fordham University (B.S. in Chem., 1954); Georgetown University Law School (LL.B., 1960). Delta Theta Phi. Patent Examiner, U.S. Patent Office, 1956-1959. *Member:* The State Bar of California; American Bar Association; American Intellectual Property Law Association; American Chemical Society; Federal Bar Association. *PRACTICE AREAS:* Intellectual Property Law; Federal Practice.

### ASSOCIATES

**NATAN EPSTEIN,** born December 8, 1947; admitted to bar, 1974, California; registered to practice before U.S. Patent and Trademark Office. *Education:* University of Cincinnati and University of California at Los Angeles (B.A., magna cum laude, 1970); University of California at Los Angeles (J.D., 1973). Phi Beta Kappa. *Member:* The State Bar of California; Los Angeles Intellectual Property Law Association. *LANGUAGES:* Spanish. *PRACTICE AREAS:* Intellectual Property Law; Federal Practice. *Email:* BPEPSTEIN@AOL.COM

**ROBERT JACOBS,** born Boston, Massachusetts, August 30, 1956; admitted to bar, 1981, Florida and Massachusetts; 1985, California; registered to practice before U.S. Patent and Trademark Office. *Education:* University of Massachusetts (B.B.A., 1978); University of California at Irvine; University of Miami (J.D., 1981). *Member:* The State Bar of California; Los Angeles Intellectual Property Association. *PRACTICE AREAS:* Intellectual Property Law; Federal Practice.

REPRESENTATIVE CLIENTS: Adelberg Laboratories, Inc.; Avantage Group, Inc.; Ben Myerson Candy Co.; Bruce Industries, Inc.; CBC Industries, Inc.; Foam Design, Inc.; Foamex L.P.; F. Gavina & Sons, Inc.; IPD Industrial Parts Depot, Inc.; Jeunique International, Inc.; K-Jack Engineering Company, Inc.; Long-Lok Fasteners Corp.; Maxim Marketing; McDonnell Douglas Helicopter Co.; O.H. Kruse Grain & Milling Co.; P.L. Porter Co.; Renco Systems, Inc.; Richmond Screw Anchor; Sato Pharmaceutical, Inc.; Selandia Designs; Soundcraft, Inc.; Sunclipse, Inc.; Velbon International Corp.; Wakunaga of America, Ltd.; Zwick Energy Research Organization.
REFERENCES: Alliance Bank (Culver City).

---

## COMSTOCK & SHARPE, INC.

*Established in 1973*

11100 WASHINGTON BOULEVARD
**CULVER CITY, CALIFORNIA 90232**
Telephone: 310-559-8820; 870-1420
Facsimile: 213-870-1421

*Estate Planning and Probate, Family Law, Real Estate and Business, General Civil and Personal Injury and Corporate Law.*

**RICHARD SHARPE,** born Dorchester, Massachusetts, March 21, 1937; admitted to bar, 1972, California. *Education:* University of Maine (B.A., 1958); Southwestern University (J.D., 1971). Chemist Non-Metallics Engineer, California, 1964-1971. Family Law Mediator and Judge-Pro-tem, Los Angeles Superior Court and Municipal Courts, 1979—. Member, Probate Volunteer Panel, 1988—. *Member:* Culver City, Santa Monica, Los Angeles County (Member, Sections on: Family Law; Probate and Real Estate Law) and American Bar Associations; State Bar of California.

**HORACE B. COMSTOCK** (Deceased).

---

## GOLLUB & GOLSAN

5839 GREEN VALLEY CIRCLE, SUITE 100
**CULVER CITY, CALIFORNIA 90230**
Telephone: 310-342-2818
Fax: 310-342-2825

*Family and Matrimonial Law.*

**LORRAINE C. GOLLUB,** born Brooklyn, New York, N.Y., December 19, 1930; admitted to bar, 1953, New York; 1969, California. *Education:* Brooklyn College; Brooklyn Law School (LL.B., 1953). Volunteer Mediator, Superior Court, Santa Monica. Arbitrator of Los Angeles County Bar Client Relations. *Member:* Los Angeles County (Trustee, 1985-1986), Culver-Marina Bar (Trustee, 1990-1992) and American (Member, Family Law Section) Bar Associations; State Bar of California; Lawyers's Club of Los Angeles County (President, 1984-1985; Delegate to State Bar Conference of Delegates, 1973-1984); Women Lawyers of Los Angeles; California Women Lawyers; Association of Certified Family Law Specialists (President, 1997). (Certified Specialist, Family Law, The State Bar of California Board of Legal Specialization). *REPORTED CASES:* In re Rabie 40 Cal. App. 3rd 917 (1974), 115 Cal. R. 594; Everett v. Everett 150 Cal. App. 3rd 1053 (1984) 201 Cal. Rptr. 351; Trope v. Katz, 11 Cal. 4th 274, Cal.Rptr. 2d, P.2d (Oct., 1995). *PRACTICE AREAS:* Marital Dissolution Law; Paternity; Child Custody; Cohabitation; Grandparents Rights and Mediation.

**MARYANNE GOLSAN,** born Atlanta, Georgia, May 1, 1951; admitted to bar, 1993, California. *Education:* California State University at Los Angeles; Southwestern University School of Law (J.D., 1993). Recipient, American Jurisprudence Awards: Property, Academic Excellence, Community Property, Law and Economics. *LANGUAGES:* French. *PRACTICE AREAS:* Family Law; Probate.

---

## THOMAS EDWARD WALL

*Established in 1977*

12063 JEFFERSON BOULEVARD
**CULVER CITY, CALIFORNIA 90230**
Telephone: 310-827-4452
Fax: 310-827-1747

*Personal Injury, Civil Trials and Appeals, Insurance Defense Disputes, Child Abuse Law, Alternative Dispute Resolution.*

**THOMAS EDWARD WALL,** born Fort Worth, Texas, March 24, 1949; admitted to bar, 1977, California, U.S. District Court, Central District of California and U.S. Court of Appeals, Ninth Circuit; 1989, U.S. Supreme Court. *Education:* Texas Wesleyan College (B.A., 1972); University of La Verne (J.D., 1975); University of California at Los Angeles (Certificate in Criminal Justice, 1978-1979). Recipient, Essay Award, Association of Trial Lawyers. Author: "Unauthorized Agency Endorsement Forgery in California", Los Angeles Lawyer, 1978; "Vacating a Probate Sale Absent Default", Journal of Beverly Hills Bar Association, 1979. Lecturer at National Linkup Heading Conference for Non-Attorneys, 1995. Managing Editor, Beverly Hills Bar Journal, Beverly Hills Bar Association, 1978-1979. Member, Los Angeles County Board of Elections 1990—. Judge Pro Temp, Los Angeles County Superior Court and Municipal Courts, 1982—. Appointed Juvenile Court Referee for the Los Angeles County Superior Court, 1993—. Appointed National Advisory Board of Mothers Against Sexual Abuse, 1995—. *Member:* Los Angeles County (Member, Professional Responsibility Section, 1988—, Childhood Sexual Abuse Panel, 1989—) and American Bar Associations; The State Bar of California (Member, Committee on Professional Responsibility, 1989—; Arbitrator, Attorney-Client Fee Dispute 1989—). *REPORTED CASES:* Brandt v. State Farm, 693 Fed. Supp. 877 (1988); Henchman v. Estate of Sapin, 203 Cal. Rptr. 712 (1983); Nationwide v. Munoz, 245 Cal. Rptr. 324 (1988); People v. Knight, 239 Cal. Rptr. 413 (1987); Bradley v. State Farm, 260 Cal. Rptr. 470 (1989); Wall v. Orange County, 272 Cal. Rptr. 702 (1990); Zepeda v. City of Los Angeles, 272 Cal. Rptr. 635 (1990); Free v. Republic Ins. Co. Cal. Rptr. 2d 296 (1992); Yamasaki v. Mercury Cas. Ins. 14 Cal. Rptr. 2d 577 (1993); Peters v. LCINA. 816 Fed. Supp. 615 (N.D. Cal 1993). *PRACTICE AREAS:* Personal Injury Law; Litigation; Insurance Law.

REFERENCE: First Federal Bank, Culver City, California.

## LINDA A. HERTZBERG

20370 TOWN CENTER LANE, SUITE 125
**CUPERTINO, CALIFORNIA 95014**
Telephone: 408-255-4900
Fax: 408-255-4906
Email: lindahertz@aol.com

*Workers Compensation Defense.*

**LINDA A. HERTZBERG,** born Palo Alto, California, August 15, 1953; admitted to bar, 1994, California; U.S. District Court, Northern District of California; U.S. Court of Appeals, Ninth Circuit. *Education:* University of California at Davis (B.A., 1975); Lincoln University (J.D., 1990). Assistant Business Editor, Lincoln University Law Review. Recipient, Corpus Juris Secundum Award. *Member:* Santa Clara County (Member, Workers' Compensation Section) and American Bar Associations.

REPRESENTATIVE CLIENTS: Argonat Insurance Company; TIG Insurance Co., Inc.

## JACKSON & ABDALAH

A PROFESSIONAL CORPORATION
Established in 1963

10455 TORRE AVENUE
**CUPERTINO, CALIFORNIA 95014**
Telephone: 408-252-5211
Fax: 408-996-7045

*General Civil and Trial Practice. Real Estate, Construction Law, Estate Planning, Probate, State and Federal Taxation Law, Corporate, Charitable Organizations, Charitable Trusts, Business, Partnerships, Start-Up Firms, Employment.*

*FIRM PROFILE: Jackson & Abdalah was founded by James E. Jackson in 1963. Mr. Jackson maintained a growing general practice and was joined by Richard K. Abdalah in 1986.*

*The firm emphasizes quality of service and responsiveness to clients. All members of the firm are active in the civic affairs and are heavily committed to continuing legal education.*

**JAMES E. JACKSON,** born Missouri, December 13, 1934; admitted to bar, 1961, California and U.S. Court of Appeals, Ninth Circuit. *Education:* University of Missouri (A.B., 1956); University of Denver (J.D., cum laude, 1959). Phi Beta Kappa; Omicron Delta Kappa. Editor-in-Chief, Law Journal Dicta, 1958-1959. Licensed Real Estate Broker, California, 1981—. Lecturer, Family Estate Planning, De Anza College, Cupertino, 1976-1979. Cupertino City Councilman, 1972-1980. Mayor, Cupertino, 1975-1976 and 1978-1979. Founding Chairman of the Board, Cupertino National Bank, 1983-1990. *Member:* Sunnyvale-Cupertino, Santa Clara County Bar Association; State Bar of California (Member, Estate Planning Committee). *REPORTED CASES:* Oki America v. Microtech International. *PRACTICE AREAS:* Estate and Business Planning; Real Estate Law; Charitable Trusts; Non-Profit Organizations.

**RICHARD K. ABDALAH,** born Bermuda, April 10, 1948; admitted to bar, 1974, California, U.S. District Court, Northern District of California and U.S. Court of Appeals, Ninth Circuit; 1981, U.S. Supreme Court. *Education:* University of California, Davis (B.A., 1970); University of Santa Clara (J.D., 1974; M.B.A., 1978). Member, Editorial Board, California Lawyer, 1983-1985. Judge Pro Tempore, Santa Clara County Municipal Court, 1981—. Judicial Arbitrator, Business Law Panel, Santa Clara County Superior Court. Superior Court Pro-Tem Settlement Judge, 1987—. Licensed Real Estate Broker, California. President, Cupertino Chamber of Commerce, 1997-1998. Board of Managers, Northwest YMCA, 1988-1991. Los Altos City Planning Commission, 1991—. *Member:* Sunnyvale-Cupertino (President, 1994) and Santa Clara County (Member, Board of Trustees, 1981-1982; President, Barristers Section, 1981-1982) Bar Associations; State Bar of California. *PRACTICE AREAS:* Real Estate Law; Business Law; Municipal Law; Employment Law; Civil Litigation.

REPRESENTATIVE CLIENTS: Cupertino National Bank; The Owen Cos.; Pan Cal Investments; Galeb Paving, Inc.; Telewave, Inc.; Pacific Pac, Inc.; All American Fitness, Inc.

## JELINCH & RENDLER

A PROFESSIONAL CORPORATION
Established in 1984

SUITE 560, 20863 STEVENS CREEK BOULEVARD
**CUPERTINO, CALIFORNIA 95014**
Telephone: 408-366-6300
Fax: 408-252-3936

*General Civil and Trial Practice. Personal Injury, Products Liability, Employment Law, Real Property and Business Law, Construction Law, Subrogation Law, Environmental, Insurance.*

**FRANK A. JELINCH,** born San Jose, California, July 22, 1943; admitted to bar, 1969, California and U.S. District Court, Northern District of California; 1972, U.S. Supreme Court. *Education:* San Jose State University (B.A., cum laude, 1965); Boalt Hall School of Law, University of California (J.D., 1968). Cupertino Chamber of Commerce (Trustee, 1992—; Vice-President, 1994-1995. San Francisco Shakespeare Trustee, 1994—. Flint Center Advisory Board, 1995—. Judge Pro Tem and Arbitrator, Superior Court of Santa Clara County, 1975—. *Member:* Sunnyvale-Cupertino (Trustee, 1986-1991; President, 1990), Santa Clara County (Trustee, 1990-1991) and American (Member, EEOC Litigation Subcommittee) Bar Associations; State Bar of California; Consumer Attorneys of Santa Clara County. *REPORTED CASES:* Hironymous v. Allison, 893 S.W. 2d 578 (Tex.App. Corpus Christi 1994); Wanland v. Los Gatos Lodge, Inc. (1991) 230 C.A. 3d 1507, 281 C.R. 890. *PRACTICE AREAS:* Personal Injury; Employment Law; Construction Law; Subrogation; Civil Litigation; Real Estate; Business Litigation.

**DEVEREAUX RENDLER,** born San Jose, California, February 6, 1959; admitted to bar, 1985, California; U.S. District Court, Northern and Eastern Districts of California. *Education:* University of Santa Clara (B.A., 1981; J.D., 1984). *Member:* Sunnyvale-Cupertino (Member, Board of Directors, 1992—; President, 1997), Santa Clara County (1997, Board of Trustees) and American Bar Associations; State Bar of California; Consumer Attorneys of Santa Clara County. *LANGUAGES:* German. *REPORTED CASES:* Joseph Gallo v. Superior Court (Sherry) App. 6th Dist. 1988) 246 Cal. Rptr. 587, 200 C.A. 3d 1375, Modified. *PRACTICE AREAS:* Personal Injury Law; Employment Law; Subrogation; Civil Litigation; Insurance Law.

REPRESENTATIVE CLIENTS: State Farm Insurance Cos.; Mercury Insurance Co.; National Semiconductor Corp. (Self Insured); Farmers Insurance Group; I.C.L., Inc. (Self Insured); California Insurance Group; Travelers Insurance Co.; Raychem Corp. (Self Insured).
REFERENCES: Cupertino National Bank; Bank of America (Cupertino Branch).

## CHARLES T. KILIAN

10320 S. DE ANZA BOULEVARD, SUITE 1-D
**CUPERTINO, CALIFORNIA 95014**
Telephone: 408-777-3403
Fax: 408-777-3401

*Civil Practice. Real Property, Municipal, Land Use, Zoning and Administrative Law.*

**CHARLES T. KILIAN,** born San Bernardino, California, March 14, 1945; admitted to bar, 1971, California; U.S. Court of Appeals, Ninth Circuit and U.S. District Court, Northern District of California. *Education:* Occidental College (cum laude, 1967); University of Michigan (J.D., 1970). Professor, Contract Law, Lincoln Law School of San Jose, 1984—. City Attorney, City of Cupertino, 1980—. District Counsel, West Valley Sanitation District of Santa Clara County, 1973—. Judge Pro Tem, Superior Court (Juvenile Division). *Member:* Sunnyvale-Cupertino and Santa Clara County Bar Associations; State Bar of California. *PRACTICE AREAS:* Municipal Law; Local Government Law; Estate and Business Planning; Real Estate Law; Probate.

REPRESENTATIVE CLIENTS: City of Cupertino; West Valley Sanitation District of Santa Clara County; Santa Cruz Seaside Co.; Decratrend Corp.

## ALICE J. MacALLISTER

20395 PACIFICA DRIVE, SUITE 103
**CUPERTINO, CALIFORNIA 95014**
Telephone: 408-255-4995
Facsimile: 408-255-1036

*Estate Planning, Probate, Conservatorships, Corporate, Business, Partnerships, Technology Law and Elder Law.*

**ALICE J. MACALLISTER,** born Philadelphia, Pennsylvania, December 31, 1945; admitted to bar, 1980, California and U.S. District Court, Northern District of California. *Education:* Pennsylvania State University (B.A., with distinction, 1967); California State University at San Diego; University of Santa Clara (J.D., 1977). Phi Beta Kappa; Pi Mu Epsilon; Alpha Lambda Delta. Lecturer, Estate Planning De Anza College, Cupertino, 1984. Author: "The Use of Volume Purchase Agreement in the Electronics Industry," Santa Clara Computer and High Technology Law Journal, 223, 1985. Vice President, Community Relations, Cupertino Chamber of Commerce, 1990-1991. Founding Member, Board of Directors, Quota International of Cupertino, Inc. 1985. Member: Board of Directors, Santa Clara County Estate Planning Council, 1993—; Board of Directors, Cupertino Chamber of Commerce, 1986-1991. Member, The Financial Planning Forum, 1994—. Who's Who of Professionals, 1995. *Member:* Sunnyvale-Cupertino, Santa Clara County (Member: Estate Planning Executive Committee, 1987—; Chair, Estate Planning, Probate Trust Section, 1994) and American Bar Associations; State Bar of California (Member: Law Office Management Committee, 1981-1983; Estate Planning, Trust and Probate Section; Business Law Section); Santa Clara County Estate Planning Council, 1983—; National Academy of Elder Law Attorneys, 1989—. (Certified Specialist, Probate, Estate Planning and Trust Law, The State Bar of California Board of Legal Specialization). *REPORTED CASES:* Precise Metals (York Fabrication, Inc.); Wood Tech Industries; Columbia Printing; Pearson Ventures, Inc.; Pfandl Metals, Inc.; Norell Prosthetics Orthotics, Inc.; Cupertino Sister City. *PRACTICE AREAS:* Estate Planning; Probate and Trust Law; Elder Law; Conservatorships; Real Estate; Business Law.

REPRESENTATIVE CLIENTS: Precise Metals (York Fabrications, Inc); Wood Tech Industries; Columbia Printing; Pearson Ventures, Inc.; Pfandi Metals, Inc.; Norell Prosthetics Orthotics Inc.; Cupertino Sister City.

## BRUCE E. PITCAITHLEY

20370 TOWN CENTER LANE, SUITE 125
**CUPERTINO, CALIFORNIA 95014**
Telephone: 408-255-4900
Fax: 408-255-4906

*Workers' Compensation, Insurance Defense and Subrogation.*

**BRUCE E. PITCAITHLEY,** born Oakland, California, June 14, 1954; admitted to bar, 1986, California; 1987, U.S. District Court, Northern District of California and U.S. Court of Appeals, Ninth Circuit. *Education:* University of California at Santa Barbara (B.A., 1976); Santa Clara University (M.B.A., 1980); Lincoln University (J.D., 1986). *Member:* Santa Clara County Bar Association; State Bar of California; California Workers Compensation Defense Attorneys Association. (Certified Specialist, Workers' Compensation Law, The State Bar of California Board of Legal Specialization). *PRACTICE AREAS:* Workers Compensation Defense Law; Insurance Defense Law; Subrogation Law.

REPRESENTATIVE CLIENTS: City of Belmont; City of Gilroy; City of Hayward; City of San Leandro; City of Milpitas; City of Salinas; City of Saratoga; Santa Clara County Transit District; Morgan Hill Unified School District; Association of Bay Area Governments; Superior National Insurance Company; National Union Fire Insurance Company; Firm Solutions, Inc.; Viking Freight System, Inc.; Stanford University; Preferred Works, Inc.; California State Automobile Association.

## SKJERVEN, MORRILL, MacPHERSON, FRANKLIN & FRIEL LLP

**CUPERTINO, CALIFORNIA**

(See San Jose)

*Intellectual Property Law, including Patents, Trademarks, Copyrights, Mask Works, Unfair Competition, Trade Secrets and Licensing; Litigation in Federal and State Courts; Corporate, Commercial and General Business Law; and International and Government Contracts Law.*

CAA172B

## DAVID MICHAEL BIGELEISEN

2171 JUNIPERO SERRA BOULEVARD
SEVENTH FLOOR
**DALY CITY, CALIFORNIA 94104**
Telephone: 415-755-1414

*Criminal Defense and Personal Injury. General Civil Trial Practice.*

**DAVID MICHAEL BIGELEISEN,** born Port Jefferson, New York, November 26, 1948; admitted to bar, 1975, New York; 1976, California. *Education:* Cornell University (A.B., 1971); University of San Diego (J.D., 1974). Recipient: Wiley Manuel Award; San Francisco Bar Association Outstanding Lawyer in Public Service Award. *Member:* State Bar of California. *LANGUAGES:* Spanish, French, German and Samoan. *REPORTED CASES:* People v. Meredith, 29 C. 3d 682 (1981).

## FOX, SHJEFLO, WOHL & NEWKOLD

Limited Liability Partnership

WESTLAKE BUILDING
375 SOUTH MAYFAIR AVENUE, SUITE 292
**DALY CITY, CALIFORNIA 94015**
Telephone: 415-994-3044
Fax: 415-994-9323

*San Mateo, California Office:* Home Savings Building, 1730 South El Camino Real, Sixth Floor. Telephone: 415-341-2900. Fax: 415-341-2258.

*General Civil, Trial and Appellate Practice. Business, Corporation, Real Estate, Construction, Family, Insurance, Toxic Tort Defense, Products Liability, Drug Liability, Personal Injury, Criminal, Estate Planning, Trust and Probate Law.*

REPRESENTATIVE CLIENTS: Brian Kangas Foulk; California Wiping Materials, Inc.; CNA Insurance Companies; Conklin Brothers; Continental Insurance Co.; C & B Construction Co.; Design Professionals Insurance Co.; Fireman's Fund Insurance Co.; Harbor Insurance Co.; Herring & Worley, Inc.
REFERENCE: Bank of America, San Mateo, California.

(For Complete Biographical Data on all Personnel, see Professional Biographies at San Mateo, California)

## CRADDICK, CANDLAND & CONTI

PROFESSIONAL CORPORATION

DANVILLE-SAN RAMON MEDICAL CENTER
915 SAN RAMON VALLEY BOULEVARD, SUITE 260
**DANVILLE, CALIFORNIA 94526-0810**
Telephone: 510-838-1100
Fax: 510-743-0729

*General Civil and Trial Practice in all State and Federal Courts. Insurance, Malpractice and Business Litigation.*

**MARRS A. CRADDICK,** born Merced, California, July 31, 1928; admitted to bar, 1959, California. *Education:* University of California, Berkeley (B.A., 1955); Boalt Hall, University of California, Berkeley (J.D., 1958). Deputy District Attorney of Sacramento County, 1959-1962. District Attorney, First Judicial District, State of Alaska, 1962-1964. Member, California Medical Legal Committee, 1977—. *Member:* Alameda County and Contra Costa County Bar Associations; Association of Defense Counsel, Northern California; The State Bar of California; Defense Research Institute.

**D. STUART CANDLAND,** born Madison, Wisconsin, September 6, 1942; admitted to bar, 1971, California. *Education:* Brigham Young University (B.A., with honors, 1967); University of California at Berkeley (J.D., 1970). Assistant Professor of Law, Armstrong College of Law, 1971-1974. Deputy Attorney General, 1970-1973. Deputy District Attorney, Solano County, 1973-1975. *Member:* Contra Costa County Bar Association; The State Bar of California; Association of Defense Counsel, Northern California. *LANGUAGES:* Spanish.

**RICHARD J. CONTI,** born Berkeley, California, December 13, 1944; admitted to bar, 1971, California. *Education:* University of California at Berkeley (B.S., 1967); Hastings College of Law, University of California (J.D., 1970). Deputy District Attorney, Alameda County, 1971-1977. *Member:* Contra Costa County and Alameda County Bar Associations; The State Bar of California; Association of Defense Counsel, Northern California.

*(This Listing Continued)*

**JUDY S. CRADDICK,** born Louisville, Kentucky; admitted to bar, 1980, California. *Education:* University of Louisville and John F. Kennedy University (J.D., 1980). *Member:* California Medical Legal Committee. *Member:* Bar Association of San Francisco; Alameda County, Contra Costa County and American Bar Associations; The State Bar of California; American Society of Law and Medicine, Inc.; Association of Defense Counsel, Northern California.

**ROBERT W. HODGES,** born Norway, Maine, February 15, 1949; admitted to bar, 1980, California. *Education:* San Francisco State University (B.A., 1977); Hastings College of Law, University of California (J.D., 1980). *Member:* Contra Costa County and American Bar Associations; The State Bar of California; Association of Defense Counsel, Northern California; American Society of Law and Medicine, Inc.; Defense Research Institute. [Major, U.S. Army, 1968-1975]

**W. DAVID WALKER,** born Morgantown, West Virginia, September 20, 1948; admitted to bar, 1976, California. *Education:* University of California (B.A., 1970); Golden Gate University (J.D., 1975). Phi Alpha Delta. *Member:* Contra Costa County Bar Association; State Bar of California; Association of Defense Counsel, Northern California.

**ROBERT W. LAMSON,** born Glendale, California, March 27, 1951; admitted to bar, 1976, California. *Education:* Stanford University (A.B., 1973); Boalt Hall School of Law, University of California (J.D., 1976). *Member:* Alameda County and Contra Costa County Bar Associations; The State Bar of California; Association of Defense Counsel, Northern California.

---

**PHILLIP J. MADDUX,** born San Francisco, California, June 20, 1944; admitted to bar, 1970, California. *Education:* University of California at Berkeley (A.B., 1966); University of San Francisco School of Law; Boalt Hall School of Law, University of California (J.D., 1969). *Member:* Contra Costa County Bar Associations; State Bar of California; California Trial Lawyers Association; The Association of Trial Lawyers of America.

**JEAN LOUISE PERRY,** born Allentown, Pennsylvania, November 17, 1950; admitted to bar, 1988, California. *Education:* University of California (B.A., 1972); San Francisco State University (M.A., 1981); University of San Francisco (J.D., 1986). Member, University of San Francisco Law Review, 1985-1986. *Member:* Contra Costa County Bar Association; State Bar of California.

**MICHAEL J. GARVIN,** born Santa Monica, California, March 15, 1962; admitted to bar, 1988, California. *Education:* University of Notre Dame (B.A., 1984); University of California at Davis (J.D., 1988). *Member:* Contra Costa County Bar Association; State Bar of California.

**DIANE C. MILLER,** born Anaheim, California, May 9, 1964; admitted to bar, 1989, California, U.S. Court of Appeals, Ninth Circuit and U.S. District Court, Northern District of California. *Education:* University of California at Santa Barbara (B.A., Bus. Econ., cum laude, 1986); University of San Francisco (J.D., 1989). Staff Member, University of San Francisco Law Review, 1986-1989. Judicial Extern, Honorable John P. Vukasin, Jr., U.S. District Court, Northern District of California, 1989. *Member:* Bar Association of San Francisco; State Bar of California (Member, Litigation Section); American Bar Association.

**STEVEN L. BROWN, JR.,** born Rapid City, South Dakota, December 1, 1964; admitted to bar, 1994, California. *Education:* Brigham Young University (B.A., 1989; J.D., magna cum laude 1993). Phi Kappa Phi. *Member:* Contra Costa County Bar Association; State Bar of California. **LANGUAGES:** Swedish.

REPRESENTATIVE CLIENTS: Kaiser Foundation Hospitals; Medical Insurance Exchange of California; The Doctor's Co.; County of Contra Costa; Farmers Insurance Group (Truck Insurance Exchange); St. Paul Fire & Marine Insurance Co.; Professional Risk Management of California, Inc.; Physician's Interindemnity; Claremont Liability Insurance Company; Program Beta.

# FRANKEL & GOLDWARE

375 DIABLO ROAD
SUITE 200
**DANVILLE, CALIFORNIA 94526**
Telephone: 510-820-8712
Fax: 510-831-0155
Email: Frankel@Danvillelaw.com
URL: http://www.Danvillelaw.com

*Business Law, Litigation, Employment, Real Property, Family Law, Personal Injury, Estate Planning and Alternative Dispute Resolution.*

## MEMBERS OF FIRM

**RICHARD A. FRANKEL,** born Los Angeles, California, July 29, 1946; admitted to bar, 1982, California. *Education:* University of California at Davis (B.A., 1972); John F. Kennedy University (J.D., 1982). Associate Professor, John F. Kennedy University, School of Law, 1982—; Golden Gate University School of Law, 1993. Instructor, California State University, Hayward, 1982-1984. Certification Review Hearing Officer, Yolo County, Woodland, California, 1983-1984. Danville Area Chamber of Commerce (Member Board of Directors, 1993—; President, 1995) *Member:* Contra Costa County (Member, Board of Directors, 1994—) and American (Member, Business Law and Employment Sections) Bar Associations; State Bar of California (Member, Sections on: Labor and Employment; Business); National Employment Lawyers Association; California Employment Lawyers Association. [With U.S. Army Security Agency, 1966-1970]. **PRACTICE AREAS:** Business; Employment Law; Civil Litigation; Alternative Dispute Resolution.

**STUART I. GOLDWARE,** born Chicago, Illinois, March 16, 1950; admitted to bar, 1977, California. *Education:* University of California, Davis (A.B., with honors, 1972); Loyola University School of Law (J.D., 1977). Instructor: Diablo Valley College, 1984-1987; California State University, Hayward, 1984-1988. Governing Board Member, 1990—, and School Board President, 1992-1993, San Ramon Valley Unified School District. Judge Pro Tem, Contra Costa County Superior Court, 1989—. *Member:* Contra Costa County Bar Association; State Bar of California; Contra Costa Barristers Association (President, 1985); Association of Family and Conciliation Courts, 1992—. **PRACTICE AREAS:** Civil Litigation; Estate Planning/Probate; Alternative Dispute Resolution.

## ASSOCIATES

**MAUREEN A. CONNEELY,** born New York, N.Y., August 31, 1954; admitted to bar, 1991, California. *Education:* University of Connecticut; John F. Kennedy University (J.D., 1991). Recipient: American Jurisprudence Awards in Business Associations; Contracts; Criminal Procedure; Civil Procedure; Evidence; Wills and Trusts; Constitutional Law and Property. Associate Professor, John F. Kennedy School of Law, 1994—. *Member:* Contra Costa County Bar Association; State Bar of California (Member, Sections on Employment and Taxation). **PRACTICE AREAS:** Business; Employment Law.

**MARCIA JENSEN LASSITER,** born Fresno, California, October 14, 1947; admitted to bar, 1989, California and U.S. Court of Appeals, Ninth Circuit. *Education:* California State University at Fresno (B.A., 1970); Golden Gate University (J.D., 1988). Recipient, American Jurisprudence Award in Conflict of Laws. Member, 1974-1979 and Chairperson, 1977-1979, Fresno County Air Pollution Control Hearing Board. Member, Golden Gate University Law School Alumni Leadership Council. Co-Chair, Advisory Council to Battered Women's Alternative Legal Advocacy Program & Family Law Indigent Client Services. Secretary, Contra Costa County Advisory Council Against Domestic Violence. *Member:* Contra Costa County Bar Association (Board Member, Women's Section); State Bar of California (Member, Family Law Section); Association of Family and Conciliation Courts. **PRACTICE AREAS:** Family Law.

CAA173B

## GAGEN, McCOY, McMAHON & ARMSTRONG

A PROFESSIONAL CORPORATION
279 FRONT STREET
P.O. BOX 218
**DANVILLE, CALIFORNIA 94526**
Telephone: 510-837-0585
Fax: 510-838-5985

Napa, California Office: 1001 Second Street, Suite 315. Telephone: 707-224-8396. Fax: 707-224-5817.

*General Civil and Criminal Trial Practice, Insurance, Financial, Family, Real Estate, Corporation Law, Estate Planning, Wine Industry Regulatory Matters and Tax Law.*

**WILLIAM E. GAGEN, JR.,** born Sonora, California, July 3, 1943; admitted to bar, 1969, California. *Education:* Georgetown University (A.B., 1965); Boalt Hall School of Law, University of California (J.D., 1968). Phi Delta Phi. Moot Court. Professor of Law, John F. Kennedy University, 1984—. Deputy District Attorney, Contra Costa County, 1970-1972. Board Member: De La Salle High School (President, Board of Trustees), John F. Kennedy University, Diablo Bank, 1984-1987, Eugene O'Neill Foundation, Danville Fire Protection District, 1976-1979. Contributing Author: CEB Publications: "Calif. Criminal Law & Procedure, Calif. Tort Damage,". co-Author: California Criminal Discovery (Bancroft, Whitney, 1995). *Member:* Contra Costa County (President, 1982) and American Bar Associations; State Bar of California; Alameda/Contra Costa Trial Lawyers Association (President, 1979); California Trial Lawyers Association. (Recognized experience as a Trial Lawyer in the field of General Personal Injury Law). Fellow, American College of Trial Lawyers. [Lt., AGC, U.S. Army, 1968-1970]. (Member of California Trial Lawyers Association, with recognized experience in the fields of Trial Lawyer and General Personal Injury) (Certified Specialist, Criminal Law, The State Bar of California Board of Legal Specialization). **PRACTICE AREAS:** Criminal Trial Practice; Personal Injury Law; Civil Litigation.

**GREGORY L. MCCOY,** born Pasadena, California, December 24, 1949; admitted to bar, 1974, California; 1975, U.S. Claims Court. *Education:* Claremont Men's College (B.A., 1971); University of California, Boalt Hall School of Law, University of California (J.D., 1974). Member, Board of Trustees, San Ramon Valley Unified School District, 1977-1985. President, East Bay Community Foundation, 1983-1987. *Member:* Contra Costa County, American (Section on Corporation, Banking and Business Law) and International Bar Associations; State Bar of California; California Trial Lawyers Association. [Lt., JAGC, USNR, 1971-1979]. **PRACTICE AREAS:** Financial Law; Real Estate Law; Business Law.

**PATRICK J. MCMAHON,** born Owatonna, Minnesota, June 2, 1942; admitted to bar, 1974, California and U.S. District Court, Northern District of California. *Education:* University of Minnesota; San Francisco State College (B.A., 1970); Boston College (J.D., 1973). Deputy District Attorney, Contra Costa County, 1974-1976. Arbitrator, Mediator, Judge Pro tem, Contra Costa County Superior Court. *Member:* Contra Costa County (Member, Board of Directors, 1983-1991; President, 1990) and American Bar Associations; State Bar of California; Alameda/Contra Costa Trial Lawyers Association (Member, Board of Governors, 1980—; President, 1985); California Trial Lawyers Association. [With U.S. Army, 1961-1964]. **PRACTICE AREAS:** General Civil Trial Practice; Business Law.

**MARK L. ARMSTRONG,** born Berkeley, California, June 19, 1951; admitted to bar, 1978, California. *Education:* University of California at Santa Barbara and University of California at Berkeley (B.A., 1974); Golden Gate University (J.D., 1978). *Member:* Contra Costa County (Member, Environmental Law Section) and American Bar Associations; State Bar of California; Alameda-Contra Costa Trial Lawyers Association. **REPORTED CASES:** DeVita v. County of Napa (1993) 28 Cal.Rptr.2d 794. **PRACTICE AREAS:** Land Use; Municipal and Environmental Law.

**LINN K. COOMBS,** born Wellington, Texas, June 8, 1945; admitted to bar, 1971, California. *Education:* Stanford University (A.B., with distinction, 1967); University of California at Los Angeles (J.D., 1970). Order of the Coif. Member, University of California at Los Angeles Law Review, 1969-1970. *Member:* State Bar of California (Member, Probate Section). (Certified Specialist, Probate, Estate Planning and Trust Law, California Board of Legal Specialization). **PRACTICE AREAS:** Estate Planning Law; Wills Law; Trusts Law.

**STEPHEN W. THOMAS,** born Richmond, California, February 5, 1949; admitted to bar, 1976, California. *Education:* University of California at Berkeley (A.B., 1971); Golden Gate University (J.D., 1976). *Member:* Alameda and Contra Costa Bar Associations; State Bar of California. **PRACTICE AREAS:** Real Estate Law; Real Property Construction Law; Administration Law; Civil Litigation.

**CHARLES A. KOSS,** born Milwaukee, Wisconsin, May 12, 1952; admitted to bar, 1981, California. *Education:* University of Wisconsin (B.B.A., 1975); Boalt Hall School of Law, University of California (J.D., 1981). *Member:* Contra Costa and American Bar Associations; State Bar of California; Wisconsin Institute of Certified Public Accountants. **PRACTICE AREAS:** Financial Law; Employment Law; Corporate Law.

**MICHAEL J. MARKOWITZ,** born Suffern, New York, January 15, 1951; admitted to bar, 1982, California. *Education:* State University of New York, College at Brockport (B.S., 1973); Golden Gate University (J.D., 1982). Deputy District Attorney, Contra Costa County, California, 1982-1985. *Member:* Contra Costa County (Member, Board of Directors) and American Bar Associations; State Bar of California; California Trial Lawyers Association; Alameda-Contra Costa Trial Lawyers Association (President, 1993); The Association of Trial Lawyers of America; California Attorneys for Criminal Justice; National Association of Criminal Defense Lawyers. (Certified Specialist, Criminal Law, The State Bar of California Board of Legal Specialization). **PRACTICE AREAS:** Criminal Trial Practice (State and Federal Courts); Juvenile Law; Personal Injury Law; General Trial Practice.

**MICHAEL W. CARTER,** born San Francisco, California, May 23, 1955; admitted to bar, 1983, California. *Education:* University of California at Berkeley (B.A., 1977); University of California at Davis (M.A., 1980); Hastings College of the Law, University of California (J.D., 1983). Phi Beta Kappa. *Member:* State Bar of California; American Bar Association. (Certified Specialist, Family Law, The State Bar of California Board of Legal Specialization). **PRACTICE AREAS:** Family Law.

**RICHARD C. RAINES,** born Philadelphia, Pennsylvania, August 20, 1946; admitted to bar, 1974, California. *Education:* University of California at Santa Barbara (A.B., 1968); Hastings College of Law, University of California (J.D., 1974). Author: "Depositions," California CEB Action Guide, Fall, 1986, revised 1990, 1992, 1994. Consultant "Meeting Statutory Deadlines", CEB Action Guide, 1990, revised 1992, 1994, 1996. Arbitrator, San Francisco and Contra Costa County Superior Court. Judge Pro Tem, San Francisco Municipal Court, Contra Costa County Superior Court. Member, State Bar Court, 1983—. Lecturer: Continuing Education of the Bar, "Compelling, Opposing & Enforcing Discovery in State Court," 1985; "Preparing Now For Discovery Under the New Act," Fall, 1986; "Discovery: New Dangers, New Weapons," Spring, 1987; "Written Discovery," Fall, 1988, 1990, 1992; "Preparing for and Taking Depositions," May, 1996. Member, State Bar Calendar Coordinating Committee, Conference of Delegates, 1984, 1985, 1986; State Bar Executive Committee, Conference of Delegates, 1995—. *Member:* State Bar of California (Member, 1984-1985 and Advisor, 1985-1986, Executive Committee, Litigation Section); California Trial Lawyers Association (Recognized experience as a Trial Lawyer and in the field of General Personal Injury Law); The Association of Trial Lawyers of America. **REPORTED CASES:** Green v. Mt. Diablo Hospital District, 207 Cal.App.3d 63; Conrad v. Ball Corporation, 24 Cal.App.4th 439. **PRACTICE AREAS:** Civil Litigation; Real Estate; Employment; Construction.

**VICTOR J. CONTI,** born Detroit, Michigan, February 25, 1956; admitted to bar, 1984, California. *Education:* San Francisco State University (B.S. in Business, 1980); University of San Francisco School of Law (J.D., 1984). Recipient: Most Outstanding Student Award, School of Business. Director, San Ramon Valley Community Service Group. President, Danville Area Chamber of Commerce, 1992. Recipient, Business Person of the Year, 1995. Director, San Ramon Valley Rotary Club. *Member:* Contra Costa County and American (Member, Sections on: Economics of Law Practice; General Practice; Real Property, Probate and Trust Law; Vice Chairperson, Law Student Division, 1983-1984) Bar Associations; State Bar of California. **PRACTICE AREAS:** Real Estate Law; Construction Law; Business Law; Civil Litigation.

**BARBARA DUVALL JEWELL,** born Cincinnati, Ohio, January 31, 1947; admitted to bar, 1981, California. *Education:* University of Texas (B.A., 1969); Loyola Law School, Los Angeles (J.D., 1981). Member, Board of Directors, 1989—; President, 1993-1994, San Ramon Valley Discovery Center, Inc. *Member:* Contra Costa County and American Bar Associations; State Bar of California; California Women Lawyers Association.

*(This Listing Continued)*

**PRACTICE AREAS:** Real Estate Litigation; Insurance Coverage Law; Design Professional Defense; Defective Construction.

**ROBERT M. FANUCCI** (for personnel and biographical data, see professional biographies at Napa, California). **PRACTICE AREAS:** Tax Law; Business Law; Real Estate Law; Estate Planning Law.

**ALLAN C. MOORE,** born Oakland, California, November 28, 1954; admitted to bar, 1979, California, U.S. District Court, Northern District of California and U.S. Court of Appeals, Ninth Circuit. *Education:* University of California at Berkeley; University of California at Davis (B.A., 1976); University of San Diego (J.D., 1979). Member, University of San Diego Law Review, 1976. Instructor, Legal Research and Writing, Merritt Junior College, Oakland, 1981-1982. *Member:* Contra Costa Bar Association; State Bar of California. **PRACTICE AREAS:** Land Use Law.

**PATRICIA E. CURTIN,** born Walnut Creek, California, June 13, 1962; admitted to bar, 1987, California; 1988, U.S. District Court, Eastern District of California; 1992, U.S. District Court, Northern District of California; 1994, U.S. Supreme Court. *Education:* California State University at Chico (B.A., 1984); McGeorge School of Law, University of the Pacific (J.D., 1987). Member: Roger J. Traynor Moot Court Competition, 1986-1987; Honor's Board, Executive Committee, Moot Court, 1987. Recipient, American Jurisprudence Award in Administrative Law, 1985-1986. Professor of Environmental Law, California State University at Sacramento, 1988-1989. Instructor, University of California, Davis, in Land Use. Co-Authoring a National Publication, "Local Government Liability for Land Use Regulation." *Member:* Contra Costa County Bar Association; State Bar of California; Contra Costa Council. **PRACTICE AREAS:** Land Use Law; Environmental Law.

**STEPHEN T. BUEHL** (for personnel and biographical data, see professional biographies at Napa, California).

---

**ALEXANDER L. SCHMID,** born St. Louis, Missouri, February 16, 1952; admitted to bar, 1980, California. *Education:* University of Pennsylvania; Antioch College (B.A., 1975); Golden Gate University (J.D., with honors, 1980; LL.M., Taxation, with highest honors, 1988). Member, Golden Gate University Law Review, 1979-1980. *Member:* Contra Costa County Bar Association; State Bar of California. (Certified Specialist, Probate, Estate Planning and Trust Law, California Board of Legal Specialization). **LANGUAGES:** French and Spanish. **PRACTICE AREAS:** Tax Law; Estate Planning; Probate Law.

**DANIEL A. MULLER,** born San Francisco, California, August 4, 1966; admitted to bar, 1994, California. *Education:* Dartmouth College; University of Virginia; University of California at Davis (B.A.;B.S., 1990; J.D., 1993). Member, Pace University National Environmental Law Moot Court Competition, 1991-1993. Instructor, and Postgraduate Researcher, Environmental Law, CEQA and Land Use, University of California, Davis, 1993. *Member:* State Bar of California (Member, Sections on: Environmental, Real Estate and Criminal Law). **PRACTICE AREAS:** Land Use; Environmental Law; Criminal Law.

REPRESENTATIVE CLIENTS: Security Pacific National Bank; Tri-Valley Bank; Bank of San Ramon Valley; Mission-Valley Bancorp; Coldwell Banker; Shell Chemical Co.; East Bay Regional Park District; Hayden, Inc.; Merrill Lynch Relocation Management, Inc.; Provimi, Inc.; Transamerica Title Insurance Co.; First American Title Co.; Title Insurance & Trust.

---

## ROGER L. GAMBATESE

*Established in 1970*

*510 FOURTH STREET*
**DAVIS, CALIFORNIA 95616**
*Telephone: 916-756-8300*
*Fax: 916-756-9165*

*Estate Planning, Trust and Probate Law.*

**ROGER L. GAMBATESE,** born East Cleveland, Ohio, January 16, 1936; admitted to bar, 1961, Ohio; 1965, California; 1967, U.S. Supreme Court. *Education:* Yale University (B.S., with honors, 1957); University of Michigan (J.D., 1960). Deputy District Attorney, Yolo County, 1965-1970. Member, 1976— and Director, 1985, Sacramento Estate Planning Council. Lecturer, Family Estate Planning, 1977-1978 and Use of Trusts in Estate Planning, 1979, University of California at Davis Extension. *Member:* Yolo County Bar Association (President, 1974); State Bar of California (Member,

*(This Listing Continued)*

---

Estate Planning, Trust and Probate Law Section). [Capt., JAGC, USAF, 1961-1965]. (Certified Specialist, Estate Planning, Trust and Probate Law, The State Bar of California Board of Legal Specialization).

REFERENCE: Bank of America; First Northern Bank of Dixon.

---

## MICHAEL J. HARRINGTON

*423 E STREET*
**DAVIS, CALIFORNIA 95616**
*Telephone: 916-759-8440*
*Fax: 916-759-8476*
*Email: avialaw@wheel.dcn.davis.ca.us*

*Airplane Crash Litigation, Aviation Law and Administrative Hearings and Appeals (Aviation).*

**MICHAEL J. HARRINGTON,** born Chicago, Illinois, July 8, 1955; admitted to bar, 1989, California and Pennsylvania; U.S. Court of Appeals, Fifth and Ninth Circuits; U.S. District Court, Southern, Central, Northern and Eastern Districts of California. *Education:* University of California at Davis (A.B., 1984); George Washington University (J.D., 1988). Author: "A Review of State, Diversity Jurisdiction, and Federal Tort Claims Act Decisions Concerning Choice of Law Rules in the United States," The Air and Space Lawyer, Forum on Air and Space Law, American Bar Association, Spring, 1991; Co-Author: with B. Coogan, "Spoliation of Evidence: The Aviation Insurance Industry and a New Tort in the 1990s," Organization of Flying Adjusters Newsletter, June 1, 1991. FAA Private Pilot Certificate and FAA Airplane and Powerplant Mechanics Certificate, Tennessee, 1976. FAA Inspection Authorization Certificate, Sacramento, 1979. Former Trial Attorney, Office of Chief Counsel, FAA, Washington, D.C. *Member:* State Bar of California; American Bar Association (Member, Air and Space Law Forum); The Association of Trial Lawyers of America; Lawyer-Pilots Bar Association; Aircraft Owners and Pilots Association (Legal Services Plan; Attorney Referral Service); National Transportation Safety Board Bar Association; Aviation Insurance Association; National Agricultural Aviation Association. **PRACTICE AREAS:** Airplane Crash Litigation; Aviation Law; Administrative Hearings and Appeals (Aviation).

REPRESENTATIVE CLIENTS: AVEMCO Insurance Company; Eastern Aviation and Marine Insurance Company; National Aviation Underwriters, Inc.; Loss Management Services, Inc.; AIG Aviation, Inc.

---

## MARK G. HENDERSON

*429 F STREET, SUITE 9*
**DAVIS, CALIFORNIA 95616-4150**
*Telephone: 916-757-1793*
*Fax: 916-757-1796*

*Estate Planning, Trusts and Probate, Civil Litigation, Business and Real Estate.*

**MARK G. HENDERSON,** born Berkeley, California, February 21, 1954; admitted to bar, 1981, California. *Education:* University of the Pacific (B.A., 1976); McGeorge School of the Law, University of the Pacific (J.D., 1981; LL.M., Bus. and Tax, 1985). Order of the Coif. Member, Traynor Honor Society. Recipient, American Jurisprudence Award in Civil Procedure. Staff Member, Pacific Law Journal, 1980-1981. President, Board of Directors of Citizens Who Care, Inc. *Member:* Sacramento County and Yolo County Bar Associations; State Bar of California. (Certified Specialist, Estate Planning, Trust and Probate Law, The State Bar of California Board of Legal Specialization). **REPORTED CASES:** Archer v. Sybert (1985) 167 Cal. App. 3d 722.

REFERENCE: Union Bank.

---

## MICHAEL R. PETERSON

*510 FOURTH STREET*
**DAVIS, CALIFORNIA 95616-4125**
*Telephone: 916-756-8300*
*Fax: 916-756-9165*

*Business and Real Estate Law. Estate Planning, Trusts and Probate.*

**MICHAEL R. PETERSON,** born Los Angeles, California, December 21, 1954; admitted to bar, 1981, California. *Education:* University of Southern California (A.B., magna cum laude, 1976; J.D., 1980) University of Cal-

*(This Listing Continued)*

**MICHAEL R. PETERSON**, *Davis—Continued*

ifornia at Davis (M.A., 1986). Member and Note Editor, Southern California Law Review, 1978-1980. *Member:* Yolo County Bar Association (President, 1995); State Bar of California.

## JOAN G. POULOS
*1723 OAK AVENUE*
**DAVIS, CALIFORNIA 95616**
*Telephone: 916-753-4450*
*Facsimile: 916-753-9457*

*Family Law, Real Estate Law, General Civil Litigation, Wills and Trusts, Labor.*

**JOAN G. POULOS,** born Almena, Kansas, June 7, 1936; admitted to bar, 1963, California. *Education:* University of Kansas (B.S., 1958); Hastings College of Law (J.D., 1962). Theta Sigma Phi; Pi Lambda Theta. Council Member, 1972 and Mayor, 1974-1976, City of Davis. *Member:* Yolo County (President) and Davis Bar Associations; National Commission on Uniform State Laws; California Elected Womens Association for Research. *PRACTICE AREAS:* Family Law; Real Estate Law; General Civil Litigation; Wills and Trusts; Labor.

### ASSOCIATE

**ALEXANDRA P. FULLERTON,** born Ukiah, California, November 7, 1967; admitted to bar, 1994, California. *Education:* University of California, Davis (B.S.B.A., 1989); University of Hastings College of the Law (J.D., 1994). *Member:* State Bar of California. *PRACTICE AREAS:* Family Law; Probate; Estate Planning.

## LAW OFFICES OF
## DAVID ROSENBERG
*503 THIRD STREET*
**DAVIS, CALIFORNIA 95616**
*Telephone: 916-750-3000*
*Telefax: 916-758-4411*

*General Civil Law, Trial Practice (State and Federal Courts), Administrative and Government Law, Business Litigation, Real Estate Litigation.*

**DAVID ROSENBERG,** born Bavaria, Germany, November 20, 1946; admitted to bar, 1974, California. *Education:* California Polytechnic State University (B.S., 1968); University of California at Davis (J.D., 1974). Order of the Coif; Law Review; Phi Kappa Phi. C.E.B. Lecturer, Recent Developments in California Litigation, 1990-1996. Deputy Executive Secretary and Chief of Staff to Governor of California, 1980-1981. Partner, Law Offices of Felderstein, Rosenberg & McManus, 1981-1986. Partner, Diepenbrock, Wulff, Plant & Hannegan, 1986-1995; Law Offices of David Rosenberg, 1996—. Commissioner and Chairman, California Law Revision Commission, 1981-1985. Mayor, City of Davis, California. Supervisor, County of Yolo, California. *PRACTICE AREAS:* General Civil Law; Trial Practice (State and Federal Courts); Administrative and Government Law; Business Litigation.

REPRESENTATIVE CLIENTS: California Rehabilitation Association; Arc-California; Gardemeyer Development Company.

## STANLEY H. WELLS
*Established in 1972*
*510 FOURTH STREET*
**DAVIS, CALIFORNIA 95616**
*Telephone: 916-758-1990*
*Fax: 916-758-1181*
*Email: shwells@den.davis.ca.us*

*Estate Planning, Trust, Probate Law, Probate Litigation, Civil Practice, Taxation, Business and Real Estate.*

**STANLEY H. WELLS,** born North Platte, Nebraska, September 19, 1931; admitted to bar, 1972, California. *Education:* McGeorge School of Law, University of the Pacific (J.D., 1971); University of Miami (LL.M. in Taxation, 1979). Phi Alpha Delta. Managing Editor, Pacific Law Journal, 1970-1971. Member, Sacramento Estate Planning Council. *Member:* Yolo County and Sacramento County Bar Associations; State Bar of California (Member, Sections on: Estate Planning, Trust and Probate). [with USAF,

*(This Listing Continued)*

1950-1968]. (Certified Specialist Estate Planning, Trust and Probate Law, The State Bar of California Legal Specialization). *PRACTICE AREAS:* Estate Planning; Probate Law; Trust Law; Business Law for the Small Business Person.

## LINNEMAN, BURGESS, TELLES,
## VAN ATTA & VIERRA
*Established in 1932*
*1820 MARGUERITE STREET*
*P.O. BOX 156*
**DOS PALOS, CALIFORNIA 93620**
*Telephone: 209-392-2141*
*Fax: 209-392-3964*
*Email: drathmann@aol.com*

*Merced, California Office:* 312 West 19th Street, P.O. Box 2263. Telephone: 209-723-2137. Fax: 209-723-0899.
*Los Banos, California Office:* 654 K Street, P.O. Box 1364. Telephone: 209-826-4911. FAX: 209-826-4766. E-Mail: 1btvv@aol.com.

*General Civil and Trial Practice. Water District and Rights Law. Real Property, Probate, Negligence, Products Liability, Agricultural Law and Personal Injury.*

### MEMBERS OF FIRM

**CARL E. VAN ATTA,** born San Francisco, California, March 6, 1919; admitted to bar, 1949, California. *Education:* Stanford University (B.A., 1940); University of San Francisco (J.D., 1948). *Member:* Merced County Bar Association; State Bar of California; The Association of Trial Lawyers of America. *PRACTICE AREAS:* Personal Injury Litigation; Probate Law; Agricultural Law.

**DIANE V. RATHMANN,** born Dos Palos, California, November 8, 1947; admitted to bar, 1979, California. *Education:* Stanford University (B.A., magna cum laude, 1969); Washington State University; University of California at Los Angeles (J.D., 1979). Phi Beta Kappa. *Member:* Merced County and Fresno County Bar Associations; The State Bar of California. *LANGUAGES:* Spanish. *PRACTICE AREAS:* Water Law; California Water District Law; Agricultural Law; Probate Law.

### OF COUNSEL

**JESS P. TELLES, JR.,** born Butte, Montana, March 7, 1920; admitted to bar, 1947, California; 1948, U.S. District Court, Southern District of California and U.S. Court of Appeals, Ninth Circuit. *Education:* University of Santa Clara (B.S., 1941); Stanford University (LL.B., 1947). Phi Delta Phi. *Member:* Merced County and Fresno County Bar Associations; The State Bar of California. *PRACTICE AREAS:* Water Law; California Water District Law; Agricultural Law.

**THOMAS J. KEENE,** born Quantico, Virginia, October 9, 1951; admitted to bar, 1977, California and U.S. Court of Appeals, Ninth Circuit; 1978, U.S. District Court, Central District of California; 1980, U.S. District Court, Eastern District of California; 1981, U.S. Tax Court. *Education:* University of California at Davis (B.A., with honors, 1973); University of California at Los Angeles (J.D., 1976). Author: "A Practical Guide To Social Security Cases," The California Legal Secretary, Fall, 1986. City Attorney, City of Arvin. Deputy City Attorney, Cities of Chowchilla, Selma and Coalinga. *Member:* Fresno County and Merced County Bar Associations; State Bar of California. *REPORTED CASES:* Doloris Villa v. Superior Court of Merced County, 124 CA 3d 1063 177 CR 752. People v. Mansfield 200 CA 3d 316 245 CR 572. *PRACTICE AREAS:* Municipal Law; Municipal Finance Law; Bond Law; Special Districts Law.

REFERENCE: The Bank of America National Trust and Savings Assn.

## GILBERT L. FLANDERS
*11510 SOUTH DOWNEY AVENUE*
*P.O. BOX 670*
**DOWNEY, CALIFORNIA 90241**
*Telephone: 310-923-9238*

*General Civil and Criminal Trial Practice. Personal Injury, Workers Compensation, Corporate, Family and Probate Law.*

**GILBERT L. FLANDERS,** born San Diego, California, September 18, 1935; admitted to bar, 1965, California. *Education:* University of San Diego; Southwestern University (J.D., 1964). Member of Board, Downey

*(This Listing Continued)*

Community Hospital Foundation, 1981—. Founding Member, Thimis Legal Society, Southwestern University, 1972. *Member:* Los Angeles County; Southeast District and American Bar Associations (Member, Sections On: Insurance; Torts); State Bar of California (Workers Compensation Section); California Applicant Attorneys Association. *LANGUAGES:* Spanish and Italian.

COUNSEL FOR: Eletrimex De Mexico; Carnevale & Lohr Marble Co., U.S.A. & Italy.
GENERAL COUNSEL: UNICO Downey Chapter.

## PAUL H. MILLER
### DOWNEY, CALIFORNIA
(See Santa Fe Springs)
*Probate, Estate Planning and Trust, Real Estate and Corporate Law.*

## CAROLYN J. SCHAUF
Established in 1986
8301 EAST FLORENCE AVENUE
SUITE 305
**DOWNEY, CALIFORNIA 90240-3970**
Telephone: 310-861-4575
FAX: 310-869-0615

*Family Law, Adoptions, Estate Planning, Probate, Debtor and Bankruptcy Law.*

**CAROLYN J. SCHAUF,** born Visalia, California, September 30, 1946; admitted to bar, 1986, California and U.S. District Court, Southern District of California. *Education:* Western State University (J.D., 1985). *Member:* Southeast District; State Bar of California. *PRACTICE AREAS:* Family Law; Estate Planning Law; Bankruptcy Law.

## TREDWAY, LUMSDAINE & DOYLE, LLP
Established in 1963
10841 PARAMOUNT BOULEVARD
**DOWNEY, CALIFORNIA 90241-3397**
Telephone: 310-923-0971; 714-750-0141
Telecopier: 310-869-4607

Irvine, California Office: Suite 1000, 1920 Main Street. Telephone: 714-756-0684. Telecopier: 714-756-0596.

*General Civil Trial Practice, Business, Corporate, Securities, Financial Institutions, Real Estate, Personal Injury, Employment, Environmental Law, Taxation, Probate, Estate Planning, and Family Law.*

FIRM PROFILE: Tredway, Lumsdaine & Doyle, was established in 1963 in the city of Downey, a suburb of Los Angeles. We have grown from modest beginnings as a small firm representing the interests of local clients to an organization which today represents a broadly based clientele throughout the entire Southern California region from our two offices. Currently our clients include national and local business engaged in manufacturing, construction, distribution, financial, "high tech", and service industries, as well as many individuals.

### MEMBERS OF FIRM

**JOSEPH A. LUMSDAINE,** born Shanghai, China, July 2, 1950; admitted to bar, 1976, California. *Education:* University of California at Berkeley (A.B., 1973); Boalt Hall School of Law, University of California (J.D., 1976). Member, Moot Court Board. Member, Ecology Law Quarterly, 1975-1976. Author: "Ocean Dumping Regulations," 4 Ecology Law Quarterly 753, 1976. *Member:* Los Angeles County, Southeast and American Bar Associations; State Bar of California. *PRACTICE AREAS:* Civil Litigation. *Email:* JAL@DOWNEY.TLDLAW.COM

**MARK C. DOYLE** (Resident, Irvine Office; see Professional Biography at Irvine, California). *PRACTICE AREAS:* Corporate Law; Real Estate Law.

**JEFFREY B. SINGER** (Resident at Irvine Office; see Irvine, California for Professional Biography). *PRACTICE AREAS:* Civil Litigation. *Email:* JBS@IRVINE.TLDLAW.COM

*(This Listing Continued)*

**MICHELE S. AHRENS,** born Lynwood, California, May 22, 1953; admitted to bar, 1982, California and U.S District Court, Central and Northern Districts of California; 1984, U.S. Court of Appeals, Ninth Circuit; 1986, U.S. District Court, Southern District of California. *Education:* California State University at Los Angeles (B.A., 1975); Loyola Law School, Los Angeles (J.D., 1982). Author: "Liability Waiting to Strike: Violation of an Employee's Privacy through Disclosure of Records," Loyola Law Review, 1981. *Member:* Los Angeles County Bar Association; State Bar of California; Women Lawyers of Los Angeles County. *REPORTED CASES:* Novar Corp. v. Bureau of Collections (1984) 160 Cal. App. 3d 1, 206 Cal. Rptr. 287. *PRACTICE AREAS:* Civil Litigation; Employment Law.

**CHERI A. KADOTANI** (Resident, Irvine Office; see Professional Biography at Irvine, California). *PRACTICE AREAS:* Family Law. *Email:* CAK@IRVINE.TLDLAW.COM

**MICHAEL A. LANPHERE** (Resident, Irvine Office; see Professional Biography at Irvine, California). *PRACTICE AREAS:* Banking Law; Civil Litigation. *Email:* MAL@IRVINE.TLDLAW.COM

**HAROLD T. TREDWAY** (Retired).

**MATTHEW L. KINLEY,** born Long Beach, California, November 14, 1962; admitted to bar, 1989, California. *Education:* University of California at Los Angeles (B.A., 1985); Loyola Law School, Los Angeles (J.D., 1989). *Member:* Orange County and Los Angeles County Bar Associations; State Bar of California. *PRACTICE AREAS:* Civil Litigation. *Email:* MLK@DOWNEY.TLDLAW.COM

**LYNN L. WALKER** (1951-1994).

**GARY LIEBERMAN,** born Los Angeles, California, April 8, 1964; admitted to bar, 1990, California. *Education:* University of California at Los Angeles (B.A., cum laude, 1987); Loyola Law School, Los Angeles (J.D., 1990). Recipient, American Jurisprudence Award in Trial Advocacy. *Member:* State Bar of California. *PRACTICE AREAS:* Civil Litigation; Corporate Law. *Email:* GAL@DOWNEY.TLDLAW.COM

**DANIEL R. GOLD,** born Glendale, California, December 4, 1961; admitted to bar, 1993, California and U.S. District Court, Eastern District of California. *Education:* University of California at Los Angeles (B.A., 1984); University of the Pacific, McGeorge School of Law (J.D., with distinction, 1993). *Member:* Los Angeles and American Bar Associations; State Bar of California. *PRACTICE AREAS:* Civil Litigation; Family Law. *Email:* DRG@DOWNEY.TLDLAW.COM

**SHARISSE E. MOLYNEUX,** born Downey, California, March 9, 1961; admitted to bar, 1992, California. *Education:* University of Southern California (B.S., 1983; J.D., 1989). *Member:* Orange County and Los Angeles Bar Associations; State Bar of California. *Email:* SEM@DOWNEY.TLDLAW.COM

**JOSEPH A. MALEKI** (Resident, Irvine Office; see Professional Biography at Irvine California).

### OF COUNSEL

**DAVID A. PASQUALINI** (Resident, Irvine Office; See Professional biography at Irvine, California).

REPRESENTATIVE CLIENTS: SBD Group, Inc.; Rockwell Federal Credit Union; CMC Builders; Culp Construction Co.; Carmenita Ford Truck Sales; Santa Fe International; Parkhouse Tire; Downey Community Hospital; Independence One of California; Michigan National Bank; Vista Federal Credit Union; Southern California Bank; Western Federal Savings & Loan; Western Financial Bank; Procom Technology, Inc.; Pella Architectural; Four Star Financial; Scher-Voit Commercial Brokerage, Lumsdaine Construction; Ameron Federal Credit Union; L.A. County-USC Medical Center Credit Union.
REFERENCE: Southern California Bank.

*(For Compete Biographical Information on all Irvine Personnel, see Professional Biographies at Irvine, California)*

## BORGERDING, PETERSON, BURNELL, GLAUSER, WATERS & ALLRED

*A PROFESSIONAL CORPORATION*

Established in 1977

**222 WEST MADISON AVENUE**
**EL CAJON, CALIFORNIA 92020-3406**
Telephone: 619-440-5242
Fax: 619-442-0198
Email: ECLAW6@AOL.COM

*General Civil Litigation. Bankruptcy, Insolvency, Corporation, Business, Administrative, Collection, Probate, Trust, Personal Injury, Family, Criminal and Real Estate Law, Workers' Compensation, Social Security.*

**C. ALBERT BORGERDING,** born San Diego, California, September 20, 1935; admitted to bar, 1962, California. *Education:* University of Santa Clara (B.S., 1957; J.D., 1961). Assistant City Attorney, 1971-1975. *Member:* Foothills and San Diego County Bar Associations; State Bar of California. **PRACTICE AREAS:** Probate; Estate Planning; Real Property.

**RICHARD M. PETERSON,** born Boston, Massachusetts, January 3, 1942; admitted to bar, 1972, California. *Education:* Miami University (B.A., 1964); University of San Diego (J.D., 1972). Chairman, Moot Court Board, 1971-1972. Lecturer, Legal Research and Writing Techniques, University of San Diego Law School, 1971-1972. Chairman, Board of Directors, Crisis House, Inc., 1979-1983. President, San Diego Power Softball ASA. *Member:* Foothills (President, 1981) and San Diego County Bar Associations; State Bar of California; Consumer attorneys of San Diego. **PRACTICE AREAS:** Domestic; Personal Injury.

**WILLIAM L. BURNELL,** born Elgin, Illinois, June 23, 1949; admitted to bar, 1974, California. *Education:* Western State University (B.S., 1971; J.D., 1974). Author: "Judicial Impeachment," Spring, 1972. *Member:* Foothills (President, 1985), San Diego County (Member, Committees on: Criminal and Juvenile Law, 1977) and American Bar Associations; State Bar of California. **PRACTICE AREAS:** Criminal; Workers Compensation; Personal Injury; Social Security Disability (SSI).

**GARY S. GLAUSER,** born Corpus Christi, Texas, September 14, 1945; admitted to bar, 1977, California. *Education:* Brigham Young University (B.A., 1969); Thomas Jefferson School of Law (J.D., 1976). Nu Beta Epsilon. *Member:* Foothills (President, 1990), San Diego County Bar Associations; State Bar of California. (Certified Family Law Specialist, California State Bar of Legal Specialization). **LANGUAGES:** Spanish. **PRACTICE AREAS:** Family.

**CHRIS J. ALLRED,** born Safford, Arizona, September 5, 1953; admitted to bar, 1982, California. *Education:* Northern Arizona University (B.A., 1979); California Western School of Law (J.D., 1982). *Member:* Foothills and San Diego County Bar Associations; American Inn of Court (Barrister, 1992-1993). **LANGUAGES:** Spanish. **PRACTICE AREAS:** Civil; Real Property; Bankruptcy; Litigation; Collection.

**DAVID W. WATERS,** born Peoria, Illinois, February 21, 1942; admitted to bar, 1971, California. *Education:* California Western University (B.S., 1964); U.S. International University (M.B.A., 1969); University of San Diego (J.D., 1970). Phi Delta Phi; Blue Key. Past President, El Cajon Chamber of Commerce, 1990. Board of Trustees, East county Economic Development Council. *Member:* San Diego County (Member, Business and Real Property Section) and Foothills (Past President) Bar Associations; State Bar of California. **PRACTICE AREAS:** Civil Litigation; Real Property; Business; Commercial Transactions.

REPRESENTATIVE CLIENTS: Parkinson Cabinet Shop; Stinnett Construction Co.; Associated Mechanical Contractors, Inc.; Baxter Drilling Co.; Delta Mechanical; Jaycraft Corp.; Custom Craft Marble; Fullerton-San Diego Enterprises; Interaction Publishers, Inc.; Aerowind Corp.; Martins Furniture, Inc.; Inova Diagnostics; North County Guinte, Inc.; Camping World, Inc.; Gull Wing, Inc.
REFERENCES: Bank of Commerce.

## THOMAS M. BUCHENAU

**275 EAST DOUGLAS AVENUE, SUITE 108**
**EL CAJON, CALIFORNIA 92020-4546**
Telephone: 619-441-1100
Fax: 619-579-5761
Email: tmbuchenau@earthlink.net

*Business Litigation, Corporate Law, Real Estate Law including Residential, Commercial Transactions and Commercial Leasing. Family Law, Probate, Estate Planning and Administration, Trusts, Civil Arbitration and Divorce Mediation.*

**THOMAS M. BUCHENAU,** born 1950; admitted to bar, 1977, California. *Education:* Trinity College (B.A., in Economics, 1972); University of San Diego (J.D., 1977). Licensed Real Estate Broker, California, 1984. Adjunct Professor, Paralegal Program, Cuyamaca Community College, 1992—. Mediator, Divorce Mediation, 1994—. Arbitrator, San Diego County Superior Court, 1990—. Settlement Conference Judge Pro Tem, Civil Division, 1991—; Judge Pro Tem, Family Support Division, 1995—, San Diego County Superior Court. Judge Pro Tem, El Cajon Judicial District, Small Claims Division, San Diego County Municipal Court, 1983—. Defense Counsel, Domestic Contempt, El Cajon Superior Court, 1994—. Conservator, California Department of Consumer Affairs, 1989-1992. Member, Institutional Review Board: Sharp Healthcare System, 1994—; Grossmont District Hospital, 1987-1994. President, Board of Directors, Grossmont-Cuyamaca College District Foundation, 1992-1994. Member, El Cajon-San Diego County Civic Center Authority, 1987-1992. President, East San Diego County Lawyer Referral Service, 1984. Pro Bono, San Diego Volunteer Lawyer Program, 1983—. Special Master, State Bar of California, 1991—. Member, Kiwanis Club of Rancho San Diego. *Member:* Foothills and San Diego County Bar Associations. **PRACTICE AREAS:** Business Law; Real Estate Law; Family Law.

## McDOUGAL, LOVE, ECKIS & GRINDLE

*A PROFESSIONAL CORPORATION*

Established in 1946

**460 NORTH MAGNOLIA AVENUE**
**P.O. DRAWER 1466**
**EL CAJON, CALIFORNIA 92022-1466**
Telephone: 619-440-4444
FAX: 619-440-4907

*General Civil and Trial Practice in all State and Federal Courts. Corporation, Probate, Personal Injury, Real Estate, Administrative and Municipal Law.*

FIRM PROFILE: McDougal, Love, Eckis & Grindle was founded in 1946. It is one of the oldest law firms in San Diego County, and has a general civil practice which includes an emphasis on municipal law. The firm represents individual and corporate clients, as well as the cities of El Cajon, Imperial Beach, Poway and La Mesa.

**C. RUPERT LINLEY** (1905-1973).

**LYNN R. MCDOUGAL,** born Colby, Kansas, February 24, 1932; admitted to bar, 1959, Colorado; 1961, California. *Education:* University of Kansas (B.A., 1954); University of Colorado (J.D., 1959). Phi Delta Phi. Recipient, Citizen of the Year Award, City of El Cajon Chamber of Commerce, 1974. Assistant City Attorney, City of El Cajon, 1962-1967; City Attorney, 1967—; City Attorney, City of Imperial Beach, 1990—. President, City Attorneys Association, San Diego County, 1974-1976. President, City Attorneys Department of the League of California Cities, 1979-1980. Member, Board of Directors, League of California Cities, 1994-1995. Deputy City Attorney, City of Poway, 1984—. *Member:* San Diego County (Member, Board of Directors, 1987-1989), Foothills (President, 1965) Bar Associations; The State Bar of California; Colorado Bar Association; Barristers Club of San Diego. **REPORTED CASES:** San Marcos Water Dist. v. San Marcos Unified School Dist. (1985) 171 Cal. App. 3d 223; San Marcos Water Dist. v. San Marcos Unified School Dist. (1986) 42 C. 3d 154; San Marcos Water Dist. v. San Marcos Unified School Dist. (1987) 190 Cal. App. 3d 1083; Estate of Maniscalco v. Cenplex Corp. (1992) 9 Cal. App.4th 520. **PRACTICE AREAS:** Municipal Law; Business Law; Real Property Law.

**S. MICHAEL LOVE,** born Kansas City, Missouri, March 28, 1943; admitted to bar, 1972, California. *Education:* Arizona State University (B.S., 1965); United States International University (J.D., 1972). Lecturer: Family Law, Continuing Education of the Bar (CEB), 1982-1996; 1994.

*(This Listing Continued)*

## PROFESSIONAL BIOGRAPHIES

## CALIFORNIA—EL CENTRO

Family Law Specialist Committee Seminar, 1982-1986; Chairman, FLSC Continuing Education Seminar, 1991; Chairman Elect of the CFLS Executive Committee of the S.D.C.B.A. Best Lawyers in America, Woodward & White, 1989-1996. *Member:* Foothills (Member, Board of Directors, 1974-1979; President, 1978) and San Diego County (Member: Permanent Committee Lawyers Referral Service, 1977-1979; Board of Directors, 1981-1983 and 1992-1995; Vice President, 1983, 1995) Bar Associations; The State Bar of California (State Delegate, State Bar Convention, 1978); Fellow, American Academy of Matrimonial Lawyers, 1987. (Certified Specialist, Family Law, The State Bar of California Board of Legal Specialization). *PRACTICE AREAS:* Family Law.

**STEPHEN M. ECKIS,** born San Diego, California, August 7, 1948; admitted to bar, 1973, California. *Education:* Pomona College (B.A., 1970); Hastings College of Law, University of California (J.D., 1973). Order of the Coif. El Cajon Citizen of the Year, 1989. City Attorney, City of Poway, 1984—. Deputy City Attorney, City of Imperial Beach, 1990—. Deputy City Attorney, City of El Cajon, 1973—. Deputy City Attorney, City of Ca Mesa, 1993—. President, City Attorneys Association, San Diego County, 1985-1986. Member, 1973— and President, 1992, City Attorneys Department of the League of California Cities. *Member:* Foothills (President, 1981-1982) and San Diego County Bar Associations; The State Bar of California. *REPORTED CASES:* Barnes v. Personnel Dept. of the city of El Cajon (1978); 87 Cal. App.3d 502; City of Poway v. City of San Diego (1991) 229 Cal.App.3d 847. *PRACTICE AREAS:* Probate Law; Estate Planning Law; Municipal Law.

**DANIEL W. GRINDLE,** born San Diego, California, June 7, 1947; admitted to bar, 1974, California. *Education:* University of California at San Diego (B.A., Economics, 1969); University of San Diego (J.D., 1973). Member, 1987-1989 Chair 1988-1989, San Diego Law Center. Member, Board of Visitors, University of San Diego Law School, 1988—. *Member:* Foothills and San Diego County (Member, Board of Directors, 1984-1986; Vice President, 1986; Member, Bench Bar 'Fast Track' Committee; Member, 1988— and Chair, 1991-1992, Lawyer Referral and Information Permanent Committee) Bar Associations; The State Bar of California (Delegate, State Bar Convention, 1983-1991; Member (1991—) and Chair, Legal Services Section Lawyer Referral and Information Service Standing Committee); San Diego Trial Lawyers Association. *PRACTICE AREAS:* Business Law; Commercial and Business Litigation; Corporate Law; Real Estate Law.

**TAMARA A. SMITH,** born Wayne, Michigan, May 16, 1948; admitted to bar, 1984, California. *Education:* San Diego State University; Western State University (J.D., 1983). Nu Beta Epsilon. City Attorney of LaMesa, 1993—. Assistant City Attorney: City of Poway, 1988—; City of Imperial Beach, 1990—; *Member:* Foothills (Member and Board of Directors, 1992—), San Diego County and American Bar Associations; State Bar of California; Lawyers Club (President, East County Chapter, 1993-1995); San Diego County City Attorneys Association (President, 1995). *PRACTICE AREAS:* Municipal Law; Real Property; Land Use.

**STEVEN E. BOEHMER,** born Oakland, California, July 19, 1961; admitted to bar, 1989, California. *Education:* San Jose State University (B.S., with honors, 1985); University of San Diego (J.D., 1989). *Member:* San Diego County and American Bar Associations. *PRACTICE AREAS:* Business Litigation; Construction Defect Litigation; Personal Injury.

**LEAH M. BOUCEK,** born Fullerton, California; admitted to bar, 1995, California. *Education:* Point Loma Nazarene College (B.A., 1991); California Western School of Law (J.D., 1995). Recipient: CFLS Excellence in Family Law Award. Listed, Who's Who in Law Students. *Member:* San Diego County and Foothills Bar Associations. *PRACTICE AREAS:* Family Law.

**REX R. ERICKSON,** born Oberlin, Kansas, February 10, 1966; admitted to bar, 1992, California. *Education:* University of Kansas (B.A., 1989; J.D., 1992). *Member:* San Diego County and Foothills Bar Associations. *PRACTICE AREAS:* Business Litigation; Personal Injury; Employment Law.

**GLENN N. SABINE,** born San Diego, California, December 24, 1961; admitted to bar, 1991, California. *Education:* University of San Diego (B.A., 1984); Ohio State University (M.C.R.P., 1986; J.D., 1990). *Member:* The State Bar of California. *PRACTICE AREAS:* Municipal; Public Law; Land Use Law; Environmental Law.

REPRESENTATIVE CLIENTS: City of El Cajon; City of Poway; City of Imperial Beach; City of La Mesa; Asphalt, Inc.; El Cajon Redevelopment Agency; Poway Redevelopment Agency; El Cajon Ford.
REFERENCE: Scripps Bank.

## JOHN E. PETZE

411 SOUTH MAGNOLIA
EL CAJON, CALIFORNIA 92020
Telephone: 619-441-9404
Telecopier: 619-441-9406

*Insurance Defense, Product Defect, Personal Injury, Construction Site Accidents, Contract Litigation, Business Formations, Civil Litigation.*

**JOHN E. PETZE,** born Wilmington, Delaware, August 5, 1953; admitted to bar, 1985, California; U.S. District Court, Southern District of California. *Education:* University of California, San Diego (B.A., magna cum laude, 1975); University of San Diego (J.D., 1984). Moot Court, Best Respondent's Brief. Graduate, 1987, College of Advocacy, San Diego Inn of Court. San Diego Municipal and Superior Court Panel of Arbitrators. *Member:* San Diego County Bar Association (Member, Monitoring and Medical/Legal Committees); State Bar of California; San Diego Trial Lawyers Association. *PRACTICE AREAS:* Insurance Defense; Product Defect; Personal Injury; Construction Site Accidents; Contract Litigation; Business Formations; Civil Litigation.

## ANDERHOLT, WALKER & ZIMMERMANN

Established in 1990

654 MAIN STREET
EL CENTRO, CALIFORNIA 92243
Telephone: 619-352-1311
Facsimile: 619-353-3410

*General Civil and Trial Practice in all State and Federal Courts. Insurance Law, Collection, Business, Corporation, Real Property, Bankruptcy, Personal Injury, Probate, Commercial Transactions and Agriculture Law.*

### MEMBERS OF FIRM

**L. BROOKS ANDERHOLT,** born Calexico, March 6, 1954; admitted to bar, 1987, California. *Education:* San Diego State University at Calexico (B.S., 1982); Western State University (J.D., 1986). *Member:* Imperial County Bar Association; State Bar of California. *LANGUAGES:* Spanish. *PRACTICE AREAS:* Insurance Law; Agricultural Law.

**STEVEN M. WALKER,** born Calexico, California, March 4, 1953; admitted to bar, 1983, California. *Education:* University of Washington (B.A., 1979); University of San Diego (J.D., 1982). *Member:* San Diego County and Imperial County Bar Associations; State Bar of California. *PRACTICE AREAS:* Civil Litigation; Governmental Defense; Local Government Law; Labor and Employment Law.

**ANN MARIE ZIMMERMANN,** born Flint, Michigan, 1963; admitted to bar, 1991, California; 1992, U.S. District Court, Southern District of California. *Education:* University of Michigan (A.B., cum laude, 1985); University of San Diego (J.D., 1990). *Member:* Imperial County Bar Association; State Bar of California. *PRACTICE AREAS:* Probate; Collections; Real Estate; Bankruptcy; Civil Litigation.

REPRESENTATIVE CLIENTS: City of Holtville; Heber Public Utility District; Irigoyen Farms; Western Farm Services, Inc.; American Medical Express; Cal. Farm Insurance Company; Carl Warren & Company for Southern California Joint Powers Authority; Farmers Insurance Exchange; Fire Insurance Exchange; Mid-Century Insurance Company; State Farm Mutual Automobile Insurance Company; Travelers Insurance Company; Truck Insurance Exchange; Twentieth Century Insurance Co.

## EWING & JOHNSON

A PROFESSIONAL LAW CORPORATION

Established in 1951

636 STATE STREET
P.O. BOX 2568
EL CENTRO, CALIFORNIA 92244
Telephone: 619-352-6371
Telecopier: 619-353-5355

*General Business, Tax and Trial Practice. Agriculture, Business, Commercial, Corporation, Geothermal and Alternative Energy, Estate Planning and Probate, Finance, Real Property and Taxation (State and Federal) Law.*

**WILLIAM J. EWING,** born Chester, Pennsylvania, August 20, 1925; admitted to bar, 1952, California. *Education:* Long Beach, California Public Schools; Long Beach College (A.A., 1948); Hastings College of Law, University of California (J.D., 1951). Delta Theta Phi. *Member:* Imperial

*(This Listing Continued)*

## EWING & JOHNSON, A PROFESSIONAL LAW CORPORATION, El Centro—Continued

County (Past President) and American (Member: Real Property, Probate and Trust Law Sections) Bar Associations; The State Bar of California. Fellow, American College of Trust and Estate Counsel. **PRACTICE AREAS:** Estate Planning Law; Probate Law; Real Property Law.

**CHARLES G. JOHNSON,** born Cheyenne, Wyoming, December 5, 1950; admitted to bar, 1976, California and U.S. District Court, Southern District of California; 1977, U.S. Tax Court. *Education:* United States International University (B.A., cum laude, 1973); California Western School of Law (J.D., 1976). Phi Alpha Delta; Blue Key. Member, Advocacy Honors Board, 1975-1976. Lead Articles Editor, California Western International Law Journal, 1975-1976. Author: "Remedies Under Maritime Law For Wrongful Death: Sea-Land Services, Inc. v. Gaudet," 5 California Western International Law Journal 446, 1975. *Member:* Imperial County and American (Member, Sections on: Corporation, Banking and Business Law; Taxation; Real Property, Probate and Trust Law) Bar Associations; The State Bar of California (Member, Sections on: Business Law; Law Office Management; Real Property Law). **LANGUAGES:** Spanish. **PRACTICE AREAS:** Business Law; Corporate Law; Real Property Law.

**JAMES K. GRAVES,** born Brawley, California, January 30, 1954; admitted to bar, 1983, California; 1984, U.S. Tax Court; 1986, U.S. District Court, Southern District of California. *Education:* University of California at San Diego (B.A., 1977); Boalt Hall School of Law, University of California (J.D., 1982); University of California at Berkeley (M.B.A., 1982). *Member:* Imperial County and American (Member: Taxation Section; Agricultural Taxation Subcommittee) Bar Associations; State Bar of California (Member, Sections on: Business Law; Real Property Law). **PRACTICE AREAS:** Business Law; Tax Law; Real Property Law.

---

**MICHAEL C. COTUGNO,** born Eatontown, New Jersey, April 12, 1971; admitted to bar, 1996, California, U.S. District Court, Southern District of California and U.S. Tax Court. *Education:* Clemson University (B.S., 1993); California Western School of Law (J.D., 1996). **PRACTICE AREAS:** Business Planning; Estate Planning; Environmental Law. **Email:** cotugno@quix.net

REPRESENTATIVE CLIENTS: Bonanza Farms, Inc.; Phillips Cattle Co.; Val Rock, Inc.; Radio Station KXO; T. C. Worthy Cash & Carry, Inc.; Imperial Printers; El Centro Drug Co.; Kandal Insurance Agency; Office Supply Co.; Foss Accountancy Corp.; Schaffner Dairy, Inc.; Hawk Farming LLC; Southland Geotechnical, Inc.; I.V. Radiology Group; Kuhn Hay; Desert Trails R.V. Park; Colmac Energy, Inc.; Heber Geothermal Company; Strahm Farms, Inc.; Superior Cattle Co.; Keithly-Williams Seeds, Inc.
REFERENCES: Bank of America (El Centro Branch); Valley Independent Bank (El Centro Branch).

## GRAY CARY WARE & FREIDENRICH

*A PROFESSIONAL CORPORATION*

Gray Cary Established in 1927

Ware & Freidenrich Established in 1969

*1224 STATE STREET*
*P.O. BOX 2890*
**EL CENTRO, CALIFORNIA 92244**
Telephone: 619-353-6140
Telecopier: 619-353-6228
Email: info@gcwf.com
URL: http://www.gcwf.com

*San Diego, California Office:* 401 "B" Street, Suite 1700. Telephone: 619-699-2700.

*San Diego/Golden Triangle, California Office:* 4365 Executive Drive, Suite 1600, 92121. Telephone: 619-677-1400. Fax: 619-677-1477.

*Palo Alto, California Office:* 400 Hamilton Avenue. Telephone: 415-328-6561.

*La Jolla, California Office:* Suite 575, 1200 Prospect Street. Telephone: 619-454-9101.

General Civil and Trial Practice in all State and Federal Courts and Administrative Agencies. Admiralty, Agribusiness, Antitrust, Aviation, Banking, Bankruptcy and Insolvency, Business, Commercial, Computer Law, Compensation and Benefits, Condemnation, Construction, Copyright and Trademark, Corporation, Corporate Securities, Customs, Eminent Domain, Employment Counseling and Litigation, Environmental, Estate Planning, Family Law,

*(This Listing Continued)*

CAA180B

Fidelity and Surety, Government Contracts, Hospital and Health Care, Immigration and Naturalization, Insurance, International Business and Litigation, Publishing, Labor, Land Use, Libel, Negligence, News Media, Pension and Profit Sharing, Privacy, Private Foundation, Probate, Products Liability, Professional Malpractice, Railroad, Real Property, Federal and State Securities, Taxation, Telecommunications, Trade Regulation, Unfair Competition, Wills and Trusts.

**JAY W. JEFFCOAT,** born Klamath Falls, Oregon, October 16, 1945; admitted to bar, 1971, California; 1974, U.S. Supreme Court. *Education:* University of California at Santa Barbara (B.A., with honors, 1967); University of California at Los Angeles (J.D., 1970). Member, Moot Court Honors Program, 1968-1969. Member, California Indian Legal Services, Law School Clinical Program, 1968-1970. Member, Board of Directors, 1977-1985 and Vice President, 1980, University of California at Santa Barbara Alumni Association. Member, Small Business Administration Advisory Council, San Diego, Riverside and Imperial Counties, 1982-1992. Member, Panel of Arbitrators, American Arbitration Association. *Member:* Imperial County (President, 1978) and American (Member, Sections on: Litigation; Tort and Insurance Practice; and Environmental Law) Bar Associations; The State Bar of California; San Diego Trial Lawyers Association. [Lt. Cmdr., JAGC, USNR, 1971-1974]. **PRACTICE AREAS:** Commercial and Environmental Litigation; Toxic Tort and Product Liability; Agricultural Law. **Email:** jjeffcoat@gcwf.com

**MERRILL F. STORMS, JR.,** born Bradenton, Florida, May 23, 1948; admitted to bar, 1977, California. *Education:* University of California at Riverside and California State University at San Bernardino (B.A., 1973); Boalt Hall School of Law, University of California (J.D., 1977). *Member:* Imperial and San Diego County Bar Associations; The State Bar of California; Associated General Contractors, San Diego Chapter (Member, Board of Directors); Building Industry Association. [USAF, 1966-1970]. **PRACTICE AREAS:** Employment Law; Construction Litigation. **Email:** mstorms@gcwf.com

Languages: Spanish, German, French, Italian and Swedish.

REPRESENTATIVE CLIENTS: Abatti Produce, Inc.; American Bankers Life; Asgrow Seed; Boise Cascade; California State Automobile Assn.; Circle K Corp.; Helena Chemical Co.; Hospital Council of San Diego and Imperial Counties; Imperial Valley Press/Brawley News; I.V. Radiology Medical Group; Jaco Oil Co.; John Deere Co.; John Elmore Farms; J.R. Simplot Co.; Maggio Farms; Petrolane, Inc.; PureGro Co.; Stevens Corp.; Unocal; Valley Independent Bank; Womack Motors, Inc.

(For Complete Biographical Data on all Partners and Associates, see Professional Biographies at San Diego, California.)

## HORTON, KNOX, CARTER & FOOTE

*Established in 1932*

*SUITE 101 LAW BUILDING*
*895 BROADWAY*
**EL CENTRO, CALIFORNIA 92243**
Telephone: 619-352-2821
Telefax: 619-352-8540
Email: hkcf@QUIX.net

*Brawley, California Office:* 195 South Second Street. Telephone: 619-344-2360. Fax: 619-344-9778.

General Civil and Trial Practice in all State and Federal Courts. Water Rights, Corporation, Insurance, Taxation, Governmental, Real Property and Probate Law.

FIRM PROFILE: The firm founded more than 50 years ago is a full service firm with the experience, resources and positive focal recognition necessary to provide effective services in southern California.

### MEMBERS OF FIRM

**HARRY W. HORTON** (1892-1966).

**JAMES H. CARTER** (1918-1978).

**ORLANDO B. FOOTE, III,** born Oakland, California, November 12, 1934; admitted to bar, 1961, California. *Education:* Stanford University (A.B., 1956; J.D., 1959). Deputy District Attorney, 1961-1963; County Counsel, 1963-1965, Imperial County. City Attorney of Imperial, California, 1965-1973. *Member:* Imperial County Bar Association; The State Bar of California. **PRACTICE AREAS:** Personal Injury Law; Construction Defect Litigation.

**JOHN PENN CARTER, III,** born El Centro, California, April 18, 1942; admitted to bar, 1967, California. *Education:* San Diego State College

*(This Listing Continued)*

# PROFESSIONAL BIOGRAPHIES

## CALIFORNIA—EL CENTRO

(A.B. 1964); California Western University (J.D., 1967). Phi Delta Phi. Author: "Acreage Limitation: Imperial Valley's New Challenge," 2 California Western Law Review, 1966; "Water Limitation: Imperial Valley's New Challenge," Valley Grower, Winter, 1985; "Water Conservation Opportunities," Valley Grower, Spring, 1985; "IID's Water Rights: The Legal and Administrative Challenges," Valley Grower, Summer, 1985. Editor-in-Chief, California Western Law Review, 1966-1967. City Attorney of Imperial, California, 1973—. Chief Counsel, Imperial Irrigation District, 1981—. *Member:* Imperial County Bar Association; The State Bar of California. *PRACTICE AREAS:* Water Law; Governmental Law; Agricultural Law.

**FRANK A. OSWALT, III,** born Palm Springs, California, July 8, 1944; admitted to bar, 1974, California. *Education:* University of California at Santa Barbara (B.A., 1967); University of San Diego (J.D., magna cum laude, 1974). *Member:* Imperial County Bar Association; The State Bar of California. *PRACTICE AREAS:* Business Law; Insurance Defense Litigation.

**DENNIS H. MORITA,** born Brawley, California, November 23, 1953; admitted to bar, 1978, California. *Education:* University of California at San Diego; University of California at Los Angeles (A.B., 1975); Loyola University of Los Angeles (J.D., 1978). Deputy County Counsel, 1979-1981 and Deputy District Attorney, 1981, Imperial County. *Member:* Imperial County Bar Association (President, 1985); The State Bar of California. *PRACTICE AREAS:* Public Law; Defense Litigation.

**PHILIP J. KRUM, JR.,** born Brawley, California, December 24, 1949; admitted to bar, 1976, California. *Education:* California State University at San Diego (B.A., with distinction, 1972); California Western School of Law (J.D., 1976). *Member:* Imperial County Bar Association; State Bar of California. (Certified Specialist, Estate Planning, Trust and Probate Law, The State Bar of California Board of Legal Specialization). *PRACTICE AREAS:* Probate Law; Estate Planning Law.

**MERCEDES Z. WHEELER,** born Mexico, September 21, 1941; admitted to bar, 1981, California. *Education:* San Diego State University (B.A. in English, 1971); Imperial Valley College (A.A., 1973); San Diego State University (B.A. in Spanish, 1975); Western State University (J.D., 1980). President: Imperial County Bar Association, 1989-1990; Brawley Economic Development Commission. Board Member, Citizens Advisory Board, California State Prison at Calipatria, California. *Member:* State Bar of California. (Resident, Brawley Office). *LANGUAGES:* Spanish. *PRACTICE AREAS:* Probate Law; Estate Planning Law; Business Law; Corporate Law.

### ASSOCIATES

**THOMAS V. BARRINGTON,** born Brawley, California, December 18, 1953; admitted to bar, 1983, California. *Education:* Imperial Valley College (A.A., 1974); University of California at Los Angeles (B.A., 1977); Southwestern University School of Law (J.D., cum laude, 1983). *Member:* Imperial County (President, 1996) and American (Member, Litigation Section) Bar Associations; State Bar of California. *PRACTICE AREAS:* Insurance Defense Litigation; Eminent Domain Law; Business Litigation.

**BRADLEY S. ELLIS,** born Birmingham, Alabama, August 3, 1959; admitted to bar, 1992, California and U.S. District Court, Southern District of California. *Education:* University of California (B.S., 1985); University of San Diego (J.D., 1991). Recipient, American Jurisprudence Award in Criminal Procedure. Senior Editor, Journal of Contemporary Legal Issues, 1990-1991. *Member:* Imperial County Bar Association; State Bar of California (Litigation Section). *PRACTICE AREAS:* Business Litigation; Health Care Law; Creditor's Rights.

**PATRICK M. PACE,** born Brawley, California, September 25, 1953; admitted to bar, 1980, California. *Education:* Brigham Young University (B.A., cum laude, 1977); Lewis & Clark College (J.D., 1980). *Member:* Imperial County and American (Member, Section of Taxation) Bar Associations; The State Bar of California. *LANGUAGES:* Spanish. *PRACTICE AREAS:* Corporations Law; Business Law; Probate Law; Trust Law.

**RUTH BERMUDEZ MONTENEGRO,** born Brawley, California, March 28, 1967; admitted to bar, 1993, California and U.S. District Court, Southern District of California. *Education:* Clarion University of Pennsylvania (B.A., summa cum laude, 1989); University of California at Los Angeles (J.D., 1992). Phi Alpha Delta. 1990-1991 President, UCLA Student Body (G-SA). Board Member, El Cendro Rotary Club; Board Member, El Centro Chamber of Commerce; Vice President, El Centro Education Foundation. *Member:* Imperial County Bar Association (President, 1995-1996; Member, Board of Directors, 1993); State Bar of California. *LANGUAGES:* Spanish. *PRACTICE AREAS:* Education Law; Corporate Law; Civil Litigation.

*(This Listing Continued)*

**JEFFREY M. GARBER,** born Neptune, New Jersey, June 9, 1961; admitted to bar, 1987, California and U.S. District Court, Ninth Circuit. *Education:* Rutgers University (B.A., 1983); California Western School of Law (J.D., 1986). Recipient, American Jurisprudence Award in Trial Practice and Legal History. Member, California Western National Trial Practice Team. *Member:* San Diego County and Imperial County Bar Associations; State Bar of California. *PRACTICE AREAS:* Litigation (Personal Injury); Construction; Industrial Defect; Insurance; Government.

**MATHEW M. McCORMICK,** born Lakewood, California, September 27, 1966; admitted to bar, 1996, California and U.S. District Court, Southern District of California. *Education:* University of California at Berkeley (B.A., with honors, 1989); Thomas Jefferson School of Law (J.D., 1995); University of San Diego School of Law. Recipient: American Jurisprudence Award, Property Law; Corpus Christie Secundum Award, Property Law; Oxford University Press Award, International Law; Moot Court, Traynor Constitutional Law, Moot Court Team Member. *Member:* Imperial County Bar Association (Member, Business Law and Taxation Section). *PRACTICE AREAS:* Business Law; Taxation; Probate; Estate Planning; Real Property Law.

### OF COUNSEL

**PAUL D. ENGSTRAND,** born Hutchinson, Kansas, April 27, 1919; admitted to bar, 1948, California; 1972, U.S. Supreme Court. *Education:* Bethany College (A.B., 1940); University of California, Berkeley (LL.B., 1948). Member: Board of Editors, California Law Review, 1947-1948; Board of Directors, San Diego County Bar Association, 1952-1955; 1965-1968. *Member:* American Judicature Society; San Diego County Bar Foundation (President, 1986-1987).

REPRESENTATIVE CLIENTS: Southern Pacific Co.; Atlantic Richfield Co.; Automobile Club of Southern California; Reliance Insurance Cos.; Surplus Lines Adjusting Co.; Bixby Land Co.; Valley Independent Bank; Transport Indemnity Co.; Beneficial Standard Life Insurance Co.; Financial Indemnity Co.; American Home Insurance Co.; Foremost Insurance Co.; Gulf Insurance Group; The Mill Mutual; Northwestern National Insurance Group; Mission Insurance Co.; Safeco Title Insurance Co.; San Diego Gas & Electric Co.; TICOR Title Insurance; Texas Industries; Chevron Chemical Co.; Chevron Geothermal; Chevron U.S.A.; Harbor Insurance Co.; South Carolina Insurance Co.; Bancomer, S.A., A National Banking Institution of Mexico; General Motors Corp.; Puregro Co.; Jordan Implement Co.
GENERAL COUNSEL FOR: Imperial Irrigation District; City of Imperial; Pioneers Memorial Hospital District; Vessey and Co., Inc.; Imperial Hardware Co.; Imperial County Superintendent of Schools: Brawley, Calexico, El Centro, Heber Holtville, Seeley, Meadows Union, Imperial, McCabe, Mulberry, San Pasqual, Westmorland School Districts; Imperial Valley Community College District.

---

## PINNEY & CALDWELL, A P.C.

*Established in 1958*

*444 SOUTH EIGHTH STREET*

*P.O. BOX 710*

**EL CENTRO, CALIFORNIA 92244**

*Telephone: 619-352-7800*

*Telefax: 619-352-7809*

*General Practice in all State and Federal Courts. Federal and State Tax Law. Estate Planning, Probate, Real Property, Insurance, Negligence and Corporation Law.*

**CLIFFORD C. CALDWELL,** born El Centro, California, January 12, 1947; admitted to bar, 1973, California; 1974, U.S. District Court, Southern District of California; 1976, U.S. Tax Court and U.S. Claims Court. *Education:* University of California at San Diego (B.A., 1969); University of California at Los Angeles (J.D., 1972). Lecturer: "Estate Planning for Farmers and Ranchers," University of California Riverside, 1985; "Changes in California Laws," California Legal Secretaries, Inc. Seminar, 1985, 1986. *Member:* Imperial County Bar Association (President, 1983-1984); The State Bar of California. *LANGUAGES:* Spanish. *PRACTICE AREAS:* Estate Planning; Probate; Real Property Taxes.

---

**MARVIN LYNN WILSON,** born Brawley, California, October 21, 1938; admitted to bar, 1988, California and U.S. District Court, Southern District of California. *Education:* University of California at Davis (B.S., 1960); Western State University (J.D., 1986). *Member:* Imperial County and San Diego Bar Associations; State Bar of California. *PRACTICE AREAS:* Estate Planning; Probate.

*(This Listing Continued)*

### PINNEY & CALDWELL, A P.C., El Centro—Continued

#### OF COUNSEL

**CHARLES A. PINNEY, JR.,** born Plymouth, Indiana, August 4, 1919; admitted to bar, 1958, California and U.S. District Court, Southern District of California; 1959, U.S. Tax Court; 1962, U.S. Supreme Court; 1966, U.S. Court of Appeals, Ninth Circuit; 1974, U.S. Court of Claims. *Education:* University of California at Los Angeles (A.B., 1941); Stanford University (J.D., 1958). Member, Faculty, American Law Institute, American Bar Association, Tax Planning for Farmers, 1974-1983. Author: "Agricultural Real Estate as a Tax Shelter," 34 USC Tax Institute, 1982; "The Farmer and Estate Tax Relief - Section 2032A Revisited," USC Tax Institute, 1985. Lecturer, University of Southern California Federal Tax Institute, 1973, 1979, 1982, 1985. *Member:* Imperial County (President, 1969), San Diego County and American (Member, Section of Taxation) Bar Associations; The State Bar of California.

REPRESENTATIVE CLIENTS: Singing Hills Country Club; Disabled American Veterans, Department of California; El Toro Land & Cattle Co.; El Centro Motors, Inc.; La Brucherie Ranch; Cattlemen's Feed & Milling; Goldfields Mining Corp.; Desert Cotton Seed Products Co.; Imperial Western Products; Torrence's Farm Implements; California Livestock Commission Co.; Fifield Land Co.; Ripley Ginning Corp.; Rain For Rent, Inc.; Duggins Construction Co.; Rancho San Diego Golf Course.

---

## PLOURD AND BREEZE

A PROFESSIONAL CORPORATION

*Established in 1972*

1005 STATE STREET
P.O. BOX 99
**EL CENTRO, CALIFORNIA 92244-0099**
Telephone: 619-352-3130
Fax: 619-352-4763

*General Civil and Criminal Trial Practice. Personal Injury, Medical Malpractice, Business, Taxation, Criminal, Family and Bankruptcy Law. Trials and Appeals.*

**LEWIS A. PLOURD** (1925-1978).

**JOHN W. BREEZE,** born Oceanside, California, October 22, 1949; admitted to bar, 1975, California and U.S. District Court, Southern District of California. *Education:* University of California at Los Angeles (B.A., 1971); Western State University (J.D., 1975). Recipient, American Jurisprudence Award, Constitutional Law. *Member:* Imperial County (Member, Board of Directors, 1988; 1989; 1990) Bar Association; State Bar of California. **PRACTICE AREAS:** Criminal Law; Medical Malpractice; General Civil Litigation; Wrongful Death; Personal Injury.

---

**MARK L. ILAGAN,** born Wilkes Barre, Pennsylvania, July 30, 1965; admitted to bar, 1995, California and U.S. District Court, Southern District of California. *Education:* Boston University (B.S.B.A., 1987); University of San Diego (M.B.A., 1990); California Western School of Law (J.D., 1995). *Member:* San Diego County and Imperial County Bar Associations. **PRACTICE AREAS:** Criminal; Family.

REPRESENTATIVE CLIENTS: Ed Mealey Construction Co., Inc.; California Teachers Association; Brooks Jewelry; Plaza Park Homeowners Association; Brock Research Center; Central Pipe Mechanical, Inc.; Abatti Produce, Inc.; Western Electrical Advertising Co., Inc.; State Farm Insurance Co.; Stoker Company.

---

## SUTHERLAND & GERBER

A PROFESSIONAL CORPORATION

*Established in 1973*

SUITE 7 THE IMPERIAL BUILDING
300 SOUTH IMPERIAL AVENUE
**EL CENTRO, CALIFORNIA 92243**
Telephone: 619-353-4444
Telefax: 619-352-2533

*General Civil and Trial Practice in all Courts. Personal Injury, Eminent Domain, Products Liability, Crop Damage, Agricultural, Business and Commercial Law.*

*(This Listing Continued)*

---

**LOWELL F. SUTHERLAND,** born Lincoln, Nebraska, December 17, 1939; admitted to bar, 1966, California. *Education:* San Diego State College (A.B., 1962); Hastings College of the Law, University of California (J.D., 1965). Member, Thurston Society. Member, Board of Editors, Hastings Law Journal, 1964-1965. *Member:* Imperial County and American Bar Associations; State Bar of California; California Trial Lawyers Association (Recognized experience in the fields of Trial Law, Personal Injury and Products Liability); The Association of Trial Lawyers of America; San Diego Trial Lawyers Association (Recipient: Outstanding Trial Lawyer Awards, April, 1981 and October, 1983; Trial Lawyer of the Year, 1982); The American Board of Trial Advocates (Associate). Certified as a Civil Trial Advocate by the National Board of Trial Advocacy. **REPORTED CASES:** Zinn v. Fred R. Bright Co., Inc.; 9 CA3d 188; 87 CR 736 (1969); Salton Bay Marina, Inc. v. Imperial Irrigation District; 172 CA3d 914; 218 CR 839 (1985); Imperial Cattle Co. v. Imperial Irrigation District; 167 CA3d 263; 213 CR 622 (1985); Beaty v. Imperial Irrigation District 186 CA3d 897; 231 CR 128 (1986); Hildre v. Imperial Irrigation District 146 CA3d 902; 194 CR 654 (1983); Wagner v. County of Imperial 145 CA3d 980; 193 CR 820 (1983). **PRACTICE AREAS:** Personal Injury Law; Business Law; Eminent Domain Litigation.

**NEIL GERBER,** born New York, N.Y., March 20, 1949; admitted to bar, 1975, California. *Education:* State University of New York at Stony Brook (B.A., summa cum laude, 1971); Hastings College of the Law, University of California (J.D., 1975). Member: Thurston Society; Order of the Coif. *Member:* State Bar of California. **LANGUAGES:** Spanish. **REPORTED CASES:** Aguirre v. Drewry Chemical Co. 162 CA3d 187; 208 CR 390 (1984); Singh v. County of Imperial Board of Retirement System 41 Cal. App. 4th 1180; 49 Cal. Rptr.2d. 220 (1996). **PRACTICE AREAS:** Business Law; Real Property Law.

**RAVINDER SAMRA,** born Calexico, California, June 2, 1953; admitted to bar, 1983, California. *Education:* University of California at Davis (B.S., 1979); Western State University (J.D., 1982). Nu Beta Epsilon. Recipient, American Jurisprudence Award in Constitutional Law. *Member:* Imperial County Bar Association; State Bar of California. **REPORTED CASES:** SKF Farms v. Superior Court, 153 CA3d 902; 200 CR 497 (1984). **PRACTICE AREAS:** Business Law; Real Property Law; Tax Law; International Law.

REFERENCES: Wells Fargo Bank National Savings and Trust Association (El Centro, California Branch).

---

## LAW OFFICES OF GARY A BACIO

EL MONTE EXECUTIVE PLAZA
11100 VALLEY BOULEVARD, SUITE 216
**EL MONTE, CALIFORNIA 91731**
Telephone: 818-452-8010
Facsimile: 818-452-1533

*General Civil Litigation, Defense of Premises, Products and Auto Liability Claims.*

**GARY A BACIO,** born Los Angeles, California, April 27, 1959; admitted to bar, 1988, California. *Education:* University of California, Los Angeles (B.A., 1981); Loyola Law School (J.D., 1984). *Member:* State Bar of California. **PRACTICE AREAS:** Insurance Defense Law (65%); Personal Injury Law (20%); Business Law (10%); Wrongful Termination-Employment at Will (5%).

#### OF COUNSEL

**DANIEL P. AGUILERA,** born Los Angeles, California, September 5, 1954; admitted to bar, 1983, California and U.S. District Court, Central District of California. *Education:* University of California at Los Angeles (B.A., 1976); Loyola Marymount University (J.D., 1982). Law Clerk to Manuel L. Real, U.S. District Court Judge, 1982-1983. *Member:* Los Angeles County, Federal and American Bar Associations; The State Bar of California.

## MICHAEL B. MONTGOMERY
A LAW CORPORATION
Established in 1963
*10501 VALLEY BOULEVARD, SUITE 121*
**EL MONTE, CALIFORNIA 91731**
Telephone: 818-452-1222
Fax: 818-452-8323

*Ft. Lauderdale, Florida Office:* Justice Building, 524 S. Andrews Avenue, Suite 320 N. Telephone: 954-522-9441. Fax: 954-522-2076.

*Civil and Trial Practice in State and Federal Courts. Eminent Domain, Municipal Bond, Community Development, Municipal and Real Property Law, Gaming Law.*

**MICHAEL B. MONTGOMERY,** born Santa Barbara, California, September 12, 1936; admitted to bar, 1963, California; 1971, U.S. Supreme Court; 1986, Hawaii; 1987, Florida. *Education:* University of California at Los Angeles (B.S., 1960); University of Southern California (J.D., 1963). Phi Delta Phi. Attorney, Division of Highways Legal Department, State of California, 1963-1965. Special Counsel, Redevelopment Agency: City of Commerce, 1969-1982; Santa Fe Springs, 1970-1982; City of Duarte, 1975-1982; Monrovia, 1977-1982; Irwindale, 1987-1988; Lake Elsinore, 1992—; Norco, 1994—. City Councilman, 1970-1974, 1980-1984; Mayor, 1980-1981, South Pasadena. Member, Redevelopment Agency, City of South Pasadena, 1972-1974; 1980-1984 and Chairman, 1982-1984. Agency Attorney, Redevelopment Agency: Monterey Park, 1973-1981; Irwindale Community, 1976-1982; Huntington Park, 1979-1992; Walnut, 1980—; South El Monte, 1988-1991. City Attorney: City of Bradbury, 1977-1980; Diamond Bar, 1993-1995. Member: Governor's State of California Infrastructure Review Task Force, 1983-1990. California Fair Political Practices Commission, 1985-1989. U.S. Commissioner, International Commission for the Conservation of Atlantic Tuna, 1985-1994. Member, Pacific Regional Fishery Management Council, 1991-1994. *Member:* Los Angeles County (Member, Committee on Condemnation Procedures), Pasadena, Hawaii State and American (Chairman, Subcommittee on Housing and Community Development, 1983-1984) Bar Associations; State Bar of California; The Florida Bar (Member, Eminent Domain Committee). (Also Of Counsel, Forman, Krehl and Montgomery, Ft. Lauderdale, Florida). **LANGUAGES:** Spanish.

COUNSEL FOR: S.A. Titan Group, Inc.; Quadreatech Corp.

## McGARRY & LAUFENBERG
*300 NORTH SEPULVEDA BOULEVARD, SUITE 2294*
**EL SEGUNDO, CALIFORNIA 90245**
Telephone: 310-335-1780
Fax: 310-335-1790

*Personal Injury Defense and Insurance Law, Probate and Estate Planning, Wills and Trusts, Taxation, Business and Commercial Litigation.*

### MEMBERS OF FIRM

**JAMES J. MCGARRY,** born Inglewood, California, April 29, 1953; admitted to bar, 1980, California; U.S. District Court, Central and Northern Districts of California. *Education:* Loyola University of Los Angeles (B.B.A., magna cum laude, 1975; J.D., 1979). Alpha Sigma Nu. Member, Scaffold Industry Association. *Member:* State Bar of California; Association of Southern California Defense Counsel. **PRACTICE AREAS:** Personal Injury Defense; Products Liability; Insurance Law.

**JEFFREY J. LAUFENBERG,** born Warren, Ohio, March 15, 1955; admitted to bar, 1980, California; 1981, U.S. District Court, Central District of California; U.S. Court of Appeals, Ninth Circuit. *Education:* Loyola University of Los Angeles (B.B.A., 1977; J.D., with honors, 1980). Recipient, Honorary Scholarship for Excellence in the Study of Law, 1979. *Member:* Los Angeles County Bar Association; State Bar of California; Association of Southern California Defense Counsel. **PRACTICE AREAS:** Personal Injury Defense; Products Liability; Insurance Law; Commercial Litigation; Real Estate.

**WILLIAM LEAMON CUMMINGS,** born Springfield, Illinois, June 22, 1954; admitted to bar, 1986, California; 1989, U.S. District Court, Central and Southern Districts of California. *Education:* University of Chicago (B.A., with honors, 1976); Johns Hopkins University (M.A., 1978); Loyola Law School (J.D., magna cum laude, 1985). Alpha Sigma Nu; St. Thomas More Law Society. Adjunct Professor, Glendale University College of Law, 1990-1992. *Member:* State Bar of California; Association of Southern Cali-

*(This Listing Continued)*

fornia Defense Counsel. **PRACTICE AREAS:** Personal Injury; Insurance Coverage; Bad Faith; Probate; Bankruptcy.

### ASSOCIATES

**DANIEL D. LAUFENBERG,** born Burbank, California, August 20, 1958; admitted to bar, 1983, California; 1984, U.S. District Court, Central District of California; 1984, U.S. Tax Court. *Education:* Stanford University (A.B., 1980); Loyola Law School, Loyola Marymount University (J.D., cum laude, 1983). Member, St. Thomas More Law Honor Society; Moot Court Honors. Recipient, American Jurisprudence Award in Real Property. Author: "Corporate Joint Ventures," NYU/RIA Conference on Corporate Tax Planning, 1984. *Member:* American Bar Association (Member: Forum Committee on Entertainment and Sports; Sections on Real Property, Probate and Trust Law, Taxation and Corporation, Banking and Business Law). **PRACTICE AREAS:** Probate and Estate Planning; Wills and Trusts; Taxation; Personal Injury; Insurance Law; Commercial Transactions; Real Estate.

**JOHN E. ZEGEL,** born East Islip, New York, October 1, 1957; admitted to bar, 1984, California. *Education:* Hofstra University (B.B.A., 1979); Southwestern University (J.D., 1982); Temple University (LL.M., 1983). *Member:* Los Angeles County Bar Association; State Bar of California. **PRACTICE AREAS:** Personal Injury Defense; Products Liability; Insurance Law; Construction Defects.

REPRESENTATIVE CLIENTS: State Farm Insurance Companies; Countrywide Services, Inc.; U.S. Scaffold & Ladder Associates, Inc.; Carl Warren & Company; Panda Inn Restaurants; Sears, Roebuck & Co.; DHL Airways, Inc.; AIG Claims Services, Inc.; California Insurance Guarantee Association; Orange County Scaffold, Inc.; Rolla Scaffold & Equipment; Sunect Ladder Company; Masterson Scaffold; Electric Insurance Company; Powermatic Power Tools; Evanston Insurance Co.; BET Plant Services, Inc.; AON Risk Services of Ohio; Homestead Insurance Company; Fontier Insurance Co.; McKesson Corp.; St. Paul Fire & Marine; A-1 Plank & Scaffold; Hunter Engineering Co.; Hill Crane Service; Allegiance Insurance Company; Horance Mann Insurance Company.

## HOWARD B. MILLER
*2101 ROSECRANS AVENUE, SUITE 5252*
**EL SEGUNDO, CALIFORNIA 90245**
Telephone: 310-607-0003
Fax: 310-607-0005
Email: hbm@netcom.com

*Mediation and Arbitration, Civil Trials, Appellate, Intellectual Property, Patents, Copyright, Trademarks, Trade Secrets, Venture Capitol, Real Estate, Bankruptcy.*

**HOWARD B. MILLER,** born Newark, New Jersey, July 11, 1937; admitted to bar, 1961, California. *Education:* Pepperdine College (B.A., 1957); University of Chicago (J.D., 1960). Order of the Coif; Phi Alpha Delta. Editor-in-Chief, University of Chicago Law Review, 1959-1960. Law Clerk to Justice Roger J. Traynor, Supreme Court of California, 1960-1961. Lecturer, 1965-1966, Associate Professor, 1966-1969, and Professor of Law, 1969-1977, University of Southern California. Principal Advocate, "The Advocates," Public Broadcasting System, 1969-1973. President, Los Angeles Board of Education, 1977-1979. Member, National Panel of Arbitrators, American Arbitration Association, 1977—. Founder and Co-Chair, USC Law Center Financial Services Institute, 1993. Instructor, Emory Law School. NITA Trial Techniques Program, 1990—. Member, Association of Attorney Mediators, 1995—. *Member:* Los Angeles County and American Bar Associations; The State Bar of California.

REFERENCE: Wells Fargo Bank (Beverly Hills).

## OHASHI & PRIVER
*222 N. SEPULVEDA BOULEVARD*
*20TH FLOOR*
**EL SEGUNDO, CALIFORNIA 90245**
Telephone: 310-364-5215
Facsimile: 310-364-5217

*Pasadena, California Office:* 215 North Marengo Avenue. Suite 225. 91101. Telephone: 818-584-1107. Facsimile: 818-356-7414.

*Business and Corporate Law. Real Estate, Federal and State Securities, Commerical and Tax Litigation.*

(For biographical data on all Personnel, see Professional Biographies at Pasadena)

## BECHERER BEERS MURPHY KANNETT & SCHWEITZER

2200 POWELL STREET, SUITE 805
**EMERYVILLE, CALIFORNIA 94608**
Telephone: 510-658-3600
Fax: 510-658-1151
URL: http://www.bechererbeers.com

*Civil Trial and Litigation.*

**FIRM PROFILE:** The firm, which was founded in 1995, engages in a general civil litigation practice with an emphasis on civil jury trials in federal and state courts. The firm's practice includes product liability, employment, toxic tort, environmental, construction, premises liability, insurance coverage, insurance bad faith, professional liability, and commercial litigation.

### MEMBERS OF FIRM

**PATRICK J. BECHERER,** born St. Louis, Missouri, June 26, 1943; admitted to bar, 1972, California. *Education:* Wabash College (A.B., 1965); University of Michigan (J.D., 1968). Law Clerk, California Superior Court, County of Alameda, Judge Robert Bostick, 1972; Judge Lionel Wilson, 1973. Associate, American Board of Trial Advocates. *Member:* The State Bar of California (Member, Litigation Section); American Bar Association (Member, Litigation and Tort and Insurance Practice Sections); Defense Research Institute; Association for the Advancement of Automotive Medicine. Fellow, American College of Trial Lawyers. **PRACTICE AREAS:** Litigation. **Email:** pjb@bechererbeers.com

**JOHN L. BEERS,** born Fort Bragg, North Carolina, June 7, 1951; admitted to bar, 1976, California. *Education:* Stanford University (B.A., 1973); University of California at Los Angeles School of Law (J.D., 1976). *Member:* Bar Association of San Francisco (Member, Labor and Employment Law Section); Alameda County Bar Association; The State Bar of California (Member, Employment Law Section). **PRACTICE AREAS:** Employment Litigation. **Email:** jlb@bechererbeers.com

**MARK S. KANNETT,** born Chicago, Illinois, January 20, 1951; admitted to bar, 1982, California. *Education:* University of Colorado (B.A., 1972); Hastings College of the Law, University of California (J.D., cum laude, 1982). Recipient, American Jurisprudence Award in Constitutional Law. *Member:* Bar Association of San Francisco; State Bar of California (Member, Litigation Section); American Bar Association (Member, Litigation and Tort and Insurance Practice Sections). **PRACTICE AREAS:** Litigation; Professional Liability; Insurance Coverage; Bad Faith Litigation; Environmental Law. **Email:** msk@bechererbeers.com

**TIMOTHY J. MURPHY,** born Longmont, Colorado, June 13, 1947; admitted to bar, 1972, California. *Education:* Stanford University (A.B., 1969); University of Colorado at Boulder (J.D., 1972). Comments Editor, University of Colorado Law Review, 1971-1972. Law Clerk to Honorable Spencer Williams, U.S. District Judge, Northern District of California, 1972-1974. *Member:* Alameda County Bar Association (Litigation and Labor and Employment Sections); The State Bar of California (Member, Employment Law Section). **PRACTICE AREAS:** Commercial Litigation; Employment Litigation. **Email:** tjm@bechererbeers.com

**LORI A. SCHWEITZER,** born Garden City, New York, October 8, 1956; admitted to bar, 1982, California. *Education:* State University of New York (B.A., 1977); Hastings College of the Law, University of California (J.D., 1982). *Member:* American Bar Association (Member, Sections on: Litigation, Tort and Insurance); The State Bar of California (Member, Litigation Section). **PRACTICE AREAS:** Product Liability Litigation; Insurance Coverage and Bad Faith Litigation. **Email:** las@bechererbeers.com

### ASSOCIATES

**KIRSTEN KOMOROSKE,** born Napa, California, April 8, 1966; admitted to bar, 1992, California. *Education:* University of California at Berkeley (B.A., 1989); Santa Clara University (J.D., 1992). **Email:** kak@bechererbeers.com

**SUSAN STOCKDALE,** born Bethesda, Maryland, August 23, 1965; admitted to bar, 1992, California. *Education:* University of Colorado, Boulder (B.A., 1987); Santa Clara University (J.D., 1991). **Email:** sls@bechererbeers.com

**SARAH VALENTINE,** born New London, Connecticut, January 14, 1961; admitted to bar, 1992, California and U.S. District Court, Northern and Central Districts of California. *Education:* Smith College (B.A., 1983); Suffolk University Law School (J.D., cum laude, 1991). Chair, 1993 and Vice-Chair, 1992, Bridging the Gap Program for Barrister's Club. *Member:*

*(This Listing Continued)*

Bar Association of San Francisco; State Bar of California. **Email:** sjv@bechererbeers.com

REPRESENTATIVE CLIENTS: The Regents of The University of California; Mazda Motor of America, Inc.; American Suzuki Motor Corporation; CNA Insurance Companies; Bridgestone/Firestone, Inc.; Hartford Insurance Co.; Pacific Gas & Electric Co.; Sybase, Inc.; AirTouch Communications; Illinois Tool Works, Inc.; The Heil Company; Tarata Corporation; Tokai Rika Co., Ltd.; Mitsubishi Motors Corporation.

## LAW OFFICES OF LYNN ANDERSON KOLLER

**EMERYVILLE, CALIFORNIA**

(See Oakland)

*Bankruptcy and Reorganization. General Civil Trial and Appellate Practice in all State and Federal Courts. Real Estate and Commercial Business Law. Civil Litigation.*

## LEGAL STRATEGIES GROUP

5905 CHRISTIE AVENUE
**EMERYVILLE, CALIFORNIA 94608**
Telephone: 510-450-9600
Fax: 510-450-9601
URL: http://www.legalstrategies.com/lsgdemoindex3.html

*Litigation, Alternative Dispute Resolution, Pre-litigation Counseling, and Intellectual Property Counseling, Licensing and Prosecution.*

**FIRM PROFILE:** Legal Strategies Group's practice is business litigation and counseling for individuals and corporations. The firm tries cases, and works closely with its clients to develop overall legal strategies which are consistent with long-term business objectives. Litigation practice areas in trial and appellate courts include: commercial disputes, antitrust, director and officer liability, professional malpractice, real estate claims, trade secrets, insurance coverage, patent, copyright and trademark claims, employment, securities disputes, environmental claims, construction disputes, financial fraud and criminal defense. Intellectual property representation includes: trademark and copyright counseling, licensing and prosecution. Special emphasis on antitrust, distribution practices and brand protection.

**TIMOTHY R. CAHN,** born Charleston, West Virginia, October 15, 1962; admitted to bar, 1992, California. *Education:* Westminster College (B.A., summa cum laude, 1984); Harvard University (J.D.,cum laude, 1990). Author: "The Law of Asylum in the United States," American Immigration Lawyers Association, 1989. Harvard Human Rights Journal, 1988-1990. Law Clerk to the Honorable Max Rosenn, U.S. Court of Appeals, Third Circuit, 1990-1991.

**JOSHUA R. FLOUM,** born Frankfurt, West Germany, May 14, 1958; admitted to bar, 1983, California. *Education:* University of California at Berkeley (A.B., with highest honors, 1980); Harvard University (J.D., cum laude, 1983). Phi Beta Kappa. Author: "Legality and Ideology," Harvard International Review, Vol. V., No. 3, December 1982; "What Role for Law in the Process of International Relations," 24 Harvard International Law Journal, 256, 1983; "The Federal Rights of Patients at Kalaupapa," 6 University of Hawaii Law Review 507, 1984; "Who's Left Standing," Recorder Environmental Law, September 1992; "Exporting Environmentalism," 3 Environmental Law News 4, 1994; "Counterfeiting in the People's Republic of China," 28 Journal of World Trade 35, 1994. Co-Author: "Theories of Attorney's Liability and Securities Transactions: The Past Year," (with Douglas M. Schwab), 359 Litigation and Practice Series 532, Practicing Law Institute 1988, Law Clerk to Hon. A. Wallace Tashima, U.S. District Court, Central District of California, 1983-1984. Litigation Counsel, Earth Island Institute, 1988—. **PRACTICE AREAS:** Antitrust, Intellectual Property, International Trade and Wildlife Litigation. **Email:** jrf@lsg.mhs.compuserve.com

**KAREN S. FRANK,** born New Haven, Connecticut, November 30, 1951; admitted to bar, 1987, California. *Education:* Connecticut College (B.A., 1973); Hastings College of the Law (J.D., 1987). Executive Articles Editor, COMM/ENT law Review, 1986-1987. *Member:* State Bar of California; American Bar Association; Copyright Society of the USA (Trustee, 1992-1996).

**GREGORY S. GILCHRIST,** born Detroit, Michigan, March 5, 1958; admitted to bar, 1983, California. *Education:* University of Michigan (B.A., 1980; J.D., 1983). Order of the Coif. Member, Michigan Law Review, 1981-

*(This Listing Continued)*

1983. *Member:* State Bar of California; American Bar Association. *Email:* gsg@lsg.mhs.compuserve.com

**PETER H. GOLDSMITH,** born Highland Park, Illinois, April 12, 1952; admitted to bar, 1979, California. *Education:* Yale University (B.A., 1974); University of California at Berkeley (J.D., 1978). Order of the Coif. California Law Review, 1976-1978. Law Clerk to the Honorable Albert C. Wollenberg, Sr., U.S. District Court, Northern District of California, 1979-1980. *Member:* State Bar of California; American Bar Association. *Email:* phg@lsg.mhs.compuserve.com

**VINCENT L. JOHNSON,** born Richmond, Virginia, August 21, 1958; admitted to bar, 1983, Virginia; 1984, District of Columbia; 1986, California. *Education:* Princeton University (B.A., 1980); University of California at Berkeley (J.D., 1983). *Member:* American Bar Association; Virginia State Bar; State Bar of California.

**LEIGH A. KIRMSSÉ,** born San Francisco, California, July 24, 1958; admitted to bar, 1992, California. *Education:* San Jose State University (B.A., 1989); Loyola Law School (J.D., 1992). Order of the Coif. Executive Editor, Loyola of Los Angeles Law Review, 1991-1992. *Member:* State Bar of California; American Bar Association (Member, Sections on: Trial Lawyers; Intellectual Property; Products Liability). *PRACTICE AREAS:* Complex Litigation; Intellectual Property; Insurance and Products Liability. *Email:* lak@lsg.mhs.compuserve.com

**LOUISE E. MA,** born Philadelphia, Pennsylvania, December 25, 1952; admitted to bar, 1978, California; 1979, Alaska. *Education:* University of California at Berkeley (A.B., College of Letters and Science, 1974; A.B., School of Journalism, 1974); University of San Francisco School of Law (J.D., 1978). Assistant Attorney General, Antitrust Division, State of Alaska, 1978-1983. Assistant Public Advocate, Office of Public Advocacy, Alaska Attorney General's Office, 1985-1987. *Member:* State Bar of California; Alaska Bar Association (Member, Alaska Committee of Bar Examiners, 1985-1987); American Bar Association; National Association of Criminal Defense Lawyers.

**HEATHER A. YOUNG,** born April 17, 1965; admitted to bar, 1991, California. *Education:* University of Virginia (B.A., 1986; J.D., 1991). Member, Editorial Board, University of Virginia Law Review, 1990-1991. *Member:* State Bar of California; American Bar Association (Member, Antitrust Section). *PRACTICE AREAS:* Intellectual Property; Antitrust; Complex Litigation; Appellate. *Email:* hay@lsg.mhs.compuserve.com

*OF COUNSEL*

**ROBERT J. VIZAS,** born Ann Arbor, Michigan, January 20, 1947; admitted to bar, 1973, California. *Education:* University of Michigan (B.A., 1968); Yale University (J.D., 1972). Law Clerk to the Honorable Charles B. Renfrew, U.S. District Court, Northern District of California, 1972. *Member:* Bar Association of San Francisco; State Bar of California.

REPRESENTATIVE CLIENTS: Levi Strauss & Co.; Raychem Corporation; Tektronix, Inc.; Telecommunications, Inc.

---

## JAMES JAY SELTZER

*WATERGATE TOWERS, TENTH FLOOR*
*2200 POWELL STREET*
**EMERYVILLE, CALIFORNIA 94608**
Telephone: 510-596-2500
Telecopier: 510-596-2519
Email: medlawline@aol.com

*Administrative Law.*

**JAMES JAY SELTZER,** born 1948; admitted to bar, 1972, California; 1983, New York; 1985, District of Columbia. *Education:* University of California; Loyola University of Los Angeles. *Member:* State Bar of California; New York State Bar Association; District of Columbia Bar. *LANGUAGES:* French and Japanese. *PRACTICE AREAS:* Administrative Law; Criminal Law; Military Law; Medicare; Medicaid; Securities Law.

---

## KEVIN K. FORRESTER

*Established in 1987*

*4403 MANCHESTER AVENUE, SUITE 205*
**ENCINITAS, CALIFORNIA 92024-7903**
Telephone: 619-944-1918
Fax: 619-944-3517
Email: kkf@cts.com

*Real Estate and Business Law, Sports Law, Alternative Dispute Resolution.*

FIRM PROFILE: Kevin K. Forrester practices exclusively in the areas of real estate, business and sports law, with emphasis upon negotiated agreements, planning, and alternative dispute resolution through mediation and arbitration.

**KEVIN K. FORRESTER,** born Beaver Dam, Wisconsin, June 14, 1957; admitted to bar, 1987, California, U.S. District Court, Southern District of California and U.S. Court of Appeals, Ninth Circuit; 1991, U.S. Supreme Court. *Education:* University of California at San Diego (B.A., 1980); University of San Diego (J.D., 1986). Member, San Diego Law Review, 1985-1986. Recipient, American Jurisprudence Award for Excellence in Contracts. Real Estate Broker, California, 1983—. Judge Pro Tem, San Diego Municipal Court, North County Judicial District. *Member:* San Diego County and Northern San Diego County Bar Associations; State Bar of California; Southern California Mediation Association; Institute of Sports Attorneys. *SPECIAL AGENCIES:* Associate, William B. Enright American Inn of Court, 1992.

REPRESENTATIVE CLIENTS: UCSD Alumni Association.
REFERENCE: Rancho Santa Fe National Bank.

---

## LARSEN & CRICKMORE

*A PROFESSIONAL ASSOCIATION*
*655 SECOND STREET*
**ENCINITAS, CALIFORNIA 92024-3507**
Telephone: 619-634-2800
Facsimile: 619-634-2569
Email: clarsen@ix.netcom.com

*Civil Litigation, Fiduciary Services, Public Agency, Probate, Estate Planning, Collections.*

**CHRISTOPHER LARSEN,** born Oakland, California, October 6, 1951; admitted to bar, 1977, California and U.S. District Court, Northern District of California; 1978, U.S. District Court, Southern District of California; 1981, U.S. Supreme Court; 1983, U.S. District Court, Central District of California; 1986, U.S. Court of Appeals, Ninth Circuit; 1987, U.S. Claims Court; 1988, U.S. District Court, Eastern District of California. *Education:* Brigham Young University (B.A., cum laude, 1974); George Washington University (J.D., with honors, 1977). Author: "You Can't Get There From Here: Service of Process Abroad and Fast Track," DICTA Magazine, December, 1992. Volunteer Commissioner Pro Tem, San Diego Municipal Court Small Claims, 1985—. *Member:* San Diego County (Chairman, Municipal Court Committee, 1989; Member, State Bar Conference of Delegates, 1990—) Bar Association; State Bar of California. *LANGUAGES:* German. *REPORTED CASES:* Bryte v. La Mesa (1989) 207 Cal.App.3d 687, 255 Cal. Rptr. 64. *PRACTICE AREAS:* Civil Litigation; Public Agency.

**JERALD D. CRICKMORE,** born La Jolla, California, November 23, 1954; admitted to bar, 1985, California. *Education:* Brigham Young University (B.A., 1980); University of San Diego (J.D., 1983). L.B.J. Scholar, U.S. House of Representatives, 1983. Co-Author: "Selected Topics in Estate Litigation," C.E.B. Course Outline, 1990. *Member:* San Diego and North San Diego County Bar Associations; State Bar of California. *LANGUAGES:* Spanish. *PRACTICE AREAS:* Fiduciary Services; Probate and Estate Planning; Transactions; Collections.

REPRESENTATIVE CLIENTS: Ramona Municipal Water District; Barratt American Incorporated; SKF Condition Monitoring, Inc.; Interspec; First Security Bank of Idaho; Pauma Valley Community Services District.

CAA185B

## CHARLES MARVIN III

*A PROFESSIONAL CORPORATION*

**120 BIRMINGHAM DRIVE, SUITE 200
ENCINITAS, CALIFORNIA 92024**
Telephone: 619-944-0123
Fax: 619-942-6176

*Real Property, Corporate, Business, Partnership and Limited Liability Companies.*

**CHARLES MARVIN III,** born New Haven, Connecticut, July 8, 1938; admitted to bar, 1968, California. *Education:* Amherst College (B.A., 1960); Boalt Hall School of Law, University of California (J.D., 1967). *Member:* Northern San Diego County (Delegate, Conference of State Bar Delegates, 1969, 1970, 1979) and American Bar Associations; State Bar of California. [Lt., USNR, active duty, 1960-1964]. **PRACTICE AREAS:** Real Property; Corporate Law; Business Law; Partnerships; Limited Liability Companies.

REPRESENTATIVE CLIENTS: Communications General Corp.; Encinitas/Carlsbad Professional Assn.; North Coast Family Medical Group, Inc.; Mitsui Fudosan (USA), Inc.; Price Costco; Santa Fe Christian Community Schools; Rancho Santa Fe Villas Condominium Association.
REFERENCE: San Dieguito National Bank.

## MITCHELL AND MURRELL

Established in 1989

**655 SECOND STREET
ENCINITAS, CALIFORNIA 92024**
Telephone: 619-753-6327
FAX: 619-753-6325

*Estate Planning, Probate, Trust Law, Business Law and Taxation.*

**DON W. MITCHELL,** born Mt. Perry, Ohio, June 22, 1928; admitted to bar, 1957, Colorado; 1958, California. *Education:* Ohio University and University of Colorado (B.S., 1954); University of Colorado (J.D., 1957). Member, 1964-1979; President, 1966-1972, San Dieguito Union High School Board of Trustees. Director, Scripps Memorial Hospital Foundation, 1981-1987. Trustee: San Dieguito Boys and Girls Clubs Foundation, 1981; Scripps Health Corp., 1989. *Member:* North San Diego County (Member, Board of Directors, 1965-1968; Vice President, 1967-1968), San Diego County and American Bar Associations; The State Bar of California. [Lt., USNR, 1948-1953]. **PRACTICE AREAS:** Estate Planning; Probate.

**GREGORY L. MURRELL,** born Portland, Oregon, September 12, 1942; admitted to bar, 1978, California and U.S. District Court, Southern District of California; 1981, U.S. Tax Court. *Education:* Oregon State University (B.S., 1965); California Western School of Law (J.D., 1977); Boston University (LL.M., in Taxation, 1978). *Member:* North San Diego County and San Diego County Bar Associations; The State Bar of California. [Lt., USN Naval Aviator, 1965-1974]. (Certified Specialist, Probate, Estate Planning and Trust Law, The State Bar of California Board of Legal Specialization). **PRACTICE AREAS:** Estate Planning; Probate; Trust Law; Tax Law.

REFERENCES: Bank of America National Trust & Savings Assn., Encinitas Branch; Union Bank, Encinitas Branch; Encinitas Chamber of Commerce.

## AARONSON & AARONSON

**16133 VENTURA BOULEVARD, SUITE 1080
ENCINO, CALIFORNIA 91436**
Telephone: 818-783-3858; 818-783-0444
Fax: 818-783-3873; 818-783-3825

*General Civil and Trial Practice. Commercial, Commercial and Industrial Leasing, Corporation, Business, Real Property, Family, Entertainment, Partnership, Pension and Profit Sharing, State and Federal Taxation, Estate Planning, Trust and Probate Law.*

### MEMBERS OF FIRM

**EDWARD D. AARONSON,** born Boston, Massachusetts, July 21, 1946; admitted to bar, 1972, California. *Education:* University of California at Los Angeles (B.A., 1968); University of New Mexico (J.D., 1971). *Member:* Los Angeles County and American Bar Associations; The State Bar of California; International Council of Shopping Centers. **PRACTICE AREAS:** Retail and Commercial Leasing; Real Estate.

*(This Listing Continued)*

**ARTHUR AARONSON,** born Los Angeles, California, March 22, 1949; admitted to bar, 1975, California. *Education:* University of California at Los Angeles (B.A. summa cum laude, 1971); University of Southern California (J.D., 1975). Phi Beta Kappa; Order of the Coif. Author: "The Disfavored Indirect Purchaser Under the Robinson-Patman Act: Can the Small Businessman Survive?" 48 University of Southern California Law Review 899, 1975; "Minimum Funding for Defined Benefit Plans," Bender's Federal Tax Service, Chapter C:11, 1989; "Prohibited Transactions and Loans From Qualified Plans," California Closely Held Corporations, Chapter 14, 1987. Member Panel of Arbitrators, Los Angeles Superior Court and American Arbitration Association. *Member:* Los Angeles County and American Bar Associations; The State Bar of California. **LANGUAGES:** Italian. **PRACTICE AREAS:** Business Law; Real Estate; Probate; Civil Litigation; Corporation.

### ASSOCIATES

**STEVEN J. BERMAN,** born Kansas City, Kansas, August 12, 1957; admitted to bar, 1985, California. *Education:* California State University at Northridge (B.A., 1980); Western State University (J.D., 1983). *Member:* State Bar of California (Member, Real Estate Section).

REPRESENTATIVE CLIENTS: Scottish & Newcastle Importers Co.; Contempo Casuals; Howard & Phil Enterprises, Inc.; Downey Glass Company; Sky Controls, Inc.; Bernini, Inc. Bertoni, Inc.; Panda Management, Inc.; L.C. Enterprises, Inc.; Food Gallery, Inc.; American Institute of Graphic Arts/L.A. Sierra Pacific Apparel Co.; Pastille, Inc.; Guess ?, Inc.; Charles David Shoes of California, Inc.; Panda Express, Inc.; Entertainment Radio Network, Inc.

## ALPERT, BARR AND GROSS

*A PROFESSIONAL LAW CORPORATION*

Established in 1976

**ENCINO OFFICE PARK I
SUITE 300, 6345 BALBOA BOULEVARD
ENCINO, CALIFORNIA 91316-1523**
Telephone: 818-881-5000
Fax: 818-881-1150

*General Civil Trial and Appellate Practice. Business, Corporate, Banking, Estate Planning and Administration, Family Law, Arbitration and Mediation, Mobile Home Residency Law, and Governmental Relations and Administrative Hearings.*

FIRM PROFILE: Alpert, Barr & Gross, A Professional Law Corporation, is a full service law firm with the emphasis on the word "service". The Firm was founded in July of 1976 and has become one of the most respected and well established firms in the Los Angeles area. Our goal is to meet the client's legal needs by providing the highest quality representation in an expeditious, professional manner and matter on a personal basis. The Firm's lawyers are experienced in various areas of the law, and clients are directed to the firm member who can best assist their particular needs.

**LEE KANON ALPERT,** born Detroit, Michigan, October 19, 1946; admitted to bar, 1972, California; 1974, U.S. District Court, Central District of California; 1984, U.S. Supreme Court. *Education:* Wayne State University; University of Southern California (B.S. in Education, 1971); Loyola University of Los Angeles School of Law (J.D., 1972). Omicron Delta Kappa. Member: National Honors Society; St. Thomas Moore Honors Society. Co-Author: "Practical Guide for Attorneys in Using Mediation to Resolve Business, Commercial and Construction Disputes," Los Angeles Lawyer, May, 1986; "Mediation: Strategies for Better Dispute Resolution," American Arbitration Association National Publication, 1987. Associate and Contributing Editor: Los Angeles County Bar Association Family Law Quarterly, 1982-1983. Lecturer, Instructor: Business Law, California State University at Northridge, 1980-1984; Los Angeles County Forum of Legal Secretaries Family Law Seminars, 1981-1985; Seminar on New Practices and Procedures in Family Law, San Fernando Valley Bar Association, 1984; San Fernando Valley Legal Secretaries Association Law Seminars, 1981, 1982 and 1987; Los Angeles Superior Court Family Law Colloquium, 1981-1983. Faculty Member: American Arbitration Association, 1981—. Chair, Los Angeles City Council Twelfth District Citizens Advisory Council, 1982—. Member, Board of Directors, Temple Ahavat Shalom, 1982-1987. Chair, Citizens Advisory Task Force for the Development of the North Campus at California State University at Northridge, 1984—. Member, California State Senate Task Force on Revisions to the Family Law Act, 1986-1988. Member, President's Constituency Board, California State University, Northridge, 1993—. Member, 1989— and President, 1995—, President's University Advisory Board, California State University, Northridge. Member, Board of Directors, 1983-1990 and President, 1987-

*(This Listing Continued)*

1989, California State University at Northridge Athletic Association. Member, Board of Directors, Los Angeles County Law Library, 1987-1989. Commissioner: City of Los Angeles Building & Safety Commission, 1996—; City of Los Angeles Bicentennial of U.S. Constitution Commission, 1986-1990. Commissioner, 1989—and Chair, 1991-1992, Los Angeles County Commission on Judicial Procedures, 1989—. President, We The People of Los Angeles Foundation, 1987-1994. Member, Board of Directors, 1988— and Vice Chair, 1991-1993, AMI/Tarzana Regional Medical Center. Member and Chair, Board of Directors, Encino-Tarzana Regional Medical Center (Hospital), 1993—. Member, 1987-1992 and Chair, 1989-1991, Van Nuys Airport Citizens Advisory Council. Member, Board of Directors: San Fernando Valley Business and Professional Association, 1989-1993; New Directions For Youth, 1991—. Member, 1992— and Chair, 1992-1996, California State Senate Small Business Advisory Commission, 1992—. Commissioner, California State Commission on the future of the Legal Profession and the State Bar, 1993-1995. Approved Member of the Faculty, California Association of Realtors, 1993—. Approved Faculty, Construction Specifications Institute, Alexandria, Virginia, 1994. Executive Producer and Host, Parallax Forum Public Affairs Weekly Los Angeles Television Program, 1993—. Member, 1993—, President, 1995—, Board of Directors, prestigious Fernando Award, Inc. Member, West Coast Advisory Council for the American Arbitration Association, 1983—. Judge Pro Tempore, Los Angeles Superior and Municipal Courts, 1982—. First West Coast Mediator, American Arbitration Association. Commercial and Construction Arbitrator and Mediator, American Arbitration Association. Founding Member, Executive Committee, San Fernando Valley Chapter Inn of Court, 1987-1991. Member, 1985—and President, 1991—, Valley Community Legal Foundation. *Member:* San Fernando Valley (President, 1985-1986; Chair, Family Law Section, 1980-1981), Los Angeles County (Trustee, 1984-1985; Member, Special Committee on Public Counsel, 1984-1985; Family Law Section, 1980—; Bench and Bar Media Liaison Committee, 1985—; Member and Secretary, Judicial Evaluations Committee, 1983-1986; Member, Committee on the Bicentennial of the United States Constitution, 1988-1992) and American (Member, Family Law Section, 1980-1992) Bar Associations; State Bar of California. *PRACTICE AREAS:* Arbitration and Mediation; Business and Civil Litigation; Commercial and Construction Law; Family Law; Governmental Relations Law.

**GARY L. BARR,** born Culver City, California, May 8, 1953; admitted to bar, 1977, California and U.S. District Court, Central, Northern, Eastern and Southern Districts of California. *Education:* University of California at Los Angeles (B.A. in Political Science, 1974); Southwestern University (J.D., 1977). Member, Moot Court: Roger Traynor Interschool Competition, Third Place; Outstanding Advocate, Schweitzer Intraschool, 1975. Staff Member, 1975-1976 and Note and Comment Editor, 1976-1977, Southwestern Law Review. Author: "Onshore Impacts of Offshore Drilling: The Police Power Alternative," 8 Sw. U.L. Rev. 967, 1976. Deputy City Attorney, Los Angeles, 1977-1979 and 1980-1982. Judge Pro Tem: Los Angeles Municipal Court, 1983—; Los Angeles Superior Court, 1993—. Family Law Mediator, 1983-1987. Judicial Clerk in Los Angeles Municipal Court, 1975. Intern for United Senate Senator Alan Cranston, 1974. Woodland Hills Chamber of Commerce, 1988-1995 (Board of Directors, 1991-1997; President, 1996; Vice President, 1993-1995; Chair of Government Affairs Committee, 1986-1994). *Member:* San Fernando Valley (Member: President 1991-1992; President Elect, 1991; Secretary, 1990-1991; Treasurer, 1989-1990; Trustee, 1986-1990; Vice Chairman, Civil Litigation Section, 1986-1987; Chairman, Law Day Program, 1985-1987, 1988-1989; Program Chairman, 1987-1988; Vice-President, Governmental Affairs, United Chamber of Commerce, 1993-1994) and Los Angeles County (Board of Trustees, 1991-1992; Member, Pre-Trial Litigation Section; Vice Chair, Executive Committee, Fee Arbitration Panel, 1995-1996) Bar Associations; State Bar of California; San Fernando Valley Legal Foundation (Board of Trustees, 1991-1992); San Fernando Valley Bar Association Settlement Services Corporation (Board of Directors, 1991-1992); California Manufactured Housing Institute (Vice Chair, 1995-1997; Treasurer, 1993-1995); Tree People of Los Angeles (Board of Directors, 1993—); Woodland Hills/West Hills Neighborhood Planning Advisory Council (Member, 1994-1996). *PRACTICE AREAS:* Civil Litigation; Commercial Trial Litigation; Creditors Rights in Bankruptcy.

**LISA W. GLAZENER,** born Los Angeles, California, July 16, 1953; admitted to bar, 1978, California; 1979, U.S. District Court, Central District of California; 1984, U.S. Supreme Court; 1985, U.S. District Court, Northern, Southern and Eastern Districts of California and U.S. Court of Appeals, Ninth Circuit. *Education:* Stanford University (B.A., 1975); Loyola University (J.D., 1978). Phi Alpha Delta. Loyola Law Review, 1977-1978. Member and President, 1993-1994, Soroptimist International. Member, Valley Industry and Commerce Association, 1992—. *Member:* San

*(This Listing Continued)*

Fernando Valley Bar Association; State Bar of California; Stanford Professional Women; Business and Professional Women of the San Fernando Valley; International Guiding Eyes (Member, Board of Directors). *PRACTICE AREAS:* Civil Trial Law; Appellate Practice.

**MARK P. GROSS,** born Brooklyn, New York, December 4, 1960; admitted to bar, 1985, New Jersey; 1986, California. *Education:* University of Florida (B.S., 1982; J.D., 1985). Alpha Lambda Delta; Omicron Delta Kappa. Law Secretary, Hon. Alexander D. Lehrer, Superior Court Matrimonial, Monmouth Court, 1985-1986. Charter Member, San Fernando Valley Chapter Inns of Court, 1987. Member, Santa Clarita Valley Chamber of Commerce, 1991-1992. *Member:* San Fernando Valley (Chairman, Mediation Program, 1991-1993; Family Law Executive Committee, 1995—), Beverly Hills, Los Angeles County, Monmouth County, New Jersey State and American Bar Associations; State Bar of California. *PRACTICE AREAS:* Family Law.

**MARK S. BLACKMAN,** born Los Angeles, California, November 16, 1960; admitted to bar, 1985, California; 1986, U.S. District Court, Central District of California; 1990, U.S. District Court, Northern, Eastern and Southern Districts of California. *Education:* University of California at Los Angeles (B.A., 1982); Loyola Marymount University (J.D., 1985). Co-Author: "Warehouseman's Lien Rights Under the Mobilehome Residency Law Amendments of 1990," WMA Reporter, July, 1992; "Multiple Bankruptcy Filings and Creditors' Rights", Westland Review, 1994. Author: "Tax Deferred Exchanges: 1991 Treasury Regulations," San Fernando Valley Bar Bulletin, Vol. 35, No. 3 March, 1992; "Bankruptcy Court Opens San Fernando Valley Office," Lawyer's World Magazine, July/August, 1996. *Member:* Board of Governors, 1984-1994 and Secretary, 1991-1992, Loyola Law School; Executive Committee, Business Section, 1990-1994, Chairperson, Business Section, San Fernando Valley Bar Association, 1994-1995, Chairperson, Law Day, 1991-1996; Program Chair, San Fernando Valley Bar Association, 1995-1996, Treasurer, San Fernando Valley Bar Association, 1996-1997, Member, Board of Trustees, 1992-1997, San Fernando Valley Bar Association. Member, San Fernando Valley Division Opening Ceremony Committee, United States Bankruptcy Court. *Member:* Los Angeles County Bar Association; State Bar of California. *PRACTICE AREAS:* Bankruptcy/Creditors Rights; Business Law and General Litigation; Real Estate Litigation; Mobilehome Financing and Mobilehome Park Law.

**MICHAEL N. BALIKIAN,** born Pasadena, California, December 16, 1957; admitted to bar, 1983, California and U.S. District Court, Eastern District of California; 1986, U.S. District Court, Southern District of California; 1994, U.S. District Court, Northern District of California and U.S. Tax Court. *Education:* University of Arizona (B.S.B.A., 1980); McGeorge School of Law (J.D., 1983; LL.M., 1984). Phi Alpha Delta. Author: "How Should You Hold Title to Real Property," Apartment Owners Association Magazine, July 1992; "How to Reduce the Property Tax You Pay," Realtor Report, April 1992 and Apartment Owners Association Magazine, June 1992; "What is Probate and Is it Worth Avoiding," Apartment Owners Association Magazine, November 1992. *Member:* Los Angeles County Bar Association (Member, Tax and Estate Planning Sections; Delegate, Conference of Delegates of California State Bar, 1991-1993) State Bar of California (Member, Tax Section); Christian Legal Society. *PRACTICE AREAS:* Estate Planning; Transactional and Business Law; Trust and Estate Administration.

**JUDITH R. SIMON,** born Gary, Indiana, June 14, 1937; admitted to bar, 1990, California. *Education:* University of California at Los Angeles (B.S., cum laude, 1960); Southwestern University School of Law (J.D., 1989). Registered Nurse, 1960-1987. *Member:* Santa Monica, San Fernando Valley and American Bar Associations; State Bar of California. *PRACTICE AREAS:* Family Law.

**JACK S. MACK,** born Sparta, New Jersey, December 1, 1954; admitted to bar, 1994, California. *Education:* California State University, Los Angeles (B.A., 1991); Southwestern University School of Law (J.D., 1994). *Member:* San Fernando Valley Bar Association. *PRACTICE AREAS:* Family Law; Civil Litigation.

*OF COUNSEL*

**CHARLES M. HUGHES,** born Los Angeles, California, August 31, 1918; admitted to bar, 1947, California. *Education:* University of California at Los Angeles (B.A., 1940); University of Southern California (LL.B., 1947). Phi Alpha Delta. Judge of Superior Court, Retired. Individual Practitioner, 1947-1961. Deputy Attorney General, State of California, 1952. Judge: Los Angeles Municipal Court, 1961-1970; Los Angeles County Superior Court, 1971-1981. President, University of Southern California Law Alumni Association, 1954. Past Member, San Fernando Valley and Desert

*(This Listing Continued)*

**ALPERT, BARR AND GROSS,** A PROFESSIONAL LAW CORPORATION, Encino—Continued

Bar Associations. [Active Duty, With U.S. Navy Reserve, Naval Intelligence Sea Duty, 1941-1945]

**LEONARD S. LEVY, (A PROFESSIONAL CORPORATION),** born Los Angeles, California, September 14, 1948; admitted to bar, 1973, California; 1974, U.S. District Court, Central District of California; 1979, U.S. District Court, Southern District of California; 1982, U.S. District Court, Eastern District of California and U.S. Court of Appeals, Ninth Circuit. *Education:* University of California at Los Angeles (B.A., 1970); Loyola University of Los Angeles (J.D., 1973). *Member:* San Fernando Valley, Los Angeles County and American (Member, Tort and Insurance Practice Section, Fidelity and Surety Committee, Section of Business Law) Bar Associations; State Bar of California. *PRACTICE AREAS:* Business Law; Insurance Law; Surety and Fidelity Law; Business, Insurance and Real Estate Litigation.

---

## ALTMAN & SCHOEMAKER

16255 VENTURA BOULEVARD, SUITE 1110
**ENCINO, CALIFORNIA 91436**
Telephone: 818-995-0080
FAX: 818-995-3419
Email: altman.a&s@mcimail.com
URL: http://www.debtcollection.com

*General Civil and Workers Compensation Defense. Trial and Appellate Practice, Commerical Collection and Enforcement of Judgements. Products Liability and Personal Injury.*

### MEMBERS OF FIRM

**REX L. ALTMAN,** born Los Angeles, California, November 23, 1950; admitted to bar, 1986, California. *Education:* University of California at Los Angeles (B.A., 1973); University of West Los Angeles (J.D., 1986). Author: "Winning Your Case Through QME Process," Workers Compensation Quarterly, Vol. 5, No. 3, Fall, 1992. Speaker at WCDAA Convention, 1992, 1994. *Member:* State Bar of California. *PRACTICE AREAS:* Workers Compensation Defense; Commercial collections.

**CHARLES SCHOEMAKER, JR.,** born New Brunswick, New Jersey, September 19, 1951; admitted to bar, 1978, California; 1979, U.S. District Court, Central District of California; 1984, U.S. District Court, Southern District of California; 1986, U.S. Court of Appeals, Ninth Circuit; 1991, U.S. Supreme Court. *Education:* Rutgers University (B.A., 1973); University of West Los Angeles (J.D., 1978). Research Editor, 1976-1977; Notes and Comments Editor, 1977-1978, University of West Los Angeles Law Review. Judge Pro Tem: Los Angeles Municipal Court; Los Angeles Superior Court. Member, Panel of Arbitrators, Los Angeles Superior Court. *Member:* Los Angeles County Bar Association; State Bar of California. *REPORTED CASES:* Cervantes v. Great American Ins. Co. (1983) 140 CA3d 763; Schlick v. Comco Management, Inc. (1987) 196 CA3d 974. *PRACTICE AREAS:* Personal Injury Law; Products Liability Law; Government Tort Liability; Subrogation Law; Commercial Collection.

### ASSOCIATES

**M. CHRISTINA RAMIREZ,** born El Paso, Texas, November 11, 1949; admitted to bar, 1985, California. *Education:* California State University at Long Beach (B.A., 1972); University of Southern California (M.S., 1974); University of California School of Law at Los Angeles (J.D., 1983). *PRACTICE AREAS:* Workers Compensation Defense; Collections.

**DANIEL J. YSABAL,** born Los Angeles, California, March 19, 1954; admitted to bar, 1986, California. *Education:* Loyola Marymount University (B.A., 1976); Glendale University (J.D., 1983). *Member:* Los Angeles County Bar Association. *PRACTICE AREAS:* Workers Compensation Defense; Collections.

REPRESENTATIVE CLIENTS: Applied Risk Management; Care America; Carl Warren & Co.; ComCo Management, Inc.; Gallagher Bassett; Los Angeles Unified School District; HCM Claim Management; Horace Mann Insurance Co.; Southern Wine and Spirits; TIG Insurance Group; Travelers Ins. Co; Twentieth Century Fox; USF Freightways.

---

## ANKER & HYMES

A LAW CORPORATION
Established in 1974

SUITE 1200, 16311 VENTURA BOULEVARD
**ENCINO, CALIFORNIA 91436-2144**
Telephone: 818-501-5800
Telecopier: 818-501-4019

*Business, Corporate and Partnership Matters, Mergers and Acquisitions, Real Estate, Taxation, Estate Planning, Probate and Civil Litigation.*

**SAMUEL H. ANKER,** born Cleveland, Ohio, December 20, 1944; admitted to bar, 1972, California and U.S. District Court, Central District of California; 1987, U.S. Tax Court. *Education:* California State University at Northridge (B.A., 1967); University of San Fernando Valley College of Law (J.D., cum laude, 1971). Instructor, Wills, Trusts and Estate Planning, Pierce College, 1981-1990. *Member:* Beverly Hills, San Fernando Valley (Member, Probate Section) and Los Angeles County Bar Associations; State Bar of California (Member, Sections on: Business Law; Estate Planning, Trust and Probate; Real Property Law). *PRACTICE AREAS:* Real Property Law; Transactional and Business Law; Mergers and Acquisitions.

**LARRY S. HYMES,** born Los Angeles, California, July 22, 1953; admitted to bar, 1977, California; 1978, U.S. Tax Court, U.S. Claims Court, U.S. District Court, Central District of California and U.S. Court of Appeals, Ninth Circuit. *Education:* University of California at Los Angeles (B.A., 1974); University of San Diego (J.D., 1977); University of San Diego at Los Angeles (LL.M., 1980). Recipient, American Jurisprudence Award for Real Property. Judge Pro Tem, Los Angeles Superior Court, 1993—. Probate Volunteer Panel Appointed Counsel, 1993—. *Member:* San Fernando Valley, Los Angeles County and American Bar Associations; State Bar of California (Member, Business Law and Taxation Sections). *PRACTICE AREAS:* Trusts; Probate and Estate Planning; Corporate; Tax Law.

---

**JONATHAN L. ROSENBLOOM,** born Los Angeles, California, September 20, 1963; admitted to bar, 1991, California, U.S. District Court, Central District. *Education:* Northwestern University; University of California at Berkeley (A.B., 1985); Northwestern University School of Law (J.D., 1989). Articles Editor, Northwestern Journal of International Law & Business, (1988-1989). *Member:* Beverly Hills and Los Angeles Bar Associations; State Bar of California. *REPORTED CASES:* Waisbren v. Peppercorn Productions, Inc., 41 Cal. App. 4th 246, 48 Cal. Rptr 2d 437 (1995). *PRACTICE AREAS:* Business Law; Business Litigation.

### OF COUNSEL

**DOUGLAS K. SCHREIBER,** born Los Angeles, California, September 16, 1953; admitted to bar, 1978, California; 1979, U.S. District Court, Central and Southern Districts of California and U.S. Court of Appeals, Ninth Circuit. *Education:* University of Southern California (B.S., cum laude, 1975); Loyola University of Los Angeles (J.D., cum laude, 1978). Recipient: American Jurisprudence Award for Remedies. *Member:* State Bar of California. *REPORTED CASES:* Waisbren v. . Peppercorn Productions Inc., (1995) 41 Cal.App.4th 246 48 Cal. Rptr. 2d 437; Lewame vs. Franchise Tax Board (1994) 9 Cal.4th 263, 36 Cal. Rptr.2d 563 Amicus Curiae. *PRACTICE AREAS:* Business; Real Estate; Litigation.

**DANIEL B. SPITZER,** born Los Angeles, California, April 9, 1953; admitted to bar, 1985, California; 1986, U.S. District Court, Central and Southern Districts of California. *Education:* University of California at Los Angeles (B.A., summa cum laude, 1976; M.A., 1983; J.D., 1985). Phi Beta Kappa. Master of Arts in Comparative Literature, University of California at Los Angeles, 1983. Author: Comment, "Contra Goff: Of Retirement Trusts and Bankruptcy Code Section 541 (c) (2)," 32 UCLA Law Review 1266, 1985. Member, Community Associations Institute, 1993—. *Member:* Beverly Hills and Los Angeles County (Member: Commercial and Bankruptcy Prejudgment Remedies Law Sections, 1985-1984) Bar Associations; State Bar of California; Barristers (Member, Board of Governors, 1986—). *LANGUAGES:* Hebrew and Yiddish. *REPORTED CASES:* In re Bosse, 122 B. R. 410 (Bkrptcy. C.D. Cal. 1990); Okrand v. City of Los Angeles, 207 Cal. App.3d 566, 254 Cal. Rptr. 913 (1989). *PRACTICE AREAS:* Business Litigation; Real Estate; Bankruptcy and Insolvency; Condominium Law; Legal Malpractice.

REFERENCE: First Los Angeles Bank; Western Bank.

## MICHAEL ROBERT BASSIN

ENCINO, CALIFORNIA

(See Los Angeles)

*General Business, Civil Litigation, Negligence and Insurance Law, Construction, Surety and Guaranty.*

---

## THE LAW OFFICES OF DAVID H. BAUM

16255 VENTURA BOULEVARD, SUITE 704
**ENCINO, CALIFORNIA 91436-2312**
Telephone: 818-501-8355
Fax: 818-501-8465
URL: http://www.adoptlaw.com

*Adoption, Probate, Family Law.*

**DAVID H. BAUM,** admitted to bar, 1978, California and U.S. District Court, Central, Southern, Northern and Eastern Districts of California; U.S. Court of Appeals, Ninth Circuit; U.S. Supreme Court. *Education:* Brandeis University (B.A., 1975); Loyola University (J.D., 1978). Author: "Selecting the Right Adoption Attorney," Counsel, A Law Quarterly, 1990; "Ethical Payment of Birth Mother Expenses," Counsel, A Law Quarterly, 1991. *Member:* Los Angeles and San Fernando Valley Bar Associations; State Bar of California. Fellow, American Academy of Adoption Attorneys; President, Academy of California Adoption Lawyers.

---

## LEONARD D. BLACK

A PROFESSIONAL CORPORATION

*Established in 1973*

16311 VENTURA BOULEVARD, SUITE 1260
**ENCINO, CALIFORNIA 91436-2152**
Telephone: 818-986-5680
Facsimile: 818-995-3422

*Civil Litigation in all State and Federal Courts, including Business, Partnership, Educational Institutions, Construction, Real Property, Commercial, Tort and Significant Family Law Matters.*

**LEONARD D. BLACK,** born 1939; admitted to bar, 1969, California. *Education:* California State University, Northridge (B.S., Accounting, 1962); University of Southern California (M.B.A., 1965); Loyola Marymount University (J.D., 1968). Phi Alpha Delta. Deputy County Counsel, Los Angeles County, 1969-1973. Former Hearing Officer, Los Angeles County Civil Service Commission. Retirement Board Referee, Los Angeles County Employee Association, 1976-1979. Arbitrator, American Arbitration Association. *Member:* Los Angeles County and San Fernando Valley Bar Associations; State Bar of California; Los Angeles Trial Lawyers Association. **PRACTICE AREAS:** Business Litigation; Tort Litigation; Real Estate Litigation; Family Law.

A list of corporate and institutional clients will be furnished with their prior consent upon request.

---

## BARRY A. BLAKE

15760 VENTURA BOULEVARD, SUITE 700
**ENCINO, CALIFORNIA 91436**
Telephone: 818-990-1457
Fax: 818-990-4006

*General Civil, Trial Practice in all California State and Federal Courts. Personal Injury, Wrongful Death, Landlord and Tenant and Creditor-Debtor Law.*

**BARRY A. BLAKE,** born Los Angeles, California, November 30, 1946; admitted to bar, 1976, California; 1977, U.S. District Court, Central District of California; 1979, U.S. Court of Appeals, Ninth Circuit; U.S. Tax Court, U.S., Court of Military Appeals and U.S. Court of Claims. *Education:* California State University at Northridge (B.A., 1969); University of San Fernando Valley (J.D., 1976). *Member:* Los Angeles County and American Bar Associations; The State Bar of California.

REFERENCE: Bank of America (Tarzana Branch).

---

## BOLDRA & KLUEGER

ENCINO, CALIFORNIA

(See Los Angeles)

*Tax Litigation and Controversies, Tax Planning, Estate Tax Planning, Estate Planning, Bankruptcy and Real Estate Law.*

---

## LAW OFFICES OF KRISTI WEILER DEAN

SUITE 230, 6345 BALBOA BOULEVARD
**ENCINO, CALIFORNIA 91316**
Telephone: 818-774-2131
FAX: 818-774-2141

*Civil Litigation including Personal Injury, Products Broker and Agent EEO Liability, Medical and Dental Malpractice, Insurance, Premises Liability, Business Litigation Defense and Construction Law.*

**KRISTI WEILER DEAN,** born San Francisco, California, April 1, 1958; admitted to bar, 1984, California and U.S. District Court, Southern, Central and Northern Districts of California. *Education:* California State University at Fresno (B.S., 1981); Pepperdine University School of Law (J.D., 1984). Certified Law Clerk, California Bar Association, 1984. Judicial Clerk to the Honorable Armand Arabian, Justice of the California Court of Appeals of Los Angeles, 1984. *Member:* San Fernando Valley, Los Angeles County and American Bar Associations.

ASSOCIATES

**FELISE L. COHEN,** born Los Angeles, California, March 7, 1960; admitted to bar, 1991, California. *Education:* California State University, Northridge; University of La Verne (J.D., 1991). Certified Law Clerk, California Bar Association, 1989. Internship, Los Angeles District Attorney's Office, 1989-1990. *Member:* San Fernando Valley Bar Association; State Bar of California. **PRACTICE AREAS:** Premises, Auto and Products.

**RAYMOND J. FEINBERG,** born New York, N.Y., September 11, 1951; admitted to bar, 1981 California and U.S. District Court, Central District of California. *Education:* Boston University (B.A., 1974); Pepperdine University (J.D., 1980). *Member:* Los Angeles County and American Bar Associations; State Bar of California; The Association of Trial Lawyers of America. **PRACTICE AREAS:** Medical Negligence; Premises Auto and Products; Construction.

**RYAN M. HERRON,** born Palms, California, August 22, 1967; admitted to bar, 1994, California. *Education:* University of California at Irvine (B.A., 1990); Southern Methodist University (J.D., 1994). **PRACTICE AREAS:** Construction.

REPRESENTATIVE CLIENTS: Lloyds of London; Illinois Insurance Exchange; Dr. F.E. Campbell, D.D.S.; Scottsdale Insurance Co.; Nautilus Insurance Co.; Penn-America Insurance Company; Alliance Insurance Company; Harry W. Gorst Co., Inc.; Compass Insurance Group; Brooks & Willmes Insurance Agency; Bliss E. Glennon; Monarch E & S; Western Security Insurance Brokers.

---

## ELLIOT, LAMB, LEIBL & SNYDER

*Established in 1988*

16501 VENTURA BOULEVARD
SUITE 301
**ENCINO, CALIFORNIA 91436**
Telephone: 818-380-0123; 310-553-5767
Fax: 818-380-0124

*Redlands, California Office:* 101 East Redlands Boulevard, Suite 285, 92373. Telephone: 909-792-8861. Fax: 909-798-6997.
*Orange County Office:* 333 South Anita Drive, Suite 660, Orange, California, 92668. Telephone: 714-978-6255. Facsimile: 714-978-9087.

*Civil Litigation. Insurance Defense and Medical Malpractice Defense.*

*FIRM PROFILE: Our law firm which specializes in the defense of professional malpractice actions against health care providers. Our cases include all types of medical malpractice, including claims involving psychiatric care, birth injuries, disputes concerning medical staff privileges and representation of physicians before the Medical Board of California. We are active in both the state and*

*(This Listing Continued)*

## ELLIOT, LAMB, LEIBL & SNYDER, Encino—Continued

federal courts, which matters pending throughout the counties of Los Angeles, Riverside, San Bernardino and Orange. We deal primarily with complex, high damage potential cases, involving claims of brain damage, paralysis and wrongful death allegedly due to medical negligence.

**MICHAEL V. LAMB,** born Fairfield, Iowa, December 23, 1952; admitted to bar, 1979, California; 1985, U.S. District Court, Central District of California. *Education:* University of Michigan (B.A., 1975); Rutgers University; Pepperdine University (J.D., 1978). *Member:* Los Angeles County and American Bar Associations; State Bar of California. *PRACTICE AREAS:* Insurance Defense; Medical Malpractice Defense.

**MICHAEL R. SNYDER,** born Downey, California, July 10, 1958; admitted to bar, 1984, California; U.S. District Court, Central District of California. *Education:* California State University at Long Beach (B.A., 1980); Western State University (J.D., 1983). *Member:* State Bar of California; American Bar Association. *PRACTICE AREAS:* Insurance Defense; Medical Malpractice Defense.

**LOREN S. LEIBL,** born Pasadena, California, July 11, 1953; admitted to bar, 1983, California and U.S. District Court, Central District of California; U.S. Court of Appeals, Ninth Circuit. *Education:* California State University at Long Beach (B.A., 1979); Southwestern University (J.D., 1983). Recipient: American Jurisprudence Award in Torts; Southwestern University Award in Torts and Legal Communication Skills. *Member:* Los Angeles County and American Bar Associations; State Bar of California. *PRACTICE AREAS:* Insurance Defense; Medical Malpractice Defense.

**D. SCOTT ELLIOT,** born Cleveland, Ohio, September 3, 1952; admitted to bar, 1977, California; 1979, U.S. District Court, Central District of California; U.S. Court of Appeals, Ninth Circuit. *Education:* California State University at Northridge (B.A., cum laude, 1974); Southwestern University (J.D., 1977). Recipient, American Jurisprudence Award in Constitutional Law. *Member:* State Bar of California; Association of Southern California Defense Counsel. *PRACTICE AREAS:* Insurance Defense; Medical Malpractice Defense.

**REBECCA J. HOGUE,** born Huntington Park, California, July 20, 1954; admitted to bar, 1984, California and U.S. District Court, Central District of California. *Education:* University of California at Irvine (B.A., 1976); Western State University (J.D., cum laude, 1983). Member, Western State University Law Review, 1982-1983. Recipient: Corpus Juris Secundum Award; American Jurisprudence Awards in Torts, Evidence, Criminal Law and Community Property. *Member:* State Bar of California. *PRACTICE AREAS:* Insurance Defense; Medical Malpractice Defense.

---

**LINDA OSTRIN,** born Alton, Illinois, April 1, 1948; admitted to bar, 1978, California. *Education:* California State University at Northridge (B.S., 1973); University of La Verne (J.D., 1978). *Member:* State Bar of California. *PRACTICE AREAS:* Insurance Defense; Medical Malpractice Defense.

**JASON J. SCUPINE,** born Burbank, California, November 3, 1965; admitted to bar, 1990, California. *Education:* University of California, Los Angeles (B.A., 1987); Loyola Marymount University (J.D., 1990). *Member:* State Bar of California; American Bar Association. *PRACTICE AREAS:* Insurance Defense; Medical Malpractice Defense.

**MICHAEL J. VAN DYKE,** born San Antonio, Texas, September 1, 1967; admitted to bar, 1993, California. *Education:* Santa Clara University (B.S., 1989); Loyola Marymount University (J.D., 1993). Member, Scott Moot Court Honors Board. Extern for the Honorable Laughlin E. Waters, Senior U.S. District Court. *Member:* State Bar of California. *PRACTICE AREAS:* Insurance Defense; Medical Malpractice Defense.

**CINDY A. SHAPIRO,** born Pasadena, California, October 27, 1966; admitted to bar, 1994, California. *Education:* University of California at Irvine (B.A.B.S., 1988); Loyola Marymount University (J.D., 1994). Phi Delta Phi. Board of Directors, Campfire Boys and Girls, 1995-1996. *Member:* State Bar of California; American Bar Association. *PRACTICE AREAS:* Insurance Defense; Medical Malpractice Defense.

### OF COUNSEL

**MICHAEL D. BROWN,** born Washington, D.C., November 28, 1946; admitted to bar, 1974, California; 1988, U.S. Supreme Court. *Education:* Fullerton Junior College (A.A., 1966); California State University at Fullerton (B.A., 1968); Southwestern University (J.D., 1974). Member, American Board of Trial Advocates. *Member:* The State Bar of California; Association of Southern California Defense Counsel. *PRACTICE AREAS:* Insurance Defense; Medical Malpractice Defense.

REPRESENTATIVE CLIENTS: The Doctors Co.; Southern California Physicians Insurance Exchange; Physicians Inter Indemnity Trust Co.; Norcal Mutual Insurance Co.; Resure, Inc.

---

## JOHN A. C. GIBSON
16000 VENTURA BOULEVARD, SUITE 1010
**ENCINO, CALIFORNIA 91436**
Telephone: 818-382-6480
FAX: 818-382-6482

*Alcoholic Beverage Licensing and Compliance, General Business and Corporate.*

**JOHN A. C. GIBSON,** born Austin, Texas, June 5, 1944; admitted to bar, 1990, California. *Education:* The University of Texas (B.A., 1965); Ohio State University (M.A., 1967); George Washington University (J.D., with honors, 1974). Co-Author: "The Real Trouble with the Government Warning," The Wine Trader, June, 1990. *Member:* Los Angeles County Bar Association. *LANGUAGES:* French, German. *PRACTICE AREAS:* Corporate; Regulatory; Administrative; Alcoholic Beverage.

---

## GOLDFARB, STURMAN & AVERBACH
**ENCINO, CALIFORNIA**
(See Los Angeles)

*General Practice. Business, Real Estate, Estate Planning, Probate, Taxation Law, Civil Litigation.*

---

## GREENBERG & BASS
Established in 1984
16000 VENTURA BOULEVARD
SUITE 1000
**ENCINO, CALIFORNIA 91436-2730**
Telephone: 818-382-6200

*General Practice.*

FIRM PROFILE: Greenberg & Bass was formed in 1984 by Arthur A. Greenberg and Robert D. Bass. The firm's practice is primarily business related with a particular emphasis on bankruptcy and insolvency related matters, commercial litigation and business planning. The firm's clients include institutional lenders, debtors, creditors, creditors' committee, trustees in bankruptcy and general business clients. The Firm has attorneys admitted to practice before all of the State and Federal Courts in California, Nevada, Arizona, New York and Missouri and is serving and represents clients in each of those jurisdictions.

### MEMBERS OF FIRM

**ARTHUR A. GREENBERG,** born Waynesville, Missouri, August 10, 1951; admitted to bar, 1976, California and U.S. Court of Appeals, Ninth Circuit. *Education:* Tel Aviv University, Tel Aviv, Israel; University of California at Los Angeles (A.B., 1972); Loyola University (J.D., 1976). *Member:* Beverly Hills, Los Angeles County (Member, Commercial Law Section) and American Bar Associations; State Bar of California (Member, Business Law Section); The Commercial Law League of America (Member, Western Region's Education Committee); American Bankruptcy Institute; Financial Lawyers Conference; California Bankruptcy Forum.

**ROBERT D. BASS,** born Los Angeles, California, October 23, 1947; admitted to bar, 1974, California, U.S. District Court, Central District of California and U.S. Court of Appeals, Ninth Circuit. *Education:* University of California at Los Angeles (B.A., 1969); University of California School of Law (J.D., 1974). Formerly Associated with, Stutman, Treister & Glatt. *Member:* Los Angeles County (Member, Commercial Law Section); State Bar of California; Financial Lawyers Conference; California Bankruptcy Forum. *PRACTICE AREAS:* Bankruptcy and Insolvency Related Matters.

**WILLIAM E. CROCKETT,** born Toledo, Ohio, June 23, 1951; admitted to bar, 1982, Missouri, U.S. District Court, Eastern District of Missouri; U.S. Court of Appeals, Eighth and Ninth Circuits; 1984, Nevada and U.S. District Court, District of Nevada; 1986, District of Columbia; 1987, California. *Education:* University of Virginia (B.A., Philosophy, 1978; Washington University (J.D., 1982). *Member:* Los Angeles Bar Association; The

*(This Listing Continued)*

Missouri Bar; State Bar of Nevada; State Bar of California; The District of Columbia Bar; American Bar Association (Member, Section on Litigation). *PRACTICE AREAS:* Real Estate Litigation; Business Litigation; Commercial Litigation.

**GARY K. SALOMONS,** born Santa Monica, California, January 7, 1961; admitted to bar, 1986, California, U.S. District Court, Central District of California and U.S. Court of Appeals, Ninth Circuit; 1987, Nevada, U.S. District Court, Northern District of California and U.S. District Court, District of Nevada. *Education:* California State University at Northridge (B.S., 1983); University of Southern California (J.D., 1986). *Member:* Los Angeles County and American (Member, Business Law Section) Bar Associations; State Bar of California; International Association of Gaming Attorneys. *PRACTICE AREAS:* Commercial Litigation; Creditor Rights; Gaming Law.

**ANDREW GOODMAN,** born New York, N.Y., February 28, 1959; admitted to bar, 1984, California and U.S. District Court, Central District of California; 1985, U.S. District Court, Northern, Southern and Eastern Districts of California and U.S. Court of Appeals, Ninth Circuit; 1988, New York. *Education:* Pitzer College (B.A., 1981); Loyola Marymount University (J.D., 1984). *Member:* Fernando Valley, Los Angeles County and American Bar Associations; State Bar of California; Financial lawyers Conference; Los Angeles Bankruptcy Forum. *PRACTICE AREAS:* Commercial Litigation; Real Estate Litigation; Bankruptcy; Insolvency Related Matters.

**JAMES R. FELTON,** born Los Angeles, California, November 11, 1963; admitted to bar, 1988, California; 1989, U.S. District Court, Central District of California and U.S. Court of Appeals, Ninth Circuit; 1992, Arizona. *Education:* Brandeis University (B.A., with high honors, 1985); University of California at Los Angeles (J.D., 1988). Member, Moot Court Honors Program. *Member:* Los Angeles County Bar Association; State Bar of California; Arizona State Bar Association. *PRACTICE AREAS:* Commercial and Real Estate Litigation; Bankruptcy and Insolvency Related Matters.

**HAROLD GUTENBERG,** born Detroit, Michigan, November 21, 1932; admitted to bar, 1972, California and U.S. Tax Court; 1978, U.S. Supreme Court. *Education:* Wayne State University (A.B., 1959); Southwestern University (J.D., 1971). *Member:* Beverly Hills (Member, Family Law Mediation Panel, 1979—), Los Angeles County (Member, Family Law Judge Pro Tem Program, 1980) and American Bar Associations; The State Bar of California.

---

## ALLAN F. GROSSMAN

Established in 1956

SUITE 304 ENCINO LAW CENTER
15915 VENTURA BOULEVARD
**ENCINO, CALIFORNIA 91436**
Telephone: 818-990-8200
FAX: 818-990-4616

*Trial and Appellate Practice in State and Federal Courts.*

**ALLAN F. GROSSMAN,** born Chicago, Illinois, July 30, 1932; admitted to bar, 1956, California; 1974, U.S. Supreme Court. *Education:* University of Chicago, University of Illinois and Northwestern University (B.S.L., 1954); University of Southern California (LL.B., 1956; LL.M., 1961). Member, Southern California Law Review, 1955-1956. Instructor: USC School of Law 1956-1959; Professor of Law: Beverly (Whittier) College of Law 1967-1970; Lecturer, Civil Jury Instructions, CEB, 1982-1986. Arbitrator: Los Angeles County Superior Court, 1976—; American Arbitration Association, 1977—. Legion Lex (President, 1977-1978). President, USC/Legion Lex American Inn of Court 1990-1992. *Member:* Los Angeles County and American Bar Associations; California Academy of Appellate Lawyers; Los Angeles Business Trial Lawyers Association; Los Angeles Trial Lawyers Association.

REFERENCE: First Los Angeles Bank, Woodland Hills.

---

## STEPHEN H. HELLER

A PROFESSIONAL CORPORATION

Established in 1976

16830 VENTURA BOULEVARD, SUITE B
**ENCINO, CALIFORNIA 91436-1714**
Telephone: 818-995-4646

*Personal Injury Litigation.*

**STEPHEN H. HELLER,** born Los Angeles, California, November 2, 1947; admitted to bar, 1974, California; U.S. District Court, Southern District of California. *Education:* University of California at Los Angeles (A.B., 1969); California Western University (J.D., 1973). Member, Million Dollar Advocates Forum. Arbitrator, American Arbitration Association. Member and Advocate, Alliance for Children's Rights, Los Angeles. *Member:* Beverly Hills, Los Angeles County and American Bar Associations; State Bar of California; California Consumer Attorneys Association (formerly California Trial Lawyers Association); The Association of Trial Lawyers of America; Consumer Attorneys Association of Los Angeles (formerly Los Angeles Trial Lawyers Association).

---

## HEMAR, ROUSSO & GARWACKI

Established in 1974

15910 VENTURA BOULEVARD, 12TH FLOOR
**ENCINO, CALIFORNIA 91436-2829**
Telephone: 818-501-3800
FAX: 818-501-2985

*Commercial Litigation, Creditors Rights, Banking, Equipment Leasing, Bankruptcy and Secured Transactions.*

### MEMBERS OF FIRM

**RICHARD P. HEMAR,** born Warsaw, Poland, July 2, 1944; admitted to bar, 1970, California and U.S. District Court, Central District of California. *Education:* University of California at Los Angeles (B.S., 1966; J.D., 1969). Member, Board of Directors, 1976-1977; 1988 and Legal Committee Chairman, 1987, Western Association of Equipment Lessors. Member, Legal Committee, American Association of Equipment Lessors, 1978. *Member:* San Fernando Valley and Los Angeles County Bar Associations; State Bar of California; California Trial Lawyers Association; Commercial Law League; United Association of Equipment Leasing; Equipment Leasing Association. *LANGUAGES:* Polish. *PRACTICE AREAS:* Creditors Rights; Banking; Equipment Leasing; Bankruptcy and Secured Transactions.

**MARTIN J. ROUSSO,** born Brooklyn, New York, February 18, 1945; admitted to bar, 1977, California; 1979, U.S. District Court, Central District of California. *Education:* California State University at Los Angeles (B.S., 1967); University of San Fernando Valley (J.D., 1977). Member, San Fernando Valley Law Review, 1976-1977. *Member:* Los Angeles County and American Bar Associations; State Bar of California; United Association of Equipment Leasing; Equipment Leasing Association; Community Bankers of Southern California. *PRACTICE AREAS:* Creditors Rights; Banking; Equipment Leasing; Bankruptcy and Secured Transactions.

**RAY D. GARWACKI, JR.,** born Los Angeles, California, June 10, 1955; admitted to bar, 1981, California and U.S. District Court, Central District of California; 1983, U.S. District Court, Northern, Southern and Eastern Districts of California. *Education:* Whittier College (B.A., 1977); Pepperdine University (J.D., 1980). Phi Alpha Delta. Author: "Prejudgment Remedies for Equipment Lessors," Western Association of Equipment Lessors Newsline, Vol. 12, Iss. 4. *Member:* Los Angeles County and American Bar Associations; State Bar of California; The Association of Trial Lawyers of America; United Association of Equipment Leasing; Equipment Leasing Association. *PRACTICE AREAS:* Creditors Rights; Banking; Equipment Leasing; Bankruptcy and Secured Transactions.

**STEPHEN E. JENKINS,** born Los Angeles, California, February 14, 1955; admitted to bar, 1981, California and U.S. District Court, Central District of California; 1983, U.S. District Court, Northern, Southern and Eastern Districts of California. *Education:* California State University at Long Beach (B.S., 1977); Western State University (J.D., 1980). Recipient, American Jurisprudence Award in Bankruptcy. Judge Pro Tem, Los Angeles Municipal Court, 1989. *Member:* State Bar of California.

**DANIEL A. HEALD, IV,** born San Diego, California, August 2, 1958; admitted to bar, 1984, California and U.S. District Court, Central, North-

*(This Listing Continued)*

### HEMAR, ROUSSO & GARWACKI, Encino—Continued

ern, Southern and Eastern Districts of California. *Education:* Claremont Men's College (B.A., 1980); McGeorge Law School (J.D., 1983). *Member:* State Bar of California.

**SAMUEL W. GORDON,** born Buffalo, New York, December 23, 1946; admitted to bar, 1972, California, U.S. Claims Court and U.S. District Court, Central District of California; 1983, U.S. District Court, Eastern, Southern and Northern Districts of California; 1984, U.S. Court of Appeals, Ninth Circuit. *Education:* University of California at Los Angeles (B.A., 1968); Loyola Law School (J.D., 1971). Phi Alpha Delta. St. Thomas More Honor Society. Member, Board of Editors, Loyola Law Review, 1970-1971. *Member:* Los Angeles County and American (Member, Ad Hoc Subcommittee, Scope of the Uniform Commercial Code) Bar Associations; State Bar of California; American Trial Lawyers Association. [Capt., USAR, 1968-1976]. *PRACTICE AREAS:* Creditors Rights; Banking; Equipment Leasing; Bankruptcy and Secured Transactions.

REPRESENTATIVE CLIENTS: AST Research; Sysco Food Service; Wells Fargo Bank.
REFERENCE: City National Bank (Westwood Office).

---

### NORMAN J. HOFFMAN, INC.
*A PROFESSIONAL CORPORATION*
**ENCINO, CALIFORNIA**
(See Los Angeles)

*Automobile Law, Tax Law, Estate Planning, Wills, Trusts, Real Estate and Probate.*

---

### JAMES W. E. HOFFMANN
**ENCINO, CALIFORNIA**
(See Los Angeles)

*Professional Malpractice, Bad Faith, Insurance Coverage, Product Liability, Insurance Defense, General Civil Litigation.*

---

### HORVITZ & LEVY
**ENCINO, CALIFORNIA**
(See Los Angeles)

*All Civil Appeals and Related Appellate Practice, including Trial Consultations, with Emphasis in the Areas of Business Law, Commercial Law, Contracts, Health Care, Hospitals, Insurance and Insurance Defense (including Coverage and Bad Faith), Legal Ethics and Professional Responsibility, Legal and Medical Malpractice, Negligence, Personal Injury, Products Liability, Professional Liability, and Torts.*

---

### J. MICHAEL HUGHES
*Established in 1978*
SUITE 700, 15760 VENTURA BOULEVARD
**ENCINO, CALIFORNIA 91436**
Telephone: 818-905-7301
Facsimile: 818-907-6848

*General Civil Trial and Appellate Practice in all State and Federal Courts. Real Estate, General Business, Corporate, Health Care and Probate Law.*

**J. MICHAEL HUGHES,** born San Diego, California, August 8, 1942; admitted to bar, 1967, California. *Education:* University of San Diego (B.A., 1964; J.D., 1967). Phi Delta Phi. Research Attorney, California Court of Appeal, 1967-1968. *Member:* Los Angeles County (Health Care Section); State Bar of California; National Health Lawyers Association.

---

### KARNO, SCHWARTZ, FRIEDMAN, SHAFRON & WARREN
A Partnership including Professional Corporations
*Established in 1961*
MANUFACTURERS BANK BUILDING
SUITE 1200, 16255 VENTURA BOULEVARD
**ENCINO, CALIFORNIA 91436**
Telephone: 818-981-3400; 213-872-1800
Telecopier: 213-872-1278

Agoura Hills, California Office: 30497 Canwood Street, Suite 102. Telephone: 818-597-7977. Telecopier: 818-597-7970.

*Real Estate, Tax, Corporate, Business, ERISA, Estate Planning and Probate Law. Litigation.*

**MARSHALL N. SCHWARTZ** (Retired).

**NORTON S. KARNO, (A PROFESSIONAL CORPORATION),** born Chicago, Illinois, June 29, 1936; admitted to bar, 1961, California, U.S. District Court, Southern District of California, U.S. Court of Appeals, Ninth Circuit, U.S. Supreme Court and U.S. Tax Court. *Education:* University of California at Los Angeles (B.S., with highest honors, 1956); University of Southern California (J.D., 1960). Phi Beta Kappa; Beta Gamma Sigma; Phi Eta Sigma; Order of the Coif. Member, Student Editorial Board, 1958-1959 and Associate Editor, 1959-1960, University of Southern California Law Review. Certified Public Accountant, California, 1961. *Member:* San Fernando Valley (Member, Sections on: Real Property, Business and Tax Law), Los Angeles County (Member, Sections on: Taxation and Real Estate Law) and American (Member, Section on Taxation) Bar Associations; State Bar of California; American Institute of Certified Public Accountants; Association of Real Estate Attorneys.

**KENNETH L. FRIEDMAN, (A PROFESSIONAL CORPORATION),** born Los Angeles, California, August 30, 1951; admitted to bar, 1976, California; 1982, U.S. District Court, Central District of California. *Education:* University of California at Los Angeles (B.A., magna cum laude, 1973; J.D., 1976). Phi Beta Kappa. Order of Barristers. Member, Moot Court Executive Board, 1975-1976. *Member:* Beverly Hills and Los Angeles County (Member, Sections on: Corporate Law; Real Estate Law) Bar Associations; State Bar of California; Association of Real Estate Attorneys; Selden Society.

**SHELLY JAY SHAFRON, (A PROFESSIONAL CORPORATION),** born Los Angeles, California, February 9, 1950; admitted to bar, 1975, California; 1976, U.S. Court of Appeals, Ninth Circuit, U.S. District Court, Southern District of California and U.S. Supreme Court; 1984, U.S. District Court, Northern District of California. *Education:* University of Southern California (B.A., 1972); Loyola University of Los Angeles (J.D., 1975). Note and Comment Editor, Loyola Law Review, 1974-1975. Author: "Back on the Road Again —The Mobility Exception in the 70's," 7 Loyola Law Review 3, 1974; "Negligence and the Commercial Landlord: A Guide to Preventive Legal Medicine," California Real Estate Directory, Vol. I, No. 4, p. 33, Winter, 1985. Approved Instructor: California Department of Real Estate Law, 1981—; Grubb and Ellis Co., 1988-1990. *Member:* State Bar of California.

**EARL W. WARREN,** born Los Angeles, California, April 9, 1940; admitted to bar, 1966, California. *Education:* University of California at Los Angeles (B.A., 1962); University California Law School (J.D., 1965). Phi Alpha Delta. *Member:* Los Angeles County Bar Association. (Resident, Agoura Hills Office). *PRACTICE AREAS:* Transactional Residential Real Estate Development; Commercial and Industrial Real Estate Development; General Corporate Law; Luxury, Sales and Use Tax Documented Vessels.

---

**KEVIN DAVID KAMMER,** born Los Angeles, California, February 25, 1959; admitted to bar, 1986, California; 1988, U.S. District Court, Central District of California. *Education:* Los Angeles Valley College (A.A., 1979); California State University at Northridge, B.A., 1981); Loyola Law School (J.D., 1984). Phi Kappa Phi. Psi Chi. *Member:* State Bar of California.

**RICHARD A. COHN, (P.C.),** born New York, N.Y., April 19, 1946; admitted to bar, 1971, New York; 1977, California. *Education:* Brandeis University (B.A., 1967); Columbia Law School (J.D., 1970). Editor, Columbia Law Review, 1969-1970. *Member:* Beverly Hills, Los Angeles County

*(This Listing Continued)*

and American (Member, Section of Taxation) Bar Associations; State Bar of California. *PRACTICE AREAS:* Taxation; Estate Planning; Business Law.

## KOLOD & WAGER
16000 VENTURA BOULEVARD, FIFTH FLOOR
ENCINO, CALIFORNIA 91436
Telephone: 818-788-4348
Fax: 818-788-4349
Email: kol-wag@pacbell.net

*Orange County, California Office:* 1551 North Tustin Avenue, Suite 195, Santa Ana, 92701. Telephone: 714-543-9300. Fax: 714-543-9400.
*San Diego, California Office:* 16476 Bernardo Center Drive, Suite 100, 92128. Telephone: 619-675-7006. Fax: 619-675-1023.
*Sonoma, California Office:* 589 First Street West, 95476. Telephone: 415-398-1092. Fax: 415-398-6009.

General Civil, Trial and Appellate Practice in State and Federal Court, emphasizing Insurance Coverage and Bad Faith, Construction Defect and Real Property, Professional Liability, General Tort Liability Defense, Products Liability and Environmental Impairment.

**SCOTT M. KOLOD,** born Las Vegas, Nevada, September 10, 1957; admitted to bar, 1982, California; 1983, U.S. Court of Appeals, Ninth Circuit. *Education:* Indiana University (B.S., 1979); University of San Diego (J.D., 1982). Phi Eta Sigma. Appellate Moot Court Board. Managing Editor of USD Woolsack. Author: "Explanation of Cumis (Independent) Counsel," SDIAA, 1995. Co-Author: "California Liability Insurance Practice, Claims and Litigation, C.E.B., 1990. *Member:* San Diego, North County and Orange County Bar Associations; Defense Research Institute; Association of Southern California Defense Counsel. **LANGUAGES:** Spanish and French. *REPORTED CASES:* Stonewall Ins. Co. v. City of Palos Verdes Estates, 46 Cal. App. 4th 1810 (1996); Jefferson-Pilot Life Ins. Co. v. Krafka, 50 Cal. App. 4th 190 (1996).

**JEROME WAGER,** born Los Angeles, California, April 20, 1957; admitted to bar, 1982, California; 1983, U.S. District Court, Central and Southern Districts of California and U.S. Court of Appeals, Ninth Circuit. *Education:* University of California at Santa Barbara (B.A., magna cum laude, 1979); University of San Diego (J.D., 1982). Phi Alpha Delta. Member: Jessup Law Society; International Law Society. Author: "Construction Defect Mediation, How to Obtain Maximum Effectiveness and Results," W.C.C., 1996. *Member:* Los Angeles, San Diego, San Francisco and Sonoma County Bar Associations; Association of Defense Counsel of Southern California.

### ASSOCIATES

**TED A. CONNOR,** born Joliet, Illinois, February 21, 1962; admitted to bar, 1987, California; 1988, U.S. District Court, Central and Southern Districts of California. *Education:* University of Notre Dame (B.A., 1984); University of San Diego (J.D., 1987). *Member:* San Diego County Bar Association; State Bar of California.

**HOLLY NOLAN,** born Morristown, New Jersey, December 19, 1962; admitted to bar, 1989, California; U.S. District Courts, Southern and Central Districts of California. *Education:* University of Redlands (B.A., 1985); University of San Diego (J.D., 1988). *Member:* San Diego County Bar Association.

**STEPHEN A. LINDSLEY,** born San Diego, California, October, 19, 1963; admitted to bar, 1990, California, U.S. District Court, Southern District of California and U.S. Court of Appeals, Ninth Circuit; 1993, U.S. District Court, Central District of California. *Education:* University of San Diego (B.A., with honors 1985; J.D., 1989). Phi Alpha Delta. Recipient: American Jurisprudence Award in Contracts; University of San Diego Scholarship. Author: "Alternate Courses of Action When Coverage is Disputed," SDIAA, 1995. *Member:* San Diego County Bar Association; State Bar of California.

**KEVIN J. HEALY,** born Boston, Massachusetts, July 10, 1962; admitted to bar, 1992, California; 1993, U.S. District Court, Central District of California and U.S. Court of Appeals, Ninth Circuit. *Education:* Brandeis University (B.A., 1985); California Western School of Law (J.D., cum laude, 1992). Staff Writer, Law Review, 1990-1991. *Member:* San Diego County Bar Association: State Bar of California.

**LALEAQUE GRAD,** born Los Angeles, California, August 6, 1970; admitted to bar, 1995, California and U.S. District Court, Southern District

*(This Listing Continued)*

of California. *Education:* University of California at San Diego (B.A., 1992); University of San Diego (J.D., cum laude, 1995).

REPRESENTATIVE CLIENTS: Acceptance Insurance Co.; Alaska Gasoline Co.; Alexander & Alexander; Alexander Hamilton Life Insurance Co.; American International Group; American States Insurance Co.; AMICA Insurance Co.; CAMICO Mutual Insurance Co.; CIGNA Property & Casualty; CNA Insurance Cos.; Criterion Gate & Manufacturing Co., Inc.; Farmers Insurance Group of Cos.; Fireman's Fund Insurance Group; Fraternal Insurance Co.; Golden Nugget Hotel & Casino; Jefferson-Pilot Life Insurance Co.; Kemper National Insurance Co.; Lindsey Morden Claims Management, Inc.; Maryland Casualty Group; Moose International, Inc,; Moselle Insurance Agency, Inc.; Ohio Casualty Insurance Co.; P.W. Stephens Contractors, Inc.; Safeco Insurance Co.; Southland Labs, Inc.; T.M. Claims Service, Inc.; Tokio Marine Management Co.; Turnberry Property Management, Inc.; Tustin-Redhill Insurance Agency; 20th Century Insurance Co.

## KRIVIS, SPILE & SIEGAL, LLP
ENCINO, CALIFORNIA
(See Spile & Siegal, LLP)

## LAW OFFICES OF
## STEVEN N. KURTZ
15760 VENTURA BOULEVARD, 16TH FLOOR
ENCINO, CALIFORNIA 91436
Telephone: 818-981-0974
Telecopier: 818-981-0984
Email: skurtz3630@aol.com

*Business and Commercial Litigation, Bankruptcy, Corporate and Personal Reorganization, Debtor-Creditor Matters and Business Law.*

**STEVEN N. KURTZ,** born Los Angeles, California, November 1, 1958; admitted to bar, 1986, California; 1987, U.S. District Court, Central District of California and U.S. Court of Appeals, Ninth Circuit; 1988, U.S. District Court, Southern and Eastern Districts of California; 1989, U.S. District Court, Northern District of California. *Education:* San Diego State University (B.A., 1981); McGeorge School of Law, University of the Pacific (J.D., 1986). *Member:* Financial Lawyers Conference; Los Angeles Bankruptcy Forum. *Member:* Los Angeles County (Commercial Law and Bankruptcy Section) and American (Business Law and Litigation Sections) Bar Associations; State Bar of California. *REPORTED CASES:* In re ZZZZ Best Carpet Cleaning Co., Inc., 921 F. 2d 968 (9th Cir. 1990).

## LEVINSON & KAPLAN
A PROFESSIONAL CORPORATION
16027 VENTURA BOULEVARD, SUITE 450
ENCINO, CALIFORNIA 91436
Telephone: 818-382-3450
Facsimile: 818-382-3445
Email: levkaplaw@aol.com
URL: http://www.levkaplaw.com

*Business Litigation, Real Estate Litigation, Employment Law and General Business Transactions.*

**ROBERT A. LEVINSON,** born Berkeley, California, November 23, 1953; admitted to bar, 1978, California; 1979, U.S. District Court, Central District of California; 1992, U.S. Tax Court. *Education:* University of Southern California (B.S., magna cum laude, 1975); University of California at Los Angeles (J.D., 1978). Member, Moot Court Honors Program. Managing Editor, U.C.L.A.-Alaska Law Review, 1977-1978. Author: "Peremptory Challenges of Judges In the Alaska Courts," 6 U.C.L.A.-Alaska Law Review 269, 1977. Co-Author: "Do Commercial Property Tenants Possess Warranties of Habitability?" 14 Real Estate Law Journal 59, 1985. Arbitrator, Los Angeles County Bar Association Fee Arbitration Panel, 1983—. Judge Pro Tem, Los Angeles County Municipal Courts, 1985—. *Member:* State Bar of California; Los Angeles County Bar Association. *PRACTICE AREAS:* Business and Real Estate Litigation; Employment Law for Management.

**STEVEN G. KAPLAN,** born San Marino, California, February 23, 1962; admitted to bar, 1988, California; 1989, U.S. District Court, Central,

*(This Listing Continued)*

**LEVINSON & KAPLAN,** A PROFESSIONAL CORPORATION, Encino—Continued

Eastern, Northern and Southern Districts of California and U.S. Court of Appeals, Ninth Circuit. *Education:* Oxford University, International Law Program; University of California at Los Angeles (B.A., 1985); Loyola Marymount University (J.D., 1988). Phi Alpha Delta (President, 1987-1988). Member, 1986-1987 and Chief Articles Editor, 1987-1988, Loyola International and Comparative Law Journal. Author: "Compensation Damage Arising From Global Nuclear Accidents: The Chernobyl Situation," 10 Loyola International and Comparative Law Journal 241, 1987. *Member:* Beverly Hills, Los Angeles County and American (Member, Section on Litigation) Bar Associations; State Bar of California; Beverly Hills Barristers; Los Angeles Trial Lawyers Association. *PRACTICE AREAS:* Business and Real Estate Litigation; Business Transactions and Consulting; Medical Practice Law; Acquisitions and Sales. *Email:* LEVKAPLAW@AOL.COM

**PATRICK CONDON,** born Washington, D.C., May 3, 1948; admitted to bar, 1989, California. *Education:* Kalamazoo College (B.A., 1970); University of California (M.A., C.Phil., 1978); Boalt Hall (J.D., 1989). Member, Editorial Board, Industrial Relations Law Journal. *Member:* State Bar of California. *PRACTICE AREAS:* Appellate; Labor; Litigation; Law and Motion.

**DANA A. KRAVETZ,** born Encino, California, May 11, 1970; admitted to bar, 1995, California and U.S. District Court, Central District of California. *Education:* University of California at San Diego (B.A., 1992); Southwestern University School of Law (J.D., 1995). *Member:* Los Angeles County and American (Member, Planning Board, Section on Arts, Entertainment and Sports) Bar Associations; State Bar of California. *PRACTICE AREAS:* Business Litigation; General Civil Litigation; Sports Law.

---

# LEWITT, HACKMAN, HOEFFLIN, SHAPIRO, MARSHALL & HARLAN

*A LAW CORPORATION*

Established in 1969

**ELEVENTH FLOOR, 16633 VENTURA BOULEVARD**
**ENCINO, CALIFORNIA 91436**

Telephone: 818-990-2120
Telecopier: 818-981-4764
Email: lhhsmh@aol.com

*Business, Corporate, Partnership and Securities Law including Syndications, Mergers and Acquisitions and Public Offerings. Real Estate, Taxation, Domestic Relations, Estate Planning, Probate, Personal Injury and Insurance Regulatory Law and related Civil Litigation and Administrative Law. Health Care and Hospital Law.*

*FIRM PROFILE: Founded in 1969, Lewitt, Hackman, Hoefflin, Shapiro, Marshall & Harlan is a full service business law and civil litigation firm. Its principals and associates pride themselves in their ability to provide high quality, personalized service to their clients.*

**LEON LEWITT,** born Paris, France, October 6, 1937; admitted to bar, 1964, California and U.S. District Court, Southern District of California; 1969, U.S. Supreme Court; 1982, U.S. District Court, Northern District of California. *Education:* Ohio State University (B.S.; B.A., 1960); University of San Diego (J.D., 1963). Phi Alpha Delta; Masters of the Roll. *Member:* Beverly Hills (Member, Sections on Business and Corporate Law), San Fernando Valley (Member, Business Section), Los Angeles County and American (Member, Section on Law Practice Management) Bar Associations; State Bar of California. *PRACTICE AREAS:* Mergers and Acquisitions; Business Law; Resolution of Business Disputes.

**MICHAEL HACKMAN,** born Orange, New Jersey, March 15, 1941; admitted to bar, 1968, California and U.S. District Court, Central District of California; 1979, U.S. Tax Court. *Education:* Wesleyan University (B.A., 1962); Stanford Graduate School of Business (M.B.A., 1964); University of California at Los Angeles (J.D., 1967). Phi Alpha Delta; Order of the Coif. Instructor Certified Public Accountant Law Review Course, University of California at Los Angeles, 1972-1975. *Member:* Beverly Hills, San Fernando Valley, Los Angeles County and American (Member, Section on Taxation) Bar Associations; State Bar of California; California Society of Hospital Attorneys; American Academy of Hospital Attorneys. (Certified Specialist, Taxation Law, The State Bar of California Board of Legal Spe-

*(This Listing Continued)*

cialization). *PRACTICE AREAS:* Taxation; Business Law; Estate Planning; Health Care.

**RICHARD M. HOEFFLIN,** born Los Angeles, California, October 20, 1949; admitted to bar, 1974, California and U.S. District Court, Central District of California; 1975, U.S. Court of Appeals, Ninth Circuit; 1976, U.S. District Court, Northern District of California; 1979, U.S. Tax Court; 1982, U.S. Supreme Court. *Education:* California State University at Northridge (B.S., cum laude, Accounting, 1971); Loyola University of Los Angeles (J.D., 1974). Phi Alpha Delta. Judge Pro Tem, Los Angeles Municipal Court, 1981-1987. Family Law Mediator, Los Angeles Superior Court, 1982. Judge Pro Tem, Los Angeles Superior Court, 1987—. Judge Pro Tem, Ventura County Superior Court, 1992—. Arbitrator, American Arbitration Association, 1992—. State Bar Fee Dispute Resolution Arbitrator, 1991—. *Member:* San Fernando Valley, Los Angeles County (Member: Real Property, Litigation, Family Law and Law Office Management Sections), Ventura County and American (Member, Section of Real Property, Probate and Trust Law) Bar Associations; State Bar of California. *PRACTICE AREAS:* Business Litigation; Real Estate Law; Estate Planning.

**ANDREW L. SHAPIRO,** born New York, N.Y., March 9, 1947; admitted to bar, 1972, California, U.S. District Court, Central District of California and U.S. Court of Appeals, Ninth Circuit; 1982, U.S. District Court, Northern District of California. *Education:* California State University at Northridge (B.A., 1968); Loyola University of Los Angeles (J.D., 1971). Phi Alpha Delta. Judge Pro Tem, Los Angeles Municipal Court, 1975—. Arbitrator: American Arbitration Association, 1974—; Los Angles Superior Court, 1974—. Settlement Conference Referee, Los Angeles Superior Court, 1987—. *Member:* San Fernando Valley, Los Angeles County and American Bar Associations; State Bar of California; Los Angeles Trial Lawyers Association; California Trial Lawyers Association; The Association of Trial Lawyers of America. *PRACTICE AREAS:* Personal Injury Law; Products Liability Litigation.

**JOHN B. MARSHALL,** born Pasadena, California, November 7, 1945; admitted to bar, 1970, California and U.S. District Court, Central District of California; 1976, U.S. District Court, Southern District of California; 1982, U.S. District Court, Northern District of California; 1983, U.S. Supreme Court. *Education:* University of Southern California (A.B., magna cum laude with honors in Political Science, 1966); Boalt Hall School of Law, University of California (J.D., 1969). Phi Beta Kappa; Phi Kappa Phi; Order of the Coif; Phi Alpha Delta (Clerk, 1968-1969). Regents Fellow in Law, 1966-1967. Special Editorial Assistant, California Continuing Education of the Bar, 1968-1969. Author, Chapter on: "Legal Forms of Organization," Financial Planning for the Independent Professional, 1978. Adjunct Professor, University of California at Los Angeles, 1975—. Judge Pro Tem, Los Angeles Superior Court, 1989—. *Member:* San Fernando Valley, Los Angeles County (Arbitrator, Dispute Resolution Services, 1989—) and American (Member, Section of Corporation, Banking and Business Law) Bar Associations; State Bar of California (Member, Corporations Committee, 1983-1985). *PRACTICE AREAS:* Real Estate; Environmental; Business; Securities; Commercial Finance Law; Health Care.

**BARRY T. HARLAN,** born Syracuse, New York, January 6, 1943; admitted to bar, 1968, California and U.S. District Court, Central District of California; 1975, U.S. Supreme Court. *Education:* University of California at Berkeley (B.A., 1964); Loyola University of Los Angeles (J.D., 1967). Judge Pro Tem and Family Law Mediator, Los Angles Superior Court, 1978—. Lecturer, Real Estate Transactions, California State University at Los Angeles, 1980-1981. *Member:* San Fernando Valley and Los Angeles County (Member, Sections on: Business and Corporation; Family Law; Real Estate) Bar Associations; State Bar of California. (Certified Specialist, Family Law, The State Bar of California Board of Legal Specialization). *PRACTICE AREAS:* Family Law; Business Litigation.

---

**THOMAS CECIL,** born Fresno, California, December 11, 1955; admitted to bar, 1983, California; 1984, U.S. District Court, Northern, Eastern, Central and Southern Districts of California; 1991, U.S. Supreme Court. *Education:* University of Southern California (B.A., 1978); University of Santa Clara (J.D., 1983). *Member:* San Fernando Valley and Los Angeles County Bar Associations; State Bar of California; Los Angeles Trial Lawyers Association. *PRACTICE AREAS:* Personal Injury; Products Liability Law; Insurance Litigation.

**CARRIE A. LEVINSON,** born Encino, California, December 2, 1959; admitted to bar, 1985, California. *Education:* University of California at Los Angeles (B.A., magna cum laude, 1981); Hastings College of the Law,

*(This Listing Continued)*

University of California (J.D., 1985). Alpha Lambda Delta. Note Editor, COMM/ENT Law Journal, 1984-1985. Author: "Carson v. Here's Johnny Portable Toilets, Inc; Plumbing the Depths of the Right of Publicity," COMM/ENT Law Journal, Vol. 7, Pg. 319. *Member:* Los Angeles County Bar Association (Member, Section on Litigation); State Bar of California. *PRACTICE AREAS:* Litigation.

**MICHELLE S. ROBINS,** born Encino, California, November 4, 1964; admitted to bar, 1989, California. *Education:* University of California at Berkeley (B.A., with high distinction, 1986); Hastings College of the Law, University of California (J.D., 1989). Phi Beta Kappa; Psi Chi. Technical Editor, Hastings Constitutional Law Quarterly, 1988-1989. *Member:* San Fernando Valley (Member, Family Law Section), Los Angeles County (Member, Family Law Section) and American (Member, Family Law Section) Bar Associations; State Bar of California (Member, Family Law Section). *PRACTICE AREAS:* Litigation; Family Law; Hospital Law; Personal Injury Law.

**HEDWIG C. SWANSON,** born Tuscaloosa, Alabama, March 11, 1950; admitted to bar, 1986, California. *Education:* University of Toronto (B.A., 1971); Loyola Marymount University (J.D., 1986). Member, Staff, 1984-1985 and Co-Managing Editor, 1985-1986, Loyola of Los Angeles International & Comparative Law Journal. Author: "U.S. Corps. Operating in Saudi Arabia and Laws Affecting Discrimination: Which Law Shall Prevail?" 8 Loy. L.A. Int'l. & Comp. L.J. 135, 1985. *Member:* San Fernando Valley, Los Angeles County and American Bar Associations; State Bar of California; Los Angeles Trial Lawyers Association; The Association of Trial Lawyers of America; Women Lawyers Association of Los Angeles. *PRACTICE AREAS:* Personal Injury Law; Products Liability Law.

**KEITH TODD ZIMMET,** born New York, N.Y., November 13, 1961; admitted to bar, 1987, California, U.S. District Court, Central District of California and U.S. Court of Appeals, Ninth Circuit. *Education:* California State University, Northridge (B.S., 1984); University of Southern California Law Center (J.D., 1987). Omicron Delta Kappa; Blue Key; Golden Key; Order of Omega; Phi Alpha Delta. Editor: USC Major Tax Planning, 1986-1987; Computer Law Journal, 1986-1987. *Member:* San Fernando Valley, Los Angeles County and American (Member, Section on Business Law) Bar Associations; State Bar of California (Member, Sections on: Business Law; Real Property Law); American Association of Equipment Lessors; Financial Lawyers Conference. *PRACTICE AREAS:* Real Estate; Business; Banking; Commercial Finance Law.

OF COUNSEL

**ROBERT L. BRENT, (A PROFESSIONAL CORPORATION),** born Baltimore, Maryland, June 30, 1932; admitted to bar, 1967, California. *Education:* University of California at Los Angeles (B.S., 1954; M.B.A., 1958); University of Southern California (J.D., 1966). Beta Gamma Sigma; Phi Kappa Phi; Order of the Coif; Phi Alpha Delta. Secretary/Treasurer, Freshman Class, 1962-1963, President, Sophomore and Senior Class, 1963-1965 and Member, Student Council, 1963-1965, University of Southern California Law School. Member, University of Southern California Law Review, 1964-1966. Certified Public Accountant, California, 1958. Author: "Widow's Allowance," University of Southern California Law Review, 1965. Member of Faculty, 1958—; Adjunct Professor of Business Law, 1958—, UCLA Extension. Arbitration American Arbitration Association, 1981—. *Member:* Los Angeles County and American Bar Associations; State Bar of California; California Society of Certified Public Accountants. [With U.S. Army Signal Corps, 1954-1956]. *PRACTICE AREAS:* Arbitration.

**DAVID S. HAMILTON,** born Riverside, California, December 1, 1955; admitted to bar, 1980, California. *Education:* University of California at Los Angeles (B.A., 1977); Loyola University of Los Angeles (J.D., magna cum laude, 1980). *Member:* Los Angeles County and San Fernando Valley Bar Associations; State Bar of California (Member, Section on Business Law). *PRACTICE AREAS:* Business Law; Securities Law.

**MAURICE LEWITT,** born Paris, France, February 9, 1931; admitted to bar, 1954; 1956, California;1976, U.S. Supreme Court. *Education:* Kent State University (B.S.) 1951 Ohio State University (J.D., 1954). *Member:* Beverly Hills, Los Angeles County (Member, Section on Voluntary Arbitration) and American Bar Associations; State Bar of California; State Bar of Ohio. *PRACTICE AREAS:* Business Law; Mergers and Acquisitions; Health Care; Arbitration and Mediation.

REPRESENTATIVE CLIENTS: Nu-Med, Inc.; Valley Health System; Hemet Valley Medical Center; Menifee Valley Medical Center; Moreno Valley Community Hospital; Islandia Hotel (San Diego); National Foundation Life Insurance Co.; National Courier Systems, Inc.; Leaseamerica, Inc.; World Media Communications, Inc.; Lieberman Research West, Inc.; California Business

*(This Listing Continued)*

Bureau, Inc.; Rochlin Baran & Balbona Inc.; Coast Plaza Doctors Hospital; Southern California Orthopedic Institute; Chartered Pension Realty Investors; Chartered Realty Advisors; Crown Disposal Co.
REFERENCES: Wells Fargo Bank.

## KENNETH MILLER
16027 VENTURA BOULEVARD, SUITE 420
**ENCINO, CALIFORNIA 91436**
Telephone: 818-386-0555
Fax: 818-386-0569
Email: wizard@sure.net

*Title Insurance, Real Property, Civil Litigation.*

**KENNETH MILLER,** born New York, N.Y., October 13, 1952; admitted to bar, 1977, California; 1978, U.S. Tax Court; 1979, U.S. District Court, Central District of California; 1983, U.S. District Court, Southern District of California; 1984, U.S. District Court, Eastern District of California; 1988, Hawaii. *Education:* California State University at Northridge (B.A., cum laude, 1974); University of California at Los Angeles (J.D., 1977). Licensed Real Estate Broker, California, 1979. Co-Author: "Living on Borrowed Land," Real Estate Today, 1981. Author: "Another Reason to Avoid Full Credit Bids," Real Property Newsletter, Los Angeles County Bar Association, Sept/Oct 1993; "Foreclosed Options," LA Lawyer Magazine, January 1996. *Member:* Beverly Hills, Los Angeles County and American Bar Associations; State Bar of California (Member, Sections on: Litigation; Real Estate); Association of Real Estate Attorneys (President, 1989-1990); California Trustees Association-Los Angeles (Director, 1988-1991, 1995—; First Vice President, Legislative Committee, 1990-1991). *PRACTICE AREAS:* Title Insurance; Real Property; Civil Litigation.

REPRESENTATIVE CLIENTS: Commonwealth Land & Title Insurance Co.; Transamerica Title Insurance Co.; Southland Title Co.; Chicago Title Insurance Co.

## IRWIN R. (ROB) MILLER
**ENCINO, CALIFORNIA**
(See Oxnard)

*General Civil and Trial Practice in State and Federal Courts. Real Estate, Family, Negligence and Malpractice Law.*

## OLDMAN & COOLEY, L.L.P.
**ENCINO, CALIFORNIA**
(See Los Angeles)

*Probate and Estate Planning, Tax, Trusts and Related Civil Trial and Appellate Practice in all State Courts.*

## PEARLMAN, BORSKA & WAX
15910 VENTURA BOULEVARD, EIGHTEENTH FLOOR
**ENCINO, CALIFORNIA 91436**
Telephone: 818-501-4343
Fax: 818-386-5700

*Employment Litigation, Workers Compensation Defense, Liability Defense, Subrogation, Insurance Coverage, Special Investigation Claims.*

**BARRY S. PEARLMAN,** born Van Nuys, California, June 17, 1956; admitted to bar, 1981, California; 1982, U.S. District Court, Central District of California. *Education:* University of California at Los Angeles (B.A., 1978); Southwestern University School of Law (J.D., 1980). Adjunct Professor, Insurance Law/Workers Compensation, Watterson College, Van Nuys, California, 1985—. President, National Association of Insurance Fraud Investigators, 1996. *Member:* Los Angeles County, San Fernando Valley and American Bar Associations; State Bar of California; California Trial Lawyers Association; Los Angeles Trial Lawyers Association; California Applicants Attorneys Association; Southern California Applicants Association; Workers' Compensation Defense Attorneys Association. (Certified Specialist, Workers's Compensation Law The State Bar of California Board of Legal Specialization). *SPECIAL AGENCIES:* National Association of Insurance Fraud Investigators. *PRACTICE AREAS:* Workers

*(This Listing Continued)*

## PEARLMAN, BORSKA & WAX, Encino—Continued

Compensation Defense; Subrogation; Employment Litigation; Employer Liability Defense; Liability Defense.

**ELLIOT F. BORSKA,** born Brooklyn, New York, January 25, 1954; admitted to bar, 1983, California; U.S. Court of Appeals, 9th Circuit. *Education:* American University (B.A., 1975); California State University at Long Beach (M.S., Criminal Justice, 1979); Southwestern University (J.D., 1982). *Member,* Workers Compensation Defense Attorney's Association, 1989—. *Member:* San Fernando Valley and American Bar Associations; State Bar of California; California Trial Lawyers Association; Association of Southern California Defense Attorneys. *PRACTICE AREAS:* Workers Compensation Defense; Subrogation; Liability Defense; Employment Litigation.

**STEVEN H. WAX,** born Los Angeles, California May 28, 1950; admitted to bar, 1976, California. *Education:* California State University (B.A., 1971); Southwestern University (J.D., 1974). Delta Thetha Phi. Member, Workers Compensation Defense Attorney Association, 1982-1996. *Member:* State Bar of California. *PRACTICE AREAS:* Workers Compensation.

**GEOFFREY H. GREENUP,** born Los Angeles, California, April 25, 1954; admitted to bar, 1982, California and U.S. District Court, Central District of California; 1983, U.S. Court of Appeals, 9th Circuit. *Education:* University of California at Los Angeles (B.A., 1977); Loyola University (J.D., Honors, 1981). Member, National Association of Fraud Investigators, 1996; Workers Compensation Defense Attorneys Association, 1988-1996. *Member:* State Bar of California. *TRANSACTIONS:* Moran v. Bradford Bldg. Maintenance. *PRACTICE AREAS:* Workers Compensation Law; Criminal Victim Restitution.

**DEAN S. BROWN,** born New York, N.Y., July 6, 1963; admitted to bar, 1990, California. *Education:* University of California, Santa Barbara (B.A., 1985); Whittier School of Law (J.D., 1989). Co-Founder of Entertainment Law Society. *Member:* State Bar of California. *PRACTICE AREAS:* Workers Compensation. *Email:* dsb@4pbw.com

### ASSOCIATES

**LOUIS PETER TRYGAR,** born New Brunswick, New Jersey, November 10, 1959; admitted to bar, 1987, California. *Education:* Rutgers University (B.A., 1982); Southwestern University School of Law (J.D., 1986). President, Delta Theta Phi, 1983-1986. Member, Los Angeles County Dispute Resolution Services. *Member:* State Bar of California. *LANGUAGES:* French. *PRACTICE AREAS:* Workers Compensation Law; Subrogation.

**THOMAS E. HANDY,** born San Diego, California, September 4, 1943; admitted to bar, 1973, California and U.S. District Court, Southern District of California; 1987, U. S. Supreme Court. *Education:* University of California at Los Angeles (B.A., 1966); University of San Diego (J.D., 1972). Delta Theta Phi. *Member:* Long Beach and Los Angeles County Bar Associations; State Bar of California. (Certified Specialist, Workers' Compensation Law The State Bar of California Board of Legal Specialization). *PRACTICE AREAS:* Workers Compensation.

**CYNTHIA ELKINS HOGAN,** born Salt Lake City, Utah, January 11, 1960; admitted to bar, 1986, California. *Education:* California State University, Northridge (B.S., 1982); Southwestern University School of Law (J.D., 1985). Phi Alpha Delta. *Member:* Los Angeles (Sections on: Labor and Employment) Bar Association; State Bar of California; Member, Women Lawyers of San Fernando Valley, 1988-1992. *PRACTICE AREAS:* Employment Law Management.

---

## MARK SCHREIBER
16501 VENTURA BOULEVARD
SUITE 401
ENCINO, CALIFORNIA 91436-2068
Telephone: 818-789-2577
Fax: 818-789-3391

*Personal Injury, Elder Abuse, and Wrongful Death Defense, Copyright, Trademark, Medical Malpractice.*

**MARK SCHREIBER,** born Butler, Pennsylvania, September 16, 1949; admitted to bar, 1984, Oregon and U.S. District Court, District of Oregon; 1986, California and U.S. District Court, Central District of California. *Education:* Reed College (B.A., 1971); Cornell University (M.P.S., cum laude, 1973); Lewis and Clark College (J.D., 1984). *Member:* Los Angeles County Bar Association; State Bar Of California; Oregon State Bar. RE-

*(This Listing Continued)*

---

PORTED CASES: Klein v. Bia Hotel Corp. 41 Cal.App.4th 1133, Cal.Rptr.2d (1996).

### ASSOCIATE

**REBECCA LYNN SMITH,** admitted to bar, 1995, California. *Education:* University of California, Riverside (B.S., 1992); Southwestern University School of Law (J.D., 1995). *Member:* State Bar of California.

REPRESENTATIVE CLIENTS: Scottsdale Insurance Co.; Cats & Dogs Music; Topa Insurance Co.
REFERENCES: Scottsdale Insurance Co; National Casualty Co.; Topa Insurance Co.

---

## SHELDEN, KULCHIN, ROSEN & FLORENCE
16130 VENTURA BOULEVARD
SUITE 650
ENCINO, CALIFORNIA 91436-2590
Telephone: 818-783-1664
Fax: 818-783-0610
Email: SKF4LAW@AOL.COM

*General Civil and Trial Practice in all Courts. Insurance Defense, Personal Injury and Family Law.*

### MEMBERS OF FIRM

**AARON E. SHELDEN,** born Detroit, Michigan, September 27, 1930; admitted to bar, 1956, Michigan; 1958, California. *Education:* University of Michigan (B.A., 1952; J.D., 1955). Judge Pro Tempore, Los Angeles County Superior Court, 1970—. Judge Pro-Tem, Los Angeles Municipal Court, 1970—. *Member:* State Bar of California; American Bar Association (Member, Tort and Insurance Practice Section); Southern California Defense Attorneys; Defense Research Institute.

**SYDNEY KULCHIN,** born New York, June 27, 1933; admitted to bar, 1961, California. *Education:* University of California at Berkeley; University of California at Los Angeles; Loyola Marymount University (J.D., 1960). *Member:* Los Angeles County Bar Association; State Bar of California.

**ARNOLD L. ROSEN,** born Philadelphia, Pennsylvania, February 8, 1938; admitted to bar, 1971, California. *Education:* Rutgers University (B.A., 1961); La Verne College of Law (J.D., 1970). *Member:* Los Angeles County Bar Association; State Bar of California.

**BARRY G. FLORENCE,** born Los Angeles, California, April 11, 1953; admitted to bar, 1981, California; U.S. Court of Appeals, Ninth Circuit. *Education:* Loyola University of Los Angeles (B.S., 1975); University of West Los Angeles (J.D., 1980). *Member:* Los Angeles County and American Bar Associations; State Bar of California.

### ASSOCIATES

**HOWARD D. SILVER,** born Detroit, Michigan, October 10, 1954; admitted to bar, 1979, California. *Education:* Arizona State University (B.S., 1976); California Western School of Law (J.D., magna cum laude, 1979). *Member:* Monterey County and Los Angeles County Bar Associations; State Bar of California.

**TERRY PORVIN,** born Detroit, Michigan, April 5, 1961; admitted to bar, 1989, California and U.S. District Court, Central District of California. *Education:* University of Michigan (B.G.S., 1984); Whittier College (J.D., 1988). *Member:* Los Angeles County and American Bar Associations; State Bar of California.

**MARIO R. RIVERA,** born Los Angeles, California, July 27, 1961; admitted to bar, 1988, California; 1991, U.S. District Court, Central and Eastern Districts of California. *Education:* Loyola Marymount University (B.A., 1983); University of Minnesota (J.D., 1986). *Member:* Los Angeles County and American Bar Associations; State Bar of California. *LANGUAGES:* Spanish.

---

## MICHAEL C. SOLNER
16000 VENTURA BOULEVARD, SUITE 500
ENCINO, CALIFORNIA 91436
Telephone: 818-995-6052
FAX: 818-995-0407

*Estate Planning, Trust and Probate Law, Civil Litigation, Professional Negligence, Business, White Collar Criminal Litigation, Elder Law.*

*(This Listing Continued)*

**MICHAEL C. SOLNER,** born San Mateo, California, April 28, 1942; admitted to bar, 1972, California, U.S. District Court, Central District of California and U.S. Court of Appeals, 9th Circuit; 1988, U.S. Tax Court; 1992, U.S. District Court, Eastern District of California. *Education:* University of Southern California (B.F.S., 1964); Loyola University (J.D., 1971). Phi Delta Phi. Assistant U.S. Attorney, Central District of California, 1972-1977. *Member:* State Bar of California. [Major, U.S. Air Force, 1964-1968]. **LANGUAGES:** Spanish.

---

## HUBERT R. SOMMERS
**SUITE 1228, 16055 VENTURA BOULEVARD**
**ENCINO, CALIFORNIA 91436**
Telephone: 818-789-0465
FAX: 818-990-6304

*General Civil and Trial Practice in all State Courts. Corporation, Real Estate, Probate, Negligence and Family Law.*

**HUBERT R. SOMMERS,** born Chattanooga, Tennessee, September 28, 1930; admitted to bar, 1960, California. *Education:* University of Missouri (B.S. in B.A., 1952); University of Southern California (J.D., 1960). *Member:* San Fernando Valley and Los Angeles County (Member, Family Law Section) Bar Associations; State Bar of California (Member, Sections on: Real Property; Business; Estate Planning, Trust and Probate Law); American Bar Association.

REFERENCE: City National Bank, Encino Office.

---

## SPILE & SIEGAL, LLP
*Established in 1986*
Formerly, Krivis, Spile and Siegal, LLP
**16501 VENTURA BOULEVARD**
**SUITE 610**
**ENCINO, CALIFORNIA 91436**
Telephone: 818-784-6899
Facsimile: 818-784-0176
Email: fsiegal@counsel.com

*Insurance Defense, Real Estate, Professional Liability, Employment Law, Criminal Defense and Alternative Dispute Resolution.*

FIRM PROFILE: *Spile & Siegal, LLP serves the insurance, real estate and other industries throughout California. The firm, which has its principal office in Encino, California, with satellite offices in San Diego, San Francisco and Ventura, has been designated preferred legal counsel in "Best's Directory of Recommended Insurance Attorneys." Our attorneys have a broad range of trial and appellate experience in both state and federal courts and have developed particular expertise in the defense of professional liability, general liability and first party claims, as well as the resolution of insurance coverage issues. We have adopted a pragmatic approach to litigation and the resolution of disputes, recognizing it is often in our client's best interest to resolve claims quickly, with minimal legal expense.*

**STEVEN D. SPILE,** born Los Angeles, California, December 6, 1955; admitted to bar, 1982, California. *Education:* University of California at Berkeley (B.A., 1978); University of Southern California (J.D., 1982). **PRACTICE AREAS:** Real Estate; Insurance Defense; Professional Liability; Alternative Dispute Resolution; Risk Management.

**FLOYD J. SIEGAL,** born Chicago, Illinois, December 21, 1952; admitted to bar, 1978, California. *Education:* California State University at San Diego (B.A., 1975); Loyola Law School (J.D., 1978). **PRACTICE AREAS:** Real Estate; Insurance Defense; Professional Liability; Employment; Appellate; Criminal Defense.

ASSOCIATES
Andrew L. Leff          Michael P West
OF COUNSEL
David I. Karp (Also practicing    Olga M. Moretti
  individually at Van Nuys)       David M. Galanti
Jeffrey L. Krivis                 Richard R. Leuthold

REPRESENTATIVE CLIENTS: State Farm Insurance Company; Republic Insurance Group; Executive Risk Management Assn.; American Modern Home Insurance; Western Mutual Insurance Company; Nobel Insurance Group; Equity Fire and Casualty Company; Homeowner's Marketing Services; Willis Corroon Administrative Services; American Real Estate Association; Polaris Insurance; Employers Reinsurance Corporation; Lawyers' Mutual Insurance Co.; The Pep Boys-Manny, Moe and Jack, American Home Shield; American Banker's Insurance Group; Northern Automotive; CRES Insurance Services; Fireman's Fund; Lancer's Claim Services; CNA, Monnex Insurance Services.

---

## STAITMAN, SNYDER & TANNENBAUM
*Established in 1961*
**SUITE 1401, 16633 VENTURA BOULEVARD**
**ENCINO, CALIFORNIA 91436-1840**
Telephone: 818-981-5300; 213-872-3530
FAX: 818-981-7104

*General Civil, Trial, Appellate Practice. Insurance Law; Litigation; Personal Injury, Products Liability, Premises Liability, Medical Malpractice, Legal Malpractice, Corporate Real Estate, Commercial and General Business.*

FIRM PROFILE: *The firm of Staitman Snyder and Tannenbaum, has actively engaged in the practice of law, within the state of California, since 1961. The firm is comprised of prominently distinguished attorneys who are assisted by a highly skilled full time staff of paralegal assistants to support each field of legal practice. They encourage continuing professional development, with all of its members participating in legal educational seminars, professional association activities and civic affairs. The firms' guiding principle is to treat the practice of law as a profession rather than a business, while striving to serve its clients in the highest professional manner.*

**JACK M. STAITMAN,** born Los Angeles, California, July 1, 1931; admitted to bar, 1960, California, U.S. District Court, Central and Southern Districts of California, U.S. Court of Appeals, Ninth Circuit and U.S. Supreme Court. *Education:* University of California at Los Angeles (B.A., 1956); University of Southern California (J.D., 1959). *Member:* State Bar of California. **PRACTICE AREAS:** Insurance Defense; Insurance Coverage; Legal Malpractice; General Civil Litigation.

**BRADLEY A. SNYDER,** born Los Angeles, California, February 12, 1957; admitted to bar, 1983, California and U.S. District Court, Central and Southern Districts of California. *Education:* University of California at Santa Barbara (B.A., with high honors, 1979); Loyola Law School (J.D., 1982). Settlement Conference Officer Van Nuys and San Fernando Branch of LASC. *Member:* State Bar of California; American Board of Trial Advocates. **PRACTICE AREAS:** Insurance Defense; Insurance Coverage; Personal Injury; Medical Malpractice; Product Liability.

**JACK J. TANNENBAUM,** born Los Angeles, California, March 5, 1942; admitted to bar, 1967, California and U.S. District Court, Central District of California. *Education:* University of California at Los Angeles (B.A., 1963); Loyola University of Los Angeles (LL.B., 1966). Judge Pro Tem, Beverly Hills Municipal Court, 1972-1976. Judge Pro Tem, Los Angeles Municipal Court, 1986—. Settlement Conference Officer Van Nuys Branch of LASC. *Member:* State Bar of California. **PRACTICE AREAS:** Personal Injury Defense; Trial Attorney.

**DAVID K. DORENFELD,** born Burbank, California, November 21, 1962; admitted to bar, 1989, California and U.S. District Court, Southern and Central Districts of California. *Education:* California State University, Northridge (B.A., 1985); Whittier College School of Law (J.D., magna cum laude, 1989). Editor, Law Review. Recipient, American Jurisprudence Award in Constitutional Law. Member, Moot Court Honors Board. *Member:* State Bar of California. **PRACTICE AREAS:** Insurance Defense; Insurance Coverage; General Civil Litigation; Bad Faith; Construction Defect; Appellate.

---

**RODGER S. GREINER,** born New York, New York, July 16, 1961; admitted to bar, 1989, California, U.S. Court of Appeals, Ninth Circuit; 1990, U.S. District Court, Central and Southern Districts of California. *Education:* University of South Florida (B.A., 1983); Pepperdine University (J.D., 1987). *Member:* American Bar Association; State Bar of California. **PRACTICE AREAS:** Insurance Defense; Insurance Coverage; Personal Injury; Product Liability; Premises Liability; Medical Malpractice; General Civil Litigation.

**GERALD P. PETERS,** born Winnipeg, Canada, March 4, 1952; admitted to bar, 1981, California. *Education:* University of Illinois (B.A., 1977); University of California at Los Angeles (J.D., 1981). *Member:* San Fernando and Los Angeles County Bar Associations; The State Bar of California. **PRACTICE AREAS:** Insurance Defense; General Civil Litigation; Appellate.

*(This Listing Continued)*

**STAITMAN, SNYDER & TANNENBAUM, Encino—Continued**

**DEBORAH K. GALER,** born Santa Monica, California, October 7, 1960; admitted to bar, 1985, California. *Education:* University of Southern California (B.A., 1982); Loyola Marymount University (J.D., 1985). Member, Loyola Entertainment Law Journal, 1984-1985. *Member:* Los Angeles County Bar Association; State Bar of California. **PRACTICE AREAS:** Civil Litigation.

REPRESENTATIVE CLIENTS: Chicago Insurance Co.; Unico American Corp.; Vanguard Insurance Co.; Blue Ridge Insurance Co.; Republic Financial Services, Inc.; Republic Insurance Co.; Snyder/Diamond, Inc.; Bedford Insurance Services, Inc.; Interstate National Insurance Corp.; Crusader Insurance Co.; Church Mutual Insurance Co.; Herald Insurance Co.; Northland Insurance Co.; Northwestern National; Concord General Insurance Co.; Zodiac of North America, Inc; Sevylor USA, Inc.; American West Insurance Co.; Farm Bureau Insurance Co.; National Union Fire Insurance Co.; American Insurance Group; General Star Insurance Co.; Allstate Insurance Co.; American International Group; Bedford Insurance Systems, Inc.; Essex Insurance Co.; GAB Insurance Services, Inc.; Martin Bayer Co.; North-West Insurance Co.; U.S. Risk Managers, Inc.; Unifax Insurance Co.; Wilshire Insurance Co.; Republic Claims Service; American States Insurance Co.; U-Haul Corporation; Republic Western Insurance Company; Nobel Insurance Company; General Star Indemnity Company.
REFERENCE: Union Bank, Los Angeles, California.

---

## STANTON LAW CORPORATION

### ENCINO, CALIFORNIA

(See Los Angeles)

*Family Law, Personal Injury, Business Litigation, Business Law, Mediation and Arbitration.*

---

## RICHARD A. STAVIN AND ASSOCIATES

**15760 VENTURA BOULEVARD, SUITE 1600**
**ENCINO, CALIFORNIA 91436**
Telephone: 818-385-1144
Fax: 818-385-1149

*Los Angeles, California Office:* 1840 Century Park East, Suite 800.
Telephone: 310-553-1144.

*Business and Fraud Litigation, Insurance Defense, Unfair Competition, Wrongful Termination, Discrimination Litigation.*

**RICHARD A. STAVIN,** born Brooklyn, New York, March 14, 1949; admitted to bar, 1975, New York and U.S. District Court, Eastern District of New York; 1982, U.S. District Court, Southern District of California; 1987, U.S. Court of Appeals, Ninth Circuit; 1989, California. *Education:* Fairleigh Dickinson University (B.A., 1971); New York Law School (J.D., 1974). *Member:* New York State Economic Crimes Counsel, 1980-1982; Mayor's Arson Task Force, New York City, N.Y., 1985-1986. *Member:* Los Angeles County, New York State and American Bar Associations; State Bar of California; So. Cal. Fraud Investigators Association; California Conference of Arson Investigators; Association of Certified Fraud Examiners.

REPRESENTATIVE CLIENTS: State Farm Insurance Co.; Allstate Insurance Co.; Farmers Insurance Group; California Casualty Group; Metro-Goldwyn Mayer, Inc.; Sizzler International, Inc.; AVI Entertainment Group, Inc.; Metropolitan Property Casualty Insurance Co.; Mercury Insurance Group; Unigard Insurance Co.; Financial Indemnity Co.; Royal Insurance Co.

---

## MICHAEL M. STEIN, INC.

**17609 VENTURA BOULEVARD, SUITE 201**
**ENCINO, CALIFORNIA 91316**
Telephone: 818-788-2700
Fax: 818-788-2788
Email: MMSTEININC@AOL.COM

*Real Estate, Taxation, Corporate, Securities, Business Litigation.*

**MICHAEL M. STEIN,** born Los Angeles, California, April 6, 1941; admitted to bar, 1967, California and U.S. Tax Court. *Education:* University of California at Los Angeles (B.A. with highest honors, 1963); Harvard University (J.D., with honors, 1966). Beta Gamma Sigma. Author: "Multiple Trust Taxation," Journal of Taxation, May, 1969. *Member:* Los Angeles County (Chairman, Federal Income Tax Committee, 1970-1971; Member,

*(This Listing Continued)*

Executive Committee, 1970-1971; Section on Taxation) and American (Member, Section on Taxation) Bar Associations; State Bar of California (Member, Tax Committee, 1970-1974).

---

## STONE & ROSENBLATT

### A PROFESSIONAL CORPORATION

**16133 VENTURA BOULEVARD**
**SUITE 855**
**ENCINO, CALIFORNIA 91436**
Telephone: 818-789-2232
Fax: 818-789-2269

*Insurance Defense Litigation, Premises Liability Defense, Construction Defect, Municipality Defense, Products, Employment, Corporate and Commercial Transactions.*

**IRA H. ROSENBLATT,** born Los Angeles, California, July 12, 1963; admitted to bar, 1989, California and U.S. District Court, Central, Southern and Eastern Districts of California and District of Arizona. *Education:* University of Arizona; University of California at Santa Barbara (B.A., 1985); McGeorge School of Law, University of the Pacific (J.D., 1989). *Member:* San Fernando Valley Bar Association (Member, Litigation Section); Association of Southern California Defense Counsel. **PRACTICE AREAS:** Insurance Defense Litigation; Construction Defect; Employment Litigation; Civil Litigation; Business Transactional.

**GREGORY E. STONE,** born Los Angeles, California, August 1, 1963; admitted to bar, 1989, California, U.S. District Court, Central District of California and District of Arizona. *Education:* University of Arizona (B.A., 1986); Southwestern University (J.D., 1989). Executive Vice President, Associated Students of the University of Arizona, 1985-1986. Business Manager, Arizona Daily Wildcat, 1984-1985. Staff Member, 1984-1985 and Managing Editor, 1985-1986, Southwestern University Law Review. *Member:* Los Angeles County and American Bar Associations; State Bar of California. **PRACTICE AREAS:** Civil Litigation; Premises Liability; Security Guard Liability; Insurance Defense; Municipality Defense; Civil Rights; Business Litigation.

---

**CAMILLE CALVERT,** born Huntsville, Alabama, March 14, 1965; admitted to bar, 1991, California and U.S. District Court, Central District of California. *Education:* University of Texas at Austin (B.A., cum laude, 1990; J.D., 1990). Recipient, Griggs-Harrison Award in Products Liability. Staff Member, 1988-1989 and Note Editor, 1989-1990, The Review of Litigation. *Member:* Los Angeles County and American Bar Associations; State Bar of California. **PRACTICE AREAS:** Insurance Defense Litigation; Premises Liability; Civil Appeals and Writs.

**RICHARD S. McGUIRE,** born Glendale, California, December 13, 1955; admitted to bar, 1985, California and Nevada. *Education:* Brigham Young University (B.S., 1981; J.D., 1984). *Member:* State Bar of California; State Bar of Nevada; Association of Southern California Defense Counsel. **PRACTICE AREAS:** Civil Litigation; Premises Liability; Insurance Defense.

**ADAM J. SOIBELMAN,** born Encino, California, October 26, 1964; admitted to bar, 1990, California and U.S. Supreme Court; 1992, U.S. District Court, Central District of California and U.S. Court of Appeals, Ninth Circuit. *Education:* California State University, Northridge (B.A., 1987); University of the Pacific, McGeorge School of Law (J.D., 1990). Moot Court Finalist, Oral Advocacy. *Member:* Beverly Hills, Los Angeles County and American Bar Associations; State Bar of California; Association of Southern California Defense Counsel. **SPECIAL AGENCIES:** Judge, Regional Client Counseling Competition, Pepperdine University, 1993, 1994, 1995. **PRACTICE AREAS:** Construction Defect; Insurance Defense; Business Litigation.

## ROBERT M. VICTOR

*Established in 1991*

**16255 VENTURA BOULEVARD, SUITE 212**
**ENCINO, CALIFORNIA 91436**
Telephone: 818-385-3744
FAX: 818-385-0410
Email: rvictor@themall.net

*Business Litigation, Personal Injury, Medical Malpractice, Product Liability, Family Law, Adoption, Corporate, Contracts and Collections.*

**ROBERT M. VICTOR,** born Philadelphia, Pennsylvania, April 12, 1966; admitted to bar, 1991, California; 1992, Pennsylvania and U.S. District Court, Central District of California. *Education:* Ursinus College (B.A., 1988); St. Josephs University; Pepperdine University (J.D., 1991). *Member:* Santa Monica, Burbank, Los Angeles County, Pennsylvania and American Bar Associations; Los Angeles Trial Lawyers Association.

## PEARL FRANKLIN VOGEL

**15760 VENTURA BOULEVARD, SUITE 700**
**ENCINO, CALIFORNIA 91436-3046**
Telephone: 818-986-6696
Fax: 818-986-3110

*Family Law and Mediation.*

**PEARL FRANKLIN VOGEL,** born Montevideo, Uruguay, October 20, 1937; admitted to bar, 1969, California. *Education:* Valley Junior College and Pierce Junior College; University of San Fernando (J.D., 1968). Member, Judge Protem and Medication Panels, San Fernando Valley Bar Association. *Member:* San Fernando Valley (Member: Board of Trustees, 1976; 1979-1981; Courts Committee, 1980—; Chairperson, Family Law Section, 1984-1995) and Los Angeles County (Dispute Resolutions Committee) Bar Associations; California Women Lawyers Association. **LANGUAGES:** Spanish and Yiddish. **PRACTICE AREAS:** Family Law (90%); Mediation; Arbitration.

## BARTLETT KIRCH & LIEVERS

**221 WEST CREST STREET**
**SUITE 200**
**ESCONDIDO, CALIFORNIA 92025-1728**
Telephone: 619-738-9789
Fax: 619-738-8733

*Personal Injury, Real Estate, Employment Law and Insurance Litigation.*

### MEMBERS OF FIRM

**BRADLEY A. BARTLETT,** born South Gate, California, August 22, 1951; admitted to bar, 1980, California. *Education:* University of California at Los Angeles (B.A., cum laude, 1973); University of San Diego (J.D., cum laude, 1980). Judge Pro Temp, Arbitrator and Mediator for the Superior Court. *Member:* North San Diego County (Member, Board of Directors), San Diego County and American Bar Associations; State Bar of California; Association of Southern California Defense Counsel.

**JACQUES J. KIRCH,** born Oxnard, California, August 19, 1959; admitted to bar, 1986, California, U.S. District Court, Northern District of California and U.S. Court of Appeals, Ninth Circuit. *Education:* University of California at San Diego (B.A., 1982); University of the Pacific, McGeorge School of Law (J.D., 1986). Member, Traynor Honor Society. Recipient, American Jurisprudence Award in Corporations. *Member:* North San Diego County, San Diego County and American Bar Associations; State Bar of California; Consumer Attorneys of San Diego.

**GREGORY Y. LIEVERS,** born Escondido, California, September 9, 1957; admitted to bar, 1983, California. *Education:* University of California at Los Angeles (B.A., 1979); University of Southern California (J.D., 1983). Co-Author: "Implied Indemnity in Breach of Contract," California Lawyer, Vol. 8, No. 2, March, 1988. Partner, Higgs, Fletcher and Mack, 1989-1995. Arbitrator, San Diego Superior Court, 1991—. *Member:* San Diego County and Northern San Diego County Bar Associations; The State Bar of California.

REPRESENTATIVE CLIENTS: American General Insurance Company; Insurance Company of the West; First Pacific National Bank; Home Depot U.S.A., Inc.

## IRA S. CARLIN

*A PROFESSIONAL CORPORATION*

*Established in 1968*

**235 EAST FOURTH AVENUE**
**ESCONDIDO, CALIFORNIA 92025**
Telephone: 619-741-8111
Fax: 619-741-4073

*Corporation, Business, Probate and Real Property Law. General Civil and Trial Practice in all State and Federal Courts. Debt Collection and Enforcement of Judgments.*

**IRA S. CARLIN,** born Boston, Massachusetts, August 11, 1936; admitted to bar, 1965, California. *Education:* Columbia University (A.B., 1958; LL.B., 1964). Instructor in Agency Law, Glendale College of Law, 1970-1971. President, Columbia University Alumni Association of Southern California, 1972-1974. President, Escondido Community Clinic, 1979-1981. Member, Escondido Public Arts Commission, 1990-1992. *Member:* North San Diego County (Chairman: Insurance Committee, 1977; Education Committee, 1978; Business Law Section, 1981-1982; Client Relations Committee, 1984; Member Sections of: Probate Law; Business Law; Civil Litigation; Real Property Law; Member, Board of Directors, 1979, 1987-1990; President, 1989) and San Diego County Bar Associations; State Bar of California. [Lt. (jg), USNR, 1958-1960]. **PRACTICE AREAS:** Civil Litigation; Probate; Corporate; Business; Real Property.

REPRESENTATIVE CLIENTS: Coast Grading Co., Inc.; TT Systems West; Joseph Webb Foods, Inc.; Zyliss U.S.A., Inc.; Sunrise Commodities; Toyota of Escondido; Monmouth Capital Management, Inc.; Hot Springs Spa of North County; Speaking From Experience, Inc.; Cocina Del Charro, Inc.; Rollin Ranches, Inc.; Ketchum Forest Products, Inc.; Quantum Communications; Benton Roof Company; Natuzzi Americas, Inc.; Burlington Northern Railroad.
REFERENCE: Rancho Santa Fe National Bank (Escondido Office).

## DOROTHY A. COLE

*Established in 1981*

**TOWN VIEW PROFESSIONAL CENTRE**
**215 SOUTH HICKORY STREET, SUITE 224**
**ESCONDIDO, CALIFORNIA 92025-4361**
Telephone: 619-745-6313

*Estate Planning, Wills, Trusts and Probate Law.*

**DOROTHY A. COLE,** born Kalispell, Montana, October 6, 1939; admitted to bar, 1974, California. *Education:* Western State University (J.D., magna cum laude, 1974). Author: "The Use and Misuse of the Marital Deduction Clause," Title Insurance and Trust Company, 29th Annual Tax and Probate Forum, 1977 and Southern California Tax Conference, Society of California Accountants, November, 1977. Lecturer on Estate Planning and Probate Law, California Continuing Education of the Bar, 1985—. *Member:* Bar Association of Northern San Diego County (Member, Board of Directors, 1978-1981; Secretary, 1978; President-Elect, 1979; President, 1979-1980; Chairman, 1976-1977 and Co-Chairman, 1978-1979, 1985-1986, Probate Section); San Diego County (Member: Fee Committee, Probate Rules Revision Committee, Arbitration Committee, Probate Section) and American Bar Associations; State Bar of California; Lawyers Club, North County Branch; California Women Lawyers Association. (Certified Specialist, Probate, Estate Planning and Trust Law, The State Bar of California Board of Legal Specialization).

## CRONIN & CRONIN

**225 EAST THIRD AVENUE**
**ESCONDIDO, CALIFORNIA 92025-4203**
Telephone: 619-745-8103
Fax: 619-739-0911

*Business and Commercial Litigation, Personal Injury Litigation with Emphasis in Accident and Injury, Criminal Defense, including matters involving White Collar Crimes, Major Felonies, Misdemeanors, Drug Trafficking, D.W.I, Domestic Violence, Probate Proceedings.*

### MEMBERS OF FIRM

**DANIEL F. CRONIN** (1922-1976).

**DANIEL J. CRONIN,** born San Diego, California, December 15, 1945; admitted to bar, 1973, California and U.S. Court of Appeals, Ninth Circuit. *Education:* Western State University (J.D., 1973). *Member:* North San

*(This Listing Continued)*

**CRONIN & CRONIN, Escondido—Continued**

Diego County Bar Association (Director, 1990—; Chairman, Criminal Law Committee, 1989—); State Bar of California; California Attorneys for Criminal Justice; California Public Defenders Association; San Diego Criminal Lawyers Club. [With U.S. Army, 1966-1968]. *PRACTICE AREAS:* Personal Injury Law; Criminal Law; Business Law; Probate Law.

**JOHN O'SHEA CRONIN,** born Escondido, California, January 6, 1961; admitted to bar, 1988, California. *Education:* Western State University (B.S.L.; J.D., 1987). *PRACTICE AREAS:* Trial Law; Civil Practice; Criminal Law; Personal Injury; Probate.

---

## BRUCE D. JAQUES, JR.
### 1520 ENCINO DRIVE
### ESCONDIDO, CALIFORNIA 92025
Telephone: 619-741-7352
Fax: 619-489-1670

*Business Litigation, Business Related Matters, Arbitration, Mediation, Computer Law, Banking, Real Estate Acquisitions and Sales.*

**BRUCE D. JAQUES, JR.,** born Pasadena, California, May 9, 1951; admitted to bar, 1979, California. *Education:* Stanford University (A.B., 1973); Duke University (J.D., 1978). Co-Author: "Implied Indemnity in Breach of Contract," California Lawyer, March 1988. Legislative Assistant, U.S. Senate, 1973-1975. Law Clerk to Hon. Hamilton Hobgood, North Carolina Superior Court, Durham, North Carolina, 1977. Assistant Counsel, Governor of Missouri, 1980. Judge Pro Tempore, California Superior Court, 1983—. Elected, Board of Directors, Palomar-Pomerado Hospital District, 1986-1992. Formerly Equity Partner and Special Counsel to Higgs, Fletcher & Mack, San Diego, California. *Member:* North San Diego County (Elected, Board of Directors, 1986-1988), San Diego County and American (Member: Section of Litigation) Bar Associations; The State Bar of California; San Diego County Computer Law Association. *REPORTED CASES:* Considime Co. v. Shadle, Hunt & Hagar, 187 Cal. App. 3d 760; 232 Cal Rptr 25 (1986).

---

## LOUNSBERY, FERGUSON, ALTONA & PEAK, LLP
### 613 WEST VALLEY PARKWAY, SUITE 345
### ESCONDIDO, CALIFORNIA 92025-2552
Telephone: 619-743-1201
Facsimile: 619-743-9926
Email: LFAPllp@aol.com

*General Civil and Trial Practice in all State and Federal Courts. Administrative, Banking, Business, Commercial, Construction, Corporation, Eminent Domain, Employment Law, Environmental, Estate Planning, Government Relations, High Tech, Land Use, Municipal, Probate, Public Contracts and Franchises, Public Finance, Real Property, Redevelopment, Federal and State Securities, Tax, Wills and Trust.*

**KENNETH H. LOUNSBERY,** born Los Angeles, California, January 2, 1940; admitted to bar, 1966, California and U.S. Supreme Court. *Education:* College of William & Mary (B.A., 1962); California Western University (J.D., 1965). Phi Alpha Delta. Recipient, Moot Court Award. Editor-in-Chief, Law School Newspaper. Co-Author: Article, "Implied Warranties In Sale of Completed House," California Western Law Review, 1965. Chief Deputy City Attorney, San Diego City Attorney's Office, 1966-1970. City Attorney: City of Escondido, 1970-1972; City of South Lake Tahoe, 1972-1976. City Manager, City of Escondido, 1976-1980. Partner, Higgs, Fletcher & Mack, 1980-1982; 1992-1996. City Attorney, City of San Marcos, 1993—. President, San Diego County City Managers Association, 1979-1980. President, Palomar-Pomerado Hospital District, 1982-1986. *Member:* North San Diego County and San Diego County Bar Associations; State Bar of California; National Institute of Municipal Law Officers; San Diego-Imperial County City Attorneys Association. *PRACTICE AREAS:* Municipal; Public Finance; Redevelopment; Land Use; Construction; Development.

**DAVID W. FERGUSON,** born Los Angeles, California, November 24, 1948; admitted to bar, 1973, California; 1974, U.S. Court of Military Appeals. *Education:* Oregon State University; University of California at Los Angeles (B.A., 1970; J.D., 1973). Chair, Escondido Downtown Revitalization Committee, 1982-1985. Chair, Escondido Chamber of Commerce,
*(This Listing Continued)*

---

1986-1987. Chair, California Center for the Arts, 1991-1994. *Member:* North San Diego County and San Diego County Bar Associations; State Bar of California. [Lt., U.S. Navy, 1970-1977]. *PRACTICE AREAS:* Local Government Transactions; Public Franchises; Public Contracts; Land Use; Development.

**ERICK R. ALTONA,** born San Diego, California, May 10, 1959; admitted to bar, 1985, California. *Education:* University of California at San Diego (B.A., in Mathematics, 1981); University of California at Davis (J.D., 1985). Recipient, American Jurisprudence Award for Equitable Remedies. *Member:* North San Diego County Bar Association; The State Bar of California. *PRACTICE AREAS:* Business; Real Estate; Commercial; Corporation; Federal and State Securities.

**HELEN HOLMES PEAK,** born Fort Irwin, California, September 9, 1957; admitted to bar, 1983, California and U.S. District Court, Southern District of California. *Education:* Stanford University (B.A., 1979); McGeorge School of Law, University of the Pacific (J.D., 1983). *Member:* North San Diego County and San Diego County Bar Associations; State Bar of California. *PRACTICE AREAS:* Environmental; Land Use; Municipal; Public Contracts; Real Property.

---

**MICHELLE J. BROWN,** born San Jose, California, June 4, 1959; admitted to bar, 1986, California. *Education:* University of California at San Diego (B.A., 1982); McGeorge School of Law, University of the Pacific (J.D., 1986). *Member:* San Diego County and American Bar Associations; State Bar of California. *PRACTICE AREAS:* Real Estate; Estate Planning; Business; Government Relations.

**KEVIN P. SULLIVAN,** born Escondido, California, December 30, 1962; admitted to bar, 1990, Texas; 1991, U.S. Court of Appeals, Fifth Circuit and U.S. District Court, Northern District of Texas; 1995, California and U.S. District Court, Western District of Texas. *Education:* University of California, San Diego (B.A., cum laude, 1986); University of San Diego (J.D., cum laude, 1990). Member, University of San Diego Law Review, 1988-1990. *Member:* American Bar Association; State Bar of California; State Bar of Texas. *REPORTED CASES:* Industrial Clearinghouse, Inc. v. Browning Manufacturing, 953 F.2d 1004 (5th Cir. 1992). *PRACTICE AREAS:* Business Litigation; Employment Law; Municipal Law.

**CHARLES A. LEPLA,** born Detroit, Michigan, January 27, 1963; admitted to bar, 1994, California. *Education:* California Polytechnic State University (B.S., cum laude, 1986); University of San Diego (J.D., 1993). Phi Kappa Phi. *Member:* State Bar of California; American Institute of Certified Planners; American Planning Association. *PRACTICE AREAS:* Land Use; Development; Public Contracts and Franchises.

**DANIEL LOUNSBERY,** born San Diego, California, February 14, 1966; admitted to bar, 1996, California. *Education:* University of Puget Sound (B.A., 1989); University of San Diego, School of Law (J.D., 1995). *PRACTICE AREAS:* General Litigation; Land Use; Municipal; Administrative.

### OF COUNSEL

**GARTH O. REID, JR.,** born Twin Falls, Idaho, March 14, 1944; admitted to bar, 1975, California; 1976, U.S. Tax Court; 1978, U.S. District Court, Southern District of California; 1978, U.S. Court of Appeals, Ninth Circuit. *Education:* University of Idaho (B.S., 1967); Hastings College of the Law, University of California (J.D., 1975). Certified Public Accountant, California, 1971. *Member:* San Diego County, North County and American Bar Associations; State Bar of California (Member, Sections on: Taxation Law; Business Law; Estate Planning Law); American Institute of Certified Public Accountants; California Society of Certified Public Accountants. [Capt., U.S. Army, 1967-1969]. (Certified Specialist, Taxation Law, The State Bar of California, Board of Legal Specialization) (Also practicing individually). *PRACTICE AREAS:* Taxation Law; Corporations Law; Estate Planning Law; Trusts Law; Business Law; Commercial Law.

**CURTIS M. FITZPATRICK,** born Rawlins, Wyoming, May 8, 1928; admitted to bar, 1964, California. *Education:* University of California at Los Angeles (A.B., 1952); University of San Diego (J.D., 1963). Assistant City Attorney, San Diego, California, 1981-1996. [Sgt, U.S. Army, 1945-1948]. *PRACTICE AREAS:* Municipal Government; Municipal Financing; Land Use and Planning; Municipal Franchising; Municipal Sports Enterprise.

## PROFESSIONAL BIOGRAPHIES
CALIFORNIA—ESCONDIDO

### JAMES E. LUND
249 EAST FOURTH AVENUE
**ESCONDIDO, CALIFORNIA 92025**
Telephone: 619-747-7800
FAX: 619-489-8423

*Corporate, Business, Real Property and Entertainment Law. Commercial and Business. Trial Practice in all State and Federal Courts, including Debt Collection and Creditor Bankruptcy Law.*

**JAMES E. LUND,** born Lynnwood, California, June 13, 1951; admitted to bar, 1979, California and U.S. District Court, Southern District of California; 1980, U.S. District Court, Central District of California. *Education:* Palomar College; Brigham Young University (B.A., 1976; J.D., cum laude, 1979). Omicron Delta Epsilon. Instructor, Legal Writing and Research, Brigham Young University, 1978-1979. Member: Escondido School Board, 1984-1990; Board of Directors, Escondido Chamber of Commerce, 1993—. *Member:* North County and San Diego County Bar Associations; State Bar of California.

### GARTH O. REID, JR.
*A PROFESSIONAL LAW CORPORATION*
Established in 1982
319 EAST SECOND AVENUE
**ESCONDIDO, CALIFORNIA 92025**
Telephone: 619-746-6420

*Taxation, Corporations, Estate Planning, Trusts, Business and Commercial Law.*

**GARTH O. REID, JR.,** born Twin Falls, Idaho, March 14, 1944; admitted to bar, 1975, California; 1976, U.S. Tax Court; 1978, U.S. District Court, Southern District of California; 1978, U.S. Court of Appeals, Ninth Circuit. *Education:* University of Idaho (B.S., 1967); Hastings College of the Law, University of California (J.D., 1975). Certified Public Accountant, California, 1971. *Member:* San Diego County, North County and American Bar Associations; State Bar of California (Member, Sections on: Taxation Law; Business Law; Estate Planning Law); American Institute of Certified Public Accountants; California Society of Certified Public Accountants. [Capt., U.S. Army, 1967-1969]. (Certified Specialist, Taxation Law, The State Bar of California, Board of Legal Specialization) (Of Counsel to Lounsbery Ferguson Altona & Peak LLP).

REFERENCE: Union Bank (La Jolla Branch).

### RODEN AND THOMPSON
Established in 1966
225 EAST THIRD AVENUE
**ESCONDIDO, CALIFORNIA 92025**
Telephone: 619-745-1484
Facsimile: 619-739-0911

*Trial Practice. Personal Injury, Wrongful Death, Insurance and Products Liability Law.*

#### MEMBERS OF FIRM

**ROBERT RODEN,** born Texarkana, Texas, January 18, 1936; admitted to bar, 1966, California. *Education:* Yuba Junior College (A.A., 1956); Chico State College (B.A., 1958); Hastings College of Law, University of California (LL.B., 1965). Phi Alpha Delta. Recipient, Outstanding Trial Lawyers Award, March, 1985. *Member:* North San Diego County Bar Association (President, 1973); State Bar of California; Consumer Attorneys of San Diego (Trial Lawyer of the Year, 1976); Consumer Attorneys of California; The Association of Trial Lawyers of America. **PRACTICE AREAS:** Negligence Law; Wrongful Death Law; Product Liability Law.

**FRANK M. THOMPSON,** born Santa Maria, California, November 6, 1951; admitted to bar, 1981, California. *Education:* California State University at Fullerton (B.A., 1974); California State University at San Diego; California Western School of Law (J.D., 1981). Recipient, Outstanding Trial Lawyers Award, February, 1987. *Member:* North San Diego County and American Bar Associations; State Bar of California; Consumer Attorneys of San Diego. [Lt. Col., USMCR, 1974—]. **PRACTICE AREAS:** Negligence Law; Wrongful Death Law; Product Liability Law.

REFERENCE: North County Bank (Escondido Branch).

### RANDALL C. STERLING
225 EAST THIRD AVENUE
**ESCONDIDO, CALIFORNIA 92025-4203**
Telephone: 619-738-1622
Facsimile: 619-738-4511

*General Civil Trial Practice.*

**RANDALL C. STERLING,** born Lynwood, California, July 22, 1958; admitted to bar, 1988, California and U.S. District Court, Southern District of California. *Education:* Pepperdine University (B.S., magna cum laude, 1979); National University (M.B.A., summa cum laude, 1985; J.D., 1988). *Member:* San Diego County Bar Association; State Bar of California.

### WHITE AND BRIGHT
*A PROFESSIONAL CORPORATION*
Established in 1981
355 WEST GRAND AVENUE
SECOND FLOOR
**ESCONDIDO, CALIFORNIA 92025**
Telephone: 619-747-3200
Fax: 619-747-5574
Email: WHITEBRIGH@aol.com

Long Beach, California Office: 3780 Kilroy Airport Way, Suite 200. Telephone: 310-490-3120. Fax: 310-981-7353.

*General Civil Litigation, Real Estate, Insurance Defense, Business, Environmental, Estate Planning, Construction Defect and Personal Injury Law.*

*FIRM PROFILE: White and Bright was founded in 1981 by Bruce H. White and David S. Bright. Our expanding firm places special emphasis on serving the legal needs of the North San Diego County business and real estate communities. Through responsive and proficient legal representation, client newsletters, seminars, continuing legal education and civic involvement, White and Bright continually endeavors to provide its clients with legal service of the highest standards.*

**DAVID S. BRIGHT,** born Los Angeles, California, July 9, 1949; admitted to bar, 1974, California. *Education:* University of California at Los Angeles (B.A., cum laude, 1971); University of San Diego (J.D., 1974). Phi Alpha Delta. Recipient, American Jurisprudence Award in Bankruptcy. *Member:* San Diego County and American Bar Associations; The State Bar of California. **PRACTICE AREAS:** Real Estate; Civil Litigation.

**LEIGH A. RAYNER,** born London, England, July 28, 1952; admitted to bar, 1985, California and U.S. District Court, Southern District of California. *Education:* Western State University (J.D., cum laude, 1985). Public Relations Editor, Criminal Justice Journal, 1985. Recipient, American Jurisprudence Awards in Contracts, Evidence, Remedies and Family Law. *Member:* San Diego County and North County Bar Associations; State Bar of California; Consumer Attorneys of San Diego. **PRACTICE AREAS:** Personal Injury; Business Litigation.

**BRUCE H. WHITE, (A P.C.),** born Evanston, Illinois, January 6, 1933; admitted to bar, 1966, California. *Education:* Whittier College (B.A., 1956); California Western University (J.D., 1966). Phi Delta Phi. Emeritus Chairman of the Board, Palomar Savings and Loan. *Member:* San Diego County, North San Diego County and American Bar Associations; State Bar of California; Consumer Attorneys of California. [With U.S. Army, 1953-1955]. **PRACTICE AREAS:** Real Estate.

**RANDOLPH W. ORTLIEB,** born San Diego, California, December 30, 1960; admitted to bar, 1987, California. *Education:* Pomona College (B.A., 1983); Washington University (J.D., 1987; M.B.A., 1987). Judge Pro-Tem, San Diego County Municipal Court, 1994-1995. *Member:* Bar Association of Northern San Diego County (Member, Lawyer Referral Service). **LANGUAGES:** Spanish. **PRACTICE AREAS:** Commercial Collections; Real Estate Litigation; Estate Planning; Construction Litigation.

**JENNIFER M. MCGAULEY,** born Santa Rosa, California, September 15, 1961; admitted to bar, 1991, California and U.S. District Court, Northern District of California; 1992, U.S. District Court, Southern District of California. *Education:* Humboldt State University (B.A., 1984); Western State University (J.D., summa cum laude, 1990). *Member:* San Diego County and American Bar Associations; Bar Association of Northern San Diego County.

*(This Listing Continued)*

**WHITE AND BRIGHT,** A PROFESSIONAL CORPORATION, *Escondido—Continued*

**MICHAEL A. FRIEDRICHS,** born Escondido, California, May 6, 1964; admitted to bar, 1995, California and U.S. District Court, Southern District of California. *Education:* University of California at Santa Cruz (B.A., Politics, 1988); Western State University (J.D., cum laude, 1995). Recipient: Outstanding Scholastic Achievement Award, Western State University, 1994-1995; American Jurisprudence Award, Contracts. Listed in Who's Who Among American Colleges and Universities, 1994-1995. Executive Editor, 1993-1995 and Editor-in-Chief, 1994-1995, San Diego Justice Journal. Author, Note, "Fast Track: A Panacea for a Cluttered and Delayed Court System?" 1 San Diego Justice Journal, 443, 1993. *Member:* Bar Association of Northern San Diego County; State Bar of California. **PRACTICE AREAS:** Civil Litigation.

REPRESENTATIVE CLIENTS: Agricultural Supply, Inc.; Coast Waste Management Co., Inc.; Escondido Escrow Co.; Escondido Ready Mix; Hollandia Dairy; Homer Heller Ford; Mission Pools of Escondido, Inc.; SKS Oil, Inc.; Wessel Construction Co., Inc.; HMS, Inc.; Federal Deposit Insurance Corporation; Vista Fire Protection Board; Northern San Diego County Association of Realtors.

---

## WILLIAM F. BARNUM
2103 MYRTLE AVENUE
P.O. BOX 173
**EUREKA, CALIFORNIA 95502**
Telephone: 707-442-6405
Fax: 707-442-1507

*Transactional Real Estate, Environmental Law, Land Use Law, Construction and Development Law, Timber and Logging.*

**WILLIAM F. BARNUM,** born Eureka, California, June 7, 1954; admitted to bar, 1979, California and U.S. District Court, Eastern District of California; 1980, U.S. District Court, Northern District of California. *Education:* Humboldt State University (B.A., Management, 1976); McGeorge School of Law, University of the Pacific (J.D., 1979). Founding Chairman, Humboldt Bay Alliance for Economic Development, 1989-1991. Member, American Arbitration Association Panel of Arbitrators. *Member:* Humboldt County Bar Association; State Bar of California (Member, Real Property Section).

REPRESENTATIVE CLIENTS: Louisiana-Pacific Corp.; Fidelity National Title Insurance Co.; 3/M National Advertising Company; Kramer Properties, Inc.; Denis E. Cosby Construction, Inc.; JLF Construction; Northern California Association of Home Builders; Barnum Timber Company.

---

## DALTON & BICKNELL
732 FIFTH STREET, SUITE H
P.O. BOX 24
**EUREKA, CALIFORNIA 95502-0024**
Telephone: 707-443-0878
Fax: 707-443-2429

*Family Law, Personal Injury, Probate, Business and Bankruptcy Law.*

### MEMBERS OF FIRM

**JOHN M. DALTON,** born Eureka, California, June 5, 1928; admitted to bar, 1957, California. *Education:* University of Santa Clara and University of California at Berkeley (B.A., 1950); University of California at Berkeley (J.D., 1957). Phi Delta Phi. *Member:* Humboldt County (President, 1971) and American Bar Associations; The State Bar of California. [With U.S. Army, 1952-1954]. (Certified Specialist, Family Law, The State Bar of California Board of Legal Specialization). **PRACTICE AREAS:** Family Law; Civil Litigation; Probate.

**DONALD W. BICKNELL,** born Indianapolis, Indiana, October 3, 1949; admitted to bar, 1974, Connecticut; 1978, California; 1994, Hawaii. *Education:* Indiana University (A.B., with high distinction, 1971); Yale University (J.D., 1974). Phi Eta Sigma; Phi Beta Kappa. *Member:* Humboldt County and American Bar Associations; The State Bar of California. (Certified Specialist, Family Law, The State Bar of California Board of Legal Specialization). **PRACTICE AREAS:** Family Law; Bankruptcy; Civil Litigation.

REFERENCE: Humboldt National Bank.

---

## DAVID P. DIBBLE
628 H STREET
**EUREKA, CALIFORNIA 95501**
Telephone: 707-444-9330

*General Civil and Trial Practice in all State and Federal Courts. Personal Injury, Products Liability, Professional Liability and Insurance Bad Faith Law. Commercial Litigation.*

**DAVID P. DIBBLE,** born San Francisco, California, September 22, 1950; admitted to bar, 1977, California and Alabama. *Education:* Ohio Wesleyan University (B.A., 1972); Cumberland School of Law (J.D., magna cum laude, 1976). Phi Alpha Delta. Member, Curia Honoris. Law Clerk to Clarence W. Allgood, Senior U.S. District Judge, Northern District of Alabama, 1976-1977. Author: "Court Cost in Alabama," Cumberland Law Review, 431 Fall, 1975. *Member:* State Bar of California; Alabama State Bar; American Bar Association; San Francisco Trial Lawyers Association; California Trial Lawyers Association. **PRACTICE AREAS:** Personal Injury; Products Liability; Professional Liability; Insurance Bad Faith; Commercial Litigation.

---

## HARLAND LAW FIRM
*Established in 1948*
622 H STREET
**EUREKA, CALIFORNIA 95501**
Telephone: 707-444-9281
Fax: 707-445-2961

*Fortuna, California Office:* 954 Main Street. Telephone: 707-725-4426. Fax: 707-725-5738.

*General Trial and Appellate Practice. Family, Probate, Estate Planning, Timber and Logging, Corporation, Personal Injury, Administrative, Construction, Labor, Education, Business and Real Property Law.*

### MEMBERS OF FIRM

**GERALD R. HARLAND,** born Clarinda, Iowa, August 21, 1922; admitted to bar, 1951, California. *Education:* Tarkio College (A.B., 1943); Stanford University (LL.B., 1951). Phi Alpha Delta. *Member:* Humboldt County Bar Association; The State Bar of California. **PRACTICE AREAS:** Estate Planning Law; Real Property Law; Probate Law; Business Law.

**RICHARD A. SMITH,** born Jacksonville, Florida, February 24, 1945; admitted to bar, 1970, South Dakota; 1971, California; 1973, U.S. Supreme Court; 1975, U.S. Claims Court. *Education:* University of California at Davis (A.B., 1967); Loyola University of Los Angeles (J.D., 1970). Member, Loyola University of Los Angeles Law Review, 1969-1970. *Member:* Humboldt County and American Bar Associations (Chairman, Forest Resources Committee, Natural Resources Section, 1991-1993); State Bar of California. **PRACTICE AREAS:** Business Law; Banking Law; Timber Law; Bankruptcy Law.

**DAVID C. MOORE,** born Conshohocken, Pennsylvania, March 7, 1943; admitted to bar, 1969, Pennsylvania; 1972, California; 1979, U.S. Supreme Court. *Education:* Villanova University (B.S., 1965; J.D., 1968). *Member:* Humboldt County Bar Association; State Bar of California. [Capt. Judge Advocate, U.S. Marine Corps, 1969-1971]. (Certified Specialist, Family Law, The State Bar of California Board of Legal Specialization). **PRACTICE AREAS:** Civil Litigation; Family Law.

**THOMAS J. BECKER,** born Cleveland, Ohio, July 7, 1939; admitted to bar, 1964, Florida; 1978, California; 1979, U.S. Supreme Court. *Education:* College of the Holy Cross and Spring Hill College (B.S., 1961); University of Florida (J.D., 1967, replaced LL.B. conferred, 1964). *Member:* Humboldt County Bar Association; State Bar of California; California Trial Lawyers Association. **PRACTICE AREAS:** Civil Litigation; Real Property Law; Administrative Law.

**WILLIAM T. KAY, JR.,** born Waynesville, Missouri, May 1, 1944; admitted to bar, 1974, California. *Education:* Seattle University (B.A., 1966); University of San Diego (J.D., 1972). Phi Alpha Delta. Member, Panel of Arbitrators, American Arbitration Association. *Member:* Humboldt County (President, 1986) and American Bar Associations; State Bar of California; Chairman, Six Rivers National Bank. **PRACTICE AREAS:** General Civil Litigation; Personal Injury Law.

**JOHN W. WARREN,** born Arcata, California, June 19, 1942; admitted to bar, 1969, California, U.S. District Court, Northern District of California and U.S. Court of Appeals, Ninth Circuit. *Education:* Humboldt State University (A.B., 1965); University of San Francisco (J.D., 1968). Member,
*(This Listing Continued)*

## PROFESSIONAL BIOGRAPHIES

McAuliffe Law Honor Society. *Member:* Humboldt County Bar Association; State Bar of California. **PRACTICE AREAS:** Business Law; Estate Planning Law; Probate Law; Maritime Law.

**GERI ANNE JOHNSON,** born Auburn, California, June 2, 1952; admitted to bar, 1980, California and U.S. District Court, Northern District of California; 1981, U.S. Court of Appeals, Ninth Circuit; 1986, U.S. Claims Court. *Education:* California State University at Chico (B.A., 1973); Golden Gate University (J.D., 1980). Consultant, Real Property Subcommittee's Joint Advisory to Continuing Education of the Bar and the State Bar of California. *Member:* Ninth Judicial Circuit Historical Society; California Supreme Court Historical Society. *Member:* Humboldt County Bar Association; State Bar of California (Member, 1988-1990 and Chair, 1990-1991, Committee on the History of Law in California). **PRACTICE AREAS:** Appellate Law; Business Law; Corporate Law; Employment Law.

### ASSOCIATE

**JULIA S. GOLD,** born San Francisco, California, April 21, 1964; admitted to bar, 1994, California. *Education:* University of California at Davis (B.S., 1989); Lewis and Clark College (J.D., 1993). *Member:* Humboldt County Bar Association; State Bar of California. **PRACTICE AREAS:** Estate Planning; Probate Law; Tax Law.

---

## LAW OFFICES OF HANS W. HERB

**EUREKA, CALIFORNIA**

(See Santa Rosa)

*Complex Environmental, Hazardous Waste and Insurance Coverage Litigation.*

---

## HUBER & GOODWIN

*Established in 1945*

HUBER-GOODWIN BUILDING
550 "I" STREET
P.O. BOX 23
**EUREKA, CALIFORNIA 95502-0023**
Telephone: 707-443-4573
Fax: 707-443-7182
Email: prior@humboldt1.com
Email: carson@humboldt1.com

*General Civil and Trial Practice. Corporation, Small Business, Probate, Estate Planning, Administrative, Personal Injury, Workers Compensation, Forestry, Agricultural, Commercial, Real Property and Environmental Law.*

### MEMBERS OF FIRM

**MILTON L. HUBER** (1914-1994).

**G. EDWARD GOODWIN** (Retired).

**DAYTON D. MURRAY, JR.** (1923-1981).

**NORMAN C. CISSNA** (1923-1989).

**ROBERT D. PRIOR,** born Fresno, California, May 22, 1932; admitted to bar, 1957, California. *Education:* Stanford University (A.B., 1954; J.D., 1957). Phi Delta Phi. *Member:* Humboldt County (President, 1974) Association; The State Bar of California. *Email:* prior@humboldt1.com

**WILLIAM H. CARSON, JR.,** born Chicago, Illinois, April 12, 1940; admitted to bar, 1970, California. *Education:* University of Illinois (B.S., 1966); University of California at Berkeley (J.D., 1969). National College of District Attorneys, 1971. Deputy District Attorney, Humboldt County, 1970-1973. Chief Trial Deputy, Humboldt County, 1972-1973. President, Humboldt County Easter Seal Society, 1972. *Member:* The State Bar of California; American Bar Association; Fellow of the American Bar Association.

REPRESENTATIVE CLIENTS: D & B Cattle Co. (livestock); Simpson Timber Co.; Miller & Rellim Redwood Cos.; Arcata Redwood Co.; Humboldt Area Foundation; Western Self Insurance Service (workers Compensation); Fresh Freeze Supply, Inc. (food services); Eureka Medical Complex; Redwood Coast Trucking; Simpson Paper Co.; Humboldt County Visitors & Convention Bureau; The Pacific Lumber Co.; Eureka Chamber of Commerce; Northern California Log Scaling and Grading Bureau; Westfall Stevedore Co.; Hilfiker Pipe Company; SHN Consulting Engineers & Surveyors; Mercer-Fraser Co.; Six Rivers National Bank.
REFERENCES: U.S. Bank of California; Humboldt Bank.

---

## JANSSEN, MALLOY, MARCHI, NEEDHAM & MORRISON

730 FIFTH STREET
P.O. DRAWER 1288
**EUREKA, CALIFORNIA 95501**
Telephone: 707-445-2071
Fax: 707-445-8305

*General Civil and Business Litigation. Products Liability, Negligence and Professional Liability. Insurance, Bankruptcy (Creditor). Medical Malpractice Defense. Insurance Coverage Litigation. General Personal Injury Litigation. Real Estate Litigation.*

### MEMBERS OF FIRM

**CLAYTON R. JANSSEN,** born San Francisco, California, November 24, 1925; admitted to bar, 1952, California. *Education:* Stanford University (B.A., 1950; J.D., 1951). Phi Delta Phi. Deputy Attorney General, State of California, 1952-1954. Member, 1961-1980 and President, 1963-1965; 1969-1971, Eureka Board of Education. Member: Board of Visitors, Stanford University Law School, 1977-1980; Judicial Council of California, 1981-1983. *Member:* Barristers Club of San Francisco (Member, Board of Directors, 1956-1957); Humboldt County (President, 1961) and American Bar Associations; The State Bar of California (Member, Board of Governors, 1973-1976; Vice President and Treasurer, 1975-1976); The Association of Defense Counsel of Northern California (Director, 1962-1963). Fellow: American College of Trial Lawyers; American Bar Foundation. Advocate, American Board of Trial Advocates. Fellow, International Academy of Trial Lawyers. **PRACTICE AREAS:** Products Liability; Personal Injury; Professional Liability; Medical Malpractice Defense; Real Estate Litigation; Insurance Defense.

**NICHOLAS R. MARCHI,** born San Francisco, California, July 19, 1949; admitted to bar, 1974, California. *Education:* University of Oregon (B.S., 1971; J.D., 1974). Phi Eta Sigma; Phi Beta Kappa. *Member:* Humboldt County Bar Association; The State Bar of California. **PRACTICE AREAS:** Professional Liability; Insurance; Medical Malpractice Defense; Insurance Coverage.

**MICHAEL F. MALLOY,** born Eureka, California, September 30, 1949; admitted to bar, 1974, California. *Education:* St. Mary's College of California (B.A., 1971); Hastings College of Law, University of California (J.D., 1974). *Member:* Humboldt County (President, 1990) and American Bar Associations; The State Bar of California. California Society of Healthcare Attorneys. **PRACTICE AREAS:** Bankruptcy; Business Litigation; Estate Planning; Probate.

**MICHAEL W. MORRISON,** born Portland, Oregon, November 11, 1950; admitted to bar, 1976, California. *Education:* California State University at Chico (B.A., 1973); Hastings College of Law, University of California (J.D., 1976). Deputy District Attorney, Humboldt County, 1977-1981. *Member:* The State Bar of California (Member, Standing Committee on The Environment, 1987-1989); Humboldt County Bar Association (Member, Lawyer Referral Service/Legal Aid Committee); California Society for Healthcare Attorneys. **PRACTICE AREAS:** Products Liability; Professional Liability; Medical Malpractice Defense; Personal Injury; Real Estate Litigation.

**W. TIMOTHY NEEDHAM,** born Placerville, California, March 13, 1953; admitted to bar, 1980, California; 1981, Alaska. *Education:* Humboldt State University (B.A., magna cum laude, 1977); University of California at Davis (J.D., 1980). Member, University of California at Davis Law Review, 1979-1980. Member, Judicial Council Committee on Uniform Local Rules. *Member:* Humboldt County and Alaska Bar Associations; The State Bar of California. **PRACTICE AREAS:** Products Liability; Professional Liability; Insurance; Personal Injury; Insurance Coverage; Real Estate Litigation.

### ASSOCIATES

**CATHERINE M. KOSHKIN,** born Buffalo, New York, February 6, 1954; admitted to bar, 1990, California. *Education:* University of Florida (B.A., 1976); McGeorge School of Law (J.D., 1990). *Member:* Humboldt County and American Bar Associations; State Bar of California (Member, General Practice Section; Estate Planning, Trust & Probate Section); California Women Lawyers. **PRACTICE AREAS:** Bankruptcy; Real Estate Litigation; Business.

COUNSEL FOR: Clinic Mutual Insurance Co.; California Casualty Insurance Co.; Allied Insurance Co.; TRW, Inc.; U.S. Bank; Caterpillar, Inc.; Nor-Cal Mutual Insurance Co.; The Travelers Insurance Co.; Pierson Investment Co. (real

*(This Listing Continued)*

**JANSSEN, MALLOY, MARCHI, NEEDHAM & MORRISON,** Eureka—*Continued*

estate); Harvey M. Harper Co. (automobile dealership); General Hospital; Pacific Bell; Humboldt Petroleum; Reichhold Chemicals, Inc.; Canevari Timber Co., Inc.; Safeco Insurance Companies of America; Safeco Select Markets; Six Rivers National Bank; American Security Insurance Company; Lawyers Mutual Insurance Company; Pacific Gas & Electric Co.

## MITCHELL, BRISSO, DELANEY & VRIEZE

814 SEVENTH STREET
P.O. DRAWER 1008
EUREKA, CALIFORNIA 95502
Telephone: 707-443-5643
Fax: 707-444-9586

*General Civil and Trial Practice in all Courts. Probate, Insurance, Corporation, Real Property, Timber and Logging Law.*

*FIRM PROFILE: The firm has been in business in Eureka since 1941, commencing under the name of Mitchell & Henderson. Clifford B. Mitchell, son of one of the founding members, is currently a partner in the firm. A total of five partners and two associates primarily serve the Northern California Counties of Humboldt, Del Norte and Trinity. Approximately 85% of the firm's work is in the field of insurance defense, accompanied by strong practices in probate, general business and municipal law.*

### MEMBERS OF FIRM

**CLIFFORD B. MITCHELL,** born San Francisco, California, July 20, 1927; admitted to bar, 1953, California. *Education:* Humboldt State College and Stanford University (A.B., 1950); Stanford University (J.D., 1953). Phi Delta Phi. Author: "Specific Performance by Partial Vendee," 4 Stanford Law Review, p. 443. Member, Board of Editors, Stanford Law Review, 1952-1953. *Member:* Humboldt County and American Bar Associations; The State Bar of California; Advocate, American Board of Trial Advocates; The Association of Defense Counsel of Northern California; Association of Insurance Attorneys. Fellow, American College of Trial Lawyers. *PRACTICE AREAS:* Insurance Defense.

**NANCY K. DELANEY,** born Eureka, California, November 17, 1950; admitted to bar, 1976, California. *Education:* Humboldt State University (A.B., 1972; M.A., 1973); Hastings College of Law, University of California (J.D., 1976). *Member:* Humboldt County and American Bar Associations; The State Bar of California; The Association of Defense Counsel of Northern California. *PRACTICE AREAS:* General Civil Litigation; Estate Planning and Probate; Personal Injury; Civil Rights; Public Entity Defense.

**PAUL A. BRISSO,** born Alhambra, California, March 21, 1952; admitted to bar, 1978, California. *Education:* California State University, Humboldt (B.A., magna cum laude, 1973); McGeorge School of Law, University of the Pacific (J.D., with great distinction, 1978). Judicial Attorney to Justice George N. Zenovich, California Fifth District Court of Appeals, 1978-1979. *Member:* Humboldt County and American Bar Associations; The State Bar of California; The Association of Defense Counsel of Northern California; American Board of Trial Advocates; Defense Research Institute. *REPORTED CASES:* Harrison v. Co. of Del Norte (1985) 168 Cal. App. 3d 1; Herring v. Peterson (1981) 116 Cal. App. 3d 608. *PRACTICE AREAS:* General Civil Litigation; Personal Injury; Construction; Wrongful Termination; Products Liability; Public Entity Defense.

**JOHN M. VRIEZE,** born Iowa City, Iowa, July 15, 1952; admitted to bar, 1984, California. *Education:* University of Miami (B.S., cum laude, 1974); Humboldt State University (M.A., 1980); University of Oregon (J.D., 1984). *Member:* Humboldt County and American Bar Associations; The State Bar of California; The Association of Defense Counsel of Northern California. *PRACTICE AREAS:* General Civil Litigation; Personal Injury; Civil Rights; Public Entity Defense.

**C. TODD ENDRES,** born Redding, California, January 9, 1964; admitted to bar, 1990, California. *Education:* Shasta Junior College (A.A., 1984); University of California at Davis (B.A., 1986); McGeorge School of Law (J.D., 1990).

### ASSOCIATES

**WILLIAM F. MITCHELL,** born Eureka, California, February 28, 1956; admitted to bar, 1992, California. *Education:* Occidental College (B.A., 1985); Santa Clara University School of Law (J.D., 1991). *Member:* Humboldt County Bar Association; State Bar of California.

*(This Listing Continued)*

CAA204B

**CHERIE L. EVANS,** born Arcadia, California, June 25, 1970; admitted to bar, 1995, California. *Education:* California Polytechnic State University (B.A., cum laude, 1992); Pepperdine University (J.D., 1995). *Member:* State Bar of California.

**RUSSELL SCOTT GANS,** born Fullerton, California, August 2, 1969; admitted to bar, 1996, California. *Education:* Saint Mary's College of California; University of Oregon (J.D., cum laude, 1996). Member, Journal of Environmental Law and Litigation. Recipient: Henry George Award. *Member:* State Bar of California. *PRACTICE AREAS:* Insurance Defense; Civil Rights.

### RETIRED PARTNER

**ROBERT C. DEDEKAM,** born San Francisco, California, April 13, 1929; admitted to bar, 1957, California; 1972, U.S. Supreme Court. *Education:* Northwestern University (B.S., 1951); Stanford University (J.D., 1956). Delta Theta Phi. Kirkwood Prize for Oral Advocacy, 1956. *Member:* Humboldt County and American Bar Associations; The State Bar of California; The Association of Defense Counsel.

REPRESENTATIVE INSURANCE COMPANY CLIENTS: Adjusting Services Unlimited; Aetna Life & Casualty; Alliance Insurance Group; Allstate Insurance Company; Cal Farm Insurance; California Capital Insurance Company; California Casualty; California State Automobile Assn.; CNA Insurance; Colonial Penn Insurance Company; Commercial Union Ins. Co.; Continental Ins. Co.; Coregis Insurance Company; Employees-Commercial Union Ins. Co.; Employer's Reinsurance Company; Farmers Insurance Company; Fireman's Fund Insurance Company; Fremont Indemnity; Golden Eagle Insurance Co.; Grange Insurance Assn.; Great American Group of Insurance Co.; HCA Parthenon Insurance Co.; Home Insurance Company; Hospital Assn. of America (Parthenon); Industrial Indemnity; Keenan & Associates; Lawyer's Mutual Insurance Company; National Chiropractic Insurance; National Union Fire Insurance Company; Nationwide Insurance Company; Northwestern National Insurance Company; Royal-Globe Insurance Company; Safeco Insurance Co.; Sequoia Insurance Company; State Farm Insurance Company; The Hartford Group; The North America Companies; The St. Paul Insurance Companies; The Travelers Insurance Companies; Transamerica Insurance Co.; Valley Insurance Co.; Viking Insurance Company; Wausau Insurance Company.
PUBLIC ENTITY/DISTRICT CLIENTS: City of Arcata; City of Crescent City; City of Eureka; City of Fortuna; City of Fort Bragg; County of Del Norte; County of Humboldt; County of Trinity; Del Norte County Local Hospital District; Housing Authority, City of Eureka; Housing Authority, County of Humboldt; Keenan & Associates; McKinleyville Community Services District; Northern Humboldt Fire Protection District No. I; Redwood Empire Municipal Ins. Fund; Trindel; Seaside Hospital District; State of Calif. Department of Corrections.
REPRESENTATIVE CLIENTS: Century 21; Eel River Sawmills; Eureka Hotel Company; General Hospital; Hertz Claim Management; Humboldt Land Title Company; Ocean View Cemetery; Peterson Tractor Company; Schmidbauer Lumber Company; St. Joseph's Hospital; Western Title Insurance Company.

## RAWLES, HINKLE, CARTER, BEHNKE & OGLESBY

EUREKA, CALIFORNIA
(See Ukiah)

*General Civil, Trial and Appellate Practice. Corporation, Real Property, Business, Probate, Negligence, Family, Criminal, Federal and State Taxation, Agricultural, Timber and Logging, Water Rights, Environmental, Zoning and Land Use Law.*

## ROBERTS, HILL, CALLIGAN, BRAGG, FEENEY & ANGELL

434 SEVENTH STREET
P.O. BOX 1248
EUREKA, CALIFORNIA 95501-1803
Telephone: 707-442-2927 95502-1248
Fax: 707-443-2747

*Insurance Defense, Personal Injury and General Civil and Trial Practice and Professional Liability Litigation, Timber and Logging, Construction Contracts and Litigation. Business, Corporation, Probate, and Real Estate Law.*

*FIRM PROFILE: The firm and its predecessor have practiced law in Eureka for more than 50 years. The firm represents clients primarily in Humboldt, Del Norte, Trinity, Mendocino and Lake Counties. Most of the work of the firm is civil and insurance defense litigation together with a significant and expanding business, municipal law and probate practice.*

*(This Listing Continued)*

## MEMBERS OF FIRM

**DONALD B. ROBERTS,** born Oakland, California, August 5, 1939; admitted to bar, 1966, California. *Education:* Bowdoin College, Brigham Young University; University of California at Berkeley (A.B., 1963); Boalt Hall School of Law (J.D., 1966). Law Clerk to Hon. Judge Lloyd H. Burke, United States District Court, 1966. Member, 1982- 1990 and Chairman, 1983-1985, Humboldt County Planning Commission. *Member:* Humboldt County (President, 1980) and American Bar Associations; State Bar of California; Association of Defense Counsel of Northern California; Defense Research Institute. **PRACTICE AREAS:** Insurance Defense; Professional Liability; General Business and Construction Litigation. **Email:** oskiz2@aol.com

**MICHAEL J. HILL,** born Eureka, California, May 25, 1938; admitted to bar, 1966, California. *Education:* Humboldt State College (A.B., 1962); Boalt Hall School of Law, University of California (LL.B., 1965). Phi Alpha Delta. *Member:* Humboldt County (President, 1987) and American Bar Associations; State Bar of California; The Association of Defense Counsel. **PRACTICE AREAS:** Civil and Insurance Defense; Defense of Environmental and Hazardous Waste Claims.

**MICHAEL D. CALLIGAN,** born Minneapolis, Minnesota, December 17, 1938; admitted to bar, 1965, California. *Education:* University of California at Los Angeles (A.B., 1960); Boalt Hall School of Law, University of California (J.D., 1964). Phi Delta Phi. *Member:* Humboldt County Bar Association (President, 1985); State Bar of California; Association of Defense Counsel of Northern California; American Board of Trial Advocates. **PRACTICE AREAS:** Insurance Defense and Defense of Municipal Liability Claims.

**WILLIAM R. BRAGG,** born Oceanside, New York, September 22, 1950; admitted to bar, 1976, California. *Education:* United States Merchant Marine Academy (B.S., 1972); Hastings College of Law, University of California (J.D., 1976). Order of the Coif. Member, Hastings Law Review, 1975-1976. *Member:* Humboldt County Bar Association; State Bar of California. **PRACTICE AREAS:** Insurance Defense and Civil Litigation; Defense of Major Felonies and White-collar Crimes.

**JOHN T. FEENEY,** born San Diego, California, January 14, 1953; admitted to bar, 1980, California. *Education:* University of California at San Diego (B.A. in Biology, 1975); California State University at Los Angeles (M.S. in Criminalistics, 1979); Loyola University (J.D., 1980). Awarded, Outstanding Master's Project, Department of Criminal Justice, California State University, 1979. Member, 1990— and Chairman, 1993, Humboldt County Planning Commission. *Member:* Humboldt County Bar Association (President, 1994); State Bar of California. **PRACTICE AREAS:** Real Estate; Business; Probate; Estate and Trusts.

**RONALD F. ANGELL,** born Santa Cruz, California, May 18, 1942; admitted to bar, 1967, California. *Education:* University of California at Berkeley (B.A., 1964); Boalt Hall School of Law, University of California (J.D., 1967). *Member:* Humboldt County Bar Association (President, 1981); State Bar of California; The Association of Defense Counsel. **PRACTICE AREAS:** General Business; Real Property; Municipal Law.

**RANDY S. PERLMAN,** born Brooklyn, New York, January 22, 1960; admitted to bar, 1987, New York; 1988, California. *Education:* Pace University (B.A., 1982); California Western School of Law (J.D., 1986). *Member:* San Diego County, New York State and American Bar Associations; State Bar of California; The Association of Defense Counsel of Northern California. **PRACTICE AREAS:** General Civil and Business Litigation; Insurance Defense.

---

**PAUL JOHN WARNER,** born San Francisco, California, November 7, 1962; admitted to bar, 1992, California; 1993, U.S. District Court, Northern District of California. *Education:* California State University, Sacramento (B.A., 1986); McGeorge School of Law (J.D., 1992). Member, Traynor Society. *Member:* Humboldt County Bar Association; State Bar of California; The Association of Defense Counsel of Northern California. **PRACTICE AREAS:** Civil Litigation; Business Litigation; Insurance Defense.

**LISA A. RUSS,** born San Diego, California, January 23, 1967; admitted to bar, 1994, California and U.S. District Court Northern and Eastern Districts of California. *Education:* University of California (B.A., 1989); McGeorge School of Law (J.D., 1994). Recipient, American Jurisprudence Award for Legal Process. Member, Pacific Law Journal, 1992-1993. *Member:* Humboldt County Bar; State Bar of California.

*(This Listing Continued)*

**REPRESENTATIVE CLIENTS:** The City of Eureka (self insured); Humboldt Bay Municipal Water District; Eel River Sawmills; McKinleyville Community Services District; Coast Central Credit Union; Wells Fargo Bank, N.A.; Fidelity National Title Co.; Eureka Title Company; Humboldt Community Services District; Oscar Larson & Associates, Inc. (Civil Engineers); Redway Community Services District; SHN Consulting Engineers and Geologists; Payless Drug Stores; Aetna Insurance; Alexis Risk Management; Allied Insurance Company; Allstate Insurance; California Insurance Group; Colonial Penn Insurance; Coregis Insurance Group; Farmers Insurance Group; Fireman's Fund Insurance; The Hartford; Home Insurance Co.; Interstate National Insurance Group; Jersey International Group; Keenan & Associates; Kemper Group; Lexington Insurance Co.; Maryland Casualty; Mercury Casualty Co.; Monarch Life Insurance Co.; Nationwide Insurance Co.; Northwest Farm Bureau Insurance, Inc.; Ohio Casualty Group; Progressive Casualty Insurance Co.; Redwood Empire Municipal Insurance; Safeco; Self-Insured Management Services; St. Paul Fire & Marine Insurance; State Farm Fire & Casualty; Travelers; Twentieth Century Insurance; Unigard; United Employers Insurance Co.; Western Greyhound; Western Surety Co.
**REFERENCE:** Humbolt Bank, Eureka, CA.

---

# STOKES, STEEVES, ROWE & HAMER
### EUREKA, CALIFORNIA
(See Arcata)

*Real Estate, Construction, Business and General Civil Litigation, Probate and Estate Planning, Business, Real Estate, Taxation, Family, Criminal and Administrative Law.*

---

# LAW FIRM OF
# W. G. WATSON, JR.

715 I STREET
P.O. BOX 1021
**EUREKA, CALIFORNIA 95501**
Telephone: 707-444-3071
Fax: 707-444-2313

*General Civil and Criminal Trial Practice, Personal Injury, Negligence, Insurance, Real Estate, Estate Planning, Probate Law, Arbitration, Mediation.*

**FIRM PROFILE:** The Law Office of W.G. Watson, Jr., was founded in 1985 by W.G. Watson, Jr., Philip G. Watson and Stephen G. Watson. Honorable W.G. Watson, Jr., served over 20 years as a Judge of the Humboldt County Superior Court, retiring in 1978 and thereafter sitting by assignment. The firm emphasizes litigation, mediations/arbitrations, juvenile law and estates.

## MEMBERS OF FIRM

**WILLIAM G. WATSON, JR.** (1918-1996).

**STEPHEN G. WATSON,** born Eureka, California, August 12, 1956; admitted to bar, 1983, California and U.S. District Court, Northern District of California. *Education:* Humboldt State University (B.A., 1980); Hastings College of Law, University of California (J.D., 1983). Deputy District Attorney, Humboldt County, 1984-1985. *Member:* Humboldt County and American Bar Associations; State Bar of California (Consultant, Continuing Education of the Bar Committee; Chair, 1989-1990); California Consumer Lawyers Association (Associate Member); Northern California Association of Defense Counsel.

**PHILIP G. WATSON,** born Eureka, California, August 12, 1956; admitted to bar, 1983, California and U.S. District Court, Northern District of California; 1985, U.S. District Court, Eastern District of California. *Education:* California State University at Humboldt (B.A., 1980); University of San Francisco (J.D., 1983). *Member:* State Bar of California; American Bar Association; California Consumer Lawyers Association (Associate Member); Northern California Association of Defense Counsel.

**JOYCE D. HINRICHS,** born Inglewood, California, October 14, 1958; admitted to bar, 1983, California and U.S. District Court, Northern District of California. *Education:* University of the Pacific (B.A., cum laude, 1980; J.D., 1983). Phi Kappa Phi. Member, Board of Editors, Pacific Law Journal, 1982-1983. Staff Writer: "Reviews of Selected 1981 California Legislation," Pacific Law Journal, Volume 13, January, 1982; "Review of Selected 1981 Nevada Legislation," Pacific Law Journal, Volume 1, October, 1981. Deputy District Attorney, Humboldt County, 1984-1986. *Member:* Humboldt County and American Bar Associations; State Bar of California (Member: Juvenile Justice Committee, 1986-1989; Rules and Procedures Committee, 1992—; Chair, 1996-1997); Humboldt Bay Business and Professional Women.

*(This Listing Continued)*

## LAW FIRM OF W. G. WATSON, JR., Eureka—Continued

REPRESENTATIVE CLIENTS: State Farm Insurance; State Farm Fire and Casualty; United Pacific Insurance Co.; Firemans Fund Insurance Co.; CUNA Mutual Insurance Group; Allstate Insurance; The Canadian Insurance; Jefferson Insurance of New York; Admiral Insurance Co.; Reliance Insurance; Planet Insurance; National General Insurance; Western/Residence Mutual Insurance.
REFERENCES: Bank of America; U.S. Bank.

---

## ZWERDLING & CROWLEY

Established in 1990

123 F STREET, SUITE C
P.O. BOX 3477
**EUREKA, CALIFORNIA 95501**
Telephone: 707-445-9628
Fax: 707-443-0442

*Plaintiff Personal Injury Litigation, Employment Litigation and Civil Rights Litigation.*

**ZACHARY E. ZWERDLING,** born Espanola, New Mexico, November 13, 1951; admitted to bar, 1976, California and U.S. District Court, Northern District of California. *Education:* Stanford University (B.A., with distinction, 1973); University of Santa Clara (J.D., 1976). Associate Editor, Santa Clara Lawyer, 1975-1976. Lecturer, Public Safety, College of the Redwoods, 1982-1990. Member, Humboldt County Legal Aid/Lawyer Referral Service Committee. Member, Bench-Bar Liaison Committee. Member, Board of Directors, Redwood Legal Assistance, 1979-1987. Attorney, Public Defender's Office, Humboldt County, 1977-1978. Partner, Diehl & Zwerdling, 1978-1988. *Member:* Humboldt County (President, 1992) and American Bar Associations; American Board of Trial Advocates; Consumer Attorneys of California; The Association of Trial Lawyers of America. Member of Consumer Attorneys of California, with recognized experience in the field of General Personal Injury, and as a Trial Lawyer. **PRACTICE AREAS:** Plaintiff Trial Practice; Personal Injury Law; Employment Litigation; Civil Rights.

**MICHAEL J. CROWLEY,** born Chicago, Illinois, June 16, 1956; admitted to bar, 1982, California and U.S. District Court, Northern District of California. *Education:* Boston College (B.A., summa cum laude, Phi Beta Kappa, 1978); University of San Francisco (J.D., with honors, 1981). Best Oral Argument, Moot Court Competition, 1979. Attorney, Rael & Young, 1982-1987. Member, Board of Directors, Pacific Art Center Theater, 1990-1993. *Member:* Humboldt County Bar Association; State Bar of California; Consumer Attorneys of California. Member of Consumer Attorneys of California, with recognized experience in the field of General Personal Injury, and as a Trial Lawyer. **PRACTICE AREAS:** Plaintiff Trial Practice; Personal Injury Law; Employment Litigation; Civil Rights.

---

## BARNETT • MATTICE

An Association of Sole Practitioners

Established in 1971

712 EMPIRE STREET
**FAIRFIELD, CALIFORNIA 94533**
Telephone: 707-425-0671
Fax: 707-425-4255

*Personal Injury and Family Law.*

**ROBERT E. BARNETT,** born New Orleans, Louisiana, November 24, 1943; admitted to bar, 1969, California. *Education:* Occidental College (B.A., with honors, 1965); Boalt Hall School of Law, University of California at Berkeley (J.D., 1968). Member, Moot Court Board, 1968. Deputy Public Defender, Solano County, 1969-1971. Chairman, Board of Directors, Solano County Legal Assistance, 1972-1974. Member, Board of Directors, Suisun Valley Bank, 1985. Member, Panel of Judicial Arbitrators, American Arbitration Association. *Member:* Solano County Bar Association (President, 1984; Chairman, Civil Litigation Committee (1993-1996); Member, Board of Directors, 1982-1986; Superior Court Panel of Judicial Arbitration); State Bar of California; Consumer Attorneys of California (Recognized Experience in: Trial Law and Personal Injury Law; Vice President, Solano County Chapter, 1974-1984); The Association of Trial Lawyers of America (Sustaining Member). (Member of California Trial Lawyers Association, with recognized experience in the fields of Trial Lawyer and General Personal Injury). **PRACTICE AREAS:** Personal Injury Law.

*(This Listing Continued)*

---

**MICHAEL C. MATTICE,** born New York, N.Y., April 18, 1948; admitted to bar, 1977, California. *Education:* Cornell University, Cerritos College and University of California at Berkeley (A.B., 1973); Hastings College of Law, University of California (J.D., 1976). Phi Beta Kappa. Author: "Family Torts: Compensable Wrongs in the No-Fault Zone," CTLA Forum, Vol. XVIII, No. 4, May, 1988; "Media in the Middle: A Study of the Mass Media Complaint Managers," Chapter 13 in No Access to Law, L. Nader, ed., Academic Press, Inc., 1980. Instructor, Legal Research and Writing, University Extension, University of California at Davis, 1982. Pro Tem Superior Court Judge, Solano County, 1991—. Pro Tem Superior Court Juvenile Referee Solano County, 1987—. Member, Solano County Panel of Judicial Arbitrators, 1988—. *Member:* Solano County Bar Association (President, 1993); State Bar of California; Consumer Attorneys of California (Sustaining Member); The Association of Trial Lawyers of America; Certified Specialist, Family Law, California Board of Legal Specialization. [Petty Officer, U.S. Navy, Hospital Corps, 1967-1970]. **PRACTICE AREAS:** Personal Injury Law; Family Law.

REFERENCES: Bank of America; Wells Fargo Bank; Bank of the West (Fairfield Branch); Westamerica Bank.

---

## CAULFIELD, DAVIES & DONAHUE

FAIRFIELD WEST PLAZA
1455 OLIVER ROAD, SUITE 130
**FAIRFIELD, CALIFORNIA 94533**
Telephone: 707-426-0223

Sacramento, California Office: 3500 American River Drive, 1st Floor.
Telephone: 916-487-7700.

*General Civil Trial, Coverage and Appellate Practice, Negligence, Professional Liability, Automotive, Products Liability, Aviation, Insurance and General Business.*

REPRESENTATIVE CLIENTS: A. Teichert & Son, Inc.; American Honda Motor Co., Inc.; B.F. Goodrich; Bridgestone/Firestone, Inc.; Chrysler Corp.; City of Folsom; City of Galt; City of Lincoln; County of El Dorado; Enserch Corp.; Game Time, Inc.; George Hills Co.; Georgia Pacific Corp.; Kawasaki Motors Corporation, U.S.A.; Makita U.S.A., Inc.; Mazda Motor of America, Inc.; Nissan Motor Corp., U.S.A.; Subaru of America, Inc.; Suzuki Motor Corp.; Textron, Inc.; Yokohama Tire Corp.
INSURANCE CLIENTS: Aetna Casualty & Surety Co.; AVEMCO Insurance Co.; Bragg & Associates; California State Automobile Assn.; CIGNA Property & Casualty; Federated Insurance Co.; Loss Management Services; Royal Insurance; St. Paul Fire & Marine Insurance Co.; State Farm Fire and Casualty Co.; State Farm Mutual Automobile Insurance Co.; Tokio Marine and Fire Insurance Co., Ltd.; Toplis & Harding, Inc.

(For Complete Biographical Data on all Personnel, see Professional Biographies at Sacramento)

---

## LAW OFFICES OF
## JOHN M. COYLE

639 KENTUCKY STREET, SUITE 210
**FAIRFIELD, CALIFORNIA 94533**
Telephone: 707-422-7300
Fax: 707-422-2637

*General Civil Litigation including Business, Real Estate, Family Law, Personal Injury and Land Use Law.*

**JOHN M. COYLE,** born Grand Junction, Colorado, July 30, 1946; admitted to bar, 1972, California, U.S. District Court, Northern District of California, U.S. Court of Appeals, Ninth Circuit and U.S. Court of Military Appeals; 1993, U.S. District Court, Eastern District of California. *Education:* University of Washington (B.A., 1968); Hastings College of Law (J.D., 1971). City Attorney, Suisun City, California, 1985-1991. Judge Pro Tem, Solano County Courts , 1992-1995. President, Board of Directors, Legal Services of Solano County, 1994. Member, Board of Directors, Legal Services of Northern California. Member, Panel of Judicial Arbitrators. *Member:* Solano County Bar Association; State Bar of California. [Capt., JAGC, USAF, 1972-1977]. **PRACTICE AREAS:** Business; Real Estate; Family Law; Personal Injury; Land Use; General Litigation; Arbitration; Mediation.

## FAVARO, LAVEZZO, GILL, CARETTI & HEPPELL

A PROFESSIONAL CORPORATION

**FAIRFIELD, CALIFORNIA**

(See Vallejo)

General Business, Civil and Criminal Trial and Appellate Practice including Corporations, Taxation, Estate Planning, Probate, Real Estate, Construction, Zoning, Municipal, Personal Injury and Family Law.

---

## GAW, VAN MALE, SMITH, MYERS & MIROGLIO

A PROFESSIONAL LAW CORPORATION

Established in 1974

CORPORATE PLAZA
1261 TRAVIS BOULEVARD, SUITE 350
**FAIRFIELD, CALIFORNIA 94533-4801**
Telephone: 707-425-1250
Fax: 707-425-1255
URL: http://www.gvmsmm.com

*Napa, California Office:* 944 Main Street. Telephone: 707-252-9000. Telecopier: 707-252-0792.

Business and Corporate Law, Real Estate, Estate Planning and Probate Administration, Family Law, Criminal Law, Corporate and Personal Taxation, Pension and Profit Sharing and Alcohol Beverage Law. General Civil Trial Practice in all State and Federal Courts. Personal Injury, Land Use, Planning and Local Government Law.

**DAVID B. GAW,** born Berkeley, California, June 2, 1945; admitted to bar, 1971, Colorado; 1972, California. *Education:* University of Colorado (A.B., 1967); Hastings College of Law, University of California (J.D., 1971). Order of the Coif; Phi Delta Phi. Member, Thurston Society. Board of Directors (Chairman, 1991-1994), The Vintage Bank. *Member:* Napa County (President, 1994; Chairman, Estate Planning, Probate and Trust Law Section, 1982-1986), Solano County and American Bar Associations; State Bar of California (Member, Estate Planning and Probate Section); National Association of Elder Law Attorneys. (Certified Specialist, Probate, Estate Planning and Trust Law, State Bar of California, Board of Legal Specialization; Certified as an Elder Law Attorney by the National Elder Law Foundation). **PRACTICE AREAS:** Estate Planning Law; Trust and Probate Law; Elder Law.

**NICHOLAS R. VAN MALE,** born Denver, Colorado, May 21, 1938; admitted to bar, 1971, Colorado and California. *Education:* University of California at Berkeley (A.B., 1962); University of California at Davis (J.D., 1970). Deputy District Attorney, Napa County, 1971-1973. *Member:* Napa County (President, 1986; Chairman, Criminal Law Section, 1982-1984) and American Bar Associations; State Bar of California. [Capt., USNR Ret.]. **PRACTICE AREAS:** Civil Litigation; Family Law; Land Use Planning Law.

**WYMAN G. SMITH, III,** born Sacramento, California, April 3, 1950; admitted to bar, 1976, California. *Education:* University of Colorado (B.A., 1972); McGeorge School of Law, University of the Pacific (J.D., 1976). Member, Traynor Society. *Member:* Napa County (Member, Real Estate and Corporate Sections) Solano County and American (Member, Business Law Section) Bar Associations; State Bar of California (Member, Real Property Law and Business Law Sections). **PRACTICE AREAS:** Business; Corporate; Real Estate Transactions.

**BRUCE A. MYERS,** born Oakland, California, November 3, 1951; admitted to bar, 1981, California and District of Columbia; 1982, U.S. Tax Court. *Education:* University of California at Berkeley (B.S., 1974); California State University at Chico (M.B.A., 1975); McGeorge School of Law, University of the Pacific (J.D., 1981; LL.M., 1984). Certified Public Accountant, 1980. *Member:* Napa County (Member, Real Estate and Corporate Sections) and American Bar Associations; State Bar of California (Member, Business Law Section); California Society of Certified Public Accountants; American Institute of Certified Public Accountants. **PRACTICE AREAS:** Taxation Law; Business Transactions; Pension Law; Profit Sharing Law.

*(This Listing Continued)*

**BRUCE A. MIROGLIO,** born St. Helena, California, September 13, 1957; admitted to bar, 1982, California. *Education:* University of California at Santa Barbara (B.A., 1979); McGeorge School of Law, University of the Pacific (J.D., 1982). Deputy District Attorney, Solano County, 1983-1984. *Member:* Napa County Bar Association; State Bar of California. **REPORTED CASES:** Vianna v. Doctors' Management Co. (1994) 27 Cal..App.4th 1186. **PRACTICE AREAS:** Civil Litigation; Personal Injury Law; Medical Malpractice Defense; Probate Litigation; Employment Litigation; Wrongful Termination.

**S. SCOTT REYNOLDS,** born Ann Arbor, Michigan, August 1, 1949; admitted to bar, 1976, California; 1979, U.S. Tax Court. *Education:* Stanford University (B.A., 1971); University of California at Berkeley (M.B.A., 1973); McGeorge School of Law, University of the Pacific (J.D., 1976). Phi Alpha Delta. Legal Intern, California Attorney General's Office, 1974-1976. *Member:* San Bernardino County and American (Member, Sections on: Taxation; Real Property, Probate and Trust Law; Corporation, Banking and Business Law; Law Office Management) Bar Associations; State Bar of California. **PRACTICE AREAS:** Estate Planning; Trust Administration; Business Law; Corporate Law; Tax Law; Real Estate; Elder Care.

*OF COUNSEL*

**MARK A. HYJEK,** born Manchester, New Hampshire, January 27, 1952; admitted to bar, 1977, California. *Education:* Raymond College; University of the Pacific, Stockton (B.A., 1973); California Western School of Law (J.D., 1976). Nominated for Root-Tilden Fellowship. Part-time Instructor, Sacramento City College, 1987-1993. Certified Elder Law Attorney, National Elder Law Foundation. *Member:* Sacramento County Bar Association; State Bar of California; National Academy of Elder Law Attorneys. (Also Practicing Individually at Fair Oaks). **PRACTICE AREAS:** Estate Planning; Elder Law.

REPRESENTATIVE CLIENTS: Bell Properties; SEDCORP; Solano Affordable Housing Foundation; Stagner Lumber Co.; Shellworth Chevrolet-Oldsmobile, Inc.; Vacaville Honda; Vacaville Mazda; West Coast Contractors; Balbi & Chang, Environmental Engineers; Pipe Shields, Inc.; Nor-Cal Concrete, Inc.; Automatic Bar Controls, Inc.; Camco International, Inc.; Control Technology; Ken Kemble, Inc.; Northbay Health Advantage; Northbay Healthcare Corp.; Premier Commercial; First Northern Bank; Penn Environmental; Parkside Dental Team.
REFERENCE: West America Bank.

(For additional biographical data, see Professional Biographies at Napa, California)

---

## HAGLER & NELSON

**FAIRFIELD, CALIFORNIA**

(See Vacaville)

General Civil and Criminal Trial Practice. Personal Injury, Business, Employment Discrimination Law, Collections, Sexual Harassment, Wrongful Termination Defense.

---

## LAW OFFICES OF M. KENDALL HILLMAN

740 TEXAS STREET, SUITE 304
**FAIRFIELD, CALIFORNIA 94533**
Telephone: 707-427-7377
Facsimile: 707-427-7370
Email: mkhlaw@aol.com

Trust and Estate Tax Planning, Probate, Real Estate, Business Sales and Acquisitions, and Land Use Planning.

**M. KENDALL HILLMAN,** born Richmond, California, November 28, 1960; admitted to bar, 1986, California. *Education:* University of California at Los Angeles (B.A., in Economics, 1983); University of Southern California (J.D., 1986). Phi Delta Phi. Member, Board of Directors, Fairfield-Suisun Chamber of Commerce. *Member:* Solano County and American Bar Associations; State Bar of California.

REPRESENTATIVE CLIENTS: Available Upon Request.

## HODSON & MULLIN

FAIRFIELD, CALIFORNIA

(See Vacaville)

General Practice with emphasis on Personal Injury, Workers Compensation, Family Law, Court-Martial Defense, Personal Bankruptcy.

---

## HONEYCHURCH AND FINKAS

Established in 1978

SUITE C, 823 JEFFERSON STREET
FAIRFIELD, CALIFORNIA 94533
Telephone: 707-429-3111
Fax: 707-429-4302

Criminal and Civil Trial Practice. Criminal Defense and Personal Injury Law.

### MEMBERS OF FIRM

**DENIS A. HONEYCHURCH,** born Berkeley, California, September 17, 1946; admitted to bar, 1972, California, U.S. District Court, Northern District of California and U.S. Court of Appeals, Ninth Circuit. *Education:* University of California at Los Angeles (B.A., 1968); Hastings College of Law, University of California (J.D., 1972). Supervising Deputy Public Defender, Public Defender's Office, Solano County, 1975-1978. Assistant Public Defender, Public Defender's Office, Sacramento County, 1973-1975. Member, President, 1982, Governing Board Fairfield Suisun Unified School District, 1979-1983. Chairman, Downtown Improvement District Board, 1981-1982. Municipal Court Judge Pro Tem, Northern Solano Judicial District, 1980—. Arbitrator, Solano County Superior Court, 1985—. Member, 1985—and President, 1988, 1992, Governing Board of Solano Community College. Member, Solano County Democratic Central Committee, 1992—. *Member:* Solano County (Director, 1987-1990; President, 1991) and American Bar Associations; State Bar of California (Member, Criminal Law Section); California Trial Lawyers Association; National Association of Criminal Defense Lawyers; California Attorneys for Criminal Justice; California Public Defenders Association. (Certified Specialist, Criminal Law, The State Bar of California Board of Legal Specialization) Certified as a Criminal Trial Advocate by the National Board of Trial Advocacy. **PRACTICE AREAS:** Criminal Defense; Felonies; Homicide; Misdemeanors; Sexual Abuse.

**R. ANTHONY FINKAS,** born Hood River, Oregon, January 14, 1946; admitted to bar, 1973, California and U.S. District Court, Northern District of California. *Education:* San Jose State University (B.A., cum laude, 1969); University of California at Davis (J.D., 1973). Adjunct Professor of Law, University of California at Davis, School of Law, 1984-1986. Directing Attorney, Solano County Legal Assistance, 1974-1975. Deputy Public Defender, Solano County Public Defender's Office, 1976-1978. Chairperson, Board of Directors, Solano County Legal Assistance, 1981-1983. Pro Tem Municipal Court Judge, Fairfield, 1981—. Pro Tem Juvenile Court Referee, Solano County Superior Court, 1981—. Arbitrator, Solano County Superior Court, 1985—. Member, 1989 and Chairman, 1993, City of Fairfield Planning Commission. *Member:* Solano County Bar Association (Secretary-Treasurer, 1979-1980); State Bar of California; California Trial Lawyers Association; California Public Defenders Association; The Association of Trial Lawyers of America; Solano County Lawyers for Criminal Justice (Director, 1983-1984; President, 1986); California Attorneys for Criminal Justice; National Association of Criminal Defense Lawyers. **PRACTICE AREAS:** Criminal Defense; Personal Injury; Felonies; Misdemeanors; Sexual Abuse.

---

## KEITGES, BANGLE & OWENSBY

A PROFESSIONAL LAW CORPORATION

1261 TRAVIS BOULEVARD, SUITE 270
FAIRFIELD, CALIFORNIA 94533
Telephone: 707-422-1301
Fax: 707-427-6677

*Sacramento, California Office:* 2150 River Plaza Drive, Suite 205. 95833. Telephone: 916-568-3400. Fax: 916-568-3404.

Governmental Entity and Insurance Defense, Insurance Coverage, Insurance Fraud, Ski and Sports Injury Litigation, Medical Malpractice, Products, Commercial and Construction. Liability, ADR Services.

(This Listing Continued)

---

**CYRIL A. KEITGES, JR.,** born Omaha, Nebraska, December 10, 1935; admitted to bar, 1962, California. *Education:* Santa Clara University (B.S., 1958; LL.B., 1961). Member, Panel of Arbitrators of Sacramento, Solano and Napa Counties. *Member:* Sacramento County and American Bar Associations; The State Bar of California; Northern California Defense Counsel Association; Sacramento Association of Defense Council; California Trial Lawyers Association; Association of Ski Defense Attorneys; California Fraud Association. **PRACTICE AREAS:** Ski and Sports Injury Litigation; Medical Malpractice; Insurance Fraud; Arbitration and Mediation Services; General Insurance Defense Matters.

**RAYMOND BANGLE, III,** born Los Angeles, California, May 21, 1949; admitted to bar, 1982, California. *Education:* University of California at Berkeley (B.A., 1971); University of California at Davis (J.D.,, 1982). *Member:* Sacramento County and Solano County Bar Associations; The State Bar of California; Northern California Defense Counsel Association. **PRACTICE AREAS:** General Insurance Defense; Insurance Coverage; Governmental Entity Defense; Construction Litigation; Medical Malpractice; Dental Malpractice Defense.

**TRACY OWENSBY,** born Fairfield, California, September 24, 1962; admitted to bar, 1987, California. *Education:* California State University at Sacramento (B.A., with high honors, 1984); University of California at Davis (J.D., 1987). Member, University of California at Davis Law Review. *Member:* Sacramento County Bar Association; State Bar of California; The California Fraud Association. **PRACTICE AREAS:** Insurance Fraud; Auto and Homeowners Litigation; Amusement and Recreation Litigation; Construction Defect and Accident Liability.

**JILL H. LATCHAW,** born Martinez, California, March 10, 1956; admitted to bar, 1987, California. *Education:* University of California at Berkeley (B.A., 1978); John F. Kennedy University (J.D., 1987). *Member:* Contra Costa, Alameda County and American Bar Associations; State Bar of California. **PRACTICE AREAS:** Insurance Defense (Personal Injury); Insurance Coverage; Construction Defects; Real Estate Errors and Omissions.

---

## WAYNE A. KNIGHT

1550 WEBSTER STREET, SUITE C
FAIRFIELD, CALIFORNIA 94533
Telephone: 707-422-5411
Fax: 707-422-0174

General Civil, Personal Injury, Business, Bankruptcy, Family Law, Real Estate.

**WAYNE A. KNIGHT,** born 1942; admitted to bar, 1979, California. *Education:* Brigham Young University (B.A., 1967); Lincoln College of Law (J.D., 1979). **PRACTICE AREAS:** Personal Injury; Family Law; Business Law; Bankruptcy; Probate.

---

## KNOX RICKSEN, LLP

CORPORATE PLAZA
SUITE 300, 1261 TRAVIS BOULEVARD
FAIRFIELD, CALIFORNIA 94533
Telephone: 707-426-3313
Fax: 707-426-0426

*Oakland, California Office:* Suite 1700, 1999 Harrison Street. Telephone: 510-893-1000. Fax: 510-446-1946.

*San Jose, Santa Clara County, California Office:* 100 Park Center Plaza, Suite 560, 95113. Telephone: 408-295-2828. Fax: 408-295-6868.

General Civil and Trial Practice. Corporate, Real Estate, Land Use, Urban Development and Environmental Law, Taxation, Estate Planning, Probate, Insurance and Medical Liability Defense Practice.

### MEMBERS OF FIRM

William C. Robbins, III      Jeffrey A. Harper
R. Patrick Snook

### ASSOCIATES

Christine A. Carringer      Dennis Earl Raglin

(For complete biographical data on all personnel and listing of representative clients, see Professional Biographies at Oakland, California)

## LUCAS & LUCAS
547 JEFFERSON STREET, SUITE A
**FAIRFIELD, CALIFORNIA 94533**
Telephone: 707-438-0210

*General Civil and Trial Practice. Insurance Defense, Negligence, Real Estate, Probate, Family and Corporate Law. Mediation and Arbitration Law.*

### MEMBERS OF FIRM

**F. RICHARD LUCAS,** born Alameda, California, August 28, 1933; admitted to bar, 1961, California. *Education:* University of Santa Clara (B.S., summa cum laude, 1955); Stanford Law School (J.D., 1960). Alpha Sigma Nu. Member, Board of Editors, Stanford Law Review, 1959-1960. Member, 1968-1985 and President, 1971-1973; 1980-1981, Solano Community College Governing Board. *Member:* Solano County Bar Association (Member, Board of Directors, 1970; President, 1978); The State Bar of California; Association of Defense Counsel (Member, Board of Directors, 1980-1982). Fellow, American College of Trial Lawyers. [1st Lt., U.S. Army Artillery, 1956-1958]. **PRACTICE AREAS:** General Practice; Civil Litigation; Insurance; Public Entity Defense.

**MATTHEW R. LUCAS,** born Fairfield, California, February 18, 1965; admitted to bar, 1990, California, U.S. District Court, Northern District of California and U.S. Court of Appeals, Ninth Circuit; 1992, U.S. District Court, Eastern District of California. *Education:* Stanford University (A.B., 1987); University of California School of Law (J.D., 1990). Member, Moot Court Honors Program. Editor, UCLA Journal of Environmental Law and Policy, 1988-89. *Member:* Solano County and American Bar Associations; Northern California Association of Defense Counsel. **LANGUAGES:** Italian. **PRACTICE AREAS:** General Practice; Personal Injury; Insurance Defense Law; Civil Litigation; Probate and Estate Planning.

**KATHERINE M. BABCOCK,** born Vallejo, California, January 20, 1953; admitted to bar, 1983, California and U.S. District Court, Eastern District of California. *Education:* University of Santa Clara (B.A., 1975) Hastings College of the Law, University of California (J.D., 1983). *Member:* Solano County and American Bar Associations; Association of Defense Counsel of Northern California. **PRACTICE AREAS:** General Practice; Insurance Defense; Construction Law; Civil Litigation.

REPRESENTATIVE CLIENTS: Farmers' Insurance Group; County of Solano; Fairfield Daily Republic; Geico Insurance Co.; City of Fairfield; City of Dixon; City of Rio Vista.

---

## McNAMARA, HOUSTON, DODGE, McCLURE & NEY
639 KENTUCKY AVENUE, SUITE 110
**FAIRFIELD, CALIFORNIA 94533-5530**
Telephone: 707-427-3998
Fax: 707-427-0268

*Walnut Creek, California Office:* 1211 Newell Avenue, Second Floor, P.O. Box 5288. Telephone: 510-939-5330. Facsimile: 510-939-0203.

*General Civil Trial Practice in all State and Federal Courts. Corporation, Insurance and Professional Liability Law.*

(For Biographical data on all Personnel, see Professional Biographies at Walnut Creek, California).

---

## WILLIAM H. McPHERSON
Established in 1953
825 WEBSTER STREET
**FAIRFIELD, CALIFORNIA 94533**
Telephone: 707-422-7706
Fax: 707-425-9331

*Family, Probate, Arbitration and Mediation. Family Law Appellate.*

**WILLIAM H. MCPHERSON,** born Bremerton, Washington, May 16, 1922; admitted to bar, 1952, California. *Education:* Stanford University (B.A., 1948; J.D., 1951). Faculty Member, Psychology Department, Sonoma State University, teaching Human Services and the Law, 1984-1987. Chairman: Solano County Republican Central Committee, 1952-1954 and 1960-1962; Solano College Site and Bond Committees, 1967. Member, Board of Governors, 1968—, Chairman, 1970-1973 and Vice Chairman, 1974-1978, California Maritime Academy. Chairman, Community Development Council, City of Vallejo, 1969-1973. Chairman, Vallejo Economic

*(This Listing Continued)*

Development Commission, 1971-1973. Pro Tem Superior Court Judge, Solano County, Panel of Judicial Arbitrators, 1979—. Author: Articles, "Casas v. Thompson," News Alert, Vol. I, No. 3, Nov. 1986, "In re Marriage of Griffis," Vol. I, No. 5, April 1987 and "Terminable Interests," Vol. II, No. 1, Aug. 1987 all published in News Alert and published by Bancroft-Whitney; "The Commingled Property Puzzle," California Lawyer, Vol. VII, No. 7, July 1987, published by California State Bar. Consultant, Bancroft-Whitney California Family Law Service, 8 Volumes, 1986. Listed in Martindale-Hubbell Bar Register of Preeminent Lawyers, 1993—. *Member:* Solano County (President, 1968; Chairman, Family Law Committee, 1990-1996) and American Bar Associations; State Bar of California; The Association of Trial Lawyers of America. [Capt., U.S. Army, Infantry, 1943-1946]. (Certified Specialist, Family Law, The State Bar of California Board of Legal Specialization). **REPORTED CASES:** IRMO Martinez (1984) 156 CA3 20; IRMO Hebbring (1989) 207 CA3 1260; IRMO Watt (1989) 214 CA 340. **PRACTICE AREAS:** Family Law; Mediation Law; Arbitration Law; Family Law Appeals; Probate Law.

---

## NANCY M. NOLTE
710 MISSOURI STREET, SUITE 3
**FAIRFIELD, CALIFORNIA 94533**
Telephone: 707-425-1058
FAX: 707-425-1059

*Benicia, California Office:* 159 East D Street, Suite G. Telephone: 707-745-8999.

*Family Law, Family Mediation.*

**NANCY M. NOLTE,** born Des Moines, Iowa, December 10, 1942; admitted to bar, 1981, California; 1982, U.S. District Court, Eastern District of California; 1992, U.S. District Court, Northern District of California. *Education:* California State University at Chico (B.A., 1972); University of California at Davis (J.D., 1981). Member, University of California at Davis Law Review, 1979-1980. *Member:* Solano County Bar Association (Secretary-Treasurer (1987); Chair, Mandatory Fee Arbitration Committee (1993-1995); Chair, ADR Committee (1994); Member Family Law Committee); State Bar of California; Women Lawyers Of Sacramento; Solano County Womens Lawyers (Life Member; Charter President, 1985; President, 1992); California Women Lawyers (Member, 1982—; Board of Directors, 1985-1986); Association of Certified Family Law Specialists; Academy of Family Law Mediators. (Certified Specialist, Family Law, The State Bar of California Board of Legal Specialization). **PRACTICE AREAS:** Family Law; Family Mediation.

### ASSOCIATE

**PASCHA R. MOLLER,** born Torrance, California, April 5, 1970; admitted to bar, 1996, California. *Education:* University of California at Santa Barbara (B.A., with highest honors); University of California at Davis (J.D., 1996). Order of the Barristers. Recipient: State Bar of California, Public Service Award; King Hall Legal Foundation Scholarship; Francis Newell Carr Scholarship Fund. Chair, King Hall School of Law Women's Caucus, 1994-1995; Founding Member of Advocates for the Rights of Children, 1993-1996; King Legal Foundation 1993-1996. *Member:* Solano County Women Lawyers; Academy of Family Mediators. **PRACTICE AREAS:** Family Law; Mediation; Child Advocacy.

---

## S. KATELIN RYAN
1143 MISSOURI STREET
**FAIRFIELD, CALIFORNIA 94533**
Telephone: 707-425-6023
Fax: 707-425-3468

*Napa, California Office:* 1370 Trancas Street, Suite 338. Telephone: 707-224-2322.

*General Civil Litigation, Employment Law, Insurance Law.*

**S. KATELIN RYAN,** born Vancouver, Washington, October 12, 1946; admitted to bar, 1988, California. *Education:* Marylhurst College (B.A., 1985); Hastings College of the Law, University of California (J.D., 1988). *Member:* Napa County and Solano County Bar Associations; State Bar of California; California Women Lawyer's Association. **PRACTICE AREAS:** Civil Litigation; Employment Law; Insurance Law.

REPRESENTATIVE CLIENTS: Available Upon Request.

## JAMES G. DONART

*Established in 1977*

SUITE 20, 300 NORTH MAIN STREET
**FALLBROOK, CALIFORNIA 92028**
*Telephone: 619-728-6670*
*FAX: 619-728-9792*

Wills, Trusts, Estate Planning and Probate Law, Serving San Diego and Riverside Counties.

**JAMES G. DONART,** born Roseburg, Oregon, October 26, 1948; admitted to bar, 1974, California. *Education:* Stanford University (A.B., 1970); University of Southern California (J.D., 1974). *Member:* San Diego County and Northern San Diego County Bar Associations; State Bar of California.

REPRESENTATIVE CLIENTS: First Interstate Bank; Union Bank; Wells Fargo Bank; Northern Trust of California N.A.; Dean Wittier Trust; Merrill Lynch Trust; First American Trust Co.
REFERENCES: Inland Empire National Bank, Fallbrook Branch.

## LAURIE, MALONEY & WHEATLEY

*Established in 1988*

1004 RIVER ROCK DRIVE, SUITE 245
**FOLSOM, CALIFORNIA 95630**
*Telephone: 916-988-3857*

*Cameron Park (El Dorado County), California Office:* 3420 Coach Lane, Suite 15. Telephone: 916-677-0245. Fax: 916-677-4802.

*Placerville (El Dorado County), California Office:* 345 Placerville Drive. Telephone: 916-622-7769.

Land Use, Business, Real Estate, Banking, Estate Planning, Municipal, Employment and Construction Law, Personal Injury and Civil Litigation, Franchising.

(For Biographical data on all Personnel, see Professional Biographies at Cameron Park, California)

## LAW OFFICES OF
## JOHN M. RAGER

8413 SIERRA AVENUE, SUITE A
**FONTANA, CALIFORNIA 92335**
*Telephone: 909-822-4445*
*Fax: 909-822-6539*

Probate Law, Family Law and Estate Planning.

**HENRY F. RAGER** (1914-1980).

**JOHN M. RAGER,** born Los Angeles, California, April 12, 1941; admitted to bar, 1966, California. *Education:* San Diego State College (B.A., 1963); Hastings College of the Law, University of California (J.D., 1966). *Member:* State Bar of California.

## JAMES L. LARSON

311 NORTH MCPHERSON STREET
P.O. BOX 1369
**FORT BRAGG, CALIFORNIA 95437**
*Telephone: 707-964-6327*
*Fax: 707-964-7559*
*Email: jlarson@mcn.org*

Estate Planning, Trust and Probate Law.

**JAMES L. LARSON,** born Crescent City, California, November 4, 1941; admitted to bar, 1966, California. *Education:* University of California at Berkeley (A.B., 1963); Boalt Hall School of Law, University of California (LL.B., 1966). Chairman, Mendocino County Air Pollution District Hearing Board, 1974-1989. *Member:* Mendocino County Bar Association (President, 1975); State Bar of California. (Certified Specialist, Estate Planning, Trust and Probate Law, The State Bar of California Board of Legal Specialization).

REFERENCE: Savings Bank of Mendocino County, Fort Bragg Branch.

## RAWLES, HINKLE, CARTER, BEHNKE & OGLESBY

**FORT BRAGG, CALIFORNIA**

(See Ukiah)

General Civil, Trial and Appellate Practice. Corporation, Real Property, Business, Probate, Negligence, Family, Criminal, Federal and State Taxation, Agricultural, Timber and Logging, Water Rights, Environmental, Zoning and Land Use Law.

## JOHN J. RUPRECHT

32670 HIGHWAY TWENTY AT SOUTH HARBOR DRIVE
P.O. BOX 1445
**FORT BRAGG, CALIFORNIA 95437**
*Telephone: 707-964-2973*
*FAX: 707-964-9255*

Civil Litigation. Personal Injury, Real Estate and Business Law.

**JOHN J. RUPRECHT,** born Chicago, Illinois, January 14, 1940; admitted to bar, 1966, California and U.S. Court of Military Appeals; 1974, U.S. Customs Court. *Education:* Claremont College (B.A., cum laude, 1962); Stanford University (J.D., 1965). Semi-Finalist, Marion Rice Kirkwood Moot Court Competition. City Attorney, Fort Bragg, California, 1978-1984. Special Counsel, City of Point Arena, 1985-1988. *Member:* Bar Association of San Francisco (Member, Ethics Committee, 1974-1977); Mendocino and American Bar Associations; State Bar of California. [Major, USMCR, active duty, 1966-1969]. **PRACTICE AREAS:** Personal Injury; Real Estate.

A list of Representative Clients will be furnished upon request.

## HARLAND LAW FIRM

*Established in 1948*

954 MAIN STREET
**FORTUNA, CALIFORNIA 95540**
*Telephone: 707-725-4426*
*Fax: 707-725-5738*

*Eureka, California Office:* 622 H Street. Telephone: 707-444-9281. Fax: 707-445-2961.

General Trial and Appellate Practice. Family, Probate, Estate Planning, Timber and Logging, Corporation, Personal Injury, Administrative, Construction, Labor, Education, Business and Real Property Law.

### MEMBER OF FIRM

**GERALD R. HARLAND,** born Clarinda, Iowa, August 21, 1922; admitted to bar, 1951, California. *Education:* Tarkio College (A.B., 1943); Stanford University (LL.B., 1951). Phi Alpha Delta. *Member:* Humboldt County Bar Association; The State Bar of California. **PRACTICE AREAS:** Estate Planning Law; Real Property Law; Probate Law; Business Law.

REFERENCES: The Bank of America (Fortuna Branch); U.S. Bank, Eureka, California.

(For complete biographical data on all personnel, see Professional Biographies at Eureka, California)

## STANLEY E. POND

563 PILGRIM DRIVE, SUITE D
**FOSTER CITY, CALIFORNIA 94404**
*Telephone: 415-341-0400*
*Facsimile: 415-578-9278*

General Civil Trial and Appellate Practice. Business, Collections, Real Estate, Insurance, Toxic Tort Defense, Products Liability, Drug Liability, Personal Injury.

**STANLEY E. POND,** born San Francisco, California, November 26, 1951; admitted to bar, 1977, California. *Education:* University of California at Davis (B.A., 1973); Hastings College of Law, University of California (J.D., 1977). *Member:* Bar Association of San Francisco; San Mateo County Bar Association; State Bar of California; Northern California Association of Defense Counsel; Defense Research Institute. **PRACTICE**

*(This Listing Continued)*

## PROFESSIONAL BIOGRAPHIES — CALIFORNIA—FREMONT

**AREAS:** Insurance Defense; Products Liability; Drug Liability; Collections; Personal Injury; General Practice.

REPRESENTATIVE CLIENTS: Abbott Laboratories; Able Freight Services, Inc.; Eastman Kodak Co.; Eastman Kodak Credit Corp.; Fireman's Fund Insurance Co.; General Electric Capital Corporation; Imaging Financial Services, Inc.; Innerworks; Lumberman's Underwriting Alliance; Peninsula Glass & Mirror.

REFERENCE: Redwood Bank, San Mateo, California.

---

## GONSALVES & KOZACHENKO
### 47460 FREMONT BOULEVARD
### FREMONT, CALIFORNIA 94538
*Telephone: 510-770-3900*
*Fax: 510-657-9876*

*General Commercial and Civil Litigation, Real Estate, Land Use and Construction, Corporate, Partnership, Securities, Environmental Compliance and Remediation, Bankruptcy and Creditor's Rights, Intellectual Property and Trade Secrets, Employment Law, Taxation, Estate Planning and Probate Law, Family Law.*

**LINDA M. GONSALVES,** born Winchester, Massachusetts, October 26, 1955; admitted to bar, 1982, California. *Education:* San Jose State University (B.A., with great distinction, 1979); University Santa Clara (J.D., summa cum laude, 1982). Recipient, Merit Scholarship. Judicial Extern to Judge Reid Ambler, Superior Court of California, Santa Clara County. Chair, Fremont Industrial and Commercial Commission, 1991-1996. Member, Fremont Committee for the Year 2000, 1985-1986. *Member:* Washington Township Bar Association (President, 1989; Director, 1987-1988); State Bar of California (Member, Section on Estate Planning and Probate). **PRACTICE AREAS:** Commercial Law; Real Estate Law; Taxation Law; Estate Planning Law; Probate Law.

**PAUL KOZACHENKO,** born San Francisco, California, February 9, 1958; admitted to bar, 1982, California. *Education:* Stanford University (B.A., Translators Certificate: Russian to English, 1979); Santa Clara University (J.D., 1982). Volunteer Pro Tem Judge, Fremont Municipal Court. President, Fremont Chamber of Commerce, 1990. Director, Fremont Chamber of Commerce, 1986-1991. *Member:* Washington Township Bar Association; State Bar of California (Member, Sections on: Litigation; Business and Real Property). **LANGUAGES:** Russian. **PRACTICE AREAS:** Real Estate Law; Business Law; Litigation.

### ASSOCIATES

**JAN O'NEAL,** born San Pedro, California, September 18, 1954; admitted to bar, 1987, California. *Education:* University of California at Irvine (A.B., cum laude, 1976) Phi Beta Kappa; Santa Clara University (J.D., 1987). Volunteer Pro Tem Judge, Fremont Municipal Court. Member, Fremont Chamber of Commerce. *Member:* State Bar of California; American Bar Association. **PRACTICE AREAS:** Business Law; Real Estate Law; Trademark.

**STEPHEN F. HELLER,** born San Francisco, California, August 28, 1948; admitted to bar, 1983, California. *Education:* Stanford University (A.B., with distinction, 1978; J.D., 1981). Phi Beta Kappa. Law Clerk to the Hon. Marilyn Hall Patel, U.S. District Judge, Northern District of California, 1981-1982. *Member:* State Bar of California. **PRACTICE AREAS:** Business Law; Business Litigation.

**DANIEL PREDDY,** born Dearborn, Michigan, July 27, 1960; admitted to bar, 1992, California and U.S. Court of Appeals, Ninth District. *Education:* San Francisco State University (B.A., 1987); Golden Gate University (J.D., 1992). *Member:* Alameda County and American Bar Associations; State Bar of California; Alameda County Family Law Association. **PRACTICE AREAS:** Family Law; Bankruptcy; Probate/Estate Planning.

**WENDY L. WAYNE,** born Castro Valley, California, June 9, 1971; (admission pending). *Education:* University of California, Davis (B.A., 1993); University of San Francisco (J.D., magna cum laude, 1996). **PRACTICE AREAS:** Litigation; Estate Planning; Bankruptcy.

### OF COUNSEL

**ALAN L. REEVES,** born Edinburgh, Scotland, January 25, 1943; admitted to bar, 1981, California. *Education:* University of Sydney (B.A., with honors class 1, Philosophy, 1963); University of New England, Australia (M.A., honors class 1, Logic, 1965); University of California at Berkeley (Ph.D., Philosophy, 1970); Stanford University (J.D., 1981). Law Clerk to Honorable Ben Duniway, United States Court of Appeals for the Ninth Circuit, 1981-1982. Instructor, Legal Writing and Research, Hastings

*(This Listing Continued)*

---

School of the Law, 1988-1989. Senior Attorney, Writs and Appeals, California Court of Appeals, Sixth Appellate District, 1988-1990. Senior Lecturer, Sydney University Law School, 1991. *Member:* Santa Clara County Bar Association (Member, Education Committee, 1994-1996; Chairman, 1996); State Bar of California (Member, Committee on Administration and Justice, 1990-1991). **PRACTICE AREAS:** Litigation.

**MARY E. JANSING,** born Cincinnati, Ohio, December 28, 1942; admitted to bar, 1982, California and U.S. Supreme Court. *Education:* California State University at San Jose (B.A., with great distinction, 1979); University of Santa Clara (J.D., cum laude, 1982); New York University (LL.M. in Taxation, 1983). Technical Editor, 1981-1982 and Chair, Santa Clara Law Review. Member, Committee of Lawyer Representatives for the United States Bankruptcy Court for the Northern District of California. *Member:* Santa Clara County Bar Association (Member: Executive Committee, 1989—); State Bar of California (Member, Bankruptcy and Commercial Law Section). (Former Partner, Logan & Jansing, San Jose, California). **REPORTED CASES:** In Re Airbeds, Inc., 92 B.R., 419, 9th Cir. BAP, 1988; Pring vs. Commissioner of Internal Revenue, 57 T.C.M. 958, 1989, CCH; Westfall vs. Commissioner of Internal Revenue, 56 T.C.M. 66, 1988, CCH; Borders vs. Commissioner of Internal Revenue, 52 T.C.M. 617, 1986, CCH. **PRACTICE AREAS:** Bankruptcy; Taxes in Bankruptcy.

---

## JAMES M. HOLLABAUGH
*Established in 1975*

### GENERAL MOTORS BUILDING, SUITE 2410
### 39465 PASEO PADRE PARKWAY
### FREMONT, CALIFORNIA 94538
*Telephone: 510-651-6100*

*Criminal, Trial and Appellate, Commercial Traffic and Personal Injury Law.*

**JAMES M. HOLLABAUGH,** born Washington, D.C., March 7, 1943; admitted to bar, 1975, California; 1976, U.S. Court of Appeals, Ninth Circuit; 1978, U.S. District Court, Northern District of California, U.S. Court of Appeals for the District of Columbia Circuit and U.S. Supreme Court. *Education:* Dartmouth College (A.B., with distinction, 1965); Golden Gate University (J.D., with honors, 1975). *Member:* Washington Township (Secretary, 1977-1978), Alameda County Bar Association; State Bar of California; California Attorneys for Criminal Justice; Christian Legal Society. [Capt., USAF, 1967-1971]

---

## KING, SNELL, MILDWURM & FOX
### A PROFESSIONAL CORPORATION
*Established in 1927*

### 39650 LIBERTY STREET, SUITE 420
### FREMONT, CALIFORNIA 94538
*Telephone: 510-770-5770*
*Fax: 510-651-8043*

*General Civil and Trial Practice. Real Estate, Construction, Landslide and Subsidence, Estate Planning, Probate, Corporate, Criminal and Family Law. Personal Injury and Business Litigation. Arbitration and Mediation Law.*

**LEROY A. BROUN** (1905-1981).

**ALLEN G. NORRIS** (1901-1978).

**BERNARD M. KING,** born Oakland, California, October 13, 1928; admitted to bar, 1953, California; 1969, U.S. Supreme Court. *Education:* University of California at Berkeley (B.S., with honors, 1949); Boalt Hall School of Law, University of California (J.D., with honors, 1952). Deputy District Attorney, Alameda County, 1953-1956. Assistant City Attorney, City of Fremont, 1956-1979. President, Fremont Civic Center Corporation, 1969-1986. President, Southern Alameda County Estate Planning Council, 1982-1983. *Member:* Washington Township (President, 1965) and Alameda County (Member, Board of Directors, 1968-1969) Bar Associations; State Bar of California. **PRACTICE AREAS:** Real Estate Law; Estate Planning Law; Corporate Law.

**JAMES C. SNELL,** born Oroville, California, October 31, 1937; admitted to bar, 1966, California. *Education:* University of California at Berkeley (B.S., 1959); Boalt Hall School of Law, University of California (LL.B., 1965). Deputy District Attorney, Alameda County, 1965-1969. Assistant Professor/Department Head, Administration of Justice, Ohlone Community College, 1967—; Azusa Pacific University, 1988—. *Member:* Washington Township (Member, Board of Directors and President, 1975; Lawyer

*(This Listing Continued)*

CAA211B

**KING, SNELL, MILDWURM & FOX,** A PROFESSIONAL CORPORATION, Fremont—Continued

Referral Service Committee, 1976—) and Alameda County Bar Associations; State Bar of California. [Col., USMCR, Ret.]. *PRACTICE AREAS:* Commercial Litigation; Construction Law.

**ALAN W. MILDWURM,** born San Francisco, California, May 16, 1952; admitted to bar, 1978, California. *Education:* University of San Francisco (B.A., 1973; M.A., 1977; J.D., 1977). Adjunct Professor, Civil Law, Ohlone Community College, 1981—. *Member:* Washington Township (Member, Board of Directors, Lawyers Referral Service Committee, 1982—; Chairman, Law Library Committee, 1982; President, 1985), Alameda County and American Bar Associations; State Bar of California. *PRACTICE AREAS:* Family Law; General Civil Law; Criminal Law.

**CRAIG S. FOX,** born San Diego, California, January 16, 1955; admitted to bar, 1980, California. *Education:* University of California at Berkeley (A.B., 1977); Hastings College of Law, University of California (J.D., 1980). *Member:* Washington Township (Member, Board of Directors, 1985-1987), Alameda County and American Bar Associations; State Bar of California. *PRACTICE AREAS:* Commercial, Construction and Real Estate Litigation.

REPRESENTATIVE CLIENTS: Central Chevrolet Co.; The Gold Hanger; Niles Electric Co.; Fremont Paving Co., Inc.; Alandale Construction Co.; PEDCOM, Inc.; McDonalds Franchise; Western Fire Chiefs Association; Arthur Beren Shoes, Inc.; Kraftile Co.; Jones-Hamilton Co.; Smoke, Fire & Water; Glacier Ice Co.; South Bay Welding Supply Co.; KKW, Inc.; Lipman Insurance Administrators; First Assembly of God; Industrial Truck Services.
REFERENCE: Comerica Bank.

---

## LEON J. MEZZETTI, JR.

Established in 1978

**COMMERCIAL BANK OF FREMONT BUILDING**
39510 PASEO PADRE PARKWAY, SUITE 190
**FREMONT, CALIFORNIA 94538**
Telephone: 510-791-1836
Fax: 510-796-1624

*Trucking Violations, Criminal Law, Family Law, Evictions, General Civil Practice.*

**LEON J. MEZZETTI, JR.,** born Muskegon, Michigan, September 14, 1951; admitted to bar, 1976, California. *Education:* University of California Davis (A.B., with honors, 1973); University of Santa Clara (J.D., 1976). *Member:* Washington Township and Alameda County Bar Associations; State Bar of California. *LANGUAGES:* Spanish, Italian and German.

---

## QUARESMA, BENYA, HALL, CONNICH, O'HARA AND NIXON

Established in 1962

SUITE 140
2201 WALNUT AVENUE
**FREMONT, CALIFORNIA 94538**
Telephone: 510-793-6400
Fax: 510-793-2086

*General Civil Trial Practice in all Courts. Corporation, Real Estate, Eminent Domain, Public Agency, Criminal, Probate, Personal Injury and Family Law.*

FIRM PROFILE: *We are the oldest-established firm in Fremont-founded in 1962. The firm has worked hard to establish a reputation for excellence among lawyers, judges and clients throughout the Bay Area. Our attorneys and professional staff understand the challenges faced by the clients with a legal problem. We work to provide legal representation at the highest levels of quality and sophistication.*

### MEMBERS OF FIRM

**E. A. QUARESMA** (1907-1985).

**ROBERT D. ELLIS** (1932-1987).

**ROBERT D. BENYA,** born Yonkers, New York, March 19, 1931; admitted to bar, 1961, California. *Education:* Syracuse University (B.S., 1953); Hastings College of Law, University of California (LL.B., 1961). Phi Alpha Delta. Trustee, 1973-1977 and President, 1976, Fremont Unified School. *Member:* Washington Township, Alameda County and Southern Alameda County Bar Associations; State Bar of California; The Association of Trial Lawyers of America; Consumers Attorneys of California; California Applicants Attorneys Association. *PRACTICE AREAS:* Personal Injury Law; Products Liability Law; Insurance Law.

**H. ROBERT HALL,** born Bakersfield, California, December 9, 1934; admitted to bar, 1965, California. *Education:* Fresno State College (A.B., 1956); Stanford University (J.D., 1964). Phi Alpha Delta. Chairman: Fremont Human Relations Commission, 1966-1971; Fremont Planning Commission, 1972-1973. Member, Panel of Arbitrators, American Arbitration Association. Member, Alameda County Retirement Board, 1983-1985. President and Chairman of Western Aerospace Museum, Oakland Airport. *Member:* Washington Township (Secretary-Treasurer, 1968) and Alameda County Bar Associations; State Bar of California; Association of Certified Family Law Specialists (Certified Specialist, Family Law, California Board of Legal Specialization). [Ret. Maj. Gen., Former Commander, Calif, ANG, 1985-1991]. (Certified Specialist, Family Law, The State Bar of California Board of Legal Specialization). *PRACTICE AREAS:* Family Law; Business Law.

**MICHAEL J. CONNICH,** born San Francisco, California, November 21, 1940; admitted to bar, 1966, California. *Education:* University of San Francisco (B.A., 1962); Hastings College of Law, University of California (J.D., 1965). *Member:* Washington Township (Secretary-Treasurer, 1980; Director, 1982-1983; President, 1984) and Alameda County Bar Associations; State Bar of California; Association of Certified Family Law Specialists. (Certified Specialist, Family Law, The State Bar of California Board of Legal Specialization). *PRACTICE AREAS:* Probate Law; Family Law; Personal Injury Law; Estate Planning.

**DAVID M. O'HARA,** born Springfield, Illinois, March 31, 1940; admitted to bar, 1970, California. *Education:* Bradley University (B.S.C.E., 1962); Hastings College of Law, University of California (J.D., 1969). Phi Delta Phi. Grand Marshal, Hastings College of Law, University of California, 1969. Instructor, Real Estate Law, Ohlone College, 1973-1984. Member, Panel of Arbitrators, American Arbitration Association; Director, Fremont Chamber of Commerce, 1992—, President, 1996-1997. Fremont Industrial-Commercial Commission, 1996. Fremont Economic Development Commission, 1996-1997. *Member:* Washington Township (President, 1986-1987) and Alameda County Bar Associations; State Bar of California. *REPORTED CASES:* New Haven v. Taco Bell 24 Cal.App.4th 1973. *PRACTICE AREAS:* Public Agency Law; Eminent Domain; Real Estate Law.

**THOMAS J. NIXON,** born Providence, Rhode Island, January 27, 1959; admitted to bar, 1984, California. *Education:* California State University at San Jose (B.S., 1981); University of Santa Clara (J.D., 1984). Beta Gamma Sigma. Judge Pro Tem and Arbitrator, Fremont-Newark-Union City Municipal Court, 1986-1996. *Member:* Washington Township (Past President) and Alameda County Bar Associations; State Bar of California. *PRACTICE AREAS:* Corporate Law; Criminal Law; Family Law.

REPRESENTATIVE CLIENTS: Union Sanitary District; Future Construction Co.; New Haven United School District; Livermore Valley Joint Unified School District Educational Facilities Corp.; Weibel, Inc.; Master Builders (Real Estate Developers); U-Haul Co.; Orchid Technology, Inc.; Bernis Industries.

---

## RIFKIND & FUERCH

A PROFESSIONAL CORPORATION

**FREMONT, CALIFORNIA**

(See Hayward)

*General Civil and Trial Practice. Insurance, Insurance Defense, Real Estate, Transportation Law, Fire Insurance, Products Liability, Automobile, Professional Liability, Landslide and Subsidence, Construction, Business, Municipal and Education Law.*

---

## J. THOMAS SHERROD

A PROFESSIONAL CORPORATION

39199 PASEO PADRE PARKWAY
**FREMONT, CALIFORNIA 94538**
Telephone: 510-796-4444
FAX: 510-791-1639

*Criminal and Administrative Law, with emphasis on Drug and Alcohol Driving Offenses. Civil Trial Matters.*

(This Listing Continued)

**J. THOMAS SHERROD,** born Provo, Utah, May 19, 1938; admitted to bar, 1964, California. *Education:* University of California at Berkeley (B.A., 1960); Boalt Hall School of Law, University of California (LL.B., 1963). Lecturer, "Trial Strategies and Techniques: Cross-Examination of the Arresting Officer in Driving Under the Influence Cases," CPDA, December 1983 (San Francisco); "Cross-Examination of the Expert Witness in Blood, Breath, and Urine Cases," CPDA, June, 1985 (Los Angeles). *Member:* Washington Township and Alameda County Bar Associations; State Bar of California; National Association of Criminal Defense Lawyers; Northern California Deuce Defenders (Co-Founder). [Capt., U.S. Army INTC, 1963-1966]

---

## SKJERVEN, MORRILL, MacPHERSON, FRANKLIN & FRIEL LLP

### FREMONT, CALIFORNIA

(See San Jose)

*Intellectual Property Law, including Patents, Trademarks, Copyrights, Mask Works, Unfair Competition, Trade Secrets and Licensing; Litigation in Federal and State Courts; Corporate, Commercial and General Business Law; and International and Government Contracts Law.*

---

## MURRAY M. ARON

*1396 WEST HERNDON, SUITE 106*
**FRESNO, CALIFORNIA 93711**
Telephone: 209-449-7601

*Civil Litigation, Insurance Defense, Personal Injury, Products Liability, Insurance Coverage Litigation, Appeals.*

**MURRAY M. ARON,** born Brooklyn, N.Y., April 2, 1945; admitted to bar, 1974, California and U. S. District Court, Eastern District of California; 1979, U.S. Supreme Court; 1982, U.S. District Court, Central District of California and U.S. Court of Appeals, Ninth Circuit. *Education:* Brooklyn College of the City University of New York (B.A., 1967); Hasting College of Law, University of California (J.D., 1974). Member, Superior Court Panel of Civil Arbitrators, Fresno and Madera Counties, 1979—. Member, Panel of Arbitrators, American Arbitration Association. Early Neutral Evaluator U.S. District Court, Eastern District of California. *Member:* Fresno County Bar Association; State Bar of California; Northern California Association of Defense Counsel. [Capt., U.S. Air Force, 1967-1971]

REPRESENTATIVE CLIENTS: Insurance Company of North America; Argonaut Insurance Co.; Progressive Companies; Superior National Insurance Co.; Allstate Insurance Co.; Merced Mutual; Hartford Accident and Indemnity; Nautilus Insurance Co.; California Insurance Group; Hanover Insurance; Borden, Inc; Crown, Cork & Seal.

---

## BAKER, MANOCK & JENSEN

*A PROFESSIONAL CORPORATION*

*5260 NORTH PALM, SUITE 421*
**FRESNO, CALIFORNIA 93704**
Telephone: 209-432-5400
Fax: 209-432-5620

*General Civil and Trial Practice. Environmental, Agricultural, Bankruptcy, Cooperative, Corporation, Medical and Malpractice Legal, Taxation, Probate and Estate Planning, Real Estate, Water Rights, Family/Domestic Relations, Oil and Gas Law, Employment, and Intellectual Property.*

FIRM PROFILE: *Baker, Manock & Jensen, a professional corporation, is a general civil practice law firm. The firm, including its predecessors, has a history dating back to the turn of the century, although its major growth has been in the last 15 years.*

*Service to clients and excellence in the practice of law are the guiding principles at Baker, Manock & Jensen. Our attorneys are graduates of leading California and national law schools. The firm encourages its attorneys to develop areas of specialization, and many are recognized experts in their fields of practice. Emphasis on continuing education is a tradition at the firm.*

**JOHN H. BAKER,** born Fresno, California, March 29, 1930; admitted to bar, 1955, California. *Education:* Fresno State College (A.B., 1952); Hastings College of The Law, University of California (J.D., 1955). Phi Alpha Delta; Thurston Society; Order of the Coif. Comment Editor, Hastings Law Journal, 1954. Member, Moot Court Board, 1954. *Member:*

*(This Listing Continued)*

Fresno County (President, 1970) and American Bar Associations; State Bar of California; American Board of Trial Advocates. (Advocate; President, San Joaquin Chapter). Fellow, American College of Trial Lawyers. *PRACTICE AREAS:* Civil Trial Practice; Business and Commercial Litigation; Professional Liability Defense.

**KENDALL L. MANOCK,** born Hanford, California, January 2, 1930; admitted to bar, 1955, California; 1958, U.S. Court of Appeals, Ninth Circuit; U.S. Supreme Court. *Education:* Fresno State College (A.B., 1951); Boalt Hall School of Law, University of California (J.D., 1954). Phi Alpha Delta. Clerk to Hon. Gilbert H. Jertberg, U.S. Court of Appeals, Ninth Circuit, 1958-1959. Assistant United States Attorney, Northern District of California, 1959-1960. *Member:* Fresno County, Federal and American (Member, Sections on: Natural Resources; Banking and Business Law; Taxation) Bar Associations; State Bar of California; American Judicature Society; National Council of Farmer Cooperatives (Member, Legal and Tax Committee). *PRACTICE AREAS:* Agriculture Law including Farmer Cooperatives; Water Law.

**DOUGLAS B. JENSEN,** born Fresno, California, February 10, 1943; admitted to bar, 1967, California. *Education:* Stanford University (A.B., cum laude, 1964; J.D., 1967). Adjunct Professor, San Joaquin College of Law, 1979-1982. Clerk to Hon. Gilbert H. Jertberg, U.S. Court of Appeals, Ninth Circuit, 1967-1968. Fellow, International Legal Center, Santiago, Chile, 1968-1970. *Member:* Fresno County (President, 1983) and American (Member: Corporation, Banking and Business Law Section; Natural Resources Energy and Environmental Law Section and Real Property, Probate and Trust Law Section) Bar Associations; State Bar of California. *LANGUAGES:* Spanish. *PRACTICE AREAS:* Water Law; Real Estate; Water Law (50%); Real Estate (30%).

**DONALD R. FISCHBACH,** born Ventura, California, September 26, 1947; admitted to bar, 1972, California. *Education:* California State Polytechnic College (B.S., with honors, 1969); Hastings College of The Law, University of California (J.D., 1972). Assistant Adjunct Professor, San Joaquin College of Law, 1980-1982. Member, Hastings Law Journal, 1971-1972. *Member:* Fresno County (President, 1985) and American (Member, Litigation Section) Bar Associations; State Bar of California (President, 1994-1995; Member, Board of Governors, Vice President and Treasurer; Commissioner, Judicial Nominees Evaluation Commission, 1983; President, 1994-1996); Young Lawyers Association (Chair, CMA/State Bar Liaison Committee, 1989). *PRACTICE AREAS:* Litigation; Medical Malpractice Defense and Personal Injury.

**ROBERT G. FISHMAN,** born Indianapolis, Indiana, February 10, 1945; admitted to bar, 1970, Indiana; 1974, U.S. Tax Court; 1975, California. *Education:* Miami University (B.A., 1967); Indiana University (J.D., 1970); New York University (LL.M., in Taxation, 1975). Author: "Revised Installment Provisions Breathe New Life Into Farmers' Deferred Payment Contracts," Vol. 54, Journal of Taxation, February, 1981; "Intentional Destruction of Tax Workpapers," Vol. 58, Journal of Taxation, April, 1983. *Member:* Fresno County and American (Member, Taxation and Real Estate Sections) Bar Associations; State Bar of California. *LANGUAGES:* German. *PRACTICE AREAS:* Taxation and Real Estate (60%).

**HOWARD M. ZIDENBERG,** born Toronto, Canada, March 1, 1949; admitted to bar, 1974, California. *Education:* California State University at Long Beach and University of California at Los Angeles (B.A., summa cum laude, 1970); University of California at Los Angeles (J.D., 1974). Phi Beta Kappa; Pi Gamma Mu. *Member:* Fresno County and American Bar Associations; State Bar of California. *PRACTICE AREAS:* Litigation; Medical Malpractice Defense.

**JOHN L. B. SMITH,** born Poughkeepsie, New York, October 10, 1945; admitted to bar, 1975, California. *Education:* United States Military Academy (B.S., 1967); Hastings College of The Law, University of California (J.D., 1975). *Member:* Fresno County and American Bar Associations; State Bar of California. [Colonel, U.S. Army Reserve]. *PRACTICE AREAS:* Environmental and Business Litigation.

**GEORGE L. STRASSER,** born San Francisco, California, October 15, 1950; admitted to bar, 1975, California. *Education:* California State University, Chico (B.A., cum laude, 1972); Boalt Hall School of Law, University of California (J.D., 1975). Phi Kappa Phi. *Member:* Fresno County (Member, Board of Directors, 1995—) and American Bar Associations; State Bar of California (Member, Advisory Committee for Continuing Education of the Bar, 1980-1983). *PRACTICE AREAS:* Business Litigation including Toxics (30%); Medical Malpractice Defense (70%).

**JOSEPH M. MARCHINI,** born Merced, California, August 19, 1953; admitted to bar, 1978, California. *Education:* University of San Francisco

*(This Listing Continued)*

## BAKER, MANOCK & JENSEN, A PROFESSIONAL CORPORATION, Fresno—Continued

(B.A., summa cum laude, 1975); Hastings College of The Law, University of California (J.D., 1978). Guest Lecturer, Agricultural-Finance, San Joaquin College of Law, 1984, 1986. *Member:* Fresno County and American (Member, Corporation, Banking and Business Law Section) Bar Associations; State Bar of California (Member, Debtor/Creditor Relations Committee, Business Law Section); American Bankruptcy Institute; Central Valley Bankruptcy Association; National Society of Accountants for Cooperatives (Co-Chair Education Committee, Far Western Chapter, 1992-1993); American Agricultural Law Association. *LANGUAGES:* Italian. *PRACTICE AREAS:* Business Litigation; Insolvency; Agribusiness.

**CRAIG A. HOUGHTON,** born Orange, California, February 9, 1954; admitted to bar, 1979, California; 1980, U.S. Tax Court. *Education:* University of California, San Diego (B.A., highest honors, 1976); Hastings College of The Law, University of California (J.D., 1979); New York University (LL.M. in Taxation, 1982). Lecturer in Law, San Joaquin College of Law, Graduate Tax Program. *Member:* Fresno County and American (Member: Corporate Tax Committee, Sales, Exchanges and Basis Committee, and Standards of Tax Practice Committee, Section of Taxation, Corporation, Banking and Business Law) Bar Associations; State Bar of California (Member: Pass - Through Entities Committee and Standards of Tax Practice Committee, Taxation Section). *PRACTICE AREAS:* Corporate Partnership and Real Estate Tax Planning; Federal and State Tax Litigation; Mergers and Acquisitions.

**ANDREW R. WEISS,** born Los Angeles, California, June 3, 1955; admitted to bar, 1980, California. *Education:* California State University, Fullerton (B.A., with honors, 1977); University of California, Davis (J.D., 1980). Associate, American Board of Trial Advocates. *Member:* Fresno County and American Bar Associations; State Bar of California. *PRACTICE AREAS:* Employment Litigation; Medical Malpractice Defense.

**MARK W. SNAUFFER,** born Colorado Springs, Colorado, August 15, 1953; admitted to bar, 1977, California. *Education:* Claremont McKenna College; University of California at Berkeley (A.B., high honors, 1974); University of California at Los Angeles (J.D., 1977). Member: Order of Barristers; Moot Court Executive Board, 1976-1977; University of California at Los Angeles-Alaska Law Review, 1976. Judge Pro Tem, Fresno County Superior Court. *Member:* Fresno County Bar Association (Member, Board of Directors, 1991-1993); State Bar of California (Member, Conference of Delegates, 1991; Member, Committee on Rules and Procedures of Court, 1993-1995 ); Fresno County Young Lawyers Association (Member, Board of Directors, 1983-1985); American Board of Trial Advocates (Associate). *PRACTICE AREAS:* Civil Litigation; Product Liability; Professional Liability Defense.

**JAMES E. SHEKOYAN,** born Fresno, California, November 12, 1940; admitted to bar, 1966, California and U.S. Court of Appeals, Ninth Circuit; 1969, U.S. Tax Court; 1971, U.S. Supreme Court. *Education:* Stanford University (A.B., 1962); Hastings College of the Law, University of California (J.D., 1965). Assistant United States Attorney, Central District of California, 1966-1970. Member, California Water Commission, 1981-1982. Chairman of City of Fresno Little Hoover Commission, 1991-1992. *Member:* Fresno County (Secretary, 1976) and American (Member, Sections on: Taxation, Economics of Law Practice; Real Property, Probate and Trust Law) Bar Associations; State Bar of California. *PRACTICE AREAS:* Estate Planning and Probate Law; Business and Real Estate Transactions.

**CARL R. REFUERZO,** born Fresno, California, July 17, 1957; admitted to bar, 1982, California. *Education:* University of California at Los Angeles (A.B., cum laude, 1979); Boalt Hall School of Law, University of California, Berkeley (J.D., 1982). Pi Gamma Mu. Co-author: "The Central Valley Project Improvement Act," Vol. 15 No. 2 Business Law News, Spring 1993; "Reclamation Law- An Overview," Vol. 2, Agricultural Law Update, May, 1985. *Member:* Fresno County and American Bar Associations; State Bar of California. *PRACTICE AREAS:* Agriculture; Business; Real Estate and Water Law.

**JOHN G. MICHAEL,** born Glen Cove, New York, November 19, 1954; admitted to bar, 1982, California, U.S. District Court, Eastern District of California; 1990, U.S. Court of Appeals Ninth Circuit; 1991, U.S. District Court, Northern District of California. *Education:* Santa Barbara City College (A.A., 1977); California State University at Northridge (B.S., magna cum laude, 1979); University of California at Davis (J.D., 1982). Order of the Coif; Phi Kappa Phi; Beta Gamma Sigma. *Member:* Fresno County and American Bar Associations; State Bar of California; Federal Bar Associa-

*(This Listing Continued)*

tion; California Trial Lawyers Association. *PRACTICE AREAS:* Business and Real Estate; Commercial Law; Litigation.

**CHRISTOPHER L. CAMPBELL,** born Tijuana B.C. Mexico, September 28, 1955; admitted to bar, 1984, California. *Education:* Deep Springs College; San Francisco State University (B.A., magna cum laude, 1979); University of California, Berkeley (M.A., City/Regional Planning, 19 84); Boalt Hall School of Law, University of California, Berkeley (J.D., 1984 ). Co-Author: "The Central Valley Project Improvement Act," Vol. 15 No. 2 Business Law News, Spring 1993. General Counsel, Deep Springs College, Mendocino Woodland Camp Association. *Member:* Fresno County (Delegate to State Bar) and American (Member, Natural Resources Energy and Environmental Law Section) Bar Associations; State Bar of California. *SPECIAL AGENCIES:* Federal Bureau of Reclamation. *TRANSACTIONS:* Financing Water Transfers. *PRACTICE AREAS:* Agriculture (Financing and Water Rights) Law (75%); Planning and Zoning.

**ROBERT D. WILKINSON,** born Van Nuys, California, January 10, 1953; admitted to bar, 1981, California and U.S. District Court, Northern and Eastern Districts of California. *Education:* Antioch College; California State University at Chico (B.A., summa cum laude, 1977); University of California at Davis (J.D., 1981). Lawyer Representative to the Ninth Circuit Court of Appeals Judicial Conference, 1995-1998. *Member:* Fresno County, Federal (President, San Joaquin Valley Chapter, 1994; National Council Member, 1993—; Vice President, San Joaquin Valley Chapter, 1993) and American (Member, Criminal Justice Section, White Collar Crime Committee) Bar Associations; California Attorneys For Criminal Justice. *LANGUAGES:* Spanish. *PRACTICE AREAS:* Business Litigation; Civil, Criminal and Medical Malpractice Defense.

**JEFFREY A. JAECH,** born Richland, Washington, August 22, 1953; admitted to bar, 1977, California; 1992, U.S. Tax Court. *Education:* Washington State University (B.A., 1974); Boalt Hall School of Law, University of California (J.D., 1977). Phi Beta Kappa; Beta Gamma Sigma. Special Agent, Federal Bureau of Investigation, 1985-1991. *Member:* Fresno County Bar Association (Chairman, 1983, Estate Planning, Income Tax and Probate Section). *PRACTICE AREAS:* Probate and Trust Administration; Estate Planning; White-collar Criminal.

**DAVID M. CAMENSON,** born Oakland, California, December 20, 1956; admitted to bar, 1985, California. *Education:* University of California at Los Angeles (B.A., magna cum laude, 1980); Indiana University (J.D./M.B.A., with honors, 1985); University of California at Davis. *Member:* State Bar of California; American Bar Association. *PRACTICE AREAS:* Business Transactions; Retirement Planning; Intellectual Property; Income Tax; Employment Taxes.

**LISA M. MARTIN,** born San Francisco, California, June 15, 1957; admitted to bar, 1982, California; 1985, U.S. District Court, Eastern District of California; 1986, U.S. District Court, Northern District of California. *Education:* California State University, Fresno (B.A., magna cum laude, 1979); University of California, Davis (J.D., 1982). *Member:* Fresno County Bar Association; State Bar of California; Santa Cruz County Defense Bar Association. *PRACTICE AREAS:* Business Litigation; Medical Malpractice Defense; White Collar Criminal Defense; Wrongful Termination.

**GAYLE D. HEARST,** born Fresno, November 9, 1962; admitted to bar, 1986, California; 1987, U.S. District Court, Eastern District of California. *Education:* California State University at Fresno (B.S., summa cum laude, 1983); University of California at Davis (J.D., 1986). Phi Theta Kappa; Beta Gamma Sigma. *Member:* State Bar of California. *PRACTICE AREAS:* Business Litigation; Medical Malpractice Defense and Construction Litigation.

**GLENN J. HOLDER,** born Dallas, Texas, November 28, 1950; admitted to bar, 1988, California. *Education:* Santa Clara University (B.S., 1971); San Joaquin College of Law (J.D., with honors, 1988). *PRACTICE AREAS:* Environmental Law; Employment Law; Civil Litigation; Bankruptcy.

**MARK B. CANEPA,** born San Francisco, California, January 26, 1959; admitted to bar, 1989, California, New Mexico, U.S. District Court, District of New Mexico and Northern District of California and U.S. Court of Appeals, Ninth and Tenth Circuits. *Education:* San Francisco State University (B.A., History, magna cum laude, 1985; B.A., Journalism, magna cum laude, 1986); Hastings College of the Law, University of California (J.D,, 1988). *Member:* Association of Defense Counsel of Northern California. *PRACTICE AREAS:* Medical Malpractice Defense; Civil Litigation.

**WILLIAM S. BARCUS,** born Fresno, California, July 20, 1963; admitted to bar, 1989, California and U.S. District Court, Eastern District of California. *Education:* California Polytechnic State University, San Luis

*(This Listing Continued)*

Obispo (B.S., 1986); University of San Diego (J.D., 1989). *PRACTICE AREAS:* Business Litigation; Real Property Litigation.

**DOUGLAS M. LARSEN,** born Provo, Utah, January 26, 1961; admitted to bar, 1989, California and U.S. District Court, Eastern District of California. *Education:* Brigham Young University (B.A., 1986; J.D., cum laude, 1989). Order of the Coif. *LANGUAGES:* French. *PRACTICE AREAS:* Employment Compliance and Litigation; False Claims Act Litigation.

**MICHAEL W. GOLDRING,** born New York, N.Y., December 21, 1959; admitted to bar, 1989, California and U.S. District Court, Eastern District of California. *Education:* University of Southern California (B.S., Entrepreneur Program, Dept. honors, 1982); San Joaquin College of Law (J.D., 1989). Delta Theta Phi. *Member:* Fresno County Bar Association (Member, Real Property Section, 1992-1995, Chairman 1992 and 1995); Los Angeles County and American Bar Associations (Member: Real Property, Probate and Trust Law; Business Law); State Bar of California (Member: Fresno County Real Estate Roundtable Steering Committee, 1992-1995, Chairman 1993-1995; Real Property, Intellectual Property, and Business Sections; San Joaquin College of Law Alumni Association Board of Directors 1990-1993, Vice President, 1992-1993). *PRACTICE AREAS:* Real Property (Secured Transactions, Workouts); Intellectual Property; Health Care Law.

**RANDALL J. KRAUSE,** born Muskegon, Michigan, May 26, 1961; admitted to bar, 1987, California; 1991, Michigan. *Education:* Calvin College (B.A., 1983); Hastings College of Law, University of California, San Francisco (J.D., 1987). *Member:* State Bar of Michigan; State Bar of California. *PRACTICE AREAS:* Environmental - Regulatory; Environmental - Litigation.

**MICHELE A. ENGNATH,** born New Orleans, Louisiana, August 18, 1963; admitted to bar, 1989, Louisiana; 1990, California; U.S. District Court, Central and Eastern Districts of California. *Education:* Newcomb College of Tulane University (B.A., magna cum laude, 1985); Tulane University School of Law (J.D., cum laude, 1989). Phi Beta Kappa. Clerk, Third Circuit Court of Appeal of Louisiana, 1989-1990. *PRACTICE AREAS:* Business and Agribusiness Litigation; Bankruptcy.

**WILLIAM M. WHITE,** born Concord, California, February 2, 1964; admitted to bar, 1991, California. *Education:* University of Missouri (B.S., 1986); Hastings College of the Law (J.D., 1990). *PRACTICE AREAS:* Professional Liability Defense; Business Litigation.

**KATHLEEN A. MEEHAN,** born Port Hueneme, California, February 16, 1953; admitted to bar, 1985, California; 1987, U.S. District Court, Central District of California; 1988, U.S. District Court, Northern and Southern Districts of California. *Education:* St. Mary's College of California (B.A., 1977); University of California, Davis (J.D., 1985). Recipient: Thomas Jefferson Award (Government Department's Outstanding Student); De La Salle Medal (School of Liberal Arts' Outstanding Student). Member, University of California at Davis Law Review, 1984-1985. Co-Author: "Attack on the Tower of Privity: The Expanding Liability of Attorneys to Non-Clients for Professional Negligence," Winter 1991, THe Brief, an ABA Publication. *Member:* Beverly Hills and Los Angeles County Bar Associations; State Bar of California. *PRACTICE AREAS:* Business Litigation; Securities Litigation.

**GARY B. WELLS,** born Salt Lake City, Utah, May 27, 1963; admitted to bar, 1991, California; 1992, U.S. District Court, Eastern District of California; 1993, U.S. District Court, Northern District of California. *Education:* Idaho State University (B.B.A., high honors, 1985); Brigham Young University (J.D., 1991). Beta Alpha Psi; Beta Gamma Sigma; Phi Kappa Phi. Journal of Public Law. American Institute of Certified Public Accountants, 1987—. Certified Public Accountant: Colorado (inactive), 1986; Utah (inactive), 1988; California, 1988. *Member:* Fresno County, Los Angeles County and American Bar Associations; Consumer Attorneys of California; The Association of Trial Lawyers of America. *PRACTICE AREAS:* Estate and Tax Planning; Family Law; Business Litigation. *Email:* gbw@cybergate.com

**RICHARD S. SALINAS,** born Indio, California, April 21, 1966; admitted to bar, 1991, California. *Education:* California State College (B.A., magna cum laude, 1988); University of California, Davis (J.D., 1991). Phi Alpha Delta. *PRACTICE AREAS:* Medical Malpractice Defense; Business Litigation.

**RICHARD A. RYAN,** born Phoenix, Arizona, June 20, 1958; admitted to bar, 1991, California and U.S. District Court, Eastern, Northern and Central Districts of California; registered to practice before the U.S. Patent and Trademark Office. *Education:* Arizona State University (B.S.C.E., 1980; J.D., 1991). Registered Professional Engineer, Texas, 1988—(inactive). *Member:* Fresno County, Los Angeles County and American Bar Associations; State Bar of California (Intellectual Property Law Section). *PRACTICE AREAS:* Patent, Trademark, Copyright and Unfair Competition Law; Litigation.

**DAVID E. HOLLAND,** born Santa Maria, California, September 3, 1968; admitted to bar, 1992, California; 1994, U.S. Tax Court. *Education:* University of California School at Davis (B.A., with honors, 1989; J.D., 1992). Phi Delta Phi. Author: "Proposed Regulations Under the Reclamation Reform Act," *Agriculture Today* (June, 1995). *Member:* State Bar of California (Member, Real Property Law Section, 1993); American Bar Association (Member, Business Law Section, 1994). *PRACTICE AREAS:* Agribusiness; Real Property; Reclamation; Water Law; Public Agency Law.

**GLEN F. DORGAN,** born Ridgecrest, California, October 20, 1966; admitted to bar, 1992, California. *Education:* California State University at Fresno (B.A., 1989); University of Oregon (J.D., 1992). Executive Editor, Oregon Law Review, 1991-1992; Distinguished Service Award, Oregon Law Review, 1992.

**CHARLES K. MANOCK,** born Fresno, California, April 19, 1963; admitted to bar, 1992, California. *Education:* University of California, Los Angeles (Pol. Sci./Hist., 1986); McGeorge School of Law, University of the Pacific (J.D., 1992).

**GLENN A. ROWLEY,** born Cedar City, Utah, June 11, 1956; admitted to bar, 1994, California. *Education:* Brigham Young University (B.A., Intercultural Communications, 1983; J.D., summa cum laude, 1994). Order of the Coif. Regional Best Oralist, Jessup International Moot Court Competition. Member, Brigham Young University Law Review, 1993-1994. Member, Board of Advocates, Trial Advocacy. Author: "Underlying Causes of the Impending U.S.-Japan Patent Wars," Journal of International and Area Studies, Fall 1993. [Capt., U.S. Air Force, 1983-1991; Capt., U.S. Air Force Reserve, 1995 —]. *LANGUAGES:* French and Japanese.

**MATTHEW EARL HOFFMAN,** born Oakland, California, May 10, 1968; admitted to bar, 1994, California. *Education:* University of California at Riverside (B.S., summa cum laude, 1990); Hastings College of the Law (J.D., cum laude, 1994). Order of the Coif. *PRACTICE AREAS:* Business; Taxation.

**COLLEEN SCHULTHIES,** born Pocatello, Idaho, February 7, 1956; admitted to bar, 1994, California; 1995, Utah. *Education:* Brigham Young University (B.A., 1978); Pepperdine University (M.B.A., 1980); University of Utah (J.D., 1994). Phi Kappa Phi; Kappa Tau Alpha.

**JAMES M. CIPOLLA,** born Van Nuys, California, January 7, 1951; admitted to bar, 1994, California. *Education:* University of Santa Clara (B.S.C., 1973; M.B.A., 1975); San Joaquin College of Law (J.D., 1994). *PRACTICE AREAS:* Real Property Transaction; Receiverships.

**MARK E. CRONE,** born Manhasset, New York, January 31, 1965; admitted to bar, 1995, California. *Education:* Trinity College (B.A., 1992); Santa Clara University (J.D., 1995).

**PAUL B. MELLO,** born Gustine, California, May 18, 1969; admitted to bar, 1995, California. *Education:* University of California at Davis (B.A., 1991., J.D., 1995). Editor, University of California at Davis Law Review. *PRACTICE AREAS:* Business Litigation; Employment Law.

**KRISTINE R. CERRO,** born Loma Linda, California, February 7, 1956; admitted to bar, 1995, California and U.S. District Court, Eastern District of California. *Education:* Pacific Union College (A.S., in Nursing, 1979); University of California, Irvine (B.A., 1991); San Joaquin College of Law (J.D., 1995). San Joaquin Agricultural Law Review, 1995. Registered Nurse, California, 1979. *Member:* State Bar of California; Association of Nurse Attorneys. *PRACTICE AREAS:* Medical Malpractice Defense; Health Care Law.

**CATHERINE M. STITES,** born St. Louis, Missouri, March 6, 1970; (admission pending). *Education:* University of California, Irvine (B.A., 1992); Washington University (J.D., 1996). Executive Notes Editor, Washington University Law Quarterly, 1995-1996. Member, Order of Barristers. Recipient: National Association of Women Lawyers 1996 Outstanding Law Graduate Award. Author: "A Palace For a Peppercorn: A Post-BFP Proposal to Resurrect Section 548 (A)(2)(A)," 73:4 Washington University Law Quarterly 1747 (1995).

*(This Listing Continued)*

CALIFORNIA—FRESNO

**BAKER, MANOCK & JENSEN,** A PROFESSIONAL
CORPORATION, Fresno—Continued

**KEITH M. WHITE,** born Chowchilla, California, May 12, 1964; (admission pending). *Education:* Sam Houston State University (B.B.A., 1987); Baylor University (J.D., 1996). Phi Alpha Delta. Notes and Comments Editor, Barylor Law Review, 1996.

**LISA A. TRAVIS,** admitted to bar, 1996, California. *Education:* California State Polytechnic University (B.A., 1992); Hastings College of the Law, University of California, San Francisco (J.D., 1996). *LANGUAGES:* Spanish.

**JEFFREY R. AHRONIAN,** admitted to bar, 1996, California. *Education:* California State University (B.S., 1993); McGeorge School of Law, University of the Pacific (J.D., 1996).

OF COUNSEL

**MICHELLE T. TUTELIAN,** born Fresno, California, December 15, 1955; admitted to bar, 1987, California and U.S. District Court, Eastern District of California. *Education:* University of Southern California (B.A., cum laude, 1977; B.S., 1979); McGeorge School of Law, University of the Pacific (J.D., 1987). *Member:* Fresno County, Los Angeles County and American (Member, Real Property, Probate and Trust Law Section) and American Bar Associations; State Bar of California; Fresno County Young Lawyers (Member, Board of Directors, 1992-1993). *PRACTICE AREAS:* Real Property.

**LEONARD I. MEYERS,** born Tulare, California, August 31, 1918; admitted to bar, 1941, California. *Education:* Fresno State College; University of Hastings College of the Law (LL.B., 1941). Instructor, California Trial Judges College, 1977 and 1978. Judge: Justice Court, 1949-1952; Municipal Court, 1952-1959; Superior Court, 1959-1987. *Member:* Fresno County Bar Association; State Bar of California; California Judges Association.

**JAMES E. GANULIN,** born Los Angeles, California, July 10, 1934; admitted to bar, 1960, California. *Education:* University of Colorado, Boulder; University of California at Los Angeles (B.S., cum laude, 1956); Boalt Hall School of Law, University of California, Berkeley (LL.B., 1959). *Member:* Fresno County Bar Association (Director, 1975-1977; Executive Council, California Conference of Barristers, 1967-1970; Secretary-Treasurer, 1969-1970); State Bar of California (Executive Committee, Public Agency Law Section, 1985-1988; Secretary-Treasurer, 1987-1988). *PRACTICE AREAS:* Water and Public Agency Law; Administrative Matters.

REPRESENTATIVE CLIENTS: Bank of America; NT & SA; Wells Fargo; Metropolitan Life Insurance Co.; Norcal Mutual Insurance; Lawyers' Mutual Insurance Company; Professional Risk Management; The Regents of the University of California; Fresno Metropolitan Flood Control District; Sunkist Growers Inc.; Western Farm Service Inc.; Challenge Dairy Products Inc.; SunMaid Growers of California; Cargill Inc.; Alta Irrigation District; Anderson-Clayton & Company; Consolidated Irrigation District; Dole Food Company; Central Title Company; The Travelers; Westcal Inc.; Kemmer Agricultural Manufacturing Company; GrayLift Inc.; Klink Citrus Association; Robb Ross Foods Inc.; Redfern Ranches; Calico - Fresno Oil Company; Kerman Telephone Company; Telstar Utilities & Construction Inc.; Hills Valley Irrigation District; Agrifim Irrigation Products Inc.; Safeco; The Doctors' Company; California Dairy Herd Improvement Association; Automated Office Systems; Boer Commodities, Inc.; Chooljian Bros. Packing Co., Inc.; Castle & Cooke, Inc.; Valley Children's Hospital-Childrens Home Care; Victor Packing Co., Inc.; CNA Insurance; Sales King International.

## BARADAT & EDWARDS

6592 NORTH FIRST STREET
FRESNO, CALIFORNIA 93710
Telephone: 209-431-5366
Fax: 209-431-1702

Practice Limited to Plaintiff's Civil Trial Litigation in all Courts, Personal Injury, Products Liability, Wrongful Death, Professional Negligence and Insurance Law.

MEMBERS OF FIRM

**DAVID G. EDWARDS,** born Fresno, California, May 27, 1955; admitted to bar, 1982, California and U.S. District Court, Eastern and Central Districts of California. *Education:* California State University at Fresno (B.A., 1978); University of Santa Clara (J.D., magna cum laude, 1982). *Member:* Fresno County and American Bar Associations; State Bar of California; Consumer Attorneys of California. *PRACTICE AREAS:* Personal Injury Law; Professional Negligence Law.

*(This Listing Continued)*

CAA216B

MARTINDALE-HUBBELL LAW DIRECTORY 1997

**DANIEL R. BARADAT,** born Tulare, California, June 21, 1950; admitted to bar, 1976, California and U.S. District Court, Eastern and Northern Districts of California; 1984, U.S. District Court, Eastern District of Oklahoma. *Education:* St. Mary's College (B.A., 1972); University of San Francisco (J.D., 1975). Judge Pro Tem, Fresno County Superior Court. *Member:* Fresno County and Merced County (Secretary-Treasurer, 1977) Bar Associations; State Bar of California; American Board of Trial Advocates; Consumer Attorneys of California. *PRACTICE AREAS:* Personal Injury Law; Legal and Medical Malpractice; Insurance Bad Faith Law.

## BARSAMIAN & SAQUI

A PROFESSIONAL CORPORATION
1141 WEST SHAW AVENUE, SUITE 104
FRESNO, CALIFORNIA 93711-3704
Telephone: 209-248-2360
Telex: 209-248-2370

Labor and Employment Law (Representing Management), including Wrongful Discharge, Employment Discrimination, Sexual Harassment, Employment Tort Actions, Labor Relations and Negotiations, Union Avoidance, OSHA and related employee injuries, Unemployment, Immigration, Wage and Hour, Drug and Alcohol Detection and Prevention, Agricultural Labor Relations, ERISA and Employee Benefits, Human Resources, Commercial Litigation, PACA and Transportation Claims.

FIRM PROFILE: Our firm is committed to providing personalized management representation in all phases of labor and employment law matters, and counsels large nationwide corporations on local issues as well as family owned businesses. We believe that true excellence in effective counsel should occur long before commencement of a union organizing campaign or litigation. We dedicate ourselves to minimizing our clients' exposure to legal harm or labor strife, and maximizing our clients' ability to withstand third party interference with their businesses.

While the firm represents companies in various industries, we place a special emphasis in representing the agricultural sector. In addition to labor and employment matters, our agricultural clientele receive experienced counsel in PACA and AG Canada claims, enforcement of PACA trust provisions, grower-shipper disputes, transportation claims, marketing transactions, and general agricultural business matters.

**RONALD H. BARSAMIAN,** born Visalia, California, May 1, 1953; admitted to bar, 1978, California and U.S. District Court, Southern District of California; 1981, U.S. District Court, Eastern and Northern Districts of California; 1993, U.S. District Court, Central District of California; 1994, U.S. Court of Appeals, Ninth Circuit. *Education:* University of California at Riverside (A.B., Pol.Sc., 1975); California Western School of Law (J.D., cum laude, 1978). Recipient: American Jurisprudence Award in Torts; Dean's Award. Staff Writer and Member, Executive Board, California Western Law Review, 1977-1978. Participant, College of Advocacy, Hastings College of the Law, University of California, 1980. Assistant General Counsel, Western Growers Association, 1979-1985. Member, United Agribusiness League Legal Forum. *Member:* Fresno County and American Bar Associations; State Bar of California (Member, Labor and Employment Law Section). *REPORTED CASES:* Maggio, Inc. v. United Farm Workers of America, AFL-CIO, 227 Cal.App.3d 847, 278 Cal.Reptr. 250 (1991), review denied, cert. denied 112 S.Ct. 187. *PRACTICE AREAS:* Labor Law; Labor Negotiations; Employment Law; Agricultural Law; Commercial Litigation; ERISA; PACA Trust Enforcement.

**MICHAEL C. SAQUI,** born Wood Ridge, New Jersey, April 22, 1963; admitted to bar, 1990, California and U.S. District Court, Eastern District of California; 1993, U.S. District Court, Southern, Northern and Central Districts of California and U.S. Court of Appeals, Ninth Circuit. *Education:* Marquette University (B.A., 1985); California Western School of Law (J.D., 1989). Member, Advocacy Honors Board National Negotiation Team. *Member:* State Bar of California (Member, Labor and Employment Law Section); American Bar Association (Member, Labor and Employment Law Section). *PRACTICE AREAS:* Labor Law; Labor Negotiations; Employment Law; Construction; Transportation; PACA Trust Enforcement; Commercial Litigation.

**PATRICK S. MOODY,** born Tiffin, Ohio, July 16, 1964; admitted to bar, 1991, California and U.S. District Court, Southern District of California; 1992, U.S. District Court, Northern and Eastern Districts of California; 1995, U.S. Court of Appeals, Ninth Circuit. *Education:* University of Florida (B.A., English Literature, 1986); California Western School of Law (J.D., with honors, 1991). Finalist, Gafford Mock Trial Competition. Re-

*(This Listing Continued)*

cipient: American Jurisprudence Awards in Torts and Pre-Trial Advocacy; Brian D. Malloy Scholarship for Excellence in Pre-Trial Advocacy. Staff Writer and Member, Executive Board, California Western Law Review and California Western International Law Journal. *Member:* Fresno County and American Bar Associations; State Bar of California. **PRACTICE AREAS:** Labor Law; Employment Law; Commercial Litigation.

---

**E. MARK HANNA,** born Nashua, New Hampshire, July 10, 1965; admitted to bar, 1994, California; 1996, U.S. District Court, Eastern and Central Districts of California. *Education:* Daniel Webster College (B.S., 1988); Bentley College (M.B.A., Finance, 1991); California Western School of Law (J.D., 1994). *Member:* Fresno, San Diego County and American Bar Associations; State Bar of California. **PRACTICE AREAS:** Labor Law; Employment Law; Agriculture Law; Workers' Compensation Discrimination.

REPRESENTATIVE CLIENTS: PPG Industries, Inc.; Butterball Turkey Co.; Grundfos Pumps; Dairyman's Cooperative Creamery Association; Consolidated Industries, Inc.; V.H. Azhderian & Co.; ATB Packing Co.; Cal-Western Farming Co.; Silver Creek Packing Co.; Hammonds Ranch; Stamoules Produce; Rose Valley Produce; Turlock Fruit Co.; Automotive Parts Exchange; Bertuccio Farms; Frieda's, Inc.; Sam Andrews' Sons; Half Moon Fruit & Produce Co.; Danna & Danna; Lindemann Produce; M. Curti & Son, Inc.; HiValue Processors; Papas & Co.; B & Z Nursery; Certified Ad Services; Gerry Smith Masonry; Gold Rush Produce; Johnson Bros. Orchards; Lettuce Processors, Inc.; Dresick Farms, Inc.; Gargiulo, Inc.; P-R Farms; Ranchers Cotton Oil; San Joaquin Valley Dairymen; Danish Creamery Association; Central Valley Dairy Products; Evangeline Seed Co., Inc.; Teledyne Ryan Aeronautical; InterTech Pharmaceuticals, Inc.

---

## BEDOYAN LAW OFFICES

2499 WEST SHAW AVENUE, SUITE 103
**FRESNO, CALIFORNIA 93711**
Telephone: 209-228-6166
FAX: 209-229-3525

*Bankruptcy and insolvency Law with emphasis on the reorganization of small to medium businesses and farms.*

**HAGOP T. BEDOYAN,** born Fresno, California, February 25, 1960; admitted to bar, 1987, California and U.S. District Court, Eastern District of California; 1988, U.S. District Court, Central and Northern Districts of California; 1989, U.S. Court of Appeals, Ninth Circuit. *Education:* University of California at Los Angeles (B.A., pol. science, 1981); McGeorge School of Law, University of the Pacific (J.D., with distinction, 1987). Traynor Honor Society. Recipient, American Jurisprudence Award in Personal Property Finance. Bankruptcy Clerk's Office Attorney, Advisory Committee, Fresno County, 1995—. *Member:* Fresno County Bar Association; State Bar of California; Central California Bankruptcy Association; American Bankruptcy Institute. (Certified Specialist, Personal and Small Business Bankruptcy Law, The State Bar of California Board of Legal Specialization). **LANGUAGES:** Armenian.

---

## BERDING & WEIL

516 WEST SHAW AVENUE, SUITE 200
**FRESNO, CALIFORNIA 93704**
Telephone: 209-221-2556
Fax: 209-221-2558

*Alamo, California Office:* 3420 Stone Valley Road West. Telephone: 510-838-2090. Fax: 510-820-5592.

*Rancho Cordova, California Office:* 2200 Sunrise Boulevard, Suite 220. 95670 Telephone: 916-851-1910. Fax: 916-851-1914.

*Santa Clara, California Office:* 3600 Pruneridge Avenue, Suite 130. 95051 Telephone: 408-556-0220. Fax: 408-556-0224.

*Construction Litigation and Community Association Law. Non-Profit Corporation Law. Appellate Practice.*

(For Complete Biographical data on all personnel, see Professional Biographies at Alamo)

---

## ALBERT J. BERRYMAN

5088 NORTH FRUIT, SUITE 102
**FRESNO, CALIFORNIA 93711**
Telephone: 209-248-4840
Facsimile: 209-248-4833

*Agricultural Law, Commercial Law, Bankruptcy (Creditors), Banking Law.*

**ALBERT J. BERRYMAN,** born Seattle, Washington, June 20, 1947; admitted to bar, 1972, California; 1992, U.S. Supreme Court. *Education:* University of Notre Dame (A.B., 1968); University of San Francisco (J.D., 1971). Phi Alpha Delta. *Member:* Fresno County Bar Association (Member: Client Relations Committee, 1979-1986; Judicial Evaluations Committee, 1981-1986; Board of Directors, 1988-1990); State Bar of California (Member, Agribusiness Committee, Business Law Section, 1992-1994; Uniform Commercial Code Committee, Business Law Section, 1985-1988); Central California Bankruptcy Association (Member, Board of Directors, 1996—); American Bankruptcy Institute; American Agricultural Law Association.

REPRESENTATIVE CLIENTS: Fresno Madera Farm Credit Services; Bank of America National Trust & Savings Assn.; Union Bank of California; Fleming Companies, Inc.; Farm Credit Leasing.

---

## BRUCE D. BICKEL

470 E. HERNDON AVENUE, SUITE 203
**FRESNO, CALIFORNIA 93720-2929**
Telephone: 209-435-7575
Facsimile: 209-435-1735
Email: brucebickel@earthlink.net

*Business and Estate Planning, Trust Administration and Probate Law.*

**BRUCE D. BICKEL,** born Berwyn, Illinois, January 12, 1952; admitted to bar, 1977, California; 1978, U.S. District Court, Eastern District of California; 1979, U.S. Court of Appeals, Ninth Circuit; 1980, U.S. Tax Court. *Education:* University of Redlands (B.A., summa cum laude, 1973); Hastings College of Law, University of California (J.D., 1977). Order of the Coif; Thurston Society. Member, Editorial Board, Hastings Law Journal, 1976-1977. Moderator and Panelist, "Drafting Wills and Related Estate Planning Documents," (1988, 1990, 1992) and "How to Administer a Decedent's Estate," (1991) California Continuing Education of the Bar. Joint Advisory Committee, "California Will Drafting," California Continuing Education of the Bar, (3d. Ed., 1992). Judge Pro Tem, Fresno County Superior Court, Probate Department, 1996—. *Member:* Fresno County Bar Association (Chairman, Estate Planning, Trust and Probate Law Section, 1997); State Bar of California; Christian Legal Society. (Certified Specialist, Estate Planning, Trust and Probate Law, The State Bar of California Board of Legal Specialization).

---

## JAN M. BIGGS

1233 WEST SHAW AVENUE, SUITE 102
**FRESNO, CALIFORNIA 93711**
Telephone: 209-221-0200
Fax: 209-221-7997

*General Civil Trial Practice. Personal Injury Litigation, Insurance Defense Coverage and Business Litigation.*

**JAN M. BIGGS,** born Denver, Colorado, April 13, 1948; admitted to bar, 1974, California. *Education:* University of California at Santa Barbara and California State University at Fresno (B.A., summa cum laude, 1971); University of the Pacific, McGeorge School of Law (J.D., 1974). Member, Clovis Unified School District Governing Board, 1987-1993. *Member:* Fresno County Bar Association; State Bar of California; Defense Research Institute; Trial Lawyers Association; Northern California Association of Defense Counsel (Director, 1987-1990).

REPRESENTATIVE CLIENTS: California Casualty; Chevron, U.S.A., Inc.; Sunvalley Farms.

CALIFORNIA—FRESNO      MARTINDALE-HUBBELL LAW DIRECTORY 1997

## BLANCO, TOMASSIAN & PIMENTEL
*A Professional Partnership*
*Established in 1991*
*3419 WEST SHAW AVENUE*
**FRESNO, CALIFORNIA 93711**
*Telephone: 209-277-7300*
*Facsimile: 209-277-7350*

General Practice, Civil Litigation, Family Domestic Relations, Business, Mergers and Acquisitions, Corporate, Partnership, Limited Liability Companies, Real Estate Transactions, Taxation, Probate and Estate Planning, Intellectual Property Rights, Franchising and Licensing, Software Licensing, Financing Law, International Law, Foreign Investment, Special Expertise in the In-Bond Maquiladora Industry, Customs, Municipal Finance, Government Affairs, Legislative, Administrative Lobbying and Public Administrative Law.

FIRM PROFILE: Founded in 1991 the firm has carved an impressive niche in the practice areas of family law, real estate transaction, corporate tax and complex international transactions. Members of the firm possess the legal acumen and the necessary presence to serve clients effectively and economically. The members of the firm are diligent, creative, thorough and personable. A unique approach to each client has consistently led our clients to rapid successes both in the United States, Latin America and Europe.

*MEMBERS OF THE FIRM*

**SALVADOR M. BLANCO,** born Chihuahua, Mexico, November 21, 1958; admitted to bar, 1988, California, U.S. District Court, Eastern District of California and U.S. Tax Court. *Education:* California State University (B.A., 1982); San Joaquin College of Law (J.D., 1987). Consultant, Continuing Education Article, "Doing Business in Mexico," CEB Business Law Reporter, Spring, 1989. Instructor: Business Law, Kings River Community College, 1989—; Economics, National University, 1990—; Real Estate, 1990; Real Estate Law, Fresno City College, 1993; Business Law, Fresno City College, 1993; International Transactions, San Joaquin College of Law, 1994. Special Counsel, Central California College of Law. Legal Counsel, Fresno Revitalization Corporation. *Member:* Fresno County Bar Association (Member: Real Property Subsection); State Bar of California (Member: Real Property Section; Business Law Section; Tax Section). LANGUAGES: Spanish. PRACTICE AREAS: Corporate Law; Real Estate Law; Taxation; Trademark Law; International Transactions; Estate Planning.

**GERALD M. TOMASSIAN,** born Milford, Massachusetts, February 11, 1961; admitted to bar, 1988, California and U.S. District Court, Eastern District of California; 1989, U.S. District Court, Northern District of California. *Education:* University of Southern California (B.A., cum laude, 1984); Hastings College of the Law, University of California (J.D., 1987). Pi Sigma Alpha; Blackstonian. Intern, Office of Presidential Personnel, White House, Washington, D.C., 1983. Extern to the Honorable Edward Dean Price, U.S. District Court, Eastern District of California, 1986. Instructor: Business Law, Kings River County College, 1989—; Business Law, Fresno City College, 1993—. Special Counsel, Central California College of Law. *Member:* Fresno County (Member, Real Property and Family Law Sections) and American (Member, Litigation and Family Law Sections) Bar Associations; State Bar of California. LANGUAGES: French. PRACTICE AREAS: Business and Real Estate Litigation; Family Law; General Civil Litigation.

**PAUL J. PIMENTEL,** born Fresno, California, December 26, 1960; admitted to bar, 1986, California and U.S. District Court, Northern and Eastern Districts of California. *Education:* University of California at Davis (B.A., 1983); McGeorge School of Law, University of the Pacific (J.D., 1986). *Member:* Fresno County and American Bar Associations; State Bar of California. PRACTICE AREAS: Municipal Tort Defense; Business Litigation; Personal Injury; Medical Malpractice; Products Liability.

**DAVID D. GOSS,** born Clovis, California, June 25, 1947; admitted to bar, 1995, California. *Education:* California State University, Northridge (B.S., 1991); Loyola Marymount University (J.D., 1995). Beta Gamma Sigma. *Member:* State Bar of California. PRACTICE AREAS: Corporate Law; Taxation; Estate Planning; Civil Litigation.

GENERAL COUNSEL FOR: Sal's Mexican Restaurant, Inc.; American Carrier Equipment Co.; AB Custom Plumbing; Robert L. Jensen & Associates; Johnny Quik Food Stores, Inc.; Beal Properties, Inc.; Pacific States Leasing; Advisory Pacific Mortgage; A&I Labor; Live Light, Inc.; VIP Classic Homes; Elite Custom Homes; ZAP Enterprises, Inc.; Americas First Mortgage, Inc.; Roadster Wheels, Inc.; Spickler Enterprises, Inc.; Thought Communications, Inc.; Mirabella Farms, Inc.; Sun Sierra Ins.; G. Mark Wells, D.V.M., Inc.; Zanontian & Sons; Lamona Towing Service, Inc.; Lamona Service Center, Inc.; Valley Wrecker Sales, Inc.; Meridian Medical Group, Inc.; Clovis Polycon, Inc.; El Cid Mexican Restaurants; Valley Small Business Development Corp.; Bargain Party Rentals; Fresno Revitalization Corporation; City of Fresno.
LOCAL COUNSEL FOR: Regency Savings Bank (Chicago, Ill.).
REFERENCE: Regency Bank, Fresno, California.

## ROBERT E. BLUE
*1180 EAST SHAW AVENUE, SUITE 214*
**FRESNO, CALIFORNIA 93710-7812**
*Telephone: 209-228-8196*
*Facsimile: 209-228-0327*

Creditor Bankruptcy, and Creditors Rights Litigation.

**ROBERT E. BLUE,** born San Jose, California, December 9, 1952; admitted to bar, 1978, Kansas and U.S. District Court, District of Kansas; 1985, California and U.S. District Court, Eastern District of California. *Education:* Brigham Young University (B.S., 1975); University of Kansas (J.D., 1978). County Attorney, Rawlins County, Kansas, 1980-1983. *Member:* Fresno County and American Bar Associations; The State Bar of California; Central California Bankruptcy Association. PRACTICE AREAS: Bankruptcy (Creditors) Law; Business Law; Probate Law.

## BLUMBERG, SENG & IKEDA
*A PROFESSIONAL CORPORATION*
*Established in 1959*
*10 RIVER PARK PLACE EAST, SUITE 220*
**FRESNO, CALIFORNIA 93720-1531**
*Telephone: 209-434-6484*
*Fax: 209-434-8240*

General Trial Practice in all Courts. Professional Malpractice Defense, Real Estate, Defense of Financial and Title Companies, Personal Injury.

FIRM PROFILE: For more than three decades, our firm has provided civil litigation services throughout Central California. The firm's practice emphasizes the defense of attorneys, accountants, insurance agents, real estate brokers and other professionals in malpractice cases and banking institutions and title companies.

**STEPHEN M. BLUMBERG,** born San Francisco, California, June 4, 1930; admitted to bar, 1959, California. *Education:* Stanford University (B.A. 1952); University of California at Los Angeles (J.D., 1958). Lecturer and Author of A.B.A. and CEB Articles on Avoiding and Defending Legal Malpractice, 1985—. Author, Book, "Preventing Legal Malpractice". *Member:* Fresno County Bar Association (President, 1977); State Bar of California (Executive Committee, Real Estate Section, 1977-1990); Association of Defense Counsel of Northern California; American Business Trial Lawyers. Fellow, American Bar Foundation. PRACTICE AREAS: Professional Malpractice Defense and Real Estate Litigation.

**MICHAEL J. SENG,** born Decatur, Alabama, December 20, 1947; admitted to bar, 1975, Tennessee; 1976, California. *Education:* University of Tennessee (B.S., 1969; J.D., 1975). Probation Monitor, State Bar Court. Lecturer and Author: "Malpractice Defense and Avoidance." Judge Pro Tem and Arbitrator, Superior Court, Fresno County. *Member:* Fresno County (Member, Client Relations Committee) and Tennessee Bar Associations; State Bar of California (Member, Litigation Section); Association of Defense Counsel of Northern California. PRACTICE AREAS: Professional Malpractice Defense; Lender Liability Defense; General Litigation.

**DALE IKEDA,** born Clovis, California, February 20, 1951; admitted to bar, 1976, California. *Education:* Stanford University (B.A., 1973); University of California at Davis (J.D., 1976). Author: "Avoiding Conflicts of Interest in Real Property Law Practice," 1993. *Member:* State Bar of California (Executive Committee, Real Property Section). PRACTICE AREAS: Business Law; Real Estate Law; Professional Malpractice Defense.

**GARY L. GREEN,** born Fresno, California, October 6, 1960; admitted to bar, 1986, Montana; 1990, District of Columbia; 1991, California. *Education:* University of Montana (B.A., with high honors, 1983); Gonzaga University (J.D., cum laude, 1986). Phi Delta Phi. Member, 1984-1986 and Technical Editor, 1985-1986, Gonzaga Law Review. Author: Note, "Journalist's Privilege in Criminal Cases," 20 Gonzaga Law Review 301, 1985. *Member:* Fresno County Bar Association; State Bar of Montana; The District of Columbia Bar; State Bar of California. PRACTICE AREAS: Professional Malpractice Defense; Civil Litigation.

**ELISE M. SHEBELUT-KRAUSE,** born Fresno, California, May 6, 1962; admitted to bar, 1987, California; 1991, Michigan. *Education:*

*(This Listing Continued)*

University of Southern California (B.S., magna cum laude, 1984); Hastings College of the Law, University of California (J.D., 1987). Phi Beta Kappa; Phi Kappa Phi. Member, National Moot Court Program. *Member:* State Bar of California; State Bar of Michigan. **PRACTICE AREAS:** Employment Law; Business Litigation; Professional Malpractice Defense; Agricultural Law.

**MICHAEL P. SLATER,** born New York, N.Y., June 15, 1963; admitted to bar, 1990, California and U.S. District Court, Eastern District of California. *Education:* University of California at Davis (B.A., 1986); University of San Diego (J.D., 1990). Phi Alpha Delta. Adjunct Instructor, San Joaquin College of Law. Delegate, Conference of Delegates, State Bar Conventions, 1996. Judge Pro Tem, Municipal Court, Fresno County. *Member:* Fresno County Bar Association; State Bar of California (Member, Board of Directors, 1996; Executive Committee, 1996); Fresno County Young Lawyers Association (Member, Board of Directors, 1994-1996; Treasurer, 1994; Vice-President, 1995, President, 1996). **PRACTICE AREAS:** Civil Litigation; Professional Malpractice Defense.

---

**MICHELLE E. KUNKEL,** born San Jose, California, October 3, 1968; admitted to bar, 1993, California. *Education:* University of California at Santa Barbara (B.A., 1990); Santa Clara University School of Law (J.D., 1993). *Member:* Santa Clara County and Fresno County Bar Associations; State Bar of California. **PRACTICE AREAS:** Professional Malpractice Defense; Civil Litigation.

**NANCY J. STEGALL,** born Lawrence, Nebraska, March 8, 1952; admitted to bar, 1996, California. *Education:* California State University at Fresno; San Joaquin College of Law (J.D., 1996). Comments Editor, 1995-1996, San Joaquin College of Law, Agricultural Law Review. (Law Clerk.) **PRACTICE AREAS:** Professional Malpractice; Business Litigation.

REPRESENTATIVE CLIENTS: Bank of America; Chicago Title Insurance Co.; Lawyers' Mutual Insurance Co.; Reliance Insurance Co.; North Atlantic Casualty and Surety Co.; California Accountants Mutual Insurance Company; REFERENCE: Regency Bank.

## BOLEN, FRANSEN & BOOSTROM LLP

*Established in 1987*
SUITE 430, EAST TOWER
GUARANTEE FINANCIAL CENTER
1322 EAST SHAW AVENUE
**FRESNO, CALIFORNIA 93710**
*Telephone: 209-226-8177*
*Fax: 209-227-4971*

*Clovis, California Office:* 414 Pollasky Avenue. Telephone: 209-226-8177. Fax: 209-322-6778.

*General Business, Banking, Creditors' Rights, Corporate, Real Estate and Taxation Law. Agricultural and Water Rights Law. Estate Planning and Probate Law.*

### PARTNERS

**HAL H. BOLEN II,** born Winchester, Virginia, October 10, 1949; admitted to bar, 1976, California. *Education:* California State University at Fresno (B.S., 1971 and M.B.A., 1973); University of California School of Law at Davis (J.D., 1976). Beta Gamma Sigma; Beta Alpha Psi. Member, Moot Court Board. Co-Managing Editor, University of California at Davis Law Review, 1976. Adjunct Professor of Law, San Joaquin College of Law, 1986—. Regional Counsel, The Prudential Insurance Company of America, 1986-1987. Director, Lawyer's Mutual Insurance Company. Trustee, Fresno Metropolitan Museum. *Member:* Fresno County Bar Association; State Bar of California (Member and Vice Chair, Legal Services Trust Fund Commission, 1983-1986). **PRACTICE AREAS:** Business Law; Real Estate; Taxation.

**KENNETH J. FRANSEN,** born Toronto, Canada, November 3, 1952; admitted to bar, 1977, California. *Education:* California State University at Fresno (B.A., summa cum laude, 1974); University of California at Los Angeles (J.D., 1977). Order of the Coif. Member, University of California at Los Angeles-Alaska Law Review, 1976. Co-Author: "Reclamation Law - An Overview," Agricultural Law Update, May 1985. Author: "Bureau of Reclamation Acreage Limitation Rules," Agricultural Law Update, September 1987; "Major Changes in ASCS Payment Limitation Law Commencing in 1989," Agricultural Law Update, March 1988. Adjunct Professor of Law, San Joaquin College of Law, 1984—. *Member:* Fresno County and American (Member: Business Law Section; Law Practice Management

*(This Listing Continued)*

Section) Bar Associations; State Bar of California; American Agricultural Law Association (Member, Board of Directors, 1986-1989). **PRACTICE AREAS:** Agricultural and Water Law; Business Law; Real Estate; Trusts and Estates.

### SENIOR ATTORNEY

**JEFFREY A. RUSSELL,** born Wilmington, Delaware, November 16, 1959; admitted to bar, 1986, California. *Education:* College of William & Mary (B.B.A., 1982); New York University (J.D., cum laude, 1986). Beta Gamma Sigma; Order of the Coif. Staff Member, 1984-1985, and Articles Editor, 1985-1986, New York University Law Review. *Member:* Fresno County Bar Association; State Bar of California. **PRACTICE AREAS:** Agricultural Law; Business Law; Real Estate.

### ASSOCIATES

**VIRGINIA MILLER PEDREIRA,** born Indianapolis, Indiana, February 20, 1961; admitted to bar, 1988, California. *Education:* Indiana University at Bloomington (B.A., with distinction, 1983); University of Southern California (J.D., 1988). Phi Beta Kappa. Staff Member, University of Southern California Computer Law Journal/Major Tax Planning, 1987-1988. *Member:* Fresno County, Los Angeles County and American Bar Associations; State Bar of California. **PRACTICE AREAS:** Real Estate; Business Law.

### OF COUNSEL

**DONNA BOOSTROM,** born Minneapolis, Minnesota, May 2, 1952; admitted to bar, 1982, California. *Education:* University of Minnesota (B.A., 1979); Hastings College of the Law, University of California (J.D., cum laude, 1982). Adjunct Professor of Law, San Joaquin College of Law, 1985-1986. *Member:* Fresno County Bar Association; State Bar of California. **PRACTICE AREAS:** Banks and Banking; Real Estate.

REPRESENTATIVE CLIENTS: ATK Custom Farm Services; Cal-West Land & Livestock, Inc.; California Controlled Atmosphere; Cantua Cooperative Gin; Capital Agricultural Property Services, Inc.; Corporate Aircraft, Inc.; Farming D; Farrior Farms, Inc.; Five Points Ranch, Inc.; Fresno Equipment Co.; Habitat for Humanity; Hewitson Cattle Company; Houck Industries; Keiser Sports Health Equipment; Kings View Mental Health Systems; London Properties; Multivision Consulting Inc.; Metzler Enterprises, Inc.; Penny Newman Grain Company; Premiere Farmland Partners; Providian Capital Management Real Estate Services, Inc.; The Prudential Insurance Company of America; Quist Dairy; Red Rock Ranch Inc.; River Park Properties; ValliWide Bank; Westchester Group, Inc.

## BORTON, PETRINI & CONRON

T. W. PATTERSON BUILDING
SUITE 830, 2014 TULARE STREET
**FRESNO, CALIFORNIA 93721**
*Telephone: 209-268-0117*
*Fax: 209-237-7995*
*Email: bpcfrs@bpclaw.com*

*Bakersfield, California Office:* The Borton, Petrini & Conron Building, 1600 Truxtun Avenue, P.O. Box 2026. Telephone: 805-322-3051. Fax: 805-322-4628. Email: bpcbak@bpclaw.com.
*San Luis Obispo, California Office:* 1114 Marsh Street. Telephone: 805-541-4340. Fax: 805-541-4558. Email: bpcslo@bpclaw.com.
*Visalia, California Office:* 206 South Mooney Boulevard, P.O. Box 1028. Telephone: 209-627-5600. Fax: 209-627-4309. Email: bpcvis@bpclaw.com.
*Sacramento, California Office:* 2233 Watt Avenue, Suite 290. Telephone: 916-484-3555. Fax: 916-484-3550. Email: bpcsac@bpclaw.com.
*Santa Barbara, California Office:* 211 East Victoria Street, Suite D. Telephone: 805-564-2404. Fax: 805-564-2176. Email: bpcsb@bpclaw.com.
*Los Angeles, California Office:* 707 Wilshire Boulevard, Suite 5100. Telephone: 213-624-2869. Fax: 213-489-3930. Email: bpcla@bpclaw.com.
*San Diego, California Office:* John Burnham Building, 610 West Ash Street, 9th Floor. Telephone: 619-232-2424. Fax: 619-531-0794. Email: bpcsd@bpclaw.com.
*Newport Beach, California Office:* 4675 MacArthur Court, Suite 1150. Telephone: 714-752-2333. Fax: 714-752-2854. Email: bpcnb@bpclaw.com.
*Modesto, California Office:* The Turner Building, 900 "H" Street, Suite D. Telephone: 209-576-1701. Fax: 209-527-9753. Email: bpcmod@bpclaw.com.
*San Francisco, California Office:* 111 Pine Street, Suite 730. Telephone: 415-981-4415. Fax: 415-391-5538. Email: bpcsf@bpclaw.com.

*(This Listing Continued)*

## BORTON, PETRINI & CONRON, Fresno—Continued

*Redding, California Office:* 280 Hemsted Drive, Suite 100. Telephone: 916-222-1530. Fax: 916-222-4498. Email: bpcred@bpclaw.com.
*San Bernardino, California Office:* 290 North "D" Street, Suite 500. Telephone: 909-381-0527. Fax: 909-381-0658. Email: bpcsbdo@bpclaw.com.
*San Jose, California Office:* 2 North Second Street. Telephone: 408-298-3997. Fax: 408-298-3365. Email: bpcsj@bpclaw.com.
*Ventura, California Office:* 1000 Hill Road, Suite 310. Telephone: 805-650-9994. Fax: 805-650-7125. Email: bpcvta@bpclaw.com.
*Santa Rosa, California Office:* 50 Santa Rosa Avenue, Suite 300. Telephone: 707-527-9477. Fax: 707-527-9488. Email: bpcsr@bpclaw.com.

*Commercial/Real Estate Litigation, Insurance Law, General Civil Trial and Appellate Practice in State and Federal Courts, Personal Injury and Casualty Defense Litigation, Insurance Bad Faith and Coverage, Labor and Employment, Toxic Torts, Real Estate, Land Use Planning, Zoning, Municipal, Professional Errors and Omissions, Healthcare Provider Malpractice Defense, Products Liability, Oil and Gas, Water, Natural Resources, Environmental, Public Entity, Administrative, Agricultural, Banking, Contracts, Corporations, Partnerships, Taxation, Creditor's Remedies, Bankruptcy, Probate, Estate Planning, Family Law.*

FIRM PROFILE: Founded by Fred E. Borton in 1899, the firm offers high quality legal services in all of the practice areas described above through its California network of sixteen regional offices. Our mission is to handle each file as if we were the client. We are responsive to the clients' need for communication, cost effectiveness and prompt evaluation.

### MEMBERS OF FIRM

**J. DAVID PETRIE,** born Kokomo, Indiana, August 1, 1955; admitted to bar, 1980, California. *Education:* University of the Pacific (B.S., 1977); University of the Pacific, McGeorge School of Law (J.D., 1980). *Member:* Fresno County and American Bar Associations; The State Bar of California; Association of Northern California Defense Counsel. **PRACTICE AREAS:** Insurance Defense; Medical Malpractice.

**DALE M. DORFMEIER,** born Fresno, California, March 27, 1949; admitted to bar, 1977, California. *Education:* California State University of Fresno (B.A., magna cum laude, 1972); San Joaquin College of Law (J.D., 1977). Instructor, State Center Community College District, 1979—. Author: "Considerations In Adjusting A Crop Loss Claim," California Defense Journal, Spring 1989. *Member:* Fresno County Bar Association; State Bar of California. **PRACTICE AREAS:** Insurance Defense; Crop Loss.

**GARY C. HARVEY,** born Reno, Nevada, June 30, 1956; admitted to bar, 1986, California. *Education:* Patten College (B.A., 1978); Whittier College School of Law (J.D., 1987). *Member:* Fresno County Bar Association; The State Bar of California. **PRACTICE AREAS:** Insurance Defense; Construction Defect.

### ASSOCIATES

**MICHAEL J. BOYAJIAN,** born La Jolla, California, February 17, 1958; admitted to bar, 1987, California. *Education:* California State University, Humboldt (B.S., 1982); Southwestern University School of Law (J.D., 1987). *Member:* The State Bar of California. **PRACTICE AREAS:** Insurance Defense; Personal Injury; Premises Liability.

**DANIEL J. TEKUNOFF,** born Fresno, California, January 3, 1965; admitted to bar, 1992, California and U.S. District Court, Central District of California; 1994, U.S. District Court, Eastern District of California; 1995, U.S. District Court, Northern District of California. *Education:* University of California at Los Angeles (B.A., 1988); Loyola Law School (J.D., 1992). *Member:* Fresno County Bar Association; State Bar of California. **PRACTICE AREAS:** Insurance Defense; Bankruptcy; Landlord Tenant.

(For a Complete Listing of Personnel and Representative Clients, please refer to our Bakersfield listing).

## BROWN & PEEL
6760 NORTH WEST AVENUE, SUITE 104
FRESNO, CALIFORNIA 93711
Telephone: 209-431-1300
Facsimile: 209-431-1442
URL: http://www.rhomberg.com/b&p

*General Civil Trial Practice in State and Federal Courts. Negligence Law, Professional Malpractice, Product Liability, Public Entities Defense, Employment Law, Construction Litigation, Coverage Opinions and Declaratory Relief Actions, Professional Errors and Omissions and Insurance Law.*

**CARL L. BROWN,** born Livermore, California, December 3, 1944; admitted to bar, 1977, California. *Education:* Foothill College (A.A., 1970); San Joaquin College of Law (J.D., 1976). Arbitrator, California Superior Court: Fresno County, 1981; and Madera County. Judge Pro Tem, Fresno County Superior Court. *Member:* Fresno County Bar Association (Member, Voluntary Services Program, 1984); Association of Defense Counsel of Northern California; The State Bar of California; Defense Research Institute; International Association of Defense Counsel; The Association of Trial Lawyers of America. **PRACTICE AREAS:** Insurance Defense; Plaintiff Personal Injury; Product Liability; Construction Litigation.

**JAMES W. PEEL,** born Livermore, California, June 26, 1959; admitted to bar, 1986, California. *Education:* Fresno State University (B.S., 1981); San Joaquin College of Law (J.D., 1985). *Member:* Fresno County Bar Association; The State Bar of California; Association of Defense Counsel of Northern California. **PRACTICE AREAS:** Insurance Defense; Subrogation; Business Litigation; Personal Injury.

---

**R. ERNEST MONTANARI, III,** born Madera, California, October 16, 1962; admitted to bar, 1991, California. *Education:* California State University at Fresno (B.S., 1986); San Joaquin, College of Law (J.D., 1990). *Member:* Fresno County and American Bar Associations; The State Bar of California. **PRACTICE AREAS:** Insurance Defense; Subrogation; Personal Injury.

REPRESENTATIVE CLIENTS: Atlantic Insurance Co.; Carl Warren & Company; CNA Insurance Companies; Continental Insurance Company; Electronic Claims Management, Inc.; Explorer Insurance Co.; GAB Insurance Services, Inc.; Great American Insurance Company; Independent Broker Services Company, Inc.; Ivex Converted Products Corporation; John Deere Transportation Company; Joint Power Insurance Authority; Midland Insurance Services; Orchard Supply Hardware; PayLess Drug Stores, Inc.; Self Insured Management Services, Inc.; Sizzler Restaurants International, Inc.; United Capitol Insurance Company; Wal-Mart Stores, Inc.
REFERENCE: Sanwa Bank California.

## KAREN A. BURT
2499 WEST SHAW AVENUE, SUITE 103
P.O. BOX 9429
FRESNO, CALIFORNIA 93792-9429
Telephone: 209-228-6172
Fax: 209-229-3525

*Landlord Tenant Law including Commercial and Residential, Common Interest Development Law, Contract Leasing and Real Estate.*

**KAREN A. BURT,** born Elgin Air Force Base, Florida, May 15, 1954; admitted to bar, 1984, California. *Education:* California State University at Long Beach (B.A., 1977); McGeorge School of the Law, University of the Pacific (J.D., 1983). *Member:* Fresno County and American Bar Associations; State Bar of California; California Women Lawyers; Fresno County Women Lawyers.

## THOMAS E. CAMPAGNE
AIRPORT OFFICE CENTER
1685 NORTH HELM AVENUE
FRESNO, CALIFORNIA 93727
Telephone: 209-255-1637
Fax: 209-252-9617

*Representing Employers in the Public, Private and Agricultural sectors regarding Labor Relations Law and Employment Discrimination and Wrongful Termination Law, Civil Trial and Appellate Practice in all State and Federal Courts, Commercial and Business Litigation, Real Property, Financial and Business Transactions and Agricultural Business Law.*

(This Listing Continued)

## PROFESSIONAL BIOGRAPHIES

## CALIFORNIA—FRESNO

**THOMAS E. CAMPAGNE,** born Fresno, California, December 21, 1950; admitted to bar, 1975, California; U.S. District Court, Eastern, Central, Southern and Northern Districts of California; U.S. Court of Appeals, Ninth Circuit; U.S. Supreme Court. *Education:* University of Santa Clara (B.S., 1971); San Joaquin College of Law (J.D., 1975). Law Clerk to the Honorable M.D. Crocker, Presiding Judge, U.S. District Court, Eastern District of California, 1975-1976. *Member:* Fresno and American (Member, Labor Law Section) Bar Associations; State Bar of California; The Association of Trial Lawyers of America; Federal Court Bar Association.

REPRESENTATIVE CLIENTS: Visalisa Community Bank; Vicom Land Development; Britz, Inc.; Britz Fertilizers, inc.; Sun-Maid Raisin Growers of California; The Housing Authorities for the City and County of Fresno; The Madera County Housing Authority; Nisei Farmers League; North Central Fire Protection District of Fresno County; RETLAW Broadcasting-KJEO Channel 47, KIMA Channel 29, KEPR Channel 19 and Channel 3 T.V.; Oberti Olive Enterprises of Madera; Rain & Hail Insurance Co.; Sunny Cove Packing House; Wileman Bros. & Elliott Packing House; Hanna & Hanna Engineering; Kash Packing Co.; United Health Centers; Hazelton Kings Rivier Packing; Silver Creek Packing Co.; Valley Dental Centers; Campos Bros. Farms; Warmerdam Packing Co.

---

## ANTHONY P. CAPOZZI

*1233 WEST SHAW AVENUE, SUITE 102*
***FRESNO, CALIFORNIA 93711***
Telephone: 209-221-0200
Facsimile: 209-221-7997

*Trial and Appellate Practice Specializing in State and Federal Criminal Defense Litigation. Personal Injury, Tax Litigation, Tax Fraud and IRS/Collections.*

**ANTHONY P. CAPOZZI,** born Buffalo, New York, June 28, 1945; admitted to bar, 1971, Ohio; 1972, Illinois and U.S. District Court, Southern District of Illinois; 1973, U.S. Court of Appeals, Ninth Circuit and U.S. District Court, Eastern District of California; 1974, U.S. Supreme Court; 1976, California; 1979, U.S. Tax Court; 1980, U.S. Court of Appeals, Fifth Circuit; 1981, U.S. District Court, Central District of California. *Education:* State University of New York at Buffalo (B.A., 1967); University of Toledo (J.D., 1970). Phi Alpha Delta. Adjunct Professor of Law, San Joaquin College of Law, 1976-1978. Lecturer, U.S. Attorney General's Advocacy Institute, Washington, D.C., 1976. Supervising Assistant U.S. Attorney, Fresno, California, 1973-1978. Member, State of California Central Regional Water Quality Control Board, 1982-1985. *Member:* Fresno County Bar Association (Member, Board of Directors, 1986-1987); State Bar of California; California Attorneys for Criminal Justice. *PRACTICE AREAS:* Civil Litigation; Civil Rights; Criminal Law; Appellate Practice; Criminal Tax Audits.

---

## CASWELL, BELL, HILLISON, BURNSIDE & GREER, L.L.P.

*Established in 1980*
*5200 NORTH PALM AVENUE, SUITE 211*
***FRESNO, CALIFORNIA 93704***
Telephone: 209-225-6550
Fax: 209-225-7912

*Business Litigation, Real Estate, Business Law, Construction, Creditors' Rights, Bankruptcy, Corporate, Taxation, Employment Law, Estate Planning and Probate.*

FIRM PROFILE: *Founded in 1980, the members of Caswell, Bell have developed a number of specialized practice areas to successfully serve a diversified business clientele in one of California's most dynamic economic regions. The firm's standards of excellence also ensure clients from outside the region in need of local counsel of the highest quality representation in both litigation and general business matters.*

### MEMBERS OF FIRM

**G. THOMAS CASWELL, JR.,** born Clinton, Oklahoma, May 12, 1931; admitted to bar, 1959, California. *Education:* Fresno State College (A.B., 1956); Stanford University (LL.B., 1959). Delta Theta Phi; Blue Key. *Member:* Fresno County Bar Association; The State Bar of California. *PRACTICE AREAS:* Real Estate; Business Transaction; Land Use; Estate Planning.

**JAMES M. BELL,** born Piggott, Arkansas, November 21, 1937; admitted to bar, 1966, California. *Education:* University of California at Berkeley (B.S., 1959); Boalt Hall School of Law, University of California at Berkeley

*(This Listing Continued)*

(LL.B., 1966). *Member:* Fresno County Bar Association (President, 1975); The State Bar of California. (Certified Specialist, Taxation Law, The State Bar of California Board of Legal Specialization). *PRACTICE AREAS:* Taxation; Real Estate; Estate Planning; Business Transactions.

**ROBERT K. HILLISON,** born Chicago, Illinois, July 27, 1939; admitted to bar, 1965, California. *Education:* University of California at Los Angeles (B.A., 1961; LL.B., 1964). Phi Delta Phi. *Member:* Fresno County and American Bar Associations; State Bar of California; American Judicature Society. *PRACTICE AREAS:* Business, Real Estate and Commercial Litigation; Real Estate.

**JAMES D. BURNSIDE, III,** born Oakland, California, March 12, 1951; admitted to bar, 1977, California; U.S. District Court, Northern District of California; 1978, U.S. District Court, Eastern District of California. *Education:* University of California at Davis (A.B., 1974); University of Santa Clara (J.D., magna cum laude, 1977). Member, Fresno County Fee Arbitration Panel. Probation Monitor, State Bar Court. Early Neutral Evaluator, U.S. District Court. *Member:* Fresno County Bar Association; The State Bar of California. *PRACTICE AREAS:* Construction; Real Estate; Business Litigation; Employment.

**RUSSELL D. GREER,** born Visalia, California, September 14, 1956; admitted to bar, 1981, California and U.S. District Court, Eastern District of California; 1984, U.S. District Court, Northern District of California; 1995, U.S. District Court, Central District of California. *Education:* California State University at Fresno (B.S., summa cum laude, 1978); University of Southern California (J.D., 1981). Alpha Kappa Psi; Phi Kappa Phi; Beta Gamma Sigma; Blue Key. *Member:* Fresno County Bar Association; The State Bar of California; Central California Bankruptcy Association (President, 1992-1993); American Bankruptcy Institute; San Joaquin Valley Ag Lenders Society (Trustee, Chapter 7 Bankruptcy Panel). *PRACTICE AREAS:* Insolvency; General Business; Real Estate; Estate Planning; Agricultural Law.

**ROBERT A. WERTH,** born San Francisco, California, November 10, 1956; admitted to bar, 1989, California. *Education:* San Jose State University (B.S., 1980); McGeorge School of Law, University of the Pacific (J.D., with great distinction, 1988). Order of the Coif. Member, Traynor Honor Society. Recipient, American Jurisprudence Awards in Remedies and Agency. *Member:* Fresno County and American Bar Associations; State Bar of California. *PRACTICE AREAS:* Litigation; Business Law; Real Estate Law.

**RANDOLF KRBECHEK,** born Ann Arbor, Michigan, March 24, 1961; admitted to bar, 1989, California and U.S. District Court, Eastern District of California. *Education:* University of Minnesota (B.A., cum laude, 1984, Phi Beta Kappa); College of William & Mary (J.D., 1989). Member, Order of the Coif. Author: "A Mix of Almonds, Marketing Orders, and First Amendment," and "State Supreme Court Decision on Usury Favors Merchants," San Francisco Daily Journal. *Member:* Fresno County and American Bar Associations; State Bar of California. *REPORTED CASES:* Estate of Berdrow (1992) 5 Cal. App. 4th 637; CTC Food International, Inc. v. PG&E (1992) 45 Cal. Public Utilities Comm. 2d 66 (CPUC). *PRACTICE AREAS:* Business Law; Contracts; Uniform Commercial Code; Real Estate; Business Litigation; Commercial Lending. *Email:* randyk@psnw.com

**BETH MAXWELL STRATTON,** born Redondo Beach, California, August 3, 1963; admitted to bar, 1988, California and U.S. District Court, Eastern District of California; 1991, U.S. District Court, Northern District of California and U.S. Court of Appeals, Ninth Circuit. *Education:* University of California at San Diego (B.A., Economics, with honors, 1985); University of San Diego (J.D., 1988). Order of the Barristers. Member, Moot Court Board. Adjunct Instructor: Discovery and Trial Preparation, Fresno City College, Paralegal Program, 1996—; Alternate Delegate Fresno County Bar Association, Conference of Delegates, 1996—. Faculty Member, University of Phoenix, 1996—. *Member:* Fresno County and American Bar Associations; State Bar of California; Fresno County Young Lawyers Association. *LANGUAGES:* Spanish. *PRACTICE AREAS:* Business and Commercial Litigation; Real Estate Litigation; Creditor's Rights; Collections.

### OF COUNSEL

**J. RUSSELL HOSE,** born Los Angeles, California, January 15, 1947; admitted to bar, 1972, California; 1973, U.S. District Court, Central District of California; 1976, U.S. Tax Court. *Education:* University of Salamanca, Salamanca, Spain; University of California at Los Angeles (B.A., 1969); Southwestern University (J.D., 1972). Member, Board of Directors, California Grape and Tree Fruit League, 1972—. Vice Chairman, California Plum Advisory Board, 1992-1993. *Member:* State Bar of California

*(This Listing Continued)*

CAA221B

## CASWELL, BELL, HILLISON, BURNSIDE & GREER, L.L.P., Fresno—Continued

(Member, Agribusiness Committee, Business Law Section, 1994). *LANGUAGES:* Spanish. *PRACTICE AREAS:* Business Transactions; Real Estate Transactions; Agricultural Law (Water PACA); Debtor/Creditor Transactions.

**O. JAMES WOODWARD III,** born Oakland, California, October 14, 1935; admitted to bar, 1965, California. *Education:* University of California at Berkeley (A.B., 1958); Stanford University (M.B.A., 1961); Boalt Hall School of Law, University of California (LL.B., 1964). Phi Delta Phi. Adjunct Faculty: California State University at Fresno, 1978-1980; Fresno Pacific College, 1994. Chairman, Board of Governors, Fresno Regional Foundation, 1987-1990. President, Fresno Convention and Visitors Bureau, 1991-1992. Member, Board of Directors, Gottschalks Inc., 1992—. *Member:* Fresno County Bar Association; State Bar of California. *PRACTICE AREAS:* Real Estate; Business Transactions.

REPRESENTATIVE CLIENTS: Wawona Frozen Foods; Lyons-Magnus; Sierra Thrift; Campos Bros. Farms; Batth Farms; Fordel, Inc.; Rogers Helicopters; Fresno Association of Realtors; Guarantee Financial Real Estate; Landmark Title Company; PrideStaff; American Ambulance; Piccadilly Inns; Fresno Motor Car Dealers Association; Fresno Dodge/Lexus; Herwaldt Pontiac/GMC/Mercedes Benz; Michael Cadillac/Toyota/Chevrolet; Quality Jeep/Eagle/Nissan; Van-G Trucking, Inc.; Densmore Engines; Fig Garden Village Shopping Center; G.L. Bruno Associates, Inc.; Industrial Refrigeration and Cooling Equipment, Inc.; Fansler Foundation; Arakelian Foundation; G.L. Bruno Foundation; Thielen & Associates Advertising; Fig Garden Golf Course; Rancho Canada Golf Course.
LOCAL COUNSEL FOR: Fresno-Madera Federal Land Bank Association; Western Farm Credit Bank; Weyerhaeuser Mortgage; Western Waste Industries; The Southland Corporation; National Advertising/3M; Ford Motor Credit Company; Pacific Theatres; GMAC; Fidelity Financial Services, Inc.; Cadiz Land Company, Inc.; Keller Industries, Inc.

## COLEMAN & HOROWITZ

Established in 1994

**499 WEST SHAW, SUITE 116**
**FRESNO, CALIFORNIA 93704**
Telephone: 209-248-4820
Facsimile: 209-248-4830

*General Civil and Trial Practice. Commercial Litigation, Corporation Law, Business, Trust, Taxation, Probate and Estate Planning, Construction, Real Estate, Banking, Appellate Advocacy, Casualty Insurance Defense, Insurance Coverage, Environmental Claims and Commercial Collections.*

### MEMBERS OF FIRM

**WILLIAM H. COLEMAN,** born Montgomery, Alabama, April 2, 1952; admitted to bar, 1977, California; 1979, U.S. District Court, Eastern District of California 1982, U.S. Tax Court. *Education:* University of Arizona (B.S., with high distinction, 1973); McGeorge School of Law (J.D., 1976). Phi Delta Phi. Member, Traynor Society. Author: "Estate Planning for Lawyers," The Bottom Line, August 1990. Panelist: CEB, NBI, FLUA. *Member:* Fresno County Bar Association; State Bar of California (Member, Probate and Real Estate Sections). *PRACTICE AREAS:* Taxation; Estate Planning; Probate and Trust; Corporate and Business; Transactions; Real Estate.

**DARRYL J. HOROWITT,** born Long Beach, California, August 23, 1956; admitted to bar, 1981, California; 1982, U.S. District Court, Central District of California and U.S. Court of Appeals, Ninth Circuit; 1989, U.S. District Court, Eastern District of California; 1993, U.S. Supreme Court and U.S. District Court, Northern District of California. *Education:* California State University, Long Beach (A.B., 1978); Western State University (J.D., 1981). Recipient, American Jurisprudence Award. Author: "Steps to Success: Goal Setting, Marketing and Servicing Your Client," The Bottom Line, February, June and August, 1990; "Goals to Remember," The Bottom Line, Law Practice Management Section, February, 1990; "How Not To Spend a Fortune on Experts," Damages, Syllabus, 1995 CAOC Seminar on Damages. Panelist: CTLA, CPA/Law Forum NAWIC. Judge Pro Tem; Fresno County Municipal Court. Arbitrator: American Arbitration Association; Fresno County; Madera County. Mediator: American Arbitration Association. *Member:* Fresno County (Member, Alternate Dispute Resolution Committee; Construction Committee) and American (Member, Sections on Litigation and Law Practice Management) Bar Associations; State Bar of California (Member: Sections on Law Practice Management and Litigation); Fresno Trial Lawyers Association; Consumer Attorneys of California. *REPORTED CASES:* In Re UFW (1989) 15 ALRB 10. *PRACTICE AREAS:* Business Litigation; Commercial Litigation; Real Estate

*(This Listing Continued)*

---

Litigation; Construction Litigation; Banking Litigation; Casualty Insurance Defense; Insurance Coverage; Environmental Claims; Commercial Collections.

**LUCILLE GOINS DIMMICK,** born Woodlake, California, August 22, 1949; admitted to bar, 1994, California and U.S. District Court, Central, Northern and Eastern Districts of California. *Education:* Fresno City College (A.S., 1991); San Joaquin College of Law (J.D., 1994). Member, National Association of Women in Construction. *Member:* Fresno County Bar Association; State Bar of California; Fresno Trial Lawyers Association. *PRACTICE AREAS:* Business Litigation; Commercial Litigation; Real Estate; Construction Law; Commercial Collections; Banking. *Email:* lucilaw@aol.com

REPRESENTATIVE CLIENTS: Hidden Villa Ranch; Utility Trailer Sales of Central California, Inc.; Martin Oil Company; Motel 6 Operating LP; Team Enterprises, Inc.; Wild Electric, Inc.; Manco Abbott; El Monte Gas Co. Inc.; Fleming Companies, Inc.; Farm Credit Leasing Services, Inc.; Marsh and McClennan, Incorporated; Ward Construction Co.; IA Construction, Inc.; Double Eagle Construction, Inc.; H&K Concrete Cutting; Honetown Realty, Inc.; Coldwell Banker Dan Blough & Assoc.; S&J Lumber Co., Inc.; WFS Financial; Acoustical Material Services.

## COOPER & HOPPE

**2444 MAIN STREET, SUITE 125**
**FRESNO, CALIFORNIA 93721-2734**
Telephone: 209-442-1650
Fax: 209-442-1659

*Monterey, California Office:* 1088 Cass Street, 93940. Telephone: 408-649-0330.

*State and Federal General Civil and Trial Practice. Insurance Defense, Business Litigation, Business Transactions, Insurance Coverage, Estate Planning and Personal Injury. Sports and Entertainment Representation.*

**JOSEPH D. COOPER,** born Fresno, California, October 30, 1960; admitted to bar, 1989, California. *Education:* University of California at Berkeley (B.S., 1982); San Joaquin College of Law (J.D., 1987). Member, NFL Players Association. Contract Advisor, NFL Players Association. *Member:* Fresno County Young Lawyers Association (Member, Board of Directors, 1989-1991); Association of Defense Counsel. *PRACTICE AREAS:* Personal Injury Defense; Business Litigation; Insurance Coverage; Crop Loss; Product Liability; Sports and Media Representation.

**THEODORE W. HOPPE,** born Staten Island, New York, August 10, 1963; admitted to bar, 1988, California; U.S. District Court, Eastern and Central Districts of California; 1989, Nebraska. *Education:* Trinity University (B.A., Psych., honors, 1985); University of Nebraska (J.D., 1988). *Member:* State Bar of California; state Bar of Nebraska; Fresno County Young Lawyers Bar Association (Member, Board of Directors). *PRACTICE AREAS:* Insurance Coverage; Personal Injury Defense; Business Litigation.

REPRESENTATIVE CLIENTS: Farmers Insurance Group; Continental Insurance Company; American States Insurance Company; Great American Insurance Company; Mid-Century Insurance Company; Truck Insurance Exchange; Travelers Insurance Company; Civil Service Employees Insurance Company; Oregon Mutual Insurance Company; Safeco Insurance Company; Aetna Life and Casualty Company; Cal Farm Insurance Company; Fireman's Fund Insurance Company; Rain and Hail Insurance Company; Sequoia Insurance Company.

## LAW OFFICES OF ROBERT D. CROSSLAND

**5200 NORTH PALM AVENUE, SUITE 209**
**FRESNO, CALIFORNIA 93704-2228**
Telephone: 209-229-6534
Fax: 209-229-2665

*San Mateo, California Office:* 177 Bovet Road, Suite 600. Telephone: 415-341-1556. Fax: 415-341-1395.

*Estate Planning, Partnership, Tax, Probate, Taxation, Corporate and Partnership Law.*

**ROBERT D. CROSSLAND,** born Upland, California, March 5, 1944; admitted to bar, 1972, California. *Education:* California State University at Fresno (B.A., 1967); American College (C.L.U., 1979); Hastings College of Law, University of California (J.D., 1970); University of Miami (LL.M. in Taxation, 1971). Estate Tax Attorney, IRS, 1972-1974. Attorney for Tax Collector, San Francisco, 1974-1976. Advanced Underwriting Consultant,

*(This Listing Continued)*

New York Life Insurance Company, 1976-1979. *Member:* San Mateo County and Fresno County Bar Associations; State Bar of California.

REPRESENTATIVE CLIENTS: De Freitas Farms Inc.; Enrico Farms Inc.; Erro Properties; Haase Equipment Co.; Krug-Bixby Associates, Inc.; Ormonde Farms; Patton Sheet Metal Inc.; Robert V. Jensen, Inc.; San Bruno Lumber Co.; Tchaney Construction Co.; Tunitas Beach Land Co.

## DIETRICH, GLASRUD & JONES

An Association of Attorneys including Law Corporations
5250 NORTH PALM AVENUE, SUITE 402
FRESNO, CALIFORNIA 93704
Telephone: 209-435-5250
Facsimile: 209-435-8776

*Business Litigation, Unfair Competition and Appellate Practice. Media Law, Environmental Litigation, Corporate, Business, Creditor Bankruptcy, Pension and Profit Sharing, Taxation, Real Property, ERISA Litigation, Health Care, Probate and Estate Planning.*

**RICHARD W. DIETRICH, (INC.),** born Lindsay, California, August 7, 1930; admitted to bar, 1959, California; 1968, U.S. Tax Court. *Education:* University of California at Berkeley (A.B., 1952); Boalt Hall School of Law, University of California (LL.B., 1958). *Member:* Fresno County and American (Member, Section on Taxation) Bar Associations; State Bar of California. (Certified Specialist, Taxation Law, The State Bar of California Board of Legal Specialization). *PRACTICE AREAS:* Estate Planning; Pension Planning; Business Transactions.

**DONALD H. GLASRUD, (INC.),** born Los Angeles, California, October 5, 1942; admitted to bar, 1969, California. *Education:* Fresno State College (A.B., summa cum laude, 1965); Boalt Hall School of Law, University of California (J.D., 1968). Law Clerk, California Court of Appeal, Fifth District, 1968-1969. *Member:* Fresno County (Member, Board of Directors, 1993—) and American (Member, Litigation Section) Bar Associations; State Bar of California (Member, Litigation Section). *PRACTICE AREAS:* Unfair Competition; Media Law; Business and Construction Litigation.

**VREELAND O. JONES, (INC.),** born Long Branch, New Jersey, November 18, 1945; admitted to bar, 1976, California. *Education:* Gettysburg College (B.A., 1967); McGeorge School of the Law, University of the Pacific (J.D., 1976). Phi Delta Phi. Member, Traynor Society. Member, Board of Editors, Pacific Law Journal, 1976. Author: "Probate Code Conservatorships: A Legislative Grant of New Procedural Protections," Pacific Law Journal, Vol. 8, 1977. *Member:* Fresno County and American (Member, Antitrust Section, Health Law Section and Section on Taxation) Bar Associations; State Bar of California (Member, 1984-1988 and Chairman, 1987-1988, Taxation Law Advisory Commission, California Board of Legal Specialization); National Health Lawyers Association; American Academy of Hospital Attorneys; California Society for Healthcare Attorneys. [Capt., U.S. Air Force, 1967-1972]. (Certified Specialist, Taxation Law, The State Bar of California Board of Legal Specialization). *PRACTICE AREAS:* Business Transactions; Health Care Law; Real Estate Law.

**ROBERT A. MALLEK JR. (INC.),** born Oakland, California, November 19, 1947; admitted to bar, 1978, California. *Education:* Stanford University (B.A., 1970); McGeorge School of the Law, University of the Pacific (J.D., 1978). Member, Traynor Society. Member, Board of Editors, Pacific Law Journal, 1977-1978. Editor, 1977 Review of Selected California Legislation. Lecturer in Law, San Joaquin College of Law, Graduate Tax Program, 1985—. Adjunct Professor, Business Law, National University, 1996—. *Member:* Fresno County and American (Member, Section on Taxation) Bar Associations; State Bar of California. [Lieut., U.S. Navy, 1970-1975]. (Certified Specialist, Taxation Law, The State Bar of California Board of Legal Specialization). *PRACTICE AREAS:* Business Transactions; Bank Workout Law; Corporate Tax; Estate Planning Law. **Email:** RAMATCAM@AOL.COM

**RICHARD E. AUNE, (INC.),** born Missoula, Montana, September 18, 1950; admitted to bar, 1977, California. *Education:* California State University (B.A., 1972); McGeorge School of the Law, University of the Pacific (J.D., 1977). *Member:* Fresno County and American Bar Associations; State Bar of California. *PRACTICE AREAS:* Employee Benefits Law.

**TIMOTHY J. BUCHANAN,** born Scranton, Pennsylvania, December 4, 1954; admitted to bar, 1981, California. *Education:* University of California at Los Angeles (B.A., magna cum laude, 1977); University of Santa Clara (J.D., 1981). Articles Editor, Santa Clara Law Review, 1980-1981. Author: "Expanding the Standard for Attempts to Monopolize: The Recommendations of the National Commission for the Review of Antitrust Laws and Procedures," 21 Santa Clara Law Review 147, 1981. Law Clerk to Hon. George A. Brown, Presiding Justice, California Court of Appeal, Fifth District, 1981-1983. Judge ProTem, Fresno County Municipal Court, 1993—. *Member:* Fresno County and American (Member, Section of Antitrust Law) Bar Associations; State Bar of California. *PRACTICE AREAS:* Unfair Competition; Business Litigation; Media and Employment Law; Securities; ERISA Litigation.

**BRUCE A. OWDOM,** born Bakersfield, California, December 14, 1948; admitted to bar, 1977, California and U.S. District Court, Eastern District of California; 1988, U.S. District Court, Central District of California. *Education:* College of Sequoias (A.A., 1969); University of Santa Clara (B.A., 1971); San Joaquin College of Law (J.D., 1977). Member, Fresno County Public Defenders Office, 1978-1985. *Member:* Fresno County Bar Association; State Bar of California. *PRACTICE AREAS:* Business; Construction; Real Property and Environmental Litigation.

**THOMAS W. ISAAC,** born Berkeley, California, August 2, 1952; admitted to bar, 1980, California and U.S. District Court, Eastern District of California. *Education:* California State University at Fresno (B.A., 1975); California Western School of Law (J.D., 1978). *Member:* Fresno County Bar Association (Business Law Section); The State Bar of California; California Bankers Association; American Bankruptcy Institute; Central California Bankruptcy Association. *PRACTICE AREAS:* Bankruptcy (Creditors) Law; Commercial Litigation; Savings and Loan Law; Title Insurance; Escrow Law.

**CHRISTOPHER E. SEYMOUR,** born Fresno, California, April 27, 1960; admitted to bar, 1986, California. *Education:* California Polytechnic State University, San Luis Obispo (B.A., magna cum laude, 1983) Phi Kappa Phi; Loyola University (J.D., 1986) Phi Alpha Delta. President, Loyola Business Law and Litigation Society, 1984-1985. *Member:* Fresno County and Los Angeles County Bar Association; State Bar of California; American Institute of Architects; Pasadena Young Lawyers Association (Past President). *PRACTICE AREAS:* Business, Construction and Design Professionals Malpractice; Litigation.

**DOUGLAS D. SCHORLING,** born Fresno, California, November 17, 1955; admitted to bar, 1980, California; 1985, U.S. Tax Court. *Education:* California State University at Fresno (B.A., magna cum laude, 1977) Phi Kappa Phi; Pi Gamma Mu; University of California at Davis (J.D., 1980). Legal Research Editor, University of California at Davis Law Review, 1979-1980. Member, Moot Court Board. Author, "Negligent Parental Supervision as Grounds for Contribution in Tort: The Case for Minimal Parental Liability," University of California at Davis Law Review, Vol. 12, No. 2, Summer, 1979. *Member:* Fresno County and American Bar Associations; State Bar of California. *PRACTICE AREAS:* Business Transactions; Health Care Law; Probate Law.

**LESLIE G. MIESSNER,** born Los Angeles, California, December 1, 1965; admitted to bar, 1992, California; U.S. District Court, Eastern District of California; U.S. Tax Court. *Education:* University of California at Los Angeles (B.A., magna cum laude, 1988) Phi Beta Kappa; University of California, Davis (J.D., 1991). Member, Trial Practice Honors Board. Adjunct Professor, National University, 1996. *Member:* Fresno County and American (Member: Health Law and Business Law Sections) Bar Associations; State Bar of California (Member, Business Law Section and Section on Taxation); California Society for Healthcare Attorneys; California Women Lawyers; Fresno County Women Lawyers (Secretary, 1994-1995); Fresno County Young Lawyers. *PRACTICE AREAS:* Business Transactions; Health Care Law; Taxation.

REPRESENTATIVE CLIENTS: American Residential Mortgage Corp.; Cadillac Plastic Group, Inc.; California Industrial Rubber; Capital Cities/ABC; Central IPA; Chicago Title Company; Coast Federal Bank; Community Medical Imaging; EMC Mortgage Corporation; Enoch Packing Corp.; Fluor Daniel, Inc.; Fresno Surgery and Recovery Care Center; Fruit Marketing, Inc.; Glendale Federal Bank; ITT/BO West Mortgage Corp.; KMSG-TV Fresno Channel 59; M.A. Hanna; McClatchy Newspapers, Inc.; Meredith Corporation; National Raisin Company; Pioneer Chlor Alkali Co., Inc.; Resolution Trust Corporation; Retlaw Broadcasting Corporation; RTC/FDIC; Schaal/Lechner Corporation; Standard Life Insurance Company; Stewart Title of Fresno County; Stewart Title Guaranty Company; U-Haul International, Inc.; ValliWide Bank; Zurich American Insurance Co.

*(This Listing Continued)*

# DOWLING, AARON & KEELER

*INCORPORATED*

Established in 1977

SUITE 200
6051 NORTH FRESNO STREET
**FRESNO, CALIFORNIA 93710**
Telephone: 209-432-4500
Fax: 209-432-4590
Email: dowling-law.com

Civil Trial and Appellate Practice, State and Federal Courts. Corporation, Banking, Creditor's Rights, Bankruptcy, Securities, Real Estate, Estate Planning, Probate, Taxation, Pension, Agricultural, Administrative, Government, Health Care, Insurance, Labor and Employment, Family Law and Sports Law.

**MICHAEL D. DOWLING,** born Richmond, California, May 20, 1942; admitted to bar, 1967, California. *Education:* Stanford University (A.B., 1963); Hastings College of The Law, University of California (J.D., 1966). Order of the Coif. Member, Thurston Society. Member, Hastings Law Journal, 1965-1966. Deputy District Attorney, Fresno County, 1967-1968. Arbitrator, Judicial Arbitration Panel, Superior Court. *Member:* Fresno County (Member, Board of Directors, 1982-1985) and American (Member, Sections on: Corporation, Banking and Business Law; Taxation) Bar Associations; State Bar of California. (Certified Specialist, Taxation Law, The State Bar of California Board of Legal Specialization). **PRACTICE AREAS:** Corporate Law; Business Transactions; Business Organization; Taxation Law; Estate Planning; Probate.

**RICHARD M. AARON,** born Fresno, California, October 24, 1954; admitted to bar, 1979, California and U.S. District Court, Eastern District of California. *Education:* University of Southern California (B.S., Business Administration, magna cum laude, 1976); Hastings College of the Law, University of California (J.D., 1979). Beta Gamma Sigma. Arbitrator, Judicial Arbitration Panel, Fresno Court, 1990—. Arbitrator, American Arbitration Association. Certified Player Agent, Major League Baseball Players Association. *Member:* Fresno County (Member: Estate Planning, Income Tax and Probate Section; Law Library Committee, 1981-1983) and American (Member: Business Law Section; Health Care Law Section) Bar Associations; State Bar of California (Member, Business Law Section). (Certified Specialist, Estate Planning, Trust and Probate Law, The State Bar of California Board of Legal Specialization). **PRACTICE AREAS:** Business Transactions; Acquisitions and Sales of Businesses; Real Estate Law; Estate Planning Law.

**BRUCE S. FRASER,** born Richmond, California, March 21, 1952; admitted to bar, 1978, California and U.S. District Court, Eastern District of California; 1981, U.S. Tax Court. *Education:* California State University, Humboldt (A.B., Political Science, 1975); Syracuse University (J.D., cum laude, 1977). Phi Delta Phi. Member, Justinian Honorary Law Society. Staff Member, Syracuse Law Review, 1976-1977. Instructor for LL.M. in Taxation Program of San Joaquin College of Law, 1983. *Member:* Fresno County (Member: Estate Planning, Income Tax and Probate Section) and American (Member, Section of Taxation) Bar Associations; State Bar of California. **PRACTICE AREAS:** Pension and Profit Sharing Law; Employee Benefits Law; Corporate Law; Qualified Domestic Relations Orders; Equipment Leasing Law.

**WILLIAM J. KEELER, JR.,** born Lockport, New York, December 14, 1948; admitted to bar, 1973, California; 1974, U.S. Court of Military Appeals; 1982, U.S. District Court, Central District of California; 1983, U.S. Tax Court. *Education:* University of Notre Dame (B.A., 1970); University of Southern California (J.D., 1973). Author: "The California Inheritance Tax Scheme: 1981 Version," Western State University Law Review, Vol. 8, No. 1, 1980. Panelist: Continuing Education of the Bar, Planning the Small Estate, 1984; Recent Developments in Estate Planning and Administration, 1985-1994; Planning for the Aging & Incapacity, 1987, 1989; Fundamentals of Estate Administration, 1988. Judge Pro Tempore, Fresno County Superior Court, Probate Dept., 1996; Judge Pro Tempore, Orange County Superior Court, Probate Dept., 1988. *Member:* Fresno County (Chairman, Estate Planning Probate and Trust Section, 1993), Orange County (Chairman, Estate Planning, Probate and Trust Law Section, 1989) and American (Member, Real Property and Trust Law Section) Bar Associations; State Bar of California (Member, Estate Planning, Trust and Probate Law Section). [Capt., U.S. Air Force Reserve; Capt., JAGD, USAF, 1974-1978]. (Certified Specialist, Estate Planning, Trust and Probate Law, The State Bar of California Board of Legal Specialization). **PRACTICE AREAS:** Estate Planning Law; Probate and Trust Law; Estate Litigation.

**JOHN C. GANAHL,** born Los Angeles, California, July 15, 1944; admitted to bar, 1970, California; 1974, U.S. District Court, Eastern District of California. *Education:* University of Notre Dame (B.B.A., 1966); University of California at Davis (J.D., 1969). Beta Alpha Psi. Deputy Legislative Counsel, California State Legislature, 1970-1972. Member, Board of Directors, 1974-1978 and Secretary, 1976-1978, Fresno County Legal Services, Inc. Alumni Senator, University of Notre Dame, 1976-1981. *Member:* Fresno County Bar Association; The State Bar of California (Member, Sections on: Business Law; Real Property Law; Delegate, Conference of Delegates, 1980-1983). **PRACTICE AREAS:** Business Transactions; Securities Law; Acquisition, Sale and Financing of Businesses; Health Care Law.

**ADOLFO M. CORONA,** born Fowler, California, April 3, 1959; admitted to bar, 1986, California and U.S. District Court, Eastern, Northern, Southern and Central Districts of California. *Education:* University of California at Berkeley (A.B. in Political Science with high honors, 1981; J.D., 1985). Member, Fowler Lions Club. *Member:* State Bar of California; American Bar Association; The Association of Trial Lawyers of America; Fresno County Bar Association (Board of Directors, 1992-1995 ); Fresno County Young Lawyers Association (Board of Directors; Secretary/-Treasurer, 1989-1990; First Vice President/President-Elect, 1990-1991; President, 1991-1992); Fresno County State Bar Delegate; Central California Bankruptcy Association; Fowler Unified School District Board of Trustees (President, 1993-1994); Fresno County School Board Trustees Association; State Center Community College District Affirmative Action Advisory Committee; Fresno and Hispanic Chamber of Commerce, Leadership Fresno, Class X; Fowler Lions Club. **LANGUAGES:** Spanish. **PRACTICE AREAS:** Business Litigation; Construction Law; Creditors Remedies; Creditor Bankruptcy Litigation; Insurance Coverage.

**PHILIP DAVID KOPP,** born Kewanee, Illinois, September 6, 1950; admitted to bar, 1979, California. *Education:* California Lutheran College (B.A., summa cum laude, 1976); University of California at Los Angeles (J.D., 1979). *Member:* Moot Court (Distinguished Advocate); U.C.L.A. Law Review, 1976-1978. Extern Law Clerk to Judge Robert J. Kelleher, U.S. District Court, Central District of California, 1977. Member, Louis M. Welsh Chapter, American Inns of Court. **PRACTICE AREAS:** Business as Commercial Litigation; Water Rights; Environmental Litigation; Intellectual Property Litigation.

**RENE LASTRETO, II,** born Portland, Oregon, May 2, 1956; admitted to bar, 1981, California, U.S. District Court, Eastern and Central Districts of California and U.S. Court of Appeals, Ninth Circuit. *Education:* California State University at Fresno; University of Utah (B.S., cum laude, 1978); University of San Francisco (J.D., 1981). Member, Moot Court Board. President, Fresno County Young Lawyers Association, 1988-1989. *Member:* Fresno County (Member, Board of Directors, 1989-1991) and American Bar Associations; The State Bar of California; Central California Bankruptcy Association. **PRACTICE AREAS:** Creditors Rights; Commercial Litigation; Bankruptcy Law; Civil Litigation.

**FRANCINE MARIE KANNE,** born Fresno, California, July 12, 1954; admitted to bar, 1988, California and U.S. District Court, Eastern District of California. *Education:* Fresno City College (A.S./R.D.H., 1977); San Joaquin College of Law (J.D., 1988). Delta Theta Phi. *Member:* Fresno County and American Bar Associations; Fresno County Women's Lawyers; California Trial Lawyers Association; Fresno County Young Lawyers (Member and President, Board of Directors, 1994). **PRACTICE AREAS:** Insurance Defense; Environmental; Business Litigation.

**CHRISTOPHER A. BROWN,** born Visalia, California, August 1, 1960; admitted to bar, 1989, California and U.S. District Court, Northern District of California; 1991, U.S. District Court, Eastern District of California. *Education:* Occidental College (B.A., 1983); Santa Clara University (J.D., 1989). *Member:* Fresno County (Member, Section on: Real Property; Environmental Law; Legislative Committee of the Environmental Law Section) and American Bar Associations; State Bar of California (Member, Section of Natural Resources, Energy and Environmental Law Legislative Committee). **PRACTICE AREAS:** Business Transactions; Real Estate Law; Environmental Law; Land Use Law; Construction Law.

---

**RICHARD E. HEATTER,** born Long Beach, California, September 2, 1944; admitted to bar, 1989, California and U.S. District Court, Eastern District of California. *Education:* St. John's University (B.A., 1966); San Joaquin College of Law (J.D., 1989). *Member:* Fresno County and American (Member, Sections on: Intellectual Property; Litigation) Bar Associa-

*(This Listing Continued)*

# PROFESSIONAL BIOGRAPHIES

## CALIFORNIA—FRESNO

tions; State Bar of California; Sports Lawyers Association. [Captain, USAF, 1969-1972]. **PRACTICE AREAS:** Business Litigation; Employment Litigation; Insurance Defense; Intellectual Property.

**JAMES C. SHERWOOD,** born Fremont, California, September 21, 1965; admitted to bar, 1990, California. *Education:* California State University, Hayward (B.S., Bus. Adm.; Fin.; Acct., 1987); University of San Diego (J.D., 1990). Phi Alpha Delta. Editor-in-Chief, Journal of Contemporary Legal Issues, 1989-1990. *Member:* Fresno County (Delegate, 1994—; Member, Board of Directors, 1995) and American Bar Associations; State Bar of California (Member, Section on Litigation); Fresno County Young Lawyers (Member, Board of Directors, 1991—; President, 1995); California Young Lawyers Association. **PRACTICE AREAS:** Employment Litigation; Construction Law; Business Litigation; Insurance Defense; Labor Law.

**MICHAEL P. DOWLING,** born Fresno, California, May 4, 1967; admitted to bar, 1995, California and U.S. District Court, Eastern District of California. *Education:* University of Redlands; California State University at Fresno (B.A., 199 0); Gonzaga University School of Law (J.D., 1994). *Member:* Fresno County Bar Association; Sports Lawyers Association. **PRACTICE AREAS:** Business Transactions; Probate and Trust Litigation; Estate Planning; Corporations; Creditor's Remedies; Personal Injury; Sports Law.

**DANIEL T. FITZPATRICK,** born Santa Rosa, California, January 20, 1958; admitted to bar, 1994, California, U.S. District Court, Eastern District of California and U.S. Court of Appeals, Ninth Circuit. *Education:* California State University at Fresno (B.S., in Physical Therapy, 1983); McGeorge School of Law (J.D., 1994). Phi Alpha Delta. Editor-in-Chief, Pacific Law Journal, 1993-1994. Author: "Antitrust and Civil RICO: The Uneven Playing Field of the Workers' Compensation Fraud Game," 25 Pac. L.J. 311 (1994); Review of Selected 1992 California Legislation, 24 Pac. L.J. 826-28, 848-52, 855-57, 919-924, 961-63, 1085-87, 1089-94 (1993). *Member:* Fresno County Bar Association (Member, Section on Real Property, Litigation, Business, Estate Planning and Agricultural); State Bar of California (Member, Section on Real Property). Fellow, Pacific Legal Foundation College of Public Interest Law. **PRACTICE AREAS:** Inverse Condemnation; Real Estate; Business Transactions; Labor Law; Probate and Trust Law.

**MARK D. KRUTHERS,** born Palo Alto, California, September 26, 1969; admitted to bar, 1995, California and U.S. District Court, Eastern District of California. *Education:* University of California at Berkeley (B.A., in Psychology, 1991); Santa Clara University (J.D., 1995). Associate Editor, Santa Clara University Law Review, 1994-1995. *Member:* Fresno County Bar Association; California Young Lawyers Association. **PRACTICE AREAS:** Business Litigation; Insurance Defense; Environmental Litigation.

### OF COUNSEL

**DANIEL K. WHITEHURST,** born Los Banos, California, October 4, 1948; admitted to bar, 1972, California. *Education:* St. Mary's College of California (A.B., 1969); Occidental College (M.A., 1973); Hastings College of the Law, University of California (J.D., 1972). Coro Foundation Fellowship in Public Affairs, 1972-1973. Fellow, Institute of Politics, John F. Kennedy School of Government, Harvard University, 1985. Mayor, City of Fresno, California, 1977-1985. Member: Fresno Metropolitan Projects Authority, 1992—; California Healthy Cities Steering Committee, 1989—; Fresno City Council, 1975-1977; Advisory Board, U.S. Conference of Mayors, 1980-1985; Board of Directors, National League of Cities, 1980-1982. *Member:* Fresno County Bar Association; State Bar of California.

**MORRIS M. SHERR,** born Marysville, California, October 3, 1930; admitted to bar, 1956, California, U.S. District Court, Northern District of California and U.S. Court of Appeals, Ninth Circuit; 1959, U.S. District Court, Southern District of California. *Education:* California State University (B.A., 1952); Hastings College of the Law, University of California (J.D., 1956). Phi Alpha Delta. Certified Public Accountant, 1961. Licensed Real Estate Broker, California, 1984. *Member:* Fresno County and American (Member, Taxation and Economics of Law Practice Sections) Bar Associations; State Bar of California (Member, Business Law, Taxation Law, Estate Planning and Probate Sections); Fresno County Estate Planning Council; National Association of Realtors; Christian Legal Society. American Institute of Certified Public Accountants; Society of Certified Public Accountants. (Certified Specialist, Taxation Law, The State Bar of California Board of Legal Specialization). **PRACTICE AREAS:** Taxation; Estate Planning; Probate; Business Law; Real Estate.

**BLAINE PETTITT,** born Chester, Montana, December 12, 1916; admitted to bar, 1942, California, U.S. Court of Appeals, Ninth Circuit and U.S.

*(This Listing Continued)*

Supreme Court. *Education:* California State University, Fresno; Hastings College of the Law, University of California (L.L.D., 1941). Recipient, Fresno County Young Lawyers Association Mentor Award, 1988. Alumnus of the Year, Fresno Chapter, Hastings Alumni Association, 1990. Deputy District Attorney, Fresno County, 1947-1948. Superior Court Judge, Fresno County, 1970-1985. Special Judicial Council Assignments, Fresno County Superior Court and Fifth Appellate District Court of Appeals, 1985—. Member, Fresno County Chapters: Past President, American Cancer Society; Former Member, Board of Directors, Salvation Army; Former Member, Board of Directors, American Red Cross. Member, Advisory Board, Social Science Department, California State University, Fresno. Member, Board of Directors, Hastings College of the Law. Chairman, Fresno Judicial Selection Advisory Board, 1983-1990. *Member:* Fresno County Bar Association; State Bar of California; California Judges Association.

REPRESENTATIVE CLIENTS: Adco Manufacturing; Bob Williams Chevrolet; Central California Kenworth/International; Chicago Title Co.; D & T Construction, Inc.; Eye Medical Clinic of Fresno, Inc.; Fresno County Economic Development Corp.; Heublein, Inc.; JE Higgins Lumber Co.; Hoosier Tire West, Inc.; Landmark Title Company; Maxco Supply Inc.; Mercedes Benz Credit Corp.; Monterey Chemical Company; Orton's Equipment Co., Inc.; Palm Village Retirement; Rain For Rent, Inc.; Regency Bank; Spencer Fruit Co.; The Loewen Group Inc.; Valley Grain Products, Inc.; Valley Yellow Pages; Walco International, Inc.; Western Oilfields Supply Company; LoBoe Bros., Inc.

## DOYLE, PENNER & BRADLEY
### 5250 NORTH PALM AVENUE, SUITE 401
### FRESNO, CALIFORNIA 93704
Telephone: 209-261-9321
Fax: 209-261-9320

*Civil Trial and Appellate Practice in all Courts with Emphasis on Federal Practice and Business, Environmental, Employment and Products Liability Litigation, Environmental Law, Employment Law, Products Liability, Corporate Law, Construction Law, Patent, Trademark and Copyright Law.*

**DAVID DOUGLAS DOYLE,** born Hamilton, Ohio, March 4, 1954; admitted to bar, 1981, California, U.S. District Court, Eastern, Northern, Central and Southern Districts of California and U.S. Court of Appeals, Ninth Circuits. *Education:* Loyola Marymount University (B.A., 1976); McGeorge School of Law, University of the Pacific (J.D., 1981). Managing Editor, Pacific Law Journal, 1979-1980. Author: Comment, "Criminal Probable Cause in Administrative Searches Under California OSHA: Mandated or Preempted?" 11 Pacific Law Journal 1019, 1980; Staff Writer, "Review of Selected 1979 California Legislation," 11 Pacific Law Journal, 324, 1980. Law Clerk to Hon. Donald R. Franson, Associate Justice, California Court of Appeal, Fifth Appellate District, 1981-1983. *Member:* Fresno County, Federal and American (Member, Sections on: Natural Resources Energy and Environmental Law; Litigation; Labor and Employment Law) Bar Associations; The State Bar of California (Member, Sections on: Environmental Law; Labor and Employment Law; Litigation). **REPORTED CASES:** Southern Pacific Land Co. v. Westlake Farms, Inc., et al., (1987) 188 Cal.App. 3d 807 (233 Cal.Rptr. 794); Selma Pressure Treating Co. v. Osmose Wood Pressuring, Inc. (1990) 221 Cal.App. 1601 (271 Cal.Rptr. 596). **PRACTICE AREAS:** Civil Litigation; Environmental Law; Employment Law; Business Law; Appellate Practice.

**RANDALL M. PENNER,** born Steinbach, Manitoba, Canada, November 13, 1953; admitted to bar, 1981, California and U.S. District Court, Eastern District of California. *Education:* Fresno Pacific College (B.A., 1976); San Joaquin College of Law (J.D., 1981). Law Clerk, California Court of Appeals, Fifth Appellate District, 1981-1983, to: Hon. George A. Brown, Presiding Justice; Presiding Justice and Robert L. Martin, Associate Justice. *Member:* Fresno County Bar Association; State Bar of California; Association of Defense Counsel of Northern California. **REPORTED CASES:** Felix v. Asai (1987) 192 Cal.App.3d 926, 237 Cal.Rptr. 718; Smith v. Royal Ins. Co. (1986) 186 Cal.App.3d 239, 230 Cal.Rptr. 495; Jimenez v. Pacific Western Construction Co. (1986) 185 Cal.App.3d. 102, 229 Cal.Rptr. 575. **PRACTICE AREAS:** Civil Litigation; Products Liability; Personal Injury; Appellate Practice.

**PETER S. BRADLEY,** born Honolulu, Hawaii, August 18, 1959; admitted to bar, 1983, California and U.S. District Court, Eastern District of California. *Education:* University of California at Davis (A.B., 1980); University of California at Los Angeles (J.D., 1983). Co-Author: "Can Science Be Inopportune? Constitutional Validity of Government Restriction On Race-I.Q. Research," University of California at Los Angeles Law Review, 1983. Adjunct Professor of Business Organization, San Joaquin College of Law, 1993—. *Member:* Fresno County and American (Member, Sections

*(This Listing Continued)*

CAA225B

CALIFORNIA—FRESNO

MARTINDALE-HUBBELL LAW DIRECTORY 1997

**DOYLE, PENNER & BRADLEY,** Fresno—Continued

on: Science and Technology; Litigation) Bar Associations; State Bar of California (Member, Sections on: Litigation; Bankruptcy). *REPORTED CASES:* Published Opinion: Serian Brothers, Inc. v. Agri Sun Nursery (1994) 25 Cal.App. 4th 306. *PRACTICE AREAS:* Civil Litigation; Employment Law; Business Litigation.

REPRESENTATIVE CLIENTS: United Pacific Securities, Inc.; Span Construction and Engineering, Inc.; Fontana Wood Preserving, Inc.; John Roth Chevrolet, Inc.; United Equipment Co., Inc.; Coast Wood Preserving, Inc.; Pistoresi Chrysler Plymouth; Institute of Aeronautical Archaeological Research; Rug Doctor L.P.; Suma Fruit International; Kraft Foods, Inc.; Giersch & Olson, Inc.; Oscar Mayer Foods; Caldwell Broadcasting Co., Inc.; GKC Broadcasting, Inc.

## *RUTHANNE EDGINTON*

6435 NORTH PALM AVENUE, SUITE 106
**FRESNO, CALIFORNIA 93704**
Telephone: 209-439-3600
Fax: 209-439-5699

*Family Law, Criminal Law, Personal Injury.*

**RUTHANNE EDGINTON,** born Los Angeles, California, August 18, 1959; admitted to bar, 1988, California and U.S. District Court, Eastern District of California. *Education:* Fresno State University (B.S., 1982); San Joaquin College of Law (J.D., 1987). Instructor, Credential in Law from Board of Governors of California Community Colleges. Member, Madera District Chamber of Commerce. *Member:* Los Angeles County, Fresno County and American Bar Associations; State Bar of California. *PRACTICE AREAS:* Family Law; Criminal Law; Personal Injury.

## *EMERICH PEDREIRA & FIKE*

*A PROFESSIONAL CORPORATION*
5220 NORTH PALM AVENUE
**FRESNO, CALIFORNIA 93704-2209**
Telephone: 209-431-1008
Facsimile: 209-431-1022

*Health Care Law, Business Litigation and Transactions, White Collar Defense, Agricultural Law, Municipal Law, Real Estate and Construction Law.*

**DAVID R. EMERICH,** born Riverside, California, May 8, 1948; admitted to bar, 1973, California and U.S. District Court, Southern District of California; 1974, U.S. District Court, Eastern District of California; 1979, U.S. Supreme Court and U.S. Tax Court. *Education:* University of Redlands (B.A., 1970); University of San Diego (J.D., 1973). Pi Gamma Mu. Member, Panel of Arbitrators, American Arbitration Association. *Member:* Fresno County and American Bar Associations; State Bar of California. *PRACTICE AREAS:* White Collar Defense; Business Litigation; Agricultural Law.

**THOMAS A. PEDREIRA,** born Merced, California, August 26, 1955; admitted to bar, 1982, California. *Education:* Stanford University (B.A., 1977); McGeorge School of Law, University of the Pacific (J.D., 1982). *Member:* Fresno County (Member, Sections on: Agricultural Law; Business Law) and American (Member, Sections on: Antitrust Law; Health Law) Bar Associations; State Bar of California; The National Health Lawyers Association; The California Society for Health Care Attorneys. *LANGUAGES:* Italian. *PRACTICE AREAS:* Health Care Law; Business Transactions; Agricultural Law.

**DAVID A. FIKE,** born Sacramento, California, April 24, 1953; admitted to bar, 1980, California and U.S. District Court, Northern and Eastern Districts of California; 1987, U.S. Court of Appeals, Ninth Circuit. *Education:* University of California at Santa Barbara (B.A., 1976); California Western School of Law (J.D., cum laude, 1980). *Member:* Fresno County Bar Association (Member, Real Property Section); State Bar of California (Member, Litigation Section). *REPORTED CASES:* Nelson v. City of Selma 881 F. 2d 836 (9th Cir. 1989). *PRACTICE AREAS:* Business Litigation; Municipal Law; Real Estate Law; Construction Law.

REPRESENTATIVE CLIENTS: United Security Bank; HMC Group Cold Storage, Inc.; Jody Cold Storage, Inc.; Produce Plastics, Inc.; Innovative Products Sales and Marketing, Inc.; OHCAL Foods; Fruit Marketing, Inc.; Stop Supply, Inc.; Giumarra Properties, Inc.; Humbolt-Del Norte Foundation for Medical Care; North Coast Physicians IPA; San Diego IPA; Central Valley Rural Dialysis; Hinds Hospice; Transwestern Insurance Administrators, Inc.; Valley Orthopedic; San Joaquin Valley Health Consortium; Central San Joaquin Valley HIV Care Consortium; San Joaquin Valley Insurance Associates; San Joaquin Valley Citizens for a Healthier Environment; Coalinga-Huron Recreation and Parks District; Valley Insurance Company.

*(This Listing Continued)*

## *ERICKSEN, ARBUTHNOT, KILDUFF, DAY & LINDSTROM, INC.*

*Established in 1950*
2440 WEST SHAW AVENUE, SUITE 101
**FRESNO, CALIFORNIA 93711-3300**
Telephone: 209-449-2600
Fax: 209-449-2603

*Oakland, California Office:* 530 Water Street, Port Building, Suite 720. Telephone: 510-832-7770. Fax: 510-832-0102.
*San Francisco, California Office:* 260 California Street, Suite 1100. Telephone: 415-362-7126. Fax: 415-362-6401.
*Sacramento, California Office:* 100 Howe Avenue, Suite 240N. Telephone: 916-483-5181. Fax: 916-483-7558.
*San Jose, California Office:* 152 North Third Street, Suite 700. Telephone: 408-286-0880. Fax: 408-286-0337.
*Walnut Creek, California Office:* 2700 Ygnacio Valley Road, Suite 280. Telephone: 510-947-1702. Fax: 510-947-4921.
*Riverside, California Office:* 1770 Iowa Avenue, Suite 210. Telephone: 909-682-3246. Fax: 909-682-4013.
*Los Angeles, California Office:* 835 Wilshire Boulevard, Suite 500. Telephone: 213-489-4411. Fax: 213-489-4332.

*General Civil, Trial and Appellate Practice in all State and Federal Courts. Corporate, Probate and Insurance Law.*

*FIRM PROFILE:* Ericksen, Arbuthnot, Kilduff, Day & Lindstrom is a statewide, civil litigation and insurance defense firm founded in 1950. This multiple office approach ensures uniform procedures and capabilities for both out-of-state and California-based clients. Experienced attorneys, backed by a well-trained paralegal staff, handle cases involving liability defense and insurance coverage and general civil litigation.

**MELVIN K. RUBE,** born Fresno, California, January 19, 1950; admitted to bar, 1978, California and U.S. District Court, Eastern District of California. *Education:* Fresno City College; University of California, Santa Barbara (B.A., 1972); Humphreys College School of Law (J.D., 1977). Fresno County Public Defender, 1979-1988. Instructor, Constitutional Law, Humphreys College School of Law, 1981-1984. *Member:* Fresno County and American Bar Associations; State Bar of California; California Attorneys for Criminal Justice; California Public Defenders Association. *PRACTICE AREAS:* Personal Injury Defense; Wills/Probate.

**R. MARC STAMPER,** born San Rafael, California, May 9, 1961; admitted to bar, 1987, California and U.S. District Court, Eastern District of California. *Education:* University of California at San Diego (B.A., 1984); University of San Diego (J.D., 1987). *Member:* Fresno County Bar Association; State Bar of California. *PRACTICE AREAS:* Insurance Defense; Business Litigation; Plaintiff Personal Injury.

**MICHAEL D. OTT,** born San Bernardino, California, June 9, 1948; admitted to bar, 1975, California; 1977, Oregon; 1982, U.S. Supreme Court. *Education:* University of California, San Diego (B.A., 1971); University of Iowa (J.D., 1974). Note & Comment Editor, Iowa Law Review, 1973-1974. Law Clerk: Hon. A. Andrew Hauk, U.S. District Court, Central District of California, 1974-1975. Author: "Pendent Jurisdiction and Minimal Diversity," 59 Iowa Law Review 197, 1973; "Close Corporations and the Federal Income Tax Laws-Should the State Label Control?" 59 Iowa Law Review 552, 1974; "Federal Law and Erosion of Sovereign Immunity," Fresno County Bar Bulletin, 1982; "The Closed Session Debate: May a Local Legislative Body Meet in closed Session in Situations Not Explicitly Authorized by the Brown Act?" 11 Public Law News, 1987; "A Tail of Two Cases, Claims Against a Public Entity," California Defense Journal, Winter, 1989. Instructor, Municipal Law, Humphreys College School of Law, Fresno County, 1982. Senior Deputy County Counsel, Lake County, 1979-1981. Senior Deputy County Counsel, Fresno County, 1981-1983. County Counsel, Madera County, 1983-1988. Judge Pro Tem, Madera County Superior Court, 1986-1988. Member, Editorial Board, Fresno County Bar Bulletin, 1986-1987. *Member:* Fresno County (Editorial Board, Fresno County Bar Bulletin, 1986-1987), Madera County (Secretary, 1986; Treasurer, 1987) and American (Member, Sections on: Urban, State and Local Government

*(This Listing Continued)*

Law; Natural Resources Law; Litigation) Bar Associations; The State Bar of California; Oregon State Bar.

(For biographical data on other personnel, see Professional Biographies at other office locations).

## FORREST & McLAUGHLIN

*A PROFESSIONAL CORPORATION*

Established in 1980

**6790 NORTH WEST AVENUE, SUITE 104**
**FRESNO, CALIFORNIA 93711**
Telephone: 209-261-9100
Telecopier: 209-261-9406

Mailing Address: P.O. Box 3317, Pinedale, California 93650-3317

*Business Law and Litigation, Insurance Law and Defense, General Civil Trial and Appellate Practice, Tax Law, Bankruptcy (Creditors); Landlord-Tenant Law, Administrative Law, Labor and Employment Law, Real Property Law, International Law; Business Planning, Corporate and Partnership Law, Commercial Law, Public Finance, Construction Law, Finance Law, Advertising Law, Agricultural Law, Environmental Law, Estate Planning and Probate, Unfair Competition, and Trade Secrets.*

FIRM PROFILE: *Forrest & McLaughlin was established in 1980 by Theodore R. Forrest, Jr. with an emphasis on general and civil litigation. The firm represents a diversified client base with emphasis on small-and medium-sized businesses, as well as representing large insurance companies such as Farmers Insurance Group of Companies.*

**THEODORE R. FORREST, JR.,** born Ferguson, Missouri, May 17, 1950; admitted to bar, 1977, California, U.S. Supreme Court and U.S. District Court, Eastern District of California. *Education:* Northeastern State University (B.S., 1973); San Joaquin College of Law (J.D., 1977). Author: "Environmental Health Law," Praeger Publishers, 1984. Adjunct Professor, San Joaquin College of Law, 1979-1983. *Member:* Fresno County and American Bar Associations; State Bar of California; California Trial Lawyers Association; American Trial Lawyers Association. *PRACTICE AREAS:* Business Litigation; Insurance Law; General Civil Trial and Appellate Practice; Unfair Competition; Labor and Employment Law; Real Property; Public Finance; Construction; Finance Law; Advertising; Administrative Law; Agricultural Law.

**WILLIAM T. McLAUGHLIN, II,** born Louisville, Kentucky, October 7, 1956; admitted to bar, 1984, California and U.S. District Court, Eastern District of California. *Education:* California Baptist College (B.A./B.S., magna cum laude, 1981); Hastings College of the Law, University of California (J.D., 1984). Phi Delta Phi. Member, 1982-1984 and Note Editor, 1983-1984, Hastings International and Comparative Law Review. Author: Note, "International Court of Justice Advisory Opinions in the Federal Court System; Critique and Proposal," 6 Hastings International and Comparative Law Review 745 (1983). *Member:* Fresno County and American Bar Associations; State Bar of California (Member, Litigation Section); Association of Defense Counsel of Northern California; Defense Research Institute; National Association of Railroad Trial Counsel. *PRACTICE AREAS:* General Civil Practice; Insurance Law and Defense; Business Law; Partnership Law; Employment Law.

---

**RONALD A. HENDERSON,** born Amarillo, Texas, January 4, 1950; admitted to bar, 1980, California and U.S. District Court, Eastern District of California; 1982, U.S. Tax Court. *Education:* California State University at Fresno (B.A., 1975); San Joaquin College of Law (J.D., 1980); McGeorge School of Law, University of the Pacific (LL.M., 1982). Tax Examiner and Employment Tax Specialist, IRS, 1971-1978. Adjunct Professor of Law, Taxation, Graduate Program, 1982-1992 and Advanced Individual Income Tax and Sales and Exchange of Property, 1983-1988, San Joaquin College of Law. Administrator, Graduate Tax Program, 1984-1986. *Member:* Fresno County Bar Association; State Bar of California. *PRACTICE AREAS:* Tax Law; Business Planning; Corporate and Partnership Law; Commercial Law; Real Property; Trade Secrets; Estate Planning and Probates.

**KENTON J. KLASSEN,** born Los Angeles, California, June 3, 1960; admitted to bar, 1986, California; 1987, U.S. District Court, Eastern District of California. *Education:* University of California at Berkeley (A.B., with honors, 1982); Hastings College of the Law, University of California (J.D., 1986). Phi Alpha Delta. Member, 1984-1986 and Note and Comment Editor, 1985-1986, Hastings Law Journal. *Member:* Fresno County Bar Association; State Bar of California. *PRACTICE AREAS:* Business Litigation; Insurance Law and Defense; Landlord-Tenant Law; Environmental Law; General Civil Trial Practice.

**JAMES F. McBREARTY,** born Philadelphia, Pennsylvania, August 25, 1952; admitted to bar, 1989, California. *Education:* St. Joseph's University (B.A., 1976); San Joaquin College of Law (J.D., 1989). *Member:* Fresno County Bar Association; The State Bar of California. *PRACTICE AREAS:* Insurance Defense; Business Litigation; Personal Injury.

**STEVEN D. HUFF,** born Grangeville, Idaho, June 5, 1950; admitted to bar, 1990, California. *Education:* Portland State University (B.A., 1972); Golden Gate University (M.B.A., 1982); University of San Diego (J.D., 1990). *Member:* Fresno County Bar Association. *PRACTICE AREAS:* Business Litigation; General Civil Trial and Appellate Practice; Insurance Law and Defense; Finance Law; Business Transactions.

**TIMOTHY R. SULLIVAN,** born Bogard, Missouri, September, 1960; admitted to bar, 1987, California. *Education:* University of Missouri-Columbia (B.A., 1983); University of Missouri-Columbia School of Law (J.D., 1986). Member, Nelson National Moot Court. *Member:* Fresno County and American Bar Associations; Association of Defense Counsel. *PRACTICE AREAS:* Insurance Coverage; Bad Faith Litigation; General Civil Trial and Appellate Practice; Business Litigation.

**JERRALD K. PICKERING,** born San Francisco, California, April 16, 1956; admitted to bar, 1982, California and U.S. District Court, Eastern District of California; 1990, U.S. District Court, Southern and Central Districts of California; 1991, U.S. District Court, Northern District of California. *Education:* University of the Pacific (B.A., 1977); McGeorge School of Law, University of the Pacific (J.D., 1982; LL.M., 1988). *Member:* Fresno County Bar Association. *PRACTICE AREAS:* Insurance Law and Defense; Business Litigation; International Law; Construction Law; Labor and Employment Law; General Civil Trial and Appellate Practice.

**JEFFREY PIERCE DAVIS,** born Fresno, California, May 16, 1955; admitted to bar, 1993, California. *Education:* University of Minnesota (B.S., 1993); San Joaquin College of Law (J.D., with honors, 1993). *PRACTICE AREAS:* General Civil and Business Litigation; Employment Law; Real Property.

**BARBARA S. HUFF,** born Albany, Oregon, November 28, 1948; admitted to bar, 1990, California and U.S. District Court, Eastern District of California. *Education:* San Jose State University (B.A., 1986); University of San Diego (J.D., 1990). Beta Gamma Sigma. Recipient, Academic Scholarship, 1987-1988. *Member:* Fresno County Bar Association; State Bar of California. *PRACTICE AREAS:* Civil Litigation; Employment Law.

REPRESENTATIVE CLIENTS: Farmers Insurance Group of Companies; Michael R. Tolladay Corp.; Allscrips Pharmaceuticals, Inc.

## FRAMPTON, HOPPE, WILLIAMS & BOEHM

*A PROFESSIONAL ASSOCIATION*

**SUITE 110, CIVIC CENTER SQUARE**
**2444 MAIN STREET**
**FRESNO, CALIFORNIA 93721-2256**
Telephone: 209-486-5730

*General Civil and Trial Practice in State and Federal Courts. Civil Appellate Practice, Personal Injury, Business and Commercial Transactions and Litigation, Bankruptcy, Antitrust, Commercial Landlord/Tenant, Criminal Defense, Environmental Law, Water Rights, Civil Rights, Equal Employment, Labor and Employment, ERISA and Health Care Law, Constitutional, Military, Negligence, Administrative.*

**MARY LOUISE FRAMPTON,** born White Plains, New York, November 26, 1946; admitted to bar, 1972, California, U.S. District Court, Eastern District of California and U.S. Court of Appeals, 9th Circuit; 1976, U.S. District Court, District of Columbia; 1977, U.S. Court of Appeals for the District of Columbia Circuit; 1978, U.S. Supreme Court; 1982, U.S. District Court, Central District of California; 1984, U.S. Court of Appeals for the Federal Circuit and U.S. Court of Military Appeals. *Education:* Brown University (B.A., magna cum laude, 1967); University College, University of London, London, England; London School of Economics and Political Science; Harvard University (J.D., cum laude, 1971). Phi Beta Kappa. Adjunct Professor, 1975-1982 and Associate Dean for Academic Affairs, 1979-1981, San Joaquin College of Law. President, San Joaquin Valley Chapter of Federal Bar Association, 1988-1989. Member: Ninth Circuit Rule 11

*(This Listing Continued)*

## FRAMPTON, HOPPE, WILLIAMS & BOEHM, A PROFESSIONAL ASSOCIATION, Fresno—Continued

Study Committee; Ninth Circuit Magistrates Advisory Committee. Judge Pro Tempore, Fresno County Superior Court. Barrister, American Inns of Court, 1992—. *Member:* Fresno County (Member, Board of Directors, 1983-1986; Chair, Judicial Selection Committee, 1981-1984; Chair, Attorneys Referral Service, 1985-1989; Resolutions Committee to the Conference of Delegates to the State Bar, 1986-1989; Member, Executive Committee of the Conference of Delegates for the State Bar, 1991; Lawyer Delegate to Ninth Circuit Conference, 1986-1989; Ninth Circuit Lawyer Representatives Coordinating Committee, 1988-1989) and American Bar Associations; State Bar of California; California Women Lawyers Association (Member, Board of Governors, 1975-1977). **PRACTICE AREAS:** Labor and Employment Law; Civil Rights; Constitutional.

**ROBERT D. HOPPE,** born Olympia, Washington, March 1, 1941; admitted to bar, 1974, California and U.S. District Court, Eastern and Central Districts of California. *Education:* University of Washington (B.A., 1965); Willamette University (J.D., 1973). *Member:* Fresno County Bar Association; State Bar of California. **PRACTICE AREAS:** Business and Agricultural Litigation; Criminal Defense.

**THOMAS BOEHM,** born Fergus Falls, Minnesota, April 4, 1948; admitted to bar, 1975, Nebraska; 1982, California. *Education:* University of Nebraska (B.S., 1970); Creighton University (J.D., 1974). *Member:* Fresno County Bar Association; State Bar of California.

**SCOTT W. WILLIAMS,** born Oakland, California, May 11, 1948; admitted to bar, 1974, Virginia, U.S. District Court, Western and Eastern Districts of Virginia and U.S. Court of Appeals, Fourth Circuit; 1981, California, U.S. District Court, Eastern District of California and U.S. Court of Appeals, Ninth Circuit. *Education:* Stanford University (B.A., 1970); Boston College of Law (J.D., cum laude, 1974). Instructor, Constitutional Law, San Joaquin College of Law, 1984-1985. *Member:* Fresno County and Federal Bar Associations; State Bar of California (Member, Labor Law Section). **PRACTICE AREAS:** Employment Law; Labor Law; Civil Rights Law; Education Law; Disability Rights.

### OF COUNSEL

**JAMES M. KAPRIELIAN,** born Dinuba, California, August 12, 1955; admitted to bar, 1982, California. *Education:* University of California at Santa Barbara (B.A., 1977); McGeorge School of Law, University of the Pacific (J.D., 1982). *Member:* Fresno County Bar Association; State Bar of California; Fresno County Young Lawyers Association (Member, Board of Directors, 1990). **PRACTICE AREAS:** Business and Agricultural Litigation; Business and Real Estate Transaction.

**TREVOR C. CLEGG,** born Fresno, California, August 9, 1947; admitted to bar, 1974, California and U.S. District Court, Eastern District of California; 1979, U.S. Court of Appeals, Ninth Circuit; 1983, U.S. District Court, Northern District of California; 1989, U.S. District Court, Southern District of California; 1991, U.S. District Court, District of Arizona. *Education:* University of California at Santa Cruz (A.B., with honors, 1969); Stanford University (J.D., 1973). Judge Pro Tem, Fresno Municipal Court, 1993—. Lecturer: " Successful Judgment Collections in California, (NBI) August 1993. *Member:* Fresno County Bar Association; State Bar of California. **REPORTED CASES:** In re Marriage of Andreen (1978) 76 Cal. App. 3d 667, 143 Cal. Rptr. 94; In re Torrez (9th Cir. BAP 1986) 63 B.R. 751,. **PRACTICE AREAS:** Bankruptcy; Civil Litigation; Appellate Practice; Insurance Coverage; ERISA Litigation; Construction Law.

**KEVIN G. LITTLE,** born New York, N.Y., February 25, 1966; admitted to bar, 1990, California and U.S. District Court, Central District of California. *Education:* Harvard University (B.A., cum laude, 1987; J.D., cum laude, 1990). Author, "Missouri v. Jenkins: Exploring the Judicial Limits of the Supremacy Clause," Harvard Blackletter Journal, Spring, 1991.

## GLEN E. GATES
*575 EAST ALLUVIAL, SUITE 105*
**FRESNO, CALIFORNIA 93720**
Telephone: 209-432-0283
Facsimile: 209-432-6321

*Business Litigation, Creditor Representation in Bankruptcy Court and Family Law and Personal Injury.*

**GLEN E. GATES,** born San Francisco, California, October 12, 1952; admitted to bar, 1979, California; U.S. District Court, Eastern District of California; 1983, U.S. District Court, Northern District of California; 1991, U.S. Court of Appeals, Ninth Circuit. *Education:* University of Northern Colorado (B.A., 1974); San Joaquin College of Law (J.D., 1978). Judge Pro Tem, Municipal and Superior Court, Fresno, California. *Member:* Fresno County and American Bar Associations; State Bar of California; The Association of Trial Lawyers of America. **PRACTICE AREAS:** Business Litigation; Bankruptcy Litigation; Personal Injury; Family Law.

REPRESENTATIVE CLIENTS: United Agri Products; Kerr Rug Company; State Center Credit Union; Calpine Containers, Inc.; Fresno Fire Department Credit Union; Fresno County Federal Credit Union; State Center Roofing; Hodges Building Materials.

## DEAN B. GORDON
*1530 EAST SHAW AVENUE, SUITE 120*
**FRESNO, CALIFORNIA 93710**
Telephone: 209-221-7777
Fax: 209-221-6812
Email: gordondb@lightspeed.net

*Personal Injury, Consumer Law, Juvenile, Criminal Defense.*

**DEAN B. GORDON,** born Los Angeles, California, October 5, 1949; admitted to bar, 1974, California; 1977, U.S. District Court, Eastern District of California. *Education:* University of California, Santa Cruz (B.A., 1971); University of California, Davis (J.D., 1974). *Member:* Fresno County Bar Association (Member, Board of Directors); State Bar of California; The Association of Trial Lawyers of America; Consumer Attorneys of California. **PRACTICE AREAS:** Personal Injury; Consumer Law; Juvenile; Criminal Defense.

## GRAHAM & JAMES LLP
*6051 NORTH FRESNO STREET, SUITE 200*
**FRESNO, CALIFORNIA 93710**
Telephone: 209-449-1400
Telecopier: 209-449-1454
Email: mcampos@gj.com
URL: http://www.gj.com

*Other offices located in:* San Francisco, Los Angeles, Orange County, Palo Alto and Sacramento, California; Seattle, Washington; Washington, D.C.; New York, New York; Milan, Italy; Beijing, China; Tokyo, Japan; London, England; Dusseldorf, Germany.

*Associated Offices:* Deacons Graham & James, Hong Kong, Sydney, Melbourne, Brisbane, Perth and Canberra, Australia.

*Affiliated Offices:* Deacons Graham & James, Hanoi and Ho Chi Minh City, Vietnam; Taipei, Taiwan and Bangkok, Thailand; In association with Dewi Soeharto & Rekan, Jakarta, Indonesia; Graham & James in affiliation with Taylor Joynson Garrett, London, England, Bucharest, Romania and Brussels, Belgium; Mishare M. Al-Ghazali & Partners, Safat, Kuwait; Law Firm of Salah, Al-Hejailan, Jeddah and Riyadh, Saudi Arabia.

*Environmental, Toxic Tort, Water Law, Natural Resources Law and Litigation.*

**MICHAEL A. CAMPOS,** born Corcoran, California, 1939; admitted to bar, 1975, California; U.S. District Court, Eastern and Northern Districts of California. *Education:* California State University at Fresno (B.S.C.E., 1963); McGeorge School of Law, University of the Pacific (J.D., 1975). Registered Civil Engineer, California, 1963; Registered Agricultural Engineer, California, 1965. Member, California State University School of Engineering Advisory Council. Deputy Executive Director, 1980-1983 and Executive Director, 1983-1985, California State Water Resources Control Board. Member, Environmental Protection Agency, Unified Environmental Statute Commission. Member: Executive Committee, 1993-1996 and Legislative Committee, 1993-1996, Environmental Law Section, State Bar of California. *Member:* Fresno County and American (Member, Sections on: Administrative Law; Urban State and Local Government Law; Natural Resources, Energy and Environmental Law) Bar Associations; California Fertilizer Association. (Also at Sacramento Office). **LANGUAGES:** Spanish. **PRACTICE AREAS:** Environmental Law; Toxic Tort; Water Law; Natural Resources Law. **Email:** mcampos@gj.com

*(This Listing Continued)*

## PROFESSIONAL BIOGRAPHIES

### RESIDENT ASSOCIATE

**LEE N. SMITH,** born Milwaukee, Wisconsin, March 29, 1959; admitted to bar, 1988, California and U.S. District Court, Eastern and Northern Districts of California; U.S. Court of Appeals, Ninth Circuit. *Education:* Brown University (A.B., 1981); University of Utah (J.D., 1988). Member, 1986-1987 and Associate Editor, 1987-1988, University of Utah Law Review. Member, Environmental Law Section, State Bar of California. *Member:* Fresno County, Sacramento County and American (Member, Natural Resources, Energy and Environmental Law Section) Bar Associations. (Also at Sacramento Office). *Email:* lsmith@gj.com

All Members and Associates Resident in California are Members of the State Bar of California except where otherwise indicated.

---

## KATHERINE L. HART
### 800 "M" STREET
### FRESNO, CALIFORNIA 93721
Telephone: 209-268-4021
Fax: 209-268-5446

*Criminal Defense and Labor and Employment Law.*

**KATHERINE L. HART,** born Salt Lake City, Utah, December 19, 1942; admitted to bar, 1977, California. *Education:* University of Utah (B.A., with honors, 1965); San Joaquin College of Law (J.D., 1977); Valedictorian. Member, Editorial Board, California Lawyer, 1992-1994. Instructor, Criminal Trial Practice, San Joaquin College of Law, 1984-1985. Member, State of California Commission on Judicial Nominees Evaluation, 1989-1992. Delegate, Ninth Circuit Court of Appeals, 1994—. President, Fresno County Bar Association, 1992. *LANGUAGES:* French. *PRACTICE AREAS:* Criminal Law; Labor and Employment.

---

## HELON & MANFREDO
*Established in 1961*

### SUITE 180, 1318 EAST SHAW AVENUE
### FRESNO, CALIFORNIA 93710
Telephone: 209-226-4420
Fax: 209-226-1524
Email: helonman@ix.netcom.com

*General Civil and Trial Practice. Agribusiness, Business, Corporate and Real Estate Law. Probate, Trusts and Estate Planning, Personal Injury, Family Law, Domestic Relations and Municipal Law.*

### MEMBERS OF FIRM

**DONALD F. MANFREDO** (Retired).

**MARVIN E. HELON,** born St. Helens, Oregon, May 21, 1920; admitted to bar, 1948, California. *Education:* University of Oregon (B.S., 1941); Stanford University (LL.B., 1948). Phi Alpha Delta. Deputy District Attorney, Fresno County, 1952-1955. City Attorney of Clovis, 1960-1985. *Member:* Fresno County and American Bar Associations; State Bar of California. *PRACTICE AREAS:* Estate Planning; Probate; Business Law; Municipal Law.

**MARVIN T. HELON,** born Fresno, California, May 2, 1953; admitted to bar, 1978, California. *Education:* California State University at Fresno (B.A., summa cum laude, 1975); San Joaquin College of Law (J.D., 1978). *Member:* Fresno County Bar Association (Director, 1984-1987); State Bar of California (Member: Business; Real Property and Estate Planning Sections). *PRACTICE AREAS:* Business Law; Real Estate Law; Estate Planning; Trusts; Probate; Guardianships.

**JOHN M. MCDANIEL,** born St. Joseph, Missouri, March 21, 1951; admitted to bar, 1976, California. *Education:* Stanford University (B.A., 1973); University of Santa Clara (J.D., summa cum laude, 1976). Judge Pro Tem, Fresno County Superior Court. *Member:* Fresno County Bar Association (Co-Chairman, 1994-1995 and Member, Family Law Section); State Bar of California (Member, Family Law Section). (Board Certified Specialist, Family Law, The State Board of California, Board of Legal Specialization). *PRACTICE AREAS:* Family Law; Domestic.

**DONALD R. FORBES,** born Fresno, California, October 20, 1951; admitted to bar, 1978, California. *Education:* University of California at Berkeley (B.A., 1974); San Joaquin College of Law (J.D., 1978). *Member:* Fresno County Bar Association; State Bar of California. *PRACTICE AREAS:* Civil Litigation; Personal Injury.

*(This Listing Continued)*

---

**NICHOLAS LOUIS LUCICH, JR.,** born San Jose, California, November 22, 1950; admitted to bar, 1976, California. *Education:* University of California at Berkeley (A.B., 1973); Hastings College of Law, University of California (J.D., 1976). Phi Beta Kappa; Order of the Coif. Member, Thurston Society. Author: "Recent Standing Cases and a Possible Alternative Approach," 27 Hastings Law Journal 213, September, 1975. Instructor, Wills & Trusts, San Joaquin College of the Law, 1993-1994. *Member:* Fresno County Bar Association; State Bar of California. (Certified Specialist, Estate Planning, Trust and Probate Law, The State Bar of California Board of Legal Specialization). *PRACTICE AREAS:* Estate Planning; Probate and Trusts; Business Transactions.

---

## *HEYMAN, KERKORIAN & MAGARIAN*

### 6425 NORTH PALM AVENUE, SUITE 104
### FRESNO, CALIFORNIA 93704
Telephone: 209-261-9300
Fax: 209-261-9305

*Civil Litigation, Employment Law and Family Law.*

**KENT F. HEYMAN,** born Stockton, California, July 29, 1955; admitted to bar, 1980, California and U.S. District Court, Eastern District of California; U.S. District Court, Northern District of California. *Education:* California State University, Fresno (B.A., cum laude, 1977); University of the Pacific (J.D., 1980). Phi Kappa Phi; Pi Gamma Mu. Lecturer: Real Estate Law, California State University, Fresno, 1984; Arbitration Day, American Arbitration Association, 1990; CEB, Law and Motion Advocacy Skills, 1990. Judge Pro Tempore, Fresno County Superior Court. Panelist: American Arbitration Association; American Business Institute; National Business Institute, 1993, 1995; Lawyers Mutual Insurance Company, 1994. *Member:* Fresno County (Member, Section of Litigation) and American (Member, Section of Litigation) Bar Associations; State Bar of California (Member, Sections on: Real Property; Business Law); Association of Business Trial Lawyers. *PRACTICE AREAS:* Agricultural Law; Airline Labor Law; Employment Litigation; Telecommunications Law.

**JOHN G. KERKORIAN,** born Inglewood, California, August 31, 1962; admitted to bar, 1988, Arizona; 1989, California. *Education:* Stanford University (A.B., 1984); Arizona State University (J.D., 1988). Recipient, Pedrick Scholar Award. Lecturer, "Avoiding Legal Malpractice," San Joaquin College of Law, 1993. *Member:* Fresno County Bar Association; State Bar of Arizona; State Bar of California; Fresno County Young Lawyers Association (Member, Board of Directors, 1993-1995); Association of Defense Counsel of Northern California; Defense Research Institute. *PRACTICE AREAS:* Professional Malpractice Defense; Business Litigation; Employment Litigation.

**MARK D. MAGARIAN,** born Fresno, California, August 20, 1966; admitted to bar, 1993, California and U.S. District Court, Eastern District of California. *Education:* University of Southern California (B.S., Business Administration, 1988); Golden Gate University (J.D., 1992). Lecturer, Madera County Employer Advisory Council, Employer Seminar, 1994. *Member:* Fresno County and American Bar Associations; State Bar of California (Member, Section on Labor and Employment Law). *PRACTICE AREAS:* Business Litigation; Employment Litigation; Labor Law Counseling.

### ASSOCIATE

**BRADY K. MCGUINNESS,** born Fresno, California, August 22, 1967; admitted to bar, 1994, California and U.S. District Court, Eastern District of California. *Education:* California State University, Fresno (B.S., cum laude, 1989); Santa Clara University School of Law (J.D., 1994; M.B.A., 1994). Beta Gamma Sigma. Recipient, American Jurisprudence Award, Business Organizations, 1994. Lecturer: Business Organizations; Fresno City College. *Member:* Fresno County and American Bar Associations; State Bar of California (Member, Real Estate Section). *PRACTICE AREAS:* Business Litigation; Business Organizations; Contracts; Employment Law.

### OF COUNSEL

**DONALD J. MAGARIAN,** born San Francisco, California, August 17, 1933; admitted to bar, 1964, California. *Education:* California State University at Fresno (A.B., 1955); Hastings College of the Law, University of California (J.D., 1963). Phi Delta Phi. Judge Pro Tempore, Superior Court Family Law, 1983—. *Member:* Fresno County Bar Association (Member, Committees on: Client Relations, 1976-1981; Family Law, 1976; Family Law Rules, 1986, 1992, 1994); State Bar of California (Member, Committee

*(This Listing Continued)*

# CALIFORNIA—FRESNO

**HEYMAN, KERKORIAN & MAGARIAN,** Fresno—
*Continued*

on Family Support, Northern California Division). [Capt., USAFR, 1956-1966]. **PRACTICE AREAS:** Family Law.

REPRESENTATIVE CLIENTS: Citgo Petroleum, Inc.; Valley Yellow Pages; NevTEL; MGC Communications, Inc.; Tandy Corporation; WestAir Commuter Airlines, Inc. (united Express).

## STEVEN R. HRDLICKA & ASSOCIATES

2115 KERN, SUITE 206
**FRESNO, CALIFORNIA 93721**
*Telephone: 209-485-1453*
*Fax: 209-485-2356*

*Landlord-Tenant, Collection, Adoption.*

**STEVEN R. HRDLICKA,** born Fresno, California, February 1958; admitted to bar, 1985, California. *Education:* Fresno State College (B.A., 1980); San Joaquin college of Law (J.D., 1984). *Member:* Fresno County Bar Association.

## JAMES M. HURLEY

1396 WEST HERNDON, SUITE 106
**FRESNO, CALIFORNIA 93711**
*Telephone: 209-449-7601*
*Facsimile: 209-449-7605*

*Civil Litigation, Insurance Defense, Personal Injury, and Products Liability.*

**JAMES M. HURLEY,** born San Francisco, California, May 27, 1955; admitted to bar, 1980, California. *Education:* Glendale Community College (A.A., 1975); University of the Pacific (B.A., cum laude, 1977); University of Southern California (J.D., 1980). Phi Kappa Phi. Adjunct Professor, San Joaquin College of Law, 1987-1989. *Member:* Fresno County and American Bar Associations; The State Bar of California; Northern California Association of Defense Counsel.

REPRESENTATIVE CLIENTS: Progressive Companies; Allstate Insurance Co.; California Insurance Group; Clovis Unified School District; Fresno Unified School District; Allied Group.

## MICHAEL G. IDIART

*Established in 1983*
2333 MERCED STREET
**FRESNO, CALIFORNIA 93721**
*Telephone: 209-442-0634*
*FAX: 209-233-6947*

*Criminal Defense and Personal Injury.*

**MICHAEL G. IDIART,** born Stockton, California, October 3, 1950; admitted to bar, 1975, California, U.S. District Court, Eastern District of California; 1991, U.S. District Court, Northern District of California. *Education:* St. Mary's College (B.A., with honors, 1972); University of California, Davis (J.D., 1975). Deputy District Attorney, Senior Deputy District Attorney, Chief Deputy District Attorney and Assistant District Attorney to Fresno County District Attorney's Office, 1975-1982. President, Fresno County Prosecutors Association, 1978, 1979, 1980. *Member:* Fresno County and American Bar Association; California Attorney's for Criminal Justice; California District Attorneys Association. (Certified Specialist, Criminal Law, The State Bar of California Board of Legal Specialization). **LANGUAGES:** Spanish.

## JACOBSON, HANSEN, NAJARIAN & FLEWALLEN

*A PROFESSIONAL CORPORATION*
6715 NORTH PALM AVENUE
SUITE 201
**FRESNO, CALIFORNIA 93704-1073**
*Telephone: 209-448-0400*
*Telephone: 209-448-0123*

*Civil Litigation emphasizing Insurance Defense.*
*(This Listing Continued)*

# MARTINDALE-HUBBELL LAW DIRECTORY 1997

**LEE M. JACOBSON,** born Chicago, Illinois, November 23, 1955; admitted to bar, 1980, California; 1981, U.S. District Court, Eastern District of California. *Education:* University of California at Davis (B.A., with honors, 1977); University of Santa Clara (J.D., 1980). Associate Editor, Santa Clara Law Review, 1979-1980. Author: "Paternity Testing With The Human Leukocyte Antigen System-A Medicolegal Breakthrough," Santa Clara Law Review 511, Vol. 20, No. 2, 1980. *Member:* Fresno County Bar Association; The State Bar of California; Fresno County Young Lawyers; Association of Defense Counsel of Northern California. **REPORTED CASES:** Haldeman v. Boise Cascade, 176 Cal. App. 3d 230 221 Cal. RPTR 412 (1985). **PRACTICE AREAS:** Civil Litigation; Insurance Defense Law.

**LEITH B. HANSEN,** born Seattle, Washington, March 29, 1956; admitted to bar, 1983, California; 1985, U.S. District Court, Eastern District of California. *Education:* Reed College (B.A., 1980); University of Washington (J.D., 1983). Member, Fresno County Voluntary Legal Services Program, 1984—. *Member:* Fresno County Bar Association; State Bar of California; Northern California Association of Defense Counsel. **REPORTED CASES:** Governing Board of the Eldorado Union High School District v. Commission on Professional Competence, 1985, 171 Cal. App. 3d 324, 217 Cal. Rptr. 457; Lopez v. Sikkema, 229 CA 3d 780, 221 Cal Rpt. 840. **PRACTICE AREAS:** Insurance Defense Law; Insurance Coverage Law; Insurance Subrogation, Interpleader and Appeals.

**JUBE J. NAJARIAN,** born Fresno, California, September 13, 1956; admitted to bar, 1981, California; 1982, U.S. District Court, Eastern District of California. *Education:* California State University at Fresno (B.A., magna cum laude, 1978); University of San Diego (J.D., 1981). Phi Kappa Phi. Recipient, American Jurisprudence Award in Agency and Partnership and Labor Law. *Member:* Fresno County Bar Association; The State Bar of California; Association of Defense Counsel of Northern California. **PRACTICE AREAS:** Insurance Defense Law; Civil Litigation; Insurance Coverage Law; Agents and Broker's Errors and Omissions.

**DAVID O. FLEWALLEN,** born Fresno, California, April 18, 1949; admitted to bar, 1979, California; U.S. District Court, Eastern District of California; U.S. Court of Appeals, Ninth Circuit. *Education:* University of California at Berkeley (A.B., 1971); University of Santa Clara (J.D., 1979). *Member:* Fresno County Bar Association; State Bar of California; Association of Defense Counsel-Northern California. **PRACTICE AREAS:** Insurance Defense Law.

**KEITH C. RICKELMAN,** born Oakdale, Illinois, September 28, 1958; admitted to bar, 1988, Illinois; 1989, California. *Education:* University of Illinois at Chicago (B.A., 1983); The John Marshall Law School (J.D., 1988). **PRACTICE AREAS:** Civil Litigation; Insurance Defense Law.

REPRESENTATIVE CLIENTS: Allstate Insurance Co.; Atlantic Mutual Insurance Co.; Circle K Corp.; Condor Insurance Co.; Financial Indemnity Co.; Fireman's Fund Insurance Co.; GAB Business Services; Hartford Insurance Co.; May Trucking Co.; MSI Insurance Co.; McDonald's Corp.; Prudential Insurance Co.; Rhone-Poulenc Ag Co.; Liberty Mutual Insurance Co.; Mutual of Enumclaw; Northbrook Property & Casualty Co.; Omaha Property & Casualty Co.; Union Carbide; Wilshire Insurance Co.; American Underwriting Managers; Great Central Insurance Co.; Home Insurance Co.; John Glenn Adjusters; Minnesota Mutual Insurance Co.; Nationwide Insurance Co.; Northland Insurance Co.; Occidental Insurance Co.; Pioneer Claim Management, Inc.; Raven Claims Service; Ryder Truck Rentals, Inc.; Utica Insurance Co.; Schools' Insurance Group; Tri County Schools' Insurance Group; Frontier Insurance Company; United Airlines, Inc.; Gold Cities Insurance; MedMarc; State Farm Insurance; Valley Insurance; Wawanesa Mutual Insurance; Western Farms Service.

## JORY, PETERSON, WATKINS & SMITH

*Established in 1982*
555 WEST SHAW, SUITE C-1
P.O. BOX 5394
**FRESNO, CALIFORNIA 93755**
*Telephone: 209-225-6700*
*Telecopier: 209-225-3416*

*Civil Trial and Appellate Practice in all State and Federal Courts. Commercial Litigation, Labor Relations Law, Agricultural Labor, Equal Employment, Wage and Hour, Wrongful Discharge Law and Insurance Coverage Litigation.*

### MEMBERS OF FIRM

**JAY V. JORY,** born Stockton, California, September 20, 1946; admitted to bar, 1972, California. *Education:* University of California at Davis (B.A., 1968; J.D., 1971). Order of the Coif; Phi Kappa Phi; Phi Delta Phi. Editor-in-Chief, University of California at Davis Law Review, 1970-1971. Moderator, Panel on the Agricultural Labor Relations Act, California State Bar Convention, 1976. Guest Lecturer, Employment Law: California Polytech-
*(This Listing Continued)*

nic State University, San Luis Obispo, 1978-1980; Agricultural Personnel Management Association, 1984-1985, 1987, 1994; California State University, Fresno, 1992-1994; California Society of Certified Public Accountants, Continuing Education Division, 1986, 1988, 1992-1994; University of California Agricultural Extension, 1994; California Bankers Association Bank Counsel Seminar, 1996. *Member:* Fresno County and American Bar Associations (Member, ABA Committee on Labor Arbitration and the Law of Collective Bargaining Agreements); State Bar of California (Member, Labor and Employment Law Section). *PRACTICE AREAS:* Labor (Management) Law; Employment Law; Labor Negotiations; Wage and Hour Law; Employment Discrimination Law; Occupational Safety and Health.

**JOHN E. PETERSON,** born Detroit, Michigan, June 23, 1941; admitted to bar, 1971, California. *Education:* Wesleyan University, Middletown Connecticut (A.B., 1963); Boalt Hall School of Law, University of California at Berkeley (J.D., 1970). Law Clerk to the Hon. Richard H. Chambers, Chief Judge, U.S. Court of Appeals for the Ninth Circuit, 1970-1971. Panelist, California Continuing Education of the Bar, Trial Practice Seminars (1993, 1995, 1996). *Member:* Fresno County (Board Member; President Elect, 1997-1998) and American Bar Associations; State Bar of California; Federal Bar Association (Member, Board of Directors, San Joaquin Valley Chapter, 1993—; President, 1993). *PRACTICE AREAS:* Unfair Competition Law; Real Property; Business Dissolutions; Banking; Construction Defect Litigation; Employment Litigation.

**CAL B. WATKINS, JR.,** born Houston, Texas, February 18, 1950; admitted to bar, 1976, California. *Education:* University of Texas (B.A., 1972; J.D., 1976). Guest Lecturer: Employee Relations Law, California Polytechnic State University, San Luis Obispo, California, 1977-1985; California State University, Fresno, 1985-1989; Agricultural Personnel Management Association 1986-1987. Legal Counsel, Western Growers Association, 1976-1979. President and General Counsel, Grower-Shipper Vegetable Association of Santa Barbara and San Luis Obispo Counties, 1980-1983. *Member:* Fresno County and American Bar Associations; State Bar of California (Member, Labor and Employment Law Section). *PRACTICE AREAS:* Labor (Management) Law; Employment Law; Labor Negotiations; Employment Discrimination Law; Sexual Harassment; Affirmative Action; Wage and Hour Law.

**MICHAEL JENS F. SMITH,** born Lincoln, Nebraska, April 13, 1955; admitted to bar, 1983, California. *Education:* University of California at Riverside (B.A., with high honors, 1977; M.A., 1979); Hastings College of Law University of California (J.D., magna cum laude, 1983). Phi Beta Kappa; Order of the Coif. Member, Thurston Society. Participant, 1981-1982 and Assistant Managing Editor, 1982-1983, Hastings Law Journal. Extern for the Honorable William W. Schwarzer, U.S. District Court, San Francisco, 1982. Law Clerk for Associate Justice Donald Franson, California Court of Appeal, Fifth Appellate District, 1983-1985. *Member:* Fresno County (Member, Board of Directors, 1990-1995) Bar Association; State Bar of California (Member, Standing Committee on Rules and Procedures of Court, 1985-1989; Co-Chair, 1987-1988); Fresno County Young Lawyers Association (Member, Board of Directors, 1986-1992; President, 1990-1991). *PRACTICE AREAS:* Insurance Coverage; Business Litigation; Employment Litigation. *Email:* MichaelJFSmith@Worldnet.ATT.com

**MARCIA A. ROSS,** born San Francisco, California, June 29, 1944; admitted to bar, 1992, California. *Education:* University of California at Berkeley (A.B, with honors, 1966; M.A., 1969); McGeorge School of Law (J.D., 1992). Order of the Coif. Moot Court Honors Board. Traynor Society. Licensed Medical Technologist, California, 1971-1993. *Member:* Fresno County and American Bar Associations; State Bar of California; Fresno County Women Lawyers. *PRACTICE AREAS:* Labor (Management) Law; Employment Discrimination Law; Sexual Harassment; Wage and Hour Law; Occupational Safety and Health; Immigration Law.

**WILLIAM M. WOOLMAN,** born Omaha, Nebraska, March 26, 1962; admitted to bar, 1989, California. *Education:* Pomona College (B.A., 1984); University of California at Los Angeles (J.D., 1989). Adjunct Professor, Civil Procedure, San Joaquin College of Law, 1992—. *Member:* Fresno County and American Bar Associations; State Bar of California. *PRACTICE AREAS:* Commercial Litigation; Construction Litigation; Employment Litigation; Bankruptcy; Creditor Litigation.

### ASSOCIATES

**JOHN J. STANDER,** born Denver, Colorado, 1967; admitted to bar, 1993, California. *Education:* American College in Paris; New York University (B.A., 1989); University of San Francisco (J.D., magna cum laude, 1993). McAuliffe Honor Society. Recipient, American Jurisprudence Award in Constitutional Law. Executive Editor, University of San Francisco Law Review, 1992-1993.

*(This Listing Continued)*

**JEFF W. REISIG,** born Gilroy, California, September 30, 1969; admitted to bar, 1996, California. *Education:* University of California at Davis (B.A., 1991); University of The Pacific, McGeorge School of Law (J.D., with Great Distinction, 1996). Order of the Coif; Moot Court Honors Board. Recipient: American Jurisprudence and Corpus Juris Secundum Awards. *PRACTICE AREAS:* Business Litigation; Employment Litigation.

**CARLA M. McCORMACK,** born Fremont, Ohio, August 2, 1969; admitted to bar, 1994, California. *Education:* Dominican College (B.A., summa cum laude, 1991); Boalt Hall School of Law, University of California (J.D., 1994). Gamma Sigma. Kappa Gamma Pi. Recipient: Dominican College Business Department Outstanding Senior Award; ANthony F. Dragonette Memorial Award for Civil Litigation Trial Practice; American Jurisprudence Award, Civil Trial Practice; Prosser Prize, COntract Law and Theory. Senior Articles Editor, International Tax and Business Lawyer, 1993-1994. *Member:* State Bar of California. *PRACTICE AREAS:* Civil Litigation; Business Law; Real Estate.

**MATTHEW D. RUYAK,** born Buffalo, New York, January 27, 1969; admitted to bar, 1996, California and U.S. District Court, Eastern District of California. *Education:* Boston University (B.A., 1991); University of California, Hastings College of the Law (J.D., 1996). Recipient: American Jurisprudence, Trial AD. I. Member, Hastings Law Journal.

REPRESENTATIVE CLIENTS: Alliance Title Company; American Cyanamid Co.; Aderson Clayton; Atascadero Mutual Water Company; Bank of the West; Basic Vegetable Products; Cambridge Filter Corp.; Cedar Vista Hospital; City of Fresno; City of Turlock; Clovis Unified School District; Coca-Cola Bottling Co.; Community Hospitals of Central California; Fresno Unified School District; East Side Winery; Foodland Markets; Foster Farms; Foster Farms Dairy; Gangi Bros. Packing Co.; Harris Farms/Harris Ranch Beef Co.; Hershey Foods Corp.; J.G. Boswell Co.; John Deere Co.; K-Mart Corp.; Pandol and Sons, Inc.; Salyer American; Madera Community Hospital; Northwest Packing Co.; Tri-Tech Graphics, Inc.; Tuolumne Utilities District; United Security Bank; United States Cold Storage; Valliwide Bank; The Vendo Company.
REFERENCE: Valliwide Bank.

## KANE, McCLEAN & MENGSHOL
*1530 EAST SHAW AVENUE, SUITE 118*
**FRESNO, CALIFORNIA 93710**
Telephone: 209-227-7200
Fax: 209-227-4527

*General Civil, Trial and Appellate Practice, all Courts. Taxation (Federal and State). Corporation, Commercial, Securities, Trusts, Probate and Estate Planning and Real Estate Law.*

### MEMBERS OF FIRM

**JOHN G. MENGSHOL,** born Berkeley, California, February 3, 1937; admitted to bar, 1966, California; 1967, U.S. District Court, Eastern District of California; 1971, U.S. Supreme Court; 1973, U.S. Tax Court. *Education:* University of California at Berkeley (B.S., 1959); Boalt Hall School of Law, University of California at Berkeley (J.D., 1966). *Member:* Fresno County and American Bar Associations; State Bar of California. *PRACTICE AREAS:* Business Transactions; Corporate Law; Taxation Law; Trusts, Estate Planning and Probate Law; Real Estate Transactions.

**STEVEN M. MCCLEAN,** born Bakersfield, California, October 31, 1951; admitted to bar, 1977, California and U.S. District Court, Eastern, Northern and Central Districts of California; U.S. Court of Appeals, Ninth Circuit; U.S. Tax Court. *Education:* University of California at Los Angeles (A.B., magna cum laude, 1973); Hastings College of Law, University of California (J.D., 1977). Phi Beta Kappa; Order of the Coif. Member, Thurston Society. Participant, 1975-1976, and Associate Editor, 1976-1977, Hastings Law Journal. *Member:* Fresno County, Federal and American Bar Associations; State Bar of California; American Arbitration Association (Arbitrator). *REPORTED CASES:* Producers Cotton Oil v. Amstar Corp. (1988) 197 Cal.App.3d 638 (242 Cal.Rptr. 941) 5 U.C.C. R. Serv. 2d (Callaghan) 32. *PRACTICE AREAS:* Civil Litigation; Antitrust; Trade Secret; Unfair Competition; Real Estate Litigation; Commercial Law.

**JEFFREY P. KANE,** born Los Angeles, California, September 24, 1951; admitted to bar, 1977, California, U.S. Tax Court and U.S. District Court, Eastern District of California. *Education:* University of California at Berkeley (A.B., 1973); University of California at Los Angeles School of Law (J.D., 1977). Phi Beta Kappa; Order of the Coif. *Member:* Fresno County and American Bar Associations; State Bar of California. *PRACTICE AREAS:* Business Transactions; Corporate Law; Taxation Law; Trusts, Estate Planning and Probate Law; Real Estate Transactions.

*(This Listing Continued)*

CALIFORNIA—FRESNO                                                      MARTINDALE-HUBBELL LAW DIRECTORY 1997

KANE, McCLEAN & MENGSHOL, Fresno—Continued

LOCAL COUNSEL FOR: Bank of America NT&SA.
REPRESENTATIVE CLIENTS: Airway Farms, Inc.; Coast Gas, Inc.; Dodge Ridge Ski Area; Ford Motor Co. (Dealer Development); Foster Dairy Farms; Foster Poultry Farms; Marko Zaninovich, Inc.; Quinn Company; United States Cold Storage, Inc. (California Counsel); Yosemite Pathology Medical Group, Inc. (Modesto, California); Nash-DeCamp Company; Sunland Packing House Company.

---

## LAWRENCE B. KENKEL

WEST SHAW FINANCIAL PARK
2499 WEST SHAW AVENUE, SUITE 103
P.O. BOX 9429
FRESNO, CALIFORNIA 93792-9429
Telephone: 209-228-6171
Fax: 209-229-3525

*Bankruptcy Law and Debtor/Creditor Relations*

**LAWRENCE B. KENKEL,** born Cincinnati, Ohio, April 29, 1949; admitted to bar, 1980, California. *Education:* Capital University; University of Cincinnati (B.S.C.E., 1972); St. Louis University (M.B.A.; J.D., 1980). Registered Civil Engineer, California, 1982. Member, St. Louis University Law Journal, 1979-1980. Law Clerk, Bankruptcy Court, Eastern District of California, Hon. E. A. Thompson, 1981-1982. Deputy Public Defender, Fresno County, 1980-1981. Lecturer, Bankruptcy Law, Fresno City College, 1991. Judge Pro Tem, Fresno County Municipal Court, 1993—. Volunteer Mediator, Victim-Offender Reconciliation Program, 1993—. *Member:* Fresno County Bar Association; State Bar of California; Central California Bankruptcy Association.

---

## KIMBLE, MacMICHAEL & UPTON

A PROFESSIONAL CORPORATION
FIG GARDEN FINANCIAL CENTER
5260 NORTH PALM AVENUE, SUITE 221
P.O. BOX 9489
FRESNO, CALIFORNIA 93792-9489
Telephone: 209-435-5500
Telecopier: 209-435-1500
Email: kmu@primenet.com

*Civil, Trial and Appellate Practice in all Courts with Emphasis in Business, Construction and Environmental Litigation, Real Estate, Bank Securities, Lender and Creditors Rights, Bankruptcy, Secured Lending, Banking, Federal and State Income, Gift and Estate Tax, Securities, Antitrust, Corporation and Probate and Estate Planning, Patent, Trademark and Copyright, Water Rights, Environmental Law, Employee Benefits Law, Products Liability Defense, ERISA Litigation, Employment Defense, Administrative and Health Care Law.*

FIRM PROFILE: Joseph C. Kimble, a preeminent Fresno attorney, founded the firm now known as Kimble, MacMichael & Upton in 1961. Since then we have grown and broadened into one of Fresno's largest firms, serving people and businesses of the San Joaquin Valley and beyond. We understand each clients situation requires individual attention and solutions. Our goal is to solve each clients problem using our diverse legal skills. To accomplish this goal we train our lawyers and organize our practice to achieve the most effective solutions, and not just to engage in the process of lawyering regardless of cost. We staff each matter individually and assign the appropriate attorney or team of attorneys and paraprofessionals to provide the best combination of specialized expertise. This approach allows us to provide superior promptness, creativity and accessibility to meet our client's needs.

**JOSEPH C. KIMBLE** (1910-1972).

**THOMAS A. MACMICHAEL** (1920-1990).

**JON WALLACE UPTON,** born Fresno, California, August 2, 1939; admitted to bar, 1970, California; 1979, U.S. Supreme Court. *Education:* Fresno State College (B.A., 1962); Hastings College of the Law, University of California (J.D., 1969). *Member:* Fresno County and American (Member, Section of Antitrust Law) Bar Associations; The State Bar of California. [Lt., USNR, 1962-1966]. *REPORTED CASES:* Gott v. U.S. (1970) 432 F.2d 45; In Re Estate of Murphy (1971) 16 Cal.App.3d 564; Catalano, Inc. v. Target Sales, Inc. (1980) 446 U.S. 643; Danzig v. Grynberg (1984) 161 Cal.App.3d 1128; Mateo-Woodburn v. Fresno Community Hosp. (1990) 221 Cal.App.3d 1169; Selma Pressure Tr. v. Osmos Wood Presser.

*(This Listing Continued)*

CAA232B

(1990) 221 Cal.App.3d 1601; Kaljian v. Menezes (1995) 36 Cal.App.4th 5730. *PRACTICE AREAS:* Federal Court Litigation; Corporate Law; Securities Law; Antitrust Law.

**ROBERT E. BERGIN,** born Chicago Heights, Illinois, August 11, 1944; admitted to bar, 1974, California; 1978, U.S. Tax Court. *Education:* Illinois Benedictine College (B.S., 1966); Hastings College of the Law, University of California (J.D., 1974). Member: Staff, 1972-1973; Editorial Board, 1973-1974, Hastings Law Journal. Author: "The First Amendment and Teacher Reinstatement: The Remedy," 24 Hastings Law Journal 551, 1973. Trustee, Rotary Roeding Park Playland Foundation, 1985-1991. *Member:* Fresno County and American (Member, Sections on: Taxation; Corporation, Banking and Business Law) Bar Associations; The State Bar of California (Member, Tax Section). [Lt., USNR, 1966-1971]. (Certified Specialist, Taxation Law, The State Bar of California Board of Legal Specialization). *PRACTICE AREAS:* Corporate and Business Law; Taxation Law; Probate, Trusts and Estate Planning; ERISA Law.

**JEFFREY G. BOSWELL,** born Provo, Utah, March 19, 1949; admitted to bar, 1976, California; 1980, U.S. Supreme Court. *Education:* Brigham Young University (B.S., magna cum laude, 1973); J. Reuben Clark Law School, Brigham Young University (J.D., cum laude, 1976). *Member:* Fresno County and American (Member, Sections on: Real Property, Probate and Trust Law; Corporation, Banking and Business Law) Bar Associations; The State Bar of California. *LANGUAGES:* Niuean. *PRACTICE AREAS:* Banking Law; Real Estate Law; Secured Lending; Insolvency Law.

**STEVEN D. MCGEE,** born Fresno, California, July 26, 1950; admitted to bar, 1976, California and U.S. District Court, Northern, Eastern, Central and Southern Districts of California; 1978, U.S. Court of Appeals, Ninth Circuit; 1980, U.S. Supreme Court. *Education:* California State University at Fresno (B.S., 1973); University of San Diego School of Law (J.D., 1976). *Member:* Fresno County and American (Member: Section on Litigation; Forum Committee on the Construction Industry) Bar Associations; The State Bar of California (Real Estate Law Section, Construction Law Subcommittee); Associated General Contractors of California (Member, Legal Advisory Committee). *PRACTICE AREAS:* Construction Law; Commercial Litigation.

**ROBERT E. WARD,** born Lewistown, Montana, May 1, 1948; admitted to bar, 1977, California; 1978, U.S. Tax Court. *Education:* University of Idaho (B.S., cum laude, 1970); University of San Diego (J.D., cum laude, 1977). Phi Beta Kappa; Phi Kappa Phi. Member of Staff, 1975-1976 and Member, Editorial Board, 1976-1977, San Diego Law Review. Author: "The Mayaguez: The Right of Innocent Passage and the Legality of Reprisal," 13 San Diego Law Review 765, 1976. *Member:* Fresno County (Chairman, Estate Planning, Income Tax and Probate Section, 1981) and American (Member: Section of Antitrust Law; Forum Committee on Health Law, 1983—) Bar Associations; The State Bar of California; National Health Lawyers Association; California Society of Health Care Attorneys. [Lt., U.S. Navy, 1970-1974]. (Certified Specialist, Taxation Law, The State Bar of California Board of Legal Specialization). *PRACTICE AREAS:* Health Care Law; Taxation Law; Corporate Law.

**JOHN P. ELEAZARIAN,** born Fresno, California, June 16, 1951; admitted to bar, 1979, California. *Education:* University of California at Berkeley (A.B., 1973); University of California at Los Angeles (M.A., 1978; J.D., 1979). Adjunct Professor, Commercial Law and Bankruptcy Law, San Joaquin College of Law. *Member:* Fresno County and American (Member: Business Bankruptcy Committee, Secured Creditor Sub-Committee, Business Law Section; Taxation Section) Bar Associations; The State Bar of California; American Bankruptcy Institute; Central California Bankruptcy Association. *PRACTICE AREAS:* Bankruptcy Law; Reorganization Law; Commercial Law.

**ROBERT H. SCRIBNER,** born Oakland, California, April 9, 1948; admitted to bar, 1973, California, U.S. District Court, Northern District of California and U.S. Court of Appeals, Ninth Circuit; 1981, U.S. District Court, Eastern District of California;. *Education:* University of California at Berkeley (A.B., 1970); Hastings College of the Law, University of California (J.D., 1973). Instructor in Legal Research and Writing, Hastings College of the Law, University of California, 1975-1977. *Member:* Bar Association of San Francisco; Fresno County (Member, Real Property Section) and American Bar Associations; The State Bar of California. *REPORTED CASES:* Wisenburg v. Molina (1976) 58 Cal.App.3d 478. *PRACTICE AREAS:* Business Litigation; Real Property Law.

**MICHAEL E. MOSS,** born San Francisco, California, April 25, 1949; admitted to bar, 1974, California. *Education:* University of California at Santa Barbara (B.A., with high honors, 1971); University of Southern Cali-

*(This Listing Continued)*

fornia (J.D., 1974). *Member:* The State Bar of California (Member, Construction, Development and Mechanic's Lien Subcommittee, Real Estate Law Section, 1981—; Labor and Employment Law Section); American Bar Association (Member: Labor and Employment Law Section; Forum Committee on the Construction Industry, 1984); Associated General Contractors of California (Member, Legal Advisory Committee); International Foundation of Employee Benefit Plans. *PRACTICE AREAS:* Construction Law; Employment and Employee Benefits Law; Real Estate Law.

**MARK D. MILLER,** born Freeport, Texas, May 14, 1958; admitted to bar, 1984, California and U.S. District Court, Eastern District of California; 1985, U.S. District Court, Northern and Southern Districts of California and U.S. Court of Appeals, Ninth Circuit; 1988, U.S. Supreme Court; 1990, U.S. District Court, Central District of California; 1994, U.S. Court of Appeals for the Federal Circuit; registered to practice before U.S. Patent and Trademark Office. *Education:* Louisiana State University (B.S., 1979); Santa Clara University (J.D., 1984). Board Member, National Trial Competition, 1984. Litigation Instructor, Fresno City College, 1991—. Intellectual Property Instructor, San Joaquin College of Law, 1993—. *Member:* Fresno County and American (Member, Section on Patent, Trademark and Copyright Law) Bar Associations; The State Bar of California (Member, Section of Patent, Trademark and Copyright Law); San Joaquin Valley Federal Bar Association. *REPORTED CASES:* Rhône-Poulenc Agrochime S.A. v. Biagro Western Sales, Inc., 35 U.S.P.Q.2d 1203 (E.D.Cal. 1994). *PRACTICE AREAS:* Patent, Trademark and Copyright Law; Commercial Litigation.

**MICHAEL F. TATHAM,** born Pittsburg, California, July 2, 1958; admitted to bar, 1985, California, U.S. District Court, Eastern District of California and U.S. Tax Court. *Education:* California State University at Fresno (B.S., 1981); Pepperdine University (J.D., 1984). *Member:* Fresno County and American Bar Associations; The State Bar of California (Member, Section of Business and Real Estate Law). *PRACTICE AREAS:* Corporate Law; Real Estate Law; Secured Lending; Insolvency Law.

**W. RICHARD LEE,** born Bakersfield, California, February 8, 1950; admitted to bar, 1985, California, U.S. Supreme Court, U.S. District Courts, Eastern, Northern and Southern District of California and U.S. Court of Appeals, Ninth Circuit. *Education:* University of Southern California (B.S., Mechanical Engineering, 1973; M.B.A., 1974); San Joaquin College of Law (J.D., cum laude, 1985). Tau Beta Pi; Pi Tau Sigma; Delta Theta Phi. Mechanical Engineer, California, 1982. *Member:* Fresno County and American Bar Associations; The State Bar of California; American Bankruptcy Institute; Central California Bankruptcy Association (President, 1993-1994). *REPORTED CASES:* Represented Creditors Committee - In Re. Montgomery Drilling Co. 121 B.R. 34 (E.D. Cal. 1990); In Re Powerburst Corp., 154 B.R. 307 (E.D. Cal. 1993); Represented Debtor - In Re. Torrez 827 F.2d 1299 (9th Cir. 1987). *PRACTICE AREAS:* Bankruptcy Law; Commercial Law; Real Estate Foreclosures and Receiverships; Construction Law.

**D. TYLER THARPE,** born Fresno, California, January 14, 1959; admitted to bar, 1985, California and U.S. District Court, Eastern District of California; 1986, U.S. District Court, Northern, Southern and Central Districts of California and U.S. Court of Appeals, Ninth Circuit; 1990, U.S. Supreme Court; 1994, U.S. Court of Appeals for the Federal Circuit. *Education:* California State University at Fresno (B.A. and B.S., cum laude, 1981); McGeorge School of Law, University of the Pacific (J.D., with great distinction, 1985). Phi Kappa Phi; Sigma Iota Epsilon; Gamma Theta Upsilon; Order of the Coif. Member, Traynor Honor Society. Law Clerk to the Honorable Donald R. Franson, Presiding Justice, California Court of Appeal, Fifth Appellate District, 1985-1986. *Member:* Fresno County, Federal and American (Member, Section on Litigation) Bar Associations; State Bar of California. *REPORTED CASES:* Mateo-woodburn v. Fresno County Hosp. (1990) 221 Cal.App3d 1169; Rosenfeld Construction Company, Inc. v. Superior Court (1991) 235 Cal.App.3d 566; United States v. Thornburg; 835 F.Supp. 543 (E.D.Cal. 1993); Rhône-Poulenc Agrochime S.A. v. Biagro Western Sales, Inc., 35 U.S.P.Q.2d. 1203 (E.D.Cal. 1994); Kaljian v. Menezes (1995) 36 Cal.App.4th 573. *PRACTICE AREAS:* Commercial Litigation; Employee Benefits Litigation; Intellectual Property Litigation; Appellate Practice.

**SYLVIA HALKOUSIS COYLE,** born Baltimore, Maryland, November 26, 1960; admitted to bar, 1985, Maryland; 1987, District of Columbia; 1988, California and U.S. District Court, Eastern District of California. *Education:* Goucher College (A.B., 1981); University of Baltimore (M.P.A., 1985; J.D., 1985); McGeorge School of Law (LL.M., 1986). Articles Editor, The Law Forum, 1984-1985. *Member:* Fresno County and Maryland State Bar Associations; The District of Columbia Bar; State Bar of California;

*(This Listing Continued)*

California Women Lawyers; National Health Lawyers Association; California Society for Healthcare Attorneys. *LANGUAGES:* French and Greek. *PRACTICE AREAS:* Health Care Law; Corporate Law; Business Law. *Email:* kmu@primenet.com

**S. BRETT SUTTON,** born Dinuba, California, December 16, 1963; admitted to bar, 1989, California; 1990, U.S. District Court, Central District of California and U.S. Court of Appeals, Ninth Circuit; 1991, U.S. District Court, Eastern District of California. *Education:* Pepperdine University (B.A., summa cum laude, 1986; J.D., cum laude, 1989). Alpha Chi. Member: Pepperdine Law Review, 1987-1989; Moot Court Honors Board, 1988-1989; Roger J. Traynor California Moot Court Champion, 1988. Pepperdine Trial Advocacy Tournament Champion, 1988-1989. Recipient, American Jurisprudence Award in Criminal Procedure. Co-Author: "Civil Code Section 5120.110 (c): " California's New Approach to Post Separation Obligations", 25 Bev. Hills Bar Journal 27, (1991) and 23 Pac. L.J. 107 (1991). Co-Author: "Multiple Punitive Damages Awards For A Single Course of Conduct: The Need For A National Policy to Protect Due Process," 43 Ala. L. Rev. 1 (1991). Graduate: Hastings College of Trial Advocacy; National Institute of Trial Advocacy. Licensed California Real Estate Broker, 1991. Adjunct Professor of Real Estate Law and Civil Litigation, Fresno City College; Judge Pro Tempore, Fresno County Municipal Court, Small Claims Division; Judicial Arbitration Panel, Madera County Superior Court. *Member:* Fresno County, Los Angeles County, Federal (Eastern District) and American Bar Associations; State Bar of California; Defense Research Institute. *REPORTED CASES:* United States v. Thornburg, 835 F.Supp. 543 (E.D.Cal. 1993). *PRACTICE AREAS:* Commercial Litigation; Real Estate Litigation; Products Liability Defense; Civil Litigation; Trial Practice; Appellate Practice.

**MICHAEL J. JURKOVICH,** born Fresno, California, September 16, 1955; admitted to bar, 1990, California and U.S. District Court, Eastern District of California; 1992, U.S. District Court, Northern District of California. *Education:* California State University (B.S., magna cum laude 1978); San Joaquin College of Law (J.D., with distinction, 1990). *Member:* Fresno County (Chair, Construction Law Section) and American (Member, Sections On: Litigation, Construction Litigation and Business Law) Bar Associations; The Associated General Contractors of California (Member, Legal Advisory Committee); The Fresno County Real Property Law Round Table. *REPORTED CASES:* Kruser v. Bank of America NT & SA (1991) 230 Cal.App.3d 741. *PRACTICE AREAS:* General Business Litigation; Construction Law.

---

**DOUGLAS V. THORNTON,** born Visalia, California, April 9, 1963; admitted to bar, 1991, California and U.S. District Court, Eastern District of California; 1993, U.S. District Court, Central District of California. *Education:* California State University at Fresno (B.A., 1988); Brigham Young University (J.D., cum laude, 1991): Hastings College of Trial Advocacy, University of California, San Francisco (Graduate). Recipient, American Jurisprudence Award in Civil Procedure. *Member:* Fresno County and American (Member, Sections on Environmental Law and Real Property) Bar Associations; State Bar of California (Member, Section on Environmental Law and Litigation). *PRACTICE AREAS:* Environmental Litigation; Business Litigation; Real Estate Law.

**ROBERT WILLIAM BRANCH,** born Fresno, California, April 13, 1960; admitted to bar, 1991, California and U.S. District Court, Eastern District of California. *Education:* University of California at Berkeley (B.S., 1983); University of Oregon (J.D., 1991). Order of the Coif. *Member:* Fresno County and American Bar Associations; State Bar of California.

**DONALD J. POOL,** born Oakdale, California, June 2, 1965; admitted to bar, 1993, California; 1994, U.S. District Court, Eastern and Central Districts of California. *Education:* California State Polytechnic University, San Luis Obispo (B.S., cum laude, 1990); University of Southern California Law Center (J.D., 1993). Extern to the Hon. Kathleen P. March, Bankruptcy Judge, Central District of California, 1992. *Member:* Fresno County and American Bar Associations; State Bar of California; Central California Bankruptcy Association; La Raza Lawyers Association. [U.S.M.C., 1983-1986]. *PRACTICE AREAS:* Commercial Litigation; Bankruptcy; Real Property; Collections; Receiverships; Products Liability Defense.

**SUSAN KING HATMAKER,** born Fresno, California, December 28, 1968; admitted to bar, 1994, California. *Education:* California State University Fresno (B.S., cum laude, 1991); McGeorge School of Law, University of the Pacific (J.D., with distinction, 1994). *Member:* Fresno County and American Bar Associations; State Bar of California (Member, Labor and

*(This Listing Continued)*

**KIMBLE, MacMICHAEL & UPTON,** A PROFESSIONAL CORPORATION, Fresno—Continued

Employment Section). *PRACTICE AREAS:* Business Litigation; Employment Defense.

**LAWRENCE J. SALISBURY,** born Santa Clara, California, August 21, 1969; admitted to bar, 1995, California and U.S. District Court, Eastern District of California. *Education:* California State University at San Jose (B.A., with honors, 1992); University of California at Davis (J.D., 1995). *Member:* Fresno County and American Bar Associations; State Bar of California. *PRACTICE AREAS:* Business Litigation.

**DANIEL R. FOSTER,** born Encino, California, August 28, 1968; admitted to bar, 1995, California and U.S. District Court, Eastern District of California. *Education:* University of California at Los Angeles (B.A., 1990); University of Illinois (J.D., cum laude, 1995). *Member:* Fresno County and American Bar Associations; State Bar of California. *PRACTICE AREAS:* Business Litigation; Corporate Law.

**MEREDITH E. ALLEN,** born Oakland, California, March 24, 1971; admitted to bar, 1996, California. *Education:* Benedictine College (B.A., summa cum laude, 1993); University of California, Berkeley Boalt Hall (J.D., 1996). Phi Sigma Alpha; Delta Epsilon Sigma. *Member:* State Bar of California.

*OF COUNSEL*

**MARY ANN BLUHM,** born Fresno, California, May 8, 1952; admitted to bar, 1978, California and U.S. District Court, Eastern District of California; 1979, U.S. Tax Court; 1980, U.S. District Court, Central District of California; 1992, U.S. Court of Appeals, Ninth Circuit; 1993, U.S. District Court, Northern District of California. *Education:* Westmont College; California State University at Fresno (B.A., Mathematics, summa cum laude, 1974); San Joaquin College of Law (J.D., valedictorian, 1978). Governor's Appointee, Sequoia Area VIII, Developmental Disabilities Board, 1994. *Member:* Fresno County Bar Association; State Bar of California. *LANGUAGES:* French and Armenian. *REPORTED CASES:* Kaljian v. Menezes (1995) 36 Cal.App.4th 573. *PRACTICE AREAS:* Appellate Practice; Business Litigation; Estate Planning; Probate.

GENERAL COUNSEL FOR: Bank of the Sierra; California Foundation for Medical Care; Key Health System; Eye Care Specialists; California Eye Institute; Drip-In Irrigation Co.; Pierce Lathing Co.; Air Operations, Inc.; Pierce Enterprises; IBEW Local Union No. 100 Employee Benefits Trusts; Pipe Trades District Council No. 36 Employee Benefits Trust Funds; Fresno Builders Exchange; Howe Electric, Inc.; Valley Engineers, Inc.; Mechanical Contractors of Central California; Fresno County Economic Opportunities Commission; Fresno City Employees Health and Welfare Trust; California Professional Firefighters Insurance Trust; The Twining Laboratories, Inc.; Western Farm Credit Bank; Rx Net, Inc.; Sonte Community Physicians Medical Group; Horizon Credit Union; Educational Employees Credit Union; Fresno County Employees Credit Union; Scn Jocquin Power Employees Credit Union.
REGIONAL COUNSEL FOR: Federal Insurance Co.; J.R. Simplot Company.
LOCAL COUNSEL FOR: USX; USX Credit Corp; CIGNA; Connecticut General Life Insurance Co.; Connecticut Mutual Life Insurance Co; Farmers Insurance; Broadcast Music, Inc.; Compass Maps, Inc.; Western Investment Real Estate Trust; National Credit Union Administration; Merrill Lynch, Pierce, Fenner & Smith, Inc.; Industrial Leasing Corporation; Elf Atochem of North America, Inc.; TCBY Enterprises, Inc.; Stella Foods, Inc.; Mitsubishi Motor Sales of America, Inc.; Boston Capitol.

---

## DAVID N. KNUDSON

A PROFESSIONAL CORPORATION

EAST SHAW COURT
1180 EAST SHAW, SUITE 214
**FRESNO, CALIFORNIA 93710-7812**
Telephone: 209-228-8196
Facsimile: 209-228-0327

*Estate Planning, Probate and Trust Law.*

**DAVID N. KNUDSON,** born Mount Shasta, California, August 21, 1951; admitted to bar, 1981, California. *Education:* California State University at San Francisco (B.A., summa cum laude, 1977); Hastings College of Law, University of California (J.D., 1981). Articles Editor, Hastings Constitutional Law Quarterly, 1980-1981. Author: "Federal Refugee Resettlement Policy: Asserting the States Tenth Amendment Defense," Hastings Constitutional Law Quarterly, Vol. 8, No. 4, 1981. *Member:* Fresno County Bar Association; The State Bar of California. (Certified Specialist, Probate,

*(This Listing Continued)*

Estate Planning and Trust Law, The State Bar of California Board of Legal Specialization). *PRACTICE AREAS:* Estate Planning; Probate; Taxation and Corporate Law.

---

## LANG, RICHERT & PATCH

A PROFESSIONAL CORPORATION

FIG GARDEN FINANCIAL CENTER
5200 NORTH PALM AVENUE, 4TH FLOOR
P.O. BOX 40012
**FRESNO, CALIFORNIA 93755**
Telephone: 209-228-6700
Fax: 209-228-6727

*General Civil and Trial Practice in all Courts. Appeals. Business, Corporation, Bankruptcy, Insolvency, Construction, Real Property, Probate and Estate Planning, Trusts, Personal Injury and Insurance Law.*

FIRM PROFILE: This firm was founded in 1963 Its business consists of serving sophisticated local concerns and clientele from out of the region who need or prefer independent counsel. The firm's reputation for communication with clients and creative solutions to the clients problem is nonpareil. High academic standards for admission to the firm have enabled it to provide innovative service with outstanding results.

**FRANK H. LANG,** born Modesto, California, June 27, 1936; admitted to bar, 1962, California; 1976, U.S. Supreme Court. *Education:* Fresno State College (B.A., 1958); Hastings College of Law, University of California; University of California at Berkeley (LL.B., 1961). Associate Editor, California Law Review, 1960-1961. *Member:* Fresno County and American Bar Associations; State Bar of California; American Bankruptcy Institute; Central California Bankruptcy Association (Director and Past President, 1989); California Bankruptcy Forum (Director and Past President, 1995). *PRACTICE AREAS:* Insolvency Law; Debtor Creditor Practice.

**WILLIAM T. RICHERT** (1937-1993).

**ROBERT L. PATCH, II,** born Fresno, California, April 14, 1943; admitted to bar, 1972, California; 1976, U.S. Supreme Court. *Education:* Fresno State College (B.A., 1968); University of California at Davis (J.D., 1971). President, University of California at Davis Law Student Association, 1970-1971. Member, University of California at Davis Moot Court Board, 1970-1971. President, University of California at Davis Law School Alumni Association, 1973-1974. Deputy District Attorney, Fresno County, 1972. *Member:* Fresno County Bar Association; The State Bar of California; Fresno County Young Lawyers Association (Member, Board of Directors, 1973-1974); Consumer Attorneys of California. *PRACTICE AREAS:* Personal Injury Law; Medical Malpractice; Construction Litigation.

**VAL W. SALDAÑA,** born Selma, California, October 25, 1951; admitted to bar, 1977, California, U.S. District Court, Eastern and Northern Districts of California, U.S. Supreme Court and U.S. District Court, Northern District of Texas. *Education:* California State University at Fresno (B.A., magna cum laude, 1974); University of California at Davis (J.D., 1977). *Member:* Fresno County Bar Association (Member, Board of Directors, 1994-1995; President-Elect, 1995-1996; President, 1996-1997; Lawyer Delegate to the U.S. Ninth Circuit Court of Appeals); The State Bar of California; Consumer Attorneys of California; Association of Trial Lawyers of America. *PRACTICE AREAS:* Construction Litigation; Insurance Law; Financial Litigation; Lender Liability Litigation.

**DOUGLAS E. NOLL,** born Pasadena, California, October 13, 1950; admitted to bar, 1977, California, U.S. Supreme Court and U.S. District Court, Eastern, Southern, Northern and Central Districts of California. *Education:* Dartmouth College (B.A., 1973); McGeorge School of Law (J.D., 1977). Member, Traynor Society. Associate Legislation Editor, 8 Pacific Law Journal, 1977. Author: Comment, "California's New General Corporation Law: Quasi-Foreign Corporations," 7 Pacific Law Journal 673, 1976; "Review of Selected 1975 California Legislation," 7 Pacific Law Journal 258, General Corporation Law and 503, Real Property, 1976. Adjunct Professor, Civil Remedies, San Joaquin College of Law, 1987—. Law Clerk to Hon. George A. Hopper, Associate Justice, California Court of Appeals, Fifth Appellate District, 1977-1978. Co-Founder and Secretary, San Joaquin Inn, American Inns of Court. President, San Joaquin Chapter, Federal Bar Association, 1989-1992. Attorney Delegate, Ninth Circuit and Judicial Conference. *Member:* Fresno County and American (Member, Sections on: Litigation; Economics of Law Practice) Bar Associations; State Bar of California. *PRACTICE AREAS:* Complex Civil Litigation.

*(This Listing Continued)*

**MICHAEL T. HERTZ,** born New York, N.Y., May 4, 1944; admitted to bar, 1971, Massachusetts and U.S. Court of Appeals, First Circuit; 1978, Maine; 1981, California, U.S. District Court, Eastern, Central and Northern Districts of California and U.S. Court of Appeals, Ninth Circuit. *Education:* Pomona College (B.S., cum laude, 1966); Harvard University (J.D., cum laude, 1970). Author: Introduction to Conflict of Laws, 1978; "The Constitutionality of the United States Trustee Program," 21 California Bankruptcy Journal, 289, 1993; "Liquor License Transfer Restrictions in Bankruptcy," 19 California Bankruptcy Journal 97, 1991; "Loretto Winery: Undermining Section 545," 18 California Bankruptcy Journal 205, 1990; "Bankruptcy Code Exemption: Notes on the Effect of State Law," 54 American Bankruptcy Law Journal 339, 1980. Law Clerk to Hon. Edward M. McEntee, U.S. Court of Appeals, 1st Circuit, 1970-1971. *Member:* Fresno County Bar Association; State Bar of California; Central California Bankruptcy Association; California Bankruptcy Forum. **PRACTICE AREAS:** Bankruptcy Law; Debtor-Creditor Practice.

**VICTORIA J. SALISCH,** born Carmel, California, December 20, 1942; admitted to bar, 1972, California, U.S. District Court, Eastern, Central and Northern Districts of California and U.S. Court of Appeals, Ninth Circuit; 1976, U.S. Tax Court. *Education:* University of California at Davis; McGeorge School of Law, University of the Pacific (J.D., summa cum laude, 1971). Member, Traynor Honor Society. Author: "Workmen's Compensation —Diseases Arising Out of Employment —A Problem of Proof," 2 Pacific Law Journal 678, 1971. Professor, San Joaquin College of Law, 1976-1979. Lecturer in Business Law, California State University, Fresno, 1976-1978. *Member:* Fresno County Bar Association; State Bar of California (Member, Section on Business Law; Real Property Law). **PRACTICE AREAS:** Real Property Law; Development and Finance; Business Law.

**BRADLEY A. SILVA,** born Tracy, California, July 9, 1958; admitted to bar, 1983, California and U.S. District Court, Eastern, Northern, Central and Southern Districts of California; U.S. Supreme Court. *Education:* California State University at Fresno (B.S., cum laude, 1980); University of Santa Clara (J.D., cum laude, 1983). *Member:* Fresno County and American Bar Associations; The State Bar of California; National Association of Railroad Trial Counsel. **PRACTICE AREAS:** Construction Litigation; Commercial Law; Agriculture Law; Railroad Law Practice.

**CHARLES TRUDRUNG TAYLOR,** born Wellington, Kansas, April 24, 1954; admitted to bar, 1986, California, U.S. District Court, Northern District of California and U.S. Court of Appeals, Ninth Circuit; 1987, U.S. Court of Appeals, Ninth Circuit and U.S. District Court, Central and Eastern Districts of California; 1990, U.S. Supreme Court. *Education:* California State University at Fresno (B.A., cum laude, 1983); Santa Clara University (J.D., 1986). Associate Editor, Santa Clara Law Review, 1985-1986. Author: "The Changing Family and the Child's Best Interest: Current Standards Discriminate Against Single Working Mothers in California Custody Modification Cases," 26 Santa Clara Law Review 759, 1986. Board of Directors, Big Brothers/Big Sisters. *Member:* Fresno County, Federal and American (Member, Section on Insurance Law) Bar Associations; State Bar of California; Consumer Attorneys of California. **PRACTICE AREAS:** Employment Law; Federal Civil Practice; Insurance Law.

**MARK L. CREEDE,** born Fresno, California, September 7, 1959; admitted to bar, 1987, California, U.S. District Court, Northern, Eastern and Southern Districts of California and U.S. Court of Appeals, Ninth Circuit. *Education:* California Polytechnic State University, San Luis Obispo (B.S., with honors, 1982); University of San Francisco (J.D., 1986). Certified Cogeneration Professional, American Association of Energy Engineers, 1988. *Member:* Fresno County (Member, Sections On: Construction; Real Property) and American (Member, Sections on: Public Contract Law; Construction Industry Forum) Bar Associations; State Bar of California (Member, Sections On: Litigation; Law Practice Management); The Construction Specifications Institute; Association of Trial Lawyers of America; American Society of Heating, Refrigerating and Air Conditioning Engineers; The American Institute of Architects; California Building Industry Association; Building Industry Association of San Joaquin Valley. **PRACTICE AREAS:** Construction Law; Commercial Litigation.

**PETER N. ZEITLER,** born Bad Axe, Michigan, May 29, 1956; admitted to bar, 1982, Texas; 1983, Ohio; 1985, California. *Education:* Albion College (B.A., summa cum laude, 1976, Phi Beta Kappa); University of Michigan (M.A., Human Genetics, 1977; J.D., cum laude, 1982). Order of the Coif. Rotary Club of Fresno. Associate Editor, University of Michigan Law Review, 1980-1981. Chairman, Fresno Real Property Roundtable. *Member:* Fresno County and American (Member, Business Law Section) Bar Associations; State Bar of California. **PRACTICE AREAS:** Business Law; Health Law.

*(This Listing Continued)*

**CHARLES L. DOERKSEN,** born Abbotsford, British Columbia, September 3, 1961; admitted to bar, 1988, California, British Columbia, U.S. District Court, Eastern District of California and U.S. Court of Appeals, Ninth Circuit. *Education:* California State University at Fresno (B.Sc., 1984); University of British Columbia (LL.B., 1987). *Member:* Fresno County and American (Member, Civil Litigation Section) Bar Associations; State Bar of California; Law Society of British Columbia; Canadian Bar Association. **PRACTICE AREAS:** Civil Litigation.

---

**LAURIE L. QUIGLEY,** born Merced, California, December 24, 1966; admitted to bar, 1991, California, U.S. District Court, Central District of California; 1992, U.S. District Court, Eastern District of California; 1996, U.S. District Court, Northern District of California. *Education:* University of California at Berkeley (B.A., 1988); University of California Hastings College of the Law (J.D., 1991). *Member:* Fresno County and American Bar Associations; Fresno County Young Lawyers Association. **PRACTICE AREAS:** Business Litigation; Construction Law; Personal Injury; Medical Malpractice.

**DOUGLAS E. GRIFFIN,** born Atlanta, Georgia, March 26, 1958; admitted to bar, 1993, California and U.S. District Court, Eastern District of California. *Education:* San Jose State University (B.A., 1981; M.B.A., 1986); Santa Clara University (J.D., 1993). *Member:* Fresno County Bar Association. **PRACTICE AREAS:** Civil Litigation; Taxation; Probate and Estate Planning.

**NABIL E. ZUMOUT,** born Amman, Jordan, May 21, 1967; admitted to bar, 1993, California and U.S. District Courts, Northern, Central and Eastern Districts of California. *Education:* University of California at Santa Cruz (B.A., 1990); Santa Clara University (J.D., 1993). Order of Barristers; Santa Clara Inn of the American Inns of Courts. Recipient, Honorable Mention Moot Court Competition. Intern Law Clerk, U.S. Magistrate Judge Patricia Trumbull, U.S. District Court, Northern District. *Member:* Fresno County and American Bar Associations; State Bar of California; Central California Bankruptcy Association. **PRACTICE AREAS:** Commercial Litigation; Bankruptcy; Business Reorganization.

**SHAWN H. ALIKIAN,** born Covina, California, October 5, 1970; admitted to bar, 1996, California and U.S. District Court, Eastern District of California. *Education:* University of California, Los Angeles (B.A., 1992; JD/MBA, 1995). *Member:* Fresno County Bar Association; State Bar of California.

**THOMAS E. GAUTHIER,** born Portsmouth, Virginia, January 3, 1970; admitted to bar, 1996, California and U.S. District Court, Eastern District of California. *Education:* University of California, Riverside (B.A., 1992); University of California, Davis (J.D., 1996). Phi Betta Kappa. Editor, Law Review, University of California. *Member:* Fresno County Bar Association; State Bar of California.

REPRESENTATIVE CLIENTS: Valley Production Credit Association; Valley Federal Land Bank Association; Mauldin-Dorfmeier Construction Co.; Community Hospitals of Central California; Kyle Railways, Inc..
REFERENCES: Wells Fargo Bank (Fresno Main Office).

---

## J. STEVEN LEMPEL

PROFESSIONAL LAW CORPORATION

Established in 1981

800 "M" STREET
**FRESNO, CALIFORNIA 93721**
*Telephone: 209-268-4021*
*Fax: 209-268-5446*

*Real Property, Eminent Domain, Land Use, and Municipal Law Litigation and Transactions.*

FIRM PROFILE: *Personal legal services of the highest quality.*

**J. STEVEN LEMPEL,** born New York, N.Y., September 3, 1945; admitted to bar, 1972, District of Columbia; 1976, California. *Education:* University of Pennsylvania (B.S., 1967); Georgetown University (J.D., 1971). City Attorney, City of Sanger, 1983-1995. Chief Deputy County Counsel, County of Fresno, 1976-1981. Judge Pro Tem, Fresno County Superior Court, 1992-. Commercial Arbitrator, American Arbitration Association. *Member:* Fresno County Bar Association; The District of Columbia Bar;

*(This Listing Continued)*

**J. STEVEN LEMPEL** PROFESSIONAL LAW CORPORATION, Fresno—Continued

State Bar of California; California City Attorneys Association; American Inns of Court (Master Attorney).

REPRESENTATIVE CLIENTS: Fresno County Employees Credit Union; Contel Cellular of California; City of Visilia.
REFERENCES: Fresno County Employees Credit Union.

## DONALD R. LEVITT, INC.
3585 WEST BEECHWOOD AVENUE, SUITE 103
FRESNO, CALIFORNIA 93711
Telephone: 209-447-1182; 800-347-9634
Fax: 209-439-4633

*Commercial Debt Collection, Family Law, Matrimonial Disputes, Bankruptcy and Criminal Defense.*

**DONALD R. LEVITT,** born Fresno, California, September 3, 1955; admitted to bar, 1981, California and U.S. District Court, Eastern District of California. *Education:* Claremont McKenna College (B.A., 1977); California Western School of Law (J.D., 1980). *Member:* Fresno County Bar Association; Commercial Law League of America; American Lawyers Quarterly; The General Bar; The Columbia List. **PRACTICE AREAS:** Commercial Debt Collection; Family Law/Matrimonial Disputes; Bankruptcy; Criminal Defense.

## LINNEMAN, BURGESS, TELLES, VAN ATTA & VIERRA
FRESNO, CALIFORNIA
(See Merced)

*General Civil and Trial Practice. Water District and Rights Law. Real Property, Probate, Negligence, Products Liability, Agricultural Law and Personal Injury.*

## LITTLER, MENDELSON, FASTIFF, TICHY & MATHIASON
A PROFESSIONAL CORPORATION
Established in 1942
1690 WEST SHAW, SUITE 201
FRESNO, CALIFORNIA 93711
Telephone: 209-431-8300
Facsimile: 209-431-8329
URL: http://www.littler.com

Offices located in: California -- Bakersfield, Long Beach, Los Angeles, Menlo Park, Oakland, Sacramento, San Diego, San Francisco, San Jose, Santa Maria, Santa Rosa and Stockton; Denver, Colorado; Washington, D.C.; Atlanta, Georgia; Baltimore, Maryland; Reno and Las Vegas, Nevada (a partnership with the Law Offices of Hicks & Walt); Morristown, New Jersey; New York, New York; and Dallas and Houston, Texas.

**FIRM PROFILE:** Littler, Mendelson, Fastiff, Tichy & Mathiason is the largest law firm in the United States engaged exclusively in the practice of employment and labor law. The firm has over 250 attorneys in 23 offices nationwide who represent and advise management in all the major sub-specialities of employment and labor law including: wage and hour law; NLRB cases and collective bargaining; workers' compensation; sex, race, and age discrimination; wrongful termination; unemployment benefits; workplace violence; substance abuse; employee privacy rights; occupational safety and health; the ADA; ERISA, employee benefits, tax issues; and immigration.

**MICHAEL J. HOGAN,** born Los Angeles, California, September 18, 1948; admitted to bar, 1975, California. *Education:* University of San Francisco (B.A., 1973; J.D., 1975). Member, University of San Francisco Law Review, 1974-1975.

**SPENCER H. HIPP,** born Kearney, New Jersey, May 25, 1947; admitted to bar, 1979, California. *Education:* Haverford College (B.A., 1969); Old Dominion University (M.A., 1976); McGeorge School of Law, University of the Pacific (J.D., 1979). Staff Member, Pacific Law Journal, 1977-1978. [Lt., USN, 1969-1976]

*(This Listing Continued)*

**GARY W. BETHEL,** born Fort Worth, Texas, October 4, 1955; admitted to bar, 1985, California. *Education:* University of California (B.A., cum laude, 1978; M.P.A., 1985); McGeorge School of Law, University of the Pacific (J.D., 1984). (Also at Santa Maria Office).

**GREGORY J. SMITH,** born Sacramento, California, September 20, 1960; admitted to bar, 1986, California. *Education:* California State University at Sacramento (B.S., with honors, 1982); McGeorge School of Law, University of the Pacific (J.D., with distinction, 1986).

**DANIEL K. KLINGENBERGER,** born Albuquerque, New Mexico, November 25, 1956; admitted to bar, 1987, California. *Education:* Creighton University (B.S.B.A., 1978); McGeorge School of Law, University of the Pacific (J.D., 1986).

---

**SHELLINE KAY BENNETT,** born Corcoran, California, February 14, 1965; admitted to bar, 1993, California. *Education:* California State University at Fresno (B.A., 1988); Hastings College of the Law, University of California (J.D., 1992).

**DEBORAH L. MARTIN,** born Fresno, California, February 26, 1968; admitted to bar, 1994, California; 1995, U.S. District Court, Eastern District of California. *Education:* University of California at San Diego (B.A., 1991); Hastings College of the Law, University of California (J.D., 1994).

**GREGORY A. HENDERSHOTT,** born Pontiac, Michigan, March 12, 1966; admitted to bar, 1995, California. *Education:* Michigan State University (B.A., 1989); University of Oregon (J.D., 1995).

(For biographical data on personnel at other locations, see Professional Biographies at those cities.)

## LOZANO SMITH
## SMITH WOLIVER & BEHRENS
A PROFESSIONAL CORPORATION
Established in 1988
2444 MAIN STREET, SUITE 260
FRESNO, CALIFORNIA 93721
Telephone: 209-445-1352
Fax: 209-233-5013

*San Rafael, California Office:* 1010 B Street, Suite 200. Telephone: 415-459-3008. Fax: 415-456-3826.
*Monterey, California Office:* One Harris Court, Building A, Suite 200. Telephone: 408-646-1501. Fax: 408-646-1801.
*San Luis Obispo, California Office:* 987 Osos Street. Telephone: 805-549-9541. Fax: 805-549-0740.

*Education, Labor and Employment, Civil Rights and Disability, Local Government, Land Use, Eminent Domain, Public Finance, Business and Insurance Litigation.*

**FIRM PROFILE:** *Lozano Smith Smith Woliver & Behrens is a law firm specializing in labor, public agency, private employment and business law. The firm began the practice of law on January 1, 1988, and has offices in Fresno, San Rafael, Monterey and San Luis Obispo.*

*Lozano Smith Smith Woliver & Behrens emphasizes representation of public agencies in all areas, private sector employment and business law and litigation. The firm's attorneys have special expertise in representing school districts, cities and other public agencies and business.*

**MAX EDWARD ROBINSON** (Retired).

**LOUIS T. LOZANO,** born Fresno, California, September 18, 1948; admitted to bar, 1975, California; 1976, U.S. District Court, Northern and Eastern Districts of California and U.S. Court of Appeals, Ninth Circuit. *Education:* University of California at Berkeley (B.A., 1970); Boalt Hall School of Law, University of California (J.D., 1975). Law Clerk, Contra Costa County Superior Court. Author: "Grossmont: A Victory for School Districts," California School Boards, Vol. 44, No., Fall 1985. Senior Deputy County Counsel for Schools, Fresno County, 1975-1980. President, Schools Legal Defense Association, 1987-1988, 1990-1991, 1992-1993. *Member:* Fresno County and Monterey County Bar Associations; State Bar of California. (Resident, Monterey Office). **LANGUAGES:** French and Armenian. **REPORTED CASES:** Trend v. Central Unified School Dist (1990) 220 Cal. App. 3d 102; N. State v. Pittsburg Unified School Dist. (1990) 220 Cal. App. 3d 1418; San Francisco Unified S.D. v. Superior Court (1981) 116 Cal. App. 3d 231. **PRACTICE AREAS:** Public Facilities Finance; La-

*(This Listing Continued)*

bor Relations; Employment; Education Law. **Email:** lou@lozanom.mhs.compuserve.com

**DIANA K. SMITH,** born San Bernardino, California, October 18, 1944; admitted to bar, 1978, California; 1980, U.S. District Court, Northern District of California; 1985, U.S. District Court, Eastern District of California; 1986, U.S. Court of Appeals, Ninth Circuit. *Education:* Smith College (A.B., cum laude, 1966); University of California at Berkeley (M.A., 1967); Loyola University at Los Angeles (J.D., cum laude, 1978). Law Clerk, General Counsel of Los Angeles Community College District. *Member:* Marin County Bar Association; State Bar of California. (Resident, San Rafael Office). *REPORTED CASES:* Clovis v. Shorey (US Ct. of Appeals, 9th Circuit); Abu Sahyun v. Palo Alto Unified School District (US Ct. of Appeals, 9th Circuit); Board of Education of the Round Valley School District v. Round Valley Teachers Association (April 29, 1996, S047491) Cal. 4th. *PRACTICE AREAS:* School Law; Employment Law; Disability Law; Special Education; Labor Law. **Email:** ds@lozanos.mhs.compuserve.com

**MICHAEL E. SMITH,** born Brawley, California, July 9, 1954; admitted to bar, 1980, California, U.S. District Court, Eastern District of California, U.S. Court of Appeals, Ninth Circuit and U.S. Supreme Court. *Education:* Claremont Mens College (B.A., magna cum laude, 1976); University of California at Davis (J.D., 1980). Associate, Baker, Manock & Jensen, 1980-1982. Senior Deputy County Counsel for Schools, Fresno County, 1982-1987. Adjunct Professor: San Joaquin College of Law, 1983-1988; California State University at Fresno, 1987. Secretary, 1985-1986 and President, 1986-1987, County Counsel Association, School Law Study Section. *Member:* Fresno County and American Bar Associations; State Bar of California. (Resident). *REPORTED CASES:* Clarence Dilts v. Cantua Elementary School District (1987) 189 Cal. App. 3d 27, 234 Cal. Rptr. 612; Belanger v. Madera Unified School District (9th Cir. 1992) 963 F. 2d 248. *PRACTICE AREAS:* Local Government; School Law; Labor Law; Employment Law; Contract Law; Elections Law; School/Education Law. **Email:** mes@lozanof.mhs.compuserve.com

**SANDRA WOLIVER,** admitted to bar, 1977, California and U.S. District Court, Northern District of California. *Education:* Bowling Green State University (B.A., magna cum laude, 1968); State University of New York at Stony Brook (M.A., 1970); Boalt Hall School of Law, University of California (J.D., 1977). In-house Counsel for Oakland Unified School District, 1977-1980. *Member:* State Bar of California. (Managing Shareholder) (Resident San Rafael Office). **LANGUAGES:** Spanish. *REPORTED CASES:* Pink v. Mt. Diablo U.S.D., Cal. App.; United Teachers of Ukiah v. Ukiah Unified School Dist.; Martin v. Kentfield. *PRACTICE AREAS:* Employment; Labor Relations; Education; Special Education; Elections. **Email:** sw@lozanos.mhs.compuserve.com

**THOMAS J. RIGGS,** born Jacksonville, Illinois, August 9, 1944; admitted to bar, 1974, California, U.S. Court of Appeals, Ninth Circuit and U.S. District Court, Eastern District of California. *Education:* California State University (B.S., distinction in Zoology, 1968); University of San Diego (J.D., cum laude, 1974). Editor, San Diego Law Review, 1973-1974. Author: "Implications of Roe v. Wade," 10 San Diego Law Review 844, 1973. Professor of Law, Contracts, Administrative Law, San Joaquin College of Law, 1979-1987. Deputy County Counsel and Chief Deputy County Counsel, Fresno County, 1975-1985. Assistant County Counsel, Fresno County, 1986-1989. Present City Attorney for Clovis and Fowler, California. *Member:* Fresno County Bar Association; State Bar of California (Member, Committee on Condemnation Law, 1985-1987); California League of Cities Legal Advocacy Committee (1995-1996). [Lt. U.S. Coast Guard, 1968-1971]. (Resident). *REPORTED CASES:* U.S. v. Fresno Unified School District (1976) 412 F. Supp. 392 (1979) 592 P.2d 1088; Rosato v. Superior Court (1975) 51 Cal. App. 3d 190; Drum v. Fresno County Dept. of Public Works (1983) 144 Cal. App. 3d 777; Fig Gordon Park No. 2 Assn. v. LAFCO (1984) 162 Cal. App. 3d 336. *PRACTICE AREAS:* Municipal Law; Local Government; Land Use; Eminent Domain. **Email:** tjr@lozanof.mhs.compuserve.com

**JEROME M. BEHRENS,** born Cornwall, New York, November 24, 1944; admitted to bar, 1974, California and U.S. District Court, Northern District of California; 1980, U.S. District Court, Eastern District of California; 1984, U.S. Tax Court; 1989, U.S. Court of Appeals, 9th Circuit. *Education:* University of California at Berkeley (B.A., 1967); Hastings College of the Law, University of California (J.D., 1974). Deputy Attorney General, State of California, 1974-1976. Senior Deputy District Attorney, Fresno County, 1976-1978. Chief Deputy County Counsel, Fresno County, 1978-1982. Municipal Bond Counsel, 1984—. Bond Counsel, Municipal Bond Attorneys of the United States, 1987. *Member:* Fresno County Bar Association; State Bar of California. (Resident, Fresno). **LANGUAGES:** French.

*(This Listing Continued)*

**REPORTED CASES:** Tripp v. Swoap (1976) 17 Cal. 3d 671; McClatchy Newspapers v. Superior Court (1988) 44 Cal. 3d 1162; Morgan Hill Unified S.D. v. Kaufman & Broad (1992) 9 Cal. App. 4th 464; Anderson v. Superior Court (1995) 11 Cal. 4th 1152. *PRACTICE AREAS:* Business; Real Property; Eminent Domain; Environmental Law; General Civil Litigation; Discrimination Claims; Civil Rights Defense. **Email:** jmb@lozanof.mhs.compuserve.com

**CHRISTINE A. GOODRICH,** born San Francisco, California, June 12, 1958; admitted to bar, 1983, California. *Education:* University of California at Berkeley (B.A., 1980); University of California at Los Angeles (J.D., 1983). Phi Beta Kappa. Staff Member, University of California at Los Angeles Law Review, 1982-1983. Staff Member, 1981-1983 and Co-comment Editor, 1981-1983, University of California at Los Angeles Pacific Basin Law Journal. Adjunct Professor of Law, San Joaquin College of Law, 1989—. Extern Law Clerk to the Hon. Robert J. Kelleher, U.S. District Court, Central District of California, 1981. Advisory Board Member for San Joaquin Valley College, Legal Secretaries Program 1986-1989. *Member:* Fresno County Bar Association; State Bar of California. (Resident). *REPORTED CASES:* American National Bank v. Peacock (1985) 165 Cal. App. 3d 1206. *PRACTICE AREAS:* Business Litigation; Creditors' Rights; Creditor Bankruptcy. **Email:** cag@lozanof.mhs.compuserve.com

**LOREN A. CARJULIA,** born Los Angeles, California, August 17, 1957; admitted to bar, 1983, California. *Education:* University of California at Los Angeles (B.A., cum laude, 1980); Hastings College of Law, University of California (J.D., 1983). Research Attorney, Marin County Superior Court, 1984-1986. Trustee, Marin County Law Library, 1987—. Extern Law Clerk to the Honorable Spencer Williams, U.S. District Court, Northern District of California, 1982. Associate Professor, Sonoma State University, 1991—. *Member:* State Bar of California. (Resident, San Rafael Office). *PRACTICE AREAS:* School Law; Personnel; Students; Constitutional Law; Special Education. **Email:** lc@lozanos.mhs.compuserve.com

**ELLEN M. JAHN,** born Chicago, Illinois, February 26, 1953; admitted to bar, 1988, California; 1989, U.S. District Court, Eastern District of California. *Education:* Illinois State University; Indiana University (B.S., with distinction, 1977); San Joaquin College of Law (J.D., with high honors, 1988). Fourth Place, Roger Traynor State Moot Court Tournament. Adjunct Professor, Contracts, Legal Research and Writing, San Joaquin College of Law, 1988-1994. Member, San Joaquin College of Law Faculty Committee, 1993-1994. *Member:* Fresno County Bar Association; State Bar of California; Fresno County Women Lawyers. (Resident, Monterey Office). *REPORTED CASES:* Belanger v. Madera, Unified School District 963 F. 2d 248 (9th Cir, 1992). *PRACTICE AREAS:* Personnel; Employment Discrimination; Collective Bargaining; Federal Litigation. **Email:** emj@lozanom.mhs.compuserve.com

**PETER K. FAGEN,** born Sigourney, Iowa, December 5, 1960; admitted to bar, 1989, California and U.S. District Court, Eastern District of California; 1990, U.S. District Court, Central, Southern and Northern Districts of California. *Education:* University of Northern Iowa (B.A., 1983); University of Iowa (J.D., 1988). *Member:* Fresno County and American (Member, Sections on: Tort and Insurance Practice; Sports and Entertainment Law) Bar Associations; State Bar of California; Fresno County Young Lawyers Association; California Young Lawyers Association. (Resident). *PRACTICE AREAS:* Insurance; Civil Rights; Labor and Employment; Public Agency Law. **Email:** pkf@lozanof.mhs.compuserve.com

---

**NANCY LU KLEIN,** born Portland, Oregon, January 15, 1961; admitted to bar, 1987, California. *Education:* Pitzer College (B.A., 1983); National Law Center, George Washington University (J.D., 1986). *Member:* State Bar of California. (Resident, San Rafael Office). **Email:** nk@lozanos.mhs.compuserve.com

**DAVID J. WOLFE,** born Stamford, Connecticut, February 19, 1962; admitted to bar, 1988, California, U.S. District Court, Eastern District of California. *Education:* University of Connecticut (B.A., magna cum laude, 1983); University of the Pacific (J.D., 1988). Order of the Coif. The Traynor Society. Staff Attorney, California Court of Appeals, Third Appellate District, 1988-1990. *Member:* Fresno County Bar Association; State Bar of California. (Resident). *REPORTED CASES:* Kaufman & Broad South Bay v. Morgan Hill Unified School Dist. (1992) 9 Cal. App. 4th 464. *PRACTICE AREAS:* Municipal Law; Zoning and Land Use; Municipal Code Enforcement; Appellate Practice. **Email:** djw@lozanof.mhs.compuserve.com

*(This Listing Continued)*

## LOZANO SMITH SMITH WOLIVER & BEHRENS, A PROFESSIONAL CORPORATION, Fresno—Continued

**HAROLD M. FREIMAN,** born Brooklyn, New York, August 19, 1964; admitted to bar, 1990, California and U.S. District Court, Northern District of California; 1991, U.S. Court of Appeals, Ninth Circuit; 1993, U.S. District Court, Eastern District of California. *Education:* University of California at Berkeley (A.B., 1987); Columbia University (J.D., 1990). Harlan Fiske Stone Scholar. Member, Columbia Human Rights Law Review, 1988-1990. Law Clerk to Justice Lloyd Doggett, Texas Supreme Court, 1991-1992. Author: "Some Get a Little and Some Get None: When is Process Due Through Fair Hearings Under P.L. 96-272," 20 Columbia Human Rights Law Review 343 (1989). Co-Author: "Standards for Interoperability and the Copyright Protection of Computer Programs", in 365 Intellectual Property/Antitrust 1993, 891 (P.L.I. 1993). *Member:* State Bar of California; American Bar Association. (Resident, Monterey). **PRACTICE AREAS:** Litigation; Education Law. *Email:* harold@lozanom.mhs.compuserve.com

**ERIC E. HILL,** born Rockford, Illinois, April 15, 1967; admitted to bar, 1994, California. *Education:* Stanford University (B.A., 1989); American University College of Law (J.D., summa cum laude, 1994). (Resident, San Rafael Office). **PRACTICE AREAS:** Employment Law; Labor Law; Education Law. *Email:* eeh@lozanos.mhs.compuserve.com

**CHRISTOPHER D. KEELER,** born La Jolla, California, November 10, 1966; admitted to bar, 1994, California. *Education:* Stanford University (B.A., 1991); Brigham Young University (J.D., cum laude, 1994). Member, Law Review, 1993-1994. Author: Casenote BYU Education and Law Journal, Spring, 1994. *Member:* American Bar Association; The State Bar of California. (Resident, Monterey Office). **LANGUAGES:** Spanish. **PRACTICE AREAS:** Education Law; Construction Law; Public Entity Law. *Email:* chris@lozanom.mhs.compuserve.com

**JAN E. TOMSKY,** born Grand Rapids, Minnesota, July 25, 1954; admitted to bar, 1994, California, U.S. District Court, Northern District of California and U.S. Court of Appeals, Ninth Circuit. *Education:* Dominican College (B.A., summa cum laude 1976; M.S. Ed., 1984); Boalt Hall School of Law (J.D., 1994). (Resident, San Rafael Office). **PRACTICE AREAS:** Education Law. *Email:* jet@lozanos.mhs.compuserve.com

**EILEEN M. O'HARE,** born Salt Lake City, Utah, June 28, 1960; admitted to bar, 1992, California and U.S. District Court Central District of California; 1995, U.S. District Court Eastern District of California and U.S. court of Appeals, Ninth Circuit. *Education:* California State University, San Jose (B.A., 1983); University of California, Davis (J.D., 1991). Senior Research Editor, University of California at Davis Law Review, 1990-1991. *REPORTED CASES:* In Re: Estate of Wernicke 16 Cal. App. 4th 1069; Hill v. City of Long Beach 33 Cal. App. 4th 1684; Anderson v. Superior Court 11 Cal. 4th 1152. **PRACTICE AREAS:** Employment Litigation; complex Business Litigation; General Civil Litigation. *Email:* emo@loznof.mhs.compuserve.com

**RUTH E. MENDYK,** born Sioux Falls, South Dakota, August 26, 1966; admitted to bar, 1992, California. *Education:* Saint Olaf College (B.A., 1988); University of Nebraska, Lincoln (J.D., 1991). *Member:* Fresno County Bar Association; State Bar of California. *Email:* rem@lozanof.mhs.compuserve.com

**KAREN SEGAR SALTY,** born Detroit, Michigan, May 5, 1961; admitted to bar, 1994, California. *Education:* Tulane University of Louisiana (B.A., 1983); University of San Francisco (J.D., 1993). (Resident, Monterey Office). **LANGUAGES:** French. *Email:* karen@lozanom.mhs.compuserve.com

**TREVIN E. SIMS,** born Los Angeles, California, August 16, 1968; admitted to bar, 1993, California. *Education:* Oral Roberts University (B.S., cum laude, 1990); University of California, Los Angeles (J.D., 1993). **PRACTICE AREAS:** Litigation; Education Law. *Email:* tes@lozanof.mhs.compuserve.com

**SUSAN LANDON MARKS,** born Englewood, New Jersey, October 11, 1951; admitted to bar, 1978, California. *Education:* Raymond College of the University of the Pacific (B.A., 1973); McGeorge School of Law, University of the Pacific (J.D., with great distinction, 1978). Member: Moot Court Honors Board; Traynor Society. Member, Board of Trustees, Mill Valley School District, 1991-1995. *Member:* Marin County Bar Association; The State Bar of California. (Resident, San Rafael Office). **PRACTICE AREAS:** Education Law; Litigation; Employment Law.

*(This Listing Continued)*

CAA238B

**RICHARD B. GALTMAN,** born Philadelphia, Pennsylvania, April 23, 1963; admitted to bar, 1988, Pennsylvania; 1989, U.S. District Court, Eastern District of Pennsylvania; 1990, California and U.S. District Court, Eastern District of California; 1993, U.S. District Court, Central District of California and U.S. Court of Appeals, Ninth Circuit. *Education:* LaSalle University (B.S., 1985); Boston University (J.D., 1988). Phi Alpha Delta. *Member:* Philadelphia, Fresno County, Pennsylvania and American Bar Associations; State Bar of California. **PRACTICE AREAS:** Labor Law; Employment Law; ERISA; Agricultural Law; PACA Trust Enforcement; Commercial Litigation.

**JAMES B. FERNOW,** born Charleston, South Carolina, June 13, 1968; admitted to bar, 1993, California and U.S. District Court, Eastern District of California. *Education:* University of Arizona (P.S., 1990; J.D., 1993). *Member:* Fresno County Bar Association; State Bar of California; Fresno Young Lawyers Association.

### OF COUNSEL

**PAUL R. DELAY,** born Beresford, South Dakota, November 12, 1919; admitted to bar, 1949, District of Columbia; 1965, California. *Education:* University of Notre Dame (A.B., 1941); Georgetown University (LL.B., 1949). *Member:* State Bar of California (Panelist); The District of Columbia Bar (Panelist). (Resident, Monterey Office). *REPORTED CASES:* Monterey County Deputy Sheriff's Association v. County of Monterey (1979) 23 Cal. 3d 296; CSEA v. King City Unified School District (1981) 116 Cal. App. 3d 695; MPUSD v. Certificated Employees Council (1974) 42 Cal. App. 3d 328; Sheehan v. Eldridge (1970) 5 Cal. App. 3d 77. **PRACTICE AREAS:** Government Law; Litigation. *Email:* paul@lozanom.mhs.compuserve.com

**PATRICIA ANDREEN,** born Philadelphia, Pennsylvania, June 3, 1949; admitted to bar, 1978, California. *Education:* Smith College (B.A., 1971); San Joaquin College of Law (J.D., 1978). Legal Research, San Joaquin College of Law, 1991. Barpassers Review, 1985-1995. Senior Deputy County Counsel, Fresno County Counsel's Office. (Resident, San Luis Obispo). **LANGUAGES:** German. *REPORTED CASES:* CTA v. Governing Board (1983) 191 Cal App 606. **PRACTICE AREAS:** Employment Law; Construction Law; Public Agency; Appellate.

**JUDD L. JORDAN,** born Glendale, California, December 27, 1950; admitted to bar, 1976, California; 1977, U.S. District Court, Central and Northern Districts of California; 1978, U.S. Court of Appeals, Ninth Circuit; 1982, U.S. Supreme Court; 1991, U.S. District Court, Eastern District of California. *Education:* University of California, Berkeley (B.A., 1973); University of California, Los Angeles (J.D., 1976). Comment Editor, UCLA Law Review, 1975-1976. *Member:* American Bar Association; The State Bar of California; American Institute of Mining, Metallurgical and Petroleum Engineers (Chairman, Southern California Mining Section, 1990-1991). (Resident, Monterey Office). **PRACTICE AREAS:** Litigation. *Email:* judd@lozanom.mhs.compuserve.com

REPRESENTATIVE CLIENTS: Alameda Unified School District; Amador County Unified School District; Antioch Unified School District; Carmel Unified School District; Clovis Unified School District; Fresno Unified School District; Madera Unified School District; Martinez Unified School District; Mendocino Community College District; Mt. View-Los Altos Union High School District; Norwalk-La Mirada; Novato Unified School District; Pleasonton Unified School District; Salinas City Schools; Salinas Union High School District; San Ramon Valley Unified School District; San Francisco Unified School District; Santa Cruz City School District; Palo Alto Unified School District; Palos Verdes Peninsula Unified School District; San Jose Unified School District; Tulare County Department of Education; Tamalpais Union High School District; Visalia Unified School District; City of Kingsburg; Marin County Office of Education; Yuba City Unified School District; Central California Schools Risk Management Authority, Principal Financial Group; Principal Mutual Life Insurance Co.; Principal Casualty Insurance Co.; Industrial Indemnity; City of Fowler; INAPRO; City of Clovis; City of Fresno; Tulare County.

## MAGILL LAW OFFICES

Established in 1989

2377 WEST SHAW-104
FRESNO, CALIFORNIA 93711
Telephone: 209-229-3333
Fax: 209-229-4234

*Personal Injury, Wrongful Death, Insurance Bad Faith, Trial Practice, Appellate Practice.*

**TIMOTHY V. MAGILL,** born Terre Haute, Indiana, September 14, 1952; admitted to bar, 1978, California and U.S. District Court, Eastern District of California; 1980, U.S. Court of Appeals, Ninth Circuit; 1981, U.S. District Court, Central District of California; 1982, U.S. District

*(This Listing Continued)*

## PROFESSIONAL BIOGRAPHIES
### CALIFORNIA—FRESNO

Court, Northern District of California; 1983, U.S. Supreme Court. *Education:* California State University at Hayward (B.A., 1974); San Joaquin College of Law (J.D., 1978). *Member:* Fresno County Bar Association; State Bar of California; Consumer Attorneys of California (Member, Board of Directors, 1990—); Fresno Trial Lawyers Association (President, 1989-1991; Co-Treasurer, 1994—).

---

## MARDEROSIAN, SWANSON & OREN
*A PROFESSIONAL CORPORATION*
### 1260 FULTON MALL
### FRESNO, CALIFORNIA 93721-1783
Telephone: 209-441-7991
Facsimilie: 209-441-8170

*Insurance Defense including Products Liability Defense, Insurance Bad Faith Defense and Personal Injury Law.*

**FIRM PROFILE:** *The Law firm of Marderosian, Swanson & Oren represents such insurance carriers as Liberty Mutual Insurance Company, United States Fidelity & Guaranty Company, Pacific National Insurance Company, Commercial Union Insurance Company, Sequoia Insurance Company, Maryland Casualty Insurance Company, Teachers Insurance Company, Hanover Insurance Company, Allianz Insurance Company, Merced Mutual Insurance Company, Atlantic Insurance Company, United Pacific Reliance Insurance Company, Wausau Insurance Company, Zurich American, Guaranty National Companies, Alliance Insurance Group, Industrial Indemnity Insurance Company, We are also local counsel for City of Fresno, Sears Roebuck & Co., and General Tire Company in regard to general liability matters.*

**C. SAM TITUS** (1957-1990).

**MICHAEL G. MARDEROSIAN,** born Fowler, California, August 30, 1950; admitted to bar, 1977, California. *Education:* University of California at Berkeley (B.A., 1973); San Joaquin College of Law (J.D., 1977). *Member:* Fresno County Bar Association; State Bar of California; Northern California Defense Counsel Association; Defense Research Institute; American Board of Trial Advocates. ***PRACTICE AREAS:*** Insurance Defense; Bad Faith; Personal Injury; Business Litigation; Employment Litigation; Civil Rights Litigation; Entertainment Law.

**JAMES W. SWANSON,** born Rochester, Minnesota, October 8, 1946; admitted to bar, 1977, California. *Education:* California State University at Fresno (B.S., 1972; M.S., 1973); San Joaquin College of Law (J.D., 1977). Instructor, Department of Criminology, California State University at Fresno, 1977-1983. *Member:* Fresno County Bar Association; State Bar of California; Northern California Association of Defense Counsel. [Sgt. Military Police, U.S. Army, 1967-1969]. ***PRACTICE AREAS:*** Insurance Defense; Bad Faith; Personal Injury.

**ERIC P. OREN,** born Merced, California, August 23, 1956; admitted to bar, 1982, California. *Education:* University of California at Los Angeles (B.A., 1978); Western State University (J.D., 1982). *Member:* Fresno County Bar Association; State Bar of California; Association of Defense Counsel of Northern California. ***PRACTICE AREAS:*** Insurance Defense; Bad Faith; Personal Injury.

**BRETT L. RUNYON,** born Fresno, California, October 20, 1959; admitted to bar, 1988, California. *Education:* Fresno City College (A.A., 1981); California State University at Fresno (B.S., 1982); San Joaquin College of Law (J.D., 1986). *Member:* Fresno County and American Bar Associations; State Bar of California; The Association of Trial Lawyers of America; Association of Defense Counsel of Northern California. ***PRACTICE AREAS:*** Insurance Defense; Bad Faith; Personal Injury; Construction Law; Libel Slander; Business Litigation.

**ALAN M. SIMPSON,** born Fresno, California, August 1, 1955; admitted to bar, 1986, California. *Education:* Fresno City College (A.A., 1975); California State University at Fresno (B.A., 1977); San Joaquin College of Law (J.D., 1983). *Member:* Fresno County (Member, Board of Directors, 1992-1996) and Goodwin Bar Associations; State Bar of California; Association of Defense Counsel; California Association of Black Lawyers. ***PRACTICE AREAS:*** Insurance Defense; Bad Faith; Personal Injury.

**WARREN R. PABOOJIAN,** born Fresno, California, May 18, 1957; admitted to bar, 1987, California. *Education:* California State University at Fresno (B.A., 1980); San Joaquin College of Law (J.D., 1985). Editor: DICTA, 1982. *Member:* Fresno County Bar Association; California; Association of Defense Counsel of Northern California. ***PRACTICE AREAS:*** Insurance Defense; Bad Faith; Personal Injury; Business Litigation; Wrongful Termination.

*(This Listing Continued)*

---

**SUE ANN CERCONE,** born Billings, Montana, April 22, 1955; admitted to bar, 1989, California. *Education:* Colorado State University (B.A., 1977); San Joaquin College of Law (J.D., with distinction, 1989). *Member:* Fresno County, Kings County and American Bar Associations; State Bar of California. ***PRACTICE AREAS:*** Insurance Defense; Bad Faith; Personal Injury.

**STEVEN D. AVERY,** born San Jose, California, June 28, 1964; admitted to bar, 1994, California. *Education:* California State University at Fresno (B.S., 1987); San Joaquin College of Law (J.D., 1994). *Member:* Fresno County Bar Association; State Bar of California. ***PRACTICE AREAS:*** Insurance Defense; Bad Faith; Personal Injury.

**STEVEN C. CLARK,** born Tucson Arizona, January 30, 1961; admitted to bar, 1995, California. *Education:* California State University at Fresno (B.A., 1988); San Joaquin College of Law (J.D., 1995). San Joaquin College Law Review, 1994-1995. *Member:* Fresno County Bar Association; State Bar of California. ***PRACTICE AREAS:*** Insurance Defense; Bad Faith; Environmental Law; Personal Injury.

REPRESENTATIVE CLIENTS: Liberty Mutual Insurance Co.; United States Fidelity Insurance Co.; Commercial Union Insurance Co.; Pacific National Insurance Co.; Allianz Insurance Co.; Wausau Insurance Co.; Hanover Insurance Co.; Atlantic Insurance Co.; Guaranty National Insurance Co. Merced Mutual Insurance Co.; Sequoia Insurance Co.; Industrial Indemnity Co.; City of Fresno, General Corp.; United Pacific Reliance; Allstate; CIGNA; Ohio Casualty Group.

---

## THOMAS C. MATYCHOWIAK
### 4321 N. WEST AVENUE, SUITE 101
### FRESNO, CALIFORNIA 93705
Telephone: 209-221-6303
Fax: 209-225-1731
Email: tmatycho@ix.netcom.com

*Civil Trial Practice. Insurance and Casualty Law.*

**THOMAS C. MATYCHOWIAK,** born Mendota, Illinois, August 25, 1943; admitted to bar, 1977, California. *Education:* University of the Pacific (A.B., 1966); McGeorge School of Law, University of the Pacific (J.D., 1977). Phi Sigma Tau. Member, Traynor Honor Society. Recipient, American Jurisprudence Award in Insurance Law. *Member:* Fresno County Bar Association; State Bar of California; The Association of Defense Counsel of Northern California.

REPRESENTATIVE CLIENTS: Caronia Corporation; Oregon Mutual Insurance Co.; Premier Claims Management; Seaboard Underwriters; Vanliner Insurance.

---

## McCOLLUM AND BUNCH
*A PROFESSIONAL CORPORATION*
### 1520 EAST SHAW AVENUE, SUITE 103
### FRESNO, CALIFORNIA 93710
Telephone: 209-222-4400
FAX: 209-222-3544

*Advertising and Marketing, Agencies and Distributorships, Antitrust and Trade Regulation, Appellate Practice, Business Law, Civil Practice, Complex and Multi-District Litigation, Contracts, Copyrights, Corporate Law, Environmental Law, Franchises and Franchising, Intellectual Property, International Law, Leases and Leasing, Litigation, Racketeer Influence and Corrupt Organizations, Real Estate and Real Property, Tax Matters, Health Care, ERISA, Construction, UCC and Securities.*

**TIMOTHY D. MCCOLLUM, (A.P.C.),** born Los Angeles, California, July 10, 1938; admitted to bar, 1976, California; 1980, U.S. Court of Appeals, Ninth Circuit; 1981, U.S. Supreme Court; 1985, U.S. District Court, Central, Eastern, Southern and Northern Districts of California; 1986, U.S. Court of Federal Claims and U.S. Court of International Trade. *Education:* Los Angeles Valley College (A.A., with honors, 1963); California State University at Los Angeles; University of California at Los Angeles and Glendale University (B.S., 1974); Glendale University (J.D., 1975). Tau Alpha Epsilon; Nu Beta Epsilon. Author: "Commercial Arbitration--Safeguards Needed," CEB Business Law Reporter; "The Family in Business," 1979. Lecturer: Commercial Arbitration, California State Bar Convention, 1983; CSUN, Business Law. Chief Counsel, Vivitar Corporation, Santa Monica, 1974-1979. *Member:* Fresno County Bar Association; State Bar of California (Member, Business and International

*(This Listing Continued)*

## McCOLLUM AND BUNCH, A PROFESSIONAL CORPORATION, Fresno—Continued

Sections). **REPORTED CASES:** Baar v. Tigerman and the American Arbitration Association (1983) 140 Cal.App.3d 979, 189 Cal.Rptr. 834, cited: 41 ALR 4th 1004, 1013; ALR 3d 815 supp.; Domke, Commercial Arbitration 23:01, et seq.; 67 Marquette L.R. Fall 1983; 21 Cal West L.R. 564, 1985; Witkin Summary, 9th Ed. Torts and Equity, P.717; CEB Partnerships, 2d 7.105 Comment. **PRACTICE AREAS:** Unfair Competition Law; International Law; Business Torts; Environmental Law.

**KENNETH S. BAYER,** born Los Angeles, California, April 14, 1956; admitted to bar, 1981, California; 1984, U.S. District Court, Southern District of California; 1991, U.S. District Court, Northern and Eastern Districts of California; 1995, Utah. *Education:* University of California at Los Angeles (B.A., 1978; J.D. 1981). *Member:* Riverside County Bar Association; State Bar of California. **LANGUAGES:** German. **REPORTED CASES:** McIntosh v. Aubry 14 Cal App 4th 1576; San Diego County v. Superior Court 176 Cal App 3d 1009. **PRACTICE AREAS:** Bankruptcy; Business Litigation; Health Care.

---

**JOSEPH A. WEBER,** born La Mirada, California, September 25, 1963; admitted to bar, 1991, California; 1992, Alaska and U.S. District Court, District of Alaska. *Education:* University of California at Los Angeles (B.A., cum laude, 1986); Hastings School of Law, University of California (J.D., 1991). *Member:* Juneau, Fresno County and Alaska Bar Associations; State Bar of California. **PRACTICE AREAS:** Corporate; Contract; Environmental; Real Estate; Land Use; Gas and Oil.

REFERENCE: 1st Interstate Bank, Encino, Ca.

---

## McCORMICK, BARSTOW, SHEPPARD, WAYTE & CARRUTH LLP

FIVE RIVER PARK PLACE EAST
**FRESNO, CALIFORNIA 93720-1501**
Telephone: 209-433-1300
Fax: 209-433-2300

Mailing Address: P.O. Box 28912, 93729-8912

*Modesto, California Office:* Centre Plaza Office Tower, 1150 Ninth Street, Suite 1510. Telephone: 209-524-1100. Fax: 209-524-1188.

*General Civil and Trial Practice. Agricultural and Water Law, Banking Law, Bankruptcy and Reorganization, Civil Rights Litigation, Civil Practice, Commodities Law, Condemnation Law, Construction Law, Corporate Law, Employment Law, Environmental Law, Estate Planning, Family Law, Franchise Law, Health Care Law, Insurance Law Legal Malpractice, Medical Malpractice, Municipal Law, Probate, Public Entity, Real Estate Agent Malpractice, Real Estate Law, Securities and Taxation Law.*

FIRM PROFILE: *McCormick, Barstow, Sheppard, Wayte & Carruth LLP was founded in the early 1950's and has grown to be one of the largest law firms in central California.*

*McCormick, Barstow's experience and statewide reputation is reflected in its clientele, and is demonstrated by the frequent appearances of its attorneys as lecturers and panelists on programs sponsored by national, state and local bar associations and professional organizations. In addition, several of the firm's partners have been appointed as judges to the federal and state courts. Most importantly, the attorneys at McCormick, Barstow believe that excellence begins with quality and timely responsiveness to the needs of its clients.*

**RICHARD A. MCCORMICK** (1915-1981).
**STEPHEN BARNETT** (1931-1988).
**DUDLEY W. SHEPPARD** (Retired).
**JAMES H. BARSTOW** (Retired).

### MEMBERS OF FIRM

**LAWRENCE E. WAYTE,** born San Mateo, California, November 4, 1936; admitted to bar, 1962, California. *Education:* Stanford University (A.B., 1958); Hastings College of Law, University of California (J.D., 1961). Phi Delta Phi. Law Clerk, Justice Frederick E. Stone, California 5th District Court of Appeals, 1961-1962. Deputy District Attorney, Fresno County, California, 1963. *Member:* Fresno County (Member, 1992-1994 and President, 1994, Board of Directors) and American Bar Associations; The State Bar of California; American Board of Trial Advocates (Diplomate); International Association of Defense Counsel. Fellow, American College of Trial Lawyers. **Email:** lwayte@mbswc.com

**LOWELL T. CARRUTH,** born Oakland, California, April 11, 1938; admitted to bar, 1963, California. *Education:* Stanford University (A.B., magna cum laude, 1959), Phi Beta Kappa; University of California at Berkeley (LL.B., 1962). Phi Delta Phi. Associate Editor, California Law Review, 1961-1962. Deputy District Attorney, Fresno County, California, 1964-1966. *Member:* Fresno County (Secretary, 1964) and American Bar Associations; The State Bar of California; Association of Defense Counsel (President, 1982; 1st Vice President, 1981; 2nd Vice President, 1980; Secretary-Treasurer, 1979); American Board of Trial Advocates (Diplomate; President San Joaquin Valley Chapter, 1973-1974). Fellow, American College of Trial Lawyers. [Capt., U.S. Army Reserve, 1964-1968] **Email:** lcarruth@mbswc.com

**JAMES H. PERKINS,** born Sacramento, California, April 30, 1928; admitted to bar, 1954, California. *Education:* Stanford University (A.B., 1950); Stanford Law School (J.D., 1953). Phi Delta Phi. *Member:* Fresno County and American Bar Associations; The State Bar of California (Member, Executive Council, Conference of Barristers, 1963); Fresno Estate Planning Council (President, 1977-1978). Fellow, American College of Trust and Estate Counsel. (Certified Specialist, Probate, Estate Planning and Trust Law, The State Bar of California Board of Legal Specialization). **Email:** jperkins@mbswc.com

**STEPHEN R. CORNWELL,** born Berkeley, California, February 12, 1942; admitted to bar, 1967, California; 1975, U.S. Supreme Court; U.S. District Court, Eastern, Central and Northern Districts of California. *Education:* San Jose State College (B.S., 1964); Boalt Hall School of Law, University of California at Berkeley (J.D., 1967). Deputy District Attorney, Ventura County, 1967-1970. *Member:* Fresno County (Member, Board of Directors, 1973-1974) and American (Member, Sections on Tort Law and Litigation) Bar Associations; American Board of Trial Advocates (Member, National Board of Directors, 1973-1978; Advocate rank); Northern California Association of Defense Counsel (Member, Board of Directors, 1990-1994). **PRACTICE AREAS:** Trial Practice; Products Liability; Engineering; Electricity; Chemistry; Oil; Flood; Construction; Employment. **Email:** scornwel@mbswc.com

**ANDREW W. WRIGHT,** born St. John, New Brunswick, Canada, September 4, 1946; admitted to bar, 1972, California. *Education:* Claremont Men's College (B.A., magna cum laude, 1968); Stanford Law School (J.D., 1971). Past Trustee and Vice-President, and current Collections Committee Chairman, Fresno Metropolitan Museum. Past President, Fresno County Easter Seal Society and Past President of the Stanford Club of Central California. Member, Panel of Arbitrators, American Arbitration Association. *Member:* Fresno County (Past Chairman, Business Law Section) and American Bar Associations; The State Bar of California. **Email:** awright@mbswc.com

**MARIO LOUIS BELTRAMO, JR.,** born San Francisco, California, February 4, 1947; admitted to bar, 1972, California. *Education:* University of San Francisco (B.A., 1969); University of Notre Dame (J.D., cum laude, 1972). Administrative Editor, Vol. 47, Notre Dame Lawyer, 1971-1972. Author: Case Comment, "Riley v. State Farm Auto Insurance," Vol. 46. Notre Dame Lawyer, Winter Issue. *Member:* Fresno County and American Bar Associations; The State Bar of California; Association of Defense Counsel; American Board of Trial Advocates; International Association of Defense Counsel; California Medical/Legal Committee.

**MICHAEL G. WOODS,** born Fresno, California, April 17, 1948; admitted to bar, 1973, California. *Education:* Fresno State University (B.A., summa cum laude, 1970); University of California at Davis (J.D., 1973). Phi Kappa Phi. *Member:* Fresno County and American Bar Associations; The State Bar of California; Association of Defense Counsel; American Board of Trial Advocates. **PRACTICE AREAS:** Trial Practice, Employment (Chairman of Employment Law Practice Group); Defense of Public Entities; Civil Rights; Products Liability.

**JAMES P. WAGONER,** born September 21, 1948; admitted to bar, 1973, California. *Education:* St. Mary's College of California (B.A., 1970); University of Santa Clara (J.D., cum laude, 1973). Law Clerk to Hon. George A. Brown, Presiding Justice, 5th District Court of Appeals, Fresno, California, 1973-1974. Member, Board of Directors, Fresno-Merced Counties Legal Services, 1976-1992. *Member:* Fresno County and American Bar Associations; The State Bar of California; Association of Defense Counsel (Member, Board of Directors, 1987-1988); Defense Research Institute.

*(This Listing Continued)*

**STEVEN G. RAU,** born Madera, California, March 1, 1950; admitted to bar, 1975, California. *Education:* University of California at Berkeley (B.A., 1972); University of California at Davis (J.D., 1975); New York University (LL.M., Taxation, 1977). Phi Beta Kappa; Order of the Coif. *Member:* Fresno County Bar Association; The State Bar of California. **PRACTICE AREAS:** Real Estate Development and Finance; General Business.

**GORDON M. PARK,** born Culver City, California, June 24, 1951; admitted to bar, 1976, California, U.S. District Court, Eastern and Northern Districts of California and U.S. Court of Appeals, Ninth Circuit. *Education:* California State University at Long Beach (B.A., summa cum laude, 1973); University of California at Los Angeles (J.D., 1976). Member, National Order of Barristers. Distinguished Advocate, UCLA Moot Court Honors Program. Co-Author: "The Coverage Trigger In Environmental Contamination Property Claims: Who Gets Shot For The Loss," ABA Property Insurance Law mid-year meeting, 1989; "The Insurance Agent: Friend or Foe," ABA Property Insurance Law mid-year meeting, 1990. Lecturer, Handling Arson and Insurance Fraud Claims and Litigation: California Conference of Arson Investigators, Fresno, June, 1984 and June, 1986; Property Insurance Forum, Fresno, December, 1985-1990. Member, Board of Directors, Fresno County Young Lawyers, 1980-1983. *Member:* Fresno County, American (Member, Torts and Insurance Practice Section and Property Insurance Law Committees) and Federal Bar Associations; The State Bar of California; Association of Defense Counsel of Northern California; Defense Research Institute; American Board of Trial Advocates (ABOTA); Northern California Fraud Investigators Association; Property Claims Association of the Pacific.

**WADE M. HANSARD,** born Los Angeles, California, August 18, 1951; admitted to bar, 1977, California. *Education:* California State University at Fresno (B.S., summa cum laude, 1974); Hastings College of Law, University of California (J.D., 1977). Phi Kappa Phi. *Member:* Fresno County and American Bar Associations; The State Bar of California; Association of Defense Counsel (Board of Directors, 1997—); Defense Research Institute. **PRACTICE AREAS:** Representing Insurers in coverage Disputes and Bad Faith Litigation; Agent Errors and Omissions; Complex Litigation.

**W. F. DOCKER,** born Fresno, California, December 7, 1949; admitted to bar, 1977, California. *Education:* Stanford University (B.A., 1972); University of Santa Clara (M.B.A., 1977; J.D., cum laude, 1977). *Member:* Fresno County and American Bar Associations; The State Bar of California; California Society for Healthcare Attorneys; National Health Lawyers Association; Fresno Estate Planning Council; American Agricultural Law Association. **PRACTICE AREAS:** Health Care; Estate Planning; Business and Agricultural Transactions.

**JUSTUS C. SPILLNER,** born Oakland, California, November 2, 1950; admitted to bar, 1975, California. *Education:* California State University at Hayward (B.A., with honors, 1972); University of San Diego (J.D., 1975). Deputy District Attorney, Alameda County, 1975-1979. *Member:* Alameda County, Fresno County and American Bar Associations; The State Bar of California; California District Attorney Association; Association of Defense Counsel of Northern California; American Board of Trial Advocates. **Email:** jspillne@mbswc.com

**HILTON A. RYDER,** born Freeport, Illinois, January 13, 1940; admitted to bar, 1972, California, U.S. District Court, Eastern District of California and U.S. Court of Appeals, Ninth Circuit. *Education:* Iowa State University (B.S., 1962; M.S., 1964); University of Santa Clara (J.D., magna cum laude, 1972). *Member:* Fresno County Bar Association; State Bar of California. **PRACTICE AREAS:** Bankruptcy and Insolvency Workouts. **Email:** hryder@mbswc.com

**D. GREG DURBIN,** born Reno, Nevada, May 28, 1953; admitted to bar, 1978, California; U.S. District Court, Eastern, Northern and Southern Districts of California; U.S. Court of Appeals, Ninth Circuit. *Education:* University of California at Berkeley (A.B., with distinction, 1975); Hastings College of Law, University of California (J.D., 1978). Phi Alpha Delta. Author: "Broach of Duty: The U.S. Foreign Trade Zones Program in Transition," 1 Hastings International and Comparative Law Review, 1977. Adjunct Professor, San Joaquin College of Law, 1990—. Member, Panel of Arbitrators, American Arbitration Association; and Neutral Evaluator, Eastern Neutral Evaluation Program, Eastern District of California. *Member:* Fresno County, Federal and American Bar Associations; State Bar of California. **PRACTICE AREAS:** Real Estate, Commercial and Water Litigation. **Email:** gdurbin@mbswc.com

**MARSHALL C. WHITNEY,** born Vallejo, California, July 5, 1951; admitted to bar, 1978, California. *Education:* University of California at Santa Barbara (B.A., Mathematics with high honors, 1973); Trinity College, Dublin, Ireland (1972-1973); Hastings College of Law, University of California (J.D., 1978). Member, Civil Justice Reform Act Advisory Committee for the U.S. District Court, Eastern District of California. Lawyer Delegate, Ninth Circuit Judicial Conference, 1992-1995. Evaluator, Early Neutral Evaluation Program for the U.S. District Court, Eastern District of California. Co-Administrator, Fresno County Bar Association Fee Dispute Program, 1992—. Attorney Arbitrator, Fresno County Superior Court Judicial Arbitration Program. *Member:* Fresno County, Federal (Executive Committee Member, Fresno Chapter) and American (Construction and Business Litigation Sections) Bar Associations; State Bar of California; Association of General Counsel. **PRACTICE AREAS:** Legal and Accounting Malpractice Defense; Business and Commercial Litigation; Construction Law. **Email:** mwhitney@mbswc.com

**DONALD S. BLACK,** born Boston, Massachusetts, July 21, 1954; admitted to bar, 1980, California. *Education:* Middlebury College (A.B., cum laude, 1976); University of Santa Clara (J.D., 1980). Associate Editor, Santa Clara Law Review, 1979-1980. Author: "The Highway Cases: Noise as a Taking or Damaging of Property in California," Vol. 20, No. 2; "Subordination Agreements: What is First May Be Last," *The Law Journal,* September, 1996. Member, Panel of Arbitrators, American Arbitration Association. Neutral Evaluator for U.S. District Court, Eastern District of California. Member, Board of Directors, Fresno Philharmonic Orchestra, 1995—. Member, Board of Governors, Association of Business Trial Lawyers *Member:* Fresno County and American (Member, Sections on Litigation and Real Property Law) and Federal Bar Associations; The State Bar of California; Association of Business Trial Lawyers (Member, Board of Governors, 1996—). **PRACTICE AREAS:** Real Estate Litigation including Brokers and Agents Liability; Creditors Rights and Remedies; Trust and Probate Litigation. **Email:** dblack@mbswc.com

**DANIEL P. LYONS,** born Seattle, Washington, September 11, 1953; admitted to bar, 1980, California. *Education:* Santa Barbara City Community College (A.A., 1975); California State University at Chico (B.S., 1977); Hastings College of Law, University of California (J.D., 1980). Phi Kappa Phi; Beta Gamma Sigma. Recipient, Financial Executives Institute Award. *Member:* Fresno County and American Bar Associations; The State Bar of California; Northern California Association of Defense Council; Northern California Fraud Investigations Association. **Email:** dlyons@mbswc.com

**RILEY C. WALTER,** born Evansville, Indiana, December 3, 1951; admitted to bar, 1980, California, U.S. District Court, Eastern and Northern District of California and District of Arizona, U.S. Court of Appeals, Ninth Circuit and U.S. Supreme Court. *Education:* California Polytechnic State University (B.A., with honors, 1973; M.S., 1974); Western State University (J.D., 1980). Gamma Sigma Delta. Alpha Gamma Rho (Faculty Advisor). Associate Professor: Agricultural Business, California State University-Fresno, 1981-1983; California Polytechnic State University/Pomona, 1976-1980, 1974-1975, San Luis Obispo. Adjunct Professor of Agricultural Law, San Joaquin College of Law, 1989-1993. Author: "A Case for Avoidance of Secret Farmer Liens: The California Producer's Lien," *San Joaquin Agricultural Law Review,* , 1994. Co-Author: "Contents of Fee Applications," *Annual Survey of Bankruptcy Law,* 1990. Contributing Author: *Advanced Chapter 11 Practice,* John Wiley Publisher (1991, Revised, 1993). *Member:* Fresno County (Chairman, Business Law Section, 1989) and American (Member, Business Bankruptcy Section) Bar Associations; State Bar of California; American Bankruptcy Institute; Central California Bankruptcy Association (President, 1989-1990); California Bankruptcy Forum (Director, 1992-1993 and 1995—); San Joaquin Valley Inn of Court (1993-1995). Certified Business Bankruptcy Specialist by American Board of Bankruptcy Certification. **PRACTICE AREAS:** Bankruptcy, Business Reorganization and Agricultural Law. **Email:** rwalter@mbswc.com

**MICHAEL L. WILHELM,** born Delano, California, November 1, 1955; admitted to bar, 1981, California. *Education:* California State College at Bakersfield (B.S., summa cum laude, 1978); University of California at Los Angeles (J.D., 1981). Beta Gamma Sigma. Member, Board of Directors, 1987— and President, 1990-1991, Central California Bankruptcy Association. *Member:* Fresno County and American Bar Associations; The State Bar of California; American Bankruptcy Institute. **Email:** mwilhelm@mbswc.com

**JOHN A. DROLSHAGEN,** born Oakland, California, June 5, 1955; admitted to bar, 1982, California. *Education:* University of California at Davis (B.A., 1978); University of Santa Clara (J.D., 1982). *Member:* Fresno County and American Bar Associations; The State Bar of California; Association of Defense Counsel; Defense Research Institute. **PRACTICE AREAS:** Environmental, Product Liability; Professional Malpractice. **Email:** jdrolsha@mbswc.com

*(This Listing Continued)*

## McCORMICK, BARSTOW, SHEPPARD, WAYTE & CARRUTH LLP, Fresno—Continued

**BRIAN M. ARAX,** born Fresno, California, February 7, 1958; admitted to bar, 1983, California; U.S. District Court, Northern and Eastern Districts of California. *Education:* University of California at Santa Barbara (B.A., 1980); University Southern California (J.D., 1983). *Member:* Fresno County Bar Association; The State Bar of California; Association of Defense Counsel; Defense Research Institute. **Email:** barax@mbswc.com

**WALTER W. WHELAN,** born Porterville, California, February 8, 1957; admitted to bar, 1982, California, U.S. District Court, Central and Eastern Districts of California and U.S. Court of Appeals, Ninth Circuit. *Education:* Stanford University (B.A., 1979); University of California at Los Angeles (J.D., 1982). Member, UCLA Moot Court Honors Program, 1980-1981. Member, State Bar Committee on Rules and Procedures of Court, 1989-1992. *Member:* Fresno County (President, Agricultural Law Section, 1992) and American Bar Associations; The State Bar of California. *LANGUAGES:* Spanish and French. **PRACTICE AREAS:** Commercial Litigation; Employment Litigation. **Email:** wwhelan@mbswc.com

**MICHAEL F. BALL,** born Chicago, Illinois, December 31, 1960; admitted to bar, 1984, California; 1985, Illinois. *Education:* University of Miami (A.B., cum laude, 1981); University of Illinois (J.D., cum laude, 1984). Phi Delta Phi (Magister, Langdell Inn, 1982-1983); Phi Kappa Phi. Member, Board of Directors, Fresno County Young Lawyers Association, 1988-1990. *Member:* Fresno County, Illinois State and American Bar Associations; The State Bar of California; Northern California Association of Defense Counsel; Defense Research Institute. **Email:** mball@mbswc.com

**STEPHEN E. CARROLL,** born San Jose, California, October 15, 1958; admitted to bar, 1984, California. *Education:* University of Santa Clara (B.A., magna cum laude, 1981); University of California at Los Angeles (J.D., 1984). Member, National Order of Barristers; UCLA Moot Court Honors Program Executive Board of Judges. *Member:* Fresno County, American and Federal (San Joaquin Chapter) Bar Associations; The State Bar of California. **Email:** scarroll@mbswc.com

**JAMES H. WILKINS,** born Potsdam, New York, May 11, 1958; admitted to bar, 1984, California. *Education:* Arizona State University (B.S., 1980; J.D., 1984). Member, National Order of Barristers; Arizona State University National Moot Court, 1983-1984; Arizona State National Moot Court Team. Recipient, American Jurisprudence Award in Remedies. *Member:* Fresno County and American Bar Associations; The State Bar of California; Association of Defense Counsel. **Email:** jwilkins@mbswc.com

**TIMOTHY JONES,** born Fresno, California, April 16, 1959; admitted to bar, 1985, California and U.S. District Court, Eastern District of California; 1986, U.S. District Court, Northern District of California; 1987, Washington. *Education:* California State University at Fresno (B.S., 1981); University of San Diego (J.D., cum laude, 1985). Recipient, American Jurisprudence Award in Constitutional Law. *Member:* Fresno County and American Bar Associations. **PRACTICE AREAS:** Environmental Litigation. **Email:** tjones@mbswc.com

**KEVIN D. HANSEN,** born Fresno, California, July 23, 1957; admitted to bar, 1985, California; 1986, U.S. District Court, Eastern District of California; 1990, U.S. District Court, Northern District of California. *Education:* University of Southern California; Fresno State University (B.S., 1980); San Joaquin College of Law (J.D., 1985). Corpus Juris Scholar, 1981-1983; Bailey National Moot Court; Student Association President, 1983-1984. Co-Author: "The Coverage Trigger In Environmental Contamination Property Claims: Who Gets Shot For The Loss," ABA Property Insurance Law Committee, mid-year meeting, 1989; "Bad Faith and Punitive Damages," Regional Editor, 1st Supplement, ABA, 1990; "How Do You Plead So You Won't Get Burned," ABA Section of Tort and Insurance Practice, National Institute, "Litigation The Civil Arson Case: Winning Without Getting Burned," 1993; "Fighting Fraus: A Team Effort: A Discussion of several Topics Relevant to the Investigation and Litigation of Fraudulent Insurance Claims," Northern California Fraud Investigators Association, Fifth Annual Training Conference, 1994. *Member:* Fresno County and American (Member, Torts and Insurance Practice Section and Property Insurance Law Committee) Bar Associations; The State Bar of California; Association of Defense Counsel of Northern California; Property Insurance Claims Association of the Pacific; California Conference of Arson Investigators; Northern California Fraud Investigators Association. **PRACTICE AREAS:** First and Third Party Insurance Fraud; Bad Faith Law and Defense; First Party Insurance Coverage and Litigation; Arson, Tort and Insurance Defense; Product and Premises Liability Defense. **Email:** khansen@mbswc.com

*(This Listing Continued)*

**PHILIP M. FLANIGAN,** born Tuscola, Illinois, December 26, 1959; admitted to bar, 1986, California and U.S. District Court, Eastern District of California; 1988, U.S. Court of Appeals, Ninth Circuit; 1990, U.S. District Court, Central and Northern Districts of California; 1992, U.S. District Court, Southern District of California. *Education:* California State University at Fresno (B.S., 1983); Pepperdine University (J.D., cum laude, 1986). Phi Delta Phi. *Member:* Fresno County and American Bar Associations; California Association of Defense Counsel; Defense Research Institute; Shanna Zerpoli Foundation (Director). **PRACTICE AREAS:** Commercial Litigation; Insurance Coverage and Insurance Bad Faith. **Email:** pflaniga@mbswc.com

**MATTHEW K. HAWKINS,** born Melbourne, Florida, February 22, 1962; admitted to bar, 1987, California and U.S. District Court, Eastern District of California; 1989, U.S. Court of Appeals, Ninth Circuit. *Education:* Brigham Young University (B.A., 1984; J.D., 1987); Regent's College, London, England, 1987. Member: Brigham Young University Board of Advocates; Jessup International Moot Court Team. *Member:* Stanislaus County, Fresno County and American Bar Associations; State Bar of California; Fresno County Young Lawyer's Association (Member, Board of Directors, 1990-1991). Resident, Modesto Office). *LANGUAGES:* Spanish.

**KENNETH A. BALDWIN,** born Sacramento, California, March 2, 1962; admitted to bar, 1987, California; U.S. District Court, Eastern and Central Districts of California. *Education:* University of California, Davis (B.A., 1984; J.D., 1987).

**DAVID R. MCNAMARA,** born Portage, Wisconsin, July 10, 1962; admitted to bar, 1987, Wisconsin; 1988, California, U.S. Court of Appeals, Ninth Circuit and U.S. District Court, Eastern and Central Districts of California and Western Districts of Wisconsin. *Education:* University of Wisconsin-Oshkosh (B.S., magna cum laude, 1984); University of Wisconsin (J.D., 1987). *Member:* Fresno County, American and Federal Bar Associations; State Bar of California; State Bar of Wisconsin. **PRACTICE AREAS:** Commercial Litigation; Employment; Real Estate. **Email:** dmcnamar@mbswc.com

**TIMOTHY L. THOMPSON,** born Fort Ord, California, July 24, 1962; admitted to bar, 1988, California, U.S. District Court, Eastern District of California and U.S. Court of Appeals, Ninth Circuit. *Education:* Loma Linda University (B.S., 1984); Santa Clara University (J.D., 1987). Chairman, Santa Clara University Moot Court Board, 1986-1987. *Member:* Fresno County and American Bar Associations; State Bar of California. **PRACTICE AREAS:** Commerical Litigation. **Email:** tthompso@mbswc.com

**WENDY S. LLOYD,** born Oak Harbor, Washington, December 6, 1962; admitted to bar, 1988, California and U.S. District Court, Eastern District of California. *Education:* University of California, Los Angeles (B.A., 1985); University of Arkansas, Fayetteville (J.D., with high honors, 1987). Member: University of Arkansas Moot Court Board; University of Arkansas Law Review, 1986-1987. *Member:* Fresno County Bar Association; State Bar of California. **Email:** wlloyd@mbswc.com

**MICHAEL J. CZESHINSKI,** born Wausau, Wisconsin, November 4, 1962; admitted to bar, 1988, California, Wisconsin and U.S. District Court, Eastern District of California. *Education:* University of Wisconsin-Madison (B.S., 1985; J.D., 1988). Member, Wisconsin International Law Journal, 1987-1988. *Member:* Fresno County and American Bar Associations; Fresno County Young Lawyers Association; Northern California Association of Defense Counsel. **PRACTICE AREAS:** Professional Errors and Omissions; Civil Litigation. **Email:** mczeshin@mbswc.com

**JOHN A. LEONARD,** born Lincoln, Nebraska, February 4, 1960; admitted to bar, 1989, California; U.S. District Court, Eastern District of California. *Education:* University of Nebraska at Lincoln (B.S., 1982; J.D., 1988); American Graduate School of International Management - Thunderbird (M.I.M., 1985). *Member:* Fresno County Bar Association; San Joaquin Valley International Trade Association.

**GREGORY S. MASON,** born San Diego, California, December 27, 1961; admitted to bar, 1990, California; 1991, U.S. District Court, Eastern and Central Districts of California. *Education:* San Diego State University (A.B., with distinction in Economics, 1987); University of San Diego (J.D., 1990). Phi Delta Phi. *Member:* Fresno County and American Bar Associations; State Bar of California (Delegate to State Bar, 1995—); Northern California Association of Defense Counsel; Fresno County Young Lawyers Association (Member, Board of Directors, 1993—). **PRACTICE AREAS:** Civil Litigation; Products Liability; Professional Liability Defense.

*(This Listing Continued)*

**MART B. OLLER, IV,** born Modesto, California, April 2, 1965; admitted to bar, 1990, California and U.S. District Court, Eastern District of California. *Education:* University of California, Irvine (B.S., cum laude, 1987); University of California, Davis (J.D., 1990). Phi Delta Phi. Member, Jessup International Moot Court Team. *Member:* Fresno County and American Bar Associations; State Bar of California; Northern California Association of Defense Counsel. *Email:* moller@mbswc.com

**PAUL J. O'ROURKE, JR.,** born Coral Gables, Florida, December 3, 1964; admitted to bar, 1989, California. *Education:* University of California at Los Angeles (B.A., 1986); Loyola Marymount University (J.D., cum laude, 1989). Order of the Coif; Alpha Sigma Nu. Member, St. Thomas Moore Honor Society. Member, Loyola Law Review, 1988-1989. *Member:* Fresno County Bar Association; Association of Defense Counsel. *Email:* porourke@mbswc.com

**TODD W. BAXTER,** born Racine, Wisconsin, May 3, 1958; admitted to bar, 1991, California. *Education:* University of Wisconsin-Parkside; University of Wisconsin (B.S., 1985); University of Nebraska (J.D., 1990). Recipient: American Jurisprudence Award for Civil Clinical Program, International Academy of Trial Lawyers Distinguished Achievement Award for Advocacy. *Member:* Fresno County, Federal and American Bar Associations; State Bar of California. *Email:* tbaxter@mbswc.com

*ASSOCIATES*

**ROBERT K. LANDEN,** born Hanover, New Hampshire, January 21, 1962; admitted to bar, 1990, California; 1991, Wisconsin. *Education:* College of William & Mary (B.A., 1984); University of Hawaii (M.A., 1987); University of Wisconsin at Madison (J.D., cum laude, 1990). Note and Comment Editor, Wisconsin International Law Journal, 1988-1990. *Member:* State Bar of Wisconsin; State Bar of California; American Bar Association. *PRACTICE AREAS:* Insurance Coverage. *Email:* rlanden@mbswc.com

**KURT F. VOTE,** born Mission Hills, California, April 9, 1967; admitted to bar, 1992, California. *Education:* University of California, Irvine (B.S., magna cum laude, 1989) Engineer of the Year; University of Southern California (J.D., 1992). Chair, Hale Moot Court Honors Program. Chair, Board of Directors, Fresno County Chapter, American Diabetes Association, 1996-1997. Secretary, Board of Directors, California Affiliate, American Diabetes Association, 1996-1997. *Member:* Fresno County, American and Federal Bar Associations. *PRACTICE AREAS:* Business Litigation; Environmental and Construction Defect Litigation. *Email:* kvote@mbswc.com

**BLAKE A. MEYEN,** born Iowa City, Iowa, August 24, 1967; admitted to bar, 1993, California. *Education:* University of Kansas (B.G.S., Crime and Delinquency Studies, 1990; J.D., 1993). Phi Delta Phi. *Member:* Fresno County and American Bar Associations; Central California Bankruptcy Association. *PRACTICE AREAS:* Creditor-Debtor; Bankruptcy; Receiverships; Agricultural Law; General Business Transactions. *Email:* bmeyen@mbswc.com

**JULIE A. NOBLE,** born Rochester, New York, December 23, 1966; admitted to bar, 1993, California. *Education:* Albertson College of Idaho (B.A., summa cum laude, 1989); University of San Diego (J.D., magna cum laude, 1993). Staff Member, 1991-1992 and Comments Editor, 1992-1993, San Diego Law Review. Recipient, American Jurisprudence Awards in Criminal Procedure and Professional Responsibility. *Member:* Fresno County Bar Association; Fresno County Lawyers Association; Fresno County Women Lawyers. *Email:* jnoble@mbswc.com

**BRUCE W. KELLEY,** born Waterloo, Iowa, September 16, 1964; admitted to bar, 1993, California. *Education:* University of Nebraska (B.A., 1987; J.D., 1993). Member, National Moot Court Team. Member, University of Nebraska Law Review. *Member:* Fresno County Bar Association; State Bar of California. *LANGUAGES:* Spanish. *PRACTICE AREAS:* Tort, Copyright and Water Law. *Email:* bkelley@mbswc.com

**PATRICK M. MARTUCCI,** born Fresno, California, September 22, 1967; admitted to bar, 1993, California. *Education:* University of California, Davis (B.A., highest honors, 1990); Santa Clara University Law School (J.D., cum laude, 1993). Phi Kappa Phi. Recipient, Certificate of Excellence in Legal Research and Writing finalist in Moot Court Competition. *Email:* pmartucc@mbswc.com

**JOHN M. DUNN,** born Lawton, Oklahoma, August 8, 1968; admitted to bar, 1993, California. *Education:* University of Notre Dame (B.A., 1990); Notre Dame Law School (J.D., 1993). Staff Member, 1991-1992 and Editor, 1992-1993, Journal of College and University Law. *Member:* Stanislaus County and Fresno County Bar Associations; Fresno County Young Lawyers Association. (Resident, Modesto Office). *PRACTICE AREAS:* General Civil Litigation.

**GREGORY A. FLOYD,** born Fullerton, California, October 5, 1969; admitted to bar, 1994, California. *Education:* University of California (B.A., 1991); University of California, Hastings College of The Law (J.D., 1994). Recipient, American Jurisprudence Award for Products Liability. Co-Author: Coverage Trigger Update for First and Third Party Insurance Cases: Who Gets Shot for The Loss? (An Analysis of Prudential-LMI v. Superior Court and Montrose Chemical Corp. v. Admiral Ins. Co.). *Member:* Fresno County, Federal and American Bar Associations; Fresno County Law Library Attorney's Advisory Committee. *PRACTICE AREAS:* Insurance Coverage and Bad Faith.

**DIRK B. PALOUTZIAN,** born Fresno, California, April 6, 1969; admitted to bar, 1994, California. *Education:* University of California, Berkeley (B.A., 1991); University of California, Davis (J.D., 1994). *Member:* State Bar of California; American Bar Association. *PRACTICE AREAS:* Insurance Coverage; Insurance Defense. *Email:* dpaloutz@mbswc.com

**DAVID T. WILSON,** born Seattle, Washington, April 18, 1962; admitted to bar, 1994, California. *Education:* University of Arizona (B.S., 1987; J.D., cum laude, 1994). Articles Editor, Arizona Journal of International & Comparative Law, 1993-1994. Author: Foreign Owned Subsidiaries and National Origin Discrimination: Can Federal Employment Discrimination Law and Employer Choice Provisions Be Reconciled?, 10 Ariz. J. Int'l & Comp. L. 507 Fall, 1993. *Member:* Fresno County Bar Association; State Bar of California (Member, Business Law and Real Property Law Sections); National Health Lawyers Association. *LANGUAGES:* Spanish. *PRACTICE AREAS:* Health Care; Real Estate; Corporate; Business; Political Law. *Email:* dwilson@mbswc.com

**SCOTT M. REDDIE,** born Encino, California, January 8, 1968; admitted to bar, 1994, California. *Education:* University of California, Los Angeles (B.A., 1991); Pepperdine University (J.D., 1994). Phi Delta Phi. Author: Section 546 (a) of the Bankruptcy Code: A Plea for Predictability, 4 Journal of Bankruptcy Law and Practice 3 (1994); Home Mortgage Strip Down in Chapter 13 Bankruptcy - A Contextual Approach to Sections 1322 (b)(2) and (b)(5), 20 Pepperdine Law Review 425 (1993). *Member:* Fresno County Bar Association; Fresno County Young Lawyers Association; Central California Bankruptcy Association. *PRACTICE AREAS:* Business Workouts; Bankruptcy Reorganizations; Creditors Remedies. *Email:* sreddie@mbswc.com

**KRISTIN L. ICHISHTA,** born San Jose, California, September 19, 1969; admitted to bar, 1994, California. *Education:* University of California, Los Angeles (B.A., cum laude, 1991); Santa Clara University (J.D., 1994). Moot Court Honors Board. Vice President, Student Bar Association. *Member:* Fresno County and Federal Bar Associations; State Bar of California; Fresno County Young Lawyers Association. *PRACTICE AREAS:* Insurance Coverage; Bad Faith; Insurance Defense. *Email:* kichisht@mbswc.com

**KAREN E. LINTOTT,** born Los Angeles, California, October 9, 1966; admitted to bar, 1995, California. *Education:* University of Southern California (B.A., 1989); University of San Diego (J.D., 1995). Member, University of San Diego Law Review, 1993-1995. *Member:* Fresno County and Federal Bar Associations; Fresno County Young Lawyers Association; State Bar of California. *PRACTICE AREAS:* Insurance Defense; General Litigation; Family Law. *Email:* klintott@mbswc.com

**ANTHONY N. DEMARIA,** born New York, New York, August 3, 1969; admitted to bar, 1995, California. *Education:* University of Southern California, Davis (B.A., 1991); University of San Diego (J.D., cum laude, 1995). President, St. Thomas More Society, 1994-1995; Honor Court Counsel, 1994-1995. Recipient, American Jurisprudence Awards: Torts, Legal Writing, Advanced Trial Advocacy. Co-Author: "Coverage Trigger Update For First and Third Party Insurance Cases: Who Gets Shot for the Loss? An Analysis of *Prudential-LMI v. Superior Court* and *Montrose Chemical Corp. v. Admiral Ins. Co.*. Tab 4, Tort and Insurance Practice Section of the ABA, April, 1996. *Member:* Fresno County and American Bar Associations; State Bar of California. *PRACTICE AREAS:* Insurance Defense; Bad Faith; Insurance Coverage; Business Litigation. *Email:* ademaria@mbswc.com

**PETER L.D. SIMON,** born Walnut Creek, California, November 22, 1968; admitted to bar, 1995, California and U.S. District Court, Eastern District of California; 1996, U.S. District Court, Southern and Northern Districts of California; U.S. Court of Appeals for the Federal Circuit and U.S. Court of Appeals, Ninth Circuit. *Education:* University of California, Los Angeles (B.A., 1992); Santa Clara University (J.D., cum laude, 1995).

*(This Listing Continued)*

**McCORMICK, BARSTOW, SHEPPARD, WAYTE & CARRUTH LLP,** Fresno—Continued

Recipient, American Jurisprudence Award, Commercial Transactions II, 1995. *Member:* Fresno County, Federal (Member, Intellectual Property and Environmental Subsections) and American (Member, Intellectual Property and Environmental Subsections) Bar Associations; State Bar of California; Fresno County Young Lawyers Association. **PRACTICE AREAS:** Business Litigation; Environmental Litigation; Intellectual Property Litigation. *Email:* psimon@mbswc.com

**STEPHANIE A. SCHRANDT,** born Ft. Leonard Wood, Missouri, July 6, 1969; admitted to bar, 1995, California. *Education:* University of Kansas (B.S.J., 1992; J.D., 1995). **PRACTICE AREAS:** Civil Litigation. *Email:* sschrand@mbswc.com

**DAVID A. EVANS,** born Torrance, California, March 4, 1970; admitted to bar, 1996, California. *Education:* University of California, Santa Barbara (B.A., 1992); University of California, Los Angeles (J.D., 1995). *Member:* Fresno County and American Bar Associations. **PRACTICE AREAS:** Insurance Coverage. *Email:* devans@mbswc.com

**LISA A. SONDERGAARD,** born Fresno, California, October 20, 1969; admitted to bar, 1996, California and U.S. District Court, Eastern District of California. *Education:* University of Southern California (B.A., 1991); San Joaquin College of Law (J.D., 1995). Professor, Paralegal Program, San Joaquin College of law, 1993-1996. **PRACTICE AREAS:** Insurance; General Civil Litigation. *Email:* lsonderg@mbswc.com

**EDMUND H. MIZUMOTO,** born Misawa, Japan, November 23, 1966; admitted to bar, 1996, California and U.S. District Court, Eastern District of California. *Education:* Johns Hopkins University (B.A., 1988); University of Washington (B.A., 1992); Northwestern University (J.D., 1995); Associate Articles Editor, Journal of Criminal and Criminology, 1994-1995. *Member:* Fresno County and American Bar Associations. **LANGUAGES:** Japanese and Spanish. **PRACTICE AREAS:** Insurance Defense Litigation; Business Litigation. *Email:* misawa@mbswc.com

**AMY L. LOPEZ,** born San Francisco, California, October 3, 1960; admitted to bar, 1996, California. *Education:* University of the Pacific (B.A., 1984); San Joaquin College of Law (J.D., 1995). Fresno County Bar Association. **PRACTICE AREAS:** Tort Litigation; Business Litigation. *Email:* alopez@mbswc.com

**JOY D. COTHRAN,** born Selma, California, November 27, 1951; admitted to bar, 1995, California. *Education:* California Polytechnic State University (B.S., with honors, 1974); Pepperdine University School of Law (J.D., 1995). **LANGUAGES:** Spanish and French. **PRACTICE AREAS:** Insurance Coverage; Business Litigation. *Email:* jcothran@mbswc.com

**JOAN JACOBS LEVIE,** born New York, New York, April 26, 1939; admitted to bar, 1995, California and U.S. District Court, Eastern District of California. *Education:* Hofstra University (B.A., 1960); San Joaquin College of law (J.D., high honors, 1995). Delta Theta Phi (Excellence in Scholarship Key, 1992-1995). Recipient: American Jurisprudence Awards for Criminal Law and Procedure, 1993; Corpus Juris Secundum Awards for Criminal Law and Procedure, 1993. Student Bar Association Scholarship. Hopper Moot Court Competition: Best Brief; Semifinalist Oral Argument, 1992. Member, National Moot Court Team, 1995. Member, San Joaquin Agricultural Law Review, 1992-1995. Extern to the Hon. Oliver W. Wanger, U.S. District Court, Eastern District, 1993. Teaching Assistant, Legal Research and Writing, San Joaquin College of law, 1992-1995. Author: "Health Claims in Wine Labeling and Advertising: Has Government Regulation Taken the Veritas Out of the Vino?", San Joaquin Agricultural Law Review, Summer, 1993. Member, Advisory Board, 1991-1996 and Member, Ethics Committee, 1992-1996, Valley Medical Center. *Fresno County, Federal and American Bar Associations; Fresno County Young Lawyers Association; Fresno County Women Lawyers Association; State Bar of California.* **PRACTICE AREAS:** Insurance Defense; Civil Litigation; Appeals. *Email:* jlevie@mbswc.com

**MICHAEL R. FIELDS,** born Ellensburg, Washington, December 20, 1969; admitted to bar, 1996, California. *Education:* San Diego State University (B.S., 1992); University of San Diego (J.D., 1996). Assistant Editor, San Diego Law Review. **PRACTICE AREAS:** General Litigation; Wrongful Termination; Third Party Insurance Defense. *Email:* mfields@mbswc.com

**JASON A. DECKER,** born Roseville, California, May 27, 1970; admitted to bar, 1996, California. *Education:* University of California (B.A., 
*(This Listing Continued)*

1993); McGeorge School of Law (J.D., 1996). Order of the Coif. *Email:* jdecker@mbswc.com

**ALYSON A. CARR,** born Lansdale, Pennsylvania, April 20, 1972; admitted to bar, 1996, California. *Education:* University of San Francisco (B.A., summa cum laude, 1993); Hastings College of the Law (J.D., 1996). Order of the Coif. Thurston Society. Recipient, American Jurisprudence Award in Evidence and Remedies. Managing Editor, Hastings International and Comparative Law Review. **PRACTICE AREAS:** Insurance Coverage; Bad Faith Defense. *Email:* acar@mbswc.com

**JUDD A. GENDA,** born Appleton, Wisconsin, May 28, 1970; admitted to bar, 1996, Wisconsin, California and U.S. District Court, Eastern District of California. *Education:* University of Wisconsin, Madison (B.A., 1992; J.D., 1996). Phi Alpha Delta. **PRACTICE AREAS:** Insurance Coverage; Bad Faith Litigation. *Email:* jgenda@mbswc.com

**GARY B. KRAFT,** born San Diego, California, February 17, 1966; admitted to bar, 1996, California. *Education:* University of Arizona (B.A., 1992; J.D., 1996). Member, Moot Court Board. Member, Arizona Law Review. **PRACTICE AREAS:** Business Litigation; Insurance Defense. *Email:* gkraft@mbswc.com

**CHRIS SCHEITHAUER,** born Vandenberg Air Force Base, March 30, 1971; admitted to bar, 1996, California. *Education:* University of Southern California (B.A./B.A., 1993; J.D., 1996). Member, USC Interdisciplinary Law Journal. Member, Federalist Society, 1993—. **PRACTICE AREAS:** Business Litigation; Insurance Defense. *Email:* cscheit@mbswc.com

**SEAN P. REIS,** born Torrance, California, August 23, 1971; admitted to bar, 1996, California. *Education:* University of California, San Diego (B.A., 1993); Rutgers University School of Law (J.D., 1996). Recipient, Nathan D. Schildkraut Award for Appellate Advocacy. Editor, Rutgers Law Review, 1995-1996. Associate Instructor, Legal Research and Writing Program, 1995-1996. **LANGUAGES:** Spanish. **PRACTICE AREAS:** Insurance Coverage; Bad Faith Litigation. *Email:* sreis@mbswc.com

**REYNOLD M. MARTINEZ,** born Oakland, California, March 17, 1971; admitted to bar, 1996, California. *Education:* University of California (B.S., 1993); University of California, Hastings College of the Law (J.D., 1996). Phi Delta Phi (Vice Magister, 1994-1995). *Member:* Fresno County Bar Association. **PRACTICE AREAS:** Insurance Coverage. *Email:* rmartine@mbswc.com

### OF COUNSEL

**DEBORAH A. BYRON,** born Fresno, California, February 24, 1951; admitted to bar, 1982, California and U.S. District Court, Eastern and Central Districts of California; 1987, U.S. Court of Appeals, Ninth Circuit; 1988, U.S. District Court, Northern District of California. *Education:* California State University at Fresno (B.A., cum laude, 1974); San Joaquin, College of Law (J.D., valedictorian, 1982). Senior Research Attorney, Fifth District Court of Appeals. *Member:* Fresno County and American Bar Associations; The State Bar of California. **PRACTICE AREAS:** Employment Law. *Email:* dbyron@mbswc.com

GENERAL COUNSEL FOR: ValliWide Bank; Bank of Stockton; ValliCorp.; Kings River State Bank; Deniz Packing Incorporated; Setton Pistachio of Terra Bella, Inc.; Farmers Firebaugh Ginning Company; TVK Containers, Inc.; Ranchwood Homes; Granville Homes; Trend Homes; McCaffrey Development LP; Diversified Development; Piccolo's Franchising Corp.; California State University Fresno Foundation; Central California Blood Center; Valley Children's Hospital; O.P.C. Farms.
LOCAL COUNSEL FOR: Helena Chemical Co.; Patriot Homes; Wilbur-Ellis (Chemicals); Setton International Foods, Inc.; Fruehauf Corp.; U S Homes; Dentel; Stewart Enterprises; Santa Ana and Fresno Land Co.
TRIAL COUNSEL FOR: Aetna Life and Casualty Co.; Allstate Insurance Co.; American States Insurance Co.; Colonial Penn; CNA; Crum & Forster Insurance CSE Insurance Group; The Dentist's Insurance Co.;Farmer's Insurance Group; Fireman's Fund Insurance Co.; Hartford Accident & Indemnity Co.; Industrial Indemnity; Insurance Company of the West; Kemper Insurance Group; Maryland Casualty Co.; Nationwide Ins. Co.; Nobel Insurance Co.; Northland Insurance Co.; Oregon Mutual Insurance Co.; Pioneer Life Insurance Co.; Prudential Property & Casualty Ins. Co.; Republic Insurance Co.; The Travelers Insurance Co.; State Farm Fire & Casualty Co.; Special District Risk Management Authority; County of Fresno; FMA Corp.; Chicago Title Insurance Co.; First American Title Insurance Company; GS Roofing Product Company, Inc.; U-Haul International Corporation; Save Mart Supermarkets, Inc.; California Bankers Association; California State Automobile Assn.; American International Group; Lawyers Mutual Insurance Co.; St. Agnes Hospital; Norcal Ins. Co.; Physicians & Surgeons Ins. Co.; CAMICO; American Sentinel Ins. Co.; Zurich American; Reliance Ins. Co.; Mercury Ins. Co.; CIGNA.

## PAMELA J. McFARLAND
*600 WEST SHAW AVENUE, SUITE 210*
*FRESNO, CALIFORNIA 93704*
Telephone: 209-225-8895
Fax: 209-225-5908

*Family Law, Domestic Relations and Child Custody.*

**PAMELA J. MCFARLAND,** admitted to bar, 1985, California; U.S. District Court, Eastern District of California. *Education:* San Joaquin College; San Joaquin College of Law (J.D., 1985). *Member:* Fresno County and American Bar Associations; State Bar of California. *PRACTICE AREAS:* Family Law; Domestic Relations; Child Custody.

## McGREGOR, DAHL, SULLIVAN & KLUG
*7080 NORTH WHITNEY AVENUE, SUITE 105*
*FRESNO, CALIFORNIA 93720-0154*
Telephone: 209-322-9292
FAX: 209-322-9191

*Estate Planning, Trust and Estate Administration, Taxation, Business Transactions, Real Estate, Water and Environmental Law.*

**WILLIAM A. DAHL,** born Evanston, Illinois, February 5, 1947; admitted to bar, 1972, California. *Education:* Yale University (A.B., cum laude, 1969); Stanford University (J.D., 1972). Co-Author: "San Jose, The Sprawling City," Stanford Environmental Law Society, 1970. Moderator: "California Boundary Law," 1993, National Business Institute. *Member:* Fresno County and American (Member, Real Property, Probate and Trust Law Section) Bar Associations; State Bar of California. [Capt., USMC, 1972-1976]. *REPORTED CASES:* Menefee v. County of Fresno (Brewer-Kalar) 163 C.A. 3d 1175. *PRACTICE AREAS:* Estate Planning Law; Real Estate Law; Water Law; Environmental Law.

**KENNETH M. KLUG,** born New York, N.Y., June 15, 1947; admitted to bar, 1973, California. *Education:* University of California at Santa Barbara (A.B., 1969); Hastings College of Law, University of California (J.D., 1972). Speaker on Estate Tax Planning at: 1982 Texas Tax Institute-ABA Joint Seminar on Post-Mortem Tax Planning; 1983 and 1991 UCLA-CEB Estate Planning Institutes; 1987 and 1990 USC Tax Institutes; 1991 Southern California Tax and Estate Planning Forum; 1994 Hawaii Tax Institute. Author: "Estate Planning for Farmers," California Continuing Education for the Bar, 1987. *Member:* Fresno County (Chair, Estate Planning, Probate and Trust Law Section, 1980) and American (Chair, Task Force on Special Valuation, 1984-1988; Chair, Forum Committee on Rural Lawyers and Agribusiness, 1988-1990; Section of Real Property, Probate and Trust Law) Bar Associations; State Bar of California (Chair, Estate Planning, Trust and Probate Law Section, 1984-1985; Member, Probate and Trust Law Advisory Commission, California Board of Legal Specialization, 1988-1991); Fellow, American College of Trust and Estate Counsel; American Law Institute. [Capt., USAR, 1972-1980]. (Certified Specialist, Probate, Estate Planning and Trust Law, The State Bar of California Board of Legal Specialization). *PRACTICE AREAS:* Probate Law; Estate Planning Law; Trust Administration Law.

**JOHN J. MCGREGOR,** born Fort Knox, Kentucky, November 18, 1946; admitted to bar, 1972, California. *Education:* University of San Francisco (A.B., 1968); Hastings College of Law, University of California (J.D., 1971); New York University (LL.M. in Taxation, 1974). Author: "Taxation of Real Property Transfers," California Continuing Education of the Bar, 1981, and supplements; "Collection of Delinquent Federal Taxes," 28 U.S.C. Tax. Inst. 589, 1976. Member, Fresno County Assessment Appeals Board, 1993–. Fresno County Assessment Appeals Board, 1993–. *Member:* Fresno County Bar Association (Director, 1983-1986; President, Young Lawyers Association, 1982); State Bar of California (Member, Executive Committee, 1983-1986 and Chair, Standards of Tax Practice Committee, 1994-1995, Taxation Section); American Law Institute. (Certified Specialist, Taxation Law, The State Bar of California Board of Legal Specialization). *REPORTED CASES:* Zaninovich v. Commissioner 616 F2d 429; Giannini Packing Corp. v. Commissioner 83 TC 526; Salwasser v. Commissioner, 1991-466. *PRACTICE AREAS:* Tax Planning; Tax Litigation; Business Transactions.

**ROBERT L. SULLIVAN, JR.,** born Hanford, California, October 16, 1942; admitted to bar, 1968, California. *Education:* University of California at Berkeley (B.S., 1964); University of San Francisco (J.D., 1967). Member, McAuliffe Law Honor Society. Editor-in-Chief, University of San Francisco Law Review, 1966-1967. Fresno Estate Planning Council, President,

*(This Listing Continued)*

1982-1983. Member, California Taxation Law Advisory Commission, California Board of Legal Specialization, 1988-1989. *Member:* Fresno County Bar Association; State Bar of California (Chair, Estate Planning, Trust and Probate Law Section Executive Committee, 1994-1995); Fellow, American College of Trust and Estate Counsel. (Certified Specialist, Taxation Law and Estate Planning, Trust and Probate Law, The State of California Board of Legal Specialization). *PRACTICE AREAS:* Estate and Tax Planning Law; Trust and Estate Administration Law; Taxation Law.

REPRESENTATIVE CLIENTS: Albrecht Farms; Angiola Water District; Bank of America NT&SA Trust Department; Bidart Bros.; Central California Faculty Medical Group; Community Emergency Medical Group; Corrin Produce Sales, Inc.; Danish Creamery Cooperative Assoc.; Foster Poultry Farms; Fresno Imaging Center; Gary L. McDonald Construction Co., Inc.; George Bros., Inc.; Gertrude and Mortimer May Foundation; MJW Storage, Inc.; Producers Packing Corporation; Regency Bank; Recency Services Corp.; Sadoian Bros., Inc.; Valley Children's Emergency Medical Group; Wells Fargo Bank, N.A. Trust Department.

## WILLIAM R. McPIKE
*4270 N. BLACKSTONE AVENUE, SUITE 315*
*FRESNO, CALIFORNIA 93726*
Telephone: 209-224-6363
Facsimile: 209-224-3239
Email: Mcpike@pacbell.net

*Civil Trial Practice. Unlawful Detainers, Bankruptcy Filings, Personal Injury, Estate Planning, Probate, Collections, Offshore Banking and Asset Protection.*

**WILLIAM R. MCPIKE,** born 1951; admitted to bar, 1980, California. *Education:* Fresno State College (B.A.); Humphreys College (J.D.). *PRACTICE AREAS:* Personal Injury Law (50); Bankruptcy Law (40); Real Property Law (300); Creditor-Debtor (150); Probate-Estate Law (20).

*ASSOCIATE*

**JUDITH TUTTLE,** born Fullerton, California, April 21, 1950; admitted to bar, 1995, California. *Education:* San Joaquin College of Law (J.D., 1995). *PRACTICE AREAS:* Civil Litigation; Unlawful Detainers; BankruptcyChapter 7 and 13; Family Trusts.

REPRESENTATIVE CLIENTS: Central Valley Commercial Corporation; Biola Recycling.

## MILES, SEARS & EANNI
*A PROFESSIONAL CORPORATION*
Established in 1956
*2844 FRESNO STREET*
*P.O. BOX 1432*
*FRESNO, CALIFORNIA 93716*
Telephone: 209-486-5200
Fax: 209-486-5240

*Practice limited to Plaintiff's Civil Litigation, Personal Injury, Product Liability and Wrongful Death.*

FIRM PROFILE: The Law Firm of Miles, Sears & Eanni, A Professional Corporation, has been in the practice of Plaintiff Civil Litigation, with an emphasis on Personal Injury Litigation on behalf of injured persons, since 1956. The Firm's offices are located in one of Fresno, California's unique Registered Historic Landmarks, the Brix Mansion, built in 1910.

*The Firm primarily represents victims of various types of accidents, as well as those who have suffered damages because of other wrongful conduct.*

*Clients of Miles, Sears & Eanni can expect that they will receive the best possible representation, settlement or verdict because of the Firm's diligence, experience, reputation and respect in the legal community, the courts and the insurance industry.*

**WM. M. MILES** (1909-1991).

**ROBERT E. SEARS** (1918-1992).

**CARMEN A. EANNI,** born Dover, New Jersey, July 16, 1934; admitted to bar, 1964, California and U.S. Court of Appeals, Ninth Circuit; 1965, U.S. District Court, Eastern District of California. *Education:* Fresno City College (A.A., 1959); San Francisco State College (B.A., 1960); Hastings College of Law, University of California (J.D., 1963). Deputy District Attorney, Fresno County, 1964-1965. *Member:* Fresno County and American Bar Associations; The State Bar of California (Member, Disciplinary Review Department of the State Bar Court, 1979-1984); Fresno Barristers Club (Secretary, 1965); California Trial Lawyers Association (President,

*(This Listing Continued)*

**MILES, SEARS & EANNI,** A PROFESSIONAL CORPORATION, Fresno—Continued

Fresno Chapter, 1969-1971; Chairman, Recognition of Experience Committee, Fresno Chapter, 1979-1980; Recognized Experience as a Trial Lawyer in the fields of General Personal Injury, Products Liability and Professional Negligence); American Board of Trial Advocates (Advocate; President, San Joaquin Valley Chapter, 1982-1983). [U.S. Army, 1955-1958]. *PRACTICE AREAS:* Personal Injury (Plaintiff) Law; Litigation; Crop Damage; Agricultural Law.

**RICHARD C. WATTERS,** born Fresno, California, August 9, 1947; admitted to bar, 1974, California and U.S. District Court, Eastern District of California; 1976, U.S. District Court, Northern District of California; 1981, U.S. Court of Appeals, Ninth Circuit; 1982, U.S. Supreme Court. *Education:* Fresno State College (B.S., cum laude, 1969; M.B.A., 1970); University of Santa Clara (J.D., 1973). Moot Court Board, 1972-1973. *Member:* Fresno County and American Bar Associations; The State Bar of California; The Association of Trial Lawyers of America; American Board of Trial Advocates (Advocate; President, San Joaquin Valley Chapter, 1994-1996). Fellow: International Society of Barristers; American College of Trial Lawyers. Board Certified Civil Trial Advocate by the National Board of Trial Advocacy. [Sgt., California Air National Guard, 1966-1972]. *PRACTICE AREAS:* Personal Injury (Plaintiff) Law; Litigation.

**GERALD J. MAGLIO,** born San Francisco, California, July 3, 1942; admitted to bar, 1971, California. *Education:* Fresno State College (A.B., 1966); Boalt Hall School of Law, University of California (J.D., 1970). *Member:* Fresno County Bar Association; The State Bar of California; California Trial Lawyers Association; American Board of Trial Advocates (Associate). *PRACTICE AREAS:* Personal Injury (Plaintiff) Law and related Litigation.

**WILLIAM J. SEILER,** born Reno, Nevada, October 22, 1947; admitted to bar, 1975, California. *Education:* Chico State University (B.A., summa cum laude, 1969); University of California at Davis (J.D., 1975). Phi Eta Sigma. Professor, Legal Methods, San Joaquin College of Law, 1978-1982. *Member:* Fresno County Bar Association; The State Bar of California. [Lt., U.S. Army, 1969-1972]. *PRACTICE AREAS:* Plaintiffs Personal Injury Law and Related Litigation.

**DOUGLAS L. GORDON,** born Florence, South Carolina, January 27, 1961; admitted to bar, 1993, California. *Education:* Wake Forest University (B.A., cum laude, 1983); University of South Carolina (M.A., 1987); University of California, Hastings College of Law (J.D., 1992). Note Editor, Hastings Comm/Ent Law Journal. Member, Moot Court Board. *Member:* Fresno County Bar Association; State Bar of California. *PRACTICE AREAS:* Plaintiffs Personal Injury Law and related Litigation.

---

## JOHN H. MISSIRLIAN
*6435 NORTH PALM AVENUE, SUITE 106*
**FRESNO, CALIFORNIA 93704**
Telephone: 209-439-3600
Fax: 209-439-5699
Email: missirlian@world.net.att.net

*Business, Business Transactions, Taxation, Probate and Estate Planning, Real Estate and Commercial Law.*

**JOHN H. MISSIRLIAN,** born Chicago, Illinois, August 21, 1950; admitted to bar, 1975, California and U.S. District Court, Eastern District of California; 1982, U.S. Tax Court. *Education:* University of California at Los Angeles (B.A., 1972); Southwestern University (J.D., 1975); McGeorge School of Law, University of the Pacific (LL.M., 1982). Instructor: Business Law, General Law and Real Estate Law, Fresno City College, 1976-1978; Legal Research, Moot Court, Professional Responsibility, Legal Analysis, San Joaquin College of Law, 1976-1980; Tax Research, San Joaquin College of Law, 1985-1988. Member, Fresno County Tax Assessment Appeals Board, 1979-1980. *Member:* Fresno County (Member: Estate Planning, Income Tax and Probate Section; Business Law Section) and American Bar Associations; State Bar of California (Member, Taxation Section).

---

## MOTSCHIEDLER, MICHAELIDES & WISHON
*Established in 1977*
*1690 WEST SHAW AVENUE*
**SUITE 200**
**FRESNO, CALIFORNIA 93711**
Telephone: 209-439-4000
Telecopier: 209-439-5654

*Civil Trial Litigation in all State and Federal Courts, Construction, Environmental, Real Estate, Real Property, Finance, Banking, Land Use Planning, Business Transactions, Corporate, Partnership, Probate and Estate Planning, Administrative, Government, Commercial Litigation, Agricultural Law, Bankruptcy, Insolvency and Employment Law.*

*FIRM PROFILE:* Motschiedler, Michaelides & Wishon is a Fresno, California law firm established in 1977. Since its existence the firm emphasizes real property, land use law, finance, business transaction, commercial litigation and estate planning. The firm has now expanded its practice to include bankruptcy, insolvency and employment law. The firm's clients include local, state and national entities in connection with transactional services and representation in state or federal courts.

**J. CARL MOTSCHIEDLER,** born Baltimore, Maryland, October 2, 1942; admitted to bar, 1969, California. *Education:* Pacific Union College; California State University at Fresno (B.S., summa cum laude, 1965); Boalt Hall School of Law, University of California (J.D., 1968). Beta Gamma Sigma; Phi Kappa Phi. *Member:* Fresno County and American Bar Associations; State Bar of California. *PRACTICE AREAS:* Land Use Development; Real Property; Business Law; Finance.

**PHILLIP G. MICHAELIDES,** born Fresno, California, October 9, 1952; admitted to bar, 1977, California. *Education:* University of Southern California (B.S., cum laude, 1974); University of Santa Clara (J.D., summa cum laude, Phi Kappa Phi, 1977). *Member:* Fresno County and American Bar Associations; State Bar of California. *PRACTICE AREAS:* Real Property Transactions; Real Property Finance; Business Transactions.

**A. EMORY WISHON, III,** born San Mateo, California, July 27, 1945; admitted to bar, 1980, California. *Education:* Brown University (A.B., 1967); University of California at Berkeley (M.B.A., 1968); Stanford University (J.D., 1980). *Member:* Fresno County Bar Association; The State Bar of California. *PRACTICE AREAS:* Real Property Law; Business Law; Partnership; Corporate Law; Probate; Estate Planning.

**JAMES A. McKELVEY,** born Greeley, Colorado, January 20, 1940; admitted to bar, 1966, California. *Education:* Fresno State College (B.S.); University of California, Boalt Hall School of Law (J.D.). Fresno City Attorney, 1978-1987. *Member:* State Bar of California. *PRACTICE AREAS:* Real Estate Law.

**C. WILLIAM BREWER,** born July 9, 1945; admitted to bar, 1976, California. *Education:* United States Naval Academy (B.S., 1967); College of Law at San Joaquin (J.D., 1976). *Member:* Fresno County Bar Association; State Bar of California (Member, Real Property Law Section). *PRACTICE AREAS:* Real Estate Law/Land Use Development; Civil Litigation; Eminent Domain Law; Inverse Condemnation Law; Regulatory Takings Law.

**MYRON F. SMITH,** born Kansas City, Missouri, December 29, 1947; admitted to bar, 1976, California. *Education:* University of Missouri (B.A., 1970); McGeorge School of Law, University of the Pacific (J.D., 1976). Deputy District Attorney, San Joaquin County, California, 1976-1980. *Member:* Fresno County Bar Associations; State Bar of California. *PRACTICE AREAS:* Business Law; Construction Litigation; Insurance Coverage Litigation.

**DAVID R. JENKINS,** born Hammond, Louisiana, September 6, 1955; admitted to bar, 1980, California; 1988, U.S. Supreme Court. *Education:* St. Mary's College of California (B.A., 1977); University of California at Davis (J.D., 1980). Law Clerk to Hon. J.W. Hedrick, Jr., Bankruptcy Judge, U.S. Bankruptcy Court Eastern District of California, 1981-1983. *Member:* Fresno County Bar Association; State Bar of California; Central Valley Bankruptcy Association. *PRACTICE AREAS:* Bankruptcy Law; Debtor/-Creditor Practice.

**RUSSELL K. RYAN,** born Porterville, California, September 28, 1961; admitted to bar, 1989, California. *Education:* Brigham Young University (B.S., cum laude, 1985); Boalt Hall School of Law, University of California at Berkeley (J.D., 1988). Psi Chi. Law Clerk to Honorable Aldon J. Anderson, U.S. District Court, District of Utah, 1988-1989. Adjunct Professor,

*(This Listing Continued)*

Commercial and Insurance Law, San Joaquin College of Law, 1992—. *Member:* Madera County (President, 1994), Fresno County and American Bar Associations; State Bar of California. **PRACTICE AREAS:** Labor and Employment Law; Business and Employment Litigation; Real Estate Law; Unfair Competition; Appellate Practice.

**BARBARA A. MCAULIFFE,** born September 8, 1958; admitted to bar, 1989, California. *Education:* Louisiana State University (B.S., 1980); University of San Diego (J.D., magna cum laude, 1989). Member, 1987-1989 and Executive Editor, 1988-1989, San Diego Law Review. *Member:* Fresno County Bar Association; State Bar of California. **PRACTICE AREAS:** Business Litigation; Construction Law; Employment Law.

REPRESENTATIVE CLIENTS: Stanley Spano; Civic Center Square, Inc.; Assemi Development; ValliWide Bank; Spencer Enterprises, Inc.; Harris Construction Company; Derrel's Mini Storage, Inc.; the Ball Family; Robert M. Mochizuki; McDonald's; Coombs, Inc.; Graham Development Company; The Mutual Life Insurance Company of New York; Sienna Corporation; Wathen-Castanos, Inc.; Madera Community Hospital; Berry Construction; Dole Dried Fruit and Nut Company; Hershey Foods; Costco.
REFERENCES: Regency Bank, Fresno, CA.

## MUSICK, PEELER & GARRETT LLP

*Established in 1954*

**6041 NORTH FIRST STREET**
**FRESNO, CALIFORNIA 93710-5444**
*Telephone: 209-228-1000*
*Facsimile: 209-447-4670*

*Los Angeles, California Office:* Suite 2000, One Wilshire Boulevard. Telephone: 213-629-7600. Facsimile: 213-624-1376.
*San Diego, California Office:* 1900 Home Savings Tower, 225 Broadway. Telephone: 619-231-2500. Facsimile: 619-231-1234.
*San Francisco, California Office:* Suite 1300, Steuart Street Tower, One Market Plaza. Telephone: 415-281-2000. Facsimile: 415-281-2010.
*Sacramento, California Office:* Wells Fargo Center, Suite 1280, 400 Capitol Mall. Telephone: 916-557-8300. Facsimile: 916-442-8629.
*Irvine, California Office:* 2603 Main Street, Suite 1025. Telephone: 714-852-5122. Facsimile: 714-852-5128.

*General Practice. Trial and Appellate Practice. Corporation, Securities and Antitrust Law. Healthcare, Hospital, College and University Law. Insurance, Excess, Reinsurance and Coverage. Labor, Real Estate, Land Use, Environmental, Eminent Domain, Oil and Gas and Mining Law. Taxation, Trust, Probate, Estate Planning, Bankruptcy and Pension and Profit Sharing.*

### MEMBERS OF FIRM

**DONALD P. ASPERGER,** born Fresno, California, June 2, 1955; admitted to bar, 1980, California; 1983, U.S. Tax Court. *Education:* University of California at Davis (A.B., with honors, 1977); University of California, Boalt Hall School of Law (J.D., 1980). **PRACTICE AREAS:** Business Transactions; Corporate Law; Estate Planning; Securities Regulation.

**JAMES B. BETTS,** born Oxnard, California, December 10, 1957; admitted to bar, 1983, California. *Education:* University of California, San Diego (B.A., 1980); University of Santa Clara (J.D., 1983). **PRACTICE AREAS:** Litigation; Labor and Employment.

**STEPHEN A. HANSEN,** born Lodi, California, December 9, 1943; admitted to bar, 1974, California; 1975, U.S. Tax Court. *Education:* University of California at Berkeley (B.A., 1966; M. Crim., 1969); University of Southern California (M.B.A., 1972); University of San Francisco (J.D., cum laude, 1974). **PRACTICE AREAS:** Healthcare; Hospitals; Corporate Law.

**JANET L. WRIGHT,** born Missoula, Montana, November 11, 1946; admitted to bar, 1972, California. *Education:* University of California at Santa Barbara (B.A., 1968); University of Southern California (J.D., 1971). **PRACTICE AREAS:** Estate Planning and Administration; Agricultural Law; Taxation; Tax Exempt Entities; General Business Law.

### ASSOCIATES

**Heather Bussing; Kathleen A. McKnight.**

## MYERS & OVERSTREET

*A PROFESSIONAL CORPORATION*

*Established in 1984*

**1130 EAST SHAW AVENUE, SUITE 200**
**FRESNO, CALIFORNIA 93710-1592**
*Telephone: 209-222-1005*
*Fax: 209-222-0702*
*URL: http://www.MyersAndOverstreet.com*

*General Civil and Trial Practice in State and Federal Courts. Insurance Litigation, including Defense, Bad Faith and Coverage, Construction Litigation, Business Litigation, Civil Rights Litigation, Public Entity Defense, Employment Law, including Discrimination and Americans with Disabilities Act (ADA) Litigation, Environmental Law, including Toxic Tort Litigation, and Products Liability.*

**GREGORY L. MYERS,** born Los Angeles, California, March 17, 1947; admitted to bar, 1980, California and U.S. District Court, Eastern and Northern Districts of California; 1981, U.S. Court of Appeals, Ninth Circuit; U.S. Supreme Court. *Education:* Fresno City College (A.A., 1974); California State University of Fresno; San Joaquin College of Law (J.D., 1980). President, San Joaquin College of Law Student Association, 1979-1980. San Joaquin College of Law Alumni Association. Adjunct Professor, Civil Litigation, San Joaquin College of Law School of Legal Assistants, 1987-1989. Faculty Member, Hastings College of Law, Center for Trial and Appellate Advocacy, 1987—. Lecturer: Bad Faith Law, Central California Adjuster's Association; Contractual Indemnity, Public Agency Risk Manager's Association; Investigating and the Civil Lawsuit and ADA Litigation, Central California Adjuster's Association. *Member:* Fresno County and American Bar Associations; State Bar of California; Northern California Defense Counsel. [With U.S. Army, 1967-1970]

**DAVID M. OVERSTREET, IV,** born Marysville, California, October 19, 1955; admitted to bar, 1982, California, U.S. Court of Appeals, Ninth Circuit and U.S. District Court, Eastern, Northern, Southern and Central Districts of California; U.S. Supreme Court. *Education:* California State University at Fresno (B.S., 1977); San Joaquin College of Law (J.D., 1981); Hastings College of Trial Advocacy, University of California (1984). San Joaquin College of Law Alumni Association. Author: "Pre-Judgement Interest," The Minute Book, the Association of Municipal Court Clerks of California, Vol. 29, No. 4, December, 1983. Adjunct Professor, Evidence, San Joaquin College of Law School of Legal Assistants, 1986-1998. *Member:* Fresno County Bar Association; State Bar of California; Association of Defense Counsel (Member, Board of Directors, 1995-1997).

**MICHAEL E. LEHMAN,** born Los Angeles, California, November 25, 1956; admitted to bar, 1988, California; U.S. District Court, Eastern, Northern and Central Districts of California; U.S. Court of Appeals, Ninth Circuit and U.S. Supreme Court. *Education:* California State University at Fresno (B.A., 1978); Cleveland Marshall College of Law (J.D., 1987). Phi Alpha Delta. *Member:* Fresno County and American Bar Associations; State Bar of California.

**THOMAS P. GUARINO,** born Hanover, New Hampshire, April 22, 1960; admitted to bar, 1989, Arkansas and U.S. District Court, Eastern and Western Districts of Arkansas; 1990, California, U.S. District Court, Eastern, Northern and Southern Districts of California; U.S. Court of Appeals, Ninth Circuit; U.S. Supreme Court. *Education:* American Institute of Banking (Diploma, 1982); Vermont Law Enforcement Training Program (1985); Castleton State College (B.A. with greatest distinction, 1985); Marshall-Wythe School of Law, International Law, Summer Program at London, England and Exeter Universities, England; University of Arkansas (J.D., 1988; LL.M., 1990); Hastings College of Advocacy (1995). Delta Theta Phi. Author: "Update on Veterinarian Malpractice," Agricultural Law Update, Vol. 7, December, 1989; "Renewal of Water Contracts," Agricultural Law Update, Vol. 10, June. 1993. *Member:* Fresno County, Arkansas and American Bar Associations; The State Bar of California.; American Agricultural Association. [U.S.N., 1977-1979]

**HARVIE RUTH SCHNITZER,** born Las Vegas, Nevada, March 17, 1965; admitted to bar, 1992, California and U.S. District Court, Eastern, Northern, Central and Southern Districts of California; U.S. Court of Appeals, Ninth Circuit. *Education:* California State University at Fresno (B.A. cum laude in Journalism and English, 1989); Golden Gate University (J.D., cum laude, 1992). Recipient, American Jurisprudence Award, Torts and Remedies. *Member:* Fresno County and American Bar Associations; Fresno County Women Lawyers; San Joaquin Valley Inn, American Inns of Court.

*(This Listing Continued)*

**MYERS & OVERSTREET, A PROFESSIONAL CORPORATION,**
Fresno—Continued

**C. MICHAEL CARRIGAN,** born Wichita, Kansas, March 18, 1960; admitted to bar, 1992, California; U.S. District Court, Eastern District of California and U.S. Court of Appeals, Ninth Circuit. *Education:* San Joaquin College of Law (Certificate, Paralegal Training, 1988; J.D., 1992). Quarterfinalist, Annual George Hopper Moot Court Competition, 1989. Judge, Annual George Hopper Moot Court Competition. Instructor, Adjunct Faculty, San Jaoquin College of Law Paralegal. San Joaquin College of Law Alumni Association. *Member:* Fresno County Bar Association; State Bar of California.

**BARBARA L. SCHARTON,** born Blythe, California, March 16, 1961; admitted to bar, 1994, California; U.S. District Court, Eastern and Southern Districts of California. *Education:* San Joaquin College of Law (J.D., 1993). *Member:* Fresno County and American Bar Associations; State Bar of California; Fresno County Young Lawyers Association.

**LORI R. MAYFIELD,** born Del Rio, Texas, June 11, 1963; admitted to bar, 1994, California and U.S. District Court, Eastern District of California. *Education:* Western Washington University-Bellingham (B.A. in Journalism, 1985); San Joaquin College of Law (J.D. with distinction, 1994). *Member:* Fresno County and American Bar Associations; State Bar of California; Fresno County Young Lawyers Association.

## NUTTALL BERMAN ATTORNEYS

A Partnership including a Professional Corporation

*Established in 1980*

2333 MERCED STREET
**FRESNO, CALIFORNIA 93721**
Telephone: 209-233-2333
Fax: 209-233-6947
Email: dfndr@cybergate.com

*Criminal Trial and Appellate Practice and Plaintiffs Personal Injury Law.*

### MEMBERS OF FIRM

**ROGER T. NUTTALL, (INC.),** born Fresno, California, December 19, 1939; admitted to bar, 1969, California; 1981, Utah. *Education:* San Francisco State University (B.A., 1962); Hastings College of Law, University of California (J.D., 1968). *Member:* Fresno County Bar Association; Utah State Bar; State Bar of California; California Trial Lawyers Association; Utah Trial Lawyers Association; Fresno Trial Lawyers Association (President, 1978); California Attorneys for Criminal Justice. Fellow, American Board of Criminal Lawyers. *REPORTED CASES:* Robert Owen Stewart vs. The Justice Court for Avenal Judicial District of Kings County, 74 CA 3d 607; 141 Cal.Rptr. 589. *PRACTICE AREAS:* Accident and Personal Injury; Plaintiff's Trial Practice; Criminal Trial Practice; White Collar Criminal Defense; Professional Disciplinary Matters.

**RICHARD P. BERMAN,** born Los Angeles, California, October 26, 1946; admitted to bar, 1973, California. *Education:* University of California at Los Angeles (B.A., 1968); (Distinguished Military Graduate); Hastings College of Law, University of California (J.D., 1972). Phi Alpha Delta. Listed, Best Lawyers in America, Criminal Defense, 1987. Instructor, Criminal Law, Fresno City College and State Center Peace Officers Academy, 1974-1979. Deputy District Attorney, 1972-1977 and Chief Deputy, 1977, Fresno County. Dean's Advisory Council, California State University, Fresno, School of Social Sciences, 1986—. *Member:* Fresno County Bar Association (Director, 1992-1994; President, 1994-1995; Chair, Criminal Law Section, 1982, 1984. Chair, Bench, Bar and Media Committee, 1990. Member, Blue Ribbon Committee on Court Coordination); State Bar of California (Member, State Bar Public Affairs Committee, 1986-1989); California Trial Lawyers Association (Recognized Experience as a Trial Lawyer and in the Field of Criminal Defense); Fresno Trial Lawyers Association (Director, 1979-1985); California Attorneys for Criminal Justice (Member and Patron, Board of Governors, 1983-1989, 1992—); National Association of Criminal Defense Lawyers (Life Member); Federal Bar Association; American Inns of Court (Master). [Capt., USAR, Medical Service Corps, 1975-1979]. *PRACTICE AREAS:* Criminal Law; White Collar Criminal Defense; Sexual Assault Law; Drug Traffic Offenses; Homicides.

*(This Listing Continued)*

### ASSOCIATES

**MARK W. COLEMAN,** born Reedley, California, July 4, 1956; admitted to bar, 1984, California; 1986, U.S. District Court, Eastern District of California and U.S. Court of Appeals, Ninth Circuit. *Education:* University of California at San Diego; San Joaquin College of Law (J.D., 1984). Assistant Federal Defender, 1988-1990. *Member:* Fresno County Bar Association; State Bar of California; California Attorneys for Criminal Justice; Fresno Attorneys for Criminal Justice; California Trial Lawyers Association; National Association of Criminal Defense Attorneys. *PRACTICE AREAS:* Personal Injury Law; Plaintiffs Trial Practice; Criminal Defense Trial Practice (with emphasis on Defense of Federal Prosecutions).

## LAW OFFICE OF
## JOHN K. ORMOND

5151 NORTH PALM, SUITE 10
P.O. BOX 28532
**FRESNO, CALIFORNIA 93729-8532**
Telephone: 209-221-8100
Fax: 209-226-8024

*Personal Injury (Plaintiff and Defense), Products Liability, Construction Disputes, Defamation, Agents and Brokers Liability.*

**JOHN K. ORMOND,** born Reno, Nevada, September 21, 1949; admitted to bar, 1979, California; 1980, U.S. District Court, Eastern District of California; 1981, U.S. Court of Appeals, Ninth Circuit; 1982, U.S. District Court, Southern District of California; 1983, U.S. District Court, Northern District of California. *Education:* University of California at Irvine (B.A., 1975); University of California at Los Angeles (J.D., 1978). *Member:* State Bar of California. *PRACTICE AREAS:* Personal Injury (Plaintiff and Defense); Products Liability; Construction Disputes; Defamation; Agents and Brokers Liability.

## PARICHAN, RENBERG, CROSSMAN & HARVEY

LAW CORPORATION
*Established in 1975*

SUITE 130, 2350 WEST SHAW AVENUE
P.O. BOX 9950
**FRESNO, CALIFORNIA 93794-0950**
Telephone: 209-431-6300
Fax: 209-432-1018

*Civil Litigation. Insurance Defense, Personal Injury, Products Liability, Business, Corporate, Probate and Estate Planning, Agricultural Law, Environmental Law.*

**HAROLD A. PARICHAN,** born Reedley, California, November 23, 1923; admitted to bar, 1949, California and U.S. District Court, Northern and Eastern Districts of California. *Education:* University of California at Berkeley (B.S., 1944); Harvard University and Stanford University (J.D., 1948). Member, Board of Visitors, Stanford University, 1977-1980. *Member:* Fresno County, American and International Bar Associations; State Bar of California; American Board of Trial Advocates; Association of Defense Counsel of Northern California. Fellow, American Bar Foundation. *PRACTICE AREAS:* Products Liability Law.

**CHARLES L. RENBERG,** born Orangeville, Utah, September 18, 1932; admitted to bar, 1963, California and U.S. Court of Appeals, Ninth Circuit; 1967, U.S. District Court, Eastern District of California. *Education:* University of California at San Francisco (B.A., 1959); Hastings College of Law, University of California (J.D., 1962). *Member:* Fresno County Bar Association; State Bar of California; American Bar Association (Member Sections on: Litigation; Tort and Insurance); Defense Research Institute; Association of Defense Counsel of Northern California. *PRACTICE AREAS:* Insurance Defense Law and Coverage; Environmental; Products Liability and Litigation.

**RICHARD C. CROSSMAN,** born Boston, Massachusetts, December 29, 1941; admitted to bar, 1971, California and U.S. District Court, Eastern District of California; 1981, U.S. District Court, Northern District of California and U.S. Court of Appeals, Ninth Circuit. *Education:* California State University at Fresno (B.A., 1966); Hastings College of Law, University of California (J.D., 1970). *Member:* Fresno County and American

*(This Listing Continued)*

# PROFESSIONAL BIOGRAPHIES

(Member, Sections on: Litigation; Tort and Insurance Practice) Bar Associations; State Bar of California; American Board of Trial Advocates; Association of Defense Counsel of Northern California. *PRACTICE AREAS:* Insurance Defense and Coverage; Products Liability; Business; Environmental and General Litigation.

**IMA JEAN HARVEY,** born Ninnekah, Oklahoma, September 12, 1927; admitted to bar, 1975, California and U.S. District Court, Eastern District of California and U.S. Court of Appeals, Ninth Circuit; 1977, U.S. District Court, Central District of California; 1981, U.S. District Court, Northern District of California. *Education:* University of California at Los Angeles; San Joaquin College of Law (J.D., 1975). Member, San Joaquin College of Law Agricultural Law Review Advisory Committee. *Member:* Fresno County and American (Member: Section of Real Property, Probate and Trust Law, Business Law and Taxation; Member, Subcommittee on Agricultural and Agri-Business Financing; Agriculture Committee Taxation Section) Bar Associations; State Bar of California (Member, Committee on Ag Law and Agri- Business; Commercial Financial Services; Sections on: Business Law; Estate Planning, Probate and Real Property); California Women Lawyers Association; Fresno County Women Lawyers. *PRACTICE AREAS:* Corporate; Business; Property; Agri-Business; Estate Planning.

**STEPHEN T. KNUDSEN,** born Winona, Minnesota, June 27, 1947; admitted to bar, 1973, California. *Education:* Claremont Men's College (B.A., 1969); University of California at Berkeley (LL.B., 1973). *Member:* Fresno County Bar Association; State Bar of California. *PRACTICE AREAS:* Insurance Defense Law; Products Liability Law.

**LARRY C. GOLLMER,** born San Diego, California, May 25, 1945; admitted to bar, 1971, California. *Education:* University of California at Los Angeles (B.A., 1967); University of Southern California (J.D., 1970). Phi Alpha Delta. *Member:* Fresno County Bar Association (Member, Attorney-Client Relations Committee, 1983—; The Arbitration Program, 1982—; Estate Planning, Probate and Real Property Section, 1983—); State Bar of California. *PRACTICE AREAS:* Corporate Law; Business Law; Probate Law.

**ROBERT G. ELIASON,** born San Jose, California, December 4, 1953; admitted to bar, 1982, California; 1983, U.S. District Court, Northern and Eastern Districts of California. *Education:* University of California at Berkeley (B.A., 1977); Hastings School of Law, University of California (J.D., 1982). *Member:* Fresno County Bar Association; State Bar of California; Association of Defense Counsel of Northern California; Defense Research Institute. *PRACTICE AREAS:* Products Liability Law; Consumer Warranty Defense Law.

**STEVEN M. MCQUILLAN,** born San Francisco, California, July 13, 1956; admitted to bar, 1982, California; 1983, U.S. District Court, Northern, Eastern, Central and Southern Districts of California and U.S. Court of Appeals, Ninth Circuit. *Education:* California State University at Chico (B.A., 1979); University of Santa Clara School of Law (J.D., 1982). *Member:* Fresno County and American (Member, Sections on: Tort and Insurance Practice Law; Litigation) Bar Associations; State Bar of California (Member, Litigation Section); Association of Defense Counsel of Northern California; Defense Research Institute (Member, ERISA-Life, Health Disability Section). *LANGUAGES:* German. *PRACTICE AREAS:* Insurance Defense and Coverage; ERISA Litigation; Environmental Litigation.

---

**DEBORAH A. COE,** born Boise, Idaho, October 24, 1951; admitted to bar, 1991, California and U.S. District Court, Eastern District of California. *Education:* Fresno City College (A.A., 1976); University of California; San Joaquin College of Law (J.D., 1991). *Member:* Fresno County and American (Member, Litigation, Torts and Personal Injury Sections) Bar Associations; State Bar of California (Member, Litigation Section); Fresno County Women Lawyers; Fresno Women's Network; Association of Defense Counsel of Northern California; Defense Research Institute. *PRACTICE AREAS:* Products Liability; Personal Injury Defense.

**MAUREEN P. HOLFORD,** born Evergreen Park, Illinois, August 20, 1951; admitted to bar, 1992, California and U.S. District Court, Eastern District of California. *Education:* San Joaquin College of Law (J.D., 1992). *Member:* Fresno County and American Bar Associations; State Bar of California; Fresno County Women Lawyer's Association; Fresno Women's Network. *PRACTICE AREAS:* Products Liability; Insurance Defense.

**KAREN L. LYNCH,** born Merced, California, December 20, 1958; admitted to bar, 1992, California and U.S. District Court, Eastern District of California; 1993, U.S. District Court, Northern District of California. *Education:* California State University, Fresno (B.A., 1981; M.A., 1989); University of Nebraska, Lincoln College of Law (J.D., 1990). Psi Chi; Delta Theta Phi; Blue Key. Listed in Who's Who Among American Law Students. Member: SABA, Environmental Law Society, 1987-1990; National Association of Public Interest Law, 1987-1990; American Psychological Association, 1980—. *Member:* Fresno County, American and Federal (Member, Young Lawyers Section) Bar Associations; State Bar of California; Fresno County Women Lawyers Association; American Trial Lawyers Association; Association of Defense Counsel of Northern California; Fresno Women's Network. *PRACTICE AREAS:* Insurance Defense; Products Liability; Federal Appeals.

**MICHAEL L. RENBERG,** born San Francisco, California, April 9, 1962; admitted to bar, 1988, California, U.S. District Court, Northern District of California and U.S. Court of Appeals, Ninth Circuit; 1989, U.S. District Court, Central and Eastern Districts of California. *Education:* University of California at Los Angeles (B.A., 1985); University of San Francisco School of Law (J.D., with honors, 1988). Extern to the Honorable David Eagleson, California Supreme Court, 1987. Law Clerk to the Honorable Robert Coyle, U.S. District Court, Eastern District of California, 1988-1989. *Member:* Fresno County (Member, Litigation Section, 1988—) and American Bar Associations; State Bar of California. *PRACTICE AREAS:* Environmental Law; Insurance Law.

REPRESENTATIVE CLIENTS: General Motors Corporation; Nissan Motor Corporation in U.S.A.; Allied Products, Corp.; Royal Insurance; National General Insurance Co.; St. Paul Insurance Co.; Safeway Stores, Inc.; Electric Motor Shop, Inc.; Orange Avenue Disposal Co.; Fowler Packing Co.; Western Pioneer Insurance Co.; The Hertz Corp.; Argonaut Insurance Co.; Continental Eagle Corp.; Data Consultants; Subaru of America; Mazda Motor of America; Makita U.S.A., Inc.; Great Dane Trailers, Inc.; Westinghouse Electric, Corp.; MBTechnology; Honda Motor Co.; A.F. Mendes & Sons Dairies; Guardsman Products, Inc.; Thrifty Payless, Inc.; Hyundai Motor America; Aon Risk Services, Inc. of Central California; Warnors Theatre; Desert Publications, Inc.; Cal Eagle Insurance; L & H Administrators; Baker & McKenzie; Motors Insurance Company; Ford New Holland; Federated Insurance Company; Fruehauf Trailer Corporation; Clark Equipment Company; Fresh Quest Produce; Case Credit Corp.; Suma Fruit; Curran Ranch; Netafim.

---

## *PERKINS, MANN & EVERETT*

*Established in 1985*

*2222 WEST SHAW, SUITE 202*
**FRESNO, CALIFORNIA 93711-3407**
*Telephone: 209-447-5700*
*Facsimile: 209-447-5600*

*General Civil and Trial Practice in State and Federal Courts. Agricultural Matters, Business, Corporation, Federal and State Taxation, Probate and Estate Planning, Real Estate, Securities Law, Commercial Law, Creditors Rights, Construction Law, Bond Law and Water Law.*

**JAN T. PERKINS,** born Long Beach, California, January 2, 1946; admitted to bar, 1973, California. *Education:* Brigham Young University (B.A., 1970); University of Utah (J.D., 1973). Vice-Chancellor, Moot Court Honor Society, 1972-1973. *Member:* Fresno County and American (Member, Sections on: Taxation, Real Property, Trust and Probate Law) Bar Associations; State Bar of California; Fresno Estate Planning Council. *LANGUAGES:* Japanese. *PRACTICE AREAS:* Real Estate; Business Organization; Taxation Law; Probate; Estate Planning; Agricultural Law.

**JERRY H. MANN,** born Los Angeles, California, June 23, 1954; admitted to bar, 1980, California and U.S. District Court Eastern and Northern Districts of California. *Education:* University of California at Berkeley (B.A., with honors, 1977); Loyola Law School (J.D., cum laude, 1980). Member, St. Thomas More Honor Society. Law Clerk to Hon. George Hopper and Hon. George N. Zenovich, Associate Justices, California Court of Appeal, Fifth District, 1980-1982. *Member:* Fresno County Bar Association (Member, Sections on: Business Law; Real Property Law); State Bar of California (Member, Litigation Section). *PRACTICE AREAS:* Civil Trial; Construction; Business; Employment; Bond Law.

**REID H. EVERETT,** born Fresno, California, April 12, 1954; admitted to bar, 1981, California, U.S. District Court, Eastern, Central, Northern and Southern Districts of California and U.S. Court of Appeals, Ninth Circuit. *Education:* Brigham Young University (B.A., magna cum laude, 1978; J.D., cum laude, 1981). Phi Kappa Phi; Phi Delta Phi. Member, Brigham Young University Journal of Legal Studies, 1980. Co-author: "Summary of Utah Family Law," Brigham Young University Journal of Legal Studies, 1980. *Member:* Fresno County (Member, Co-Founder, 1988 and Co-Chair, 1989, Business Law Section; Member, Real Property Section) and American (Member, Section on Business Law) Bar Associations; State Bar of California (Member: Section on Business Law; Appointed member, Debtor/-

*(This Listing Continued)*

### PERKINS, MANN & EVERETT, Fresno—Continued

Creditor Relations and Bankruptcy Committee, 1990-1992); American Bankruptcy Institute; Central California Bankruptcy Association; California Bankruptcy Forum; American Agricultural Law Association. *LANGUAGES:* German. *PRACTICE AREAS:* Agricultural Law; Real Property Law; Commercial Law; Secured Transactions; Creditors Rights.

#### ASSOCIATE

**LARRY B. LINDENAU,** born Concord, California, August 2, 1967; admitted to bar, 1992, California and U.S. District Court, Eastern District of California. *Education:* Brigham Young University (B.S., 1989; J.D., magna cum laude, 1992). Order of the Coif. Member, Brigham Young Law Review, 1990-1992. *Member:* Fresno County (Member, Sections on: Business Law; Real Property; Estate Planning and Probate) and American Bar Associations. *PRACTICE AREAS:* Business Law; Corporate Law; Real Estate Law; Estate Planning; Probate.

REPRESENTATIVE CLIENTS: A & M Carpet, Inc.; Agricultural Agronomics, Inc.; Agricultural Priority Pollutants Laboratories, Inc.; American Grape Harvesters, Inc; Benefit Administration Corporation; DiBuduo Land Management Co., Inc.; Fleet Bank N.A.; Gage Bros. Construction Company, Inc; Ilex Computer Corporation; James G. Parker Insurance Associates; Lincoln Mutual Life Insurance Company; Old West Ranch Company; PB Loader Corporation; Protective Life Insurance Company; Richard Heath & Associates, Inc.; Wood Recovery Systems, Inc.

---

## PHILLIPS & SPALLAS, LLP
### MAUBRIDGE BUILDING
### 2344 TULARE STREET
### FRESNO, CALIFORNIA 93721
*Telephone: 209-237-8805*
*Fax: 209-237-8812*

*San Francisco Office:* 225 Bush Street, 16th Floor. 94104. Telephone: 415-439-8870. Fax: 415-439-8822.

*San Luis Obispo Office:* 972 Santa Rosa Street. 93401. Telephone: 805-544-4875. Fax: 805-544-4877.

*General Civil Trial Practice in all State and Federal Courts.*

FIRM PROFILE: Phillips & Spallas serves the entire state and specializes in defending civil litigation lawsuits. The firm maintains fully-staffed offices in San Francisco, San Luis Obispo and Fresno and is devoted not only to defending clients in civil litigation, but to providing seminars for clients on a regular basis and encouraging partners and associates to participate in continued legal education, association activities and civic affairs.

**ROBERT K. PHILLIPS,** born Evanston, Illinois, April 22, 1958; admitted to bar, 1986, Indiana; 1988, California. *Education:* University of Arizona (B.A., 1980); Boston University (M.Th., 1982); University of Notre Dame (J.D., 1985); London School of Economics and Political Science (LL.M., 1986). *Member:* San Luis Obispo County and Fresno County Bar Associations; California State Bar; Indiana State Bar Association; International Bar Association; Association of Defense Counsel. (Also at San Luis Obispo.) *REPORTED CASES:* Creditors' Collection Service v. Hanzell Vineyards, Ltd., 5 Cal. App. 4th Supp. 1 (1992); State Farm Fire and Casualty Company v. Yu Kiyo, Ltd., et al., 870 Fed. Supp. 292 (1994); Edwards v. A.L. Lease & Co. (1st Dist., Div. 5) 46 Cal. App. 4th 1029 (1996).

REPRESENTATIVE CLIENTS: Atlas Insurance Co.; Cincinnati Insurance Cos.; Frito-Lay, Inc.; Holiday Inns, Inc.; The Kemper Insurance Group; Leader Insurance; Parnelli Jones, Inc.; Pepsi-Cola, Inc.; Pizza Hut of America, Inc.; Wal-Mart Stores, Inc.

*(For complete biographical data on all personnel, see Professional Biographies at San Francisco)*

---

## DONALD D. POGOLOFF
### 2650 WEST SHAW AVENUE, SUITE 103
### FRESNO, CALIFORNIA 93711
*Telephone: 209-432-2650*
*Telefax: 209-432-2653*

*Mental Health Law, Health Care, Hospital Law and Non-Profit Organizations.*

**DONALD D. POGOLOFF,** born San Diego, California, March 11, 1948; admitted to bar, 1972, California; 1973, U.S. District Court, Southern District of California; 1976, U.S. Supreme Court. *Education:* University of California at San Diego (B.A., 1969); University of San Diego (J.D., 1972).

*(This Listing Continued)*

Recipient: University of California Alumni Association Scholarship; U.S. Public Health Service Tuition Grant. Lecturer: Law and Nursing, College of the Sequoias, 1981—; Professor, Law and Healthcare Administration, California State University, 1987—; Lecturer, Chapman University, 1992—. Member: State Advisory Council on Family Planning, 1981-1986; Tulare County Maternal, Child and Adolescent Health Board, 1978-1986. Member, Panel of Arbitrators, American Arbitration Association, 1992. *Member:* State Bar of California (Hearing Officer, Mandatory Fee Arbitration Committee, Mandatory Fee Arbitration Division); American Bar Association (Member, Health Law Section); American Hospital Association; American Academy of Hospital Counsel; National Health Lawyers (Hearing Officer, Alternate Dispute Resolution Panel); California Association of Hospitals and Health Systems; California Healthcare Attorneys Association; Association of Mental Health Administrators; American Society of Law and Medicine; American College of Health Care Executives.

---

## RICHARDSON, JONES & ESRAELIAN
### A Partnership including a Professional Corporation
### 2660 WEST SHAW, SUITE 100
### FRESNO, CALIFORNIA 93711
*Telephone: 209-449-1028*
*Fax: 209-449-8744*

*Taxation, Probate and Estate Planning. General Corporate Practice. Pension and Profit Sharing, Real Property Law.*

#### MEMBERS OF FIRM

**BAXTER K. RICHARDSON** (1921-1992).

**ROBERT L. JONES, JR., (INC.),** born St. Louis, Missouri, June 20, 1947; admitted to bar, 1972, California; 1975, U.S. Tax Court. *Education:* University of the Pacific (B.A., 1969); University of California School of Law (J.D., 1972). *Member:* Fresno County (Member, Board of Directors, 1982-1985) and American (Member, Section on Taxation) Bar Associations; State Bar of California (Member, Sections on: Taxation; Real Property, Probate and Trust Laws). *PRACTICE AREAS:* Taxation; Probate and Estate Planning; Corporate; Pension and Profit Sharing; Real Property.

**ROBYN L. ESRAELIAN,** born Fresno, California, April 18, 1955; admitted to bar, 1980, California; 1981, U.S. Tax Court. *Education:* California State University at Fresno (B.S., 1977); McGeorge School of Law, University of the Pacific (J.D., 1980). Phi Alpha Delta. Member, Traynor Society. *Member:* Fresno County and American Bar Associations; State Bar of California. *PRACTICE AREAS:* Probate; Estate Planning; Corporate; Real Property Law.

REPRESENTATIVE CLIENTS: Hematology-Oncology Medical Group of Fresno, Inc.; Cinco Farms, Inc.; Farmers Lumber & Supply Co.; Valley Pipe and Supply, Inc.; Melkonian Enterprises, Inc.; Los Banos Gravel Company, Inc.; Wawona Frozen Foods; J. Oberti, Inc.; G. Oberti & Sons; Stamoules Produce.

---

## ROBERT J. ROSATI
### 800 M STREET
### FRESNO, CALIFORNIA 93721
*Telephone: 209-268-4021*
*Facsimile: 209-268-5446*

*Civil Trial and Appellate Practice in all Courts, Business Litigation, Insurance Coverage and Litigation, Labor and Employment, Personal Injury, Environmental and Land Use.*

**ROBERT J. ROSATI,** born Rochester, New York, September 30, 1954; admitted to bar, 1983, California; 1984, U.S. District Court, Northern District of California; U.S. District Court, Eastern District of California and U.S. Court of Appeals, Ninth Circuit. *Education:* State University of New York at Albany (B.A., magna cum laude, 1977); San Francisco State University; Hastings College of Law, University of California (J.D., 1983). *Member:* Fresno County Bar Associations; State Bar of California (Member, Labor Law and Litigation Sections).

REPRESENTATIVE CLIENTS: Garringer Adjusting Company; Yosemite Lakes' Owners Association.

## DANIEL W. ROWLEY
GUARANTEE FINANCIAL CENTER
1320 EAST SHAW AVENUE, SUITE 126
**FRESNO, CALIFORNIA 93710**
Telephone: 209-244-6940
Facsimile: 209-244-6950

*Commercial, Business and Employment Law Litigation, Civil Appeals and Writs.*

**DANIEL W. ROWLEY,** born Bell, California, November 11, 1955; admitted to bar, 1983, California; 1986, U.S. District Court, Eastern District of California; 1988, U.S. Court of Appeals, Ninth Circuit. *Education:* California State University at San Jose (B.A., 1977); Southwestern University School of Law (J.D., cum laude, 1983). Member, Moot Court Honors Program, 1981-1982. Staff Member, 1981 and Managing Editor, 1982-1983, Southwestern University Law Review. Author: Comment, "California Code of Civil Procedure Section 340.5: The Discovery Rule Codified?" 13 Southwestern University Law Review 759. Research Attorney for Honorable George A. Brown, Presiding Justice, Fifth District Court of Appeal, 1983-1985. *Member:* Fresno County and American Bar Associations; State Bar of California. *PRACTICE AREAS:* Commercial Litigation; Business Litigation; Employment Litigation.

---

## DARREL R. RUSTIGIAN
545 EAST ALLUVIAL AVENUE, SUITE 107
**FRESNO, CALIFORNIA 93720**
Telephone: 209-438-8732
Fax: 209-438-7219

*Personal Injury, Civil Litigation, Real Estate and Business Law.*

**DARREL R. RUSTIGIAN,** born Fresno, California, November 3, 1958; admitted to bar, 1985, California. *Education:* California State University at Fresno (B.A., 1980); University of San Francisco (J.D., 1984). *Member:* Fresno County Bar Association; State Bar of California; California Young Lawyers Association; Fresno County Young Lawyers Association. *PRACTICE AREAS:* Business Law; Personal Injury.

---

## SAGASER, HANSEN, FRANSON & JAMISON
A PROFESSIONAL CORPORATION
2445 CAPITOL STREET, SECOND FLOOR
P.O. BOX 1632
**FRESNO, CALIFORNIA 93717-1632**
Telephone: 209-233-4800
Fax: 209-233-9330

*Civil Trial and Appellate Practice in all State and Federal Courts. Commercial, Agricultural and Employment Litigation, Labor Relations Law (Management). Agricultural Labor, Equal Employment, Wage and Hour, Wrongful Discharge Law and Litigation and Health Care Litigation.*

**ERIC K. HANSEN** (1952-1996).

**HOWARD A. SAGASER,** born Hanford, California, January 30, 1950; admitted to bar, 1976, California. *Education:* California State Polytechnic University (B.S., 1973); Hastings College of Law, University of California (J.D., 1976). Order of the Coif; Phi Kappa Phi. Member, Thurston Society. Editorial Associate, Hastings Law Journal, 1975-1976. Extern Law Clerk to the Honorable William P. Clark, Jr., Associate Justice, California Supreme Court, 1975. Guest Speaker, "Labor Issues Affecting California Employers," California Agricultural Leadership Foundation, 1981-1994. *Member:* Fresno County Bar Association; State Bar of California. *REPORTED CASES:* Holcomb v. Bingham Toyota, 871 F.2d 109 (1989); J.R. Norton Co. Inc. v. Agricultural Labor Relations Board, 26 Cal. 3d 1, 160 Cal. Rptr. 710 (Amicus) (1979); Joe A. Freitas & Sons v. Food Packers, Processors and Warehousemen Local 865, International Brotherhood of Teamsters, 164 Cal. App. 3d 1210, 211 Cal. Rptr. 157 (1985); Quinn Company, 273 NLRB No. 107, 118 LRRM 1239 (1984); Harris Farms, Inc. v. Superior Court of Fresno County, 285 Cal. Rptr. 659, 234 Cal. App. 3d 415 (1991). *PRACTICE AREAS:* Labor (Management) Law; Labor Negotiations; Agricultural Law; Civil Rights Law; Employment Discrimination Law; Employment Law.

*(This Listing Continued)*

**DONALD R. FRANSON, JR.,** born Fresno, California, February 6, 1952; admitted to bar, 1978, California. *Education:* University of California (A.B., 1974); Hastings College of Law, University of California (J.D., 1978). Deputy District Attorney, Fresno County District Attorney's Office, 1979-1980. Executive Vice President and General Counsel, Producers Cotton Oil Co., 1988-1991. Arbitrator and Mediator, American Arbitration Association. *Member:* Fresno County Bar Association; State Bar of California (Member, Rules and Procedures of Court Committee, 1987-1989). *REPORTED CASES:* All-West Design, Inc. v. Boozer (1986); 183 Cal. App. 3d 1499, 228 Cal. Rptr. 736; Rose v. City of Coalinga (1987), 190 Ca. App. 3d 1627, 236 Cal. Rptr. 124; Stokes v. Dole Nut Co. (1995) 41 Cal.App. 4th 285; San Benito Foods v. Director of the Dept. of Food and Agricultural, State of Calif. (1996) 96 DAR 14097. *PRACTICE AREAS:* Agricultural Law; Business Litigation; Crop Damage Law; Lender Liability; Employment Litigation.

**DANIEL O. JAMISON,** born Fresno, California, November 28, 1952; admitted to bar, 1977, California and U.S. District Court, Eastern District of California; 1982, U.S. District Court, Northern District of California. *Education:* Claremont Men's College and University of California at Berkeley (A.B., 1974); University of California School of Law at Davis (J.D., 1977). Member, National Moot Court Team and Honors Moot Court Board. Law Clerk to Judge M.D. Crocker, U.S. District Court, Eastern District of California, 1977-1978. *Member:* Fresno County and American Bar Associations; State Bar of California; Northern California Association of Defense Counsel; Defense Research Institute. *REPORTED CASES:* Madera Community Hospital v. County of Madera, 155 Cal. App. 3d 136 (1984); Turpin v. Sortini, 31 Cal. 3d 220 (1982); Mateo-Woodburn v. Fresno Community Hospital 221 Cal. App. 3d 1169 (1990); Paredes v. County of Fresno 203 Cal. App. 3d 1 (1988). *PRACTICE AREAS:* Hospital Law; Health Care Law; Antitrust Law; Real Estate; Business Litigation.

**NANCY A. MALER,** born Los Angeles, California, July 9, 1962; admitted to bar, 1992, California. *Education:* University of California at San Diego (B.A., cum laude, 1984); University of California School of Law, Davis (J.D., 1992). Order of the Coif, *Member:* State Bar of California.

**KIMBERLY A. GAAB,** born Fresno, California, June 25, 1967; admitted to bar, 1993, California. *Education:* University of California at Berkeley (B.S., with high honors, 1989); Haas School of Business, University of California, Berkeley (M.B.A., 1993); University of California, Boalt Hall School of Law (J.D., Certificate in Environmental Law, 1993). Phi Beta Kappa; Beta Gamma Sigma. *Member:* Fresno County and American Bar Associations; State Bar of California.

**PATTI L. WILLIAMS,** born Oakland, California, March 27, 1962; admitted to bar, 1992, California. *Education:* University of California at Davis (B.A., 1988; J.D., 1992). *Member:* State Bar of California.

**K. PONCHO BAKER,** born Spirit, Lake, Iowa, September 25, 1960; admitted to bar, 1991, California. *Education:* Briar Cliff College (B.S., summa cum laude, 1983); University of Hastings College of the Law (J.D., 1991). *Member:* Fresno County Bar Association; Fresno County Young Lawyers (Board of Directors).

**KRISTI R. CULVER,** born Chico, California, August 1, 1963; admitted to bar, 1988, California and Nebraska; 1990, U.S. District Court, Southern, Central and Eastern Districts of California. *Education:* California State University at Chico (B.A., 1985); University of the Pacific, McGeorge School of Law (J.D., summa cum laude, 1988). Member: Order of the Coif; Traynor Honor Society. Comment and Note Editor, Pacific Law Journal, 1987-1988. Law Clerk: Hon. C.T. White, Chief Justice, Supreme Court of Nebraska, 1988-1989; Hon. Dennis L. Beck, U.S. District Court, Eastern District of California, 1993-1995. Author: "Civil RICO: Should Private Litigants Be Granted Equitable Relief?" 18 Pacific Law Journal, 1199, 1987. *Member:* Fresno County Women Lawyers.

**CATHERINE J. CERNA,** born Los Angeles, California, March 28, 1961; admitted to bar, 1995, California. *Education:* University of California at Los Angeles (B.A., 1992); Hasting College of Law (J.D, 1995). Associate Articles Editor, 45 Hasting Law Journal, 1994. Author: "Economic Theory Applied to Civil Forfeiture: Efficiency and Deference Through Reallocation of External Costs," 46 Hastings Law Journal, 1939. Extern to Judge Alex Kozinski, 9th Circuit Court of Appeals, 1993. *Member:* State Bar of California. *PRACTICE AREAS:* Business and Employment Litigation.

REPRESENTATIVE CLIENTS: Agri-Sun Nursery; Airway Farms, Inc.; Central Valley General Hospitals; City of Fresno; Community Hospitals of Central California; County of Kings; Dole Food Company; Dunavant Enterprises, Inc.; Foster Farms; Fresno Equipment Company; Fresno Unified School District; Granite Construction Company; Kings View Mental Health; Kraft General Foods; Los Gatos Tomato Products; Northwest Packing; Pandol & Sons, Inc.; Pioneer Equipment Company; Pizza Hut; Prudential Insurance Company of

*(This Listing Continued)*

## CALIFORNIA—FRESNO — MARTINDALE-HUBBELL LAW DIRECTORY 1997

**SAGASER, HANSEN, FRANSON & JAMISON,** A PROFESSIONAL CORPORATION, Fresno—Continued

America; Quinn Company; San Benito Foods; Shell Oil Company; Taco Bell Corp.; TomaTek, Inc.; Universal Foods Corp.; Unocal; Western Farm Service; Westlands Water District; Woolf Enterprises.
REFERENCE: Sanwa Bank California.

---

## SANDELL & YOUNG

An Association of Attorneys including a Professional Corporation

**SUITE B, 929 "L" STREET**
**FRESNO, CALIFORNIA 93721-2699**
Telephone: 209-445-1500
Fax: 209-445-1509

*General Civil and Trial Practice. Insurance Defense, Casualty, Surety, Personal Injury, Negligence, Probate and Estate Planning, Insurance, Appellate Practice, Products Liability, Premises Liability and Probate Law.*

**HAROLD D. SANDELL, (INC.)** (1927-1991).

**WILLIAM M. YOUNG, (INC.),** born San Francisco, California, June 10, 1931; admitted to bar, 1959, California. *Education:* University of California at Berkeley (A.B., 1953); Hastings College of the Law, University of California (J.D., 1958). Phi Alpha Delta. Assistant District Attorney, Madera County, California, 1959-1960. *Member:* Fresno County and American Bar Associations; State Bar of California; Association of Defense Counsel —Northern California. (Member, Sandell and Young, A Partnership including Professional Corporations). **PRACTICE AREAS:** Litigation; Insurance Defense; Personal Injury; Products Liability; Premises Liability; Appellate Practice.

**ROBERTA J. DUFFY,** born Fresno, California, January 23, 1957; admitted to bar, 1987, California. *Education:* California State University (B.S., 1979); San Joaquin College of Law (J.D., 1987). *Member:* Fresno County and American Bar Associations; State Bar of California; Consumer Attorneys of California; Association of Defense Counsel - Northern California. **PRACTICE AREAS:** Insurance Defense; Litigation; Personal Injury; Appellate Practice; Insurance.

REPRESENTATIVE CLIENTS: Aetna Casualty and Surety Company; American Fire and Casualty; Allstate Insurance; Avis Rent A Car System Insurance; California Casualty Indemnity Exchange; Carolina Casualty; Electric Mutual; Empire Insurance Company; Fireman's Fund American Insurance Cos.; Grange Insurance Association; Great Falls; Hanover of California; The Hartford Insurance Group; Horace Mann Insurance Company; Motors Insurance; National Auto and Casualty Insurance Co.; Stanley Works; USF&G; United Pacific/Reliance Insurance Cos.; United Service Automobile Association; West American; National General Insurance Company.

---

## GARY W. SAWYERS

**1180 EAST SHAW AVENUE**
**SUITE 214**
**FRESNO, CALIFORNIA 93710-7812**
Telephone: 209-228-8190
Facsimile: 209-225-8955
Email: gsawyers@aol.com

*Water Law, Water Rights, Agricultural Matters, Public Agency Representation, Business Law and Real Estate Transactions.*

**GARY W. SAWYERS,** born Santa Monica, California, November 24, 1955; admitted to bar, 1980, California. *Education:* University of California at San Diego, Revelle College (B.A., summa cum laude, 1977); University of California at Los Angeles (J.D., 1980). Phi Beta Kappa. Adjunct Professor of Law, San Joaquin College of Law, 1987-1989. *Member:* Fresno County Bar Association; American Agricultural Law Association.

**MELANIE J. ALDRIDGE,** born Lake Charles, Louisiana, May 28, 1963; admitted to bar, 1991, California. *Education:* California State University at Fresno (B.A., magna cum laude, 1987); University of California at Davis (J.D., 1991). *Email:* melholly@aol.com

REPRESENTATIVE CLIENTS: American West Aviation; Borba Farms, Inc.; California Farm Water Coalition; Devine and Wood Farming, Inc.; Dudley Ridge Water District; Errotabere Ranches; Family Farm Alliance; Farm Credit Services of Southern California; Friant Water Users Authority; Harris Farms, Inc.; Kings River Water Association; Lone Tree Mutual Water Company; Madera Water District; Neves Bros. Farms; The Newhall Land and Farming Company; Provost and Pritchard, Inc.; Sunny Cove Citrus Association; Westchester Group, Inc.; Western Farm Credit Bank.

CAA252B

---

## PHILIP S. SETRAKIAN

**2350 WEST SHAW AVENUE, SUITE 106**
**FRESNO, CALIFORNIA 93711**
Telephone: 209-439-7000
Fax: 209-439-7087

*Personal Injury, Plaintiff, Criminal Defense, Adult, Juvenile, Federal and State.*

**PHILIP S. SETRAKIAN,** born Fresno, California, April 6, 1947; admitted to bar, 1974, California; 1976, U.S. District Court, Eastern District of California; 1980, U.S. District Court, Southern District of California. *Education:* University of California at Santa Barbara (B.A., 1969); University of the Pacific, McGeorge School of Law (J.D., 1973). Member, Fig Garden Rotary. Board Member, Fresno County Legal Services, 1978-1979. Co-author: "Three Strikes and Your Out," Criminal Legislation. *Member:* Fresno County Bar Association; Fresno County Trial Lawyers Association.

---

## STAMMER, McKNIGHT, BARNUM & BAILEY

Established in 1916

**2540 WEST SHAW LANE, SUITE 110**
**P.O. BOX 9789**
**FRESNO, CALIFORNIA 93794-9789**
Telephone: 209-449-0571
Fax: 209-432-2619

*General Civil and Trial Practice. Insurance, Water Rights Law.*

FIRM PROFILE: *The firm was founded by Walter Stammer in 1916. He was joined by Galen McKnight in 1931. As the area's population has grown, the firm has increased in size. It began doing and still engages in general practice in State and Federal Courts including trials and appeals. The firm's practice has emphasized the fields of general negligence, products liability, insurance, all areas of professional liability, transportation, public utilities, hospital, real estate, water law and business law.*

**W. H. STAMMER** (1891-1969).

**JAMES K. BARNUM** (1918-1987).

**DEAN A. BAILEY** (1924-1995).

**GALEN McKNIGHT** (1904-1991).

**JAMES N. HAYS,** born Fresno, California, April 9, 1925; admitted to bar, 1951, California. *Education:* Stanford University (A.B., 1948; LL.B., 1950). Delta Theta Phi. *Member:* Fresno County Bar Association; State Bar of California; Association of Defense Counsel; Defense Research and Trial Lawyers Association. **PRACTICE AREAS:** Products Liability Law; Insurance Coverage Law; Real Estate; Professional Liability; Construction Litigation.

**CAREY H. JOHNSON,** born Cleveland, Ohio, April 14, 1942; admitted to bar, 1967, California. *Education:* University of San Francisco (B.S., 1964; LL.B., 1967). *Member:* Fresno County Bar Association; State Bar of California; Northern California Association of Defense Counsel (Director, 1982-1984; California Medical/Legal Committee); American Board of Trial Advocates. [Capt., USMC, 1968-1971]. **PRACTICE AREAS:** Medical Malpractice; Civil Trial Practice; Personal Injury Law; Insurance Defense.

**FRANK D. MAUL,** born Fresno, California, February 20, 1950; admitted to bar, 1975, California. *Education:* California State University at Fresno (B.A., 1972); Hastings College of Law, University of California (J.D., 1975). Phi Kappa Phi. *Member:* Fresno County Bar Association; State Bar of California; Defense Research and Trial Lawyers Association; Northern California Association of Defense Counsel (Director); American Board of Trial Advocates; Association of Defense Trial Attorneys. **PRACTICE AREAS:** Products Liability Law; Insurance Coverage; Professional Liability; Personal Injury Law; Construction Litigation.

**CRAIG M. MORTENSEN,** born Whittier, California, September 8, 1953; admitted to bar, 1980, California. *Education:* Brigham Young University (B.S., 1977; J.D., cum laude, 1980). *Member:* Fresno County Bar Association; State Bar of California; Northern California Association of Defense Counsel; Ameican Board of Trial Advocates. **LANGUAGES:** Japanese. **PRACTICE AREAS:** Water Law; Personal Injury Law; Medical Malpractice.

*(This Listing Continued)*

**JERRY D. JONES,** born San Francisco, California, March 2, 1951; admitted to bar, 1976, California. *Education:* California State University at Fresno (B.A., summa cum laude, 1973); University of Notre Dame (J.D., 1976). Phi Kappa Phi. Chief Deputy District Attorney, County of Fresno, 1983-1986. *Member:* Fresno County and American Bar Associations; State Bar of California; Northern California Association of Defense Counsel; Defense Research Institute. *PRACTICE AREAS:* Professional Liability; Health Care Law; Business Litigation; Products Liability; Criminal Law.

**MICHAEL P. MALLERY,** born Long Beach, California, July 15, 1959; admitted to bar, 1984, California. *Education:* University of California at Davis (B.A., 1981); McGeorge School of Law, University of the Pacific (J.D., 1984). Comment Staff Writer, 1982-1983 and Managing Editor, 1983-1984, Pacific Law Journal. Board Member, Central California Legal Service, Inc. Adjunct Professor of Law, San Joaquin College of Law, 1993—. *Member:* Fresno County Bar Association; State Bar of California; Northern California Association of Defense Counsel. *PRACTICE AREAS:* Professional Liability; Health Care Law; Discrimination (Employee and Housing); Business Litigation.

**M. BRUCE SMITH,** born Los Angeles, California, October 9, 1956; admitted to bar, 1981, California and U.S. District Court, Eastern District of California. *Education:* University of California at Santa Barbara (B.A., 1978); Hastings College of the Law, University of California (J.D., 1981). Deputy District Attorney: Sacramento County, 1981; Fresno County, 1983-1988. *Member:* Fresno County Bar Association; State Bar of California; Northern California Association of Defense Counsel. *PRACTICE AREAS:* Insurance Defense; Employment Discrimination; Sexual Harassment; Criminal Law.

**THOMAS J. GEORGOUSES,** born Phoenix, Arizona, September 27, 1962; admitted to bar, 1990, California and U.S. District Court, Eastern District of California. *Education:* California State University at Fresno (B.S., 1985); San Joaquin College of Law (J.D., 1990). Adjunct Professor, San Joaquin College of Law, 1993—. *Member:* Fresno County Bar Association; State Bar of California; Northern California Association of Defense Counsel; American Inns of Court. *PRACTICE AREAS:* Insurance Defense; Premises Liability; Professional Liability.

### ASSOCIATES

**STEVEN R. STOKER,** born St. Louis, Missouri, May 25, 1963; admitted to bar, 1991, California and U.S. District Court, Eastern District of California. *Education:* Brigham Young University (B.A., 1987; J.D., 1991; M.B.A., 1991). *Member:* Fresno County Bar Association; State Bar of California; Association of Defense Counsel. *LANGUAGES:* Spanish. *PRACTICE AREAS:* Negligence Law; Litigation; Construction Law; Business Litigation; Health Care Law.

**M. JAQUELINE YATES,** born Crestline, Ohio, March 5, 1963; admitted to bar, 1992, California. *Education:* California State University, Fresno (B.A., cum laude, 1987); San Joaquin College of Law (J.D., with distinction, 1992). *Member:* Fresno County Bar Association; State Bar of California; Association of Defense Counsel of Northern California; California Women Lawyers. *PRACTICE AREAS:* Insurance Defense; Professional Liability; Family Law; Children's Rights.

**BRUCE J. BERGER,** born Glendale, California, August 13, 1957; admitted to bar, 1988, California, U.S. District Court, Eastern District of California and U.S. Tax Court. *Education:* California State University (B.S., 1980); Whittier College School of Law (J.D., 1984). Phi Alpha Delta. Certified Public Accountant, California, 1982. Instructor, Business Law and Accounting, Fresno City College, 1987. *Member:* Fresno County and American Bar Associations; State Bar of California; California Society of Certified Public Accountants; American Institute of Certified Public Accountants; California Society of Healthcare Attorneys; National Health Lawyers Association. *PRACTICE AREAS:* Health Law; Taxation.

**CELENE M.E. BOGGS,** born Philadelphia, Pennsylvania, January 3, 1969; admitted to bar, 1994, California. *Education:* Saint Josephs University (B.S., 1991) University of California, Hastings College of Law (J.D., 1994). *Member:* Fresno County Bar Association; State Bar of California; Association of Defense Counsel. *PRACTICE AREAS:* Negligence Law; Litigation.

REPRESENTATIVE CLIENTS: Pacific Bell; Pacific Gas & Electric Co.; Chevron, U.S.A.; Goodyear Tire & Rubber Co.; John Deere Co.; Caterpillar, Inc.; County of Fresno; Fresno Irrigation District; Community Hospitals of Central California; Madera Community Hospital; Sherwin-Williams Corp.; The Travelers Insurance Group; Truck Insurance Exchange; State Farm Insurance Cos.; Grocers Insurance Co.; Golden Eagle Insurance Company; CHAIS.
REFERENCE: Bank of America National Trust & Savings Assn. (Fresno Main Office).

# THOMAS, SNELL, JAMISON, RUSSELL AND ASPERGER

*A PROFESSIONAL CORPORATION*

Established in 1939

2445 CAPITOL STREET
P.O. BOX 1461
**FRESNO, CALIFORNIA 93716**
Telephone: 209-442-0600; 800-559-9009
Telecopier: 209-442-5078
Email: tsnell@cybergate.com

Civil Trial and Appellate Practice, all State and Federal Courts. Taxation (Federal and State). Corporation, Securities, Probate and Estate Planning, Labor and Employment, Condominium, Real Estate, Administrative, Environmental, Natural Resources, Creditors' Rights and Government Law.

FIRM PROFILE: The firm was founded just prior to World War II and began as a group of tax specialists. Since that time, the firm's practice has expanded to encompass a broad range of litigation, agricultural, manufacturing, financial, development, and professional concerns. The firm maintains a full-service business practice emphasizing business organization and planning, property transactions, tax planning, agricultural law, estate planning, trust and probate administration, commercial law, bankruptcy, environmental and public resources law and a full-service litigation practice in all federal and state trial and appellate courts.

**HOWARD B. THOMAS** (1912-1993).

**FENTON WILLIAMSON, JR.** (1926-1993).

**ROGER E. FIPPS,** born Long Beach, California, December 29, 1929; admitted to bar, 1957, California. *Education:* University of California (A.B., 1951); University of California at Berkeley (J.D., 1957). *Member:* State Bar of California; Fresno County and American Bar Associations. (Certified Specialist, Taxation Law, The State Bar of California Board of Legal Specialization). *PRACTICE AREAS:* Trusts and Estates; Estate Planning; Estate and Gift Taxation.

**SAMUEL C. PALMER, III,** born Philadelphia, Pennsylvania, June 9, 1934; admitted to bar, 1959, California. *Education:* Yale University; Stanford University (A.B., 1956); Loyola University of Los Angeles (J.D., 1958). Phi Delta Phi. Author: "A National Legal Services Corporation; The Legal Profession's Responsibility," State Bar Journal, 1971. Adjunct Professor, Agriculture Law, California State University, Fresno, 1982—. Member: Chancery Club, 1969; Member, Fresno Ag Roundtable, 1994; Member, Fresno Business Council, 1995; Member, Board of Directors, Legal Aid Foundation, 1969-1976; Member, Board of Directors, Volunteers in Parole. Chairman and Delegate for Eastern District of California, Ninth Circuit Conference, 1989-1992. Representative of Los Angeles Bar on Board of Trustees, Western Center on Law and Poverty, 1969-1981. Member, 1969-1981, and Chairman, 1971-1976, Subcommittee of Committee of State Bar Examiners. *Member:* Fresno County (President, 1992; Vice President and President-Elect, 1991; Treasurer, 1987-1988; Member, Board of Directors, 1987-1993; Chair, Court Liaison and Rules Committees, 1985), Los Angeles County (Member, Executive Committee, Junior Barristers, 1964-1965; Vice Chairman, Bar Membership Recruitment Committee, 1968-1969; Member, 1966-1969, and Chairman, 1969, Committee on Group Legal Services) and American Bar Associations; State Bar of California. *PRACTICE AREAS:* Business Litigation.

**JAMES O. DEMSEY,** born New York, N.Y., May 29, 1938; admitted to bar, 1965, California. *Education:* University of California at Berkeley (B.S., 1960; J.D., 1964). Phi Delta Phi. Member, Executive Council, Conference of Barristers, 1970-1973. *Member:* Fresno County (Director, 1982-1984) and American Bar Associations; State Bar of California. [Capt., U.S.A.R., 1960-1969]. *PRACTICE AREAS:* Real Estate Transactions; Business Transactions; State and Local Taxation Law.

**ROBERT J. TYLER,** born Hartford, Connecticut, March 28, 1938; admitted to bar, 1963, California. *Education:* San Diego State College (A.B., 1959); Stanford University (J.D., 1962). Phi Alpha Delta. Clerk to J. Schauer, California Supreme Court, 1963-1964. *Member:* Fresno County and American Bar Associations; State Bar of California (Member, Committee on Taxation, 1969-1972). *PRACTICE AREAS:* Estate Planning; Probate; Reclamation Law; Taxation Law.

*(This Listing Continued)*

**THOMAS, SNELL, JAMISON, RUSSELL AND ASPERGER,** A PROFESSIONAL CORPORATION, Fresno— Continued

**GERALD D. VINNARD,** born New Orleans, Louisiana, September 11, 1944; admitted to bar, 1970, California. *Education:* Pacific Union College and Fresno State College (B.S., summa cum laude, 1966); Harvard University (J.D., cum laude, 1969). Assistant Professor, Contracts, Taxation and Negotiable Instruments, Loyola University School of Law, 1969-1970. Arbitrator, American Arbitration Association. *Member:* Fresno County and American Bar Associations; State Bar of California. [Lt., JAGC, U.S. Naval Reserve, 1970-1974]. *PRACTICE AREAS:* Bankruptcy Law; Business Litigation; Real Estate.

**E. ROBERT WRIGHT,** born Oakland, California, July 9, 1944; admitted to bar, 1972, California; 1977, U.S. Court of Appeals, Ninth Circuit; 1979, U.S. Supreme Court and U.S. District Court, Eastern District of California; 1981, District of Columbia. *Education:* University of California at Berkeley (B.S., 1966); Harvard University (J.D., 1971). Adjunct Professor, Environmental Law, Constitutional Law and Water Law, San Joaquin College of Law, 1991—. Principal Author: "The Attorney General's Asbestos Liability Report To The Congress," U.S. Department of Justice, 1981. Co-Author: "Transfer of Development Rights: A Remedy For Prior Excessive Subdivision," 10 University of California at Davis Law Review 1, 1977. Senior Trial Attorney, Policy, Legislation, and Special Litigation Section, Land and Natural Resources Division, U.S. Department of Justice, Washington, D.C., 1980-1982. Deputy Attorney General, State of California, Public Resources and Environmental Sections, 1972-1980. General Counsel, California Tahoe Regional Planning Agency, 1974-1977. *Member:* Fresno County, Federal and American Bar Associations; State Bar of California; District of Columbia Bar. [Capt., U.S Army, 1966-1968]. *REPORTED CASES:* California v. Bergland, 483 F. Supp. 465 (E.D. Cal. 1980), aff'd, 690 F.2d 753 (9th Cir. 1982); City of South Lake Tahoe v. California Tahoe Regional Planning Agency, 625 F.2d 231 (9th Cir. 1980), cert. denied, 101 S. Ct. 619 (1980); Horn v. County of Ventura, 24 Cal. 3d 605 (1979). *PRACTICE AREAS:* Civil Litigation; Environmental Litigation.

**DAVID M. GILMORE,** born Seattle, Washington, March 14, 1958; admitted to bar, 1982, California and U.S. District Court, Eastern District of California; 1983, U.S. District Court, Northern District of California; 1992, U.S. Tax Court; 1994, U.S. Court of Appeals, Ninth Circuit. *Education:* University of California at Davis (A.B., with honors, 1979); McGeorge School of Law, University of the Pacific (J.D., with great distinction, 1982). Order of the Coif. Member, Traynor Honor Society. Associate Articles Editor, Pacific Law Journal, 1981-1982. Author, Comment, "Creation of Life: A New Frontier for Liability," 13 Pacific Law Journal 99, 1981. *Member:* Fresno County, Federal and American Bar Associations; State Bar of California. *REPORTED CASES:* Estate of Berdrow (1992) 5 Cal. App. 4th 637; Mosesian v. Pennwalt Corp. (1987) 191 Cal. App. 3d 851; Producers Cotton Oil Co. v. Amstar Corp. (1988) 197 Cal. App. 3d 638. *PRACTICE AREAS:* Litigation; Appellate Practice; Business Law; Securities Litigation; Commercial Law.

**RUSSELL O. WOOD,** born Fresno, California, January 27, 1957; admitted to bar, 1983, California; 1984, U.S. District Court, Southern and Eastern Districts of California. *Education:* California State University at Fresno (A.B., with honors, 1979); University of California at Berkeley (J.D., and M.B.A., 1983). Order of the Coif. Law Clerk to Honorable Edward J. Schwartz, U.S. District Judge, Southern District of California, 1983-1984. *Member:* Fresno County Bar Association; State Bar of California. *PRACTICE AREAS:* Real Estate; Trusts and Estates; Business and Financing Transactions.

**SCOTT R. SHEWAN,** born Olean, New York, June 1, 1958; admitted to bar, 1983, New York; 1985, California and U.S. District Court, Western District of New York and U.S. District Court, Northern District of California; 1986, U.S. District Court, Eastern District of California; 1991, U.S. Court of Appeals, Ninth Circuit. *Education:* Roberts Wesleyan College (B.A., magna cum laude, 1979); Columbia University (J.D., 1982). Alpha Kappa Sigma. *Member:* Fresno County and American Bar Associations; State Bar of California. *PRACTICE AREAS:* Civil Litigation; Securities Arbitration.

**HILARY A. CHITTICK,** born Palo Alto, California, October 2, 1953; admitted to bar, 1979, California. *Education:* University of Madrid, Madrid, Spain; University of California at San Diego (B.A., 1975); Hastings College of Law, University of California (J.D., 1979). *Member:* Fresno County, Federal and American Bar Associations; State Bar of California; Leadership Fresno; Fresno County Juvenile Justice Commission; State Board of Governors, California Women Lawyers; Fresno County Women Lawyers; Fresno Business and Professional Women. *LANGUAGES:* Spanish. *PRACTICE AREAS:* Civil Litigation; Business Litigation; Federal Criminal Defense.

*OF COUNSEL*

**WILLIAM N. SNELL,** born Nevada City, California, February 23, 1916; admitted to bar, 1940, California. *Education:* Stanford University (A.B., 1937; J.D., 1940). Order of the Coif; Delta Theta Phi. Author: "Reflections on the Practical Aspects of 'The Sale of Corporate Control'," Duke Law Journal 1193 (Latty Symposium on Corporate and Securities Law), 1972. Secretary and General Counsel, The Vendo Company, 1981-1988. *Member:* Fresno County Bar Association; State Bar of California; American Law Institute; American Judicature Society. [Lieut., U.S.N.R., 1942-1945]. *REPORTED CASES:* Brown v. Halbert, 271 Cal. App. 2d 252; 38 ALR 3d 718. *PRACTICE AREAS:* Corporate Law; Business Law; Products Liability; Securities.

**T. NEWTON RUSSELL,** born Diamondville, Wyoming, March 17, 1918; admitted to bar, 1943, California. *Education:* Stanford University (A.B., 1940; J.D., 1943). Order of the Coif; Phi Delta Phi. *Member:* Fresno County (Director, 1980-1982) and American Bar Associations; State Bar of California (Member, Committee on Taxation, 1962-1965); American Law Institute. Fellow, American College of Trust and Estate Counsel. *PRACTICE AREAS:* Estate Planning Law; Probate Law; Trust Administration Law.

**CHARLES E. SMALL,** born Portland, Oregon, August 16, 1928; admitted to bar, 1957, California. *Education:* University of California at Los Angeles (B.S., 1950; J.D., 1956). Nu Beta Epsilon; Order of the Coif. Member, University of California at Los Angeles Law Review, 1955-1956. *Member:* Fresno County Bar Association; State Bar of California.

**JAMES E. LAFOLLETTE,** born Concord, Massachusetts, March 27, 1928; admitted to bar, 1959, California. *Education:* Fresno State College (A.B., 1951); Hastings College of Law, University of California (J.D., 1958). *Member:* Fresno County and American Bar Associations; State Bar of California. [Lieut., U.S.A.F. (pilot), 1952-1955]. *PRACTICE AREAS:* Business Litigation; Products Liability Litigation; Appellate Practice.

*RETIRED*

**PAUL ASPERGER,** born Tucson, Arizona, April 26, 1928; admitted to bar, 1953, California. *Education:* University of California at Berkeley (A.B., 1949; J.D., 1952). Phi Alpha Delta. Fellow, American College of Probate Counsel. (Retired).

**OLIVER M. JAMISON,** born Portland, Oregon, August 1, 1916; admitted to bar, 1941, California. *Education:* Fresno State College and Stanford University (A.B., 1938); Stanford University (J.D., 1941). Order of the Coif; Phi Alpha Delta. [Capt., A.U.S., 1942-1946]. (Retired).

---

**MARCUS DON MAGNESS,** born Oklahoma City, Oklahoma, May 26, 1965; admitted to bar, 1990, California. *Education:* McGill University (B.Eng., 1987); University of Oklahoma (J.D., 1990); University of Miami (LL.M., Taxation, 1994). Phi Delta Phi. *Member:* Fresno County and American Bar Associations; State Bar of California. *PRACTICE AREAS:* Taxation; Real Property; Business Litigation.

**ANGELA E. TAYLOR,** born Logan, Utah, June 29, 1970; admitted to bar, 1995, California; 1996, U.S. District Court, Northern and Eastern Districts of California. *Education:* University of California, Santa Cruz (B.A., with honors, 1992); Santa Clara University (J.D., 1995). *Member:* Fresno County Bar Association; State Bar of California.

REPRESENTATIVE CLIENTS: California Table Grape Commission; Cedar Vista Hospital; D.B.O. Development Company; Giannini Farms; Giannini Packing Company; Gottschalk's, Inc.; Hansen Ranches; Lyles Diversified, Inc.; New England Sheet Metal Works, Inc.; Pelco; Simonian Fruit Company; Spano Enterprises, Inc.; Valley Engineers, Inc.
LOCAL COUNSEL FOR: Equitable Life Assurance Society of the United States; Halsey Drug Co., Inc.; Metropolitan Life Insurance Co.; PPG Industries; Unocal; The Vendo Company; Wallpapers to Go, Inc.
REFERENCE: The Bank of California.

## WAGNER & WAGNER, A PROFESSIONAL CORPORATION
1322 EAST SHAW AVENUE, SUITE 340
FRESNO, CALIFORNIA 93710
Telephone: 209-224-0871
Telecopier: 209-224-0885

*Estate Planning, Trusts and Probate Law. General Business including Partnerships, Corporation, Complex Business Transactions, Real Estate and Related Tax Issues.*

**BRYAN N. WAGNER,** born Fresno, California, June 29, 1956; admitted to bar, 1984, California and U.S. District Court, Eastern District of California. *Education:* Dartmouth College (B.A., 1979); McGeorge School of Law (J.D., 1984). Order of the Coif. *Member:* Fresno and American Bar Associations; State Bar of California. **PRACTICE AREAS:** General Business Law; Real Estate; Land Use; Taxation; Corporate Law.

**JAMES F. WAGNER,** born Denver, Colorado, July 25, 1929; admitted to bar, 1955, California. *Education:* University of California (B.S., 1951); Boalt Hall School of Law (J.D., 1954). **PRACTICE AREAS:** Trusts and Estates; Probate; Business Law.

**MATTHEW C. WAGNER,** born Fresno, California, January 16, 1962; admitted to bar, 1989, California. *Education:* Dartmouth College (B.A., 1985); University of California at Los Angeles (J.D., 1989). **PRACTICE AREAS:** Trusts and Estates; Probate; Business Law; Taxation Litigation.

## WILD, CARTER & TIPTON
A PROFESSIONAL CORPORATION
246 WEST SHAW AVENUE
P.O. BOX 16339
FRESNO, CALIFORNIA 93755-6339
Telephone: 209-224-2131
Telecopier: 209-224-8462

*General Civil, Trial and Appellate Practice. Business, Real Estate, Corporation, Construction, Banking, Environmental, Agriculture, Insurance, Trademark, Probate and Estate Planning, Oil and Gas, Taxation, Bankruptcy and Employment Law.*

**FIRM PROFILE:** *Founded in 1893, Wild, Carter & Tipton is the oldest firm in Fresno. The firm offers a full range of business and litigation services and has developed practice groups to meet the specialized needs of its clients.*

**MOUNT K. WILD** (1890-1959).

**M. GORDON WILD** (1922-1972).

**ARTHUR L. BLANK** (1906-1983).

**JACK M. TIPTON** (1933-1990).

**M. BRUCE WILD** (1946-1990).

**ROBERT G. CARTER,** born Detroit, Michigan, October 1, 1927; admitted to bar, 1955, California and U.S. District Court, Northern and Eastern Districts of California. *Education:* University of California at Los Angeles (B.A., 1951; LL.B., 1954). Phi Delta Phi. Law Clerk, U.S. District Court, 1955. Assistant U.S. Attorney, U.S. Attorney's Office, Los Angeles, 1956. Deputy District Attorney, Fresno County District Attorney's Office, 1957-1959. Federal Commissioner, Condemnation, 1959-1961. Fresno Chamber of Commerce Board of Directors, 1987—. President, Fresno Chamber of Commerce, 1992. Vice-Chair, Fresno Regional Medical Center, 1993. President, Fresno Business Council, 1993; President and Chairman of the Board, Fresno Revitalization Corporation, 1993; President and Chairman Better Business Bureau, 1991; President, North Fresno Rotary Club, 1972-1973; Board Member, Economic Development Corporation, 1991—. *Member:* Fresno County and American Bar Associations; State Bar of California; California Trial Lawyers Association; The Association of Trial Lawyers of America. **PRACTICE AREAS:** Business and Commercial Law.

**BRUCE M. BROWN,** born Long Beach, California, January 5, 1952; admitted to bar, 1977, California and U.S. District Court, Eastern District of California. *Education:* Riverside City College and University of California at Davis (A.B., 1974); Hastings College of Law, University of California (J.D., 1977). Phi Delta Phi. *Member:* Fresno County Bar Association; State Bar of California. **SPECIAL AGENCIES:** Agribusiness Committee of the Business Law Section of the State Bar of California. **PRACTICE AREAS:** Real Estate; Finance; Agricultural Law.

*(This Listing Continued)*

**WILLIAM H. LEIFER,** born Brooklyn, New York, June 21, 1948; admitted to bar, 1974, California, U.S. District Court, Northern, Southern, Central and Eastern Districts of California; U.S. District Court, District of Arizona; and U.S. Court of Appeals, Ninth Circuit; 1976, U.S. Tax Court. *Education:* University of California at Los Angeles (B.A., 1970); Hastings College of Law, University of California (J.D., 1973). Co-Author: "California Rental Housing Reference Book," California Apartment Association, 1985, 1987, 1989 and 1990. Lecturer: Continuing Education for Real Estate Licensees, Fresno City College, 1983-1986; Landlord/Tenant Law, California Continuing Education of the Bar, 1985 and 1987. President, Apartment Association of Greater Fresno, 1989-1991. *Member:* Fresno County Bar Association; State Bar of California; Association of Trial Lawyers of America. **SPECIAL AGENCIES:** Commissioner, Fresno City Housing Authority. **PRACTICE AREAS:** Landlord/Tenant; Health Insurance; Civil Litigation.

**G. DANA FRENCH,** born Glen Ridge, New Jersey, March 28, 1951; admitted to bar, 1977, California; 1978, U.S. Tax Court. *Education:* Clark University (B.A., 1973); University of Toledo (J.D., cum laude, 1977); New York University (LL.M., Taxation, 1978). Member, University of Toledo Law Review, 1976-1977. *Member:* Fresno County (Secretary, 1986; Treasurer, 1987; Vice President, 1988; President, 1989) and American (Member, Tax and Real Property Section) Bar Associations; State Bar of California (Member, Sections on: Business Law, Real Property and Tax). **PRACTICE AREAS:** Business Transactions; Estate Planning; Tax; Real Estate; Corporations.

**RICHARD A. HARRIS,** born Fresno, California, April 12, 1947; admitted to bar, 1972, California; U.S. District Court, Eastern District of California; U.S. Court of Appeals, Ninth Circuit; U.S. Supreme Court; U.S. Tax Court. *Education:* California State University, Fresno (B.S., cum laude, 1972); Golden Gate University (J.D., 1972); University of Florida (LL.M., in Taxation, 1978). Assistant U.S. Attorney, U.S. Attorney's Office, Fresno, California, 1974-1977. Licensed California Real Estate Broker, 1973. Instructor, San Joaquin College of Law, Tax Program, 1981; Humphreys College of Law, 1973-1978. Lecturer, "Continuing Education of Real Estate Licensees Courses," Fresno City College, 1985-1986. *Member:* Fresno County and American Bar Associations; State Bar of California. **PRACTICE AREAS:** Tax; Family Law; Civil and Criminal Litigation.

**RUSSELL G. VANROZEBOOM,** born Fresno, California, September 24, 1948; admitted to bar, 1974, California; U.S. District Court, Central and Eastern Districts of California; U.S. Court of Appeals, Ninth Circuit. *Education:* University of California at Santa Barbara; Fresno State University; Humphreys College (LL.B., 1974). Instructor, Humphreys College School of Law, Legal Research and Trial Practice, 1976-1978. *Member:* Fresno County and American (Member, Litigation Section) Bar Associations; State Bar of California; California Trial Lawyers Association. **PRACTICE AREAS:** Business and Agricultural Litigation; Insurance Policy Interpretation; General Civil Litigation.

**TRACY A. AGRALL,** born Fresno, California, December 22, 1956; admitted to bar, 1981, California and U.S. District Court, Eastern District of California; 1982, U.S. District Court, Central District of California; 1983, U.S. District Court, Northern District of California. *Education:* California State University, Fresno (B.A., magna cum laude, 1978); Pepperdine University (J.D., 1981). Delta Theta Phi. Member, Pepperdine Law Review, 1979-1981. *Member:* Fresno County and American (Member: Labor and Employment, and Intellectual Property Law Sections) Bar Associations; State Bar of California; California Women Lawyers. **PRACTICE AREAS:** Employment and Business Law.

**GARY L. HUSS,** born Carrington, North Dakota, February 11, 1947; admitted to bar, 1973, California. *Education:* California State University of San Jose (B.A., 1965); University of Santa Clara (J.D., 1973). Member, Editorial Staff, Bar Bulletin, 1984-1987. President, Fresno County Prosecutor's Association, 1984-1986. Panel Member, American Arbitration Association. *Member:* Fresno County Bar Association (Member, Judicial Evaluations Committee); State Bar of California; Alameda County Trial Lawyers Association. **SPECIAL AGENCIES:** State Bar Commission on Criminal Law Specialization. **PRACTICE AREAS:** White Collar Criminal Defense; Department of Motor Vehicles Litigation; General Business Litigation; Agricultural Litigation; Administrative Licensing Litigation; Employment Litigation.

**PATRICK J. GORMAN,** born Los Angeles, California, August 15, 1961; admitted to bar, 1987, California and U.S. District Court, Eastern District of California; 1993, U.S. District Court, Central District of California. *Education:* Fresno City College (A.A., 1982); California State University at Fresno (B.S., 1984); Santa Clara University (J.D., cum laude, 1987).

*(This Listing Continued)*

**WILD, CARTER & TIPTON,** A PROFESSIONAL CORPORATION, Fresno—Continued

Associate Editor, Santa Clara Law Review, 1986-1987. *Member:* Fresno County and American (Member, Sections on Litigation and Construction Industry) Bar Associations; State Bar of California; California Trial Lawyers Association. *PRACTICE AREAS:* Construction and Business Litigation.

**STEVEN E. PAGANETTI,** born Port Chester, New York, June 20, 1951; admitted to bar, 1979, California, U.S. District Court, Eastern and Northern Districts of California and U.S. Court of Appeals, Ninth Circuit. *Education:* Massachusetts State College (B.A., 1974); San Joaquin College of Law (J.D., 1979). *Member:* Fresno County Bar Association; State Bar of California; Panel Member, American Arbitration Association. *PRACTICE AREAS:* Trials, Business and Environmental Litigation.

**ROBERT C. SCHMALLE,** born Hanford, California, March 19, 1960; admitted to bar, 1991, California. *Education:* Fresno City College (A.A.); San Joaquin College (J.D., 1991). Phi Delta Phi. *Member:* Fresno County Bar Association (Member, Young Lawyers Division); State Bar of California; San Joaquin Valley Inns of Court. *PRACTICE AREAS:* Business Litigation; Environmental Law; Entertainment Law (Music).

**BERTRAM T. KAUFMANN,** born Pasadena, California, October 23, 1962; admitted to bar, 1990, California and U.S. District Court, Eastern District of California. *Education:* Embry-Riddle Aeronautical University (B.S.), magna cum laude, 1983); Boalt Hall School of Law, University of California (J.D., 1990). Omicron Delta Kappa; Sigma Tau Delta. *Member:* Los Angeles County, Fresno County and American Bar Associations. [1st Lt., U.S.A.F., 1983-1987]. *PRACTICE AREAS:* Agribusiness; Aviation; Business Transactions; Commercial Law; Real Property.

**WESLEY J. HAMMOND,** born Fresno, California, October 3, 1955; admitted to bar, 1994, California. *Education:* University of California, Berkeley (A.B., 1977); San Joaquin College of Law (J.D., 1993). Delta Theta Phi. Real Estate Broker, California, 1978—. *Member:* State Bar of California. *PRACTICE AREAS:* Real Estate Law.

### OF COUNSEL

**RICHARD L. HARRIMAN,** born 1944; admitted to bar, 1975, California. *Education:* Stanford University (B.A.); University of California School of Law at Davis (J.D.). *Member:* State Bar of California. *LANGUAGES:* French.

REPRESENTATIVE CLIENTS: A. Duda & Sons, Inc.; Apartment Association of Greater Fresno; A. Zahner Company, Inc.; Balcor Property Management, Inc.; Bedminster Bioconversion Corporation; BMC West; Bridgestone/Firestone, Inc.; BSK & Associates; Buckingham Property Management, Inc.; Butterfield Brewing Company, Inc.; Clovis Community Bank; Cole Financial Group; Cribari Vineyards, Inc.; Dan Gamel, Inc.; Donaghy Sales, Inc.; Duncan Enterprises; Eagle Creek Mining & Drilling, Inc.; Federal Deposit Insurance Corp.; Ford New Holland; Fresno Valves & Castings, Inc.; Geoservices, Inc.; Geotechnical Consultants, Inc.; Great Western Bank; Grupe Management Co.; Harry S. Aslan, Inc.; Inland Star Distribution Centers, Inc.; Jeffrey-Scott Advertising, Inc.; Johnny Quick Food Stores, Inc.; Jordan Management Company; Jorgenson & Co.; Kaprielian Bros. Packing Co.; Lincoln Properties; Lummus Industries, Inc.; MaceRich California Associates; Manco Abbott, Inc.; Maximus Recording Studios; Merrill, Lynch, Pierce, Fenner & Smith; Pearson Realty; Phoenix Coatings, Inc.; Picker Parts, Inc.; P-R Farms, Inc.; Puritan Insurance Co.; Regency Bank; Remington Arms Company, Inc.; Resolution Trust Corporation; Schoenwald-Oba-Mogensen-Pohill-Miller, Inc.; Scrimco, Inc.; Southland Produce Co.; Spieker Partners; Sun Life Assurance Company of Canada; S&W Firesprinklers, Inc.; Telles Farms; T-H Agriculture & Nutrition Co., Inc.; The Pengad Co.; U.S. West, Inc.; Utility Trailer Sales; Valley Stairway, Inc.; Volkswagon of America; Wasco Hardfacing; Wells Fargo Bank; West Hills Cooperative, Inc.; Worthington Corp.; Zacky Farms; Zarn, Inc.; Zurn Industries, Inc.; Fowler Packing Co.; Visalia Produce.

REFERENCE: Regency Bank (Branches at Fresno, California).

## ADRIAN S. WILLIAMS
*1665 WEST SHAW, SUITE 108*
**FRESNO, CALIFORNIA 93711**
Telephone: 209-226-7767
Facsimile: 209-224-4960
*Email: Available Upon Request*

Business Law (Debtors and Creditors), Bankruptcy, Farming (Debtors and Creditors) and Real Property.

**ADRIAN S. WILLIAMS,** born Detroit, Michigan, September 25, 1936; admitted to bar, 1961, Michigan; 1972, California. *Education:* University of Michigan (A.B., 1957); Wayne State University (J.D., 1961). Junior and Senior Editor, Wayne State University Law Review. Recipient: Arthur L.

*(This Listing Continued)*

CAA256B

---

Robbins Moot Court Award. *Member:* Fresno County and Central California Bar Associations; State Bar of California; State Bar of Michigan; American Bankruptcy Law Institute; American Society of Computer Lawyers; Christian Legal Society. *REPORTED CASES:* Dettman v. Fresno Madera Production Credit Assn. B.A.P. No. EC-87-1203 Docket #88-15197; Christensen v. EMC BAP. No. EC-932082. *PRACTICE AREAS:* Bankruptcy Reorganization (Chapter 11 & 12); Debtors and Creditors; Bankruptcy-Chapter 7 Insolvencies; Real Property Law; Small Business and Corporate Law.

## WORREL & WORREL
*Established in 1946*
**SUITE 130, CIVIC CENTER SQUARE
2444 MAIN STREET
FRESNO, CALIFORNIA 93721-1984**
Telephone: 209-486-4526
Fax: 209-486-6948

*Domestic and Foreign Patent, Trademark and Copyright and Related Intellectual Property Law. Trials in all Federal Courts.*

**RICHARD M. WORREL** (1913-1995).

**RODNEY K. WORREL,** born Fresno, California, June 29, 1943; admitted to bar, 1972, California; 1976, U.S. Supreme Court; 1983, U.S. Court of Appeals for the Federal Circuit; U.S. Court of Appeals, Ninth Circuit; registered to practice before U.S. Patent and Trademark Office. *Education:* California State University at Fresno (B.A., 1966); University of California at Davis (J.D., 1969). Author: "The Wright Brothers' Pioneer Patent," American Bar Association Journal, October, 1979. Law Clerk for Honorable M.D. Crocker, U.S. District Court Judge for Eastern District of California, 1969-1971. President, Fresno County Young Lawyers, 1973-1974. *Member:* Fresno County (Member, Board of Directors, 1974, Secretary, 1977 and President, 1984) and American (Member, Patent, Trademark and Copyright Section) Bar Associations; The State Bar of California; American Intellectual Property Law Association.

REPRESENTATIVE CLIENTS: Anderson Clayton Corp.; The Ansel Adams Gallery; Bank of America; BAP Software, Inc.; J.G. Boswell Co.; Bowsmith, Inc.; Buckner, Inc.; N.A. Chislett & Co. (Australia); Danair, Inc.; Duncan Enterprises; California State University, Fresno; California State University, Bakersfield; Community Hospitals of Central California; FMS Manufacturing Co.; Fresno Pacific College; Gottschalk's Inc.; Hagan Electronics International; HIT Products Corp.; Keiser Corporation; Koda Farms, Inc.; Metropolitan Life Insurance Company; Weir Floway, Inc.; Pappas Telecasting Incorporated; Paramount Farming Company; Star Fruits (France); Sun-Glo of Idaho Inc.; The Vendo Company; City of Visalia; Warren & Baerg Manufacturing, Inc.; Weather Tec Corp.

REFERENCES: Bank One; Merrill Lynch, Pierce, Fenner & Smith, Inc.

## BALLARD, WIMER, BROCKETT & EDWARDS
*An Association of Attorneys*
**SUITE 200, 1235 NORTH HARBOR BOULEVARD
FULLERTON, CALIFORNIA 92632**
Telephone: 714-871-1132
Facsimile: 714-871-5620

*Business, Civil and Trial Practice in all State and Federal Courts. Corporate, Mergers and Acquisitions, Antitrust, Unfair Trade Practices, Probate, Estate Planning, Taxation and Real Estate Law, Earth Movement and Construction Defect, Family Law, Custody, Support, UCCJA Matters.*

**J. LARRY BALLARD,** born Bakersfield, California, April 4, 1937; admitted to bar, 1964, California. *Education:* University of California at Los Angeles (B.S., 1959); University of Southern California (J.D., 1964). Member, 1968-1973 and Chairman, 1970-1973; 1991—, and Chairman, 1994—, , Fullerton City Planning Commission. *Member:* Orange County Bar Association; The State Bar of California. (Certified Specialist, Taxation Law and Probate, Estate Planning and Trust Law, The State Bar of California Board of Legal Specialization). *PRACTICE AREAS:* Estate Planning Law; Real Estate Law; Transactional Law.

**WARREN B. WIMER,** born Philadelphia, Pennsylvania, June 20, 1939; admitted to bar, 1967, California. *Education:* University of Maryland (B.S., 1962); Georgetown Law Center and Loyola University of Los Angeles (J.D., 1967). Judge Pro Tem, Orange County Superior Court, 1977-1994. *Member:* Orange County Bar Association (Member, Sections on Business

*(This Listing Continued)*

Litigation, Real Property, Federal Courts); State Bar of California; Orange County Trial Lawyers Association. *PRACTICE AREAS:* Earth Movement; Construction Defects; Real Estate; Business Litigation; Mergers, Acquisitions and Business Purchases.

**LEE H. BROCKETT,** born Maywood, California, August 19, 1946; admitted to bar, 1972, California. *Education:* Occidental College (A.B., 1968); California Western University (J.D., 1972); New York University (LL.M., in taxation, 1973). *Member:* Orange County and American (Member, Sections on: Taxation; Law Office Management) Bar Associations; The State Bar of California. (Certified Specialist, Taxation Law, The State Bar of California Board of Legal Specialization). *PRACTICE AREAS:* Taxation Law; Estate Planning Law; Real Estate; Pension Law; Transactional Law. *Email:* BrockettL@aol.com

**THOMAS C. EDWARDS,** born West Orange, New Jersey, May 2, 1946; admitted to bar, 1972, District of Columbia; 1973, California. *Education:* University of California at Los Angeles (B.A., 1968); George Washington University (J.D., 1971). Member, Blue Key. Member, Newport Beach City Planning Commission, 1988-1994; Chairman, 1992-1993; Newport Beach City Councilman, 1994—. Judge Pro Tem, Orange County Municipal Courts, 1978—. Special Compliance Counsel, Department of Corporations, 1989-1991. General Counsel, Orange County Airport Site Coalition, 1987-1989. Arbitrator, American Arbitration Association. *Member:* Orange County Bar Association; State Bar of California; District of Columbia Bar. *PRACTICE AREAS:* Real Estate; Business Law. *Email:* TEdwa.60265@aol.com

**RICHARD S. PRICE II,** born Whittier, California, July 9, 1957; admitted to bar, 1982, California. *Education:* University of California at Riverside (B.A., with high honors, 1979); University of California at Davis (J.D., 1982). Judge Pro Tem, Orange County Municipal Court, 1987—. Arbitrator, Orange County Superior Court, 1994—. *Member:* Orange County and American Bar Associations; State Bar of California. *REPORTED CASES:* In Re: Arm (1994) 175 B.R. 349. *PRACTICE AREAS:* Real Estate and Business Litigation; Collections; Real Estate Law.

**CHRISTOPHER J. KOORSTAD,** born Long Beach, California, October 10, 1956; admitted to bar, 1982, California; 1987, U.S. Tax Court. *Education:* California State University at Fullerton (B.A., with honors, 1979); University of California at Davis (J.D., 1982). National Finalist, National Moot Court Team. *Member:* Orange County Bar Association; State Bar of California. *LANGUAGES:* Spanish. *PRACTICE AREAS:* Business Law; Real Estate Litigation; Unfair Competition Law; Wrongful Termination Law.

**SARA STEWART BERGSTROM,** born Butte, Montana, October 26, 1937; admitted to bar, 1986, California. *Education:* University of California at Los Angeles (B.A., 1959); California State University at Fullerton (M.S., 1977); Western State University (J.D., cum laude, 1986). Member, Western State University Law Review, 1985-1986. Extern, U.S. Court of Appeals, Ninth Circuit, 1985. Author: Notes and Comments, Volume 12, Number 2, Western State University Law Review, 1985. *Member:* Orange County (Member, Family Law Section) and American Bar Associations; State Bar of California; National Academy of Elder Law Attorneys. *PRACTICE AREAS:* Family Law; Elder Law; Probate; Guardianship; Conservatorships.

**RANDALL J. FRIEND,** born Minneapolis, Minnesota, March 29, 1960; admitted to bar, 1986, California. *Education:* California State University at Fullerton (B.A., accounting, 1983); California Western School of Law (J.D., cum laude, 1986); New York University (LL.M. in Taxation, 1987). Editor, California Western Law Review, 1984-1986. Author: "Civil Rico: The Resolution of the Racketeering Enterprise Injury Requirement," 21 Cal. W. L. Rev. 364, 1985. *Member:* Orange County Bar Association; State Bar of California. *PRACTICE AREAS:* Taxation Law; Real Estate Law; Construction Defect; Business Law.

REFERENCE: California State Bank (Anaheim, California Office).

# WILLIAM M. BUSH
*110 EAST WILSHIRE AVENUE, SUITE 210*
*FULLERTON, CALIFORNIA 92632-1998*
*Telephone: 714-992-0800*
*Fax: 714-879-5811*
*Email: wmbushesq@aol.com*

*Practice limited to Family Law, Litigation and Mediation.*

**WILLIAM M. BUSH,** born Long Beach, California, June 23, 1941; admitted to bar, 1967, California. *Education:* Stanford University (A.B., 1963); Hastings College of the Law, University of California (J.D., 1966). *Member:* Orange County (Member, Family Law Section; Chairman, Committee on Administration of Justice, 1982) and American Bar Associations; State Bar of California (Member, Family Law Advisory Commission, 1979-1985; Chairman, 1982-1985; Member, Board of Legal Specialization, 1982-1989). Fellow, American Academy of Matrimonial Lawyers. (Certified Specialist, Family Law, The State Bar of California Board of Legal Specialization).

# CURRAN AND WATSON
*Established in 1975*
*SUITE 290, 1235 NORTH HARBOR BOULEVARD*
*FULLERTON, CALIFORNIA 92632*
*Telephone: 714-871-1138*
*Facsimile: 714-871-5620*

*General Criminal Trial Practice in all State and Federal Courts. Administrative and Family Law.*

## MEMBERS OF FIRM

**RICHARD J. CURRAN,** born Weymouth, Massachusetts, October 25, 1942; admitted to bar, 1973, California; 1974, U.S. District Court, Central District of California; 1985, U.S. Court of Appeals, Ninth Circuit, U.S. Supreme Court and U.S. Court of Military Appeals. *Education:* California State College; California State University, Long Beach (B.A., 1970); University of Southern California (J.D., 1973). Pi Kappa Phi. Instructor, Criminal Law and Criminal Procedure, Administration and Criminal Justice Departments, California State University at Fullerton, 1978—. Referee, Orange County Juvenile Court, 1980—. *Member:* Orange County Bar Association; State Bar of California. *PRACTICE AREAS:* Criminal Law.

**WILLIAM G. WATSON,** born Syracuse, New York, March 22, 1947; admitted to bar, 1972, California. *Education:* University of Hawaii; University of Southern California (B.S., 1968; J.D., 1972). Phi Alpha Delta. Instructor, Criminal Law, California State University at Fullerton, 1983. Referee, Orange County Juvenile Court, 1980—. *Member:* Orange County Bar Association; State Bar of California. [With U.S. Army Reserve, 1969-1975]. *PRACTICE AREAS:* Criminal Law; Family Law.

# ELENBAAS & SCHOEMAN
*Established in 1982*
*SUITE 235*
*1370 N. BREA BOULEVARD*
*FULLERTON, CALIFORNIA 92635*
*Telephone: 714-871-7100*
*Fax: 714-871-7142*

*General Civil and Trial practice in all State and Federal Courts, Landlord/Tenant, Business and Corporate Law, Employment Law and Construction Law.*

*FIRM PROFILE: Elenbaas & Schoeman is listed in the Bar Register of Preeminent Lawyers. Our philosophy is to provide the highest quality of legal service, and by remaining small, we are able to maintain our commitment to cost effective representation and personal attention to each of our clients. Over the years we have achieved consistently excellent results for our clients. The firm handles cases in all state and federal courts in California, and our clients have included companies throughout the United States.*

**THOMAS E. ELENBAAS,** born Monrovia, California, August 5, 1952; admitted to bar, 1977, California; U.S. District Court, Central, Northern, Southern and Eastern Districts of California; U.S. Court of Appeals, Fifth, Seventh and Ninth Circuits; U.S. Supreme Court. *Education:* California State University at Fullerton; Western State University (B.S.L., 1975; J.D., 1977). Associate Executive Editor, Western State University Law Review,

*(This Listing Continued)*

*ELENBAAS & SCHOEMAN, Fullerton—Continued*

1976-1977. *Member:* Orange County and Los Angeles County Bar Associations; State Bar of California. **PRACTICE AREAS:** Landlord Tenant; Employment Law; Real Estate; Civil Litigation; Business Litigation; Appellate Practice.

**CARA HAGAN SCHOEMAN,** born Inglewood, California, February 23, 1962; admitted to bar, 1990, California; U.S. District Court, Central, Southern, Northern and Eastern Districts of California; U.S. Court of Appeals, Ninth Circuit. *Education:* University of Southern California (B.S., 1983); Loyola Marymount University (M.B.A., 1985); Western State University (J.D., 1989). *Member:* Orange County and Los Angeles County Bar Associations; Orange County Women Lawyers Association. **PRACTICE AREAS:** Civil Litigation; Business Law; Landlord Tenant; Real Estate; Construction Law.

---

## EDWARD D. GOLDSTEIN
### SUITE 305, 110 EAST WILSHIRE AVENUE
### FULLERTON, CALIFORNIA 92632
Telephone: 714-525-5055
Telecopier: 714-525-6654

*Corporation, Health Care and Business Law.*

**EDWARD D. GOLDSTEIN,** born New York, N.Y., July 12, 1927; admitted to bar, 1953, California, U.S. Court of Appeals, Ninth Circuit and U.S. District Court, Northern District of California; 1957, U.S. District Court, Central District of California. *Education:* Adelphi University; University of Michigan (A.B., 1950; J.D., with distinction, 1952). Phi Kappa Phi; Order of the Coif. Assistant Editor, University of Michigan Law Review, 1951-1952. Member, State of California Solid Waste Management and Resources Recovery Advisory Council, 1972-1973. Chairman of the Board, Knox Glass Co. & Fairmont Glass Co., 1967-1968. Pres. & Chief Executive Officer, Glass Containers Corp., 1968-1982. Member, Board of Trustees, 1982-1988 and Chairman, 1984-1988, St. Jude Hospital & Rehabilitation Center. Chairman, 1995, St. Jude Medical Center Memorial Foundation. Outside General Counsel, FHP International and FHP, Inc., 1985-1987. *Member:* Orange County (Member, Sections on: Business Litigation; Real Estate; OCBA/OCMA) and American (Member: Sections on Antitrust Law and Corporation, Banking and Business Law; Forum Committee on Health Law) Bar Associations; State Bar of California; National Health Lawyers Association; American College of Legal Medicine (Associate-in-Law). **PRACTICE AREAS:** Health Care; Business; Corporate Law.

---

## STANLEY L. MOERBEEK
### 1370 NORTH BREA BOULEVARD, SUITE 210
### FULLERTON, CALIFORNIA 92835-4128
Telephone: 714-773-5396
FAX: 714-773-5837

*Real Estate, Civil Litigation, Personal Injury, Business Representation, Collections and Estates and Estate Litigation.*

**STANLEY L. MOERBEEK,** born Toronto, Canada, November 12, 1951; admitted to bar, 1980, California and U.S. District Court, Central District of California; 1981, U.S. Court of Appeals, Ninth Circuit; 1994, U.S. District Court, District of Arizona. *Education:* California State University at Fullerton (B.A., magna cum laude, 1974); International Business Transactions, Sorbonne and University of San Diego, Paris, France (1977); Loyola Marymount University (J.D., 100% honor roll, 1979); Bankruptcy and Business Rehabilitation Law, University of Southern California Law Center (1982); Orange County Bar Association College of Trial Advocacy. Phi Kappa Phi. Lt. Governor, American Bar Association Ninth Circuit Law Student Division, 1979. Judge Pro Tem, Orange County Superior Court, 1984-. Member, California Association of Realtors Attorney Referral Panel, 1985-. Notary Public. *Member:* Orange County and Los Angeles County Bar Associations.

---

## ROSEMARY NIXON
### *Established in 1978*
### SUITE 240, 1235 NORTH HARBOR BOULEVARD
### FULLERTON, CALIFORNIA 92632
Telephone: 714-773-1938
Fax: 714-773-0986
Email: MISSBRUIN@aol.com

*Family Law, Support & Custody, Bankruptcy and Probate Law and Trust.*

**ROSEMARY NIXON,** born Bloomington, Illinois, July 11, 1937; admitted to bar, 1978, California; 1979, U.S. District Court, Central District of California; 1984, U.S. Supreme Court. *Education:* University of California at Los Angeles (B.A., 1960); Western State University, School of Law (J.D., 1978). Instructor, Community Property, Western State University, College of Law, 1980. Court Appointed Master, Orange County Superior Court, 1987. *Member:* Orange County Bar Association (Member, Sections on: Family Law; Bankruptcy and Chairman, Bankruptcy Section, 1984); State Bar of California.

---

## JAMES A. STEARMAN
### *Established in 1977*
### SUITE 200, 1235 NORTH HARBOR BOULEVARD
### FULLERTON, CALIFORNIA 92632
Telephone: 714-871-1132; 870-8501
Facsimile: 714-871-5620

*General Civil Trial Practice. Collections, Real Estate, Business, Corporate and Partnership Law.*

**JAMES A. STEARMAN,** born Los Angeles, California, June 24, 1951; admitted to bar, 1977, California; 1978, U.S. District Court, Central District of California; 1989, U.S. Supreme Court. *Education:* University of California at Irvine (B.A., 1973); Pepperdine University (J.D., 1977). Recipient, American Jurisprudence Award. Licensed Real Estate Broker, California, 1978. Judge Pro Tem, Orange County, California, 1983-1996. Arbitrator, Professional Standards Committee of G.N.O.C., Association of Realtors. *Member:* Orange County Bar Association (Member, Real Estate Section); State Bar of California (Member, Real Estate Section); National Association of Realtors; California Association of Realtors. **REPORTED CASES:** Ross v. City of Yorba Linda (1991); Calif. Ct. of Appeal-4th Dist. 1 C.A. 4th 954, 2 Cal. Rptr. 2d 638 (Zoning Law-Writ of Mandate).

REPRESENTATIVE CLIENTS: Caesars Palace; Caesars Tahoe; Las Vegas Hilton; Reno Hilton; Mirage Casino-Hotel; Golden Nugget; Paris Blues; Sheraton Anaheim Hotel; MGM Grand Hotel; Treasure Island.

---

## WHEATLEY OSAKI & ASSOCIATES
### 2600 EAST NUTWOOD AVENUE, SUITE 101
### FULLERTON, CALIFORNIA 92831
Telephone: 714-992-6300
FAX: 714-441-1652

Long Beach, California Office: 3780 Kilroy Airport Way, Suite 200, 90806. Telephone: 1-800-422-2090.

*Construction Law, Insurance Defense, Civil Litigation and Collections.*

**JEFF R. WHEATLEY** (1927-1994).

**KERRY G. OSAKI,** born Greeley, Colorado, October 14, 1953; admitted to bar, 1978, California; 1980, U.S. District Court, District of California, U.S. Tax Court and U.S. Circuit Court, Ninth Circuit. *Education:* University of California, Santa Barbara (B.A., 1975); Loyola Law School (J.D., 1978). Author: "Notice Changes Lien Timing," Contractors Advocate, 1st Quarter, 1990; "Collecting Your Money," Geogram, January, 1992. Speaker: "Improving Client Relations, Orange County Japanese American Lawyers Association, October 1992. Mediator, Los Angeles County Bar Attorney, Client Relations Office, 1985—. *Member:* Orange County and Los Angeles County Bar Associations; State Bar of California (Member Sections on: Business Law, 1991—; Estate Planning, Trust and Probate, 1980-1982); Orange County Japanese American Lawyers Association (Member and Board of Directors); Construction Financial Managers Association; Asian Business Association (Member and Board of Directors); Southern California Builders Association. **PRACTICE AREAS:** Construction Law; Contracts/Corporations; Insurance Defense and Collections.

## NEUMILLER & BEARDSLEE
*A PROFESSIONAL CORPORATION*
### GALT, CALIFORNIA
(See Stockton)

*General Civil Practice and Litigation in all State and Federal Courts, Real Property, Condominium, Land Use, Natural Resources, Environmental, Water and Water Rights, Mining, Agricultural, Corporation, Partnership, Business Planning, Securities, Creditor's Rights in Bankruptcy, Taxation, Employee Benefits, Insurance, Administrative, Health Care, Governmental and Legislative, Trusts, Estate Planning, Probate and Municipal Law.*

---

## ERNEST L. HAYWARD
12371 LEWIS STREET
SUITE 102
### GARDEN GROVE, CALIFORNIA 92840-4687
Telephone: 714-750-1414
Fax: 714-750-7743

*Probate and Probate Litigation. Guardianship, Conservatorship and Conservatorship Litigation.*

**ERNEST L. HAYWARD,** born Waltham, Massachusetts, August 16, 1943; admitted to bar, 1975, California; 1978, U.S. District Court, Central District of California. *Education:* California State University at Fullerton (B.A., 1966); California State University at Long Beach; Southwestern University (J.D., 1975); University of Southern California. *Member:* Orange County Bar Association (Member, Elder Law and Probate and Trust Law Sections; Chair, Estate Planning, Probate and Trust Section, 1994); State Bar of California.

REFERENCE: Bank of America.

---

## BAKER, OLSON, LeCROY & DANIELIAN
*A LAW CORPORATION*
144 NORTH BRAND BOULEVARD
P.O. BOX 29062
### GLENDALE, CALIFORNIA 91209-9062
Telephone: 818-502-5600
Facsimile: 818-241-2653

*General Civil and Trial Practice in all State and Federal Courts. Federal and State Tax, Corporation, Partnership, Real Estate, Trust, Estate Planning, Probate, General Business Law, Immigration and Naturalization. Business and Probate Litigation.*

FIRM PROFILE: *Baker, Olson, LeCroy & Danielian, A Law Corporation, is a Glendale law firm presently comprised of highly seasoned lawyers. We are large enough to satisfy the diverse and specialized needs of a wide range of individual and business clients, yet small enough to maintain close and personalized legal representation. We are able to apply the services and talents of our lawyers, the ranks of whom include attorneys/CPAs, certified tax specialists, and litigation specialists, to client matters wherever necessary.*

*Finally, we pride ourselves in keeping current. Every lawyer in our firm participates in continuing legal education programs and seminars to sharpen existing skills and stay on top of current legal developments.*

**SHELDON S. BAKER,** born St. Paul, Minnesota, December 4, 1936; admitted to bar, 1962, California. *Education:* Rutgers University (B.A., summa cum laude, 1958); Stanford University (J.D., 1961). Order of the Coif; Phi Beta Kappa; Pi Sigma Alpha. Revising Editor, Stanford Law Review, 1960-1961. Co-author: "Post Mortem Tax Planning," 1966 and "California Inheritance Tax Practice," 1973, California Continuing Education of the Bar, University of California. Member, Glendale City Council, 1993—. Chairman, Glendale City Housing Authority, 1993-1994. Chairmen Glendale Redevelopment Agency, 1995. Member, Housing & Economic Development Committee, California League of Cities, 1995—. Member, 1965-1981 and President, 1967-1968; 1972-1973; 1979-1980, Glendale Unified School District Board of Education, Glendale, California. Member, 1965-1981 and President, 1967-1968; 1971-1972; 1975-1976; 1980-1981, Glendale Community College District, Board of Education, Glendale, California. President, Los Angeles County School Trustees Association, 1976-1978. President, California School Boards Association, 1980. *Member:* Glendale, Los Angeles County and American (Member, Sections of: Business Law; Taxation; Corporation, Banking and Business Law; Member, Committee

*(This Listing Continued)*

on Pension and Profit Sharing Trusts, Real Property, Probate and Trust Law Section, 1976-1977) Bar Associations; State Bar of California (Member, Sections on Taxation; Real Property). (Certified Specialist, Taxation Law, The State Bar of California Board of Legal Specialization).

**ERIC OLSON,** born Los Angeles, California, December 8, 1940; admitted to bar, 1966, California, U.S. Court of Appeals, Ninth Circuit, U.S. District Court, Northern District of California, U.S. District Court, Southern District of California (now Central District) and U.S. Tax Court; 1971, U.S. Supreme Court; 1982, U.S. District Court, Southern and Eastern Districts of California. *Education:* Pomona College (B.A., 1962); Harvard University (J.D., 1965); Stanford University. Teaching Fellow, Stanford Law School, 1965-1966. Los Angeles County Deputy County Counsel, Schools Division, 1968-1969. *Member:* Los Angeles County Bar Association (Member, Sections on: Law of Local Government, 1970—; Trial Lawyers, 1970—; Commercial Law and Bankruptcy, 1970—; Vice President and Director, Credit Union, 1978-1981). *PRACTICE AREAS:* Business Law; Real Property; Commercial; Business Litigation; Probate Litigation.

**CHARLES L. LECROY, III,** born Louisville, Kentucky, June 4, 1953; admitted to bar, 1978, California; 1984, U.S. Tax Court. *Education:* University of California at Los Angeles (B.A., magna cum laude, 1975); University of California at Davis (J.D., 1978). Member, University of California at Davis Law Review, 1977-1978. *Member:* Los Angeles County Bar Association (Member, Sections on: Taxation; Real Property; Probate and Trust Law); The State Bar of California (Member, Sections on: Real Property Law; Estate Planning, Probate and Trust Law and Business Law). (Certified Specialist, Taxation Law, The State Bar of California Board of Legal Specialization).

**ARSEN DANIELIAN,** born Tehran, Iran, May 17, 1954; admitted to bar, 1985, California and U.S. District Court, Central District of California; 1986, U.S. District Court, Eastern, Southern and Northern Districts of California and U.S. Court of Appeals, Ninth Circuit; 1989, U.S. Supreme Court. *Education:* National University of Iran (LL.B., 1978) University of La Verne (M.A., 1982; J.D., 1984). Chairman, Executive Board, Garikian Scholarship Fund, Western Prelacy of the Armenian Apostolic Church of America, 1981—. Secretary, Board of Trustees, Holy Martyrs Armenian Apostolic Church and Ferrahian School, 1982-1983. Chairman, Education Council, Western Prelacy of the Armenian Apostolic Church of America, 1987-1991. Chairman, Eighteenth National Representative Assembly, Western Prelacy of the Armenian Apostolic Church of America, 1990. Secretary, (1990-1992), Vice-Chairman, (1992—); Executive Council, Western Prelacy of the Armenian Apostolic Church of America. Member, Board of Trustees and Executive Committee of the Board of Trustees, American Armenian International College, University of La Verne, 1990-1991. Chairman, Glendale Schools 2000 Action Planning Team (GUSD), 1992-1993. Member, Board of Directors, Armenian Educational Foundation, 1992—. Secretary, Board of Directors, United American Fund, (1994—). Member, Board of Directors, Glendale Symphony Orchestra Association, (1994—). *Member:* Los Angeles County (Member, Immigration Law Section), American and International Bar Associations; State Bar of California (Member, International Law Section). *LANGUAGES:* Armenian and Persian (Farsi).

---

**MICHAEL S. SIMON,** born Philadelphia, Pennsylvania, November 9, 1960; admitted to bar, 1987, California; 1988, U.S. Tax Court and U.S. District Court, Central District of California; 1990, U.S. Court of Appeals, Ninth Circuit; 1991, U.S. District Court, Northern District of California. *Education:* University of California at Los Angeles (B.A., Economics, 1983); Loyola Law School (J.D., 1986). Settlement Officer, Los Angeles Municipal Court, 1991—. *Member:* Beverly Hills (Member, Sections on Litigation, Probate, Trusts and Estate Planning and Taxation) and Los Angeles County (Member, Sections on: Litigation; Taxation; Trust and Estates) Bar Associations; State Bar of California (Member, Sections on: Litigation; Taxation; Estate Planning, Trust and Probate).

### OF COUNSEL

**JOHN J. JACOBSON,** born Los Angeles, California, October 22, 1950; admitted to bar, 1981, California. *Education:* California State University at Northridge (B.S., 1972; M.S., 1976); University of Southern California (M.B.T., 1980); University of California at Los Angeles (J.D., 1981). Certified Public Accountant, California, 1975. *Member:* Los Angeles County (Member, Sections on: Probate; Taxation) Bar Association; State Bar of California (Member, Sections on: Estate Planning, Trust and Probate; Taxation); California Society of Certified Public Accountants.

## BENJAMIN, LUGOSI & BENJAMIN, LLP

520 NORTH CENTRAL AVENUE, SUITE 800
### GLENDALE, CALIFORNIA 91203-1919
Telephone: 818-502-8400
Fax: 818-956-1099
Email: INFO@BENJILULAW.COM

*Entertainment Law, Licensing, Rights of Publicity and Privacy, General, Civil and Business Litigation including Bad Faith.*

**BELA G. LUGOSI,** born Los Angeles, California, January 5, 1938; admitted to bar, 1964, California and U.S. District Court, Central District of California; 1973, U.S. District Court, Southern District of California; 1979, U.S. District Court, Eastern District of California; 1985, U.S. Supreme Court. *Education:* University of Southern California (B.S., 1960; LL.B., 1964). Phi Delta Phi. *Member:* Los Angeles County (Member, Executive Committee, and Chairman, Alternative Dispute Resolution Section, 1995-1996; Member, Executive Committee, 1975-1983 and Chairman, Trial Lawyers Section, 1975-1976; Member, Committees on: Judiciary, 1980; Judicial Appointments, 1980-1981; Member, 1980-1985 and Chairman, 1983-1985, Fair Judicial Election Practices) and American (Member, Litigation Section) Bar Associations; The State Bar of California; Chancery Club (Los Angeles Chapter); Association of Business Trial Lawyers; Association of Attorney-Mediators. **PRACTICE AREAS:** Business Litigation; Entertainment Law; Alternative Dispute Resolution. **Email:** BELAL@BENJILULAW.COM

**ROBERT N. BENJAMIN,** born Cleveland, Ohio, November 7, 1946; admitted to bar, 1979, California, U.S. District Court, Central and Northern Districts of California and U.S. Court of Appeals, Ninth Circuit. *Education:* California State University at Northridge (B.S., 1971); Southwestern University (J.D., cum laude, 1979). Phi Alpha Delta. Editor, Southwestern Law Review, 1978-1979. *Member:* Burbank and Los Angeles (Member, Litigation Section) Bar Associations; State Bar of California. **PRACTICE AREAS:** Entertainment Law; Licensing; Business Litigation; Insurance Bad Faith.

**EARL M. BENJAMIN,** born Bay Village, Ohio, January 14, 1952; admitted to bar, 1979, California. *Education:* Ohio University (A.B., cum laude, 1975); University of San Diego (J.D., cum laude, 1979). Phi Beta Kappa. Member, San Diego Law Review, 1978-1979.

**MARK W. YOCCA,** born Los Angeles, California, July 15, 1963; admitted to bar, 1988, California, U.S. District Court, Central District of California and U.S. Court of Appeals, Ninth Circuit. *Education:* University of California, Santa Barbara (B.A., 1985); Loyola Law School, Los Angeles (J.D., 1988). St. Thomas More Law Honor Society. Member, Loyola of Los Angeles Law Review, 1986-1987. *Member:* Los Angeles County and Intellectual Property Bar Associations. **PRACTICE AREAS:** Business Litigation; Entertainment Law; Insurance Coverage; Insurance Bad Faith.

**FRANK LUPO,** born Brooklyn, New York, April 20, 1955; admitted to bar, 1986, California; 1988, U.S. District Court, Central District of California. *Education:* University of California at Santa Cruz (B.A., 1982); Loyola University of Los Angeles (J.D., 1985). Staff Writer, 1983-1984; Articles Editor, 1984-1985, Loyola Entertainment Law Journal. Law Clerk, 1984-1986; Associate, 1986-1988, Girardi, Keene and Crane. *Member:* Burbank, Los Angeles County and Media District Intellectual Property Bar Associations; State Bar of California. **PRACTICE AREAS:** Entertainment Law; Licensing; Business Litigation; Insurance Coverage; Insurance Bad Faith. **Email:** FLUPO@BENJILULAW.COM

**TAVI B. BENJAMIN,** born New Orleans, Louisiana, January 8, 1966; admitted to bar, 1993, Louisiana; 1995, California. *Education:* Louisiana State University (B.A., 1988); Loyola University, School of Law (J.D., 1993). Phi Delta Phi (President). *Member:* Los Angeles County Bar Association; State Bar of California; Louisiana State Bar Association. **PRACTICE AREAS:** Entertainment; General Business. **Email:** TAVIB@BENJILULAW.COM

REPRESENTATIVE CLIENTS: Comedy 111 Productions, Inc.; Classic Characters Entertainment Group; Republic Indemnity Company of America; Pacific Rim, Assurance Co.

## BRIGHT AND BROWN

550 NORTH BRAND BOULEVARD, SUITE 2100
### GLENDALE, CALIFORNIA 91203
Telephone: 818-243-2121; 213-489-1414
Facsimile: 818-243-3225

*Business Litigation, Oil, Gas and Energy Law and Environmental Law.*

FIRM PROFILE: Since its inception in 1981, the law firm of Bright and Brown has specialized in complex business and commercial litigation. The firms areas of expertize in litigation include business torts, contracts disputes, a wide range of energy and energy related matters, federal and state environmental disputes (involving the Federal Superfund Act, the Resources Conservation and Recovery Act and similar state statues), and defense of criminal prosecution alleging environmental violations. The firm also has general litigation expertise in the area of land use regulation. While the business and commercial litigation is the core of the firm's practice, the firm also has a high level of expertise representing clients in oil and gas matters, and in state and federal administrative proceedings relating to land use and environmental regulation.

The firm's partners and senior associates have substantial experience in both state and federal courts at trial and appellate levels. Certain members of the firm also have substantial experience with methods of alternative dispute resolution, including arbitration, mediation and private settlement conferences.

**JAMES S. BRIGHT,** born Glendale, California, 1949; admitted to bar, 1975, California; 1976, U.S. District Court, Central District of California; 1980, U.S. District Court, Northern, Eastern and Southern Districts of California; 1987, U.S. Court of Appeals, Ninth Circuit; 1989, U.S. District Court, Northern District of Texas. *Education:* University of Southern California (B.S., 1971); Loyola University of Los Angeles (J.D., 1975). *Member:* Los Angeles County (Member, Section on: Litigation) and American (Member, Sections on: Litigation; Natural Resources Law) Bar Associations; State Bar of California. Fellow, American College of Trial Lawyers. **PRACTICE AREAS:** Business Litigation; Oil and Gas; Environmental.

**GREGORY C. BROWN,** born Glendale, California, 1951; admitted to bar, 1976, California; 1977, U.S. Court of Appeals Ninth Circuit and U.S. District Court, Central District of California; 1991, U.S. District Court, Eastern and Northern Circuits of California. *Education:* George Washington University (B.A., with honors, 1973); University of California at Los Angeles (J.D., 1976). Phi Beta Kappa. Member, The Order of Barristers. Member, Executive Board, UCLA Moot Court Honors Program, 1975-1976. *Member:* Los Angeles County (Member, Section on: Litigation) and American (Member, Sections on: Natural Resources Law; Litigation) Bar Associations; State Bar of California. **PRACTICE AREAS:** Business Litigation; Oil and Gas; Environmental.

**MAUREEN J. BRIGHT,** born Hollywood, California, 1950; admitted to bar, 1978, California; 1979, U.S. District Court, Central District of California; 1989, U.S. District Court, Southern District of California and U.S. Court of Appeals, Ninth Circuit. *Education:* University of Southern California (B.S., cum laude, 1972); Loyola University of Los Angeles (J.D., 1978). *Member:* Los Angeles County (Member, Section on: Litigation) and American (Member, Section on: Litigation) Bar Associations; State Bar of California; Catholic Health Association. **PRACTICE AREAS:** Business Litigation; Environmental.

**JOHN QUIRK,** born Ridgecrest, California, 1949; admitted to bar, 1979, California; 1980, U.S. District Court, Central District of California; 1981, U.S. District Court, Eastern District of California; 1989, U.S. District Court, Northern and Southern Districts of California and U.S. Court of Appeals, Ninth Circuit. *Education:* California State University at Northridge (B.A., summa cum laude, 1976); Loyola University of Los Angeles (J.D., cum laude, 1979). Visiting Lecturer: Jurisprudence, California State University at Northridge, 1980; "An Overview of California Oil and Gas Law, Leasing and Division Order Practice," The National Association of Lease and Title Analysts, August 1990; "Purchasing and Selling Marginal Properties," American Association of Petroleum Landmen, 1989 West Coast Institute; "California Well Abandonment: DOG Compliance Oversight and Enforcement, and Abandonment Bond Requirements," American Association of Professional Landmen, 1994 West Coast Institute; "Preferential Purchase Rights, Perpetuities and Marketable Record Title," American Association of Professional Landmen, 1996 West Coast Institute. Volunteer Judge Pro Tempore, Los Angeles County Superior Court. *Member:* Los Angeles County and American Bar Associations; The State Bar of California (Member, Section on Natural Resources Law); American Association of Petroleum Landmen. **PRACTICE AREAS:** Oil and Gas Transactions and Title; Land Use Regulation and Permitting.

*(This Listing Continued)*

**BRIAN L. BECKER,** born Manhattan, Kansas, 1959; admitted to bar, 1984, California; 1985, U.S. District Court, Central District of California; U.S. Court of Appeals, Ninth Circuit; U.S. District Court, Eastern and Northern Districts of California; U.S. District Court, District of Arizona. *Education:* Washburn University (B.A., summa cum laude, 1981); Kansas University (J.D., 1984). Order of the Coif. Member, Kansas Law Review, 1983-1984. *Member:* Los Angeles County (Member, Section on Alternative Dispute Resolution) and American (Member, Section on Litigation) Bar Associations; State Bar of California (Member, Section on Litigation). *PRACTICE AREAS:* Business Litigation.

### ASSOCIATES

**ANTHONY S. BRILL,** born Los Angeles, California, 1963; admitted to bar, 1990, California; California Supreme Court; U.S. District Court, Central, Northern, Southern and Eastern Districts of California; U.S. Court of Appeals, Ninth Judicial Circuit. *Education:* University of California at Los Angeles (B.A., 1986); University of Southern California (J.D., 1990). Phi Alpha Delta. *Member:* Los Angeles County (Member, Sections on: Environmental Law, Natural Resources and Business Litigation) and American Bar Associations; State Bar of California. *PRACTICE AREAS:* Business Litigation; Oil and Gas; Environmental.

**DORIS A. MENDENHALL,** born Los Angeles, California, October 12, 1956; admitted to bar, 1994, California. *Education:* Stanford University (A.B., 1978); University of California at Los Angeles (J.D., 1994). Phi Beta Kappa. *Member:* Los Angeles Bar Association; State Bar of California (Member, Environmental Section). *PRACTICE AREAS:* Business Litigation; Environmental.

## CALENDO, PUCKETT, SHEEDY & DiCORRADO

701 NORTH BRAND BOULEVARD, SUITE 300
**GLENDALE, CALIFORNIA 91203**
Telephone: 818-549-1935
Facsimile: 818-549-0337

*General Defense Litigation in all Courts and Tribunals. Personal Injury, Premises Liability, Products Liability, Property Damage and Virtually every type of Tort Claim.*

FIRM PROFILE: *The law firm of Calendo, Puckett, Sheedy & DiCorrado is an active civil litigation firm representing insurance carriers and insureds in all areas of general defense litigation. This includes insurance fraud detection and defense, automobile losses, premises liability, products liability, property damage, uninsured motorist, and virtually every type of tort claim. The firm's attorneys are successful and well respected lawyers who have extensive litigation experience.*

*The partners of Calendo, Puckett, Sheedy & DiCorrado have extensive litigation experience in all superior and municipal courts, along with arbitration experience in all courts and in front of all private tribunals. The firm has a diverse civil litigation case load with emphasis on general insurance defense with a specialty in insurance fraud detection and defense. This includes direct responsibility for cases involving all aspects of medical fraud, property, arson, premises and all aspects of fraudulent claims involving automobile losses.*

*In addition to the litigation experience, members of the firm have presented seminars and claims training programs to carriers and organizations both in California and nationwide with respect to fraud recognition, medical and clinic practices, litigation strategies, attorney and investigator roles in fraud deterrence.*

### MEMBERS OF FIRM

**STEPHEN P. CALENDO,** born Maywood, Illinois, February 2, 1957; admitted to bar, 1982, Arizona; 1984, California and U.S. District Court, Central District of California and District of Arizona. *Education:* Arizona State University (B.S., 1979); Pepperdine University School of Law (J.D., 1982). *Member:* Los Angeles County and American Bar Associations; State Bar of Arizona; State Bar of California; Association of Southern California Defense Counsel; Southern California Fraud Investigators Association. *PRACTICE AREAS:* Civil Litigation; Insurance Defense.

**KIM B. PUCKETT, (MR.),** born Beech Grove, Indiana, December 23, 1953; admitted to bar, 1979, California, Colorado and U.S. District Court, Central District of California. *Education:* Indiana University (B.A.,1976); Loyola Marymount University (J.D., 1979). *Member:* Los Angeles County, Colorado and American Bar Associations; State Bar of California; Association of Southern California Defense Counsel. *PRACTICE AREAS:* Civil Litigation; Insurance Defense.

*(This Listing Continued)*

**CHRISTOPHER M. SHEEDY,** born Buffalo, New York, March 13, 1954; admitted to bar, 1984, California and U.S. District Court, Central District of California. *Education:* San Francisco State University; California State University at Long Beach (B.A., 1980); Southwestern University (J.D., 1983). Member, Moot Court Honors Program. Public Defender, Los Angeles, 1984-1986. *Member:* Los Angeles County and American Bar Associations; State Bar of California; Association of Southern California Defense Counsel. *PRACTICE AREAS:* Civil Litigation; Insurance Defense.

**RICHARD A. DiCORRADO,** born Mineola, New York, January 1, 1957; admitted to bar, 1985, California and U.S. District Court, Central District of California. *Education:* Rutgers University (B.A., 1979); Pepperdine University (J.D., 1983). *Member:* Los Angeles County and American Bar Associations; State Bar of California; Association of Southern California Defense Counsel. *PRACTICE AREAS:* Civil Litigation; Insurance Defense.

**CHRISTOPHER E. DWYER,** born San Francisco, California, April 11, 1960; admitted to bar, 1987, California and U.S. Court of Appeals, Ninth Circuit. *Education:* University of California at Irvine (B.A., 1982); Southwestern University School of Law (J.D., 1986). *Member:* Los Angeles County and American Bar Associations; State Bar of California; Association of Southern California Defense Counsel. *PRACTICE AREAS:* Civil Litigation; Insurance Defense.

### ASSOCIATES

**PATRICIA ARIANA DUPRE,** born Los Angeles, California, March 11, 1949; admitted to bar, 1985, California, U.S. District Court, Central District of California and U.S. Court of Appeals, Ninth Circuit. *Education:* Los Angeles City College (A.A., 1982); California State College at Los Angeles; Southwestern University School of Law (J.D., 1985). *Member:* Los Angeles County (Member, Client Relations Committee, 1986—) and American Bar Associations; State Bar of California; Los Angeles Women Lawyers; Association of Southern California Defense Counsel. *LANGUAGES:* Italian. *PRACTICE AREAS:* Civil Litigation; Insurance Defense.

**ADRIENNE R. BERNSTEIN-HAHN,** born Manhattan, New York, October 11, 1961; admitted to bar, 1988, California, U.S. District Court, Central District of California and U.S. Court of Appeals, Ninth Circuit. *Education:* University of California at Los Angeles (B.A., 1985); Loyola Marymount University (J.D., 1988). *Member:* Los Angeles County and American Bar Association; State Bar of California; Women Lawyers of Los Angeles; Association of Southern California Defense Counsel. *LANGUAGES:* Spanish and French. *PRACTICE AREAS:* Civil Litigation; Insurance Defense.

**BRIAN C. O'HARA,** born Washington, D.C., October 3, 1955; admitted to bar, 1988, California and U.S. District Court, Central, Southern and Eastern Districts of California. *Education:* University of Colorado; University of California at Los Angeles (B.A., 1979); Loyola University at Los Angeles (J.D., 1987). *Member:* Los Angeles County and American Bar Associations; The State Bar of California; Association of Southern California Defense Counsel. *PRACTICE AREAS:* Civil Litigation; Insurance Defense Law.

**MARY ANN BURKIN,** born Kansas City, Kansas, August 9, 1949; admitted to bar, 1992, California and U.S. District Court, Central District of California. *Education:* University of Southern California (B.A., 1970); California State University, Long Beach (M.A., 1977); Loyola Law School (J.D., 1992). *Member:* Los Angeles County Bar Association; State Bar of California. *PRACTICE AREAS:* Civil Litigation; Insurance Defense.

**MARK L. RUSSAKOW,** born Henrietta, New York, June 13, 1967; admitted to bar, 1992, California. *Education:* University of California, Irvine (B.A., 1989); Loyola Law School (J.D., 1992). *Member:* Los Angeles County Bar Association; State Bar of California; Association of Southern California Defense Counsel. *PRACTICE AREAS:* Civil Litigation; Insurance Defense.

**JAMES L. MEIER,** born Phoenix, Arizona, May 3, 1967; admitted to bar, 1993, California. *Education:* Indiana University (B.S., 1989); De Paul University College of Law (J.D., 1993). Order of the Coif. *Member:* Los Angeles County Bar Association; State Bar of California; Association of Southern California Defense Association. *PRACTICE AREAS:* Civil Litigation; Insurance Defense.

**MICHAEL J. RILEY,** born Los Angeles, California, April 22, 1966; admitted to bar, 1994, California. *Education:* California State University at Northridge (B.A., 1990); Loyola University of Los Angeles (J.D., 1993).

*(This Listing Continued)*

**CALENDO, PUCKETT, SHEEDY & DiCORRADO,**
Glendale—Continued

*Member:* Los Angeles County Bar Association; State Bar of California.
**PRACTICE AREAS:** Civil Litigation; Insurance Defense.

**GREGORY M. CRIBBS,** born Lakewood, California, October 14, 1965; admitted to bar, 1995, California. *Education:* University of California, Los Angeles (B.A., 1988); University of San Diego (J.D., 1994). *Member:* Los Angeles County Bar Association (Barristers). **PRACTICE AREAS:** Civil Litigation; Insurance Defense.

REPRESENTATIVE CLIENTS: Allstate Insurance Co.; Atlantic Mutual Insurance Co.; Avis World Headquarters; Baker, Monk & Elliston; Budget Rent-a-Car; CalFarm Insurance Co.; Colonial Penn Insurance Co.; Fireman's Fund Insurance Co.; Maryland Casualty Insurance Co.; May Dept. Stores; Progressive Insurance Co.; Safeco Insurance Co.; State Farm Insurance Co.; Wawanesa Insurance Co.; Automobile Club of Southern California; CNA.

## DENNEY & OTHS
*130 NORTH BRAND BOULEVARD*
*FOURTH FLOOR*
**GLENDALE, CALIFORNIA 91203**
*Telephone: 818-500-9030*
*Fax: 818-500-8079*
*Email: 71361@compuserve.com*

*Environmental Law and Litigation.*

**RICHARD J. DENNEY, JR.,** born Kansas City, Missouri, July 27, 1939; admitted to bar, 1965, California; 1969, District of Columbia; 1985, Illinois. *Education:* Stanford University (B.S., 1961); Harvard University (J.D., 1964). Co-Editor, *California Environmental Law Handbook, Ninth Edition,* Government Institutes, Inc., 1995. Assistant General Counsel, East African Community, 1966-1968; Assistant General Counsel, Air, Noise and Radiation Division, 1971-1976; Associate General Counsel, Pesticides and Toxic Substances Division, 1976-1978 and Associate General Counsel, Toxic Substances Division, 1978-1980, U.S. Environmental Protection Agency. Listed In The Best Lawyers in America, Woodward White, 1997-1998. **PRACTICE AREAS:** Environmental; Litigation.

**ELEANOR F. OTHS,** born New Rochelle, New York, July 11, 1964; admitted to bar, 1989, California. *Education:* Indiana University (B.A., 1985; J.D., 1989). Phi Beta Kappa. Co-Author: *California Environmental Law Handbook, Ninth Edition,* Government Institutes, Inc., 1995. Co-Chairman, California State Bar, Environmental Section, Subcommittee on Hazardous Waste Remediation, 1995. *Member:* Los Angeles County (Environmental Law Section); American Bar Association; State Bar of California (Environmental Law Section). **LANGUAGES:** French. **PRACTICE AREAS:** Environmental; Litigation.

*OF COUNSEL*

**JOSEPH J. O'MALLEY,** born Wilkes-Barre, Pennsylvania, October 24, 1923; admitted to bar, 1956, District of Columbia; 1977, California. *Education:* University of Scranton (B.A., 1946); Georgetown University (J.D., 1956). Trial Attorney, Antitrust Division, Department of Justice, 1957-1965. Associate Chief Counsel, Merger and Branch Litigation and Antitrust, Office of Comptroller of the Currency, U.S. Treasury Department, 1965-1968. Assistant Director Litigation, Bureau of Competition, Federal Trade Commission, Washington, D.C., 1968-1976. **PRACTICE AREAS:** Corporate Litigation; Antitrust; Environmental.

## EDWARDS, EDWARDS & ASHTON
*A PROFESSIONAL CORPORATION*
*Established in 1952*
*SUITE 500 WELLS FARGO BANK BUILDING*
*420 NORTH BRAND BOULEVARD*
**GLENDALE, CALIFORNIA 91203**
*Telephone: 818-247-7380*
*Los Angeles: 213-245-9451*
*FAX: 818-247-7025*

*General Civil and Trial Practice. Wills, Trusts, Probate, Estate Planning, Taxation, Corporations, Business, Commercial, Real Property, Family and Personal Injury Law.*

*(This Listing Continued)*

*FIRM PROFILE: Edwards, Edwards & Ashton has served Glendale and its neighboring communities for more than forty years as a general civil law practice. The firm began in 1952 as a partnership of brothers John and Mark Edwards, who remain active in the firm's practice. The firm strives to provide high quality legal services in the following areas of emphasis: Probate, Estate Planning and Trust Law, Corporate and Business Planning; Family law; Real Estate Transactional work; General Civil Trial practice; and Business and Real Estate Litigation.*

*The firm believes strongly in demonstrating a commitment to the community it serves and encourages its attorneys to contribute their time and experience to local service clubs, the chamber of commerce, and community agencies and charities.*

**JOHN U. EDWARDS,** born Kobe, Japan, April 23, 1919; admitted to bar, 1946, California; 1953, U.S. District Court, Southern District of California. *Education:* University of California at Berkeley (B.A., 1939); University of California, Boalt Hall (LL.B., 1946). Member, National Panel, American Arbitration Association. *Member:* Glendale (President, 1951), Los Angeles County (Member: Board of Trustees, 1963-1964; Probate and Trust Law Section) and American Bar Associations; State Bar of California (Member, Section on Estate Planning, Trust and Probate). **PRACTICE AREAS:** Probate and Estate Planning; General Business; Civil Litigation.

**MARK U. EDWARDS,** born Chicago, Illinois, January 25, 1921; admitted to bar, 1952, California; 1954, U.S. District Court, Southern District of California; 1971, U.S. Supreme Court. *Education:* University of California at Berkeley (B.A., 1942); Hastings College of Law (LL.B., 1951). *Member:* Glendale (President, 1964-1965), Los Angeles County (Member, Family Law Section) and American (Member, Family Law Section) Bar Associations; State Bar of California (Member, Family Law Section); Los Angeles Trial Lawyers Association; California Trial Lawyers Association; The Association of Trial Lawyers of America. (Certified Specialist, Family Law, The State Bar of California Board of Legal Specialization). **PRACTICE AREAS:** Family Law; Personal Injury and Property Damage Litigation.

**ERIC A. ASHTON,** born New York, N.Y., February 24, 1931; admitted to bar, 1959, California. *Education:* University of Southern California (B.S., 1953; M.A., 1954; J.D., 1958). Certified Public Accountant, California, 1959. *Member:* Glendale, Los Angeles County and American Bar Associations; State Bar of California. Fellow: American College of Trust and Estate Counsel; International Academy of Estate and Trust Law. **PRACTICE AREAS:** Estate Planning; Probate and Trust Law; General Business; Tax Planning.

**JEFFREY P. BRANDT,** born Los Angeles, California, March 11, 1953; admitted to bar, 1978, California; 1982, U.S. Tax Court; 1989, U.S. District Court, Central District of California. *Education:* University of California at Irvine (B.A., 1975); University of California at Berkeley (J.D., 1978); New York University (LL.M. in Taxation, 1979). Phi Beta Kappa. Author: "Change in Ownership," California Taxation, Chapter 88, Matthew Bender, 1989; "Appointment of Trustees" and "Trustees Powers," California Wills and Trusts, Matthew Bender 1992. *Member:* Los Angeles County and American (Member, Sections on: Taxation; Real Property, Probate and Trust Law) Bar Associations; State Bar of California (Member, Estate Planning, Trust and Probate Section). (Certified Specialist, Estate Planning, Trust and Probate Law, California Board of Legal Specialization). **PRACTICE AREAS:** Estate Planning; Probate and Trust Law.

**WILBUR GIN,** born Los Angeles, California, September 11, 1955; admitted to bar, 1980, California; 1982, U.S. District Court, Central District of California and U.S. Tax Court. *Education:* University of California at Los Angeles (B.A., summa cum laude, 1977; J.D., 1980). Phi Beta Kappa. Member, University of California at Los Angeles International Law Journal, 1978-1980. *Member:* Los Angeles County (Member, Sections on: Taxation, Business, Real Property and Estate Planning; Trust and Probate) and Glendale Bar Associations; State Bar of California (Member, Sections on: Taxation, Business, Real Property and Estate Planning; Trust and Probate). **PRACTICE AREAS:** Real Estate Transactions; General Business and Corporate; Estate Planning.

**DONNA M. ENCINAS,** born Los Angeles, California, September 23, 1961; admitted to bar, 1989, California and U.S. District Court, Central District of California. *Education:* University of California at Santa Barbara (B.A., 1983); Southwestern University (J.D., 1988). Phi Alpha Delta. *Member:* Glendale, Los Angeles County and San Fernando Valley (Member, Sections on: Barristers; Family Law) Bar Associations; State Bar of California. **PRACTICE AREAS:** Family Law.

**ERIC ANDREW ASHTON,** born Glendale, California, November 7, 1964; admitted to bar, 1990, California; 1991, U.S. District Court, Central

*(This Listing Continued)*

District of California. *Education:* University of California, Berkeley (A.B., 1986); University of Southern California (J.D., 1990; M.B.A., 1990). *Member:* Glendale, Los Angeles County Bar Associations; State Bar of California. *PRACTICE AREAS:* Estate Planning; Taxation; Real Estate Transactions.

### OF COUNSEL

**BRIAN D. COCHRAN,** born San Diego, California, October 26, 1946; admitted to bar, 1974, California and U.S. District Court, Central District of California; 1986, New York. *Education:* University of California at Los Angeles (B.A., 1968; M.B.A., with honors, 1970); Southwestern University (J.D., cum laude, 1974). Note and Comments Editor, Southwestern University Law Review, 1974. Author: "Appellate Review of Sentences: A Survey," 17 St. Louis University Law Journal 221, 1972; "Book Reviews," 17 St. Louis University Law Journal 298, 1972, 17 St. Louis University Law Journal 430, 1973 and 18 St. Louis University Law Journal 170, 1974; "Time Sharing Ownership of Condominiums," 8 Beverly Hills Bar Journal 41, March-April, 1974; "Emerging Products Liability Under Section 2-318 of the Uniform Commercial Code: A Survey," 29 The Business Lawyer 975, April, 1974; "California Insurance Information and Privacy Protection Act," 4 Los Angeles Lawyer 14, March, 1981; "How to Introduce A Computer Into Your Law Office," Interface Age, Feb., 1983. *Member:* Los Angeles County and American Bar Associations; State Bar of California (Delegate, 1981; Member, 1982—, Vice Chair, 1983-1984 and Chair, 1984-1985, Group Insurance Committee). *PRACTICE AREAS:* Insurance; Business and Commercial Litigation.

REFERENCES: Bank of America; Central Bank of Glendale; Wells Fargo Bank.

---

## FLANAGAN, BOOTH, UNGER & MOSES

*Established in 1979*

**1156 NORTH BRAND BOULEVARD**
**GLENDALE, CALIFORNIA 91202-2582**
*Telephone: 818-244-8694*
*Fax: 818-244-1852*

Santa Ana, California Office: 1851 East First Street, Suite 805. 92705. Telephone: 714-835-2607. Fax: 714-835-4825.

*General Civil and Trial Practice in all Courts. Criminal, Driving While Intoxicated and Personal Injury Law.*

### MEMBERS OF FIRM

**J. MICHAEL FLANAGAN,** born Fullerton, California, December 30, 1941; admitted to bar, 1970, California; 1973, U.S. Supreme Court. *Education:* University of Southern California (B.S., 1965; M.B.A., 1968; J.D., 1969). Phi Delta Phi. Instructor, Trial of Drunk Driving Cases, University of Southern California, 1983—. *Member:* Glendale (President, 1984-1985) and Los Angeles County Bar Associations; The State Bar of California; California Trial Lawyers Association; The Association of Trial Lawyers of America; Criminal Courts Bar Association (Member, Board of Trustees, 1980-1983). *PRACTICE AREAS:* Criminal Law; Personal Injury Law.

**DOUGLAS M. BOOTH,** born California, March 16, 1944; admitted to bar, 1975, California. *Education:* University of Nevada; Western State University (B.S., 1973; J.D., 1975). *Member:* Orange County and American Bar Associations; The State Bar of California; Orange County Trial Lawyers Association. *PRACTICE AREAS:* Personal Injury.

**CHARLES J. UNGER,** born Alexandria, Virginia, October 30, 1955; admitted to bar, 1981, California. *Education:* Northwestern University (B.A., 1977); University of Illinois (J.D., 1980). Instructor on Criminal Defense Tactics, Emphasis on DUI Defense, A Continuing Education Course at University at Southern California, 1984-1987. *Member:* Glendale and Los Angeles County Bar Associations; The State Bar of California. *PRACTICE AREAS:* Criminal Law; Personal Injury Law.

**J. BARRY MOSES,** born Corona, California, September 5, 1953; admitted to bar, 1984, California. *Education:* Western State University (B.S., 1982; J.D., 1982). *Member:* Orange County and American Bar Associations; The State Bar of California; Orange County Trial Lawyers Association. *PRACTICE AREAS:* Personal Injury.

*(This Listing Continued)*

### ASSOCIATES

**MICHAEL T. DANIS,** born Covina, California, May 15, 1959; admitted to bar, 1984, California. *Education:* California State Polytechnic University (B.A., 1980); University of California at Los Angeles (J.D., 1983). Phi Kappa Phi. Outstanding Scholar. *Member:* The State Bar of California. *PRACTICE AREAS:* Personal Injury.

**JAMES A. GROVER,** born Los Angeles, California, August 14, 1959; admitted to bar, 1988, California. *Education:* University of California at Los Angeles (B.A., 1982); Santa Clara University (J.D., 1987). *Member:* Glendale and Los Angeles County Bar Associations; State Bar of California. *PRACTICE AREAS:* Criminal; Personal Injury Law.

---

## GILL AND BALDWIN

*Established in 1962*

**130 NORTH BRAND BOULEVARD**
**FOURTH FLOOR**
**GLENDALE, CALIFORNIA 91203**
*Telephone: 818-500-7755; 213-245-3131*
*Fax: 818-242-4305*

*General Civil and Trial Practice in all State and Federal Courts. Public Contract and Construction Law, Tax and Administrative Law, Estate Planning and Probate.*

### MEMBERS OF FIRM

**SAMUEL S. GILL** (1912-1965).

**JOHN M. CARMACK,** born Los Angeles, California, September 6, 1937; admitted to bar, 1964, California. *Education:* University of California at Los Angeles (B.S., 1960; LL.B., 1963). Phi Delta Phi. Member, Board of Editors, U.C.L.A. Law Review, 1962-1963. *Member:* Los Angeles County and American Bar Associations; The State Bar of California. *PRACTICE AREAS:* Corporate; Business; Transactions; Estate Planning.

**JOSEPH C. MALPASUTO,** born Beverly Hills, California, January 11, 1938; admitted to bar, 1975, California. *Education:* University of the Pacific (B.A., 1960); University of San Fernando Valley (J.D., 1974). Blue Key. Salutatorian. Member of Staff, University of San Fernando Valley Law Review, 1974. *Member:* Los Angeles County and American Bar Associations; The State Bar of California. *PRACTICE AREAS:* Construction Litigation; Mediation; Arbitrator.

**KIRK S. MACDONALD,** born Glendale, California, October 24, 1948; admitted to bar, 1982, California. *Education:* University of Southern California (B.S.C.E., cum laude, 1970); Western State University (J.D., cum laude, 1982). Tau Beta Pi. Editorial Board Member, 1979 and Executive Editor, 1980, Western State University Law Review. *Member:* Los Angeles County and American Bar Associations; The State Bar of California; Water Pollution Control Federation; California Water Pollution Control Association; American Society of Civil Engineers. *PRACTICE AREAS:* Construction Litigation; Mediation; Arbitration.

### OF COUNSEL

**ERNEST R. BALDWIN,** born Detroit, Michigan, July 12, 1925; admitted to bar, 1958, California. *Education:* Michigan State University (B.S., 1948); University of California at Los Angeles (LL.B., 1957). Phi Alpha Delta. Member, Board of Editors, U.C.L.A. Law Review, 1956-1957. *Member:* Bar Association of San Francisco; Los Angeles County and American (Member, Section of Public Contract Law) Bar Associations; The State Bar of California. *PRACTICE AREAS:* Corporate; Business; Transactions; Estate Planning.

REPRESENTATIVE CLIENTS: Amelco Corp.; Bireley Foundation; Boral Resources; Builders Fence Co., Alcorn Fence Company, Inc.; Calex Engineering; Calmat; Cass and Johansing; Clarke Contracting Corp.; Curtis Sand & Gravel; Howard Building Corp.; Industrial Asphalt; Kasler Corp.; Manhole Adjusting Contractors, Inc.; McCoy Construction Co.; Pacific Lightweight Products Co.; Rolleze, Inc.; Roofmaster Products Co.; Southern California Contractors Assn.; Steiny and Co., Inc.; U.S. Equipment Co., Inc.; Vinnell Foundation; REFERENCE: American West Bank.

## GREENWALD, HOFFMAN & MEYER

Established in 1927

**500 NORTH BRAND BOULEVARD, SUITE 920**
**GLENDALE, CALIFORNIA 91203-1904**
Telephone: 818-507-8100; 213-381-1131
Fax: 818-507-8484

General Civil Trial and Appellate Practice. Probate, Trust, Estate Planning, Real Property, Environmental, Condominium, Corporation, Banking, Business and Family Law.

### MEMBERS OF FIRM

**GUY PRESTON GREENWALD, JR.** (1914-1984).

**DONALD M. HOFFMAN,** born Los Angeles, California, August 27, 1935; admitted to bar, 1961, California and U.S. District Court, Southern District of California. *Education:* University of California at Los Angeles (B.S., 1957; LL.B., 1960). Beta Gamma Sigma; Phi Alpha Delta. Member, Board of Directors, Hollygrove, Los Angeles Orphans Home Society. *Member:* Los Angeles County and American Bar Associations; State Bar of California. **PRACTICE AREAS:** Probate Law; Estate Planning Law; Real Property Law; Corporation Law; Business Law.

**LAWRENCE F. MEYER,** born Montebello, California, June 6, 1947; admitted to bar, 1972, California and U.S. District Court, Central District of California; 1973, U.S. District Court, Eastern District of California. *Education:* Whittier College, University of Cambridge, Cambridge, England and University of Southern California (A.B., cum laude, 1969); University College Faculty of Laws, University of London, England and University of Notre Dame (J.D., 1972). Judge Pro-Tem, Los Angeles Municipal Court, 1982—; Los Angeles Superior Court, 1989—. Board of Directors, Blind Childrens Center Los Angeles and Big Sisters of Los Angeles. *Member:* Los Angeles County and American Bar Associations; State Bar of California. **PRACTICE AREAS:** Probate Law; Estate Planning Law; Real Property Law; Corporation Law; Business Law; Litigation.

**RAUL M. MONTES,** born Queretaro, Mexico, January 23, 1956; admitted to bar, 1981, California; 1982, U.S. District Court, Central District of California and U.S. Court of Appeals, Ninth Circuit. *Education:* University of California at Los Angeles (B.S., 1978; J.D., 1981). *Member:* Los Angeles County and American Bar Associations; State Bar of California; The Association of Trial Lawyers of America. **LANGUAGES:** Spanish. **PRACTICE AREAS:** General Civil Litigation; Environmental; Real Property Law; Probate Law; Estate Planning Law; Business Law.

### ASSOCIATES

**JEANNE BURNS-HAINDEL,** born Arcadia, California, June 25, 1957; admitted to bar, 1987, California, U.S. Court of Appeals, Ninth Circuit and U.S. District Court, Central District of California. *Education:* Pasadena City College (A.A., 1977); University of Southern California (B.A., magna cum laude, 1979; J.D., 1987). Phi Beta Kappa; Phi Kappa Phi. *Member:* Los Angeles County Bar Association; State Bar of California. **PRACTICE AREAS:** Probate Law; Estate Planning Law; Real Property; Corporation Law; Business Law; Litigation.

REFERENCES: Bank of America (Los Angeles and Pasadena Trust Offices); Northern Trust of California (Headquarters Office); Bank of America (Glendale Main Branch).

## HAGENBAUGH & MURPHY

A Partnership including Professional Corporations

Established in 1954

**700 NORTH CENTRAL AVENUE, SUITE 500**
**GLENDALE, CALIFORNIA 91203**
Telephone: 818-240-2600
Fax: 818-240-1253
Email: hmurphy@interserv.com
URL: http://www.seamless.com/hm/

*Orange County, California Office:* 701 South Parker Street, Suite 8200, Orange. Telephone: 714-835-5406. Fax: 714-835-5949.
*San Bernardino, California Office:* 301 Vanderbilt Way, Suite 220. Telephone: 909-884-5331. FAX: 909-889-1250.

General Civil and Trial Practice in all State and Federal Courts. Insurance, Casualty, Life, Health, Accident and Disability Insurance, Malpractice, Surety and Aviation Law, Employment Law, Business Litigation (including

*(This Listing Continued)*

Commercial and Advertising Disputes), Trademark and Copyright Litigation and Workers Compensation Subrogation.

*FIRM PROFILE:* From its beginning in 1954, the firm has retained its identity as a full service civil litigation firm, including appellate work. There is an emphasis on cost-effective resolution of cases, not simply endless "litigation." The firm has offices in Los Angeles, Orange and San Bernardino counties, and serves all of Southern California.

Demonstrated strengths exist in these and related areas: Products Liability: Automotive products, heavy equipment, machinery, landslide and water damage, construction defect claims, medical devices, toxic torts, drugs and blood products; Professional Liability: physician and hospital liability, staff privileges, chiropractic and osteopathic, dental, rehabilitation and nursing home injuries, insurance agents and brokers, business litigation, elder abuse and attorney malpractice; Property Related Liability: premises injuries, fires and property damage, mass disaster litigation, real estate fraud, construction, homeowner's associations, landfill and toxic waste, commercial lease disputes; Other Personal Injury: major personal injuries whether caused by automobiles, travel injuries, assault and battery, employment terminations, civil rights violations, defamation, sports injuries, malicious prosecution; Coverage And Bad Faith: defense of bad faith actions, coverage opinions and litigation, including complex multicarrier cases, declaratory relief actions; development of insurer's position on cases statewide; Employment Law: civil rights, wrongful termination, sexual harassment, contract disputes and employer counseling; Intellectual Property: trademark and copyright infringement.

**VAN A. HAGENBAUGH** (1914-1980).

**SIGURD E. MURPHY** (1903-1976).

**WILLIAM D. STEWART, (A P.C.),** born Warren, Ohio, January 19, 1943; admitted to bar, 1968, California. *Education:* University of California at Los Angeles (A.B., 1963); Southwestern University (J.D., 1967). *Member:* Los Angeles County and American Bar Associations; The State Bar of California; Association of Southern California Defense Counsel; Defense Research Institute.

**JOHN J. TARY, (A P.C.),** born Szolnok, Hungary, September 2, 1938; admitted to bar, 1973, California. *Education:* California State University at Los Angeles (B.S., 1963); University of Southern California (M.B.A., 1970); Loyola University of Los Angeles (J.D., 1973). *Member:* Los Angeles County Bar Association; State Bar of California; Association of Southern California Defense Counsel; Defense Research Institute.

**RAYMOND R. MOORE, (A P.C.),** born Los Angeles, California, October 15, 1943; admitted to bar, 1969, California. *Education:* California State University-Northridge (A.B., 1965); University of Southern California (J.D., 1968). Phi Delta Phi. *Member:* Los Angeles County and American Bar Associations; State Bar of California; American Board of Trial Advocates; Association of Southern California Defense Counsel.

**NEIL R. GUNNY,** born Los Angeles, California, February 10, 1951; admitted to bar, 1977, California; 1979, U.S. District Court, Central District of California; 1983, U.S. Court of Appeals, Ninth Circuit. *Education:* University of California at Los Angeles (B.A., 1973); University of Santa Clara (J.D., summa cum laude, 1977). *Member:* State Bar of California; Association of Southern California Defense Counsel (Committee Chairman, 1991-1994); Community Associations Institute. (Resident, Orange County Office). **PRACTICE AREAS:** Appraisal Malpractice; Homeowners Association Litigation; General Tort Litigation.

**ALAN R. ZUCKERMAN,** born Long Island, New York, August 1, 1951; admitted to bar, 1977, California. *Education:* University of Southern California (B.A., cum laude, 1973); Loyola University of Los Angeles (J.D., cum laude, 1977). *Member:* Los Angeles County and American (Member, Sections on: Litigation; Tort and Insurance Practice) Bar Associations; State Bar of California; Association of Southern California Defense Counsel; Defense Research Institute.

**DAVID L. WINTER,** born Chicago, Illinois, August 22, 1954; admitted to bar, 1979, California. *Education:* Miami University (B.A., 1976); McGeorge School of Law, University of the Pacific (J.D., 1979). Comment, "Social Host Liability for Furnishing Alcohol: A Legal Hangover?" 10 Pacific Law Journal 95. *Member:* State Bar of California; Association of Southern California Defense Counsel; Defense Research Institute.

**MARY E. PORTER,** born Bemidji, Minnesota, February 15, 1946; admitted to bar, 1977, California. *Education:* California State University at Long Beach (A.B., 1973); Loyola University of Los Angeles (J.D., 1977). *Member:* Los Angeles County Bar Association; State Bar of California; Association of Southern California Defense Counsel.

*(This Listing Continued)*

**DANIEL A. LEIPOLD,** born Berwyn, Illinois, December 22, 1947; admitted to bar, 1977, California. *Education:* St. Mary's College (B.A., 1970); Western State University (J.D., 1977). Author: *Law & Motion Manual*, Orange County Bar Association, 1980. *Member:* Orange County and American Bar Associations; The State Bar of California; Association of Southern California Defense Counsel. (Resident, Orange County Office). *PRACTICE AREAS:* Serious Injury Cases; Malpractice Defense; First Amendment Defense; Elder Abuse Defense; Slapp Suite Defense.

**CRAIG D. ARONSON,** born New York, N.Y., June 10, 1956; admitted to bar, 1982, California. *Education:* Dartmouth College (B.A., summa cum laude, 1977); University of Chicago (J.D., 1980). Phi Beta Kappa. Rufus Choate Scholar. *Member:* The State Bar of California. *PRACTICE AREAS:* Coverage; Bad Faith; Advertising Injury; Business Litigation.

**PAUL G. SZUMIAK,** born Detroit, Michigan, May 22, 1954; admitted to bar, 1983, California. *Education:* Michigan State University (B.A., 1976); Southwestern University (J.D., 1983). Recipient, American Jurisprudence Award in Corporations Law. *Member:* State Bar of California; Association of Southern California Defense Counsel.

**ROBERT F. DONOHUE,** born Philadelphia, Pennsylvania, April 9, 1951; admitted to bar, 1983, California. *Education:* Western Michigan University (B.A., 1973); University of Toledo (J.D., 1983). *Member:* State Bar of California; State Bar of Arizona. (Resident, Orange County Office). *PRACTICE AREAS:* Civil Rights Defense; Serious Bicycle Accident; Accounting Malpractice; Partnership; Business Litigation.

**KATHARINE L. SPANIAC,** born Long Beach, California, October 16, 1957; admitted to bar, 1983, California. *Education:* Pomona College (B.A., 1979); McGeorge School of the Law, University of the Pacific (J.D., 1983). Phi Delta Phi. Recipient, American Jurisprudence Award in Agency. Staff Writer, Pacific Law Journal Review, 1982-1983. *Member:* State Bar of California; Association of Southern California Defense Counsel. (Resident, San Bernardino Office).

**ALAN H. BOON,** born Los Angeles, California, July 2, 1954; admitted to bar, 1983, California. *Education:* University of California at Berkeley (B.A., with distinction, 1976); Loyola Marymount University (J.D., cum laude, 1983). Member, St. Thomas More Law Honor Society. *Member:* State Bar of California. (Resident, Orange County Office).

**JAMIE B. SKEBBA,** born Waukesha, Wisconsin, June 9, 1960; admitted to bar, 1986, California. *Education:* Washington and Lee University; University of Wisconsin-Milwaukee (B.A., 1982); Pepperdine University (J.D., 1985); McGeorge School of the Law, University of the Pacific (LL.M., 1986). *Member:* State Bar of California; American Bar Association; Association of Southern California Defense Counsel; National Health Lawyers Association.

---

**RAYMOND T. GAIL,** born Santa Monica, California, September 10, 1936; admitted to bar, 1965, California. *Education:* University of California at Los Angeles (B.S., 1961; J.D., 1964). Mediator, District Court of Appeals. *Member:* State Bar of California; Association of Southern California Defense Counsel; Defense Research Institute; American Board of Trial Advocates. (Resident, San Bernardino Office).

**KIRK G. NEIBERGER,** born Van Nuys, California, December 30, 1952; admitted to bar, 1980, California. *Education:* Cerritos Junior College (A.A., 1973); California State University at Long Beach (B.A., cum laude, 1976); Western State University College of Law (J.D., 1980). Phi Kappa Phi; Pi Sigma Alpha. Executive Editor, Western State University Law Review, 1980. *Member:* State Bar of California; American Bar Association; Association of Southern California Defense Counsel.

**MEREDITH A. MUSICANT,** born Los Angeles, California, May 5, 1959; admitted to bar, 1986, California. *Education:* Waseda University, Tokyo; Occidental College (A.B., magna cum laude, 1981); University of California at Davis (J.D., 1986). Phi Delta Phi. *Member:* Los Angeles County Bar Association; State Bar of California.

**DAVID M. CHUTE,** born Kansas City, Missouri, May 6, 1963; admitted to bar, 1988, California; 1989, U.S. District Court, Central District of California. *Education:* University of California at Irvine (B.A., 1985); Loyola Marymount University (J.D., 1988). *Member:* State Bar of California. (Resident, Orange County Office).

**LUANNE WALSH,** born Hobart, Oklahoma, September 15, 1946; admitted to bar, 1989, California. *Education:* Baylor University (B.A., 1968); Southwestern University School of Law (J.D., 1988). Recipient: American Jurisprudence Award in Corporation and Federal Tax Administration and Litigation. Who's Who Among American Law Students, 8th and 9th Editions. *Member:* Los Angeles County and American Bar Associations; State Bar of California.

**RHONDA L. ETZWILER,** born Ashland, Ohio, December 1, 1962; admitted to bar, 1990, California. *Education:* The University of Akron (B.S.N., summa cum laude, 1985); California Western School of Law (J.D., 1989). *Member:* Los Angeles County and American Bar Associations; State Bar of California; The Association of Trial Lawyers of America; Association of Southern California Defense Counsel; American Society of Law and Medicine. *PRACTICE AREAS:* Medical Malpractice Defense Law.

**STEVEN M. SCHUETZE,** born Seattle, Washington, November 4, 1963; admitted to bar, 1989, California; 1990, Washington and U.S. Court of Appeals, Ninth Circuit. *Education:* University of Washington (B.A., 1986); Pepperdine School of Law (J.D., cum laude, 1989). Associate Editor, Pepperdine Law Review. *Member:* State Bar of California.

**THOMAS J. HEATLY,** born Des Moines, Iowa, August 16, 1952; admitted to bar, 1990, California. *Education:* San Diego State University (B.A., with honors, 1975); University of San Diego (J.D., 1990). *Member:* State Bar of California.

**MATTHEW R. RUNGAITIS,** born Los Angeles, California, June 7, 1964; admitted to bar, 1990, California; 1991, Arizona and U.S. District Court, Central District of California. *Education:* University of Minnesota (B.I.S., 1987); McGeorge School of Law (J.D., 1990). Who's Who Among American Law Students. Recipient: Raymond Henry Biele II Memorial Scholarship; American Jurisprudence Award for Remedies. *Member:* Los Angeles County and American Bar Associations; State Bar of California; State Bar of Arizona; Association of Southern California Defense Counsel.

**STEPHEN BARRY,** born Monterey, California, January 22, 1953; admitted to bar, 1979, California; 1980, U.S. District Court, Central District of California; 1982, U.S. Court of Appeals, Ninth Circuit and U.S. District Court, Northern District of California. *Education:* Stanford University (B.A., 1974); University of California at Los Angeles (J.D., 1978). *Member:* State Bar of California.

**JULIE M. DEROSE,** born Syracuse, New York, September 15, 1957; admitted to bar, 1991, California, U.S. District Court, Central District of California and U.S. Court of Appeals, Ninth Circuit. *Education:* Cornell University (B.S., in Industrial and Labor Relations, 1979); Loyola Law School (J.D., 1990). *Member:* Los Angeles County and American Bar Associations; State Bar of California; Pasadena Young Lawyers Association; California Young Lawyers.

**RANDAL A. WHITECOTTON,** born Torrance, California, March 14, 1964; admitted to bar, 1991, California. *Education:* University of California, Irvine (B.A., 1986); Whittier College School of Law (J.D., 1989). *Member:* Los Angeles County (Member, Litigation Section) and Orange County (Member, Litigation Section) Bar Associations; State Bar of California. (Resident, San Bernardino Office).

**CATHY L. SHIPE,** born California, November 20, 1960; admitted to bar, 1991, California. *Education:* National University (B.B.A., cum laude, 1982; M.B.A., 1985); California Western School of Law (J.D., magna cum laude, 1991). Phi Alpha Delta. Notes and Comments Editor, California Western Law Review/International Law Journal, 1990-1991. Recipient: American Jurisprudence Awards: Contracts and Trial Practice; National Telecommunications Law Moot Court Competition; First Place Oral Argument, Best Brief Award. *Member:* Los Angeles County Bar Association; State Bar of California; Association of Southern California Defense Counsel. (Resident, Orange County Office).

**KERI LYNN BUSH,** born Burbank, California, August 23, 1963; admitted to bar, 1992, California and District of Columbia. *Education:* University of the Pacific (B.S., 1985); McGeorge School of Law (J.D., 1991). Phi Delta Phi; Lambda Kappa Sigma; Delta Sigma Phi. Moot Court Top Oralist. Clerk, Hon. Ira A. Brown, Jr., Superior Court of San Francisco. *Member:* State Bar of California; American Bar Association (Vice-President, Professional Activities Committee, 1988-1991).

**MICHAEL A. TONYA,** born Columbus, Ohio, December 27, 1952; admitted to bar, 1992, California. *Education:* University of Missouri at Columbia (B.A., 1975); Case Western Reserve University (J.D., 1992); University of San Diego. Recipient: American Jurisprudence Award, Research and Writing; Randolph Read Law and Psychiatry Award. Member, Dean's Tutorial Society. Associate, Case Western Reserve Journal of International Law. Author: "Baby Steps Toward Fair Labor Standards: Evaluating The Child Labor Deterring Act," Case Western Reserve Journal of International Law, Spring, 1992. *Member:* State Bar of California.

*(This Listing Continued)*

## HAGENBAUGH & MURPHY, Glendale—Continued

**LAURA C. MCLENNAN,** born Peoria, Illinois, October 23, 1957; admitted to bar, 1986, California; 1987, U.S. District Court, Central District of California. *Education:* University of Illinois (B.S.N., 1979); Loyola Marymount University (J.D., with honors, 1986). Recipient, American Jurisprudence Award in Remedies. Member: Illinois Board of Registered Nursing, 1979; California Board of Registered Nursing, 1980; Minnesota Board of Registered Nursing, 1980. *Member:* Los Angeles County and American Bar Associations; State Bar of California; California. *LANGUAGES:* Spanish.

**GRACIELA L. FREIXES,** born Habana, Cuba, September 7, 1955; admitted to bar, 1981, California and U.S. District Court, Central District of California; 1982, U.S. District Court, Northern District of California. *Education:* California State University at Northridge (B.A., magna cum laude, 1977); Loyola Law School Los Angeles (J.D., 1980). Phi Alpha Delta. *Member:* Los Angeles County and American Bar Associations; State Bar of California; SCAHRM, ASHRM, SUCA Defense Counsel; Mexican-American Bar Association; Hispanic National Bar Association; Cuban American Bar Association. *LANGUAGES:* Spanish.

**MELINDA W. EBELHAR,** born Irondequoit, New York, May 3, 1957; admitted to bar, 1983, California; 1990, Colorado; 1992, New York. *Education:* Occidental College (A.B., cum laude, 1979); University of California, Boalt Hall School of Law (J.D., 1983). Psi Chi. Temporary Judge, Los Angeles Municipal Court, 1992-1993. *Member:* State Bar of California; Association of Southern California Defense Counsel. *PRACTICE AREAS:* Appellate Practice; Insurance Coverage; General Litigation.

**KIRK N. SULLIVAN,** born Tupelo, Mississippi, November 19, 1957; admitted to bar, 1984, California and U.S. District Court, Central, Northern and Eastern Districts of California; 1987, U.S. Court of Appeals, Fourth and Tenth Circuits; 1988, U.S. Court of Appeals, Ninth Circuit; 1993, Colorado. *Education:* University of Wyoming; London School of Economics (B.S., 1981); Pepperdine University (J.D., 1984). Phi Alpha Delta. *Member:* Beverly Hills, Los Angeles County, Colorado and American (Forum Committee on Entertainment and Sports Industries; Section on Intellectual Property Law; Section on Tort and Insurance Practice (Member, Fidelity and Surety Law Committee)) Bar Associations; State Bar of California (Section on Intellectual Property Law). *REPORTED CASES:* Dworkin v. Hustler Magazine, 668 F. Supp. 1408 (C.D. Cal. 1987); Dworkin v. LFP, 839 P.2d 903 (Wyo. 1992); Spence v. Flynt, 816 P. 2d 771 (Wyo. 1991); Aguayo v. Tomco Carburetor Co., 853 F.2d 744 (9th Cir. 1988); Leidoldt v. LFP, 647 F.Supp. 1283 (D.C. Wyo. 1986). *PRACTICE AREAS:* Intellectual Property; Fidelity and Surety; Business Litigation; Insurance Coverage.

**GARY P. SIMONIAN,** born Los Angeles, California, March 17, 1965; admitted to bar, 1995, California and U.S. District Court, Central District of California; 1996, U.S. Court of Appeals, Sixth Circuit. *Education:* Occidental College (B.A., 1989); Southwestern University (J.D., 1993). Highest Achievement Award, Copyright Law. *PRACTICE AREAS:* Intellectual Property; Insurance Coverage.

**MARK HABEEB,** born Detroit, Michigan, March 16, 1966; admitted to bar, 1995, California. *Education:* Pepperdine University (B.S., 1988; J.D., 1994); American Graduate School of International Management (Thunderbird), Glendale, Arizona (Master of International Management, 1989). Phi Alpha Delta. *Member:* Beverly Hills Bar Association. *LANGUAGES:* German. *PRACTICE AREAS:* Medical Malpractice.

**HOWARD J. HIRSCH,** born New York, N.Y., April 19, 1964; admitted to bar, 1995, California and U.S. District Court, Central District of California. *Education:* University of Arizona (B.F.A., 1987); University of Southern California; Western State University, College of Law (J.D., 1994). Delta Theta Phi (Vice Dean). Associate Planning Editor, 1992-1993 and Lead Articles/Planning Editor, 1993-1994, Western State University Law Review. *Member:* Orange County Bar Association; State Bar of California. (Resident, Orange County Office).

**MICHELLE MANN,** born Glendale, California, October 21, 1967; admitted to bar, 1993, California and U.S. District Court, Central District of California. *Education:* California State University at Northridge (B.A., cum laude, 1989); University of the Pacific, McGeorge School of Law (J.D., 1992). Pi Sigma Alpha. Political Science Honor Society. *Member:* San Fernando Valley Bar Association (Member, Family and General Insurance Sections); State Bar of California (Member, Insurance and General Civil Sections).

*(This Listing Continued)*

REPRESENTATIVE CLIENTS: Farmers Insurance Group; Truck Insurance Exchange; Fire Insurance Exchange; St. Paul Cos.; Mid-Century Insurance Co.; Employers Self Insurance Service; Michigan Millers Mutual Insurance Co.; Cooperative of America Physicians, Inc.; Aetna Insurance Co.; Sequoia Insurance Co.; Southern California Physicians Insurance Exchange; California Compensation Insurance Co.; State Farm Insurance Co.; Transamerica; St. Paul Fire & Marine Insurance Co.; County of San Bernardino; Chubbs; Commercial Union; Markel-Rhulin.

## HEMER, BARKUS & CLARK

Established in 1984

550 NORTH BRAND BOULEVARD, SUITE 1800
P.O. BOX 293
**GLENDALE, CALIFORNIA 91202**
Telephone: 818-241-8999
Fax: 818-241-2014
Email: Kallwyr@aol.com

*Ontario, California Office:* 3401 Centrelake Drive, Suite 400. Telephone: 714-467-0660. Fax: 909-390-3628.

*Civil Trial and Appellate Practice. Medical and Legal Professional Liability, Products Liability, Negligence and Insurance Law.*

FIRM PROFILE: *Mr. Hemer first started working for Allstate Insurance Company when he attended Claims School and worked in their house counsel firm. Thereafter, he was general counsel for the Financial Indemnity Company, another auto carrier, for five years before forming the firm of Bolton & Hemer. The latter firm was in existence until 1983. The present firm was established in 1984 and is dedicated to the aggressive defense of civil litigation.*

*We have found that very early contact with the insured and the claims representative is conductive to establishing a good working relationship. The insured is contacted shortly after assignment, and is urged to work with counsel in successful defense of the litigation. Every effort is used to work with the claims personnel to bring about the earliest resolution to litigation.*

**RALPH S. HEMER,** born Leipzig, Germany, July 3, 1931; admitted to bar, 1962, California and U.S. District Court, Central District of California. *Education:* Los Angeles Valley College (A.A., 1956); Southwestern University (LL.B., 1961). Tau Alpha Epsilon; Delta Theta Phi. Member, Panel of Arbitrators, American Arbitration Association. *Member:* Los Angeles County and American (Member, Section on Insurance, Negligence and Compensation Law) Bar Associations; The State Bar of California; Association of Southern California Defense Counsel; Defense Research and Trial Lawyers Association; American Judicature Society; Federation of Insurance and Corporate Counsel; Defense Research Institute. *LANGUAGES:* German.

**RAMUNE E. BARKUS,** born Cowra, Australia, November 9, 1949; admitted to bar, 1979, California and U.S. District Court, Central District of California. *Education:* Barat College of the Sacred Heart (B.A., 1971); Southwestern University (J.D., 1979). *Member:* Los Angeles County and American Bar Associations; The State Bar of California; The Baltic Lawyers Association. *LANGUAGES:* Lithuanian and French. *PRACTICE AREAS:* Medical Malpractice Defense.

**BRADLEY C. CLARK,** born Santa Barbara, California, August 1, 1955; admitted to bar, 1983, California; 1987, U.S. District Court, Central District of California. *Education:* Santa Barbara City College (A.A., 1979); University of Redlands (B.S.); Santa Barbara College of Law (J.D., 1983). *Member:* State Bar of California; Association of Southern California Defense Counsel; Southern California Association of Hospital Risk Managers. *PRACTICE AREAS:* Medical Malpractice Defense.

### ASSOCIATES

**CATHY L. PATRENOS,** born Fukuoka, Japan, October 3, 1953; admitted to bar, 1989, California; U.S. District Court, Central District of California; U.S. Court of Appeals, Ninth Circuit. *Education:* Phoenix College (A.A., 1974); Citrus Belt College (B.S., 1984); Citrus Belt Law School (J.D., 1986). Registered Nurse, California, 1974. *Member:* State Bar of California; American Bar Association. *PRACTICE AREAS:* Medical Malpractice Defense.

**LAURENCE Y. WONG,** born Santa Monica, California, February 17, 1956; admitted to bar, 1982, California. *Education:* Santa Monica City College (A.A., 1976); California State University at Long Beach (B.A., 1978); Western State University College of Law (J.D., 1981). *Member:* Orange County Bar Association; State Bar of California; Association of Southern California Defense Counsel; Orange County Insurance Defense Association. *PRACTICE AREAS:* Medical Malpractice Defense.

*(This Listing Continued)*

**KRISTEN L. CHESNUT,** born Key West, Florida, December 27, 1948; admitted to bar, 1990, California. *Education:* Boise State University (A.S., 1974); St. Mary's College (B.A., 1987); Golden Gate University (J.D., 1990). Editor, Golden Gate University Law Review, 1990. Author: Article, "Reflections on a Jewel: U.S. v. Alvarado, "Ninth Circuit Survey, Golden Gate University Law Review, 1990. Registered Nurse, California, 1974. *Member:* State Bar of California; California Nurses Association. *PRACTICE AREAS:* Medical Malpractice Defense.

**JOHN P. FREEMAN,** born Pasadena, California, January 18, 1961; admitted to bar, 1991, California. *Education:* University of California at Los Angeles (B.A., 1986); Southwestern University (J.D., 1990). *Member:* Los Angeles and American Bar Associations. *PRACTICE AREAS:* Medical Malpractice Defense.

**DAVID A. ARKUSS,** born Brooklyn, New York, May 27, 1954; admitted to bar, 1978, California; U.S. District Court, Central District of California; U.S. Court of Appeals, Ninth Circuit; U.S. Supreme Court. *Education:* University of Rochester, New York (B.A., cum laude, 1975); Southwestern School of Law at Los Angeles (J.D., 1978). Delta Theta Phi. Arbitrator of the Los Angeles Superior Court Arbitration Program, 1985—. *Member:* Los Angeles County Bar Association; State Bar of California; Association of Southern California Defense Counsel. *PRACTICE AREAS:* Medical Malpractice Defense.

**TOM M ALLEN,** born Long Beach, California, August 8, 1946; admitted to bar, 1977, California. *Education:* Western State University, College of Law (Fullerton Campus) (B.S.L., 1976; J.D., 1977). *Member:* Riverside County and Orange County Bar Associations. *PRACTICE AREAS:* Medical Malpractice Defense.

**RICHARD I. GONZALEZ,** born San Bernardino, California, June 14, 1967; admitted to bar, 1991, California. *Education:* California State University at San Bernardino (B.A., 1988); Pepperdine University (J.D., 1991). *Member:* State Bar of California; Association of Southern California Defense Counsel. *PRACTICE AREAS:* Medical Malpractice Defense.

**JOANN G. HOUSMAN,** born Syracuse, New York, August 10, 1957; admitted to bar, 1987, California. *Education:* D'Youville College, Buffalo, New York (B.S., Nursing, 1979); Southwestern University School of Law (J.D., 1986). *Member:* State Bar of California; Association of Southern California Defense Counsel; American Nurses Association.

**JACK ROSENBAUM,** born Philadelphia, Pennsylvania; admitted to bar, 1996, California; U.S. District Court, Central District of California; U.S. Court of Appeals, Ninth Circuit. *Education:* University of Pennsylvania (B.A., 1971; Villanova University School of Law, (1972); Temple University School of Dental Medicine (D.M.D., 1976); Southwest ern University (J.D., 1995). Alpha Omega. Licensed to practice Dentistry, 1978—. Member, American Dental Association; Tri-County Dental Association; American Society of Dentistry for Children. *Member:* Los Angeles County and Federal Bar Associations; State Bar of California; Association of Southern California Defense Counsel. *PRACTICE AREAS:* Medical Malpractice Defense.

REPRESENTATIVE CLIENTS: The Doctors Co.; Southern California Physicians Insurance Exchange; Physicians Interindemnity; Hartford Insurance Group; Home Insurance; Kaiser Foundation Health Plan, Inc.; Professional Underwriters Liability Insurance Co.
REFERENCE: One Central Bank, Glendale, California.

## JOHN HILL & ASSOCIATES

*801 NORTH BRAND BOULEVARD, SUITE 240*
**GLENDALE, CALIFORNIA 91203**
*Telephone: 818-552-2400*
*Fax: 818-552-4444*

Torrance, California Office: 2050 West 190th Street, Suite 200. Telephone: 310-782-2500. Fax: 310-782-0200.

*General Civil Litigation. Insurance Defense, Products Liability, Toxic Torts, Environmental, Medical Malpractice, Government Liability, Warranty Action, Real Estate, Corporate and Construction Law, Wills and Trusts, Banking.*

**JOHN W. HILL,** born Pittsburg, Kansas, December 5, 1935; admitted to bar, 1968, California. *Education:* University of Illinois (B.S., 1957); Southwestern University (J.D., 1966). Psi Chi; Sigma Lambda Sigma; Phi Alpha Delta. Member and Chairman, California State Bar Calendar Coordinating Committee, 1983-1987. Appointed by Los Angeles Superior Court as Arbitrator for the Los Angeles Attorney's Special Arbitration Plan, 1982-1990. Judge ProTem for Los Angeles Municipal Court, 1983-1984.

*(This Listing Continued)*

Settlement Officer for the Los Angeles Superior Court, 1984. *Member:* Los Angeles County (Member, Los Angeles Delegation Executive Committee, 1981-1984; Chairman, Legislative Review Committee of the Litigation Section) and American Bar Associations; The State Bar of California; Association of Southern California Defense Counsel; American Board of Trial Advocates. *PRACTICE AREAS:* Civil Litigation; Toxic Torts; Insurance Defense; Medical Malpractice; Products Liability.

## IRSFELD, IRSFELD & YOUNGER LLP

*A Partnership including Professional Corporations*
*Established in 1908*
*SUITE 900, 100 WEST BROADWAY*
**GLENDALE, CALIFORNIA 91210-1296**
*Telephone: 818-242-6859*
*Fax: 818-240-7728*
*Email: 104736.1745@compuserver.com*

*General Civil, Business and Real Estate Litigation and Arbitration in all State and Federal Courts. Corporations, Securities, Commercial, Municipal, Estate Planning, Real Property, Personal Injury Litigation, Taxation, Probate, Eminent Domain, Construction Law, Bankruptcy (Creditor) and Debt Collection.*

*FIRM PROFILE: Irsfeld, Irsfeld & Younger is a full service law firm established in 1908. The goal of the firm is to provide quality legal services to our clients by combining academic excellence and creativity with a practical approach to the client's legal needs. Our clients range from large real estate development companies, industrial manufacturers, insurance companies and financial concerns to a variety of smaller businesses and individuals.*

*In 1984, the firm moved to its present offices in Glendale, California, which allows easy access to all Southern California courts. The firm also regularly handles matters in San Diego, Riverside, Orange, San Bernardino and Ventura Counties as well as in Northern California. Over the years, the firm has been retained by clients located throughout the United States to handle their litigation and transactional needs.*

### MEMBERS OF FIRM

**JAMES B. IRSFELD** (1880-1966).

**KENNETH C. YOUNGER** (1922-1996).

**JOHN H. BRINK, (P.C.),** born Los Angeles, California, July 25, 1933; admitted to bar, 1957, California. *Education:* University of Notre Dame and Loyola University of Los Angeles (LL.B., cum laude, 1957). Alpha Sigma Nu; Phi Delta Phi. Instructor in Law, Loyola University of Los Angeles, 1960-1968. Member, Board of Directors, 1965— and President, 1968-1969, Financial Lawyers Conference. Member and Chair, 1971, Commercial Law and Bankruptcy Section, Los Angeles County Bar Association. Member, National Panel of Arbitrators, American Arbitration Association. *Member:* American Bar Association (Member, Section of Corporation, Banking and Business Law). *PRACTICE AREAS:* Business Law; Real Property Law; Estate Planning.

**PETER J. IRSFELD, (P.C.),** born Hollywood, California, July 21, 1939; admitted to bar, 1966, California. *Education:* Stanford University (B.S., 1961); University of California at Los Angeles (LL.B., 1965). Phi Delta Phi; Order of the Coif. Production Editor, University of California at Los Angeles Law Review, 1964-1965. *Member:* Hollywood Bar Association (Member, Board of Governors, 1967-1978; President, 1976-1977). *PRACTICE AREAS:* Bankruptcy (Creditor) Law; Debt Collection Law; Civil Litigation.

**JAMES J. WALDORF, (P.C.),** born Wilmar, California, January 8, 1938; admitted to bar, 1966, California; 1973, U.S. Supreme Court. *Education:* Loyola University of Los Angeles (B.B.A., 1962; J.D., 1965). Alpha Sigma Nu; Phi Delta Phi. Recipient, William Tell Aggeler Award, 1965. *Member:* San Fernando Valley and American Bar Associations; American Society of Heating, Refrigerating and Air Conditioning Engineers; Association of Business Trial Lawyers; Financial Lawyers Conference. *PRACTICE AREAS:* Real Estate Law; Construction Law; Litigation; Real Estate.

**C. PHILLIP JACKSON, (P.C.),** born Rifle, Colorado, May 25, 1948; admitted to bar, 1974, California. *Education:* University of California at Los Angeles (B.A., cum laude, 1970); University of Bordeaux, France; Loyola University of Los Angeles (J.D., cum laude, 1974). Member, Litigation and Alternative Dispute Resolution Sections, Los Angeles County Bar Association. Member, National Panel of Arbitrators, American Arbitration Association. *Member:* American Bar Association (Member, Sections of: Litigation; Business Law; Antitrust Law); Association of

*(This Listing Continued)*

## IRSFELD, IRSFELD & YOUNGER LLP, Glendale—Continued

Business Trial Lawyers. *PRACTICE AREAS:* Construction Law; Business Law; Real Estate; Litigation; Arbitration Law.

**NORMAN H. GREEN, (P.C.),** born Los Angeles, California, November 11, 1952; admitted to bar, 1979, California. *Education:* University of California at Irvine (A.B., 1974); University of California at Los Angeles (J.D., 1979). Phi Alpha Delta (Clerk, 1978). Tax Auditor, Internal Revenue Service, 1974-1976. Adjunct Professor of Taxation, Northrop University Law Center, 1986. Member: Los Angeles County Bar Association (Member, Sections on: Taxation and Real Property; Chair, Arbitration Committee, 1995—); State Bar of California (Member: Sections on: Estate Planning, Probate and Trust Law; Business Law). *Member:* Glendale and American Bar Associations. (Certified Specialist, Taxation Law, The State Bar of California Board of Legal Specialization). *PRACTICE AREAS:* Taxation Law; Business Law; Estate Planning and Probate Law.

**KATHRYN E. VAN HOUTEN,** born Trenton, Michigan, June 6, 1959; admitted to bar, 1989, California, U.S. District Court, Central and Northern Districts of California and U.S. Court of Appeals, Ninth Circuit. *Education:* West Los Angeles College; University of California at Los Angeles (B.A., magna cum laude, 1983); Loyola University of Los Angeles (J.D., 1989). *PRACTICE AREAS:* Business Litigation; Family Law; Probate Law.

### ASSOCIATES

**PETER C. WRIGHT,** born Bucks County, Pennsylvania, April 30, 1943; admitted to bar, 1973, California. *Education:* Indiana University (A.B., 1970; J.D., 1972). Senior Assistant City Attorney, Glendale, 1974-1979. General Counsel, Housing Authority, City of Los Angeles, 1982-1984. Special Counsel, 1984-1985. *Member:* Glendale and American Bar Associations. *PRACTICE AREAS:* General Civil Litigation; Business; Tort; Real Property; Extraordinary Writs.

**DIANE L. WALKER,** born Columbus, Ohio, July 1, 1959; admitted to bar, 1985, California; 1986, U.S. District Court, Central District of California and U.S. Court of Appeals, Ninth Circuit; 1992, U.S. District Court, Northern District of California. *Education:* California State University at Northridge (B.A., magna cum laude, 1982); Pepperdine University (J.D., magna cum laude, 1985). Pi Sigma Alpha; Phi Delta Phi. Member, 1983-1985, and Managing Editor, 1984-1985, Pepperdine Law Review. Author: Note, "Marsh v. Chambers: The Supreme Court Takes a New Look at the Establishment Clause," 11 Pepperdine Law Review 591, 1984. *Member:* Glendale Bar Association. *PRACTICE AREAS:* Business Litigation; Real Property Law; Probate Law.

### RETIRED

**JAMES B. IRSFELD, JR.**

All Members and Associates are members of the Los Angeles County Bar Association and The State Bar of California.

REPRESENTATIVE CLIENTS: Lear Siegler, Inc.; M. J. Brock & Sons, Inc.; Chrysler Credit Corp.; V.W. Credit Corp; Ticor Title Insurance Company; INA Corp.; California Land Title Co.; Asphalt Recycling and Reclaiming Association; American Arbitration Assn.; Liberty Mutual Insurance Company; The Bank of Hollywood; Airline & Reporting Corporation; Chartered Construction Corporation; Ryland Group, Inc.; Glenborough; Realty Trust Incorporated; Pacific Greystone Corporation; Volwood Corporation; Chrysler Corp.; Ebensteiner Co.; Toyota Motor Credit Corp.; Great Western Bank.
REFERENCES: Glendale Federal Bank; Bank of Hollywood.

## JOBE & STOTERAU

Established in 1996

330 NORTH BRAND BOULEVARD, SUITE 590
**GLENDALE, CALIFORNIA 91203**
Telephone: 818-246-7413
FAX: 818-246-7414
Email: 76324.1372@compuserve.com

*Real Estate, Estate Planning, Corporate Law and Nonprofit Organizations.*

**MEREDITH JOBE,** born Glendale, California, 1956; admitted to bar, 1981, California. *Education:* Loma Linda University (B.A., 1977); University of Southern California (M.B.A., 1981; J.D., 1981). Vice Chair, Board of Trustees, La Sierra University. Author: Chapter on Incorporated Associations for California Transactions Forms (Bancroft-/Whitney 12/96). FIRPTA: Taxation of Foreign Investors in U.S. Real Property (The American College of Mortgage Attorneys Abstract, September 1983. *Member:*
*(This Listing Continued)*

State Bar of California (Member, Committee on Nonprofit Organizations and Unincorporated Associations, 1989-1995; Chairman, 1992-1993). *PRACTICE AREAS:* Real Estate; Estate Planning; Corporations; Nonprofit Organizations.

**H. PETER STOTERAU,** born Coeur d'Alene, Idaho, June 2, 1938; admitted to bar, 1968, California. *Education:* San Fernando Valley State College (B.S., 1964); University of California, Los Angeles (J.D., 1967). *Member:* Los Angeles County and American Bar Associations; The State Bar of California; International Council of Shopping Centers; California Business Properties Association. *PRACTICE AREAS:* Business; Real Estate; Corporations; Government Business.

## KLEIN & ROSENBAUM

Established in 1985

121 WEST LEXINGTON DRIVE, FIFTH FLOOR
**GLENDALE, CALIFORNIA 91203**
Telephone: 818-243-1366
Fax: 818-246-5780

*Practice emphasizing: Representing Management and Plaintiffs in Labor and Employment Law including appearances before State and Federal Agencies and Courts.*

**ALFRED KLEIN,** born Stuttgart, Germany, October 22, 1946; admitted to bar, 1972, California; 1975, U.S. District Court, Central District of California; 1979, U.S. Court of Appeals, Ninth Circuit; 1996, U.S. Supreme Court. *Education:* University of Michigan (B.A., 1968); University of California Boalt Hall School of Law (J.D., 1971). Listed in: Who's Who in American Law; Who's Who in California. Author: "Solicitation Rules Will Need Revision," Journal of The American Hospital Association, August 16, 1975, reprinted, Hospital Organization and Management, Rakich and Darr, Second Edition; "Why You Can't Afford to Ignore ERISA," Personnel Journal, June, 1986; "Screening Employees for Alcohol and Drug Abuse: Legal Problems and Legislative Solutions," Vol. 5, No. 1, Labor and Employment Law News (State Bar of California), Spring, 1986; "Employees Under the Influence-Outside the Law?" Personnel Journal, September, 1986; "A Basic Primer on California Labor Code Section 132a," Vol. 5, No. 4, Labor and Employment Law News, Winter, 1987; "The Current Legal Status of Employment Tests," Los Angeles Lawyer, July/August, 1987; "An Overview of the Current Legal Status of Employment Tests," Vol. 10, No. 2, Business Law News, Summer, 1987. Contributor: Antitrust and Labor Committee Report, Labor and Employment Law Section, American Bar Association, 1977, 1978; "Alcohol & Drugs in the Workplace: Costs, Controls and Controversies," BNA Special Report, pp. 59-77, 1986. Contributing Editor, The Developing Labor Law, Second Edition and First Supplement. Instructor, Legal Writing and Research, University of California, Hastings College of the Law, San Francisco, California, 1973-1974. Lecturer and Moderator: UCLA Extension; American Arbitration Association; Town Hall of California, Industrial Relations Section; Orange County Industrial Relations Research Association; San Gabriel Valley Bar Association; Merchants and Manufacturers Association; Bureau of National Affairs; 1985 Southern California Labor Law Symposium; 15th Annual ALMACA Convention; Institute of Business Management & Entrepreneurship; Executive Circles; Society for Professionals in Dispute Resolution, 1988 Annual Conference. Senior Labor Attorney for Products Operations, ARCO Petroleum Products Company, a division of Atlantic Richfield Company, 1979-1985. Assistant to Corporate Employee Relations Counsel, Atlantic Richfield Company, 1975-1979. Associate, Musick, Peeler & Garrett, 1973-1975. Field Attorney, National Labor Relations Board, West Los Angeles and San Francisco offices, 1971-1973. Judge Pro Tem, Los Angeles Municipal Court, Small Claims, 1987. *Member:* Los Angeles County Bar Association (Member: Executive Committee, 1985-1988; Symposium Planning Committee, 1985; Chair, Legislature Monitoring Committee, 1985-1988; Vice Chair, Retreat Committee, 1987-1988; Labor and Employment Law Section; Labor and Employment Law Section); State Bar of California. *REPORTED CASES:* Monard v. FDIC 62 F. 3d 1169.

**DAVID E. ROSENBAUM,** born Kansas City, Missouri, September 28, 1942; admitted to bar, 1967, Missouri; 1971, California; 1972, U.S. District Court, Central District of California; 1974, Pennsylvania; 1975, U.S. District Court, Eastern and Western Districts of Pennsylvania; 1981, New Jersey and U.S. Court of Appeals, 3rd Circuit; 1982, U.S. Supreme Court. *Education:* University of Missouri (B.A., 1964; J.D., 1967). Order of the Coif. Member, Editorial Board, Missouri Law Review, 1966-1967. Law Clerk, Hon. John W. Oliver, Chief Judge, Western District of Missouri, 1967-1969. Trials and Appeals Attorney, National Relations Board, Appellate
*(This Listing Continued)*

Court Branch, Washington, D.C., 1969-1970. Associate, Labor Section, Mitchell, Silberberg & Knupp, Los Angeles, 1970-1973. Senior Attorney, Labor and Employee Relations, Atlantic Richfield Company, Philadelphia, Pennsylvania, 1973-1984. Senior Associate, Pechner, Dorfman, Wolff, Rounick & Cabot, Philadelphia, 1984-1986. *Member:* Los Angeles County (Member, Labor and Employment Law Section), Philadelphia (Member, Labor and Employment Law Committee) and American (Member, Labor and Employment Law Section) Bar Associations; Maritime Law Association of the United States. *PRACTICE AREAS:* Labor and Employment; OSHA and Environmental; Government Contracts.

REPRESENTATIVE CLIENTS: Pennoyer-Dodge Co.; The Hedman Co.; Reinhold Industries; Gilmore Envelope Corp.; Bon Appetit Danish, Inc.; Hair Club for Men; Family Restaurants, Inc.; Health Care Partners; Molding Corporation of America; HXM Terminals Transport, Inc.

---

## KNAPP, PETERSEN & CLARKE

*A PROFESSIONAL CORPORATION*

**500 NORTH BRAND BOULEVARD, 20TH FLOOR**
**GLENDALE, CALIFORNIA 91203-1904**
Telephone: 818-547-5000; 213-245-9400
Telecopier: 818-547-5329

*Palm Springs, California Office:* 960 East Tahquitz Canyon Way, Suite 101. Telephone: 619-325-8500. Telecopier: 619-325-2454.

*General Civil, Trial and Appellate Practice in all State and Federal Courts, Arbitration Tribunals and Administrative Agencies. General Insurance, Professional Liability, Product Liability, Environmental, Corporate and General Business, State, Federal and Local Taxation, Real Estate, Escrow Errors and Omissions Defense, Construction and Land Use, Construction Defect Litigation, Estate Planning, Probate, Labor and Employment, Administrative and Regulatory Insurance Law and Title Banking.*

**RYAN C. KNAPP** (Retired, 1992).

**LAURENCE R. CLARKE** (Retired).

**DONALD C. PETERSEN,** born Minneapolis, Minnesota, May 7, 1934; admitted to bar, 1960, Minnesota; 1963, California. *Education:* University of Minnesota (B.S.L., 1958; LL.B., 1960). Phi Delta Phi. Member, University of Minnesota Law Review, 1957-1959. *Member:* American Board of Trial Advocates; International Association of Insurance Counsel; American Board of Professional Liability Attorneys.

**DAVID C. HABER,** born Corpus Christi, Texas, November 11, 1941; admitted to bar, 1972, California. *Education:* Claremont-McKenna College (B.A., 1963); Loyola University of Los Angeles (J.D., 1971).

**KEVIN J. STACK,** born New York, N.Y., August 12, 1951; admitted to bar, 1976, California; 1977, U.S. District Court, Central District of California. *Education:* University of California, Los Angeles (B.A., cum laude, 1973); Loyola University of Los Angeles (J.D., cum laude, 1976).

**ANDRÉ E. JARDINI,** born Los Angeles, California, June 14, 1951; admitted to bar, 1976, California; 1978, U.S. District Court, Central District of California; 1980, U.S. Court of Appeals, Ninth Circuit. *Education:* University of Notre Dame (B.A., 1973); University of California, Hastings College of the Law (J.D., 1976). Law Clerk to Hon. Robert Firth, U.S. District Court, Central District of California, 1977-1978.

**PETER J. SENUTY,** born Bellingham, Washington, March 28, 1950; admitted to bar, 1975, California; 1976, U.S. District Court, Central District of California; 1980, U.S. Court of Appeals, 9th Circuit. *Education:* Stanford University (A.B., with distinction, 1972; J.D., 1975). *Member:* Los Angeles County and American (Member, Tort and Insurance Practice Section) Bar Associations; Conference of Insurance Counsel; Defense Research Institute.

**DAVID I. BELL,** born London, England, May 15, 1954; admitted to bar, 1979, California, U.S. District Court, Central District of California and U.S. Court of Appeals, Ninth Circuit; 1983, U.S. Supreme Court. *Education:* University of California at Irvine (B.S., 1975); Southwestern University (J.D., 1978); Harvard Law School (PIL, 1982). Co-Author: "Civil Consequences of Nuclear Power," Article 6, The Insurance Law Journal, p. 727-747, December, 1978. Member, President's Advisory Council, City of Hope National Medical Center, 1981. *Member:* American Bar Association (Member: Forum Committee on Health Law, 1979—); American Society of Law and Medicine.

**CYNTHIA A. TRANGSRUD,** born Thief River Falls, Minnesota, October 28, 1954; admitted to bar, 1982, California, U.S. District Court, North-

*(This Listing Continued)*

ern, Eastern, Southern and Central Districts of California and U.S. Court of Appeals, Ninth Circuit. *Education:* Hamline University (B.A., magna cum laude, 1977); University of Minnesota (J.D., 1980).

**GWEN FREEMAN,** born Alexandria, Virginia, June 27, 1956; admitted to bar, 1981, Pennsylvania; 1982, California and U.S. District Court, Central District of California. *Education:* University of Virginia (B.A., with honors, 1978; J.D., 1981). Law Clerk to the Hon. Paul A. Mueller, Jr., Court of Common Pleas, Pennsylvania, 1981-1982. *Member:* Pennsylvania Bar Association; Conference of Insurance Counsel.

**STEPHEN C. PASAROW,** born Los Angeles, California, September 30, 1952; admitted to bar, 1980, California. *Education:* University of California at Los Angeles (B.A., 1974); Southwestern University (J.D., 1978). Recipient, 1992 Defense Trial Lawyer of the Year by O'Brien's Verdictum Juris Publications. *Member:* American Board of Trial Advocates.

**NANCY MENZIES VAESSEN,** born Everett, Washington, July 29, 1946; admitted to bar, 1975, California, U.S. District Court, Central District of California and U.S. Court of Appeals, Ninth Circuit; 1984, U.S. District Court, Northern District of California. *Education:* Everett Junior College (A.A., 1966); Eastern Washington State College (B.A., cum laude, 1970); Loyola Law School, Los Angeles (J.D., 1975). Member, Products Liability Committee, National Spa and Pool Institute, 1984-1988. *Member:* Desert and Riverside County Bar Associations. (Resident, Palm Springs Office).

**JAMES M. PHILLIPPI,** born Spokane, Washington, February 15, 1953; admitted to bar, 1981, California and U.S. District Court, Southern, Central and Northern Districts of California. *Education:* California State University (B.A., 1975); Loyola Marymount University (J.D., 1981). Member, City of Santa Rosa General Plan Committee, 1972. *Member:* American Arbitration Association; American Institute of Architects (Affiliate Member).

**NANCY L. NEWMAN,** born Downey, California, September 29, 1955; admitted to bar, 1982, California; 1983, U.S. District Court, Central District of California. *Education:* University of California at Los Angeles (B.A., 1978); Southwestern University School of Law (J.D., 1981).

**K. STEPHEN TANG,** born Los Angeles, California, February 27, 1956; admitted to bar, 1981, California and U.S. District Court, Northern and Central Districts of California; 1982, U.S. District Court, Southern District of California; 1983, U.S. Court of Appeals, Ninth Circuit; 1986, U.S. District Court, Eastern District of California. *Education:* University of California at Davis (A.B., 1976); Loyola University of Los Angeles (J.D., 1980). *Member:* Association of Southern California Defense Counsel; Southern California Chinese Lawyers Association.

**STEPHEN M. HARRIS,** born Yakima, Washington, November 26, 1956; admitted to bar, 1983, California. *Education:* University of Washington (B.A., 1980); DePaul University (J.D., 1983).

**CLIFFORD R. COHEN,** born San Francisco, California, June 13, 1960; admitted to bar, 1985, California. *Education:* University of California at Berkeley (A.B., with highest honors, 1982) Phi Beta Kappa; University of California; Hastings College of the Law (J.D., 1985). Phi Delta Phi.

**SHAHEN HAIRAPETIAN,** born Montebello, California, April 21, 1959; admitted to bar, 1983, California; 1984, U.S. Tax Court; 1987, U.S. District Court, Central District of California. *Education:* University of California at Riverside (B.A., 1980); DePaul University (M.B.A., with distinction, 1983; J.D., with honors, 1983). Beta Gamma Sigma. Licensed Real Estate Broker, California, 1985. Commissioner, 1986-1988 and Chairman, 1989, Montebello Housing Mediation Board. Member, Educational Committee, Armenian Mesrobian School, 1986-1989. Member, Board of Trustees, Armenian Apostolic Holy Cross Church of Los Angeles, 1989. Member, Board of Trustees, JD/MBA Association of Los Angeles, 1986-1989. (Certified Specialist, Taxation Law, The State Bar of California, Board of Legal Specialization). *LANGUAGES:* Armenian and Russian.

**GLENN K. GILSLEIDER,** born Torrance, California, June 5, 1961; admitted to bar, 1986, California. *Education:* University of California at Berkeley (A.B., 1983); Pepperdine University (J.D., 1986). Member, Interschool Moot Court Team. Trial Advocacy Tournament Winner.

**JOHN J. HIGGINS,** born Lompoc, California, September 30, 1959; admitted to bar, 1987, California. *Education:* Oakland University (A.S., 1980); Michigan State University (B.A., 1983); University of London, London, England; Pepperdine University (J.D., 1987). First Place Gray's Inn-International Moot Court Competition, London, England, 1985. Recipient, American Jurisprudence Award in Insurance Law. *Member:* Association of Southern California Defense Counsel.

*(This Listing Continued)*

**KNAPP, PETERSEN & CLARKE,** A PROFESSIONAL
CORPORATION, Glendale—Continued

**WILLIAM J. ROHR,** born San Diego, California, July 1, 1945; admitted to bar, 1976, California; 1977, U.S. District Court, Central District of California; 1983, U.S. Court of Appeals, Ninth Circuit. *Education:* Cerritos College (A.A., 1973); Western State University (B.S.L., 1975; J.D., 1976). *Member:* Los Angeles County, Orange County and American Bar Associations; State Bar of California; Lawyers Club of Los Angeles County; Southern California Defense Counsel Association. [Sgt., USAR, 1965-1971]. (Resident, Palm Springs Office).

**PHILIP R. HOMSEY, II,** born Sacramento, California, January 6, 1948; admitted to bar, 1976, California; 1986, U.S. Tax Court. *Education:* University of Hawaii (B.A., 1973); McGeorge School of Law, University of the Pacific (J.D., 1976); University of San Diego (LL.M., 1988). Roger Traynor Honor Society. Member, Executive Committee and Honor Board, Moot Court. Recipient, American Jurisprudence Award, Contracts. Licensed Real Estate Broker, California, 1991. Professor of Law, Glendale University College of Law, 1976-1979. Adjunct Professor: Whittier University College of Law, 1992—; California State University, Los Angeles School of Business, 1980-1983. Member: Greek Theatre Advisory Commission, 1988—; Los Feliz Citizens Traffic Mobility Task Force, 1989—; Olympic Advisory Committee, 1984; Los Feliz Improvement Association, 1988—.

**ALEXANDER LEVY,** born Philadelphia, Pennsylvania, October 1, 1946; admitted to bar, 1974, California. *Education:* University of California at Los Angeles (B.A., 1969); Southwestern University (J.D., 1974). Founding Chairman, Real Estate Litigation Subsection, Real Estate Section, State Bar of California, 1984-1985. *Member:* Los Angeles County Bar Association (Member, Title Insurance Subsection); California Land Title Association.

**STEVEN RAY GARCIA,** born San Gabriel, California, October 20, 1957; admitted to bar, 1983, California; 1985, U.S District Court, Central District of California; 1990, U.S. District Court, Southern District of California. *Education:* Claremont McKenna College (B.A., 1979); University of California at Los Angeles (J.D., 1983). *Member:* American Bar Association (Member, Sections on: Tort and Insurance Law Practice; Real Property; Probate and Trust Law; Litigation).

**CYRIL CZAJKOWSKYJ,** born Erlangen, West Germany, February 22, 1951; admitted to bar, 1978, California and U.S. District Court, Northern District of California; 1983, U.S. District Court, Central District of California. *Education:* Northwestern University (B.A., 1972); University of Chicago (M.A., 1973); University of San Francisco (J.D., 1977).

**JO ANN MONTOYA,** born Los Angeles, California, May 23, 1962; admitted to bar, 1987, California. *Education:* University of California at Los Angeles (B.A., cum laude, 1984); University of California, Hastings College of the Law (J.D., 1987). Member, Hastings Law Journal, 1986-1987.

**MARIA A. GROVER,** born San Francisco, California, July 29, 1962; admitted to bar, 1987, California. *Education:* Santa Clara University (B.S., 1984; J.D., 1987).

**CONSTANCE G. ZANGLIS,** born Los Angeles, California, March 30, 1959; admitted to bar, 1985, California. *Education:* University of Redlands (B.A., 1981); University of California at Davis (J.D., 1985). Phi Beta Kappa. Co-Chairman, Moot Court Board, 1984-1985. *Member:* Association of Southern California Defense Counsel.

**MARA L. WEBER,** born Fredericksburg, Virginia, December 3, 1951; admitted to bar, 1981, California; 1982, U.S. District Court, Central District of California and U.S. Court of Appeals, Ninth Circuit. *Education:* University of California at Santa Cruz; University of Southern California (B.S., magna cum laude, 1974); University of California at Los Angeles (J.D., 1981). Phi Beta Kappa; Phi Kappa Phi. Member, Mortar Board. Registered Occupational Therapist, California, 1975—.

**GAIL S. COOPER-FOLB,** born Newark, New Jersey, August 19, 1958; admitted to bar, 1983, California; 1985, U.S. District Court, Central District of California. *Education:* University of California at Davis (B.A., with highest honors, 1980); University of California at Los Angeles (J.D., 1983). Phi Beta Kappa. Recipient, American Jurisprudence Award, 1983. Member, UCLA Law Review, 1981-1983. Adjunct Professor, University of La Verne School of Law, 1993—. *LANGUAGES:* French.

**DAPHNE B. SUBAR,** admitted to bar, 1990, California. *Education:* University of California at Santa Barbara (B.A., 1986); Washington College of Law of American University (J.D., 1989). *Member:* Illinois State Bar Association.

**DIRON M. OHANIAN,** admitted to bar, 1991, California. *Education:* University of California at Los Angeles (B.A., cum laude, 1988); University of Southern California (J.D., 1991).

**TIMOTHY K. CUTLER,** admitted to bar, 1988, California. *Education:* California State University, Fullerton (B.A., 1984); Loyola Law School (J.D., Cum Laude, 1988).

**KRISTINA ANN TENNER,** admitted to bar, 1988, California. *Education:* Indiana University (B.A., 1983); Hastings College of the Law, University of California (J.D., 1988).

**MITCHELL B. LUDWIG,** admitted to bar, 1984, California; 1985, U.S. District Court, Central District of California. *Education:* Hofstra University (B.B.A., 1981); Southwestern University (J.D., cum laude, 1984). Recipient, American Jurisprudence Book Awards in Criminal Law, Criminal Procedure and Debtor-Creditor Relations. Staff Member, 1982-1983 and Managing Editor, 1983-1984, Southwestern University Law Review. *Member:* Beverly Hills and Los Angeles County Bar Associations.

**ALAN J. CARNEGIE,** admitted to bar, 1985, California. *Education:* University of Arizona (B.A., 1981; J.D., 1985). Kappa Tau Alpha; Phi Alpha Delta. *Member:* American Bar Association.

**PENNY L. WHEAT,** admitted to bar, 1977, Nevada; 1978, California; 1984, U.S. Supreme Court and U.S. Tax Court; 1986, U.S. District Court, Central District of California. *Education:* Syracuse University (B.A., 1968); Southwestern University (J.D., cum laude, 1976); Georgetown University (LL.M., 1984). Delta Theta Phi. Editor, Southwestern University Law Review, 1975-1976. Listed in: Who's Who in California, 1987. Real Estate Broker, California, 1976, Nevada, 1981. Author, "The Rights and Obligations of Child Support," Southwestern University Law Review, Volume 7, Spring, 1975. *Member:* Los Angeles County, Clark County and American Bar Associations; State Bar of Nevada.

**YU-FENG (FRANCES) CHOU,** admitted to bar, 1990, California. *Education:* National Taiwan University, Taipei, Taiwan (LL.B., 1985); George Washington University (M.C.L., 1987); Hastings College of Law, University of California (J.D., 1990). *LANGUAGES:* Chinese (Mandarin).

**CATHERINE A. GAYER,** admitted to bar, 1991, California. *Education:* L.A. Pierce Junior College (A.A., 1984); San Diego State University (B.S., 1987); Northern Illinois University (J.D., 1990). *Member:* Desert Bar Association. (Resident, Palm Springs Office).

**ANTOINETTE S. WALLER,** admitted to bar, 1991, California. *Education:* University of California at Los Angeles (B.A., 1985); Loyola University Law School (J.D., 1990).

**GRETA T. HUTTON,** admitted to bar, 1982, California. *Education:* Stanford University (B.A., 1978); Columbia University (J.D., 1981).

**BARRY R. GAMMELL,** born Pasadena, California, November 17, 1949; admitted to bar, 1982, California and U.S. District Court, Central District of California; 1988, U.S. District Court, Southern and Northern Districts of California; 1989, U.S. District Court, Eastern District of California. *Education:* California State Polytechnic University, Pomona (B.S., 1972); San Francisco State University; Western State University at Fullerton (J.D., 1981). *Member:* Eastern Bar Association. **PRACTICE AREAS:** Insurance Coverage Litigation.

**DAVID I. GORNEY,** admitted to bar, 1981, California; 1982, U.S. District Court, Central, Southern, Northern and Eastern Districts of California. *Education:* University of California at Los Angeles (B.A., 1978); Southwestern University (J.D., 1981). Recipient, American Jurisprudence Award in Torts. Judge Pro Tem, Los Angeles Municipal Court. Designated as Special Master, Los Angeles Superior Court re Cal. Penal Code §1524 (c) matters. *Member:* American Bar Association; State Bar of California; Association of Southern California Defense Counsel; Lawyers-Pilots Bar Association.

**ANASTASIA BAUMEISTER,** admitted to bar, 1990, California. *Education:* University of California at Berkeley (A.B., 1987); University of San Francisco (J.D., 1990).

**DANIEL T. MOSIER,** admitted to bar, 1987, California, U.S. District Court, Eastern and Northern Districts of California and U.S. Court of Appeals, Ninth Circuit; 1988, U.S. District Court, Southern District of California; 1994, U.S. District Court, Central District of California. *Education:* University of California at Santa Cruz (B.A., 1980; M.S., 1982); Southwest-

*(This Listing Continued)*

ern University (J.D., 1986). *Member:* Association of Southern California Defense Counsel. *LANGUAGES:* Spanish.

**STEVEN E. CREAMER,** admitted to bar, 1994, California. *Education:* University of California at Los Angeles (B.A., 1988); Loyola Marymount University (J.D., 1994).

**JAMES L. HSU,** admitted to bar, 1994, California, U.S. District Court, Central District of California and U.S. Court of Appeals, Ninth Circuit. *Education:* University of California at Los Angeles (B.A., 1991; J.D., 1994).

**CLAIRE WONG,** admitted to bar, 1980, Singapore; 1990, California. *Education:* National University of Singapore (LL.B., 1979); University of London (LL.M., 1987).

**DEBBIE S. HARRIS SHERMAN,** born Los Angeles, California, May 26, 1961; admitted to bar, 1995, California and U.S. District Court, Central District of California. *Education:* University of Southern California (B.A., cum laude, 1983); University of Madrid, Madrid, Spain; Western State University (J.D., 1994). Recipient, American Jurisprudence Award, Legal Writing II. Charter Member, Western State University Tax Law Society. *Member:* Desert Bar Association. (Resident, Palm Springs Office). *LANGUAGES:* Spanish.

**PAUL R. KASSABIAN,** born Pasadena, California, July 9, 1966; admitted to bar, 1995, California. *Education:* Occidental College (B.A., 1988); University of California, Los Angeles (J.D., 1995). *Member:* Los Angeles County and American Bar Associations. *PRACTICE AREAS:* Appellate; Insurance Coverage; Probate.

**PHILLIP T. S. TUKIA,** born Auckland, New Zealand, February 9, 1966; admitted to bar, 1996, California. *Education:* California State University at Northridge (B.A., 1989); Loyola Marymount University (J.D., 1995).

All attorneys are admitted to the State Bar of California unless otherwise noted.

REFERENCE: Wells Fargo Bank (Glendale, California).

---

## LASKIN & GRAHAM
SUITE 840
800 NORTH BRAND BOULEVARD
**GLENDALE, CALIFORNIA 91203**
*Telephone: 213-665-6955; 818-547-4800; 714-957-3031*
*Telecopier: 818-547-3100*

*General Civil and Trial Practice in all State and Federal Courts, Eminent Domain, Municipal Law, Environmental Law, Real Property Damage, Employment Law, Construction Law, Land Use, Insurance Law, Professional Liability, Banking, Leasing, Bankruptcy, Financial Institutions Law, Commercial Documentation, Business Law and Litigation.*

*FIRM PROFILE: The law firm of Laskin & Graham is located in the new Glendale Corporate and Financial District, a few minutes from Downtown Los Angeles. Laskin & Graham's law practice emphasizes eminent domain, redevelopment law, inverse condemnation, real property matters and creditors' rights litigation. The firm assists owners, business tenants and occupants and public agencies when property may be impacted by an eminent domain or redevelopment project and has a prominent banking, bankruptcy and commercial litigation section with extensive experience in representing major financial institutions. The firm is an actively qualified member of the California Minority Counsel Program. The firm encourages continuing professional development and legal education, professional association activities and civic affairs. The firm members regularly author articles and lecture in the areas of their specialties, including matters dealing with real property, eminent domain, inverse condemnation, landslide litigation, property litigation, creditors' rights and related issues of concern to financial institutions regarding regulatory, documentation and litigation matters.*

### OF COUNSEL

**RICHARD LASKIN,** born Philadelphia, Pennsylvania, August 2, 1933; admitted to bar, 1959, California. *Education:* Los Angeles State College of Applied Arts and Sciences (B.A., 1955); University of California at Los Angeles (J.D., 1958). Nu Beta Epsilon. Lecturer: "The New Eminent Domain Law," California Continuing Education of the Bar Program, 1976; ALI/ABA Study Course, "Eminent Domain and Land Valuation Litigation," 1986. Judge Pro Tem: Los Angeles Municipal Courts, 1980-1985; Pasadena Municipal Court, 1975-1985. Assistant City Attorney, City of Los Angeles, 1960-1970. City Attorney, Cudahy, 1971-1982, 1986-1990 and Maywood, 1976-1980. Deputy City Attorney, San Dimas, 1970-1976, and Covina, 1971-1986. *Member:* Glendale, Los Angeles County (Member,

*(This Listing Continued)*

Condemnation Procedures Committee, 1969-1970; 1974-1990) and American Bar Associations; The State Bar of California; American Judicature Society. [U.S. Army, 1958-1960]. *PRACTICE AREAS:* Eminent Domain; Inverse Condemnation; Municipal Law; Real Property; General Civil Litigation.

### MEMBERS OF FIRM

**ARNOLD K. GRAHAM,** born Almena, Kansas, January 30, 1944; admitted to bar, 1970, California and U.S. District Court, Central District of California; 1975, U.S. Court of Appeals, Ninth Circuit; 1976, U.S. Supreme Court; 1990, U.S. Court of Claims. *Education:* Kansas State University (B.A., 1966); University of California at Los Angeles (J.D., 1969). Author: "Landslide & Subsidence Liability," CEB Supp., 1982; "Legal Issues in Emergency Management," Office of Programs and Academics, National Emergency Training Center (FEMA), 1984. Judge Pro Tem, Los Angeles Municipal Court, 1982-1992. Attorney, Office of the County Counsel, Los Angeles, 1970-1985. Principal Deputy County Counsel, 1978-1985. Deputy City Attorney, Covina, 1985-1986; Cudahy, 1986-1990. Vice President, 1978-1979, and President, 1980-1984, Los Angeles County Counsel Association. Los Angeles Assessment Appeals Board Legal Advisor, 1975-1984. Member, International Right-of-Way Association. Lecturer: American Institute of Real Estate Appraisers; American Society of Appraisers; Association of Engineering Geologists. *Member:* Glendale, Los Angeles County (Member: Sections on Eminent Domain, Real Property and Local Government; Condemnation Committee) and American Bar Associations; State Bar of California (Member, Committee on Zoning, Land Use and Environmental Regulations, Real Property Section, 1981-1984); The Association of Trial Lawyers of America. *PRACTICE AREAS:* Litigation; Eminent Domain; Inverse Condemnation; Land Use Law; Zoning and Planning, Environmental; Municipal; School Law; General Civil Practice.

**SUSAN L. VAAGE,** born Pasadena, California, July 7, 1953; admitted to bar, 1978, California; 1979, U.S. District Court, Central District of California; 1980, U.S. District Court, Northern, Southern and Eastern Districts of California; 1986; U.S. Supreme Court; 1987, U.S. Supreme Court and U.S. Court of Appeals, Ninth Circuit. *Education:* University of California at Irvine (B.A., 1975); Loyola University of Los Angeles (J.D., 1978). Judge Pro Tem, Los Angeles Superior Court, 1989—. Lecturer: California Credit Union Collectors' Council; California Bankers Association. *Member:* Los Angeles County Bar Association; State Bar of California; Los Angeles Bankruptcy Forum; Financial Lawyers Conference; Women Lawyers Association of Los Angeles; Mexican-American Bar Association of Los Angeles; Federal Bar Association of Los Angeles. *LANGUAGES:* Spanish. *PRACTICE AREAS:* Commercial Litigation; Bankruptcy; Insolvency; Creditors' Rights; Financial Institution Law; Business Litigation.

**JOHN S. PETERSON,** born Glendale, California, December 14, 1956; admitted to bar, 1981, California; 1982, U.S. District Court, Central District of California and U.S. Court of Appeals, Ninth Circuit. *Education:* University of California at Los Angeles (A.B., magna cum laude, 1978); University of California at Los Angeles, School of Law (J.D., 1981). Phi Beta Kappa; Omicron Delta Epsilon. Special Condemnation Counsel: Southern California Rapid Transit District, 1989-1993; City of Costa Mesa, 1992-1993; Costa Mesa Redevelopment Agency, 1992-1993; City of Newport Beach, 1990-1993; Burbank-Glendale-Pasadena Airport Authority, 1990-1991; City of Adelanto, 1992-1993. *Member:* Pasadena, Los Angeles County (Member, Real Property Section; Condemnation Committee) and American (Member, Real Property, Probate and Trust Section) Bar Associations; State Bar of California (Member, Real Property Section). *PRACTICE AREAS:* Litigation; Eminent Domain; Inverse Condemnation; Land Use Law; Zoning and Planning; Environmental; Municipal; General Civil Practice.

**MICHAEL ANTHONY CISNEROS,** born Los Angeles, California, January 1, 1956; admitted to bar, 1982, California; 1983, U.S. District Court, Central District of California; 1988, U.S. Court of Appeals, Ninth Circuit; 1989, U.S. District Court, Southern, Northern and Eastern Districts of California. *Education:* University of Southern California (B.A., 1978); Pepperdine University (J.D., 1982). Phi Delta Phi. Judge Pro Tempore, East Los Angeles Municipal Court, 1988—. *Member:* Los Angeles County Bar Association; State Bar of California; Mexican-American Bar Association; Financial Lawyers Conference; Los Angeles Bankruptcy Forum; American Bankruptcy Institute. *LANGUAGES:* Spanish. *PRACTICE AREAS:* Bankruptcy; Commercial Litigation; Creditors' Rights.

**GREGSON M. PERRY,** born Los Angeles, California, August 18, 1961; admitted to bar, 1986, California. *Education:* Menlo College (A.A., 1980); University of California at Berkeley (B.A., Legal Studies, 1982); McGeorge School of Law (J.D., 1985). *Member:* Beverly Hills, Los Angeles County

*(This Listing Continued)*

## LASKIN & GRAHAM, Glendale—Continued

and American Bar Associations; State Bar of California; California Trial Lawyers Association. *PRACTICE AREAS:* Eminent Domain; Condemnation; Real Property; Municipal Law; General Civil Practice.

**LYNN I. IBARA,** born Waimea, Kauai, Hawaii, September 19, 1953; admitted to bar, 1984, California. *Education:* University of Hawaii (B.A., 1976); Hastings College of Law, University of California (J.D., 1984). Phi Alpha Delta. Executive Publishing Editor, COMM/ENT Law Journal, 1983-1984. *Member:* Los Angeles County Bar Association; State Bar of California; Women In Business. *LANGUAGES:* Hawaiian. *PRACTICE AREAS:* Eminent Domain; Real Property Litigation; Municipal Law; General Civil Practice.

REPRESENTATIVE SPECIAL COUNSEL REFERENCES: Culver City Redevelopment Agency; South Gate Redevelopment Agency; Burbank Redevelopment Agency; Bell Gardens Redevelopment Agency; Inglewood Redevelopment Agency; Long Beach Redevelopment Agency; La Mirada Redevelopment Agency; City of Adelanto; City of Culver City; City of Redondo Beach; City of Simi Valley; City of Cudahy; City of Inglewood; City of Long Beach; County of Los Angeles; Lynwood Unified School District; Las Virgenes Unified School District; Long Beach Unified School District; Oxnard Union High School District; Keppel Union School District; Southern California Rapid Transit District.
REPRESENTATIVE CORPORATE COUNSEL REFERENCES: Bank of California; Bank of the West; Crown Books; Dollar Rent A Car; Dynamic Finance Corporation; Geosoils, Inc.; Hopkins Development Company; International Bank of California; Mobil Oil; North American Development Corp.; Pacific Southwest Realty Corporation; Sanwa Bank California; Seeley Company; So. Cal. Gas Co.; Southern California Bank; Southern Pacific Transportation Company; Sunbelt Management Company; Texaco Inc.; Tokai Credit Corp.; Trak Auto; Union Bank; Wells Fargo Bank.

## RICHARD W. McLAIN
### A PROFESSIONAL CORPORATION

700 NORTH BRAND BOULEVARD, SUITE 630
**GLENDALE, CALIFORNIA 91203**
Telephone: 818-549-3930
Fax: 818-549-3939

*Trial and Appellate Practice in all State and Federal Courts, Insurance Law, Bad Faith Defense, Negligence, Products Liability, Casualty and Fire Insurance Law, Professional Negligence, Landslide and Subsidence Law, Environmental Law, Professional Liability, Municipalities and Public Entities, Excess and Surplus Lines.*

**RICHARD W. MCLAIN,** born Pittsburgh, Pennsylvania, May 30, 1938; admitted to bar, 1969, California. *Education:* Loyola University of Los Angeles (B.A., 1962; J.D., 1968). *Member:* Los Angeles County Bar Association; The State Bar of California; Association of Southern California Defense Counsel; American Board of Trial Advocates; Defense Research Institute. (Also Of Counsel to Sacino, Bertolino & Hallissy, Sacramento).

**CHARLES H. STOKES,** born Los Angeles, California, April 7, 1942; admitted to bar, 1973, California. *Education:* University of California at Los Angeles; Southwestern University School of Law (J.D., 1973). Phi Alpha Delta. Member, Southwestern University Law Review, 1971-1972. Judge Pro Tem, Municipal Court, Los Angeles Judicial District, 1982-1983. *Member:* Los Angeles County and American Bar Associations; State Bar of California. [With U.S. Army (National Guard), 1965-1971]

### OF COUNSEL

**D. F. SACINO,** born Los Angeles, California, October 21, 1930; admitted to bar, 1962, California; 1967, U.S. District Court, Eastern District of California. *Education:* University of Southern California (B.A., 1953); Southwestern University (J.D., cum laude, 1962). Who's Who in American Law. *Member:* State Bar of California; American Bar Association; Pacific Claim Executives Association; Association of Northern California Defense Counsel. [Staff Sgt., U.S. Army, 1953-1955]. (Also at Sacino, Bertolino & Hallissy, Sacramento). *LANGUAGES:* Spanish and Italian.

## MELBY & ANDERSON
FIFTH FLOOR, 121 WEST LEXINGTON DRIVE
**GLENDALE, CALIFORNIA 91203**
Telephone: 818-246-5644
Los Angeles: 213-245-2606
Fax: 818-246-5780

*General Civil and Trial Practice in State Courts. Trials and Appeals. Probate, Estate Planning, Real Property, Business, Corporation Litigation, Family Law, Water Rights, Municipal Law and Banking.*

### MEMBERS OF FIRM

**HENRY MELBY,** born Los Angeles, California, August 21, 1919; admitted to bar, 1948, California; 1950, U.S. District Court, Central District of California. *Education:* University of California (A.B., 1941); University of Southern California (J.D., 1948). Order of the Coif; Phi Delta Phi. Member, Los Angeles County Commission on Judicial Procedure, 1963-1973. *Member:* Glendale (President, 1954), Los Angeles County (Member, Board of Trustees, 1956-1958) and American Bar Associations; The State Bar of California (Member, Executive Committee, Conference of State Bar Delegates, 1968-1972; Chairman, 1972; Member, Committee on Administrative Justice, 1961-1963). *PRACTICE AREAS:* Probate; Estate Planning.

**JARRETT S. ANDERSON,** born Provo, Utah, May 22, 1936; admitted to bar, 1961, California and Utah. *Education:* Utah State University (B.S., 1958); University of Southern California (J.D., 1961). *Member:* Glendale (President, 1970-1971), Los Angeles County (Member, Board of Trustees, 1977-1979) and American Bar Associations; The State Bar of California. [Capt., J.A.G.C., U.S. Army, active duty, 1961-1964]. *PRACTICE AREAS:* Civil Litigation; Family Law.

**RANDALL MELBY,** born Glendale, California, June 13, 1950; admitted to bar, 1977, California; U.S. District Court, Central District of California. *Education:* United States International University (B.A., 1972); California Western School of Law (J.D., 1977). *Member:* Glendale (Member, Board of Trustees, 1980-1989; President, 1987-1988), Los Angeles County and American Bar Associations; The State Bar of California. *PRACTICE AREAS:* Probate and Estate Planning.

**PATRICK A. LIDDELL,** born Long Branch, New Jersey, July 30, 1945; admitted to bar, 1978, California; 1979, U.S. District Court, Central District of California. *Education:* California State University at Northridge (B.S., 1971; M.S., 1973); University of San Fernando Valley (J.D., 1978). *Member:* Glendale (Member, Board of Trustees, 1984-1991; President, 1991-1992), Los Angeles County and American Bar Associations; The State Bar of California. *PRACTICE AREAS:* Business; Real estate.

**MICHAEL W. DEAKTOR,** born Pittsburgh, Pennsylvania, November 14, 1957; admitted to bar, 1986, California; 1987, U.S. District Court, Central District of California. *Education:* Arizona State University (B.S., 1979); Pepperdine University (J.D., cum laude, 1986). Beta Alpha Psi; Phi Delta Phi. Certified Public Accountant, Arizona, 1982. *Member:* Glendale, Los Angeles County and American Bar Associations; The State Bar of California; Arizona Society of Certified Public Accountants. *PRACTICE AREAS:* Probate and Estate Planning.

**VALERIE K. BYER,** born Huntington Park, California, February 4, 1949; admitted to bar, 1990, California and U.S. District Court, Central District of California. *Education:* University of Southern California (B.A., magna cum laude, 1986); Loyola University of Los Angeles (J.D., 1990). Phi Beta Kappa. *Member:* Glendale, Los Angeles County and American Bar Associations; State Bar of California. *PRACTICE AREAS:* Civil Litigation; Family Law.

REPRESENTATIVE CLIENTS: Glendale Motor Car Dealer's Assn.; Crescenta County Water District; Foothill Municipal Water District; Thermal Products, Inc. (Refrigerator Equipment); Western Pioneers Sales, Inc. (Restaurant Equipment).
REFERENCES: Trust & Savings Assn.; Wells Fargo Bank all Glendale, Calif. Main Offices.

## MESSINA, LALAFARIAN & MANNING
SUITE 1670
550 NORTH BRAND BOULEVARD
**GLENDALE, CALIFORNIA 91203-1900**
Telephone: 818-242-5250
FAX: 818-242-4828

*General Liability Defense, Products Liability, Insurance Defense, Insurance Coverage.*

*(This Listing Continued)*

# PROFESSIONAL BIOGRAPHIES

## CALIFORNIA—GLENDALE

*FIRM PROFILE:* The Law Offices of Messina, Lalafarian & Manning is a general trial practice law firm engaged primarily in the defense of civil litigation matters. Originally established in 1983 as House Defense Counsel to The Hertz Corporation, the Firm was re-organized in 1987 as a private defense firm.

The Law Offices of Messina, Lalafarian & Manning handles defense litigation for a variety of insurance carriers, self-insureds, public entities, non profit corporations and car rental companies. The firm handles liability matters including motor vehicle, premises liability, equipment, product and maintenance defect, construction losses and intentional torts. The firm also handles Appeals, insurance coverage, Declaratory Relief Actions, insurance and self-insurance liability questions and contract interpretation issues. As a wholly owned woman's business, the firm is certified pursuant to 49 CFR, Part 23 of the U.S. Department of Transportation Rules and Regulations as a "Woman's Business Enterprise." Members of the firm serve as arbitrators of the Los Angeles County Superior Court Arbitration Panel.

**NINA R. MESSINA,** born New York, N.Y., April 27, 1944; admitted to bar, 1980, California, 1981, U.S. District Court, Central District of California and U.S. Court of Appeals, Ninth Circuit. *Education:* Queen of Angels School of Nursing (R.N., 1968); University of California at Los Angeles (B.A., cum laude, Political Science, 1977); Southwestern University (J.D., 1979). Phi Gamma Mu; Pi Sigma Alpha. Lead Articles Editor, Computer Law Journal, 1979. Registered Nurse, California, 1968. Arbitrator, Los Angeles County Superior Court Panel of Arbitrators. Judge Pro Tem, Los Angeles County Superior Court. *Member:* Los Angeles County and American Bar Associations; State Bar of California; Association of Southern California Defense Counsel; California Women Lawyers Association.

**DANIEL LALAFARIAN,** admitted to bar, 1981, California. *Education:* California State University, Los Angeles (B.A., Journalism, 1973); Western State University (J.D., 1981). Phi Alpha Delta. Arbitrator, Los Angeles County Superior Court Arbitration Panel. *Member:* Los Angeles County Bar Association; The Association of Southern California Defense Counsel. [U.S. Army, 1967-1969, serving in Vietnam]

**MARY VANOSDEL MANNING,** born Santa Monica California, October 10, 1952; admitted to bar, 1981, California; U.S. District Court, Central District of California. *Education:* University of Arizona; University of California at Los Angeles (B.A., Political Science, 1974); Southwestern University (J.D., cum laude, 1981). Recipient: American Jurisprudence Award in Family Law; Excellence in Product Liability. Graduate, U.C.L.A. Attorney Assistant Training Program. Note and Comment Editor, Southwestern University Law Review, 1980-1981. Author: "Economic Injury to Third Parties," 12 SW L. Rev. 87 (1981), cited by California Supreme Court in landmark decision in Moradi-Shalal v. Fireman's Fund (1988) 46 Cal. 3d 287. Judge Pro Tempore, Los Angeles Superior Court. *Member:* Los Angeles County (Chairman, Insurance Committee) and American Bar Associations; Association of Southern California Defense Counsel.

**WILLIAM P. RYAN,** admitted to bar, 1989, California; U.S. District Court, Central District of California. *Education:* California State University at Northridge (B.A., Speech Communication, 1979); University of LaVerne (J.D., 1989). *Member:* Los Angeles County and American Bar Associations; Southern California Defense Counsel; Trial Advocacy Institute.

---

## O'FLAHERTY & BELGUM

Established in 1983

1000 NORTH CENTRAL, SUITE 300
**GLENDALE, CALIFORNIA 91202-2957**
Telephone: 818-242-9229
Fax: 818-242-9114
Email: oandb&primenet.com
URL: http://www.oandb-law/oandb

*Long Beach, California Office:* 100 Oceangate, Suite 500, 90802-4312. Telephone: 310-437-0090. Fax: 310-437-5550.

*Orange County, California Office:* 222 South Harbor Boulevard, Suite 600, Anaheim, CA 92805-3701. Telephone: 714-533-3373. Fax: 714-533-2607.

*Riverside, California Office:* 3880 Lemon Street, Suite 450, 92501-3301. Telephone: 909-341-0049. Fax: 909-341-3919.

*Ventura, California Office:* 840 County Square Drive, Suite 200, 93003-5406. Telephone: 805-650-2600. Fax: 805-650-2658.

General Civil, Trial and Appellate Practice in State and Federal Courts. Medical and Dental Malpractice, Products Liability, General Insurance Law, Insurance Coverage, Wrongful Termination, Workers' Compensation, Business and Environmental Litigation.

*(This Listing Continued)*

---

### MEMBERS OF FIRM

**MICHAEL A. O'FLAHERTY,** born Chicago, Illinois, July 28, 1947; admitted to bar, 1973, California and U.S. District Court, Central District of California; 1985, U.S. District Court, Northern District of California. *Education:* University of California at Santa Barbara (B.A., 1969); University of Southern California (J.D., 1972). Member, Southern California Law Review, 1970-1971. Author: Article 44 Southern California Law Review 1092, 1971. Member, Panel of Arbitrators, Los Angeles Superior Court Arbitration Program. *Member:* Los Angeles County Bar Association; The State Bar of California (Principal Referee, 1982-1987); Association of Southern California Defense Counsel; American Board of Trial Advocates. [Capt., U.S. Army Reserve, 1970-1979]. (Resident, Glendale Office).

**STEPHEN L. BELGUM,** born Fort Meade, South Dakota, May 24, 1943; admitted to bar, 1972, California; 1973, U.S. District Court, Central District of California. *Education:* Whittier College (B.A., 1965); University of Southern California (J.D., 1972). Member, Panel of Arbitrators, Los Angeles Superior Court Arbitration Program. *Member:* Long Beach and Los Angeles County Bar Associations; State Bar of California. [Captain, U.S. Army, 1966-1969]. (Resident, Glendale Office) (Managing Partner).
**PRACTICE AREAS:** Trials.

**TODD C. THEODORA,** born Paterson, New Jersey, June 30, 1960; admitted to bar, 1985, California, U.S. District Court, Central District of California and U.S. District Court, District of Minnesota. *Education:* California State University at Long Beach (B.A., 1982); University of San Diego (J.D., 1985). Phi Beta Kappa; Kappa Tau Alpha. Author: Manual, "Handling Complex Litigation"; Staff Writer, "California Regulatory Law Reporter," 1983-1984. National Coordinating Counsel, Dunlop Tire Corporation, 1986—. Member, Panel of Arbitrators, Los Angeles Superior Court Arbitration Program. *Member:* Los Angeles County, Long Beach and American Bar Associations; State Bar of California; Association of Southern California Defense Counsel; American Board of Trial Advocates; American College of Legal Medicine; National Association of Railroad Trial Counsel. (Resident, Long Beach Office).

**JOHN J. WEBER,** born Los Angeles, California, May 19, 1947; admitted to bar, 1972, California; 1973, U.S. District Court, Central District of California; 1975, U.S. Court of Appeals, Ninth Circuit and U.S. District Court, Northern and Eastern Districts of California; 1983, U.S. District Court, Southern District of California. *Education:* Loyola University of Los Angeles (B.A., 1969); University of Southern California (J.D., 1972). *Member:* Los Angeles County Bar Association; State Bar of California; Association of Southern California Defense Counsel; Southern California for Healthcare Risk Management. (Resident, Long Beach Office).

**GREGORY M. HATTON,** born Grand Rapids, Michigan, July 10, 1955; admitted to bar, 1985, California. *Education:* Phillips Academy, Andover, Massachusetts; University of California (B.A., 1982); University of San Diego (J.D., 1985). Author: Manual, "How to Handle Commercial Trucking Litigation," 1989. Columnist, "California Regulatory Law Reporter," 1983-1984; "Comprehensive Litigation Management Plans," for Self-Insured Corporations, 1993. Chairman, Curriculum Committee for American Studies, University of California at Santa Cruz; Planning Consultant, Third Party Claims Administration, Metrolink Commuter Rail System, 1992. *Member:* Orange County, Los Angeles County and American Bar Associations; The State Bar of California; National Association of Railroad Trial Counsel; Association of Southern California Defense Counsel. (Resident, Orange County Office).

**LYNN E. OVANDO,** born Ann Arbor, Michigan, December 10, 1957; admitted to bar, 1983, California, U.S. Court of Appeals, Ninth Circuit and U.S. District Court, Central District of California. *Education:* St. Marys College (B.A., summa cum laude, 1980); Rutgers University (J.D., 1983). Phi Alpha Theta; Kappa Gamma Pi. Adjunct Professor, Lawyering Skills, Western State University College of Law, 1988—. *Member:* Orange County and American (Member, Health Care Section) Bar Associations; State Bar of California; The Association of Southern California Defense Counsel; California Association of Healthcare Attorneys; California Association of Hospitals and Health Systems; Southern California Association of Healthcare Risk Management. (Resident, Long Beach Office).

**STEPHEN L. SCHUMM,** born Glendale, California, April 12, 1950; admitted to bar, 1983, California, U.S. District Court, Central District of California and U.S. Court of Appeals, Ninth Circuit. *Education:* California State University at Los Angeles (B.A., 1980); Southwestern University School of Law (J.D., 1983). *Member:* Los Angeles County and American (Vice-Chair, Tort and Insurance Committee Section of General Practice, 1985-1986) Bar Associations; State Bar of California; The Association of Southern California Defense Counsel. (Resident, Long Beach Office).

*(This Listing Continued)*

CAA273B

## O'FLAHERTY & BELGUM, Glendale—Continued

**ERNEST C. CHEN,** born New York, N.Y., September 3, 1946; admitted to bar, 1972, Louisiana; 1975, U.S. Supreme Court; 1979, California; U.S. Court of Appeals, Fifth and Ninth Circuits. *Education:* Loyola University (A.B., 1968; J.D., 1971); University of San Diego (LL.M., 1984). Instructor, U.S. Attorney General's Trial Advocacy Institute, 1978. Assistant District Attorney, New Orleans, Louisiana, 1972-1975. Assistant U.S. Attorney, New Orleans, Louisiana, 1975-1978. Special Prosecutor, Jan Department of Justice, Organized Crime Section, 1979-1980. *Member:* Orange County and Los Angeles County Bar Associations; State Bar of California. (Resident, Orange County Office).

**LISA A. CROSS,** born Kansas City, Missouri, July 27, 1959; admitted to bar, 1988, California. *Education:* University of California at Santa Barbara (B.A., 1981); Pepperdine University (J.D., 1987). Paralegal Certification, UCLA, 1982. *Member:* Los Angeles County Bar Association; State Bar of California; Association of Southern California Defense Counsel; Southern California Association of Hospital Risk Managers. (Resident, Orange County Office).

**NANCY G. WANSKI,** born Luverne, Alabama, November 15, 1950; admitted to bar, 1988, California and U.S. Court of Appeals, Ninth Circuit. *Education:* University of Alabama at Birmingham (B.S., Nursing, 1974); California State University at Long Beach (M.S. Critical Care Nursing, 1981); University of Southern California (J.D., 1988). Finalist, Hale Moot Court Competition. Registered Nurse, California, 1977. *Member:* State Bar of California; The Association of Southern California Defense Counsel; Southern California Association of Hospital Risk Managers; American Association of Critical Care Nurses. (Resident, Glendale Office).

**LEE M. THIES,** born Cleveland, Ohio, January 21, 1955; admitted to bar, 1987, California. *Education:* California State University at Fullerton (B.A., 1978); Western State University (J.D., 1981). Recipient, American Jurisprudence Award in Constitutional Law. Author: "Informed Consent, The Physician's Increasing Burden," 8 Western State University Law Review 113, 1980. Member, Board of Directors, California State University at Fullerton Alumni Association, 1981-1983. Associate Division Counsel, Emerson Electric, 1987-1989. Corporate Counsel, South California Association Hospital Risk Managers, 1991—. *Member:* State Bar of California; Association of Southern California Defense Counsel; National Association of Healthcare Lawyers. (Resident, Riverside Office).

**KRISTEN J. HEIM,** born Redlands, California, April 13, 1959; admitted to bar, 1987, California and U.S. District COurt, Central District of California. *Education:* University of California at Irvine (B.A., 1981); University of San Diego (Paralegal Certification, 1981); Pepperdine University (J.D., 1987). Member, Moot Court Board. Recipient: American Jurisprudence Award in Advanced Civil Procedure. *Member:* State Bar of California; Association of Southern California Defense Counsel. (Resident, Long Beach Office).

**MIKE MARTINEZ,** born San Pedro, California, May 25, 1962; admitted to bar, 1989, California and U.S. District Court, Central District of California. *Education:* University of Southern California (B.A., 1985); Boston College (J.D., 1988). Skull and Dagger; Order of Troy; Blue Key. *Member:* Los Angeles County, Ventura, Santa Barbara and American Bar Associations; State Bar of California, Association of Southern California Defense Counsel; Defense Research Institute; Ventura Trial Lawyers Association. (Resident, Ventura Office).

### OF COUNSEL

**LEE T. BELGUM,** born Decorah, Iowa, October 30, 1953; admitted to bar, 1978, California. *Education:* California Lutheran College (B.A., magna cum laude, 1975); University of California at Los Angeles (J.D., 1978). *Member:* Long Beach and Los Angeles County Bar Associations; State Bar of California. (Resident, Orange County Office).

**C. SNYDER PATIN,** born Opelousas, Louisiana, September 26, 1930; admitted to bar, 1975, California; 1976, U.S. District Court, Central District of California. *Education:* Columbia University (B.S., 1960); Whittier College School of Law (J.D., cum laude, 1975). Phi Alpha Delta. Member, Whittier College Law Review, 1974-1975. *Member:* Los Angeles County and American Bar Associations; Medical-Legal Society; Association of Southern California Defense Counsel; Defense Research Institute. (Resident, Anaheim Office). *LANGUAGES:* Greek, Latin, French and German. *REPORTED CASES:* Arato v. Avedon, 5 Cal 4th 1172. *PRACTICE AREAS:* Medical Malpractice; Dental Malpractice; Products Liability; Staff Privileges Issues.

*(This Listing Continued)*

### ASSOCIATES

**PAMELA A. BENBEN,** born Medina, New York, February 18, 1955; admitted to bar, 1981, California; 1984, U.S. District Court, Central District of California. *Education:* State University of New York at Buffalo (B.A., summa cum laude, 1977); Loyola Marymount University (J.D., 1981). *Member:* State Bar of California; American Bar Association; Southern California Association of Defense Counsel. (Resident, Glendale Office). *REPORTED CASES:* Ramos v. Valley Vista Hosp., 234 Cal.Rptr. 608, Ordered Not Published, (Rule 976, Cal. Rules of Ct.) (Cal.App. 2 Dist., Jan 30, 1987) (NO CIV. B019781, CIV. B016746); Grant v. Avis Rent A Car System, Inc., 158 Cal.App.3d 813, 204 Cal.Rptr. 869 (Cal.App. 2 Dist., Jul 26, 1984) (NO. B004006).

**ROBERT M. DATO,** born San Diego, California, April 6, 1958; admitted to bar, 1983, California; 1984, U.S. Court of Appeals, Ninth Circuit; 1986, U.S. District Court, Central District of California; 1987, U.S. Supreme Court and U.S. Court of Appeals, Tenth Circuit; 1988, U.S. Court of Appeals, Fifth Circuit; 1989, U.S. Court of Appeals, Seventh Circuit and U.S. District Court, Southern, Northern and Eastern Districts of California. *Education:* California State University at San Diego (B.A., magna cum laude, 1980); Hastings College of Law, University of California; University of San Diego (J.D., 1983). Lead Articles Editor, San Diego Law Review, 1982-1983. Author: "The Effect of Passage of Time on the Status of Inactive Public Figures," Federal Communications Law Journal, 1983. Senior Research Attorney to Presiding Justice David G. Sills, California Court of Appeal, Fourth District, Division Three, 1991-1993. *Member:* Orange County (Chair: Appellate Law Section, 1992; Orange County Lawyer Board of Advisors, 1993) and American Bar Associations; State Bar of California. (Resident, Long Beach Office).

**DONNA R. EVANS,** born Springfield, Missouri, September 14, 1954; admitted to bar, 1983, California; 1984, U.S. District Court, Southern District of California. *Education:* University of Colorado (B.S., 1975); Western State University College of Law (J.D. with honors, 1981). Member, Western State Law Review Board, 1979-1980. Recipient: American Jurisprudence Awards in Trial Practice and Torts. *Member:* Los Angeles County and American Bar Associations; State Bar of California; Los Angeles County Trial Lawyers Association; California Trial Lawyers Association; The Association of Trial Lawyers of America. (Resident, Long Beach Office). *PRACTICE AREAS:* Medical Malpractice.

**SUZANNE BOYLE,** born Los Angeles, California, January 31, 1949; admitted to bar, 1989, California. *Education:* Mount St. Mary's College (B.A., 1971); Western State University (J.D., summa cum laude, 1989). Recipient, American Jurisprudence Awards. (Resident, Glendale Office).

**SHARON A. BRAHMS,** born Los Angeles, California; admitted to bar, 1989, California, U.S. District Court, Central District of California and U.S. Court of Appeals, Ninth Circuit. *Education:* St. Vincent's College (R.N., 1967); Southwestern University School of Law (J.D., 1988). Recipient, Best Brief Award, 1986 Intramural Moot Court Competition. Registered Nurse: Minnesota, 1967; California, 1972. Judicial Clerkship to Honorable Fred Woods, Los Angeles Superior Court. *Member:* State Bar of California. (Resident, Long Beach Office).

**TODD E. CROUTCH,** born Northridge, California, March 18, 1963; admitted to bar, 1989, California; U.S. District Court, Central District of California and U.S. Court of Appeals, Ninth Circuit. *Education:* San Diego State University (B.S., 1986); University of New Hampshire; Loyola Law School (J.D., 1989). Scott Moot Court Participant. Legal Intern for Honorable Arnold Gold, Robert Letteau and Thomas Schneider, Superior Court, Northridge. *Member:* State Bar of California; American Bar Association. (Resident, Glendale Office). *REPORTED CASES:* Stevenson v. Superior Court (1996) 42 Cal. App. 4th 1288. *PRACTICE AREAS:* Employment; General Liability; Product Liability Defense Litigation.

**D. ELIZABETH NASH,** born Los Angeles, California, July 5, 1961; admitted to bar, 1988, California, U.S. District Court, Central District of California and U.S. Tax Court. *Education:* California State University at Fullerton (B.A., 1985); Pepperdine University (J.D., 1988). Recipient, American Jurisprudence Award, Agency and Partnership Law. Author: "Sex Based Employment Discrimination," Orange County Bar Journal. *Member:* Orange County and American Bar Associations; State Bar of California; Orange County Barrister. (Resident, Riverside Office).

**STEPHEN C. FRASER,** born Aledo, Illinois, August 31, 1956; admitted to bar, 1991, California. *Education:* Knox College (B.A., 1978); Southwestern University School of Law (J.D., cum laude, 1990). Recipient, American Jurisprudence Award in Evidence and Family Law. *Member:* State Bar of California. (Resident, Glendale Office).

*(This Listing Continued)*

**JOHANNA A. SCHLEUTER,** born Martins Ferry, Ohio; admitted to bar, 1989, California; 1990, U.S. District Court, Central District of California. *Education:* Ohio University (B.S., 1964); Western State University (J.D., 1988). Recipient, American Jurisprudence Award. *Member:* Orange County and American Bar Associations; State Bar of California; Orange County Barristers. (Resident, Long Beach Office).

**CHERYL P. NESSEL,** born Brooklyn, New York, September 12, 1955; admitted to bar, 1982, California and U.S. District Court, Central District of California. *Education:* California State University at Northridge (B.A., 1978); Southwestern University School of Law (J.D., 1981). Adjunct Professor, Lawyering Skills Western State University College of Law, 1993. *Member:* State Bar of California; American Bar Association. (Resident, Long Beach Office).

**RONALD A. CHAVEZ,** born San Pedro, California, October 17, 1954; admitted to bar, 1986, California, U.S. District Court, Central District of California and U.S. Court of Appeals, Ninth Circuit. *Education:* University of California at Santa Cruz (B.A., with honors, 1977); University of California at Los Angeles (J.D., 1984). Co-Author: "Can Science Be Inopportune? Constitutional Validity of Governmental Restrictions on Race-IQ Research," 31 UCLA L.Rev. 1, 1983. *Member:* Long Beach County, American and Mexican American Bar Associations; Association of Southern California Defense Counsel. (Resident, Long Beach Office). **LANGUAGES:** Spanish.

**ALEXANDER M. WATSON,** born Bloomington, Minnesota, December 16, 1964; admitted to bar, 1991, California. *Education:* Grinnell College (B.A., 1987); Hamline University School of Law (J.D., 1991). Recipient, American Jurisprudence Award for Evidence. Associate Editor, Hamline Law Review, 1990-1991. *Member:* State Bar of California; American Bar Association. (Resident, Glendale Office).

**KELLI L. BAKER,** born Detroit, Michigan, November 19, 1965; admitted to bar, 1991, California and U.S. District Court, Central District of California; 1993, Michigan. *Education:* Indiana University (B.A., 1987); Northern Illinois University (J.D., 1991). *Member:* State Bar of California. (Resident, Orange County Office).

**DAVID E. MEAD,** born Santa Maria, California, July 20, 1965; admitted to bar, 1991, California; 1992, U.S. District Court, Central District of California. *Education:* University of California at Los Angeles (B.A., 1988); Loyola Law School of Los Angeles (J.D., 1991). Phi Alpha Delta. Member, St. Thomas More Law Honor Society. Executive Editor, Loyola of Los Angeles International and Comparative Law Journal, 1990-1991. *Member:* State Bar of California. (Resident, Glendale Office).

**ARTHUR R. PETRIE, II,** born Santa Monica, California, September 16, 1959; admitted to bar, 1992, California, U.S. District Court, Central District of California and U.S. Court of Appeals, Ninth Circuit. *Education:* University of California at Los Angeles (B.A., 1982); Western State University (J.D., magna cum laude, 1991). *Member:* Orange County and American Bar Associations; State Bar of California. (Resident, Orange County Office).

**BARBARA S. BOARNET,** born Los Angeles, California, August 3, 1966; admitted to bar, 1992, California; 1995, District of Columbia. *Education:* University of California at San Diego (B.A., 1989); Loyola University of Los Angeles (J.D., 1992). Author: Casenote, "Narell v. Freeman: The Ninth Circuit has Delusions about Illusions of Love," Loyola Entertainment Law Journal, Vol. 11, Nov. 1, 1991. *Member:* Orange County and American Bar Associations; District of Columbia Bar; State Bar of California; Orange County Women Lawyers. (Resident, Orange County Office).

**JOSEPH A. MAHONEY,** born Boston, Massachusetts, January 23, 1951; admitted to bar, 1978, California and U.S. District Court, Central District of California. *Education:* University of Massachusetts (B.A., 1973); Southwestern University (J.D., 1978). *Member:* Orange County Bar Association; State Bar of California. (Resident, Orange County Office).

**KATHLEEN E. BARNETT,** born Ames, Iowa, March 20, 1957; admitted to bar, 1987, California; 1988, U.S. District Court, Central District of California; 1995, Idaho and U.S. District Court, District of Idaho. *Education:* University of California at Santa Barbara (B.A., 1979); University of San Diego (J.D., 1986). *Member:* Los Angeles County, Orange County and American Bar Associations; State Bar of California. (Resident, Long Beach Office).

**SUSAN E. SHUBE,** born Encino, California, March 31, 1965; admitted to bar, 1990, California and U.S. District Court, Central District of California. *Education:* University of California at Los Angeles (B.A., 1987); University of Southern California (J.D., 1990). Moot Court Honors Program. *Member:* American Bar Association. (Resident, Orange County Office).

**DANIEL K. DIK,** born Long Beach, California, April 1, 1959; admitted to bar, 1991, California, U.S. District Court, Central District of California and U.S. Court of Appeals, Ninth Circuit; 1995, Colorado; registered to practice before U.S. Patent and Trademark Office. *Education:* California State University, Long Beach (B.S., 1982); University of Southern California (J.D., 1991). Phi Alpha Delta. Editor: Computer Law Journal; Major Tax Planning Journal. Clinical Laboratory Technologist, California, 1982—. Author, "Copyrighted Software and Tying Arrangements: A Fresh Appreciation for per se Illegality," 10 Computer L.J. 413 1990. *Member:* Los Angeles County and American Bar Associations; State Bar of California; California Association for Medical Laboratory Technology; American Society of Clinical Pathologists. (Resident, Long Beach Office). **LANGUAGES:** Spanish.

**DEBRA L. DENTON,** born Cocoa, Florida, January 11, 1954; admitted to bar, 1993, California; 1994, U.S. District Court, Central District of California. *Education:* University of Southern California (B.S., 1987); Western State University (J.D., 1992). *Member:* Los Angeles County Bar Association; National Attorneys' Committee for Transplant Awareness, Inc.; California Women Lawyers; United Liver Association (Attorneys Division). (Resident, Long Beach Office).

**SHERYL A. RAGEN,** born Boston, Massachusetts, December 12, 1963; admitted to bar, 1992, California; 1993, U.S. District Court, Central District of California. *Education:* Mount Saint Mary's College at Los Angeles (B.A., 1988); Loyola University of Los Angeles (J.D., 1992). Psi Chi National Honor Society. Recipient: International Law Scholarship, 1990. Student Bar Association Speaker Chairperson, 1990. *Member:* State Bar of California. (Resident, Glendale Office).

**JOSEPH M. ACIERNO,** born Idaho Falls, Idaho, October 25, 1961; admitted to bar, 1993, California; 1994, U.S. District Court, Central District of California. *Education:* Creighton University (B.S., cum laude, 1983; M.D., 1987; J.D., 1993). Pi Mu Epsilon. Medical Doctor, Nebraska, 1988. *Member:* Los Angeles County Bar Association; State Bar of California (Member, Health Law Section); American Medical Association. American College of Legal Medicine (Fellow). (Resident, Glendale Office). **PRACTICE AREAS:** Medical Malpractice Defense.

**KATHLEEN M. WYNEN,** born Long Beach, California, August 25, 1951; admitted to bar, 1993, California. *Education:* University of La Verne (B.S., magna cum laude, 1989); Loyola School of Law (J.D., 1993). Member, Loyola Law School, Law Review, 1993. (Resident, Orange County Office).

**DONALD W. ORMSBY,** born Hermosa Beach, California, September 6, 1964; admitted to bar, 1993, California, U.S. District Court, Central and Southern Districts of California and U.S. Court of Appeals, Ninth Circuit. *Education:* El Camino College (A.A., 1984); University of California at Los Angeles (B.A., with honors, 1987); University of Southern California (J.D., 1993). Alpha Gamma Sigma; Phi Alpha Delta; Golden Key Honor Society. *Member:* American Bar Association (Member, Litigation Section). (Resident, Orange County Office).

**ERIK L. JACKSON,** born Los Angeles, California, February 7, 1965; admitted to bar, 1993, California; 1994, U.S. District Court, Central District of California. *Education:* University of California at Los Angeles (B.A., 1988); University of Southern California (J.D., 1992). Recipient: Fulbright Fellowship, Helsinki, Finland, 1992-1993; Carl Mason Franklin Award for International Law; California State Fellowship Award; Law Merit Scholar Award. *Member:* State Bar of California. (Resident, Orange County Office).

**JOSEPH M. ELGGUINDY,** born Montreal, Quebec, Canada, December 14, 1969; admitted to bar, 1994, California and U.S. District Court, Central District of California. *Education:* University of California at Berkeley (B.A., 1991); Pepperdine University (J.D., cum laude, 1994). Recipient: Dean's Merit Scholarship Award. *Member:* State Bar of California; American Bar Association. (Resident, Orange County Office).

**RICHARD G. KOLOSTIAN, JR,** born Los Angeles, California, July 25, 1967; admitted to bar, 1994, California and U.S. District Court, Central District of California. *Education:* University of California at Irvine (B.A., 1989); Whittier Law School (J.D., 1994). Phi Alpha Delta. Chief Justice, Whittier Moot Court Honors Board. Recipient: Whittier Law School General Scholarship. (Resident, Long Beach Office).

**MARK H. SHPALL,** born El Paso, Texas, October 10, 1967; admitted to bar, 1994, California. *Education:* University of California at Santa Bar-

*(This Listing Continued)*

## O'FLAHERTY & BELGUM, Glendale—Continued

bara (B.A., 1990); University of Southern California (J.D., 1994). *Member:* State Bar of California. (Resident, Glendale Office).

**STEPHEN Z. VEGH,** born Encino, California, November 12, 1967; admitted to bar, 1994, California and U.S. District Court, Central District of California. *Education:* University of California at Los Angeles (B.S., Biology, 1990); McGeorge School of Law (J.D., 1994). Recipient: Best Brief Award, Jessup International Moot Court Competition, 1992-1993. *Member:* Los Angeles County; State Bar of California. (Resident, Orange County Office). *LANGUAGES:* Hungarian.

**WILLIAM D. HARDY,** born Sierra Madre, California, August 15, 1966; admitted to bar, 1995, California. *Education:* University of California at La Jolla (B.S., 1988); Southern University (J.D., 1994). (Resident, Long Beach Office).

**PETER S. KRAVITZ,** born New York, N.Y., December 9, 1969; admitted to bar, 1995, California. *Education:* Lehigh University (B.A., 1992); Rutgers University School of Law (J.D., 1995). Member, Rutgers Law Journal. (Resident, Long Beach Office).

**CYNTHIA D. ROGERS,** born Hayward, California, September 30, 1959; admitted to bar, 1995, California. *Education:* California State University (B.A., 1989); Whittier Law School (J.D., 1995). Recipient: American Jurisprudence Award in Criminal Law. Moot Court Honors Board. Registered Respiratory Therapist, 1981; Respiratory Care Practitioner, 1988. *Member:* Los Angeles County Bar Association; State Bar of California.

**MARCEL R. PIDOUX,** born Montevideo, Uruguay, June 15, 1967; admitted to bar, 1993, California. *Education:* University of Southern California (B.A., cum laude, 1989; J.D., 1993). (Resident, Glendale Office). *LANGUAGES:* Spanish. *PRACTICE AREAS:* Medical Malpractice Defense.

**BRIAN P. BARROW,** born Long Beach, California, August 28, 1968; admitted to bar, 1995, California. *Education:* University of California at Santa Cruz (B.A., 1990); Whittier College School of Law (J.D., cum laude, 1995). Recipient: American Jurisprudence Award-Civil Procedure; Associate of Southern California Defense Counsel Scholarship, 1994. Member, 1993-1995 and Lead Articles Editor, 1994-1995, Whittier Law Review. Author: "Buckley v. Fitzsimmons: Tradition Pays A Price For The Reduction of Prosecutorial Misconduct," 15 Whittier Law Review 301, 1995. (Resident, Long Beach Office).

**MICHAEL P. SANDLER,** born Los Angeles, California, February 19, 1970; admitted to bar, 1995, California. *Education:* University of California at San Diego (B.A., 1992); Loyola University of Los Angeles (J.D., 1995). Staff Member, International and Comparative Law Journal, 1994-1995. (Resident, Anaheim Office).

**DR. PAUL D. SLATER,** born New Haven, Connecticut, March 24, 1962; admitted to bar, 1995, California. *Education:* Stanford University (B.S., 1984); University of Utah (M.D., 1988; J.D., 1995). William H. Leary Scholar. Recipient, American Jurisprudence Award, Commercial Law, Fall, 1993. Staff Member, University of Utah Law Review, 1993-1994. Licensed Physician, State of Utah, 1989—. Member: American Medical Association; Utah Medical Association; Salt Lake County Medical Association, 1989-1992. *Member:* State Bar of California. (Resident, Anaheim Office). *PRACTICE AREAS:* Medical Malpractice Defense.

REPRESENTATIVE CLIENTS: Farmers Insurance Group of Companies; Dunlop Tire Corporation; INA/Aetna Insurance Corp.; McDonnell Douglas Corp.; Occidental Fire and Casualty Company of North Carolina; Royal Insurance Co.; Wilshire Insurance Co.; The Travelers Companies; Multi-Systems Agency Limited (MMI); UniHealth; Truck Insurance Exchange; Adventist Health System; Daughters of Charity; H.M.S Bierly; Yellow Cab of North Orange County; Orange County Transit District; Orange County Transit Authority; Orange County Dial-A-Ride; Metrolink (SCRRA); Rockwell International; General Dynamics; INA; TOPA; CHAIS; FHP; Caronia Corp.; SCPIE; Hyatt Corp.; County of Los Angeles; PRM; ACIC; American City Mortgage Corp.

---

## O'ROURKE, ALLAN & FONG

*Established in 1978*

3RD FLOOR, 104 NORTH BELMONT
P.O. BOX 10220
**GLENDALE, CALIFORNIA 91209-3220**
Telephone: 818-247-4303
Fax: 818-247-1451

*General Civil and Trial Practice in all State and Federal Courts. Real Estate, Construction, Business, Probate, Personal Injury, Family Law and Negligence Law, Entertainment Law.*

### MEMBERS OF FIRM

**DENIS M. O'ROURKE,** born Los Angeles, California, July 10, 1939; admitted to bar, 1968, California. *Education:* California State University at Los Angeles (B.S., 1961); University of Southern California (J.D., 1967). Deputy City Attorney, Los Angeles, 1968-1971. Member: Panel of Arbitrators, American Arbitration Association; Los Angeles Superior Court Panel of Arbitrators. *Member:* Glendale (Member, Board of Trustees, 1980-1987; President, 1985-1986), Los Angeles County and American Bar Associations; The State Bar of California; California Trial Lawyers Association; Los Angeles Trial Lawyers Association. *PRACTICE AREAS:* Complex Civil Litigation; Construction; Real Estate Litigation.

**JOAN H. ALLAN,** born Cleveland, Ohio, March 20, 1944; admitted to bar, 1979, California. *Education:* Bowling Green State University (B.A., 1965; M.A., 1968); Southwestern University (J.D., 1979). Member, Board of Directors, Glendale Lawyer Referral Service, 1987-1990. Past President, Soroptimist International of Glendale. Member, Advisory Board, Glendale YWCA. Member, Business and Professional Women. *Member:* Glendale (Member, Board of Trustees, 1989-1994; Officer, 1994—), Los Angeles County and American Bar Associations; The State Bar of California; Women's Lawyers Association; Los Angeles Trial Lawyers Association. *PRACTICE AREAS:* Personal Injury; Family Law; Business Litigation.

**RODERICK D. FONG,** born Los Angeles, California, June 30, 1956; admitted to bar, 1989, California. *Education:* University of California at Los Angeles (B.A., cum laude, 1978); University of Southern California (M.B.A., 1978); Loyola Marymount University (J.D., 1988). Omicron Delta Epsilon; Beta Gamma Sigma. Certified Public Accountant, California, 1982. Member: Los Angeles County and American Bar Associations; The State Bar of California. *PRACTICE AREAS:* Corporate; Business Litigation; Probate; Construction.

### ASSOCIATES

**DENISE MICHELLE O'ROURKE,** born Los Angeles, California, October 26, 1965; admitted to bar, 1992, California, U.S. District Court, Central District of California and U.S. Court of Appeals, Ninth Circuit. *Education:* Santa Monica College (A.A., 1987); University of Southern California at Los Angeles (B.A., 1988); Whittier College School of Law (J.D., cum laude, 1992). Phi Alpha Delta. Moot Court Honors Board. Member, Whittier College School of Law Law Review, 1991-1992. *Member:* Los Angeles County, Glendale, American and Federal Bar Associations; State Bar of California; Irish American Bar Association. *PRACTICE AREAS:* General Civil Litigation; Entertainment Law; Business Litigation; Municipal Litigation.

REPRESENTATIVE CLIENTS: Baker Protective Services; The Bicycle Club Casino; Kenco Construction, Inc.; KFI/KOST Radio; LSI Financial Group; Pacific Tractor and Equipment Co.; Patrick Media Group, Inc.; TEMPCO Disaster Services, Inc.; Tractorland, Inc.; Wells Fargo Guard Services; Pacific Electric & Power, Inc.; United Towing Services, Inc.
REFERENCES: Verdugo Banking Company (Glendale, California); Community Bank (Glendale, California).

---

## OTT & HOROWITZ

*A PROFESSIONAL CORPORATION*

700 NORTH CENTRAL AVENUE
8TH FLOOR, SUITE 850
**GLENDALE, CALIFORNIA 91203**
Telephone: 818-242-3100
Fax: 818-242-3102
Email: ohlaw@aol.com

*General Civil, Trial and Appellate Practice in State and Federal Courts and Arbitration Tribunals, Commercial Litigation, Labor, Real Estate and Corporate.*

*(This Listing Continued)*

**FIRM PROFILE:** *Ott & Horowitz is a litigation firm which represents a select group of financial institution, labor and employment, insurance, education, and municipal entity clients. The firm is committed to providing top quality legal services on a cost effective basis.*

*The firm has considerable experience in the defense of casualty matters, professional liability and lender liability suits. Appellate law is an equally strong facet of the firm's practice and the firm's principals have argued appeals in most of the California Courts of Appeal, including the California Supreme Court. Representation of financial institutions, particularly credit unions, is an important element of the firm's practice.*

*Labor and employment law is an important area of specialization, and the firm has successfully defended multiple cases of wrongful termination, discrimination and harassment. Familiarity with ongoing developments in this area, and an ability to advise its clients accordingly, is a firm hallmark.*

**THOMAS H. OTT,** born Kansas City, Kansas, November 4, 1947; admitted to bar, 1979, California, U.S. District Court, Central District of California and U.S. Court of Appeals, Ninth Circuit. *Education:* California State Polytechnic University (B.S., 1970); Southwestern University (J.D., 1979). Past Member, Editorial Board, Los Angeles Lawyer Magazine. *Member:* Los Angeles County and American Bar Associations; State Bar of California; Association of Southern California Defense Counsel; California Trial Lawyers Association. **PRACTICE AREAS:** Labor; Employment; Credit Union; Insurance Coverage.

**CRAIG A. HOROWITZ,** born Ellenville, New York, February 13, 1961; admitted to bar, 1986, California, U.S. District Court, Central and Northern Districts of California and U.S. Court of Appeals, Ninth Circuit. *Education:* Brown University (B.A., magna cum laude, 1983; Phi Beta Kappa); University of California at Los Angeles (J.D., 1986). Member, 1984-1985 and Editor, 1985-1986, UCLA Law Review. Extern to Judge Joseph T. Sneed, U.S. Court of Appeals, Ninth Circuit, 1985. Adjunct Professor, Personnel and Labor Law, The Claremont Graduate School, The Peter F. Drucker Management Center. *Member:* Los Angeles County (Member, Labor and Employment Law Section) and American Bar Associations. **PRACTICE AREAS:** Employment Law; Labor Law; Wrongful Termination.

**WAYNE D. CLAYTON,** born Lynwood, California, April 6, 1959; admitted to bar, 1988, California; 1989, U.S. District Court, Central District of California and U.S. Court of Appeals, Ninth Circuit. *Education:* Reed College (B.A., 1982); Loyola Marymount University (J.D., cum laude, 1988). Order of the Coif. Member, St. Thomas More Law Honor Society. Member, 1986-1987 and Articles Editor, 1987-1988, Loyola of Los Angeles International and Comparative Law Journal. *Member:* Santa Monica and Los Angeles County (Member: Sections on Litigation; Labor Law; Homeless Committee, 1989-1990; Legislative Activity Committee, 1989-1990; Barristers-Executive Committee, 1990-1991; Chair, Oral History Project, 1990-1991; Education Committee, 1989-1991; Neighborhood Law School, 1989-1990; Landlord Tenant Dispute Settlement Office, 1988-1990) Bar Associations; State Bar of California (Member, Sections on: Litigation; Labor). **PRACTICE AREAS:** Employment Law; Labor Law; Wrongful Termination.

---

**STEVEN H. TAYLOR,** born Santa Monica, California, April 11, 1962; admitted to bar, 1992, California. *Education:* University of Southern California (B.S., 1984); Hastings College of Law, University of California, San Francisco (J.D., 1991). Phi Delta Phi. *Member:* State Bar of California. **LANGUAGES:** Spanish. **PRACTICE AREAS:** Litigation.

**JANINE R. MENHENNET,** born San Francisco, California, October 6, 1966; admitted to bar, 1992, California, U.S. District Court, Central District of California and Court of Appeals, Ninth Circuit; 1995, U.S. District Court, Southern District of California. *Education:* University of California (B.A., 1988); Loyola University of Los Angeles (J.D., 1992). Member, Loyola of Los Angeles Entertainment Law Journal, Vol. 12, No. 2, 1992. Member, Barristers South Central Legal Services Committee, 1994—. *Member:* State Bar of California. **PRACTICE AREAS:** Employment; Financial Institutions; Labor; Business Litigation.

**PATRICK CAREY,** born Long Beach, California, October 12, 1961; admitted to bar, 1993, California. *Education:* California State University, Long Beach (B.A., 1986); Loyola University of Los Angeles (J.D., 1993). *Member:* Los Angeles County Bar Association (Member, Sections on: Labor and Employment; Commercial Law); State Bar of California. **PRACTICE AREAS:** Financial Institutions; Employment; Labor.

*(This Listing Continued)*

---

REPRESENTATIVE CLIENTS: Alhambra Unified School District; Arise Associates; California Credit Union League; Cigna HealthCare; City of Redondo Beach; Clipper Express; Colorado State Employees Credit Union; Cuna Mutual Insurance Group/Cumis Insurance Society; Landry Service Co., Inc.; First Financial Federal Credit Union; Flintridge Riding Club; Hughes Aircraft Corporation; Hughes Aircraft Employees Federal Credit Union; Ketchum Communications; Lockheed Corp.; Lockheed Federal Credit Union; Los Angeles Federal Credit Union; The California Credit Union; Lumen Electronics; Management Health Services; Orthopedic & Surgical Associates Medical Group; Pasadena School Employees Federal Credit Union; Rehab Data, Inc.; SCE Employees Federal Credit Union; South Bay Union High School District; State Farm Mutual Automobile Insurance Co.; State Farm Fire and Casualty Insurance Co.; St. Jude Emergency Medical Group; The Regents of the University of California; TTC, Illinois, Inc.; United Defense Credit Union.

---

## JAMES J. PAGLIUSO

801 NORTH BRAND BOULEVARD
SUITE 320
**GLENDALE, CALIFORNIA 91203**
*Telephone: 818-244-2253; 213-744-1330*
*Fax: 818-547-0283*

*Negligence Law. Trials and Appeals, Medical Malpractice and Products Liability Law.*

**JAMES J. PAGLIUSO,** born Glendale, California, November 10, 1945; admitted to bar, 1971, California. *Education:* University of California at Los Angeles (B.A., 1967; J.D., 1971). Author: "Situations To Avoid If You Don't Want To Be Sued," Contemporary OB/GYN, March, 1982. Sole research attorney, *Medical Malpractice,* David M. Harney, 1973. Listed in: Best Lawyers in America, 1983-1985; Most Respected Lawyers; California Lawyer Magazine, September, 1989; Bar Register of Preeminent Lawyers, 1995; Associate, Partner, Harney, Wolfe, Pagliuso, Shaller & Carr, 1971-1987; Solo Practice, 1987—. Glendale Bar Association, President, 1995-1996. Glendale UNICO Italians, President, 1991-1992. Foundation of Glendale Association for the Retarded, President, 1992-1993. Salvation Army Advisory Board, Member. Glendale Family YMCA Board, Member. Glendale Youth Alliance Board, Member. *Member:* Los Angeles County and Glendale Bar Associations; Italian American Lawyers Association; American Board of Trial Advocates. Fellow, International Academy of Trial Lawyers.

REFERENCE: Bank of America, West Glenoaks Branch.

---

## MICHAEL N. STAFFORD

104 NORTH BELMONT
THIRD FLOOR
**GLENDALE, CALIFORNIA 91206**
*Telephone: 818-247-4303*
*Fax: 818-247-1451*

*General Civil and Trial Practice in all State and Federal Courts, Real Estate, Corporate and Business Law, Probate and Estate Planning, Arbitration and Mediation.*

**MICHAEL N. STAFFORD,** born Detroit, Michigan, August 2, 1938; admitted to bar, 1972, California; 1973, U.S. Tax Court. *Education:* Wayne State University and California State University at Los Angeles (B.A., 1962); Loyola University of Los Angeles (J.D., 1971). Staff Member, Loyola University of Los Angeles Law Review, 1970-1971. Member, St. Thomas More Law Honor Society. Judge Pro Temp, Glendale Municipal Court, and Glendale Superior Court. *Member:* Glendale (Trustee, 1984-1991; President, 1989-1990) and Los Angeles County (Trustee, 1987-1989; Member, Real Estate and Business Law Sections) Bar Associations; State Bar of California. **PRACTICE AREAS:** Real Estate; Corporate; Business Law; Probate; Estate Planning.

---

## STYSKAL, WIESE & MELCHIONE

*Established in 1974*

550 NORTH BRAND BOULEVARD, SUITE 550
**GLENDALE, CALIFORNIA 91203**
*Telephone: 818-241-0103*
*Fax: 818-241-5733*

*General Corporate, Commercial and Consumer, Insurance and Computer Law as it affects Credit Unions.*

*(This Listing Continued)*

# CALIFORNIA—GLENDALE

## STYSKAL, WIESE & MELCHIONE, Glendale—Continued

FIRM PROFILE: Styskal, Wiese & Melchione was founded in 1974 by L. J. Styskal, Alvin O. Wiese Jr., and Edgar J. Melchione, bringing together three of the area's leading practitioners of general corporate, commercial and consumer law. In 1987, with a long history of banking law, the firm began devoting a substantial portion of its practice to the representation of credit unions. The firm now represents credit unions on a nationwide basis, emphasizing a philosophy of preventative law. The firm encourages continuing professional development and all partners and associates participate in continuing legal education seminars, professional associations and civic affairs.

### MEMBERS OF FIRM

**JOSEPH S. MELCHIONE,** born Los Angeles, California, February 16, 1948; admitted to bar, 1974, California, U.S. District Court, Northern and Central Districts of California and U.S. Supreme Court; 1987, U.S. Tax Court. *Education:* University of California at Santa Barbara (B.A., with high honors, 1970), Phi Beta Kappa; University of California at Davis School of Law (J.D., 1974). Adjunct Professor, Glendale College of Law. Faculty, Western CUNA Management School. *Member:* State Bar of California; American Bar Association (Member, Credit Union Committee). **SPECIAL AGENCIES:** California Department of Corporations Commissioner's Credit Union Advisory Committee. **PRACTICE AREAS:** General Corporate, Commercial and Consumer Law; Insurance; Computer; Credit Union Law.

**WILLIAM J. ADLER,** born Boston, Massachusetts, June 2, 1959; admitted to bar, 1986, California, U.S District Court, Central District of California and U.S. Tax Court. *Education:* University of Notre Dame (B.B.A., 1981); Loyola University of Los Angeles, School of Law (J.D., 1986). Certified Public Accountant, California, 1983. Member, Credit Union Committee of the California Society of Certified Public Accountants. *Member:* State Bar of California. **PRACTICE AREAS:** General Corporate, Commercial and Consumer Law; Insurance; Computer; Credit Union Law.

**BRUCE A. PEARSON,** born Watseka, Illinois, January 22, 1963; admitted to bar, 1992, California. *Education:* University of Illinois (B.A., cum laude, 1986); Southwestern University School of Law (J.D., summa cum laude, 1992). Phi Beta Kappa. *Member:* Los Angeles County Bar Association; State Bar of California. **LANGUAGES:** Russian. **PRACTICE AREAS:** General Corporate, Commercial and Consumer Law; Insurance; Computer; Credit Union Law.

### ASSOCIATE

**DONNA M. WHOOLEY,** born San Francisco, California, December 4, 1968; admitted to bar, 1995, California. *Education:* University of California at Los Angeles (B.A., 1992); Loyola Law School - Los Angeles (J.D., 1995). Phi Alpha Delta. St. Thomas Moore Society. **PRACTICE AREAS:** Corporate Law; Consumer Law; Credit Union Law.

REPRESENTATIVE CLIENTS: Beckman Employees Credit Union; Cal-Tech Employees Federal Credit Union; Coast Central Credit Union; Courts & Records Federal Credit Union; Digital Employees Federal Credit Union; F & A Federal Credit Union; 1st City Savings Federal Credit Union; Hudson Valley Federal Credit Union; Hughes Aircraft Employees Federal Credit Union; H.P. Employees Federal Credit Union; Wescom Credit Union.

---

## THOMAS & PRICE

Established in 1980

**535 NORTH BRAND BOULEVARD, 7TH FLOOR**
**GLENDALE, CALIFORNIA 91203**
Telephone: 213-387-4800; 818-500-4800
FAX: 818-500-4822

*Ventura, California Office:* 1655 Mesa Verde Avenue, Suite 230. Telephone: 805-642-6255. Fax: 805-642-4580.

Insurance Defense, Medical Accounting, Legal Malpractice, Automobile Law, Product Liability, Construction and Premise Liability Law, Oilfield Exploration and Production Accidents, Wrongful Termination, Sexual Discrimination, Intellectual Property Law.

### MEMBERS OF FIRM

**MICHAEL THOMAS,** admitted to bar, 1968, California. *Education:* University of California at Los Angeles (B.A., 1962); Southwestern University (LL.B., 1967). *Member:* Los Angeles County and American Bar Associations; American Board of Trial Advocates; Inns of Court; Association of Southern California Defense Counsel. **PRACTICE AREAS:** Civil Litigation; Personal Injury; Medical Malpractice; Legal Malpractice; Wrongful Termination; Sexual Harassment; Intellectual Property; Insurance Defense.

**BONNIE R. LOUIS,** admitted to bar, 1978, California. *Education:* California State University at Los Angeles (B.S., in Accounting, 1973); Southwestern University (J.D., cum laude, 1978). Certified Public Accountant, California, 1978. Member, California State Board of Accounting. *Member:* Association of Southern California Defense Counsel. **PRACTICE AREAS:** Accounting; Malpractice; Civil Litigation; Personal Injury; Medical Malpractice; Insurance Defense.

**CRAIG R. DONAHUE,** admitted to bar, 1977, California. *Education:* University of California at Los Angeles; University of California at Berkeley (A.B., 1973); Loyola Marymount University (J.D., 1977). *Member:* Wilshire, Beverly Hills, South Bay and Los Angeles County Bar Associations; Southern California Association of Health Care Risk Managers. **PRACTICE AREAS:** Civil Litigation; Medical Malpractice; Insurance Defense.

**MAUREEN F. THOMAS,** admitted to bar, 1982, California. *Education:* University of California at Santa Barbara (B.A., 1979); McGeorge School of Law, University of the Pacific (J.D., 1982). **PRACTICE AREAS:** Construction; Civil Litigation; Personal Injury; Medical Malpractice; Insurance Defense.

### ASSOCIATES

**JOHN P. DEGOMEZ,** admitted to bar, 1981, California. *Education:* California State University at Northridge (B.A., 1974); Wadsworth School of Radiology (A.R.R.T., 1971); Golden West University (J.D., 1980). *Member:* Southern California Defense Counsel. **PRACTICE AREAS:** Civil Litigation.

**TIMOTHY A. HODGE,** admitted to bar, 1985, California. *Education:* Los Angeles Valley College (A.A., 1977); California State University at Northridge (B.A., 1979); Southwestern University (J.D., 1982). **PRACTICE AREAS:** Civil Litigation.

**LINDA B. HUREVITZ,** admitted to bar, 1986, California. *Education:* American College in Paris, Paris, France; George Washington University (B.A., 1971); Golden Gate University; Thomas Jefferson College of Law (J.D., 1985). **PRACTICE AREAS:** Civil Litigation.

**CHRISTIAN E. SANNE,** admitted to bar, 1982, California. *Education:* University of California at Los Angeles (B.A., 1976); Southwestern University (J.D., 1981). **PRACTICE AREAS:** Civil Litigation.

**BENJIMIN M. BREES,** admitted to bar, 1990, California. *Education:* University of Notre Dame (B.A., 1972); University of La Verne (J.D., 1990). **PRACTICE AREAS:** Civil Litigation.

**JANET L. KEUPER,** admitted to bar, 1987, California and U.S. Court of Appeals, 9th Circuit. *Education:* San Jose State University (B.A., 1982); Pepperdine University School of Law (J.D., 1986). **PRACTICE AREAS:** Civil Litigation.

**KEVIN M. MCCORMICK,** admitted to bar, 1984, California. *Education:* California State University at Los Angeles (B.A., 1980); Loyola Marymount University School of Law (J.D., 1984). **PRACTICE AREAS:** Civil Litigation.

### OF COUNSEL

**LAWRENCE E. PRICE,** admitted to bar, 1973, California; 1975, Florida. *Education:* Lamar University (B.S., in E.E., 1965); Loyola University of California (J.D., 1973). *Member:* Los Angeles County and American Bar Associations; American Board of Trial Advocates; Association of Southern California Defense Counsel. **PRACTICE AREAS:** Product Liability; Construction; Civil Litigation; Personal Injury; Medical Malpractice; Insurance Defense.

REPRESENTATIVE CLIENTS: Farmers Insurance Group; The Vons Companies, Inc.; Kemper Insurance Group; Pool OffShore Co.; Pool Well Servicing; County of Los Angeles; Mobil Oil Corp.; Kemper Insurance Group of Companies; Reliance Insurance Company; Professional Risk Management; Hanover Insurance Co.; Santa Fe Energy; Associated Oiltools International; Kaneb Co.

---

## TILEM WHITE & WEINTRAUB LLP

**701 NORTH BRAND BOULEVARD**
**SUITE 440**
**GLENDALE, CALIFORNIA 91203**
Telephone: 818-507-6000
Fax: 818-507-6800

Bankruptcy, Workouts, Related Litigation, Creditor Rights in Marital Dissolution Proceedings, Bankruptcy Appellate Practice.

*(This Listing Continued)*

FIRM PROFILE: Tilem White & Weintraub LLP has represented Debtors, Creditors, Chapter 7 Trustees, Creditor Committees, Lessors, spouses of Debtors and others having business before the Bankruptcy Court. The firm emphasizes its Chapter 11 Reorganization practice, but also maintains a solid foundation in Chapter 7 Liquidation cases and Chapter 13 Consumer cases.

**DAVID A. TILEM,** born Santa Monica, California, November 12, 1955; admitted to bar, 1982, California; 1983, Massachusetts and U.S. Tax Court; U.S. District Court, Northern, Southern, Central and Eastern Districts of California; U.S. Court of Federal Claims. *Education:* Brown University (A.B. Political Science, 1978); Loyola University at Los Angeles (J.D., 1981). Member, Financial Lawyers Conference, 1985-1995; Conference on Local Rules, U.S. Bankruptcy Court, Central District of California, 1990-1992, 1995; Ninth Circuit Gender Bias Task Force, Bankruptcy Advisory Committee, 1993-1995. Chair, Bankruptcy and Family Law Working Group, 1992-1994. *Member:* Los Angeles County Bar Association (Commercial Law and Insolvency Section); American Bankruptcy Institute; Los Angeles Bankruptcy Forum; Commercial Law League of America (Member, Bankruptcy and Insolvency Section). (Board Certified, Business Bankruptcy Specialist, Commercial Law League of America Academy of Commercial and Bankruptcy Law Specialists). *LANGUAGES:* Spanish. *PRACTICE AREAS:* Bankruptcy; Workouts; Bankruptcy Litigation.

**C. CASEY WHITE,** born Cleveland, Ohio, November 10, 1942; admitted to bar, 1984, Nevada; 1985, California; 1990, U.S. Court of Appeals, 9th Circuit. *Education:* University of California at Los Angeles (B.A., 1975); University of San Diego (J.D., 1984). *Member:* Los Angeles County Bar Association (Co-Chair, 1993-1994 and Chair, 1995-1996, Individual and Consumer Bankruptcy Subcommittee of the Bankruptcy and Commercial Law Section); American Bankruptcy Institute; State Bar of Nevada; Los Angeles Bankruptcy Forum. *PRACTICE AREAS:* Bankruptcy; Litigation; Bankruptcy Appellate Practice.

**DANIEL J. WEINTRAUB,** born New York, N.Y., April 10, 1960; admitted to bar, 1987, California and U.S. Court of Appeals, Ninth Circuit. *Education:* University of California at Los Angeles (B.A., cum laude, with departmental highest honors, 1982); University of Southern California (J.D., 1987). Chair, Hale Moot Court Honors Program. In-house Counsel, City National Bank, 1991-1993. Associate, Sheppard, Mullin, Richter & Hampton, 1988-1991. *Member:* Beverly Hills and Los Angeles County Bar Associations; State Bar of California; Financial Lawyers Conference; Los Angeles Bankruptcy Forum. *PRACTICE AREAS:* Bankruptcy Law; Foreclosure Law; Business Law; Collections.

**JEANNE C. WANLASS,** born Newport Beach, California, March 9, 1968; admitted to bar, 1993, California. *Education:* Stanford University (B.A., with honors and distinction, 1990); Boalt Hall School of Law, University of California, Berkeley (J.D., 1993). Judicial Extern to the Honorable Randall J. Newsome, U.S. Bankruptcy Court, Oakland, California, 1993. *Member:* Orange County Bar Association; State Bar of California; Orange County Barristers. *LANGUAGES:* French. *PRACTICE AREAS:* Bankruptcy Law.

## GERALD A. TOMSIC

Established in 1977

625 WEST BROADWAY, SUITE D
**GLENDALE, CALIFORNIA 91204-1997**
Telephone: 818-500-4888; Fax: 818-241-2842

*Estate Planning, Wills and Trusts, Probate, Taxation, Business, Corporate and Partnership Law, Real Estate, Limited Liability Companies.*

**GERALD A. TOMSIC,** born Harvey, Illinois, March 5, 1950; admitted to bar, 1976, California; 1977, U.S. District Court, Central District of California; 1978, U.S. Tax Court. *Education:* Wharton School of Finance; University of Pennsylvania (B.S., 1972); Loyola University (J.D., 1976). Certified Public Accountant, California, 1975. Instructor in Law, Glendale College, 1979-1983. *Member:* Los Angeles County Bar Association; State Bar of California (Member, Sections on: Taxation; Business Law; Real Property; Estate Planning, Trust and Probate Law); American Association of Attorney-Certified Public Accountants; Los Angeles Estate Planning Council; Glendale Rotary Club.

## STEVEN E. TRYTTEN

A PROFESSIONAL LAW CORPORATION

Established in 1985

500 NORTH BRAND BOULEVARD, SUITE 1030
**GLENDALE, CALIFORNIA 91203**
Telephone: 818-500-9969
Fax: 818-500-9979

*Advanced Estate Planning, Trust, Probate and Taxation.*

**STEVEN E. TRYTTEN,** born Ann Arbor, Michigan, November 11, 1952; admitted to bar, 1978, Illinois; 1983, California; 1987, U.S. Tax Court. *Education:* University of Illinois (B.S., 1974; J.D., 1978; M.B.A., 1978). C.P.A., State of Illinois, 1979. Co-Author: "Grantor Trusts," 18th Annual CEB-UCLA Estate Planning Institute, 1996; "Turning Sand Into Glass: Clarifying Retirement Benefits in The Estate Plan", 47th Annual USC Institute on Federal Taxation (1995); "A Second Look At Spousal Rights in An IRA", California State Bar Estate Planning Trust and Probate News (1994). Director: Glendale Estate Planning Council, 1994—. *Member:* Glendale, San Fernando Valley, Los Angeles County (Member: Taxation; Trusts & Estates Sections, 1984—) and American (Member: Taxation; Law Practice Management; Real Property, Probate and Trust Law Sections, 1995—) Bar Associations; State Bar of California (Member and Chair-Elect, Executive Committee on Estate and Gift Taxation, Taxation Section, 1993—; Committee on Taxation, Estate Planning, Trust and Probate Section, 1994—); American Institute of CPAs; California Society of CPAs. (Certified Specialist, Taxation Law, Estate Planning, Trust and Probate Law, The State Bar of California Board of Legal Specialization). *PRACTICE AREAS:* Advanced Estate Planning (40%); Estate Planning (30%); Probate and Trust Administration (10%); Taxation (20%).

REPRESENTATIVE CLIENTS: Lockheed Martin Corporation; Walt Disney Company; PacifiCare Health Systems, Inc.; Merrill Lynch, Inc.

## WAGNER & MIDDLEBROOK

Established in 1985

3541 OCEAN VIEW BOULEVARD
**GLENDALE, CALIFORNIA 91208**
Telephone: 818-957-3340
Fax: 818-957-8123

*Patent, Trademark and Copyright Law. Unfair Competition, Trade Secrets, Computer Law and related causes (transactional, administrative, prosecution and litigation in all state and federal courts).*

### MEMBERS OF FIRM

**JOHN E. WAGNER,** born Sioux Falls, South Dakota, September 19, 1926; admitted to bar, 1951, Iowa; 1955, New York; 1959, U.S. Supreme Court; 1961, California; registered to practice before U.S. Patent and Trademark Office. *Education:* Iowa State University (B.S.G.E., 1948); University of Iowa (J.D., 1951). University of Iowa Law Review, 1949-1951. Lecturer in Business and Intellectual Property Law, Engineering Graduate School, University of California at Los Angeles, 1977-1987.

**THERESA W. MIDDLEBROOK,** born Summit, New Jersey, November 8, 1953; admitted to bar, 1979, California; 1980, U.S. District Court, Central District of California; 1983, U.S. District Court, Southern District of California; 1984, U.S. Court of Appeals, Ninth and Federal Circuits and U.S. District Court, Northern District of California; 1989, U.S. Supreme Court. *Education:* University of California at Irvine (B.A., 1975); Southwestern University (J.D., 1979).

**ROBERT C. SMITH,** born Brookings, South Dakota, July 29, 1926; admitted to bar, 1952, South Dakota; 1973, U.S. Claims Court; registered to practice before U.S. Patent and Trademark Office (Not admitted in California). *Education:* South Dakota State University (B.S.E.E., 1949); South Dakota University (J.D., 1952). [U.S. Army Air Corps, 1945]

REPRESENTATIVE CLIENTS: Bianchi International; Focus on the Family; Hitachi Chemical Research Center, Inc.; Mitsubishi International Corp.; Pacific-Sierra Research Corp.; World Service Office, Inc. of Narcotics Anonymous; J.L. Shepard & Associates.
REFERENCE: First Interstate Bank.

CALIFORNIA—GLENDALE

## WESIERSKI & ZUREK

Established in 1987

800 NORTH BRAND BOULEVARD, SUITE 250
**GLENDALE, CALIFORNIA 91203**
Telephone: 818-543-6100
Telecopier: 818-543-6101

*Irvine, California Office:* Suite 1500, 5 Park Plaza. Telephone: 714-975-1000. Telecopier: 714-756-0517.

General Civil Litigation, Insurance Bad Faith, Defense and Coverage, Appellate Practice, Insurance Defense, Products Liability, Professional Liability, Representation of Employers and Employees, Premises Liability, Real Property (Land Subsidence), Toxic Torts and Intellectual Property.

FIRM PROFILE: *Wesierski & Zurek has an extensive litigation background. The law firm engages in a variety of legal practice at both the state and federal levels. The firm selects its lawyers carefully and trains them to become proficient in their areas of specialization. The firm supports continuing legal education for its lawyers in order to keep them current in their ares of specialization and to enable them to meet the changing needs of the firm's clients.*

*The philosophy of the firm includes a strong emphasis on the close personal relationship that should develop between legal professionals and their clients. We have an extremely high success rate for favorable jury verdicts and we also have more trial experience than many other firms our size.*

REPRESENTATIVE CLIENTS: Marriott Corp.; Wausau Insurance Co.; General Accident Insurance Co.; State Farm Insurance Co.; Balboa Insurance Group; PepsiCo, Inc.; Pepsi-Cola Bottling Company of Los Angeles; The Atlantic Cos.; Kraft, Inc.; Westfield Insurance Co.; Aetna Insurance Co.; Liberty Mutual Insurance Co.; Taco Bell Corp.; Saga Corp.; Mercury Insurance Co.; Liberty National Co.; Twentieth Century Insurance Co.; Esco Elevators, Inc.; Pacific National Insurance Co.; Pizza Hut Corp.; Ecolab Inc.; St. Paul Insurance Co.; Safeco Insurance Co.; Restaurant Enterprises Group; Allstate Insurance Company; Fireman's Fund Insurance Company; Pearle Vision, Inc.; Home Insurance Co.; McKesson Corp.; CNA Insurance Co.

(For biographical data on all personnel, see Professional Biographies at Irvine, California)

## WOLFLICK & SIMPSON

130 NORTH BRAND BOULEVARD, 4TH FLOOR
**GLENDALE, CALIFORNIA 91203**
Telephone: 818-243-8300

Labor, Employment Law.

### MEMBERS OF FIRM

**GREGORY D. WOLFLICK,** born Chicago, Illinois, May 24, 1956; admitted to bar, 1983, California; 1985, U.S. District Court, Central District of California. *Education:* University of Arizona (B.S., 1977); Southwestern University (J.D., 1982). Instructor, Labor and Employment Law, California State University at Northridge, 1986. *Member:* Los Angeles County and American Bar Associations; State Bar of California. **PRACTICE AREAS:** Labor; Employment Law. **Email:** GDWOLF@ix.netcom.com

**DAVID B. SIMPSON,** born Sunnyvale, California, April 2, 1957; admitted to bar, 1982, California. *Education:* University of California at Los Angeles (B.A., summa cum laude, 1979); University of California School of Law, Los Angeles (J.D., 1982). Member, Moot Court. *Member:* State Bar of California. **PRACTICE AREAS:** Labor; Employment Law. **Email:** DBSWS@ix.netcom.com

**WILHELM ISAIAH VARGAS,** born New York, New York, February 10, 1961; admitted to bar, 1995, California and U.S. District Court, Central District of California. *Education:* New Mexico Military Institute (A.A., 1981); California State University at Long Beach (B.S., 1983); Southwestern University, School of Law (J.D., 1995). *Member:* Puerto Rican and American Bar Associations; State Bar of California; National Notary Association. [(1st Lt. U.S. Army, Armor, Airborne Ranger, 1983-1986]. **LANGUAGES:** Spanish. **PRACTICE AREAS:** Employment Law; Labor Law.

## STETTNER, EISENBERG & MORRIS

1433 EAST ALOSTA AVENUE
**GLENDORA, CALIFORNIA 91740-3747**
Telephone: 818-914-2791
Facsimile: 818-914-3946

Family Law, including Dissolutions, Prenuptials, Cohabitation Agreements, Spousal Support, Custody and Adoptions, International Custody Disputes.

(This Listing Continued)

CAA280B

MARTINDALE-HUBBELL LAW DIRECTORY 1997

FIRM PROFILE: *The Law Office of Stettner, Eisenberg & Morris exclusively specializes in all aspects of Family Law representing Parents and Children, Guardians ad litem, Independent and Step-Parent Adoptions and contested Child Custody Litigation.*

### MEMBERS OF FIRM

**PAMELA P. STETTNER,** born 1948; admitted to bar, 1977, California. *Education:* University of Southern California (B.A., cum laude, 1969; M.A., in Philosophy, 1971); Southwestern University School of Law (J.D., 1977). Editor, SCALE Program, Southwestern University School of Law, 1977. Adjunct Professor, Paralegal Program, University of La Verne, 1995. Visiting Adjunct Professor, Client Interviewing and Control, SCALE Program, Southwestern School of Law, 1982. Program Coordinator and Lecturer: Minors' Counsel Mandatory Training Program, Los Angeles County Bar Association, September 1995. Lecturer: Gender Bias and the Law, California Mandatory Continuing Legal Education Program, Italian American Bar Association, May 1995; Problems in Bias and Ethics, California Mandatory Continuing Legal Education Program, Whittier Family Law Bar Study Group, June 1994; Overview of New Legislation Dealing with Move Away Orders, California Mandatory Continuing Legal Education Program, Orange County Family Law Bar Association, March 1994; Ethical Considerations in Child Custody Cases, California Mandatory Continuing Legal Education Program, Western San Bernardino County and East-West Family Law Counsel Bar Associations, February 1994. *Member:* Los Angeles County and American Bar Associations; State Bar of California; California Women Lawyers; Association of Family and Conciliation Courts; East-West Family Law Counsel Bar Association (President, 1993; Program Chair, 1992). **PRACTICE AREAS:** Family Law.

**DONALD S. EISENBERG,** born Los Angeles, California, November 8, 1947; admitted to bar, 1976, California and U.S. District Court, Central District of California. *Education:* California State University at Long Beach (A.B., 1968); University of California at Los Angeles (J.D., 1975). Lecturer, Psychology and Counseling Aspects of Family Law, CEB, 1984. *Member:* Specialist-Certification Examination Drafting Committee, 1982, 1984, 1987; Seal Beach Environmental Quality Control Board, 1985-1990. Member, Association of Family and Conciliation Courts. *Member:* Beverly Hills (Member, Family Law Section); Los Angeles County (Member, Family Law Section) and Orange County Bar Associations; State Bar of California (Member; Family Law Section; Custody and Visitation Committee-South, 1986-1989). [Staff Sgt., USAF, 1969-1973]. (Certified Specialist, Family Law, The State Bar of California Board of Legal Specialization) (Also Practicing Individually, Los Angeles, California).

**CHARLES J. MORRIS, JR.,** born Montgomery, Alabama, May 16, 1956; admitted to bar, 1989, California, U.S. Court of Appeals, Ninth Circuit and U.S. District Court, Central District of California. *Education:* Mississippi State University (B.A., magna cum laude, 1980); Harvard University (M.Div., 1983); University of Southern California (J.D., 1989). Phi Kappa Phi; Phi Alpha Delta; Phi Alpha Theta. *Member:* Pasadena, Los Angeles County (Member, Sections on: Litigation; Real Property) and American (Member, Litigation Section) Bar Associations; State Bar of California (Member, Litigation Section). [With USAF, 1976-1980; 2nd Lt., USAFR, 1980-1986]. **PRACTICE AREAS:** Litigation; Family Law.

### ASSOCIATES

**HARVEY A. SILBERMAN,** born New York, N.Y., January 10, 1957; admitted to bar, 1992, California. *Education:* Wesleyan University (B.A., 1978); University of Southern California (J.D., 1992). Author: "Beyond Living Wills," National Rotary, September, 1994. Member, Writers Guild of America, 1988—. *Member:* State Bar of California. **PRACTICE AREAS:** Family Law; Testamentary; Civil; Probate.

**WENDY M. DEWEESE,** born Boston, Massachusetts, July 3, 1965; admitted to bar, 1993, California. *Education:* Pomona College (B.A., magna cum laude, 1987); Southwestern University Law School (J.D., 1993). Phi Delta Phi (Vice-Magister, 1992-1993). Member, Southwestern University Law Review. *Member:* Los Angeles County and American Bar Associations. **LANGUAGES:** Dutch; German and French. **PRACTICE AREAS:** Family Law.

## BULLIVANT, HOUSER, BAILEY, PENDERGRASS & HOFFMAN

*A PROFESSIONAL CORPORATION*
*11335 GOLD EXPRESS DRIVE, SUITE 105*
**GOLD RIVER, CALIFORNIA 95670**
Telephone: 916-852-9100
FAX: 916-852-5777
URL: http://www.bullivant.com

*Portland, Oregon Office:* 300 Pioneer Tower, 888 S.W. Fifth Avenue, 97204-2089. Telephone: 503-228-6351. Facsimile: 503-295-0915.

*Seattle, Washington Office:* 2400 Westlake Office Tower, 1601 Fifth Avenue, 98101-1618. Telephone: 206-292-8930. Facsimile: 206-386-5130. Cable Address: Sealaw.

*Vancouver, Washington Office:* 300 First Independence Place, 1220 Main Street. 98660-2962. Telephones: 360-693-2424; 360-225-1100. Facsimile: 206-695-8504.

Insurance Coverage; Insurance Defense; General Litigation; Environmental and Related Areas of Litigation.

**JAMES G. DRISCOLL**, born Boston, Massachusetts, June 17, 1948; admitted to bar, 1977, Oregon and U.S. District Court, District of Oregon; 1980, U.S. Court of Appeals, Ninth Circuit; 1989, U.S. Supreme Court; 1992, California and U.S. District Court, Eastern, Northern, Central and Southern Districts of California. *Education:* Columbia College, Columbia University (B.A., 1971); Northwestern School of Law, Lewis and Clark College (J.D., 1977). *Member:* State Bar of California (Member, Environmental Law Section; Litigation Section); Oregon State Bar (Member, Sections on: Alternative Dispute Resolution (Past-Chair); Government Law; Environmental and Natural Resource Law; Real Estate and Land Use); Sacramento County, Multnomah County and American Bar Associations. **PRACTICE AREAS:** Insurance Coverage; Environmental Litigation; Insurance Defense Litigation; Commercial Litigation. *Email:* Jim.Driscoll@Bullivant.com

**M. TAYLOR FLORENCE**, born Salt Lake City, Utah, June 16, 1960; admitted to bar, 1986, Utah and U.S. District Court, District of Utah; 1987, U.S. Court of Appeals, Tenth Circuit; 1988, Colorado; 1990, Oregon and U.S. District Court, District of Oregon; 1992, California and U.S. District Court, Eastern, Northern, Central and Southern Districts of California. *Education:* University of Utah (B.A., with honors, 1983; J.D., 1986). Pi Sigma Alpha. Leary Scholar. Member, Journal of Contemporary Law, University of Utah, 1985-1986. Author: Comment, "Failure to Specify All Grounds for Disclaimer of Coverage in Disclaimer Letter," Recurring Issues in Insurance Disputes - A Guide for Insurers and Insureds, Tort and Insurance Practice Section, American Bar Association (1996); "Using the Interstate Compact to Control Regional Acid Deposition," 6 Journal of Energy Law & Policy 413, 1985. *Member:* Sacramento County, Multnomah County and American Bar Associations; State Bar of California; Utah State Bar; Oregon State Bar; Association of Defense Counsel for Northern California. **PRACTICE AREAS:** Environmental, Insurance and Commercial Litigation. *Email:* Taylor.Florence@Bullivant.com

---

**ROBERT E. ASPERGER**, born Fresno, California, August 4, 1958; admitted to bar, 1984, California and U.S. District Court, Eastern District of California; 1985, U.S. District Court, Northern District of California; 1986, U.S. District Court, Central District of California and U.S. Court of Appeals, Ninth Circuit; 1990, U.S. District Court, Southern District of California. *Education:* University of California at Davis (B.A., with honors, 1980; J.D., 1984). Recipient, American Jurisprudence Award in Contracts. *Member:* Sacramento County Bar Association; The State Bar of California. **PRACTICE AREAS:** Insurance Defense Litigation; Professional Liability. *Email:* Bob.Asperger@Bullivant.com

**TAMARA L. BOECK**, born Fresno, California, May 19, 1967; admitted to bar, 1993, California and U.S. District Court, Eastern District of California; 1994, U.S. District Court, Northern, Central and Southern Districts of California; 1994, Nevada and U.S. Court of Appeals, Ninth Circuit. *Education:* California State University, Fresno (B.S., cum laude, 1990); McGeorge School of Law, University of the Pacific (J.D., with distinction, 1993). Comment Writer, 1991-1992, Comment Editor, 1992-1993, Pacific Law Journal. Author: "Transactional Immunity Under the California Water Code: Advance Pardon For Crimes Revealed?" 24 Pac. L.J. 505, 1993. *Member:* Sacramento County Bar Association; Women Lawyers of Sacramento; State Bar of California; State Bar of Nevada. **PRACTICE AREAS:** *(This Listing Continued)*

Coverage Litigation; Insurance Defense Litigation; Environmental Litigation; Product Liability. *Email:* Tami.Boeck@Bullivant.com

**GAIL E. GEARIN**, born Spokane, Washington, February 17, 1947; admitted to bar, 1988, Oregon; 1990, Washington; 1992, California. *Education:* Portland State University (B.S., 1979; M.B.A.,, 1981); Lewis & Clark College (J.D., 1988). *Member:* Sacramento County, Multnomah County and Washington State and Bar Associations; State Bar of California (Member, Litigation Committee); Oregon State Bar (Member, Litigation Section). **PRACTICE AREAS:** Environmental Coverage and Defense Litigation; Insurance Defense Litigation; Insurance Coverage. *Email:* Gail.Gearin@Bullivant.com

**DAVID R. LANE**, born Boulder, Colorado, January 14, 1951; admitted to bar, 1978, California and U.S. District Court, Eastern District of California; 1983, U.S. District Court, Northern District of California; 1995, U.S. Court of Appeals, Ninth Circuit. *Education:* University of California at Davis (A.B., 1972); McGeorge School of Law, University of the Pacific (J.D., 1978). Member, Moot Court Honors Board. Moot Court Award of Excellence. *Member:* State Bar of California; American Bar Association (Member, Section on Tort and Insurance Practice); Defense Research Institute. **PRACTICE AREAS:** Insurance Coverage; Insurance Litigation. *Email:* David.Lane@Bullivant.com

**KATHLEEN ANN LYNCH**, born Patchogue, New York, September 30, 1965; admitted to bar, 1994, California and U.S. District Court, Eastern District of California. *Education:* California State University at Sacramento (B.S., 1988; McGeorge School of Law, University of the Pacific (J.D., 1994). **PRACTICE AREAS:** Insurance Defense; Insurance Coverage; Coverage Litigation. *Email:* Kathleen.Lynch@Bullivant.com

**KEVIN S. MAPES**, born Portland, Oregon, January 5, 1967; admitted to bar, 1994, California. *Education:* University of Puget Sound (B.A., 1989); Lewis & Clark College (J.D., cum laude, 1994). Phi Beta Kappa. *Member:* Sacramento County Bar Association; State Bar of California. **PRACTICE AREAS:** Insurance Coverage; Coverage Litigation; Environmental Litigation. *Email:* Kevin.Mapes@Bullivant.com

*OF COUNSEL*

**JANE O'DONNELL**, born Stockton, California; admitted to bar, 1981, California and U.S. District Court, Central, Northern, Eastern and Western Districts of California; U.S. Court of Appeals, Ninth Circuit; U.S. Supreme Court. *Education:* University of Southern California (B.A., 1973); Southwestern University (J.D., 1981). *Member:* Sacramento County Bar Association; The State Bar of California; Defense Research Institute; Association of Northern California Defense Counsel. **PRACTICE AREAS:** Litigation. *Email:* Jane.O'Donnell@Bullivant.com

REPRESENTATIVE CLIENTS: Reliance Insurance Co.; The Hanover Insurance Co.; United States Fidelity & Guaranty.; Federated Insurance Co.; Dean's & Homer; Houston General Insurance Co.; Grocers Insurance Co.; Standard Insurance Co.

---

## DENNIS N. WESTERBERG

*LAW CORPORATION*

SUITE 525
*11344 COLOMA ROAD*
**GOLD RIVER, CALIFORNIA 95670-4462**
Telephone: 916-638-1506
Fax: 916-638-7833

General Negligence Law. Professional Liability, Products Liability and Aviation Law. Trial Practice.

**DENNIS N. WESTERBERG**, born Sacramento, California, December 18, 1944; admitted to bar, 1974, California. *Education:* University of California at Davis (B.S., 1971); McGeorge College of the Law (J.D., 1974). Phi Alpha Delta. Judicial Arbitrator, Sacramento County, 1979—. *Member:* Sacramento County and American Bar Associations; State Bar of California; California Trial Lawyers Association.

## GROKENBERGER & WILSON

A PROFESSIONAL CORPORATION

Established in 1984

160 NORTH FAIRVIEW AVENUE
SUITE 4
GOLETA, CALIFORNIA 93117
Telephone: 805-964-4761
FAX: 805-967-0186

Santa Barbara, California Office: La Rinconada Building. 1004 Santa Barbara Street. Telephone: 805-564-1230. Fax: 805-965-2685.

*Family Law, Real Estate, Creditor work in Bankruptcy Court, Landlord-Tenant, Shopping Center and Condominium Law. General Business and Civil Litigation, Personal Injury Law, Probate and Estate Planning.*

FIRM PROFILE: For more than twelve years, Grokenberger & Wilson has been a prominent name in the Santa Barbara legal community. Founded in 1984 and nurtured by the combined talents of David M. Grokenberger and Rachel Lindenbaum Wilson, Grokenberger & Wilson has grown into a full service law firm, becoming a recognized leader in Real Estate, Landlord-Tenant, Family Law and Civil Litigation matters. With the addition of experienced attorneys with diverse backgrounds and training, Grokenberger & Wilson has expanded its practice to include General Business Representation, Estate Planning and Probate, Personal Injury and Appeals.

The attorneys of Grokenberger & Wilson consider it a privilege to take on the responsibility of meeting their clients' legal needs. This strong, motivated team of partner and associate attorneys, and trained staff, is dedicated to providing the best possible level of service and furnishing top quality legal representation according to high professional and ethical standards. Grokenberger & Wilson believes that its clients are its greatest asset. The firm's commitment to excellence is a commitment to its clients.

**JAMES H. SMITH,** born Santa Barbara, California, April 12, 1951; admitted to bar, 1978, California and U.S. District Court, Central District of California. *Education:* Sacramento State University (B.A., 1975); California Western University (J.D., 1978). Recipient, American Jurisprudence Award. Director, Attorney Referral Service, 1981-1989. *Member:* Santa Barbara County Bar Association; The State Bar of California. **REPORTED CASES:** Otanez v. Blue Skies Mobile Home Park (1991) 1 Cal App 4th 1521, 3 Cal. Rptr 2nd 210. **PRACTICE AREAS:** Real Estate; Construction Defects; Civil Litigation.

REPRESENTATIVE CLIENTS: Santa Barbara Rental Property Assn.; Pacifica Property Management; The Alternative Copy Shops; Beneficial California Inc.; Rosen Investments; The Tennis Club of Santa Barbara; Firenze Designs; Allstate Worldwide, Inc.; Alternative Graphics; Goleta National Bank; Encina Royale Homeowners Association; Cushman Contracting Corp.; Pacifica Commercial Reality.

(For Complete Biographical Data on all Personnel see Professional Biographies at Santa Barbara)

---

## O'GORMAN & O'GORMAN

SUITE B-2, 5901 ENCINA ROAD
GOLETA, CALIFORNIA 93117
Telephone: 805-967-1215
FAX: 805-683-2058

*Business, Probate, Finance and Bankruptcy Law.*

**C. BRIAN O'GORMAN,** born Oakland, California, February 26, 1941; admitted to bar, 1966, California. *Education:* Columbia College (A.B., 1962); University of California at Berkeley (LL.B., 1965). *Member:* Santa Barbara County Bar Association (Director, 1977-1978); State Bar of California. **PRACTICE AREAS:** Business Law; Probate; Finance; Bankruptcy Law.

**BARRETT PATRICK O'GORMAN,** born Oakland, California, January 12, 1964; admitted to bar, 1990, California. *Education:* University of California at Los Angeles (B.A., 1986); Loyola Marymount University (J.D., 1989). *Member:* Santa Barbara County Bar Association; State Bar of California. **PRACTICE AREAS:** Business Law; Finance; Bankruptcy Law; Consumer Finance.

CAA282B

---

## LAW OFFICES OF
## CHARLES R. FARRAR, JR.

120 RICHARDSON STREET, SUITE D
GRASS VALLEY, CALIFORNIA 95945
Telephone: 916-273-0800
Fax: 916-273-0777
Email: crflawgodl@aol.com
Email: cflawgld@oro.net

*Business and Commercial Transactions and Agreements, General Civil Trial and Appellate Practice, Easements and Real Property Law, Land Use and Environmental Law (C.E.Q.A.), Computer Law, Administrative and Municipal Law and Mediation Law.*

**CHARLES R. FARRAR, JR.,** born Santa Cruz, California, September 15, 1946; admitted to bar, 1972, California. *Education:* University of Vienna; University of California at Berkeley (A.B., 1968); Boalt Hall School of Law, University of California, Berkeley (J.D., 1972). Order of the Coif. Associate Editor, California Law Review, 1970-1972. Partner, Morrison & Foerster, Litigation and Business Departments, 1972-1986. Assistant General Counsel, Diasonics, Inc., 1986-1988. Partner, Roach & Farrar, Nevada City, California, 1991-1993. *Member:* Nevada County and American Bar Associations; State Bar of California.

REFERENCES: A list of Representative Clients and References will be furnished upon request.

---

## RICHARD M. HAWKINS

A PROFESSIONAL CORPORATION

Established in 1974

SUITE 2, 10563 BRUNSWICK ROAD
GRASS VALLEY, CALIFORNIA 95945
Telephone: 916-272-6733
Fax: 916-272-7861
Email: rhawk53@aol.com

*General Civil Practice, Probate, Estate Administration, Estate Planning, Wills, Trusts, Taxation and Corporate Law.*

**RICHARD M. HAWKINS,** born Nevada City, California, July 23, 1949; admitted to bar, 1974, California and U.S. District Court, Eastern District of California; 1982, U.S. District Court, Northern District of California, U.S. Court of Appeals, Ninth Circuit, U.S. Tax Court, U.S. Claims Court and U.S. Supreme Court. *Education:* University of California at Davis (B.S., 1971); Hastings College of Law, University of California (J.D., 1974); McGeorge School of Law, University of Pacific (LL.M. in Taxation, 1983). Order of the Coif; Phi Kappa Phi. Member, Thurston Society. *Member:* State Bar of California; American Bar Association. (Certified Specialist, Estate Planning, Trust and Probate Law, The State Bar of California Board of Legal Specialization).

REFERENCE: Bank of America (Nevada City Branch).

---

## TERRY A. ROACH

GRASS VALLEY, CALIFORNIA

(See Nevada City)

*Real Property, Land Use, Environmental, Business Law, Estate Planning and Probate, Computer Law, General Civil Trial and Appellate Practice and Alternative Dispute Resolution.*

---

## SHINE, COMPTON & NELDER-ADAMS

131 SOUTH AUBURN STREET
GRASS VALLEY, CALIFORNIA 95945
Telephone: 916-272-2686
Fax: 916-272-5570

*General Civil and Real Estate Litigation, Environmental, Land Use, Family Law, Estate Planning/Probate, Business Law, Employment, Government and Public Agency Law and Personal Injury.*

**RAYMOND E. SHINE,** born Berkeley, California, August 21, 1948; admitted to bar, 1973, California and U.S. District Court, Northern District of California; 1976, U.S. District Court, Eastern District of California.

*(This Listing Continued)*

*Education:* University of California at Berkeley (B.A., 1970; J.D., 1973). Lecturer, Real Estate Law, Sierra College, 1976—. Legal Authorship: "California Civil Procedure Before Trial," 3rd Edition CEB. *Member:* Nevada County Bar Association (President, 1978); State Bar of California. **PRACTICE AREAS:** Civil Litigation; Real Estate; Business; Local Government; Land Use; Environmental. *Email:* rshine@nccn.net

**CHARLES A. COMPTON,** born San Francisco, California, July 11, 1945; admitted to bar, 1976, California and U.S. District Court, Northern District of California; 1988, U.S. District Court, Eastern District of California. *Education:* Stanford University (B.A., 1967); Hastings College of Law, University of California (J.D., 1974). Legal Authorship: "California Trial Practice: Civil Procedure During Trial," 3rd Edition CEB; "California Civil Procedure Before Trial," 3rd Edition CEB. *Member:* Nevada County Bar Association; State Bar of California. **PRACTICE AREAS:** Estate Planning/Probate; Business; Personal Injury; Real Estate. *Email:* ccompton@nccn.net

**MARALEE NELDER-ADAMS,** born San Francisco, California, January 12, 1956; admitted to bar, 1981, California and U.S. District Court, Eastern District of California. *Education:* University of California at Davis (A.B., 1976; M.A., 1978); McGeorge School of Law (J.D., 1981). Author and Editor (with Pamela Pierson, CFLS, Rebecca Prater, CFLS, and Jeffrey Wilson), of *Family Law Module for Law Practice Management Sourcebook,* published by the Law Practice Management Section, State Bar of California, 1989. *Member:* Nevada County (President, 1985; Chair, Fee Arbitration Committee, 1987—); State Bar of California. (Certified Specialist, Family Law, The State Bar of California Board of Legal Specialization). **LANGUAGES:** French. **PRACTICE AREAS:** Family Law. *Email:* mneldera@nccn.net

**JAMES A. CURTIS,** born San Gabriel, California, July 25, 1948; admitted to bar, 1976, California; 1977, U.S. District Court, Southern District of California; 1981, U.S. District Court, Eastern District of California; 1983, U.S. Court of Appeals, Ninth Circuit. *Education:* University of California at Santa Barbara (B.A., 1971); Western State University, San Diego (J.D., 1976). *Member:* State Bar of California; California County Counsel's Association (Member, 1989-1996; President, 1994-1995; Member, Board of Directors, 1989-1996; Member, Continuing Legal Education Committee, 1986-1996). **PRACTICE AREAS:** Local Government (Public Agency); Land Use; Environmental; Employment.

---

## BREKHUS, WILLIAMS, WESTER & HALL
*1000 DRAKES LANDING ROAD*
**GREENBRAE, CALIFORNIA 94904**
*Telephone: 415-461-1000*
*Fax: 415-461-7356*

San Francisco, California Office: 44 Montgomery Street, Suite 1000, 94104-4612. Telephone: 415-296-9962.

*Civil Litigation and Appellate Practice. Insurance, Construction, Landslide and Subsidence, Personal Injury, Inverse Condemnation and Eminent Domain, Municipal and Zoning Law.*

### MEMBERS OF FIRM

**PETER B. BREKHUS,** born Rapid City, South Dakota, January 1, 1939; admitted to bar, 1965, California. *Education:* University of San Francisco (B.S., 1961); University of San Francisco Law School (J.D., 1964). Assistant City Trial Attorney, 1967-1972 and City Attorney, 1973, Larkspur, California. Assistant Trial Attorney, Marin Municipal Water District, Town of Ross, 1967-1973. Mayor of Ross, 1982-1983, 1988-1989, 1993-1994. Councilman, Town of Ross, 1978-1994. Member, Marin County Council of Mayors and Councilmen, 1980. *Member:* Marin County and American Bar Associations; State Bar of California; Association of Defense Counsel.

**SCOTT A. WILLIAMS,** born Minneapolis, Minnesota, January 23, 1948; admitted to bar, 1977, California. *Education:* Chico State College (B.A., 1971); McGeorge School of Law, University of the Pacific (J.D., 1977). *Member:* Marin County Bar Association; State Bar of California; Association of Defense Counsel; Executive Council of Home Owners; Community Associations Institute; Council of Condominium Homeowner Associations.

**BARRY F. WESTER,** born San Francisco, California, April 27, 1953; admitted to bar, 1982, California. *Education:* Santa Clara University (B.A., 1975); Hastings College of Law, University of California (J.D., 1980). *Member:* Marin County Bar Association; State Bar of California; Association of Defense Counsel.

*(This Listing Continued)*

**ROBERT P. HALL, JR.,** born Redwood City, California, October 31, 1952; admitted to bar, 1981, California. *Education:* University of California at Berkeley (B.S., 1975); London School of Economics, London, England; San Francisco Law School (J.D., 1979). Recipient, Bancroft-Whitney Award. *Member:* Bar Association of San Francisco; Marin County and American Bar Associations; State Bar of California (Member, Real Property Law Section); Consumer Attorneys of California: Association of Defense Counsel; Executive Council of Home Owners; Community Associations Institute; Council of Condominium Homeowner Associations; Building Industry Association.

### ASSOCIATES

**MATTHEW D. BREKHUS,** born Covina, California, October 15, 1960; admitted to bar, 1985, California. *Education:* University of California at Los Angeles (B.A., 1982); McGeorge School of Law, University of the Pacific (J.D., 1985). Member, Traynor Society. *Member:* Marin County Bar Association; State Bar of California; Association of Defense Counsel.

**LINDA J. PHILIPPS,** born Cincinnati, Ohio, February 13, 1949; admitted to bar, 1983, California. *Education:* University of California at Santa Cruz (A.B., with honors, 1973); Boalt Hall School of Law, University of California (J.D., 1982). Co-Author with Thomas C. Given: "Equality in the Eye of the Beholder - Classification of Claims and Interests in Chapter 11 Reorganizations," Ohio State Law Journal, Vol. 43. No. 4, 1982. *Member:* Marin County Bar Association; State Bar of California.

**PAULA M. WEAVER,** born San Francisco, California, December 18, 1953; admitted to bar, 1980, California. *Education:* University of California at Berkeley (A.B., with honors, 1976); University of San Francisco School of Law (J.D., 1979). *Member:* Marin County Bar Association (Board of Directors); The State Bar of California; Marin County Women Lawyers Association.

**STACEY ANN LUCAS,** born Grand Rapids, Michigan, May 9, 1957; admitted to bar, 1991, California. *Education:* University of California (B.A., 1979); New York University (M.A., 1983); University of San Francisco (J.D., 1991). *Member:* Bar Association of San Francisco; Marin County (Board of Directors) and American Bar Associations; Marin County Womens Lawyers Association.

REPRESENTATIVE CLIENTS: Fireman's Fund Insurance Co.; Golden Eagle Insurance Co.; Classic Syndicate Insurance Co.; Bay Area Rentals; Van Beurden & Associates, Insurance Brokers; Commercial Transfer Trucking Co., Inc.; Hendricks Development Co.; Seaport Co.; Horne Enterprises; Cheda Knolls Homeowners' Assn.; Marin Somerset Homeowners' Assn.; De Soto Cab Co.; Sunshine Cab Co.; Bluebird Cab Co.; Pacific Cab Co.; Fara Estates Homeowners Assn.; The Oceana Marin Assn.; Buena Vista Gardens Homeowners' Assn.; Cedarbrook Homeowners' Assn.; Cheda Knolls Homeowners' Assn.; Eucalyptus Knoll Homeowners' Assn.; Fara Estates Homeowners' Assn.; Hillside Park East Homeowners' Assn.; Lighthouse at Bridgeport Owners' Assn.; Marin Somerset Place Homeowners' Assn.; Oceana Marin Assn.; Shoreview House Condo Assn.; Teresita Homeowners' Assn.; Villa Ignacio Homeowners' Assn.

---

## THE MILLS FIRM
*300 DRAKES LANDING, SUITE 155*
**GREENBRAE, CALIFORNIA 94904**
*Telephone: 415-464-4770*
*Fax: 415-464-4777*
*Email: millsfrm@microweb.com*

*Class Actions in Partnerships, Trusts, Securities, Consumer Fraud, Mass Torts, and Environmental Cases. General Civil and Trial Practice in all courts.*

**ROBERT W. MILLS,** born Raleigh, North Carolina, January 12, 1949; admitted to bar, 1974, California. *Education:* University of California at Berkeley (B.A., with honors, 1971); Golden Gate University (J.D., 1974). Technical Certifications: NASD Series 22, 39, 7, 63 and 24 (Securities Licenses) 1982-1991. Registered Investment Advisor, 1984-1991. Licensed Real Estate Broker, California, 1980-1988. Faculty Member, San Francisco State University, 1976-1979. Member: NASD Arbitration Panel, 1991—; Panel of Arbitrators, American Arbitration Association, 1991—. *Member:* The Association of Trial Lawyers of America; Association of Business Trial Lawyers; Consumer Attorneys of California; National Association of Consumer Advocates. **PRACTICE AREAS:** Consumer Class Actions; Business Fraud; Fiduciary Law; Business Litigation.

**DEREK G. HOWARD,** born Bryn Mawr, Pennsylvania, September 30, 1958; admitted to bar, 1985, California. *Education:* University of Pennsylvania (B.A., 1980); Golden Gate University (J.D., 1984). Extern to the Honorable John H. Dimond, Supreme Court of the State of Alaska, 1983.

*(This Listing Continued)*

CAA283B

## THE MILLS FIRM, Greenbrae—Continued

Legal Research Attorney, San Francisco County Superior Court, 1985. Litigation Associate, Pillsbury, Madison & Sutro, 1986-1991. Author, Comment: "Nuclear Plant Construction After Pacific Gas: A Pyrrhic Victory for the States?" 14 Golden Gate University Law Rev. 359 (1984). Co-Author, Survey, "Interference Torts," American Bar Association, 1996. *Member:* Bar Association of San Francisco; Marin County and American (Member, Antitrust Section Committee on Business Torts and Unfair Competition) Bar Associations; State Bar of California. *LANGUAGES:* German. *PRACTICE AREAS:* Unfair Competition; Unfair Trade; Business Fraud; Consumer Class Actions; Civil Litigation.

**RICHARD S. KOHN,** born New York, N.Y., September 22, 1942; admitted to bar, 1968, district of Columbia (Not admitted in California). *Education:* University of Vermont (B.A., with honors, 1965); Boston University School of Law (LL.B., 1968. Senior Editor, Boston University Law Review, 1967-1968. Law Clerk to Hon. Edward M. McEntee, United States Court of Appeals for the First Circuit, 1968-1970. Vermont Legal Aid Inc., 1970-1973. Litigation Director, American Civil Liberties Union for Vermont and New Hampshire, 1973-1975. Staff Attorney, Lawyers' Committee for Civil Rights Under Law, Washington, D.C., 1975-1980. Levitt & Kohn, Washington, D.C., 1980-1982. Director of Litigation, Migrant Farmworker Project, California Rural Legal Assistance, San Francisco, CA., 1982-1995. Faculty, Stanford Law School and University of San Francisco Law School Advocacy Skills Workshops. Supreme Court Arguments: United States v. Bailey, 444 U.S. 394 (1980); Wooley v. Maynard, 430 U.S. 705 (1977); Philbrook v. Glodgett and Weinberger v. Glodgett, 421 U.S. 707 (1975). Author: Alternative Methods of Piercing the Corporate Veil in Contract and Tort Cases, 48 B.U.L.Rev. 123 (1968); The Arrest Warrant in Massachusetts: A Legal Placebo?, 47 B.U.L. Rev. 244 (1967). *Member:* Vermont State; The District of Columbia Bar; State Bar of California. *PRACTICE AREAS:* Appellate Practice; Constitutional Law; Civil Rights; Consumer Fraud.

**GILMUR R. MURRAY,** born Oak Park, Illinois, April 26, 1954; admitted to bar, 1983, California. *Education:* University of Chicago (A.B., 1975); University of California at Berkeley (M.A., Economics, 1983); Boalt Hall School of Law, University of California (J.D., 1983). Litigation Associate, McCutchen, Doyle, Brown & Enersen, 1984-1989. Partner, Carr & Mussman (1989-1993). *Member:* Bar Association of San Francisco; State Bar of California; American Bar Association. *PRACTICE AREAS:* Unfair Competition; Unfair Trade; Business Fraud; Consumer Class Actions; Contract Fraud; Oil Pollution.

**LLOYD S. LEVENSON,** born Boston, Massachusetts, February 5, 1959; admitted to bar, 1986, California. *Education:* Harvard University (A.B., cum laude, 1981); Boston College (J.D., cum laude, 1986). Legal Extern to Judge William G. Young, District of Massachusetts, 1985. Litigation Associate, McCutchen, Doyle, Brown & Enersen, 1986-1989. *LANGUAGES:* French. *PRACTICE AREAS:* Commercial Litigation; Consumer Class Actions; Securities Class Action.

**NICOLE A. DILLER,** born Toledo, Ohio, September 18, 1966; admitted to bar, 1991, California. *Education:* University of Michigan (B.G.S., with distinction, 1987); Stanford University (J.D., 1991). Litigation Associate, Heller, Ehrman, White & McAuliffe, 1991-1993. *Member:* District of Columbia Bar; State Bar of California. *PRACTICE AREAS:* Civil RICO; Trust Litigation; Fiduciary Law; Consumer Class Action; Unfair Competition.

**STEVEN R. RHOADS,** born Denver, Colorado, March 24, 1957; admitted to bar, 1982, California. *Education:* University of California at Berkeley (A.B., 1979); Golden Gate University (J.D., 1982). Recipient: 1985, Bar of San Francisco Award of Merit; 1985, Barristers Club Certificate of Appreciation; 1986, American Bar Association Services to The Bar Award. Litigation Associate: Boornazian, Jensen & Garthe; Herron & Herron. Sole Practitioner, 1982-1995. Author: "Getting Credit When Credit is Due-New Legal Options for Women," Vogue Magazine, 1985; "Elements of a Journal," American Bar Association, Membernet, 1986; Producing a Substantial Law Journal," American Bar Association, 1986; "A Delicate Balance-Drug Testing at the Workplace," High Times Magazine, 1987; "Maternity Leave Rights-Motherhood and Livelihood: Are They Compatible?", Working Woman Magazine, 1987. Founding Editor in Chief, San Francisco Barrister Law Journal, 1985-1986; Trials Digest Magazine, 1991-1994. Founder, The ADR Clearinghouse, Inc. Director, First District Appellate Project, 1995—. Consultant, State Bar of California Commission on the Future of the Practice of Law, 1994-1995. MCLE Lecturer, Legal Journals, American Bar Association, New Orleans, 1987; Lawyers and Media, Bar Association of San Francisco, 1987; Providing Psychological Damages, Bar Association of San Francisco, 1995. Guest Speaker, Employment Law Rights, KALW Radio, 1993. Arbitrator, San Mateo County Superior Court, 1988-1992. *Member:* Bar Association of San Francisco State Bar of California; Consumer Attorneys of California. *PRACTICE AREAS:* Unfair Business Practices; Business Litigation; Business Torts; Consumer Class Actions; Civil Litigation.

**ALEXANDER J. LUCHENITSER,** born Kiev, Ukraine, October 6, 1969; admitted to bar, 1995, California. *Education:* Harvard University (A.B., magna cum laude, 1991); Stanford Law School (J.D., with distinction, 1994). Law Clerk To: Justice Warren W. MAtthews, Alaska Supreme Court, 1994-1995; U.S. MAgistrate Judge Wayne D. Brazil, U.S. District Court, Northern District of California, 1996. Member, Student Steering Committee, East Palo Alto Community Law Project, 1992-1994. *Member:* State Bar of California. *LANGUAGES:* Russian.

---

## STOCKWELL, HARRIS, WIDOM & WOOLVERTON

*A PROFESSIONAL CORPORATION*

Established in 1957

**SUITE 307, 200 SOUTH 13TH STREET**
**GROVER BEACH, CALIFORNIA 93433**
Telephone: 805-473-0720
Fax: 805-473-0635

*Los Angeles, California Office:* 6222 Wilshire Boulevard, Sixth Floor, P.O. Box 48917. Telephone: 213-935-6669; 818-784-6222; 310-277-6669. Fax: 213-935-0198.
*San Bernardino, California Office:* Suite 303, 215 North "D" Street. Telephone: 909-381-5553. Fax: 909-384-9981.
*Santa Ana, California Office:* Suite 500, 2551 N. Tustin Avenue, P.O. Box 11979. Telephone: 714-479-1180. Fax: 714-479-1190.
*Ventura, California Office:* 2021 Sperry Avenue, Suite 46. Telephone: 805-654-8994; 213-617-7290. Fax: 805-654-1546.
*San Diego, California Office:* Suite 400, 402 West Broadway. Telephone: 619-235-6054. Fax: 619-231-0129.

*Workers Compensation Insurance and Employment Matters.*

(See Professional Biographies at Los Angeles)

---

## GRISWOLD, LaSALLE, COBB, DOWD & GIN, L.L.P.

Established in 1945

**311 NORTH DOUTY STREET**
**HANFORD, CALIFORNIA 93230**
Telephone: 209-584-6656
Facsimile: 209-582-3106

*General Civil, Criminal, Trial and Appellate Practice in all State, Federal and Military Courts. Administrative, Environmental Law, Agricultural, Bankruptcy, Corporation, Creditors Rights, Estate Planning, Family Law, Insurance, Land Use, Oil and Gas, Personal Injury, Probate, Real Estate, Taxation, Water Rights, Workers Compensation and Zoning Law.*

FIRM PROFILE: *Founded in 1945 by Lyman D. Griswold and the late Roger Walch, Griswold, LaSalle, Cobb, Dowd & Gin, L.L.P., is recognized by the nationwide legal community by its inclusion in the Martindale-Hubbell Bar Register of Preeminent Lawyers. The Bar Register serves as a directive for the legal profession's top lawyers, selecting lawyers who have been rated by their colleagues as exceptional in their field. King County Superior Court Judge Louis F. Bissig was a longtime partner in the firm.*

*The firm is a sustaining member of the California Agricultural Leadership Program and the Agricultural Council of California. Also, the firm represents approximately 50 farmer cooperatives.*

**LYMAN D. GRISWOLD,** born Hanford, California, September 14, 1914; admitted to bar, 1940, California. *Education:* University of California (A.B., 1937; LL.B., 1940). Phi Alpha Delta. Assistant District Attorney, Kings County, 1942-1947. *Member:* Kings County and American Bar Associations; The State Bar of California. Fellow, American College of Trial Lawyers. (Retired).

**STEVEN W. COBB** (1947-1993).

*(This Listing Continued)*

## MEMBERS OF FIRM

**MICHAEL E. LASALLE,** born Downey, California, September 10, 1945; admitted to bar, 1971, California. *Education:* Fresno State College (B.S., summa cum laude, 1967); University of California at Davis (J.D., 1970). Phi Kappa Phi; Blue Key. *Member:* Kings County (President, 1973) and American Bar Associations; The State Bar of California. **PRACTICE AREAS:** Estate, Probate and Trust Planning; Business Transactions (Agriculture).

**ROBERT M. DOWD,** born Hanford, California, October 12, 1946; admitted to bar, 1976, California and U.S. Court of Military Appeals. *Education:* San Francisco State University (B.A., 1968); California Western School of Law (J.D., magna cum laude, 1976). Phi Alpha Delta. *Member:* Kings County (President, 1987) and American Bar Associations; The State Bar of California; California Trial Lawyers Associations; The Association of Trial Lawyers of America; Association of Business Trial Lawyers of Central California. [Col., USMCR (USMC, 1968-1981)]. **PRACTICE AREAS:** Civil Litigation; Agricultural Cooperative Law.

**ROBERT W. GIN,** born Los Angeles, California, July 25, 1948; admitted to bar, 1982, California. *Education:* California Polytechnic University (B.S., cum laude, 1971); McGeorge School of Law, University of the Pacific (J.D., with distinction, 1982). Member, Order of the Coif; Traynor Honor Society. Editor, Pacific Law Journal, 1981-1982. Author: Comment, "Prenatal Fraud, Untruth and the Consequences for the Drug Manufacturer," Pacific Law Journal, Vol. 13, October, 1981. *Member:* Fresno County, Kings County (President, 1992) and American Bar Associations; The State Bar of California. **REPORTED CASES:** Tos v. Mayfair Packing Co., 160 Cal App. 3rd 67, 206 Cal Rptr. 459; Plaza Tulare v. Tradewell Stores, Inc., 207 Cal App. 3rd 522, 254 Cal Rptr. 792. **PRACTICE AREAS:** Environmental Law; Corporate and Administrative Law; Business Transactions; Probate and Trusts.

**RANDY L. EDWARDS,** born Phoenix, Arizona, July 27, 1953; admitted to bar, 1982, California; 1990, Colorado. *Education:* Colorado State University (B.A., 1975); Pepperdine University (M.A., 1979); McGeorge School of Law, University of The Pacific (J.D., 1982). *Member:* Kings County and American Bar Associations; State Bar of California; California Trial Lawyers Association; The Association of Trial Lawyers of America. [Lt. Col. USMCR (USMC 1975-1991)]. **PRACTICE AREAS:** Criminal; Civil Litigation.

**CRAIG GRISWOLD,** born Hanford, California, April 27, 1945; admitted to bar, 1984, California. *Education:* University of California at Berkeley (B.A., 1967); Lincoln Law School (J.D., 1984). *Member:* Kings County and American Bar Associations; State Bar of California. **LANGUAGES:** French. **PRACTICE AREAS:** Water Law; Agricultural Cooperative Law; Business Law.

## ASSOCIATES

**JACK G. WILLIS,** born Hanford, California, February 19, 1947; admitted to bar, 1990, California. *Education:* Stanford University (B.A., 1969); San Joaquin College of Law (J.D., 1982). *Member:* Kings County Bar Association; State Bar of California. **PRACTICE AREAS:** Business Law; Civil Litigation.

**JIM D. LEE,** born Carnegie, Oklahoma, August 24, 1950; admitted to bar, 1992, California. *Education:* U.S. Air Force Academy; California State University, Fresno (B.A., 1989); William Howard Taft (J.D., 1991). *Member:* State Bar of California. **LANGUAGES:** French. **PRACTICE AREAS:** Business Law; Civil Litigation.

**JEFFREY L. LEVINSON,** born San Pedro, California, February 14, 1955; admitted to bar, 1993, California. *Education:* University of California, Berkeley (B.A., 1977); San Joaquin College of Law (J.D., 1991). Trustee, 1985— and President, 1990-1991, West Hills Community College District. *Member:* Kings County and American Bar Associations; State Bar of California. **PRACTICE AREAS:** Civil Litigation; Creditor's Rights; Business Law.

**A. DAVID MEDEIROS,** born Hanford, California, February 14, 1962; admitted to bar, 1988, California. *Education:* California Polytechnic State University (B.A., 1985); McGeorge School of Law, University of the Pacific (J.D., 1988). Phi Delta Phi. Member, National Moot Court Competition Team. Judge Pro Tempore, San Luis Obispo County Superior Court. *Member:* Kings County and American Bar Associations; State Bar of California; Consumer Attorneys of California; The Association of Trial Lawyers of America. **PRACTICE AREAS:** Civil Litigation; Business Litigation; Insurance; Personal Injury.

*(This Listing Continued)*

## OF COUNSEL

**JULIENNE L. RYNDA,** born Hawthorne, California, September 20, 1953; admitted to bar, 1979, California and U.S. District Court, Eastern District of California; 1980 U.S. District Court, Central District of California. *Education:* California State University at Long Beach (B.A., magna cum laude, 1976); University of California at Davis (J.D., 1979). Phi Delta Phi. Member, University of California, Davis Alumni Association. *Member:* Kings County Bar Association (Secretary/Treasurer, 1983-1984; President, 1985-1986); State Bar of California (Member, Family Law Section); California Women Lawyers' Association. **PRACTICE AREAS:** Family Law; Children; Wills; Probate; Contracts.

REPRESENTATIVE CLIENTS: A & M Livestock; Armona Community Services District; Badasci Land Leveling, Inc.; David A. Bush, Inc.; Calcot, Ltd.; Chicago Title Insurance Co.; Federal Land Bank; Food Services of America; Gibson Wine Co.; Gilkey Farms; GWF Power Systems Co., Inc.; Hanford Title Co.; Guest Services, Inc.; Justo's Basque Restaurant; Kings County Housing Authority; Kings County Water District; Kings Country Club; Laton Community Services District; Martella Auction Co.; Paul Mueller Co.; Richard's Chevrolet-Pontiac-Buick-Olds, Inc.; Souza's Enterprises; Stone Land Co.; Toyota Motor Co.; U.S. Genes, Inc. Western Waste Industries. Wood Brothers Excavation; World-Wide Sires, Inc.; Verdegaal Brothers, Inc.

---

## NEIL A. HELDING

Established in 1967

623 WEST GRANGEVILLE BOULEVARD
P.O. BOX 1190
**HANFORD, CALIFORNIA 93232**
Telephone: 209-584-6601
Fax: 209-584-6375

*General Civil and Trial Practice in all Courts. Personal Injury, Family, Corporation, Real Property, Estate Planning, Probate, Water Rights, Creditors Rights and Bankruptcy Law.*

**NEIL A. HELDING,** born Racine, Wisconsin, March 13, 1934; admitted to bar, 1960, California. *Education:* College of the Sequoias (A.A., 1954); Fresno State College (A.B., 1956); Hastings College of Law, University of California (J.D., 1959). Order of the Coif. Contributing Author: *Exploring Government in Tulare County,* Brown Co., 1966. Deputy Legislative Counsel, State of California, 1963-1964. Deputy and Assistant District Attorney, Tulare County, 1964-1967. *Member:* Kings County Bar Association (President, 1969); The State Bar of California. [Capt., J.A.G., Air Force, 1960-1963]

REPRESENTATIVE CLIENTS: Joe G., Inc.; Robert's Chevrolet, Inc.; Roe Oil Co.; King's Orchards, Inc.; Pirelli-Armstrong Tire Corp.; South Fork Ranch, Inc.; Sippel Construction, Inc.
REFERENCE: Union Bank of California; Hanford, California.

---

## KAHN, SOARES & CONWAY

OLD PHONE BUILDING
219 NORTH DOUTY STREET
P.O. BOX 1376
**HANFORD, CALIFORNIA 93230**
Telephone: 209-584-3337
Fax: 209-584-3348

Sacramento, California Office: Suite 200, 1112 "I" Street. Telephone: 916-448-3826. Fax: 916-448-3850.

*General Civil and Trial Practice in State and Federal Courts. Personal Injury, Agricultural, Water, Environmental, Business, Corporation, Administrative, Real Property, Municipal Law, Land Use, Labor and Employment, Estate Planning and Probate Law, Government Relations.*
In addition to the partners listed below, the firm currently employs four associates in the Hanford office, and three associates in the Sacramento office. The firm also retains Jack C. Parnell, former Deputy Secretary, United States Department of Agriculture, as a government relations advisor, resident in Sacramento and Washington, D.C.

**FIRM PROFILE:** Affiliated, in Washington D.C., with Fleishman-Hillard, Inc., international public relations firm.

## MEMBERS OF FIRM

**JAN L. KAHN,** born Fresno, California, April 1, 1944; admitted to bar, 1972, California, U.S. District Court, Northern, Central and Eastern Districts of California, U.S. Court of Appeals, Ninth and Eleventh Circuits and U.S. Supreme Court. *Education:* Fresno State College (B.A., 1969); McGeorge College of the Law, University of the Pacific (J.D., 1972). Phi

*(This Listing Continued)*

## KAHN, SOARES & CONWAY, Hanford—Continued

Delta Phi. *Member:* Kings County (President, 1979) and American (Vice-Chairman, General Practice Section; Agricultural Law Committee) Bar Associations; State Bar of California. (Resident).

**GEORGE H. SOARES,** born San Luis Obispo, California, August 20, 1944; admitted to bar, 1978, California, U.S. District Court, Eastern District of California and U.S. Supreme Court. *Education:* California Polytechnic State University (B.S., 1966); McGeorge College of the Law, University of the Pacific (J.D., 1973). Phi Alpha Delta. President, Student Body, 1966. Consultant to California Assembly Agriculture Committee, 1971-1978. *Member:* Kings County Bar Association; State Bar of California. (Resident, Sacramento Office).

**RICHARD C. CONWAY,** born Fort Ord, California, July 9, 1953; admitted to bar, 1978, California and U.S. District Court, Eastern District of California. *Education:* University of California at Santa Barbara (B.A., cum laude, 1975); Western State University (J.D., 1978). President, Student Bar Association, Western State University, 1977-1978. *Member:* Kings County, Tulare County and American Bar Associations; State Bar of California; California Trial Lawyers Association; Association of Trial Lawyers of America.

**MICHAEL J. NOLAND,** born San Francisco, California, March 22, 1953; admitted to bar, 1978, California and U.S. District Court, Northern, Eastern and Central Districts of California. *Education:* University of the Pacific (B.A., 1975); Western State University (J.D., 1978). Member, Kings County Fair Board, 1985—. *Member:* Kings County (Member, Sections on: Business Law; Estate Planning and Probate) and American Bar Associations; State Bar of California.

**DALE A. STERN,** born La Verne, California, September 12, 1957; admitted to bar, 1987, California and U.S. District Court, Northern, Central and Eastern Districts of California, U.S. Court of Appeals, Ninth Circuit and U.S. Supreme Court. *Education:* University of La Verne; California State Polytechnic University (B.S., 1984); University of California at Davis (J.D., 1987). *Member:* Sacramento and American (Member Section on Real Property) Bar Associations; State Bar of California; American Agricultural Law Association. (Resident, Sacramento Office).

REPRESENTATIVE CLIENTS: City of Hanford; Chemical Waste Management, Inc.; Tulare Land Basin Water Storage District; Ashwood Enterprises; California Avocado Commission; Overland Stockyards, Inc.; California Grocers Association; Pest Control Operators of California; California Citrus Mutual; California Strawberry Commission; California Cotton Ginners Association; The Allen Group; Valley Ford-Lincoln-Mercury, Inc.; Westlake Farms, Inc.; Central Valley General Hospital; St. Elizabeth Community Hospital; Harris Farms, Inc.; Wood & Devine Cattle Co.; Mid-Cal Farms, Inc.; Dresick Farms, Inc.; Anderson Farms, Inc.; Biagro Western Sales, Inc.; Bret's Auto Center; Valley Orthopedics Assoc.; King's Medical Group, Inc.; McLean Chemical Sales; Kaweah Sierra Medical Group, Inc.; VandenBerghe Companies; Razzari Ford and Merle Stone Chevrolet.

---

## KIMBLE, MacMICHAEL & UPTON
### A PROFESSIONAL CORPORATION
### HANFORD, CALIFORNIA
(See Fresno)

*Civil, Trial and Appellate Practice in all Courts with Emphasis in Business, Construction and Environmental Litigation, Real Estate, Bank Securities, Lender and Creditors Rights, Bankruptcy, Secured Lending, Banking, Federal and State Income, Gift and Estate Tax, Securities, Antitrust, Corporation and Probate and Estate Planning, Patent, Trademark and Copyright, Water Rights, Environmental Law, Employee Benefits Law, Products Liability Defense, ERISA Litigation, Employment Defense, Administrative and Health Care Law.*

---

## MAROOT, HARDCASTLE & HATHERLEY
### 429 NORTH REDINGTON STREET
### P.O. BOX 1759
### HANFORD, CALIFORNIA 93232-1759
Telephone: 209-584-0131
Fax: 209-584-7625

Visalia, California Office: 1001 North Demaree. Telephone: 209-734-3540.
*(This Listing Continued)*

---

*General Civil, Criminal, Trial and Appellate Practice. Estate Planning, Probate, Corporation, Partnerships, Family, Creditors Rights, Personal Injury and Water Rights Law. Employment Litigation, Bankruptcy, Domestic Relations, Real Property Law.*

**K. PHILLIP MAROOT,** born Corcoran, California, April 22, 1936; admitted to bar, 1962, California. *Education:* Pomona College (B.A., 1958); Stanford University (J.D., 1961). Assistant District Attorney, Kings County, 1962-1964. Hanford School District Trustee, 1971-1982. *Member:* Kings County (President, 1967) and American Bar Associations; The State Bar of California. *PRACTICE AREAS:* Estate Planning; Probate Law; Corporate and Business Law; Real Estate Law.

**V. WAYNE HARDCASTLE,** born Hanford, California, September 28, 1951; admitted to bar, 1977, California and U.S. District Court, Northern and Eastern Districts of California; 1989, U.S. Court of Appeals, Ninth Circuit. *Education:* College of Sequoias (A.A., 1971); California State College, Bakersfield (B.A., 1973); University of San Diego (J.D., 1977). *Member:* Kings County Bar Association; State Bar of California. *PRACTICE AREAS:* Personal Injury Law; Civil Litigation; Criminal Defense Law; Family Law.

**DALE J. HATHERLEY,** born 1950; admitted to bar, 1977, California; 1979, U.S. District Court, Eastern District of California. *Education:* University of California at San Diego (B.A., 1972); University of San Diego (J.D., 1977). *Member:* State Bar of California. (Certified Specialist, Family Law, The State Bar of California Board of Legal Specialization). *PRACTICE AREAS:* Family Law; Bankruptcy Law; Personal Injury Law.

### ASSOCIATE

**JOHN M. MELIKIAN,** born Fresno, California, April 7, 1961; admitted to bar, 1990, California and U.S. District Court, Eastern District of California. *Education:* California State University of Fresno (B.S., with honors, 1984); University of California, Davis (J.D., 1990). Certified Public Accountant, California, 1987. *Member:* Kings County Bar Association (President, 1996); State Bar of California. *PRACTICE AREAS:* Civil Litigation; Family Law; Corporate Law.

---

## ROBINSON, PALMER & LOGAN
### HANFORD, CALIFORNIA
(See Bakersfield)

*General Civil and Trial Practice. Insurance Defense, Water Rights, Public, Land Use and Business Law.*

---

## WILD, CARTER & TIPTON
### HANFORD, CALIFORNIA
(See Fresno)

*General Civil, Trial and Appellate Practice. Business, Real Estate, Corporation, Construction, Banking, Environmental, Agriculture, Insurance, Trademark, Probate and Estate Planning, Oil and Gas, Taxation, Bankruptcy and Employment Law.*

---

## LAW OFFICES OF JANET L. NATHANSON
### 13731 SOUTH ROSSBURN AVENUE
### HAWTHORNE, CALIFORNIA 90250-6461
Telephone: 310-643-6247
Fax: 310-643-7271

*Elder Law, Public Benefits, Probate and Estate Planning.*

**JANET L. NATHANSON,** born Los Angeles, California, December 13, 1928; admitted to bar, 1982, California; 1983, U.S. District Court, Central District of California and U.S. Court of Appeals, Ninth Circuit. *Education:* University of California at Los Angeles (B.A., 1951); Northrop University (J.D., 1980). Delta Theta Phi. *Member:* Los Angeles County (Member, Government Benefits Section) and American Bar Associations; State Bar of California; California Women Lawyers. *PRACTICE AREAS:* Elder Law; Estate Planning; Wills; Trust Law; Government Law.

## PROFESSIONAL BIOGRAPHIES

CALIFORNIA—HAYWARD

### RICHARD H. BAILIN
21790 HESPERIAN BOULEVARD
HAYWARD, CALIFORNIA 94541-7003
Telephone: 510-783-5300
Fax: 510-782-3082

*Real Estate, Business, Corporate, Estate Planning and Probate Law.*

**RICHARD H. BAILIN,** born Sioux City, Iowa, June 28, 1935; admitted to bar, 1961, California. *Education:* University of Michigan (B.B.A., 1957); Harvard Law School (LL.B., 1960). *Member:* Alameda County Bar Association; The State Bar of California (Member, Sections on: Business Law; Real Property; Taxation; Estate Planning; Trust and Probate).

### KEVIN D. FLYNN
SUITE 209, 21573 FOOTHILL BOULEVARD
HAYWARD, CALIFORNIA 94541
Telephone: 510-886-1166

*Family Law.*

**KEVIN D. FLYNN,** born Brooklyn, New York, December 15, 1950; admitted to bar, 1976, California. *Education:* California State University at San Jose (B.A., 1973); University of San Francisco (J.D., 1976). *Member:* Alameda County and American (Member, Family Law Section) Bar Associations; State Bar of California.

### HALEY, PURCHIO, SAKAI & SMITH
P.O. BOX 450
22320 FOOTHILL BOULEVARD, SUITE 620
HAYWARD, CALIFORNIA 94543
Telephone: 510-538-6400
Oakland: 510-351-1932

*General Civil and Trial Practice. Business, Corporation, Real Property, Construction, Land Use, Municipal and Probate Law.*

#### MEMBERS OF FIRM

**J. KENNETH BIRCHFIELD** (1920-1978).

**JOHN K. SMITH,** born Oakland, California, October 18, 1926; admitted to bar, 1955, California. *Education:* Stanford University (B.A., 1949); Hastings College of Law (LL.B., 1954). Mayor, City of Hayward, 1966-1970. *Member:* Alameda County and American Bar Associations; State Bar of California.

**ROBERT SAKAI,** born Albany, California, August 6, 1945; admitted to bar, 1974, California. *Education:* University of California at Berkeley (B.S., 1967; M.S., 1969); Hastings College of Law, University of California (J.D., 1974). California Probate Referee. *Member:* Alameda County and American Bar Associations; State Bar of California; Asian American Bar Association.

**CYNTHIA K. SMITH,** born Castro Valley, California, May 21, 1957; admitted to bar, 1983, California. *Education:* Santa Clara University (B.S., cum laude, 1979); Hastings College of Law, University of California (J.D., 1983). *Member:* Alameda County and American Bar Associations; State Bar of California.

#### OF COUNSEL

**JOHN J. PURCHIO,** born New York, N.Y., 1915; admitted to bar, 1946, New York; 1947, California. *Education:* Fordham University (B.S., 1938; LL.B., 1946). Superior Court Judge, Alameda County, 1961-1983. Mayor, City of Hayward, 1957-1958.

**DONALD A. PEARCE** (1898-1982).

**MARLIN W. HALEY** (1910-1993).

REPRESENTATIVE CLIENTS: City Center Commercial (Shopping Center); Oak Hills, Walnut Hills, Creekwood (Apartment Complexes); R. Zaballos & Sons (General Contractors); Hospital Associates; Wolf Investment Co.; Chicago Title Company of Alameda County; Mission Valley Rock Co. (quarry), LaVista Quarry; MW Associates (realtors); Currin Construction Co. (developers); Sunol Golf & Recreation Company; Industrial Boxboard Corporation; Rowell Ranch Rodeo, Inc.; Chabot Medical Building Associates (Medical Offices).

### WILLIAM W. HASKELL & ASSOCIATES
*Established in 1977*
22320 FOOTHILL BOULEVARD
SUITE 330
HAYWARD, CALIFORNIA 94541
Telephone: 510-785-7400
Fax: 510-783-1501

*General Civil and Trial Practice in State and Federal Courts. General Civil Litigation including Insurance Defense, Personal Injury, Construction, Real Property, Landslide, Subsidence and Business Litigation.*

**WILLIAM W. HASKELL,** born New York, N.Y., April 3, 1942; admitted to bar, 1971, California. *Education:* Stanford University (A.B., 1966); Hastings College of Law, University of California (J.D., 1970). Recipient, David E. Snodgrass Fellowship, 1969-1970. *Member:* Alameda County and Southern Alameda County Bar Associations; State Bar of California; Association of Defense Counsel; Consumer Attorneys of California; National Association of Securities Dealers Arbitration Panel. **PRACTICE AREAS:** Insurance Defense Law; Personal Injury Law; Public Entity Law; Construction Litigation; Insurance Coverage Law.

#### ASSOCIATES

**MARK ALAN GOODMAN,** born Chicago, Illinois, April 29, 1950; admitted to bar, 1987, California. *Education:* University of California at Berkeley (B.S., 1978); John F. Kennedy School of Law (J.D., 1983). Adjunct Faculty Member, John F. Kennedy School of Law, Construction Law. *Member:* Alameda County and San Francisco Bar Associations; State Bar of California; Consumer Attorneys of California. **PRACTICE AREAS:** Insurance Defense; Construction and Business Litigation; Insurance Fraud; Personal Injury; General Civil.

**G. RANDY KASTEN,** born Oakland, California, April 11, 1955; admitted to bar, 1984, California; 1991, U.S. Tax Court. *Education:* Reed College (B.A., 1978); Golden Gate University (J.D., 1982). *Member:* Alameda County and Eastern Alameda County Bar Associations; State Bar of California. **PRACTICE AREAS:** Insurance Defense Law; General Civil and Construction Litigation; Products Liability; Taxation; Real Property; Business Formations and Transactions.

**KENNETH R. VAN VLECK,** born Fremont, California, August 31, 1965; admitted to bar, 1993, California and U.S. District Court, Northern District of California; U.S. Court of Appeals, Ninth Circuit. *Education:* Stanford University (A.B., 1990); Hastings College of Law, University of California (J.D., 1993). *Member:* Alameda County Bar Association; State Bar of California. **PRACTICE AREAS:** Insurance Defense; General Civil and Construction Management Litigation.

**ARMAND P. ADKINS,** born Los Angeles, California, March 11, 1969; admitted to bar, 1995, California. *Education:* University of California at Berkeley (B.A., 1991); University of California, Hastings College of the Law (J.D., 1995). **PRACTICE AREAS:** Insurance Defense; General Civil Litigation; Insurance Coverage Law.

**LYN DAVALY TADLOCK,** born San Francisco, California; admitted to bar, 1993, California. *Education:* Universite De Paris Faculte De Droit; Golden Gate University (J.D., 1987). *Member:* State Bar of California. **PRACTICE AREAS:** Insurance Defense; General Civil Litigation.

REPRESENTATIVE CLIENTS: Allstate Insurance Co.; Farmers Insurance Group; City of Fremont; Aetna Insurance Co.; Horace Mann Insurance Co.; Utica Mutual Insurance Co.; G.A.B.; Colonial Penn Insurance Co.; U.S.F. & G.; Leasing, U.S.A.; Fidelity American Bank; Northwest Insurance Co.; First State Insurance Co.; National Union Fire Insurance; Insurance Company of the State of Pennsylvania; ARIES, Inc.; Leaseway of Northern California, Inc.; Northbrook Insurance Co.; Agricultural Excess & Surplus Insurance Co.; Grain Dealers Mutual Insurance Co.; TransAmerica Insurance; Republic Financial Services, Inc.; American Bankers Insurance of Florida; Auto Owners Insurance Co. of Michigan.
REFERENCES: Wells Fargo Bank (Hayward Main); Allstate Insurance Co. (Martinez and Pleasanton); Farmers Insurance Group (Pleasanton).

### JAMES J. PHILLIPS
*A PROFESSIONAL CORPORATION*
1331 B STREET, SUITE 4
HAYWARD, CALIFORNIA 94541
Telephone: 510-886-2120
Fax: 510-463-8656

*Pleasanton, California Office:* 4900 Hopyard Road, Suite 260, 94588.
Telephone: 510-463-1980.

*(This Listing Continued)*

## JAMES J. PHILLIPS A PROFESSIONAL CORPORATION, Hayward—Continued

*Estate Planning, Trust and Probate Law.*

**JAMES J. PHILLIPS,** born Oakland, California, April 16, 1954; admitted to bar, 1980, California and U.S. Court of Appeals, Ninth Circuit. *Education:* University of California at Davis (B.S., magna cum laude, 1976); Hastings College of Law (J.D., 1980); Golden Gate University School of Law (LL.M. in Taxation, 1988). First Place, David E. Snodgrass Moot Court Competition, 1979. Author of estate planning articles for the California Continuing Education of the Bar. *Member:* Eastern Alameda County (President, 1990) and Alameda County Bar Associations; State Bar of California (Member, Executive Committee, Section on Estate Planning, Trust and Probate Law, 1991-1992). (Certified Specialist, Estate Planning, Trust and Probate Law, The State Bar of California Board of Legal Specialization).

REFERENCES: Community First National Bank; Wells Fargo Bank; Com Core Realty; Hometown Brokers.

## RIFKIND & FUERCH
### A PROFESSIONAL CORPORATION
SUITE 614, 24301 SOUTHLAND DRIVE
**HAYWARD, CALIFORNIA 94545**
Telephone: 510-785-3101
Fax: 510-785-6828

*General Civil and Trial Practice. Insurance, Insurance Defense, Real Estate, Transportation Law, Fire Insurance, Products Liability, Automobile, Professional Liability, Landslide and Subsidence, Construction, Business, Municipal and Education Law.*

**RICHARD D. RIFKIND,** born Los Angeles, California, May 19, 1937; admitted to bar, 1963, California. *Education:* University of California, Los Angeles (A.B., 1959); Boalt Hall, University of California, Berkeley (LL.B., 1962). Judge, State Bar Courts, 1979. *Member:* Alameda County and Southern Alameda County Bar Associations; State Bar of California; Defense Research Institute; Association of Defense Counsel.

**STEPHEN M. FUERCH,** born Alameda, California, March 17, 1945; admitted to bar, 1975, California. *Education:* California State University at Chico (B.S., 1970); McGeorge School of Law, University of the Pacific (J.D., 1975). *Member:* Alameda County and Southern Alameda County Bar Associations; State Bar of California; Defense Research Institute; Association of Defense Counsel. *PRACTICE AREAS:* Construction Law; Government Tort Liability; Products Liability; Personal Injury; Real Property; Civil Liability.

**MICHAEL J. GREATHOUSE,** born Clovis, New Mexico, June 8, 1956; admitted to bar, 1981, California. *Education:* California Polytechnic State University, San Luis Obispo (B.A., 1978); Pepperdine University (J.D., 1981). *Member:* Alameda County Bar Association; State Bar of California.

REPRESENTATIVE CLIENTS: Fireman's Fund American Insurance Co.; Royal Insurance Co.; City of Fremont (Self-Insured); Briggs & Stratton Inc. (Northern California Counsel); National Auto Recovery Bureau; Colonial-Penn Insurance Co.; J.C. Penney Insurance Co.; Orion Group Insurance Co.; East Bay Regional Park Dist. (Self Insured); Hayward Unified School District (Self Insured); State Farm Insurance Co.; Chabot-Las Positas Community College District-General Counsel.
REFERENCE: Sanwa Bank California, Hayward (Southland Office).

## SCHENONE & PECK
1260 B STREET, SUITE 350
**HAYWARD, CALIFORNIA 94541**
Telephone: 510-581-6611
Fax: 510-581-6174

*Civil and Trial Practice Law. Real Property, Construction, Land Use, Estate Planning, Probate, Trusts, Business, Corporation and Commercial Law.*

### MEMBERS OF FIRM

**BART J. SCHENONE,** born Livermore, California, February 17, 1949; admitted to bar, 1974, California. *Education:* Stanford University (B.A., with distinction, 1971); University of Michigan (J.D., 1974). *Member:* Alameda County (Member, Board of Directors, 1990-1991; Chair of Estate Planning, Trust and Probate Law Section, 1996) and American (Member,

*(This Listing Continued)*

Real Property, Probate and Trust Law Section) Bar Associations; State Bar of California (Member, Resolutions Committee, 1990-1995 and Chair, 1995, Member, Sections on: Estate Planning, Trust and Probate; Real Property). (Certified Specialist, Probate, Estate Planning and Trust Law, The State Bar of California Board of Legal Specialization). *PRACTICE AREAS:* Estate Planning; Trust; Probate; Real Property.

**RONALD G. PECK,** born Oakland, California, December 26, 1951; admitted to bar, 1977, California. *Education:* University of the Pacific (B.A., with distinction, 1974); McGeorge College of the Law, University of the Pacific (J.D., 1977). Member, Traynor Society. Law Clerk to Hon. Procter Hug, Jr., U.S. Court of Appeals, Ninth Circuit, 1977-1978. Judge Pro Tem, Fremont Municipal Court, 1985—. Member, City of Hayward Planning Commission, 1984-1992. *Member:* Alameda County and American Bar (Member, Litigation Section) Associations; State Bar of California (Member, Sections on: Real Property; Business Law; Estate Planning, Trust and Probate). *PRACTICE AREAS:* Commercial Litigation; Real Property; Construction Disputes; Collection; Business Disputes; Trusts, Wills & Estates.

REPRESENTATIVE CLIENTS: Cooper and Cook Insurance Services, Inc.; United Brokers Co.; REMAX Realty; State Shingle Co.; Castlewood Properties, Inc.; Ardenwood Development Associates; Ardenbrooks, Inc.; BSR Realty; Abco Heating & Air Conditioning; Fuller Enterprises Property Management Co.; Lewis Construction Co.

## VARNI, FRASER, HARTWELL & RODGERS
Established in 1971
22771 MAIN STREET
P.O. BOX 570
**HAYWARD, CALIFORNIA 94543-0570**
Telephone: 510-886-5000; 352-4500
Fax: 510-538-8797

Livermore, California Office: 2109 Fourth Street, P.O. Box 511, 94550-0511. Telephone: 510-447-1222. Fax: 510-443-7831.

*State and Federal Court Business Litigation, Real Estate Development and Land Use, Environmental and Eminent Domain, Estate Planning and Probate Practice.*

FIRM PROFILE: *The partnership was formed in 1971 and since its inception has maintained a small, influential, Northern California practice with emphasis on business, land use, condemnation, agriculture, administrative agencies, probate, trusts and estate planning. The firm has established and maintained a quality practice by providing personalized and prompt service at sensible rates. The firm represents large clients in business transactions and well-situated, influential public agencies. The firm is recognized as an authority in the areas of land use, transit, solid waste and liquid waste disposal, inverse condemnation, estate planning and probate. Public agencies and landowners have been represented in trials and appeals in a significant number of reported land use and inverse condemnation cases.*

### MEMBERS OF FIRM

**ANTHONY B. VARNI,** born Hayward, California, February 15, 1939; admitted to bar, 1964, California and U.S District Court, Northern and Eastern Districts of California; U.S. Court of Appeals, Ninth Circuit. *Education:* University of Santa Clara (B.A., 1961); Santa Clara Law School (LL.B., 1963). Editor, Santa Clara Law Review. Lecturer, Current Real Estate Issues, California Continuing Education of the Bar, 1971-1993. *Member:* Alameda County (Former Member, Board of Directors) and American (Member, Real Property and Probate Section) Bar Associations; State Bar of California (Member, Agri-Business Section; Former Member, Eminent Domain Section); Lawyers Panel for California Association of Sanitary Agencies. *PRACTICE AREAS:* Real Estate; Land Use; Eminent Domain; Inverse Condemnation.

**KEITH S. FRASER,** born Livermore, California, May 31, 1936; admitted to bar, 1961, California. *Education:* Stanford University (B.S., 1958); Hastings College of the Law, University of California (LL.B., 1961). Phi Delta Phi. Deputy District Attorney, Alameda County, 1961-1963. Member, 1983-1984 and Chairman, 1985, State Bar Commission on Judicial Nominees Evaluation; Member, 1987, 1988 and Chairman, 1989, Review Committee. *Member:* Alameda County, Eastern Alameda County and American Bar Associations; State Bar of California (Member, Real Property and Probate Sections); Tri-Valley Business and Estate Planning Council. *PRACTICE AREAS:* Real Estate; Land Use; Probate.

**ELIZABETH E. TRUTNER,** born Oakland, California, March 3, 1958; admitted to bar, 1989, California. *Education:* University of California at

*(This Listing Continued)*

Davis (B.A., 1980); University of San Diego (International Law Program, Paris, 1986); San Francisco Law School (J.D., with honors, 1989). Recipient: American Jurisprudence Award in Corporations and Remedies; West Publishing Award. *Member:* Alameda County and Eastern Alameda County Bar Associations; State Bar of California (Member, Probate and Estate Planning Section); Tri-Valley Business and Estate Planning Council. (Resident, Livermore Office) (Certified Specialist, Estate Planning, Trust and Probate Law, The State Bar of California Board of Legal Specialization). *LANGUAGES:* French. *PRACTICE AREAS:* Probate; Estate Planning; Guardianship and Conservatorship.

**JOHN S. HARTWELL** (1924-1993).

**LIONEL A. RODGERS** (1942-1989).

### ASSOCIATE

**CHRISTINE KASUN MORUZA,** born Camp Pendleton, California, October 12, 1951; admitted to bar, 1976, California. *Education:* University of California at Santa Barbara (B.A., summa cum laude, 1973); University of California, Hastings College of Law (J.D., 1976). Assistant District Attorney, City and County, San Francisco, 1977-1983. *Member:* Eastern Alameda County Bar Association; State Bar of California. *PRACTICE AREAS:* Business Litigation.

REPRESENTATIVE CLIENTS: Agricultural Clients: Hunt-Wesson, Inc. (Tomato Products); Glad-A-Way Gardens, Inc. (Flower Production); Mohr-Fry Ranches (Wine); Raspo Farms (Apricots and Nuts); Dittmer Trust (Grazing); Lamb-Weston, Inc. (Potatoes); Devor Nurseries, Inc. (Plants); Garms Estate (Soft Shell Wheat). Development Clients: Kaufman & Broad of Northern California (Housing); Golden State Development (Housing); Britannia Developments, Inc. (R & D Construction); Balch Enterprises, Inc. (Industrial Construction); The O'Brien Group (Housing). Government Agencies: City of Newark (Special Counsel); Castro Valley Sanitary District; Livermore-Amador Valley Transit Authority. Title Insurance Companies: First American Title Guaranty Co.; Chicago Title Co. Insurance Companies: Travelers Insurance; The Ohio Casualty Insurance Co.; CIGNA Insurance; Fireman's Fund; Scottsdale Insurance Co. Telecommunications: Channel 14. Business: Mack Truck, Inc.; Nokia-Kinex Corp.; Livermore Stockmen's Rodeo Assn.; Livermore-Pleasanton Rod and Gun Club; Callaghan Mortuary; Groth Bros.; Chevrolet-Oldsmobile-Geo.

---

## BLOOM, RUDIBAUGH & GUNN

Established in 1953

**805 EAST FLORIDA AVENUE**
**HEMET, CALIFORNIA 92543**
Telephone: 909-652-1400
Fax: 909-652-3990

*Temecula, California Office:* 43517 Ridge Park Drive, Suite 100. Telephone: 909-676-2112. Fax: 909-694-0418.

*General Civil and Trial Practice. Family, Estate Planning, Probate, Bankruptcy and Criminal Law.*

### MEMBERS OF FIRM

**KATHLYN J. BLOOM-RUDIBAUGH,** born Los Angeles, California, November 21, 1951; admitted to bar, 1977, California; 1978, U.S. District Court, Southern District of California; 1982, U.S. District Court, Central District of California. *Education:* California State University, San Diego (B.A., 1973); Western State University (J.D., 1977). Trustee, Hemet Unified School District, 1994—. *Member:* Hemet/San Jacinto, Riverside County and American Bar Associations; State Bar of California. *PRACTICE AREAS:* Family Law; Real Estate.

**C. SCOTT RUDIBAUGH,** born Youngstown, Ohio, June 3, 1950; admitted to bar, 1980, California and U.S. District Court, Southern, Central and Eastern Districts of California. *Education:* Grove City College (B.S., 1972); Western State University (J.D., 1977). Judge Pro Tem, Family Law, Riverside Superior Court. *Member:* Hemet/San Jacinto, Riverside County and American Bar Associations; State Bar of California. *PRACTICE AREAS:* Family Law; Bankruptcy.

**REBECCA L. GUNN,** born Fort Dodge, Iowa, March 16, 1951; admitted to bar, 1980, California; 1981, Colorado, U.S. District Court, District of Colorado, U.S. District Court, Central and Southern Districts, California and U.S. Tax Court. *Education:* University of Minnesota (B.E.S., 1976); Loyola University (J.D., 1980); Denver University School of Law (M.L., Taxation, 1986). Assistant Municipal Judge, Loveland, Colorado. Board Member, Aspiring Angels. *Member:* Hemet/San Jacinto, Colorado and American Bar Associations; The State Bar of California. *PRACTICE AREAS:* Estate Planning, Probate and Tax.

---

## SWAN, CARPENTER, WALLIS & McKENZIE

A Partnership including Professional Corporations

Established in 1961

**1600 EAST FLORIDA AVENUE, SUITE 211**
**HEMET, CALIFORNIA 92544**
Telephone: 909-658-7162
Facsimile No.: 909-658-2231

*Sun City, California Office:* 26858 Cherry Hills Boulevard. Telephone: 909-672-1881. Facsimile: 909-672-3164.

*General Civil Trial Practice. Corporate, Estate Planning, Probate, Real Property, Family and Commercial Law.*

**D. RICHARD SWAN, (P.C.),** born York, Nebraska, July 10, 1934; admitted to bar, 1961, California. *Education:* University of Colorado (B.A., 1957; LL.B., 1960). Phi Delta Phi. *Member:* Riverside County Bar Association (President, 1977-1978); The State Bar of California. (Certified Specialist, Family Law, The State Bar of California Board of Legal Specialization). *PRACTICE AREAS:* Commercial Law; Family Law.

**THOMAS M. CARPENTER, (P.C.),** born Chicago, Illinois, August 22, 1933; admitted to bar, 1966, California. *Education:* Loyola University, Chicago (B.S., 1958; J.D., 1961). Instructor, Trusts and Estates, Citrus Belt Law School, 1976-1989. President, Riverside County Estate Planning Council, 1978-1980. *Member:* Riverside County Bar Association; The State Bar of California. (Certified Specialist, Probate, Estate Planning and Trust Law, The State Bar of California Board of Legal Specialization). *PRACTICE AREAS:* Estate Planning Law; Probate Law.

**BRUCE M. WALLIS, (P.C.),** born Colfax, Washington, December 22, 1945; admitted to bar, 1975, California; 1978, Nevada. *Education:* University of California at Santa Barbara (B.A., 1967); McGeorge College of the Law (J.D., 1975). District Counsel, U.S. Small Business Administration, 1977-1979. *Member:* Riverside County Bar Association; The State Bar of California; State Bar of Nevada. *PRACTICE AREAS:* Real Property Law; Commercial Law; Banking Law; General Civil Litigation.

**KEVIN A. McKENZIE,** born Hollywood, California, April 24, 1957; admitted to bar, 1984, California. *Education:* California Lutheran College (B.A., summa cum laude, 1979); University of Southern California (J.D., 1984). *Member:* State Bar of California. *PRACTICE AREAS:* Estate Planning; Probate and Conservatorships; Real Estate; General Civil Litigation; Aviation Law; Insurance Defense.

REPRESENTATIVE CLIENTS: First Mountain Bank; AIG Insurance Co.; Hemet Community Medical Group; Valley Merchants Bank.
REFERENCES: United California Saving Bank, Bank of America.

---

## WELEBIR & McCUNE

A PROFESSIONAL LAW CORPORATION

**HEMET, CALIFORNIA**

(See Redlands)

*Practice limited to Catastrophic Personal Injury and Wrongful Death, Products Liability, Aviation, Railroad and Toxic Torts. Class Actions related to Defective Products and Mass Torts.*

---

## NORMAN D. JAMES

**49 PIER AVENUE**
**2ND FLOOR**
**HERMOSA BEACH, CALIFORNIA 90254**
Telephone: 310-798-4131
Fax: 310-798-4136

*Civil Trials and Appellate Practice in all State and Federal Courts, Business Litigation and Federal Criminal Law.*

**NORMAN D. JAMES,** born Neenah, Wisconsin, November 10, 1943; admitted to bar, 1969, Illinois; 1970, U.S. Court of Military Appeals; 1973, U.S. District Court, Central District of California and U.S. Court of Appeals, Ninth Circuit; 1976, California; 1987, U.S. Court of Appeals, Eighth and Eleventh Circuits. *Education:* University of Illinois (A.B., 1965; J.D., 1969). Assistant U.S. Attorney, Criminal Division, Central District of California, 1973-1979. *Member:* Los Angeles County, Illinois State and Federal Bar Associations; State Bar of California. [CPT, JAGC, U.S. Army, 1969-1973]. *REPORTED CASES:* United States v. Salerno 902 F.2d 1429 (9th

*(This Listing Continued)*

NORMAN D. JAMES, Hermosa Beach—Continued

Circuit 1990); Firstmark Capital Corp. v. Hempel Financial Corp. 859 F.2d 92 (9th Circuit 1988); United States v. Noti 731 F.2d 610 (9th Circuit 1984).

## LAW OFFICES OF
## MATTHEW W. MONROE

*2200 PACIFIC COAST HIGHWAY*
*SUITE 312*
**HERMOSA BEACH, CALIFORNIA 90254-2757**
*Telephone: 310-318-3595*
*Fax: 310-318-1257*

*General Practice.*

**MATTHEW W. MONROE,** born Milwaukee, Wisconsin, November 1, 1948; admitted to bar, 1990, California; 1991, U.S. District Court, Southern, Eastern and Central Districts of California and U.S. Court of Military Appeals. *Education:* Campbell College (B.S., 1975); Pepperdine University (M.B.A., 1979); National University School of Law (J.D., 1989). Professor, Law Review, University of North Carolina and Golden Gate University, 1987. *Member:* State Bar of California; American Bar Association. [U.S. Marine Corp. Counterintelligence Agent, U.S. Naval Investigative Service, 1967-1987]. *LANGUAGES:* Japanese, Vietnamese and French. *PRACTICE AREAS:* Insurance Defense; Admiralty Law; Business Law; Civil Litigation; Military Law.

### ASSOCIATES

**TOM R. SHAPIRO,** born New Brunswick, New Jersey, January 9, 1962; admitted to bar, 1986, California; 1987, U.S. District Court, Central District of California; 1992 U.S. Court of Appeals, Ninth Circuit. *Education:* Ithaca College (B.S., 1983); Catholic University of America (J.D., 1986). *PRACTICE AREAS:* Civil Litigation; Civil Rights Litigation; Business Litigation.

**DEANNA R. HARWOOD,** born Torrance, California, July 21, 1960; admitted to bar, 1994, California and U.S. District Court, Central District of California; 1996, U.S. District Court, Eastern District of California and District of Arizona. *Education:* California State University, Northridge (B.S., 1982); Southwestern University School of Law (J.D., 1994). Recipient, Exceptional Achievement Award in International Environmental Law. *Member:* Los Angeles County Bar Association; State Bar of California. *PRACTICE AREAS:* Insurance Defense; Admiralty; Trademark; Corporate Litigation.

**STEVEN D. SMELSER,** born Torrance, California, May 5, 1969; admitted to bar, 1995, California and U.S. District Court, Central District of California; 1996, Hawaii, U.S. District Court, Eastern, Northern and Southern Districts of California and District of Arizona. *Education:* University of California at Los Angeles (B.S., in Political Science/History, 1992); Loyola Law School at Los Angeles (J.D., 1995). *Member:* State Bar of California. *PRACTICE AREAS:* Insurance Defense; Admiralty; Corporate Litigation.

**DARA S. NIAD,** born Wiesbaden, Germany, May 10, 1970; admitted to bar, 1995, California and U.S. District Court, Central District of California; 1996, U.S. District Court, District of Hawaii. *Education:* Russell Sage College (B.S., 1991); Southwestern University (J.D., 1995). Recipient, McComb Scholarship. Dean, Delta Theta Phi, 1994-1995. *Member:* Los Angeles County Bar Association; State Bar of California. *PRACTICE AREAS:* Insurance Defense; Admiralty; Civil Litigation; Civil Rights Defense.

**DANIEL A. SCHUCH,** born Palos Verdes Estates, California, August 17, 1955; admitted to bar, 1988, California and U.S. District Court, Central District of California. *Education:* University of Tennessee at Knoxville (B.A., with honors, 1984; J.D., 1987). Phi Alpha Delta. *Member:* Beverly Hills and Los Angeles County Bar Associations; State Bar of California. *PRACTICE AREAS:* Insurance Defense; Admiralty; Trademark/Copyright; Civil Litigation.

### OF COUNSEL

**RALPH M. SINGER, JR.,** born Portland, Oregon, April 6, 1930; admitted to bar, 1977, California; 1978, U.S. District Court, Central District of California. *Education:* Loyola Marymount University (B.B.A., 1952; J.D., 1977). *Member:* Los Angeles County Bar Association; State Bar of

*(This Listing Continued)*

California; Los Angeles Trial Lawyers Association. *PRACTICE AREAS:* Business Law; Insurance Defense Law; Real Property Law.

**K. D. JOHNSON,** born Fresno, California, August 26, 1952; admitted to bar, 1980, California; 1981, Nevada; 1983, Arizona. *Education:* Tulsa Junior College (A.A., 1973); Northeastern Oklahoma State University (B.S., 1975); University of California at Davis (J.D., 1980). Judicial Clerkship, Reno, Nevada. Clerk, Yolo County District Attorney. *Member:* State Bars of Arizona, California and Nevada. [With U.S. Air Force, Air National Guard, 1973-1975]. *PRACTICE AREAS:* Admiralty/Maritime; Insurance Defense, Business and Real Estate Litigation.

REPRESENTATIVE CLIENTS: Jardine Rolfe, Ltd.; All Risk Claims Services, Inc. ; General Star Management Co.; Generali Insurance; Fairclaim Adjusting Services, Inc.; Nautilus Insurance Co.; National Association of Underwater Instructors (NAUI); American Nitrox Divers International (ANDI); Scuba Schools International (SSI); Oceanic Industries; Modern Nuclear; Lido Sailing Club; Diamond W Floor Covering, Inc.; Anza Borrego Foundation; Diving Technologies International, Inc.; Lloyds of London; Miller North American at Lloyds of London; Mumford Underwriters at Lloyds of London; Anglo American at Lloyds; Toplis & Harding; Illinois Insurance Exchange; Pelagic; 2001 Design Group; Destination Oceanic; National Association of Scuba Diving Schools (NASDS); Florida Association of Dive Operators (FADO); National Association of Scuba Educators (NASE); Professional Association of Dive Instructors (PADI); SBJ Regis Lowe at Lloyds of London; SBJ Marine & Energy at Lloyds of London; Gale Smith & Co.; Insurance Management Services; Royal Insurance Co.; Scuba Retailers Association (SRA); Sherwood Scuba; Destination Oceanic Travel, Oceanic etc.; Oceanic Singapore; Romney; Philagic Industries; Continental Ins. Co.; T.H.E. Insurance Company; American General Insurance Company.

## NASH & EDGERTON

A Limited Liability Partnership
*2615 PACIFIC COAST HIGHWAY, SUITE 322*
**HERMOSA BEACH, CALIFORNIA 90254**
*Telephone: 310-937-2066*
*Fax: 310-937-2063*

*Torrance, California Office:* 3625 Del Amo Boulevard, suite 360. Telephone: 310-370-8272. Fax: 310-214-9677.

*Commercial and Securities Litigation, Broker-Dealer Defense. General Business Practice. Corporate, Contract, Finance, Real Property Law, New Ventures and Partnership Law.*

**SAVERY L. NASH,** born Ruston, Louisiana, April 19, 1933; admitted to bar, 1960, California and U.S. District Court, Central District of California. *Education:* University of Oklahoma; University of California at Los Angeles (B.A., 1956; LL.B., 1959). *Member:* State Bar of California. *PRACTICE AREAS:* General Business Practice; Corporate; Contract; Finance; Real Property; New Ventures and Partnership.

**SAMUEL Y. EDGERTON, III,** born Bryn Mawr, Pennsylvania, April 27, 1956; admitted to bar, 1982, Massachusetts and District of Columbia; 1986, California and U.S. District Court, Central District of California. *Education:* Boston University (B.S., cum laude, 1978); Catholic University of America (J.D., 1982). Attorney, Office of Enforcement, U.S. Securities Commission, Los Angeles, California, 1982-1986. Special Assistant U.S. Attorney, U.S. Attorney's Office, Los Angeles, California, 1984-1986. Councilman, 1991—, Mayor, 1993-1994, Hermosa Beach, California. *Member:* Los Angeles County and American Bar Associations; State Bar of California. *PRACTICE AREAS:* Securities Brokerage Defense; Bankruptcy; Real Estate and Commercial Litigation.

**SHELLEY NASH,** born Los Angeles, California, November 28, 1959; admitted to bar, 1986, California and U.S. District Court, Southern District of California. *Education:* University of California at Berkeley (B.A., 1981); University of San Diego (J.D., 1985). *Member:* Los Angeles County and American Bar Associations; State Bar of California.

**DAVID MAURER,** born Los Angeles, California, March 8, 1951; admitted to bar, 1983, California and U.S. District Court, Central District of California; 1985, U.S. District Court, Northern District of California; 1986, U.S. Court of Appeals, Ninth Circuit and U.S. District Court, Southern District of California; 1989, U.S. Court of Appeals, District of Columbia Circuit. *Education:* University of California at Berkeley (B.A., 1972); University of Southern California (M.A., 1975); Loyola Law School (J.D., 1983). Member: Scott Moot Court Honors Board; Loyola Law School State Moot Court Team. Judicial Extern to the Honorable Terry J. Hatter, Jr. U.S., District Court, Central District of California, 1982. Temporary Judge, Los Angeles Municipal Court, 1995—. *Member:* Los Angeles County and American Bar Associations; State Bar of California. *PRACTICE AREAS:* Securities; Business; Commercial Litigation.

*(This Listing Continued)*

**DAMON RUBIN,** born Johannesburg, South Africa, December 17, 1970; admitted to bar, 1996, California. *Education:* Loyola Marymount University (B.S., cum laude, 1993); Syracuse University College of Law (J.D., cum laude, 1996). Recipient: CALI Award for Excellence in the Study of Commercial Transactions. Editor, Syracuse Journal of Legislation and Policy. Judicial Extern to Judge Frederick J. Scullin, U.S. District Court, Northern District of New York, 1994-1995; Chief Judge Stephen D. Gerling, U.S. Bankruptcy Court, Northern District of New York, 1995-1996; Judge Candace Cooper, Los Angeles Superior Court (Summer 1994). Clerk for the Federal Deposit Insurance Corporation, Litigation Division (Summer 1995). *Member:* State Bar of California. **PRACTICE AREAS:** Civil Litigation.

REPRESENTATIVE CLIENTS: American Express Financial Services, Inc.; American Express Assurance Company; American Express Tax and Business Services, Inc.; BHH Management, Inc.; Brentwood Medical Products, Inc.; DXL USA, Inc.; Financial Network Investment Corporation; Learned Lumber; Marymount College; Rasmussen Iron Works, Inc.; Staff Control, Inc.

## LAW OFFICE OF
## LEONARD L. SCHAPIRA

555 PIER AVENUE, SUITE 4
HERMOSA BEACH, CALIFORNIA 90254
Telephone: 310-318-9050
Fax: 310-376-3531

*Real Estate, Lender Liability, Debt Restructuring, Business, Consumer and Commercial Law.*

**LEONARD L. SCHAPIRA,** born New York City, N.Y., 1952; admitted to bar, 1990, California and U.S. District Court, Central District of California; 1991, U.S. District Court, Northern District of California and U.S. Court of Appeals, Ninth Circuit. *Education:* University of California at Los Angeles; Stanford University (A.B., 1974); Loyola University at Los Angeles (J.D., 1990). Co-Author: "Lender Liability Against Ailing Banks and Thrifts," Chapter 20, 1990 edition, Lender Liability, Cappello & Komoroske, Parker & Son Publishers; "Builder Beware: How To Protect Yourself During and After the Credit Crunch," California Builder Magazine, March, 1991 Edition; "Lender Liability Chapter 4B Law of Distressed Real Estate," Dunaway, Clark, Boardman Publishers, 1991 Edition; "Stare Decisis, Politics Over Precedent," CTLA Forum Magazine, 1991. Banking, Real Estate, Insurance and Investment Frauds Analyst, Better Business Bureau of Los Angeles and Orange Counties, 1985-1986. Licensed California Realtor, 1987. Legal Intern, Consumer Law Division, California Office of Attorney General. Southern California Anti-Fraud Task Force, 1988. Judicial Extern: Hon. William J. Lasarow, Presiding Judge U.S. Bankruptcy Court, Central District of California, 1989; Judge Extern: Hon. Cynthia Holcomb Hall, Judge, U.S. Court of Appeals, Ninth Circuit, 1990. Panelist, California Bar, Los Angeles City Attorney's Program on Foreclosure Avoidance, 1993.

## BRUCE LINDSEY

HOLLISTER, CALIFORNIA
(See Salinas)

*Bankruptcy, Commercial and Insolvency Law.*

## ANTHONY LOMBARDO & ASSOCIATES

HOLLISTER, CALIFORNIA
(See Salinas)

*Real Estate Acquisitions and Development, Civil Trial and Litigation.*

## NOLAND, HAMERLY, ETIENNE & HOSS

A PROFESSIONAL CORPORATION
HOLLISTER, CALIFORNIA
(See Salinas)

*Business and Commercial Litigation. Construction Litigation. General Business, Corporation, Probate, Estate Planning, Real Property, Land Use, Administrative Law, Tax Law and Family Law.*

## ALAN LEIGH ARMSTRONG

18652 FLORIDA STREET, SUITE 225
HUNTINGTON BEACH, CALIFORNIA 92648-6006
Telephone: 714-375-1147
Fax: 714-375-1149
Email: armstrng@deltanet.com
URL: http://users.deltanet.com/armstrng/

*Probate, Trust and Estate, Real Estate, Commercial Real Estate, Admiralty, Small Business Law.*

**ALAN LEIGH ARMSTRONG,** born Los Angeles, California, April 25, 1945; admitted to bar, 1984, California; 1985 U.S. District Court, Central District of California and U.S. Court of Appeals, Ninth Circuit; 1987, U.S. Tax Court; 1988, U.S. Supreme Court; 1995, U.S. District Court, Southern District of California. *Education:* University of California (B.A., 1967); Western State University (J.D., 1984). *Member:* State Bar of California.

## HOOD, WETZLER & REED

18141 BEACH BOULEVARD, SUITE 300
HUNTINGTON BEACH, CALIFORNIA 92648
Telephone: 714-842-6837
Fax: 714-841-6216
Email: INFO@HWRLAW.COM

*Civil Practice and Appellate practice including Real Property, Financial Institutions, Banking, Mortgage Lending, Title Insurance, Insurance Defense and Coverage, Transactional Matters, Commercial Litigation, Creditors' Rights, Bankruptcy, General Corporate, Probate.*

### MEMBERS OF FIRM

**THOMAS W. HOOD,** admitted to bar, 1974, California and U.S. District Court, Southern and Central Districts of California. *Education:* California State University at Long Beach (B.A., 1971); University of San Diego (J.D., 1974). Judge Pro-Tem. *Member:* Orange County Bar Association (Member, Sections on: Real Property; Commercial Law); State Bar of California; Royal Barrister Society. **REPORTED CASES:** Harbour Landing-Dolfann, Ltd. v. Stanley C. Anderson (1996) 48 Cal.App.4th 260. **PRACTICE AREAS:** Real Property; Commercial Transactional Matters; Title Insurance Defense; General Business Negotiations.

**SANDRA S. WETZLER,** admitted to bar, 1982, California and U.S. District Court, Northern, Southern, Eastern and Central Districts of California; U.S. Court of Appeals, Ninth Circuit. *Education:* University of Michigan (B.A., 1969); California State University at Sacramento (M.B.A., 1977); McGeorge School of Law, University of the Pacific (J.D., 1981). *Member:* Orange County and American Bar Associations; The State Bar of California. **PRACTICE AREAS:** Civil Litigation and Appellate Practice; Corporate; Financial Litigation; Real Property; Commercial Litigation; Title Insurance and Insurance Defense; Coverage Litigation.

**JAMES T. REED, JR.,** admitted to bar, 1978, Tennessee; 1981, U.S. Tax Court and U.S. Supreme Court; 1984, California; 1985, U.S. Court of Appeals, Ninth Circuit, U.S. District Court, Northern, Southern, Eastern and Central Districts of California. *Education:* University of Tennessee at Knoxville (B.S., 1971); Memphis State University (J.D., 1978). Omicron Delta Kappa. Associate Editor, 1977 and Administrative Editor, 1977-1978, Memphis State University Law Review. Author: "Federal Courts: Abstention and The Expansion of The Federalism Concept," 8 Memphis State University Law Review 853, 1978. *Member:* Orange County and Tennessee Bar Associations; State Bar of California; Orange County Bankruptcy Forum; Financial Lawyers Conference of Los Angeles. **PRACTICE AREAS:** Financial Litigation; Creditors' Rights; Real Estate and Commercial Litigation.

## GEORGE L. ROGERS
*A LAW CORPORATION*

Established in 1976

SUITE 103, 17111 BEACH BOULEVARD
**HUNTINGTON BEACH, CALIFORNIA 92647-5999**
Telephone: 714-847-6041
Fax: 714-842-2151
Email: glralaw@1change.com

*General Civil, Trial and Appellate Practice in all State and Federal Courts. Probate, Estate Planning, Tax, Business, Real Property, Domestic Relations and ERISA Transactions.*

**GEORGE L ROGERS,** born Pasadena, California, July 23, 1943; admitted to bar, 1969, California and U.S. Tax Court; 1970, U.S. District Court, Central District of California; 1975, U.S. Court of Appeals, Ninth Circuit; 1982, U.S. Supreme Court. *Education:* University of California at Los Angeles (B.A., 1965; J.D., 1968); New York University (LL.M., in Taxation, 1969). Licensed Real Estate Broker, California, 1982. *Member:* Orange County Bar Association (Chairman, Tax Section, 1975); State Bar of California; Orange County Trial Lawyers Association; Consumer Trial Lawyers Association. **PRACTICE AREAS:** Probate Law; Estate Planning; Taxation Law.

---

**L. EUGENE HALLSTED,** born Muskogee, Oklahoma, October 28, 1945; admitted to bar, 1971, California. *Education:* Loma Linda University (B.A., 1967); Willamette University (J.D., 1970). Delta Theta Phi. Judge Pro-Tem, Orange County Superior Court, 1980—. *Member:* Orange County and American Bar Associations; State Bar of California; Orange County Trial Lawyers Association; Consumer Trial Lawyers Association; The Association of Trial Lawyers of America.

**RALPH R. LOYD,** born Ulm, Germany, July 25, 1952; admitted to bar, 1980, California; 1981, U.S. District Court, Central District of California and U.S. Court of Appeals, Ninth Circuit. *Education:* University of Texas; California State University at Long Beach (B.A., 1976); Western State University College of Law (J.D., 1979). *Member:* State Bar of California. **PRACTICE AREAS:** ERISA; General Trial Practice.

## STUTZ, GALLAGHER, ARTIANO, SHINOFF & HOLTZ
*A PROFESSIONAL CORPORATION*

**IMPERIAL, CALIFORNIA**

(See San Diego)

*General Civil Trial Practice with Special Emphasis in Product Liability, Employment, Environmental, Professional Liability, Construction Defect Litigation, Public Entity, Commercial Litigation, Insurance Coverage, Defense of the Hospitality Industry and Medical Providers.*

## RUSSELL L. DAVIS
Established in 1968

74900 HIGHWAY 111
**INDIAN WELLS, CALIFORNIA 92210**
Telephone: 619-341-1040
Fax: 619-341-8084

*Federal and State Taxation, Tax Litigation and Tax Controversies, Estate Planning, Probate and Probate Litigation.*

**RUSSELL L. DAVIS,** born Chicago, Illinois, October 15, 1939; admitted to bar, 1962, Illinois; 1974, California; 1967, U.S. Supreme Court and U.S. Claims Court; 1969, U.S. Tax Court; 1987, U.S. District Court, Southern District of California; 1988, U.S. District Court, Central District of California; 1988, U.S. Court of Appeals, Ninth Circuit. *Education:* University of Illinois (1956-1959); De Paul University (J.D., 1962); New York University (L.L.M., Taxation, 1963). Trial Attorney: U.S. Department of Justice, Tax Division, Refund Trial Section, Washington, D.C., 1963-1968. *Member:* State Bar of California (Member, Taxation Section, Estate and Gift Tax Committee, Executive Committee and Chair); American Bar Association (Member, Sections on: Taxation and Real Property, Probate and Trust Law).

*(This Listing Continued)*

## JOSEPH A. GIBBS
74-900 HIGHWAY 111, SUITE 211
**INDIAN WELLS, CALIFORNIA 92210**
Telephone: 619-779-1790
Fax: 619-779-1780

Palm Springs California Office: 901 E. Tahquitz Canyon Way, Suite C-203. Telephone: 619-320-7111. Fax: 619-320-6392.

*Civil Litigation, Real Estate, Business, Commercial, Corporate and Partnership Law.*

**FIRM PROFILE:** *Articles written by the Palm Desert Newspaper, "It is critically important that a lawyer have complete knowledge of all aspects of his client's business", says Joe Gibbs. Whether its planning a car dealership expansion or inspecting the progress of a bib lettuce crop, a hands on approach and the knowledge gained with it is the foundation for good sound legal advice. Joe Gibbs of Indian Wells is the youngest member of the Board of Directors that Eisenhower Medical Center has ever had. He is one of the most experienced and ethical trial attorneys in the desert. Why write a story about him? Well, because whether you know the legal profession or not, he can serve as a sort of benchmark for selecting attorneys. He's a good example of a good example.*

**JOSEPH A. GIBBS,** born Los Angeles, California, November 24, 1951; admitted to bar, 1978, California and U.S. District Court, Southern District of California; 1983, U.S. Court of Appeals, Ninth Circuit; 1988, U.S. Supreme Court. *Education:* Loyola University of Chicago; University of San Diego (B.A., 1974); Western State University (J.D., 1977). Deputy District Attorney, Riverside County, 1979-1981. Member, Schlecht, Shevlin and Shoenberger, A Law Corporation, 1981-1993. Judge Pro Tem, Riverside Superior Court and Municipal Courts, 1981—. Member, Rent Review Commission, 1986-1988 and Chairman and Hearing Officer, 1986-1987, City of Palm Desert. Member, Board of Trustees: Eisenhower Medical Center; Palm Springs Bank Advisory Board; Riverside County District Attorney Advisory Board; Palm Desert High School Foundation. *Member:* Desert (President, 1988-1989; Board of Trustees, 1986-1990) and Riverside County Bar Associations; State Bar of California (Special Master); California Trial Lawyers Association; Palm Springs Trial Lawyers Association; The Association of Trial Lawyers of America; Arbitrator and Mediator, American Arbitration Association. **PRACTICE AREAS:** Civil Litigation; Real Estate; Business; Commercial.

### ASSOCIATE

**GREGORY R. OLESON,** born Boston, Massachusetts, August 4, 1967; admitted to bar, 1993, California. *Education:* Elmira College (B.A., 1989); Marquette University (J.D., 1993). *Member:* Desert Bar Association; State Bar of California. **PRACTICE AREAS:** Civil Litigation; Real Estate; Business Litigation.

REPRESENTATIVE CLIENTS: Weston Waste Industries; Rancho Mirage Country Club; YMCA; Hightech Irrigation; Maple Leaf Plumbing; Price Nurseries; Carl Karcher; Fury Investments, Inc.; Heathman Inc.; Desert Orthopedic Group; Outdoor Media Group, A California Corp.; Palm Springs Motors, Inc.; Sleep N' Den, Inc.; Wells Fargo Bank; Independent Credit Card Assn.; Remax Realty; Valley Fair Management Corp.; Golden Acre Farms, Inc.

## HEALEY & HEALEY
**INDIAN WELLS, CALIFORNIA**

(See Palm Desert)

*Estate Planning, Probate, Wills and Trust, Real Estate, Personal Injury and General Business.*

## RONALD W. JOHNSON
Established in 1974

45-025 MANITOU DRIVE AT HIGHWAY 111
**INDIAN WELLS, CALIFORNIA 92210**
Telephone: 619-360-8675
Fax: 619-360-1211

*Family Law, Divorce, Child and Spousal Support, Child Custody Disputes, Premarital and Separation Agreements, Living Arrangement Agreements.*

*(This Listing Continued)*

**RONALD W. JOHNSON,** born Casa Grande, Arizona, November 28, 1939; admitted to bar, 1968, California; 1975, Colorado. *Education:* University of Arizona (B.S., 1961); Hastings College of the Law, University of California (J.D., 1967). Member, Moot Court Board. *Member:* State Bar of California; Colorado (Member: Ethics Committee, 1979—; Family Law Section) and American Bar Associations. (Certified Specialist, Family Law, The State Bar of California Board of Legal Specialization). *LANGUAGES:* Spanish. *PRACTICE AREAS:* Family Law; Divorce; Adoptions; Child Custody; Premarital Agreements; Separation Agreements; Living Arrangement Agreements.

---

## DOUGLAS MARTIN

*A LAW CORPORATION*

Established in 1982

WALL STREET WEST
74-785 HIGHWAY 111, SUITE 201
**INDIAN WELLS, CALIFORNIA 92210**
Telephone: 619-776-1377
Fax: 619-776-1380

*Estate Planning, Probate, Real Estate, Corporate, Taxation and Business Law.*

FIRM PROFILE: *Established in 1982, the firm's emphasis in the areas of estate and tax planning, family and charitable trusts, ancillary probate and probate administration, commercial and residential real estate and small closely held businesses. The firm currently has a number of Canadian clients and is now listed in The Martindale-Hubbell Canadian Law Directory. The firm believes in providing the highest quality legal services in a timely and cost-effective manner. Mr. Martin takes great pride in being listed in The Martindale-Hubbell Bar Register of Preeminent Lawyers in the Probate and Estate Planning and Real Estate sections.*

**DOUGLAS MARTIN,** born Oakland, California, October 22, 1937; admitted to bar, 1963, California. *Education:* Stanford University (A.B., 1959); Loyola University of Los Angeles (LL.B., 1962); University of Southern California (Certificate of Graduate Study in Taxation). Phi Delta Phi. *Member:* Los Angeles County (Member, Sections on: Trusts and Estates; Real Property; Business and Corporations), Desert and American (Member, Sections on: Real Property, Probate and Trust Law; Business Law; Taxation; General Practice) Bar Associations; State Bar of California (Member, Sections on: Estate Planning, Trust and Probate; Real Property Law; Business Law; Taxation). *PRACTICE AREAS:* Estate Planning; Probate; Real Estate; Corporate Law; Taxation Law.

### LEGAL SUPPORT PERSONNEL

**CAROL A. MORENO,** born Chicago Heights, Illinois, July 20, 1946. *Education:* California State University at Los Angeles (Paralegal certificates, 1977 - General and Corporate). *PRACTICE AREAS:* Estate Planning; Probate; Real Estate; Corporate; Drafting Wills; Trusts; Property Agreements; Probate Pleadings; Purchase, Sale and Loan Documents; Articles, Minutes and Corporate Agreements; Probate Administration; Tax.

REPRESENTATIVE CLIENTS: Association of Air Medical Services; Bank of America National Trust and Savings Association as Trustee; Braille Institute of America Inc.; California Amforge Corp.; Caregivers Home Health; Bob and Marie Evans Foundation; Heart Institute of the Desert Foundation; Nissan Motor Corporation in U.S.A.; Northern Trust Bank of California N.A. as Trustee; Rayne of the Valley, Inc.; Sierra Leasing Co.; West Coast Turf.

---

## THOMAS T. ANDERSON, P.C.

45-926 OASIS STREET
**INDIO, CALIFORNIA 92201**
Telephone: 619-347-3364
Fax: 619-347-5572

*Negligence Law, Highway Safety, Products Liability, Insurance Bad Faith, Legal Malpractice and Consumer Fraud.*

FIRM PROFILE: *The Anderson Firm is a full service law firm. Clients are provided with top quality, cost efficient legal services with close personal contact. The firm is listed in the Bar Register Preeminent Law Directory under General Practice.*

**THOMAS T. ANDERSON,** born Seattle, Washington, July 9, 1928; admitted to bar, 1955, California. *Education:* University of Oregon (B.B.A., 1949); Willamette University (B.S., 1954); University of San Francisco (LL.B., 1955). Co-author: *Anatomy of a Personal Injury Law Suit, A Hand-*
(This Listing Continued)

book of Basic Trial Advocacy, published 1968. Member, Judicial Council, State of California, 1977-1979. *Member:* Desert (Member, Board of Trustees, 1959-1960; President, 1963-1965) and Riverside County Bar Associations; State Bar of California; Consumer Attorneys of California (Member, Board of Governors, 1963-1966; Vice President, 1966-1969; President, 1970-1971); Western Trial Lawyers Association (Member, Board of Governors, 1965-1970); The Association of Trial Lawyers of America (Associate Editor, 1965—; Member, Board of Governors, 1971-1977; Chairman, Membership Committee, 1971; Member, Executive Committee, 1974-1976; Trustee, Attorney's Congressional Campaign Trust, 1975-1979); International Academy of Trial Lawyers; American Board of Trial Advocates. Fellow: International Society of Barristers; Inner Circle of Advocates. *PRACTICE AREAS:* Personal Injury; Highway Safety; Consumer Fraud; Insurance Bad Faith.

---

**DAVID M. CHAPMAN,** born Anchorage, Alaska, March 1, 1950; admitted to bar, 1977, California. *Education:* Arizona State University (B.S., 1973); University of San Fernando Valley (J.D., 1977). Delta Theta Phi. Managing Editor, San Fernando Valley Law Review, 1976-1977. *Member:* Desert (Trustee; President, 1996-1997), Riverside County Bar Association (Member, Board of Trustees); State Bar of California; Consumer Attorneys of California; The Association of Trial Lawyers of America; Palm Springs Trial Lawyers Association. *PRACTICE AREAS:* Personal Injury Law; Products Liability Law; Insurance Law.

**SAMUEL F. TRUSSELL,** born Gadsden, Alabama, October 26, 1947; admitted to bar, 1985, California. *Education:* San Francisco State University (B.A., 1972; M.A., 1975); Southwestern University (J.D., 1985). Recipient, American Jurisprudence Book Awards: Criminal Law, Wills and Trusts; Professional Ethics. *Member:* Desert Bar Association; State Bar of California; Consumer Attorneys of California; The Association of Trial Lawyers of America. *LANGUAGES:* Spanish. *PRACTICE AREAS:* Personal Injury; Consumer Fraud; Products Liability Law; Insurance Law.

**GREGORY T. ANDERSON,** born Santa Monica, California,; admitted to bar, 1993, California. *Education:* University of Maryland; Golden Gate University (J.D., 1992). *Member:* State Bar of California; Consumer Attorneys of California; Consumer Attorneys of Los Angeles. *PRACTICE AREAS:* Plaintiffs Civil Trial; Plaintiffs Medical Malpractice.

REFERENCE: City National Bank.

---

## CLARK HEAD

82-500 HIGHWAY 111, SUITE 5
**INDIO, CALIFORNIA 92201**
Telephone: 619-347-3173
Fax: 619-347-0046

*Criminal Defense, Felonies, Civil Litigation.*

**CLARK HEAD,** born Grand Junction, Colorado, June 4, 1945; admitted to bar, 1976, California. *Education:* Sacramento State College (B.A., 1971); University of Arkansas (J.D., 1975). Public Defender, Calaveras County, 1981-1989. Calavera County Law library, Board of Trustees; Delegate to Bar Convention. *Member:* State Bar of California. *PRACTICE AREAS:* Criminal Defense; Felonies; Civil Litigation.

---

## IVES, KIRWAN & DIBBLE

*A PROFESSIONAL CORPORATION*

**INDIO, CALIFORNIA**

(See Palm Springs)

---

## KINKLE, RODIGER AND SPRIGGS

*PROFESSIONAL CORPORATION*

**INDIO, CALIFORNIA**

(See Riverside)

*General Trial Practice. Negligence, Malpractice, Products Liability, Construction and Insurance Law.*

## CHARLES J. KOOSED

82-500 HIGHWAY 111, SUITE 5
INDIO, CALIFORNIA 92201
Telephone: 619-347-6579

*Juvenile Law, Juvenile Dependency, Criminal Defense, Felonies, Criminal Defense, DUI.*

**CHARLES J. KOOSED,** born Torrance, California, December 27, 1967; admitted to bar, 1994, California. *Education:* University of California at Los Angeles (B.A., political science, 1990); Southwestern University, School of Law (J.D., 1994). *Member:* State Bar of California (Criminal Law Section); California Public Defenders Association; Desert Bar Association (Criminal Law Committee). **PRACTICE AREAS:** Juvenile Law; Juvenile Dependency; Criminal Defence; Felonies; DUI.

## JERRY SHUFORD

SUITE 111
82500 HIGHWAY III
P.O. BOX 10370
INDIO, CALIFORNIA 92202
Telephone: 619-347-3635
Fax: 619-347-0046

*Practice Limited to Major Felonies and Drunk Driving Defense. Criminal Writs and Appeals.*

**JERRY SHUFORD,** born Valdese, North Carolina, October 18, 1936; admitted to bar, 1970, California and U.S. District Court, Central District of California; 1977, U.S. Supreme Court. *Education:* San Francisco State College (B.A., 1963); Southwestern University (J.D., 1970); University of Southern California Law Center. Advanced Criminal Law Certificate, 1972. City Attorney, Coachella, 1976-1979. Judge, Pro Tem, Municipal and Superior Courts, 1975-1981. Chairman, United Way of the Desert, 1975. *Member:* Desert Bar Association (Member, Board of Trustees, 1978-1980); The State Bar of California; California Attorneys for Criminal Justice; California Public Defender's Association. [HM2, U.S. Navy, 1954-1957]. **PRACTICE AREAS:** Criminal Defense; Writs and Appeals; Drunk Driving Defense.

REFERENCE: El Dorado Bank.

## WELEBIR & McCUNE

A PROFESSIONAL LAW CORPORATION

INDIO, CALIFORNIA

(See Redlands)

*Practice limited to Catastrophic Personal Injury and Wrongful Death, Products Liability, Aviation, Railroad and Toxic Torts. Class Actions related to Defective Products and Mass Torts.*

## JOHN CLARK BROWN, JR.

Established in 1982
407 EAST FLORENCE AVENUE
INGLEWOOD, CALIFORNIA 90301
Telephone: 310-419-2214

*Real Estate, Business and Bankruptcy Litigation and Trial Practice in all Courts.*

**JOHN CLARK BROWN, JR.,** born Montclair, New Jersey, August 11, 1943; admitted to bar, 1971, California and U.S. District Court, Central District of California; 1980, U.S. Court of Appeals, Ninth Circuit. *Education:* Stanford University (B.A., 1966); University of California School of Law at Los Angeles (J.D., 1971). Author: "To Sue or Not to Sue, Which is the More Profitable Question?" Los Angeles Business Journal, 1982; "Are Housing Caps 'Necessary' " California Lawyer, February, 1989; "Gimme a Break (From the Full Credit Bid)," CTA Newsletter, Fall, 1995; "Lets Outlaw The Full Credit Bed Rule", CTA Newsletter, Winter, 1996; "How Much Should Lenders Credit Bid at Foreclosure Sales,? CTA Newsletter, Spring, 1996. Instructor: Arbitration, Fall, 1981 and Damages, Winter, 1983, Spring, 1985, Trial Preparation, Winter, 1986, Breach of Contract Remedies, Fall, 1987, California Continuing Education of the Bar, Program for Legal Paraprofessionals, 1980, University of Southern California School of Law. Law Clerk to Honorable James A. Cobey, Associate Justice, California Court of Appeal, 1971-1972. Arbitrator, Los Angeles Superior Court. Member, Panel of Arbitrators, American Arbitration Association. *Member:* Los Angeles County (Member, Sections on: Trial; Real Estate Law; Member, Committees on: Legal Services, 1982-1984; Legislative Activity, 1982-1983; Public Counsel, 1983-1984) and American (Member, Section on Litigation) Bar Associations; The State Bar of California (Member, Sections on Litigation and Real Estate); Association of Business Trial Lawyers.

REPRESENTATIVE CLIENTS: Home Savings of America; Federal Home Loan Mortgage Corp.; Glendale Federal Bank; First Independent Trust Deed Services; Calwide Trust Deed Services, Inc.; Torrance Bank; Norwest Mortgage Corporation; Kinetics Technology International Corp.; Carlisle Realty Holdings, Ltd.; Barristers Executive Suites, Inc.; Nationwide Title Clearing Inc.; National Enterprises, Inc.

## ALBRECHT & BARNEY

1 PARK PLAZA, SUITE 300
IRVINE, CALIFORNIA 92614
Telephone: 714-263-1040
Fax: 714-263-1099

*Estate and Gift Tax Law, Estate Planning, Trust and Estate Administration, Asset Protection Planning.*

*FIRM PROFILE: The firm practices exclusively in the following areas: estate planning, including wills, living trusts, irrevocable trusts, charitable remainder and charitable lead trusts, insurance trusts, asset protection planning, international estate planning, trust and estate administration and estate and gift tax audits and appeals.*

**RICHARD J. ALBRECHT,** born St. Paul, Minnesota, 1948; admitted to bar, 1973, Minnesota; 1974, California; 1977, U.S. Tax Court. *Education:* University of Minnesota (B.S., 1970; J.D., 1973); New York University (LL.M. in Taxation, 1974). Author: Application of The Active Business Requirement to the Tax-Free Spin-Off of Corporate Real Estate, Pepperdine Law Review; IRS Concedes Personal Holding Company Issue, and Section 333; Problems and Practical Solutions, Orange County Bar Journal. Instructor, U.S.C. Graduate Tax Program. Adjunct Professor of Law, American College of Law and Irvine University College of Law. Former Chairman, Taxation Section of the Orange County Bar Association. Lecturer: California Education for the Bar (CEB) for the Following: Estate Planning for Owners of Closely-Held Businesses", "Advising Real Estate Investors", "Taxation For The General Practitioner and Non- Tax Specialist". Given the Following Seminars for the Center for Professional Education (CPE): "Asset Protection Techniques for Today's Litigious Society" and "Limited Liability Companies: Current & Future Uses". **PRACTICE AREAS:** Estate and Gift Tax Law; Estate and Business Planning; Asset Protection Planning.

**COLLEEN BARNEY,** born Jamaica, New York, 1966; admitted to bar, 1993, California. *Education:* Central Michigan University (B.S., magna cum laude, 1990); University of Michigan (J.D., 1993); University of San Diego (LL.M., in Taxation, cum laude, 1994). **PRACTICE AREAS:** Estate and Gift Tax Law; Estate Planning; Tax Law; Trust and Estate Administration.

ASSOCIATE

**COMMIE STEVENS,** born Orange, California, 1970; admitted to bar, 1996, California. *Education:* University of California at Irvine (B.A., 1992); Pepperdine University (J.D., cum laude, 1995). **PRACTICE AREAS:** Estate and Gift Tax Law; Estate Planning; Trust and Estate Administration.

## ALDRICH & BONNEFIN, P.L.C.

18200 VON KARMAN AVENUE, SUITE 730
P.O. BOX 19686
IRVINE, CALIFORNIA 92623
Telephone: 714-474-1944
Telecopier: 714-474-0617
Email: 103132.2601@compuserve.com

*Banking, Business and Financial Law.*

*FIRM PROFILE: Aldrich & Bonnefin, A Professional Law Corporation, was founded in 1984 by Mark E. Aldrich. Since its formation, the firm has concentrated on every major aspect of banking law, including regulatory compliance, corporate, environmental, labor and litigation. Our clients include commercial banks, bank holding companies, savings associations, industrial loan companies and other financial institutions. The firm specializes in a "preventive law" approach at cost-effective prices, including an innovative group legal service,*

(This Listing Continued)

the Bankers' Compliance Group, which is currently comprised of over 145 financial institutions throughout California. The law firm is listed in the Bar Register of Preeminent lawyers.

**MARK E. ALDRICH,** born Whittier, California, October 20, 1953; admitted to bar, 1979, California and U.S. District Court, Central District of California. *Education:* University of Notre Dame; Loyola University of Los Angeles (B.A., cum laude, 1975); University of Southern California (J.D., 1979). Pi Gamma Mu; Legion Lex. Speaker and Panelist: Bankers' Compliance Group; California Bankers Association; Robert Morris Associates; Western Independent Bankers Association, 1981—. Formed, Bankers Compliance Group, 160 Member Cooperative Legal Service Group for Banks, 1981. *Member:* Orange County, Los Angeles County and American (Member, Commercial Finances Service Committee, Corporation, Banking and Business Law Section, 1982—) Bar Associations; State Bar of California (Secretary, Financial Institutions Committee, 1995). *PRACTICE AREAS:* Banking; Commercial Code, Articles 3 & 4; Corporate and Securities.

**JANET M. BONNEFIN,** born Lancaster, California, October 12, 1957; admitted to bar, 1982, California; 1983, U.S. Court of Appeals, Ninth Circuit. *Education:* El Camino College (A.A., 1976); California State University at Long Beach (B.A., 1979); Loyola Law School of Los Angeles (J.D., 1982). *Member:* Orange County and American Bar Associations; State Bar of California. *PRACTICE AREAS:* Consumer Financial Services (100%).

**MARK ALAN MOORE,** born Fairfield, California, October 13, 1952; admitted to bar, 1983, California. *Education:* University of California, Irvine (B.A., magna cum laude, 1975); University of Chicago Law School (J.D., 1983). Moot Court. Instructor, 1995 FFIEC Payment Systems Risk Conferences. *Member:* State Bar of California (Member, Consumer Financial Services Committee, 1991-1994). *PRACTICE AREAS:* Consumer Financial Services; Financial Institutions; Payment Systems; Computer Law.

**DAVID BUSTAMANTE,** born El Paso, Texas, November 9, 1955; admitted to bar, 1980, California. *Education:* United States International University; Whittier College (B.A., 1977); Loyola University of Los Angeles (J.D., 1980). *Member:* State Bar of California. *PRACTICE AREAS:* Litigation; Regulatory Compliance - Operations; Negotiable Instruments; Contracts; Writs and Attachments (20%).

---

**ERIC G. BARON,** born Pasadena, California, February 19, 1951; admitted to bar, 1987, California; 1991, U.S. District Court, Northern, Eastern, Central and Southern Districts of California. *Education:* Georgetown University (B.S.F.S., 1973); American Graduate School of International Management (M.I.M., with distinction, 1979); Georgetown University (J.D., magna cum laude, 1987). Order of the Coif. Certified Public Accountant, Washington, D.C., 1984. Member, The Tax Lawyer, 1985-1986. *Member:* State Bar of California. *LANGUAGES:* German and Hebrew. *PRACTICE AREAS:* Commercial Transactions; Real Estate Transactions; Documentary and Standby Letters of Credit; Environmental Law; Litigation.

**KEITH R. FORRESTER,** born Neptune, New Jersey, November 25, 1961; admitted to bar, 1987, California; 1988, New Jersey and U.S. District Court, District of New Jersey; 1992, U.S. District Court, Central District of California; 1993, U.S. District Court, Southern District of California. *Education:* Villanova University (B.A., 1984); Pepperdine University (J.D., 1987). Co-Author: "Basic Real Estate Law in New Jersey", National Business Institute, 1992. Member, Real Estate and Business Law Sections, Orange County Bar Association, 1992. *Member:* State Bar of California. *PRACTICE AREAS:* Commercial Litigation; Writs and Attachments; Commercial Transactions; Loan Workouts; Bank Regulatory Compliance; Negotiable Instruments.

**ANNE M. MCEACHRAN,** born Inglewood, California, February 23, 1966; admitted to bar, 1993, California. *Education:* California State University at Long Beach (B.S., 1989); Whittier College School of Law (J.D., 1993). *Member:* State Bar of California.

**KRISTEN WELLES LANHAM,** born Lubbock, Texas, May 27, 1967; admitted to bar, 1992, California, U.S. District Court, Central District of California and U.S. Court of Appeals, Ninth Circuit. *Education:* University of California, Davis (B.A., 1988); Whittier College School of Law (J.D., 1991). Phi Delta Phi. *Member:* Orange County and American Bar Associations; State Bar of California. *LANGUAGES:* Spanish. *PRACTICE AREAS:* Corporate Banking; Business Litigation.

**ROBERT K. OLSEN,** born Chicago, Illinois, June 8, 1958; admitted to bar, 1983, California; 1990, District of Columbia. *Education:* University of California, Irvine (B.A., magna cum laude, 1980); University of California, Los Angeles (J.D., 1983). Phi Beta Kappa. Order of the Coif. Faculty, University of California Extension, 1991-1992. *Member:* Orange County Bar Association; The State Bar of California. *PRACTICE AREAS:* Banking.

REPRESENTATIVE CLIENTS: Bankers Compliance Group; Alliance Bank; American River Bank; Bank Leumi Le Israel, B.M.; Brentwood Bank of California; California Commerce Bank; California Korea Bank; Fallwood National Bank; High Desert National Bank; State Bank of India (California); Valley Independent Bank; Valliwide Bank.
REFERENCES: S. Suresh Kumar, President, Brentwood Bank of California; Donald G. Stebbins, CEO, High Desert National Bank; Curtis Reis, President, Alliance Bank; William Young, CEO, American River Bank.

---

## ALLEN, MATKINS, LECK, GAMBLE & MALLORY LLP

A Limited Liability Partnership including Professional Corporations

Established in 1977

*FOURTH FLOOR, 18400 VON KARMAN*
**IRVINE, CALIFORNIA 92715**
*Telephone: 714-553-1313*
*Telecopier: 714-553-8354*

*Los Angeles, California Office:* Seventh Floor, 515 South Figueroa Street, 90071. Telephone: 213-622-5555. Telecopier: 213-620-8816.
*San Diego, California Office:* 501 West Broadway, Suite 900, 92101. Telephone: 619-233-1155. Facsimile: 619-233-1158.
*West Los Angeles, California Office:* 1999 Avenue of the Stars, 90067. Telephone: 310-788-2400. Fax: 310-788-2410.

*General Civil, Trial and Appellate Practice in all State and Federal Courts. Real Property and Construction Law. Land Use and Environmental Law, including Administrative and Regulatory Practice. Corporations, Securities, Partnerships and Public Bond Financings. Federal, State and Local Taxation. Labor and Employment Law (Management) and Wrongful Termination. Bankruptcy, Creditors Rights, Receiverships and Restructuring. Estate Planning and Trusts.*

*FIRM PROFILE: Allen, Matkins, Leck, Gamble & Mallory LLP is recognized as one of the premier commercial real estate, business and finance law firms in the United States, providing legal services in connection with complex projects including high-rise office buildings, industrial parks, shopping centers, planned communities, mixed-use developments, hotels and resorts. In addition to its real estate practice, the firm has a pre-eminent business practice centered on business litigation, corporate, tax, environmental, bankruptcy and creditors' rights and labor departments.*

*Allen, Matkins has offices in downtown Los Angeles, West Los Angeles, Orange County and San Diego and enjoys a prestigious regional, national and international clientele. The firm is committed to the highest standards of professional excellence in the delivery of legal services.*

### PARTNERS

**JOHN C. GAMBLE,** born Los Angeles, California, September 16, 1945; admitted to bar, 1971, California. *Education:* Stanford University (B.A., 1967); Loyola University of Los Angeles (J.D., 1971). Member, St. Thomas More Law Honor Society. Member, Loyola University of Los Angeles Law Review, 1969-1970. *Member:* Los Angeles County, Orange County and American Bar Associations; State Bar of California. (Resident). *PRACTICE AREAS:* Real Estate.

**THOMAS C. FOSTER,** born Santa Monica, California, October 17, 1948; admitted to bar, 1975, California; 1977, U.S. Tax Court. *Education:* University of Southern California (B.S., 1970; J.D., 1975). Certified Public Accountant, California, 1976. *Member:* Los Angeles County, Orange County and American Bar Associations; State Bar of California. (Resident). *PRACTICE AREAS:* Tax; Partnerships; General Corporate.

**R. MICHAEL JOYCE,** born Los Angeles, California, December 13, 1951; admitted to bar, 1977, California; 1978, U.S. District Court, Central District of California; 1979, U.S. Court of Appeals, Ninth Circuit. *Education:* Princeton University (A.B., 1974); University of Southern California (J.D., 1977). Order of the Coif. Panelist, CEB Programs on Real Property Remedies, 1984. Moderator, CEB Program on Real Property Leases, 1984. *Member:* Orange County and American Bar Associations; State Bar of California. (Resident). *PRACTICE AREAS:* Real Estate.

**LAWRENCE D. LEWIS, (P.C.),** born Los Angeles, California, February 25, 1946; admitted to bar, 1972, California; U.S. District Court, Central, Southern, Northern and Eastern Districts of California; U.S. Court of Appeals, Ninth Circuit; U.S. Supreme Court. *Education:* University of California at Berkeley (A.B., 1968); Boalt Hall School of Law, University of

*(This Listing Continued)*

## ALLEN, MATKINS, LECK, GAMBLE & MALLORY LLP, Irvine—Continued

California (J.D., 1972). Phi Beta Kappa. *Member:* Orange County, San Diego County and American Bar Associations; State Bar of California. (Resident). **PRACTICE AREAS:** Litigation.

**MONICA E. OLSON,** born Redwood City, California, October 30, 1954; admitted to bar, 1980, California. *Education:* University of California at Los Angeles (B.A., magna cum laude, 1976; J.D., 1980). *Member:* Orange County and American Bar Associations; State Bar of California. (Resident). **PRACTICE AREAS:** Real Estate.

**THOMAS E. GIBBS,** born Munich, Germany, September 8, 1955; admitted to bar, 1980, California and U.S. District Court, Central and Southern Districts of California. *Education:* University of California at Irvine (B.A., summa cum laude, 1977); University of California at Los Angeles (J.D., 1980). Phi Beta Kappa; Order of the Coif. Comments Editor, Federal Communications Law Journal, 1979-1980. *Member:* Orange County and American Bar Associations; State Bar of California. (Resident). **PRACTICE AREAS:** Litigation.

**DWIGHT L. ARMSTRONG,** born Lancaster, Pennsylvania, July 11, 1952; admitted to bar, 1977, California. *Education:* Stanford University (B.A., with departmental honors, 1974); University of Southern California (J.D., 1977). Member, 1975-1977 and Articles Editor, 1976-1977, Southern California Law Review. Author: Note, "Products Liability, Comparative Negligence and the Allocation of Damages Among Multiple Defendants," 50 Southern California Law Review, 73, 1976. Law Clerk to Hon. E. Avery Crary, U.S. District Court, Central District of California, 1977-1978. Panelist, American bar Association, General Practice Section 1995 Spring Meeting, "Complying with the Americans with Disabilities Act: The Employer's Perspective." Guest Lecturer, University of California, Irvine Extension, Human Resources Certificate Program, 1995. Author: "Take it Lying Down (Liability for Misrepresentation)," The Los Angeles Daily Journal, July 18, 1996; "Stereotyping Dress Codes in Tatters," The National Law Journal, January 16, 1995. Speaker: American Electronics Association, "Steps to Prevent Wrongful Termination Lawsuits," November 7, 1996; Council on Education in Management, "Managing Mangers (and Providing the 10 Top Legal Problems they can cause)," July 18, 1996; National Human Resources Association, Orange County Affiliate, "Current Issues involving Sexual Harassment Claims," 1994. Arbitration Panel Member under National Rules for the Resolution of Employment Disputes (American Arbitration Association). *Member:* Orange County (Former Chair, Labor Law Section) and American (Member, Section on Labor and Employment Law) Bar Associations; State Bar of California (Labor and Employment Law Section). (Resident). **PRACTICE AREAS:** Labor and Employment Law (Management).

**PAUL D. O'CONNOR,** born Columbus, Ohio, September 19, 1955; admitted to bar, 1980, California. *Education:* California State University at Fullerton (B.S., 1977); Loyola University of Los Angeles (J.D., cum laude, 1980); New York University (LL.M., 1981). Law Clerk to Senior Judge William M. Drennan, U.S. Tax Court, 1981-1983. *Member:* Los Angeles County, Orange County and American Bar Associations; State Bar of California. (Resident). **PRACTICE AREAS:** Business Organization and Tax Planning.

**S. LEE HANCOCK,** born Knoxville, Tennessee, August 11, 1955; admitted to bar, 1979, Missouri; 1982, U.S. Tax Court; 1983, U.S. Claims Court; 1988, California. *Education:* Southwest Missouri State University (B.S., summa cum laude, 1975); Southern Methodist University (J.D., cum laude, 1979). Phi Delta Phi; Order of the Coif. Associate Editor, Journal of Air Law and Commerce, 1978-1979. Certified Public Accountant, Missouri, 1977. Speaker and Co-Author: National Business Institute on Considerations in Buying or Selling a Business, 1987. Co-Author: "Tax Planning for the Ownership and Operation of General Aviation Aircraft," 45 J. Air L. and Commerce 275, 1979. *Member:* Orange County and American (Member, Section on Business Law) Bar Associations; The Missouri Bar; State Bar of California. (Resident). **PRACTICE AREAS:** Securities; Corporate.

**RICHARD E. STINEHART,** born Los Angeles, California, August 5, 1956; admitted to bar, 1982, California, U.S. District Court, Central District of California and U.S. Court of Appeals, Ninth Circuit. *Education:* University of California at Irvine (B.A., magna cum laude, 1978); University of Southern California (J.D., 1982). Phi Beta Kappa; Order of the Coif. *Member:* Los Angeles County, Orange County and American Bar Associations; State Bar of California. (Resident). **PRACTICE AREAS:** Real Estate.

**STEPHEN R. THAMES,** born Escondido, California, July 18, 1956; admitted to bar, 1982, California. *Education:* University of California at Davis (B.A., cum laude, 1978); University of California at Los Angeles (J.D., 1982). Member, Moot Court Honor Society. *Member:* Los Angeles County, Orange County and American Bar Associations; State Bar of California. (Resident). **PRACTICE AREAS:** Litigation.

**ANNE E. KLOKOW,** born Boston, Massachusetts, May 26, 1954; admitted to bar, 1980, California, U.S. District Court, Central District of California and U.S. Court of Appeals, Ninth Circuit. *Education:* University of California at Santa Barbara (B.A., summa cum laude, 1976); University of Southern California (J.D., 1980). *Member:* Orange County Bar Association; State Bar of California. (Resident). **PRACTICE AREAS:** Real Estate.

**DAVID W. WENSLEY,** born Holyoke, Massachusetts, February 20, 1958; admitted to bar, 1984, California. *Education:* University of Southern California (B.S., cum laude, 1981); Hastings College of the Law, University of California (J.D., cum laude, 1984). Beta Gamma Sigma; Phi Delta Phi. Member, Thurston Society. *Member:* American Bar Association; State Bar of California (Member, Real Property Law Section); International Council of Shopping Centers; Institute of Real Estate Management; Commercial Industrial Developers Association. (Resident). **PRACTICE AREAS:** Real Estate; Environmental Law.

**GARY S. MCKITTERICK,** born Mexico, Missouri, December 20, 1958; admitted to bar, 1984, California. *Education:* Stanford University (A.B., 1981); Loyola University of Los Angeles (J.D., 1984). Author, "Organizing and Planning the Project," Chapter 415, Volume 12, California Real Estate Law and Practice (Matthew Bender). *Member:* Orange County (Member, Construction Section) and American (Member, Forum Committee on the Construction Industry) Bar Associations; State Bar of California (Member, Real Property Section); International Council of Shopping Centers; National Association of Industrial and Office Properties; Urban Land Institute. (Resident). **PRACTICE AREAS:** Real Estate.

**PATRICK J. GRADY,** born White Plains, New York, April 28, 1959; admitted to bar, 1984, California and U.S. Court of Appeals, Ninth Circuit; 1989, U.S. Supreme Court. *Education:* California State University, Long Beach (B.S., with great distinction, 1981) Beta Gamma Sigma; University of Southern California (J.D., 1984). *Member:* Orange County (Member, Labor Law Section) and American Bar Associations; State Bar of California (Member, Labor Law Section). (Resident). **PRACTICE AREAS:** Labor (Management).

**ROBERT M. HAMILTON,** born Inglewood, California, April 11, 1959; admitted to bar, 1984, California. *Education:* University of Southern California (B.S., magna cum laude, 1981); Loyola University of Los Angeles (J.D., 1984); New York University (LL.M. in Taxation, 1985). Beta Gamma Sigma; Beta Alpha Psi. Editor, Loyola of Los Angeles International and Comparative Law Journal, 1983-1984. Law Clerk to Hon. Jules G. Korner, III, U.S. Tax Court, 1985-1987. *Member:* Los Angeles County, Orange County and American Bar Associations; State Bar of California. (Resident). **PRACTICE AREAS:** Business Organizations; Tax Planning.

**VINCENT M. COSCINO,** born Chicago, Illinois, September 6, 1960; admitted to bar, 1985, California; U.S. District Court, Central, Eastern, Northern and Southern Districts of California and U.S. Court of Appeals, Ninth Circuit. *Education:* Occidental College (B.A., 1982); University of San Diego (J.D., 1985). Author of three-Part Series entitled: "So You Always Wanted a Chapter 11 Practice...A Road Map Through The Reorganization Process," Orange County Bar Association, Commercial Law and Bankruptcy Section, 1996. Co-Author: "Relief from Stay: A Survey of Judicial Practice," California Bankruptcy Forum Conference, 1994. Panelist: CEB February 1995 "Taking and Enforcing Security Interests in Personal Property." Director, Orange County Bankruptcy Court, Central District of California. *Member:* San Diego County, Orange County and American Bar Associations; State Bar of California; San Diego, Orange County and Los Angeles and Inland Empire Bankruptcy Forums; Financial Lawyers Conference; American Bankruptcy Institute. **PRACTICE AREAS:** Bankruptcy Law; Insolvency Law; Commercial Law.

### RESIDENT ASSOCIATES

**BRADLEY N. SCHWEITZER,** born San Jose, California, May 18, 1957; admitted to bar, 1987, California. *Education:* University of California at Los Angeles (B.A., 1979); Loyola University of Los Angeles (J.D., cum laude, 1986). Member, St. Thomas More Law Honor Society. *Member:* State Bar of California. **PRACTICE AREAS:** Real Estate.

**ALAN J. GORDEE,** born Boston, Massachusetts, January 5, 1961; admitted to bar, 1987, California; 1988, U.S. District Court, Central District of California; 1989, U.S. Court of Appeals, Ninth Circuit; 1992, U.S. Dis-

*(This Listing Continued)*

trict Court, Southern District of California; 1993, Massachusetts. *Education:* Yale University (B.A., 1983); Boston University (J.D., cum laude, 1987). Associate Editor, American Journal of Law and Medicine, 1985-1987. *Member:* Orange County and American Bar Associations; State Bar of California. **PRACTICE AREAS:** Litigation.

**PAMELA L. ANDES,** born Anaheim, California, June 25, 1963; admitted to bar, 1988, California. *Education:* University of Southern California (B.S., magna cum laude, 1985); Loyola University of Los Angeles (J.D., magna cum laude, 1988). Member: Order of the Coif; St. Thomas More Law Honor Society. Member: 1986-1988, Executive Editor, 1987-1988, Loyola of Los Angeles Law Review. *Member:* State Bar of California. **PRACTICE AREAS:** Real Estate and Environmental.

**CATHERINE M. PAGE,** born Kirkbymoorside, England, March 22, 1957; admitted to bar, 1990, California. *Education:* University of Hull, England (B.Sc., with honors, 1978); University of Toledo (J.D., summa cum laude, 1990). Order of the Coif. Member, 1988-1990 and Editor-in-Chief, 1989-1990, University of Toledo Law Review. Author: Note, "United States v. Kozminski: Involuntary Servitude - A Standard at Last," 20 University of Toledo Law Review 1023 (1989). *Member:* Orange County and American Bar Associations; State Bar of California. **PRACTICE AREAS:** Litigation.

**LESLIE TUCKER FISCHER,** born Durham, North Carolina, July 15, 1965; admitted to bar, 1990, California. *Education:* Stanford University (A.B., 1987); University of California School of Law, Los Angeles (J.D., 1990). *Member:* Orange County and American Bar Associations; State Bar of California. **PRACTICE AREAS:** Corporate Securities; General Corporate.

**RALPH H. WINTER,** born Santa Monica, California, March 3, 1962; admitted to bar, 1991, California. *Education:* Santa Clara University (B.S.C., 1984); Notre Dame University (J.D., cum laude, 1991); The Concannon Programme of International Law, Notre Dame University, London, England (1990). Articles Editor, Notre Dame Journal of Law, Ethics and Public Policy, 1990-1991. Certified Public Accountant, California, 1987. *Member:* Orange County and American Bar Associations; State Bar of California. **PRACTICE AREAS:** Corporate; Tax.

**MICHAEL S. GREGER,** born Lynwood, California, January 27, 1966; admitted to bar, 1991, California, U.S. District Court, Central, Eastern and Southern Districts of California and U.S. Court of Appeals, Ninth Circuit. *Education:* California State University at Fullerton (B.A., 1988); Southwestern University School of Law (J.D., magna cum laude, 1991). Articles Editor, Southwestern University Law Review, 1990-1991. Southwestern Moot Court Honors Program, 1989-1990. Author: "Preliminary Questions of Fact for the Judge: The Standard of Proof for Pretrial Admissibility Problems," 20 Southwestern L. Rev. 453 (1991). *Member:* Orange County and American Bar Associations; State Bar of California. **PRACTICE AREAS:** Litigation; Bankruptcy.

**A. KRISTINE FLOYD,** born Sacramento, California, March 31, 1966; admitted to bar, 1991, California. *Education:* University of Southern California (B.A., magna cum laude, 1988); Duke University (J.D., with high honors, 1991). Phi Beta Kappa. *Member:* Orange County Bar Association; State Bar of California. **PRACTICE AREAS:** Litigation.

**STEPHEN J. KEPLER,** born Palo Alto, California, September 16, 1965; admitted to bar, 1991, California. *Education:* University of California at Los Angeles (B.A., 1987); Boalt Hall School of Law, University of California at Berkeley (J.D., 1991). Recipient: Jurisprudence Award in Contracts. Adjunct Professor, University of California at Irvine, Graduate School of Management, 1995—. Adjunct Professor, Western State Law School, 1993-1995. **PRACTICE AREAS:** Litigation and Employment Law.

**MICHAEL A. ALVARADO,** born Los Angeles, California, December 30, 1965; admitted to bar, 1992, California. *Education:* University of California at Los Angeles (B.A., 1989); Stanford University (J.D., 1992). *Member:* Orange County Bar Association; State Bar of California. **PRACTICE AREAS:** Real Estate.

**MARY KAY RUCK,** born Massillon, Ohio, October 1, 1965; admitted to bar, 1992, Georgia and U.S. District Court, Northern and Middle Districts of Georgia; 1993, California; U.S. District Court, Central and Southern Districts of California; 1995, Colorado. *Education:* Wittenberg University (B.A., 1987); University of Michigan (J.D., 1992). *Member:* State Bar of Georgia; State Bar of California; Orange County, Colorado and American Bar Associations. **PRACTICE AREAS:** Employment Law.

**SUSAN E. GRAHAM,** born Newport Beach, California, June 27, 1964; admitted to bar, 1989, California. *Education:* University of California, Los

*(This Listing Continued)*

Angeles (B.A. Economics, 1986); Loyola Law School (J.D., 1989). *Member:* Orange County and American Bar Assns.; State Bar of California (Member, Real Property Section). **PRACTICE AREAS:** Real Estate Transactional Practice.

**CHRISTOPHER G. LUND,** born Brooklyn, New York, November 2, 1962; admitted to bar, 1992, California. *Education:* University of Southern California (B.S., 1986); Loyola Law School (J.D., 1992). Certified Public Accountant, California, 1990. *Member:* Los Angeles County and American Bar Associations; State Bar of California. **PRACTICE AREAS:** Real Estate Transactions.

**SALLY S. COSTANZO,** born Philadelphia, Pennsylvania, March 30, 1958; admitted to bar, 1994, California. *Education:* University of California at Santa Cruz (B.A., with highest honors, 1980; Ph.D., 1990); University of California at San Diego (M.A., 1982); University of California at Los Angeles School of Law (J.D., 1994). Law Review. American Jurisprudence Award in Constitutional Law. Author: *"Jury Decision Making in the Capital Penalty Phase: Legal Assumptions, Empirical Findings, and a Research Agenda,"* Law and Human Behavior (1992); *"The Death Penalty: Public Opinions, Supreme Court Decisions, and Juror Perspectives,"* Chapter in Violence and the Law (1994); *"Life or Death Decisions: An Analysis of Capital Jury Decision-Making Under the Special Issues Sentencing Framework,"* Law and Human Behavior (1994); *"Deciding to Take a Life: Capital Juries, Sentencing Instructions, and the Jurisprudenceof Death,"* Journal of Social Issues (1994). **PRACTICE AREAS:** Employment Law.

**ALLISON FONG GREENBERG,** born Los Angeles, California, February 8, 1964; admitted to bar, 1995, California. *Education:* University of California, Los Angeles (B.S.Ch.E., cum laude, 1986); Loyola Law School, Los Angeles (J.D., cum laude, 1995). Order of the Coif. *Member:* State Bar of California. **PRACTICE AREAS:** Real Estate; Environmental.

**JEFFREY MANNISTO,** born Sandusky, Ohio, September 13, 1966; admitted to bar, 1996, California. *Education:* University of Texas (B.B.A., 1989); University of Mississippi (J.D., magna cum laude, 1995); New York University (LL.M. in Taxation, 1996). Certified Public Accountant, Texas, 1991. Phi Kappa Phi. Robert C. Khayat Scholarship Award. Managing Editor, Mississippi Law Journal, 1994-1995. Author: Comment, *Mississippi Limited Liability Companies: Potential Exposure Under Federal and State Securities Laws,* 64 Mississippi Law Journal 173 (1994). *Member:* State Bar of California. **PRACTICE AREAS:** Taxation, Estate Planning and Business Organization.

**TRACY L SILVA,** born Oklahoma City, Oklahoma, May 30, 1963; admitted to bar, 1996, California. *Education:* University of Texas, Austin (B.A., 1986); Southern Methodist University (J.D., cum laude, 1996). Order of the Coif; Phi Delta Phi. Member, 1994-1996 and Articles Editor, 1995-1996, Southern Methodist University Law Review. Author: Comment, "Dial '1-900-Pervert' and Other Statutory Measures That Provide Public Notification of Sex Offenders," 48 Southern Methodist University Law Review 1962 (1995). *Member:* American Bar Association. **PRACTICE AREAS:** Litigation.

---

## ALLEN, ROSS & MOONEY

*A PROFESSIONAL CORPORATION*
2603 MAIN STREET, SUITE 1000
**IRVINE, CALIFORNIA 92614**
Telephone: 714-955-3334
Fax: 714-955-3723

*Civil Litigation, Banking, Business, Real Estate.*

### MEMBERS OF FIRM

**STEPHANIE E. ALLEN,** born Covina, California, June 20, 1954; admitted to bar, 1980, California. *Education:* University of California at Irvine (B.A., 1977); California Western School of Law (J.D., cum laude, 1980). Member, California Western Law Review, 1978-1980. Formerly with the Office of the Comptroller of the Currency. *Member:* Orange County Bar Association. **PRACTICE AREAS:** Banking; Corporate; Mergers and Acquisitions.

**JAMES L. ROSS,** born Cleveland, Ohio, May 1, 1957; admitted to bar, 1982, California. *Education:* University of California at Davis (A.B., with honors, Phi Beta Kappa, 1979); University of Southern California (J.D., 1982). Member, Southern California Law Review, 1980-1981. Author: "Regulation of Campaign Contributions: Maintaining the Integrity of the Political Process Through an Appearance of Fairness," 56 Southern Califor-

*(This Listing Continued)*

**ALLEN, ROSS & MOONEY** *A PROFESSIONAL CORPORATION, Irvine—Continued*

nia Law Review 669, 1983. *Member:* Orange County Bar Association. **PRACTICE AREAS:** Real Estate.

**W. ERNEST MOONEY,** born Chicago, Illinois, September 9, 1953; admitted to bar, 1978, California and U.S. District Court, Central District of California. *Education:* Illinois State University (B.S., with honors, 1975); University of Southern California (J.D., 1978). Finalist, Hale Moot Court Competition, 1977. Member, University of Southern California Moot Court Team, 1978. *Member:* Orange County Bar Association. **PRACTICE AREAS:** Litigation.

---

## ALVARADO, SMITH, VILLA & SANCHEZ

A PROFESSIONAL CORPORATION

IRVINE, CALIFORNIA

(See Newport Beach)

*Sophisticated Business Transactions and Complex Litigation.*

---

## THE AMANTE LAW FIRM

Established in 1994

19800 MACARTHUR BOULEVARD
SUITE 1450
**IRVINE, CALIFORNIA 92715-2442**
Telephone: 714-724-4510
Telecopier: 714-724-4504

*General Civil and Trial Practice in all California State and Federal Courts. Business, Real Estate, Construction, Employment, Homeowner Association, Banking, Mortgage Brokerage, Partnership and Commercial Law. Bankruptcy, Insolvency, Corporate and Partnership Reorganization and Debtor and Creditor Rights Law.*

FIRM PROFILE: *The Amante Law Firm specializes in complex trial practice, including all aspects of trial preparation and pre-trial motions. The Amante Law Firm frequently associates with other firms in preparing for and presenting complex lawsuits at trial, and providing strategic planning and trial consultation for complicated matters.*

**JEROME L. AMANTE,** born Montebello, California, November 16, 1948; admitted to bar, 1983, California; 1984, U.S. District Court, Central, Eastern, Southern and Northern Districts of California and U.S. Court of Appeals, Ninth Circuit. *Education:* University of California at Los Angeles (B.A., 1979); Southwestern University School of Law (J.D., 1982). Phi Alpha Delta (Sammis Chapter); Order of the Barristers. Member, 1980-1981 and Chairman, 1981-1982, and Chairman, Board of Governors, Moot Court Honors Program. Member: Kaufman Securities Moot Court Competition, 1982; American Bar Association National Appellate Advocacy Competition, 1981. *Member:* Los Angeles County, Orange County (Member, Business Litigation and Law Practice Management Sections) and American (Member, Litigation Section) Bar Associations; State Bar of California (Member, Litigation and Law Practice Management Sections); Orange County Trial Lawyers Association. **PRACTICE AREAS:** Business; Real Estate; Construction Litigation; Civil Trial Advocacy; Trial Consultation.

### ASSOCIATES

**CATHERINE STARK SHIEL,** born Phoenix, Arizona, September 4, 1953; admitted to bar, 1979, California and U.S. District Court, Southern and Central Districts of California; 1981, U.S. District Court for the District of Columbia. *Education:* Stanford University (A.B., 1975); Arizona State University (J.D., 1978). Member, 1976-1978 and Managing and Comment Editor, 1977-1978, Arizona State Law Journal. Federal Clerkship, U.S. District Court for the Eastern District of Missouri, James H. Meredith, Chief Judge, 1978-1979. *Member:* State Bar of California. **PRACTICE AREAS:** Civil Litigation; Legal Writing; Trial and Appellate Practice; Bankruptcy Law.

*(This Listing Continued)*

---

### OF COUNSEL

**HEIDI KNAPP LEANDERS,** born Encino, California, June 30, 1955; admitted to bar, 1980, California. *Education:* University of Southern California (B.S., summa cum laude, 1977); University of California at Los Angeles (J.D., magna cum laude, 1980). Member: Bankruptcy Mediation Panel for the Central District of California; Ethics Panel for the U.S. Bankruptcy Courts, Central District. Director, Orange County Bankruptcy Forum. Master, Peter Elliott Inn of Court. *Member:* Orange County (Member: Sections on: Real Estate and Litigation; Client Relations Committee; Commercial Law and Bankruptcy Section; Bankruptcy Forum; Judicial Liaison Committee-Bankruptcy; Bankruptcy Section Liaison to Federal Bar Committee for the Construction of the Orange County Federal Courthouse) and American Bar Associations; State Bar of California. **PRACTICE AREAS:** Bankruptcy-Debtors; Creditors; Creditors Committees; Trustee Representation; Civil and Bankruptcy Litigation.

**JANICE M. PATRONITE,** born Whittier, California, October 18, 1951; admitted to bar, 1976, California, U.S. District Court, Central, Southern and Eastern Districts of California and U.S. Court of Appeals, Ninth Circuit. *Education:* University of California at Santa Barbara (B.A., magna cum laude, 1973); Loyola University (J.D., cum laude, 1976). Member, St. Thomas More Law Honor Society. Member, Loyola Law Review, 1974-1975. Author: "Agreed Boundaries and Boundaries by Acquiescence-The Need for a Straight Line from the Courts," 9 Loyola Law Review 637, 1976. Teaching Fellow, Loyola Law School, 1975-1976. *Member:* Los Angeles County and Orange County Bar Associations; State Bar of California. **PRACTICE AREAS:** Corporate; Business; Real Estate Law; Civil Litigation; Appellate Practice.

REPRESENTATIVE CLIENTS: Advanced Medical Applications, Inc.; Agee & Strawn, C.P.A.; Alliance Real Properties, Inc.; Certified International Corp.; Charles Kober Associates, Inc.; Chenbro America, Inc.; Crown Realty and Development, Inc.; CSP International, Inc.; De-Carbon Australia Pty. Ltd.; Enterprise Systems Consulting; Equipment Technology Co.; Global Computer Technologies, Inc.; Global Data Center, Inc.; Hippe & Arlen Associates, Inc.; Hoffman Sheet Metal; ITD Industries, Inc.; Laser Rite, Inc.; MBA Consultants; Northern Continental Funding, Inc.; Novo Industries, Inc.; Phoneby Co.; Sheppard Construction, Inc.; Southwestern Paving Co.; Strategic Placement Group; Voit Commercial Brokerage, Inc.; Weinraub Enterprises, Inc.; Wholesale Capital Corporation.

---

## ANDRADE & MUZI

MARINE NATIONAL BANK BUILDING
18401 VON KARMAN, SUITE 350
**IRVINE, CALIFORNIA 92715**
Telephone: 714-553-1951
Telecopier: 714-553-0655

*San Diego, California Office:* Tokia Bank Building, 3111 Camino Del Rio North, Suite 1100. Telephone: 619-291-2481.

*Civil Trial and Appellate Practice, Construction Law, Insurance and Surety Litigation, General, Commercial, Civil Litigation, Bankruptcy, Real Estate and Business Law.*

### MEMBERS OF FIRM

**RICHARD B. ANDRADE,** born San Diego, California, May 8, 1951; admitted to bar, 1977, California, U.S. Court of Appeals, Ninth Circuit and U.S. District Court, Northern, Eastern, Central and Southern Districts of California and Federal Bar. *Education:* San Diego State University (B.S., 1973); California Western School of Law (J.D., cum laude, 1977). Legal Counsel for Engineering Contractors Association. Licensed General Engineering Contractor, State of California. *Member:* Los Angeles County, Orange County (Member, Sections on: Construction; Real Property) and American (Member, Sections on: Labor Law Management Committee; Public Contract Law) Bar Associations; State Bar of California (Member, Construction, Labor and Public Works Sections); The Association of Trial Lawyers of America. **PRACTICE AREAS:** Construction Litigation; Maritime Law; Labor Law and Environmental Law.

**ANDREW C. MUZI,** born Salamanca, New York, April 15, 1961; admitted to bar, 1987, California and U.S. Court Appeals, Ninth Circuit; Federal Bar. *Education:* Alfred State College (A.A.S., Acct., 1981); State University of New York at Buffalo (B.S., Bus. Adm., cum laude, 1983); Western State University (J.D., 1987). Certified Public Accountant, California, 1986. Member, Engineering Contractors Association. *Member:* Orange County and American Bar Associations; State Bar of California; California Trial Lawyers Association; The Association of Trial Lawyers of America; Association of Attorneys-Certified Public Accountants. **PRACTICE AREAS:** Construction Litigation; Environmental Law; Business Litigation.

*(This Listing Continued)*

# PROFESSIONAL BIOGRAPHIES

CALIFORNIA—IRVINE

**RONALD G. HOLBERT,** born Portsmouth, Virginia, June 6, 1948; admitted to bar, 1979, California; 1980, Nevada and U.S. District Court, District of Nevada. *Education:* San Diego State University (B.A., 1974); California Western School of Law (J.D., 1977). Author: "Foreclosures and Evictions in California and Nevada," Mortgage Servicers Manual, 1984 Edition. Real Estate Brokers License, California. *Member:* Los Angeles County Bar Association (Member, Real Property and Trust Law Section); State Bar of California; State Bar of Nevada; Nevada Trial Lawyers Association; California Trial Lawyers Association; The Association of Trial Lawyers of America. *PRACTICE AREAS:* Real Estate.

**ABILIO TAVARES, JR.,** born Jersey City, New Jersey, April 21, 1956; admitted to bar, 1982, New York; 1985, U.S. District Court, Northern District of New York; 1988, California; 1990, U.S. District Court, Central District of California and U.S. Court of Appeals, Second and Ninth Circuits. *Education:* Boston University (B.A., magna cum laude with distinction, 1978); Albany Law School of Union University (J.D., 1981). Confidential Judicial Clerk, Hon. Joseph Harris, State of New York, 1982. Member, Editorial Board, Los Angeles Lawyer Magazine. *Member:* Long Beach, Los Angeles County (Member, Sections on: Intellectual Property; Entertainment), New York State (Member, Entertainment Section) and American Bar Associations; State Bar of California. *PRACTICE AREAS:* Contract; Construction; Entertainment; Insurance; Intellectual Property and Tort Litigation.

**SAMUEL G. BROYLES, JR.,** born Battle Mountain, Nevada, May 16, 1961; admitted to bar, 1987, California and U.S. District Court, Northern, Southern and Central Districts of California. *Education:* University of Nevada, Reno (B.S., with high distinction, 1983); University of Santa Clara (J.D., 1987). Phi Kappa Phi. Santa Clara County Superior Court Research Attorney, 1987-1988. *Member:* Los Angeles County and Orange County Bar Associations; State Bar of California. *PRACTICE AREAS:* Business Litigation; Mobile Home Park Litigation; Construction Litigation; Real Estate Litigation; Certain Transactional Matters.

**FRANK A. SATALINO,** born Syracuse, New York, December 30, 1963; admitted to bar, 1989, California; 1990, U.S. District Court, Southern and Central Districts of California and U.S. Court of Appeals, Ninth Circuit. *Education:* State University of New York at Oswego (B.A., 1986); Hastings College of Law, University of California (J.D., 1989). Phi Delta Phi. Member, Hastings Constitutional Law Quarterly. *Member:* Los Angeles County, Orange County and American Bar Associations; State Bar of California. *PRACTICE AREAS:* Construction Claims; Mechanic's Liens; Public and Private Projects; Construction Defect Actions; Insurance Litigation.

## OF COUNSEL

**KURT KUPFERMAN,** born 1922; admitted to bar, 1986, California. *Education:* New Jersey Institute of Technology (B.S., 1950; M.S. 1956); Western State University (J.D., 1975). *Member:* Orange County/Harbor Bar Association; State Bar of California; California Trial Lawyers; Orange County Trial Lawyers. *LANGUAGES:* German. *PRACTICE AREAS:* Criminal Law; Family Law; Business Law.

REPRESENTATIVE CLIENTS: American International Cos.; American Home Assurance; Insurance Company of North America (INA); National Union Fire Insurance of Pittsburgh, PA; Aetna Insurance Co.; Fremont Insurance Co.; Maryland Casualty; Commercial Union Insurance Co.; Superior National Insurance Co.; Fireman's Fund; CIGNA; Advanco Constructors, Inc.; Capitan Enterprises, Inc.; Gentosi Brothers, Inc.; R.D. Olson Construction; Griffith Company; Mladen Buntich Construction Co.; Steve Bubalo Construction; Veco International.

## ARTER & HADDEN

**FIVE PARK PLAZA, 10TH FLOOR, JAMBOREE CENTER**
**IRVINE, CALIFORNIA 92714**
*Telephone: 714-252-7500*
*Facsimile: 714-833-9604*

**REVISERS OF THE OHIO LAW DIGEST FOR THIS DIRECTORY.**

*In Cleveland, Ohio:* 1100 Huntington Building, 925 Euclid Avenue. Telephone: 216-696-1100. Fax: 216-696-2645.
*In Columbus, Ohio:* 21st Floor, One Columbus, 10 West Broad Street. Telephone: 614-221-3155. Fax: 614-221-0479.
*In Washington, D.C.:* 1801 K Street, N.W., Suite 400K. Telephone: 202-775-7100. Fax: 202-857-0172.
*In Dallas, Texas:* 1717 Main Street, Suite 4100. Telephone: 214-761-2100. Fax: 214-741-7139.
*In Los Angeles, California:* 700 South Flower Street, 30th Floor. Telephone: 213-629-9300. Fax: 213-617-9255.

*(This Listing Continued)*

*In Austin, Texas:* 100 Congress Avenue, Suite 1800. Telephone: 512-479-6403. Fax: 512-469-5505.
*In San Antonio, Texas:* 7710 Jones Maltsberger, Harte-Hanks Tower, Suite 540. Telephone: 210-805-8497. Fax: 210-805-8519.
*In San Francisco, California:* 201 California Street, 14th Floor, 94111. Telephone: 415-912-3600. Fax: 415-912-3636.
*In San Diego, California:* 402 West Broadway, Fourth Floor, 92101. Telephone: 619-238-0001. Fax: 619-238-8333.
*In Woodland Hills, California:* 5959 Topanga Canyon Boulevard, Suite 244, 91367. Telephone: 818-712-0036. Fax: 818-346-6502.

*General Civil and Trial Practice. Antitrust, Banking, Corporation, Corporate Financing, Creditors' Rights, Estate Planning, Trust, Probate, Government Contract, International Business, Labor and Employment, Oil and Gas, Products Liability, Negligence, Admiralty, Maritime, Workers Compensation, Public Utility, General Real Estate, Finance, Securities and Taxation Law.*

## MEMBERS OF FIRM

**JACK W. FLEMING,** born Lakewood, Ohio, May 18, 1950; admitted to bar, 1975, Virginia; 1976, U.S. Court of Federal Claims; 1979, District of Columbia and California. *Education:* University of Michigan (B.S.I.E., magna cum laude, 1972); Cornell University (J.D., 1975). Tau Beta Pi. Author: "Bid Protests on California Public Works Projects," Construction Law Manual, Vol. III, AGC of California, 1990; "Coping With the New AIA A201: A Challenge for Contractors," Construction Law Manual Vol. III, AGC of California, 1988; "Recent Developments Concerning the Liability of Architects and Engineers," Construction Law Manual Vol. II, AGC of California, 1986; "A Guide to the Use of Computers in Litigation to Estimate Damages in Complex Litigation," 2 Computer Law Journal 863, Fall 1980; "Calculating Damages in Complex Litigation," Legal Times of Washington, November, 1979. Co-author: "Cardinal Changes," Construction Change Order Claims, Wiley Law Publications, 1994; "Bid Protest Suits in Federal Courts," Briefing Paper, Federal Publications, Inc., April 1983. Chairman, Legal Advisory Committee, AGC of California, 1989. *Member:* District of Columbia Bar; Virginia State Bar; State Bar of California; Los Angeles County (Member: Real Property Section; Construction Law Subsection), Orange County (Member, Construction Law Subsection) and American (Member, Public Contract Law Section) Bar Associations. *PRACTICE AREAS:* Construction Law; Public Contract Law; Business Litigation.

**BRUCE G. HOLDEN,** born Grand Rapids, Michigan, May 5, 1951; admitted to bar, 1981, California and U.S. District Court, Central District of California; 1986, U.S. Tax Court. *Education:* University of Michigan (B.S., 1973; M.S., 1974); Pepperdine University (J.D., 1981). Alpha Pi Mu. *Member:* State Bar of California. *PRACTICE AREAS:* Finance; Corporate Law; Real Estate Law. *Email:* BHolden@arterhadden.com

**CURTISS L. ISLER,** born Warren, Ohio, June 11, 1945; admitted to bar, 1975, Ohio; 1990, California. *Education:* Miami University (A.B., 1967); Ohio State University (J.D., summa cum laude, 1975). Associate Editor, Ohio State Law Journal, 1974-1975. Order of the Coif. *Member:* Ohio State and American Bar Associations; State Bar of California; National Association of Railroad Trial Counsel; Federation of Insurance and Corporate Counsel; Cleveland Association of Civil Trial Attorneys (President, 1984-1985); Defense Research Institute. *Email:* CIsler@arterhadden.com

**RANDOLF W. KATZ,** born New York, New York, November 5, 1953; admitted to bar, 1979, California. *Education:* Northwestern University; University of California at Berkeley (A.B., 1975); University of California at Los Angeles (J.D., 1978). *Member:* American Bar Association. *PRACTICE AREAS:* Corporate Law; Securities Law. *Email:* RKatz@arterhadden.com

**STEPHEN H. LACOUNT,** born Brockton, Massachusetts, September 2, 1950; admitted to bar, 1977, New York; 1987, California. *Education:* Boston University (B.A., cum laude, 1972); New York Law School (J.D., 1976); New York University School of Law (LL.M., Trade Regulation, 1979). Author: "Penetrating the Japanese PC Market--An AST Case Study," World Computer Law Congress, Los Angeles, 1991. Faculty, USC Computer Law Institute, Los Angeles, 1991, 1994. Adjunct Faculty, California State University at Fullerton, International Business Law Program, 1992-1966. Co-Chairman, Computer Law Association's 1995 Pacific Rim Computer Law Conference, San Francisco, 1995. Corporate Counsel, AST Computers, 1987-1991. Director, Computer Law Association, 1992—. Chairman, AEA Orange County Software Forum, 1992—. Advisor, Southern California District Export Council of United States Department of Commerce, 1994—. Advisor, University of California Irvine Accelerate Technology SBDC. *Member:* Orange County and New York State Bar Associations; State Bar of California; Computer Law Association; America

*(This Listing Continued)*

CAA299B

## ARTER & HADDEN, Irvine—Continued

Electronics Association (Member, Orange County Executive Council). *PRACTICE AREAS:* Commercial Transactions; Business Law; Computer and Technology; Proprietary Rights; Licensing. *Email:* SLaCount@arterhadden.com

**JOSEPH J. NARDULLI,** born Tustin, California, December 29, 1947; admitted to bar, 1974, California; 1977, U.S. District Court, Central District of California; 1981, U.S. Supreme Court; 1988, U.S. District Court, Southern, Eastern and Northern Districts of California. *Education:* University of California at Los Angeles (B.A., 1970); University of San Diego (J.D., 1973). Phi Delta Phi. *Member:* Orange County Bar Association (Member, Section of Real Property); State Bar of California. *Email:* JNardull@arterhadden.com

**MICHAEL P. RIDLEY,** born Long Beach, California, March 8, 1947; admitted to bar, 1972, California and U.S. District Court, Central District of California; 1973, U.S. District Court, Northern District of California. *Education:* Stanford University (A.B., with great distinction, 1969); Yale University (J.D., 1972). Phi Beta Kappa. Contributing Author: "Pratt's Guide to Venture Capital Sources," Venture Economics, Inc., 1985-1995; "Laymen's Guide to Legal Documentation," 2nd and 3rd Edition, National Association of Small Business Investment Companies. Member, Board of Directors, New Cap Partners, Inc.; Trustee, Stanford University, 1980-1985. *Member:* State Bar of California; American Electronics Association of Orange County; National Association of Small Business Investment Companies; Western Regional Association of Small Business Investment Companies (Secretary). *Email:* MRidley@arterhadden.com

**H. NEAL WELLS III,** born Los Angeles, California, September 10, 1936; admitted to bar, 1962, California; 1971, U.S. Supreme Court; U.S. Tax Court. *Education:* Pomona College and Stanford University (A.B., 1958); Stanford University (J.D., 1961). Trustee, Placentia Library District, 1966-1970. *Member:* Los Angeles County, Orange County and American Bar Associations; The State Bar of California (Co-chairman, Probate Law and Administration Committee, Estate Planning, Trust and Probate Section, 1977-1979; Member, 1979-1985, Vice President, 1982-1983, President, 1983-1984 and Advisor, 1985-1988, Executive Committee, Estate Planning Trust and Probate Section; Member, California Board of Legal Specialization Probate, Estate Planning and Trust Law Advisory Committee, 1989-1991). Fellow, American College of Trust and Estate Counsel. (Certified Specialist, Estate Planning, Trust and Probate, The State Bar of California Board of Legal Specialization). *Email:* HNWells@arterhadden.com

### ASSOCIATES

**RODNEY W. BELL,** born Los Angeles, California, October 23, 1957; admitted to bar, 1986, California; 1987, U.S. District Court, Central District of California; 1991, U.S. Court of Appeals, Ninth Circuit. *Education:* California State University, Northridge (B.A., 1982); Southwestern University School of Law (J.D., 1986). *PRACTICE AREAS:* Business Law; Securities; Commercial Law. *Email:* RBell@arterhadden.com

**MARIE A. CIOTH,** born Milwaukee, Wisconsin, May 15, 1964; admitted to bar, 1991, California, Wisconsin (inactive) and U.S. District Court, Western District of Wisconsin; 1995, New Mexico. *Education:* California State University, Fullerton (B.A., 1987; M.S., Taxation, 1994); University of Wisconsin-Madison (J.D., cum laude, 1990). *Member:* State Bar of California (Member, Taxation Section). *PRACTICE AREAS:* Corporate. *Email:* MCoith@arterhadden.com

**JAMES K. DIERKING,** born Long Beach, California, March 8, 1961; admitted to bar, 1990, California, U.S. District Court, Southern, Central, Eastern and Northern Districts of California and U.S. Court of Appeals, Ninth Circuit; 1991, District of Columbia; 1992, U.S. Claims Court. *Education:* California State University at Fullerton (B.A., with honors, 1984); University of San Diego (M.A., 1988; J.D., 1988); London School of Economics, England (LL.M., 1989). Member: American Friends of the London School of Economics, LSE Club; Convocation Member, University of London, 1989—. Associate Professor of Law and Business, The American College in London, 1994-1995. Foreign Service Intern, U.S. Department of State, Bureau of East Asian and Pacific Affairs, American Embassy, Seoul, South Korea, 1986. *Member:* Orange County, Los Angeles County and American Bar Associations; State Bar of California. *PRACTICE AREAS:* Construction; Commercial Litigation; Complex Contract Disputes; International Business. *Email:* JDierkin@arterhadden.com

**CHRISTINE E. HOWSON,** born Long Beach, California, September 30, 1963; admitted to bar, 1988, California and U.S. District Court, Southern District of California; 1989, U.S. District Court, Central District of California. *Education:* Marquette University (B.A., 1985); McGeorge School of Law, University of the Pacific (J.D., 1988). *Member:* State Bar of California.

**DAVID K. MARION,** born Pompton Plains, New Jersey, March 24, 1965; admitted to bar, 1993, Florida; 1994, District of Columbia; 1995, California. *Education:* Shippensburg University (B.A., 1987); Capital University (J.D., 1991). Phi Alpha Delta. Judicial Extern to: Honorable George C. Smith, U.S. District Court, Southern District of Ohio; Honorable William A. Sweeney, The Supreme Court of Ohio. Associate to W. Vincent Rakestraw, Former Assistant U.S. Attorney General. Assistant General Counsel, Scherer Companies. *Member:* Orange County, Ohio State and American Bar Associations; The Florida Bar; The District of Columbia Bar; State Bar of California. *PRACTICE AREAS:* Commercial Litigation. *Email:* DMarion@arterhadden.com

**MARK T. PALIN,** born Providence, Rhode Island, April 14, 1953; admitted to bar, 1985, Arizona and U.S. Court of Appeals, Ninth Circuit; 1988, California. *Education:* California State University at Fullerton (B.A., 1976); Hastings College of the Law, University of California (J.D., 1985). Senior Research Editor, Board of Editors, Hastings Constitutional Law Quarterly, 1984-1985. Listed in Who's Who International. Author: "Securities Fraud Litigation," Orange County Lawyer, May 1993. *Member:* State Bar of Arizona; State Bar of California; Orange County (Member, Business Litigation Section) and Orange County Federal (President, 1994) Bar Associations. *PRACTICE AREAS:* Business Law; Personal Injury Litigation. *Email:* MPalin@arterhadden.com

**JOSEPH P. QUINBY,** born Palo Alto, California, June 11, 1956; admitted to bar, 1982, California. *Education:* Occidental College (A.B., 1979); University of Santa Clara School of Law (J.D., 1982). Adjunct Professor: Saddleback College Business Science Division (Business Law). *PRACTICE AREAS:* Real Property Litigation; Civil Practice. *Email:* JQuinby@arterhadden.com

**PETER K. RUNDLE,** born Riverside, California, December 30, 1959; admitted to bar, 1985, California; 1986, U.S. District Court, Central District of California and U.S. Court of Appeals, Ninth Circuit; 1988, U.S. District Court, Northern, Eastern and Southern Districts of California. *Education:* University of California at Irvine (B.A., cum laude, 1982); Hastings College of the Law, University of California (J.D., 1985). Phi Beta Kappa. *Member:* Orange County (Member, Resolutions Committee, 1992—; Member/Arbitrator, Mandatory Fee Arbitration Committee, 1993—; Delegate, State Bar Conference, 1993—; Member, Sections on: Financial Services and Institutions, 1993-1995; Business Litigation, 1988-1995; Business Law, 1992-1995) and Los Angeles County (Member, Amicus Briefs Committee, 1988—) Bar Associations; The State Bar of California (Member, Sections on: Litigation, 1990—, Business Law, 1990—, Real Estate, 1995—; Appointed Special Master in Penal Code § 1524 Search Warrant Proceedings, 1991—). *PRACTICE AREAS:* Litigation; Real Estate; Title Insurance. *Email:* PRundle@arterhadden.com

### OF COUNSEL

**HENRY G. KOHLMANN,** born Lincoln, Nebraska, 1939; admitted to bar, 1974, California. *Education:* San Jose State College, San Jose (B.S.E.E., 1971); University of California, Hastings College of the Law (J.D., 1974). Member, U.S. Patent Bar, 1972—. *Email:* HKohlman@arterhadden.com

REVISERS OF THE OHIO LAW DIGEST FOR THIS DIRECTORY.

---

## *AULT, DEUPREY, JONES AND GORMAN*

A Law Partnership including Professional Corporations

*Established in 1978*

**AT&T TOWER**
**8001 IRVINE CENTER DRIVE, SUITE 980**
**IRVINE, CALIFORNIA 92718-2921**
Telephone: 714-450-8345
Facsimile: 714-450-8353

*San Diego, California Office:* 402 West Broadway, 16th Floor. Telephone: 619-544-8300. Fax: 619-338-0017.

*Vista, California Office:* 202 West Vista Way. Telephone: 619-631-1800. Fax: 619-631-1915.

*General Civil and Trial Practice in all State and Federal Courts. Appellate Practice, Family, Negligence, Insurance and Medical and Legal Malpractice Law.*

*(This Listing Continued)*

**FIRM PROFILE:** The law firm of Ault, Deuprey, Jones and Gorman was originally formed in August of 1978 by attorneys with a strong background in defense litigation. Since that time, the primary business of the firm has continued to be in a wide variety of defense litigation, including both third-party and first-party matters.

**THOMAS H. AULT, (INC.),** born San Diego, California, September 22, 1945; admitted to bar, 1972, California. *Education:* California State University at San Diego (B.A., 1968); University of San Diego (J.D., 1972). President, San Diego County Bar Association, 1982. *Member:* Association of Southern California Defense Counsel; Defense Research Institute; Association of Trial Attorneys of America; American Board of Trial Advocates.

**JOSEPH P. PRICE,** born Carbondale, Pennsylvania, September 20, 1958; admitted to bar, 1984, Minnesota; 1987, California and U.S. District Court, Southern District of California. *Education:* University of Scranton (B.S., 1981); Hamline University School of Law (J.D., 1984). *Member:* Minnesota State and American Bar Associations. [Lieut., JAGC, U.S. Navy, 1985-1988]

(For Complete Biographical Data on all Personnel, see Professional Biographies at San Diego, California)

---

## LAW OFFICES OF ROBERT L. BACHMAN

Established in 1986

THE ATRIUM
19100 VON KARMAN AVENUE
SUITE 380
**IRVINE, CALIFORNIA 92715**
Telephone: 714-955-0221
Telecopier: 714-955-0324

Construction Defect, Mechanics Lien, Construction Claims, Bankruptcy, Transactional Matters and Labor Law.

**FIRM PROFILE:** The Law Offices of Robert L. Bachman provides service in the construction industry on all matters related to the construction industry from labor law, licensing, incorporation, transaction work, collections, bankruptcy, mechanic's lien, stop notice and bond claims. In addition, the firm does general business litigation.

**ROBERT L. BACHMAN,** born Los Angeles, California, February 20, 1949; admitted to bar, 1973, California and U.S. District Court, Southern District of California; U.S Supreme Court. *Education:* California State University at Fullerton (B.A., summa cum laude, 1970); University of California at Davis (J.D., 1973). Order of the Coif; Phi Delta Phi (Magister, 1972-1973). Author: "Licensing A Broker Dealer Firm for Real Estate Syndication Purposes," Securities Regulation Law Journal, Spring, 1976. *Member:* Orange County and American Bar Associations. **REPORTED CASES:** Valley Circle Estates v. VTN Corporation.

REPRESENTATIVE CLIENTS: The Austin Co.; Hensel Phelps; Savala Construction; Al Shankle Construction; Steve P. Rados; The Griffith Co.; DSL Transportation Services, Inc.
REFERENCES: DSL Transportation Services, Inc.; Al Shankle Construction.

---

## BAINBRIDGE GROUP

A LAW CORPORATION

18301 VON KARMAN AVENUE, SUITE 410
**IRVINE, CALIFORNIA 92612**
Telephone: 714-442-6600
FAX: 714-442-6609

General Business, Corporate, Partnership and Real Estate, Finance, Mergers and Acquisitions, Strategic Alliances and Technology Licensing.

**MICHAEL E. JOHNSON,** born Orange, California, November 9, 1960; admitted to bar, 1987, California and New York. *Education:* San Diego State University (B.S., Finance, 1983); University of California, Los Angeles (J.D., 1986). President, Associated Students. Recipient, Most Outstanding Student Award. Member, UCLA Law Review. Editor, California Legislative Bulletin, 1992-1994. Author: "California Corporate Securities Law: 1996 Changes and the Continuing Evolution," Business Law News (Summer, 1996). *Member:* Orange County; Technology Law) and American (Member, Negotiated Acquisitions Committee, 1996—; Business Law Section; International Law and Practice Section) Bar Associations; State Bar of California (Member, Corporations Committee, 1993—; Education Com-

*(This Listing Continued)*

---

mittee, 1992-1994, Business Law Section). **PRACTICE AREAS:** Mergers and Acquisitions; Strategic Alliances; Corporate Finance; Technology Licensing. *Email:* mej@ix.netcom.com

**DAVID W. GREENMAN,** born Pittsburgh, Pennsylvania, August 30, 1952; admitted to bar, 1981, Wisconsin; 1984, Texas; 1991, California. *Education:* Colorado State University (B.S., Physical Sciences, 1975); University of Illinois (J.D., with honors, 1981). *Member:* State Bar of California. **PRACTICE AREAS:** Real Estate; Real Estate Finance; Partnerships; General Corporate.

**RANDY MCDONALD,** born San Francisco, California, April 4, 1949; admitted to bar, 1976, Texas and U.S. Court of Appeals, Fifth Circuit; 1978, California; 1981, U.S. District Court, Central District of California; 1982, U.S. Supreme Court and U.S. Court of Appeals, Ninth Circuit; 1987, U.S. District Court, Southern District of California; 1993, U.S. Tax Court; 1995, U.S. District Court, Northern District of California. *Education:* University of California, Los Angeles (B.A., summa cum laude, 1971); Duke University (J.D., 1975). Phi Beta Kappa; Phi Delta Phi. Editor, Duke Law Journal. Arbitrator, American Arbitration Association. *Member:* Orange County (Executive Committee, Real Estate Section, 1990-1992) and American Bar Associations; American Inns of Court. **PRACTICE AREAS:** General Business; Corporate and Partnerships; Real Estate; Real Estate and Corporate Finance; Technology Licensing; Intellectual Property; Strategic Alliances and Technology Transfers; Alternative Dispute Resolution.

**SAMUEL M. HUNG,** born New York, N.Y., March 15, 1960; admitted to bar, 1985, New York (Not admitted in California). *Education:* University of Tennessee (B.A., 1981); University of Chicago (J.D., 1984). Phi Beta Kappa. (Also of Counsel, Eaton & Van Winkle, New York, N.Y.). **LANGUAGES:** Mandarin Chinese and French. **PRACTICE AREAS:** Corporate; Securities.

---

## BAKER, SILBERBERG & KEENER

NEWPORT GATEWAY, SUITE 850
19900 MACARTHUR BOULEVARD
**IRVINE, CALIFORNIA 92612**
Telephone: 714-955-0900
Fax: 714-955-0909

Santa Monica, California Office: Suite 300, 2850 Ocean Park Boulevard. Telephone: 310-399-0900. Fax: 310-399-1644.

General Civil and Business Litigation. Appellate, Professional Malpractice, Insurance Coverage/Bad Faith, Toxic Torts, Personal Injury and Products Liability Law, Architectural & Engineering, Legal Ethics.

A list of Representative Clients will be furnished upon request.

(For biographical data, see Professional Biographies at Santa Monica, California)

---

## BARNES, CROSBY, FITZGERALD & ZEMAN

Established in 1989

2030 MAIN STREET, SUITE 1050
**IRVINE, CALIFORNIA 92614**
Telephone: 714-852-1100
Fax: 714-852-1501

Construction, Labor, Tort and Commercial Law.

**FIRM PROFILE:** Barnes, Crosby, Fitzgerald & Zeman LLP is a commercial law firm serving local, regional and national clients in all areas of business and civil litigation, real estate and labor law.

### MEMBERS OF FIRM

**ROBERT SAMUEL BARNES,** born Anaheim, California, November 2, 1922; admitted to bar, 1950, California. *Education:* Stanford University (LL.B., 1950). Member, Orange County Superior Court Arbitration Panel. *Member:* Orange County (President, 1970-1972) and American (Member and Delegate for Orange County, 1993—) Bar Associations; State Bar of California; American Board of Trial Advocates; American Inns of Courts; Fellows of the American Bar Association; Orange County Bar Foundation (Director, 1980—; President, 1990-1993). **PRACTICE AREAS:** Business Related Matters; Civil Litigation.

**WILLIAM M. CROSBY,** born Pasadena, California, January 26, 1945; admitted to bar, 1971, California; 1974, U.S. District Court, Northern Dis-

*(This Listing Continued)*

## BARNES, CROSBY, FITZGERALD & ZEMAN, Irvine—Continued

trict of California and U.S. Court of Appeals, Ninth Circuit; 1977, U.S. District Court, Central District of California. *Education:* University of California at Berkeley (A.B., cum laude, 1967); Loyola University of Los Angeles (J.D., 1970). Phi Delta Phi; Pi Sigma Alpha. Author: "Presenting the Plaintiffs Case," Wrongful Termination Practice, CEB, 1987. Lecturer, "Wrongful Termination of Employment," CEB, 1986. *Member:* Orange County (Board Member, 1988-1991) and American Bar Associations; State Bar of California (Referee, 1978—); Consumer Attorneys of California; California Employment Lawyers Association (Founder and Board Member, 1986-1994); National Employment Lawyers Association; American Board of Trial Advocates. **PRACTICE AREAS:** Employment Law; Civil Litigation.

**MICHAEL J. FITZGERALD,** born Denver, Colorado, January 4, 1951; admitted to bar, 1976, California and U.S. District Court, Northern District of California; 1980, U.S. District Court, Southern District of California; 1977, U.S. Court of Appeals, Ninth Circuit. *Education:* California State University (B.A., 1973); University of San Francisco (J.D., 1976). *Member:* Orange County Bar Association (Member, Litigation Section, Public Relations); State Bar of California; American Board of Trial Advocacy, Moot Court Judge U.S.F. **PRACTICE AREAS:** Commercial; Business Litigation.

**LARRY S. ZEMAN,** born Chicago, Illinois, July 19, 1950; admitted to bar, 1975, Illinois; 1976, California. *Education:* Miami University, Oxford, Ohio (B.A., cum laude, 1972); Northwestern University, School of Law (J.D., cum laude, 1975). Phi Beta Kappa. Member, Editorial Board of the Journal of Criminal Law and Criminology, 1974-1975. Lecturer, California State University, Long Beach, Department of Finance, Real Estate and Law, 1978-1985. Author: "Mechanic's Lien Abuse vs. The Lis Pendens Solution: A Property Owner's Case for Mechanic's Lien Reform and Practical Suggestions Until That Occurs," California Real Property Law Reporter, Vol. 16 No. 10, (Nov., 1993). *Member:* Orange County (Member, Construction Law and Real Estate Law Sections) and Illinois State Bar Associations; State Bar of California; Orange County Asian American Bar Association. **PRACTICE AREAS:** Real Estate; Construction; Business Litigation; Tort Litigation.

**MARK H. CHEUNG,** born Hong Kong, August 5, 1961; admitted to bar, 1989, Massachusetts; 1990, California. *Education:* Brandeis University (B.A. 1985); Boston College (J.D., 1989). Member and Editor, Boston College Environmental Affairs Law Review, 1987-1989. Author: "Dockominiums: An Expansion of Riparian Rights that Violates the Public Trust Doctrine," 16 Boston College Environmental Affairs Law Review 821, 1989; "Rethinking the History of the Seventeenth-Century Colonial Ordinance: A Reinterpretation of an Ancient Statute," 42 Maine Law Review 115, 1990. *Member:* Orange County, Massachusetts and American Bar Associations; Orange County Asian American Bar Association (President, 1996-1997); State Bar of California. **PRACTICE AREAS:** Real Estate; Construction; Business Litigation; Tort Litigation.

**ALKA N. PATEL,** born India, July 17, 1960; admitted to bar, 1994, California and U.S. District Court, Central District of California. *Education:* California State University at Northridge (B.S. Bus. Adm., 1985); University of Southern California (M.B.T., 1992); Southwestern University School of Law (J.D., 1994). Moot Court Honors Program. Recipient: American Jurisprudence Award-Conflict of Laws; Exceptional Achievement Award-Crimes Transactions. Certified Public Accountant, California, 1987. *Member:* Los Angeles County Bar Association; State Bar of California; New York State Bar. **PRACTICE AREAS:** Business Litigation; Tax; Bankruptcy; Estate Planning; Probate.

### OF COUNSEL

**FREDERICK J. STEMMLER,** born Pittsburg, Pennsylvania, August 14, 1948; admitted to bar, 1973, California; 1990, Colorado. *Education:* University of California (B.A., 1969); University of Southern California (J.D., 1973). Counsel Member, Urban Land Institute. Member, International Council Shopping Centers. *Member:* Colorado Bar Association; State Bar of California; Orange County Asian American Bar Association. **PRACTICE AREAS:** Real Estate; Commercial Transactions.

REPRESENTATIVE CLIENTS: The Equitable Life Insurance Company Assurance of The U.S.; The Koll Company; ABC Entertainment Center; Waymire Drum Company; Layton Belling & Associates; United Pacific Construction, Inc.; California Mart; Nationwide Insurance Company; Vilie Circuits; Ranger Insurance Company; First American Title Insurance Company; Electronic Circuits, Inc.; Carter International; Huber Photo; Ionspec Corporation; Roque Center; Hopkins Realty Group; Shoe City Companies.

## BARNETT & RUBIN

A PROFESSIONAL CORPORATION

2 PARK PLAZA, SUITE 980

**IRVINE, CALIFORNIA 92614**

Telephone: 714-261-9700
Facsimile: 714-261-9799
Email: Lawyers@Pacbell.net

*Civil Litigation, Receiverships and Bankruptcy.*

**RICHARD L. BARNETT,** born Berkeley, California, May 9, 1953; admitted to bar, 1979, California; U.S. Supreme Court. *Education:* San Jose State University (B.S, in accounting, 1976); Pepperdine University (J.D., 1979). Beta Alpha Psi. Judge Pro Tem, Orange County Municipal Court. Former Director, Saratoga Savings and Loan Association. *Member:* Orange County Bar Association; State Bar of California; Federal Bar Association; Orange County Bankruptcy Forum; Orange County Trial Lawyers Association. (Certified Specialist, Personal and Small Business Bankruptcy Law, The California Board of Legal Specialization). **PRACTICE AREAS:** Bankruptcy Law.

**JEFFREY D. RUBIN,** born Philadelphia, Pennsylvania, March 19, 1952; admitted to bar, 1979, California; U.S. Supreme court. *Education:* California State University (B.A., 1975); Western State University (J.D., 1978). *Member:* Orange County Bar Association; Orange County Trial Lawyers Association. **PRACTICE AREAS:** Civil Practice; Commercial Law; Real Estate; Receivership Law.

---

**KATHRYN B. SALMOND,** born Stanford, California, May 28, 1963; admitted to bar, 1988, California; U.S. District Court, Central and Southern Districts of California; U.S. Supreme Court. *Education:* University of California at Berkeley (B.A., 1985); University of Southern California (J.D., 1988). *Member:* Orange County and American Associations; Orange County Legion Lex Inns of Court. **PRACTICE AREAS:** Commercial Litigation; Real Estate; Receivership; Bankruptcy Law.

## BERGER, KAHN, SHAFTON, MOSS, FIGLER, SIMON & GLADSTONE

A Professional Corporation including a Professional Corporation

SUITE 650, 2 PARK PLAZA

**IRVINE, CALIFORNIA 92714**

Telephone: 714-474-1880
Telecopier: 714-474-7265

*Los Angeles, California Office:* 4215 Glencoe Avenue (Marina L.C. Del Rey), 90292-5634. Telephone: 310-821-9000. Telecopier: 310-578-6178.

*Novato, California Office:* Suite 304, 1701 Novato Boulevard, 94947. Telephone: 415-899-1770. Telecopier: 415-899-1769.

*San Diego, California Office:* 402 W. Broadway, Suite 400, 92101. Telephone: 619-236-8602. Telecopier: 619-236-0812.

*Bend, Oregon Office:* P.O. Box 1407, 97709. Telephone: 541-388-1400. Telecopier: 541-388-4731.

*Insurance and Environmental Law, Real Estate, Tax and Probate, Music and Entertainment Law and Intellectual Property, General Civil and Trial Practice in all State and Federal Courts.*

(For complete biographical data on all personnel, see Professional Biographies at Los Angeles, California).

## BIESTY, McCOOL & GARRETTY

A PROFESSIONAL CORPORATION

**IRVINE, CALIFORNIA**

(See Los Angeles)

*Insurance Defense. Legal, Real Estate, Insurance Agents and Brokers' Errors & Omissions. Construction Defect and Family Law. Governmental Tort Liability. General Civil Litigation, Alternate Dispute Resolution.*

## RICHARD P. BOOTH, JR.

2030 MAIN STREET, SUITE 1600
**IRVINE, CALIFORNIA 92714**
Telephone: 714-752-2145
FAX: 714-622-0206

*Medical Malpractice, Personal Injury Law, Employment Law.*

**RICHARD P. BOOTH, JR.,** born Ft. Smith, Arkansas, July 1, 1944; admitted to bar, 1974, California, U.S. District Court, Central District of California and U.S. Court of Appeals, Ninth Circuit; 1979, U.S. Tax Court. *Education:* University of Southern California (B.S., in Accounting, 1968); Loyola University of Los Angeles (J.D., 1973). *Member:* Orange County and American Bar Associations; State Bar of California; Advocate, American Board of Trial Advocates (Chapter President, 1990). **PRACTICE AREAS:** Medical Malpractice; Personal Injury Law; Employment Law.

## BORCHARD & WILLOUGHBY

A PROFESSIONAL CORPORATION
18881 VON KARMAN AVENUE, SUITE 1400
**IRVINE, CALIFORNIA 92612**
Telephone: 714-644-6161
Fax: 714-263-1913

*Civil Litigation.*

**FIRM PROFILE:** *Borchard & Willoughby was formed by former attorneys of one of the most respected law firms in the country, and it focuses on civil trial and appellate practice in state and federal courts. Despite its comparatively small size, Borchard & Willoughby has represented clients in complex, multiparty litigation, including massive securities disputes. Borchard & Willoughby believes in the productive use of high technology and, by virtue of the experience each attorney brings, provides sophisticated legal services with efficiency and excellence.*

**MICHAEL D. BORCHARD,** born Ft. Walton Beach, Florida, November 11, 1961; admitted to bar, 1988, California and U.S. District Court, Northern, Southern and Central Districts of California. *Education:* Middlebury College (B.A., 1983); Boston University (J.D., cum laude, 1987). Editor, Annual Review of Banking Law, 1985-1987. *Member:* Orange County Bar Association; State Bar of California. **PRACTICE AREAS:** Civil Litigation; Securities Litigation; Real Estate Litigation; Appellate Practice.

**MICHAEL L. WILLOUGHBY,** born Marion, Ohio, 1949; admitted to bar, 1981, California and U.S. District Court, Northern District of California; 1983, U.S. District Court, Eastern District of California; 1984, U.S. Court of Appeals, Ninth Circuit; 1985, U.S. District Court, Central and Southern Districts of California. *Education:* University of Southern California (B.S., cum laude, 1971); Boalt Hall School of Law, University of California (J.D., 1981). Order of the Coif. *Member:* State Bar of California (Member, Litigation Section). [Lt., U.S.N., 1971-1978]. **PRACTICE AREAS:** Civil Litigation; Securities Litigation; Real Estate Litigation; Appellate Practice.

**MARK A. RODRIGUEZ,** born Los Angeles, California, May 23, 1959; admitted to bar, 1987, California and U.S. District Court, Central District of California; 1989, U.S. District Court, Northern and Southern Districts of California; 1990, U.S. Court of Appeals, Ninth Circuit. *Education:* Loyola Marymount University (B.A., 1980); Harvard University (J.D., 1987). Member, Harvard Journal of International Law, 1986-1987. *Member:* State Bar of California. **PRACTICE AREAS:** Civil Litigation; Securities Litigation; Real Estate Litigation; Appellate Practice.

---

**STEPHANIE A. PITTALUGA,** born Lubbock, Texas, April 16, 1969; admitted to bar, 1996, California and U.S. District Court, Central and Southern Districts of California. *Education:* California State University at Fullerton (B.A., with high honors, 1992); Western State University (J.D., magna cum laude, 1995). Member, Western State University, Irvine, Journal of Law, 1993-1995. *Member:* State Bar of California. **LANGUAGES:** French.

REPRESENTATIVE CLIENTS: Surfer Magazine; Delta Net Internet Services; International Food and Beverage; City of Orange (California); Weld County (Colorado).

## BOUTWELL, BEHRENDT & ENNOR

1 PARK PLAZA, SUITE 490
**IRVINE, CALIFORNIA 92714**
Telephone: 714-251-2888
Fax: 714-251-2889

*Los Angeles, California Office:* 333 South Grand Avenue, 37th Floor. Telephone: 213-346-0070. Fax: 213-346-0071.
*San Francisco, California Office:* 221 Sansome Street, Suite 3. Telephone: 415-274-8511. Fax: 415-274-8513.

*Banking, Finance, Mortgage Banking, Pensions/ERISA, Tax Exempt Entities, Corporate and Municipal Finance Law.*

**FIRM PROFILE:** *Boutwell, Behrendt & Ennor is a certified majority womenowned law firm specializing in banking, corporate finance, public finance, employee benefits, corporate and environmental law. The background of the firm's partners includes practice at national law firms and within major corporations. These attorneys bring to their practice a high degree of sophistication coupled with a unique sensitivity to their client's overall business and legal needs. While the firm provides a quality of legal services normally associated with large law firms, the smaller size of the firm allows it to be more accessible to its clients, and more responsive to their needs.*

### MEMBERS OF FIRM

**SHERRIE M. BOUTWELL,** born Kirkwood, Missouri, November 26, 1957; admitted to bar, 1983, California; 1984, U.S. District Court, Central District of California and U.S. Tax Court. *Education:* University of California, Irvine (B.A., magna cum laude, 1979); University of California, Los Angeles (J.D., 1983). Phi Beta Kappa. Member, UCLA/Alaska Law Review, 1982-1983. Member, Western Pension Conference, 1988-1994. *Member:* Orange County Bar Association (Member, Section on Law Practice Management); State Bar of California (Member: Employee Benefits Committee; Tax Section); Christian Legal Society. **PRACTICE AREAS:** Pension/ERISA; Employee Benefits; Executive Compensation.

**LAWRENCE B. BEHRENDT,** born New York, N.Y., August 28, 1955; admitted to bar, 1981, New York; 1987, California. *Education:* University of California at Berkeley (A.B., summa cum laude, 1976); Duke University; Georgetown University (J.D., 1980). Phi Beta Kappa. Editor, Journal of Law and Policy in International Business, 1979-1980. *Member:* Orange County, New York State and American (Member: Business Law Section; Uniform Commercial Code Committee; Investment Securities Subcommittee) Bar Associations; State Bar of California. **PRACTICE AREAS:** Banking and Finance; Environmental; Corporate.

**SARA LANGFORD ENNOR,** born San Francisco, California, June 7, 1952; admitted to bar, 1981, California. *Education:* University of the Pacific, Stockton (B.A., 1976); University of San Francisco (J.D., 1980). Lecturer, ERISA, National Institute of Pension Administrators. *Member:* San Francisco County Bar Association; State Bar of California (Member, Sections on: Business and Corporate Law; Tax and Employee Benefits Subsection); Western Pension Conference; National Institute of Pension Administrators. **PRACTICE AREAS:** Pension Plans; ERISA; Fiduciary Law.

## JOHN J. BRANDLIN, JR.

Established in 1974
SUITE 730
7700 IRVINE CENTER DRIVE
**IRVINE, CALIFORNIA 92718-2929**
Telephone: 714-453-2100
Fax: 714-453-7393; E-Mail: JBrandlin@earthlink.net
Email: JBrandlin@aol.com

*Business, Corporate, Civil Litigation, Computers and Software, Bankruptcy, Estate Planning and Probate Law.*

**JOHN J. BRANDLIN, JR.,** born Ann Arbor, Michigan, November 22, 1944; admitted to bar, 1974, California and U.S. District Court, Central District of California. *Education:* University of Arizona (B.A., 1967); Southwestern University School of Law (J.D., 1974). Member, Board of Directors, Buena Park Chamber of Commerce, 1985-1988. *Member:* Orange County, Los Angeles County and American Bar Associations; State Bar of California. **PRACTICE AREAS:** Business Law; Computers and Software; Litigation; Estate Planning and Probate; Bankruptcy; Corporate Law.

REPRESENTATIVE CLIENTS: Smith Micro Software, Inc.; Micro Trim, Inc.; Preproduction Plastics, Inc.; Stein Industries, Inc.

## LAW OFFICES OF
## HUGH BRECKENRIDGE

4199 CAMPUS DRIVE, SUITE 700
**IRVINE, CALIFORNIA 92715**
Telephone: 714-854-2520
FAX: 714-854-4897
Email: HUGHBRECK@PRODIGY.COM

*Real Estate and Business Transactions and Litigation, Settlement, Arbitration and Mediation.*

**HUGH BRECKENRIDGE,** born Santa Monica, California, December 2, 1946; admitted to bar, 1975, California; 1976, U.S. District Court, Central District of California; 1978, U.S. Court of Appeals, Ninth Circuit; 1984, U.S. District Court, Southern District of California. *Education:* Stanford University (B.A., 1968); Pepperdine University (J.D., 1975). Staff Member, Pepperdine Law Review, 1974-1975. Author: "Zoning and the Vested Right to Use Property: There Ought to be a Right," 2 Pepperdine Law Review, S219. *Member:* Orange County Bar Association; The State Bar of California. **PRACTICE AREAS:** Contract Law; Corporate Law; Real Estate Law; Partnership Law; Civil Litigation.

## BROWN, PISTONE, HURLEY
## & VAN VLEAR

A PROFESSIONAL CORPORATION
*Established in 1989*
SUITE 900 AT&T BUILDING
8001 IRVINE CENTER DRIVE
**IRVINE, CALIFORNIA 92618-2921**
Telephone: 714-727-0559
Fax: 714-727-0656
Email: BPHVLAW@AOL.COM

*Phoenix, Arizona Office:* 2999 North 44th Street, Suite 300. Telephone: 602-968-2427. Fax: 602-840-0794.
*San Diego, California Office:* 4350 La Jolla Village Drive, Suite 300. Telephone: 619-546-4368. Fax: 619-453-2839.
*Sacramento, California Office:* 980 Ninth Street, 16th Floor. Telephone: 916-449-9541. Fax: 916-446-7104.

*Construction, Environmental and Technology Trial Practice, Public Works, Contractor Professional Licensing and Bonding, Mechanics Liens, Insurance Coverage, Malpractice, International Projects, Arbitration, Environmental Law, Air and Water Permits, Trial and Appellate Practice.*

*FIRM PROFILE: Brown, Pistone, Hurley & Van Vlear serves as project counsel and trial lawyers on construction, environmental and technology disputes worldwide, including many of the largest public works projects in the United States. Attorneys in the firm have degrees and practical experience in civil, mechanical, electrical and nuclear engineering and computer science.*

*The Project Counsel Group acts as legal counsel for owners, designers, and contractors during the course of major construction projects. Pre-project legal services include contracts drafting and bid packages, insurance and bonding, evaluation of project and site risks.*

*The Environmental Group engages in counseling and representation of clients in administrative proceedings and litigation. The emphasis of this practice is underground contamination, OSHA violations, asbestos removal, air quality permitting and associated civil fines and penalties.*

*The Technology Group provides counsel and trial representation in a broad range of technology development and commercial applications including software, medical devices, semiconductor and computer hardware, and associated high technology.*

*The Trial & Arbitration Group deals with litigated cases involving catastrophic failures, construction delay and overrun claims, construction and products defects, engineer and architect malpractice and performance problems on major projects.*

**ERNEST C. BROWN,** born Reno, Nevada, December 12, 1953; admitted to bar, 1978, California and U.S. District Court, Northern District of California; 1981, U.S. District Court, Central District of California; 1989, U.S. District Court, Eastern District of California; 1991, U.S. District Court, District of Arizona. *Education:* Massachusetts Institute of Technology (B.S.C.E., 1975); University of California at Berkeley (M.S.C.E., 1978); Boalt Hall School of Law, University of California (J.D., 1978). Chi Epsilon. Licensed Professional Engineer, California, 1980. Co-Author: Architect/Engineer Malpractice, Federal Publications, 1980; "Opportunities and Risks in Asbestos Abatement and Hazardous Waste Management," PSMA Management Report, Jan. 1987; "What Lawyers Must Know About Asbestos," ABA Journal, Nov. 1987; "Architect/Engineer Liability Under California Law", Cambridge Institute; " California Public Works: Contracts & Litigation." Author and Statewide Program Chair, CEB Program, (May 1995). Adjunct Faculty, Construction Law, University of California, 1979-1985. Corporate Counsel, Fluor Corporation, 1980-1984. *Member:* Orange County (Chairman, Construction Section, 1987-1992) and American (Member, Forum Committee on the Construction Industry) Bar Associations; State Bar of California (Co-Chairman, Construction Section of Real Estate Section, 1988-1990); National Society of Professional Engineers; California Society of Professional Engineers; AGC Legal Advisory Committee (Chairman, 1992-1993). **PRACTICE AREAS:** Construction; Public Works; Environmental; Mediation.

**THOMAS A. PISTONE,** born Yonkers, New York, February 22, 1949; admitted to bar, 1977, California and U.S. District Court, Central District of California; 1982, U.S. District Court, Eastern, Northern and Southern Districts of California and U.S. Court of Appeals, Ninth Circuit; 1984, District of Columbia. *Education:* St. Mary's College; California State University at Long Beach (B.A., 1973); Hastings College of Law, University of California (J.D., 1977). Order of the Coif. Member, Thurston Society. Member, Hastings Law Journal, 1975-1976. Instructor: Evidence, Western State University College of Law, 1978-1982; Legal Research, Civil Litigation, University of California, Irvine, 1982-1994. Judge Pro Tem, Orange County Superior Court. Arbitrator, Mediator and Member of Orange County Advisory Board, American Arbitration Association. *Member:* Orange County (Member: Business Litigation, Technology, Construction and Real Estate Sections; Judiciary Committee, Federal Courts Committee), Federal and American (Member Litigation Section, Intellectual Property Law Section; Technology Section) Bar Associations; The State Bar of California (Member: Business Law Section; Litigation Section; Environmental Law Section; Intellectual Property Section). **PRACTICE AREAS:** Construction Litigation; Real Estate and Title Litigation; Business Litigation; Computer Products Litigation; Environmental Litigation.

**GREGORY F. HURLEY,** born Clifton, New Jersey, December 6, 1958; admitted to bar, 1986, California and U.S. Court of Appeals, Ninth Circuit; 1987, Colorado and Minnesota; 1988, District of Columbia. *Education:* Occidental College; University of California at Berkeley (B.S., 1982); University of Colorado (J.D., 1986). Psi Chi. Registered Environmental Assessor, State of California. *Member:* Federal Bar Association; The Association of Trial Lawyers of America; Colorado Trial Lawyers Association. **PRACTICE AREAS:** Construction Litigation; Business Litigation; Construction Project Insurance Coverage; Disabled Access Litigation; Environmental Law; Pollution Site Insurance Coverage; Asbestos Remediation.

**JOHN E. VAN VLEAR,** born Pasadena, California, April 20, 1962; admitted to bar, 1987, California; 1988, U.S. District Court, Central District of California. *Education:* University of California at Irvine (B.A., magna cum laude, 1984) Phi Beta Kappa; Pepperdine University (J.D., cum laude, 1987). Recipient: Sorenson Memorial Award for Literary Excellence; West Publishing Company Award, Most Significant Contribution to Overall Legal Scholarship, Pepperdine Class of 1987. Staff Member, Pepperdine Law Review, 1986-1987. Registered Environmental Assessor, State of California, 1992. Adjunct Professor, Environmental Law, Western State University School of Law, 1991. Author: The Environmental Handbook (1996); "Environmental Trends and the Precious Metal Industry: Understanding Liabilities/Adopting Effective Strategies," Precious Metals, 1995 (IPMI, 1995); "Effective Handling of Environmental Consultants: A Practical Approach," California Environmental Law Reporter, November 1992; "CERCLA Section 107 Private Cause of Action and The Revised National Contingency Plan," *Environmental Waste Management*, August, 1990; Comment, "Land Use Aesthetics: A Citizen Survey Approach to Decision Making," 15 Pepperdine Law Review 207, 1988. *Member:* Orange County Bar Association (Co-Chair, Toxic and Environmental Section, 1996); State Bar of California; Environmental Professionals Organization (Founding President, 1991-1994; Executive Director, 1994—). **SPECIAL AGENCIES:** Federal Environmental Protection Agency (EPA), Region IX; California Department of Toxic Substances Control (DTSC) and Regional Water Quality Control Boards (RWQCB). **TRANSACTIONS:** Brownfields Redevelopment of Kaiser Ventures California Speedway; Waste disposal Inc.; Superfund Site; Roche Estate Oil Production Site. **PRACTICE AREAS:** Environmental Law; Cost Recovery Litigation; Regulatory Compliance; Site Assessment and Remediation; Real estate.

*(This Listing Continued)*

# PROFESSIONAL BIOGRAPHIES

## CALIFORNIA—IRVINE

**MICHAEL K. WOLDER,** born Long Beach, California, May 11, 1960; admitted to bar, 1989, California; 1990, U.S. District Court, Central and Southern Districts of California. *Education:* California State University at Long Beach (B.S.M.E., 1983); Western State University (J.D., 1989). *Member:* Orange County (Chairman, Construction Law Subsection) Bar Association; State Bar of California; American Society of Mechanical Engineers. *PRACTICE AREAS:* Private Development; Public Works; Construction Litigation; Engineering.

---

**FRANCIS T. DONOHUE, III,** born Albany, New York, August 23, 1954; admitted to bar, 1982, California; 1983, U.S. Court of Appeals, Ninth Circuit and U.S. District Court, Central, Northern, Southern and Eastern Districts of California; 1984, New York. *Education:* St. John Fisher College (B.S., 1976); Pace University School of Law (J.D., cum laude, 1982); University of California (M.A., Environmental Analysis, 1993). Member, Pace University Law Review, 1981-1982. Articles and Presentations: "Criminal Liability of Safety Managers: The Increase Use of 'Be A Manager Go to Jail' Legislation," (1992); Keynote: "Expanded Contractor Liability for Pollution Cleanup," (1993); "Is YIMBY the Answer to NIMBY? Possible Solutions to the Political and Economic Problems in Siting Hazardous Waste Facilities," Conference on the Political Aspects of Environmentalism (1992); "Environmental and Hazardous Law/Regulations Overview," (1992); "Impacts of Environmental Law and Regulation on Risk Management," (1991). Instructor, Environmental Law and Policy, University of California at Irvine, 1992-1994. *Member:* State Bar of California; New York State Bar Association. *PRACTICE AREAS:* Environmental Law; Construction Law; General Litigation.

**ROBERT C. SCHNEIDER,** born Cedarburg, Wisconsin, August 3, 1948; admitted to bar, 1973, California; 1974, U.S. District Court, Central, Southern and Eastern Districts of California; 1989, Arizona; 1991, U.S. District Court, District of Arizona. *Education:* Luther College (B.A., summa cum laude, valedictorian, 1970); Stanford University (J.D., 1973). Recipient: National Merit Scholarship; Regents Scholarship. Real Estate Broker, California, 1983—. Lecturer: Bechtel Corporation Seminars, 1975-1980; Coastline Community College, 1976-1983. *Member:* Los Angeles County, Orange County, Maricopa County and American Bar Associations; State Bar of California; State Bar of Arizona. (Resident, Phoenix, Arizona Office). *PRACTICE AREAS:* Engineering; Construction Law; Real Estate; Corporate Law; Contract Law; Computer Software.

**SHEILA I. PATTERSON,** born Los Angeles, California, January 25, 1954; admitted to bar, 1982, California; 1984, U.S. District Court, Central District of California. *Education:* University of California at Santa Barbara; University of California at Irvine (B.A., 1978); Loyola University at Los Angeles (J.D., 1982). *Member:* Los Angeles County and Orange County (Member, Business Law Section) Bar Associations; State Bar of California; Orange County Women Lawyers Association (Past Member, Board of Directors). *PRACTICE AREAS:* Civil and Environmental Litigation; Land Use.

**MICHAEL R. GANDEE,** born Charleston, West Virginia, August 12, 1962; admitted to bar, 1993, California and U.S. District Court, Central District of California; 1994, U.S. District Court, Eastern District of California. *Education:* University of Maryland (B.S., Civil Engineering, 1985; B.S., Computer Science, 1987); Pepperdine University (J.D., 1993). *Member:* Orange County Bar Association; State Bar of California. *PRACTICE AREAS:* Construction Law; Public Works.

**JULIA E. KRESS,** born Dhahran, Saudi Arabia, August 22, 1966; admitted to bar, 1991, California; 1995, U.S. District Court, Central District of California. *Education:* Loyola University of Chicago (B.B.A., 1988); Loyola Law School (J.D., 1991). *Member:* Los Angeles County and American Bar Associations; State Bar of California. *SPECIAL AGENCIES:* California Air Resources Board, South Coast Air Quality Management District; Department of Toxic Substances Control; State Water Quality Control Board; Office of Health Hazard Assessment; Cal-OSHA and The U.S. Environmental Protection Agency. *PRACTICE AREAS:* Environmental and Business Litigation; Environmental Compliance.

*OF COUNSEL*

**ROBERT G. MAHAN,** born Worcester, Massachusetts, October 19, 1939; admitted to bar, 1980, California. *Education:* University of Southern California (B.S., 1961; M.S., 1969); Western States University (J.D., 1979). Blue Key; Skull & Dagger. *Member:* State Bar of California. Western Association of Insurance Brokers; Associated General Contractors of California. [With U.S. Navy, 1961-1965 active/USNR, 1965—]

*(This Listing Continued)*

**STEPHEN M. WONTROBSKI,** born New York, N.Y., May 1, 1947; admitted to bar, 1976, Texas; 1990, California. *Education:* Boston College (B.S., 1968); Syracuse University (M.B.A., 1970); University of Houston (J.D., 1975). Certified Public Accountant, Texas 1972. *Member:* State Bar of Texas; State Bar of California. *PRACTICE AREAS:* Construction Law; Environmental Law; Engineering; Insurance Law.

**BRIAN A. RUNKEL,** born Dayton, Ohio, October 27, 1961; admitted to bar, 1987, Maryland; 1988, District of Columbia, U.S. Court of Appeals, District of Columbia Appeals and U.S. District Court, District of Maryland (Not admitted in California). *Education:* George Washington University (B.A., 1984); Harvard Law School (J.D., cum laude, 1987). Phi Beta Kappa. Member, Environmental Law Institute, 1988. Deputy Secretary, California Environmental Agency, 1991-1993. *Member:* Bar Association of the District of Columbia; Maryland State and American Bar Associations; The District of Columbia Bar. *PRACTICE AREAS:* Environmental Law.

REPRESENTATIVE CLIENTS: Air Products & Chemicals, Inc.; City of Anaheim; Anaheim Convention Center Authority; American Arbitration Association; Ameron; Bank of America; Birtcher, CHZ2M Hill; Chicago Title; Disposal Control/Laidlaw Environmental; Ebasco Services; Ebasco Constructors, Inc.; Fluor Daniel; Illinois Tool Works; International Technology Corporation; Irvine Co.; County of Los Angeles; County of Orange; John Wayne Airport; City of Newport Beach; Kaiser Ventures; Regency Health Services, Inc.; Thrifty Corporation; Worldwide Environmental Products.

---

## BRYAN CAVE LLP

A Partnership including a Professional Corporation

*Established in 1873*

18881 VON KARMAN, SUITE 1500
**IRVINE, CALIFORNIA 92715-1500**
Telephone: (714) 223-7000
Facsimile: (714) 223-7100

*For attorney e-mails use: First initial, last name, firm name, e.g., rsmith@bryancavellp.com*

*St. Louis, Missouri Office:* One Metropolitan Square, 211 North Broadway, Suite 3600, 63102-2750. Telephone: (314) 259-2000. Facsimile: (314) 259-2020.

*Washington, D.C. Office:* 700 Thirteenth Street, N.W., 20005-3960. Telephone: (202) 508-6000. Facsimile: (202) 508-6200.

*New York, N.Y. Office:* 245 Park Avenue, 10167-0034. Telephone: (212) 692-1800. Facsimile: (212) 692-1900.

*Kansas City, Missouri Office:* 3500 One Kansas City Place, 1200 Main Street, 64141-6914. Telephone: (816) 374-3200. Facsimile: (816) 374-3300.

*Overland Park, Kansas Office:* 7500 College Boulevard, Suite 1100, 66210-4035. Telephone: (913) 338-7700. Facsimile: (913) 338-7777.

*Phoenix, Arizona Office:* 2800 North Central Avenue, Twenty-First Floor, 85004-1098. Telephone: (602) 230-7000. Facsimile: (602) 266-5938.

*Los Angeles, California Office:* 777 South Figueroa Street, Suite 2700, 90017-5418. Telephone: (213) 243-4300. Facsimile: (213) 243-4343.

*Santa Monica, California Office:* 120 Broadway, Suite 500, 90401-2305. Telephone: (310) 576-2100. Facsimile: (310) 576-2200.

*London SW1H 9BU England Office:* 29 Queen Anne's Gate. Telephone: 171-896-1900. Facsimile: 171-896-1919.

*Riyadh 11465 Saudi Arabia Office:* In Cooperation with Kadasah Law Firm, P.O. Box 20883. Telephone: 966-1-474-0888. Facsimile: 966-1-476-2881.

*Kuwait City, Kuwait Office:* Mashora Advocates & Legal Consultants, Sheraton Towers, Second Floor, P.O. Box 5902 Safat, 13060. Telephone: 965-240-4470/240-600. Facsimile: 965-245-9000.

*Dubai, U.A.E. Office:* Al-Mahairi Legal Consultants - Bryan Cave LLP, Dubai, Holiday Centre, Commercial Tower, Suite 1103, P.O. Box 13677, UAE. Telephone: 971-4-314-123. Facsimile: 971-4-318-287.

*Abu Dhabi, U.A.E. Office:* Al-Mehairi Legal Consultants - Bryan Cave LLP, Abu Dhabi, Dhabi Tower, Suite 304, P.O. Box 47645. Telephone: 971-2-260-335. Facsimile: 971-2-260-332.

*Hong Kong Office:* Suite 2106, Lippo Tower, 21/F, Lippo Centre, 89 Queensway. Telephone: 852-2522-2821. Facsimile: 852-2522-3830.

*Shanghai, People's Republic of China Associated Office:* 100 Fu Xing Xi Lu, 3C, 200031. Telephone: 86-21-6466-3845. Facsimile: 86-21-6466-4280.

*Administrative and General Civil Practice. Antitrust, Aviation, Banking, Computer, Corporate Financing, Corporation, Environmental, Estate Planning, Government Contracts, Immigrations, International, Labor, Probate, Products Liability, Real Estate, Securities, Taxation, Technology, Transportation, Trust and University Law; U.S. Visa Law and Practice. General Civil Trial and Appellate Practice.*

*(This Listing Continued)*

## BRYAN CAVE LLP, Irvine—Continued

### PARTNERS

**WAYNE C. ARNOLD,** born Mississippi, 1953; admitted to bar, 1977, Mississippi; 1978, U.S. District Court, Northern District of Mississippi; 1982, California; 1983, U.S. District Court, Central District of California; 1984, Arizona; 1985, U.S. District Court, District of Arizona; 1986, U.S. Court of Appeals, Ninth Circuit; 1994, U.S. Court of Appeals, Eleventh Circuit. *Education:* California State University at Long Beach (B.A., 1975); University of Mississippi (J.D., 1977). Member: Education, ADR, and Lawyer Referral and Information Services Committees, Orange County Bar Association, 1995—; Continuing Legal Education Committee, 1985-1989, State Bar of Arizona. Member, 1987— and Chairman, 1988-1991, Board of Legal Specialization, State Bar of Arizona. *PRACTICE AREAS:* Commercial Litigation; Products Liability; Employment Litigation.

**PETER C. BRONSON,** born New York, 1950; admitted to bar, 1974, California; U.S. District Court, Central, Southern, Northern and Eastern Districts of California; U.S. Court of Appeals, Ninth Circuit; U.S. Supreme Court. *Education:* University of California at Los Angeles (A.B., magna cum laude, 1971; J.D., 1974). Phi Beta Kappa; Member, Moot Court. Managing Editor, UCLA Law Review, 1973-1974. Author: Comment, 21 UCLA Law Review 181, 1973. Law Clerk to the Hon. Rodney K. Potter, California Court of Appeal, 1974-1975. Judge Pro Tempore, Los Angeles Municipal Court, 1987-1993. *Member:* Orange County, (Member, Resolutions Committee, 1994-1996), Los Angeles County (Member, Executive Committee, Provisional and Post-Judgement Remedies Section, 1986-1994; Chair, 1991-1992) and Federal Bar Associations. [Lt., USNR, 1973-1979]. (Also at Santa Monica Office). *PRACTICE AREAS:* Bankruptcy; Commercial Litigation.

**PETER T. FAGAN,** born Illinois, 1948; admitted to bar, 1973, Illinois, Indiana, U.S. District Court, Southern District of Indiana, U.S. Court of Claims and U.S. Court of Military Appeals; 1979, U.S. District Court, Northern District of Illinois and U.S. Claims Court; 1983, U.S. District Court, Northern District of Indiana and U.S. Court of Appeals, Seventh Circuit; 1994, California and U.S. District Court, Central District of California. *Education:* University of Notre Dame (B.B.A., 1970; J.D., 1973); George Washington University (LL.M., with highest honors, 1976). Beta Alpha Psi. Co-author: "The Federal Tort Claims Act As It Relates to Aviation," Insurance Counsel Journal, 1981. [Capt., U.S. Army, JAGC, 1973-1979]. *PRACTICE AREAS:* Government Contracts; Construction Law; Civil Litigation.

**GARY J. HIGHLAND,** born Illinois, 1955; admitted to bar, 1979, California and U.S. District Court, Central District of California. *Education:* University of Illinois; University of California, Irvine (B.A., 1976); University of Southern California (J.D., 1979). Notes Editor and Member, Southern California Law Review, 1977-1979. Licensed California Real Estate Broker, 1980. Author: "Sales of Defective Used Products: Should Strict Liability Apply?" 52 Southern California Law Review 805-28, 1979. *Member:* Orange County (Member, Section on: Real Estate Law) and American (Member, Section on: Real Property, Probate and Trust Law) Bar Associations; State Bar of California (Member, Real Property Section).

**WILBUR D. LAYMAN,** born New York, 1931; admitted to bar, 1960, California. *Education:* Tufts University (A.B., 1953); Boalt Hall School of Law, University of California (J.D., 1959). Order of the Coif; Phi Delta Phi. Assistant Editor, California Law Review, 1958-1959. *Member:* Los Angeles County (Member, Real Property Committee, 1963—) and Orange County (Member, Taxation Committee, 1974—) Bar Associations.

**JAMES B. O'NEAL,** born Mississippi, 1944; admitted to bar, 1969, Texas; 1972, California; 1976, U.S. Tax Court; 1978, District of Columbia. *Education:* University of Mississippi (B.B.A., 1966); University of Texas (J.D., 1969); University of Florida (LL.M. in Taxation, 1976). Phi Alpha Delta; Beta Gamma Sigma. Member, Editorial Board, Texas International Law Journal, 1968-1969. Adjunct Professor in Taxation, Graduate School of Taxation, Golden Gate University, 1981—. *Member:* State Bar of California (Member, International Law and Taxes Section); International Bar Association (Member, Taxes Committee of Section on Business Law; Vice Chair, Committee on Closely Held Business Enterprises, Section on General Practice, 1993—); International Fiscal Association.

**ANGELO A. PAPARELLI,** born Michigan, 1949; admitted to bar, 1976, Michigan; 1980, U.S. Supreme Court; 1982, California. *Education:* University of Michigan (B.A., 1971); Wayne State University (J.D., 1976). Co-Author: *Business Metamorphosis:* The Effect of Changed Circumstances on U.S. Employers and Nonimmigrant Workers, American Immigration Lawyers Association (1994); *Avoiding or Accepting Risks in H-1B/LCA Practice, Immigration Briefings,* Nov. & Dec., 1992; "The *Quasar* Case: Hidden Problems of Employment, Immigration and Tax Law," American Bar Association, Section of International Law and Practice, March 1992; "The Immigration Act of 1990; Death Knell for the H-1B?" Federal Publications Inc., 1991; "Life After Mergers and Acquisitions: The Immigration Impact on U.S. Employers and Alien Workers," International Quarterly (October, 1990). Chairman, Immigration and Nationality Committee, Section of International Law and Practice, American Bar Association, 1991—. Immigration Section Executive Board Member, 1985—, Los Angeles County Bar Association. *Member:* American Immigration Lawyers Association (Member, Board of Governors, 1988-1994; Chair, E Visa Investors and Traders Committee, 1988-1989 , 1990-1991 and 1993-1994, and Chair, 1987-1988 Southern California Chapter). Law Clerk to Judge Dorothy C. Riley, Michigan Court of Appeals, 1976-1978. (Also at Los Angeles Office) (Co-Leader, Immigration Department) (Certified Specialist, Immigration and Nationality Law, The State Bar of California Board of Legal Specialization).

**JEFFREY W. SHIELDS,** born California, 1957; admitted to bar, 1983, California and U.S. District Court, Central District of California; 1984, U.S. District Court, Southern and Northern Districts of California; 1987, U.S. Supreme Court and U.S. District Court, Eastern District of California; 1988, U.S. Court of Appeals, Ninth Circuit. *Education:* Brigham Young University (B.A., summa cum laude, 1980; J.D., cum laude, 1983). *Member:* Federal, International and Inter-Pacific Bar Associations. *LANGUAGES:* Japanese. *PRACTICE AREAS:* International Litigation; Real Estate Litigation; Employment Litigation; Financial Transactions Litigation; Bankruptcy Litigation.

**STEVEN H. SUNSHINE,** born California, 1951; admitted to bar, 1976, California. *Education:* University of California at Los Angeles (B.A., magna cum laude, 1973); University of California at Los Angeles (J.D., 1976). Phi Beta Kappa.

### OF COUNSEL

**MONICA E. BARAJAS,** born New Jersey, 1961; admitted to bar, 1987, California; 1988, U.S. District Court, Central District of California. *Education:* University of California at Los Angeles (B.A., 1984); Hastings College of Law, University of California (J.D., cum laude, 1987). *LANGUAGES:* Spanish. *PRACTICE AREAS:* Business Immigration.

**ROBERT E. DYE,** born California, 1948; admitted to bar, 1973, California. *Education:* Whittier College (B.A., with high honors, 1969; M.A., 1970); University of Southern California (J.D., 1973). Order of the Coif; Delta Sigma Rho; Tau Kappa Alpha; Phi Alpha Delta. Co-winner, University of Southern California Hale Moot Court Honors Program, 1971-1972. Executive Editor, Southern California Law Review, 1972-1973.

### COUNSEL

**KEVIN P. BJERREGAARD,** born Wisconsin, 1959; admitted to bar, 1987, California; 1988, U.S. District Court, Central District of California; U.S. Court of Appeals, Ninth Circuit. *Education:* University of Wisconsin-Madison (B.A., 1980); Johns Hopkins University (M.A., 1981); University of Minnesota (J.D., cum laude, 1986). *Member:* Riverside Bar Association (Chairman, Publications Committee, 1987-1988). *PRACTICE AREAS:* Litigation.

**REN R HAYHURST,** born California, 1962; admitted to bar, 1987, Arizona; 1989, California; U.S. District Court, District of Arizona; U.S. District Court, Central, Southern and Eastern Districts of California; U.S. Court of Appeals, Ninth Circuit. *Education:* University of Utah (A.A., International Relations, 1984; B.S., Psychology, magna cum laude, 1984; B.S., Political Science, magna cum laude, 1984; J.D., 1987). Phi Beta Kappa; Phi Kappa Phi; Psi Chi; Phi Eta Sigma; Order of the Coif. William H. Leary Scholar. Recipient: American Jurisprudence Awards in Constitutional Law I and II. Legal Teaching Assistant: Constitutional Law, University of Utah Law School, 1986; "Street Law," University of Utah/Skyline, 1987. Law Clerk for Justice Christine Durham, Utah Supreme Court, 1986. *Member:* Federal Bar Association; California Trial Lawyers Association. *LANGUAGES:* German.

### RESIDENT ASSOCIATES

**EDWARD G. BECKER,** born Missouri, 1965; admitted to bar, 1990, Missouri, 1991, District of Columbia (Not admitted in California). *Education:* University of Missouri (B.S., cum laude, A.B., 1987); Georgetown University (J.D., cum laude, 1990). *PRACTICE AREAS:* International Law; Government Contracts; Litigation.

*(This Listing Continued)*

**J. IRA BURKEMPER,** born Missouri, 1962; admitted to bar, 1994, California. *Education:* Tufts University (B.A., 1985); American Graduate School of International Management (M.I.M., 1987); University of Southern California (J.D., 1994). Associate Editor, 1993-1994, USC Law Review. **LANGUAGES:** German and Italian. **PRACTICE AREAS:** Immigration.

**MARY LYNN K. COFFEE,** born Oklahoma, 1963; admitted to bar, 1989, California. *Education:* Trinity University (B.S. in Business/Finance, summa cum laude, 1985); University of Texas (J.D., with honors, 1989). Alpha Lambda Delta. Wall Street Journal Outstanding Business Student. Constitutional Rights Foundation Legal Advisory Board and Mock Trial Coach, 1990—. Note Author, Texas Review of Litigation, Spring, 1989. Field Study Instructor and Guest Lecturer, University of California, Irvine, 1991-1994. **PRACTICE AREAS:** Real Estate; Endangered Species; Wetlands Protection.

**MYNETTE M. DUFRESNE,** born California, 1965; admitted to bar, 1991, California; 1992, U.S. District Court, Southern, Central and Eastern Districts of California. *Education:* Mt. Vernon College (B.A., 1986); Loyola Marymount University (J.D., 1991). Articles Editor, Loyola of Los Angeles Law Review, 1990-1991.

**ADAM J. GILLMAN,** born New Mexico, 1969; admitted to bar, 1993, California; 1994, U.S. District Court, Southern, Central and Eastern Districts of California. *Education:* University of California, Berkeley, (B.A., 1990); Hastings College of the Law, University of California (J.D., 1993). Assistant Editor, Hastings Constitutional Law Directory, 1991-1993.

**JAMES R. ROUSE,** born Alabama, 1943; admitted to bar, 1989, California; 1990, U.S. District Court, Central, Eastern, Southern and Northern Districts of California and U.S. Court of Appeals, Ninth Circuit. *Education:* United States Naval Academy (B.S., with distinction, 1965); Golden Gate University (M.B.A., 1971); George Washington University (J.D., with honors, 1989). Peter M. Elliot Inn of Court. [Captain, U.S. Navy, 1965-1989]. **PRACTICE AREAS:** Products Liability; Business Litigation.

All Partners and Associates of the Firm are members of the American Bar Association.

(For a complete list of representative clients, see St. Louis, Missouri, listing)

# THE BUSCH FIRM
*2532 DUPONT DRIVE*
**IRVINE, CALIFORNIA 92612**
*Telephone: 714-474-7368*
*Fax: 714-474-7732*
*Email: trb@buschfirm.com*
*URL: http://www.buschfirm.com*

*Las Vegas, Nevada Office:* Hughes Center Executive Suites, 3753 Howard Hughes Parkway, Suite 200, 89109. Telephone: 702-892-3789. Fax: 702-892-3992.

*Estate Planning and Trusts, Probate, Federal, State and Local Tax Planning, Real Estate Transactional, Corporate Transactional and Reorganization, Partnerships, and Limited Liability Companies.*

*FIRM PROFILE:* The Busch Firm is one of the largest law firms with a professional staff composed of principally J.D., C.P.A.'s. It specializes in the area of tax, financial and legal matters which utilize the professional disciplines of accounting and law.

*The Firm was founded in Southfield, Michigan in 1979, and relocated to Irvine, California in 1984.*

**TIMOTHY R. BUSCH,** born Clinton, Michigan, November 23, 1954; admitted to bar, 1978, Michigan; 1984, California; 1992, Texas; 1995, District of Columbia. *Education:* Western Michigan University (B.B.A., 1975); Wayne State University (J.D., 1978). Certified Public Accountant, Michigan, 1978 and California, 1982. *Member:* Orange County Bar Association (Member, Managing Partner's Section); American Association of Attorneys-Certified Public Accountants. **PRACTICE AREAS:** Estate; Tax; Business Law.

**RUDOLPH J. FUCHS,** born Los Angeles, California, April 13, 1957; admitted to bar, 1992, California, U.S. District Court, Central District of California and U.S. Tax Court. *Education:* California State University, Long Beach (B.S., with great distinction, Finance, 1980; B.S., with great distinction, Accounting, 1982); Southwestern University School of Law (J.D., 1992). Beta Gamma Sigma. Recipient: Exceptional Achievement Award, Tax Litigation and Administration, 1991; American Jurisprudence Award, Insurance Law, 1991. Certified Public Accountant, California, 1985. *Member:* Orange County Bar Association (Member, Tax Law Section); State Bar of California (Member, Sections on: Tax; Probate/Estate Planning); American Institute of Certified Public Accountants (Member, Tax Section); California Society of Certified Public Accountants. **PRACTICE AREAS:** Tax Law.

**DAVID L. KELIGIAN,** born Los Angeles, California, April 10, 1956; admitted to bar, 1980, California, U.S. District Court, Central District of California and U.S. Court of Appeals, Ninth Circuit; 1983, U.S. Tax Court; 1986, U.S. Claims Court. *Education:* University of Southern California, Los Angeles (B.S. in Accounting, 1977; M.B.A., magna cum laude, 1980; J.D., 1980). Certified Public Accountant, California, 1982. Instructor: Accounting for Lawyers, California Continuing Education of the Bar, 1986-1994; Advising California Professional Partnerships and Corporations, California Continuing Education of the Bar, 1990; Recent Developments in Business Law, 1990-1991. Author: "Agreements Among Founders," and "Tax Electing," Capitalizing and Protecting New Business, California; Continuing Education of the Bar, 1996; Consultant, Materials on Limited Partnerships, "Selecting and Forming Business Entities," California Continuing Education of the Bar, 1996. Business Valuation for "Business Buyout Agreements," Continuing Education of the Bar, 1991. Administrative Office of U.S. Federal Courts, 1988-1992; California CPA Foundation, Real Estate Tax, Family Limited Partnerships, Valuation Planning, IRS Procedure, and Bankruptcy Tax, 1988-1990. Author: "GRATs and GRUTs: What They Are and How To Draft Them," The Practical Tax Lawyer, Winter, 1995; Appraisal Issues Now Require Greater Attention For Tax Planning to be Effective," The Journal of Taxation, February, 1994; "A Primer on the New Passive Loss Rules," The Practical Tax Lawyer, 1987; "A Weaker U.S. Dollar-Influx of Foreign Entertainment Companies," Los Angeles Business Journal, April, 1988; "Deal Making Protocol With The Japanese," Hollywood Reporter, August, 1988; "Passive Activity Regulations Bookkeeping," Taxation For Accountants, October, 1988, reprinted in Taxation for Lawyers, November/December, 1988; "Wait Before You Open Your Files To IRS," Los Angeles Business Journal, September, 1989; "Liability of Tax Return Preparers," Los Angeles Daily Journal, November, 1989; "Financing Laws Transform Corporate Landscapes," Los Angeles Business Journal, December, 1989; "IRS Hits Independent Contractor Issue," Los Angeles Business Journal, 1990; "Avoiding Tax Disasters," San Fernando Valley Construction Journal, 1991; "Using Exchanges Effectively," San Fernando Valley Construction Journal, 1991. Co-Author: "Tax Practice in California," Supplement, California Continuing Education of the Bar, 1986-1990; "FIRPTA—A Manual For Escrow Officers," California Escrow Association, November, 1988. Panelist: "Corporate Tax Planning and Drafting for the Acquisition and Disposition of Corporate Business," Tax Section of the State Bar, 1990; "New Developments in Estate and Gift Planning," Tax Section of the State Bar, 1991; "Tax Planning For Real Estate Dispositions and Exchanges," 1991. Guest Lecturer, UCLA Extension, Real Estate Tax, 1989-1990. *Member:* Los Angeles County (Member, Tax Section) and American (Member, Sections on: Taxation; Corporate Law) Bar Associations; State Bar of California; California Society of Certified Public Accountants. **PRACTICE AREAS:** Estate; Tax; Business Law.

**GEORGE P. MULCAIRE,** born San Antonio, Texas, August 20, 1956; admitted to bar, 1984, California. *Education:* University of California at Davis (B.A., 1979); Santa Clara University (M.B.A., 1984; J.D., 1984). Licensed Real Estate Broker, California, 1995. *Member:* Orange County Bar Association; State Bar of California (Member, Sections on: Real Property; Taxation); Young Tax Lawyers (Member, Orange County Section). **PRACTICE AREAS:** Real Estate; Business and Tax Law.

**LAYNE T. RUSHFORTH,** born Salt Lake City, Utah, October 15, 1951; admitted to bar, 1978, Utah; 1981, Nevada. *Education:* Brigham Young University (B.A., cum laude, 1975; J.D., cum laude, 1978). Author: "Nevada Estate Planning and Probate Handbook," Nevada Estate Planning Institute, 1983. Co-Author: "An Analysis of the Final GST Regulations: Certain Planning Issues Still Remain," Tax Management Estates, Gifts and Trusts Journal, Vol. 21, No. 6, November 14, 1996. *Member:* Utah State Bar; State Bar of Nevada; Southern Nevada Estate Planning Counsel (President, 1986-1988); American College of Trust and Estate Council. (Resident, Las Vegas, Nevada Office). **PRACTICE AREAS:** Probate Law; Trusts and Estate Law; Business Formation.

**JAMES J. SCHEINKMAN,** born New Rochelle, New York, September 29, 1958; admitted to bar, 1983, Massachusetts (inactive); 1984, New York; 1991, California; 1994, U.S. District Court, Central District of California; 1995, U.S. District Court, Southern District of California. *Education:* State University of New York at Binghamton (B.A., with distinction in Economics and Environmental Studies, 1980); New York University School of Law (J.D., 1983). Phi Beta Kappa. Recipient, Moot Court Advocacy Award, 1981. Senior Research Editor, Annual Survey of American Law, 1982-1983.

*(This Listing Continued)*

## THE BUSCH FIRM, Irvine—Continued

Certificate in Personal Financial Planning, University of California, Irvine, 1994. Lecturer: "Dealing With The New Kids on the Block: LLCs and LLPs," Orange County Bar Association, Corporate Counsel Section, April 1996; "According to Plan? Selling and Purchasing Companies through Chapter 11," Orange County Bar Association, Business and Corporate Section, October 1995; "Selected Topics in Commercial Law," Orange County Bar Association, Financial Practices Section, May 1994; "A Primer in the Secondary Mortgage Market," Orange County Bar Association, Financial Practices Section, January 1994 (Co-Panelist). Author: "Federal Practice and Jurisdiction" 1982 Ann. Sur. Am. L. 625. *Member:* Orange County Bar Association (Officer, Business and Corporate Section, 1996; Co-Chair, Corporate Counsel Section, 1994-1995; Member, Sections on: Business and Corporate; Financial Practices); State Bar of California (Member, Business Law Section); Orange County Bankruptcy Forum; Young Executives of America (Board of Directors, Orange County Chapter, 1996). PRACTICE AREAS: Corporate; Securities; Commercial; Real Estate Transactional and Finance; Creditors Rights; Business Reorganizations.

**CLAY STEVENS,** born Poughkeepsie, New York, July 28, 1969; admitted to bar, 1996, California. *Education:* Occidental College (A.B., 1991); Pepperdine University (J.D., magna cum laude, 1995); New York University School of Law (LL.M., Tax, 1996). Recipient, American Jurisprudence Award for Legal and Research and Writing, 1993. Note and Comment Editor, Pepperdine Law Review, 1994-1995. Author: "Killing Two Birds with One Stone' Elimination of the Punitive Damage Exemption of Section 104(a)(2) Leads to Greater Efficiency and Raises Revenue," 28 Beverly Hills Bar Association Journal 168, 1994; "Split-Recovery: A Constitutional Answer to the Punitive Damage Dilemma," 21 Pepperdine Law Review 857, 1994; "California Supreme Court Survey, Lennane v. Franchise Tax Board," 23 Pepperdine Law Review 746, 1996; "The Geostationary Orbit: The Need for an Integrated Global Policy," 23 Journal of Space Law 183, 1995. *Member:* Orange County Bar Association; California State Bar. PRACTICE AREAS: Estate; Tax; Business Planning.

**DOUGLAS M. STEVENS,** born Detroit, Michigan, June 21, 1964; admitted to bar, 1989, California. *Education:* University of Southern California (B.S., 1986; J.D., 1989). Recipient: American Jurisprudence award in Bankruptcy. Executive Notes Editor, Computer Law Journal, Major Tax Planning, 1988-1989. Author: "Return to the Stone Age-The Regulation of Program Trading," 8 Computer/Law Journal 479. *Member:* State Bar of California; American Bar Association. PRACTICE AREAS: Business and Tax; Real Estate.

**ALLEN B. WALBURN,** born Hartford, Connecticut, September 27, 1960; admitted to bar, 1995, California. *Education:* San Diego State University (B.S., cum laude, 1982); University of San Diego (J.D., magna cum laude, 1994; LL.M. in Taxation, summa cum laude, 1995). Beta Gamma Sigma. Order of the Coif. Recipient: American Jurisprudence Awards in Trusts and Estates and Evidence; Am Jur-Bancroft Whitney Award in Estate Planning, 1995; Ralph Gano Miller Taxation Award; 1995 RIA Annual Taxation Award. Member, San Diego Law Review. Author: "Depreciation of Intangibles: An Area of the Tax Law in Need of Change," 30 San Diego Law Review 453, 1993. Co-Author: "An Analysis of the Final GST Regulations: Certain Planning Issues Still Remain," Tax Management Estates, Gifts and Trusts Journal, Vol. 21, No. 6, November 14, 1996. Certified Public Accountant, California, 1985. *Member:* Orange County and San Diego County Bar Associations; State Bar of California; American Institute of Certified Public Accountants; American Association of Attorney-Certified Public Accountants. PRACTICE AREAS: Estate, Tax and Business Planning.

**RICK S. WEINER,** born Chicago, Illinois, February 15, 1962; admitted to bar, 1990, California; 1994, Nevada. *Education:* University of California at Los Angeles (B.A. in Economics, 1983); Arizona State University (J.D., 1989). Licensed Real Estate Broker, California, 1991 and Nevada, 1995. Certified Public Accountant, Arizona, 1988 and California, 1990. *Member:* Clark County and American (Member, Section on Real Property, Probate and Trust Law) Bar Associations; State Bar of California; State Bar of Nevada; American Institute of Certified Public Accountants. PRACTICE AREAS: Real Estate Transactional and Finance; Corporate and Business Planning Law.

CAA308B

## BYE, HATCHER & ROBINSON
A Partnership including a Professional Corporation

**SUITE 1100, FIVE PARK PLAZA**
**IRVINE, CALIFORNIA 92714**
Telephone: 714-553-2404
Telecopier: 714-660-7212

*General Trial Practice in all State and Federal Courts emphasizing Business, Real Estate and Products Liability Litigation.*

*FIRM PROFILE: The Bye, Hatcher & Robinson are an established firm who takes pride in their achievements. The firm is listed in the Preeminent Law Directory.*

**ROLAND E. BYE,** born Valley City, North Dakota, June 21, 1946; admitted to bar, 1972, California. *Education:* Harvard University (B.A., cum laude, 1968); Boalt Hall School of Law, University of California (J.D., 1971). Clerk to Justice John W. Kerrigan, California Court of Appeals, 1971-1972. *Member:* Orange County (Chairman, Business Litigation Section, 1978) and American Bar Associations; State Bar of California (Member: Litigation and Real Estate Sections); California Trial Lawyers Association. REPORTED CASES: Stewart Development IV v. Superior Court (1980) 108 Cal.App.3rd 266 (leading case on expungement of lis pendens under C.C.P. §409.1). PRACTICE AREAS: Business Litigation; Real Estate Litigation.

**PATRICK G. HATCHER, (P.C.),** born Mexico City, D.F. Mexico, August 29, 1944; admitted to bar, 1973, California; 1974, U.S. District Court, Central District of California. *Education:* California State University at Los Angeles (B.A., with highest honors, 1970); University of California at Los Angeles (J.D., 1973). Formerly name partner, Murtaugh, Hatcher & Miller. *Member:* Los Angeles County and Orange County Bar Associations; State Bar of California; Association of Southern California Defense Counsel; Defense Research and Trial Lawyers Association. PRACTICE AREAS: Products Liability; Business Litigation.

**DAVID A. ROBINSON,** born San Bernardino, California, October 13, 1957; admitted to bar, 1982, California. *Education:* University of California, Riverside (A.B., magna cum laude, 1979); University of California, Hastings College of the Law (J.D., 1982). Clerk to Associate Justice Joseph R. Grodin, California Supreme Court, 1982-1983. Counsel, Volunteer Center of Greater Orange County. Litigation of Counsel, Jones, Day, Reavis & Pogue, Irvine, California, 1990-1995. Litigation Partner, Wyman Bautzer Kuchel & Silbert, 1989-1990. General Counsel, K-Lath Division of Georgetown Wire Co., Inc. *Member:* Orange County Bar Association (Member, Board of Directors).

**MICHAEL S. WINSTEN,** born Brooklyn, New York, September 14, 1958; admitted to bar, 1986, California, U.S. District Court, Central District of California and U.S. Court of Appeals, Ninth Circuit; 1992, U.S. District Court, Southern, Eastern and Northern Districts of California. *Education:* Cornell University (B.S., 1982); University of Southern California (J.D., 1986). Phi Delta Phi. Recipient, American Jurisprudence Award in Torts. Member, Computer Law Journal, 1984-1985. Member, Major Tax Planning, 1984-1985. Extern to Judge William J. Rea, U.S. District Court, Central District of California, 1985. Formerly with, Matkins, Leck, Gamble & Mallory and Kindel & Anderson. *Member:* Orange County and American Bar Associations; State Bar of California. PRACTICE AREAS: Business Litigation.

**JONATHAN S. PINK,** born Los Angeles, California, 1961; admitted to bar, 1995, California and U.S. District Court, Central District of California. *Education:* University of California, Berkeley (B.A., 1983); University of California, Los Angeles, School of Motion Picture and Television (M.F.A., 1987); Southwestern University School of Law (J.D., 1995). Recipient: Exceptional Achievement Awards in Criminal Law Theory; Interviewing Counseling and Negotiation. Member, 1993-1994; Editor-in-Chief, 1994-1995, Southwestern Journal of Law and Trade in the Americas. Clerk to NAFTA Binational Panelist Robert Lutz, 1994-1995. Extern to Justice Earl Johnson, California Court of Appeal, Second Appellate District, 1995. Author: Comment, "Moral Rights: A Copyright Conflict Between the United States and Canada," 1 Southwestern Journal of Law and Trade in the Americas 171. *Member:* Beverly Hills and Los Angeles Bar Associations. LANGUAGES: Business. PRACTICE AREAS: Business Litigation.

REPRESENTATIVE CLIENTS: American Honda Motor Co.; Dresser Industries, Inc.; E & J Gallo Winery; Sears, Roebuck and Co.; Burgundy Insurance Co.; Dresser-Rand Co.; Georgetown Wire Co., Inc.; Trammell Crow Company.

# CALLAHAN & BLAINE
### A PROFESSIONAL LAW CORPORATION
*Established in 1984*

**SUITE 800, 18500 VON KARMAN**
**IRVINE, CALIFORNIA 92612**
Telephone: 714-553-1155
Fax: 714-553-0784
Email: info@callahan-law.com

General Civil and Trial Practice in all State and Federal Courts including Banking, Commercial, Construction, Environmental, Insurance Coverage and Bad Faith, Intellectual Property, Real Property, Corporate and Securities Litigation, Transactional Representation in Corporate, Real Estate and Commercial Law.

*FIRM PROFILE:* Callahan & Blaine is a professional law corporation comprised of 3 principals, 7 associates and 2 attorneys Of Counsel. Our lawyers outstanding skills, top academic credentials and backgrounds which include experience with major national law firms. Members of the firm participate in continuing legal education and professional association activities as frequent speakers and contributing authors. Our goal is to represent our clients as we would want to be represented, always putting their interests first and diligently working to fully understand and serve their needs. In short, to do whatever it takes for the successful resolution of their cases.

Nationally recognized for setting precedent in Insurance Coverage Law representing policyholders, Callahan & Blaine specializes in Complex Business Litigation including Insurance Coverage and Bad Faith, Intellectual Property, Real and Corporate Property, Banking, Commercial Construction, Environmental, and Securities Litigation as well as Transactional Representation in Corporate, Real Estate and Commercial Law. The law firm is listed in the Bar Register of Preeminent lawyers.

REPORTED CASES: Hall v. Easy Rest, No. 96-1021, Fed.Cir. (1996); Sentex Systems v. Hartford Accident and Indemnity, 93 F.3d 578 (9th Cir. 1996); Fonovisa v. Cherry Auction, et al., 76 F.3d 259 (9th Cir. 1996); Kurisu v. Michigan Millers Mutual Insurance Co., 28 U.S.P.Q.2d. 1430 (Ct.App.Cal.1993 (unpub.); TKB International, Inc. v. United States of America, 995 F.2d 1460 (9th Cir. 1993).

**DANIEL J. CALLAHAN, (A PROFESSIONAL CORPORATION),** born Chicago, Illinois, September 13, 1949; admitted to bar, 1980, California and Hawaii; 1981, U.S. Tax Court and U.S. District Court, District of Hawaii; 1983, U.S. District Court, Northern, Eastern, Central and Southern Districts of California. *Education:* Western Illinois University (B.A., magna cum laude, 1976); University of California School of Law at Davis (J.D., with honors, 1979). Phi Kappa Phi; Pi Sigma Alpha. Editor, University of California at Davis Law Review, 1978. Author: "The Effect of Express Warranties On Seed Sales With An Eye To The U.C.C., Unconscionability and The California Agricultural Code," ll U.C.D. Law Review 335, 1978. Recipient: California State Bar 1994 President's Pro Bono Award. *Member:* Los Angeles County, Orange County (Chair, 1996, Business Litigation Section; Member, Executive Committee, Insurance Section), Hawaii State, Federal and American Bar Associations; State Bar of California (Member, Litigation and Law Practice Management Sections); Orange County Trial Lawyers Association; Consumer Attorneys of California; The Association of Trial Lawyers of America (Member, Insurance Section); Association of Business Trial Lawyers. **PRACTICE AREAS:** Complex Business Litigation; Insurance Coverage; Unfair Competition; Bad Faith; Banking; Real Estate; Commercial and Construction Law.

**STEPHEN E. BLAINE,** born Los Angeles, California, June 27, 1953; admitted to bar, 1980, California; 1981, U.S. Tax Court and U.S. District Court, Southern District of California; 1984, U.S. District Court, Northern District of California; 1986, U.S. District Court, Central District of California; 1995, U.S. District Court, Eastern District of California and U.S. Court of Appeals, Federal Circuit; 1996, U.S. Supreme Court. *Education:* California State University at Northridge (B.A., 1976); Loyola Marymount University (J.D., 1980). Member, Board of Directors, Women's Transitional Living Center, 1982-1983. *Member:* Orange County (Member, Sections on: Real Estate; Business and Corporations; Business Litigation) and Federal Bar Associations; State Bar of California. **PRACTICE AREAS:** Corporate Law; Business and Transactional Law; Real Property; Intellectual Property Litigation; Entertainment Law.

*(This Listing Continued)*

**KATHLEEN L. DUNHAM,** born Los Angeles, California, May 2, 1950; admitted to bar, 1981, California. *Education:* University of California at Berkeley (B.A., 1972); University of California at Los Angeles (J.D., 1978); University of California at Irvine (Teaching Certificate, 1988). *Member:* State Bar of California; Hispanic Bar Association. **LANGUAGES:** Spanish. **PRACTICE AREAS:** Civil Litigation; Business Law; Insurance Coverage Litigation; Creditors Rights.

**JIM P. MAHACEK,** born Sioux Falls, South Dakota, June 15, 1947; admitted to bar, 1977, California and U.S. District Court, Southern District of California; 1978, U.S. District Court, Central District of California and U.S. Court of Military Appeals; 1981, U.S. Court of Appeals, Ninth Circuit; U.S. District Court, Northern District of California; 1994, U.S. Supreme Court; 1995, U.S. District Court, Eastern District of California and U.S. District Court, District of Arizona. *Education:* University of South Dakota (B.A., 1969); Pepperdine University (J.D., 1977). Recipient: American Jurisprudence Award, Tort Practice. Instructor, Legal Writing, University of California, Irvine. Extension Division Lecturer, Real Estate Industry, Manufactured Housing Regulations. Judge Pro Tem, South Orange County Municipal Court, 1979-1984. Director, California Chapter of the National Neurofibromatosis Foundation, 1982-1985. *Member:* Orange County (Member, Business Litigation Section), South Orange County and American Bar Associations; State Bar of California. [Lt. Col., USMCR, Ret.]. **PRACTICE AREAS:** Administrative Law; Price Control Regulation; Civil Litigation; Appellate Practice.

**MICHAEL J. SACHS,** born Cleveland, Ohio, April 6, 1962; admitted to bar, 1987, Illinois; 1988, California and U.S. District Court, Central District of California; 1993, U.S. Court of Appeals, Fourth Circuit; 1994, U.S. District Court, Eastern District of California. *Education:* Washington University (A.B., 1984); Boston University (J.D., 1987; M.B.A., 1988). Intern, U.S. Securities and Exchange Commission, 1986-1988. *Member:* Los Angeles County, Orange County, Illinois State and American Bar Associations; State Bar of California. **PRACTICE AREAS:** Business Litigation; Insurance Coverage Litigation; Securities Litigation. *Email:* lawboy714@aol.com

**ANDREW A. SMITS,** born Harvey, Illinois, May 18, 1963; admitted to bar, 1990, California; U.S. District Court, Central, Eastern, Northern and Southern Districts of California; U.S. Court of Appeals, Ninth Circuit. *Education:* University of California at San Diego (B.A., 1986); Loyola Law School (J.D., 1989). *Member:* Orange County Bar Association (Member: Commercial Law; Bankruptcy and Business Litigation Sections); State Bar of California. **PRACTICE AREAS:** Business Litigation; Bankruptcy.

**GARY S. SPITZER,** born Redondo Beach, California, April 11, 1965; admitted to bar, 1991, California; 1994, U.S. District Court, Central District of California. *Education:* University of Southern California (B.A., History and International Relations, with honors, 1987); University of Bonn, Germany; Loyola Marymount Law School (J.D., Dean's list, 1991). Member, National History Honors Society. *Member:* Los Angeles County Bar Association; State Bar of California; California Business Trial Lawyers Association. **LANGUAGES:** German. **PRACTICE AREAS:** Business Litigation.

**EDWARD SUSOLIK,** born Trnava, Czechoslovakia, December 15, 1962; admitted to bar, 1990, California and U.S. District Court, Central, Southern, Northern and Eastern Districts of California. *Education:* University of Southern California at Los Angeles (B.A., Phil., Eng., Hist., 1986); University of Southern California School of Law (J.D., 1990). Order of the Coif. Recipient: American Jurisprudence Award, Constitutional Law I and II. Staff Member, 1988-1989 and Articles Editor, 1989-1990, University of Southern California Law Review. *Member:* Orange County (Member, Business Litigation Section) and American Bar Associations; State Bar of California. **PRACTICE AREAS:** Complex Business Litigation; Insurance Bad Faith; Insurance Coverage; Constitutional Law.

**GRAIG R. WOODBURN,** born Brighton, Massachusetts, June 19, 1960; admitted to bar, 1988, Massachusetts and California; 1993, U.S. District Court, Central and Northern Districts of California; 1995, U.S. Court of Appeals, Federal Circuit. *Education:* Hartwick College (B.A., with honors, Economics and Political Science, 1982); Georgetown University Law Center (J.D., 1987). *Member:* Massachusetts Bar Association; State Bar of California. **PRACTICE AREAS:** Securities Litigation; Intellectual Property Litigation; Business Litigation.

*(This Listing Continued)*

**CALLAHAN & BLAINE, A PROFESSIONAL LAW CORPORATION, Irvine—Continued**

*OF COUNSEL*

**SHELLEY M. LIBERTO,** born San Diego, California, February 6, 1953; admitted to bar, 1987, California; 1988, U.S. District Court, Central, Southern, Eastern and Northern Districts of California and U.S. Court of Appeals, Ninth Circuit. *Education:* University of California at Berkeley (B.A., 1975); University of Arizona (M.A., 1980); McGeorge School of Law, University of the Pacific (J.D., 1987). Order of the Coif; Traynor Honor Society. Recipient, American Jurisprudence Award in Conflict of Laws. Assistant Editor, Pacific Law Journal. California Real Estate Broker. Author: "Preferred Communications v. City of Los Angeles: First Amendment Rights and Cable Television Franchise Procedures," 17 Pac. L.J. 965 (1986); "Renfrew v. Loysen: Fee Awards for Attorneys Appearing In Propria Persona," 17 Pac. L.J. 614, 616, 711, 756, 758 and 789 (1985); "Review of Selected Nevada Legislation, 1985," 17 Pac. L.J. Nev. Legis. 59, 171, and 193 (1985). *Member:* Orange County Bar Association (Member, Business Litigation Section); State Bar of California. [U.S. Peace Corps, Morocco, 1976-1979]. **LANGUAGES:** Arabic and French. **PRACTICE AREAS:** Business Litigation; Computers and Software; Insurance Coverage; Legal Malpractices; Real Estate. **Email:** liberto@msn.com

**WALT D. MAHAFFA,** born New London, Connecticut, October 29, 1954; admitted to bar, 1980, California and U.S. District Court, Central District of California. *Education:* Loyola University of Los Angeles (B.A., 1976); Pepperdine University (J.D., 1979). Phi Alpha Delta. *Member:* Orange County (Member, Business Litigation Section) and American Bar Associations; State Bar of California. **PRACTICE AREAS:** Litigation; Business Law; Real Estate Law.

REPRESENTATIVE CLIENTS: Aqua Queen Mfg., Inc.; Arbek Manufacturing, Inc.; California; Citibank Corp., Classic Corporation; Communications Satellite Corporation of America; Fiber-Tech Engineering; Fonovisa, Inc.; Helionetics, Inc.; International Tory; Intex Recreation Corporation; Laserscope, Inc.; IS Enterprises; The Limited Stores, Inc.; MCI Communications Corporation; Media Deput; Northrup Gruman; Omnitel, Inc.; Orange County Museum of Art; Pick Systems; Pizza Hut, Inc., a subsidiary of Pepsico, Inc.; Playboy Enterprises, Inc.; Proxima Corporation; PTS/Polyseal; Reebok, International; Sentex, Inc.; Robinson Internation; Sandwell Enterprises; Signature Spas; Soldermask Corp.; SolderMask Technology, Inc.; Styles for Less; Sunglass Products, Inc.; Surgin Surgical Instrumentation, Inc.; Taco Bell, a subsidiary of Pepsico, Inc.; TKB International; Universal Protection Services; Verteq, Inc.; Western Digital Corp.

---

# BENJAMIN F. CARD

19800 MACARTHUR BOULEVARD, SUITE 370
**IRVINE, CALIFORNIA 92715**
Telephone: 714-851-6900
FAX: 714-955-1626

*Civil Litigation and Arbitration.*

**BENJAMIN F. CARD,** born Los Angeles, California, November 14, 1939; admitted to bar, 1971, California. *Education:* University of California at Berkeley (B.A., 1962); Western State University (J.D., 1970). Principal Attorney's Arbitration Service, 1988. *Member:* American Board of Trial Advocates (Past President, Orange County Chapter); Robert A. Banyard Inn of Court (Master Bencher). [Lt. USNR]

REFERENCE: Bank of America.

---

# CASE, KNOWLSON, BURNETT & WRIGHT

A Partnership including Professional Corporations

*Established in 1987*

5 PARK PLAZA, SUITE 800
**IRVINE, CALIFORNIA 92614**
Telephone: 714-955-1050
Telecopier: 714-851-9112

*Los Angeles, California Office:* Suite 1700, 2121 Avenue Of The Stars. Telephone: 213-552-2766. Telecopier: 213-552-3229.

*General Civil Trial and Appellate Practice in all State and Federal Courts. Corporate, Real Estate, Real Estate Finance, Taxation, Estate Planning, Trusts and Probate Law.*

FIRM PROFILE: *Case, Knowlson, Burnett & Wright, a Partnership including Professional Corporations, is a full-service law firm specializing in real estate, corporate transactions, civil litigation, and taxation, with substantial activity in estate planning and probate and bankruptcy matters. Members of our firm have been practicing law since 1974 with substantial experience at major Los Angeles law firms prior to the formation of the firm in 1986. The firm has 15 attorneys and maintains offices in Los Angeles and Irvine.*

**DANIEL A. CASE, (P.C.),** born Los Angeles, California, April 22, 1951; admitted to bar, 1976, California; 1977, U.S. District Court, Central District of California. *Education:* Massachusetts Institute of Technology (B.S., 1973; M.S., 1973); University of California at Berkeley (J.D., 1976). Notes and Comments Editor, Industrial Relations Law Journal, 1975-1976. *Member:* The State Bar of California. (Resident, Los Angeles Office). **PRACTICE AREAS:** Corporate; Real Estate.

**ARTHUR R. KNOWLSON, JR., (P.C.),** born Teaneck, New Jersey, November 18, 1948; admitted to bar, 1974, California and U.S. District Court, Central District of California; 1977, U.S. Tax Court. *Education:* Rutgers University (B.A., 1971); University of San Diego (J.D., 1974); University of Miami (LL.M. in Taxation, 1977). Adjunct Professor, Federal Income Taxation of Partners and Partnerships and Employee Retirement Plans, Graduate School of Taxation, Golden Gate University 1979—. *Member:* Orange County (Member, Sections on: Estate Planning, Probate and Trust Law, Real Estate and Tax) and American (Member, Taxation Section) Bar Associations; The State Bar of California (Member, Taxation Section). **PRACTICE AREAS:** Tax; Estate Planning; Trust; Probate.

**MICHAEL W. BURNETT, (P.C.),** born San Pedro, California, November 27, 1953; admitted to bar, 1980, Oregon; 1981, California; U.S. District Court, Central and Southern Districts of California. *Education:* University of California at Irvine (B.A., cum laude, 1977); University of the Pacific, McGeorge School of Law (J.D., with distinction, 1980). Member, Order of the Coif. Comment Editor, Pacific Law Journal, 1979-1980. Author: "The California Judiciary and Mandatory Sentencing," Vol. 11 Pacific Law Journal. *Member:* The State Bar of California (Member, Real Estate Section). **PRACTICE AREAS:** Real Estate.

**BARRY A. YOCH,** born Indianapolis, Indiana, August 21, 1953; admitted to bar, 1978, California; 1979, U.S. District Court, Central District of California; 1984, U.S. District Court, Southern District of California and U.S. Tax Court. *Education:* University of California at Riverside (B.S., with high honors, 1975); University of California at Los Angeles (J.D., 1978). *Member:* Orange County (Member: Sections on Estate Planning, Probate and Trust Law and Taxation) and American Bar Associations; The State Bar of California. **PRACTICE AREAS:** Estate Planning; Tax Law.

**RICK A. CIGEL,** born Stevens Point, Wisconsin, June 14, 1956; admitted to bar, 1982, California; 1983, U.S Court of Appeals, Ninth Circuit and U.S. District Court, Northern, Southern, Eastern and Central Districts of California. *Education:* University of Malaya, Kuala Lumpur, Malaysia; Jagiellonian University, Krakow, Poland; University of Wisconsin (B.S., with high honors, 1979); Northwestern University (J.D., 1982). *Member:* The State Bar of California. (Resident, Los Angeles Office).

**MICHAEL F. WRIGHT,** born Jackson, Mississippi, September 14, 1954; admitted to bar, 1979, California; 1989, U.S. Court of Appeals, Federal Circuit and Ninth Circuit. *Education:* Stanford University (B.A., 1976; J.D., 1979). Phi Beta Kappa. Law Clerk to the Honorable Lawrence T. Lydick, U.S. District Court, Central District of California, 1979-1980. *Member:* The State Bar of California. (Resident, Los Angeles Office).

**PATRICK W. WALSH,** born Brooklyn, New York, June 1, 1949; admitted to bar, 1974, California; 1980, District of Columbia. *Education:* Stanford University (B.A., with distinction, 1971); Boalt Hall School of Law, University of California (J.D., 1974). Associate Editor, 1972-1973 and Research Editor, 1973-1974, California Law Review. *Member:* The State Bar of California; District of Columbia Bar. (Resident, Los Angeles Office). **PRACTICE AREAS:** Civil Trial; Real Estate; Health.

*ASSOCIATES*

**RICK AUGUSTINI,** born Berkeley, California, August 30, 1967; admitted to bar, 1992, California, U.S. District Court, Central and Southern Districts of California and U.S. Court of Appeals, Ninth Circuit. *Education:* University of California, Irvine (B.A., 1989); Loyola Law School (J.D., 1992). Member, Loyola Law Review, 1991-1992. *Member:* State Bar of California.

*OF COUNSEL*

**DAVID M. LUBER,** born Los Angeles, California, July 5, 1950; admitted to bar, 1977, California. *Education:* University of California at Los Angeles (B.A., magna cum laude, 1973); Boalt Hall School of Law, University of California (J.D., 1976). Member, Environmental Law Quarterly, 1975-

*(This Listing Continued)*

1976. Member, Century City Chamber of Commerce Real Estate Advisory Cabinet. *Member:* Century City, Los Angeles County and American (Member, Sections on: Real Estate; Real Estate Financing) Bar Associations; The State Bar of California. (Resident, Los Angeles Office). *PRACTICE AREAS:* Real Estate; Real Estate Financing.

**EDWIN I. LASMAN,** born Los Angeles, California, March 5, 1955; admitted to bar, 1982, California; 1983, U.S. District Court, Central District of California and U.S. Court of Appeals, Ninth Circuit; 1987, U.S. District Court, Southern, Northern and Eastern Districts of California. *Education:* University of California at Berkeley (B.A., summa cum laude, 1976); University of California at Los Angeles (M.B.A., 1981; J.D., 1981). Phi Beta Kappa. Member, Moot Court Honors Program. Executive Editor, University of California at Los Angeles Journal of International Law, 1986-1987. Professor, Corporations, University of West Los Angeles School of Paralegal Studies, 1986. Member, French-American Chamber of Commerce, 1986-1987. *Member:* Los Angeles County and American (Member, Sections on: Business Law; Litigation) Bar Associations; State Bar of California. *LANGUAGES:* French. *PRACTICE AREAS:* Corporate Law; Real Estate; Civil Litigation.

**DANIEL G. JORDAN,** born Los Angeles, California, June 29, 1954; admitted to bar, 1981, California and U.S. District Court, Central District of California. *Education:* University of California at Los Angeles (A.B., 1978); Boalt Hall School of Law, University of California (J.D., 1981). *Member:* Los Angeles County and American Bar Associations; State Bar of California.

## CATES & HAN

19800 MACARTHUR BOULEVARD, SUITE 1450
**IRVINE, CALIFORNIA 92612**
Telephone: 714-757-4104
Facsimile: 714-757-4107
Email: cateshan@aol.com

*Business Transactions, Estate Planning, Litigation and Arbitration involving Franchising, Distribution, Unfair Competition, Trade Secrets and Business Torts.*

**JAMES W. HAN,** born Seoul, Korea, August 5, 1954; admitted to bar, 1983, California, U.S. District Court, Central District of California and U.S. District Court of Appeals, Ninth Circuit; 1985, U.S. District Court, Southern District of California. *Education:* University of California, Berkeley (A.B., 1980); Hastings College of Law (J.D., 1983). Instructor, Franchise Law, University of California at Irvine Extention, 1995. Judge Pro Tem, Orange County Superior Court, 1991—. Judge Pro Tem, Municipal Court West Orange County, 1991—. *Member:* Orange County, Los Angeles County and American (Forum Committee on Franchising, Litigation and Dispute Resolution Division, 1988—) Bar Associations; State Bar of California (Member, Business Law Section; Co-Chairman, Franchise Law Committee, 1992—); Federal Bar Association; Orange County Asian American Bar Association.

**WILLIAM L. CATES,** born Los Angeles, California, June 23, 1959; admitted to bar, 1985, California; 1987, U.S Tax Court. *Education:* California State University at Fullerton (B.A., 1981); University of California, Hastings College of Law (J.D., 1984). Phi Alpha Delta (Member, 1981-1984; President, 1984). Tax Professional, Peat Marwick & Company, 1985-1987. *Member:* Los Angeles County and American Bar Associations; Orange Coast Estate Planning Council. *PRACTICE AREAS:* Corporate Transactions; Probate; Estate Planning Law; Tax.

## CHAPMAN, FULLER & BOLLARD

Established in 1987

2010 MAIN STREET, SUITE 400
**IRVINE, CALIFORNIA 92714**
Telephone: 714-752-1455
Telecopier: 714-752-1485

*General Civil, Trial and Appellate Practice, State and Federal Courts, Business and Real Estate Law, Products Liability, Construction Defect, Personal Injury, Employment Law, Trade Secrets, Trademark and Unfair Competition Litigation.*

*(This Listing Continued)*

### MEMBERS OF FIRM

**WILLIAM D. CHAPMAN,** born Long Beach, California, March 26, 1954; admitted to bar, 1981, California; 1987, U.S. District Court, Central, Northern and Southern Districts of California. *Education:* Brigham Young University (B.S., 1978); Pepperdine University (J.D., 1981). Phi Delta Phi. Semi-finalist, Oral Advocacy, Vincent Dalsimer Moot Court Competition, 1980. Best Brief Award and Best Oralist Team, Phillip C. Jessup International Law Moot Court Competition, Pacific Region, 1981. *Member:* Orange County Bar Association (Member, Business Litigation Section, Business and Corporate Law, Construction Law, Creditors' Rights); State Bar of California. *LANGUAGES:* Spanish. *PRACTICE AREAS:* Litigation.

**H. DANIEL FULLER,** born Salt Lake City, Utah, March 11, 1955; admitted to bar, 1982, California and U.S. District Court, Central District of California; 1984, U.S. Court of Appeals, Ninth Circuit; 1985, U.S. District Court, Southern District of California. *Education:* University of California at Los Angeles (B.A., magna cum laude, 1979); Brigham Young University (J.D., cum laude, 1982). Member, Moot Court Board of Advocates. *Member:* Orange County Bar Association; State Bar of California (Trade Secrets Sub-Committee). *LANGUAGES:* Spanish. *PRACTICE AREAS:* Litigation.

**WILLIAM C. BOLLARD,** born Van Nuys, California, December 24, 1954; admitted to bar, 1982, California; 1983, U.S. District Court, Central District of California. *Education:* Brigham Young University (B.A., with honors, 1979); Pepperdine University (J.D., cum laude, 1982). Phi Delta Phi. Articles Editor, Pepperdine University Law Review, 1982. Member, Panel of Arbitrators, American Arbitration Association. *Member:* Orange County Bar Association (Member, Commercial Litigation Section); State Bar of California. *LANGUAGES:* Spanish. *PRACTICE AREAS:* Litigation.

### ASSOCIATE

**ROBERT J. HADLOCK,** born Long Beach, California, May 31, 1961; admitted to bar, 1994, California; 1995, U.S. District Court, Central District of California. *Education:* California State University, Fullerton (B.A., with honors, 1988); Hastings College of the Law, University of California (J.D., 1994). Member, 1992-1994 and Note Editor, 1993, 1994, Hastings Constitutional Law Quarterly. American Jurisprudence Award Winner in Evidence Workshop. Legal Research Instructor, Southern California College of Business and Law, 1994. Founding Member and President, Hastings Educational Alliance for the Rights of the Disabled, 1992-1994. *Member:* Orange County Bar Association; State Bar of California. *PRACTICE AREAS:* Litigation.

### OF COUNSEL

**RICHARD L. BROWN,** born American Fork, Utah, January 26, 1952; admitted to bar, 1979, California. *Education:* Brigham Young University (B.S., cum laude, 1976; J.D., cum laude, 1979). Member, Moot Court Board. Recipient, International Academy of Trial Lawyers Outstanding Advocate Award. *Member:* Orange County Bar Association; State Bar of California. *PRACTICE AREAS:* General Civil Practice; Corporate Law; Probate; Professional Liability Defense; Environmental Law.

REPRESENTATIVE CLIENTS: Albertsons Inc.; Alumax, Inc.; Dana Corp.; Merrill Lynch; Owens-Corning Fiberglass Corp.; Sinclair Paint Co.; Wet Design.

## CHEVALIER, ALLEN & LICHMAN, LLP

5 PARK PLAZA, SUITE 1500
**IRVINE, CALIFORNIA 92614**
Telephone: 714-474-6967
Fax: 714-474-9606

Torrance, California Office: 23430 Hawthorne Boulevard, Skypark 3, Suite 200. Telephone: 310-378-0975. Fax: 310-791-1546.

*Commercial Litigation, Aviation Law and Litigation, Environmental Law and Litigation.*

FIRM PROFILE: *At Chevalier, Allen & Lichman, we provide clients the personalized services and attention of a small firm and professional acumen usually associated with major national law firms, but at more realist costs.*

**GARY MIKEL ALLEN,** born Cairo, West Virginia, December 22, 1939; admitted to bar, 1992, California. *Education:* (California Western University (PH.D., aviation environmental studies, 1981); (California State University (J.D., 1987).

**ROGER P. FREEMAN,** born Pomona, California, 1946; admitted to bar, 1972, California; 1973, Arizona and U.S. Court of Appeals, Ninth Cir-

*(This Listing Continued)*

### CHEVALIER, ALLEN & LICHMAN, LLP, Irvine—Continued

cuit. *Education:* University of Redlands (B.A., cum laude, 1968); University of California at Los Angeles (J.D., 1971). Author: "Construction and Application of Military Function Exception to Notice and Comment Requirements of Administrative Procedure Act" 133 ALR Fed. 537 (1996); "Application of State and Local Construction and Building Regulations to Contractors Engaged in Construction Projects for the Federal Government" 131 ALR Fed. 583 (1996); "FAA Review of Noise Rules Under ANCA and Part 161", 6 Airport Noise Report 141 (1994); "Noise Notes-FAA Review of Requests for Waivers of Fleet Compliance Deadlines," Airport Highlights, Feb 6, 1995; "Noise Note: Is Noise a Dead Issue?" Airport Highlights, May 22, 1995; "Noise and Environmental Law, An Update for Airports", Airports West, June 1995; Noise Note: Airport Noise and the DNL Debate" Airport Highlights, July 24, 1995; "Noise Note: Neighbors Using Financial Approaches to Pressure Airports to Regulate Noise" Airport Highlights, February 5, 1996; "Commentary: Recent Events May Change Tactics Communities Use", Airport Noise Report 23 (Feb. 19, 1996). Co-Author: "The Environmental Consequences of Municipal Airports: A Subject of Federal Mandate?" 53 Journal of Air Law Commerce 375 (1987). Editorial Board, Airport Environmental Management Handbook, Airport Council International (1992, 1994). Adjunct Professor, Land Use Law, Thomas Jefferson College of Law, 1996. Local Government Law, University of La Verne College of Law. Aviation Law, California State University, Los Angeles, 1995. Deputy City Attorney, City of Long Beach 1980-1994. Deputy City Attorney, City of Torrance, 1972-1980. Chairman, Legal Committee, Airport Council, International (1992). El Toro Airport Reuse Citizens Advisory Commission, Alternative (1996). *Member:* Orange County Bar Association (Member, Aviation and Real Estate Sections); The State Bar of California (Member Real Estate Section); National Association of Security Dealers; Building Industry Association; Transportation Association.

**BERNE C. HART,** born Biglerville, Pennsylvania, September 2, 1940; admitted to bar, 1991, California and U.S. Court of Appeals, Ninth Circuit; 1992, U.S. District Court, Northern, Eastern and Southern Districts of California. *Education:* Western State University (B.S.L., 1984; J.D., 1987). *Member:* State Bar of California; American Bar Association. (Resident). *PRACTICE AREAS:* Civil Practice.

**BARBARA E. LICHMAN,** born New York, N.Y., April 27, 1946; admitted to bar, 1988, California. *Education:* University of Southern California (Ph.D., 1986; J.D., 1988). Member, Computer/Tax Journal, University of Southern California Law School, 1986-1987. Author: "The Courts v. Planning: The Anatomy of Four Conflicts," Western State Law Review, Volume XV, Number 1, Fall, 1987. *Member:* American Planning Association. *PRACTICE AREAS:* Aviation and Airport Access Regulation; Commercial Litigation; Environmental.

**FREDERICK C. WOODRUFF,** born Utica, New York, September 5, 1937; admitted to bar, 1963, New York (Not admitted in California). *Education:* Syracuse University (LL.B., 1962); George Washington University (LLM., public law, 1968). *PRACTICE AREAS:* Aviation law (50%); Environmental Law (25%); Administrative Law (25%).

---

### VIVIEN M. CHIU

2603 SOUTH MAIN STREET, SUITE 800
IRVINE, CALIFORNIA 92714
Telephone: 714-833-8239

*Family Law, Immigration Law.*

**VIVIEN M. CHIU,** born Hong Hong, Hong Kong, August 27, 1957; admitted to bar, 1992, California. *Education:* University of Waterloo (B.S., 1979); Western State University (J.D., 1992). *PRACTICE AREAS:* Family Law; Immigration Law.

CAA312B

---

### CHRISTIE, PARKER & HALE, LLP

SUITE 1440
5 PARK PLAZA
IRVINE, CALIFORNIA 92714
Telephone: 714-476-0757
Los Angeles: 213-681-1800
Cable Address: "Patlaw"
Telex: ITT 4995129 (CP&H PSD)
Telecopier: 714-476-8640

*Pasadena, California Office:* Fifth Floor, Wells Fargo Bank Building, 350 West Colorado Boulevard. Telephone: 818-795-9900.

*Patent, Trademark and Copyright Law. Unfair Competition, Trade Secrets, Computer Law, Biotechnology, Licensing, Antitrust and Complex Business Litigation.*

(For Personnel and Biographical Data, see Professional Biographies at Pasadena, California)

---

### DOUGLAS D. CICIONE

A PROFESSIONAL CORPORATION
Established in 1985

SUITE 300, 19762 MACARTHUR BOULEVARD
IRVINE, CALIFORNIA 92612-2478
Telephone: 714-253-3499; 310-379-8602
Fax: 714-474-9392

*Federal and State Taxation. Estate Planning, Trust and Probate. Tax Collection, Audit and Litigation. Corporate, Partnership and Business Tax Planning.*

**DOUGLAS D. CICIONE,** born Jamaica, New York, March 28, 1951; admitted to bar, 1978, California. *Education:* St. Lawrence University (B.A., summa cum laude, with highest distinction in Economics, 1973); Stanford University (J.D., 1977); Stanford Graduate School of Business (M.B.A., 1977); University of San Diego School of Law (LL.M. in Taxation, 1984). Phi Beta Kappa. Recipient: Wall Street Journal Award for Outstanding Economics Thesis. Licensed Real Estate Broker, California, 1986. *Member:* Los Angeles County and Orange County Bar Associations; State Bar of California. (Certified Specialist, Taxation Law, Estate Planning, Trust and Probate Law, The State Bar of California Board of Legal Specialization).

---

### COLLINS & BELLENGHI

18401 VON KARMAN AVENUE, SUITE 220
IRVINE, CALIFORNIA 92612-1542
Telephone: 714-851-9311
Fax: 714-851-9333

*Labor and Employment Law, Banking and Financial Institution Law, Complex Litigation, Consumer Law, Contract Disputes, Business Torts and Professional Liability Law.*

**MICHAEL J. COLLINS,** born Lynwood, California, March 19, 1950; admitted to bar, 1975, California. *Education:* Seattle University (B.A., 1972); Loyola University of Los Angeles (J.D., 1975). *Member:* State Bar of California; California Trial Lawyers Association (Recognized Experience as a Trial Lawyer); American Board of Trial Advocates (Associate). (Certified as a Civil Trial Advocate by the National Board of Trial Advocacy).

**JULIAN B. BELLENGHI,** born Philadelphia, Pennsylvania, March 9, 1948; admitted to bar, 1981, District of Columbia, U.S. District Court for the District of Columbia and U.S. Court of Appeals for the District of Columbia Circuit; 1987, California; 1988, U.S. District Court, Central District of California and U.S. Court of Appeals, Ninth Circuit; 1991, U.S. District Court, Northern, Southern and Eastern Districts of California. *Education:* University of Madrid, Madrid, Spain; Georgetown University (B.S., cum laude, 1970); Antioch College (J.D., 1981). Alumni Admissions Consultant for Georgetown University. Co-Author: "Employment Law Bulletin," 1988—. Staff Attorney: National Labor Relations Board, Division of Judges, Washington, D.C., 1982-1984; Association of Flight Attendants, 1984-1987. Court appointed Arbitrator, Los Angeles Superior Court, 1993—. Judge Pro Tem, Los Angeles Municipal Court, 1994—. *Member:* Los Angeles County and San Fernando Valley (Member, Litigation Section) Bar Associations; The District of Columbia Bar; State Bar of California (Member, Labor Law Section); Italian American Lawyers Association (President Elect). *LANGUAGES:* Spanish and Italian. *REPORTED*

*(This Listing Continued)*

CASES: Barnes v. Litton Systems, Inc., 28 Cal.App 4th. 681, 33 Cal.Rptr.2d 652 (1994).

### ASSOCIATES

**DEBORAH S. ROBBINS,** born Gordon, Nebraska, August 12, 1961; admitted to bar, 1993, California and U.S. District Court, Central District of California. *Education:* Mid-America Nazarene College (B.A., 1983); Washburn University of Topeka (J.D., 1992). *Member:* Orange County Bar Association; State Bar of California; Christian Legal Society (President, 1989—).

## A. BENNETT COMBS

### A PROFESSIONAL CORPORATION

14988 SAND CANYON, SUITE 1-8
**IRVINE, CALIFORNIA 92618**
Telephone: 714-786-0023
Fax: 714-786-3864

*Insurance Defense, Products Liability, Church and Clergy, Premises, Automobile.*

**A. BENNETT COMBS,** born Paola, Kansas, March 1, 1945; admitted to bar, 1976, California; U.S. District Court, Central, Southern, Eastern and Northern Districts of California and U.S. Court of Appeals, Ninth Circuit. *Education:* Los Angeles State College; Glendale College (LL.B., 1975). *Member:* Orange and Los Angeles County Bar Associations; State Bar of California; American Board of Trial Advocates; Association of Southern California Defense Counsel; Defense Research Institute. **PRACTICE AREAS:** Insurance Defense; Products Liability; Church/Clergy; Premises; Automobile.

REPRESENTATIVE CLIENTS: Church Mutual Insurance Company; Invacare Corporation; Hamilton Resources/MEDMARC; Empire Fire & Marine; Farmers Home Group.

## CONNOR, CULVER, BLAKE & GRIFFIN LLP

2600 MICHELSON DRIVE, SUITE 1450
**IRVINE, CALIFORNIA 92612**
Telephone: 714-622-2600
Fax: 714-622-2626

*Business Litigation, with Areas of Concentration in Land Use, Construction Defect, Real Estate, Financial Institutions, Securities, Bankruptcy, Employment Law, including Sexual Harassment and Discrimination.*

**EDMOND M. CONNOR,** born September 1, 1950; admitted to bar, 1975, California. *Education:* Georgetown University (B.A., summa cum laude, 1972); Stanford University (J.D., 1975). Phi Beta Kappa. *Member:* Orange County (Member: Board of Directors, 1987-1989, 1991-1993; Executive Committee, 1995—; Board of Directors of Public Law Center, 1987—; Chair, 1991-1993. Recipient, 1995 PLC Attorney of the Year Award. Co-Chair, Civic Center Homeless Task Force, 1992; Recipient, 1991 OCBA Liberty Bell Award); Federal (Delegate, Ninth Circuit Judicial Conference, 1993-1995) and American (Recipient, 1991 ABA Pro Bono Publico Award) Bar Associations; State Bar of California (Recipient, President's Pro Bono Service Award, 1991).

**MARILYN MARTIN CULVER,** born December 5, 1957; admitted to bar, 1983, California. *Education:* University of California at Los Angeles (B.A., cum laude, 1980; J.D., 1983).

**LAURA LEE BLAKE,** born December 12, 1962; admitted to bar, 1990, California. *Education:* University of Iowa (B.A., with highest distinction, 1986); University of Iowa College of Law (J.D., with distinction, 1989). Staff Member, Iowa Law Review, 1987-1989. Law Clerk to the Honorable C. Arlen Beam, U.S. Court of Appeals, Eighth Circuit, 1989-1990. Chair, State Bar of California Court Rules Committee, 1995—; Chair, State Bar of California Subcommittee on Proposed Legislation, 1994-1995.

**CRAIG L. GRIFFIN,** born August 11, 1957; admitted to bar, 1989, California. *Education:* California State University, Long Beach (B.S., 1982); Brigham Young University (J.D., summa cum laude, 1989). Order of the Coif. Lead Articles Editor, Brigham Young University Law Review, 1988-1989. Law Clerk to the Honorable Thomas Gibbs Gee, U.S. Court of Appeals, Fifth Circuit, 1989-1990.

*(This Listing Continued)*

**ROMA R. HANLON,** born October 31, 1964; admitted to bar, 1993, California. *Education:* University of California at Los Angeles (B.A., 1987); Santa Clara University (J.D., 1992). Associate Editor, Santa Clara University Law Review, 1992. Extern to the Honorable James Ware, U.S. District Court, Northern District of California, 1992. Public Law Center, New Attorney of the Year, 1994.

**DAVID J. HASSELTIME,** born Upland, California, January 23, 1970; admitted to bar, 1996, California. *Education:* University of California at Irvine (B.A., cum laude, 1992); University of San Diego School of Law (J.D., magna cum laude, 1996) Phi Beta Kappa. Order of the Coif. Executive Comments and Notes Editor, San Diego Law Review, 1995-1996. Comment, The Evolution of the Capital Punishment Jurisprudence of the United States Supreme Court and the Impact of Tuilaepa v. California on That Evolution, 32 San Diego L. Rev. 593 (1995).

## CORBETT & STEELMAN

### A PROFESSIONAL LAW CORPORATION

SUITE 200, 18200 VON KARMAN
**IRVINE, CALIFORNIA 92612**
Telephone: 714-553-9266
Telecopier: 714-553-8454

*General Practice including Trial and Appellate Litigation in all State and Federal Courts. Corporate, Banking, Franchise, Real Property, Insurance, Antitrust, Trade Secret, Bankruptcy and Insolvency Matters.*

**BRUCE R. CORBETT,** born Rochester, New York, July 29, 1944; admitted to bar, 1970, California. *Education:* Hamilton College and University of Pennsylvania (B.A., 1966); Cornell University (J.D., 1969). *Member:* Orange County (Member: Business Litigation Section; Committee on Administration of Justice, 1977-1979) and American (Member, Sections on: Litigation; Corporation, Banking and Business Law; Patent, Trademark and Copyright Law; Antitrust Law; Insurance. Negligence and Compensation Law) Bar Associations; State Bar of California; Orange County Trial Lawyers Association.

**KEN E. STEELMAN,** born Ames, Iowa, September 28, 1945; admitted to bar, 1972, California. *Education:* University of Iowa (B.S., 1967); California Western University (J.D., 1972). Phi Delta Phi. Deputy District Attorney, County of Orange, 1973-1975. *Member:* Orange County (Member: Insurance Committee, 1976; Committee on Administration of Justice, 1978-1979; Fee Arbitration Committee, 1979-1983; Judiciary Committee, 1982-1983; Business Litigation, Commercial and Bankruptcy Sections) and American Bar Associations; State Bar of California; Orange County Trial Lawyers Association.

**RICHARD B. SPECTER,** born Philadelphia, Pennsylvania, September 6, 1952; admitted to bar, 1977, Missouri; 1978, Illinois and Pennsylvania; 1984, California. *Education:* Washington University (B.A., cum laude, 1974); George Washington University (J.D., 1977). Instructor, George Washington University National Law Center, 1975. *Member:* Orange County (Member: Business Litigation Section), Illinois State, Pennsylvania and American (Member, Litigation Section and Committee on Entertainment and Sports Industries) Bar Associations; The Missouri Bar; The State Bar of California.

**DAVID F. BROWN,** born Orange, New Jersey, September 22, 1955; admitted to bar, 1981, California. *Education:* University of California, Irvine (B.S., cum laude, 1977); University of California, Los Angeles (J.D., 1981). Phi Beta Kappa. *Member:* Orange County (Member: Business Litigation and Real Estate Law Sections; Federal Court Committee, 1983) and American (Member: Section of Litigation) Bar Associations; State Bar of California.

---

**MARK M. MONACHINO,** born Passaic, New Jersey, December 1, 1963; admitted to bar, 1989, California, U.S. District Court, Central District of California and U.S. Court of Appeals, Ninth Circuit. *Education:* University of Notre Dame (B.S.EE., 1985; B.A., Philosophy, 1986); Loyola Law School (J.D., cum laude, 1989). Chief Note and Comment Editor, International and Comparative Law Journal. Member, St. Thomas Moore Honor Society. *Member:* Orange County and American Bar Associations; State Bar of California.

*(This Listing Continued)*

## CORBETT & STEELMAN, A PROFESSIONAL LAW CORPORATION, Irvine—Continued

**DEBRA L. BARBIN,** born Anaheim, California, October 28, 1966; admitted to bar, 1991, California; 1992, U.S. District Court, Central District of California. *Education:* Texas Christian University; University of California at Los Angeles (B.A., 1988); University of California, Hastings College of Law (J.D., 1991). Phi Beta Kappa; Phi Delta Phi (Vice Magister, 1990-1991). Associate Editor of Research and Development, Hastings Journal of Communications and Entertainment Law. Recipient, American Jurisprudence Award in Wills and Trusts. *Member:* San Bernardino County, Western San Bernardino County and American Bar Associations; State Bar of California; Association of Southern California Defense Counsel.

**ANTHONY L. LANZA,** born El Centro, California, September 21, 1964; admitted to bar, 1991, California; 1993, U.S. District Court, Central District of California. *Education:* University of Notre Dame (B.A., magna cum laude, 1987); Hastings College of the Law, University of California (J.D., 1991). Member, Hastings Law Review, 1990-1991. Mock Trial Coach, Constitutional Rights Foundation of Orange County, 1992—. *Member:* Orange County Bar Association; State Bar of California. [First Lieut., U.S. Army, 1987—]

**ROBERT H. FEIGENBAUM,** born Middletown, New York, February 6, 1969; admitted to bar, 1996, California. *Education:* State University of New York at Albany (B.A., 1991); University of San Diego School of Law (J.D., 1995).

REPRESENTATIVE CLIENTS: Beatrice/Hunt-Wesson Foods, Inc.; First American Title Insurance Co.; Fluor Corp.; Ortega Properties; Coscan Davidson Homes; Colorbus, Inc.; Fibertron Corp.; Sho Air International; Corporate Bank; BKM Total Office; Little Caesar Enterprises; Rancho Mission Viejo; Red Robin International; Lawyers' Mutual Insurance Co.; Resolution Trust Corporation; City of Newport Beach.
REFERENCE: Marine National Bank.

---

## COREY, CROUDACE, DIETRICH & DRAGUN

Established in 1992

5 PARK PLAZA, SUITE 1050
**IRVINE, CALIFORNIA 92714**
Telephone: 714-251-2777
Fax: 714-251-2779

*Real Estate, Finance, Land Use and Business.*

FIRM PROFILE: *Corey, Croudace, Dietrich & Dragun is composed primarily of attorneys from the Real Estate and Finance Departments of Latham & Watkins. Corey, Croudace, Dietrich & Dragun specializes in real estate, finance, land use, bankruptcy and general business law, and is committed to delivering high-quality, cost effective legal services.*

### MEMBERS

**VIRGINIA P. CROUDACE,** born Worcester, Massachusetts, November 27, 1954; admitted to bar, 1985, California. *Education:* Bates College (B.A., 1976); University of Southern California (J.D., 1985). Staff Member, 1983-1984 and Articles Editor, 1984-1985, Southern California Law Review. Author: Note, "Where the Boys Are: Can Separate Be Equal in School Sports?", 58 Southern California Law Review (1985). Attorney, Latham & Watkins, 1985-1992. *Member:* State Bar of California.

**DEBRA M. DIETRICH,** born Pasadena, California, August 27, 1960; admitted to bar, 1986, California. *Education:* University of California at Los Angeles (B.A., 1982); Haas School of Business, University of California at Berkeley (M.B.A., 1985); Boalt Hall School of Law, University of California (J.D., 1985). Attorney, Latham & Watkins, 1986-1992. *Member:* State Bar of California (Vice-Chair, Affordable Housing Subsection, Real Property Section).

**ANTHONY J. DRAGUN,** born Fontana, California, November 3, 1957; admitted to bar, 1986, California. *Education:* University of California at Riverside (B.S., honors, 1981); Haas School of Business, University of California at Berkeley (M.B.A., 1985); Boalt Hall School of Law, University of California (J.D., 1985). Beta Gamma Sigma. Attorney, Latham & Watkins, 1985-1992. *Member:* State Bar of California. (Also Of Counsel to Songstad, Randall & Ulich, Irvine, California).

*(This Listing Continued)*

---

### ASSOCIATES

**MARK A. NITIKMAN,** born Santa Monica, California, January 31, 1958; admitted to bar, 1988, California. *Education:* University of California at Los Angeles (B.A., 1978); University of Southern California (M.P.A., 1980; J.D., 1988). Order of the Coif. Staff Member, Southern California Law Review, 1986-1988. Legal Extern to Hon. Wm. Rea. Central District of California, 1987. Author: "Instant Planning-Land Use Regulation by Initiative in California," 61 Southern California Law Review. 497 (1988). Legal Writing Instructor, USC, 1987-1988. Member, Federalist Society, 1987—. *Member:* State Bar of California (Member: Steering Committee, Real Property Section; Affordable Housing Subsection, Orange County Chapter).

**JOSEPH L. COLEMAN,** born Pikeville, Kentucky, January 13, 1959; admitted to bar, 1986, New York; 1989, California. *Education:* University of Chicago (A.B., 1980); Temple University School of Law (J.D., magna cum laude, 1985). Co-Author: "Pledges of Partnership Interests: Panacea or Pandora's Box?" Vol. 368 Real Estate Workouts and Bankruptcies 1991, 23, 121 (PLI 1991); "Pledges of Partnership Interests," Los Angeles Lawyer (June 1992). *Member:* Orange County and American (Member, Real Property, Probate and Trust Law Section) Bar Associations. **PRACTICE AREAS:** Real Estate Finance; Real Estate; Business Law; Public Finance.

### OF COUNSEL

**CHRISTIANNE F. KERNS,** born Inglewood, California, August 11, 1958; admitted to bar, 1985, California. *Education:* California State University at Fullerton (B.A., cum laude, 1980); University of Southern California Law Center (J.D., 1985). Editor-in-Chief, Major Tax Planning and Computer Law Journal, University of Southern California, 1984-1985. *Member:* Los Angeles County, Orange County and American (Member, Commercial Financial Services Committee) Bar Associations; State Bar of California; Financial Lawyers Conference. (Also Of Counsel to Armstrong, Hirsch, Jackoway, Tyerman & Wertheimer at Los Angeles). **PRACTICE AREAS:** Real Estate Finance; Real Estate Workouts; Commercial Law; Business Law.

---

## COX, CASTLE & NICHOLSON, LLP

A Limited Liability Partnership including Professional Corporations

19800 MACARTHUR BOULEVARD, SUITE 600
**IRVINE, CALIFORNIA 92715**
Telephone: 714-476-2111
Fax: 714-476-0256

*Los Angeles, California Office:* 28th Floor, Two Century Plaza, 2049 Century Park East. Telephone: 310-277-4222. Fax: 310-277-7889.

*General Civil, Trial and Appellate Practice in all State and Federal Courts. Real Property and Construction Law. Land Use and Environmental Law. Public Bond Financing. International Law. Labor Relations Bankruptcy, Receiverships and Creditors Rights. Taxation, Trusts, Estate Planning and Probate Law.*

FIRM PROFILE: *Cox, Castle & Nicholson, LLP was founded over 40 years ago and has consistently focused its practice on the representation of businesses and individuals involved in all aspects of the real estate, construction and financial services industries. With offices in both Los Angeles and Irvine, California, Cox, Castle & Nicholson, LLP is one of the largest firms serving the real estate industry in the United States. The firm provides the breadth and depth of legal services typically required by developers, builders, investors, landlords, tenants, lenders and others who are involved in a wide range of commercial, industrial, residential, hotel and resort projects.*

### RESIDENT PARTNERS

**ARTHUR O. SPAULDING, JR.,** born Pasadena, California, April 17, 1948; admitted to bar, 1973, California; 1976, Nevada; 1979, U.S. Court of Appeals, Ninth Circuit; 1980, U.S. Supreme Court. *Education:* Yale University (B.A., 1970); University of California at Los Angeles (J.D., 1973). Admitted to practice before the Nevada Gaming Commission and State Gaming Control Board, 1978. Director: American Resort Development Association Board of Directors, 1989-1991. Director, 1984-1989 and Vice President, 1987-1988, International Foundation for Timesharing. Lecturer: American Resort Development Association Annual Conferences, 1981-1996. **PRACTICE AREAS:** Resort and Residential Development Law; Real Estate and Receivables Finance Law; Real Property Law.

**LORA LEE MOORE,** born Whittier, California, June 5, 1952; admitted to bar, 1977, California and U.S. District Court, Central and Southern Districts of California. *Education:* Whittier College (B.A., 1974); Loyola Uni-

*(This Listing Continued)*

versity of Los Angeles (J.D., cum laude, 1977). Member, St. Thomas More Law Honor Society. Managing Editor, Loyola University of Los Angeles Law Review, 1976-1977. *Member:* Orange County Bar Association; State Bar of California. **PRACTICE AREAS:** Construction Law; Civil Litigation.

**P. JEROLD WALSH,** born Youngstown, Ohio, October 13, 1937; admitted to bar, 1977, Texas; 1979, California; 1982, U.S. District Court, Central District of California. *Education:* University of Florida (B.S., with high honors, 1961; M.S., 1963); University of Houston (J.D., cum laude, 1976). Phi Beta Kappa; Sigma Pi Sigma. Member, Order of the Barons. *Member:* State Bar of Texas; State Bar of California; American Bar Association. **PRACTICE AREAS:** Environmental Law; Hazardous and Toxic Substances Law; Real Property Law.

**MARK P. MCCLANATHAN,** born Winona, Minnesota, May 10, 1952; admitted to bar, 1977, California; 1980, U.S. Tax Court. *Education:* University of Wisconsin-Madison (B.B.A., magna cum laude, 1974); University of Southern California (J.D., 1977). Phi Kappa Phi; Beta Gamma Sigma; Beta Alpha Psi; Order of the Coif. *Member:* Orange County Bar Association (Member, Real Estate Section); The State Bar of California (Member, Real Property Section). **PRACTICE AREAS:** Real Property Law; Corporate Law; Taxation Law.

**JOHN A. KINCANNON,** born San Pedro Beach, California, September 13, 1955; admitted to bar, 1980, Arkansas; 1982, Texas; 1986, California. *Education:* University of Arkansas (B.S.B.A., with honors, 1977; J.D., 1980); New York University (LL.M., in Taxation, 1981). Beta Gamma Sigma; Beta Alpha Psi; Phi Alpha Delta. Certified Public Accountant, Arkansas, 1980. *Member:* Orange County and American Bar Associations; State Bar of California (Member, Real Estate Section). **PRACTICE AREAS:** Real Property Law; Partnerships Law; Public Finance.

**JESS R. BRESSI,** born Philadelphia, Pennsylvania, March 23, 1957; admitted to bar, 1983, California. *Education:* California State University at Northridge (B.S., 1979); Southwestern University School of Law (J.D., 1983). Member, Moot Court Honors Program. First Place Oralist and Best Brief Award, Intellectual Property Moot Court Competition, Los Angeles County Bar Association, 1982. Law Clerk to the Honorable Geraldine Mund, U.S. Bankruptcy Judge, Central District of California, 1984-1985. *Member:* State Bar of California; Financial Lawyers Conference; Orange County Bankruptcy Forum. **PRACTICE AREAS:** Bankruptcy Law; Real Estate, Construction and Commercial Litigation; Creditor Rights Law.

**D. SCOTT TURNER,** born San Jose, California, January 2, 1952; admitted to bar, 1982, California; 1983, U.S. District Court, Eastern District of California. *Education:* University of California at Davis (B.S., 1975); McGeorge School of the Law, University of the Pacific (J.D., 1982). Deputy Real Estate Commissioner, California Department of Real Estate, 1980-1984. *Member:* State Bar of California (Member, Real Property Section); American Resort and Residential Development Association (Member, State Legislative Committee; Director, International Foundation for Timesharing, 1988—); California Building Industry Association (Member, Home Builders Council); Asociacion Mexicana De Desarroll adores Turisticos, A.C. **PRACTICE AREAS:** Real Property Law.

### RESIDENT ASSOCIATES

Stathi George Marcopulos; Camellia Kuo Schuk; Colin C. Swainston; Robert J. Sykes.

---

# CROWELL & MORING LLP

*Established in 1979*

**2010 MAIN STREET, SUITE 1200**
**IRVINE, CALIFORNIA 92714-7217**
*Telephone: 714-263-8400*
*Fax: 714-263-8414*

*Washington, D.C. Office:* 1001 Pennsylvania Avenue, N.W. Telephone: 202-624-2500. Fax: 202-628-5116.
*London, England Office:* 180 Fleet Street, EC4A 2HD. Telephone: 011-44-171-413-0011. Fax: 011-44-171-413-0333.

*General Practice.*

### MEMBERS OF FIRM

**DONALD E. SOVIE,** born Tacoma, Washington, October 16, 1944; admitted to bar, 1970, California. *Education:* Seattle University (B.A., 1966); University of San Francisco (J.D., 1969). Assistant Procurement Legal Advisor, Judge Advocate, Assistant Procurement Counsel, Claims

*(This Listing Continued)*

Officer and Counsel, Legal Officer in Charge, U.S. Army, 1969-1974. Senior Trial Attorney, Army Contract Appeals Division, 1975-1977. Labor Advisor, Office of the Assistant Secretary of the Army for Research, Development and Acquisition, 1977-1978. **PRACTICE AREAS:** Government Contract Law; International Business Law; Federal Practice; Commercial Law. *Email:* dsovie@cromor.com

**RANDALL L. ERICKSON,** born Eau Claire, Wisconsin, January 17, 1943; admitted to bar, 1971, Wisconsin; 1972, California. *Education:* University of Wisconsin (B.S., 1965); Duke University (J.D., 1971). Research Editor, Duke Law Journal, 1970-1971. **PRACTICE AREAS:** Construction Law; Commercial Banking Law; Antitrust Law.

**MICHAEL D. NEWMAN,** born New York, N.Y., July 9, 1952; admitted to bar, 1985, Maryland (inactive); 1986, District of Columbia; 1991, California. *Education:* Oberlin College (A.B., 1974); Purdue University (M.A., 1975; Ph.D., 1980); George Washington University (J.D., 1985).

### OF COUNSEL

**LINDA M. CIPRIANI,** born New York, N.Y., 1954; admitted to bar, 1979, Texas; 1995, California. *Education:* State University of New York at Albany (B.A., 1974); Northeastern University (J.D., 1979). Attorney, Office of Special Counsel, Department of Energy, 1979-1982. Assistant United States Attorney, United States Attorney's Office, Southern District of Texas, 1982-1986. **PRACTICE AREAS:** Insurance Coverage; First and Third Party Insurance Defense; Toxic Tort Defense; Superfund.

**STEVEN A. FINK,** born New York, New York, December 7, 1954; admitted to bar, 1980, California. *Education:* Tulane University (B.A., 1976; J.D., 1980). **PRACTICE AREAS:** Business Litigation; Construction Law; Labor Law.

**STEVEN P. RICE,** born Glendale, California, February 9, 1956; admitted to bar, 1980, California. *Education:* Occidental College (B.A., 1977); Harvard University (J.D., 1980). Phi Beta Kappa. **PRACTICE AREAS:** Commercial Litigation; Unfair Business Practices; Real Estate Litigation. *Email:* srice@cromor.com

### ASSOCIATES

**CECELIA A. TRIPI,** born Los Angeles, California, June 14, 1959; admitted to bar, 1985, California. *Education:* University of Southern California (B.A., 1981); Loyola Law School (J.D., 1984). *Email:* ctripi@cromor.com

**DONALD E. BRADLEY,** born Los Angeles, California, February 15, 1963; admitted to bar, 1989, California. *Education:* California State University at Fullerton (B.A., 1986); University of California at Davis (J.D., 1989). *Email:* dbradley@cromor.com

**STUART EINBINDER,** born Los Angeles, California, February 8, 1964; admitted to bar, 1991, California. *Education:* University of California at Santa Barbara (B.A., 1986); Hastings College of the Law, University of California (J.D., 1991). Order of the Coif. Member, Hastings Constitutional Law Quarterly, 1990-1991.

**DIANE SMITH DARUTY,** born Chicago, Illinois, November 3, 1963; admitted to bar, 1993, California. *Education:* University of Illinois, Urbana-Champaign (B.S., 1985); University of California-Davis (J.D., 1992). Certified Public Accountant, California, 1989.

**DEBORAH E. COLANER,** born Cincinnati, Ohio, August 9, 1968; admitted to bar, 1993, California. *Education:* Miami University, Oxford, Ohio (B.A., 1990); University of Southern California (J.D., 1993). Senior Editor, 1991-1992 and Executive Notes Editor, 1992-1993, Interdisciplinary Law Journal. *Email:* dcolaner@cromor.com

**JOHN F. WALSH,** born Ottawa, Ontario, Canada, January 9, 1962; admitted to bar, 1996, California. *Education:* Queen's University at Kingston, Canada (B.A., 1988); American University (M.A., 1985); Claremont Graduate School (Ph.D., 1992); Loyola Law School (J.D., 1996). Order of the Coif. Staff Member, Loyola of Los Angeles International and Comparative Law Journal, 1995-1996. *Email:* jwalsh@cromor.com

(For complete biographical data on personnel at Washington, D.C. and London, England, see Professional Biographies at those locations)

## JOSEPH S. D'ANTONY, & ASSOCIATES

100 PACIFICA, SUITE 200
IRVINE, CALIFORNIA 92718-3320
Telephone: 714-727-7077
Fax: 714-727-1284

*Los Angeles, California Office:* 2049 Century Park East, Suite 880, 90067-3110. Telephone: 310-843-2800. Facsimile: 310-843-2820.

*Insurance Defense, Personal Injury, Medical Malpractice Defense.*

**JOSEPH S. D'ANTONY,** born Akron, Ohio, January 1, 1939; admitted to bar, 1973, California. *Education:* Ohio Northern University (B.A., in Pharm., 1962); Pepperdine University (J.D., 1973). Phi Alpha Delta. Registered Pharmacist: Ohio, 1963; California, 1965. *Member:* Orange County and American Bar Associations; The State Bar of California; American Society for Pharmacy Law; Association of Southern California Defense Counsel. (Also Of Counsel to DiCaro, Lacey & Nield, San Diego). *PRACTICE AREAS:* Malpractice Law; Personal Injury Law; Dental Malpractice Law; Alternative Dispute Resolution; Insurance Defense.

**DANIEL W. DOYLE,** born New Haven, Connecticut, August 20, 1963; admitted to bar, 1989, California. *Education:* Southern Connecticut State University (B.A., Political Science, 1985); University of San Diego School of Law (J.D., 1989). Law Clerk to: District Attorney's Office, San Diego County; Honorable Donald W. Cellotto, New Haven, Connecticut, 1989-1990. *Member:* San Diego County and Orange County Bar Associations; State Bar of California. *PRACTICE AREAS:* Personal Injury; Medical Malpractice; Construction Defects; Criminal Matters.

*ASSOCIATES*

**KELLY A. FORTIN,** born Windsor, Ontario, December 22, 1966; admitted to bar, 1992, California. *Education:* Oakland University (B.A., Departmental Honors, English, 1988); Wayne State University (J.D., 1991). Law Clerk for Judge Stewart Newblatt, U.S. District Court, Flint, Michigan. *Member:* Orange County Bar Association; State Bar of California; Orange County Barristers. *PRACTICE AREAS:* Civil Litigation; Professional Liability; Medical Malpractice.

## DiPINTO & SHIMOKAJI, P.C.

2192 MARTIN STREET, SUITE 260
IRVINE, CALIFORNIA 92715
Telephone: 714-223-0838
Fax: 714-223-0845

*Toxic Tort Defense, Construction Litigation, Products Liability, General Civil Litigation, Negligence, Intellectual Property, General Business.*

**ILSE HARLE DiPINTO,** born Linz, Austria, April 8, 1953; admitted to bar, 1977, California; U.S. District Court, Southern, Central and Northern Districts of California; U.S. Court of Appeals, Ninth Circuit; U.S. Supreme Court. *Education:* California State University at Fullerton (B.A., 1974); University of California at Los Angeles (J.D., 1977). Phi Kappa Phi; Phi Alpha Theta. Member, Order of the Barristers. Member: Moot Court Honors Program, 1975-1976 and Executive Board of Judges, 1976-1977. Recipient: Moot Court Distinguished Advocate Award. Author: "The College Legal Clinic— Why, Where and Who," published in Orange County Bar Journal, Summer, 1973. Arbitrator, Orange County Superior Court, 1987-1989. *Member:* Orange County and American (Member, Tort and Insurance Practice Section) Bar Associations; State Bar of California; Association of Southern California Defense Counsel; Defense Research Institute. *PRACTICE AREAS:* Toxic Tort Defense Law; Construction Litigation; Products Liability Law; General Civil Litigation.

**MICHAEL A. SHIMOKAJI,** born Los Angeles, California, October 18, 1954; admitted to bar, 1980, California; registered to practice before the U.S. Patent and Trademark Office. *Education:* University of California at Irvine (B.A., Chemistry, 1976); Southwestern University (J.D., 1980). Executive Editor, Southwestern University Law Review, 1979-1980. Extern Clerk, Hon. Robert M. Takasugi, U.S. District Court, Central District of California, 1979. Instructor, Legal Research, University of California at Irvine. Past Vice-President, Orange County Japanese American Lawyers. Licensed California Real Estate Broker. *Member:* State Bar of California; Defense Research Institute. *PRACTICE AREAS:* Products Liability; Negligence; Intellectual Property; General Business.

*(This Listing Continued)*

REPRESENTATIVE CLIENTS: Allstate Insurance; Bartron Corp.; Mazda Motor of America, Inc.; Standard Pacific Corp.; State Farm Fire & Casualty Insurance; TCO Insurance Services; Toyota Motor Sales, U.S.A., Inc.
REFERENCE: Sumitomo Bank.

## JOHN A. DUNCAN

A PROFESSIONAL CORPORATION

IRVINE, CALIFORNIA

(See Orange)

*Estate and Trust Litigation. Probate Litigation, Conservatorship Litigation, Estate Planning, Estate and Trust Law, Estate and Trust Professional Negligence Litigation, Legal Malpractice Litigation and Consulting in these fields.*

## JACK M. EARLEY

19100 VON KARMAN AVENUE, SUITE 950
IRVINE, CALIFORNIA 92715
Telephone: 714-476-8900
Fax: 714-476-0900

*Criminal Defense and Environmental White Collar Civil Litigation.*

**JACK M. EARLEY,** born Hampton, Virginia, May 2, 1948; admitted to bar, 1974, California; 1983, U.S. District Court, Southern District of California; 1985, U.S. District Court, Central District of California. *Education:* California State University, Long Beach (B.A., 1970); Loyola University of Los Angeles (J.D., 1973). Attorney of The Year, Public Law Center of Orange County, 1996. Faculty Member: Orange County Bar Association College of Trial Advocacy; California Death Penalty College; California Attorneys for Criminal Justice Trial Advocacy Skills and Annual Death Penalty Seminars; California Public Defenders Association Annual Death Penalty Seminar; American Bar Association Battered Women Seminar. Senior Trial Attorney, Riverside County Public Defender's Office, 1974-1978. Deputy Public Defender IV, Orange County Public Defender's Office, 1978-1982. *Member:* Orange County Bar Association; State Bar of California; California Attorneys for Criminal Justice (Member, Board of Governors); California Public Defenders Association; The Association of Trial Lawyers of America. (Certified Specialist, Criminal Law, The State Bar of California Board of Legal Specialization). *REPORTED CASES:* People v. Broderick; People v. Strawn; People v. Lee. *PRACTICE AREAS:* Criminal Defense; Environmental; White Collar; Civil Litigation.

## LAWRENCE S. EISENBERG

8001 IRVINE CENTER DRIVE, SUITE 1500
IRVINE, CALIFORNIA 92718
Telephone: 714-753-1500
FAX: 714-753-1516

*Civil Trial Practice, Negligence, Products and Premises Liability, Professional Malpractice and Business Litigation, Wills and Trusts.*

**LAWRENCE S. EISENBERG,** born Brooklyn, New York, August 7, 1954; admitted to bar, 1983, Washington; 1984, California, New York and Massachusetts; U.S. Court of Appeals, Ninth Circuit; U.S. District Court, Central, Northern and Eastern Districts of California; U.S. District Court, Western District of Washington; 1990, U.S. Supreme Court. *Education:* University of Buffalo, State University of New York (B.A., cum laude, 1976); Southwestern University School of Law (J.D., 1981). Author: "The Care and Treatment of Handicapped Children," Journal of Dentistry for Children, Vol. 43, 1976; "The Media and Public "Misperception" of the Civil Justice System," CTLA Forum, July/August, 1993. *Member:* Orange County Bar Association; State Bar of California; Orange County Trial Lawyers Association (Member, Board of Directors, 1987-1994; President, 1993; President-Elect, 1992; Vice-President, 1989-1991); Los Angeles Trial Lawyers Association; California Trial Lawyers Association (Member, Board of Governors, 1990, 1993-1995; Recognition of Experience Certificates: Trial Lawyer; General Personal Injury; Professional Negligence; Products Liability); Association of Trial Lawyers of America.

## FAUSTMAN, CARLTON, DiSANTE & FREUDENBERGER LLP

*2600 MICHELSON DRIVE*
*SUITE 800*
**IRVINE, CALIFORNIA 92612**
*Telephone: 714-622-1661*
*Facsimile: 714-622-1669*

*Los Angeles, California Office:* 700 South Flower Street. Eleventh Floor, 90017. Telephone: 213-892-6308. Fax: 213-892-2263.

*Sacramento, California Office:* 711 9th Street, Suite 100, 95814. Telephone: 916-443-0999. Fax: 916-442-5140.

*San Francisco, California Office:* 388 Market Street, Suite 400, 94111. Telephone: 415-296-3813. Fax: 415-296-3814.

*San Diego, California Office:* 8910 University Center Lane, Suite 500, 92122. Telephone: 619-678-8446. Fax: 619-678-8447.

*On behalf of Employers, Employment Discrimination, Wrongful Discharge, Sexual Harassment and ERISA Litigation. Union Organizing Campaigns, Unfair Labor Practice Proceedings, Collective Bargaining Negotiations, Grievance Arbitration and other Labor Management Relations Issues. Wage and Hour and Occupational Safety and Health Proceedings. Trade Secrets and Unfair Competition Litigation. Employee Handbooks and Advice on Personnel Issues.*

### MEMBERS OF FIRM

**DAVID F. FAUSTMAN,** born Swindon, England, April 23, 1952; admitted to bar, 1978, California. *Education:* University of Southern California (B.S., with honors, 1975); University of California at Los Angeles (J.D., 1978). Order of the Coif. Index Editor, UCLA Law Review, 1977-1978. Moot Court Distinguished Advocate. *Member:* Sacramento County and San Francisco County (Member, Labor and Employment Law Section) Bar Associations; State Bar of California. (Also at San Francisco and Sacramento Offices). **PRACTICE AREAS:** Employment Law; Labor Law; Business Litigation.

**CHRISTOPHER W. CARLTON,** born Seattle, Washington, November, 18, 1956; admitted to bar, 1983, California. *Education:* Duke University (A.B., magna cum laude, 1979); Cornell University (J.D., 1982). Senior Note Editor, Cornell Law Review, 1981-1982, Member, 1980-1981. Law Clerk to the Honorable Cynthia Holcomb Hall, U.S. District Judge, Central District of California, 1982-1983. *Member:* Los Angeles County and Orange County (Member, Labor and Employment Law Section) Bar Associations; State Bar of California. (Also at Los Angeles). **PRACTICE AREAS:** Employment Law; Labor Law; Business Litigation.

**MARIE D. DiSANTE,** born Allentown, Pennsylvania, August 8, 1963; admitted to bar, 1988, California. *Education:* Texas Christian University (B.S., summa cum laude, 1985); Southern Methodist University (J.D., 1988). Phi Beta Kappa. Order of the Coif. Notes and Comments Editor, Journal of Air Law and Commerce, 1987-1988. *Member:* Orange County Bar Association (Member, Labor and Employment Law Section; Chairperson, Labor Law Section, 1993); State Bar of California. **PRACTICE AREAS:** Employment Law; Labor Law.

**TIMOTHY M. FREUDENBERGER,** born Downey, California, January 20, 1962; admitted to bar, 1988, California. *Education:* University of California at San Diego (B.A., 1985); University of California, Hastings College of Law (J.D., 1988). Phi Delta Phi. Member, Hastings Law Journal, 1986-1987. Author: "Privacy in the Workplace," The California Labor Letter, Volume II, Nos. 4 and 5, 1991. Co-Author: The Legal Aspects of Occupational Violence, The Complete Workplace Violence Prevention Manual, 1994. *Member:* Orange County Bar Association (Member, Labor and Employment Law Section); State Bar of California. (Also at San Diego). **REPORTED CASES:** Lee v. Bank of America NT&SA, 27 Cal.App.4th 197, 32 Cal.Rptr.2d 388 (1994). **PRACTICE AREAS:** Employment Law; Labor Law.

### ASSOCIATES

**LAURA L. SAADEH,** born Burbank, California, September 2, 1954; admitted to bar, 1987, California. *Education:* California State University at Northridge; California State University at Fullerton (B.A., 1981); Loyola Law School, Los Angeles (J.D., cum laude 1987). Alpha Sigma Nu; St. Thomas Moore Honor Society. Chief Note and Comment Editor, Loyola Law Review, 1986-1987. *Member:* Orange County Bar Association (Member, Labor and Employment Law Section); State Bar of California. **PRACTICE AREAS:** Employment Law; Labor Law.

*(This Listing Continued)*

**CHRISTOPHER M. ROBERTSON,** born Kalamazoo, Michigan, December 31, 1962; admitted to bar, 1989, California. *Education:* Princeton University (B.A., 1985); University of Michigan (J.D., 1988). *Member:* State Bar of California. **PRACTICE AREAS:** Employment Law; Labor Law.

**ALYSSA J. ALLEN,** born Los Angeles, California, May 6, 1966; admitted to bar, 1992, California. *Education:* Pepperdine University (B.A., magna cum laude, 1988); University of California, Hastings College of Law (J.D., cum laude, 1991). Associate Editor, Hastings International and Comparative Law Review, 1990-1991. Phi Alpha Delta (Vice President); Alpha Chi, Member, 1989-1991. *Member:* San Francisco and Los Angeles County Bar Associations; State Bar of California. (Also at San Francisco). **PRACTICE AREAS:** Employment Law; Labor Law; Business Litigation. **Email:** alyssa@FCDF.com

**LEIGH A. WHITE,** born Dumas, Arkansas, December 28, 1967; admitted to bar, 1993, California. *Education:* University of Arkansas at Fayetteville (B.S.B.A., 1990); Southern Methodist University (J.D., 1993). Order of the Coif. Notes and Comments Editor, So. Methodist U. Law Review, 1992-1993. Author: "TSB Reports, The War Over Admissibility", 58 Journal of Air Law and Commerce, 903. *Member:* Orange County and American (Member, Employment & Labor Relations Commission 1995) Bar Associations; State Bar of California. **PRACTICE AREAS:** Employment Law; Labor Law; Business Litigation.

**DIANE L. SCHLESINGER,** born Los Angeles, California, March 5, 1963; admitted to bar, 1988, California. *Education:* University of California at Los Angeles (B.A., summa cum laude, 1984); Boalt Hall School of Law, University of California (J.D., 1988). Phi Beta Kappa. Associate Editor, California Law Review, 1987-1988. *Member:* American Bar Association; State Bar of California. (Also at Los Angeles). **PRACTICE AREAS:** Employment Law; Labor Law; Business Litigation.

**JASON L. HOFFMAN,** born Los Angeles, California, February 7, 1969; admitted to bar, 1995, California. *Education:* University of California at San Diego (B.A., with honors, 1992); University of the Pacific, McGeorge School of Law (J.D., 1995). McGeorge National Moot Court Competition participant, 1993. McGeorge School of Law, Trial Advocacy, participant, 1994. Judicial Extern, Honorable Lynne Riddle, United States Bankruptcy Court, Central District of California, Santa Ana, 1994. *Member:* Beverly Hills, Los Angeles and San Francisco (Member, Labor and Employment Law Section) Bar Associations; State Bar of California. (Also at San Francisco Office). **PRACTICE AREAS:** Employment Law; Labor Law.

**ANN H. QUSHAIR,** born Newport Beach, California, October 4, 1969; admitted to bar, 1995, California. *Education:* University of California at Irvine (B.A., cum laude, 1991); Cornell University (J.D., 1994). Finalist, Cornell Upper-Class Moot Court Competition, Spring, 1993. Quarterfinalist, Cornell First Year Moot Court Competition, 1992. Editor, 1993-1994, Member, 1992-1993, Cornell Journal of Law and Public Policy. Bench Brief Editor, Cornell Moot Court Board, 1993-1994. Judicial Extern, Honorable David G. Sills, Presiding Justice, California Court of Appeals, Fourth Appellate District, Division Three. *Member:* Orange County Bar Association (Member, Labor and Employment Law Section); State Bar of California. **PRACTICE AREAS:** Employment Law; Labor Law.

### OF COUNSEL

**RONNA S. REED,** born Whittier, California, May 10, 1955; admitted to bar, 1984, California. *Education:* University of California at Berkeley (B.A., with highest honors, 1977); University of Southern California (J.D., 1984). Phi Beta Kappa. Staff Member, University of Southern California Law Review, 1982-1983. *Member:* State Bar of California. (Also at Sacramento) (Also Of Counsel to Kohut & Kohut LLP, Santa Rosa, California). **PRACTICE AREAS:** Employment Law; Labor Law.

**KRISTINE P. NESTHUS,** born Fort Eustis, Virginia, October 11, 1955; admitted to bar, 1985, California. *Education:* University of Wisconsin (B.A., with high honors, 1977); University of Kansas (J.D., 1985). Order of the Coif. Member, Kansas Law Review, 1983-1984. Kansas University, Legal Research and Writing, 1983-1985. *Member:* San Diego County and American Bar Associations; State Bar of California. (Also at San Diego). **PRACTICE AREAS:** Employment Law; Labor Law; Business Litigation.

## FEDER, GOODMAN & SCHWARTZ
INCORPORATED

2 PARK PLAZA, SUITE 450
**IRVINE, CALIFORNIA 92614**
Telephone: 714-251-2800
Telecopier: 714-251-2801

*General Business and Taxation Law including Profit-Sharing, Employee Stock Ownership Plans and Employee Benefits, Estate Planning, Corporations, Business Sales and Acquisitions, Health Care, Finance, Securities, Tax Audits and Disputes, Tax Exempt Organizations and Real Estate Transactions and Related Litigation.*

*FIRM PROFILE: The firms approach in solving business and legal issues, has earned a well developed reputation for being a strong, creative and cost sensitive in its representation of clients. The firm is dedicated to providing legal services of the highest quality to its clients.*

**JON C. FEDER,** born Los Angeles, California, January 27, 1941; admitted to bar, 1966, California. *Education:* University of California at Berkeley (B.S., 1962); Hastings College of the Law, University of California (J.D., 1965); New York University (LL.M., 1974). Member, Hastings College of the Law, University of California Law Review, 1964-1965. Instructor, Estate Planning, University of California Extension, 1979-1984. *Member:* Los Angeles County, Orange County (Member, Tax Section) and American (Member, Sections on: Taxation; Real Property, Probate and Trust Law) Bar Associations; State Bar of California; Orange County Estate Planning Council. (Certified Specialist, Taxation Law, The State Bar of California Board of Legal Specialization). **PRACTICE AREAS:** Estate Planning.

**RANDOLPH M. GOODMAN,** born New York, N.Y., July 25, 1948; admitted to bar, 1974, New York; 1977, District of Columbia; 1981, California. *Education:* Franklin & Marshall College (B.A., 1970); Rutgers University (J.D., 1973); New York University (LL.M., 1974). Editor, Rutgers University Law Review, 1972-1973. Editor, The Tax Lawyer, 1977-1979. Author: "Exempt Compensation Arrangements Under ERISA," 28 Catholic University Law Review 445, 1979; "Employee Medical and Other Fringe Benefits," California Society of Certified Public Accountants, 1989; "Retirement and Benefit Planning." Butterworth Legal Publishers, 1991. *Member:* Los Angeles County, Orange County and American (Member, Section of Taxation) Bar Associations; State Bar of California; The District of Columbia Bar; National Association of College and University Attorneys (Co-Chair, Section on Taxation, 1990—); Board of Advisors, University of California (Irvine) Graduate School of Management (Health Care Programs, 1991—); National Board of Advisors, Financial and Estate Planning (1990—).

**JOHN W. SCHWARTZ,** born New York, N.Y., March 22, 1949; admitted to bar, 1975, New York; 1983, California. *Education:* Cornell University (B.A., 1968); Cornell Law School (J.D., 1974). Chancellor, Cornell Law School Moot Court Board. Louis Kaiser Award. *Member:* Los Angeles County (Member, Sections on: Taxation; Business Law), Orange County, New York State and American Bar Associations; State Bar of California.

**DAVID I. LESSER,** born New York, N.Y., May 21, 1953; admitted to bar, 1979, California. *Education:* University of Rochester (B.A., with honors and distinction, 1975); Columbia University (J.D., 1979). *Member:* Los Angeles County (Member, Business and Corporations Law Section) Orange County (Member, Real Estate Law Section) and American Bar Associations; State Bar of California.

**ALISON SMITH FAY,** born October 2, 1953; admitted to bar, 1981, California. *Education:* Stanford University (A.B., 1975); Hastings College of Law, University of California (J.D., 1981). Order of the Coif. Member, 1979-1980 and Associate Managing Editor, 1980-1981, Hastings Law Journal. **PRACTICE AREAS:** Employee Benefits.

**MICHELLE A. WAKINO,** born Arcadia, California, December 6, 1960; admitted to bar, 1989, California. *Education:* California State University at Fullerton (B.A., with honors, 1981); University of Southern California (M.B.T., 1984); Loyola Law School (J.D., cum laude, 1989). Certified Public Accountant, California, 1983. Part-time Lecturer: Masters of Business Tax, University of Southern California, 1992—. *Member:* State Bar of California; American Bar Association; American Institute of Certified Public Accountants; California Society of Certified Public Accountants.

**STEVEN M. DRISCOLL,** born Long Beach, California, October 23, 1956; admitted to bar, 1990, California. *Education:* Loyola Marymount University (B.S., cum laude, 1978); University of Southern California

*(This Listing Continued)*

(M.B.T., 1982); Loyola Law School (J.D., 1990). Order of the Coif. American Jurisprudence Award: Federal Income Tax, Corporations & Constitutional Law, Alpha Sigma Nu Honor Society Staff Member (1988-1989) Loyola Law Review. Assistant Professor, California State University, 1983-1990. *Member:* Orange County and American (Member: Estate Planning, Probate and Trust Section) Bar Associations; Certified Public Accountant, California, 1981. **PRACTICE AREAS:** Estate Planning; Administrative; Probate.

**DONNA T. TONKON,** born Philadelphia, Pennsylvania, July 8, 1950; admitted to bar, 1976, Pennsylvania; 1979, California. *Education:* Barnard College (B.A., cum laude, 1972); Washington College of Law of American University (J.D., 1976); University of San Diego. Member: Long Beach Bar Association, Estate Planning Section, 1990-1994; Pennsylvania Bar Association, Estate Planning Section, 1976-1980. *Member:* State Bar of California (Member, Estate Planning Section). **PRACTICE AREAS:** Estate Planning; Trust Planning; Estate Administration; Probate.

**DEBORAH FABRICANT,** born New York, N.Y., January 12, 1952; admitted to bar, 1980, New York and U.S. District Court, Southern District of New York; 1988, California. *Education:* Barnard College (A.B., cum laude, 1974); New York University (J.D., cum laude, 1979). Order of the Coif. *Member:* The Association of the Bar of the City of New York; Orange County and New York State Bar Associations. **PRACTICE AREAS:** Litigation.

## FIORE, WALKER, RACOBS & POWERS
A PROFESSIONAL LAW CORPORATION

Established in 1979

KOLL CENTER IRVINE
18400 VON KARMEN, SUITE 600
**IRVINE, CALIFORNIA 92612-1514**
Telephone: 714-955-0560
Fax: 714-955-2894

*Riverside, California Office:* 6670 Alessandro, Suite B. Telephone: 909-789-8100. Fax: 909-789-8105.
*Palm Desert, California Office:* 74-361 Highway III, Suite 1. Telephone: 619-776-6511. Fax: 619-776-6517.

*Community Association, Real Property, Civil Litigation, Construction and Business.*

*FIRM PROFILE: Fiore, Walker, Racobs & Powers, A Professional Law Corporation, has been in existence since August, 1972, and has established the practice of law in the fields of community association law, real property and civil litigation.*

*Our mission is to: Provide quality legal services to our clients; set a positive example for the legal profession; contribute to the continuing success of community associations through education, legislation and legal services.*

**RICHARD S. FIORE,** born Hackensack, New Jersey, February 26, 1942; admitted to bar, 1968, California. *Education:* Occidental College (A.B., 1963); Hastings College of the Law, University of California (J.D., 1967).

**BRADLEY D. WALKER,** born Milwaukee, Wisconsin, December 3, 1955; admitted to bar, 1981, Wisconsin; 1982, California. *Education:* University of Wisconsin (B.S., with distinction, 1977); Pepperdine University School of Law (J.D., 1981).

**PETER E. RACOBS,** born Lucerne Valley, California, November 4, 1957; admitted to bar, 1983, California. *Education:* University of California at Riverside (B.A., 1979); University of California at Davis (J.D., 1983).

**JANET L. S. POWERS,** born Pasadena, California, September 1, 1955; admitted to bar, 1985, California. *Education:* University of California at Los Angeles (B.A., 1977); Southwestern University School of Law (J.D., 1984).

**STEPHEN D. MCNAMARA,** born Culver City, California, August 26, 1954; admitted to bar, 1987, California. *Education:* San Diego State University (B.A., Psychology, 1977); California Western School of Law (J.D., 1986).

**DAVID E. CANE,** born Los Angeles, California, November 12, 1961; admitted to bar, 1987, California. *Education:* University of California at Los Angeles (B.A., 1983); Southwestern University School of Law (J.D., 1986).

*(This Listing Continued)*

**CHESTER A. PUCHALSKI,** born Morristown, New Jersey, December 29, 1962; admitted to bar, 1988, California. *Education:* George Washington University (B.A., 1984); Georgetown University Law Center (J.D., 1987).

**MARK HOPKINS,** born Fort Worth, Texas, December 20, 1947; admitted to bar, 1978, California; 1979, Federal Central District. *Education:* Southern Methodist University (B.B.A., 1970); Pepperdine University (J.D., 1978).

**JAMES C. HARKINS, IV,** born New York, N.Y., April 7, 1963; admitted to bar, 1989, Massachusetts; 1991, California and District of Columbia. *Education:* University of Maryland (B.A., 1985); American University, Washington College of Law (J.D., 1988).

**TRACY ANN STEVENSON,** born Newport Beach, California, November 2, 1960; admitted to bar, 1992, California and U.S. District Court, Central District of California. *Education:* California State University (B.S., 1982); Western State University (J.D., 1992). *Member:* Orange County Bar Association. **PRACTICE AREAS:** Construction Defect; Business Litigation; Probate.

A List of Representative Clients will be furnished upon request.
REFERENCES: Commerce Bank; Wells Fargo Bank.

---

## LACHLAN FOSTER

SUITE 1250, ONE PARK PLAZA
**IRVINE, CALIFORNIA 92614**
Telephone: 714-263-1010
Telecopier: 714-263-1693

*Corporate, Securities and Business Practice.*

**LACHLAN FOSTER,** born Hastings, Michigan, January 8, 1931; admitted to bar, 1958, California. *Education:* Michigan State University (B.A., with high honor, 1952; M.A., 1956); Yale Law School (J.D., 1958). Phi Kappa Phi. *Member:* Orange County (Member, Corporations Section) and American (Member, Corporation, Banking and Business Law Section) Bar Associations.

---

## FRANKEL & TENNANT

PROFESSIONAL CORPORATION

17875 VON KARMAN, SUITE 350
**IRVINE, CALIFORNIA 92614-6257**
Telephone: 714-252-4700
Fax: 714-252-5597

*Real Property, Banking, Creditors' Rights, Loan Workouts/Foreclosure/Bankruptcy and Litigation.*

*FIRM PROFILE:* The Firm's litigation practice emphasizes representation of secured creditors in state and federal court actions relating to real estate issues, including foreclosures, receiverships and bankruptcies. Its attorneys have handled sophisticated litigation for financial institutions, contractors, real estate developers and other businesses and individuals, including lender liability and construction litigation, as well as a broad array of general business litigation matters.

The Firm has particular expertise in real estate loan portfolio management and servicing, specifically including loan workouts, forbearances, discounted payoffs, deeds in lieu and foreclosed real estate management and disposition, in connection with residential and commercial real estate loans. The Firm handles the purchase and sale of loans, including participation agreements and loan servicing agreements. The Firm's real estate finance practice also includes all areas of residential and commercial real estate loan origination.

The Firm also has significant experience handling general transactions relating to retail, commercial, industrial and residential real properties, both improved and unimproved. Typical transactions involve acquisition, development, management and disposition of real properties, as well as negotiation, preparation and implementation of related agreements and leases. All sides of transactions, including buyers and sellers, landlords and tenants, are represented.

**BENJAMIN W. FRANKEL,** born Chelsea, Massachusetts, January 8, 1942; admitted to bar, 1966, California. *Education:* Stanford University (A.B., 1962; J.D., 1965). Member, Attorneys Committee, California League of Savings Institutions, 1980-1990. *Member:* Orange County Bar Association (Member, Real Estate Section); State Bar of California (Member, Real Property Law Section). [Lieut., USCGR, 1965-1968]

(This Listing Continued)

---

**DOUGLAS G. TENNANT,** born New Rochelle, New York, October, 13, 1956; admitted to bar, 1983, New York and U.S. District Court, Southern and Eastern Districts of New York; 1985, California, U.S. District Court, Southern, Northern and Central Districts of California and U.S. Court of Appeals, Ninth Circuit; 1986, U.S. District Court, Eastern District of California; 1989, District of Columbia; 1993, Texas. *Education:* Yale University (B.A., cum laude, in history, 1978); Columbia University (J.D., 1982). *Member:* Orange County Bar Association (Member, Sections on: Business Litigation; Commercial Law and Bankruptcy; Creditors' Rights; Insurance Law and Real Estate Law); State Bar of California (Member, Real Property Law Section).

---

**MARC C. FORSYTHE,** born San Francisco, California, January 4, 1961; admitted to bar, 1990, California; U.S. District Court, Central District of California. *Education:* University of Nevada-Reno (B.S., 1984); McGeorge School of Law (J.D., 1990). Recipient: American Jurisprudence Awards in Reorganizations, Recapitalizations and Insolvencies and Decedents Estates and Trusts. Staff Writer, 1989-1990 and Casenote Editor, 1990-1991, Pacific Law Journal. Certified Public Accountant, Nevada, 1987. Author: "Undercollateralized Creditors Cry Timber to the Right to Compensation for Interest on the Value of Collateral," 20 Pacific Law Review 1309, 1989. Law Clerk to the Honorable Judge James N. Barr, U.S. Bankruptcy Court, Central District of California, 1990-1991. *Member:* Orange County Bar Association (Member, Commercial Law and Bankruptcy Section); Orange County Bankruptcy Forum; American Bankruptcy Institute; Nevada Society of Certified Public Accountants; American Institute of Certified Public Accountants; Association of Insolvency Accountants.

---

## FRASCA & ASSOCIATES

5 PARK PLAZA, SUITE 1500
**IRVINE, CALIFORNIA 92614**
Telephone: 714-553-8193
Fax: 714-553-8195

*General Commercial Litigation Practice in both State and Federal Courts.*

*FIRM PROFILE:* Ms. Frasca, formerly a partner of Jones, Day, Reavis & Pogue for over 10 years, will continue her practice in both state & federal court matters. Ms. Frasca has represented and continues to represent some of the largest companies in the world. Firm resume available upon request.

**JOANNE M. FRASCA,** born Montclair, New Jersey, October 24, 1953; admitted to bar, 1977, Arizona; 1979, Illinois; 1982, California. *Education:* University of Connecticut (B.A., 1974); University of Notre Dame (J.D., 1977). Phi Beta Kappa. *Member:* State Bar of California. **PRACTICE AREAS:** Business Litigation.

---

## FREEMAN, FREEMAN & SMILEY, LLP

A Limited Liability Partnership including Law Corporations

Established in 1976

2010 MAIN STREET, SUITE 580
**IRVINE, CALIFORNIA 92614**
Telephone: 714-833-7966
Facsimile: 714-833-9584

*Los Angeles, California Office:* Penthouse, Suite 1200, 3415 Sepulveda Boulevard. Telephone: 310-398-6227. Facsimile: 310-391-4042.
*San Francisco, California Office:* One Market, Steuart Tower, 16th Floor. Telephone: 415-974-1930.

*Estate and Gift Planning, Probate, Real Estate, Corporate, Business Succession Planning, Civil Trial and Appellate Litigation.*

(For complete biographical data on all personnel, see Professional Biographies at Los Angeles, California)

---

## FRIEDMAN PETERSON & STROFFE

A Partnership including Law Corporations
19800 MACARTHUR BOULEVARD, SUITE 1100
**IRVINE, CALIFORNIA 92612-2425**
Telephone: 714-955-1086
Facsimile: 714-833-9436

*General Business, Corporate, Real Property, Construction, Unfair Competition, Licensing and Trademark Law. Litigation.*

(This Listing Continued)

*FRIEDMAN PETERSON & STROFFE, Irvine—Continued*

**BRYAN M. FRIEDMAN, (A PROFESSIONAL CORPORATION),** born South Africa, October 20, 1946; admitted to bar, 1970, South Africa; 1984, California and U.S District Court, Central District of California. *Education:* University of Witwatersrand Faculty of Law (Dip. Law, 1968). *Member:* Orange County Bar Association; State Bar of California. *PRACTICE AREAS:* Domestic and International Business Transactions; Licensing and Trademarks; Copyright.

**ROBERT A. PETERSON, (A PROFESSIONAL CORPORATION),** born Los Angeles, California, August 18, 1947; admitted to bar, 1973, California and U.S. District Court, Northern, Central and Southern Districts of California. *Education:* University of California at Berkeley (B.A., 1969); Hastings College of Law, University of California (J.D., 1973). *Member:* Orange County and American Bar Associations; State Bar of California. *PRACTICE AREAS:* State and Federal Court Litigation; General Business; Real Property Law.

**JAMES D. STROFFE,** born Moline, Illinois, August 29, 1951; admitted to bar, 1977, California and U.S. District Court, Central and Southern Districts of California; 1981, U.S. Court of Appeals, Ninth Circuit. *Education:* Harvard University (B.A., magna cum laude, 1973); University of San Diego School of Law (J.D., magna cum laude, 1976). *Member:* State Bar of California; American Bar Association (Member, Law Office Management, Real Property Probate and Trusts Sections). *PRACTICE AREAS:* Real Property Law; Construction Law; Litigation.

---

**BRIAN F. SEGALL,** born Durban, South Africa, June 15, 1946; admitted to bar, 1970, South Africa; 1972, Swaziland; 1991, New York and U.S. District Court, Eastern and Southern Districts of New York; 1996, California; 1997, U.S. District Court, Central District of California. *Education:* University of Witwatersrand Faculty of Law (Dip. Law, cum laude, 1968); New York University (M.A., cum laude, 1982). *Member:* Orange County, New York State and American Bar Associations; State Bar of California. *PRACTICE AREAS:* Domestic and International Business Transactions; Licensing and Trademarks; Copyright.

**LAWRENCE H. BINDEROW,** born New York, New York, July 27, 1956; admitted to bar, 1982, Illinois and U.S. District Court, Northern District of Illinois; 1989, California and U.S. District Court, Southern District of California. *Education:* University of Wisconsin-Madison (B.A., 1978); John Marshall Law School (J.D., 1982). *Member:* San Diego County, Illinois State and American Bar Associations; State Bar of California. *PRACTICE AREAS:* Trademarks; Copyright and Domestic and International Licensing.

---

## *LAWRENCE J. GALARDI*

Established in 1959

*WELLS FARGO TOWER*
*2030 MAIN STREET*
*SUITE 1050*
***IRVINE, CALIFORNIA 92714***
*Telephone: 714-852-1100*
*Telecopier: 714-252-7780*

*General Civil Litigation, Construction Defect, Business Disputes, Aviation and Products Liability Law. Trial Practice in all State and Federal Courts.*

*FIRM PROFILE: Mr. Galardi has 36 years of litigation and trial experience, complex and multiple party litigation involving construction defect, landslide and subsidence, aviation, products liability, real property, contract and fraud cases and the defense of general tort litigation.*

*Mr. Galardi has prepared and tried and supervised the preparation and trial of air cases in jurisdictions throughout the country.*

*In private practice his broad litigation and trial experience includes court assignments as lead counsel and as liaison counsel in multiple suit litigation involving both commercial and general aviation category aircraft. Mr. Galardi in listed in the Preeminent Law Directory.*

**LAWRENCE J. GALARDI,** born New York, N.Y., February 15, 1935; admitted to bar, 1959, New York; 1960, U.S. District Court, Southern and Eastern Districts of New York; 1962, U.S. District Court, Central and Northern Districts of California and U.S. Court of Appeals, Second and Ninth Circuits; 1971, California; 1974, U.S. Supreme Court. *Education:* Seton Hall University (B.A., 1955); Brooklyn Law School (LL.B., 1959).

*(This Listing Continued)*

---

Delta Theta Phi. Author: "Use of Investigation Materials in Aircraft Accident Litigation," Brooklyn Law Review, December, 1965; "Freedom of Information Act," American Trial Lawyers Digest, 1968; "Choosing the Defendant in Aircraft Accident Litigation," Practicing Law Institute, 1970; "Rights of Servicemen Under the Tort Claims Act," University of Southern California, 1970. Instructor, Aviation Law, University of Southern California, 1970-1971. Assistant U.S. Attorney, New York, 1959-1962. Chief, Aviation Tort Litigation Section, 1962-64, Assistant Chief, Tort Section, 1968-1970 and Chief, Aviation Tort Section, 1968-1970, U.S. Department of Justice. Assistant Member, U.S. Civil Aeronautics Board, 1964-1968. Magana and Cathcart, Los Angeles, 1970-1973. *Member:* Beverly Hills, Los Angeles, Orange County and San Diego County, Federal, New York State and American (Member: Forum on Construction Industry; Section of Insurance, Negligence and Compensation Law; Standing Committee, Aeronautical Law, 1972—) Bar Associations; State Bar of California; California Trial Lawyers Association; The Association of Trial Lawyers of America (Member: Section of Aviation Law; Military Aviation Committee, 1970—; International Aviation Committee, 1974—); Lawyers-Pilots Bar Association; Law-Science Academy of America; Orange County Asian American Bar Association; Italian American Lawyers Association; Community Associations Institute. [(Captain, U.A. Army)]. *PRACTICE AREAS:* Construction Defect; Aviation Law; Business Disputes; Products Liability Law; Civil Trial Practice.

---

## *GAUNTLETT & ASSOCIATES*

*18400 VON KARMAN, SUITE 300*
***IRVINE, CALIFORNIA 92612***
*Telephone: 714-553-1010*
*Fax: 714-553-2050*
*Email: ugauntlett@aol.com*

*Policyholder Insurance-Coverage Representation, Patent, Trademark, Copyright, Trade Secret, Antitrust, Business, Environmental and Labor Litigation as well as Business and Estate Planning.*

*FIRM PROFILE: Gauntlett & Associates maintains an international practice representing fortune 1000 companies in insurance coverage as well as intellectual property disputes. David A. Gauntlett also serves as an expert on insurance coverage issues.*

**DAVID A. GAUNTLETT,** born Long Beach, California, May 16, 1954; admitted to bar, 1980, California and U.S. District Court, Central District of California; 1982, U.S. District Court, Northern, Eastern and Southern Districts of California; 1987, U.S. Court of Appeals, Ninth Circuit; 1993, U.S. Court of Appeals, Fourth Circuit; 1994, U.S. District Court, District of Connecticut; U.S. Court of Appeals for the Federal Circuit; U.S. Supreme Court. *Education:* University of California at Irvine (B.A., magna cum laude, 1976); Boalt Hall School of Law, University of California (J.D., 1979). Associate Editor and Production Manager, California Law Review, 1978-1979. Author: "Wellenkamp v. Bank of America: Invalidation of Automatically Enforceable Due-on-Sale Clause,: 67 California Law Review 886, 1979; "Establishing Intellectual Property Defense Coverage," Practical Lawyer, Vol. 38, No. 2, March, 1992; "Insurance Coverage for Intellectual Property Lawsuits," Intellectual Property Litigation and Counseling, Ch. 29 Matthew Bender & Co., Inc., Pub. 5/94; "Potential Coverage for Patent Infrigement Lawsuits Still Exists Dispite the Courts Ruling in Watercloud and Iolab," New Matter, Vol. 19, Issue 1, Spring 1994; "Coverage for Wrongful Termination, Sexual Harassment and Discrimination Claims," Risk Management Letter, Vol. 13, Issue 3, June 1994; "Strategies for Corporate and IP Counsel in Obtaining Coverage for IP Lawsuits," Licensing Law Business Report, Vol. 17, Issue 3, Sept/Oct. 1994; "Recent Developments in Intellectual Property Coverage Torts and Insurance Law Jorunal," Vol.XXX, No. 2, Winter 1995; "No Advertising Injury Exclusion in Commercial General Liability Polcies Bar Coverage For Intellectual Property Lawsuits," Intellectual Property Newsletter, Spring 1996, Vol. 14, No. 3. *Member:* Los Angeles County, Orange County and American (Chair, Special Committee on Insurance, Intellectual Property Law Section; Vice-Chair, Insurance Coverage Committee, Litigation Section; Vice-Chair, and Chair Emeritus, Intellectual Property Committee, Tort and Insurance Practice Section, 1995-1996) Bar Associations; State Bar of California; The Association of Trial Lawyers of America. *LANGUAGES:* French. *PRACTICE AREAS:* Insurance Coverage; Intellectual Property; Antitrust; Business; Environmental; Tort; Labor Law.

*(This Listing Continued)*

**DAVID A. STALL,** born Chicago, Illinois, January 20, 1944; admitted to bar, 1969, Illinois, District of Columbia, U.S. District Court, Northern District of Illinois and U.S. Court of Appeals, Seventh Circuit; 1986, California; 1990, U.S. District Court, Central and Southern Districts of California; 1991, U.S. Court of Appeals, Ninth Circuit. *Education:* Marquette University (A.B., 1965); John Marshall Law School (J.D., 1968). Author: "Relief in a Single Document," California Bar Journal, June, 1995; "Know Your Probate Order," OCBA Estate Planning, Probate & Trust Law and Elder Law Sections Newsletter, Vol. 2, No. 1, Spring, 1995. *Member:* Chicago, San Diego, Orange County and Illinois State Bar Associations; State Bar of California.

**LEO E. LUNDBERG, JR.,** born Gridley, California, October 7, 1955; admitted to bar, 1986, California; 1987, U.S. District Court, Central District of California and U.S. Court of Appeals, Ninth Circuit; 1988, U.S. Court of International Trade; 1994, U.S. District Court, Eastern District of California; 1995, U.S. District Court, Southern and Northern Districts of California. *Education:* California Lutheran College (B.S., cum laude, 1978); Loyola Law School (J.D., cum laude, 1986). St. Thomas More Honor Society. Recipient, American Jurisprudence Award in Evidence and Criminal Procedure. *Member:* Orange County Bar Association (Member, Business Litigation Section); State Bar of California (Member, Litigation Section).

**MICHAEL DANTON RICHARDSON,** born Baton Rouge, Louisiana, December 4, 1959; admitted to bar, 1987, Louisiana; 1988, Texas and U.S. District Court, Southern District of Texas; 1989, California and U.S. District Court, Northern and Eastern Districts of Texas; 1990, District of Columbia and U.S. District Court, Western District of Texas; 1992, U.S. District Court, Central District of California; 1994, U.S. Court of Appeals, Ninth Circuit and U.S. District Court, Northern District of California; 1996, U.S. Court of Appeals for the Federal Circuit and U.S. District Court, Eastern and Southern Districts of California. *Education:* Southeastern Louisiana University (B.A., 1983); Louisiana State University (J.D., 1986). Recipient: American Jurisprudence Award in Entertainment Law; Best Memorial, Southern Regional, 1986 Philip C. Jessup International Law Moot Court Competition. *Member:* Orange County (Member, Technology, Business Litigation and Insurance Sections), Louisiana State and American (Member, Intellectual Property Law and Law Forum Committee on Entertainment and Sports Industries) Bar Associations; State Bar of California; State Bar of Texas; District of Columbia Bar; California Copyright Conference.

**WILLIAM P. WARDEN,** born San Antonio, Texas, May 9, 1948; admitted to bar, 1974, Oklahoma; 1993, New York; 1994, California. *Education:* Trinity University (B.A., 1970); University of Oklahoma (J.D., 1973).

**STANLEY H. SHURE,** born Los Angeles, California, January 21, 1954; admitted to bar, 1984, California; 1989, U.S. District Court, Central District of California. *Education:* Occidental College (A.B., 1977); Loyola University (J.D., 1984). Recipient, Departmental Distinction in Biochemistry. Beta Beta Beta. *LANGUAGES:* French. *Email:* 72612.1331@Compuserve.com

**ELIZABETH A. GILLIS,** born Boston, Massachusetts, July 11, 1960; admitted to bar, 1988, Massachusetts; 1989, Connecticut; 1990, New York; 1991, Colorado; 1993, Louisiana (Not admitted in California). *Education:* Harvard University (B.A., 1982); Suffolk University Law School (J.D., cum laude, 1986). Member, Suffolk University Law Review. Author: Comment, "The Privileges and Immunities Clause: A Strenghtened Standard with a Clarified Analysis-Supreme Court of New Hampshire v. Piper," 20 Suffolk University Law Review 93, 1986; "Voice Identification by Spectrographic Analysis," 20 Suffolk University Law Review 264, 1986. *Member:* The Association of the Bar of the City of New York; Boston, Massachusetts, Connecticut and American Bar Associations. *LANGUAGES:* Italian.

**MARK H. PLAGER,** born Newark, New Jersey, December 3, 1964; admitted to bar, 1990, New Jersey and U.S. District Court, District of New Jersey; 1991, Colorado and U.S. Court of Appeals, Third Circuit; registered to practice before the U.S. Patent and Trademark Office (Not admitted in California). *Education:* Lafayette College (B.S., 1987) Quinnipiac College School of Law (J.D., 199 0). Recipient: Moot Court Honor Society, Quinnipiac College, School of Law, 1989-1990. Author: "Intellectual Property Infringement Claims: Are You Covered?," The Law Works, Vol 3, No. 4 (April, 1996); "$100,000 For A Photocopy-Part II: The Appeal" The Law Works, Vol. 2, No. 1 (January, 1995). *Member:* American Bar Association (Member, Intellectual Property Law Section); American Intellectual Property Law Section.

*(This Listing Continued)*

**JEFFREY S. ALLISON,** born Albuquerque, New Mexico, November 10, 1967; admitted to bar, 1994, California and U.S. Court of Appeals, Federal Circuit. *Education:* University of California at Irvine (B.A., 1990); University of the Pacific, McGeorge School of Law (J.D., 1994). Judicial Externship, The Honorable Robert W. Alberts, U.S. Bankruptcy Court, Central District of California, 1993. *Member:* Los Angeles County, Orange County, Sacramento County and American Bar Associations; State Bar of California; California Young Lawyers Association.

*OF COUNSEL*

**GARY L. HINMAN,** born Lincoln, Illinois, December 28, 1940; admitted to bar, 1966, Illinois; 1976, California. *Education:* University of Illinois (B.S., 1963; J.D., 1966); Golden Gate University (M.B.A., 1980). Instructor, Graduate Tax Program, Golden Gate University, 1981. States Attorney, Logan County, Illinois, 1968-1972. *Member:* Orange County Bar Association; State Bar of California. *PRACTICE AREAS:* Business; Corporate; Partnerships; Real Estate; Franchise; Taxation; International Law; Business Litigation.

**JOSE ZORRILLA, JR.,** born Havana, Cuba, September 26, 1948; admitted to bar, 1971, California; 1974, U.S. Supreme Court. *Education:* University of Southern California (A.B., 1971); California Western School of Law (J.D., Departmental Honor, 1974). Deputy District Attorney, Orange County, 1975-1979. U.S. Department General Attorney, 1975. Naturalization Examiner, 1974-1975. (Also practicing individually at the same address). *LANGUAGES:* Spanish. *PRACTICE AREAS:* Contract Law; Corporations Law; Patent, Trademark and Copyright.

REPRESENTATIVE CLIENTS: Avery Dennison Corporation; Callaway Golf Company; Fonovisa, Inc.; The Limited, Inc.; MCI Communications Corporation; McFadden Systems, Inc.; Micron Technology, Inc.; Reebok International; Unocal.

## DENNIS L. GEILER, INC., A P.C.

*19900 MAC ARTHUR BOULEVARD, SUITE 700*
**IRVINE, CALIFORNIA 92715**
*Telephone: 714-660-1040*
*Fax: 714-660-0342*

*Business and Estate Planning including Corporation, Partnerships and Real Estate Business and Civil Litigation.*

**DENNIS L. GEILER,** born Los Angeles, California, April 17, 1942; admitted to bar, 1968, California and U.S. Court of Appeals, Ninth Circuit. *Education:* University of Southern California (B.S., 1964; J.D., 1967). Phi Delta Phi. Recipient, American Jurisprudence Award in Real Estate Finance. Lecturer, Business Law, Woodbury Business College, Los Angeles, California, 1967-1968. Member, Board of Arbitrators, American Arbitration Association. *Member:* Orange County and American Bar Associations; State Bar of California. *PRACTICE AREAS:* Business Law; Estate Planning Law; Real Estate Law.

**WARREN WORTH,** born California; admitted to bar, 1989, California. *Education:* Western State University (B.S.L.; 1987; J.D., 1988), Trinity College, Cambridge University, Cambridge, England. *Member:* Orange County Bar Association (Member, Real Estate Section). *PRACTICE AREAS:* Tort Law; Real Estate (Property) Law; Contract Law.

## GENSON, EVEN, CRANDALL & WADE

*A PROFESSIONAL CORPORATION*
*7700 IRVINE CENTER DRIVE, #700*
**IRVINE, CALIFORNIA 92718**
*Telephone: 714-753-1000*
*FAX: 714-753-1039*

*Woodland Hills, California Office:* 21031 Ventura Boulevard, Suite 801. Telephone: 818-999-4811. FAX: 818-999-1782.
*Rancho Cucamonga, California Office:* 9483 Haven Avenue, Suite 102. Telephone: 909-390-4811. FAX: 909-390-1907.
*San Diego, California Office:* 9988 Hibert Street, Suite 300. Telephone: 619-635-6300. FAX: 619-635-6306.

*Trial practice in State and Federal Courts: Employment Practices Liability, Third Party Violent Crime/Premises Security, Product Liability, Warranty Litigation, Insurance Coverage, Insurance Bad Faith, Insurance Fraud, HMO/Managed Care Defense, Medical Malpractice, Directors and Officers Liability, Professional Malpractice, Construction Defect, Government Liability, Premises Liability, Transportation Liability, Vehicle Liability, Environ-*

*(This Listing Continued)*

*GENSON, EVEN, CRANDALL & WADE, A PROFESSIONAL CORPORATION, Irvine—Continued*

mental Liability, Recreational Sports and Leisure Activities Liability, Appellate Practice, Business Litigation (Class Action, Fraud, Misrepresentation, Breach of Contract, etc.).

(For complete Biographical data on all personnel, see Professional Biographies at Woodland Hills, California).

## GEORGE & SHIELDS, LLP

Established in 1989

30 CORPORATE PARK, SUITE 300
**IRVINE, CALIFORNIA 92714-5133**
Telephone: 714-263-1085
Fax: 714-263-0585

*General Civil and Trial Practice in State and Federal Courts. Business, Real Estate, Construction, Insurance, Surety, Contract, Personal Injury and Negligence Litigation. Corporate, Partnership, and Limited Liability Company Formation and Maintenance. Business, Finance and Real Estate Transactions, including Secured Transactions. Special Counsel on Legal Ethics and Conflicts of Interest including Attorney-Client Fee Agreements and Disputes.*

FIRM PROFILE: *George & Shields was founded in 1989 by Robert K. George and Timothy F. Shields who had worked together in a general civil litigation and transaction firm for five years previously. From its inception, the firm has represented both local and national clients in a wide range of litigation, creditor's rights, business formation, acquisition, financing and other transactional matters. Members of the firm serve as judges pro tempore in the local superior courts, as arbitrators for the local bar association, and are active in business, social, civil, charitable and political affairs.*

### MEMBERS OF FIRM

**ROBERT K. GEORGE,** born Roanoke, Virginia, 1949; admitted to bar, 1974, California. *Education:* University of California at Irvine (B.A., Social Sciences, 1971); Pepperdine University (J.D., 1974). State President, California Junior Chamber of Commerce, 1979. Director and General Counsel, California Jaycees Foundation, 1979-1992. Director and General Counsel, Universal Care, Inc., 1992—. Secretary and Director, Bank of Lakewood. Treasurer, Director and General Counsel, Greater Long Beach Girl Scouts, 1986-1993. *Member:* State Bar of California. **PRACTICE AREAS:** Business; Business Acquisitions; Real Estate; Personal Injury Litigation; Employment Law; Estate Planning.

**TIMOTHY F. SHIELDS,** born Laguna Beach, California, April 18, 1957; admitted to bar, 1985, California, U.S. Court of Appeals, Ninth and Federal Circuits, U.S. Tax Court and U.S. Supreme Court. *Education:* Eastern Washington University (B.A., with honors, 1982); Pepperdine University (J.D., 1985). Recipient Wilson Medallion. Moot Court Medalist, Oral Advocacy and Brief Writing. Externship, Hon. Justice Edward J. Wallin, California Court of Appeals, 1985. Judge Pro Tempore, Orange County Superior Court. *Member:* Orange County (Member, Business Litigation Section; Arbitrator, Client Relations Committee), Los Angeles County and American Bar Associations; State Bar of California. **PRACTICE AREAS:** Business; Real Estate; General Civil Litigation; Construction Claims; Labor and Employment Law; Creditor's Rights; Enforcement of Judgements; Estate Planning; Commercial Transactions.

**DAVID W. SPARKS,** born Ontario, California, 1968; admitted to bar, 1993, California, U.S. District Court, Central District of California and U.S. Court of Appeals, Ninth Circuit. *Education:* California State Polytechnic University at Pomona (B.A., Political Science, 1990); Pepperdine University (J.D., 1993). Externship, Hon. Judge Ronald Lew, U.S. District Court, Central District of California. *Member:* Orange County (Member, Litigation Section; Legislative Affairs Committee) and American Bar Associations; State Bar of California. **PRACTICE AREAS:** Civil Litigation; Business Law; Corporate Law; Torts; Personal Injury; Enforcement of Judgements; Employment; Labor Law.

## GIBSON, DUNN & CRUTCHER LLP

Established in 1890

4 PARK PLAZA, SUITES 1400, 1500, 1700 AND 1800
**IRVINE, CALIFORNIA 92614-8557**
Telephone: 714-451-3800
Telecopier: 714-451-4220

*Los Angeles, California Office:* 333 South Grand Avenue. Telephone: 213-229-7000. Telex: 188171 GIBTRASK LSA (TRT), 674930 GIBTRASK LSA (WUT). Telecopier: 213-229-7520. Cable Address: GIBTRASK LOS ANGELES.

*General Civil, Trial and Appellate Practice, State and Federal Courts. Antitrust Law, Specialized Criminal Defense. General Corporation, Securities, Administrative, Labor and Employment, Real Estate, Taxation, Estate Planning, Probate and Trust, International Business, Entertainment, Commercial, Insolvency, Bankruptcy and Reorganization, Natural Resources, Oil and Gas, Environmental Energy, Municipal and Public Utility Law.*

FIRM PROFILE: *Gibson, Dunn & Crutcher, originating in Los Angeles, has been providing legal services to clients since 1890. Today, the firm has grown to one of the largest law firms in the world with approximately 600 active attorneys in 15 offices situated in most of the world's important business centers. The firm has experts in virtually every area of the law, particularly those which relate to commercial transactions and disputes, and has more effective geographical coverage in the United States than any other major firm. The firm's lawyers and staff are dedicated to providing quality service on a timely and cost effective basis.*

*Our Irvine office was originally established in 1964 to serve Orange County's growing real estate developments. It now has grown to approximately 75 lawyers involved in most practice areas, representing large businesses as well as emerging and small entrepreneurial companies and individuals. This office offers particular expertise in venture capital financings, mergers and acquisitions and public offerings, antitrust, unfair competition, trade secrets, insolvency, ERISA, real estate development and finance, estate planning, employment, environmental and commercial litigation matters.*

### PARTNERS

**KENNETH E. RISTAU, JR.,** born February 14, 1939; admitted to bar, 1965, California. *Education:* Colgate University (B.A., magna cum laude, high honors, 1961); New York University (J.D., cum laude, 1964). Phi Beta Kappa; Order of the Coif. Member, New York University Law Review, 1963-1964. *Member:* Los Angeles County, Orange County and American Bar Associations. **PRACTICE AREAS:** Management Labor Law; N.L.R.B. Practice; Equal Employment and Labor Law; Wrongful Termination Litigation; General Litigation. *Email:* kristau@gdclaw.com

**RICHARD G. DUNCAN, JR.,** born August 2, 1938; admitted to bar, 1967, California. *Education:* Stanford University (A.B., 1960); University of California School of Law, Los Angeles (LL.B., 1966). Order of the Coif. Senior Editor, U.C.L.A. Law Review, 1965-1966. *Member:* Orange County and American Bar Associations. Fellow, American College of Trial Lawyers. [Active Duty, Second and First Lieutenant, U.S. Marine Corps, 1960-1963]. **PRACTICE AREAS:** Business, Corporate, Real Estate and Land Use Litigation. *Email:* rduncan@gdclaw.com

**RALPH C. WINTRODE,** born December 21, 1942; admitted to bar, 1967, California; 1984, New York; 1989-1992, Japan (Gaikokuho Jimu Bengoshi); 1990, District of Columbia. *Education:* University of Southern California (B.S., 1966; J.D., 1967). Order of the Coif. Associate Editor, University of Southern California Law Review, 1966. *Member:* Los Angeles County, Orange County, New York State, American and Inter-Pacific Bar Associations; District of Columbia Bar; State Bar of California. **PRACTICE AREAS:** Real Estate; Land Use; Corporate; Mergers and Acquisitions; Bankruptcy. *Email:* rwintrode@gdclaw.com

**BLAKE T. FRANKLIN,** born September 28, 1942; admitted to bar, 1966, California; 1969, District of Columbia; 1976, New York. *Education:* Dartmouth College (A.B., cum laude, 1963); Harvard Law School (J.D., 1966). Visiting Professor of Commercial Law, University of Costa Rica, 1967-1968. International Legal Advisor, Government of Bolivia, 1993. *Member:* The Association of the Bar of the City of New York; District of Columbia Bar; American and Interamerican Bar Associations; American Society of International Law. (Irvine, California and New York City Offices). **LANGUAGES:** Spanish. **PRACTICE AREAS:** International Transactions (project finance, etc.); Banking Law; Corporate Law.

**JOHN C. WELLS,** born October 19, 1941; admitted to bar, 1967, California; 1969, Oregon. *Education:* Stanford University (B.A., 1963); Boalt

*(This Listing Continued)*

Hall School of Law, University of California (J.D., 1966). *Email:* jwells@gdclaw.com

**J. MICHAEL BRENNAN,** born December 31, 1939; admitted to bar, 1972, California. *Education:* Fordham University (A.B., 1961); Boalt Hall School of Law, University of California (J.D., 1971). Order of the Coif. Member, 1969-1971 and Book Review Editor, 1970-1971, California Law Review. [Captain, U.S. Marine Corps, 1961-1968]. *LANGUAGES:* French. *PRACTICE AREAS:* Securities Litigation; Proceedings Before the Securities and Exchange Commission; Class Actions and Derivative Suits; Corporate and Partnership Takeover, Control and Dissolution Matters. *Email:* mbrennan@gdclaw.com

**WAYNE W. SMITH,** born June 8, 1942; admitted to bar, 1972, California. *Education:* California State College at Long Beach (B.A., cum laude, 1965); University of California at Los Angeles (J.D., 1972). Order of the Coif. (Los Angeles and Irvine Offices). *PRACTICE AREAS:* Business and Securities Litigation; Entertainment Litigation. *Email:* wsmith@gdclaw.com

**DENNIS A. GLADWELL,** born October 27, 1943; admitted to bar, 1970, Utah; 1971, California. *Education:* University of Utah (B.S., 1966; J.D., 1970). Order of the Coif. Editor-in-Chief, Utah Law Review, 1969-1970. *Member:* Orange County (Chairman, Labor Section, 1982-1983) and American Bar Associations; Utah State Bar. [Capt., JAG, USMC, 1971-1974]. *PRACTICE AREAS:* Employment Law; Labor Law. *Email:* dgladwell@gdclaw.com

**S. DAVID BLINN,** born March 7, 1945; admitted to bar, 1970, California. *Education:* Wesleyan University (B.A., 1967); Southern Methodist University (J.D., 1970). Order of the Coif. Member, 1968-1970 and Casenote Editor, 1969-1970, Southwestern Law Journal. (Los Angeles and Irvine Offices). *Email:* dblinn@gdclaw.com

**GERARD J. KENNY,** born May 30, 1943; admitted to bar, 1973, California. *Education:* Brooklyn College (B.A., 1966); University of Southern California (J.D., 1973). Order of the Coif. Executive Editor, University of Southern California Law Review, 1972-1973. Law Clerk to Chief Justice Donald R. Wright, California Supreme Court, 1973-1974. *Member:* American Bar Association. *PRACTICE AREAS:* Taxation (Corporate, Partnership and Personal Income Tax); Federal and State Tax Controversies; Employee Compensation Programs; Mergers, Acquisitions and Divestitures; Partnerships. *Email:* gkenny@gdclaw.com

**GORDON A. SCHALLER,** born August 27, 1949; admitted to bar, 1973, California; 1980, Washington. *Education:* Iowa State University (B.S., with distinction, 1970); University of Minnesota (J.D., magna cum laude, 1973). Order of the Coif. Member and Editor, Minnesota Law Review, 1971-1973. *Member:* Washington State Bar Association. Fellow, American College of Trust and Estate Counsel. *PRACTICE AREAS:* Estate Planning, Trust and Probate Administration; Tax Exempt Organizations; Charitable Tax Planning. *Email:* gschaller@gdclaw.com

**ROBERT W. LOEWEN,** born April 27, 1948; admitted to bar, 1975, California. *Education:* Pomona College (B.A., 1970); University of Southern California (J.D., 1975). Order of the Coif. Executive Editor of Lead Articles, Southern California Law Review, 1974-1975. Law Clerk to Honorable Walter Ely, U.S. Circuit Judge, Ninth Circuit, 1975-1976; Honorable Byron R. White, U.S. Supreme Court, 1976-1977. [U.S. Army, 1970-1972]. *PRACTICE AREAS:* Business Litigation; Toxic Tort Litigation; Trade Secrets; Land Use and Real Estate Litigation; Insurance Coverage. *Email:* rloewen@gdclaw.com

**ROBERT EVERETT DEAN,** born April 26, 1951; admitted to bar, 1976, California. *Education:* University of California at Irvine (B.A., magna cum laude, 1973); University of Minnesota (J.D., magna cum laude, 1976). *PRACTICE AREAS:* General Corporate Law; Securities Law; Banking. *Email:* rdean@gdclaw.com

**THOMAS D. MAGILL,** born January 22, 1950; admitted to bar, 1976, California. *Education:* Dickinson College (B.A., 1972); Duke University (J.D., 1976). Phi Beta Kappa; Order of the Coif. Member, Editorial Board, Duke Law Journal, 1975-1976. *PRACTICE AREAS:* Mergers, Acquisitions and Divestitures; Securities; Corporate Law. *Email:* tmagill@gdclaw.com

**WILLIAM D. CLASTER,** born April 9, 1952; admitted to bar, 1976, California. *Education:* Stanford University (B.A., 1973); University of California at Los Angeles (J.D., 1976). Managing Editor, U.C.L.A. Law Review, 1975-1976. Contributing Author: "California CEB, Wrongful Employment Termination Practice" (1987). *PRACTICE AREAS:* Labor and Employment Law; Employment Discrimination; Wrongful Discharge and Privacy Litigation; Federal and State Wage and Hour Law; Non-Competition Agreements; Collective Bargaining Agreements and Arbitrations. *Email:* wclaster@gdclaw.com

**JOSEPH P. BUSCH III,** born July 26, 1948; admitted to bar, 1976, California. *Education:* Claremont Men's College (B.A., summa cum laude, 1970); Boalt Hall School of Law, University of California (J.D., 1976). Associate Editor, California Law Review, 1975-1976. [United States Navy, 1970-1972]. *PRACTICE AREAS:* ERISA Litigation; Accounting Liability Litigation; Securities Litigation. *Email:* jbusch@gdclaw.com

**LARRY C. BOYD,** born March 21, 1952; admitted to bar, 1977, California. *Education:* Stanford University (A.B., with distinction, 1974; J.D., 1977). Phi Beta Kappa. Member, 1975-1976 and Note Editor, 1976-1977, Stanford Law Review. *Member:* Orange County and American Bar Associations. *PRACTICE AREAS:* Intellectual Property and Business Litigation. *Email:* lboyd@gdclaw.com

**E. MICHAEL GREANEY,** born June 15, 1952; admitted to bar, 1977, California. *Education:* Loyola University (B.A., 1974); University of Southern California (J.D., 1977). Member, Southern California Law Review, 1975-1976. (Irvine, California and New York, N.Y. Offices). *PRACTICE AREAS:* Corporate Securities; Mergers and Acquisitions; General Business Law. *Email:* mgreaney@gdclaw.com

**KAREN H. CLARK,** born December 17, 1944; admitted to bar, 1978, California. *Education:* Pomona College, Stanford University (B.A., 1966); University of Washington (M.A., History, 1968); University of Michigan (J.D., magna cum laude, 1977). Order of the Coif. Associate Editor, Michigan Law Review, 1976-1977. *Member:* Orange County and American Bar Associations. *PRACTICE AREAS:* Real Property and Business Transactions; Real Property Finance and Workouts; Commercial Leasing. *Email:* kclark@gdclaw.com

**MARK W. SHURTLEFF,** born September 1, 1953; admitted to bar, 1978, California. *Education:* Stanford University (B.A., 1975); University of Southern California (J.D., 1978). Order of the Coif. Executive Editor of Lead Articles, Southern California Law Review, 1977-1978. Law Clerk to Honorable Walter Ely, U.S. Court of Appeals, Ninth Circuit, 1978-1979. *PRACTICE AREAS:* Securities; Intellectual Property; Software; General Corporate. *Email:* mshurtleff@gdclaw.com

**WALTER L. SCHINDLER,** born June 23, 1951; admitted to bar, 1980, California. *Education:* Yale University (B.A., magna cum laude, 1973; M.A., 1976; Ph.D., 1977); Harvard University (J.D., cum laude, 1980). Fulbright Scholar, Italy, 1974-1975. *PRACTICE AREAS:* Corporate Law; Securities Law. *Email:* wschindler@gdclaw.com

**MICHELE C. COYLE,** born August 12, 1951; admitted to bar, 1978, Washington; 1995, California. *Education:* University of Nebraska (B.A., 1972); Franklin Pierce Law Center (J.D., 1978); University of Washington (LL.M., 1982). Member, Mortar Board. Attorney, U.S. Environmental Protection Agency, Seattle, Washington, 1978-1983. Special Assistant U.S. Attorney, 1982-1983. LR 39.1 Mediator, Western District Washington. Member, Natural Resources, Energy and Environmental Section and Environmental Crimes Sub Committee, American Bar Association. *PRACTICE AREAS:* Environmental Law; Toxics; Product Liability; Labor and Employment. *Email:* mcoyle@gdclaw.com

**JEFFREY T. THOMAS,** born November 15, 1957; admitted to bar, 1982, California. *Education:* University of California, San Diego (B.A., 1979) University of San Diego (J.D., magna cum laude, 1982). Notes and Comments Editor, San Diego Law Review, 1981-1982. Law Clerk to Honorable Gerald Brown, Presiding Justice, California Court of Appeal, Fourth District, 1982-1983. *PRACTICE AREAS:* Business Litigation; Land Use Litigation; Antitrust; Intellectual Property Litigation; Real Estate Litigation. *Email:* jthomas@gdclaw.com

**CRAIG H. MILLET,** born June 2, 1954; admitted to bar, 1982, California. *Education:* University of Southern California (B.A., 1978); Pepperdine University (J.D., summa cum laude, 1982). Best Team and Best Advocate, Vincent S. Dalsimer Moot Court Competition, 1981. Editor-in-Chief, Pepperdine Law Review, 1980-1982. *Member:* International Bar Association (Member, Subcommittee J). *PRACTICE AREAS:* Bankruptcy Litigation; Insolvency; Creditors' Rights; International Bankruptcy. *Email:* cmillet@gdclaw.com

**ROBERT E. PALMER,** born December 11, 1956; admitted to bar, 1984, California. *Education:* University of Nebraska (B.A., with honors, 1978); Pepperdine University (J.D., magna cum laude, 1984). Editor-in-Chief, Pepperdine Law Review, 1983-1984. Executive Member, Moot Court Board, 1983-1984. President, Federal Bar Association, Orange

*(This Listing Continued)*

## GIBSON, DUNN & CRUTCHER LLP, Irvine—Continued

County Chapter, 1996-1997. Director, Orange County Bar Association, 1994. Chair, Business Litigation Section, Orange County Bar Association, 1994—. President, Constitutional Rights Foundation of Orange County, 1993-1995. Co-Chair, New Associates Reception, Orange County Bar Association, 1996. *PRACTICE AREAS:* Litigation, with a focus on Complex Business Litigation including Intellectual Property; Environmental Counseling and Litigation. *Email:* rpalmer@gdclaw.com

**BRIAN W. COPPLE,** born September 28, 1960; admitted to bar, 1987, California; 1988, Arizona. *Education:* Stanford University (A.B., 1982); University of California at Los Angeles (M.B.A., 1987; J.D., 1987). Member, Order of the Coif. Member, UCLA Law Review, 1984-1986. *LANGUAGES:* German. *PRACTICE AREAS:* Corporate Law; Securities; Venture Capital; Contracts; Technology and Science. *Email:* bcopple@gdclaw.com

**TIMOTHY J. KAY,** born October 31, 1953; admitted to bar, 1987, California. *Education:* University of San Francisco (B.A., 1975); Hastings College of the Law, University of California; Stanford Law School (J.D., with distinction, 1987). Member, 1985-1986, and Note Editor, 1986-1987, Stanford Law Review. *PRACTICE AREAS:* Trusts and Estates; Estate and Gift Tax Controversies; Nonprofit and Charitable Organizations; Taxation; Guardianship and Conservatorship. *Email:* tkay@gdclaw.com

**GENIENE B. STILLWELL,** born November 10, 1962; admitted to bar, 1988, California. *Education:* Texas A & M University (B.B.A., 1985); University of Texas at Austin (J.D., 1988). Order of the Coif. Member, Texas Law Review, 1986-1987. *PRACTICE AREAS:* Labor and Employment Law; Trade Secrets. *Email:* gstillwell@gdclaw.com

### ADVISORY COUNSELS

**THOMAS B. PITCHER,** born November 28, 1938; admitted to bar, 1967, California. *Education:* University of Florida (B.S., in B.A., 1960); Duke University (J.D., 1966). Order of the Coif. Note Editor, Duke Law Journal, 1965-1966. *Member:* American Bar Association. *PRACTICE AREAS:* Business Law; Corporate Law; Securities; Mergers, Acquisitions and Divestitures; Commercial Law.

**FRANK L. MALLORY,** born May 5, 1920; admitted to bar, 1948, California (Inactive). *Education:* Stanford University (A.B., cum laude, 1941; LL.B., 1947). Phi Beta Kappa; Order of the Coif. *Member:* Los Angeles County, Orange County and American Bar Associations.

**GUY K. CLAIRE,** born February 14, 1925; admitted to bar, 1958, California. *Education:* University of Southern California (A.B., 1954; LL.B., 1957). Order of the Coif. Editor-in-Chief, Southern California Law Review, 1956-1957. *Member:* Orange County and American Bar Associations.

### OF COUNSELS

**JOHN A. ARGUELLES,** born August 22, 1927; admitted to bar, 1955, California. *Education:* University of California at Los Angeles (B.A., 1950; LL.B., 1954). Councilman, City of Montebello, 1962-1963. East Los Angeles Municipal Court Judge, 1963-1969. Los Angeles County Superior Court Judge, 1969-1984. Justice: California Court of Appeals, 1984-1987; California Supreme Court, 1987-1989. *Member:* Los Angeles and Orange County Bar Associations. *PRACTICE AREAS:* Alternative Dispute Resolution. *Email:* jarguelles@gdclaw.com

**W. RICHARD SMITH, JR.,** born September 24, 1960; admitted to bar, 1986, Georgia and California. *Education:* University of Virginia (B.S., 1982); Emory University (J.D., 1985). Editorial Board, Emory Law Journal, 1984-1985. Founding Editor-in-Chief, Emory International Law Review, 1984-1985. *PRACTICE AREAS:* Computers and Software; Intellectual Property. *Email:* rsmith@gdclaw.com

### SPECIAL COUNSEL

**TERESA JOANNING FARRELL,** born September 17, 1958; admitted to bar, 1986, California. *Education:* University of California, San Diego (B.A., 1980); University of California, Hastings College of the Law (J.D., magna cum laude, 1986). Order of the Coif. Staff Member, 1984-1985 and Executive Editor, 1985-1986, Hastings Law Journal. Extern to the Honorable Eugene F. Lynch, U.S. District Court, Northern District of California, 1986. *PRACTICE AREAS:* Real Estate; Finance. *Email:* tfarrell@gdclaw.com

### ASSOCIATES

**MARIANNE SHIPP,** born April 17, 1952; admitted to bar, 1987, California. *Education:* Youngstown State University (B.S., 1975); University of San Diego (J.D., 1987). Member, University of San Diego Law Review, 1986-1987. *PRACTICE AREAS:* Labor and Employment; ERISA Litigation. *Email:* mshipp@gdclaw.com

**LIISA ANSELMI STITH,** born April 4, 1963; admitted to bar, 1988, California and Colorado. *Education:* University of Notre Dame (B.A., 1985); Duke University (J.D., 1988). Member, Moot Court Board. Member, Alaska Law Review, 1987-1988. *PRACTICE AREAS:* General Corporate and Securities. *Email:* lstith@gdclaw.com

**GUNNAR BLAISE GOODING,** born May 6, 1963; admitted to bar, 1989, California. *Education:* University of California at Berkeley (B.A., 1985); University of Southern California Law Center (J.D., 1989). Executive Articles Editor, Southern California Law Review, 1988-1989. *PRACTICE AREAS:* Employment Litigation; Labor. *Email:* ggooding@gdclaw.com

**OSCAR GARZA,** born July 23, 1963; admitted to bar, 1990, California. *Education:* California State University (B.S., 1985); University of Arizona (J.D., 1990). Member, University of Arizona Law Review, 1989-1990. *PRACTICE AREAS:* Debtor and Creditor's Rights; Bankruptcy Litigation. *Email:* ogarza@gdclaw.com

**ALAN N. BICK,** born March 16, 1961; admitted to bar, 1990, California. *Education:* Dartmouth College (B.A., summa cum laude, 1983); Stanford University Law School (J.D., 1990). Senior Editor, Stanford Environmental Law Journal, 1990. *PRACTICE AREAS:* Environmental; Intellectual Property. *Email:* abick@gdclaw.com

**ANDREA E. NEUMAN,** born May 20, 1965; admitted to bar, 1990, California. *Education:* University of Virginia (B.S., 1987; J.D., 1990). *PRACTICE AREAS:* Trust/Probate Litigation and General Commercial Litigation. *Email:* aneuman@gdclaw.com

**CLARK D. STITH,** born May 19, 1961; admitted to bar, 1991, New York; 1992, District of Columbia; 1994, California. *Education:* University of Kansas (B.S., B.A., 1985); University of Erlangen-Nuremberg, Erlangen, Germany (Fulbright Scholar, 1985-1986); Georgetown University Law Center (J.D., cum laude, 1990); Georgetown University School of Foreign Service (M.S., 1992). Articles Editor, The Georgetown Law Journal, 1990. *LANGUAGES:* German and French. *PRACTICE AREAS:* Litigation; Intellectual Property. *Email:* cstith@gdclaw.com

**J. FRED NEUMAN,** born July 15, 1965; admitted to bar, 1990, California. *Education:* Kansas State University (B.S., magna cum laude, 1987); University of Virginia (J.D., 1990). *PRACTICE AREAS:* Antitrust; Litigation. *Email:* fneuman@gdclaw.com

**SCOTT M. KNUTSON,** born November 15, 1960; admitted to bar, 1992, California. *Education:* Washington State University (B.A., 1985); Pepperdine University (M.B.A., 1988); University of Minnesota (M.B.T., 1991; J.D., cum laude, 1991). Rho Chi National Pharmaceutical Honor Society. Registered Pharmacist, State of Washington, 1986. *PRACTICE AREAS:* Tax Law. *Email:* sknutson@gdclaw.com

**JEFFREY H. REEVES,** born May 23, 1966; admitted to bar, 1991, California. *Education:* Texas A & M University (B.S., 1988); University of Houston (J.D., cum laude, 1991). Research Editor, Houston Law Review, 1989-1991. *PRACTICE AREAS:* Commercial Litigation; Bankruptcy Litigation. *Email:* jreeves@gdclaw.com

**JOHN M. WILLIAMS, III,** born April 16, 1963; admitted to bar, 1991, California; 1993, District of Columbia. *Education:* University of California at Irvine (B.A., 1985); University of Southern California (M.P.A., 1987); Georgetown University (J.D., cum laude, 1991). Editor-in-Chief, Journal of Law and Policy in International Business, 1990-1991. *PRACTICE AREAS:* Securities; Mergers, Acquisitions and Divestitures. *Email:* jwilliams@gdclaw.com

**GREGG P. GOLDMAN,** born October 27, 1965; admitted to bar, 1991, California. *Education:* Arizona State University (B.S., 1987; J.D., magna cum laude, 1991). Note and Comment Editor, Arizona State University Law Review, 1990-1991. *Email:* ggoldman@gdclaw.com

**PETER M. STONE,** born July 16, 1967; admitted to bar, 1992, California. *Education:* University of California at Berkeley (B.A., magna cum laude, 1988); University of California, Boalt Hall School of Law (J.D., 1991). Phi Beta Kappa. Order of the Coif. Topics and Research Editor, International Tax & Business Lawyer, 1990-1991. Law Clerk, Hon. James L. Buckley, United States Court of Appeals for the D.C. Circuit, 1991-

*(This Listing Continued)*

1992. *PRACTICE AREAS:* Real Estate and Securities Litigation. *Email:* pstone@gdclaw.com

**MARK J. PAYNE,** born June 16, 1964; admitted to bar, 1992, California. *Education:* Mary Washington College (B.S., cum laude, 1986); College of William & Mary (J.D., 1991). Order of the Coif. Managing Editor, William & Mary Law Review, 1990-1991. Law Clerk for the Honorable Rebecca Beach Smith, U.S. District Judge, Eastern District of Virginia. *PRACTICE AREAS:* Labor and Employment. *Email:* mpayne@gdclaw.com

**TRYGVE M. THORESEN,** born March 11, 1964; admitted to bar, 1993, California. *Education:* University of California, Santa Barbara (B.A., magna cum laude, 1987); University of California, Hastings College of the Law (J.D., magna cum laude, 1992). Order of the Coif. Thurston Society. Member, Hastings Law Journal. *PRACTICE AREAS:* Mergers, Acquisitions and Divestitures; Securities. *Email:* tthoresen@gdclaw.com

**MARYN L. MILLER,** born October 21, 1966; admitted to bar, 1992, California. *Education:* University of California at Los Angeles (B.A., 1988); University of California, Boalt Hall School of Law (J.D., 1992). *Email:* mmiller@gdclaw.com

**MICHELLE D. LUSTIG,** born April 13, 1966; admitted to bar, 1992, California. *Education:* University of California at Los Angeles (B.A., 1988); Loyola Law School (J.D., 1992). Order of the Coif. Member, 1990-1992 and Production Editor, 1991-1992, Loyola Law School International & Comparative Law Journal. *PRACTICE AREAS:* Corporations. *Email:* mlustig@gdclaw.com

**SHARYL P. BILAS,** born April 21, 1967; admitted to bar, 1992, California. *Education:* University of California at Los Angeles (B.A., magna cum laude, 1989); Georgetown Law School (J.D., cum laude, 1992). Phi Beta Kappa. *PRACTICE AREAS:* Labor and Employment Law. *Email:* sbilas@gdclaw.com

**DAVID A. SEGAL,** born January 18, 1967; admitted to bar, 1993, New York and California. *Education:* Massachusetts Institute of Technology (S.B., 1989); Fordham University School of Law (J.D., magna cum laude, 1992). Annual Survey Editor, Fordham Law Review, 1991-1992. Order of the Coif. Clerk to the late Hon. J. Daniel Mahoney, U.S. Court of Appeals for the Second Circuit, 1992-1993. *PRACTICE AREAS:* Intellectual Property Litigation and Counseling; Business Litigation. *Email:* dsegal@gdclaw.com

**LESLIE R. OLSON,** born November 6, 1964; admitted to bar, 1993, California; 1995, Colorado. *Education:* Colorado College (B.A., 1987); University of San Diego School of Law (J.D., magna cum laude, 1993). Member, 1991-1993 and Executive Editor, 1992-1993, San Diego Law Review. *PRACTICE AREAS:* Corporate Law. *Email:* lolson@gdclaw.com

**DONNA M. BIGI,** born June 24, 1959; admitted to bar, 1993, California. *Education:* University of California (B.A., 1983); University of Southern California (J.D., 1993). Order of the Coif. Executive Editor, Southern California Law Review, 1992-1993. Law Clerk, Hon. Alfred T. Goodwin, Ninth Circuit Court of Appeals, Pasadena, California, 1993-1994. *PRACTICE AREAS:* Labor and Employment; Litigation. *Email:* dbigi@gdclaw.com

**THOMAS S. JONES,** born March 29, 1967; admitted to bar, 1993, California; 1994, Pennsylvania. *Education:* College of William & Mary (B.A., 1989; J.D., 1992). Order of the Coif. Staff Member and Business Editor, William & Mary Law Review, 1991-1992. Law Clerk, Honorable William D. Hutchinson, U.S. Court of Appeals, Third Circuit, 1992-1994. *PRACTICE AREAS:* Litigation. *Email:* tjones@gdclaw.com

**TORREY A. OLINS,** born April 15, 1969; admitted to bar, 1993, California. *Education:* University of Pennsylvania (B.A., 1989); Stanford Law School (J.D., 1993). Phi Beta Kappa. *PRACTICE AREAS:* Employee Benefits. *Email:* tolins@gdclaw.com

**COSMAS N. LYKOS,** born May 4, 1968; admitted to bar, 1994, California. *Education:* Dickinson College (B.A., 1990); Duke University School of Law (J.D., with honors, 1993). Senior Editor, Law and Contemporary Problems, 1992-1993. *PRACTICE AREAS:* Corporate Law. *Email:* clykos@gdclaw.com

**ADAM E. MUCHNICK,** born January 15, 1969; admitted to bar, 1995, California; 1996, Florida. *Education:* Stanford University (A.B., 1991); University of Chicago (J.D., 1994). Order of the Coif. Law Clerk to the Honorable Jesse E. Eschbach, U.S. Court of Appeals, Seventh Circuit, 1994-1995. *LANGUAGES:* Spanish. *PRACTICE AREAS:* Corporate Law; International Law. *Email:* amuchnick@gdclaw.com

*(This Listing Continued)*

**MARK N. MAZDA,** born August 26, 1968; admitted to bar, 1995, California. *Education:* Brigham Young University (B.A., magna cum laude, 1992); Columbia University (J.D., 1995). Harlan Fiske Stone Scholar. *LANGUAGES:* Portuguese. *Email:* mmazda@gdclaw.com

**PAUL A. ANDRONICO,** born March 6, 1967; admitted to bar, 1995, California. *Education:* University of California at Santa Barbara (B.A., with honors, 1989); University of San Diego (J.D., magna cum laude, 1995). Executive Editor, San Diego Law Review, 1994-1995. *Email:* pandronico@gdclaw.com

**MICHAEL E. SANDERS,** born April 15, 1958; admitted to bar, 1996, California. *Education:* University of Arkansas (B.S.B.A., summa cum laude, 1992); Stanford University (J.D., 1995). Executive Editor, Stanford Journal of International Law, 1994-1995. *Email:* msanders@gdclaw.com

**JEFF AUGUSTINI,** born June 24, 1969; admitted to bar, 1995, California. *Education:* University of California at Los Angeles (B.A., cum laude, 1987); Georgetown University Law Center (J.D., cum laude, 1995). Member, Georgetown Journal of Law and Policy in International Business, Winter 1995. *Email:* jaugustini@gdclaw.com

**DANIEL H. BAREN,** born August 8, 1966; admitted to bar, 1995, California. *Education:* Northwestern University (B.S., 1988); University of Southern California (J.D., 1995). Order of the Coif. Articles Editor, USC Law Review, 1994-1995. *Email:* dbaren@gdclaw.com

**JESSE S. FINLAYSON,** born August 15, 1970; admitted to bar, 1995, California. *Education:* Arizona State University (B.A., cum laude, 1992); University of San Diego (J.D., magna cum laude, 1995). Order of the Coif. *Email:* jfinlayson@gdlaw.com

**MICHAEL A. BARMETTLER,** born June 24, 1969; admitted to bar, 1996, California. *Education:* Northern Arizona University (B.S.B.A., 1992); University of San Diego (J.D., magna cum laude, 1995). Order of the Coif. Executive Comments Editor, San Diego Law Review, 1993-1995. Judicial Clerk to the Honorable C. Thomas White, Supreme Court of Nebraska, 1995-1996. *Email:* mbarmettler@gdclaw.com

**JEAN DE FOREST BILLYOU,** born September 6, 1966; admitted to bar, 1995, California; 1996, Hawaii. *Education:* Wellesley College (B.A., 1988); Duke University School of Law (J.D., 1995). *Email:* jbillyou@gcdlaw.com

### STAFF ATTORNEYS

**MELINDA DALTON WATERMAN,** born April 17, 1968; admitted to bar, 1995, California. *Education:* University of Southern California (B.A., 1990); Pepperdine University School of Law (J.D., 1995). *PRACTICE AREAS:* Estate Planning. *Email:* mdalton@gdclaw.com

**BRIAN R. KIRCHOFF,** born January 31, 1950; admitted to bar, 1979, California. *Education:* San Francisco State University (B.A., 1972; M.A., 1974); McGeorge School of Law, University of the Pacific (J.D., 1979). Member, Moot Court Honors Board. *PRACTICE AREAS:* Real Estate. *Email:* bkirchoff@gdclaw.com

Unless Otherwise Indicated All Members and Associates of the firm are members of The State Bar of California.

(For information on firm personnel, address and telephone information regarding the firm's offices located in Century City, San Diego, San Francisco and Menlo Park, California; Denver, Colorado; Washington, D.C.; New York, N.Y.; Dallas, Texas; Paris, France; London, England; Hong Kong; Jeddah and Riyadh, Saudi Arabia (Affiliated Offices), see professional biographies at Los Angeles, California)

---

# GIBSON, HAGLUND & JOHNSON
*2010 MAIN STREET, SUITE 400*
**IRVINE, CALIFORNIA 92714**
Telephone: 714-752-1100
Fax: 714-752-1144

*Business, Corporate and Securities. Franchising, Real Estate, Municipal Finance, Investment Management and Financial Services, Mergers and Acquisitions.*

### MEMBERS OF FIRM

**ROBERT V. GIBSON,** born Indianapolis, Indiana, February 7, 1921; admitted to bar, 1950, California and U.S. District Court, Southern District of California. *Education:* Wayne State University; North Carolina State University; Stanford University; University of San Francisco (LL.B., 1950). *Member:* Los Angeles Bar Association; State Bar of California.

*(This Listing Continued)*

## GIBSON, HAGLUND & JOHNSON, Irvine—Continued

**BRUCE H. HAGLUND,** born Idaho Falls, Idaho, May 13, 1951; admitted to bar, 1980, California; 1981, U.S. District Court, Central District of California. *Education:* University of Utah (B.A., 1975; J.D., 1979). *Member:* State Bar of California; American Bar Association. *LANGUAGES:* Japanese. *PRACTICE AREAS:* Corporate Law; Securities.

**PAUL H. JOHNSON,** born Provo, Utah, November 4, 1942; admitted to bar, 1974, California. *Education:* California State University, Long Beach (B.A., 1965); Western State University (J.D., 1973). *PRACTICE AREAS:* Corporate Law; Estate Planning.

---

## GRACE, BRANDON, HOLLIS AND RAMIREZ

7700 IRVINE CENTER DRIVE, SUITE 800
**IRVINE, CALIFORNIA 92718**
Telephone: 714-753-2860
Fax: 714-753-2899

San Diego, California Office: 1010 Second Avenue, Suite 1800, 92101.
Telephone: 619-595-0800. Fax: 619-595-0328.

*General Civil and Trial Practice with an emphasis on providing a defense in the following areas: Medical Negligence, Hospital Liability, Personal Injury, Construction Defect, Product Liability, Real Estate and Creditor's Remedies.*

(For complete biographical data on all personnel see Professional Biographies at San Diego, California)

---

## GRANT & LAUBSCHER

A Partnership including a Professional Corporation

Established in 1991

2030 MAIN STREET, SUITE 1600
**IRVINE, CALIFORNIA 92714**
Telephone: 714-660-1600
Telecopier: 714-660-6060

*General Civil Trial Practice, with Emphasis in Areas of Antitrust, Business, Real Estate and Securities Litigation.*

FIRM PROFILE: *Grant & Laubscher was founded in 1991 for the purpose of providing litigation and dispute resolution services. Its attorneys are well-seasoned in complex civil trial practice at all levels of the state and federal courts. Grant & Laubscher enjoys an exceptional reputation for achieving successful resolutions for its clients, and is committed to providing the highest caliber of services in a cost-effective manner.*

**DAVID C. GRANT, (P.C.),** born Culver City, California, May 18, 1947; admitted to bar, 1972, California; 1981, U.S. Tax Court. *Education:* Colgate University (A.B., 1969); Loyola University of Los Angeles (J.D., cum laude, 1972). Alpha Sigma Nu. Member, St. Thomas More Law Honor Society. Member: 1970-1972, and Editor-in-Chief, 1971-1972, Loyola University of Los Angeles Law Review. Author: "Note," 5 Loy. L.A. L. Rev. 611. Moderator, CEB Program on Provisional Remedies, 1976. Panelist: CEB Program on Real Estate Broker Practice, 1981; CEB Program on Civil Trial Practice, 1985, 1987, 1989; CEB Real Property Institute Program, 1989. Moderator: CEB Program on Real Property Remedies, 1991; CEB Program on Construction Law, Contracts and Disputes, 1989. Judge Pro Tem, Orange County Superior Court, 1983-1996. *Member:* Orange County, San Diego County and American Bar Associations; State Bar of California. *PRACTICE AREAS:* Litigation.

**BARRY R. LAUBSCHER,** born Los Angeles, California, April 26, 1946; admitted to bar, 1972, California. *Education:* Case-Western Reserve University and John Carroll University (B.S., magna cum laude, 1969); Cornell University (J.D., 1972). Omicron Delta Epsilon. Panelist, CEB Program on Business Torts, 1981. Judge Pro Tem, Orange County Municipal Court, 1976-1978, Orange County Superior Court, 1981-1996. *Member:* Los Angeles County, Orange County, Federal and American Bar Associations; State Bar of California. *PRACTICE AREAS:* Litigation; Antitrust.

**JAMES R. PERCIVAL,** born Des Moines, Iowa, October 19, 1955; admitted to bar, 1981, California. *Education:* University of Iowa (B.B.A., special honors with high distinction, 1977); Stanford University (J.D., 1980). Beta Gamma Sigma. Law Clerk to Hon. Lawrence T. Lydick, U.S. District Court, Central District of California, 1980-1981. *Member:* Los Angeles County, Orange County and American Bar Associations; State Bar of California. *PRACTICE AREAS:* Litigation.

**MARK A. SCHADRACK,** born Seattle, Washington, October 23, 1959; admitted to bar, 1985, California. *Education:* University of California at Berkeley (A.B., 1981); Loyola University of Los Angeles (J.D., 1985). Staff Member, 1983-1984 and Note and Comment Editor, 1984-1985, Loyola University of Los Angeles Law Review. *Member:* Orange County and American Bar Associations; State Bar of California. *PRACTICE AREAS:* Litigation.

**DENISE L. MCKINNEY,** born Oakland, California, March 20, 1965; admitted to bar, 1990, California. *Education:* University of California at Los Angeles (B.A., with high honors, magna cum laude, 1987); University of California, Boalt Hall School of Law (J.D., 1990). Phi Beta Kappa. Moot Court Board. McBaine Honors Competition Winner. Attorney Coach, Constitutional Rights Foundation Annual Mock Trial Competition. *Member:* Orange County and American Bar Associations; State Bar of California. *PRACTICE AREAS:* Litigation.

**DEEANN M. TAYLOR,** born San Fernando, California, March 29, 1966; admitted to bar, 1992, California. *Education:* University of California at Los Angeles (B.A., magna cum laude, 1988); New York University School of Law (J.D., magna cum laude, 1992). Phi Beta Kappa. Order of the Coif. Recipient: American Jurisprudence Award in Professional Responsibility, 1992. Member, 1990-1991; Editor and Board Member, 1991-1992, Annual Survey of American Law. Author: Hepps, Dunn & Bradstreet and Milkovich The Lingering Confusion in Defamation Law, Annual Survey of American Law, 1992/1993 Vol., Issue 1. *Member:* Orange County Bar Association; State Bar of California. *PRACTICE AREAS:* Litigation.

**GORDON G. MAY,** born Salt Lake City, Utah, September 20, 1966; admitted to bar, 1993, California; 1994, U. S. District Court, Central District of California. *Education:* Pepperdine University (B.A., Economics, cum laude, 1990); Loyola Law School, Los Angeles (J.D., 1993). Recipient: American Jurisprudence Award in Trial Advocacy, 1992. Extern, Federal Trade Commission, Los Angeles, California. *Member:* Orange County Bar Association; State Bar of California. *PRACTICE AREAS:* Litigation.

**LEA B. WILLIAMS,** born Phoenix, Arizona, October 14, 1968; admitted to bar, 1993, California; 1994, U.S. District Court, Central District of California and U.S. Court of Appeals, Ninth Circuit. *Education:* Arizona State University (B.A., summa cum laude, 1990); University of Texas at Austin (J.D., with honors, 1993). Phi Beta Kappa. *Member:* Orange County Bar Association; State Bar of California. *LANGUAGES:* Spanish. *PRACTICE AREAS:* Litigation.

---

## GRECO, MOLLIS & O'HARA

A PROFESSIONAL CORPORATION

18400 VON KARMAN, SUITE 500
**IRVINE, CALIFORNIA 92612-1514**
Telephone: 714-263-0600
Fax: 714-263-1513

*Taxation, Federal (State and Local), Real Estate Law, Corporate, Business Law, Bankruptcy, Probate, Wills and Trusts, and Trials and Appeals.*

**THOMAS A. GRECO,** born New York, N.Y., September 11, 1948; admitted to bar, 1977, California and U.S. Tax Court. *Education:* University of California at Los Angeles and California State University at Fullerton (B.A., 1973); Pepperdine University (J.D., 1976); New York University (LL.M., in Taxation, 1977). Phi Alpha Delta. Member, Pepperdine University Law Review, 1975-1976. *Member:* Orange County and American Bar Associations; The State Bar of California. [With U.S. Army, 1968-1970]. *PRACTICE AREAS:* Business and Real Estate Transactions; Partnerships and Corporations; Federal and State Taxation; Civil Litigation; Bankruptcy.

**RONALD A. MOLLIS,** born Martins Ferry, Ohio, May 18, 1955; admitted to bar, 1981, California; 1982, U.S. Tax Court, U.S. District Court, Southern, Central, Eastern and Northern Districts of California, U.S. Court of Appeals, Ninth Circuit and U.S. Claims Court; 1985, U.S. Supreme Court. *Education:* Golden West Junior College (A.A., 1975); California State University at Long Beach (B.S., 1977); Western State University College at Law (J.D., 1980). Delta Theta Phi. Real Estate Broker, California, 1988. California Teaching Credential, 1982—. *Member:* Orange County (Member, Sections on: Taxation; Wills, Trust and Probate), Los Angeles County (Member, Sections on: Taxation; Corporate; Business) and American (Member, Corporations Committee, Taxation Section) Bar Associa-

*(This Listing Continued)*

tions; State Bar of California (Member: Board of Legal Specialization Taxation Law Advisory Committee, 1989-1994; Business Law Section Committee, 1995—); American Society of International Law. (Certified Specialist, Taxation Law, The State Bar of California Board of Legal Specialization). *PRACTICE AREAS:* Tax Law; Business Law; Federal, State and Local Taxation Law; Estate Planning; Business and Real Estate Transaction; Partnerships; Corporation Law.

**KEVIN O'HARA,** born Santa Monica, California, April 6, 1958; admitted to bar, 1983, California. *Education:* University of California at Santa Barbara (B.A., with honors, magna cum laude, 1980); Loyola Marymount University (J.D., 1983); University of San Diego (LL.M., in Tax, 1984). *Member:* Los Angeles County (Member Sections on: Taxation, Corporate, Business), Orange County (Member, Taxation, Wills, Trusts and Probate) and American (Member, Section of Taxation) Bar Associations; State Bar of California. *PRACTICE AREAS:* Tax; Estate Planning; Probate; Corporate; Business; Real Estate.

**CHARLES A. MOLLIS,** born Weirton, West Virginia, February 19, 1959; admitted to bar, 1985, California; 1986, U.S. District Court, Eastern, Northern, Southern and Central Districts of California and U.S. Court of Appeals, Ninth Circuit; 1987, U.S. Claims Court and U.S. Tax Court; 1989, U.S. Supreme Court. *Education:* California State University at Long Beach (B.A., with honors, 1980); Western State University (J.D., 1985). Recipient, American Jurisprudence Award in Corporations. *Member:* State Bar of California; American Bar Association. *REPORTED CASES:* Nanfito vs. Superior Court (1991) 2 C.A. 4th 315; 2 C.R. 2nd 876. *PRACTICE AREAS:* General Civil Trial Practice; Insurance Law; Construction Law; Products Liability Law; Environmental Law.

## GROH, CARROLL, STERN & ROBINSON

*A PROFESSIONAL CORPORATION*
*2600 MICHELSON, SUITE 270*
**IRVINE, CALIFORNIA 92715**
*Telephone: 714-752-7600*
*Fax: 714-752-7661*

*General Business Law, with an emphasis in: Corporate, Tax, Real Estate and Employment Transactions; Business, Real Estate and Personal Tort/Contract Litigation; Business and Personal Tax Planning and Appeals; Conservatorship and Probate Proceedings.*

**MARTIN C. GROH,** born Trenton, New Jersey, December 24, 1950; admitted to bar, 1977, Delaware; 1979, Pennsylvania, U.S. Tax Court and U.S. Claims Court; 1982, California and U.S. District Court, Central District of California. *Education:* Drexel University (B.S.B.A., in Finance and Accounting, 1973); New York University (M.B.A., with distinction, 1974; LL.M., in Taxation, 1980); Villanova University (J.D., 1977). Author: "A Checklist for Preparing Opinion Letters in Standard Corporate Transactions," CEB California Business Law Practitioner, Vol. IV, No. 4, Fall 1989. Tax Instructor, California Society of Certified Public Accountants, 1983-1986. Instructor/Panel Member: "A Special Program on Legal Opinions," State Bar of California Business Law Section, December 1989. *Member:* Orange County (Member, Sections on: Taxation; Business and Corporation Law) and American Bar Associations (Member, Sections on: Business Law; International Law; Taxation); State Bar of California (Member, Sections on: Business Law; International Law; Taxation). *PRACTICE AREAS:* Business; Tax; Corporate Transactional Law; Executive Employment. *Email:* MartyGCSR@aol.com

**DAVID B. CARROLL,** born Rossland, British Columbia, Canada, June 14, 1942; admitted to bar, 1981, California. *Education:* University of British Columbia (A.B., 1964); University of California at Riverside (M.A., 1967); Rice University (Ph.D., 1971); Loyola Law School (J.D., 1980). Phi Kappa Phi. Recipient, John W. Gardner Award, Rice University. *Member:* Orange County and American Bar Associations; State Bar of California. *PRACTICE AREAS:* Business Litigation; Real Estate Litigation; Personal Tort-/Contract Litigation.

**W. ROD STERN,** born Bellflower, California, December 18, 1955; admitted to bar, 1983, California; 1984, U.S. District Court, Central District of California; 1989, U.S. Supreme Court, U.S. Tax Court and U.S. Claims Court; 1995, U.S. District Court, Southern District of California. *Education:* University of California at Los Angeles (A.B., 1977); Hastings College of the Law, University of California (J.D., 1983); New York University (LL.M., in Taxation, 1989). *Member:* Orange County and American (Member, Section on Taxation) Bar Associations; State Bar of California. *PRACTICE AREAS:* Business Law; Tax Law; Conservatorships; Probate.

*(This Listing Continued)*

**GREGORY E. ROBINSON,** born Bremerhaven, Germany, March 25, 1956; admitted to bar, 1983, California; 1984, U.S. District Court, Central District of California. *Education:* Brigham Young University (B.A., cum laude, 1980), Phi Kappa Phi; Hinckley Scholar; University of Utah (J.D., 1983). Staff Member: Utah Law Review, 1982-1983. Speaker, CEB Program, Secured Real Property Transactions, May, 1990 and November, 1992. Author: Note, "Charitable Lobbying Restraints and Tax Exempt Organizations: Old Problems, New Directions?" 1984 Utah Law Review 337. *Member:* Orange County Bar Association (Board Member, Business and Corporate Law Section). *LANGUAGES:* Italian. *PRACTICE AREAS:* Corporate; Real Estate; Real Estate Finance; Commercial Law.

## GREGORY R. GULLSTRAND

*Established in 1980*
*18022 COWAN*
*SUITE 203 D*
**IRVINE, CALIFORNIA 92714**
*Telephone: 714-474-8501*
*Fax: 714-474-9883*

*General Civil Trial Practice in all State and Federal Courts. Construction, and Business Litigation.*

**GREGORY R. GULLSTRAND,** born Los Angeles, California, November 30, 1953; admitted to bar, 1980, California; U.S. District Court, Central and Northern Districts of California. *Education:* University of California, Santa Cruz (B.A., with honors, 1975); University of California School of Law at Davis (J.D., 1980). Law Clerk for Justice Roger G. Connor, Supreme Court of Alaska, 1980. *Member:* Orange County Bar Association; State Bar of California.

REPRESENTATIVE CLIENTS: Allied International; Analysis Group; Concrete Reinforcing Steel Institute; Conergics Corp.; Conveyor Corporation of America; Design Build Associates; Gateway Pacific Construction; Inland Empire Steel; JD Steel Co.; Mayfran International; Mai Steel Services; McMillen Builders; Mid-West Conveyor Corp.; Midwest Mechanical Contractors; MW Builders of Kansas; Orange Coast Electric Supply Co.; PKM Steel Services; Progressive Shoring Systems; SGB Construction; South Coast Builders; Stone Construction Equipment; Tomkins Industries; Westside Electric.

## HANLEY & PATCH

*A Partnership including Professional Corporations*
*19900 MACARTHUR BOULEVARD, SUITE 650*
**IRVINE, CALIFORNIA 92715-2445**
*Telephone: 714-253-0800*
*Fax: 714-253-0870*

*General Civil Litigation Practice in State and Federal Courts. Commercial, Business, Complex and High Technology Litigation, Toxic and Hazardous Substance, Real Estate, Environmental and Employment.*

*FIRM PROFILE: Hanley & Patch believes that "Bigger isn't always Better", However "Performance is Best". The lesson is taught by experience. Larger firms run as some kind of machines, the small firm gives client a lot of control.*

*The firm has achieved a position of uncommon respect and reputation. A recent survey of clients by the "American Lawyers" resulted in citations of excellence for 262 litigations firms. The Hanley & Patch firm was chosen. The firm is listed in the Preeminent Law Directory.*

**WILLIAM B. HANLEY, (P.C.),** born Sharpsville, Pennsylvania, March 14, 1946; admitted to bar, 1974, California; 1977, U.S. Court of Appeals, Ninth Circuit; 1985, U.S. Supreme Court and U.S. District Court, Central, Southern, Eastern and Northern Districts of California. *Education:* Duquesne University (B.A., 1968); Pepperdine University School of Law (J.D., 1974). Member, Pepperdine University Law Review, 1973-1974. Author: "Lis Pendens and Procedural Due Process," Vol. 1, No. 3, Pepperdine Law Review, 1974. *Member:* Orange County and American (Member, Section of Litigation) Bar Associations; The State Bar of California (Member, Committee on Jury Instruction, 1978-1980); Orange County Trial Lawyers Association; California Trial Lawyers Association; The Association of Trial Lawyers of America. [CPT., U.S. Army, 1968-1971]. *REPORTED CASES:* Dawes v. Superior Court, 111 Cal. App. 3d 82; State Farm v. Davis, 937 F. 2d 1415. *PRACTICE AREAS:* Trials.

**RYAN MARK PATCH, (P.C.),** born North Conway, New Hampshire, March 22, 1960; admitted to bar, 1987, California and U.S. District Court, Central, Southern and Northern Districts of California. *Education:* Massachusetts Maritime Academy (B.S., Marine Eng., 1983); Southwestern Uni-

*(This Listing Continued)*

## HANLEY & PATCH, Irvine—Continued

versity School of Law (J.D., 1986). Recipient: American Jurisprudence Award: Torts and Exceptional Achievement Award in Admiralty Law. Third Engineers License, U.S. Coast Guard, 1983. *Member:* Orange County (Member, Environmental Law and Real Estate Section) and American Bar Associations; State Bar of California. [Lt. JG., Naval Officer, 1983-1987]. *PRACTICE AREAS:* Civil Litigation; Real Estate Loan Transactions.

**JOSHUA M. WOLFF**, born Los Angeles, California, October 29, 1959; admitted to bar, 1988, California and U.S. District Court, Central District of California. *Education:* University of California, Berkeley (A.B., with honors, 1982); University o f Freiburg, Germany; George Washington University, National Law Center (J.D., 1987). Member, Journal of International Law & Economics. Member, Moot Court Board. *Member:* Orange County Bar Association; State Bar of California. *LANGUAGES:* German. *REPORTED CASES:* Denney v. Lawrence (1994) 22 Cal. App 4th 927 (libel).

**PAUL KIM**, born Seoul, Korea, November 22, 1966; admitted to bar, 1991, California; 1992, U.S. Supreme Court. *Education:* Rensselaer Polytechnic Institute (B.S.M.E., 1988), Pi Tau Sigma; Georgetown University (J.D., 1991). Pi Tau Sigma. *Member:* State Bar of California; Orange County Bar Association; Orange County Patent Law Association; Orange County Barristers. *PRACTICE AREAS:* Business Law; Intellectual Property; Employment Law.

**JOHANNA Y. HSU**, born Fort Collins, Colorado; admitted to bar, 1993, California and U.S. District Court, Central District of California; 1994, U.S. District Court, Southern District of California; 1996, U.S. Court of Appeals, Ninth Circuit. *Education:* University of California, Irvine (B.A., 1988); Loyola Marymount University (J.D., 1992). *Member:* Orange County Bar Association; State Bar of California. *LANGUAGES:* Taiwanese. *PRACTICE AREAS:* Employment Litigation; Complex Business Litigation.

**DIMITRI P. GROSS**, born Pasadena, California, March 29, 1966; admitted to bar, 1994, California. *Education:* University of California at Los Angeles (B.A. Political Science, 1991); University of the Pacific, McGeorge School of Law (J.D., 1994). *Member:* California State Bar. *PRACTICE AREAS:* Business Litigation.

REPRESENTATIVE CLIENTS: BP Oil Company; BE Aerospace, Inc.; Westco Real Estate Finance Corp.
REFERENCE: National Bank of Southern California, Newport Beach, California.

## RODNEY R. HATTER AND ASSOCIATES

Established in 1985

19800 MACARTHUR BOULEVARD, SUITE 1450
**IRVINE, CALIFORNIA 92715**
Telephone: 714-724-4558
Fax: 714-724-4551

*Franchise, Corporate, Business, Real Estate and Civil Litigation.*

**RODNEY R. HATTER**, born Marysville, Kansas, February 9, 1944; admitted to bar, 1970, New York; 1972, Kansas; 1979, California. *Education:* Harvard University (A.B., cum laude, 1966); Columbia University (J.D., 1969). *Member:* Orange County and American (Member, Forum Committee on Franchising, 1980—; Member, Franchising Subcommittee, Small Business Committee, 1987—) Bar Associations; State Bar of California (Member, Franchise Legislation Committee, 1983—; Franchise Law Committee, 1995—); International Franchise Association (Member, Legal Legislative Committee, 1983—).

### ASSOCIATES

**ERIC J. STOOP**, born Orlando, Florida, October 7, 1966; admitted to bar, 1993, California. *Education:* Westmont College (B.A., 1988); Willamette University (J.D., 1993). *Member:* Orange County Bar Association; State Bar of California.

**PATRICIA L. STOOP**, born Oakland, California, January 20, 1969; admitted to bar, 1994, California. *Education:* Virginia Tech University (B.A., 1991); Willamette University College of Law (J.D., 1994). *Member:* Orange County and American Bar Associations; State Bar of California.

*(This Listing Continued)*

REPRESENTATIVE CLIENTS: KFC Southern California Franchise Associations; La Salsa Franchise Corp.; Oil Can Henry's; One Stop Undercar, Inc.; Pick Up Stix, Inc.; Rodjean Barbeques, Inc.; Sperry Van Ness, Inc.; Star Franchise Assn.; Taco Bell Corp. and FRANMAC; Tire Pros Francorp; Window-Wear, Inc.

## RAY HENDRICKSON

UNIVERSITY TOWER, SUITE 700
4199 CAMPUS DRIVE
**IRVINE, CALIFORNIA 92612**
Telephone: 714-833-0101; 854-8800
Fax: 714-854-4897

*Divorce, Custody, Family and Negligence Law. Personal Injury, Civil and Business Litigation and actions relating to Psychic Trauma.*

**RAY HENDRICKSON**, born Valley City, North Dakota, November 10, 1937; admitted to bar, 1973, California and U.S. District Court, Northern, Southern, Eastern and Central Districts of California; 1978, U.S. Supreme Court; 1979, U.S. Court of Appeals, Ninth Circuit. *Education:* North Dakota State University (B.S. in chemistry, 1962); Western State University (J.D., 1973); Pepperdine University (M.A. in psychology, 1981); United States International University (Ph.D. in psychology, 1991). Phi Kappa Phi; Blue Key. Counsel, Libertarian Party of California, 1978—. Counsel and Member, Board of Directors, Irvine Community Theatre, 1974—. Judge Pro Tem and Arbitrator, Superior Court of California, 1979—. Member, Board of Directors: College Legal Clinic, 1981—; Center for Creative Alternatives, 1987—. Adjunct Professor: Psychology, United States International University, 1993—; University of California, Irvine, California Extension Division. Arbitrator, Fee Arbitration Panel, Orange County Bar Association, 1981—. Member, 1987—and Instructor, 1988—, Civil Air Patrol. Certified Flight Instructor, 1990—. Member, Accrediting Team, Pacific Association of Schools and Colleges. Psychological Assistant, Lake Forest Psychological Clinic, 1992. *Member:* Orange County and American Bar Associations; State Bar of California; Lawyer-Pilots Bar Association. [U.S. Army, 1955-1958]

REFERENCES: Mitsui Manufacturers Bank, Newport Beach, California; Bank of California, Newport Beach, California; Home Fed, Irvine, California.

## HEWITT & McGUIRE

19900 MACARTHUR BOULEVARD, SUITE 1050
**IRVINE, CALIFORNIA 92715**
Telephone: 714-798-0500
FAX: 714-798-0511
Email: HMLAW@INTERNETMCI.COM

*Corporate, Business, Securities Law, Real Estate, Land Use, Natural Resources, Environmental, Public Finance Law, Corporate Finance.*

### MEMBERS OF FIRM

**DEAN DUNN-RANKIN**, born Sarasota, Florida, November 23, 1958; admitted to bar, 1985, Texas; 1988, California. *Education:* University of Hawaii (B.A., with distinction, 1981); University of Southern California (J.D., 1985). Order of the Coif. Member, Southern California Law Review, 1983-1984. *PRACTICE AREAS:* Real Estate Law.

**CHARLES S. EXON**, born New Orleans, Louisiana, June 1, 1949; admitted to bar, 1983, California. *Education:* University of Missouri (B.A., 1971); University of Southern California (M.F.A., 1977; J.D., 1983). Phi Beta Kappa; Order of the Coif. *PRACTICE AREAS:* Corporate Law; Securities Law; Business Law.

**ANDREW K. HARTZELL**, born Carlisle, Pennsylvania, April 16, 1963; admitted to bar, 1990, California. *Education:* University of Pennsylvania (B.A., summa cum laude, 1985); Stanford University (J.D., with distinction, 1988). Phi Beta Kappa. Law Clerk to the Hon. Edith H. Jones, U.S. Court of Appeals, Fifth Circuit, 1988-1989. *PRACTICE AREAS:* Natural Resources Law; Environmental Law; Land Use Law.

**HUGH HEWITT**, born Warren, Ohio, February 22, 1956; admitted to bar, 1983, District of Columbia; 1989, California. *Education:* Harvard College (A.B., cum laude, 1978); University of Michigan (J.D., magna cum laude, 1983). Order of the Coif. Law Clerk to Hon. Roger Robb, U.S. Court of Appeals, District of Columbia Circuit, 1983-1984. Assistant White House Counsel, 1985-1986. General Counsel and Deputy Director, The U.S. Office of Personnel Management, 1986-1989. Member, The Administrative Conference of the United States, 1987-1989. Member, Board of Governors, The South Coast Air Quality Management District, 1995-1996.

*(This Listing Continued)*

**PRACTICE AREAS:** Natural Resources Law; Land Use Law; Environmental Law.

**MARK R. MCGUIRE,** born Glendale, California, September 25, 1964; admitted to bar, 1990, California. *Education:* University of California at Santa Barbara (B.A., with highest honors, 1986); Stanford University (J.D., 1989). Law Clerk to Hon. Herbert Y.C. Choy, U.S. Court of Appeals, Ninth Circuit, 1989-1990. **PRACTICE AREAS:** Real Estate Law; Land Use Law; Environmental Law.

**DENNIS D. O'NEIL,** born Oakland, California, January 27, 1938; admitted to bar, 1966, California. *Education:* University of Southern California (B.A., 1960); Hastings College of the Law, University of California (J.D., 1966). Assistant City Attorney, City of Newport Beach, 1969-1971. City Attorney, City of Newport Beach, 1972-1979. **PRACTICE AREAS:** Real Estate Law; Land Use Law; Health Law.

**JAY F. PALCHIKOFF,** born Culver City, California, August 21, 1955; admitted to bar, 1982, California. *Education:* University of California at Los Angeles (B.A., magna cum laude, 1977); University of California at Los Angeles School of Law (J.D., 1982). **PRACTICE AREAS:** Real Estate Law; Business Law.

**PAUL A. ROWE,** born Muncie, Indiana, February 8, 1958; admitted to bar, 1985, California; 1987, Minnesota. *Education:* University of North Dakota (B.A., 1980); University of Minnesota (J.D., 1985). Order of the Coif. Associate Editor, Minnesota Law Review, 1984-1985. Certified Public Accountant, Minnesota, 1980. **PRACTICE AREAS:** Corporate Law; Securities Law; Real Estate Law; Business Law.

**WILLIAM L. TWOMEY,** born Inglewood, California, February 8, 1955; admitted to bar, 1981, California. *Education:* University of California at Santa Barbara (B.A., with high honors, 1977); University of California at Los Angeles (J.D., 1981). Order of the Coif. **PRACTICE AREAS:** Corporate Law; Securities Law; Business Law.

**JOHN P. YEAGER,** born Peoria, Illinois, September 14, 1958; admitted to bar, 1983, California. *Education:* University of California at Santa Barbara (B.A., 1980); University of California at Los Angeles (J.D., 1983). Phi Beta Kappa. **PRACTICE AREAS:** Real Estate Law; Land Use Law; Public Finance Law.

---

# HINCHY, WITTE, WOOD, ANDERSON & HODGES

*A LAW CORPORATION*

Established in 1965

*2030 MAIN STREET, SUITE 1300*
**IRVINE, CALIFORNIA 92614**
Telephone: 714-260-4710
FAX: 714-260-4711

*Rancho Bernardo, California Office:* 11440 West Bernardo Court, Suite 280. Telephone: 619-487-7948; 586-7696. FAX: 619-487-2177.

*San Diego, California Office:* 525 B Street, Suite 1500. Telephone: 619-239-1901. FAX: 619-696-0555.

*Palm Desert, California Office:* 74-010 El Paseo, Suite 200. Telephone: 619-779-8569. FAX: 619-568-6175.

*General Civil Litigation, General Commercial, including Corporations, Limited Liability Companies, Partnerships and Taxation; Real Estate, Estate Planning and Probate; Financial Institutions, Mortgage Banking, Collection, Bankruptcy, Family Law, Labor Relations and Employment Law and Related Litigation, Agricultural Labor Relations, Employee Stock Ownership Plans (ESOPs), ERISA, Pension and Profit Sharing, Employee Benefits Law and Litigation.*

Wayne A. Hersh        Jon G. Miller (Resident)

REFERENCE: Scripps Bank.

(For complete Biographical Data on all Personnel see Professional Biographies at San Diego, California)

---

# HIRSON WEXLER PERL & STARK

*A PROFESSIONAL CORPORATION*

*JAMBOREE CENTER*
*ONE PARK PLAZA, SUITE 950*
**IRVINE, CALIFORNIA 92614**
Telephone: 714-251-8844
Fax: 714-251-1545
Email: immigration_law@msn.com
URL: http://www.immig.com

*Los Angeles, California Office:* 6310 San Vicente Boulevard, Suite 415, 90048. Telephone: 213-936-0200. Fax: 213-936-4488. E-Mail: 73411.37@compuserve.com. Web-Site: http://www.immig.com.

*San Diego, California Office:* 4275 Executive Square, Suite 800, 92037. Telephone: 619-452-5700. Fax: 619-452-1911. E-Mail: hkps@immiglaw.com. Web-Site: http://www.immig.com.

*Phoenix, Arizona Office:* 3443 North Central Avenue, Suite 706, 85012. Telephone: 602-266-4700. Fax: 602-265-8108. E-Mail: 73344.21@compuserve.com. Web-Site: http://www.immig.com.

*Dallas, Texas Office:* Heritage Square Tower II, 7th Floor, 5001 L.B.J. Freeway, 75244. Telephone: 214-991-7400. Fax: 214-991-1501. E-Mail: hkps@immig-law.com. Web-Site: http://www.immig.com.

*Immigration and International Law Firm.*

**FIRM PROFILE:** *Our attorneys are regular speakers at seminars and Attorney Bar Associations, private organizations and the public.*

*Hirson Wexler Perl & Stark concentrates on permanent and temporary business and investor visas, and work visas for professional, high-tec, executive and managerial personnel.*

*We provide a highly professional service in assisting with all facets of the immigration process. Our specialization and combined years of experience make us one of the most successful Immigration Law Offices in the U.S. We can help you, your company, and your clients work through the extensive red tape surrounding immigration cases. We are committed to excellence in our work product and promise to handle your cases effectively and cost efficiently.*

**DAVID HIRSON,** born Johannesburg, South Africa, May 14, 1947; admitted to bar, 1980, California; 1988, District of Columbia. *Education:* University of Witwatersrand, South Africa (Law, 1967). *Member:* Orange County (Chairman, Immigration Law Section, 1987), Los Angeles County and American Bar Associations; State Bar of California (Vice-Chair, International Section, 1997-1998); American Immigration Lawyers Association (Chapter Chairs, California Chapter, 1989-1990); INS (Immigration Naturalization Service) Liaison Committee, California Service Center, 1990-1992; Vice Chair, Liaison Committee, Immigration Naturalization Service Headquarters, Washington, D.C., 1992-1993, 1995-1997; Co-Chair Committee on Permanent Investor Visas, 1993-1994); American Electronic Association (Member, Orange County Legal and International Committees, 1990). (Certified Specialist, Immigration and Nationality Law, The State Bar of California Board of Legal Specialization) (Also at Los Angeles). **PRACTICE AREAS:** Immigration Law; International Law. **Email:** immigration_law@msn.com

**MITCHELL L. WEXLER,** born Brooklyn, New York, August 17, 1960; admitted to bar, 1985, California; 1986, U.S. District Court, Central District of California. *Education:* Hofstra University (B.A., Business, 1982); Southwestern University School of Law (J.D., 1985). *Member:* Beverly Hills (Member, Immigration Section, 1987) and Los Angeles County (Member, Executive Committee, Immigration Section, 1986) Bar Associations; State Bar of California (Member, Immigration and Nationality Law Advisory Commission, 1996); American Immigration Lawyers Association. (Certified Specialist, Immigration and Nationality Law, The State Bar of California Board of Legal Specialization). **PRACTICE AREAS:** Immigration and Naturalization Law; Nationality Law. **Email:** 73344.61@Compuserve.com

**GARY B. PERL,** born East-London, South Africa, February 17, 1952; admitted to bar, 1979, South Africa; 1986, California and U.S. District Court, Southern, Central, Northern and Eastern Districts of California; 1991, Texas. *Education:* University of The Witwatersrand, Johannesburg, South Africa (B.Com., 1974; LL.B., 1978). *Member:* San Diego County Bar Association (Member, Immigration, International and Business Law Sections; Co-Chair, Program Planning Committee, International Law Section; Member, Advocacy Committee, San Diego World Trade Center Association, 1995); State Bar of California; State Bar of Texas. (Resident, San Diego, California and Dallas, Texas Offices). **LANGUAGES:** Afrikaans. **PRACTICE AREAS:** Immigration Law; International Law.

*(This Listing Continued)*

**HIRSON WEXLER PERL & STARK,** *A PROFESSIONAL CORPORATION, Irvine—Continued*

**JOANNE TRIFILO STARK,** born Buffalo, New York, July 12, 1949; admitted to bar, 1982, Arizona and U.S. District Court, District of Arizona; 1986, U.S. Court of Appeals, Ninth Circuit. *Education:* University of Madrid, Madrid, Spain; Cornell University (A.B., 1971); Arizona State University (M.A., 1975; J.D., 1982). Cornell National Scholar. *Member:* Maricopa County and American Bar Associations; State Bar of Arizona (Member, Immigration Naturalization Service, California Service Center, Liaison Committee Co-Chair, 1991-1992; International Law Section, 1996); American Immigration Lawyers Association; Arizona Women Lawyers Association; Chair and Vice Chair: American Immigration Lawyers Association, Arizona Chapter 1987-1990; Arizona State Bar Immigration Section, 1988-1989). (Resident, Phoenix, Arizona Office). *LANGUAGES:* Spanish. *PRACTICE AREAS:* Immigration and Naturalization.

OF COUNSEL

**LANCE KAPLAN**

---

## HORWITZ & BEAM

TWO VENTURE PLAZA, SUITE 380
**IRVINE, CALIFORNIA 92618**
Telephone: 714-453-0300; 310-842-8574
Fax: 714-453-9416
Email: HOROWITZBEAM@EARTHLINK.NET

*General Business Practice. Corporate, Securities Offerings, Partnerships, Business Acquisitions and Dispositions. General Civil Litigation Practice in State and Federal Courts, Real Estate, Mobilehome Park, Administrative and Bankruptcy Law.*

FIRM PROFILE: *The Horwitz & Bean firm is an aggressive law firm who get the job done. The firm provides professional service and believes that the client comes first. The firm speaks several languages, German, French, Polish and Russian.*

MEMBERS OF FIRM

**LAWRENCE W. HORWITZ,** born San Bernardino, California, September 9, 1959; admitted to bar, 1984, Texas and California; 1987, U.S. District Court, Central District of California and U.S. Court of Appeals, Ninth Circuit. *Education:* University of California at Berkeley (B.S., 1981); Boalt Hall School of Law, University of California, Berkeley (J.D., 1984). Phi Beta Kappa; Phi Delta Phi (President, 1983). Associate Editor, International Tax and Business Lawyer, 1983. *Member:* Orange County and Los Angeles County Bar Associations. *PRACTICE AREAS:* General Business; Civil Litigation.

**GREGORY B. BEAM,** born Los Angeles, California, December 12, 1948; admitted to bar, 1982, California; 1984, U.S. District Court, Central District of California; 1985, U.S. District Court, Northern, Southern and Eastern Districts of California and U.S. Court of Appeals, Ninth Circuit; 1986; U.S. Supreme Court. *Education:* San Diego State University (B.A., 1972); University of San Diego (J.D., 1981). Phi Delta Phi. *Member:* Orange County and American (Member, Section on: Business Litigation) Bar Associations; State Bar of California. *PRACTICE AREAS:* Civil Litigation; Banking Law; Real Estate.

ASSOCIATES

**LAWRENCE R. BUJOLD,** born Wurzburg, West Germany, December 16, 1956; admitted to bar, 1985, California and U.S. District Court, Southern District of California; 1988, U.S. District Court, Central District of California. *Education:* University of California at San Diego (B.A., 1978); University of San Diego (J.D., 1983). *Member:* Orange County Bar Association; State Bar of California. *REPORTED CASES:* Rubin v. Green (1993) 4 Cal. 4th 1187. *PRACTICE AREAS:* Litigation; Real Estate; Banking; Intellectual Property.

**LAWRENCE M. CRON,** born Montebello, California, April 25, 1963; admitted to bar, 1989, California and U.S. District Court, Southern District of California; 1992, U.S. District Court, Central District of California; U.S. District Court, Northern District of California. *Education:* University of California, Los Angeles (B.A., 1986); University of Pacific, McGeorge School of Law (J.D., with distinction, 1989). Recipient, Verne Adriane and Annable McGeorge Academic Achievement Scholarship. *Member:* Orange County and American (Member, Business Section) Bar Associations. *PRACTICE AREAS:* Business Litigation; Commercial Litigation; Bankruptcy; Creditors Rights.

*(This Listing Continued)*

---

**LYNNE BOLDUC,** born Medford, Massachusetts, May 17, 1966; admitted to bar, 1995, California and U.S. District Court, Central District of California. *Education:* Newbury College, Western State University College of Law (J.D., salutation, summa cum laude, 1994). Author: *My Two Moms: The Dimensions of Surrogate Motherhood as Determined by the California Supreme Court in Johnson v. Calvert,* Western State University Law Review, 1993; *Time for a Change: Problems with the American Jury System,* Women Lawyers Journal, 1995; *A Case Without A Client: The Private Securities Litigation Reform Act of 1995,* The Federal Lawyer, 1996. *Member:* Beverly Hills and Federal (Member: Corporate and Association Counsels Division and Financial Institutions & The Economy Section) Bar Associations; State Bar of California (Member, Business Section). *PRACTICE AREAS:* Securities Law and Business Transactions.

**PHILIP N. FRIEDMAN,** born Philadelphia, Pennsylvania, June 18 1956; admitted to bar, 1983, California; 1984, U.S. District Court, Northern District of California and U.S. Court of Appeals, Ninth Circuit; 1989, U.S. District Court, Central District of California; 1990, District of Columbia. *Education:* University of Georgia; University of California at Irvine (B.A., in History, 1980); Hastings College of Law, University of California (J.D., 1983); University of California at Berkeley (M.A., 1985). *Member:* State Bar of California. *PRACTICE AREAS:* Civil Litigation; Real Estate and Broker Law; Business Transactions.

**THOMAS B. GRIFFEN,** born Newport Beach, California, August 14, 1963; admitted to bar, 1988, California. *Education:* University of Southern California (B.A., summa cum laude, 1985; J.D., 1988). Phi Beta Kappa; Phi Kappa Phi; Golden Key; Order of the Coif. Recipient, American Jurisprudence Awards: Contracts; Property; Criminal Procedure; Criminal Law. Member, Senior Staff, Southern California Law Review, 1986-1988. Author: Note, "Zoning Away the Evils of Alcohol," 61 Southern California Law Review 1373, 1988. *Member:* State Bar of California.

REPRESENTATIVE CLIENTS: Sanwa Bank; Cruttenden & Company; Dun & Bradstreet Software Systems; Brookstreet Securities; UnionBank of California; Citizens Mortgage; VR Business Brokers; Generation Capital Associates; I/O Magic, Inc.; CD Interactive, Inc.; Tobishima Development; Valor Computer Systems; Robert F. Kennedy Medical Center; Computer Products Center; Beta Capital Group; Advanced Micro Systems; Saddlbock R.V.; Westport Capital; The Star Companies; InnovaCom, Inc.; Novamed, Inc.

---

## HYMAN, PHELPS & McNAMARA

Established in 1989

2603 MAIN STREET
**IRVINE, CALIFORNIA 92614**
Telephone: 714-553-7400
Telecopier: 714-553-7433

*Washington, D.C. Office:* 700 Thirteenth Street, N.W., Suite 1200, 20005. Telephone: 202-737-5600. Telecopier: 202-737-9329.

*Practice before all Courts, Government Agencies and International Regulatory Authorities involving Foods, Drugs, Cosmetics, Medical Devices, Pesticides, Controlled Substances and Consumer Products.*

(For Complete Biographical Data on all Personnel, see Professional Biographies at Washington, D.C.)

---

## WARREN S. INOUYE

2212 DUPONT DRIVE, SUITE B
**IRVINE, CALIFORNIA 92715**
Telephone: 714-757-0757
Fax: 714-757-0759

*Real Estate Development, Contracts and Business Law.*

**WARREN S. INOUYE,** born Richfield, Utah, March 27, 1951; admitted to bar, 1979, California; 1980, Utah. *Education:* Brigham Young University (B.S., magna cum laude, 1976; J.D., 1979). J. Rueben Clark Society of International Law (President, 1978-1979). *Member:* Orange County (Member, Business and Corporate Law Section) and American (Member, Corporation, Banking and Business Law Section) Bar Associations; Japanese-American Bar Association of Greater Los Angeles. *LANGUAGES:* Japanese. *PRACTICE AREAS:* Real Estate Development; Contracts; Business Law.

## IVANJACK & LAMBIRTH

A Partnership including Professional Corporations

*Established in 1972*

5 PARK PLAZA, SUITE 800
**IRVINE, CALIFORNIA 92614**
Telephone: 714-475-4477
Telecopier: 714-475-4475
Email: ivanjack@AOL.com

Los Angeles, California Office: 12301 Wilshire Boulevard, Suite 600. 90025-1000. Telephone: 310-820-7211. Telecopier: 310-820-0687.

*General Civil Trial and Appellate Practice in all State and Federal Courts, Commercial, Banking and Financial Institutions, Real Estate, Secured Transactions, Equipment Leasing, Creditors' Rights and Bankruptcy, Transactional Documentation, Operational and Regulatory Compliance Advice, Business and Construction.*

*FIRM PROFILE: The firm specializes in representing financial institutions, finance lessors and other corporate clients in every major area of commercial law. The firm offers extensive experience in litigating commercial disputes as well as in structuring and negotiating banking, business and real estate workouts. Although the firm has been historically identified with lending institutions, its clients are engaged in many types of commercial businesses and ventures.*

REPRESENTATIVE CLIENTS: Bank of America; Citibank N.A.; Union Bank of California, N.A.; Sanwa Bank California; Great Western Bank; Imperial Bank; First Republic Thrift and Loan; General Electric Capital Corp.; Fleet Credit Corp.; Western Bank; Siemens Credit Corp.; International Bank of California; Center Capital Corp.; Linotype-Hell Co.; Mercedes-Benz Credit Corp.; American Honda Finance Corp.; Don Kott Auto Center; Aggreko, Inc.; AAF-McQuay, Inc.; Chase Manhattan Bank; Citizens Business Bank; Downey National Bank; National Bank of Southern California; The Money Store; One Central Bank; Sunwest Bank; Lee Servicing Co.; Wendover Funding; National Enterprises, Inc.; First Bank and Trust; El Dorado Bank.

(For biographical data on all personnel, see Professional Biographies at Los Angeles, California)

---

## IVES, KIRWAN & DIBBLE

A PROFESSIONAL CORPORATION

*Established in 1939*

101 PACIFICA, SUITE 250
**IRVINE, CALIFORNIA 92718**
Telephone: 714-450-8900
FAX: 714-450-8908

Los Angeles, California Office: The Biltmore Court, Fourth Floor, 520 South Grand Avenue. Telephone: 213-627-0113. FAX: 213-627-1545.

Ventura-Santa Barbara Office: 5210 Carpinteria Avenue, P.O. Box 360, Carpinteria, California. Telephone: 805-684-7641. FAX: 805-684-9649.

San Bernardino-Riverside Office: 777 Tahquitz Way, Suite 23, Palm Springs, California. Telephone: 619-788-2611. FAX: 619-778-2612.

*FIRM PROFILE: Ives, Kirwan & Dibble specializes in general civil litigation in both State and Federal Courts. For many years we have practiced in the traditional area of general liability defense, including but not limited to products liability, premises liability, professional liability, auto liability, truckers liability, cargo loss and damage, fire loss and damage, construction defect litigation, general negligence, international torts, insurance coverage (primary, excess, and reinsurance), and workers' compensation. In more recent years, our practice has grown in several developing areas such as business torts, directors and officers errors and omissions, trademark and copyright infringement, business transactional work and litigation, wrongful termination, legal malpractice, child abuse, insurance bad faith, toxic torts, environmental pollution litigation, Americans with Disabilities Act claims, and municipal liability and Federal civil rights litigation.*

**ROGER ERIK MARKEN,** born Seattle, Washington, December 27, 1944; admitted to bar, 1972, California, U.S. District Court, Central District of California, U.S. District Court, Northern District of California and U.S. Court of Appeals, Ninth Circuit. *Education:* University of Washington (B.S., 1967); Southwestern University (J.D., 1972). *Member:* State Bar of California; American Bar Association; Association of Interstate Commerce Commission Practitioners.

**STEVEN S. MARKEN,** born Torrance, California, May 6, 1965; admitted to bar, 1991, California and U.S. District Court, Central District of California. *Education:* Arizona State University (B.S., 1987); Southwestern

*(This Listing Continued)*

---

University of Law at Los Angeles (J.D., 1991). *Member:* Orange County and American Bar Associations; State Bar of California.

MAJOR INSURANCE COMPANY CLIENTS: Acceptance Insurance Companies; Allianz Insurance Company; Allianz Underwriters Insurance Company; American International Group, Inc.; American Mutual Insurance Company; American States Insurance Company; Amica Mutual Insurance Company; The Canadian Insurance Company of California; Citation Insurance Group; The Chubb Group of Insurance Companies; California Insurance Guaranty Association; First State Insurance Company; Government Employees Insurance Company; Harbor Insurance Company; The Hartford Specialty Company; Home & Automobile Insurance Company; Houston General Insurance Company; Industrial Fire & Casualty; Industrial Indemnity Company; Industrial Underwriters, Inc.; Jefferson Insurance Group; Monticello Insurance Co.; National Indemnity Company; National Union Fire Insurance Company; Planet Insurance Company; Preferred Risk Mutual Insurance Company; Prudential-LMI Mutual Insurance Company; Reliance Insurance Company; Safeco Insurance Company; Stonewall Insurance Company; Tokio Marine & Fire Insurance Company; Transport Insurance Company; Union Bankers Insurance Company; Utica Mutual Insurance Company; Westchester Specialty Group.

(For Complete Biographical Data on all Personnel, see Los Angeles, California Professional Biographies).

---

## JACKSON, DeMARCO & PECKENPAUGH

A LAW CORPORATION

4 PARK PLAZA, 16TH FLOOR
P.O. BOX 19704
**IRVINE, CALIFORNIA 92714**
Telephone: 714-752-8585
Fax: 714-752-0597

*Business and Real Estate Transactions, Financing and Construction, Taxation, Estate Planning, Corporate, Subdivision Law, Condominiums and Planned Developments, General Litigation, Land Use, Employment, Partnership, and Construction Defect Litigation and Appellate Practice.*

**LANCE A. ADAIR,** born Orange, California, 1959; admitted to bar, 1985, California; 1986, U.S. District Court, Central District of California and U.S. Court of Appeals, Ninth Circuit. *Education:* University of California, Riverside (B.S., 1982); Hastings College of the Law, University of California (J.D., 1985). Symposium Editor and Editorial Board Member, Hastings Constitutional Law Quarterly, 1984-1985. **PRACTICE AREAS:** Litigation. *Email:* laa194@jdplaw.com

**MARC D. ALEXANDER,** born Los Angeles, California, 1951; admitted to bar, 1981, California. *Education:* University of California at Santa Cruz (B.A., 1972); John Hopkins University (M.A., 1974; Ph.D., 1976); University of California at Los Angeles (J.D., 1981). Phi Beta Kappa. Articles Editor, UCLA Law Review, 1980-1981. Law Clerk to the Hon. Warren J. Ferguson, U.S. Court of Appeals, 9th Circuit, 1981-1982. **LANGUAGES:** French. **PRACTICE AREAS:** Litigation. *Email:* mda002@jdplaw.com

**THOMAS D. ARNOLD,** born Bellflower, California, 1958; admitted to bar, 1992, California; U.S. District Court, Central District of California. *Education:* University of California, Los Angeles (B.S., 1981); University of Southern California (M.B.A., 1984); Loyola Marymount University (J.D., 1991). Member, St. Thomas More Law Honor Society. **PRACTICE AREAS:** Litigation. *Email:* tda237@jdplaw.com

**DIANE P. CAREY,** born Pittsburgh, Pennsylvania, 1957; admitted to bar, 1983, California. *Education:* University of Notre Dame (B.A., 1979); Washington & Lee University (J.D., 1983). Lead Articles Editor, Washington and Lee Law Review, 1982-1983. **PRACTICE AREAS:** Real Estate. *Email:* dpc156@jdplaw.com

**BRIAN W. CASSERLY,** born Orange, California, 1949; admitted to bar, 1976, California and U.S. District Court, Central District of California. *Education:* University of California at Los Angeles (B.A., 1971); Hastings College of Law, University of California (J.D., 1976). *Member:* Los Angeles and Orange County Bar Associations; State Bar of California. **PRACTICE AREAS:** Real Estate Law; Real Estate Finance Law; Corporate Law. *Email:* bwc257@jdplaw.com

**JOHN W. COCHRANE,** born Cleveland, Ohio, 1955; admitted to bar, 1981, California, U.S. District Court, Northern, Eastern, Central and Southern Districts of California, U.S. Supreme Court and U.S. Court of Appeals, Ninth Circuit. *Education:* University of California, Davis (A.B., 1977); University of California, Los Angeles (J.D., 1980). Law Clerk to Judge Schwartz, U.S. District Court, Eastern District of California, 1980-1981. **PRACTICE AREAS:** Business Litigation. *Email:* jwc246@jdplaw.com

*(This Listing Continued)*

## JACKSON, DeMARCO & PECKENPAUGH, A LAW CORPORATION, Irvine—Continued

**JOHN C. CONDAS,** born Salt Lake City, Utah, 1961; admitted to bar, 1989, California. *Education:* University of Chicago (A.B., 1983); University of California at Los Angeles (M.A., Urban Planning, 1985); University of Southern California (J.D., 1988); University of California (Advanced to Candidacy, Ph.D. Program, Urban and Regional Planning, 1988). Extern Law Clerk to the Honorable Alex Kozinski, U.S. Court of Appeals, Ninth Circuit, 1988. Staff Lecturer, University of Southern California Graduate School of Business Administration. Instructor, Real Estate Development and Finance, U.S.C. Graduate School of Business Administration Minority and CCEDA Programs. Co-author: "The California Two-Step: Evasion of the Takings Clause by the California Courts," Western State University Law Journal, Vol. 3, No. 1, 1994. Author: "County Congestion Management Program: Developers' Indigestion," San Jose Business Journal, October 1992; "Ehrlich: One Step Forward and Two Steps Sideways," Orange County Lawyer, June 1996. *PRACTICE AREAS:* Land Use and Environmental Law and Litigation; Real Estate and Financial Institutions Litigation. *Email:* jcc258@jdplaw.com

**JAMES R. DeMARCO,** born North Adams, Massachusetts, 1940; admitted to bar, 1966, District of Columbia; 1970, California. *Education:* Boston College (B.S., 1962); Georgetown University (LL.B., 1965). *PRACTICE AREAS:* Litigation. *Email:* jrd023@jdplaw.com

**STEVEN J. DZIDA,** born Fresno, California, 1950; admitted to bar, 1974, California. *Education:* Loyola University of Los Angeles (B.A., 1971; J.D., 1974); University of Utah (M.B.A., 1979). [Capt., U.S. Air Force, 1975-1979]. *PRACTICE AREAS:* Real Estate. *Email:* sjd024@jdplaw.com

**ROGER M. FRANKS,** born Johannesburg, South Africa, 1968; admitted to bar, 1993, California. *Education:* University of California at Berkeley (B.S., 1990); Loyola Marymount University (J.D., 1993). Staff Member, 1991-1992 and Note and Comment Editor, 1992-1993, Entertainment Law Journal. *Member:* State Bar of California. *PRACTICE AREAS:* Real Estate and Commercial Litigation; Land Use. *Email:* rmf261@jdplaw.com

**HELENE Z. FRANSZ,** born Los Angeles, California, 1960; admitted to bar, 1985, California. *Education:* Boston College (B.A., summa cum laude, 1982); Georgetown University (J.D., cum laude, 1985). Phi Beta Kappa. Articles and Notes Editor, American Criminal Law Review, 1984-1985. Author: "Administrative Summons," White Collar Crime Survey, American Criminal Law Review, 1984. *PRACTICE AREAS:* General Business and Real Estate. *Email:* hmz113@jdplaw.com

**EDWARD A. GALLOWAY,** born Abilene, Texas, 1956; admitted to bar, 1982, Texas; 1987, California. *Education:* University of Texas (B.A., 1978); Southern Methodist University (J.D., 1982). *LANGUAGES:* Russian and German. *PRACTICE AREAS:* Litigation. *Email:* eag115@jdplaw.com

**ROGER A. GRAD,** born Brooklyn, New York, 1958; admitted to bar, 1985, California; 1986, U.S. District Court, Central District of California and U.S. Court of Appeals, Ninth Circuit. *Education:* University of California at Los Angeles (B.A., 1980); McGeorge School of the Law, University of the Pacific (J.D. in Taxation, 1984); University of San Diego (LL.M., 1985). *Member,* Moot Court Honors Board; International Moot Court Honors Board. Member, board of Directors, Advocacy Arts Foundation, 1995—. *PRACTICE AREAS:* Tax Planning and Litigation; Estate Planning; Corporate and Partnerships; Business Transactional. *Email:* rag268@jdplaw.com

**WILLIAM MICHAEL HENSLEY,** born Fresno, California, 1954; admitted to bar, 1979, California; U.S. District Court, Central, Eastern, Northern and Southern Districts of California; U.S. Court of Appeals, Ninth Circuit. *Education:* University of Southern California (B.A., summa cum laude, 1976); Rutgers University (J.D., with honors, 1979). *PRACTICE AREAS:* Real Property; Commercial Banks; Commercial Bankruptcy; Construction Defect; Liens; Securities Litigation. *Email:* wmh260@jdplaw.com

**DARREN L. HEREFORD,** born Taipei, Taiwan, 1967; admitted to bar, 1993, California. *Education:* University of Pittsburgh (B.A., in Economics and Business, 1989); Loyola University of Los Angeles (J.D., 1993). Managing Editor, Loyola International and Comparative Law Journal, 1992-1993. *Member:* Los Angeles County and American Bar Associations; State Bar of California; Southern California Chinese Lawyers Association. *PRACTICE AREAS:* Real Estate Development and Subdivisions Law; Nonprofit Corporate Law; Contract. *Email:* dlh266@jdplaw.com

**JOAN M. HUCKABONE,** born Riverside, California, 1969; admitted to bar, 1994, California. *Education:* University of California at Riverside (B.A., summa cum laude, 1991); Hastings College of Law, University of California (J.D., 1994). *PRACTICE AREAS:* Business Litigation. *Email:* jmh271@jdplaw.com

**F. SCOTT JACKSON,** born Chicago, Illinois, 1945; admitted to bar, 1972, California. *Education:* United States Air Force Academy (B.S., 1967); University of Denver (J.D., cum laude, 1971). Managing Editor, Denver Law Journal, 1970-1971. President, Community Associations Institute, 1982-1983. Author: "Commercial and Mixed Use Condominiums and PUD's," Practicing Law Institute, Spring, 1982; Co-author: "Business Condominiums," National Association of Home Builders, 1985; "Condominiums and Cooperatives," 2nd Ed., John Wiley & Sons, 1984; "California Condominiums and Planned Development Practice," California Continuing Education of the Bar, 1984. *Member:* American College of Real Estate Lawyers; College of Community Association Lawyers. *PRACTICE AREAS:* Real Estate. *Email:* fsj037@jdplaw.com

**ANDREW V. LEITCH,** born Las Vegas, Nevada, 1964; admitted to bar, 1989, California. *Education:* Pomona College (B.A., 1986); Pepperdine University (J.D., cum laude, 1989). Member, Pepperdine University Law Review, 1988-1989. *PRACTICE AREAS:* Real Estate; Corporate; Business Transactions. *Email:* avl1274@jdplaw.com

**THOMAS D. PECKENPAUGH,** born Chicago, Illinois, 1939; admitted to bar, 1966, California. *Education:* California State University, Long Beach (B.A., 1961); University of California at Los Angeles (J.D., 1965). *PRACTICE AREAS:* Business and Real Estate. *Email:* tdp071@jdplaw.com

**JOHN PETRASICH,** born Long Beach, California, 1945; admitted to bar, 1971, California. *Education:* University of Southern California (B.A., cum laude, 1967) ; University of Southern California (J.D., 1970). Order of the Coif. Associate Editor, University of Southern California Law Review, 1969-1970. *PRACTICE AREAS:* Litigation. *Email:* jp072@jdplaw.com

**ANDREW C. SCHUTZ,** born Los Angeles, California, 1943; admitted to bar, 1970, California. *Education:* University of California at Los Angeles (B.A., 1966; J.D., 1969). *PRACTICE AREAS:* Business; Real Estate. *Email:* acs243@jdplaw.com

**DAVID C. SMITH,** born Long Beach, California, 1966; admitted to bar, 1995, California. *Education:* University of California at Los Angeles (B.A., 1988); Pepperdine University School of Law (J.D., magna cum laude, 1995). Associate Editor, Pepperdine Law Review, 1993-1995. *PRACTICE AREAS:* Litigation. *Email:* dcs278@jdplaw.com

**DOUGLAS P. SMITH,** born Los Angeles, California, March 5, 1956; admitted to bar, 1981, California and U.S. District Court, Southern and Central Districts of California. *Education:* University of Southern California (B.A., 1978); Loyola Law School, Los Angeles (J.D., cum laude, 1981). Member: Loyola Law Review, 1980-1981; St. Thomas More Law Honor Society. *PRACTICE AREAS:* Commercial; Business; Probate; Environmental Litigation. *Email:* dps272@jdplaw.com

**JAY R. STEINMAN,** born Los Angeles, California, 1950; admitted to bar, 1977, California. *Education:* California Polytechnic University (B.A., 1973); University of Southern California (J.D., 1977). *PRACTICE AREAS:* Real Estate Acquisition; Development and Financing. *Email:* jrs095@jdplaw.com

**MICHAEL L. TIDUS,** born Los Angeles, California, 1961; admitted to bar, 1986, California, U.S. District Court, Central District of California and U.S. Court of Appeals, Ninth Circuit; 1987, U.S. District Court, Northern, Southern and Eastern Districts of California. *Education:* University of California at San Diego (B.A. in Economics, 1982); University of Southern California (M.B.A., 1986; J.D., 1986). Phi Delta Phi. Lecturer, School of Business Administration, University of Southern California, 1984-1986. Extern, Hon. Stephen Reinhardt, U.S. Court of Appeals, Ninth Circuit, Summer, 1984. Intern: U.S. Attorneys Office, Civil Division, Summer, 1984; Securities and Exchange Commission, Enforcement Staff, Spring, 1986. Author: "Developers Get Bad News on Impact Fees," National Law Journal, January, 1993. Lecturer: "Billboards and Commercial Signs: Design, Development and Legal Challenges to Regulation," Harvard University Schools of Law, Government, Business and Design, Real Estate and Urban Development Forum, Distinguished Speaker Series, 1992. *Member:* Los Angeles County and American Bar Associations; State Bar of California. *PRAC-*

*(This Listing Continued)*

TICE AREAS: Land Use Litigation; Eminent Domain. *Email:* mlt259@jdplaw.com

### LEGAL SUPPORT PERSONNEL

**LAVON DEGRAW** (Office Administrator).

## JACKSON & WILSON

VENTURA PLAZA
2 VENTURA, SUITE 280
**IRVINE, CALIFORNIA 92618**
Telephone: 714-450-1103
Fax: 714-450-1105
URL: http://www.jacksonwilson.com

San Jose, California Office: 1228 Lincoln Avenue, Suite 102, 95125.

Civil Settlement, Mediation, Trial and Appellate service at the State and Federal Court level. Wrongful Death, Serious Personal Injury, Business Litigation, Products Liability, Professional Malpractice, Maritime, Aviation, Negligence, Professional Practice Disputes and Resolutions, Commercial Collections, and Insurance Matters involving Bad Faith. Litigation, including Bench and Jury Trials, Appeals, Writs, Arbitrations, Depositions, Law and Motion and Petitions for Injunctive Relief.

FIRM PROFILE: A respected trial firm with an outstanding reputation in both the Northern and Southern California Communities, Jackson & Wilson has provided sophisticated legal services to individual and corporate clients with personalized care and concern. Large-firm senior attorney experience without large-firm overhead has resulted in consistent client satisfaction, at a reasonable cost, without compromising excellence or timeliness. Although a litigation firm, Jackson & Wilson practices preventive law by constantly seeking to anticipate and avoid legal problems. The firm also has a major commitment to pro-bono representation and community service. Its members are deeply committed to serving their clients and the profession.

**JON MITCHELL JACKSON,** born Tucson, Arizona, August 27, 1957; admitted to bar, 1986, California, U.S. Court of Appeals, Ninth Circuit and U.S. District Court, Central District of California. *Education:* University of Arizona (B.S., 1980); Western State University (J.D., 1985). Past President of Monarch Beach Rotary. *Member:* Orange County and American Bar Associations; State Bar of California (Member, Business and Tort Sections); Orange County Trial Lawyers Association; American Trial Lawyers Association; California Trial Lawyers Association (Consumer Attorney Association); The Association of Trial Lawyers of America. **PRACTICE AREAS:** Tort Law; Business Law. *Email:* firm@jacksonwilson.com

**LISA M. WILSON,** born Upland, California, January 13, 1960; admitted to bar, 1986, California and U.S. District Court, Central District of California. *Education:* University of Southern California (B.A., 1982); Cambridge University, England; Western State University (J.D., 1986). *Member:* Orange County and American Bar Associations; State Bar of California (Member, Business and Tort Sections); California Trial Lawyers Association (Consumer Attorney Association); Orange County Women Lawyers; Orange County Trial Lawyers Association; The Association of Trial Lawyers of America. **PRACTICE AREAS:** Tort Law; Business Law. *Email:* firm@jacksonwilson.com

## JASPER & JASPER

A PROFESSIONAL CORPORATION
Established in 1985
19900 MACARTHUR BOULEVARD, SUITE 1120
**IRVINE, CALIFORNIA 92612**
Telephone: 714-756-1560
Fax: 714-756-2251

General Civil Trial Practice in all State and Federal Courts. Business, Franchise and Employment Litigation, Restaurant Industry Litigation.

**STUART P. JASPER,** born Brooklyn, New York, December 23, 1947; admitted to bar, 1973, Florida and District of Columbia; 1980, California, U.S. District Court, Central, Southern, Northern and Eastern Districts of California and U.S. Court of Appeals, Ninth Circuit. *Education:* University of Miami (B.A., 1969; J.D., 1973). Master, Peter M. Elliott Inn of Court. Lecturer, "Trial Preparation," The Rutter Group, 1991. "Depositions," Continuing Education of the Bar, 1992. Trial Attorney, U.S. Department of Justice, Washington, D.C., 1973-1975 and Los Angeles, 1976-1978. Special Assistant U.S. Attorney, Phoenix, Arizona, 1978. Editor, Orange County

*(This Listing Continued)*

Bar Association Bulletin, 1988. *Member:* Orange County Bar Association (Member, Board of Directors, 1987-1995; Chairman, Judiciary Committee, 1992-1993; Chairman, Business Litigation Section, 1986).

**CATHERINE R. JASPER,** born Moorhead, Minnesota, July 27, 1951; admitted to bar, 1981, California and U.S. District Court, Central and Southern Districts of California. *Education:* University of California at Irvine (B.A., 1973); Western State University at Fullerton (J.D., 1980). Member, Western State University Law Review, 1979-1980.

REPRESENTATIVE CLIENTS: PepsiCo., Inc.; Taco Bell Corp.; Pizza Hut, Inc.; Frito Lay, Inc.; Family Restaurants, Inc.; El Torito Restaurants, Inc.; Coco's Restaurants, Inc.; Carrows Restaurants, Inc.; Sir Speedy, Inc.; Fountain Valley Body Works, Inc.; Armored Transport, Inc.; Baskin-Robbins USA, Co.; Paisa, Inc. (Purrfect Auto Service); Omega Optical Co.; Flag Star Corporation.

## JEFFERS, WILSON & SHAFF, LLP

TOWER 17
18881 VON KARMAN AVENUE
SUITE 1400
**IRVINE, CALIFORNIA 92715**
Telephone: 714-660-7700
Facsimile: 714-660-7799

Corporate Law, Securities, Mergers and Acquisitions, and Taxation.

FIRM PROFILE: We formed our new firm in April 1994 with the goal of serving the corporate, securities and tax law needs of emerging companies on a cost-effective basis. All of our lawyers have legal backgrounds with larger Los Angeles, Orange County, San Francisco and New York based law firms, and have extensive experience in corporate and securities law, corporate and partnership finance, federal and state taxation, mergers and acquisitions, venture capital, investment company formation and regulation, real estate investment trusts and business litigation. Accordingly, the firm offers growing companies the opportunity to reduce their legal costs without any sacrifice in quality, responsiveness or expertise.

### MEMBERS OF FIRM

**MICHAEL B. JEFFERS,** born Wenatchee, Washington, July 10, 1940; admitted to bar, 1964, Washington; 1970, New York; 1988, California. *Education:* University of Washington (B.A., 1962; LL.B., 1964); New York University (LL.M., Taxation, 1970). Phi Delta Phi. *Member:* The Association of the Bar of the City of New York; State Bar of California; Washington State and American Bar Associations; Judge Advocates Association. [Captain, USAF, JAGC, 1965-1968]. **PRACTICE AREAS:** Corporate and Securities Law.

**CHRISTOPHER A. WILSON,** born New Kensington, Pennsylvania, October 14, 1959; admitted to bar, 1987, California; 1988, U.S. District Court, Central District of California. *Education:* Brigham Young University (B.A., 1985; J.D., magna cum laude, 1987). Phi Alpha Delta (Marshall, 1986-1987). Order of the Coif. Member, 1985-1986; Executive Editor, 1986-1987, Brigham Young University Law Review. *Member:* State Bar of California. **LANGUAGES:** French. **PRACTICE AREAS:** Corporate and Securities Law; Mergers and Acquisitions.

**MICHAEL E. SHAFF,** born Boston, Massachusetts, July 31, 1954; admitted to bar, 1979, Massachusetts; 1980, New York and U.S. Tax Court; 1981, U.S. District Court, Eastern and Southern Districts of New York; 1991, California and U.S. District Court, Southern District of California; 1992, U.S. District Court, Central District of California. *Education:* Columbia University (B.A., 1976); New York University (J.D., 1979; LL.M., in Taxation, 1987). Staff Member, Review of Law and Social Change, 1978-1979. Co-Author: "Real Estate Investment Trusts Handbook," Clark Boardman Callaghan, 1988-1995. *Member:* Orange County (Member, Tax Section, Secretary, 1996), New York State, and American (Member: Taxation Section; Real Estate Taxation Committee; Financial Transactions Committee) Bar Associations; State Bar of California. (Certified Specialist, Taxation Law, The State Bar of California Board of Legal Specialization). **PRACTICE AREAS:** Taxation.

**BARRY D. FALK,** born Perth Amboy, New Jersey, June 6, 1962; admitted to bar, 1988, California. *Education:* Kean College (B.S., in Accounting, 1985); Loyola Law School (J.D., 1988). Omicron Delta Epsilon. Member, U.S. Securities and Exchange Commission, Division of Enforcement, 1988-1990; Division of Corporation Finance, 1991-1993. *Member:* Orange County and American Bar Associations (Vice Chairman, Securities Law

*(This Listing Continued)*

## JEFFERS, WILSON & SHAFF, LLP, Irvine—Continued

Committee, 1992-1993); State Bar of California (Member, Corporation Committee, Business Law Section, 1996). *PRACTICE AREAS:* Corporate and Securities Law.

---

## JENNINGS & HAUG

*1920 MAIN STREET, SUITE EIGHT-THIRTY*
**IRVINE, CALIFORNIA 92714**
*Telephone: 714-250-7800*
*Fax: 714-250-4913*
*Email: jhlaw@syspac.com*

Phoenix, Arizona Office: 2800 North Central Avenue, Suite Eighteen Hundred. Telephone: 602-234-7800.

*General Practice in State and Federal Courts and before Administrative Agencies. Commercial, Bankruptcy, Creditors Rights, Construction, Corporate, Labor and Employment Law, Estate Planning, Fidelity and Surety, Insurance, Personal Injury. Trials and Appeals.*

**ROBERT A. SCHEFFING,** born Overland, Missouri, September 23, 1942; admitted to bar, 1967, Arizona; 1974, U.S. Supreme Court; 1984, U.S. Claims Court; 1990, California. *Education:* University of Notre Dame (A.B., 1964); University of Vienna, Vienna, Austria; University of Arizona (J.D., cum laude, 1967). Phi Delta Phi. Recent Decisions Editor, Arizona Law Review, 1966-1967. Charter Member, Curia Regis. Judge Pro Tempore, Superior Court, 1984-1990. Member, Tort and Insurance Practice Section, American Bar Association. *Member:* Orange County Bar Association (Construction Law Section); State Bar of California (Real Property Section, Construction Subsection); Fidelity and Surety Law Committee, Forum on the Construction Industry and Public Contract Law; Southern California Association of Defense Counsel; Legal Advisory Committee of the Associated General Contractors of California; Defense Research Institute; and DRI Construction Law Committee. Founding Fellow, Arizona Bar Foundation, 1984—. *PRACTICE AREAS:* Surety; Construction; Product Liability; Personal Injury; Design Professional Liability; Insurance Coverage.

### ASSOCIATE

**PAUL D. KRAMER,** born Pasadena, California, July 16, 1963; admitted to bar, 1990, California. *Education:* University of California (B.A., psychology, 1985); Loyola Law School (J.D., 1990). *Member:* Orange County Bar Association (Construction Law Committee); State Bar of California (Construction Law Subcommittee, under Real Estate Committee); Orange County Barristers; California Surety Association. (Resident). *PRACTICE AREAS:* Commercial and Construction Litigation; Surety, Contract and Real Property Litigation.

(For complete biographical data on all personnel see Professional Biographies at Phoenix, Arizona)

---

## JACQUELINE M. JENSEN, INC.

*Established in 1978*
*18006 SKY PARK CIRCLE, SUITE 109*
**IRVINE, CALIFORNIA 92614**
*Telephone: 714-261-0100*
*Fax: 714-261-0176*

*Estate Planning, Estate Tax, Trusts, Asset Protection, Probate, Business Law and Elder Care.*

**JACQUELINE M. JENSEN,** born New York, New York, July 22, 1938; admitted to bar, 1978, California. *Education:* Trinity College (B.A., 1960); University of Tulsa (J.D., 1977). Author: "Form 706/709 Estate and Gift Taxes Planning and Compliance 1992," Gear Up Tax Seminars, 1992; "Nursing Home Care: Will it Impoverish your Family," Connections to Excellence, pp. 67-70, Aug. 1990; "Benefits of Charitable Trusts," Business to Business, pp. 58-60, Nov. 1989; "Revocable Living Trusts: What they Offer California Residents," Business to Business, pp. 54-59, Aug. 1989. Adjunct Professor, Western State University, College of Law. National Speaker, Gear Up Tax Seminars. Past Member, Board of Directors, Universal Care, Long Beach, California. Past Member, Board of Directors, YWCA. Past President, Lions Club. Legal Counsel, Women in Business, Orange County, 1988. Past Vice-President, Trinity College Alumni, Orange County. Member: Orange County Bar Association; State Bar of California; Orange County Estate Planning Council. (Board Certified, Probate, Estate Planning and Trust Law, California Board of Legal Specialization).

A List of References will be available upon request.

---

## TIMOTHY L. JOENS & ASSOCIATES

*A PROFESSIONAL CORPORATION*
*Established in 1986*
*JAMBOREE CENTER*
*FIVE PARK PLAZA, SUITE 1480*
**IRVINE, CALIFORNIA 92714**
*Telephone: 714-553-1950*
*Fax: 714-553-8835*

*Trial and Appellate Litigation for Civil Matters in all State and Federal Courts, including Business, Real Property, Contract, Will Contests, Collection, Personal Injury, Professional Malpractice, Corporate, Partnership, Franchise, Surety, Lien and Construction Matters.*

*FIRM PROFILE:* Timothy L. Joens and Associates, A Professional Corporation, was formed in 1986. Since its formation, the firm has concentrated on trial, appellate, arbitration, and general litigation practice, with special emphasis on franchise, business and corporate, general contract, real estate sales and brokerage, construction and lien, will contests, personal injury and professional malpractice matters. By remaining small, the firm seeks to maintain its commitment to quality and cost effectiveness. Clients from other parts of the United States and world frequently have called upon the firm's attorneys for assistance in Southern California litigation matters. Mr. Jones is listed in The Preeminent Law Directory.

**TIMOTHY L. JOENS,** born Inglewood, California, January 23, 1951; admitted to bar, 1979, California. *Education:* University of Southern California (B.A., 1973); Loyola University of Los Angeles (J.D., cum laude, 1979). Recipient, American Jurisprudence Award on Evidence. *Member:* Orange County and American Bar Associations; State Bar of California; Christian Legal Society (President, Orange County Chapter, 1983-1985). *PRACTICE AREAS:* Civil Litigation; Franchise Law; Personal Injury; Professional Liability Law.

REPRESENTATIVE CLIENTS: Alii Drive Continuation Limited Partnership; Century 21 of the Pacific, Inc.; Century 21 Real Estate Corporation; Century 21 Region V, Inc.
REFERENCE: First Business Bank, Irvine, California.

---

## JONES, DAY, REAVIS & POGUE

*2603 MAIN STREET, SUITE 900*
**IRVINE, CALIFORNIA 92714-6232**
*Telephone: 714-851-3939*
*Telex: 194911 Lawyers LSA*
*Telecopier: 714-553-7539*

*In Los Angeles, California:* 555 West Fifth Street, Suite 4600. Telephone: 213-489-3939. Telex: 181439 UD. Telecopier: 213-243-2539.
*In Atlanta, Georgia:* 3500 One Peachtree Center, 303 Peachtree Street, N.E. Telephone: 404-521-3939. Cable Address: "Attorneys Atlanta". Telex: 54-2711. Telecopier: 404-581-8330.
*In Brussels, Belgium:* Avenue Louise 480, 7th Floor, B-1050 Brussels. Telephone: 32-2-645-14-11. Telecopier: 32-2-645-14-45.
*In Chicago, Illinois:* 77 West Wacker. Telephone: 312-782-3939. Telecopier: 312-782-8585.
*In Cleveland, Ohio:* North Point, 901 Lakeside Avenue. Telephone: 216-586-3939. Cable Address: "Attorneys Cleveland." Telex: 980389. Telecopier: 216-579-0212.
*In Columbus, Ohio:* 1900 Huntington Center. Telephone: 614-469-3939. Cable Address: "Attorneys Columbus." Telecopier: 614-461-4198.
*In Dallas, Texas:* 2300 Trammell Crow Center, 2001 Ross Avenue. Telephone: 214-220-3939. Cable Address: "Attorneys Dallas." Telex: 730852. Telecopier: 214-969-5100.
*In Frankfurt, Germany:* Triton Haus, Bockenheimer Landstrasse 42, 60323 Frankfurt am Main. Telephone: 49-69-9726-3939. Telecopier: 49-69-9726-3993.
*In Geneva, Switzerland:* 20, rue de Candolle. Telephone: 41-22-320-2339. Telecopier: 41-22-320-1232.
*In Hong Kong:* 29th Floor, Entertainment Building, 30 Queen's Road Central. Telephone: 852-2526-6895. Telecopier: 852-2868-5871.

*(This Listing Continued)*

*In London, England:* Bucklersbury House, 3 Queen Victoria Street. Telephone: 44-171-236-3939. Telecopier: 44-171-236-1113.

*In New Delhi, India:* Pathak & Associates, 13th Floor, Dr. Gopal Das Bhavan, 28 Barakhamba Road. Telephone: 91-11-373-8793. Telecopy: 91-11-335-3761.

*In New York, New York:* 599 Lexington Avenue. Telephone: 212-326-3939. Cable Address: "JONESDAY NEWYORK." Telex: 237013 JDRP UR. Telecopier: 212-755-7306.

*In Paris, France:* 62, rue du Faubourg Saint-Honore. Telephone: 33-1-44-71-3939. Telex: 290156 Surgoe. Telecopier: 33-1-49-24-0471.

*In Pittsburgh, Pennsylvania:* 500 Grant Street, 31st Floor. Telephone: 412-391-3939. Cable Address: "Attorneys Pittsburgh." Telecopier: 412-394-7959.

*In Riyadh, Saudi Arabia:* The International Law Firm, Sulaymaniyah Center, Tahlia Street, P.O. Box 22166. Telephone: (966-1) 462-8866. Telecopier: (966-1) 462-9001.

*In Taipei, Taiwan:* 8th Floor, 2 Tun Hwa South Road, Section 2. Telephone: (886-2) 704-6808. Telecopier: (886-2) 704-6791.

*In Tokyo, Japan:* Toranomon MT Building, 4th Floor, 10-3, Toranomon 3-Chome, Minato-ku, Tokyo 105, Japan. Telephone: 81-3-3433-3939. Telecopier: 81-3-5401-2725.

*In Washington, D.C.:* Metropolitan Square, 1450 G Street, N.W. Telephone: 202-879-3939. Cable Address: "Attorneys Washington." Telex: 89-2410 ATTORNEYS WASH. Telecopier: 202-737-2832.

*General Practice.*

### MEMBERS OF FIRM IN IRVINE

**THOMAS R. MALCOLM,** born Los Angeles, California, January 2, 1939; admitted to bar, 1966, California. *Education:* University of California, Berkeley (A.B., 1962); University of California, Hastings College of the Law (LL.B., 1966). Fellow, American College of Trial Lawyers. *Email:* trmalcolm@jonesday.com

**DULCIE D. BRAND,** born Fort Worth, Texas, September 24, 1955; admitted to bar, 1981, District of Columbia; 1984, Illinois; 1986, Texas; 1995, California. *Education:* Texas A & M University (B.A., 1976); George Washington University (J.D., 1981). Order of the Coif. *Email:* ddbrand@jonesday.com

**RICHARD J. GRABOWSKI,** born Los Angeles, California, January 1, 1961; admitted to bar, 1986, California. *Education:* California State University, Long Beach (B.A., 1983); University of California, Los Angeles (J.D., 1986). Order of the Coif. *Email:* rgrabowski@jonesday.com

### ASSOCIATES

**J. SCOTT SCHOEFFEL,** born Long Beach, California, October 25, 1954; admitted to bar, 1980, California. *Education:* University of California, Santa Barbara (B.A., 1976); University of California, Berkeley (Boalt Hall) (J.D., 1980). *Email:* sschoeffel@jonesday.com

**MARK D. KEMPLE,** born Montclair, New Jersey, February 27, 1962; admitted to bar, 1989, California. *Education:* University of California, Los Angeles (B.A., 1984); University of Southern California (J.D., 1989). Order of the Coif. Law Clerk to Judge Rafeedie, U.S. District Court, Central District of California, 1989-1990. *Email:* mkemple@jonesday.com

**WILLIAM E. HALLE,** born Metairie, Louisiana, July 30, 1963; admitted to bar, 1990, California. *Education:* University of California, Los Angeles (B.A., 1986); University of Michigan (J.D., 1990). *Email:* wehalle@jonesday.com

**MARC K. CALLAHAN,** born Long Beach, California, January 22, 1967; admitted to bar, 1991, California. *Education:* University of California, Los Angeles (B.A., 1988); University of California, Hastings College of the Law (J.D., 1991). Phi Beta Kappa; Order of the Coif. *Email:* mkcallahan@jonesday.com

**JEFFREY B. KIRZNER,** born Portsmouth, New Hampshire, July 3, 1966; admitted to bar, 1991, California. *Education:* University of California, Los Angeles (B.A., 1988); University of California, Hastings College of the Law (J.D., 1991). Order of the Coif. *Email:* jkirzner@jonesday.com

**MICHELLE M. NUSZKIEWICZ,** born Crescent City, California, September 26, 1966; admitted to bar, 1992, California. *Education:* University of Southern California (B.A., 1989; J.D., 1992). *Email:* mnuszkiewicz@jonesday.com

**MICHAEL D. FABIANO,** born Washington, D.C., November 19, 1964; admitted to bar, 1993, California. *Education:* Rice University (B.A., 1986); University of California, Berkeley (M.S., 1988); University of California, Hastings College of the Law (J.D., 1993). Order of the Coif. Law Clerk to

*(This Listing Continued)*

Judge McLaughlin, U.S. District Court, Central District of California, 1993-1994. *Email:* mikefabiano@jonesday.com

**JAMES L. POTH,** born Abilene, Texas, September 16, 1967; admitted to bar, 1994, Pennsylvania; 1996, California. *Education:* University of California, Berkeley (B.A., 1990); University of California, Hastings College of the Law (J.D., 1994). *Email:* jlpoth@jonesday.com

**HEATHER A. MCCONNELL,** born Glendale, California, April 11, 1970; admitted to bar, 1996, California. *Education:* University of California, Irvine (B.A., 1993); Loyola Law School, Los Angeles (J.D., 1996). Order of the Coif. *Email:* hmcconne@jonesday.com

---

## LAW OFFICES OF JONES & DONOVAN

*A PROFESSIONAL CORPORATION*

CENTERPOINTE 6, SUITE 230
19782 MACARTHUR BOULEVARD
IRVINE, CALIFORNIA 92715
Telephone: 714-833-8893
Telecopier: 714-833-7555

*Government Contracts and related Commercial Contracts, including Litigation before all Courts and Boards of Contract Appeals.*

**PETER BEST JONES,** born New York, N.Y., September 25, 1943; admitted to bar, 1968, New Jersey; 1969, District of Columbia; 1975, California. *Education:* Dartmouth College (A.B., cum laude, 1965); Columbia Law School (LL.B., 1968). *Member:* The District of Columbia Bar; Orange County, Federal and American Bar Associations; State Bar of California. **PRACTICE AREAS:** Government Contracts; Contracts.

**BRIAN J. DONOVAN,** born Buffalo, New York, June 28, 1945; admitted to bar, 1975, California; 1976, District of Columbia. *Education:* United States Air Force Academy (B.S., 1967); Loyola University of Los Angeles (J.D., cum laude, 1974). Phi Delta Phi. Note and Comment Editor, Loyola University of Los Angeles Law Review, 1973-1974. Law Clerk, Hon. E. Avery Crary, U.S. District Court, Los Angeles. *Member:* The District of Columbia Bar; Orange County, Federal and American Bar Associations; State Bar of California. [Capt., U.S. Air Force (OSI), 1967-1971]. **PRACTICE AREAS:** Government Contracts; Contracts.

---

**TONI L. DEGASPERIN,** born Fairmount, West Virginia, December 31, 1955; admitted to bar, 1983, California. *Education:* Ohio State University (B.S., 1979); University of San Diego School of Law (J.D., 1982). Adjunct Professor, Northrop University School of Law, 1987. *Member:* Orange County and Federal Bar Associations; State Bar of California. [Capt., J.A.G.C., U.S. Air Force, 1984-1989]. **PRACTICE AREAS:** Government Contracts; Contracts.

---

## KASDAN, SIMONDS, McINTYRE, EPSTEIN & MARTIN

*Established in 1978*

2600 MICHELSON DRIVE, TENTH FLOOR
IRVINE, CALIFORNIA 92715
Telephone: 714-851-9000
Fax: 714-833-9455

*General Civil and Trial Practice, State and Federal Courts. Business, Real Property, Financial Institutions, Product Liability, Corporate, Creditors Rights, Property Tax Assessment Appeals, Public Law and Construction Law.*

*FIRM PROFILE: The Law Firm's trial practice focuses on major construction defect litigation. Kasdan Simonds utilizes a state-of-the-art computerized data base and case management system, and has a full professional support staff. The firm emphasizes innovative solutions to achieve client goals. The firm is noted for its zealous, creative advocacy. Kasdan Simonds strives to provide quality service in a responsive and timely manner, at a competitive cost.*

### MEMBERS OF FIRM

**KENNETH S. KASDAN,** born New York, N.Y., February 14, 1951; admitted to bar, 1976, California; 1978, U.S. District Court, Central District of California; 1979, U.S. Court of Appeals, 9th Circuit; 1986, U.S. District Court, Southern and Northern Districts of California; 1987, U.S.

*(This Listing Continued)*

## KASDAN, SIMONDS, McINTYRE, EPSTEIN & MARTIN, Irvine—Continued

Court of Appeals, 5th and 10th Circuits. *Education:* Bernard M. Baruch College of the City University of New York (B.A., cum laude, 1973); State University of New York at Buffalo (J.D., 1976). *Member:* Orange County and American (Member, Business Law and Litigation Sections) Bar Associations; State Bar of California (Member, Business Law Section); Orange County Trial Lawyers Association (Member, Business Litigation Section). *PRACTICE AREAS:* Construction Defect Litigation; Business Litigation.

**VANCE C. SIMONDS, JR.,** born Ann Arbor, Michigan, February 17, 1947; admitted to bar, 1978, California; 1979, U.S. District Court, Central District of California; 1983, U.S. Court of Appeals, 9th Circuit; 1986, U.S. District Court, Southern District of California; 1988, U.S. District Court, Western District of Pennsylvania. *Education:* Stanford University (A.B., in History, 1968); Loyola University of Los Angeles (J.D., 1978). *Member:* Orange County and American Bar Associations; State Bar of California; California Trial Lawyers Association. *PRACTICE AREAS:* Medical Products Liability; Business Litigation.

**R. DONALD McINTYRE,** born Detroit, Michigan, April 20, 1949; admitted to bar, 1975, California; 1977, U.S. District Court, Central District of California; 1986, U.S. District Court, Southern District of California; 1987, U.S. Court of Appeals, 5th and 10th Circuits; 1990, U.S. Court of Appeals, Ninth Circuit; 1992, U.S. District Court, Eastern and Northern Districts of California. *Education:* University of California at Irvine (B.A., cum laude, 1971); University of California at Los Angeles (J.D., 1975). Licensed Real Estate Broker, California, 1976. *Member:* Orange County Bar Association (Member, Sections on: Real Estate; Construction); State Bar of California (Member, Real Property Law and Law Practice Management Sections). *PRACTICE AREAS:* Real Estate Law; Construction; Real Property Tax and Assessment Appeals.

**DAVID G. EPSTEIN,** born New York, N.Y., April 29, 1943; admitted to bar, 1978, California. *Education:* Columbia University (B.A., summa cum laude, 1963; Ph.D., 1969); University of California at Los Angeles (J.D., 1978). Phi Beta Kappa. Recipient, American Jurisprudence Award in Labor Law. Member, Federal Communication Law Journal, 1977-1978. Member, Santa Monica City Council, 1983-1987. Member: Arbitration and Mediation Panels, Orange County Superior Court, 1991—; Commercial Arbitration Panel, American Arbitration Association. *Member:* Orange County Bar Association; State Bar of California (Member, Public Law Section). *LANGUAGES:* Portuguese, Spanish and French. *PRACTICE AREAS:* Construction Defect Litigation; Civil Litigation.

**RONALD B. MARTIN,** born Santa Ana, California, June 5, 1952; admitted to bar, 1978, California. *Education:* University of California at Los Angeles (B.A., 1974); Loyola Marymount University (J.D., 1978). *Member:* Orange County and American Bar Associations; State Bar of California. *PRACTICE AREAS:* Construction Defect Litigation; Real Estate Law.

**ANDREW D. WEISS,** born Montclair, New Jersey, July 18, 1960; admitted to bar, 1985, California and U.S. District Court, Northern District of California; 1986, U.S. Tax Court; 1988, U.S. District Court, Eastern District of California; 1990, U.S. District Court, Central and Southern Districts of California. *Education:* University of California at Los Angeles (B.A., 1982) California State University at San Diego (J.D., 1985). *Member:* Orange County Bar Association; State Bar of California. *PRACTICE AREAS:* Construction Defect Litigation; Civil Litigation.

### ASSOCIATE

**HENRY P. SCHRENKER,** born Anderson, Indiana, June 9, 1956; admitted to bar, 1978, California; 1987, U.S. District Court, Central and Southern Districts of California; 1988, U.S. Court of Appeals, Ninth Circuit. *Education:* Indiana University (B.A., 1978); Western State University (J.D., 1984). Judge Pro Tem, Orange County Municipal and Superior Courts. Mediator, HOAMS (Homeowners Association Mediation Service. *Member:* Orange County and American Bar Associations. *PRACTICE AREAS:* Construction Defects; Real Estate Litigation.

**STEVEN S. HANAGAMI,** born Los Angeles, California, July 10, 1959; admitted to bar, 1993, California and U.S. District Court, Southern District. *Education:* University of California at Los Angeles (B.S., 1982); George Washington University National Law Center (J.D., 1992). Phi Eta

*(This Listing Continued)*

CAA336B

Sigma. National Society of Professional Engineers, 1980-1984. *Member:* State Bar of California. *PRACTICE AREAS:* Construction Defect; Business Litigation.

REFERENCES: Marine National Bank; California State Bank.

## KATTEN MUCHIN & ZAVIS

A Partnership including Professional Corporations

Katten Muchin & Zavis Established in 1974

**TWO PARK PLAZA, SUITE 800**
**IRVINE, CALIFORNIA 92714-5976**
*Telephone: 714-263-3500*
*Telecopier: 714-263-3533*

*Chicago, Illinois Office:* 525 West Monroe Street, Suite 1600. Telephone: 312-902-5200. Telecopier: 312-902-1061. Telex: 298264 ATLAW UR.
*Los Angeles, California Office:* 1999 Avenue of the Stars, Suite 1400. Telephone: 310-788-4400. Telecopier: 310-788-4471.
*New York, New York Office:* 40 Broad Street, Suite 2000. Telephone: 212-612-9500. Telecopier: 212-425-0266.
*Washington, D.C. Office:* 1025 Thomas Jefferson Street, N.W., East Lobby, Suite 700. Telephone: 202-625-3500. Telecopier: 202-298-7570. Telex: 211195 KMZ UR.

*Creditor's Rights, Environmental, Intellectual Property, Labor and Employment Law, Litigation and Trial Practice, Real Estate.*

### MEMBER OF FIRM

**THOMAS S. MAHR,** born Reedsburg, Wisconsin, June 23, 1954; admitted to bar, 1981, California and U.S. District Court, Central District of California; 1990, U.S. District Court, Northern District of California; 1991, U.S. court of Appeals, Ninth Circuit; 1994, U.S. District Court, Southern District of California. *Education:* University of Miami (B.M., magna cum laude, 1978; J.D., cum laude, 1981). Member, University of Miami Law Review, 1979-1981. *Member:* Orange County, Los Angeles County and American Bar Associations; State Bar of California. *PRACTICE AREAS:* Business, Entertainment and Commercial Litigation. *Email:* 6014779@mcimail.com

**FREDERICK H. KRANZ,** born Los Angeles, California, February 2, 1947; admitted to bar, 1972, California; U.S. Court of Appeals, Ninth, Seventh and District of Columbia Circuits; U.S. District Court, Eastern, Southern, Central and Northern Districts of California. *Education:* Loyola University-Los Angeles (B.A., 1969); University of California School of Law at Los Angeles (J.D., 1972). Judge Pro Tem, Orange County Superior Court, 1989—. *Member:* State Bar of California; American Bar Association. *PRACTICE AREAS:* Commercial and High-Tech Litigation.

**STUART M. RICHTER,** born Bethlehem, Pennsylvania, July 17, 1961; admitted to bar, 1986, California and U.S. District Court, Central and Southern Districts of California. *Education:* University of Virginia (B.S., 1983); Pepperdine University (J.D., magna cum laude, 1986). *Member:* Orange County and Los Angeles County Bar Associations; State Bar of California. *PRACTICE AREAS:* Litigation.

### ASSOCIATES

Thia M. Cochran; Michelle A. Curtis; Melody Williams Dapp; Eoin L. Kreditor.

## KAYAJANIAN & BREWSAUGH

**18500 VON KARMAN AVENUE, SUITE 430**
**IRVINE, CALIFORNIA 92715**
*Telephone: 714-955-2254*
*Facsimile: 714-833-1556*

*Personal Injury, Business Law, Civil Litigation, Family Law, Construction.*

FIRM PROFILE: *The law firm of Kayajanian & Brewsaugh consists of the named partners of Jack J. Kayajanian and Gary D. Brewsaugh.*

*The firm specializes in family law cases, with an emphasis on child and spousal support collection and defense. The firm currently services the Alternate Defense contract for Orange County Superior Court for indigent paternity and civil contempt (family law) defendants, handling over 100 cases per year under the contract. Mr. Kayajanian is one of Orange County's leading experts on family law contempt cases, has published an article for the Orange County Lawyer detailing the issues regarding the successful prosecution of family law contempt cases, and has been asked to speak on the subject several times.*

*(This Listing Continued)*

In addition to the family law practice, Mr. Brewsaugh performs corporate and business transactions, and practices business and personal injury litigation.

Mr. Kayajanian is also involved in sports law. Representative clients include the former Los Angeles Rams, Chuck Knox, Jack Faulkner, N.F.L. Alumni, N.F.L. Retired Players Association, Bob Welch, and Jerry Tarkanian.

The solid family law practice, together with the personal injury, business, sports and criminal legal work done by the partners, makes the firm a full-service provider of legal services.

### MEMBERS OF FIRM

**JACK J. KAYAJANIAN,** born Fresno, California, August 22, 1950; admitted to bar, 1977, California. *Education:* California State University at Fresno (B.A., 1973); Western State University (J.D., 1976). Member, Western State University Law Review, 1975-1976. Full Professor, Western State University, 1985—. Judge Pro Tempor, Orange County Superior Court, 1985-1989. *Member:* Orange County (Member, Family Law Panel) and West Orange County Bar Associations; State Bar of California; California Trial Lawyers Association. (Certified Specialist, Family Law, The State Bar of California Board of Legal Specialization). **PRACTICE AREAS:** Criminal Law; Personal Injury; Business Law.

**GARY D. BREWSAUGH,** born 1953; admitted to bar, 1978, California. *Education:* Yale University (B.A., 1975); Western State University (J.D., 1978). *Member:* State Bar of California. **PRACTICE AREAS:** Civil Litigation; Family Law; Personal Injury; Business Law; Construction.

---

## LAW OFFICES OF
## JENNIFER L. KELLER

*19100 VON KARMAN AVENUE, SUITE 950*
**IRVINE, CALIFORNIA 92612**
Telephone: 714-476-8700
Fax: 714-476-0900
Email: HVDE71A@PRODIGY.COM

*Criminal Defense and Related Civil Litigation.*

**JENNIFER L. KELLER,** born Fort Wayne, Indiana, February 26, 1953; admitted to bar, 1978, California; 1984, U.S. District Court, Central and Southern Districts of California and U.S. Court of Appeals, Ninth Circuit. *Education:* University of California, Berkeley (A.B., 1975); Hastings College of Law, University of California (J.D., 1978). Member, Hastings Constitutional Law Quarterly, 1977-1978. Attorney of the Year, Public Law Center of Orange County, 1996. Lawyer of the Year, Constitutional Rights Foundation of Orange County, 1983. Faculty: OCBA College of Trial Advocacy, 1982, 1984, 1990, 1991. CACJ Faculty: Prop 115, Preliminary Hearings, 1990; Trial Advocacy Workshop, 1992; Trial & Appellate Advocacy Workshop, 1993; "Three Strikes Seminar", 1994; Fall Seminar, "Oral Argument," 1995. CPDA Faculty: Homicide Seminar, 1986; Sentencing Seminar, 1989; Trial Skills Institute, 1990; Advanced Trial Skills Institute, 1992, 1996, 1997; Annual Seminar, 1992. Chair, 1993-1994; Vice-Chair, 1992-1993 and Commissioner, 1990-1992, California State Bar Board of Legal Specialization, Criminal Law Advisory Commission. Senior Deputy Public Defender, Orange County, 1978-1983, 1989-1991. Senior Research Attorney, Justice Edward Wallin, California Court of Appeal, Fourth District, Division 3, 1986-1989. Lawyer Representative, Ninth Circuit Judicial Conference, 1996-1999. *Member:* Orange County Bar Association (President, 1996; Officer, 1993-1995; Board of Directors, 1991-1993) National Association of Criminal Defense Lawyers; California Attorneys for Criminal Justice (Member, Board of Governors, 1992-1993). (Certified Specialist, Criminal Law, The State Bar of California Board of Legal Specialization). **REPORTED CASES:** United States v. Stites, 56 F.3d 1020 (1995); People v. Sellers (1988) 203 Cal. App. 3d 1042; Betsworth v. WCAB (1994) 26 Cal. App. 4th 586. **PRACTICE AREAS:** Criminal Defense; Civil Litigation.

---

## KENDRICK & JACKSON

*19800 MACARTHUR BOULEVARD*
*SUITE 270*
**IRVINE, CALIFORNIA 92612**
Telephone: 714-261-6440
Facsimile: 714-261-5758

*Business and Civil Litigation including Real Property, Insurance Banking, Construction and Employment Disputes.*

*(This Listing Continued)*

---

**JOHN J. KENDRICK, JR.,** born Covina, California, May 26, 1946; admitted to bar, 1974, California, U.S. Supreme Court and U.S. District Court, Southern, Northern and Central Districts of California. *Education:* University of California at Los Angeles (B.A., 1968); University of the Pacific, McGeorge School of Law (J.D., with distinction, 1974). Phi Delta Phi. Member, Traynor Society. Member, Pacific Law Journal, 1973-1974. *Member:* Orange County (Member, Sections on: Real Property; Business Litigation) Bar Association; State Bar of California (Member, Landlord-Tenant and Residential Housing Committee, Real Property Law Section).

**C. BENNETT JACKSON, JR.,** born New Haven, Connecticut, February 13, 1939; admitted to bar, 1969, California and U.S. District Court, Central District of California; 1978, U.S. Supreme Court; 1984, U.S. District Court, Central, Southern, Northern and Eastern Districts of California. *Education:* Stanford University (A.B., 1960); University of Southern California (J.D., 1968). Phi Delta Phi. *Member:* Orange County Bar Association (Member, Business Litigation, Elder Law, Probate and Estate Planning Sections); State Bar of California. Newport Beach Public Library, Board of Trustees, 1986-1997.

**JANE GRILLIOT KEARL,** born Celina, Ohio, November 30, 1965; admitted to bar, 1991, California and U.S. District Court, Central District of California. *Education:* Ohio Northern University (B.A., with high honors, 1988); Ohio State University (J.D., with honors, 1991). Judicial Extern for Honorable George P. Smith, U.S. District Court, Central District of Ohio. *Member:* Orange County (Member, Business Litigation Section) and American Bar Associations; State Bar of California.

---

## DALE A. KIKEN

*18400 VON KARMAN AVENUE, SUITE 500*
**IRVINE, CALIFORNIA 92715**
Telephone: 714-476-0270
Fax: 714-476-2883

*Business Litigation.*

**DALE A. KIKEN,** born Denver, Colorado, April 19, 1953; admitted to bar, 1981, California, U.S. Tax Court, U.S. District Court, Central District of California and U.S. Court of Appeals, 9th Circuit; 1989, U.S. District Court, Northern and Southern Districts of California. *Education:* University of Colorado at Boulder (B.A., 1975); Pepperdine University (J.D., 1980). Phi Alpha Delta. *Member:* Orange County and American Bar Associations; State Bar of California. **PRACTICE AREAS:** Business Litigation.

---

## LAW OFFICES OF
## C. WILLIAM KIRCHER, JR.

*A PROFESSIONAL CORPORATION*
*Established in 1985*

*19800 MACARTHUR BOULEVARD, SUITE 1450*
**IRVINE, CALIFORNIA 92612-2442**
Telephone: 714-720-9752
Fax: 714-720-8752

*Civil Business, Commercial and Securities Litigation in Federal and State Courts.*

**C. WILLIAM KIRCHER, JR., (PROFESSIONAL CORPORATION),** born Los Angeles, California, June 7, 1946; admitted to bar, 1972, California; 1976, U.S. District Court, Central District of California and U.S. Court of Appeals, Ninth Circuit; 1981, U.S. District Court, Northern District of California; 1983, U.S. District Court, Southern District of California and U.S. Claims Court; 1984, U.S. District Court, Eastern District of California; 1988, U.S. Supreme Court. *Education:* Stanford University (B.A., with distinction, 1968); Stanford Law School (J.D., 1971). Associate Consultant, California Senate Committee on Health and Welfare, 1975-1976. Assistant United States Attorney, Central District of California, 1976-1981. *Member:* Orange County, Federal and American (Member, Litigation Section) Bar Associations; State Bar of California. **PRACTICE AREAS:** Business Litigation; Securities Litigation; Commercial Litigation.

REFERENCE: First Los Angeles Bank (Main Branch).

## KIRTLAND & PACKARD LLP

18101 VON KARMAN AVENUE
NINETEENTH FLOOR
**IRVINE, CALIFORNIA 92715-1041**
Telephone: 714-263-9700
Fax: 714-263-9090

*Los Angeles, California Office:* 1900 Avenue of the Stars, Twenty-Fifth and Twenty-Sixth Floors. Telephone: 310-552-9700. Cable Address: "Kirtpack". Fax: 310-552-0957.

*General Civil and Trial Practice in State and Federal Courts. Aviation, Employment and Labor Law, Environmental, Insurance, Medical Malpractice, Professional and Product Liability and Toxic Torts Law.*

### MEMBERS OF FIRM

**MARK P. POLIQUIN,** born Los Angeles, California, October 30, 1955; admitted to bar, 1980, California; 1981, U.S. Tax Court; 1994, U.S. Supreme Court; 1996, U.S. District Court, Southern District of California. *Education:* University of Southern California (B.S., 1977); Loyola Marymount University, Los Angeles (J.D., 1980). Co-Editor: California Law Digest; Best's Directory of Recommended Insurance Attorneys, A.M. Best Company, Inc., 1992. *Member:* Orange County Bar Association (Member, Tort and Insurance Practice Section); State Bar of California; Association of Southern California Defense Counsel; American Board of Trial Advocates.

**JOHN M. GOODSPEED,** born Milwaukee, Wisconsin, March 24, 1950; admitted to bar, 1979, California. *Education:* University of Michigan; Albion College (B.A., 1972); University of Notre Dame; Pepperdine University (J.D., 1978). Author: "The Standard of Care FAA Air Traffic Controller Must Exercise with Respect to the Hazard of Wing Tip Vortices," June, 1977; "The Theory, Appropriateness, Determination, and Disparity of Exemplary Awards in Aviation Accident Law," June, 1978. Special Agent, Federal Bureau of Investigation, United States Department of Justice, 1983-1987. *Member:* Orange County, Los Angeles County and American Bar Associations; State Bar of California; Association of Southern California Defense Counsel.

**JEFFREY M. ANIELSKI,** born Akron, Ohio, July 20, 1956; admitted to bar, 1986, California; 1993, Maryland. *Education:* Ohio University (B.A., 1980); Southwestern University (J.D., 1986). *Member:* State Bar of California; Association of Southern California Defense Counsel.

### RESIDENT ASSOCIATES
### IRVINE OFFICE

| | |
|---|---|
| Robert W. Skripko, Jr. | Timothy D. Otte |
| C. Christopher Mulder | Layne M. Bukovskis |
| Curtis C. Holmes II | Paul R. Cotter |
| Joseph Stephen McMillen | Ronald J. Thommarson |

### RESIDENT PARTNERS
### LOS ANGELES OFFICE

| | |
|---|---|
| Harold J. Hunter, Jr. | Robert M. Churella |
| Jacques E. Soiret | Scott M. Schutz |
| Michael L. Kelly | Steven M. Maslauski |
| Joseph E. Gregorich | John M. Caron |
| Robert A. Muhlbach | Terrence J. Schafer |

(For complete biographical data on all Members and Of Counsel, see Professional Biographies at Los Angeles, California)

## KITAGAWA & EBERT, P.C.

Formerly known as Kitsuta & Ebert, P.C.

8001 IRVINE CENTER DRIVE, SUITE 850
**IRVINE, CALIFORNIA 92718**
Telephone: 714-727-0290
Fax: 714-727-0607

*Atlanta, Georgia Office:* 400 Colony Square, Suite 200. 1201 Peachtree Street, N.E. Telephone: 404-870-0290. Fax: 404-870-0079.

*General Business, Corporate, International, Business and Tax Litigation, Employment Law, Employment Litigation, Collection Litigation, Estate Planning, Probate, Real Estate, Sports, Entertainment, Licensing. Restructuring, Mergers and Acquisitions.*

(This Listing Continued)

*FIRM PROFILE: Kitagawa & Ebert, P.C. represents Japan businesses throughout the U.S.A. Lisa M. Kitagawa, Esq. is a graduate of Kyoto University and is fluent in Japanese. James R. Ebert, Esq. is an attorney and a California Certified Public Accountant. The firm's pleasant professional staff is also fluent in Japanese. The firm strives to provide high quality legal services at reasonable rates. Both Ms. Kitagawa and Mr. Ebert are admitted to practice in California and Georgia. The firm is experienced in serving the business needs which are unique to Japanese businesses.*

**LISA M. KITAGAWA,** born Los Angeles, California, 1959; admitted to bar, 1982, California; 1995, Georgia. *Education:* University of Southern California (B.S., Business Finance, 1979); Tokyo University, Japan, (1981); Loyola Law School (J.D., 1982); Kyoto University, Japan (LL.M., 1986). Japanese Ministry of Education Scholar, 1982-1984. College Women's Association of Japan Scholar, 1985-1986. Founder and First President, Japan-U.S. Business Alliance. *Member:* Atlanta, Orange County and American Bar Associations; State Bar of California (Executive Committee Advisor, International Law Section, 1992, 1993; Member, Business Section); Orange County Japanese American Lawyers Association (Founder and First President); Orange County Japanese American Association; Orange County Japan America Society; Georgia Japan America Society. **LANGUAGES:** Japanese.

**JAMES R. EBERT,** born Los Angeles, California, 1956; admitted to bar, 1982, California; 1996, Georgia. *Education:* Santa Clara University (B.S.C., 1979); Loyola Law School (J.D., 1982). Certified Public Accountant, California, 1988. *Member:* Atlanta, Orange County and American Bar Associations; American Association of Attorneys Certified Public Accountants.

REPRESENTATIVE CLIENTS: All Nippon Airways Co., Ltd. (ANA); Cyber Entertainment, Inc.; Hakuba U.S.A., Inc.; Noevir U.S.A., Inc.; Plaza Homes, Ltd.; Sakura Bank; SMK Manufacturing, Inc.; Southland Box Company (Tomoku, Ltd.); Sunrise Co., Ltd.; Zett Corporation.

## KLEIN & SZEKERES

Established in 1982

4199 CAMPUS DRIVE, SUITE 700
**IRVINE, CALIFORNIA 92715**
Telephone: 714-854-5502
FAX: 714-854-4897
Email: hjklein@mail.calypso.com

*Patent, Trademark and Copyright Law. Unfair Competition Law. Election Law.*

### MEMBERS OF FIRM

**HOWARD J. KLEIN,** born New York, N.Y., April 25, 1950; admitted to bar, 1976, New York and U.S. District Court, Southern and Eastern Districts of New York; 1977, California; 1978, U.S. District Court, Central District of California; 1984, U.S. Court of Appeals, Federal and Ninth Circuits; registered to practice before U.S. Patent and Trademark Office. *Education:* Massachusetts Institute of Technology (B.S., 1972); Duke University (J.D., 1975). Phi Alpha Delta. *Member:* Orange County Bar Association; State Bar of California (Member, Patent, Trademark and Copyright Section); Orange County Patent Law Association (President, 1988); American Intellectual Property Law Association. **SPECIAL AGENCIES:** Federal Election Commission. **PRACTICE AREAS:** Intellectual Property Law; Election Law.

**GABOR L. SZEKERES,** born Budapest, Hungary, January 1, 1944; admitted to bar, 1977, California; 1981, U.S. District Court, Central District of California; 1989, U.S. Court of Appeals for the Federal Circuit; registered to practice before U.S. Patent and Trademark Office. *Education:* State University of New York at Buffalo (Ph.D., Medicinal Chemistry, 1971); Western State University at Fullerton (J.D., 1977). Recipient, American Jurisprudence Award in Torts and Property. *Member:* State Bar of California; American Chemical Society. **LANGUAGES:** Hungarian, German and Spanish. **PRACTICE AREAS:** Intellectual Property Law.

REPRESENTED CLIENTS: Allergan, Inc.; Epoch Pharmaceuticals, Inc.; Healthcomm, Inc,; A/S Nunc; Bourns, Inc.; I-Flow Corp.; Taylor-Dunn Manufacturing, Inc.; Viennatone Ges. m.b.h.; Advanced Surgical Intervention, Inc.; Systemed, Inc.; Allied Healthcare Products, Inc.; BTR, plc; Gretson International Ltd.; Max Planck Institute; Nalge Nuna Inc.; Bioglan, Inc.

## CARL J. KLUNDER

108 PACIFICA, 3RD FLOOR
P.O. BOX 19799
**IRVINE, CALIFORNIA 92623-9799**
Telephone: 714-753-1229
Fax: 714-753-1413

*Insurance Coverage, Casualty Insurance Law, Environmental Insurance Litigation, Bad Faith; Excess Insurance Law, Insurance Agents, Errors and Omissions, Life Insurance Law.*

**CARL J. KLUNDER,** born Chicago, Illinois, June 8, 1945; admitted to bar, 1977, California, U.S. District Court, Central and Southern Districts of California and U.S. Court of Appeals, 9th Circuit. *Education:* Chaminade College and Brown University (B.G.S., with distinction, 1969); University of Hawaii (M.B.A., 1972); University of California at Los Angeles (J.D., 1977). Intern, Hon. H. Baird Kidwell, Associate Justice, Hawaii State Supreme Court, 1977. *Member:* Orange County (Secretary/Treasurer, 1985-1986, Co-Chairman, 1986-1987 and Chairman, 1987-1989, Insurance Law Section), Federal and American Bar (Co-Chair, Publication Subcommittee and Co-Editor, Newsletter, 1989—; Member, Insurance Coverage Litigation Committee, Section of Litigation) Associations; State Bar of California; Conference of Insurance Counsel; Association of Southern California Defense Counsel; Defense Research Institute (Member, Arbitration Panel for Insurance Disputes). **PRACTICE AREAS:** Insurance Coverage; Casualty Insurance Law; Environmental Insurance Litigation; Bad Faith; Excess Insurance Law; Insurance Agents Errors and Omissions; Life Insurance Law.

## PHILLIP J. KOLCZYNSKI

LAKESHORE TOWERS
18101 VON KARMAN AVENUE, SUITE 1800
**IRVINE, CALIFORNIA 92715**
Telephone: 714-833-8999
Fax: 714-833-7878
Email: Klawcorp@aol.com

*Aviation, Products Liability, Insurance, Business Litigation.*

**PHILLIP J. KOLCZYNSKI,** born Cleveland, Ohio, December 9, 1947; admitted to bar, 1977, Ohio; 1978, District of Columbia; 1984, California. *Education:* Marquette University (B.A., 1969); Case Western Reserve University (J.D., 1977). Recipient, Navy ROTC Full Scholarship. Commercial Instrument Pilot. Author: *Preparing for Trial in Federal Court,* 2 Ed., James Pub. 1996. Trial Attorney: Office of the Chief Counsel, F.A.A., Washington, D.C., 1977-1978; Trial Attorney: Aviation Unit, Torts Branch, U.S. Department of Justice, Washington, D.C., 1980-1983. [Major, USMCR, active flight duty, 1969-1974]

## MARK A. KOMPA

Established in 1989
2603 MAIN STREET, SUITE 1170
**IRVINE, CALIFORNIA 92714**
Telephone: 714-250-9500
Facsimile: 714-250-9515

*Real Estate, Landlord-Tenant, Creditors' Rights and Bankruptcy, Commercial and Business Law and Appellate Practice.*

**MARK A. KOMPA,** born Nashville, Tennessee, February 26, 1955; admitted to bar, 1980, Pennsylvania; 1984, U.S. District Court, Eastern District of Pennsylvania; 1987, California and U.S. District Court, Central District of California; 1988, U.S. District Court, Southern District of California. *Education:* Samford University; University of Southern California (B.A., 1977); Syracuse University (J.D., 1980). Phi Beta Kappa. Recipient, American Jurisprudence Award in Administrative Law. Assistant District Attorney, Philadelphia District Attorney's Office, 1980-1984. *Member:* Los Angeles County and Orange County Bar Associations; State Bar of California. **REPORTED CASES:** In re Victor Dye Works, Inc., 48 B.R. 943 (Bkrptcy.E.D. Pa. 1985); In re Zerodec Megacorp, Inc., 54 B.R. 814 (Bkrptcy.E.D. Pa. 1985); In re Oxford Royal Mushroom Products, Inc., 59 B.R. 926 (Bkrptcy.E.D. Pa. 1986); In re McCombs Properties VIII, Ltd., 91 B.R. 907 (Bkrptcy. C.D. Cal. 1988). **PRACTICE AREAS:** Landlord and Tenant Law; Civil Litigation.

*(This Listing Continued)*

REPRESENTATIVE CLIENTS: Children's Hospital of Orange County (CHOC); Connecticut General Life Insurance Co. (CIGNA); Core-Mark International, Inc.; Dana Commercial Credit Corp.; First American Title Insurance Co.; First American Real Estate Information Services, Inc.; Fleet Credit Corp.; The Irvine Co.; McDonnell Douglas Realty Company; The Mutual Life Insurance Company of New York (MONY);Nippon Landic (U.S.A.), Inc.; Signal Capital Corp.; State Farm Insurance company; West Publishing Co.

## KOPENY & POWELL

8001 IRVINE CENTER DRIVE, SUITE 1170
**IRVINE, CALIFORNIA 92618**
Telephone: 714-453-2243
Facsimile: 714-453-1916
Email: KPATKP@AOL.COM

*Writs and Appeals in all State and Federal Courts, Tax Controversies and Defense of White Collar Crimes, Business Litigation, Tax and Estate Planning.*

FIRM PROFILE: *The Kopeny & Powell firm is listed in The Preeminent Lawyers.*

**WILLIAM J. KOPENY,** born Chicago, Illinois, September 28, 1950; admitted to bar, 1974, California, U.S. District Court, Central District of California; 1984, U.S. Supreme Court; 1989, U.S. Court of Appeals, Ninth Circuit. *Education:* California State University; University of California at Santa Barbara (B.A., 1971); University of Southern California (J.D., 1974). Contributing Author: California Criminal Law, Procedure and Practice, Supplement, 1989, 1990, 1992. Author: *Rost Motions Manual,* published by California Attorneys for Criminal Justice, 1974; "In re Yurko," Orange County Bar Journal, Spring, 1974; "Capital Punishment-Who Should Choose?" Western State Law Review, Volume 22, No. 2 and "The Impact of Proposition 8 on Statements," Volume 13, No. 1, Western State Law Review; Chapter 55 "Death Penalty Cases," California Criminal Law Procedure & Practice, CEB, 1986. Instructor, Criminal Law Procedure, California State College at Fullerton, 1981-1982; Criminal Procedure, 1983-1984 and Legal Analysis, 1984, Western State University College of Law. Orange County Public Defender, 1980-1985. Listed in The Best Lawyers in America, 1993-1994, 1994-1995. *Member:* Orange County (Member, Appellate Law Section), Federal and American Bar Associations ; State Bar of California (Member, Criminal Law Section); California Attorneys for Criminal Justice; National Association of Criminal Defense Lawyers; California Academy of Appellate Lawyers; American Inns of Court, Orange County. (Certified Specialist, Criminal Law, The State Bar of California Board of Legal Specialization) (Also practicing individually at Santa Ana, California). **REPORTED CASES:** Powell v. Superior Court (People), 232 Cal.App.3d 785, 283 Cal.Rptr. 777 (1991); In Re Robinson, 216 Cal.App.3d 1510, 265 Cal.Rptr. 574 (1990); People P.2d 905, 229 Cal.Rptr. 131 1986); Freedom Newspapper, Inc. v. Superior Court (Orange County), 186 Cal.App.3d 1102, 231 Cal.Rptr. 189 (1986); Koon v. U.S., - U.S.-, 116 S.Ct.2035, 135 L.Ed.2d 392 (1996). **PRACTICE AREAS:** Appellate Practice; White Collar Trials Trials. **Email:** WJKATKP@AOL.COM

**JOHN W. POWELL,** born Brooklyn, New York, January 19, 1947; admitted to bar, 1974, California. *Education:* Loyola University of Los Angeles (B.A., 1969); University of California at Los Angeles (J.D., 1974); New York University (LL.M., Taxation, 1986). *Member:* Orange County (Member, Appellate Law Section), Federal and American (Member, Section of Taxation) Bar Associations; State Bar of California. **REPORTED CASES:** In Re: Edgar M., 14 Cal.3d 727, 122 Cal. Rptr. 574, 537 Pal 406 (19750; Manier v. Anaheim Business Center Co., 161 Cal. App. 3d 503, 207 Cal. Rptr. 508 (1984). **PRACTICE AREAS:** Appellate Practice; Taxation; Litigation.

## GEORGE M. KORNIEVSKY

A PROFESSIONAL CORPORATION
Established in 1986
18881 VON KARMAN AVENUE, SUITE 1260
**IRVINE, CALIFORNIA 92612-1578**
Telephone: 714-724-0888
Fax: 714-752-7035
Email: gmkapc@quick.com

*Practice limited to Family Law.*

**GEORGE M. KORNIEVSKY,** born San Francisco, California, November 29, 1953; admitted to bar, 1978, California. *Education:* University of Santa Clara (B.A., magna cum laude, 1975); Institut Fuer Europaische Studien, Vienna, Austria; Hastings College of the Law, University of Cali-

*(This Listing Continued)*

CALIFORNIA—IRVINE                                                                    MARTINDALE-HUBBELL LAW DIRECTORY 1997

**GEORGE M. KORNIEVSKY** *A PROFESSIONAL CORPORATION, Irvine—Continued*

fornia (J.D., 1978). Phi Delta Phi. *Member:* Orange County Bar Association (Member, Family Law Section); State Bar of California; Association of Certified Family Law Specialists. (Certified Specialist, Family Law, The State Bar of California Board of Legal Specialization). *LANGUAGES:* German. *REPORTED CASES:* In Re: Marriage of McCann (1996) 41 Cal. App. 4th 978. *PRACTICE AREAS:* Dissolution of Marriage; Support and Visitation; Pre-Nuptial Agreements; Appeals.

## KRING & BROWN

Established in 1988

38 CORPORATE PARK, SUITE 200
P.O. BOX 19782

**IRVINE, CALIFORNIA 92623-9782**

Telephone: 714-261-7895
Telecopier: 714-261-7545

*Riverside, California Office:* 5225 Canyon Crest Drive, Building 100, Suite 166. Telephone: 909-684-0332. Fax: 909-684-4376.

*San Diego, California Office:* 225 Broadway, Suite 2100. Telephone: 619-236-0668. Fax: 619-236-0809.

General Civil and Commercial Trial Practice in all State and Federal Courts, Construction, General Business, Corporate, Real Estate, Estate Planning, Insurance, Immigration.

FIRM PROFILE: Kring & Brown, with offices in Irvine, Riverside and San Diego, California, is a full-service law firm. The firm is dedicated to providing high-quality, economical and responsive legal services to clients throughout the continental U.S. and around the world.

The firm's growth since 1988, together with the diversity and quality of its clients, exemplifies the confidence Kring & Brown clients place in the firm's legal services. The firm's members have distinguished themselves, both in practice and in their respective academic arenas, as the attached biographies indicate.

The firm brings to its practice thorough preparation and coordination, thoughtful strategy, and strong courtroom advocacy, while at all times controlling costs and fees.

### MEMBERS OF FIRM

**KYLE D. KRING**, born Long Beach, California, January 9, 1960; admitted to bar, 1986, California and U.S. District Court, Central District of California. *Education:* Long Beach City College (A.A., 1980); University of California at Irvine (B.A., 1982); Loyola University of Los Angeles (J.D., 1984). *Member:* Orange County and American Bar Associations; State Bar of California; Southern California Defense Council. *PRACTICE AREAS:* Civil and Business Litigation; Personal Injury Defense; Construction Defect; Insurance Fraud.

**GREGORY G. BROWN**, born La Jolla, California, March 23, 1962; admitted to bar, 1987, California; 1988, Arizona; U.S. District Court, Central District of California; U.S. Court of Appeals, Ninth Circuit. *Education:* Arizona State University (B.S., 1984); University of San Diego (J.D., 1987). Member, University of San Diego Law Review, 1985-1987. Member, Board of Editors, Journal of Contemporary Legal Issues, 1986-1987. *Member:* Orange County Bar Association; State Bar of California (Member, Business Law Section); State Bar of Arizona; Southern California Defense Counsel. *PRACTICE AREAS:* Civil and Business Litigation; Corporate Law; Real Estate; Estate Planning.

**STUART A. SMITH**, born Salt Lake City, Utah, January 18, 1959; admitted to bar, 1986, California, U.S. District Court, Central District of California and U.S. Court of Appeals, Ninth Circuit. *Education:* University of California at Los Angeles (B.A., History, 1982); Loyola Law School (J.D., 1985). *Member:* Orange County and American Bar Associations; State Bar of California; American Trial Lawyers Association. *PRACTICE AREAS:* Civil and Business Litigation; Plaintiff Personal Injury; Subrogation.

**NICOLE WHYTE**, born Johannesburg, South Africa, February 20, 1965; admitted to bar, 1990, South African Supreme Court; 1991, California. *Education:* University of the Witwatersrand (B.A., 1986; LL.B., 1988). Member, British American Chamber of Commerce. *Member:* Orange County Bar Association (Member, Construction and Immigration Sections); State Bar of California; American Immigration Lawyers' Association; Robert A. Banyard Inns of Court (Barrister). *LANGUAGES:* Afrikaans, French, Latin. *PRACTICE AREAS:* Construction; Civil Litigation; Immigration.

*(This Listing Continued)*

**KEITH G. BREMER**, born Los Angeles, California, May 24, 1964; admitted to bar, 1991, California and U.S. District Court, Central District of California. *Education:* San Diego State University (B.S., 1987); Western State University (J.D., 1991). *Member:* Orange County Bar Association. (Also at Riverside Office). *PRACTICE AREAS:* Civil Litigation; Business Litigation; Construction.

Louis T. Antosh, Jr.
Russell R. Arens
Kenneth W. Chung
Anna M. D'Alessandro
Jeffrey D. Farrow
Robert B. Gibson
Nina D. Klawunder
Jeffrey A. Lake
 (Resident at San Diego Office)
Benjamin T. Ladinig
Jeffrey R. Marquart
Michelle McWhorter
 (Resident, Irvine Office)
Raymond Meyer, Jr.
 (Resident at Riverside Office)
Robert Mougin
 (Resident at San Diego Office)
Mary Ann Noiroux
Rina K. Rai
Laurie Rau
Brent Reden
 (Resident at San Diego Office)
Paul A. Rianda
Joseph A. Robertson
Dirk E. Silva
 (Resident at Riverside Office)
Craig J. Silver
Paul N. Stam
Kere K. Tickner
 (Resident at Riverside Office)
Tonia Tompkins
Jon H. Van De Grift
 (Resident at San Diego Office)

REPRESENTATIVE CLIENTS: American States Insurance Company, Santa Ana, California; Farmers Group of Insurance Companies; Golden Bear Insurance Company, Stockton, California; Golden Eagle Insurance Company, San Diego, California; Guaranty National Insurance Company, Englewood, Colorado; Liberty Mutual Insurance Company, Boston, Massachusetts; LMI Insurance Company, Van Nuys, California; M.A. Hanna Company, Cleveland, Ohio; National Union Insurance Company; Old Republic Insurance Company, Chicago, Illinois; Reliance Insurance Company, Irvine, California; Royal Insurance, Walnut Creek, California; Ryder Truck Rental, Inc., Littleton, Colorado; Scottsdale Insurance Company, Scotsdale, Arizona; Sentry Insurance Co., Stevens Point, Wisconsin; Strasbaugh Inc. San Luis Obispo, California; Utah Home Fire Insurance Company, Salt Lake City, Utah.

## DONALD R. KURTZ

8001 IRVINE CENTER DRIVE, SUITE 1140
**IRVINE, CALIFORNIA 92718**

Telephone: 714-753-8122
Facsimile: 714-753-8120

Business Law, Corporate Law, Estate Planning, Taxation, Bankruptcy.

**DONALD R. KURTZ**, born Caldwell, Idaho, July 25, 1955; admitted to bar, 1980, Oregon; 1981, California and U.S. Tax court; 1983, U.S. District Court, Central District of California. *Education:* Walla Walla College (B.A., 1977); University of Oregon (J.D., 1980); University of San Diego (LL.M., Taxation, 1984). *PRACTICE AREAS:* Trusts and Estates; Corporate Law; Taxation Law; Bankruptcy.

**GREGORY J. ANDERSON**, born Portland, Oregon, January 24, 1967; admitted to bar, 1992, California and U.S. District Court, Central District of California; 1993, Oregon. *Education:* Biola University (B.S., 1989); University of Oregon (J.D., 1992). *Member:* Orange County Bar Association; State Bar of California; Oregon State Bar. *PRACTICE AREAS:* Estate Planning, Probate and Trusts; Business and Corporate Law; Business Litigation; General Litigation.

## WILLIAM G. LANE

18400 VON KARMAN AVENUE
SUITE 500
**IRVINE, CALIFORNIA 92715**

Telephone: 714-474-9961
Fax: 714-474-9973

Intellectual Property Law.

**WILLIAM G. LANE**, born Oakland, California, March 12, 1937; admitted to bar, 1969, California, U.S. District Court, Northern and Central Districts of California and U.S. Court of Appeals, Ninth Circuit; registered to practice before U.S. Patent and Trademark Office. *Education:* University of California at Berkeley (B.A., 1962); Golden Gate University (J.D, 1968). *Member:* Orange County (Chairman, Business and Corporate Section, 1990; Co-Chairman, International Law Section, 1989), Federal (Orange

*(This Listing Continued)*

County Chapter, President, 1993—) and American Bar Associations; State Bar of California; Los Angeles Patent Law Association; Orange County Patent Law Association (President, 1992—); American Chemical Society. **PRACTICE AREAS:** Patents; Trademark Litigation; Intellectual Property.

# LAUGHLIN, FALBO, LEVY & MORESI LLP

A Partnership including Professional Corporations

3 PARK PLAZA, SUITE 1400
P.O. BOX 17659
**IRVINE, CALIFORNIA 92713**
Telephone: 714-251-0120
Fax: 714-251-0125
Email: lflm@lflm.com
URL: http://lflm.com/

*San Francisco, California Office:* Two Embarcadero Center, Fifth Floor. Telephone: 415-781-6676. Fax: 415-781-6823.
*Sacramento, California Office:* 106 K Street - Second Floor. Telephone: 916-441-6045. Fax: 916-441-7067.
*Redding, California Office:* 930 Executive Way, Second Floor. Telephone: 916-222-0268. Fax: 916-222-5705.
*Pasadena, California Office:* 200 South Los Robles, Suite 500. Telephone: 818-568-9700. Fax: 818-568-3905.
*Walnut Creek, California Office:* 100 Pringle Avenue, Suite 630. Telephone: 510-210-0210. Fax: 510-210-0105.
*San Jose, California Office:* 1570 The Alameda, Suite 100. Telephone: 408-286-8801. Fax: 408-286-1935.

*General Civil and Trial Practice. Workers' Compensation Defense (State and Federal), Labor Relations and Employment Discrimination.*

**GERALD R. BURKE,** born San Francisco, California, January 21, 1950; admitted to bar, 1975, California; 1978, U.S. Tax Court. *Education:* University of Oregon (B.S. in Economics and Business Administration, 1972); California Western School of Law (J.D., 1975); Georgetown University Law Center (LL.M in Labor Law, 976). Author: "Labor Relations in the Postal Service," West Federal Practice Manual, 1976. Instructor: University of San Francisco, 1978-1980; Golden Gate University, 1980; California State University, Hayward, 1981. **PRACTICE AREAS:** Workers' Compensation. **Email:** gburke@lflm.com

**JEFFREY M. ADELSON,** born Burbank, California, January 21, 1952; admitted to bar, 1977, California. *Education:* California State University at Fullerton (B.A., 1973); Western State University (J.D., 1976). **PRACTICE AREAS:** Workers' Compensation Defense; Employment Law. **Email:** jadelson@lflm.com

---

**PRISCILLA W. LLOYD,** born Red Bank, New Jersey, December 22, 1948; admitted to bar, 1979, Pennsylvania; 1992, California. *Education:* Temple University (A.B., 1992; J.D., 1979). Assistant District Attorney, 1980-1991. **PRACTICE AREAS:** Subrogation. **Email:** plloyd@lflm.com

**STEPHANIE H. PROFFITT,** born San Antonio, Texas, May 23, 1947; admitted to bar, 1981, California. *Education:* California State University at Long Beach (B.A., with high distinction, 1977); Whittier College (J.D., 1980). Phi Alpha Delta. **PRACTICE AREAS:** Workers' Compensation. **Email:** sproffitt@lflm.com

**ALICE O. BURDEN,** born Sugar Creek, Missouri, October 21, 1956; admitted to bar, 1982, California. *Education:* University of Missouri at Kansas City (B.A., 1978); Southwestern University (J.D., 1982). *Member:* Orange County Bar Association. **PRACTICE AREAS:** Workers' Compensation. **Email:** aburden@lflm.com

**MANUEL GARCIA,** born Bakersfield, California, November 29, 1963; admitted to bar, 1991, California. *Education:* California State Polytechnic University (B.A., 1986); Western State University College of Law (J.D., 1990). President, Hispanic Law Students Association, 1988-1989. **PRACTICE AREAS:** Workers' Compensation. **Email:** mgarcia@lflm.com

**CYNTHIA J. BROWN,** born Inglewood, California, December 3, 1958; admitted to bar, 1988, California. *Education:* Fullerton College (A.A., 1978); Fresno State College (B.S., 1980; M.S., 1981, M.S.); Western State University (J.D., 1986). *Member:* Orange County Bar Association. **PRACTICE AREAS:** Workers' Compensation. **Email:** cbrown@lflm.com

**TIMOTHY G. KELLER,** born Lima, Ohio, August 1, 1949; admitted to bar, 1984, California. *Education:* University of California at Berkeley (B.A., 1975); John F. Kennedy University (J.D., 1984). **PRACTICE AREAS:**
*(This Listing Continued)*

Longshoremen; Harbor Workers' Act; Workers' Compensation. **Email:** tkeller@lflm.com

**MARY-CAY GALLAGHER,** born Cleveland, Ohio, May 4, 1948; admitted to bar, 1985, California. *Education:* University of California at Riverside and Irvine (B.A., 1975); Western State University (J.D., 1984). **Email:** mgallagh@lflm.com

**DAVIL R. VASQUEZ,** born Encino, California, April 7, 1960; admitted to bar, 1989, California. *Education:* University of California at Davis (B.A., 1985); University of California at Davis (J.D., 1988). Member, Robert Banyard Inns of Court. **PRACTICE AREAS:** Subrogation Law; Insurance Defense Law; Liability Defense Law; Business Litigation. **Email:** dvasquez@lflm.com

Unless Otherwise Indicated All Partners and Associates are Members of the State Bar of California.

REPRESENTATIVE CLIENTS: AC Transit; Aetna Casualty & Surety Co.; Alameda County Schools; Allianz Insurance Co.; Alta Bates Hospital; American Hardware Mutual; American International Adjustment Co.; American International Underwriters; American Protective Services; Argonaut Insurance; Bank of America; California Casualty Insurance Co.; City of Anaheim; Continental Co.; Continental Loss Adjusting Service; Crawford and Co.; Eagle Marine Insurance Co.; Eagle Pacific Ins. Co.; Electric Mutual; Employers Insurance of Wausau; Fireman's Fund; Fremont Indemnity; GAB Business Services; Gates, McDonald & Co.; General Electric Co.; Hartford Accident & Indemnity; Hewlett-Packard; Industrial Indemnity Co.; Insurance Company of the West; Liberty Mutual Insurance; Majestic Insurance Co.; McKesson Corp.; MHG Adjusting Co.; Regents of the University of California; Royal Globe Group; Safeway Stores; San Francisco Newspaper Agency; Sequoia Hospital; Standard Oil Co.; Todd Shipyards Corp.; TOSCO; United Airlines, Inc.; U.S. Sprint Communications; USX; Wells Fargo Bank; Zenith National Insurance; Zurich-American Insurance.

(For biographical data on other personnel, see Professional Biographies at San Francisco, Sacramento, Redding, Walnut Creek, San Jose and Pasadena)

---

# LAYMAN, JONES & DYE
**IRVINE, CALIFORNIA**

(See Bryan Cave LLP)

*Administrative and General Civil Practice. Antitrust, Aviation, Banking, Computer, Corporate Financing, Corporation, Environmental, Estate Planning, Government Contracts, Immigrations, International, Labor, Probate, Products Liability, Real Estate, Securities, Taxation, Technology, Transportation, Trust and University Law; U.S. Visa Law and Practice. General Civil Trial and Appellate Practice.*

---

# LOBEL & OPERA
PROFESSIONAL CORPORATION

Established in 1987

SUITE 1100
19800 MACARTHUR BOULEVARD
P.O. BOX 19588
**IRVINE, CALIFORNIA 92713**
Telephone: 714-476-7400
Fax: 714-476-7444

*Bankruptcy, Insolvency, Corporate Reorganization and Commercial Litigation Matters.*

FIRM PROFILE: *Lobel & Opera is the successor firm to Lobel, Winthrop & Broker which was established in 1987. The Firm is the largest of its kind in Orange County specializing in bankruptcy, insolvency, business reorganization, debtor/creditor matters and related litigation. The Firm provides workout and bankruptcy representation to businesses in a variety of fields including, aerospace, apparel, architecture, automotive dealerships, computer equipment and software, construction, electronics, energy, engineering, entertainment, equipment leasing, government, health providers, hotels and motels, manufacturing, radio, real estate, restaurants, retailing and transportation. The Firm, and its predecessor, confirmed plans of reorganization in over 51 cases in the past five years.*

**WILLIAM N. LOBEL,** born Philadelphia, Pennsylvania, December 25, 1943; admitted to bar, 1969, Florida; 1970, U.S. District Court, Southern District of Florida; 1980, California and U.S. District Court, Northern, Central and Southern Districts of California. *Education:* University of Miami (B.B.A., 1966; J.D., cum laude, 1969). Member: Bar and Gavel; Wig and Robe. Member, Editorial Board, University of Miami Law Review,
*(This Listing Continued)*

**LOBEL & OPERA, PROFESSIONAL CORPORATION,** *Irvine— Continued*

1968-1969. Executive Editor, Amicus Curia. Student Instructor, Research and Writing, University of Miami Law School, 1968-1969. Law Clerk to Hon. William O. Mehrtens, U.S. District Court, Southern District of Florida, 1969. Lecturer: "Foreclosure and Repossession in California - How To Do It Right," National Business Institute, 1989; "Strategies For Dealing With Customers and Suppliers In Bankruptcy," Orange County CFO Forum, 1989. Panel Member, "Financial Concerns of the Health Care Industry," Whittier Law School Health Symposium, 1987; "Claims in Bankruptcy," National Convention of Federal Bar Association, 1993. Director, University of Miami Law Alumni Association, 1971-1972. Founder, Past President and Chairman of the Board, Current Director, Orange County Bankruptcy Forum, 1988-1991. Director, California Bankruptcy Journal, 1989-1991. Director, California Bankruptcy Journal, 1989-1991. Chairman, Liaison Committee Commercial Law and Bankruptcy Section, Orange County Bar Association, 1989-1991. Chairman, California Bankruptcy Forum State Conference, 1991-1992. Lawyer Delegate, Ninth Circuit Judicial Conference, 1991—. *PRACTICE AREAS:* Bankruptcy Law; Insolvency Law; Reorganization.

**ROBERT E. OPERA,** born Long Beach, New York, 1956; admitted to bar, 1981, California. *Education:* University of Pennsylvania (B.A., summa cum laude, 1978), Phi Beta Kappa; University of California at Los Angeles (J.D., 1981). Member, Moot Court Executive Board. Lecturer: "Fundamentals of Bankruptcy," California Continuing Education of the Bar, 1988-1989, 1991; "Chapter 11 Plan Confirmation Issues," Orange County Bar Association, Bankruptcy Section; "Current Issues in Bankruptcy," 1996 Annual Orange County Bar Association Seminar. Member, Judicial Liaison Committee on Revision of Local Bankruptcy Rules. Member, Editorial Board, California Bankruptcy Journal, 1989-1990. *Member:* Los Angeles County and Orange County (Member, Commercial Law and Bankruptcy Section) Bar Associations. *PRACTICE AREAS:* Reorganization; Bankruptcy Law.

**ALAN J. FRIEDMAN,** born Los Angeles, California, March 26, 1961; admitted to bar, 1987, California and U.S. District Court, Central District of California; 1988, U.S. Court of Appeals, Ninth Circuit, U.S. District Court, Northern and Southern Districts of California. *Education:* University of California at San Diego (B.A., 1983); Hastings College of the Law, University of California (J.D., cum laude, 1987). Phi Delta Phi. Recipient, American Jurisprudence Award in Criminal Law. Extern, United States District Court, Honorable Richard A. Gadbois, Jr. *Member:* Orange County (Member, Commercial Section) and American (Commercial Section) Bar Associations. *PRACTICE AREAS:* Bankruptcy Law; Reorganization.

**PAMELA Z. KARGER,** born LaPorte, Indiana, December 20, 1953; admitted to bar, 1986, Texas; 1987, Illinois; 1988, U.S. District Court, Northern District of Illinois; 1990, California and U.S. District Court, Central and Southern Districts of California. *Education:* Indiana University (B.S., 1975); South Texas College of Law (J.D., 1986). Law Clerk, to Hon. John J. Wilson, U.S. Bankruptcy Judge, 1988-1990. *Member:* Orange County Bar Association; Orange County Bankruptcy Forum; Bankruptcy Mediation Program for Central District of California. *PRACTICE AREAS:* Bankruptcy Law; Reorganization.

**CHERYL A. SKIGIN,** born Cleveland, Ohio, June 8, 1951; admitted to bar, 1976, California; 1977, Nevada; 1978, District of Columbia. *Education:* Johns Hopkins University (B.A., 1973) Phi Beta Kappa; Emory University (J.D., with distinction, 1976). Order of the Coif. *Member:* Washoe County, Orange County and Federal Bar Associations; State Bar of California; District of Columbia Bar; State Bar of Nevada; Orange County Bankruptcy Forum; California Women Lawyers Association. *PRACTICE AREAS:* Bankruptcy.

**TAVI CLAIRE STANLEY,** born New York, N.Y., March 10, 1966; admitted to bar, 1993, California and U.S. District Court, District of California; 1995, U.S. District Court, Northern and Southern Districts of California. *Education:* University of California-Irvine (B.A., cum laude, 1989); University of Southern California (J.D., 1993). Senior Editor, Southern California Interdisciplinary Law Journal and Major Tax Planning Journal. Recipient, American Jurisprudence Award in Real Property. Law Clerk to the Honorable John E. Ryan, U.S. Bankruptcy Judge, Central District of California, 1993-1994. Contributor, "The New Value Defense in Preference Actions," Orange County Bar Association, Commercial Law and Bankruptcy Section; Contributor, "Bankruptcy Litigation: A Workshop in Trial Strategy," Orange County Bankruptcy Forum Special Projects Committee.

*(This Listing Continued)*

*Member:* Orange County and American Bar Associations; State Bar of California; Orange County Bankruptcy Forum. *PRACTICE AREAS:* Bankruptcy Law; Reorganization.

**METINER G. KIMEL,** born Philadelphia, Pennsylvania, October 23, 1958; admitted to bar, 1991, Washington; 1993, California; 1994, U.S. District Court, Eastern and Western Districts of Washington; 1995, U.S. District Court, Central and Southern Districts of California. *Education:* University of Pennsylvania (B.A., 1980); Baruch College (M.B.A., in Accounting, 1987); University of Washington (J.D., 1991); New York University (LL.M., in Taxation, 1995). Law Clerk to the Hon. John F. Ryan, U.S. Bankruptcy Court, Central District of California, 1991-1992 and to the Hon. John A. Rossmeissl, U.S. Bankruptcy Court, Eastern District of Washington, 1992-1994. Certified Public Accountant, New York, 1987, Washington, 1988. *Member:* Washington State Bar Association; State Bar of California; American Institute of Certified Public Accountants.

**EDWARD P. CHRISTIAN,** born Lakewood, California, June 23, 1965; admitted to bar, 1995, California. *Education:* University of California (B.A., 1987); University of Southern California (J.D., 1995). Commercial Pilot License, 1990. [Lt., U.S. Navy, Naval Aviator, 1987-1991]. *PRACTICE AREAS:* Insolvency Law; Reorganization; Workouts.

**ROBERT J. MROFKA,** born South Bend, Indiana, July 28, 1951; admitted to bar, 1986, Texas; 1991, California. *Education:* Purdue University (B.S.Ch.E., 1973); The University of Chicago Law School (J.D., with honors, 1986). *Member:* State Bar of California; State Bar of Texas; American Bankruptcy Institute.

**HAMID R. RAFATJOO,** born Tehran, Iran, June 8, 1970; admitted to bar, 1995, California. *Education:* University of California at Irvine (B.A., cum laude, 1992); Loyola Marymount University (J.D., 1995). Phi Alpha Delta (Treasurer, 1992-1994); Golden Key National Honor Society. Law Clerk to the Hon. John E. Ryan, U.S. Bankruptcy Court, 1995-1996. Law Clerk to the Hon. James N. Barr, Hon. Lynne Riddle, Hon. John E. Ryan, Hon. John J. Wilson, U.S. Bankruptcy Court, Central District of California, 1996. *Member:* Orange County (Member, Programs Committee, Commercial Law and Bankruptcy Section, 1995-1996) and American Bar Associations; Orange County Bankruptcy Forum. *LANGUAGES:* Farsi and French. *PRACTICE AREAS:* Reorganization; Creditors' Rights; Litigation.

---

## MAHER, LEE & GODDARD, LLP
*18500 VON KARMAN AVENUE, SUITE 700*
**IRVINE, CALIFORNIA 92715**
Telephone: 714-721-7555
Facsimile: 714-721-7444

*General Civil and Business Practice, Environmental Law, Employment Law, Insurance Coverage, Trial and Appellate Practice.*

**MICHAEL K. MAHER,** born Long Branch, New Jersey, July 19, 1949; admitted to bar, 1975, California and U.S. District Court, Central District of California; 1978, U.S. District Court, f California, Eastern District of California; 1980, U.S. Court of Appeals, Ninth Circuit; 1987, U.S. District Court, Northern and Southern Districts of California; 1989, U.S. Tax Court and U.S. Court of International Trade; 1991, U.S. District Court, District of Arizona. *Education:* University of Dayton (B.A., 1971); Loyola University of Los Angeles (J.D., cum laude, 1975). Member, St. Thomas More Law Honor Society. *Member:* Los Angeles County, Orange County and American Bar Associations; State Bar of California; Association of Business Trial Lawyers. *PRACTICE AREAS:* Business Law; Civil Practice; Employment Law; Insurance; General Practice.

**RAYMOND A. LEE,** born Mitchell Air Force Base, Long Island, New York, August 23, 1951; admitted to bar, 1981, California; 1982, U.S. Tax Court. *Education:* University of Miami (B.A., magna cum laude, 1976); University of Florida School of Law (J.D., with honors, 1980). *Member:* State Bar of California. [Capt., U.S. Army, 1970-1975]. *PRACTICE AREAS:* Corporate Law; Corporate (Corporation) Financing Law; Business Acquisitions Law; Real Estate (Property) Law.

**WILLIAM A. GODDARD, IV,** born Los Angeles, California, March 20, 1959; admitted to bar, 1987, California. *Education:* University of California at Los Angeles (B.A., 1981); Hastings College of Law, University of California (J.D, 1984). Phi Delta Phi. *Member:* Los Angeles County and American Bar Associations; The State Bar of California. *PRACTICE AREAS:* Federal Income Tax Law and California Income; Franchise and ad valorem Property Tax Law; Corporate; Partnership; Real Estate and International Tax Planning.

*(This Listing Continued)*

**CYNTHIA R. MAHER,** born La Habra, California, November 30, 1958; admitted to bar, 1982, California. *Education:* University of California at Los Angeles (B.A., 1979); Loyola University of Los Angeles (J.D., 1982). Member, Loyola Law Review, 1980-1981. Author: "The Sixth Amendment Right to Present a Defense," 14 Loyola Law Review 571, 1981; "Bail," 14 Loyola Law Review 618, 1981. *Member:* Los Angeles County, Orange County and American Bar Associations; State Bar of California. *PRACTICE AREAS:* Environmental Law; Real Estate Litigation; Land Use; Construction Litigation; Labor Law.

**SHERMAN O. HALSTEAD, JR.,** born Hopewell, Virginia, June 17, 1960; admitted to bar, 1985, Texas and U.S. District Court, Southern District of Texas; 1986, U.S. District Court, Western District of Texas; 1988, California. *Education:* University of Virginia (B.A., with highest distinction, 1982); Stanford University (J.D., 1985). Phi Beta Kappa. *Member:* State Bar of California; State Bar of Texas; American Bar Association.

**MAUREEN M. ALPIN,** born Sheridan, Wyoming, November 29, 1965; admitted to bar, 1992, California. *Education:* University of Wyoming (B.S., 1987); U.S. International University (M.A., 1988); McGeorge School of Law (J.D., 1992). *Member:* Orange County (Member: Real Property Law Section; Business Law Section; Employment Law Section) and Riverside County Bar Associations; State Bar of California. *PRACTICE AREAS:* Financial Institutions Law; Transactions; Business Litigation; Construction Litigation; Commercial Law; Employment Law.

---

## GUY E. MAILLY

7700 IRVINE CENTER DRIVE
**IRVINE, CALIFORNIA 92618**
*Telephone: 714-753-1676*

*General Practice.*

**GUY E. MAILLY,** born Cincinnati, Ohio, August 21, 1954; admitted to bar, 1983, Colorado; 1987, Texas; 1988, California. *Education:* Beloit College; University of Chicago (A.B., with honors, 1980); University of Texas (J.D., 1983). *Member:* State Bar of Texas; State Bar of California.

---

## MALCOLM, CISNEROS & HOUSER

A Partnership including a Professional Corporation

JAMBOREE CENTER
5 PARK PLAZA, SUITE 830
**IRVINE, CALIFORNIA 92714**
*Telephone: 714-252-9400*
*Telecopier: 714-252-1032*

*San Bernardino, California Office:* 290 North "D" Street, Suite 723. 92401. Telephone: 909-884-6882. Fax: 909-884-8189.

*Commercial and Business Litigation in the Bankruptcy, District and State Courts. Creditors' Rights and Trustee Representation.*

### MEMBERS OF FIRM

**WILLIAM G. MALCOLM, (A PROFESSIONAL CORPORATION),** born Palo Alto, California, December 22, 1959; admitted to bar, 1987, California. *Education:* University of Santa Clara (B.Sc., 1982; J.D., 1985); Loyola Marymount University. Senior Law Clerk to the Honorable Richard Mednick, United States Bankruptcy Judge for the Central District of California, Los Angeles Division and to the Honorable John E. Ryan, U.S. Bankruptcy Judge, Central District of California, Santa Ana Division. *Member:* Orange County Bar Association; State Bar of California; Orange County Bankruptcy Forum (Member, Special Projects Committee); American Bankruptcy Institute. *PRACTICE AREAS:* Bankruptcy; Reorganization; Creditors Rights; Bankruptcy Court Litigation.

**ARTURO M. CISNEROS,** born San Bernardino, California, October 23, 1959; admitted to bar, 1985, California. *Education:* University of California at Los Angeles (B.A., 1981; J.D., 1984). Law Clerk to The Honorable William J. Lasarow, U.S. Bankruptcy Chief Judge, Central District of California, Los Angeles Division and The Honorable John J. Wilson, U.S. Bankruptcy Judge, Central District of California, San Bernardino Division. U.S. Central District Bankruptcy Trustee Panel Member, San Bernardino. *Member:* San Bernardino County, Orange County, Federal and American Bar Associations; State Bar of California; Hispanic Bar Association (President, 1993); Los Angeles County Bankruptcy Forum; Inland Empire Bankruptcy Forum (Vice-President); American Inns of Court. *PRACTICE AREAS:* Bankruptcy; Creditor and Trustee Representation.

*(This Listing Continued)*

**ERIC D. HOUSER,** born St. Louis, Missouri, April 30, 1962; admitted to bar, 1987, California. *Education:* University of California at San Diego (B.A., 1984); University of San Diego (J.D., 1987). Senior Editor, The Journal of Contemporary Legal Issues, 1986-1987. Staff Member/Contributor, "California Regulatory Law Reporter," Vols. 5-6, 1985-1987. Co-Author: "Bankruptcy and Complex Civil Litigation: Practice and Procedures, California Continuing Education of the Bar, Program on Advocacy and Management in Complex Litigation, 1991 Trial Practice Institute." *Member:* Orange County (Member, Sections on: Commercial Law and Bankruptcy; Business Litigation) and Federal Bar Associations; State Bar of California (Orange County Delegate Member, Resolutions Committee); Orange County Bankruptcy Forum. *PRACTICE AREAS:* Commercial and Business Litigation; Bankruptcy.

### ASSOCIATES

**SHAWN R. MILLER,** born New York, N.Y., January 6, 1966; admitted to bar, 1993, California. *Education:* University of California, San Diego (B.A. in Political Science and History, 1987); American University (M.A. in International Affairs, 1990); Southwestern University School of Law (J.D., 1992). Law Clerk to the Honorable Calvin K. Ashland, U.S. Bankruptcy Chief Judge, Central District of California. *Member:* Orange County, Los Angeles County and American Bar Associations; State Bar of California; Orange County Bankruptcy Forum (Member, Bankruptcy Local Rules Bench/Bar Committee); Los Angeles County Bankruptcy Forum. *LANGUAGES:* Italian and Spanish. *PRACTICE AREAS:* Bankruptcy; Creditors Rights; Commercial Litigation.

**MICHAEL R. BROOKS,** born Minot, North Dakota, July 18, 1966; admitted to bar, 1993, California. *Education:* California State University, Long Beach (B.S. in Economics, cum laude, 1990); University of Southern California Law Center (J.D., 1993). Extern to the Honorable John E. Ryan, U.S. Bankruptcy Court, Central District of California. *Member:* Orange County Bar Association (Member, Resolution Committee); State Bar of California (Orange County Delegate); Orange County Bankruptcy Forum. *LANGUAGES:* French. *PRACTICE AREAS:* Commercial Litigation; Bankruptcy.

**YVONNE RAMIREZ,** born Sacramento, California, May 25, 1966; admitted to bar, 1992, Texas and U.S. District Court, Northern District of Texas; 1993, California and U.S. District Court, Central District of California; 1994, U.S. District Court, Southern, Eastern and Northern Districts of California. *Education:* University of Texas at Austin (B.A., 1988; J.D., 1991). Phi Eta Sigma. Briefing Attorney, The Honorable Lawrence E. Meyers, Court of Appeals, Second District of Texas, 1991-1992. Briefing Intern, The Honorable Raul Gonzalez, The Supreme Court of Texas, 1991. *Member:* Orange County (Member, Commercial Law and Bankruptcy Section), Riverside County and San Bernardino Bar Associations; State Bar of Texas; State Bar of California; Association of Southern California Defense Counsel; Hispanic Bar Association; Orange County Bankruptcy Forum; Peter M. Elliot Inns of Court. *PRACTICE AREAS:* Bankruptcy; Creditors Rights; Commercial Litigation.

**DONNA A. GOLEM,** born Whittier, California, March 1, 1963; admitted to bar, 1996, California. *Education:* University of California, Los Angeles (B.A., 1985); Loyola Law School (J.D., 1991). Staff Member, Loyola of Los Angeles Law Review, 1989-1990. Member, St. Thomas Moore Law Honor Society. Author: Note, "The Public Trust Doctrine Unprecedentedly Gains New Ground in Phillips Petroleum v. Mississippi," 22 Loy L.A.L. 1319 (1989). Judicial Extern to the Honorable Kathleen T. Lax, U.S. Bankruptcy Court, Central District of California. *Member:* Orange County Bar Association; State Bar of California. *PRACTICE AREAS:* Commercial and Business Litigation; Bankruptcy.

**ZACHARY J. ZAHAREK,** born Arcadia, California, December 30, 1968; admitted to bar, 1995, California. *Education:* University of Santa Clara (B.S., 1991; J.D., 1994; M.B.A., Argibusiness, 1994). Member of the University of California J.D./M.B.A. Association. Law Clerk to Honorable Timothy McCoy, Superior Court of Los Angeles County. *Member:* Orange County and San Bernardino County Bar Associations; State Bar of California. *PRACTICE AREAS:* Bankruptcy; Creditors Rights; Commercial Litigation.

**KUSHAL S. BHAKTA,** born Surat, India, June 7, 1970; admitted to bar, 1996, California. *Education:* University of California, Los Angeles (B.A., 1992); University of California, Hastings College of Law (J.D., 1995). Extern to the Honorable John E. Ryan, U.S. Bankruptcy Court, Central District of California. *Member:* Orange County Bar Association; State Bar of California. *PRACTICE AREAS:* Bankruptcy; Creditor's Rights; Commercial Litigation.

*(This Listing Continued)*

## MALCOLM, CISNEROS & HOUSER, Irvine—Continued

REPRESENTATIVE CLIENTS: Great Western Bank; Ocwen Federal Bank & Trust; Bank of America; Aames Home Loan; EMC Mortgage Corp.; Southern Pacific Thrift & Loan; Ingram Micro; Freddie Mac; Home Savings of America; American Savings Bank; Southern California Federal Savings & Loan; First Nationwide Bank; Countrywide; First Plus Financial; Omni Bank.

## MALPASS & GENTILE

19800 MACARTHUR BOULEVARD
SUITE 350
IRVINE, CALIFORNIA 92715
Telephone: 714-553-2000
Facsimile: 714-553-2080

*Bankruptcy, Corporate Reorganization, Commercial, Banking and Business Law. Business, Real Estate and Bankruptcy Litigation and Appeals.*

FIRM PROFILE: *Malpass & Gentile dedicated themselves to providing the highest quality legal representation. The firm provides a wide range of legal services with local, state and Canada. We believe we have retained our original commitment while benefitting for those less & experience.*

### MEMBERS OF FIRM

**T. EDWARD MALPASS,** born Petoskey, Michigan, March 14, 1953; admitted to bar, 1977, Colorado; 1978, Michigan; 1982, Illinois; 1983, California; 1986, U.S. Court of Appeals, Ninth Circuit. *Education:* University of Colorado at Boulder (B.A., 1974; J.D., 1977). Phi Delta Phi. Author: "A Bankruptcy Debtor's Right to Turnover of Property Held by Creditors: A Perspective on Sections 542 and 543 of the Bankruptcy Code," 88 Commercial Law Journal 242, 1983; "Employment and Compensation of Counsel for the Debtor When the Debtor is Not in Possession," Clark, Boardman Callaghan, Annual Survey of Bankruptcy Law, p. 339, 1991. Law Clerk to the Honorable David Patton, U.S. Bankruptcy Court, Detroit, Michigan, 1980-1981. *Member:* Orange County (Chair, Commercial Law and Bankruptcy Section, 1988), Federal (Secretary, 1991) and American (Member, Chapter 11 Subcommittee, Business Law Section) Bar Associations; State Bar of California; American Bankruptcy Institute. (Certified Specialist, Personal and Small Business Bankruptcy Law, The State Bar of California Board of Legal Specialization) (Certified Specialist, Business Bankruptcy Law, American Bankruptcy Board of Certification). **PRACTICE AREAS:** Bankruptcy; Business and Commercial Litigation.

**SUSAN E. GENTILE,** born Washington, D.C., September 28, 1959; admitted to bar, 1985, California, U.S. District Court, Central and Southern Districts of California and U.S. Court of Appeals, Ninth Circuit; 1995, Colorado. *Education:* University of California at Los Angeles (B.A., 1981); Loyola Law School (J.D., 1985). Phi Alpha Delta. Member, Scott Moot Court Honors Board, 1983-1985. *Member:* Orange County, Colorado and American Bar Associations; State Bar of California; Orange County Bankruptcy Forum. **PRACTICE AREAS:** Banking Law; Bankruptcy Litigation.

**MELISSA C. ALEXANDER,** born St. Paul, Minnesota, December 25, 1965; admitted to bar, 1992, California and U.S. District Court, Central District of California. *Education:* University of California, Berkeley (B.A., 1987); University of Southern California (J.D., 1991). *Member:* Orange County and Los Angeles County Bar Associations; State Bar of California; Orange County Women Lawyers Association; Orange County Bankruptcy Women Lawyers; Orange County Barristers Association (Member, Board of Directors, 1995-1996); Orange County Bankruptcy Forum. **LANGUAGES:** French. **PRACTICE AREAS:** Bankruptcy; Business Litigation.

### LEGAL SUPPORT PERSONNEL

**TAMMY L. VALVERDE**

## MANNING, MARDER & WOLFE

SUITE 1450
19800 MACARTHUR BOULEVARD
IRVINE, CALIFORNIA 92715
Telephone: 714-556-0552
Email: rfs@mmw.com
URL: http://www.mmw.com

*Los Angeles, California Office:* 45th Floor at First Interstate Tower, 707 Wilshire Boulevard. Telephone: 213-624-6900. Fax: 213-624-6999.
*San Diego, California Office:* 964 Fifth Avenue, Suite 214. Telephone: 619-699-5933.

*(This Listing Continued)*

CAA344B

*Insurance Defense, Police Civil Liability, General Civil Litigation, Private Security Litigation, Corporate Law, Business Formation and Securities Offerings, Employment Litigation, Entertainment Law, Workers' Compensation Defense, Professional Liability (Medical Malpractice, Legal Malpractice, Construction Malpractice), Appellate Law, Health Law, Bad Faith, Insurance Coverage, Loss Prevention and Risk Management.*

(For complete biographical data on all personnel, see Professional Biographies at Los Angeles)

## RALPH G. MARTINEZ

8001 IRVINE CENTER DRIVE, #1550
IRVINE, CALIFORNIA 92618
Telephone: 714-450-0123
Fax: 714-753-8069

*Business Litigation, Real Estate Litigation and Personal Injury.*

**RALPH G. MARTINEZ,** born Culver City, California, January 27, 1953; admitted to bar, 1978, California and U.S. District Court, Southern District of California; 1986, U.S. Supreme Court; 1988, U.S. District Court, Eastern District of California; 1989, U.S. District Court, Central District of California. *Education:* Azusa Pacific College (B.A., cum laude, 1975); California Western School of Law (J.D., 1978). Executive Editor, California Western International Law Journal, 1977-1978. Author: "Fifth Amendment and International Comity As A Basis for Avoiding Choice Between Conflicting Demands of Two Sovereigns; A Critical Look at United States v. Field," 8 California Western International Law Journal 368, 1978. Former Adjunct Professor of Communication, Bakersfield Community College. Member, Toastmasters International. *Member:* Orange County Bar Association; State Bar of California; Orange County Trial Lawyers Association (Member, Board of Directors, 1996—); Christian Legal Society. **PRACTICE AREAS:** Business Litigation; Real Estate Litigation; Personal Injury.

## ANDREW K. MAUTHE

18500 VON KARMAN, SUITE 700
IRVINE, CALIFORNIA 92612-0504
Telephone: 714-833-7035
Fax: 714-721-7444
Email: amauthe@aol.com

*Bankruptcy and Creditors Rights, Insolvency and Reorganization.*

**ANDREW K. MAUTHE,** born Pasadena, California, June 11, 1943; admitted to bar, 1982, California. *Education:* University of California at Los Angeles (A.B., 1966); California State University at Long Beach (M.A., 1972); University of Southern California (J.D., 1982). Member, University of Southern California Law Review, 1980-1982. *Member:* Orange County (Member, Commercial Law Section), and Federal (Director, Orange County Chapter, 1986-1989; President, 1991-1992) Bar Associations; State Bar of California.

## McKENNA & STAHL

2603 MAIN STREET, SUITE 1010
IRVINE, CALIFORNIA 92614-6232
Telephone: 714-752-2800
Facsimile: 714-752-6723

*Corporations, Corporate Finance And Securities, Real Estate, Real Estate Finance, Land Use, Partnerships, Limited Liability Companies and Taxation.*

**CHARLES A. MCKENNA, JR.,** born Green Bay, Wisconsin, March 10, 1938; admitted to bar, 1974, California. *Education:* Marquette University (A.B., 1960); The American University (M.A., 1969); University of Virginia (J.D., 1974). Chairman, Moot Court Board. **PRACTICE AREAS:** Real Estate; Real Estate Finance.

**HARRY S. STAHL,** born East Orange, New Jersey, November 25, 1943; admitted to bar, 1973, California. *Education:* College of the Holy Cross (B.S., 1965); Northeastern University (M.S., 1967); The Washington College of Law, of The American University (J.D., 1972). Member of Staff, Securities and Exchange Commission, 1970-1972. **PRACTICE AREAS:** Corporate Law; Securities Law.

*(This Listing Continued)*

## PROFESSIONAL BIOGRAPHIES

### CALIFORNIA—IRVINE

*OF COUNSEL*

**CHRISTOPHER E. CALL,** born Long Beach, California. November 29, 1951; admitted to bar, 1976, California; 1978, District of Columbia. *Education:* University of Southern California (B.A., 1973); University of California at Berkley (J.D., 1976). Instructor, Real Estate and Tax Law, University of California at Irvine, School of Business, 1989-1992. *PRACTICE AREAS:* Securities; Real Estate.

---

### CHRISTOPHER B. MEARS, A P.C.

OLD TOWN IRVINE
14988 SAND CANYON AVENUE, SUITE 1-8
**IRVINE, CALIFORNIA 92618**
Telephone: 714-551-2250
Fax: 714-551-0887
Email: CMEARS1031@AOL.COM

*General Tort Litigation. Medical and Legal Malpractice, Insurance, Negligence, Civil Rights, Personal Injury, Government, Products Liability and Wrongful Termination.*

**CHRISTOPHER B. MEARS,** born Santa Ana, California, August 9, 1951; admitted to bar, 1982, California; U.S. District Court, Central and Eastern Districts of California; U.S. Court of Appeals, Ninth Circuit. *Education:* California State University at Fullerton (B.A., with honors, 1975); Western State University (J.D., 1981). Member, Western State University Law Review, 1980-1981. Member, Western State University Hall of Fame. OCTLA Trial Lawyer of The Year, 1995. *Member:* Orange County, Federal and American Bar Associations; State Bar of California; Orange County Trial Lawyers Association (Member, Board of Directors); California Trial Lawyers Association; American Board of Trial Advocates.

---

### MESERVE, MUMPER & HUGHES

A Partnership
Established in 1889

2301 DUPONT DRIVE, SUITE 410
**IRVINE, CALIFORNIA 92612**
Telephone: 714-474-8995
Telecopier: 714-975-1065
Email: mmhir@ix.netcom.com

Los Angeles, California Office: 555 South Flower Street, 18th Floor. Telephone: 213-620-0300. Telecopier: 213-625-1930.
San Diego, California Office: 701 "B" Street, Suite 1080. Telephone: 619-237-0500. Telecopier: 619-237-0073.

*General Civil and Trial Practice in all State and Federal Courts. Banking, Corporate, Real Estate, Labor, Life Insurance, Probate, Estate Planning, Family Law and Bankruptcy.*

*MEMBERS OF FIRM*

**EDWIN A. MESERVE** (1863-1955).

**SHIRLEY E. MESERVE** (1889-1959).

**HEWLINGS MUMPER** (1889-1968).

**CLIFFORD E. HUGHES** (1894-1981).

**BERNARD A. LECKIE,** born Los Angeles, California, December 10, 1932; admitted to bar, 1960, California; 1979, U.S. Supreme Court and U.S. Court of Appeals, 9th Circuit. *Education:* University of Southern California (B.S., 1957; LL.B., 1959). Phi Delta Phi. Recipient, Law Week Award, University of Southern California Law School, for highest scholastic progress in senior year, 1959. Member, National Panel of Arbitrators, American Arbitration Association. Weekly Chairman for Indigent Defense Panel, 1964-1967. Examiner for State Bar, 1967-1968. Examiner in disciplinary proceedings, 1967-1968; Member, Disciplinary Committee #16, 1969-1971 and Chairman, 1972-1973; Local Administrative Committee #2, 1973-1980; Member and Chairman, Preliminary Investigation Panel #7, 1978-1980, State Bar of California. Special Master, Orange County, 1981—. *Member:* Orange County, Los Angeles County and American Bar Associations; The Association of Trial Lawyers of America; American Judicature Society; California Trial Lawyers Association; Los Angeles Trial Lawyers Association; Association of Deputy District Attorneys of Los Angeles County; Orange County Trial Lawyers Association.

**DAVID R. EICHTEN,** born New Ulm, Minnesota, November 8, 1948; admitted to bar, 1973, California, U.S. District Court, Southern District of California and U.S. Supreme Court; 1984, Minnesota. *Education:* University of Minnesota (B.A., cum laude, 1970); University of San Diego (J.D., cum laude, 1973).

**TIMOTHY A. GRAVITT,** born Los Angeles, California, January 28, 1957; admitted to bar, 1984, California; 1985, U.S. District Court, Central District of California and U.S. Court of Appeals, Ninth Circuit. *Education:* University of California at San Diego (B.A., 1981) Hastings College of Law, University of California (J.D., 1984). *Member:* Orange County, San Diego County, Los Angeles County and American Bar Associations.

**E. AVERY CRARY,** born 1939; admitted to bar, 1968, California. *Education:* Georgetown University (B.S., 1961); Southwestern University (LL.B., 1967). Phi Delta Phi. *Member:* Los Angeles County, Orange County and American Bar Associations.

**LISA A. ROQUEMORE,** born Ridgecrest, California, July 10, 1962; admitted to bar, 1989, California and U.S. District Court, Central District of California; 1992, U.S. District Court, Southern and Northern Districts of California; 1994, U.S. Court of Appeals, Ninth Circuit; 1996, U.S. District Court, Eastern District of California; U.S. Supreme Court. *Education:* San Diego State University (B.A., with distinction in Psychology, 1985); California Western School of Law (J.D., 1988). Sigma Nu Phi. William P. Gray Legion Lex Inns of Court. Intern to Hon. Louise DeCarl Malugen, U.S. Bankruptcy Judge, Southern District of California. Lecturer: Ethics in Bankruptcy, Orange County Bankruptcy Forum, June 12, 1993 (Participant and Contributor); The Most Important Thing You Need to Know About Bankruptcy, Orange County Women Lawyers Association, September 12, 1994 (Panel Member and General Bankruptcy Lectures to Practitioners). Member, Orange County Bankruptcy Forum. *Member:* Orange County (Publicity Chairperson, Commercial Law and Bankruptcy Section, 1995, 1996) and Federal (Orange County Section) Bar Associations; Orange County Bankruptcy Forum. *PRACTICE AREAS:* Bankruptcy; Commercial and Business Litigation.

*OF COUNSEL*

**J. ROBERT MESERVE,** born 1916; admitted to bar, 1942, California. *Education:* University of California (A.B., 1938); Hastings College of Law (LL.B., 1941). Phi Delta Phi. *Member:* Orange County, Los Angeles County and American Bar Associations; American College of Trust and Estate Counsel; International Academy of Estate and Trust Law.

**GARY V. SPENCER,** born Vernon, Texas, September 2, 1944; admitted to bar, 1970, California and U.S. District Court, Central District of California; 1976, U.S. District Court, Southern District of California; 1989, U.S. District Court, Eastern District of California. *Education:* University of Southern California (B.A., cum laude, 1966); Boalt Hall School of Law, University of California (J.D., 1969). Instructor, La Verne College of Law, 1972-1974. *Member:* San Bernardino County, San Bernardino County West End (Member, Board of Directors, 1972-1974), Orange County and American Bar Associations; California Trial Lawyers Association; Orange County Trial Lawyers Association (Member, Board of Directors, 1980-1981); Society of Professionals in Dispute Resolution; Southern California Mediation Association. *PRACTICE AREAS:* Construction Law; Mediation; Trademark Licensing; General Business.

*ASSOCIATES*

**JOSEPH B. MCGINLEY,** born Lynwood, California, December 18, 1955; admitted to bar, 1982, California, U.S. Court of Appeals, Ninth Circuit and U.S. District Court, Central District of California; 1983, U.S. District Court, Northern and Southern Districts of California. *Education:* University of Southern California (A.B., 1979; J.D., 1982). Quarter Finalist, Hale Moot Court Honors Program, 1980-1981. Publications Editor, Major Tax Planning Journal, Volume 33, 1981. Notes and Articles Editor, Major Tax Planning Journal, Volume 34, 1981-1982. Publications Editor, Computer Law Journal, 1981-1982. Board of Directors, 1989-1990, Legion Lex. Legion Lex, Inns of Court. Law Clerk Extern for Justice Lynn Compton, California Court of Appeals, Second District, 1981. *Member:* Orange County Bar Association.

**WENDY C. SATULOFF,** born Van Nuys, California, August 5, 1966; admitted to bar, 1992, California, U.S. District Court, Central District of California and U.S. Court of Appeals, Ninth Circuit; 1994, U.S. District Court, Southern District of California; 1996, U.S. District Court, Eastern District of California. *Education:* University of California at Los Angeles (B.A., 1988); Loyola Law School of Los Angeles (J.D., 1992). *Member:* Orange County (Commercial Law and Bankruptcy Section; Publicity Committee, Commercial Law and Bankruptcy Section; Law and Technology Committee) and American Bar Associations; Orange County Bankruptcy Forum; Peter M. Elliot Inn of Court. *PRACTICE AREAS:* Bankruptcy.

*(This Listing Continued)*

MESERVE, MUMPER & HUGHES, Irvine—Continued

All Members and Associates of the Firm are Members of the State Bar of California.

(For Biographical Data of all Firm Personnel, see Los Angeles, California Professional Biographies).

## MEUERS, DRESSLER & KEATON, LLP
Established in 1989
17620 FITCH STREET
IRVINE, CALIFORNIA 92614
Telephone: 714-260-6665
Fax: 714-260-6666

*Naples, Florida Office:* 2590 Golden Gate Parkway, Suite 109. telephone: 941-649-6100. Fax: 941-649-5414.

*Perishable Agricultural Commodities Act, Agricultural Law, Bankruptcy and Creditors' Rights, Commercial Law and Litigation, Employment Law.*

FIRM PROFILE: *The firm was founded in 1989 to provide legal services to the fresh and frozen produce industry. Meuers, Dressler & Keaton is one of the largest national firms that limits its practice to representing the produce industry. Our services include: enforcing produce sellers' rights under the Perishable Agricultural Commodities Act (PACA) trust provisions in all federal district and bankruptcy courts; litigating complex contractual disputes in administrative proceedings before the USDA, Ag Canada and civil courts; defense of PACA regulatory matters; drafting commercial documents; and employment law. The firm has offices in Naples, Florida and Irvine, California.*

**DONALD G. DRESSLER,** born Lyons, Kansas, October 25, 1945; admitted to bar, 1970, California and U.S. District Court, Central District of California. *Education:* Kansas State University (B.A., 1996); Stanford University (J.D., 1969). Phi Delta Phi. Recipient, Association Executive of the Year, Southern California Society of Association Executives, 1994. Author, "Surprise, You May Be a Farm Labor Contractor," Agricultural Law Journal, 1980. Instructor, Employment Law, University of California at Irvine Extension, 1990—. Member, American Society of Association Executives, 1977—. Chairman, Financial Commission, City of Irvine, 1993—. *Member:* State Bar of California. **PRACTICE AREAS:** Labor and Employment; Corporate Law.

**DOUGLAS B. KERR,** born New Castle, Pennsylvania, October 26, 1956; admitted to bar, 1983, California; 1995, Arizona and U.S. District Court, District of Arizona. *Education:* University of California at Irvine (B.A., 1979); McGeorge School of Law, University of the Pacific (J.D., 1983). Member, National Moot Court Honors Board. President, Village of Westpark, 1987-1995. *Member:* Orange County Bar Association (Member, Labor Law Section, 1983-1984); State Bar of California. **PRACTICE AREAS:** Labor and Employment Law; Perishable Commodities; Corporate Law; ERISA.

REPRESENTATIVE CLIENTS: Adams Brothers Produce Co., Inc.; Collier Enterprises; Coloma Frozen Foods, Inc.; Dean Foods Vegetable Company; Dole Fresh Vegetables Company; Gargiulo, L.P.; Giumarra Vineyards Corp.; Inn Foods Incorporated; Tom Lange Company, Inc.; Mills Distributing Co.; Naturipe Berry Growers; NuChief Sales, Inc.; Plantation Produce Co.; Roland Marketing, Inc.; Six L's Packing Company, Inc.; Turbana Corporation; Western Growers Association; Wholesale Produce Supply Co., Inc.; Zellwin Farms, Inc.

## MORRISON & FOERSTER LLP
Established in 1883
TWELFTH FLOOR, 19900 MACARTHUR BOULEVARD
IRVINE, CALIFORNIA 92715-2445
Telephone: 714-251-7500
Facsimile: 714-251-0900
URL: http://www.mofo.com

*Other offices located in:* San Francisco, Los Angeles, New York, Washington, D.C., London, Brussels, Hong Kong, Tokyo, Sacramento, Palo Alto, Walnut Creek and Denver.

FIRM PROFILE: *Morrison & Foerster is one of the world's largest international law firms with over 500 lawyers in 13 offices worldwide. The firm's legal practice encompasses every major area of commercial law, including corporate finance, project finance, institutional lending, financial services, real estate, environmental and land use planning, mining and natural resources, multimedia, intellectual property, energy, communications, computer technology, insurance, alternative dispute resolution, product liability, bankruptcy and workouts, estate planning, probate, trust administration, financial transactions, labor and employment, immigration, civil, criminal and securities litigation, entertainment and sports, food and beverage, health care, hotel and resort, antitrust, international business, international litigation and arbitration, trade regulation, transportation and tax.*

### MEMBERS OF FIRM

**ANDREW P. BERNSTEIN,** born September 29, 1955; admitted to bar, 1980, California. *Education:* University of California, Los Angeles (B.A., summa cum laude, 1977); University of California, Los Angeles School of Law (J.D., 1980). Phi Beta Kappa; Order of the Coif. **PRACTICE AREAS:** Real Estate. *Email:* abernstein@mofo.com

**RONALD J. DEFELICE,** born February 28, 1943; admitted to bar, 1969, California; 1988, District of Columbia; 1989, New York. *Education:* Stanford University (A.B., with great distinction, 1965); Harvard Law School (J.D., cum laude, 1968). Phi Beta Kappa. **PRACTICE AREAS:** Real Estate; Environmental; Land Use. *Email:* rjdefelice@mofo.com

**LAWRENCE P. EBINER,** born July 8, 1953; admitted to bar, 1985, California. *Education:* Loyola-Marymount University (B.A., cum laude, 1975); University of California, Los Angeles School of Law (J.D., 1985). Co-Author: "Discovery of Computer Records," California Deposition and Discovery Practice, Matthew Bender, 1995; "Closing Argument in Construction Cases," Trying a Complex Construction Case, Prentice Hall, 1994. Judicial Extern to Hon. Stephen Reinhardt, U.S. Court of Appeals, Ninth Circuit, 1984. Law Clerk to Hon. Lawrence K. Karlton, U.S. District Court, Eastern District of California, 1985-1987. **PRACTICE AREAS:** Litigation; Alternative Dispute Resolution; Real Property; Insurance; Energy; General Business Litigation. *Email:* lebiner@mofo.com

**MICHAEL L. HAWKINS,** born Barberton, Ohio, March 26, 1954; admitted to bar, 1985, California. *Education:* The Ohio State University (B.A., 1976); California State University at Fullerton (M.B.A., 1982); Villanova University School of Law (J.D., cum laude, 1985). Order of the Coif. Case and Comment Editor, Villanova Law Review, 1984-1985. **PRACTICE AREAS:** Securities; Corporate Finance; Business Practice. *Email:* mhawkins@mofo.com

**GARY P. LONG,** born December 16, 1948; admitted to bar, 1979, California. *Education:* Pomona College (B.A., cum laude, 1971); University of California, Los Angeles School of Law (J.D., 1979). Order of the Coif. **PRACTICE AREAS:** Real Estate; Financial Transactions; Financial Restructurings and Workouts. *Email:* glong@mofo.com

**ELLEN R. MARSHALL,** born April 23, 1949; admitted to bar, 1975, California; 1981, District of Columbia; 1989, New York. *Education:* Yale University (A.B., magna cum laude, with highest departmental honors in Philosophy, 1971); Harvard Law School (J.D., cum laude, 1974). **PRACTICE AREAS:** Corporate Finance; Financial Services and Transactions; Employee Benefit Plans. *Email:* emarshall@mofo.com

**ROBERT M. MATTSON, JR.,** born May 13, 1948; admitted to bar, 1975, California. *Education:* Stanford University (A.B., 1971); Northwestern University Graduate School of Management (M.M., 1975); Northwestern University School of Law (J.D., cum laude, 1975). Chair, Corporation, Banking and Business Law Section, The Bar Association of San Francisco, 1983-1986. Chair, Corporations Committee, 1987-1988, and Member, Executive Committee, 1995-1997, Business Law Section, State Bar of California. **PRACTICE AREAS:** Corporate Finance; Securities. *Email:* rmattson@mofo.com

**ROBERT A. NAEVE,** born March 1, 1955; admitted to bar, 1982, California. *Education:* University of Southern California (B.M., magna cum laude, 1977); Stanford Law School (J.D., 1982). Author: "Managing Laboratory Personnel: The CLIA and OSHA Manual," Thompson Publishing Group, 1994; Managing the ADA: The Complete Compliance Guide," John Wiley & Sons, 1992; "Wrongful Termination: Reliable Policies to Avoid Lawsuits and Maintain At-Will Employment Today," Borgman & Associates, 1990; "Pre-Employment Testing: Employee Selection Techniques in a Legal Context," Borgman & Associates, 1990; "Maintaining a Drug Free Workplace," American Sommerset, 1989. Law Clerk to the Honorable Judith N. Keep, U.S. District Court, Southern District of California, 1981-1982. **PRACTICE AREAS:** Labor and Employment; Litigation; Alternative Dispute Resolution. *Email:* rnaeve@mofo.com

**JANE M. SAMSON,** born February 7, 1958; admitted to bar, 1985, California. *Education:* St. Mary's College, Notre Dame (B.Mus., summa cum laude, 1980); University of Notre Dame Law School (J.D., cum laude, 1985). **PRACTICE AREAS:** Land Use; Environmental; Real Estate. *Email:* jsamson@mofo.com

*(This Listing Continued)*

**CHARLES E. SCHWENCK,** born June 19, 1945; admitted to bar, 1972, California. *Education:* University of California, Berkeley (A.B., 1968; J.D., 1971). *Member:* Federal Energy and American (Member, Business Law, International, Public Utility and Natural Resources, Energy and Environmental Sections) Bar Associations; State Bar of California. **PRACTICE AREAS:** International Project Development; International Project Finance; Construction; Public Utility. *Email:* cschwenck@mofo.com

**CARL R. STEEN,** born 1958; admitted to bar, 1986, New York; 1989, District of Columbia; 1996, California. *Education:* State University of New York at Plattsburgh (B.A., 1981); Washington College of Law, The American University (J.D., 1984). *Member:* New York State, District of Columbia, Federal Energy and American (Vice-Chairman, Alternate Energy Sources Committee, Natural Resources Section, 1986-1989; Chairman, Alternate Energy Sources Committee, 1989-1991) Bar Associations. **PRACTICE AREAS:** International Project Development; International Project Finance. *Email:* csteen@mofo.com

**JOSEPHINE STATON TUCKER,** born September 19, 1961; admitted to bar, 1986, Missouri; 1988, California. *Education:* William Jewell College (B.A., summa cum laude, 1983); Harvard Law School (J.D., 1986). Co-Author: "California Employer's Guide to Employee Handbooks and Personnel Policy Manuals," Matthew Bender. Author: "Designation of Leave Under the Family and Medical Leave Act: Is the Clock Running?" California Employment Law Reporter, 1995; "Sexual Harassment in Professional Relationships: What Does New Civil Code Section 51.9 Mean for Employers?" California Employment Law Reporter, 1994. Law Clerk to Hon. John R. Gibson, U.S. Court of Appeals, Eighth Circuit, 1986-1987. **PRACTICE AREAS:** Labor and Employment. *Email:* jtucker@mofo.com

**THOMAS J. UMBERG,** born September 25, 1955; admitted to bar, 1980, California. *Education:* University of California, Los Angeles (B.A., cum laude, 1977); University of California, Hastings College of the Law (J.D., 1980). Member, California State Assembly, 1990-1994. Chairman, Assembly Committee on Environmental Safety and Toxic Materials, 1992-1994. Assistant U.S. Attorney, Criminal Division, Central District of California, 1987-1990. Adjunct Professor of Law, Southwestern University, 1995—. Member, California Council on Criminal Justice, 1991—. [Lt. Col., U.S. Army Reserve, Active Duty, 1980-1985]. **PRACTICE AREAS:** Litigation; Land Use and Environmental Law; Regulatory Law; Legislative. *Email:* tumberg@mofo.com

**DEAN J. ZIPSER,** born June 1, 1955; admitted to bar, 1980, California. *Education:* University of California, Los Angeles (B.A., summa cum laude, 1977); Stanford Law School (J.D., 1980). Phi Beta Kappa. Associate Editor, Stanford Law Review, 1979-1980. Co-Author: *California Lis Pendens Practice*, California Continuing Education of the Bar, (2d ed.), and Yearly Supplements, first and second editions, 1985—. **PRACTICE AREAS:** Litigation; Real Estate; Construction; Intellectual Property. *Email:* dzipser@mofo.com

*OF COUNSEL*

**KAREN J. LEE,** born May 29, 1944; admitted to bar, 1981, California. *Education:* University of Minnesota (B.A., B.S., with distinction, 1966); California State University at Long Beach (M.A., 1971); Loyola University of Los Angeles (J.D., cum laude, 1981). Phi Kappa Phi. St. Thomas More Law Society. Note and Comment Editor, Loyola Law Review, 1980-1981. Author: Note, "Conviction of Non-Charged Offenses," 13 Loyola Law Review 521, 1980; "L.A. La Vina: Developer-Prepared Environmental Impact Reports," Orange County Lawyer, June 1991. Life, California Standard Secondary Teaching Credential. *Member:* Los Angeles County, Orange County and American Bar Associations; State Bar of California; Commercial Real Estate Women; Condemnation Attorneys Group; The Urban Land Institute. **PRACTICE AREAS:** Land Use and Entitlement Litigation; Business Litigation. *Email:* klee@mofo.com

**PAUL M. SMITH,** born September 29, 1952; admitted to bar, 1977, California. *Education:* University of Southern California (B.A., 1973); Loyola Marymount University (J.D., 1977). **PRACTICE AREAS:** Commercial Litigation. *Email:* psmith@mofo.com

*ASSOCIATES*

**JOSEPH H. CHI,** born September 6, 1966; admitted to bar, 1993, California; registered to practice before U.S. Patent and Trademark Office. *Education:* University of California, Los Angeles (B.S.E.E., cum laude, 1987); University of Southern California Law Center (J.D., 1993). Extern to the Hon. Barry Russell, U.S. Bankruptcy Judge, Central District of California, 1991. **LANGUAGES:** Mandarin. *Email:* jchi@mofo.com

*(This Listing Continued)*

**SALLY P. ENRIQUEZ,** born September 28, 1959; admitted to bar, 1995, California. *Education:* Michigan State University (B.A., summa cum laude, 1981); University of California, Los Angeles School of Law (J.D., 1995). *Email:* senriquez@mofo.com

**WILLIAM B. GRENNER,** born February 17, 1962; admitted to bar, 1989, California. *Education:* University of California, Irvine (B.A., Political Science, magna cum laude, 1984; B.A., Social Ecology, magna cum laude, 1984); Georgetown University Law Center (J.D., 1988). Phi Beta Kappa. Member, Board of Directors, Legal Aid Society of Orange County, 1996—. *Member:* Orange County Bar Association (Member, Board of Directors, 1992-1995; Chair, Pro Bono Committee, 1991-1995); Orange County Bar Foundation (Secretary, 1993; Trustee, 1991—); Public Law Center (Member, Board of Directors, 1993—). *Email:* wgrenner@mofo.com

**KRISTINA M. JODIS,** born July 17, 1967; admitted to bar, 1992, California. *Education:* University of Notre Dame (B.A., 1989); University of Michigan Law School (J.D., 1991). *Member:* American Inns of Court (Legion Lex Chapter). *Email:* kjodis@mofo.com

**ROBERT J. KEENAN,** born November 16, 1965; admitted to bar, 1990, California. *Education:* California State University, Fullerton (B.A., with high honors, 1987); University of Southern California Law Center (J.D., with honors, 1990). Law Clerk to Honorable Alicemarie H. Stotler, U.S. District Court, Central District of California, 1990-1991. *Email:* rkeenan@mofo.com

**JACK A. KHOURI,** born April 1, 1969; (admission pending). *Education:* Stanford University (A.B., with distinction, 1991); Hastings College of the Law, University of California (J.D., 1996). *Email:* jkhouri@mofo.com

**PHILIP J. KOEHLER,** born October 29, 1951; admitted to bar, 1991, California; U.S. District Court, Central District of California and U.S. Court of Appeals, Ninth Circuit. *Education:* University of Texas at Austin (B.A., 1972); University of Southern California (J.D., 1991). Member, Moot Court. *Member:* International Society of Certified Employee Benefit Specialists. *Email:* pkoehler@mofo.com

**SONIA A. LISTER,** born May 11, 1967; admitted to bar, 1992, California. *Education:* University of California, Irvine (B.A., 1988); University of California, Davis School of Law (J.D., 1992). *Email:* slister@mofo.com

**H. MARK MERSEL,** born July 17, 1962; admitted to bar, 1987, California. *Education:* University of Pennsylvania, Wharton School of Finance (B.S., magna cum laude, 1984); University of California, Hastings College of the Law (J.D., 1987). Extern to the Honorable Mariana R. Pfaelzer, U.S. District Court Judge, Central District of California, 1985, 1987. *Email:* hmersel@mofo.com

**C KEITH MOSLEY,** born January 4, 1964; admitted to bar, 1993, California. *Education:* Arizona State University (B.S., magna cum laude, 1989); Columbia University School of Law (J.D., 1993). Editor, Columbia Business Law Review, 1992-1993. *Email:* ckmosley@mofo.com

**JEREMY T. NAFTEL,** born March 8, 1971; admitted to bar, 1996, California. *Education:* Pomona College (B.A., 1993); University of Southern California Law Center (J.D., 1996). *Email:* jnaftel@mofo.com

**RONALD P. OINES,** born May 28, 1963; admitted to bar, 1990, California. *Education:* California State University, Fullerton (B.A., 1986); Arizona State University College of Law (J.D., cum laude, 1989). Editor, Arizona State University Law Journal, 1988-1989. Extern to Judge Stephen Reinhardt, U.S. Court of Appeals, Ninth Circuit, 1988. *Email:* roines@mofo.com

**CAROLE E. REAGAN,** born August 11, 1967; admitted to bar, 1992, California. *Education:* University of California, Berkeley (B.A., magna cum laude, 1989); University of California, Berkeley, Boalt Hall School of Law (J.D., 1992). *Email:* creagan@mofo.com

**JENNIFER A. RIEL,** born July 4, 1969; admitted to bar, 1995, California. *Education:* California State University, Long Beach (B.M., cum laude, 1992); University of California, Berkeley, Boalt Hall School of Law (J.D., 1995). Executive Editor, Ecology Law Quarterly, 1994-1995. *Email:* jriel@mofo.com

**BRIAN C. SINCLAIR,** born April 14, 1969; admitted to bar, 1995, California and U.S. District Court, Central, Southern, Northern and Eastern Districts of California. *Education:* University of California, Los Angeles (B.A., 1992); University of California, Davis (J.D., 1995). Order of the Coif. Articles Editor, University of California, Davis Law Review, 1994-1995. *Member:* Orange County and American Bar Associations. *Email:* bsinclair@mofo.com

*(This Listing Continued)*

## MORRISON & FOERSTER LLP, Irvine—Continued

**TAMARA POWELL TATE,** born April 15, 1965; admitted to bar, 1989, California. *Education:* University of California at Irvine (B.A., cum laude, 1986); University of California, Berkeley, Boalt Hall School of Law (J.D., 1989). *Email:* tptate@mofo.com

**WILLIAM B. TATE, II,** born March 28, 1965; admitted to bar, 1988, California. *Education:* University of Southern California (A.B., 1985); Stanford University (J.D., 1988). *Email:* wtate@mofo.com

**PETER D. TAYLOR,** born June 14, 1965; admitted to bar, 1995, California. *Education:* University of California, Santa Barbara (B.A., 1987); University of California, Los Angeles School of Law (J.D., 1995). Phi Beta Kappa. *LANGUAGES:* Japanese. *Email:* ptaylor@mofo.com

(For biographical data on San Francisco, Los Angeles, Sacramento, Walnut Creek and Palo Alto, CA, New York, NY, Washington, DC, Denver, CO, London, England, Brussels, Belgium, Hong Kong and Tokyo, Japan see professional biographies at each of those cities.)

## MORRISON & LESPIER

3333 MICHELSON DRIVE
SUITE 605
**IRVINE, CALIFORNIA 92715-1685**
Telephone: 714-474-7755
Email: 74014.2126@compuserve.com
URL: http://www.cal__law.com

*Civil and Business Litigation, Banking Litigation, Real Estate Litigation, Bankruptcy Litigation (Creditors), Commercial Litigation, Personal Injury, Title Insurance Litigation.*

### MEMBERS OF FIRM

**STEVEN C. MORRISON,** born Indianapolis, Indiana, September 3, 1953; admitted to bar, 1979, Indiana and U.S. District Court, Southern District of Indiana; 1981, Ohio; 1985, California and U.S. District Court, Central, Eastern and Southern Districts of California; 1986, U.S. Court of Appeals for the Federal Circuit and U.S. District Court, Western District of Michigan; U.S. Court of Appeals, 9th and 6th Circuits. *Education:* Indiana University (B.S., 1975; J.D., cum laude, 1979). Member, Order of the Barristers. *Member:* Orange County Bar Association; State Bar of California; The Association of Trial Lawyers of America. *PRACTICE AREAS:* Banking Litigation; Real Estate Litigation; Personal Injury; Title Insurance Litigation; Commercial.

**MANFREDO E. LESPIER,** born Fort Polk, Louisiana, March 14, 1958; admitted to bar, 1990, California and U.S. District Court, Central and Southern Districts of California; U.S. Court of Appeals, 9th Circuit. *Education:* University of California at Irvine (B.A., 1981); Western State University (J.D., 1988). *Member:* Orange County and American Bar Associations; State Bar of California; Hispanic National Bar Association; Orange County Hispanic Bar Association. *LANGUAGES:* Spanish. *PRACTICE AREAS:* Commercial Litigation; Bankruptcy Law (Creditors); Personal Injury; Civil Litigation; Banking Litigation; Real Estate.

---

**CARL P. LUCKADOO,** born Morganton, North Carolina, January 3, 1954; admitted to bar, 1989, Illinois and U.S. District Court, Northern District of Illinois; 1992, California and U.S. District Court, Central and Southern Districts of California; 1995, U.S. Court of Appeals, 9th Circuit. *Education:* University of North Carolina (B.A., 1974); University of Minnesota (J.D., cum laude, 1989). Phi Beta Kappa. *Member:* Orange County Bar Association; State Bar of California. *PRACTICE AREAS:* Real Estate Law; Creditors Bankruptcy Law; Banking Litigation; Corporate Law.

**MARY DURBIN,** born Athens, Greece, May 5, 1960; admitted to bar, 1994, California and U.S. District Court, Central and Southern Districts of California; 1995, U.S. Court of Appeals, 9th Circuit. *Education:* Pensacola Junior College (Legal Secretarial Science, 1979); The Way College of Emporia, Emporia, Kansas (A.A., 1984); Western State University (J.D., magna cum laude, 1993). *Member:* Orange County Bar Association; State Bar of California. *LANGUAGES:* Greek. *PRACTICE AREAS:* Real Estate Litigation; Business Litigation; Civil Litigation; Personal Injury.

## MOWER, KOELLER, NEBEKER, CARLSON & HALUCK

*Established in 1986*
108 PACIFICA
P.O. BOX 19799
**IRVINE, CALIFORNIA 92713-9799**
Telephone: 714-753-1229
Fax: 714-753-1413

*San Bernardino, California Office:* 412 West Hospitality Lane, Suite 300, 92408. Telephone: 909-381-3334. Fax: 909-889-2007.
*San Diego, California Office:* 225 Broadway, 21st Floor. Telephone: 619-233-1600. Fax: 619-236-0527.
*Yuma, Arizona Office:* 212 South 2nd Avenue, P.O. Bin 11791. Telephone: 520-782-2531. Fax: 520-782-5319.

*General Liability, Construction Defect, Environmental Law, Medical Malpractice, Product Liability, Business Litigation, Governmental Tort Liability, Insurance and Insurance Bad Faith Law.*

*FIRM PROFILE:* Mower, Koeller, Nebeker, Carlson & Haluck specializes in the handling of complex litigation matters and business tort claims. The firm has expanded rapidly since its formation in 1986 and now includes thirty three lawyers covering the Southern California and Western Arizona area. We are extremely proud of the results we have obtained and look forward to developing new client relationship while we continue to excel at servicing the needs of existing clients.

### MEMBERS OF FIRM

**JON R. MOWER,** born Los Angeles, California, May 14, 1950; admitted to bar, 1976, California. *Education:* Stanford University (B.A., with honors, 1972); University of California at Los Angeles (J.D., 1976). Member, U.C.L.A. Law Review, 1975-1976. *Member:* Orange County and American Bar Associations; The State Bar of California; Association of Southern California Defense Counsel. *PRACTICE AREAS:* Insurance Defense; Medical Malpractice Law; Government Law; Bad Faith Law; Civil Trial.

**KEITH D. KOELLER,** born Urbana, Illinois, September 5, 1956; admitted to bar, 1981, California. *Education:* University of Southern California (B.A., 1978); Loyola University of Los Angeles (J.D., with honors, 1981). Phi Beta Kappa. *Member:* Orange County (Member, Insurance Law Section), San Diego County and American Bar Associations; The State Bar of California; Association of Southern California Defense Counsel. *PRACTICE AREAS:* Insurance Coverage; Insurance Defense; Bad Faith Law; Construction Defect Litigation; Construction Accidents.

**WILLIAM L. HALUCK,** born Michigan City, Indiana, September 2, 1952; admitted to bar, 1978, California. *Education:* Loyola University of Los Angeles (B.B.A., 1974; J.D., 1978). Alpha Sigma Nu. Judge Pro Tem, Orange County Superior Court, 1986-1987. *Member:* Orange County Bar Association; The State Bar of California; Association of Southern California Defense Counsel. *PRACTICE AREAS:* Civil Trial; Insurance Coverage; Construction Defect Litigation; Medical Malpractice Law; Government Law.

**JOSEPH J. CULLEN,** born New York, N.Y., September 2, 1952; admitted to bar, 1981, California. *Education:* Loyola University (B.A., 1974); Southwestern University School of Law (J.D., 1980). *Member:* Orange County Bar Association; State Bar of California. *LANGUAGES:* Swedish. *PRACTICE AREAS:* Construction Defect Litigation; Bad Faith Law; Insurance Coverage; Insurance Defense Law; Construction Accidents.

**PATRICK A. CARREON,** born Los Angeles, California, December 4, 1958; admitted to bar, 1985, California. *Education:* Harvard University (B.A., 1981); University of California at Los Angeles (J.D., 1984). *Member:* Orange County Bar Association; The State Bar of California; Association of Southern California Defense Counsel.

**LYNN M. BOUSLOG,** born Macomb, Illinois, March 19, 1953; admitted to bar, 1985, California. *Education:* Western Illinois University (B.S.Ed., 1975); Drake University (J.D., 1984). *Member:* Orange County and American Bar Associations; The State Bar of California; Association of Southern California Defense Counsel.

**EDWARD W. SCHMITT,** born Youngstown, Ohio, March 13, 1956; admitted to bar, 1981, California. *Education:* University of California at Santa Barbara (B.A., summa cum laude, 1978); Hastings College of Law, University of California (J.D., 1981). Member, Moot Court Board. Instructor, Moot Court, Hastings College of the Law, University of California,

*(This Listing Continued)*

1980-1981. *Member:* Orange County Bar Association; State Bar of California; Association of Southern California Defense Counsel.

**ELLEN E. HUNTER,** born Gastonia, North Carolina, June 11, 1957; admitted to bar, 1987, California. *Education:* Agnes Scott College (B.A., 1979); Western State University (J.D., 1986). *Member:* Orange County and American Bar Associations; State Bar of California. **PRACTICE AREAS:** Insurance Defense; Construction Defect.

---

Nancy J. Altman
Mark D. Newcomb
Terrence J. Giannone
Ferdinand M. Trampe
James A. Burton
Eric W. Smith
Steven G. Holett

REPRESENTATIVE CLIENTS: Aetna Casualty & Surety; Allstate Insurance Company; American International Insurance Group; Armstrong World Industries; City of Brawley; CNA Insurance; Doctors Company; City of El Centro; Farm Credit Banks; Fireman's Fund Insurance Companies; Fremont Indemnity Company; Great Southwest Fire Insurance Company; Home Insurance Group; Horace Mann Insurance Company; City of Imperial; City of La Mesa; City of Norwalk; County of Orange; Oxy-Dry Corporation; Reliance Insurance Company; Royal Insurance Company; City of San Clemente; Scottsdale Insurance Company; Sentry Claims Service; Southern California Joint Powers Insurance Authority; State Farm Mutual Automobile Insurance Company; State Farm Fire and Casualty Insurance Company; Tuftex Carpet Mills Inc.; United States Automobile Association; City of Yuma; Winnebago Industries; American Golf Corporation.

---

## JOSEPH E. MUDD, P.L.C.

*8001 IRVINE CENTER DRIVE, SUITE 1170*
***IRVINE, CALIFORNIA 92618***
*Telephone: 714-453-1012*
*Fax: 714-453-1516*

*Corporate and Business Transactions and Representation with emphasis in the area of Taxation and Tax Controversy.*

**JOSEPH E. MUDD,** born St. Louis, Missouri, May 16, 1947; admitted to bar, 1972, Montana; 1987, New York; 1989, California. *Education:* Carroll College; University of Montana (B.A., 1969; J.D., 1972); New York University (LL.M., Tax, 1986). Associate Editor, University of Montana Law Review, 1971-1972. Author: "Planning for the 100% Penalty," and "Discharge of Taxes in Bankruptcy," Orange County Bar Journal, 1990. Professor, Masters in Tax Program, Golden Gate University, 1987-1988. Former Senior Attorney, IRS District Counsel, Laguna Niguel, California. Member, Orange County Industrial League. *Member:* Orange County Bar Association (President, Tax Section, 1993); South Orange County Bar Association (Vice-President); State Bar of Montana; State Bar of California. (Certified Specialist, Taxation Law, The State Bar of California Board of Legal Specialization). **PRACTICE AREAS:** Taxation Law; IRS Representation; Business Transactions; Corporate Planning; Business Reorganization; Estate Planning.

---

**JERI L. GARTSIDE,** born Royal Oak, Michigan, January 6, 1960; admitted to bar, 1986, Michigan; 1987, California. *Education:* Michigan State University (B.A., 1982); Thomas M. Cooley (J.D., cum laude, 1986). *Member:* Orange County Bar Association. **PRACTICE AREAS:** Tax Controversy; Bankruptcy.

**DENNIS M. SANDOVAL,** born Riverside, California, April 3, 1958; admitted to bar, 1996, California, U.S. District Court, Central and Southern Districts of California and U.S. Tax Court. *Education:* California State University (B.A., cum laude, 1983); Western State University (J.D., cum laude, 1996). Member, Law Review. Member, Western State University Tax Law Society, 1994-1996. Recipient: AmJur Awards in Community Property; Legal Writing; Wills; Trusts; Corporations. Author: "The Search for the Holy Grail: The Quest to Preserve the Benefits of Community Property Ownership Under California's Transmutation Statute," Western State University Law Review, Fall, 1996. Member, Institute of Certified Financial Planners, 1985—. Certified Financial Planner, 1984. Enrolled Agent, 1986. Registered Financial Consultant, 1993. *Member:* State Bar of California. **PRACTICE AREAS:** Estate Planning; Tax Controversy; Probate Administration; Retirement Planning/Pension Distributions; Charitable Planning/Planned Giving.

*(This Listing Continued)*

---

### LEGAL SUPPORT PERSONNEL

**CLA TONI M. STOREY,** born San Diego, California, November 12, 1952. *Education:* University of California, Irvine (Certificate in Legal Assistantship, with honors, 1991). Certified Legal Assistant, National Association of Legal Assistants, 1995. Associate Member: Tax Section, Orange County Bar Association. Member: Orange County Paralegal Association; National Association of Legal Assistants; Aircraft Owners and Pilots Association (Airplane Single Engine Land, 1981). **PRACTICE AREAS:** Taxation; Bankruptcy; Litigation.

REPRESENTATIVE CLIENTS: Metagenics, Inc.; Par-Way Group, Inc.; Venus Labs, Inc.; Cristek Interconnects, Inc.; Wish Enterprises.

---

## MUSICK, PEELER & GARRETT LLP

Established in 1954

*2603 MAIN STREET, SUITE 1025*
***IRVINE, CALIFORNIA 92614-6232***
*Telephone: 714-852-5122*
*Facsimile: 714-852-5128*

*Los Angeles, California Office:* Suite 2000, One Wilshire Boulevard. Telephone: 213-629-7600. Facsimile: 213-624-1376.

*San Diego, California Office:* 1900 Home Savings Tower, 225 Broadway. Telephone: 619-231-2500. Facsimile: 619-231-1234.

*San Francisco, California Office:* Suite 1300, Steuart Street Tower, One Market Plaza. Telephone: 415-281-2000. Facsimile: 415-281-2010.

*Sacramento, California Office:* Wells Fargo Center, Suite 1280, 400 Capitol Mall. Telephone: 916-557-8300. Facsimile: 916-442-8629.

*Fresno, California Office:* 6041 North First Street. Telephone: 209-228-1000. Facsimile: 209-447-4670.

*General Practice. Trial and Appellate Practice. Corporation, Securities and Antitrust Law. Healthcare, Hospital, College and University Law. Insurance, Excess, Reinsurance and Coverage. Labor, Real Estate, Land Use, Environmental, Eminent Domain, Oil and Gas and Mining Law. Taxation, Trust, Probate, Estate Planning, Bankruptcy and Pension and Profit Sharing.*

### MEMBERS OF FIRM

**HAL G. BLOCK,** born Chicago, Illinois, February 14, 1953; admitted to bar, 1982, Illinois; 1985, California. *Education:* Illinois Institute of Technology (B.Arch., 1977); John Marshall Law School (J.D., 1982). **PRACTICE AREAS:** Construction and Design Defect Litigation; Insurance Coverage; Business and Commercial Litigation.

**EDUARDO GUERINI BOLT,** born Panama City, Republic of Panama, September 24, 1948; admitted to bar, 1977, California. *Education:* California State University at Northridge (B.S., 1972); University of San Fernando Valley School of Law (J.D., summa cum laude, 1976). **LANGUAGES:** Spanish, Italian and Portuguese. **PRACTICE AREAS:** Corporate; Business; Real Estate Transactions.

### ASSOCIATE

Robin L. Hayward.

---

## NEULAND & NORDBERG

*A PROFESSIONAL LAW CORPORATION*

*ONE TECHNOLOGY DRIVE*
*SUITE I-803*
***IRVINE, CALIFORNIA 92718***
*Telephone: 714-453-7200*
*Fax: 714-453-7212*

*Homeowner Association and Condominium Law, Real Property, Civil Litigation, Construction Law, Business, Personal Injury, Probate.*

**RICHARD P. NEULAND,** born New York, N.Y., August 4, 1946; admitted to bar, 1975, California. *Education:* University of Notre Dame; California State University at Long Beach (B.S., 1971); Pepperdine University (J.D., 1975). California DRE approved educator to teach California Community Association Managers (CACM) designation courses. Lecturer, Homeowners Association/Condominium Law, Orange County Continuing Education. *Member:* Orange County Bar Association; State Bar of California; College of Community Association Lawyers; California Association of Community Managers; Community Association Institute (President, Southern Counties Chapter, 1989). [With U.S. Army, 1966-1969]. **PRAC-**

*(This Listing Continued)*

**NEULAND & NORDBERG, A PROFESSIONAL LAW CORPORATION, Irvine—Continued**

TICE AREAS: Homeowner Association; Condominium Law; Real Estate; Business; Personal Injury.

**DANIEL A. NORDBERG,** born Pasadena, California, February 16, 1952; admitted to bar, 1977, California. *Education:* University of California at Irvine (B.A., 1974); Pepperdine University School of Law (J.D., 1977). California DRE approved educator to teach California Community Association Managers (CACM) designation courses. Lecturer, Homeowner Association/Condominium Law, Orange County Continuing Education. *Member:* Orange County Bar Association; State Bar of California; Orange County Trial Lawyers Association; Community Association Institute (President, Southern Counties Chapter, 1984-1985). *PRACTICE AREAS:* Homeowner Association; Condominium Law and Litigation; Construction Defect Litigation; Real Estate; Personal Injury.

---

**DENVER R. ANDREWS, JR.,** born Richmond, Virginia, August 7, 1949; admitted to bar, 1982, California and U.S. District Court, Central District of California. *Education:* University of North Carolina (B.A., 1971); Southwestern University (J.D., 1982). *Member:* State Bar of California. *PRACTICE AREAS:* Civil Litigation; Business; Construction; Community Associations; Personal Torts.

**DAVID E. HICKEY,** born Burbank, California, 1964; admitted to bar, 1989, California and U.S. District Court, Southern District of California. *Education:* University of California, Los Angeles (B.A., 1986); Hastings College of the Law (J.D., 1989). *Member:* Orange County Bar Association; State Bar of California. *PRACTICE AREAS:* Community Association Law; Real Property/Civil Litigation; Business.

**ROBERT F. WILSON,** born San Bernardino, California, April 9, 1951; admitted to bar, 1978, California and U.S. District Court, Northern District of California; 1981, U.S. District Court, Central District of California. *Education:* University of Southern California; University of California at Irvine (B.A., 1974); California Western School of Law (J.D., 1977). *Member:* Orange County Bar Association; State Bar of California; Association of Southern California Defense Counsel (Member, Board of Directors, 1984-1992; Amicus Chairman, 1984; Public Relations Chairman, 1992; Director for San Bernardino County, 1986-1991); Community Association Institute; California Association of Community Managers. *PRACTICE AREAS:* Personal Injury; Insurance Defense; Corporation; Business; Real Estate; Construction Law; Homeowners Association Law; General Civil Litigation.

**DEAN E. SMART,** born Kingston, Jamaica, March 26, 1959; admitted to bar, 1987, California; 1988, U.S. District Court, Central District of California. *Education:* California State University at Fullerton (B.A., 1984); Pepperdine University (J.D., 1987). Lecturer: "Home Owners Construction Defect Litigation"; "Disclosure Requirements in Residential Real Estate Transfer." Sexual Assault Victim Counselor, 1991-1992; Mentor, 1993—, City of Santa Ana sponsored Project Pride. *Member:* Orange County Bar Association (Member, Alternative Disputes Resolution Committee, 1996—); State Bar of California; The Association of Trial Lawyers of America; International Law Society (Member and Secretary, 1985-1987); Christian Legal Society. *LANGUAGES:* Spanish. *PRACTICE AREAS:* Construction Defect; Community Association; Personal Injury; Commercial.

*OF COUNSEL*

**WILLIAM P. HICKEY,** born Pittsburgh, Pennsylvania, March 4, 1938; admitted to bar, 1967, California. *Education:* University of California at Los Angeles (B.S., 1960; J.D., 1966). Phi Delta Phi. Member Emeritus, California Legislative Action Committee. *Member:* Orange County and American Bar Associations; State Bar of California; Community Association Institute. *PRACTICE AREAS:* Community Association Law; Probate.

REFERENCE: Bank of America (Laguna Hills Branch).

---

## NICHOLS & ANDREWS
*A PROFESSIONAL LAW CORPORATION*
Established in 1985

5 PARK PLAZA, SUITE 800
IRVINE, CALIFORNIA 92614-6501
Telephone: 714-475-4477
Fax: 714-475-4475

General Civil and Trial Practice. Commercial Law, Banking, Business, Creditor Bankruptcy, Construction, Real Estate, Personal Injury.

*FIRM PROFILE: Nichols & Andrews was founded in 1985 as a firm specializing in business and banking law. The firm serves all Southern California Counties and offers a wide range of legal services, with an emphasis on prompt, practical and cost efficient resolution of disputes. The law firm is listed in the Bar Register of Preeminent Lawyers.*

**ROBERT F. NICHOLS, JR.,** born Oak Park, Illinois, July 17, 1927; admitted to bar, 1966, California and U.S. District Court, Central, Southern, Eastern and Northern Districts. *Education:* St. John's College (B.A., 1949); Loyola University of Los Angeles (LL.B., 1965). *Member:* Orange County Bar Association; The State Bar of California. *PRACTICE AREAS:* Commercial Banking Law; Business Law; Real Estate Law; Corporate Law; Creditor's Rights; Appeals.

**CAMILLA N. ANDREWS,** born Los Angeles, California, March 14, 1958; admitted to bar, 1986, California; 1987, U.S. District Court, Central District of California and U.S. District Court, Southern, Eastern and Northern Districts of California. *Education:* University of Santa Clara (B.A., 1980); Loyola Marymount University (J.D., 1986). Member, Board of directors, French American Chamber of Commerce. *Member:* Los Angeles County and Orange County (Financial Institutions, Commercial Law and Bankruptcy, Creditors Rights, Real Estate and Business Litigation Sections) Bar Associations; State Bar of California; Financial Women International; National Association of Women Lawyers. *LANGUAGES:* French. *PRACTICE AREAS:* Commercial Litigation; Creditors' Rights; Contract Disputes; Financial Institution Litigation; Creditor Bankruptcy; Judicial and Nonjudicial Foreclosures; Collections; Business Litigation; Appellate Practice; Real Estate; Wrongful Termination; Sexual Harassment; Personal Injury.

REPRESENTATIVE CLIENTS: Bank of America, NT & SA; California State Bank; Downey National Bank; National Bank of Southern California; The Money Store; One Central Bank; Sunwest Bank; Lee Servicing Co.; Telacu/Carpenter; Wendover Funding; Chase Manhattan Bank; Citizens Business Bank; Eldorado Bank; FDIC; First Bank & Trust.

---

## NOSSAMAN, GUTHNER, KNOX & ELLIOTT, LLP

SUITE 1800, 18101 VON KARMAN AVENUE
IRVINE, CALIFORNIA 92715-1007
Telephone: 714-833-7800
Telefacsimile: 714-833-7878

*Los Angeles, California Office:* Thirty-First Floor, Union Bank Square, 445 South Figueroa Street. Telephone: 213-612-7800.

*San Francisco, California Office:* Thirty-Fourth Floor, 50 California Street. Telephone: 415-398-3600.

*Sacramento, California Office:* Suite 1000, 915 L Street. Telephone: 916-442-8888.

*Washington, D.C. Office:* c/o French & Company, The Homer Building, Suite 370-S, 601 13th Street, N.W. Telephone: 202-783-7272.

*General Civil Practice, including Real Estate, Corporations and Litigation in all State and Federal Courts. Transportation, Land Use, Environmental, Hazardous Waste, Solid Waste and Regulatory Law.*

*MEMBERS OF FIRM*

**HOWARD F. HARRISON,** born Los Angeles, California, May 15, 1937; admitted to bar, 1963, California. *Education:* University of California at Los Angeles (A.B., 1959); Boalt Hall School of Law, University of California (LL.B., 1962). *Member:* Orange County Bar Association (President, 1979); State Bar of California; American Board of Trial Advocates; American College of Trial Lawyers. *PRACTICE AREAS:* Civil Litigation. *Email:* hfh@ngke.com

**ROBERT D. THORNTON,** born Hayward, California, November 17, 1950; admitted to bar, 1976, California; 1978, District of Columbia. *Education:* University of California at Berkeley (A.B., with distinction, 1972);

*(This Listing Continued)*

University of San Francisco (J.D., 1976). Member, McAuliffe Law Honor Society. Member, University of San Francisco Law Review, 1975-1976. Counsel, Subcommittee on Fisheries and Wildlife Conservation and the Environment, Committee on Merchant Marine and Fisheries, U.S. House of Representatives, 1977-1980. Lecturer, Legal Systems in Environmental Planning and Management, University of Southern California School of Planning and Urban Studies, 1982—. *Member:* State Bar of California; District of Columbia Bar. *PRACTICE AREAS:* Environmental Law; Land Use Law; Hazardous Waste Law; Endangered Species; Transportation Law. *Email:* rdt@ngke.com

*GREGORY W. SANDERS,* born Alameda, California, June 30, 1947; admitted to bar, 1977, California; 1979, District of Columbia. *Education:* California State University, Fullerton (B.A., 1972); Pepperdine University (J.D., 1977). Chief Administrative Assistant to Congressman, Jerry M. Patterson, 1978-1980. Chief Administrative Assistant to Orange County Supervisor Ralph B. Clark, 1972-1978. *Member:* State Bar of California; District of Columbia Bar. [Lt. U.S. Army, 1967-1971]. *PRACTICE AREAS:* Land Use Law; Real Property Law; Legislative Law. *Email:* gws@ngke.com

*JOHN J. FLYNN III,* born Los Angeles, California, March 4, 1952; admitted to bar, 1977, California. *Education:* University of California at Los Angeles (B.A., magna cum laude, 1974); Boalt Hall School of Law, University of California (J.D., 1977). *Member:* State Bar of California. *PRACTICE AREAS:* Litigation. *Email:* jjf@ngke.com

*RENSSELAER J. SMITH IV,* born Loma Linda, California, January 8, 1956; admitted to bar, 1981, California. *Education:* University of California at Riverside (B.A., with highest honors, 1978); University of California at Los Angeles (J.D., 1981). *Member:* State Bar of California. *PRACTICE AREAS:* Real Property Law. *Email:* rs@ngke.com

*JOHN C. MURPHY,* born Pasadena, California, December 4, 1954; admitted to bar, 1980, California. *Education:* Brown University; University of California at Riverside (B.A., with honors, 1976); University of Southern California (J.D., 1980). Member, Hale Moot Court Honors Program. *Member:* State Bar of California. *PRACTICE AREAS:* Litigation. *Email:* jcm@ngke.com

*JOHN P. ERSKINE,* born Los Angeles, California, July 22, 1951; admitted to bar, 1978, California. *Education:* California State University at Fullerton (B.A., 1974); Pepperdine University (J.D., 1978). Executive Assistant, Orange County Board of Supervisors, 1977-1982. Director, Governmental Affairs, 1982-1983. Executive Director, Orange County Region, Building Industry Association of Southern California, 1983-1989. *Member:* State Bar of California. *PRACTICE AREAS:* Real Property Law; Land Use Law; Environmental Law. *Email:* jpe@ngke.com

*E. GEORGE JOSEPH,* born New York, N.Y., February 22, 1958; admitted to bar, 1983, California. *Education:* Cornell University (A.B., 1980); University of California at Los Angeles (J.D., 1983). Order of the Coif. Extern to Hon. William Matthew Byrne, U.S. District Court, Central District of California, 1982. *Member:* State Bar of California. *PRACTICE AREAS:* Litigation. *Email:* egj@ngke.com

*ADAM H. RELIN,* born Los Angeles, California, June 8, 1962; admitted to bar, 1987, California. *Education:* University of California, Berkeley (A.B., with distinction, 1983); University of California at Los Angeles (M.A., Urban Planning, 1987; J.D., 1987). Editor, UCLA Journal of Environmental Law and Policy, 1986-1987. *Member:* State Bar of California. *PRACTICE AREAS:* Environmental Law. *Email:* ahr@ngke.com

*JAMES M. PICOZZI,* born Schenectady, New York, April 15, 1959; admitted to bar, 1988, New York; 1990, District of Columbia; 1991, California. *Education:* Yale University (B.A., 1981; J.D., 1987). Editor, Yale Law Journal, 1986-1987. Clerk to Hon. Anthony J. Scirica, U.S. Court of Appeals, Third Circuit, 1988-1989. *Member:* State Bar of California; New York State Bar Association; District of Columbia Bar. *PRACTICE AREAS:* Litigation. *Email:* jmp@ngke.com

*DAVID L. COLGAN,* born Kansas City, Missouri, 1949; admitted to bar, 1975, Missouri; 1976, California. *Education:* University of Kansas (B.A., 1971); University of Missouri-Kansas City (J.D., 1974). Member, UKMC Law Review, 1973-1974. Student Editor-in-Chief, The Urban Lawyer, 1974. *Member:* State Bar of California. *PRACTICE AREAS:* Real Property and Land Use Law. *Email:* dlc@ngke.com

*(This Listing Continued)*

### RESIDENT ASSOCIATES

*SUE S. OKUDA,* born Orange, California, August 11, 1954; admitted to bar, 1989, California. *Education:* California State University at Fullerton (B.A., 1976; M.A., 1981); Boalt Hall School of Law, University of California (J.D., 1989). Phi Beta Kappa. *Member:* State Bar of California. *PRACTICE AREAS:* Litigation. *Email:* sso@ngke.com

*K. ERIK FRIESS,* born Newport Beach, California, July 23, 1965; admitted to bar, 1990, California. *Education:* University of California at San Diego (B.A., 1987); Hastings College of the Law (J.D., 1990). *Member:* State Bar of California. *PRACTICE AREAS:* Litigation. *Email:* kef@ngke.com

*RICK E. RAYL,* born Ravenna, Ohio, April 11, 1969; admitted to bar, 1994, California. *Education:* University of California at Irvine (B.A., magna cum laude, 1991); Boalt Hall School of Law, University of California (J.D., 1994). Member and Associate Editor, California Law Review, 1992-1994. Member, Moot Court Board, 1993-1994. *Member:* State Bar of California. *PRACTICE AREAS:* Litigation. *Email:* rer@ngke.com

*FRANCIS D. LOGAN, JR.,* born New York, N.Y., August 30, 1963; admitted to bar, 1992, California. *Education:* Dartmouth College (B.A., 1986); University of Southern California (J.D., 1992). Editor, Computer/-Tax Journal, 1990-1991. *Member:* State Bar of California. *PRACTICE AREAS:* Litigation. *Email:* fdl@ngke.com

### OF COUNSEL

*JEAN O. MELIOUS,* born Canandaigua, New York, October 3, 1957; admitted to bar, 1984, California. *Education:* St. Lawrence University (B.A., summa cum laude, 1979); University of Edinburgh, Scotland (M.Ph., 1981); Harvard University (J.D., cum laude, 1984). Phi Beta Kappa. Marshall Scholar, Articles Editor, Harvard Environmental Law Review, 1982-1983. *Member:* State Bar of California. *PRACTICE AREAS:* Land Use Law; Environmental Law.

REFERENCE: Union Bank (Los Angeles Headquarters Office).

(For Biographical Data of other Firm Personnel, see Professional Biographies at Los Angeles, San Francisco, Sacramento, California and Washington, D.C.).

## YOLITA J. NOWAK
*18400 VON KARMAN AVENUE, SUITE 500*
**IRVINE, CALIFORNIA 92715-1514**
*Telephone: 714-851-5948*
*Facsimile: 714-851-0936*

*Corporate, Business Transactions, Partnerships and Securities and Investments.*

*YOLITA J. NOWAK,* born San Francisco, California, December 24, 1960; admitted to bar, 1986, California. *Education:* Fullerton Community College; California State University at Chico; Western State University College of Law (J.D., 1986). *Member:* State Bar of California; American Bar Association (Member, Sections on: Corporation Law; Securities; International Law). *PRACTICE AREAS:* Securities Law.

## OPPENHEIMER POMS SMITH
*1920 MAIN STREET, SUITE 1050*
**IRVINE, CALIFORNIA 92714**
*Telephone: 714-263-8250*
*FAX: 714-263-8260*
*Email: owdlaw.com*

*Los Angeles, California Office:* 2029 Century Park East, 38th Floor, 90067. Telephone: 310-788-5000. FAX: 310-277-1297.

*San Jose, California Office:* 333 West Santa Clara Street, Suite 1000, 95113. Telephone: 408-275-8790. FAX: 408-275-8793.

*Oppenheimer Wolff & Donnelly:*

*Brussels, Belgium Office:* Avenue Louise 250, Box 31, 1050. Telephone: 32-2-626-0500. FAX: 32-2-626-0510.

*Chicago, Illinois Office:* Two Prudential Plaza, 45th Floor, 180 North Stetson Avenue, 60601.

*Minneapolis, Minnesota Office:* 3400 Plaza VII, 45 South Seventh Street, 55401. Telephone: 612-344-9300. FAX: 612-344-9376.

*New York, N.Y. Office:* Citicorp Center, 153 East 53rd Street, 10022. Telephone: 212-826-5000. Telecopier: 212-486-0708.

*Paris, France Office:* 53 Avenue Montaigne, 75008. Telephone: (33/1) 44 95 03 50. FAX: (33/1) 44 95 03 40.

*(This Listing Continued)*

## OPPENHEIMER POMS SMITH, Irvine—Continued

*St. Paul, Minnesota Office:* 1700 First Bank Building, 55101. Telephone: 612-223-2500. FAX: 612-223-2596.

*Washington, D.C. Office:* 1020 Nineteenth Street, N.W., Suite 400, 20036. Telephone: 202-293-6300. FAX: 202-293-6200.

*Detroit, Michigan Office:* Timberland Office Park, Suite 250, 5445 Corporate Drive, 48098. Telephone: 810-267-8500. FAX: 810-267-8559.

*Affiliated Offices:*

*Goudsmit & Branbergen, J.J. Viottastraat, 46 Amsterdam 1071.* Telephone: 31-20-662-30-31. FAX: 31-20-673-65-58.

*Pisano, DeVito, Maiano & Catucci, Piazza Del Duomo, 20, Milan 20122.* Telephone: 39-2-878281. FAX: 39-2-861275.

*Pisano, DeVito, Maiano & Catucci, Via G. Borsi, 3, Rome 00197.* Telephone: 39-6-8079087. FAX: 39-6-8078407.

*Medical Device, Health Care, Business/Technology, Labor and Employment, Antitrust, professional Liability and Securities, Banking and Finance, Real Estate, Corporate Finance, Employee Benefits, International Corporate, Tax-/Trust and Estate, Environmental Law and Toxic Torts, Insurance, Products Liability, Transportation, Dispute Resolution/Arbitration, European Community, International Tax.*

(For complete biographical data on all personnel, see Professional Biographies at Los Angeles, California)

## OSWALD & YAP

A PROFESSIONAL CORPORATION

Established in 1985

19900 MACARTHUR BOULEVARD, SUITE 700
IRVINE, CALIFORNIA 92715
Telephone: 714-756-6000
Telefax: 714-756-6020

*General Civil and Trial Practice, Banking, Real Estate, Equipment Leasing, Secured Transactions, Securities and Commodities Litigation, Bankruptcy and Immigration.*

**MICHAEL A. OSWALD,** born Artesia, California, July 17, 1949; admitted to bar, 1979, California and U.S. District Court, Central District of California; 1981, U.S. Court of Appeals, Fifth and Ninth Circuits; 1985, U.S. District Court, Southern District of California. *Education:* University of Notre Dame (B.A., 1971); Loyola Law School (J.D., 1978). Member, Loyola University of Los Angeles Law Review, 1977-1978. Chairman, Industrial Development Authority, City of Irvine, 1982-1983. Member, Executive Committee, Friends Committee on Legislation, 1985-1989. With United States Army Security Agency, 1971-1974. *Member:* Orange County, Los Angeles County and American (Member, Securities Litigation Committee) Bar Associations; State Bar of California.

**CALVIN C.S. YAP,** born Manila, Philippines, October 25, 1956; admitted to bar, 1982, California and U.S. District Court, Central, Southern and Eastern Districts of California; 1983, U.S. Court of Appeals, Ninth Circuit. *Education:* University of Illinois (B.S., 1978); Northwestern University (J.D., 1981). Instructor, University of California at Irvine, 1982-1983. *Member:* Orange County (Member, Real Estate Section), Los Angeles County and American (Member, Corporation, Banking and Business Law Section) Bar Associations; State Bar of California. *LANGUAGES:* Taiwanese.

**GERALD L. GREENGARD,** born Santa Monica, California, January 21, 1961; admitted to bar, 1986, California. *Education:* University of California at Berkeley (B.A., with honors, 1983); University of Michigan (J.D., 1986). Recipient, Certificate of Merit Award. Honorary Membership, Society of Writers on Legal Subjects. Author: "Obstacles to Implementation of the Treaty of Rome Provisions for Transnational Legal Practice.". *PRACTICE AREAS:* Commercial Litigation.

**JEFFREY E. THOMAS,** admitted to bar, 1983, California. *Education:* California State University at Long Beach (B.A., 1978); Western State University (J.D., 1982). *PRACTICE AREAS:* Commercial Litigation.

**NIALL SWEETNAM,** admitted to bar, 1983, England (Barrister); 1984, Hong Kong (Barrister); 1990, California; 1994, Cayman Islands. *Education:* Trinity College; Cambridge University; Inns of Court School of Law, London. *PRACTICE AREAS:* Commercial Litigation.

**GARY R. WHITE,** born Glendale, California, November 3, 1952; admitted to bar, 1985, California. *Education:* University of California, Berke-

*(This Listing Continued)*

ley (A.B., 1974); University of British Columbia (M.A., 1978); University of Washington (Ph.C., 1981; J.D., 1984). *PRACTICE AREAS:* Commercial Litigation.

**TZONG-BING TSAI,** admitted to bar, 1994, California. *Education:* Grinnell College (B.A., 1988); University of California at Los Angeles (M.A., 1991); Golden Gate University (J.D., 1994). Recipient: First Prize of 1994 National Energy Law Policy Institute Writing Competition; Fourth Prize of 1993 Roger Traynor Moot Court Competition. *PRACTICE AREAS:* Commercial Litigation.

**JOHN Y. IGARASHI,** born 1969; admitted to bar, 1995, California. *Education:* University of California, San Diego (B.A., 1992); Loyola Law School of Los Angeles (J.D., 1995). Recipient, First Place District Award of Second Place National Award, Japanese American Citizens League Speech Competition. *PRACTICE AREAS:* Commercial Litigation.

REPRESENTATIVE CLIENTS: Bank of America; BMG Victor, Inc.; Citizens Thrift & Loan; Federal Deposit Insurance Corporation (FDIC); First Security Thrift; Freedom Financial Thrift & Loan; Lasergraphics; Resolution Trust Corporation (RTC); TAWA Supermarkets, Inc.; Tustin Thrift & Loan; Wells Fargo Bank.

## PALMIERI, TYLER, WIENER, WILHELM & WALDRON, LLP

A Limited Liability Partnership including Professional Corporations

Established in 1986

EAST TOWER - SUITE 1300
2603 MAIN STREET
P.O. BOX 19712
IRVINE, CALIFORNIA 92614-6228
Telephone: 714-851-9400
Telecopier: 714-851-1554; 851-3844; 757-1225
Email: general@ptwww.com

*General Civil and Trial Practice in all State and Federal Courts. Condemnation, Corporation, Estate Planning, Probate, Product Liability Defense, Real Property, Securities, Tax and Trust Law.*

### MEMBERS OF FIRM

**ANGELO J. PALMIERI,** (A PROFESSIONAL CORPORATION) (1926-1996).

**ROBERT F. WALDRON,** (A PROFESSIONAL CORPORATION), born Los Angeles, California, July 3, 1927; admitted to bar, 1955, California. *Education:* University of Oslo (Norway) and University of California at Los Angeles (B.A., 1951); University of California at Los Angeles (J.D., 1954). Phi Delta Phi. Instructor, Legal Aspects of Real Estate, University of California at Los Angeles, 1959-1963. Deputy County Counsel, Los Angeles County, 1955-1957. Assistant County Counsel, Orange County, 1957-1959. Judge Pro Tem, Orange County Superior Court, 1975-1978. *Member:* Orange County and American (Member: Committee on Condemnation Law, Section on Real Property, Probate and Trust Law, 1975—; Section of Litigation) Bar Associations; The State Bar of California (Member, Committee on Condemnation Law, 1975-1977); Diplomate, American Board of Trial Advocates. Fellow, American College of Trial Lawyers. *PRACTICE AREAS:* Condemnation Law; Litigation.

**ALAN H. WIENER,** (A PROFESSIONAL CORPORATION), born Hackensack, New Jersey, May 20, 1941; admitted to bar, 1967, California. *Education:* Wesleyan University (B.A., 1963); Stanford University (LL.B., 1966). Phi Beta Kappa. *Member:* Orange County (Member, Business and Corporate Law Section), and American Bar Associations. *PRACTICE AREAS:* Corporate Law; Real Estate Law; Tax Law.

**ROBERT C. IHRKE,** (A PROFESSIONAL CORPORATION), born Ames, Iowa, January 26, 1941; admitted to bar, 1966, California. *Education:* Purdue University (B.A., 1963); Stanford University (LL.B., 1966). *Member:* Orange County (Member, Business and Corporate Law Section), and American Bar Associations. *PRACTICE AREAS:* Corporate Law; Real Estate Law.

**JAMES E. WILHELM,** (A PROFESSIONAL CORPORATION), born South Gate, California, November 2, 1940; admitted to bar, 1969, California. *Education:* California State College at Long Beach (A.B., 1964); University of California at Los Angeles (J.D., 1968). Order of the Coif; Phi Delta Phi. *Member:* Orange County (Member, Estate Planning Section), and American Bar Associations. *PRACTICE AREAS:* Estate Planning Law; Estate Administration Law.

*(This Listing Continued)*

**DENNIS G. TYLER, (A PROFESSIONAL CORPORATION),** born Pendleton, Oregon, April 27, 1943; admitted to bar, 1970, California. *Education:* University of California at Los Angeles (B.A., 1966); University of California at Davis (J.D., 1969). *Member:* Orange County (Member, Real Estate Section), and American Bar Associations. **PRACTICE AREAS:** Real Estate Law.

**MICHAEL J. GREENE, (A PROFESSIONAL CORPORATION),** born Watsonville, California, May 28, 1946; admitted to bar, 1972, California. *Education:* Stanford University (A.B., 1968); Harvard University (J.D., cum laude, 1972). *Member:* Orange County (Member, Real Estate Section), and American Bar Associations. **PRACTICE AREAS:** Real Estate Law; Partnership Law.

**FRANK C. ROTHROCK, (A PROFESSIONAL CORPORATION),** born Pomona, California, August 8, 1947; admitted to bar, 1972, California; 1986, U.S. Supreme Court. *Education:* Occidental College (A.B., cum laude, 1969); Boalt Hall School of Law, University of California at Berkeley (J.D., 1972). Phi Beta Kappa; Order of the Coif. *Member:* Orange County (Member, Business Litigation Section; Chairman, College of Trial Advocacy, 1983-1984), American and Federal Bar Associations; Association of Southern California Defense Counsel; Defense Research Institute; Federation of Insurance and Corporate Counsel. **REPORTED CASES:** San Diego Gas & Electric Co. v. Superior Court, 13 Cal.3d 893 (1996); San Diego Gas & Electric Co. v. Superior Court, 38 Cal. Rptr. 2d 811 (1995); Ministry of Health v. Shiley, 858 F.Supp. 1426 (C.D. Cal. 1994); Artiglio v. Superior Court, 22 Cal.App.4th 1388 (1994); McGhan Medical Corp. v. Superior Court, 11 Cal.App.4th 804 (1992); Shiley Inc. v. Superior Court, 4 Cal.App. 4th 126 (1992); Stangvik v. Shiley Inc., 54 Cal.3d 744 (1991); Stangvik v. Shiley Inc., 273 Cal. Rptr. 179 (1990); Khan v. Shiley Inc., 217 Cal.App.3d 846 (1990); Shiley Inc. v. Superior Court, 250 Cal.Rptr. 793 (1988); Corrigan v. Bjork-Shiley Corp., 182 Ca.App.3d 166 (1986); Landscape Specialities v. Laborers' Intern., 477 F.Supp. 17 (C.D.Cal. 1979). **PRACTICE AREAS:** Pharmaceutical and Medical Device Product Liability; General Product Litigation; Civil Writs and Appeals.

**DENNIS W. GHAN, (A PROFESSIONAL CORPORATION),** born Bakersfield, California, February 5, 1952; admitted to bar, 1977, California. *Education:* University of California at Santa Barbara (B.A., 1974); Hastings College of Law, University of California (J.D., 1977). Member: Order of the Coif; Thurston Society. Participant, 1975-1976 and Developments Editor, 1976-1977, Hastings Constitutional Law Quarterly. *Member:* Orange County (Member, Real Estate Section) and American Bar Associations. **PRACTICE AREAS:** Real Estate Law.

**DAVID D. PARR, (A PROFESSIONAL CORPORATION),** born Trenton, New Jersey, July 17, 1951; admitted to bar, 1978, California. *Education:* Duke University (A.B., magna cum laude, 1973); Georgetown University (J.D., 1977). Member, 1975-1976 and Editor, 1976-1977, Law and Policy in International Business. Author: Comment, "Qualification as a Selected Purchaser in Customs Valuation," 9 Law and Policy In International Business 697, 1977; "Export-Import Bank Section of: Administrative Survey October 1974-September 1975," 8 Law and Policy in International Business 279, 1976. Law Clerk to Trial Division, U.S. Court of Claims, 1977-1978. *Member:* Orange County (Member, Sections on: Tax; Corporate Law) and American Bar Associations. **PRACTICE AREAS:** Corporate Law; Real Estate Law; Tax Law.

**CHARLES H. KANTER, (A PROFESSIONAL CORPORATION),** born Los Angeles, California, March 2, 1951; admitted to bar, 1976, California. *Education:* University of California at Santa Barbara (B.A., 1972); University of California at Davis (J.D., 1976). Member, University of California at Davis Law Review, 1975-1976. Court Law Clerk, U.S. Court of Appeals, 9th Circuit, 1976-1977. Panelist, C.E.B. Programs on Fundamentals of Civil Litigation, 1986-1987. *Member:* Orange County (Member, Business Litigation Section) and American Bar Associations. **PRACTICE AREAS:** Litigation.

**GEORGE J. WALL,** born Boston, Massachusetts, December 15, 1948; admitted to bar, 1974, Florida and New Jersey; 1979, California. *Education:* University of Virginia (B.A., 1971); University of Miami (J.D., 1974). Member, Endowment Committee, Orange County Performing Arts Center, 1985-1993. *Member:* The Florida Bar. **PRACTICE AREAS:** Corporate Law; Real Estate Law.

**L. RICHARD RAWLS,** born Hagerstown, Maryland, January 17, 1952; admitted to bar, 1977, California; 1988, U.S. Supreme Court. *Education:* Oberlin College and University of Southern California (B.A., magna cum laude, 1974); Georgetown University (J.D., 1977). Phi Beta Kappa. *Member:* Orange County (Member, Business Litigation Section) and American

*(This Listing Continued)*

Bar Associations; Defense Research Institute. **PRACTICE AREAS:** Litigation; Product Liability Defense.

**PATRICK A. HENNESSEY,** born Culver City, California, November 15, 1952; admitted to bar, 1978, California. *Education:* University of California at Berkeley (B.A., with distinction, 1975); University of San Diego (J.D., 1978). Member, Committee on Condemnation Law, State Bar of California, 1989-1991. *Member:* Orange County (Member, Real Estate Section) and American Bar Associations. **PRACTICE AREAS:** Condemnation Law; Litigation.

**DON FISHER,** born Fort Wayne, Indiana, July 31, 1952; admitted to bar, 1980, California. *Education:* Northern Illinois University (B.A., magna cum laude, 1974); Boalt Hall School of Law, University of California at Berkeley (J.D., 1980). Associate Editor, California Law Review, 1979-1980. Panelist, Mechanic's Lien Law, C.E.B. Programs. *Member:* Orange County (Member, Business Litigation Section) and American Bar Associations. **PRACTICE AREAS:** Litigation.

**GREGORY N. WEILER,** born Corona, California, August 16, 1956; admitted to bar, 1981, California. *Education:* California State University, Long Beach (B.A., with honors, 1978); University of California, Hastings College of Law (J.D., 1981). Member, Hastings International and Comparative Law Review, 1980-1981. Licensed Real Estate Broker, California, 1982. Member, Zoning, Land Use and Environmental Regulation Section, State Bar of California. *Member:* Orange County Bar Association (Member, Real Estate Section). **PRACTICE AREAS:** Real Estate and Land Use.

**WARREN A. WILLIAMS,** born Los Angeles, California, February 10, 1953; admitted to bar, 1978, California; 1980, U.S. Tax Court. *Education:* Yale University (B.A., with honors in Philosophy, 1975); University of Southern California (J.D., 1978). Member, 1976-1977, and Note and Article Editor, 1977-1978, University of Southern California Law Review. *Member:* Orange County (Member, Business and Corporate Law, Real Estate and Tax Sections) and American Bar Associations. **PRACTICE AREAS:** Real Estate Law; Corporate Law.

**JOHN R. LISTER,** born Long Beach, California, November 24, 1956; admitted to bar, 1982, California. *Education:* University of California at Irvine (B.A., 1979); Boalt Hall School of Law, University of California at Berkeley (J.D., 1982). Associate Editor, 1980-1981 and Executive Editor, 1981-1982, The Ecology Law Quarterly. Member, Boalt Hall Moot Court Board. *Member:* Orange County (Member, Business Litigation Section) and American Bar Associations. **PRACTICE AREAS:** Litigation.

**BRUCE W. DANNEMEYER,** born Santa Barbara, California, July 5, 1957; admitted to bar, 1982, California. *Education:* Valparaiso University (B.A., with high honors, 1979); Boalt Hall School of Law, University of California (J.D., 1982). *Member:* Orange County Bar Association (Member, Business Litigation Section). **PRACTICE AREAS:** Litigation.

**CYNTHIA M. WOLCOTT,** born Claremont, New Hampshire, February 5, 1954; admitted to bar, 1985, California. *Education:* Dartmouth College (B.A., magna cum laude, 1976); University of Southern California (J.D., 1985). Certified Public Accountant, California, 1983. *Member:* Orange County (Member, Business and Corporate Law, and Real Estate Sections) and American Bar Associations. **PRACTICE AREAS:** Corporate Law; Real Estate Law.

**JOEL P. KEW,** born Edwards Air Force Base, California, November 25, 1956; admitted to bar, 1982, California. *Education:* University of California at Berkeley (B.A., 1978); University of San Francisco (J.D., 1981). *Member:* Orange County (Member, Business Litigation Section) and American Bar Associations. **PRACTICE AREAS:** Litigation.

**MICHELLE M. FUJIMOTO,** born Fort Campbell, Kentucky, January 31, 1962; admitted to bar, 1986, California. *Education:* Pepperdine University (B.A., magna cum laude, 1983); University of Southern California Law Center (J.D., 1986). Author: "Computers: The Link to Missing Children," (1985), USC Computer Law Journal, Summer, 1986. *Member:* Orange County (Member, Business Litigation Section) and American Bar Associations; California Women Lawyers Association. **PRACTICE AREAS:** Product Liability; Commercial Litigation.

**GARY C. WEISBERG,** born Redlands, California, October 1, 1960; admitted to bar, 1987, California. *Education:* University of California at Irvine (B.A., magna cum laude, 1982); Hastings College of Law, University of California (J.D., 1987). Recipient, American Jurisprudence Award in Criminal Procedure. Participant, 1985-1986 and Articles Editor, 1986-1987, Hastings Constitutional Law Quarterly. Judicial Extern to the Honorable Spencer Williams, U.S. District Court, Northern District of California. Author: "Compensation for Loss of Business Goodwill in California Condem-

*(This Listing Continued)*

**PALMIERI, TYLER, WIENER, WILHELM & WALDRON, LLP,** *Irvine—Continued*

nation Cases," Cal. Bus. Law Rptr. (Apr. 1992). Adjunct Professor, Constitutional Law, Western State University College of Law. *Member:* Orange County (Member, Business Litigation Section) and American Bar Associations. **PRACTICE AREAS:** Litigation; Condemnation Law.

**MICHAEL H. LEIFER,** born Trenton, New Jersey, October 22, 1962; admitted to bar, 1988, California. *Education:* University of California at Los Angeles (B.A., 1985); Loyola Marymount University (J.D., 1988). Phi Delta Phi. *Member:* Los Angeles County, Orange County (Member, Business Litigation Section) and American Bar Associations. **PRACTICE AREAS:** Real Estate Litigation; Business Litigation; Condemnation; Public Agency.

---

**NORMAN J. RODICH,** born Travis A.F.B., Fairfield, California, August 3, 1961; admitted to bar, 1986, California. *Education:* University of California at Davis (A.B., with honors, 1983; J.D., 1986). Member, University of California at Davis Law Review, 1985-1986. Judicial Extern, California Supreme Court Justice Cruz Reynoso, Spring, 1985. *Member:* Orange County (Member, Business Litigation Section), Federal and American Bar Associations; State Bar of California (Member, Orange County Education Committee, Litigation Section). **PRACTICE AREAS:** Litigation.

**MICHELE D. MURPHY,** born Ellwood City, Pennsylvania, November 9, 1957; admitted to bar, 1988, California. *Education:* University of California at Los Angeles (B.A., cum laude, 1979); Loyola University of Los Angeles (J.D., 1988). Recipient, American Jurisprudence Awards in Evidence and Conflict of Laws. Staff Writer, 1987 and Executive Editor, 1988, Loyola Entertainment Law Journal. Author: Note, "United States v. MacDonald: Congress Acts to Make Sure that Crime Doesn't Pay-Sometimes," 7 Loy. Ent. L.J. 201, 1987. *Member:* Orange County (Member, Business Litigation Section), and American Bar Associations. **PRACTICE AREAS:** Litigation.

**SCOTT R. CARPENTER,** born Newport Beach, California, March 7, 1962; admitted to bar, 1989, California. *Education:* Stanford University (B.A., 1985); University of California at Los Angeles (J.D., 1989). Judicial Extern to the Honorable J. Spencer Letts, U.S. District Court, 1988. *Member:* Orange County (Member, Business Litigation Section) and American Bar Associations; State Bar of California. American Inns of Court, 1990-1991. **PRACTICE AREAS:** Litigation.

**RICHARD A. SALUS,** born Pasadena, California, November 20, 1964; admitted to bar, 1989, California. *Education:* University of California at Riverside (B.A., with honors, History, 1986); Hastings College of the Law (J.D., 1989). Recipient, Thomas Broadbent Award. Technical Editor, Hastings Constitutional Law Quarterly, 1989. Member, Board of Directors and Legal Advisor, Orange County Chapter, March of Dimes. *Member:* Orange County (Member, Sections on: Toxics and Estate Planning) and American Bar Associations. **PRACTICE AREAS:** Corporate Law; Environmental; Estate Planning Law; Estate Administration Law.

**D. SUSAN WIENS,** born Los Alamos, New Mexico, May 24, 1950; admitted to bar, 1989, California. *Education:* University of California at Irvine (B.A., 1972); California State University (M.A., 1974); Loyola Marymount University Law School (J.D., 1989). Scott Moot Court; Honors Board, Traynor Moot Court. *Member:* Orange County (Business Litigation Section) and American Bar Associations. **PRACTICE AREAS:** Litigation; Product Liability Defense.

**RONALD M. COLE,** born San Mateo, California, July 12, 1947; admitted to bar, 1990, California. *Education:* University of California at Los Angeles (B.A., 1975); Loyola Law School (J.D., 1990). *Member:* Orange County (Member, Business Litigation Section) and American Bar Associations. **PRACTICE AREAS:** Business Litigation.

**CYNTHIA B. PAULSEN,** born Covina, California, July 30, 1965; admitted to bar, 1990, California. *Education:* University of California at Los Angeles (B.A. in Economics, 1987); University of San Diego (J.D., 1990). Phi Delta Phi. Associate Editor, Journal of Contemporary Legal Issues, 1989-1990. *Member:* Orange County and American Bar Associations; American Inns of Court. **PRACTICE AREAS:** Corporate Law; Real Estate Law.

**SEAN P. O'CONNOR,** born Los Angeles, California, March 11, 1965; admitted to bar, 1991, California. *Education:* University of California at Los Angeles; Hastings College of Law, University of California (J.D., 1991). Phi Delta Phi. *Member:* Orange County (Member, Business Litigation Section) and American Bar Associations. **PRACTICE AREAS:** Litigation; Condemnation Law.

**SUSAN T. SAKURA,** born Saigon, Vietnam, August 28, 1967; admitted to bar, 1993, California. *Education:* Stanford University (B.A., with honors, 1989); George Washington University (J.D., 1992). Regional Winner, National Moot Court Competition. *Member:* Orange County and Asian-American (Orange County Chapter) Bar Associations; Orange County Barristers (Member, Board of Directors). **PRACTICE AREAS:** Business Litigation.

**JENNIFER ANNE KIM,** born Seoul, South Korea, May 19, 1968; admitted to bar, 1994, New York; 1995, Illinois; 1996, California. *Education:* Brown University (A.B., magna cum laude, 1990), Phi Beta Kappa; Harvard University (J.D., 1993). Member, 1990-1993 and Co-Chair, 1992-1993, Harvard Real Estate and Urban Development Forum. Co-Chair, Harvard Real Estate and Urban Development Journal, 1991-1992. *Member:* Orange County and American Bar Associations. **PRACTICE AREAS:** Real Estate.

**MATTHEW W. PASKERIAN,** born Hollywood, California, October 10, 1966; admitted to bar, 1996, California. *Education:* University of California at Berkeley (B.S., 1989); University of San Diego (J.D., 1995). Recipient: American Jurisprudence Award in Business Planning. Certified Public Accountant, California, 1993. Extern, to Justice Armand Arabian, California Supreme Court, 1994. *Member:* California Society of Certified Public Accountants. **PRACTICE AREAS:** Corporate; Business Law.

**PAUL B. LA SCALLA,** born Fullerton, California, November 13, 1971; admitted to bar, 1996, California. *Education:* University of San Diego (B.B.A., 1992); Loyola Marymount University (J.D., 1996). Member, St. Thomas More Society. *Member:* Orange County Bar Association; State Bar of California. **PRACTICE AREAS:** Products Liability; Business Litigation; Eminent Domain.

All Members and Associates are Members of the State Bar of California.

---

## PAONE, CALLAHAN, McHOLM & WINTON

*Established in 1981*

EIGHTH FLOOR, 19100 VON KARMAN AVENUE
P.O. BOX 19613
**IRVINE, CALIFORNIA 92713-9613**
*Telephone: 714-955-2900*
*Facsimile: 714-955-9009*
*Email: info@paone.com*
*URL: http://www.paone.com*

Westlake Village, California Office: 200 North Westlake Boulevard, Suite 100. Telephone: 805-371-5755. Fax: 805-446-1915.

*Real Property, Land Use, Environmental, Partnership, Business, Commercial and Public Law, Banking, Business, Real Property, Land Use, Redevelopment and Family Law Litigation. General Civil Trial and Appellate Practice, State and Federal Courts. Sports Law.*

*FIRM PROFILE: We can never change the way the world views lawyers, but we want our clients to, know that we are different. We recognize that the lawyer serves the client and that our livelihood depends upon the quality of that service and the fairness of our billing practices. We believe that the best service for the lowest price will be delivered by the most experienced attorneys. We also believe that clients prefer knowing that their lawyers has "been down this road before" and understand the practical needs of their business.*

*We do not "leverage" our profitability by hiring untrained and untested attorneys to learn at our clients expensive, As a result, we bring a sophistication and dept to the handling of our clients' needs which even the largest of firms often cannot match. We are successful because we know that our clients want specialization, as well as personal service and efficiency. They are willing to pay for quality, but are tired of paying for training, overhead costs and inefficiency.*

*Our firm is listed in the preeminent directory of lawyers. Because of our philosophy and expertise, we are fortunate to handle some of the most sophisticated and challenging projects found in our practice areas.*

### MEMBERS OF FIRM

**ROBERT E. CALLAHAN,** born New York, N.Y., August 17, 1949; admitted to bar, 1975, California, U.S. District Court, Central, Southern, Northern and Eastern Districts of California and U.S. Court of Appeals, Ninth Circuit. *Education:* University of California, Santa Barbara (B.A., 1971); University of Santa Clara (J.D., cum laude, 1975). Business Editor, Santa Clara Law Review, 1974-1975. Judicial Clerk, California Court of

*(This Listing Continued)*

Appeal, Fourth District, 1974. *Member:* Orange County Bar Association (Member, Business Litigation and Family Law Sections); State Bar of California (Member, Family Law Section); Sports Lawyers Association; Association of College Conference Counsel. *PRACTICE AREAS:* Family Law; Business; Real Property; Litigation; Sports Law.

**RICHARD J. FOSTER,** born San Gabriel, California, September 10, 1951; admitted to bar, 1981, California. *Education:* California State University at Long Beach (B.A., 1974); University of Southern California (M.P.A., 1977); Loyola University of Los Angeles (J.D., 1981). Member, Loyola University of Los Angeles Law Review, 1980-1981. *Member:* Orange County and American (Member, Litigation Section) Bar Associations; The State Bar of California. *PRACTICE AREAS:* Business Law; Real Estate Litigation; Construction; Eminent Domain.

**SUSAN K. HORI,** born Seattle, Washington, June 17, 1955; admitted to bar, 1980, California; 1982, District of Columbia. *Education:* University of Washington (B.A., magna cum laude, 1976); Boalt Hall School of Law, University of California, Berkeley (J.D., 1979). Phi Beta Kappa. Managing Editor, Ecology Law Quarterly, 1978-1979. Contributing Editor, Land Use Forum, Continuing Education of the California Bar. Author: "Protecting Wetlands: Agency Approaches to Mitigation," Land Use Forum, Continuing Education of the Bar, 1992; "The Future of the Endangered Species Act," Land Use Forum, Continuing Education of the Bar, 1991; "Extending the Rule of Reason: New Limits on the Range of Alternatives Required in an EIR," California Real Property Journal, State Bar of California, 1989. Co-Author: "Multiagency/Interest Agreements: Bridging the Chasm," Institute on Planning, Zoning, and Eminent Domain, Southwestern Legal Foundation, 1985. Law Clerk to Justice Burke, Alaska Supreme Court, 1979 Term. Staff Attorney, Office of the Solicitor, U.S. Department of the Interior, 1980-1982. *Member:* Orange County (Member, Real Estate Section), Los Angeles County and American (Member: Natural Resources Section; Environmental Quality Committee) Bar Associations; The District of Columbia Bar; State Bar of California (Member, Real Property Law Section Executive Committee, 1987-1991; Legislation Co-Chair, 1984-1986). *PRACTICE AREAS:* Land Use and Environmental Law.

**ALAN JULES KESSEL,** born Boston, Massachusetts, July 2, 1962; admitted to bar, 1987, California and U.S. District Court, Central District of California; 1989, U.S. District Court, Eastern and Southern Districts of California and U.S. Court of Appeals, Ninth Circuit; 1990, U.S. District Court, Northern District of California. *Education:* Tulane University (B.A., cum laude, 1984); New York University (J.D., 1987). Phi Beta Kappa; Phi Eta Sigma. Member, Annual Survey of American Law, 1985-1986. Author: "Prisoner's Rights: Unconstitutional Prison Overcrowding," Annual Survey of American Law, Volume 4, 1984; "Limited Nuclear War: A Critical Analysis," Hamline Journal of Public Law and Policy, Volume 10:2, June 1990. *Member:* Orange County and American Bar Associations; State Bar of California; Federal Bar Association. *LANGUAGES:* Spanish. *PRACTICE AREAS:* Business; Real Estate; Land Use; Environmental Litigation. *Email:* ajk@paone.com

**KENNETH S. KRAMER,** born Troy, New York, November 7, 1957; admitted to bar, 1982, California; 1984, New York. *Education:* University of Pennsylvania (B.A., 1979); University of Southern California (J.D., 1982). Lecturer, Practice Under the Subdivision Map Act, Pilot Practice Skills Training Program, California Continuing Education of the Bar, 1986-1987. Author: "Hazardous Waste Considerations," *California Real Property Sales Transactions,* CEB, 1993. *Member:* Orange County, New York State and American Bar Associations; State Bar of California. *PRACTICE AREAS:* Real Property Transactions and Finance; Commercial Leasing.

**STEVEN A. MCHOLM,** born Long Beach, California, December 28, 1949; admitted to bar, 1975, California; 1982, U.S. Court of Appeals, Ninth Circuit and U.S. District Court, Central District of California. *Education:* University of California, Irvine (B.A., cum laude, 1972); Loyola Marymount University (J.D., 1975). Instructor, Business Law and Contracts, University of California, Irvine, 1984—. Member, National Association of Real Estate Investment Trusts, Inc., 1986—. *Member:* Orange County (Member, Real Estate Section) Bar Association; State Bar of California (Member, Real Property Section). *PRACTICE AREAS:* Real Property Transactions and Finance; Commercial Leasing. *Email:* sam@paone.com

**TIM PAONE,** born Batavia, New York, December 21, 1949; admitted to bar, 1976, California; 1977, U.S. District Court, Central District of California and U.S. Court of Appeals, Ninth Circuit. *Education:* University of California, Santa Barbara (B.A., 1972); University of Southern California (J.D., 1975). Member, California Law Revision Commission, appointed by Governor George Deukmejian, 1985-1989. Member, 1978-1979, 1981-1983 and Chairman, 1979, 1982-1983, City of Huntington Beach Planning Commission. *Member:* Orange County (Member, Real Estate Section), Los Angeles County and American (Member: Urban, State and Local Government Committee; Committee on Land Use, Planning and Zoning, Subcommittee on Innovative Growth Controls, 1977—) Bar Associations; State Bar of California (Member, Real Property Section). *PRACTICE AREAS:* Land Use and Environmental Law. *Email:* tp@paone.com

**JOHN F. SIMONIS,** born January 27, 1961; admitted to bar, 1986, California. *Education:* Marquette University (B.S., magna cum laude, 1983); University of Michigan (J.D., cum laude, 1986). Phi Delta Phi; Order of the Coif. *Member:* State Bar of California. *PRACTICE AREAS:* Real Property Transactions and Finance; Commercial Leasing; Land Use. *Email:* jfs@paone.com

**MARTIN J. STEIN,** born Chicago, Illinois, January 22, 1950; admitted to bar, 1975, California. *Education:* University of Southern California (B.A., with honors, 1972); Southwestern University School of Law (J.D., 1975). Member and Chairperson, Department of Real Estate Task Force, California Building and Industry Association. *Member:* Orange County and American Bar Associations; State Bar of California; Community Associations Institute; California Building Industry Association (Chairperson, Department of Real Estate Task Force). *PRACTICE AREAS:* Real Estate Development; Subdivisions.

**DANIEL K. WINTON,** born Turlock, California, February 14, 1947; admitted to bar, 1973, California. *Education:* University of California, Santa Barbara (B.A., 1969); University of California, Berkeley (M.B.A., 1973); Boalt Hall School of Law, University of California, Berkeley (J.D., 1973). Vice President, Residential Development, The Sickels Group, 1984-1985. Counsel, Commercial Industrial Development Association, Inc., 1988—. Member, Board of Directors, 1992—, and Vice President, Southern California, 1995—, California Business Properties Association, 1992—; Member, Board of Directors: Orange County Business Council, 1993—; Industrial League of Orange County, 1993-1995; Orange County Private Sector Task Force, 1991—; Chair, 1994. *Member:* Orange County (Member, Real Estate Section), Los Angeles County and American (Member, Real Property Section) Bar Associations; State Bar of California (Member, Real Property, Tax Law and Business Law Sections). *PRACTICE AREAS:* Business and Real Property Transactions; Real Property Finance; Strategic Alliances; Joint Ventures and Partnerships. *Email:* dkw@paone.com

## ASSOCIATE

**KENNETH D. JOHNSON,** born Kansas City, October 4, 1957; admitted to bar, 1985, California. *Education:* Ohio State University (B.A., 1978); Case Western Reserve University (J.D., cum laude, 1985). *Member:* Orange County (Member, Sections on: Real Property; Public and International Law) and American Bar Associations; State Bar of California. [U.S. Marine Corp., 1978-1982]. *LANGUAGES:* French, Spanish and Russian. *PRACTICE AREAS:* Redevelopment; Affordable Housing; Real Property; Environmental Law. *Email:* kdj@paone.com

## OF COUNSEL

**JAMES R. CAVANAUGH,** born Washington, D.C., June 11, 1949; admitted to bar, 1974, Pennsylvania and Maryland; 1975, U.S. Court of Military Appeals; 1976, District of Columbia; 1977, California; 1986, Washington. *Education:* University of Notre Dame (A.B., magna cum laude, History, 1971; J.D., 1974). Phi Alpha Theta. Executive Director, Notre Dame Legal Aid and Defender Association, 1973-1974. *Member:* Orange County (Member, Real Property Law Section), Maryland State, Pennsylvania and Washington State Bar Associations; District of Columbia Bar; State Bar of California. [Captain, USAF (Assistant Staff Judge Advocate), 1975-1978]. *PRACTICE AREAS:* Real Property Transactions; Land Use.

**WILLIAM R. DEVINE,** born Lynwood, California, December 24, 1951; admitted to bar, 1981, Colorado; 1983, California; 1992, Washington. *Education:* California Polytechnic State University (B.S., Zoology, magna cum laude, 1974); Brigham Young University (M.S., Wildlife Ecology, 1978); J. Reuben Clark Law School, Brigham Young University (J.D., cum laude, 1981); University of Oregon. Tri Beta; Phi Kappa Phi. Member: Urban Land Institute; California Building Industry Association. *Member:* Orange County (Member, Real Estate and Environmental Law Sections) and American (Member, Urban, State and Local Government and Natural Resources Law Sections) Bar Associations; State Bar of California (Member, Environmental and Real Property Law Sections). *PRACTICE AREAS:* Real Estate Development; Land Use; Environmental; Natural Resources.

**ROGER A. GRABLE,** born Akron, Ohio, September 19, 1944; admitted to bar, 1971, California. *Education:* Brigham Young University (B.A.,

*(This Listing Continued)*

## PAONE, CALLAHAN, McHOLM & WINTON, Irvine—Continued

1967); Hastings College of Law, University of California (J.D., 1970). Phi Delta Phi; Order of the Coif. Member, Thurston Society. Editor, Hastings Law Journal, 1969-1970. Author: "Compensation for Possibilities of Reverter and Powers of Termination under Condemnation Law," 20 Hastings Law Journal 787, 1969; "Legal Limits of Government Land Use Regulations-An Expanding Concept," 2 Symposium Pepperdine Law Review 527, 1975. Co-Author: "Growth Control in California: Prospects for Local Implementation of Timing and Sequential Control of Residential Development," 5 Pacific Law Journal 570, 1974; "Tools for Local Growth Management: An Update," League of California Cities, Spring, 1987. City Attorney: Irvine, 1980-1990; La Palma, 1976-1986. *Member:* Orange County Bar Association (President, 1986); The State Bar of California (Chairman, State Bar Resolutions Committee, 1986; State Bar Conference of Delegates Executive Committee, 1988-1991). **PRACTICE AREAS:** Land Use; Environmental; Public Law.

**CARY D. LOWE,** born Linz, Austria, October 5, 1948; admitted to bar, 1974, California, U.S. District Court, Southern District of California, U.S. Court of Appeals, Ninth Circuit and U.S. Supreme Court. *Education:* University of Southern California (B.A., 1969; M.A., International Relations, 1970; J.D., 1974; Ph.D., Urban Planning, 1980). Lecturer: School of Architecture and Urban Planning, University of California at Los Angeles, 1980-1983; Law Center, University of Southern California, 1981-1983; School of Urban and Regional Planning, University of Southern California, 1984-1987; Center for Real Estate Development, University of Southern California, 1987-1990. Member: California Building Industry Association, 1984—; San Bernardino Downtown Task Force, 1992-1993; Governor's Public Investment Task Force, 1980-1981; Governor's Housing Task Force, 1978-1979; Los Angeles City Council Rent Stabilization Committee, 1978; Los Angeles Mayor's Task Force on Mortgage Lending, 1975-1976. *Member:* Orange County and San Bernardino County Bar Associations; State Bar of California (Member, Real Property Law Section, 1985—). **PRACTICE AREAS:** Land Use Regulation; Real Estate; Environmental; Corporate; Nonprofit Organizations. *Email:* cdl@paone.com

**KATHLEEN CAROTHERS PAONE,** born Pittsburgh, Pennsylvania, May 10, 1955; admitted to bar, 1980, California; U.S. District Court, Central, Southern, Northern and Eastern Districts of California; U.S. Court of Appeals, Ninth Circuit. *Education:* University of California at Los Angeles (A.B., cum laude, 1977); Loyola Law School, Los Angeles (J.D., 1980). Member, St. Thomas More Law Honor Society. Recipient, TICOR Foundation Scholarship. *Member:* Orange County and American Bar Associations; State Bar of California; The Association of Trial Lawyers of America. **PRACTICE AREAS:** Business, Real Estate and Land Use Litigation. *Email:* kcp@paone.com

**CARLA K. RYHAL,** born Colorado Springs, Colorado, July 5, 1959; admitted to bar, 1982, California; 1983, Texas; 1986, New York. *Education:* Pepperdine University (B.A., summa cum laude, 1979); University of California at Los Angeles (J.D., 1982). *Member:* State Bar of California. (Resident, Westlake Village). **PRACTICE AREAS:** Land Use.

**JOHN E. TAWA, JR.,** born Trois-Rivieres, Quebec, Canada, August 7, 1962; admitted to bar, 1987, California. *Education:* Colby College (B.A., magna cum laude, 1984); University of Virginia (J.D., 1987). Phi Beta Kappa. Governor, Wilshire Bar Association, 1993-1994. *Member:* State Bar of California. **LANGUAGES:** French. **PRACTICE AREAS:** Civil Litigation. *Email:* jet@paone.com

---

## JON PIERRE PARADIS, INC.

*A LAW CORPORATION*

*Established in 1980*

**18002 COWAN, FIRST FLOOR**
**IRVINE, CALIFORNIA 92614-6812**
*Telephone: 714-477-2400*
*Facsimile: 714-851-0108*

*Civil and Appellate Litigation in Business, Commercial, Landlord and Tenant and Real Estate Law.*

**JON PIERRE PARADIS,** born Canton, Ohio, February 15, 1942; admitted to bar, 1968, California and U.S. District Court, Central District of California; 1977, U.S. Court of Appeals, Ninth Circuit. *Education:* Long Beach State College (B.A., cum laude, 1964); University of California at Los Angeles (J.D., 1967). Member, Moot Court, University of California at Los Angeles. *Member:* Orange County Bar Association; State Bar of California; Consumer Attorneys of California; Orange County Trial Lawyers Association. (Member of Consumer Attorneys of California with recognized experience as a Trial Lawyer). **PRACTICE AREAS:** Contracts; Business Litigation; Real Estate; Real Estate Litigation.

REPRESENTATIVE CLIENTS: Himes-Peters Architects & Associates; Genlabs, Inc.; Craig Construction Co.; Hexcel Corp.; Tri-Level, Inc. Lithographers; J.F.M. Developers Inc.; Petrominerals Corp.; South Coast Helicopters, Inc.; Lil' Pickle, Inc.; Hoffman Sheet Metal; Westcliff Jewelers; Option One Mortgage Corporation; Van Deusen, Youmans & Walmsley, Inc., A Professional Law Corporation.

---

## PARILLA, MILITZOK & SHEDDEN, LLP

*Established in 1989*

**SUITE 1250, 1 PARK PLAZA**
**IRVINE, CALIFORNIA 92614-8509**
*Telephone: 714-263-1010*
*Telecopier: 714-263-1693*

*General Civil and Trial Practice in all California State and Federal Courts. Real Estate and Homeowner Association Law. Corporate, Business, Partnership and Commercial Law. and Creditor Rights Law.*

### MEMBERS OF FIRM

**MARC ETTINGER,** born Encino, California, December 11, 1957; admitted to bar, 1988, California, U.S. District Court, Central, Northern and Southern Districts of California and U.S. Court of Appeals, Ninth Circuit. *Education:* San Diego State University (B.A., 1979); Western State University (J.D., 1983). *Member:* Orange County and American (Member, Section on Business Litigation) Bar Associations; State Bar of California. **PRACTICE AREAS:** Condominium Law; Contract Law; Real Estate Property Law; Civil Litigation; Construction Law.

**BRADLEY N. GARBER,** born Canton, Ohio, July 3, 1958; admitted to bar, 1984, California; U.S. Court of Military Appeals; 1988, U.S. District Court, Central, Northern and Southern Districts of California; U.S. Court of Appeals, Ninth Circuit. *Education:* Ashland College (B.A., cum laude, 1980); Pepperdine University (J.D., 1983). Phi Alpha Theta; Omicron Delta Epsilon. *Member:* Orange County (Member, Sections on Real Estate and Business Litigation) and American (Member, Sections on: Corporation, Banking and Business Law; Labor and Employment Law) Bar Associations; State Bar of California. [Major, USMCR]. **PRACTICE AREAS:** General Business Litigation; Real Estate Property Litigation.

**STEVEN MILITZOK,** born Manhattan, New York, April 26, 1952; admitted to bar, 1978, California; 1979, New York; 1980, District of Columbia, U.S. Court of Appeals for the District of Columbia Circuit, U.S. Court of Appeals, Ninth Circuit, U.S. Tax Court, U.S. District Court, Central District and U.S. Court of Claims. *Education:* Franklin & Marshall College; University of Southern California (B.A., 1973); University of San Diego (J.D., cum laude, 1977); Georgetown University (M.L.T., 1980). *Member:* The District of Columbia Bar; The State Bar of California. **PRACTICE AREAS:** Real Estate Development Law; Partnership Law; Business Law.

**PAUL H. PARILLA,** born Chicago, Illinois, September 17, 1948; admitted to bar, 1973, Wisconsin; 1974, U.S. Court of Military Appeals; 1977, California and U.S. District Court, Central, Northern and Southern Districts of California; U.S. Supreme Court. *Education:* Carthage College (B.A., 1970); Marquette University (J.D., 1973). Delta Theta Phi. *Member:* Orange County and American Bar Associations; State Bar of California; Orange County Trial Lawyers Association; Los Angeles County Trial Lawyers Association. [Colonel, USMCR; Military Judge, 1975-1977]. **PRACTICE AREAS:** Real Estate Law; Business and Real Estate Trial Practice.

**RHEA S. SHEDDEN,** born Oil City, Pennsylvania, February 20, 1949; admitted to bar, 1982, California, U.S. District Court, Central District of California and U.S. Court of Appeals, Ninth Circuit. *Education:* Cornell University (A.B., 1971); University of Southern California (J.D., 1982). Legion Lex. Staff Member, University of Southern California Law Review, 1981-1982. *Member:* Orange County and American Bar Associations; State Bar of California (Member, Real Estate Section). **PRACTICE AREAS:** Construction Law; Real Estate Property Law; Shopping Center Law.

REPRESENTATIVE CLIENTS: AM Homes; Beauchamp Enterprises; California Title Reporting Service; Catellus Development Corp.; Century Homes; Children's Discovery Centers of America, Inc.; Crowell Industries; Greystone Homes, Inc.; Kenneth Leventhal & Co.; Lewis Homes Management Corp.; Mission Equity, Inc.; Monarch Business Forms, Inc.; Northern Counties Title Insurance Company; Pacific National Bank; Parducci Winery, Ltd.; The Penn-

*(This Listing Continued)*

hill Co.; Premier Group, Inc.; Prime Care Health Network, Inc.; South Coast Title Company; State Wide Investors, Inc.; T&B Planning Consultants, Inc.; Ticon General Contractors; Transcorp Pension Services, Inc.; Western Dental Services.

## PAYNE & FEARS

*Established in 1992*

**4 PARK PLAZA, SUITE 1100**
**IRVINE, CALIFORNIA 92714**
*Telephone: 714-851-1101*
*Fax: 714-851-1212*

*FIRM PROFILE: The firm specializes in representing companies in all aspects of Labor and Employment Law and General Business Litigation including Wrongful Termination Litigation, Civil Rights/Discrimination Litigation, Trade Secret and Unfair Competition Disputes, Management/Union Relations, Wage/Hour Matters, advising employers regarding Personal Issues, and Business Litigation involving Real Property, Contracts, Construction, Insurance Coverage, Construction Defect, Product Liability, Business Tort, Corporate and Fiduciary Relations Disputes.*

### MEMBERS OF FIRM

**JAMES L. PAYNE,** born San Bernardino, California, December 23, 1951; admitted to bar, 1982, California. *Education:* University of California at Irvine (B.A., 1975); Loyola Law School, Los Angeles (J.D., cum laude, 1982). Member, St. Thomas More Law Honor Society. Member, 1980-1981 and Articles Editor, 1981-1982, Loyola Law Review. Law Clerk to the Hon. Thomas Tang, Circuit Judge, U.S. Court of Appeals, Ninth Circuit, 1982-1983. Author and Lecturer: California Continuing Education of the Bar, 1983-1995. *Member:* Orange County (Member, Labor Law Section) and American (Member, Labor and Employment Law Section) Bar Associations; State Bar of California (Member, Intellectual Property Section). *PRACTICE AREAS:* Employment Law and Related Litigation; Wrongful Termination Law; Employment Discrimination Law; Civil Rights Law; Wage and Hour Law; Trade Secrets Law.

**DANIEL F. FEARS,** born Los Angeles, California, November 8, 1955; admitted to bar, 1983, California. *Education:* California State Polytechnic University (B.S., 1979); University of San Diego (J.D., magna cum laude, 1983). Research Editor, San Diego Law Review, 1982-1983. Staff Writer, Public Interest Law Journal, 1982-1983. Co-Author: "Avoiding Wrongful Termination in the 1990's," American Somerset, Inc., 1989. Lecturer, California Continuing Education of the Bar, 1989—. Delegate, California State Bar Association Convention, 1991-1994. *Member:* Orange County (Chairman, Labor Law Section, 1989; Member, Business Litigation Section) and American Bar Associations; State Bar of California. *PRACTICE AREAS:* Labor Law; Employment Law and Related Litigation; Wrongful Termination Law; Employment and Housing Discrimination Law; Civil Rights Law; Trade Secrets Litigation.

**DANIEL M. LIVINGSTON,** born Salt Lake City, Utah, July 6, 1957; admitted to bar, 1982, California; 1987, U.S. Supreme Court. *Education:* Stanford University (A.B., with honors, 1979); Brigham Young University (J.D., 1982). Associate Editor, Brigham Young University Law Review, 1981-1982. Author: Note, "Implied Warranties of Security in Residential Leases," 1980 B.Y.U. Law Review 681. Associate, O'Melveny & Myers, Los Angeles, California, 1982-1987. Shareholder, Call, Clayton & Jensen, Newport Beach, California, 1988-1994. *Member:* Orange County Bar Association; State Bar of California. *PRACTICE AREAS:* Business; Construction Litigation.

**DANIEL L. RASMUSSEN,** born Orange, California, March 27, 1959; admitted to bar, 1985, California. *Education:* Brigham Young University (B.S., magna cum laude, 1982); Boalt Hall School of Law, University of California, Berkeley (J.D., 1985). *Member:* Orange County Bar Association; State Bar of California; Association of Business Trial Lawyers. *PRACTICE AREAS:* Business Litigation.

**SCOTT S. THOMAS,** born Preston, Idaho, October 5, 1954; admitted to bar, 1982, California. *Education:* Brigham Young University (B.A., 1979; J.D., 1982). Member, Brigham Young University Journal of Legal Studies, 1981-1982. Co-Author: Comparative and Reverse Bad Faith: Insured's Breach of Implied Covenant of Good Faith and Fair Dealing as an Affirmative Defense or Counterclaim," Tort & Insurance Law Journal, Vol. 23 No. 1, Fall 1987. *Member:* Orange County (Chairman, Insurance Law Section, 1989-1990) and American Bar Associations; State Bar of California. *PRACTICE AREAS:* Business Litigation; Insurance Coverage.

*(This Listing Continued)*

**KAREN O. STRAUSS,** born Danville, Illinois, April 15, 1963; admitted to bar, 1988, California. *Education:* University of California at Los Angeles (B.A., magna cum laude, 1984); University of California, Boalt Hall (J.D., 1988). Phi Beta Kappa. *Member:* Orange County Bar Association (Member, Labor and Employment Law Section). *PRACTICE AREAS:* Employment Law; Wrongful Termination; Employment Discrimination; Trade Secrets and Unfair Competition; Labor Law.

**BENJAMIN A. NIX,** born Framingham, Massachusetts, December 18, 1961; admitted to bar, 1988, California. *Education:* California State University, Fullerton (B.S., with high honors, 1985); University of California, Hastings (J.D., magna cum laude, 1988). Order of the Coif. Member, 1986-1987 and Note and Articles Editor, 1987-1988, Hastings Law Journal. Extern for Hon. Stanley Mosk, California Supreme Court, 1988. *Member:* Orange County and American Bar Associations; State Bar of California; American Inns of Court. *PRACTICE AREAS:* Business Litigation; Civil Litigation; Trade Secrets; Unfair Competition.

---

**VALERIE L. MCNAMARA,** born Redondo Beach, California, August 13, 1960; admitted to bar, 1986, California. *Education:* University of California at Irvine; University of California at Berkeley (A.B., with distinction, 1982) Phi Beta Kappa; University of California, Hastings College of Law (J.D., cum laude, 1986). Phi Beta Kappa; Order of the Coif. Thurston Honor Society. *Member:* Orange County (Member, Labor and Employment Law Section) and Federal Bar Associations. *PRACTICE AREAS:* Employment Law; Labor Law.

**DOUGLAS A. BARRITT,** born Denver, Colorado, June 4, 1962; admitted to bar, 1990, California. *Education:* California State Polytechnic University (B.S., 1985); Loyola Marymount University (J.D., 1990). St. Thomas More Law Honor Society. Chief Articles Editor, Loyola of Los Angeles Int'l. & Comp. Law Journal. *Member:* Orange County Bar Association (Member, Labor and Employment Law Section). *PRACTICE AREAS:* Employment Law; Wrongful Termination; Employment Discrimination; Unfair Competition Law.

**THOMAS L. VINCENT,** born Pacoima, California, July 27, 1962; admitted to bar, 1990, California. *Education:* University of California at Santa Barbara (B.A. with highest honors, 1987); Stanford University (J.D., 1990). Phi Beta Kappa. Recipient, Robert Wilson Award for Outstanding Senior in Spanish and Portuguese Studies. Associate, Call, Clayton & Jensen, Newport Beach, California, 1990-1994. *Member:* Orange County Bar Association; State Bar of California. *LANGUAGES:* Portuguese. *PRACTICE AREAS:* Business; Real Estate; Construction Litigation.

**MARK A. SACKS,** born Pomona, California, April 30, 1964; admitted to bar, 1991, California. *Education:* University of California, Santa Barbara (B.A., summa cum laude, 1986); Harvard University (J.D., 1991). *Member:* Orange County Bar Association (Member, Labor and Employment Law Section). *PRACTICE AREAS:* Labor and Employment Law; Wrongful Termination; Employment Discrimination.

**JAMES G. KAY,** born Austin, Texas, March 15, 1950; admitted to bar, 1991, California and U.S. District Court, Central, Southern and Eastern Districts of California; 1992, U.S. Court of Appeals, Ninth Circuit. *Education:* University of Texas at Austin (B.B.A., with honors, 1971); Georgetown University (J.D., magna cum laude, 1991). Phi Kappa Phi; Beta Gamma Sigma; Beta Alpha Psi; Order of the Coif. Recipient, Lawyers Edition Awards, Evidence and Trial Practice. Associate Editor, Georgetown Law Journal, 1989-1991. Certified Public Accountant, Texas, 1972-1991. *Member:* Orange County Bar Association (Member, Business Litigation Section); State Bar of California. *PRACTICE AREAS:* Business Litigation; Construction Litigation; Insurance Coverage Litigation.

**DANIEL J. PAYNE,** born Long Beach, California, May 16, 1957; admitted to bar, 1988, California; 1990, U.S. District Court, Central District of California. *Education:* University of California at Santa Barbara (B.A., with high honors, 1979); Trinity College, University of Dublin, Dublin, Ireland; University of California at Los Angeles (J.D., 1988). Member, Moot Court Honors Program. *Member:* Long Beach and Orange County (Member, Business Law Section) Bar Associations. *PRACTICE AREAS:* Business; Land Use; Environmental; Construction Litigation.

**ERIC C. SOHLGREN,** born Los Angeles, California, October 16, 1955; admitted to bar, 1992, California. *Education:* Whitman College (B.A., 1978); Pepperdine University (M.B.A., 1985); Loyola University of Los Angeles (J.D., cum laude, 1992). Order of the Coif; Alpha Sigma Nu. Member, St. Thomas More Honor Society. Editor-in-Chief, Loyola of Los Angeles Law Review. Author: "Group Health Benefits Discrimination Against AIDS Victims: Falling Through the Gaps of Federal law -- ERISA, the

*(This Listing Continued)*

*PAYNE & FEARS, Irvine—Continued*

Rehabilitation Act and the Americans with Disabilities Act," Loy. L.A. L. Rev. 1247 (1991). *Member:* Orange County (Member, Labor and Employment Law Section) and American (Member, Labor Law Section) Bar Associations; State Bar of California (Member, Labor and Employment Law Section). *PRACTICE AREAS:* Employment Law; Wrongful Termination; Employment Discrimination; Employee Benefits.

**JEFFREY K. BROWN,** born Long Beach, California, March 13, 1965; admitted to bar, 1992, California. *Education:* Yale University (B.A., 1989); Boalt Hall School of Law, University of California (J.D., 1992). *PRACTICE AREAS:* Labor and Employment Law; Wrongful Termination Defense; Employment Litigation; Employment Discrimination; Wage and Hour Law.

**JANE M. FLYNN,** born Palo Alto, California, March 27, 1964; admitted to bar, 1993, California. *Education:* University of California, Santa Cruz (B.A., with honors, 1987); University of California, Hastings College of the Law (J.D., 1993). *Member:* Orange County Bar Association (Member, Labor and Employment Law Section); State Bar of California.

---

## PERKINS, ZARIAN & DUNCAN, P.C.
2030 MAIN STREET, SUITE 660
IRVINE, CALIFORNIA 92614
Telephone: 714-475-1700
Fax: 714-475-1800

Los Angeles, California Office: 1801 Century Park East, Suite 1100.
Telephone: 310-203-4646. Fax: 310-203-4647.

*Business Litigation including Securities, Real Estate, Construction, Insurance, Antitrust, Environmental and Commercial Disputes.*

**KENNETH L. PERKINS, JR.,** born St. Louis, Missouri, June 19, 1956; admitted to bar, 1984, California, U.S. District Court, Northern, Southern and Eastern Districts of California and U.S Court of Appeals, Ninth Circuit. *Education:* University of California at Irvine (B.A., 1980); University of Southern California (J.D., 1983). Member, 1981-1982, and Editor, 1982-1983, Hale Honors Moot Court Program. Former Partner, Wyman, Bautzor, Kuchel & Silbert (1990-1991); Katten, Muchin & Zavis (1991-1994); Allen, Matkins, Leck, Gamble & Mallory (1994-1996). *Member:* Orange County (Section on Business Litigation), Los Angeles and American Bar Associations; State Bar of California. *PRACTICE AREAS:* Business, Real Estate, Construction and Insurance Litigation.

**JOHN N. ZARIAN,** born Las Vegas, Nevada, November 23, 1962; admitted to bar, 1989, California; 1992, District of Columbia, U.S. District Court, Central, Southern, Northern and Eastern Districts of California and U.S. Court of Appeals, Ninth Circuit. *Education:* University of Utah (B.A., with honors, in Political Science, 1984; M.S., in Finance, 1989); University of Southern California (J.D., 1989). Phi Delta Phi. Marriner S. Eccles Fellowship in Political Economy, 1985-1986. Member: Hale Moot Court Honors Program; Jessup International Moot Court Team. Staff Member, Southern California Law Review, 1988-1989. Inn of Court, Legion Lex Chapter, 1989-1992. *Member:* Orange County, Los Angeles and American Bar Associations; State Bar of California; District of Columbia Bar; Armenian Bar Association. *LANGUAGES:* Spanish and Italian. *PRACTICE AREAS:* Securities, General Business and Commercial Litigation.

**ADAM D. DUNCAN, JR.,** born Salt Lake City, Utah, January 4, 1964; admitted to bar, 1990, California. *Education:* University of Utah (B.A., cum laude, 1986); University of Southern California (J.D., 1990). Phi Beta Kappa; Phi Kappa Phi. Member, University of Southern California Law Review, 1988-1990. Commissioner, City of Los Angeles, Department of Public Works, 1993-1995. *Member:* Los Angeles County Bar Association; State Bar of California. (Resident, Los Angeles Office). *PRACTICE AREAS:* Real Estate, Environmental, Securities and Commercial Litigation.

**DAN E. CHAMBERS,** born Davenport, Iowa, July 13, 1966; admitted to bar, 1991, California; U.S. District Court, Northern, Southern, Central and Easter Districts of California; U.S. Court of Appeals, Ninth Circuit. *Education:* University of Iowa (B.A., summa cum laude, 1988); Southwestern University, School of Law (J.D., 1991). Phi Beta Kappa. Member, 1989-1990 and Editor-In-Chief, 1990-1991, Southwestern University Law Review. Second Place Oralist, Western Region. National Moot Court Competition. Wiloman Scholar. Deputy District Attorney, Los Angeles County (1991-1996). *Member:* Los Angeles, Orange County and American Bar Associations; State Bar of California;. *LANGUAGES:* Spanish, Italian. *PRACTICE AREAS:* Business, Real Estate, Construction and Insurance Litigation.

---

## LAW OFFICES OF
## MARK D. PETERSON
NEWPORT GATEWAY TOWERS
19800 MACARTHUR BOULEVARD, SUITE 1450
IRVINE, CALIFORNIA 92612
Telephone: 714-757-4143
Facsimile: 714-757-4148
Email: mpeterson2@aol.com

*Business Litigation, Insurance Coverage.*

FIRM PROFILE: *The firm strives to provide its clients with high quality, creative and cost-effective legal services in business litigation and insurance coverage matters. Mark D. Peterson, formerly a partner in the Trial Division of the Litigation Department of Manatt, Phelps & Phillips has a broad litigation background which includes state and federal court actions, as well as private mediation and arbitration. He handles matters relating to real estate, banking, lender liability, directors and officers liability, health care, partnerships, real property secured loan transactions and landlord-tenant liability. Mr. Peterson also has extensive experience litigating insurance "bad faith" and other insurance matters, as well as providing advice regarding insurance coverage under various contracts, including general liability policies, directors and officers policies, title insurance policies, and financial institution bonds.*

**MARK D. PETERSON,** born Montebello, California, February 28, 1961; admitted to bar, 1986, California and U.S. District Court, Central District of California; 1988, U.S. District Court, Southern District of California; 1992, U.S. District Court, Northern District of California. *Education:* Stanford University (A.B., with distinction, 1983); University of California, Los Angeles (J.D., 1986). Guest Lecturer, "Pre-Trial Advocacy: Fundamentals of Insurance Coverage for the Litigator," University of Southern California Law Center, 1994-1996. *Member:* Orange County Bar Association (Insurance Law Section); State Bar of California. *LANGUAGES:* Spanish. *REPORTED CASES:* Daniel E. Dyer v. Northbrook Property & Casualty Insurance Company, 210 Cal.App. 3d 1540 (1989); Allstate Insurance Company v. Interbank Financial Services, 215 Cal. App. 3d 825 (1989); Roger Marsh v. Stanley K. Burrell, a/k/a M.C. Hammer, 805 F. Supp. 1493 (1992).

---

## PINTO & DUBIA, LLP
Established in 1987
2 PARK PLAZA, SUITE 300
IRVINE, CALIFORNIA 92614
Telephone: 714-955-1177
FAX: 714-833-2067

*Commercial, Industrial and Residential Real Estate. Real Property Acquisition, Development, Leasing and Finance. Toxic Substances, Property Management, Common Interest Communities, Foreclosure Law and Lender Workouts. Partnership, Corporation and Limited Liability Company Law. General Business Transactions. General Civil and Trial Practice, Complex Litigation, Unfair Competition and Business Torts. Construction Defect and Brokerage Litigation. Bankruptcy and Debtor-Creditor Reorganization.*

### MEMBERS OF FIRM

**SAUL B. PINTO,** born Saskatoon, Saskatchewan, Canada, January 4, 1954; admitted to bar, 1979, California. *Education:* University of California at Berkeley (A.B., with honors, 1976); University of Southern California (J.D., 1979).

**CHRISTIAN F. DUBIA, JR.,** born Duluth, Minnesota, May 21, 1948; admitted to bar, 1978, California. *Education:* United States Naval Academy (B.S., 1970); Pepperdine University (M.B.A., 1974; J.D., Valedictorian, 1978). Managing Editor, Pepperdine Law Review, 1977-1978. [Lieutenant Colonel, USMCR, Certified as Military Judge]

**MICHAEL R. TENERELLI,** born Glendale, California, November 12, 1951; admitted to bar, 1977, California. *Education:* Loyola University of Los Angeles (B.B.A., 1973); Loyola Law School (J.D., 1977). Member, Loyola University of Los Angeles Law Review, 1975-1976.

**KENNETH A. RYDER,** born New Haven, Connecticut, February 27, 1957; admitted to bar, 1982, California. *Education:* University of Notre

*(This Listing Continued)*

Dame (B.A., with high honors, 1979); New York University (J.D., 1982). Member, New York University Review of Law and Social Change, 1981.

**MARK K. WORCESTER,** born Burbank, California, September 9, 1955; admitted to bar, 1980, California. *Education:* University of Southern California (B.A., magna cum laude, 1977; J.D., 1980). Program Chairperson, 1992, Member and Director, California Bankruptcy Forum.

**MARK D. ERICKSON,** born Milwaukee, Wisconsin, May 6, 1957; admitted to bar, 1982, California. *Education:* University of California, Davis (B.A., 1979); Hastings College of the Law, University of California (J.D., 1982). Phi Kappa Phi. Member, Hastings Constitutional Law Quarterly, 1980-1981. [Capt., US Army, Trial Defense Service, 1983-1986]

**SHELLI J. BLACK,** born Torrance, California, December 25, 1961; admitted to bar, 1986, California. *Education:* University of California at Los Angeles (B.A., 1983); Loyola Law School (J.D., 1986).

### ASSOCIATES

**LYNNDA A. MCGLINN,** born St. Petersburg, Florida, October 23, 1967; admitted to bar, 1992, California. *Education:* University of Southern California (B.S., cum laude, 1989); Loyola Law School (J.D., 1992).

**J. SCOTT RUSSO,** born Santa Monica, California, July 24, 1965; admitted to bar, 1991, California. *Education:* University of California at Davis (B.S., 1987); Loyola Law School (J.D., 1991).

**JOHN M. LEVERETT,** born Springfield, Missouri, November 28, 1959; admitted to bar, 1993, California. *Education:* University of California at Irvine (B.S., 1982); Loyola Law School (J.D., 1993).

**LORI L. HEIMERL,** born Pasadena, California, December 30, 1969; admitted to bar, 1994, California. *Education:* University of Southern California (B.S., 1991); McGeorge University School of Law (J.D., 1994). Order of the Coif. Recipient, AmJur, Real Property. *Member:* Orange County Bar Association; State Bar of California. *PRACTICE AREAS:* Real Estate.

**ERIN A. OWEN,** born Fullerton, California, May 20, 1966; admitted to bar, 1996, California. *Education:* University of Southern California (B.A., 1989); Pepperdine University, School of Law (J.D., 1996). Pepperdine University Law Review and Inter-School Trial Team, 1995-1996.

---

## PIVO & HALBREICH
*Established in 1985*

**1920 MAIN STREET, SUITE 800**
**IRVINE, CALIFORNIA 92714**
*Telephone: 714-253-2000*

*General Civil and Trial Practice in State and Federal Courts. Professional and Products Liability, Medical Malpractice, Insurance, Disability Law and Elder Law, Conservatorships, Environmental and Employment Law, Trade Secrets. Social Security and Medi-Cal Appeals, Hospital Privileges Matters and Professional Medical Boards.*

*FIRM PROFILE: The Pivo and Halbreich firm offers high quality service and prides themselves in hands on firm management. All documents are intensively reviewed by the partners. The firm is listed in the Preeminent Law Directory.*

**KENNETH R. PIVO,** born Los Angeles, California, November 2, 1953; admitted to bar, 1978, California; 1979, U.S. District Court, Central District of California. *Education:* University of California at Irvine (B.S., cum laude, 1975); Hastings College of Law, University of California (J.D., 1978). Phi Delta Phi. Editor: Hastings Law News, 1975-1976; Constitution Law Quarterly, 1976-1978. Lectures and Presentations: Podiatric Risk Management Seminar, Sheraton La Reina Plaza Hotel, Los Angeles, Ca., January 14, 1989; Podiatric Risk Management Seminar, San Francisco, January 28, 1989; Interpreting and Analyzing Medical Records, UC Irvine, Extension, February 11, 1989; Diabetic Foot and Malpractice, O.C. Podiatric Medical Assoc. Seminar, Newport Sheraton, April 1, 1989; American Bar Assoc./Young Lawyers Div., Memphis, Tennessee, April 27, 1989; Interpreting and Analyzing Medical Records, UC San Diego, Extension, November 11, 1989; Risk Management and AIDS, East Los Angeles Regional Center, January 14, 1988; "Counter-Suits" and "DPM-Ortho Relations," Podiatric Risk Management Seminar, Los Angeles, January 23, 1988; "Counter-Suits" and DPM-Ortho Relations," Podiatric Risk Management Seminar, San Francisco, January 30, 1988; Risk Management and AIDS, Orange County Disability Center, March 16, 1988; American Postgraduate Podiatric Med. Assoc., Los Angeles, May 22, 1988; Board Presentations re: AIDS policy, Orange County Disability Center, May 26, 1988; AIDS, Harbor Regional Center, June 5, 1988; New Bar Admittee Presentations, June 14, 1988; AIDS Symposium, East Los Angeles Regional Center,

*(This Listing Continued)*

August 5, 1988; Risk Management, Orange County Developmental Disability Center, October 5, 1988; Risk Management, North Los Angeles Regional Center, October 13, 1988; "AIDS" and "Confidentiality and Client's Rights," American Assoc. Mental Retardation, October 20, 1988; New Bar Admittee Presentation, December 12, 1988; New Bar Admittee Presentation, June 17, 1987; Disability Section of State Bar, Los Angeles, June 20, 1987; Legal Rights of the Developmentally Disabled, Los Angeles, May 1, 1986; State Bar Affiliate Outreach Program, September 27, 1986; Paralegals in Medical Malpractice Litigation, UC Irvine, November 22, 1986; Paralegals in Medical Malpractice Litigation, UC Santa Barbara, December 6, 1986; Risk Management, Lanterman Regional Center, June 20, 1985. Member, Liaison Committee, Orange County Podiatric Association, 1986-1987. *Member:* Long Beach (Member: Superior Court Committee; Legislative Committee; Scholarship Committee, 1986-1988; Member, 1986-1988 and Chairperson, 1987-1988, Municipal Court Committee; Member: Board of Directors, 1985-1987; Legal Aid Pro Bono Committee, 1985-1986; Co-Chair, Sports Committee, 1984-1985), Los Angeles County, Orange County (Member, Orange County Medical Association/Bar Association Liaison Committee) and American Bar Associations; State Bar of California (Liaison: Board of Governors Committee on Access, 1988-1989; Board of Governors Committee on Discipline, 1988-1989; Board of Governors Committee on Administration & Finance, 1987-1988; Board of Governors Committee on Communication and Bar Relations, 1987-1988); California Young Lawyers Association (President, 1989-1990; Member, 2nd Vice President, 1988-1989 and Treasurer, 1987-1988, Board of Directors; Chair, Statewide Barristers' Presidents Council, 1988-1989; Chairperson: Roger Traynor Moot Court Competition, 1987-1988; Presidents Council, 1987-1988); California Judges Association (Member, Statewide Coordinating Committee on Public Forum Workshops); Long Beach Barrister Association (President, 1986-1987; Vice President, 1985-1986; Secretary-Treasurer, 1984-1985; Director, Legal Aid Counseling, 1984-1985); Orange County Medical Association (Member, Orange County Medical Association/Bar Association Liaison Committee). Member, Board of Directors: California College of Podiatric Medicine; The Wellness Community.

**EVA S. HALBREICH,** born Cracow, Poland, October 9, 1948; admitted to bar, 1975, California; 1976, U.S. District Court, Central District of California and U.S. Court of Appeals, Ninth Circuit; 1980, U.S. Supreme Court. *Education:* Sarah Lawrence College (B.A., 1970); Sorbonne University and L'Institute d'Etudes Politiques, Paris, France; Boalt Hall, University of California at Berkeley (J.D., 1975). Instructor, Trial Advocacy, U.S. Department of Justice, Washington, D.C., 1979, 1980. Assistant United States Attorney, Central District of California, 1975-1981. Judge Pro Tem, Los Angeles County Municipal Courts, 1986—. *Member:* Los Angeles County (Member, Judicial Committee) and Orange County Bar Associations; The State Bar of California; Association of Business Trial Lawyers; Association of Southern California Defense Counsel. *LANGUAGES:* French, Hebrew and Polish.

**DOUGLAS A. AMO,** born Los Angeles, California, April 12, 1957; admitted to bar, 1985, California and U.S. District Court, Central District of California; 1986, U.S. Court of Appeals, Ninth Circuit; 1991, U.S. Supreme Court. *Education:* University of California at Davis (B.A., 1979); McGeorge School of the Law, University of the Pacific (J.D., 1983). Member, Robert A. Banyard Inn of Court, Orange County. Judge Pro Tem, Orange County Superior Court, 1991—. Judge, Constitutional Rights Formulation of Orange County, 1989—. *Member:* Orange County and American Bar Associations; State Bar of California.

**RICHARD O. SCHWARTZ,** born New York, N.Y., November 3, 1952; admitted to bar, 1979, New York; 1980, U.S. District Court, Southern District of New York; 1983, California; 1994, U.S. District Court, Eastern District of California. *Education:* Boston University (B.A., 1974); Hofstra University; New York Law School (J.D., 1979). Author: "Do Constitutional Rights Exist if No One is Listening? The Legacy of In Re Hop," California Regional Centers Journal, Fall 1987. *Member:* Orange County and New York State Bar Associations; State Bar of California.

**MONA Z. HANNA,** born Cairo, Egypt, September 5, 1962; admitted to bar, 1987, California and U.S. District Court, Central District of California; 1994, U.S. District Court, Eastern District of California. *Education:* California State University at Los Angeles (B.A., 1984); Hastings College of the Law, University of California (J.D., 1987). *Member:* Orange County and Los Angeles County Bar Associations; The Barristers; California Women Lawyers; Orange County Women Lawyers. *LANGUAGES:* Arabic.

*(This Listing Continued)*

## PIVO & HALBREICH, Irvine—Continued

### ASSOCIATES

**CHARLES A. PALMER,** born Long Beach, California, March 3, 1949; admitted to bar, 1977, California; 1978, U.S. District Court, Central District of California. *Education:* California State University at Long Beach (B.A., 1972); Pepperdine University (J.D., 1977). Arbitrator, Superior Court Arbitration Program. LASC South District Settlement Officer. Member, Joseph A. Ball, Clarence S. Hunt, Inn of Court, Long Beach. *Member:* Long Beach (Member, Board of Governors, Legislative Committee) and Los Angeles County Bar Associations; State Bar of California; Association of Southern California Defense Counsel. *PRACTICE AREAS:* Construction Accident; Construction Defect; Trucking Accident; Toxic Injuries; Product Liability.

**WILLIAM J. MALL, III,** born Salina, Kansas, May 30, 1965; admitted to bar, 1990, California. *Education:* The Citadel (B.A., magna cum laude, 1987); Temple University (J.D., cum laude, 1990). *Member:* State Bar of California. *PRACTICE AREAS:* Medical Malpractice.

**KATHLEEN E. WILCOX,** born Upland, California, February 2, 1962; admitted to bar, 1990, California. *Education:* University of California, San Diego (B.A.,1985); California Western School of Law (J.D., 1988). Recipient, American Jurisprudence Award, Criminal Procedure. *Member:* Orange County Bar and American Bar Associations; State Bar of California.

**TIMOTHY J. LIPPERT,** born Washington, D.C., April 8, 1965; admitted to bar, 1992, California and U.S. District Court, Central District of California. *Education:* Villanova University; University of California at Los Angeles (B.A., 1987); Pepperdine University School of Law (J.D., 1991). *Member:* Los Angeles and Orange County Bar Associations. *PRACTICE AREAS:* Medical Malpractice.

**MICHAEL A. BRODIE,** born Pittsburgh, Pennsylvania, January 19, 1944; admitted to bar, 1969, Virginia; 1973, District of Columbia; 1975, Pennsylvania; 1984, California. *Education:* College of William & Mary (A.B., 1967; J.D., 1969); George Washington University (LL.M., 1975). Member, College of William & Mary Law Review, 1967-1969. *Member:* State Bar of California; Federal, American and International Bar Associations. [Major, Army JAGC, 1969-1973]. *PRACTICE AREAS:* Medical Malpractice.

**LANCE GORDON GREENE,** born Springfield, Ohio, March 21, 1961; admitted to bar, 1993, California. *Education:* Arizona State University (B.S., 1983); University of Minnesota (J.D., 1992). *Member:* State Bar of California. [Lt., U.S. Navy, 1985-1989]. *PRACTICE AREAS:* Medical Malpractice.

**ANNIE GLASS HENSHEL,** born New York, N.Y., April 19, 1943; admitted to bar, 1977, California. *Education:* University of California at Los Angeles (B.A., cum laude, 1973); Southwestern University (J.D., 1976). *Member:* State Bar of California; Association of Southern California Defense Counsel.

**JENNIFER BATLINER,** born Chicago, Illinois, March 12, 1969; admitted to bar, 1995, California. *Education:* California State University, Fullerton (B.A., 1992); University of San Diego (J.D., 1995). *Member:* State Bar of California.

REPRESENTATIVE CLIENTS: Physicians and Surgeons Underwriters Corp.; Fremont Indemnity; Kaiser Foundation Health Plan, Inc.; Kaiser Hospitals and related Medical Groups; American Continental Insurance Co.; The Doctors' Co.; Harbor Regional Center; Developmental Disabilities Regional Center; South Central Los Angeles Regional Center and Related Entities; The Travelers; Rockwell International Corp.; California National Physicians Insurance Company; Southern California Physicians Insurance Exchange; Daniel Freeman Memorial Hospital; Long Beach Memorial Center; Farmers Insurance Group of Cos.; Mateon Navigation Co., Inc.; MMI Companies, Inc.

## POMS, SMITH, LANDE & ROSE
### IRVINE, CALIFORNIA
(See Oppenheimer Poms Smith, Los Angeles)

## PRICE, GESS & UBELL, P.C.
Established in 1985

2100 S.E. MAIN STREET, SUITE 250
**IRVINE, CALIFORNIA 92714**
Telephone: 714-261-8433
Telecopier: 714-261-9072
Email: pgu@ix.netcom.com

*Patent, Trademark, Copyright, Trade Secret and Antitrust Causes and Related Litigation and Counseling.*

**JOSEPH W. PRICE, JR.,** born Philadelphia, Pennsylvania, November 25, 1941; admitted to bar, 1968, District of Columbia; 1970-1982, U.S. Court of Custom and Patent Appeals; 1971, U.S. Supreme Court; 1972, California; 1982, U.S. Court of Appeals for the Federal Circuit; registered to practice before U.S. Patent and Trademark Office. *Education:* Villanova University (B.M.E., 1964); Georgetown University (J.D., 1967); Golden Gate University (M.S., Tax, 1987). Delta Theta Phi. Recipient: 1992 Achievement Award, Orange County Patent Law Association. Author: "Price Restrictive Patent Licenses," Journal of Patent Office Society, February 1968; "Practical Guidelines to U.S. Patent Prosecution for the Japanese Practitioner", Patent Management, April, 1992. *Member:* Orange County and American Bar Associations; The State Bar of California; Orange County Patent Law Association (Founding President, 1982); Los Angeles Intellectual Property Law Association. *REPORTED CASES:* Angres v. Dioptics Medical Products, Inc., 2 USPQ 2d 1041 (C.D. Cal 1986). *PRACTICE AREAS:* Patent; Trademark; Copyright.

**ALBIN H. GESS,** born April 22, 1942; admitted to bar, 1972, California; 1977, U.S. Supreme Court; 1982, U.S. Court of Appeals for the Federal Circuit; registered to practice before U.S. Patent and Trademark Office. *Education:* University of Detroit (B.E.E., 1966); American University (J.D., 1971). Listed in Who's Who Worldwide, 1993. Author: "Competitive Product Design In The Face Of Valid Patents" New Matter, vol. 20, no. 1 Winter, 1995. *Member:* Orange County, Federal and American (Chairman, 1973-1974, Subcommittee of Patent Enforcement Section of Patent Trademark and Copyright Law Section) Bar Associations; State Bar of California, Senior Member; Institute of Electrical and Electronics Engineers (Chair, Orange County Section, 1994-1996; Board Member, Los Angeles Council, 1995-1997); Orange County Patent Law Association (President, 1989) Orange County Engineering Council. Secretary, 1995-1996); Los Angeles Intellectual Property Law Association. American Intellectual Property Law Association; Licensing Executive Society; Fellow: Institute for the Advancement of Engineering. *REPORTED CASES:* In re VE Holding v. Johnson Cos. Appliance, 917 F.2d 1574 (CAFC 1990). The U.S. Court of Appeals for the Federal Circuit cited Mr. Gess's writings in support of its decision; California Irrigation Services, Inc. v. Bartron Corp. 9 USPQ 2d 1859 (C.D. Cal. 1988). *PRACTICE AREAS:* Patent; Trademark; Copyright.

**FRANKLIN D. UBELL,** born Canton, Illinois, January 15, 1949; admitted to bar, 1975, California; U.S. Court of Appeals for the Federal Circuit; registered to practice before U.S. Patent and Trademark Office. *Education:* University of Illinois (B.S.E.E., with highest honors, 1971); George Washington University (J.D., with honors, 1975). Eta Kappa Nu; Tau Beta Pi. Member: Bronze Tablet; Knight of St. Patrick. Author: "Electronic Funds Transfer and Antitrust Laws," 93 Banking Law Journal 43, 1976; "Assignor Estoppel: A Wrong Turn From Lear," 71 Journal of the Patent Office Society 26, 1989. *Member:* Orange County and American Bar Associations; The State Bar of California; American Intellectual Property Law Association (Chairman, Computer Software Judicial Developments Subcommittee, 1989); Orange County Patent Law Association; International Trademark Association. *REPORTED CASES:* Adray v. Adrayhart, Inc. 68 F.3d 362 (9th cir. 1995). *PRACTICE AREAS:* Patent; Trademark; Copyright.

**STEFAN J. KIRCHANSKI,** born Berkeley, California, January 26, 1949; admitted to bar, 1992, California; registered to practice before U.S. Patent and Trademark Office. *Education:* University of California (B.A., with great distinction and honors, 1969; PhD., 1974); Southwestern University; Loyola University (J.D., 1992). Phi Beta Kappa. *Member:* State Bar of California; Orange Patent Law Association; American Society for Cell Biology; Society for Analytic Cytology. *PRACTICE AREAS:* Patent; Trademark; Copyright.

**DOYLE B. JOHNSON,** born Concord, California, June 3, 1966; admitted to bar, 1995, California. *Education:* University of California at Berkley (BSEE, 1988); Pepperdine University School of Law (J.D., summa cum laude, 1995). *Member:* American Intellectual Property Law Association; Orange County Patent Law Association.

*(This Listing Continued)*

**MICHAEL J. MOFFATT,** born Anaheim, California, April 3, 1962; admitted to bar, 1995, California. *Education:* California State University at Long Beach (BSME, 1986; MSME, 1992); Pepperdine University (J.D., cum laude, 1995). Law Review Editor, Pepperdine University 1994-1995. Author: "The Death Of The Voting Rights Act Or An Exercise In Geometry: Shaw Answers" 22 Pepperdine Law Review. *Member:* Orange County and American Bar Associations; Orange County Patent Lawyers Association. *PRACTICE AREAS:* Patents; Litigation; Trademarks.

**GORDON E. GRAY, III,** born Norfolk, Virginia, September 25, 1969; admitted to bar, 1994, California; 1995, U.S. District Court, District of Arizona. *Education:* University of Illinois (B.S., 1990); Loyola Law School (J.D., 1994). *Member:* Los Angeles County; The State Bar of California (Member, Intellectual Property Section); Orange County Patent Law Association. *PRACTICE AREAS:* Intellectual Property.

---

## RAITT & MORASSE

A PROFESSIONAL CORPORATION

Established in 1991

17320 REDHILL AVENUE, SUITE 370
**IRVINE, CALIFORNIA 92614-5644**
Telephone: 714-261-1700
Fax: 714-261-2073

*General Civil Litigation and Appellate Practice in all Courts. Real Estate, Corporation, Insurance and Business Law.*

**G. EMMETT RAITT, JR.,** born Santa Ana, California, May 26, 1951; admitted to bar, 1975, California. *Education:* Pomona College (B.A., 1972); University of Southern California (J.D., 1975). Phi Alpha Delta. Senior Staff Member, Southern California Law Review, 1974-1975. Author: "The Minor's Right to Consent to Medical Treatment: A Corollary of the Constitutional Right of Privacy," 48 Southern California Law Review 1417. *Member:* State Bar of California; American Bar Association; Los Angeles Trial Lawyers Association. *PRACTICE AREAS:* Real Estate Litigation; Business Litigation; Insurance Litigation.

**STEVEN R. MORASSE,** born Lynwood, California, October 25, 1958; admitted to bar, 1985, California. *Education:* Loyola Marymount University (B.A., 1981); University of San Diego (J.D., 1984). Clerk for the Honorable Irving Shimer, Los Angeles Superior Court and Motion Department, 1984. *Member:* Orange County Bar Association; State Bar of California. *PRACTICE AREAS:* Business Law; Real Estate Law; Insurance Law; Litigation.

---

**DESMOND J. COLLINS,** born San Pimas, California, July 11, 1967; admitted to bar, 1995, California; U.S. District Court, Central District of California. *Education:* University of California, Santa Barbara (B.A., 1990); Southwestern University School of Law (J.D., 1995). *Member:* Orange County Bar Association; State Bar of California. *PRACTICE AREAS:* Real Estate Litigation; Business Litigation; Insurance Law.

---

## RAMSAY & JOHNSON

A LAW CORPORATION

Established in 1984

SUITE 750, 19800 MACARTHUR BOULEVARD
**IRVINE, CALIFORNIA 92715**
Telephone: 714-476-5070
Fax: 714-851-8659

*Insurance Law and Civil Litigation. Insurance Coverage and Bad Faith, Subrogation and Insurance Defense.*

*FIRM PROFILE: Ramsay & Johnson's special expertise is in advising insurers on the handling, investigating, analyzing and/or litigating of insurance coverage questions. The lawyers of Ramsay & Johnson, ALC, are particularly experienced in property, casualty, environmental, errors and omissions, and life insurance coverage issues. Some of the firm members testify as expert witnesses on insurance issues. The firm also handles general civil litigation and appellate work emphasizing the representation of defendants in lawsuits involving defective construction and professional malpractice.*

**JANICE A. RAMSAY,** born Muskegon, Michigan, October 23, 1942; admitted to bar, 1970, California. *Education:* Indiana University (A.B.,
*(This Listing Continued)*

1964); Indiana University and University of San Francisco (J.D., 1969). Member, University of San Francisco Law Review, 1968-1969. Member, McAuliffe Law Honor Society, 1969. Member, National Moot Court Team, University of San Francisco, 1968-1969. Author: "Witherspoon v. Illinois: The Future of Capital Case Juries in California," 3 University of San Francisco Law Review 75, 1968; "Regulation of Sexual Conduct By Withholding Government Benefits and Privileges," 3 University of San Francisco Law Review 372, 1969; "The Spoliation of Evidence in a Subrogation Context: An Ounce of Prevention is Worth a Pound of Cure," Property Insurance Subrogation from A to Z, American Bar Association National Institute on Property Insurance Subrogation. *Member:* Orange County and American Bar Associations; State Bar of California; California Women Lawyers; Orange County Women Lawyers; Association of Southern California Defense Counsel; Defense Research Institute. *REPORTED CASES:* State Farm Fire & Casualty Company v. Tan, 690 F.Supp 886 (D.C. Cal. 1988); 690 F.Supp 886; Prudential - LMI Commercial Insurance Co. v. Superior Court of San Diego County, 51 Cal. 3d 674 (1990); Carty v. American States, 7 Cal. App. 4th 399 (1992). *PRACTICE AREAS:* Insurance Coverage/Bad Faith Litigation; Property Claim Coverage Issues; Environmental Insurance; Litigation; Insurance Fraud; Insurance Subrogation.

**JUDY J. JOHNSON,** born Minneapolis, Minnesota, May 4, 1952; admitted to bar, 1977, California. *Education:* Stanford University (B.A., with distinction, 1974); University of Southern California (J.D., 1977). *Member:* Orange County (Member, Insurance Law Section) and American (Member, Property Insurance Law and Litigation Sections) Bar Associations; The State Bar of California; Orange County Women Lawyers; American Inns of Court (Master Bencher). *PRACTICE AREAS:* Insurance Coverage/Bad Faith Law; Professional Errors and Omissions Law; Insurance Defense Law.

**PHILLIP E. SMITH,** born Minneapolis, Minnesota, March 3, 1960; admitted to bar, 1985, California. *Education:* California Lutheran College (B.A., summa cum laude, 1982); Loyola Law School (J.D., 1985). Alpha Mu Gamma. *Member:* Orange County (Secretary/Treasurer, Insurance Law Section, 1989—) and American Bar Associations; State Bar of California. *REPORTED CASES:* Nationwide Mutual Insurance Co.. v. Devlin, 11 Cal. App. 4th 81 (1992). *PRACTICE AREAS:* Insurance Coverage; Bad Faith Law; Environmental Insurance Litigation; Excess Insurance Law; Casualty Insurance Law.

**STEPHEN E. SMITH,** born Minneapolis, Minnesota, March 3, 1960; admitted to bar, 1985, California. *Education:* California Lutheran College (B.A., summa cum laude, 1982); University of Southern California (J.D., 1985). Alpha Mu Gamma. Recipient, American Jurisprudence Award for Professional Responsibility. *Member:* Orange County and American Bar Associations; The State Bar of California; Association of Southern California Defense Counsel. *PRACTICE AREAS:* Insurance Coverage; Bad Faith Law; Litigation.

**KAREN A. GRUBER,** born Cleveland, Ohio, October 16, 1951; admitted to bar, 1987, California and U.S. District Court, Southern District of California; 1988, U.S. District Court, Central District of California. *Education:* University of California at Irvine (B.A., cum laude, 1982); University of San Diego (J.D., 1987). Recipient, American Jurisprudence Award, Professional Responsibility. Internship: University of San Diego Institute on International and Comparative Law, London; University of San Diego Environmental Law Clinic. *Member:* Orange County and American Bar Associations; State Bar of California. *REPORTED CASES:* Zands v. Nelson, 779 F.Supp. 1254 (S.D. Cal. 1991); Zands v. Nelson, 797 F.Supp. 805 (S.D. Cal. 1992). *PRACTICE AREAS:* Environmental Insurance Litigation; Environmental Law; Environmental Liability Law; Insurance Coverage; Insurance Defense Law.

**JAMES P. CARTER,** born Provo, Utah, November 25, 1963; admitted to bar, 1990, California. *Education:* Brigham Young University (B.A., 1987; J.D., 1990). Phi Delta Phi. Member: Order of Barristers; American Inns of Court; Moot Court Board of Advocates. *Member:* Orange County Bar Association (Member, Insurance Law Section); State Bar of California. *LANGUAGES:* French. *REPORTED CASES:* Carty v. American States Insurance Co., 7 Cal. App. 4th 399 (1992); Zands v. Nelson, 797 F.Supp. 805 (S.D. Cal. 1992). *PRACTICE AREAS:* Insurance Coverage and Defense; Civil Litigation; Bad Faith.

**CYNTHIA CARUSO PALIN,** born Norfolk, Virginia, March 30, 1959; admitted to bar, 1986, Arizona and U.S. District Court, District of Arizona; 1989, California and U.S. Court of Appeals, Ninth Circuit. *Education:* Arizona State University (B.S., 1980; J.D., 1986); Georgetown University Law Center. Recipient, Regents Academic Scholarship. *Member:* Orange County and American Bar Associations; State Bar of Arizona; State
*(This Listing Continued)*

**RAMSAY & JOHNSON, A LAW CORPORATION, Irvine—Continued**

Bar of California. *REPORTED CASES:* Martinez v. State Workman's Compensation Insurance Fund of the State of Arizona. *PRACTICE AREAS:* Property and Commercial Insurance Coverage and Defense; Legal Malpractice Defense; Personal Injury Law.

**KIMBERLY H. CORNWELL,** born Buffalo, New York, May 11, 1961; admitted to bar, 1987, New Jersey, New York and U.S. District Court, District of New Jersey; 1988, U.S. District Court, Eastern and Southern Districts of New York; 1992, California. *Education:* Northwestern University (1978-1980); Syracuse University (B.S., 1982); New York Law School (J.D., 1987). *Member:* Orange County, New Jersey State, New York State and American Bar Associations; State Bar of California. *PRACTICE AREAS:* Insurance Coverage and Defense.

**VICTORIA L. GUNTHER,** born Minneapolis, Minnesota, August 2, 1962; admitted to bar, 1989, California. *Education:* California State University at Northridge (B.A., 1986); Loyola Marymount University (J.D., 1989). Phi Delta Phi. American Jurisprudence Award in Development of Legal Thought. Mabel Wilson Richards Scholarship. *Member:* Orange County Bar Association; State Bar of California; California Women Lawyers. *PRACTICE AREAS:* Insurance Coverage.

**MICHAEL J. LOGAN,** born Los Angeles, California, July 28, 1942; admitted to bar, 1973, California. *Education:* University of Southern California (B.S., 1965); Southwestern University (J.D., 1972). *Member:* State Bar of California. *PRACTICE AREAS:* Insurance Defense and Coverage.

**RENEE FRIEND GURWITZ,** born Carmichael, California, June 20, 1970; admitted to bar, 1994, California. *Education:* California State University, Sacramento (B.A., 1991); McGeorge School of Law (J.D., 1994). Phi Alpha Delta. Member, Order of Barristers. Recipient, William D. James Foundation Scholarship. *Member:* Orange County and American Bar Associations; State Bar of California. *PRACTICE AREAS:* Insurance Coverage; Insurance Defense.

**JOSEPH C. GEBARA,** born Lincoln, Nebraska, October 17, 1963; admitted to bar, 1990, Arizona; 1991, California; 1992, U.S. District Court, Central and Southern Districts of California and U.S. Court of Appeals, Ninth Circuit. *Education:* University of Southern California (B.S., 1986); Brigham Young University (J.D., cum laude, 1990). Law Clerk, The Honorable Jefferson L. Lankford, Arizona Court of Appeals, 1990-1991. *Member:* Orange County Bar Association; State Bar of Arizona; State Bar of California. *PRACTICE AREAS:* Insurance Coverage; Insurance Defense; Civil Litigation.

**TODD E. WENDEL,** born Las Vegas, Nevada, July 1, 1962; admitted to bar, 1992, Utah and U.S. District Court, District of Utah; 1995, California. *Education:* Brigham Young University (B.S., 1986); University of Utah (M.B.A., 1989; J.D., 1992). *Member:* Orange County Bar Association; State Bar of California; Utah State Bar. *PRACTICE AREAS:* Insurance Coverage; Insurance Defense.

**KIM G. DUNNING,** born Cleveland, Ohio, September 16, 1949; admitted to bar, 1977, Texas; 1978, California and U.S. District Court, Central District of California. *Education:* Stanford University (B.A., 1971); Southern Methodist University (J.D., with honors, 1977); University of California, at Davis (M.A., 1992). Phi Delta Phi. *Member:* Los Angeles County and Orange County Bar Association; State Bar of California; State Bar of Texas. *PRACTICE AREAS:* First Party Insurance; Appellate Practice.

**CHRISTOPHER S. ANDRE,** born Sanitarium, California, August 16, 1964; admitted to bar, 1995, California and U.S. District Court, Central District of California. *Education:* California State University, Fullerton (B.A., with high honors, 1990); Loyola Marymount University (J.D., 1995). *Member:* Orange County and American Bar Association; State Bar of California. *PRACTICE AREAS:* First and Third Party Insurance Defense; Insurance Coverage.

**JOAN C. DONNELLAN,** born Whittier, California, January 4, 1952; admitted to bar, 1978, California, U.S. District Court, Northern, Southern and Central Districts of California and U.S. Supreme Court. *Education:* Whittier College (B.A., 1974); Pepperdine University (J.D., 1977; M.B.A., 1989). Phi Alpha Delta. Co-Author, "Secured Transactions," Bancroft Whitney. *Member:* State Bar of California (Member: Corporations Committee; Business Law Section, 1985-1988; UCC Committee, 1989-1994 and Chair, UCC Committee, 1992-1993); American Bar Association (Member: Business Law Section; Commercial Law Section; Employment Law Section). *PRACTICE AREAS:* Commercial Law; Employment Law; Banking Law; Insurance Law.

REPRESENTATIVE CLIENTS: State Farm Fire and Casualty Co.; Nationwide Insurance Cos.; 20th Century Insurance Co.; Fireman's Fund Insurance Cos.; American States Insurance Co.; Lawyers Mutual Insurance Co.; Wausau Insurance Cos.; ITT Hartford Insurance Group; Ohio Casualty Insurance Co.; Zurich American Group.

---

## TERRY L. RHODES
*19762 MACARTHUR BOULEVARD, SUITE 100*
**IRVINE, CALIFORNIA 92715**
*Telephone: 714-752-2285*

*General Business, Real Estate and Estate and Tax Planning.*

**TERRY L. RHODES,** born Los Angeles, California, April 23, 1940; admitted to bar, 1969, California. *Education:* California State University at Long Beach (B.S., 1963); University of California, Los Angeles (J.D., 1968). Order of the Coif. Certified Public Accountant, California, 1965. *Member:* Los Angeles County, Orange County and American Bar Associations; State Bar of California; California Society of Certified Public Accountants (Orange County Chapter).

---

## JEFFREY A. ROBINSON
*2301 DUPONT DRIVE, SUITE 410*
**IRVINE, CALIFORNIA 92612**
*Telephone: 714-752-7007*
*Fax: 714-752-7023*

*Specializing in the representation of domestic and foreign businesses in all aspects of commercial and administrative litigation, including trial, appellate and administrative proceedings in both state and federal courts.*

**JEFFREY A. ROBINSON,** born Bremerhaven, Germany, March 25, 1956; admitted to bar, 1983, District of Columbia; 1987, California. *Education:* University of Utah (B.A., magna cum laude, 1980); Brigham Young University (J.D., summa cum laude, 1983). Phi Beta Kappa; J. Reuben Clark Scholar. Lead Article Editor, Brigham Young University Law Review, 1982-1983. Author: Automatic Recovery of Attorneys Fees For the Prevailing Party; Ending the Conflict Between Principles and Pocketbook, 35 Orange County Lawyer 33 (June 1993); "The Use of A Rule 37 (b) (2) (A) Sanction to Establish In Personam Jurisdiction," 1982 BYU Law Review 103; "An Assessment of State and Federal Jurisdiction to Regulate Access Charges After the AT&T Divestiture," 1983 BYU Law Review 376. Judicial Clerk to Judge Malcolm R. Wilkey, U.S. Court of Appeals for the District of Columbia Circuit, 1983-1984. Legal Assistant, Judge Charles N. Brower, Iran-United States Claims Tribunal, The Hague, 1985-1987. Associate: Gibson, Dunn & Crutcher 1984-1985, 1987-1990; Associate and Partner, Chapman, Fuller & Bollard, 1991-1993. *Member:* Orange County and American Bar Associations. *REPORTED CASES:* Golden Cheese Company of California v. Voss, 230 Cal. App. 3d 547 & 727 (1991). *PRACTICE AREAS:* General Civil Litigation; Dispute Resolutions; Trials; Appellate and Administrative Proceedings.

REPRESENTATIVE CLIENTS: Golden Cheese Company of California; JDL Corporation.

---

## ROBINSON & CAMPBELL
*ONE PARK PLAZA, SUITE 1250*
**IRVINE, CALIFORNIA 92714**
*Telephone: 714-263-8790*
*Fax: 714-263-1793*

*Trials and Appeals in State and Federal Courts and Alternative Dispute Resolution involving Real Estate, Finance and Construction Litigation, Partnership, Corporate, Business and Employment Disputes. Commercial Fraud, Business Torts, Breach of Contract, Collection and Insurance, Sexual Harassment, Wrongful Termination, Civil Rights and Discrimination.*

**ROBERT C. ROBINSON,** born New York, N.Y., April 7, 1956; admitted to bar, 1980, New York; 1981, U.S. Court of Military Appeals; 1983, California; 1984, U.S. District Court, Central and Southern Districts of California. *Education:* State University of New York, College at Buffalo (B.S., summa cum laude, 1977); Brooklyn Law School (J.D., 1980). American Jurisprudence in Contracts at Brooklyn Law. Editor, The Orange County Lawyer, 1990. *Member:* Orange County Bar Association (Member, Board of Directors 1991-1992; Member, Labor, Business Litigation and

*(This Listing Continued)*

Appellate Law Sections); California Employment Lawyers Association; The Association of Trial Lawyers of America. [Lieut. Col., USMCR, Judge Advocate]. *PRACTICE AREAS:* Employment Litigation; Business Litigation; General Commercial Law; Real Estate; Litigation.

**WARREN B. CAMPBELL,** born Greeley, Colorado, May 13, 1949; admitted to bar, 1976, California; 1977, U.S. Court of Military Appeals; 1981, Texas; 1982, U.S. District Court, Southern District of Texas; 1986, U.S. District Court, Central District of California. *Education:* California State University at Los Angeles (B.A., 1972); Pepperdine University (J.D., 1976). *Member:* Orange County Bar Association; State Bar of California; State Bar of Texas. [Major, USMCR, Judge Advocate]. *PRACTICE AREAS:* General Commercial; Construction; Insurance and Real Estate Litigation.

---

## ROSENBAUM & DEIHL

A PROFESSIONAL CORPORATION

8001 IRVINE CENTER DRIVE, SUITE 1500
**IRVINE, CALIFORNIA 92718**
Telephone: 714-753-1990
Fax: 714-753-1888

*General Business, Corporate Law, Tax Law, Business Litigation, Estate Planning, Mergers and Acquisitions, Real Estate Law.*

FIRM PROFILE: *The Firm is a general business practice. The Firm has an additional special emphasis on mergers and acquisitions, and business continuation planning for closely-held businesses. The Firm serves as corporate counsel to numerous domestic corporations, as well as corporations based outside the United States, and business owners. Mr. Rosenbaum is an experienced speaker and lecturer in the areas of business and estate planning, frequently speaking throughout California. Mr. Rosenbaum has also served as an expert witness in litigation matters involving issues of California general corporate law.*

**KEITH A. ROSENBAUM,** born Brooklyn, New York, December 23, 1958; admitted to bar, 1982, California; 1984, U.S. Tax Court; 1987, U.S. Supreme Court. *Education:* Brooklyn College; California State University at Fullerton (B.A., 1979); California Western School of Law (J.D., magna cum laude, 1982); New York University (LL.M., in Taxation, 1984). Founder, California Badge & Gavel Society. Author: "An Introduction to the Mexican Maquiladoro Program," California Business Law Practitioner, Vol. IV, No. 2, Spring, 1989; "Due Diligence for Buying or Selling a Business," Inc. Magazine, February 1996. Adjunct Law Professor, Corporations and Federal Income Tax, Western State University College of Law, 1985—. Instructor, Legal Research and Writing, California Western School of Law, 1980-1981. Senior Reserve Police Officer, City of Irvine, 1983—.

**RICHARD T. DEIHL,** born Whittier, California, May 11, 1951; admitted to bar, 1977, California. *Education:* Whittier College (B.A., 1973); Pepperdine University College of Law (J.D., 1977). General Counsel and Vice President, The Lusk Company, Irvine, California, 1978-1993. *Member:* Los Angeles County, Orange County and American Bar Associations; State Bar of California. *PRACTICE AREAS:* General Business; Corporate Law; Real Estate; Corporate Finance.

---

**PAUL R. HUBER,** born Los Angeles, California, April 4, 1956; admitted to bar, 1989, California. *Education:* University of California at Los Angeles (B.A., 1977); Western State University (J.D., 1989). *Member:* Orange County and American Bar Associations. *PRACTICE AREAS:* Business Litigation; General Business.

---

## ROSS, DIXON & MASBACK, L.L.P.

5 PARK PLAZA, SUITE 1200
**IRVINE, CALIFORNIA 92614-8529**
Telephone: 714-622-2700
Fax: 714-622-2739

Washington, D.C. Office: 601 Pennsylvania Avenue, N.W., North Building, 20004-2688. Telephone: 202-662-2000.

*General Trial and Appellate Practice before State and Federal Courts, Insurance Coverage Litigation and Counseling, Directors and Officers Liability, Professional Liability, Corporate, First Amendment, Media and Intellectual Property Litigation.*

(This Listing Continued)

---

### RESIDENT MEMBER

**ROBERT M. POZIN,** born Chicago, Illinois, November 2, 1954; admitted to bar, 1980, District of Columbia; 1994, California; U.S. District Court, Central, Southern, Northern and Eastern Districts of California; U.S. Court of Appeals, Ninth, Fourth, Seventh, Eighth and District of Columbia Circuits. *Education:* Yale University (B.A., cum laude, 1976); Harvard University (J.D., cum laude, 1979). Developments Editor, Harvard Law Review, 1978-1979. Co-Author: "Internal Corporate Investigations," Securities Law Techniques, Matthew Bender, 1985; "Bankruptcy Trustee and Examiner Investigations," Securities Law Techniques, Matthew Bender, 1985; "Computer Evidence at Trial," ABA National Institutes, 1985. Author: Note, "Intracorporate Conspiracies Under 42 U.S.C. Section 1985 (c)," 92 Harvard Law Review 470, 1978. Law Clerk to Chief Judge Lloyd F. MacMahon, U.S. District Court, Southern District of New York, 1979-1980. *Member:* Orange County and American Bar Associations; The District of Columbia Bar; State Bar of California.

---

**PASCAL W. DI FRONZO,** born Los Angeles, California, April 11, 1964; admitted to bar, 1989, California; U.S. District Court, Northern, Central and Southern Districts of California and U.S. Court of Appeals, Ninth Circuit. *Education:* University of California at Los Angeles (B.A., with honors, 1986); University of California, Hastings College of the Law (J.D., 1989). Associate Editor, Research and Development, The Hastings International & Comparative Law Review, 1988-1989. Author: "The Hague Evidence Convention in the Aftermath of *Societe Nationale Industrielle Aerospatiale,*" Hastings International and Comparative Law Review, Vol. 12:3, 1989. *Member:* Orange County, Santa Clara County and American (Member, Sections on: Business Law; Intellectual Property Law) Bar Associations; State Bar of California.

**MICHELE L. LYNCH,** born Stanford, California, October 3, 1968; admitted to bar, 1993, California; U.S. District Court, Central and Southern Districts of California. *Education:* University of California at Los Angeles (B.A., 1990); University of California, Hastings College of the Law (J.D., magna cum laude, 1993). Order of the Coif. Recipient, American Jurisprudence Awards. Member, 1991-1992 and Production Editor, 1992-1993, Hastings Law Journal. Author: "The Right to Write In: Voting Rights and the First Amendment," 44 Hastings L. J. 727 (1993). *Member:* Orange County and American Bar Associations; State Bar of California.

### RESIDENT OF COUNSEL

**ALEC M. BARINHOLTZ,** born Chicago, Illinois, October 20, 1957; admitted to bar, 1988, California; U.S. District Court, Central, Southern, Northern and Eastern Districts of California and District of Arizona. *Education:* Northern Illinois University (B.S., 1979); Southwestern University School of Law (J.D. magna cum laude, 1988). Recipient, American Jurisprudence Awards. Member, 1986-1987 and Articles Editor, 1987-1988, Southwestern University Law Review. Author: "False Light Invasion of Privacy: False Tort?" 17 Southwestern University Law Review 135, 1987. *Member:* Orange County and American Bar Associations; State Bar of California.

(For complete biographical data on all personnel, see Professional Biographies at Washington, D.C.)

---

## THE RUDOLPH LAW GROUP

A PROFESSIONAL CORPORATION

**IRVINE, CALIFORNIA**
(See Costa Mesa)

*General Trial and Appellate Practice in State and Federal Courts, including General Business and Commercial Litigation, Real Estate Litigation, Product Liability, Intellectual Property, Trade Secrets and Unfair Competition, Environmental, Employment and Partnership, Corporate and Trust Disputes.*

---

## RUS, MILIBAND, WILLIAMS & SMITH

SUITE 700
2600 MICHELSON DRIVE
**IRVINE, CALIFORNIA 92612**
Telephone: 714-752-7100
Fax: 714-252-1514

*General Civil and Trial Practice. Complex Commercial Litigation, Bankruptcy, Insolvency, Corporate Reorganization and Creditors Rights.*

(This Listing Continued)

**RUS, MILIBAND, WILLIAMS & SMITH, Irvine—**
*Continued*

**RONALD RUS,** born Denver, Colorado, March 20, 1950; admitted to bar, 1975, California and U.S. District Court, Central, Southern and Eastern Districts of California; U.S. Court of Appeals, Ninth Circuit. *Education:* University of Southern California (B.A., 1972); Pepperdine University (J.D., 1975). Phi Alpha Delta. Author: "Bankruptcy and Complex Civil Litigation," CEB and State Bar Trial Practice Institute Manual, 1991. Visiting Lecturer, Complex Litigation, Stanford Law School, 1992. Co-Lead Counsel ACC/Lincoln Savings Securities Litigation. Director, 1988-1994 and President, 1989-1990, Orange County Bankruptcy Forum. Director, California Bankruptcy Forum, 1988-1994. Chairman, Annual Conference, California Bankruptcy Forum, 1994. *Member:* Orange County (Member, Sections on: Commercial Law and Bankruptcy; Business Litigation; appointed to Judiciary Committee, 1993) Federal and American Bar Associations; State Bar of California; The Association of Business Trial Lawyers; American Bankruptcy Institute; American Inns of Court (Master of the Bench, Peter M. Elliott Chapter). *REPORTED CASES:* In re Fietz, 852 F.2d 455, (9th Cir. 1988); In re American Continental Corporation/Lincoln Sav. & Loan Securities Litigation, 794 F.supp. 1424, (D.Ariz., 1992); In re County of Orange, 183 B.R. 594, (Bankr. C.D. Cal 1995); In re Walters, 136 B.R. 256, (Bkrptcy. C.D. Cal., 1992). *PRACTICE AREAS:* Complex Litigation; Creditors Rights; Bankruptcy Litigation.

**JOEL S. MILIBAND,** born Bronx, New York, October 12, 1952; admitted to bar, 1977, California and U.S. District Court, Southern District of California; 1982, U.S. District Court, Central District of California and U.S. Court of Appeals, Ninth Circuit. *Education:* University of California at Riverside (B.A., with honors, 1973); University of San Diego (J.D., magna cum laude, 1977). Judge Pro Tem, Riverside Superior and Municipal Courts, 1981-1990. *Member:* Desert (President, 1987-1988), Orange County (Member, Board of Directors; Chair, Modest Means Committee; Chair, Lawyer Referral and Information Service; Member, Sections on: Commercial Law and Bankruptcy; Business Litigation), Federal and American Bar Associations; State Bar of California (Chair, Committee on Mandatory Fee Arbitration, 1991; Presiding Arbitrator, 1993—); Commercial Law League of America; American Bankruptcy Institute; Orange County Bankruptcy Forum; American Inns of Court (Master of the Bench, Peter M. Elliott Chapter). *REPORTED CASES:* Hydrotech Systems, Ltd. v. Oasis Water Park, 52 Cal 3d. 488 (1991). *PRACTICE AREAS:* Business Litigation; Commercial Litigation; Bankruptcy Litigation; Real Estate Law. *Email:* miliband@rmws.com

**J. SCOTT WILLIAMS,** born Birmingham, Alabama, July 6, 1956; admitted to bar, 1983, California; 1984, U.S. District Court, Central District of California; 1985, U.S. District Court, Southern District of California. *Education:* Brigham Young University (B.A., 1979; J.D., 1983). Phi Delta Phi. Law Clerk to the Honorable Peter M. Elliot, U.S. Bankruptcy Judge, Central District of California. Author: "Non-Business Liquidation Under Chapter 13 of the Bankruptcy Code: A Tool to Prevent The Loss of Homeowner Equity," The American Bankruptcy Law Journal, Volume 59, Summer, 1985; Class Proofs of Claim in Bankruptcy: A Once Discredited Concept Gains Favor," California Bankruptcy Journal, Volume 18, Winter, 1990. Member, Editorial Board, California Bankruptcy Journal, 1989-1991. Member, Orange County Bankruptcy Forum. Director, Inland Empire Bankruptcy Forum. *Member:* Orange County (Member, Commercial Law & Bankruptcy Section) and Federal (President, Orange County Chapter, 1995-1996) Bar Associations. *LANGUAGES:* German. *PRACTICE AREAS:* Bankruptcy, Insolvency and Commercial Litigation. *Email:* swilliam@rmws.com

**RANDALL A. SMITH,** born Long Beach, California, December 8, 1958; admitted to bar, 1984, California; 1985, U.S. District Court, Southern and Central Districts of California and U.S. Court of Appeals, Ninth Circuit. *Education:* Occidental College (B.A., cum laude, 1981); University of California at Los Angeles (J.D., 1984). Recipient, American Jurisprudence Award in Criminal Law and Labor Law. *Member:* Orange County (Program Chairman, 1989; Chairman, 1990; and Director, 1995-1996, Commercial Law and Bankruptcy Section) and American Bar Associations; State Bar of California; Orange County Trial Lawyers Association. *PRACTICE AREAS:* Complex Litigation; Business Litigation; Creditors Rights; Bankruptcy Litigation. *Email:* rsmith@rmws.com

**LAUREL ZAESKE,** born Shreveport, Louisiana, February 16, 1960; admitted to bar, 1988, California and U.S. Court of Appeals, Ninth Circuit. *Education:* University of Colorado at Boulder (B.S., 1981); University of Southern California (J.D., 1988). Certified Public Accountant: Colorado, *(This Listing Continued)*

1982; California, 1986. *Member:* Orange County and Federal Bar Associations; Orange County Bankruptcy Forum (Treasurer, Board of Directors); Orange County Chapter of Legion Lex (Member, Board of Directors); California Bankruptcy Forum (Member, Board of Directors); American Inns of Court. *PRACTICE AREAS:* Civil Litigation; Bankruptcy Litigation. *Email:* zaeske@rmws.com

**M. PETER CRINELLA,** born Petaluma, California, August 25, 1964; admitted to bar, 1989, California. *Education:* University of San Diego (B.A., 1986); University of Southern California (J.D., 1989). *Member:* State Bar of California. *PRACTICE AREAS:* Civil Litigation; Bankruptcy. *Email:* mpcrinella@rmws.com

**JEFFREY H. SUSSMAN,** born Aberdeen, Maryland, December 25, 1965; admitted to bar, 1991, California and U.S. District Court, Central and Southern Districts of California; 1994, U.S. Court of Appeals, Ninth Circuit. *Education:* University of California at Berkeley (B.A., 1987); University of Southern California (J.D., M.B.A., 1990). Beta Gamma Sigma; Phi Delta Phi. Recipient: American Jurisprudence Award in Bankruptcy. Judicial Extern to the Honorable Barry Russell, U.S. Bankruptcy Judge, Central District of California, 1990. Author: " An Imperfect Answer to a Question of Perfection: The 1993 Amendment to California Civil Code Section 2924h(c) and The Avoidability of Nonjudicial Foreclosure Sales Under Sections 544(a)(3), 549, and 362 of the Bankruptcy Code," 22 Cal. Bankr. J. 287 (1995). Member, Orange County Bankruptcy Forum, 1991—. *Member:* Orange County Bar Association (Commercial Law and Bankruptcy Section, 1991—); State Bar of California; Peter M. Elliott Inn of Court. *PRACTICE AREAS:* Bankruptcy. *Email:* jsussman@rmws.com

**CATHRINE M. CASTALDI,** born San Pedro, California, July 6, 1965; admitted to bar, 1991, California. *Education:* University of California at Los Angeles (B.A., 1987); University of San Diego (J.D., 1991). Phi Alpha Delta. Member, Orange County Bankruptcy Forum. Inland Empire Bankruptcy Forum. *Member:* Orange County (Commercial Law and Bankruptcy Section) and Federal Bar Associations; State Bar of California; American Inns of Court (Associate, Peter M. Elliott). *PRACTICE AREAS:* Corporate Bankruptcy; Complex Business Litigation. *Email:* ccastaldi@rmws.com

**DAVID EDWARD HAYS,** born Los Angeles, California, February 16, 1966; admitted to bar, 1992, California. *Education:* California State University at Fullerton (B.A., with honors, 1989); University of Southern California (J.D., 1992). Phi Alpha Delta. Hale Moot Court Honors Program. Member, Commercial Law and Bankruptcy Section: Orange County Bankruptcy Forum; Inland Empire Bankruptcy Forum. *Member:* Los Angeles (Member, Commercial Law and Bankruptcy Section), Orange County and Federal Bar Associations; State Bar of California; American Inns of Court, William P. Gray Legion Lex Chapter. *REPORTED CASES:* In re Continental Capital & Credit, Inc., 158 B.R. 828 (Bankr. C.D.Cal. 1993, J. Wilson); In re Turner, 186 B.R. 108 (9th Cir. BAP 1995); In re National Environmental Waste Corporation, 191 B.R. 832 (Bankr. C.D.Cal. 1996, J. Wilson). *PRACTICE AREAS:* Complex Litigation; Creditors Rights; Bankruptcy Law. *Email:* ehays@rmws.com

**STEVEN JOSEPH KRAEMER,** born Chicago, Illinois, February 1, 1966; admitted to bar, 1992, California. *Education:* University of California at Santa Barbara (B.A., 1989); University of Southern California (J.D., 1992). Phi Delta Phi. *Member:* Orange County and Federal Bar Associations; State Bar of California. *PRACTICE AREAS:* Complex Litigation; Creditors Rights Law; Bankruptcy Law. *Email:* skraemer@rmws.com

**LEO J. PRESIADO,** born Inglewood, California, July 25, 1968; admitted to bar, 1993, California. *Education:* University of California, Berkeley (B.A., 1990); University of California, Los Angeles (J.D., 1993). Judicial Extern: to the Honorable Calvin K. Ashland, Chief Judge; Bankruptcy Appellate Panel, U.S. Bankruptcy Court, Central District of California. Member, Orange County Bankruptcy Forum. *Member:* Orange County and Federal Bar Associations; State Bar of California. *PRACTICE AREAS:* Corporate; Bankruptcy Law; Complex Business Litigation; Creditor's Rights. *Email:* lpresiad@rmws.com

## SAMUELS & STEEL, LLP
*18881 VON KARMAN AVENUE*
*SUITE 1400*
**IRVINE, CALIFORNIA 92612**
*Telephone: 714-224-0140*
*FAX: 714-224-0141*
*Email: SamSteel@aol.com*
*General Practice.*

**HERBERT N. SAMUELS,** born Brooklyn, New York, June 1, 1930; admitted to bar, 1955, New York; 1957, Florida; 1958, California. *Education:* College of the City of New York (B.B.A., 1951); Brooklyn Law School (LL.B., 1954). Speaker: Real Property Matters, Continuing Education of the Bar, Los Angeles County Bar Association; University of Southern California Real Estate Institute, 1991. *Member:* Los Angeles County, Orange County, New York State and American Bar Associations; State Bar of California; The Florida Bar; Building Industry Association. **PRACTICE AREAS:** Corporate and Business; Real Estate Development; Commercial Development Law; Land Use Entitlement Law; Joint Ventures and Financing.

**WILLIAM L. STEEL,** born Newport Beach, California, May 20, 1957; admitted to bar, 1982, California. *Education:* University of California at Los Angeles (B.A., cum laude, 1979); University of Southern California (J.D., 1982). Member, Hale Moot Court Honors Program, 1980-1981. Notes and Articles Editor, U.S.C. Tax Institute Major Tax Planning Journal, 1981-1982. General Counsel, The Zond Group, 1986. *Member:* Los Angeles County and Orange County (Member, Real Estate Section) Bar Associations; State Bar of California. **PRACTICE AREAS:** Business Law; Real Property Transactions; Financing Law.

**HILARY B. GLEN-GROSSMAN,** born San Mateo, California, May 19, 1960; admitted to bar, 1986, California. *Education:* University of California at Berkeley (B.A., 1982); Hastings College of the Law, University of California (J.D., 1986). Real Estate Broker, California, 1992. *Member:* State Bar of California. **LANGUAGES:** Spanish. **PRACTICE AREAS:** Real Estate Transactional.

---

## JACK L. SCHOELLERMAN
*2030 MAIN STREET, SUITE 1600*
**IRVINE, CALIFORNIA 92614**
*Telephone: 714-660-7000*
*Fax: 714-660-6096*

*Corporate, Partnership, Taxation and Estate Planning Law.*

**JACK L. SCHOELLERMAN,** born Los Angeles, California, June 27, 1946; admitted to bar, 1972, California. *Education:* Claremont Men's College (B.A., 1968); University of San Diego (J.D., cum laude, 1971). Member of Staff, 1969-1970; Articles Editor, 1970-1971, San Diego Law Review. Author: "A Reevaluation of the Decision Not to Adopt the Unconscionability Provision of the Uniform Commercial Code in California," San Diego Law Review, Vol. 7, 1970; "Property—Wharfing Out—Riparian Owner Permitted to Use Filled-In Swamp as a Wharf to Real Navigable Water," San Diego Law Review, Vol. 7, No. 3, 1970. *Member:* Orange County and American (Member, Sections on: Taxation; Corporation, Banking and Business Law; Real Property, Probate and Trust Law) Bar Associations; State Bar of California.

---

## STEPHEN J. SCHUMACHER
*Established in 1979*
*18201 VON KARMAN, SUITE 220*
**IRVINE, CALIFORNIA 92612-1005**
*Telephone: 714-752-9425*
*Telecopier: 714-752-8170*

*Business, Tax and Estate Planning Practice. Corporation, Real Property, Probate, Trusts, Wills, Securities and Federal and State Taxation Law.*

**STEPHEN J. SCHUMACHER,** born Los Angeles, California, February 5, 1942; admitted to bar, 1968, California. *Education:* University of Southern California (A.B., 1963); Hastings College of Law, University of California (J.D., 1967); New York University (LL.M., in Taxation, 1969). Phi Delta Phi. *Member:* Orange County and American (Member, Sections on: Taxation; Real Property, Probate and Trust; Corporation and Banking Law) Bar Associations; The State Bar of California (Member, Taxation Section and Member, Estate Planning, Probate and Trust Committee).

REFERENCE: Bank of America (Irvine Industrial Branch).

---

## SEDGWICK, DETERT, MORAN & ARNOLD
*A Partnership including Professional Corporations*
*17TH FLOOR, 3 PARK PLAZA*
**IRVINE, CALIFORNIA 92714**
*Telephone: 714-852-8200*
*Fax: 714-852-8282*
*Email: E-Mail@SDMA.com*

*San Francisco, California Office:* 16th Floor, One Embarcadero Center. Telephone: 415-781-7900. Cable Address: "Sedma". Fax: 415-781-2635.
*Los Angeles, California Office:* 801 South Figueroa Street, 18th Floor. Telephone: 213-426-6900. Fax: 213-426-6921.
*New York, New York Office:* 41st Floor, 59 Maiden Lane. Telephone: 212-422-0202. Fax: 212-422-0925.
*Chicago, Illinois Office:* The Rookery Building, Seventh Floor, 209 South La Salle Street. Telephone: 312-641-9050. Fax: 312-641-9530.
*London, England Office:* Lloyds Avenue House, 6 Lloyds Avenue, EC3N 3AX. Telephone: 0171-929-1829. Fax: 0171-929-1808.
*Zurich, Switzerland Office:* Spluegenstrasse 3, CH-8002. Telephone: 011-411-201-1730. Fax: 011-411-201-4404.

*General Civil Litigation and Trial Practice. Aviation, Business, Construction, Directors and Officers Liability, Employment and Labor, Entertainment, Environmental, Fidelity and Surety, General Liability, Health Care, Pharmaceuticals, Insurance and Reinsurance, Intellectual Property, Products Liability, and Professional Malpractice.*

### MEMBERS OF FIRM

**GREGORY H. HALLIDAY,** born Washington, D.C., March 29, 1952; admitted to bar, 1978, California. *Education:* Stanford University (B.A., with distinction, 1974); Hastings College of Law, University of California (J.D., 1978).

**ALAN J. FREISLEBEN,** born Los Angeles, California, December 9, 1952; admitted to bar, 1978, California. *Education:* University of Southern California (B.A., 1975); Loyola University of Los Angeles (J.D., 1978). Co-Author: California Unfair Claims Settlement Practices Regulations Desk Book (1993).

**CURTIS D. PARVIN,** born Avalon, California, December 16, 1956; admitted to bar, 1984, California. *Education:* University of California at Irvine (B.A., 1980); Pepperdine University (J.D., cum laude, 1984). Co-Editor: "Cable Franchising and Production," Symposium Syllabus, 1983; "Independent Film Production in the Eighties," Symposium Syllabus, 1984.

**JOHN E. FEELEY,** born Brooklyn, New York, January 16, 1959; admitted to bar, 1984, California. *Education:* Fairfield University (B.S., 1981); Southwestern University School of Law (J.D., 1984).

**TODD ANDREW PICKER,** born Milwaukee, Wisconsin, October 17, 1962; admitted to bar, 1987, California. *Education:* University of Washington (B.A., 1984); McGeorge School of Law, University of the Pacific (J.D., 1987).

**LILY CHOW,** born Hong Kong, August 19, 1962; admitted to bar, 1988, California. *Education:* University of California at Los Angeles (B.A., 1984; J.D., 1987). President, Orange County Asian American Bar Association, 1995-1996. **LANGUAGES:** Cantonese.

### SPECIAL COUNSEL

**DALE A. HUDSON,** born San Jose, California, March 13, 1953; admitted to bar, 1978, California. *Education:* University of California at Santa Cruz (B.A., 1975); Boalt Hall School of Law, University of California (J.D., 1978). Author: "The Family Rights Act of 1991," CYLA Quarterly News, 1992; "EEOC Regulations on Americans With Disabilities Act Leave Many Questions Unanswered," Orange County Lawyer Magazine, May 1992; How to Withdraw from Representation," Los Angeles Lawyer, March 1994; Note, "Sierra Club v. Department of Interior," Ecology Law Quarterly, vol. 7, no. 3.

**RONALD B. PIERCE,** born Oceanside, California, October 28, 1954; admitted to bar, 1979, California. *Education:* Ventura College; University of California at Berkeley (A.B., 1976); University of California at Los Angeles (J.D., 1979). Phi Beta Kappa. Member, Moot Court Honors Program.

*(This Listing Continued)*

## SEDGWICK, DETERT, MORAN & ARNOLD, Irvine— Continued

*Member:* Orange County Bar Association (Sections on Business Litigation, Construction and Law Management); State Bar of California (Sections on Litigation and Law Office Management); Christian Legal Society.

**MICHAEL J. KHOURI,** born San Francisco, California, August 19, 1956; admitted to bar, 1981, California; 1984, U.S. Supreme Court. *Education:* Loyola Marymount University (B.A., cum laude, 1977); California State University, Long Beach (M.P.A., magna cum laude, 1978); Loyola Law School, Los Angeles ( J.D., 1981). Deputy District Attorney, Orange County California, 1982-1986.

**THOMAS J. BOIS, II, (P.C.),** born Manchester, New Hampshire, November 9, 1955; admitted to bar, 1982, Missouri; 1983, California; 1993, District of Columbia. *Education:* St. Michael's College (A.B., magna cum laude, 1977); St. Louis University (J.D., 1981). Hosser-Wagner Scholar. Certified Environmental Inspector, California. Registered Environmental Assessor, California, 1991. Author: *California Groundwater & Soil Contamination:* Technical Preparation & Litigation Management, 1st ED. 1994, Wiley Law Publications; "California Environmental Statutes" California Construction Defect and Land Subsidence Litigation, 1st Ed 1989, Ch. 14, Wiley Law Publications; "Financial Responsibilities for Environmental Liabilities" 18 W. St. U. L. Rev. 1983, 1990; "How to Survive an Administrative Environmental Investigation" Orange County Lawyer, Vol. 33, No. 5, June, 1991; "A Business Guide to the Regulation Jungle", Orange County Business Journal, Vol. 14, No. 30, July, 1991; "Hazardous Wastes and Environmental Issues," California Construction Defect Litigation: Residential and Commercial, 2d Ed 1992, Ch 5, Wiley Law Publications; "An Insurer's Defense and Indemnity Obligations After AIV Insurance Company v. Superior Court," 27 Tort & Ins. L.J. 764 (1992); "Defending Against Environmental Claims," 22, The Brief 6 (1992). Member, National Advisory Board Environmental Assessment Association, 1991—.

### OF COUNSEL

**IRENE E. ZIEBARTH,** born Los Angeles, California, March 5, 1943; admitted to bar, 1985, California. *Education:* California State University at Fullerton (B.A., 1980); Loyola Law School (J.D., 1984).

### ASSOCIATES

**RICHARD WM. ZEVNIK,** born Neenah, Wisconsin, July 19, 1953; admitted to bar, 1985, California. *Education:* University of California at Los Angeles (B.A., 1976); Tulane University School of Public Health; Loyola Marymount University (J.D., 1985).

**KELLY LEE FIDONE,** born Los Angeles, July 30, 1963; admitted to bar, 1988, California. *Education:* University of California at Los Angeles (B.A., 1985); Loyola Marymount University (J.D., 1988).

**RALPH A. GUIRGIS,** born Dundee, Scotland, March 18, 1965; admitted to bar, 1989, California. *Education:* California State University at Fullerton (B.A., cum laude, 1986); McGeorge School of Law, University of the Pacific (J.D., 1989).

**ANGELA L. BALL,** born San Francisco, California, August 23, 1964; admitted to bar, 1991, California. *Education:* University of California, Berkeley (A.B., 1987); University of Southern California (J.D., 1991).

**ALLEN B. GRESHAM, II,** born San Bernardino, California, May 7, 1964; admitted to bar, 1991, California. *Education:* Occidental College (A.B., 1986); Loyola Law School (J.D., 1991).

**DEBORAH L. O'CONNOR,** born San Jose, California, July 13, 1965; admitted to bar, 1991, California. *Education:* California State University at Chico (B.A., magna cum laude, 1987); Hastings College of the Law, University of California (J.D., 1991).

**ALAN B. UNTERMAN,** born Long Beach, California, July 8, 1965; admitted to bar, 1991, California. *Education:* University of California, Berkeley (B.S., Business Administration, 1987); University of California at Los Angeles (J.D., 1991). *LANGUAGES:* Dutch.

**JEFFREY I. BRAUN,** born Jaffa, Israel, May 28, 1967; admitted to bar, 1992, California. *Education:* University of California at Irvine (B.A., 1989); McGeorge School of Law (J.D., 1992).

**JILL A. TRACY,** born Willingboro, New Jersey, November 9, 1965; admitted to bar, 1992, New Jersey; 1993, New York; 1996, California. *Education:* Vassar College (B.A., 1987); Franklin Pierce Law Center (J.D., 1992).

*(This Listing Continued)*

**CHARLES R. GOSSAGE,** born Redwood City, California, January 9, 1967; admitted to bar, 1993, California. *Education:* Arizona State University (B.S., 1990); Pepperdine University (J.D., 1993).

**BRIAN D. JONES,** born Stockton, California, May 31, 1967; admitted to bar, 1995, California. *Education:* University of California, Los Angeles (B.A., with honors, 1991); Pepperdine School of Law (J.D., cum laude, 1995).

All Partners and Associates are members of the State Bar of California.

(For complete biographical data on all personnel at San Francisco and Los Angeles, California, Chicago, Illinois, New York, New York, London, England and Zurich, Switzerland, see Professional Biographies at those locations).

## SIKORA AND PRICE

INCORPORATED

Established in 1971

10 CORPORATE PARK
SUITE 300
**IRVINE, CALIFORNIA 92606**
Telephone: 714-261-2233
Telecopier: 714-261-6935

*Federal and State Taxation Law. Estate Planning, Probate, Business and Real Estate Transactions, Partnerships, Corporation Law. Trials and Appeals.*

**WARREN SIKORA,** born Chicago, Illinois, May 6, 1921; admitted to bar, 1953, California and U.S. Tax Court; 1962, U.S. Supreme Court; 1965, U.S. Court of Appeals, Ninth Circuit. *Education:* University of Chicago (B.A., 1942; M.B.A., 1946); University of California at Los Angeles (J.D., 1952). Phi Alpha Delta. Lecturer, Continuing Education of The Bar, State Bar of California. Certified Public Accountant, California, 1949. *Member:* Orange County (Member, Sections on: Taxation; Probate) and American (Member: Professional Service Corporations Committee, Section of Taxation, 1978-1981; Sales and Financial Transactions Committee, Section of Taxation, 1981—; Chairman, 1987-1988; Section of Real Property, Probate and Trust Law) Bar Associations; State Bar of California. (Certified Specialist, Taxation Law, The State Bar of California Board of Legal Specialization). *PRACTICE AREAS:* Estate Planning; Real Estate Law; Business Law.

**DONALD R. PRICE,** born Inglewood, California, July 24, 1940; admitted to bar, 1966, California. *Education:* Long Beach State College (B.S., 1963); University of California at Los Angeles (LL.B., 1966). Phi Delta Phi. Judge Pro-Tem, Orange County Municipal and Superior Courts, 1981—. *Member:* Orange County and American Bar Associations; State Bar of California. *PRACTICE AREAS:* Litigation; Business Law; Real Property Transactions.

**STEVEN C. CROOKE,** born Berkeley, California, April 19, 1951; admitted to bar, 1977, California. *Education:* University of California at Santa Barbara (B.A., cum laude, 1973); University of Santa Clara (J.D., magna cum laude, 1977). *Member:* Orange County and American (Member, Sections on: Real Property, Probate and Trust Law; Corporation, Banking and Business Law) Bar Associations; State Bar of California. *PRACTICE AREAS:* Real Estate Transactions; Business Law; Litigation.

**BRUCE J. GARY,** born Minneapolis, Minnesota, February 14, 1954; admitted to bar, 1980, California. *Education:* University of Minnesota (B.S., with honors, 1976; J.D., 1980). Beta Alpha Psi; Beta Gamma Sigma. Certified Public Accountant: Minnesota, 1977; California, 1981. Lecturer, Buy-Sell Agreements, Continuing Education of the Bar, 1993. Instructor in Paralegal Studies of Coastline Community College, 1981-1983. Judge Pro Tem, Orange County Superior and Municipal Courts. *Member:* Orange County Bar Association; State Bar of California; American Institute of Certified Public Accountants. (Certified Specialist, Estate Planning, Trust and Probate Law, The State Bar of California Board of Legal Specialization). *PRACTICE AREAS:* Business Law; Real Estate Transactions; Probate Law; Estate Planning Law.

## SIMON, McKINSEY, MILLER, ZOMMICK, SANDOR & DUNDAS

*A LAW CORPORATION*
*Established in 1951*
SUITE 670, 4199 CAMPUS DRIVE
**IRVINE, CALIFORNIA 92715**
Telephone: 714-856-1916
Facsimile: 714-856-3834

Long Beach, California Office: 2750 Bellflower Boulevard. Telephone: 213-421-9354. Facsimile: 213-420-6455.

*General Civil and Civil Trial Practice. Corporation, Real Estate, Estate Planning, Trust, Taxation, Probate, Negligence, Family Law, Local Government Administrative Hearings and Appeals.*

REFERENCE: Farmers and Merchants Bank.

(For Complete Biographical Data on all Personnel, see Professional Biographies at Long Beach, California)

---

## SMITH, BRENNAN & DICKERSON

*A PROFESSIONAL CORPORATION*
19900 MACARTHUR BOULEVARD
SEVENTH FLOOR
**IRVINE, CALIFORNIA 92612**
Telephone: 714-442-1500
Facsimile: 714-442-1515

*Business and Civil Litigation in all State and Federal Courts, including Real Estate, Environmental, Land Use, Banking, Employment, Insurance, Construction, Contract, Antitrust, and Securities Litigation; Real Estate Transactions and Land Use.*

**PHILIP E. SMITH,** born Flushing, New York, November 21, 1956; admitted to bar, 1981, District of Columbia; 1985, California. *Education:* University of Virginia (B.A., with high distinction, 1978; J.D., 1981). Phi Beta Kappa. Chair, 1994, Delegate, 1985-1994, Orange County Bar Association, State Bar Conference of Delegates. *Member:* Orange County Bar Association. **PRACTICE AREAS:** Civil Litigation; Environmental; Antitrust; Real Estate; Insurance.

**DONALD D. DICKERSON,** born Fort Leavenworth, Kansas, October 8, 1956; admitted to bar, 1982, California; 1985, Arizona. *Education:* California State Polytechnic University (B.A. cum laude, 1979); University of Southern California (J.D., 1982). Delegate, Orange County Bar Association, State Bar Conference of Delegates, 1985-1993. *Member:* Orange County Bar Association. **PRACTICE AREAS:** Business Litigation; Real Estate; Land Use; Environmental; Construction.

**STERLING A. BRENNAN,** born Clovis, New Mexico, July 26, 1959; admitted to bar, 1986, California; 1995, U.S. Supreme Court. *Education:* University of California at Irvine; Brigham Young University (B.A., 1983); J. Reuben Clark Law School, Brigham Young University (J.D., cum laude, 1986). National Order of Barristers. Law Clerk to the Honorable A. Andrew Hauk, U.S. District Court, Central District of California, 1986-1987. *Member:* Orange County, Federal and American Bar Associations; Peter M. Elliott Inn of Court. **PRACTICE AREAS:** Business Litigation; Real Estate; Environmental; Land Use; Construction.

**JAY W. DEVERICH,** born San Francisco, California, January 5, 1955; admitted to bar, 1986, California. *Education:* Brigham Young University (B.S., cum laude, 1980); Boalt Hall School of Law, University of California, Berkeley (J.D.,1986). Order of the Coif. Member, 1984-1985 and Associate Editor, 1985-1986, International Tax and Business Lawyer. Certified Public Accountant, California, 1982. *Member:* Orange County Bar Association. **LANGUAGES:** Japanese. **PRACTICE AREAS:** Real Estate Transactional; Land Use. *Email:* JayWD@aol.com

**JOSEPH G. HARRAKA, JR.,** born Paterson, New Jersey, November 26, 1960; admitted to bar, 1985, California; 1990, New York and New Jersey. *Education:* Seton Hall University (B.A., magna cum laude, with highest departmental honors in History, 1982); University of Notre Dame (J.D., cum laude, 1985). Phi Alpha Theta. Pindar Scholar, 1982-1985. Director, Notre Dame Moot Court Board, 1984-1985. *Member:* Orange County Bar Association (Member, Investment Committee, 1996); American Inn of Court. **PRACTICE AREAS:** Commercial Litigation; Environmental; Bankruptcy; Securities Arbitration.

*(This Listing Continued)*

---

**MICHAEL W. ELLISON,** born Binghamton, New York, September 6, 1963; admitted to bar, 1989, California; 1990 U.S. District Court, Central District of California; 1992, U.S. Court of Appeals, Ninth Circuit. *Education:* Cornell University (B.A., cum laude, 1985); University of Michigan (M.A., 1989; J.D. cum laude, 1989). *Member:* Orange County (Chair, Pro Bono Committee, 1996) and American (Member, Executive Ethics Committee, 1990-1992) Bar Associations. **PRACTICE AREAS:** Business Litigation; Environmental Litigation.

**DAVID G. HAGOPIAN,** born Inglewood, California, August 23, 1963; admitted to bar, 1989, California and U.S. District Court, Central District of California; 1992, U.S. District Court, Northern, Southern and Eastern Districts of California. *Education:* University of California at Irvine (B.A., magna cum laude, 1985); University of Southern California (J.D., 1989). Phi Beta Kappa. Order of the Coif. Recipient: Hale Moot Court Best Brief Award; Distinguished Student Scholar. Commencement Speaker, 1985. Legal Writing Instructor, University of Southern California, 1987-1989. *Member:* Orange County and American Bar Associations. **PRACTICE AREAS:** Business Litigation; Employment Law; Insurance Coverage; Construction.

**CAROLINE MCINTYRE,** born New York, N.Y., March 8, 1966; admitted to bar, 1992, California. *Education:* Vassar College (B.A. cum laude, 1988); University of Notre Dame (J.D., 1991). Staff Member, 1989-1990 and Assistant Lead Articles Editor, 1990-1991, Journal of College and University Law. Co-Author: "Parate v. Isidor: Resolving the Conflict Between the Academic Freedom of the University and the Academic Freedom of the Professor," Journal of College and University Law, 1990. *Member:* Orange County and American (Barristers; Business Litigation Section; Labor and Employment Law Section) Bar Associations. **LANGUAGES:** Spanish. **PRACTICE AREAS:** Business Litigation.

---

## SMITH, SILBAR, DUFFY, PARKER & WOFFINDEN

19100 VON KARMAN AVENUE
SUITE 400
**IRVINE, CALIFORNIA 92715**
Telephone: 714-263-8066
Fax: 714-263-8073

*Alternate Dispute Resolution; Business Law, Commercial Law, Complex and Multi District Litigation, Litigation Defense, Government Contracts, Real Estate, Probate, Property Taxation, Corporate, Domestic Relations, Federal Tax, Non-Profit and Charitable Organizations, Taxation, Trademarks and Wills.*

### MEMBERS OF FIRM

**CAMERON M. SMITH, JR.,** born Ann Arbor, Michigan, February 24, 1945; admitted to bar, 1973, California. *Education:* Yale University (B.A., 1966); University of Virginia (J.D., 1973). Order of the Coif. Notes and Comments Editor, University of Virginia Law Review, 1972-1973. *Member:* Orange County (Member, Client Relations Committee, 1992-1993) and American Bar Associations; State Bar of California. [Capt., USMC, 1966-1970]

**LISA WELCH SILBAR,** born Nashville, Tennessee, June 9, 1958; admitted to bar, 1985, California. *Education:* University of North Carolina (B.S., 1980); Vanderbilt University (J.D., 1984). *Member:* Orange County (Member, Sections on: Estate Planning, Probate and Trust; Taxation) and American (Member: Section of Taxation; Committee on Sales, Exchanges and Basis; Member, Sub-Committee on Pass-Through Entities/Real Estate; Member, Committee on Estate and Gift Taxes) Bar Associations; State Bar of California (Co-Chair, Young Tax Lawyers Committee, Orange County Chapter); California Women Lawyers; Orange County Women Lawyers.

**ANTHONY C. DUFFY,** born Seattle, Washington, February 4, 1947; admitted to bar, 1972, California, U.S. Court of Appeals, Ninth Circuit and U.S. District Court, Northern District of California; 1976, U.S. District Court, Central District of California; 1986, U.S. District Court, Southern District of California. *Education:* Stanford University (B.A., with great distinction, 1968); Yale University (J.D., 1971). Phi Beta Kappa. *Member:* Orange County (Member, Litigation Section) and American (Member, Litigation Section) Bar Associations; State Bar of California; Orange County Trial Lawyers Association; The California Trial Lawyers Association; Association of Trial Lawyers of America; American Inns of Court.

**KEITH M. PARKER,** born Los Angeles, California, July 2, 1952; admitted to bar, 1983, California. *Education:* University of California at Los

*(This Listing Continued)*

## SMITH, SILBAR, DUFFY, PARKER & WOFFINDEN,
*Irvine—Continued*

Angeles (B.S., summa cum laude, 1974); Northwestern University (J.D., summa cum laude, 1982). Order of the Coif. Coordinating Executive Editor, Northwestern University Law Review, 1981-1982. Law Clerk to the Honorable George E. MacKinnon, U.S. Court of Appeals, D.C. Circuit, 1982-1983. *Member:* Orange County (Member, Business Litigation Section) and American (Member, Public Contract Law Section) Bar Associations; State Bar of California.

**ARLEN D. WOFFINDEN**, born Honolulu, Hawaii, March 5, 1950; admitted to bar, 1977, California. *Education:* Brigham Young University (B.A., 1974; J.D., cum laude, 1977). Casenote and Comment Editor, Brigham Young University Law Review, 1976-1977. *Member:* Orange County (Member, Sections on: Estate Planning, Probate and Trust; Tax Law) and American (Member: Real Property, Probate and Trust Law Section; Committee on State and Local Taxation) Bar Associations; State Bar of California.

---

**RACHELLE SINGER**, born Detroit, Michigan, January 25, 1964; admitted to bar, 1989, California; 1990, U.S. District Court, Central and Northern Districts of California and U.S. Court of Appeals, Ninth Circuit. *Education:* The Ohio State University (B.A., with honors, 1986; J.D., with honors, 1989). Order of the Coif. Articles Editor, The Ohio State University Law Journal, 1988-1989. Law Clerk to the Honorable Procter Hug, Jr., Judge of the U.S. Court of Appeals, Ninth Circuit, 1989-1990. *Member:* Orange County Bar Association; State Bar of California.

**GREGORY S. LANE**, born Los Angeles, California, September 7, 1962; admitted to bar, 1989, California; 1991, District of Columbia. *Education:* University of California at Berkeley (B.S., 1986); Pepperdine University (J.D., magna cum laude, 1989). Lead Articles Editor, Pepperdine Law Review, 1988-1989. Associated with: Latham & Watkins, 1989-1991; Wilmer, Cutler & Pickering, 1991-1993. *Member:* Orange County Bar Association; District of Columbia Bar; State Bar of California.

---

## SNELL & WILMER, L.L.P.
*Established in 1938*

*1920 MAIN STREET, SUITE 1200*
**IRVINE, CALIFORNIA 92614**
*Telephone: 714-253-2700*
*FAX: 714-955-2507*

*Phoenix, Arizona Office:* One Arizona Center, 85004-0001. Telephone: 602-382-6000. Fax: 602-382-6070.

*Tucson, Arizona Office:* Norwest Tower, Suite 1500, One South Church Avenue, 85701-1612. Telephone: 520-882-1200. Fax: 520-884-1294.

*Salt Lake City, Utah Office:* Broadway Centre, 111 East Broadway, Suite 900, 84111-1004. Telephone: 801-237-1900. Fax: 801-237-1950.

*General Civil Practice. Trials and Appeals before State and Federal Courts. Bankruptcy and Insolvency, Commercial Litigation, Corporate and Securities, Franchising, Labor and Employment, Product Liability Litigation. Construction, Real Estate, Environmental and Natural Resources, Computer and High Technology, Health Care, Estate Planning.*

### MEMBERS OF FIRM

**ROBERT J. GIBSON**, born San Antonio, Texas, September 22, 1946; admitted to bar, 1977, Arizona and U.S. District Court, District of Arizona; 1978, U.S. Court of Appeals, Ninth Circuit; 1980, U.S. Supreme Court; 1989, California; 1990, U.S. District Court, Central, Eastern and Southern Districts of California. *Education:* Arizona State University (B.S., 1973); University of Arizona (J.D., 1977). Beta Gamma Sigma. Member, University of Arizona Law Review, 1976-1977. Clerk to Justice Frank X Gordon, Jr., Arizona Supreme Court, 1977-1978. *Member:* Orange County and American (Member, Environmental Law Section and Product Liability Subcommittee) Bar Associations; State Bar of Arizona; Product Liability Advisory Council (Sustaining Member); Defense Research Institute, Inc. [Capt., U.S. Army, 1966-1971]. (Resident). *PRACTICE AREAS:* Product Liability Litigation; Environmental Litigation. *Email:* gibsonh@swlaw.com

**ARTHUR P. GREENFIELD**, born Washington, D.C., April 30, 1936; admitted to bar, 1964, California and Arizona. *Education:* University of California at Los Angeles (A.B., 1959); University of Arizona (LL.B., 1964). Phi Delta Phi. Listed in 1991-1996 edition of Best Lawyers in America. *Member:* State Bar of Arizona; Product Liability Advisory Council (Sustaining Member). Fellow: American College of Trial Lawyers; International Society of Barristers. *PRACTICE AREAS:* Civil Litigation; Product Liability Litigation; Commercial Litigation.

**CREIGHTON D. MILLS**, born Kansas City, Missouri, June 28, 1955; admitted to bar, 1981, California. *Education:* University of California, Irvine (B.A., magna cum laude, 1977); University of California at Los Angeles (M.B.A., 1981; J.D., 1981). Phi Beta Kappa; Beta Gamma Sigma. *Member:* Orange County Bar Association (Member, Section of Real Property). (Resident). *PRACTICE AREAS:* Real Estate Law; Commercial Finance.

**STEVEN T. GRAHAM**, born Orange, California, August 16, 1956; admitted to bar, 1982, California; 1983, U.S. District Court, Central District of California; 1984, U.S. District Court, Southern, Northern and Eastern Districts of California. *Education:* University of California at Santa Barbara (B.A., 1979); Pepperdine University (J.D., cum laude, 1982). Recipient: Corpus Juris Secundum Award, 1979-1980; American Jurisprudence Award in Torts. Articles Editor, Pepperdine Law Review, 1981-1982. (Resident). *PRACTICE AREAS:* Commercial; Environmental; Construction; Litigation.

**CHRISTY D. JOSEPH**, born Oakland, California, November 1, 1960; admitted to bar, 1988, California and U.S. District Court, Central District of California; U.S. District Court, Northern and Southern Districts of California. *Education:* University of California at Irvine (B.A., magna cum laude, 1985); Hastings College of Law, University of California (J.D., 1988). Phi Beta Kappa. *Member:* Orange County and American Bar Associations. *PRACTICE AREAS:* Employment Litigation; Commercial Litigation; Product Liability Litigation.

**WILLIAM S. O'HARE, JR.**, born Baltimore, Maryland, December 21, 1952; admitted to bar, 1978, California. *Education:* Loyola College of Maryland (A.B., 1974); Hastings College of Law, University of California (J.D., 1978). Order of the Coif. Member, Thurston Society. Lawyer Representative, Ninth Circuit Judicial Conference, 1992—. *Member:* Orange County (Chair: Business Litigation Section, 1991; Resolutions Committee, 1990; Member, Board of Directors, 1989—), American (Member, Sections on: Litigation and Tort and Insurance Practice; Forum on Franchising) and Federal Bar Associations; The State Bar of California (Conference of Delegates, 1985—; Member, Sections on: Litigation; Labor and Employment Law; Chair, Orange County Delegation, 1990). (Resident). *PRACTICE AREAS:* Commercial Litigation. *Email:* oharew@swlaw.com

**DIANE R. SMITH**, born New Orleans, Louisiana, October 10, 1946; admitted to bar, 1975, California. *Education:* University of California, Berkeley (A.B., 1972, Phi Beta Kappa, Distinction in Scholarship); Boalt Hall School of Law, University of California (J.D., 1975). Co-author: with Robert J. Gibson, "Environmental Litigation," a module of Bancroft Whitney's California Civil Litigation set (26 volumes), 1993. Member, Panel of Arbitrators, American Arbitration Association. *Member:* Orange County (Chairman, Environmental Law Section, 1990-1992) and American Bar Associations. (Resident). *PRACTICE AREAS:* Environmental Law; High Technology, Engineering and Construction Contracts.

**GARY A. WOLENSKY**, born Allentown, Pennsylvania, January 7, 1954; admitted to bar, 1978, Pennsylvania and U.S. District Court, Eastern District of Pennsylvania; 1988, New Jersey; 1991, California; U.S. District Court, Central District of California. *Education:* Villanova University (B.A., 1975; J.D., 1978). Phi Kappa Phi. Law Clerk to Honorable William W. Vogel of the Montgomery County Court of Common Pleas, 1978-1979. *Member:* Pennsylvania Bar Association (Member, Medicolegal Committee, 1981); Defense Research Institute; Association of Southern California Defense Counsel; Society of Automotive Engineers. (Resident). *PRACTICE AREAS:* Product Liability Litigation.

**GILBERT N. KRUGER**, born Bronx, New York, May 15, 1941; admitted to bar, 1967, New York; 1980, California. *Education:* Brooklyn College (B.S., 1963); Hastings College of Law, University of California (LL.B., 1966). Member: Order of the Coif; Thurston Society. Member, Hastings Law Review, 1966. Author: "Service Bureau Contracts," Computers and the Law, 3d Edition, 1981; "Stock Transfer Restrictions and The Close Corporation: A Statutory Proposal," 17 Hastings Law Journal 583, 1966. Staff Vice President and Assistant General Counsel, Automatic Data Processing, Inc., 1970-1979. Mediator, U.S. Bankruptcy Court, Central District of California. Member, Panel of Arbitrators, American Arbitration Association. *Member:* Computer Law Association (Board of Directors, 1979-1986). (Resident). *PRACTICE AREAS:* Corporate Law; Securities Law; Emerging Business Law; Technology Law.

*(This Listing Continued)*

**CHARLES W. HURST,** born Salt Lake City, Utah, July 4, 1957; admitted to bar, 1983, Pennsylvania; 1986, California. *Education:* The University of Chicago; Wesleyan University (B.A., cum laude, 1979); Duke University (J.D., 1983). Recipient, American Jurisprudence Award in Civil Procedure. *Member:* Orange County (Real Estate Section) and American (Real Property, Probate and Trust Law Section) Bar Associations. (Resident). *PRACTICE AREAS:* Real Estate Law; Commercial Finance.

**DAVID W. EVANS,** born Bridgeport, California, September 25, 1939; admitted to bar, 1971, California. *Education:* University of Santa Clara (B.S., 1960); Loyola University of Los Angeles (J.D., 1970). Lecturer: "Handling a Decedent's Estate," Continuing Education of the Bar; "Procedural Aspects of Probate Litigation," Orange County Bar Association Seminars. *Member:* Orange County (Member, Sections on: Probate; Trust Law) and American (Member, Real Property, Probate and Trust Law Section) Bar Associations; Orange Coast Estate Planning Council. (Resident). *PRACTICE AREAS:* Estate Planning, Probate and Trust Law; Guardianship and Conservatorship; Estate and Gift Taxation.

**RICHARD A. DEREVAN,** born Pasadena, California, June 4, 1949; admitted to bar, 1974, California. *Education:* University of California at Irvine (B.A., 1971); Hastings College of Law, University of California (J.D., 1974). Order of the Coif. Law Clerk Extern to the Hon. Louis H. Burke, California Supreme Court, 1974. Law Clerk to the Hon. Philip C. Wilkins, U.S. District Court, Eastern District of California, 1974-1976. Lawyer Representative to Ninth Circuit Judicial Conference, 1990-1992. *Member:* Orange County (Board of Directors, 1991-1993; Chair, Federal Court Committee, 1991-1992; Chair, Business Litigation Section, 1988) and American (Litigation Section) Bar Associations; The State Bar of California (Appellate Courts Committee, 1979-1983, Vice-Chair, 1981-1982 and Chair, 1982-1983); California Academy of Appellate Lawyers; Scribes, The American Society of Writers on Legal Subjects. *PRACTICE AREAS:* Appellate Law. *Email:* derevar@swlaw.com

**RANDOLPH T. MOORE,** born Bennington, Vermont, May 6, 1955; admitted to bar, 1985, California and U.S. District Court, Central District of California; 1988, U.S. District Court, Eastern District of California and U.S. Court of Appeals, Ninth Circuit; 1989, U.S. District Court, Southern District of California. *Education:* Boston University (B.A., 1980); Rensselaer Polytechnic Institute (M.S., 1982); Boston College (J.D., cum laude, 1985). Recipient, American Jurisprudence Award in Contract. Associate Editor, Uniform Commercial Code Reporter-Digest, 1983-1985. *Member:* Orange County and American Bar Associations. *PRACTICE AREAS:* Commercial Litigation; Product Liability Litigation.

**NANETTE D. SANDERS,** born Los Angeles, California, May 22, 1958; admitted to bar, 1985, California; 1986, U.S. District Court, Northern, Central and Southern Districts of California. *Education:* California State Polytechnic University at Pomona (B.S., Accounting, 1981); Loyola Law School, Los Angeles (J.D., 1985). *Member:* Orange County and American Bar Associations; Orange County Bankruptcy Forum. *PRACTICE AREAS:* Bankruptcy; Reorganization; Commercial Litigation. *Email:* sandern@swalw.com

**LUKE A. TORRES,** born Bakersfield, California, November 13, 1957; admitted to bar, 1982, California. *Education:* University of California at Santa Barbara (B.A., 1979); University of California at Davis (J.D., 1982). Order of the Coif. *Member:* Orange County and American Bar Associations; Defense Research Institute. (Resident). *PRACTICE AREAS:* Product Liability Litigation.

**GREGG AMBER,** born Fort Sill, Oklahoma, May 14, 1956; admitted to bar, 1981, California; 1982, Colorado; 1984, Massachusetts. *Education:* The Principia College (B.A., 1978); Stanford University (J.D., 1981). *Member:* Orange County and American Bar Associations. *PRACTICE AREAS:* Corporate; Securities. *Email:* amberg@swlaw.com

**PENELOPE PARMES,** born Great Neck, New York, December 1, 1947; admitted to bar, 1982, California. *Education:* University of Denver; San Francisco Law School (J.D., with highest honors, 1982). *Member:* Los Angeles County, Orange County and American Bar Associations; Los Angeles Bankruptcy Forum (Member, Board of Directors, 1992—; Vice President, 1996-1997); California Bankruptcy Forum (Member, Board of Directors, 1992—). *PRACTICE AREAS:* Bankruptcy Law; Creditors' Remedies Law.

**FRANK CRONIN,** born Boston, Massachusetts, May 26, 1944; admitted to bar, 1971, Massachusetts; 1972, District of Columbia; 1976, California. *Education:* Boston College (A.B., 1966); Boston College Law School (J.D., 1971). Trial Attorney, Civil Rights Division, U.S. Department of Justice, 1971-1976. *Member:* Orange County and Los Angeles County (Member, Litigation and Labor Law Sections) Bar Associations; State Bar of California (Member, Sections on: Labor and Employment; Litigation). [Lt., U.S. Army, Medical Service Corps, 1966-1968]. *PRACTICE AREAS:* Labor and Employment Law.

## ASSOCIATES

**SHARA C. BERAL,** born Newport Beach, California, August 1, 1971; admitted to bar, 1996, California. *Education:* University of California at Los Angeles (A.B., honors, 1993); University of Chicago (J.D., 1996). *PRACTICE AREAS:* Litigation.

**TIFFANNY BROSNAN,** born Santa Monica, California, March 5, 1971; admitted to bar, 1996, California. *Education:* University of California at Los Angeles (B.A., summa cum laude, 1993; J.D., 1996). Phi Beta Kappa; Phi Alpha Theta; Golden Key.

**LARRY A. CERUTTI,** born Los Angeles, California, 1957; admitted to bar, 1987, California. *Education:* Occidental College (A.B., 1979); Northeastern University (M.B.A., 1982); McGeorge School of Law, University of the Pacific (J.D., 1987). Member, Pacific Law Journal, 1985-1986. Author: "SEC Rule 10b-16: Should the Federal Courts Allow Sophisticated Investors to Recover?" 18 Pac. L.J. 171 (1986). *PRACTICE AREAS:* Securities; Corporate.

**KENT M. CLAYTON,** born Phoenix, Arizona, May 7, 1961; admitted to bar, 1990, California. *Education:* University of Miami (B.M., magna cum laude, 1986); University of Virginia (J.D., 1990). Author: "The Necessity of Expressly Designating Copyright Ownership in Software Development and Licensing Agreements," 10 The Computer Lawyer 18 (January 1993, Prentice Hall Law and Business); "Halting the Spread of Sega: The Unreasonableness of The European Model in the U.S. Software Industry," 2 The International Computer Lawyer 10 (February 1994, Prentice Hall Law and Business). Member: American Bar Association, sections on Business Law and Patent, Trademark and Copyright Law, 1990—; Orange County Bar Association, 1993—; National Notary Association, 1994—. *PRACTICE AREAS:* Securities; Business; Finance Law; Multimedia; Computer Law.

**ALEXANDER L. CONTI,** born Rochester, New York, November 1, 1965; admitted to bar, 1991, California. *Education:* Northwestern University (B.A., 1987); University of San Diego (J.D., 1991). *PRACTICE AREAS:* Business and Product Liability Litigation.

**ELLEN L. DARLING,** born Tucson, Arizona, July 5, 1964; admitted to bar, 1990, California and U.S. District Court, Southern and Central Districts of California. *Education:* University of Arizona (B.A., 1986), Mortar Board; University of San Diego (J.D., 1990). *Member:* Orange County and American Bar Associations. *PRACTICE AREAS:* Product Liability Litigation; Commercial Litigation; Environmental Litigation.

**LISA M. FARRINGTON,** born Long Beach, California, February 20, 1966; admitted to bar, 1993, California. *Education:* California State University, Long Beach (B.S., 1988); Loyola Law School (J.D., 1993). *Member:* Orange County and Federal Bar Associations; Orange County Bankruptcy Forum. *PRACTICE AREAS:* Bankruptcy Law; Commercial Litigation.

**CHARLISA HOLLOWAY,** born Waukegan, Illinois, November 6, 1968; (admission pending). *Education:* Howard University (B.A., cum laude, 1990; J.D., 1996). Member, Howard Law Journal. *PRACTICE AREAS:* Litigation.

**JON J. JANECEK,** born Long Beach, California, October 17, 1962; admitted to bar, 1988, California. *Education:* University of California at Los Angeles (B.S., cum laude, 1985); Hastings College of the Law, University of California (J.D., cum laude, 1988). Member, Thurston Society. Assistant Executive Editor, Hastings Constitutional Law Quarterly, 1987-1988. *Member:* Orange County and American Bar Associations. *PRACTICE AREAS:* Real Estate Law; Commercial Finance.

**RONALD T. LABRIOLA,** born Whittier, California, December 7, 1965; admitted to bar, 1993, California; U.S. District Court, Central District of California; U.S. Court of Appeals, Ninth Circuit. *Education:* Princeton University (B.S.E., 1988); Loyola University of Los Angeles (J.D., 1992). Phi Delta Phi. *Member:* Orange County and American Bar Associations. *PRACTICE AREAS:* Product Liability Litigation.

**CRISTY G. LOMENZO,** born Downey, California; admitted to bar, 1995, California. *Education:* California State University, Fullerton (B.A., summa cum laude, 1992); Hastings College of the Law, University of California (J.D., cum laude, 1995). Phi Kappa Phi. President's Scholar. Member, Hastings Law Journal. *Member:* Orange County and American Bar Associations. *PRACTICE AREAS:* Corporate and Securities Law; Real Estate and Commercial Finance.

*(This Listing Continued)*

## SNELL & WILMER, L.L.P., Irvine—Continued

**JEFFREY SCOTT MARKS,** born Los Angeles, California, November 13, 1969; admitted to bar, 1995, California. *Education:* University of California, Santa Barbara (B.A., 1991); Loyola Law School (J.D., 1995). Order of the Coif; Alpha Sigma Nu; St. Thomas More Honor Society. Member, Loyola Entertainment Law Journal. *PRACTICE AREAS:* Litigation.

**ROBERT J. MURILLO,** born Milwaukee, Wisconsin, June 11, 1974; (admission pending). *Education:* University of Chicago (B.A., 1993; M.A., 1993); Fordham University (J.D., 1996). *LANGUAGES:* Spanish. *PRACTICE AREAS:* Business and Finance.

**MICHAEL B. REYNOLDS,** born Fresno, California, September 6, 1969; admitted to bar, 1994, California. *Education:* University of California at Davis (B.A., with highest honors, 1991), Phi Beta Kappa; University of California at Los Angeles School of Law (J.D., 1994). Moot Court Honors Program. *PRACTICE AREAS:* Bankruptcy Law.

**DANIEL S. RODMAN,** born Anaheim, California, February 25, 1966; admitted to bar, 1991, California; U.S. District Court, Central, Northern, Eastern and Southern Districts of California and U.S. Court of Appeals, Ninth Circuit. *Education:* University of Southern California (B.S., 1988); Loyola Law School (J.D., 1991). *Member:* Beverly Hills, Los Angeles County, Orange County, Federal and American Bar Associations. *PRACTICE AREAS:* Product Liability Litigation.

**GERDA M. ROY,** born Los Angeles, California, March 16, 1962; admitted to bar, 1987, California and U.S. District Court, Central District of California; 1989, District of Columbia; 1991, U.S. District Court, Eastern District of California; U.S. District Court, Southern District of California; U.S. Court of Appeals, Ninth Circuit; 1992, U.S. District Court, Northern District of California. *Education:* University of California at Davis (B.A., high honors, 1984); Boalt Hall School of Law, University of California (J.D., 1987). Phi Beta Kappa. Member, 1985-1986 and Executive Editor, 1986-1987, California Law Review. *Member:* Orange County and American Bar Associations; District of Columbia Bar. *PRACTICE AREAS:* Business Litigation; State and Federal Appeals.

**JULIANNE SARTAIN,** born Long Beach, California; admitted to bar, 1990, California; U.S. Court of Appeals, Ninth Circuit; U.S. District Court, Central, Eastern, Southern and Northern Districts of California; U.S. District Court, District of Arizona. *Education:* University of California at Berkeley (A.B., 1987); University of California, Los Angeles (J.D., 1990). Managing Editor, UCLA Law Review. Law Clerk to the Hon. Melvin Brunetti, Ninth Circuit Court of Appeals. *Member:* Orange County, Federal and American Bar Associations. *PRACTICE AREAS:* Commercial Litigation.

**SEAN MICHAEL SHERLOCK,** born Green Bay, Wisconsin, June 9, 1964; admitted to bar, 1992, California; U.S. District Court, Central, Southern, Northern and Eastern Districts of California. *Education:* Michigan Technological University (B.S., 1986); Loyola Law School (J.D., 1992). *Member:* Orange County and American Bar Associations.. *PRACTICE AREAS:* Environmental Law.

**MARTIN W. TAYLOR,** admitted to bar, 1990, California, U.S. District Court, Central, Eastern, Northern and Southern, Districts of California and U.S. Court of Appeals, Ninth Circuit. *Education:* California State University at Fullerton (B.A., 1987); McGeorge School of Law, University of the Pacific (J.D., with great distinction, 1990). Order of the Coif. *Member:* Los Angeles and Orange County (Member Busines Law and Bankruptcy Section) Bar Associations. *PRACTICE AREAS:* Bankruptcy Law; Reorganization Law; Commercial Litigation.

(All Attorneys are Members of the State Bar of California unless otherwise indicated)
The Firm is a member of LEX MUNDI, a Global Association of 120 independent Firms.

REPRESENTATIVE CLIENTS: AirTouch Cellular; Allergan, Inc.; Chrysler Motors Corp.; Coast Federal Savings; Coopers & Lybrand; First Interstate Bank; Ford Motor Co.; General Motors Corp.; Honda North America, Inc.; Nissan Motor Corp.; The Prudential Real Estate Affiliates, Inc.; Family Restaurants, Inc.; Toyota Motor Sales, U.S.A., Inc.; UCI Foundation; Wells Fargo Bank, N.A.; BHP Copper, Inc.; Arthur Andersen & Co.; The Hartford; Del Webb Corp.; Mayo Clinic; CIGNA Healthplan, Inc.; Lincoln Health Resources Corp.; Baxter Healthcare Corp.; Household Finance Corp.; Perini Land & Development; Honeywell, Inc.; Emerson Electric Company; Southern Pacific Railroad Co.; El Paso Natural Gas Co.; ASARCO, Inc.; Allstate Insurance Co.; Mutual Life Insurance Company of New York; Mutual of Omaha insurance Co.; Goodwill Industries; Burr-Brown Corp.; Duval Mining Co.; Maya Construction Co.; Richmond American Homes; U.S. Home Corp.; E.I. du Pont de Nemours and Company, Inc.; Alphagraphics, Inc.; Outboard Marine Co.; Automatic Data Processing, Inc.; Graphix Zone, Inc.; Navistar International Corp.; Plummers' International; Phillips Petroleum Co.

## SPEISER, KRAUSE, MADOLE & COOK

Established in 1979
ONE PARK PLAZA
SUITE 470
**IRVINE, CALIFORNIA 92614-8520**
Telephone: 714-553-1421
Fax: 714-553-1346

*New York, N.Y. Office:* Speiser, Krause, Madole & Nolan, Two Grand Central Tower, 140 East 45th Street. Telephone: 212-661-0011. Fax: 212-953-6483.

*Rosslyn, Virginia Office:* Speiser, Krause, Madole & Lear, 1300 North Seventeenth Street, Suite 310. Telephone: 703-522-7500. Fax: 703-522-7905.

*Dallas, Texas Office:* Speiser, Krause & Madole, P.C., Three Lincoln Centre, 5430 LBJ Freeway - Suite 1575. Telephone: 972-404-1401. Fax: 972-404-9797.

General Civil Trial and Appellate Practice in State and Federal Courts, Aviation, Negligence, Products Liability, Medical Malpractice, Commercial Law and Complex Tort Litigation.

FIRM PROFILE: Speiser, Krause, Madole has over forty years experience in complex litigation matters involving aviation, maritime, fire and other disasters. We strive to give personal attention to our clients and put our national resources to work in dealing with today's increasingly complex litigation. The Firm's practice serves clients throughout the world.

**JOSEPH T. COOK,** born Jersey City, New Jersey, June 2, 1941; admitted to bar, 1972, Virginia; 1973, District of Columbia; 1977, California; 1988, U.S. Supreme Court; U.S. District Court for the District of Columbia; U.S. District Court, Northern, Central and Southern Districts of California; U.S. District Court, District of Arizona; U.S. Court of Appeals, Ninth Circuit; U.S. Court of Federal Claims. *Education:* United States Naval Academy (B.S., 1963); George Washington University National Law Center (J.D., cum laude, 1972). Author: "The Liability of The United States For Negligent Inspection 1983," 48 Journal of Air Law and Commerce 725, 1983; "Multi-Party/Multi-Jurisdiction Litigation: Practical Considerations," Personal Injury Defense Techniques, Matthew Bender, 1987. Judge Protem, Los Angeles Municipal Court, 1982-1985. Commercial pilot, single engine, land, instrument ratings, 1969. Graduate, Navy Accident Investigation Course, Naval Post-Graduate School, Monterey, California, 1971; University of Southern California Aircraft Accident Investigation Course, 1980. Instructor, Attorney General's Advocacy Institute, 1977-1978. Lecturer, University of Southern California Institute of Safety and System Management, 1979—. Trial Attorney, Aviation Litigation Unit, U.S. Department of Justice, 1972-1976. Assistant U.S. Attorney, Civil Division, Southern District of California, 1976-1979. *Member:* Orange County (Chair, Air Law Section, 1992-1993), Virginia and American Bar Associations; District of Columbia Bar; State Bar of California; The Association of Trial Lawyers of America; Lawyer-Pilots Bar Association (Member, Board of Directors, 1986-1994; Secretary, 1994, 1995; President-Elect, 1996). [U.S. Naval Aviator, active flight duty, 1965-1969; Commander, U.S. Naval Reserve, Retired]. *REPORTED CASES:* Finley v. U.S., 490 U.S. 545 (1989); Estrada v. U.S., 967 F.2d 1421 (9th Cir. 1992); Steering Committee, et al. v. U.S., 6 F.3d 572 (9th Cir. 1993). *PRACTICE AREAS:* Aviation Accidents; International Aviation Law; Personal Injury and Wrongful Death Litigation; Mass Disaster Litigation; Products Liability.

**JUANITA M. MADOLE,** born Port Arthur, Texas, May 2, 1949; admitted to bar, 1974, Texas; 1975, District of Columbia, U.S. Court of Appeals, for the District of Columbia Circuit and U.S. Court of Appeals, Ninth Circuit; 1976, U.S. District Court, District of Columbia; 1977, U.S. Court of Appeals, First Circuit; 1978, U.S. Court of Appeals, Fifth and Tenth Circuits; 1980, U.S. Supreme Court; 1981, U.S. Court of Appeals, Eleventh Circuit; 1982, U.S. Court of Appeals, Sixth Circuit; 1984, U.S. Court of Appeals, Fourth Circuit; 1988, Colorado; 1989, California. *Education:* Tulane University (B.S., cum laude, 1971); University of Houston (J.D., magna cum laude, 1974). Delta Theta Phi. Member, Order of the Barons. Co-Author: *Recovery For Wrongful Death III,* 1992; *Negligence Litigation Handbook,* 1986. Editor: The Government Defense Contractor, 1986; Litigating the Aviation Case, 1987. Trial Attorney, U.S. Department of Justice, Aviation Litigation Unit, 1974-1975. Member, Board of Advisors to the Southern Methodist University Journal of Air Law and Commerce, 1994—. *Member:* District of Columbia Bar (Member, Aircraft Accident Law Committee, 1978—); State Bar of Texas; State Bar of California (Member, Federal Courts Committee); Colorado, Federal and American

*(This Listing Continued)*

(Chairman, Aviation and Space Law Committee, Section on Tort and Insurance Practice, 1986-1987; Senior Vice Chairman, 1987—; Editor, Aviation and Space Law Newsletter, 1984-1986; Member, Aviation Law Committee, Litigation Section, 1984—) Bar Associations; The Association of Trial Lawyers of America; Lawyer-Pilots Bar Association. *PRACTICE AREAS:* Aviation Accidents; International Aviation Law; Personal Injury and Wrongful Death Litigation; Mass Disaster Litigation; Products Liability.

**JOHN J. VETH,** born New York, N.Y., August 18, 1941; admitted to bar, 1987, California; 1988, U.S. District Court, Central, Southern, Eastern and Northern Districts of California; 1995, U.S. District Court, District of Arizona and U.S. Court of Appeals, District of Columbia Circuit. *Education:* New York University (B.S., 1963); Troy State University (M.S., 1973); Auburn University (M.P.A., 1975); Western State University (J.D., 1987); University of Southern California Institute of Safety and Systems Management, 1983. Phi Delta Phi. Member, Editorial Board, Western State University Law Review, 1986-1987. Recipient: American Jurisprudence Award in Uniform Commercial Code; Brief Writing Award, Ferguson Honors Moot Court Competition; 1987 Fellowship in Trial Advocacy, Orange County Chapter of American Board of Trial Advocates (ABOTA). Associate Director, Ferguson Honors Moot Court. Commercial Pilot, Multi/Single Engine Land and Instrument Ratings, 1968. Author: "Military Retirement Pay, The California Legislature and the Recalcitrant California Judiciary: The Odyssey Continues,: Western State University Law Review, Vol. 18, pp. 243, Fall, 1990. Book Reviews: "Across State Lines: Applying the Conflict of Laws to Your Practice," Western State University Law Review, Vol. 18, pp. 893, Spring 1991; "Practical Aviation Law," Western State University Law Review, Vol. 19, pp. 369, Fall 1991. Lecturer, Western State University, College of Law, 1988; University of Southern California Institute of Safety and Systems Management, 1989—. *Member:* Orange County (Director, 1992-1993; Member, Aviation Section) and American (Member, Sections on: Litigation; Tort and Insurance Practice) Bar Associations; State Bar of California (Member, Litigation Section); The Association of Trial Lawyers of America; Lawyer-Pilots Bar Association. President, Orange County Barristers (1993). Director, Orange County Trial Lawyers (1993—). [Lt. Col. U.S. Air Force, 1963-1984 (Ret)]. *PRACTICE AREAS:* Aviation Accidents; International Aviation Law; Personal Injury and Wrongful Death Litigation; Mass Disaster Litigation; Products Liability.

**GERARD R. LEAR,** born Elizabeth, New Jersey, August 19, 1939; admitted to bar, 1970, Virginia; 1972, District of Columbia; 1974, U.S. District Court, Eastern District of Virginia; 1975, U.S. Supreme Court; 1976, U.S. Court of Appeals, Fourth Circuit. *Education:* Mount St. Mary's College (B.S., 1961); American University (J.D., 1970). Member, Editorial Board and Articles Editor, The American University Law Review, 1969-1970. Trial Attorney, Aviation Litigation Unit, Torts Section, U.S. Department of Justice, 1970-1973. Counsel for the U.S. Government in numerous aviation disaster cases, including the 1972 Eastern Airlines L-1011 crash in the Florida Everglades. Member, Plaintiffs' Steering Committee (PSC): Eastern Airlines DC-9 crash at Charlotte, North Carolina, 1974; TWA 727 crash near Upperville, Virginia, 1974; Air Canada DC-9 fire at Cincinnati, Ohio, 1983; Arrow Air DC-8 crash at Gander, Newfoundland, 1985; Northwest Airlines MD-80 air crash at Detroit Metropolitan Airport, 1987; USAir disaster, La Guardia Airport, 1992; USAir 737 disaster near Pittsburgh, Pennsylvania, 1994; American Airlines 757 disaster near Cali, Colombia, 1995. Counsel: Varig 707 fire disaster near Paris, France, 1973; Pan Am and KLM 747 collision on the Island of Tenerife, 1977; Air Florida 737 disaster at Washington, D.C., 1982; Air India 747 bombing over the Irish Sea, 1985; Independent Air 707 crash at Santa Maria, The Azores, 1989; United Airlines DC-10 crash at Sioux City, Iowa, 1989; American Eagle ATR72 icing crash near Roselawn, Indiana, 1994. *Member:* District of Columbia Bar; American Bar Association (Member, Sections on: Tort and Insurance Practice; Litigation; Member, Forum Committee on Air and Space Law, 1983—); Virginia State Bar; Virginia Trial Lawyers Association; The Association of Trial Lawyers of America. Commercial Pilot with Multiengine, Helicopter and Instrument Ratings, 1965. [Capt., USMCR, active flight duty, 1963-1967]. (Resident, Rosslyn, Virginia Office). *PRACTICE AREAS:* Aviation Accidents; International Aviation Law; Personal Injury and Wrongful Death Litigation; Mass Disaster Litigation; Products Liability.

**KENNETH P. NOLAN,** born Brooklyn, New York, June 11, 1949; admitted to bar, 1978, New York, U.S. District Court, Southern and Eastern Districts of New York, U.S. Court of Appeals, Second Circuit and U.S. Supreme Court; 1993, District of Columbia. *Education:* Brooklyn College of the City University of New York (B.A., 1971); Brooklyn Law School (J.D., 1977). Author: "Construction Accidents and the Labor Law," Vol. 29, No. 7, Brooklyn Barrister, May, 1978; "Material Misrepresentation and the Insurance Law," Vol. 52, No. 4, New York State Bar Journal, June, 1980; "Handling Identification Problems in Product Liability Cases," Vol. 87, No. 1, Case and Comment, Jan-Feb., 1982 and Vol. 32, No. 7, Brooklyn Barrister, May, 1981; "All About Litigation," Vol. 10, No. 3, Litigation, Spring, 1984; "Interview with Simon H. Rifkind," Vol. 10, No. 4, Litigation, Summer, 1984; "Settlement Negotiations," Vol. 11, No. 4, Litigation, Summer, 1985; "Jury Selection," Vol. 16, No. 3, Litigation, Spring, 1990; "Weinstein On The Courts," Vol. 18, No. 3, Litigation, Spring, 1992; "Direct Examination - For Real," Vol. 19, No. 3 Litigation, Spring, 1993; "Closing Argument," Vol. 20, No. 4 Litigation, Summer, 1994; "Judge or Jury: The Lawyer's Perspective," Vol. 21, No. 1, Litigation, Fall, 1994; "Litigating in the Limelight: Milton Gould," Vol. 21, No. 2, Litigation, Winter, 1995; "The Client's Suffering," Vol. 21, No. 3, Litigation, Spring, 1995; "Interview with Floyd Abrams," Vol. 23, No. 1, Litigation, Fall, 1996. Co-Author: "Statute of Limitations Distinguishes Between 'Medical Devise' and 'Toxic Substance' Cases," Vol. 33, No. 2, Brooklyn Barrister, January, 1982; "All About Litigation," Vol. 11, No. 3, Litigation, Spring, 1985; "Judges Compare Courts," Vol. 11, No. 3, Litigation, Spring, 1985. Medical Malpractice Panelist, Supreme Court, Kings County, 1986-1992. *Member:* The Association of the Bar of the City of New York (Member, Committee on Aeronautics, 1985-1988); Brooklyn (Member, Judiciary Committee, 1990—), New York State (Member, Committee on Tort Reparations, 1979-1985; Member, Board of Editors, "New York State Bar Journal," 1995—) and American (Associate Editor, "Litigation," 1982-1994; Executive Editor, "Litigation," 1994-1996; Editor-in-Chief, "Litigation," 1996—, Journal of the Section of Litigation) Bar Associations; Bay Ridge Lawyers Association (President, 1991-1992); New York State Trial Lawyers (Member, Board of Directors, 1992-1995); Brehon Law Society; Lawyer-Pilot Bar Association; The Association of Trial Lawyers of America; Association of Personal Injury Lawyers, Great Britain (Non-Resident Member). (Resident, New York, N.Y. Office). *PRACTICE AREAS:* Aviation Accidents; International Aviation Law; Personal Injury and Wrongful Death Litigation; Mass Disaster Litigation; Products Liability; Medical Malpractice; Corporate Litigation.

**JAMES TEAGUE CROUSE,** born Asheville, North Carolina, August 12, 1949; admitted to bar, 1981, Louisiana and U.S. District Court, Eastern District of Louisiana; 1982, U.S. Court of Appeals, Second and Fifth Circuits; 1983, New York and U.S. District Court, Southern and Eastern Districts of New York; 1986, District of Columbia; 1990, Texas; 1991, Wisconsin; 1994, U.S. District Court, Southern District of Texas; 1996, North Carolina and U.S. District Court, Northern District of Texas. *Education:* Davidson College (B.A., 1971); Duke University (J.D., 1980). Commercial Helicopter Pilot with Instrument Ratings, United States, 1973. Graduate, United States Army Helicopter Maintenance Test Pilot School, 1974. *Member:* The Association of the Bar of the City of New York; San Antonio, New York State, Louisiana State and American Bar Associations; District of Columbia Bar; State Bar of Texas; The Association of Trial Lawyers of America; Lawyer-Pilots Bar Association. [Capt., U.S. Army Aviator, Active Flight Duty, 1973-1977; Lieutenant Colonel, U.S. Army National Guard and U.S. Army Reserve Aviator, Active Flight Duty, 1977—]. (Resident, Rosslyn, Virginia Office). *PRACTICE AREAS:* Aviation Accidents; International Aviation Law; Personal Injury and Wrongful Death Litigation; Mass Disaster Litigation; Products Liability.

**FRANK H. GRANITO, III,** born New York, N.Y., January 25, 1959; admitted to bar, 1987, New York and New Jersey; 1988, U.S. District Court, Eastern District of New York; 1995, U.S. Supreme Court; U.S. District Court, Southern District of New York, U.S. Court of Appeals, Second Circuit and U.S. District Court, District of New Jersey. *Education:* Franklin & Marshall College (B.A., 1982); St. John's University (J.D., 1987). Author: "New York's Choice of Law," Aviation Litigation News, Vol. I, No. II, March 1991. *Member:* The Association of the Bar of the City of New York (Member, Committee on Aeronautics, 1991-1993; 1995—); American Bar Association (Member, Committee on Aeronautics, Litigation Section, 1991-1993; Vice-Chairman, Aviation and Space Law Committee, Section on Tort and Insurance Practice, 1995—); New York State Trial Lawyers Association; New York County Trial Lawyers Association (Member, Committee on Aeronautical Law, 1990—); The Association of Trial Lawyers of America; Lawyer-Pilots Bar Association. (Resident, New York, N.Y. Office). *PRACTICE AREAS:* Aviation Accidents; International Aviation Law; Personal Injury and Wrongful Death Litigation; Mass Disaster Litigation; Products Liability; Medical Malpractice.

*(This Listing Continued)*

## SPEISER, KRAUSE, MADOLE & COOK, Irvine—Continued

### OF COUNSEL

**STUART M. SPEISER,** born New York, N.Y., June 4, 1923; admitted to bar, 1948, New York; 1971, District of Columbia (Not admitted in California). *Education:* University of Pennsylvania; Columbia University (LL.B., 1948). Commercial Pilot, single and multi engine land rating, U.S., 1945. Author: *Preparation Manual for Aviation Negligence Cases,* 1958; "Death in the Air," 1957; *Speiser's Negligence Jury Charges,* 1961; *"Speiser's Aviation Law Guide,"* 1962; *"Lawyers Aviation Handbook,"* 1964, 1965; "Airline Passenger Death Cases," 8 American Jurisprudence Trials 173, 1965; *Recovery For Wrongful Death,* 1966, 2nd Edition, 1975; "Light Aircraft Accident Litigation," 13 *American Jurisprudence Trials* 557, 1967; *Lawyers' Economic Handbook,* 1969, 2nd Edition, 1979; *Res Ipsa Loquitor,* 1973; *"Attorney Fees,"* 1973. Co-author: *How to Handle the Big Negligence Case,* Practising Law Institute, 1968; *Aviation Tort Law,* 1978; *Lawsuit,* 1980; *The American Law of Torts,* 1983. Member of Faculty, National College of Advocacy, 1978—. James Smithson Medalist, Smithsonian Institution, 1979. *Member:* The Association of the Bar of the City of New York; New York State and American Bar Associations; Federal Bar Council (Member, Committee on Aeronautical Law, 1957—); The Association of Trial Lawyers of America (Chairman, Aviation Law Committee, 1955-1958; Chairman, Aviation Law Section, 1958-1964); American Society of International Law. Fellow: International Academy of Law and Science; International Society of Barristers (Director, 1967-1970). [Active flight duty, U.S. Air Force, 1943-1946]

**CHARLES F. KRAUSE,** born Chicago, Illinois, August 28, 1931; admitted to bar, 1961, New York; 1971, District of Columbia and U.S. Supreme Court; 1980, U.S. Court of Appeals, Second and Seventh Circuits and District of Columbia Circuit; 1983, Texas (Not admitted in California). *Education:* Valparaiso University (B.A., 1957); Rutgers University Law School (J.D., 1960). Case Editor, Rutgers Law Review. Commercial Pilot with Multi-Engine and Instrument Ratings, 1957. Author: "Helicopter Accident Litigation," 22 American Jurisprudence Trials 517, 1975. Co-Author: *Aviation Tort Law,* 1978; *The American Law of Torts,* 1983; *Recovery for Wrongful Death,* 1992; "Structured Settlements," p. 1527, American Bar Association Journal, December, 1980. Member, Board of Editors, New York State Bar Journal, 1972-1995. Adjunct Professor, St. Mary's University School of Law, 1992-1995. Member of Faculty, National College of Advocacy, 1974. Chairman, Aviation Accident Litigation, Law Journal Seminars, 1980. *Member:* The Association of the Bar of the City of New York; New York State and American Bar Associations; State Bar of Texas (Chairman, Aviation Law Section, 1991-1993); Texas Trial Lawyers Association; The Association of Trial Lawyers of America (Chairman, Aviation Law Section, 1972-1974). Fellow, American College of Trial Lawyers. [Captain, U.S. Marine Corps Air Reserve, active flight duty, 1952-1956]

---

## LAW OFFICE OF LISA STAIGHT

2172 DUPONT DRIVE, SUITE 17
**IRVINE, CALIFORNIA 92715**
*Telephone: 714-851-2111*
*Fax: 714-851-0161*

*Certified Family Law Specialist.*

**LISA STAIGHT,** born Alexandria, Louisiana, February 8, 1950; admitted to bar, 1977, California. *Education:* Tulane University (B.A., cum laude, 1971); Pepperdine University School of Law (J.D., cum laude, 1977). Member, Pepperdine University Law Review, 1976-1977. *Member:* Orange County Bar Association (Family Law Section; Education Committee); State Bar of California; Association of Certified Family Law Specialists. (Certified Specialist, Family Law, The State Bar of California Board of Legal Specialization). *LANGUAGES:* Spanish. *PRACTICE AREAS:* Family Law; Divorce; Paternity; Child Custody; Child and Spousal Support; Enforcement; Premarital Agreements.

---

## STEPONOVICH & ASSOCIATES

A PROFESSIONAL LAW CORPORATION
Established in 1979
KOLL CENTER IRVINE - TRANSAMERICA TOWER
18201 VON KARMAN AVENUE, SUITE 650
**IRVINE, CALIFORNIA 92612-1005**
*Telephone: 714-852-1073*
*Fax: 714-852-1276*
*Email: STEPOLAW@aol.com*

*Litigation Practice in Banking, Business, Commercial, Family Law, Financial, Real Estate and Tort Matters.*

**MICHAEL J. STEPONOVICH, JR.,** born Los Angeles, California, October 7, 1946; admitted to bar, 1977, California and U.S. District Court, Central District of California; 1981, U.S. District Court, Southern District of California and U.S. Court of Appeals, Ninth Circuit; 1984, U.S. District Court, Eastern District of California, U.S. Supreme Court and U.S. Tax Court; 1985, U.S. District Court Northern District of California; 1990, District of Columbia; 1992, U.S. District Court, Eastern District of Michigan; 1993, U.S. District Court, District of Arizona. *Education:* California State University at Long Beach (B.S., 1970); Western State University (J.D., 1975). Phi Beta Delta. *Member:* Orange County and Los Angeles County Bar Associations; The Association of Trial Lawyers of America; Consumer Attorneys of California. Robert A. Banyard Inn of Court. [Sergeant, USMC, 1969-1975]. *REPORTED CASES:* Will v. Engebretson & Company, Inc. (1989) 213 CA 3d 1033; Douglas v. Superior Court of Orange County (1989) 215 CA 3d 155; Kelly-Zurian v. Wohl Shoe Company (1994) 22 CA 4th 397; Saltarelli & Steponovich v. Douglas (1995) 40 CA 4th 1. *PRACTICE AREAS:* Banking; Business and Commercial Litigation; Real Estate Litigation; Tort Litigation.

---

## STEVENS, KRAMER, AVERBUCK & HARRIS

A PROFESSIONAL CORPORATION
Established in 1994
18400 VON KARMAN AVENUE, SUITE 615
**IRVINE, CALIFORNIA 92612**
*Telephone: 714-253-9553*
*Fax: 714-253-9643*

*Los Angeles, California Office:* 1990 S. Bundy Drive, Suite 340, 90025. Telephone: 310-442-8435. Fax: 310-442-8441.

*General Civil Litigation Defense in all State and Federal Courts. Commercial and Personal Lines, Construction Defect, Bad Faith, Insurance Coverage and Declaratory Relief, Medical Malpractice, Environmental Law, Legal Malpractice, Wrongful Termination, Governmental Entity Defense.*

(For Complete Biographical Data on all Personnel, see Professional Biographies at Los Angeles)

---

## SUCHMAN, GALFIN & PASSON, LLP

18101 VON KARMAN AVENUE, SUITE 1400
**IRVINE, CALIFORNIA 92612-1043**
*Telephone: 714-752-2444*
*Facsimile: 714-833-8256*
*Email: sgplaw1@aol.com*

*Santa Ana, California Office:* 2122 North Broadway, Suite 100. Telephone: 714-752-2444.

*General Civil and Trial Practice, Commercial Litigation. Financial Institutions including Banks and Savings & Loan Associations, Corporate, Business, Real Estate, Title Insurance, Bankruptcy (Creditor Representation), Equipment Leasing, Construction, Mobilehome Law, Probate, Estate Planning and Trust Law.*

### MEMBERS OF FIRM

**STEWART R. SUCHMAN,** born New York, N.Y., May 18, 1942; admitted to bar, 1970, California and U.S. District Court, Central District of California; 1973, U.S. District Court, Eastern and Southern Districts of California. *Education:* University of California at Los Angeles (B.A., 1966); Hastings College of Law, University of California (J.D., 1969). Lecturer, The Rutter Group, Enforcing Judgements, 1987-1989. Vice President,

*(This Listing Continued)*

## PROFESSIONAL BIOGRAPHIES

## CALIFORNIA—IRVINE

Hastings Alumni Association, Greater Los Angeles Chapter, 1974-1975. Corporations Counsel, California Department of Corporations, 1970-1971. *Member:* Orange County (Member, Judiciary Committee) Bar Association; State Bar of California. **PRACTICE AREAS:** Corporate Law; Commercial Law; Litigation; Banking Law; Construction Law.

**TED A. GALFIN,** born Brooklyn, New York, November 30, 1953; admitted to bar, 1980, California and U.S. District Court, Northern, Southern and Central Districts of California. *Education:* University of California at Berkeley (B.A., 1976); Golden Gate University (J.D., 1980). Judge Pro Tempore, Municipal Court, Orange County Harbor Judicial District, 1985. *Member:* Orange County Bar Association; State Bar of California. **PRACTICE AREAS:** Litigation; Bankruptcy (Creditor Representation); Commercial Law; Landlord and Tenant Law; Banking Law; Mobilehome Law.

**KENNETH D. PASSON,** born Los Angeles, California, November 8, 1953; admitted to bar, 1978, California and U.S. District Court, Central, Eastern, Northern and Southern Districts of California. *Education:* University of California at Los Angeles (B.A., cum laude, 1975); Loyola Marymount University (J.D., 1978). Member, St. Thomas More Law Honor Society. *Member:* Orange County Bar Association; State Bar of California. **REPORTED CASES:** Dodd v. Citizens Bank of California (1990) 222 Cal. App. 3d 1624; Symonds v. Mercury Savings and Loan Assn. (1990) 225 Cal. App. 3d 1458. **PRACTICE AREAS:** Title Insurance Law; Commercial Law; Litigation; Banking Law; Receivership Law; Equipment Leasing Law.

**LORRAINE KAY SMYTH,** born Glendale, California, March 16, 1957; admitted to bar, 1982, California; U.S. District Court, Southern District of California. *Education:* California Polytechnic State University (B.A., 1979); California Western School of Law (J.D., 1982). Past President, Orange County Chapter of Financial Women International. *Member:* Orange County Bar Association; State Bar of California. **PRACTICE AREAS:** Litigation; Landslide and Subsidence Law; Construction Law; Commercial Law.

**MICHAEL R. ADAMS,** born Santa Barbara, California, February 1, 1960; admitted to bar, 1985, California and U.S. District Court, Southern District of California; 1986, U.S District Court, Central and Northern Districts of California and U.S. Tax Court. *Education:* University of California at Riverside (A.B., 1982); University of San Diego (J.D., 1985). *Member:* Orange County Bar Association; State Bar of California. **PRACTICE AREAS:** Business Law; Corporate Law; Estate Planning and Trust Law; Probate Law.

**WILLIAM E. ALSNAUER, JR.,** born Sharon, Pennsylvania, November 12, 1957; admitted to bar, 1982, Pennsylvania; 1984, California; U.S. District Court, Central, Eastern, Northern and Southern Districts of California; U.S. District Court, Western District of Pennsylvania. *Education:* Grove City College (A.B., 1979); Ohio Northern University (J.D., 1982). Pi Gamma Mu; Phi Alpha Delta. Associate Technical Editor, Ohio Northern University Law Review, 1981-1982. *Member:* Orange County Bar Association; State Bar of California. **PRACTICE AREAS:** Bankruptcy (Creditor Representation); Litigation; Commercial Law; Collection Law; Landlord and Tenant Law.

**MARCELLE SUZANNE STRAUSS,** born Detroit, Michigan, April 10, 1960; admitted to bar, 1986, California; 1987, U.S. Court of Appeals, Ninth Circuit and U.S. District Court, Southern, Northern, Eastern and Central Districts of California. *Education:* University of California at Berkeley (B.A., 1982); McGeorge School of Law, University of the Pacific (J.D., 1986). Honors in Oral Advocacy, International Moot Court. Instructor, Legal Writing, McGeorge School of Law, University of the Pacific, 1985-1986. *Member:* Orange County Bar Association ; State Bar of California. **PRACTICE AREAS:** Litigation; Construction Law; Insurance Defense Law; Employment Law; Title Insurance Law.

**ADAM M. GREELY,** born Los Angeles, California, August 7, 1964; admitted to bar, 1991, California; 1992, U.S. District Court, Northern, Southern, Eastern and Central Districts of California. *Education:* Pomona College (B.A., 1987); Loyola Law School Los Angeles (J.D., 1991). Saint Thomas More Law Honor Society. *Member:* Orange County Bar Association; State Bar of California. **PRACTICE AREAS:** Litigation; Bankruptcy (Creditor Representation); Commercial Law; Collection Law.

---

### SUTTON AND MURPHY

7700 IRVINE CENTER DRIVE, SUITE 830
**IRVINE, CALIFORNIA 92718**
Telephone: 714-753-5057

*Insurance Defense, Plaintiffs' Personal Injury, Civil Litigation.*

(This Listing Continued)

---

*MEMBERS OF FIRM*

**MICHAEL S. SUTTON,** born Hampton, Virginia, August 20, 1955; admitted to bar, 1980, California. *Education:* California State University at Fullerton (B.A., 1977); Loyola University (J.D., 1980). Instructor: Fundamentals of Civil Litigation, Continuing Education of Bar. Judge Pro Tem, Orange County Superior Court and Los Angeles County Superior Court. *Member:* Orange County and American Bar Associations; State Bar of California; Southern California Defense Counsel. **PRACTICE AREAS:** Personal Injury Law; Insurance Defense.

**THOMAS M. MURPHY,** born Sioux City, Iowa, March 12, 1962; admitted to bar, 1987, California. *Education:* University of California at Los Angeles (B.A., 1984); Loyola University (J.D., 1987). *Member:* Orange County Bar Association; State Bar of California; Southern California Defense Association. **PRACTICE AREAS:** Personal Injury Law; Insurance Defense.

**STEVEN G. PRATT,** born Long Beach, California, August 13, 1965; admitted to bar, 1993, California. *Education:* University of California at Santa Barbara; California Western School of Law (J.D., 1992). *Member:* Orange County Bar Association; State Bar of California. **PRACTICE AREAS:** Personal Injury Law; Insurance Defense.

REPRESENTATIVE CLIENTS: Aetna Casualty & Surety Co.; Fireman's Fund Insurance Co.; Fleetwood Enterprises, Inc.; Winnebago Industries, Inc.; Textron, Inc.; R & B Realty Group; Bernard Warschaw Insurance Sales Agency, Inc.; GAB Business Services, Inc.; Pizza Hut; UCA Risk Management, Inc.; Precision Risk Management, Inc.; Sterling Casualty Insurance Co.; Dependable Insurance Co.; The Clorox Co.; Pacific Pioneer Insurance Company of Oklahoma; Royal Insurance Company of Canada; American Bonding Co.; Home Insurance Co.; Countrywide Services Corp.; A.R.D.I. Exchange - A Risk Retention Company; Dynamics Corporation of America; Get Smart Scaffold Co.; Westinghouse Air Brake Co.; Gulf Stream Coach, Inc.; The Prime-Mover Co.; Sunnybrook R.V., Inc.; Whirlpool Corp.; Southcorp U.S.A., Inc.; American Appliance Manufacturing Corp.

---

### LAWRENCE TAYLOR

IRVINE, CALIFORNIA

(See Long Beach)

*Criminal Defense practice limited to Drunk Driving Defense.*

---

### THROCKMORTON, BECKSTROM, OAKES & TOMASSIAN LLP

A Partnership

19800 MACARTHUR BOULEVARD, SUITE 350
**IRVINE, CALIFORNIA 92612**
Telephone: 714-955-2280
Fax: 714-467-8081

*Pasadena, California Office:* Corporate Center Pasadena, 225 South Lake Avenue, Suite 500. Telephone: 818-568-2500; 213-681-2321. Fax: 818-405-0786.

*Construction (claims and defects), Real Estate, Insurance, Business, Commercial and Medical Legal Law. General Civil Litigation, Defense of Religious Institutions. All aspects of Trial and Appellate Work.*

(For Complete Biographical Data on all Personnel, see Professional Biographies at Pasadena, California)

## LAW OFFICES OF
## SUSAN M. TRAGER

A PROFESSIONAL CORPORATION

Established in 1980

THE LANDMARK BUILDING
SUITE 104, 2100 S. E. MAIN STREET
**IRVINE, CALIFORNIA 92614**
Telephone: 714-752-8971
Telefax: 714-863-9804

*Administrative Proceedings and Civil Litigation relating to Water Rights, Species and Habitat Protection, Natural Resources, Hazardous Materials, Municipal Law, Eminent Domain, Land Use Planning and Environmental Law.*

FIRM PROFILE: *The Firm advises and represents clients before administrative agencies and before state and federal courts in matters involving water rights, and water resources management, in California and Nevada, land use, municipal law, eminent domain, wetlands, and endangered species.*

*The Firm serves as special counsel to cities, counties, water districts, community services districts, and other public agencies. The firm represents and advises agricultural businesses, land owners, land developers, mutual water companies and manufacturers on these issues.*

*The Firm is frequently called upon to draft and review legislation, to provide testimony to legislative and administrative bodies, and to engage in policy analysis, planning and implementation.*

**SUSAN M. TRAGER,** born New York, N.Y., September 11, 1947; admitted to bar, 1973, California; 1974, Nevada. *Education:* Colorado Woman's College; University of Colorado (B.S., 1970); Golden Gate University (J.D., 1973). Member, Editorial Board and Contributing Editor, Shepard's California Water Law and Policy Reporter, 1991—. Member, Advisory Board, Shepard's California Environmental Law and Regulation Reporter, 1992—. Author: "California's Ground Water: Who's in Charge?" Shepard's California Water Law and Policy Reporter, January 1992; "Emerging Forums for Groundwater Dispute Resolution in California: A Glimpse at the Second Generation of Groundwater Issues and How Agencies Work Toward Problem Resolution," Pacific Law Journal, 1988. Co-Author: "The New Age Land Grab: Habitat Protection as the Politically Correct (and Cheap) Taking of Private Property," Shepard's California Water Law and Policy Reporter, August, 1994; "Wet Windfall," Club Management, September-October, 1994; "Safe Drinking Water Act Reauthorization: In the Eye of the Storm," ABA Natural Resources & Environment Magazine (Summer 1994); "CEQA Mitigation Measures; Can They Be Relied on - By Themselves--as Protection from Adverse Impacts?" Shepard's California Environmental Law & Regulation Reporter, October 1993; "Water, Water Everywhere But...Species Protection Regulations as Water Rights Takings After Nollan and Lucas," Shepard's California Water Law and Policy Reporter, November 1992. Faculty Member: CLE International, Conference on California Water Law; September 5, 6, 1991 (Los Angeles), March 25-27, 1992 (San Francisco), March 18-19, 1993 (San Francisco), September 23-24, 1993 (Coronado), October 27-28, 1994 (Coronado), July 27-28, 1995 (San Francisco), March 28-29, 1996 (San Francisco). 19th Biennial Groundwater Conference, University of California Water Resources Center, California Department of Water Resources, State Water Resources Control Board, September 13-14, 1993 (Sacramento); Natural Resources Law Center, University of Colorado School of Law, Boulder, Colorado, "Uncovering the Hidden Resource: Groundwater Law, Hydrology and Policy in the 1990's," June 13-17, 1992; 24th Annual Rocky Mountain Groundwater Conference, September 27, 1994 (Las Vegas); Association of State Dam Safety Officials, September 8-11, 1996 (Seattle). Member: Citizens Advisory Committee, Southern California Hazardous Waste Management Authority, 1986—; California Planning Roundtable, 1985—; Board of Trustees, Nevada Indian Legal Services, Inc., 1975-1976; Congressman Duncan Hunter's Advisory Committee on Water Resources, 1985-1986. Deputy Attorney General, Nevada, 1975-1977. Judge Pro Tem, Harbor Municipal Court, Newport Beach, 1982-1984. *Member:* Orange County and American (Member, Natural Resources and Environmental Law Section) Bar Associations; State Bar of California (Member: Environmental Law; Public Law; Real Property Law); State Bar of Nevada; The Association of Trial Lawyers of America. **SPECIAL AGENCIES:** California Water Resources Control Board; California Department of Toxic Substances Control; California Department of Fish and Game; Regional Water Quality Control Boards; County Boards of Supervisors; City Councils; City and County Planning Commissions; U.S. Army Corp of Engineers; U.S. Bureau of Reclamation; U.S. Bureau of Land Management; U.S. Fish and Wildlife Service; Local Agency Formation Commissions; Legislative Committees; Water Districts; Local and Regional Sanitation Districts. **PRACTICE AREAS:** Water Rights Law; Land Use; Municipal Law; Environmental Law; Eminent Domain.

---

**MICHELE A. STAPLES,** born Glen Ridge, New Jersey, April 30, 1960; admitted to bar, 1989, California. *Education:* Montclair State College (B.S., 1982); University of San Diego (J.D., 1989). Recipient: Best Paper Presented, National Water Supply Improvement Association 1992 Biennial Conference, Desalting and Recycling, August, 1992. Listed in: Who's Who Among American Law Students, 1987-1988; Who's Who in American Law, 1994-1995. Intern to Hon. J. Clifford Wallace, U.S. Court of Appeals, Ninth Circuit, 1988. Author: "How to Promote Water Reclamation and Reuse Through the California Water Rights System," 88 Desalination 189, 1992. Co-Author: "The New Age Land Grab: Habitat Protection as the Politically Correct (and Cheap) Taking of Private Property," Shepard's California Water Law and Policy Reporter, August, 1994; "Safe Drinking Water Act Reauthorization: In the Eye of the Storm," ABA Natural Resources & Environment Magazine (Summer 1994); "CEQA Mitigation Measures: Can They Be Relied on By Themselves--as Protection from Adverse Impacts?" Shepard's California Environmental Law & Regulation Reporter, October 1993. "Water, Water Everywhere But...Species Protection Regulations as Water Rights Takings After Nollan and Lucas," Shepard's California Water Law and Policy Reporter, November 1992. Faculty Member: West-Northwest Symposium on Environmental Law, February 4, 1995 (San Francisco); CLE International Conference on Regulatory Takings, March 2, 1995 (San Francisco); CLE International Conference on California Water Law, September 23-24, 1993 (Coronado); April 14-15, 1994 (San Francisco); October 27-28, 1994 (Coronado); July 27-28, 1995 (San Francisco); March 28-29, 1996 (San Francisco). *Member:* Orange County (Member, Environmental Law Section) and American Bar Associations (Member, Natural Resources and Environmental Section); State Bar of California. **SPECIAL AGENCIES:** U.S. Fish and Wildlife Service; California State Water Resources Control Board; Regional Water Quality Control Boards; Local Agency Formation Commissions; County Boards of Supervisors; City Councils; City and County Planning Commissions; Water Districts. **PRACTICE AREAS:** Endangered Species; Transactional Environmental Law; Water Rights; Reclaimed Water Contracts.

**LAURA PAVLOFF COUCH,** born Camp Lejeune, North Carolina, October 1, 1969; admitted to bar, 1996, California. *Education:* University of California at Berkley (B.A., 1981); University of the Pacific, McGeorge School of Law (J.D., 1996). *Member:* Orange County (Member, Environmental Law Section) and American Bar Associations; State Bar of California.

REPRESENTATIVE CLIENTS: Hi-Desert Water District; SAMDA, Inc.; Glencrest; Sunworld; San Luis Rey Municipal Water District; Fluidmaster; Santa Ana Heights Water Co.; Cameo Homes; Hermann-Jensen Nursery, Inc.; Warren Valley Basin Watermaster; C. R. Energy, Inc.; Foothill Properties; Water Advisory Committee of Orange County; Ahmanson Developments, Inc.; Mission Viejo Company; The Chambers Group; Windsong Development; Rose Hills Co.; Rancon Hemet Properties; Lyon Communities, Inc.; Domenigoni Family Trust; Hermes Development Int'l Inc.; Las Flores Group, Inc.; John Boere Dairy; The Diamond Brothers Five and Six Partnerships.
SPECIAL COUNSEL TO: Orange County Water District; Capistrano Valley Water District; Rancho Pauma Mutual Water Co.; Santa Ana Watershed Project Authority; Emerald Bay Service District; County of Tehama; Cities of Orange, Norco, Big Bear Lake, Pismo Beach, Chino, Rialto, and Redlands.
REFERENCE: Sanwa Bank California.

---

## TREDWAY, LUMSDAINE & DOYLE, LLP

Established in 1963

SUITE 1000
1920 MAIN STREET
**IRVINE, CALIFORNIA 92714**
Telephone: 714-756-0684
Telecopier: 714-756-0596

*Downey, California Office:* 10841 Paramount Boulevard. Telephone: 310-923-0971; 714-750-0141. Telecopier: 310-869-4607.

*General Civil Trial Practice, Business, Corporate, Securities, Financial Institutions, Real Estate, Personal Injury, Employment, Environmental Law, Taxation, Probate, Estate Planning, and Family Law.*

FIRM PROFILE: *Tredway, Lumsdaine & Doyle, was established in 1963 in the city of Downey, a suburb of Los Angeles. We have grown from modest beginnings as a small firm representing the interests of local clients to an organization which today represents a broadly based clientele throughout the entire*

*(This Listing Continued)*

# PROFESSIONAL BIOGRAPHIES

## CALIFORNIA—IRVINE

Southern California region from our two offices. Currently our clients include national and local business engaged in manufacturing, construction, distribution, financial, "high tech", and service industries, as well as many individuals.

### MEMBERS OF FIRM

**JOSEPH A. LUMSDAINE** (Resident at Downey Office; see Downey, California for Professional Biography). *PRACTICE AREAS:* Civil Litigation. *Email:* JAL@DOWNEY.TLDLAW.COM

**MARK C. DOYLE,** born Hollywood, California, July 2, 1958; admitted to bar, 1983, California. *Education:* Loyola Marymount University (B.A., cum laude, 1980); Loyola Law School, Los Angeles (J.D., 1983). Pi Gamma Mu. Recipient, American Jurisprudence Award. *Member:* Orange County and American Bar Associations; State Bar of California. *PRACTICE AREAS:* Corporate Law; Real Estate Law. *Email:* MCD@IRVINE.TLDLAW.COM

**JEFFREY B. SINGER,** born Chicago, Illinois, July 1, 1956; admitted to bar, 1981, California. *Education:* University of Wisconsin-Madison (B.A., with distinction, 1978); University of San Diego (J.D., cum laude, 1981). *Member:* Orange County and American Bar Associations; State Bar of California. *REPORTED CASES:* Eisenbaum v. Western Energy Resources, Inc. (1990) 218 Cal. App. 3d 314; Wu v. Interstate Consolidated Industries (1991) 226 Cal. App. 3d 1511. *PRACTICE AREAS:* Civil Litigation. *Email:* JBS@IRVINE.TLDLAW.COM

**MICHELE S. AHRENS** (Resident at Downey Office; see Downey, California for Professional Biography). *REPORTED CASES:* Novar Corp. v. Bureau of Collections (1984) 160 Cal. App. 3d 1, 206 Cal. Rptr. 287. *PRACTICE AREAS:* Civil Litigation; Employment Law. *Email:* MSA@DOWNEY.TLDLAW.COM

**CHERI A. KADOTANI,** born Watsonville, California, August 12, 1959; admitted to bar, 1985, California. *Education:* University of California at Irvine (B.A., 1981); Western State University College of Law (J.D., 1984). Associate and Technical Editor, Western State University Law Review, 1983-1984. Member, Board of Directors, Orange County Japanese-American Lawyers Association, 1990-1991. *Member:* Orange County Bar Association (Member, Family Law Section); State Bar of California. *REPORTED CASES:* In re Marriage of Simpson, 92 Daily Journal D.A.R. 18002 (1992). *PRACTICE AREAS:* Family Law. *Email:* CAK@IRVINE.TLDLAW.COM

**MICHAEL A. LANPHERE,** born Albuquerque, New Mexico, July 1, 1959; admitted to bar, 1985, California and U.S. District Court, Central District of California. *Education:* Arizona State University (B.S., 1981); Loyola Law School, Los Angeles (J.D., 1984). *Member:* Orange (Member, Business Litigation Section) and Los Angeles County Bar Associations; State Bar of California (Member, Litigation Section). *PRACTICE AREAS:* Banking Law; Civil Litigation. *Email:* MAL@IRVINEW.TLDLAW.COM

**HAROLD T. TREDWAY** (Retired).

**MATTHEW L. KINLEY** (Resident at Downey Office; see Downey, California for Professional Biography). *PRACTICE AREAS:* Civil Litigation. *Email:* MLK@DOWNEY.TLDLAW.COM

**LYNN L. WALKER** (1951-1994).

**GARY LIEBERMAN** (Resident at Downey Office; see Downey, California for Professional Biography). *PRACTICE AREAS:* Civil Litigation; Corporate Law. *Email:* GAL@DOWNEY.TLDLAW.COM

**DANIEL R. GOLD** (Resident at Downey Office; See Downey, California for Professional Biography). *PRACTICE AREAS:* Civil Litigation; Family Law. *Email:* DRG@DOWNEY.TLDLAW.COM

**SHARISSE E. MOLYNEUX** (Resident at Downey Office; see Downey California for Professional Biography).

**JOSEPH A. MALEKI,** born Tehran, Iran, April 17, 1969; admitted to bar, 1995, California. *Education:* California State University at Long Beach (B.S., 1991); Western State University, College of Law (J.D., 1995). Recipient, American Jurisprudence Award in Contracts and Civil Procedure. *Member:* American Bar Association; State Bar of California. *PRACTICE AREAS:* Civil Litigation. *Email:* JAM@IRVINE.TLDLAW.COM

### OF COUNSEL

**DAVID A. PASQUALINI,** born Sandusky, Ohio, June 15, 1948; admitted to bar, 1986, Massachusetts; 1987, U.S. District Court, District of Massachusetts; 1992, California and U.S. District Court, Central District of California. *Education:* Miami University (B.S.Ed., 1970); Bowling Green State University (M.A., 1983); Cornell University (J.D., 1986). *Member:*

*(This Listing Continued)*

State Bar of California; American Bar Association. *PRACTICE AREAS:* Estate Planning; Probate; Business Law. *Email:* DAP@IRVINE.TLDLAW.COM

REPRESENTATIVE CLIENTS: SBD Group, Inc.; Rockwell Federal Credit Union; CMC Builders; Culp Construction Co.; Carmenita Ford Truck Sales; Santa Fe International; Parkhouse Tire; Downey Community Hospital; Independence One of California; Michigan National Bank; Vista Federal Credit Union; Southern California Bank; Western Federal Savings & Loan; Western Financial Bank; Procom Technology, Inc.; Pella Architectural; Four Star Financial; Scher-Voit Commercial Brokerage, Lumsdaine Construction; Ameron Federal Credit Union; L.A. County-USC Medical Center Credit Union.
REFERENCE: Southern California Bank.

(For Compete Biographical Information on all Downey Personnel, see Professional Biographies at Downey, California)

---

## CONRAD G. TUOHEY

A PROFESSIONAL LAW CORPORATION

Established in 1969

8001 IRVINE CENTER DRIVE, SUITE 1000

**IRVINE, CALIFORNIA 92718-2996**

Telephone: 714-453-1255

Fax: 714-453-9566

*Toxic/Environmental Law and International Trials and Appeals.*

**CONRAD G. TUOHEY,** born Brooklyn, New York, December 27, 1933; admitted to bar, 1962, California and U.S. District Court, Central District of California; 1977, U.S. Supreme Court; 1979, U.S. Court of Appeals, Ninth Circuit and U.S. District Court, Southern District of California; 1980, New York, District of Columbia, U.S. District Court, Northern District of California, U.S. Court of Appeals for the District of Columbia and U.S. Court of International Trade; 1981, U.S. Court of Claims; 1982, U.S. District Court, District of Columbia and Eastern District of California. *Education:* George Washington University (B.A., 1957); University of Michigan (J.D., 1960). Phi Delta Phi. Author: "Toxic Torts As Absolute Nuisances," 16 Western State University Law Review 5, 1988; "Corporate Director Resignation," 33 Arkansas Law Review 106, 1979; "Negligent Infliction of Emotional Distress Arising From a Breach of Contract," 8 Southwestern University Law Review 665, 1976; "Kickbacks, Rebates and Tying Arrangements in Real Estate Transaction; RESPA; Antitrust and Unfair Practices," 2 Pepperdine University School of Law Review 309, 1975; "Comprehensive Health Planning and Procedures: The California Experience," 11 University of San Diego Law Review 353, 1974. Legal Counsel/Consultant, California State Senate, 1981-1987; Committee Counsel, Senate Select Committee on the Pacific Rim, 1986-1987. Member: Orange County Transit District Committee, 1966-1968; Board of Directors, Partners of the Alliance for Progress (National and Inter-American), 1970-1972; Public Interest Director, Federal Home Loan Bank Board, San Francisco, 1980-1983. President: Friends of the University, California State University, Fullerton, 1969-1971; California Partners of the Americas, Alliance for Progress, 1969-1972. *Member:* Orange County (Founder/First Chair: Toxic-Environmental Law Section; International Law Section), New York State and American (Member, International Law Section) Bar Associations; The State Bar of California (Member: International Law Section; Environmental Law Section); The District of Columbia Bar. [Rifle Squad Leader, Regular Army of the U.S., 1951-1954]. *PRACTICE AREAS:* Toxic Torts; Environmental Law; International Law.

---

**FERDINAND DE VEYRA GONZALEZ,** born Manila, Philippines, March 9, 1958; admitted to bar, 1983, Philippines; 1988, California. *Education:* University of the Philippines (B.A., 1978); Ateneo de Manila University (J.D., 1982). *Member:* Orange County Bar Association. *LANGUAGES:* Tagalog. *PRACTICE AREAS:* Toxic Torts; Environmental Law; International Law.

References will be furnished upon request.

## TURNER AND REYNOLDS
*A LAW CORPORATION*
Established in 1985
18400 VON KARMAN AVENUE, SUITE 500
**IRVINE, CALIFORNIA 92612-1584**
Telephone: 714-474-6900
Fax: 714-474-6907

General Civil Trial Practice. Business, Construction, Securities, Commodities, Real Property, Bankruptcy, Banking, Insurance, Environmental, Eminent Domain and Personal Injury Litigation.

FIRM PROFILE: Since 1985 we have represented Southern California businesses, their owners, subsidiaries and divisions of national companies in a variety of industries. Currently our clients include national and local businesses engaged in manufacturing, construction, insurance, real estate, "high tech" and service industries, health care providers and institutions, as well as many individuals. The firm represents clients in every aspect of civil litigation before all California state and federal courts, including real estate, construction defect, securities, commodities, employment, business litigation and bankruptcy.

**FREDERICK E. TURNER,** born Long Beach, California, December 6, 1953; admitted to bar, 1980, California; U.S. Court of Appeals, Ninth Circuit; U.S. District Court, Central and Southern Districts of California. *Education:* California State University, Long Beach (B.S., with high distinction, 1977); Loyola Law School (J.D., cum laude, 1980). *Member:* Orange County (Member, Business Litigation Section) and Los Angeles County Bar Associations; The State Bar of California. **REPORTED CASES:** The City v. Hart, (1985) 175 Cal. App. 3d 92. **PRACTICE AREAS:** Commercial Litigation; Business Litigation; Real Estate Litigation; Insurance Litigation; Construction Litigation.

**RICHARD J. REYNOLDS,** born Los Angeles, California, July 4, 1954; admitted to bar, 1979, California; U.S. Court of Appeals, Ninth Circuit; U.S. District Court, Central, Eastern and Southern Districts of California. *Education:* Loyola University of Los Angeles (B.A., cum laude, 1976); Loyola Law School (J.D., 1979). Staff Member, Loyola Law School International and Comparative Law Annual, 1978. *Member:* Orange County (Member, Real Estate, Bankruptcy and Commercial Law Sections), Los Angeles County and American Bar Associations; The State Bar of California; Orange County Bankruptcy Forum; Financial Lawyers Conference. **PRACTICE AREAS:** Bankruptcy Law; Business Litigation; Real Estate Litigation.

---

**CHARLES W. LOSNESS,** born Portland, Oregon, March 16, 1950; admitted to bar, 1991, California and U.S. District Court, Central District of California. *Education:* San Diego State University (B.S., 1972); Western State University (J.D., 1990). Technical Editor, Western State University Law Review, 1989-1990. Recipient: American Jurisprudence Awards-Torts I and Trusts; James M. Brower Achievement Award. Author, Comment: "Growth Control Regulations: What Does It Take to Withstand Judicial Scrutiny?" Western State University Law Review, Volume 17, Number 1, Fall, 1989, Page 157. *Member:* Orange County Bar Association (Member, Construction Law Section, 1991—); State Bar of California. **PRACTICE AREAS:** Construction Litigation; Eminent Domain/Condemnation Litigation; Real Estate Litigation.

**ROBERT F. ZWIERLEIN,** born Los Angeles, California, May 19, 1963; admitted to bar, 1988, California, U.S. District Court, Central District of California and U.S. Court of Appeals, Ninth Circuit. *Education:* San Diego State University (B.A., 1985); University of Southern California (J.D., 1988). Phi Alpha Delta (Marshall, 1987). Member, 1986 and Editor, 1987, Environmental Law Journal. Recipient, American Jurisprudence Award in Labor Law. *Member:* Los Angeles County, Orange County and American (Member, Sections on: Litigation; Environmental Law) Bar Associations; State Bar of California; Association of Southern California Defense Counsel; Defense Research Institute, Inc. **LANGUAGES:** German. **PRACTICE AREAS:** Business Law; Commercial Law; Real Estate Litigation; Personal Injury.

REPRESENTATIVE CLIENTS: El Dorado Bank; Haskell and White; Leon Richman Design; Liberty Capital Markets Inc.; Monex; Pioneer Bank; Newport Pacific Corporation; Southern California Builders Association; Web Service Company, Inc.; Z. Cavaracci.

---

## MICHAEL V. VOLLMER
IRVINE, CALIFORNIA
(See Newport Beach)
Practice limited to Estate Planning, Probate, Trust and Taxation Law.

---

## WAGNER & ASSOCIATES
5 PARK PLAZA, SUITE 1500
**IRVINE, CALIFORNIA 92714**
Telephone: 714-474-6964
Fax: 714-756-0517

General Civil Litigation, Commercial Law, Securities Arbitration, Landlord/Tenant Law.

FIRM PROFILE: The Wagner firm is a highly qualified legal service. The Wagners both come from large firms which allows them to give their client, large firm experience at a low rate.

**DONALD P. WAGNER,** born Pittsburgh, Pennsylvania, December 3, 1960; admitted to bar, 1987, California; 1988, U.S. Court of Appeals, Ninth Circuit and U.S. District Court, Central, Southern, Eastern and Northern Districts of California. *Education:* University of California at Los Angeles (B.A., 1983); Hastings College of Law, University of California (J.D., 1987). Senior Production Editor, Hastings Constitutional Law Quarterly, 1986-1987. Extern, Hon. Joseph T. Sneed, Ninth Circuit Court of Appeals. *Member:* Orange County Bar Association; American Inns of Court, Orange County Legion Lex Chapter.

**MEGAN L. WAGNER,** born Mountain Home, Idaho, July 7, 1962; admitted to bar, 1987, California; 1988, U.S. District Court, Central District of California. *Education:* University of California at Los Angeles (B.A., cum laude, 1983); University of California at Berkeley (J.D., 1987). Order of the Coif. Associate Editor, California Law Review. Member, Legion Lex, American Inns of Court, 1992-1993; 1994-1995. *Member:* Orange County Bar Association (Member, Appellate Law Section, 1992-1995). (Resident). **PRACTICE AREAS:** Civil Litigation; Civil Appeals.

---

## WATT, TIEDER & HOFFAR, L.L.P.
3 PARK PLAZA, SUITE 1530
**IRVINE, CALIFORNIA 92714**
Telephone: 714-852-6700
Telecopier: 714-261-0771

*McLean Virginia Office:* 7929 Westpark Drive, Suite 400, Telephone: 703-749-1000. Telecopier: 703-893-8029.
*Washington, D.C. Office:* 601 Pennsylvania Avenue, N.W. Suite 900, Telephone: 202-462-4697.

Government Contracts, Construction, Surety, Environmental, Commercial Litigation, International Business, Toxic Waste and Real Estate Law.

FIRM PROFILE: In our construction, surety, business and transactional practices, we offer the expertise and attention of a specialist with the resources of a larger firm. In our construction and surety practices, our attorneys advise clients nationally and internationally on all phases of the construction process, particularly in the litigation of construction claims, including the innovative use of alternative dispute resolution techniques. In our business and transactional practices, our services include business planning, commercial litigation and negotiation and drafting of documents for a variety of commercial transactions nationally and internationally.

### MEMBERS OF FIRM
**JOHN B. TIEDER, JR.,** born Albany, New York, May 8, 1946; admitted to bar, 1971, Virginia; 1972, District of Columbia and U.S. Claims Court (Not admitted in California). *Education:* Johns Hopkins University (A.B., 1968); Syracuse University and American University (J.D., 1971). Lecturer and Co-Author: "Proving Construction Contract Damages," Federal Publications, Inc., 1982—; "Successful Techniques for Project Control and Construction Risk and Claims Management: Recognizing and Avoiding Claims," and "Resolving the Claim," State Electricity Commission of Victoria/CEMC, 1985; Advanced Course on Construction Claims for Owners and Contractors in Australia & The Pacific Basin: "Pricing and Damages for Construction Claims in the Commonwealth Countries, The United States and Under Civil Law," and "Legal Considerations for Interna-

*(This Listing Continued)*

tional Construction Contracts in the Pacific Rim," Engineering News Record, August, 1985; Construction Litigation/Representing the Owner: "Suing the Construction Manager," Wiley Law Publications, 1984, 1990; "The Employer in International Construction," Lion International, 1985—; "Construction Litigation Superconference," Andrews Publications, Inc. 1986—; Construction Litigation/Representing the Contractor: "Suing the Construction Manager," Wiley Law Publications, 1986, 1992; Construction Law: "Bidding," Matthew Bender & Co., 1986; "Reducing & Resolving Construction Contract Claims," Lion International/Center for Management, Development and Training, 1988—; "Proving Claims Under the FIDIC Conditions of Contract," Lion International, 1989—; American Bar Association Forum on the Construction Industry: "The Special Risks Inherent in Design/Build Fast Track Projects - The Contractor's Perspective," 1989; George Washington University, "International Construction Program Management & Contract Claims - Claims by Owners," 1989—; Construction Contract Claims in the Middle East," Lion International, 1990—; "Construction's Newest Old Problem: Claims for Non-Payment and Late Payment of the Contract Price," Construction Technology International, 1990; "Risk-Shifting Clauses in Construction Contracts," Construction Briefings, August 1991; Forbes Magazine: "Project Financing and Construction in the 1990's-Bridges and Tunnels," 1992; "Pricing of Construction Claims," Lion International/Center for Management, Development and Training, 1992—; American Bar Association Forum on the Construction Industry: "International Dispute Resolution," 1992; "Contract Planning and Administration," Center for Management, Development and Training, 1994. Lecturer in Law, Marshall-Wythe School of Law, College of William & Mary, 1977—. Member: The District of Columbia Bar; Virginia, Federal, American and Inter-Pacific Bar Associations; Virginia State Bar; American College of Construction Lawyers (Charter Member).

**ROBERT M. FITZGERALD,** born West Chester, Pennsylvania, October 15, 1947; admitted to bar, 1975, Virginia; 1976, District of Columbia and U.S. Claims Court (Not admitted in California). Education: College of William & Mary (B.A., 1969); Marshall-Wythe School of Law, College of William & Mary (J.D., 1975). Omicron Delta Kappa. Articles Editor, William & Mary Law Review, 1974-1975. Author: Comment, "Mandatory Maternity Leave: Title VII and Equal Protection," 14 William & Mary Law Review 1026, 1973; Note, "Federal Legislation to Enhance Competition in the Securities Industry," 16 William & Mary Law Review 621, 1975; Article, "Performance Problems and Remedies," Federal Publications, Inc., 1978; "Challenging Arbitration Awards," Construction Briefings No. 89-4, March 1989; "Alternative Dispute Resolution in the Construction Industry," Wiley Law Publication, 1990. Lecturer: Claim Avoidance, CPM Scheduling, Contract Administration, Engineering News Record Seminars, 1980, 1981, 1982, 1988, 1989, 1990; Performance Problems and Remedies, Federal Publication Seminar, 1977-1984; Standard Form 23-A, Federal Publication Seminar, 1979-1981. Speaker: Construction Litigation, Super Conference, 1988; Association of General Contractors of Alaska, 1989; County Engineers Association of Maryland, 1984. Lecturer in Law, Marshall-Wythe School of Law, College of William & Mary, 1977-1980, 1989. Member: Bar Association of the District of Columbia; The District of Columbia Bar; Fairfax County and American (Member, Public Contract Law Section) Bar Associations; Virginia State Bar. *PRACTICE AREAS:* Public Construction Law; Private Construction Law; Zoning.

**MICHAEL G. LONG,** born Encino, California, October 31, 1962; admitted to bar, 1987, California, U.S. District Court, Northern District of California and U.S. Court of Appeals, Ninth Circuit; 1989, District of Columbia. Education: Georgetown University (B.A., in Theology, cum laude, 1984); Hastings College of Law, University of California (J.D., 1987). Member, Moot Court Board. National Appellate Advocacy Competition, Regional Champions. Author: "Waiver of the Contract Completion Date in Government Contracts," The Construction Lawyer, Volume 12, Number 2, April 1992. Co-Author: "Construction Claims Under California Law"; "California Construction Law: Preserving and Pursuing Payment Rights." Member: State Bar of California; California Associated General Contractors (Member, Legal Advisory Committee). *PRACTICE AREAS:* Construction Law; Government Contracts; Surety Law.

**CHRISTOPHER P. PAPPAS,** born Worcester, Massachusetts, March 13, 1960; admitted to bar, 1990, California and U.S. District Court, Central and Southern Districts of California. Education: Carnegie-Mellon University (B.S., 1982); Hastings College of Law, University of California; Vermont Law School (J.D., cum laude, 1989). Author: "California Construction Law: Preserving and Pursuing Payment Rights." Guest Lecturer, "Engineering and the Law," California State Polytechnic University, 1992. Member: Orange County (Construction Law Section) and American (Public

*(This Listing Continued)*

Contract Law Section) Bar Associations. *PRACTICE AREAS:* Construction Contract Litigation; Commercial Litigation.

### ASSOCIATE

**GREGORY JOHN DUKELLIS,** born Los Angeles, California, August 13, 1964; admitted to bar, 1991, California; U.S. District Court, Central and Southern Districts of California. Education: University of Southern California (B.S., 1986); Loyola University Law School (J.D., 1991). Member: Orange County (Member, Construction Law Section), Los Angeles County and Wilshire (Member, Board of Governors, 1994-1995) Bar Associations. *PRACTICE AREAS:* Construction Law; Commercial Litigation; Government Contracts; Surety Law.

(For Complete Biographical data on all Personnel, see Professional Biographies at McLean, Virginia).

## WESIERSKI & ZUREK
*Established in 1987*

SUITE 1500, 5 PARK PLAZA
**IRVINE, CALIFORNIA 92714**
Telephone: 714-975-1000
Telecopier: 714-756-0517

Glendale, California Office: 800 North Brand Boulevard, Suite 250.
Telephone: 818-543-6100. Telecopier: 818-543-6101.

*General Civil Litigation, Insurance Bad Faith, Defense and Coverage, Appellate Practice, Insurance Defense, Products Liability, Professional Liability, Representation of Employers and Employees, Premises Liability, Real Property (Land Subsidence), Toxic Torts and Intellectual Property.*

FIRM PROFILE: *Wesierski & Zurek has an extensive litigation background. The law firm engages in a variety of legal practice at both the state and federal levels.*

*The firm selects its lawyers carefully and trains them to become proficient in their areas of specialization. The firm supports continuing legal education for its lawyers in order to keep them current in their areas of specialization and to enable them to meet the changing needs of the firm's clients.*

*The philosophy of the firm includes a strong emphasis on the close personal relationship that should develop between legal professionals and their clients. We have an extremely high success rate for favorable jury verdicts and we also have more trial experience than many other firms our size.*

### PARTNERS

**CHRISTOPHER P. WESIERSKI,** born Los Angeles, California, October 20, 1953; admitted to bar, 1979, California and U.S. District Court, Central District of California; 1980, U.S. Court of Appeals, Ninth Circuit and U.S. District Court, Southern and Eastern Districts of California; 1981, U.S. District Court, Northern District of California. Education: Long Beach City College (A.A., cum laude, 1973); California State University at Long Beach (B.A., cum laude, 1975); University of San Diego (J.D., 1978). Who's Who in American Law. Outstanding Young Men in America. Who's Who in Emerging Lawyers. Author: "Mary Carter Agreements and Good Faith Settlements: Are They Both Possible in California?" Insurance Counsel Journal, October, 1981. Member: Los Angeles County, Orange County and American Bar Associations; The State Bar of California; Association of Southern California Defense Counsel; Defense Research Institute; American Board of Trial Advocates. *PRACTICE AREAS:* Wrongful Termination Law; Medical Malpractice Law; Insurance Coverage Law; Premises Liability Law; Auto Liability; Disputes Including Sexual Harassment Charges; Product Liability.

**RONALD ZUREK,** born Los Angeles, California, September 6, 1952; admitted to bar, 1977, California; 1981, U.S. District Court, Central and Eastern Districts of California. Education: University of California at Los Angeles (B.A. in Economics, cum laude, 1974); Loyola University of Los Angeles (J.D., cum laude, 1977). Member, Loyola Law Review, 1975-1976. Recipient, Defense Trial Lawyer of the Year, O'Brien's Publications, 1992. Member: Los Angeles County, Orange County and American Bar Associations; State Bar of California; Association of Southern California Defense Trial Counsel; American Board of Trial Advocates. (Resident, Glendale Office). *PRACTICE AREAS:* Wrongful Termination; Medical Malpractice; Insurance Coverage; Premises Liability; Automobile Liability.

**DANIEL J. FORD, JR.,** born Middletown, Connecticut, April 15, 1957; admitted to bar, 1982, California, U.S. Court of Appeals, Ninth Circuit and U.S. District Court, Southern District of California; 1983, U.S. District Court, Central District of California. Education: University of California at

*(This Listing Continued)*

## WESIERSKI & ZUREK, Irvine—Continued

Davis (B.S. in Agricultural and Managerial Economics, 1979); University of San Diego (J.D., 1982). Member, 1980-1982 and Vice Magister, 1981-1982, Phi Delta Phi. *Member:* Orange County Bar Association; State Bar of California; Association of Southern California Defense Counsel. *PRACTICE AREAS:* Civil Litigation Law; Auto Liability Law; Insurance Law; Bad Faith Law.

**TERENCE P. CARNEY,** born Detroit, Michigan, November 21, 1957; admitted to bar, 1982, California; 1983, U.S. District Court, Central District of California. *Education:* University of the Pacific (B.A. in Political Science and Political Economy, cum laude, 1979); Loyola University of Los Angeles (J.D., with honors, 1982). Recipient, President's Scholar Athlete of the Year, University of the Pacific, 1979. *Member:* Long Beach, Los Angeles County and Orange County Bar Associations; State Bar of California; Association of Southern California Defense Counsel. *PRACTICE AREAS:* Land Subsidence Law; Auto Law; Premises Liability Law; Products Liability; Sexual Harassment; Wrongful Termination.

**THOMAS G. WIANECKI,** born Huntington Park, California, May 19, 1951; admitted to bar, 1976, California; 1977, U.S. District Court, Central District of California. *Education:* University of California at Los Angeles (B.A., cum laude, 1973); Loyola University of Los Angeles (J.D., 1976). *Member:* Orange County Bar Association; State Bar of California. *PRACTICE AREAS:* Personal Injury Law; Construction Defect Litigation; Dental Malpractice; Premises Liability.

**STEPHEN M. ZIEMANN,** born Los Angeles, California, January 10, 1959; admitted to bar, 1987, California, U.S. District Court, Northern, Eastern, Central and Southern Districts of California and U.S. Court of Appeals, Ninth Circuit. *Education:* Brigham Young University (B.S., 1984); University of Southern California (J.D., 1987). Phi Delta Phi. Hale Moot Court Honors Program. Recipient, American Jurisprudence Award in Federal Courts. Instructor, Glendale Career College. Who's Who in Law. *Member:* Legion Lex and Glendale and Orange County Bar Associations; State Bar of California. *LANGUAGES:* Japanese. *PRACTICE AREAS:* Civil Litigation; Product Liability; Premises Liability; Wrongful Termination; Unlawful Detainer; Contract Law; Real Property Issues.

**MARK E. BRUBAKER,** born Cortez, Colorado, July 15, 1955; admitted to bar, 1987, California; 1989, U.S. District Court, Eastern District of California; 1993, U.S. District Court, Central District of California; 1995, Colorado. *Education:* Fort Lewis College (B.S. in Geology, 1980); Southwestern University School of Law (J.D., 1987). Phi Alpha Delta. Recipient, American Jurisprudence Award in Contracts Seminar. *Member:* Orange County, Colorado and American Bar Associations; State Bar of California;. *PRACTICE AREAS:* Environmental Law; Construction Defect Litigation; Contract Law; Insurance Defense Law.

### ASSOCIATES

**CHRISTOPHER M. FISHER,** born Washington, Indiana, January 25, 1961; admitted to bar, 1989, California; U.S. District Court, Northern and Central Districts of California; U.S. Court of Appeals, Ninth Circuit. *Education:* University of Maryland (B.S., Biochemistry, 1984); Golden Gate University (J.D., 1989). Associate Editor, Golden Gate Law Review, 1988-1989. Recipient, American Jurisprudence Award in Corporations, 1988. *Member:* Orange County Bar Association; State Bar of California. *PRACTICE AREAS:* Personal Injury Law; Insurance Defense Law.

**MARK J. GIANNAMORE,** born Pittsburgh, Pennsylvania, January 6, 1959; admitted to bar, 1986, California; 1988, U.S. District Court, Central District of California. *Education:* University of California at Los Angeles (B.A. in Psychology, 1981); Southwestern University (J.D., 1985). *Member:* Los Angeles County, Orange County and American Bar Associations; State Bar of California. *PRACTICE AREAS:* Insurance Defense; Products Liability; Medical Malpractice Defense.

**PAUL J. LIPMAN,** born Los Angeles, California, January 5, 1961; admitted to bar, 1991, California and U.S. District Court, Central and Southern Districts of California. *Education:* University of California at Los Angeles (B.A. environmental science, 1986) ; Washington University; Loyola University of Los Angeles (J.D., 1990). Author: "Plaintiffs New Burden of Proof on Summary Judgement," Orange County Lawyer, May 1995; "Price of Admission: Getting Medical Records into (and out of) Evidence," LA Daily Journal 11-27-95; Contributing Editor, Civil Procedure Before Trial (CEB 1996). *Member:* State Bar of California. *PRACTICE AREAS:* Premises Liability; General Civil Trials and Appeals; Business Litigation; Toxic Torts; Insurance Defense Law; Products Liability; Bankruptcy Law.

*(This Listing Continued)*

CAA378B

**DAVID F. MASTAN,** born Baltimore, Maryland, May 1, 1963; admitted to bar, 1991, California. *Education:* University of California, Los Angeles (B.A., Political Science, 1986); Loyola Law School (J.D., 1989). *Member:* Los Angeles County and American Bar Associations; State Bar of California; Association of Southern California Defense Counsel. *PRACTICE AREAS:* Civil Litigation.

**STEVEN D. TURNER,** born Northridge, California, June 24, 1967; admitted to bar, 1994, California. *Education:* Brigham Young University (B.A., International Relations, 1991); Pepperdine University School of Law (J.D., 1994). First Place, Pepperdine Moot Court Negotiation Tournament, 1994. Judicial Clerk, Honorable Lawrence Waddington, Los Angeles Superior Court, 1993. *Member:* Orange County and American Bar Associations; State Bar of California. *LANGUAGES:* Spanish. *PRACTICE AREAS:* Insurance Defense; Bad Faith; Alternative Dispute Resolution.

**ROBERT M. BINAM,** born Los Angeles, California, November 22, 1968; admitted to bar, 1995, California; U.S. District Court, Central District of California. *Education:* University of Southern California (B.A., 1992); Loyola La w School (J.D., 1995).

**DIANE E. JACOBS,** born Lancaster, California, November 16, 1959; admitted to bar, 1995, California. *Education:* University of California at Irvine (B.A., social ecology, 1988); Western State University (J.D., 1995). *Member:* Orange County and American Bar Associations; State Bar of California.

**BRUCE V. RORTY,** born Orange, California, April 1, 1957; admitted to bar, 1986, California; 1989, U.S. District Court, Central District of California. *Education:* Dartmouth College; University of California at Santa Cruz (B.A., with honors, 1981); Institute of International and Comparative Law, Oxford, England; University of San Diego (J.D., 1985). Phi Alpha Delta. *Member:* Orange County and American Bar Associations; State Bar of California. *PRACTICE AREAS:* Insurance Bad Faith; Employment Law; Civil Litigation; Medical Malpractice.

REPRESENTATIVE CLIENTS: Marriott Corp.; Wausau Insurance Co.; General Accident Insurance Co.; State Farm Insurance Co.; Balboa Insurance Group; Pepsico, Inc.; Pepsi-Cola Bottling Company of Los Angeles; The Atlantic Cos.; Kraft, Inc.; Westfield Insurance Co.; Aetna Insurance Co.; Liberty Mutual Insurance Co.; Taco Bell Corp.; Saga Corp.; Mercury Insurance Co.; Liberty National Co.; Twentieth Century Insurance Co.; Esco Elevators, Inc.; Pacific National Insurance Co.; Pizza Hut Corp.; Ecolab Inc.; St. Paul Insurance Co.; Safeco Insurance Co.; Restaurant Enterprises Group; Allstate Insurance Co.; Fireman's Fund Insurance Company; Pearle Vision, Inc.; Home Insurance Company; McKesson Corp.; Midland Risk Insurance Co.; CNA Insurance Co.

## WILLIS, KENDIG & ALPERT

5 PARK PLAZA
SUITE 800
**IRVINE, CALIFORNIA 92714-8501**
Telephone: 714-440-7000

*Civil Litigation and Administrative Proceedings relating to Hazardous Materials, Land Use Planning, Municipal Law, Air Quality, Wetlands and General Environmental Law, as well as related Real Estate Issues and Business Litigation.*

FIRM PROFILE: *The Willis, Kendig & Alpert law firm focuses on environmental, litigation and compliance law. Because of the firm size its clients are able to receive hands on experience without paying large firm fees.*

### MEMBERS OF FIRM

**GEOFFREY K. WILLIS,** born Fullerton, California, March 15, 1961; admitted to bar, 1986, California, U.S. District Court, Central and Southern Districts of California and U.S. Court of Appeals, Ninth Circuit. *Education:* Pomona College (B.A., 1983); Hastings College of the Law, University of California (J.D., 1986). Mortarboard. *Member:* Orange County (Member, Toxics & Environmental Section), Riverside County (Editor, Riverside County Bar Association "Bar Bulletin," 1987-1989; Member Board of Directors, 1990-1992) and American Bar Associations; The State Bar of California (Member, Sections on: Environmental Law, Litigation, Urban, State and Local Government Law); Riverside County Barristers Association (Vice-President, 1989-1990; President, 1990-1991). *SPECIAL AGENCIES:* California Department of Toxic Substances Control; California Department of Fish and Game; South Coast Air Quality Management District; Orange County Health Services Agency; U.S. Fish and Wildlife Service; U.S. Forest Service; Regional Water Quality Control Board - Santa Ana Region. *REPORTED CASES:* KOLA v. U.S., 882 F. 2d 361 (9th cir. 1989); City of Rancho Cucamonga, et al v. Mackzum, 286 Cal. Rept. 39 (1991). *PRACTICE AREAS:* Environmental Litigation; Air Quality; Hazardous Waste; Land Use; Municipal Litigation.

*(This Listing Continued)*

**DAVID E. KENDIG,** born Long Beach, California, April 19, 1966; admitted to bar, 1991, California, U.S. District Court, Central District of California and U.S. Court of Appeals, Ninth Circuit. *Education:* University of Southern California (B.A., cum laude, 1988); University of Southern California Law Center (J.D., 1991). Phi Delta Phi. Author: "Clearing the Hurdles: Insurance and Environmental Claims in California," Shepard's California Environmental Law and Regulation Reporter, April, 1992. *Member:* Los Angeles County, Orange County and American Bar Associations; State Bar of California (Member, Environmental Law Section). **SPECIAL AGENCIES:** Regional Water Quality Control Board - Santa Ana Region; California Department of Toxic Substances Control; Orange County Health Services Agency, Environmental Health; U.S. Army Corp of Engineers; California Water Resources Control Board. **PRACTICE AREAS:** Environmental Litigation; Environmental Insurance; Lender/Trustee Environmental Liability; Real Estate Transactions; Wetlands Regulation; Land Use.

**MARK D. ALPERT,** born Berkeley, California, April 17, 1963; admitted to bar, 1988, California, U.S. District Court, Central District of California and U.S. Court of Appeals, Ninth Circuit. *Education:* University of California at Irvine (B.A., cum laude, 1985); Vanderbilt University (J.D., 1988). Phi Beta Kappa. *Member:* Orange County (Member, Business Litigation Section) and American Bar Associations; State Bar of California. **PRACTICE AREAS:** Business; Real Estate and Land Use Litigation; Environmental Litigation.

REPRESENTATIVE CLIENTS: Sato-Kogyo, Ltd.; Spanish Hills Development Company; The City of Redlands; The City of Rialto; Velie Circuits, Inc.; KOLA, Inc.; Rare and Tasty, Inc.; Philton Properties; Communications for America, Inc.; Karen Elliott & Associates; The Fudge Trust; The Bostock-Leek Family Trust.

## WOLDT & HAM
### A PROFESSIONAL LAW CORPORATION
2151 MICHELSON DRIVE, SUITE 136
**IRVINE, CALIFORNIA 92612-1311**
Telephone: 714-833-5000
Fax: 714-833-5300

*Representing Management in the Defense of Employment Litigation and Labor Disputes and the Development and Implementation of Employment Policies and Procedures.*

*FIRM PROFILE: Woldt & Ham is comprised of attorneys with transactional and litigation experience in the resolution of employment and labor law issues. The scope of the firm's representation encompasses the identification, analysis and resolution of legal issues arising in all phases of the employment relationship, including: The establishment or modification of the structure of the employment relationship; the negotiation and preparation of appropriate documentation memorializing the terms and conditions of the employment relationship; the development and maintenance of a strong and productive work force; the challenge of resolving employment disputes in a timely, efficient and cost-effective manner; and the identification, analysis and resolution of other matters arising in the employment and labor law areas.*

**WENDY A. WOLDT,** born Tachikawa, Japan, April 22, 1956; admitted to bar, 1981, California and U.S. District Court, Northern District of California; 1982, U.S. District Court, Central District of California and U.S. Court of Appeals, Ninth Circuit; 1995, U.S. District Court, Eastern District of California. *Education:* University of Southern California (A.B., 1978); Hastings College of Law, University of California (J.D., 1981). Order of Laurel; Phi Kappa Phi; Phi Beta Kappa. Member, Mortar Board. Extern to Marc Poche, Associate Justice, California Court of Appeal, 1st Appellate District, 1981. Seminars: "Selected Issues in Employment Law," California Continuing Education of the Bar, Panelist, 1991—; "Workplace Harassment and Discrimination-What Employers Need to Know," California Continuing Education of the Bar, Panelist, 1992; "Recent Developments in Wrongful Termination and Employment Discrimination Law," California Continuing Education of the Bar, Panelist, 1993—. Publications: "Insurance Coverage for Wrongful Termination," Los Angeles Lawyer Magazine, June 1990; Sexual Harassment in the Workplace: A Practical Guide for Employers, California Continuing Education of the Bar, 1992, Revised, 1995. *Member:* Los Angeles County (Member, Litigation and Employment Law Sections), Orange County and American (Member, Labor and Employment Law Section) Bar Associations. **REPORTED CASES:** Foreman vs. Knapp Press (1985) 173 Cal.App.3d 200, 218 Cal.Rptr. 815.

**SCOTT W. HAM,** born Charlottesville, Virginia, September 11, 1963; admitted to bar, 1989, California, Pennsylvania and U.S. District Court, *(This Listing Continued)*

Central District of California; 1994, United States Court of Appeals, Ninth Circuit; 1995, U.S. District Court, Eastern District of California. *Education:* Pennsylvania State University (B.A., 1985); Pepperdine University School of Law (J.D., 1988). Delta Theta Phi (Vice-Dean, 1987-1988). Publications: "Teaching an Old Dog A New Trick: Utilizing the Separate Trial of Special Defenses In Employment Discrimination Actions," California Labor and Employment Law Quarterly, Summer 1994. *Member:* Los Angeles County (Member, Labor and Employment Section), Orange County and American (Member, Labor and Employment Sections) Bar Associations.

**KATHLEEN O. PETERSON,** born Staten Island, New York, January 29, 1960; admitted to bar, 1986, California, U.S. District Court, Central, Northern, Southern and Eastern Districts of California and U.S. Court of Appeals, Ninth Circuit. *Education:* Stanford University (A.B., 1982); University of California at Los Angeles (J.D., 1986). *Member:* Los Angeles and Orange County Bar Associations; State Bar of California. **REPORTED CASES:** Nurmi v. Peterson, 10 U.S.P.Q. 2d 1775 (C.D. Cal. 1989); Microsoft Corp. v. A-Tech., 855 F.Supp. 308 (C.D. Cal. 1994); Fennessy v. Southwest Airlines, 91 F.3d 1359 (9th Cir. 1996). *Email:* KPeterson@aol.com

**MARIANNE VAN RIPER,** born Lynwood, California, May 27, 1963; admitted to bar, 1988, California. *Education:* University of California, Los Angeles (B.A., 1985); Pepperdine University School of Law (J.D., cum laude, 1988). Pepperdine University, School of Law, Law Review, 1987-1988. *Member:* Orange County Bar Association (Member, Labor and Employment Law Section).

**LIGIA G. CIMPOERU,** born Bucharest, Romania, November 17, 1969; admitted to bar, 1994, California and U.S. District Court, Central District of California. *Education:* Loma Linda University (B.A., psychology, 1991); Southwestern University School of Law (J.D., 1994). *Member:* State Bar of California; American Bar Association. **LANGUAGES:** Romanian. **PRACTICE AREAS:** Employment.

**STEFAN RESS MILLER,** born Washington, D.C., April 18, 1968; (admission pending). *Education:* Vanderbilt University (B.A., 1990); University of Pittsburgh (J.D., 1995). Publications: "NAFTA: A Model for Reconciling the Conflict Between Free Trade and International Environmental Protection," University of Pittsburgh Law Review, Winter 1994, 56 U. Pitt. L.Rev. 483.

**DEBORA A. CAPPUCCI,** born Ithaca, New York, October 28, 1971; admitted to bar, 1996, California; 1987, U.S. District Court, Central District of California. *Education:* Cornell University, School of Industrial and Labor Relations (B.S., 1993); University of Denver, College of Law (J.D., 1996). *Member:* University of Denver Law Review, 1994-1996. *Member:* Orange County and American (Member, Labor and Employment Law Sections) Bar Associations.

## CHARLES C.H. WU & ASSOCIATES
2603 S.E. MAIN STREET, SUITE 800
**IRVINE, CALIFORNIA 92614-6232**
Telephone: 714-251-0111
Fax: 714-251-1588
Email: CWU@ODONT.CON

*Business Litigation, Business Transactions, Intellectual Property.*

**CHARLES C.H. WU,** born Tai Pei, Taiwan, July 26, 1961; admitted to bar, 1993, California and U.S. District Court, Central District of California; 1994, U.S. District Court, Northern and Southern Districts of California. *Education:* University of Southern California (B.S.E.E., 1984; M.S.E.E., 1986); Western State University (J.D., 1993). Tau Beta Pi; Alpha Epsilon Delta; Golden Key. Recipient: American Jurisprudence Award: Constitutional Law; Torts and Remedies. Member, California Department of Real Estate, 1987. Author: Orange County Asian American Bar Association, Newsletter, 1994-1996. Orange County Asian American Bar Association (Secretary, 1993-1996; Board of Governors). *Member:* Orange County and Los Angeles County Bar Associations. **PRACTICE AREAS:** Business Litigation; Business Transactions; Intellectual Property.

## STEPHEN R. ZALKIND
833 VOGAN TOLL ROAD
**JACKSON, CALIFORNIA 95642**
*Telephone: 209-223-2244*
*Fax: 209-223-5458*

General Civil, Real Estate, Municipal, Business, Family Law, Probate and Related Litigation.

**STEPHEN R. ZALKIND,** born Sacramento, California, September 25, 1942; admitted to bar, 1968, District of Columbia; 1970, California. *Education:* University of California at Berkeley (A.B., 1965); Howard University (J.D., cum laude, 1968). Law Clerk to Hon. William B. Bryant, U.S. District Judge, District of Columbia, 1968-1969. Member of Faculty, San Francisco Law School, 1972-1976. *Member:* Amador County and American Bar Associations; State Bar of California.

REPRESENTATIVE CLIENTS: ACES Waste Services, Inc.; Toma & Anderson Surveying; Amador Economic Development Corporation; Sutter Creek Fire Protection District; Prospect Motors, Inc.; Kreth, Inc.

---

## LAW OFFICES OF
## JOHN L. FALLAT
SUITE 100
907 SIR FRANCIS DRAKE BOULEVARD
**KENTFIELD, CALIFORNIA 94904-1502**
*Telephone: 415-457-3773*
*Fax: 415-457-2667*

*San Francisco, California Office:* One Sansome Street, Suite 2100. 94104. Telephone: 415-399-1180; Fax: 415-951-4660.

*Pasadena, California Office:* 225 South Lake Avenue, Suite 300, 91101. Telephone: 818-296-0155. Fax: 818-432-5401.

General trial and civil practice including insurance and surety defense, administrative law, transportation, collections, bankruptcy, probate and consumer class actions.

**JOHN L. FALLAT,** born Allentown, Pennsylvania, July 14, 1955; admitted to bar, 1984, California and U.S. District Court, Northern District of California; 1988, U.S. District Court, Southern District of California; 1989, U.S. District Court, Central District of California. *Education:* University of California at Santa Barbara (B.A., 1980); California Western School of Law (J.D., cum laude, 1984). Recipient: American Jurisprudence Award for: Criminal Law, 1982; Trial Practice, 1983; Faculty Academic Excellence Awards: International Business Transactions, 1983; Mexican Law, 1984; Special Commendation for Outstanding Achievement in legal research and writing Legal Skills Course, 1982. Sophister Appellate Advocacy Instructor, 1983. Member, Santa Clara World Trade Association, 1988-1989. *Member:* Bar Association of San Francisco; Marin County Bar Association; State Bar of California.

### ASSOCIATES

**STEVEN D. SCHROEDER,** born Berlin, Wisconsin, June 11, 1956; admitted to bar, 1985, California. *Education:* University of Wisconsin-Madison (B.S., 1978); California Western School of Law (J.D., 1984). Phi Delta Phi. President's Scholarship. Lead Articles Editor, California Western School of Law. Author: "Patenting Microorganisms: Working the Bugs Out of the International Depository Authority," 14 California Western International Law Journal 49, Winter, 1984. Arbitrator, Contractor's Disputes. *Member:* San Diego County and American Bar Associations; State Bar of California. *PRACTICE AREAS:* Surety Defense; Real Estate; Personal Injury; Business.

**SUSANNAH M. DUDLEY,** born Greenwich, Connecticut, October 13, 1968; admitted to bar, 1996, California. *Education:* University of California, San Diego (B.A., 1990); Chicago-Kent College of Law (J.D., 1994). *Member:* Bar Association of San Francisco (Member, Family Law Section, 1996—); State Bar of California. *PRACTICE AREAS:* Insurance Defense; Family Law.

REPRESENTATIVE CLIENTS: Highlands Insurance Co.; St. Paul Seaboard Company; Lawyers Surety Corp.; California Compensation Insurance Co.; Old Republic Surety Co.; Amwest Surety Insurance Co.; PST Van Lines; U.S. Department of Justice; Office of the United States Trustee; California State Department of Consumer Affairs; Policyholders for Automobile Insurance Reform.

---

## NOLAND, HAMERLY, ETIENNE & HOSS
A PROFESSIONAL CORPORATION
104 SOUTH VANDERHURST, SUITE D
**KING CITY, CALIFORNIA 93930**
*Telephone: 408-386-1080*
*Fax: 408-386-1083*

*Salinas, California Office:* Civic Center Building, 333 Salinas Street. Telephones: 408-424-1414; 372-7525. Fax: 408-424-1975.

*Monterey, California Office:* Heritage Harbor, 99 Pacific Street, Building 200, Suite C, 93940. Telephone: 408-424-1414. Fax: 408-373-4797.

Business and Commercial Litigation. Construction Litigation. General Business, Corporation, Probate, Estate Planning, Real Property, Land Use, Administrative Law, Tax Law and Family Law.

(For Personnel and Biographical Data, see Professional Biographies, Salinas, California)

---

## BELZER, HULCHIY & MURRAY
3650 MT. DIABLO BOULEVARD
SUITE 130
**LAFAYETTE, CALIFORNIA 94549-3765**
*Telephone: 510-284-9600*
*Fax: 510-284-9630*

Civil Trial and Appellate Practice, Business, Real Estate, Landslide and Subsidence, Real Estate Syndications, Construction, Personal Injury, Professional Negligence, Insurance, Estate Planning and Probate Law.

### MEMBERS OF FIRM

**ROBERT A. BELZER,** born Oakland, California, October 29, 1943; admitted to bar, 1969, California. *Education:* University of California at Berkeley (B.A., 1965); Hastings College of Law, University of California (J.D., 1968). Member: Order of the Coif; Thurston Society. Member, Editorial Staff, Hastings Law Journal, 1967-1968. Law Clerk to Associate Justice Raymond L. Sullivan, Supreme Court of California, 1968-1969. Instructor, Legal Aspects of Real Estate, Diablo Valley College, 1971-1975. Vice President and General Counsel, R.J. Hill Company, 1990-1993. *Member:* Alameda County and Contra Costa County Bar Associations; State Bar of California. *PRACTICE AREAS:* Real Estate Law; Estate Planning; Probate.

**NICHOLAS P. HULCHIY,** born Chicago, Illinois, April 9, 1949; admitted to bar, 1973, Illinois; 1974, California. *Education:* University of Michigan (B.A., 1970); DePaul University (J.D., 1973). *Member:* Alameda County, Contra Costa County and Illinois State Bar Associations; State Bar of California. *PRACTICE AREAS:* Real Estate Transactions; Real Estate Law; Construction Law; Civil Litigation.

**WILLIAM J. MURRAY,** born Los Gatos, California, August 27, 1953; admitted to bar, 1979, California. *Education:* California State University at San Jose (B.S., summa cum laude, 1976); University of Santa Clara (J.D., cum laude, 1979). Phi Kappa Phi; Beta Alpha Psi. Law Clerk to Judge Seymour J. Abrahams, U.S. Bankruptcy Court, San Jose, 1979-1980. *Member:* Alameda County and Contra Costa County Bar Associations; State Bar of California. *PRACTICE AREAS:* Business Litigation; Real Estate Litigation; Construction Law; Insurance Litigation.

### ASSOCIATES

**ROBERT P. RICH,** born New York, N.Y., June 8, 1957; admitted to bar, 1982, California and U.S. District Court, Northern District of California. *Education:* Swarthmore College (B.A.,1978); Hastings College of the Law, University of California (J.D., 1982). Law Clerk, 1983-1985; Research Attorney, 1983-1985; Hearing Officer, 1991—, Alameda County Superior Court. Assistant Public Defender, Alameda County, 1985-1988. *Member:* Alameda County Bar Association; State Bar of California; Society Professionals in Dispute Resolution. *PRACTICE AREAS:* Litigation; Mediation.

## FOLEY McINTOSH & FOLEY

*PROFESSIONAL CORPORATION*

*Established in 1950*

SUITE 250, 3675 MT. DIABLO BOULEVARD
**LAFAYETTE, CALIFORNIA 94549**
Telephone: 510-284-3020
Fax: 510-284-3029

*General Civil and Trial Practice in all Courts. Corporate, Business, Real Property, Tax and Probate Law.*

**FIRM PROFILE:** Foley McIntosh & Foley was founded in 1950. The Firm specializes in providing sophisticated legal services and advice to individuals and businesses of all sizes on a broad range of subjects, including: commercial and real estate litigation, tax, business entity (corporation, partnership, limited liability company) formation, operation, purchase or sale, real estate acquisition and sale, leases, employment law and related disputes, commercial law, environmental law, insurance coverage, estate planning and probate. The Firm is dedicated to providing these services expeditiously - always with a view toward minimizing legal expenses.

**JAMES D. CLAYTOR,** born Berkeley, California, September 17, 1947; admitted to bar, 1972, California. *Education:* Claremont McKenna College (B.A., cum laude, 1969); Stanford University (J.D., 1972). Deputy Attorney General, State of California, 1972-1979. *Member:* Contra Costa County Bar Association; The State Bar of California. **PRACTICE AREAS:** Business Litigation including Employment; Real Estate; Environmental Law; Insurance Coverage.

**WILLIAM R. FOLEY,** born Albany, California, September 8, 1942; admitted to bar, 1969, California. *Education:* University of San Francisco (B.S., 1965; J.D., 1968). Member, McAuliffe Law Honor Society. Assistant Managing Editor, 1967 and Managing Editor, 1968, University of San Francisco Law Review. *Member:* Alameda County Bar Association; The State Bar of California. **PRACTICE AREAS:** Real Property; Business Law; Estate Planning; Probate and Trust Administration.

**DAVID L. FREY, JR.,** born Berkeley, California, May 23, 1945; admitted to bar, 1971, California. *Education:* University of California at Berkeley (B.A., 1967); University of California at Davis (J.D., 1970); Golden Gate University (LL.M., in Taxation, with honors, 1983). Recipient: American Jurisprudence Award in Estate and Gift Tax. *Member:* Alameda County Bar Association; The State Bar of California (Member, Section on Taxation). **PRACTICE AREAS:** Business Law and Transactions; Taxation; Estate Planning; Probate Administration.

**THOMAS J. McINTOSH,** born San Gabriel, California, January 19, 1930; admitted to bar, 1966, California. *Education:* Chico State College (B.A., 1957); University of California, Hastings College of the Law (J.D., 1966). *Member:* Alameda County Bar Association; The State Bar of California; American Institute of Certified Public Accountants. **PRACTICE AREAS:** Business Law and Transactions; Taxation; Estate Planning; Probate Administration.

**JAY RICHARD STRAUSS,** born New York, N.Y., June 20, 1944; admitted to bar, 1973, California. *Education:* Binghamton University (Harpur College) (B.A., 1966); Golden Gate University (J.D., summa cum laude, 1973). *Member:* Contra Costa County Bar Association; The State Bar of California. **SPECIAL AGENCIES:** City of Lafayette Traffic Commission, 1991-1993; Lafayette Planning Commission, 1993—; President, Lafayette Chamber of Commerce, 1994. **PRACTICE AREAS:** Business and Real Estate Transactions; Civil Litigation.

---

**WILLIAM H. CURTIS,** born Springfield, Illinois, June 5, 1957; admitted to bar, 1989, California. *Education:* University of California at Berkeley (B.A., cum laude, 1985); Hastings College of the Law, University of California (J.D., 1988). Phi Beta Kappa; Member, Hastings Moot Court Board, 1987-1988. **REPORTED CASES:** Diamond Heights HOA v. Nat. Am. Ins. Co., (1991), 227 Cal. App. 3d 563; Patricia H. v. Berkeley Unified School Dist. (1993) 830 F. Supp. 1288. **PRACTICE AREAS:** Business; Commercial; Real Estate; Personal Injury; Insurance Coverage.

**KENNETH W. PRITIKIN,** born Chicago, Illinois, November 17, 1956; admitted to bar, 1983, California. *Education:* University of California at Berkeley (B.A., 1978; M.B.A., 1983); Hastings College of the Law, University of California (J.D., 1983). *Member:* State Bar of California. **PRACTICE AREAS:** Business Litigation including Real Estate; Environmental Law; Insurance Coverage.

*(This Listing Continued)*

**REPRESENTATIVE CLIENTS:** Alger Consulting Group, Inc.; Andronico's Markets; Engineered Air Systems, Inc.; Fabricated Metals, Inc.; Fleming Companies, Inc.; Fry's Electronics, Inc.; Independent Acceptance Co., Inc.; Independent Owner's Health Service, Inc.; Quality Care; Noll Manufacturing Company; Northwest Metal Products Company; Pacific Coast-Trane Service Agency; Pet Club; Schnitzer Steel Co.; Pacific Coast Sales & Services, Inc.; The Noll Foundation, Inc.; USA Petroleum Company; Western States Design, Inc.
**REFERENCES:** Mechanics Bank, Albany; Lamorinda National Bank, Lafayette.

---

## LORENZ ALHADEFF CANNON & ROSE

LAFAYETTE TERRACE
3697 MOUNT DIABLO BOULEVARD, SUITE 100
**LAFAYETTE, CALIFORNIA 94549**
Telephone: 510-283-1599
Facsimile: 510-283-5847

*San Diego, California Office:* 550 West "C" Street, Nineteenth Floor, 92101-3540. Telephone: 619-231-8700. Facsimile: 619-231-8323.

*Temecula, California Office:* The Tower Plaza, 27555 Ynez Road, Suite 203, 92591-4677. Telephone: 909-699-9088. Facsimile: 909-699-9878.

*Riverside, California Office:* The Orleans Building, 3638 University Avenue, Suite 256, 92501. Telephone: 909-369-3281. Facsimile: 909-683-4307.

*General Civil and Trial Practice in all State and Federal Courts, Administrative Law, Antitrust, Banking, Bankruptcy, Reorganization and Creditors Rights, Business, Construction, Corporations, Environmental, International Business and Litigation, Public Finance, Real Estate Litigation, Real Estate Transactions, Federal and State Securities and Trade Regulation, White Collar Crime, Estate Planning, Probate, Criminal.*

(For complete biographical data on all personnel, see Professional Biographies at San Diego, California)

---

## DIANE G. MICHELSEN

3190 OLD TUNNEL ROAD
**LAFAYETTE, CALIFORNIA 94549-4133**
Telephone: 510-945-1880
Fax: 510-933-6807

*Agency Adoption, Private Adoption, Independent Adoption and Surrogate Parenting Law.*

**DIANE G. MICHELSEN,** born Jersey City, New Jersey, November 7, 1945; admitted to bar, 1980, California and U.S. District Court, Northern District of California. *Education:* University of California at Berkeley (B.A., 1968); San Francisco State University (M.S.W.; 1974); Golden Gate University (J.D., 1979). Therapist, Family Systems, Specializing in Adoption and Surrogacy Related Issues, 1985—. Consultant, State of California Department of Social Services, 1985—. Social Worker/Adoption Worker, State of California, 1985—. Adoption Worker, Los Angeles County, 1985. President, Academy of California Adoption Lawyers, 1987-1993. Chairman of the Board, Post-Adoption Center for Education and Research, 1990-1992. Board Member, 1990, 1991, 1994, 1995, Vice-President, 1995 and President-Elect, 1996, The American Academy of Adoption Attorneys. *Member:* Contra Costa County Bar Association; State Bar of California (Member, Family Law/Adoption Section). **PRACTICE AREAS:** Adoptions; Surrogacy Law.

---

## PEDDER, STOVER, HESSELTINE & WALKER, LLP

*Established in 1956*

3445 GOLDEN GATE WAY
P.O. BOX 479
**LAFAYETTE, CALIFORNIA 94549-0479**
Telephone: 510-283-6816
Fax: 510-283-3683

*Emphasis in Estate and Will Contests. General Civil, Trial and Criminal Practice. Real Property, Personal Injury, Business, Taxation, Domestic Relations, Estate Planning, Probate, Livestock, Appellate Law.*

*(This Listing Continued)*

## PEDDER, STOVER, HESSELTINE & WALKER, LLP,
*Lafayette—Continued*

### MEMBERS OF FIRM

**STANLEY PEDDER,** born Berkeley, California, February 19, 1935; admitted to bar, 1961, California. *Education:* College of the Pacific (B.A., Econ., 1957); Boalt Hall School of Law, University of California (J.D., 1960). Arbitrator/Mediator, American Arbitration Association. *Member:* Contra Costa County and American Bar Associations; The State Bar of California; California Trial Lawyers Association. **PRACTICE AREAS:** Personal Injury Law; General Civil Litigation; Estate and Will Contests.

**JOHN A. STOVER,** born Idaho, June 14, 1924; admitted to bar, 1956, Idaho; 1966, California. *Education:* University of Idaho (B.S., 1950; LL.B., 1952); New York University (LL.M., in Taxation, 1953). Phi Alpha Delta. Instructor in Law, John F. Kennedy University, 1970-1974. *Member:* Contra Costa County Bar Association; The State Bar of California. **PRACTICE AREAS:** Wills Law; Trusts Law; Probate Law.

**W. G. HESSELTINE,** born Chico, California, July 22, 1943; admitted to bar, 1970, California. *Education:* University of Southern California (B.S., 1966); Golden Gate University (J.D., 1969). Member, Golden Gate University Law Review, 1968-1969. Deputy District Attorney, San Bernardino County, 1970-1973. *Member:* Contra Costa County Bar Association; The State Bar of California. **PRACTICE AREAS:** Criminal Law; General Civil Trial Practice; Domestic Relations.

**TIMOTHY B. WALKER,** born Martinez, California, March 25, 1955; admitted to bar, 1980, California. *Education:* Humboldt State University (A.B., 1977); Hastings College of Law, University of California (J.D., 1980). *Member:* Contra Costa County Bar Association; The State Bar of California. **PRACTICE AREAS:** Real Property Law; Business Law; Conservatorships; General Civil Litigation.

---

**ROBERT R. HALL,** born Rockford, Illinois, June 26, 1921; admitted to bar, 1952, California. *Education:* Principia College (B.A., 1942); University of Michigan (LL.B., 1951). *Member:* Contra Costa County Bar Association; The State Bar of California. [Lieutenant, U.S. Navy, 1942-1946]. **PRACTICE AREAS:** Estate and Will Contests; General Civil Practice.

**STEWART W. LENZ,** born King City, California, April 8, 1957; admitted to bar, 1987, California. *Education:* University of California at Berkeley (B.S.M.E., 1980); Cornell University (J.D., cum laude, 1987). Registered Mechanical Engineer, California, 1984. *Member:* Contra Costa Bar Association; The State Bar of California. **PRACTICE AREAS:** General Practice; Estate Planning Law; Contested Trusts and Estates; Business Law.

**MELINDA R. SELF,** born San Pablo, California, September 28, 1959; admitted to bar, 1991, California. *Education:* University of Phoenix (B.S.B.A., 1987); John F. Kennedy University School of Law (J.D., 1991). Member, 1989-1991 and Editor-in-Chief, 1991, John F. Kennedy Law Review. Member, Advisory Council, Battered Women's Alternatives Legal Advocacy Program. *Member:* Contra Costa County Bar Association; State Bar of California; Association of Legal Administrators. **PRACTICE AREAS:** Domestic Relations.

REPRESENTATIVE CLIENTS: Contra Costa County Farm Bureau; First American Title; Von Bokkelen Bonds and Insurance Agency.
REFERENCE: Bank of America, Lafayette Branch.

---

## EVA-MARIE BOYD
1160 CATALINA
LAGUNA BEACH, CALIFORNIA 92651-2952
Telephone: 714-494-0374
Fax: 714-497-3148

*Trademarks, Copyrights, Contracts, Business Law, Art Law.*

**EVA-MARIE BOYD,** born Breslau, Germany, November 7, 1941; admitted to bar, 1988, California. *Education:* Texas Christian University (B.A., magna cum laude, 1968); Western State University (J.D., 1988). Recipient, Orange County Public Law Center Advocate of the Year, 1993. Member, California Lawyers for the Arts, 1989—. Past Secretary and Treasurer; Member, 1990—, Western State Alumni Association. Member, Board of Directors, City of Laguna Beach Chamber of Commerce, 1993-1995. Member, Legal Aid of Orange County Board of Directors, 1994—. *Member:* Orange County Bar Association (Member: 1989—, Board of Directors, 1995—; Lawyer Referral Service Executive Committee, 1990—; Pro Bono Committee, 1992—); State Bar of California; Orange County Barristers (Past President; Member, 1989—). **LANGUAGES:** German. **PRACTICE AREAS:** Civil Litigation; Trademarks; Landlord Tenant; Contracts; Copyrights.

---

## DONALD L. DROZD
401 GLENNEYRE STREET, SUITE H
LAGUNA BEACH, CALIFORNIA 92651-2401
Telephone: 714-497-2453
Fax: 714-376-2618
Email: DDROZD@aol.com

*Estate Planning, Probate, Trust, Real Property, Business and Elder Law.*

**DONALD L. DROZD,** born Long Beach, California, August 24, 1949; admitted to bar, 1974, California and U.S. Tax Court. *Education:* University of California at Santa Barbara (B.A., cum laude, 1971); University of California at Los Angeles (J.D., 1974). Member, Blue Key. Co-Author, "Checklist for the Evaluation of a 100% Penalty Case," Orange County Bar Journal, Vol. 4, No. 2, Summer, 1977. *Member:* Orange County Bar Association; State Bar of California (Member, Estate Planning, Trust and Probate Law Section). (Certified Specialist, Estate Planning, Trust and Probate Law, The State Bar of California Board of Legal Specialization).

---

## WARREN FINLEY
564 VISTA LANE
LAGUNA BEACH, CALIFORNIA 92651
Telephone: 714-494-8960
Facsimile: 714-497-8477
Email: WFinley@SurEmail.com
URL: http://www.SurEmail.com/finley

*Commercial, Corporate, Real Estate, Partnership, Taxation and Estate Planning, Probate, Wills and Trust.*

FIRM PROFILE: Warren Finley has been a Certified Public Accountant, a Certified Tax Specialist and has been a partner in law firms located in Orange County, California. He created his own firm in 1992 in order to provide sophisticated service to a select group of clients. Mr. Finley endeavors to keep his clients free from the concerns of litigation. Mr. Finley is listed in the Preeminent Law Directory.

**WARREN FINLEY,** born New York, N.Y., January 28, 1932; admitted to bar, 1960, California; 1965, U.S. Tax Court; 1973, U.S. Supreme Court. *Education:* Stanford University (B.A., with honors, 1952; M.B.A., 1954); University of Southern California (LL.B., 1959). Certified Public Accountant, California, 1955. Director, Orange County Fair, 1970-1975. *Member:* Orange County Bar Association (Member, Tax, Real Estate, Business and Estate Planning Law Sections); The State Bar of California. **PRACTICE AREAS:** Corporate Law; Real Estate; Taxation; Wills; Trust; Probate.

---

## A. JANE FULTON LAW OFFICES
SUITE C, 301 FOREST AVENUE
LAGUNA BEACH, CALIFORNIA 92651
Telephone: 714-494-9411; 714-494-5844.

*General Practice. Concentrating in Family Law and Criminal Law. Writs and Appeals in all Courts.*

**A. JANE FULTON,** born Inglewood, California, December 3, 1938; admitted to bar, 1966, California; 1974, U.S. Supreme Court. *Education:* Holy Names College; San Francisco State University (A.B., 1960); University of the Pacific (J.D., 1966). *Member:* Orange County (Member, Family Law Section) and American (Member, Family Law Section) Bar Associations; The State Bar of California (Member, Family Law Section).

---

## LEVIN & GLUCK
384 FOREST AVENUE, SUITE 13
LAGUNA BEACH, CALIFORNIA 92651
Telephone: 714-497-7676
Facsimile: 714-497-7679
URL: http://www.lagunalaw.com

*Patent, Trademark, Copyright, Trade Dress and Unfair Competition Law and Related Litigation.*

*(This Listing Continued)*

**FIRM PROFILE:** Levin & Gluck is a rapidly growing, intellectual property law firm, located in internationally known Laguna Beach, California. The firm emphasizes litigation of patent, trademark and copyright cases, particularly temporary restraining orders and preliminary injunctions. Mr. Levin is one of the leading experts in the country in the field of trade dress law, having written the first single author treatise Trade Dress Protection, published by Clark Boardman Callaghan in 1996. Mr. Gluck leads the firm's patent department, including its new biotechnology group.

Levin & Gluck has a national law practice, handling cases in California, New York and Florida, among other areas. It competes on an efficiency and effectiveness level with much larger intellectual property law firms. The firm prides itself on its results and track record in the litigation it has handled. Levin & Gluck also works with many other law firms, including intellectual property firms, as local counsel in Southern California, and as experts in certain areas of intellectual property law. The firm also utilizes very skilled intellectual property attorneys who work with Levin & Gluck on an independent or "Of Counsel" basis, including one with over 30 years of trademark and patent litigation experience.

Reported Cases: A.T. Cross Company v. Cross Electronics, Inc., 213 U.S.P.Q. 181 (S.D.Fla. 1981); Baracuda International Corp., v. F.N.D. Enterprise, Inc. 222 U.S.P.Q. 134 (S.D. Fla. 1982); Carol Cable Company, Inc. v. Grand Auto Inc., F.Supp., 4 U.S.P.Q.2d 1056 (N.D. Cal. 1987); CPC International, Inc. v. Albury Sales Company, 504 F.Supp. 549 (S.D. Fla. 1980); Ellison Educational Equipment, Inc. v. Tekservices, Inc., 903 F.Supp. 1350, 37 U.S.P.Q. 2d 1563 (D.Neb. 1995); Fimab-Finanziarian Magnificio Biellese Fratelli Fila S.p.A. v. Kitchen, 548 F.Supp. 248 (S.D.Fla. 1982), 219 U.S.P.Q. 40; Fimab-Finanziaria Maglificio Biellesa Fratelli Fila S.p.A. v. Helio Import/Export, Inc., 601 F.Supp. 1, 223 U.S.P.Q. 795 (S.D.Fla. 1983); Hewlett-Packard v. Repeat-O-Type Stencil Mfg. Corp., 1995 WL 552168 (N.D.Cal. 1995); Judith Ripka Designs, Ltd. v. Penny Preville, 1996 WL 32509 (S.D.N.Y. January 26, 1996); Kelley Blue Book v. Car-Smarts, Inc., 802 F.Supp. 278, U.S.P.Q. 1481 (C.D. Cal. 1992); Kransco Manufacturing, Inc. v. Markwitz, 656 F.2d 1376 (9th Cir. 1981); Massachusetts Bay Insurance Company v. Penny Preville, 38 U.S.P.Q.2d (S.D.N.Y. 1996); Minuteman Press International, Inc., v. Minute-Men Press, Inc., 219 U.S.P.Q. 426 (N.D.Cal. 1983); Pony Express Courier Corp. v. Pony Express Delivery Service, 10 U.S.P.Q.2d 1475 (9th Cir. 1988); Scientific Technology v. Stanford Telecommunications, 9 U.S.P.Q.2d 1567 (N.D.Cal. 1988); In re Sasson Licensing Corp. 35 U.S.P.Q.2d 1511 (Commissioner of Patents 1995); Wing Industries, Inc. v. Korach, 213 U.S.P.Q.886 (S.D.Fla. 1981).

## MEMBERS OF FIRM

**WILLIAM E. LEVIN,** born Miami, Florida, June 13, 1954; admitted to bar, 1979, Florida; 1982, California; U.S. District Court, Eastern, Central and Northern Districts of California; U.S. Court of Appeals, Fifth, Ninth and Eleventh Circuits; U.S. Trademark Trial and Appeal Board. *Education:* Connecticut College; Emory University (B.A., political science, 1976); University of Miami Law School (J.D., 1979). Member, Editorial Board, Trademark World, 1986-1989. Editorial Board, The Trademark Reporter, 1987-1988, 1993—. Editorial Committee, San Francisco Attorney Magazine, 1986-1989. Program Materials Editor, American Bar Association, Patent, Trademark and Copyright Section, Second Annual continuing education program. Licensed Real Estate Broker, California, 1987. Author: "Trade Dress Protection," Clark Boardman Callaghan, 1996; "Judging Likelihood of Confusion in the United States," Trademark World," Nov. 86 (Part I) and January 1987 (Part II); "What's In A Name: Music to My Ears," San Francisco Attorney (1987); "On The Area (Code) of Phone Marks", Remarks, Vol. 5, No. 3, United States Trademark Association, November 1992. Speaker, Orange County Patent Law Association, "Trade Dress Protection (MCLE)," June, 1995. Program Organizer and Plaintiff's Counsel, Mock Temporary Restraining Order Hearing, San Francisco Patent and Trademark Law Association, May 1985. Program Organizer and Plaintiff's Counsel, Mock Temporary Restraining Order Hearing, San Francisco Bar Association Barristers Club, March 1986. Member, International Trademark Association, 1982—. *Member:* Orange County Bar Association (Member, Patent, Trademark and Copyright Section; Committee Chairperson and Program Editor); State Bar of California; Orange County Patent Law Association; American Arbitration Association (former Arbitrator in Trademark Cases); Los Angeles Complex Inns of Court, (Member, Executive Committee, 1994-1996). *PRACTICE AREAS:* Trademark; Trade Dress; Copyright and Related Litigation.

**PETER J. GLUCK,** born Savannah, Georgia, August 4, 1964; admitted to bar, 1993, New York, U.S. District Court, Southern and Eastern Districts of New York and Court of Appeals, Ninth, Eleventh and Federal Circuits; registered to practice before U.S. Patent and Trademark Office (Not admitted in California). *Education:* Bates College (A.B., biology and philosophy, 1986); Franklin Pierce Law Center (J.D., 1991; M.I.P., 1994). Issues Editor, Idea: The Journal of Law and Technology, 1989-1992. Senior Issues Editor, Idea: The Journal of Law and Technology, 1991-1992. Teaching Assistant: Patent Practice, Franklin Pierce Law Center, 1991-1993; Immunology-The HIV Virus Research Seminar, The New School for Social Research, 1994-1995. *Member:* New York State and American Bar Associations; New York County Lawyers Association; New York Intellectual Property Lawyers Association; American Intellectual Property Law Association; Licensing Executive Society. *LANGUAGES:* French. *PRACTICE AREAS:* Patent; Trademark Law; Copyright Law; Biotechnology.

## ASSOCIATES

**OWEN J. BATES,** born St. Louis, Missouri, December 28, 1949; admitted to bar, 1995, California. *Education:* St. Louis University (B.A., chemistry, 1974); Western State University, College of Law (J.D., 1994). Recipient, American Jurisprudence Award, Torts 1. Patent Administrator, Cortex Pharmaceuticals, Irvine, California. Senior Development Engineer, Biological Chemistry Department, University of California at Irvine. *Member:* Orange County and American Bar Associations; Intellectual Property Law Association (Founding Member, at Western State Law); American Trial Lawyers Association; Orange County Patent Lawyers Association; Los Angeles Intellectual Property Law Association; American Society of Clinical Pathologist. *PRACTICE AREAS:* Intellectual Property Law; Litigation.

**SERGIO A. GUTIERREZ,** born Miami, Florida, October 21, 1968; admitted to bar, 1996, California; U.S. District Court, Central and Southern Districts of California. *Education:* University of California at Los Angeles (B.A., economics and political science, 1990); Loyola Marymount University (J.D., 1996). *Member:* Orange County and Los Angeles County Bar Associations. *LANGUAGES:* Spanish. *PRACTICE AREAS:* Intellectual Property Law; Litigation.

## OF COUNSEL

**JAMES E. HAWES,** born Harvey, Illinois, July 5, 1934; admitted to bar, 1962, District of Columbia; 1962-1982, U.S. Court of Customs and Patent Appeals; 1963, Massachusetts; 1973, California; 1973, U.S. Court of Appeals, Ninth Circuit; 1976, U.S. Supreme Court; 1982, U.S. Court of Appeals for the Federal Circuit; registered to practice before U.S. Patent and Trademark Office. *Education:* University of Illinois (B.S.E.E., 1957); George Washington University (J.D., 1961); Boston University (M.B.A., 1970). Author: *Trademark Registration Practice, Copyright Registration Practice,* and *Patent Application Practice.* Clark Boardman Callaghan, Ltd., Patent Application Practice and Practitioner, Trademark Manuel, New York. Examiner, U.S. Patent and Trademark Office, 1957-1960. *Member:* Orange County Bar Association; State Bar of California (Board Member, Intellectual Property Law Section, 1990-1994); Los Angeles Intellectual Property Law Association (President, 1989); American Intellectual Property Law Association (Chair, CLE Committee, 1992—); Orange County Patent Law Association (Board Member, 1991-1995); Copyright Society of the U.S.A.; National Inventors Hall of Fame Foundation (President, 1996-1997). *PRACTICE AREAS:* Patent, Trademark and Copyright Law.

## LEGAL SUPPORT PERSONNEL

**PATRICIA E. ANDERSON,** born Los Angeles, California, February 18, 1963. *Education:* University of California at Los Angeles, (B.A., political science, emphasizing international governments, 1988); Whittier College (J.D., 1993). Clerk, California Trial Court, The Superior Court in Orange County. *Member:* American Bar Association. (Law Clerk). *PRACTICE AREAS:* Intellectual Property Law Litigation.

**ROBERT Z. EVORA,** born Lynwood, California, August 8, 1969. *Education:* University of California at Los Angeles (B.S.M.E, 1993); Thomas Jefferson School of Law, San Diego, California. *Member:* San Diego Intellectual Property Bar Association (Member, 1996—). (Patent Clerk). *PRACTICE AREAS:* Patent, Trademark, Copyright Litigation.

**MERRITT L. MCKEON,** born Newport Beach, California, August 9, 1957. *Education:* Regents College, SUNY Albany, New York, (B.S., political science and sociology, 1992); New York University, Gallatin School (M.A., 1993); Benjamin N. Cardozo, School of Law (J.D., 1996). Recipient, ABA Family Law Section Schwab Writing Award. Author: "International Parental Kidnaping: A New Law A New Solution", ABA Family Law Quarterly, 30 Family L. Q 235 (Spring, 1996). Co-Author: Stop Domestic Violence, An Action Plan for Saving Lives, Spring, 1997, St. Martins Press. *Member:* Orange County Women Lawyers Association. (Law Clerk).

**MANFRED E. WOLFF,** born Berlin, Germany, February 14, 1930. *Education:* University of California at Berkley (B.S., pharmacy, 1951; M.S.,

*(This Listing Continued)*

**LEVIN & GLUCK, Laguna Beach—Continued**

pharmaceutical chemistry, 1953; PH.D., pharmaceutical chemistry, 1955). Senior Vice-President, Research Department, ImmunoPharmaceutics, Inc., San Diego, California. Vice-President of Discovery Research, Allergan, Irvine, California. Certified Paralegal, California. *Member:* Licensing Executives Society; American Association for the Advancement of Science; American Association of Pharmaceutical Scientist; American Chemical Society. (Certified Paralegal). *LANGUAGES:* German. *PRACTICE AREAS:* Patent Prosecution; Intellectual Property Litigation.

---

## ROBERT S. LEWIN

*A LAW CORPORATION*

Established in 1972

105 CRESCENT BAY DRIVE, SUITE F
**LAGUNA BEACH, CALIFORNIA 92651**
Telephone: 714-497-8897
FAX: 714-497-1714

*Business Litigation State and Federal, Legal Malpractice, Real Estate, Collections and Appellate.*

**ROBERT S. LEWIN,** born Staten Island, New York, June 21, 1942; admitted to bar, 1972, California. *Education:* Cornell University; University of California at Irvine (B.A., 1969); University of California at Los Angeles (J.D., 1972). National Order of Barristers. Chief Justice, Moot Court Honors Program, 1971-1972. *Member:* Orange County Bar Association (Past Director); State Bar of California; Orange County Barristers (Past President). *LANGUAGES:* Chinese.

LEGAL SUPPORT PERSONNEL

**DIANE E. FEDDEN** (Legal Assistant).

---

## ROBERT W. LUPPI

401 GLENNERYE, SUITE A
**LAGUNA BEACH, CALIFORNIA 96251**
Telephone: 714-494-8553

*Personal Injury.*

**ROBERT W. LUPPI,** born Los Angeles, California, November 29, 1945; admitted to bar, 1971, California; 1992, Colorado. *Education:* University of California at Santa Barbara (B.A., 1967); Loyola Marymount University (J.D., 1970). *PRACTICE AREAS:* Personal Injury Law.

---

## McCLUNG & DAVIS

A Partnership including a Professional Corporation

Established in 1989

32392 PACIFIC COAST HIGHWAY, SUITE 250
**LAGUNA BEACH, CALIFORNIA 92677**
Telephone: 714-499-8424
Facsimile: 714-499-8423
Email: 76530.556@compuserve.com

*Northern California Office:* Pioneer Hotel, 2925 Woodside Road, Woodside, California. Telephone: 415-851-9700. Fax: 415-851-9701.

*General Civil Practice. Business, Family Law, Real Property, Environmental, Administrative, Eminent Domain and Redevelopment, Government Relations Law, Civil Rights, Health Care, Probate and Estate Planning Law.*

**CHARLES E. McCLUNG, (A PROFESSIONAL CORPORATION),** born Evanston, Illinois, July 17, 1927; admitted to bar, 1952, California, U.S. Court of Appeals, 9th Circuit and U.S. District Court, Northern District of California; 1957, U.S. Tax Court; 1974, U.S. Supreme Court. *Education:* Stanford University (A.B., 1949; J.D., 1951). Phi Delta Phi. Deputy Attorney General of California, 1952-1954. *Member:* Orange County, Los Angeles County and American (Member, Sections on: Real Property, Probate and Trust Law; Litigation) Bar Associations; The State Bar of California. *PRACTICE AREAS:* Health Care Law; Real Property Law; Probate Law; Estate Planning Law.

**CHARLES E. McCLUNG, JR.,** born Palo Alto, California, July 8, 1953; admitted to bar, 1979, California; 1981, U.S. District Court, Southern District of California; 1983, U.S. Court of Appeals, Ninth Circuit and U.S.

*(This Listing Continued)*

---

District Court, Central District of California; 1984, U.S. Court of Appeals, District of Columbia Circuit; U.S. District Court, Northern and Eastern Districts of California. *Education:* Stanford University (A.B., 1976); University of California at Davis (J.D., 1979). Phi Kappa Phi; Order of the Coif. Recipient, Neumiller Moot Court Top Competitor, First Place Team and Best Brief, 1978. Editor, King Hall Advocate, 1978 and 1979. *Member:* Orange County and Los Angeles County Bar Associations; The State Bar of California. *PRACTICE AREAS:* Family Law; Eminent Domain Law; Civil Rights Law; Litigation.

**PAUL W. DAVIS,** born Duncan, Oklahoma, June 27, 1953; admitted to bar, 1979, California and U.S. District Court, Eastern District of California; 1982, U.S. District Court, Northern District of California; 1987, U.S. District Court, Central District of California. *Education:* Stanford University (A.B., 1975); University of California at Davis (J.D., 1979). Deputy City Attorney of Napa, 1980-1981. *Member:* Orange County Bar Association; State Bar of California. *PRACTICE AREAS:* Business Law; Real Property Law; Estate Planning Law; Appeals.

REPRESENTATIVE CLIENTS: Saddleback Valley Radiology Medical Associates; Murphy-Rodgers, Inc.; Perfection Machine and Tool Works; Ace Muffler and Transmission; Calthorpe Associates; ACLU of Southern California; Great Leap, Inc.; Pacifica Foundation; Pioneer Center; O'Neill Properties, Inc.

---

## McMAHON & McMAHON

SUITE E, 401 GLENNEYRE STREET
**LAGUNA BEACH, CALIFORNIA 92651**
Telephone: 714-494-9785
Fax: 714-494-5970

*General Civil and Criminal Trial Practice. Real Estate, Construction, Mechanics Lien, Commercial Collections and Personal Injury Law. Construction Defect Litigation.*

MEMBERS OF FIRM

**PETER C. McMAHON,** born Pasadena, California, February 9, 1949; admitted to bar, 1976, California. *Education:* University of California at Santa Barbara (B.A., 1971); Western State University (J.D., 1976). *Member:* South Orange County Bar Association; State Bar of California. *PRACTICE AREAS:* Real Estate; Construction Litigation; Personal Injury Law; Construction Defects.

**ROBERT V. McMAHON,** born Pasadena, California, January 31, 1960; admitted to bar, 1984, California. *Education:* University of California at Santa Barbara (1981); Southwestern University School of Law (J.D., 1983). *Member:* Orange County and South Orange County (President, 1991-1992) Bar Associations; State Bar of California. *PRACTICE AREAS:* Personal Injury Law; Civil Trial; Criminal Law.

REFERENCES: Orange National Bank; Great American Savings and Loan.

---

## NOKES, DAVIS & QUINN

*A PROFESSIONAL CORPORATION*

450 OCEAN AVENUE
**LAGUNA BEACH, CALIFORNIA 92651**
Telephone: 714-376-3055
FAX: 714-376-3070

*Insurance Coverage, Construction Litigation, Commercial Litigation, Real Estate Litigation, Civil Litigation, Family Law and Business Litigation.*

**LAURENCE P. NOKES,** born Hutchinson, Kansas, October 19, 1954; admitted to bar, 1982, California; 1983, U.S. District Court, Central, Northern, Southern and Eastern Districts of California. *Education:* University of Utah (B.A., 1979); McGeorge School of Law, University of the Pacific (J.D., 1982). *Member:* South Coast, Orange County, Los Angeles County Bar Associations; State Bar of California; Consumer Attorneys of California. *LANGUAGES:* Italian. *REPORTED CASES:* Marsh & McLennan v. Superior Court, 49 C 3d 1, 1989. *PRACTICE AREAS:* Insurance Coverage; Construction Litigation; Real Estate Litigation.

**THOMAS P. DAVIS,** born Glendale, California, June 7, 1950; admitted to bar, 1975, Oregon; 1976, California and U.S. District Court, Central District of California; 1988, U.S. District Court, Eastern District of California; 1989, U.S. District Court, Southern District of California. *Education:* University of Southern California (B.A., 1972); Duke University (J.D., 1975). Phi Beta Kappa. Associate Professor, Lewis and Clark Northwestern College of Law, 1975-1976. *Member:* South Coast, Orange County, Los Angeles County and American Bar Associations; State Bar of California;

*(This Listing Continued)*

State Bar of Oregon (Inactive). *PRACTICE AREAS:* Business Litigation; Real Estate Litigation; Civil Litigation; Family Law; Probate Litigation.

**THOMAS P. QUINN, JR.,** born Evanston, Illinois, May 9, 1962; admitted to bar, 1987, California; 1988, U.S. District Court, Central and Southern Districts of California; 1989, U.S. District Court, Eastern District of California. *Education:* University of Notre Dame (B.A., 1984); McGeorge School of Law, University of the Pacific (J.D., 1987). Order of the Coif; Traynor Society. Recipient, American Jurisdiction Award, Contracts, Civil Procedure Federal Courts, Family Law. *Member:* South Coast, Orange County and Los Angeles County Bar Associations. *PRACTICE AREAS:* Construction Litigation; Insurance Litigation; Real Estate Litigation; Business Litigation.

REPRESENTATIVE CLIENTS: U.S.F.& G. Insurance; FFF Enterprises; Utah Home Fire Insurance Co.; Standard Corp; Hunsaker & Associates, Irvine, California.

## THOMAS A. REILLY
Established in 1965
**1400 SOUTH COAST HIGHWAY, PENTHOUSE SUITE
LAGUNA BEACH, CALIFORNIA 92651**
Telephone: 714-494-8575

*General Civil and Criminal Trial Practice.*

**THOMAS A. REILLY,** born San Francisco, California, August 13, 1933; admitted to bar, 1963, California. *Education:* University of San Francisco (B.S., 1955); Hastings College of Law, University of California (J.D., 1962). Deputy District Attorney, Orange County, 1963-1965. *Member:* Orange County and South Orange County (President, 1981-1982, 1988-1989; Member, Board of Directors, 1988-1989; 1991-1992, 1995-1996) Bar Associations; The State Bar of California.

## JAMES G. ROURKE
**633 ALTA VISTA
LAGUNA BEACH, CALIFORNIA 92651-4040**
Telephone: 714-497-9652
Facsimile: 714-494-5570

*Municipal Law, Business Law.*

**JAMES G. ROURKE,** born Santa Monica, California, May 16, 1926; admitted to bar, 1954, California, U.S. Supreme Court and U.S. Tax Court. *Education:* University of California at Berkeley (A.B., 1950); Boalt Hall School of Law, University of California (J.D., 1953). Phi Delta Phi. Author: "Fifield Manor Tax Refund Cases," University of Southern California Law Review, 1962. Attorney, Consulting Tax Counsel, California State Board of Equalization, 1953-1954. Attorney, California Franchise Tax Board, 1954-1955. City Attorney, Tustin, 1960-1994. Special Counsel, Assessment Practices, District Attorney, County of Butte, 1964-1965. Member, Board of Directors, Orange County Legal Aid Society, 1960-1964. Judge Pro Tempore, Orange County Superior Court, 1975—. State Bar Court Referee, 1978—. Member, City Attorneys Department, League of California Cities, 1960—. Member, Panel of Arbitrators, American Arbitration Association. *Member:* Orange County and Los Angeles County Bar Associations; State Bar of California (Chairman, Committee on Lawyer Reference and Legal Aid Services, 1963-1964); National Association of Railroad Trial Counsel; Orange County City Attorneys Association (President, 1980). *PRACTICE AREAS:* Municipal Law; Business Law.

## SHERNOFF, BIDART & DARRAS
A Partnership including Professional Corporations
**130 CLEO STREET
LAGUNA BEACH, CALIFORNIA 92651**
Telephone: 714-494-6714
Fax: 714-497-0825

Claremont, California Office: 600 South Indian Hill Boulevard. Telephone: 909-621-4935. Fax: 909-625-6915.

Palm Desert, California Office: 73-111 El Paseo, Suite 208. Telephone: 619-568-9944.

*Practice Limited to Plaintiff's Insurance Bad Faith, Automobile Insurance, Fire Insurance, Commercial Liability Insurance, Homeowners Insurance, Accident and Health Insurance, Catastrophic Personal Injury, Wrongful*
(This Listing Continued)

*Death, Wrongful Termination, Lender's Liability and Consumer Law Litigation.*

### MEMBERS OF FIRM

**WILLIAM M. SHERNOFF, (P.C.),** born Chicago, Illinois, October 26, 1937; admitted to bar, 1962, Wisconsin; 1966, California. *Education:* University of Miami (B.B.A., 1959); University of Wisconsin (J.D., 1962). Co-Author: Legal Treatise, "Insurance Bad Faith Litigation," published by Matthew Bender, 1984; "How to Make Insurance Companies Pay Your Claims and What to do if They Don't," Hastings House, 1990. Author: "Payment Refused," published by Richardson & Steirman, 1986. *Member:* State Bar of California; Los Angeles Trial Lawyers Association (Trial Lawyer of the Year, 1975); California Trial Lawyers Association (President, 1981); The Association of Trial Lawyers of America. *PRACTICE AREAS:* Insurance Bad Faith.

**MICHAEL J. BIDART, (P.C.),** born Chino, California, September 15, 1950; admitted to bar, 1974, California; 1980, U.S. District Court, Eastern, Central and Southern Districts of California; 1980, U.S. Supreme Court. *Education:* California State Polytechnic University (B.S., 1971); Pepperdine University (J.D., 1974). Phi Alpha Delta. Author: CTLA Article, "The Appropriate Use of Assignments In Insurance Bad Faith Actions: Do's and Don't's". Rutter Group Lecturer, Insurance Bad Faith, 1989. Lecturer/Panelist: CTLA Continuing Legal Education, Insurance Bad Faith, 1989; First Party Bad Faith Cases, Rutter Group, 1993. *Member:* Western San Bernardino County and San Bernardino County Bar Associations; State Bar of California; California Trial Lawyers Association; The Association of Trial Lawyers of America; Trial Lawyers for Public Justice; Los Angeles Trial Lawyers Association. *LANGUAGES:* Basque. *PRACTICE AREAS:* Insurance Bad Faith.

**FRANK N. DARRAS,** born Chicago, Illinois, April 15, 1954; admitted to bar, 1987, California; U.S. District Court, Eastern, Central, Northern and Southern Districts of California. *Education:* Oakton Community Junior College; Emory University (1977); Western State University (J.D., 1986). Certified Paramedic, Illinois, 1973. Trial Attorney Project, Hastings College of Advocacy, 1987. Lecturer/Panelist: "Discovery in Bad Faith Law Suit," ATLA National Convention, 1989; "A Discovery Checklist for Bad Faith Litigation," ATLA, National Convention, 1990; "Medical Life & Disability Fraud," ATLA Convention, 1991; "First Party Bad Faith Cases," Rutter Group, 1993. *Member:* Los Angeles County, San Bernardino County and American Bar Associations; State Bar of California; Los Angeles Trial Lawyers Association; California Trial Lawyers Association (Board Member, PAC Drive); The Association of Trial Lawyers of America (Member, Insurance Section Executive Board, 1991—); Trial Lawyers for Public Justice. *LANGUAGES:* Greek. *PRACTICE AREAS:* Insurance Bad Faith.

(For Complete Biographical Data on all personnel, see Professional Biographies at Claremont, California).

## BARRY T. SIMONS
*LAWYERS COURT*
**260 ST. ANN'S DRIVE
LAGUNA BEACH, CALIFORNIA 92651**
Telephone: 714-497-1729
FAX: 714-497-3971
Email: simmslaw@primenet.com
Email: simonslaw@aol.com

*Criminal Defense in State and Federal Courts, DUI/DWI, Juvenile Law and Appeals.*

**BARRY T. SIMONS,** born 1946; admitted to bar, 1972, California; 1973, U.S. Supreme Court. *Education:* American University (B.S.); New York Law School (J.D.). Notes Editor, Law Review N.Y. Law Forum, 1970. Founding Member, National College DUI Defense (Recognized Export in Drunk Driving Defense). Co-Chair, Municipal Court, California Attorneys Criminal Justice. *Member:* Orange County (Board of Directors, 1981) and South Orange County (Board of Directors, 1980-1995; President, 1986) Bar Association; State Bar of California; National Association of Criminal Defense Attorneys.

### LEGAL SUPPORT PERSONNEL
**LINDA M. SMITH**

## LINDA GUNDERSON
OAKBROOK PLAZA, SUITE 385
24422 AVENIDA DE LA CARLOTA
**LAGUNA HILLS, CALIFORNIA 92653**
Telephone: 714-837-1060
Telecopier: 714-837-4594

*Probate and Trust Law.*

**LINDA GUNDERSON,** born Minneapolis, Minnesota, July 31, 1950; admitted to bar, 1978, California. *Education:* University of Oregon and California College of Arts and Crafts (B.F.A., with distinction, 1973); University of the Pacific (J.D., 1978). Panelist, Continuing Education of the Bar: Fundamentals of Estate Planning, 1982-1983; Inheritance and Gift Tax Law, 1981. Director, 1980— and President, 1983-1994, Legal Aid Society of Orange County. *Member:* Orange County (Director, 1982-1984; Vice Chair, Probate Section, 1993) and South Orange County (President, 1981-1982; Director, 1985-1989) Bar Associations; State Bar of California; Orange County Women Lawyers. (Certified Specialist, Probate, Estate Planning and Trust Law, The State Bar of California Board of Legal Specialization).

## JACQUELINE M. JENSEN, INC.
**LAGUNA HILLS, CALIFORNIA**
(See Irvine)

*Estate Planning, Estate Tax, Trusts, Asset Protection, Probate, Business Law and Elder Care.*

## JAMES W. LENT
24031 EL TORO ROAD, SUITE 130
**LAGUNA HILLS, CALIFORNIA 92653**
Telephone: 714-829-8009
Fax: 714-829-8209

*Corporate Law, Business Law, Estate Planning, Probate, Elder Law.*

**JAMES W. LENT,** born Tiverton, Rhode Island, July 18, 1936; admitted to bar, 1989, California and U.S. Court of Appeals, Ninth Circuit. *Education:* College of the Holy Cross (B.S., 1958); University of Southern California (M.S., 1975); Suffolk University (J.D., 1987); McGeorge School of Law, University of the Pacific (LL.M., 1988). Phi Delta Phi. Member: Rotary Club, Board of Directors, 1994-1995; World Trade Center of Orange County, 1989. Nominee President, California AARP, 1995. Member, Board of Directors, The Retired Officers Association. Board of Directors, Newport Irvine Rotary Club. *Member:* Orange County Bar Association; State Bar of California. [Lt. Col., U.S. Marine Corps, 1960-1981]. **PRACTICE AREAS:** Probate and Estate Planning; Business; Elder Law.

## THE LAW OFFICES OF STANTON T. MATHEWS & ASSOCIATES
24012 CALLE DE LA PLATA, SUITE 320
**LAGUNA HILLS, CALIFORNIA 92653**
Telephone: 714-586-2235

*Civil Trial and Appellate Practice, Personal Injury, Insurance Bad Faith, Professional Negligence, Products Liability, Wrongful Death, Premise Liability, Trucking Liability.*

**STANTON T. MATHEWS,** born May 28, 1952; admitted to bar, 1981, California; 1982, U.S. Court of Appeals, Ninth and Tenth Circuits and U.S. District Court, Eastern, Central and Southern Districts of California and District of Colorado. *Education:* Brigham Young University (B.A., 1976); Pepperdine School of Law; Western State University (J.D., 1981). Recipient, Certificate in Aviation Litigation, National Judicial College, Reno, Nevada. Certification OB/Gyn, Pediatric Malpractice, 1986. Lecturer: "Trial Practice," Orange County Bar Association, 1990—. *Member:* Orange County Bar Association; State Bar of California; Association of Trial Lawyers of America; California Consumer Attorneys Association; Los Angeles Trial Lawyers Association; Orange County Trial Lawyers; Orange County College of Trial Advocacy; Western Trial Lawyers Association. **LANGUAGES:** Spanish. **REPORTED CASES:** Budd v. American Excess Ins.

*(This Listing Continued)*

Co. **PRACTICE AREAS:** Personal Injury; Trial Practice; Professional Negligence; Products Liability; Insurance Coverage.

### ASSOCIATES

**PAUL W. RALPH,** born Compton, California, December 31, 1962; admitted to bar, 1991, California; U.S. District Court, Central and Eastern Districts of California. *Education:* California State University at Fullerton (B.A., 1986); Southwestern University School of Law (J.D., 1990). *Member:* Orange County and American Bar Associations; California State Bar; Orange County Trial Lawyers Association; California Consumer Attorneys Association; Western Trial Lawyers Association. **PRACTICE AREAS:** Personal Injury; Medical Malpractice; Construction Defects.

### LEGAL SUPPORT PERSONNEL
### PARALEGALS

**PATRICIA TONTI-MACE**

**SHARING GARRETT-CHAPMAN**

## LAW OFFICES OF ROBERT T. MATTHEWS
23382 MILL CREEK DRIVE
SUITE 120
**LAGUNA HILLS, CALIFORNIA 92653**
Telephone: 714-470-1390
Fax: 714-470-1337

*Probate and Estate Planning, Probate and Trust Litigation and Trust Law.*

**ROBERT T. MATTHEWS,** born Baltimore, Maryland, July 2, 1954; admitted to bar, 1982, California. *Education:* Western Maryland College (B.A., 1976); Irvine University (J.D., 1981). Delta Pi Alpha. Instructor: Fundamental Evidence in Trials, Orange County Bar Association, 1994. Lecturer: Estates and Trusts, Dispute Resolution and Litigation, California Continuing Education of the Bar, 1989, 1991; Estate Planning and Probate Clinic, Orange County Bar Association, 1986; Discovery Strategies in Estate and Trust Litigation, Orange County Bar Association, 1992. Moderator, Orange County Bar Association Probate Clinic, 1988. *Member:* Orange County (Chairman, Estate Planning, Probate and Trust Law Section, 1991) and American Bar Associations; State Bar of California; California Trial Lawyers Association; Orange County Trial Lawyers Association. (Certified Specialist, Estate Planning, Trust and Probate Law, The State Bar of California Board of Legal Specialization). **PRACTICE AREAS:** Probate Law; Probate and Trust Litigation; Civil Law; Trial Practice; Estate Planning; Trust Administration.

### ASSOCIATE

**STEPHEN C. KIMBALL,** born St. Louis, Missouri, March 11, 1963; admitted to bar, 1991, California and U.S. District Court, Central District of California. *Education:* University of Paris, Sorbonne; Brigham Young University (B.A., 1987); University of San Diego (J.D., 1990). *Member:* Orange County (Member, Estate Planning, Probate & Trust Section) and American Bar Associations; State Bar of California; Orange County Trial Lawyers Association. **LANGUAGES:** French. **PRACTICE AREAS:** Civil Litigation; Probate Litigation; Trust Litigation; Probate Administration; Estate Planning.

## SUSAN R. MEDWIED
23046 AVENIDA DE LA CARLOTA, SUITE 600
**LAGUNA HILLS, CALIFORNIA 92653**
Telephone: 714-588-5703
Facsimile: 714-588-5777

*Breach of Contract, Mechanics Lien, Stop Notice, Attachment, Claim and Delivery, Judgement Enforcement, Business Planning.*

**SUSAN R. MEDWIED,** born Newark, New Jersey, April 15, 1953; admitted to bar, 1977, Kansas; 1985, California. *Education:* University of Bridgeport (B.A., 1972); Seton Hall University (J.D., 1976). Speaker and Panel Member, "Psychiatry and the Law," Conference jointly sponsored by the Kansas Bar Association and the Menninger Foundation, 1981; Trainer and Conference Coordinator, "Basic Lawyering Skills," Sponsored by L.S.C. Western U.S., 1979-1980. *Member:* Topeka (Member, Ethics and Grievance Committee, 1979-1982), Orange County (Member: Client Relations Committee, 1988—; Business Litigation Section, 1989—) and Kansas Bar Asso-

*(This Listing Continued)*

ciations; State Bar of California; Orange County Women Lawyers. *PRACTICE AREAS:* Business Planning; Constructions Liens; Mechanics Liens; Construction Contracts.

## MICHELLE A. REINGLASS
SUITE 170
23161 MILLCREEK ROAD
**LAGUNA HILLS, CALIFORNIA 92653**
Telephone: 714-587-0460
FAX: 714-587-1004

*Business, Civil and Employment Litigation, Employment Discrimination, Sexual Harassment, Wrongful Termination.*

**MICHELLE A. REINGLASS,** born Los Angeles, California, December 9, 1954; admitted to bar, 1979, California; 1981, U.S. District Court, Central District of California; 1990, U.S. District Court, Southern District of California. *Education:* University of California, Irvine; Western State University (B.S., 1977; J.D., 1978). Phi Alpha Delta. Best Brief, Second Place Team, Moot Court, 1978. Recipient, American Jurisprudence Award for Evidence. Author: "The New Enforcement of Judgments Act," Orange County Bar Association Bulletin, September, 1983; Sexual Harassment-The Evolution & The Revolution (Women in the Workplace, Nov 1993; "You're Served, What to do When Served with a Subpoena," O.C. Psychologist, July 1994; Co-Author: Rutter Group/CJA, Wrongful Termination and Employment Discrimination Program Update, January, 1995. Instructor, Professional Responsibility, Western State College of Law, 1991; Oral Advocacy Workshops, 1988 and 1990 and Evidence for Business Lawyers, 1990, Surviving Attorneys Fees Disputes, 1993 and 1994, California Continuing Education of the Bar; Rutter Group/CJA Tort Litigation Program, "Wrongful Termination, Employment Discrimination, January 1995. Lecturer, Law and Motion Seminar, California State Bar Convention, 1990-1991; Bridging the Gap, Law and Motion, 1987-1993, College of Trial Advocacy, 1989-1991; 1989-1992, 1995, Orange County Bar Association. Advisor, Action Guide on Establishing Good Client Relations, California Continuing Education of the Bar, 1990. *Member:* Orange County Bar Association (President, 1993; Treasurer, 1991; Secretary, 1990, Member, Board of Directors, 1984-1989; Chairman, Business Litigation Section, 1989); State Bar of California; Orange County Trial Lawyers Association (Member, Board of Directors, 1987-1989); Volunteers in Parole (Chair, Advisory Committee, 1990-1991). Listed Who's Who in American Law, 1994 and 1995. *LANGUAGES:* Spanish and French.

### ASSOCIATE

**MICHELLE M. LENTS,** born Omaha, Nebraska, September 2, 1966; admitted to bar, 1993, California and U.S. District Court, Southern District of California; 1996, U.S. District Court, Central District of California. *Education:* San Diego State University (B.A. magna cum laude, with distinction, 1990); International and Comparative Law Institute, Oxford England (1992); University of San Diego (J.D., 1993). Phi Beta Kappa; Phi Beta Phi; Phi Delta Phi. Peter M. Elliot Inn of Court. Judicial Extern, Justice Patricia Benke, California Court of Appeal, Fourth District, 1993. Chair, Student Committee, Lawyer's Club of San Diego, 1994-1996. Attorney Volunteer, San Diego Volunteer Lawyer's Program, 1995-1996. *Member:* Orange County Bar Association; State Bar of California; California Employment Lawyers Association. *PRACTICE AREAS:* Business, Civil and Employment Litigation; Employment Discrimination; Sexual Harassment both State and Federal Courts.

## REYNOLDS & DEILY
Established in 1990
TAJ MAHAL, SUITE 115
23521 PASEO DE VALENCIA
**LAGUNA HILLS, CALIFORNIA 92653-3138**
Telephone: 714-454-8800
FAX: 714-454-9207

*Estate Planning, Probate and Civil Litigation.*

FIRM PROFILE: *The firm specializes in estate and tax planning, probate, conservatorships, trust administration and related litigation. Mrs. Reynolds brings to the firm over forty years experience in the estate and tax planning area. Mr. Deily complements the practice with an extensive background in general civil, conservatorship and estate litigation. The firm strives to provide quality services in a cost effective and timely manner, while conducting themselves in accordance with the highest moral and ethical standards. The office is dedicated to being responsive to the needs of their clients, while treating them with kindness, understanding, compassion and respect.*

### MEMBERS OF FIRM

**SALLIE TIERNAN REYNOLDS,** born Santa Ana, California, September 13, 1923; admitted to bar, 1953, California. *Education:* Scripps College and Stanford University (B.A., with distinction, 1945); Boalt Hall School of Law, University of California and University of California at Los Angeles School of Law (J.D., 1953). Phi Beta Kappa. Trustee, 1961—; Chairman of the Board, 1980-1986, Scripps College. *Member:* Orange County (Chairman, Estate Planning, Probate and Trust Law Section, 1982), Los Angeles County and American Bar Associations; State Bar of California. (Certified Specialist, Probate, Estate Planning and Trust Law, The State Bar of California Board of Legal Specialization). *PRACTICE AREAS:* Estate and Tax Planning and Trust Law; Probate Law.

**JOHN P. DEILY,** born Albuquerque, New Mexico, July 4, 1953; admitted to bar, 1980, California. *Education:* Notre Dame University; University of California at Long Beach (B.A., magna cum laude, 1976); Hastings College of the Law, University of California (J.D., 1980). Instructor, Family Law, Saddleback College, 1984. Municipal Court Judge Pro Tem, Orange County, 1986—. *Member:* Ventura County (Chairman, Law Day, 1983), South Orange County, Los Angeles County and Orange County (Member, Executive Committee, Estate Planning, Probate and Trust Law Section, 1994—) Bar Associations; State Bar of California. *PRACTICE AREAS:* Probate, Estate Planning and Trust Law; Probate, Trust and Conservatorship Litigation; Trial Practice.

### ASSOCIATES

**KRISTA LEE POWERS,** born West Covina, California, May 10, 1968; admitted to bar, 1993, California. *Education:* University of California, Los Angeles (B.A., with honors, 1990); University of San Diego (J.D., with honors in Estate Planning, 1993). *Member:* Los Angeles County, Orange County (Estate Planning, Probate and Trust Law and Elder Law Sections) and American Bar Associations; State Bar of California. *PRACTICE AREAS:* Estate and Tax Planning; Trust Law; Probate Law; Trust and Conservatorship Litigation.

## LAWRENCE S. ROSS
A LAW CORPORATION
OAKBROOK PLAZA
24422 AVENIDA DE LA CARLOTA, SUITE 365
**LAGUNA HILLS, CALIFORNIA 92653**
Telephone: 714-581-3360
Fax: 714-581-2649

*Family Law, Probate, Estate Planning, Trust Law.*

**LAWRENCE S. ROSS,** born New York, N.Y., February 24, 1948; admitted to bar, 1975, California. *Education:* University of Chicago (B.S., 1969); University of California at Los Angeles (J.D., 1975). Phi Beta Kappa; Sigma Xi. Licensed Real Estate Broker, California, 1980. *Member:* Orange County Bar Association; State Bar of California. (Certified Specialist, Family Law; Estate Planning, Trust and Probate Law, The State Bar of California Board of Legal Specialization) (Also Member, Ross and Lightholder). *PRACTICE AREAS:* Family Law; Estate Planning; Probate.

## SMALL, HENSTRIDGE & CABODI
24422 AVENIDA DE LA CARLOTA, SUITE 460
**LAGUNA HILLS, CALIFORNIA 92653**
Telephone: 714-837-5534
Fax: 714-837-6160

*Insurance Defense.*

**WALTER S. SMALL** (1972-1992).

**ROBERT M. HENSTRIDGE,** born Cleveland, Ohio, March 7, 1949; admitted to bar, 1976, California. *Education:* California State University at Fullerton (B.A., magna cum laude, 1972); University of San Diego (J.D., 1976). *Member:* Orange County Bar Association; State Bar of California. *PRACTICE AREAS:* Construction Defects; Insurance; Personal Injury; Products Liability; Business Law.

**K. J. CABODI,** born Spring Valley, Illinois, August 5, 1953; admitted to bar, 1980, California. *Education:* University of Illinois (B.A., 1975); Pepperdine University (J.D., 1978). *Member:* Orange County Bar Association;

(This Listing Continued)

**SMALL, HENSTRIDGE & CABODI,** Laguna Hills—
*Continued*

State Bar of California; California Trial Lawyers Association; American Chemical Society. *PRACTICE AREAS:* Personal Injury; Construction Law; Insurance Defense.

ASSOCIATES

Bryan D. Pyles                James L. Chase

## STETINA BRUNDA & BUYAN

A PROFESSIONAL CORPORATION

Established in 1980

SUITE 401, 24221 CALLE DE LA LOUISA
**LAGUNA HILLS, CALIFORNIA 92653**
Telephone: 714-855-1246
Telex: 704355
Facsimile: 714-855-6371
Email: 104052.1330@compuserve.com

*Intellectual Property Law including Patent, Trademark, Copyright, Unfair Competition, Trade Secret, Licensing, Computer Law and Related Antitrust Law, Hands-On Computer Law.*

FIRM PROFILE: *Stetina Brunda & Buyan was founded in 1980 and serves the intellectual property needs of the greater Southern California area through its strategically located offices in South Orange County. The firm concentrates on both domestic and foreign intellectual property prosecution, litigation and licensing. The firm encourages its personnel to engage in continuing professional development through continuing legal education and professional association activities.*

*Stetina Brunda & Buyan is a member of the Bar Register of Preeminent Lawyers. The firm received the highest rating available from Martindale-Hubbell.*

**KIT M. STETINA, (MR.),** born Compton, California, December 4, 1952; admitted to bar, 1978, California, U.S. District Court, Central, Northern and Southern Districts of California, U.S. Court of Appeals, Ninth and Federal Circuits and U.S. Claims Court; registered to practice before U.S. Patent and Trademark Office, 1979. *Education:* Arizona State University (B.S. in Mech. Eng., 1974); Pepperdine University (J.D., cum laude, 1978). Phi Alpha Delta. Staff Member, 1976-1977 and Editor, 1977-1978, Pepperdine University Law Review. *Member:* Orange County Bar Association; State Bar of California; Orange County Patent Law Association; Los Angeles Patent Law Association. *REPORTED CASES:* No Fear, Inc. v. Imagine Films, Inc., 38 U.S.P.Q.2d 1374; Big Ball Sports, Inc. v. No Fear, Inc., 38 U.S.P.Q. 2d 1383. *PRACTICE AREAS:* Patent, Trademark, Copyright, Unfair Competition; Antitrust; Commercial Litigation; Computer.

**BRUCE B. BRUNDA,** born Staten Island, New York, January 15, 1951; admitted to bar, 1978, New York, U.S. District Court, Southern and Eastern Districts of New York and U.S. Court of Appeals for the Federal Circuit; 1981, U.S. Court of Customs and Patent Appeals; 1983, California, U.S. District Court, Northern, Central and Southern Districts of California and U.S. Claims Court; registered to practice before U.S. Patent and Trademark Office, 1978. *Education:* New Jersey Institute of Technology (B.S.E.E., 1972); Franklin Pierce Law Center (J.D., 1977). Author: "Patent Preliminary Injunction," 65 Journal Patent Office Soc'y 632, (1983); "Resolution of Patent Disputes by Non-Litigation Procedures," 15 A.I.P.L.A. Quar. Jour. 73 (1987). Judicial Law Clerk to Chief Judge Howard T. Markey, U.S. Court of Appeals for the Federal Circuit, 1980-1982. Director/Officer, Orange County Patent Law Association, 1984—. Director/Officer, Orange County Barristers Association, 1984-1986. *Member:* Orange County and American Bar Associations; State Bar of California; American Intellectual Property Law Association; Los Angeles Patent Law Association. [With U.S. Army (Special Forces), 1972-1974]

**ROBERT DEAN BUYAN,** born Rochester, Pennsylvania, January 27, 1953; admitted to bar, 1985, Ohio and U.S. District Court, Northern District of Ohio and U.S. Court of Appeals for the Federal Circuit; 1987, California; 1988, U.S. District Court, Central, Northern and Southern Districts of California and U.S. Court of Appeals, Ninth Circuit; 1995, U.S. Supreme Court; registered to practice before U.S. Patent and Trademark Office, 1986. *Education:* Gannon College (B.S., Biology, 1974); Ohio State University; Capital University (J.D., 1985). Staff Member, Capital University Law Review, 1982-1983. *Member:* American Bar Association; State Bar of California; American Chemical Society; Orange County Patent Law Association; Lawyer-Pilots Bar Association.

*(This Listing Continued)*

**MARK B. GARRED,** born Euclid, Ohio, July 19, 1964; admitted to bar, 1990, Ohio, California and U.S. District Court, Northern District of California and Northern District of Ohio; 1991, U.S. District Court, Central and Southern Districts of California; 1995, U.S. Court of Appeals, Ninth Circuit and U.S. Court of Appeals for the Federal Circuit; registered to practice before U.S. Patent and Trademark Office, 1991. *Education:* Gannon University (B.M.E., 1986); Cleveland State University (J.D., 1989). *Member:* Orange County and American Bar Associations; State Bar of California; Orange County Patent Law Association.

**WILLIAM J. BRUCKER,** born Pittsburgh, Pennsylvania, February 21, 1964; admitted to bar, 1990, Ohio and U.S. District Court, Northern District of California and Northern District of Ohio; 1994, California and U.S. District Court, Central and Southern Districts of California; 1995, U.S. Court of Appeals, Ninth Circuit and U.S. Court of Appeals for the Federal Circuit; registered to practice before U.S. Patent and Trademark Office, 1992. *Education:* Gannon University (B.E.E., 1986); Case Western Reserve University (J.D., 1990). *Member:* American Bar Association; State Bar of California; American Intellectual Property Law Association; Orange County Patent Law Association.

**MATTHEW A. NEWBOLES,** born Bakersfield, California, September 5, 1965; admitted to bar, 1993, California; 1994, U.S. District Court, Central, Northern and Southern Districts of California; 1995, U.S. Court of Appeals, Ninth and Federal Circuits; registered to practice before U.S. Patent and Trademark Office, 1994. *Education:* California Polytechnic State University (B.S., Biochemistry, cum laude, 1988); Santa Clara University (J.D., 1993). Research Editor, Santa Clara Computer and High Technology Law Journal, 1992-1993. *Member:* State Bar of California; Orange County Patent Law Association.

**THOMAS C. NABER,** born Omaha, Nebraska, September 20, 1941; admitted to bar, 1972, Colorado and U.S. District Court, District of Colorado; registered to practice before U.S. Patent and Trademark Office, 1973 (Not admitted in California). *Education:* University of Denver (B.S., 1964; J.D., 1971). *Member:* Orange County Patent Law Association.

**DARREN S. RIMER,** born Los Angeles, California, October 16, 1969; admitted to bar, 1995, California and U.S. District Court, Central District of California. *Education:* University of California at Irvine (B.A., Psychology, 1991); Southwestern University School of Law (J.D., magna cum laude, 1995). Recipient: American Jurisprudence Book Awards in Constitutional Criminal Procedure, Contracts, Federal Courts, Legal Research and Writing and Torts. Staff Member and Special Projects Editor, Southwestern University Law Review, 1993-1995. Oralist, Moot Court Honors Program, 1993-1994. Law Clerk to the Honorable Charles F. Eick, United States Magistrate Judge, U.S. District Court for the Central District of California, 1995-1996. *Member:* Orange County and American Bar Associations; State Bar of California; Orange County Patent Law Association.

*LEGAL SUPPORT PERSONNEL*

**NORMAN E. CARTE,** born Hampton, Virginia, February 9, 1955; admitted to bar, registered to practice before U.S. Patent and Trademark Office, 1981. *Education:* University of Central Florida (B.S., 1979); California State University at Fullerton (M.B.A., 1991). Intellectual Property Section, State Bar of California. *Member:* Los Angeles and Orange County Patent Law Association. (Patent Agent).

**KRISTY KAY MOORE.** *Education:* University of Minnesota; Moorhead University; American Institute for Paralegal Studies, Paralegal Program Certificate (1989-1990). (Paralegal and Foreign Filing Specialist).

REPRESENTATIVE CLIENTS: Arnette Optic Illusions; Baxter Healthcare Corp.; Bird Products Corp.; Calico Industries, Inc.; Dana Innovations/Sonance, Inc.; Dinamation Intl. Inc.; Dunn-Edwards Corp.; Energy Suspension; Field Mfg. Corp.; Flojet Corp.; Gecko Trading Co.; G.T. Bicycles, Inc.; H.C. Power, Inc.; Inland Empire Foods; Innova Electronics Corp.; Innovation Sports, Inc.; Johnson & Johnson/Critikon Div.; Luther Medical Products, Inc.; No Fear, Inc.; Norm Reeves, Inc.; Northrop-Grumman Corp.; No Touch North America, Inc.; PacFab Fabrication, Inc.; Panavise Prods., Inc.; PharmaBotanixx, Pick Systems, Inc.; Prince Lionheart, Inc.; Shaw & Sons; Sparta, Inc.; Spy Optic Ltd.; Sterling Electric, Inc.; Sun Ten Labs; The Ink Co.; 3-Day Blinds, Inc.; Tyco Industries, Inc.; W.E. Hall Co./Pacific Corrugated Pipe Co.

## EDWARD H. STONE, P.C.
**LAGUNA HILLS, CALIFORNIA**
(See Newport Beach)
*Estate Planning, Probate and Business Planning.*

---

## NANCY BOXLEY TEPPER
*A PROFESSIONAL CORPORATION*
Established in 1977
24031 EL TORO ROAD, SUITE 130
**LAGUNA HILLS, CALIFORNIA 92653**
Telephone: 714-830-6660
Fax: 714-830-6123

*Tax and Estate Planning, Trust Administration, Probate Administration, Trust and Probate Litigation, Estate Administration, Will Contests.*

**NANCY BOXLEY TEPPER,** born Richmond, Virginia, March 7, 1933; admitted to bar, 1958, New York; 1969, California. *Education:* University of Richmond; Radcliffe College (B.A., magna cum laude, 1953); Harvard University (LL.B., magna cum laude, 1958). Phi Beta Kappa. Editor, Harvard Law Review, 1956-1958. Author: "Estate Planning Considerations," *Business Buy-Out Agreements,* (C.E.B. 1976, Supp. 1982); "Estate Planning for Second Marriages," *Trusts and Estates,* 1981, updated and reprinted, 1982. Associate, Simpson, Thacher & Bartlett, N.Y.C., 1958-1963. Freelance Legal Editor and Writer, Columbia Law School, N.Y.C., Prentice-Hall, Inc., Englewood, N.J., 1963-1969. Associate, Kindel & Anderson, Laguna Hills, 1969-1977. Endowment Counsel, Orange County Performing Arts Ctr., 1985—. Member, Fund-Raising Committee, Saddleback Hospital. *Member:* Orange County, New York State and American Bar Associations; State Bar of California; Orange County Estate Planning Council.

---

## MELVIN D. THOMAS
*ELDORADO BANK BUILDING*
24012 CALLE DE LA PLATA, SUITE 480
**LAGUNA HILLS, CALIFORNIA 92653-7625**
Telephone: 714-458-6700
Fax: 714-458-1362

*Civil Litigation, Real Estate, Corporate/Business Counsel, Corporate Formation, Dissolutions, Franchise Law, Shareholder Disputes, Complex or Unusual Tax/Business Matters, Family Law, Probate, Multi-State Tax Return Preparation, Tax Audit/Appeal Representation, Forensic Accounting Issues, Investment/Tax Fraud Issues, General Tax Compliance, Trusts and Estates.*

**MELVIN D. THOMAS,** born Edmond, Oklahoma, September 29, 1939; admitted to bar, 1978, California; 1979 U.S. Tax Court. *Education:* Oklahoma City University (B.S., 1966); Western State University J.D., 1978). Certified Public Accountant, California, 1971. Real Estate Broker, California, 1986. **PRACTICE AREAS:** Civil Practice (40%, 10); Taxation Law (20%, 15); Real Estate Law (10%, 15); Family Law (20%, 10); Corporate Law (10%, 5).

---

## LAW OFFICES OF CRAIG S. WALTON
23151 MOULTON PARKWAY
**LAGUNA HILLS, CALIFORNIA 92653**
Telephone: 714-699-0177
Fax: 714-699-6792

*civil Litigation including Medical Malpractice and Personal Injury.*

**CRAIG S. WALKON,** born Detroit, Michigan, December 31, 1962; admitted to bar, 1989, California and Arizona. *Education:* Michigan State University (B.A., with honors, 1985); Wayne State University (J.D., 1988). *Member:* Orange County Bar Association; State Bar of California; State Bar of Arizona; Consumer Attorney Association of Los Angeles. **PRACTICE AREAS:** Medical Malpractice; Personal Injury; Employment Litigation; Hospital Law; Premises Liability; Products Liability.

---

## GENEVIEVE WALL
*A LAW CORPORATION*
Established in 1984
23521 PASEO DE VALENCIA, SUITE 201-B
**LAGUNA HILLS, CALIFORNIA 92653**
Telephone: 714-859-0861

*Estate Planning, Wills and Trusts, Estate Litigation, Guardianships.*

**GENEVIEVE WALL,** born New York, N.Y., August 17, 1950; admitted to bar, 1981, California. *Education:* University of California at Los Angeles (B.A., 1973); Western State University (J.D., 1981). Recipient, American Jurisprudence Award in Torts. *Member:* Orange County (Member, Estate Planning and Elder Law Sections); State Bar of California. **PRACTICE AREAS:** Trust Law; Estate Planning Law; Probate Law; Wills Law.

---

## LAW OFFICES OF
## HARRY G. WEISSENBERGER, INC.
*GLENDALE FEDERAL BUILDING, SUITE 309*
24221 CALLE DE LA LOUISA
**LAGUNA HILLS, CALIFORNIA 92653-7602**
Telephone: 714-380-4046
Fax: 714-380-1179
Email: weisspat@aol.com

*Patent, Trademark, Copyright and Unfair Competition Law. Trials in Federal and State Courts.*

**HARRY G. WEISSENBERGER,** born Berlin, Germany, August 20, 1928; admitted to bar, 1952, Georgia; 1956, U.S. Supreme Court; 1957, Missouri; 1961, Michigan; 1964, California; 1982, U.S. Court of Appeals for the Federal Circuit; registered to practice before U.S. Patent and Trademark Office. *Education:* Swiss Institute of Technology; Georgia Institute of Technology (B.E.E., with honors, 1950); Emory University (J.D., 1952); George Washington University (LL.M., 1956). Phi Alpha Delta; Tau Beta Pi; Eta Kappa Nu. Member, Panel of Arbitrators, American Arbitration Association. *Member:* Orange County Bar Association; State Bar of California; American Intellectual Property Law Association; Orange County Patent Law Association (Secretary, 1983-1984; Vice President, 1984-1985; President, 1985-1986). **LANGUAGES:** German, French. **PRACTICE AREAS:** Intellectual Property Law.

*LEGAL SUPPORT PERSONNEL*

**LOUISE C. MARRONE** (Legal Assistant).

REPRESENTATIVE CLIENTS: Loral Aerospace Corp.; Medtronic Inc.; First Byte; Nimbus, Inc.; Folsom Research, Inc.; Continuos Coating Corp.; Western Exterminator Co.; Knight Equipment International, Inc.; Axa Corp.

---

## ASHWORTH & MORAN
28202 CABOT ROAD, SUITE 300
**LAGUNA NIGUEL, CALIFORNIA 92677-1249**
Telephone: 714-365-5776
Fax: 714-365-5720

*Newport Beach, California Office:* 18 Corporate Plaza, Suite 114. Telephone: 714-720-1477. Fax: 714-720-1478.

*Corporation, Business and Real Estate Law, General Civil, Trial and Appellate Practice. State and Federal Courts, Estate Planning.*

**BERNARD L. MORAN,** born Los Angeles, California, June 27, 1949; admitted to bar, 1979, California and U.S. Tax Court. *Education:* University of Southern California (B.A., with honors, 1971); Brigham Young University (J.D., 1978). Delta Theta Phi. Senior Articles Editor, Utah Bar Journal, 1977-1978. *Member:* The State Bar of California; American Bar Association. [Capt., USMC, 1971-1974]. **PRACTICE AREAS:** Commercial Law; Business Transactions.

**ERIC K. BILLINGS,** born Orange, California, April 4, 1958; admitted to bar, 1985, California. *Education:* Brigham Young University; Western State University (B.S., 1982; J.D., 1985). Licensed General Contractor, California, 1982. Member, Associated Institute of Architects (AIA), 1990. *Member:* Orange County and American Bar Associations; State Bar of Cali-

*(This Listing Continued)*

**ASHWORTH & MORAN, Laguna Niguel**—Continued

fornia. LANGUAGES: Norwegian. PRACTICE AREAS: Business Litigation; Construction; Collections; Personal Injury; Torts.

(For biographical data on firm other personnel, See Professional Biographies at Newport Beach, California)

---

## CHARLENE L. BAILLIE

27762 FORKES ROAD, SUITE 1
LAGUNA NIGUEL, CALIFORNIA 92677
Telephone: 714-348-2929
Fax: 714-348-2987

*Workers Compensation Defense.*

**CHARLENE L. BAILLIE,** born Long Beach, California, September 15, 1954; admitted to bar, 1983, California. *Education:* Southwestern University School of Law (J.D., with distinction, 1982). Recipient, American Juris Prudence Award for Scholastic Achievement, 1982. Coordinator, Curriculum Development in Workers' Compensation State Certification Program, University of California System. Adjunct Faculty Member: Office of Continuing Education, California State Polytechnic University, Pomona, California, 1995; Advanced Workers' Compensation, Insurance Education Association, 1995. *Member:* Orange County (Member, Workers' Compensation Section); State Bar of California (Member, Subsections on: Workers' Compensation and Employment; Labor Law); Orange County Workers' Compensation Defense Attorneys Association; California Compensation Defense Attorneys' Association; Title I, Association of ADA Professionals.

---

## DAVID L. BELZ

28202 CABOT ROAD #215
LAGUNA NIGUEL, CALIFORNIA 92677
Telephone: 714-347-0447
Fax: 714-364-0606

*civil, Personal Injury.*

**DAVID L. BELZ,** born 1950; admitted to bar, 1975, California. *Education:* California State University, Fullerton (B.A., 1972) Pepperdine University (J.D.,1975). PRACTICE AREAS: Personal Injury Law (100%).

---

## MICHAEL GOODE

30101 TOWN CENTER DRIVE, SUITE 100
LAGUNA NIGUEL, CALIFORNIA 92677
Telephone: 714-249-2260
Fax: 714-495-3867

*General Civil and Trial Practice. Franchise and Corporation Law.*

**MICHAEL GOODE,** born Chicago, Illinois, January 19, 1950; admitted to bar, 1977, California and U.S. District Court, Central District of California. *Education:* Loyola University, Chicago Illinois (B.A., 1972); Pepperdine University (J.D., 1977). *Member:* Orange County, South Orange County and American Bar Associations; State Bar of California; The Association of Trial Lawyers of America. PRACTICE AREAS: Civil Litigation; Franchises and Franchising.

REPRESENTATIVE CLIENTS: Honey Baked Ham, Inc.; Health Benefits Inc.; Creative Health Programs; W.S. Circuits, Inc.; National Union Insurance.
REFERENCES: Monarch Bank; Bank of America (Laguna Beach Office).

---

## GRADY LAW FIRM

A PROFESSIONAL CORPORATION

28202 CABOT ROAD, SUITE 300
LAGUNA NIGUEL, CALIFORNIA 92677
Telephone: 714-752-1222

San Diego, California Office: Aventine, 8910 University Center Lane, Suite 500, 92122-1085. Telephone: 619-535-1222. Fax: 619-535-0222.

*Construction Defect and Land Subsidence Litigation, Personal Injury, General Business and Litigation Practices.*

**THOMAS GRADY,** born Newark, New Jersey, November 28, 1945; admitted to bar, 1976, California and U.S. District Court, Southern District

*(This Listing Continued)*

---

of California; 1981, U.S. Court of Appeals, Ninth Circuit; 1983, U.S. District Court, Central District of California; 1984, U.S. Supreme Court. *Education:* California State University at San Diego (B.A., 1973); University of San Diego (J.D., 1976). PRACTICE AREAS: Construction Defect Litigation; Insurance; Personal Injury; Wrongful Death.

**MICHAEL DREW DICKS,** born Brooklyn, New York, April 1, 1963; admitted to bar, 1989, California. *Education:* San Diego State University (B.S., cum laude, 1986); California Western School of Law (J.D., 1989). PRACTICE AREAS: Plaintiff Construction; Defect Litigation.

**CHRISTOPHER J. COGLIANESE,** born Hoboken, New Jersey, November 25, 1961; admitted to bar, 1990, California. *Education:* Rutgers University (B.A., 1985); University of San Diego (J.D., 1989). Member, International Law Society, University of San Diego Law School, 1987-1988. *Member:* American Bar Association; American Trial Lawyers Association. PRACTICE AREAS: Plaintiff Construction Defects.

**DARLENE ROHR KOWALCZYK,** born San Diego, California, June 13, 1962; admitted to bar, 1988, California and U.S. District Court, Southern District of California. *Education:* San Diego State University (B.A., cum laude, 1985); Loyola Marymount University (J.D., 1988). Phi Beta Kappa. *Member:* State Bar of California; American Bar Association.

---

## HIGHAM, McCONNELL & DUNNING

28202 CABOT ROAD, SUITE 450
LAGUNA NIGUEL, CALIFORNIA 92677-1250
Telephone: 714-365-5515
FAX: 714-365-5522
Email: HMDTI@AOL.com

*Corporate, Public and Private Securities, Venture Capital, Tax, Partnership, Technology Transfer, Real Estate and General Business Law, as well as Leveraged Buyouts and other Mergers and Acquisitions.*

**DOUGLAS F. HIGHAM,** born Berkeley, California, March 19, 1951; admitted to bar, 1978, California; 1980, U.S. Tax Court. *Education:* Brigham Young University (B.S. in Accounting, cum laude, 1975; J.D., cum laude, 1978). Member, Brigham Young University Law Review, 1976-1977. *Member:* Orange County Bar Association (Member, Sections on: Corporate; Real Estate; Taxation); The State Bar of California; American Institute of Certified Public Accountants. PRACTICE AREAS: Business Law; Corporate Law; Securities; Partnership Law; Taxation Law; Mergers and Acquisitions.

**SCOTT E. MCCONNELL,** born Lansing, Michigan, October 3, 1952; admitted to bar, 1978, California; 1979, U.S. District Court, Central District of California. *Education:* University of Southern California (B.S. in Business Administration, magna cum laude, 1974); University of California at Los Angeles (J.D., 1978). Recipient, American Jurisprudence Award, 1977. *Member:* The State Bar of California; American Bar Association (Member, Sections on: Business Law; International Law; Science and Technology Law). PRACTICE AREAS: Corporate Law; Securities; Mergers and Acquisitions; Technology Transfer; Business Law.

**STEVEN J. DUNNING,** born Denver, Colorado, May 15, 1949; admitted to bar, 1981, California. *Education:* Stanford University (B.A., 1973); Loyola University of Los Angeles (J.D., cum laude, 1981). *Member:* Orange County (Business and Corporate Law Section, Chairman, 1988-1989) and American (Member, Business Law Section) Bar Associations; The State Bar of California. PRACTICE AREAS: Corporate Law; Securities; Mergers and Acquisitions; Business Law; Real Estate Law.

---

## ROBINSON, PHILLIPS & CALCAGNIE

A PROFESSIONAL CORPORATION

Incorporated 1986
Established in 1978

28202 CABOT ROAD
SUITE 200
LAGUNA NIGUEL, CALIFORNIA 92677
Telephone: 714-347-8855
Fax: 714-347-8774
Email: rpc@robinson-pilaw.com

San Diego, California Office: 110 Laurel Street. Telephone: 619-338-4060. Fax: 619-338-0423.

*(This Listing Continued)*

*Automobile Product Liability Litigation, Toxic Tort, Corporate Fraud, Serious Injury and Death Cases.*

*FIRM PROFILE: The firm prides itself on being one of the preeminent plaintiff automobile product litigation practices in the United States. The firm has been involved in over 150 automobile fuel system fire cases since Mark P. Robinson, Jr. was co-counsel in the trial of the landmark Grimshaw vs. Ford case, which resulted in a $128 million dollar verdict. In addition, the firm is handling a variety of automotive crashworthiness cases including seat and occupant restraint system design, automobile roof design, and vehicle rollovers, as well as design defect litigation involving utility vehicles, ATV's, motorcycles and roadways. Mark P. Robinson, Jr. has handled automobile product liability litigation in over thirty states, including the landmark "Kentucky School Bus" fire case trial in 1992. The Law firm is listed in Bar Register of Preeminent Lawyers. The Law firm is able to communicate in the following languages: Spanish, Italian and French.*

*Grimshaw vs. Ford Motor Co., 119 Cal App 757, 1981; Bangert vs. Narmco, 163 Cal App 3d 207, 1984; Fisher vs. Superior Court, 103 Cal App 3rd 434, 1980; In re Air Crash in Bali, Indonesia, 871 Fed 2d 812 (9th Cir. 1989).*

**MARK P. ROBINSON, JR.,** born Pasadena, California, March 10, 1945; admitted to bar, 1972, California. *Education:* Stanford University (B.A., 1968); Loyola University of Los Angeles (J.D., cum laude, 1972). Member, National Moot Court Society. Member, Los Angeles County District Attorney's Office, 1972-1973. Author and Lecturer: "Punitive Damages in Product Liability Cases," Pepperdine Law Review, 1978; "A Futuristic Look at Products Liability Law & Closing Argument," Southern Methodist University Products Liability Institute, 1985; "Proving a Difficult Punitive Damages Case," California Trial Lawyers Association, 29th Annual Convention, 1990; "Proving Damages: Special Cases with Unique Problems of Proof," San Diego Trial Lawyers Seminar, 1991; "Obtaining Discovery from Auto Manufacturers," The Association of Trial Lawyers of America, Seminar 1986; "Product Liability Litigation: Overcoming Defenses of Alteration, Misuse and Superseding Causes," CTLA Forum, April 1991; "Product Liability Litigation: Discovery Relating to Other Products, Complaints, Injuries and Subsequent Conduct," CTLA Forum, October 1992. *Member:* State Bar of California; American Bar Association; California Trial Lawyers Association (Member, Board of Governors, 1978 and 1983); Orange County Trial Lawyers Association (Recipient, Orange County Trial Lawyer of the Year Award, 1978; President, 1981); International Society of Barristers; American Board of Trial Advocates. (Also at San Diego Office). *PRACTICE AREAS:* Products Liability Law; Civil Litigation; Personal Injury Law.

**GORDON G. PHILLIPS, JR.,** born Detroit, Michigan, August 16, 1953; admitted to bar, 1979, California. *Education:* University of Southern California (B.S., in Accounting, 1975); Loyola University of Los Angeles (J.D., 1979). Member, Jessup International Moot Court Team. Lecturer: Cost Containment in Complex Product Liability Litigation, Western Trial Lawyers Association, 1995; Biomechanics in Product Liability Litigation, Society of Automotive Engineers, 1994. *Member:* State Bar of California; American Bar Association; The Association of Trial Lawyers of America; California Trial Lawyers Association; Los Angeles Trial Lawyers Association; Orange County Trial Lawyers Association. (Also at San Diego Office). *PRACTICE AREAS:* Products Liability Law; Civil Litigation; Personal Injury Law.

**KEVIN F. CALCAGNIE,** born Glendale, California, February 27, 1955; admitted to bar, 1983, California; 1987, U.S. Supreme Court and U.S. Court of Appeals, Ninth Circuit; U.S. Court of Appeals, Fifth Circuit. *Education:* California State University at Fullerton (B.A., 1977; Western State University (J.D., 1983). Associate Editor, 1981 and Editor-in-Chief, 1982, Western State University Law Review. Recipient, American Jurisprudence Awards in Evidence and Uniform Commercial Code. Contributing Author: "Products Liability Litigation: Product Studies," Clark Boardman, Callaghan, 1996; "A Guide to Toxic Torts," Matthew Bender and Company, 1987. Author: "Automotive Fuel System Crashworthiness Litigation," Trial, November 1996; "Selection of Experts in Auto Crashworthiness Cases," Trial, May 1995; "Product Liability Litigation: Overcoming Defenses of Alteration, Misuse and Superseding Causes," CTLA Forum, April 1991; "Product Liability Litigation: Discovery Relating to Other Products, Complaints, Injuries and Subsequent Conduct," Western State University Consumer Law Journal, 1992; "Occupant Restraint System Litigation," CTLA Forum, October 1993; "Roadway Design Litigation: Essential Statutory and Decisional Law," CTLA Forum, November 1994. *Member:* Orange County Bar Association; State Bar of California; Consumer Attorneys of California (Member, Board of Governors at Large, 1996; Education Chair, 1996); California Trial Lawyers Association (Member, Board of Governors at-

*(This Listing Continued)*

Large 1993-1994); Orange County Trial Lawyers Association. (Also at San Diego Office). *PRACTICE AREAS:* Products Liability Law; Civil Litigation; Personal Injury Law.

---

**ALLAN F. DAVIS,** born Portsmouth, Virginia, September 3, 1954; admitted to bar, 1983, California. *Education:* University of Wyoming (B.S., 1976; J.D., 1982). Author: "California Code of Civil Procedures Section 340.1 and the Delayed Discovery Doctrine," CTLA Forum, July/August 1994. Lecturer, "Determining Damages in Personal Injury Actions," Continuing Education of the Bar, May 1995. *Member:* State Bar of California; Orange County Trial Lawyers Association (Member, Board of Directors); The Association of Trial Lawyers of America; California Trial Lawyers Association. (Also at San Diego Office). *PRACTICE AREAS:* Products Liability Law; Personal Injury Law.

**SUSAN LEE GUINN,** born Langhorne, Pennsylvania, July 22, 1965; admitted to bar, 1992, California and U.S. District Court, Southern and Central Districts of California. *Education:* University of New Mexico (B.S.N., 1987); University of Denver (J.D., 1991). Member, Science and Law Subcommittee, California Plaintiff Steering Committee, Breast Implant Litigation. *Member:* Consumer Attorneys of California (Board Member); The San Diego Trial Lawyers Association; The Lawyers Club of San Diego; The Western Trial Lawyer Association (Education Chairperson, 1995-1996; Board Member); The Attorneys Information Group; Trial Lawyers for Public Justice; Association of Trial Lawyers of America (Member: Political Action Management Committee; Publications Committee). (Also at San Diego Office). *PRACTICE AREAS:* Products Liability Law; Personal Injury Law; Medical Malpractice Law; Civil Litigation; Toxic Torts.

**JEOFFREY L. ROBINSON,** born Los Angeles, California, May 29, 1955; admitted to bar, 1981, California and U.S. District Court, Central District of California. *Education:* University of the Pacific (B.A., 1977); Southwestern School of Law (J.D., 1980). Lecturer: "Trial Tactics," MCLE, 1992; "Final Argument," CDAA, 1989; "Art of Voir Dire," 1987. *Member:* Orange County Bar Association; State Bar of California; Association of Trial Lawyers of America; Orange County Trial Lawyers Association; California Consumer Attorneys; California District Attorney's Association. *PRACTICE AREAS:* Products Liability; Personal Injury; Civil Litigation.

*LEGAL SUPPORT PERSONNEL*

| Lin Moen | Darleen Perkins |
| Donna Hosea | Francine Teer |
| Linda Audeoud | |

---

## GARY D. STEVENS
30011 IVY GLENN DRIVE, SUITE 109
**LAGUNA NIGUEL, CALIFORNIA 92677-5014**
Telephone: 714-249-9295

*Family Law, Business Law, Personal Injury Law, Civil Litigation.*

**GARY D. STEVENS,** born 1935; admitted to bar, 1975, California. *Education:* University of California, Berkeley (B.S., 1958) University of Southern California (M.S., 1963) Pepperdine University (J.D., 1974). (Certified Specialist, Family Law, The State Bar of California Board of Legal Specialization).

---

## C. LARRY FANCHER
440 EAST LA HABRA BOULEVARD
**LA HABRA, CALIFORNIA 90631**
Telephone: 714-870-9972; 310-691-1300

*Family Law and Related Litigation.*

**C. LARRY FANCHER,** born Auburn, Washington, August 6, 1942; admitted to bar, 1982, California and U.S. District Court, Central District of California. *Education:* Central Washington University (B.A., 1964); California State University at Long Beach (M.A., 1969); Western State University (J.D., 1981). *Member:* Orange County Bar Association; State Bar of California. (Certified Specialist, Family Law, The State Bar of California Board of Legal Specialization). *PRACTICE AREAS:* Family Law.

## GOLDSTEIN & WARD, INC.

Established in 1982

440 EAST LA HABRA BOULEVARD
**LA HABRA, CALIFORNIA 90631**
Telephone: 310-694-3821; 714-870-9972
Fax: 310-697-8477

*Business Litigation and Bankruptcy Law.*

**BURTON H. WARD,** born Los Angeles, California, February 14, 1940; admitted to bar, 1970, California; 1974, U.S. Supreme Court. *Education:* San Diego State College (B.S., 1965); Loyola University of Los Angeles (J.D., 1969). Phi Alpha Delta. Lecturer, Business Law, Chapman College, Orange, California, 1970-1972. *Member:* Los Angeles County, Orange County and American Bar Associations; State Bar of California; Commercial Law League of America. **PRACTICE AREAS:** Business Litigation; Bankruptcy.

**JONATHAN A. GOLDSTEIN,** born Brooklyn, New York, July 20, 1950; admitted to bar, 1975, California. *Education:* Syracuse University (B.A., 1972); University of San Diego (J.D., 1975). Adjunct Professor of Law, (Contracts), Western State University, School of Law, Fullerton, California, 1994—. *Member:* Orange County Bar Association; State Bar of California. **PRACTICE AREAS:** Business Litigation; Bankruptcy.

---

**DAVID T. WARD,** born Glendale, Arizona, April 5, 1962; admitted to bar, 1989, California. *Education:* Brigham Young University (B.A., magna cum laude, 1985); Cornell University (J.D., cum laude, 1989). Phi Kappa Phi. *Member:* Orange County Bar Association; State Bar of California. **LANGUAGES:** Spanish. **PRACTICE AREAS:** Business Litigation; Bankruptcy.

REPRESENTATIVE CLIENTS: Union Bank of California; California State Bank; Citizens Bank; Don Steves Chevrolet; Burch Ford; Toyota of Orange; Lyle Parks, Jr., Construction; Franklin Reinforcing Steel Company.
REFERENCE: The Bank of California.

---

## MICHAEL R. McDONNELL, INC.

A PROFESSIONAL CORPORATION

440 EAST LA HABRA BOULEVARD
**LA HABRA, CALIFORNIA 90631**
Telephone: 310-694-3827; 714-870-9972
Fax: 310-694-4280

*Criminal Trial Practice in State and Federal Courts, Juvenile Law.*

**MICHAEL R. MCDONNELL,** born Chicago, Illinois, November 6, 1942; admitted to bar, 1968, California; 1974, U.S. Supreme Court. *Education:* University of San Diego (B.A., 1964; J.D., 1967). *Member:* Orange County Bar Association; State Bar of California; California Trial Lawyers Association; California Attorneys for Criminal Justice; National Association of Criminal Defense Lawyers. **PRACTICE AREAS:** Criminal; Juvenile; Federal and State.

---

**JEFFREY D. KENT,** born Whittier, California, April 30, 1967; admitted to bar, 1992, California; 1993, U.S. District Court, Central and Eastern Districts of California; 1995, U.S. District Court, Southern District of California and U.S. Court of Appeals, Ninth Circuit. *Education:* University of California, Irvine (B.A. in Economics and Political Science, 1989); Western State University (J.D., 1992). *Member:* Orange County Bar Association; State Bar of California; California Public Defenders Association; California Deuce Defenders. **PRACTICE AREAS:** Criminal Law; Juvenile; Federal and State.

REFERENCE: Landmark Bank.

## ARMSTRONG, FISCH AND ASSOCIATES, P.C.

4250 EXECUTIVE SQUARE
SUITE 900
**LA JOLLA, CALIFORNIA 92037**
Telephone: 1-800-846-1666
Fax: 619-453-1147

*Estate Planning, Probate, Trust Planning and Taxation Law.*

**ROBERT G. ARMSTRONG,** born 1947; admitted to bar, 1976, California. *Education:* University of California at San Diego (B.A., 1973); University of San Diego (J.D., 1976). *Member:* State Bar of California. **PRACTICE AREAS:** Estate Planning Law.

**SANFORD FISCH,** born Newark, New Jersey, July 27, 1955; admitted to bar, 1980, California. *Education:* Boston University (B.A., cum laude, 1977); University of San Diego (J.D., 1980); Georgetown Law Center (LL.M., 1982). *Member:* State Bar of California. **PRACTICE AREAS:** Estate Planning; Probate; Trust Planning; Taxation Law.

---

## BLANCHARD, KRASNER & FRENCH

A PROFESSIONAL CORPORATION

7724 GIRARD AVENUE, 3RD FLOOR
**LA JOLLA, CALIFORNIA 92037**
Telephone: 619-551-2440
FAX: 619-551-2434
Email: bkfl@aol.com

*General Civil Trial Practice. General Corporate and Commercial Law, Tax Estate Planning, International Transactions, Securities, Regulation, Financial Institutions, Copyright, Trademark and Licensing and Bankruptcy.*

**ROBERT W. BLANCHARD,** born Denver, Colorado, January 27, 1953; admitted to bar, 1980, California. *Education:* University of Denver (B.S.B.A., 1975); University of San Diego (J.D., magna cum laude, 1980). Contributing Author: "Commercial Real Estate Finance," American Bar Association, 1993. Author: "Applying the Rule of Reason: A Survey of Recent Cases and Comments," Vol. 17, No. 2, San Diego Law Review, 1979; "Introduction to Asset Securitization", American Bar Association, 1991; "Money Laundering andthe Transactional Lawyer", Probate and Property Magazine, March/April 1991; Co-Author: "Cleaning the Environment in the Money Laundry," American Banker, July, 1992. *Member:* San Diego County and American Bar Associations; State Bar of California. **PRACTICE AREAS:** Financial Institutions Law; Securities Regulation Law; Corporate Law; Real Estate Law.

**MARK A. KRASNER,** born Bad Kreuznach, Germany, September 4, 1954; admitted to bar, 1981, California; U.S. Tax Court. *Education:* San Diego State University (B.S. in Accounting, summa cum laude, 1974); University of San Diego (J.D., magna cum laude, 1981). Beta Alpha Psi; Beta Gamma Sigma; Phi Kappa Phi. Certified Public Accountant, California, 1977. Faculty, California Continuing Education of the Bar and California Society of Certified Accountants, 1982—. Big Brothers of San Diego (Executive Committee; Board Member and Officer). San Diego Jewish Academy (Former Executive Committee; Board Member and Officer). San Diego State University Alumni Association (Board Member). *Member:* San Diego County and American Bar Associations; State Bar of California; American Institute of Certified Public Accountants; California Society of Certified Public Accountants; National Association of Accountants. **LANGUAGES:** Spanish. **PRACTICE AREAS:** Real Property Law; Business Law; Taxation Law.

**ALAN W. FRENCH,** born Wooster, Ohio, March 9, 1964; admitted to bar, 1989, California. *Education:* University of the Pacific (B.S., magna cum laude, Bus. Adm. & Finance, 1986); Boston University (J.D., cum laude, 1989). Phi Kappa Phi; Beta Gamma Sigma. Note and Comment Editor, Annual Review of Banking Law, 1988-1989. Author: Comment, "Accounting for Third World Debt: Mandated Reserve Requirements," 9 Annual Review of Banking Law 465, 1990. *Member:* San Diego County and American Bar Associations; State Bar of California; Community Associations Institute. **PRACTICE AREAS:** Business Law; Banking Law; Real Estate Law.

*(This Listing Continued)*

**BRAD RODRIGUEZ BOHRER,** born Hollywood, California, June 8, 1968; admitted to bar, 1993, California and U.S. District Court, Southern and Central Districts of California. *Education:* Southern Methodist University (B.B.A., Finance, 1990; B.B.A., Real Estate and Urban Land Economics, 1990); Pepperdine University (J.D., 1993). Member: Boarder Trade Alliance, 1996—; Institute of the Americas, 1996—. *Member:* San Diego County (Member, Sections on: International Law; Litigation) and American (Member, Sections on: International Law; Litigation) Bar Associations; State Bar of California (Member, Sections on: International Law; Litigation). *PRACTICE AREAS:* International Sales and Trade Law; General Business Litigation; Real Estate; Tax.

**GLENN T. MACALUSO,** admitted to bar, 1996, California. *Education:* New York University (B.A., 1992); University of San Diego (J.D., 1996). *Member:* State Bar of California.

REPRESENTATIVE CLIENTS: Bank of Coronado; First National Bank; Investment Placement Group; Delimex; Gasmaster International Inc.; La Jolla Diagnostics, Inc.; Midtown Niki Group; People Feeders; Windemere Homeowners Association; Caywood-Scholl Capital Management; Real Property Services Corp.; SenDx Medical, Inc.; Ventana Growth Funds.

## MICHELE M. BURGART
*Established in 1982*

THE WALL STREET BUILDING
7855 IVANHOE AVENUE, SUITE 320
LA JOLLA, CALIFORNIA 92037
*Telephone: 619-456-1190*
*FAX: 619-456-1244*

*Estate Planning and Administration.*

**MICHELE M. BURGART,** born 1944; admitted to bar, 1971, Tennessee; 1975, California. *Education:* Montclair State College (B.A., 1961); University of Tennessee at Knoxville (J.D., 1971). *Member:* San Diego County Bar Association; State Bar of California. *PRACTICE AREAS:* Wills; Trust Law; Probate Law.

## CIRCUIT, McKELLOGG, KINNEY & ROSS LLP
*Established in 1987*

1205 PROSPECT STREET
SUITE 400
LA JOLLA, CALIFORNIA 92037
*Telephone: 619-459-0581*
*Fax: 619-459-0690*

*General Civil, Trial, Arbitration and Appellate Practice. Antitrust, Bankruptcy, Corporation and Business Law, Employment, Estate Planning, Probate, Pension and Profit Sharing, Real Property, Taxation, Trusts, Health Care, Insurance Defense, Copyright and Trademark Law.*

### MEMBERS OF FIRM

**RICHARD K. CIRCUIT,** born Salt Lake City, Utah, February 25, 1943; admitted to bar, 1970, Utah; 1972, California. *Education:* Brigham Young University (B.A., 1967); University of Utah (J.D., 1970); New York University (LL.M., in Taxation, 1971). Order of the Coif; Phi Alpha Delta; Blue Key. Member, Bar and Gavel. Author: "What You Have Always Wanted to Know About the IRS but Were Afraid to Ask," 51 Taxes 389, 1973. Law Clerk to Justice F. Henri Henriod, Utah Supreme Court, 1969-1970. *Member:* San Diego County Bar Association; State Bar of California. *PRACTICE AREAS:* Corporate Law; Business Law; Intellectual Property Law.

**R. KEITH MCKELLOGG,** born Lorain, Ohio, June 1, 1947; admitted to bar, 1973, California and U.S. District Court, Southern District of California; 1980, U.S. Supreme Court. *Education:* California State University at Fullerton (B.A., 1969); University of San Diego (J.D., 1973). Beta Gamma Sigma. Recipient: Gordon Fife Memorial Award. *Member:* San Diego County Bar Association; State Bar of California; The Association of Business Trial Lawyers. *PRACTICE AREAS:* Civil Litigation; Real Estate Law; Bankruptcy Law; Corporate Law.

**RICHARD R. KINNEY, JR.,** born Columbus, Ohio, December 8, 1943; admitted to bar, 1969, Ohio; 1972, California. *Education:* Ohio Wesleyan University (B.A., 1966); The Ohio State University (J.D., 1969). Co-author

*(This Listing Continued)*

"California Inheritance Taxation of Inter-Spousal Transfers," 2 Community Property Journal 6, 1975. Instructor: California Western School of Law, 1974-1977; California Continuing Education of the Bar, "Tax Reform Act of 1976 Revisited," 1978. *Member:* San Diego County Bar Association (Chairman, Legislative Subcommittee on Probate and Estate Planning, 1975); State Bar of California; National Health Lawyers Association; California Society for Healthcare Lawyers. *PRACTICE AREAS:* Estate Planning Law; Probate Law; Trust Law; Taxation Law; Health Care Law.

**SCOTT HUNTER ROSS,** born Santa Barbara, California, March 16, 1950; admitted to bar, 1979, California. *Education:* Seattle University (B.A., magna cum laude, 1975); University of San Diego (J.D., 1979). Phi Delta Phi. *Member:* La Jolla, San Diego County and American Bar Associations; State Bar of California; San Diego Trial Lawyers Association; Association of Southern California Defense Counsel. *PRACTICE AREAS:* Civil Litigation; Business Litigation; Employment Law; Family Law.

**DARL R. DANFORD,** born Fort Morgan, Colorado, June 4, 1958; admitted to bar, 1984, California. *Education:* University of Colorado (B.A., with distinction, 1980); University of Oklahoma College of Law (J.D., 1983). Phi Alpha Delta. Editor and Research Editor, Oklahoma Law Review, 1982. Author: "Liens: Laborer's Liens: Encumbering Real Property with Super-Priority," 35 Oklahoma Law Review 629, 1982. Instructor, Legal Research and Writing, University of Oklahoma College of Law, 1982-1983. *Member:* La Jolla (President, 1990) and San Diego County Bar Associations; State Bar of California; California Society for Healthcare Attorneys. *PRACTICE AREAS:* Business Civil Litigation; Intellectual Property Litigation; Employment Law; Health Care Law.

**PHILLIP C. WING,** born Phoenix, Arizona, May 22, 1957; admitted to bar, 1985, California and U.S. District Court, Southern District of California; 1989, U.S. Tax Court; 1991, U.S. District Court, Northern, Eastern and Central Districts of California and U.S. Court of Appeals, Ninth Circuit; 1992, U.S. Supreme Court. *Education:* Brigham Young University (B.S., 1981); University of San Diego (J.D., 1985). *Member:* La Jolla, San Diego County and American Bar Associations; State Bar of California. *LANGUAGES:* Spanish. *PRACTICE AREAS:* Civil Litigation; Business Litigation; Employment Law; Insurance Law; Real Estate Law; Personal Injury Law.

**DANIEL PEARL,** born San Diego, California, December 13, 1965; admitted to bar, 1994, California. *Education:* University of California at Los Angeles (B.A., 1988); California Western School of Law (J.D., 1994). *Member:* San Diego and LaJolla Bar Associations; State Bar of California. *PRACTICE AREAS:* General Civil Litigation; Real Estate; Business Litigation; Real Property Transactions.

**SHERI LYNNE PERLMAN,** born Anaheim, California, July 8, 1967; admitted to bar, 1996, California. *Education:* San Diego Stet University (B.S., 1992); Thomas Jefferson School of Law (J.D., 1995). *Member:* State Bar of California. *PRACTICE AREAS:* Estate Planning; Probate Law; Trust Law.

REPRESENTATIVE CLIENTS: Ahntech; Esscor; California Emergency Physicians; Chicago Title Insurance Company; Commonwealth Title Insurance Co.; Desert Hospital Emergency Physicians; Diebold, Inc.; Gryphon Software Corporation; Great Western Mortgage Co.; LG InfoComm, Inc.; Michigan Healthcare Network, Inc.; National General Insurance; RCP Co.; REMEC, Inc.; Scripps Bank; Suzy's Zoo; The Chicago Corp.; Torrey Enterprises; Unigard Security Insurance Group; Union Bank Trust Division; Viasat; Zurich-American Insurance Group.

## DARVY MACK COHAN
*Established in 1975*

SUITE 550, 1200 PROSPECT STREET
LA JOLLA, CALIFORNIA 92037
*Telephone: 619-459-4432*
*Fax: 619-454-3548*

*Civil, Business Law, Bankruptcy Law, Commercial Litigation, Insurance Law and Corporate Law.*

**DARVY MACK COHAN,** born Inglewood, California, September 22, 1943; admitted to bar, 1973, California and U.S. District Court, Southern District of California; 1982, U.S. District Court, Central District of California; 1983, U.S. District Court, Northern and Eastern Districts of California; 1985, U.S. Court of Appeals, Ninth Circuit. *Education:* United States Coast Guard Academy (B.S., 1965); California Western School of Law (J.D., 1973). Executive Editor, California Western Law Review, 1972-1973. Author: "Associated Home Builders v. City of Walnut Creek: California's Misdirected Quest for Park and Recreation Space," 8 Cal. West. Law Rev.

*(This Listing Continued)*

## DARVY MACK COHAN, La Jolla—Continued

129, 1972. *Member:* La Jolla Bar Association; State Bar of California. [Capt., USCG, 1965-1970; USCGR, 1970-1988]. *PRACTICE AREAS:* Civil Litigation; Commercial Litigation; Business and Corporate Litigation.

REPRESENTATIVE CLIENTS: Citibank; Seattle First National Bank; Chevy Chase Bank.
REFERENCE: Scripps Bank, La Jolla, CA.

---

## WILLIAM A. COHAN, P.C.

7746 HERSCHEL AVENUE
LA JOLLA, CALIFORNIA 92037-4403
Telephone: 619-551-0939
Fax: 619-551-0193
Email: wcohan@aol.com

*Complex Civil and Criminal Litigation.*

FIRM PROFILE: *For the past sixteen years the majority of Bill Cohan's practice has been devoted to defending federal criminal tax cases, conspiracies to defraud the United States, money laundering and related criminal charges, including searches and seizures, forfeitures, grand jury proceedings and summons enforcement litigation. Thus far in his career he has achieved dismissals or acquittals of all or substantially all charges in 34 of 64 cases. He has obtained reversals on appeal in 7 criminal cases and 7 civil actions. He has also persuaded the government not to file criminal charges against at least 12 clients In addition to these accomplishments, he has had more than 50 reported decisions.*

**WILLIAM A. COHAN,** born Palo Alto, California, March 16, 1947; admitted to bar, 1976, Colorado; 1989, California. *Education:* Stanford University (B.A., 1970); University of Washington (J.D., 1976). *Member:* State Bar of California. *LANGUAGES:* German; French; Spanish. *PRACTICE AREAS:* Complex Litigation; Criminal Tax Litigation; White Collar Defense Law.

---

## FERGUSON, NEWBURN & WESTON

A PROFESSIONAL CORPORATION
*Established in 1931*

SUITE 260, 7777 FAY AVENUE
LA JOLLA, CALIFORNIA 92037
Telephone: 619-454-4233
Facsimile: 619-454-3052

*Estate Planning, Trust and Probate Law.*

**KEITH M. FERGUSON** (1903-1965).

**JOHN L. NEWBURN** (Retired, 1989).

**WILLIAM E. FERGUSON,** born Denver, Colorado, 1923; admitted to bar, 1950, California. *Education:* Pomona College (B.A.); Boalt Hall, University of California (LL.B.). *Member:* San Diego County and American Bar Associations; State Bar of California (Member: Unauthorized Practice Committee, 1972-1973; Executive Committee, Estate Planning, Trust and Probate Section, 1975-1982); International Academy of Estate and Trust Law (Academician, Executive Council Member). Fellow, American College of Trust and Estate Counsel (State Chairman, 1986-1992). *PRACTICE AREAS:* Estate Planning; Trust Law; Probate.

**DAVID WESTON,** born La Jolla, California, November 22, 1948; admitted to bar, 1977, California. *Education:* San Diego State College (A.B., 1972); Hastings College of the Law, University of California (J.D., 1977). Member: Order of the Coif; Thurston Society. Member and Editor, Hastings Law Journal, 1975-1977. *Member:* San Diego County and American Bar Associations; State Bar of California (Member, Executive Committee, Estate Planning, Trust and Probate Section). Fellow, American College of Trust and Estate Counsel. (Certified Specialist, Estate Planning, Trust and Probate Law, The State Bar of California Board of Legal Specialization). *PRACTICE AREAS:* Estate Planning; Trust Law; Probate.

REFERENCES: Union Bank (La Jolla Office); Scripps Bank (La Jolla Office).

---

## FISH & RICHARDSON P.C.

4225 EXECUTIVE SQUARE, SUITE 1400
LA JOLLA, CALIFORNIA 92037
Telephone: 619-678-5070
Fax: 619-678-5099
Email: info@fr.com
URL: http://www.fr.com

*Boston, Massachusetts Office:* 225 Franklin Street. Telephone: 617-542-5070. Fax: 617-542-8906.
*Washington, D.C. Office:* 601 13th Street, N.W. Telephone: 202-783-5070. Fax: 202-783-2331.
*Houston, Texas Office:* One Riverway, Suite 1200. Telephone: 713-629-5070. Fax: 713-629-7811.
*Menlo Park, California Office:* 2200 Sand Hill Road, Suite 100. Telephone: 415-322-5070. Fax: 415-854-0875.
*Minneapolis, Minnesota Office:* Fish & Richardson P.C., P.A., 60 South Sixth Street, Suite 3300. Telephone: 612-335-5070. Fax: 612-288-9696.
*New York, N.Y. Office:* 45 Rockefeller Plaza, Suite 2800. Telephone: 212-765-5070. Fax: 212-258-2291.

*Intellectual Property Law: Trials, Transactions, Patents, Trademarks, Copyrights, Trade Secrets, Entertainment Law, Telecommunications Law, Drug and Medical Device and Antitrust Law.*

**JOHN F. LAND,** born 1953; admitted to bar, 1978, California; registered to practice before U.S. Patent and Trademark Office. *Education:* California Institute of Technology (B.S., with honors, 1975); University of Southern California (J.D., 1978). Author: "Protection of Computer Software by Copyrights, Trade Secrets and Patents," 1984; "Liability for Software Failure," 1984. *PRACTICE AREAS:* Intellectual Property; Copyrights; Patents; Trademarks; Trade Secrets. *Email:* land@fr.com

**JOHN R. WETHERELL, JR.,** born 1948; admitted to bar, 1985, District of Columbia; registered to practice before U.S. Patent and Trademark Office (Not admitted in California). *Education:* University of Florida (B.S., Chemistry, 1972; Ph.D., Microbiology, 1977); Seton Hall University (J.D., 1984). *PRACTICE AREAS:* Intellectual Property; Patents; Trade Secrets; Unfair Trade Practices. *Email:* wetherell@fr.com

**SCOTT C. HARRIS,** born 1957; admitted to bar, 1987, Pennsylvania; 1988, District of Columbia; registered to practice before U.S. Patent and Trademark Office (Not admitted in California). *Education:* George Washington University (B.S.E.E., with highest honors, 1979; J.D., 1987). Order of the Coif. *PRACTICE AREAS:* Intellectual Property; Patents. *Email:* harris@fr.com

---

**MONIQUE L. CORDRAY,** born 1964; admitted to bar, 1989, Florida; 1990, District of Columbia; registered to practice before U.S. Patent and Trademark Office (Not admitted in California). *Education:* West Virginia University (B.S.Ch.E., 1986); University of Florida (J.D., with honors, 1989); Georgetown University Law Center (LL.M., with distinction, 1993). *PRACTICE AREAS:* Intellectual Property; International Trade Commission Practice. *Email:* cordray@fr.com

**STACY L. TAYLOR,** born 1959; admitted to bar, 1986, California; registered to practice before U.S. Patent and Trademark Office. *Education:* California Polytechnic State University (B.S., 1982); California Western School of Law (J.D., cum laude, 1985). *PRACTICE AREAS:* Intellectual Property; Litigation; Trademarks; Copyrights. *Email:* taylor@fr.com

**JUNE MARIE LEARN,** born 1937; admitted to bar, 1988, California; registered to practice before U.S. Patent and Trademark Office. *Education:* University of California, Riverside (Ph.D., English, 1971); California State Polytechnic University (B.S., Chemical Engineering, 1981); Loyola Law School (J.D., 1987). *PRACTICE AREAS:* Intellectual Property; Patents. *Email:* learn@fr.com

**LISA A. HAILE,** born 1960; admitted to bar, 1992, California; registered to practice before U.S. Patent and Trademark Office. *Education:* Rollins College (B.A., Biology, 1982); Georgetown University Schools of Medicine and Dentistry (Ph.D., Medical Microbiology and Immunology, 1987); California Western School of Law (J.D., 1991). *PRACTICE AREAS:* Intellectual Property; Patents. *Email:* haile@fr.com

**CHRISTOPHER S. MARCHESE,** born 1964; admitted to bar, 1992, Pennsylvania; 1993, District of Columbia; 1994, California; registered to practice before U.S. Patent and Trademark Office. *Education:* Centre College (B.A., Mathematics, 1987); University of Kentucky (B.S.E.E., 1987); George Washington University (J.D., 1992). *PRACTICE AREAS:* Intellec-

*(This Listing Continued)*

tual Property; Patents; Copyrights; Trademarks; Trade Secrets. *Email:* marchese@fr.com

**DONALD L. WENSKAY,** born 1954; admitted to bar, 1988, Michigan; 1995, California; registered to practice before U.S. Patent and Trademark Office. *Education:* University of Michigan (B.S., in Physics, 1979); Wayne State University (J.D., 1987). *PRACTICE AREAS:* Patent; Trademark; Intellectual Property. *Email:* wenskay@fr.com

REFERENCE: First National Bank of Boston, Boston, Massachusetts.

(For Biographical Data on Personnel at Boston, Massachusetts, Menlo Park, California, Washington, D.C., Minneapolis, Minnesota, Houston, Texas and New York, N.Y., see Professional Biographies at those locations)

---

## FISHER THURBER LLP

*Established in 1980*

LA JOLLA EXECUTIVE TOWER
4225 EXECUTIVE SQUARE
SUITE 1600
**LA JOLLA, CALIFORNIA 92037-1483**
Telephone: 619-535-9400
Fax: 619-535-1616

*Finance, Securities, Real Estate, Tax, Corporate Law, Franchise.*

FIRM PROFILE: Fisher Thurber, LLP's practice emphasizes the representation of entrepreneurial growth companies in a wide range of fields. The firm is involved primarily in business organization and finance matters, and provides services in securities law, corporate law, real estate, tax, franchise and related specialties.

**DAVID A. FISHER,** born Pasadena, California, June 25, 1951; admitted to bar, 1977, California and U.S. District Court, Southern District of California; U.S. Tax Court; U.S. Court of Claims. *Education:* University of California at San Diego (B.A., 1973); Thomas Jefferson School of Law (J.D., 1976). Executive Editor, Law Review, University of San Diego Postgraduate Diploma in Taxation, 1982. Editor, Syndication Advisor, 1982-1988. Instructor, Real Estate Investment/Syndication, University of California at San Diego, 1980-1993. *Member:* San Diego County and American Bar Associations; State Bar of California. (Also Of Counsel to Law Offices of Jack A. Donenfeld, Cincinnati, Ohio). *PRACTICE AREAS:* Corporate; Securities; Real Estate; Taxation.

*OF COUNSEL*

**MARSHALL THURBER,** born St. Johnsbury, Vermont, April 3, 1943; admitted to bar, 1970, California. *Education:* Union College (B.A., 1966); Hastings College of Law, University of California (J.D., 1969). *Member:* State Bar of California. *PRACTICE AREAS:* Business; Management Practices.

---

**TIMOTHY J. FITZPATRICK,** born Los Angeles, California, August 7, 1950; admitted to bar, 1979, California. *Education:* University of California at San Diego (B.A., 1973;) University of San Diego School of Law (LL.M. in Tax, 1988); Thomas Jefferson School of Law (J.D., 1978). Staff Member, Law Review, 1976-1977. Corporation Counsel, Department of Corporations, State of California, 1980-1986. *Member:* State Bar of California; American Bar Association. *PRACTICE AREAS:* Securities; Corporate; Franchise.

**NANCY L. MAURIELLO,** born Glendale, California, August 27, 1958; admitted to bar, 1994, California. *Education:* University of California at Los Angeles (B.A., 1979); Thomas Jefferson School of Law (J.D., 1993). Business Editor, Law Review, 1991-1992. Extern Law Clerk: U.S. Bankruptcy Court; U.S. Attorney's Office. *Member:* San Diego County and American Bar Associations; State Bar of California. *PRACTICE AREAS:* Securities; Corporate; Real Estate.

*LEGAL SUPPORT PERSONNEL*

**MERRILL R. CANNON,** born Medicine Hat, Alberta, Canada, May 2, 1954. *Education:* University of California at San Diego (1991, with honors, Legal Assistant Program). Member, Association of Legal Assistants, 1992—.

---

## THOMAS J. GALVIN

7825 FAY AVENUE, SUITE 200
**LA JOLLA, CALIFORNIA 92037**
Telephone: 619-456-3590
Fax: 619-456-1835
Email: tgalvin@ix.netcom.com

*Commercial Real Estate, Commercial Leasing for Retail Office and Industrial Property, Multi-State, Multi-Property Purchase and Sales Transactions. General Business Law.*

FIRM PROFILE: *After serving as a corporate counsel for national landlords and tenants for 15 years, Mr. Galvin specializes in providing low cost representation on a project or long term basis.*

**THOMAS J. GALVIN,** born Yonkers, New York, May 7, 1951; admitted to bar, 1978, Michigan; 1983, Colorado; 1989, California. *Education:* Michigan State University (B.A. in Political Science, 1973); Detroit College of Law (J.D., cum laude, 1978). Corporate Counsel: E.N. Maisel & Associates, Southfield, Michigan, 1979-1983; Burger King Corp., 1984-1987; Price Company (Price Costco, Inc.), 1990-1993. *Member:* San Diego Bar Association (Member, Real Estate Section); State Bar of California (Member, Real Estate Section). *TRANSACTIONS:* Taco Bell Corp. 1988 (Comprehensive Properties Audit); Marriott Corp. 1989 (Conversion of Big Boy Restaurants to Allies); The Price Company, 1991 (Formation of Price REIT); Price Costco, Inc., 1994-1995 (Sale of 85 shopping centers); Pepsico 1994-1996 (Counsel for California Pizza Kitchens).

REPRESENTATIVE CLIENTS: Price Costco, Inc.; Pepsico.
REFERENCE: Bank of America.

---

## GRAY CARY WARE & FREIDENRICH

*A PROFESSIONAL CORPORATION*

SUITE 575, 1200 PROSPECT STREET
**LA JOLLA, CALIFORNIA 92037**
Telephone: 619-454-9101
Telecopier: 619-456-3075
Email: info@gcwf.com
URL: http://www.gcwf.com

*San Diego, California Office:* 401 "B" Street, Suite 1700. Telephone: 619-699-2700.

*San Diego/Golden Triangle, California Office:* 4365 Executive Drive, Suite 1600, 92121. Telephone: 619-677-1400. Fax: 619-677-1477.

*Palo Alto, California Office:* 400 Hamilton Avenue. Telephone: 415-328-6561.

*El Centro, California Office:* 1224 State Street, P.O. Box 2890. Telephone: 619-353-6140.

*General Civil and Trial Practice in all State and Federal Courts and Administrative Agencies. Admiralty, Agribusiness, Antitrust, Aviation, Banking, Bankruptcy and Insolvency, Business, Commercial, Computer Law, Compensation and Benefits, Condemnation, Construction, Copyright and Trademark, Corporation, Corporate Securities, Customs, Eminent Domain, Employment Counseling and Litigation, Environmental, Estate Planning, Family Law, Fidelity and Surety, Government Contracts, Hospital and Health Care, Immigration and Naturalization, Insurance, Intellectual Property, International Business and Litigation, Publishing, Labor, Land Use, Libel, Licensing, Multimedia Negligence, News Media, Pension and Profit Sharing, Privacy, Private Foundation, Probate, Products Liability, Professional Malpractice, Railroad, Real Property, Federal and State Securities, Taxation, Telecommunications, Trade Regulation, Unfair Competition, Wills and Trusts.*

**THEODORE J. CRANSTON,** born San Diego, California, October 27, 1939; admitted to bar, 1965, California. *Education:* Stanford University (B.A., 1961; J.D., 1964). Order of the Coif. Member, Board of Editors, Stanford Law Review, 1963-1964. *Member:* San Diego County and American Bar Associations; The State Bar of California (Member, Estate Planning, Trust and Probate Section). Fellow, American College of Trust and Estate Counsel. (Resident, San Diego/Golden Triangle Office). *PRACTICE AREAS:* Taxation Law; Real Estate Law; Trusts Law; Estates Law. *Email:* tcranston@gcwf.com

**MELITTA FLECK,** born Bayreuth, West Germany, March 20, 1948; admitted to bar, 1979, California. *Education:* Mount St. Mary's College (B.A., 1970); San Diego State University (M.S., 1976); Hastings College of the Law, University of California (J.D., 1979). Order of the Coif. Member and Editor, Hastings Law Journal, 1977-1979. *Member:* San Diego County and American (Member, Section on Real Property, Probate and Trust Law)

*(This Listing Continued)*

**GRAY CARY WARE & FREIDENRICH,** A PROFESSIONAL CORPORATION, La Jolla—Continued

Bar Associations; The State Bar of California (Member: Estate Planning, Trust and Probate Section; Executive Committee, Estate Planning, Trust and Probate Law Section). Fellow: The American College of Trust and Estate Counsel. (Resident, San Diego/Golden Triangle Office). *PRACTICE AREAS:* Estate Planning; Estate and Gift Taxation; Trust Administration; Probate Law; Fiduciary Law. **Email:** mfleck@gcwf.com

**ELLEN H. WHELAN,** born Cleveland, Ohio, November 26, 1956; admitted to bar, 1984, California and U.S. District Court, Southern District of California. *Education:* Mt. Holyoke College; University of California at Davis (B.A., summa cum laude, 1981); Stanford University (J.D., 1984). Phi Beta Kappa. *Member:* San Diego County and American Bar Associations; The State Bar of California (Chair, LaJolla Estate Planning, Trust and Estates Section). (Resident, San Diego/Golden Triangle Office). *PRACTICE AREAS:* Trusts Law; Estates Law. **Email:** ewhelan@gcwf.com

**KARL ZOBELL,** born La Jolla, California, January 9, 1932; admitted to bar, 1959, California. *Education:* Utah State University and Columbia University (A.B., 1953); Columbia University and Stanford University (J.D., 1958). Chairman, City of San Diego Planning Commission, 1988-1991. *Member:* San Diego County and American (Member, Real Property, Probate and Trust Law Section) Bar Associations; The State Bar of California. Fellow, American College of Trust and Estates. (Resident, La Jolla Office). *PRACTICE AREAS:* Real Estate Transactions; Land Use Law; Trusts Law; Estates Law. **Email:** kzobell@gcwf.com

---

**MILDRED BASDEN,** born Galveston, Texas, October 9, 1949; admitted to bar, 1989, California and U.S. District Court, Southern District of California. *Education:* University of Texas (B.S.N., 1975); University of San Diego (J.D., magna cum laude, 1989). Member, San Diego Law Review. *Member:* San Diego County Bar Association; The State Bar of California (Member, Estate Planning, Trust and Probate Section). Resident, San Diego/Golden Triangle Office). *PRACTICE AREAS:* Trusts Law; Estates Law. **Email:** mbasden@gcwf.com

Languages: Spanish, German, French, Italian and Swedish.

REPRESENTATIVE CLIENTS: Dr. Seuss Foundation; Ernest W. Hahn, Inc.; Home Capital Corp.; Home Federal Savings & Loan; Imperial Corporation of America; La Jolla Bank & Trust Company; La Jolla Real Estate Brokers Assn.; McKellar Development Corp.; Merrill, Lynch, Pierce, Fenner & Smith; Nexus Development Co.; Planning Research Corp.; Pro Kennex, Inc.; Putnam Foundation; San Diego Community Foundation; Science Applications International Corp.; Scripps Bank; Scripps Clinic and Research Foundation; Scripps Memorial Hospital; The Copley Press, Inc.; Timken-Sturgis Foundation; Warren Properties.

(For complete Biographical Data on all Partners and Associates, See Professional Biographies at San Diego, California.)

---

## LAW OFFICES OF
## THOMAS A. HENRY, JR.

SUITE 315, 875 PROSPECT STREET
P.O. BOX 1168
**LA JOLLA, CALIFORNIA 92038**
Telephone: 619-454-1780
Fax: 619-454-1792

*Estate Planning, Probate, Trust Administration and Conservatorship Law.*

**THOMAS A. HENRY, JR.,** born Evanston, Illinois, August 7, 1938; admitted to bar, 1963, Colorado; 1966, California; 1992, U.S. Supreme Court. *Education:* University of Colorado (B.A., 1960; LL.B., 1963). *Member:* San Diego County and Colorado Bar Associations; State Bar of California.

---

**SARA A. HENRY,** born Englewood, Colorado, May 4, 1965; admitted to bar, 1991, California. *Education:* University of Colorado (B.A., 1987); California Western University (J.D., 1991). *Member:* San Diego County Bar Association; State Bar of California.

REPRESENTATIVE CLIENTS: Scripps Bank; Vista Valley Country Club; Scripps Memorial Hospitals Foundation.
REFERENCE: Scripps Bank.

CAA396B

---

## LAUTANEN & STANLEY

A PROFESSIONAL LAW CORPORATION
4225 EXECUTIVE SQUARE, SUITE 525
**LA JOLLA, CALIFORNIA 92037**
Telephone: 619-554-1091
FAX: 619-554-1093
Email: stanley0@counsel.com

*Federal, State and Local Tax Law, Administrative Tax Appeals and Tax Litigation.*

**W. ALAN LAUTANEN,** born Ashtabula, Ohio, May 31, 1953; admitted to bar, 1980, California; 1981, U.S. Tax Court, U.S. Claims Court and U.S. District Court, Southern District of California; 1985, Supreme Court, Federated States of Micronesia. *Education:* Kent State University (B.B.A., 1975); Duke University (J.D., 1980). Beta Alpha Psi; Beta Gamma Sigma. Member, Editorial Board, Duke Law Journal, 1979-1980. Certified Public Accountant: Ohio, 1977; California, 1981. Assistant Attorney General, Tax Matters, Government of the Federated States of Micronesia, 1984-1985. *Member:* San Diego County Bar Association; The State Bar of California. *PRACTICE AREAS:* State and Local Tax Controversies (50%, 16); Federal Tax Controversies (50%, 16).

**KIMBERLY S. STANLEY,** born Long Beach, California, December 10, 1956; admitted to bar, 1985, California; 1988, District of Columbia; 1989, U.S. Court of Appeals, Second, Third, Fourth, Sixth, Eighth, Ninth and Tenth Circuits; 1993, U.S. Tax Court. *Education:* Brigham Young University (B.S., magna cum laude, 1978); George Washington University (J.D., with honors, 1985); Georgetown University (LL.M., Taxation, 1988). Articles Editor, George Washington Journal of International Law and Economics, 1983-1985. Editorial Advisor, The Tax Lawyer, 1988-1989. Attorney-Advisor, U.S. Tax Court, Hon. Stephen J. Swift, 1985-1987. Trial Attorney, U.S. Department of Justice, Tax Division, 1987-1992. *Member:* San Diego County and American (Member, Taxation Section) Bar Associations; State Bar of California (Member, Taxation Section). *PRACTICE AREAS:* Federal Tax Controversies (75%, 11); State Tax Controversies (25%, 4). **Email:** stanley0@counsel.com

REPRESENTATIVE CLIENTS: American Airlines; Anheuser-Busch Companies; The Scripps Research Institute; Rusty Pelican Restaurants; The McMillin Companies; Proctor & Gamble.

---

## LUCE, FORWARD, HAMILTON & SCRIPPS LLP

A Partnership including Professional Corporations

*Established in 1873*

LA JOLLA GOLDEN TRIANGLE
4275 EXECUTIVE SQUARE, SUITE 800
**LA JOLLA, CALIFORNIA 92037**
Telephone: 619-535-2639
Fax: 619-453-2812
URL: http://www.luce.com

*San Diego, California Office:* 600 West Broadway, Suite 2600, 92101. Telephone: 619-236-1414. Fax: 619-232-8311.
*Los Angeles, California Office:* 777 South Figueroa, Suite 3600, 90017. Telephone: 213-892-4992. Fax: 213-892-7731.
*San Francisco, California Office:* 100 Bush Street, 20th Floor, 94104. Telephone: 415-395-7900. Fax: 415-395-7949.
*New York, N.Y. Office:* Citicorp Center, 153 East 53rd Street, 26th Floor, 10022. Telephone: 212-754-1414. Fax: 212-644-9727.
*Chicago, Illinois Office:* 180 North La Salle Street, Suite 1125, 60601. Telephone: 312-641-0580. Fax: 312-641-0380.

*General Civil Practice and Litigation in all State and Federal Courts. Antitrust, Banking, Bankruptcy, Business, Commercial, Copyright, Corporate Finance, Corporations, Energy and Resource, Environmental, Estate Planning, Family, Fidelity and Surety, First Amendment, Foreign Investment, Health Care Organizations, Immigration and Naturalization, Insurance and Reinsurance, Intellectual Property, International Financial Transactions, Labor, Land Use, Mergers and Acquisitions, Municipal Finance, Partnership, Patent, Pension and Profit-Sharing, Probate, Probate Litigation, Product Liability and Warranty, Professional Responsibility, Public Utility, Real Property, Securities, Taxation, Trademark, Trust and Venture Financing Law, Water Law.*

(This Listing Continued)

## MEMBERS OF FIRM

**JACK G. CHARNEY,** born Augusta, Georgia, July 3, 1946; admitted to bar, 1972, California. *Education:* Vanderbilt University (B.A., 1968); Stanford University (J.D., 1971). Recipient, Bancroft-Whitney American Jurisprudence Award. Author: "New Charitable Contribution Appraisal Regulations," Estate Planning and California Probate Reporter (CEB, 1985); "Estate Planning for Copyrights," Estate Planning and California Probate Reporter (CEB, 1990). *Member:* San Diego County (Chairman, Probate Section, 1981) and American Bar Associations. San Diego Estate Planning Council (President, 1995-1996). Fellow, American College of Trust and Estate Counsel (Member, Practice, Professional Standards and Demographics Committee). [1st Lt., U.S. Army, 1972]. *PRACTICE AREAS:* Estate Law; Personal Tax Planning Law; Probate Law; Trust Administration Law. *Email:* jcharney@luce.com

**ROBERT J. DURHAM, JR.,** born Kansas City, Missouri, February 27, 1941; admitted to bar, 1975, California. *Education:* Williams College (B.A., 1962); Yale University (M.A., 1963; Ph.D., 1969); Stanford University (J.D., 1975). Phi Beta Kappa. Lecturer, Probate, Wills and Estate Planning, California Western Law School, 1978-1985. Adjunct Professor, LL.M. Tax Program, University of San Diego Law School, 1979-1985. Member: Executive Committee, Estate Planning, Trust and Probate Section, The State Bar of California; Advisory Board, UCLA-CEB Estate Planning Institute. *Member:* American Bar Association. Fellow and Regent, American College of Trust and Estate Counsel (Editor, ACTEC NOTES, 1992-1993; Member: Estate and Gift Tax Committee; Editorial Board Technology Committee); International Academy of Estate and Trust Law (Academician). *PRACTICE AREAS:* Estate Planning; Tax Planning; Probate Law; Estate and Trust Administration. *Email:* rdurham@luce.com

**FREDERICK R. VANDEVEER,** born Butte, Montana, January 5, 1951; admitted to bar, 1980, California. *Education:* University of Utah (B.A., magna cum laude, 1973); Brigham Young University (J.D., magna cum laude, 1980). Executive Editor, Brigham Young University Law Review, 1979-1980. Chair, Tax Exempt Organizations Committee, Taxation Section, State Bar of California. *Member:* American Bar Association (Member, Exempt Organizations Committee). *PRACTICE AREAS:* Estate Planning; Estate Administration; Trust Administration; Charitable Giving; Charitable Trusts and Foundations; Tax Exempt Organizations. *Email:* fvandeve@luce.com

**MARY F. GILLICK,** born Yokohama, Japan, September 8, 1950; admitted to bar, 1984, California. *Education:* Texas Christian University; University of Maryland (B.S., 1972); University of San Diego (J.D., magna cum laude, 1984). Lead Articles Editor, San Diego Law Review, 1982-1983. Co-Author: "Civil Practice," Probate and Trust Proceedings, Bancroft Whitney, Vols. I-IV, 1993. Clerk to Honorable Eugene Wright, Senior Circuit Judge for the Ninth Circuit Court of Appeals, 1984-1985. Member, Executive Committee and Chair, Litigation Committee, Estate Planning, Trust and Probate Section, State Bar of California. *PRACTICE AREAS:* Trust and Estate Litigation. *Email:* mgillick@luce.com

**DANIEL N. RIESENBERG,** born Berkeley, California, June 9, 1949; admitted to bar, 1979, California. *Education:* Brown University (A.B., 1971); Ohio State University (M.A., 1974); Georgetown University (J.D., 1979). Associate Editor, Tax Lawyer, 1978-1979. President, Western Pension & Benefits Conference, San Diego Chapter, 1988-1990. Author: "Minimum Coverage and Participation Requirements," CEB Course Outline, Advanced Pension and Benefits Planning After the 1986 Tax Reform Act, 1987. *Member:* State Bar of California; American Bar Association (Member, Employee Benefits Committee, Taxation Section, 1986—). *PRACTICE AREAS:* Employee Benefits; ERISA; Pension and Profit Sharing Plans; Employee Stock Ownership Plans; Deferred Compensation; Flexible Benefit Plans; COBRA; Employee Health Benefits; Executive Compensation; Flexible Benefit Plans; Pension and Profit Sharing Plans. *Email:* driesenb@luce.com

## ASSOCIATES

**CAROL K. KAO,** born Taiwan, October 11, 1963; admitted to bar, 1991, California. *Education:* University of California, Los Angeles (B.A., cum laude, 1985); University of Southern California (J.D., 1991). Staff: Southern California Interdisciplinary Law Journal; Major Tax Planning Journal. Licensed Certified Public Accountant, California, 1989. *PRACTICE AREAS:* Estate Planning; Probate; Trust Administration. *Email:* ckao@luce.com

**PHILIP J. SULLIVAN,** born New York, N.Y., January 31, 1963; admitted to bar, 1988, New Jersey, Pennsylvania and U.S. District Court, District of New Jersey; 1990, California, U.S. District Court, Southern District of California and U.S. District Court, Eastern District of Pennsylvania. *Education:* Seton Hall University (B.S., magna cum laude, 1985); Villanova University (J.D., cum laude, 1988); New York University (LL.M., Taxation, 1995). *Member:* San Diego County Bar Association; State Bar of California. *PRACTICE AREAS:* Estate Planning. *Email:* psullivan@luce.com

All Members of the Firm and Associates are Members of the San Diego County Bar Association and The State Bar of California.

(For complete Biographical Data on all Personnel, see Professional Biographies at San Diego).

---

# LYON & LYON LLP

A Limited Liability Partnership Including Professional Corporations

*Established in 1911*

SUITE 660, 4250 EXECUTIVE SQUARE
**LA JOLLA, CALIFORNIA 92037**
Telephone: 619-552-8400
FAX: 619-552-0159
Email: lyon@lyonlyon.com
URL: http://www.lyonlyon.com

*Los Angeles, California Office:* First Interstate World Center, 47th Floor, 633 West Fifth Street. Telephone: 213-489-1600.

*Costa Mesa, California Office:* Suite 1200, 3200 Park Center Drive. Telephone: 714-751-6606.

*San Jose, California Office:* Suite 1150, 303 Almaden Boulevard. Telephone: 408-993-1555.

*Intellectual Property Law including Patent, Trademark, Copyright, Trade Regulation, Unfair Competition and Antitrust Law. Litigation.*

## RESIDENT PARTNERS

**DOUGLAS E. OLSON, (A PROFESSIONAL CORPORATION),** born Madison, Wisconsin, March 23, 1937; admitted to bar, 1965, Virginia; 1966, California; registered to practice before the U.S. Patent and Trademark Office. *Education:* University of Wisconsin (B.S. in Ch.E., 1959; M.S. in Ch.E., 1960); George Washington University (LL.B., 1965). Tau Beta Pi; Order of the Coif. Member, Editorial Staff, George Washington Law Review, 1964-1965. Law Clerk, U.S. Court of Customs and Patent Appeals, 1964-1965. *Member:* Los Angeles County and American Bar Associations; Virginia State Bar; American Intellectual Property Law Association; Los Angeles Intellectual Property Law Association. *PRACTICE AREAS:* Patent, Trademark, Unfair Competition; Intellectual Property.

**JOHN M. BENASSI,** born Florence, Italy, September 21, 1948; admitted to bar, 1975, District of Columbia; 1976, Illinois; 1977, California; registered to practice before the U.S. Patent and Trademark Office. *Education:* University of Illinois (B.S., 1971); George Washington University (J.D., cum laude, 1974). Law Clerk to: Hon. Hal D. Cooper and Hon. Joseph V. Colaianni, U.S. Court of Claims, Washington, D.C., 1974-1975. Volunteer Criminal Prosecutor, Tap Program, City of Los Angeles, 1989-1990. *Member:* Los Angeles County, Illinois State and American (Member, Sections on: Antitrust; Litigation; Intellectual Property Law) Bar Associations; The District of Columbia Bar; American Intellectual Property Law Association; The Association of Business Trial Lawyers; Los Angeles Intellectual Property Law Association. *PRACTICE AREAS:* Intellectual Property.

**MARY S. CONSALVI,** born Chicago, Illinois, August 3, 1958; admitted to bar, 1983, Illinois and U.S. District Court, Northern District of Illinois; 1987, California, U.S. District Court, Northern, Central and Southern Districts of California and U.S. Court of Appeals, Seventh and Ninth Circuits; registered to practice before the U.S. Patent and Trademark Office. *Education:* Purdue University (B.S., 1980); L'Universita Per Stranieri, Perugia, Italy; De Paul University (J.D., 1983); University of Southern California (M.B.A., 1992). Co-Author: "De-Vexing Prejudgment Interest Awards in Patent Cases," 67 J. Pat. Off. Soc'y, 1985. *Member:* Illinois State and American Bar Associations; International Trademark Association; American Intellectual Property Law Association. *LANGUAGES:* Italian and French. *PRACTICE AREAS:* Patent, Trademark, Unfair Competition; Intellectual Property.

**ROBERT C. LAURENSON,** born Canton, Ohio, May 17, 1953; admitted to bar, 1987, Virginia; 1988, California; 1990, District of Columbia; registered to practice before the U.S. Patent and Trademark Office. *Education:* Massachusetts Institute of Technology (S.B., Electrical Engineering, 1975; S.M., Electrical Engineering and Computer Science, 1977; S.M., Management, 1981); George Washington University National Law Center

*(This Listing Continued)*

## LYON & LYON LLP, La Jolla—Continued

(J.D., 1987). Tau Beta Pi; Eta Kappa Nu. Clerk, 1992-1994, Hon. S. Jay Plager, Circuit Judge, United States Court of Appeals for the Federal Circuit. Author: "Computer Software 'Article of Manufacture' Patents," JPTOS, October 1995, at 811; "The Application of 35 U.S.C. §271 (g) To U.S. Manufactured Products," New Matter, Vol. 20, No. 1, at 13. *Member:* Los Angeles County, San Diego County and American Bar Associations; State Bar of Virginia; District of Columbia Bar; American Intellectual Property Law Association; Federal Circuit Bar Association; Los Angeles Intellectual Property Law Association; San Diego Intellectual Property Law Association. *PRACTICE AREAS:* Litigation; Patent, Trademark, Copyright; Intellectual Property.

### RESIDENT ASSOCIATES

**RICHARD WARBURG,** born Rickmansworth, England, April 12, 1957; admitted to bar, 1990, Massachusetts; 1991, California and U.S. Court of Appeals, Ninth and Federal Circuits; registered to practice before the U.S. Patent and Trademark Office. *Education:* Birmingham University, England (B.Sc. 1978; Ph.D., Molecular Biology, 1981); Suffolk University (J.D., magna cum laude, Valedictorian, 1990). Phi Delta Phi. Recipient: American Jurisprudence Award in Wills and Trusts and Commercial Law. Member, Suffolk University Law Review, 1989-1990. Author: Suffolk Law Review XXIV, 951-973, 1990; Suffolk Law Review XXIV, 155-188, 1990; American Society For Microbiology News 53, 267-269, 1987; American Society For Microbiology News 52, 389-393, 1986. Member: American Society For Microbiology, 1981-1991; Genetics Society, 1978-1991. *Member:* Boston, Massachusetts, Federal Circuit and American Bar Associations; San Diego Patent Law Association; American Intellectual Property Law Association. *PRACTICE AREAS:* Patent, Trademark, Copyright; Intellectual Property. *Email:* patent@cts.com

**WAYNE B. BROWN,** born New York, New York, November 17, 1963; admitted to bar, 1992, California; 1993, U.S. District Court, Central and Southern Districts of California. *Education:* Harvard University (B.A., Chemistry, 1985); University of California, Berkeley (M.P.P., Public Policy, 1992); Boalt Hall School of Law, University of California, Berkeley (J.D., 1992). Harvard Dean's Honor List, 1984-1985. Member, High Technology Law Journal, 1990. Awarded Certificate of Merit for Contribution to the Congressional Sub-Committee on Infant Mortality, 1991. Co-Author: "Analysis of a Leprosy-Specific Antibody Epitope," Lepr. Rev. (1986) 57, Suppl. 2 157-62. *Member:* Los Angeles County (Member, Litigation Section); State Bar of California; American Bar Association (Member, Litigation Section); Inn of Court. *PRACTICE AREAS:* Patent, Trademark, Trade Secret, Unfair Competition and Business Tort Counseling and; Litigation; Trademark Prosecution; Intellectual Property.

**JESSICA R. WOLFF,** born Oak Ridge, Tennessee, October 6, 1964; admitted to bar, 1992, California and U.S. District Court, Southern District of California; registered to practice before the U.S. Patent and Trademark Office. *Education:* Bryn Mawr College (A.B. in Chemistry with Concentration in Cell Biology, magna cum laude, 1986); Massachusetts Institute of Technology (M.S. in Synthetic Organic Chemistry, 1988); University of California at Los Angeles (J.D., 1992). Member and Editor, Journal of Environmental Law and Policy, 1990-1992. Co-Author: "Patent Appeals Court Addresses Obviousness and Enablement/Utility in Biotech Cases," San Diego Daily Transcript, Wednesday, June 21, 1995, page 4A. *Member:* American Intellectual Property Lawyers Association; San Diego Intellectual Property Lawyers Association; American Chemical Society. *PRACTICE AREAS:* Patent, Trademark, Copyright, Unfair Competition, Trade Secret; Intellectual Property.

**SHELDON O. HEBER,** born New York, N.Y., July 19, 1960; admitted to bar, 1993, California and U.S. District Court, Southern District of California; registered to practice before the U.S. Patent and Trademark Office. *Education:* City University of New York (Ph.D., 1990); California Western University (J.D., 1992). *PRACTICE AREAS:* Patent; Intellectual Property.

**JEFFREY WILLIAM GUISE,** born Maquoketa, Iowa, March 9, 1959; admitted to bar, 1993, California and U.S. District Court, Central and Eastern Districts of California; registered to practice before the U.S. Patent and Trademark Office. *Education:* University of Iowa (B.S., in Microbiology, (1981); Southwestern Medical School (Ph.D., in Microbiology and Immunology, 1982); University of San Diego (J.D., cum laude, 1992). Member, 1989-1992; Executive Editor, 1991-1992, San Diego Law Review. Extern for Circuit Judge Alan D. Lourie, Court of Appeals for the Federal Circuit, 1992. Author: "Controlling Biotech Babies Following the Transfer of Self-Replicating Inventions," San Diego Law Review, Vol. 28, P. 939, 1991; "Expansion of the Scope of Disclosure Required Under the Informed Consent Doctrine: Moore v. The Regents of The University of California," San Diego Law Review, Vol. 28, P. 455, 1991. Member, Federation of American Societies For Experimental Biology. *Member:* American and Federal Circuit Bar Associations; American Intellectual Property Association; American Society for Microbiology; American Association for The Advancement of Science. *PRACTICE AREAS:* Patent, Trademark, Copyright; Intellectual Property.

**CHARLES S. BERKMAN,** born Anaheim, California, November 22, 1968; admitted to bar, 1993, California; 1994, U.S. District Court, Southern District of California; registered to practice before U.S. Patent and Trademark Office. *Education:* University of Texas, Austin (B.S. in Chemistry, 1990; J.D., 1993). Article Editor, Texas Intellectual Property Law Journal, 1992-1993. *Member:* American Bar Association (Patent, Copyright and Trademark Section; Committee on Patent Legislation, 1992-1993); San Diego Intellectual Property Law Association; American Intellectual Property Law Association. *PRACTICE AREAS:* Patent, Unfair Competition, Antitrust; Intellectual Property.

**SHERYL RUBINSTEIN SILVERSTEIN,** born Los Angeles, California, September 21, 1961; admitted to bar, 1993, California, U.S. District Court, Central, Southern and Northern Districts of California and U.S. Court of Appeals, Ninth Circuit. *Education:* University of California at Berkeley (A.B., Molecular Biology, with honors, 1983); University of California at Los Angeles (Ph.D., Molecular biology, 1990); University of Southern California (J.D., 1993). Order of the Coif. Recipient: Peter Knecht Memorial Award. Articles Editor, Southern California Law Review. Author: "Biotechnology Patents and the Deposit Requirement," 66 Southern California Law Review, 937, 1993. Co-Founder, U.S.C. Intellectual Property Law Society, 1990-1993. Legal Writing/Lawyering Skills Instructor, University of Southern California, 1992-1993. *Member:* San Diego Intellectual Property Law Association. *LANGUAGES:* French. *PRACTICE AREAS:* Patent; Unfair Competition; Antitrust; Intellectual Property.

**ANTHONY C. CHEN,** born NanChang, Jiang Xi, P.R. China, March 31, 1966; admitted to bar, 1993, California; registered before the U.S. Patent and Trademark Office. *Education:* University of Science and Technology of China, P.R., China (B.Sc., in Cell Biology, 1987); Harvard Law School (J.D., 1993). *Member:* State Bar of California; American Bar Association; San Diego Intellectual Property Law Association; American Intellectual Property Law Association. *LANGUAGES:* Mandarin, Chinese. *PRACTICE AREAS:* Patent, Trademark, Trade Secret, Technology Licensing; Biotechnology Patent Prosecution; Litigation; Opinion Analysis. *Email:* GetApatent@aol.com

**CLARKE W. NEUMANN, JR.,** born Hartford, Connecticut, August 4, 1963; admitted to bar, 1993, California; registered to practice before the U.S. Patent and Trademark Office. *Education:* The Pennsylvania State University (B.S., Chemical Engineering, 1985); Tau Beta Pi, Loyola Law School (J.D., 1993). *PRACTICE AREAS:* Intellectual Property.

**VICKI GEE NORTON,** born Inglewood, California, May 27, 1960; admitted to bar, 1994, California. *Education:* University of California at Davis (Ph.D., in Biochemistry, 1990); University of California at Los Angeles (J.D., 1994). Order of the Coif. Managing Editor, UCLA Law Review Vol. 41. *PRACTICE AREAS:* Patent; Intellectual Property.

**TIMOTHY J. LITHGOW,** born Oroville, California, July 11, 1962; admitted to bar, 1991, California; registered to practice before the U.S. Patent and Trademark Office. *Education:* Port Loma College (B.A., summa cum laude, 1984); University of Southern California (M.D., 1988); University of California, Boalt Hall School of Law (J.D., 1991). *Member:* San Diego Intellectual Property Law Association; Biocom. *PRACTICE AREAS:* Patent Law; Trademark Law; Intellectual Property.

**GARY H. SILVERSTEIN,** born New York, N.Y., August 24, 1955; admitted to bar, 1996, California; registered to practice before the U.S. Patent and Trademark Office. *Education:* Colgate University (A.B., magna cum laude, Honors in Biology, 1977); University of Michigan (Ph.D. in Cellular and Molecular Biology, 1991); University of San Diego (J.D., 1995). Phi Beta Kappa. Freshman Psychology Honors Program, Colgate University. Recipient, Michigan Cancer Research Institute Fellowship, University of Michigan, 1987-1988. *Member:* San Diego Intellectual Property Law Association. *PRACTICE AREAS:* Intellectual Property.

**AMY STARK HELLENKAMP,** born Pittsburgh, Pennsylvania, June 21, 1966; admitted to bar, 1996, California; registered to practice before the U.S. Patent and Trademark Office. *Education:* Pennsylvania State University (B.S., 1988); University of San Diego (J.D., 1995). Order of the Coif.

*(This Listing Continued)*

Member, San Diego Law Review, 1993-1995. *PRACTICE AREAS:* Patent; Intellectual Property.

**WILLIAM J. KOLEGRAFF,** born Huron, South Dakota, March 19, 1959; admitted to bar, 1996, California. *Education:* South Dakota School of Mines and Technology (B.S.E.E., 1981); University of San Diego (J.D., 1996). Order of the Coif. Member, San Diego Law Review, 1995-1996. *Member:* San Diego Intellectual Property Association. *PRACTICE AREAS:* Patent; Trademark; Intellectual Property.

**JONATHAN HALLMAN,** born Encino, California, April 20, 1959; admitted to bar, 1996, California. *Education:* Illinois State University (B.S., 1983); University of Illinois (M.S.E.E., 1988); University of California at Los Angeles (J.D., 1996). Recipient, American Jurisprudence Award in Community Property. *Member:* San Diego Intellectual Property Law Association. *PRACTICE AREAS:* Intellectual Property.

**HOWARD N. WISNIA,** born Paterson, New Jersey, July 23, 1969; admitted to bar, 1996, California; registered to practice before the U.S. Patent and Trademark Office. *Education:* George Washington University (B.S.E.E., 1991; J.D., 1996). Former Patent Examiner, U.S. Patent and Trademark Office. *Member:* San Diego Intellectual Property Association. *PRACTICE AREAS:* Intellectual Property.

*RESIDENT OF COUNSEL*

**BRADFORD J. DUFT,** born Summit, New Jersey, November 19, 1954; admitted to bar, 1980, California, 1981-1982, U.S. Court of Customs and Patent Appeals; 1982, U.S. Court of Appeals for the Federal Circuit; 1985, U.S. Court of Appeals, Ninth Circuit; registered to practice before the U.S. Patent and Trademark Office. *Education:* University of Colorado (B.A., Molecular Biology, 1977); California Western School of Law (J.D., cum laude, 1980); George Washington University (LL.M., with highest honors, Patent and Trade Regulation, 1983). Member, California Western Law Review, 1978-1980. Law Clerk and Technical Advisor to Judge Giles S. Rich, U.S. Court of Customs and Patent Appeals, 1980-1982 and U.S. Court of Appeals for the Federal Circuit, 1982-1983. Member: Los Angeles County and American Bar Associations; American Intellectual Property Law Association; Los Angeles Intellectual Property Law Association; San Diego Intellectual Property Law Association; Federal Circuit Bar Association. *PRACTICE AREAS:* Intellectual Property.

**SUZANNE L. BIGGS,** born Glendale, California, July 26, 1948; admitted to bar, 1978, New York and U.S. District Court, Southern and Eastern Districts of New York; 1981, California, U.S. District Court, Northern District of California and U.S. Court of Appeals, Ninth Circuit; 1983, U.S. Court of Appeals for the Federal Circuit; 1989, U.S. District Court, Central and Southern Districts of California; registered to practice before the U.S. Patent and Trademark Office. *Education:* Pomona College (B.A., 1970); Stanford University; University of Virginia; University of Southern California (J.D., 1977). Phi Alpha Delta (Justice, Jefferson Chapter). *Member:* American Bar Association (Member, Sections on: Antitrust; Business Law; Patent, Trademark and Copyright Law; Litigation); American Intellectual Property Law Association; San Diego Intellectual Property Law Association. *LANGUAGES:* (Reading) German, French. *PRACTICE AREAS:* Patent, Trademark, Copyright, Unfair Competition, Licensing; Intellectual Property.

**F.T. ALEXANDRA MAHANEY,** born Washington, D.C., December 3, 1959; admitted to bar, 1986, California and U.S. District Court, Southern and Central Districts of California; registered to practice before the U.S. Patent and Trademark Office. *Education:* Brown University (B.S., Mechanical Engineering, 1981); Phi Beta Kappa; University of California at Los Angeles (J.D., 1986). Order of the Coif. Associate Editor, UCLA Law Review. Author: Comment, " Incontestability: The Park 'N Fly Decision," 33 UCLA L. Rev. 114g (1986). Extern to the Hon. W. Matthew Byrne, U.S. District Court, Central District of California. *Member:* American Bar Association (Member, Patent, Trademark and Copyright Section; Amicus Brief Committee); American Intellectual Property Law Association; Lawyers Club. *PRACTICE AREAS:* Intellectual Property Litigation; Patent, Trademark, Copyright, Unfair Competition, Antitrust.

**STEPHEN S. KORNICZKY,** born New York, N.Y., January 31, 1963; admitted to bar, 1988, California; registered to practice before the U.S. Patent and Trademark Office. *Education:* Polytechnic Institute of New York (B.S.M.E., 1984); State University of New York at Buffalo (J.D., 1987). Co-Author: "Verdict Forms: A Peek Into The 'Black Box'," Jury Trials in Patent and Other High Tech Litigation § V (1995) and 23 AIPLA Quarterly Journal (1996); "Proving Infringement In View Of Markman v. Westview Instruments, Inc. And Hilton Davis Chemical Co. v. Warner-Jenkinson Co.: Who Does What And When?" ABA's Advanced Intellectual

*(This Listing Continued)*

Property Litigation Techniques 101-119 (1995). Judicial Law Clerk to the Honorable Giles Sutherland Rich, U.S. Court of Appeals, Federal Circuit, 1991-1993. *Member:* Orange County and American (Member, Amicus Brief Committee) Bar Associations; American Intellectual Property Law Association. *PRACTICE AREAS:* Litigation; Patent; Trademark; Copyright; Unfair Competition; Intellectual Property.

(For Complete Biographical Data on all Personnel, see Professional Biographies at Los Angeles)

---

## MAURER LAW FIRM

Established in 1978

7825 FAY AVENUE, SUITE 200
**LA JOLLA, CALIFORNIA 92037**
*Telephone: 619-456-5570*
*Fax: 619-551-8919*

Trial Practice, Professional Liability, Personal Injury, Products Liability, Insurance Law, Business Law and Sports Law.

FIRM PROFILE: *The firm specializes in malpractice and business litigation involving substantial damages or other consequences.*

**CHARLES D. MAURER, JR.,** born Jamestown, North Dakota, February 13, 1946; admitted to bar, 1973, Arizona; 1975, Washington; 1976, California and U.S. Supreme Court. *Education:* North Dakota State University (B.A., 1968); St. John's University; Arizona State University (J.D., 1973). Deputy Public Defender, Phoenix, Arizona, 1973-1975. General Counsel and Assistant Vice President, Risk Analysis and Research Corporation, 1975-1978. California Appellate Project Habeas Corpus Death Row Counsel, 1989. *Member:* State Bar of California; State Bar of Arizona; Washington State and American Bar Associations. *PRACTICE AREAS:* Malpractice; Personal Injury; Insurance; Construction Defect; Business Litigation.

REPRESENTATIVE CLIENTS: Ace Machine Co.; Alpine Insurance Co.; Bruck-Allen Architects; Carrier, Johnson, Wu; CNA Insurance; Commercial Insurance Resources, Inc.; C.W. Kim; Design Professionals Insurance Co.; Galvin-Cristilli Architects; Gulf Insurance Co.; J.B. Young & Associates, Ltd.; Krommenhoek-McKeown Architects; Lexington Insurance Company; Lloyds of London; Lyons, Warren & Assoc.; James M. Montgomery, Consulting Engineers, Inc.; J. Muller International; The Perkins & Will Group, Inc.; Project Design Consultants; RBF/Sholders &. Sanford, Inc.; SGPA, Architects; Stichler Design Group, Inc.; Tectonics; Travis, Verdugo, Curry & Associates; Turner Construction; TCO Insurance Services.

---

## STEPHEN V. McCUE

Established in 1983

SUITE 240, 4180 LA JOLLA VILLAGE DRIVE
**LA JOLLA, CALIFORNIA 92037-1471**
*Telephone: 619-455-5015*
*Fax: 619-455-7924*

General Civil and Trial Practice. Real Estate and Business Law.

**STEPHEN V. MCCUE,** born Casper, Wyoming, February 22, 1956; admitted to bar, 1983, California; 1985, Nevada. *Education:* University of California at Santa Barbara (B.A., 1978); University of San Diego (J.D., 1983). Author: "Professionalism In The Courtroom: A Perspective From A Business Law Firm," Trial News, November-December, 1984. Law Clerk to Hon. John F. Mendoza-Eighth Judicial District, Las Vegas, Nevada, 1984. *Member:* La Jolla Bar Association (Treasurer, 1990-1991); State Bar of California; State Bar of Nevada. *LANGUAGES:* Spanish and French. *REPORTED CASES:* Carver v. Teitsworth (1991), 1 Cal. App. 4th 845, 2 Cal. Rptr. 2d 446.

---

## NUGENT & NEWNHAM

*A PROFESSIONAL CORPORATION*

Established in 1965

875 PROSPECT STREET, SUITE 305
**LA JOLLA, CALIFORNIA 92037**
*Telephone: 619-459-3821*
*Fax: 619-459-6358*

*San Diego, California Office:* Suite 2200, 1010 Second Avenue. Telephone: 619-236-1323. Fax: 619-238-0465.

General Civil Trial Practice. Negligence, Taxation, Corporation, Real Property, Trusts and Estates, Pension and Profit Sharing, Employee Benefits, Health Care Law, Employer-Employee Relations, and Appellate Law.

*(This Listing Continued)*

NUGENT & NEWNHAM, A PROFESSIONAL CORPORATION,
La Jolla—Continued

**STEPHEN L. NEWNHAM,** born Philadelphia, Pennsylvania, April 29, 1934; admitted to bar, 1963, California. *Education:* Dartmouth College (A.B., 1956); University of Pennsylvania (LL.B., magna cum laude, 1962). Order of the Coif. Associate Editor, University of Pennsylvania Law Review, 1961-1962. Lecturer on Wills and Estate Planning, California Western Law School, 1971-1982. Member, Advisory Board, UCLA-CEB Estate Planning Institute, 1977-1987. *Member:* State Bar of California. Fellow, American College of Trust and Estate Counsel. (Certified Specialist, Estate Planning, Trust and Probate Law, The State Bar of California Board of Legal Specialization). ***PRACTICE AREAS:*** Trusts and Estates.

---

**M. KATHRYN NEWNHAM,** born San Diego, California, November 30, 1963; admitted to bar, 1991, California. *Education:* University of San Diego (B.A., 1988); Ohio State University (J.D., with honors, 1991). *Member:* State Bar of California (Member, La Jolla Probate Section). ***PRACTICE AREAS:*** Trusts and Estates.

REPRESENTATIVE CLIENTS: Pacific Theatres Corp.; Lottery Enterprises Inc.; Anesthesia Service Medical Group; San Diego County Medical Society; San Diego Private Practice Association; Specialty Medical Clinic, Inc.; Visiting Nurse Assn.; California Western School of Law; Coleman College; Greene International West, Inc.; Jassoy, Graff & Douglas C.P.A.'S; Peterson & Co C.P.A.'S; Royal Life Insurance Co. of N.Y.; Fuller Ford; Trevellyan Oldsmobile Co.; Weseloh Chevrolet; Rancho Santa Fe Escrow Corp.; The Newland Group Inc.
REFERENCE: Union Bank.

(For complete biographical data on all personnel, see Professional Biographies at San Diego, California)

---

## ROBERT J. PECORA

Established in 1986

SUITE 550, 1200 PROSPECT STREET
**LA JOLLA, CALIFORNIA 92037**
Telephone: 619-454-4014
Fax: 619-454-3548
Email: rjpecora@rplaw.alphapacnet.com

*Personal Injury, Civil Litigation.*

**ROBERT J. PECORA,** born Rochester, New York, March 8, 1954; admitted to bar, 1982, California. *Education:* University of Rochester (B.A., 1976); California Western School of Law (J.D., 1981). *Member:* San Diego County Bar Association; State Bar of California; Consumer Attorneys of California; American Trial Lawyers Association.

REFERENCE: Wells Fargo Bank.

---

## STEVEN SCHORR

Established in 1987

5398 LA JOLLA MESA DRIVE
**LA JOLLA, CALIFORNIA 92037-8038**
Telephone: 619-454-2261
Fax: 619-459-7187

*Appellate Litigation, Criminal Appellate.*

**STEVEN SCHORR,** born New York, N.Y., September 28, 1956; admitted to bar, 1983, New York; 1986, California. *Education:* Harvard University (A.B., 1978; J.D., 1982). Associate, Szold & Brandwen, New York, N.Y., 1982-1984. *Member:* San Diego County (Member, Appellate Court Committee) and American (Member, Criminal Law Section) Bar Associations; American Civil Liberties Union. ***REPORTED CASES:*** People v. Ivans (1992), 2 Cal. App. 4th 1654, 4 Cal. Rptr. 2d 66; People v. Brown (1991) 234 Cal. App. 3d 918; 285 Cal. Rptr. 824; People v. McGee (1993) 15 Cal. App. 4th 107, 19 Cal. Rptr. 2d 12; People v. Maestas (1993) 20 Cal. App. 4th 1482. ***PRACTICE AREAS:*** Appellate Litigation; Criminal Law.

---

## THOMAS & TEAFF

Established in 1976

SUITE 2212, 8950 VILLA LA JOLLA DRIVE
**LA JOLLA, CALIFORNIA 92037**
Telephone: 619-457-2330; 457-2470
Telecopier: 619-452-9484

*General Civil and Trial Practice. Estates, Business, Real Property, Negligence, Enforcement of Judgments, Family, Entertainment and Sports Law.*

### MEMBERS OF FIRM

**JOHN H. THOMAS,** born El Paso, Texas, October 24, 1934; admitted to bar, 1964, Virginia; 1966, California. *Education:* University of Virginia (B.A., 1956; LL.B., 1964). Phi Beta Kappa; Order of the Coif; Phi Alpha Delta. Law Clerk to Gerald Brown, Presiding Justice, Fourth District Court of Appeal, 1965-1966. Member, Board of Trustees, Rancho Santa Fe School District, 1968-1974. Instructor, Western State University College of Law, 1972-1974. *Member:* San Diego, Virginia State and American Bar Associations; State Bar of California; The Association of Trial Lawyers of America. [LCDR, USNR]. ***PRACTICE AREAS:*** Negligence; Real Estate; Trusts and Estates; Collections; Family Law.

**ROBERT F. TEAFF,** born Louisville, Kentucky, August 13, 1943; admitted to bar, 1968, Kentucky and Massachusetts; 1976, California. *Education:* Bellarmine College (B.A., magna cum laude); Boston College Law School (J.D., 1968). Presidential Scholar, Boston College Law School, 1965-1968. Instructor, Real Estate, City Colleges of Chicago, 1974-1975. Trustee, The Bishop's School, 1994—. Panelist, Sports Law Symposium, California Western School of Law, 1987, 1994. *Member:* San Diego (Member, Sections on: Business Law; Real Estate; Probate) and Kentucky Bar Associations; State Bar of California; Consumer Attorneys of San Diego County. [LCDR, JAGC, USNR, 1968-1975]. ***PRACTICE AREAS:*** Real Estate; Trusts and Estates; Contracts; Sports Law; Business Law.

REFERENCES: Union Bank (La Jolla Branch); First Interstate Bank (La Jolla Branch); City National Bank (La Jolla Branch).

---

## TOOTHACRE & PEDERSON

Established in 1978

4225 EXECUTIVE SQUARE, SUITE 260
**LA JOLLA, CALIFORNIA 92037**
Telephone: 619-457-4240
Telecopier: 619-457-0303

*General Civil and Trial Practice. Real Estate, Corporation, Business, Domestic Relations, Probate, Personal Injury, Wrongful Termination, and Dental Malpractice Law.*

**ROD M. TOOTHACRE,** born Burlington, Iowa, July 28, 1935; admitted to bar, 1961, Iowa; 1962, California. *Education:* Burlington College (A.A., 1955); State University of Iowa (B.S.C., 1957; J.D., 1960). Phi Alpha Delta. *Member:* San Diego County, Iowa State and American Bar Associations; State Bar of California; San Diego Trial Lawyers Association.

**CHARLES B. PEDERSON,** born San Diego, California, July 16, 1948; admitted to bar, 1977, California. *Education:* University of California at San Diego (B.A., 1970); University of San Diego (J.D., 1976). *Member:* San Diego County Bar Association; State Bar of California.

**SCOTT H. TOOTHACRE,** born San Diego, California, November 25, 1962; admitted to bar, 1990, California. *Education:* San Diego State University (B.A., 1987); Western State University (J.D., 1990). Delta Theta Phi (Vice-Dean, 1989; Dean, 1989-1990). Recipient, American Jurisprudence Award. Listed in Who's Who, 1990 and 1992. *Member:* San Diego County Bar Association; San Diego Trial Lawyers Association.

REFERENCES: Scottsdale Auto Lease; Pacific Nissan; United Cerebral Palsy Association of San Diego.

## LAW OFFICES OF
## MAURILE C. TREMBLAY

*A PROFESSIONAL CORPORATION*

*Established in 1987*

4180 LA JOLLA VILLAGE DRIVE, SUITE 210
**LA JOLLA, CALIFORNIA 92037**
Telephone: 619-558-3030
FAX: 619-558-2502

*General Civil, Trial and Appellate Practice. Title Insurance Defense, Business and Securities Litigation, Insurance, Real Estate, Commercial and Creditor Rights Law.*

**MAURILE C. TREMBLAY,** born Bridgeport, Connecticut, August 26, 1944; admitted to bar, 1969, Connecticut and U.S. Claims Court; 1971, California. *Education:* University of Connecticut (B.A., 1966); Georgetown University (J.D., 1969). Editor, Georgetown Law Journal, 1967-1969. Law Clerk to Chief Judge Wilson Cowen, U.S. Court of Claims, 1969-1970. *Member:* San Diego County Bar Association; State Bar of California. **REPORTED CASES:** La Jolla Mesa Vista Improvement Association v. La Jolla Mesa Vista Homeowners Association, 220 Cal. App. 3d 1187 (1990). **PRACTICE AREAS:** Civil Litigation; Title Insurance Law; Real Estate Law. **Email:** maurile@aol.com

**MARK D. ESTLE,** born Urbana, Illinois, November 20, 1955; admitted to bar, 1981, Texas; 1988, California. *Education:* Texas A & M University (B.A., 1978); Baylor University School of Law (J.D., 1981). Phi Alpha Delta. *Member:* San Diego County Bar Association; State Bar of Texas; State Bar of California. **PRACTICE AREAS:** Business Litigation; Real Estate; Creditor Rights Law; Business; Real Estate Litigation.

---

## CHRISTOPHER J. WALT

2223 AVENIDA DE LA PLAYA, SUITE 100
**LA JOLLA, CALIFORNIA 92037**
Telephone: 619-459-5940
Fax: 619-459-7210

*General Business Law, Real Estate Law, Corporate Law, Securities Law, Mergers and Acquisitions Law.*

**CHRISTOPHER J. WALT,** born Los Angeles, California, September 1, 1950; admitted to bar, 1979, California. *Education:* Stanford University (B.A., with honors, 1973; M.A., 1973); University of California at Berkeley (J.D., 1979). Phi Beta Kappa. Member, Moot Court Board. Associate Editor, California Law Review, 1977-1979. Consultant, California State Assembly, 1973-1976. **PRACTICE AREAS:** General Business Law; Real Estate; Corporate Law; Securities Law; Mergers and Acquisitions Law.

---

## GYORKOS & FENTON

*A LAW CORPORATION*

*Established in 1973*

LAKE FOREST PLAZA
23072 LAKE CENTER DRIVE
SUITE 104
**LAKE FOREST, CALIFORNIA 92630**
Telephone: 714-837-7750
Fax: 714-837-6242

*General Civil and Trial Practice. Insurance, Business, Corporate and Family Law. Environmental and Toxic Substance Law.*

**FRED C. FENTON** (1908-1987).

**JOHN W. GYORKOS,** born River Rouge, Michigan, May 6, 1943; admitted to bar, 1973, California. *Education:* Orange Coast College (A.A., 1967); Western States University (B.S., 1969; J.D., 1973). *Member:* Orange County, West Orange County (Chairman, Bench and Bar Committee, 1979-1985) and American Bar Associations; State Bar of California. **PRACTICE AREAS:** Business and Tort Litigation.

---

**DAVID L. RUKSTALIS,** born South Gate, California, March 5, 1956; admitted to bar, 1995, California. *Education:* National University (B.B.A., summa cum laude, 1983); Loyola Marymount University School of Law (J.D., 1987). Contracts Manager, British Petroleum, 1988-1991. *Member:*

*(This Listing Continued)*

---

Orange County Bar Association; State Bar of California. **PRACTICE AREAS:** Contracts; Business Law; Family Law; Environmental Law; Toxic Substances Law; General Litigation.

**CLAYTON B. HUNTINGTON,** born Los Angeles, September 7, 1966; admitted to bar, 1995, California. *Education:* University of California at Irvine (B.S., 1990); Western State University at Irvine (J.D., 1994). Recipient: Excellence in Research Award; American Jurisprudence Award in Bankruptcy. Author: "Wrongful Termination: The Rising Cost of Employee Litigation to Small Business, Mainstreet Business & Venture," April, 1995. *Member:* State Bar of California. **PRACTICE AREAS:** Labor Law; Tort Litigation; Business and Tax Litigation; Family Law; General Litigation.

REPRESENTATIVE CLIENTS: United States Fidelity and Guaranty Co.; American Fidelity Fire Insurance Co.; Central National Insurance Co.; Central States Health & Life Company of Omaha; Fremont Indemnity Co.; Republic National Life Insurance; Bently Labs; Holland Automation, Inc.; Equitable Mortgage Insurance Company, Inc.

---

## ROUP, LOOMIS & JOHNSON LLP

SUITE 310, 23101 LAKE CENTER DRIVE
**LAKE FOREST, CALIFORNIA 92630-6819**
Telephone: 714-472-2377

*Real Estate, Civil Litigation and Bankruptcy.*

**RONALD D. ROUP,** born Beaver Falls, Pennsylvania, October 8, 1948; admitted to bar, 1980, California and U.S. District Court, Central, Northern, Eastern and Southern Districts of California. *Education:* West Virginia University (B.S.A.E., 1970); Western State University (J.D., 1980). *Member:* Orange County Bar Association; The State Bar of California (Member, Real Estate Section); Orange County Bankruptcy Forum; Community Associations Institute.

**TARY C. LOOMIS-THERRIEN,** born Maryland, February 26, 1961; admitted to bar, 1988, California. *Education:* California State University at Fullerton (B.A., 1985); Western State University at Fullerton (J.D., 1988). Delta Theta Phi. Instructor, Community Associations Institute, 1994-1995. *Member:* Orange County Bar Association (Member: Business and Litigation Sections); State Bar of California; Community Associations Institute.

**MICHAEL W. JOHNSON,** born Whittier, California, January 16, 1965; admitted to bar, 1990, California and U.S. District Court, Southern District of California; 1991, U.S. District Court, Central District of California; 1993, U.S. District Court, Northern and Eastern Districts of California. *Education:* St. Mary's College of California (B.S., 1987); University of San Diego (J.D., 1990). *Member:* Orange County Bar Association (Real Estate Section); California State Bar; Orange County Bankruptcy Forum; Orange County Escrow Association; California Land Title Association.

---

**KELLY A. BEALL,** born Austin, Texas, October 30, 1964; admitted to bar, 1992, California and U.S. District Court, Central District of California; 1994, U.S. District Court, Northern, Southern and Central Districts of California. *Education:* University of California at Santa Barbara (B.A., 1988); McGeorge School of Law, University of the Pacific (J.D., 1992). Phi Delta Phi. *Member:* State Bar of California.

---

## BRIGHAM & GAUSTAD

**LAKEPORT, CALIFORNIA**

(See Ukiah)

*Business, Real Property and General Civil Litigation, Family Law, Will Contest and Probate.*

---

## RAWLES, HINKLE, CARTER, BEHNKE & OGLESBY

**LAKEPORT, CALIFORNIA**

(See Ukiah)

*General Civil, Trial and Appellate Practice. Corporation, Real Property, Business, Probate, Negligence, Family, Criminal, Federal and State Taxation, Agricultural, Timber and Logging, Water Rights, Environmental, Zoning and Land Use Law.*

## JOSEPHINE A. FITZPATRICK

*Established in 1979*

4909 LAKEWOOD BOULEVARD, SUITE 303
**LAKEWOOD, CALIFORNIA 90712**
*Telephone: 310-630-1616*
*FAX: 310-360-2026*

*Family, Adoption and Probate Law.*

**JOSEPHINE A. FITZPATRICK,** born May 11, 1942; admitted to bar, 1979, California. *Education:* Long Beach City College (A.A., 1976); Western State University (J.D., 1979). Instructor, Family Law, California State University at Long Beach, 1985-1990. Member: State Bar Custody and Visitation Committee, 1986—; Board of Directors, Lakewood-Weingart YMCA, 1980—. Member: American Academy of Family Mediators, 1993—; Academy of Family Mediators, 1993—. *Member:* Long Beach (Member, Family Law Section, 1980—), Los Angeles County (Member, Family Law Section, 1980—) and American (Member, Family Law Section, 1980—) Bar Associations; State Bar of California (Member: Family Law Section, 1980—; Child Custody Committee); Long Beach Women Lawyers Association (Member, 1979—; President, 1984-1985); Christian Legal Society. (Certified Specialist, Family Law, The State Bar of California Board of Legal Specialization).

## CLARENCE BENDER

*Established in 1978*

9001 GROSSMONT BOULEVARD
**LA MESA, CALIFORNIA 91941-4031**
*Telephone: 619-463-5500*
*FAX: 619-463-0701*
*Email: kucal57@aol.com*

*General Civil Trial Practice in both State and Federal Courts. Aviation Law, business Law, Workers Compensation, Personal Injury, Probate, and Family Law.*

**CLARENCE BENDER,** born Russell, Kansas, March 1, 1932; admitted to bar, 1964, Kansas and U.S. District Court, District of Kansas; 1971, California; 1973, U.S. District Court, Southern District of California; 1977, U.S. Court of Appeals, Ninth Circuit. *Education:* University of Kansas (B.S., 1957; J.D., 1964). Delta Tau Delta; Phi Delta Phi. President, Student Bar Association, University of Kansas. City Attorney, Goodland, Kansas, 1965-1966. Member, Aircraft Owners and Pilots Association Prepaid Legal Services Panel. *Member:* Foothills (President, 1976), San Diego County (Member: Family, Business, Probate Law, Workers' Compensation and Aviation Law Sections; Client Relations Committee, 1977-1988) and Kansas (Inactive) Bar Associations; State Bar of California; Lawyer-Pilot Bar Association. [U.S. Army, 1953-1955]

## PATRICK F. O'CONNOR

WELLS FARGO BANK BUILDING
5464 GROSSMONT CENTER DRIVE, THIRD FLOOR
**LA MESA, CALIFORNIA 91942**
*Telephone: 619-463-4284*
*Facsimile: 619-464-6471*

*Employment Law, Serious Personal Injury, Business Litigation.*

**PATRICK F. O'CONNOR,** born Seymour, Indiana, March 4, 1947; admitted to bar, 1973, California. *Education:* DePauw University (B.A., 1969); Georgetown University (J.D., 1973). Deputy District Attorney, County of San Diego, 1974-1978. Assistant City Attorney, City of El Cajon, 1984-1992. Assistant City Attorney, City of Poway, 1984-1986. Board of Directors, San Diego Mediation Center, 1991-1992. *Member:* Foothills (Member, Board of Directors, 1985-1993; President, 1991) and San Diego County (Board of Directors, 1990-1992) Bar Associations; The State Bar of California; The Association of Trial Lawyers of America; California Trial Lawyers Association; Consumer Attorneys of San Diego (Board of Directors, 1989-1990). *PRACTICE AREAS:* Employment Law-Discrimination; Serious Personal Injury; Business Litigation.

CAA402B

## DAVID EDWARD AMBILL

936 WEST AVENUE J-4, SUITE 203
**LANCASTER, CALIFORNIA 93534-4246**
*Telephone: 805-945-8733*
*Fax: 805-723-0160*
*Email: daveambill@aol.com*

*Real Estate.*

**DAVID EDWARD AMBILL,** born Torrance, California, December 22, 1948; admitted to bar, 1981, California and U.S. District Court, Southern District of California; 1982, U.S. District Court, Central District of California; 1988, U.S. District Court, Eastern District of California. *Education:* University of California at Santa Barbara (B.A., with honors, 1970); Western State University College of Law (J.D., with high honors, 1980). *Member:* Antelope Valley Bar Association (President, 1994); State Bar of California (Member, Real Property Section); California Association of Realtors (Member, Legal Affairs Forum). *PRACTICE AREAS:* Real Property; Residential; Brokers and Agents; Commercial Leasing; Partnerships and Joint Ventures; Creditors Rights.

REPRESENTATIVE CLIENTS: Palmdale Association of Realtors; Great Western Bank; Fannie Mae; Freddie Mac; Hartwig Realty; Antelope Valley Country Club; Equity Management Services; Credit Bureau of Lancaster and Palmdale.

## COSGROVE, MICHELIZZI, SCHWABACHER, WARD & BIANCHI

*A PROFESSIONAL CORPORATION*

*Established in 1962*

767 WEST LANCASTER BOULEVARD
**LANCASTER, CALIFORNIA 93534-3135**
*Telephone: 805-948-5021*
*Telecopier: 805-948-5395*

*General Civil and Trial Practice. Probate, Estate Planning, Commercial, Business Law, Personal Injury, Workers Compensation, Real Estate, Family Law and Adoptions.*

**PHILIP M. SCHWABACHER** (1913-1993).

**LEONARD A. COSGROVE,** born San Diego, California, August 2, 1924; admitted to bar, 1952, California and U.S. District Court, Northern and Southern Districts of California. *Education:* San Diego State University (A.B., 1948); Loyola Law School (J.D. 1952). United States Magistrate Judge, 1970-1994. *Member:* Antelope Valley Bar Association (President, 1959); State Bar of California. [with U.S. Army, 1943-1946]. *PRACTICE AREAS:* Probate Law; Estate Planning Law; Living Trusts.

**FRANK G. MICHELIZZI,** born Rockford, Illinois, September 13, 1929; admitted to bar, 1954, California and U.S. District Court, Southern District of California. *Education:* Wright College (A.A., 1949); DePaul University (LL.B., 1952). Chairman of Board, 1967-1968 and Secretary of Board, 1963-1966, Antelope Valley Hospital District. *Member:* Antelope Valley Bar Association (President, 1969); State Bar of California; The Association of Trial Lawyers of America; California Trial Lawyers Association; Los Angeles Trial Lawyers Association; American Hospital Attorneys Association; California District Hospital Attorneys Association. *PRACTICE AREAS:* Personal Injury Law; Hospital Law.

**THOMAS J. WARD,** born Chicago, Illinois, February 22, 1942; admitted to bar, 1968, California; 1974, U.S. District Court, Central and Eastern Districts of California. *Education:* University of San Francisco (B.A., 1964); University of California at Los Angeles (J.D., 1967). City Attorney, City of Lancaster, California, 1978-1987. Attorney, Antelope Valley Transit Authority, 1992—. *Member:* Antelope Valley (President, 1974) and American Bar Associations; State Bar of California. *PRACTICE AREAS:* Municipal Law; Real Property Law; Business Law.

**DAVID W. BIANCHI,** born Amsterdam, New York, June 12, 1950; admitted to bar, 1979, California; 1981, U.S. District Court, Central and Eastern Districts of California. *Education:* Florida State University (B.S., 1972); San Fernando Valley College of Law (J.D., 1979). Instructor, Business Law, Antelope Valley College, 1983—. Deputy City Attorney, City of Lancaster, 1984-1987. Listed in Who's Who in American Law, 1994-1995. Judge Pro Tem, Los Angeles County Superior and Municipal Court. *Member:* Antelope Valley Bar Association (President, 1988; Chairman, Fee Arbitration Committee, 1994—); State Bar of California. (Certified Specialist,

*(This Listing Continued)*

Family Law, The State Bar of California Board of Legal Specialization). **PRACTICE AREAS:** Family Law; Adoptions; Estate Planning Law; Probate Law.

**DAVID T. COLLINS,** born Cheyenne, Wyoming, August 16, 1956; admitted to bar, 1983, California. *Education:* California State University at Northridge (B.A., 1978); University of Idaho (J.D., 1982). Member, Board of Editors, University of Idaho Law Review, 1982-1983. *Member:* Antelope Valley Bar Association (President, 1993); State Bar of California. **PRACTICE AREAS:** Worker's Compensation; Personal Injury.

---

**JAMES LILLICRAP,** born Newport, Vermont, October 26, 1962; admitted to bar, 1990, California. *Education:* University of Vermont (B.A., 1985); Whittier College School of Law (J.D., 1990). Judge Pro-Tem, Los Angeles Superior Court. *Member:* Antelope Valley Bar Association (Vice-President, 1995); State Bar of California. **PRACTICE AREAS:** Family Law.

**KEVIN L. VON TUNGELN,** born Farmington, New Mexico, October 30, 1964; admitted to bar, 1991, District of Columbia; 1992, California and U.S. District Court, Central and Eastern Districts of California. *Education:* New Mexico State University (B.S.E.E., 1987); University of New Mexico (J.D., 1990). Member, University of New Mexico Law Review, 1989-1990. *Member:* Antelope Valley Bar Association; State Bar of California; District of Columbia Bar. **PRACTICE AREAS:** Business Law.

REPRESENTATIVE CLIENTS: Antelope Valley Hospital Medical Center; Antelope Valley Health Ventures; Letcher Mint; Wickes Corp.; Weston Builders Supply Company, Inc.; Ridgetop Ranch Properties, Inc.; Desert Moving & Storage, Inc.; Lancaster Old Town Site; Antelope Valley Transportation Agency; Lancaster Auto-Mart, Inc.; U.A.W., California School Employees Assn.

## GILLON, LEPORE, MENEFEE & BAIRD

*Established in 1979*

*43825 NORTH 10TH STREET WEST*
*P.O. BOX 4379*
**LANCASTER, CALIFORNIA 93539**
Telephone: 805-948-1618
Facsimile: 805-948-4989
Email: avlaw@qnet.com

*Personal Injury, General Civil and Trial Practice. Probate and Real Estate Law. Insurance, Corporation, Commercial and Estate Planning Law.*

### MEMBERS OF FIRM

**ROBERT GILLON,** born Montreal, Quebec, February 3, 1946; admitted to bar, 1979, California. *Education:* University of California at Los Angeles (B.A., 1969); Whittier College (J.D., 1973). *Member:* State Bar of California; American Bar Association. **PRACTICE AREAS:** Real Estate; Representing Creditors in Bankruptcy, Condemnation; General Civil Practice. *Email:* avlaw@qnet.com

**ROBERT T. LEPORE,** born Camden, New Jersey, May 9, 1951; admitted to bar, 1981, California, U.S. District Court, Central, Eastern, Northern and Southern Districts of California and U.S. Court of Appeals, Ninth Circuit. *Education:* St. Joseph's College (B.S., 1973); Southwestern University (J.D., 1980). *Member:* Antelope Valley, Los Angeles County and American Bar Associations; State Bar of California; California Trial Lawyers Association; The Association of Trial Lawyers of America. **PRACTICE AREAS:** Personal Injury. *Email:* avlaw@qnet.com

**TERRY R. MENEFEE,** born Champaign, Illinois, July 11, 1943; admitted to bar, 1977, California; 1979, District of Columbia; 1986, Hawaii. *Education:* San Francisco State College (B.A., 1970); McGeorge School of Law, University of the Pacific (J.D., 1976); Georgetown University Law Center (LL.M., 1978). Phi Delta Phi. Recipient, The McGeorge School of Law Faculty Award for Outstanding Student Achievement, 1976. Best Memorial (Brief), McGeorge International Law Moot Court Competition, 1975. Member: Traynor Honor Society; International Law Moot Court Honors Board, 1975-1976; Jessup International Law Moot Court Competition Team, 1975. Author: "Admiralty Jurisdiction in Brokers Action for Premiums," Journal of Maritime Law and Commerce, Vol. 10, No. 4, July, 1979. *Member:* The State Bar of California; Hawaii State Bar Association (Associate); The District of Columbia Bar; American Bar Association; Defense Research Institute; Society of Chartered Property and Casualty Underwriters. **PRACTICE AREAS:** Insurance Law; Real Property Litigation; Personal Injury; Product Liability; Defamation; Wrongful Termination; Civil Appeals. *Email:* avlaw@qnet.com

*(This Listing Continued)*

**TERENCE A. BAIRD,** born Albuquerque, New Mexico, April 3, 1950; admitted to bar, 1983, California and U.S. District Court, Central and Eastern Districts of California. *Education:* Brigham Young University (B.S., 1978); University of the Pacific, McGeorge School of Law (J.D., 1983). Adjunct Assistant Professor, Business and Real Estate Law, Antelope Valley College, Lancaster, California, 1984—. *Member:* Antelope Valley (President, 1991), Los Angeles County and American Bar Associations. **LANGUAGES:** German. **PRACTICE AREAS:** Business Law; Real Estate Law; Construction Law; Municipal Law; Land Use Law; Probate; Estate Planning. *Email:* avlaw@qnet.com

REFERENCES: Antelope Valley Bank; California Republic Bank; First Interstate Bank; Wells Fargo Bank.

## RANDOLPH A. ROGERS

*857 WEST LANCASTER BOULEVARD*
**LANCASTER, CALIFORNIA 93534**
Telephone: 805-945-4404
Facsimile: 805-723-7089

*Civil Litigation and Trial Practice with emphasis on Business Partnership, Real Estate, Construction, Consumer, Civil Rights, Wrongful Death and Insurance Law.*

**RANDOLPH A. ROGERS,** born Gowanda, New York, November 3, 1954; admitted to bar, 1978, Georgia; 1979, Florida and U.S. District Court, Northern District of Georgia; 1980, U.S. Court of Appeals, Fifth Circuit; 1981, U.S. District Court, Middle District of Florida and U.S. Court of Appeals, Eleventh Circuit; 1982, U.S. District Court, Southern District of Florida; 1984, California; 1988, U.S. District Court, Eastern and Central Districts of California. *Education:* University of Colorado at Boulder; University of Florida (B.A., 1975; J.D., cum laude, 1978). Phi Kappa Phi. Member, 1976-1978 and Articles Editor, 1977, University of Florida Law Review. *Member:* Antelope Valley (Bar President, 1995; Vice-President, 1993-1994; President Elect, 1994—) and Los Angeles County Bar Associations; State Bar of Georgia; The Florida Bar; State Bar of California.

## MARK E. THOMPSON

*A PROFESSIONAL CORPORATION*

*Established in 1981*

*857 WEST LANCASTER BOULEVARD*
**LANCASTER, CALIFORNIA 93534**
Telephone: 805-945-5868
Fax: 805-723-7089

*Probate, Wills, Trusts, Estate Planning, Conservatorships, and Elder Law.*

FIRM PROFILE: *Mark E. Thompson limits his practice to probate, wills, trusts, estate planning, conservatorships, and elder law. The firm employs an assistant attorney and a full time experienced support staff and serves an area comprised of North Los Angeles, East Kern and North San Bernardino Counties. Mark E. Thompson is a Certified Specialist in Probate, Estate Planning and Trust Law, and participates in advanced continuing legal education at the highest levels, local bar activities and numerous civic affairs. This firm is a contractor for Valley Caregiver Resource Center, serving families and caregivers of brain-impaired adults.*

**MARK E. THOMPSON,** born San Fernando Valley, California, August 7, 1947; admitted to bar, 1977, California and U.S. District Court, Central District of California; 1978, U.S. District Court, Eastern District of California. *Education:* Antelope Valley College (A.A., 1971); University of San Fernando Valley - La Verne College of Law (J.D., cum laude, 1976). Member, Board of Directors, 1983-1991 and Chapter President, 1988-1990, Antelope Valley Chapter of American Red Cross. Member, Professional Advisory Council, 1989—, Member, Board of Directors, 1990— and Treasurer, 1992-1996, Gift Foundation of Antelope Valley Hospital. Board of Directors and President, 1996-1997, Rotary Club of Lancaster. Associate Member, A.V. Chapter of Life Underwriters. Member, Board of Directors, Lancaster Chamber of Commerce. *Member:* Antelope Valley (Member, Board of Directors, 1978-1982; President, 1982; Chairman, Lawyer Referral Service, 1982-1983), Los Angeles County and American Bar Associations; State Bar of California (Member: Estate Planning, Trust and Probate Law Section; Past Member, Subcommittee on Estate Planning); National Academy of Elder Law Attorneys. (Certified Specialist, Probate, Estate Planning and Trust Law, The State Bar of California Board of Legal Specialization).

*(This Listing Continued)*

**MARK E. THOMPSON** A PROFESSIONAL CORPORATION, Lancaster—Continued

*PRACTICE AREAS:* Probate; Wills; Trust Law; Estate Planning; Elder Law; Conservatorships.

---

**CYNTHIA R. POLLOCK,** born Jefferson City, Missouri, January 16, 1961; admitted to bar, 1991, California. *Education:* Central Missouri State University (B.S., 1984); Loyola University Law School (J.D., 1990). Member, Board of Directors, Antelope Valley Chapter of American Red Cross. *Member:* Los Angeles County (Member, Estate Planning, Trust and Probate Section and Past Member of Senior Outreach Committee) and American (Member, Real Property and Probate Sections) Bar Associations; State Bar of California; National Academy of Elder Law Attorneys. *PRACTICE AREAS:* Probate; Wills; Trust Law; Estate Planning; Elder Law; Conservatorships.

REFERENCE: Antelope Valley Bank, Lancaster, California.

---

## *MYRON S. GREENBERG*
### A PROFESSIONAL CORPORATION
#### 700 LARKSPUR LANDING CIRCLE, SUITE 205
#### **LARKSPUR, CALIFORNIA 94939**
Telephone: 415-461-5844
Fax: 415-461-5873
Email: taxlaw700@aol.com

*Federal and State Taxation Law. Probate and Estate Planning.*

**MYRON S. GREENBERG,** born Los Angeles, California, October 17, 1945; admitted to bar, 1971, California. *Education:* University of California at Los Angeles (B.S., 1967); University of California at Los Angeles School of Law (J.D., 1970). Phi Delta Phi. Articles Editor, U.C.L.A. Law Review, 1969-1970. Certified Public Accountant, California, 1971. Author: "Guaranteed Loans and Direct Loans: Equal Treatment Under The Tax Law," 16 U.C.L.A. Law Review 421, 1969; "Cattle and Taxes Under the 1969 Tax Reform Act," 17 U.C.L.A. Law Review 1251, 1970; "The Widow's Election: A Sale or Disposition of Community Property?" 24 Title Insurance Tax and Probate Forum 59, 1972. Co-Author: Attorney's Guide to California Professional Corporations, 3rd Edition, 1977. Professorial Lecturer, Golden Gate University Graduate School of Taxation, 1978-1982. Instructor, Estate Planning, University of California, Berkeley Extension, 1989—. Member, Planning Committee, CEB Institute on Advanced Tax Planning For Real Property Transactions, 1981—. Member, Advisory Committee For Curriculum Development, Certificate in Personal Financial Planning, University of California, Berkeley, 1990—. *Member:* Marin County (Member, Board of Directors, 1994—; Treasurer, 1996—) and American (Member: Taxation Section: Committee on Depreciation and Amortization, 1973-1974; Committee on Employee Benefits, 1976-1979) Bar Associations; State Bar of California. (Certified Specialist, Taxation Law, The State Bar of California Board of Legal Specialization).

---

## *JACKSON, LEWIS, SCHNITZLER & KRUPMAN*
#### 700 LARKSPUR LANDING CIRCLE
#### SUITE 167
#### **LARKSPUR, CALIFORNIA 94939-1754**
Telephone: 415-461-5899
Facsimile: 415-461-5898

Other offices located in: Atlanta, Georgia; Boston, Massachusetts; Chicago, Illinois; Dallas, Texas; Greenville, South Carolina; Hartford, Connecticut; Los Angeles, California; Miami, Florida; Morristown, New Jersey; New York, New York; Orlando, Florida; Pittsburgh, Pennsylvania; San Francisco, California; Stamford, Connecticut; Washington, D.C.; White Plains, New York; Woodbury, New York.

*Labor Relations, Employment Discrimination, Wrongful Discharge and Other Employment-Related Litigation, Employee Benefits and Pension Law, Wage and Hour, OSHA, Immigration Law, Public Sector and State Labor Relations Law, On Behalf of Management.*

*(This Listing Continued)*

---

### MEMBERS OF FIRM

**JOHN V. NORDLUND,** born Brooklyn, New York, August 20, 1948; admitted to bar, 1979, New York; 1983, California. *Education:* Ithaca College (B.A., 1974); New York Law School (J.D., magna cum laude, 1979). Member, New York Law School Law Review, 1978-1979. Co-author: "The Antipathies of Organized Labor," Labor Law Journal, May, 1982. *Member:* Bar Association of San Francisco; State Bar of California; New York State and American Bar Associations.

### ASSOCIATES

**TYLER A. BROWN,** born Oakland, California, January 2, 1960; admitted to bar, 1985, California and U.S. District Court, Northern District of California. *Education:* University of Notre Dame (B.A., 1982); Hastings College of the Law, University of California (J.D., cum laude, 1985).

**WILLIAM T. HEARNE,** born Tulsa, Oklahoma, June 18, 1969; admitted to bar, 1994, Minnesota (Not admitted in California). *Education:* University of Tulsa (B.A., 1991); Tulane University Law School (J.D., cum laude, 1994). Phi Beta Kappa.

---

## *KATZ, BIERER & BRADY*
### A PROFESSIONAL CORPORATION
Established in 1971
#### 101 LARKSPUR LANDING CIRCLE, SUITE 223
#### **LARKSPUR, CALIFORNIA 94939**
Telephone: 415-925-1600
FAX: 415-925-0940

*General Civil Trial Practice. Negligence, Product Liability, Legal and Medical Malpractice, Business Litigation, Wrongful Termination, Insurance Bad Faith, and Will Contests.*

**RICHARD L. KATZ,** born Bronx, New York, November 4, 1938; admitted to bar, 1969, California. *Education:* University of Florida (B.S.B.A., 1960); Golden Gate College (J.D., summa cum laude, 1968). Beta Alpha Psi. Certified Public Accountant: Florida, 1962; California, 1964. Professional Lecturer in Trial Practice, 1970-1971 and Professional Negligence, 1971-1974, Golden Gate University School of Law. Member, Panel of Arbitrators, American Arbitration Association. *Member:* Marron County and American Bar Associations; Bar Association of San Francisco (Chairman, 1973; Trial Lawyers Section); State Bar of California; San Francisco Trial Lawyers Association (Member, Board of Directors, 1971-1977; Parliamentarian, 1978); Consumer Attorneys of California; The Association of Trial Lawyers of America. (Member of Consumer Attorneys of California, with recognized experience in the fields of General Personal Injury and Professional Negligence).

**JOEL D. BIERER,** born Brooklyn, New York, March 14, 1949; admitted to bar, 1981, California. *Education:* State University of New York at Cortland (B.A., Pol. Sc., 1970; M.S., 1974); University of San Francisco (J.D., 1980). Recipient, Best Brief Award, Moot Court Competition. Instructor, Legal Research and Writing, University of San Francisco, 1980. *Member:* Bar Association of San Francisco; Marin County Bar Association; State Bar of California; The Association of Trial Lawyers of America; Consumer Attorneys of California; Marin County Trial Lawyers Association.

**STEVEN J. BRADY,** born Chicago, Illinois, March 29, 1960; admitted to bar, 1984, California. *Education:* Northwestern University (B.A. in Philosophy, with honors, 1981); Loyola University School of Law (J.D., 1984). Volunteer: National Eagle Scout Association; National Veteran's Foundation (formerly Vietnam Veteran's Association). *Member:* Bar Association of San Francisco; Marin County Bar Association; State Bar of California; San Francisco Trial Lawyers Association; Marin County Trial Lawyers Association; The Association of Trial Lawyers of America; Consumer Attorneys of California (Member, Board of Governors).

### OF COUNSEL

**ALVIN J. SCHIFRIN,** born July 31, 1940; admitted to bar, 1965, New York; 1971, California. *Education:* Columbia University (A.B., 1961); University of Pennsylvania (J.D., 1964). Adjunct Professor, Trial Practice, University of San Francisco, 1983-1986. *Member:* Marin County Bar Association; Bar Association of San Francisco; State Bar of California; New York State Bar Association.

## WEINBERG, HOFFMAN & CASEY

A Partnership including a Professional Corporation
*Established in 1992*
**900 LARKSPUR LANDING CIRCLE, SUITE 155**
**LARKSPUR, CALIFORNIA 94939**
Telephone: 415-461-9666
Fax: 415-461-9681

*General Civil and Trial Practice. Insurance Defense, Plaintiff Trial Practice. Medical Legal Practice including Medical Malpractice.*

**IVAN WEINBERG,** born Los Angeles, California, March 29, 1943; admitted to bar, 1968, California. *Education:* Stanford University (A.B., 1964); University of California at Los Angeles (J.D., 1967); University of California at Berkeley, Health and Medical Sciences Department (M.S., 1984). Phi Delta Phi. Assistant Public Defender, Alameda County, 1972-1974. Member: Panel of Arbitrators, Marin County and American Arbitration Association. Judge Pro Tem and Settlement Judge, Marin County Superior Court. *Member:* Bar Association of San Francisco; Marin County and American Bar Associations; State Bar of California; San Francisco Trial Lawyers Association; The American Society of Law and Medicine, Inc.; Association of Defense Counsel; American College of Legal Medicine. **PRACTICE AREAS:** Medical-Legal; Medical Malpractice; Personal Injury; Insurance Defense; Medical Board Actions Defense.

**JOSEPH HOFFMAN,** born Easton, Maryland, February 12, 1954; admitted to bar, 1984, California. *Education:* Babson College (B.S., 1975); American Graduate School of International Management (M.I.M., 1977); University of San Francisco (J.D., 1983). *Member:* Bar Association of San Francisco; State Bar of California; California Trial Lawyers Association; Association of Defense Counsel of Northern California. **LANGUAGES:** German, Spanish and Portuguese. **PRACTICE AREAS:** Insurance Defense; Products Liability; Medical Malpractice Defense; Litigation; Personal Injury.

**A. MICHAEL CASEY,** born San Francisco, California, July 7, 1942; admitted to bar, 1967, California. *Education:* University of California at Berkeley (B.A., 1964); Hastings College of Law, University of California (J.D., 1967). Member: San Francisco Superior Court Arbitration Panel; Marin County Superior Court Arbitration Panel; Charter Member of Marin County Civil Action Early Disposition Program. **PRACTICE AREAS:** Insurance Defense; Litigation; Personal Injury.

*OF COUNSEL*

**MARK ROPERS,** born Auburn, California, August 8, 1938; admitted to bar, 1973, California and U.S. District Court, Northern District of California; 1975, U.S. District Court, Central and Southern Districts of California. *Education:* Menlo College (A.A., 1960); Stanford University (B.A., 1964); Hastings College of the Law, University of California (J.D., 1972). Judge Pro Tem, 1990—. *Member:* Marin County Bar Association; State Bar of California; Association of Defense Counsel. [With USMC, 1956-1958]. **PRACTICE AREAS:** Insurance Defense Law; Litigation.

---

## CULLEY * GOODWIN

**2162 FIFTH STREET**
**LIVERMORE, CALIFORNIA 94550**
Telephone: 510-443-0822

*Business Law and Family Law.*

**PATRICIA CULLEY,** born Portland, Oregon, September 27, 1942; admitted to bar, 1978, California. *Education:* California State University at Hayward (B.A., 1975); Western State University (J.D., 1978). Recipient: Corpus Juris Secundum; American Jurisprudence Conflicts of Law. *Member:* Eastern Alameda County Bar Association, President (1989).

**ROBERT E. GOODWIN,** born Palo Alto, California, April 28, 1943; admitted to bar, 1967, California. *Education:* University of San Francisco (B.S., 1964; J.D., 1967). Managing Editor, University of San Francisco Law Review, 1966-1967. Member, McAuliffe Law Honor Society. Examiner, California State Bar Examinations, 1968. President, Livimore Chapter of Commerce, 1996—. *Member:* Eastern Alameda County and American Bar Associations; State Bar of California. **PRACTICE AREAS:** Business Law; Real Estate Law; Civil Litigation.

---

## RIFKIND & FUERCH

*A PROFESSIONAL CORPORATION*
**LIVERMORE, CALIFORNIA**
(See Hayward)

*General Civil and Trial Practice. Insurance, Insurance Defense, Real Estate, Transportation Law, Fire Insurance, Products Liability, Automobile, Professional Liability, Landslide and Subsidence, Construction, Business, Municipal and Education Law.*

---

## VARNI, FRASER, HARTWELL & RODGERS

*Established in 1971*
**2109 FOURTH STREET**
**P.O. BOX 511**
**LIVERMORE, CALIFORNIA 94550-0511**
Telephone: 510-447-1222
Fax: 510-443-7831

Hayward, California Office: 22771 Main Street, P.O. Box 570, 94543. Telephone: 510-886-5000. Fax: 510-538-8797.

*Estate Planning, Trusts, Probate, Real Estate Development and Land Use, Business Transactions, Environmental and Eminent Domain, State and Federal Court Business Litigation.*

**FIRM PROFILE:** *The partnership was formed in 1971 and since its inception has maintained a small, influential, Northern California practice with emphasis on estate planning, trusts, probate, business, land use, condemnation, agriculture and administrative agencies. The firm has established and maintained a quality practice by providing personalized and prompt service at sensible rates. The firm represents large clients in business transaction and well-situated, influential public agencies. The firm is recognized as an authority in the areas of estate planning and probate, land use, transit, solid and liquid waste disposal and inverse condemnation. Public agencies and landowners have been represented in trials and appeals in a significant number of reported land use and condemnation cases.*

*MEMBERS OF FIRM*

**ANTHONY B. VARNI,** born Hayward, California, February 15, 1939; admitted to bar, 1964, California and U.S District Court, Northern and Eastern Districts of California; U.S. Court of Appeals, Ninth Circuit. *Education:* University of Santa Clara (B.A., 1961); Santa Clara Law School (LL.B., 1963). Editor, Santa Clara Law Review. Lecturer, Current Real Estate Issues, California Continuing Education of the Bar, 1971-1993. *Member:* Alameda County (Former Member, Board of Directors) and American (Member, Real Property and Probate Section) Bar Associations; State Bar of California (Member, Agri-Business Section; Former Member, Eminent Domain Section); Lawyers Panel for California Association of Sanitary Agencies. **PRACTICE AREAS:** Real Estate; Land Use; Eminent Domain; Inverse Condemnation.

**KEITH S. FRASER,** born Livermore, California, May 31, 1936; admitted to bar, 1961, California. *Education:* Stanford University (B.S., 1958); Hastings College of the Law, University of California (LL.B., 1961). Phi Delta Phi. Deputy District Attorney, Alameda County, 1961-1963. Member, 1983-1984 and Chairman, 1985, State Bar Commission on Judicial Nominees Evaluation; Member, 1987, 1988 and Chairman, 1989, Review Committee. *Member:* Alameda County, Eastern Alameda County and American Bar Associations; State Bar of California (Member, Real Property and Probate Sections); Tri-Valley Business and Estate Planning Council. **PRACTICE AREAS:** Real Estate; Land Use; Probate.

**ELIZABETH E. TRUTNER,** born Oakland, California, March 3, 1958; admitted to bar, 1989, California. *Education:* University of California at Davis (B.A., 1980); University of San Diego (International Law Program, Paris, 1986); San Francisco Law School (J.D., with honors, 1989). Recipient: American Jurisprudence Award in Corporations and Remedies; West Publishing Award. *Member:* Alameda County and Eastern Alameda County Bar Associations; State Bar of California (Member, Probate and Estate Planning Section); Tri-Valley Business and Estate Planning Council. (Resident) (Certified Specialist, Estate Planning, Trust and Probate Law, The State Bar of California Board of Legal Specialization). **LANGUAGES:** French.

**JOHN S. HARTWELL** (1924-1993).

**LIONEL A. RODGERS** (1942-1989).

*(This Listing Continued)*

*VARNI, FRASER, HARTWELL & RODGERS,*
Livermore—Continued

### ASSOCIATE

**CHRISTINE KASUN MORUZA,** born Camp Pendleton, California, October 12, 1951; admitted to bar, 1976, California. *Education:* University of California at Santa Barbara (B.A., summa cum laude, 1973); University of California, Hastings College of Law (J.D., 1976). Assistant District Attorney, City and County, San Francisco, 1977-1983. *Member:* Eastern Alameda County Bar Association; State Bar of California. **PRACTICE AREAS:** Business Litigation.

REPRESENTATIVE CLIENTS: Agricultural Clients: Hunt-Wesson, Inc. (Tomato Products); Glad-A-Way Gardens, Inc. (Flower Production); Mohr-Fry Ranches (Wine); Raspo Farms (Apricots and Nuts); Dittmer Trust (Grazing); Lamb-Weston, Inc. (Potatoes); Devor Nurseries, Inc. (Plants); Garms Estate (Soft Shell Wheat). Development Clients: Kaufman & Broad of Northern California (Housing); Golden State Development (Housing); Britannia Developments, Inc. (R & D Construction); Balch Enterprises, Inc. (Industrial Construction); The O'Brien Group (Housing). Government Agencies: City of Newark (Special Counsel); Castro Valley Sanitary District; Livermore-Amador Valley Transit Authority. Title Insurance Companies: First American Title Guaranty Co.; Chicago Title Co. Insurance Companies: Travelers Insurance; The Ohio Casualty Insurance Co.; CIGNA Insurance; Fireman's Fund; Scottsdale Insurance Co. Telecommunications: Channel 14. Business: Mack Truck, Inc.; Nokia-Kinex Corp.; Livermore Stockmen's Rodeo Assn.; Livermore-Pleasanton Rod and Gun Club; Callaghan Mortuary; Groth Bros.; Chevrolet-Oldsmobile-Geo.

(For complete Biographical Data on all Personnel, see Professional Biographies at Hayward, California)

## ADAMS, HORSTMANN & EDWARDS

*PROFESSIONAL CORPORATION*

Established in 1968

*25 NORTH SCHOOL STREET*
**LODI, CALIFORNIA 95240**
*Telephone: 209-333-1414; 478-5356*
*Fax: 209-333-0104*

*General Civil Practice, Agricultural Water Rights, Probate, Estate Planning, Corporate, Construction, Commercial and Real Estate, Bankruptcy, Personal Injury, and Criminal Law in all Courts.*

**STEWART C. ADAMS, JR.,** born Stockton, California, August 27, 1937; admitted to bar, 1963, California. *Education:* Stanford University (B.A., 1959); Boalt Hall School of Law, University of California (LL.B., 1962). Phi Delta Phi. *Member:* San Joaquin County and American Bar Associations; State Bar of California. **PRACTICE AREAS:** Estate Planning Law; Probate Law; Living Trust Law; Real Estate Law; Water Rights Law.

**HERBERT E. HORSTMANN,** born Oakland, California, March 19, 1938; admitted to bar, 1963, California. *Education:* Claremont Mens College (B.A., 1959); Boalt Hall School of Law, University of California (LL.B., 1962). Phi Delta Phi. *Member:* San Joaquin County Bar Association; State Bar of California. **PRACTICE AREAS:** Business Law; Construction; Family Law; Corporate Law; Litigation.

**ROY D. EDWARDS,** born Mesa, Arizona, July 24, 1940; admitted to bar, 1973, California; 1982, U.S. Claims Court. *Education:* California State University at Sacramento (B.A., 1964); McGeorge College of the Law, University of the Pacific (J.D., 1973). *Member:* San Joaquin County Bar Association; State Bar of California. **PRACTICE AREAS:** Accident and Personal Injury; Bankruptcy, Criminal Law; Family Law.

REPRESENTATIVE CLIENTS: Farmers & Merchants Bank; North San Joaquin Water Conservation District; Muller Supply Co.; Valley Material Transport; Ledbetter Farms; Vino Farms; Lodi Drug Company; Herman Ehlers & Sons, Inc.; D & R Orthopedic Laboratories, Inc.

## DRISCOLL & ASSOCIATES

*801 SOUTH HAM LANE, SUITE H*
**LODI, CALIFORNIA 95242**
*Telephone: 209-334-1935*
*Fax: 209-334-0178*

*Civil Litigation and Transaction Practice in Business, Real Estate, Government, Estate Planning and Family Law.*

**THOMAS J. DRISCOLL, JR.,** born Glendale, California, May 22, 1955; admitted to bar, 1980, California, U.S. Court of Appeals, Ninth Circuit and U.S. District Court, Eastern and Central Districts of California. *Education:* Claremont Men's College (B.A., summa cum laude, 1977); University of California at Davis (J.D., 1980). Outstanding Advocate, Neumiller Honors Moot Court Competition, 1979. Vice President and Board of Directors Member, 1987-1991, United Way. Judicial Arbitrator in Superior and Municipal Courts, San Joaquin County. *Member:* State Bar of California; San Joaquin County (Member, Client Relations and Mandatory Fee Arbitration Committee, 1984-1988; Chairman, 1986-1987) and American Bar Associations;. **PRACTICE AREAS:** Business; Real Estate; Construction Litigation; Education; Government.

**SUZANNE B. BROWN,** born Huntington, New York, 1970; admitted to bar, 1995, California, U.S. District Court, Eastern and Central Districts of California and U.S. Court of Appeals, Ninth Circuit. *Education:* University of California at Davis (B.A., with honors, 1992; J.D., 1995). Phi Delta Phi. Pi Sigma Alpha. Member, Prytanean Honor Society. Member Golden Key National Honor Society. *Member:* San Joaquin County and American Bar Associations; State Bar of California. **PRACTICE AREAS:** Family Law; Education; Government.

REPRESENTATIVE CLIENTS: Overhead Door Corp.; Robertson-Ceco Corp.; Ceco Building Systems; Star Building Systems; General Aluminum Corporation; California Teachers Assoc.; Stockton Teachers Assoc.; San Joaquin County Coordinating Council; Sturman, Jacobson, Arbios Properties, Inc.; McCarty Construction; Manteca-Lathrop Fire Protection District; K&K Tire and Wheel, Inc.; St. Anne's Parish; St. Anne's Endowment.

## MULLEN, SULLIVAN & NEWTON

Established in 1940

*1111 WEST TOKAY STREET*
*P.O. BOX 560*
**LODI, CALIFORNIA 95241-0560**
*Telephone: 209-334-5144*
*Fax: 209-333-1034*

*Civil Practice with emphasis in Business, Real Estate, Construction, Agriculture, Commercial, Bankruptcy, Education, Municipal/Government, Estate Planning and Probate, Torts and Family Law. Trials and Appeals in all State and Federal Courts.*

**FIRM PROFILE:** *The firm was established originally as Litts & Perovich in 1940, and with the addition of Robert H. Mullen, became Litts, Mullen & Perovich in 1942. Subsequent additions, and the retirement of three partners, brought the firm to its present complement of 5 (five) attorneys. In 1984, Mullen, Sullivan & Newton was established as the permanent name. As the largest firm in Northern San Joaquin County, its clientele extends through the several mid-central valley counties, from Sacramento to Merced, and from Tuolumne to Contra Costa.*

### MEMBERS OF FIRM

**THOMAS J. NEWTON,** born Millen, Georgia, July 24, 1942; admitted to bar, 1973, California, U.S. Court of Appeals, Ninth Circuit and U.S. District Court, Eastern District of California. *Education:* Emory University (B.A., 1964); University of the Pacific (J.D., with distinction, 1973). Phi Alpha Delta. Taynor Society. Recipient, American Jurisprudence Award. President, District Chamber of Commerce, Lodi, 1977-1978. *Member:* San Joaquin County and American Bar Associations; State Bar of California; California Trial Lawyers Association. [USAF: Outstanding Young Officer, 36TAS, 1966; Distinguished Flying Cross, 1968]. **PRACTICE AREAS:** Personal Injury Law; Litigation.

**CRAIG RASMUSSEN,** born Sacramento, California, September 13, 1953; admitted to bar, 1978, California, U.S. Court of Appeals, Ninth Circuit and U.S. District Court, Northern and Eastern Districts of California. *Education:* University of California at Berkeley (A.B., magna cum laude, 1975); University of the Pacific (J.D., 1978). City of Lodi Planning Commission, 1984—. *Member:* San Joaquin County and American Bar Associations; State Bar of California; San Francisco Trial Lawyers Association; California Trial Lawyers Association. **PRACTICE AREAS:** Real Estate Law; Business Litigation.

**STEPHEN C. SNIDER,** born Modesto, California, January 15, 1956; admitted to bar, 1981, California, U.S. Court of Appeals, Ninth Circuit and U.S. District Court, Northern and Eastern Districts of California, U.S. Claims Court. *Education:* University of the Pacific (B.A., 1978; J.D., 1981; LL.M., 1983). Phi Delta Phi. Traynor Honor Society, 1981. *Member:* San Joaquin County Bar Association; State Bar of California; California Trial

*(This Listing Continued)*

Lawyers Association; Defense Research Institute. *PRACTICE AREAS:* General Practice.

**JAMES V. DEMERA, III,** born Fresno, California, March 13, 1954; admitted to bar, 1989, California, U.S. Court of Appeals, Ninth Circuit and U.S. District Court, Northern and Eastern Districts of California. *Education:* California State University (B.S., 1984); University of the Pacific, Mc George School of Law (J.D., 1988). Phi Delta Phi. *Member:* San Joaquin County Bar Association; State Bar of California. *PRACTICE AREAS:* General Law; Civil Law; Business Law; Litigation; Construction Law; Environmental; Agricultural Law.

**JENNIFER DAVENA JORDAN,** born Whittier, California, March 20, 1954; admitted to bar, 1981, New York; 1982, California; U.S Court of Appeals, Ninth Circuit and U.S. District Court, Northern and Southern Districts of California. *Education:* San Diego State University (B.A., with honors and distinction, 1978); Fordham University; California Western School of Law (J.D., 1981). *Member:* San Joaquin County Bar Association (Member, Program Committee; Chairperson, Mandatory Continuing Legal Education Committee, 1994); State Bar of California. *PRACTICE AREAS:* Civil Practice; Insurance Defense; Construction Defects; Litigation.

### OF COUNSEL

**ROBERT H. MULLEN,** born Redwood City, California, August 8, 1914; admitted to bar, 1938, California, U.S. Court of Appeals, Ninth Circuit and U.S. District Court, Northern and Eastern Districts of California. *Education:* University of California at Berkeley (J.C., 1934); Hastings College of Law, San Francisco (J.D., 1938). Phi Alpha Delta. School Board Member, Lodi U.H.S., 1946-1956. City Attorney, Lodi, 1952-1978. *Member:* San Joaquin County Bar Association (Chairman, Probate Policy Committee, 1984—; Superior Court Judicial Liaison, 1985—); State Bar of California. *PRACTICE AREAS:* Estate Planning Law; Probate Law; Real Estate Law; Railroad Law.

**CORNELIUS M. (BUD) SULLIVAN, JR.,** born Lodi, California, October 2, 1933; admitted to bar, 1961, California, U.S. Court of Appeals, Ninth Circuit and U.S. District Court, Northern and Eastern Districts of California. *Education:* University of the Pacific (A.B., with honors, 1955); University of California at Berkeley (LL.B., J.D., 1960). Phi Delta Phi. Member, Moot Court Board, 1959-1960. Assistant City Attorney, Lodi, 1964-1979. President, Board of Trustees, Lodi Public Library, 1969—. Recipient, San Joaquin County Distinguished Service to Education Award, 1977. *Member:* San Joaquin County (President, 1970) and American Bar Associations; State Bar of California. *PRACTICE AREAS:* Real Estate Development Law; Education Law; Public Law.

REPRESENTATIVE CLIENTS: California Teachers Association; City of Lodi; J.R. Simplot Co.; Lodi Association of Realtors; All State Packers; California Association of Realtors Legal Referral Panel; Pacoast Chemical Co.; Simplot Land and Cattle Co.; Cal-Agri Financial Interchange, Inc.; California Concrete Pipe Co.; Foster Lumber Co.; Ripon Farm Service Inc.; S.S.I. Food Services, Inc.; Plummer Pontiac; Cadillac G.M. Truck; Canandaigua Wine Co., Inc.; Guild Wineries & Distilleries, Inc.; Pizza World Supreme, Inc.; Ameron International.

## NEUMILLER & BEARDSLEE

*A PROFESSIONAL CORPORATION*

**LODI, CALIFORNIA**

(See Stockton)

*General Civil Practice and Litigation in all State and Federal Courts. Real Property, Condominium, Land Use, Natural Resources, Environmental, Water and Water Rights, Mining, Agricultural, Corporation, Partnership, Business Planning, Securities, Creditor's Rights in Bankruptcy, Taxation, Employee Benefits, Insurance, Administrative, Healthy Care, Governmental and Legislative, Trusts, Estate Planning, Probate and Municipal Law.*

## GROSSMAN, COX & JOHNSON

Established in 1941

121 NORTH H STREET

P.O. BOX 458

**LOMPOC, CALIFORNIA 93438**

Telephone: 805-736-8555

FAX: 805-736-6647

*General Practice. Probate, Estate Planning, Real Estate, Corporation, Banking, Business, Personal Injury, Family Law and Criminal Law.*

**LAWRENCE C. GROSSMAN** (1914-1983).

*(This Listing Continued)*

**TERRILL F. COX,** born North Platte, Nebraska, October 26, 1931; admitted to bar, 1958, California. *Education:* University of California at Los Angeles (B.A., 1953; J.D., 1958). Phi Delta Phi. Lompoc Justice Court Judge, 1966-1976. Lompoc Municipal Court Judge, 1966-1978. *Member:* Santa Maria-Lompoc Bar Association (President, 1970); State Bar of California. *PRACTICE AREAS:* Probate; Estate Planning; Personal Injury; Criminal; Banking Law; Family Law.

**LESLIE E. JOHNSON, II,** born Lompoc, California, June 1, 1952; admitted to bar, 1981, California and U.S. District Court, Central District of California. *Education:* Harvard University (A.B., cum laude, 1974); University of Santa Clara (J.D.; M.B.A., 1980). *Member:* Santa Maria-Lompoc Bar Association; State Bar of California. *PRACTICE AREAS:* Probate; Estate Planning; Corporation; Business; Real Estate Law; Family Law.

REPRESENTATIVE CLIENTS: First Valley Bank; Santa Barbara County Housing Authority; Lompoc Hospital District; Lompoc Oil Developing Co.; Vandenberg Community Service District; Lompoc Warehouse Corp.; Robert M. Witt Ranch; Valley Medical Group of Lompoc, Inc.

## LAW OFFICES OF JAMES H. ACKERMAN

SUITE 1440

ONE WORLD TRADE CENTER

**LONG BEACH, CALIFORNIA 90831-1440**

Telephone: 310-436-9911

Cable Address: "Jimack"

Telecopier: 310-436-1897

*Admiralty, General Maritime, Personal Injury and International Law. Trial Practice.*

**JAMES H. ACKERMAN,** born Los Angeles, California, March 21, 1917; admitted to bar, 1949, California and U.S. Court of Appeals, Ninth Circuit; 1958, U.S. Supreme Court. *Education:* University of Southern California (B.A., 1940; J.D., 1948); United States Merchant Marine Academy (B.S., in Marine Transportation, 1944). Phi Alpha Delta. Member, Board of Councillors, University of Southern California Law Center, 1976—. *Member:* Long Beach (Chairman, Ethics Committee, 1964-1967; Chairman, Committee on Lawyer Referral, 1966-1967; Chairman, Judicial Liaison Committee, 1973-1975; President, 1980-1981); Los Angeles County (Trustee, 1975-1978; Member, Judicial Evaluation Committee, 1976-1977) and American Bar Associations; The State Bar of California (Member, Legislative Committee, 1970-1973; Consultant, California Pleasure Boating Law, 1963 Cal. C.E.B.); California Trial Lawyers Association (Founding Member; Vice President, 1963-1966; Member: Legislative Committee, 1965-1967; Board of Governors, 1966-1973; Associate Editor, Law Journal, 1964-1974; Chairman, Admiralty Section, 1966-1973); Western Trial Lawyers Association (Member, Board of Governors, 1965-1970; Chairman, Annual Convention, 1968); The Association of Trial Lawyers of America ; Member, Committee on Insurance, 1964-1965; Chairman, California State Seminars Committee, 1964-1965; Member, Board of Governors, 1964-1971; Associate Editor in Admiralty, Law Journal, 1962-1972; Member, Committees on: Ethics, 1964-1967; Appellate Amicus Curiae, 1966-1968; Chairman, National Convention, Los Angeles, 1966; Chairman, Labor Liaison Committee, 1966-1968; Trustee, Roscoe Pound Foundation, 1985—; Chairman, International Law Committee, 1971-1974; Chairman, Delegation, World Peace Through Law Conference, Abidjan, Ivory Coast, 1973; Member, President's Advisory Committee, 1971-1973, 1986-1987; Chairman, Investment Committee, 1971-1975; Chairman, National Midwinter Convention, Acapulco, 1974; Chairman West Coast Admiralty Section, 1975-1985); Maritime Law Association of the United States. Fellow, International Academy of Trial Lawyers (Member, Board of Directors, 1982-1991; International Relations, Secretary, 1987-1989; President, 1991-1992; President of the Foundation 1993—); American Inns of Court (Master of the Bench).

REFERENCES: Farmers and Merchants Bank (Long Beach Main Office); Sumitomo Bank of California (Long Beach Main Office).

CALIFORNIA—LONG BEACH                                                MARTINDALE-HUBBELL LAW DIRECTORY 1997

## BAKER & HOSTETLER
*Established in 1916*
300 OCEANGATE, SUITE 620
**LONG BEACH, CALIFORNIA 90802-6807**
Telephone: 310-432-2827
FAX: 310-432-6698

*In Cleveland, Ohio:* 3200 National City Center, 1900 East Ninth Street. Telephone: 216-621-0200.

*In Columbus, Ohio:* Capitol Square, Suite 2100, 65 East State Street. Telephone: 614-228-1541.

*In Denver, Colorado:* 303 East 17th Avenue, Suite 1100. Telephone: 303-861-0600.

*In Houston, Texas:* 1000 Louisiana, Suite 2000. Telephone: 713-236-0020.

*In Los Angeles, California:* 600 Wilshire Boulevard. Telephone: 213-624-2400.

*In Orlando, Florida:* SunBank Center, Suite 2300, 200 South Orange Avenue. Telephone: 407-649-4000.

*In Washington, D. C.:* Washington Square, Suite 1100, 1050 Connecticut Avenue, N. W. Telephone: 202-861-1500.

*In College Park, Maryland:* 9658 Baltimore Boulevard, Suite 206. Telephone: 301-441-2781.

*In Alexandria, Virginia:* 437 North Lee Street. Telephone: 703-549-1294.

*In San Francisco, California:* One Sansome Street, Suite 2000. Telephone: 415-951-4705.

*General Practice.*

### MEMBERS OF FIRM IN LONG BEACH, CALIFORNIA

**SHELDON A. GEBB,** born Long Beach, California, January 12, 1935; admitted to bar, 1964, California. *Education:* University of California, Berkeley (A.B., 1957); Boalt Hall School of Law, University of California (LL.B., 1963). Chairman, Board of Trustees, Southwestern University School of Law, 1985-1991. *Member:* The State Bar of California; American Bar Association; Maritime Law Association of the United States. (Managing Partner, Los Angeles and Long Beach, California and Houston, Texas Offices). *PRACTICE AREAS:* Admiralty; Litigation; Insurance.

### PARTNERS

**ROBERT E. COPPOLA,** born New York, N.Y., April 11, 1939; admitted to bar, 1966, District of Columbia; 1968, New York; 1970, California. *Education:* Columbia University (A.B., 1960); Georgetown University (LL.B., 1965). *Member:* The State Bar of California; Maritime Law Association of the United States. (Partner in Charge). *PRACTICE AREAS:* Admiralty; Litigation; Insurance.

**DAVID A. KETTEL,** born New York, N.Y., May 5, 1960; admitted to bar, 1986, California and U.S. District Court, Central, Northern and Southern Districts of California. *Education:* University of California at Davis (B.A., cum laude, 1982); Tulane University (J.D., 1985). Phi Alpha Delta. Maritime Scholar. *Member:* Los Angeles County, Long Beach and American Bar Associations; State Bar of California; Association of Southern California Defense Counsel; Los Angeles Barristers; Propellor Club. *PRACTICE AREAS:* Admiralty; Oil and Gas; General Litigation.

**GEORGE T. MOORADIAN,** born Detroit, Michigan, May 24, 1954; admitted to bar, 1979, Michigan and District of Columbia; 1983, California; 1984, U.S. Tax Court; 1986, U.S. District Court, Central District of California; 1989, U.S. Court of Appeals, Ninth Circuit. *Education:* University of Michigan (B.A., with high distinction, 1976; J.D., 1978); New York University (LL.M., in Taxation, 1980). Certified Public Accountant, Michigan, 1982. Author: "Characterization of Contingent Payments on Shared Appreciation Mortgages," 57 Journal of Taxation 20, July, 1982. *Member:* State Bar of California; State Bar of Michigan; District of Columbia Bar; American Bar Association (Member, Taxation Section); American Institute of Certified Public Accountants; Michigan Association of Certified Public Accountants. *PRACTICE AREAS:* Tax Law; Estate Planning Law.

**CHRISTINA L. OWEN,** born Oakland, California, September 22, 1946; admitted to bar, 1972, California. *Education:* University of California, Berkeley (B.S., 1968); University of Southern California (J.D., 1971). *Member:* State Bar of California; Maritime Law Association of the United States. *PRACTICE AREAS:* Admiralty; Litigation; Insurance Coverage.

### ASSOCIATES

**KENNETH E. JOHNSON,** born Staten Island, New York, November 23, 1952; admitted to bar, 1979, New York; 1981, California. *Education:* St. Lawrence University (B.S., 1974); Brooklyn Law School (J.D., 1978). *Member:* The State Bar of California; Maritime Law Association of the United States; Foreign Trade Association. [LCDR, USCGR]. *PRACTICE AREAS:* Admiralty; Customs and Trade Law.

**GEORGE M. JONES,** born Youngstown, Ohio, April 5, 1956; admitted to bar, 1992, California, U.S. District Court, Northern, Eastern, Southern and Central Districts of California and U.S. Court of Appeals, Ninth Circuit. *Education:* University of Hawaii (B.A., 1980); University of San Francisco (J.D., 1992). Editor-in-Chief, University of San Francisco Maritime Law Journal, 1991-1992. *Member:* Long Beach Bar Association; State Bar of California; Maritime Law Association of the United States; Propellor Club of the United States. *PRACTICE AREAS:* Civil Litigation.

**STEVEN Y. OTERA,** born Los Angeles, California, September 19, 1965; admitted to bar, 1991, California; U.S. District Court, Northern, Eastern, Central and Southern Districts of California and U.S. Court of Appeals, Ninth Circuit. *Education:* University of California at Los Angeles (B.A., 1987); Loyola University of Los Angeles (J.D., 1991). Note & Comment Editor, Loyola University of Los Angeles International and Comparative Law Journal, 1990-1991. Author, Comment: "International Extradition and the Medellin Cocaine Cartel: Surgical Removal of Colombian Cocaine Traffickers for Trial in the United States," 13 Loyola University of Los Angeles International and Comp. L.J., 1991. *Member:* State Bar of California. *PRACTICE AREAS:* Admiralty Personal Injury Defense; Insurance Coverage and Defense; General Business Litigation.

**ROBERT M. WHITE, JR.,** born Memphis, Tennessee, March 31, 1953; admitted to bar, 1990, California; U.S. District Court, Central, Northern, Eastern and Southern Districts of California and U.S. Court of Appeals, Ninth Circuit; 1992, U.S. Court of Appeals, Seventh Circuit. *Education:* University of Tennessee at Knoxville (B.S.B.A., 1980); University of Manitoba, Faculty of Law (LL.B., 1987). *Member:* State Bar of California. *PRACTICE AREAS:* Admiralty; Marine Construction; Personal Injury Defense.

### OF COUNSEL

**HERBERT W. KALMBACH,** born Port Huron, Michigan, October 19, 1921; admitted to bar, 1952, California. *Education:* University of Southern California (B.S., 1949; J.D., 1951). Phi Delta Phi. *Member:* Los Angeles County, Orange County and American Bar Associations; The State Bar of California. [Lt. (jg), U.S.N.R., 1942-1947]

## BLUMBERG LAW CORPORATION
*Established in 1954*
100 OCEANGATE
SUITE 1100
**LONG BEACH, CALIFORNIA 90802**
Telephone: 310-437-0403
Fax: 310-432-0107

*Mammoth Lakes Office:* 1196 Majestic Pines Drive. P.O. Box 368, Mammoth Lakes, California, 93546. Telephone: 619-934-2907. Fax: 619-934-5499.

*General Civil Trial and Appellate Practice. Professional Liability and Mediation.*

**MYRON BLUMBERG,** born February 2, 1919; admitted to bar, 1954, California. *Education:* University of Minnesota (B.B.A., 1940); University of Southern California (J.D., 1954). Mediator, Dispute Resolution Center of California. Legal Counsel, Mammoth Lakes Fire Protection District. *Member:* State Bar of California; Mono County Bar Association. *PRACTICE AREAS:* Municipal Law; Dispute Resolution and Mediation.

**JOHN P. BLUMBERG,** born December 6, 1949; admitted to bar, 1976, California. *Education:* California State University, Long Beach (B.A., 1972); Western State University (J.D., 1976). Arbitrator and Mediator. *Member:* Long Beach, Los Angeles County and Orange County Bar Associations; State Bar of California (Chair, Committee on Rules and Procedures of Court, 1993); Consumer Attorneys Association of California and Los Angeles; Long Beach Bar Association Trial Advocacy Institute (Director); National Board of Trial Advocacy, American Board of Trial Advocates (Diplomate). (Certified as a Civil Trial Advocate by the NAtional Board of Trial Advocacy). *PRACTICE AREAS:* Legal and Medical Malpractice; Personal Injury; Business Litigation; Mediation.

**AVE BUCHWALD,** born March 6, 1951; admitted to bar, 1976, California. *Education:* University of California at Los Angeles (B.S., 1973); State University of New York at Buffalo (J.D., 1976). *Member:* Long Beach Bar

*(This Listing Continued)*                                                                     *(This Listing Continued)*

Association; State Bar of California. *PRACTICE AREAS:* Real Estate; Civil Litigation; Appeals.

REPRESENTATIVE CLIENTS: Mammoth Lakes Fire Protection District.
REFERENCES: Furnished Upon Request.

## LAW OFFICES OF
## BRIAN K. BRANDMEYER

*Established in 1995*

ONE WORLD TRADE CENTER, SUITE 1600
**LONG BEACH, CALIFORNIA 90831-1600**
Telephone: 310-499-2131
Fax: 310-499-2132

*Family Law, Personal Injury.*

**BRIAN K. BRANDMEYER,** born Spokane, Washington, July 6, 1937; admitted to bar, 1963, California. *Education:* Loyola University at Los Angeles (B.A., 1959; J.D., 1962). Phi Delta Phi. *Member:* Los Angeles County, Southeast and American Bar Associations; State Bar of California (Member, Family Law Section). *PRACTICE AREAS:* Family Law; Personal Injury.

## LISA E. BRANDON

200 OCEANGATE, SUITE 1580
**LONG BEACH, CALIFORNIA 90802**
Telephone: 310-901-9800
FAX: 310-983-9383

*Family Practice emphasizing Dissolution, Marital Contracts, Custody Issues, Wills, Trusts and Related Civil Litigation.*

**LISA E. BRANDON,** born Whittier, California, July 29, 1960; admitted to bar, 1987, California and U.S. Court of Appeals, Ninth Circuit; 1991, Oklahoma. *Education:* California State University at Fullerton (B.A., 1983); Southwestern University School of Law (J.D., 1987). Recipient, American Jurisprudence Award in Civil Procedure. Consultant, "Practice under the California Family Law Act," CEB, 1992. *Member:* Beverly Hills (Member, Family Law Section), Long Beach (Member, Family Law Section), Los Angeles County (Member, Family Law Section) and American (Member, Family Law Section) Bar Associations; State Bar of California; California Women Lawyers Association (Governor, 1990-1992; Treasurer, 1991-1992; President-Elect, 1992-1993; President, 1993-1994); CEB Family Law Advisory Committee. (Certified Specialist, Family Law, The State Bar of California, Board of Legal Specialization). *PRACTICE AREAS:* Family Law; Civil Litigation.

## FRANKLIN J. BRUMMETT

111 W. OCEAN BOULEVARD, SUITE 1300
P.O. BOX 2210
**LONG BEACH, CALIFORNIA 90802**
Telephone: 310-437-2926
Fax: 310-590-7909

*Civil Litigation and Business Matters.*

**FRANKLIN J. BRUMMETT,** born Wahpeton, North Dakota, October 6, 1934; admitted to bar, 1964, California and U.S. District Court, Central District of California; 1980, U.S. Supreme Court. *Education:* University of Portland (B.S. Gen.Eng., 1956); University of Southern California (LL.B., 1963). Order of the Coif. Member, Editorial Board, Southern California Law Review, 1962-1963. Author: "Outline for Use in the Preparatory Course: California Real Estate Salesman License," "Outline for Use in the Preparatory Course: California Real Estate Broker License,"; "New Stature for Land Sale Contracts," Long Beach Bar Bulletin, December, 1974. Adjunct Associate Professor, California State University at Long Beach, Legal Assistant Program, 1989-1993. Instructor, Long Beach Trial Advocacy Institute, Los Angeles Superior Court, 1990. *Member:* Long Beach (Member, Real Property Section), Los Angeles County (Member, Executive Committee, Real Property Section, 1974-1975) and American (Member, Litigation Section) Bar Associations; State Bar of California (Member, Litigation Section); American Inns of Court.

## BURNS, AMMIRATO, PALUMBO, MILAM & BARONIAN

*A PROFESSIONAL LAW CORPORATION*

*Established in 1989*

ONE WORLD TRADE CENTER, SUITE 1200
**LONG BEACH, CALIFORNIA 90831-1200**
Telephone: 310-436-8338; 714-952-1047
Fax: 310-432-6049

*Pasadena, California Office:* 65 North Raymond Avenue, 2nd Floor.
Telephone: 818-796-5053; 213-258-8282. Fax: 818-792-3078.

*General Civil and Trial Practice in all Courts. Insurance Defense, Products Liability, Toxic Torts, Construction Litigation, Medical Malpractice, Personal Injury, Tort, Subrogation and Wrongful Termination.*

(For Complete Biographical Data on all Personnel see Professional Biographies at Pasadena)

## STEVAN R. CALVILLO

200 OCEANGATE, SUITE 430
**LONG BEACH, CALIFORNIA 90802**
Telephone: 310-983-6624
Facsimile: 310-983-6628

*Business, Real Estate Litigation and Shareholder Litigation.*

**STEVAN R. CALVILLO,** born Los Angeles, California, December 3, 1947; admitted to bar, 1975, California, U.S. District Court, Central and Southern Districts of California and U.S. Court of Appeals, Ninth Circuit; U.S. Supreme Court. *Education:* San Diego State University (B.S., 1971); Western State University College of Law (J.D., 1975). Voluntary Member, Settlement Conference (Judge Pro Temps). *Member:* Long Beach, Los Angeles County and American (Member, Section on Litigation) Bar Associations; State Bar of California; The Association of Trial Lawyers of America.

## CAMERON, MADDEN, PEARLSON, GALE & SELLARS

ONE WORLD TRADE CENTER SUITE 1600
**LONG BEACH, CALIFORNIA 90831-1600**
Telephone: 310-436-3888
Telecopier: 310-437-1967

*General Civil Trial and Appellate Practice, State and Federal Courts, Real Estate, Land Use, Environmental, Administrative, Corporate, Partnership, Taxation, Estate Planning, Trust and Employment Law.*

FIRM PROFILE: *Cameron, Madden, Pearlson, Gale & Sellars is based in Long Beach, California. The firm's practice encompasses a broad spectrum of the law with specific expertise in the areas listed below.*

*The environmental practice includes the purchasing, selling, leasing, and financing of real property.*

*The real estate practice includes land acquisition, development, financing, single and multi-phase commercial and residential subdivisions.*

*The litigation practice includes trial and appellate work in the prosecution and defense of a wide variety of complex cases.*

*The general business practice includes the formation and dissolution of corporations, partnerships and other business entities, reorganizations, lending transactions, secured transactions, sales and acquisitions of businesses and professional practices, and general contract matters.*

*The tax practice includes expertise in all local, state and federal tax matters.*

*The estate planning practice includes all aspects of estate planning and probate matters including the preparation of wills and trusts, estate and tax planning, and all related litigation.*

*The employment practice includes employment contracts, employee handbooks, personnel policies, taxation, wage and hour issues, discrimination and harassment issues, employment termination matters, and all related litigation.*

(This Listing Continued)

## CAMERON, MADDEN, PEARLSON, GALE & SELLARS,
Long Beach—Continued

### MEMBERS OF THE FIRM

**TIMOTHY C. CAMERON**, born Long Beach, California, December 18, 1943; admitted to bar, 1973, California; U.S. Court of Appeals, Ninth Circuit. *Education:* University of California, Berkeley (A.B., 1966); U.S. International University (J.D., 1973). *Member:* Long Beach and Los Angeles County Bar Associations; The State Bar of California.

**CHARLES M. GALE**, born St. Paul, Minnesota, May 23, 1955; admitted to bar, 1980, California; 1981, Arizona, U.S. District Court, District of Arizona and U.S. Court of Appeals, 9th Circuit; 1986, U.S. District Court, Central, Eastern and Southern Districts of California. *Education:* Indiana University (A.B, with honors, 1977); Stanford University (J.D., 1980). Phi Beta Kappa. Law Clerk to the Honorable Winston E. Arnow, Chief Judge, U.S. District Court, Northern District of Florida, 1980-1981. Author: "Supplementing the Administrative Record in CEQA Cases," 9 California Real Property Journal, No. 4, Fall, 1991; "Ten Common Environmental Myths When Selling, Buying or Leasing Real Property," Los Angeles Business Journal, Oct. 5, 1992; "Feasible and Future Mitigation Measures Under CEQA," 12 California Real Property Journal, No. 4, Fall, 1994. *Member:* Long Beach and Los Angeles County (Member, Real Property and Environmental Law Sections) Bar Associations; State Bar of Arizona; The State Bar of California; Inter-Pacific Bar Association; International Bar Association. *PRACTICE AREAS:* Environmental Law; Real Estate.

**PATRICK T. MADDEN**, born Long Beach, California, September 7, 1944; admitted to bar, 1972, California; U.S. Court of Appeals, Ninth Circuit and U.S. District Court, Central, Eastern, Northern and Southern Districts of California. *Education:* University of California, Los Angeles (A.B., 1967); University of Southern California (J.D., 1972). Law Clerk to Hon. Malcolm M. Lucas, U.S. District Court, Central District of California, 1972-1973. Commissioner, State Bar Legal Services Trust Fund, 1988-1992. *Member:* Long Beach and Los Angeles County Bar Associations; The State Bar of California (Member, Board of Governors, 1980-1981); California Young Lawyers Association (Member, Board of Directors, 1977-1981; President, 1979-1980).

**PAUL R. PEARLSON**, born Los Angeles, California, March 13, 1955; admitted to bar, 1980, California; U.S Court of Appeals, Ninth Circuit. *Education:* University of California, Berkeley (A.B. in Economics, magna cum laude, 1977); Stanford University (J.D., 1980). Phi Beta Kappa. *Member:* Long Beach and Los Angeles County Bar Associations; The State Bar of California. *PRACTICE AREAS:* Business Litigation.

**JAMES D. SELLARS**, born Ann Arbor, Michigan, September 1, 1952; admitted to bar, 1978, California and U.S. District Court, Central District of California; U.S. Tax Court. *Education:* California State University at Long Beach (B.S., 1975); Pepperdine University (J.D., 1978); New York University (LL.M. in Taxation, 1984). *Member:* Long Beach and Los Angeles County Bar Associations; The State Bar of California (Member: Tax Section; Business Law Section; Committee on: Partnerships and Unincorporated Associations, 1980-1983, 1986-1989; Non-Profit and Unincorporated Associations, 1990-1993). *PRACTICE AREAS:* Taxation; Estate Planning; Commercial Law; Corporate Law.

### ASSOCIATE

**LILLIAN D. SALINGER**, born Redwood City, California, September 30, 1967; admitted to bar, 1992, California; 1994, U.S. District Court, Central, Eastern, Northern and Southern Districts of California. *Education:* University of California, Los Angeles (B.A., magna cum laude, 1989); Boalt Hall School of Law, University of California at Berkeley (J.D., 1992). Phi Beta Kappa. Author: "Poverty Law: What Is It?", 12 Legal Reference Services Quarterly, No. 2/3 (1992). *Member:* Long Beach and Los Angeles County Bar Associations; The State Bar of California.

---

## GARY R. CARLIN
*A PROFESSIONAL CORPORATION*

Established in 1970

SUITE 918, 555 EAST OCEAN BOULEVARD
**LONG BEACH, CALIFORNIA 90802**
Telephone: 310-432-8933
Fax: 310-435-1656

*Civil Trials and Appeals. Wrongful Termination, Personal Injury, Business Litigation and Family Law.*

*(This Listing Continued)*

**GARY R. CARLIN**, born Los Angeles, California, October 16, 1942; admitted to bar, 1970, California, U.S. District Court, Central District of California and U.S. Court of Appeals, Ninth Circuit. *Education:* University of California at Los Angeles (A.B., 1964); Hastings College of Law, University of California (J.D., 1969). Judge Pro Tem: Municipal Court, Long Beach Judicial District, 1975-1976; Superior Court, County of Los Angeles, 1975-1977. Superior Court Arbitrator, County of Los Angeles, Personal Injury Panel, 1979-1993. Family Law Mediator, Los Angeles Superior Court Mandatory Mediation Program, County of Los Angeles, South District, 1980—. Referee: Hearing Department of the State Bar Court, 1984-1990 (Supervising Referee, Master Calendar, 1986-1990); Compensated Referee of the State Bar Court, 1986-1988; Review Department Referee, 1988-1989; Probation Monitor, 1984-1989. Member, National Panel of Arbitrators, American Arbitration Association. *Member:* Long Beach (Member, Arbitration Committee, 1980-1984), Los Angeles County and American Bar Associations; State Bar of California; The Association of Trial Lawyers of America; California Trial Lawyers Association; Los Angeles Trial Lawyers Association.

REPRESENTATIVE CLIENTS: Tee Cee Feed Co., Inc.; Parkford Petroleum, Inc.; Imperial Petroleum, Inc.; Moberly and Jones Construction Co., Inc.; Superior Transportation Services, Inc.; Gary M. Schmidt Construction Co.; Collection Control Bureau; InterNet; Newcastle Enterprises, Ltd.
REFERENCE: Bank of America.

---

## CAYER, KILSTOFTE & CRATON
*A PROFESSIONAL LAW CORPORATION*

Established in 1955

SUITE 700, 444 WEST OCEAN BOULEVARD
**LONG BEACH, CALIFORNIA 90802**
Telephone: 310-435-6008
Fax: 310-435-3704
Email: CKCCRC@AOL.COM

*General Business and Civil Trial Practice before all Federal and State Courts. Banking and Bank Litigation, Business Litigation, Corporations, Corporate Securities, Federal and State Taxation, Estate Planning, Probate, Real Property Sales and Financing, Equine Law and Syndication, Family Law, Personal Injury and Workers Compensation Law.*

**JOHN J. CAYER**, born Lynwood, California, August 29, 1928; admitted to bar, 1955, California and U.S. District Court, Southern District of California; 1973, U.S. Court of Appeals, Ninth Circuit and U.S. Supreme Court. *Education:* Compton College (A.B., 1950); Loyola Marymount University (J.D., 1954). Phi Alpha Delta. City Attorney, City of Lynwood, 1974-1976. *Member:* State Bar of California. *PRACTICE AREAS:* Banking; Corporation; Estate Planning; Probate; Equine and Securities Law.

**STEPHEN R. KILSTOFTE**, born Long Beach, California, June 17, 1951; admitted to bar, 1978, California, U.S. District Court, Central and Southern Districts of California and U.S. Court of Appeals, Ninth Circuit. *Education:* California State University at Long Beach (B.A., cum laude, 1974); Southwestern University (J.D., 1978). *Member:* State Bar of California; American Bar Association. *PRACTICE AREAS:* Business Litigation; Family; Personal Injury; Workers Compensation.

**CURT R. CRATON**, born New Orleans, Louisiana, October 30, 1954; admitted to bar, 1985, California, U.S. District Court, Central and Southern Districts of California, U.S. Court of Appeals, Ninth Circuit and U.S. Tax Court. *Education:* Harvey Mudd College (B.S., 1976); Loyola Marymount University (J.D., 1985). *Member:* State Bar of California. *PRACTICE AREAS:* Banking; Corporation; Tax; Estate Planning; Real Property Law.

---

**CORTLEN R. HAUGE**, born Faribault, Minnesota, May 15, 1945; admitted to bar, 1993, California and U.S. District Court, Central District of California; 1995, Minnesota. *Education:* Winona State University (B.A., 1986); Loyola Law School (J.D., 1993). *Member:* Los Angeles County, Long Beach and Minnesota State Bar Associations; State Bar of California. *PRACTICE AREAS:* Civil Litigation; Bankruptcy; Banking; General Business Law.

REPRESENTATIVE CLIENTS: First State Bank of Southern California; Culver National Bank; U.S. Amada Ltd.; Old English Rancho; Nowell Steel & Supply Co., Inc.; Standard Catering, Inc.; Custom Bilt Metals; Gateway Mattress Co., Inc.; Maness Industries, Inc.; Maness Environmental Services, Inc.; New Har-

*(This Listing Continued)*

vest Christian Fellowship; Industrial Printing Group; Lucky Installations, Inc.; Chanil Foundation; Palmco Corporation; Santa Fe Importers, Inc.; Transit Sales International; Mori Seiki Co., Ltd.; Mori Seiki U.S.A., Inc.; Yamazen, Inc.; Complete Coach Works; Commuter Bus Lines, Inc.

## CHURCHILL & BOSKOVICH

401 EAST OCEAN BOULEVARD, SUITE 507
**LONG BEACH, CALIFORNIA 90802**
Telephone: 310-437-1559
Telecopier: 310-495-4311

*Probate, Estate Planning and Trust Law.*

### MEMBERS OF FIRM

**CAROL A. CHURCHILL,** born Louisville, Kentucky, April 11, 1953; admitted to bar, 1983, California, U.S. District Court, Central District of California, U.S. Court of Appeals, Ninth Circuit and U.S. Supreme Court. *Education:* Mesa College; Colorado State University (B.S., 1975); University of West Los Angeles (J.D., 1983). *Member:* Long Beach and Los Angeles County Bar Associations; State Bar of California; Women Lawyers of Long Beach. (Certified Specialist, Probate, Estate Planning and Trust Law, State Bar of California Board of Legal Specialization). *PRACTICE AREAS:* Probate; Estate Planning; Trust Administration; Estate Taxation.

**VIOLET M. BOSKOVICH,** born San Pedro, California, March 8, 1953; admitted to bar, 1984, California; 1986, U.S. District Court, Central District of California and U.S. Court of Appeals, Ninth Circuit. *Education:* Los Angeles Harbor College (A.A., 1972); California State University at Long Beach; Northrop University (J.D., 1983). *Member:* Long Beach and Los Angeles County Bar Associations; State Bar of California; Women Lawyers of Long Beach. *PRACTICE AREAS:* Probate; Estate Planning; Trust Administration.

## LAURA E. CLAVERAN-LOPEZ

2703 EAST SEVENTH STREET
**LONG BEACH, CALIFORNIA 90804**
Telephone: 310-433-0004
Fax: 310-433-4640
Email: lawrac@aol.com

*Personal Injury, Immigration and Naturalization, Art Law.*

**LAURA E. CLAVERAN-LOPEZ,** born Mexico; admitted to bar, 1982, California. *Education:* University of California at Los Angeles (B.A., 1975); University of Southern California (J.D., 1979). *PRACTICE AREAS:* Personal Injury; Immigration and Naturalization; Art Law.

## STEPHEN E. COCKRIEL

333 WEST BROADWAY, SUITE 306
**LONG BEACH, CALIFORNIA 90802-4440**
Telephone: 310-901-1447
FAX: 310-437-3492

*Estate Planning, Probate, Real Estate and Business Law.*

**STEPHEN E. COCKRIEL,** born Long Beach, California, June 8, 1948; admitted to bar, 1973, California. *Education:* University of Southern California (B.S., 1970); Loyola University of Los Angeles (J.D., 1973). *Member:* Long Beach Bar Association; State Bar of California.

## LAW OFFICES OF JEROME S. COHEN

301 EAST OCEAN BOULEVARD
SUITE 540
**LONG BEACH, CALIFORNIA 90802-4828**
Telephone: 310-983-1160
Fax: 310-983-1870

*Bankruptcy, Business Reorganization, Commercial Collections, Judgment Enforcement, Insolvency, Creditors' Rights, Domestic and International Commercial Law.*

**JEROME S. COHEN,** born Wilmington, Delaware, July 1939; admitted to bar, 1971, Delaware; 1977, District of Columbia; 1978, Maryland; 1989, California. *Education:* Swarthmore College (B.A., 1961); University of Pennsylvania Law School (LL.B., 1964). Law Clerk to the Honorable Walter K. Stapleton, U.S. District Court, District of Delaware, 1971. Author: "Mechanics Lien Claim in Bankruptcy: Perfecting Made Easy", McGraw-

*(This Listing Continued)*

Hill Shepard's California Construction Law Reporter, March, 1994. Employed By: Delaware Department of Natural Resources and Environmental Control, 1971-1973; U.S. Nuclear Regulatory Commission 1973-1975; U.S. Department of Labor, 1975-1979; Seifman & Lechner, 1979-1980. Member, Rotary Club International. *Member:* Long Beach and Los Angeles County Bar Associations; Financial Lawyers Conference. *LANGUAGES:* French. *PRACTICE AREAS:* Bankruptcy; Civil Litigation.

## DANNER & CHONOLES, L.L.P.

100 OCEANGATE, SUITE 840
**LONG BEACH, CALIFORNIA 90802**
Telephone: 562-983-8980
Fax: 562-983-8986

*General Civil Trial and Appellate Practice in State and Federal Courts. Products Liability, Premises Liability, Wrongful Termination, Business Litigation.*

**MICHAEL J. DANNER,** born Cedar Rapids, Iowa, April 16, 1952; admitted to bar, 1977, California; 1979, U.S. District Court, Central District of California. *Education:* University of Iowa (BB.A., 1974); Southwestern University (J.D., 1977). *Member:* Long Beach and Los Angeles County Bar Associations; State Bar of California; Association of Southern California Defense Counsel. *LANGUAGES:* Spanish. *PRACTICE AREAS:* Products Liability; Premises Liability; Construction Litigation.

**STEPHEN J. CHONOLES,** born Louisville, Kentucky, April 17, 1955; admitted to bar, 1992, California and U.S. District Court, Central District of California. *Education:* Antioch College (B.A., 1978); University of Michigan (M.A., in Telecommunication Arts; M.A., in Asian Studies, Japan Specialization, 1983); Southwestern University School of Law (J.D., 1991). Recipient: Hopwood Writing Award; Leo Burnett Filmmaking Scholarship; Foreign Language and Area Studies (Japan) Fellowship. *Member:* Long Beach and Los Angeles Bar Associations; State Bar of California. *LANGUAGES:* Japanese. *PRACTICE AREAS:* Wrongful Termination; Business Litigation; Products Liability.

### ASSOCIATE

**JANET E. GLENNY,** born Monterey Park, California, April 3, 1958; admitted to bar, 1993, California. *Education:* California State University at Northridge (B.A., 1982); Southwestern University School of Law (J.D., 1992). *Member:* Beverly Hills and Los Angeles County Bar Associations; State Bar of California. *PRACTICE AREAS:* Products Liability; Landlord-Tenant Litigation.

REPRESENTATIVE CLIENTS: Montgomery KONE, Inc.; Shelby Williams Industries, Inc.; Woodhead Industries, Inc.; The Heil Co.; Color Tile, Inc.; Allianz Insurance Co. of Canada; Guardian Insurance Co. of Canada.

## VALERIE K. DeMARTINO

100 OCEANGATE, 12TH FLOOR
**LONG BEACH, CALIFORNIA 90802**
Telephone: 310-628-5577
Fax: 310-628-5578

*Corporate, Business Transactions, Probate, Conservatorships and Estate Planning, Commercial Law, Business and Probate Litigation.*

**VALERIE K. DEMARTINO,** born Johnstown, Pennsylvania, March 13, 1954; admitted to bar, 1984, California. *Education:* California State University at Los Angeles (B.A., 1976); University of West Los Angeles (J.D., 1984). *Member:* Long Beach and Los Angeles County Bar Associations; State Bar of California; Women Lawyers Association of Long Beach; American Inns of Court. *PRACTICE AREAS:* Business; Probate; Litigation.

## LAW OFFICE OF
## MICHAEL J. EMLING

555 EAST OCEAN BOULEVARD
SUITE 500
**LONG BEACH, CALIFORNIA 90802**
Telephone: 310-491-1400
Fax: 310-491-3400
Email: emling@aol.com

*Patent, Trademark, Copyright and Business Litigation.*

*(This Listing Continued)*

## LAW OFFICE OF MICHAEL J. EMLING, Long Beach—Continued

FIRM PROFILE: Mr. Emling began his career as a trial lawyer as a criminal prosecutor in San Diego, California. After entering private practice in Long Beach, he tried both criminal defense cases and civil disputes. Mr. Emling has had primary litigation and trial responsibility for a wide variety of cases, including trademark, copyright and patent infringement claims, software piracy, antitrust, insurance coverage disputes, inverse condemnation, zoning, personal injury, civil rights, wrongful termination, construction defect, educational rights for the disabled, breach of contract, and other commercial disputes. Mr. Haymond has had responsibility for patent prosecution matters and has acted as primary attorney in several litigation matters including copyright disputes pertaining to computer software and embedded firmware. His patent prosecution practice emphasizes medical devices, computer software and mechanical inventions.

**MICHAEL J. EMLING,** born Long Beach, California, March 19, 1957; admitted to bar, 1985, California; U.S. District Court, Northern and Central Districts of California; U.S. Court of Appeals, Ninth Circuit; U.S. Court of Appeals for the Federal Circuit. *Education:* University of California at Santa Cruz (B.A. in Politics, 1981); University of San Francisco (J.D., cum laude, 1985); University of Virginia School of Law, Trial Practice Institute, 1993. Member, McAuliffe Honor Society. Recipient, American Jurisprudence Awards for: Evidence; Property. *Member:* Long Beach and American Bar Associations; State Bar of California (Member, Section on Intellectual Property). (Also Of Counsel to Moore, Rutter & Evans). **REPORTED CASES:** In Re Circuit Breaker Litigation, Cite: 852 F. Supp. 883 (C.D. Cal. 1994). **PRACTICE AREAS:** Intellectual Property Litigation.

---

**PHILIP H. HAYMOND,** born Los Angeles, California, January 26, 1957; admitted to bar, 1990, California; 1992, U.S. Court of Appeals for the Federal Circuit; U.S. District Court, Central District of California; U.S. Court of Appeals, Ninth Circuit; registered to practice before the U.S. Patent and Trademark Office. *Education:* University of California at Santa Cruz (B.A., emphasis in neurobiology and computer and information science, 1985); University of San Francisco (J.D., 1990). Recipient, State Bar Wiley M. Manuel Award, 1992. *Member:* State Bar of California (Member, Section on Intellectual Property); American Bar Association (Member, Section on Intellectual Property); Los Angeles Intellectual Property Association; San Francisco Intellectual Property Association. **PRACTICE AREAS:** Patent, Trademark and Copyright Law.

**ANNE-ELENORE E. BOGOCH,** born Brookline, Massachusetts, July 23, 1964; admitted to bar, 1989, New York and Massachusetts; 1991, California. *Education:* Dartmouth College (B.A., 1985); Boston University (J.D., magna cum laude, 1988). *Member:* State Bar of California; American Bar Association. **LANGUAGES:** French. **PRACTICE AREAS:** Intellectual Property; Copyright; Trademark; Entertainment Law.

### OF COUNSEL

**SANDRA M. PARKER,** admitted to bar, 1992, California; 1993, U.S. District Court, Central District of California; registered to practice before U.S. Patent and Trademark. *Education:* University of Southern California (M.S.E.E., 1988); Western State University (J.D., 1991). *Member:* Los Angeles and Orange County Bar Associations. (Also practicing individually, Long Beach). **LANGUAGES:** French and Russian. **PRACTICE AREAS:** Intellectual Property.

REPRESENTATIVE CLIENTS: Aetna Casualty and Surety Co.; Industrial Indemnity Co.; Alliance Research Corporation Inc.

---

## FIELDS ISRAEL & BINNING LLP

115 PINE AVENUE, SUITE 300
**LONG BEACH, CALIFORNIA 90802**
Telephone: 310-432-5111
Fax: 310-432-6333

General Civil, Trial and Appellate Practice, State and Federal, U.S. Tax and U.S. Claims Courts, including Business, Corporate, Commercial, Bankruptcy, Labor, Real Estate Transactions and Land Use, Environmental, Construction, Health Care, Insurance, Personal Injury, Product Liability, Maritime and International Law.

FIRM PROFILE: Fields Israel & Binning brings together the expertise of lawyers of diverse and distinguished backgrounds with vast experience in business and litigation matters.

The Firm's expertise extends beyond conventional areas of law to include specific expertise in the fields of banking, real estate development, administrative planning and environmental law (including representation of public and private sector clients in the permitting of complex real estate, energy and port projects), judicial review of administrative decisions, eminent domain, Los Angeles and Long Beach port facility negotiations, domestic and international business and trade financing, labor and employment law, construction defect defense, toxic tort litigation, insurance defense, professional liability defense, health care law, bankruptcy law, maritime, mediation and arbitration.

The lawyers of Fields Israel & Binning are well known and well respected in the business communities and by the judiciary not only for their commitment to quality legal work but also for their involvement and commitment to business, civic and charitable associations.

**GARY D. FIELDS,** born Los Angeles, California, August 5, 1951; admitted to bar, 1976, California; 1979, U.S. District Court, Central District of California; 1984, U.S. Court of Appeals, Ninth Circuit. *Education:* University of California, Berkeley (A.B., 1973); Southwestern University School of Law (J.D., 1976). Phi Beta Kappa. Member, Southwestern University School of Law, Law Review, 1975-1976. Extern to the Honorable Rodney Potter, California Court of Appeal, 1976. Founding Partner, Fields & Creason, Orange and Riverside Counties, 1986-1996. Member: International Conference of Building Officials; Risk and Insurance Management Society; Southern California Association of Health Care Risk Managers. Vice President, Board of Trustees, Westerly School of Long Beach. Member, Board of Directors, Long Beach Symphony. *Member:* Long Beach, Los Angeles County and Orange County (Member, Sections on: Insurance Law; Medical/Legal; Construction and Business) Bar Associations; State Bar of California; Association of Southern California Defense Counsel; Defense Research Institute; Building Industry Association, Orange County Chapter; Southern Nevada Homebuilders Association.

**ALBERT S. ISRAEL,** born Long Beach, California, March 3, 1951; admitted to bar, 1976, California and U.S. District Court, Central, Eastern, Southern and Northern Districts of California. *Education:* University of California at Los Angeles (A.B., with honors, 1973); Loyola Law School of Los Angeles (J.D., 1976). Note and Comment Editor, Loyola Law Review, 1975-1976. Partner: Carlsmith Ball Wichman Case & Ichiki, Long Beach, 1990-1995; Ball, Hunt, Hart, Brown & Baerwitz, Long Beach, 1983-1989. Law Clerk to the Honorable Manuel L. Real, U.S. District Court Judge, Central District of California, 1976-1977. Member, Board of Directors: Long Beach Area Chamber of Commerce; International Business Association of the Long Beach Area Chamber of Commerce; Torrance Area Chamber of Commerce; United Way of Greater Los Angeles, Harbor Area; Jewish Community Center of Long Beach and West Orange County; Legal Aid Foundation of Long Beach. Member, International Business Network, Junior Chamber of Commerce International. Senator, Junior Chamber of Commerce International. *Member:* Long Beach and Los Angeles County Bar Associations; State Bar of California.

**MICHAEL W. BINNING,** born Long Beach, California, August 17, 1954; admitted to bar, 1979, California and U.S. District Court, Eastern, Central and Southern Districts of California; 1983, U.S. Tax Court; 1984, U.S. Court of Claims. *Education:* University of California, Santa Barbara (B.A., summa cum laude, 1976); University of California, Davis (J.D., 1979). Extern, Honorable Robert L. Ordin, U.S. Bankruptcy Court, Central District of California, 1978. Member, Board of Directors: Legal Aid Foundation of Long Beach; American Red Cross, Greater Long Beach Chapter. Member: Long Beach Rotary Club; Leadership Long Beach, 1995 Class. *Member:* Long Beach and Los Angeles County Bar Associations; State Bar of California.

---

**JULIE H. BILLINGS,** born Anaheim, California, July 22, 1968; admitted to bar, 1993, California. *Education:* University of California, Davis (B.A., 1990); California Western School of Law (J.D., 1993). Staff Counsel, U.S. Small Business Administration, 1994-1996. *Member:* Long Beach and Los Angeles County Bar Associations; State Bar of California.

### OF COUNSEL

**CHARLES E. GREENBERG,** born New York, New York, May 30, 1933; admitted to bar, 1960, California, U.S. Supreme Court and U.S. District Court, Central District of California. *Education:* Dartmouth College (B.A., 1955); University of Southern California (LL.B., 1959). Adjunct Professor of Law, California State University, Long Beach. Partner: Calsmith

*(This Listing Continued)*

## PROFESSIONAL BIOGRAPHIES

Ball Wichman Case & Ichiki, Long Beach, 1990-1993; Ball, Hunt Hart, Brown & Baerwitz, Long Beach, 1973-1990. Deputy City Attorney: City of Long Beach, 1965-1972; City of Los Angeles, 1960-1965. Chairman, Long Beach Mayor Beverly O'Neil's Transition Team; Member, Mayor O'Neil's Blue Ribbon Advisory Committee; Board of Directors, Long Beach Economic Partnership (Chairman, Technology Committee). *Member:* Long Beach, Los Angeles County and American Bar Associations; The State Bar of California.

**SHARON P. KEE,** born Los Angeles, California, September 22, 1950; admitted to bar, 1977, California; 1982, U.S. District Court, Central and Southern Districts of California. *Education:* University of California, Berkeley (B.A., 1973); Loyola Law School of Los Angeles (J.D., 1977). Phi Beta Kappa. Adjunct Professor, Cal Poly Pomona. Partner, Bryan, Cave, Irvine, 1991-1993. Attorney, 1978-1991 and Associate General Counsel, 1989-1991, McDonnell Douglas Corporation. *Member:* Los Angeles County Bar Association (Member, Labor and Employment Law Sections); State Bar of California. ***PRACTICE AREAS:*** Labor and Employment Law; Wage and Hour Law; Employment Contracts; Wrongful Termination; WARN Act; Occupational Safety and Health; Union Labor Law; Privacy Law; Employee Drug Testing.

REPRESENTATIVE CLIENTS: Edison International; Sheraton Long Beach Hotel; Port Petroleum, Inc.; Denni Corporation; Croshaw Communications, Inc.; Pacific Roofing & Design; First Fire Systems, Inc.; Dennison Electric, Inc.; Phillip Daniel Group, Inc.; Fremont Indemnity Co.; Nationwide Insurance Co.; Planned Parenthood Federation of America; Financial Indemnity Co.; Deans and Homer; Allstate Insurance Co.; Wausau Insurance Co.; Home Insurance Company; AIG Claims Services; Torino Construction; Watt Industries; Coultrup Construction; Coregis Insurance; Recreation Technologies, Inc.; Port of Long Beach; City of El Monte; Capistrano Bay District.

---

# FISHER & PORTER

*A LAW CORPORATION*

Established in 1981

**110 PINE AVENUE, 11TH FLOOR**
P.O. BOX 22686
**LONG BEACH, CALIFORNIA 90801-5686**

Telephone: 310-435-5626
Telex: 284549 FPKLAW UR
Fax: 310-432-5399

*Admiralty, Insurance and General Business Litigation, Transportation and Aviation Law, Environmental Law.*

*FIRM PROFILE: Fisher & Porter is a full-service business and insurance litigation firm serving an international and domestic clientele. The firm's practice focuses on the defense of complex liability claims and disputes for corporate clients. The firm's primary fields of concentration include general civil and appellate practice in the following areas:*

*General Insurance: Defense of coverage and "bad faith" claims arising out of marine, inland marine, construction, products liability, property and casualty, cargo and general liability policies, defense of insured under such policies, analysis of coverage.*

*Marine: Defense of personal injury and property liability claims arising under the Jones Act, Longshore and Harbor Workers' Compensation Act, Carriage of Goods by Sea Act, marine construction losses, tug and tow, salvage, general average, hull claims, product liability claims, environmental and pollution claims and other P&I-related matters; representation before the Department of Transportation, Federal Maritime Commission, U.S. Customs Service, Coast Guard, OSHA and CalOSHA in matters of marine construction, manning, safety, licensing, regulatory issues, license suspension and revocation proceedings and trade issues.*

*Transportation: Defense of air, rail and motor carriers against claims for loss of property and personal injury including under domestic legislation and the Warsaw Convention; representation before various governmental authorities including the National Transportation Safety Board, Federal Aviation Administration, public utilities commissions, Department of Transportation and U.S. Customs Service in matters of licensing, regulation, liability issues and safety.*

*Energy and Pollution: Defense of toxic claims, including asbestos personal injury and property damage, underground storage tank claims, marine environmental losses and related insurance issues.*

*Construction Law: Defense of Property and casualty claims and losses arising from construction projects, employers' liability, general personal injury, contract review, loss prevention advice, labor law issues and other related matters.*

*(This Listing Continued)*

---

**GERALD M. FISHER,** born Los Angeles, California, November 4, 1944; admitted to bar, 1973, California; U.S. District Court, Northern, Eastern, Central and Southern Districts of California; U.S. Court of Appeals, Ninth Circuit and U.S. Supreme Court. *Education:* California State University at Long Beach (B.A., cum laude, 1970); University of San Diego (J.D., 1973). Moot Court Honors, University of London and Cambridge University. President, Propeller Club of the United States, Ports of Los Angeles and Long Beach. *Member:* State Bar of California; American Bar Association; Maritime Law Association of the United States; American Waterways Operators. ***PRACTICE AREAS:*** Complex Litigation in Admiralty; Aviation; Transportation Law; Insurance; Insurance "Bad Faith" Defense; General Business Litigation; Labor Law.

**DAVID S. PORTER,** born Long Beach, California, January 29, 1955; admitted to bar, 1980, California and U.S. District Court, Southern, Central, Eastern and Northern Districts of California; 1982, U.S. Court of Appeals, Ninth Circuit; 1992, U.S. Supreme Court. *Education:* University of California, Los Angeles (B.A., 1977); University of California at Los Angeles School of Law (J.D., 1980). Phi Beta Kappa. Extern for Judge Macklin Fleming, California Court of Appeal, 1980. *Member:* Long Beach and American Bar Associations; State Bar of California. ***REPORTED CASES:*** Foss Launch & Tug Co. v. Char Ching Shipping U.S.A., Ltd., 808 F.2d 697 (9th Cir. 1987); Interpool Limited v. Char Yigh Marine (Panama) S.A., 890 F.2d 1453 (9th Cir. 1989); Alexander v. Circus Circus Enterprises, Inc., 972 F.2d 261 (9th Cir. 1992). ***PRACTICE AREAS:*** Trials and Appeals; Insurance Coverage and "Bad Faith" Defense; Marine P & I Coverage and Defense.

**THERESE G. GROFF,** born Burbank, California, February 11, 1959; admitted to bar, 1984, California; 1985, U.S. District Court, Central and Eastern Districts of California; 1986, U.S. District Court, Southern and Northern Districts of California; 1988, U.S. Court of Appeals, Ninth Circuit; 1992, U.S. Supreme Court. *Education:* Loyola Marymount University (B.B.A., with honors, 1981); Loyola Law School (J.D., 1984). Alpha Sigma Nu. Member, International Law Journal, 1983-1984. President, Board of Managers, Long Beach YMCA. *Member:* Long Beach and American Bar Associations; State Bar of California; Transportation Lawyers Association. ***PRACTICE AREAS:*** Transportation Law; Admiralty; Aviation; "Bad Faith" Insurance Defense; ICC and FMC Tariffs; Environmental Law.

**MICHAEL W. LODWICK,** born New Orleans, Louisiana, September 21, 1946; admitted to bar, 1981, Louisiana and U.S. Court of Appeals, Fifth Circuit; 1982, U.S. Court of Appeals, District of Columbia Circuit; 1986, U.S. Court of Appeals, Eleventh Circuit; 1987, U.S. Supreme Court; 1990, California and U.S. Court of Appeals, Ninth Circuit; 1996, U.S. Court of Appeals, Second Circuit. *Education:* Louisiana State University in New Orleans (B.A., 1968); Tulane University (M.A., 1972; Ph.D., 1976); Loyola University (J.D., 1981). Recipient: American Jurisprudence Award in Contracts; Corpus Juris Secundum Award, 1979; Loyola Law Alumni Award, Best Law Review Comment, 1981. Member, 1979-1980, and Editor-in-Chief, 1980-1981, Loyola Law Review. Author: "Who Governs the Ports? A Lacuna in the Law of Shipping Regulation," 26 Loy. L. Rev. 627 (1980); "Admiralty: Fifth Circuit Symposium," 27 Loy. L. Rev. 697 (1981); "Admiralty: Fifth Circuit Symposium," 28 Loy. L. Rev. 699 (1982). *Member:* State Bar of California; Louisiana State and American (Member: Section of Tort and Insurance Practice; Committee on Corporate Counsel) Bar Associations; Maritime Law Association of the United States. ***REPORTED CASES:*** Flota Mercante Grancolombiana, S.A. v. Florida Const. Equip. Inc., 798 F.2d 143 (5th Cir. 1986); Louis Dreyfus Corp. v. Plaquemines Port, Harbor & Terminal Dist., 21 S.R.R. 1072 (F.M.C. 1982); All Pacific Trading, Inc. v. M /V Hanjin Yosu, 7 F.3d 1427 (9th Cir. 1993); TRW, Inc. v. TWI Int'l Exhibition Logistics, 29 F.3d 634 (9th Cir. 1994) (opinion at 1994 U.S. App. LEXIS 16416); Tai Ping Ins. Co. v. Northwest Airlines, Inc. 94 F.3d 29 (2d Cir. 1996). ***PRACTICE AREAS:*** Marine, Inland Marine and Property Insurance Coverage and Defense; Hull and Cargo Subrogation and Hull Defense; Toxic Torts; Maritime Administrative Law; Civil Trials and Appeals.

**GEORGE P. HASSAPIS,** born Chicago, Illinois, September 19, 1965; admitted to bar, 1990, California, U.S. District Court, Northern, Eastern, Central and Southern Districts of California and U.S. Court of Appeals, Ninth Circuit. *Education:* University of Chicago (A.B., 1986); University of San Diego (J.D., 1989). Phi Alpha Delta. Oral Advocacy Specialist, University of San Diego, 1988. Water Transportation Law Editor, Journal of Transportation Law, Logistics and Policy, 1993—. Member, Propeller Club of the United States. *Member:* Long Beach Bar Association; State Bar of California; Maritime Law Association of the United States; Association of Transportation Law, Logistics and Policy. **LANGUAGES:** Greek. ***REPORTED CASES:*** Tai Ping Ins. Co. v. Northwest Airlines, Inc., 94 F.3d

*(This Listing Continued)*

**FISHER & PORTER**, A LAW CORPORATION, Long Beach—Continued

29 (3d. Cir. 1996). *PRACTICE AREAS:* Admiralty and Transportation Litigation; Construction Litigation; Insurance Litigation and Coverage Disputes; Environmental and Toxic Tort Litigation; "Bad Faith" Defense; Appeals. *Email:* Gpascali@aol.com

OF COUNSEL

**STEPHEN C. KLAUSEN**, born Los Angeles, California, June 24, 1946; admitted to bar, 1973, California; U.S. District Court, Central District of California. *Education:* University of California at Los Angeles (B.A., 1968; J.D., 1972). *Member:* Los Angeles County Bar Association (Member, Litigation Section); State Bar of California. *PRACTICE AREAS:* Defense of Complex Personal Injury; Products Liability; Property Damage; Construction; Environmental and Commercial Claims.

**STEPHEN CHACE BASS**, born San Gabriel, California, August 9, 1952; admitted to bar, 1987, California, U.S. District Court, Central and Northern Districts of California; U.S. Court of Appeals, Ninth Circuit and U.S. Supreme Court. *Education:* California State University at Long Beach (B.A., Psychology, 1975; B.A., History, summa cum laude, 1976); University of California at Los Angeles (M.A., summa cum laude, 1981; J.D., 1986). Chancellors Fellowship. Member, UCLA Law Review, 1985-1986. Law Clerk to the Hon. Dickran M. Tevrizian, Jr., U.S. District Court, Central District of California. Associate Professor, Legal Writing, California State University at Long Beach. *Member:* Long Beach and Los Angeles County Bar Associations; State Bar of California. *PRACTICE AREAS:* Maritime Law; Insurance Law; Commercial Litigation.

**ANTHONY P. LOMBARDO**, born St. Louis, Missouri, December 21, 1961; admitted to bar, 1991, California and U.S. District Court, Central, Eastern and Southern Districts of California; U.S. Court of Appeals, Ninth Circuit; 1994, Missouri. *Education:* St. Louis University (B.A., 1985; J.D., 1989). Law Clerk to Hon. William H. Crandall, Missouri Court of Appeals, 1988. *Member:* State Bar of California; The Missouri Bar. *PRACTICE AREAS:* Insurance Coverage; Cargo Claims; Business Litigation.

---

**VICKI L. HASSMAN**, born Houston, Texas, March 12, 1966; admitted to bar, 1993, California; 1994, Colorado; U.S. District Court, Central, Northern, Eastern and Southern Districts of California; U.S. Court of Appeals, Ninth Circuit. *Education:* Southern Methodist University; University of Colorado at Boulder (B.S.B.A., 1988); Emory University School of Law (J.D., 1993). Phi Alpha Delta. Candidate, 1991-1992, and Executive Managing Editor and Executive Board Member, 1992-1993, Bankruptcy Developments Journal. Judicial Intern to the Honorable Raymond Dean Jones, Court of Appeals, State of Colorado, 1991. Extern to the Honorable A. David Kohn, Chief Judge, U.S. Bankruptcy Court, Northern District of Georgia, 1992. *Member:* Orange County Bar Association; State Bar of California; Orange County Barristers. *PRACTICE AREAS:* Commercial Litigation; Transportation Law; Insurance Coverage; Trials and Appeals.

**LINDA A. MANCINI**, born Framingham, Massachusetts, September 5, 1960; admitted to bar, 1990, California; U.S. District Court, Central District of California. *Education:* Regis College (B.A., magna cum laude, 1982); Boston College (M.A., 1984); Pepperdine University Law School (J.D., 1989). Phi Delta Phi. Judicial Intern to the Honorable Sara K. Radin, Superior Court, Los Angeles County. *Member:* Los Angeles County and American Bar Associations; State Bar of California. *PRACTICE AREAS:* Insurance Defense; Commercial Litigation; Cargo Subrogation; Environmental and Toxic Tort Litigation.

**MICHAEL J. MCLAUGHLIN**, born Long Beach, California, February 25, 1966; admitted to bar, 1992, California; 1993, U.S. District Court, Central District of California; 1996, U.S. Court of Appeals, Ninth Circuit; U.S. District Court, Southern, Eastern and Northern Districts of California. *Education:* Durham University, England; Loyola Marymount University (B.B.A., 1988); Loyola Law School (J.D., 1992). Alpha Sigma Nu; Beta Gamma Sigma. *Member:* Los Angeles and Long Beach Bar Associations; Association of Southern California Defense Counsel. *PRACTICE AREAS:* Maritime Personal Injury; Inland Marine; Transportation; Insurance Litigation.

**SANDRA L. GRYDER**, born San Pedro, California, May 24, 1959; admitted to bar, 1985, California; U.S. Court of Appeals, Ninth Circuit and U.S. District Court, Central District of California; 1986, U.S. District Court, Southern, Northern and Eastern Districts of California. *Education:* Loyola Marymount University (B.A., magna cum laude, 1981); Loyola Law School (J.D., 1984). Pi Gamma Mu. Member, Scott Moot Court Honors Program. Recipient, American Jurisprudence Award in Contracts. *Member:* Los Angeles County and Century City Bar Associations; State Bar of California (Member, Real Property and Litigation Sections); Women Lawyers Association of Los Angeles.

**KENNETH F. MATTFELD**, born Mineola, New York, November 12, 1954; admitted to bar, 1996, California. *Education:* University of Michigan (B.S. in naval architecture and marine engineering, 1976); College of William and Mary (M.B.A., 1982); University of Southern California (M.S., 1988); Loyola Law School (J.D., 1995). *PRACTICE AREAS:* Marine; Environmental and Toxic Tort Litigation.

REPRESENTATIVE CORPORATE CLIENTS: Airborne Express; Albright & Wilson; Americas and Mexico; Brink's Incorporated; Burlington Air Express, Inc.; Cargill International S.A.; Catalina Channel Express; Circus Circus Enterprises; Connolly-Pacific Co.; Distribution Auto Services (a division of Nissan Motors); Hornblower Dining Yachts; L.G. Everist Co.; Makita U.S.A., Inc.; Manson Construction & Engineering Co.; Mitsubishi Trading; Mitsui Trading; Owens-Corning; Pacific Southwest Seed & Grain; Port of Los Angeles and Worldport Los Angeles Project; Reebok, Inc.; Southern Pacific Transportation Company; Star & Crescent Boat Co.

REPRESENTATIVE INSURANCE CLIENTS: American International Group; Atlantic Mutual Companies; CNA/MOAC; Fireman's Fund Insurance Companies; International Marine Underwriters/Commercial Union; The Mitsui Marine & Fire Insurance Company, Ltd; Mutual Marine Office; The Nippon Fire & Marine Insurance Co. Ltd; The Royal Insurance Companies; The Sumitomo Marine & Fire Insurance Co. Ltd; The Taisho Marine & Fire Insurance Company, Ltd.; The Tokio Marine & Fire Insurance Company, Ltd.; Underwriters at the Institute of London Underwriters; Underwriters at Lloyd's, London; Wm. H. McGee & Co., Inc.; Yasuda Fire & Marine Insurance Company, Ltd.

---

## RICHARD L. FITZER

P.O. BOX 50053
LONG BEACH, CALIFORNIA 90815
Telephone: 310-494-4185
Fax: 310-597-7712
Email: Rollwyr@aol.com

*Entertainment, representing Musicians, Criminal Appeals.*

**RICHARD L. FITZER**, born Cheverly, Maryland, August 17, 1966; admitted to bar, 1991, California. *Education:* University of California at Irvine (B.A., 1988); De Paul University (J.D., 1991); University of Southern California (M.B.A., 1994). Author: "Do Ozzy Osborne and Judas Priest Contribute to the Market Place of I Laws?" DePaul Entertainment Law Journal, May 1991. *Member:* State Bar of California. *PRACTICE AREAS:* Intellectual Property Law; Entertainment Law; Criminal Law.

REPRESENTATIVE CLIENTS: Standing Hawthorn; Soul Scream; California Appellate Project, Standing Hawthron; Eracism.

---

## FLYNN, DELICH & WISE

ONE WORLD TRADE CENTER, SUITE 1800
LONG BEACH, CALIFORNIA 90831-1800
Telephone: 310-435-2626
Fax: 310-437-7555

*San Francisco, California Office:* Suite 1750, 580 California Street.
Telephone: 415-693-5566. Fax: 415-693-0410.

*Admiralty, Maritime, International Transportation, Insurance Coverage, Intellectual Property and Civil Litigation.*

**ERICH P. WISE**, born San Francisco, California, 1948; admitted to bar, 1974, California. *Education:* Harvard University (B.A., cum laude, 1970); University of Chicago (J.D., 1974). Law Clerk to Hon. Malcolm M. Lucas, U.S. District Judge, Central District of California, 1974-1976. *Member:* The State Bar of California. *PRACTICE AREAS:* Admiralty and Maritime Law; International Transportation; Civil Litigation; Insurance Coverage.

**NICHOLAS S. POLITIS**, born Los Angeles, California, 1954; admitted to bar, 1980, California. *Education:* University of California at Santa Barbara (B.A., summa cum laude, 1976); University of California at Los Angeles (J.D., 1980). *Member:* The State Bar of California. *PRACTICE AREAS:* Admiralty and Maritime Law; International Transportation; Civil Litigation; Insurance Coverage.

---

**THOMAS C. JORGENSEN**, born Milwaukee, Wisconsin, 1963; admitted to bar, 1991, California. *Education:* University of Wisconsin-Madison (B.A., with honors and distinction, 1985); University of Michigan (J.D., 1990). Intern, Wisconsin Court of Appeals, Second District, 1989. *Member:*

*(This Listing Continued)*

State Bar of California. *PRACTICE AREAS:* Admiralty and Maritime Law; International Transportation; Civil Litigation.

**SOOK H. LEE,** born Seoul, Korea, November 13, 1957; admitted to bar, 1992, California. *Education:* Korea University, Seoul, Korea (B.A., 1980); University of Hawaii (M.A., 1983); Southwestern University School of Law (J.D., 1992). Member, Moot Court Honor Program. *Member:* Long Beach and Los Angeles County Bar Associations; The State Bar of California; Women Lawyers of Long Beach; Korean American Bar Association. *LANGUAGES:* Korean. *PRACTICE AREAS:* Admiralty and Maritime Law.

*LEGAL SUPPORT PERSONNEL*

**DENISE C. ORR,** born Hawthorne, California, September 29, 1957. *Education:* California State University, Long Beach (B.S., with distinction, 1979); University of California at Los Angeles (Certificate in Litigation, 1981). (Legal Assistant). *PRACTICE AREAS:* Admiralty and Maritime Law; Civil Litigation.

REPRESENTATIVE CLIENTS: American Hawaii Cruises; Holland America Line; Through Transport Mutual Insurance Association, Ltd.; The Britannia Steam Ship Insurance Association Limited; The Steamship Mutual Underwriting Association (Bermuda) Ltd.; General Steamship Corp., Ltd.; Commodore Cruise Line, Ltd.; Interocean Steamship Corporation; Sea-Land Service, Inc.; Wellcraft Marine; Neptune Orient Lines; Princess Cruises; Hatteras Yachts; The Yasuda Fire & Marine Insurance Co. of America, Inc.; Lasco Shipping Co.; Matson Navigation Co.; The United Kingdom Mutual Steam Ship Assurance Association (Bermuda) Ltd.; The Standard Steamship Owners' Protection & Indemnity Association (Bermuda) Ltd.

(For Biographical data on San Francisco personnel, see Professional Biographies at San Francisco)

## FORD, WALKER, HAGGERTY & BEHAR

*PROFESSIONAL LAW CORPORATION*
*ONE WORLD TRADE CENTER*
*TWENTY SEVENTH FLOOR*
**LONG BEACH, CALIFORNIA 90831**
*Telephone: 310-983-2500*
*Telecopier: 310-983-2555*

*Alternative dispute resolution, Appellate practice, Automobile negligence, Insurance defense, Bad faith, Casualty defense, Commercial litigation, Construction defect litigation, Dental Malpractice, Declaratory relief, Employment discrimination, Civil Environmental litigation, False arrest, Fire losses, Fraudulent and suspect claims, Homeowners liability, Insurance coverage, Legal malpractice, Malicious prosecution, Mass catastrophe, Municipality defense, Pollution and toxic torts, Premises liability, Product liability, Security related litigation, Sexual harassment claims, Wrongful termination.*

FIRM PROFILE: Ford, Walker, Haggerty & Behar was formed in December of 1991 by G. Richard Ford, Timothy L. Walker, William C. Haggerty and Jeffrey S. Behar. The four founding partners, all former senior partners at the law offices of Shield & Smith, sought to build upon their longtime tradition of service to the insurance industry by creating a new firm dedicated to the aggressive, cost efficient, service-oriented practice of law with the highest standards of ethical responsibility. Although the majority of the firm's practice is concentrated in Los Angeles and Orange Counties, Ford, Walker, Haggerty & Behar also engages in all phases of litigation in federal and state courts in San Diego, San Bernardino, Ventura, Santa Barbara and Kern Counties. In addition, the firm has been retained by its insurance industry clients to act as regional and-/or national coordinating counsel with respect to interstate litigation. In order to continue to provide the legal services clients want, the firm is dedicated to remaining adaptable to the changes of the nineties and to actively promote the early efficient resolution to all litigation.

**G. RICHARD FORD,** born Los Angeles, California, June 30, 1941; admitted to bar, 1966, California. *Education:* Pomona College (B.A., 1962); Stanford University (LL.B., 1965). Phi Delta Phi. Magister, Miller Inn, 1964-1965. Arbitrator Los Angeles County Superior Courts, 1978—. *Member:* Los Angeles County and American Bar Associations; The State Bar of California; Association of Southern California Defense Counsel; American Board of Trial Advocates; International Association of Defense Counsel. *PRACTICE AREAS:* Insurance Bad Faith; Auto Negligence; Police Misconduct.

**TIMOTHY L. WALKER,** born Whittier, California, September 25, 1947; admitted to bar, 1972, California. *Education:* University of California at Santa Barbara (B.A., 1969); Loyola University of Los Angeles (J.D., 1972). Lecturer, California Continuing Education of the Bar, 1980—. Arbitrator, Los Angeles County Superior Courts, 1978—. *Member:* Los Angeles

*(This Listing Continued)*

County and American Bar Associations; State Bar of California; Association of Southern California Defense Counsel (Member, Board of Directors, 1979—); American Board of Trial Advocates; International Association of Defense Counsel; Defense Research Institute (Regional Vice President). *PRACTICE AREAS:* Construction Defects Litigation; Civil Environmental Litigation; Legal Malpractice; Bad Faith; Municipality Defense.

**WILLIAM C. HAGGERTY,** born Stamford, Connecticut, February 9, 1949; admitted to bar, 1977, California. *Education:* Brown University (B.A., with honors, 1971); University of Santa Clara (J.D., magna cum laude, 1977). Associate Editor, Santa Clara Law Review, 1976-1977. Recipient, American Jurisprudence Book Award for excellence in Torts. Author: Comment, "Wage Garnishment-Still Driving the Wage-Earning Family to the Wall," 17 Santa Clara Law Review 631, 1977. *Member:* Los Angeles County and American Bar Associations; The State Bar of California; Association of Southern California Defense Counsel. *PRACTICE AREAS:* Dental Malpractice; Professional Liability; Products Liability; Premises Liability.

**JEFFREY S. BEHAR,** born Philadelphia, Pennsylvania, November 20, 1952; admitted to bar, 1978, California. *Education:* University of California at Los Angeles (B.A., magna cum laude, 1974); University of California at Santa Barbara; Loyola University of Los Angeles (J.D., 1978). Phi Beta Kappa; Pi Gamma Mu. Recipient, American Jurisprudence Book Award for Excellence in Criminal Procedure. *Member:* State Bar of California; American Bar Association; Association of Southern California Defense Counsel; American Board of Trial Advocates; International Association of Defense Counsel; Defense Research Institute. *PRACTICE AREAS:* Construction Defect Litigation; Products Liability; Premises Liability; Security Related Litigation; Civil Environmental Litigation.

**MARK STEVEN HENNINGS,** born Denison, Iowa, December 7, 1953; admitted to bar, 1981, California. *Education:* California State University at Fullerton (B.A., with honors, 1977); Yale University; Loyola University of Los Angeles (J.D., 1981). *Member:* Los Angeles County Bar Association; American Bar Association (Member, Litigation Section); State Bar of California; Association of Southern California Defense Counsel. *PRACTICE AREAS:* Fraudulent and Suspect Claims; Automobile Negligence.

**DONNA ROGERS KIRBY,** born Detroit, Michigan, January 6, 1949; admitted to bar, 1983, California. *Education:* University of Toledo (B.A., cum laude, 1980); University of Southern California (J.D., summa cum laude, 1983). *Member:* State Bar of California; Association of Southern California Defense Counsel. *PRACTICE AREAS:* Insurance Coverage; Bad Faith Litigation.

**TINA IVANKOVIC MANGARPAN,** born San Pedro, California, October 18, 1959; admitted to bar, 1985, California. *Education:* Drew University (B.A., magna cum laude, 1981); Pepperdine University (J.D., 1984). Phi Beta Kappa; Pi Sigma Alpha; Phi Alpha Delta. *Member:* State Bar of California; Association of Southern California Defense Counsel. *PRACTICE AREAS:* Premises Liability; Security Related Litigation; Product Liability; Construction Defect Litigation.

**SUSAN D. BERGER,** born Los Angeles, California, January 19, 1960; admitted to bar, 1985, California. *Education:* University of California at Los Angeles (B.A., 1982); Southwestern University (J.D., 1985). *Member:* State Bar of California; Association of Southern California Defense Counsel. *LANGUAGES:* Italian, Spanish and French.

**JOSEPH A. HEATH,** born Burbank, California, May 29, 1958; admitted to bar, 1986, California. *Education:* University of California at Los Angeles (B.A., 1983); Southwestern University (J.D., 1986). Senior Editor, Southwestern University Law Review, 1985-1986. *Member:* State Bar of California; Association of Southern California Defense Counsel.

**ROBERT J. CHAVEZ,** born Santa Monica, California, June 9, 1961; admitted to bar, 1987, California. *Education:* University of Southern California (B.S., 1983; J.D., 1986). Phi Delta Phi. *Member:* State Bar of California; American Bar Association; Association of Southern California Defense Counsel.

**J. MICHAEL McCLURE,** born Groton, Connecticut, August 26, 1953; admitted to bar, 1986, California. *Education:* Virginia Polytechnic Institute; North Texas State University (B.A., 1984); University of West Los Angeles (J.D., 1986). Delta Theta Phi. Moot Court Finalist. Member, Sport and Entertainment Law Society, 1983-1986. *Member:* State Bar of California.

*(This Listing Continued)*

**FORD, WALKER, HAGGERTY & BEHAR,** PROFESSIONAL LAW CORPORATION, Long Beach—Continued

**ARTHUR W. SCHULTZ,** born Los Angeles, California, July 13, 1946; admitted to bar, 1977, California. *Education:* University of California at Los Angeles and University of Southern California (D.D.S., 1970); Loyola University of Los Angeles (J.D., 1977). Licensed Dentist, California, 1970. *Member:* South Bay Bar Association; State Bar of California.

**JON T. MOSELEY,** born Naha, Okinawa, November 3, 1958; admitted to bar, 1984, California. *Education:* University of California at Los Angeles (B.A., 1980); Pepperdine University (J.D., 1984). *Member:* Los Angeles County and American Bar Associations; State Bar of California; Association of Southern California Defense Counsel.

**MAXINE J. LEBOWITZ,** born Teaneck, New Jersey, August 29, 1944; admitted to bar, 1982, California; 1983, U.S. District Court, Central District of California; 1984, U.S. District Court, Eastern District of California. *Education:* Hebrew Union College (B.S., 1974; M.A., 1976); Southwestern University (J.D., 1982). Research Attorney to Justice Vaino Spencer, California Court of Appeal, 1982-1984. *Member:* Wilshire and American (Member, Accountants Liability Subcommittee, 1985—) Bar Associations; State Bar of California; Association of Southern California Defense Counsel; South Bay Women Lawyers Bar Association; California Women Lawyers Association.

**TIMOTHY P. MCDONALD,** born Camden, New Jersey, February 5, 1958; admitted to bar, 1986, California. *Education:* Fairfield University (B.A., 1980); Georgetown University; University of San Diego School of Law (J.D., 1986). *Member:* State Bar of California; American Bar Association; Irish American Bar Association; Association of Southern California Defense Counsel.

**K. MICHELE WILLIAMS,** born Chicago, Illinois, March 12, 1943; admitted to bar, 1987, California. *Education:* Mt. San Antonio Junior College; California State University at San Francisco (B.A., 1967); Whittier College School of Law (J.D., cum laude, 1987). Recipient, American Board of Trial Advocates Award for Excellence in Preparation for Trial Advocacy. *Member:* Los Angeles County Bar Association; State Bar of California; Women Lawyers Association of Los Angeles; Lawyers Club of Los Angeles; Association of Southern California Defense Counsel.

**STEPHEN WARD MOORE,** born Ann Arbor, Michigan, May 4, 1961; admitted to bar, 1989, California. *Education:* University of Southern California (B.A., 1984); McGeorge School of Law, University of California (J.D., 1988). Phi Alpha Delta. Finalist, Top Memorial Competition, Phillip C. Jessup International Moot Court. Member, International Moot Court Honors Board. *Member:* State Bar of California. *LANGUAGES:* Spanish.

**JAMES D. SAVAGE,** born San Luis Obispo, California, December 22, 1963; admitted to bar, 1989, California. *Education:* University of Arizona (B.A., 1986); University of San Diego (J.D., 1989). *Member:* State Bar of California.

**TODD D. PEARL,** born Culver City, California, July 3, 1964; admitted to bar, 1990, California. *Education:* California State University; San Diego State University; University of California, Los Angeles (B.A., 1987); Santa Clara University (J.D., 1990). Member, Moot Court Honors Board. *Member:* State Bar of California; Association of Southern California Defense Counsel.

**PATRICK J. GIBBS,** born Union, New Jersey, February 25, 1964; admitted to bar, 1989, California. *Education:* California Lutheran University (B.A., 1986); Pepperdine University (J.D., 1989).

**JAMES O. MILLER,** born Jamaica, New York, March 24, 1948; admitted to bar, 1991, California and U.S. District Court, Central District of California. *Education:* University of California, Santa Barbara (B.A., 1971); University of Southern California; Southwestern University School of Law (J.D., 1991). Recipient, American Jurisprudence Award, Administrative Law. Member, National Education and California Teachers Associations, 1973-1991. *Member:* Los Angeles County Bar Association. State Bar of California; American Bar Association.

**DAVID HUCHEL,** born Glendora, California, March 5, 1965; admitted to bar, 1990, California and U.S. District Court, Central District of California. *Education:* California State University, Sacramento (B.A., 1987); McGeorge School of Law (J.D., 1990). Phi Alpha Delta. Member, Moot Court. *Member:* State Bar of California; Association of Southern California Defense Counsel.

**ROBERT REISINGER,** born Long Beach, California, March 21, 1964; admitted to bar, 1991, California and U.S. District Court, Central District of California. *Education:* San Diego State University (B.S., 1987); California Western School of Law (J.D., 1991). Phi Delta Phi (Vice Magister, 1991). Western Athletic Scholar Athlete. Recipient, American Jurisprudence Award for Legal Skill II. Secretary, Embassy Park Homeowners Association, 1992-1993. *Member:* Los Angeles County and American Bar Associations; State Bar of California.

**THEODORE A. CLAPP,** born West Covina, California, May 13, 1964; admitted to bar, 1991, California. *Education:* Loyola Marymount University (B.S., 1986; J.D., 1991). Member, 1988-1991 and Chairman, 1989-1990, Loyola Law School Environmental Law Society. *Member:* State Bar of California.

**STANLEY L. SCARLETT,** born Daytona Beach, Florida, July 11, 1958; admitted to bar, 1987, California and U.S. District Court, Central District of California. *Education:* San Francisco State University (B.A., 1983); Boalt Hall School of Law, University of California (J.D., 1986). *Member:* Los Angeles County Bar Association; State Bar of California. [U.S. Navy, 1976-1980]

**SCOTT A. RITSEMA,** born Ann Arbor, Michigan, November 10, 1961; admitted to bar, 1988, California; 1989, U.S. District Court, Central, Southern and Northern Districts of California and U.S. Court of Appeals, Ninth Circuit. *Education:* University of California at Los Angeles (B.A., 1984); University of California at Davis (J.D., 1988). Blue Key; Order of the Coif. *Member:* Los Angeles County Bar Association; The State Bar of California. *PRACTICE AREAS:* Civil Litigation.

**MICHAEL GUY MARTIN,** born Los Angeles, California, April 29, 1959; admitted to bar, 1993, California. *Education:* San Francisco State University (B.A., Psychology, 1984); University of la Verne (J.D., 1992). Recipient, American Jurisprudence Book Award for Excellence in Civil Procedure. *Member:* Los Angeles Bar Association; State Bar of California.

**COLLEEN A. STRONG,** born Sacramento, California, August 2, 1967; admitted to bar, 1993, California and U.S. District Court, Eastern District of California; 1994, U.S. District Court, Central and Southern Districts of California. *Education:* California State University, Sacramento (B.S., 1989); University of the Pacific, McGeorge School of Law (J.D., 1992). Phi Delta Phi. Member: Order of the Barristers; National Moot Court Competition Team. Top Oralist Finalist, McGeorge School of Law, 1991. Recipient: Gary V. Schaber Memorial Scholarship, 1991; Mr. & Mrs. William D. James Foundation Scholarship, 1991. *Member:* State Bar of California; American Bar Association; Southern California Defense Counsel. *PRACTICE AREAS:* Insurance; Personal Injury Defense; Municipality Defense.

**THOMAS L. GOURDE,** born Salt Lake City, Utah, November 14, 1962; admitted to bar, 1990, California; 1991, U.S. District Court, Central District of California; 1992, District of Columbia and U.S. Court of Appeals, District of Columbia Circuit. *Education:* University of Utah (B.A., cum laude, 1987; J.D., 1990). Member, 1988-1989 and Administrative Editor, 1989-1990, Journal of Contemporary Law and Journal of Energy Law and Policy. Semi-Finalist and Best Written Brief, Roger J. Traynor Moot Court Competition, 1988-1989; Regional Semi-Finalist, National Moot Court Competition, 1989. American College of Trial Lawyers. *Member:* Los Angeles County and American Bar Associations; State Bar of California (Member, Section on Litigation); Bar Association of The District of Columbia; Association of Southern California Defense Counsel. *LANGUAGES:* French. *PRACTICE AREAS:* Litigation; Professional Malpractice Defense.

**PATRICK J. STARK,** born Caledonia, Minnesota, January 29, 1964; admitted to bar, 1989, California and U.S. Court of Appeals, Ninth Circuit; 1990, U.S. District Court, Central District of California; 1991, Minnesota. *Education:* University of Wisconsin (B.S., with honors, 1986); Pepperdine University (J.D., 1989). *Member:* State Bar of California.

**SHAYNE L. WULTERIN,** born Harbor City, California, January 17, 1966; admitted to bar, 1991, California. *Education:* Westmont College (B.A., magna cum laude, 1988); Whittier College School of Law (J.D., 1991). Phi Delta Phi; Moot Court. *Member:* State Bar of California; The Association of Trial Lawyers of America; Southern California Defense Counsel. *PRACTICE AREAS:* Automobile Fraud; Automobile Liability; Construction Defect; Police Misconduct.

**CHARLES D. JARRELL,** born Lubbock, Texas, October 12, 1967; admitted to bar, 1994, California and U.S. District Court, Central District of California. *Education:* New Mexico State University (B.A., 1991); University of Southern California (J.D., 1994). Mortar Board. Golden Key.

*(This Listing Continued)*

*Member:* Los Angeles County and American Bar Associations; State Bar of California; Association of Southern California Defense Counsel.

**CHARLES J. SCHMITT,** born Long Beach, California, August 16, 1968; admitted to bar, 1994, California. *Education:* University of California at Santa Barbara (B.A., 1990); Southwestern University School of Law (J.D., 1994). Moot Court. *Member:* State Bar of California.

**KYLE A. OSTERGRAD,** born Torrance, California, October 27, 1970; admitted to bar, 1995, California; 1996, U.S. District Court, Central District of California. *Education:* University of California (B.A., with honors, 1992); Santa Clara University (J.D., cum laude, 1995).

**TODD L. KESSLER,** born New York, N.Y., May 26, 1966; admitted to bar, 1992, California; 1995, U.S. District Court, Southern District of California. *Education:* University of Colorado at Boulder (B.S., 1988); Thomas Jefferson (J.D., 1992). Member, Southern California Defense Counsel. **PRACTICE AREAS:** Construction Defect Defense; Automobile Defense.

*OF COUNSEL*

**THEODORE P. SHIELD, P.L.C.,** born North Dakota, May 23, 1920; admitted to bar, 1949, California. *Education:* University of California; University of Southern California (LL.B., 1948). Deputy District Attorney, County of Los Angeles, 1949-1953. Member, BAJI Committee, 1978—. *Member:* Los Angeles County and American Bar Associations; The State Bar of California (Member: Board of Governors, 1977-1980; Commission on Judicial Nominee Evaluation, 1981-1983); Association of Southern California Defense Counsel; International Association of Defense Counsel (Member, Executive Committee, 1970-1973; President, 1974-1975); American Judicature Society; Defense Research Institute (Member, Board of Directors, 1974-1976). Fellow: International Academy of Trial Lawyers; American College of Trial Lawyers; International Society of Barristers; American Board of Trial Advocates (Trial Lawyer of the Year, 1974).

REPRESENTATIVE CLIENTS: Automobile Club of Southern California; California State Auto Association; Zurich-American Insurance Co.; Hertz Claim Management Corp.; Fireman's Fund; Argonaut Insurance Co.; Vasa North Atlantic Insurance Co.; Hilton Hotels Corp.

---

## FULWIDER PATTON LEE & UTECHT, LLP

*200 OCEANGATE, SUITE 1550*
**LONG BEACH, CALIFORNIA 90802-4351**
*Telephone: 310-432-0453*
*Fax: 310-435-6014*
*Email: fulwidr@primenet.com*
*Email: fulwiderlb@aol.com*

*Los Angeles, California Office:* 10877 Wilshire Boulevard, 10th Floor. Telephone: 310-824-5555. Internet: fulwidr@primenet.com; fulwidr@aol.com. FAX: 310-824-9696.

*Patent, Trademark, Copyright and Unfair Competition Law. Litigation.*

### MEMBER OF FIRM

**VERN SCHOOLEY,** born Reed City, Michigan, September 26, 1937; admitted to bar, 1967, California; registered to practice before U.S. Patent and Trademark Office. *Education:* Ferris State College and Michigan State University (B.S.M.E., 1961); University of San Diego (J.D., 1966). President, Joseph A. Ball/Clarence S. Hunt Inn of Court, 1991-1992. *Member:* Long Beach (Past President), Los Angeles County and American Bar Associations; State Bar of California; American Intellectual Property Law Association. (Resident). **PRACTICE AREAS:** Patent, Trademark, Copyright and Unfair Competition Law; Litigation.

### ASSOCIATES

**GUNTHER D. HANKE,** born Linz, Austria, June 23, 1955; admitted to bar, 1986, California; registered to practice before U.S. Patent and Trademark Office. *Education:* University of Southern California (B.S., cum laude, 1977); University of California at Los Angeles; Southwestern University School of Law (J.D., 1985). Member, Joseph A. Ball/Clarence S. Hunt Inn of Court. *Member:* Long Beach Bar Association; Los Angeles Intellectual Property Law Association; Orange County Patent Law Association. (Resident). **LANGUAGES:** German. **PRACTICE AREAS:** Patent, Trademark, Copyright and Unfair Competition Law; Litigation.

**GARY M. ANDERSON,** born Oakland, California, November 13, 1949; admitted to bar, 1981, California; U.S. District Court, Central District of California; registered to practice before U.S. Patent and Trademark Office. *Education:* University of California at Los Angeles (B.S.M.E., 1972); Southwestern University (J.D., cum laude, 1980). Phi Alpha Delta. Staff Member, 1978-1979 and Managing Editor, 1979-1980, Southwestern University Law Review. Member: American Inns of Court; Joseph A. Ball/Clarence S. Hunt Inn of Court. *Member:* Orange County and American Bar Associations; American Intellectual Property Law Association; Orange County Patent Law Association. (Resident). **PRACTICE AREAS:** Patent, Trademark, Copyright and Unfair Competition Law; Litigation.

**RUSSELL C. PANGBORN,** born Long Beach, California, December 21, 1966; admitted to bar, 1994, California; registered to practice before U.S. Patent and Trademark Office. *Education:* Stanford University (B.A., 1989); Hastings College of the Law, University of California (J.D., 1993). *Member:* Long Beach Bar Association; State Bar of California. (Resident). **PRACTICE AREAS:** Trademark; Copyright; Patent Litigation; Trade Secret.

**DERRICK W. REED,** born Santa Monica, California, October 7, 1969; admitted to bar, 1995, California; registered to practice before U.S. Patent and Trademark Office. *Education:* University of California at San Diego (B.S.E.E., 1992); Loyola University of Los Angeles (J.D., 1995). *Member:* Long Beach Bar Association; American Inns of Court; Long Beach Barristers. (Resident). **PRACTICE AREAS:** Patent Prosecution; Patent Litigation; Trademark Law; Unfair Competition Law; Intellectual Property Law.

**JOANNE M. YBABEN,** born Los Angeles, California, June 4, 1966; admitted to bar, 1994, California and U.S. District Court, Southern District of California; registered to practice before U.S. Patent and Trademark Office. *Education:* University of California at San Diego (B.A., 1989); California Western School of Law (J.D., 1994). Adjunct Professor, National University School of Management and Technology, 1995-1996. *Member:* Long Beach Bar Association; Women Lawyers Association; American Inns of Court. (Resident). **PRACTICE AREAS:** Patents and Trademark Prosecution and Litigation.

**SEAN M. CASEY,** born Port Chester, New York; admitted to bar, 1995, California; registered to practice before U.S. Patent and Trademark Office. *Education:* Boston University College of Engineering (B.S.A.E., 1988); Southwestern University School of Law (J.D., 1995). *Member:* Orange County, Long Beach County and American Bar Associations; Long Beach Barristers; American Inns of Court; American Intellectual Property Association; Patent and Trademark Office Society; Southern California Professional Engineers Association; A.I.A.A.; A.F.C.E.A. (Resident). **PRACTICE AREAS:** Patent; Copyright; Trademark Prosecution; Intellectual Property Litigation.

*OF COUNSEL*

**FRANCIS A. UTECHT,** born Minneapolis, Minnesota, March 6, 1923; admitted to bar, 1952, California; 1958, U.S. Supreme Court; 1960, U.S. Claims Court; 1970-1982, U.S. Court of Customs and Patent Appeals; registered to practice before U.S. Patent and Trademark Office. *Education:* University of Southern California (B.S.M.E., 1947); Southwestern University (J.D., 1951). *Member:* Long Beach, Los Angeles County and American Bar Associations; State Bar of California (Chairman, Patent, Trademark and Copyright Section, 1982-1983); American Intellectual Property Law Association. (Resident). **PRACTICE AREAS:** Patent; Trademark Law; Copyright Law; Unfair Competition Law; Litigation.

(For complete biographical data on all personnel see Professional Biographies at Los Angeles, California).

---

## ROBERT W. GASPER

*SHORELINE SQUARE TOWER, SHERATON PLAZA*
*301 EAST OCEAN BOULEVARD, SUITE 540*
**LONG BEACH, CALIFORNIA 90802-4828**
*Telephone: 310-436-2294*
*Fax: 310-590-8999*

*General Family Law Practice. Dissolution of Marriage, Child Custody, Support and Divorce Law.*

**ROBERT W. GASPER,** born Long Beach, California, January 18, 1955; admitted to bar, 1979, California; 1980, U.S. District Court, Southern, Central and Northern Districts of California. *Education:* University of California at Los Angeles (B.A., cum laude, 1977); University of San Diego (J.D., with high honors, 1979). Judge Pro Tem: Long Beach Municipal Court, 1980-1985; Los Angeles County Sup. Court, 1988—. Family Law Mediator, Los Angeles County Superior Court, 1983—. *Member:* Long Beach (Member, Board of Governors, 1983, 1984, 1986, 1987, 1996, 1997; Chair,

*(This Listing Continued)*

**ROBERT W. GASPER,** Long Beach—*Continued*

Professional Responsibility Committee, 1987), Los Angeles County (Member, Family Law Section, 1985—) and American (Member, Family Law Section) Bar Associations; State Bar of California.

REFERENCE: International City Bank, Long Beach, California.

---

## GAUHAN AND KING

A Partnership of Professional Corporations

Established in 1983

SUITE 610, 100 OCEANGATE
**LONG BEACH, CALIFORNIA 90802**
Telephone: 310-437-6661
Fax: 310-495-1642

*Tort Litigation, Personal Injury Law and Insurance Matters.*

**DENNIS P. GAUHAN, (A LAW CORPORATION),** born Long Beach, California, April 5, 1945; admitted to bar, 1972, California, U.S. District Court, Central District of California and U.S. Court of Appeals, 9th Circuit. *Education:* Long Beach City College (A.A., 1966); University of California at Los Angeles (B.S., 1968); Loyola University of Los Angeles (J.D., 1971). *Member:* Long Beach Bar Association; The State Bar of California. **PRACTICE AREAS:** Torts; Negligence; Premises Liability; Products Liability; Construction Accidents; Insurance Matters; Arbitration; Mediation.

**THOMAS C. KING, (A LAW CORPORATION),** born Los Angeles, California, July 17, 1945; admitted to bar, 1972, California, U.S. District Court, Central District of California and U.S. Court of Appeals, 9th Circuit. *Education:* Loyola University of Los Angeles and California State College at Los Angeles (B.S., 1968); Loyola University of Los Angeles (J.D., 1971). Phi Delta Phi. *Member:* Long Beach Bar Association; State Bar of California. **PRACTICE AREAS:** Torts; Negligence; Premises Liability; Products Liability; Construction Accidents; Insurance Matters; Arbitration; Mediation.

REFERENCE: Wells Fargo Bank.

---

## K. DOYLE GEORGE

ONE WORLD TRADE CENTER, SUITE 1600
**LONG BEACH, CALIFORNIA 90831-1600**
Telephone: 310-436-3888
Fax: 310-437-1967

*Real Estate, Business Planning and Organization, Business Transactions Matters, Alternate Dispute Resolution, General Civil Litigation.*

**K. DOYLE GEORGE,** born Alton, Illinois, 1950; admitted to bar, 1976, Pennsylvania and U.S. District Court, Western District of Pennsylvania; 1985, Arizona; 1988, California. *Education:* Lehigh University (B.A., 1972); Georgetown University Law Center (J.D., 1975). *Member:* Pennsylvania and American (Member, Sections of: Real Property, Probate and Trust Law; Business Law) Bar Associations; State Bar of Arizona (Member, Section of Real Property). [1st Lt., USAR, 1972-1980]

---

## EDWARD P. GEORGE, JR., INC.

A PROFESSIONAL CORPORATION

Established in 1975

SUITE 430
5000 EAST SPRING STREET
**LONG BEACH, CALIFORNIA 90815**
Telephone: 310-497-2900
Facsimile: 310-497-2904

*General Civil and Criminal Practice in all Courts. Trials and Appeals, Personal Injury.*

**EDWARD P. GEORGE, JR.,** born Los Angeles, California, October 10, 1932; admitted to bar, 1960, California. *Education:* Occidental College and University of California at Los Angeles (B.A., 1954); University of California at Los Angeles (LL.B., 1959). Phi Delta Phi. President, Graduating Class of 1959, University of California at Los Angeles School of Law. Deputy City Attorney, Los Angeles, 1960-1963. Co-Editor, California Jury Instructions, Criminal, West Publishing Company, 1976-1996. *Member:*

*(This Listing Continued)*

---

Long Beach (President, 1986) and Los Angeles County (Member, Board of Trustees, 1984-1985) Bar Associations; State Bar of California (Member, Committee on Jury Instructions, 1974-1975; Chairperson, Committee on Jury Instructions, 1976-1978; Advisor, Committee on Jury Instructions, 1979-1980; Member, Disciplinary Board, 1972-1987; Assistant Presiding Referee and Chairperson, Review Department of the State Bar Court, Disciplinary Board, 1981-1982; The Presiding Referee (Chairperson) of the State Bar Court, Disciplinary Board, 1983, 1984; Member, Executive Committee of the State Bar Court, 1981-1986; Chairperson, Executive Committee of the State Bar Court, 1982-1983, 1983-1984; Member: Commission for Revision of Rules of Professional Conduct, Disciplinary Board, 1986-1987; 1989-1991; Board of Governors, 1987-1990; Vice President, State Bar, 1989-1990); Member, State of California Commission on Judicial Performance, 1991-1994. Fellow, American College of Trial Lawyers. Fellow, International Academy of Trial Lawyers. **PRACTICE AREAS:** Criminal; Personal Injury; Appellate. *Email:* epg@ix.netcom.com

**TIMOTHY L. O'REILLY,** born Harbor City, California, June 19, 1964; admitted to bar, 1990, California. *Education:* California State University, Long Beach (B.A., 1986); Whittier College School of Law (J.D., 1990). Associate Editor, Whittier College Law Review. Phi Delta Phi. *Member:* Los Angeles County and Long Beach Bar Associations; State Bar of California; Long Beach Barristers (President, 1997). **PRACTICE AREAS:** Criminal; Personal Injury; Appellate.

OF COUNSEL

**ALBERT C. S. RAMSEY,** born Moose Jaw, Saskatchewan, Canada, October 3, 1912; admitted to bar, 1937, California. *Education:* University of California at Los Angeles (A.B., 1933); University of Southern California (LL.B., 1937). City Prosecutor, Long Beach, California, 1942-1948. City Attorney, Signal Hill, California, 1949-1951. *Member:* State Bar of California. **PRACTICE AREAS:** Criminal; Personal Injury; Appellate.

REFERENCE: Harbor Bank, Long Beach.

---

## LORNA C. GREENHILL

60 ELM AVENUE
**LONG BEACH, CALIFORNIA 90802**
Telephone: 310-437-2973

*General Civil Practice. Family, Real Estate, Personal Injury, Probate and Estate Planning Law.*

**LORNA C. GREENHILL,** born Long Beach, California, November 30, 1942; admitted to bar, 1978, California. *Education:* California State University at Long Beach (B.A., summa cum laude, 1975); University of California at Los Angeles (J.D., 1978). *Member:* Long Beach (President 1991), Los Angeles County and American Bar Associations; State Bar of California; Women Lawyers of Long Beach (First President, 1981-1982).

REFERENCE: Bank of America, Main Branch, Long Beach, California.

---

## HAINES & LEA

A LAW CORPORATION

100 WEST BROADWAY, #595
**LONG BEACH, CALIFORNIA 90802**
Telephone: 310-437-0400
Fax: 310-437-0206

*San Francisco, California Office:* 235 Pine St., Suite 1300. Telephone: 415-981-1050. Fax: 415-989-3561.

*General Civil and Trial Practice. Financial Institutions, Corporation, Labor Relations and Employment Law, Real Estate, Construction Law and Probate Law.*

(For complete Biographical data on all personnel, see professional Biographies at San Francisco, California)

## ERIC S. HARTMAN

*Established in 1970*

**SUITE 245, 6615 EAST PACIFIC COAST HIGHWAY**
**LONG BEACH, CALIFORNIA 90803**
Telephone: 310-598-9753
Fax: 310-430-4218

*Business, Corporate, Real Estate, Wills, Trusts and Probate Law.*

**ERIC S. HARTMAN,** born Fresno, California, November 5, 1944; admitted to bar, 1970, California and U.S. District Court, Central District of California; U.S. Court of Appeals, Ninth Circuit. *Education:* Whittier College (B.A., 1966); Boalt Hall School of Law, University of California (J.D., 1969). Member, Moot Court Board. Adjunct Professor, Business Law, California State University at Long Beach, 1973-1974. Judge Pro Tem, Long Beach Municipal Court, 1977-1983. *Member:* Long Beach (Member, Board of Governors, 1973-1974; 1978-1979; 1995—; Chairman: Arbitration Committee, 1977; Legislative Committee, 1992-1994) and Los Angeles County Bar Associations; State Bar of California (Member, Conference of Delegates, 1992-1995).

REPRESENTATIVE CLIENTS: Hamada of America, Inc.; DermaNet, Inc.; Continental Enterprises; Mesa Mechanical/Pipeline, Inc.; Pego Systems; Kerr Floors, Inc.; Heard Optical Co.; Alamitos Bay Marine; Airport Customs Service; Delray Tire & Retreading, Inc.
REFERENCE: Harbor Bank (Marina Office).

---

## HILL, BETTS & NASH LLP

A Limited Liability Partnership including Professional Corporations

**ARCO CENTER**
**200 OCEANGATE, SUITE 400**
**LONG BEACH, CALIFORNIA 90802-4302**
Telephone: 310-437-4407
Rapifax: 310-437-6057

*New York, N.Y. Office:* Suite 5215, One World Trade Center. Telephone: 212-839-7000. Telex: ITT 426284; 667170. Telecopier: 212-839-7105. Rapifax: 212-466-0514. Cable Address: "Hillbetts."

*Washington, D.C. Office:* 1615 New Hampshire Avenue, N.W. Telephone: 202-319-0800. Telex: ITT 440083. Fax: 202-319-0804.

*Newark, New Jersey Office:* One Gateway Center, Suite 1203. Telephone: 201-623-0800. Fax: 201-623-1188.

*General Practice. Admiralty, Aviation, Banking, Corporate, Employee Benefits, Environmental, Estates, Insurance, International, Securities and Taxation Law.*

### MEMBERS OF FIRM

**GEOFFREY D. FERRER,** born Valley Forge, Pennsylvania, December 14, 1955; admitted to bar, 1982, New York and U.S. District Court, Southern and Eastern Districts of New York; 1990, California; 1991, U.S. District Court, Northern District of California; 1992, U.S. Court of Appeals for the Federal Circuit and U.S. Court of Appeals, Ninth Circuit. *Education:* University of Oklahoma (B.A., 1978); Columbia University (J.D., 1981). *Member:* State Bar of California; American and International Bar Associations; Maritime Law Association of the United States. (Also at New York, N.Y. Office).

**LYNN E. MOYER,** born Detroit, Michigan, May 14, 1953; admitted to bar, 1987, California and U.S. District Court, Central District of California. *Education:* Western State University (B.S., 1984; J.D., 1987). Recipient, American Jurisprudence Awards in Contracts, Torts and Community Property. Associate Director, Moot Court, 1986. *Member:* State Bar of California (Member, Committee of Rules and Procedures in Court, 1991-1994); Long Beach Barristers Association (President, 1990); California Women Lawyers (District Governor, 1990-1992); Long Beach Women Lawyers; Joseph A. Ball, Clarence S. Hunt and American (Treasurer) Inns of Court; Arthritis National Research Foundation (President). (Resident).

### COUNSEL

**ROBERT B. FOUGNER,** born New York, N.Y., March 29, 1952; admitted to bar, 1978, New York; 1988, California. *Education:* George Washington University (B.B.A., 1974); Tulane University (J.D., 1977). *Member:* The Association of the Bar of the City of New York; State Bar of California; American Bar Association; Maritime Law Association of the United States. (Resident).

*(This Listing Continued)*

---

### ASSOCIATES

**BRIAN B.A. McALLISTER,** born New York, N.Y., October 30, 1967; admitted to bar, 1993, California; 1994, New York, U.S. District Court, Central and Northern Districts of California and U.S. Court of Appeals, 9th Circuit. *Education:* Hamilton College (B.A., cum laude, 1989); University of California, Hastings College of the Law (J.D., 1993). Phi Sigma Iota. Author: "The United Nations Conference of Environment and Development: An Opportunity to Forge a New Unity in the Work of the World Bank Among Human Rights, the Environment, and Sustainable Development," 16 Hastings Int'l & Comp L. Rev. 689 (1993). *Member:* State Bar of California. **LANGUAGES:** French.

REFERENCE: First Interstate Bank of California.

(For complete biographical data on all personnel, see Professional Biographies at New York, New York)

---

## JOHNSON, CEBULA & RYGH

*A PROFESSIONAL CORPORATION*

*Established in 1987*

**FIFTH FLOOR**
**115 PINE AVENUE**
**LONG BEACH, CALIFORNIA 90802**
Telephone: 310-437-0307
Fax: 310-495-1894

*Automobile Negligence, Insurance Defense, Bad Faith, Complex Litigation, Construction Defect Litigation, Fraudulent and Suspect Claims, Insurance Coverage, Municipality Defense, Premise Liability, Product Liability, Medical Malpractice, Wrongful Termination and Appellate Practice.*

*FIRM PROFILE: Headquartered in Long Beach, Johnson, Cebula & Rygh provides responsive and effective legal representation to insurance companies and self-insured corporations throughout California. The firm's hallmark is through aggressive litigation with an emphasis on speedy resolution of claims. The firm maintains direct and continual client contact.*

**R. SCOTT JOHNSON,** born Sonora, California, May 11, 1952; admitted to bar, 1979, California. *Education:* Harvard College (A.B., cum laude, 1974); University of Southern California (J.D., 1978). Tort Law Instructor, Insurance Educational Association, 1982—. Adjunct Professor, Chapman University School of Law, 1995—. *Member:* Los Angeles County and American Bar Associations; State Bar of California; Association of Southern California Defense Counsel. **PRACTICE AREAS:** Insurance Coverage; Bad Faith; Tort Litigation.

**T. J. CEBULA,** born Washington, D.C., March 31, 1957; admitted to bar, 1983, California. *Education:* California State University at Long Beach (B.A., 1980); Loyola Law School, Los Angeles (J.D., 1983). *Member:* State Bar of California; Long Beach, Los Angeles County and American Bar Associations; Association of Southern California Defense Counsel. **PRACTICE AREAS:** General Civil Law; Litigation; Insurance Defense Law; Fraud and Suspicious Claims.

**JOHN M. RYGH,** born Canton, South Dakota, November 1, 1953; admitted to bar, 1986, California; U.S. District Court, Central and Southern Districts of California. *Education:* Colorado State University (B.A., 1979 ); Southwestern University (J.D., 1986). Phi Alpha Delta. Moot Court Honors Program. *Member:* State Bar of California. **PRACTICE AREAS:** Construction Defect; Insurance Defense; Employment Law; Governmental Entities.

---

**DONA FAY BAUER,** born Washington, D.C., July 25, 1953; admitted to bar, 1985, California; 1986, U.S. District Court, Central District of California. *Education:* Pasadena City College (A.A., 1980; Paralegal Certificate, 1981); Whittier College (J.D., 1984). *Member:* State Bar of California. **PRACTICE AREAS:** Municipality Defense; Premises Liability; Uninsured Motorist Litigation.

**DAVID C. WILLIAMSON,** born Beatrice, Nebraska, September 27, 1956; admitted to bar, 1982, Nebraska and U.S. District Court, District of Nebraska; 1987, California; 1988, U.S. District Court, Central District of California. *Education:* University of Nebraska at Lincoln (B.A., 1979; J.D., 1982). Author: "Medical Indigency in Nebraska," Nebraska Legislative Council, 1986. *Member:* Long Beach, Los Angeles County, Nebraska State and American Bar Associations; State Bar of California (Member, Young Lawyers Section). **PRACTICE AREAS:** Entertainment Law.

*(This Listing Continued)*

### JOHNSON, CEBULA & RYGH, A PROFESSIONAL CORPORATION, Long Beach—Continued

**BARBARA M. MCANDREWS,** born Los Angeles, California, February 4, 1962; admitted to bar, 1988, California and U.S. District Court, Central District of California. *Education:* University of California at Irvine (B.S., 1985); Southwestern University (J.D., 1988). Moot Court Honors Program. *Member:* Los Angeles County and American Bar Associations; State Bar of California. *PRACTICE AREAS:* Insurance Coverage; Environmental Law; Transactional Law; Receiverships.

**MICHAEL D. LIND,** born Des Moines, Iowa, June 2, 1962; admitted to bar, 1988, California and U.S. District Court, Central and Southern Districts of California. *Education:* California State University at Long Beach (B.A., summa cum laude, 1985); Hastings College of Law, University of California (J.D., 1988). *Member:* State Bar of California; American Bar Association. *PRACTICE AREAS:* General Civil Law; Insurance Coverage; Bad Faith; General Civil Appellate Practice; Insurance Defense.

**TAMAR POLADIAN,** born Cairo, Egypt, October 25, 1964; admitted to bar, 1991, California and U.S. District Court, Central District of California. *Education:* University of California at Los Angeles (B.A., 1986); Southwestern University School of Law, (J.D., 1990). Phi Alpha Delta. *Member:* Los Angeles County, American and Armenian Bar Associations; State Bar of California. *LANGUAGES:* Armenian. *PRACTICE AREAS:* General Civil Law; Litigation; Insurance Defense; Premises Liability.

**DAVID BRIAN ROSENBERG,** born Van Nuys, California, December 4, 1960; admitted to bar, 1986, California and U.S. District Court, Central and Eastern Districts of California. *Education:* California State University at Northridge (B.A., 1983); Whittier College (J.D., 1986). Recipient, American Jurisprudence Award - Torts, 1983. *PRACTICE AREAS:* Premises Liability; Tort Litigation.

**THEODORE S. OKAZAKI,** born Los Angeles, California, January 27, 1962; admitted to bar, 1989, California and U.S. District Court, Central District of California. *Education:* University of California at Los Angeles (B.A., 1985); Southwestern University School of Law (J.D., 1988). *Member:* Los Angeles County Bar Association; State Bar of California; Japanese American Bar Association. *LANGUAGES:* Japanese. *PRACTICE AREAS:* Premises Liability; Tort Litigation; Government Entities; Insurance Defense.

**CONNIE A. MCHUGH,** born Long Beach, California, April 23, 1961; admitted to bar, 1992, California and U.S. District Court, Central District of California. *Education:* California State University, Long Beach (B.S., 1984); Western State University (J.D., 1988). *Member:* Long Beach, Los Angeles County and American Bar Associations. *PRACTICE AREAS:* Civil Law; Litigation; Insurance Defense.

---

### KAISER & SWINDELLS

*Established in 1981*

**SUITE 900 SUMITOMO TOWER
444 WEST OCEAN BOULEVARD
LONG BEACH, CALIFORNIA 90802-4516**
Telephone: 310-590-8471
Telecopier: 310-437-0903
Email: ks@kaiserlaw.com
URL: http://www.crl.com/~kaiser/

*Civil Trial Practice. Insurance Defense, Personal Injury, Products Liability, Construction, Common Carrier, Condominium and Homeowners Association Law, Insurance Fraud, Environmental, Trucking, Professional Negligence, Vertical Transportation, Business Torts and Litigation.*

*FIRM PROFILE: Integrity and excellence of work product are the two basic principles of outstanding legal service. Sensitive legal disputes require trustworthy lawyers. Accurate counseling and skillful advocacy are the hallmarks of excellent work product. We are committed to these principles.*

**RAYMOND T. KAISER,** born April 8, 1951; admitted to bar, 1976, California; 1977, U.S. District Court, Central District of California and U.S. Court of Appeals, Ninth Circuit; 1980, U.S. Supreme Court. *Education:* University of Southern California (B.A., cum laude, 1973); Loyola University of Los Angeles (J.D., cum laude, 1976). Member, St. Thomas More Law Society. Recipient, American Jurisprudence Award in Constitutional Law. Arbitrator, American Arbitration Association. LASC South District Settlement Officer. Member, Joseph A. Ball, Clarence S. Hunt, Inn of Court, Long Beach. Member, California Technology Association. Member, Association for California Tort Reform. *Member:* Long Beach, Los Angeles County and American Bar Associations; State Bar of California; Association of Southern California Defense Counsel; Southern California Association of Healthcare Risk Managers; Southern California Fraud Investigators Association. *Email:* raymond@kaiserlaw.com

**PAMELA A. SWINDELLS,** born February 5, 1949; admitted to bar, 1988, California, U.S. District Court, Central District of California and U.S. Court of Appeals, Ninth Circuit. *Education:* Rhode Island Hospital School of Nursing (R.N., 1969); University of Redlands (B.A., 1978); Pace University (J.D., 1987). Registered Nurse, California, 1974. Member, Board of Trustees, Long Beach Community Hospital Foundation. Member, Joseph A. Ball, Clarence S. Hunt, Inn of Court, Long Beach. *Member:* Long Beach Bar Association; State Bar of California; Long Beach Women Lawyers Association; Southern California Association of Healthcare Risk Managers; Southern California Fraud Investigators Association. [Capt., U.S. Air Force, 1970-1974] *Email:* pamela@kaiserlaw.com

#### ASSOCIATES

**WAYNE D. LOUVIER,** born February 6, 1957; admitted to bar, 1983, California; 1984, U.S. District Court, Central District of California. *Education:* University of California at Irvine (B.A., 1979); Western State University (J.D., 1983). *Member:* Long Beach Bar Association; State Bar of California. *Email:* wayne@kaiserlaw.com

**ERIC C. DEMLER,** born Long Beach, California, May 9, 1954; admitted to bar, 1980, California, U.S. District Court, Central District of California and U.S. Court of Appeals, Ninth Circuit. *Education:* California State University at Long Beach (B.A., with honors, 1977); Loyola University of Los Angeles (J.D., 1980). Phi Alpha Delta. *Member:* Long Beach Bar Association; State Bar of California. *Email:* eric@kaiserlaw.com

---

### KEESAL, YOUNG & LOGAN

*A PROFESSIONAL CORPORATION*

*Established in 1970*

**400 OCEANGATE**
P.O. BOX 1730
**LONG BEACH, CALIFORNIA 90802-1730**
Telephone: 310-436-2000
Telex: KEESAL LGB 656460
Telecopier: 310-436-7416

*San Francisco, California Office:* Four Embarcadero Center, Suite 1500. Telephone: 415-398-6000. Telecopier: 415-981-7729; 415-362-8535. Telex: KEESAL SF 656460.

*Anchorage, Alaska Office:* 1029 W. 3rd Avenue, Suite 650. Telephone: 907-279-9696. Telecopier: 907-279-4239. Telex: KEESAL LGB 656460.

*Seattle, Washington Office:* 1301 Fifth Avenue, Suite 2714. Telephone: 206-622-3790. Telecopier: 206-343-9529. Telex: KEESAL LGB 656460.

*Hong Kong Office:* 1603 The Centre Mark, 287 Queen's Road Central. Telephone: 852-285-41718. Telecopier: 852-254-16189.

*General Civil Trial, Appellate and Business Practice, Securities, Employment, Admiralty, Commodities, Professional Malpractice, Insurance, Real Estate, Employment, Real Estate, Corporate, Environmental, Franchise, Labor, Intellectual Property, Products Liability and Administrative Law.*

*FIRM PROFILE: Keesal, Young & Logan has developed the reputation for providing quality, results-oriented legal services to its clients. Those clients are a prestigious group from the securities, financial services, real estate, insurance, maritime and software industries. With offices in Long Beach, San Francisco, Anchorage and Seattle, KY&L attorneys routinely handle matters throughout the western United States, ranging from civil trials, arbitrations, labor disputes and regulatory proceedings to shipboard investigations and commercial transactions. The firm specializes in business, securities litigation, employment, admiralty and professional malpractice, in addition to a general business practice that includes corporate finance, securities, commercial law, intellectual property and real estate.*

**SAMUEL A. KEESAL, JR.,** born Chicago, Illinois, July 31, 1939; admitted to bar, 1966, California; 1982, Hawaii; 1991, Colorado; 1973, U.S. Supreme Court. *Education:* University of Arizona; Long Beach State College (B.S., 1962); University of Southern California (LL.B., 1965). Outstanding Law Associate. Listed in: Best Lawyers of America, Civil Litigation, all six editions and Maritime Law Association, International Academy of Trial Lawyers (Member, Board of Directors, 1994—). American Board of Trial Advocates (Advocate); Outstanding Alumnus of Business School at California State University, Long Beach, 1991. Co-Author: "Shipowners'

*(This Listing Continued)*

Liability for Longshoremen Personal Injuries: The Supreme Court Blocks The 'Importation' of Unseaworthiness," 7 U.S.F., Mar. L.J. 67, 1994; "Employment Disputes," in Securities Arbitration 1992, Vol. 2 (PLI Corporate Law and Practice Course Handbook, Series No. 781, 1992). *Member:* Los Angeles County and American (Member, Committee on Commodities Regulation, 1980-1981; Vice Chairman, Securities, Commodities and Exchange Subcommittee of the Administrative Law Section, 1985-1988) Bar Associations; State Bar of California (Member, 1968-1973 and Chairman, 1969-1973, Disciplinary Committee); Maritime Law Association of the United States (Member, Committee on Personnel, 1983—). (Also at San Francisco Office).

*J. STEPHEN YOUNG,* born Hartford, Connecticut, May 9, 1948; admitted to bar, 1973, California. *Education:* University of California at Los Angeles (B.A., 1970); University of Southern California (J.D., 1973). *Member:* State Bar of California (Member, Securities Industry Association Broker Dealer Litigation Committee). *PRACTICE AREAS:* Securities and Commodity Futures Litigation; Securities and Commodity Futures Regulatory Work and Employment Litigation.

*ROBERT H. LOGAN,* born Coco Solo, Canal Zone, March 29, 1948; admitted to bar, 1973, California. *Education:* Stanford University (A.B. 1970); University of Southern California (J.D., 1973). *Member:* State Bar of California; Maritime Law Association of the United States.

*MICHAEL M. GLESS,* born Los Angeles, California, August 1, 1940; admitted to bar, 1966, California; 1975, U.S. Supreme Court. *Education:* University of Southern California (B.S., 1962; LL.B., 1965). Member, Board of Directors, Legion Lex. Mediator, Los Angeles Superior Court, 1992-1994. *Member:* State Bar of California; American Bar Association; Maritime Law Association of the United States; American Board of Trial Advocates (National Board of Directors, 1993-1994); Southern California Defense Counsel.

*PETER R. BOUTIN,* born San Francisco, California, October 6, 1950; admitted to bar, 1975, California; 1982, U.S. Supreme Court. *Education:* Stanford University (A.B., 1972); University of Santa Clara (J.D., magna cum laude, 1975). Comments Editor, Santa Clara Law Review, 1974-1975. Author: "The Medical Malpractice Crisis: Is the Medical Review Committee a Viable and Legal Alternative?" 15 Santa Clara Law Review 405, 1975. Co-Author: "American Arbitration Association Securities Arbitration Training Materials" (1994). U.S. District Court Early Neutral Evaluator. Member: Panel of Arbitrators, San Francisco Superior Court; San Francisco Superior Court Settlement Panel; American Arbitration Association Securities Advisory Committee. *Member:* Bar Association of San Francisco; State Bar of California; Association of Business Trial Lawyers. (Resident, San Francisco Office). *REPORTED CASES:* Clifton v. Ulis, 17 Cal. 3d 99 (1976); Meier v. Texas Int'l. Drilling Funds, Inc.; 441 F. Supp 1056 (N.D. Cal., 1977); MacMurray v. Bear Stearns, Fed. Sec. L. Rep (CCH) P99, 617 (C.D. Cal ., 1983); Schetter v. Prudential-Bache Securities, Inc., 695 F. Supp 1077 (E.D. Cal., 1988); King v. Prudential-Bache Securities, Inc., 226 Cal. App. 749 (1990); Sheppard v. Morgan Keegan, 218 Cal. App. 3d 61 (1990). *PRACTICE AREAS:* Securities Litigation; Employment Litigation; Professional Malpractice Litigation.

*SCOTT T. PRATT,* born Fall River, Massachusetts, January 30, 1950; admitted to bar, 1975, California. *Education:* University of Southern California (B.S., 1972); University of California at Los Angeles (J.D., 1975). Member, 1973-1975 and Topics Editor, 1974-1975, Alaska Law Review. *Member:* State Bar of California; Maritime Law Association of the United States.

*TERRY ROSS,* born Los Angeles, California, October 11, 1948; admitted to bar, 1973, California; 1987, U.S. Supreme Court. *Education:* Stanford University (A.B., 1970); University of Southern California (J.D., 1973). *Member:* Los Angeles County Bar Association; State Bar of California; Maritime Law Association of the United States.

*JOHN D. GIFFIN,* born Stephenville, Newfoundland, Canada, March 1, 1951; admitted to bar, 1979, California. *Education:* University of Oklahoma (B.B.A., 1973); Hastings College of Law, University of California (J.D., 1979). *Member:* State Bar of California; American Bar Association; Maritime Law Association of the United States. [Lt., USN, 1972-1976]. (Resident, San Francisco Office).

*WILLIAM H. COLLIER, JR.,* born Galveston, Texas, November 1, 1952; admitted to bar, 1978, Louisiana; 1979, Texas; 1981, California. *Education:* Rice University (B.A., cum laude, 1975); Tulane University of Louisiana (J.D., 1978). *Member:* Louisiana State Bar Association; State Bar of Texas; State Bar of California; Maritime Law Association of the United States.

*(This Listing Continued)*

*ROBERT D. FEIGHNER,* born Roanoke, Virginia, January 14, 1951; admitted to bar, 1976, California. *Education:* University of Maryland (B.A., magna cum laude, 1973); University of Southern California (J.D., 1976). Phi Beta Kappa; Phi Alpha Delta. *Member:* State Bar of California.

*PHILIP MCLEOD,* born Berkeley, California, February 25, 1953; admitted to bar, 1981, California. *Education:* University of California at Santa Cruz (B.A., with honors, 1976); Hastings College of Law, University of California (J.D., 1981). *Member:* State Bar of California. (Resident, San Francisco Office).

*NEAL SCOTT ROBB,* born San Jose, California, November 13, 1957; admitted to bar, 1982, California. *Education:* University of California at Irvine (B.A., with honors, 1979); Hastings College of Law, University of California (J.D., 1982). Member, 1980-1981, and Executive Technical Editor, 1981-1982, Comm./Ent., A Journal of Communications and Entertainment Law. *Member:* State Bar of California.

*BEN SUTER,* born Sacramento, California, December 14, 1954; admitted to bar, 1982, California; 1983, Arizona; 1984, Hawaii; 1987, U.S. Supreme Court. *Education:* University of California at Santa Barbara (B.A., 1978); Hastings College of Law, University of California (J.D., 1982). Member, 1980-1982, and Articles Editor, 1981-1982, Hastings Constitutional Law Quarterly. *Member:* State Bar of California; State Bar of Arizona; Hawaii State Bar Association. (Resident, San Francisco Office). *LANGUAGES:* French. *REPORTED CASES:* Unioil, Inc. v. E.F. Hutton & Co., 809 F 2d 548 (9th Cir., 1986); Franklin v. Kaypro Corp., 884 F2d 1222 (9th Cir., 1989); Levine v. Diamanthuset, Inc., 722 F Supp 579 (N.D. Cal., 1989); Greenberg v. Shearson Lehman Brothers, Inc., 1993 WL 144856 (C.D. Cal., 1993) Aff'd 60 F 3D 834 (9th Cir., 1995); Glavor v. Shearson Lehman Hutton, Inc., 879 F Supp 1028 (N.D. Cal., 1994) Aff'd - 89 F3d 845 (9th Cir., 1996).

*STEPHEN C. CLIFFORD,* born New Haven, Connecticut, January 29, 1949; admitted to bar, 1973, District of Columbia; 1983, California. *Education:* Georgetown University (B.S.F.S., 1970); Catholic University (J.D., 1973); George Washington University (LL.M., 1980). Author: "Motor Carriers' Duty of Service in Conflict with the Protected Right of Employee-Drivers to Honor Picket Lines at Shippers' Premises," 49 ICC Practitioners Journal 142, 1982. *Member:* The District of Columbia Bar; State Bar of California. (Resident, San Francisco Office).

*E. SCOTT DOUGLAS,* born Los Angeles, California, July 10, 1958; admitted to bar, 1983, California; 1985, Hawaii. *Education:* University of Santa Clara (B.S., 1980) University of San Diego (J.D., 1983). Member, 1981-1982 and Comments Editor, 1982-1983, San Diego Law Review. Law Clerk to the Hon. A. Andrew Hauk, Senior Judge and Chief Judge Emeritus, U.S. District Court, Central District of California, 1983-1984. *Member:* Hawaii State and American Bar Associations; State Bar of California.

*SHANNON L. MCDOUGALD,* born Portland, Oregon, October 3, 1959; admitted to bar, 1985, California; 1994, Washington. *Education:* Loyola Marymount University (B.A., 1981); Alpha Sigma Nu; University of California at Los Angeles (J.D., 1984). Member, Moot Court Honors Program, Distinguished Advocate. *Member:* King County and Washington State Bar Associations; State Bar of California; Maritime Law Association of the United States. (Resident, Seattle, Washington Office). *PRACTICE AREAS:* Litigation; Securities; Admiralty and Maritime Law; Entertainment Law.

*WILLIAM E. MCDONNELL, JR.,* born San Francisco, California, June 12, 1951; admitted to bar, 1979, California; 1980, District of Columbia. *Education:* University of California at Berkeley (B.A., 1973); Hastings College of Law, University of California (J.D., 1978). Author: "The CFTC'S Large Trader Reporting System," 38 Business Lawyer 917-951, May, 1983; "Prejudgment Interest as Damages in Commodity Futures Litigation," 40 Business Lawyer, 1267-1282, August, 1985; "Recovery of Prejudgment Interest on Commodity Futures Claims: Recent Developments," Commercial Damages Reporter, Vol. 3, Issue 2, 34-37, March, 1988. *Member:* The State Bar of California. (Resident, San Francisco Office).

*MICHAEL A. THURMAN,* born Los Angeles, California, May 3, 1957; admitted to bar, 1985, Oregon; 1986, California. *Education:* Stanford University (A.B., with honors, 1979); University of Oregon (J.D., 1985). Recipient, American Jurisprudence Award for Academic Excellence in Criminal Procedure. *Member:* Long Beach and American (Member, Litigation Section) Bar Associations; Oregon State Bar; State Bar of California.

*DAWN M. SCHOCK,* born Ashley, North Dakota, February 26, 1957; admitted to bar, 1985, California. *Education:* University of North Dakota (B.A., 1979); Long Island University (M.A., 1981 ); McGeorge School of

*(This Listing Continued)*

**KEESAL, YOUNG & LOGAN,** A PROFESSIONAL CORPORATION, Long Beach—Continued

the Law, University of the Pacific (J.D., 1985). *Member:* State Bar of California; California Women's Lawyers (President-Elect).

**TIMOTHY N. WILL,** born Arcadia, California, April 17, 1959; admitted to bar, 1986, California. *Education:* University of the Pacific (B.S., 1981); University of San Diego (J.D., 1985). Member and Comment Editor, San Diego Law Review, 1984-1985. Author: "Tender Offer Defenses: The Need for National Guidelines in Light of Mobil," San Diego Law Review, Vol. 21, 1985. *Member:* Los Angeles County Bar Association; State Bar of California.

**ALBERT E. PEACOCK, III,** born Los Angeles, California, April 1, 1959; admitted to bar, 1983, Hawaii; 1988, California; 1990, U.S. Supreme Court; 1994, Alaska. *Education:* University of Southern California (B.A., magna cum laude, 1980; J.D., 1983). Phi Beta Kappa; Phi Delta Phi. *Member:* Hawaii State Bar Association; State Bar of California; Maritime Law Association of the United States. (Resident, Anchorage, Alaska Office).

**CAMERON STOUT,** born Redwood City, California, March 10, 1958; admitted to bar, 1985, California. *Education:* Princeton University (A.B., 1980); University of San Francisco (J.D., with honors, 1984). *Member:* The State Bar of California. (Resident, San Francisco Office). *LANGUAGES:* French. *REPORTED CASES:* Washington v. Baenziger, 673 F Supp. 1478 (N.D. Cal., 1987).

**JOHN R. LOFTUS,** born Paterson, New Jersey, September 17, 1958; admitted to bar, 1987, California. *Education:* St. Michaels College (B.A. in History and Spanish, 1980); Whittier College (J.D., magna cum laude, 1986). Editor-in-Chief, Whittier Law Review, 1985-1986. Recipient, American Board of Trial Advocates Award. Author: "Admiralty Jurisdiction: Tort Actions of Ship Repair and Construction Workers-Application of Locality Test and Traditional Maritime Activity Test," 7 Whittier Law Review 393, 1985. *Member:* State Bar of California.

**DAVID M. BARTHOLOMEW,** born Fairbanks, Alaska, June 23, 1959; admitted to bar, 1987, California and U.S. District Court, Central and Southern Districts of California. *Education:* Wesleyan University (B.A., 1981); University of Southern California (J.D., 1986). *Member:* State Bar of California.

**JEFFREY D. WARREN,** born New Haven, Connecticut, November 22, 1956; admitted to bar, 1981, Texas; 1988, Arizona; 1991, California. *Education:* Purdue University (B.A., honors, 1978); University of Houston (J.D., cum laude, 1981). Phi Delta Phi. Member, Order of the Barons. *Member:* State Bar of Texas; State Bar of Arizona; State Bar of California.

**ROBERT J. STEMLER,** born Detroit, Michigan, April 11, 1962; admitted to bar, 1987, California. *Education:* University of Southern California (B.A., 1984; J.D., 1987). Phi Delta Phi. *Member:* State Bar of California.

**LISA M. BERTAIN,** born San Francisco, California, May 19, 1960; admitted to bar, 1986, California. *Education:* University of California at Berkeley (A.B., 1982); University of San Francisco (J.D., with honors, 1986). Recipient, American Jurisprudence Award in Remedies. Author: "Defense Strategies For Voir Dire In A Sexual Harassment Case" (CTLA Annual Convention 1992); "California Discrimination Laws" (CEB 1996); "Economic Suicide Claims: An Emerging Trend In Securities Litigation" (PLI 1996). Panelist: "Sexual Harassment Mock Trial" (CTLA Annual Convention 1992); "Gender Bias In The Legal Profession" (CEB 1996); "Emerging Trends In Securities Arbitration" (PLI 1996). Deputy District Attorney, Alameda County District Attorney's Office, 1986-1989. California District Attorney's Association, 1986-1989. *Member:* State Bar of California. (Resident, San Francisco Office).

**JANET M. SIMMONS,** born Torrance, California, April 10, 1962; admitted to bar, 1987, California. *Education:* University of California at Los Angeles (B.A., 1984); Loyola Marymount University (J.D., 1987). *Member:* State Bar of California; California Attorneys for Criminal Justice.

**ROBERT J. BOCKO,** born Terra Haute, Indiana, May 13, 1960; admitted to bar, 1986, Washington and U.S. District Court, Western District of Washington; 1988, U.S. Court of Appeals, Ninth Circuit. *Education:* University of Maine (J.D., 1985). *Member:* King County and Washington State Bar Associations; Maritime Law Association of the United States. (Resident, Seattle, Washington Office).

**MICHELE R. FRON,** born Chicago, Illinois, July 3, 1958; admitted to bar, 1988, California. *Education:* University of California at Irvine (B.A., 1980); Western State University (J.D., cum laude, 1987). Recipient, American Jurisprudence Awards. NASD/NYSE Registered Representative, 1982-1989. Member, Western State University Law Review, 1986-1987. *Member:* State Bar of California. *LANGUAGES:* Spanish.

**ROBERT A. S. BLEICHER,** born San Francisco, California, August 4, 1958; admitted to bar, 1983, California. *Education:* University of California at Berkeley (A.B., with honors, with distinction in general scholarship, 1980); University of Santa Clara (J.D., 1983). *Member:* State Bar of California. (Resident, San Francisco Office).

**MICHAEL L. ARMITAGE,** born Weybridge, Surrey, England, November 9, 1961; admitted to bar, 1987, Louisiana; 1991, California. *Education:* Purdue University; Tulane University (B.A., magna cum laude, 1984; J.D., cum laude, 1987). Order of the Coif. Senior Fellow, Legal Research and Writing Program, Tulane University. Member, Tulane Moot Court Board. Co-Author: "Shipowners' Liability for Longshoremen Personal Injuries: The Supreme Court Blocks The Importation of Unseaworthiness," 7 U.S.F., Mar. L.J. 67, 1994. *Member:* New Orleans, Louisiana State, Federal and American Bar Associations; State Bar of California; Maritime Law Association of the United States. *LANGUAGES:* Spanish and Portuguese.

**ROBERT B. ERICSON,** born Bronxville, New York, February 16, 1958; admitted to bar, 1984, California; 1985, U.S. Court of Appeals, Ninth Circuit. *Education:* Stanford University (B.A., with honors, 1980); University of California at Los Angeles (J.D., 1984). Comments and Articles Editor, Federal Communications Law Journal, 1982-1984. Distinguished Advocate, Moot Court Honors Program. Extern Law Clerk to Hon. Frank K. Richardson, California Supreme Court, Summer, 1982. *Member:* State Bar of California.

**ELIZABETH P. BEAZLEY,** born Newport Beach, California, June 9, 1961; admitted to bar, 1988, California. *Education:* University of California at Berkeley (B.A., History and Political Science, 1983); University of San Diego (J.D., 1988). *Member:* Los Angeles County Bar Association; State Bar of California.

**PAUL J. SCHUMACHER,** born Roslyn, New York, November 11, 1951; admitted to bar, 1984, California. *Education:* Santa Clara University (B.S., 1973); Loyola Law School (J.D., cum laude, 1983). Member, St. Thomas More Law Honors Society. *Member:* State Bar of California; American Bar Association.

**BRIAN L. ZAGON,** born Los Angeles, California, December 18, 1963; admitted to bar, 1989, California. *Education:* University of California (B.A., 1985); Hastings College of Law, University of California (J.D., 1989). Order of the Coif. Member, Thurston Society. Recipient, American Jurisprudence Awards in Torts, Civil Procedure, Legal Writing Research and Secured Transactions. *Member:* State Bar of California. (Resident, San Francisco Office).

## ASSOCIATES

**DOUGLAS R. DAVIS,** born Salt Lake City, Utah, February 7, 1949; admitted to bar, 1975, Utah; 1976, Alaska. *Education:* University of Utah (B.S., 1972); Gonzaga University (J.D., 1975). *Member:* Alaska Bar Association; Maritime Law Association of the United States. (Resident, Anchorage, Alaska Office).

**ELIZABETH A. KENDRICK,** born Whittier, California, February 28, 1959; admitted to bar, 1986, California. *Education:* University of California at Los Angeles (B.A., 1982); Oxford University, England; Loyola Law School of Los Angeles (J.D., 1985). Jessup International Honors Moot Court Team. Co-Author: "Errors and Omissions Coverage For Securities Brokers," Defense Counsel Journal, Vol. 61, No. 3, July, 1994. *Member:* State Bar of California.

**JOHN A. TREPTOW,** born Fairmont, Minnesota, April 13, 1946; admitted to bar, 1972, Missouri; 1973, California; 1976, Alaska. *Education:* Washington University (A.B., 1968; J.D., 1971). Law Clerk to the Hon. Theodore McMillan, Missouri Court of Appeals, 1972-1973. Co-Author: "Broker Liability," Alaska Bar Association, 1988; "Trial Advocacy in Alaska," NBI, 1989; "Personal Injury Litigation Practice in Alaska," NBI, 1990; "How to Evaluate and Settle Personal Injury Claims in Alaska," PESI, 1992. *Member:* Alaska and American Bar Associations; State Bar of California; The Association of Trial Lawyers of America; Association of Ski Defense Attorneys; Defense Research Institute (DRI). (Resident, Anchorage, Alaska Office). *REPORTED CASES:* Basel v. Westward Trawlers, Inc., 869 P.2d 1185 (Alaska, 1994); Chevron USA, Inc. v. Hammond, 726 F.2d 483 (9th Circuit, 1984), cert. denied 471 U.S. 1140 (1985); Industrial Risk Insurers v. Creole Production Services, Inc., 746 F.2d 526 (Ninth Circuit, 1985); Webster v. Bechtel, Inc., 621 P.2d 890 (Alaska, 1980).

*(This Listing Continued)*

**SUSAN WRIGHT MASON,** born Charlotte, North Carolina, April 9, 1944; admitted to bar, 1978, North Carolina; 1979, Alaska; 1982, U.S. Supreme Court. *Education:* Hollins College (B.A., with honors, 1966); University of North Carolina, Chapel Hill (J.D., with honors, 1978). Phi Beta Kappa. Law Clerk to Justice Edmond Burke, Alaska Supreme Court, 1978-1979. Alaska Supreme Court Committee on Appellate Rules, 1988—. Co-Author: "Administrative Law: Challenging and Advising Agency Conduct," Alaska Bar Association, 1994; "Effective Appellate Practice in Alaska," NBI, 1994. *Member:* Alaska and American Bar Associations; North Carolina State Bar; National Health Lawyers Association; American Academy of Healthcare Attorneys; Anchorage Inn of Court. (Resident, Anchorage, Alaska Office).

**JON W. ZINKE,** born Mineola, New York, October 9, 1953; admitted to bar, 1981, New York and U.S. District Court, Southern and Eastern Districts of New York. *Education:* State University of New York Maritime College (B.S., 1975); Brooklyn Law School (J.D., 1980). U.S. Coast Guard Chief Mates License, Ocean Going, Unlimited Tonnage, 1992. Chairman, Law Committee, American Chamber of Commerce in Hong Kong, 1996-1997. *Member:* American Bar Association; Maritime Law Association of the United States. [Lt. (Ret.), U.S. Naval Reserve, 1975-1988]. (Resident, Hong Kong Office).

**LINDA A. LOFTUS,** born Los Angeles, California, June 12, 1956; admitted to bar, 1988, California. *Education:* University of California at Santa Barbara (B.A., 1978); Loyola Marymount University (J.D., 1987). *Member:* State Bar of California.

**ERIC SWETT,** born Los Angeles, California, March 31, 1957; admitted to bar, 1986, California. *Education:* Amherst College (B.A., 1979); University of Oregon (J.D., 1986). Member, Moot Trial Team. *Member:* American Bar Association; State Bar of California. (Resident, San Francisco Office). *LANGUAGES:* French and Spanish.

**GREGORY E. COPELAND,** born Alhambra, California, June 27, 1946; admitted to bar, 1989, California. *Education:* University of California at Santa Cruz (B.A., summa cum laude, 1977); Johns Hopkins University; Loyola Marymount University (J.D., 1989). Recipient, American Jurisprudence Award in Legal Thought. *Member:* State Bar of California.

**JOSEPH A. WALSH, II,** born Salina, Kansas, June 8, 1961; admitted to bar, 1989, California. *Education:* U.S. Merchant Marine Academy (B.S., with honors, 1983); University of Arizona (J.D., cum laude, 1989). Member, Moot Court Board. Recipient, Boris Kozolchyk Award for Best Student Note. Master, 1600 GT; Second Mate, Unlimited, U.S. Coast Guard, 1993. Author: "Documentary Maritime Fraud: Redefining the Standard," 6 Arizona Journal of International and Comparative Law. *Member:* Los Angeles County Bar Association (Member, International Law Section); State Bar of California; Maritime Law Association of the United States. [With U.S. Navy, 1983-1986; LCDR (SWO), U.S. Naval Reserve, 1986—]

**MICHAEL C. LICOSATI,** born Phoenix, Arizona, October 8, 1964; admitted to bar, 1989, California. *Education:* University of San Diego (B.A., 1986; J.D., 1989). *Member:* State Bar of California; American Bar Association.

**JODI S. COHEN,** born Brooklyn, New York, October 9, 1964; admitted to bar, 1990, California. *Education:* California State University at Fullerton (B.A., 1987); McGeorge School of Law (J.D., 1990). *Member:* American Bar Association. *PRACTICE AREAS:* Securities.

**MARK W. NELSON,** born Sacramento, California, July 28, 1965; admitted to bar, 1990, California; 1996, Colorado. *Education:* California State University, Sacramento (B.A., 1987); University of San Diego (J.D., 1990). Phi Alpha Delta. *Member:* Los Angeles County, Orange County and American Bar Associations; State Bar of California; Maritime Law Association of the United States; Propeller Club of the United States. *PRACTICE AREAS:* Maritime Litigation; Securities Litigation; General Litigation.

**PHILIP R. LEMPRIERE,** born San Francisco, California, April 11, 1961; admitted to bar, 1989, California; 1990, Washington State. *Education:* U.S. Merchant Marine Academy (B.S., 1984); University of San Francisco (J.D., 1989). Business Editor, University of San Francisco Maritime Law Journal, 1988-1989. Charter Member, University of San Francisco Admiralty and Maritime Law Society. Merchant Marine Third Officer, Unlimited Tonnage, NY, 1984. *Member:* State Bar of California; Washington State Bar Association. (Resident, Seattle, Washington Office). *PRACTICE AREAS:* Admiralty/Maritime Law; Insurance Law; Litigation.

**LESLIE M. SULLIVAN,** born Inglewood, California, May 21, 1959; admitted to bar, 1986, California. *Education:* University of California at Los Angeles (B.S., cum laude, 1981); Loyola Marymount University (J.D., 1985). Staff Member, 1983-1984, Note and Comment Editor, 1984-1985, Loyola Law Review. Author: Comment, "California Evidence Code Section 1103: Further Abuse of The Rape Victim," 18 Loy. L.A.L. Rev. 895, 1985. *Member:* Orange County and American Bar Associations; State Bar of California.

**HERBERT H. RAY, JR.,** born Tacoma, Washington, January 16, 1961; admitted to bar, 1988, Alaska. *Education:* College of William and Mary (B.S., 1982); George Mason University (M.S., 1986); University of Oregon (J.D., 1988). Articles Editor, Oregon Law Review. *Member:* Alaska and American Bar Associations; Maritime Law Association of the United States. (Resident, Anchorage, Alaska Office).

**E. SCOTT PALMER,** born Van Nuys, California, March 31, 1966; admitted to bar, 1991, California and U.S. Court of Appeals, Ninth Circuit. *Education:* University of California at Berkeley (B.S., 1988); University of Southern California (J.D., 1991). Phi Delta Phi. Co-Author: California Pollution Law Update, GARD News 124. *Member:* State Bar of California.

**JILL ELIZABETH OLOFSON,** born Cleveland, Ohio, March 21, 1965; admitted to bar, 1991, California. *Education:* University of California at Los Angeles (B.S./B.A., 1988); Loyola Law School (J.D., 1991). Phi Delta Phi. Recipient, American Jurisprudence Awards. *Member:* State Bar of California.

**JULIE LEANN TAYLOR,** born Battle Creek, Michigan, September 12, 1966; admitted to bar, 1991, California. *Education:* California Polytechnic State University (B.A., cum laude, 1988); Hastings College of Law, University of California (J.D., magna cum laude, 1991). Order of the Coif. Member, Hastings Law Journal, 1989-1991. *Member:* State Bar of California. (Resident, San Francisco Office).

**LISA KAYE DONAHUE,** born Moscow, Idaho, March 9. 1966; admitted to bar, 1991, California. *Education:* Cornell University (B.A., 1988); University of California at Los Angeles (J.D., 1991). *Member:* State Bar of California.

**STACEY MYERS GARRETT,** born York, Pennsylvania, September 24, 1966; admitted to bar, 1991, California and U.S. Court of Appeals, Ninth Circuit. *Education:* California Polytechnic State University (B.S., summa cum laude, 1987); Hastings College of Law, University of California (J.D., magna cum laude, 1991). Phi Delta Phi. Order of the Coif. Member, Thurston Society. Member, Hastings Law Journal, 1989-1991. *Member:* State Bar of California.

**MICHAEL A. SITZMAN,** born Boston, Massachusetts, October 14, 1964; admitted to bar, 1991, California. *Education:* University of California at Davis (B.S., 1986); McGeorge School of Law (J.D., with distinction, 1991). Order of the Coif. Associate Comment Editor, Pacific Law Journal, 1990-1991. Author: "Marlene F. vs. Affiliated Psychiatric Medical Clinic: Negligent Infliction of Emotional Distress Bounces Out of Bounds," 22 Pac L.J. 189, 1990; "Copyright: An Alternative within the Field of Biotechnology," April 1990. Recipient: Awarded First Prize, Nathan Burkan Memorial Competition, ASCAP. *Member:* State Bar of California. (Resident, San Francisco Office).

**GORDON CRAIG YOUNG,** born Oakland, California, January 23, 1966; admitted to bar, 1992, California. *Education:* St. Mary's College (B.A., 1988); University of San Francisco (J.D., 1991). Winner, Moot Court Advocate of the Year Competition, 1991-1992. Moot Court Board Case Counsel, 1990-1991. Assistant Articles Editor, University of San Francisco Maritime Law Journal, 1990-1991. *Member:* State Bar of California. (Resident, San Francisco Office).

**WILLIAM J. BRIDGEN,** born Coledale, Pennsylvania, June 2, 1964; admitted to bar, 1989, California; 1990, U.S. Court of Appeals, Ninth Circuit; 1991, District of Columbia. *Education:* Gettysburg College (B.A., 1986); Temple University (J.D., 1989). *Member:* Los Angeles County and American Bar Associations; Bar Association of the District of Columbia; State Bar of California.

**GREGORY A. BOSS,** born Glendale, California, July 5, 1961; admitted to bar, 1987, California. *Education:* University of Southern California (B.S., 1983; J.D., 1987). *Member:* Los Angeles County and American Bar Associations; State Bar of California.

**RICHARD WILLIAM SMIRL,** born Waukesha, Wisconsin, April 18, 1967; admitted to bar, 1992, California. *Education:* University of California (B.A., 1989); Loyola Marymount University (J.D., 1992). *Member:* Los Angeles County and American (Member, Litigation Section) Bar Associations; State Bar of California.

*(This Listing Continued)*

**KEESAL, YOUNG & LOGAN,** A PROFESSIONAL CORPORATION, Long Beach—Continued

**PAUL I. HAMADA,** born Los Angeles, California, September 4, 1964; admitted to bar, 1992, California. *Education:* University of California at Irvine (B.A., cum laude, 1986); University of Chicago (A.M., 1989); Loyola Marymount University (J.D., 1992). Recipient, Alfred P. Sloan Fellowship. Member, 1990-1992 and Note and Comment Editor, 1991-1992, Loyola of Los Angeles Law Review. *Member:* State Bar of California.

**ELIZABETH J. LINDH,** born Boston, Massachusetts, October 10, 1966; admitted to bar, 1992, California. *Education:* University of Arizona (B.A., 1988); University of California, Hastings College of Law (J.D., 1992). Phi Delta Phi. Author, "The Unconstitutionality of the Unitary Tax under the due process and commerce clauses of the U.S. Constitution," Hastings Constitutional Law Quarterly, Summer, 1992. *Member:* Los Angeles Bar Association; State Bar of California.

**LAUREN SARA FORBES,** born Bethesda, Maryland, April 17, 1967; admitted to bar, 1992, California. *Education:* University of California at Irvine (B.A., 1989); Loyola Marymount University (J.D., 1992). *Member:* State Bar of California.

**PETER J. MORGAN, III,** born New Jersey, January 19, 1964; admitted to bar, 1989, Connecticut; 1990, California; 1991, New York. *Education:* Hamilton College (B.A., 1986); University of Connecticut (J.D., with honors, 1989). Assistant District Attorney, Santa Cruz County District Attorney's Office, 1990-1993. *Member:* State Bar of California. (Resident, San Francisco Office).

**JEFFREY SCOTT SIMON,** born New York, N.Y., September 8, 1964; admitted to bar, 1993, California. *Education:* University of San Diego (B.B.A., cum laude, 1987); Boston College (J.D., cum laude, 1993). Certified Public Accountant, California, 1990. *Member:* State Bar of California; American Institute of Certified Public Accountants.

**KELLY J. MOYNIHAN,** born Albany, New York, November 6, 1966; admitted to bar, 1993, California. *Education:* University of California at Los Angeles (B.A., 1989); Hastings College of the Law, University of California (J.D., 1993). *Member:* State Bar of California. (Resident, San Francisco Office).

**ALISSA B. JANES,** born New Hartford, New York, November 12, 1962; admitted to bar, 1993, California. *Education:* Yale University (B.A., magna cum laude, 1984); University of California at Los Angeles (J.D., 1993; M.B.A., 1993). Phi Alpha Delta. Member, Yale Club of New Haven Scholar, 1980-1984. *Member:* State Bar of California. *LANGUAGES:* Italian, French.

**ELIZABETH E. ATLEE,** born San Bernardino, California, April 14, 1965; admitted to bar, 1993, California. *Education:* Yale University (B.A., 1987); University of Southern California (J.D., 1993). Hale Moot Court Winner, 1991-1992. *Member:* State Bar of California; Women Lawyers Association of Long Beach. *LANGUAGES:* Spanish.

**DANIEL J. FINNERTY,** born Mineola, New York, July 17, 1965; admitted to bar, 1993, California. *Education:* United States Merchant Marine Academy (B.S. in Marine Engineering, 1987); George Mason University (J.D., 1993). U.S.C.G. Third Assistant Engineers License, 1987. *Member:* State Bar of California.

**GABRIELLE L. WALKER,** born San Francisco, California, July 3, 1958; admitted to bar, 1993, California. *Education:* John F. Kennedy University (J.D., 1993). Recipient: John F. Kennedy University Outstanding Student Award, 1993; American Jurisprudence Award for Academic Achievement, 1992-1993; West Publishing Award for Outstanding Scholastic Achievement, 1992-1993. Member, 1990-1993 and Editor-In-Chief, 1992-1993, John F. Kennedy University Law Review. *Member:* State Bar of California. (Resident, San Francisco Office).

**THADDEUS I. PAUL,** born Minneapolis, Minnesota, September 28, 1966; admitted to bar, 1993, Washington and U.S. District Court, Western District of Washington. *Education:* University of Minnesota (B.A., 1990), Phi Beta Kappa, Mortar Board President; University of Washington (J.D., 1993). Moot Court Honor Board Vice President, American Jurisprudence Award recipient in Torts and Insurance Law I & II. *Member:* Washington State Bar Association. (Resident, Seattle, Washington Office).

**CRAIG E. HOLDEN,** born Los Angeles, California, February 3, 1970; admitted to bar, 1994, California. *Education:* University of California at Los Angeles (B.A., 1991); Hastings College of the Law, University of California (J.D., 1994). *Member:* State Bar of California.

*(This Listing Continued)*

**ESTHER S. KIM,** born Los Angeles, California, April 6, 1969; admitted to bar, 1994, California. *Education:* University of California at Los Angeles (B.A., 1991); University of San Diego (J.D., 1994). *Member:* State Bar of California. (Resident, San Francisco Office).

**KIMBERLY WONG,** born Los Angeles, California, February 13, 1970; admitted to bar, 1994, California. *Education:* California State University, Northridge (B.A., 1991); Hastings College of the Law, University of California (J.D., 1994). *Member:* State Bar of California.

**JOHN M. WHELAN,** born Jacksonville, North Carolina, June 9, 1961; admitted to bar, 1994, California. *Education:* University of Michigan (B.A., 1983); University of Southern California (J.D., 1994). *Member:* State Bar of California. [Capt., USMC, 1983-1991]

**LAUREN N. SCHWAKE,** born Los Angeles, California, May 6, 1969; admitted to bar, 1994, California. *Education:* University of Pennsylvania (B.A., 1991); Loyola Law School (J.D., 1994). *Member:* State Bar of California.

**TERESA SOLOMON MACK,** born Bakersfield, California, September 27, 1963; admitted to bar, 1994, California. *Education:* California State University, Northridge (B.S., 1986); University of Southern California (J.D., 1994). Sample Fellow, 1993. Certified Public Accountant, California, 1989. *Member:* State Bar of California.

**CHRISTINE ANN MILLER,** born Los Angeles, California, February 11, 1965; admitted to bar, 1995, California. *Education:* University of Southern California (B.S., 1987; J.D., 1995). *Member:* State Bar of California.

**ELIZABETH C. CRANDALL,** born Santa Monica, California, January 29, 1970; admitted to bar, 1995, California. *Education:* University of California at Berkeley (B.A., with high distinction, 1992); McGeorge School of Law/University of the Pacific (J.D., with great distinction, 1995). Phi Beta Kappa; Phi Delta Phi. Member, Order of the Coif. Member and Assistant Comment Editor, The Transnational Lawyer Law Journal, 1993-1995. Recipient: American Jurisprudence Award; West Publishing Award for Most Significant Contribution Toward Overall Legal Scholarships. Author: "Will Nafta's North American Agreement on Labor Cooperation Improve Enforcement of Mexican Labor Laws?" 7 Transnat'l Law, 165, 1995. *Member:* State Bar of California.

**DAVID SHANE BRUN,** born De Queen, Arkansas, February 28, 1967; admitted to bar, 1995, California. *Education:* University of Arkansas (B.S.I.E., 1990); University of California, Hastings College of the Law (J.D., 1995). Phi Alpha Delta (Vice-President, 1993—). *Member:* State Bar of California. (Resident, San Francisco Office).

**DENA L. MURPHY,** born Pasadena, California, November 30, 1969; admitted to bar, 1995, California. *Education:* California State University, Long Beach (B.S., 1992); University of San Diego (J.D., magna cum laude, 1995). Executive Editor, San Diego Law Review, 1994-1995. *Member:* State Bar of California.

**KATHLEEN N. HIROSE,** born Los Angeles, California, June 1, 1969; admitted to bar, 1995, California. *Education:* University of California at Los Angeles (B.A., 1992); Loyola Marymount University (J.D., 1995). Phi Alpha Delta. Member, St. Thomas More Honor Society, 1993-1995. *Member:* State Bar of California.

**SARAH TONG SANGMEISTER,** born Madison, Wisconsin, June 24, 1969; admitted to bar, 1994, California. *Education:* Northwestern University (B.S., 1991); Pepperdine School of Law (J.D., 1994). Phi Delta Phi.

**TED FYKE ANGUS, JR.,** born Salt Lake City, Utah, October 19, 1970; admitted to bar, 1996, California. *Education:* University of California at Los Angeles (B.A., 1992); Hastings College of the Law (J.D., cum laude, 1996). Order of the Coif; Phi Alpha Delta (President); Thurston Society. Recipient, American Jurisprudence Award in Contracts. (Resident, San Francisco Office).

**SHANNON S. WAGONER,** born San Francisco, California, January 13, 1971; admitted to bar, 1996, California. *Education:* University of California, Santa Barbara (B.A., cum laude, 1992); Hastings College of the Law (J.D., 1996). American Jurisprudence Award, Legal Writing and Research. Author, Note, "American Geophysical Union v. Texaco: Is the Second Circuit Playing Fair With the Fair Use Doctrine?" 18 Comm/Ent Law Journal 181, 1995. (Resident, San Francisco Office).

**ADYM W. RYGMYR,** born Mt. Vernon, Washington, February 19, 1969; admitted to bar, 1996, California. *Education:* University of Puget Sound (B.A., Business, with honors, 1991); University of Southern California (J.D., 1996).

*(This Listing Continued)*

# PROFESSIONAL BIOGRAPHIES

## CALIFORNIA—LONG BEACH

**PAMELA J. REEDER,** born Redwood City, California, February 27, 1971; admitted to bar, 1996, California. *Education:* University of California, Berkeley (B.A., 1993); Loyola Law School of Los Angeles (J.D., 1996). Phi Delta Phi. Articles Editor, International and Comparative Law Journal, 1994-1996. Author, "A.I.D.S. Infects The Canadian Legal Community," 18 Loyola International & Comparative Law Journal 401, 1996.

**MICHAEL W. BIARD,** born Orange, California, December 27, 1968; admitted to bar, 1996, California and U.S. District Court, Central and Southern Districts of California. *Education:* Columbia University (B.A., 1991); Loyola Law School (J.D., cum laude, 1996). Order of the Coif. St. Thomas More Law Honor Society. American Jurisprudence Awards: Trial Advocacy; Trusts and Wills. Loyola of Los Angeles International Law Journal, 1994-1996.

**JILANA L. MILLER,** born San Diego, California, June 20, 1970; admitted to bar, 1996, California. *Education:* University of Southern California (B.A., 1991); University of San Diego (J.D., 1996). Order of the Coif. Moot Court Board.

### OF COUNSEL

**MICHAEL H. WOODELL,** born Ukiah, California, April 20, 1942; admitted to bar, 1979, Alaska. *Education:* Western Washington University (B.A., 1965); Gonzaga University (J.D., magna cum laude, 1979). *Member:* Alaska Bar Association; Maritime Law Association of the United States. [Lieut., U.S. Navy, 1966-1972]. (Resident, Anchorage, Alaska Office).

**REESE H. TAYLOR, JR.,** born Los Angeles, California, May 6, 1928; admitted to bar, 1954, California and U.S. District Court, Southern District of California; 1966, Nevada and U.S. District Court, District of Nevada; 1986, U.S. Court of Appeals for the District of Columbia Circuit; 1987, U.S. Supreme Court. *Education:* Stanford University (B.A., with distinction, 1949); Cornell University (LL.B., 1952). Phi Delta Phi. Member, Order of the Coif. Chairman: Nevada Public Service Commission, 1967-1971; Interstate Commerce Commission, 1981-1985. Vice Chairman, Nevada Tax Commission, 1967-1969. Director of United States Railway Association, 1981-1985. Member: Administrative Conference of the United States and its Committee on Adjudication, 1982-1985; Council of Independent Regulatory Agencies, 1981-1985; NARUC, 1982-1985; Association of Transportation Practitioners, 1986—. *Member:* State Bar of California; State Bar of Nevada; American Bar Association; American Judicature Society. **PRACTICE AREAS:** Transportation; Railroads; Trucking.

**RICHARD A. APPELBAUM,** born Chicago, Illinois, February 6, 1940; admitted to bar, 1970 District of Columbia and Florida (Not admitted in California). *Education:* U.S. Coast Guard Academy (B.S., 1961); George Washington University (J.D., 1970). Chief of Law Faculty and Professor, U.S. Coast Guard Academy, 1973-1977. *Member:* District of Columbia Bar; The Florida Bar. [Rear Admiral, U.S. Coast Guard, 1957-1996]

REPRESENTATIVE CLIENTS: American Express Bank; American Express Inc.; American Express Travel Related Services, Inc.; Alex, Brown & Sons; American Club (The); American President Lines, Ltd.; API Security; ARCO Marine, Inc.; ARCO Products Company; ARCO Transportation; Arizona Heart Institute; Associated Securities Corp.; Assuranceforeningen Gard; Atlantic Richfield Company; Autodesk, Inc.; BHP Transport; Bank One; Bear, Stearns & Co., Inc.; Blue Star Line; Britannia Steam Ship Insurance Association Limited (The); British Marine Mutual Insurance Association Limited; CBS Records; Central Gulf Lines, Inc.; Chevron Shipping Company; Chilean Lines; City of Long Beach; City of Los Angeles; Commodore Cruise Line Ltd.; Core-Mark International, Inc.; Cowen & Co.; Craig Consumer Electronics; Crowell, Weedon & Co.; Crowley Marine Services, Inc.; Cunard Line Ltd.; D.H. Blair & Co., Inc.; Employers Reinsurance Corporation; E&O Professionals; Ericsson Inc.; EVEREN Securities, Inc.; Fairmont Shipping; Financial Network Investment Corp.; F.L. Industries; Forum Insurance Co.; Foss Maritime; Franklin Bank; Franklin Trust Company; Franklin Resources Inc.; Furman Selz; GE Capital Mortgage Services Incorporated; GRE Insurance Group; Galles Racing International; Geldermann, Inc.; General Accident Group; Great Lakes Dredge & Dock Company; Griffin Insurance Association Limited; Harlock Williams Lemon, Ltd.; Holland America Line Westours, Inc.; Hyundai Merchant Marine (America), Inc.; Interocean Transport; Itohchu (America); Japan Ship Owners Mutual P&I Association; Kayne, Anderson & Co., Inc.; Kelso & Company; Keystone Shipping Co.; J. Lauritzen A/S; Lear Siegler Diversified Holdings Corp.; Lehman Brothers Inc.; Linsco/Private Ledger Financial Services, Inc.; Liverpool & London P&I Association (The); London Steam-Ship Owners' Mutual Insurance Association Limited (The); Loomis Armored, Inc.; Lykes Brothers Steamship Co., Inc.; Maersk, Inc.; Makita USA, Inc.; Maritime Overseas Corporation; Marsh & McLennan; Merrill Lynch, Pierce, Fenner & Smith, Inc.; Montgomery Securities; Morgan Stanley & Co., Inc.; National Futures Association; Newcastle Protection & Indemnity Association; North American Shipowners Insurance Services (USA), Inc.; North of England P&I Association Limited; Olde Discount Corporation; OMI Bulk Management Corp.; Oppenheimer & Co., Inc.; Pacific Union Bank; PaineWebber Incorporated; Penn-Attransco Corporation; Pennsylvania House, Inc.; Premier Cruise Lines, Ltd.; Primerica Financial Services; Princess Cruises; Prudential Securities, Inc.; Pullman Company, Quick & Reilly, Inc.; Rapistan-Demag Corp.; Rauscher Pierce Refsnes, Inc.; Regency Cruises; Royal Alliance Associates, Inc.; Royal Caribbean Cruise Line, Inc.; Schroder Wertheim & Company, Incorporated; Shand Morahan & Co.; Smith Barney, Inc.; Sony Music Entertainment Group; St. Paul Companies; Standard Steamship Owners Protection & Indemnity Association (Bermuda), Ltd. (The); Star Shipping (USWC), Inc.; Steamship Mutual Underwriting Association, Ltd.; Sutro & Co., Incorporated; Teekay Shipping (Canada), Ltd.; Tokio Marine and Fire Insurance Co., Ltd. (The); Transport Mutual Services, Inc.; Travelers, Inc. (The); U.S. Oil; United Kingdom Mutual Steamship Assurance Association (Bermuda) Limited (The); Ultramar, Inc.; Union Carbide Corp.; Unocal Corp.; United Technologies; Van Kasper & Co.; Wah Kwong Shipping Agency; Wedbush Securities; West Coast Shipping Co.; West of England Ship Owners Mutual Insurance Association (The); Wilmington Transportation Co.; Worthington Bank and Trust; Yangming Marine Transport Co.; Zurich American.

---

## KEGEL, TOBIN & TRUCE

*A PROFESSIONAL CORPORATION*

Established in 1966

330 GOLDEN SHORE DRIVE, SUITE 150
**LONG BEACH, CALIFORNIA 90802**
Telephone: 310-437-1108
Facsimile: 310-435-3742
Email: comp-law@ktt.com

*Los Angeles, California Office:* 3580 Wilshire Boulevard, 10th Floor, P.O. Box 76907. Telephone: 213-380-3880. FAX: 213-383-8346.

*Ventura, California Office:* 5450 Ralston Street, Suite 204, P.O. Box 7779. Telephone: 805-644-2216. Facsimile: 805-644-8625.

*Rancho Cucamonga, California Office:* 10737 Laurel Street, #240, P.O. Box 3329. Telephone: 909-466-5555. Facsimile: 909-466-5562.

*San Diego, California Office:* 2535 Kettner Boulevard, Suite 2A1. Telephone: 619-696-0906.

*Van Nuys, California Office:* 14545 Friar Street, Suite 104. Telephone: 818-947-0300. Facsimile: 818-947-0303.

*Workers Compensation, Longshore and Harborworkers, Public Employment, Retirement Law. Insurance Law, Third Party Subrogation.*

(For complete biographical data on all personnel, see Professional Biographies at Los Angeles, California)

---

## KERRY, GARCIA & LEWIS

320 GOLDEN SHORE DRIVE, SUITE 480
**LONG BEACH, CALIFORNIA 90802**
Telephone: 310-436-1234
Fax: 310-495-2590

*Civil Trial and Appellate Practice emphasizing Defense and Plaintiff Personal Injury, Premises Liability, Products Liability, Professional Negligence, Construction, Aviation, Insurance, Business Litigation and Transaction matters, Commercial, Corporate and Real Estate Transactions, Alternative Dispute Resolution.*

**ANDREW GARCIA,** born New York, N.Y., December 30, 1942; admitted to bar, 1977, California; 1978, U.S. District Court, Central District of California. *Education:* California State University at Northridge (B.A., 1972); Southwestern University (J.D., 1977). Judge Pro Tem, Los Angeles and Long Beach Municipal Court, 1985—. Arbitrator, Los Angeles and Orange County Superior Court Arbitration Panel, 1981—. Member, Panel of Arbitrators, American Arbitration Association. *Member:* Long Beach and Los Angeles County Bar Associations; State Bar of California; Los Angeles Trial Lawyers Association; California Trial Lawyers Association. **LANGUAGES:** Spanish. **PRACTICE AREAS:** Civil Trial; Personal Injury Insurance; Construction; Business Litigation and Transactions.

**WILLIAM H. KERRY,** born Trona, California, August 12, 1947; admitted to bar, 1977, California. *Education:* California State University at Long Beach (B.A., 1973); University of West Los Angeles (J.D., 1977). Former Airline Pilot. Certified, Airline Transport and Flight Instructor. *Member:* State Bar of California; American Bar Association; Association of Southern California Defense Counsel. **PRACTICE AREAS:** Aviation litigation and certificate actions; Personal Injury Insurance; Business Litigation and Transactions.

**DANIEL G. LEWIS,** born Chicago, Illinois, August 6, 1958; admitted to bar, 1985, Colorado and California. *Education:* Fresno Pacific College (B.A., cum laude, 1981); Willamette University (J.D., 1984). Phi Delta Phi. Arbitrator, Los Angeles Superior and Municipal Court Arbitration Panel. *Member:* Long Beach, Los Angeles County, Continental Divide and Colorado Bar Associations; State Bar of California; Association of Southern California Defense Counsel. **PRACTICE AREAS:** Arbitration; Civil Trial; Personal Injury Insurance.

*(This Listing Continued)*

KERRY, GARCIA & LEWIS, Long Beach—Continued

**CHRISTOPHER E. BOTTI,** born Brooklyn, New York, December 11, 1964; admitted to bar, 1990, California. *Education:* State University of New York at Oneonta (B.S., 1987); Whittier School of Law (J.D., 1990). Member, Whittier College School of Law Review, 1989-1990. Member, Moot Court Honor Board. **PRACTICE AREAS:** Personal Injury Insurance; Business Litigation and Transactions.

**LEE B. MADINGER,** born Port Arthur, Texas, September 4, 1948; admitted to bar, 1990, California and U.S. District Court, Central District of California. *Education:* Washington & Lee University (B.A., 1970); Southern Methodist University (M.Th., 1973); Whittier College School of Law (J.D., summa cum laude, 1990). Phi Delta Phi. Valedictorian, Whittier Law School Class of 1990. Articles Editor, Whittier Law Review, 1989-1990. Recipient, American Jurisprudence Awards in: Criminal Law; Contracts; Torts; Civil Procedure and Remedies. Adjunct Instructor of Legal Skills, Whittier College School of Law, 1991—. Author: "Free Speech in Public Places: Application of the Perry Analysis in Picketing Cases," 1 Whittier Law Review 267 (1989). *Member:* Riverside County Bar Association; State Bar of California. [Lieut., U.S. Navy, 1982-1988]. **PRACTICE AREAS:** Personal Injury Insurance; Business Litigation and Transactions; Appellate Work.

**MARK A. SAYED,** born Los Angeles, California, March 1, 1957; admitted to bar, 1987, California and U.S. District Court, Central District of California. *Education:* University of California, Irvine (B.A., 1984); Southwestern University (J.D., 1987). Judge Pro-Tem and Judicial Settlement Officer of the Long Beach Municipal Court. *Member:* State Bar of California; Los Angeles County Bar Association. **PRACTICE AREAS:** Personal Injury Insurance; Real Estate Transactions; Federal Employer's Liability Act; Common Carrier Liability; Professional Malpractice.

REPRESENTATIVE CLIENTS: Interinsurance Exchange of the Automobile Club of Southern California; Superior National Insurance; Twentieth Century Insurance Co.; Dick Cepek, Inc.; Shell Oil; Connecticut Specialty Insurance Group; R.L. Gresha.
REFERENCE: First Interstate Bank (Market Place Branch).

## KINKLE, RODIGER AND SPRIGGS

PROFESSIONAL CORPORATION

**LONG BEACH, CALIFORNIA**

(See Santa Ana)

General Trial Practice. Negligence, Malpractice, Products Liability, Construction and Insurance Law.

## KIRLIN, CAMPBELL & KEATING

301 EAST OCEAN BOULEVARD, SUITE 540
**LONG BEACH, CALIFORNIA 90802-4804**
Telephone: 310-491-1267
Fax: 310-590-8999

Other Offices Located in: New York, New York, Washington, D.C., Stamford, Connecticut and Caldwell, New Jersey.

General Practice. General Civil Trial and Appellate Practice. Admiralty and Maritime, International, Corporate, Administrative, Finance, Labor, Trusts and Estates, Tax, Insurance Coverage and Defense, Reinsurance, Personal Injury, Environmental, Oil Pollution and Coast Guard Proceedings, Bankruptcy and Real Estate Law.

### RESIDENT PARTNERS

**DONN BORG,** born New York, New York, April 7, 1928; admitted to bar, 1959, District of Columbia; 1968, California. *Education:* United States Merchant Marine Academy (B.S., 1950); Georgetown University (LL.M., 1959).

**GEOFFREY W. GILL,** born Camden, Maine, July 20, 1946; admitted to bar, 1975, New York and U.S. Court of Appeals, 2nd Circuit; 1986, Florida; 1987, U.S. Court of Appeals, 11th Circuit; 1992, California. *Education:* United States Merchant Marine Academy (B.S., 1968); U.S. Naval War College; Fordham University School of Law (J.D., 1974).

*(This Listing Continued)*

CAA426B

### RESIDENT OF COUNSEL

**JOSEPH R. MCFAUL,** born Pomona, California, 1953; admitted to bar, 1983, Washington; 1984, California; 1986, U.S. Court of Appeals, 9th Circuit; 1987, U.S. Supreme Court; 1988, U.S. Claims Court and U.S. Court of Military Appeals. *Education:* U.S. Coast Guard Academy (B.S., 1975); University of Puget Sound (J.D., magna cum laude, 1983).

(For complete biographical data on all personnel, see Professional Biographies at other locations).

## RICHARD W. W. KLINK

444 WEST OCEAN BOULEVARD, 9TH FLOOR
**LONG BEACH, CALIFORNIA 90802-4526**
Telephone: 310-432-7838
Fax: 310-432-7455

*Criminal Defense, White Collar Crime, DUI Litigation.*

**RICHARD W. W. KLINK,** born San Francisco, California, August 20, 1936; admitted to bar, 1973, California and U.S. District Court, Central District of California; 1978, U.S. Court of Miltary Appeals. *Education:* California State University at Long Beach (B.A., economics, 1966); Pacific Coast University (J.D., 1972). Los Angeles County District Attorney, 1973-1992. *Member:* Los Angeles County (Member, Criminal Law Section) and Long Beach Bar Associations; California Attorneys for Criminal Justice. [Colonel USMCR (Ret) 1963-1996]

## LA TORRACA AND GOETTSCH

A Law Partnership
211 EAST OCEAN BOULEVARD, SUITE 400
P.O. BOX 21978
**LONG BEACH, CALIFORNIA 90801-4978**
Telephone: 310-436-1887
Telecopier: 310-436-8489

*General Civil Litigation including Insurance Coverage, Insurance Bad Faith, Insurance Defense, Insurance Fraud, Toxic Tort Law, Personal Injury, Products Liability, Malpractice, Commercial Litigation, Defamation, Unfair Competition, Real Property Litigation, Construction Defects Litigation, Complex Litigation and Civil Appeals. Trial Practice in all State and Federal Courts.*

*FIRM PROFILE: La Torraca and Goettsch, a law partnership, is a general civil litigation law firm that specializes in trial and appeals in all state and federal courts in California. The lawyers in the firm are experienced in a number of fields, including personal injury, products liability, legal malpractice, medical malpractice, commercial litigation, insurance coverage in all lines of personal and commercial insurance, Cumis litigation and Civil Code Subsection 2860 disputes, toxic tort litigation and insurance coverage for environmental claims, insurance bad faith, the defense of insureds, insurance fraud, arson claims, suspect third-party claims, real property litigation, construction defect litigation, defamation, unfair competition, and intellectual property litigation.*

### MEMBERS OF FIRM

**HENRY B. LA TORRACA,** born Long Beach, California, March 3, 1951; admitted to bar, 1976, California. *Education:* California State University at Long Beach (B.S., magna cum laude, 1973); Loyola University (J.D., 1976). *Member:* Long Beach and Los Angeles County Bar Associations; State Bar of California; Association of Southern California Defense Counsel; Defense Research Institute. **PRACTICE AREAS:** Insurance Coverage; Third Party Defense; Business Litigation; Insurance Bad Faith Law; Insurance Law; Civil Practice; Federal Practice; Intellectual Property Law; RICO; Subrogation Law.

**RAYMOND H. GOETTSCH,** born Rockford, Illinois, August 19, 1947; admitted to bar, 1982, California. *Education:* Northern Illinois University (B.A., 1969); McGeorge School of Law, University of the Pacific (J.D., with great distinction, 1982). Order of the Coif. Member, Traynor Society. Recipient, American Jurisprudence Awards, Civil Procedure, Conflicts of Law and Torts. Staff Writer, 1980-1981 and Assistant Editor, 1981-1982, Pacific Law Journal. Author: "The Right of Publicity: Premature Burial for California Property Rights In The Wake of 'Lugosi' ," 12 Pacific Law Journal 989-1011, 1981. *Member:* Long Beach, Federal and American Bar Associations; State Bar of California (Member, 42500lectual Property Section); Association of Southern California Defense Counsel; Defense Research Institute. **REPORTED CASES:** David Kleis, Inc. v. Superior Court, 37 Cal.App. 4th 1035 (2d Dist., 1995); *Safeco Insurance Company of America vs. Pemcon International, Inc., d.b.a. General Magnetics,* 935 F2d 275 (9th

*(This Listing Continued)*

Cir., 1991); *Safeco Insurance Company of America vs. Andrews,* 915 F2d 500 (9th Cir., 1990). **PRACTICE AREAS:** Personal Injury Law; Products Liability Law; Malpractice Law; Commercial Litigation; Bad Faith Law; Civil Appeals; Civil Practice; Federal Practice; Insurance Coverage; Intellectual Property Law; Intentional Torts; Legal Malpractice; RICO; Subrogation Law.

*ASSOCIATES*

**TERESA CHO,** born Seoul, South Korea, May 4, 1964; admitted to bar, 1992, California. *Education:* University of California, Berkeley (B.S., 1986); University of California, Los Angeles School of Law (J.D., 1991). Assistant Business Editor, Federal Communications Law Journal. Moot Court Participant. Summer Extern, Ninth Circuit Court of Appeals. El Centro Legal Volunteer. *Member:* Los Angeles County Bar Association; State Bar of California.

**ANDRES C. HURWITZ,** born Boston, Massachusetts, July 19, 1965; admitted to bar, 1990, California, U.S. District Court, Central, Eastern, Northern and Southern Districts of California and U.S. Court of Appeals, Ninth Circuit. *Education:* Duke University; Boston College (B.A., cum laude, 1987); Georgetown University (J.D., 1990). Phi Alpha Theta. *Member:* Los Angeles County (Member, Litigation Section) and American Bar Associations; State Bar of California; Association of Southern California Defense Counsel. **PRACTICE AREAS:** Civil Practice; Accident and Personal Injury Law; Insurance Defense Law; Bad Faith Law; Product Liability Law.

**SUSAN KOEHLER SULLIVAN,** born Seattle, Washington, December 19, 1965; admitted to bar, 1991, California; 1992, Washington. *Education:* University of Washington (B.A., with honors, 1987); University of California at Los Angeles (J.D., 1991). Moot Court Honors Program. Managing Editor, Pacific Basin Law Journal. Summer Extern, U.S. District Court, Central District of California. *Member:* Los Angeles County (Member, Domestic Violence Counseling Project) and Washington State Bar Associations; State Bar of California. **PRACTICE AREAS:** Bad Faith Law; Insurance Law.

**ERIC R. LITTLE,** born Chicago, Illinois, July 18, 1963; admitted to bar, 1993, California and U.S. District Court, Central District of California; 1994, U.S. District Court, Northern District of California. *Education:* University of the Pacific (B.A., 1985); University of San Francisco (J.D., 1993). *Member:* State Bar of California.

**NICOLA MIGLIACCIO,** born Ischia, Italy, September 15, 1963; admitted to bar, 1992, California; 1994, U.S. District Court, Central District of California. *Education:* California State University at Long Beach (B.A., 1989); McGeorge School of Law (J.D., 1992); Georgetown University Law Center (LL.M., 1993). *Member:* State Bar of California.

**JONATHAN A. HENDRICKS,** born Los Angeles, California, June 9, 1966; admitted to bar, 1994, California and U.S. District Court, Eastern District of California. *Education:* Pomona College (B.A., 1988); McGeorge School of Law (J.D., 1994). Recipient, American Jurisprudence Awards for Constitutional Law and Legal Theory and Policy. *Member:* State Bar of California.

**SCOTT K. MURCH,** born Redondo Beach, California, June 13, 1968; admitted to bar, 1994, California and U.S. District Court, Central District of California. *Education:* University of California at San Diego (B.A., 1990); Hastings College of Law, University of California (J.D. cum laude, 1994). *Member:* State Bar of California.

**DAVID JAMES REINARD,** born Sewickley, Pennsylvania, September 10, 1961; admitted to bar, 1991, California. *Education:* Loyola Marymount University (B.A., 1984); Southwestern University School of Law (J.D., 1991). *Member:* State Bar of California. **PRACTICE AREAS:** General Liability.

REPRESENTATIVE CLIENTS: Safeco Insurance Cos.; The Chubb Group of Insurance Cos.; CNA Insurance Companies; Farmers Insurance Group of Companies; Great American Insurance Co.; Northwestern Insurance Group; Colonial Penn Insurance Co.; Reliance Insurance Company of Illinois; General Accident Group; Kemper Insurance Group; Balboa Insurance Co.; California Insurance Group.

## *CHARLES J. LIBERTO*
*4201 LONG BEACH BOULEVARD, SUITE 327*
*P.O. BOX 7737*
**LONG BEACH, CALIFORNIA 90807-0737**
*Telephone: 310-424-7441*
*Fax: 310-424-2231*

*Practice limited to Estate Planning, Trust and Probate Law.*

**CHARLES J. LIBERTO,** born Los Angeles, California, 1940; admitted to bar, 1965, California and U.S. District Court, Southern District of California; 1969, U.S. Tax Court; 1979, U.S. Supreme Court. *Education:* Occidental College (B.A., 1961); Loyola University of Los Angeles (J.D., 1964). Phi Alpha Delta. Member, National Moot Court Team. City Attorney, City of Arcadia, California, 1976-1983. *Member:* Los Angeles County Bar Association (Chairman, Governmental Law Section, 1981-1982; Member, Tax and Probate Law Sections, 1987—); State Bar of California.

REFERENCE: Queen City Bank (Long Beach Main Office).

## *LILLICK & CHARLES LLP*
*ONE WORLD TRADE CENTER*
*SUITE 950*
**LONG BEACH, CALIFORNIA 90831-0950**
*Telephone: 310-499-7000*
*Cable Address: "Lillickchs LGB"*
*Telex: 188652 LILLICKCHS LGB*
*FAX: 310-437-5957*

*San Francisco, California Office:* Two Embarcadero Center, Suite 2600, 94111-3996. Telephone: 415-984-8200. Cable Address: "Lillickchs SF." Telex: 184983 LILLICKCHS SF. FAX: 415-984-8300.

*Parsippany, New Jersey Office:* 119 Cherry Hill Road, Second Floor, 07054-1114. Telephone: 201-334-8100. Telex: 178727 LILLICKCHS NJ. FAX: 201-334-9559.

*General Civil and Trial Practice. Aviation, Banking, Bankruptcy/Creditors' Rights, Commercial, Computer Law, Construction, Corporate, Environmental, Estate and Trust, Finance, Governmental Regulation, Independent Power, Insurance, International Business, Labor, Maritime, Products Liability, Project Finance, Real Estate, Tax, Toxic Tort, Trademark, Visa and Immigration.*

*LONG BEACH PARTNERS*

**PHILLIP S. DALTON,** born Long Beach, California, January 26, 1948; admitted to bar, 1975, California, California Supreme Court and U.S. District Court, Northern District of California; 1977, U.S. District Court, Central District of California; 1992, U.S. District Court, Eastern District of California. *Education:* University of California at Los Angeles (B.A., 1970; J.D., 1975). *Member:* Maritime Law Association of the United States. **PRACTICE AREAS:** Maritime; Defense of Shipowner Interests in Personal Injury and Cargo Matters; Construction; Products Liability Defense.

**KATHLEEN MAHON ISAAC,** born Washington, Missouri, January 18, 1947; admitted to bar, 1977, District of Columbia; 1982, U.S. Supreme Court; 1988, California. *Education:* University of Missouri (B.A., 1968); Georgetown University (J.D., 1977). Phi Beta Kappa. Research Editor, American Criminal Law Review, 1976-1977. Law Clerk to Judge J. Dudley Digges, Court of Appeals of Maryland, 1977-1978. *Member:* Los Angeles County and American Bar Associations; The District of Columbia Bar; Maritime Law Association of the United States. **PRACTICE AREAS:** Transportation Regulation; Maritime; Immigration; Corporate.

**WILLIAM L. ROBINSON,** born Washington, D.C., December 11, 1946; admitted to bar, 1979, California; 1983, U.S. Supreme Court. *Education:* United States Naval Academy (B.S.E.E., 1969); George Washington University (M.S.A., 1975); Boalt Hall School of Law, University of California (J.D., 1979). *Member:* American Bar Association. [Capt., USNR (Retired 1994, Active Duty 1969-1976]. (Managing Partner). **PRACTICE AREAS:** Aviation; Products Liability; Toxic Tort; Environmental and Commercial Litigation.

**ROBERT B. YOSHITOMI,** born Ontario, Oregon, October 19, 1944; admitted to bar, 1973, California; 1992, New Jersey; 1993, District of Columbia. *Education:* Princeton University (A.B., 1970); Boalt Hall School of Law, University of California (J.D., 1973). *Member:* Maritime Law Association of the United States. **PRACTICE AREAS:** Trade and Transportation Regulation; Maritime; Immigration; Corporate.

*(This Listing Continued)*

## LILLICK & CHARLES LLP, Long Beach—Continued

### OF COUNSEL

**PHILIP L. JOHNSON,** born Beloit, Wisconsin, January 24, 1939; admitted to bar, 1973, California; 1978, U.S. Court of Military Appeals; 1980, U.S. Supreme Court. *Education:* Princeton University (A.B., 1961); University of Southern California (J.D., 1973). Author: Journal of Air Law & Commerce, "Privileged Information: A Manufacturer's Critical Self-Analysis," 1993. Lecturer: California Continuing Education of the Bar, "Effective Direct and Cross-Examination," 1995; "Ethics for Litigators," 1995; "Federal Practice Institute: Litigating in the Northern and Central Districts of California, 1995 and 1996, "How to Present and Attack Documentary and Demonstrative Evidence," 1996; "Preparing a Case for Trial," 1996; "Truth or Consequences: Ethical Issues in the Settlement of Litigation," 1996. Princeton University, "The Profession of Law: Does Race Matter," 1994; ATLA National College of Advocacy "Defense Perspective," 1995. Judge Pro Tem, California State Bar Court, 1990-1995. *Member:* Defense Research Institute; Association of Southern California Defense Counsel. [Col., USMCR (Retired), active duty, 1961-1970]. **PRACTICE AREAS:** Aviation; Products Liability; Insurance Defense.

### LONG BEACH ASSOCIATES

**JOHN C. ASHBY,** born Chicago, Illinois, September 24, 1961; admitted to bar, 1989, California. *Education:* University of Michigan (A.B., 1983; M.B.A., 1985; J.D., 1988).

**BRIAN R. FAULKNER,** born Los Angeles, California, October 31, 1953; admitted to bar, 1983, California. *Education:* University of California at Los Angeles (B.A., 1975); University of San Diego (J.D., 1983). *Member:* Los Angeles County and American Bar Associations; Maritime Law Association of the United States. **PRACTICE AREAS:** Product Liability; Insurance; Admiralty; Construction Litigation.

All Members and Associates are members of The State Bar of California.

(For Complete Biographical Data on Personnel at San Francisco and Parsippany see Professional Biographies at those locations)

---

## LITTLER, MENDELSON, FASTIFF, TICHY & MATHIASON

*A PROFESSIONAL CORPORATION*

*Established in 1942*

**401 E. OCEAN BOULEVARD, SUITE 204**
**LONG BEACH, CALIFORNIA 90802**
Telephone: 310-437-2441
Facsimile: 310-435-0406
URL: http://www.littler.com

*Offices located in:* California -- Bakersfield, Fresno, Los Angeles, Menlo Park, Oakland, Sacramento, San Diego, San Francisco, San Jose, Santa Maria, Santa Rosa and Stockton; Denver, Colorado; Washington, D.C.; Atlanta, Georgia; Baltimore, Maryland; Reno and Las Vegas, Nevada (a partnership with the Law Offices of Hicks & Walt); Morristown, New Jersey; New York, New York; and Dallas and Houston, Texas.

FIRM PROFILE: Littler, Mendelson, Fastiff, Tichy & Mathiason is the largest law firm in the United States engaged exclusively in the practice of employment and labor law. The firm has over 250 attorneys in 23 offices nationwide who represent and advise management in all the major sub-specialities of employment and labor law including: wage and hour law; NLRB cases and collective bargaining; workers' compensation; sex, race, and age discrimination; wrongful termination; unemployment benefits; workplace violence; substance abuse; employee privacy rights; occupational safety and health; the ADA; ERISA, employee benefits, tax issues; and immigration.

---

**EUGENE L. CHRZANOWSKI,** born Bayonne, New Jersey, October 22, 1948; admitted to bar, 1973, District of Columbia; 1985, Virginia; 1990, California. *Education:* College of the Holy Cross (B.A., 1970); Georgetown University Law Center (J.D., 1973).

(For biographical data on personnel at other locations, see Professional Biographies at those cities)

---

## LOMBARDI & PERRY, LLP

**110 PINE AVENUE, 12TH FLOOR**
**LONG BEACH, CALIFORNIA 90802**
Telephone: 310-983-3616
Fax: 310-983-3618

*Personal Injury including Insurance Defense.*

**CHRISTOPHER LOMBARDI,** born Gander, Newfoundland, December 13, 1949; admitted to bar, 1980, California. *Education:* California State University at Long Beach (B.A., 1976); Western State University (J.D., 1979). Delta Theta Phi. *Member:* Los Angeles County Bar Association; State Bar of California.

**SCOTT D. PERRY,** born Sacramento, California, February 18, 1962; admitted to bar, 1994, California. *Education:* Saddleback College (A.A., 1984); California State University at Fullerton (B.A., 1987); Western State University (J.D., 1993). *Member:* State Bar of California.

REPRESENTATIVE CLIENTS: A-Best Products; Combustion Engineering Inc.; Stauffer Chemical; Connecticut Valley Claim Service Co., Inc.

---

## JAY B. LONG

**GREATER LOS ANGELES WORLD TRADE CENTER**
**ONE WORLD TRADE CENTER, SUITE 800**
**LONG BEACH, CALIFORNIA 90831-0800**
Telephone: 310-983-8146; Fax: 310-983-8199
Email: jayblong@ix.netcom.com

*Monterey, California Office:* 500 Camino El Estero, Suite 200, 93940.
Telephone: 408-649-3877. Fax: 408-649-4705.

*Environmental and Energy Law, including Regulatory and Legislative Matters; Insurance Coverage Law; Construction and Design Law; Sports, Sponsorship and Event Law; Advertising, Marketing and Distribution Law; Select Business, Real Estate, other Civil Litigation and Trial Practice in all State and Federal Courts; Alternate Dispute Resolution.*

**JAY B. LONG,** born Long Beach, California, December 24, 1953; admitted to bar, 1982, California, U.S. District Court, Central, Southern, Northern and Eastern Districts of California and U.S. Court of Appeals, Ninth Circuit. *Education:* University of California at Davis (B.S., Environmental Planning and Management, with honors, 1976; J.D., 1982). Judicial Extern to the Honorable Raul E. Ramirez, U.S. District Court, Eastern District of California, 1982. Judge pro tem, Long Beach Unified Courts. Certified Mediator. Staff Member, California Energy Commission, 1976-1979. *Member:* Long Beach, Los Angeles, Orange, Monterey Counties and American Bar Associations; State Bar of California.

---

## MADDEN, JONES, COLE & JOHNSON

*A PROFESSIONAL CORPORATION*

*Established in 1976*

**SUITE 1300**
**111 WEST OCEAN BOULEVARD**
**LONG BEACH, CALIFORNIA 90802**
Telephone: 310-435-6565
Fax: 310-590-7909
Email: MJCJLAW@AOL.COM

*Civil Litigation, Business, Corporate, Healthcare, Construction, Personal Injury, Real Estate, Probate, Tax and Estate Planning Matters.*

**PHILIP M. MADDEN,** born Long Beach, California, July 22, 1937; admitted to bar, 1963, California. *Education:* University of California at Berkeley (A.B., 1959; LL.B., 1962). Deputy District Attorney, Los Angeles County, 1963-1965. Deputy City Attorney, Long Beach, 1965-1967. *Member:* Long Beach (President, 1988) and Los Angeles County Bar Associations; State Bar of California. **PRACTICE AREAS:** Business Law; Civil Litigation.

**STEVEN A. JONES,** born Bell, California, March 17, 1953; admitted to bar, 1979, California. *Education:* Long Beach City College (A.S., 1974); Long Beach State University (B.S., 1976); Pepperdine University (J.D., 1979). *Member:* Long Beach and Los Angeles County Bar Associations; State Bar of California. **PRACTICE AREAS:** Healthcare; Business Law; Real Estate.

*(This Listing Continued)*

**MONTGOMERY COLE,** born Long Beach, California, June 7, 1955; admitted to bar, 1980, California. *Education:* California State University at Long Beach (B.S., 1977); Loyola University of Los Angeles (J.D., 1980). Founding Member, Joseph A. Ball/Clarence S. Hunt Inn of Court. *Member:* Long Beach and Los Angeles County Bar Associations; State Bar of California; Consumer Attorneys of California; Consumer Attorneys of Los Angeles. **PRACTICE AREAS:** Personal Injury Litigation; Civil and Commercial Litigation.

**ROBERT R. JOHNSON,** born Long Beach, California, July 10, 1943; admitted to bar, 1968, California. *Education:* University of California, Santa Barbara (B.A., 1965); University of Southern California (J.D., 1968); New York University (LL.M., taxation, 1969). *Member:* Long Beach, Los Angeles County and American Bar Associations; State Bar of California. (Also Member of Johnson & Johnson). **PRACTICE AREAS:** Estate Planning; Business; Tax Law.

---

**JOHN VITA,** born New York, N.Y., September 6, 1953; admitted to bar, 1989, California. *Education:* Brooklyn College (B.S., 1974); Pepperdine University (M.B.A., 1984); Loyola University of Los Angeles (J.D., 1989). *Member:* Long Beach, Los Angeles County and American Bar Associations; State Bar of California. **PRACTICE AREAS:** Civil Litigation; Commercial Litigation; Securities Litigation.

**MARY E. FRANKART,** born Conneaut, Ohio, November 12, 1956; admitted to bar, 1988, California. *Education:* Loyola Marymount University (B.A., 1978); Loyola Marymount University School of Law (J.D., 1988). *Member:* Long Beach Bar Association; State Bar of California. **PRACTICE AREAS:** Healthcare; Civil and Commercial Litigation.

**SUSIE E. KIM,** born Seoul, S. Korea, October 17, 1967; admitted to bar, 1994, California. *Education:* University of California, Davis (B.A., 1990); University of California at Davis (J.D., 1993). *Member:* Long Beach and Los Angeles Bar Associations; State Bar of California. **PRACTICE AREAS:** Estate Planning; Probate; Civil Litigation.

REPRESENTATIVE CLIENTS: All City Electric Supply; Allied Refrigeration, Inc.; Askew Hardware & Supply Co.; Beach City Chevrolet; B&B Pipe & Tool Co.; Damis Construction; Farmers & Merchants Trust Co.; John Bloeser Carpet Co.; Long Beach Public Transportation Co.; Mack Trucks, Inc.; Pipe Sales Company; Pro Health Partners Medical Group; Sisters of Charity of the Incarnate Word; St. Bernardine Medical Center; St. Mary Medical Center; Walters Wholesale Electric Co.; Wells Fargo Bank and Trust Co.

---

## MOORE, RUTTER & EVANS

A Partnership including a Professional Corporation

**555 EAST OCEAN BOULEVARD, SUITE 500**
**LONG BEACH, CALIFORNIA 90802-5090**
Telephone: 310-494-6667; 435-4499
Facsimile: 310-495-4229

*Huntington Beach, California Office:* 2100 Main Street, Suite 280, 92648. Telephone: 714-374-3333.

*General Civil, Maritime and Trial Practice in all State and Federal Courts, Appellate Practice, Automobile Negligence, Business Torts, Casualty Defense, Commercial Litigation, Construction Defect Litigation, Environmental Torts, Estate Planning, Insurance Coverage, Inverse Condemnation, Law Enforcement Defense, Municipality Defense, Premises Liability, Products Liability and Wrongful Termination.*

### RESIDENT PARTNERS

**NEAL MOORE,** born Downey, California, September 5, 1945; admitted to bar, 1971, California and U.S. District Court, Central District of California; 1975, U.S. Court of Appeals, Ninth Circuit. *Education:* University of Southern California (A.B., 1967; J.D., 1971). Phi Delta Phi. Deputy County Counsel, County of Los Angeles, 1971-1976. *Member:* Long Beach, Orange County, Los Angeles County and Federal Bar Associations; The State Bar of California; Association of Southern California Defense Counsel; Association of Business Trial Lawyers; American Board of Trial Advocates. **PRACTICE AREAS:** Public Entity Defense; Law Enforcement Defense; Insurance Defense.

**MARK D. RUTTER,** born Santa Monica, California, November 25, 1948; admitted to bar, 1973, California; 1974, U.S. District Court, Central District of California; 1984, U.S. Court of Appeals, Ninth Circuit. *Education:* University of California at Los Angeles (B.A., 1970); Loyola University of Los Angeles (J.D., 1973). *Member:* South Bay and Long Beach Bar Associations; The State Bar of California; Association of Southern Califor-

*(This Listing Continued)*

nia Defense Counsel; Defense Research Institute; American Board of Trial Advocates. **REPORTED CASES:** Cooper v. Bray 21 Cal. 3d 841, 148 Cal. Rptr. 148, 1978; Tri-Chem, Inc. v. County of Los Angeles 60 Cal. App. 3d 306, 132 Cal. Rptr. 142, 1976; Garcia v. Joseph Vince Company 84 Cal. App. 3d 868, 148 Cal. Rptr. 743, 1978; Huizar v. Albex Corp. 156 Cal. App. 3d 534, 203 Cal. Rptr. 47, 1984; Cowing v. City of Torrance 60 Cal. App. 3d 757, 131 Cal. Rptr. 830, 1976; Garza v. Kantor 54 Cal. App. 3d 1025, 127 Cal. Rptr. 164, 1976; Glenwood Homeowners Assoc., Inc. v. Prosher Development, Ltd., 111 Cal. App. 3d 1002, 169 Cal. Rptr. 48, 1980. **PRACTICE AREAS:** Insurance Defense; Public Entity Defense; Products Liability; Premises Liability.

**WILLIAM D. EVANS, (P.C.),** born Hazleton, Pennsylvania, January 12, 1953; admitted to bar, 1978, California. *Education:* Pennsylvania State University (B.A., 1974); Pepperdine University (J.D., cum laude, 1978). Editor, Pepperdine Law Review, 1977-1978. Author: "Massachusetts Board of Retirement v. Murgia: A Fifty Year Old Policeman and Traditional Equal Protection Analysis: Are They Both Past Their Prime?," 4 Pepperdine Law Review 369, 1977. Teaching Fellow, Legal Research and Writing, Pepperdine University, 1977. *Member:* Long Beach (Member: Board of Governors, 1987-1990; Arbitration Committee, 1990) and American Bar Associations; State Bar of California; California Public Defenders Association; Los Angeles Trial Lawyers Association (Member, Federal Courts Committee); Orange County Trial Lawyers Association (Member, Criminal Law Committee, 1979—); The Association of Trial Lawyers of America; California Public Defenders Association; Los Angeles Criminal Courts Bar Association; California Attorneys for Criminal Justice; National Association of Criminal Defense Lawyers. **PRACTICE AREAS:** Civil Trial Practice; Criminal Trial Practice.

### OF COUNSEL

**MICHAEL J. EMLING,** born Long Beach, California, March 19, 1957; admitted to bar, 1985, California. *Education:* University of California at Santa Cruz (B.A., 1981); University of San Francisco (J.D., cum laude, 1985). Member, McAuliffe Honor Society. Deputy City Attorney, City of San Diego, 1985-1986. *Member:* Long Beach Bar Association; State Bar of California. (Also Practicing Individually, Long Beach). **PRACTICE AREAS:** Copyright; Trademark; Estate Planning; Business Torts; Insurance Defense.

REPRESENTATIVE CLIENTS: City of Hawthorne; City of Huntington Beach; County of Los Angeles; Hartford Accident & Indemnity; Louisiana-Pacific Corp.; Professional Risk Management; Aetna Casualty & Surety Co.; Nationwide/Wausau Insurance Company; City of Costa Mesa; Independent Cities Risk Management Authority.

---

## O'FLAHERTY & BELGUM

**100 OCEANGATE SUITE 500**
**LONG BEACH, CALIFORNIA 90802-4312**
Telephone: 310-437-0090
Fax: 310-437-5550
Email: oandb&primenet.com
URL: http://www.oandb-law/oandb

*Glendale, California Office:* 1000 North Central, Suite 300, 91202-2957. Telephone: 818-242-9229. Fax: 818-242-9114.

*Orange County, California Office:* 222 South Harbor Boulevard, Suite 600, Anaheim, 92805-3701. Telephone: 714-533-3373. Fax: 714-533-2607.

*Riverside, California Office:* 3880 Lemon Street, Suite 450, 92501-3301. Telephone: 909-341-0049. Fax: 909-341-3919.

*Ventura, California Office:* 840 County Square Drive, Suite 200, 93003-5406. Telephone: 805-650-2600. Fax: 805-650-2658.

*General Civil, Trial and Appellate Practice in State and Federal Courts. Medical and Dental Malpractice, Products Liability, General Insurance Law, Insurance Coverage, Wrongful Termination, Worker's Compensation, Business and Environmental Litigation.*

(For Complete Biographical Data on all Personnel, see Professional Biographies at Glendale).

## LARRY H. PARKER

3605 LONG BEACH BOULEVARD
SUITE 100
**LONG BEACH, CALIFORNIA 90807**
Telephone: 800-872-0000
Fax: 310-595-4908

*Environmental Law, Asbestos Toxic Torts, Chemical Exposure, Hazardous Materials and Substances, Management, Hazardous Waste, Toxic Injuries, Toxic Exposure, Construction Defects, Insurance Bad Faith, Personal Injury, Medical Malpractice, Maritime Accidents, Aviation Accidents, Automobile, Bus and Train Accidents.*

FIRM PROFILE: The Asbestos/Hazardous Materials Division of the Parker Law Firm is engaged in the Asbestos Property Damage/Personal Injury (asbestos bodily injury) aspects of the ongoing asbestos litigation on behalf of building owners and individuals who have worked in the manufacturing or application of Asbestos Containing Materials.

The Hazardous Materials Division in association with the nations top Asbestos Litigating Law Firms offer you the finest representation available anywhere. A property owner may be able to recover all his past, present and future Asbestos Removal Costs including all associated expenses such as Tenant Relocation and Loss Rental Income.

An individual who has been diagnosed with asbestosis, Pleural thickening or Plaques, Cancers such as mesothelioma is also blanketed under Strict Liability.

The Asbestos/Hazardous Materials and Personal Injury Division is under the direction of Attorney Larry H. Parker. Mr. Parker established The Law Offices Of Larry H. Parker, Inc. in 1976 and has enjoyed a healthy growth and diversification from its inception. In addition to Mr. Parkers involvement in the area of Hazardous Materials, the Parker Law Firm continues to be a dominating name in the area of Personal Injury Law. Through the years the Parker Law Firm has represented a discriminating group of Clients who benefit from the highest levels of Service. The Firm is recognized and distinguished for its expertise, high standards of work and attention to detail regarding highly sophisticated legal matters.

**LARRY H. PARKER,** born 1948; admitted to bar, 1973, California. *Education:* California State University, Los Angeles (B.A., 1970); Southwestern University School of Law (J.D., 1973). *Member:* State Bar of California. **PRACTICE AREAS:** Personal Injury.

## PERONA, LANGER & BECK

A PROFESSIONAL CORPORATION
Established in 1979
300 EAST SAN ANTONIO
**LONG BEACH, CALIFORNIA 90807**
Telephone: 310-426-6155
Facsimile: 310-490-9823

Los Angeles, California Office: 9255 Sunset Boulevard, Suite 920. Telephone: 800-435-7542.

*Personal Injury, Products Liability, Malpractice, Insurance (Bad Faith), Commercial Litigation and Trial Practice in all Courts and Administrative Agencies. Landslide and Subsidence Law. Construction Defect.*

**JAMES T. PERONA,** born Des Moines, Iowa, December 10, 1935; admitted to bar, 1963, California. *Education:* La Sierra College and Willamette University (B.S., 1961); Willamette University (LL.B., 1962). Editor, Willamette Law Journal, 1961-1962. *Member:* Long Beach and Los Angeles County Bar Associations; State Bar of California.

**MAJOR A. LANGER,** born Liberty, New York, July 11, 1942; admitted to bar, 1966, New York; 1967, California. *Education:* University of North Carolina and State University of New York (B.A., 1963); St. John's University (LL.B., 1966). *Member:* Long Beach Bar Association; State Bar of California.

**RONALD BECK,** born Los Angeles, California, November 18, 1953; admitted to bar, 1978, California. *Education:* Claremont Men's College (B.A., cum laude, 1975); University of San Diego (J.D., 1978). Phi Alpha Delta. Recipient, American Jurisprudence Award, Civil Procedure. *Member:* Long Beach Bar Association; State Bar of California.

**WAYNE M. ROBERTSHAW,** born Long Beach, California, July 1, 1949; admitted to bar, 1974, California. *Education:* Whittier College (B.A.,
*(This Listing Continued)*

1971); Loyola University of Los Angeles (J.D., 1974). *Member:* Long Beach Bar Association; State Bar of California; Long Beach Barristers.

**JOHN C. THORNTON,** born Terre Haute, Indiana, May 5, 1950; admitted to bar, 1978, California. *Education:* California State College (B.A., cum laude, 1973); Indiana University; Southwestern University (J.D., 1977). *Member:* State Bar of California.

**M. LAWRENCE LALLANDE,** born Puerto Rico, November 20, 1957; admitted to bar, 1984, California; 1985, U.S. Tax Court. *Education:* Pepperdine University (B.S., 1980; J.D., 1983). Phi Alpha Delta. *Member:* Long Beach, Los Angeles County, Orange County and American Bar Associations; State Bar of California. **LANGUAGES:** Spanish.

**ELLEN R. SERBIN,** born Selma, Alabama, September 22, 1959; admitted to bar, 1987, California and Arizona. *Education:* Pitzer College (B.A., 1981); University of San Diego (J.D., 1986). Order of Barristers. Member, Moot Court Board. *Member:* Orange County, Los Angeles County and American Bar Associations; State Bar of California; State Bar of Arizona; California Trial Lawyers Association; The Association of Trial Lawyers of America.

---

**NELSON L. COHEN,** born Long Beach, California, May 26, 1960; admitted to bar, 1991, California. *Education:* University of Southern California (B.S., 1983); Whittier College School of Law (J.D., 1990). *Member:* Long Beach Bar Association.

**R. PAUL KATRINAK,** born Reading, Pennsylvania, November 29, 1963; admitted to bar, 1993, California. *Education:* University of Maryland (B.S., 1988); University of San Diego (J.D., 1992). Order of the Barristers. Member, Moot Court Board, 1991-1992. Recipient, American Jurisprudence Awards, Property and Civil Procedure. *Member:* State Bar of California.

**SUSAN GRAHAM,** born Boston, Massachusetts, November 29, 1963; admitted to bar, 1992, California. *Education:* University of Massachusetts (B.A., 1985); Loyola University of Los Angeles (J.D., 1992). *Member:* State Bar of California.

**EDWARD T. TRUMPER,** born Washington, D.C., July 21, 1965; admitted to bar, 1992, California. *Education:* Loma Linda University (B.B.A., cum laude, 1988); University of San Diego (J.D., 1992). Executive Comments Editor, San Diego Law Review, 1991-1992. *Member:* State Bar of California.

**RICHARD L. STUHLBARG,** born Long Beach, California, November 6, 1964; admitted to bar, 1995, California. *Education:* Bowdoin College (A.B., magna cum laude, 1987); University of Paris, Paris, France (CPLF and DES, French and Art History, 1986); Loyola Law School (J.D., 1995). James Bowdoin Scholar. Recipient, Edgar Oakes Achorn Prize, 1985. Chief Note and Comment Editor, International and Comparative Law Journal, 1994-1995. **LANGUAGES:** Japanese, Spanish and French.

**RHONDA ANN VISNISKI,** born Mullenburg, New Jersey, July 1, 1966; admitted to bar, 1995, California. *Education:* Pennsylvania State University (B.A., 1988); Loyola Law School (J.D., 1995). Psi Chi; Alpha Phi Omega. Member: Mortar Board Honor Society; Pennsylvania State University Choir, 1985-1988.

## PRAY, PRICE, WILLIAMS & RUSSELL

Established in 1929
810 FIDELITY FEDERAL PLAZA BUILDING
555 EAST OCEAN BOULEVARD
**LONG BEACH, CALIFORNIA 90802**
Telephone: 310-436-1231
Facsimile: 310-435-6384

*General Civil and Criminal Trial Practice. Corporation, Real Estate, Estate Planning, Trust, Taxation, Probate, Negligence and Family Law.*

FIRM PROFILE: The firm had its origins with Russell H. Pray in the early 1920's in Long Beach. Many prominent lawyers who entered practice privately were employed by the firm. All the members of the firm participate in continuing education. The firm offers legal services in the areas in which the firm practices, and is in the general practice of the law.

### MEMBERS OF FIRM

**RUSSELL H. PRAY** (1892-1971).
*(This Listing Continued)*

# PROFESSIONAL BIOGRAPHIES

## CALIFORNIA—LONG BEACH

**WM. A. WILLIAMS,** born Long Beach, California, July 3, 1927; admitted to bar, 1954, California and U.S. District Court, Central District of California; 1971, U.S. Supreme Court; 1978, U.S. District Court, Southern and Eastern Districts of California; 1979, U.S. Court of International Trade and U.S. Court of Military Appeals. *Education:* University of Southern California and California Institute of Technology; Southwestern University (J.D., 1953). *Member:* Long Beach (Member, Board of Governors, 1966-1967; 1974-1975; President, 1979), Los Angeles County (Member, Board of Trustees, 1977-1978) and American Bar Associations; The State Bar of California; The Association of Trial Lawyers of America; The American Inns of Court. **PRACTICE AREAS:** Commercial Law; Litigation; Real Property Law; Construction Law; Cooperative Housing Law.

**JAMES B. RUSSELL, JR.,** born Clinton, Oklahoma, August 11, 1929; admitted to bar, 1959, California and U.S. District Court, Central District of California. *Education:* Long Beach City College (A.A., 1950); Long Beach State College (B.A., 1953); University of Southern California (LL.B., 1958). Phi Delta Phi. *Member:* Long Beach (President, 1987; Member, Board of Governors, 1986) and Los Angeles County (Member, Board of Trustees, 1986) Bar Associations; The State Bar of California; The American Inns of Court. **PRACTICE AREAS:** Litigation Related to Negligence Law; Injury Accidents both Plaintiff and Defense; Family Law; Construction Law; Criminal Defense Law.

**WILLIAM C. PRICE,** born Long Beach, California, February 12, 1947; admitted to bar, 1973, California and U.S. District Court, Central District of California. *Education:* Brigham Young University (A.B., 1970); University of California at Los Angeles (J.D., 1973). Order of the Coif. *Member:* Long Beach Bar Association; The State Bar of California. **LANGUAGES:** French and Tahitian. **PRACTICE AREAS:** Probate and Estate Planning Law; Family Law; Litigation; Construction Law; Personal Injury.

**JAY H. PICKING,** born Cleveland, Ohio, January 8, 1954; admitted to bar, 1980, California; U.S. District Court, Northern, Southern, Central and Eastern Districts of California. *Education:* Ohio State University (B.A., 1976); California Western School of Law (J.D., 1979). Chairman of the Board, Goodwill Industries of Southern Los Angeles County, 1987-1988. *Member:* Long Beach (Member, Board of Governors, 1985) and American Bar Associations; The State Bar of California. **PRACTICE AREAS:** Litigation; Construction Law; Personal Injury Law; Family Law.

**BRUCE E. BOTHWELL,** born Long Beach, California, January 30, 1954; admitted to bar, 1980, California and U.S. District Court, Southern and Central Districts of California. *Education:* Long Beach City College; University of California at Los Angeles (B.A., magna cum laude, 1976); University of San Diego (J.D., 1980). Pi Gamma Mu. Member, Long Beach Barristers. *Member:* Long Beach (Member, Board of Governors, 1988) and American Bar Associations; State Bar of California. **PRACTICE AREAS:** Litigation; Personal Injury Law; Family Law; Business Law; Real Estate Law.

**DAVID M. PRICE,** born Long Beach, California, November 10, 1958; admitted to bar, 1985, California. *Education:* Brigham Young University (B.A., magna cum laude, 1982); University of California at Davis (J.D., 1985). Member, University of California at Davis Law Review, 1984-1985. *Member:* Long Beach, Los Angeles County and American Bar Associations; State Bar of California. **LANGUAGES:** German. **PRACTICE AREAS:** Litigation; Commercial Law; Construction Law; Corporations Law; Family Law.

REFERENCES: Bank of America National Trust & Savings Assn.; Farmers & Merchants Bank (Long Beach Main Offices).

---

## PRINDLE, DECKER & AMARO

Established in 1990

310 GOLDEN SHORE
4TH FLOOR
P.O. BOX 22711
**LONG BEACH, CALIFORNIA 90801-5511**
Telephone: 310-436-3946
Fax: 310-495-0564
Email: LAWPDA1@aol.com

*San Francisco, California Office:* 369 Pine Street, Suite 800. 94104. Telephone: 415-788-8354. Fax: 415-788-3625.

*General Litigation Practice including Insurance Defense, Asbestos Personal Injury and Property Damage, Personal Injury, Products Liability, Recreation and Amusement Park Litigation, Environmental, Admiralty, Business Transaction, Real Estate Transaction, Superfund, Workers Compensation, Construction Litigation and Coverage.*

FIRM PROFILE: *The firm was established in 1990. A focus is Insurance Defense emphasizing Asbestos Personal Injury, Property Damages and including Environmental Litigation. Another focus is Amusement Park Litigation, Skating Rinks, Water Parks, Batting Cages, Fitness Facilities and Grand Prix Parks. The firm's practice is nationwide with a Branch Office in San Francisco, California.*

### MEMBERS OF FIRM

**KENNETH B. PRINDLE,** born Los Angeles, California, October 27, 1953; admitted to bar, 1978, California; 1990, Colorado, Hawaii and U.S. District Court, Northern, Eastern Central and Southern Districts of California. *Education:* University of California at Santa Barbara (B.A., 1975); Southwestern University School of Law (J.D., 1978). Phi Delta Phi. *Member:* South Bay, Long Beach and Los Angeles County Bar Associations; State Bar of California; Association of Southern California Defense Counsel; Defense Research Institute (Lecturer); International Association of Defense Counsel. **PRACTICE AREAS:** Environmental; Asbestos Personal Injury; Property Damage; Insurance Coverage Defense.

**R. JOSEPH DECKER,** born Omaha, Nebraska, November 2, 1947; admitted to bar, 1978, California, U.S. District Court, Northern, Central and Southern Districts of California, U.S. District Court, Northern District of Texas, U.S. District Court, Northern District of Washington. *Education:* California State University, Fullerton (B.A., 1974); Southwestern University School of Law (J.D., 1978). Phi Delta Phi. *Member:* Long Beach and Los Angeles County Bar Associations; State Bar of California; California Workers' Compensation Defense Attorneys' Association; Association of Southern California Defense Counsel; U.S. Supreme Court Bar Association. **PRACTICE AREAS:** Admiralty; Real Estate Transactions; Business Transactions; Personal Injury; Property Damage; Workers Compensation.

**MICHAEL L. AMARO,** born Los Angeles, California, July 17, 1958; admitted to bar, 1983, California; 1984, U.S. District Court, Central District of California. *Education:* California State University at Fullerton (B.A., 1980); Southwestern University School of Law (J.D., cum laude, 1983). *Member:* Long Beach, Los Angeles County and American (Member, Sports Law Committee) Bar Associations; State Bar of California; Defense Research Institute; Association of Southern California Defense Counsel; International Amusement and Leisure Defense Association (Founding Member); World Water Association; Roller Skating Association; International Association of Amusement Parks. **PRACTICE AREAS:** Insurance Defense; Amusement Park Litigation; Product Liability.

**ANDY J. GOETZ,** born Torrance, California, April 20, 1961; admitted to bar, 1986, California and U.S. District Court, Central District of California. *Education:* University of California at Berkeley (B.A., 1983); Loyola Law School (J.D., 1986). *Member:* Long Beach, Los Angeles and American Bar Associations; State Bar of California; Association of Southern California Defense Counsel. **PRACTICE AREAS:** Environmental; Asbestos Personal Injury; Property Damage; Insurance Defense.

**MARY KIRK HILLYARD,** born Coronado, California, August 24, 1950; admitted to bar, 1980, California and U.S. District Court, Northern District of California. *Education:* San Diego State University (B.A., 1972); Hastings Law School ( J.D., 1979). *Member:* San Francisco Bar Association; State Bar of California; Association of Northern California Defense Counsel. (Resident, San Francisco Office). **PRACTICE AREAS:** Insurance Defense; Asbestos Personal Injury; Property Damage; Environmental; Construction Litigation.

**GARY E. YARDUMIAN,** born Berkeley, California, August 18, 1961; admitted to bar, 1987, California and U.S. District Court, Central District of California. *Education:* California Polytechnic State University (B.S., 1984); Southwestern University School of Law (J.D., 1987). *Member:* Los Angeles County and American Bar Associations; State Bar of California; Southern California Defense Counsel. **PRACTICE AREAS:** Construction Litigation; Coverage; Insurance Defense.

**MONTE H. MACHIT,** born Los Angeles, California, September 3, 1957; admitted to bar, 1989, California and U.S. District Court, Central District of California. *Education:* California State University at Long Beach (B.A., 1980); Loyola Law School (J.D., 1988); University of Southern California Law Center. General Counsel, California Workers' Compensation Enquirer. *Member:* Long Beach, Los Angeles County and American Bar Associations; State Bar of California; Association of Southern California Defense Counsel; California Workers' Compensation Defense Attorneys Association. **PRACTICE AREAS:** Insurance Coverage Defense; Amusement Park Litigation.

*(This Listing Continued)*

CAA431B

**PRINDLE, DECKER & AMARO, Long Beach—**Continued

*ASSOCIATES*

**TAHEREH K. BARNES,** born Long Beach, California, January 21, 1966; admitted to bar, 1991, California; U.S. District Court, Central District of California. *Education:* University of California at San Diego (B.A., 1988); Southern University School of Law (J.D., 1990). *Member:* Long Beach, Los Angeles and American Bar Associations; State Bar of California; Association of Southern California Defense Counsel; California Workers' Compensation Defense Attorneys Association; California Young Trial Lawyers Association. *PRACTICE AREAS:* Insurance Coverage Defense; Environmental; Workers Compensation.

**JACK R. REINHOLTZ,** born Lynwood, California, November 19, 1962; admitted to bar, 1990, California; U.S. District Court, Central District o f California. *Education:* Loyola Marymount University (B.S., 1986); Santa Clara University School of Law (J.D., 1990). *Member:* Los Angeles County and American Bar Associations; State Bar of California; Association of Southern California Defense Counsel; California Young Trial Lawyers Association. *PRACTICE AREAS:* Insurance Defense; Construction Litigation.

**JACK C. NICK,** born Los Angeles, California, March 16, 1967; admitted to bar, 1992, California. *Education:* University of California at Santa Barbara (B.A., 1989); Loyola Law School (J.D., 1992). *Member:* Los Angeles County and American Bar Associations; State Bar of California; Association of Southern California Defense Counsel; California Young Trial Lawyers Association. *PRACTICE AREAS:* Insurance Defense; Amusement Park Litigation; Product Liability.

**KRISTIN E.D. DUNN,** born Honolulu, Hawaii, December 15, 1967; admitted to bar, 1992, California. *Education:* University of Southern California (B.S., 1989); Loyola Law School (J.D., 1992). *Member:* Los Angeles County and American Bar Associations; State Bar of California; Association of Southern California Defense Counsel; California Young Trial Lawyers Association. *PRACTICE AREAS:* Insurance Coverage; Environmental.

**JAMES G. MURRAY,** born Van Nuys, California, February 6, 1960; admitted to bar, 1985, California; U.S. District Court, Central District of California and U.S. Court of Appeals, Ninth Circuit. *Education:* University of California at Irvine (B.A., 1982); Loyola Law School (J.D., 1985). *Member:* Los Angeles County and American Bar Associations; State Bar of California; Association of Southern California Defense Counsel. *PRACTICE AREAS:* Insurance Defense; Environmental; Product Liability.

**ANNA M. FERGUSON,** born Seal Beach, California, July 12, 1968; admitted to bar, 1993, California. *Education:* University of California, Santa Barbara (B.A., with high honors, 1990); Pepperdine Law School (J.D., cum laude, 1993). Phi Delta Phi. *Member:* Los Angeles County and American Bar Associations; State Bar of California; Association of Southern California Defense Counsel. *PRACTICE AREAS:* Insurance Defense.

**THOMAS A. STEIG,** born Ukiah, California, June 21, 1959; admitted to bar, 1985, California; U.S. District Court, Northern District of California. *Education:* University of California at Berkeley (A.B., 1981); McGeorge School of Law (J.D., 1985). *Member:* Contra Costa County Bar Association; State Bar of California; Association of Northern California Defense Counsel. (Resident, San Francisco Office). *PRACTICE AREAS:* Insurance Defense; Asbestos Personal Injury; Construction.

**THOMAS P. GMELICH,** born San Antonio, Texas, October 4, 1967; admitted to bar, 1993, California. *Education:* University of California, Berkeley (B.A., 1989); Loyola Law School (J.D., 1993). *Member:* State Bar of California; Association of Southern California Defense Counsel. *PRACTICE AREAS:* Insurance Defense.

**PETER A. POGUE,** born Evanston, Illinois; admitted to bar, 1994, California. *Education:* Purdue University (B.S., Business Administration and Finance, 1989); Golden Gate University (J.D., 1993; M.B.A., 1994). (Resident, San Francisco Office). *PRACTICE AREAS:* Insurance Defense; Asbestos Personal Injury.

**DWAYNE S. BECK,** born Santa Ana, California, September 18, 1961; admitted to bar, 1992, California. *Education:* Institute of European Studies; University of Redlands (B.A., 1983); Western State University (J.D., 1992). *Member:* Orange County Bar Association; State Bar of California; Association of Southern California Defense Counsel. *PRACTICE AREAS:* Insurance Defense; Amusement Park Litigation.

*(This Listing Continued)*

**DARREN B. ROSENBERG,** born Los Angeles, California, January 5, 1970; admitted to bar, 1995, California. *Education:* Brown University (A.B., 1992); Southwestern University School of Law (J.D., 1995). Member, Clarence S. Hunt-Joseph A. Ball Inn of Court, 1995—.

**AMY E. AHLERS,** born Palo Alto, California, July 21, 1966; admitted to bar, 1993, California. *Education:* University of California, Berkeley (B.A., 1988); University of San Francisco (J.D., 1993). Member, USF Law Review, 1991-1993. *Member:* State Bar of California. (Resident, San Francisco Office). *PRACTICE AREAS:* Litigation.

**HALEH RAHIMZADEH,** born Tehran, Iran, October 30, 1971; admitted to bar, 1996, California. *Education:* New York University (B.A., summa cum laude, 1993); University of Southern California (J.D., 1996). Phi Beta Kappa; Phi Sigma Alpha. Recipient: Founders Day Award. Member, Moot Court honors program. *LANGUAGES:* Persian and French. *PRACTICE AREAS:* Litigation.

*OF COUNSEL*

**WILLIAM MURRAY HAKE,** born Oakland, California, December 18, 1951; admitted to bar, 1983, California, U.S. District Court, Eastern, Northern, Southern and Central Districts of California, U.S. District Court, Southern, Northern and Eastern Districts of Texas, U.S. District Court, District of Hawaii and U.S. Court of Appeals, Ninth Circuit. *Education:* California State University, San Jose (B.S., 1977); McGeorge School of Law, University of the Pacific (J.D., 1983). Recipient, Gary V. Schaber Award. Adjunct Professor, Trial Practice, University of San Francisco School of Law, 1994-1995. Faculty, Trial Advocacy, Harvard Law School, Cambridge, Massachusetts. Member, Executive Committee, U.S. District Court, Northern California District Federal Practice Program. *Member:* Bar Association of San Francisco (Member, Litigation Section); Marin County and American (Member, Forum Committee on the Construction Industry) Bar Associations; Association of Defense Counsel of Northern California; Defense Research Institute. *PRACTICE AREAS:* Trials; Professional Liability; Complex and Multi-District Litigation; Asbestos Toxic Torts; Insurance Defense; Federal Litigation.

**MARK B. PEPYS,** born Los Angeles, California, August 5, 1937; admitted to bar, 1964, California. *Education:* University of California at Berkeley (B.A., 1959); Boalt Hall, School of Law, University of California (LL.B., 1963). Phi Delta Phi. *Member:* Los Angeles County (Chairman, Trial Lawyers Section, 1978-1979) and American Bar Associations; The State Bar of California; American Board of Trial Advocates; Association of Southern California Defense Counsel (Secretary-Treasurer, 1975-1976). Fellow, American College of Trial Lawyers. *PRACTICE AREAS:* Products Liability; Professional Liability; Construction Defects.

REPRESENTATIVE CLIENTS: A C & S, Inc.; Admiral Insurance Co.; Aetna; American Empire Surplus Lines Insurance Co.; American International Group, Inc.; Chubb Group; Distribution Services, Ltd.; Employers Insurance of Wausau; Fansteel, Inc.; Fireman's Fund Insurance Co.; GAB; Great American Insurance Co.; ITT; The Hartford; INA/Cigna; K & K Insurance Group; Malibu Grand Prix Corp.; Multimodal Container Lines; Nationwide Insurance; Nautilus Insurance Co.; The Noetics Group; Raging Waters; Scanwell/SCL Shipping; Scottsdale Insurance Co.; Texaco Inc.; Travelers; USF&G; Utah Fire Insurance Co.; Wild Rivers; Zurich Insurance Co.

---

# RIEDMAN, DALESSI & DYBENS

Established in 1931

200 OCEANGATE, SUITE 440
**LONG BEACH, CALIFORNIA 90802**
Telephone: 310-436-5203; 435-5608
Fax: 310-437-8225

*General Civil and Trial Practice in all Courts. Business and Corporate, Real Property, Estate Planning, Trust and Probate Law. Family Law. Personal Injury.*

FIRM PROFILE: *The firm of Riedman, Dalessi & Dybens is the successor law firm to that established by Fred M. Riedman in the 1930's. For a period of years George Deukmejian, former attorney general and governor of California, was a partner in the firm.*

*The firm is proud of its historical background and of the fact that its clientele consist of many who have been clients and friends for a period of many years. The firm desires to impress upon everyone associated with it the importance of maintaining its reputation and the good relationship which exists between the firm and its clientele.*

*(This Listing Continued)*

## PROFESSIONAL BIOGRAPHIES

### MEMBERS OF FIRM

**WILLIAM T. DALESSI,** born Santa Maria, California, December 11, 1922; admitted to bar, 1948, California; 1957, U.S. Supreme Court. *Education:* Santa Maria Junior College; University of Southern California (J.D., 1948). Phi Alpha Delta. City Councilman, 1957-1960 and Chairman, Legislative Committee, 1957-1960, City of Long Beach. President, Long Beach Estate Planning and Trust Council, 1964-1965. Member, Charter Revision Committee, 1960-1963 and Marina Advisory Committee, 1966-1972, City of Long Beach. Special Representative from State of California to the Commission of the California (USA-Mexico), 1972-1980. Member, Joseph A. Ball/Clarence S. Hunt Inn of Court. *Member:* Long Beach (Member: Public Relations Committee, 1959; Board of Governors, 1966; Arbitration and Ethics Committee, 1971; Chairman; Law Office Management and Economics Committee, 1972), Los Angeles County and American Bar Associations; The State Bar of California. **PRACTICE AREAS:** Estate Planning; Probate Law; Business Law; Real Estate Law.

**FRED L. RIEDMAN,** born Long Beach, California, August 15, 1930; admitted to bar, 1957, California. *Education:* University of Redlands (A.B., 1952); University of Southern California (J.D., 1957). Phi Delta Phi. Member, Board of Directors, California Museum of Science and Industry, 1984-1993. Member, Board of Directors, Aquarium of the Pacific at Long Beach, California, 1995—. *Member:* Long Beach, Los Angeles County and American Bar Associations; The State Bar of California. **PRACTICE AREAS:** Real Estate Law.

**BRUCE A. DYBENS,** born Long Beach, California, December 26, 1950; admitted to bar, 1976, California; 1981, U.S. Supreme Court. *Education:* University of California at Los Angeles (B.A., cum laude, 1973); Loyola University (J.D., 1976). Judge Pro Tem, Long Beach Municipal Court, 1981-1995. Family Law Mediator, Superior Court, County of Los Angeles South District, 1981-1995. Member, Joseph A. Ball/Clarence S. Hunt Inn of Court. *Member:* Long Beach (Member, Board of Governors, 1981-1982, 1993-1994), Los Angeles County and American Bar Associations; The State Bar of California; Long Beach Barristers Club (Secretary-Treasurer, 1980; Vice President, 1981, President, 1982). **PRACTICE AREAS:** Litigation; Personal Injury Law; Real Estate Law; Family Law.

---

### LAW OFFICES OF
### MICHELLE M. RODENBORN

ONE WORLD TRADE CENTER, SUITE 1600
**LONG BEACH, CALIFORNIA 90831-1600**
Telephone: 562-436-5456
Fax: 562-437-1967
Email: customs@rodenborn.com
URL: http://www.rodenborn.com

*Customs, International Trade and Transportation Law. Trial and Appellate Practice in all State and Federal Courts. Practice before Federal Administrative Agencies. Export Licensing.*

**MICHELLE M. RODENBORN,** born Fort Dodge, Iowa, 1948; admitted to bar, 1974, California; U.S. District Court, Northern, Central and Southern Districts of California; U.S. Court of International Trade; U.S. Court of Appeals for The Federal Circuit; U.S. Court of Appeals, Ninth Circuit. *Education:* University of Iowa (B.A., 1970; J.D., 1973). Member, Iowa Law Review, 1971-1972. Licensed Customs Broker, 1985. Judge Pro Tem, Los Angeles County Superior Court, 1980-1983. Founder and Past President, 1990-1991, The Organization of Women in International Trade. *Member:* Los Angeles County Bar Association (Member, Executive Committee, International Law Section, 1993—; Member, 1987— and Chair, 1988-1990, Customs Law Committee); State Bar of California (Member, International Law Section); Customs and International Trade Bar Association. **LANGUAGES:** Russian, French and Spanish.

---

### RUSSELL & MIRKOVICH

ONE WORLD TRADE CENTER
SUITE 1450
**LONG BEACH, CALIFORNIA 90831-1450**
Telephone: 310-436-9911
FAX: 310-436-1897

*General Civil, Trial and Appellate Practice in State and Federal Courts, Admiralty, Maritime, International, Environmental and Commercial Law, Personal Injury and Business Litigation.*

(This Listing Continued)

---

**CARLTON E. RUSSELL,** born Corona, California, January 10, 1928; admitted to bar, 1960, District of Columbia; 1962, California. *Education:* Chaffey College and United States Coast Guard Academy (B.S., 1952); George Washington University (J.D., 1960). Order of the Coif; Phi Delta Phi. Legislation Editor, George Washington Law Review, 1959-1960. Author: "Regulation," Chapter 2, California Pleasure Boating Law, 1963 Cal C.E.B. Special Assistant to Chief Counsel, U.S. Coast Guard, Washington, D.C., 1960. District Legal Officer, 11th Coast Guard District, Long Beach California, 1961-1963. *Member:* Long Beach (Chairman, Military Affairs Committee, 1990-1991; Member, Board of Governors, 1977-1978), Los Angeles County, Orange County, Federal and American Bar Associations; The State Bar of California; Maritime Law Association of the United States; Judge Advocates Association; The Association of Trial Lawyers of America. [Captain, U.S. Coast Guard Reserve]. **PRACTICE AREAS:** Maritime; Environmental; Personal Injury.

**JOSEPH N. MIRKOVICH,** born San Pedro, California, December 11, 1939; admitted to bar, 1970, California. *Education:* Georgetown University and University of California at Los Angeles (B.S., 1962); University of San Francisco (J.D., 1969). Phi Delta Phi. *Member:* Long Beach (Member, Board of Governors, 1981-1982), Los Angeles County, Harbor (Secretary-Treasurer, 1973-1974; Vice President, 1974-1975; President, 1975-1977) and American Bar Associations; The State Bar of California; Maritime Law Association of the United States. [Capt., U.S. Naval Reserve]. **PRACTICE AREAS:** Maritime; International; Commercial; Business Litigation.

---

### SAMUEL M. SALMON

SUITE 520, 200 OCEANGATE, ARCO CENTER
**LONG BEACH, CALIFORNIA 90802**
Telephone: 310-437-0841
Fax: 310-432-3610

*Trial Litigation Matters in State and Federal Courts and Arbitration Proceedings in Business, Contract, Fraud, Legal Malpractice and Bankruptcy Reorganization.*

**SAMUEL M. SALMON,** born California, August 30, 1931; admitted to bar, 1957, California, U.S. Court of Appeals, Ninth Circuit and U.S. District Court, Northern, Southern, Central, Eastern and Western Districts of California. *Education:* University of California at Berkeley; Hastings College of Law, University of California (J.D., 1957). Phi Alpha Delta. Trustee, Hastings College of Law Foundation, 1985. *Member:* Long Beach (Board of Governors, 1980-1982, 1993-1994; President, 1985) and Los Angeles County (Trustee, 1983-1984; Member, Federal Courts Committee, 1986—) Bar Associations; State Bar of California (Member, Administration of Justice Committee, 1986-1989; Delegate, State Bar Convention, 1981—).

REPRESENTATIVE CLIENTS: Progressive Custom Wheels, Inc.; MHT Luxury Alloys.

---

### WILLIAM H. SHIBLEY

555 EAST OCEAN BOULEVARD, SUITE 500
P.O. BOX 1731
**LONG BEACH, CALIFORNIA 90801-1731**
Telephone: 213-437-6654
Telecopier: 310-491-5400
Email: shib@ix.netcom.com

*General Civil, Business Intellectual Property and Criminal Trial Practice with emphasis on Plaintiff Personal Injury, Criminal Defense, Maritime Injury, Longshore Compensation.*

**WILLIAM H. SHIBLEY,** born Los Angeles, California, February 27, 1946; admitted to bar, 1973, California and Idaho; 1975, U.S. District Court, Central District of California; 1993, U.S. District Court, Northern District of California and U.S. Court of Appeals, Ninth Circuit; 1995, U.S. District Court, Southern District of California. *Education:* Long Beach City College; Stanford University (B.S., 1969); University of Texas (J.D., 1972). Staff and Managing Editor, American Journal of Criminal Law, 1972. Law Clerk, Travis County Legal Aid and Defender Society, Austin, Texas 1972. Author: "The Attorney Client Privilege and The Right to Uncensored Mail," American Journal of Criminal Law, 1972; Distant Forum Abuse in Consumer Transactions: A Proposed Solution, 51 Tex.L.Rev. 268, 1973. Member, Central Neighborhood Facilities Center, Advisory Committee, 1975-1980; Member, Economic Development Commission of the City of Long Beach, 1984-1992. Long Beach Legal Aid Foundation, Board 1983-1985. Board of Directors and Executive Committee, 1987-1994; 1995 —, Alumni Association, University of Texas at Austin Law School. *Member:*

(This Listing Continued)

**WILLIAM H. SHIBLEY, Long Beach—Continued**

Long Beach (Member, Board of Governors, 1976-1977, 1983-1984, 1988-1990), Los Angeles County and American (Young Lawyers Section, Affiliate Outreach Program, 1975-1977; Section on: Litigation, General Practice, Criminal) Bar Associations; State Bar of California (Conference of Delegates, 1978; 1994-1995; Conference of State Bar and Young Lawyer Presidents, 1976-1982); Long Beach Barristers Club (President, 1977); California Young Lawyers Association (Board of Directors, 1979-1982; Secretary, 1981-1982). *LANGUAGES:* German, Spanish, Portuguese and Arabic.

---

## *GREGORY S. SILVER*

SUITE 410, 200 OCEANGATE
P.O. BOX 1967
**LONG BEACH, CALIFORNIA 90801**
Telephone: 310-491-1212
Fax: 310-590-8181

*General Civil and Criminal Trial Practice, Real Estate, Commercial, Workers Compensation, Personal Injury and Family Law.*

**GREGORY S. SILVER,** born Orange, California, September 11, 1953; admitted to bar, 1982, California. *Education:* California State University at Long Beach (B.S., 1977); University of Southern California; Western State University (J.D., 1982). Adjunct Professor, Workers Compensation, California State University at Long Beach, 1986-1987. *Member:* Long Beach and American Bar Associations; State Bar of California. **REPORTED CASES:** In re the Marriage of Roberta J. & D. Michael Trainotti, 212 CAL App. 3d, 381, 1072.

---

## *LAWRENCE SILVER & ASSOCIATES*

*A LAW CORPORATION*
111 WEST OCEAN BOULEVARD
SUITE 1900
**LONG BEACH, CALIFORNIA 90802-4649**
Telephone: 310-901-4500
Facsimile: 310-901-4520
Email: lsilver@lsilver.com

*General Civil and Trial Practice before all Federal and State Administrative Agencies and Courts. Business, Real Estate, Antitrust, Securities, Commodities, Labor, Corporate, Automotive Dealer Law, Physicians/Hospital Relations Law and Health Law, Computer and Internet Law.*

**LAWRENCE SILVER,** born Uniontown, Pennsylvania, July 1, 1944; admitted to bar, 1968, Pennsylvania; 1972, U.S. Supreme Court; 1976, California. *Education:* University of Wisconsin (B.S., 1964; J.D., 1968). Research Editor, Wisconsin Law Review, 1968. Co-author, with Mark E. Field, *The Route To The Summit:* Jurisdiction Under The Sherman Act , 4 De Paul Business L.J. 429, 1992. Author, "Anxiety and The First Semester of Law School," Wisconsin Law Review 1201, 1968. Law Clerk to the late Hon. David Stahl, Court of Appeals for the Third Circuit, 1968-1969. Deputy Attorney General, Chief Civil Litigation, Commonwealth of Pennsylvania, 1972-1976. Adjunct Professor of Law, Loyola Law School, 1978—. Instructor, National Institute of Trial Advocacy, 1979—. Arbitrator, National Futures Association. *Member:* Beverly Hills (Member, Fee Arbitration Panel), Los Angeles County (Member, Fee Arbitration Panel) and American Bar Associations; State Bar of California. **REPORTED CASES:** Summit Health v. Pinhas, 500 U.S. 322, 111 S.Ct. 1842, (1991) affirming; Pinhas v. Summit Health, Ltd., 894 F.2d 1024 (9th Cir. 1989); Pennsylvania v. New Jersey, 426 U.S. 660, 96 C.Ct. 2333, (1976); First National Monetary Corp. v. Commodity Futures Trading Commission, 677 F2d 522 (6th Cir. 1982), cert. denied sub nom., Monex International v. Commodity Futures Trading Commission 459 U.S. 1016; Aldens Inc. v. Packel, 524 F2d 38 (3d Cir. 1975), cert. denied, 425 U.S. 943 (1976); Shapp v. Simon, 510 F2d 379 (T.E.C.A. 1975), cert denied 424 U.S. 911 (1976); Congress Financial Corp. v. Sterling Coin-Op Machinery Corp., 456 F 2d 451 (3d Cir. 1972); Lebowitz v. Forbes Leasing and Finance Corp., 326 F.Supp. 1335 (E.D. Pa. 1971), aff'd 456 F.2d 979 (3d Cir. 1972), cert. denied 409 U.S. 843, rehearing denied 409 U.S. 1049; Undergraduate Student Assoc. v. Peltason, 359 F.Supp. 320 (N.D. Ill. 1973) (Motion to Dismiss), 367 F.Supp. 1055 (N.D. Ill. 1973) (Summary Judgement); Pennsylvania ex rel Rafferty v. Philadelphia Psychiatric Center, 356 F.Supp. 500 (E.D. Pa. 1973); In the Matter of First National Monetary Corp. (Monex) (1984-1986 Transfer Binder) COMM.FURT.L.REP. (cch) ¶22,698 (August 7, 1985); Haverford College v. Reeher, 329 F.Supp. 1196. (E.D. Pa. 1971); Ford Dealers Association v. Department of Motor Vehicles, 32 Cal.3d 347, 185 Cal.Rptr. 453 (1982); Oyakawa v. Gillett, 8 Cal.App.4th 628, 10 Cal.Rptr.2d 469 (1992); Doe vs. Polaski, 222 Cal.App.3d 1406, 272 Cal. Rptr. 474 (1990), petition for review denied; Shurpin v. Elmhirst, 148 Cal.App.3d 94, 195 Cal.Rptr. 737 (1983); Writers Guild of America v. Merrick, 130 Cal.App.3d 212, 181 Cal.Rptr. 530 (1982); Addison v. Department of Motor Vehicles, 69 Cal. App.3d 486, 138 Cal.Rptr. 185 (1977); Addison v. Department of Motor Vehicles, 69 Cal.App.3d 484, 138 Cal.Rptr. 185 (1977); Oyakawa v. Gillett, 140 Ariz. 29, 854 P.2d 1212 (Ariz. App. 1993); Upper St. Clair Township v. Commonwealth of Pennsylvania, 478 Pa. 546, 387 A.2d 456 (1977), aff'g 13 Pa. Commonwealth Ct. 71, 317 A.2d 906 (1974); Commonwealth of Pennsylvania v. Monumental Properties Inc., 459 Pa. 450, 329 A.2d 812 (1974), rev'g 10 Pa. Commonwealth Ct. 596, 314 A.2d 333 (1973); Hetherington v. McHale, 458 Pa. 479, 329 A.2d 250 (1974), rev'g 10 Pa. Commonwealth Ct. 501, 311 A.2d 162 (1973); People v. Witzkowski, 53 Ill.2d 216, 290 N.E.2d 236 (1972); People v. Witzkowski, 44 Ill.App.3d 152, 357 n.E.2d 1348 ---(1976), pet. for hearing denied ---Ill.2d--,--. N.E.2d-------(1976), appeal dismissed, 434 U.S. 883 (1977). *PRACTICE AREAS:* Litigation; Business Litigation.

---

**MARK E. FIELD,** born Ames, Iowa, September 27, 1953; admitted to bar, 1977, California; 1978, U.S. District Court, Central District of California; 1980, U.S. Court of Appeals, Ninth Circuit. *Education:* University of California at Riverside (B.A., cum laude, 1974); University of California at Berkeley (J.D., 1977). Associate Editor, Industrial Relations Law Journal, 1976-1977. Co-Author, with Lawrence Silver, *The Route To The Summit:* Jurisdiction Under The Sherman Act , 4 De Paul Business L.J. 429, (Spring-/Summer, 1992). *Member:* Los Angeles County Bar Association (Member, Fee Arbitration Panel); State Bar of California. **REPORTED CASES:** Felt v. Atchison, Topeka & Santa Fe Railroad, 831 F.Supp. 780 (C.D. Cal. 1993), rev'd 60 F3d 1416 (9th Cir. 1995); Docksider, Ltd. v. Sea Technology, Ltd., 875 F.2d 762 (9th Cir. 1989); Excess & Cas. Reinsurance Assn. v. Insurance Comr. etc., 656 F.2d 497 (9th Cir. 1981). *PRACTICE AREAS:* Litigation; Business Litigation.

**VICTORIA PYNCHON,** born San Diego, California, May 1, 1952; admitted to bar, 1980, California and U.S. District Court, Eastern District of California; 1985, U.S. District Court, Central, Southern and Northern Districts of California. *Education:* University of California at San Diego (B.A., magna cum laude, 1975); University of California at Davis (J.D., 1980). Order of the Coif. Co-Author, with Victor Rabinowitz and Donald McCormick, "Environmental Disclosure vs. Insurance Coverage: Damned if You Do, Damned if You Don't", Environmental Finance, Summer, 1991. Lecturer, Business Law, School of Business and Economics, California State University at Northridge, 1984-1986. Instructor, National Institute of Trial Advocacy, 1994—. Participant, Los Angeles County Bar Association Barristers Hospice/AIDS Project, 1990-1991. *Member:* State Bar of California. **REPORTED CASES:** Harris v. Smith, 157 Cal.App. 3d 100 (1984); Ziller Electronics Lab v. Superior Court, 206 Cal.App. 3d 1222 (1988); Geophysical Systems Corp. v. Seismograph Service Corp., 738 F.Supp. 348 (1990). *PRACTICE AREAS:* Litigation; Business Litigation.

**JEFFREY M. TANZER,** born New York, N.Y., August 30, 1952; admitted to bar, 1984, Montana; 1987, California. *Education:* University of California at Santa Cruz (B.A., 1974); University of Montana (J.D., high honors, 1984). Editor-in-Chief, Montana Law Review, 1983-1984. *Member:* State Bar of California. *PRACTICE AREAS:* Business Litigation.

**FRED GALANTE,** born Mexico City, Mexico, June 2, 1969; admitted to bar, 1995, California. *Education:* California State University, Northridge (B.A., 1992); Loyola Marymount University (J.D., 1995). St. Thomas More Law Honor Society. Recipient: Academic Incentive Scholarship. Member, 1993-1994 and Staff Writer, Note and Comment Editor, 1994-1995, International and Comparative Law Journal. *Member; Los Angeles County Bar Association. LANGUAGES:* Spanish.

REFERENCE: The Bank of California (Los Angeles Branch).

## SIMON, McKINSEY, MILLER, ZOMMICK, SANDOR & DUNDAS
*A LAW CORPORATION*
Established in 1951

**2750 BELLFLOWER BOULEVARD**
**LONG BEACH, CALIFORNIA 90815**
Telephone: 310-421-9354
Facsimile: 310-420-6455

Irvine, California Office: Suite 670, 4199 Campus Drive. Telephone: 714-856-1916. Facsimile: 714-856-3834.

General Civil and Civil Trial Practice. Corporation, Real Estate, Estate Planning, Trust, Taxation, Probate, Negligence, Family Law, Local Government Administrative Hearings and Appeals.

FIRM PROFILE: The firm of SIMON, McKINSEY, MILLER, ZOMMICK, SANDOR & DUNDAS was established in Long Beach in 1951 by Harry J. Simon and Thomas W. McKinsey as a general law practice. In 1953 they were joined by Arthur W. Miller and together the founders built a solid reputation within their community.

The continuing success of the firm led to the acquisition of the Long Beach office in 1964. Since that time, the firm has grown and expanded. A civil litigation department has been in place since 1978. Another stride was made two years later with the establishment of a full-service office in Irvine.

The firm now offers expertise in the primary areas of family, corporate, business and tax law; matters involving estate planning and the management of trusts, probate, guardianships and conservatorships; and a diverse litigation practice including business matters, personal injury and malpractice proceedings.

Today Simon, McKinsey, Miller, Zommick, Sandor & Dundas offers a strong network of legal professionals helping to meet clients' needs.

**HARRY J. SIMON** (1922-1977).

**THOMAS W. McKINSEY** (1920-1990).

**ARTHUR W. MILLER** (Retired).

**KENNETH ZOMMICK,** admitted to bar, 1965, California. *Education:* University of California at Los Angeles (B.A., 1960); Boalt Hall School of Law, University of California at Berkeley (J.D., 1964). *Member:* Long Beach Bar Association (President, 1981-1982); State Bar of California (Member, Litigation Section Committee); California Trial Lawyers Association; Long Beach Inn of Court (Charter Member). **PRACTICE AREAS:** Estate Planning; Personal Injury; Medical Malpractice.

**DAVID L. SANDOR,** admitted to bar, 1968, California. *Education:* Yale University (B.A., 1964); Boalt Hall School of Law, University of California at Berkeley (J.D., 1967). (Certified Specialist, Family Law, The State Bar of California Board of Legal Specialization). **PRACTICE AREAS:** Family Law.

**GERALDINE G. SANDOR,** admitted to bar, 1975, California. *Education:* University of California at Berkeley (B.A., 1964); Boalt Hall School of Law, University of California at Berkeley (J.D., 1967). (Certified Specialist, Family Law, The State Bar of California Board of Legal Specialization) (Resident, Irvine Office). **PRACTICE AREAS:** Family Law.

**DAVID G. DUNDAS,** admitted to bar, 1969, California. *Education:* University of California at Santa Barbara (B.A., 1964); Southwestern University (LL.B., 1968). *Member:* State Bar of California (Member, Section on Probate and Trust Law). (Resident, Irvine Office). **PRACTICE AREAS:** Estate Planning; Business Law.

---

**ROBERT M. STONE,** admitted to bar, 1982, California. *Education:* University of California at Los Angeles (B.A., 1978); Hastings College of Law, University of California (J.D., 1982). **PRACTICE AREAS:** Business Law.

**CARRIE BLOCK,** born New York, N.Y., September 23, 1968; admitted to bar, 1993, California. *Education:* University of California, Los Angeles (B.A., 1990); Loyola Marymount University (J.D., 1993). Order of the Coif; Phi Delta Phi. *Member:* State Bar of California. (Resident, Irvine Office). **PRACTICE AREAS:** Family Law.

REFERENCE: Farmers and Merchants Bank.

## SPALTRO & LAMHOFER
**3760 KILROY AIRPORT WAY, SUITE 260**
**LONG BEACH, CALIFORNIA 90806-2455**
Telephone: 310-988-1027
Facsimile: 310-988-1163

*Insurance Defense, Automobile and Premises Liability, Commercial Trucking Accidents, Insurance Coverage, Product Liability, Insurance Fraud Law, Construction Defect and Subrogation.*

FIRM PROFILE: Spaltro & Lamhofer, Attorneys at Law, provide responsive and effective legal representation to insurance companies and self-insured entities throughout Los Angeles, Orange, Riverside, San Bernardino, San Diego, Ventura and Santa Barbara counties. Our commitment to exceptional representation is backed by having an experienced attorney handle a case from inception through settlement, arbitration or trial while maintaining direct client contact. The firm strives to meet each client's individualized litigation needs. Our overall success rate at trial exceeds 90%, which includes cases defensed, won on pre-trial motions, or verdicts below the pre-trial offer.

**JAMES P. SPALTRO,** born Portland, Maine, May 29, 1950; admitted to bar, 1982, California; 1987, U.S. District Court, Central District of California; 1989, U.S. District Court, Southern District of California. *Education:* University of Southern Maine (B.A. in Psychology, magna cum laude, 1978); University of San Diego (J.D., 1981). Awarded Outstanding Achievement in Torts. Judge Pro Tem, Los Angeles County, California. *Member:* Long Beach and Los Angeles County Bar Associations; State Bar of California. [SSgt. (E-5), USAF, 1969-1973]. **REPORTED CASES:** Weinrot and Son, Inc. vs. Jackson, (1985) 40 Cal. 3d 327. **TRANSACTIONS:** Authored Resolution 9-5-85 to amend California Civil Code 49, Legislative Committee, Long Beach Bar Association. **PRACTICE AREAS:** Insurance Defense; Automobile and Premises Liability; Commercial Trucking Accidents; Insurance Coverage; Product Liability; Insurance Fraud; Construction Defect; Subrogation.

**ERIC T. LAMHOFER,** born Norwalk, California, January 29, 1959; admitted to bar, 1984, California; 1986, U.S. District Court, Central District of California. *Education:* University of California at Santa Barbara (B.A., 1981) Dean's Honor List; McGeorge School of Law, University of the Pacific (J.D., 1984). *Member:* Long Beach, Los Angeles County and American Bar Associations; State Bar of California; Association of Southern California Defense Counsel. **PRACTICE AREAS:** Insurance Defense; Automobile and Premises Liability; Commercial Trucking Accidents; Insurance Coverage; Product Liability; Construction Defect; Subrogation.

**LISA ANN HOLLINGWORTH,** born Lynwood, California, May 18, 1954; admitted to bar, 1985, California, U.S. District Court, Central and Southern Districts of California. *Education:* California State University, Long Beach (B.S., cum laude, 1976); Loyola Marymount University (J.D., 1984). Special Agent, U.S. Department of State, Foreign Services, 1976-1981. Judge Pro Tem, Orange County, California. *Member:* State Bar of California; American Bar Association. (Also Member, Law Offices of Sharon Lybeck Hartmann, Los Angeles). **REPORTED CASES:** Santa Monica Hospital Medical Center v. Superior Court (1988), 203 Cal. App. 3rd 1026. **PRACTICE AREAS:** Civil Rights; Insurance Defense; Premises Liability; Products Liability; Insurance Fraud Defense.

## PATRICK C. STACKER
**ONE WORLD TRADE CENTER**
**SUITE 1600**
**LONG BEACH, CALIFORNIA 90831-1600**
Telephone: 310-436-7963
Fax: 310-437-1967

*Real Estate, Corporate, Estate Planning and Dispute Resolution.*

**PATRICK C. STACKER,** admitted to bar, 1976, California. *Education:* Auburn University (B.S.I.E., 1967); Southwestern University (J.D., 1976). House Counsel, C.B. Commercial, 1978-1989. General Counsel, C.B. Commercial Investment Banking, 1989-1991. National Reconciler, Lutheran Church Missouri Synod, 1992-1996. *Member:* Los Angeles County Bar Association (Member, Sections on: Real Property, Estate and Probate and Health Care); State Bar of California (Delegate, 1990; Member, Real Property Section); National Association of Realtors (Member: License Law
*(This Listing Continued)*

## PATRICK C. STACKER, Long Beach—Continued

Committee; State and Municipal Legislation Committee, 1983, 1985, 1989). [Lieutenant, U.S. Navy]

REPRESENTATIVE CLIENTS: Newman Tonks Quality Hardware; Falcon Locks; Balboa Investment Group; Christian Reformed Church Board of Home Missions.

---

## STOLPMAN • KRISSMAN • ELBER • MANDEL & KATZMAN LLP

A Partnership including Professional Corporations

*Established in 1952*

NINETEENTH FLOOR
111 WEST OCEAN BOULEVARD
LONG BEACH, CALIFORNIA 90802-4649

Telephone: 310-435-8300
Telecopier: 310-435-8304

Los Angeles (Westwood) Office: Suite 1800, 10880 Wilshire Boulevard.

*Tort Litigation, Trials, Appeals and Workers Compensation.*

FIRM PROFILE: Stolpman, Krissman (formerly Silver, McWilliams) is an established law firm of highly talented, results-oriented specialists who work as a team in the preparation and litigation of tort claims.

Since 1952, we have served thousands of injury victims, obtaining hundreds of awards in six and seven figures—often in cases of highly disputed, difficult liability.

Stolpman, Krissman's considerable expertise in the areas of Product Liability, Construction Accidents, Industrial Accidents, Professional Negligence, Maritime Accidents and Insurance Bad Faith can help your clients obtain a full recovery.

Within Stolpman, Krissman our attorneys specialize in the many different aspects of preparation and trial of substantial cases. Experience shows that our system, utilizing each attorney's talents to maximum advantage, achieves the best results possible for our clients.

Our team includes successful trial attorneys, Certified Specialists in Workers' Compensation, an engineer/lawyer, and others who have demonstrated the special ability necessary to obtain full value in settlement or trial.

Our team approach—focusing talent on particular aspects of major cases—helps account for the consistently high verdicts and settlements we obtain for our clients. Team approach, detailed case preparation, and dynamic trial presentation works—we get results!.

### MEMBERS OF FIRM

**THOMAS G. STOLPMAN, (INC.),** born Cleveland, Ohio, June 2, 1949; admitted to bar, 1976, California and U.S. District Court, Central District of California; 1985, U.S. District Court, Eastern District of California. *Education:* University of California at Los Angeles (B.A., 1972); University of Southern California (J.D., 1976). Editor, 1984-1987 and Editor Emeritus, 1988—, The Advocate, Los Angeles Trial Lawyers Monthly Law Journal. Author, *Negotiating Successful Settlements*, Bankcroft Whitney, 1991. Recipient, Ted Horn Memorial Award for Outstanding Service to the Profession, 1992. President, State Bar of California, 1996-1997. Board of Governors, State Bar of California, 1993-1996. Director, Miralesta Recreation and Park District, Rancho Palos Verdes, California, 1982—. *Member:* Los Angeles County Bar Association (Trustee, 1987-1988; Executive Committee, Litigation Section, 1990—); State Bar of California (Member, Litigation Section); Consumer Attorneys Association of Los Angeles (President, 1989; Member, Board of Governors, 1978—); Consumer Attorneys of California (Board of Governors, 1987-1990); American Board of Trial Advocates (Advocate); The Association of Trial Lawyers of America. (Certifications of Experience as Trial Lawyer, General Personal Injury, Professional Negligence, Product Liability, Public Entity Liability, Appellate Law and Motion and Insurance Bad Faith by the California Trial Lawyers Association). Certified as a Civil Trial Advocate by the National Board of Trial Advocacy. *PRACTICE AREAS:* Products Liability Law; Professional Negligence Law; Maritime Accidents Law.

**LEONARD H. MANDEL,** born Los Angeles, California, October 20, 1938; admitted to bar, 1967, California and U.S. District Court, Central District of California. *Education:* Stanford University (B.S., 1960; M.S., 1961); University of Southern California (J.D., 1966). Phi Alpha Delta; Order of the Coif. Professional Engineer, Mechanical Engineering, Ca., 1966. Author: "Automobile Seat Belts: Protection for Defendants as well as for Motorists?" Southern California Law Review, 1965, reprinted, Frumer & Friedman, "Personal Injury Annual," 1966; "Defendant's Employees as Plaintiff's Experts," California Trial Lawyers Association Journal, Spring, 1974. Professor, UCLA Law School, Trial Tactics and Techniques, 1974-1982. *Member:* State Bar of California; Consumer Attorneys of California; Consumer Attorneys Association of Los Angeles (Board of Governors, 1974-1979). *LANGUAGES:* Spanish. *PRACTICE AREAS:* Products Liability Law; Construction Accident Law.

**BERNARD KATZMAN, (INC.),** born Omaha, Nebraska, March 17, 1935; admitted to bar, 1964, California. *Education:* University of California at Los Angeles (B.A., 1957; LL.B., 1963). Phi Alpha Delta. *Member:* Long Beach (Member, Workers Compensation Section; Board of Governors) and Los Angeles County Bar Associations; State Bar of California; California Applicants Attorneys Association (President, 1987-1988). [1st Lt., USAF, 1958-1960]. *LANGUAGES:* Spanish. *PRACTICE AREAS:* Workers Compensation Law.

**JOEL KRISSMAN,** born Chicago, Illinois, May 6, 1948; admitted to bar, 1973, California; 1974, U.S. District Court, Central District of California. *Education:* University of California at Los Angeles (B.A., 1970); University of San Diego (J.D., 1973). Verdictum Juris Trial Lawyer of the Year, 1994. Consumer Attorneys Association of Los Angeles, Trial Lawyer of the Year, 1994. *Member:* Los Angeles County Bar Association; State Bar of California; Consumer Attorneys Association of Los Angeles (Board of Governors); Consumer Attorneys of California; The Association of Trial Lawyers of America. *PRACTICE AREAS:* Products Liability Law; Maritime Accidents Law; Premises/Construction Accidents.

**MARY NIELSEN ABBOTT,** born San Rafael, California, March 8, 1951; admitted to bar, 1977, California and U.S. District Court, Central District of California. *Education:* University of California, Davis (A.B., 1973); McGeorge School of Law, University of the Pacific (J.D., 1976). *Member:* Los Angeles County Bar Association; State Bar of California; Consumer Attorneys of California; Consumer Attorneys Association of Los Angeles. *PRACTICE AREAS:* Premises/Construction Accident Law; Products Liability Law.

**DONNA SILVER,** born Los Angeles, California, January 11, 1954; admitted to bar, 1979, California. *Education:* University of California at Los Angeles (A.B., summa cum laude, 1976); University of Southern California (J.D., 1979). Phi Beta Kappa. *Member:* Los Angeles County Bar Association; State Bar of California; Consumer Attorneys Association of Los Angeles. *PRACTICE AREAS:* Appellate Practice.

**DENNIS M. ELBER,** born October 20, 1951; admitted to bar, 1976, California. *Education:* University of California at Los Angeles (B.A., summa cum laude, 1973; J.D., 1976). Phi Beta Kappa. Deputy, Los Angeles County Public Defenders Office, 1978-1984. Verdictum Juris Trial Lawyer of the Year, 1993. *Member:* State Bar of California; Consumer Attorneys Association of Los Angeles; Consumer Attorneys of California. *PRACTICE AREAS:* Construction Accidents Law; Products Liability Law; Maritime Accidents Law.

### ASSOCIATES

**EDWIN SILVER,** born Los Angeles, California, 1922; admitted to bar, 1950, California. *Education:* University of California at Los Angeles; University of Southern California (LL.B., 1949). *Member:* State Bar of California; California Applicants Attorneys Association. *PRACTICE AREAS:* Workers Compensation Law.

**LYNNE RASMUSSEN,** born Los Angeles, California, March 28, 1953; admitted to bar, 1984, California. *Education:* California State University, Long Beach (B.A., 1976); San Diego State University (M.S.W., 1978); Loyola University (J.D., 1984). *Member:* State Bar of California; American Bar Association; Consumer Attorneys Association of Los Angeles. *PRACTICE AREAS:* Appeals; Construction Accidents Law; Products Liability Law; Maritime Accidents Law.

**ELAINE MANDEL,** born Los Angeles, California, October 18, 1967; admitted to bar, 1992, California and U.S. District Court, Central District of California; 1993, U.S. District Court, Eastern District of California. *Education:* University of California, Los Angeles (B.A., magna cum laude, 1989; J.D., 1992). Phi Beta Kappa; Phi Alpha Delta. Regents Scholar; Alumni Scholar; Fishbaugh Scholar. Moot Court National Team and Moot Court Board of Directors. Judicial Extern, the Hon. Harry L. Hupp, U.S. District Court, Central District of California. *Member:* Consumer Attorneys Association of Los Angeles. *LANGUAGES:* Spanish. *PRACTICE AREAS:* Construction Accidents Law; Products Liability Law.

*(This Listing Continued)*

## STRAIN & ROSENBERGER

A LAW CORPORATION

UNION BANK BUILDING
400 OCEANGATE, SUITE 520
**LONG BEACH, CALIFORNIA 90802-4356**
Telephone: 310-436-2900
Fax: 310-436-5393
Email: 103504.312@compuserve.com

*International, Federal and State Taxation Law. Pension and Profit Sharing Law. Employee Benefit Law. Estate Planning.*

FIRM PROFILE: *Strain & Rosenberger, a Law Corporation, provides legal advice with respect to a broad spectrum of tax matters.*

*We commonly work in conjunction with certified public accountants and other counsel who provide specialized advice in related areas such as corporate acquisitions, real estate exchanges, and partnership syndications.*

**JOHN A. STRAIN,** born Waterloo, Iowa, October 15, 1948; admitted to bar, 1974, California; 1979, U.S. Tax Court; 1995, U.S. Court of Federal Claims. *Education:* Claremont Men's College (B.A., summa cum laude, 1971); University of Chicago (J.D., with honors, 1974). Order of the Coif. Member, 1972-1973 and Associate Editor, 1973-1974, University of Chicago Law Review. *Member:* Long Beach, Los Angeles County and American (Member, Taxation Section) Bar Associations; State Bar of California. (Certified Specialist, Taxation Law, The State Bar of California Board of Legal Specialization). *LANGUAGES:* Spanish. *PRACTICE AREAS:* International, Federal and State Taxation Law; Estate Planning; Pension and Profit Sharing Law; Employee Benefit Law.

**PAUL D. ROSENBERGER,** born Los Angeles, California, August 1, 1963; admitted to bar, 1989, California; 1995, U.S. Court of Federal Claims. *Education:* University of California at Los Angeles (B.A., 1986); Southwestern University School of Law (J.D., 1989). Member, 1987-1988 and Research Editor, 1988-1989, Southwestern University Law Review. *Member:* Long Beach, Los Angeles County (Member, Section on Taxation) and American (Member, Real Property, Probate and Trust Law Section) Bar Associations; State Bar of California (Member, Tax Section). *PRACTICE AREAS:* International, Federal and State Taxation Law; Probate and Estate Planning.

---

## SWAIN & DIPOLITO

Established in 1993

555 EAST OCEAN BOULEVARD
SUITE 400
**LONG BEACH, CALIFORNIA 90802-5051**
Telephone: 310-983-7833
Fax: 310-983-7835

*General Civil, Trial and Appellate Practice in all State and Federal Courts. Admiralty and Maritime, Transportation, Labor and Employment, General Liability and Insurance Law.*

### MEMBERS OF FIRM

**MICHAEL L. SWAIN,** born Lake Charles, Louisiana, July 22, 1958; admitted to bar, 1983, Louisiana; 1987, California. *Education:* Franklin and Marshall College (B.A., 1980); Tulane University (J.D., cum laude, 1983). Tulane University Post-Graduate Studies in Admiralty, 1985-1986. Law Clerk to Chief Judge Nauman S. Scott, U.S. District Court, Western District of Louisiana, 1983-1985. *Member:* State Bar of California; Louisiana State Bar Association; Maritime Law Association of the United States (Proctor; Member, Carriage of Goods Committee). *PRACTICE AREAS:* Admiralty and Maritime; Transportation; General Liability; Business.

**FRANK X. DIPOLITO,** born New York, N.Y., October 27, 1951; admitted to bar, 1988, California. *Education:* State University of New York Maritime College (B.S., 1972); Loyola Law School (J.D., 1988). St. Thomas More Honor Society. U.S. Coast Guard Master's License, 1978. Council Member, American Master Mariners. California State Bar Probation Monitor. *Member:* Los Angeles County Bar Association; State Bar of California; Maritime Law Association of the United States. *PRACTICE AREAS:* Admiralty and Maritime; Insurance Defense Coverage.

**JOHN G. NURSALL,** born Alhambra, California, February 25, 1953; admitted to bar, 1988, California. *Education:* University of Southern California (B.A., 1975; M.A., 1978, Ph.D., 1987); Pepperdine University (J.D.,
*(This Listing Continued)*

---

1987). *Member:* State Bar of California. *PRACTICE AREAS:* Admiralty and Maritime; Labor and Employment.

### OF COUNSEL

**CHERYL F. GERTLER,** born San Francisco, California, December 22, 1957; admitted to bar, 1982, California; 1987, Illinois. *Education:* University of California at Los Angeles (B.A., 1979); University of California, Davis, School of Law (J.D., 1982). *Member:* State Bar of California; American Immigration Lawyers Association. *LANGUAGES:* Japanese. *PRACTICE AREAS:* Corporate; Commercial; Real Estate; Immigration.

REPRESENTATIVE CLIENTS: Australia-New Zealand Direct Line; Hapag-Lloyd Aktiengeselschaft; Interocean Ugland Management Corporations; Keihin Ocean Line; Keihin America Corporation; Mammoet Western, Inc.; Ocean Marine Mutual Protection & Indemnity Association Limited; St. Paul Fire & Marine Insurance Company; Sea-Land Service, Inc.; Scuko Container Line; United Kingdom Mutual Shipowner's Assurance Assn.

---

## TABRISKY BRUCCULERI & STEIN, LLP

301 EAST OCEAN BOULEVARD
SUITE 270
**LONG BEACH, CALIFORNIA 90802**
Telephone: 310-901-4852
Fax: 310-901-4854
Email: marlaw@tbsllp.com
URL: http://www.tbsllp.com

*Commercial Litigation and Transactions, International Business, Aviation, Maritime, Insurance, Defense of Bad Faith, Personal Injury, Maritime Products Liability, Environmental cases and Appellate Practice in all Courts.*

FIRM PROFILE: *Tabrisky Brucculeri & Stein LLP is a boutique law firm providing its clients with expertise in a wide range of legal matters. The firm's effective use of advanced technology and experienced paraprofessional staff allow it to provide legal services that are narrowly tailored to meet its clients' needs and objectives in the most cost effective and efficient manner possible. Tabrisky Brucculeri & Stein LLP combines a strong and diversified domestic practice that is national in scope with a practice that has a substantial international character. The firm has special experience representing national and multi-national companies who sell and distribute their products and services over extensive territories, and who require multi-faceted and wide-ranging legal services.*

**JOSEPH P. TABRISKY,** born Denver, Colorado, March 29, 1960; admitted to bar, 1985, California; 1986, U.S. District Court, Central District of California and U.S. Court of Appeals, Ninth Circuit; 1987, U.S. District Court, Northern District of California; 1990, U.S. District Court, District of Arizona; 1992, U.S. District Court, Southern District of California and U.S. Supreme Court; 1994, Florida and U.S. District Court, Middle District of Florida; 1995, U.S. District Court, Northern District of Florida. *Education:* University of California at Berkley (B.A., 1982); University of Santa Clara (J.D., 1985). Note Editor, Santa Clara Computer and High-Technology Law Journal, 1984-1985. Author: "Recent Developments in Cargo Litigation," 18 Tulane Maritime Law Journal, 1994; Note, "Copyright Law: Substantial Compliance," Videotronics Inc. v. Bend Electronics, 586 F.Supp. 478, D.C., Nov. 1984; 1 Santa Clara Computer and High-Technology Law Journal 175, 1985. *Member:* Jacksonville and American (Member, Litigation Section) Bar Associations; State Bar of California; The Florida Bar (Admiralty Committee); Maritime Law Association of the United States (Proctor Member; Secretary, Young Lawyers Committee, 1996—; Recreational Boating Committee; Electronics Communications and Commerce). (Board Certified Admiralty and Maritime Specialist, Florida Bar Board of Legal Specialization and Education). *REPORTED CASES:* All Pacific Trading, Inc. v. M/V Hanjin Yosu, 7F.3d 1427, 1994 AMC 365 (9th Cir. 1993), cert. denied, U.S. 127 L.Ed.2d 693, 114 S.Ct. 1301 (1994); In re Korea Shipping Corp. Ltd., 1990 AMC 190 (C.D.Cal. 1989), 919 F.2d. 601, 1991 AMC 499 (9th Cir. 1990), cert. denied; Hanjin Container Lines v. Tokio Marine & Fire Insurance Co., Ltd., 499 U.S. 961, 113 L.Ed.2d 651, 111 S.Ct. 1586 (1991); Tokio Marine & Fire Insurance Co., Ltd. v. M/V Sammi Aurora, 903 F.2d 1244, 1990 AMC 2235 (9th Cir. 1990); In re M/V F.P. Clipper, SMA No. 3119 (1994). *PRACTICE AREAS:* Commercial Litigation and Transactions; International Business and Maritime Litigation; Environmental and Toxic Tort Claim; Insurance; Maritime Personal Injury. *Email:* jtabrisky@tbsllp.com

**FRANK C. BRUCCULERI,** born Port Jefferson, New York, March 8, 1963; admitted to bar, 1988, California; 1989, U.S. District Court, Central, Southern and Northern Districts of California and U.S. Court of Appeals, Ninth Circuit; 1992, U.S. Court of Appeals, Seventh Circuit. *Education:*
*(This Listing Continued)*

### TABRISKY BRUCCULERI & STEIN, LLP, Long Beach—Continued

Williams College (B.A., 1985); Tulane University (J.D., 1988). *Member:* State Bar of California; Maritime Law Association of the United States (Passenger and Cruise Ship Liability Committee). *REPORTED CASES:* Griffith v. Martech Int'l, Inc., 754 F. Supp. 166 (C.D. Cal. 1989). *PRACTICE AREAS:* Jones Act; Longshore; Personal Injury Defense; Maritime Insurance; Property Casualty Litigation and Coverage; Labor Law; Environmental and Toxic Tort Claims.

**KATHY W. STEIN,** born Washington, D.C., August 23, 1952; admitted to bar, 1987, California and U.S. District Court, Central District of California; 1988, U.S. District Court, Northern, Eastern and Southern Districts of California and U.S. Court of Appeals. *Education:* University of California at Irvine (B.A., 1978); Whittier College School of Law (J.D., magna cum laude, 1987). Author: "Recent Developments in Maritime Law;" "Update on Forum Selection Clauses in Maritime Documents," Tulane Maritime Law Journal, Vol 20, No. 2, 1996; "Federal Product Liability Proposal: Effect of Adoption on California Plaintiffs," Whittier Law Review, Vol. 7, No. 4, 1985. *Member:* State Bar of California; Federal Bar Association; Maritime Law Association of the United States (Procter Member); Propellor Club of the United States. *REPORTED CASES:* North End Oil, Ltd. v. M/V Ocean Confidence, 777 F.Supp. 12 (C.D. Ca. 19910); Trent v. Princess Cruises, Inc. 50 F.3d 16 (9th Cir. 1995). *PRACTICE AREAS:* Maritime Personal Injury; Passenger Cruise Ship Work; Charter Parties; Cargo Disputes; Commercial and General Business Litigation; Products Liability Litigation; Marine Financing; Vessel Foreclosure; Bankruptcy and Creditor Representation; Drafting and Preparation of Air and Maritime Bills of Lading.

---

### TAUBMAN, SIMPSON, YOUNG & SULENTOR

Established in 1891

249 EAST OCEAN BOULEVARD, SUITE 700
P.O. BOX 22670
**LONG BEACH, CALIFORNIA 90801-5670**
Telephone: 310-436-9201
FAX: 310-590-9695

*General Civil and Criminal Trial Practice. Business, Taxation, Real Estate, Environmental, Oil and Gas, Eminent Domain, Estate Planning and Probate, Commercial.*

**E. C. DENIO** (1864-1952).

**GEO. A. HART** (1881-1967).

**GEO. P. TAUBMAN, JR.** (1897-1970).

**MATTHEW C. SIMPSON** (1900-1988).

**RICHARD G. WILSON** (1928-1993).

**ROGER W. YOUNG,** born New York, N.Y., January 21, 1921; admitted to bar, 1949, California. *Education:* University of Notre Dame (A.B., magna cum laude, 1942); Harvard University (J.D., 1949); University of Southern California (LL.M. in Taxation, 1954). *Member:* Long Beach and Los Angeles County Bar Associations; State Bar of California. *PRACTICE AREAS:* Taxation; Estate Planning and Probate.

**WILLIAM J. SULENTOR,** born San Pedro, California, March 16, 1946; admitted to bar, 1972, California. *Education:* Loyola University of Los Angeles (B.B.A., 1967; J.D., magna cum laude, 1972). Alpha Sigma Nu. Recipient of William Tell Aggeler Award, Loyola University of Los Angeles, 1972. *Member:* Long Beach and Los Angeles County Bar Associations; State Bar of California. *PRACTICE AREAS:* Business; Real Estate; Environmental; Oil and Gas.

**PETER M. WILLIAMS,** born Houston, Texas, October 2, 1944; admitted to bar, 1970, California. *Education:* Stanford University (B.A., 1966); University of Southern California (J.D., with highest honors, 1969). Recipient, Justin Dart Award. Deputy Public Defender, 1970-1981 and Head Deputy Public Defender, 1981-1989, Los Angeles County. Member: Los Angeles County Task Force on Drug Abuse, 1987-1989; Child Abuse Consortium, 1984-1986. *Member:* Long Beach and Los Angeles County Bar Associations; State Bar of California. *PRACTICE AREAS:* Trial Practice.

**SCOTT R. MAGEE,** born Sussex, New Jersey, December 25, 1957; admitted to bar, 1985, California. *Education:* California State University,

*(This Listing Continued)*

---

Long Beach (B.S., 1981); Pepperdine University (J.D., 1984); Georgetown University (LL.M., in Taxation, 1985). *Member:* Long Beach and Los Angeles County Bar Associations; State Bar of California. *PRACTICE AREAS:* Business; Taxation; Estate Planning.

**MARIA M. ROHAIDY,** born Placitas, Cuba, June 13, 1963; admitted to bar, 1989, California. *Education:* University of Miami (B.A., with honors, 1984); University of Miami Law School; Whittier College (J.D., with honors, 1988). Pi Sigma Alpha. *Member:* Long Beach and Los Angeles County Bar Associations; State Bar of California; American Inns of Court; Los Angeles Trial Lawyers Association. *LANGUAGES:* Spanish. *PRACTICE AREAS:* Litigation.

**STUART C. TALLEY,** born Santa Monica, California, December 9, 1969; admitted to bar, 1995, California. *Education:* University of California at Santa Barbara (B.A., with highest honors, 1992); Pepperdine School of Law (J.D., magna cum laude, 1995). Recipient, First Place I.H. Prinzmetal Writing Competition. Author: "Per Formula In Sound Recordings: Is There Justification In The Age Of Digital Broadcasting," 27 Beverly Hills Bar Association Law Journal 79 (1995). *Member:* Long Beach and Los Angeles County Bar Associations; State Bar of California. *PRACTICE AREAS:* Business; Litigation.

ATTORNEYS FOR: Bixby Land Co.; Renick Cadillac, Inc.; Stricklin/Snively Mortuary; The Termo Co.; Oil Operators Inc.; Astro Aluminum Treating Co. Inc.; Aerocraft Heat Treating Co.; CAL American Insurance Co.; City of Long Beach; Mercado Latino, Inc.
LOCAL COUNSEL: Crown Cork & Seal Co., Inc.
REFERENCE: 1st Business Bank (Torrance Office).

---

### LAWRENCE TAYLOR

3780 KILROY AIRPORT WAY, SUITE 200
**LONG BEACH, CALIFORNIA 90806**
Telephone: 310-594-6278; 714-752-1550
Facsimile: 310-598-4603
Email: letaylor@msn.com
URL: http://law.net/sponsors/taylor/

*Criminal Defense practice limited to Drunk Driving Defense.*

**FIRM PROFILE:** Lawrence Taylor is nationally recognized as "one of the most respected drunk driving attorneys in the country" (editor, DWI JOURNAL). The author of the standard textbook in the field, he has lectured at CLE seminars in 34 states: "Taylor excels at trial preparation and tactics. His expertise is incomparable" (TRIAL). Mr. Taylor's practice is limited to DUI/DWI criminal litigation nationwide, with a primary caseload in Los Angeles and Orange Counties.

**LAWRENCE TAYLOR,** born Los Angeles, California, April 1, 1942; admitted to bar, 1970, California and U.S. Court of Appeals, Ninth Circuit; 1975, U.S. Supreme Court; 1993, Washington. *Education:* University of California, Berkeley (B.A., 1966); University of California School of Law, Los Angeles, (J.D., 1969). Author: *Drunk Driving Defense*, 4th ed. (Boston: Little, Brown & Co.), 1996; *California Drunk Driving Defense, 2nd ed.* (San Francisco: Bancroft-Whitney), 1995. Board of Regents, National College of DUI Defense, Atlanta (Dean, 1995-1996); Board of Editors, *California DUI Report*. Associate Professor, Gonzaga University School of Law, Spokane Washington, 1982-1985. Fullbright Professor of Law, Osaka University, Japan, 1985. Deputy District Attorney, Los Angeles, 1970-1971. Deputy Public Defender, Los Angeles, 1971-1972. Special Prosecutor, Attorney General of Montana, 1975-1976. *Member:* Los Angeles County, Orange County and Washington State Bar Associations; State Bar of California. [With U.S.M.C., 1961-1964.]. *PRACTICE AREAS:* Drunk Driving Defense.

---

### D. MICHAEL TRAINOTTI

A PROFESSIONAL LAW CORPORATION

SUITE 410, 200 OCEANGATE
**LONG BEACH, CALIFORNIA 90802**
Telephone: 310-590-8621
Fax: 310-590-8181

*General Tax Practice. Real Estate, Trust and Probate Law, Estate Planning, Corporation and Partnership Law. Real Estate Pass Through Entities.*

**D. MICHAEL TRAINOTTI,** born San Pedro, California, July 29, 1944; admitted to bar, 1974, California; 1985, U.S. Tax Court. *Education:* California State University at Long Beach (B.A., 1967); Southwestern University (J.D., 1973); Golden Gate University (M.S., Taxation, 1983). *Member:*

*(This Listing Continued)*

Long Beach (Member, Sections on: Real Estate; Probate), Los Angeles County (Member, Taxation Section) and American (Member, Taxation Section) Bar Associations; State Bar of California (Member, Sections on: Tax; Business Law; Chairman, Tax Section, Washington, D.C. Trip, 1993); Estate Planning Council of Long Beach. [First Lt., U.S. Army, 1967-1970]

REFERENCE: Farmers & Merchants Bank; Harbor Bank.

## VANDENBERG, NEWELL, CURTIS, NELSON & SCHUUR

*A PROFESSIONAL CORPORATION*
*SUITE 400 HARBOR BANK BUILDING*
*11 GOLDEN SHORE DRIVE*
**LONG BEACH, CALIFORNIA 90802**
Telephone: 310-435-7471
Facsimile: 310-435-7405
Email: VNCNS@earthlink.net

*General Civil and Trial Practice. Corporation, Real Estate, Estate Planning, Trust and Probate Law. Tax Litigation. Trials and Appeals. Negligence and Family Law.*

FIRM PROFILE: The law firm of Vandenberg, Newell, Curtis, Nelson & Schuur has a long history of providing professional legal services to the Long Beach community. The firm provides a variety of general civil legal services with emphasis on real estate, estate planning and probate, family law, personal injury and corporation law, both transactional and litigation. The firm has represented insured parties of the Interinsurance Exchange of the Automobile Club of Southern California, as well as other national carriers, in uninsured motorist claims and other tort claims for two decades.

Members of the law firm have a long history of civic, community and charitable involvement and have been active within local, county and state bar associations. In community government, members of the firm have served as city councilmen and city mayors. The law firm is proud to have a former member as a California Appellate Court Justice (Honorable Justice Michael Nott) and two former members presiding as Superior Court Judges.

**JACK M. VANDENBERG** (1921-1986).

**FRANK R. NEWELL**, born Tacoma, Washington, January 20, 1950; admitted to bar, 1975, California and U.S. District Court, Central District of California. *Education:* Long Beach State University (B.A., 1972); University of Southern California (J.D., 1975). Phi Kappa Phi. Arbitrator, Los Angeles County Arbitration Panel. *Member:* Long Beach (Member, Board of Governors, 1990-1991; Secretary/Treasurer, 1993; Vice President, 1994; President-Elect, 1995; President, 1996), Los Angeles County (Trustee, 1994) and American Bar Associations; State Bar of California (Delegate, State Bar Convention, 1978-1980); Long Beach Bar Foundation (Treasurer and Director). *PRACTICE AREAS:* Probate; Real Estate Law; Business and Corporations; Estate Planning.

**MARK CURTIS**, born Long Beach, California, April 16, 1954; admitted to bar, 1980, California. *Education:* Long Beach City College and University of California at Los Angeles (B.A., 1976); Pepperdine University (J.D., 1979). *Member:* Orange County, Los Angeles County and Long Beach (Member, Family Law Mediation Panel, 1983—) Bar Associations; State Bar of California; Christian Legal Society. *PRACTICE AREAS:* Family Law; Probate Law; Estate Planning; Personal Injury Law.

**KEITH A. NELSON**, born Duluth, Minnesota, August 18, 1945; admitted to bar, 1975, California and U.S. District Court, Central District of California. *Education:* Western State University (J.D., 1975). Member, La Palma City Council, 1984-1992. Arbitrator, Los Angeles County Arbitration Panel, 1982—. *Member:* Long Beach and Los Angeles County Bar Associations; State Bar of California; Association of Southern California Defense Counsel; Defense Research Institute. *PRACTICE AREAS:* Personal Injury Law; Negligence and Trials; Civil Trial Law.

**PAMELA BOURETTE SCHUUR,** born Lakewood, California, July 17, 1959; admitted to bar, 1985, California; 1986, U.S. Tax Court; 1987, U.S. District Court, Southern District of California. *Education:* University of Southern California (B.S., 1981); Whittier College (J.D., 1985); National Institute of Trial Advocacy. Phi Alpha Delta. American Inns of Court. *Member:* Long Beach (Board of Governors), Orange County and American Bar Associations; State Bar of California; Women Lawyers of Long Beach (President-Elect, 1994-1995; President, 1995-1996); California Women Lawyers. *PRACTICE AREAS:* Probate Litigation; Estate Planning; Conservatorships; Construction Law; Tax Litigation.

*(This Listing Continued)*

**GREGORY J. BURNIGHT,** born Long Beach, California, May 30, 1966; admitted to bar, 1991, California. *Education:* University of California at Berkeley (B.A., 1988); University of Southern California (J.D., 1991). Inns of Court. *Member:* Long Beach and American Bar Associations; State Bar of California; Long Beach Barristers (Vice-President); American Inns of Court. *PRACTICE AREAS:* Business and Corporations; Personal Injury; Estate Planning; Family Law; Probate Litigation.

REPRESENTATIVE CLIENTS: Automobile Club of Southern California; National Automobile and Casualty Insurance Co.; Gemological Institute of America; Economy Reconveyance Corp.; Shoreline Properties (Real Estate); Anchor Seaport Escrow Co.; Firstline Mortgage, Inc. (Real Estate Loan Brokers); Pacific Sporting Goods; HCM (Commercial Real Estate Brokers); L.B. Brokerage, Inc. (Real Estate); Bourette Machine Company, Inc.; Keystone Machine Company, Inc.; Greater Long Beach Christian Schools, Inc.; Rancho Car Wash; Big Penny Car Wash; Robert Hatch & Associates (Professional Fiduciaries); Schaap, Miller, Stahlburg (Professional Fiduciaries).
REFERENCES: Harbor Bank; Farmers and Merchants Trust Co.

## WALSH, DONOVAN, LINDH & KEECH

*301 EAST OCEAN BOULEVARD, SUITE 1200*
**LONG BEACH, CALIFORNIA 90802-4828**
Telephone: 310-901-4848
Telefax: 310-901-4850;
Telex: 384-831

*San Francisco, California Office:* Suite 2000, 595 Market Street. Telephone: 415-957-8700. Telefax: 415-543-9388. Telex: WU 384831 WADINH SFO; RCA 286833 WDL UR; ESL 62756007.
*Los Angeles, California Office:* Suite 2600, 445 South Figueroa Street. Telephone: 213-612-7757. Telefax: 213-612-7797. Telex: WU 401760 WADINH LSA ESL 62949341.

*General Civil and Trial Practice. Admiralty, Commercial, Construction, Bankruptcy, Franchising, International Practice and Insurance Law.*

(For Complete Biographical Data on all Personnel, see San Francisco, California Professional Biographies)

## ROBERT A. WEINBERG

*Established in 1986*
*4335 ATLANTIC AVENUE*
**LONG BEACH, CALIFORNIA 90807**
Telephone: 310-424-1798
Fax: 310-424-0047

*Collections, Business and Construction Law. Estate Planning, Banks Receivables.*

**ROBERT A. WEINBERG,** born Los Angeles, California, February 27, 1957; admitted to bar, 1983, California. *Education:* University of California at Los Angeles (B.A., 1980); Pepperdine University (J.D., 1983). Phi Alpha Delta. *Member:* Los Angeles County (Member: Steering Committee; Construction Law Subcommittee) Bar Association; State Bar of California; Engineering Contractors Association. *PRACTICE AREAS:* Collections; Construction; General Business; Estate Planning.

REPRESENTATIVE CLIENTS: ASK Financial, Inc.; Blue Sky; Blue Sea, Inc.; Trench Shoring Company; Lawrence Diamant, Bankruptcy Trustee; Curtis Danning, Bankruptcy Trustee; Republic Bank.

## ALLAN B. WEISS AND ASSOCIATES

*5000 E. SPRING STREET*
*SUITE 430*
**LONG BEACH, CALIFORNIA 90815-1270**
Telephone: 310-421-6333
Telecopier: 310-421-6903

*General Civil and Trial Practice. Corporation, Real Estate, General Business, Probate, International, Hazardous Waste, Negligence, Employment, Insurance (coverage and defense), and Domestic Relations.*

**ALLAN B. WEISS (A PROFESSIONAL LAW CORPORATION),** born Long Beach, California, March 27, 1944; admitted to bar, 1969, California. *Education:* Stanford University (A.B., 1965); University of Southern California (J.D., 1968). Phi Delta Phi. *Member:* Long Beach, Los Angeles County and American Bar Associations; The State Bar of California. *PRACTICE AREAS:* Civil Litigation; Real Estate; Corporate Law; Inter-

*(This Listing Continued)*

**ALLAN B. WEISS AND ASSOCIATES,** Long Beach—
*Continued*

national Law; Hazardous Waste; Business Law; Probate Law; Negligence Law; Employment Law; Insurance Coverage Law; Insurance Defense.

---

**JOCK R. DAVIDSON, (INC., A PROFESSIONAL LAW CORPORATION),** born San Diego, California, September 15, 1943; admitted to bar, 1971, California. *Education:* Long Beach City College (A.A., 1963); University of California at Los Angeles (B.S., 1966; J.D., 1969). Phi Delta Phi. Family Law Mediator, Superior Court, South District, 1984—. Judge Pro Tem, Los Angeles County Superior Court, South District, 1994—. Judge Pro Tem, Long Beach Municipal Court, 1986—. *Member:* Long Beach and Los Angeles County Bar Associations; State Bar of California. *PRACTICE AREAS:* Civil Litigation; Probate Law; Negligence Law; Family Law.

**RYAN K. HIROTA (A PROFESSIONAL LAW CORPORATION),** born Los Angeles, California, September 12, 1952; admitted to bar, 1981, California; 1982, U.S. District Court, Central and Southern Districts of California; 1985, U.S. District Court, Eastern District of California; 1986, U.S. Court of Appeals, Ninth Circuit; 1987, U.S. District Court, Northern District of California. *Education:* University of California, Irvine (B.S., 1974); Western State University (J.D., 1981). Judge Pro Tem, Long Beach Municipal Court, 1987—. *Member:* Long Beach (Member, Board of Governors, 1987-1989; Secretary/Treasurer, 1994-1995; Vice-President, 1996; President-Elect, 1996; President, 1997), Los Angeles County (Member, Real Estate Section) and American Bar Associations; State Bar of California (Member, Real Estate Section, 1993—); Women Lawyers of Long Beach; Joseph A. Ball, Clarence S. Hunt Inn of Court (Member, Development Contact, 1996-1997). Fellow, Long Beach Bar Foundation (Member, Board of Directors, 1993—; Secretary, 1995-1996). *PRACTICE AREAS:* Real Estate; Business Litigation.

**JAMES R. FLATEBO,** born Rockford, Illinois, March 24, 1959; admitted to bar, 1992, California and U.S. District Court, Central and Eastern Districts of California. *Education:* San Diego State University (B.A., 1984); Whittier College School of Law (J.D., magna cum laude, 1992). Associate Editor, Whittier Law Review, 1992. Instructor, Business Law, Cerritos College, 1996. Arbitrator, Better Business Bureau, 1994-1996. *Member:* Long Beach and Los Angeles County Bar Associations; State Bar of California. *PRACTICE AREAS:* Civil Litigation; Real Estate.

**MIRA SUSAN WOLFF,** born Inglewood, California, January 11, 1966; admitted to bar, 1992, California. *Education:* California State University, Long Beach (B.A., 1989); Southwestern University School of Law (J.D., 1992). American Trial Lawyers Association (ATLA) Student Trial Advocacy Team. *Member:* Long Beach Bar Association; State Bar of California; Long Beach Women Lawyers Association. *PRACTICE AREAS:* Business Litigation; Employment; Civil Litigation.

*OF COUNSEL*

**JAMES D. TURNER,** born Long Beach, California, August 5, 1950; admitted to bar, 1976, California. *Education:* California State University at Dominguez Hills (B.A., 1972); Southwestern University (J.D., 1976). *Member:* Long Beach Bar Association; State Bar of California. *PRACTICE AREAS:* Civil Litigation; Insurance Coverage; Personal Injury Defense.

REPRESENTATIVE CLIENTS: Mitchell Land & Improvement Co. (Real Estate Development, Hazardous Waste); Irwin Industries, Inc. (Petrochemical Construction, insurance coverage, defense); Bed, Bath & Beyond, Inc. (Retailing); Purple Heart Veterans Rehabilitation Services, Inc.; TLC CORPORATION (Labor Leasing); WEB Vocational Consultants; Executive Office Concepts; Hotel Cabo San Lucas, Cabo San Lucas, B.C. Mexico.
REFERENCES: Wells Fargo Bank, Long Beach Main Branch; Bank of America, Belmont and Bixby Knolls Branches; Comerica Bank-California (formerly National Bank of Long Beach).

---

## WILLIAM B. WELDEN

*Established in 1990*

**5150 EAST PACIFIC COAST HIGHWAY**
**LONG BEACH, CALIFORNIA 90804-3393**
*Telephone: 310-986-1201*
*Fax: 310-597-2174*

*General Civil and Trial Practice in all Courts. Insurance Bad Faith, Insurance Coverage, Arbitrator.*

*(This Listing Continued)*

CAA440B

---

**WILLIAM B. WELDEN,** born Hampton, Iowa, June 1, 1950; admitted to bar, 1977, Iowa; 1985, California. *Education:* Iowa State University (B.S., 1972); Drake University (J.D., 1976); University of Nottingham, Nottingham, England (M. Phil., Laws, 1978). Barrister Member: American Inns of Court; Louis Welch, Robert Banyard and Ball-Hunt Inns, 1986-1992. Instructor, Appellate Advocacy and Legal Writing, University of Puget Sound Law School, 1982-1984. Adjunct Professor: Western State University Law School, 1984-1986; California Western School of Law, 1985-1987. Judicial Magistrate, Iowa, 1980-1981. Member, Education Appeals Board, U.S. Department of Education, 1982-1987. *Member:* Los Angeles County Bar Association; State Bar of California; American Arbitration Association (Arbitrator). *PRACTICE AREAS:* General Civil and Trial Practice; Insurance Bad Faith; Insurance Coverage; Arbitrator.

REPRESENTATIVE CLIENTS: CDI Corp., Philadelphia, PA; Country Cos., Bloomington, IL; Minnehoma Insurance Co., Tulsa OK; Adesco Inc., Tulsa, OK; Ohio Indemnity Co., Columbus, OH.
REFERENCE: Bank of America (Seal Beach Branch).

---

## WILLIAMS WOOLLEY COGSWELL NAKAZAWA & RUSSELL

**111 WEST OCEAN BOULEVARD, SUITE 2000**
**LONG BEACH, CALIFORNIA 90802-4614**
*Telephone: 310-495-6000*
*Telecopier: 310-435-1359; 310-435-6812*
*Telex: ITT: 4933872; WU: 984929*
*Email: wwlaw@msn.com*

*Rancho Santa Fe, California Office:* P.O. Box 9120, 16236 San Dieguito Road, Building 3, Suite 3-15, 92067. Telephone: 619-497-0284. Fax: 619-759-9938.

*Port Hueneme, California Office:* 237 E. Hueneme Road, Suite A, 93041. Telephone: 805-488-8560. Fax: 805-488-7896.

*Commercial Transactions and Litigation, Maritime Law, Transportation and International Law, Environmental Law, Immigration Law, Personal Injury and Product Liability Litigation.*

*FIRM PROFILE: The law firm of Williams Woolley Cogswell Nakazawa & Russell ("Williams Woolley") began operations in Long Beach in February of 1988. The founding partners came from two of the largest firms in California, Lillick McHose & Charles (now known as Pillsbury, Madison & Sutro) and Graham & James. The formation of Williams Woolley represents the joinder of attorneys with reputations for excellence and aggressiveness in representing clients, with special care being paid to the particular needs and interests of each client.*

*Williams Woolley is known internationally for its expertise in the field of maritime and transportation law, as well as environmental law. In this regard, Williams Woolley represents all sectors of the maritime transportation industry, including financial institutions, ocean carriers, terminal operators, cruise lines and international maritime insurance associations. We advise clients on United States and international maritime transportation, commercial and environmental law, and represent them in litigation before federal and state courts and administrative agencies.*

*Williams Woolley also handles regulatory and policy matters before the Federal Maritime Commission, Department of Transportation, Coast Guard, Customs Service and other U.S., foreign and international agencies.*

*MEMBERS OF FIRM*

**REED M. WILLIAMS,** born Pasadena, California, December 18, 1926; admitted to bar, 1954, California. *Education:* California Maritime Academy (B.S., 1947); University of California at Berkeley; University of California, Hastings College of Law (LL.B., 1954). Associate Editor, American Maritime Cases, 1968—. Member, Board of Governors, California Maritime Academy, 1968-1972; Board of Harbor Commissioners, City of Long Beach, 1977-1978. Formerly with: U.S. Department of Justice, Admiralty and Shipping Section; Graham & James (Senior Maritime Partner). *Member:* Long Beach (Member, Board of Governors, 1976-1978) and Los Angeles County Bar Associations; State Bar of California; The Maritime Law Association of the United States (Proctor Member; Member, Executive Committee, 1972-1975). *REPORTED CASES:* Orient Steam Navigation Co., Ltd. v. United States of America (Kearsarge-Oriana), 231 F.Supp. 469, 1964 AMC 2163 (S.D. Cal. 1964); Chervy v. Peninsular & Oriental Steam Navigation Co., Ltd. (Arcadia), 364 F.2d 908, 1966 AMC 226 (9th Cir. 1966); Waterman Steamship Corp. v. Gay Cottons (Chickasaw) 414 F.2d 724, 1969 AMC 1682 (9th Cir. 1969); Japan Line, Ltd. v. County of Los Angeles, 441 U.S. 434, 99 S.Ct. 1813, 16 L.Ed.2d 336, 1979 AMC 881

*(This Listing Continued)*

(1979); Lubick v. Travel Service, Inc., 573 F.Supp. 904 (D.V.I. 1983); and Matter of Bowoon Sangsa Co., Ltd., 720 F.2d 595, 1984 AMC 97 (9th Cir. 1983). *PRACTICE AREAS:* Maritime Law; Transportation and International Law; Commercial Transactions and Litigation; Personal Injury. *Email:* wwlaw@msn.com

***DAVID E. R. WOOLLEY,*** born Westminster, England, November 7, 1946; admitted to bar, 1973, California. *Education:* Britannia Royal Naval College; Oxford University, Eng land (B.A., with honors, 1970); University of California at Berkeley, Boalt Hall (J.D., 1973). Member, Moot Court. Adjunct Professor of Law, University of Southern California, 1994—. Editor, Benedict on Admiralty. *Member:* Los Angeles County and American Bar Associations; State Bar of California; The Maritime Law Association of the United States (Proctor Member, Maritime Arbitration Committee); International Association of Defense Counsel; Center for International Legal Studies, Salzburg, Austria. *REPORTED CASES:* Melwire Trading Co., Inc. v. M/C Cape Antibes, 811 F.2d 1271, 1987 AMC 1217 (9th Cir. 1986); Flexi-Van Leasing, Inc. v. M/V C.C. San Francisco, 808 F.2d 697 (9th Cir. 1987); and GF Company v. Pan Ocean Shipping Co., Ltd., 23 F.3d 1498 (9th Cir. 1994); All Pacific Trading, Inc. v. M/V Hanjin Yosu 7 F.3d 1427, 1994 AMC 365 (9th Cir. 1994); Slaven v. BP America, Inc., 973 F.2d 1468, 1993 AMC 9, 22 ELR 21500 (9th Cir. 1992); Tongil Co. Ltd. v. M/V Hyundai Innovator, 968 F.2d 999, 1992 AMC 2440 (9th Cir. 1992); C-Art Ltd. v. Hong Kong Islands Line America S.A., 940 F.2d 530, 1991 AMC 2888 (9th Cir. 1991); Tokio Marine & Fire Ins. Co. Ltd. v. M/V Sammi Aurora 903 F.2d 1244, 1990 AMC 2235 (9th Cir. 1990); Interpool Limited v. Char Yigh Marine (Panama) S.A., 890 F.2d 1453, 1990 AMC 1 (9th Cir. 1989); Genetics International v. Comorant Bulk Carriers, Inc., 877 F.2d 806, 1989 AMC 1725 (9th Cir. 1989). *PRACTICE AREAS:* Maritime Law; Environmental Law; Transportation and International Law; Commercial Transactions and Litigation; Personal Injury; Product Liability. *Email:* wwlaw@msn.com

***FORREST R. COGSWELL,*** born Chicago, Illinois, August 18, 1946; admitted to bar, 1975, California. *Education:* Dartmouth College (A.B., cum laude, highest distinction, 1968); University of Chicago (J.D., 1975). Recipient, Pray Modern Language Prize. Member Moot Court Honors Program. Formerly Partner, Lillick McHose & Charles. Licensed Private Pilot. *Member:* Los Angeles County and American Bar Associations; State Bar of California; The Maritime Law Association of the United States (Proctor Member: Member, Uniformity Committee); Dartmouth Lawyers' Association; Dartmouth College Alumni Association. *LANGUAGES:* Spanish. *REPORTED CASES:* Amando Martinez v. Korean Shipping Corp., Ltd., et al., 903 F.2d 606 (9th Cir. 1990); Katherine E. Rumberg, et al. v. Weber Aircraft Corporation, et al., 424 F. Supp. 294 (1976); Eliud A. Torres v. Johnson Lines and NYK Lines, 1989 AMC 1009; United Kingdom Mutual Steamship Assurance Association (Bermuda) Limited v. Continental Maritime of San Francisco, Inc., Inc., 1993 AMC 542. *PRACTICE AREAS:* Maritime Law; Transportation and International Law; Commercial Transactions and Litigation; Personal Injury; Product Liability. *Email:* wwlaw@msn.com

***ALAN NAKAZAWA,*** born Tokyo, Japan, December 12, 1951; admitted to bar, 1978, California; U.S. District Court, Northern, Southern, Eastern and Central Districts of California; U.S. Court of Appeals, Ninth Circuit; U.S. Supreme Court. *Education:* Yale University (B.A., 1974); University of Southern California (J.D., 1978). Author: "COGSA and Choice of Foreign Law Clauses in Bills of Lading," Tulane L.J. Vol. 17, No. 1, Fall 1992. Lecturer, Norwegian Shipping Academy, International Bunker Conference, Oslo, Norway, November, 1992. *Member:* State Bar of California; The Maritime Law Association of the United States (Proctor Member); Japanese-American Bar Association; Yale Alumni Club of Southern California; Japan American Society. *REPORTED CASES:* North River Ins. Company v. Fed Sea/Fed Pac, 647 F.2d 985 (9th Cir. 1981); Mobil Sales & Supply Corporation v. Panamax Venus, 804 F.2d 541, 1987 AMC 305 (9th Cir. 1986); Carman Tool & Abrasives, Inc. v. Evergreen Lines, 871 F.2d 897 (9th Cir. 1989); Mori Seiki USA, Inc. v. M.V. Alligator Triumph, 990 F.2d 444 (9th Cir. 1993); North End Oil v. Norman Spirit, 1993 AMC 88 (C.D. Cal. 1992); Oman Refinery v. M.T. Bertina, 1993 AMC 147 (C.D. Cal. 1992). *PRACTICE AREAS:* Maritime Law; Transportation and International Law; Commercial Transactions and Litigation; Immigration. *Email:* wwlaw@msn.com

***BLAKE W. LARKIN,*** born San Francisco, California, November 14, 1955; admitted to bar, 1979, Supreme Court of New South Wales, Australia and Federal Courts of Australia; 1982, Supreme Court of Papua New Guinea; 1986, California. *Education:* University of Wollongong, Australia (G.D.Ph.); Australian National University (LL.B., 1978); London Institute of World Affairs (Dip. Air and Space Law); University of London (LL.M.,

*(This Listing Continued)*

International Law, 1985). Formerly with, Lillick McHose & Charles. Member, American Association of Arbitrators. *Member:* Los Angeles County and American Bar Associations (Member, Admiralty and Maritime Law Committee; Charter Member, Forum Committee on Air and Space Law International Law) and State Bar of California (Member, International Law Section); Law Society of New South Wales; The Maritime Law Association of the United States (Proctor Member, Marine Ecology and Vice-Chair, Marine Insurance and General Average Committee); Law Council of Australia; Maritime Law Association of Australia and New Zealand; Australian-American Chamber of Commerce (Member, Board of Directors, 1992—). *PRACTICE AREAS:* Maritime Law; Environmental Law; Transportation and International Law; Commercial Transactions and Litigation; Personal Injury; Products Liability.

***THOMAS A. RUSSELL,*** born Corona, California, August 2, 1953; admitted to bar, 1983, California. *Education:* University of California at Berkeley (B.S., 1976); University of Southern California (J.D., 1982). Law Clerk to Justice Robert Kingsley, Associate Justice, California Court of Appeals, 1981. Formerly with Graham & James. Contributing Author: *Benedict on Admiralty,* Ch. 2-5 in Vol. 2 and Ch. 12 in Vol. 8, (Matthew Bender, 1995); *Recreational Boating Law,* Ch. 12 (Matthew Bender, 1992). Author: "Nonjudicial Foreclosure Under the Ship Mortgage Act," 18 J.Mar.L.Com. 555 (1987); "The Foreclosure of Preferred Ship Mortgages," 48 Consumer Fin. L.Q. Rep. 136 (1994). Co-Author: "Current Topics in the Law of Recreational Boating," 5 U.S.F. Mar. L.J. 107 (1992). Lecturer, Pacific Admiralty Seminar, 1992, 1996; Pacific Multimodal International Expo, 1992. Editor: *Boating Briefs,* 1991-1996. Chairman, Planning Committee for the Symposium, "Energy and The Oceans: A Legal Perspective," in 1 L & Envir. 3-156, (1985). Formerly with Graham & James. *Member:* Los Angeles County and American (Chairman, Maritime Financing Subcommittee, 1994—) Bar Associations; State Bar of California; The Maritime Law Association of the United States (Proctor Member; Vice-Chairman, Recreational Boating Committee, 1996—); The Center for International Commercial Arbitration (Member, Board of Directors, 1990—); International Business Association of Southern California (Member, Board of Directors, 1989—; President, 1994-1995); Greater Los Angeles World Trade Center Association (Member, Board of Directors, 1996—). *REPORTED CASES:* Sea-Land Service, Inc. v. Murrey & Son's Co., 824 F.2d 740, 1988 AMC 1, 24 SRR 393 (9th Cir. 1987); Hong Kong Islands Line America S.A. v. Distribution Services Limited, 795 F.Supp. 983, 1992 AMC 82, 25 SRR 1601 (1991) aff'd 963 F.2d 378 (9th Cir. 1992); Key Bank of Maine v. M/V Asever, 1993 AMC 263 (C.D. Cal. 1992); Maryland National Bank v. The Vessel Madam Chapel, 46 F.3d 895, 1995 AMC 850, 27 SRR 279 (9th Cir. 1995); Dietrich v. Key Bank, N.A. 72 F.3d 1509, 1996 AMC 609, 27 SRR 448 (11th Cir, 1996), Logistics Management, Inc. v. Pyramid Tent Arena, 86 F.3d 908 1996 AMC 1826, 27 SRR 838 (9th Cir. 1996). *PRACTICE AREAS:* Maritime Law; Commercial Transactions and Litigation; Business; Regulatory; Immigration; Labor and Employment. *Email:* wwlaw@msn.com

*ASSOCIATES*

***TODD A. VALDES,*** born Redondo Beach, California, August 22, 1963; admitted to bar, 1993, California and U.S. District Court, Central and Southern Districts of California. *Education:* Harvard University (A.B., 1985); University of Southern California (J.D., 1993). *Member:* Los Angeles County Bar Association; State Bar of California. [Lieut. Cmdr., U.S. Navy, 1985-1990; U.S. Naval Reserve, 1990—]. *PRACTICE AREAS:* Business Litigation; Commercial Litigation; Admiralty and Maritime Law.

***THOMAS G. WALSH,*** born Oak Park, Illinois, March 8, 1967; admitted to bar, 1994, California. *Education:* University of Notre Dame (B.A., 1989); University of Southern California Law Center (J.D., 1994). *Member:* Los Angeles County Bar Association; State Bar of California; American Society of International Law; Southern California Chinese Lawyers Association. *LANGUAGES:* Mandarin and Spanish. *PRACTICE AREAS:* Admiralty and Maritime Law; International Law; Commercial Law; Litigation. *Email:* wwlaw@msn.com

***RICHARD J. NIKAS,*** born Long Beach, California, September 9, 1968; admitted to bar, 1996, California; U.S District Court, Central and Eastern Districts of California. *Education:* University of Southern California (B.A., 1991; J.D., 1995). Phi Alpha Delta. Member and Finalist, Hale Moot Court Honors Program. Member, Hale Moot Court National Honors Team. Recipient: Best Oralist, Spong National Invitational Moot Court; The Judge E. Avery Crary Award for Excellence in Oral Advocacy. Assistant Editor, *Boating Briefs* of the Maritime Law Association, 1994-1996. Author: "Foreign Arbitration Clause in Salvage Agreement May Not Be Enforced Absent Reasonable Relationship with the Foreign State," *Boating Briefs,* Vol.

*(This Listing Continued)*

## WILLIAMS WOOLLEY COGSWELL NAKAZAWA & RUSSELL, Long Beach—Continued

3, No. 2, 1994; Federal Safety Act Precludes State Tort Claims on Injuries From Unguarded Boat Propeller, *Boating Briefs*, Vol. 5, No. 1.; Boxing The Compass: The Origin and Development of Admiralty Tort Jurisdiction in The United States; Testing the Limits: The Limitation of Shipowner Liability Under The Limitation Act, The Fire Statute and OPA 90, USC Law Center. Co-Author: The Effects of Recent Case Law on the Recreational Boating Industry, 9 U.S.F. Mar. L.J. Vol. 2 (1997); Recent Developments in Recreational Boating Law, Pacific Admiralty Seminar (1996). Contributing Author: *Benedict on Admiralty*, Ch IX-X in Vol. 2 (Matthew Bender 1996). Research Assistant, Benedict on Admiralty, Matthew Bender Publishing Co., Vol. 2, Ch. 2, 3, 4, 5, 1995-1996; Vol. 8, Ch. 12, 1995-1996. President: First Year Law Students Association, 1992-1993; University of Southern California Admiralty and Maritime Law Society, 1992-1995. President, 1993-1994; President Emeritus, 1994-1995, University of Southern California International Law Society. President, 1993-1994; Captain, 1994-1995, University of Southern California Jessup International Moot Court. Board of Advisors, Hale Moot Court Advisory Board. Member, Hellenic-American Council. **LANGUAGES:** Greek, Russian and Spanish. **PRACTICE AREAS:** Admiralty and Maritime Law; International Law; Litigation. **Email:** wwlaw@msn.com

---

## WISE, WIEZOREK, TIMMONS & WISE

A PROFESSIONAL CORPORATION

Established in 1949

3700 SANTA FE AVENUE, SUITE 300
P.O. BOX 2190
**LONG BEACH, CALIFORNIA 90810**
Telephone: 310-834-5028
Fax: 310-834-8018

*Redding, California Office:* 443 Redcliff Drive, Suite 230. Telephone: 916-221-7632. Fax: 916-221-8832.

General Civil and Trial Practice in State and Federal Courts. Corporation, International Business, Insurance, Real Property, Immigration, Estate Planning, Probate and Tax Law.

**GEORGE E. WISE,** born Chicago, Illinois, February 26, 1924; admitted to bar, 1949, California; 1955, U.S. Supreme Court. *Education:* Lake Forest College; Northwestern University; University of Chicago (J.D., 1948). Member, Board of Editors, University of Chicago Law Review, 1947-1948. Research Attorney for Hon. John W. Shenk, Justice of the California Supreme Court, 1948-1949. *Member:* Los Angeles, Long Beach (President, 1970; "Attorney of the Year, 1990") and American Bar Associations; The State Bar of California. Fellow, American College of Trial Lawyers. **PRACTICE AREAS:** General Civil Practice; Corporate; Real Property; Probate; Estate Planning.

**DUANE H. TIMMONS,** born Dubuque, Iowa, December 21, 1945; admitted to bar, 1972, California. *Education:* Harvard University (A.B., 1968); Stanford University (J.D., 1971). *Member:* The State Bar of California. **PRACTICE AREAS:** Insurance Law; Litigation; Medical Malpractice; Personal Injury; Products Liability; Torts Law.

**ANTHONY F. WIEZOREK,** born Dubuque, Iowa, December 1, 1941; admitted to bar, 1972, California. *Education:* University of California at Los Angeles (B.A., 1965); California State College at Long Beach (M.A., 1968); Loyola University of Los Angeles (J.D., 1972). *Member:* Long Beach and American Bar Associations; The State Bar of California. **PRACTICE AREAS:** Insurance Law; Litigation.

**SUSAN E. ANDERSON WISE,** born Chicago, Illinois, December 27, 1948; admitted to bar, 1974, California. *Education:* Lawrence University (B.A., cum laude, 1970); University of Chicago (J.D., 1974). Phi Beta Kappa. *Member:* Long Beach (President, 1994), Los Angeles County and American Bar Associations; The State Bar of California. **PRACTICE AREAS:** Civil Litigation; Employment Law; General Business Litigation; Insurance Coverage; Real Property Law.

**ALBERT F. PADLEY, III,** born Pasadena, California, August 20, 1953; admitted to bar, 1978, California. *Education:* University of Notre Dame (B.A., 1975); Loyola University of Los Angeles (J.D., 1978). Phi Alpha Delta. *Member:* The State Bar of California; American Bar Association. **PRACTICE AREAS:** Insurance Coverage; Insurance Defense.

*(This Listing Continued)*

---

**MICHAEL J. PEARCE,** born Newcastle upon Tyne, England, July 17, 1952; admitted to bar, 1979, California. *Education:* Oxford University, England (B.A., 1973); Cambridge University, England (M.Phil., 1975); Duke University (J.D., 1979). *Member:* Long Beach, Los Angeles County and American Bar Associations; The State Bar of California; Association of Business Trial Lawyers. **PRACTICE AREAS:** Contract Law; Insurance Law; International Law; Litigation.

**MARK C. ALLEN, III,** born Santa Monica, California, December 9, 1949; admitted to bar, 1974, California. *Education:* Grinnell College (B.A., 1971); Loyola University of Los Angeles, (J.D., 1974). *Member:* State Bar of California (Member, Special State Bar Committee on Courts, 1985; Vice Chairman Law Section, 1981; Business, Public Law, Litigation Sections). **PRACTICE AREAS:** Contract Law; Insurance Law; Litigation; Probate Law.

**RICHARD P. DIEFFENBACH,** born Seattle, Washington, July 7, 1955; admitted to bar, 1982, California. *Education:* Albright College (B.A., cum laude, 1978); Washington University (J.D., 1981). Member, Urban Law Review, 1980, 1981. Author/Lecturer, *Mixed Collateral Foreclosure*, Cal. CEB, January 1993. *Member:* Los Angeles County Bar Association; The State Bar of California. **PRACTICE AREAS:** Insurance Law; Real Property; Litigation.

**STEVEN C. RICE,** born Grand Forks, North Dakota, April 14, 1959; admitted to bar, 1983, California. *Education:* Harvard University (A.B., 1980); University of California at Davis (J.D., 1983). *Member:* Long Beach and Los Angeles County Bar Associations; The State Bar of California. **PRACTICE AREAS:** Insurance Law; Litigation.

**STEPHEN M. SMITH,** born Los Angeles, California, June 7, 1958; admitted to bar, 1983, California. *Education:* University of Southern California (A.B., 1980); Loyola Marymount University (J.D., 1983). *Member:* The State Bar of California; American Bar Association. **PRACTICE AREAS:** Insurance Coverage.

**THOMAS J. YOCIS,** born February 20, 1956; admitted to bar, 1981, Illinois; 1984, California. *Education:* Lewis University (B.A., 1978); University of Chicago (J.D., 1981); University of San Diego (LL.M., 1984). *Member:* Los Angeles County Bar Association; State Bar of California. **PRACTICE AREAS:** Contract Law; Corporate Law; Estate Planning; Probate Law; Tax Planning.

**JAMES M. COX,** born Whittier, California, June 17, 1960; admitted to bar, 1984, California. *Education:* California State University at Fullerton (B.A., cum laude, 1981); University of Southern California (J.D., 1984). *Member:* Los Angeles County Bar Association; The State Bar of California. **PRACTICE AREAS:** Insurance Law; Litigation.

**MATHEW J. VANDE WYDEVEN,** born Santa Monica, California, October 13, 1963; admitted to bar, 1988, California. *Education:* University of California at Los Angeles (B.A., Economics, 1985); Loyola Marymount University (J.D., 1988). *Member:* Los Angeles County and American Bar Associations; State Bar of California. **PRACTICE AREAS:** Insurance Defense.

**TAE J. IM,** born Seoul, South Korea, February 19, 1963; admitted to bar, 1988, California. *Education:* Johns Hopkins University (B.A. Economics, 1985); University of California at Los Angeles (J.D., 1988). *Member:* Los Angeles County and American Bar Associations. **PRACTICE AREAS:** Insurance Coverage; Insurance Defense.

---

## GEORGE S. ZUGSMITH

A PROFESSIONAL LAW CORPORATION

Established in 1982

SUITE 430
5000 EAST SPRING STREET
**LONG BEACH, CALIFORNIA 90815-1270**
Telephone: 310-420-6164
Fax Number: By Request

Family Law, Child Support, Spousal Support, Divorce, Custody and Visitation.

**GEORGE S. ZUGSMITH, JR.,** born Pittsburgh, Pennsylvania, October 19, 1939; admitted to bar, 1969, California and U.S. District Court, Central District of California; 1975, U.S. Supreme Court. *Education:* Menlo College (B.S., cum laude, 1964); California Western University and University of San Fernando Valley (J.D., cum laude, 1968). Lecturer, Child and Spousal Support, Long Beach Library Series, Long Beach Bar. Guest Lecturer, "The Management of a Family Law Practice," a Continuing Legal

*(This Listing Continued)*

Education Program, University of Southern California Law School, 1994, 1995. Deputy City Attorney, Los Angeles, 1969-1971. Deputy District Attorney, County of Los Angeles, 1971-1973. Private Practice, 1973—. Judge Pro Tem, Mediator, Los Angeles County Superior Court, Family Law Department, 1990—. Volunteer: Lawyers in the Library; Long Beach Legal Aid, Domestic Violence. Mediator, Superior Court. *Member:* Long Beach (Member: Family Law Section; Chair, 1994-1995; Vice Chair, 1992-1993; Secretary, 1991-1992), Beverly Hills, Orange County (Member, Family Law Section), Los Angeles County (Member Sections on: Family Law and Arbitration) and Orange County Bar Associations; State Bar of California (Member, Family Law Section and Committee on Custody).

REFERENCE: Farmers & Merchants Bank, Long Beach.

## KENNETH B. SABO
*A PROFESSIONAL CORPORATION*
Established in 1967
3551 FLORISTA AVENUE, SUITE 1A
**LOS ALAMITOS, CALIFORNIA 90720**
Telephone: 310-594-8787
Fax: 310-594-8780

General Business, Corporate, Partnership, Insurance, Real Estate, Commercial Law and Related Litigation. Civil Trials and Appeals in all State and Federal Courts.

**KENNETH B. SABO,** born Akron, Ohio, March 5, 1938; admitted to bar, 1967, California and U.S. District Court, Central District of California; 1971, U.S. Supreme Court; 1976, U.S. District Court, Northern District of California; 1985, U.S. District Court, Eastern District of California. *Education:* Compton College (A.A., 1958); University of Southern California (A.B., 1960); Southwestern University (J.D., 1966). Instructor of Law, South Bay University, 1969-1972. *Member:* Los Angeles County and Orange County Bar Associations; State Bar of California.

REPRESENTATIVE CLIENTS: Upon Request.

## ROBERT L. DENEBEIM
885 NORTH SAN ANTONIO ROAD, SUITE K
**LOS ALTOS, CALIFORNIA 94022-1305**
Telephone: 415-941-7327
Facsimile: 415-941-7328

*General Practice/Family Law.*

**ROBERT L. DENEBEIM,** born Columbia, Missouri, August 5, 1953; admitted to bar, 1980, California. *Education:* University of California at Berkeley (B.A., 1975); San Francisco Law School (J.D., 1980). Deputy District Attorney, San Mateo County, 1981-1982. *Member:* San Mateo County Bar Association; State Bar of California. **REPORTED CASES:** Henslee v. DMV, 168CA3d 445; Marvin v. DMV, 191CA3d 171. **PRACTICE AREAS:** Family Law; Civil Litigation; Business Law.

## KENNETH R. KAYE
Established in 1972
SUITE A, 220 STATE STREET
**LOS ALTOS, CALIFORNIA 94022**
Telephone: 415-949-1660
Fax: 415-949-5024

*Real Estate, Taxation, Tax Deferred Exchanges, Estate Planning, Trusts, Corporate and Business Law.*

**KENNETH R. KAYE,** born Milwaukee, Wisconsin, December 27, 1943; admitted to bar, 1970, California; 1972, U.S. Court of Appeals, Ninth Circuit. *Education:* University of Pennsylvania (B.S., cum laude, 1966); Stanford University (J.D., 1969). Beta Gamma Sigma. Director, 1976-1986 and President, 1983-1984, Miramonte Mental Health Services. Instructor, Tax Aspects of Real Estate, Foothill College and De Anza College, 1979-1982. Director, 1983-1989 and President, 1987-1989, Los Altos Chamber of Commerce. Director, 1995—and Vice-President, 1996-1997, Community Services Agency of Mountain View and Los Altos. *Member:* Palo Alto and Santa Clara County Bar Associations; State Bar of California (Member,

*(This Listing Continued)*

Sections of: Real Estate; Taxation). [1st Lt., U.S. Army, 1970-1972]. **PRACTICE AREAS:** Real Estate Law; Real Estate Transactions; Tax Deferred Exchanges; Estate Planning; Trusts and Probate.

## LANGLEY, LAMBERTO, KREGER & MOHER
Established in 1982
4984 EL CAMINO REAL, SECOND FLOOR
**LOS ALTOS, CALIFORNIA 94022-1433**
Telephone: 415-428-1100
Fax: 415-428-1102

San Francisco, California Office: 465 California Street, Suite 1285, 94104. Telephone: 415-394-9900. Fax: 415-394-9997.
Santa Rosa, California Office: 404 Mendocino Avenue, Suite 200, 95401. Telephone: 707-577-0895. Fax: 707-526-5864.

*Trial and Appellate Practice, Insurance Defense, Insurance Law and Coverage, Environmental and Toxic Tort Claims, Business Litigation, Personal Injury, Bad Faith, Products Liability, Professional Liability, Landslide/Subsidence Claims, Construction, Arson and Fraud Claims, Insurance Appraisals.*

### MEMBERS OF FIRM

**LARRY D. LANGLEY,** born Tulsa, Oklahoma, February 7, 1942; admitted to bar, 1973, California. *Education:* Oklahoma State University (B.Arch.E., 1966); University of San Francisco (J.D., 1973). Chi Epsilon. Member, McAuliffe Law Honor Society. Registered Civil Engineer, California, 1969. Instructor, Evidence and Civil Procedure, San Mateo Law School, 1977-1979. Lecturer in Bad Faith, California Continuing Education of the Bar, 1985, 1987 and 1989. Judge Pro Tem, San Mateo County Superior Court, 1989—. Member, Panel of Arbitrators, American Arbitration Association. *Member:* Santa Clara, San Mateo County (Delegate, State Bar Convention, 1981; Member, Board of Directors, 1982) and American Bar Associations; State Bar of California; Defense Research Institute; Association of Defense Council of Northern California; California Conference of Arson Investigators; Property Claims Association of the Pacific. **REPORTED CASES:** Magnolia Square HOA v. Safeco Insurance Company of America (1990) 221 CA 3d 1049; National Union v. Siliconix (1989) 729 Fed. Supp. 77; State Farm Mutual Automobile Insurance Co., Becker v., 52 Cal. App. 3d 282, 124 Cal. Rptr. 739 (1975). **PRACTICE AREAS:** Product Liability; Personal Injury; Construction; Environmental; Business and Employment Litigation; Insurance Coverage;; Arson/Fraud Law; Bad Faith.

**PETER N. LAMBERTO,** born Des Moines, Iowa, December 4, 1947; admitted to bar, 1974, California; 1976, Hawaii. *Education:* University of San Francisco (B.A., 1970; J.D., 1974). Member, Panel of Arbitrators, Santa Clara Superior Court. *Member:* Santa Clara County, San Mateo County, Hawaii State and American Bar Associations; State Bar of California; Association of Defense Counsel of Northern California; Defense Research Institute. **REPORTED CASES:** Mid-Century Insurance Co. v. Hartford Casualty Insurance Co., 26 Cal. App. 4th 1783. **PRACTICE AREAS:** Civil Litigation; Defense of Toxic Torts; Personal Injury; Product Liability; Construction Law; Commercial and Business Torts.

**BRIAN S. KREGER,** born Chicago, Illinois, May 27, 1954; admitted to bar, 1982, California. *Education:* University of Wisconsin-Madison; University of California at Santa Barbara (B.A., 1978); University of Santa Clara (J.D., 1982). *Member:* Santa Clara County Bar Association; State Bar of California; Association of Defense Counsel of Northern California. **REPORTED CASES:** Kohn v. Superior Court (1983, 1st Dist) 142 Cal. App. 3d 323; Mid-Century Insurance Co. v. Hartford Casualty Insurance Co., 26 Cal. App. 4th 1783; Worthington v. Rusconi, et al, 29 Cal App 4th 1488 (1994). **PRACTICE AREAS:** Trials and Appeals; Defense of Personal Injury; Wrongful Termination; Product Liability; Construction Defect Cases.

**JAMES P. MOHER,** born New Haven, Connecticut, July 2, 1954; admitted to bar, 1982, California and U.S. District Court, Northern, Eastern and Southern Districts of California. *Education:* University of California at Santa Cruz (B.A., 1979); Hastings College of Law, University of California (J.D., 1982). Author: "Resolving Multiparty Tort Litigation," California Torts, Matthew Bender Co., 1985; "Cumis: A Liability Insurer's Duty to Pay for Its Insured's Independent Counsel," CTLA Forum, May, 1985; "New Standards for Determining Good Faith Settlements," San Mateo Bar Association Journal, July/August, 1985. *Member:* Bar Association of San Francisco; State Bar of California; American Bar Association; Barristers Club of San Francisco. **PRACTICE AREAS:** Business Litigation; Com-

*(This Listing Continued)*

## LANGLEY, LAMBERTO, KREGER & MOHER, Los Altos—Continued

mercial Litigation; Personal Injury Law; Construction Law; Insurance Coverage.

**JOYCE D. ANDREWS,** born Brooklyn, New York, January 26, 1949; admitted to bar, 1985, California and U.S. District Court, Northern and Eastern Districts of California. *Education:* Hofstra University (B.A., cum laude, 1970); Adelphi University (M.A., 1975); University of Santa Clara (J.D., cum laude, 1985). Author: "Good Faith Settlements: Pointers and Pitfalls," In Brief, Fall 1986; "Effectively Using CCP 998," Times & Trials, November, 1989; "Getting the Benefit of the Bargain: How to Tender Defense to an Insurance Company and Make it Stick," In Brief, Winter, 1995. *Member:* Santa Clara County and American Bar Associations; State Bar of California; Association of Defense Counsel of Northern California. *LANGUAGES:* French, Spanish and German. *PRACTICE AREAS:* Trials and Appeals; Defense of Personal Injury; Insurance Coverage; Litigation.

### ASSOCIATES

**BONNIE L. MILLER,** born Palo Alto, California, May 3, 1950; admitted to bar, 1984, California and U.S. District Court, Northern District of California; 1986, U.S. District Court, Eastern District of California. *Education:* San Francisco Law School (J.D., 1983). Arbitrator, San Mateo County, 1987-1995. *Member:* San Mateo County and Santa Clara County Bar Associations; The State Bar of California; San Mateo County Barristers (Member, Board of Directors, 1986-1990; Vice President, 1988; Member, ADR Committee, 1991-1995; Board of Directors, Legal Aid Society, San Mateo County, 1991-1995; Consumer Attorneys of San Mateo County. *PRACTICE AREAS:* Construction; Personal Injury Litigation; Juvenile; Family Law.

**PHILIP R. SODERQUIST,** born New Ulm, Minnesota, April 26, 1954; admitted to bar, 1986, California. *Education:* University of California at Berkeley (B.A., with high honors, 1982); Hastings College of the Law, University of California (J.D., 1986). Judge Pro Tem, Santa Clara County Superior Court. Certified General Contractor, California, 1981. *Member:* Santa Clara County Bar Association; State Bar of California; Association of Defense Counsel of Northern California. *PRACTICE AREAS:* Trials and Appeals; Complex Construction Litigation; Personal Injury.

**J. PENNY OLIVER,** born Seattle, Washington, January 12, 1949; admitted to bar, 1987, California. *Education:* Montana State University (B.A., with honors, 1972); Western Illinois University (M.A., with honors, 1978); Santa Clara University (J.D., with honors, 1987). Phi Beta Kappa; Phi Kappa Phi. Member, Support Network for Battered Women. *Member:* Santa Clara County Bar Association; State Bar of California; Association of Defense Counsel of Northern California; Central Coast Claims Association. *LANGUAGES:* French. *REPORTED CASES:* Magnolia Square HOA v. Safeco Insurance Company of America (1990) 221 CA3d 1049. *PRACTICE AREAS:* Trials and Appeals; Defense of Personal Injury; Insurance Coverage.

**KRISTI J. SPIERING,** born Tacoma, Washington, August 8, 1963; admitted to bar, 1991, Arizona; 1995, California. *Education:* Lewis and Clark College (B.A., 1985); University of Cincinnati (J.D., 1991). Order of the Coif. Author: "Irrebuttable Exile Under the Immigration Marriage Fraud Amendments: A Perspective From the Eighth Amendment and International Human Rights Law," 58 U. Cinn. L. Rev. 1397, 1990. *PRACTICE AREAS:* Tort Litigation; Insurance Coverage; Insurance Defense.

**ALAN J. ZACHARIN,** born Oakland, California, October 3, 1947; admitted to bar, 1990, California; 1993, Montana. *Education:* University of California at Berkeley (B.S., 1969) McGeorge School of Law, Sacramento (J.D., 1990). Order of the Coif. *Member:* Alameda County Bar Association and Bar Association of San Francisco. *PRACTICE AREAS:* Civil Litigation.

**ELIZABETH VAN DER TOORREN,** born Los Gatos, California, December 3, 1966; admitted to bar, 1992, California. *Education:* University of California at Los Angeles (B.A., 1988); University of San Francisco (J.D., cum laude, 1992). *Member:* Bar Association of San Francisco; State Bar of California.

**JASON H. ANDERSON,** born Harbor City, California, January 16, 1969; admitted to bar, 1994, California. *Education:* University of San Diego (B.A., 1991); Southern Methodist University (J.D., cum laude, 1994). Member, Moot Court Justice Team; Notes and Comments Editor, Southern Methodist Law Review, 1993-1994. *Member:* Santa Clara County and American Bar Associations; State Bar of California. *PRACTICE AREAS:*

*(This Listing Continued)*

Civil Litigation; Business Litigation; Products Liability; Personal Injury; Wrongful Termination.

**ERIC L. GRAVES,** born West Germany, September 20, 1969; admitted to bar, 1995, California. *Education:* California State University at Fullerton (B.A., 1992); McGeorge School of Law (J.D., 1995). Order of the Coif; Traynor Honor Society. Writer and Primary Editor, Pacific Law Journal, 1993-1995.

**LISA A. LANGLEY,** born San Francisco, California, February 13, 1970; admitted to bar, 1996, California and Massachusetts. *Education:* University of California (B.A., 1992); New England School of Law (J.D., 1995). *Member:* Boston and Massachusetts Bar Associations.

REPRESENTATIVE CLIENTS: California Insurance Group; California State Automobile Association; Chubb Group of Insurance Companies; Erie Insurance Group; Frontier Adjusters of San Jose; ITT/ Hartford Insurance Group; Minnehoma Insurance Co.; Paramount Parks, Inc.; Penn-America Insurance Co.; Precision Risk Management, Inc.; Republic Western Insurance Co.; Safeco Insurance Company of America; San Jose Water Company; Sportmart, Inc.; Toplis & Harding, Inc.; Transamerica Insurance Group; Utica National Insurance Group; Willis Corroon Administrative Services; Zurich-American Insurance Group.

---

## *MALOVOS & KONEVICH*

Established in 1983

*LOS ALTOS PLAZA*
*5150 EL CAMINO REAL, SUITE A-22*
**LOS ALTOS, CALIFORNIA 94022**
Telephone: 415-988-9700
Facsimile: 415-988-9639

*General Civil Practice. Real Property, Probate and Estate Planning, Corporation, Business and Family Law.*

**MARIAN MALOVOS KONEVICH,** born Palo Alto, California, September 26, 1949; admitted to bar, 1975, California. *Education:* University of California at Berkeley (B.A. in Anthropology, 1971); McGeorge School of Law, University of the Pacific (J.D., 1975). Member, International Moot Court Honors Board. Recipient, American Jurisprudence Award for Remedies, 1974. Instructor, De Anza Community College, 1979—. Member, Board of Directors, 1979-1984 and President, 1983-1984, Mountain View Senior Coordinating Council. Member, Steering Committee, El Camino Hospital Associates, 1983-1991. President, El Camino Hospital Associates, 1990-1991; Member, Camino Healthcare Foundation, Planned Giving Council, 1995—. *Member:* Santa Clara County (Member, Board of Directors, Committee on Women Lawyers, 1980-1985) and Palo Alto Area (Chair Client Relations Committee, 1982-1985) Bar Associations; The State Bar of California (Member, Estate Planning, Trust and Probate Law Section). (Certified Specialist, Probate, Estate Planning and Trust Law, The State Bar of California Board of Legal Specialization). *PRACTICE AREAS:* Probate; Estate Planning; Trust Law; Corporation.

**ROBERT W. KONEVICH,** born San Francisco, California, December 20, 1947; admitted to bar, 1982, California. *Education:* University of California at Santa Cruz (B.A. in Politics, 1979); University of Santa Clara (J.D., 1982). Associate Editor, University of Santa Clara Law Review, 1981-1982. Recipient, American Jurisprudence Award for Real Property, 1980. Founding President, Steering Committee, El Camino Hospital Associates, 1983-1987. *Member:* Santa Clara County and American Bar Associations; The State Bar of California (Member, Real Property Law Section). *PRACTICE AREAS:* Real Property; Business; Family Law.

### RETIRED FOUNDING PARTNER

**KENNETH R. MALOVOS,** born San Jose, California, October 2, 1908; admitted to bar, 1933, California; 1944, U.S. Supreme Court. *Education:* University of Santa Clara; Stanford University (A.B. in Economics, 1930; J.D., 1933). Phi Beta Kappa. *Member:* Santa Clara County, Palo Alto Area and American Bar Associations; The State Bar of California (Member, Committee on Administration of Justice, 1955-1959). [With U.S. Naval Reserve, active duty, Bu Aer, 1943-1945]

REFERENCES: Great Western Bank, Los Altos, California Branch; Citibank, Los Altos, California.

## MYERS, HAWLEY, MORLEY, MYERS & McDONNELL

An Association of Attorneys
Established in 1963
166 MAIN STREET
P.O. BOX 280
LOS ALTOS, CALIFORNIA 94022
Telephone: 415-948-1600
Fax: 415-949-3581

*General Civil and Trial Practice. Taxation, Corporate, Family, Real Property, Business, Estate Planning, Trusts and Probate.*

**PAUL I. MYERS, JR.** (1928-1991).

**SAM R. MORLEY,** born Pasadena, California, May 12, 1932; admitted to bar, 1960, California. *Education:* Stanford University (A.B., 1954; LL.B., 1959). Phi Delta Phi. Member, Stanford Law Review, 1957-1959. *Member:* Santa Clara County and Palo Alto Bar Associations; State Bar of California. [USNR, active duty, 1955-1957]

**PAUL I. "CHICO" MYERS, III,** born San Jose, California, June 16, 1950; admitted to bar, 1976, California. *Education:* University of California at Santa Barbara and Stanford University (B.A., 1972); Armstrong College (J.D., 1976). *Member:* Palo Alto (President, 1985-1986; Board of Trustees, 1992-1993) Bar Association; State Bar of California (Member, Litigation, Business and Estate Planning, Trusts and Probate Sections). **REPORTED CASES:** People v. Phillips (1985) 41 Cal. 3d 29.

**JOHN P. MCDONNELL,** born San Francisco, California, December 31, 1950; admitted to bar, 1977, California. *Education:* University of San Francisco (B.A., 1974); Boalt Hall School of Law, University of California (J.D., 1977); New York University (LL.M. in Taxation, 1978). Author: "Foreign Exchange and the Indirect Foreign Tax Credit," 10 Jour. Corp. Tax. 301, 1984; "An Overview of Outbound Foreign Investment," 5 Hastings Int'l. Comp. Law Rev. 579, 1982; "Tax Aspects of Currency Fluctuations," 5 Hastings Int'l. Comp. Law Rev. 649, 1982. *Member:* State Bar of California (Member, Section on Taxation); American Bar Association (Member, Section on Taxation; Committee on Standards of Tax Practice, 1983—). **REPORTED CASES:** Lettieri v. Equitable Life Assur. Soc. 627 F.2d 930 (9th Cir. 1980).

**ALEXANDER P. MYERS,** born Mountain View, California, November 9, 1962; admitted to bar, 1988, California. *Education:* University of California at Los Angeles (B.A., 1985); University of San Francisco (J.D., 1988). Recipient, American Jurisprudence Award, Comparative Law. *Member:* Palo Alto Bar Association; State Bar of California.

*OF COUNSEL*

**MELVIN L. HAWLEY,** born Chicago, Illinois, June 21, 1920; admitted to bar, 1952, California. *Education:* Yale University (B.A., 1942); Stanford University (LL.B., 1951). Sheriff, Santa Clara County, 1955-1959. Deputy Director, California State Department of Justice, 1959-1961. *Member:* Palo Alto and Santa Clara Bar Associations; State Bar of California. [Capt., U.S. Air Force, 1942-1945]

REFERENCE: Wells Fargo Bank.

## NELSON, PERLOV & LEE

A PROFESSIONAL CORPORATION
339 SOUTH SAN ANTONIO ROAD
LOS ALTOS, CALIFORNIA 94022
Telephone: 415-941-6161
Fax: 415-949-0695

*General Civil and Trial Practice. Insurance, Products Liability, Malpractice and Personal Injury Law.*

**THOMAS F. NELSON,** born Gothenburg, Nebraska, June 19, 1935; admitted to bar, 1963, California. *Education:* University of San Francisco (B.S., 1957; LL.B., 1962). Recipient, American Jurisprudence Award. *Member:* Santa Clara County Bar Association; State Bar of California; Association of Defense Counsel of Northern California; Trial Attorneys of America; Federation of Insurance and Corporate Counsel; Association of Insurance Attorneys; American Board of Trial Advocates. **PRACTICE AREAS:** Insurance Defense; Products Liability; Professional Malpractice; Personal Injury; Civil Litigation.

*(This Listing Continued)*

**FLORENCE T. PERLOV** (Retired).

**MARK S. LEE,** born San Francisco, California, March 13, 1954; admitted to bar, 1979, California. *Education:* Pepperdine University (B.A., 1976); University of Santa Clara (J.D., 1979). *Member:* Santa Clara County Bar Association; State Bar of California; Association of Defense Counsel of Northern California. **PRACTICE AREAS:** Insurance Defense; Products Liability; Professional Malpractice; Personal Injury; Civil Litigation.

**KIM JAMES,** born Berkeley, California; admitted to bar, 1982, California. *Education:* California State University at Sacramento (B.A., 1977); McGeorge School of Law, University of California (J.D., 1981). *Member:* Santa Clara County Bar Association; State Bar of California; Association of Defense Counsel of Northern California (Board of Directors, 1995—). **PRACTICE AREAS:** Insurance Defense; Products Liability; Professional Malpractice; Personal Injury; Civil Litigation.

**PATRICIA M. LEARY,** born St. Columbus, Cornwall, Great Britain, December 2, 1951; admitted to bar, 1980, California. *Education:* Lanchester University, Coventry, England (B.A., 1974); San Francisco Law School (J.D., 1980). *Member:* Santa Clara County Bar Association; The State Bar of California. **PRACTICE AREAS:** Insurance Defense; Products Liability; Professional Malpractice; Personal Injury; Civil Litigation.

**MARY ACQUESTA,** born Phoenix, Arizona, November 6, 1958; admitted to bar, 1983, California. *Education:* University of California at Los Angeles (B.A., 1980); University of Santa Clara (J.D., 1983). *Member:* Santa Clara County Bar Association; The State Bar of California. **PRACTICE AREAS:** Insurance Defense; Products Liability; Professional Malpractice; Personal Injury; Civil Litigation.

REPRESENTATIVE CLIENTS: Liberty Mutual Insurance Co.; Traveler's Insurance; Industrial Indemnity Co.; State Farm Insurance Co.; Chubb Insurance Group. Self Insured: K-Mart Stores; County of Santa Cruz; City of Mountain View; Lucky Stores, Inc.; Pier 39; Breuners; Cala Foods; Pacific Telesis; Marriott Corp.

## AARONSON & AARONSON

LOS ANGELES, CALIFORNIA
(See Encino)

*General Civil and Trial Practice. Commercial, Commercial and Industrial Leasing, Corporation, Business, Real Property, Construction, Family, Mortgage, Entertainment, Partnership, Pension and Profit Sharing, State and Federal Taxation, Estate Planning, Trust and Probate Law.*

## ABROLAT & TEREN

5777 WEST CENTURY BOULEVARD, SUITE 1550
LOS ANGELES, CALIFORNIA 90045
Telephone: 310-410-9111
Facsimile: 310-410-1687

*Employment Litigation, Representing Employees and Employers, Sexual Harassment, Discrimination, Wrongful Termination, Disability Discrimination, Whistle Blower Cases, Civil Rights Litigation.*

FIRM PROFILE: *Dynamic, aggressive law firm focusing on employment litigation and trials, representing both employers and employees. Both partners have earned valuable experience and knowledge by working at a firm which only represents employers and then a firm that only represents employees. This extensive exposure to both sides of employment litigation provides a unique dual prospective which works to the advantage of all clients, plaintiffs and defendants alike.*

*MEMBERS OF FIRM*

**NANCY L. ABROLAT,** born Marietta, Ohio, September 30, 1965; admitted to bar, 1990, California and U.S. District Court, Central District of California. *Education:* University of the Pacific (B.A., cum laude, 1987); Hastings College of Law, University of California (J.D., magna cum laude, 1990). 00i Kappa Phi; Order of the Coif; Thurston Honor Society. Recipient, American Jurisprudence Award-Real Property. Participant, Hastings Mock Trial. Member, 1988-1989, and Associate Managing, 1989-1990, Hastings Law Journal. Associate, Paul, Hastings, Janofsky and Walker, Santa Monica/Los Angeles, 1990-1994. Participant, Trial Attorney Project, Los Angeles County Bar, Spring 1995. Speaker, "Current Topics in employment Law," Legion Lex, Spring 1996. *Member:* Los Angeles County Bar Association; State Bar of California; National Employment Lawyers Association (NELA), 1995—.

*(This Listing Continued)*

### ABROLAT & TEREN, Los Angeles—Continued

**PAMELA MCKIBBIN TEREN,** born Downey, California, July 6, 1963; admitted to bar, 1990, California and U.S. District Court, Central District of California. *Education:* University of California at Los Angeles (B.A., 1985); California State University at Fullerton (M.A., 1987); Loyola Law School, Los Angeles (J.D., cum laude, 1990). Order of the Coif. St. Thomas More Law Honor Society. Recipient, American Jurisprudence Award-Civil Procedure. Participant, Loyola Moot Court. Member, 1988-1989 and Note and Comment Editor, 1989-1990, International and Comparative Law Journal. Associate, Paul, Hastings, Janofsky and Walker, Santa Monica/Los Angeles, 1990-1993. Member, National Employment Lawyers Association (NELA), 1994—. Speaker, "Sexual Harassment Update," Lorman Business Center, Inc., April 1996. *Member:* Los Angeles County Bar Association; State Bar of California.

#### ASSOCIATE

**KEVIN P. BERG,** born Cortland, New York, March 1, 1968; admitted to bar, 1996, California and U.S. District Court, Central District of California. *Education:* University of Southern California (B.A., cum laude, 1990); Pepperdine University School of Law (J.D., 1996). Recipient, University of Merit Scholarship, 1995-1996. Client Counsel Tournament, 1995. Participant, Negotiations Tournament, 1995. *Member:* State Bar of California. *PRACTICE AREAS:* Employment Litigation; Sexual Harassment; Discrimination; Whistle-Blower Cases; Wrongful Termination.

---

## ACKER, KOWALICK & WHIPPLE

A PROFESSIONAL CORPORATION
WORLD TRADE CENTER
SUITE 900
350 SOUTH FIGUEROA STREET
**LOS ANGELES, CALIFORNIA 90071**
Telephone: 213-687-3933
Fax: 213-626-3561

*Civil Trial Practice in State and Federal Courts. Insurance Law. Products Liability, Personal Injury, Malpractice, Subrogation and Business Litigation.*

*FIRM PROFILE: Acker, Kowalick & Whipple is a firm which maintains a diverse litigation practice representing businesses, professional persons and governmental entities in the defense of civil liability claims in California state and federal courts. While the firm's practice is primarily devoted to the representation of insured entities on assignment as approved counsel by certain insurers, we also represent self-insured litigants in the manufacturing, construction and service industries.*

*Since the firm's founding in 1979, our attorneys have represented clients engaged in nearly all standard industrial classifications of manufacturing and sales as well as many of the professions and financial services in the resolution of disputed liability claims.*

**STEPHEN ACKER,** born Pasadena, California, September 1, 1951; admitted to bar, 1975, California; 1985, Maryland and District of Columbia. *Education:* University of California at Santa Barbara (B.A., with high honors, 1972); Hastings College of the Law, University of California (J.D., 1975). Member, Board of Directors (City Council) City of Pasadena, California, 1979-1983. Commissioner, Burbank, Glendale, Pasadena Airport Authority, 1981-1983. Consular Officer, U.S. Department of State, American Embassy, Buenos Aires, Argentina, 1986-1988. *Member:* Los Angeles County and American Bar Associations; State Bar of California; Association of Southern California Defense Counsel. *LANGUAGES:* Spanish. *PRACTICE AREAS:* Professional Liability; Products Liability.

**W. FREDERICK KOWALICK,** born Rochester, Pennsylvania, July 18, 1948; admitted to bar, 1973, California; 1974, U.S. District Court, Central District of California; 1975, U.S. Court of Military Appeals; 1981, U.S. District Court, Southern District of California. *Education:* California State University at Northridge (B.A., magna cum laude, 1970); University of California at Los Angeles School of Law (J.D., 1973). Executive Editor, U.C.L.A.-Alaska Law Review, 1972-1973. *Member:* State Bar of California; Association of Southern Defense Counsel; Defense Research Institute. [CDR JAGC, USNR; Active Duty, 1974-1977]. *PRACTICE AREAS:* Insurance Coverage Law and Litigation.

**ANTHONY HENRY WHIPPLE,** born Los Angeles, California, October 29, 1948; admitted to bar, 1979, California; 1981, U.S. District Court, Central District of California. *Education:* University of California at Los Angeles (B.A., 1974); Whittier College School of Law (J.D., 1979). Arbitra-

*(This Listing Continued)*

---

tor, Los Angeles Superior Court. *Member:* Los Angeles County Bar Association; State Bar of California; Association of Southern California Defense Counsel. *PRACTICE AREAS:* Tort and Insurance Coverage Litigation.

**BRIAN F. DRAZICH,** born East Chicago, Indiana, September 3, 1942; admitted to bar, 1980, Wisconsin; 1982, California and U.S. District Court, Central District of California. *Education:* Idaho State University (B.S., in Physics, 1966); University of Wisconsin at Madison (J.D., 1980). *Member:* Los Angeles County Bar Association; State Bar of California; Association of Southern California Defense Counsel.

---

**D. ALTON KELLY,** born Attleboro, Massachusetts, February 26, 1951; admitted to bar, 1991, California. *Education:* Metropolitan State College (B.A., 1980); Southwestern University School of Law (J.D., 1985). *Member:* Los Angeles County Bar Association; State Bar of California. *PRACTICE AREAS:* Business Litigation; Civil Litigation; Construction Defects; Insurance Coverage.

**BERNHARD E. BIHR,** born Los Angeles, California, December 14, 1947; admitted to bar, 1974, California. *Education:* Los Angeles Valley College and California State University at Los Angeles (B.A., 1969); Loyola University of Los Angeles (J.D., 1973). Arbitrator, Los Angeles Superior Court, 1982—. *Member:* Los Angeles County Bar Association; State Bar of California; Association of Southern California Defense Counsel. *PRACTICE AREAS:* Construction Defect; Professional Liability; Insurance Defense.

**JERRI L. JOHNSON,** born Ames, Iowa, September 27, 1963; admitted to bar, 1989, California and U.S. District Court, Central District of California. *Education:* Drake University (B.S., 1986); Pepperdine University (J.D., 1989). Phi Alpha Delta. *PRACTICE AREAS:* Personal Injury Defense; Products Liability; Medical Malpractice; Professional Malpractice.

**CATHERINE L. RHODES,** born New York, N.Y., February 3, 1964; admitted to bar, 1991, California and U.S. District Court, Central District of California. *Education:* Stanford University (B.A., 1986); Southwestern University School of Law (J.D., 1989). Phi Alpha Delta. Recipient, Jurisprudence Award in Civil Procedure. *Member:* Los Angeles County and American Bar Associations; State Bar of California. *LANGUAGES:* French and Spanish. *PRACTICE AREAS:* Business Litigation; Conservatorships; Probate; Civil Litigation.

**A. GINA HOGTANIAN,** born Yerevan, Armenia, September 7, 1965; admitted to bar, 1994, California, U.S. District Court, Central District of California and U.S. Court of Appeals, Ninth Circuit. *Education:* University of California, Los Angeles (B.A., 1988); Whittier Law School (J.D., 1993). Recipient: American Jurisprudence Award in Legal Research and Writing; Moot Court Honors. *Member:* Los Angeles and American Bar Association; State Bar of California. *LANGUAGES:* Armenian, Russian and French.

**TAWNYA L. SOUTHERN,** born Willits, California, February 1, 1967; admitted to bar, 1994, California. *Education:* University of California at Los Angeles (B.A., Political Science, 1990); Southwestern University School of Law (J.D., 1994). Dean's List, University of California at Los Angeles. Recipient: American Jurisprudence Award - International Human Rights. *Member:* Beverly Hills, Los Angeles County (Member, Sections on: Litigation and International Law) Bar Associations; Consumer Attorneys of Los Angeles. *PRACTICE AREAS:* Civil Litigation; Construction Defect.

REPRESENTATIVE CLIENTS: American International Group; Tokio Marine and Fire Insurance Co., Ltd.; Northbrook Property and Casualty Insurance Co.; Argonaut Ins., Co.; Unigard Insurance Co.; Metropolitan Transportation Authority of Los Angeles County; City of Hawthorne, Ca.; Torrance Unified School District; Crawford & Co.; Burson Concrete Contractors.

---

## SIDNEY A. ADAIR

SUITE 104, 444 NORTH LARCHMONT BOULEVARD
**LOS ANGELES, CALIFORNIA 90004-3030**
Telephone: 213-464-4875
Fax: 213-464-1817

*Trust, Estate Planning, Probate and Taxation Law. Corporation, Real Property.*

**SIDNEY A. ADAIR,** born Los Angeles, California, February 16, 1928; admitted to bar, 1960, California. *Education:* University of Southern California; Babson College (B.S., 1951); University of Pennsylvania (M.B.A., 1954); University of Southern California (J.D., 1960). Phi Alpha Delta;

*(This Listing Continued)*

Blue Key. Deputy Public Defender, Los Angeles County, 1960-1961. Chairman, 1976-1978 and Trustee, 1976-1994, Windsor Square-Hancock Park Historical Society (Rancho La Brea). Member of Board: Children's Bureau of Southern California Foundation; Vice-President, Opera Guild of Southern California, 1975—. *Member:* Wilshire (Member, Board of Governors, 1985-1986, 1989—), Los Angeles County (Member, Sections on: Probate and Trust Law; Business and Corporation Law) and American (Member, Committee on Environmental Law, General Practice Section, 1972—) Bar Associations; The State Bar of California. [Capt., U.S. Air Force, 1951-1953]

REFERENCES: Union Bank of California, N.A. (Los Angeles Main Office) Wells Fargo Bank (Larchmont Branch).

## BRUCE ADELSTEIN
11661 SAN VICENTE BOULEVARD, SUITE 1015
**LOS ANGELES, CALIFORNIA 90049**
Telephone: 310-979-3565
Fax: 310-826-8242
Email: adelstein@appellatelaw.com

*Appellate Practice, Civil and Criminal in all State and Federal Courts.*

**BRUCE ADELSTEIN,** born Los Angeles, California, September 4, 1964; admitted to bar, 1992, California and U.S. District Court, Central District of California. *Education:* University of California, Los Angeles (B.A., magna cum laude, 1986; M.A., 1986); University of Chicago (J.D., with honors, 1990). Phi Beta Kappa. *Member:* Los Angeles County and American (Member, Antitrust Section) Bar Associations; State Bar of California.

## AGAJANIAN & McFALL
346 NORTH LARCHMONT BOULEVARD
**LOS ANGELES, CALIFORNIA 90006-3012**
Telephone: 213-993-0198

*Defense of Medical and Hospital Malpractice, Motor Sports Litigation, Governmental Litigation, Products Liability, General Insurance, Hospital, and Business Litigation.*

### MEMBERS OF FIRM

**CARY J. C. AGAJANIAN,** born Los Angeles, California, October 14, 1941; admitted to bar, 1967, California. *Education:* University of Southern California (B.S., 1963; LL.B., 1966). Phi Delta Phi. Deputy City Attorney, 1968-1977. *Member:* Los Angeles County Bar Association; State Bar of California. *REPORTED CASES:* Hoffman v. Sports Car Club of America, et al. (1986), 180 Cal. App. 3d 119, Cite as 225 Cal. Rptr. 359, Dummit & Agajanian, Cary Agajanian, Los Angeles, for amicus curiae K & K Ins. Co.; National and International Brotherhood of Street Racers Inc. v. Superior Court of Los Angeles County (1989), 215 Cal. App. 3d 943, 264 Cal. Rptr. 44, Agajanian and McFall, Cary Agajanian, Universal City for K & K Ins. Co.; Ford v. Gouin (1992), 3 Cal. 4th 339, 11 Cal. Rptr. 2d 30, 834 P2d 724, Agajanian, McFall & Tomlinson, Cary Agajanian, Universal City for amicus curiae K & K Ins. Co.

**SCOTT B. McFALL,** born Sacramento, California, September 4, 1951; admitted to bar, 1978, California; U.S. District Court, Southern District of California. *Education:* University of Southern California (B.S., 1972); Southwestern University School of Law (J.D., 1977). *Member:* Los Angeles County Bar Association; State Bar of California; Association of Southern California Defense Counsel.

**PHILIP D. WEISS,** born Hollywood, California, July 23, 1961; admitted to bar, 1988, California; U.S. District Court, Central and Southern Districts of California. *Education:* California State University, Northridge (B.A., 1985); Loyola Law School (J.D., 1988). *Member:* State Bar of California; Association of Southern California Defense Counsel.

---

**CHRISTINE M. YOCCA,** born Los Angeles, California, March 24, 1964; admitted to bar, 1988, California; U.S. District Court, Central District of California. *Education:* Loyola Marymount University (B.A., with honors, 1985); Loyola Law School (J.D., 1988). Alpha Sigma Nu. *Member:* Los Angeles County Bar Association; State Bar of California; Association of Southern California Defense Counsel; Women Lawyers' Association of Los Angeles.

*(This Listing Continued)*

**ABBIE CRIST,** born Rochester, Minnesota, February 5, 1958; admitted to bar, 1985, California. *Education:* University of California, Davis (B.A., with honors, 1980); Loyola Law School (J.D., 1985). *Member:* State Bar of California; Association of Southern California Defense Counsel.

**PAUL L. TETREAULT,** born Lowell, Massachusetts, March 12, 1955; admitted to bar, 1984, California and U.S. District Court, Central District of California. *Education:* Pepperdine University (B.A., 1978); Southwestern University School of Law (J.D., 1983). *Member:* Los Angeles County Bar Association; State Bar of California; Association of Southern California Defense Counsel.

**KENNETH M. VON HELMOLT,** born Winnipeg, Manitoba, Canada, December 28, 1958; admitted to bar, 1994, California. *Education:* University of California at Los Angeles (B.A., 1984); Loyola Law School (J.D., 1994). Commencement Speaker, Loyola Law School. Member, Motor Press Guild, 1986-1995. *Member:* State Bar of California; American Bar Association; Association of Southern California Defense Counsel.

REPRESENTATIVE CLIENTS: Tenet Healthcare Corp.; County of Los Angeles; TIG Insurance Company; Transamerica Insurance Group; Hospital Underwriting Group, Inc.; K & K Insurance Group, Inc.; North American Van Lines; Richwell Insurance Agency; American Specialty Claims Services, Inc.; Essex Insurance Company; Reliance National Insurance Company; John Deere Insurance Company.

## AGAPAY, LEVYN & HALLING
*A PROFESSIONAL CORPORATION*
Established in 1974
FOURTH FLOOR, 10801 NATIONAL BOULEVARD
**LOS ANGELES, CALIFORNIA 90064**
Telephone: 310-470-1700
Fax: 310-470-2602

*Orange, California Office:* One City Boulevard West, Suite 835, 92668. Telephone: 714-634-1744. Fax: 714-634-0417.

*General Civil Practice. Real Estate, Construction, Corporation, Computer Law, Business, Banking, Unfair Competition, Taxation, Commercial Law and Related Litigation and Risk Management.*

**JOE M. AGAPAY, JR.,** born Upland, California, January 20, 1936; admitted to bar, 1962, California and U.S. District Court, Central District of California. *Education:* University of Southern California (A.B. in Political Science, 1958; LL.B., 1961). Phi Alpha Delta (President, 1960-1961). President, Trojan Football Alumni Club, 1983-1984. President, National Football Foundation and College Hall of Fame, L.A. Chapter, 1991-1993. *Member:* Century City and Los Angeles County Bar Associations; State Bar of California. *PRACTICE AREAS:* Complex Civil Litigation; Construction. *Email:* JMA@AGAPAY.COM

**THOMAS S. LEVYN,** born Los Angeles, California, April 2, 1949; admitted to bar, 1974, California and U.S. District Court, Central District of California. *Education:* University of Southern California (B.S. in Business, cum laude, 1971; J.D., 1974). Beta Gamma Sigma. Outstanding Graduating Senior. Mayor, City of Beverly Hills, 1996—. Vice Mayor, City of Beverly Hills, 1995-1996. Member of City Council, City of Beverly Hills, 1992—. General Counsel, The Prudential Jon Douglas Company, 1995—. Member, Board of Governors, Cedars Sinai Medical Center, 1986—. Member, Board of Trustees, Temple Isaiah, 1991-1992. Member, Board of Directors, Beverly Hills Public Access Corporation, 1989-1992. Panel Member: Institute of Real Estate Management Annual Conferences, 1994 and 1995, "Complex Lease Issues," ; Institute of Real Estate Management, Los Angeles Chapter, 1996, "The Relationship Between Property Managers and Asset Managers". Judge, Trial Advocacy Program, University of Southern California Law Center, 1982-1983. Landlord-Tenant Settlement Officer and Judge Pro Tempore, Los Angeles Municipal Court, 1984-1986. *Member:* Beverly Hills, Century City, Los Angeles County (Member, Real Property Section) and American Bar Associations; State Bar of California. *PRACTICE AREAS:* Real Estate; Risk Management; Business Law.

**CHRIS W. HALLING,** born Los Angeles, California, June 28, 1953; admitted to bar, 1979, California, U.S. District Court, Central District of California and U.S. Court of Appeals, Ninth Circuit. *Education:* University of California at Los Angeles (B.A. in Economics, cum laude, 1975); University of Southern California (J.D., 1979). Member, 1977-1978; Notes Editor, 1978-1979, Southern California Law Review. Author: Note, "The Federal False Claims Act: A 'Remedial' Alternative for Protecting the Government from Fraudulent Practices," 52 Southern California Law Review 159, 1978. *Member:* Los Angeles County and American (Member, Committee on Con-

*(This Listing Continued)*

**AGAPAY, LEVYN & HALLING,** A PROFESSIONAL CORPORATION, Los Angeles—Continued

tracting for Computers, Section of Science & Technology) Bar Associations; State Bar of California. **PRACTICE AREAS:** Business Litigation; Corporations; Computer Law; Intellectual Property; Real Estate. **Email:** CWH@AGAPAY.COM

---

**GLEN R. SEGAL,** born Bellflower, California, June 12, 1961; admitted to bar, 1986, California, U.S. District Court, Central District of California and U.S. Court of Appeals, Ninth Circuit. *Education:* California State University at Fullerton (B.A., with honors, 1983); University of Southern California (J.D., 1986). Publications Editor, Computer/Law Journal and Major Tax Planning, 1985-1986. Author: Note, "The Threat from Within - Cable Television and the Invasion of Privacy," 7 Computer/Law Journal 89, 1986. *Member:* Los Angeles County and American Bar Associations; State Bar of California. (Resident Member, Orange Office).

**PETER J. KRUPINSKY,** born Hartford, Connecticut, June 12, 1954; admitted to bar, 1979, California; 1980, U.S. District Court, District of California. *Education:* Worcester Polytechnic Institute (B.S. Math., 1976); Loyola Law School (J.D., 1979). Recipient, American Jurisprudence Award for Study of Corporate Law. *Member:* Los Angeles County Bar Association; State Bar of California.

**LAURIE J. BERGREN,** born Worthington, Minnesota, July 20, 1958; admitted to bar, 1985, California. *Education:* Iowa State University (B.A., 1981); University of Vienna, Austria; Drake University School of Law (J.D., 1984). Delta Phi Alpha. Recipient: American Jurisprudence Award for Criminal Practice and Procedure. *Member:* Los Angeles County Bar Association; State Bar of California.

**TRACEY P. HOM,** born Los Angeles, California, October 22, 1956; admitted to bar, 1990, California. *Education:* University of Southern California (B.S., cum laude, 1978); Loyola Law School, Los Angeles (J.D., 1990). Assistant Professor of Ethics, University of Southern California, 1990—. *Member:* Los Angeles County and American Bar Associations; State Bar of California; Women Lawyers Association. **Email:** TPH@AGAPAY.COM

**RICHARD D. COATS,** born Yuba City, California, August 20, 1954; admitted to bar, 1984, California. *Education:* University of California at Los Angeles (B.A., 1981); McGeorge School of the Law, University of the Pacific (J.D., with distinction, 1984); New York University (LL.M., 1985). Recipient, American Jurisprudence Awards in Corporations and Remedies. Author, "Negotiating Lease Termination Agreements," American Bar Association's The Practical Real Estate Lawyer. Board Member, Los Angeles Lawyer Magazine, 1993-1995. *Member:* Los Angeles County Bar Association (Member, Real Property Law Section); State Bar of California (Member, Subcommittee on Landlord/Tenant Law). **PRACTICE AREAS:** Commercial Leasing Transactions.

**STEVEN A. SOKOL,** born 1950; admitted to bar, 1978, California, U.S. District Court, Central, Northern, Southern and Eastern Districts of California, U.S. Supreme Court, California Supreme Court, U.S. Court of Appeals, Ninth Circuit, U.S. Court of Military Appeals, Washington, D.C., U.S. Tax Court, Washington, D.C. *Education:* University of California at Los Angeles (B.A., Political Science, 1974); Southwestern University School of Law (J.D., 1977). Author, "A Guide to Real Property Taxation: Federal State and Local," Legal Issues in Real Estate, 1984; "A Closer Look at Tax Reform - Impact of the Tax Reform on Real Estate," Legal Issues in Real Estate, 1986. Judge Pro Tempore, Los Angeles Judicial Court, 1990—. *Member:* Los Angeles County and American Bar Associations; State Bar of California; Association of Real Estate Attorneys. **Email:** SAS@AGAPAY.COM

**PAMELA J. PALUGA,** born Chicago, Illinois, October 1, 1963; admitted to bar, 1989, California; 1990, U.S. District Court, Central District of California. *Education:* University of California, Los Angeles (B.A., 1986); Suffolk University (J.D., cum laude, 1989). Phi Delta Phi. *Member:* Los Angeles County Bar Association; State Bar of California; Women's Lawyers of Los Angeles. **PRACTICE AREAS:** Real Estate Litigation; Business Litigation. **Email:** PJP@AGAPAY.COM

OF COUNSEL

**ALAN B. GRASS,** born Detroit, Michigan, December 13, 1942; admitted to bar, 1968, Michigan; 1980, California. *Education:* University of Michigan (B.A., 1964); Harvard University (J.D., 1967). Phi Beta Kappa; Phi Kappa Phi; Pi Sigma Alpha. Chairman, Honors Council Steering Com-

*(This Listing Continued)*

mittee, 1963-1964. Panelist, "Employee Benefit Plans Under ERISA," November, 1981, "First Annual Business Law Institute," May, 1982 and "Introduction to Qualified Plans," November, 1983, California Continuing Education of the Bar. Associate Professor of Law, Whittier College School of Law, Los Angeles, California, 1983-1987. Assistant Professor of Clinical Accounting, School of Business Administration, University of Southern California, 1990—. *Member:* Beverly Hills, Los Angeles County and American (Member, Sections on: Corporation, Banking and Business Law; Taxation, Member, Personal Service Corporation Committee, 1977—) Bar Associations; State Bar of California; State Bar of Michigan.

**GLEN DRESSER,** born Los Angeles, California, May 8, 1949; admitted to bar, 1974, California and U.S. District Court, Central, Southern, Northern and Eastern Districts of California. *Education:* University of Southern California (B.A. in History, magna cum laude, 1971; J.D., 1974). Phi Beta Kappa; Phi Kappa Phi. Member, 1972-1973; Note and Article Editor, 1973-1974, Southern California Law Review. Author: Note, "First Amendment Protection Against Libel Actions-Distinguishing Media and Non-Media Defendants," 47 Southern California Law Review 902, 1974. *Member:* Los Angeles County Bar Association (Member, Sections on: Commercial Law and Bankruptcy); State Bar of California. (Also practicing individually). **PRACTICE AREAS:** Commercial Law; Bankruptcy; Banking.

**NANCI E. MURDOCK,** born Los Angeles, California; admitted to bar, 1983, California; 1984, U.S. District Court, Central District of California and U.S. Court of Appeals, Ninth Circuit; 1990, Massachusetts; 1993, U.S. Supreme Court. *Education:* University of Southern California (B.A., 1971); Loyola Marymount University (J.D., 1983). Member, National Moot Court Team. Recipient, Moot Court Best Brief Award; Outstanding Brief Writing Award, West Publishing Company. Law Clerk and Senior Attorney for presiding Justice Joan Dempsey Klein, California Court of Appeals, 1983-1987. Urban Planner, Mayor's Office, Los Angeles, 1973-1980. *Member:* Beverly Hills (Member, Entertainment Section) and Los Angeles County (Chairperson, Barristers' Artists and the Law Committee, 1989-1990) Bar Associations; State Bar of California. **REPORTED CASES:** Musick, Peeler & Garrett v. Employers Insurance of Wausau, 113 S.Ct. 2085, 124 L.Ed. 2d 194, 61 U.S.L.W. 4520 (1993). **PRACTICE AREAS:** Appellate; Business Litigation; Intellectual Property. **Email:** NEM@AGAPAY.COM

REPRESENTATIVE CLIENTS: Aetna Realty Advisors; Amsted Corp.; Bank of America; Charles Dunn Co.; Cigna Real Estate; El Camino Resources; Farmers Insurance Group Real Estate; G.E. Realty Group; Hersch & Co.; Hewlett Packard Co.; Irvine Co.; Koll Management Services; Prudential Jon Douglas Co.; R&B Realty Group; Trident Group; The Voit Cos.; William Lyon Property Management Co.; Pinnacle Realty; Century Life of America; GE Capitol ReoCom.

---

## AGNEW & BRUSAVICH
### LOS ANGELES, CALIFORNIA
(See Torrance)

*Practice limited to Civil Litigation including Personal Injury, Medical Malpractice, Product Liability, Elder Abuse, General Negligence, Wrongful Death, Insurance Bad Faith, Business Tort and Fraud Cases.*

---

## MICHAEL C. AGRAN
SUITE 1225, 10960 WILSHIRE BOULEVARD
### LOS ANGELES, CALIFORNIA 90024
Telephone: 310-477-5544
FAX: 310-477-8768

*Federal and State Taxation, Business, Trusts and Estate Planning and Probate Law.*

**MICHAEL C. AGRAN,** born Chicago, Illinois, March 25, 1942; admitted to bar, 1967, California. *Education:* University of California at Los Angeles (B.S., magna cum laude, 1963); Harvard University (J.D., cum laude, 1966). Author: "How to Avoid or Handle Foreign Personal Holding Company Status," Prentice-Hall, U.S. Taxation of International Operations. Beta Gamma Sigma. *Member:* Beverly Hills, Los Angeles County and American Bar Associations; The State Bar of California. (Certified Specialist, Taxation Law, The State Bar of California Board of Legal Specialization).

# PROFESSIONAL BIOGRAPHIES

CALIFORNIA—LOS ANGELES

## AIDIKOFF & KESLUK

9255 SUNSET BOULEVARD
SUITE 411
**LOS ANGELES, CALIFORNIA 90069**
Telephone: 310-273-3180
Fax: 310-273-6137
Email: paidi@aol.com

*Securities Arbitration and Civil Litigation, Plaintiff Personal Injury.*

FIRM PROFILE: Aidikoff & Kesluk has been in practice since 1977 in the same location with an established, well-known presence in the community. The firm specializes in securities litigation with particular emphasis on the rights and remedies of the individual investor.

### MEMBERS OF FIRM

**PHILIP M. AIDIKOFF,** born 1948; admitted to bar, 1975, California and U.S. District Court, Central District of California; 1981, U.S. Supreme Court. *Education:* University of California (B.A., 1969); Southwestern University School of Law (J.D., 1975). Member, Southwestern University Law Review, 1974-1975. Faculty Member, Practicing Law Institute, Securities Arbitration, 1995. *Member:* Beverly Hills and Los Angeles County Bar Associations; State Bar of California; San Francisco Trial Lawyers Association; The Association of Trial Lawyers of America; Consumer Attorneys Association of Los Angeles; Consumer Attorneys of California; Public Investors Arbitration Bar Association. **PRACTICE AREAS:** Securities Arbitration.

**BRIAN S. KESLUK,** born 1956; admitted to bar, 1984, California. *Education:* Pennsylvania State University (B.A., 1977); Southwestern University of Los Angeles (J.D., 1982). *Member:* Los Angeles County Bar Association; State Bar of California; Consumer Attorneys Association of Los Angeles; Consumer Attorneys Association of California. **PRACTICE AREAS:** Civil Litigation; Business Litigation; Plaintiff Personal Injury.

### OF COUNSEL

**ROBERT A. UHL,** born New York, N.Y., December 15, 1946; admitted to bar, 1976, New York and U.S. District Court, Southern and Eastern Districts of New York; 1977, California and U.S. District Court, Northern District of California; 1979, U.S. District Court, Central District of California; 1982, U.S. Court of Appeals, Ninth Circuit; 1983, U.S. Court of Appeals, Seventh Circuit. *Education:* University of Pittsburgh (B.A., 1968); Fordham University (J.D., 1975). Member, Fordham University Law Review, 1975. Judge Pro Tem, Los Angeles Municipal Court, 1986-1988. *Member:* Beverly Hills Bar Association; State Bar of California (Disciplinary Referee, 1985-1986); American Bar Association; Public Investors Arbitration Bar Association. (Also practicing individually). **PRACTICE AREAS:** Securities Arbitration.

## AIKENHEAD, CIPES & SUPANICH

EQUITABLE PLAZA, 30TH FLOOR
3435 WILSHIRE BOULEVARD
**LOS ANGELES, CALIFORNIA 90010-2050**
Telephone: 213-738-9700
Fax: 213-380-3308

*General Business, including formation and counseling of corporations, partnerships and limited liability companies, mergers and acquisitions, estate and succession planning, probate, estate and trust administration, commercial lending, creditor bankruptcy representation, environmental law and real estate law.*

### MEMBERS OF FIRM

**DAVID S. AIKENHEAD,** born Kalamazoo, Michigan, March 28, 1946; admitted to bar, 1972, California. *Education:* Bucknell University (A.B., 1968); University of Pittsburgh (J.D., 1971). Phi Alpha Delta. Member, University of Pittsburgh Law Review, 1969-1971. *Member:* Wilshire, Los Angeles County and American (Member, Sections on: Real Property, Probate and Trust Law; Corporation, Banking and Business Law; Economics of Law Practice) Bar Associations; State Bar of California.

**ANDREW P. CIPES,** born Mt. Vernon, New York, February 16, 1950; admitted to bar, 1976, California. *Education:* University of California at Los Angeles (B.A., 1972); Loyola University of Los Angeles (J.D., 1976). *Member:* Wilshire (Member, Board of Governors, 1983-1987) and Los Angeles County Bar Associations; State Bar of California.

*(This Listing Continued)*

**DENNIS M. SUPANICH,** born Detroit, Michigan, September 30, 1953; admitted to bar, 1978, California. *Education:* Marquette University (B.S., 1975); University of Southern California (J.D., 1978). Beta Gamma Sigma. *Member:* State Bar of California (Member, Sections on: Real Property; Business Law; Intellectual Property Practice; Estate Planning, Trust and Probate).

REPRESENTATIVE CLIENTS: Los Angeles Convention & Visitors Bureau; United Aeronautical Corp.; USA Properties Fund, Inc.; American Feed & Farm Supply, Inc.; Bank United of Texas, FSB; Bloomfilm; Freedom Management Co.; AHT Architects, Inc.

## AJALAT, POLLEY & AYOOB

A Partnership including Professional Corporations

Established in 1975

SUITE 200, 643 SOUTH OLIVE STREET
**LOS ANGELES, CALIFORNIA 90014**
Telephone: 213-622-7400
Fax: 213-622-4738

*State and Local Taxation Law: Real and Personal Property Taxes, Franchise and Income Taxes, Sales and Use Taxes, Gross Receipts Taxes.*

### MEMBERS OF FIRM

**CHARLES R. AJALAT, (A PROFESSIONAL CORPORATION),** born Chicago, Illinois, March 4, 1947; admitted to bar, 1972, California; 1973, U.S. Tax Court; 1975, U.S. Supreme Court. *Education:* Harvard University (B.A., magna cum laude, 1968); Boalt Hall School of Law, University of California (J.D., 1971). Author: "The Los Angeles Business License Tax and The Property Tax Statute of Limitations," Journal of Property Tax Management, Vol. 8, Issue 1, Winter, 1996. Co-Author with Terry L. Polley: "California's Water's Edge Legislation," 1987 So. California Tax Institute, 5-1. Co-Author: "California Taxes," California Continuing Education of the Bar, 1978. Co-Author with Frank Keesling: "Recent Limitations on the Taxing Jurisdiction of California State and Local Governments - Governments Proposition 13 and Before," The Los Angeles Lawyer, 1978. Co-Author with Alexander Pope: "Proposition 13 Section 2(a): Base Years, Changes of Ownership and New Construction," California State Bar Journal, December, 1979. Adjunct Professor, Master of Taxation Program, University of Southern, California, 1975—. Law Clerk to Chief Justice Donald R. Wright, Supreme Court of California, 1971-1972. Chairman, National Association of State Bar Tax Sections, 1981-1983. Commission Member, Governor's Tax Reform Advisory Commission, 1984-1985. Recipient, V. Judson Klein Award, Taxation Section, State Bar of California. *Member:* Los Angeles County (Chairman, State and Local Tax Committee, 1975-1976; Member, Executive Committee, Taxation Section, 1975-1976; 1982-1983, 1987-1988) and American (Member, State and Local Tax Committee, Section of Taxation, 1975-1992) Bar Associations; State Bar of California (Member, Executive Committee, Taxation Section, 1975-1977; Chairman, Property, Sales and Local Tax Committee, 1975-1976; Chairman, State Tax Court Committee, 1976-1980; 1989). (Certified Specialist, Taxation Law, The State Bar of California Board of Legal Specialization). **SPECIAL AGENCIES:** Assessment Appeals Boards; State Board of Equalization; Franchise Tax Board; City Tax Boards, Employment Development Department. **PRACTICE AREAS:** State and Local Tax Law.

**TERRY L. POLLEY, (A PROFESSIONAL CORPORATION),** born Long Beach, California, June 2, 1947; admitted to bar, 1973, California; 1974, U.S. Tax Court; 1987, U.S. Supreme Court. *Education:* University of California at Los Angeles (A.B., 1970); College of William & Mary (J.D., 1973). Research Editor and Member, Board of Editors, William & Mary Law Review, 1972-1973. Co-Author with Charles R. Ajalat: "California's Water's Edge Legislation," 1987 So. California Tax Institute, 5-1. Author: "California Sales and Use Tax Implications of Corporate Capital Restructuring and Reorganizations: Special Application of the Occasional Sales Exemption" 15 Tax Section News 2, 1989; "Assessment and Taxation of Possessory Interests," 1985 Assessment and Valuation Law in the 80's 105 (IAAO). Lecturer on Tax Law, Master of Taxation Program, University of Southern California, 1978-1994. Member, National Association of State Bar Tax Sections (Chair, 1995-1996; Executive Committee, 1991—). *Member:* Los Angeles County (Chair, Taxation Section, 1985-1986; Chair, State and Local Tax Committee, 1981-1982; Member: Executive Committee, Taxation Section, 1980-1987; Executive Committee, Probate and Trust Law Section, 1981-1984) and American (Member, State and Local Tax Committee, Section of Taxation, 1975-1992) Bar Associations; The State Bar of California (Recipient, V. Judson Klein Award, Taxation Section; Chair, Taxation Section, 1990-1991; Member: Executive Committee, Taxation

*(This Listing Continued)*

CAA449B

CALIFORNIA—LOS ANGELES

## AJALAT, POLLEY & AYOOB, Los Angeles—Continued

Section, 1987-1992; State and Local Committee, Taxation Section, 1975—). (Certified Specialist, Taxation Law, The State Bar of California Board of Legal Specialization). **SPECIAL AGENCIES:** Franchise Tax Board; Assessment Appeals Boards; State Board of Equalization; City Tax Boards; Employment Development Department. **PRACTICE AREAS:** State and Local Tax Law.

**RICHARD J. AYOOB,** born Los Angeles, California, April 16, 1953; admitted to bar, 1978, California. *Education:* University of Southern California (B.S., 1975); Hastings College of the Law, University of California (J.D., 1978). Author: "Sales Tax Consequences in Selling a Business," Los Angeles Lawyer, Vol. 6, No. 10, January, 1984; "The Tax Climate in the City of Los Angeles," Journal of Property Tax Management, Vol. 4, Issue 2, Fall, 1992. Co-Author: "California Closely Held Corporations: Tax Planning and Practice Guide," Matthew Bender & Co., Inc., 1987; with Kathleen K. Wright, *Manual of California Taxes,* Tax Institute, 1993. Member, State Board of Equalization Tax Advisory Group, 1993. Member, Institute of Property Taxation (Co-Chair, Legal Committee, 1994-1995). Member, Board of Advisors, The Journal of California Taxation, Faulkner & Gray, Inc., 1989-1992. Lecturer on Tax Law: Golden Gate University Graduate School of Taxation, 1985-1991; Master of Taxation Program, University of Southern California, 1986—. Judge Pro Tem, Los Angeles Municipal Court, 1985-1988. *Member:* Los Angeles County (Chairman, State and Local Tax Committee, 1986-1987; Member, Executive Committee, Taxation Section, 1985-1987) and American (Member, State and Local Tax Committee, Section of Taxation, 1984—) Bar Associations; The State Bar of California (Chairman, State and Local Tax Committee, Taxation Section, 1987-1990; Executive Committee, 1993—). **SPECIAL AGENCIES:** State Board of Equalization; Franchise Tax Board; Assessment Appeals Boards; City Tax Board; Employment Development Department. **PRACTICE AREAS:** State and Local Tax Law.

REPRESENTATIVE CLIENTS: Air France; American President Companies, Ltd.; ARCO; Black & Decker Manufacturing Company; The Coca-Cola Company; Dayton Hudson Corporation; E.I. Du Pont De Nemours & Company; Gencorp.; General Motors Corp.; Holiday Corporation; InterVarsity Press; C. Itoh Electronics, Inc.; Kimberly-Clark Corp.; Lockheed Martin Corporation; MCA, Inc.; R.H. Macy & Co., Inc.; Maguire/Thomas Partners; Marriott Corp.; Masco Building Products Corp.; Mitsubishi Electric America, Inc.; National Academy of Sciences; Shuwa Investments Co.; Sony Corporation of America; Teledyne, Inc.; Tenet Healthcare Corporation; Tenneco, Inc.; Town of Chino Valley; Transamerica Financial Services; Union Pacific Corp.; University of Southern California; The Walt Disney Company; Xerox Corporation; Zell/Chilmark Fund, L.P.
REFERENCE: Bank of America (Los Angeles Main Office).

---

## AKRE, BRYAN & CHANG

355 SOUTH GRAND AVENUE
SUITE 4100
LOS ANGELES, CALIFORNIA 90071-3103
Telephone: 213-626-0100
Fax: 213-626-1428

*Banking and Financial Institutions, Corporate, Corporate Finance, Employment Law, Business Litigation, International Law, Intellectual Property and Real Estate.*

**FIRM PROFILE:** Akre, Bryan & Chang is a law firm which provides a full range of corporate, financial, real estate, employment, intellectual property and litigation services to the banking, manufacturing, real estate and general services industries. The firm was formed by seasoned, exceptionally talented attorneys who had practiced with such premier law firms as: Latham & Watkins; Milbank, Tweed, Hadley & McCloy; Paul, Hastings, Janofsky & Walker; O'Melveny & Myers, and Whitman & Ransom. The firm's litigation team is staffed by legal professionals with a broad range of experience in civil practice and expertise in highly technical areas such as electronics, defense, electrical engineering, molecular and cell biology, genetics, computer science, aerospace, telecommunications and construction. The firm's attorneys are also experienced in international transactions, including inbound and outbound investment, labor and finance issues, regulatory compliance, insurance coverage (including fidelity bond, bad faith and director and officer liability) and the representation of Pacific Rim businesses. The principal objective of the firm is to provide professional, comprehensive, cost effective legal services in a competitive business environment,

**M. JAN AKRE,** born San Diego, California, 1947; admitted to bar, 1975, California; 1992, U.S. Supreme Court. *Education:* Loyola University of Los Angeles (B.A., 1969); Harvard University and Boston College (J.D.,

*(This Listing Continued)*

CAA450B

MARTINDALE-HUBBELL LAW DIRECTORY 1997

1975). Managing Editor, Boston College Law Review, 1974-1975. Author: "Urban Homesteading: Once More Down the Yellow Brick Road," 3 Environmental Affairs 563, 1974. Editor, International Court of Justice Opinion Briefs, 1978. Member, Board of Advisors, American Council of State Savings Supervisors, 1987—. *Member:* State Bar of California; Bar of the Supreme Court of the United States. [Capt., U.S. Marine Corps, 1969-1972}. **PRACTICE AREAS:** Banking Law; Financial Transactions; General Corporate.

**GEOFFREY L. BRYAN,** born Long Beach, California, 1952; admitted to bar, 1980, California; 1981, District of Columbia. *Education:* Carnegie-Mellon University (B.S., 1975); Stanford University (J.D., 1980). Order of the Coif. Article Editor, Stanford Law Review, 1979-1980. Law Clerk to Hon. Dorothy W. Nelson, U.S. Court of Appeals, Ninth Circuit, 1980-1981. Recipient, State Bar Board of Governors Commendation for pro bono legal service to low-income Californians, 1990. Co-author, "The Use of Expert Witnesses in Complex Economic and Financial Litigation," chapter in Starr & McCormick, *Witness Preparation* (Little, Brown & Co., 1996). *Member:* Los Angeles County (Member, Sections on: Labor; Litigation) and American (Member, Sections on: Business Law; Labor; Litigation) Bar Associations; State Bar of California (Member, Sections on: Labor; Litigation); District of Columbia Bar; Association of Business Trial Lawyers. **LANGUAGES:** French. **REPORTED CASES:** Ziello v. Superior Court (First Fed'l Bank) (1995) 36 Cal. App. 4th 321, 42 Cal. Reptr. 2d 251. **PRACTICE AREAS:** Commercial Litigation; Appellate; Employment Law; Trade Secrets; Intellectual Property. **Email:** GLBryan@AOL.COM

**WOOJIN (EUGENE) CHANG,** born Seoul, Korea, 1959; admitted to bar, 1988, California. *Education:* Massachusetts Institute of Technology (B.S., 1980); Sloan School of Management, M.I.T. (M.S., 1983); Boalt Hall School of Law, University of California (J.D., 1988). Eta Kappa Nu; Tau Beta Pi. Recipient, American Jurisprudence Award for Corporate Tax Class. Associate Editor, International Tax and Business Lawyer, 1986-1988. *Member:* State Bar of California; Korean Bar Association. **LANGUAGES:** Korean and Japanese. **PRACTICE AREAS:** International Law; High Technology.

**STEVEN K. HAZEN,** born Boulder City, Nevada, 1949; admitted to bar, 1976, California. *Education:* Pepperdine University (B.A., magna cum laude, 1970); University of Chicago (J.D., 1975). Comment Editor, University of Chicago Law Review, 1974-1975. Member, Visiting Committee, Pepperdine University, 1982-1985. Director, Educational Services Exchange with China Incorporated, 1982-1988. *Member:* State Bar of California (Member, Corporations Committee, 1996—); American Bar Association (Member, Sections 0n: Corporation, Banking and Business Law; International Law and Practice ; Chairman, 1985-1986 and Vice Chairman, 1984-1985, Far Eastern Law Committee; Chairman, 1986-1987, Peoples Republic of China Committee). **PRACTICE AREAS:** Corporate; International Business. **Email:** SKHazen@AOL.COM

**RONALD J. SELGRATH,** born Los Angeles, California, 1945; admitted to bar, 1972, California and U.S. District Court, Central District of California; 1973, U.S. District Court, Southern District of California and U.S. Court of Appeals, Ninth Circuit. *Education:* University of California at Los Angeles (A.B., with honors, 1967); University of California School of Law (J.D., 1971). Phi Delta Phi. *Member:* Los Angeles County Bar Association (Member, Federal Practice and Procedures Committee, 1980-1981); State Bar of California. **REPORTED CASES:** Beaudreau v. Superior Court 14 C 3 448, 121 CR 585; Cole v. Los Angeles Community College District 137 CR 588, 68 CA 2 26; In re. Larry P 201 CA 3 888, 247 CR 472; In re. Marianne R 113 CA 3 423, 169 CR. **PRACTICE AREAS:** Litigation; Insurance Coverage.

**JOSEPH F. DANIELS,** born Merced, California, April 9, 1970; admitted to bar, 1996, California and U.S. District Court, Central District of California; U.S. Court of Appeals for the 4th Circuit. *Education:* University of California, Berkeley (A.B., 1992); University of Southern California (J.D., 1996). Member, Southern California Law Review, 1994-1995. Managing Articles Editor, Southern California Interdisciplinary Law Journal, 1995-1996. Author, "Comparing U.S. and Hong Kong Public Offering Regulation: How Cost Effective is China's Primary Capital Market," Vol 69, So. Cal Law Review.

### OF COUNSEL

**RONALD H. MALIN,** born California, 1934; admitted to bar, 1960, California and Colorado; 1978, District of Columbia. *Education:* University of Southern California (B.S., 1956); University of Denver (J.D., 1959). Phi Alpha Delta. Member, Board of Editors, University of Denver Law Review, 1958-1959. Law Clerk, Justice Albert T. Frantz, Colorado Supreme Court, 1959. Former Chairman of the World Trade Bank and World Trade

*(This Listing Continued)*

Bancorp Beverly Hills, California, 1981-1985. Member/Secretary, Countywide Citizens Planning Council for Los Angeles County Department of Regional Planning. *Member:* Beverly Hills, Los Angeles County, Colorado and American Bar Associations; District of Columbia Bar. *PRACTICE AREAS:* Real Estate Law; Real Estate Finance and Development Law; Syndications Law; Agricultural Law. *Email:* RHMalin@AOL.COM

## LAW OFFICES OF JOHN R. ALCORN
### LOS ANGELES, CALIFORNIA
(See Newport Beach)

*U.S. Immigration and Nationality Law.*

## ALEXANDER & YONG
Established in 1992
### 10940 WILSHIRE BOULEVARD, SUITE 2200
### LOS ANGELES, CALIFORNIA 90024
Telephone: 310-824-5254
Fax: 310-208-3493

*Business Litigation, Insurance Defense, Real Property, Bankruptcy, Trust and Estate Planning, Taxation, Probate, Conservatorships, China Trade and Investments, Corporate Transactions.*

### MEMBERS OF FIRM

**J. BERNARD ALEXANDER, III,** born Los Angeles, California, October 19, 1960; admitted to bar, 1987, California and U.S. District Court, Central District of California. *Education:* University of California at Los Angeles (B.A., English and Political Science, 1983); Southwestern University (J.D., 1986). Barristers' Landlord-Tenant Settlement Officer, 1988-1990. Arbitrator, Superior and Municipal Court. *Member:* Los Angeles County Bar Association; State Bar of California (Member, Real Property Section); Association of Southern California Defense Counsel. *PRACTICE AREAS:* Civil Litigation; Insurance Defense; Insurance Fraud; Municipality and Peace Officer Defense; Business; Real Estate; Employment Litigation.

**JEFFREY S. YONG,** born Singapore, September 8, 1961; admitted to bar, 1988, California and U.S. District Court, Central District of California. *Education:* University of California, Los Angeles (B.A., Political Science, 1983); University of California, Hastings College of Law (J.D., 1986). *Member:* State Bar of California (Member, Real Property Section). *LANGUAGES:* Mandarin Chinese. *PRACTICE AREAS:* Business and Real Property Litigation; Environmental Law; Bankruptcy; Securities; China Trade; Estate Planning.

**MARY C. ALEXANDER,** born San Fernando, California, September 23, 1959; admitted to bar, 1988, California; 1989, U.S. Tax Court. *Education:* University of California at Los Angeles (B.A., 1982); Southwestern School of Law (J.D., 1988). *Member:* Los Angeles County Bar Association (Member: Family and Estate Planning Sections); State Bar of California. *LANGUAGES:* Spanish. *PRACTICE AREAS:* Probate, Trusts, Wills, Estate; Real Estate Transactions; Family Law.

### ASSOCIATES

**ARTURO D. SANCHEZ,** born Los Angeles, California, May 12, 1965; admitted to bar, 1994, California and U.S. District Court, Central District of California. *Education:* University of California, Berkeley (B.A., Political Economics, Natural Resources, 1988); Western State University College of Law (J.D., 1993). *Member:* Los Angeles County Bar Association; State Bar of California. *LANGUAGES:* Spanish. *PRACTICE AREAS:* Civil Litigation; Business and Real Estate Litigation; Insurance Fraud.

## EUGENE S. ALKANA
### LOS ANGELES, CALIFORNIA
(See Pasadena)

*General Civil Practice. Equine Law and Syndications. Litigation. Business, Commercial, Real Estate, Construction, Collections, Non-Profit Organizations.*

## ALLDERDICE AND DENMAN
### WILSHIRE PARK PLACE
### SUITE 820
### 3700 WILSHIRE BOULEVARD
### LOS ANGELES, CALIFORNIA 90010-3085
Telephone: 213-383-9500
Facsimile: 213-383-9666
Email: allden@aol.com

*Labor and Employment Law (Management), Entertainment and Intellectual Property Law and Related Litigation.*

### MEMBERS OF FIRM

**LINDA AUERBACH ALLDERDICE,** born Madison, Wisconsin, 1949; admitted to bar, 1973, District of Columbia and U.S. District Court, District of Columbia; 1975, U.S. Court of Appeals for the District of Columbia Circuit; 1978, California, U.S. Court of Appeals, Fourth, Fifth, Seventh, Eighth and Tenth Circuits and U.S. District Court, Central District of California; 1982, U.S. Court of Appeals, Ninth Circuit and U.S. District Court, Southern District of California; 1986, U.S. District Court, Northern District of California. *Education:* University of Wisconsin (B.A., with distinction, 1970); National Law Center, George Washington University (J.D., with honors, 1973). Counsel to Member Jenkins and Attorney for Appellate Court Division Office of the General Counsel, National Labor Relations Board, 1973-1978. Litigation Associate, Wyman, Bautzer, Rothman, Kuchel & Silbert, 1978-1981. Litigation Associate, 1981-1984 and Partner, 1985-1990, Petit and Martin. Partner, Ballard, Rosenberg & Golper, 1990-1994. *Member:* Los Angeles County (Member, Labor Law Section) and American (Member: Labor and Employment Law Section; Committee on Employee Rights and Responsibilities in the Work Place, 1987—) Bar Associations; State Bar of California; District of Columbia Bar. *PRACTICE AREAS:* Labor and Employment Law (Management) and Related Litigation; Intellectual Property Litigation.

**ALEXANDRA DENMAN,** born Oklahoma City, Oklahoma, 1947; admitted to bar, 1973, District of Columbia; 1978, California; U.S. Supreme Court; U.S. Court of Appeals for the District of Columbia Circuit and U.S. District Court for the District of Columbia. *Education:* Vassar College (B.A., 1969); George Washington University (J.D., with honors, 1973). Litigation Associate, Donovan, Leisure, Newton & Irvine, Washington, D.C., 1973-1976. Senior Attorney, Motion Picture Division, Paramount Pictures Corporation, 1981-1985. Vice President, Theatrical Legal Affairs, United Artists, 1985-1987. *Member:* Los Angeles County (Member, Intellectual Property Section) and Beverly Hills Bar Associations; State Bar of California; Copyright Society of the USA (Former Board of Trustees Member). *PRACTICE AREAS:* Entertainment Law; Intellectual Property.

### OF COUNSEL

**FLORAN L. FINK,** born Queens, New York, 1949; admitted to bar, 1975, New York; U.S. District Court, Southern and Eastern Districts of New York; 1976, U.S. Court of Appeals, Second Circuit; 1985, California and U.S. District Court Central and Northern Districts of California; 1986, U.S. Court of Appeals, Ninth Circuit. *Education:* Sarah Lawrence College (B.A.,1971); Dartmouth College; George Washington University (J.D., with honors, 1974); New York University. Order of the Coif. Rufus Choate Scholar. Member, Journal of International Law and Economics. Lecturer: Federal Bar Association Winter Meeting, 1982, "Employment Discrimination;" CEB "Preparing and Examination Expert Witnesses In Civil Litigation," 1990. Litigation Associate, Finley, Kumble, Heine, Underberg & Grutman, 1974-1976. Litigation Associate, 1976-1982 and Litigation Partner, 1982-1985, Robinson, Silverman, Pearce, Aronshon & Berman. Senior Litigation Associate, L.A. Office, 1985-1987 and Special Counsel in Litigation, 1987-1989, Skadden, Arps, Slate, Meagher & Flom. Partner, Gold, Marks, Ring & Pepper, 1989-1993. Of Counsel, Kramer & Goldwasser, 1993-1995. *Member:* Los Angeles County (Member, Litigation Section), New York State and American (Member, Sections on: Labor Law; Litigation; Patent, Trademark and Copyright Law) Bar Associations; State Bar of California. *PRACTICE AREAS:* Labor; Employment Law; Business Litigation; Intellectual Property Litigation.

### LEGAL SUPPORT PERSONNEL

**PAMELA L. MOSES,** born San Francisco, California, 1945. *Education:* Los Angeles Pierce College (A.A., 1965). (Office Administrator).

## ALLEN, MATKINS, LECK, GAMBLE & MALLORY LLP

A Limited Liability Partnership including Professional Corporations

*Established in 1977*

**SEVENTH FLOOR, 515 SOUTH FIGUEROA STREET
LOS ANGELES, CALIFORNIA 90071**
Telephone: 213-622-5555
Telecopier: 213-620-8816

*Irvine, California Office:* Fourth Floor, 18400 Von Karman, 92715. Telephone: 714-553-1313. Telecopier: 714-553-8354.

*San Diego, California Office:* 501 West Broadway, Suite 900, 92101. Telephone: 619-233-1155. Facsimile: 619-233-1158.

*West Los Angeles, California Office:* 1999 Avenue of the Stars, Suite 1800, 90067. Telephone: 310-788-2400. Fax: 310-788-2410.

*General Civil, Trial and Appellate Practice in all State and Federal Courts. Real Property and Construction Law. Land Use and Environmental Law, including Administrative and Regulatory Practice. Corporations, Securities, Partnerships and Public Bond Financings. Federal, State and Local Taxation. Labor and Employment Law (Management) and Wrongful Termination. Bankruptcy, Creditors Rights, Receiverships and Restructuring. Estate Planning and Trusts.*

*FIRM PROFILE: Allen, Matkins, Leck, Gamble & Mallory LLP is recognized as one of the premier commercial real estate, business and finance law firms in the United States, providing legal services in connection with complex projects including high-rise office buildings, industrial parks, shopping centers, planned communities, mixed-use developments, hotels and resorts. In addition to its real estate practice, the firm has a pre-eminent business practice centered on business litigation, corporate, tax, environmental, bankruptcy and creditors' rights and labor departments.*

*Allen, Matkins has offices in downtown Los Angeles, West Los Angeles, Orange County and San Diego and enjoys a prestigious regional, national and international clientele. The firm is committed to the highest standards of professional excellence in the delivery of legal services.*

### PARTNERS

**FREDERICK L. ALLEN,** born Kansas City, Missouri, July 2, 1939; admitted to bar, 1967, California. *Education:* Stanford University (A.B., 1961); Hastings College of Law, University of California (LL.B., 1966). Phi Delta Phi. *Member:* Los Angeles County and American Bar Associations; State Bar of California (Member, Real Property Section, Executive Committee, 1984-1987; Vice-Chair, 1987; Chairman, Commercial and Industrial Development Subsection, 1982-1984). [U.S. Naval Officer, 1961-1963]. **PRACTICE AREAS:** Real Estate.

**JOHN C. GAMBLE,** born Los Angeles, California, September 16, 1945; admitted to bar, 1971, California. *Education:* Stanford University (B.A., 1967); Loyola University of Los Angeles (J.D., 1971). Member, St. Thomas More Law Honor Society. Member, Loyola University of Los Angeles Law Review, 1969-1970. *Member:* Los Angeles County, Orange County and American Bar Associations; State Bar of California. (Resident, Irvine Office). **PRACTICE AREAS:** Real Estate.

**BRIAN C. LECK,** born Los Angeles, California, May 21, 1945; admitted to bar, 1971, California. *Education:* Stanford University (B.A., 1967); University of California at Los Angeles (J.D., 1970). Member, U.C.L.A. Law Review, 1968-1970. *Member:* Los Angeles County and American Bar Associations; State Bar of California. **PRACTICE AREAS:** Corporate.

**RICHARD C. MALLORY,** born Rapid City, South Dakota, July 3, 1945; admitted to bar, 1970, California. *Education:* University of Southern California (B.S., magna cum laude, 1966); Stanford University (J.D., 1969). Beta Gamma Sigma; Phi Kappa Phi. Editor, CEB Commercial Real Property Lease Practice Guide, Second Edition, 1996. Panelist, CEB Programs on: Commercial Leasing, 1976; Secured Real Property Transactions, 1980; Purchase and Sale Agreements, 1980; Recent Developments in Real Property Law, 1982; 3rd Annual CEB Real Property Practice Institute on Leasing, 1986; 7th Annual CEB; Real Property Practice Institute on Issues in Management and Operations of Commercial Real Property, 1990; Commercial Real Property Leases, 1991; 9th Annual CEB Real Property Practice Institute on Selected Issues in Commercial Lease Practice, 1992; Commercial Real Property Leases, 1994; 12th Annual CEB Real Property Practice Institute on Acquiring, Enhancing and Disposing of Real Property, 1995; Advanced Course of Study: Office Leasing, 1996. Board of Visitors, Stanford Law School, 1992-1994. *Member:* Los Angeles County and American Bar Associations; State Bar of California. **PRACTICE AREAS:** Real Estate.

*(This Listing Continued)*

**MICHAEL L. MATKINS,** born Los Angeles, California, May 18, 1945; admitted to bar, 1971, California. *Education:* Stanford University (A.B., 1967); University of Southern California (J.D., 1970). CEB Annual Real Property Institute, Capital Formation in Real Property Development, 1984. Benjamin S. Crocker Symposium, Critical and Emerging Issues in Real Estate Development, 1994. *Member:* Los Angeles County and American Bar Associations; State Bar of California. **PRACTICE AREAS:** Real Estate.

**MARVIN E. GARRETT,** born Hollywood, California, August 4, 1941; admitted to bar, 1970, California. *Education:* Northwestern University (B.S.I.E., 1963; M.B.A., 1965); University of Southern California (J.D., 1970). Phi Delta Phi; Beta Gamma Sigma; Order of the Coif. Member, Southern California Law Review, 1968-1970. Article: Appellate Courts Turn Back Clock on Malpractice Claims, December, 1993; Article: For Whom it Tolls, April, 1995; Article: Operating Pass-Through Expenses: A Legal Hotbutton, April, 1995; Article: Where Did Everybody Come From? November, 1995. *Member:* Los Angeles County (Member: Superior Courts Committee, 1976-1978; Attorney Arbitration Panel, 1977-1993; Lawyers Professional Liability Committee, 1990-1994) and American Bar Associations; State Bar of California. Los Angeles Business Trial Lawyers. **PRACTICE AREAS:** Litigation.

**MICHAEL E. GLEASON, (P.C.),** born Peoria, Illinois, October 27, 1936; admitted to bar, 1963, Utah; 1965, California. *Education:* Loyola University of Los Angeles (B.B.A., 1959; LL.B., 1963). Phi Delta Phi; Alpha Sigma Nu. Recipient, William Tell Aggeler Award for Legal Scholarship, 1963. *Member:* San Diego County and American Bar Associations; Utah State Bar; State Bar of California; International Council of Shopping Centers (Member and Past Chairman, Law Conference Planning Committee); Urban Land Institute (Member, Development Regulations Council). (Resident, San Diego Office). **PRACTICE AREAS:** Real Estate.

**THOMAS C. FOSTER,** born Santa Monica, California, October 17, 1948; admitted to bar, 1975, California; 1977, U.S. Tax Court. *Education:* University of Southern California (B.S., 1970; J.D., 1975). Certified Public Accountant, California, 1976. *Member:* Los Angeles County, Orange County and American Bar Associations; State Bar of California. (Resident, Irvine Office). **PRACTICE AREAS:** Tax; Partnerships; General Corporate.

**ROBERT J. CATHCART,** born Palo Alto, California, September 28, 1945; admitted to bar, 1972, California; 1973, Washington. *Education:* Stanford University (A.B., 1968); University of Washington (J.D., 1972). Editor, Comments Department, Washington Law Review, 1971-1972. Clerk to Judge David W. Soukup, Superior Court of Washington, Seattle, Washington, 1972-1973. Judge Pro Tem, Los Angeles Municipal Court, 1982— and Los Angeles Superior Court, 1989—. Panelist: CEB Program on Real Property Remedies, 1991. Moderator, 13th Annual CEB Real Property Institute on Minimizing Real Property Liabilities (Construction, 1996). *Member:* Los Angeles County, Washington State and American Bar Associations; State Bar of California (Member, Committee on Administration of Justice, 1977-1980); Association of Business Trial Lawyers. **PRACTICE AREAS:** Litigation; Construction Law.

**R. MICHAEL JOYCE,** born Los Angeles, California, December 13, 1951; admitted to bar, 1977, California; 1978, U.S. District Court, Central District of California; 1979, U.S. Court of Appeals, Ninth Circuit. *Education:* Princeton University (A.B., with honor, 1974); University of Southern California (J.D., 1977). Order of the Coif. Panelist, CEB Programs on Real Property Remedies, 1984. Moderator, CEB Program on Real Property Leases, 1984. *Member:* Los Angeles, Orange County and American Bar Associations; State Bar of California. (Resident, Irvine Office). **PRACTICE AREAS:** Real Estate.

**GERBEN HOEKSMA,** born Los Angeles, California, February 18, 1947; admitted to bar, 1972, California and U.S. District Court, Central District of California. *Education:* University of Southern California (B.A., 1968; J.D., 1971). *Member:* Los Angeles County (Member: Real Property Section; Real Estate Finance Subsection) and American Bar Associations; State Bar of California (Member, Real Estate Section). (Resident, West Los Angeles Office). **PRACTICE AREAS:** Real Estate.

**THOMAS W. HENNING,** born Los Angeles, California, October 27, 1949; admitted to bar, 1976, California. *Education:* University of California at Los Angeles (B.A., 1970); Georgetown University (J.D., 1975); New York University (LL.M., 1976). Kenneson Fellow, 1975-1976. Editor, Law & Policy in International Business, 1974-1975. Graduate Editor, Tax Law Review, 1975-1976. Author: Financing, Refinancing and Work-Outs of

*(This Listing Continued)*

California Property: Tax Planning for Recourse and Nonrecourse Debt, 48th U.S.C. Tax Institute, 1996; "The Receipt of a Partnership Interest for Services," 44th U.S.C. Tax Institute, 1992; "Partnership Allocations-Sailing Beyond the Safe Harbor," 41st U.S.C. Tax Institute, 1989; "Tax Shelters After the 1984 Tax Reform Act," 37th U.S.C. Tax Institute, 1985; "Tax Planning for the Receipt of an Equity Interest for Services," CEB Advanced Real Property Tax Planning, 1984; "New and Emerging Issues Under the Motion Picture and Television Investment Tax Credit" 36th U.S.C. Tax Institute 800, 1984. "Personal Residences -- Planning for Tax-Free and Tax-Deferred Sales and Exchanges," 14 Review of Taxation of Individuals 22, 1980; "Treatment of the Grantor Trust as a Separate Entity," 32 Tax Law Review 409, 1977. "Tax Planning for Partners and Partnerships Affected by TRA's Far Reaching Changes," 18 Taxation for Accountants 260, 1976; 8 Taxation for Lawyers 524, 1976. Adjunct Professor, University of San Diego Law School, Graduate Tax Program, 1987-1988. *Member:* Beverly Hills (Chair, Tax Section), Los Angeles County (Former Chair, Foreign Tax Committee) and American Bar Associations; State Bar of California (Former Chair, Real Estate Tax Subcommittee). *PRACTICE AREAS:* Tax, Joint Ventures and Business Organizations.

*PATRICK E. BREEN,* born Los Angeles, California, May 6, 1953; admitted to bar, 1978, California. *Education:* University of Santa Clara (B.S.C, summa cum laude, 1975); Boalt Hall School of Law, University of California (J.D., 1978). *Member:* Los Angeles County and American Bar Associations; State Bar of California. *PRACTICE AREAS:* Trials; Litigation; Land Use; Environmental; Bankruptcy; Creditors Rights and Workouts.

*LAWRENCE D. LEWIS, (P.C.),* born Los Angeles, California, February 25, 1946; admitted to bar, 1972, California; U.S. District Court, Central, Southern, Northern and Eastern Districts of California; U.S. Court of Appeals, Ninth Circuit; U.S. Supreme Court. *Education:* University of California at Berkeley (A.B., 1968); Boalt Hall School of Law, University of California (J.D., 1972). Phi Beta Kappa. *Member:* Orange County, San Diego County and American Bar Associations; State Bar of California. (Resident, Irvine Office). *PRACTICE AREAS:* Litigation.

*GEORGE T. MCDONNELL,* born Palo Alto, California, August 31, 1953; admitted to bar, 1979, California. *Education:* University of California at Los Angeles (B.A., cum laude, 1976); Hastings College of Law, University of California (J.D., 1979). Phi Delta Phi; Order of the Coif. Member, Thurston Society. *Member:* Los Angeles County and American Bar Associations; State Bar of California. *PRACTICE AREAS:* Litigation.

*MICHAEL F. SFREGOLA,* born Orange, California, February 27, 1954; admitted to bar, 1979, California; 1982, U.S. Tax Court. *Education:* University of California at Irvine (B.A., summa cum laude, 1976); University of Southern California (J.D., 1979). Phi Beta Kappa; Order of the Coif. *Member:* Los Angeles County, Orange County and American Bar Associations; State Bar of California. *PRACTICE AREAS:* Tax and Real Estate.

*DAVID A. B. BURTON, (P.C.),* born Pittsburgh, Pennsylvania, December 13, 1955; admitted to bar, 1981, California. *Education:* Amherst College (B.A., summa cum laude, 1977); Stanford University (J.D., 1980). Phi Beta Kappa. Panelist, Infocast Programs on Commercial Loan Documentation, 1988, 1989, 1990. Panelist, Benjamin Crocker Symposium on The Troubled Real Estate Project, 1991. Panelist, Los Angeles County Bar, Real Estate Section Program on Renegotiating Loan Documents in the Current Environment, 1991. Panelist, CEB Program on Representing the Borrower in a Real Property Foreclosure or Workout, 1992. Panelist, Beverly Hills Bar Association annual Real Estate Seminar on Real Estate Loan Workouts, 1993. Moderator and Panelist, CEB Program on Real Property Workouts, 1994. Author: "Controlling Risk in Fee Management," Journal of Property Management, September/October 1993; "Documenting a Successful Real Estate Loan Workout for the Borrower," Corporate Real Estate Executive, October 1993. *Member:* Los Angeles County and American Bar Associations; State Bar of California. *PRACTICE AREAS:* Real Estate.

*MONICA E. OLSON,* born Redwood City, California, October 30, 1954; admitted to bar, 1980, California. *Education:* University of California at Los Angeles (B.A., magna cum laude, 1976; J.D., 1980). *Member:* Orange County and American Bar Associations; State Bar of California. (Resident, Irvine Office). *PRACTICE AREAS:* Real Estate.

*THOMAS E. GIBBS,* born Munich, Germany, September 8, 1955; admitted to bar, 1980, California and U.S. District Court, Central and Southern Districts of California. *Education:* University of California at Irvine (B.A., summa cum laude, 1977); University of California at Los Angeles (J.D., 1980). Phi Beta Kappa; Order of the Coif. Comments Editor, Federal Communications Law Journal, 1979-1980. Judge Pro Tem, Orange County Superior Court. *Member:* Orange County and American Bar Associations;

*(This Listing Continued)*

State Bar of California. (Resident, Irvine Office). *PRACTICE AREAS:* Litigation.

*VERNON C. GAUNTT,* born Long Beach, California, January 13, 1950; admitted to bar, 1975, California. *Education:* University of Southern California (B.S., 1972; M.B.A., 1975; J.D., 1975). Phi Kappa Psi; Beta Gamma Sigma. *Member:* San Diego County and American Bar Associations; State Bar of California. (Resident, San Diego Office). *PRACTICE AREAS:* Real Estate.

*DWIGHT L. ARMSTRONG,* born Lancaster, Pennsylvania, July 11, 1952; admitted to bar, 1977, California. *Education:* Stanford University (B.A., with departmental honors, 1974); University of Southern California (J.D., 1977). Member, 1975-1977 and Articles Editor, 1976-1977, Southern California Law Review. Author: Note, "Products Liability, Comparative Negligence and the Allocation of Damages Among Multiple Defendants," 50 Southern California Law Review, 73, 1976. Law Clerk to Hon. E. Avery Crary, U.S. District Court, Central District of California, 1977-1978. Panelist, American bar Association, General Practice Section 1995 Spring Meeting, "Complying with the Americans with Disabilities Act: The Employer's Perspective." Guest Lecturer, University of California, Irvine Extension, Human Resources Certificate Program, 1995. Author: "Take it Lying Down (Liability for Misrepresentation)," The Los Angeles Daily Journal, July 18, 1996; "Stereotyping Dress Codes in Tatters," The National Law Journal, January 16, 1995. Speaker: American Electronics Association, "Steps to Prevent Wrongful Termination Lawsuits," November 7, 1996; Council on Education in Management, "Managing Mangers (and Providing the 10 Top Legal Problems they can cause)," July 18, 1996; National Human Resources Association, Orange County Affiliate, "Current Issues involving Sexual Harassment Claims," 1994. Arbitration Panel Member under National Rules for the Resolution of Employment Disputes (American Arbitration Association). *Member:* Orange County (Former Chair, Labor Law Section) and American (Member, Section on Labor and Employment Law) Bar Associations; State Bar of California (Labor and Employment Law Section). (Resident, Irvine Office). *PRACTICE AREAS:* Labor and Employment Law (Management).

*PAUL D. O'CONNOR,* born Columbus, Ohio, September 19, 1955; admitted to bar, 1980, California. *Education:* California State University at Fullerton (B.S., 1977); Loyola University of Los Angeles (J.D., cum laude, 1980); New York University (LL.M., 1981). Law Clerk to Senior Judge William M. Drennan, U.S. Tax Court, 1981-1983. *Member:* Los Angeles County, Orange County and American Bar Associations; State Bar of California. (Resident, Irvine Office). *PRACTICE AREAS:* Business Organization and Tax Planning.

*S. LEE HANCOCK,* born Knoxville, Tennessee, August 11, 1955; admitted to bar, 1979, Missouri; 1982, U.S. Tax Court; 1983, U.S. Claims Court; 1988, California. *Education:* Southwest Missouri State University (B.S., summa cum laude, 1975); Southern Methodist University (J.D., cum laude, 1979). Phi Delta Phi; Order of the Coif. Associate Editor, Journal of Air Law and Commerce, 1978-1979. Certified Public Accountant, Missouri, 1977. Speaker and Co-Author: National Business Institute on Considerations in Buying or Selling a Business, 1987. Co-Author: "Tax Planning for the Ownership and Operation of General Aviation Aircraft," 45 J. Air L. and Commerce 275, 1979. *Member:* Orange County and American (Member, Section on Business Law) Bar Associations; The Missouri Bar; State Bar of California. (Resident, Irvine Office). *PRACTICE AREAS:* Securities; Corporate.

*DAVID L. OSIAS,* born Hayward, California, April 10, 1954; admitted to bar, 1979, California and U.S. District Court, Southern, Central, Northern and Eastern Districts of California. *Education:* University of California at Davis (B.S., with honors, 1976); Boalt Hall School of Law, University of California (J.D., 1979). Phi Kappa Phi. Adjunct Professor of Law, University of San Diego, 1989-1991. *Member:* San Diego County (Member, Bankruptcy and Commercial Law Sections) and American (Member, Section of Business Law; Natural Resources Water Committee) Bar Associations; The State Bar of California; Financial Lawyers Conference; Commercial Law League; American Bankruptcy Institute; California Bankruptcy Forum (President, 1995); San Diego Bankruptcy Forum (Immediate Past President; Ex Officio Director). (San Diego and Los Angeles Offices). *PRACTICE AREAS:* Bankruptcy; Creditors' Rights; Water Rights and Resources.

*WILLIAM R. HARMSEN,* born Pomona, California, July 24, 1946; admitted to bar, 1972, California; U.S. District Court, Central Southern and Northern Districts of California and District of Columbia; U.S. Court of Appeals, Ninth Circuit. *Education:* Claremont Men's College (B.A., 1968); Hastings College of Law, University of California (J.D., 1971).

*(This Listing Continued)*

**ALLEN, MATKINS, LECK, GAMBLE & MALLORY LLP,**
Los Angeles—Continued

*Member:* Los Angeles County (Member, Federal Courts and Federal Appointments Committees) and American Bar Associations; American Bar Association Savings Institutions (Subcommittee on Regulation and Legislation and Litigation Section). *PRACTICE AREAS:* Litigation.

**DEBRA DISON HALL,** born Los Angeles, California, June 12, 1952; admitted to bar, 1981, California. *Education:* California Institute of Technology (B.S., 1974); University of Southern California (J.D., 1981). Member, Southern California Law Review, 1979-1981. Author: Note, "Pretrial Discovery of Net Worth in Punitive Damage Cases," 54 S. Cal. L. Rev. 1141, 1981. *Member:* Los Angeles County and American Bar Associations; State Bar of California; National Association of College and University Attorneys. *PRACTICE AREAS:* Corporate.

**ANTON N. NATSIS,** born Detroit, Michigan, August 11, 1958; admitted to bar, 1983, California. *Education:* University of Michigan at Ann Arbor (B.B.A., 1980; J.D., 1983). Beta Gamma Sigma. Chief Consultant, CEB California Leasing Series, 1996. Chairman, California State Bar Southern California Landlord/Tenant Subsection, 1994-1996. (Resident, West Los Angeles Office). *PRACTICE AREAS:* Real Estate Development Law; Finance Law.

**GEORGE J. BERGER,** born Berlin, Germany, November 3, 1944; admitted to bar, 1973, California; U.S. District Court, Central and Southern Districts of California; U.S. Court of Appeals, Ninth Circuit; U.S. Supreme Court. *Education:* Webb Institute of Naval Architecture (B.S., 1966); University of Southern California (J.D., 1973). Member, Southern California Law Review, 1971-1973. Author, "Retaliatory Eviction In California--The Legislature Slams the Door and Boards Up The Windows," So. Cal. Law Review Vol. 46, 1973; "Flood Warnings," ULI Urban Land Magazine, March 1994. Instructor, National Institute for Trial Advocacy, 1991—. *Member:* San Diego County and American Bar Associations; State Bar of California; San Diego Trial Lawyers Association; Association of Business Trial Lawyers. (Resident, San Diego Office). *PRACTICE AREAS:* Litigation.

**MICHAEL C. PRUTER,** born Houston, Texas, February 21, 1955; admitted to bar, 1980, Texas; 1983, California; 1984, U.S. Tax Court. *Education:* University of Texas (B.A., 1977); Southern Methodist University (J.D., 1980). *Member:* San Diego County and American (Member, Section of Taxation) Bar Associations; State Bar of Texas; State Bar of California. (Resident, San Diego Office). *PRACTICE AREAS:* Tax/Real Estate.

**MICHAEL H. CERRINA,** born Bakersfield, California, April 4, 1957; admitted to bar, 1982, California. *Education:* University of Southern California (B.S., cum laude, 1979); Loyola University of Los Angeles (J.D., cum laude, 1982). Beta Gamma Sigma; Alpha Lambda Delta. Member: Loyola of Los Angeles Law Review, 1980-1981; St. Thomas More Law Honor Society. *Member:* Los Angeles County and American Bar Associations; State Bar of California. *PRACTICE AREAS:* Real Estate.

**RICHARD E. STINEHART,** born Los Angeles, California, August 5, 1956; admitted to bar, 1982, California, U.S. District Court, Central District of California and U.S. Court of Appeals, Ninth Circuit. *Education:* University of California at Irvine (B.A., magna cum laude, 1978); University of Southern California (J.D., 1982). Phi Beta Kappa; Order of the Coif. *Member:* Los Angeles County, Orange County and American Bar Associations; State Bar of California. (Resident, Irvine Office). *PRACTICE AREAS:* Real Estate.

**STEPHEN R. THAMES,** born Escondido, California, July 18, 1956; admitted to bar, 1982, California. *Education:* University of California at Davis (B.A., cum laude, 1978); University of California at Los Angeles (J.D., 1982). Member, Moot Court Honor Society. *Member:* Los Angeles County, Orange County and American Bar Associations; State Bar of California. (Resident, Irvine Office). *PRACTICE AREAS:* Litigation.

**JOHN K. MCKAY,** born Eugene, Oregon, March 24, 1953; admitted to bar, 1982, Florida; 1986, California. *Education:* University of Southern California (B.A., 1975); Stetson University (J.D., 1982). *Member:* Los Angeles County and American Bar Associations; The Florida Bar; State Bar of California. *PRACTICE AREAS:* Real Estate Litigation; Land Use; Environmental Litigation; Employment Litigation.

**DANA I. SCHIFFMAN,** born Los Angeles, California, June 7, 1956; admitted to bar, 1982, California. *Education:* University of California at Los Angeles (B.A. and B.S., magna cum laude, 1978; M.B.A., 1982; J.D., 1982). Phi Beta Kappa; Beta Gamma Sigma. Co-Author: "A Practical

*(This Listing Continued)*

Guide to Environmental Investigations and the Use of Environmental Consultants in Real Property Transactions," California Real Property Law Journal, Spring, 1988. *Member:* San Diego County and American Bar Associations; State Bar of California (Co-Chairman, Environmental Law Subsection, Real Property Section, 1988-1991); International Council of Shopping Centers. (Resident, San Diego Office). *PRACTICE AREAS:* Real Estate; Hazardous Substances.

**ANNE E. KLOKOW,** born Boston, Massachusetts, May 26, 1954; admitted to bar, 1980, California, U.S. District Court, Central District of California and U.S. Court of Appeals, Ninth Circuit. *Education:* University of California at Santa Barbara (B.A., summa cum laude, 1976); University of Southern California (J.D., 1980). *Member:* Orange County Bar Association; State Bar of California. (Resident, Irvine Office). *PRACTICE AREAS:* Real Estate.

**NEIL N. GLUCK,** born Brooklyn, New York, June 12, 1958; admitted to bar, 1983, California. *Education:* University of Massachusetts (B.B.A., cum laude, 1980); Stanford University (J.D., 1983). Beta Gamma Sigma; Beta Alpha Psi. Co-Author, Chapter 5A, Lease Takeover Agreements, Current Leasing Law and Techniques (Matthew Bender 1995). Contributing Consultant Lease Action Guideline, 1st Edition (CEB). Co-Author, Negotiating Expansion Rights in Multi-Tenant Projects; Real Estate Finance, Spring, 1992. *Member:* Los Angeles County and American Bar Associations; State Bar of California (Member, Real Property Law Section); NACORE International (Los Angeles Chapter). *PRACTICE AREAS:* Real Estate.

**DAVID W. WENSLEY,** born Holyoke, Massachusetts, February 20, 1958; admitted to bar, 1984, California. *Education:* University of Southern California (B.S., cum laude, 1981); Hastings College of the Law, University of California (J.D., cum laude, 1984). Beta Gamma Sigma; Phi Delta Phi. Member, Thurston Society. *Member:* American Bar Association; State Bar of California (Member, Real Property Law Section); International Council of Shopping Centers; Institute of Real Estate Management; Commercial Industrial Developers Association. (Resident, Irvine Office). *PRACTICE AREAS:* Real Estate; Environmental Law.

**GARY S. MCKITTERICK,** born Mexico, Missouri, December 20, 1958; admitted to bar, 1984, California. *Education:* Stanford University (A.B., 1981); Loyola University of Los Angeles (J.D., 1984). Author, "Organizing and Planning the Project," Chapter 315, Volume 12, California Real Estate Law and Practice (Matthew Bender). *Member:* Orange County (Member, Construction Section) and American (Member, Forum Committee on the Construction Industry) Bar Associations; State Bar of California (Member, Real Property Law Section); International Council of Shopping Centers; National Association of Industrial and Office Properties; Urban Land Institute. (Resident, Irvine Office). *PRACTICE AREAS:* Real Estate; Construction Law.

**PATRICK J. GRADY,** born White Plains, New York, April 28, 1959; admitted to bar, 1984, California and U.S. Court of Appeals, Ninth Circuit; 1989, U.S. Supreme Court. *Education:* California State University, Long Beach (B.S., with great distinction, 1981) Beta Gamma Sigma; University of Southern California (J.D., 1984). *Member:* Orange County (Member, Labor Law Section) and American Bar Associations; State Bar of California (Member, Labor Law Section). (Resident, Irvine Office). *PRACTICE AREAS:* Labor (Management).

**RAY B. GLINER,** born St. Louis, Missouri, April 3, 1960; admitted to bar, 1985, California. *Education:* University of Illinois (B.S., with highest honors, 1982); Boalt Hall School of Law, University of California (J.D., 1985). Beta Alpha Psi; Beta Gamma Sigma. Certified Public Accountant, Illinois, 1982. Author, "Negotiating Expansion Rights in Multi-Tenant Projects," Real Estate Finance, Spring 1992. *Member:* Los Angeles County, San Diego County and American Bar Associations; State Bar of California. (Resident, San Diego Office). *PRACTICE AREAS:* Real Estate.

**ANTHONY S. BOUZA,** born Brooklyn, New York, October 2, 1960; admitted to bar, 1985, California and U.S. District Court, Central District of California. *Education:* Amherst College (B.A., 1982); University of Chicago (J.D., 1985). *Member:* Los Angeles County (Executive Committee of the Real Property Section) and American Bar Associations; State Bar of California; Southern California Chapter of NAIOP (Board of Directors); Los Angeles Headquarters Association (Board of Directors). *PRACTICE AREAS:* Real Estate.

**CHARLES N. KENWORTHY,** born Los Angeles, California, December 10, 1957; admitted to bar, 1985, California; 1986, U.S. District Court, Central, Eastern, Southern and Northern Districts of California and U.S. Court of Appeals, Ninth Circuit; 1989, District of Columbia. *Education:*

*(This Listing Continued)*

University of California at Los Angeles (B.A., 1980); University of San Diego School of Law (J.D., magna cum laude, 1985). Recipient, American Jurisprudence Awards. Licensed Real Estate Broker, California, 1982. Instructor of Law, University of San Diego School of Law, 1984-1985. *Member:* Beverly Hills, Los Angeles County and American Bar Associations; State Bar of California; California Trial Lawyers Association; The Association of Trial Lawyers of America. (Resident, West Los Angeles Office). ***PRACTICE AREAS:*** Business Litigation and Entertainment Law.

**ANTHONY J. OLIVA,** born San Francisco, California, July 20, 1960; admitted to bar, 1986, Florida, California and U.S. District Court, Southern District of Florida; 1988, Connecticut and U.S. District Court, District of Connecticut; 1990, U.S. District Court, Central District of California; 1993, U.S. District Court, Southern District of California and U.S. Court of Appeals, Ninth Circuit. *Education:* Princeton University (B.A., cum laude, 1982); Boalt Hall School of Law, University of California at Berkeley (J.D., 1985). *Member:* State Bar of California; The Florida Bar; American Bar Association. ***PRACTICE AREAS:*** Litigation.

**ROBERT M. HAMILTON,** born Inglewood, California, April 11, 1959; admitted to bar, 1984, California. *Education:* University of Southern California (B.S., magna cum laude, 1981); Loyola University of Los Angeles (J.D., 1984); New York University (LL.M. in Taxation, 1985). Beta Gamma Sigma; Beta Alpha Psi. Editor, Loyola of Los Angeles International and Comparative Law Journal, 1983-1984. Law Clerk to Hon. Jules G. Korner, III, U.S. Tax Court, 1985-1987. *Member:* Los Angeles County, Orange County and American Bar Associations; State Bar of California. (Resident, Irvine Office). ***PRACTICE AREAS:*** Business Organizations; Tax Planning.

**DAVID R. ZARO,** born Los Angeles, California, January 23, 1959; admitted to bar, 1986, California, U.S. District Court, Central and Northern Districts of California and U.S. Court of Appeals, Ninth Circuit. *Education:* Stanford University (B.A., 1981); Hastings College of the Law, University of California (J.D., 1986). *Member:* American Bar Association; State Bar of California; Financial Lawyers Conference; American Bankruptcy Institute. ***PRACTICE AREAS:*** Litigation; Bankruptcy; Creditors Rights.

**JANET A. WINNICK,** born Shelton, Connecticut, March 16, 1961; admitted to bar, 1986, California and U.S. District Court, Central District of California. *Education:* Stanford University (B.A., 1983); University of California at Los Angeles (J.D., 1986). *Member:* Los Angeles County and American Bar Associations; State Bar of California. ***PRACTICE AREAS:*** Real Estate.

**ROBERT R. BARNES,** born Joliet, Illinois, June 29, 1960; admitted to bar, 1985, Illinois and U.S. District Court, Northern District of Illinois; 1986, U.S. Court of Appeals, 7th Circuit; 1988, U.S. Supreme Court; 1989, California, U.S. Court of Appeals, 9th Circuit and U.S. District Court, Southern and Central Districts of California. *Education:* University of Chicago (A.B., with honors, Phi Beta Kappa, 1982; J.D., 1985). Co-Author: "District Court Reverses Bankruptcy Decision that Threatened RTC Asset Sales," 15 CEB Real Property Law Reporter 181 (May 1992); "Creditors'-/Debtors' Rights," Annual Survey of Illinois Law, Illinois Institute of Continuing Legal Education, 1989. Director, San Diego and California Bankruptcy Forums. *Member:* State Bar of California; Financial Lawyers Conference of Southern California; American Bankruptcy Institute. (Resident, San Diego Office). ***PRACTICE AREAS:*** Bankruptcy Law; Insolvency Law; Commercial Law.

**VINCENT M. COSCINO,** born Chicago, Illinois, September 6, 1960; admitted to bar, 1985, California; U.S. District Court, Central, Eastern, Northern and Southern Districts of California and U.S. Court of Appeals, Ninth Circuit. *Education:* Occidental College (B.A., 1982); University of San Diego (J.D., 1985). Author of three-Part Series entitled: "So You Always Wanted a Chapter 11 Practice...A Road Map Through The Reorganization Process," Orange County Bar Association, Commercial Law and Bankruptcy Section, 1996. Co-Author: "Relief From Stay: A Survey of Judicial Practices," California Bankruptcy Forum Conference, 1994; Panelist: CEB February 1995 "Taking and Enforcing Security Interests in Personal Property." Director, Orange County Bankruptcy Court, Central District of California. *Member:* San Diego County, Orange County and American Bar Associations; State Bar of California; San Diego, Orange County, Los Angeles and Inland Empire Bankruptcy Forums; Financial Lawyers Conference; American Bankruptcy Institute. ***PRACTICE AREAS:*** Bankruptcy Law; Insolvency Law; Commercial Law.

**JEFFREY R. PATTERSON,** born Trenton, New Jersey, November 17, 1960; admitted to bar, 1986, California, U.S. District Court, Central and Southern Districts of California and U.S. Court of Appeals, Ninth Circuit. *Education:* Duke University (A.B., cum laude, 1982); University of Southern California (J.D., 1986). Co-Author: "Relief From Stay: A Survey of Judicial Practices," California Bankruptcy Forum Conference, 1994; "The Allowed Secured Claim: Accounting For Payments of Net Rents," California Bankruptcy Journal, 1996. *Member:* San Diego County and American Bar Associations; State Bar of California; Association of Business Trial Lawyers; San Diego and Orange County Bankruptcy Forums; American Bankruptcy Institute; Financial Lawyers Conference. (Resident, San Diego Office). ***PRACTICE AREAS:*** Litigation; Bankruptcy and Creditors Rights.

**MARK R. HARTNEY,** born Evanston, Illinois, June 10, 1962; admitted to bar, 1988, California. *Education:* University of California at Los Angeles (B.A., 1984); University of California at Davis (J.D., 1988). *Member:* Los Angeles County and American Bar Associations; State Bar of California. ***PRACTICE AREAS:*** Litigation; Environmental; Land Use.

**JOHN M. TIPTON,** born Louisville, Kentucky, March 27, 1962; admitted to bar, 1988, California. *Education:* Miami University (A.B., magna cum laude, 1985); Harvard University (J.D., cum laude, 1988). Phi Beta Kappa. *Member:* Beverly Hills, Los Angeles and American Bar Associations; State Bar of California. (Resident, West Los Angeles Office). ***PRACTICE AREAS:*** Real Estate Development Law; Finance Law.

## ASSOCIATES

**CHERYL S. RIVERS,** born Los Angeles, California, February 19, 1954; admitted to bar, 1980, California and U.S. District Court, Central District of California. *Education:* University of California at Santa Barbara (B.A., 1976); California State University at Northridge; Southwestern University School of Law; University of Southern California (J.D., 1980). Recipient: American Jurisprudence Awards for Real Property and Civil Procedure; West Publishing Award. Notes Editor, Southern California Law Review, 1979-1980. Author: "California's Pilot Project in Economical Litigation," Southern California Law Review, Vol. 53. No. 5, July 1980. *Member:* Los Angeles County Bar Association; The State Bar of California (Current Co-Chair, The Landlord Tenant Subsection of the Real Property Law Section). (Resident West Los Angeles Office). ***PRACTICE AREAS:*** Real Estate.

**CRAIG D. SWANSON,** born Denison, Iowa, September 25, 1959; admitted to bar, 1986, California and Arizona. *Education:* University of San Diego (B.B.A., magna cum laude, 1982); University of San Diego Law School (J.D., magna cum laude, 1985). Beta Gamma Sigma. Member, San Diego Law Review, 1984-1985. *Member:* State Bar of California; State Bar of Arizona. (Resident, San Diego Office). ***PRACTICE AREAS:*** Real Estate.

**BRADLEY N. SCHWEITZER,** born San Jose, California, May 18, 1957; admitted to bar, 1987, California. *Education:* University of California at Los Angeles (B.A., 1979); Loyola University of Los Angeles (J.D., cum laude, 1986). Member, St. Thomas More Law Honor Society. *Member:* State Bar of California. (Resident, Irvine Office). ***PRACTICE AREAS:*** Real Estate.

**GREGORY G. GORMAN,** born Sacramento, California, February 5, 1962; admitted to bar, 1987, California; 1988, U.S. District Court, Central District of California. *Education:* Northwestern University (B.S., Journalism, 1984; J.D., 1987). *Member:* Los Angeles County Bar Association (Member, Barristers; Barristers Executive Committee, 1989-1991; Co-Chair, Judicial Forum Steering Committee, 1988-1989); State Bar of California (Member, Sections on: Litigation; Business Law); Sickle Cell Research Foundation (Member, Board of Directors, 1992—; Second Vice President, 1994—). ***PRACTICE AREAS:*** Litigation; Real Estate Law; Attorney Malpractice; Unfair Trade Practices; Trade Secrets Law.

**ALAN J. GORDEE,** born Boston, Massachusetts, January 5, 1961; admitted to bar, 1987, California; 1988, U.S. District Court, Central District of California; 1989, U.S. Court of Appeals, Ninth Circuit; 1992, U.S. District Court, Southern District of California; 1993, Massachusetts. *Education:* Yale University (B.A., 1983); Boston University (J.D., cum laude, 1987). Associate Editor, American Journal of Law and Medicine, 1985-1987. *Member:* Orange County and American Bar Associations; State Bar of California. (Resident, Irvine Office). ***PRACTICE AREAS:*** Litigation.

**PAMELA L. ANDES,** born Anaheim, California, June 25, 1963; admitted to bar, 1988, California. *Education:* University of Southern California (B.S., magna cum laude, 1985); Loyola University of Los Angeles (J.D., magna cum laude, 1988). Member: Order of the Coif; St. Thomas More Law Honor Society. Member: 1986-1988, Executive Editor, 1987-1988, Loyola of Los Angeles Law Review. *Member:* State Bar of California. (Resident, Irvine Office). ***PRACTICE AREAS:*** Real Estate and Environmental.

*(This Listing Continued)*

**ALLEN, MATKINS, LECK, GAMBLE & MALLORY LLP,**
Los Angeles—Continued

**REBECCA L. GUNDZIK,** born Redstone Arsenal, Alabama, November 15, 1963; admitted to bar, 1988, California. *Education:* University of California at Berkeley (B.A., 1985); University of Southern California (J.D., 1988). Quarter Finalist, Hale Moot Court Honors Competition. *Member:* Los Angeles County Bar Association; State Bar of California. *PRACTICE AREAS:* Litigation.

**ADELA CARRASCO,** born Los Angeles, California, May 22, 1963; admitted to bar, 1989, California; 1992, U.S. District Court, Central District of California. *Education:* Stanford University (B.A., 1985); Boalt Hall School of Law, University of California (J.D., 1988). *Member:* Los Angeles, Orange County and American Bar Associations; Hispanic Bar Association of Orange County (Board of Directors, 1992). (Resident, West Los Angeles Office). *LANGUAGES:* Spanish. *PRACTICE AREAS:* Commercial Litigation.

**MARTHA K. GUY,** born Muskogee, Oklahoma, June 4, 1957; admitted to bar, 1983, California. *Education:* University of California at Santa Barbara (B.A., with honors, 1979); Hastings College of Law, University of California (J.D., 1983). Note and Comment Editor, Hastings Law Journal, 1982-1983. Author: "The Public Trust Doctrine and California Water Law: National Audubon Society v. Department of Water and Power," 33 Hastings Law Journal 653. Extern to Hon. Allen E. Broussard, Justice, California Supreme Court, 1982-1983. Clerkship, Hon. Peter W. Bowie, Bankruptcy Court, 1992. *Member:* San Diego County and American Bar Associations; The State Bar of California; San Diego Bankruptcy Forum. (Resident, San Diego Office). *PRACTICE AREAS:* Commercial Real Estate Leasing; Secured Real Estate Financing; Bankruptcy and Creditor's Rights; Real Estate.

**GEORGE W. KUNEY,** born San Francisco, California, July 20, 1964; admitted to bar, 1989, California, U.S. District Courts, Northern, Eastern, Central and Southern Districts of California, U.S. District Court, District of Arizona and U.S. Court of Appeals, Ninth Circuit. *Education:* University of California at Santa Cruz (B.A., with honors in Economics, 1986); Hastings College of Law, University of California (J.D., cum laude, 1989). Adjunct Instructor, Legal Writing and Research and Moot Court, Hastings College of Law, 1991-1993. *Member:* State Bar of California; Bar Association of San Diego; American Bar Association (Sections of Business Law and Litigation); San Diego Bankruptcy Forum; American Bankruptcy Institute; Commercial Law League; Financial Lawyers Conference; California Bankruptcy Journal Editorial Board. (Resident, San Diego Office). *PRACTICE AREAS:* Bankruptcy, Insolvency, Reorganization; Commercial Law and Litigation.

**DANIEL L. GOODKIN,** born Los Angeles, California, January 18, 1961; admitted to bar, 1987, California and U.S. District Court, Central District of California. *Education:* Claremont Men's College; University of California at Los Angeles (B.A., 1983); Loyola Marymount University (J.D., 1987). *Member:* Beverly Hills, Los Angeles County and American Bar Associations; State Bar of California. *PRACTICE AREAS:* General Real Estate Litigation; Construction Litigation; Real Estate Finance Litigation; Landlord Tenant Litigation; Bankruptcy.

**CATHERINE M. PAGE,** born Kirkbymoorside, England, March 22, 1957; admitted to bar, 1990, California. *Education:* University of Hull, England (B.Sc., with honors, 1978); University of Toledo (J.D., summa cum laude, 1990). Order of the Coif. Member, 1988-1990 and Editor-in-Chief, 1989-1990, University of Toledo Law Review. Author: Note, "United States v. Kozminski: Involuntary Servitude - A Standard at Last," 20 University of Toledo Law Review 1023 (1989). *Member:* Orange County and American Bar Associations; State Bar of California. (Resident, Irvine Office). *PRACTICE AREAS:* Litigation.

**SCOTT P. SCHOMER,** born Nantucket Island, Massachusetts, August 29, 1962; admitted to bar, 1990, California. *Education:* Western Michigan University (B.S., 1985); Boston University (J.D., 1990). *Member:* State Bar of California; American Bar Association (Member, Litigation Section). *PRACTICE AREAS:* Commercial Litigation.

**KELLI L. FULLER,** born Evanston, Illinois, December 21, 1959; admitted to bar, 1989, California and U.S. District Court, Southern, Central and Eastern Districts of California. *Education:* Sonoma State University (B.S., 1986); McGeorge School of Law (J.D., with Great Distinction, 1989). Order of the Coif. Member, Order of the Barristers. Recipient, American Jurisprudence Awards in Criminal Law and Evidence. *Member:* San Diego County and American Bar Associations; California and San Diego Bankruptcy Forums. (Resident, San Diego Office). *PRACTICE AREAS:* Commercial Litigation; Bankruptcy and Creditor's Rights.

**LESLIE TUCKER FISCHER,** born Durham, North Carolina, July 15, 1965; admitted to bar, 1990, California. *Education:* Stanford University (A.B., 1987); University of California School of Law, Los Angeles (J.D., 1990). *Member:* Orange County and American Bar Associations; State Bar of California. (Resident, Irvine Office). *PRACTICE AREAS:* Corporate Securities; General Corporate.

**MICHAEL J. KIELY,** born Phoenix, Arizona, March 14, 1964; admitted to bar, 1989, California. *Education:* Georgetown University (B.S.B.A., 1986); University of California School of Law, Los Angeles (J.D., cum laude, 1989). Associate Editor, University of California at Los Angeles Law Review. Co-Author: Chapter 5A, Lease Takeover Agreements, Current Leasing Law and Techniques (Matthew Bender 1995); "Organizing and Planning the Project," (California Real Estate and Law Practice, Vol. 12, Ch. 415, 1996). *Member:* Los Angeles County Bar Association; State Bar of California. *PRACTICE AREAS:* Real Estate Transactions.

**DAVID ADAM SWARTZ,** born Great Neck, New York, March 4, 1966; admitted to bar, 1991, California and U.S. District Court, Central District of California. *Education:* Wharton School, University of Pennsylvania (B.S., in Economics, 1988); University of California at Los Angeles (J.D., 1991). *Member:* Los Angeles County, Beverly Hills and American Bar Associations; State Bar of California. (Resident, West Los Angeles Office). *PRACTICE AREAS:* Litigation; Transactional Real Estate; Leasing.

**RALPH H. WINTER,** born Santa Monica, California, March 3, 1962; admitted to bar, 1991, California. *Education:* Santa Clara University (B.S.C., 1984); Notre Dame University (J.D., cum laude, 1991); The Concannon Programme of International Law, Notre Dame University, London, England (1990). Articles Editor, Notre Dame Journal of Law, Ethics and Public Policy, 1990-1991. Certified Public Accountant, California, 1987. *Member:* Orange County and American Bar Associations; State Bar of California. (Resident, Irvine Office). *PRACTICE AREAS:* Corporate; Tax.

**MICHAEL S. GREGER,** born Lynwood, California, January 27, 1966; admitted to bar, 1991, California, U.S. District Court, Central, Eastern and Southern District of California and U.S. Court of Appeals, Ninth Circuit. *Education:* California State University at Fullerton (B.A., 1988); Southwestern University School of Law (J.D., magna cum laude, 1991). Articles Editor, Southwestern University Law Review, 1990-1991. Southwestern Moot Court Honors Program, 1989-1990. Author: "Preliminary Questions of Fact for the Judge: The Standard of Proof for Pretrial Admissibility Problems," 20 Southwestern L. Rev. 453 (1991). *Member:* Orange County and American Bar Associations; State Bar of California. (Resident, Irvine Office). *PRACTICE AREAS:* Litigation; Bankruptcy.

**A. KRISTINE FLOYD,** born Sacramento, California, March 31, 1966; admitted to bar, 1991, California. *Education:* University of Southern California (B.A., magna cum laude, 1988); Duke University (J.D., with high honors, 1991). Phi Beta Kappa. *Member:* Orange County Bar Association; State Bar of California. (Resident, Irvine Office). *PRACTICE AREAS:* Litigation.

**ROBERT A. LURIE,** born Los Angeles, California, October 2, 1965; admitted to bar, 1991, California. *Education:* University of California at Berkeley (B.S. with high honors, 1987); University of California at Los Angeles School of Law (J.D., 1991). Order of the Coif; Phi Beta Kappa; Beta Gamma Sigma. Recipient, American Jurisprudence Award in Bankruptcy. *Member:* Los Angeles County and Beverly Hills Bar Associations; State Bar of California. (Resident, West Los Angeles Office). *PRACTICE AREAS:* Real Estate.

**SUSAN G. SPIRA,** born Houston, Texas, February 11, 1963; admitted to bar, 1990, California and U.S. District Court, Central and Northern Districts of California. *Education:* University of California, Los Angeles (B.A., 1985); University of Pittsburgh, Institute of Shipboard Education (Semester at Sea); Loyola University of Los Angeles (J.D., 1989); University of San Diego, Institute of International and Comparative Law, London, England. *Member:* Los Angeles County and American Bar Associations; State Bar of California; Los Angeles Bankruptcy Forum; Financial Lawyers' Conference; Women Lawyers of Los Angeles Association. *PRACTICE AREAS:* Bankruptcy/Creditors' Rights (80%, 40); Receiverships (20%, 10).

**CYNTHIA ANN EDER,** born New York, N.Y., August 23, 1962; admitted to bar, 1992, California. *Education:* Pace University (B.A., 1984); University of Southern California (J.D., 1992). *Member:* Los Angeles County (Chair, General Real Estate Law Subsection) and American Bar Associations; State Bar of California. *PRACTICE AREAS:* Real Estate.

*(This Listing Continued)*

**MICHAEL A. ALVARADO,** born Los Angeles, California, December 30, 1965; admitted to bar, 1992, California. *Education:* University of California at Los Angeles (B.A., 1989); Stanford University (J.D., 1992). *Member:* Orange County Bar Association; State Bar of California. (Resident, Irvine Office). **PRACTICE AREAS:** Real Estate.

**HADAR GONEN GOLDSTEIN,** born Los Angeles, California, December 10, 1967; admitted to bar, 1992, California. *Education:* University of California at Los Angeles (B.A., 1989); University of Southern California (J.D., 1992). Member, Computer/Tax Journal. **PRACTICE AREAS:** Real Estate Transactions.

**MARY KAY RUCK,** born Massillon, Ohio, October 1, 1965; admitted to bar, 1992, Georgia and U.S. District Court, Northern and Middle Districts of Georgia; 1993, California; U.S. District Court, Central and Southern Districts of California; 1995, Colorado. *Education:* Wittenberg University (B.A., 1987); University of Michigan (J.D., 1992). *Member:* State Bar of Georgia; State Bar of California; Orange County, Colorado and American Bar Associations. (Resident, Irvine Office). **PRACTICE AREAS:** Employment Law.

**ERIC J. SHELBY,** born Mill Valley, California, February 19, 1966; admitted to bar, 1992, California. *Education:* University of California at Berkeley (B.A., 1988); University of California at Davis (J.D., 1992). Extern to the Honorable Richard Gadbois, U.S. District Court, Central District of California. *Member:* Los Angeles County and Beverly Hills Bar Associations; State Bar of California. (Resident, West Los Angeles Office). **PRACTICE AREAS:** Real Estate.

**SUSAN E. GRAHAM,** born Newport Beach, California, June 27, 1964; admitted to bar, 1989, California. *Education:* University of California, Los Angeles (B.A. Economics, 1986); Loyola Law School (J.D., 1989). *Member:* Orange County and American Bar Assns.; State Bar of California (Member, Real Property Section). (Resident, Irvine Office). **PRACTICE AREAS:** Real Estate Transactional Practice.

**MARTIN L. TOGNI,** born King City, California, March 13; admitted to bar, 1988, California; U.S. District Court, Central, Northern, Southern and Eastern Districts of California; U.S. Court of Appeals, Ninth Circuit. *Education:* California State University at Fresno (B.A., 1985); University of Notre Dame (J.D., 1988). Phi Kappa Phi. Member, Federalist Society, 1986-1988. Co-Author: Subletting and Assignments, After Kendall," Los Angeles Daily Journal, March, 10, 1989. *Member:* San Diego County Bar Association; State Bar of California; International Council of Shopping Centers. (Resident, San Diego Office). **LANGUAGES:** Romansch and Spanish. **PRACTICE AREAS:** Real Estate.

**DAVID T. HATHAWAY,** born Pasadena, California, May 16, 1967; admitted to bar, 1993, California. *Education:* London School of Economics, London, England; University of California at Berkeley (B.A., with honors, 1989); Loyola Law School (J.D., 1993). Semi-finalist, Scott Moot Court Competition, 1992. Member 1990-1993, Officer 1992 and Co-Chair 1993, Environmental Law Society. *Member:* Los Angeles County and American Bar Associations; State Bar of California. **PRACTICE AREAS:** Litigation.

**CHRISTOPHER G. LUND,** born Brooklyn, New York, November 2, 1962; admitted to bar, 1992, California. *Education:* University of Southern California (B.S., 1986); Loyola Law School (J.D., 1992). Certified Public Accountant, California, 1990. *Member:* Los Angeles County and American Bar Associations; State Bar of California. (Resident, Irvine Office). **PRACTICE AREAS:** Real Estate Transactions.

**LORAINE L. PEDOWITZ,** born Santa Monica, California, August 7, 1959; admitted to bar, 1985, California and U.S. District Court, Southern District of California; 1987, U.S. District Court, Central District of California. *Education:* University of California at San Diego (B.A., cum laude, 1981); Boalt Hall School of Law, University of California at Berkeley (J.D., 1985). Regent's Scholar. *Member:* San Diego County Bar Association; State Bar of California; Lawyers Club of San Diego. (Resident, San Diego Office). **PRACTICE AREAS:** Bankruptcy/Creditors' Rights.

**RANDY J. MYRICKS,** born Milwaukee, Wisconsin, January 20, 1965; admitted to bar, 1993, California. *Education:* University of Wisconsin at Madison (B.B.A., 1986); University of Minnesota at Minneapolis (J.D., 1992). Journal of Law & Inequality. **PRACTICE AREAS:** Real Property.

**JOHN G. PIANO,** born Rochester, New York, March 11, 1967; admitted to bar, 1992, California and U.S. District Court, Central District of California. *Education:* State University of New York at Buffalo (B.A., magna cum laude, 1989); Cornell University (J.D., 1992). Phi Beta Kappa; Phi Alpha Delta. *Member:* Los Angeles County (Member: Business and Corporations Law; Barristers) and American (Member, Business Law Section) Bar Associations; State Bar of California.

**MARK J. HATTAM,** born Oakland, California, April 30, 1957; admitted to bar, 1994, California. *Education:* University of Colorado (B.A., 1982); Loyola University of Los Angeles (J.D., 1994). Order of the Coif. Member, St. Thomas More Law Honor Society. *Member:* San Diego County Bar Association; State Bar of California. (Resident, San Diego Office). **PRACTICE AREAS:** Litigation.

**MICHAEL R. FARRELL,** born Flushing, New York, June 2, 1967; admitted to bar, 1994, California. *Education:* Yale University (B.A., 1989); University of Southern California (J.D., 1994). Interdisciplinary Law Journal. Major Tax Planning Journal. *Member:* Los Angeles County Bar Association; State Bar of California. **PRACTICE AREAS:** Litigation.

**STEPHEN J. KEPLER,** born Palo Alto, California, September 16, 1965; admitted to bar, 1991, California. *Education:* University of California at Los Angeles (B.A., 1987); Boalt Hall School of Law, University of California at Berkeley (J.D., 1991). Recipient: Jurisprudence Award in Contracts. Adjunct Professor, University of California at Irvine, Graduate School of Management, 1995—. Adjunct Professor, Western State Law School, 1993-1995. (Resident, Irvine Office). **PRACTICE AREAS:** Litigation and Employment Law.

**STEVE WELLINGTON,** born St. Louis, Missouri, April 2, 1961; admitted to bar, 1994, California. *Education:* San Diego State University (B.S., summa cum laude, 1984); University of San Diego (J.D., magna cum laude, 1994). *Member:* San Diego County Bar Association; State Bar of California. (Resident, San Diego Office). **PRACTICE AREAS:** Real Estate.

**SALLY S. COSTANZO,** born Philadelphia, Pennsylvania, March 30, 1958; admitted to bar, 1994, California. *Education:* University of California at Santa Cruz (B.A., with highest honors, 1980; Ph.D., 1990); University of California at San Diego (M.A., 1982); University of California at Los Angeles School of Law (J.D., 1994). Law Review. American Jurisprudence Award in Constitutional Law. Author: *"Jury Decision Making in the Capital Penalty Phase:* Legal Assumptions, Empirical Findings, and a Research Agenda," Law and Human Behavior (1992); *"The Death Penalty:* Public Opinions, Supreme Court Decisions, and Juror Perspectives," Chapter in Violence and the Law (1994); *"Life or Death Decisions:* An Analysis of Capital Jury Decision-Making Under the Special Issues Sentencing Framework," Law and Human Behavior (1994); *"Deciding to Take a Life:* Capital Juries, Sentencing Instructions, and the Jurisprudence of Death," Journal of Social Issues (1994). (Resident, Irvine Office). **PRACTICE AREAS:** Employment Law.

**ANN MARIE MAAS,** born La Mesa, California, January 17, 1967; admitted to bar, 1990, California and U.S. District Court, Southern District of California. *Education:* Brigham Young University (B.A., 1987; J.D., 1990). Phi Delta Phi. Order of the Barrister. Member, Board of Advocates. Director, Second Year Moot Court Program, 1989-1990. *Member:* State Bar of California. (Resident, San Diego Office). **PRACTICE AREAS:** Real Estate.

**TODD E. WHITMAN,** born New York, N.Y., December 28, 1967; admitted to bar, 1994, California. *Education:* University of Michigan (B.B.A., with distinction, 1989); University of Southern California (J.D., 1994). *Member:* Los Angeles County Bar Association. **PRACTICE AREAS:** Litigation.

**ALLISON L. MALIN,** born Los Angeles, California, January 16, 1965; admitted to bar, 1990, California, U.S. Court of Appeals, Ninth Circuit and U.S. District Court, Central District of California; 1992, Colorado and District of Columbia; 1993, U.S. Court of Appeals, Tenth Circuit and U.S. District Court, District of Colorado; 1995, U.S. District Court, Southern, Northern and Eastern Districts of California. *Education:* University of California at Berkeley (B.A., 1986); University of Southern California (J.D., 1990). Phi Alpha Delta. Recipient, American Jurisprudence Award for Civil Procedure. *Member:* Beverly Hills (Member, Litigation Section), Los Angeles County (Member, Litigation Section) and American (Member, Sections on: Litigation; Environmental; Trademark; Business Law; Securities) Bar Associations; State Bar of California; Los Angeles Women Lawyers Association. (Resident, West Los Angeles Office). **PRACTICE AREAS:** Real Estate; Natural Resources; Civil Trial; Environmental Law; General Practice.

**REON ROSKI-AMENDOLA,** born Los Angeles, California, March 6, 1964; admitted to bar, 1994, California and U.S. District Court, Southern District of California. *Education:* University of Southern California (B.A., 1986); Loyola University of Los Angeles (J.D., 1994). (Resident, West Los

*(This Listing Continued)*

**ALLEN, MATKINS, LECK, GAMBLE & MALLORY LLP,**
Los Angeles—Continued

Angeles Office). **LANGUAGES:** Chinese. **PRACTICE AREAS:** Real Estate.

**ALLISON FONG GREENBERG,** born Los Angeles, California, February 8, 1964; admitted to bar, 1995, California. *Education:* University of California, Los Angeles (B.S.Ch.E., cum laude, 1986); Loyola Law School, Los Angeles (J.D., cum laude, 1995). Order of the Coif. *Member:* State Bar of California. (Resident, Irvine Office). **PRACTICE AREAS:** Real Estate; Environmental.

**JEFFREY MANNISTO,** born Sandusky, Ohio, September 13, 1966; admitted to bar, 1996, California. *Education:* University of Texas (B.B.A., 1989); University of Mississippi (J.D., magna cum laude, 1995); New York University (LL.M. in Taxation, 1996). Certified Public Accountant, Texas, 1991. Phi Kappa Phi. Robert C. Khayat Scholarship Award. Managing Editor, Mississippi Law Journal, 1994-1995. Author: Comment, *Mississippi Limited Liability Companies: Potential Exposure Under Federal and State Securities Laws,* 64 Mississippi Law Journal 173 (1994). *Member:* State Bar of California. (Resident, Irvine Office). **PRACTICE AREAS:** Taxation, Estate Planning and Business Organization.

**PAMELA M. EVERETT,** born Los Angeles, California, September 26, 1962; admitted to bar, 1996, California. *Education:* University of Nevada (B.A., 1992); University of San Diego (J.D., 1995). *Member,* San Diego Law Review. 1st Place John M. Winters Moot Court Competition. Oral Advocacy Specialist. **PRACTICE AREAS:** Real Estate; Bankruptcy.

**JEFFREY N. STRUG,** born Halifax, Nova Scotia, Canada, October 11, 1969; admitted to bar, 1995, Nova Scotia; 1997, California. *Education:* University of Western Ontario, Canada (B.A., 1990); Dalhousie University (LL.B., 1994); New York University (LL.M., Tax, 1996). Member, Domus Legis Society, 1991-1994. License: Nova Scotia Barrister and Solicitor (June 1994) (Licensed under the Nova Scotia Barristers' Society) Nova Scotia, Canada. *Member:* Nova Scotia Barristers' Society; Canadian Bar Association. **PRACTICE AREAS:** Tax.

**KATHRYN D. HORNING,** born Altadena, California, July 7, 1959; admitted to bar, 1996, California. *Education:* University of California, San Diego (B.A., 1982); University of San Diego 9J.D., 1996). Order of the Coif. Editor-in-Chief, San Diego Law Review, 1995-1996. Author: "The End of Innocence: The Effect of California's Recreational Use Statute on Children at Play," San Diego Law Review, Vol. 32:3 (1995). **PRACTICE AREAS:** Litigation; Bankruptcy.

**JORDAN FISHMAN,** born Los Angeles, California, December 19, 1968; admitted to bar, 1996, California. *Education:* University of Pennsylvania (B.S., 1991); Yale University School of Management (M.P.P.M., 1994); Hastings College of the Law, University of California, San Francisco (J.D., 1996). (Resident, West Los Angeles Office). **PRACTICE AREAS:** Real Estate.

**TRACY L SILVA,** born Oklahoma City, Oklahoma, May 30, 1963; admitted to bar, 1996, California. *Education:* University of Texas, Austin (B.A., 1986); Southern Methodist University (J.D., cum laude, 1996). Order of the Coif; Phi Delta Phi. Member, 1994-1996 and Articles Editor, 1995-1996, Southern Methodist University Law Review. Author: Comment, "Dial '1-900-Pervert' and Other Statutory Measures That Provide Public Notification of Sex Offenders," 48 Southern Methodist University Law Review 1962 (1995). *Member:* American Bar Association. (Resident, Irvine Office). **PRACTICE AREAS:** Litigation.

**FRANCIS N. SCOLLAN,** born Scott AFB, Illinois, December 30, 1969; admitted to bar, 1996, California. *Education:* University of California at Berkeley (B.A., 1992); Boalt Hall School of Law, University of California, Berkeley (J.D., 1996). *Member:* State Bar of California. **PRACTICE AREAS:** Litigation.

**DARREN A. MANIBOG,** born Los Angeles, California, July 3, 1970; admitted to bar, 1996, California. *Education:* University of Southern California (B.A., 1993); Boalt Hall school of Law, University of California, Berkeley (J.D., 1996). Senior Editor, Asian Law Journal. Member, Moot Court Board.

**VEENA D. PERSAUD,** born San Francisco, California, August 22, 1967; admitted to bar, 1996, California. *Education:* University of California, Davis (B.S., 1990); University of California, Berkeley (J.D., 1996). **LANGUAGES:** French. **PRACTICE AREAS:** Land Use; Real Estate; Environmental Law.

*(This Listing Continued)*

CAA458B

*OF COUNSEL*

**JOHN G. DAVIES,** born San Diego, California, June 28, 1934; admitted to bar, 1963, California. *Education:* University of Southern California (B.A., 1956); University of California at Berkeley (LL.B., 1962). Order of the Coif; Phi Delta Phi; Lambda Alpha. Note and Comment Editor, California Law Review, 1961-1962. Law Clerk to the Hon. Roger J. Traynor, Associate Justice of the California Supreme Court, 1962-1963. Adjunct Professor/Professor, Western State Law School, 1970-1977. Chairman, San Diego Planning Commission, 1980-1983. President, San Diego Centre City Development Corporation, 1987-1992. Member, The Regents of the University of California, 1992—. Judicial Appointments Secretary to Governor Pete Wilson, Jan. 1995—. [With U.S. Navy, 1956-1959]. (Resident, San Diego Office). **PRACTICE AREAS:** Probate and Estates.

**JOE M. DAVIDSON,** born Lubbock, Texas, May 26, 1955; admitted to bar, 1979, California and U.S. District Court, Central District of California; 1992, U.S. District Court, Southern District of California. *Education:* University of Southern California (B.S. magna cum laude, 1976); Loyola University of Los Angeles (J.D., 1979). Beta Gamma Sigma. *Member:* San Diego County (Business Law Section) and American (Corporate, Banking and Business Law Sections) Bar Associations; State Bar of California (Business Law Section). (Resident, San Diego Office). **PRACTICE AREAS:** Corporate Law.

**MICHAEL J. MURPHY,** born Inglewood, California, August 7, 1957; admitted to bar, 1984, California. *Education:* Whittier College (B.A., with honors, 1979); Stanford University (M.B.A., 1983; J.D., 1983); New York University (LL.M., 1989). *Member:* State Bar of California; American Bar Association. **PRACTICE AREAS:** Tax.

REFERENCE: Wells Fargo Bank (Los Angeles Main Office).

---

## ALLEN, RHODES, SOBELSOHN & JOHNSON, LLP

*Established in 1973*

**10866 WILSHIRE BOULEVARD, SUITE 200**
**LOS ANGELES, CALIFORNIA 90024**
*Telephone: 310-475-0875; 213-879-9660*

*Santa Barbara, California Office:* 125 East De La Guerra, 2nd Floor.
Telephone: 805-965-5236.

*Workers Compensation, Subrogation, Insurance Law. Employment Law and Appellate Practice.*

*MEMBERS OF FIRM*

**BERNARD SOBELSOHN,** born Brooklyn, New York, October 27, 1943; admitted to bar, 1968, California. *Education:* Columbia University (A.B., 1964; LL.B., 1967); Columbia Business School (M.B.A., 1967). Member, Columbia Law School Board of Visitors. *Member:* Los Angeles County and American (Chairman, ABA Committee on Workers' Compensation, 1979-1981) Bar Associations; State Bar of California. (Certified Specialist, Workers Compensation Law, The State Bar of California Board of Legal Specialization).

**MICHAEL E. JOHNSON,** born Oakland, California, June 26, 1948; admitted to bar, 1973, California and U.S. District Court, Northern District of California. *Education:* University of San Francisco (B.S., 1970); Hastings College of Law, University of California (J.D., 1973). Member, Moot Court Board, 1972-1973. *Member:* Santa Barbara County and American Bar Associations; State Bar of California. (Resident, Santa Barbara Office).

*OF COUNSEL*

**DAVID B. ALLEN,** born Hyrum, Utah, June 9, 1931; admitted to bar, 1959, California, U.S. District Court, Southern District of California and Utah. *Education:* Utah State University; University of Utah (B.A., with honors, 1955); Stanford University (LL.B., 1958). Deputy Attorney General of State of California, 1958-1960. *Member:* Los Angeles County and American Bar Associations; State Bar of California; Utah State Bar. (Also practicing individually, Lexington, Kentucky).

**J. RICHARD RHODES,** born Glendale, California, September 27, 1929; admitted to bar, 1968, California. *Education:* University of California at Los Angeles (B.A., 1951); University of San Fernando Valley (J. D., 1967). *Member:* State Bar of California; American Bar Association. (Certified Specialist, Workers' Compensation Law, The State Bar of California Board of Legal Specialization).

*(This Listing Continued)*

# PROFESSIONAL BIOGRAPHIES

## CALIFORNIA—LOS ANGELES

REPRESENTATIVE CLIENTS: Aetna Casualty & Surety Co.; Traveler's Insurance Co.; Golden Eagle Insurance Co.; Firm Solutions; Republic Indemnity Co.; Industrial Indemnity Co.; Highlands Insurance Co.; Transamerica Insurance Co.; Fireman's Fund Insurance Co.; Crawford & Co.; Home Insurance Co.; Regents of the University of California; Los Angeles Community College District; Las Virgenes Unified School District; Keenan & Associates; Kemper Insurance Co.; Rockwell International; Metropolitan Transit Authority; Marriott Corp.; United States Fidelity & Guaranty; County of Orange; County of San Luis Obispo; City of Los Angeles; City of Santa Maria; City of San Luis Obispo.
REFERENCE: Wells Fargo Bank.

## ALPERT, BARR AND GROSS
### A PROFESSIONAL LAW CORPORATION
### LOS ANGELES, CALIFORNIA
(See Encino)

*General Civil Trial and Appellate Practice. Business, Corporate, Banking, Estate Planning and Administration, Family Law, Arbitration and Mediation, Mobile Home Residency Law, and Governmental Relations and Administrative Hearings.*

## ALSCHULER GROSSMAN & PINES LLP
Established in 1952

**2049 CENTURY PARK EAST, THIRTY-NINTH FLOOR**
**LOS ANGELES, CALIFORNIA 90067-3213**
Telephone: 310-277-1226
Fax: 310-552-6077
Email: info@agplaw.com
URL: http://www.agplaw.com

*General Civil and Trial Practice in all State and Federal Courts. Corporation, Securities, Real Estate, Land Use, Entertainment Law, Taxation, Antitrust, Administrative, Financial Institutions, Insurance, Municipal, Probate and Professional Liability Defense.*

FIRM PROFILE: *For over 40 years Alschuler Grossman & Pines LLP has enjoyed a national reputation for vigorous and creative advocacy in complex business litigation and business transactions. This select group of professionals is committed to finding practical solutions which produce tangible and cost-effective results for clients. Their "hands-on" commitment to the practice of law sets Alschuler Grossman & Pines LLP apart from many other leading law firms. The scope of the firm's practice has led Alschuler Grossman & Pines LLP to establish relationships with leading law firms throughout the world through its founding membership in the Association of Commercial Lawyers International. These relationships give the firm the access necessary to represent clients' interests effectively in out-of-state and foreign jurisdictions.*

### MEMBERS OF FIRM

**LEON S. ALSCHULER** (1910-1987).

**DANIEL ALBERSTONE,** born Los Angeles, California, September 26, 1956; admitted to bar, 1982, California. *Education:* University of California at Los Angeles (B.A. in Economics, 1979); Southwestern University (J.D., 1982). *Member:* Century City, Los Angeles County and American Bar Associations; State Bar of California. *Email:* dalberstone@agplaw.com

**BRUCE D. ANDELSON,** born Los Angeles, California, May 4, 1950; admitted to bar, 1974, California. *Education:* Brown University, Phi Beta Kappa, Manning Scholar (A.B., magna cum laude, 1971); Stanford University (J.D., 1974). California State Fellow. Author: "Usury and Third-Party Transactions," Beverly Hills Bar Journal, 1975. *Member:* Beverly Hills and Century City Bar Associations; State Bar of California. *Email:* bandelson@agplaw.com

**JEFFREY C. BRIGGS,** born September 21, 1956; admitted to bar, 1981, California. *Education:* University of Minnesota (B.A., summa cum laude, 1978; J.D., cum laude, 1981). Phi Beta Kappa. Member, 1979-1980, and Note and Comment Editor, 1980-1981, University of Minnesota Law Review. President, Century City Bar Association, 1997—. *Member:* Los Angeles County and American Bar Associations; Association of Business Trial Lawyers (Treasurer, 1996-1997); State Bar of California. *Email:* jbriggs@agplaw.com

**MICHAEL J. BRILL, (P.C.),** born New York, N.Y., July 17, 1945; admitted to bar, 1974, New York; 1976, U.S. Tax Court; 1977, California. *Education:* Clark University (B.A., with honors, 1967); Brooklyn Law School (J.D., 1973). Member, Brooklyn Law Review, 1972-1973. *Member:* Beverly Hills, Century City (President, 1989; Governor, 1985-1990), Los Angeles County (Trustee, 1990) and American Bar Associations; State Bar of California. *Email:* mbrill@agplaw.com

**MICHAEL L. CYPERS,** born Los Angeles, California, August 17, 1956; admitted to bar, 1981, California. *Education:* University of California at Berkeley (A.B., with great distinction in general scholarship, 1978); Boalt Hall School of Law, University of California (J.D., 1981). Phi Beta Kappa. Member, Moot Court Board. Member, Advisory Board, The Fulfillment Fund. *Member:* Beverly Hills (Chair, Appellate Practice Committee, 1984-1986), Century City (Co-Chair, Professional Liability Section) and American (Member, Committee on Professional Liability Litigation) Bar Associations; State Bar of California. *Email:* mcypers@agplaw.com

**MELVYN B. FLIEGEL, (P.C.),** born Chelsea, Massachusetts, June 29, 1936; admitted to bar, 1962, California. *Education:* University of California at Los Angeles (A.B., with honors, 1958); Harvard University (J.D., 1961). Pi Gamma Mu. Author: "Delays, Interruptions & Suspensions of Work by the Government Under Fixed-Price Contracts," 36 Southern California Law Review 323, 1961. Attorney, U.S. Atomic Energy Commission, 1961-1963. Member, Panel of Arbitrators, American Arbitration Association. *Member:* Beverly Hills, Century City, Los Angeles County and American Bar Associations; State Bar of California; Association of Business Trial Lawyers. *Email:* mfliegel@agplaw.com

**ANDREW D. FRIEDMAN,** born Honolulu, Hawaii, December 4, 1958; admitted to bar, 1983, District of Columbia; 1986, California. *Education:* Wake Forest University (B.A., cum laude, 1980); George Washington University (J.D., with high honors, 1983). Order of the Coif. *Member:* Century City, Los Angeles County and American Bar Associations; State Bar of California. *Email:* afriedman@agplaw.com

**BRUCE A. FRIEDMAN, (P.C.),** born Los Angeles, California, May 22, 1950; admitted to bar, 1976, California. *Education:* Claremont Mens College (B.A., cum laude, 1972); George Washington University (J.D., with honors, 1975). Author: "Allocation Under Directors' and Officers' Liability Insurance," 6 International Ins. Law Review, 1995; "Insurance Fraud: Why It Might Be the S&L Scandal of the Nineties," Risk Management Magazine, 1993; "The Right to Independent Counsel," Litigation Journal, Section of Litigation, ABA, Vol. 12, No. 4, 1986. Contributing Author: California Continuing Education of the Bar, *Civil Procedure Before Trial,* 3d, "Involuntary Dismissal". *Member:* Century City and American Bar Associations; State Bar of California; Association of Business Trial Lawyers (President, 1993-1994 and Member, Board of Governors, 1986-1994). *Email:* bfriedman@agplaw.com

**DALE J. GOLDSMITH,** born Santa Monica, California, July 26, 1960; admitted to bar, 1985, California. *Education:* Yale University (B.A., cum laude, 1982); University of Chicago (J.D., 1985). Special Counsel, Mayor Richard Riordan's Real Estate Development Reform Committee, 1994. Member, Volunteer Lawyer's Committee of Progress, L.A. *Member:* Century City and Los Angeles County Bar Associations; State Bar of California. *Email:* dgoldsmith@agplaw.com

**MARSHALL B. GROSSMAN, (P.C.),** born Omaha, Nebraska, March 24, 1939; admitted to bar, 1965, California. *Education:* University of California at Los Angeles; University of Southern California (B.S.L. and LL.B., 1964). Order of the Coif; Phi Alpha Delta. Production Editor, Southern California Law Review, 1963-1964. Lecturer in Law, University of Southern California Law Center, 1966-1969. Author: "Class Actions: Prosecution and Defense," Continuing Education of The Bar, 1979. Commissioner, California Coastal Commission, 1981-1986. Member, Board of Directors: Public Counsel, 1973-1980; Bet Tzedek Legal Services, 1990—; United Way, 1992-1995; Jewish Big Brothers, 1995—. *Member:* Beverly Hills (Chair, Civil Practice and Procedure Committee, 1969-1970; Member, Board of Governors, 1970-1976), Century City, Los Angeles County and American Bar Associations; State Bar of California; Beverly Hills Barristers (President, 1972-1973); Association of Business Trial Lawyers (Member, Board of Governors, 1973-1975). *Email:* mgrossman@agplaw.com

**CAROLE E. HANDLER,** born New York, New York; admitted to bar, 1975, Pennsylvania; 1987, California. *Education:* Radcliffe College (A.B., 1957); University of Pennsylvania (M.S., 1963; J.D., 1975). Law Clerk to Judge Edmund B. Spaeth, Jr., Superior Court of Pennsylvania, 1975-1976. Author: "A Reconsideration of the Relevance and Materiality of the Preamble in Constitutional Interpretation," Cardozo Law Review, 1990; "The Information Superhighway in 1995: Proceeding With Caution," The Communications Lawyer, 1995. *Member:* Beverly Hills, Century City (Chair, Entertainment Section, 1996-1997), Los Angeles County (Chair, Antitrust Section, 1993-1994; Executive Committee, Antitrust Section, 1986—), New York State, Federal and American Bar Associations; State Bar of Califor-

*(This Listing Continued)*

CAA459B

**ALSCHULER GROSSMAN & PINES LLP, Los Angeles—**
*Continued*

nia; Association of Business Trial Lawyers; Copyright Society. *Email:* cehandler@agplaw.com

**GERALD B. KAGAN,** *(P.C.),* born Boston, Massachusetts, January 31, 1943; admitted to bar, 1967, Virginia and District of Columbia; 1969, California. *Education:* University of Massachusetts (A.B., cum laude with distinction, 1964); George Washington University School of Law (J.D., with honors, 1967). Trustee Scholar. Order of the Coif; Pi Sigma Alpha. Member, Board of Directors, United States-Mexico Chamber of Commerce (Pacific Chapter), 1993—. Member, Board of Directors, Los Angeles Venture Association, 1992—. President, Association of Commercial Lawyers International, 1994-1995. *Member:* Beverly Hills (Chairman, Environmental Law Committee, 1974-1976), Century City, Los Angeles County and American Bar Associations; State Bar of California. *Email:* jkagan@agplaw.com

**FRANK KAPLAN,** *(P.C.),* born New York, N.Y., December 15, 1946; admitted to bar, 1972, California. *Education:* University of Cincinnati (B.A., with high honors, 1968); University of Michigan (J.D., 1971). Phi Beta Kappa. Member, Pacific Southwest Regional Board of Anti-Defamation League. *Member:* Century City, Los Angeles County and American Bar Associations; State Bar of California; Association of Business Trial Lawyers. *Email:* fkaplan@agplaw.com

**KAREN KAPLOWITZ,** *(P.C.),* born New Haven, Connecticut, November 27, 1946; admitted to bar, 1972, California. *Education:* Barnard College (B.A., cum laude, 1968); University of Chicago (J.D., 1971). Phi Beta Kappa. *Member:* Century City, Los Angeles County and American (Chair, Employer-Employee Relations Committee, Torts and Insurance Practice Section) Bar Associations; State Bar of California; Women Lawyers Association of Los Angeles; Association of Business Trial Lawyers (President, 1996—; Member, Board of Governors, 1990—). *Email:* kkaplowitz@agplaw.com

**DANA N. LEVITT,** *(P.C.),* born Los Alamos, New Mexico, November 1, 1949; admitted to bar, 1977, California. *Education:* University of Massachusetts (B.A., summa cum laude, 1974); Duke University (J.D., 1977). Finalist, National Moot Court Championships. Recipient, Justice Lewis F. Powell, Jr. Medal for Excellence in Advocacy. *Member:* Century City, Los Angeles County and American Bar Associations; State Bar of California. *Email:* dlevitt@agplaw.com

**KENNETH S. MEYERS,** born Los Angeles, California, April 23, 1956; admitted to bar, 1981, California. *Education:* Pomona College (B.A., cum laude, 1978); University of California, Boalt Hall School of Law at Berkeley (J.D., 1981). Author: "Allocation Under Directors' and Officers' Liability Insurance," 6 International Ins. Law Review, 1995. *Member:* Century City Bar Association; State Bar of California. *Email:* kmeyers@agplaw.com

**BURT PINES,** *(P.C.),* born Burbank, California, May 16, 1939; admitted to bar, 1964, California. *Education:* University of Southern California (B.A., magna cum laude, 1960); New York University (J.D., 1963). Phi Beta Kappa; Order of the Coif. Root-Tilden Scholar. Associate Editor, New York University Law Review, 1962-1963. Author: "Obscenity Quagmire," 49 California State Bar Journal 509, 1974; "California Governmental Conflict of Interest Act: The Public Interest vs. The Right to Privacy," 49 Los Angeles Bar Journal 321, 1974; "More Active Role for Local Government in Anti-Trust Enforcement," 8 Southwestern University Law Review 505, 1976; "Non-Criminal Solutions for Minor Misdemeanor Complaints," 63 American Bar Association Journal 1208, 1977. Assistant U.S. Attorney, Los Angeles, California, 1964-1966. Los Angeles City Attorney, 1973-1981. Member: California Council on Criminal Justice, 1974-1981; California Crime Resistance Task Force, 1979-1981. Chair, California Commission on Personal Privacy, 1981-1982. Member, Board of Directors, Public Counsel, 1985-1987. *Member:* Century City, Los Angeles County and American (Member, Legal Advisory Committee on Television and Motion Pictures, 1973-1980) Bar Associations; State Bar of California; National Institute of Municipal Law Officers (Trustee, 1973-1981); California District Attorneys Association (Member, Board of Directors, 1979-1980). *Email:* bpines@agplaw.com

**GWYN QUILLEN,** born Los Angeles, California, July 18, 1962; admitted to bar, 1988, California. *Education:* University of Southern California (B.A., Economics, 1985; J.D., 1988). Order of the Coif. Executive Articles Editor, University of Southern California Law Review, 1987-1988. Law Clerk, Honorable Robert Boocheever, U.S. Court of Appeals, Ninth Circuit, 1988-1989. *Member:* Century City (Co-Chair, Professional Liability Section), Los Angeles County and American (Member, Committee on Law and Accounting, Business Law Section, 1994—) Bar Associations; State Bar of California. *Email:* gquillen@agplaw.com

**PAUL H. ROCHMES,** born Washington, D.C., October 28, 1946; admitted to bar, 1977, California. *Education:* University of Chicago (B.A., with honors, 1968; J.D., 1977). Order of the Coif. Author: "Amendment to 18 U.S.C. §3237 (b) Limits Ability of Federal Criminal Tax Defendants to Obtain Mandatory Change of Venue," Business Crime Commentary, No. 7, Sept. 1985. Faculty, Hastings Trial Advocacy Institute, 1985-1988. Member, Federal Indigent Defense Panel, 1990—. Assistant U.S. Attorney, Los Angeles, 1980-1983. *Member:* Century City and Los Angeles County Bar Associations; State Bar of California. *Email:* phrochmes@agplaw.com

**JOHN A. SCHWIMMER,** born New York, N.Y., February 14, 1958; admitted to bar, 1983, California. *Education:* Brown University (B.A., magna cum laude, 1980); Boalt Hall School of Law, University of California (J.D., 1983). Phi Beta Kappa; Order of the Coif. *Member:* Beverly Hills, Century City and Los Angeles County Bar Associations; State Bar of California; Association of Business Trial Lawyers. *Email:* jschwimmer@agplaw.com

**MICHAEL A. SHERMAN,** born New York, N.Y., August 23, 1956; admitted to bar, 1980, California; 1993, Arizona. *Education:* Columbia College (B.A., 1977); Boalt Hall School of Law, University of California (J.D., 1980). Harlan Fiske Stone Scholar. Co-author, Article, "Plaintiff's Counsel's Role in Representative Litigation", ABA Section of Litigation, 1982. Author: "Special Concerns of Class Action Plaintiffs in Bankruptcy Cases," Financial Lawyers Conference, November 1992. *Member:* Century City and Los Angeles County (Vice Chair, Subsection on Pre-Judgment Remedies) Bar Associations; Financial Lawyers Conference; Bankruptcy Study Group; Association of Business Trial Lawyers (Chair, Technology Litigation Section). *Email:* masherman@agplaw.com

**SANDRA G. SLON,** born New York, N.Y., June 25, 1948; admitted to bar, 1984, California. *Education:* Miami University, Ohio (B.A., cum laude, 1970); University of Colorado (M.A., 1974); Boalt Hall School of Law, University of California (J.D., 1984). Phi Beta Kappa. Officer and Director, Women's Network, Beverly Hills Chamber of Commerce. *Member:* Beverly Hills and Century City Bar Associations; State Bar of California; Women Lawyers Association of Los Angeles. *Email:* sslon@agplaw.com

**WILLIAM S. SMALL,** *(P.C.),* born Detroit, Michigan, December 7, 1949; admitted to bar, 1977, California. *Education:* Harvard University (A.B., cum laude, 1972); University of California at Los Angeles (J.D., 1977). Phi Beta Kappa. Author: "Real Estate Seller-Buyer," California Attorney's Damages Guide (California CEB 1984, 1986, 1987). Member, Advisory Commission on Real Property Insurance to the California State Senate Committee on Insurance and Indemnity, 1982-1989. *Member:* Beverly Hills, Century City, Los Angeles County and American Bar Associations; State Bar of California. *Email:* wsmall@agplaw.com

**PIERRE VOGELENZANG,** *(P.C.),* born Noordwijk, Netherlands; admitted to bar, 1972, Netherlands; 1981, California. *Education:* Harvard University; University of Leiden, Netherlands (LL.M., 1969); Tulane University of Louisiana (LL.M., 1970); Stanford University (J.D., 1980). Recipient, Hilman Oehlman Jr. Award. Member, Stanford Law Review, 1979-1980. Author: "Intercompany Transactions in California Combined Reports," 52 Tax Notes 343 (1991); "Second-Stage Apportionment of Unitary Income," 49 Tax Notes 335 (1990); "The Resequencing Aspect of Rev. Rul. 87-66: Applying Kimbell-Diamond to Reorganizations," Parts 1 & 2, 15 Intl. Tax J. 197, 335 (1989), published in revised form in 18 J. Real Est. Tax., 219, 332 (1991); "Notice 88-89: The Impact of the Uniform Capitalization Rules on the Foreign Investor's Interest Deduction," 18 Tax Mgt. Intl. J. 24 (1989); "Two Aspects of Article 115 E.C.C. Treaty," 18 Common Mkt. L. Rev. 169 (1981); "Foreign Sovereign Compulsion in American Antitrust Law," 33 Stanford Law Review 131, (1980). *Member:* Century City, Los Angeles County (Member, Executive Committee, Tax Section, 1992-1993; Chair, Subcommittee on Passthrough Entities, Tax Section, 1992-1993) and American Bar Associations; State Bar of California. *Email:* pvogelenzang@agplaw.com

**BRUCE WARNER,** *(P.C.),* born Los Angeles, California, January 15, 1944; admitted to bar, 1970, California. *Education:* University of California at Los Angeles (B.A., 1966); University of Southern California (J.D., 1969). Order of the Coif; Phi Alpha Delta. Associate Editor, Southern California Law Review, 1967-1969. Co-Author: "Uses and Abuses of Asset Protection Trusts," 41 Major Tax Planning, 1993. Editor, "Recent Developments in Bankruptcy," State Bar of California Annual Survey of Business Law, 1988—. *Member:* Beverly Hills (Member, Board of Governors, 1974-1975), Century City (Co-Chair, Debtor/Creditor Relations and Bankruptcy Com-

*(This Listing Continued)*

mittee, 1991—), Los Angeles County (Member, Executive Committee, Law Office Management Section, 1984-1986) and American Bar Associations; State Bar of California (Member, Standing Committee for Maintenance of Professional Competence, 1974-1978; Chair, 1977-1978; Member, Debtor/-Creditor Relations and Bankruptcy Subcommittee, Business Law Section, 1980-1981; 1990-1993); Beverly Hills Barristers, (Member, Board of Governors, 1970-1979); California Young Lawyers Association (Member, Board of Governors, 1974-1977; Vice-President, 1976-1977); Association of Business Trial Lawyers; Financial Lawyers Conference. *Email:* bwarner@agplaw.com

**KAREN AFRICK WOLFEN,** born Los Angeles, California, November 14, 1960; admitted to bar, 1986, California. *Education:* University of California at Los Angeles (B.A., magna cum laude, 1982; J.D., 1985). Member, University of California at Los Angeles Law Review, 1983-1985. *Member:* Century City and Los Angeles County Bar Associations; State Bar of California. *Email:* kwolfen@agplaw.com

**JOAN A. WOLFF,** born New York, N.Y., July 17, 1957; admitted to bar, 1983, California. *Education:* Brown University (A.B., 1979); University of California at Los Angeles (J.D., 1983). *Member:* Century City (Treasurer, 1996—) and Los Angeles County Bar Associations; State Bar of California. *Email:* jwolff@agplaw.com

## ASSOCIATES

**M. CRIS ARMENTA,** born Brooklyn, New York; admitted to bar, 1995, California. *Education:* University of California, Berkeley (B.A., 1989); Loyola Law School (J.D., 1994). Order of the Coif; Alpha Sigma Mu. Managing Editor, Loyola Law School Review, 1993-1994. Recipient, Dean's Service Award; National Hispanic Scholarship Fund Scholar; Law Clerk to the Honorable Robert J. Kelleher, U.S. District Court, Central District of California, 1994-1995. *Member:* Century City and American Bar Associations; State Bar of California; Mexican-American Bar Association; Women Lawyers Association of Los Angeles. *Email:* carmenta@agplaw.com

**BETTY BALES,** born Athens, Greece, March 9, 1963; admitted to bar, 1991, California. *Education:* University of California at Los Angeles (B.A., 1986; M.A., 1988); New York University (J.D., 1991). Phi Beta Kappa; Root-Tilden-Snow Scholar; Blaustein Fellow. *Member:* Century City Bar Association; State Bar of California. *Email:* bbales@agplaw.com

**JULIAN BREW,** born Durham, North Carolina, November 11, 1966; admitted to bar, 1990, California. *Education:* University of Miami (B.A., cum laude, 1987); University of Chicago (J.D., 1990). Phi Beta Kappa. *Member:* Century City and Los Angeles County Bar Associations; State Bar of California. *Email:* jbrew@agplaw.com

**REBECCA EDELSON,** born Fort Leavenworth, Kansas, February 26, 1961; admitted to bar, 1990, California. *Education:* University of Pennsylvania (B.A., 1983); University of Kent at Canterbury, England; University of California at Los Angeles School of Law (J.D., 1990). Member, Moot Court Team. *Member:* Beverly Hills, Century City, Los Angeles County and American Bar Associations; State Bar of California. *Email:* bedelson@agplaw.com

**YAEL FEINREICH,** born Petach-Tikva, Israel, February 11, 1970; admitted to bar, 1995, California. *Education:* University of California at Los Angeles (B.A., summa cum laude, 1992); University of California School of Law, Los Angeles (J.D., 1995). Phi Beta Kappa. Recipient: Florence Wilson Merit Scholarship. *Member:* Century City Bar Association; State Bar of California. *Email:* yael@agplaw.com

**GRANT E. FINKLE,** born Los Angeles, California, April 27, 1968; admitted to bar, 1994, California. *Education:* University of California at Los Angeles (B.A., magna cum laude, 1991; J.D., 1994). Order of the Coif. *Member:* Century City Bar Association; State Bar of California. *Email:* gfinkle@agplaw.com

**DONALD P. HARRIS,** born Queens, New York, December 1, 1964; admitted to bar, 1994, California. *Education:* California State University, Northridge (B.S., 1991); Loyola University of Los Angeles (J.D., 1994). *Member:* Century City and Langston Bar Associations; State Bar of California. *Email:* dharris@agplaw.com

**JOHNNIE A. JAMES,** born Compton, California, January 26, 1963; admitted to bar, 1989, California. *Education:* University of California at Los Angeles (B.A., 1986); New York University (J.D., 1989). Recipient, Ralph J. Bunche Academic Scholarship. Member, Mortar Board National Honor Society. Root-Tilden-Snow Scholar. Member, Board of Directors, 1996—, Executive Committee, 1996— and Co-Chair, Technology Committee, 1996—, Public Counsel. *Member:* Beverly Hills, Century City and Langston Bar Associations; State Bar of California. *Email:* jjames@agplaw.com

**CAROLINE S. LEE,** born Honolulu, Hawaii, April 23, 1968; admitted to bar, 1992, California. *Education:* Yale University (B.A., magna cum laude, with distinction, 1989); Boalt Hall School of Law, University of California (J.D., 1992). Associate Editor, California Law Review. *Member:* Century City, Los Angeles County and Korean-American Bar Associations; State Bar of California. *Email:* clee@agplaw.com

**JONATHAN A. LOEB,** born Los Angeles, California, September 2, 1967; admitted to bar, 1992, California. *Education:* University of California at Berkeley (B.A., 1989); University of Southern California (J.D., 1992). Phi Beta Kappa. Member, Southern California Law Review, 1990-1991. Extern, Honorable William Matthew Byrne, Jr., United States District Court Judge, 1991. *Member:* Century City, Los Angeles County and American Bar Associations; State Bar of California. *Email:* jloeb@agplaw.com

**DANA MILMEISTER,** born Hollywood, California, August 30, 1966; admitted to bar, 1993, California. *Education:* University of California at Los Angeles (B.A., 1988); University of Southern California (J.D., 1993). Semi-Finalist, Hale Moot Court Honors Program; Quarter-Finalist, National Moot Court Competition. *Member:* Century City and Los Angeles County Bar Associations; State Bar of California. *Email:* dmilmeister@agplaw.com

**JEFFREY H. MINTZ,** born Elizabeth, New Jersey, January 17, 1970; admitted to bar, 1994, California. *Education:* University of California at Berkeley (B.A., magna cum laude, 1991); University of California at Los Angeles School of Law (J.D., 1994). Phi Beta Kappa. *Member:* Century City and American Bar Associations; State Bar of California. *Email:* jmintz@agplaw.com

**MICHAEL A. TAITELMAN,** born Milwaukee, Wisconsin, June 22, 1966; admitted to bar, 1991, California. *Education:* University of California at Berkeley (B.A., 1988); Boalt Hall School of Law, University of California (J.D., 1991). *Member:* Century City, Los Angeles County and American Bar Associations; State Bar of California. *Email:* mtaitelman@agplaw.com

## OF COUNSEL

**STANLEY S. ARKIN,** born Los Angeles, California, February 28, 1938; admitted to bar, 1963, New York; 1973, California; 198 2, District of Columbia. *Education:* University of Southern California (A.B., magna cum laude, 1959); Harvard Law School (J.D., cum laude, 1962). Phi Beta Kappa; Phi Kappa Phi; Blue Key. Regular Columnist, "Business Crime," New York Law Journal, 1985—. Author: "The Presumption of General Damages in the Law of Constitutional Libel," 68 Columbia Law Review, December 1968; "Self-Regulation and Approaches To Maintaining Standards of Professional Integrity," 30 University of Miami Law Review, Summer, 1976, No. 4. Lead Author: *Business Crime,* (Six Volumes) Matthew Bender, 1981; *The Prevention and Prosecution of Computer and High Technology Crime* Matthew Bender, 1988. Contributing Author: Rico: Civil and Criminal Law and Strategy, Law Journal Seminars-Press, 1989-1991. Adjunct Associate Professor, New York University School of Law, Criminal Trial Advocacy, 1975-1985. Special Prosecutor in Connection with 1970 Prison Riots, New York City Department of Corrections, 1971-1972. Member, Advisory Committee on the Criminal Procedure Law, Judicial Conference of the State of New York, 1973-1980. *Member:* Association of the Bar of the City of New York (Chairman, Committee on Professional Discipline, 1986-1988; Chairman, 1970-1972, Committee on Criminal Courts, Law and Procedure); Century City, New York State (Chairman, Committee on Standards for Judicial Competence, 1975-1980) and American Bar Associations; State Bar of California; New York County Lawyers Association. Fellow, American College of Trial Lawyers. (Also Member, Arkin Schaffer & Kaplan, New York, New York).

**ERIC VAN GINKEL,** born Breda, The Netherlands, May 10, 1939; admitted to bar, 1973, New York; 1989, California. *Education:* University of Leyden Law School (J.D., 1964); Columbia University School of Law (J.D., 1969). Assistant Lecturer, University of Leyden Law School, 1964-1965, 1967. Associate, Project on European Legal Institutions, Columbia University School of Law, 1966. Member, Europa Institute, University of Leyden Law School, 1964-1967. Co-author: "Les Monopoles dans le Marche Commun, L'Article 37 du Traite de Rome," 1968. *Member:* Century City and American Bar Associations; State Bar of California. *LANGUAGES:* Dutch, French, German, Italian. *Email:* evanginkel@agplaw.com

*(This Listing Continued)*

ALSCHULER GROSSMAN & PINES LLP, Los Angeles—Continued

### LEGAL SUPPORT PERSONNEL

**DENISE J. GRIGST,** born Columbus, Ohio, August 3, 1952. *Education:* University of Cincinnati (B.A., 1974); Western State University, San Diego (J.D., 1978). Member: American Association of Law Libraries, 1981—; Southern California Association of Law Libraries, 1981—. Chair, Westside Law Librarians, 1986-1987. (Librarian). *Email:* dgrigst@agplaw.com

**W. JACK KESSLER,** born Seattle, Washington, April 8, 1950; admitted to bar, 1977, California. *Education:* Ambassador University (B.A., 1972); University of Southern California (M.B.A., 1977; J.D., 1977). Editor-in-Chief, Southern California Law Review, 1977. Editor, Major Tax Planning, 1981-1985. Recipient: Elijah Watts Sells Award; John F. Forbes Gold Medal. Certified Public Accountant, California, 1974. *Member:* Century City and American Bar Associations; State Bar of California; American Institute of CPAs; California Society of CPAs; Association of Professional Law Firm Managers (Secretary, 1994-1995). (Executive Director). *Email:* wjkessler@agplaw.com

---

## ALTMAN & SCHOEMAKER
### LOS ANGELES, CALIFORNIA
(See Encino)

*General Civil and Workers Compensation Defense, Trail and Appellate Practice. Commercial Collection and Enforcement of Judgements. Products Liability and Personal Injury.*

---

## ALVARADO, SMITH, VILLA & SANCHEZ
A PROFESSIONAL CORPORATION
611 WEST SIXTH STREET, SUITE 2650
**LOS ANGELES, CALIFORNIA 90017**
Telephone: 213-229-2554
Facsimile: 213-617-8966
URL: http://www.Alvarado-Smith.com

Newport Beach, California Office, 4695 MacArthur Court, Suite 800. 92658. Telephone: 714-955-1433. Fax: 714-955-1704.

*Sophisticated Business Transactions and Complex Litigation.*

FIRM PROFILE: *Alvarado, Smith, Villa & Sanchez is a diversified law firm made up of highly-skilled and experienced attorneys, representing clients engaged in sophisticated business transactions and complex litigation. The firm maintains offices in Newport Beach and Los Angeles and is well-positioned to service clients throughout the entire Southern California region.*

*The Firm's transactional department represents numerous real estate developers, corporate clients, governmental entities, financial institutions and mortgage lenders in connection with all aspects of commercial and residential real estate matters, loan originations, documentation and loan portfolio management. The Firm also represents various real estate developers, investors and manufacturers relative to transactions in Mexico. In addition, the Firm's litigation department has extensive experience handling routine and complex litigation matters pertaining to general commercial disputes, franchise, employment, construction defect litigation and financial institution actions, including director and officer professional liability, loan defaults, and foreclosure actions.*

*The Firm has achieved additional prominence through the extensive involvement of the Firm's attorneys in civic and philanthropic activities throughout Southern California.*

### RESIDENTS

**RAYMOND G. ALVARADO,** born Los Angeles, California, July 2, 1936; admitted to bar, 1972, California; U.S. District Court, Central District of California; U.S. Court of Appeals, Ninth Circuit; U.S. Supreme Court. *Education:* University of Southern California (B.A., 1961); London School of Economics; Southwestern University (J.D., 1970). Recipient, American Jurisprudence Awards for Evidence and Civil Procedure. Member: Mexican American Political Action Committee; Orange County Hispanic Chamber of Commerce; California Minority Counsel Program; Orange County Voting Inspires Participation; Board of Trustees of California Minority Counsel. *Member:* Los Angeles County, Orange County, Federal and American Bar Associations; State Bar of California; Los Angeles

*(This Listing Continued)*

County Mexican American Bar Association; Orange County Hispanic Bar Association. *PRACTICE AREAS:* Secured Transaction Litigation; Business Litigation.

**FERNANDO VILLA,** born Mazatlan, Mexico, March 23, 1957; admitted to bar, 1985, California and U.S. Court of Appeals, Ninth Circuit; 1987, U.S. District Court, Central District of California. *Education:* University of California at Los Angeles (B.A., magna cum laude, 1980); Boalt Hall School of Law, University of California (J.D., 1984). Pi Gamma Mu. *Member:* Los Angeles County and American Bar Associations; State Bar of California. *LANGUAGES:* Spanish. *SPECIAL AGENCIES:* California Department of Health Services; Los Angeles County Department of Public Works; Community Redevelopment Agency of Los Angeles; City of Los Angeles Fire Commission. *PRACTICE AREAS:* Environmental Law; Land Use Law; Local Government Law; Commercial Litigation; Real Estate Litigation.

**RAÚL F. SALINAS,** born Los Angeles, California, January 12, 1960; admitted to bar, 1986, California; 1987, U.S. District Court, Central District of California; 1991, U.S. Court of Appeals, Ninth Circuit and U.S. District Court, Northern and Southern Districts of California. *Education:* Loyola Marymount University (B.B.A., 1982); Georgetown University Law Center (J.D., 1985). Member and Team Captain, National Moot Court Team, Regional Championship, 1984-1985. Member, Jessup International Moot Court Team, 1983-1984. Extern, Justice Cruz Reynoso, California Supreme Court, 1984. Commissioner, State Bar Judicial Nominees Evaluation Commission, 1993—. *Member:* Los Angeles County and American (Member, Litigation Section) Bar Associations; State Bar of California; Mexican-American Bar Association; Association of Business Trial Lawyers. *LANGUAGES:* Spanish. *PRACTICE AREAS:* Commercial Law; Business Litigation.

**J. MICHELLE HICKEY,** admitted to bar, 1989, California, U.S. District Court, Central District of California and U.S. Court of Appeals, Ninth Circuit. *Education:* University of California at Los Angeles (B.A., cum laude, 1986); Boalt Hall School of Law, University of California (J.D., 1989). *PRACTICE AREAS:* Environmental Law; Litigation.

**FRANCES Q. JETT,** admitted to bar, 1995, California. *Education:* University of California (B.A., 1990); University of San Diego (J.D., 1994). *PRACTICE AREAS:* Business Litigation.

**SUSAN BADE HULL,** admitted to bar, 1991, California. *Education:* Claremont McKenna College (B.A. in Latin American Studies-Spanish, with honors, 1985); Loyola Law School, Los Angeles (J.D., 1990). *PRACTICE AREAS:* Environmental Law; Land Use Law.

---

**STEVEN M. LAWRENCE,** admitted to bar, 1990, California and U.S. District Court, Northern, Central and Eastern Districts of California; 1994, U.S. District Court, Southern District of California. *Education:* California State University at Los Angeles (B.A., 1981); University of California at Los Angeles (J.D., 1985). *PRACTICE AREAS:* Bankruptcy; Creditor Rights; Commercial Litigation.

**ROBERT W. BROWN, JR.,** born Los Angeles, California, June 13, 1949; admitted to bar, 1977, California. *Education:* Los Angeles City College (A.A., 1972); California State University at Los Angeles (B.S., 1974); University of California School of Law at Los Angeles (J.D., 1977). *PRACTICE AREAS:* Real Estate; Business; Banking.

**STEVEN C. YUNG,** born Hon Kong, November 5, 1966; admitted to bar, 1994, California, U.S. District Court, Central District of California and U.S. Court of Appeals, Ninth Circuit. *Education:* California State University at Los Angeles (B.S. cum laude, 1991); University of Southern California (J.D., 1994). *Member:* State Bar of California; Los Angeles County Bar Association. *PRACTICE AREAS:* Civil Litigation; Business Transactional.

(For biographical data on all personnel, see Professional Biographies at Newport Beach, California)

## DEAN V. AMBROSE
**1901 AVENUE OF THE STARS**
**SUITE 1551**
**LOS ANGELES, CALIFORNIA 90067**
Telephone: 310-785-9700
Fax: 310-556-1266

*Partnership, Real Estate, Corporate, Securities and General Business Law.*

**DEAN V. AMBROSE,** born Denver, Colorado, August 15, 1938; admitted to bar, 1965, California. *Education:* University of Denver (B.S., 1961; J.D., 1964). Phi Delta Phi. Member, University of Denver Law Journal, 1963-1964. Contributor "Advising California Partnerships," California Continuing Education of the Bar, 1975. *Member:* Beverly Hills (Member, Barristers Board of Governors, 1967-1970), Los Angeles County (Member: Executive Committee, Business and Corporations Law Section, 1984-1990; Chairman, Committee on Partnerships, 1984-1990) and American Bar Associations; The State Bar of California (Member, 1978-1981 and Chairman, 1980-1981), Partnerships and Unincorporated Business Associations Committee; Member, 1981-1984 and Secretary/Treasurer, 1983-1984, Executive Committee, Business Law Section. (Also of Counsel to Stein & Kahan, Santa Monica, California).

## ANANDA & KRAUSE
**LOS ANGELES, CALIFORNIA**
(See Westlake Village)

*Commercial Collections, Business and Real Estate Litigation, Creditors Rights, Bankruptcy and Estate Planning.*

## ANDERSEN, KELEHER & SPATA
**LOS ANGELES, CALIFORNIA**
(See Manhattan Beach)

*General Civil Litigation and Trial Practice, Eminent Domain, Inverse Condemnation, Land Use, Zoning, Environmental and Mobile Home Park Law, Real Property Litigation, General Liability and Insurance Law.*

## SANDRA JONES ANDERSON
**THIRTY SEVENTH FLOOR**
**777 SOUTH FIGUEROA STREET**
**LOS ANGELES, CALIFORNIA 90017-5800**
Telephone: 213-892-7478
Facsimile: 213-892-7481
Email: sanderson@greenheart.com

*Probate, Trusts, and Estate Planning, Tax Exempt Organizations, Real Estate, Elder Law.*

**SANDRA JONES ANDERSON,** born Fort Worth, Texas; admitted to bar, 1980, California. *Education:* University of California at Berkeley (B.A., 1961); Atlanta University (M.A., 1962); University of California at Los Angeles (M.S.W, 1971); Whittier College School of Law (J.D., 1980). *Member:* Beverly Hills, Los Angeles County, National and American Bar Associations; State Bar of California; Women Lawyers Association of Los Angeles; Black Women Lawyers. *PRACTICE AREAS:* Health Care; Elder Law; Probate; Nonprofit and Charitable Organizations.

## ANDERSON, ABLON, LEWIS & GALE, LLP
**SUITE 2000 EQUITABLE PLAZA BUILDING**
**3435 WILSHIRE BOULEVARD**
**LOS ANGELES, CALIFORNIA 90010**
Telephone: 213-388-3385
Telecopier: 213-388-8432

Thousand Oaks, California Office: 220-H Briarwood Building, 299 West Hillcrest Drive, 91360. Telephone: 805-373-5273. Fax: 805-495-1456.

*Civil Trial Practice, State and Federal Courts. Business Law, Commercial, Corporation, Taxation, Securities, Trusts, Probate and Real Property Law.*

(This Listing Continued)

*FIRM PROFILE: Anderson, Ablon, Lewis & Gale has been a business oriented law firm for more than 30 years. Industries in which the firm's clients are involved include the automotive aftermarket, manufacturing, oil & gas, retailing, title insurance, high technology research and development, and real estate development, construction and syndication.*

### MEMBERS OF FIRM

**ROBERT E. LEWIS,** born Long Beach, California, July 29, 1944; admitted to bar, 1970, California and U.S. Court of Military Appeals; 1975, U.S. Supreme Court. *Education:* University of California at Los Angeles (B.S. in Accounting, 1966; J.D., 1969). Beta Gamma Sigma; Phi Delta Phi. Planning Commissioner, 1980-1989; City Councilman, 1989-1992; Mayor, 1991-1992, City of Thousand Oaks, California; Member, Board of Trustees, HCA Los Robles Regional Medical Center, 1993-1996; Member, Board of Directors, Senior Concerns; Chairman, Board of Directors, Alliance for the Arts. *Member:* Los Angeles County Bar Association (Member, Commercial Law Section); State Bar of California. [Capt., U.S. Army, JAGC, 1967-1975]. *PRACTICE AREAS:* Commercial and Secured Transactions; Real Estate; Corporate.

**JERALD E. GALE,** born Hollywood, California, February 9, 1954; admitted to bar, 1981, California and U.S. District Court, Central District of California; 1989, U.S. District Court, Eastern District of California. *Education:* University of California at Berkeley (B.A., magna cum laude, 1976); Hastings College of Law (J.D., 1979). Member, Moot Court. Law Clerk to Honorable Frederick J. Woelflen, Magistrate, U.S. District Court, Northern District of California. Contributing Author: "Damages in Business Litigation," Association of Business Trial Lawyers, 1987. Co-Author: "Compensatory Damages in Business Litigation" and "Damages for Misrepresentation and Fraud in Business Litigation," Los Angeles County Bar Association and The Rutter Group, 1989. Member, California Land Title Association. Member, Board of Trustees, JCCA of Greater Los Angeles, 1989—. Member, Board of Directors, VCJCC, 1988—; Vice President, 1990—. *Member:* Los Angeles County (Member, Sections on: Real Property and Title Insurance) and American (Member, Sections on: Corporation, Banking, Business Law; Real Property; Probate and Trust Law; Litigation) Bar Associations; State Bar of California (Member, Litigation Section); Association of Business Trial Lawyers. *PRACTICE AREAS:* Litigation; Business; Commercial; Real Property; Escrow and Title Litigation; Partnership and Corporate Litigation; Secured Transaction Litigation; Unfair Competition; Petroleum Marketing Practices Act.

**HARRIS D. BASS,** born Hartford, Connecticut, August 27, 1952; admitted to bar, 1977, California; 1979, Connecticut; 1981, U.S. Tax Court. *Education:* University of Connecticut (B.S., summa cum laude, 1974); University of California at Los Angeles (J.D., 1977). Beta Gamma Sigma. *Member:* Los Angeles County (Member, Sections on: Corporation; Taxation) and Connecticut Bar Associations; State Bar of California. *PRACTICE AREAS:* Corporate; Tax; Estate Planning; Real Estate; Trust and Probate Law.

### ASSOCIATES

**FARHAD KAZEMZADEH,** born Tehran, Iran, February 24, 1942; admitted to bar, 1970, California. *Education:* Yale University (B.A., 1964); Vanderbilt University Law School (J.D., 1967). *Member:* Los Angeles County Bar Association; State Bar of California. [U.S. Army, 1967-1969]. *LANGUAGES:* Persian, Russian. *PRACTICE AREAS:* Real Estate; Title Insurance; Litigation.

**CANDACE CONNART BLEIFER,** born Jackson, Mississippi, April 16, 1960; admitted to bar, 1992, California; 1993, U.S. District Court, Central and Northern Districts of California; 1994, Florida. *Education:* University of Texas at Austin (B.B.A., summa cum laude, 1982); Loyola Law School of Los Angeles (J.D., 1992). Phi Kappa Phi. Beta Gamma Sigma. Recipient, American Jurisprudence Awards in Family Law, Community Property and Ethics, Counseling and Negotiation. *Member:* Los Angeles County Bar Association; State Bar of California; Women Lawyers Association of Los Angeles. *PRACTICE AREAS:* Business Litigation.

**ROBERT DAVID SCHWARTZ,** born Mountain View, California, December 19, 1964; admitted to bar, 1993, California. *Education:* University of California at Los Angeles (B.S., 1988); McGeorge School of Law (J.D., with distinction, 1993). Phi Delta Phi. Traynor Honor Society. Staff Writer, "The Transnational Lawyer." Recipient, American Jurisprudence Award in Sales. *Member:* Ventura County Bar Association; State Bar of California.

(This Listing Continued)

**ANDERSON, ABLON, LEWIS & GALE, LLP,** Los Angeles—*Continued*

## OF COUNSEL

**CHARLES R. ANDERSON,** born Walla Walla, Washington, May 15, 1927; admitted to bar, 1953, Indiana; 1957, California. *Education:* Indiana University (B.S., 1951; J.D., 1953). Beta Gamma Sigma; Phi Delta Phi. Author: "Stop Payment and Uniform Commercial Code," Indiana Law Journal, 1953. *Member:* Los Angeles County and Wilshire (Member, Board of Governors, 1985—) Bar Associations; State Bar of California. (Retired). ***PRACTICE AREAS:*** Corporate; Tax; Business.

**HERMAN ABLON,** born New York, N.Y., February 3, 1931; admitted to bar, 1961, California. *Education:* City University of New York (B.B.A., 1952); University of Southern California (LL.B., 1960). Beta Gamma Sigma; Phi Alpha Delta. Licensed Certified Public Accountant. *Member:* Los Angeles County and American Bar Associations; State Bar of California. (Retired). ***LANGUAGES:*** French. ***PRACTICE AREAS:*** Real Estate; Tax; Corporate.

REPRESENTATIVE CLIENTS: Abco Construction Co.; Atlantic Richfield Co.; Maremont Corp.; Sealed Power Corp.; Standard Motor Products; Stewart Title Guaranty Co.; Stewart Title Co.; Cahn Instruments, Inc.; Holmes-Halley Industries, Inc.; Ticor Title Insurance Company of California; Chicago Title Insurance Co.; Transamerica Title Insurance; Commonwealth Title Insurance; Highlands Insurance Co.; Chubb Group of Insurance Companies; Crane Veyor Corp.; Computer Aided Systems, Inc.; Bentley Manufacturing Co., Inc.
REFERENCE: Bank of America (Wilshire & Harvard Branch).

# ANDERSON, McPHARLIN & CONNERS

A Partnership including Professional Corporations
*ONE WILSHIRE BUILDING, NINETEENTH FLOOR*
*624 SOUTH GRAND AVENUE*
**LOS ANGELES, CALIFORNIA 90017-3320**
Telephone: 213-688-0080; 714-669-1609
Telecopier: 213-622-7594

Riverside, California Office: 3750 University Avenue, Suite 225. Telephone: 909-787-1900. Telecopier: 909-787-6749.

*General Civil and Trial Practice in all State and Federal Courts. Fidelity and Surety, Environmental Litigation (Hazardous Waste, Toxic Torts), Products Liability, Property Insurance, Title Insurance, Maritime, Fire Insurance, Commercial and General Liability Insurance Defense, Insurance Coverage, Bad Faith Litigation, Business Torts, Architects' and Engineers' Errors and Omissions, Construction Litigation, Commercial Litigation, Banking, Labor and Professional Malpractice Law.*

FIRM PROFILE: *Anderson, McPharlin & Conners was founded in 1947 by the three named partners. Since that date the firm has grown to its present size of 21 partners and 21 associates. When founded, the firm limited its practice to surety bond and fidelity insurance litigation and claims resolution, fields in which Anderson, McPharlin & Conners has earned a national reputation. In the past 25 years, however, the firm has expanded its practice to include the areas stated above.*

**NEWTON E. ANDERSON** (1897-1967).

**WILLIAM J. CONNERS** (1911-1986).

**KENNETH E. LEWIS** (1919-1990).

## MEMBERS OF FIRM

**MICHAEL C. PHILLIPS, (P.C.),** born Santa Barbara, California, June 15, 1945; admitted to bar, 1971, California, U.S. District Court, Northern, Central and Southern District of California and U.S. Court of Appeals, 9th Circuit; 1976, U.S. Supreme Court. *Education:* University of Colorado (B.A., 1967); Loyola University (J.D., 1970). Phi Delta Phi. *Member:* Los Angeles County and American Bar Associations; State Bar of California; Federation of Insurance and Corporate Counsel; Maritime Law Association of the United States. ***PRACTICE AREAS:*** Toxic Torts; Products Liability Litigation; Construction Defect Litigation; Insurance Coverage; Maritime Litigation. ***Email:*** MCP@AMCLAW.COM

**THOMAS J. CASAMASSIMA,** born New York, N.Y., December 16, 1941; admitted to bar, 1968, California; 1972, U.S. Supreme Court; 1973, U.S. Court of Appeals, 9th Circuit and U.S. District Court, Central and Southern Districts of California. *Education:* California State University (B.A., 1964); University of California at Los Angeles (LL.B., 1967). Author: "Student Financial Aid Termination-Analysis and Application of the Federal Riders," The College Counsel, Vol. VI, No. I, 1971; "The Expanding Discovery of Expert Opinions and Reports," DRI, Apr., 1986; "Defining Insurable Risk in The Commercial General Liability Insurance Policy: Guidelines for Interpreting The Work Product Exclusion," The Construction Lawyer, Jan. 1992 Vol. 12 #1; "Defining 'Sudden and Accidental,'" The Risks and Benefits Journal, Jan./Feb. 1992; "Insurance for Environmental Accidents," The Risks and Benefits Journal, Nov./Dec. 1991; "Chapter 25 Extra Contractual Damages," in a book entitled "Law of Suretyship," published by Tort and Insurance Practice Section, American Bar Association, 1993. *Member:* Los Angeles County (Member: Superior Courts Committee; Superior Courts Committee, 1987-1989) and American (Member, Tort and Insurance Practice Section) Bar Associations; State Bar of California; The Association of Southern California Defense Counsel; Defense Research Institute. ***PRACTICE AREAS:*** Trial Practice; Environmental Litigation; Insurance Coverage; Construction Law; Surety Law; Products Liability; Professional Liability. ***Email:*** TJC@AMCLAW.COM

**DAVID T. DiBIASE,** born Los Angeles, California, June 14, 1948; admitted to bar, 1973, California. *Education:* University of Southern California (B.A., cum laude, 1970); University of California at Los Angeles (J.D., 1973). Contributing Author, ABA Annotated Bankers Blanket Bond and Annotated Commercial Blanket Bond, 1985. Panelist/Author, ABA National Institute on Commercial Blanket Bonds, 1985. Panelist/Author, ABA National Institute on Fidelity Bonds, 1989. Panelist/Author, ABA National Institute on Financial Institution Bonds, 1989 and 1992. Panelist/Author, ABA Fidelity and Surety Law Committee, "Fidelity Bonds" Program, 1996. *Member:* Los Angeles County (Member, Title Insurance Sub-Section) and American (Chair, Fidelity and Surety Law Committee, 1992-1993) Bar Associations; State Bar of California; International Association of Defense Counsel. ***PRACTICE AREAS:*** Surety and Fidelity Bond Law; Legal Professional Liability Defense; Title Insurance Law; Real Estate (Property) Law; Bad Faith Litigation; Insurance Coverage; Professional Liability Law. ***Email:*** DTD@AMCLAW.COM

**ERIC A. SCHNEIDER,** born Los Angeles, California, May 12, 1954; admitted to bar, 1980, California. *Education:* University of California at Santa Barbara (B.A., cum laude in Economics, 1976); University of California at Los Angeles (J.D., 1980). Member, Executive Board Moot Court Honors Program; National Trial Advocacy Team. Past President, Surety Claims Association of Los Angeles, 1987-1988. *Member:* State Bar of California; Association of Real Estate Attorneys (President, 1993-1994); California Land Title Association (Associate Member). ***PRACTICE AREAS:*** Personal Injury Defense; Business Torts; Construction Litigation. ***Email:*** EAS@AMCLAW.COM

**GARY J. VALERIANO,** born Sharon, Pennsylvania, September 20, 1952; admitted to bar, 1979, California; 1982, U.S. District Court, Central District of California. *Education:* California State University at Northridge (B.A., cum laude, 1974); Loyola University of Los Angeles (J.D., magna cum laude, 1979). Member, 1977-1978 and Managing Editor, 1978-1979, Loyola Law Review. Adjunct Professor of Law, Loyola University of Los Angeles, 1985-1987. Author: "Pitfalls in Insurance Coverage for 'Computer Crimes'," 59 Defense Counsel Journal No. 4, 1992; "Statutory Fidelity Bonds - Do They Mean What They Say," FSLC Mid-Winter (ABA 1989). Co-Author: with David T. DiBiase, "Trial Strategy from the Defendant's Viewpoint," Financial Institution Bonds (ABA 1989). Co-Contributor, "First Supplement to the Commercial Blanket Bond Annotated," (ABA 1991); "Fidelity Law Topical Outline and Bibliography (1989 ABA-TIPS, Fidelity & Surety Law Committee). *Member:* Los Angeles County and American Bar Associations; State Bar of California. ***Email:*** GJV@AMCLAW.COM

**JESSE S. HERNANDEZ,** born San Francisco, California, October 1, 1951; admitted to bar, 1980, California, U.S. District Court, Central District of California, U.S. Court of Appeals, Ninth Circuit and U.S. Supreme Court. *Education:* University of California at Los Angeles (B.A., 1974; Loyola Marymount University (J.D., 1979). *Member:* Los Angeles County (Real Estate, Title Insurance and Probate Subsections) and American (TIPS; Title Insurance Claims) Bar Associations; Association of Southern California Defense Counsel. ***Email:*** JSH@AMCLAW.COM

**JOEL A. OSMAN,** born Los Angeles, California, October 16, 1956; admitted to bar, 1982, California, U.S. District Court, Northern, Central and Southern Districts of California and U.S. Court of Appeals, Ninth Circuit. *Education:* University of California at San Diego (B.A., magna cum laude, 1978); UCLA School of Law (J.D., 1981). *Member:* Los Angeles County and American Bar Associations; State Bar of California; Association of Southern California Defense Counsel. ***PRACTICE AREAS:*** Civil Litigation; Environmental Litigation. ***Email:*** JAO@AMCLAW.COM

*(This Listing Continued)*

# PROFESSIONAL BIOGRAPHIES

**PAUL F. SCHIMLEY,** born Niagara Falls, New York, July 13, 1955; admitted to bar, 1981, California and U.S. District Court, Southern District of California; 1984, U.S. District Court, Central District of California; 1989, U.S. Court of Appeals, Ninth Circuit. *Education:* Niagara University (B.A., Political Science, magna cum laude, 1977); University of San Diego (J.D., 1981). *Member:* Los Angeles County Bar Association; State Bar of California. *PRACTICE AREAS:* Employment Litigation; Real Estate Litigation. *Email:* PFS@AMCLAW.COM

**MICHAEL S. ROBINSON,** born Los Angeles, California, August 4, 1959; admitted to bar, 1984, California, U.S. District Court, Central District of California and U.S. Court of Appeals, Ninth Circuit; 1986, U.S. Court of International Trade. *Education:* Linfield College (B.A., cum laude, 1981); Loyola Marymount University (J.D., 1984). *Member:* Los Angeles County Bar Association (Member, Real Property Section, Title Insurance Sub Section); State Bar of California. *Email:* MSR@AMCLAW.COM

**MARK E. ARONSON,** born Brooklyn, New York, April 9, 1954; admitted to bar, 1979, California; 1983, U.S. District Court, Northern, Central and Southern Districts of California and U.S. Court of Appeals, Ninth Circuit; 1990 U.S. Supreme Court; 1995, U.S. District Court, District of Arizona. *Education:* State University of New York at Buffalo (B.A., 1975); Ohio Northern University (J.D., 1978). Member, Ohio Northern Law Review, 1976-1978. *Member:* Los Angeles County and American Bar Associations; State Bar of California. *Email:* MEA@AMCLAW.COM

**ANN GRAUPMANN ZUCKERMAN,** born Minneapolis, Minnesota, February 26, 1957; admitted to bar, 1986, California; 1989, Minnesota; 1990, U.S. District Court, Central District of California. *Education:* Gustavus Adolphus College (B.A., 1979); Loyola Marymount University (J.D., 1985). *Member:* Los Angeles County and Minnesota State Bar Associations; State Bar of California; California Women Lawyers. *PRACTICE AREAS:* Civil and Environmental Litigation; Insurance Coverage; Employment Law. *Email:* AGZ@AMCLAW.COM

**BRIAN S. MIZELL,** born San Jose, California, April 28, 1962; admitted to bar, 1988, California; 1990, U.S. District Courts, Northern, Southern and Central Districts of California. *Education:* San Jose State University (B.A., 1985); Pepperdine University (J.D., 1988). *Member:* State Bar of California. (Resident, Riverside Office). *Email:* BSM@AMCLAW.COM

**JANE ELLEN RANDOLPH,** born Twin Falls, Idaho, January 15, 1962; admitted to bar, 1988, California; 1989, U.S. District Court, Northern, Eastern, Southern and Central Districts of California and U.S. Court of Appeals, Ninth Circuit. *Education:* Colorado State University (B.A., 1984); McGeorge School of Law, University of the Pacific (J.D., 1988). Phi Alpha Delta (Engle Chapter Vice Justice, 1989; San Fernando Chapter Marshall, 1993). Staff Writer, Pacific Law Journal, Vol. 18, No. 2, Review of Selected 1986 California Legislation. Associate Editor, Pacific Law Journal, Vol. 19, No. 2, Review of Selected 1987 California Legislation. *Member:* State Bar of California. *Email:* JER@AMCLAW.COM

**CARLETON R. BURCH,** born Rantoul, Illinois, November 2, 1961; admitted to bar, 1987, California; 1988, U.S. District Court, Central District of California; 1994, Colorado. *Education:* The Colorado College (B.A., cum laude, 1984); Hastings College of the Law, University of California (J.D., 1987). Pi Gamma Mu. *LANGUAGES:* Japanese and Spanish. *PRACTICE AREAS:* Commercial Law; Business Litigation; Fidelity and Insurance Coverage Matters. *Email:* CRB@AMCLAW.COM

**LISA MARIE LE NAY COPLEN,** born Los Angeles, California, December 28, 1963; admitted to bar, 1989, California and U.S. Court of Appeals, Ninth Circuit; 1990, U.S. District Court, Central District of California; 1994, U.S. District Court, Southern District of California. *Education:* University of Southern California (B.S., Finance, 1986); Loyola Law School (J.D., 1989). Chief Justice, Scott Moot Court Honors Board, 1989. *Member:* Los Angeles County and American Bar Associations; State Bar of California. *Email:* LLC@AMCLAW.COM

## ASSOCIATES

**G. WAYNE MURPHY, (P.C.),** born Torrance, California, January 21, 1942; admitted to bar, 1969, California; 1973, U.S. Supreme Court. *Education:* San Fernando State College (B.A., 1965); Loyola University of Los Angeles (J.D., 1968). *Member:* Los Angeles County and American (Member, Fidelity and Surety Law Committee, Tort and Insurance Practice Section, 1973—) Bar Associations; The State Bar of California; International Association of Defense Counsel. *PRACTICE AREAS:* Contract Law; Construction Law; Public Contract Law; Surety Law. *Email:* GWM@AMCLAW.COM

*(This Listing Continued)*

**JOHN J. IMMORDINO,** born Los Angeles, California, September 10, 1952; admitted to bar, 1980, California; 1985, U.S. District Court, Central District of California; 1986, U.S. District Court, Southern District of California; 1987, U.S. District Court, Eastern and Northern Districts of California. *Education:* California State University, Northridge (B.A., 1975); Southwestern University School of Law (J.D., 1979). *Member:* State Bar of California. *PRACTICE AREAS:* Surety; Construction Litigation; Commercial Litigation; Real Estate Litigation; Insurance Defense. *Email:* JJI@AMCLAW.COM

**WAYNE B. DUCHARME,** born Winnipeg, Canada, June 19, 1943; admitted to bar, 1986, Arizona; 1988, California; 1989, U.S. District Court, Central District of California. *Education:* California State University at Northridge (B.S.B.A., summa cum laude, 1979); Hastings College of Law, University of California (J.D., 1986); University of Illinois (Certificate in Public Accounting, 1996). Beta Alpha Psi; Beta Gamma Sigma; Phi Kappa Phi; Alpha Gamma Sigma. Licensed Real Estate Broker, California, 1991. Certified Public Accountant, Illinois, 1996. Certificate in Mediation, Dispute Resolution Services, 1996. Author: "Copyright Protection and Unauthorized Use of Architectural Drawings," 2 Construction Practice Newsletter, 1993. Lecturer in Law: "Locating Errors and Omissions in Design Professionals' Plans and Specifications," Surety Claims Association, 1995. *Member:* Los Angeles Bar Association (Real Property Section); State Bar of Arizona; State Bar of California; American Institute of Certified Public Accountants; Toastmasters' International CTM. *PRACTICE AREAS:* Construction; Real Estate; Business Litigation; Surety Law. *Email:* WBD@AMCLAW.COM

**PAULA G. TRIPP,** born Bakersfield, California, November 26, 1958; admitted to bar, 1984, California and U.S. District Court, Southern, Central and Eastern Districts of California. *Education:* University of Southern California (B.A., 1980); McGeorge School of Law, University of the Pacific (J.D., 1983). Phi Alpha Delta. *Member:* Los Angeles County (Member, Amicus Curiae Briefs Committee; Delegate to State Bar Convention, 1989) and American Bar Associations; State Bar of California; Association of Southern California Defense Counsel; The Association of Trial Lawyers of America. *PRACTICE AREAS:* Aviation; Motor Carrier and Truck Liability; Premises Liability; Construction Defect and Accident Litigation. *Email:* PGT@AMCLAW.COM

**MARCI L. BOLTER,** born Los Angeles, California, September 30, 1964; admitted to bar, 1989, California, U.S. District Court, Central District of California and U.S. Court of Appeals, Ninth Circuit. *Education:* California State University at Northridge (B.A., 1986); University of Southern California Law Center (J.D., 1989). Phi Alpha Delta. International Officer, 1989—. *Member:* Los Angeles County Bar Association; State Bar of California; California Women Lawyers. *PRACTICE AREAS:* General Litigation; Personal Injury; Construction Defect; Product Liability; Toxic Torts. *Email:* MLB@AMCLAW.COM

**JEANETTE E. JERLES,** born Arcadia, California, September 15, 1964; admitted to bar, 1990, California, U.S. District Court, Federal District of California and U.S. District Court, Central District of California. *Education:* University of California (B.A., 1987); Pepperdine University (J.D., cum laude, 1990). Associate Editor, Pepperdine Law Review, 1989-1990. Co-Author: "Defining Insurable Risk in the Commercial General Liability Insurance Policy: Guidelines for Interpreting the Work Product Exclusion," The Construction Lawyer. *Member:* State Bar of California. *Email:* JEJ@AMCLAW.COM

**ERNEST J. BARTLETT,** born Los Angeles, California, December 6, 1959; admitted to bar, 1991, California and U.S. Court of Appeals, Ninth Circuit; 1993, U.S. District Court, Northern, Central and Southern Districts of California. *Education:* University of California at Santa Cruz (B.A., 1984); University of San Francisco (J.D., 1991). Recipient, American Jurisprudence Award, Appellate Advocacy. *Member:* Los Angeles County and American Bar Associations; State Bar of California. *PRACTICE AREAS:* Environmental, Surety and Probate Litigation; Bankruptcy. *Email:* EJB@AMCLAW.COM

**STEVEN R. YEE,** born San Francisco, California, August 9, 1966; admitted to bar, 1991, California. *Education:* University of California at Irvine (B.A., cum laude, Political Science and Social Ecology, 1988); University of California, Hastings College of the Law, (J.D., 1991). Member, Board of Governors, Hastings Moot Court Program. *Member:* Los Angeles County and American Bar Associations; State Bar of California. *Email:* SRY@AMCLAW.COM

**ARNOLD W. HOLADAY,** born Dover, Delaware, December 29, 1963; admitted to bar, 1993, California. *Education:* University of California at Irvine (B.A., 1986; M.B.A., 1987); University of San Francisco (J.D., cum

*(This Listing Continued)*

CAA465B

## ANDERSON, McPHARLIN & CONNERS, Los Angeles— Continued

laude, 1993). Staff Member, University of San Francisco Law Review, 1991-1993. Article Editor, University of San Francisco Maritime Law Journal, 1992-1993. *Member:* State Bar of California. (Resident, Riverside Office). *Email:* AWH@AMCLAW.COM

**MICHAEL S. BARRETT,** born Omaha, Nebraska, March 3, 1965; admitted to bar, 1994, California. *Education:* University of Nebraska at Lincoln (B.S., 1988); Creighton University (J.D., 1994). Phi Delta Phi. Intra-School Tournament Director, Creighton Moot Court Board, 1993-1994. Recipient: American Jurisprudence Award In Trial Practice, 1993; David A. Svoboda Trial Advocacy Award, Creighton Law School, 1994. Quarterfinalist, ATLA National Student Trial Advocacy Competition, 1994. *Member:* State Bar of California. *PRACTICE AREAS:* Surety Litigation. *Email:* MSB@AMCLAW.COM

**STEWART DENNIS REID,** born Fresno, California, February 6, 1966; admitted to bar, 1995, California. *Education:* University of California at Los Angeles (B.A., 1989); University of La Verne (J.D., 1995). General Contractors License, California, 1991. *Member:* State Bar of California. (Resident, Riverside Office). *Email:* SDR@AMCLAW.COM

**JUDY HAWTHORNE-WATERS,** born Los Angeles, California, Mary 19, 1968; admitted to bar, 1996, California. *Education:* University of California, Berkeley (B.A., 1990); Loyola Law School (J.D., 1996).

**REGINA R. WONG,** born Inglewood, California, September 16, 1971; admitted to bar, 1996, California. *Education:* University of California, Berkeley (B.A., 1993); University of Los Angeles, Los Angeles (J.D., 1996). Phi Delta Phi. Member, Pacific Basin Law Journal.

### OF COUNSEL

**ELDON V. McPHARLIN,** born O'Neill, Nebraska, June 16, 1910; admitted to bar, 1937, Iowa; 1938, California. *Education:* Creighton University and State University of Iowa (B.A., 1935); State University of Iowa (J.D., 1937). Phi Delta Phi. *Member:* Los Angeles County and American Bar Associations; The State Bar of California; International Association of Insurance Counsel (Chairman, Fidelity and Surety Committee, 1968-1969); Federation of Insurance Counsel.

**NELSON P. STEITZ,** born Springfield, Massachusetts, November 26, 1919; admitted to bar, 1953, California. *Education:* Trinity College (A.B., 1943); University of Southern California (LL.B., 1952). *Member:* Los Angeles County and American Bar Associations; The State Bar of California.

REPRESENTATIVE CLIENTS: Aetna Casualty & Surety Co.; Alliance Insurance Co.; American International Group; American Reinsurance Co.; Chicago Title Insurance Co.; Chubb Group of Companies; CIGNA Companies; Commercial Union Insurance; Continental Guaranty & Credit Co.; Continental Insurance Co.; Employers Reinsurance Corp.; Fireman's Fund Insurance Co.; First Business Bank; General Bank of Commerce; General Insurance Company of America; Globe Indemnity; Harbor Insurance Co.; Hartford Companies; Highlands Insurance Co.; Indemnity Company of California; Industrial Indemnity Co.; Insurance Company of North America; Maryland Casualty Co.; Mid Century Insurance Co.; New Hampshire Insurance Co.; Northbrook Insurance Co.; Ohio Casualty Insurance Co.; Pacific Indemnity Co.; Peerless Insurance Co.; Royal Indemnity Co.; Shand Morahan; State Farm Insurance Group; Ticor Title Co.; Transamerica Insurance Co.; Transamerica Title Co.; Underwriters at Lloyds of London; United Pacific Insurance Co.; U.S. Fidelity & Guaranty Co.; U.S. Fire Insurance Co.

---

## ANDERSON & SALISBURY
### LOS ANGELES, CALIFORNIA
(See Pasadena)

*Family Law.*

---

## ANDREWS & HENSLEIGH, LLP
### 700 SOUTH FLOWER STREET
### 11TH FLOOR
### LOS ANGELES, CALIFORNIA 90017
Telephone: 213-892-6364
Fax: 213-892-2265

*General Civil Trial, Business Litigation, Commercial Litigation, Insurance Law and Tort.*

*(This Listing Continued)*

---

### MEMBERS OF FIRM

**JOSEPH M. ANDREWS,** born Lafayette, Indiana, June 5, 1951; admitted to bar, 1978, California and U.S. District Court, Northern District of California; 1979, U.S. District Court, Central District of California; 1988, U.S. Court of Appeals, Ninth Circuit; 1989, U.S. District Court, Southern and Eastern Districts of California. *Education:* University of California at Riverside (B.A., cum laude, 1973); Hastings College of the Law, University of California (J.D., 1978). Research Editor, Hastings Law Journal, 1977-1978. Adjunct Professor, University of Laverne College of Law, 1988-1990. *Member:* Los Angeles County and American Bar Associations; The Association of Trial Lawyers of America; California Trial Lawyers Association. *REPORTED CASES:* Employers Reinsurance Corp. v. Phoenix Insurance Co., 186 Cal. App. 3d 545, 230 Cal. Rptr. 792 (1986); Kane, Kane & Kritzer v. Altagen, 107 Cal. App. 3d 36, 165 Cal. Rptr. 534 (1980). *PRACTICE AREAS:* Civil Litigation.

**BARBARA J. HENSLEIGH,** born Cedar Rapids, Iowa, September 21, 1955; admitted to bar, 1985, California. *Education:* University of Texas (B.S.N., 1978; J.D., 1985). Arbitrator, Los Angeles Superior and Municipal Courts. *Member:* American Bar Association (Member, Litigation Management and Economics Committee, Litigation Section); California Women Lawyers; The State Bar of California. *PRACTICE AREAS:* Litigation; Commercial.

### ASSOCIATE

**JOHN J. AUMER,** born Hawthorne, California, February 9, 1959; admitted to bar, 1987, California and U.S. District Court, Central and Eastern Districts of California. *Education:* University of California at Los Angeles (B.A., 1983); Hastings College of the Law, University of California (J.D., 1987). Judicial Externship, Justice Carl Anderson, Presiding Justice, California Court of Appeals, First Appellate District, Division Four, 1987. *Member:* Los Angeles County Bar Association; State Bar of California. *PRACTICE AREAS:* Civil Litigation.

---

## ANDREWS & KURTH L.L.P.
### SUITE 4200, 601 S. FIGUEROA STREET
### LOS ANGELES, CALIFORNIA 90017
Telephone: 213-896-3100
Telecopier: 213-896-3137

*Houston, Texas Office:* Suite 4200, 600 Travis, 77002. Telephone: 713-220-4200. Telecopier: 713-220-4285. E-Mail: webmaster@andrews-kurth.com.

*Washington, D.C. Office:* Suite 200, 1701 Pennsylvania Avenue, N.W. Telephone: 202-662-2700. Telecopier: 213-896-3137.

*Dallas, Texas Office:* Suite 4400, 1601 Elm Street. Telephone: 214-979-4400. Telecopier: 214-979-4401.

*The Woodlands, Texas Office:* Suite 150, 2170 Buckthorne Place, 77380. Telephone: 713-220-4801. Telecopier: 713-364-9538. E-Mail: hightech@andrews-kurth.com.

*New York, N.Y. Office:* 425 Lexington Avenue. Telephone: 212-850-2800. Telecopier: 212-850-2929.

*London, England Office:* 2 Creed Court, 5-11 Ludgate Hill, EC4M 7AA. Telephone: 0171-236-3456. Telefax: 0171-236-4276.

*General Civil Practice, Antitrust, Asset Securitization, Bankruptcy and Business Reorganization, Biotechnology, Corporate and Securities, Energy Regulatory, Environmental, Natural Resources, Health and Safety, Finance, Intellectual Property, International, Labor and Employment, Litigation, Oil and Gas, Real Estate, Taxation, Utility. Trial of Civil Cases in all Courts.*

FIRM PROFILE: *Andrews & Kurth L.L.P. is a national law firm with approximately 250 attorneys. Founded in 1902 in Houston, Texas, the firm is one of the oldest and largest law firms in Texas. The firm represents a wide variety of local, national and international concerns from its offices in New York, Washington, D.C., Los Angeles, Dallas and Houston. Many of the attorneys of Andrews & Kurth have national and international reputations as leaders in their respective practice areas.*

*Proud of the firm's tradition, Andrews & Kurth is strongly committed to providing quality legal services with individual attention and personal concern.*

### MEMBERS OF FIRM

**STEVEN H. HANEY,** born Pasadena, California, 1957; admitted to bar, 1985, California; 1986, U.S. District Court, Central District of California. *Education:* California State University at Sacramento (B.A., magna cum laude, 1982); University of California at Davis (J.D., 1985). Winner, Neumiller Moot Court Competition, 1984. Member, University of California at

*(This Listing Continued)*

Davis Trial Practice Honors Board, 1984-1985. Extern to Frances Newell Carr, Associate Justice, California Court of Appeal, 1984. Participant, Trial Attorney's Project, 1986. *Member:* Los Angeles County and American (Member, Criminal Justice Section, White Collar Crime Committee) Bar Associations; State Bar of California. [With USAF, 1976-1980]. *PRACTICE AREAS:* Civil Litigation; White Collar Criminal Defense; Contract Law; Real Estate Law.

**DAVID J. JOHNSON, JR.,** born Huntington, New York, 1956; admitted to bar, 1985, California and U.S. District Court, Central District of California. *Education:* University of Virginia (B.A., 1979; M.B.A., 1985; J.D., 1985). *PRACTICE AREAS:* Corporate Law; Securities.

**WILLIAM H. LANCASTER,** born Oakland, California, 1951; admitted to bar, 1986, California. *Education:* University of Maryland (B.A., 1973); University of Virginia (M.A., 1974; Ph.D., A.B.D., 1978; J.D., 1985). Phi Beta Kappa; Phi Kappa Phi. *Member:* Los Angeles County Bar Association; State Bar of California. *PRACTICE AREAS:* Business Litigation.

**CARL B. PHELPS,** born Brooklyn, New York, 1939; admitted to bar, 1965, California. *Education:* Colgate University (A.B., 1961); Harvard University (LL.B., 1964). Chair, Harvard Law School Association of Southern California, 1983-1985. *Member:* Beverly Hills, Los Angeles County (Trustee, 1996-1997; Real Property Section: Executive Committee, 1985-1997, Chair, 1995-1996) and American Bar Associations; The State Bar of California. *PRACTICE AREAS:* Real Estate Law; Corporate Law.

**SHELLY ROTHSCHILD,** born Brooklyn, New York, 1949; admitted to bar, 1977, New York; 1985, California. *Education:* Smith College (B.A., 1970); Boston University (J.D., 1976). *Member:* Los Angeles County and American Bar Associations; State Bar of California. *PRACTICE AREAS:* Bankruptcy Law.

**RALPH W. TARR,** born Bakersfield, California, 1948; admitted to bar, 1976, California; 1982, U.S. Supreme Court; 1990, District of Columbia. *Education:* Dartmouth College (A.B., magna cum laude, 1970); California State University, Sacramento (M.P.A., 1973); University of California, Hastings College of Law (J.D., 1976). Phi Beta Kappa; Phi Kappa Phi; Order of the Coif. Editorial Review Board, Hasting Law Journal. *Member:* State Bar of California; District of Columbia Bar; American Bar Association. *PRACTICE AREAS:* General Practice; Natural Resources Law; Environmental Law.

**MICHAEL T. WILLIAMS,** born Boston, Massachusetts, 1953; admitted to bar, 1982, California and U.S. District Court, Northern and Central Districts of California; 1983, U.S. District Court, Southern District of California and U.S. Court of Appeals, Ninth Circuit; 1985, U.S. District Court, Eastern District of California; 1993, U.S. Court of Appeals, Fifth Circuit. *Education:* Ithaca College (B.A., magna cum laude, 1975); University of San Diego (J.D., cum laude, 1982). Managing and Research Editor, San Diego Law Review, 1981-1982. Co-Author: "The National Cooperative Production Amendments of 1993," International Legal Strategy, Legal Risk Management for Japanese Corporation, Vol. II-6, June, 1993. Moderator and Panelist: "Temporary Restraining Orders and Preliminary Injunctions in Trade Secret and Unfair Competition Cases," Provisional and Post-Judgement Remedies Section, presented to the Los Angeles County Bar Association, October, 1995; "The Art of War: Contested Confirmation of a Plan in a Single Asset Bankruptcy Case," presented at the Annual Meeting of the California State Bar, September, 1995; "War and Peace: the Use of Arbitration and Mediation in Commercial Dispute and Bankruptcy," sponsored by Debtor-Creditor Relations and Bankruptcy Committee and UCC Committee, presented at the Section Education Institute, California State Bar, June 1995. Speeches: "Practical Solutions for Ethical Dilemmas Facing Corporate Counsel," presented to Corporate Counsel Committee and Corporate Law Department Section of Los Angeles County Bar Association, January, 1993; "Product Liability: Representing Aviation Component Manufacturers," presented to Kansas Bar Association, Overland Park, Kansas, April, 1992. Judge, Pro Tempore, Los Angeles County Municipal Court, Los Angeles Judicial District, 1992—. Panel Mediator, United States Bankruptcy Court, Central District of California, 1995—. Volunteer Pilot, Angel Flight. *Member:* Los Angeles County (Member, Executive Committee of Provisional and Post-Judgement Remedies Section, 1994—; Co-Chair, Real Property Litigation Subsection; Real Property Section, 1993-1994) and American (Member, Antitrust Section and Business Law Section) Bar Associations; State Bar of California (Member, Real Property Law Section). [Officer, USMC, 1975-1979]. *PRACTICE AREAS:* Civil Litigation; Appellate; Aviation; Antitrust; Bankruptcy; Commercial Law; Real Estate.

*(This Listing Continued)*

*OF COUNSEL*

**MARTA THOERNER KURLAND,** born Los Angeles, California, 1958; admitted to bar, 1983, California. *Education:* Loyola Marymount University (B.B.A., summa cum laude, 1980); University of California at Berkeley-Boalt Hall (J.D., 1983). *Member:* Los Angeles County Bar Association. *PRACTICE AREAS:* Real Estate Law; Real Estate Finance Law; Business Law.

**DIANE C. WEIL,** born Los Angeles, California, 1956; admitted to bar, 1981, Nevada; 1982, California. *Education:* Occidental College (A.B., 1977); University of Southern California (J.D., 1980). Phi Alpha Delta. *Member:* Washoe County Bar Association; State Bar of California; State Bar of Nevada. *PRACTICE AREAS:* Bankruptcy Law; Debtor Creditor Law; Real Estate Law.

*ASSOCIATES*

**DAMON C. ANASTASIA,** born Santa Monica, California, 1966; admitted to bar, 1992, California, U.S. District Court, Central District of California and U.S. Court of Appeals, Ninth Circuit; 1993, U.S. District Court, Eastern, Northern and Southern Districts of California and U.S. Court of Appeals, First Circuit. *Education:* University of California at Los Angeles (B.A., with honors, 1989); Georgetown University; Boston College (J.D., 1992). Phi Alpha Theta; Pi Sigma Alpha. Staff Writer, 1990-1991 and Notes and Comments Editor, 1991-1992, Boston College International and Comparative Law Review. Judicial Extern to the Honorable Stephen Reinhardt, U.S. Circuit Judge, U.S. Court of Appeals, Ninth Circuit, 1990. Law Clerk, 1992-1993 and Judicial Extern, 1991, to the Honorable David S. Nelson, Senior U.S. District Judge, U.S. District Court, District of Massachusetts. Law Clerk to the Honorable James L. Watson, Senior Judge, U.S. Court of International Trade, while sitting by designation to the U.S. District Court for the District of Massachusetts, 1992-1993. *Member:* Los Angeles County (Litigation Section) and American (Litigation Section) Bar Associations; Association of Business Troal Lawyers; Defense Research Institute. *PRACTICE AREAS:* General Civil Litigation; Insurance Litigation; Commercial Litigation.

**GRAEME LAWRENCE CURRIE,** born Rochester, New York, 1959; admitted to bar, 1985, New York; 1988, California. *Education:* University of Vermont (B.A., 1981); Washington and Lee University School of Law (J.D., 1984). Phi Delta Phi, 1981-1984. *Member:* Los Angeles and American Bar Associations; State Bar of California. [Lieutenant, JAGC, USNR, 1984-1988]. *PRACTICE AREAS:* Contract Law; Real Estate Law; Patent, Trademark and Copyright Law; Bankruptcy Law.

**JON L. R. DALBERG,** born Republic of South Africa, 1955; admitted to bar, 1987, California. *Education:* University of Natal (B.A., 1978; M.A., 1982; LL.B., 1983); Yale University (LL.M., 1984). *PRACTICE AREAS:* Bankruptcy Law.

**JOHN L. HOUSE,** born Monterey, California, 1950; admitted to bar, 1984, Texas; 1986, U.S. District Court, Northern District of Texas; 1989, California. *Education:* Texas Tech University (B.A., with honors, 1974); University of Southern California (M.A., with distinction, 1976); University of Texas at Austin (J.D., 1983). Phi Delta Phi. Author "Regulation of Oil and Natural Gas Pipeline Transportation and Utility Sales," California Oil and Gas Newsletter, Fall 1994; "Water Law," 40 Southwestern Law Journal, April 1986; "Water Law," Southwestern Law Journal, April 1995. *Member:* Dallas and American (Member, Natural Resources Section) Bar Associations; State Bar of Texas; State Bar of California (Member, Real Estate; Natural Resources Subsection); Rocky Mountain Mineral Law Foundation. *LANGUAGES:* French and Spanish. *PRACTICE AREAS:* Energy; Oil and Gas; Real Estate; Corporate.

**DIANA J. HUNT,** born Lakewood, California, 1962; admitted to bar, 1993, California; 1994, U.S. District Court, Central District of California; 1996, U.S. District Court, Northern District of California. *Education:* University of California at Los Angeles (B.A., 1985); Loyola Marymount University (J.D., 1993). Law Clerk to Honorable Robin L. Ribet, Bankruptcy Judge, U.S. District Court, Central District of California, 1993-1994. *Member:* Los Angeles County, Federal and American Bar Associations. *PRACTICE AREAS:* Litigation; Bankruptcy.

**CHARLES GUSTAF KLINK,** born New York, New York, 1965; admitted to bar, 1993, New York and U.S. District Court, Eastern District of New York (Not admitted in California). *Education:* Pomona College (B.A., 1987); University of California at Los Angeles (J.D., 1992). Author: Book Chapter, "Bankruptcy and Intangible Holdings: Redeeming Your Investment When Disaster Strikes," The New Role of Intellectual Property in Commercial Transactions (John Wiley & Sons, Inc. 1994). *LANGUAGES:*

*(This Listing Continued)*

## ANDREWS & KURTH L.L.P., Los Angeles—Continued

Spanish. **PRACTICE AREAS:** Asset Securitization; Corporate Securities; Bankruptcy and Reorganization.

**GREGG J. LOUBIER,** born Worcester, Massachusetts, 1956; admitted to bar, 1986, California. *Education:* Trinity College; Hampshire College (B.A., 1979); University of California at Davis (J.D., 1986). **PRACTICE AREAS:** Real Estate.

**DAVID W. MEADOWS,** born Los Angeles, California, 1957; admitted to bar, 1988, California. *Education:* University of California at Los Angeles (B.A., 1980); University of St. Andrews, Scotland (Diploma in Philosophy, 1981); Loyola Law School of Los Angeles (J.D., 1988). Chief Articles Editor, 1987-1988 and Staff Member, 1986-1987, Loyola of Los Angeles Law Review. Author: "Bankruptcy Code Section 362(d) (2): Protecting Turnkey Sale Values in Liquidations Under the Bankruptcy Code," 21 Loyola of Los Angeles Law Review 893, (1988). *Member:* Los Angeles County Bar Association; State Bar of California. **PRACTICE AREAS:** Bankruptcy Law.

**GABRIELA MEJIA,** born Los Angeles, California, 1966; admitted to bar, 1992, California. *Education:* University of California at Los Angeles (B.A., 1989) University of California at Los Angeles School of Law (J.D., 1992). *Member:* Mexican-American Bar Association; Women's Lawyers Association of Los Angeles Bar. **LANGUAGES:** Spanish. **PRACTICE AREAS:** Litigation and International Law.

**AUDRA M. MORI,** born Los Angeles, California, 1967; admitted to bar, 1992, California. *Education:* University of California at Los Angeles (B.A., 1989); Cornell University (J.D., 1992). Law Clerk, Honorable Richard W. Goldberg, U.S. Court of International Trade. *Member:* State Bar of California; Japanese American Bar Association. **PRACTICE AREAS:** Litigation.

**REBECCA O'MALLEY,** born Corpus Christi, Texas, 1965; admitted to bar, 1990, California. *Education:* Yale University (B.A., 1987); Columbia University (J.D., 1990). **PRACTICE AREAS:** General Business Litigation.

**DANIEL F. PASSAGE,** born Rochester, New York, 1966; admitted to bar, 1992, New York (Not admitted in California). *Education:* University of California at Irvine (B.A., 1989); Columbia University (J.D., 1992). **PRACTICE AREAS:** Corporate Securitization; Securities.

**STEVEN L. SATZ,** born St. Louis, Missouri, 1950; admitted to bar, 1978, Missouri; 1993, California. *Education:* Indiana University (B.A., 1972); University of Missouri (J.D., 1978). *Member,* University of Missouri Law Review. Author: "Computer Software," 41 Journal of Missouri Bar 104 (1985); "Motor Fuel, Special Fuel and Cigarette Taxes," Missouri Taxation Law and Practice, Chapter 20, The Missouri Bar (1981). **PRACTICE AREAS:** Real Estate.

(For Biographical data of Houston, Dallas and The Woodlands, Texas, Washington, D.C. and New York, New York Personnel see Professional Biographies at Houston, Dallas and The Woodlands, Texas, Washington, D.C. and New York, New York)

---

## ANGEL AND NEISTAT
### A PROFESSIONAL CORPORATION
*Established in 1978*

28TH FLOOR
555 SOUTH FLOWER STREET
**LOS ANGELES, CALIFORNIA 90017-2205**
Telephone: 213-689-4500
Fax: 213-689-4651

*Civil Litigation in State and Federal Courts. Business, Real Property, Secured Transactions, Bankruptcy, Insolvency, Corporation and Banking Law.*

**MICHAEL A. ANGEL,** born September 8, 1947; admitted to bar, 1973, California and U.S. District Court, Central District of California. *Education:* University of California at Los Angeles (B.A., 1969); University of San Diego (J.D., 1972). Delta Theta Phi (President). *Member:* Los Angeles County Bar Association; State Bar of California; California League of Savings Institutions (Member, Attorneys Committee); Mortgage Bankers Association of America. **PRACTICE AREAS:** Civil Litigation; Corporate.

**DOUGLAS M. NEISTAT,** born Melbourne, Australia, October 22, 1946; admitted to bar, 1973, California and U.S. District Court, Central District of California. *Education:* California State University at Northridge (B.A., 1969); University of San Diego (J.D., 1972). Director, Australian

*(This Listing Continued)*

CAA468B

American Chamber of Commerce. *Member:* Beverly Hills and Los Angeles County (Member, Commercial Law and Bankruptcy Section) Bar Associations; State Bar of California; Los Angeles Bankruptcy Forum. **PRACTICE AREAS:** Bankruptcy; Corporate.

**ALAN HOLMBERG,** born March 29, 1949; admitted to bar, 1975, California and U.S. District Court, Central District of California. *Education:* Oberlin College (B.A., 1971); University of Southern California (J.D., 1975). Member, University of Southern California Law Review, 1984-1985. *Member:* Beverly Hills (Member, Bankruptcy Section) and Los Angeles County (Member, Commercial Law and Bankruptcy Section) Bar Associations; State Bar of California; Los Angeles Bankruptcy Forum. **PRACTICE AREAS:** Civil Litigation; Bankruptcy.

**STEVEN L. CRANE,** born Chicago, Illinois, November 13, 1952; admitted to bar, 1981, California; 1983, U.S. District Court, Central District of California. *Education:* University of California at Santa Cruz (B.A., with honors, 1976); University of California at Los Angeles (J.D., 1981). Comments Editor, Federal Communications Law Journal, 1980-1981. *Member:* Los Angeles County Bar Association; State Bar of California. **PRACTICE AREAS:** Civil Litigation; Bankruptcy.

**STEVEN A. SCHWABER,** born New York, N.Y., November 13, 1942; admitted to bar, 1969, California, U.S. District Court, Central District of California and U.S. Court of Appeals, Ninth Circuit; 1972, U.S. Supreme Court. *Education:* University of California at Los Angeles (B.A., 1965); Loyola University of Los Angeles (J.D., 1968). Phi Alpha Delta (Treasurer, Ford Chapter, 1967-1968). Author: "The Realities of Chapter 7 Trustee Compensation," *1991 Annual Survey of Bankruptcy Law,* Callaghan & Company, 1991. Associate Editor, *Journal of the American Bankruptcy Institute.* Deputy City Attorney, Los Angeles, California, 1969-1972 and 1974-1976. Law Clerk to California Court of Appeals, Justice John F. Aiso, 1969. Arbitrator, Los Angeles Superior Court, Business Litigation Panel, 1984—. Court appointed Trustee in Chapter 11 and Chapter 7 Bankruptcy Cases, 1986-1990. Los Angeles County Superior Court Approved Receiver in Business Cases. Member, Small Business Advisory Board to the Senate Select Committee on Small Business Enterprises, 1981. *Member:* State Bar of California (Member: Business Law Section; Legislation Committee, 1984-1985); Council of Certified Bankruptcy Specialists (Founding Director); Association of Business Trial Lawyers; American Bankruptcy Institute; Financial Lawyers Conference; Los Angeles Bankruptcy Forum. (Certified in Commercial Bankruptcy Law by the American Board of Bankruptcy Certification). **PRACTICE AREAS:** Bankruptcy; Receiverships.

**ALAN J. STOMEL,** born Los Angeles, California, January 25, 1956; admitted to bar, 1986, California. *Education:* Pomona College (B.A., 1977); University of California at Los Angeles (M.A., 1982); Loyola University (J.D., 1986). Extern, Office of the United States Trustee, 1986. *Member:* Financial Lawyers Conference; Los Angeles Bankruptcy Forum. **PRACTICE AREAS:** Bankruptcy.

**GARY R. WALLACE,** born Jersey City, New Jersey, September 4, 1961; admitted to bar, 1987, California and U.S. District Court, Central District of California. *Education:* Boston University (B.A., 1983); University of Southern California (J.D., 1987). Member, University of Southern California Journal of Law and the Environment, 1986-1987. *Member:* Los Angeles County Bar Association; State Bar of California. **PRACTICE AREAS:** Civil Litigation.

**DANIEL H. REISS,** born Los Angeles, California, April 19, 1962; admitted to bar, 1990, California and U.S. District Court, Central, Eastern, Northern and Southern Districts of California. *Education:* California State University at Northridge (B.S. magna cum laude , 1984); Loyola Law School (J.D., 1990). St. Thomas More Society. Note and Comment Editor, 1989-90, Staff Member, 1988-89, Loyola of Los Angeles Law Review. Certified Public Accountant, California, 1987. *Member:* State Bar of California; Federal Bar Association; Financial Lawyers Conference; Los Angeles Bankruptcy Forum. **PRACTICE AREAS:** Bankruptcy Law.

REPRESENTATIVE CLIENTS: USA Great Western Bank; Coast Federal Bank; TransOhio Savings Bank; Sears Mortgage Corp.; City of Oxnard; Certified Grocers of California, Ltd.; First Union National Bank; First Union Mortgage Corp.; Federal Deposit Insurance Corp.; Resolution Trust Corp.; Stewart Title Guarantee Co.; Chicago Title. AUSTRALIA Australian Consulate; Australian Trade Commission (Austrade); Queensland Government Office; Queensland Tourist and Travel Corp.; Victorian Government Office; Lustig and Moar; Minter Ellison; Phoenix Communications, Ltd; AIDC, Ltd.; Commonwealth Bank of Australia.

## ANGLEA & BANNON
### A PROFESSIONAL CORPORATION
**LOS ANGELES, CALIFORNIA**
(See Pasadena)

*Estate Planning, Probate and Trust Law, General Tax Matters, General Business Matters, Real Estate and Environmental Law; Fiduciary and Tax Litigation.*

---

## ANKER & HYMES
### A LAW CORPORATION
**LOS ANGELES, CALIFORNIA**
(See Encino)

*Business, Corporate and Partnership Matters, Mergers and Acquisitions, Real Estate, Taxation, Estate Planning, Probate and Civil Litigation.*

---

## ANTIN & TAYLOR
1875 CENTURY PARK EAST, SUITE 700
**LOS ANGELES, CALIFORNIA 90067**
Telephone: 310-788-2733
Fax: 310-788-0754
Email: mantin@ix.netcom.com

*Taxation, Estate Planning, Pension and Profit Sharing and General Business Law.*

FIRM PROFILE: *The Firm of Antin & Taylor, is involved in wealth and financial planning and in the preparation of wills, trust and estate planning for individuals and their families, including charitable and life insurance planning and business property agreements. In addition, the firm handles all matters relating to probate, estates, trusts and Federal and State gift and death taxes.*

*Mr. Antin and Mr. Taylor specialize in Federal and State income taxation, ERISA qualified pension and profit sharing plans, non-qualified deferred compensation plans, welfare benefit plans, fringe benefits, cafeteria plans, health reimbursement plans, life and disability insurance planning. The firm represents clients in tax litigation before the IRS, Franchise Tax Board, State Board of Equalization and other tax and regulatory agencies as well as before California and Federal Courts.*

### MEMBERS OF FIRM

**MICHAEL ANTIN,** born Milwaukee, Wisconsin, November 30, 1938; admitted to bar, 1964, California, U.S. District Court, Southern District of California and U.S. Tax Court. *Education:* University of California at Los Angeles (B.S., 1960); University of California at Berkeley (J.D., 1963). Author: "Taxation of Stock Rights," 51 California Law Review, 46, 1963; "Let's Adopt the Independent Executor," 1 Journal of the Beverly Hills Bar Association 29, September, 1967; "Recent Developments in Medical Reimbursement Plans," 3 Journal of the Beverly Hills Bar Association 20, October, 1969; "The Vanishing Marital Trust—After the Tax Reform Act," 3 The Tax Advisor 218, April, 1972; "Relating Your Retirement Plan Benefits to Your Estate Plan," 6 Journal of the Beverly Hills Bar Association 15, May-June, 1972; "The Horrors of the Individual Trustee of a Retirement Plan," 8 Pension & Welfare News 72, November, 1972; "Pension Reform Bill," 8 Journal of the Beverly Hills Bar Association 12, September 1974; "How to Handle Break-up of Professional Corporation," Taxation for Lawyers, Nov./Dec., 1979; "Economics of Buy-Sell Planning, Putting the Package Together," 1981 U.S.C., Tax Inst. 500; "How to Operate Your Trust or Probate", Layman Publishing Company, 309 pages, 1983. Lecturer, Continuing Education of the Bar: "Marital Deduction," 1996; "Trust Administration," 1993; "Selected Issues in Advising California Professional Partnerships and Corporations," 1990; "Real Property Transactions After the 1986 Tax Reform," 1986; "Income Tax Consequences of Real Property Transactions," 1985; "Tax and Financial Planning for Individuals," 1985; "Impact of the Economic Recovery Tax Act of 1981 on Estate Planning and Administration," 1982; "Personal Tax and Financial Planning for Professionals," 1981; "Estate Administration: A Basic Practice Course," 1973; "Professional Corporations," 1969; "VEBA's in the 90's," 13th Annual National Institute of Pension Administrators, 1995; "Reasonable Compensation: Pushing the (Pay) Envelope," Southern Federal Tax Institute, 1996. *Member:* Beverly Hills (Chairman: Sub-Committee to Reform the Probate Code, 1966-1968; Probate Committee, 1969; Vice Chairman, Tax Committee, 1970), Los An-

*(This Listing Continued)*

geles County and American (Chairman Professional Service Corporations Committee, Section of Taxation, 1984-1986) Bar Associations; The State Bar of California. Fellow: American College of Tax Counsel; American College of Trust and Estate Counsel; Western Pension Conference. (Certified Specialist, Taxation Law, The State Bar of California Board of Legal Specialization). *PRACTICE AREAS:* Taxation Law; Estate Planning Law; Corporate Planning Law; Probate Law.

**MICHAEL L. TAYLOR,** born Santa Monica, California, June 25, 1949; admitted to bar, 1975, California and U.S. District Court, Central District of California; 1984, U.S. Supreme Court; 1985, U.S. Court of Appeals for the Ninth Circuit; 1991, U.S. Tax Court. *Education:* University of Santa Clara (B.A., 1971; J.D., 1974); Wharton School of Economics, University of Pennsylvania. Certified Employee Benefit Specialist, 1985. Lecturer, San Jose State University, 1975. Member, Advisory Board, Tax and Legal Consultant, American Lupus Foundation, 1983—. Member, Alumni Board of Directors, University of Santa Clara, 1984—. Publications: "Reasonable Compensation: Pushing the (Pay) Envelope," Southern Federal Tax Institute, 1996; Discrimination in Benefits and Coverage: 410(a)(26), 410(b) and 401(a)(4); 17th Advanced Pension Seminar materials, Corbel & Co., (1990). Participant Loans; Plan Horizons, The Official Publication of the National Institute of Pension Administrators, (1989). Lecturer/Panelist: IRS Audits of Qualified Plans and section 414(m)(n)(o) Concerns. Current Regulation of Retirement Plans. Member, Steering Committee of the Employee Benefits Committee of the State Bar on Taxation, 1991. *Member:* Los Angeles Bar Association; State Bar of California (Member, Sections on: Labor and Employment Law; Estate Planning, Trust and Probate); International Foundation of Employee Benefit Plans. Fellow, International Society of Certified Employee Benefit Specialists. *PRACTICE AREAS:* Employee Benefit Law; Tax Exempt Organizations; Taxation; Estate Planning; Probate Law; Trust Law; Estate Probate; Income Tax; Gift Taxation.

---

## APPLETON, PASTERNAK & PASTERNAK
### A LAW CORPORATION
1925 CENTURY PARK EAST, SUITE 2140
**LOS ANGELES, CALIFORNIA 90067-2722**
Telephone: 310-553-1500
Facsimile: 310-553-1540

*The Firm Practice includes Receiverships and Litigation in the areas of Complex Business, Employment, Environmental Law, Family Law, Personal Injury, Real Estate, Unfair Competition and Alternative Dispute Resolution.*

**PETER M. APPLETON,** born Los Angeles, California, August 5, 1942; admitted to bar, 1967, California. *Education:* University of California at Los Angeles (A.B., 1964; J.D., 1967). Order of the Coif. Senior Editor, UCLA Law Review, 1966-1967. Author: Note: "The 11th Amendment prevents the United States from Impleading a State: Parks v. United States," 13 UCLA Law Review 433, 1966; Note: "Judicial Retraction of Standing Limitations in Review of NLRB Actions: UAW v. Scofield," 13 UCLA Law Review 1408, 1966. Co-Author: Article, "Advertisers Too, Have Constitutional Rights," 19 Publishing, Entertainment, Advertising and Allied Fields Law Quarterly, 393, 1981. *Member:* Beverly Hills (Member, Board of Governors, 1973-1985; President, 1984-1985; Editor, 1973-1976, Beverly Hills Bar Journal), Los Angeles County (Trustee, 1983-1984) and American (Member, Litigation Section) Bar Associations; State Bar of California (Member, Executive Committee of Conference of Delegates, 1985-1987; Chair, 1988-1989; Member, Judicial Nominees Evaluation Commission, 1993-1996).

**CYNTHIA F. PASTERNAK,** born New York, N.Y., May 14, 1952; admitted to bar, 1977, California; 1979, U.S. District Court, Central District of California; 1981, U.S. Court of Appeals, Ninth Circuit. *Education:* University of California at Los Angeles (B.A., cum laude, 1973); Loyola University at Los Angeles (J.D., 1976). Phi Alpha Delta. Chancellor's Marshal, Mortar Board, Political Science Department Special Honors. Ninth Circuit Editor, Loyola Law Review, 1975-1976. Author: "Insufficient Guidelines and the Legal Consequences for Youth Service Bureaus," and "Juvenile Offenders and the Police Dispositional Process," State of California Department of the Youth Authority, 1973. Lecturer: Mentor Program, Oct, 1994, Dec., 1994; MCLE Extravaganza, 1995-1996. Settlement Officer, VAST, 1995-1996. Listed: International Who's Who of Professionals; National Association of Who's Who; Strathmore's Who's Who Registry; National Association for Female Executives. *Member:* Beverly Hills (Member, Family Law Section; Vice-Chair, Legislation Committee, 1995-1996; Litigation Section; Real Estate Section; Resolutions Committee), Century City (Co-Chair, Tort Litigation Section, 1996-1997), Los Angeles County

*(This Listing Continued)*

## APPLETON, PASTERNAK & PASTERNAK, A LAW CORPORATION, Los Angeles—Continued

(Member: Family Law Section; Litigation Section; Co-Chairperson, Economics of Law Practice Committee, 1982-1983; Chairperson, Artists and the Law Committee, 1983-1984) and American (Member, Sections on: Family Law; Litigation; Torts and Insurance Practice) Bar Associations; State Bar of California; The Association of Trial Lawyers of America; California Women Lawyers; Consumer Attorneys Association of Los Angeles; Women Lawyers Association of Los Angeles.

**DAVID J. PASTERNAK,** born New York, N.Y., March 5, 1951; admitted to bar, 1976, California. *Education:* University of California at Los Angeles (B.A., cum laude, 1973); Loyola University of Los Angeles (J.D., cum laude, 1976). Member, St. Thomas More Law Honor Society. Associate Editor, Loyola Law Review, 1975-1976. Co-Author: Case Note, "United Housing Foundation, Inc. v. Forman," Loyola Law Review 206, 1975. Lecturer, California Continuing Education of the Bar, 1984. Staff Counsel, California Department of Corporations, 1976-1979. California Deputy Attorney General, 1979-1980. Founding Co-Chair, California Receivers Forum, 1995-1996. *Member:* Beverly Hills (Board of Governors, 1982-1984 and 1988-1992), Los Angeles County (President-Elect, 1996—; Senior Vice-President, 1995-1996; Vice-President, 1994-1995; Alternative Dispute Resolution Section; Executive Committee, 1994-1995; Environmental Law Section; Chair, Litigation Section, 1994-1995; Executive Committee, 1983-1985 and 1994-1995; Trustee, 1983-1985, 1989-1991, 1994-1996; Barristers Officer, 1982-1984; Barristers President, 1984-1985) and American (Member: House of Delegates, 1986-1987; Judicial Administrative Division; Litigation Section) Bar Associations; State Bar of California; Association of Business Trial Lawyers (Member, Board of Governors, 1985-1987); Chancery Club.

**HEATHER APPLETON,** born Los Angeles, California, September 1, 1967; admitted to bar, 1992, California; 1993, U.S. District Court, Northern, Eastern and Central Districts of California; 1994, U.S. District Court, Southern District of California. *Education:* University of California at Davis (B.A., 1989); Loyola Law School (J.D., 1992). Author: "The First Amendment: Is the Freedom of Speech More Important Than the Protection of Human Life?" Loyola of Los Angeles Entertainment Law Journal, Volume 12, Issue 2, 1992. *Member:* Beverly Hills, Century City, Los Angeles County and American Bar Associations; State Bar of California (Member, Labor and Employment Section).

## ARANT, KLEINBERG, LERNER & RAM, LLP

SUITE 1080, 2049 CENTURY PARK EAST (CENTURY CITY)
LOS ANGELES, CALIFORNIA 90067-3112
Telephone: 310-557-1511
Telex: 5101012414 AKL LAX
Cable Address: "PTCLAW"
Facsimile: 310-557-1540

*Civil Trial and Appellate Practice in All State and Federal Courts Regarding Patents, Trademarks, Copyrights, Antitrust, Unfair Competition and Intellectual Property Law, Entertainment and Music Litigation and General Business Litigation. Transactional Matters For Corporate and Entertainment Law.*

FIRM PROFILE: *Arant, Kleinberg, Lerner & Ram, LLP provides full intellectual property services in a broad range of technologies. Particular areas of emphasis are prosecution and defense of patent, trademark, copyright, trade dress and unfair competition claims, entertainment and business litigation, protection of multi-media, computer, electronics, and medical technology and business transactions relating to the protection, commercialization and licensing of copyrights, trademarks, patents and trade secret property, United States and international patent and trademark prosecution.*

### MEMBERS OF FIRM

**GENE W. ARANT,** born North Powder, Oregon, December 21, 1920; admitted to bar, 1950, California; 1972, Alabama; registered to practice before U.S. Patent and Trademark Office. *Education:* Oregon State University (B.S.E.E., 1943); Harvard University Graduate School of Physics, Advanced Electronics Course, with honors, 1944; University of Southern California (J.D., 1949). Delta Theta Phi (Dean, Field Senate, 1948-1949; Dean, Los Angeles Alumni Senate, 1966-1967); Eta Kappa Nu; Tau Beta Pi; Pi Mu Epsilon. Author: "What Every Lawyer Should Know About Patents," Los Angeles Bar Bulletin, January, 1961; "The Cue for Mr. Lise," American Bar Association Journal, March, 1972; "New Integrity for Patent Law,"
*(This Listing Continued)*

California Lawyer, November, 1984. Lecturer in Engineering, University of Southern California, 1947-1951. *Member:* State Bar of California; Alabama State Bar; American Bar Association; Los Angeles Intellectual Property Law Association; American Intellectual Property Law Association. **PRACTICE AREAS:** Counseling; Alternative Dispute Resolution; Licensing; Domestic and Foreign Patent and Trademark Prosecution.

**MARVIN H. KLEINBERG,** born Bronx, New York, August 17, 1927; admitted to bar, 1954, California; 1957, U.S. Supreme Court; U.S. Court of Appeals, Third, Fifth, Ninth and Federal Circuits; registered to practice before U.S. Patent and Trademark Office. *Education:* University of California at Los Angeles (B.A., 1949); Boalt Hall School of Law, University of California (J.D., 1953). Deputy Public Defender, Los Angeles County, 1954. Adjunct Lecturer on Patent Law, 1975— and Member, Innovative Clinic Advisory Council, 1975—, Franklin Pierce Law Center. Member, Advisory Council, P.T.C., Research Foundation, Franklin Pierce Law Center, 1981—. *Member:* Los Angeles County and American (Member, Section on Patent, Trademark and Copyright Law) Bar Associations; State Bar of California; American Intellectual Property Law Association; Los Angeles Intellectual Property Law Association; Academy of Applied Sciences. **PRACTICE AREAS:** Domestic and International Patent Prosecution; Intellectual Property; Patents; Trademarks; Intellectual Property Litigation; Business Counseling.

**MARSHALL A. LERNER,** born Newark, New Jersey, July 19, 1941; admitted to bar, 1966, District of Columbia and U.S. Court of Appeals, District of Columbia Circuit; 1969, U.S. Supreme Court; 1973, California and U.S. Court of Appeals, Ninth Circuit; 1982, U.S. Court of Appeals for the Federal Circuit; 1967, registered to practice before U.S. Patent and Trademark Office. *Education:* New Jersey Institute of Technology (B.S.E.E., with honors, 1962); George Washington University (J.D., with honors, 1965). Tau Beta Pi; Eta Kappa Nu; Phi Eta Sigma. Instructor, Patent Law Fundamentals, University of California at Los Angeles Extension Center, Spring, 1976. Examiner, U.S. Patent and Trademark Office, 1963-1965. Patent Adviser, Office of Naval Research, 1965-1967. *Member:* Los Angeles County and Beverly Hills Bar Associations; State Bar of California; District of Columbia Bar; Los Angeles Patent Law Association; Los Angeles Copyright Law Association. **PRACTICE AREAS:** Intellectual Property Litigation; Patent and Trademark Prosecution; Advertising Injury; Trade Secrets.

**MICHAEL J. RAM,** born Newark, New Jersey, December 18, 1940; admitted to bar, 1972, New Jersey; 1973, New York; 1986, California; U.S. District Court, Central District of California; registered to practice before the U.S. Patent and Trademark Office. *Education:* Lafayette College (B.S.Ch.E., 1962); Newark College of Engineers (M.S.Ch.E, 1963; D.S.Ch.E., 1966); Seton Hall University (J.D., 1972). Author: "Patent Fraud; A New Defense?," Journal of the Patent Office Society, Vol. 54, No. 6, pp. 363-382, June, 1972; Collaborator on Paper: U.S. Government Policies Relating to Technology Licensing, Practicing Law Institute Symposium on Current Trends in Domestic and International Licensing, 1974; "Noninfringing Sales of An Infringing Medical Device - Lilly v. Medtronics," Medical Device & Diagnostic Industry, Vol. 12, No. 9, pp. 36-39, September, 1990; "U.S. Patent System - Important Differences to Non-U.S. Manufacturers," - International Medical & Diagnostic Industry, Vol. 1, No. 4, pp. 22-25, Nov.-Dec., 1990; "Managing Intellectual Property: Fourjays Publications, London, England, Editorial Advisory Board; "Noninfringing Sales of Infringing Medical Devices - Lilly v. Medtronics," Patent World, May 1991; "Due Diligence Clauses - Damned If You Do, Damned If You Don't," AUTM Western Regional Meeting, July 1992. Speaker: "Licensing Your Invention to a Corporation," Invention Convention, September 1990, September 1991 and September, 1992; "Recent Changes in International Licensing," Orange County World Trade Center, February, 1991. Guest Lecturer: "Licensing for Entrepreneurs," UCLA Extension Division, April 1991 and April 1992; Legal Aspects of Technology Transfer, U.C. Berkley Extension Division, Fall, 1994, Spring/Fall, 1995. Co-Chair, Publications Committee LES, 1991. Chapter Author, Drafting Business Contracts, CEB, 1994, 1996; Practice Consultant, California Civil Practice, Bancroft Whitney, 1993; Contributing Editor, Trade Secret Law, CEB, 1996. Subcommittee Chairman, Intellectual Property Section, ABA. Workshop Leader, LES National Meeting, "Valuing New Technology for Licensing," October, 1996. *Member:* New Jersey State and American Bar Associations; State Bar of California; Licensing Executives Society; American Chemical Society; American Institute of Chemical Engineers; Los Angeles Intellectual Property Law Association. [Capt., U.S. Army, 1965-1967]. **PRACTICE AREAS:** Domestic and International Patent Prosecution; Domestic and International Trademark Prosecution; Trade Secrets; Medical Patents and Technology; Licensing; Corporate Law.
*(This Listing Continued)*

**BRADFORD E. MATTES,** born Opelousas, Louisiana, February 4, 1956; admitted to bar, 1992, California; U.S. Court of Appeals, Ninth and Federal Circuits; U.S. District Court, Northern, Eastern, Southern and Central Districts of California; registered to practice before the U.S. Patent and Trademark Office. *Education:* University of Houston (B.S.M.E., 1986); Pepperdine University School of Law at Malibu (J.D., 1991). *Member:* State Bar of California; American Intellectual Property Law Association; Los Angeles Intellectual Property Law Association. **PRACTICE AREAS:** Intellectual Property Litigation; Patent and Trademark Prosecution; Trade Secrets.

**MICHAEL R. DILIBERTO,** born Miami, Florida, February 17, 1958; admitted to bar, 1987, Florida; 1988, California and U.S. District Court, Southern District of Florida; 1989, District of Columbia; U.S. Court of Appeals, Ninth and Federal Circuits; U.S. District Court, Northern, Eastern, Southern and Central Districts of California. *Education:* University of Miami at Coral Gables (B.M., 1981); Temple University School of Law, Rome, Italy, (1985); University of Miami (J.D., 1987). Recipient, Two Performance Awards, Downbeat Magazine. Adjunct Professor, Entertainment Industry Contracts, Trebas Institute of Recording Arts, 1990—. Author: "Looking Through the 'Rear Window': A Review of the United States Supreme Court Decision in Stewart v. Abend," Managing Intellectual Property, London, England, Nov. 1991 and Loyola of Los Angeles Entertainment Law Journal, Vol 12, Issue 2, 1992. Deputy City Attorney, Van Nuys City Attorney's Office, 1994. Member, Screen Actors Guild, 1986—. *Member:* State Bar of California; The Florida Bar; District of Columbia Bar; American Bar Association (Member, Forum on the Entertainment and Sports Industries, 1988—); Los Angeles Copyright Society; California Copyright Conference (1990—). **LANGUAGES:** Spanish. **PRACTICE AREAS:** Intellectual Property Litigation; Intellectual Property Law; Copyright Law; Trademark Law; Entertainment Law; Business Law; Trade Secrets; Alternative Dispute Resolution.

### ASSOCIATE

**MICHAEL T. SMITH,** born San Gabriel, California, May 28, 1965; admitted to bar, 1994, California. *Education:* California State Polytechnic University (B.A., 1983); Southwestern University School of Law (J.D., 1992). **PRACTICE AREAS:** Trademark; Copyright; Intellectual Property; Litigation Support.

REPRESENTATIVE CLIENTS: Alexander Steele Systems Technologies; Allied Insurance Co.; American International Industries; AML Communications, Inc.; Atlantic Mutual Insurance Co.; Berney-Karp; Calcor Space Facility, Inc.; Calavo Growers; Cardinal Laboratories, Inc.; Charles Jerome Broquard; Chick E. Boom Publishing; Chubb Insurance Co.; Constitution State Insurance Co.; Datametrics Corp.; Design Solange Ltd., Inc.; Durabag Co., Inc.; Earth Science, Inc.; EDnet; EPS Technologies; Euro-Products; Federal Insurance; Fireman's Fund Insurance Co.; Greif & Co.; Harbor Insurance Co.; Industries Indemnity Co.; Infoconnect, Ltd.; Interplast Group; J.B. Research; J. Robert Scott; Kaiser Aerospace and Electronics; Kaiser Electronics; Kaiser Electroprecision; Kaiser Electro-Optics; Karate Angels; L'Anza Research Laboratories; Liqui-Box Corp.; MK Diamond Products; MSI Insurance Co.; National Technical Systems; Northbrook Insurance Co.; Oasis Medical, Inc.; Ohio Casualty Group; Optima Technologies; Pacific Andrology, Inc.; Performance Products; Royal Insurance; Safeco; Scottsdale Insurance Co.; SEGA Gameworks, Ltd.; Skechers, U.S.A., Inc.; Steadfast Insurance; Summer Communications, Inc.; Uncle Milton Industries, Inc.; University of California-Los Angeles; Uptime Integrated Systems, Inc.; UroHealth, Inc.; Vision Biology; West American Ins. Co.; XPlain Corp.; Zurich-American.

---

## *ARGUE PEARSON HARBISON & MYERS*

A Partnership including a Professional Corporation

*Established in 1972*

*801 SOUTH FLOWER STREET*
*SUITE 500*
**LOS ANGELES, CALIFORNIA 90017-4699**
*Telephone: 213-622-3100*
*Telecopier: 213-622-7575*

General Business and Civil Litigation Practice. Corporation, Securities, Real Estate and Partnership Law. Finance, Regulatory, International, Federal and State Taxation, Pension and Profit Sharing, Labor and Employment, Estate Planning, Trust and Probate Law, Insurance Coverage, Nonprofit Corporation.

FIRM PROFILE: *Argue Pearson Harbison & Myers is firmly established in the Southern California community, and committed to civic involvement; the majority of our lawyers are native Southern Californians. Firm members have held or now hold positions of leadership in such organizations as: The Los Angeles Area Chamber of Commerce, Rotary International, The Los Angeles Olympic Organizing Committee, Town Hall, City of Glendale Planning Commission, and the Los Angeles County Bar Association.*

*Further involvement in the community is evidenced by the participation of firm members in teaching Continuing Education programs. Additionally, several members of Argue Pearson have authored books and articles on such subjects as: California corporate securities laws, pension and profit sharing plans, and probate and estate planning.*

*In order to assure responsiveness and accountability, typically one partner supervises and coordinates all matters relating to given client. This continuing personal responsibility guarantees quality legal services, continuity, and responsiveness.*

### *MEMBERS OF FIRM*

**LOUIS W. MYERS** (1943-1993).

**DON M. PEARSON (A PROFESSIONAL CORPORATION),** born Elk City, Oklahoma, May 25, 1941; admitted to bar, 1969, California. *Education:* Brigham Young University (B.S., magna cum laude, 1965); Harvard Law School (J.D., cum laude, 1968). Author: "Attorney's Guide to California Stock Qualification and Exemption," California Continuing Education of the Bar, 1969, revised and republished, 1978. Lecturer, Taxation, The Real Estate and Partnerships Master of Business Taxation Program, University of Southern California, 1976-1986. *Member:* Los Angeles County (Member, Executive Committee, Business and Corporations Law Section, 1972-1980; Executive Committee, Taxation Section, 1977-1985; Chairman, 1983-1984) and American Bar Associations; State Bar of California. **PRACTICE AREAS:** Business Law.

**STEPHEN F. HARBISON,** born Santa Monica, California, December 28, 1943; admitted to bar, 1969, California. *Education:* Stanford University (A.B., 1965; LL.B., 1968). Arbitrator, Los Angeles Municipal Court. *Member:* Los Angeles County Bar Association (Member: Committee on Ethics and Professional Responsibility, 1991-1994; Committee on the Judiciary, 1991-1992; Labor Law and Real Property Sections; Arbitrator, Dispute Resolutions Services; Attorney Client Relations Services); State Bar of California (Member: Labor Law and Litigation Sections). **PRACTICE AREAS:** Civil Litigation.

**WILLIAM A. JONES,** born Boston, Massachusetts, April 20, 1945; admitted to bar, 1974, California. *Education:* Princeton University (A.B., 1967); George Washington University (J.D., cum laude, 1974). *Member:* Los Angeles County (Member, Taxation, Business and Corporations Law Sections) and American Bar Associations; State Bar of California. **PRACTICE AREAS:** Business Transactions.

**JERRY K. STAUB,** born Glendale, California, August 2, 1942; admitted to bar, 1967, California. *Education:* Cambridge University, Cambridge, England (Special Certificate, 1962); University of Southern California (B.A., magna cum laude, 1964; J.D., 1967). Associate Editor, University of Southern California Law Review, 1966-1967. Phi Beta Kappa; Phi Kappa Phi; Order of the Coif. Author, "California Surface Waters," University of Southern California Law Review, 1967. Professor, Northrop University Law School, 1977-1978. Judge Pro Tempore of the Los Angeles Municipal Court, 1975 and 1976. *Member:* Los Angeles County Bar Association; State Bar of California. **PRACTICE AREAS:** Civil Litigation.

**DOUGLAS F. GALANTER,** born Long Branch, New Jersey, April 8, 1955; admitted to bar, 1980, California, U.S. Court of Appeals, Ninth Circuit and U.S. District Court, Central District of California; 1981, U.S. District Court, Northern District of California; 1988, U.S. District Court, Southern District of California; 1989, New York. *Education:* State University of New York at Albany (B.S., 1977); University of Southern California (J.D., 1980). Member, Board of Editors, Los Angeles Lawyer, 1992—. Author: "Pilot Life Insurance Co. v. Dedeaux: A Reprieve for Insurers of Employee Benefit Plans", California Continuing Education of the Bar Civil Litigation Reporter, Vol. 9, No. 5, July 1987. *Member:* Los Angeles County (Member: Panel of Arbitrators, Fee Dispute Resolution Program, 1985—; Amicus Briefs Committee, 1988—), New York State and American Bar Associations; State Bar of California (Delegation of Los Angeles County Bar Association to Conference of Delegates, 1987-1990). **PRACTICE AREAS:** Civil Litigation; Business Litigation.

**ANTHONY M. VIENNA,** born Long Beach, California, January 5, 1943; admitted to bar, 1970, California. *Education:* University of California at Berkeley; California State College at Long Beach (B.S., 1964); University of Southern California (J.D., 1969). Member, Southern California Law Review, 1968-1969. Author: "Preserving Unused Operating Losses in Liquidation and Merger of Subsidiaries," The Los Angeles Bar Bulletin, Vol. 49, No. 12, October, 1974; "Effect of a Multi-Corporate F Reorganization on Loss Carryovers and Carrybacks," Vol. 42, The Journal of Taxation, Page

*(This Listing Continued)*

## ARGUE PEARSON HARBISON & MYERS, Los Angeles—Continued

130, March, 1975; "ESOPS - The Nation of Leveraging in Qualified Plans," 28 U.S.C. Tax Institute 875 (1976); "Tax-Free Rollovers: Enhanced Leveraging for ESOPS," 36 Major Tax Planning (USC) 13-1 (1986); "Mature ESOPs" "Crisis or Transition?" Journal of Employee Ownership Law and FInance, January 1993. Certified Public Accountant, California, 1969. Program Chairman, Western Pension Conference, 1978. Internal Revenue Agent and Internal Revenue Service Estate Examiner, 1965-1968. *Member:* Los Angeles County (Editor, Newsletter, 1975-1977; Chairman, Employee Benefits Committee, 1976-1978; Treasurer, 1978-1979 and Secretary, 1979-1980, Vice-Chairperson, 1980-1981 and Chairperson, 1982-1983, Chairperson, Legislative Advisory Committee, 1983-1984, Taxation Section) and American Bar Associations; State Bar of California (Member, Taxation Section); Foreign Trade Association of Southern California. **PRACTICE AREAS:** Probate and Estate Planning; Tax.

**PHILIP J. KAPLAN,** born Washington, D.C., November 17, 1954; admitted to bar, 1984, Louisiana; 1988, California. *Education:* The Hotchkiss School; Washington and Lee University (B.A., magna cum laude, 1978); Brasenose College, Oxford University, Oxford, England (Visiting Scholar, 1978-1979); Tulane University (J.D., 1984). Phi Beta Kappa. *Member:* Los Angeles County and American Bar Associations; Louisiana State Bar Association; State Bar of California; Bar Association of the Fifth Federal Circuit. **LANGUAGES:** Spanish. **PRACTICE AREAS:** Civil Litigation; Entertainment Law.

**RICHARD G. RASMUSSEN,** born Chicago, Illinois, April 5, 1958; admitted to bar, 1987, California. *Education:* Biola College (B.A., 1980); Loyola Law School, Los Angeles (J.D., cum laude, 1987). Phi Delta Phi. Member, St. Thomas More Law Honor Society. Editor, Loyola Entertainment Law Journal, 1986-1987. *Member:* Los Angeles County (Member, Sections on: Business and Corporations Law; Real Estate and Intellectual Property Law) and American Bar Associations; State Bar of California. **PRACTICE AREAS:** Real Estate; Finance; Business Transactions.

### ASSOCIATES

**THOMAS SCHALOW,** born Milwaukee, Wisconsin, July 12, 1949; admitted to bar, 1982, California. *Education:* Yale University (B.A., cum laude, 1975); University of Southern California (J.D., 1981). Member, Southern California Law Review, 1980-1981. *Member:* Los Angeles County Bar Association; State Bar of California. **PRACTICE AREAS:** Civil Litigation.

**PATRICIA VENEGAS,** born Los Angeles, California, March 30, 1958; admitted to bar, 1988, California. *Education:* California State University at Los Angeles (B.S., 1981); University of California at Los Angeles (J.D., 1987). Certified Public Accountant, California, 1984. *Member:* American Bar Association; Mexican-American Bar Association; American Institute of Certified Public Accountants; California Society of Certified Public Accountants. **PRACTICE AREAS:** Civil Litigation.

**SCOTT CHAPLAN,** born Los Angeles, California, January 31, 1964; admitted to bar, 1991, California. *Education:* University of Southern California (B.S., 1987); Pepperdine University (J.D., 1991). Phi Alpha Delta. Licensed Real Estate Broker. Member, Pepperdine Law Review, 1989-1991. Member: Town Hall; World Affairs Council. *Member:* American Bar Association (Member, Litigation, Real Property and Entertainment Law Sections); Los Angeles Trial Lawyers Association; Los Angeles Chamber of Commerce Ambassadors. **PRACTICE AREAS:** Civil Litigation; Business Transactions.

**ANDREA L. ESTERSON,** born Philadelphia, Pennsylvania, December 26, 1963; admitted to bar, 1992, California, U.S. Tax Court, U.S. District Court, Central District of California and U.S. Court of Appeals, Ninth Circuit. *Education:* University of Southern California (B.S., magna cum laude, in Accounting, 1986); Loyola Marymount University (J.D., 1991). Beta Gamma Sigma. Certified Public Accountant, 1989. *Member:* Los Angeles County (Member Sections on: Business Law; Taxation; Probate and Trust Law), Beverly Hills (Member, Sections on: Taxation; Probate and Trust Law; Business Law) and American (Member, Sections on: Business Law; Taxation; Probate and Trust Law) Bar Associations; State Bar of California (Member Sections on: Taxation; Probate and Trust Law; Business Law) California Society of Certified Public Accountants; American Association of Attorneys Certified Public Accountants.

*(This Listing Continued)*

### OF COUNSEL

**JOHN C. ARGUE,** born Glendale, California, January 25, 1932; admitted to bar, 1957, California. *Education:* Occidental College (A.B., 1953); University of Southern California (LL.B., 1956). Phi Delta Phi. Founding Chairman, Los Angeles Olympic Organizing Committee. President, Southern California Committee for the Olympic Games, 1972—. Chairman: Los Angeles Area Chamber of Commerce, 1989; Los Angeles Chamber of Commerce Law and Justice Committee. Vice Chairman and Trustee, Pomona College, 1979. Trustee, University of Southern California, 1985—. Trustee: Occidental College, 1992—, (Director); Avery Dennison, 1988—. Director, CalMat, Inc.; Director, TCW/DW and TCW Galileo Mutual Funds; Chairman, Rose Hills Memorial Park. Chairman: Amateur Athletic Foundation, 1995; Criminal Justice Legal Foundation, 1995. *Member:* Los Angeles County Bar Association (Member, Section of Taxation Law); State Bar of California; Chancery Club (President, 1986).

REPRESENTATIVE CLIENTS: Aaron Brother Art Marts, Inc.; Armstrong World Industries, Inc.; Beverly Enterprises; Beverly Foundation; California Manufacturing Enterprises; Calstrip Steel Corporation; Conrad Hilton, III; ColorGraphics, Inc.; Direct Capital Corporation; Downey Auto Center; Electronic Conventions Management; Executive Equity Companies; 1st Business Bank; Forest Lawn Company; Friendly Ford, Las Vegas; Frontier Ford; Hayward Lumber Company; IBM; Insul-Acoustics, Inc.; IntriPlex Technologies, Inc.; Jones Brothers Construction; Kaiser Steel-VEBA; Lexus of Glendale; LTC Properties Inc.; Magic Johnson; McDonnell Douglas Finance Corporation; Metro Auto Group; Nationwide Health Properties, Inc.; Omega Healthcare Investors, Inc.; One-Central Bank; ORCO Construction Supply; Piel, Inc.; Prudential-Stevenson Real Estate Services; Rose Hills Mortuary; Salsbury Industries; Sir Speedy, Inc.; Smoking Car Productions; Steve Garvey; The United Methodist Church; Thomasville Furniture Industries, Inc.; Troxel Cycling & Fitness Co.; Verdugo Escrow Company; Westland Graphics; Windsurfing International, Inc.

---

## ARIAS & OZZELLO
### A PROFESSIONAL CORPORATION
### 11766 WILSHIRE BOULEVARD
### SUITE 720
### LOS ANGELES, CALIFORNIA 90025-6538
Telephone: 310-478-1212
Fax: 310-474-8884

*Civil Litigation, Corporate, Business and Entertainment Litigation, Real Estate and Investment Fraud, Major Personal Injury, Product Liability, Negligence, Insurance Law and Class Action Litigation. Construction Defect, Wrongful Death, Harassment, Discrimination, Premises and Product Liability, Breach of Contract, Insurance Defense.*

FIRM PROFILE: *Arias & Ozzello's clients include not only large corporations and small businesses, but individuals, families and professional athletes. The firm has a national practice, which includes many large verdicts and class action litigation. The principals of Arias & Ozzello possess over 25 years of combined legal experience. The firm's attorneys are admitted to practice before State and Federal courts in California, New York, New Jersey and Washington, D.C. Arias & Ozzello's philosophy is to provide comprehensive and aggressive legal services in a cost effective and efficient manner. The firms experience in business transactions has given it a reputation as thorough and meticulous as well as practical.*

**MICKEL M. ARIAS,** born Torrance, California, 1959; admitted to bar, 1984, California; 1986, New York and New Jersey; 1989, District of Columbia. *Education:* Southern Connecticut State University (B.S., 1981); Pepperdine University (J.D., 1984). Member, Moot Court Board. Chairman, Trial Advocacy Board. Past Associate, Condon & Forsyth. Managing Attorney, Sayre, Moreno, Purcell & Boucher. Arbitrator, Beverly Hills/Los Angeles County Bar Association Fee Dispute Program. *Member:* Los County, New York State, New Jersey State and American Bar Associations; District of Columbia Bar; The Association of Trial Lawyers of America; California Consumer Attorneys Association; Consumer Attorneys Association of Los Angeles; Sports Lawyers Association. **PRACTICE AREAS:** Business Litigation; Entertainment Litigation; Personal Injury; Negligence; Sports Law.

**MARK A. OZZELLO,** born Pueblo, Colorado, 1956; admitted to bar, 1984, California. *Education:* Georgetown University (B.A., 1981) Pepperdine University (J.D., 1984). Editor: Pepperdine Law Review; American Bar Association Symposium on Victims Right's. Author: Articles, "Enjoining Politically Motivated Strikes In Federal Courts: The Jacksonville Bulk Terminal Case," 10 Pepperdine L.Rev. 489, 1983; "The California Supreme Court Survey: A Review of Decisions," 10 Pepperdine L. Rev. 835, 1983. Past Associate: Tipler & Tipler; Dezes & Caiafa. Judge Pro Tem for the Orange County Municipal Court. *Member:* American Bar Association;

*(This Listing Continued)*

Consumer Attorneys Association of Los Angeles. *PRACTICE AREAS:* Corporate Law; Business Litigation; Real Estate.

*REPRESENTATIVE CLIENTS:* Airport Propane; Aliso Hills Dental Associates; Beetley & Beetley Properties, Inc.; Dental Associates of Irvine; E.H. Butland Development Corporation; Gateway State Bank, a New York Banking Institution; Greentyre, Inc. of Great Britain; Hilliger Cabinets, Inc.; International Model Management, Inc.; Lemans Auto Body, Inc.; Los Angeles Pottery, Inc.; NRG Enterprises Corp.; Orca Yacht Charters, Inc.; Peanut Butter & Jelly - Childrens Apparel; Public Parking, Inc.; Viramontes International, Inc.

## *ARMSTRONG HIRSCH JACKOWAY TYERMAN & WERTHEIMER*

A PROFESSIONAL CORPORATION

Established in 1976

SUITE 1800, 1888 CENTURY PARK EAST (CENTURY CITY)
**LOS ANGELES, CALIFORNIA 90067**
Telephone: 310-553-0305
Fax: 310-553-5036

*Entertainment, Corporation, Taxation, Real Estate, Estate Planning and Securities Law.*

FIRM PROFILE: *Armstrong Hirsch Jackoway Tyerman & Wertheimer is a full service law firm with 25 attorneys. The firm specializes in all aspects of entertainment law.*

**ALLAN L. ALEXANDER,** born Watsonville, California, October 28, 1940; admitted to bar, 1966, California. *Education:* Stanford University (A.B., cum laude, 1962); Harvard University (LL.B., 1965). Phi Beta Kappa. Council Member, Beverly Hills City Council, 1988—. Mayor, City of Beverly Hills, 1989-1990; 1995-1996. Commissioner, 1983-1988 and Chairman, 1985-1986, Beverly Hills Planning Commission. Lecturer in Law and Economics, Faculty of Law and Economics, University Gabriel Rene Moreno, Santa Cruz, Bolivia, S.A. (University Educator, Peace Corps), 1966-1967. Co-Author: "Rule 144—The Sale of Restricted and Control Securities," Vol. 47, No. 2, California State Bar Journal. Director, 1976-1981 and President, 1981, Public Counsel; Director, Economic Resources Corporation, 1974—; Director, 1977-1987 and President, 1981, SOS Exceptional Youth Foundation. Member, Advisory Committee to California Continuing Education of the Bar, 1981-1985. *Member:* Beverly Hills, Los Angeles County and American Bar Associations; The State Bar of California (Chairman, Education Committee, 1983-1985 and Member, Executive Committee, 1984-1986, Business Law Section). *PRACTICE AREAS:* Real Estate; Corporate; Business Law.

**KARL R. AUSTEN,** born Boston, Massachusetts, August 29, 1964; admitted to bar, 1989, California. *Education:* Amherst College (B.A., magna cum laude, 1986); Harvard Law School (J.D., cum laude, 1989). *Member:* Beverly Hills (Member, Entertainment Section), Los Angeles County and American Bar Associations; State Bar of California. Fellow, John Woodruff Simpson. *LANGUAGES:* French. *PRACTICE AREAS:* Entertainment.

**JOSEPH D'ONOFRIO,** born New York, N.Y., January 29, 1956; admitted to bar, 1982, California. *Education:* Princeton University (A.B., summa cum laude, 1978); University of Pennsylvania (J.D., 1981); Wharton Graduate School of Business. Phi Beta Kappa. *Member:* American Bar Association; The State Bar of California (Member, Real Property Section). *PRACTICE AREAS:* Real Estate.

**ALAN J. EPSTEIN,** born Green Bay, Wisconsin, May 18, 1960; admitted to bar, 1987, California, U.S. Tax Court, U.S. District Court, Central District of California and U.S. Court of Appeals, Ninth Circuit. *Education:* University of Wisconsin (B.B.A., with distinction, 1982); University of California at Los Angeles (J.D., 1987). Order of the Coif; Phi Kappa Phi. Author: "Foreign Expropriation Losses of Personal Assets: Should a Deduction be Allowed Under Internal Revenue Code Section 165(c)(3)?" 40 Tax Lawyer 211, 1986. *Member:* Beverly Hills (Chairman, Taxation Section, 1990) and Los Angeles County (Chairman, Entertainment Tax Subcommittee, Taxation Section, 1995) Bar Associations; The State Bar of California. *PRACTICE AREAS:* Taxation; Business Law.

**J. GUNNAR ERICKSON,** born Washington, D.C., December 2, 1946; admitted to bar, 1975, California. *Education:* Stanford University (B.A., 1969); Yale Law School (J.D., 1975). Co-Author: Musician's Guide to Copyright, 1983. Member, Steering Committee of UCLA Entertainment Law Symposium. Member, Academy of Television Arts and Sciences. *Member:* State Bar of California. *PRACTICE AREAS:* Entertainment.

*(This Listing Continued)*

**ANDREW L. GALKER,** born Brooklyn, New York, March 13, 1965; admitted to bar, 1992, California and U.S. District Court, Central District of California. *Education:* Yale University (B.A., summa cum laude, 1987); Stanford University Law School (J.D., 1992). Phi Beta Kappa. *Member:* Beverly Hills Bar Association (Member, Sections on: Business Law; Entertainment Law; Patent, Trademark and Trade Secrets); State Bar of California (Member, Intellectual Property Section). *PRACTICE AREAS:* Entertainment.

**ROBERT S. GETMAN,** born New York, N.Y., July 16, 1956; admitted to bar, 1981, California and U.S. District Court, Central District of California. *Education:* State University of New York at Albany (B.A., summa cum laude, 1978) Phi Beta Kappa; Cornell University (J.D., 1981). Cornell Law Review. *PRACTICE AREAS:* Entertainment; Intellectual Property.

**GEORGE T. HAYUM,** born New York, N.Y., February 21, 1945; admitted to bar, 1973, New York; 1975, District of Columbia; 1980, California. *Education:* Princeton University (A.B., cum laude, 1967); Woodrow Wilson School of Public and International Affairs; Université de Bordeaux, Bordeaux, France; Yale University (J.D., 1972). Fullbright Scholar. *LANGUAGES:* French. *PRACTICE AREAS:* Entertainment.

**BARRY L. HIRSCH,** born Chicago, Illinois, November 11, 1933; admitted to bar, 1957, California; 1985, New York. *Education:* University of California at Los Angeles; University of Southern California (LL.B., 1957). Co-author: "Piracy and Privilege In Literary Titles," University of Southern California Law Review, Winter, 1959. *Member:* Beverly Hills and Los Angeles County Bar Associations; State Bar of California; Los Angeles Copyright Society. *PRACTICE AREAS:* Entertainment.

**JAMES R. JACKOWAY,** born Richmond, Virginia, April 16, 1952; admitted to bar, 1978, New York; 1986, California. *Education:* Ohio University (B.A., summa cum laude, 1974; M.A., 1974); Yale University (J.D., 1977). Law Clerk to the Honorable Inzer B. Wyatt, U.S. District Judge, Southern District of New York, 1978. *Member:* The Association of the Bar of the City of New York; The State Bar of California. *PRACTICE AREAS:* Entertainment.

**JONATHAN D. KAUFELT,** born Highland Park, New Jersey, March 25, 1952; admitted to bar, 1976, New Jersey; 1978, New York; 1979, District of Columbia; 1980, U.S. Tax Court; 1987, California. *Education:* University of Pennsylvania (B.A., 1973); Georgetown University (J.D., 1976); New York University (LL.M., 1977). *Member:* State Bar of California. *PRACTICE AREAS:* Business Law; Entertainment; Taxation.

**CHRISTIANNE F. KERNS,** born Inglewood, California, August 11, 1958; admitted to bar, 1985, California and U.S. District Court, Central District of California. *Education:* California State University at Fullerton (B.A., cum laude, 1980); University of Southern California Law Center (J.D., 1985). Editor-in-Chief, Major Tax Planning and Computer Law Journal, University of Southern California, 1984-1985. *Member:* Los Angeles County, Orange County and American (Member, Commercial Financial Services Committee; Business Law Section) Bar Associations; State Bar of California; Financial Lawyers Conference. (Also Of Counsel to Corey, Croudace, Dietrich & Dragun at Irvine). *PRACTICE AREAS:* Real Estate Finance; General Business; Finance.

**JAMES C. MANDELBAUM,** born New York, N.Y., April 27, 1959; admitted to bar, 1986, New York; 1987, California. *Education:* Yale University (B.A., cum laude, 1981); New York University (J.D., 1985). Walter J. Derenberg Fellow in Copyright, 1984-1985. Frist Prize, Nathan Burkan Competition, 1985. Recipient, American Jurisprudence Award. Staff Member, Annual Survey of American Law, 1984. Member, Editorial Staff, Journal of the Copyright Society of U.S.A., 1985. Author: "The Nation: Overprotection of the First Amendment in Fair Use Analysis," Journal of the Copyright Society of the U.S.A., Vol. 32 #2, Dec., 1984. *Member:* The State Bar of California; New York State Bar Association. *PRACTICE AREAS:* Entertainment.

**MARCY S. MORRIS,** born Brooklyn, New York, February 5, 1955; admitted to bar, 1981, California. *Education:* State University of New York at Buffalo (B.A., Theatre & Communications, magna cum laude, 1975); University of California at Los Angeles (J.D., 1981). Editor-in-Chief, UCLA Journal of Environmental Law & Policy, 1979-1980. Author: "Hazardous Wastes: Regulatory Protection and the Government as Good Samaritan," TRIAL, January, 1982. Member, Hollywood Women's Political Committee, Women in Film. Member, Board of Directors, Earth Communications Office (ECO), 1989-1991. *Member:* Los Angeles County Bar Association (First Vice Chair, 1989-1990, Second Vice Chair, 1988-1989, Third Vice Chair, 1987-1988 and Secretary-Treasurer, 1986-1987, Intellec-

*(This Listing Continued)*

***ARMSTRONG HIRSCH JACKOWAY TYERMAN &
WERTHEIMER,*** A PROFESSIONAL CORPORATION, *Los
Angeles—Continued*

tual Property and Unfair Competition Section); State Bar of California. ***PRACTICE AREAS:*** Entertainment.

**MICHELE M. MULROONEY,** born November 3, 1960; admitted to bar, 1985, California. *Education:* University of Southern California (B.S., magna cum laude, 1982; J.D., 1985); Georgetown University. Order of the Coif; Beta Gamma Sigma. ***PRACTICE AREAS:*** Probate and Estate Planning.

**GEOFFRY W. OBLATH,** born San Francisco, California, July 5, 1949; admitted to bar, 1974, California. *Education:* University of California at Los Angeles (B.A., magna cum laude, 1971); Harvard University (J.D., cum laude, 1974). Phi Beta Kappa. *Member:* The State Bar of California. ***PRACTICE AREAS:*** Entertainment.

**RANDY M. SCHIENBERG,** born Chicago, Illinois, March 27, 1958; admitted to bar, 1985, California; 1986, U.S. District Court, Central District of California. *Education:* Stanford University (B.A., with distinction, 1980); Harvard Graduate School of Business Administration (M.B.A., 1983); University of California School of Law at Los Angeles (J.D., 1985). Member, 1983-1984 and Chief Articles Editor, 1985-1986, Federal Communications Law Journal. *Member:* Beverly Hills, Los Angeles County and American Bar Associations; State Bar of California. ***PRACTICE AREAS:*** Entertainment.

**SCOTT A. STEIN,** born Freeport, New York, November 12, 1966; admitted to bar, 1991 California. *Education:* Emory University (B.B.A., 1988); University of Southern California (J.D., 1991). ***PRACTICE AREAS:*** Entertainment Law.

**ROBERT STULBERG,** born Los Angeles, California, April 28, 1959; admitted to bar, 1986, California. *Education:* Brown University (A.B., magna cum laude, 1982); Harvard University (J.D., magna cum laude, 1985). Phi Beta Kappa. Member, 1983-1984 and Executive Editor, 1984-1985, Harvard Law Review. Author: Note, "Employment Discrimination Against the Handicapped and Section 504 of the Rehabilitation Act," 97 Harvard Law Review 997 (1984). Teaching Fellow, Harvard College, 1985. Law Clerk to Judge Joseph T. Sneed, U.S. Court of Appeals for the Ninth Circuit, 1985-1986. *Member:* Los Angeles County Bar Association; The State Bar of California. ***PRACTICE AREAS:*** Entertainment.

**BARRY W. TYERMAN,** born Chilliwack, British Columbia, Canada, November 3, 1947; admitted to bar, 1972, California. *Education:* University of California at Los Angeles (B.S., 1967; M.B.A., 1971; J.D., 1971). Order of the Coif. Note and Comment Editor, UCLA Law Review, 1970-1971. Awarded 1971 Nathan Burkan Memorial Competition National Award First Prize by The American Society of Composers, Authors and Publishers. *Member:* Beverly Hills and Los Angeles County Bar Associations; The State Bar of California; Los Angeles Copyright Society. ***PRACTICE AREAS:*** Motion Pictures; Music; Interactive Media.

**ROBERT S. WALLERSTEIN,** born Paducah, Kentucky, Dec. 9, 1948; admitted to bar, 1973, California. *Education:* University of Southern California (B.A., 1970); University of the Pacific, McGeorge School of Law (J.D., 1973). *Member:* Beverly Hills and American Bar Associations; The State Bar of California. ***PRACTICE AREAS:*** Entertainment.

**ERIC C. WEISSLER,** born New York, N.Y., February 22, 1954; admitted to bar, 1981, New York; 1988, California. *Education:* Yale University (B.A., summa cum laude, 1975); Harvard University (J.D., cum laude, 1980). Phi Beta Kappa. *Member:* American Bar Association. ***PRACTICE AREAS:*** Entertainment.

**ALAN S. WERTHEIMER,** born Los Angeles, California, October 26, 1948; admitted to bar, 1972, California. *Education:* Brandeis University and Stanford University (A.B., with great distinction, 1969); Stanford University (J.D., 1972). Phi Beta Kappa. Member, Board of Editors, 1970-1971 and Note Editor, 1971-1972, Stanford Law Review. Author: "The Diminished Capacity Defense to Felony-Murder," 23 Stanford Law Review 799, 1971. Law Clerk to Judge George W. Phillips, Jr., Alameda County Superior Court, Criminal Division, 1971. Member and Chairman, 1978-1983, Judge Pro Tem Panel, Small Claims Court, Beverly Hills Barristers, 1976-1983. Member, Panel of Arbitrators, Producers-Writers Guild Basic Agreement of 1981. *Member:* Beverly Hills, Century City, Los Angeles County and American Bar Associations; The State Bar of California. ***PRACTICE AREAS:*** Entertainment.

*(This Listing Continued)*

*OF COUNSEL*

**RONALD J. BASS,** born Los Angeles, California, March 26, 1942; admitted to bar, 1968, California. *Education:* Stanford University (A.B., magna cum laude, 1963); Yale University (M.A., 1964); Harvard University (J.D., cum laude, 1967). Phi Beta Kappa. Woodrow Wilson Fellow, Yale University. *Member:* Beverly Hills and Los Angeles County Bar Associations; The State Bar of California; Los Angeles Copyright Society. ***PRACTICE AREAS:*** Entertainment.

**GERALDINE S. HEMMERLING,** born Los Angeles, California, 1928; admitted to bar, 1953, California; 1960, U.S. Supreme Court. *Education:* University of California at Los Angeles (B.S., 1949); Boalt Hall School of Law, University of California and University of California at Los Angeles (J.D., 1952). Co-author and Co-editor: "Inter Vivos Trusts," McGraw Hill, 1975. President, UCLA Law Alumni Association, 1974. Chairman, Advisory Board, UCLA-CEB Estate Planning Institute, 1978-1985. Trustee, UCLA Foundation. *Member:* Los Angeles County and American (Council Member, Real Property, Probate and Trust Section, 1979-1985; Co-Chairman, National Conference of Lawyers and Corporate Fiduciaries, 1984-1987) Bar Associations; State Bar of California. Fellow: American College of Trust and Estate Counsel (President, 1989); International Academy of Estate and Trust Law (Member, Executive Committee, 1987-1989). ***PRACTICE AREAS:*** Probate and Estate Planning.

**ARTHUR O. ARMSTRONG,** born Seattle, Washington, November 28, 1929; admitted to bar, 1959, California. *Education:* University of Washington and San Diego State College (B.S., 1955); University of California Berkeley (LL.B., 1958). Order of the Coif. Editor-in-Chief, California Law Review, 1957-1958. *Member:* The State Bar of California. ***PRACTICE AREAS:*** Corporate; Securities Law; Taxation.

---

## *ARMSTRONG & TABOR*

*Established in 1990*

*1901 AVENUE OF THE STARS, SUITE 1050*
**LOS ANGELES, CALIFORNIA 90067**
*Telephone: 310-203-0005*
*Fax: 310-553-0851*

*General Civil and Trial Practice in all State and Federal Courts. Commercial, Corporate, Insurance, Mergers and Acquisitions, Surety and Real Property Law, Insurance Brokers and Agencies.*

*MEMBERS OF FIRM*

**JAMES S. ARMSTRONG, JR.,** born Chicago, Illinois, December 19, 1943; admitted to bar, 1972, California; 1995, Colorado. *Education:* Stanford University (B.A., 1965); Hastings College of Law, University of California (J.D., 1970). Member, Moot Court Board, 1970. Judge Pro Tem, Los Angels Superior and Municipal Courts. Member, Panel of Arbitrators, Los Angeles Superior Court, 1985—. *Member:* Los Angeles County (Member, Insurance Programs Committee, 1976-1983), Colorado and American (Member, Sections on: Litigation; Insurance, Negligence and Compensation Law) Bar Associations; The Defense Research Institute; Association of Southern California Defense Counsel; State Bar of California. ***REPORTED CASES:*** Lee v. Takao Building Development Co. Ltd. 175 Cal. App. 3d 565, 220 Cal. Rptr. 782 (1986). ***PRACTICE AREAS:*** Civil Trial; Commercial; Corporate; Insurance; Surety.

**STEPHEN H. TABOR,** born Long Beach, California, November 15, 1946; admitted to bar, 1972, California; 1979, U.S. Supreme Court and U.S. Tax Court. *Education:* Menlo College (A.A., 1966); University of California at Berkeley (A.B., 1968); Hastings College of Law, University of California (J.D., 1971). Judge Pro Tem: Los Angeles Municipal Court, 1981—; Los Angeles Superior Court, 1994—. Member, 1979 and Past President and Director, 1995, Conference of Insurance Council. Member: Panel of Arbitrators, American Arbitration Association; Panel of Arbitrators, Los Angeles Superior Court, 1983—. *Member:* State Bar of California; American Bar Association; The Defense Research Institute; Association of Southern California Defense Counsel. ***REPORTED CASES:*** Hilb, Rogal and Hamilton Insurance Services of Orange County, Inc. vs. Stanley P. Robb; Schwalbe vs. Jones (1976) 16 Cal.3d 514, 516 (546 P.2d 1033; 128 Cal. Rptr. 321); Daar vs. Alvord (1980) 101 Cal.App.3d 480, 481-482 (161 Cal.Rptr. 658). ***PRACTICE AREAS:*** Civil Trial; Commercial; Corporate; Insurance; Surety.

*(This Listing Continued)*

REPRESENTATIVE CLIENTS: American Ambassador Insurance Co.; California Insurance Guarantee Association; Hilb, Rogal and Hamilton; Times Mirror Company; CIGNA Cos. (ESIS); The Pep Boys Manny Moe & Jack of CA.; Safeco Insurance Co.; Human Services Insurance; Alliance Insurance Services; American Business Insurance; Brokers Los Angeles Inc.; United Artist Theatre Circuit, Inc.; Thorson & Associates Insurance Services, Inc.

## ARNBERGER, KIM, BUXBAUM & CHOY
515 SOUTH FLOWER STREET, SUITE 3500
**LOS ANGELES, CALIFORNIA 90071-2201**
Telephone: (213) 426-6255; (213) 426-4355
Facsimile: (213) 426-6222

*REVISER OF THE PEOPLE'S REPUBLIC OF CHINA AND MONGOLIA LAW DIGESTS FOR THIS DIRECTORY.*

*Other Los Angeles, California Office:* 3731 Wilshire Boulevard, Suite 910, West Tower, Los Angeles, California, 90010. Telephone: (213) 380-7780. Facsimile: (213) 380-5798.

*New York Office:* 100 Maiden Lane, 16th Floor, Suite 1600B, New York, New York, 10038. Telephone: (212) 504-6109. Fax: (212) 412-7016. E-Mail: akbc.ny@juno.com; Choylaw@earthlink.net.

*San Francisco, California Office:* 555 Montgomery Street, Suite 1405, San Francisco, California, 94111. Telephone: (415) 362-7601. Fax: (415) 753-4512. E-Mail: jurisprude@aol.com.

*Hong Kong Office:* 3201 Citibank Tower, 3 Garden Road, Central, Hong Kong. Telephone: (852) 2523-7001. Fax: (852) 2845-0947. E-Mail: AKBC@hk.super.net.

*Beijing (Peking), People's Republic of China Office:* China World Trade Centre, Suite 2518, No. 1 Jian Guo Men Wai Avenue, Beijing, P.R.C. Telephone: (86)(10) 6505-2288 Ext: 2523/2518. Fax: (86)(10) 6505-2538. E-Mail: akbcbjo@public.bta.net.cn.

*Guangzhou (Canton), People's Republic of China Office:* China Hotel Office Tower, Suite 512, Guangzhou, P.R.C. Telephone: (86)(20) 86663388 Ext: 2512. Fax: (86)(20) 8669-1217. Email:gzakbcgz@public1.guangzhou.gd.cn.

*Xiamen, People's Republic of China Office:* Foreign Trade Centre, Suite 519, No. 15 Hu Bing North Road, Xiamen City, P.R.C. Telephone: (86)(592) 506-3059. Facsimile: (86)(592) 511-1044 Ext: 519. E-Mail: akbcxmo@xpublic.fz.fj.cn.

*Shenzhen, People's Republic of China Office:* Shenzhen Development Center, Suite 2103, Renmin Nan Lu, Shenzhen, P.R.C. Telephone: (86)(755) 229-8009. Facsimile: (86)(755) 229-8011. E-Mail: szakbcsz@public.szptt.net.cn.

*Shanghai, People's Republic of China Office:* Room 1907, Astronaut Building, No. 525 Sichuan Bei Road, Shanghai 200085, P.R.C. Telephone: (86)(21) 6357-5676; (86)(21) 6357-5677. Fax: (86)(21) 6357-5679. E-Mail: akbcsho@public.sta.net.cn.

*Ulaanbaatar, Mongolia Office:* Mongolian Business Development Agency, Prime Minister Amar's Street, Ulaanbatar, Mongolia. Telephone: (976)(1) 31-3492. Facsimile: (976)(1) 32-5102. E-Mail: akbc@magicnet.mn.

*General Business, Corporate and Commercial Transaction and Civil Litigation Practice involving Foreign Trade and International Business Transactions, Intellectual Property and Technology Transfers, Corporate Formation and other Start-Ups, Securities and Commodities, Mergers and Acquisitions, Real Estate and Construction, Regulatory and Insurance Matters, Products Liability and General Casualty, Employment Law and Immigration, Cross-border Financing and International Taxation, Natural Resources, and Environmental Law, Aircraft and Equipment Leasing, Admiralty and Maritime, and Complex Commercial Litigation and Arbitration.*

*FIRM PROFILE:* ARNBERGER, KIM, BUXBAUM & CHOY *is an international law firm with offices on the east and west coasts of the U.S.A. (New York City, Los Angeles and San Francisco) and in Hong Kong, China and Mongolia. The Firm's international division maintains five offices inside China, including the capital at Beijing and the cities of Guangzhou (Canton), Shanghai, Shenzhen, and Xiamen. Each of the Firm's partners are recognized international practitioners, several of whom are prominent in their respective legal fields and some of whom have extensively published and frequently lectured on current legal issues. The Firm's attorneys include several prominent American, Asian and European-trained attorneys, along with attorneys who are of counsel to the Firm and assist it from associated offices in Tokyo, Seoul, Taipei, Bangkok, Jakarta and Sydney.*

*Established in 1969 the Firm traces its roots in Asia to 1972, when one of its attorneys became the first American attorney to represent foreign parties in China. It has since become one of the largest American firms in East Asia. The Firm's international practice is also supported by experienced attorneys in the*

*(This Listing Continued)*

*Firm's state-side offices, who provide expertise and work closely to coordinate overseas representations with client management and in-house counsel in North America and Europe. The firm opened the first foreign law office in Mongolia in 1992, and is active in legal work, including arbitration, in Russia and some Eastern European countries. The Firm's legal prominence in Northeast Asia is recognized in its appointment as the official reviser of Martindale-Hubbell's China and Mongolia Law Digests. The Firm's attorneys have handled challenging cross-border cases and international transactions, ranging from leading copyright infringement and antipiracy victories in China on behalf of foreign software and literary publishers, through the negotiation of natural resource concession rights in Myanmar (Burma), to obtaining one of the largest product liability settlements in the Commonwealth of the Northern Marianna Islands on behalf of Japan's largest construction contractor. The firm undertakes numerous major transactional matters including drafting the first insurance joint venture contracts in China; establishing major power plant contracts, handling major loan agreements and leasing transactions and assisting in public offerings. The Firm handles numerous transactions on behalf of major international banks. The Firm also handles all corporate work and other legal work on behalf of overseas divisions of European, Asian and American Corporations.*

*The Firm is active in the representation of parties in the U.S.A., including foreign parties doing business in the U.S. Attorneys in the American offices actively handle all aspects of domestic-based litigation, complex business transactions and corporate matters, securities and commodities, admiralty law, employment law and international transactions. Attorneys in the Firm's U.S. offices also routinely counsel businesses and entrepreneurs in their investment matters and day-to-day corporate and business activities. Attorneys in the Firm's U.S.-based litigation division routinely handle a variety of cases, including securities and commodities, breach of contract, employment discrimination, insurance disputes, marine law, product liability, unfair competition, and intellectual property infringement litigation. The Firm has handled appeals all the way to the U.S. Supreme Court, including a successful landmark case (Butz v. Economou 438 US 478, 1978). The Firm's U.S.-based attorneys are frequently called upon to represent clients in significant transactions, example of which includes the US$60 million acquisition of America's third largest ski resort by a major foreign investor and the first ever negotiated license of patent rights between the National Institute of Health and a major Japanese manufacturer. The Firm has been very active in securities and commodities compliance and litigation, as well as public offerings in the U.S.A.*

*The Firm's partners and associates bring extensive international and domestic legal experience that few firms of its size can equal. The Firm therefore offers the expertise and diversity of a big-Firm, while simultaneously providing the personalized service and responsiveness found in smaller firms. The Firm has thus been favored with a broad client base comprised of many of the world's foremost multinational companies from the U.S., Canada, Asia and Europe. Various attorneys of the Firm are admitted to practice in New York, California, and other U.S. jurisdictions, as well as in foreign jurisdictions such as China, Mongolia, Hong Kong, Japan, Korea, Thailand, Indonesia and Australia. In addition to English, attorneys of the Firm are fluent in numerous foreign languages, including Mandarin, Shanghainese, Hokkien, Cantonese and other Chinese dialects, Japanese, Thai, Indonesian Bahasa, Korean, French, Spanish and Swedish.*

### MEMBERS OF THE FIRM

**DAVID S. KIM**, born Seoul, South Korea, February, 1961; admitted to bar, 1990, California and U.S. District Court, Northern and Central Districts of California. *Education:* Western Illinois University (B.B.A., 1983; M.B.A., 1985); Southwestern University School of Law, Los Angeles (J.D., 1989). Recipient, Bradley and Pollack Scholarship, 1990. *Member:* State Bar of California; California Trial Lawyers Association; Los Angeles Trial Lawyers Association; California Korean Bar Association. **LANGUAGES:** English and Korean. **PRACTICE AREAS:** Litigation; Real Estate; Construction; Arbitration.

**H. BENNETT ARNBERGER**, born Globe, Arizona, July, 1953; admitted to bar, 1983, California and U.S. District Court, Northern and Central Districts of California. *Education:* University of California at Berkeley (A.B., with honors and distinction, 1977); University of San Francisco (J.D., 1983). Phi Delta Phi. Author: "The Developing Intellectual Property Regime in China, AIPLA Computer Law Institute (1996)"; "Ensuring Compliance Through Intellectual Property Audits," 5 International Legal Strategy 54 (1994); "Avoiding The Hidden Liabilities of Independent Contractors," I Foreign Assignments (Kaigai Chuzai) 99 (1994); "Proactive Prevention of Cross-Cultural Disputes," 6 International Legal Strategy 60 (1994); "Protecting Against Misappropriation of Trade Secrets," 10 International Legal Strategy 63 (1993); "Taxation and Legal Requirements of California Corporations," 16 International Business Law Journal (Kokusai

*(This Listing Continued)*

## ARNBERGER, KIM, BUXBAUM & CHOY, Los Angeles—Continued

Shoji Homu) 202 (1988). Associate, Yuasa & Hara, Tokyo, Japan, 1987-1989. Contract Administrator, Chemsult AG, Saudi Arabia, 1977-1980. *Member:* San Francisco, Los Angeles County and American (Member, Section on International Law) Bar Associations; State Bar of California; International Bar Association (Member, Section on Business Law); The Association of Trial Lawyers of America; Japan Society of Northern California; California-Southeast Asia Business Association; American Chamber of Commerce in Japan (Member, Committee on Licensing, Patents & Trademarks, 1987-1989). (San Francisco Office). *PRACTICE AREAS:* Business and Commercial Transactions; Intellectual Property Transactions; Corporate Law; Employment Law; International Transactions; Litigation and Arbitration.

**DAVID C. BUXBAUM,** born New York, N.Y., July, 1933; admitted to bar, 1970, New York and U.S. District Court, Southern, Eastern, Northern and Western Districts of New York; 1971, U.S. Court of Appeals, Second Circuit; 1974, U.S. Supreme Court; 1975, U.S. Court of Appeals, Seventh and Fourth Circuits; 1978, U.S. Court of Appeals, Eighth Circuit; 1979, U.S. Court of Appeals, First Circuit; 1981, California; 1989, U.S. District Court, Central District of California; 1991, U.S. District Court, Northern District of California; U.S. Court of Appeals, Ninth Circuit. *Education:* New York University (B.A., 1954); University of Michigan (J.D., 1959) concurrent graduate studies, University of Michigan Graduate School; graduate study, Harvard University and University of Washington (M.A., 1963; Ph.D., 1968). Member, Far East Honor Society, University of Michigan. Author: *Articles:* "Preliminary Trends in the Development of the Legal Institutions of Communist China and the Nature of the Criminal Law," International and Comparative Law Quarterly, January, 1962, reprinted in *Government of Communist China,* Chandler, San Francisco, 1966; "Horizontal and Vertical Influences Upon the Substantive Criminal Law of Mainland Chinese, Some Preliminary Observations," Osteuropa Recht, No. 1, 1964; "Chinese Family Law in Common Law Setting: A Note on the Institutional Environment and the Substantive Family Law of the Chinese in Malaysia and Singapore," Journal of Asian Studies, August, 1966; "Some Aspects of Civil Procedure and Practice at the Trial Level in Tanshui and Hsinchu...," XXX Journal of Asian Studies, 1971; *Lawyer's Challenge in China Trade: New and Developing Legal System,* New York Law Journal, International Law Finance and Trade, February, 1979; *Commodities Trade with China,* New York Law Journal, December, 1978; *Regulation of Commodity Futures Exchanges in Japan,* New York Law Journal, October, 1978; *Commodities Transactions in China and Hong Kong,* New York Law Journal, June, 1978; *Jurisdiction Over Foreign Transactions and Foreign Nationals,* New York Law Journal, April, 1978; *Two Cases of Dispute Settlement,* U.S.-China Business Review, Vol. 1, No. 2, March/April, 1974; *Two Cases of Dispute Settlement,* Arbitration and Dispute Settlement in Trade with China, Special Report No. 4 for Members of the National Council for United States-China Trade, February, 1974; *Negotiation with the Chinese,* Trade with China, 1973; *American Trade with the People's Republic of China: Some Preliminary Perspectives,* Columbia Journal of Transnational Law, Vol. 12, No. 1, 1973; *Liability of Federal Officials in Damage for Acts Unconstitutional or in Excess of their Authority; Expanding the Concept of the Rule of Law,* Capital University Law Review, Vol. 8, Issue 4, 1979; *Taking on the Government Alone; Sole Practitioner Battles Way to Supreme Court and Wins,* Legal Times of Washington, December, 1978; *Disclosure of Management Remuneration, Transaction, Litigation and Employment History,* Los Angeles Daily Journal, March, 1979; *Contracts in China,* China Trade, Praeger, 1982. Monthly Columnist, New York Law Journal on Commodities Law, 1976-1982; *Contract Law in China, The Dynamics of Statutory Development and Practice,* Doing Business in China, 1990, Streng et al, ed. Contracts in China during the Qing Dynasty: Key to the Civil Law XXI No. 2, Journal of Oriental Studies, University of Hong Kong, 1995. *The Commercial Laws of China,* and *Patents Law and Practice, Trademark Law and Practice, The People's Republic of China,* Digest of the Commercial Laws of the World, 1982-1993. *M.A. Dissertation:* "Legal Institutions of Contemporary Mainland China," University of Washington, 1962. *Ph.D. Dissertation:* Some Aspects of Substantive Family Law and Social Change in Rural China, 1896-1967," University of Washington, 1968. *Case Note:* "Freedom of Marriage in a Pluralistic Society," Malaya Law Review, 1963. Editor: *Traditional and Modern Legal Institutions in Asia and Africa,* Journal of Asian and African Studies, Supplement Edition, 1967; *Family Law and Customary Law in Asia: A Contemporary Legal Perspective,* 1968; *Law and Social Change: A Case Study of Family Law and Social Change in China and Other Developing Areas,* University of Washington Press, 1978; *Transition and Permanence: Chinese History and Culture, A Festschrift in Honor of Dr. Kung-Chan Hsiao,* 1971; *Chinese Family Law and Social Change in Historic and Comparative Perspective,* University of Washington Press, 1978; *China Trade: Prospects and Perspectives,* Prager, 1982; *Articles:* IP Enforcement and Education, The *New Gazette* (Hong Kong), January 1995; A Program for IP Rights Enforcement, The *New Gazette* (Hong Kong), February 1995; Scope of Trademark Protection Extended, The *New Gazette (Hong Kong),* March 1995; Action Plan to Avert Trade War, The *New Gazette (Hong Kong),* April 1995; Judge's Law Enhances IP Enforcement, The *New Gazette* (Hong Kong), 1995; Enforcement of Sino-US IP Agreement, The *New Gazette* Hong Kong, June 1995; Recent IP Cases in China, The *New Gazette* (Hong Kong), July 1995; Functioning Task Forces, The *New Gazette* (Hong Kong), August 1995; Protection of Famous Products and Famous Brands, The *New Gazette* (Hong Kong), September 1995; The Status of IP in China, The *New Gazette* (Hong Kong), October 1995; Leading Copyright Cases in Beijing, The *New Gazette* (Hong Kong), November 1995; Foreign Investment in China, The *Asian Investment Law Directory* 1995; Recent Developments of Intellectual Property Protection in China, *Hong Kong Law Year Book (1994); "Securities Regulations:* China: (to appear in) *International Securities Regulations:* Pacific Rim (N.Y. 1996). Criminal Law Regime Sees Progress After 17 Years, *China Law & Practice,* May 1996; Landmark Judgment against Juren Computer Co., *IP Asia,* June 1996; Trade War Averted, *IP Asia,* July/August 1996. Do We Meet the Mark? *Hong Kong Lawyer,* October 1996. Protecting IP Post-97, *Hong Kong Lawyer,* November 1996; "Extending Protection" *Hong Kong Lawyer,* December, 1996. Sole Counsel for Successful Respondents, *Butz v. Economou,* 438 US 478, 1978. Counsel for Successful Claimants, *Microsoft, Autodesk and Wordperfect v. Juren,* Beijing Intermediate Court, 1996. Associate Professor, Chinese Law, Comparative Law and Domestic Relations, University of Washington, 1968-1969. Assistant Lecturer, Chinese Law, Domestic Relations, Labor Law, Jurisprudence, Comparative Law, University of Singapore, 1963-1964. Adjunct Professor of Law: Touro Law School, 1980; Southwestern University School of Law, 1983-1988. Member, Commission on Labor Law, Singapore, 1963-1964. Member, Panel of Arbitrators, American Arbitration Association. *Member:* American Bar Association (Member, Committee on Far Eastern Law, Section of International and Comparative Law, 1965-1971); New York Trial Lawyers Association (Member, Liaison Committee with Judicial Conference, 1971-1978). (Hong Kong Office). *LANGUAGES:* Chinese. *PRACTICE AREAS:* International Law; Complex International Litigation; Complex International Contracts; Joint Ventures; Investment Law; Intellectual Property Protection an Enforcement; Commodities and Securities.

**KENNETH Y. CHOY,** born Hong Kong, May, 1956; admitted to bar, 1987, New York; U.S. District Court, Southern and Eastern Districts of New York; 1990, California; 1991, U.S. District Court, Central and Northern Districts of California and U.S. Court of Appeals, Ninth Circuit. *Education:* San Francisco State University (B.A., 1977); Northeastern University (J.D., 1986). Judicial Intern to Hon. Dolores K. Sloviter, U.S. Court of Appeals for the Third Circuit, 1985-1986. *Member:* State Bar of California (International Section). (New York Office). *LANGUAGES:* Chinese (Cantonese and Mandarin). *PRACTICE AREAS:* Transactions; Investments; Business Planning; Joint Ventures involving U.S. and Greater China (China, Taiwan, Hong Kong); International Litigation; Dispute Resolution.

**DOUGLAS L. BRYAN,** born Whittier, California, September, 1960; admitted to bar, 1991, California and U.S. District Court, Central District of California; 1992, U.S. Court of Appeals, Ninth Circuit. *Education:* California Polytechnic State University (B.S., 1983); Southwestern University School of Law (J.D., 1991). *Member:* State Bar of California; American Bar Association. *PRACTICE AREAS:* Tax Law; Corporate Law; Corporate Reorganizations; Constitutional Law; Insurance.

### OF COUNSEL

**MICHAEL A. BRAND,** born Phoenix, Arizona, August 29, 1952; admitted to bar, 1977, Colorado; 1978, California. *Education:* Indiana University (A.B., 1974); Harvard University (J.D., 1977). Phi Beta Kappa; Wendel Wilkie Scholar. Partner: Brobeck, Phleger & Harrison, 1992-1993; Baker & McKenzie, 1981-1992. *Member:* State Bar of California; American Bar Association. (Also Member of Brand Farrar Dziubla Freilich & Kolstad, Los Angeles). *PRACTICE AREAS:* Real Estate Law; International Transactions; Loan Workouts.

**ROBERT W. DZIUBLA,** born Chicago, Illinois, July 18, 1952; admitted to bar, 1980, Illinois; 1988, California. *Education:* Northwestern University (B.A., 1974; J.D., 1980); University of Chicago (M.A., 1978); University of Washington (LL.M., 1983). 1979 Jessup International Moot Court Competition: World Championship Team; National Championship Team; Best

*(This Listing Continued)*

Brief in National Competition. Professor of International Finance Law and International Business Law (Adjunct), University of Southern California, 1994—. Senior Fulbright Fellow in Japanese Corporate and Securities Law, 1983-1984, Faculty of Law, University of Kyoto. Author: "Hotel Bankruptcies and Restructurings in the 1990s (Part: 1) (in Japanese: Iza to iu toki no tame ni)" Vol. 1-4, 60 (Nov. 1992); "Japan's New Tax System," Venture Japan, Vol. 1, No. 3, 56 (1989); "Enforcing Corporate Responsibility: Japanese Corporate Directors' Liability to Third Parties for Failure to Supervise," 18 Law in Japan 55 (1986); "The Impotent Sword of Japanese Justice: the Doctrine of Shobunsei as a Barrier to Administrative Litigation," 18 Cornell International Law Journal 37 (1985); "International Trading Companies: Building on the Japanese Model," 4 Northwestern Journal International Law & Business 422 (1982); "Zenith Radio Corp. v. United States: The Demise of Congressionally Mandated Countervailing Duties," 1 Northwestern Journal International Law and Business 318 (1979). East Asian Affairs Advisor to Senator Paul Simon, 1982, 1988 and Senator Alan Dixon, 1982. Partner: Jones, Day, Reavis & Pogue, 1990-1993; Baker & McKenzie, Los Angeles, 1988-1990, Tokyo, Japan, 1985-1988. *Member:* Illinois State Bar Association; State Bar of California. (Also Member of Brand Farrar Dziubla Freilich & Kolstad, Los Angeles). *LANGUAGES:* English and Japanese. *PRACTICE AREAS:* International Transactions; Finance; Trade; Technology; Transfers; Real Estate; Aircraft and Equipment Leasings.

**CHARLES K. KOLSTAD,** born West Lafayette, Indiana, September 6, 1953; admitted to bar, 1980, New York; 1992, California. *Education:* University of Villanova (B.S., cum laude, 1975); Columbia University (M.B.A., 1978); University of Notre Dame (J.D., 1979). Professor, Columbia University Graduate School of Business Administration (Adjunct Assistant, 1984). Partner: Coopers & Lybrand, 1979-1992 (Managing Director, Financial Services Group, Tokyo, Japan, 1985-1990). *Member:* State Bar of California; New York State and American Bar Associations. (Also Member of Brand Farrar Dziubla Freilich & Kolstad, Los Angeles). *PRACTICE AREAS:* International Taxation; Business Transactions; Mergers and Acquisitions; Aircraft and Equipment Leasings.

**ROGER S. SAXTON,** born Martins Ferry, Ohio, April, 1952; admitted to bar, 1979, Sweden (as Jurist); 1980, Pennsylvania and U.S. District Court, Western District of Pennsylvania; 1992, New South Wales, Australia (Not admitted in California). *Education:* Case Western Reserve University (J.D., 1979). Studies in Japanese Law, Sophia University and University of Tokyo, Tokyo, Japan (1977-1980); Studies in Australian Law, University of Sydney (1989-1991). *Member:* Pennsylvania Bar Association; Law Society of New South Wales; Inter Pacific Bar Association. (Of Counsel, Sydney, Australia). *LANGUAGES:* English, Swedish and Japanese. *PRACTICE AREAS:* Litigation and Business Transactions between Australia, U.S. and Asia.

**KAZUKO ITOH,** born Tokyo, Japan, January, 1923; admitted to bar, 1959, Japan. *Education:* Tsuda College; Tokyo Bunrika University. Legal Advisor to Her Britanic Majesty's Ambassador, Tokyo, 1976—. Legal Consultant to the American Embassy, Tokyo, 1976—. *Member:* Tokyo Bar Association; International Bar Association. (Of Counsel, Tokyo, Japan). *LANGUAGES:* Japanese, English, French and Spanish. *PRACTICE AREAS:* General Civil and Trial Practice; International Arbitration; Patent Litigation and Business Transactions between Japan, Asia and U.S..

**DUCK-SOON CHANG,** born Korea, July, 1960; admitted to bar, 1985, Korea and Korea Patent Bar; 1991, New York; 1992, California. *Education:* Judicial Training and Research Institute of the Supreme Court of Korea (198 3-1984); College of Law, Seoul National University (B.Jur,. 1983); Harvard Law School (LL.M., 1990). Author: "Technology Transfer, Cooperation and Joint Venture Agreements with Korea," Chapter 4 of Legal Aspects of Business Transactions and Investment in the Far East (Kluwer, 1988); "Arbitration Procedures in Korea," Vol. 1, Asia Law and Practice 7 (1989); "Arbitration in South Korea," Vol. 14 East Asian Executive Reports 1 (1992). Lecturer, International Patent Training and Research Institute of the Korean Industrial Property Office. Arbitrator, Korean Commercial Arbitration Board. *Member:* New York State and American Bar Associations; State Bar of California; Korean Bar Association; Korean Patent Bar Association; International Trademark Association. *LANGUAGES:* Korean, English, Japanese (reads only). *PRACTICE AREAS:* Litigation and Business Transactions between S. Korea, Asia and U.S..

**DEBORAH S. CHEW,** born Singapore, May, 1964; admitted to bar, 1988, Singapore; 1991, California. *Education:* National University of Singapore (LL.B., with honors, 1987). Associate, Arthur Loke & Partners, Singapore, 1988-1991. *Member:* State Bar of California; American Immigration Lawyers Association; Singapore American Business Association (Founding

*(This Listing Continued)*

Member and Director); Hong Kong Association of California (Director); Asian Business Association; Law Society of Singapore and Academy of Law of Singapore. (Of Counsel, San Francisco Office). *LANGUAGES:* English and Chinese (Mandarin, Cantonese, Taiwanese and Chiu-chow dialect). *PRACTICE AREAS:* In-Bound Transactions and U.S. Immigration Matters.

**CHRISTINA Y. CHEN,** born Canton, China, May 2, 1943; admitted to bar, 1983, California. *Education:* San Francisco State University (B.A., 1969); Hastings College of the Law, University of California (J.D., 1979). (Of Counsel, San Francisco Office). *LANGUAGES:* English and Chinese (Mandarin, Cantonese and Toisan dialect). *PRACTICE AREAS:* Business Transactions and Litigation between Asia and U.S..

**LI ZHUOGEN,** born Shunde, Guangdong Province, PRC, October, 1935. *Education:* Yue Xue Teachers Training College. 1985-1991, Judge (ret.) Guangzhou Middle People's Court, Civil Division and Director of Administration. Recipient, 1984, 1985 Guangzhou City Court Systems Advance Specialist of the Year; 1988, Guangdong Province Outstanding Judge of the year; 1989 Third Degree Honor awarded by the Guangdong Province High Court. (Hong Kong Office). *LANGUAGES:* Chinese (Mandarin and Cantonese). *PRACTICE AREAS:* Litigation; Civil Law; Arbitration; Admiralty; Commercial Law; Securities Law; Real Estate Law; Intellectual Property.

**CONSTANCE M. BURKE,** born Queens, New York, November 5, 1944; admitted to bar, 1982, New York and U.S. District Court, Southern and Eastern Districts of New York (Not admitted in California). *Education:* Mount St. Mary's College (B.A., 1966); Hunter College of the City University of New York (M.S.W., 1976); Brooklyn Law School (J.D., 1981). Order of Barristers. *Member,* 1978-1979, Senior Editor, 1978-1980 and Book Review Editor, 1980-1981, Brooklyn Law Review. Author: Comment, "Blurring the Arrest-Search Dichotomy," 45 Brooklyn Law Review 901, 1979. *Member:* New York County Lawyers Association. *PRACTICE AREAS:* Trial and Appellate Litigation in all Courts.

**MICHAEL J. ORLOFSKY,** born Brooklyn, New York, August 24, 1963; admitted to bar, 1989, New York, New Jersey; 1991, District of Columbia and U.S. District Court, Southern and Eastern Districts of New York and New Jersey; U.S. Court of Appeals, Second Circuit; U.S. Supreme Court (Not admitted in California). *Education:* Rutgers University (B.A., summa cum laude, 1985); New York University (J.D., 1989). Phi Beta Kappa. *PRACTICE AREAS:* Trial and Appellate Litigation in all Courts.

## HONG KONG ASSOCIATES

**LEE KUI LAM,** born Hong Kong, May, 1949 (Not Admitted in United States); admitted to bar, 1980, Supreme Court of England and Wales, United Kingdom; Supreme Court of Hong Kong, Hong Kong. *Education:* University of London (LL.B., 1977); University of East Asia, Macau (DIP in Chinese Law). (Also Member of S.K. Wong & Lee, Hong Kong). *LANGUAGES:* Cantonese, English and Mandarin. *PRACTICE AREAS:* Litigation; Arbitration; Company Law; Commercial; Conveyancing; Intellectual Property; P.R.C. Conveyancing; Notarization and Commercial; Overseas Notarization.

**WONG SUI KWAN,** born Hong Kong, February, 1952 (Not Admitted in United States); admitted to bar, 1977, Supreme Court of Hong Kong; 1983, Supreme Court of England and Wales; 1989, Notary Public; 1990, the Chartered Institute of Arbitrators ; 1995, China-Appointed Attesting Officer. (Also Member of S.K. Wong & Lee, Hong Kong). *LANGUAGES:* Cantonese, English and Mandarin. *PRACTICE AREAS:* Litigation; Arbitration; Company Law; Commercial Law; Conveyancing; Notarization and Commercial; Overseas Notarization.

**PANG KA KWONG,** born Hong Kong, April, 1958 (Not Admitted in United States); admitted to bar, 1991, Supreme Court of Hong Kong, Hong Kong; 1996, Supreme Court of England and Wales, United Kingdom. *Education:* Chinese University of Hong Kong ((B.Soc.Sc., 1982); University of London (LL.B., 1988). *LANGUAGES:* Cantonese, English and Mandarin. *PRACTICE AREAS:* Litigation; Arbitration; Company and Commercial Law.

**CHOW SIU WO ANTHONY,** born Hong Kong, June, 1956; admitted to bar, 1991, New York and Florida (Not admitted in California). *Education:* University of Waterloo, Ontario Canada (B.A.S., Civil Eng.); University of Western Ontario (LL.B., 1987); University of Miami (J.D., 1984). *Member:* The Law Society of Upper Canada; The Law Society of England and Wales; The Law Society of Hong Kong. *LANGUAGES:* Cantonese, English and Mandarin. *PRACTICE AREAS:* Corporate and Commerical; Litigation; Real Estate and Mortgage Remedies.

*(This Listing Continued)*

**ARNBERGER, KIM, BUXBAUM & CHOY,** Los Angeles—
*Continued*

**FUNG TIK LUNG,** born Hong Kong, October, 1996 (Not Admitted in United States); admitted to bar, 1992, Supreme Court of Hong Kong, Hong Kong. *Education:* University of Hong Kong (LL.B., P.C.LL.). *LANGUAGES:* Chinese and English. *PRACTICE AREAS:* Commercial Law; Real Estate Law; Civil Litigation.

**FONG CHUN KWONG,** born Hong Kong, August, 1954 (Not Admitted in United States); admitted to bar, 1993, Supreme Court of Hong Kong, Hong Kong; 1995, Supreme Court of England and Wales. *LANGUAGES:* Chinese English and Mandarin. *PRACTICE AREAS:* Wills and Probate; Conveyancing and Tenancy; Matrimonial Proceedings.

**CHAN SHING CHE PHILEAS,** born Hong Kong, December, 1962 (Not Admitted in United States); admitted to bar, 1994, Supreme Court of Hong Kong; 1995, Supreme Court of England and Wales. (Also Member of S.K. Wong & Lee, Hong Kong). *LANGUAGES:* Chinese, English and Mandarin. *PRACTICE AREAS:* Conveyancing including Tenancy Matters; Family Law; General Litigation including Enforcement for Arbitration Awards; Personal Injury; Contractual Disputes.

**WONG SHUN FOON,** born Hong Kong, March, 1958 (Not Admitted in United States); admitted to bar, 1995, Supreme Court of Hong Kong. *Education:* The Chinese University of Hong Kong (B.A., 1982); University of London (LL.B., Part I, 1991) University of Hong Kong (P.C.LL., 1992). (Also Member of S.K. Wong & Lee, Hong Kong). *LANGUAGES:* Chinese, English and Mandarin. *PRACTICE AREAS:* Conveyancing; Civil and Criminal Litigation; Divorce; Intellectual Property; Employment Law.

**WONG SUK HAR,** born Hong Kong, June, 1956 (Not Admitted in United States); admitted to bar, 1986, The Institute of Chartered Secretaries and Administrators; 1996, Supreme Court of Hong Kong, Hong Kong. *Education:* London School of Accountancy (A.C.I.S., 1983); University of Central England in Birmingham (Certificate of Common Professional Examination, 1992); University of Central England in Birmingham (Law Society Final, 1993). (Also Member of S.K. Wong & Lee, Hong Kong). *PRACTICE AREAS:* Company Law; Conveyancing and Litigation.

**SZE WAI SHAN,** born Hong Kong, September, 1970 (Not Admitted in United States); admitted to bar, 1996, Supreme Court of Hong Kong. *Education:* University of Hong Kong (LL.B., P.C.LL.). *LANGUAGES:* Chinese, English and Mandarin. *PRACTICE AREAS:* Litigation; Conveyancing; Family Law; Intellectual Property Law; Probate.

**ZHOU JIAN HONG,** born Zhejiang Province, China, August, 1965 (Not Admitted in United States); admitted to bar, 1990, Peoples Republic of China. *Education:* Hangzhou University (LL.B., 1986); Peking University (LL.M., 1989). *LANGUAGES:* Chinese and English. *PRACTICE AREAS:* P.R.C.; Commercial Law; Securities Law; Real Estate Law; Intellectual Property; Arbitration.

### ASSOCIATES

**LAN MINGLIANG,** born Hainan Province, China, August, 1927; admitted to bar, 1989, China. *Education:* China University of Political Science & Law & Foreign Affairs College (1954- 1958). Publications: Outline of Administrative Law; General Situation of International Organization; International Constitution (Teaching Material); Outline and Guidance on International Law. Standing Vice-President of China International Economy, Science-Technology, Legal Personal Society. Vice President of China Commerce Federation Commercial Affairs Promoting Commission; Advisor of Asian-African Development and Communication Society of China; Standing Council Member of China Society of International Law; Council Member of all-China Lawyer's Association. Council Member of China research Committee of Hong Kong Law; Specialist of the Specialist Committee of CICCI Council; Member of Legal Council Committee of All-China Federation of Returned Overseas Chinese. (Beijing Office). *LANGUAGES:* Chinese, English. *PRACTICE AREAS:* Public International Law; Private International Law; Intellectual Property.

**C. SOPHIA NG,** born Jiangsu, China, April, 1970; admitted to bar, 1995, California; U.S. District Court, Northern District of California and U.S. Court of Appeals, Ninth Circuit. *Education:* University of California at Davis (B.A., 1992); University of California, Hastings College of the Law, San Francisco (J.D., 1995). Judicial Extern to California Supreme Court Criminal Central Staff, 1994. Public Interest Scholar, Public Interest Clearing House, 1995. *Member:* State Bar of California; American Bar Association. (San Francisco Office). *LANGUAGES:* English and Chinese (Cantonese and Mandarin). *PRACTICE AREAS:* Civil Litigation; Commercial Transactions; Nationality and Immigration Law.

**PING YE,** born Jiangsu, China, May, 1967; admitted to bar, 1988, China; 1995, Hawaii. *Education:* Law School of Fudan University (Batchelor of Law, 1987); William S. Richardson School of Law (J.D., 1994). Assistant Professor of Law, Shanghai University, Finance and Economics, 1988-1991. (San Francisco Office). *LANGUAGES:* Mandarin and Chinese Dialect, English. *PRACTICE AREAS:* International Trade Law; Business and Commercial Law; Commercial Transactions and Litigation between Asia and U.S..

**ROBERT M. SHANNON,** born Chicago, USA, December 1962; admitted to bar, 1995, California. *Education:* University of California, Los Angeles (B.A., Communication Studies, 1986); Hastings College of the Law, University of San Francisco (J.D., 1994). Member, Hastings Law Journal, 1992-1994. (Hong Kong Office). *LANGUAGES:* English. *PRACTICE AREAS:* General Commercial Transactions.

**HAO XIAODONG,** born Inner Mongolia, China, March, 1965; admitted to bar, 1990, China. *Education:* Inner Mongolia University (B.S.); China University of Political Science and Law (LL.B., 1991). (Beijing Office). *LANGUAGES:* Chinese, English, Japanese. *PRACTICE AREAS:* Litigation; Business Law; Intellectual Property.

**LIN JIA,** born Guangdong Province, China, October, 1962; admitted to bar, 1989, China. *Education:* Zhongshan University, Guangzhou, China (LL.B.); People University, Beijing, China (LL.M.). (Beijing Office). *LANGUAGES:* English, Chinese. *PRACTICE AREAS:* Chinese Law; Contracts; Trademark Arbitration.

**BYAMBAA BAYARMAA,** born Moscow, Russia, November 6, 1960; admitted to bar, 1982, Mongolia. *Education:* Moldova State University, Law Faculty, 1982; Passed State Examination on Bar Practice, March, 1994. (Mongolia Office). *LANGUAGES:* Russian, German, Romania, English. *PRACTICE AREAS:* Commercial and Contract Law; Arbitration; Litigation.

**HUANG JIANG-XIONG,** born Rongyan City, Fujian, January, 1964; admitted to bar, 1987, China. *Education:* South-West Politics & Law College (B.A., 1984); College of Xiamen University (Master of Law, 1990). (Xiamen Office). *LANGUAGES:* Chinese, Taiwanese, English. *PRACTICE AREAS:* Civil Law; Commercial Law; Investment Law; Real Estate Law.

**LIN YONG,** born Fuzhou, China, October, 1969; admitted to bar, 1993, China. *Education:* Xiamen University Law Department (B.A., 1992). (Shanghai Office). *LANGUAGES:* Chinese, English and Fuzhou. *PRACTICE AREAS:* General Civil Law; International Investment; Corporation Law; Civil Litigation.

**WU HONGLIANG,** born Shanghai, China, 1935; admitted to bar, 1985, China; registered patent agent. *Education:* Beijing Iron and Steel Institute (B.S., 1960). (Shanghai Office). *LANGUAGES:* Chinese and English (shanghai dialect). *PRACTICE AREAS:* Patent and Trademark Law; Intellectual Property.

**WANG XIAOGANG,** born Hebei, China, October, 1971; admitted to bar, 1993, China. *Education:* China University (M.A., LL.B., Political and Law, 1993). *Member:* China Bar Association. *LANGUAGES:* English, Chinese. *PRACTICE AREAS:* International Investment Law; Company and Security Law; Intellectual Property Law.

**LIN CHANG,** born Shantou City, China, November, 1971; admitted to bar, 1993, China. *Education:* Law Department Shantou University (1989-1993). (Guangzhou Office). *LANGUAGES:* English, Chinese (Mandarin and Cantonese). *PRACTICE AREAS:* Intellectual Property Litigation; Contracts; Real Estate; Trade; Insurance; Adoption Law.

**FENG RUIDING,** born Luzhou City, Sichuan Province, December, 1961; admitted to bar, 1989, China. *Education:* Law Department Southwest College of Politics and Law (1986-1988, 1991-1993). (Guangzhou Office). *LANGUAGES:* Chinese (Mandarin). *PRACTICE AREAS:* Trade; Intellectual Property; Company Law; Marriage; Real Property; Contracts; Insurance Law.

**ZHONG WENYA,** born Shenzhen, China, December, 1970; admitted to bar, 1994, China. *Education:* Shenzhen University of Law (Graduate Student, 1993; M.B.A., Business & Administration, 1996). *Member:* Shenzhen Lawyer's Association. (Shenzhen Office). *LANGUAGES:* English, Chinese. *PRACTICE AREAS:* International Securities.

**DU LEI,** born Xiamen, Fujian Province, China, February 3, 1972 (Not Admitted in United States). *Education:* Xiamen University (LL.B., 1994).

*(This Listing Continued)*

**LANGUAGES:** Mandarin, English and Taiwanese. **PRACTICE AREAS:** International Business Law; Overseas Financial Market.

**STEVEN P. LEAVENWORTH,** born Harbor City, California, May 28, 1965; admitted to bar, 1995, California; 1996, Illinois. *Education:* University of California at Berkeley (A.B., 1988); University of Michigan (J.D., 1992). (Beijing Office). **PRACTICE AREAS:** Joint Venture; Intellectual Property; International Litigation and Commercial Transactions between U.S. and Asia.

**DASHSAMBUU ODONGUA,** born Ulaanbaatar, Mongolia, January, 1968 (Not Admitted in United States). *Education:* Invanovo State University (LL.B., 1993); Sorbonne, Paris (Commerical Law). **LANGUAGES:** Mongolian, Russian, French and English. **PRACTICE AREAS:** Commercial Law; Business Law; Intellectual Property.

**WANG XINHUA,** born Changchun, China, 1964 (Not Admitted in United States). *Education:* Jilin University (LL.B., 1986); Korea Maritime University (LL.M., 1996). **LANGUAGES:** Chinese and English. **PRACTICE AREAS:** International Law; International Trade; Maritime Law; Aviation Law.

**WEI ZHENG,** born Beijing, China, 1969 (Not Admitted in United States); admitted to bar, 1995, Beijing, China. *Education:* Xiamen University (LL.B., 1993). **LANGUAGES:** Chinese and English.

**WU FANXIANG,** born Shanghai, China, December, 1968 (Not Admitted in United States); admitted to bar, 1994, China. *Education:* Shanghai University (LL.B.). **LANGUAGES:** Chinese. **PRACTICE AREAS:** Company Law; Contract Law.

**LI ZHIGUANG,** born Shanghai, China, November, 1968 (Not Admitted in United States); admitted to bar, 1994, China. *Education:* Shanghai University Law Institute (LL.B.). *Member:* Chinese Bar Association. **LANGUAGES:** Chinese and English. **PRACTICE AREAS:** Economical Contract Law; Insurance Law; Criminal Law; Foreign Contract Law.

**TERENCE J. DENIGAN,** born Newport Beach, California, October, 1966; admitted to bar, 1996, Washington (Not admitted in California). *Education:* University of California, Berkeley (B.A., 1989); Charles University, Czechoslovakia (International Law Program. 1993); Golden Gate University School of Law, San Francisco (J.D., 1993). **LANGUAGES:** English, Spanish and Turkish. **PRACTICE AREAS:** International Corporate Law (Foreign Investment); Civil Litigation; Criminal Defense.

**LEI SHANYING,** born Guangzhou, China, 1973; admitted to bar, 1995, China (Not Admitted in United States). *Education:* Zhongshan University (LL.B.). **LANGUAGES:** Mandarin, Cantonese and English. **PRACTICE AREAS:** Economic Law; Contracts; Real Estate Dispute.

**HU JIE,** born Shanghai, China, July, 1968; admitted to bar, 1993, China (Not Admitted in United States). *Education:* Shanghai University (LL.B.). **LANGUAGES:** Chinese and English. **PRACTICE AREAS:** Economic Law; International Economic Law; Company Law.

**TENG LI,** born Liaoning, China, January, 1971 (Not Admitted in United States); admitted to bar, 1993, China. *Education:* Liaoning University, Shenyang, China (LL.B., 1992); Huaqiao University (Quanzhou, China (LL.M., 1995). **LANGUAGES:** Chinese and English. **PRACTICE AREAS:** International Investment Law; China Intellectual Property Law; China Contract Law.

**WU HONG LIANG,** born Shanghai, China, 1935; admitted to patent bar 1985, China, registered patent agent (Not Admitted in United States). *Education:* Beijing Iron and Steel Institute (B.S., 1960). **LANGUAGES:** Chinese, English and Shanghai dialect. **PRACTICE AREAS:** Patent and Trademark Law; Intellectual Property.

*LEGAL SUPPORT PERSONNEL*

**WU ZHANGOING,** born Shantou, Guangdong Province, China, October, 1967. *Education:* Shenzhen University (LL.B., 1991). (Shenzhen Office). **LANGUAGES:** English, Chinese. **PRACTICE AREAS:** Business Litigation.

**LIU XIAOXUN,** born Hunan, China, December, 1963. *Education:* Renmin University of China (M.B.A., International Law, 1993). (Beijing Office). **LANGUAGES:** English, Chinese. **PRACTICE AREAS:** Chinese Law; Commercial Law.

**LEE YAN,** born China, November, 1971. *Education:* Shenzhen University (LL.B., LL.M., Political Sciences and Law). *Member:* Shenzhen Lawyer's Association. (Shenzhen Office). **LANGUAGES:** English, Chinese (Mandarin and Cantonese). **PRACTICE AREAS:** Litigation and Contracts; Intellectual Property.

*(This Listing Continued)*

**IAN C. FORSYTH,** born Bendigo, Australia, July, 1969. *Education:* Syracuse University, College of Law (J.D.); International Relations, The Maxwell School of Citizenship & Public Affairs, Syracuse University (M.A.); A.B. East Asian Studies, University of California at Davis. **LANGUAGES:** English, Chinese and Mandarin. **PRACTICE AREAS:** General International.

REVISER OF THE PEOPLE'S REPUBLIC OF CHINA AND MONGOLIA LAW DIGESTS FOR THIS DIRECTORY.

---

## ARNDT & VAN PATTEN

A Law Partnership of Professional Corporations
*523 WEST SIXTH STREET*
*SUITE 310*
**LOS ANGELES, CALIFORNIA 90014**
Telephone: 213-622-7174
Fax: 213-622-8026

*Bangkok, Thailand Office:* Associated Lawyers & Consultants Ltd., 4th Floor, Panunee Building, 518/3 Ploenchit Road. Telephone: 662-252-0177; 251-9832. Fax: 662-251-2323. E-Mail: arndt@ksc.av.ac.th.
*Yangon, Myanmar Affiliated Office:* Maw Htoon & Partners Law Offices, 49/51 31st Street. Telephone: (951) 71919. Facsimile: (951) 34586.

*General Commercial and Corporate Law. International Law.*

*MEMBERS OF FIRM*

**CRAIG R. ARNDT, (P.C.),** born Ashtabula, Ohio, 1937; admitted to bar, 1963, California. *Education:* Yale University (B.A., magna cum laude, 1959); Yale Law School (LL.B., 1962). *Member:* Los Angeles County Bar Association; State Bar of California. (Also with Pacific Legal Group, Bangkok, Thailand; Also with Associated Lawyers & Consultants, Ltd., Bangkok, Thailand). **LANGUAGES:** French. **PRACTICE AREAS:** Commercial Law; Corporate Law; International Law.

**ANTHONY J. VAN PATTEN, (P.C.),** born Stockton, California, December 16, 1932; admitted to bar, 1963, California. *Education:* University of California at Berkeley (A.B., 1953); Boalt Hall School of Law, University of California at Berkeley (LL.B., 1962). Author, "Planning for Business with China," Long Range Planning Journal 27, August 1974. Co-author, "Foreign Investments in the Republic of Korea," 20 Hastings Law Journal 245, November 1968. *Member:* State Bar of California. **LANGUAGES:** Japanese, Chinese. **REPORTED CASES:** Ministry of Defense of Islamic Republic of Iran v. Gould, Inc. 969 F.2d 764, 9th Cir., 1992. Counsel for Republic of Iran. **PRACTICE AREAS:** Intellectual Property; Corporate Law; International Law.

*OF COUNSEL*

**ROBERT H. TAKEUCHI (P.C.),** born Tacoma, Washington, June 3, 1937; admitted to bar, 1964, California. *Education:* University of California at Los Angeles (A.B., 1959); University of Southern California (LL.B., 1963). Phi Alpha Delta. Lead Articles Editor, University of Southern California Law Review, 1962-1963. Vice Chair, Board of Trustees, Pomona College. President, Japan America Society of Southern California, 1982-1983. Member, Japan/California Advisory Council, State of California, 1979-1982. Chair, Los Angeles--Nagoya Sister City Affiliation, 1972-1973. Co-Author: "Setting Up Enterprises in the U.S.A./Japan's Guide to Business in America," Press International, Ltd., 1976. Author: "Japanese Businesses: New Clients, Old Traditions," Los Angeles Lawyer, Vol. 2, No. 3, May, 1979. *Member:* State Bar of California (Member, Executive Committee, International Law Section, 1993-1995); Los Angeles County (Chair, Pacific Rim Committee, 1990-1991 and Member, Executive Committee, International Law Section, 1990-1993) and American Bar Associations; Japanese American Bar Association; Chancery Club. **PRACTICE AREAS:** International Business Law.

REFERENCE: First Los Angeles Bank (Downtown Branch).

---

## ARNELLE, HASTIE, McGEE, WILLIS & GREENE

*2049 CENTURY PARK EAST, SUITE 800*
**LOS ANGELES, CALIFORNIA 90067**
Telephone: 310-552-3200
Fax: 310-552-3214

*San Francisco, California Office:* One Market, Steuart Street Tower, 9th Floor. 94105-1310. Telephone: 415-495-4747. Telecopier: 415-495-5123.

*(This Listing Continued)*

### ARNELLE, HASTIE, McGEE, WILLIS & GREENE, Los Angeles—Continued

Civil Litigation. Bankruptcy. Business. The Civil Litigation Practice includes Commercial, Construction, Environmental, Toxic, Insurance, Intellectual Property, Labor and Employment, Products Liability and Professional Malpractice.

FIRM PROFILE: Arnelle, Hastie, McGee, Willis & Greene is a regional minority-owned firm with a practice emphasizing litigation on behalf of corporations and public entities. The firm also has expertise in the areas of Patent, Trademark, Copyright and Computer Laws and represents creditors in bankruptcy and insolvency matters. Arnelle, Hastie, McGee, Willis & Greene, which has engaged in numerous joint ventures with non-minority owned law firms, is an original participant in the American Bar Association, Minority Counsel Demonstration Program.

#### MEMBERS OF FIRM

**REGINALD D. GREENE,** born Tuskegee, Alabama, August 9, 1951; admitted to bar, 1978, California; 1980, U.S. District Court, Central District of California. *Education:* United States Military Academy; Georgia Institute of Technology (B.E.E.S., 1974); University of Michigan (J.D., 1977). Attorney, Office of the District Attorney, Los Angeles County, 1978-1979. *Member:* Los Angeles County and American Bar Associations; State Bar of California; Association of Southern California Defense Counsel; National Bar Association. [With US Army, 1969-1971]. (Resident). *PRACTICE AREAS:* Litigation; Products Liability; Intellectual Property; Construction; Structural Defects.

**WILLIAM H. HASTIE,** born St. Thomas, U.S. Virgin Islands, March 5, 1947; admitted to bar, 1973, Pennsylvania and U.S. District Court, Eastern District of Pennsylvania; 1974, California, U.S. Court of Appeals, Ninth Circuit and U.S. District Court, Northern District of California; 1990, U.S. District Court, Central District of California. *Education:* Amherst College (B.A., 1968); University of Strasbourg, Strasbourg, France; Boalt Hall School of Law, University of California (J.D., 1971). Editor and Annotator, "California Civil Rights Laws," California Fair Employment and Housing Commission, 1978. Author: "Wrongful Discharge: New Plaintiff's Tool," Current Trends in Housing and Employment, University of Missouri-KC, CLE, 1987; "Protecting the Individual Corporate Defendant in Wrongful Termination Cases," Employment Relations Today, 1987. Visiting Law Professor: Graduate School of Public Policy, University of California at Berkeley, 1981-1982 and 1983-1985; American Bar Association Model Trial Institute, 1978. Court-appointed lawyer representative: U.S. Ninth Circuit Judicial Conference, 1976-1978; Ninth Circuit Committee on Evaluation of Lawyers, 1979-1981. Pro Tem, United States Trial Commissioner, 1985-1987. Director, Blue Cross of California, 1994—. Recipient: Legal Defense Fund NAACP Pro Bono Legal Service Award, 1989; Bar Association of San Francisco, Distinguished Service Award, 1990; Charles Houston Bar, Clinton White Trial Advocacy Award, 1991; National Bar Association, Commercial Law Award, 1992; California Association of Black Lawyers, Lawyer of the Year Award, 1993. Undersecretary and General Counsel, California State and Consumer Services Agency, 1979-1982. Executive and Chief Legal Officer, California Fair Employment and Housing Commission, 1976-1978. *Member:* Bar Association of San Francisco (Member, Committee on Federal Practice, 1976-1977); Pennsylvania and American (Member: Legal Education Section, 1974-1976; Committee on Bar Examinations and Clinical Legal Education, 1974-1977; Labor and Employment Law, 1986-1992; Economics of the Practice of Law, 1988-1993) Bar Associations; State Bar of California (Member: Disciplinary Hearing Subcommittee, 1977-1979; Advisory Panel on Bar Examinations, 1978-1979; Steering Committee, California Minority Counsel Program, 1989-1993, Chair, 1992-1993); National Bar Association (Chair, National Task Force on Economic Development, 1988-1989; Member, Commercial Law Section; Chair, Corporate Counsel Conference, 1992—); California Association of Black Lawyers (Co-Chair, Corporate Counsel Conference, 1988-1989); Charles Houston Bar Association; William Hastie Lawyers Association. (Also at San Francisco, California Office). *PRACTICE AREAS:* Commercial Litigation; Employment Law; Business.

#### SPECIAL COUNSEL

**JOHN A. MINOR III,** born Oakland, California, February 14, 1951; admitted to bar, 1977, California and U.S. District Court, Eastern and Northern Districts of California; 1978, District of Columbia; 1981, U.S. District Court, Central District of California and U.S. Court of Appeals, Ninth Circuit. *Education:* Stanford University (B.A., 1972); University of California, Berkeley (Boalt Hall) (J.D., 1976). Staff Counsel, U.S. Senate

*(This Listing Continued)*

Judiciary Committee, 96th Congress, 1979-1981. *Member:* State Bar of California. (Resident). *PRACTICE AREAS:* Real Estate; Banking; Corporate Law.

#### ASSOCIATES

**ROBERT SHAYNE FIGGINS,** born Phoenix, Arizona, July 5, 1966; admitted to bar, 1992, California and U.S. District Court, Central District of California. *Education:* Pepperdine University (B.S., 1988; J.D., 1991). *Member:* State Bar of California. (Resident).

**MICHAEL V. LEE,** born Saigon, Vietnam, 1969; admitted to bar, 1994, California, U.S. District Court, Central District of California and U.S. Court of Appeals, 9th Circuit. *Education:* University of California, Irvine (B.A., cum laude, 1991); University of California, Los Angeles (J.D., 1994). Phi Beta Kappa; Phi Delta Phi. Member, UCLA Moot Court Honors Program, 1994. Law Clerk to: Honorable James Barr, U.S. Bankruptcy Court, Central District of California, 1992. Law Clerk to: Hon. William Burby, 1994; Hon. William Huss, 1994-1995; Hon. Ernest Hiroshige, 1994-1996; Hon. Fumiko Wasserman, 1995-1996; Los Angeles County Superior Court. *Member:* State Bar of California. (Resident). *LANGUAGES:* Vietnamese. *PRACTICE AREAS:* Products Liability Litigation; Commercial Law; Warranty Litigation.

**SCOTT K. LINER,** born Burlingame, California, June 19, 1964; admitted to bar, 1989, California; 1992, U.S. District Court, Central District of California. *Education:* University of California (B.S., with honors, 1986); Loyola Marymount University (J.D., 1989). *Member:* Los Angeles County Bar Association; State Bar of California. (Resident). *PRACTICE AREAS:* Products Liability; Insurance Coverage.

**BRANDON M. TESSER,** born Rochester, New York, August 20, 1968; admitted to bar, 1993, California; 1994, U.S. District Court, Central District of California. *Education:* University of California, Santa Barbara (B.A., 1990); University of California, San Diego; Loyola Marymount University (J.D., 1993). Law Clerk to: Hon. Volney V. Brown, Jr., 1991; Hon. Lisa Hill Fenning, 1991. *Member:* Los Angeles County, Beverly Hills and Century City Bar Associations; State Bar of California. (Resident). *PRACTICE AREAS:* Civil Litigation; Business Litigation.

REPRESENTATIVE CLIENTS: American Telephone & Telegraph; Bank of America; Atlantic Richfield Co.; Baxter HealthCare Corp.; California Public Employees Retirement System; Chevron Corporation; City & County of San Francisco; City of Los Angeles; Eastman Kodak; Eaton Corporation; E.I. du Pont de Nemours & Co.; Federal Deposit Insurance Corp.; Ford Motor Company; Frito-Lay, Inc.; General Motors Corporation; Grumann Air Co.; Lockheed Corp.; Levi Strauss & Co.; NationsBank; Pacific Bell; Pacific Gas & Electric Co.; Shell Oil Co.; State Farm Companies; State of California; Teachers Insurance & Annuity Association; United Airlines; University of California; Wells Fargo Bank; WMX Technologies; Xerox Corporation.

(For Complete Biographical Data on all Personnel, see Professional Biographies at San Francisco, California)

---

### ARNOLD & PORTER
#### 44TH FLOOR, 777 FIGUEROA STREET
#### LOS ANGELES, CALIFORNIA 90017-2513
*Telephone: 213-243-4000*
*Telecopy: 213-243-4199*

*Washington, D.C. Office:* Thurmond Arnold Building, 555 Twelfth Street, N.W., 20004-1202. Telephone 202-942-5000. Telecopy: 202-942-5999.
*Denver, Colorado Office:* 1700 Lincoln Street, 80203-4540. Telephone: 303-863-1000. Telecopy: 303-832-0428.
*New York, N.Y. Office:* 399 Park Avenue, 10022-4690. Telephone: 212-715-1000. Telecopy: 212-715-1399.
*The United Kingdom Office:* One, St. Paul's Churchyard, London, England, EC4M 8SH. Telephone: 011-44-171-236-3626. FAX: 011-44-171-236-3610.

*General Practice.*

#### PARTNERS

**BRIAN K. CONDON,** born Los Angeles, California, August 31, 1963; admitted to bar, 1988, California. *Education:* University of California at Los Angeles (B.A., cum laude, 1985); Hastings College of Law, University of California (J.D., magna cum laude, 1988). Order of the Coif. *Member:* State Bar of California. *PRACTICE AREAS:* Litigation. *Email:* condobr@aporter.com

**LAWRENCE A. COX,** born Salt Lake City, Utah, August 1, 1952; admitted to bar, 1977, California. *Education:* University of California at Irvine (A.B., magna cum laude, 1974); Boalt Hall School of Law, University of California (J.D., 1977). Phi Beta Kappa. Chairman, Moot Court Board.

*(This Listing Continued)*

*Member:* State Bar of California. **REPORTED CASES:** Keating v. National Union, 754 F. Supp. 1431 (C.D.Cal. 1990); Smith v. Montoro, 648 F. 2d 602 (9th Cir. 1981). **PRACTICE AREAS:** Litigation; Litigation of Securities; Health Care; Insurance; Legal Malpractice; Environmental. **Email:** coxla@aporter.com

**ERIC L. DOBBERTEEN,** born Battle Creek, Michigan, October 22, 1948; admitted to bar, 1973, Michigan; 1978, California. *Education:* Western Michigan University (B.A., cum laude, 1970); College of William and Mary (J.D., 1973). Assistant U.S. Attorney, Central District of California, 1977-1983. [Lt. U.S. Navy, JAGC, 1974-1977]. **PRACTICE AREAS:** White Collar Criminal Defense Law; Complex Civil Litigation. **Email:** dobbeer@aporter.com

**DAVID S. EISEN,** born Los Angeles, California, February 18, 1956; admitted to bar, 1981, California. *Education:* University of California at San Diego (B.A., cum laude, 1978); University of Southern California (J.D., 1981). Chairman, Hale Moot Court Honors Program. *Member:* State Bar of California. **PRACTICE AREAS:** Law Firm and Other Partnership Disputes; Complex Business Litigation; Legal Malpractice Litigation Defense; Employment Law. **Email:** eisenda@aporter.com

**GREGORY C. FANT,** born Los Angeles, California, August 26, 1951; admitted to bar, 1976, California; 1980, U.S. Supreme Court. *Education:* University of California at Irvine (B.A., summa cum laude, 1973); University of California at Los Angeles (J.D., 1976). Order of the Coif. Managing Editor, UCLA-Alaska Law Review, 1975-1976. *Member:* Los Angeles County Bar Association (Editor, Newsletter, 1984-1987, Member, 1986-1991 and Chair, 1991, Steering Committee, Annual Securities Regulation Seminar and Member, 1984— and Chair, 1992-1993, Executive Committee, Business and Corporations Law Section); Financial Lawyers Conference. **PRACTICE AREAS:** Corporation Law; Business Law; Banking Law; Real Estate Law. **Email:** fantgr@aporter.com

**JAMES I. HAM,** born Fresno, California, June 29, 1956; admitted to bar, 1981, California. *Education:* University of Southern California (A.B., magna cum laude, 1978); University of California at Los Angeles (J.D., 1981). Executive Editor, UCLA Law Review, 1980-1981. *Member:* Los Angeles County Bar Association (Secretary, 1987-1988 and Chairman, 1988-1989, Professional Responsibility and Ethics Committee; Delegate to the State Bar Convention, 1988, 1992); State Bar of California (Member, Committee on Professional Responsibility and Conduct, 1987-1990). **REPORTED CASES:** Hartbrodt v. Burke (1996) 42 Cal.App.4th 168, 49 Cal. Rptr. 2d 562. **PRACTICE AREAS:** Commercial Litigation; Products Litigation; Employment Law; Legal Ethics. **Email:** hamja@aporter.com

**MATTHEW T. HEARTNEY,** born Des Moines, Iowa, February 25, 1953; admitted to bar, 1979, New York; 1986, California. *Education:* Oberlin College (B.A., with honors, 1975); Yale Law School (J.D., 1978). Phi Beta Kappa. Editor, 1977, Note Editor, 1977-1978, Yale Law Journal. **PRACTICE AREAS:** Litigation; Antitrust. **Email:** heartma@aporter.com

**CRAIG N. HENTSCHEL,** born Santa Monica, California, June 26, 1950; admitted to bar, 1975, California; 1980, U.S. Supreme Court. *Education:* University of California at Los Angeles (A.B., cum laude, 1972); Loyola University of Los Angeles (J.D., cum laude, 1975). *Member:* State Bar of California. **Email:** hentscr@aporter.com

**POLLY HORN,** born Schenectady, New York, January 31, 1935; admitted to bar, 1978, California. *Education:* Vanderbilt University (A.B., cum laude, 1956); University of Southern California (J.D., 1978). *Member:* State Bar of California. **PRACTICE AREAS:** Commercial Litigation; Legal Malpractice. **Email:** hornpo@aporter.com

**LAURENCE J. HUTT,** born New York, N.Y., December 15, 1950; admitted to bar, 1975, California; 1995, Colorado. *Education:* University of Pennsylvania (B.A., cum laude, 1972); Stanford University (J.D., 1975). Phi Beta Kappa; Order of the Coif. Judge Pro Tem, Los Angeles Municipal Court, 1985-1988. Joint Settlement Officer Program, Los Angeles Superior Court, 1990. Judge Pro Tem, Los Angeles Superior Court, 1994. *Member:* Los Angeles County Bar Association (Delegate to State Bar Convention, 1981-1992; Member: Delegation Executive Committee, 1986-1992; Delegation Officer, 1989-1992; Delegation Chair, 1992; Chair, Superior Courts Subcommittee, 1988-1989; State Courts Committee, 1989-1993, Vice Chair, 1989-1990); State Bar of California (Elected Member, Executive Committee of the Conference of Delegates, District 7, 1992-1995, Vice Chair and Legislative Chair, 1994-1995). **PRACTICE AREAS:** Real Estate and Banking Litigation; Sports Litigation; Commercial Litigation. **Email:** huttla@aporter.com

**THEODORE G. JOHNSEN,** born Evanston, Illinois, March 4, 1943; admitted to bar, 1969, California. *Education:* University of California at *(This Listing Continued)*

Los Angeles (B.A., 1965; J.D., 1968). Order of the Coif. Associate Editor, 1966-1967 and Note and Comment Editor, 1967-1968, University of California at Los Angeles Law Review. Instructor of Law, University of Michigan Law School, 1968-1969. *Member:* Los Angeles County (Member, Executive Committee of the Business and Corporations Law Section, 1982-1989) and American Bar Associations; State Bar of California. **PRACTICE AREAS:** Corporate; Securities. **Email:** johnsth@aporter.com

**MAURICE A. LEITER,** born Boston, Massachusetts, February 10, 1958; admitted to bar, 1982, Massachusetts; 1983, New York; 1986, California. *Education:* Harvard University (B.A., cum laude, 1979); Georgetown University (J.D., cum laude, 1982). Editor, American Criminal Law Review, 1981-1982. Assistant U.S. Attorney, Central District of California, 1986-1991; Assistant Chief, Criminal Division, 1989-1990. **PRACTICE AREAS:** Civil Litigation; Products Liability; White Collar Criminal Defense. **Email:** leiterma@aporter.com

**MARGARET M. MORROW,** born Columbus, Nebraska, October 29, 1950; admitted to bar, 1974, California. *Education:* Bryn Mawr College (B.A., magna cum laude, 1971); Harvard University (J.D., cum laude, 1974). Recipient: Los Angeles County Bar Association Shattuck-Price Award, 1997; Judicial Council of California, Bernard E. Witkin Amicus Curiae Award, 1995; Women Lawyers Association of Los Angeles, Ernestine Stahlhut Award, 1994; Legal Aid Foundation of Los Angeles, Maynard Toll Award, 1990. President, 1993-1994, Vice-President, 1992-1993, Board of Governors, 1990-1994 and Conference of Delegates Executive Committee, 1985-1988, State Bar of California. Member: USC Law School Board of Councillors, 1985-1991; Commission to Draft an Ethics Code for Los Angeles City Government, 1989-1990. Lawyer Representative, Ninth Circuit Judicial Conference, 1990-1993. *Member:* Los Angeles County (President, 1988-1989, Member, Board of Trustees, 1981-1983, 1984-1989 and President, Barristers, 1982-1983) and American (Member, House of Delegates, 1990-1992; Director, Young Lawyers Division, 1984-1985) Bar Associations; Association of Business Trial Lawyers (Member, Board of Governors, 1982-1983). **REPORTED CASES:** American States Insurance Co. v. Borbor, 826 F2d 888 (9th Cir. 1987); McKeown v. First Interstate Bank, 194 Cal App. 3d 1225 (1987); University of Southern California v. Superior Court, 222 Cal. App. 3d, 1028 (1990); The Crane v. The Arizona Republic, 972 F. 2d 1511 (9th Cir. 1992). **PRACTICE AREAS:** Appellate Practice; Arbitration and Mediation; Insurance Coverage Law; Commercial Litigation. **Email:** morroma@aporter.com

**J. DAVID OSWALT,** born Pampa, Texas, September 23, 1947; admitted to bar, 1976, California. *Education:* University of Arizona (B.A., with high distinction, 1969); University of California at Los Angeles (J.D., 1976). Order of the Coif; Phi Beta Kappa. Member, U.C.L.A. Law Review, 1974-1976. **PRACTICE AREAS:** Commercial Litigation. **Email:** oswalda@aporter.com

**JOHN J. QUINN,** born San Francisco, California, September 19, 1932; admitted to bar, 1959, California; 1965, U.S. Supreme Court. *Education:* University of Southern California (A.B., 1954; J.D., 1959). Phi Delta Phi (President, 1958-1959); Order of the Coif. Member, Editorial Board, University of Southern California Law Review, 1958-1959. Member, Trojan Barristers (President, 1964). Lawyer Representative, Ninth Circuit Judicial Conference, 1965-1980, 1984-1987, 1992-1996. *Member:* Los Angeles County (President, 1976-1977; Member, Board of Trustees, 1968-1970; 1973-1977; Barristers, President, 1968-1969) and American (Member, House of Delegates, 1977-1982) Bar Associations; Los Angeles Trial Lawyers Association; California Trial Lawyers Association; American Board of Trial Advocates; American College of Trial Lawyers. **PRACTICE AREAS:** Litigation. **Email:** quinnjo@aporter.com

**ELLEN KELLY REISMAN,** born Waterbury, Connecticut, October 24, 1959; admitted to bar, 1984, District of Columbia (Not admitted in California). *Education:* Boston College (B.A., summa cum laude, 1981); University of Chicago (J.D., cum laude, 1984). Phi Beta Kappa. Member, University of Chicago Law Review, 1983-1984. **PRACTICE AREAS:** Food and Drug; Products Liability. **Email:** reismel@aporter.com

**RICHARD C. SMITH,** born Berkeley, California, January 18, 1943; admitted to bar, 1969, California. *Education:* Claremont McKenna College (A.B., 1965); Hastings College of Law (J.D., 1968). Member, Editorial Board, Hastings Law Journal, 1967-1968. Author: *Condominiums and Planned Developments*, CEB, 1984. Author or Speaker: "Redesigning Blackacre: Acquiring, Enhancing and Disposing of Real Property," CEB, 1995; "Airport Retail Leasing," International Conference of Shopping Centers, 1995; "Planned Developments and Condominiums," CEB, 1994; "Coping With Governmental Regulation of Real Property," CEB, 1993; "Title Insurance: Obtaining The Coverage You Want," PLI, 1993; "Development Re- *(This Listing Continued)*

## ARNOLD & PORTER, Los Angeles—Continued

strictions Related to Airports and Aircraft Operations," CEB, 1992; "Airport Privatization," Pacific Rim Council on Urban Development, 1991; "Planned Developments and Condominiums: The Development Stage," CEB, 1990; "Issues in Management and Operations of Commercial Real Property," CEB, 1990; "Legal Issues in Airport Development and Operations," CEB, 1989; "Liability Issues in Connection with Airport Fueling Operations," American Association of Airport Executives, 1989; "Acquiring and Disposing of Real Property in the 90's: Current Issues and Emerging Trends," CEB, 1989; "REMICS and CMO's," L.A.C.B.A., 1987; "Leasing," CEB, 1986; "Condominium Management Issues," C.A.I., 1985; "Construction Law," CEB, 1985; "Capital Formation," CEB, 1984; "Condominiums in the 1980's," CEB, 1979, 1981, 1982; "FHLMC and FNMA Warranty Requirements," L.A.C.B.A., 1979; "Condominiums and Planned Developments," CEB, 1977. Faculty Member, U.S.C. School of Urban Planning and Development Graduate Programs in Real Estate Development and Planning, 1989—. Member: California Department of Real Estate, Subdivision Advisory Committee, 1979-1987; C.E.B. Annual Real Property Practice Institute, Planning Committee, 1983—(Chairman, 1989-1990); Legal Committee Airport Operators Council International, 1987—. *Member:* State Bar of California (Member, Executive Committee, Real Property Section, 1985-1988). *PRACTICE AREAS:* Real Estate Law; Airport Law. *Email:* smitric@aporter.com

**JAMES F. SPEYER,** born New York, N.Y., September 5, 1959; admitted to bar, 1985, New York; 1987, California. *Education:* Williams College (B.A., 1981); George Washington University (J.D., 1985). Phi Beta Kappa. Member, George Washington University Law Review, 1984-1985. *Email:* speyeja@aporter.com

**MARK J. SPOONER,** born Norfolk, Virginia, November 11, 1945; admitted to bar, 1970, Virginia; 1971, District of Columbia; 1977, U.S. Supreme Court; 1994, California. *Education:* Georgetown University (A.B., 1967); University of Virginia (J.D., 1970). Order of the Coif. Virginia Editor, University of Virginia Law Review, 1969-1970. Co-Author: "International Joint Ventures," Federal Publications, 1988; "Joint Ventures with International Partners," Butterworth, 1994. *PRACTICE AREAS:* Complex Civil Litigation; Antitrust; Franchising/Distribution. *Email:* spoonma@aporter.com

**JULIE M. WARD,** born Pasadena, California, August 2, 1955; admitted to bar, 1984, California. *Education:* University of California at Santa Cruz (B.A., with honors, 1977); Boalt Hall School of Law, University of California (J.D., 1984). Member, Moot Court Board. *Member:* State Bar of California. *PRACTICE AREAS:* Commercial Litigation; Employment Law Litigation. *Email:* wardju@aporter.com

**EDWARD W. ZAELKE,** born Lynwood, California, June 19, 1958; admitted to bar, 1983, California. *Education:* California State University at Long Beach (B.A., 1980); University of California at Los Angeles (J.D., 1983). Order of the Coif. Managing Editor, UCLA Law Review, 1982-1983. *PRACTICE AREAS:* Real Estate. *Email:* zaelked@aporter.com

### OF COUNSEL

**SUSAN J. ELIOT,** born Los Angeles, California, November 2, 1957; admitted to bar, 1981, California; 1985, New York. *Education:* University of Southern California (B.S., 1978; J.D., 1981). *PRACTICE AREAS:* Civil Litigation; Financial Institutions. *Email:* eliotsu@aporter.com

**RUSSEL I. KULLY,** born Omaha, Nebraska, August 17, 1932; admitted to bar, 1960, California. *Education:* Wharton School, University of Pennsylvania (B.S., 1954); Stanford University (J.D., 1959). Member, Board of Editors, Stanford Law Review, 1957-1958. Member, Board of Directors, Public Broadcasting Systems/NAPTS, 1977-1983. Chairman of Board, Community Television of Southern California (KCET), 1978-1982. *Member:* State Bar of California (Member, Committee on Corporations, 1972-1975). *PRACTICE AREAS:* Corporation Law; Non-Profit Law; Health Care Law. *Email:* kullyru@aporter.com

### ASSOCIATES

**HILARY ADEL,** born Buffalo, New York, July 30, 1967; admitted to bar, 1995, California. *Education:* University of Vermont (B.A., 1990); Northeastern University (J.D., 1995). Law Clerk to Hon. Barefoot Sanders, U.S. District Court, Northern District of Texas, 1995-1996. *Member:* State Bar of California. *PRACTICE AREAS:* Litigation. *Email:* adelhi@aporter.com

**JOHN D. BANDIERA,** born Montreal, Quebec, Canada, September 30, 1950; admitted to bar, 1994, California. *Education:* McGill University (B.A., 1972); New York University (Ph.D., 1982); Stanford Law School (J.D., 1993). *Member:* State Bar of California. *PRACTICE AREAS:* Business Litigation. *Email:* bandijo@aporter.com

**STEVEN H. BERGMAN,** born Queens, New York, June 28, 1963; admitted to bar, 1995, California. *Education:* University of California, Berkeley (B.S., 1984); University of California at Los Angeles School of Law (J.D., 1995). Order of the Coif. Editor-in-Chief. U.C.L.A. Journal of Environmental Law and Policy, 1994-1995. *PRACTICE AREAS:* Litigation. *Email:* bergmst@aporter.com

**THEODORE J. BRO,** born Los Angeles, California, February 25, 1969; admitted to bar, 1995, California. *Education:* University of Michigan (B.G.S., with high honors, 1992); Georgetown University Law Center (J.D., magna cum laude, 1995). Golden Key; Order of the Coif. Senior Editor, Journal of Law and Policy in International Business. *PRACTICE AREAS:* Litigation. *Email:* broth@aporter.com

**CAREY C. CHERN,** born Poughkeepsie, New York, September 26, 1966; admitted to bar, 1993, California. *Education:* Harvard University (A.B., 1988); Stanford Law School (J.D., 1993). *Email:* chernca@aporter.com

**MARTHA JEANNETTE CLARK,** born Bronxville, New York, October 6, 1956; admitted to bar, 1984, California. *Education:* Stanford University (B.A., 1978); Hastings College of the Law, University of California (J.D., 1984). *Member:* State Bar of California. *Email:* clarkje@aporter.com

**SHARON L. DOUGLASS,** born Portland, Oregon, December 10, 1964; admitted to bar, 1990, California. *Education:* Claremont McKenna College (B.A., cum laude in History and Political Science , 1986); Loyola Law School (J.D., 1990). *Member:* State Bar of California. *PRACTICE AREAS:* Business Litigation. *Email:* douglsh@aporter.com

**MARK R. DROZDOWSKI,** born Camden, New Jersey, April 9, 1962; admitted to bar, 1993, California. *Education:* George Washington University (B.A., with distinction and special honors, 1984); Yale University (M.A., 1987); University of California at Los Angeles (J.D., 1993). Phi Beta Kappa. Member, 1991-1992 and Editor, 1992-1993, UCLA Law Review. *Email:* drozdma@aporter.com

**WILLIAM H. FORMAN,** born Philadelphia, Pennsylvania, January 7, 1965; admitted to bar, 1990, California. *Education:* Princeton University (A.B., summa cum laude, 1987); Harvard University (J.D., cum laude, 1990). *PRACTICE AREAS:* Litigation. *Email:* formawi@aporter.com

**JAMES D. LAYDEN,** born Whitehall, New York, March 1, 1962; admitted to bar, 1988, California. *Education:* Colgate University (B.A., cum laude, 1985); University of Notre Dame (J.D., cum laude, 1988). Phi Beta Kappa. *PRACTICE AREAS:* Commercial Litigation. *Email:* laydeja@aporter.com

**PATRICIA A. LIBBY,** born Hempstead, New York, February 8, 1961; admitted to bar, 1987, California; 1989, District of Columbia. *Education:* Stanford University (B.A., 1982); University of California at Los Angeles School of Law (J.D., 1987). Member and Editor, U.C.L.A. Law Review, 1985-1987. *Member:* State Bar of California. *Email:* libbypa@aporter.com

**JOHN D. LOMBARDO,** born Bellflower, California, May 26, 1971; admitted to bar, 1996, California. *Education:* Claremont McKenna College (B.A., magna cum laude, 1993); University of California School of Law, Los Angeles (J.D., 1996). Phi Beta Kappa; Order of the Coif. Chief Comments Editor, UCLA Law Review, 1995-1996. Assistant Editor, UCLA Pacific Basin Law Journal, 1994-1996. *PRACTICE AREAS:* Litigation. *Email:* lombajo@aporter.com

**TRACY L. MERRITT,** born Seattle, Washington, May 27, 1962; admitted to bar, 1988, California. *Education:* Occidental College (A.B., summa cum laude, 1984); Stanford Law School (J.D., 1987). Phi Beta Kappa; Order of the Coif. Senior Book Review Editor, Stanford Law Review, 1986-1987. Law Clerk to the Hon. Charles E. Wiggins, 1987-1988. Attorney, Civil Division, U.S. Department of Justice, 1988-1991. *PRACTICE AREAS:* Litigation. *Email:* merritr@aporter.com

**DIANE S. PONCE-GOMEZ,** born Santa Paula, California, July 31, 1970; admitted to bar, 1996, California. *Education:* University of California, Los Angeles (B.A., cum laude, 1992; J.D., 1996). *PRACTICE AREAS:* Litigation.

**KELLEY P. POTTER,** born Palo Alto, California, September 19, 1966; admitted to bar, 1992, California. *Education:* University of California at Los Angeles (B.A., 1989); Southwestern University School of Law (J.D., 1992). *Member:* State Bar of California. *Email:* potteke@aporter.com

*(This Listing Continued)*

**MICHAEL H. WALIZER,** born Erie, Pennsylvania, October 29, 1943; admitted to bar, 1988, California. *Education:* State University of New York at Buffalo (B.A., 1965; Ed.M., 1967); Florida State University (Ph.D., 1970); University of California at Los Angeles (J.D., 1987). Member, Moot Court Honors Program. Staff, The Federal Communications Law Journal. Mediator/Settlement Officer, Dispute Resolution Services, Los Angeles Municipal and Superior Courts, 1989—. Member, Board of Directors, American Youth Soccer Association, 1993—. Los Angeles Superior Court Arbitrator, 1993—. Member, Mediation Panel, Bankruptcy Court, Central District of California, 1995—. *Member:* Los Angeles County (Member: Homeless Task Force, 1989-1990; Committee on the Homeless, 1990-1991; Homeless Assistance Project Committee, 1991-1992) and American Bar Associations; State Bar of California; American Arbitration Association; Southern California Mediation Association. **PRACTICE AREAS:** Real Estate and Banking Litigation; Bankruptcy; Legal Ethics and Discipline; Construction Defects; General Business Litigation. *Email:* walizmi@aporter.com

**MINA S. YANG,** born Seoul, Korea, November 29, 1969; admitted to bar, 1996, California. *Education:* University of California, Berkeley (B.A., 1991); University of California School of Law, Los Angeles (J.D., 1995). Order of the Coif. Member and Editor, UCLA Law Review, 1993-1995. Judicial Clerk to Hon. Edward Rafeedie, 1995-1996. **LANGUAGES:** Korean. **PRACTICE AREAS:** Corporate; Real Estate.

(For biographical data of the Washington, D.C. personnel, see Professional Biographies at Washington, D.C.)
(For biographical data of the Denver personnel, see Professional Biographies at Denver, Colorado)
(For biographical data of the New York personnel, see Professional Biographies at New York, New York)
(For biographical date of the London personnel, see Professional Biographies at London, England)

## ARONOFF & SOUKUP
*A PROFESSIONAL LAW CORPORATION*
Established in 1989

*11726 SAN VICENTE BOULEVARD, SUITE 600*
**LOS ANGELES, CALIFORNIA 90049**
Telephone: 310-207-6700
Fax: 310-207-6714

*Real Estate, Bankruptcy, Commercial Litigation, Transactions, and Landlord-Tenant Law.*

**FIRM PROFILE:** *Aronoff & Soukup is a merger of Aronoff & Associates, founded in 1985 and Soukup & Associates, established in 1979. The firm specializes in commercial and real estate transactions and litigation, bankruptcy, business planning and appeals. The firm's clientele consists mainly of real estate developers, mid-size banks, and other mid-sized businesses. Bankruptcy work is concentrated in Chapter 11 reorganizations, and is equally divided between debtor and creditor representation. The firm encourages writing and publishing of articles on legal issues, as well as participation in bar association activities and continuing legal eduction seminars. The firm also has major commitment to pro-bono representation and community service.*

**JOHN F. SOUKUP,** born Burbank, California, March 4, 1948; admitted to bar, 1974, California and U.S. District Court, Central District of California. *Education:* University of Southern California (B.A., 1970; J.D., 1973). Member, University of Southern California Law Review, 1972-1973. Author: "California Real Property Sale Transactions, Chapter 3, The Purchase and Sale Agreement," California Continuing Education of the State Bar (CEB), 1981; also 2nd edition 1993-revision of prior book. *Member:* The State Bar of California. **PRACTICE AREAS:** Real Estate - Transactional; Business - Transactional.

**ROBERT C. ARONOFF,** born Toledo, Ohio, March 15, 1951; admitted to bar, 1976, California. *Education:* University of California at Berkeley (B.A., magna cum laude, 1973); University of Denver (J.D., 1976). Senior Editor, Denver Law Forum, 1975-1976. Recipient: Lawyer of the Year Award, Los Angeles County Bar Association, 1984; Lawyer of the Year Award, Constitutional Rights Foundation, 1984. Author: "Creative Financing Enters the Bankruptcy Courts Under the Cram Down Provisions of the Bankruptcy Code: Compulsory Refinancing of Balloon Payments," 16 Beverly Hills Bar Association Journal 127; "New Entities and Bankruptcy," Los Angeles Lawyer, Vol. 6, No. 2, page 22, April, 1983; "Discovery in the Bankruptcy Court: Depositions v. Rule 2004 Examinations," Beverly Hills Bar Journal, 1984. Co-Author, "Filing Bankruptcy For Existing Clients," Los Angeles Daily Journal Report, No. 89-5, April 28, 1989; "Appointing

*(This Listing Continued)*

and Organizing Official Creditors' Committees with Model By-Laws," California Bankruptcy Journal, Vol. 20, No. 4, 1992. Judge Pro Tem: Los Angeles Municipal Court, 1981—; Beverly Hills Municipal Court, 1981—; Santa Monica Municipal Court, 1987—; Culver City Municipal Court, 1989—. Delegate to U.S./China Joint Session on Trade, Economic and Investment Law, 1987. Commissioner, Parks, Recreation and Community Resources, City of Hermosa Beach, California, 1995—. *Member:* Beverly Hills (Chairman, Bankruptcy Section, 1993-1995; Board of Governors, 1994—), Los Angeles County and American Bar Associations; The State Bar of California; Constitutional Rights Foundation (Associates Vice-President, 1983-1985; Member, Lawyers' Advisory Council, 1992—; Board of Directors, 1996—); Trustee Jewish Big Brothers Association of Los Angeles (Vice President, 1988-1992; Secretary, 1993—). (Certified Specialist, Business Bankruptcy Law, American Bankruptcy Board of Certification). (Certified Specialist, Personal and Small Business Bankruptcy Law, The State Bar of California Board of Legal Specialization). **PRACTICE AREAS:** Commercial Litigation; Real Estate Litigation; Landlord and Tenant Law; Bankruptcy Law.

---

**SCOTT A. SCHIFF,** born Los Angeles, California, January 25, 1963; admitted to bar, 1988, California; 1989, U.S. District Court, Central, Eastern, Southern and Northern Districts of California; 1992, U.S. Supreme Court. *Education:* University of California at Berkeley (B.A., with distinction, 1985); Hastings College of Law, University of California (J.D., 1988). Phi Delta Phi. Member and Associate Articles Editor, Hastings International and Comparative Law Journal, 1986-1988. Author: "Settlement Offers Under C.C.P. Section 998 Determining the More Favorable Judgment" Beverly Hills Bar Association Journal, Vol. 26, No. 2 P.77, Spring, 1992; "Who Is Liable For Trust Fund Taxes In Bankruptcy?" The Management Gazette, Vol. VI, No. 1 P.1, Winter/Spring, 1993; "Recent Cases Read Homestead Exemption Laws Differently" Los Angeles and San Francisco Daily Journals, 1993. Executive Editor, Beverly Hills Bar Association Journal, 1991-1993. *Member:* Beverly Hills (Member, Executive Committee, Bankruptcy Section), Los Angeles County and American Bar Associations; State Bar of California. **PRACTICE AREAS:** Real Estate; Business Transactional; Bankruptcy Law; Civil Litigation.

**EDWARD J. CANDELARIA, II** (1965-1995).

**ADAM S. ROSSMAN,** born Los Angeles, California, October 11, 1966; admitted to bar, 1995, California and U.S. District Court, Central District of California. *Education:* University of California at Berkeley (B.A., with honors, 1988; M.A., 1990); Loyola Marymount University Law School (J.D., 1994). **LANGUAGES:** French. **PRACTICE AREAS:** Commercial Litigation; Bankruptcy; Real Estate Litigation; Transactions.

REPRESENTATIVE CLIENTS: Alliance Bank; Bank One Texas; Billcon International: California Cellular Dealers' Association; City National Bank; Comar Acquisitions, Inc.; Costa Mesa Servicing Center; Dixie Farms, Inc.; First Charter Bank; Glendale Health Care; Hanmi Bank; Kalnex Foods Corporation; Key Financial Services; LLB Development Company; NCNB Texas National Bank; The Pratt Company; Quest Fitness; Resolution Trust Corporation; Restaurant Services; Riley Pearlman Mitchell Company; Servistar Corporation; Turnberry Property Management; Vinton, Waller, Slivka & Panasci.
APPROVED ATTORNEYS FOR: Resolution Trust Corporation.
REFERENCES: First Interstate Bank, N.A.

## MICHAEL H. ARTAN
*445 SOUTH FIGUEROA STREET*
*TWENTY-SEVENTH FLOOR*
**LOS ANGELES, CALIFORNIA 90071**
Telephone: 213-688-0370
Facsimile: 213-627-9201

*Criminal Defense in all Federal and State Courts, including White Collar Crime, Civil and Licensing Defense.*

**MICHAEL H. ARTAN,** born Los Angeles, California, January 13, 1956; admitted to bar, 1981, California, U.S. District Court, Central District of California and U.S. Court of Appeals, Ninth Circuit; 1989, U.S. Tax Court. *Education:* University of California at Los Angeles (B.A., magna cum laude, 1977); University of California at Los Angeles School of Law (J.D., 1980). Author: "Temporary Employment of Foreign Nationals: The 'H' Visa," The International Lawyer, Volume 14, pp. 235-256, Spring, 1980. *Member:* Los Angeles County Bar Association; National Association of Criminal Defense Lawyers; California Attorneys for Criminal Justice. **LANGUAGES:** Armenian. **PRACTICE AREAS:** Criminal Defense; Civil Litigation.

## ARTER & HADDEN
**700 SOUTH FLOWER STREET, 30TH FLOOR**
**LOS ANGELES, CALIFORNIA 90017-4101**
Telephone: 213-629-9300
Cable Address: "Oslaw"
Facsimile: 213-617-9255

*REVISERS OF THE OHIO LAW DIGEST FOR THIS DIRECTORY.*

*In Cleveland, Ohio:* 1100 Huntington Building, 925 Euclid Avenue. Telephone: 216-696-1100. Fax: 216-696-2645.

*In Columbus, Ohio:* 21st Floor, One Columbus, 10 West Broad Street. Fax: 614-221-0479. Telephone: 614-221-3155.

*In Washington, D.C.:* 1801 K Street, N.W., Suite 400K. Telephone: 202-775-7100. Fax: 202-857-0172.

*In Dallas, Texas:* 1717 Main Street, Suite 4100. Telephone: 214-761-2100. Fax: 214-741-7139.

*In Irvine, California:* Five Park Plaza, 10th Floor, Jamboree Center. Telephone: 714-252-7500. Fax: 714-833-9604.

*In Austin, Texas:* 100 Congress Avenue, Suite 1800. Telephone: 512-479-6403. Fax: 512-469-5505.

*In San Antonio, Texas:* 7710 Jones Maltsberger, Harte-Hanks Tower, Suite 540. Telephone: 210-805-8497. Fax: 210-805-8519.

*In San Francisco, California:* 201 California Street, 14th Floor, 94111. Telephone: 415-912-3600. Fax: 415-912-3636.

*In San Diego, California:* 402 West Broadway, Fourth Floor, 92101. Telephone: 619-238-0001. Fax: 619-238-8333.

*In Woodland Hills, California:* 5959 Topanga Canyon Boulevard, Suite 244, 91367. Telephone: 818-712-0036. Fax: 818-346-6502.

*General Civil and Trial Practice. Antitrust, Banking, Bankruptcy and Commercial Transactions, Corporation, Corporate Financing, Creditors Remedies, Environmental, Estate Planning, Trust, Probate, Government Contract, Intellectual Property, International Business, Labor and Employment, Oil and Gas, Products Liability, Negligence, Admiralty, Maritime, Workers Compensation, Public Utility, General Real Estate, Finance, Securities and Taxation Law.*

### MEMBERS OF FIRM

**ROBERT P. ANDREANI**, born New Brunswick, New Jersey, 1955; admitted to bar, 1980, California, U.S. District Court, Central District of California and U.S. Court of Appeals, Ninth Circuit. *Education:* Stanford University (B.A., with distinction, 1977); University of Southern California Law Center (J.D., 1980). Author: "Independent Panels to Choose Publishable Opinions: A Solution to the Problems of California's Selective Publication System," The Pacific Law Journal, Vol. 12, No. 3, April, 1981. Extern to the Hon. Justice Mildred L. Lillie, California Court of Appeal, Second District, Los Angeles, 1979. *Member:* Los Angeles County and American Bar Associations; The State Bar of California. **LANGUAGES:** Italian, French, Spanish. *PRACTICE AREAS:* Real Estate; Corporate and Commercial Law; Environmental Law. *Email:* RAndrean@arterhadden.com

**KATHLEEN M. K. BRAHN,** born Milwaukee, Wisconsin, August 18, 1954; admitted to bar, 1982, Massachusetts and U.S. District Court, District of Massachusetts; 1983, U.S. Court of Appeals, First Circuit; 1986, California and U.S. District Court, Central District of California. *Education:* University of Wisconsin (B.F.A., with honors, 1975); University of San Francisco (J.D., 1981). Staff Member, 1979-1980 and Topics Editor, 1980-1981, University of San Francisco Law Review. Author: "Diethylstilbestrol: Extension of Class Action Procedures to Generic Drug Litigation," 14 University of San Francisco Law Review 461, 1980. *Member:* Los Angeles County and American Bar Associations; State Bar of California (Member, Sections on: Business Law; Litigation). *PRACTICE AREAS:* Business Litigation. *Email:* KBrahn@arterhadden.com

**JAMES S. BRYAN,** born Pittsburgh, Pennsylvania, October 26, 1944; admitted to bar, 1972, California. *Education:* Harvard University (A.B., cum laude, 1966); University of Pennsylvania (J.D., cum laude, 1971). Order of the Coif. Managing Editor, University of Pennsylvania Law Review, 1970-1971. Author: "Shifting the Burdens in Disparate Impact Cases: Wards Cove Packing v. Atonio," 6 Labor Lawyer 233, 1990; "The Applicable Statute of Limitations in Wrongful Termination Cases, Labor & Employment," Law News, Winter, At 6, 1987; "Sexual Harassment As Unlawful Discrimination Under Title VII of the Civil Rights Act of 1964," 14 Loy. L.A.L. Rev. 25 (1980). Law Clerk to Hon. Marvin E. Frankel, U.S. District Court, Southern District of New York, 1971-1972. *Member:* Los Angeles County and American Bar Associations; The State Bar of California. *PRACTICE AREAS:* Labor and Employment Law; Civil Litigation. *Email:* JBryan@arterhadden.com

*(This Listing Continued)*

**STEVEN J. COTÉ,** born Waterbury, Connecticut, February 19, 1957; admitted to bar, 1983, California and U.S. District Court, Southern District of California. *Education:* Seton Hall University (B.S., magna cum laude, Economics, 1980); University of San Diego (J.D., cum laude, 1983). Omicron Delta Epsilon. Member, University of San Diego Law Review, 1982-1983. Recipient, American Jurisprudence Awards in Corporation and Torts. *Member:* San Diego County, Los Angeles County and American Bar Associations; State Bar of California. *Email:* SCote@arterhadden.com

**JAY M. DAVIS,** born Santa Barbara, California, November 21, 1946; admitted to bar, 1972, California; 1974, U.S. District Court, Central District of California. *Education:* Menlo School of Business Administration (B.S., 1968); University of San Diego (J.D., 1971). Chairman, Legal Affairs Committee, California Bankers Association, 1984-1986. Member of California Bankers Association Task Force to rewrite the California Banking Law, 1985-1989. President and Director, Los Angeles Headquarters Association, 1980-1989. Member, Financial Lawyers Conference. Affiliate Member, International Bankers Association, 1990—. Member, British American Chamber of Commerce. *Member:* Los Angeles County (Member, Sections on: Corporate Law 1993-1995; Commercial Law and Bankruptcy) and American (Member, Corporate Counsel Section) Bar Associations; State Bar of California (Member, Financial Institutions Committee, Business Law Section, 1985-1987). *Email:* JDavis@arterhadden.com

**WILLIAM S. DAVIS,** born Altadena, California, February 28, 1949; admitted to bar, 1974, California; U.S. District Court, Northern, Central, Eastern and Southern Districts of California, U.S. Court of Appeals, Ninth Circuit and U.S. Supreme Court. *Education:* University of Redlands (B.A., with distinction, 1971); University of California at Los Angeles (J.D., 1974). Member, Moot Court. Legal Intern, Center for Law and Social Policy, Washington, D.C., 1973. Panelist, 1984, 1992, 1994 and Consultant, 1989—, California Continuing Education of the Bar. *Member:* Los Angeles County, American (Member, Litigation Section) and Federal Bar Associations; The State Bar of California. *Email:* WDavis@arterhadden.com

**ERIC D. DEAN,** born New York, N.Y., June 27, 1948; admitted to bar, 1973, California; U.S. District Court, Central District of California. *Education:* University of California at Los Angeles (B.S., 1970; J.D., 1973). Order of the Coif. *Member:* State Bar of California. *Email:* EDean@arterhadden.com

**DAVID R. DECKER,** born New Rochelle, NY., December 6, 1942; admitted to bar, 1967, Virginia; 1968, New York and U.S. Court of Military Appeals; 1970, California. *Education:* Lehigh Univ. (B.A., 1964); Univ. of Virginia (LL.B., 1967). [Capt., JAGC, USNR-Retired]. *PRACTICE AREAS:* Corporate Law; Securities Regulation Law; Mergers and Acquisitions Law. *Email:* DDecker@arterhadden.com

**RICHARD D. DE LUCE,** born Nanaimo, British Columbia, October 3, 1928; admitted to bar, 1955, California; 1963, U.S. Supreme Court. *Education:* University of California at Los Angeles (A.B., with honors, 1950); Stanford University (J.D., 1955). Phi Delta Phi; Phi Beta Kappa. Member, Stanford Law Review, 1954-1955. Law Clerk to Justice Homer R. Spence, Associate Justice California Supreme Court, 1955-1956. Co-Author: "California Civil Writ Practice," 2nd ed., California CEB, 1987. *Member:* Los Angeles County (Chairman, Legislation Committee, 1970-1973) and American (Co-Chairman, Committee on Labor Arbitration and the Law of Collective Bargaining Agreements, Section of Labor Relations Law, 1969-1973) Bar Associations; The State Bar of California (Member, Committee on Administration of Justice, 1971-1974). Fellow: American College of Trial Lawyers; American Bar Foundation. [Captain, U.S. Army Reserve (Korean War)] *Email:* RDeLuce@arterhadden.com

**EDWIN W. DUNCAN,** born Oakland, California, May 11, 1945; admitted to bar, 1970, California. *Education:* University of California at Berkeley (A.B., 1966); Hastings College of Law, University of California (J.D., 1969). Member: Order of the Coif; Thurston Society. Member, Hastings Law Journal, 1968-1969. Member, Executive Committee, Los Angeles Barristers, 1971-1973. Member, Board of Directors, 1972-1975 and Vice-President, 1974-1975, California Barristers. Chairman, 1985-1987, Member, Board of Directors, 1983—, Southern California Swimming Inc. Chairman, Counselors Committee, United States Swimming, Inc., 1994—. *Member:* Los Angeles County, Federal and American (Editor of Law Notes, Young Lawyers Section, 1970-1972; Member, Section on Tort and Insurance Practice) Bar Associations; The State Bar of California (Member, Litigation Section). *REPORTED CASES:* Western Electric Company v. LaHoma Smith, 99 Cal. App.3d 629 (1979); Pacific Telephone and Telegraph Company v. Workers' Compensation Appeals Board and Thomas Blackburn 112 Cal. App.3d 241 (1980); Chevron U.S.A. vs. Bragg Crane & Rigging, 180 Cal. App.3d 639 (1986); Bartram vs. FDIC, 235 Cal. App. 3d 1749

*(This Listing Continued)*

(1991); Twenty-Nine Pals Band Mission Indians v. Pete Wilson, 925 F.Supp.1470 (C.D.CA 1996). **PRACTICE AREAS:** Commercial; Tort; Product Liability Litigation. **Email:** EDuncan@arterhadden.com

**JAMES E. DURBIN,** born Racine, Wisconsin, December 9, 1944; admitted to bar, 1973, California. *Education:* United States Air Force Academy (B.S., 1967); University of Southern California (M.B.A., 1970); Loyola University of Los Angeles (J.D., cum laude, 1973). Member, St. Thomas More Law Society. Articles Editor, Loyola of Los Angeles Law Review, 1972-1973. *Member:* The State Bar of California. [Capt., USAF, 1963-1971] **Email:** JDurbin@arterhadden.com

**RICHARD N. ELLNER,** born New York, N.Y., April 12, 1929; admitted to bar, 1954, New York; 1962, District of Columbia; 1966, California. *Education:* Harvard University (A.B., cum laude, 1951; LL.B., 1954). Trial Attorney, Branch of Enforcement, New York Regional Office, 1957-1959 and Senior Branch Attorney, Division of Corporation Finance, Washington, D.C., 1959-1961, Securities and Exchange Commission. Author: "Rule 144," L.A. County Bar Bull., April 1972. Co-Author: "Antitrust Advisor," 1st ed., McGraw-Hill, Inc., 1971; "Business Buy-Out Agreements," 1st ed., California CEB, 1976. *Member:* Los Angeles County and American Bar Associations; The State Bar of California. **Email:** REllner@arterhadden.com

**DONALD C. ERICKSON,** born Darby, Pennsylvania, June 17, 1950; admitted to bar, 1976, California; 1977, U.S. District Court, Eastern District of California; 1983, U.S. District Court, Central District of California. *Education:* University of California at Santa Barbara (B.A., 1972); University of Southern California (J.D., 1976). Member, Southern California Law Review, 1974-1975. *Member:* Los Angeles County and American (Vice-Chairman, Torts and Insurance Practice Section; Committee on Insurance Coverage Litigation, 1995-1996; 1996-1997) Bar Associations; State Bar of California; Association of Southern California Defense Counsel. **Email:** DErickso@arterhadden.com

**JACK GOLDMAN,** born New York, N.Y., November 18, 1940; admitted to bar, 1966, California and U.S. District Court, Central District of California; 1986, U.s. District Court, Northern and Southern Districts of California. *Education:* Lafayette College (B.A., 1962); University of California at Los Angeles (J.D., 1965). Moot Court Honors. *Member:* Beverly Hills, Los Angeles County and American Bar Associations; State Bar of California. **PRACTICE AREAS:** Corporate and Securities; Trade Regulations; Mergers and Acquisitions; Asset Based Lending; Health Law. **Email:** JGoldman@arterhadden.com

**WAYNE S. GRAJEWSKI,** born Lynwood, California, July 28, 1951; admitted to bar, 1976, California. *Education:* Stanford University (A.B., 1973, Phi Beta Kappa ); Boalt Hall School of Law, University of California (J.D., 1976). First Place, McBaine Moot Court Competition. Chairman, Boalt Hall Moot Court Board, 1975-1976. Author: "Prohibiting Cruel or Unusual Punishment: California's Requirement of Proportionate Sentencing," 10 USF L. R. 524, 1976. *Member:* Los Angeles County and American Bar Associations; The State Bar of California. **Email:** WGrajews@arterhadden.com

**JOHN L. HOSACK,** born Tacoma, Washington, January 3, 1944; admitted to bar, 1969, California. *Education:* University of Washington; University of San Francisco (J.D., 1968). Phi Delta Phi (Magister of Stephens Inn, 1966-1968). Author: "California Title Insurance Practice," California Continuing Education of the Bar, 1980. Consultant on *California Mortgage and Deed of Trust Practice,* published by the California Continuing Education of the Bar, 1979; *California Real Property Sales Transactions,* published by California Continuing Education of the Bar, 1981. Visiting Lecturer, University of California Berkeley, (Boalt Hall) School of Law, 1979-1994. Chairman, Real Property Section, The Bar Association of San Francisco, 1978. *Member:* American College of Real Estate Lawyers; American Land Title Association (Member, Lender's Counsel Group); Bank Attorneys Association. Fellow, American College of Mortgage Attorneys. **Email:** JHosack@arterhadden.com

**CURTISS L. ISLER,** born Warren, Ohio, June 11, 1945; admitted to bar, 1975, Ohio; 1990, California. *Education:* Miami University (A.B., 1967); Ohio State University (J.D., summa cum laude, 1975). Associate Editor, Ohio State Law Journal, 1974-1975. Order of the Coif. *Member:* Ohio State and American Bar Associations; State Bar of California; National Association of Railroad Trial Counsel; Federation of Insurance and Corporate Counsel; Cleveland Association of Civil Trial Attorneys (President, 1984-1985); Defense Research Institute. **Email:** CIsler@arterhadden.com

**JOHN E. JAMES,** born Davenport, Iowa, February 7, 1951; admitted to bar, 1976, California. *Education:* California State University at Fullerton (B.A., with honors, 1973); Loyola University of Los Angeles (J.D., cum laude, 1976); New York University (LL.M., in Taxation, 1977). Member, St. Thomas More Law Society. Co-Author: "Planning Guide for Receipt of Lump Sum Distributions from Qualified Plans," CCH Financial & Estate Planning Reporter, Vol. 2, Forms & Planning Aids, Paragraph 6310, 1980; "Reassessing Medical Reimbursement After Change in the Law and Regulations," 54 Journal of Taxation 30, January, 1981; "Consequences of Discriminatory Medical Reimbursement Plans," 54 Journal of Taxation 89, February, 1981; "Final Regs. on Medical Reimbursement Generally Tougher than Proposed Rules," 54 Journal of Taxation 348, June, 1981. Instructor, Program for Legal Paraprofessionals, University of California, Los Angeles, 1979-1981. *Member:* Los Angeles County, Orange County (Member, Taxation Section) and American (Chairman, Subcommittee on Exclusions from Gross Income of the Committee on General Tax Problems, 1981-1983) Bar Associations. **PRACTICE AREAS:** Taxation Law; Partnership Law. **Email:** JJames@arterhadden.com

**BART L. KESSEL,** born San Diego, California, November 3, 1960; admitted to bar, 1986, California; 1987, U.S. District Court, Central, Eastern, Northern and Southern District of California; U.S. District Court, Northern District of Texas. *Education:* Vanderbilt University (B.S., cum laude, 1982); University of California School of Law at Davis (J.D., 1986). Phi Delta Phi. *Member:* State Bar of California.

**CRAIG G. KLINE,** born Chicago, Illinois, July 9, 1951; admitted to bar, 1979, California, U.S. District Court, Central District of California and U.S. Court of Appeals, Ninth Circuit; 1982, U.S. District Court, Northern District of California; 1983, U.S. District Court, Southern District of California. *Education:* University of Pennsylvania (A.B., A.M., cum laude, with honors in History, 1973); Wadham College, University of Oxford, Oxford, England (M.Litt., 1975); Hastings College of the Law, University of California (J.D., 1978). Editorial Advisory Board Member and U.S. Correspondent for the International Insurance Law Review. *Member:* State Bar of California. **PRACTICE AREAS:** Direct Insurance and Reinsurance; Environmental Law. **Email:** CKline@arterhadden.com

**MICHAEL S. KOGAN,** born New York, N.Y., February 10, 1955; admitted to bar, 1985, Florida and U.S. Tax Court; 1987, California. *Education:* Colgate University; University of Denver (B.A., 1976; M.B.A., 1979); Southwestern University School of Law (J.D., cum laude, 1984); New York University ( LL.M. in Taxation, 1985). Adjunct Professor of Law, Western State University School of Law. *Member:* The Florida Bar; State Bar of California; American Bar Association. **Email:** MKogan@arterhadden.com

**JULIE DEAN LARSEN,** born Fremont, Nebraska, April 13, 1959; admitted to bar, 1984, California and Nebraska. *Education:* University of Nebraska (B.A., 1980; J.D., 1984). Law Clerk for the Honorable John T. Grant, Nebraska Supreme Court, 1984-1985. *Member:* State Bar of California; Nebraska State and American Bar Associations; The Association of Trial Lawyers of America. **Email:** JDLarsen@arterhadden.com

**KENNETH J. MURPHY,** born Los Angeles, California, January 23, 1937; admitted to bar, 1964, California and U.S. District Court, Central District of California; 1966, U.S. Tax Court; 1972, U.S. Supreme Court; 1977, U.S. Court of Appeals, Ninth Circuit. *Education:* University of Santa Clara (B.S., 1958); University of Southern California (J.D., 1964). Phi Delta Phi. Chairperson, United Way, Inc., Los Angeles, 1993-1995. *Member:* Los Angeles County and American Bar Associations; The State Bar of California. [U.S. Marine Corps, 1958-1961] **Email:** KMurphy@arterhadden.com

**BRUCE H. NEWMAN,** born Minneapolis, Minnesota, August 15, 1935; admitted to bar, 1961, California. *Education:* University of California at Los Angeles (A.B., 1957; LL.D., 1960). *Member:* Los Angeles County Bar Association; State Bar of California. **Email:** BNewman@arterhadden.com

**RICHARD R. PACE,** born Chicago, Illinois, December 19, 1940; admitted to bar, 1970, Illinois; 1977, California. *Education:* United States Naval Academy (B.S., 1963); University of Illinois (J.D., 1970). Co-Author: "Equal Employment Practices," Chapter 2, Advising California Employers, 1981. Lecturer on Labor and Employment Law, University of Southern California Graduate School of Business Administration, 1988-1994. *Member:* Chicago, Los Angeles County (Member, Section on Labor Law) and Illinois State Bar Associations. [LT., U.S. Navy, 1963-1968]. **PRACTICE AREAS:** Labor and Employment Law. **Email:** RPace@arterhadden.com

**J. DOUGLAS POST,** born Frankfurt-am-Main, West Germany, December 14, 1952; admitted to bar, 1978, California. *Education:* Stanford University (B.A., with distinction, 1975; J.D., 1978); Cambridge University, Cambridge, England (LL.M., 1979). Phi Beta Kappa. Vice-President, Stan-

*(This Listing Continued)*

*ARTER & HADDEN, Los Angeles—Continued*

ford Environmental Law Society, 1977. Co-Author, "National Forest Land Management," Published by Ford Foundation, 1978. Member, Board of Directors, Marine Exchange of Los Angeles-Long Beach Harbor, 1988—. *Member:* Los Angeles County Bar Association; State Bar of California. *Email:* DPost@arterhadden.com

**KAY RUSTAND,** born Fergus Falls, Minnesota, March 9, 1948; admitted to bar, 1978, California. *Education:* University of California at Los Angeles (B.A., cum laude, 1970; J.D., 1978); San Diego State University. Member, Moot Court. Extern to the Honorable J. Clifford Wallace, Judge, U.S. Court of Appeals, 9th Circuit, 1977. Court Law Clerk, U.S. Court of Appeals, 9th Circuit, 1978-1979. Law Clerk to the Honorable Herbert Y.C. Choy, Judge, U.S. Court of Appeals, 9th Circuit, 1979-1980. *Member:* Los Angeles County and American Bar Associations; The State Bar of California; Christian Legal Society. *PRACTICE AREAS:* Securities; Corporate and Commercial Law; Real Estate. *Email:* KRustand@arterhadden.com

**ANDREA Y. SLADE,** born Detroit, Michigan, January 5, 1943; admitted to bar, 1978, California. *Education:* University of California at Los Angeles (A.B., 1975); Southwestern University School of Law (J.D., cum laude, 1978). *Member:* Los Angeles County Bar Association (Member: Committee on, Legislative Review, 1985—; Ethics Committee, 1984-1987); The State Bar of California; Association of Business Trial Lawyers. *Email:* ASlade@arterhadden.com

**STEPHEN T. SWANSON,** born Los Angeles, California, January 19, 1942; admitted to bar, 1970, California; U.S. Court of Appeals, Ninth Circuit; U.S. Supreme Court. *Education:* University of California at Los Angeles (A.B., 1964); Loyola University (J.D., 1969). Member, Loyola University of Los Angeles Law Journal, 1968-1969. Teaching Fellow, Loyola Law School, 1967-1969. Lecturer: Continuing Education of the Bar, Series on Trial Practice and Procedure, 1984—; "Acquiring and Selling Real Property, Environmental Problems," P.L.I., 1981-1993. Judge Pro Tem. Arbitrator, Los Angeles Superior Court, Los Angeles County Bar Association. *Member:* Los Angeles County and American (Member: Litigation Section; Torts and Insurance Practice Section; Toxic and Hazardous Substances Committee) Bar Associations; The State Bar of California; American Judicature Society; Defense Research Institute. [USNR, 1964-1966] *Email:* SSwanson@arterhadden.com

**JOHN R. TATE,** born Palo Alto, California, March 15, 1951; admitted to bar, 1976, California; 1977, U.S. District Court, Central District of California; 1978, U.S. Court of Appeals, Ninth Circuit; 1985, U.S. Supreme Court; 1992, U.S. District Court, District of Arizona. *Education:* Dartmouth College (A.B., 1973); Vanderbilt University (J.D., 1976). Lecturer: "Creditor's Remedies and Debtor's Rights," CEB, 1986 and 1988. *Member:* The State Bar of California; American Bar Association; American Business Trial Lawyers. *Email:* JTate@arterhadden.com

**JACQUELINE I. VALENZUELA,** born San Diego, California, August 24, 1952; admitted to bar, 1976, California; 1977, New Mexico and Navajo Nation; 1985, U.S. District Court, Southern and Northern Districts of California; 1988, U.S. District Court, Central District of California; 1992, Arizona; 1994, Texas. *Education:* University of California (B.A., 1973); University of San Diego (J.D., 1976). *Member:* State Bar of California; State Bar of New Mexico; State Bar of Texas. *Email:* JValenzu@arterhadden.com

**RONALD WARNER,** born New York, N.Y., April 15, 1944; admitted to bar, 1969, New York; 1972, California; 1979, District of Columbia. *Education:* Tulane University (B.A., 1965); New York University (J.D., 1968). Order of the Coif. Business Manager and Editor, New York University Law Review, 1967-1968. *Member:* American Bar Association (Committee on Federal Regulation of Securities, 1978—). *Email:* RWarner@arterhadden.com

**KIM W. WEST,** born Charleston, West Virginia, December 2, 1950; admitted to bar, 1977, California. *Education:* West Virginia University (B.S., cum laude, 1973); Duke University (J.D., 1977). *Member:* Los Angeles County and American (Member, Section on Tort and Insurance Practice) Bar Associations; State Bar of California. *Email:* KWest@arterhadden.com

**MICHAEL C. ZELLERS,** born Cleveland, Ohio, August 31, 1955; admitted to bar, 1980, Ohio; 1990, California. *Education:* Grove City College (A.B., 1977); The Ohio State University College of Law (J.D., 1980). *Member:* Ohio State and American Bar Associations; State Bar of California; International Association of Defense Counsel; National Health Lawyers Association; Cleveland Association of Civil Attorneys (President, 1989-1990). *Email:* MZellers@arterhadden.com

*(This Listing Continued)*

*RETIRED PARTNERS*

**ROBERT HENIGSON,** born Los Angeles, California, December 27, 1925; admitted to bar, 1956, California. *Education:* California Institute of Technology (B.S., with honor, 1948; M.S., 1949); Harvard Law School (LL.B., cum laude, 1955). Phi Delta Phi; Tau Beta Pi. Adjunct Professor, Loyola University School of Law, 1958-1975. *Member:* State Bar of California; American Bar Association; American Judicature Society.

**RICHARD F. OUTCAULT, JR.,** born Chicago, Illinois, April 25, 1924; admitted to bar, 1951, California. *Education:* Stanford University (A.B., 1947; LL.B., 1950). Phi Beta Kappa; Phi Alpha Delta. Member, Chancery Club, 1957. *Member:* Los Angeles County (Member, Board of Trustees, 1968-1970) and American Bar Associations; The State Bar of California (Member, 1969-1971 and Chairman, 1971, State Bar Disciplinary Board; Chairman, Clients Security Fund Committee, 1972-1975). Fellow, American Bar Foundation.

**REED A. STOUT,** born Mt. Pleasant, Utah, December 14, 1911; admitted to bar, 1937, District of Columbia; 1947, California. *Education:* University of Utah (A.B., 1933); George Washington University (J.D., 1937). Delta Theta Phi. *Member:* Los Angeles County and American Bar Associations; The State Bar of California. Fellow, American College of Trial Lawyers.

*OF COUNSEL*

**MICHAEL L. COATES,** born Inglewood, California, July 4, 1960; admitted to bar, 1987, California, U.S. District Court, Central District of California and U.S. Court of Appeals, Ninth Circuit. *Education:* University of Southern California (B.S., 1983); McGeorge School of the Law, University of the Pacific (J.D., 1987). Author: "Cianci v. Superior Courts: RICO, A Runaway Statute Now Running Into State Court," 18 Pac. L.J. 1267, 1987. *Member:* Los Angeles County and Orange County (Member, Sections on: Real Estate Law, Business Litigation; Toxic and Environmental Law) Bar Associations; State Bar of California. *Email:* MCoates@arterhadden.com

**BARBARA R. DIAMOND,** born New York, N.Y., September 13, 1929; admitted to bar, 1975, New Jersey; 1981, California and U.S. District Court, Central District of California. *Education:* Beaver College (B.A., 1950); Rutgers University (J.D., 1975). *Member:* Los Angeles County Bar Association; The State Bar of California; Women Lawyers Association of Los Angeles.

**JUDITH A. GILBERT,** born Los Angeles, California, January 9, 1946; admitted to bar, 1971, California Supreme Court and U.S. District Court Central District of California; 1974, U.S. District Court Southern District of California; 1975, U.S. Court of Appeals for the Ninth Circuit and U.S. Supreme Court; 1977, U.S. District Court, Northern District of California and U.S. Tax Court; 1978, U.S. District Court, Eastern District of California; 1992, U.S. Court of Appeals, Sixth Circuit. *Education:* University of California at Los Angeles (A.B., magna cum laude, 1967) Harvard Law School (J.D., 1970). Phi Beta Kappa. Editor, Harvard Journal on Legislation, 1970. Author: "Emanations of the 'Shift of Emphasis' Theory - the 'Improper Purposes' Doctrine Revisited: Tax Payers' Rights to Challenge Special Agents' Summons of 'Third Party' Bank Records," 5 Suffolk University Law Review 35, 1970; "California's State Bar," 19 Beverly Hills Bar Association J. 189, 1985; "Alternative Answers," 20 Beverly Hills Bar Association J. 65, 1986; "Retention Election," 20 Beverly Hills Bar Association J. 145, 1986; "Film Industry Bankruptcy: Securing the Right to Payment Before It Happens," Beverly Hills Bar Association Journal, 1992. Frequent speaker at seminars on Bankruptcy and Finance (including financing and insolvency in the entertainment industry). Member, Board of Governors, Southern California Chapter of the Arthritis Foundation, 1988—. Judge Pro Tem Municipal and Small Claims Court, 1974-1984. Member, UCLA Alumni Advisory Board, 1972-1978. Member of Panel: Los Angeles County Superior Court and Beverly Hills Bar Association Arbitration and Mediation. Member, Executive Committee to Conference of Delegates of State Bar, 1991-1996; Chair, 1994-1995; Ex Officio Member, 1995-1996. California State Bar Resolutions Committee, 1986, 1988-1990; Delegate to State Bar Conference, 1972—. Member, Governance, 1995-1996, ADR, 1994-1996, Active/Inactive Membership, 1996 and Structure, 1996—, Task Forces of Board of Governors, State Bar of California; Coalition to Save the Unified Bar (Executive and Steering Committees 1995-1996). Attorney, Fee Disputes Resolution Panel, Beverly Hills Bar Association and Los Angeles County Bar Association. Public Counsel, Member, Board of Directors, 1986-1989. Member, Steering Committee and Co-Chair of Fundraising Sub-Committee, 1986, Los Angeles County Bar Association and Affiliates Committee in Opposition to Proposition 61; California State Bar Conference on Living Wills and the Right to Die (Vice Chair, 1977); California

*(This Listing Continued)*

State and Assembly Task Forces on Living Wills and the Right to Die, 1978-1979; California State Bar Conference Committees on Rights and Obligations of Unmarried Cohabitators (Marvin v. Marvin), 1978-1980, and on Legal Specialization, 1980-1981; State Bar of California Annual Meeting Planning Committee and 1987 Annual Meeting of State Bar Host Committee, 1986-1987. *Member:* Los Angeles County Bar Association (Board of Trustees, 1984-1985); Beverly Hills Bar Association (Ex-Officio Member, Board of Governors and Executive Committee, 1986-1987; President, 1985-1986; Member, Board of Governors, 1980-1987; Chair Women and the Law Committee, 1986-1989; Chair, Individual Rights Committee, 1990-1993; Resolutions Committee and Delegate to State Bar Conference, 1973-1991; Chair, 1980-1981); Beverly Hills Bar Association Foundation (Member of Board of Directors, 1983-1985); American Bar Association (Member, Litigation and Banking, Corporate and Commercial Sections; ABA Task Force on International Perfection of Securities Interests, 1996—); Federal Bar Association; California Women Lawyers Association; Women Lawyers Association of Los Angeles; Financial Lawyers Conference; Los Angeles Bankruptcy Forum; Commercial Law League of America; Copyright Society; Women in Business. *PRACTICE AREAS:* Finance and Insolvency; Entertainment Finance; Insolvency; Copyright; Entertainment; Business Transactions.

**RONALD M. GRIFFITH,** born Philadelphia, Pennsylvania, March 7, 1946; admitted to bar, 1973, California and U.S. District Court, Central District of California. *Education:* Tufts University (B.A., magna cum laude, 1968); University of Pennsylvania (J.D., 1973). Assistant U.S. Attorney, Antitrust Division, U.S. Department of Justice, 1973-1977. Member, Attorneys Committee, Western League of Savings Institutions, 1989—. *Member:* The State Bar of California (Member, Real Property Section). *PRACTICE AREAS:* Real Estate; Banks and Banking.

**STEVEN T. GUBNER,** born Encino, California, March 14, 1966; admitted to bar, 1991, California; 1992, Nevada; U.S. District Courts, Southern Central, Eastern and Northern Districts of California and U.S. of Appeals, Ninth Circuit. *Education:* University of California at Santa Barbara (B.A., 1988); McGeorge School of Law (J.D., 1991). Staff Writer, Transnational Lawyer, 1990. Author: Note, *The European Economic Community And Effects Doctrine Jurisdiction:* The Community's New Weapon, 3 Transnat'l Law. 759 (1990); *Transnational Lawyer,* (1991). Speaker, Southern California Mortgage Bankers Association on Bankruptcy Law and Foreclosure Process. Judicial Extern to the Honorable David E. Russell, U.S. Bankruptcy Court, Eastern District of California. *Member:* Los Angeles County and Orange County (Member, Commercial Law and Bankruptcy Program Committee Section) Bar Associations; State Bar of California; State Bar of Nevada; Los Angeles, Inland Empire, Orange County Bankruptcy Forum. *PRACTICE AREAS:* Commercial Bankruptcy Law; Appellate Law; Real Estate Litigation; Asset Based Financing; Commercial Collection Actions. *Email:* SGubner@arterhadden.com

## ASSOCIATES

**JULIAN BACH,** born Los Angeles, California, October 14, 1964; admitted to bar, 1992, California. *Education:* University of California at Davis (B.S., 1987); McGeorge School of Law (J.D., 1992). *Member:* Los Angeles and Orange County Bar Associations. *Email:* JBach@arterhadden.com

**VICTOR M. BARTHOLETTI,** born North Hollywood, California, July 20, 1962; admitted to bar, 1988, California; U.S. Supreme Court; U.S. District Court, Central, Northern, Southern and Eastern Districts of California; U.S. Court of Appeals, Ninth Circuit. *Education:* University of Southern California (B.A., 1984; J.D., 1988). Article Editor, Computer Law Journal, 1987-1988, Major Tax Planning, 1987-1988. *Member:* The State Bar of California; Los Angeles County and American Associations; Japanese American Bar Association. *Email:* VBarthol@arterhadden.com

**MOLLIE F. BENEDICT,** born Boulder, Colorado, September 8, 1971; (admission pending). *Education:* Northwestern University (B.A., 1993); University of California at Los Angeles School of Law (J.D., 1996). *Email:* MBenedict@arterhadden.com

**SUSAN C. BERGEMANN,** born Cedar Rapids, Iowa, November 26, 1956; admitted to bar, 1982, District of Columbia, U.S. District Court for the District of Columbia, Virginia and U.S. District Court, Eastern District of Virginia; 1989, Florida; 1993, U.S. District Court, Southern District of Florida; 1996, California. *Education:* University of Iowa (B.A., 1977); Washington College of Law of American University (J.D., 1981). *Member:* The District of Columbia Bar; The Florida Bar; State Bar of California. *PRACTICE AREAS:* Civil Litigation; Products Liability; Insurance. *Email:* SBergema@arterhadden.com

*(This Listing Continued)*

**LINLEY CLARE BIZIK,** born Tucson, Arizona, May 24, 1970; admitted to bar, 1995, California. *Education:* University of Arizona (B.S.B.A., magna cum laude, 1992); University of California at Los Angeles (J.D., 1995). Beta Gamma Sigma; Phi Eta Sigma. Member, UCLA Moot Court Honors Board. Recipient: UCLA Graduate Student Association Jeffrey L. Hanson Distinguished Service Award; 1992 University of Arizona Award for Most Outstanding Graduate of the College of Business and Public Administration. Member, UCLA Pacific Basin Law Journal. *Email:* LBizik@arterhadden.com

**KATESSA M. CHARLES,** born Los Angeles, California, July 14, 1963; admitted to bar, 1990, California; 1991, District of Columbia. *Education:* University of California at Santa Barbara (B.A., 1985); Georgetown University Law Center (J.D., 1989). Member, Senior Staff, The Tax Lawyer, 1987-1989. Author: Note, "The Elimination of Estate Tax Exemption for Project Notes: United States v. Wells Fargo Bank," 42 Tax Lawyer 423 (1989). *Member:* State Bar of California; District of Columbia Bar. *PRACTICE AREAS:* Business and Employment Litigation. *Email:* KCharles@arterhadden.com

**SANDRA FLORES,** born Ventura, California, December 9, 1970; (admission pending). *Education:* University of California at Los Angeles (B.A., 1993); Boalt Hall School of Law, University of California (J.D., 1996). *PRACTICE AREAS:* Litigation. *Email:* SFlores@arterhadden.com

**ROBERT M. FORESTER,** born Chicago, Illinois, April 18, 1969; admitted to bar, 1995, California. *Education:* Tulane University, School of Architecture (B.Arch., 1991); University of Southern California (J.D., 1994). *Member:* State Bar of California. *PRACTICE AREAS:* Business Litigation. *Email:* RForeste@arterhadden.com

**ADAM GUBNER,** born Los Angeles, California, February 14, 1968; admitted to bar, 1993, California and U.S. District Court, Central District of California. *Education:* University of California at Santa Barbara (B.A., 1990); McGeorge School of Law (J.D., with distinction, 1993). Assistant Comment Editor, Pacific Law Journal. *Member:* Los Angeles County Bar Association; State Bar of California. *PRACTICE AREAS:* Bankruptcy; Corporate Reorganization; Creditors Rights. *Email:* AGubner@arterhadden.com

**HOLLY A. HAYES,** born Los Angeles, California, July 31, 1952; admitted to bar, 1989, California. *Education:* Mills College (B.A., 1974); Loyola Law School (J.D., 1987). Member, California Minority Counsel Program Steering Committee. *Member:* Los Angeles County and American Bar Associations; State Bar of California; Black Women Lawyers Association. *Email:* HHayes@arterhadden.com

**DAVID M. HERSHORIN,** born Atlanta, Georgia, November 12, 1964; admitted to bar, 1990, California; 1991, District of Columbia and U.S. District Court, Central, Southern, Northern and Eastern Districts of California. *Education:* University of Southern California (B.S., 1987); Whittier College School of Law (J.D., 1990). Phi Delta Phi. Licensed Real Estate Broker, California, 1988—. *Member:* Los Angeles County (Member, Commercial and Bankruptcy Law Sections) and Orange County (Member, Commercial and Bankruptcy Law Sections) Bar Associations; District of Columbia Bar; Orange County Bankruptcy Forum. *PRACTICE AREAS:* Commercial Litigation; Real Estate Litigation. *Email:* DHershor@arterhadden.com

**TAMMY L. KAHANE,** born Los Angeles, California, March 23, 1964; admitted to bar, 1989, California. *Education:* University of California at Los Angeles (B.A., 1986); Loyola Law School (J.D., 1989). Judicial Extern to the Honorable William M. Byrne, Jr., U.S. Bankruptcy Court, Central District of California. *Member:* Orange County and American Bar Associations; State Bar of California; Financial Women International. *PRACTICE AREAS:* Commercial Litigation; Real Estate Litigation; Banking Law. *Email:* TKahane@arterhadden.com

**KATHRYN L. KEMPTON,** born Davenport, Iowa, August 30, 1969; admitted to bar, 1994, California; 1995, U.S. District Court, Eastern District of California. *Education:* University of Iowa (B.A., 1991; J.D., with honors, 1994). Recipient, American Jurisprudence Award. Member: Jessup International Moot Court Team; Moot Court Board; Van Oosterhout Memorial Moot Court Competition. Presidential Scholar, University of Iowa. Member, American Inns of Court, 1993. *Member:* Los Angeles County and Sacramento County (Board Member, International Law Section) Bar Associations; State Bar of California (Member, Litigation and International Law Sections); Barristers Club (Board Member). *LANGUAGES:* Spanish. *Email:* KKempton@arterhadden.com

**WENDY L. LINDER,** born Camden, New Jersey, October 3, 1958; admitted to bar, 1990, California. *Education:* San Diego State University

*(This Listing Continued)*

## ARTER & HADDEN, Los Angeles—Continued

(A.B., 1984); Southwestern University (J.D., 1990). *Member:* Los Angeles County Bar Association (Member, Real Property Section and Real Estate Litigation and Personal and Post-Judgement Remedies Sections); State Bar of California (Member Real Property Law Section). *Email:* WLinder@arterhadden.com

**BRENDA J. LOGAN,** born Omaha, Nebraska; admitted to bar, 1991, California. *Education:* University of Nebraska at Omaha (B.S., 1979); Georgetown University Law Center (J.D./M.B.A., 1990). *Member:* Los Angeles County Bar Association (Member, Commercial Law and Bankruptcy Sections); Black Women Lawyers Association of Los Angeles, Inc.; Women Lawyers Association of Los Angeles. *PRACTICE AREAS:* Bankruptcy; Creditors Rights; Commercial Litigation. *Email:* BLogan@arterhadden.com

**MARY DEVEREAUX MACKEY,** born Pittsburgh, Pennsylvania, July 22, 1961; admitted to bar, 1990, California and U.S. District Court, Central, Southern, Northern and Eastern Districts of California; 1991, Pennsylvania. *Education:* Duquesne University (B.S., 1983); Loyola Law School (J.D., 1990). Author: "Battle Over A Monet: The Requirement of Due Diligence in a Lawsuit by the Owner Against a Good Faith Purchaser & Possessor," 9 Loy. Ent. L. J. 57. *PRACTICE AREAS:* Labor and Employment; Business Litigation. *Email:* MMackey@arterhadden.com

**MICHELLE MCALOON,** born Staten Island, New York, March 30, 1970; admitted to bar, 1995, California. *Education:* University of California, Irvine (B.A., 1992); University of California, Los Angeles (J.D., 1995). Author: "Working But Not 'Available to Work': Reconciling the Rights of Undocumented Laborers with the IRCA of 1984," UCLA Chicano & Latino L. Rev. May 1994. *PRACTICE AREAS:* Litigation. *Email:* MMcAloon@arterhadden.com

**MAURA B. O'CONNOR,** born St. Paul, Minnesota, February 6, 1960; admitted to bar, 1988, California. *Education:* Carleton College (B.A., 1981); University of Minnesota (J.D., cum laude, 1988). Director, National Moot Court Competition Team. Member, University of Minnesota Law School Board of Visitors. *Member:* Los Angeles County and American Bar Associations; State Bar of California. *PRACTICE AREAS:* Real Estate Law; Corporate Law.

**JOHN M. ORR,** born Bryan, Texas, July 19, 1965; admitted to bar, 1990, California, U.S. District Court, Central, Eastern, Northern and Southern Districts of California and U.S. Court of Appeals, Ninth Circuit. *Education:* University of Kent at Canterbury, Great Britain; University of Southern California (B.A., 1987; J.D., 1990). *Member:* State Bar of California (Member, Litigation Section); American Bar Association. *Email:* JOrr@arterhadden.com

**JANE H. ROOT,** born Chicago, Illinois, August 27, 1965; admitted to bar, 1991, California and U.S. District Court, Central District of California. *Education:* Brown University (B.A., 1988); University of California at Los Angeles (J.D., 1991). Member, Moot Court Honors Program. Extern to the Honorable David V. Kenyon, United States District Court, Central District of California. *Member:* Los Angeles County Bar Association; State Bar of California. *PRACTICE AREAS:* Litigation. *Email:* JRoot@arterhadden.com

**ALEXANDER G. RUFUS-ISAACS,** born Sussex, England, April 25, 1957; admitted to bar, 1982, England; 1988, California; 1989, U.S. District Court, Central District of California and U.S. Court of Appeals, Ninth Circuit. *Education:* Inns of Court School of Law, London, England; City University, London, England; Oriel College, Oxford, England (B.A., 1979; M.A., 1987). Author: "The Fee-Shifting Experiment," Los Angeles Daily Journal, April 8, 1992. *Member:* Los Angeles County and American Bar Associations; State Bar of California; Middle Temple, England. *LANGUAGES:* French, German and Portuguese. *Email:* ARufus@arterhadden.com

**HELEN A. SABO,** born Los Angeles, California, October 2, 1962; admitted to bar, 1988, California. *Education:* University of California at Los Angeles (B.A., magna cum laude, 1984); Stanford University (J.D., 1988). Phi Beta Kappa. *Email:* HSabo@arterhadden.com

**MICHAEL D. SCHWARZMANN,** born Pasadena, California, August 4, 1963; admitted to bar, 1995, California and U.S. District Court, Central and Southern Districts of California. *Education:* University of Southern California (B.S., 1988); Loyola Law School, Los Angeles (J.D., 1994). *PRACTICE AREAS:* Bankruptcy; Corporate Reorganization; Creditors Rights. *Email:* MSchwarz@arterhadden.com

*(This Listing Continued)*

**ROBERT G. SOPER,** born Los Angeles, California, August 27, 1957; admitted to bar, 1984, California; U.S. District Court, Central District of California. *Education:* University of California at Berkeley (A.B., 1980); University of California at Los Angeles (J.D., 1984). Extern, 1983 and Law Clerk, 1986, to the Honorable Consuelo B. Marshall, U.S. District Court, Central District of California. *Member:* The State Bar of California. *Email:* RSoper@arterhadden.com

**JULIANA STAMATO,** born Red Bank, New Jersey, June 19, 1956; admitted to bar, 1984, California and U.S. District Court, Central District of California. *Education:* Rutgers College (B.A., 1978); Loyola University of Los Angeles (J.D., 1984). Member, St. Thomas More Law Honor Society. Member, Loyola Law Review, 1982-1984. Author: "Labor Law in the Ninth Circuit: Sex Discrimination Under Title VII," Los Angeles Law Review, Vol. 17, No. 2, 1984. *Member:* Los Angeles County Bar Association; State Bar of California; Los Angeles Women Lawyers Association; Southern California Association of Non-Profit Housing. *PRACTICE AREAS:* Secured Transactions; Real Estate Transactions; Affordable Housing. *Email:* JStamato@arterhadden.com

**KAREN M. STUCKEY,** born New York, N.Y., August 10, 1964; admitted to bar, 1989, California. *Education:* University of Missouri-Columbia (B.J., 1986); University of San Diego (J.D., 1989). Member, San Diego Law Review, 1988-1989. *Member:* San Diego County and American Bar Associations. *Email:* KStuckey@arterhadden.com

**NEIL M. SUNKIN,** born New York, N.Y., March 23, 1959; admitted to bar, 1985, Texas; 1986, U.S. District Court, Northern District of Texas; 1987, U.S. Court of Appeals, Fifth Circuit; 1990, U.S. District Court, Southern District of Texas; 1991, California and U.S. District Court, Central District of California. *Education:* Brandeis University (B.A., cum laude, 1981); Emory University (J.D., 1985). Co-Author: "Banks and Thrifts: Government Enforcement and Receivership," (Matthew Bender, 1991). *Member:* Los Angeles County (Member, Litigation Section), Dallas and American Bar Associations; State Bar of Texas; State Bar of California (Member, Litigation Section); Dallas Association of Young Lawyers (Chairman, Grants Committee, 1988-1989; Chairman, "Scared Straight" Project, 1988-1989; Vice Chairman, Continuing Legal Education Committee, 1989-1990). *REPORTED CASES:* Federal Deposits Insurance Corp. v. Claycomb, 945 F.2d 853 (5th Cir. 1991), cert. den'd, 504 U.S. 955; Federal Deposit Insurance Corp. v. Selaiden Builders, Inc., 973 F.2d 1249 (5th Cir. 1992), cert. den'd, 507 U.S. 1051. *Email:* NSunkin@arterhadden.com

**DANIEL R. VILLEGAS,** born Apple Valley, California, September 27, 1960; admitted to bar, 1990, Oregon; 1992, California and U.S. District Court, Central District of California. *Education:* University of Redlands (B.A., 1983); Northwestern School of Law of Lewis & Clark College (J.D., 1988). *Member:* Los Angeles County and Mexican American Bar Associations; State Bar of California; Oregon State Bar; Southern California Defense Counsel. *Email:* DVillega@arterhadden.com

**DAVID B. ZOLKIN,** born Los Angeles, California, August 17, 1965; admitted to bar, 1991, California, U.S. District Court, Central, Northern, Southern and Eastern Districts of California and U.S. Court of Appeals, Ninth Circuit. *Education:* University of California at Los Angeles (B.A., 1988); University of Southern California (J.D., 1991). *Member:* Los Angeles County and American Bar Associations; State Bar of California. *Email:* DZolkin@arterhadden.com

REPRESENTATIVE CLIENTS: Chevron Corp.; Pac Tel Properties; Western Union Corporation; The Bank of California, National Association; Brunswick Corp.; Reliance Steel & Aluminum Co.; Scope Industries; Huntington Beach Co.; American International Group ("AIG"); National Railroad Passenger Car; American Brands; CBI Industries; ADT, Inc.; Boral Industries; Federal Home Loan Bank Board; Federal Savings & Loan Assn.; Federal Savings & Loan Insurance Corp.; NMB Corp.; The Travelers; AT&T Technologies; Nutri/System; Warner Bros.

REVISERS OF THE OHIO LAW DIGEST FOR THIS DIRECTORY.

## ASHEN, GOLANT & LIPPMAN

*Established in 1975*

*2029 CENTURY PARK EAST, SUITE 2610*
**LOS ANGELES, CALIFORNIA 90067**
*Telephone: 310-203-0303*
*Fax: 310-203-8803*

*Beverly Hills, California Office:* 1737 Franklin Canyon Drive, 90210. Telephone: 310-274-8060. Fax: 310-858-1922.

*Chicago, Illinois Office:* 70 West Madison Street, 1700, 60602. Telephone: 312-422-0729. Fax: 312-422-0730.

*(This Listing Continued)*

Montrose, California Office: 4385 Ocean View Boulevard. Telephone: 818-249-5961. Fax: 818-249-8384.

Patent, Trademark and Copyright Law. Intellectual Property Litigation and Licensing. Unfair Competition, Trade-Secret, Computer and High-Technology Law.

### MEMBERS OF FIRM

**ROBERT M. ASHEN,** born Chicago, Illinois, March 14, 1934; admitted to bar, 1958, Illinois; 1962, California; 1963, U.S. Court of Appeals, Ninth Circuit; registered to practice before U.S. Patent and Trademark Office. *Education:* Purdue University (B.S.M.E., 1956); Harvard University (J.D., 1958). Pi Tau Sigma; Tau Beta Pi. Author: "Lawyers Need Love--and ADR," Beverly Hills Bar Association Bar Brief, March, 1994. Lecturer, Continuing Education of the Bar. Arbitrator: American Arbitration Association, 1964—. Settlement Officer, Beverly Hills Municipal Court. *Member:* Beverly Hills Bar Association; State Bar of California; Los Angeles Intellectual Property Law Association; American Intellectual Property Law Association.

**JOSEPH H. GOLANT,** born Chicago, Illinois, January 20, 1941; admitted to bar, 1966, California; U.S. Supreme Court; U.S. Court of Appeals, Ninth and Federal Circuits; registered to practice before U.S. Patent and Trademark Office. *Education:* University of Illinois (B.S.M.E., 1962); University of Chicago (J.D., 1965). Phi Delta Phi. Author: "Monopolization of A Color?" Law Works, (May, 1995); "A Seventeen Year Monopoly for a Financial Product? Welcome to the Wonderful World of Patents," Beverly Hills Bar Journal, Winter, (1993); "Patenting Coverages," Best's Review, April, (1993); "Patents for Financial Products," 208 New York Law Journal 112 (1992). Seminar Speaker: Patent Damages; Jury Selection; Trademark Counterfeiting; Trade Secrets and Intellectual Property Rights-Fundamentals and Recent Trends. Instructor, Patent, Trademark and Copyright Law, University of Southern California Law School, 1973, UCLA Extension, 1986-1992. Assistant U.S. Attorney, 1971-1973. Visiting Committee, University of Chicago Law School, 1986-1989. Editor, Beverly Hills Bar Journal, 1972-1977. *Member:* Beverly Hills (Board of Governors, 1977-1978, 1993-1995), Los Angeles County and American Bar Associations; State Bar of California; Los Angeles Intellectual Property Law Association (Board of Governors, 1969-1971); American Intellectual Property Law Association; Association of Business Trial Lawyers.

**PETER I. LIPPMAN,** born Chicago, Illinois, April 17, 1939; admitted to bar, 1964, U.S. Patent and Trademark Office; 1982, California; 1983, U.S. District Court, Central District of California and U.S. Court of Appeals, Ninth Circuit. *Education:* California Institute of Technology (B.S., 1961); Southwestern University School of Law (J.D., magna cum laude, 1982). Chief Lead Articles Editor, Southwestern University Law Review, 1981-1982. Recipient, American Jurisprudence Awards. Member, Monrovia Planning Commission, 1976-1977. *Member:* Beverly Hills (Member, Board of Governors; Volunteer Arbitration Panelist; Chairman and Membership Co-Chairman, Patent Trademark-Copyright Section), Los Angeles County Bar Associations; Los Angeles Intellectual Property Law Association.

**ELIZABETH L. SWANSON,** born Hastings, Nebraska, October 26, 1955; admitted to bar, 1990, California; 1991, U.S. District Court, Central District of California; 1992, U.S. Court of Appeals for the Federal Circuit. *Education:* University of Utah (B.S., cum laude, 1977; J.D., 1985). Phi Delta Phi (Secretary of Local Chapter, 1984-1985; Treasurer, 1983-1985). Staff Member, University of Utah Law Review. Author: "The Work-Product Doctrine and Attorney-Client Privileges As Applied to Patent Attorneys," European Intellectual Property Review, Vol. 13, Issue 2, February, 1991; "A Study of Iopanoate Metabolism and Toxicity in Isolated Cell Cultures," Investigative Radiology, Supp. to Vol. 15, No. 6, November-December, 1980. . *Member:* State Bar of California; Los Angeles Intellectual Property Law Association. **PRACTICE AREAS:** Litigation.

REFERENCE: City National Bank (Beverly Hills Office).

## RAYMOND L. ASHER
*A PROFESSIONAL CORPORATION*
2040 AVENUE OF THE STARS, SUITE 400
**LOS ANGELES, CALIFORNIA 90067**
Telephone: 310-277-4510
Fax: 310-277-7623
Email: ASHERLAW@Loop.com

Civil Trial and Appellate Practice in State and Federal Courts. Real Estate, Taxation, Corporation, Partnership, Entertainment, Intellectual Property and Computer Law.

**RAYMOND L. ASHER,** born Pittsburgh, Pennsylvania, October 3, 1945; admitted to bar, 1972, California; 1973, U.S. District Court, Central District of California; 1976, U.S. District Court, Southern and Eastern Districts of California, U.S. Tax Court and U.S. Supreme Court; 1980, U.S. Court of Appeals, Ninth Circuit. *Education:* University of California, Berkeley (A.B., 1967); University of California, Los Angeles (M.A., 1971; J.D., 1972). Phi Beta Kappa. Member, UCLA Law Review. *Member:* Century City, Los Angeles County and American Bar Associations; State Bar of California.

## MARGALO ASHLEY-FARRAND
**LOS ANGELES, CALIFORNIA**
(See Pasadena)

Family Law, Mediation, Family Trusts and Wills, Probate, Small Business, Bankruptcy.

## ASTOR & PHILLIPS
*A PROFESSIONAL LAW CORPORATION*
Established in 1963

800 WILSHIRE BOULEVARD, FIFTEENTH FLOOR
**LOS ANGELES, CALIFORNIA 90017-2619**
Telephone: 213-680-9212
Facsimile: 213-891-2910
Email: astorphill@aol.com

*Orange County Office:* 333 City Boulevard West, 17th Floor. Orange, California. Telephone: 714-634-8050.

Business, Real Estate, Corporate, Estate Planning, Probate, Taxation, Solid Waste Management/Environmental Law. General Trial Practice in Business, Real Estate, Eminent Domain, Commercial and Trust Litigation, Governmental Affairs, Family Law.

**GEORGE R. PHILLIPS,** born Los Angeles, California, April 2, 1928; admitted to bar, 1957, California and U.S District Court, Southern District of California; 1958, U.S. Tax Court. *Education:* University of California, Los Angeles (B.S., with honors in Accounting, 1950); University of California School of Law (J.D., 1956). Beta Gama Sigma; National Business Administration Honorary Society. Certified Public Accountant, 1957. *Member:* State Bar of California; American Bar Association. [U.S. Army (Finance) S.F.C., 1950-1552]. **PRACTICE AREAS:** Taxation Law; Real Estate Law; Business Law; Estate Planning.

**MARK E. LABOUNTY,** born Pomona, California, May 9, 1953; admitted to bar, 1979, California; 1985, U.S. Tax Court. *Education:* California State University at Long Beach (B.S., summa cum laude, 1976); Loyola Law School (J.D., cum laude, 1979). Beta Gamma Sigma. Certified Public Accountant, 1981. *Member:* Los Angeles County and American Bar Associations. **PRACTICE AREAS:** Estate Planning; Probate; Real Estate Law; Corporate Law.

**JOHN KELLY ASTOR,** born Inglewood, California, October 18, 1957; admitted to bar, 1983, California and U.S. District Court, Central District of California; 1989, U.S. Supreme Court. *Education:* California State University; University of Southern California (B.A., 1979); Western State University (J.D., 1982). Recipient, American Jurisprudence Award in Corporations. *Member:* Orange and American Bar Associations; State Bar of California. (Resident at Orange Office). **PRACTICE AREAS:** Solid and Hazardous Waste; Environmental Law; Governmental Affairs; Corporate Law; Family Law.

*(This Listing Continued)*

## ASTOR & PHILLIPS, A PROFESSIONAL LAW CORPORATION, Los Angeles—Continued

**GARY R. PHILLIPS,** born Pasadena, California, March 13, 1958; admitted to bar, 1986, California; 1987, U.S. District Court, Central District Court of California. *Education:* University of Southern California (B.S., 1980; J.D., 1985). Certified Public Accountant, 1987. Real Estate Broker's License, California, 1991. *Member:* Los Angeles County and American Bar Associations; State Bar of California. **PRACTICE AREAS:** Real Estate Law; Trial Practice; Business; Real Estate; Commercial; Trust Litigation; Estate Planning.

### OF COUNSEL

**Z. HARRY ASTOR,** born Fresno, California, April 16, 1922; admitted to bar, 1949, California and U.S. District Court, Southern District of California. *Education:* University of California at Los Angeles; University of Southern California (A.B., 1947; J.D., 1948). *Member:* State Bar of California. [2nd Lt., U.S. Air Force, 1942-1945]. (Resident at Orange Office). **PRACTICE AREAS:** Corporate Law; Business Law; Probate Law; Governmental Affairs.

---

**RONALD N. SARIAN,** born Philadelphia, Pennsylvania, November 7, 1957; admitted to bar, 1986, California; 1987, U.S. Court of Appeals, Ninth Circuit and U.S. District Court, Central and Eastern Districts of California. *Education:* University of California at Los Angeles (B.A., 1980) College of Letters and Science Honors Program, Omicron Delta Epsilon; Loyola Marymount University (J.D., 1985). Phi Alpha Delta. *Member:* American Bar Association. **PRACTICE AREAS:** Business, Real Estate, Tort and Construction Litigation.

**GARY Y. TANAKA,** born Torrance, California, March 16, 1963; admitted to bar, 1991, California. *Education:* California State University at Long Beach; Western State University (B.S., 1989; J.D., 1990). *Member:* State Bar of California. **PRACTICE AREAS:** Real Estate Law; Corporate Law; Estate Planning.

**LYA KINGSLAND-CANADA,** born Santa Monica, California, April 27, 1961; admitted to bar, 1988, California; 1989, U.S. District Court, Central District of California. *Education:* California State University at Fullerton (B.S., 1985); Western State University (J.D., with honors, 1988). *Member:* Orange County and American Bar Associations; State Bar of California. (Resident at Orange Office). **PRACTICE AREAS:** Family Law; Probate; Corporate Law.

**ERIC B. LABOUNTY,** born Glendora, California, January 16, 1963; admitted to bar, 1994, California. *Education:* California State University, Chico (B.A., 1985); Western State University (J.D., 1994).

---

## ATKINS & EVANS

**5900 WILSHIRE BOULEVARD, SUITE 2750**
**LOS ANGELES, CALIFORNIA 90036**
Telephone: 213-933-4100
Fax: 213-933-4157

General Casualty Litigation, Products Liability, Government Agencies, Tort Liability, Employment Litigation, Commercial Litigation and Criminal Defense, Taxation and Entertainment, Construction, Real Estate.

FIRM PROFILE: Atkins & Evans was originally established in 1978 and is one of the longest tenured minority professional service firms in the city. The firm has emphasized civil litigation particularly in negligence, commercial, employment, real estate and entertainment law. Although the size of the firm has varied over the years, we have found that communication and efficiency is at its optimum with a small firm. Through the judicious use of advanced computer and word processing capabilities, we have been able to deliver prompt, effective and quality legal services to our clients.

As lawyers, we feel that we have an obligation not only to our clients, but also to the community at large.

**NELSON L. ATKINS,** born Los Angeles, California, May 27, 1939; admitted to bar, 1965, California. *Education:* California State University, Los Angeles (B.A., 1961); Loyola University of Los Angeles (LL.B., 1964). Alpha Delta. Thomas Moore Law Society. *Member:* State Bar of California. **PRACTICE AREAS:** Personal Injury Defense Law; Employment Law; Construction Law; Business Litigation; Labor and Employment.

**IRWIN S. EVANS,** born Beaumont, Texas, November 26, 1938; admitted to bar, 1966, California; 1985 U.S. Supreme Court; 1994, U.S. Court of Appeals, Ninth Circuit. *Education:* California State University, Los Angeles (B.A., 1960); Loyola University of Los Angeles (J.D., 1965). Phi Alpha Delta. Recipient Bancroft Whitney Award, Torts, Corporations. *Member:* Los Angeles County and American Bar Associations; State Bar of California; Association of Southern California Defense Counsel. **PRACTICE AREAS:** Product Liability Law; Personal Injury Law; Commercial Law.

### ASSOCIATES

**KAREN LABAT WELLS,** born New Orleans, Louisiana, May 6, 1961; admitted to bar, 1986, California. *Education:* California State University (B.S., 1982); Loyola University of Los Angeles (J.D., 1985). *Member:* Los Angeles County Bar Association; State Bar of California; California Women Lawyers Association. **PRACTICE AREAS:** Civil Litigation; Commercial Litigation.

**SYNA N. DENNIS,** born Chicago, Illinois, July 3, 1962; admitted to bar, 1988, California; 1989, U.S. District Court, Central District of California. *Education:* University of California at Los Angeles (B.A., 1984); Boalt Hall School of Law, University of California (J.D., 1987). *Member:* Langston and Los Angeles County Bar Associations; State Bar of California. **PRACTICE AREAS:** Civil Litigation.

**HERBERT N. WIGGINS,** born Los Angeles, California, July 3, 1959; admitted to bar, 1986, California, U.S. District Court, Northern District of California; 1988, U.S. District Court, Eastern District of California; 1989, U.S. District Court, Southern and Central Districts of California. *Education:* Dartmouth College (A.B., cum laude, 1981); Boalt Hall School of Law, University of California (J.D., 1985). *Member:* Bar Association of San Francisco; Los Angeles County Bar Association (Member, Steering Committee on: Construction Law; Financial Institution; International Law); State Bar of California. **LANGUAGES:** Spanish and Portuguese. **REPORTED CASES:** G. Monchette v. Oakland Unified School District, 217 Cal.App. 3d 303, 266 Cal. P.appl. (1990). **PRACTICE AREAS:** Government Liability; Premises Liability; Automobile Accidents and Injuries; International; Products Liability (10%).

**DARLENE DIANE GARTRELL,** born Los Angeles, May 9, 1962; admitted to bar, 1993, California; 1994, U.S. District Court, Central District of California. *Education:* California Polytechnic State University; University of Nevada (B.A., 1984); Arizona State University (J.D., 1992). *Member:* State Bar of California. **PRACTICE AREAS:** Civil Litigation, Insurance Defense; Governmental Defense; Employment Law.

**HENRY L. HEINS, III,** born Los Angeles, California, April 10, 1965; admitted to bar, 1994, California, U.S. District Court, Central District of California and U.S. Court of Appeals, Ninth Circuit. *Education:* Morehouse College (B.A., 1988); University of West Los Angeles (J.D., 1993). *Member:* Los Angeles County Bar Association (President, 1992—); Los Angeles Trial Lawyers Association.

### OF COUNSEL

**ANTHONY E. ALEXANDER,** born Los Angeles, California, August 4, 1945; admitted to bar, 1974, California; 1976, U.S. District Court, Central District of California; 1989, U.S. Supreme Court. *Education:* University of California at Los Angeles (B.S., 1968; M.B.A., 1970); University of Southern California. Chairman of the Board of Directors of Pacific Coast Regional Urban Small Business Development Corporations, 1982. President, Minority Bar Association. Member, 1974-1984, President, 1981-1982, John M. Langston Bar Association. *Member:* Los Angeles County (Trustee, 1983-1985) and American Bar Associations; California Association of Black Lawyers; California Trial Lawyers. **PRACTICE AREAS:** Civil Litigation; Criminal Litigation.

**LEE R. YOUNG, JR.,** born Los Angeles, California, December 15, 1937; admitted to bar, 1966, California. *Education:* California State University at Los Angeles (B.A., 1960); Loyola University of Los Angeles; Southwestern University (J.D., 1965). Deputy City Attorney, City of Los Angeles, 1966. General Counsel's Office, MCA, Inc. 1969. General Counsel, ABC Records, 1972. Vice President of Business Affairs, Motown Records, 1976. President, Motown Music Group, 1987. *Member:* Beverly Hills Bar Association; State Bar of California; National Bar Association. **PRACTICE AREAS:** Entertainment Law.

REPRESENTATIVE CLIENTS: Argonaut Insurance Co.; Beneficial Corp. City of Compton; City of Inglewood; City of Los Angeles, Department of Airports; The Community Redevelopment Agency of the City of Los Angeles; County of Los Angeles: Eastman Kodak Co.; Elitegroup Computer Systems, Inc.; Family Restaurants; Federal Deposit Insurance Corp. (FDIC); Ford Motor Co.; Kaiser Foundation Health Plan, Inc.; Los Angeles County Metropolitan Transportation Authority (LACMTA); Los Angeles Metro Rail; Los Angeles Unified School

*(This Listing Continued)*

District; McDonnell Douglas Corp.; Memphis Light, Gas & Water; Motorola, Inc.; Mutual of Omaha Insurance Co.; State Farm Insurance Co.; Tandem Computer Co.; Tupperware, Inc.; U.S.A.A. Casualty Insurance Co.; Wells Fargo Bank.

## ATKINSON, ANDELSON, LOYA, RUUD & ROMO

*A PROFESSIONAL CORPORATION*

### LOS ANGELES, CALIFORNIA

(See Cerritos)

*Labor Relations representing Management. School Law. Construction and Real Estate Law. Civil Litigation. Corporate, Securities and Tax Law. Estate Planning Law.*

## AUGUSTINI, WHEELER & DILLMAN, LLP

PACIFIC CENTER, SUITE 300
523 WEST SIXTH STREET
### LOS ANGELES, CALIFORNIA 90014
Telephone: 213-629-8888
Telecopier: 213-688-7600

*General Civil Trial and Appellate Litigation in all State and Federal Courts and Arbitrations; with emphasis on Business Contract and Tort Litigation; including real estate and real property matters; hazardous waste, pollution and environmental matters; RTC matters, banking and lender liability; and corporate and partnership litigation.*

FIRM PROFILE: *Augustini, Wheeler & Dillman is a boutique business litigation firm whose founders developed their trial skills at major Los Angeles law firms, but preferred the atmosphere of a small firm. The Firm handles all varieties of business litigation and arbitration for both plaintiffs and defendants, but the Firm specializes in cases involving real estate and business disputes.*

### MEMBERS OF FIRM

**ALFRED E. AUGUSTINI,** born Framingham, Massachusetts, October 24, 1942; admitted to bar, 1969, California; 1970, U.S. District Court, Central and Northern Districts of California and U.S. Court of Appeals, 9th Circuit; 1977, U.S. Supreme Court. *Education:* Boston College (A.B., with honors, 1964); Georgetown University (J.D., 1967). Recent Decisions Editor, Georgetown Law Journal, Vol. 55, 1967. Law Clerk, United States Court of Appeals, 9th Circuit, 1967-1968. *Member:* Los Angeles County and American Bar Associations; State Bar of California; Association of Business Trial Lawyers.

**DAVID C. WHEELER,** born Bloomington, Indiana, February 22, 1947; admitted to bar, 1974, Illinois; 1977, California. *Education:* Indiana University (B.A., 1969); The Ohio State University (M.A., 1971); Northwestern University (J.D., with honors, 1974). Member, Editorial Board, Northwestern University Law Review, 1973-1974. *Member:* Los Angeles County and American Bar Associations; State Bar of California; Association of Business Trial Lawyers.

**KIRK D. DILLMAN,** born Oak Park, Illinois, April 27, 1956; admitted to bar, 1983, California. *Education:* Reed College (B.A., summa cum laude, 1979); University of California at Los Angeles (J.D., 1983). Member: Executive Board, Moot Court Honors Program. Law Clerk, Hon. Judge Laughlin E. Waters, United States District Court, Central District of California, 1983-1985. *Member:* Los Angeles County and American Bar Associations; State Bar of California; Association of Business Trial Lawyers.

### ASSOCIATES

**JOHN M. BOWERS,** born Marietta, Georgia, December 31, 1956; admitted to bar, 1991, California and U.S. District Court, Central District of California. *Education:* University of Florida (B.S., 1978); Pepperdine University (J.D., magna cum laude, 1991). *Member:* American Bar Association. **PRACTICE AREAS:** Litigation.

**LAWRENCE C. JONES,** born Atlanta, Georgia, June 2, 1953; admitted to bar, 1992, California. *Education:* Reed College (B.A., 1980); University of Southern California (J.D., 1992).

### OF COUNSEL

**PETER H. STRONG,** born Ann Arbor, Michigan, March 1, 1952; admitted to bar, 1975, California; 1979, U.S. District Court, Central and Northern Districts of California; 1980, U.S. Court of Appeals, Ninth Circuit; 1981, U.S. District Court, Eastern District of California. *Education:*

*(This Listing Continued)*

University of Arizona (A.B., with high distinction, 1972); Stanford University (J.D., 1975). Judge Pro Tem, Los Angeles Municipal Court, 1982—. *Member:* State Bar of California.

REPRESENTATIVE CLIENTS: Toyota Motor Sales, U.S.A., Inc.; Home Savings and Loan Assn.; Watt Industries, Inc.; Trammell Crow Co.; U.S. Bank Note; Goldrich & Kest Industries; The Hewson Co.; The Larwin Co.; Tiger Real Estate Partners.

## BACON & MILLS, LLP

800 WILSHIRE BOULEVARD, SUITE 950
### LOS ANGELES, CALIFORNIA 90017
Telephone: 213-486-6500
Fax: 213-486-6552

*West Covina, California Office:* 100 North Barranca Street, 11th Floor. Telephone: 818-915-6555. Fax: 818-915-8855.

*General Civil Trial and Appellate Practice in Federal and State Courts. Insurance Defense, Employment, Corporate, Federal and State Taxation Law, Environmental, Probate and Estate Planning.*

FIRM PROFILE: *While formed in 1995, the firm of Bacon & Mills offers its clients the services of attorneys with years of experience and a proven record of superior legal representation of its clients. The firm is headed by senior partners Robert Parker Mills and Robert L. Bacon who possess a combined 65 years of legal experience. The firm serves your needs in the areas of general civil litigation, complex and multi-party litigation, corporate and business matters (including acquisitions and dissolutions), federal, state and local tax matters, construction defect litigation, employment law, product liability, environmental law, probate, and estate planning. The firm is very proud of its reputation in the legal community for providing exemplary services in a timely and cost effective manner.*

**ROBERT PARKER MILLS,** born St. Louis, Missouri, July 27, 1945; admitted to bar, 1971, California; 1985, U.S. Supreme Court; 1987, District of Columbia; 1996, Missouri. *Education:* University of Missouri (B.A., English and History, 1967; J.D., 1970). Phi Delta Phi. Licensed Real Estate Broker, California, 1983. Author: "Proposition 51: The Ramifications and Potential Applications," The Verdict, 1986; "Recent Cases Affecting Insurer's Liability," The Verdict, 1987; "The Defense of the Rock Hudson Estate in an Alleged Sexually Transmitted Disease Case," The Verdict, 1991. *Member:* Pasadena and Los Angeles County Bar Associations; District of Columbia Bar; Southern California Defense Counsel (Former Director); Defense Research Institute; Inns of Court. **PRACTICE AREAS:** General Civil Trial Litigation; Insurance Defense Law; Sexually Transmitted Disease (AIDS) Litigation; Employment Law; Construction Defect Litigation; Product Liability Litigation.

**ROBERT L. BACON,** born Ontario, California, October 25, 1928; admitted to bar, 1952, California; 1974, U.S. Tax Court; 1983, U.S. Supreme Court. *Education:* Pasadena City College (A.A., 1948); Hastings College of the Law, University of California (J.D., 1951). Revising Editor, Hastings Law Journal, 1951. Co-Author: "Hazardous Waste Facility Siting In So. California," U.S.C. Journal of Law and Environment, 1987. Member, So. California Hazardous Waste Authority, 1985-1990. Member, State of California Hazardous Waste Appeals Board, 1989-1990. Member and Chair, 1989-1990, Environmental Quality Committee, League of California Cities. Founding President, San Gabriel Neighborhood Legal Aid Society, 1966. *Member:* San Gabriel Valley (President, 1963-1964), Eastern and Los Angeles County Bar Associations; State Bar of California; Inns of Court (President, 1996-1997). **PRACTICE AREAS:** Corporations; Tax; Transactions; Estate Planning; Real Estate; Environmental.

**THEODORE E. BACON,** born Pasadena, California, July 3, 1959; admitted to bar, 1984, California; U.S. District Court, Central and Southern Districts of California. *Education:* Occidental College (A.B., 1981); McGeorge School of Law, University of the Pacific (J.D., 1984). Arbitrator, Los Angeles County Superior Court. *Member:* Eastern and Los Angeles County Bar Associations; State Bar of California. (Resident at West Covina Office). **PRACTICE AREAS:** Business Litigation; Corporate; Labor; Probate and Estate Planning.

**JAMES W. COLFER,** born Oak Lawn, Illinois, December 26, 1962; admitted to bar, 1988, California. *Education:* University of California at Riverside (B.A., 1985); Boalt Hall School of Law, University of California (J.D., 1988). *Member:* Eastern and Los Angeles County Bar Associations; State Bar of California. **PRACTICE AREAS:** Business; Insurance Defense; Employment Law.

*(This Listing Continued)*

BACON & MILLS, LLP, Los Angeles—Continued

**CARL ANDREW BOTTERUD,** born Loma Linda, California, April 10, 1956; admitted to bar, 1992, California, U.S. District Court, Central District of California and U.S. Court of Appeals, Ninth Circuit. *Education:* Occidental College (A.B., 1979); Whittier College School of Law (J.D., cum laude, 1992). Staff Member, Whittier College School of Law, Law Review, 1990-1992; Senior Editor, 1991-1992. Extern to Honorable Harry Pregerson, Court of Appeals, Ninth Circuit. Adjunct Professor, Whittier College School of Law, 1992; Visiting Assistant Professor of Law, Evidence, Corporations, Public Interest Law, 1993-1994. President, National Association for Public Interest Law, 1991-1992. *Member:* Pasadena, Eastern, Los Angeles County (Co-Chair, Legal Services to the Poor Committee, 1994—) and American (Member, Sections on: Litigation; Individuals Rights; Responsibilities) Bar Associations; State Bar of California; National Association for Public Interest Law (President, 1991-1992). **PRACTICE AREAS:** Business Litigation; Employment Law; Insurance Defense.

**ADAM J. GERARD,** born Hawthorne, California, October 6, 1963; admitted to bar, 1993, California; 1994, U.S. Tax Court. *Education:* California State University Fullerton (B.A. in Political Science, 1989); Pepperdine University (J.D., 1993). Chairperson, Moot Court Honor Board, Interschool Program. Judicial Extern to The Honorable John E. Ryan, U.S. Bankruptcy Court Judge, Central District of California. *Member:* Los Angeles County Bar Association; State Bar of California; Southern California Defense Counsel. **PRACTICE AREAS:** Business and Civil Litigation; Insurance Defense.

**HOWARD S. HOU,** born Morristown, New Jersey, October 15, 1966; admitted to bar, 1992, California. *Education:* University of Connecticut (B.S., magna cum laude, 1988); University of California School of Law, Davis (J.D., 1992); McGeorge School of Law, University of the Pacific (LL.M., 1994). Beta Gamma Sigma. *Member:* Los Angeles County Bar Association (Member, Taxation Section). **LANGUAGES:** Mandarin Chinese. **PRACTICE AREAS:** Taxation; Estate Planning; Corporate.

REPRESENTATIVE CLIENTS: Lucas Industries, Inc.; Lucas Aviation; Lucas Aerospace; Nationwide/Wausau Insurance Company; Weyerhauser Corporation; Federated Holdings, Inc.; Federated Auction Systems, Inc.; Crawford & Company; Ralph M. Parsons; Dillingham North American; PacCar Leasing; California State Bank; Columbia Showcase & Cabinet Co.; Cannon Fabriction, Inc.; Cornerstone Systems, Inc.; ; Singer, Lewak, Greenbaum & Goldstein, CPAs; Optical Components, Inc.; Femino Foundation; Coleman Foundation; Excel Technology, Inc.

---

## LAW OFFICES OF
## BRUCE R. BAILEY
**1900 AVENUE OF THE STARS, SUITE 1630**
**LOS ANGELES, CALIFORNIA 90067**
Telephone: 310-286-9900
Telecopier: 310-286-9907
Email: brbailey@netcom.com
URL: http://www.baileyfirm.com

*International Transactions, Taxation, Corporate Law, Real Estate, Promotion, Marketing and Advertising Law, Employee Benefits.*

**BRUCE R. BAILEY,** born Grand Island, Nebraska, April 7, 1941; admitted to bar, 1966, California and U.S. District Court, Central District of California; 1968, U.S. Tax Court; 1969, U.S. Claims Court; 1971, U.S. Court of Appeals, Ninth Circuit. *Education:* University of California at Los Angeles (B.A., 1962; J.D., 1965). Order of the Coif. Associate Editor, UCLA Law Review, 1964-1965. *Member:* Los Angeles County (Member, Sections on Taxation, Business and Corporations) and American (Member, Taxation Section) Bar Associations. (Certified Specialist, Taxation Law, The State Bar of California Board of Legal Specialization).

### ASSOCIATES

**GREGORY R. SCHENZ,** born Barberton, Ohio, April 17, 1965; admitted to bar, 1993, California. *Education:* George Washington University (B.A., cum laude, 1987); Loyola University of Los Angeles (J.D., 1993). Order of the Coif; Phi Delta Phi (Exchequer, 1992-1993). Editor-in-Chief, Loyola of Los Angeles Entertainment Law Journal, 1992-1993. *Member:* Beverly Hills and Los Angeles County Bar Associations; State Bar of California.

**JOHN R. DENNY,** born Santa Monica, California, February 5, 1957; admitted to bar, 1994, California and U.S. District Court, Central District of California. *Education:* University of California at Los Angeles (B.A.,

*(This Listing Continued)*

---

1980); Loyola Law School (J.D., 1994). Order of the Coif. Editor, Loyola of Los Angeles Law Review, 1993-1994. *Member:* State Bar of California. **PRACTICE AREAS:** Litigation.

**RICHARD CHARLES HERMAN,** born Los Angeles, California, March 6, 1963; admitted to bar, 1995, California. *Education:* University of Colorado at Boulder (B.A., 1986); Loyola University of Los Angeles (J.D., 1995). Phi Delta Phi. Editor-in-Chief, Loyola of Los Angeles International and Comparative Law Journal, 1994-1995. Chapter President, Federalist Society, 1994-1995. *Member:* Los Angeles County, Orange County and American (Member, Litigation Section, 1995-1996) Bar Associations; State Bar of California.

### OF COUNSEL

**CLAUDIO O. WOLFF,** born Buenos Aires, Argentina, August 11, 1958; admitted to bar, 1983, California. *Education:* University of California at Los Angeles (B.A., magna cum laude, 1980; J.D., 1983). Omicron Delta Epsilon; Phi Gamma Mu; Order of the Barristers Moot Court. Lecturer: "Recent Developments in Business Law Practice," California Continuing Education of the Bar, State Bar of California, March, 1989. *Member:* Los Angeles County (Member, Limited Liability Companies Committee) and American Bar Associations; State Bar of California (Member, Partnership Committee, Business Law Section, 1989-1991). **PRACTICE AREAS:** General Corporate and Securities Law; Real Estate Law; International Transactions.

**STEVEN U. ROSS,** born New York, N.Y., February 14, 1955; admitted to bar, 1981, California; 1982, U.S. District Court, Central District of California; 1983, U.S. District Court, Southern District of California. *Education:* University of California at Berkeley (B.A., with high honors, 1977); Loyola University of Los Angeles (J.D., 1981). *Member:* Los Angeles County and American Bar Associations; State Bar of California. **PRACTICE AREAS:** Business Litigation; Real Estate Law.

REPRESENTATIVE CLIENTS: Simon Marketing, Inc.; Yaohan Department Stores; Cohen-Brown Management Group; Metropolitan Transportation Authority; San Francisco Culinary, Bartenders and Service Employees Benefit Funds.

---

## ROBERT K. BAKER
**601 SOUTH FIGUEROA STREET, 41ST FLOOR**
**LOS ANGELES, CALIFORNIA 90017-5758**
Telephone: 213-612-0800
Facsimile: 213-689-7607

*General Civil Trial, Criminal Antitrust, Securities and Tax, Commercial Litigation, Trademark, Trade Secrets.*

**ROBERT K. BAKER,** born Anderson, Indiana, March 20, 1940; admitted to bar, 1966, California; 1971, New York; U.S. Court of Appeals, Second Circuit; 1976, U.S. Supreme Court and U.S. Court of Appeals, Ninth Circuit. *Education:* Stanford University (B.A., 1962; LL.B., 1965). Order of the Coif. Articles Editor, Stanford Law Review, 1964-1965. Author: "Extraterritorial Enforcement of Exchange Regulations," 16 Stanford Law Review 202, 1968; "Antitrust and Trade Regulation Statutory and Agency Overview," in Antitrust and Trade Regulation Compliance, CEB, 1980. Instructor in Law, Columbia University, 1965-1966. Member, Policy Planning Staff, Antitrust Division, 1966-1967 and Special Assistant to the Deputy Attorney General, 1967-1968, U.S. Department of Justice. Deputy General Counsel and Co-Director, Media Task Force, National Commission on the Causes and Prevention of Violence, Washington, D.C., 1968-1969. *Member:* Los Angeles County and American Bar Associations. **PRACTICE AREAS:** Complex Litigation; Antitrust Law; Securities Litigation; Trade Secrets Law.

---

## SCOTT L. BAKER
**2029 CENTURY PARK EAST, SUITE 2750**
**LOS ANGELES, CALIFORNIA 90067**
Telephone: 310-553-2253
Fax: 310-553-2254
Email: bake@earthlink.net

*General Civil Practice including Business, Contract, Art and Entertainment, Insurance Defense and Accident Litigation.*

**SCOTT L. BAKER,** born Columbus, Ohio, January 22, 1959; admitted to bar, 1985, Ohio; 1987, California; 1988, District of Columbia. *Education:* The Ohio State University (B.S., 1981); Case Western Reserve University School of Law (J.D., 1985). Member, Moot Court Executive Board, 1984-

*(This Listing Continued)*

1985. Law Clerk to the Honorable Robert B. Krupansky, U.S. Court of Appeals, Sixth Circuit, 1985-1986. Former Chief West Coast Counsel, Agency Rent-A-Car. *Member:* Beverly Hills and Los Angeles County Bar Associations; State Bar of California; District of Columbia Bar; Ohio State Bar Association.

## *BAKER & HOSTETLER*

Established in 1916

600 WILSHIRE BOULEVARD
LOS ANGELES, CALIFORNIA 90017-3212

Telephone: 213-624-2400
FAX: 213-975-1740

*In Cleveland, Ohio:* 3200 National City Center, 1900 East Ninth Street. Telephone: 216-621-0200.

*In Columbus, Ohio:* Capitol Square, Suite 2100, 65 East State Street. Telephone: 614-228-1541.

*In Denver, Colorado:* 303 East 17th Avenue, Suite 1100. Telephone: 303-861-0600.

*In Houston, Texas:* 1000 Louisiana, Suite 2000. Telephone: 713-236-0020.

*In Long Beach, California:* 300 Oceangate, Suite 620. Telephone: 310-432-2827.

*In Orlando, Florida:* SunBank Center, Suite 2300, 200 South Orange Avenue. Telephone: 407-649-4000.

*In Washington, D. C.:* Washington Square, Suite 1100, 1050 Connecticut Avenue, N. W. Telephone: 202-861-1500.

*In College Park, Maryland:* 9658 Baltimore Boulevard, Suite 206. Telephone: 301-441-2781.

*In Alexandria, Virginia:* 437 North Lee Street. Telephone: 703-549-1294.

*In San Francisco, California:* One Sansome Street, Suite 2000. Telephone: 415-951-4705.

General Practice.

MEMBERS OF FIRM IN LOS ANGELES, CALIFORNIA

**EDWARD J. MCCUTCHEN** (1857-1933).

**HAROLD A. BLACK** (1895-1970).

**GEORGE HARNAGEL** (1903-1962).

**G. WILLIAM SHEA** (1911-1986).

**SHELDON A. GEBB,** born Long Beach, California, January 12, 1935; admitted to bar, 1964, California. *Education:* University of California, Berkeley (A.B., 1957); Boalt Hall School of Law, University of California (LL.B., 1963). Chairman, Board of Trustees, Southwestern University School of Law, 1985-1991. *Member:* The State Bar of California; American Bar Association; Maritime Law Association of the United States. (Managing Partner-Los Angeles, Long Beach, California and Houston, Texas Offices). *PRACTICE AREAS:* Admiralty; Litigation; Insurance.

PARTNERS

**ANGELA C. AGRUSA,** born Los Angeles, California, May 6, 1962; admitted to bar, 1987, California. *Education:* University of California, Los Angeles (B.A., 1984); Loyola Law School (J.D., 1987). Recipient, American Jurisprudence Award in International Law. *Member:* Los Angeles County and American Bar Association; State Bar of California. *PRACTICE AREAS:* Litigation.

**WILLIAM P. BARRY,** born Bethesda, Maryland, January 11, 1948; admitted to bar, 1978, California. *Education:* United States Naval Academy (B.S., 1970); Catholic University of America (J.D., 1978). Production Editor, Catholic University of America Law Review, 1977-1978. *Member:* Los Angeles and American Bar Associations; The State Bar of California; Maritime Law Association of the United States; Southern California Marine Underwriters Association. *PRACTICE AREAS:* Admiralty Law; Maritime Litigation; Environmental Litigation.

**PATRICK J. CAIN,** born San Fernando, California, March 22, 1957; admitted to bar, 1982, California. *Education:* Loyola Marymount University (B.A., magna cum laude, 1979); University of California at Los Angeles School of Law (J.D., 1982). Judge Pro Tem, Los Angeles County Municipal Court, 1989-1990. Member, UCLA Law Review, 1980-1981. Member and Distinguished Advocate, 1980-1981 and Chief Justice, 1981-1982, UCLA Moot Court Honors Program. *Member:* Los Angeles County and American Bar Associations; State Bar of California. *PRACTICE AREAS:* Employment Litigation; Wrongful Termination; Unfair Competition; Workplace Violence. *Email:* pcain@baker-hostetler.com

*(This Listing Continued)*

**PENNY M. COSTA,** born Oakland, California, December 4, 1951; admitted to bar, 1983, California. *Education:* Holy Names College (B.A., summa cum laude, 1973); Marquette University (M.A., 1976); University of California, Los Angeles (J.D., 1983). Distinguished Advocate, UCLA Moot Court Honors Program. Member, UCLA National Moot Court Team. *Member:* The State Bar of California. *PRACTICE AREAS:* Litigation.

**RICHARD A. DEEB,** born Glendale, California, February 8, 1963; admitted to bar, 1987, California. *Education:* Loyola Marymount University (B.A., 1984; J.D., 1987). Editor: Loyola Law Review, 1986-1987; Board of Editors, Leader's Product Liability Law and Strategy Journal, 1991—. *Member:* Los Angeles County Bar Association; State Bar of California. *PRACTICE AREAS:* Litigation and Product Liability.

**DAVID A. DESTINO,** born Providence, Rhode Island, January 24, 1944; admitted to bar, 1970, California. *Education:* University of Connecticut (B.S., 1966); Boston University (J.D., magna cum laude, 1969). Editor, Boston University Law Review, 1968-1969. Law Clerk to T. Emmet Clarie, U.S. District Court, 1969-1970. *Member:* American Bar Association; The State Bar of California. *PRACTICE AREAS:* Litigation; Antitrust.

**JACK D. FUDGE,** born Zion, Arkansas, August 15, 1934; admitted to bar, 1964, California. *Education:* University of Southern California and San Jose State College (B.A., 1956); Hastings College of Law, University of California (LL.B., 1963). Order of the Coif. *Member:* The State Bar of California; Federal and American Bar Associations. *PRACTICE AREAS:* Litigation.

**RICHARD A. GOETTE,** born Rochester, New York, December 22, 1948; admitted to bar, 1975, California; 1980, District of Columbia. *Education:* St. Lawrence University (B.A., 1971); Southwestern University (J.D., 1975). *Member:* American Bar Association; The State Bar of California; The District of Columbia Bar. *PRACTICE AREAS:* Litigation.

**BYRON HAYES, JR.,** born Los Angeles, California, July 9, 1934; admitted to bar, 1960, California; 1963, U.S. Supreme Court. *Education:* Pomona College (B.A., magna cum laude, 1956); Harvard University (LL.B., cum laude, 1959). Phi Beta Kappa. President, Pomona College Alumni Association, 1984-1985. *Member:* Los Angeles County (Chairman, Real Property Section, 1982-1983) and American Bar Associations; The State Bar of California; Association of Real Estate Attorneys; Financial Lawyers Conference; American College of Mortgage Attorneys (Regent, 1984-1990; 1991-1993; President, 1993-1994). *PRACTICE AREAS:* Business Transactions; Real Estate Law; Financial Institutions Law. *Email:* bhayes@baker-hostetler.com

**EMIL W. HERICH,** born Twenty Nine Palms, California, August 20, 1957; admitted to bar, 1984, California. *Education:* University of California, Berkeley (B.A., with highest honors, with great distinction, 1979); University of California, Los Angeles (J.D, 1984). Phi Beta Kappa. *Member:* Los Angeles County Bar Association; The State Bar of California. *PRACTICE AREAS:* Litigation.

**DENNIS F. HERNANDEZ,** born Redlands, California, January 16, 1953; admitted to bar, 1981, California. *Education:* Loyola Marymount University (B.A., 1975); Georgetown University (J.D., 1981). Editor, American Criminal Law Review, 1980-1981. Law Clerk, California Supreme Court. *Member:* The State Bar of California; American Bar Association. *LANGUAGES:* Spanish. *PRACTICE AREAS:* First Amendment Law and Litigation; Intellectual Property. *Email:* dhernandez@baker-hostetler.com

**BRADLEY R. HOGIN,** born Summit, New Jersey, September 5, 1958; admitted to bar, 1989, California and U.S. District Court, Central District of California;1992, U.S. District Court, Eastern District of California; U.S. District Court of Appeals, District of Columbia and Ninth Circuits. *Education:* University of California at Berkeley (A.B., with high honors, 1984); Washington College of Law, American University (J.D., 1988). Phi Beta Kappa. Senior Articles Editor, American University Law Review, 1987-1988. Author: "Update on State Superfund Reforms," feature article for California Environmental Law and Regulation Reporter (November 1995); "The Underground Storage Tank Corrective Action Process," California Environmental Insider (December 1994); "Post-Cleanup Stigma Damage Claims; The Latest Front in the War Over Hazardous Waste Cost Recovery," BNA California Environmental Law Reporter (December 1994); Member of Advisory Board, for California Environmental Law and Regulation Reporter (May 1992 to 1996); Columnist for Impact, California Business Environmental Assistance Center bi-monthly newsletter (January 1993 to 1996); Author: "Use of Contingent Valuation in Natural Resource Damage Assessments," feature article for Shepard's California Environmental Law and Regulation Reporter (August 1993); "Local Regulation of Oil Pro-

*(This Listing Continued)*

**BAKER & HOSTETLER, Los Angeles—Continued**

duction in California," Pacific Oil World (May 1992); California Environmental Law Handbook, (Government Institutes, Inc.) (5th-9th editions 1991-1995) (Co-Author). I Member: Los Angeles County (Member, Executive Committee of Environmental Law Section, 1995-1996), and American (Vice Chair, Marine Resources Committee, Section on Natural Resources, Energy and Environmental Law, 1992-1995) Bar Associations; State Bar of California. *PRACTICE AREAS:* Environmental and Natural Resources Law; Litigation.

**JOSEPH B. HUDSON, JR.,** born California, December 30, 1939; admitted to bar, 1976, New York; 1978, U.S. District Court, Southern and Eastern Districts of New York; 1979, California; 1980, U.S. District Court, Northern District of California; 1981, U.S. District Court, Southern District of California. *Education:* Stanford University (B.A., 1962); Yale University (M.Phil, 1974); New York University (M.A., 1971; J.D., 1974). *PRACTICE AREAS:* Business.

**PETER W. JAMES,** born Irvington, New York, August 23, 1941; admitted to bar, 1968, California. *Education:* Stanford University (B.A., 1963); Yale University (LL.B., 1966). Law Clerk to Gus J. Solomon, U.S. District Court, 1966-1967. *Member:* Los Angeles County and American Bar Associations; The State Bar of California. *PRACTICE AREAS:* Business Litigation; School Equal Protection Litigation.

**MICHAEL M. JOHNSON,** born Long Beach, California, February 12, 1951; admitted to bar, 1976, California. *Education:* University of California, Los Angeles (B.A., 1973); Hastings College of Law, University of California (J.D., 1976). Phi Beta Kappa. Commissioner, California Fair Employment and Housing Commission, 1995—and 1987-1991. *Member:* Los Angeles County and American Bar Associations; The State Bar of California (Chair, Labor and Employment Section, 1995-1996; Member, Executive Committee, 1991—). *PRACTICE AREAS:* Employment Law; Litigation. *Email:* mikejohn@baker-hostetler.com

**ANTHONY M. KEATS,** born Newark, New Jersey, January 2, 1955; admitted to bar, 1986, California and U.S. District Court, Northern, Central, Southern and Eastern Districts of California. *Education:* Brown University (B.A., 1977; M.A., 1978); University of San Francisco (J.D., 1984). Director, Moot Court Board, 1984. *Member:* Beverly Hills and American (Member, Section on Patents, Trademark and Copyrights) Bar Associations; State Bar of California (Member, Section on Patents and Trademarks); U.S. Trademark Association; San Francisco Patent and Trademark Law Association; International Anti-Counterfeiting Coalition. *PRACTICE AREAS:* Intellectual Property.

**LYNN S. LOEB,** born Los Angeles, California, November 27, 1962; admitted to bar, 1988, California; 1991, District of Columbia. *Education:* University of California, Los Angeles (B.A., 1984); George Washington University (J.D., with honors, 1988). *Member:* State Bar of California; The District of Columbia Bar. *PRACTICE AREAS:* Intellectual Property Litigation.

**LARRY W. MCFARLAND,** born Houston, Texas, December 23, 1958; admitted to bar, 1987, California and Texas. *Education:* University of Texas at Austin (B.A., 1983); University of Houston (J.D., 1986). Member, University of Houston Law Review, 1984-1986. *Member:* Los Angeles Bar Association (Member, Intellectual Property Section); State Bar of California (Member, Intellectual Property Section). *PRACTICE AREAS:* Intellectual Property; Litigation and Counseling.

**JOHN C. MUELLER,** born Los Angeles, California, September 19, 1952; admitted to bar, 1977, California. *Education:* Stanford University (A.B., 1974); University of Southern California (J.D., 1977). *Member:* Los Angeles County and American Bar Associations; The State Bar of California. *PRACTICE AREAS:* Environmental and Natural Resources Law.

**DEAN G. RALLIS JR.,** born Sioux Falls, South Dakota, February 4, 1955; admitted to bar, 1980, California, U.S. District Court, Central, Eastern, Southern and Northern Districts of California and U.S. Court of Appeals, Ninth Circuit. *Education:* University of Arizona; University of Southern California (B.S.B.A., cum laude, 1977); University of Southern California (J.D., 1980). Beta Gamma Sigma; Beta Alpha Psi; Phi Alpha Delta. *Member:* Los Angeles County (Member, Board of Trustees, 1988-1989; Member, Sections on: Commercial Law and Bankruptcy; Business and Corporate Law; Member, Prejudgment Remedies Executive Committee, 1985) and American (Member, Sections on: Corporation, Banking and Business Law; Real Property, Probate and Trust Law; Taxation) Bar Associations; Lawyer's Club of Los Angeles (Member, Board of Governors, 1982-1989; President, 1986-1987; Delegate, State Bar Conference of Delegates, 1980-1989); Financial Lawyers Conference; Turnaround Management Association; California Young Lawyers Association (Member, Board of Directors, 1987-1990). *PRACTICE AREAS:* Insolvency Law; Bankruptcy Litigation; Reorganization Law; Secured Transactions; Real Estate Finance. *Email:* drallis@baker-hostetler.com

**JILL SARNOFF RIOLA,** born New York, New York, March 18, 1954; admitted to bar, 1980, New York; 1984, California. *Education:* University of Rochester (B.A., 1976); New York University (J.D., 1979). Phi Beta Kappa. *Member:* Beverly Hills, Los Angeles County (Member, Intellectual Property and Unfair Competition Law Sections), New York State and American (Member, Patent, Trademark and Copyright Law Section) Bar Associations; State Bar of California. *PRACTICE AREAS:* Trademark; Copyright; Advertising; Marketing Services.

**THOMAS G. ROBERTS,** born Bakersfield, California, May 25, 1949; admitted to bar, 1974, California. *Education:* University of Southern California (B.A., 1971; J.D., 1974). Order of the Coif. Member, Board of Editors, Southern California Law Review, 1973-1974. *Member:* Los Angeles County and American Bar Associations; The State Bar of California. *PRACTICE AREAS:* Business Law; Real Estate Law.

**JACK I. SAMET,** born New York, N.Y., August 6, 1940; admitted to bar, 1965, New York; 1973, California. *Education:* Columbia University (B.A., magna cum laude, 1961); Harvard University (J.D., 1964). Phi Beta Kappa. *Member:* Los Angeles County, New York State and American (Member, Business Torts Committee and Civil R.I.C.O. Subcommittee) Bar Associations; The State Bar of California; United States Supreme Court Bar. *REPORTED CASES:* Holmes vs. S.I.P.C., U.S. Supreme Court, 1991; S.E.C. vs. Korocorp, 9th Circuit, 1978; Hanly vs. S.E.C., 2nd Circuit, 1969; Rollins Burdick Hunter vs. Alexander & Alexander, Cal. Ct. of Appeal, 1988; In Re ZZZZ Best Litigation, Cal. Dist. Court, 1995; In Re Executive Life Conservatorship, Cal. Appellate Court, 1995. *PRACTICE AREAS:* Securities Litigation; Corporate Control Disputes; Legal Malpractice; Business; Unfair Competition.

**DAVID C. SAMPSON,** born Bakersfield, California, February 3, 1952; admitted to bar, 1985, California. *Education:* University of Maryland; San Diego State University (B.S.B.A., summa cum laude, 1982); University of California, Los Angeles (J.D., 1985). *Member:* Los Angles County Bar Association; State Bar of California. *LANGUAGES:* German and Czech. *PRACTICE AREAS:* Land Use; Real Estate.

**BILL E. SCHROEDER,** born Long Beach, California, January 16, 1942; admitted to bar, 1967, California. *Education:* Stanford University (B.A., 1963); Boalt Hall School of Law, University of California (LL.B., 1966). Order of the Coif. *Member:* Los Angeles County and American Bar Associations; The State Bar of California. *PRACTICE AREAS:* Litigation.

**DIANE C. STANFIELD,** born Columbia, South Carolina, January 25, 1956; admitted to bar, 1982, California. *Education:* California State University at Northridge (B.A., 1979); University of California, Los Angeles (J.D., 1982). *Member:* Los Angeles County Bar Association; The State Bar of California. *PRACTICE AREAS:* Real Estate Litigation. *Email:* dstanfield@baker-hostetler.com

**TERESA R. TRACY,** born Granite City, Illinois, July 21, 1952; admitted to bar, 1979, California; 1980, U.S. District Court, Central and Eastern Districts of California. *Education:* California State University at Northridge (B.A., in Psychology, magna cum laude, 1974); Loyola University of Los Angeles (J.D., cum laude, 1979). Member, Loyola University of Los Angeles Law Review, 1977-1978. Author: "Comparative Fault and Intentional Torts," 12 Loyola University of Los Angeles Law Review, 1978. Member, Merchants & Manufacturers, 1985—. *Member:* Los Angeles County (Member, Labor Law Section) and American (Member, Labor and Employment Law Section) Bar Associations; State Bar of California; California Women Lawyers Association; Association of Human Resource Professionals; Los Angeles Human Resources Association; Los Angeles Urban League (Member, Board of Directors, 1991—). *PRACTICE AREAS:* Management Labor and Employment Law (Private and Public).

**RALPH ZAREFSKY,** born Houston, Texas, April 9, 1950; admitted to bar, 1976, California; 1993, District of Columbia. *Education:* Northwestern University (B.A., cum laude, 1972); Stanford University (J.D., 1976). Phi Beta Kappa. Law Clerk to Hon. Lawrence T. Lydick, U.S. District Court, 1976-1978. *Member:* The State Bar of California; American Bar Association. *PRACTICE AREAS:* Litigation.

*(This Listing Continued)*

## ASSOCIATES

**STEVE W. ACKERMAN,** born New York, N.Y., March 31, 1959; admitted to bar, 1984, California and U.S. District Court, Central and Northern Districts of California; 1986, U.S. District Court, Southern District of California and U.S. Court of Appeals for the Federal Circuit; registered to practice before U.S. Patent and Trademark Office. *Education:* Cornell University (B.S., 1980); Hofstra University (J.D., 1983). Member, 1981-1983 and Research Editor, 1982-1983, Hofstra University Law Review. Author: "Protection of the Design of Useful Articles: Current Inadequacies and Proposed Solutions," Hofstra Law Review, Vol. 11, No. 3, 1983. *Member:* Los Angeles County (Member, Intellectual Property Section), Beverly Hills (Member, Sections on: Entertainment; Litigation; Patent, Trademark and Copyright) and American (Member, Patent, Trademark and Copyright Law Section) Bar Associations; State Bar of California; United States Trademark Association. *PRACTICE AREAS:* Intellectual Property. *Email:* sackerman@baker-hostetler.com

**DAVID W. AMMONS,** born Cleveland, Ohio, January 23, 1969; admitted to bar, 1994, Ohio (Not admitted in California). *Education:* University of Southern California (B.A., 1991); University of Michigan (J.D., 1994). *PRACTICE AREAS:* Litigation.

**ROGER L. ARMSTRONG,** born Mason City, Iowa, July 19, 1957; admitted to bar, 1995, California and U.S. District Court, Central District of California. *Education:* University of California, San Diego (B.A., 1979); Loyola University (J.D., cum laude, 1995). Order of the Coif; Phi Alpha Phi; St. Thomas More Law Honor Society; Alpha Sigma Nu. Editor-in-Chief, Loyola of Los Angeles Law Review, 1994-1995. Author: "CERCLA's Petroleum Exclusion: Bad Policy in a Problematic Statute," 27 Loyola of Los Angeles Law Review, 1994. Vice President: Universal Pictures, 1987-1991; TriStar Pictures, 1991-1992. *Member:* Beverly Hills, Los Angeles County, Federal and American Bar Associations. *PRACTICE AREAS:* Business Law; Entertainment Law.

**KATHLEEN E. BAILEY,** born Galveston, Texas, March 23, 1958; admitted to bar, 1992, California. *Education:* University of Houston (B.S., summa cum laude, Business, 1989; J.D., cum laude, 1992). Order of the Coif; Order of the Barrons. Appropriations Committee Chairperson, American Red Cross, 1983-1984. *Member:* State Bar of California; American Bar Association (Member; Tort and Insurance Section); Public Counsel. *PRACTICE AREAS:* Litigation; Insurance Coverage.

**DAVID CAPLAN,** born Boston, Massachusetts, December 25, 1969; admitted to bar, 1995, California. *Education:* Williams College (B.A., 1992); Northeastern University (J.D., 1995). *PRACTICE AREAS:* Intellectual Property. *Email:* dcaplan@baker-hostetler.com

**MARIA T. CELOCRUZ,** born New York, N.Y., August 11, 1946; admitted to bar, 1993, Massachusetts; 1994, California. *Education:* Smith College (A.B., 1969); Harvard University (A.M., 1972); Boston University School of Law (J.D., 1993). Edward F. Hennessey Distinguished Scholar. Articles Editor, American Journal of Law and Medicine, 1992-1993. Author: "Aid-in-Dying: Should We Decriminalize Physician-Assisted Suicide And Physician-Committed Euthanasia?," 18 Am. J. L. & Med. 369 (1992). Law Clerk to the Hon. Zachary R. Karol, U.S. District Court, District of Massachusetts, 1993-1994. *PRACTICE AREAS:* Labor and Employment Law.

**NORMAN C. DAVIS,** born Los Angeles, California, June 18, 1942; admitted to bar, 1993, California. *Education:* California State University, Fullerton (M.B.A., 1970); Western State University, College of Law (J.D., 1978). *Member:* California Society for Healthcare Attorneys. *PRACTICE AREAS:* Healthcare Law; Business Law.

**ANDREW J. DURKOVIC,** born Takoma Park, Maryland, September 1, 1960; admitted to bar, 1993, California. *Education:* University of California (B.A., 1989); Loyola Law School (J.D., 1992). Articles Editor, Loyola of Los Angeles Law Review. *LANGUAGES:* Spanish. *Email:* adurkovi@baker-hostetler.com

**KEITH A. FINK,** born Santa Monica, California, March 11, 1962; admitted to bar, 1990, California and U.S. District Court, Central, Southern and Eastern Districts of California, U.S. Court of Appeals, Ninth Circuit. *Education:* University of California at Los Angeles (B.A., 1985); Southwestern University School of Law (J.D., cum laude, 1989). National Cross-Examination Debate Association Champion, 1982-1984. Author: "Scylla and Charybdis: Charting a Course for Law Enforcement Officers Caught Between 42 U.S.C. §1983 & 18 U.S.C. & §241 and 242," Federal Bar News and Journal, Vol 41, No 5, pp 370-380, June 1994; "Admissibility of Expert Testimony on The Code of Silence," Federal Evidence Practice Guide Reporter, Vol. 2, Issue 16, pp 263-367, June 1993; "Demonstrative Evidence,"

*(This Listing Continued)*

Federal Evidence Guide, Chapter 5, 1993; "Considerations for Admitting Photographic Evidence," Federal Evidence Practice Guide Reporter, Vol 2, pp 171-175, August 1992; "Defending Depositions," Federal Litigation Guide, Chapter 18, 1991. Adjunct Professor of Law Southwestern University School of Law 1993— (Employment Discrimination Law, Civil Rights & Civil Liberties & Pre-Trial Civil Practice). Lecturer: Expert Witness Seminar, Lorman Business Center, "Use of Experts in Employment Cases," Sept 13, 1996; "Basic Personnel Law," Employers Group,, 1995-1996; "Federal Appeals: Avoiding Traps for the Unwary Trial Attorney," Wilshire Bar Association, April 29, 1993; "Attorneys Fees in Civil Rights Cases: Understanding The Supreme Court's Technical and Deminimus Language," PLI, New York, October 30, 1991. *Member:* Beverly Hills and Los Angeles County Bar Associations. *REPORTED CASES:* Brooks v. Cook 938 F.2d 1038 (9th Cir. 1991); Romberg v. Nichols 970 F.2d 1152 (9th Cir. 1992); Alliance v. Coleella 995 F.2d (9th Cir. 1993); Wilkes v. Reyes 5 F.3d (9th Cir. 1993); Credit Manager's Association v. Kennesaw 25 F.3d (9th Cir 1993); Romberg v. Nichols II 48 F.3d 453 (9th Cir. 1995); Williams v. Superior Court (1993) 5 Cal. 4th 337; Williams v. Superior Court (1992) 15 Cal. App. 4th 913. *PRACTICE AREAS:* Labor Law; Civil Rights; Business Litigation; Appellate Law; Personal Injury Defense.

**MEGAN E. GRAY,** born Houston, Texas, August 8, 1969; admitted to bar, 1995, California. *Education:* University of Texas (B.A. cum laude, , 1991; J.D., 1995); LBJ School of Public Affairs (M.A., 1995). Member, Texas International Law Journal. Member, Board of Advocates. *Member:* Los Angeles County (Member: Committee of Intellectual Property; Entertainment Law (Executive Committee, 1996—; Program Chair, 1996—)) and American (Member, Intellectual Property Litigation Section, 1996—) Bar Associations; American Intellectual Property Association; Women Lawyers Association of Los Angeles;. *LANGUAGES:* Russian. *PRACTICE AREAS:* Intellectual Property; Litigation.

**JAMES E. HOUPT,** born Pittsburg, California, July 9, 1951; admitted to bar, 1992, Virginia and U.S. Court of Appeals, 4th Circuit; 1993, District of Columbia, Maryland, U.S. District Court for the District of Columbia and U.S. District Court, Eastern District of Virginia; 1994, U.S. District Court, District of Maryland (Not admitted in California). *Education:* California State University (B.A., with distinction, 1976); Harvard University (J.D., cum laude, 1992). Member, Harvard Law School Association, 1992—. Author: "Access to Electronic Records: A Guide to Reporting on State and Local Government in the Computer Age," Reporter's Committee of Freedom of the Press (1990). Co-Author: "The libel Curtain: A Comparison of Canadian and American Libel Law," Institute of Continuing Legal Education, Canadian Bar Association (1994). *Member:* The District of Columbia Bar; Virginia State Bar; American Bar Association. [With USN, 1970-1974]. *PRACTICE AREAS:* General Litigation; First Amendment; Freedom of Information. *Email:* jhoupt@baker-hostetler.com

**LISA F. HINCHLIFFE,** born Torrance, California, December 17, 1960; admitted to bar, 1987, California. *Education:* Wellesley College (B.A., 1982); University of Southern California (J.D., 1987). Wellesley Scholar. *Member:* Los Angeles County and American Bar Associations; State Bar of California. *LANGUAGES:* Spanish. *PRACTICE AREAS:* Employment Litigation; Business Law; Constitutional Law.

**SUSAN HORWITZ,** born Oakland, California, April 1, 1951; admitted to bar, 1993, Florida 1995, Georgia (Not admitted in California). *Education:* Sonoma State University (B.A., magna cum laude, 1978); Hastings School of Law (J.D., 1981). *PRACTICE AREAS:* Intellectual Property; Litigation.

**THOMAS JOHNSON,** admitted to bar, 1992, California. *Education:* Hillsdale College (B.A., 1984); Golden Gate University (J.D., 1992). *PRACTICE AREAS:* Bankruptcy Law.

**JEFFREY K. JOYNER,** born Lawton, Oklahoma, May 27, 1969; admitted to bar, 1995, California. *Education:* George Washington University (B.A., 1989); Southwestern University (J.D., 1995). *PRACTICE AREAS:* Litigation; Intellectual Property.

**KIRSTIN M. LARSON,** born Washington, D.C., February 20, 1970; admitted to bar, 1995, California. *Education:* University of California at Santa Barbara (B.A., cum laude, 1992); Southwestern University School of Law (J.D., 1995). Assistant Editor, Southwestern University Law Review Extern for the Honorable Harry L. Hupp, Central District of California. *PRACTICE AREAS:* General Litigation.

**MARCIA T. LAW,** born Los Angeles, California, November 18, 1963; admitted to bar, 1989, California, U.S. District Court, Central District of California and U.S. Court of Appeals, Ninth Circuit. *Education:* University

*(This Listing Continued)*

CALIFORNIA—LOS ANGELES

**BAKER & HOSTETLER, Los Angeles—Continued**

of California at Los Angeles (B.A., 1985); University of California at Davis (J.D., 1989). *PRACTICE AREAS:* Litigation; Employment.

**STEPHEN NAKATA,** admitted to bar, 1993, California. *Education:* University of California, Los Angeles (B.A., 1989); University of San Francisco School of Law (J.D., 1992). *PRACTICE AREAS:* Product Liability; Workers Compensation.

**PEGGY A. PROPPER,** born St. Paul Minnesota, November 10, 1944; admitted to bar, 1988, California; U.S. District Court, Central, Southern and Eastern Districts of California and U.S. Court of Appeals, Ninth Circuit. *Education:* Western State University (B.S., 1985; J.D., 1987). *PRACTICE AREAS:* Bankruptcy; Business.

**GREGG A. RAPOPORT,** born Los Angeles, California, August 19, 1962; admitted to bar, 1988, California, U.S. Court of Appeals, Ninth Circuit and U.S. District Court, Central and Northern Districts of California. *Education:* University of California, Los Angeles (B.A., magna cum laude, 1984; J.D., 1988). Phi Beta Kappa. *Member:* Los Angeles County and American Bar Associations; State Bar of California. *LANGUAGES:* Russian. *PRACTICE AREAS:* Business and Real Estate Litigation.

**MARC I. SELTZER,** born New York, N.Y., November 10, 1962; admitted to bar, 1992, California. *Education:* University of California, Berkeley (B.A., 1986); Boston University (J.D., 1991). Member, American Journal of Law and Medicine, Boston University, 1990-1991. *PRACTICE AREAS:* Intellectual property; National and International Anticounterfeiting Enforcement and Litigation; Internet Monitoring and Enforcement.

**CRANSTON J. WILLIAMS,** born London, England, August 4, 1963; admitted to bar, 1992, California. *Education:* Lehman College (B.S., 1989); University of California at Los Angeles (J.D., 1992). *Member:* State Bar of California.

**DENNIS L. WILSON,** born Fresno, California, May 26, 1966; admitted to bar, 1991, California. *Education:* California State University, Fresno (B.A., 1988); University of Southern California (J.D., 1991). *Member:* Beverly Hills Bar Association; International Trademark Association; International Anti-Counterfeiting Coalition. *PRACTICE AREAS:* Intellectual Property.

OF COUNSEL

**JANET S. HOFFMAN,** born Cambridge, Massachusetts, March 3, 1955; admitted to bar, 1983, Ohio; 1985, California. *Education:* Bryn Mawr College (A.B., magna cum laude, 1977); University of Illinois (M.S., 1979); University of Michigan (J.D., cum laude, 1983). *Member:* State Bar of California; American Bar Association. *LANGUAGES:* French and Spanish. *PRACTICE AREAS:* Business. *Email:* jhoffman@baker-hostetler.com

**GLEN A. SMITH,** born Bakersfield, California, June 7, 1955; admitted to bar, 1982, California and U.S. District Court, Central District of California; 1987, U.S. Court of Appeals, Ninth Circuit. *Education:* University of California at Los Angeles (B.A., cum laude, 1979); Loyola Law School (J.D., 1982). Member, St. Thomas More Law Honor Society. Adjunct Professor of Law, Loyola Law School, 1990-1991. Senior Lecturer, USC School of Journalism, 1993-1996. *Member:* Los Angeles County and American (Member, Sections on: Litigation; Communications) Bar Associations; State Bar of California.

**JOHN R. SOMMER,** born Fort Wayne, Indiana, March 12, 1958; admitted to bar, 1982, California; 1983, District of Columbia. *Education:* Indiana University (A.B., cum laude, 1979); University of California, Los Angeles (J.D., 1982). Member, UCLA Law Review. Associate Member, Federal Communications Law Journal. Recipient, American Jurisprudence Award for Legal Profession. Author: Editor, *Central District Manual* (1992), *Northern District Manual* (1995), *Eastern District Manual* (1995), *Southern District Manual* (1995), *California Judges' Rules and General Orders,* ; "California: Penalty Interest Is Not Usury," *Pacific Basin Legal Developments Bulletin* (January 1991); "Study and Recommendation: Which Municipal Court District for the City of Sierra Madre, California," May 1990; "Judicial System," Chapter VI of *Doing Business in California* (2d Edition 1989); "Insurers To Pay for Pollution Clean-Up," *Pacific Basin Legal Developments Bulletin* (October 1989); "The Volunteer Prosecutor Program: One Route To Jury Trial Experience," *Inter Alia,* Vol. 27, No. 2 (March 1989) (State Bar of Michigan); "Attorney Disqualification: Conflicts Under Model Rules of Professional Conduct," *Current Problems in Federal Civil Practice 1983,* 653 (B. Garfinkel ed. 1983). Judge Pro Tem, 1989— and Judicial Arbitrator, 1991—. Los Angeles Superior Court. Judge Pro Tem, East Los Angeles Municipal Court, 1988—. Extern to Hon. Eugene A.

*(This Listing Continued)*

CAA496B

MARTINDALE-HUBBELL LAW DIRECTORY 1997

Wright, U.S. Court of Appeals, Ninth Circuit, 1981. Legal Extern, Federal Communications Commission, Common Carrier Bureau, Washington, D.C., 1981. *Member:* State Bar of California (Delegate, State Bar Convention, 1990-1991, 1993-1994); Federal Bar Association (President, Los Angeles Chapter, 1993-1994; Vice President, 1992-1993; Secretary, 1991-1992; Meetings Chairperson, 1989-1992; Member, Board of Directors, 1989—; National Council Member, 1993—). *LANGUAGES:* Spanish. *REPORTED CASES:* Acuson Corp. v. Aloka Co., Ltd., 10 USPQ 1814 (Cal. App., 6th Dist. 1989). *PRACTICE AREAS:* Intellectual Property Litigation; Business Advice and Litigation. *Email:* jsommer@baker-hostetler.com

---

## BAKER AND JACOBSON

*A PROFESSIONAL CORPORATION*

SUITE 500
11377 WEST OLYMPIC BOULEVARD
**LOS ANGELES, CALIFORNIA 90064-1683**
Telephone: 310-914-7990
Fax: 310-914-7913

*General Business and Commercial Litigation, including Complex Financial and Securities Fraud, Litigation under the Racketeer Influenced and Corrupt Organizations Act, Shareholders' Disputes, Wrongful Termination, Construction Matters, Bankruptcy Practice, Accountant's and Lawyer's Collections and Liability, and Real Estate Litigation of all types, including representation of Sellers, Purchasers, Developers, Lenders, Landlords, Contractors and Brokers.*

FIRM PROFILE: *The Law Offices of Baker & Jacobson was founded in 1989 as a firm exclusively devoted to real estate, business and commercial litigation. The firm is comprised entirely of experienced litigators with outstanding academic credentials, and who were trained at large firms. The members of the firm believe that litigation is most effectively handled by one senior attorney being directly and continuously involved in the management of each action. The team approach to litigation is avoided.*

**ROBERT P. BAKER,** born Bridgeport, Connecticut, December 21, 1950; admitted to bar, 1975, Massachusetts; 1977, California, U.S. District Court, Central and Southern Districts of California and U.S. Court of Appeals, Ninth Circuit. *Education:* Boston College (A.B., 1972); Harvard University (J.D., 1975). *Member:* Los Angeles County, Massachusetts and American Bar Associations. *PRACTICE AREAS:* Business; Commercial; Real Estate Litigation.

**LAWRENCE M. JACOBSON,** born Los Angeles, California, June 4, 1956; admitted to bar, 1981, California and U.S. District Court, Central District of California; 1982, U.S. Court of Appeals, Ninth Circuit; 1983, U.S. District Court, Northern and Southern Districts of California; 1986, U.S. District Court, Eastern District of California. *Education:* University of California at Berkeley (A.B., 1978); University of California at Los Angeles (J.D., 1981). Member, Moot Court Honors Program. *Member:* Los Angeles County and American Bar Associations; State Bar of California. (Also Of Counsel to Glickfeld, Fields & Jaffe). *PRACTICE AREAS:* Bankruptcy Law; Commercial Litigation; Business Litigation; Creditors' Rights.

---

## BAKER, MANOCK & JENSEN

*A PROFESSIONAL CORPORATION*

**LOS ANGELES, CALIFORNIA**

(See Fresno)

*General Civil and Trial Practice. Environmental, Agricultural, Bankruptcy, Cooperative, Corporation, Medical and Malpractice Legal, Taxation, Probate and Estate Planning, Real Estate, Water Rights, Family/Domestic Relations, Oil and Gas Law, Intellectual Property, and Employment Law.*

---

## BAKER, SILBERBERG & KEENER

**LOS ANGELES, CALIFORNIA**

(See Santa Monica)

*General Civil and Business Litigation. Appellate, Professional Malpractice, Insurance Coverage/Bad Faith, Toxic Torts, Personal Injury and Products Liability Law.*

## BANNAN, GREEN, SMITH & FRANK

555 SOUTH FLOWER STREET
FORTY FOURTH FLOOR
**LOS ANGELES, CALIFORNIA 90071**
Telephone: 213-362-1177
Fax: 213-362-1188
Email: BGSF.com

General Civil Trial and Appellate Practice in all State and Federal Courts, Product Liability, Environmental, Employment Law, Securities, Commercial Litigation, White Collar Criminal Defense including Antitrust.

### MEMBERS OF FIRM

**C. FORREST BANNAN,** born Seattle, Washington, January 5, 1946; admitted to bar, 1970, California; 1979, U.S. Supreme Court. *Education:* University of Santa Clara (B.S.C., 1967; J.D., cum laude, 1970); University of California at Los Angeles (M.B.A., 1972). Trial Attorney, U.S. Department of Justice, Antitrust Section Foreign Commerce Division, 1973-1979. Special Assistant U.S. Attorney, Eastern District of Virginia, 1978-1979. *Member:* Los Angeles County and American Bar Associations; State Bar of California. *PRACTICE AREAS:* Trial Practice; Antitrust; Employment Law; White Collar Criminal Defense; Commercial Litigation. *Email:* Forrest@BGSF.com

**WARD D. SMITH,** born San Francisco, California, April 13, 1953; admitted to bar, 1981, California; 1982, U.S. District Court, Eastern District of California and U.S. Court of Appeals, Ninth Circuit; 1983, U.S. District Court, Southern District of California; 1984, U.S. District Court, Northern District of California. *Education:* University of California at Berkeley (A.B., 1977); McGeorge School of the Law, University of the Pacific (J.D., 1981). Staff Member, Pacific Law Journal, 1980-1981. Author: "Reservation of Rights Notices and Non-Waiver Agreements," 12 Pacific Law Journal 763. Co-Author: "California Civil Practice Torts," Pacific Law Journal, 1993. *Member:* Los Angeles County (Member, Trial Lawyers Section) and American Bar Associations; State Bar of California; Southern California Defense Counsel. *PRACTICE AREAS:* Environmental Law; Products Liability; Commercial Law. *Email:* Ward@BGSF.com

**LESLEY C. GREEN,** born Pasadena, California, June 22, 1947; admitted to bar, 1983, California. *Education:* Pasadena City College (A.A., with honors, 1980); University of Southern California (J.D., 1983). Executive Editor, U.S.C. Major Tax Planning and Computer Law Journal, 1982-1983. Recipient, American Jurisprudence Award for Excellence in Community Property. *Member:* Los Angeles County and American Bar Associations; State Bar of California. *PRACTICE AREAS:* Employment Law; First Party Insurance Bad Faith; ERISA Litigation. *Email:* Lesley@BGSF.com

**RONALD F. FRANK,** born Newark, New Jersey, July 17, 1957; admitted to bar, 1982, Texas; 1983, California. *Education:* Bucknell University (B.A., summa cum laude, with honors in Psychology, 1979); University of Virginia (J.D., 1982). Phi Beta Kappa; Omicron Delta Epsilon; Psi Chi; Phi Eta Sigma. Articles Editor, Virginia Journal of International Law, 1981-1982. Author: "Power of Congress Under the Property Clause To Give Extraterritorial Effect to Federal Lands Law," 15 Natural Resources Lawyer 663, 1983; "The Convention on the Conservation of Antarctic Marine Living Resources," 13 Ocean Develop. and Intl. Law 291, 1983. *Member:* Los Angeles County and American (Member, Litigation Section) Bar Associations. *PRACTICE AREAS:* Product Liability; Asbestos Defense; Mass Toxic Torts; General Trial Practice. *Email:* Ron@BGSF.com

### ASSOCIATES

**GREGG M. AUDET,** born Meriden, Connecticut, November 29, 1965; admitted to bar, 1992, California; U.S. District Court, Central, Southern, Northern and Eastern Districts of California. *Education:* College of the Holy Cross (B.A., 1988); University of Michigan (J.D., 1991). Executive Editor, 1990-1991 and Associate Editor, 1989-1990, Michigan Law Review. *Member:* State Bar of California; American Bar Association. *PRACTICE AREAS:* Civil Litigation; Products Liability. *Email:* Greg@BGSF.com

**GARY J. GOODSTEIN,** born New York, N.Y., September 3, 1966; admitted to bar, 1993, California and U.S. District Court, Central District of California. *Education:* San Francisco State University (B.A., 1988); Loyola Law School (J.D., cum laude, 1993). Order of the Coif; Phi Delta Phi. Golden Key National Honor Society. *Member:* Los Angeles County Bar Association; State Bar of California. *PRACTICE AREAS:* Business Litigation; Professional Liability; Insurance Coverage. *Email:* Gary@BGSF.com

*(This Listing Continued)*

**RUSSELL G. PETTI,** born Point Pleasant, New Jersey, February 6, 1955; admitted to bar, 1988, California; 1989, U.S. District Court, Northern and Central Districts of California. *Education:* Lehigh University (B.A., 1978); Emory University (J.D., 1988). Order of the Coif. First Honor Graduate, 1988. Assistant U.S. Attorney, Central District of California, 1990-1994. [Major, U.S. Marine Corps, 1978-1985] *Email:* Russell@BGSF.com

**KRISTINA E. WEAVER,** born Lancaster, California, June 26, 1971; admitted to bar, 1994, California, U.S. District Court, Central and Southern Districts of California and U.S. Court of Appeals, Ninth Circuit; 1995, U.S. District Court, Eastern and Northern Districts of California. *Education:* University of California at Santa Barbara (B.A., Political Science, 1991); Loyola Law School, Los Angeles (J.D., 1994). St. Thomas More Law Honor Society (President, 1993-1994). Recipient, American Jurisprudence Award, Remedies. Staff Member, 1992-1993 and Articles Editor, 1993-1994, Loyola Law Review. *Member:* Los Angeles County Bar Association; State Bar of California. *PRACTICE AREAS:* Insurance Defense Litigation; Products Liability Litigation; Commercial Litigation. *Email:* Kristina@BGSF.com

## BARBOSA GARCIA & BARNES

A Partnership including a Professional Corporation

*Established in 1983*

SUITE 390, 500 CITADEL DRIVE
**LOS ANGELES, CALIFORNIA 90040**
Telephone: 213-889-6600
FAX: 213-889-6605

Education, Municipal, Administrative, Land Use, Real Estate, Corporate, Banking and Commercial, Employment, Environmental, Public Finance, Public Sector Labor. General Business and Commercial Litigation, State and Federal Civil and Appellate Litigation.

*FIRM PROFILE:* Barbosa Garcia & Barnes, a Fifteen-attorney firm, has a sophisticated practice representing both private clients and public entities. The firm has an established corporate clientele ranging from Fortune 500 corporations to small family businesses. For many years, the firm has represented governmental clients as city attorney to several cities and as general and special counsel to counties, school districts, and other public entities. The firm's specialization and the expertise of its attorneys, balanced between litigation and transactional work, has allowed the firm to combine the resources of a large firm with the accessibility and responsiveness of a small firm. Members of the firm actively participate in professional and civic affairs, including pro-bono representation.

**HENRY S. BARBOSA, (P.C.),** born Covina, California, May 3, 1948; admitted to bar, 1974, California; U.S. District Court, Central District of California; and U.S. Court of Appeals, Ninth Circuit. *Education:* University of California at Santa Barbara; University of California at Los Angeles (B.A., 1970; J.D., 1973). Deputy District Attorney, Los Angeles County, 1974-1975. City Attorney: Monrovia, California, 1976-1980; Montebello, California, 1980—; Lynwood, California, 1987-1993; Azusa, California, 1992—. Member, State Solid Waste Clean-up Advisory Committee, 1989—. Member, State Bar Legal Trust Fund Commission, 1987-1989. Member, Board of Directors, Three Valleys Municipal Water District, 1993—. *Member:* Los Angeles County Bar Association (Member, Judiciary Committee); State Bar of California (Member, Executive Committee, Public Law Section); American Bar Association; Mexican American Bar Association; National Institute of Municipal Law Officers (Judge Pro Tempore, Municipal Court); Los Angeles County City Attorneys Association; National Hispanic Media Coalition (National Vice Chair). *REPORTED CASES:* Campbell v. City of Monrovia (1978) 84 Cal.App.3d 341; Doyle v. City of Chino (1981) 117 Cal.App.3d 673; Salvaty v. Falcon Cable TV (1985) 165 Cal.App.3d 798; Salazar v. City of Montebello (1987) 190 Cal.App.3d 953. *PRACTICE AREAS:* Municipal Law; Land Use and Zoning Law; Redevelopment Law; Environmental Law; CATV Law; Civil Rights.

**BONIFACIO BONNY GARCIA,** born Fresno, California, October 27, 1956; admitted to bar, 1981, California, U.S. District Court, Central District of California, U.S. Court of Appeals, Ninth Circuit and U.S. District Court, Eastern District of California. *Education:* Loyola Marymount University (B.A., magna cum laude, 1978); Harvard Law School (J.D., 1981). Alpha Sigma Nu. Author: "The Uses of History in Law: Some Aspects of the Process," 92/93 Law & Justice 127, Hilary/Easter, 1987. Adjunct Professor, Legal History, Loyola Marymount University, 1984. Member: Archdiocese of Los Angeles, Catholic Life Issues Commission. Chairperson: Blue Ribbon Commission on Advancement of Women at East Los

*(This Listing Continued)*

## BARBOSA GARCIA & BARNES, Los Angeles—Continued

Angeles College; Chairperson, Board of Regents, Verbum Dei High School. *Member:* Los Angeles County Bar Association; State Bar of California. *PRACTICE AREAS:* Negotiations; Commercial; Corporate; Real Estate; General Business; Governmental Relations.

**DOUGLAS D. BARNES,** born Sacramento, California, August 17, 1952; admitted to bar, 1979, California, U. S. District Court, Central District of California; and U.S. Court of Appeals, Ninth Circuit. *Education:* University of London, London, England; Pomona College (B.A., 1974); University of California at Irvine (M.A., 1976); University of California at Los Angeles (J.D., 1979). Legal Authorship: The California Municipal Law Handbook, League of California Cities, Chapter re: California Government Tort Liability, 1993. *Member:* State Bar of California; Los Angeles County City Attorneys Association. *REPORTED CASES:* Sounhein v. City of San Dimas, 11 Cal.App. 4th 1255. *PRACTICE AREAS:* Municipal Law; Personnel Law; Civil Rights Law; Tort Liability.

**PETER E. LANGSFELD,** born Budapest, Hungary, September 27, 1947; admitted to bar, 1988, California. *Education:* California State University at Los Angeles (B.S., 1973; M.B.A., 1980); Southwestern University (J.D., 1988). Judge Pro Tempore, Superior and Municipal Court. *Member:* Los Angeles County and American Bar Associations; State Bar of California (Probation Monitor); California Trial Lawyers Association; The Association of Trial Lawyers of America. *LANGUAGES:* Hungarian and Spanish. *PRACTICE AREAS:* Municipal Tort Defense Law; Eminent Domain Law; Criminal Law.

**KENNETH T. FONG,** born Los Angeles, February 9, 1961; admitted to bar, 1989, California. *Education:* California State University at Los Angeles (B.S., 1984); Loyola Law School (J.D., 1988). Articles Editor, 1987-1988, Loyola of Los Angeles Law Review. Articles Editor, California Real Property Journal, 1994-1996. Author: "Shell Oil Co. v. Santa Monica: The Sticky Business of Setting Oil Pipeline Franchise Fees Under the Dormant Commerce Clause," 21 Loy. L.A. L. Rev. 581, 1988; "An Introduction to Drafting Redevelopment Agreements," 19 Pub. L.J., No. 1, Spring, 1995. Co-Author: "What's Right With Redevelopment," 13 Calif. Real. Prop. J., No. 2, Spring, 1995. Member: Board of Directors, Asian Youth Center, 1988-1996. *Member:* State Bar of California (Executive Committee, Real Property Section); Southern California Chinese Lawyers Association (Member, Board of Governors). *PRACTICE AREAS:* Redevelopment Law; Corporate Law; Real Estate Law.

**JONATHAN B. STONE,** born Evanston, Illinois, March 12, 1958; admitted to bar, 1985, California. *Education:* University of California, Berkeley (A.B., 1980; J.D., 1985); University of California at Los Angeles (M.A., 1991). Phi Beta Kappa. Recipient, California Planning Foundation Academic Achievement Award, 1991. Contributing Editor, Industrial Relations Law Journal, 1984-1985. Author: "A Path of No Return: Employer Overpayments into Employee Benefit Plans." Indus. Rel. L. Rev. 68, 1986. Co-Author: "Holding Companies Could Hold the Future," Fed Home Loan Bank J, April, 1989. Member. American Planning Association, (California Chapter). *Member:* American Bar Association; The State Bar of California. *PRACTICE AREAS:* Municipal Law; Planning, Zoning and Land Use Law; Bonds and Securities Law.

---

**AUGUSTIN R. JIMENEZ,** born Los Angeles, California, April 3, 1953; admitted to bar, 1980, Washington and U.S. District Court, Western District of Washington; 1991, California; 1992, U.S. District Court, Central District of California; 1995, U.S. Court of Appeals, Ninth Circuit. *Education:* California State University at Long Beach (B.A., 1976) University of Washington School of Law (J.D., 1979); Anderson Graduate School of Management, University of California at Los Angeles (M.B.A., 1989). Author: "Search and Seizure Update", Legal Notes, No. 432 (Municipal Research and Services Center of Washington), March 1985. Member, Board of Directors, United Way of Greater Los Angeles, 1995. *Member:* Los Angeles County, Washington State and American Bar Associations; The State Bar of California. *REPORTED CASES:* Supreme Court of the State of Washington: Seattle v. Williams, 101 Wn2d 445, 680 P2d 1051 (1984); Court of Appeals of the State of Washington: Seattle v. Gordon, 39 Wash. App. 437, 693 P2d 741 (1985); Seattle v. Tolliver, 31 Wash. App. 299, 641 P2d 719 (1982). *PRACTICE AREAS:* Municipal Law; Employment and Personnel Law; Litigation; Air Quality Law.

**RAJEEV M. TALWANI,** born Englewood, New Jersey, April 11, 1959; admitted to bar, 1986, New York; 1988, California. *Education:* Columbia

*(This Listing Continued)*

College (B.A., 1981); Harvard University (J.D., cum laude, 1985). *PRACTICE AREAS:* Commercial Law; Corporate Law; General Business Law.

**ERICK L. SOLARES,** born Guatemala City, Guatemala, April 17, 1962; admitted to bar, 1989, California and U.S. District Court, Central District of California. *Education:* University of California at Los Angeles (B.A., 1984); University of San Diego (J.D., 1988). Deputy Attorney for the California Department of Transportation, 1989-1994. *Member:* State Bar of California; State Bar of California; The Mexican-American Bar Association. *LANGUAGES:* Spanish. *PRACTICE AREAS:* Personal Injury Law; Tort Liability; Civil Rights.

**LORIE A. CAMPOS,** born Long Beach, California, June 5, 1967; admitted to bar, 1993, California. *Education:* University of California at Berkeley (B.S., 1989); Stanford University (J.D., 1992). Member, Articles Committee, Stanford Law Review, 1991-1992. *Member:* State Bar of California. *PRACTICE AREAS:* Education Law; Litigation.

**CHARISMA T. TAN-SANCHEZ,** born Basilan, Philippines, November 19, 1971; admitted to bar, 1995, California. *Education:* University of California at Berkeley (B.S., high honors, 1992); University of California, Boalt Hall School of Law (J.D., 1995). Editor, Asian Law Journal, 1992-1995. Co-Chair, Treasurer, Asian Pacific American Law Students Association, 1992-1995. Third-Year Representative, Boalt Hall Students Association, 1994-1995. *Member:* San Fernando Valley and Los Angeles County Bar Associations; State Bar of California; Philippine American Bar Association; Southern California Chinese Lawyers Association. *PRACTICE AREAS:* Litigation; Education Law.

**DIANA M. CARBAJAL,** born Los Angeles, California, May 30, 1963; admitted to bar, 1995, California. *Education:* California State University, Fullerton (B.A., 1986); Loyola Law School (J.D., 1995). Member, Byrne Trial Advocacy Team. *Member:* State Bar of California; Mexican-American Bar Association. *PRACTICE AREAS:* Litigation; Criminal.

**SYLVIA J. TRUJILLO,** born Raton, New Mexico, April 5, 1969; admitted to bar, 1996, California. *Education:* Bryn Mawr College (B.A., 1991); Kennedy School of Government, Harvard University (M.P.P., 1993); University of California Boalt Hall School of Law (J.D., 1996). La Raza Law Journal, 1995-1996.

### OF COUNSEL

**NORMAN LIEBERMAN,** born Jersey City, New Jersey, November 11, 1922; admitted to bar, 1968, California. *Education:* University of California at Berkeley (B.A., 1950); Whittier College School of Law (J.D., 1968). City Attorney, Monterey Park, California, 1973-1984. *Member:* State Bar of California. *PRACTICE AREAS:* Municipal Law; Land Use Law; Personnel Law; Eminent Domain Law.

**JOHN F. LAGLE,** born Kansas City, Missouri, January 22, 1938; admitted to bar, 1967, California. *Education:* University of California at Los Angeles (B.S., Bus. Adm., 1961); University of California at Los Angeles School of Law (J.D., 1967). Author: First Supplement to Practice Under the California Corporate Securities Law of 1968, Marsh & Volk (1972). *Member:* Los Angeles County (Member, Business Law Section) and American (Member, Sections on: Business Law; Taxation) Bar Associations; The State Bar of California. *PRACTICE AREAS:* Real Property Law; Corporations Law; Finance Law; Securities Law.

### LEGAL SUPPORT PERSONNEL

**GABRIEL MEDINA,** born Hollywood, California, December 13, 1966. *Education:* California State University at Fullerton (B.A., 1994); University of California at Los Angeles (Certificate, 1995). *Member:* Los Angeles Paralegal Association. (Paralegal).

**JANICE MINAMOTO,** born Los Angeles, California, May 1, 1971. *Education:* University of California at Los Angeles (B.A., 1994); University of California at Los Angeles (Certificate, 1996). (Paralegal).

**ELISABETH OYAKAWA,** born Manchester, Iowa, January 12, 1966. *Education:* California State University (B.A., 1991); University of California at Los Angeles Attorney Assistant Training Program (Paralegal Certificate, 1996). (Paralegal).

REPRESENTATIVE CLIENTS: City of Los Angeles; Los Angeles Community Redevelopment Agency; California Health Facilities Finance Authority; County of Los Angeles; City of Montebello; Azusa, Commerce; Los Angeles Unified School District; Garvey School District; South Coast Air Quality Management District Hearing Board; Metropolitan Transportation Authority; ARCO; BuenaVision; CB Commercial Real Estate Group, Inc.; Granko Development Corp.; BKK Corp.; Texaco; Northrop Grumman Corporation; Bank of America; Wells Fargo Bank; Perdomo & Sons, Inc.; I.T & E. Overseas, Inc.; Gruma Corporation; Pico Water District.

## BARGER & WOLEN
**515 SOUTH FLOWER STREET, 34TH FLOOR**
**LOS ANGELES, CALIFORNIA 90071**
Telephone: 213-680-2800
Facsimile: 213-614-7399
Email: barwol@ix.netcom.com

*San Francisco, California Office:* 47th Floor, 101 California Street, 94111. Telephone: 415-434-2800. FAX: 415-434-2533.
*Newport Beach, California Office:* 19800 MacArthur Boulevard, Suite 800, Irvine, California, 92715. Telephone: 714-757-2800. FAX: 714-752-6313.
*Sacramento, California Office:* 925 "L" Street, Suite 1100, 95814. Telephone: 916-448-2800. FAX: 916-442-5961.
*New York, N.Y. Office:* 100 Park Avenue, 23rd Floor, 10017. Telephone: 212-557-2800. FAX: 212-213-1199.

*General Civil and Trial Practice in State and Federal Courts. Corporation, Securities, Real Estate, Real Estate Financing, Insurance, Banking, Probate, Trademark, Antitrust and Administrative Law. General Business, Legislative and Appellate Practice.*

### MEMBERS OF FIRM

**RICHARDS D. BARGER,** born Los Angeles, California, August 10, 1928; admitted to bar, 1954, California and U.S. District Court, Central District of California; 1957, U.S. Court of Appeals, Ninth Circuit; 1960, U.S. Supreme Court; 1972, District of Columbia. *Education:* Indiana University (B.S., 1950); University of Southern California (LL.B., 1953). Phi Delta Phi. Author: "Insolvency of Insurers," California Insurance Law & Practice, Matthew Bender, 1986. Co-Author: "The Life Insurance Law of California," The Association of Life Insurance Counsel (1990). Insurance Commissioner, State of California, 1968-1972. Member, Advisory Committee to Secretary of HUD under Federal Reinsurance Act of 1968, 1969-1972. President, National Association of Insurance Commissioners, 1971-1972. Member, California Commission on Uniform State Laws, 1972-1977. Member, Los Angeles County Board of Supervisors' Blue Ribbon Commission on Territorial Rating in the Automobile Insurance Industry, 1982-1984. Commissioner, Los Angeles County Citizens Economy and Efficiency Commission, 1992—. Member, Board of Councilors of the University of Southern California Law Center, 1993—. President, California Young Lawyers Association, 1961-1962. *Member:* The Association of the Bar of the City of New York; Los Angeles County (President, Barristers, 1960-1961; Member, Board of Trustees, 1960-1961) and American (Chairman, Committee on Public Regulation of Insurance, 1972-1974) Bar Associations; The State Bar of California; The District of Columbia Bar; American Council of Life Insurance, Legal Section. Fellow, American Bar Foundation (California Chair). **PRACTICE AREAS:** General Corporate Law; Insurance Law; Regulatory Law.

**KENT KELLER,** born Springfield, Missouri, March 13, 1943; admitted to bar, 1969, California, U.S. District Court, Northern, Central and Southern Districts of California and U.S. Court of Appeals, Ninth and Eleventh Circuits; U.S. Supreme Court. *Education:* Southwest Missouri State College (B.A., 1965); Washington University (J.D., 1968). Order of the Coif. Editor, Washington University Law Quarterly, 1967-1968. Author: "The Evolving Doctrine of Wrongful Termination of Employment: Practical Considerations Regarding Employment and Insurance Agent Relationships," 32 Insurance Federation Quarterly 105, 1982; "Antirebate Law, Standing And Judicial Review of Administrative Policymaking: Recent Developments," 1 Journal of Insurance Regulation 123, 1982. Co-Author: "Identifying and Using Insurance Coverage in Business Litigation," Continuing Education of the Bar, 1984, 1986, 1989, 1991 and 1993; "Business General Liability Policies," California Insurance Law & Practice, Matthew Bender, 1992; "Analyzing Coverage: Reading and Interpreting Insurance Policies" and "Claims Involving Excess Insurance," California Liability Insurance Practice, CEB, 1991. Lecturer, California Continuing Education of the Bar, 1984, 1986, 1989, 1991 and 1993; Practicing Law Institute, 1989; American Bar Association, 1991; Association of Business Trial Lawyers, 1992; Association of California Insurance Companies, 1995. *Member:* Los Angeles County and American Bar Associations; The State Bar of California. Fellow: American College of Trial Lawyers; American Bar Foundation. **PRACTICE AREAS:** Litigation; Insurance Law; Insurance Regulation.

**THOMAS B. ACKLAND,** born Cleveland, Ohio, November 22, 1940; admitted to bar, 1971, California, U.S. District Court, Southern and Central Districts of California and U.S. Court of Appeals, Ninth Circuit. *Education:* Dartmouth College (A.B., 1962; M.B.A., 1963); Case Western Reserve University (J.D., 1970). Order of the Coif. Recent Developments Editor, Case Western Reserve Law Review, 1969-1970. Author: "The Evolving Doctrine of Wrongful Termination of Employment: Practical Considerations Regarding Employment and Insurance Agent Relationships," 32 Insurance Federation Quarterly 105, Winter, 1982, Reprinted 3 Insurance Litigation Reporter 158, 1982. *Member:* Los Angeles County, Federal and American Bar Associations; The State Bar of California; Lawyer-Pilots and Inter-Pacific Bar Associations. **PRACTICE AREAS:** Aviation Law; Securities Litigation; Insurance Law.

**ROBERT WOOD HOGEBOOM,** born Joplin, Missouri, December 28, 1947; admitted to bar, 1974, California and U.S. District Court, Central District of California. *Education:* Stanford University (B.A., 1970); California Western School of Law (J.D., 1974). Author: "Understanding the Risk Retention Act," 5 Underwriter's Reports 16, 1987; "The California Insurance Company Holding Act", "The Regulation of Insurer Investments" and "Operation of Life and Disability Insurance Carriers," California Insurance Law & Practice, Matthew Bender, 1986; "Life Insurance in Partnerships and Close Corporations," Business Insurance Law and Practice Guide, Matthew Bender, 1989; "Avoiding Pitfalls In Insurance Department Investigations," 9 Underwriter's Rept. 22, 1982. President, Conference of Insurance Counsel, 1990. Director, Federation of Insurance Counsel. *Member:* Los Angeles County and American (Member: Torts and Insurance Practice Law Section; Insurance Law Committee) Bar Associations; The State Bar of California (Member, Insurance Law Committee). **PRACTICE AREAS:** Insurance Law; Corporate Law; Administrative Law.

**STEPHEN C. KLEIN,** born Los Angeles, California, May 11, 1951; admitted to bar, 1975, California; 1976, U.S. District Court, Central, Southern, Northern and Eastern Districts of California; 1978, U.S. Court of Appeals, Ninth Circuit. *Education:* University of California at Los Angeles (B.A., 1972); Southwestern University (J.D., 1975). Co-Author: "Legal Perspectives," Risk & Benefits Management, 1987. Author: "Issuance of Insurance Policies," California Insurance Law & Practice, Matthew Bender, 1986; "Reinsurance," California Law and Practice, Matthew Bender, 1991. *Member:* Los Angeles County and American (Member, Section of Tort and Insurance Practice; Committee on Insurance Coverage Litigation, Vice Chair, 1991-1993, 1996, National Institute Program Chair, 1990-1991) Bar Associations; Conference of Insurance Counsel; The State Bar of California; International Association of Defense Counsel; Defense Research Institute. **PRACTICE AREAS:** Litigation; Insurance Coverage; Reinsurance.

**S. STUART SOLDATE,** born Pasadena, California, May 24, 1951; admitted to bar, 1976, California. *Education:* Harvard College (B.A., magna cum laude, 1973) Phi Beta Kappa; Stanford University (J.D., 1976). Author: "The Regulation of Insurer Investments," California Insurance Law & Practice, Matthew Bender, 1986. *Member:* Los Angeles County and American Bar Associations; The State Bar of California. **PRACTICE AREAS:** Insurance Regulatory Law; Securities Law; Corporate Tax Law.

**ROYAL FOREST OAKES,** born Los Angeles, California, November 19, 1952; admitted to bar, 1978, California. *Education:* University of California, Los Angeles (B.A., summa cum laude, 1974; J.D., 1977). Phi Beta Kappa. Distinguished Advocate, UCLA Moot Court Honors Program, 1975-1977. Member, UCLA Law Review, 1975-1977. Author: "The Health and Disability Insurance Contract," California Insurance Law & Practice, Matthew Bender, 1986; "Fear of Firing," 8 Los Angeles Lawyer 12, March, 1985; "Avoiding Employee Lawsuits," Air Play, June, 1985; "Damage Control: Discovery of Expert Witnesses," 7 Los Angeles Lawyer 40, September, 1984; "Board of Equalization Insurance Tax Hike Ripe for Challenge," Underwriters Report, 1991. Columnist, "Business Litigation," Los Angeles Daily Journal, 1986—. Editor: quarterly newsletters, "Employer Alert", "Bad Faith Alert" and "Media Alert," 1986—. Extern, Associate Justice William P. Clark, Jr., Supreme Court of California, 1976. Lecturer: Hastings College of Law Center for Trial & Appellate Advocacy, 1987—; Stanford Bar Institute, 1988—; American Bar Association, General Practice Section, 1991; American Council of Life Insurance, 1989. Commentator, KFWB Radio (Los Angeles) and WMAQ Radio (Chicago), 1988—; Host, "Air Talk - The Legal Edition," KPCC-FM (Pasadena, California) 1988—. Member: Board of Directors, Association of Southern California Defense Counsel (1993); President, Insurance Council of the City of Hope (1996); Board of Directors, University Club of Los Angeles (1993). *Member:* Los Angeles County (Member: Bioethics Committee, 1984—; Speakers Bureau Committee, 1982—) and American (Member: Section on Tort and Insurance Practice; Section on Litigation) Bar Associations; The State Bar of California; Defense Research Institute; Conference of Insurance Counsel. **PRACTICE AREAS:** Business Litigation; Wrongful Discharge Law; Employment Law; Reinsurance Law.

**JOHN J. RICHMOND,** born St. Louis, Missouri, October 22, 1951; admitted to bar, 1977, California. *Education:* California State University,

*(This Listing Continued)*

## BARGER & WOLEN, Los Angeles—Continued

Long Beach (B.A., magna cum laude, 1973); Loyola University, Los Angeles (J.D., cum laude, 1977). Member, St. Thomas More Law Honor Society. Member, 1975-1977 and Note and Comment Editor, 1976-1977, Loyola of Los Angeles Law Review. Author: "Nature and Types of Life Insurance," California Insurance Law & Practice, Matthew Bender, 1986. *Member:* Los Angeles County and American Bar Associations; The State Bar of California. **PRACTICE AREAS:** Real Estate Finance Law; Insurance Regulatory Law.

**STEVEN H. WEINSTEIN,** born New York, N.Y., May 22, 1953; admitted to bar, 1979, California and U.S. District Court, Central and Northern Districts of California, U.S. Court of Appeals, Ninth Circuit and U.S. Supreme Court. *Education:* University of California, Los Angeles (B.A., 1975); Southwestern University (J.D., cum laude, 1978). Member, Moot Court Honors Program, 1977-1978. Note and Comment Editor, Southwestern University Law Review, 1977-1978. Staff Editor, Southwestern Nevada Law Review, 1977-1978. Author: "Ratemaking & Rate Regulation," *California Insurance Law & Practice,* (Mathew Bender, 1993); "Proposition 103 Generic Hearings, A Casualty Actuarial Showcase," Vol. 17 No. 2 The Actuarial Review 1 (May 1990); "Proposition 103: Back to the Future," Vol. 18, No. 2 The Actuarial Review 1 (May 1991). "Limitations on Judicial Relief After Hills v. Gautreaux: A Metropolitan-Wide Remedy For Housing Segregation," 9 Southwestern University Law Review 815, 1977. *Member:* Los Angeles County and American Bar Association; The State Bar of California. **PRACTICE AREAS:** Insurance Regulatory Litigation; Environmental Law; Litigation; Business Litigation; Construction Law.

**GAIL E. COHEN,** born Boston, Massachusetts, March 3, 1953; admitted to bar, 1979, New Jersey and Pennsylvania; 1980, California; 1983, U.S. District Court, Central District of California. *Education:* Clark University (B.A., 1975); Rutgers University (J.D., with honors, 1979). Article Editor, Rutgers-Camden Law Journal, 1978-1979. Law Clerk to Judge Mitchell H. Cohen, U.S. District Court, New Jersey, 1979-1980. *Member:* Los Angeles County Bar Association; State Bar of California; Women Lawyers Association. **PRACTICE AREAS:** Litigation; Insurance Law.

**SANDRA I. WEISHART,** born Santa Ana, California, September 27, 1954; admitted to bar, 1979, California and U.S. District Court, Central, Northern, Eastern and Southern Districts of California. *Education:* University of California, Los Angeles (B.A., summa cum laude, 1976; J.D., 1979). Phi Beta Kappa. Member, UCLA Law Review, 1977-1979. Author: "Availability of Immediate Newborn Coverage in Group Health Policies," 9 California Broker 38, June, 1987; "Professional Responsibilities of Brokers and Agents," 48 The Broker, May/June, 1985. *Member:* Los Angeles County Bar Association; The State Bar of California; California Women Lawyers. **PRACTICE AREAS:** Business Litigation; Insurance Coverage Law; Banking Law.

**MARTIN E. ROSEN,** born Princeton, New Jersey, January 8, 1957; admitted to bar, 1983, California; 1984, U.S. District Court, Central District of California and U.S. Court of Appeals, Ninth Circuit; 1991, U.S. District Court, Northern, Southern and Eastern Districts of California. *Education:* University of California at Los Angeles (B.A., summa cum laude, 1978; M.B.A., 1982; J.D., 1982). Phi Beta Kappa. Member, U.C.-L.A. Moot Court Honors Program, 1980-1982. Author: "Insolvency of Insurers," California Insurance Law & Practice, Matthew Bender, 1986; "Pilot Life's Dramatic Impact," 10 Los Angeles Lawyer 37, October, 1987; "Whose Book Is It Anyway," Insurance Journal (1992). *Member:* The State Bar of California. **PRACTICE AREAS:** Business Litigation; Insurance Bad Faith.

**LARRY M. GOLUB,** born Los Angeles, California, December 3, 1957; admitted to bar, 1983, California, U.S. District Court, Northern, Central and Southern Districts of California, U.S. Court of Appeals, Ninth Circuit, U.S. Supreme Court and U.S. Tax Court. *Education:* University of California at Los Angeles (B.A., magna cum laude, 1979); Hastings College of Law, University of California (J.D., magna cum laude, 1983). Phi Alpha Delta. Member, Thurston Society. Note and Comment Editor, Hastings Law Journal, 1982-1983. Author: "Business General Liability Policies," California Insurance Law & Practice, Matthew Bender, 1992; "Products Liability Insurance," California Insurance Law & Practice, Matthew Bender, 1994. "Identifying and Using Insurance Coverage in Business Litigation," Continuing Education of the Bar, 1984, 1986, 1989, 1991 and 1993; "Analyzing Coverage: Reading & Interpreting Insurance Policies" and "Claims Involving Excess Insurance," California Liability Insurance Practice: Claims & Litigation, California Continuing Education of the Bar, 1991—; "Insurance Coverage for Employee Claims," CA Employment Law Practice,

*(This Listing Continued)*

CEB (1996). Judicial Extern to California Supreme Court Justice Joseph Grodin, Court of Appeal, First District, 1982. *Member:* Los Angeles County and American Bar Associations; The State Bar of California; Association of Business Trial Lawyers. **PRACTICE AREAS:** Insurance Coverage Law; Employment Law; Construction Law.

**JOHN C. HOLMES,** born Glendale, California, January 17, 1959; admitted to bar, 1985, California, U.S. District Court, Central, Northern and Eastern Districts of California and U.S. Court of Appeals, Ninth Circuit. *Education:* University of California at San Diego (B.A., 1982); University of Southern California (J.D., 1985). Member, Hale Moot Court Honors Program, 1983-1984. Co-Author: "Delinquency Proceedings," California Law of Life Insurance, Association of Life Insurance Counsel, 1990; "Formation and Issuance of Life Insurance Policies," California Law of Life Insurance, Association of Life Insurance Counsel, 1990; "Issuance of Insurance Policies," California Insurance Law & Practice, Matthew Bender, 1986; "Insolvency of Insurers," California Insurance Law and Practice, Matthew Bender, 1990. *Member:* Los Angeles County and American Bar Associations; The State Bar of California. **PRACTICE AREAS:** Insurance Coverage Law; Insurance Insolvency Law; Business Litigation.

**DAVID C. PARK,** born Boston, Massachusetts, March 7, 1960; admitted to bar, 1986, California and U.S. District Court, Central, Eastern and Southern Districts of California. *Education:* University of California at Los Angeles (B.A., 1982); Boston College School of Law (J.D., 1985). Recipient, Thomas Macken Joyce Award. Chairman and Writer, Boston College Moot Court and Mock Trial Program, 1984-1985. Teaching Assistant, Legal Research and Writing, Boston College, 1983-1984. Co-Author: "Issuance of Insurance Policies," California Insurance Law & Practice, Matthew Bender, 1986. *Member:* Los Angeles County Bar Association; The State Bar of California; Korean American Bar Association of Southern California. **PRACTICE AREAS:** Business Litigation; Real Estate Litigation; Insurance Litigation; Banking Litigation; Architecture Law.

**ROBERT J. MCKENNON,** born Los Angeles, California, July 13, 1959; admitted to bar, 1986, California, U.S. District Court, Central, Northern, Southern and Eastern Districts of California and U.S. Court of Appeals, Ninth Circuit. *Education:* California State University of Fullerton (B.A., with honors, 1982); Loyola Marymount University; University of Southern California (J.D., 1985). Member: St. Thomas More Law Honor Society; Scott Moot Court Honors Program. Co-Author: "Delinquency Proceedings," California Law of Life Insurance," Association of Life Insurance Counsel, 1990; "Formation and Insurance of Life Insurance Policies," California Law of Life Insurance Counsel, 1990. Author: "Insolvency of Insurers," California Insurance Law and Practice, Matthew Bender, 1991, "Insurance Issues in Bankruptcy: An Insurer's Perspective," ABA's Tort & Insurance Law Journal. *Member:* Los Angeles County and American Bar Associations; The State Bar of California. **PRACTICE AREAS:** Business Litigation; Insurance Insolvency and Litigation; Bankruptcy Law.

**RICHARD G. DE LA MORA,** born Oceanside, California, June 11, 1958; admitted to bar, 1985, California; 1986, U.S. District Court, Central District of California. *Education:* University of California at Santa Barbara (B.A., 1980); University of Southern California (J.D., 1985). Author: "Relationship Between the Insurance and Financial Services Industries," CA Insurance Law & Practice, Mathew Bender (1991). *Member:* State Bar of California. **PRACTICE AREAS:** General Corporate Law; Insurance Regulation Law; Reinsurance; Administrative Law.

**JOHN E. MCPHERSON,** born San Diego, California, December 14, 1954; admitted to bar, 1986, California. *Education:* San Diego State University (B.A., summa cum laude, 1977) Phi Beta Kappa; University of California at Los Angeles (M.A., 1982); Hastings College of the Law, University of California (J.D., 1986). Order of the Coif. Member, Moot Court Board. *Member:* State Bar of California. **PRACTICE AREAS:** General Corporate Law; Business Law; Insurance Regulation Law.

**MICHAEL L. ROSENFIELD,** born Winnipeg, Manitoba, July 12, 1958; admitted to bar, 1987, California. *Education:* Arizona State University (B.A., 1981); Pepperdine University (J.D., cum laude, 1987). Author: "Insurance and Employee Benefits," Business Insurance Law and Practice, Matthew Bender, 1989; "State of Confusion," The Review, May 1989. *Member:* State Bar of California; American Bar Association; The Conference of Insurance Counsel. **PRACTICE AREAS:** Insurance Regulatory Law; General Corporate Law.

*(This Listing Continued)*

## ASSOCIATES

**RANDALL A. DOCTOR,** born Augsburg, Germany, January 28, 1962; admitted to bar, 1987, California. *Education:* University of California at Los Angeles (B.A., 1984); Hastings College of the Law, University of California (J.D., 1987); Stockholm Universitet Stockholm, Sweden (Diploma of International Law Program, 1991). Phi Delta Phi. Member, Hastings International and Comparative Law Review, 1986-1987. Judicial Extern to Arthur Alarcon, U.S. Court of Appeals, Ninth Circuit. Author: "Life Insurance in Partnerships and Close Corporations," Chapter 12, Business Insurance & Practice Guide, Mathew Bender (1991). *Member:* Los Angeles County and American Bar Associations; State Bar of California. *PRACTICE AREAS:* General Corporate Law; Insurance Regulatory Law.

**SCOTT J. THERRIEN,** born Manchester, New Hampshire, July 4, 1962; admitted to bar, 1988, California, U.S. District Court, Central District of California and U.S. Court of Appeals, 9th Circuit. *Education:* Pennsylvania State University (B.B.A., 1983); Southwestern University School of Law (J.D., cum laude, 1988). Member: Moot Court Honors Program; Phillip P. Jessup International Law Competition, 1987-1988. Member, 1986-1987, Chief Note and Comment Editor and Member, Executive Board, 1987-1988, Southwestern University Law Review. *Member:* State Bar of California.

**GREGORY B. SCARLETT,** born Daytona Beach, Florida, July 10, 1952; admitted to bar, 1987, California. *Education:* Florida State University (B.S., 1977); University of California, Los Angeles (J.D., 1987). Judicial Extern to the Hon. Stephen Reinhardt, U.S. Court of Appeals, 9th Circuit. *Member:* Los Angeles County and American Bar Associations; State Bar of California. *PRACTICE AREAS:* General Litigation.

**LINDA R. CARUSO,** born Hartford, Connecticut, April 25, 1964; admitted to bar, 1989, California and U.S. District Court, Central District of California. *Education:* College of the Holy Cross (B.A., 1986); George Washington University (J.D., 1989). Member, The George Washington University Consumer Protection Reporting Service (spring 1989). Author: "Formation and Structure of Domestic Life Insurance," The Life Insurance Law of California, 1990. *Member:* State Bar of California.

**AUDREY M. LYNESS,** born Oakland, California, October 31, 1961; admitted to bar, 1989, California, U.S. District Court, Northern, Southern and Central District of California, U.S. Court of Appeals, Ninth Circuit. *Education:* Carleton College (B.A., magna cum laude, with distinction in Political Science, 1983); University of California, Hastings College of Law (J.D., cum laude, 1989). Hastings International and Comparative Law Review Participant, 1987-1988; Associate Articles Editor, 1988-1989. *Member:* State Bar of California.

**HEATHER PETERS,** born Manhasset, N.Y., November 30, 1965; admitted to bar, 1990, Pennsylvania; 1991, California, U.S. District Court, Eastern District of Pennsylvania and Central District of California; 1992, U.S. District Court, Northern, Southern and Eastern Districts of California. *Education:* Nova University (B.S., with distinction, 1987); Southwestern University School of Law (J.D., 1990). Phi Alpha Delta. Recipient, American Jurisprudence Award in Constitutional Law. Member, Southwestern Law Review, 1988-1989. *Member:* Pennsylvania and American Bar Associations; State Bar of California. *PRACTICE AREAS:* Insurance Bad Faith; Employment Law.

**JOHN M. LE BLANC,** born Long Beach, California, December 21, 1959; admitted to bar, 1991, California. *Education:* California State University at Long Beach (B.A., 1983); Biola University (M.Div., with high honors, 1987); Southwestern University School of Law (J.D., cum laude, 1991). Staff Member, Southwestern University Law Review, 1989-1990. Articles Editor, Executive Board Member, Southwestern University Law Review, 1990-1991. Author: "The Emancipated Courtroom: Ending Federally Coerced Attorney Appointments," 20 Southwestern University Law Review, Vol. 1. *Member:* The State Bar of California.

**J. STEVEN BINGMAN,** born Tiffin, Ohio, November 6, 1960; admitted to bar, 1991, California. *Education:* Indiana University School of Music (B.S., 1985); Pepperdine University School of Law (J.D., cum laude, 1991). Phi Delta Phi. Member, 1989-1991 and Managing Editor, 1990-1991, Pepperdine Law Review. Judicial Extern to the Honorable William J. Rea, U.S. District Court, Central District of California, 1990. Author: "The Descendible Right of Publicity: Has the Time Finally Come for a National Standard?" 17 Pepp. L. Rev. 933 (1990). *Member:* Los Angeles and American Bar Associations; The State Bar of California.

**ROBERT J. CERNY,** born Los Angeles, California, May 24, 1966; admitted to bar, 1992, California. *Education:* Boston College (B.A., 1988; J.D., 1992). Co-Author: "Strategic Environmental Assessment: Amending

*(This Listing Continued)*

the EA Directive," Environmental Policy and Law, Volume 22, No. 3 (1992). *Member:* State Bar of California.

**MARINA M. MANIATIS,** born Skokie, Illinois, September 9, 1964; admitted to bar, 1991, Illinois; 1994, California. *Education:* University of Chicago (B.A., with distinction in Political Science, 1986); John Marshall Law School (J.D., summa cum laude, 1991). *Member:* Los Angeles, Illinois State and American Bar Associations; State Bar of California.

**GREGORY O. EISENRICH,** born Burbank, California, November 20, 1966; admitted to bar, 1992, California. *Education:* University of California at Davis (A.B., 1989); Boalt Hall School of Law, University of California (J.D., 1992). *Member:* State Bar of California.

**RUSSELL H. BIRNER,** born Lawrence, Kansas, July 27, 1963; admitted to bar, 1991, Texas; 1995, California. *Education:* University of Texas (B.A., 1985); Tulane University of Louisiana (J.D., cum laude, 1991). Member and Administrative Justice for Academic Programs: Moot Court Board. Senior Fellow, Legal Research and Writing Program.

**MICHAEL J. ROTHMAN,** born Minneapolis, Minnesota, June 7, 1962; admitted to bar, 1988, Minnesota; 1993, California. *Education:* Carleton College (B.A., magna cum laude, 1984); University of Minnesota Law School (J.D., cum laude, 1988). President, Moot Courts Board and Director International Moot Court. Law Clerk for The Honorable Gary L. Crippen on the Minnesota Court of Appeals. *Member:* State Bar of California; Los Angeles and American bar Associations.

**PABLO M. ZYLBERGLAIT,** born Buenos Aires, Argentina, June 12, 1968; admitted to bar, 1994, California. *Education:* California State University, Northridge (B.S., cum laude, 1991); Georgetown University Law Center (J.D., 1994). Author: "OPIC's Investment Insurance, The Platypus of Governmental Programs and Its Jurisprudence," *Law and Policy in International Business,* Vol. 25:1 (October 1993); Interrelationship Between Insurance and Financial Services Industries," CA Insurance Law & Practice, Matthew Bender (1995).

**ERIN E. MARTENS,** born Ann Arbor, Michigan, November 26, 1969; admitted to bar, 1994, California. *Education:* University of California at Berkeley (B.A., 1991); Santa Clara University (J.D., 1994). Research Editor, Santa Clara University Law Review, 1993-1994. *Member:* State Bar of California. *PRACTICE AREAS:* Environmental Insurance Coverage; Insurance Bad Faith.

**JOHN P. NEWELL,** born Huntington, New York, September 2, 1963; admitted to bar, 1995, California. *Education:* State University of New York at Stony Brook (B.A., 1986); Southwestern University (J.D., magna cum laude, 1995). Editor: Southwestern Law Review. Member: Southwestern Interscholastic Trial Advocacy Team.

## OF COUNSEL

**ALAN R. WOLEN,** born Los Angeles, California, February 18, 1941; admitted to bar, 1966, California, U.S. District Court, Southern and Central Districts of California and U.S. Court of Appeals, Ninth Circuit; 1969, U.S. Supreme Court and U.S. Court of Military Appeals; 1976, U.S. Tax Court. *Education:* University of California, Los Angeles (B.S., Accounting Finance, 1962); University of Southern California (J.D., 1965). Phi Alpha Delta. Board of Editors, Southern California Law Review, 1964-1965. Author: "Vertical Restraints on Territorial Distribution," 37 Southern California Law Review 332, 1964. Co-Author: "Indebtedness and the Serviceman," X Air Force JAG Law Review 25, 1968. Author: "The California Insurance Holding Company Act," California Insurance Law & Practice, Matthew Bender, 1986. Lecturer: Corporate Indemnification of Directors and Officers, University of California, Los Angeles, 1972, 1974 and Stanford University, 1973; Executive Compensation —Tax and Other Limits, University of California, Los Angeles, 1979. Instructor, Legal Aspects of Contracts and Construction Law, University of California, Los Angeles, 1985-1986. Deputy Attorney General, State of California, 1966. *Member:* Los Angeles County (Chair, Financial Institutions Committee of the Business and Corporations Law Section, 1993-1994) and American Bar Associations; The State Bar of California (Member, Financial Institutions Committee, 1983-1986. [Deputy Staff Judge Advocate, U.S. Air Force, 1966-1969]. *PRACTICE AREAS:* General Corporate Law; Insurance Law; Real Estate Law.

**WILLIAM A. KURLANDER,** born Los Angeles, California, February 7, 1926; admitted to bar, 1950, California. *Education:* Washburn University of Topeka, University of New Mexico and University of California at Los Angeles (B.A., 1947); Loyola University of Los Angeles (LL.B., 1950). Author: "Supreme Court's Responsibility for Court Congestion," California State Bar Journal, 1981; "Allocation of Defense Costs Between Primary and Specific Excess Carriers," Defense Research Institute, 1979. Co-Author:

*(This Listing Continued)*

CALIFORNIA—LOS ANGELES

### BARGER & WOLEN, Los Angeles—Continued

Matthew Bender's California Insurance Law & Practice, Chapter 47, "Products Liability Insurance," August 1994. *Member:* Los Angeles County (Member, Board of Trustees, 1968-1970), Santa Monica Bay District (President, 1964) and American Bar Associations; State Bar of California (Chairman and Presiding Officer of Conference of Delegates, 1975; Member, Executive Committee of the Conference of Delegates, 1972-1975, Member, Board of Governors, 1978-1981; Vice President, 1980-1981). Fellow, American College of Trial Lawyers. Diplomate, American Board of Trial Advocates (National President, 1967). **PRACTICE AREAS:** Litigation, Insurance Coverage.

REFERENCES: Bank of America (Los Angeles Main Office); Security Pacific National Bank (Los Angeles Main Office).

---

## BARKER & ROMNEY
*A PROFESSIONAL CORPORATION*

**LOS ANGELES, CALIFORNIA**

(See Pasadena)

*Construction, Construction Defect, Business, Real Estate, Land Use, Environmental Law, Eminent Domain, General Civil Litigation, Community Association Law, Insurance Law and Appellate Law.*

---

## BARLOW & KOBATA

*2029 CENTURY PARK EAST, SUITE 3230*
**LOS ANGELES, CALIFORNIA 90067**
Telephone: 310-277-7556
Fax: 310-277-2982

*Management Labor, Employment, Personnel, Discrimination and Administrative Law. Litigation.*

### MEMBERS OF FIRM

**WAYNE E. BARLOW,** born Philadelphia, Pennsylvania, September 11, 1942; admitted to bar, 1968, California and U.S. District Court, Central District of California; 1974, U.S. Tax Court; 1976, District of Columbia and U.S. District Court, Northern and Southern Districts of California; 1981, U.S. Court of Appeals, Ninth Circuit; 1982, U.S. Supreme Court; 1984, New York, U.S. Court of Appeals, Tenth Circuit and U.S. Claims Court. *Education:* Hartnell College (A.A., 1962); New York University; University of California at Santa Barbara (B.A., 1964); University of Southern California (J.D., 1967). *Member:* Beverly Hills (Member, Labor Section), Los Angeles County (Member, Labor Section), New York State and American (Member, Labor and Employment Law Section) Bar Associations; State Bar of California; District of Columbia Bar. **LANGUAGES:** Spanish, Italian. **PRACTICE AREAS:** Management Labor Law; Employment Law; Discrimination Law.

**MARK T. KOBATA,** born Long Beach, California, September 1, 1950; admitted to bar, 1977, California; 1978, U.S. District Court, Central District of California; 1980, U.S. Court of Appeals, Ninth Circuit and U.S. District Court, Southern District of California; 1981, U.S. District Court, Northern District of California; 1984, U.S. Claims Court; 1987, U.S. Supreme Court. *Education:* University of California at Los Angeles (B.A., 1972); Southwestern University (J.D., 1976). *Member:* Los Angeles County and American (Member, Labor and Employment Law Section) Bar Associations; State Bar of California. **PRACTICE AREAS:** Management Labor Law; Employment Law; Discrimination Law.

### ASSOCIATES

**JAMES E. HALL,** born San Rafael, California, June 26, 1954; admitted to bar, 1980, California, U.S. District Court, Central District of California and U.S. Court of Appeals, Ninth Circuit. *Education:* University of California at Santa Cruz (B.A., honors in History, 1976); California Western School of Law (J.D., 1980); Georgetown University (LL.M., Labor Law, 1981). Co-Author: "Recent Development in Public Employee Labor Relations," The Urban Lawyer, Vol. 16, Number 4, Fall, 1984. *Member:* Century City, Los Angeles County and American (Member, Labor and Employment Law Section) Bar Associations; State Bar of California. **PRACTICE AREAS:** Management Labor Law; Employment Law; Discrimination Law.

CAA502B

---

MARTINDALE-HUBBELL LAW DIRECTORY 1997

## MARILYN BARRETT

*1900 AVENUE OF THE STARS*
*SUITE 1450*
**LOS ANGELES, CALIFORNIA 90067**
Telephone: 310-788-0028
Fax: 310-788-0215
E-Mail: mbarr@counsel.com
Email: mbarr@Counsel.com

*Business Law. State and Federal Tax Law.*

**MARILYN BARRETT,** born Hoisington, Kansas, August 23, 1952; admitted to bar, 1978, California; 1979, District of Columbia and U.S. Tax Court. *Education:* University of Kansas (B.S., with highest distinction, 1973); University of California at Los Angeles (J.D., 1977). Beta Gamma Sigma. Associate Editor, University of California at Los Angeles Law Review, 1976-1977. Certified Public Accountant, Maryland, 1978. Author: "Stock Options: Court Rules That Employees Must Pay Ordinary Income Tax When Their Options Were Sold As Part Of Company's Acquisition," CEB California Business Law Reporter, January 1996; "Loan Out Corporations: Ninth Circuit Rides To The Rescue As The IRS Continues Its Assault On Loan-Out Corporations," CEB California Business Law Reporter, November 1995; "U.S. Supreme Court Holds That ADEA Damages Are Taxable, But Its Decision Creates New Uncertainty," CEB California Business Law Reporter, September 1995; "When Is The Sale Of A Business Subject to Sales Tax Like an Over-the-Counter Retail Sale? In California, Most of the Time," CEB California Business Law Reporter, June 1995; "Ninth Circuit Disallows Corporation's Deduction of Interest Accrued on Deferred Compensation," CEB California Business Law Reporter, March, 1995; "The Not-So-Friendly Skies For Victims of Age Discrimination: The IRS Attacks Exclusion of ADEA Damages," CEB California Business Law Reporter, January, 1995; "Has The Insanity Stopped? IRS Partially Reserves Punitive Policy Denying Deductibility of Clean-up Costs-But Questions Remain," California Environmental Law Reporter, July, 1994; "Tax Issues Concerning Independent Contractors and Loan-Out Corporations," Tax Management Compensation Planning Journal, (In Two Parts), September 3, 1993 and October 1, 1993; "Is the Loan-Out Corporation Dead or Alive? Is the Independent Contractor an Endangered Species?" distributed by the Los Angeles County Bar Association Taxation Section (1992); "Rust vs. Sullivan: New Limits on Choice Imposed by the Supreme Court," Westside Woman, July 17, 1991; "Claim of Right: A Tax Doctrine Unjustly Applied to Accrued Income Subject to Litigation," 24 University of California at Los Angeles Law Review, 877, 1977; "The Recently Proposed Regulations under I.R.C. §704 (b); A Brief Review," 9 Tax Section News, No. 3, Spring, 1983. Co-Author: "Independent Contractors, Employees, the Entertainment Industry and the IRS: Tax Administration Problem Heads for Hollywood," The ABA Entertainment and Sports Lawyer, Fall, 1993; "Proposal On The Taxation of Escrow and Settlement Funds Under I.R.C. §468 B (g), Tax Notes Today, June 13, 1991; "Section 482 and Non-recognition Transfers," Tax Notes, December 1989. Contributing Editor (Taxation), CEB California Business Law Reporter. *Member:* Los Angeles County (Member, Taxation, Business and Corporations Law Sections; Chair-Elect, Taxation Section, 1996-1997; Member At Large, Executive Committee of Taxation Section, 1992-1993; Chair, Entertainment Tax Committee, 1991-1992; Chair, Ad Hoc Disaster Recovery Tax Relief Committee, 1992-1993) and American (Member, Committee on Affiliated and Related Corporations, 1981-1992; Chair, Subcommittee on Intercompany Allocations, 1989-1990) Bar Associations; State Bar of California (Chair, Taxation Section, 1996-1997, Member, 1992—, Executive Committee of Taxation Section); District of Columbia Bar; American Institute of Certified Public Accountants (Member, Tax Section). (Also Of Counsel to Kelly & Lytton). **PRACTICE AREAS:** Business Law; State and Federal Tax Law.

---

## BARTON, KLUGMAN & OETTING

A Partnership including Professional Corporations

*Established in 1958*

*37TH FLOOR, 333 SOUTH GRAND AVENUE*
**LOS ANGELES, CALIFORNIA 90071-1599**
Telephone: 213-621-4000
Telecopier: 213-625-1832

*Newport Beach Office:* Suite 700, 4400 MacArthur Boulevard, P.O. Box 2350, 92660. Telephone: 714-752-7551. Telecopier: 714-752-0288.

*(This Listing Continued)*

General Civil and Trial Practice. Taxation, Corporation, Banking, Probate and Trust Law. Antitrust, Corporate Securities, Real Property, Environmental, Oil and Gas, Labor and International Business Law. Professional Liability Defense, Insurance Coverage, Directors and Officers Defense and Coverage.

FIRM PROFILE: Barton, Klugman & Oetting is a full service law partnership with offices in Los Angeles and Orange Counties. Our attorneys are trained at a wide variety of law schools, including Boalt Hall, Cornell, Harvard, Hastings, Illinois, Michigan, Northwestern, UCLA, USC and Wisconsin. The Firm has engaged in a diversified general civil law practice for over 30 years and has developed a reputation for high quality, responsive legal work.

### COUNSEL TO FIRM

†**ROBERT M. BARTON,** born Jacksonville, Florida, April 4, 1922; admitted to bar, 1945, California. *Education:* University of Kansas (A.B., 1942); University of Michigan (J.D., 1944). Phi Delta Phi. Member, Board of Editors, Michigan Law Review, 1944. Author: "Terminating an Interest in a Close Corporation," published by New York University, 1974; "Trusts: Some Nontestamentary Uses," Trust & Estates, January, 1981, Lecturer, "Tax Highlights of 1975," 1975 at New York University Tax Institute; Title Insurance and Trust Tax Forum, 1981. Special Assistant to the Attorney General of the U.S., 1954-1965. *Member:* Los Angeles County (Member, Board of Trustees, 1949; 1960-1963), Orange County and American Bar Associations; The State Bar of California (Secretary, Committee on Rules of Professional Conduct, 1953-1959; Chairman, Committee on Bar Examiners, 1967-1968); Chancery Club; American Law Institute (Life Member). *PRACTICE AREAS:* Business Law; Taxation; Estate Planning; Estate Administration.

†**ROBERT H. KLUGMAN,** born Ottawa, Illinois, May 20, 1926; admitted to bar, 1950, Illinois; 1958, California. *Education:* Yale University (B.A., 1947); Northwestern University (J.D., 1950). Delta Theta Phi; Order of the Coif. Member, Editorial Board, Illinois Law Review, 1949. Instructor in Taxes, University of Southern California Law Graduate School, 1963-1967. *Member:* Los Angeles County and American Bar Associations; The State Bar of California; Association of Tax Counsel. [Lt., U.S.N.R., active duty, 1946-1947; 1950-1952]. *PRACTICE AREAS:* Business Law; Taxation; Real Estate; Environmental Law; Construction Law.

†**RICHARD F. OETTING,** born Wyandotte, Michigan, July 25, 1931; admitted to bar, 1960, California. *Education:* University of Michigan and University of California at Berkeley (A.B., with honors, 1953); University of Southern California (LL.B., 1959). Phi Alpha Delta; Phi Kappa Phi; Order of the Coif. Associate Editor, U.S.C. Law Review, 1958-1959. *Member:* Los Angeles County Bar Association (Chair, Executive Committee, Trial Lawyers Section, 1983-1984; Chair, Delegation to the State Bar Conference, 1975-1976; Member, Insurance Programs Committee, 1984-1989); State Bar of California (Member, Executive Committee California Conference of Delegates, 1976-1979); Association of Business Trial Lawyers; Chancery Club; Founding Member, Los Angeles County Bar Association Inn of Court (President, 1991-1992). *PRACTICE AREAS:* Securities Litigation; Professional Liability Defense; Directors and Officers Insurance Defense; Banking Litigation; Federal Practice.

### MEMBERS OF FIRM

†**DAVID F. MORGAN,** born New York, N.Y., August 9, 1931; admitted to bar, 1961, California. *Education:* Swarthmore College (B.A., 1953); Harvard University (J.D., 1960). Phi Beta Kappa. *Member:* Los Angeles County Bar Association (Chairman, International Law Section, 1969-1971; Chair, Business and Corporations Law Section, 1982-1983); The State Bar of California (Member, Local Administrative Committee No. 2, 1969-1972; Hearing Examiner, Committee of Bar Examiners, 1973-1978; Referee, State Bar Court, 1979-1982). [Lt., USNR, active duty, 1953-1957]. *PRACTICE AREAS:* Corporate Law; Securities; Mergers, Acquisitions & Divestitures; Finance. *Email:* MORGANLWYR@AOL.COM

†**WILLIAM D. HERZ,** born Detroit, Michigan, October 30, 1943; admitted to bar, 1969, California. *Education:* Michigan State University (B.A., magna cum laude, 1965); University of Michigan (J.D., cum laude, 1968). Phi Delta Phi; Phi Kappa Phi; Beta Gamma Sigma. *Member:* Los Angeles County Bar Association; State Bar of California. *PRACTICE AREAS:* Real Estate; Corporate Law; Probate; Estate Planning.

†**CHARLES J. SCHUFREIDER,** born Chicago, Illinois, February 27, 1945; admitted to bar, 1970, California. *Education:* Northwestern University (B.A., 1966); University of Illinois (J.D., 1969). Order of the Coif. Assistant Editor, University of Illinois Law Forum, 1968-1969. *Member:* State Bar of California (Member, Committee on Rules and Procedures of Court, 1983-1986). *PRACTICE AREAS:* Trial Practice; Employment Law; Commercial Banking Litigation; Professional Liability Defense; Insurance Coverage; Bad Faith Litigation.

†**ROBERT LOUIS FISHER,** born Long Beach, California, February 8, 1944; admitted to bar, 1972, California. *Education:* University of California, Berkeley (A.B., 1965); University of California at Los Angeles (J.D., 1972). Phi Alpha Delta. Senior Editor, U.C.L.A., Alaska Law Review, 1971-1972. Master of the Bench, Association for California Tort Reform, 1991—. *Member:* State Bar of California (Member, Committee on Administration of Justice, 1994—); Los Angeles Complex Litigation Inn of Court (Member, Executive Committee, 1994—). [Lt., USNR, 1966-1970]. *PRACTICE AREAS:* General Civil Practice; Trial Practice; Real Property Litigation; Commercial Litigation. *Email:* 73653.2445@Compuserve.com

†**GILBERT D. JENSEN,** born Los Angeles, California, May 30, 1946; admitted to bar, 1974, California. *Education:* University of California at Los Angeles (B.S., 1968; M.S., Business Administration, 1969); Boalt Hall School of Law, University of California (J.D., 1974). *Member:* Los Angeles County (Member, Litigation Section) and American Bar Associations; State Bar of California. *PRACTICE AREAS:* International Law; Insurance Coverage; Securities; General Civil Practice; Trial Practice.

†**DAVID J. CARTANO,** born Seattle, Washington, November 6, 1949; admitted to bar, 1976, California; 1983, U.S. Tax Court. *Education:* University of Washington (B.A., magna cum laude, 1972); Cornell University (J.D., 1976); University of Southern California (Masters in Taxation, 1989). Phi Beta Kappa. Member, Board of Editors, Cornell International Law Journal, 1975-1976. Author: "Incentive Stock Options— The Sequential Exercise Restriction," TAXES-The Tax Magazine, August, 1982; "The Tax Benefit Rule in Corporate Liquidations," The Journal of Corporate Taxation, Autumn, 1983; "ESOPs and Restricted Securities," Journal of Pension Planning and Compliance, November, 1977; "Meeting the New IRS Requirements," Financial Operations, Fall, 1987. Panelist on Partnership Law, California Continuing Education of the Bar, 1987-1988. *Member:* Los Angeles County Bar Association (Member, Section on Taxation); State Bar of California. *PRACTICE AREAS:* Taxation; Corporate Law. *Email:* CARTANO@MSN.com

**MARTIN J. SPEAR,** born Chicago, Illinois, April 9, 1943; admitted to bar, 1971, California and U.S. District Court, Central, Southern and Northern Districts of California; 1976, U.S. Supreme Court; 1977, U.S. Court of Appeals, Ninth Circuit. *Education:* California State University at Northridge (B.A., 1966); Southwestern University (J.D., 1970). Member, Editorial Board, Los Angeles County Bar Journal, 1978-1979. *Member:* Beverly Hills (Secretary, Commercial Law Section, 1973-1974), Los Angeles County and American (Lecturer, Forum on Construction Law, 1984—) Bar Associations; State Bar of California (Secretary, Education Committee, Business Law Section; Liaison Member, Financial Institutions and Insurance Committees of Business Law Section). *PRACTICE AREAS:* Trial Practice; Corporate Law; Banking; Loan Restructuring; Commercial Finance.

†**TOD V. BEEBE,** born Albuquerque, New Mexico, October 1, 1956; admitted to bar, 1981, California. *Education:* University of Southern California (B.A., cum laude, 1978); Boalt Hall School of Law, University of California at Berkeley (J.D., 1981). *Member:* State Bar of California (Member, Business Law Section Committee on Financial Institutions). *PRACTICE AREAS:* Trial Practice; Insurance Coverage; Securities; Banking; Entertainment; Professional Liability. *Email:* 72741.2750@Compuserve.com

**RONALD R. ST. JOHN,** born Fort Huachuca, Arizona, June 13, 1956; admitted to bar, 1981, California. *Education:* University of Southern California (A.B., 1978; J.D., 1981). Executive Managing Editor, Southern California Law Review, 1980-1981. Honorary Member, Scribes, 1981-1982. Author: "Aggressive Innovation and Antitrust Liability," 53 Southern California Law Review 1369, 1980; "Shifting Compliance Costs in Commercial Tenancies," 18 Los Angeles Lawyer, Sept. 1995. Co-Author: "Supreme Court's Badaracco Decision Defines "Return"; Bad News for Tax Evaders," 60 Journal of Taxation 202, 1984; "Federal Estate and Gift Taxes--Past, Present and Future," 64 Taxes, The Tax Magazine 634, 1986. *Member:* Los Angeles County Bar Association; State Bar of California. *PRACTICE AREAS:* Real Estate; Environmental Law; Taxation; Estate Planning; Probate.

†**MARK A. NEWTON,** born Longview, Washington, November 19, 1958; admitted to bar, 1986, California. *Education:* University of Nebraska (B.S., 1982); University of California, Hastings College of the Law (J.D., 1986). *Member:* State Bar of California. *PRACTICE AREAS:* General Business Litigation; Banking Litigation; Insurance Coverage; Professional Liability Defense; Real Estate Litigation.

*(This Listing Continued)*

# CALIFORNIA—LOS ANGELES

## BARTON, KLUGMAN & OETTING, Los Angeles—Continued

**MARGOT I. MCLEAY,** born Timaru, New Zealand, October 26, 1960; admitted to bar, 1989, California. *Education:* Canterbury University (LL.B., 1983). Barrister and Solicitor of High Court of New Zealand, 1984. Solicitor of High Court of England and Wales, 1988. Member, English Law Society, 1989-1992. Member, New Zealand Law Society, 1984-1987. *Member:* State Bar of California. **PRACTICE AREAS:** General Civil Practice; Business Litigation; Banking Law; International Law; Insurance Coverage.

### ASSOCIATES

**BARBARA W. G. CROWLEY,** born Sewanee, Tennessee, March 19, 1924; admitted to bar, 1974, California. *Education:* University of Chicago (B.A., 1944); Loyola University (J.D., 1974). Phi Beta Kappa. Member, Los Angeles County Commission on Historical Landmarks, 1972-1974. *Member:* Los Angeles County and American (Member, Sections on: Real Property, Probate and Trust Law; Taxation; Family Law) Bar Associations; State Bar of California. **PRACTICE AREAS:** Probate; Estate Planning; Nonprofit and Charitable Organizations.

**REIKO L. FURUTA,** born Oakland, California, April 26, 1966; admitted to bar, 1993, California. *Education:* University of California, Berkeley (B.A., with honors, 1988); Hastings College of the Law, University of California (J.D., 1993). Publications Editor, Hastings Constitutional Law Quarterly, 1992-1993. *Member:* Los Angeles County Bar Association; State Bar of California. **PRACTICE AREAS:** Business Litigation; Probate Administration; Estate Planning.

**JALEEN NELSON,** born Pomona, California, March 19, 1968; admitted to bar, 1994, California. *Education:* Brigham Young University (B.A., 1990; M.A., 1991); University of California at Los Angeles (J.D., 1994). Articles Editor, University of California at Los Angeles, 1993-1994. Author: "Sledge Hammers and Scalpels: The FBI Digital Wiretap Bill and Its Effect of Free Flow of Information and Privacy," 41 U.C.L.A. Law Review 1541. *Member:* Los Angeles County and American Bar Associations; State Bar of California (Member, Sections on: Litigation and International); Women Lawyers Association of Los Angeles. **PRACTICE AREAS:** General Civil Practice; Banking Litigation; Business Litigation; Insurance Coverage.

†Denotes a lawyer whose Professional Corporation is a member of the partnership or is Counsel to the Firm

REPRESENTATIVE CLIENTS: ANZ Bank; Alcan Aluminium Corp.; American Home Assurance Co.; Bank of America; The BOC Group, Inc. (Airco); The Chubb Group of Insurance Companies; Connecting Devices, Inc.; Credito Italiano; Crum & Forster Managers Corp.; Daiwa Corporation; Fluor Corporation; First Interstate Bank of California; First State Insurance Co.; Geofon Incorporated; Hartford Specialty Co.; Hirsch Pipe & Supply Co.; International Insurance Co.; International Surplus Lines Insurance Co.; Jacobs Engineering Group Inc.; J. Walter Thompson Co.; Los Angeles Chemical Co.; Mikuni American Corp.; National Union Fire Insurance Co.; New England Reinsurance; Omnichrome; The Pines Resorts; Bank of Scotland; Sanwa Bank California; Staub Metals Corporation; Wells Fargo Bank, N.A.; Western Allied Corporation.
REFERENCES: Bank of America, N.T. & S.A.; The Bank of California (Southern California Headquarters); Wells Fargo Bank, N.A. (Wells Fargo Center, Los Angeles).

## BASILE & LANE, L.L.P.

11400 WEST OLYMPIC BOULEVARD, 9TH FLOOR
**LOS ANGELES, CALIFORNIA 90064-1565**
Telephone: 310-478-2114
Fax: 310-478-0229

*Taxation, Estate Planning, Corporate and International Law.*

### MEMBERS OF FIRM

**PAUL L. BASILE, JR.,** born Oakland, California, December 27, 1945; admitted to bar, 1972, California, U.S. District Court, Central District of California and U.S. Court of Appeals, Ninth Circuit; 1977, U.S. Supreme Court and U.S. Tax Court; 1978, U.S. Claims Court; 1979, U.S. Customs Court and U.S. Court of Customs and Patent Appeals; 1981, U.S. Court of International Trade; 1985, U.S. District Court, Northern District of California. *Education:* Occidental College (B.A., 1968); University of Washington; University of California at Los Angeles (J.D., 1971). Phi Alpha Delta. Moot Court Award. Author: "Liability of Directors Under the New California Nonprofit Corporation Law," University of San Francisco Law Review, Summer 1979. Consultant, Advising California Nonprofit Corporations, CEB (1984). *Member:* Beverly Hills (Member, Sections on: Probate,

*(This Listing Continued)*

Trust and Estate Planning, Taxation and Law Practice Management), Los Angeles County (Member: Sections on Business, Corporations Law and Taxation, Trusts and Estates, Small Firm and Solo Practitioner) and American (Chair, 1994—, Vice Chair, 1992-1994, Closely-Held Business Committee, Corporate Tax Committee, Tax Practice Management Committee and Small Firm Lawyers Committee; Section of Taxation; Special Problems of Business Owners and Estate Planning and Drafting: Pre-Death Planning Issues Committees, Section of Real Property, Probate and Trust Law; Section of Business Law; Taxation Committee; Law Practice Management Section) Bar Associations; State Bar of California (Vice Chair, 1995—, Member: Taxation Law Advisory Commission, 1994—; Nonprofit and Unincorporated Organizations Committee, 1989-1992, Business Law Section; Sections on Taxation and Estate Planning, Trust and Probate). (Certified Specialist, Taxation Law, The State Bar of California Board of Legal Specialization).

**JEFF W. LANE,** born New York, N.Y., October 9, 1950; admitted to bar, 1976, New York; 1978, California. *Education:* City College of the City University of New York (B.A., magna cum laude, 1972); New York University (J.D., 1975). Phi Beta Kappa. *Member:* Los Angeles County Bar Association; State Bar of California. **PRACTICE AREAS:** Taxation Law; Estate Planning; Business Law.

## MICHAEL ROBERT BASSIN

CITY NATIONAL BANK BUILDING
16133 VENTURA BOULEVARD
SUITE 1175 (ENCINO)
**LOS ANGELES, CALIFORNIA 91436-2415**
Telephone: 818-905-6096
Fax: 818-905-9145

*General Business, Civil Litigation, Negligence and Insurance Law, Construction, Surety and Guaranty.*

**MICHAEL ROBERT BASSIN,** born Burbank, California, October 6, 1948; admitted to bar, 1976, California and U.S. District Court, Central District of California; 1980, U.S. District Court, Northern, Southern and Eastern Districts of California; 1981, U.S. Court of Appeals, Ninth Circuit. *Education:* San Fernando Valley State College (B.A., 1970); Loyola University at Los Angeles (J.D., 1975). *Member:* The State Bar of California. **REPORTED CASES:** Elder v. Carlisle 1987, 2nd App. Dist. 193 Cal App. 3rd 1313; United Electric v. National Bonding 1983, 711 P.2d 131; Cornish v. Superior Court (Capital Bond & Insurance Co., real party interest) (1989) 209 Cal.App.3d 467.

## BATTLE FOWLER LLP

A Limited Liability Partnership
1999 AVENUE OF THE STARS, SUITE 2700
**LOS ANGELES, CALIFORNIA 90067**
Telephone: 310-277-9090

*New York, N.Y. Office:* Park Avenue Tower, 75 East 55th Street, 10022. Telephone: 212-856-7000.

*General and International Practice.*

### MEMBERS OF FIRM

**GEORGE GORDON BATTLE** (1897-1949).

**LUDLOW S. FOWLER** (1924-1961).

**SANFORD C. PRESANT,** admitted to bar, 1977, New York, District of Columbia and U.S. Tax Court; 1978, U.S. Claims Court; 1982, U.S. Supreme Court; 1992, California. *Education:* Cornell University (B.A., 1973); State University of New York at Buffalo (J.D., 1976); Georgetown University (LL.M., in Taxation, 1981). Kripke Securities Law Fellowship, New York University, 1976. Options Task Force, U.S. Securities and Exchange Commission, 1976-1978. Co-Author: with Leslie H. Loffman, "Contributions of Property to Partnership: The Proposed Regulations Under Section 704(c)(1)(A)," Journal of Taxation, April-May, 1993; "Avoiding Minimum Gain Recapture in Workouts Under the Final Section 704(b) Regulations," 20 Journal of Real Estate Taxation 237 Spring, 1993; "Tax Consequences of Restructuring the Real Estate Partnership in Default," Tax Aspects of Loan Workouts and Bankruptcies, California Continuing Education of the Bar Fall, 1992; "The Final Regulations Under Section 752," 19 Journal of Real Estate Taxation 267 (Summer 1992); "Proposed Regulations Create Self-Charged Interest Exceptions Under the Passive Loss Rules," 19 Journal of Real Estate Taxation 121 (Winter 1992); "Notice 90-41 Expands Ability to

*(This Listing Continued)*

Use Borrowings in Real Estate Partnerships Having Tax-Exempt Partners," 18 Journal of Real Estate Taxation 314 (Summer 1991); "Leveraged Partnerships with Tax-Exempt Entities--Qualified Allocations and the Fractions Rule," NYU 48th Annual Institute on Federal Taxation (Feb. 1990); "A Practical Guide to the Section 752 Temp. Regs.," 70 Journal of Taxation 196, 260, April-May, 1989; "The Effect of IRS Notice 88-75 on Publicly Traded Partnerships," 40 Tax Notes 747, August, 1988; "Treasury Issues Final Partnership Allocation Regulations, ABA Sect. Tax'n Newsletter, Spring, 1986; "The Final Partnership Noncourse Debt Allocation Regulations," Taxes Mag., Feb., 1987; "How ACRS Anti-Churning Rules Affect Real Estate Partnerships and Their Partners," 57 Journal of Taxation 148, September, 1982 and "Interest Accruals Under the Rule of 78's — A Postmortem," Real Estate Review, Fall, 1984; with Peter M. Fass, "Special Tax Problems of Resyndications"; with Peter M. Fass and Leslie H. Loffman, "The Effect of the Tax Reform Act of 1984 on Tax Shelters," Clark Boardman Co., 1984; with Leslie H. Loffman, "Real Estate Syndication Tax Handbook," Clark Boardman Co., 1986; with Peter M. Fass, R.J. Haft and L.H. Loffman, "The Tax Reform Act of 1986," and "Tax Aspects of Real Estate Investments," Clark Boardman Callahan Co., 1992. Adjunct Associate Professor, New York University, 1983—. Co-Chairman: "Partnerships and S Corporations," NYU Institute on Federal Taxation, Summer 1992; 9th Annual New York University Conferences on Federal Taxation of Real Estate Transactions, 1987; "Sophisticated Tax Planning for Real Estate Transactions," Practising Law Institute, 1988—. Commentator: The Nightly Business Report, Public Broadcasting System, 1986-1988; "Inside Real Estate," Public Broadcasting System, 1988. Presenter, California Economic Summit, 1993. *Member:* The Association of the Bar of the City of New York; New York State (Member, Tax Section Committees on Partnerships, 1980—; Income From Real Property, 1980—; Financial Institutions and Financial Futures, 1979-1982) and American (Chairman, ABA Tax Section Committee on Partnerships; Taxation, 1992-1994; Vice Chairman, 1990-1993; Chairman: ABA Tax Section Subcommittee on Partnership Tax Allocations, 1986-1990; ABA Tax Section Subcommittee on Partnership Audit Procedures, 1984-1986; Task Force on Workouts and Debt Restructurings, 1990—; Member, ABA Task Forces on Section 108: Bankruptcy and Workouts, 1991 and on President's Tax Proposals to Congress, 1985) Bar Associations.

(For Biographical data on all personnel, see Professional Biographies at New York, New York)

---

## BAUM, HEDLUND, ARISTEI, GUILFORD & DOWNEY

*A PROFESSIONAL CORPORATION*

Established in 1973

SUITE 950, 12100 WILSHIRE BOULEVARD
**LOS ANGELES, CALIFORNIA 90025**
*Telephone:* 310-207-3233; 800-827-0087
*Facsimile:* 310-820-7444
*Email:* bhagd@bhagd.com
*URL:* http://www.bhagd.com/attorneys/

Washington, D.C. Office: 1250 24th Street, N.W., Suite 300. Telephone: 202-466-0513; 800-827-0097. Facsimile: 202-466-0527.

*Limited only to Plaintiff's Serious Personal Injury and Wrongful Death Accident Litigation nationwide and worldwide; including Aviation Accident Litigation, Airplane Accidents, Bus Accidents, Tractor-Trailer Accidents, Train Accidents, Public Transportation Accidents, General Tort, Mass Disaster Litigation, Multi-District Litigation and Product Liability including Drug Litigation.*

*FIRM PROFILE: Baum, Hedlund, Aristei, Guilford & Downey (previously named Kananack, Murgatroyd, Baum & Hedlund) focuses its nationwide practice on commercial aviation, bus and train litigation. The firm routinely handles the complex evidence and choices of law issues involved in such cases throughout the United States in both state and federal courts. As can be seen on the list of our noteworthy cases, we have worked on many of the most prominent accidents in recent history. Other areas of our practice include general aviation, product liability and mass disaster litigation. The firm was established in 1973 and is now comprised of 30 staff, including 10 attorneys, two of whom are commercial pilots and another a mechanical engineer. We have two offices, one in Los Angeles, California and the other in Washington, D.C. The firm is listed in Martindale-Hubbell's Bar Register of Preeminent Lawyers, which represents the top nine percent of attorneys in terms of legal competence and ethics.*

*The following is a partial listing of the more noteworthy cases in which the firm*
(This Listing Continued)

---

has been involved: *Arrow Air Crash, Gander Newfoundland, 1985; Dupont Plaza Hotel Fire, San Juan, Puerto Rico, 1986; Amtrak/Conrail Train Crash, Chase, Maryland, 1987; Northwest Airlines Crash, Detroit, 1987; Continental Express Crash, Durango, Colorado, 1988; Ford Motor Company School Bus Crash, Carrollton, Kentucky, 1988; Delta Airlines Crash, Dallas, Texas, 1988; Three Rivers Boat Regatta Disaster, Pittsburgh, Pennsylvania, 1988; Hatchie River Bridge Collapse, Covington, Tennessee, 1989; Scenic Air Tours Airline Crash, Hawaii, 1989; United Airlines Crash, Sioux City, Iowa, 1989; Grand Canyon Airlines Crash, Phoenix, Arizona, 1989; Building Collapse, San Francisco Earthquake, 1989; Northwest Airlines Runway Collision, Detroit, 1990; Hot Air Balloon Tour Crash, Phoenix, Arizona, 1990; Aeroperlas Air Crash, Panama City, Panama, 1990; L-Tryptophan Drug Litigation, 1990; Prozac Drug Litigation, 1990; USAir/Skywest Airlines Crash, Los Angeles, 1991; United Airlines Crash, Colorado Springs, Colorado, 1991; Tropic Air Crash, Belize, 1991; Amtrak Train Crash, Camden, South Carolina, 1991; Girl Scouts Bus Crash, Palm Springs, California, 1991; CommutAir (USAir) Airlines Crash, Saranac Lake, New York, 1992; USAir Crash, Flushing, New York, 1992; Adventure Airlines Crash, Grand Canyon, Arizona, 1992; Perris Valley Skydivers Crash, Perris, California, 1992; TWA Jet Fire, JFK Airport, New York, 1992; Hawaii Helicopters Crash, Maui, 1992; Fialuridine - Hepatitis B Drug Litigation, 1992; Cancun Tour Bus Accident, Mexico, 1993; American Stage Lines Tour Bus Accident, Grays Harbor, Washington, 1993; Amtrak Train Derailment, Saraland, Alabama, 1993; U.S. Air Force Bus Accident, Thousand Oaks, California, 1993; Taca Airlines Crash, Guatemala, 1993; China Eastern Airlines Accident, Shemya, Alaska, 1993; Skydive Long Island Crash, East Moriches, New York, 1993; British Tour Bus Accident, Faversham, England, 1993; Northwest Airlink Crash, Hibbing, Minnesota, 1993; Apartment Collapse, Northridge, California Earthquake, 1994; USAir Crash, Charlotte, North Carolina, 1994; Amtrak Train Derailment, near Batavia, New York, 1994; USAir Crash, near Aliquippa, Pennsylvania, 1994; Alfred P. Murrah Building Bombing, Oklahoma City, Oklahoma, 1995; Atlantic Southeast Airlines Crash, near Carrollton, Georgia, 1995; American Airlines Crash, near Cali Colombia, 1995; Amtrak/MARC collision, Silver Spring, Maryland, 1996; ValuJet Airlines Crash, near Miami, Florida, 1996; TWA Explosion, Near East Moriches, New York, 1996.*

**MICHAEL L. BAUM,** born Clinton, Oklahoma, April 10, 1952; admitted to bar, 1985, California; 1986, U.S. District Court, Central District of California; 1989, U.S. District Court, Eastern and Northern Districts of California; 1990, U.S. Court of Appeals, 9th Circuit; 1991, U.S. District Court, Western District of Michigan and U.S. Supreme Court; 1993, District of Columbia; U.S. District Court, Northern District of Ohio. *Education:* University of California at Los Angeles (B.A., summa cum laude, 1982; J.D., 1985). Listed, Bar Register of Preeminent Lawyers; Who's Who in American Law; Who's Who in the World. Member, Plaintiff Steering Committee, United Airlines Crash, Sioux City, Iowa, 1989. Trial Counsel, United Airlines Crash, Sioux City, Iowa; Plaintiff Steering Committee, Northwest Airlines Crash, Detroit, 1990; Plaintiff Steering Committee, USAir 1016 Air Crash at Charlotte, 1994; Plaintiff Steering Committee, Illinois State Court Proceedings for USAir 427 Air Crash near Aliquippa, Pennsylvania, 1994. *Member:* State Bar of California; The District of Columbia Bar; Bar Association of the District of Columbia; Consumer Attorneys of California. **PRACTICE AREAS:** Aviation Accidents and Injuries; Complex and Multi-District Litigation; Products Liability; Mass Disaster Litigation; Wrongful Death; Railroad Accidents and Injuries; Personal Injury.

**PAUL J. HEDLUND,** born Abington, Pennsylvania, June 26, 1946; admitted to bar, 1973, California; 1977, U.S. District Court, Central District of California; 1991, U.S. District Court, Eastern District of California; 1994, U.S. District Court, Northern District of New York and U.S. Court of Appeals, Ninth Circuit and District of Columbia; registered to practice before U.S. Patent and Trademark Office. *Education:* University of Michigan (B.S.M.E., 1968); University of California School of Law at Los Angeles (J.D., 1973). Listed: Bar Register of Preeminent Lawyers; Who's Who in American Law; Who's Who in the World. Member, Trial Counsel, United Airlines Crash, Sioux City, Iowa. *Member:* District of Columbia Bar; Bar Association of the District of Columbia; State Bar of California. **REPORTED CASES:** Sigala v. Anaheim City School District, 15 Cal. App. 4th 661, 19 Cal. Rptr. 2d 38 (1993); Curry v. Continental Airlines, 513 F.2d 45 (9th Cir. 1975). **PRACTICE AREAS:** Airplane Crash Litigation; Aviation Accidents and Injuries; Mass Disaster Litigation; Railroad Accidents and Injuries; School Bus Accidents; Wrongful Death Law; Catastrophic Injury; Complex and Multi-District Litigation.

**J. CLARK ARISTEI,** born Washington, D.C., September 6, 1948; admitted to bar, 1975, California and U.S. District Court, Southern District of California; 1979, U.S. District Court, Central District of California; 1993,
(This Listing Continued)

## BAUM, HEDLUND, ARISTEI, GUILFORD & DOWNEY,
A PROFESSIONAL CORPORATION, Los Angeles—Continued

U.S. District Court, Eastern District of California. *Education:* Los Angeles Harbor College (A.A., 1968); California State University at Long Beach (B.A., cum laude, 1971); University of San Diego (J.D., 1975). Recipient, American Jurisprudence Award in Constitutional Law, 1973. Adjunct Professor of Law, University of West Los Angeles School of Law, 1986—. Listed, Bar Register of Preeminent Lawyers, Participant, Landlord-Tenant Court Settlement Officer Program, 1979, 1981. *Member:* State Bar of California; Consumer Attorneys Association of Los Angeles. **REPORTED CASES:** Penner v. Falk, 153 Cal. App. 3d 858, 200 Cal. Rptr. 661 (1984); Geffen v. County of Los Angeles, 197 Cal. App. 3d 188, 242 Cal. Rptr. 492 (1987). *PRACTICE AREAS:* Catastrophic Injury; School Bus Accidents; Wrongful Death; Products Liability; Railroad Accidents and Injuries; Mass Disaster Litigation; Complex and Multi-District Litigation.

**ROBERT E. GUILFORD,** born Cleveland, Ohio, April 14, 1933; admitted to bar, 1959, California, U.S. District Court, Central District of California and U.S. Court of Appeals, Ninth Circuit; 1964, U.S. District Court, Northern District of California. *Education:* University of Virginia (B.A., with honors in Philosophy); Harvard University (J.D., 1958). Phi Eta Sigma. Raven Society. Jefferson Society. Listed, Bar Register of Preeminent Lawyers. Commercial Pilot's License with Instrument Rating. Former Assistant U.S. Attorney, Central District of California. Chairman, Classic Jet Aircraft Association. Co-Founder, Warbirds of America. V.P., Hunter Flight Test, Ltd. *Member:* State Bar of California; Lawyer-Pilots Bar Association. **REPORTED CASES:** Curry v. Continental Airlines, 513 F.2d 691 (9th Cir. 1975); Baker v. Kipnis, 547 F.2d 1174 (9th Cir. 1976); Pratali v. Gates, 4 Cal. App. 4th 632, 5 Cal. Rptr. 2d 733 (1992); Datner v. Mann Theatres Corp., 145 Call, App. 3d 768, 193 Cal. Rptr. 676 (1983); The People exrel, Department of Public Works v. Salem Dev. Co., 216 Cal,App. 2d 652, 31 Cal Rptr. 193 (1963). *PRACTICE AREAS:* Airplane Crash Litigation; Aviation Accidents and Injuries; Aviation Products Liability; Aviation Torts; Helicopter Crash Litigation; Personal Injury; Wrongful Death.

**WILLIAM J. DOWNEY III,** born Newton, Massachusetts, July 27, 1947; admitted to bar, 1988, California; 1992, U.S. District Court, Central District of California and U.S. District Court, Southern District of California; 1995, U.S. District Court, Eastern District of California. *Education:* Northeastern University (B.S., magna cum laude, 1983); Suffolk University (J.D., cum laude, 1988). Phi Delta Phi. Recipient, American Jurisprudence Award. Listed, Bar Register of Preeminent Lawyers; Who's Who in American Law; Who's Who in the East. Member, Plaintiff Steering Committee, Prozac Product Liability Cases, Indianapolis, Indiana; Plaintiff Steering Committee, Perris Skydivers Crash, Perris, California, 1992; Plaintiff Steering Committee, Fialuridine Product Liability Cases, Washington, D.C.; Plaintiff Steering Committee, Northridge Meadows Apartment collapse, Northridge, California Earthquake, 1994. *Member:* State Bar of California; Consumer Attorneys of California. *PRACTICE AREAS:* Catastrophic Injury; Products Liability - Drugs and Medical Devices; Products Liability; Construction Accidents; Mass Disaster Litigation; Wrongful Death.

---

**JOHN A. GREAVES,** born Kansas City, Missouri, February 18, 1948; admitted to bar, 1992, Iowa, and U.S. District Court, Southern District of Iowa; 1994, California and U.S. District Court, Northern District of California; 1995, U.S. District Court, Central, Eastern and Southern Districts of California and U.S. Court of Appeals, Ninth Circuit. *Education:* University of Missouri at Kansas City (B.A., 1976); Drake University Law School (J.D., with honors, 1992); Drake University College of Business and Public Administration (M.P.A., 1992). Delta Theta Phi. Listed, Bar Register of Preeminent Lawyers; Who's Who in American Law. Airline Transport Pilot Licence, USA, 1982. Member, Plaintiff Steering Committee, Atlantic Southeast Airlines Crash, near Carrollton, Georgia, 1995. *Member:* Iowa State and American Bar Associations; State Bar of California; Iowa Trial Lawyers Association; Association of Trial Lawyers of America; Lawyer-Pilots Bar Association; Consumer Attorneys of California. *PRACTICE AREAS:* Airplane Crash litigation; Aviation Accidents and Injuries; Aviation Products Liability; Helicopter Crash Litigation; Complex and Multi-District Litigation.

**CARA L. BELLE,** born Asheboro, North Carolina, February 8, 1945; admitted to bar, 1988, Pennsylvania; 1989, District of Columbia; 1991, Maryland; 1994, U.S. District Court for the District of Columbia (Not admitted in California). *Education:* University of North Carolina (B.A., Biology, 1968); University of Maryland School of Law (J.D., 1986). Registered Medical Technologist and Registered Specialist, Hematology, American Society of Clinical Pathologists, 1979- 1983. Licensed Insurance Agent, Health Annuities, Maryland, 1986-1989. License, National Association of Securities Dealers, 1987-1989. Listed, Bar Register of Preeminent Lawyers and Strathmore's Who's Who. *Member:* Pennsylvania Bar Association; District of Columbia Bar (Member, Personal Injury and Property Insurance Section); Maryland State Bar Association, Inc.; Bar Association of the District of Columbia; Women's Bar Association of the District of Columbia; American Immigration Lawyers Association. (Resident, Washington, D.C. Office). *PRACTICE AREAS:* Personal Injury Law; Wrongful Death Law; Railroad Accidents and Injuries; Mass Disaster Litigation; Truck Accidents.

**ROBERT F. FOSS,** born Portland, Maine, November 21, 1952; admitted to bar, 1994, California; 1995, U.S. District Court, Central District of California. *Education:* No. Virginia Community College; University of Honolulu (J.D., 1994). Listed, Bar Register of Preeminent Lawyers. *Member:* Los Angeles County Bar Association; State Bar of California. *PRACTICE AREAS:* Wrongful Death; Personal Injury; Mass Disaster Litigation; Aviation Accidents and Injuries; Products Liability.

**KAREN A. BARTH,** born Dubuque, Iowa, December 8, 1966; admitted to bar, 1995, California and U.S. District Court, Central District of California. *Education:* Colorado State University (B.A., 1989); University of California School of Law, Davis (J.D., 1995). Member, Moot Court Board. National Moot Court and Trial Competitions. Legal Intern, California Court of Appeal, Third District. Member, The Barristers. The South Central Legal Services Committee. Member, Barristers Partners for Success Committee. Member, Trial Practice Inn of Court. *Member:* Los Angeles County and American Bar Associations; Women's Lawyers Association of Los Angeles; National Association of Women Lawyers. *PRACTICE AREAS:* Class Actions; Complex and Multi-District Litigation; Wrongful Death; Products Liability; Mass Disaster Litigation; Personal Injury.

**V. NEIL FORN, II,** born Cincinnati, Ohio, July 8, 1957; admitted to bar, 1996, California. *Education:* University of Southern California (M.A., 1986); Pepperdine University School of Law (J.D., 1995). *Member:* Environmental Law Society; Entertainment Law Society. *PRACTICE AREAS:* Personal Injury; Wrongful Death; Mass Disaster Litigation; Complex and Multi-District Litigation.

Languages: Spanish, German and French

REFERENCE: Union Bank.

---

## JOAN S. BAUMAN

Established in 1977

2029 CENTURY PARK EAST, SUITE 2610
**LOS ANGELES, CALIFORNIA 90067**
Telephone: 310-203-8267
Fax: 310-203-8644
Email: JoanBauman@aol.com

*Family and Divorce Law, Premarital Agreements, Arbitration and Mediation.*

**JOAN S. BAUMAN,** born New Jersey, October 9, 1950; admitted to bar, 1977, California. *Education:* California State University at Northridge (B.A., 1972); University of La Verne (J.D., 1977). Board Member, 1980-1986 and President, Board of Directors, 1984, San Fernando Valley Community Mental Health Center, Inc. *Member:* San Fernando Valley (Member, Board of Trustees, 1985-1988; Chairperson, Membership Benefits Committee, 1985-1987) and Los Angeles County (Member, Family Law Section) Bar Associations; State Bar of California (Member, Family Law Section). (Certified Specialist, Family Law, The State Bar of California Board of Legal Specialization). *REPORTED CASES:* In Re Marriage of White, 1987, 192 CA3d 1022.

---

## BEAM, BROBECK & WEST

**LOS ANGELES, CALIFORNIA**

(See Santa Ana)

*Civil Litigation. Trial and Appellate Practice. Health Care Provider Malpractice, Construction, Environmental Litigation, Government Tort Liability, Products Liability and General Personal Injury Liability.*

# PROFESSIONAL BIOGRAPHIES

## BECK, DE CORSO, DALY, BARRERA & OH
*A PROFESSIONAL LAW CORPORATION*
Established in 1984
**601 WEST FIFTH STREET, 12TH FLOOR**
**LOS ANGELES, CALIFORNIA 90071-2025**
Telephone: 213-688-1198
Fax: 213-489-7532
Email: beckdecorso@earthlink.net
URL: http://www.earthlink.net/~beckdecorso

*Civil and Criminal Litigation in State and Federal Courts and before Administrative Agencies.*

FIRM PROFILE: Beck, De Corso, Daly, Barrera & Oh was founded in 1984 by Mark Beck and Anthony De Corso. The firm practices in both state and federal courts, concentrating on litigation including civil and criminal trials and appeals, administrative proceedings, and other alternative dispute resolutions proceedings.

In its criminal practice, the firm represents individuals and businesses from the pre-indictment, investigatory phase (including grand jury and corporate internal investigations) through any sentencing and appeal, in various discrete practice areas, including but not limited to the following: financial and securities crimes, bribery and public corruption, defense contracting crimes, import/export violations, environmental offenses, and fraud and abuse in health care.

In its civil practice, the firm represents plaintiffs and defendants in complex business litigation (often parallel to criminal proceedings) involving matters such as forfeitures, unfair competition, anti-trust, RICO, fraud, defamation, contract claims, and defense of qui tam (False Claims Act) suits.

In its administrative practice, the firm represents individuals and companies in licensing and permit revocations, security clearance reviews, forfeiture actions, and actions to debar or suspend government contractors.

**MARK E. BECK,** born Los Angeles, California, September 4, 1950; admitted to bar, 1975, California; 1976, U.S. District Court, Central District of California; 1977, U.S. Court of Appeals, Ninth Circuit; 1980, U.S. Supreme Court; 1983, U.S. Court of Appeals, Federal Circuit. *Education:* Stanford University (B.A., 1972); Georgetown University (J.D., 1975). Phi Beta Kappa. President, Georgetown University Student Bar Association, 1974-1975. Assistant U.S. Attorney, 1977-1981 and Assistant Chief, Criminal Division, 1981, Central District of California. Co-Author with Jennifer B. Smith: "Representing Government Contractors Accused of Misconduct," California Lawyer Magazine, May, 1987. *Member:* Los Angeles County and American Bar Associations; State Bar of California.

**ANTHONY A. DE CORSO,** born Allentown, Pennsylvania, February 13, 1953; admitted to bar, 1983, California and U.S. District Court, District of California; 1984, U.S. Court of Appeals, Ninth Circuit; 1985, U.S. Court of Appeals for the Federal Circuit. *Education:* Purdue University (B.A., 1974; Ph.D., 1980); Loyola Marymount University (J.D., cum laude, 1983). Phi Beta Kappa. *Member:* Los Angeles County and American Bar Associations; State Bar of California; California Attorneys for Criminal Justice.

**BRYAN D. DALY,** born Suffern, New York, January 15, 1959; admitted to bar, 1985, California and U.S. District Court, Central District of California; 1990, U.S. Court of Appeals, Ninth Circuit. *Education:* Ramapo College (B.A., with high honors, 1982); Rutgers University (J.D., with honors, 1985). With U.S. Attorneys Office, Criminal Division, Central District of California, 1990-1995. Director, Southern California Defense Procurement Fraud Task Force, 1991-1995. *Member:* Los Angeles County and American Bar Associations; State Bar of California.

**TERESA R. BARRERA,** born Portland, Oregon, December 6, 1959; admitted to bar, 1987, California; 1988, U.S. District Court, Central District of California. *Education:* Harvard University (A.B., 1982); University of California at Davis (J.D., 1987). *Member:* Los Angeles County and American Bar Associations; State Bar of California; Mexican-American Bar Association of Los Angeles.

**ANGELA E. OH,** born Los Angeles, California, September 8, 1955; admitted to bar, 1986, California. *Education:* University of California at Los Angeles (B.A., 1977; M.P.H., 1981); University of California at Davis (J.D., 1986). President, Korean American Bar Association of Southern California, 1993. Chair, Federal Judicial Nominations Committee, 1993-1995. Lawyer Representative, 9th Circuit Judicial Conference, 1995-1996. *Member:* Los Angeles County and American Bar Associations; State Bar of California;

*(This Listing Continued)*

Korean-American Bar Association of Southern California. **LANGUAGES:** Korean.

---

**PETER J. DIEDRICH,** born San Francisco, California, November 8, 1955; admitted to bar, 1981, California. *Education:* University of California at San Diego (B.A., magna cum laude, 1977); Georgetown University (J.D., 1981). Editor, Law and Policy in International Business, 1980-1981. *Member:* Los Angeles County and American Bar Associations; The State Bar of California. *PRACTICE AREAS:* Business and Commercial Litigation; Real Estate Litigation; Construction Litigation.

**JOAN M. STEINMANN,** born Minneapolis, Minnesota, February 21, 1961; admitted to bar, 1989, California, U.S. District Court, Central District of California and U.S. Court of Appeals, Ninth Circuit; 1994, U.S. District Court, District of Arizona; 1995, U.S. District Court, Southern District of California; 1996, U.S. District Court, Northern District of California. *Education:* University of Minnesota (B.A., 1986; J.D., cum laude, 1989). Phi Kappa Phi. Member, 1987-1988, and Managing Editor, 1988-1989, University of Minnesota Law Review. *Member:* Century City, Los Angeles County and American Bar Associations; State Bar of California.

**EVAN SCHEFFEL,** born New York, N.Y., August 7, 1969; admitted to bar, 1996, California and U.S. District Court, Central District of California. *Education:* University of South Florida (B.A., cum laude, 1990); Nova University (M.B.A., 1992); Thomas M. Cooley Law School (J.D., cum laude, 1995); Georgetown University (LL.M., in White Collar Criminal and Employment Law, 1996). Recipient: American Jurisprudence Award: Certificate of Merit: Constitutional Law I, Advocacy, Lawyering Before Trial, Alternative Dispute Resolution, Scholarly Writing I, Entertainment Law. Assistant Editor, Thomas M. Cooley Law Review, 1995. Association of Trial Lawyers of America National Trial Advocacy Competition, 1994.

### OF COUNSEL

**GODFREY ISAAC,** born Chicago, Illinois, April 25, 1925; admitted to bar, 1952, California; 1972, District of Columbia; 1974, U.S. Court of Appeals, Ninth Circuit; 1975, U.S. Supreme Court. *Education:* University of Southern California; Loyola University (J.D., cum laude, 1951). Phi Delta Phi. Author: "Writ of Administrative Mandamus" PLI Course Handbook Series (1982); "I'll See You in Court" (1979); Alternative Fee Arrangements In a Competitive Market," Los Angeles Lawyer, 1994. *Member:* Los Angeles County and American (Chairman, Sub-Committee on Small Firm and Complex Litigation, 1978-1979) Bar Associations; American Academy of Forensic Sciences (Chairman: Jurisprudence Section, 1979-1981; Program Committee, Jurisprudence Section, 1976-1977). *PRACTICE AREAS:* Trial Practice; Medical Law; White Collar Law; Criminal Defense Law; Wrongful Termination/Employment at Will; Injunctions; Entertainment Litigation; Administrative Mandamus; Arbitrations and Mediations.

---

## BECKMAN, DAVIS, SMITH & RUDDY LLP
**601 SOUTH FIGUEROA STREET, SUITE 2600**
**LOS ANGELES, CALIFORNIA 90017-5704**
Telephone: 213-624-4900
Facsimile: 213-624-5300

*General Civil Trial and Appellate Practice, Insurance, Employment and Discrimination, Products Liability, Environmental and Probate Law.*

### MEMBERS OF FIRM

**BRUCE A. BECKMAN,** born Lomita, California, April 25, 1930; admitted to bar, 1959, California; 1985, U.S. Supreme Court. *Education:* University of California at Los Angeles (B.A., 1953; LL.B., 1958). Order of the Coif. Member, Board of Editors, U.C.L.A. Law Review, 1957-1958. Co-Author: "A Guide to Obtaining Regulatory Approvals For New Industrial Facilities in California," 17 San Diego Law Review 979, 1980; "Problem Areas in the Exemption Process Under the Powerplant and Industrial Fuel Use Act of 1978," 29 Kansas Law Review, 1981. Author: "Constitutional Issues In Insurance Claim Litigation," 22 Tort & Ins. Prac. J. 244, 1987. Author: "Liability of Non-Life Insurance companies for Punitive Damages Claims in the United States," 56 Non-Life Insurance Journal, 195 (oral presentation), 235 [article] (August, 1994), Journal of the Non-Life Insurance Institute of Japan, Article in English. Member, California Attorney General's Environmental Task Force, 1972-1978. Member, Los Angeles County Watershed Commission, 1981-1990. Member, Los Angeles City Attorney's Regulatory Reform Task Force, 1982-1985. *Member:* Los Angeles County (Member, Environmental Law Section) and American (Member, Sections on: Natural Resources; Urban, State and Local Government Law; Chair,

*(This Listing Continued)*

## BECKMAN, DAVIS, SMITH & RUDDY LLP, Los Angeles—Continued

Life Insurance Law Committee, Tort and Insurance Practice, 1992-1993; Business Law) Bar Associations; State Bar of California (Member: Public Law Section; Real Estate Section); Conference of Insurance Counsel. *PRACTICE AREAS:* Life, Health and Disability Insurance Law; Appellate Practice; Constitutional Law; Environmental Law; Real Estate.

**RICHARD T. DAVIS, JR.,** born Houston, Texas, April 26, 1945; admitted to bar, 1971, California. *Education:* University of Texas (B.A., with honors, 1968; J.D., with high honors, 1970). Phi Delta Phi; Chancellors; Order of the Coif. Associate Editor, Texas Law Review, 1969-1970. *Member:* Los Angeles County and American Bar Associations; State Bar of California. *PRACTICE AREAS:* Professional Liability Defense and Insurance Coverage; Life, Health and Disability Insurance Law; Products Liability; Real Estate and Commercial Litigation.

**JEFFREY P. SMITH,** born Cambridge, Massachusetts, July 24, 1947; admitted to bar, 1976, California. *Education:* Pomona College (B.A., 1969); University of Southern California (J.D., 1976). *Member:* Los Angeles County and American Bar Associations; State Bar of California. *PRACTICE AREAS:* Life, Health and Disability Insurance Law; ERISA; Civil Litigation; General Practice.

**CATHERINE HUNT RUDDY,** born San Bernardino, California, June 25, 1953; admitted to bar, 1977, California. *Education:* University of Southern California (B.S., magna cum laude, 1974; J.D., 1977). Member, Southern California Law Review, 1975-1976. Alpha Lambda Delta; Phi Kappa Phi; Beta Gamma Sigma. *Member:* Los Angeles County and American Bar Associations; State Bar of California. *PRACTICE AREAS:* Life, Health and Disability Insurance Law; ERISA; Contract Dispute Resolution; Employment.

### OF COUNSEL

**SIDNEY W. BISHOP,** born Denver, Colorado, October 28, 1926; admitted to bar, 1950, Colorado; 1958, California. *Education:* Regis College (B.S., 1949); University of Denver (Westminster) (J.D., 1950). Assistant Postmaster General of the United States, 1962-1963. Deputy Postmaster General of the United States, 1963-1964. *Member:* Los Angeles County (Member: Corporate Law Departments Section, Executive Committee, 1975-1991; Chair, 1978-1979; Continuing Legal Education Committee, 1991-1992), Federal and American (Member: Tort and Insurance Practice Section; Life Insurance Law Committee; Health Insurance Law Committee, Chair, 1978-1979; Public Regulation of Insurance Committee) Bar Associations; State Bar of California (Chair, 1992-1993, Insurance Law Committee); Association of Life Insurance Counsel; American Counsel of Life Insurance (Member, Legal Section); Institute for Corporate Counsel Emeritus (Member, Board of Governors); Conference of Insurance Counsel (Chair, 1980); Prudential Insurance Company of America (House Counsel, 1956-1961; 1964-1968); American Insurance Association (General Counsel, 1968-1970); Beneficial Standard Life Insurance Company (General Counsel, 1973-1991). *PRACTICE AREAS:* Disability Insurance; Insurance Regulation; Life and Health Insurance; Unfair Insurance Practices; Reinsurance.

**CHERYL A. DE BARI,** born Jersey City, New Jersey, September 9, 1959; admitted to bar, 1984, California. *Education:* Dickinson College (B.A., cum laude, 1981); University of San Francisco (J.D., with honors, 1984). Recipient, American Jurisprudence Award. *Member:* Los Angeles County Bar Association; The State Bar of California. *PRACTICE AREAS:* Insurance Law; ERISA; Subrogation; Products Liability.

### ASSOCIATES

**LAURA L. CHAPMAN,** born New Orleans, Louisiana, October 7, 1964; admitted to bar, 1993, California. *Education:* Smith College (A.B., 1986); University of Southern California (J.D., 1993). *Member:* State Bar of California. *PRACTICE AREAS:* Insurance Litigation; Employment Litigation; Commercial Litigation.

**BRIAN F. ROWE,** born Corvallis, Oregon, September 22, 1962; admitted to bar, 1993, California and U.S. District Court, Central District of California; Registered to Practice Before U.S. Patent Office. *Education:* University of California at Davis (B.S., 1986); Loyola University of Los Angeles (J.D., 1993). *Member:* Los Angeles County Bar Association. *PRACTICE AREAS:* Insurance; Bankruptcy; General Practice.

## BEEHLER & PAVITT
### LOS ANGELES, CALIFORNIA
(See Culver City)

*Patent, Trademark and Copyright Law. Unfair Competition Law. Trial Practice in the Federal Courts.*

## BEHR AND ABRAMSON

A Partnership including A Professional Corporation

2049 CENTURY PARK EAST, 26TH FLOOR
### LOS ANGELES, CALIFORNIA 90067
Telephone: 310-556-9200
Telecopier: 310-556-9229

*Entertainment and Technology Transactions.*

**JOEL BEHR, (A P.C.),** born Rockford, Illinois, October 22, 1942; admitted to bar, 1968, California. *Education:* University of Southern California (B.S., 1964); University of Chicago (J.D., 1967). Beta Gamma Sigma. Member, Board of Directors, University of Chicago Alumni Association, 1971-1974. *Member:* Beverly Hills (Co-Chairman, Entertainment Law Committee, 1981-1983; Co-Director, Beverly Hills Bar/USC Entertainment Law Institute Symposia, 1981-1983; Continuing Member of Planning Board), Century City, Los Angeles County and American (Member, Forum Committee on the Entertainment and Sports Industries, 1982-1983) Bar Associations; State Bar of California; Los Angeles Copyright Society (President, 1986-1987 and Member, Board of Trustees, 1981-1988). *PRACTICE AREAS:* Entertainment Law. *Email:* JAYBEEJD@aol.com

**HOWARD ANDREW ABRAMSON,** born Brooklyn, New York, October 19, 1963; admitted to bar, 1988, New Jersey; 1989, New York and California. *Education:* University of Pennsylvania (B.A., summa cum laude, 1985); Harvard Law School (J.D., cum laude, 1988). Phi Beta Kappa. Law Clerk for Justice Daniel J. O'Hern, Supreme Court of New Jersey, 1988-1989. *Member:* Beverly Hills and Los Angeles County Bar Associations; State Bar of California. *PRACTICE AREAS:* Entertainment Law.

**DENNIS N. CLINE,** born Orange, California, August 10, 1954; admitted to bar, 1987, California. *Education:* University of California at Los Angeles (B.A., summa cum laude, 1977); Boalt Hall School of Law, University of California (J.D., 1987). Associate Editor, California Law Review, 1986-1987. Recipient: American Jurisprudence Award for Computer Law, 1986; The Thelen-Marrin Memorial Award, 1987. Author: Comment, "Copyright Protection of Software in the EEC: The Competing Policies Underlying Community and National Law and the Case for Harmonization," 75 California Law Review 633, 1987. *Member:* Los Angeles County Bar Association; State Bar of California. *LANGUAGES:* Spanish. *PRACTICE AREAS:* Entertainment Law.

**NORMAN H. BECKER,** born Los Angeles, California, December 3, 1967; admitted to bar, 1992, California; 1993, U.S. District Court, Central District of California and U.S. Court of Appeals, Ninth Circuit. *Education:* University of California, Berkeley (A.B., with honors, 1989); University of California, Los Angeles (J.D., 1992). Assistant Managing Editor, Federal Communications Law Journal, 1991-1992. *Member:* Los Angeles County, Beverly Hills and American Bar Associations; State Bar of California; Constitutional Rights Foundation (Member, Advisory Council; Sports and Law Committee). *PRACTICE AREAS:* Entertainment Law.

**ADAM DAVID KALLER,** born Flint, Michigan, September 15, 1966; admitted to bar, 1991, California, U.S. District Court, Central District and Southern Districts of California and U.S. Court of Appeals, Ninth Circuit. *Education:* University of Southern California (B.S., 1988); Whittier College School of Law (J.D., 1991). President, Student Division, The Association of Trial Lawyers of America, 1990-1991. *Member:* Beverly Hills and Los Angeles County Bar Associations; State Bar of California. *PRACTICE AREAS:* Entertainment Law.

## BELCHER, HENZIE & BIEGENZAHN
*A PROFESSIONAL CORPORATION*
Established in 1950

333 SOUTH HOPE STREET, SUITE 3650
**LOS ANGELES, CALIFORNIA 90071-1479**
Telephone: 213-624-8293
Telecopier: 213-895-6082

*Aviation, Product Liability, General Civil Trial and Appellate Practice, Insurance Defense, Personal Injury.*

*FIRM PROFILE: Belcher, Henzie & Biegenzahn specializes in defending insured and uninsured clients in a wide range of tort and business matters. Members of the firm litigate throughout the State of California in both Federal and State Courts, and in other jurisdictions throughout the United States.*

**FRANK B. BELCHER** (1891-1979).

**DAVID BERNARD** (1931-1978).

**JOHN S. CURTIS,** born Glen Cove, New York, October 15, 1945; admitted to bar, 1972, California. *Education:* University of Redlands (B.A., 1967); Hastings College of Law, University of California (J.D., 1971). Phi Delta Phi; Order of the Coif. *Member:* Los Angeles County and American Bar Associations; The State Bar of California; Association of Southern California Defense Counsel. **PRACTICE AREAS:** General Negligence Trials & Appeals; Insurance Defense Law; Products Liability Law (Defective Products); Casualty Insurance Law; Federal Practice.

**E. LEE HORTON,** born Fort Worth, Texas, May 16, 1944; admitted to bar, 1973, California. *Education:* Texas A. & M. University and University of California at Santa Barbara (B.A., 1967); Southwestern University (J.D., magna cum laude, 1973). Editor, Southwestern University Law Review, 1972-1973. *Member:* Los Angeles County and American Bar Associations; The State Bar of California; Lawyer-Pilot Bar Association. Fellow, American College of Trial Lawyers. [Capt., U.S. Army Reserve, Active Duty, 1967-1970]. **PRACTICE AREAS:** Airplane Crash Litigation; Aviation Law; Products Liability Law; Labor Law; Business Law; Defective Products.

**WILLIAM T. DELHAGEN,** born Larchmont, New York, August 13, 1944; admitted to bar, 1975, California; 1976, U.S. District Court, Southern and Central Districts of California; 1977, U.S. Court of Appeals, Ninth Circuit; 1983, U.S. Supreme Court; 1989, U.S. District Court, Northern and Eastern Districts of California. *Education:* Massachusetts Institute of Technology (B.S.A.E., 1966); University of Southern California (M.S.A.E., 1969); Loyola University of Los Angeles (J.D., 1975). Advanced Systems Project Engineer, Rockwell International, 1966-1975. *Member:* Los Angeles County and American (Member, Litigation Section) Bar Associations; American Board of Trial Advocates; Association of Southern California Defense Counsel; Lawyers-Pilots Bar Association. **PRACTICE AREAS:** Airplane Crash Litigation; Products Liability Law; Litigation Defense Law; Accident and Personal Injury Law; Business Law.

**JULIA AZRAEL,** born Seattle, Washington, June 15, 1950; admitted to bar, 1982, District of Columbia; 1983, California. *Education:* Stanford University (B.A., 1968); Fordham University (J.D., 1982). Clerk to Judge Richard Salzman, D.C. Superior Court. *Member:* Los Angeles County Bar Association; The District of Columbia Bar; State Bar of California; Association of Southern California Defense Counsel. **LANGUAGES:** Russian and French. **PRACTICE AREAS:** Civil Trials.

---

**JEFFREY L. HORWITH,** born Stamford, Connecticut, April 30, 1956; admitted to bar, 1983, California, U.S. District Court, Central and Southern Districts of California and U.S. Court of Appeals, Ninth Circuit. *Education:* University of Southern California (B.S., cum laude, 1978; J.D., 1983). *Member:* Los Angeles County and American Bar Associations; Association of Southern California Defense Counsel. **PRACTICE AREAS:** Litigation; Products Liability Law; Insurance Defense Law; Motor Vehicle Litigation; Aviation Law.

**GEORGETTE RENATA HERGET,** born Brooklyn, New York, February 28, 1949; admitted to bar, 1980, California; 1981, U.S. District Court, Central, Southern and Northern Districts of California and U.S. Court of Appeals, Ninth Circuit; 1984, U.S. Supreme Court. *Education:* State University of New York at Albany (B.A., cum laude, 1970); Whittier College (J.D., cum laude, 1980). Member, 1977-1980 and Chairperson, 1979-1980, Moot Court Honors Board. Regional Director, ABA National Appellate Advocacy Competition, 1979-1980. Recipient: ABA Silver Key Award; American Jurisprudence Award for Outstanding Achievement in the Study of Wills. Adjunct Professor of Law, Whittier College School of Law, 1981-1982. Contributing Author: *Insurance Handbook for Business Litigators,* 1989. *Member:* Los Angeles County (Member, Conference of Delegates to State Bar Convention, 1983) and American (Member, Sections on: Tort and Insurance Practice) Bar Associations; State Bar of California; Lawyer-Pilots Bar Association. **PRACTICE AREAS:** Insurance Defense Law; Aviation Law; General Civil Practice; Accident and Personal Injury Law; Insurance Coverage Law.

**DAVID L. BONAR,** born Durham, North Carolina, October 9, 1957; admitted to bar, 1990, California, U.S. District Court, Eastern, Central, Northern and Southern Districts of California and U.S. Court of Appeals, Ninth Circuit. *Education:* Claremont McKenna College (B.A., 1981); Loyola University of Los Angeles (J.D., 1990). Recipient, Jurisprudence Award in Federal Taxation. Member: Association of U.S. Army; Army Aviation Association of America; American Helicopter Society; Helicopter Association International; Airborne Law Enforcement Association. Commercial Pilot, 1981. *Member:* Los Angeles County and American Bar Associations; State Bar of California (Member, Litigation Section). [Captain, U.S. Army, 1981-1987; U.S. Army Reserve, 1987-1994]. **PRACTICE AREAS:** Aviation Products Liability Litigation.

**RAYMOND E. HANE, III,** born Torrance, California, May 11, 1960; admitted to bar, 1990, California; 1991, U.S. District Court, Central, Eastern, Southern and Northern Districts of California and U.S. Court of Appeals, Ninth Circuit. *Education:* University of California (B.A., 1982) Southwestern University School of Law (J.D., cum laude, 1990). Editor, Southwestern University Law Review, 1989-1990; Dean's Scholar, 1987-1990. Author: "Boyle v. United Technologies: The Military Contractor Defense Expands the Scope of Tort Immunity for Design Defects in Military Equipment," Southwestern University Law Review, Volume 19, No. 3, 1990. *Member:* Los Angeles County and American (Member, Section on Litigation) Bar Associations; State Bar of California. **LANGUAGES:** Spanish. **PRACTICE AREAS:** General Civil Trials and Appellate Practice; Aviation Law; Products Liability Law.

**JAMES C. HILDEBRAND,** born Los Angeles, California, July 19, 1955; admitted to bar, 1990, California. *Education:* University of California at Santa Cruz (B.A., 1978); Southwestern University (J.D., cum laude, 1990). Member, 1988-1989, and Research Editor, 1989-1990, Southwestern University Law Review. *Member:* Los Angeles County Bar Association; State Bar of California. **PRACTICE AREAS:** Civil Trials; Appellate Practice; Aviation Law; Products Liability; Insurance Defense.

**ROBERT S. COOPER,** born Palo Alto, California, March 6, 1960; admitted to bar, 1992, California and U.S. District Court, Central District of California. *Education:* University of California at Berkeley (B.A., 1982); Lewis & Clark-Northwestern College of Law; Loyola University of Los Angeles (J.D., 1992). Judicial Extern, U.S. District Court, Central District of California, and the Honorable Magistrate John R. Kronenberg, 1991. **LANGUAGES:** Spanish. **PRACTICE AREAS:** Civil Trials; Appellate Practice; Aviation Law; Products Liability; Toxic Tort Law; Accident and Personal Injury Law.

**WUN-EE CHELSEA CHEN,** born Dover, New Jersey, February 24, 1964; admitted to bar, 1992, California, U.S. District Court, Central, Southern, Northern and Eastern Districts of California and U.S. Court of Appeals, Ninth Circuit. *Education:* Harvard University (B.A., cum laude, 1987); Loyola Law School of Los Angeles (J.D., 1992). Recipient, American Jurisprudence Award for Excellent Achievement in Civil Procedure Writing. Editor-in-Chief, Loyola of Los Angeles Entertainment Law Journal, 1991-1992. Author: "Pinning Opinion to the First Amendment Mat," Loyola of Los Angeles Entertainment Law Journal, Vol. 11, No. 2, p. 567, 1991. *Member:* Los Angeles County and American Bar Associations; State Bar of California. **LANGUAGES:** Taiwanese; Mandarin. **REPORTED CASES:** Continental Airlines, Inc. v. Intra Brokers, Inc., 24 F.3d 1099 (9th Cir. 1994). **PRACTICE AREAS:** Civil (General Civil) Practice; Appellate Practice; Aviation Law; Products Liability Defense; Business Law.

**JOHN ERIN MCOSKER,** born Harbor City, California, February 15, 1967; admitted to bar, 1993, California and U.S. District Court, Central District of California. *Education:* Loyola Marymount University; University of Notre Dame (B.A., 1989); Santa Clara University (J.D., 1993). *Member:* State Bar of California.

**MARY E. GRAM,** born Ann Arbor, Michigan, September 21, 1956; admitted to bar, 1993, California and U.S. District Court, Central District of California. *Education:* University of Oklahoma (B.F.A., with honors, 1978); Southwestern University School of Law (J.D., summa cum laude, 1993). Phi Delta Phi. Moot Court Honors Program, 1992-1993. Member,

*(This Listing Continued)*

**BELCHER, HENZIE & BIEGENZAHN,** A PROFESSIONAL CORPORATION, Los Angeles—Continued

Southwestern University Law Review, 1992-1993. *Member:* State Bar of California; California Association of Trial Lawyers. **PRACTICE AREAS:** Civil Trial; Appellate Practice; Products Liability.

*OF COUNSEL*

**GEORGE M. HENZIE,** born Pomona, California, November 5, 1920; admitted to bar, 1949, California. *Education:* Stanford University (B.A., 1942; J.D., 1949). Member, Board of Editors, Stanford Law Review. Lecturer in Law, Stanford University Law School, 1955-1978. *Member:* Los Angeles County (Trustee, 1966-1968) and American Bar Associations; The State Bar of California (Member, Board of Bar Examiners, 1971-1978). Fellow, American College of Trial Lawyers.

**LEO J. BIEGENZAHN,** born Seattle, Washington, February 14, 1926; admitted to bar, 1954, California. *Education:* Stanford University (A.B., 1951; J.D., 1954). Phi Delta Phi. Order of the Coif. *Member:* Los Angeles County (Chairman, Members Insurance Committee, 1971-1973) and American Bar Associations; The State Bar of California (Member, State Bar Disciplinary Board, 1974-1980). Fellow, American College of Trial Lawyers.

**JAMES M. DERR,** born Santa Monica, California, November 11, 1945; admitted to bar, 1980, California; 1993, Virgin Islands. *Education:* California State University at Northridge (B.A., 1970); Southwestern University (J.D., magna cum laude, 1980). Member: Order of the Barristers; Moot Court Board of Governors. Airline Transport Pilot, Certified Flight Instructor, single and multi-engine, Ground Instructor, advanced and instrument and Airframe and Powerplant Mechanic. Director of Charter Operations and Chief Pilot, Golden West Skyways. Director of Operations and Maintenance and Chief Pilot, All Island Air. *Member:* Los Angeles County Bar Association; The State Bar of California. [With U.S. Air Force, 1964-1967]. (Also Practicing Individually at 5-6 Kongens Gade, Suite B4, P.O. Box 664, Charlotte Amalie, St. Thomas, U.S. Virgin Islands 00804). **PRACTICE AREAS:** Business Law; Aviation Law; Airplane Crash Litigation; Civil Practice; Insurance Defense Law.

REPRESENTATIVE CLIENTS: Alaska Airlines; Allied Signal/Bendix; Allison Engine Company; American Airlines; Beech Acceptance; Beech Aerospace Services, Inc.; Beech Aircraft; Beechcraft West; Burt Rutan; Cessna Aircraft; Caloric, Inc.; Continental Airlines; Northwest Airlines; Southwest Airlines; Trans World Airlines; United Airlines; Aluminum Company of America (ALCOA); Benton Harbor Engineering; C.E.& M. Co./PACECO; Fruehauf Trailer; Inland Surgery Center; Kelly Springfield; Kelsey-Hayes; Kocks Crane & Marine; Koehring Cranes; Mark C. Bloome; Mobay Chemical; Monsanto; Raytheon Co.; TEREX; Wysong & Miles; Associated Aviation Underwriters; Aviation Adjustment Bureau; Aviation Claims Center; Chubb Insurance; Commercial Union Insurance; Fidelity Bankers Life Insurance; Fireman's Fund; Lumbermen's Underwriting Alliance; North Pacific Insurance; Progressive Casualty Insurance; Ranger Insurance; State Farm Mutual; Shand, Morahan & Co.; Signal Aviation Underwriters; United States Fire Insurance; General Motors Corp.; Hecny Transportation; Puritan-Bennett Corp.; Temcor; Tnemec Co., Inc.; Western Wheel; The May Department Stores Co.; The Timken Co.; Montgomery Ward.; Civil Air Patrol; Crum & Forster; US Air, Inc.; Hobart Brothers Co.; Preferred Physicians Mutual; McCauley Propellers.
REFERENCE: Bank of America (Los Angeles Main Office).

---

# BELIN RAWLINGS & BADAL

Established in 1990

11601 WILSHIRE BOULEVARD, SUITE 2200
**LOS ANGELES, CALIFORNIA 90025-1758**
Telephone: 310-575-5300
Fax: 310-445-0884

*General Commercial Litigation Practice in all State and Federal Courts. Arbitration, Mediation and Dispute Resolutions. Administrative Hearings and Appeals, International Litigation. Firm Specialties include: securities, antitrust, financial institutions, real estate and construction defect litigation.*

FIRM PROFILE: *Belin Rawlings & Badal is a Los Angeles law firm which was formed in July, 1990. The principal areas of the firm's practice are complex commercial litigation and dispute resolution and the counseling of clients in the avoidance of commercial disputes. The firm's guiding principles are to provide its clients with legal services of the highest quality, to employ efficiencies and economies which allow the work to be performed at a fair price, and to emphasize a high degree of personal service in connection with its client relationships. Quality, creativity, integrity, efficiency, and an uncompromising accessibility to clients are the backbone of Belin Rawlings & Badal's approach. The firm believes that its greatest assets are a talented group of lawyers committed to the practice of law, and a satisfied group of clients. The law firm is listed in the Bar Register of Preeminent Lawyers.*

(This Listing Continued)

CAA510B

---

*MEMBERS OF FIRM*

**DANIEL N. BELIN,** born Washington, D.C., February 28, 1938; admitted to bar, 1962, Iowa; 1963, California; 1969, District of Columbia. *Education:* University of Michigan (B.S., cum laude, 1959); Harvard University (LL.B., 1962). Phi Beta Kappa; Phi Kappa Phi. Recipient, Honorary Fellowship, The Hebrew University of Jerusalem, 1980. Member, 1978—, President, 1986-1990, Chairman, 1990-1994, Board of Trustees, Los Angeles County Museum of Art. Member, Board of Governors, The Music Center of Los Angeles County, 1980—. Member, Board of Directors, Los Angeles Philharmonic Association, 1986—. Member, University of California at Los Angeles School of Medicine Board of Visitors, 1984—. Member, Board of Trustees, The Ahmanson Foundation, 1980—. Member, Board of Trustees, Samuel H. Kress Foundation, 1991—. *Member:* Los Angeles County, Iowa State and American Bar Associations; District of Columbia Bar; State Bar of California.

**DOUGLAS M. RAWLINGS,** born Oakland, California, April 3, 1947; admitted to bar, 1974, California. *Education:* Duke University (B.A., magna cum laude, 1971); Yale University (J.D., 1974). Phi Beta Kappa. President, 1992—, Member, 1990—, Board of Trustees, South Bay/Harbor Interreligious Council. *Member:* Los Angeles County (Member, Section on Barristers and International Law), American (Member, Sections on International Law; Litigation) and International (Member, Section on Business Law) Bar Associations; State Bar of California. [Capt., U.S. Air Force, Department of Judge Advocate General, 1975-1979]. **LANGUAGES:** Finnish, German (Read).

**ROBERT G. BADAL,** born Albuquerque, New Mexico, May 1, 1947; admitted to bar, 1974, District of Columbia; 1978, California. *Education:* University of Pennsylvania (B.A., cum laude, 1969); Harvard University (J.D., 1973). Phi Beta Kappa. Attorney, Federal Trade Commission, Washington, D.C., 1973-1976; Acting Regional Director, Federal Trade Commission, Los Angeles, California, 1978. Member, California State Bar Council of Delegates, Los Angeles County Delegates, 1982-1983. *Member:* Los Angeles County Bar Association (Member: Barristers Executive Committee, 1979-1981; Antitrust Executive Committee, 1981-1990; Chairman, Committee on the Legal Problems of the Elderly, 1980-1981); State Bar of California.

**PAUL N. SORRELL,** born Emporia, Kansas, January 14, 1961; admitted to bar, 1986, California. *Education:* Whittier College (B.A., 1983); University of California at Los Angeles (J.D., 1986). Co-Author: "Attacks on Medical Staff Self-Governance Intensify," Vol. 37, No. 8 Southern California Psychiatrist, p.3, April, 1989. *Member:* Los Angeles County (Member, Litigation Section) and American (Member, Litigation Section) Bar Associations; State Bar of California. **PRACTICE AREAS:** Business Litigation; Real Estate; Construction Defect; Financial Institution Litigation.

**BURTON FALK,** born Chicago, Illinois, January 5, 1957; admitted to bar, 1981, California; 1982, U.S. District Court, Central, Northern, Southern and Eastern Districts of California. *Education:* University of Illinois (B.A., magna cum laude, 1978); Phi Beta Kappa; Phi Kappa Phi; University of Michigan (J.D., 1981). Judge Pro Tem, 1987-1988. *Member:* Beverly Hills and Los Angeles County Bar Associations; State Bar of California (Member, Intellectual Property Division); Association of Business Trial Lawyers. **PRACTICE AREAS:** Business; Entertainment Litigation; Family Law.

*ASSOCIATES*

**STEPHANIE BLACKMAN,** born San Diego, California, February 18, 1961; admitted to bar, 1987, California. *Education:* University of Colorado (B.A., magna cum laude, 1983); University of California at Los Angeles (J.D., 1987). Phi Beta Kappa. Member, University of California at Los Angeles Law Review, 1985-1987. *Member:* Beverly Hills, Los Angeles County and American Bar Associations; State Bar of California.

**JOHN A. SCHLAFF,** born Santa Monica, California, March 1, 1959; admitted to bar, 1988, California. *Education:* University of California at Los Angeles (A.B., summa cum laude, 1983; M.A., 1983); Harvard University (J.D., 1987). Phi Beta Kappa. Recipient, Harvard Entrepreneur of the Year Award. Member, Board of Directors, Harvard Prison Legal Assistance Project, 1985-1987. *Member:* State Bar of California.

*OF COUNSEL*

**MARTIN S. SCHWARTZ,** born Brooklyn, New York, August 30, 1935; admitted to bar, 1961, New York; 1962, California. *Education:* University of Pennsylvania and College of the City of New York (B.B.A., cum laude, 1955); New York University (LL.B., cum laude, 1961; LL.M., 1962). Beta Gamma Sigma. Pomeroy Scholar, New York University Law School,

(This Listing Continued)

1959-1961. Kenneson Fellowship, New York University Graduate Tax School, 1962. Associate Editor, New York University Law Review, 1961. Student Editor, New York University Tax Law Review, 1962. *Member:* Los Angeles County and American (Chairman, Committee on Banking Institutions, Section of Taxation, 1974-1977; Vice Chairman, Committee on Banking Institutions, Section of Taxation, 1977-1979) Bar Associations; The State Bar of California. (Certified Specialist, Taxation Law, The State Bar of California Board of Legal Specialization).

**JAMES EDWARD DOROSHOW,** born Chicago, Illinois, April 16, 1953; admitted to bar, 1979, Illinois and U.S. District Court, Northern District of Illinois; 1981, California; 1982, U.S. District Court, Central District of California. *Education:* Washington University (B.A. cum laude, 1975); Stanford University (J.D., 1979). Member, Stanford International Law Journal. Member: Board of Trustees, Max and Anna Levinson Foundation, 1979—; Board of Directors, American Jewish Congress, 1992—. *Member:* Illinois State and American Bar Associations; State Bar of California. *PRACTICE AREAS:* Litigation; Business; Construction Defect; Real Estate; Financial Institutions.

## THEODORE M. BELL
### 1901 AVENUE OF THE STARS, 11TH FLOOR
### LOS ANGELES, CALIFORNIA 90067
Telephone: 310-553-5572
Fax: 310-277-7947
Email: tedbell9@aol.com

*Corporations, Partnerships, Taxation, International Investments and Taxation, Securities, Real Estate, Estate Planning.*

**THEODORE M. BELL,** born Shanghai, China, January 11, 1941; admitted to bar, 1967, California and U.S. District Court, Central District of California; 1982, U.S. Tax Court. *Education:* University of California at Berkeley (A.B., 1961); Boalt Hall School of Law, University of California (J.D., 1964). Author: "Covenants Not to Compete and Goodwill in the Sale of Corporate Stock," Vol. 46, No. 5, The Los Angeles Bar Bulletin, March, 1971; "Internal Revenue Code Section 1244: Its Benefits and Its Pitfalls," Vol. 48, No. 10, The Los Angeles Bar Bulletin, August, 1973; "Corporate Plan Can Change Investor's Potential Capital Loss into Ordinary Loss at No Cost," Vol. 4, No. 1, Taxation for Lawyers, July/August, 1975; "Drafting Sale Contract to Avoid Tax Conflicts Over Goodwill and Covenants Not to Compete," Vol. 5, No. 1, Taxation for Lawyers, July/August, 1976. *Member:* Los Angeles (Member, Real Estate, Corporation and Taxation Committee, 1967-1976) and American Bar Associations; State Bar of California (Member: Taxation Section; Corporations Section).

## STANTON P. BELLAND, P.C.
### 10 UNIVERSAL CITY PLAZA, SUITE 2000
### LOS ANGELES, CALIFORNIA 91608-7806
Telephone: 818-754-3770
Telecopier: 818-754-3780

*General Corporate and Business Practice with emphasis on Closely Held Business Planning, Acquisitions and Finance and International Business Transactions.*

**STANTON P. BELLAND,** born Chicago, Illinois, December 12, 1931; admitted to bar, 1960, California. *Education:* University of California at Los Angeles (A.B., 1953; LL.B., 1959). Phi Delta Phi; Order of the Coif. Author: "The Iran-United States Claims Tribunal," Journal of International Arbitration, 1984. *Member:* The State Bar of California; American Bar Association (Member, Sections of: Corporation, Banking and Business Law; International Law); International Bar Association (Member, Sections on: Closely Held and Growing Business Enterprises; International Arbitration). *PRACTICE AREAS:* Closely Held Businesses; Corporate Reorganizations; International Corporate Law; Strategic Business Planning.

## DAVID R. BENCE
### LOS ANGELES, CALIFORNIA
(See Torrance)

*Business Litigation, Insurance, Real Estate, Contracts, General Corporate and Partnership Law, Estate Planning and Probate, Alternative Dispute Resolution.*

## BENJAMIN, LUGOSI & BENJAMIN, LLP
### LOS ANGELES, CALIFORNIA
(See Glendale)

*Entertainment Law, Licensing Rights of Publicity and Privacy, General Civil and Business Litigation including Bad Faith.*

## JOEL R. BENNETT
### LOS ANGELES, CALIFORNIA
(See Pasadena)

*Civil Litigation & Jury Trials in all State & Federal Courts, Antitrust, Unfair Competition, Trade Regulation, Trade Secrets, Breach of Contract, Unfair Trade Practices, Health Care Litigation, Telecommunications Antitrust, Intellectual Property, Trademark, Copyright, Patent.*

## LEON F. BENNETT
### LOS ANGELES, CALIFORNIA
(See Woodland Hills)

*Practice Limited to Family Law and Entertainment and Litigation Law.*

## BENOIT LAW CORPORATION
Established in 1970
### 2551 COLORADO BOULEVARD
### LOS ANGELES, CALIFORNIA 90041-1040
Telephone: 213-255-0000; 213-254-9307
Telecopier: 213-254-4538

**LUC P. BENOIT,** born Berne, Switzerland; admitted to bar, 1968, California; 1971, U.S. Supreme Court; registered to practice before U.S. Patent and Trademark Office. *Education:* Zurich State College of Technology, Switzerland (Diploma, Department of Telecommunication); Loyola University of Los Angeles (J.D., 1967). Alpha Sigma Nu; Phi Alpha Delta. *Member:* Los Angeles County (Chairperson, Law and Technology Section, 1980-1982; Arbitrator, Attorney-Client Relationships, 1980-1994) and American Bar Associations; State Bar of California (Trial Examiner, 1974-1979); Los Angeles Intellectual Property Law Association (Chairman, International Law Committee, 1973-1980; Director, 1977-1979).

## BENSINGER, GRAYSON & RITT
### LOS ANGELES, CALIFORNIA
(See Pasadena)

*Criminal Defense in State and Federal Courts, General Civil and Appellate Practice in all State and Federal Courts. Business Litigation, Entertainment Law, Employment Discrimination, Sexual Harassment, and Mediation of Family, Divorce and Community Disputes.*

## BENTON, ORR, DUVAL & BUCKINGHAM
A PROFESSIONAL CORPORATION
### LOS ANGELES, CALIFORNIA
(See Ventura)

*General and Trial Practice in State and Federal Courts and most Agencies and Governmental Bodies. Insurance and Appeals, Real Property, Corporations, Estate Planning, Trusts, Probate, Bankruptcy and Environmental Law.*

## BERGER, KAHN, SHAFTON, MOSS, FIGLER, SIMON & GLADSTONE

A Professional Corporation including a Professional Corporation

**4215 GLENCOE AVENUE (MARINA DEL REY)**
**LOS ANGELES, CALIFORNIA 90292-5634**
Telephone: 310-821-9000
Telecopier: 310-578-6178
Email: lawyers@bergerkahn.com

*Irvine, California Office:* Suite 650, 2 Park Plaza. Telephone: 714-474-1880. Telecopier: 714-474-7265.

*Novato, California Office:* Suite 304, 1701 Novato Boulevard. Telephone: 415-899-1770. Telecopier: 415-899-1769.

*San Diego, California Office:* 402 W. Broadway, Suite 400. Telephone: 619-236-8602. Telecopier: 619-236-0812.

*Bend, Oregon Office:* P.O. Box 1409, 97709. Telephone: 541-388-1400. Telecopier: 541-388-4731.

*Insurance Law, Real Estate, Music and Entertainment Law; Tax, Probate, Intellectual Property, General Civil and Trial Practice in all State and Federal Courts.*

**WILLIAM BERGER** (1903-1974).

**DOUGLAS C. BERARD,** born Lynn, Massachusetts, August 30, 1945; admitted to bar, 1979, California; 1980, U.S. Court of Appeals, Ninth Circuit and U.S. District Court, Central District of California. *Education:* The Citadel (B.A., 1968); Southwestern University (J.D., 1978). *Member:* Los Angeles County and American Bar Associations; International Association of Property Insurance Counsel (Founding Member and Past President). [Capt. USAF, 1968-1973]

**CAROLE J. BUCKNER,** born Fresno, California, April 30, 1959; admitted to bar, 1984, California; U.S. District Court, Central District of California and U.S. Court of Appeals, Ninth Circuit. *Education:* University of California at Berkeley (B.A., with honors, 1980); Hastings College of Law, University of California (J.D., 1984). Member, Steering Committee, California Minority Counsel Program, 1993-1996. *Member:* Orange County Bar Association (Member, Sections on: Business Litigation and Labor and Employment Litigation; Minority Issues Committee); State Bar of California (Member, Sections on: Litigation; Labor and Employment Law). (Resident, Irvine Office).

**STEPHAN S. COHN,** born Brooklyn, New York, May 6, 1959; admitted to bar, 1986, California; 1987, U.S. District Court, Central, Southern, Eastern and Northern Districts of California. *Education:* University of California at Berkeley (B.A., 1981); University of San Diego (J.D., 1985). *Member:* Orange County and American Bar Associations; Orange County Insurance Defense Association. (Resident, Irvine Office).

**SAMUEL M. DANSKIN,** born El Centro, California, August 21, 1963; admitted to bar, 1988, California, U.S. Court of Appeals, Ninth Circuit and U.S. District Court, Northern, Eastern and Central Districts of California. *Education:* University of California at San Diego (B.A., 1985); University of San Diego (J.D., 1988). Co-Author: "Emotional Distress: Minor Issue Muddies the Duty to Defend," Defense Counsel Journal, Vol. 57, April, 1990. *Member:* Orange County Bar Association. (Resident, Irvine Office).

**PAUL FIGLER,** born Natrona, Pennsylvania, October 18, 1941; admitted to bar, 1971, California. *Education:* Los Angeles City College and University of California at Los Angeles; Southwestern University, Los Angeles (J.D., 1970). *Member:* Los Angeles County and American (Member Sections on Real Property, Probate and Trust Law and Corporation, Banking and Business Law) Bar Associations.

**STEVEN H. GENTRY,** born Kansas City, Missouri, October 6, 1943; admitted to bar, 1976, California and U.S. District Court, Central District of California; 1981, U.S. Court of Appeals, Ninth Circuit and U.S. District Court, Eastern, Northern and Southern Districts of California. *Education:* Princeton University (B.S.E., 1965); Loyola University of Los Angeles (J.D., 1975). *Member:* Orange County Bar Association (Business Litigation Section); American Electronics Association. (Resident, Irvine Office).

**LEON J. GLADSTONE,** born Brooklyn, New York, March 26, 1951; admitted to bar, 1976, California. *Education:* University of California at Irvine (A.B., cum laude, 1973); Hastings College of Law, University of California (J.D., 1976). *Member:* Beverly Hills (Member, Sections on: Corporation, Banking and Business Law; Intellectual Property and Entertainment Law; Insurance) and Los Angeles County Bar Associations; Association of Southern California Defense Counsel.

*(This Listing Continued)*

**WILLIAM J. GLAZER,** born Los Angeles, California, May 4, 1950; admitted to bar, 1975, California and U.S. District Court, Central District of California; 1982, U.S. Supreme Court. *Education:* University of California at Los Angeles (B.A., cum laude, 1972); Loyola Marymount University (J.D., cum laude, 1975). Deputy Attorney General, California, 1975-1979. Judge ProTem, Los Angeles Municipal Court, 1981—. Special Master for Los Angeles Superior Court, 1991—. Tort and Insurance Arbitrator, Los Angeles Superior Court, 1980-1982. Member, Panel of Arbitrators, American Arbitration Association. *Member:* Los Angeles County and American (Member, Sections on: Tort and Insurance Practice Law; Intellectual Property) Bar Associations; Defense Research Institute; Association of Southern California Defense Counsel.

**DAVID A. HELFANT,** born New York, N.Y., March 5, 1955; admitted to bar, 1980, California; 1981, U.S. District Court, Central District of California and U.S. Court of Appeals, Ninth Circuit; 1982, U.S. District Courts, Eastern, Southern and Northern Districts of California. *Education:* State University of New York at Binghamton (B.A., 1977); Southwestern University (J.D., 1980). Deputy City Attorney, Santa Monica, 1980-1981. *Member:* Santa Monica Bay District, Beverly Hills, Century City (Chairman, Family Law Committee, 1982-1983; Delegate, California State Bar Convention, 1982, 1983 and 1984), Los Angeles County and American Bar Associations; The Association of Trial Lawyers of America.

**JAMES F. HENSHALL, JR.,** born Meriden, Connecticut, October 1, 1962; admitted to bar, 1987, California and U.S. District Court, Southern District of California; 1988, U.S. District Court, Central District of California. *Education:* San Diego State University (B.A., magna cum laude, 1984); University of San Diego (J.D., 1987). *Member:* Orange County Bar Association; Orange County Insurance Defense Association. (Resident, Irvine Office).

**HARRI J. KETO,** born Kuortane, Finland, April 14, 1949; admitted to bar, 1976, California and U.S. District Court, Southern District of California; 1977, U.S. District Court, Central District of California. *Education:* University of California at Irvine (B.A., 1971); University of San Diego (J.D., 1976). *Member:* Orange County (Member, Sections on Real Estate and Business) and American (Member, Sections on: Corporation, Banking and Business Law; Economics of Law Practice) Bar Associations; State Bar of California. (Resident, Irvine Office). *LANGUAGES:* Finnish.

**HOWARD F. KLINE,** born New York, N.Y., September 20, 1951; admitted to bar, 1976, California; 1977, U.S. District Court, Central District of California; 1980, U.S. District Court, Southern District of California and U.S. Court of Appeals, Ninth Circuit; 1987, U.S. District Court, Northern District of California. *Education:* Bowling Green State University; Oneonta State (B.A., 1973); Western State (J.D., 1976). *Member:* Orange County Bar Association (Member, Board of Directors, Real Estate Section). (Resident, Irvine Office).

**LANCE A. LABELLE,** born Minneapolis, Minnesota, January 18, 1955; admitted to bar, 1982, Minnesota; 1984, California; 1985, U.S. District Court, District of Minnesota and Central District of California; 1987, U.S. District Court, Southern and Northern Districts of California and U.S. Court of Appeals, Ninth Circuit. *Education:* University of Minnesota (B.A., 1978); Hamline University (J.D., 1982). Judicial Clerk to the Honorable Chester Durda, Minneapolis, Minnesota, 1983-1985. *Member:* Orange County and Minnesota State Bar Associations; Defense Research Institute; Association of Southern California Defense Counsel. (Resident, Irvine Office).

**ALAN H. LAZAR,** born Oakland, California, June 7, 1941; admitted to bar, 1970, California and U.S. District Court, Northern District of California; U.S. Court of Appeals, Ninth Circuit; 1973, U.S. District Court, Central District of California; 1975, U.S. District Court, Southern District of California. *Education:* University of California at Berkeley (A.B., 1962); University of California at Los Angeles (J.D., 1969); Institut de Hautes Etudes Internationales, Geneva, Switzerland. Judge Pro Tem, Los Angeles Municipal Court, 1979-1989. *Member:* Century City (Member, Board of Governors, 1984-1989), Los Angeles County (Member, Professional Liability Insurance Committee, 1989-1990) and American (Member, Accountants Liability Committee, Litigation Section, 1985-1988; Chairman, Sub-Committee, Insurance Agents and Brokers Liability, Litigation Section, 1989) Bar Associations; State Bar of California (Member, Professional Liability Insurance Committee, 1992—); Professional Liability Underwriting Society.

**ROBERT W. MEHR,** born Princeton, New Jersey, November 2, 1961; admitted to bar, 1987, California; 1988, U.S. District Court, Southern District of California; 1990, U.S. District Court, Central, Eastern and Northern Districts of California. *Education:* California State University at Chico

*(This Listing Continued)*

(B.A., 1984); Southwestern University (J.D., cum laude, 1987). (Resident, Novato Office).

**G. ARTHUR MENESES,** born Burbank, California, April 7, 1958; admitted to bar, 1982, California; 1985, U.S. District Court, Central and Southern Districts of California; 1986, U.S. Supreme Court. *Education:* University of California, Los Angeles (B.A., cum laude, 1979; J.D., 1982). Associate Editor, UCLA Chicano Law Review, 1981-1982. *Member:* Los Angeles County, San Bernardino County, Riverside County and American Bar Associations; Defense Research Institute; Legal Aid Society of San Bernardino, Inc. Inland Empire Future Leaders Program Mock Trial Program.

**ALLEN L. MICHEL,** born Chicago, Illinois, May 26, 1950; admitted to bar, 1975, California; 1976, U.S. District Court, Central and Southern Districts of California; 1991, U.S. District Court, Eastern District of California; 1992, U.S. District Court, Northern District of California. *Education:* University of California at Santa Barbara; University of California at Los Angeles (B.A., 1971); University of California at Los Angeles School of Law (J.D., 1975). Member, Moot Court Honors Program. *Member:* Beverly Hills and American Bar Associations; Association of Business Trial Lawyers; Association of Southern California Defense Counsel.

**MELODY S. MOSLEY,** born West Palm Beach, Florida, March 12, 1954; admitted to bar, 1984, California; 1985, U.S. District Court, Central District of California; U.S. District Court, Northern and Southern Districts of California; U.S. Court of Appeals, Ninth Circuit. *Education:* California State University at Long Beach (B.A., 1978); Southwestern University School of Law Scale Program (J.D., 1984). Author: "Valuation of the Community-Separation or Trial-Which is Preferable Time," Family Law News, State Bar of California Family Law Section, 1984. *Member:* Orange County Bar Association; Orange County Insurance Defense Association. (Resident, Irvine Office).

**JON ROGER MOSS,** born Los Angeles, California, October 20, 1937; admitted to bar, 1965, California; 1985, U.S. Tax Court; U.S. District Court, Central, Southern, Eastern and Northern Districts of California and Northern District of Alabama; U.S. Court of Appeals, Ninth and Fourth Circuits; U.S. Supreme Court. *Education:* University of California at Los Angeles (B.A., 1959; J.D., 1964). Phi Delta Phi. [Lt. (j.g.), U.S.N.R.; 1959-1961]

**PATRICK E. NAUGHTON,** born Peoria, Illinois, July 15, 1950; admitted to bar, 1978, California; 1984, U.S. District Court, Central District of California. *Education:* California State University at Fresno (B.A., cum laude, 1973); Pepperdine University (J.D., 1976). Member, Moot Court Honor Board, 1975-1976. *Member:* Orange County and American Bar Associations. (Resident, Irvine Office).

**ROBERT W. NELMS,** born Houston, Texas, February 4, 1958; admitted to bar, 1984, Virginia and U.S. Court of Appeals, Fourth Circuit; 1985, California, U.S. District Court, Central District of California and U.S. Court of Appeals, Ninth Circuit. *Education:* University of Virginia (B.A., 1980); Pepperdine University (J.D., 1984). Author: "Chapter 13 and the Classification of Unsecured Claims," Campbell University Law Review, Campbell University School of Law, 1986. Chairman, Board of Professional Standards, Pepperdine University School of Law, 1983-1984. (Resident, Irvine Office).

**TIMOTHY A. NICHOLSON,** born Redlands, California, January 9, 1962; admitted to bar, 1989, California. *Education:* California State University at San Bernardino (B.A., 1984); Western State University School of Law (J.D., cum laude, 1988). Associate Editor, Book Review Editor and Member, Board of Editors, Western State University Law Review, 1986-1988. Recipient: American Jurisprudence Awards in Torts and Evidence; Corpus Juris Secundum Award. Member, Barristers Moot Court Competition Committee. *Member:* Orange County, Los Angeles County and American Bar Associations; Orange County Barristers; Orange County Insurance Defense Association. (Resident, Irvine Office).

**TERESA RANSOM PONDER,** born Columbia, South Carolina, September 18, 1953; admitted to bar, 1987, California and U.S. District Court, Central, Eastern and Southern Districts of California. *Education:* University of South Carolina (A.S., 1975); Georgia State University; Oglethorpe University; Western State University College of Law (J.D., 1987). Member, Western State University Law Review, 1985-1986. *Member:* Orange County Bar Association; Orange County Insurance Defense Association; Orange County Women Lawyers. (Resident, Irvine Office).

**ERIC N. RIEZMAN,** born Brooklyn, New York, April 21, 1954; admitted to bar, 1980, California; U.S. District Court, Central District of California. *Education:* George Washington University (B.A., 1976); Western States

*(This Listing Continued)*

University College of Law (J.D., 1980). *Member:* Orange County Bar Association. (Resident, Irvine Office).

**CAROL PESKOE SCHANER,** born Long Branch, New Jersey, April 19, 1955; admitted to bar, 1982, California, U.S. District Court, Southern and Central Districts of California and U.S. Tax Court. *Education:* Cornell University (B.S., 1977); University of San Diego School of Law (J.D., 1982; LL.M., cum laude, 1994). Certified Public Accountant, California, 1981. (Certified Specialist, Taxation Law, The State Bar of California Board of Legal Specialization) (Resident, Irvine Office).

**ANTHONY E. SHAFTON,** born St. Louis, Missouri, July 17, 1941; admitted to bar, 1967, California. *Education:* University of California at Los Angeles (A.B., 1963; LL.B., 1966). Co-author: "Protective Orders," Chapter in California Discovery, 1975. *Member:* Los Angeles County and American Bar Associations; International Association of Property Insurance Counsel (Founding Member and Past President); Association for California Tort Reform (Senior Counsel Panel Member).

**CRAIG S. SIMON,** born Los Angeles, California, April 23, 1953; admitted to bar, 1977, California; U.S. District Court, Central, Southern and Northern Districts of California; U.S. Court of Appeals, Ninth Circuit. *Education:* University of California at Los Angeles (B.A., cum laude, 1974); Loyola University of Los Angeles (J.D., 1977). Member, St. Thomas More Law Honor Society, 1975. *Member:* Los Angeles County, Orange County, San Diego County and American Bar Associations; Defense Research Institute; Association of Southern California Defense Counsel; Orange County Insurance Defense Association. (Resident, Irvine Office).

**OWEN J. SLOANE,** born Brooklyn, New York, December 28, 1941; admitted to bar, 1966, California. *Education:* Cornell University (B.A., with distinction, 1962); Yale University (J.D., cum laude, 1965). Order of the Coif. Member, Editorial Staff, 1963-1965 and Notes and Comment Editor, 1964-1965, Yale Law Journal. Instructor, University of Southern California Law School, 1967-1968. Member, Planning Committee, University of Southern California Entertainment Law Institute, 1973. Co-Editor, Syllabus & Forms, 1974-1975. *Member:* Beverly Hills (Program Co-Chairman, Entertainment Law Section, 1969-1971), Los Angeles County and American (Member: Section on Patent, Trademark and Copyright Law; Committee on Neighboring Rights, 1974—) Bar Associations; Los Angeles Copyright Society.

**SHERMAN M. SPITZ,** born East Liverpool, Ohio, November 22, 1952; admitted to bar, 1978, California; U.S. District Court, Central and Southern Districts of California; U.S. Court of Appeals, Ninth Circuit. *Education:* University of California at Los Angeles (B.A., in Economics, 1974); Southwestern University (J.D., 1978). Member, Moot Court. Member, Law Review Staff, Southwestern University, 1977-1978. Deputy District Attorney, 1979-1981. *Member:* Orange County and American Bar Associations; Orange County Insurance Defense Association. (Resident, Irvine Office).

**JEFFREY M. SPURLOCK,** born Laguna Beach, California, September 18, 1963; admitted to bar, 1989, California; U.S. District Court, Central District of California. *Education:* Pepperdine University (B.S., summa cum laude, 1985; J.D., cum laude, 1988). Co-Author: "Are You Really Ready to Testify?", The National Fire and Arson Report, Vol. 10, No. 3 (1992). *Member:* Orange County and American Bar Associations; Orange County Insurance Defense Association. (Resident, Irvine Office).

**JEFFREY A. SWEDO,** born Chicago, Illinois, March 25, 1953; admitted to bar, 1977, California; U.S. District Court, Central and Southern Districts of California. *Education:* Valparaiso University (B.S.B.A., 1973); Cornell University (J.D., cum laude, 1977). Author: "Ruzicka v. General Motors Corporation: Negligence, Exhaustion of Remedies and Relief in Duty of Fair Representation Cases," 33 Arbitration Journal, June, 1978. *Member:* Orange County Bar Association. (Resident, Irvine Office).

**ARTHUR J. SWERDLOFF,** born Pomona, California, January 10, 1939; admitted to bar, 1964, California; 1980, U.S. District Court, Central District of California. *Education:* Claremont Men's College (B.A., 1960); Boalt Hall School of Law, University of California (J.D., 1963). *Member:* Westwood Bar Association (President, 1982). [Capt., U.S. Army, Infantry, 1963-1966]

**ROBERTA S. TAYLOR,** born Pontiac, Michigan, May 18, 1961; admitted to bar, 1986, Nevada; 1987, California and U.S. District Court, Southern District of California. *Education:* Michigan State University (B.A., 1983); University of San Diego (J.D., 1986). Instructor, Advanced Business Law, University of Nevada, 1986. *Member:* San Diego County and American Bar Associations; State Bar of Nevada; American Inns of Court; San Diego Defense Lawyers. (Resident, San Diego Office).

*(This Listing Continued)*

## BERGER, KAHN, SHAFTON, MOSS, FIGLER, SIMON & GLADSTONE, Los Angeles—Continued

**SARA SCHWAB TRASK,** born Orange, California, September 25, 1960; admitted to bar, 1986, California and U.S. District Court, Southern and Central Districts of California. *Education:* University of California at Davis (B.A., 1982); McGeorge School of Law, University of the Pacific (J.D., 1986). Best Brief Finalist, National Moot Court Competition. (Resident, Irvine Office).

**ROGER M. VOSBURG,** born Long Beach, California, December 1, 1952; admitted to bar, 1980, California. *Education:* California State University (B.A., magna cum laude, 1978); Southwestern University (J.D., 1980). Staff Member, Southwestern Law Review, 1979-1980. *Member:* Bar Association of San Francisco; Marin County, Los Angeles County and American Bar Associations; State Bar of California. (Resident, Novato Office).

**BRUCE M. WARREN,** born Cleveland, Ohio, August 22, 1957; admitted to bar, 1982, California and U.S. District Court, Southern District of California; 1985, U.S. District Court, Central District of California. *Education:* University of California at Irvine (B.A., 1979); California Western University School of Law (J.D., magna cum laude, 1982). Member, California Western Law Review, 1981-1982. Law Clerk to U.S. Magistrate, U.S. District Court, Southern District of California, 1982-1983. Judge Pro Temp in LA Municipal Court. *Member:* Los Angeles County Bar Association; International Association of Property Insurance Counsel.

---

**MICHAEL J. AIKEN,** born Los Angeles, California, March 13, 1955; admitted to bar, 1981, California; U.S. District Court, Northern and Central Districts of California. *Education:* University of Southern California (A.B., 1977; J.D., 1980).

**DALE A. AMATO,** born San Diego, California, March 28, 1961; admitted to bar, 1988, California; 1989, U.S. District Court, Southern District of California. *Education:* San Diego State University (B.S., with distinction, 1985); University of San Diego (J.D., 1988). Member, San Diego Law Review. *Member:* San Diego County and American Bar Associations; State Bar of California; San Diego Defense Lawyers. (Resident, San Diego Office).

**JON D. ANDERSEN,** born Glendale, California, September 22, 1962; admitted to bar, 1994, California; 1995, U.S. District Court, Central and Northern Districts of California. *Education:* California State University, Northridge (A.A.A.S., 1988); California State University, Fullerton (J.D., 1993). (Resident, Irvine Office).

**SHIREEN G. BANKI,** born Minneapolis, Minnesota, June 8, 1967; admitted to bar, 1992, California and U.S. Court of Appeals, Ninth Circuit; 1995, Minnesota. *Education:* University of California at Santa Barbara (B.A., with honors, 1989); Southwestern University (J.D., 1992). *Member:* Mortar Board Society; Order of Omega. Recipient: American Jurisprudence Book Award for Uniform Commercial Code; Tom Bradley Scholarship; Southwestern Exceptional Achievement Award - Contracts. Staff Member, 1990-1991 and Note and Comment Editor, 1991-1992, Southwestern University School of Law, Law Review. (Resident, Irvine Office).

**JULIE R. BEATON,** born Philadelphia, Pennsylvania, August 9, 1961; admitted to bar, 1994, California. *Education:* LaSalle University (B.A., 1983); Southwestern University School of Law (J.D., 1994). Member: The National Order of the Barristers; Moot Court Honor Society. Recipient, Schumacher Full Merit Scholarship. Member, Black Law Students Association. *Member:* Orange County and American Bar Associations. (Resident, Irvine Office).

**JAMES K. BERIKER,** born 1965; admitted to bar, 1993, California. *Education:* Trinity College, University of Toronto (B.A., with distinction, 1988); Dalhousie University (LL.B., 1991). *LANGUAGES:* French.

**LAURA FARREL BUCHER,** born Orange, California, September 9, 1961; admitted to bar, 1987, California; 1990, U.S. District Court, Central District of California. *Education:* California State University at Fullerton (B.S., 1984); Pepperdine University (J.D., 1987). Member, Moot Court. Member, Women's Legal Association, 1984-1987; California Women Lawyers, 1993-1995. (Resident, Irvine Office).

**PATRICIA J. CAMPBELL,** born Los Angeles, California, September 27, 1957; admitted to bar, 1991, California, U.S. District Court, Central District of California and U.S. Court of Appeals, Ninth Circuit. *Education:* California State University at Los Angeles (B.A., cum laude, 1988); University of Southern California (J.D., 1991). Phi Kappa Phi; Phi Alpha Delta; Golden Key. Best Oralist, Siegal National Moot Court Competition.

**ANNE BARDEN CLEELAND,** born Pasadena, California, March 13, 1956; admitted to bar, 1981, California; 1982, U.S. District Court, Central District of California and U.S. Court of Appeals, Ninth Circuit. *Education:* University of California at Los Angeles (B.A., 1978); Pepperdine University (J.D., 1981). (Resident, Irvine Office).

**KERI FLYNN CORFIELD,** born Long Beach, California, May 15, 1962; admitted to bar, 1989, California and U.S. District Court, Central District of California; U.S. Court of Appeals, Ninth Circuit. *Education:* University of California at Santa Barbara (B.A., 1985); University of San Diego (J.D., 1988). *Member:* Los Angeles County and Orange County Bar Associations; Legion Lex Inn of Court. (Resident, Irvine Office).

**RENEE C. D'AGOSTINO,** born Weirton, West Virginia, December 20, 1963; admitted to bar, 1991, California; 1992, U.S. District Court, Central District of California. *Education:* University of Nevada at Las Vegas (B.S., in Bus. Admin., 1985); Loyola Law School (J.D., 1991). Certified Public Accountant, California, 1987. (Resident, Irvine Office).

**KIMBERLY A. DONLON,** born Santa Monica, California, June 1, 1961; admitted to bar, 1993, California and U.S. District Court, Central District of California. *Education:* University of Southern California (B.A., 1983); Southwestern University School of Law (J.D., 1992). *Member:* Los Angeles County and American Bar Associations.

**MARGARET M. DRUGAN,** born Queens, New York, August 14, 1969; admitted to bar, 1994, California. *Education:* Boston University (B.A.; B.S., 1991); Southwestern University School of Law (J.D., 1994). (Resident, Irvine Office).

**RIVA I. EDWARDS,** born Calgary, Alberta, Canada, September 19, 1964; admitted to bar, 1989, California. *Education:* Chapman College (B.A., cum laude, 1986); University of San Diego (J.D., 1989). Phi Alpha Delta. *Member:* Los Angeles County and American Bar Associations; State Bar of California. (Resident, Irvine Office).

**PHILIP T. EMMONS,** born Culver City, California, October 19, 1954; admitted to bar, 1986, California, U.S. District Court, Northern District of California and U.S. Court of Appeals, Ninth Circuit. *Education:* University of California at Davis (B.S., Zoology, with honors, 1981); McGeorge School of Law, University of the Pacific (J.D., 1986). *Member:* State Bar of California. [With USAF, 1974-1978]. (Resident, Irvine Office).

**DAVID B. EZRA,** born Downey, California, November 14, 1963; admitted to bar, 1990, California and U.S. District Court, Central and Southern Districts of California. *Education:* California State University at Fullerton (B.A., with honors, 1987); University of Southern California (J.D., 1990). Order of the Coif. Recipient, American Jurisprudence Awards in Development of Legal Thought; Evidence; Gifts, Wills and Trusts. Editor, University of Southern California Law Review, 1989-1990. Author: "Smoker Battery: An Antidote to Second-Hand Smoke," 63 So. California Law Review 1061 (1990) reprinted in Daily Journal Report, October 26, 1990; "Get Off Your Butts: The Employer's Right to Regulate Employee Smoking," 60 Tennessee Law Review 905 (1993); "Sticks and Stones Can Break My Bones, But Tobacco Smoke Can Kill Me: Can We Protect Children From Parents That Smoke?" 13 Saint Louis University Public Law Review 547 (1994) (Symposium on Smokers' and Non-Smokers' Rights); "Separate But Not Equal: Gender - Specific Dress Codes and Employment Discrimination," 3 Western State University Journal of Law 119 (1994). Co-Author: "Insureds Should Think Twice Before Rejecting Defense Offers," Los Angeles Daily Journal (August 1994). (Resident, Irvine Office).

**LINDSEY S. FELDMAN,** born Suffern, New York, May 5, 1952; admitted to bar, 1977, California. *Education:* McGill University, Montréal, Québec (Collegial, 1971); Alvescot College, Oxfordshire, England; Syracuse University (B.S., 1973); University of California at Los Angeles (J.D., 1976); Hastings College of the Law, University of California. Articles Editor, Hastings College of the Law Communications/Entertainment Law Journal, 1976.

**GARY GANCHROW,** born Brooklyn, New York, February 17, 1968; admitted to bar, 1993, California. *Education:* Yeshiva University (B.A., magna cum laude, 1989); Fordham University (J.D., cum laude, 1992).

**DANIEL J. GOODSTEIN,** born Chicago, Illinois, October 27, 1953; admitted to bar, 1981, California and U.S. District Court, Central District of California. *Education:* California State University (B.A., 1976); San Fernando Valley College of Law (J.D., 1980).

*(This Listing Continued)*

**ARETA KAY GUTHREY,** born Castro Valley, California, May 8, 1959; admitted to bar, 1985, California; 1986, Washington; 1988, U.S. District Court, Northern and Central Districts of California. *Education:* Pepperdine University (B.A., 1981); McGeorge School of Law, University of the Pacific (J.D., with distinction, 1985). Adjunct Professor, Western State University, Irvine, California, 1992. (Resident, Irvine Office).

**REID S. HONJIYO,** born Honolulu, Hawaii, July 27, 1962; admitted to bar, 1987, California. *Education:* University of California at Davis (A.B., 1984); University of California at Los Angeles (J.D., 1987). Phi Beta Kappa. Lecturer, Contracts, Peoples College of Law, Fall, 1990. Los Angeles County Bar Association; Japanese American Bar Association.

**AMY HSIEH,** born Taipei, Taiwan, February 5, 1969; admitted to bar, 1994, California. *Education:* University of California at Berkeley (B.A., 1991); University of San Francisco (J.D., 1994).

**ERIC B. JOHNSON,** born St. Paul, Minnesota, August 30, 1956; admitted to bar, 1985, Minnesota; 1986, U.S. District Court, Western District of Washington; 1990, Washington, California and U.S. District Court, Central District of California. *Education:* St. Olaf College; University of Minnesota (B.A., 1978); University of Minnesota, Graduate School of Journalism and Mass Communication (1980-1982); William Mitchell College of Law (J.D., 1985). Member, William Mitchell Law Review, 1984-1985. Judicial Law Clerk to the Honorable Henry W. McCarr, Minneapolis, Minnesota, 1985. Special Assistant U.S. Attorney, Western District of Washington, 1986-1988. *Member:* Orange County, Minnesota State, Washington State and American (Member, Sections on: Litigation; Patent, Trademark and Copyright) Bar Associations. [Major, United States Air Force, 1986-1990; Major, California Air National Guard, 1992—]. (Resident, Irvine Office).

**SUSANNE BERRY JOHNSON,** born Shreveport, Louisiana, February 28, 1964; admitted to bar, 1989, California, U.S. District Court, Central District of California and U.S. Court of Appeals, Ninth Circuit. *Education:* Newcomb College of Tulane University (B.A., 1986); Pepperdine University School of Law (J.D., 1989).

**ANN K. JOHNSTON,** born Chicago, Illinois, December 31, 1964; admitted to bar, 1989, California and U.S. District Court, Central and Southern Districts of California; U.S. Court of Appeals, Ninth Circuit. *Education:* University of California at Irvine (B.A., 1986); Pepperdine University (J.D., 1989). (Resident, Irvine Office).

**RICHARD O. KNAPP,** born Los Angeles, California, March 1, 1964; admitted to bar, 1989, California, U.S. District Court, Southern District of California and U.S. Court of Appeals, Ninth Circuit. *Education:* University of California at Santa Barbara (B.A., 1986); University of San Diego (J.D., 1989). Phi Alpha Delta. (Resident, Irvine Office).

**CATHERINE K. LA TEMPA,** born Long Beach, California, August 23, 1955; admitted to bar, 1992, California and U.S. District Court, Central District of California. *Education:* San Diego State University (B.A., 1978); Loyola Law School, Los Angeles (J.D., 1992). Phi Delta Phi; Order of the Coif; St. Thomas More Honor Society. Recipient, American Jurisprudence Award in Torts, Evidence, Sales and Payments. Editor, Loyola Law School International and Comparative Law Journal, 1990-1992. (Resident, Irvine Office).

**JEFFREY B. LEHRMAN,** born New York, N.Y., June 11, 1963; admitted to bar, 1989, California and U.S. District Court, Central and Southern Districts of California. *Education:* State University of New York at Binghamton (B.S., 1985); Boston University (J.D., 1988). Recipient, American Jurisprudence Award. Paul J. Liacos Scholar. (Resident, Irvine Office).

**DENISE A. MACRAE,** born Paterson, New Jersey, July 3, 1960; admitted to bar, 1987, California and U.S. District Court, Central District of California. *Education:* St. Louis University, Madrid, Spain; Trinity College (B.A., 1982); Southwestern University School of Law (J.D., 1987). Judge Pro Tem, Municipal Court of California, Los Angeles Judicial District, 1992-1993. *Member:* Los Angeles County (Member, Sections on: Provisional & Post Judgement Remedies; Commercial Law; Bankruptcy; Barristers' Committees: Executive Committee, 1992-1994; Bench and Bar Relations, 1991-1992; Co-Chair, Homeless Advocacy Project, 1991-1994; Committee on The State Bar, 1991-1993) and American Bar Associations; State Bar of California; Association of Business Trial Lawyers; Financial Lawyers Conference; Women Lawyers Association. *LANGUAGES:* Spanish.

**MARK F. MARNELL,** born Lynwood, California, September 3, 1953; admitted to bar, 1981, California and U.S. District Court, Eastern, Southern, Central and Northern Districts of California; 1986, U.S. Court of Appeals, Ninth Circuit. *Education:* University of Santa Clara (B.A., magna cum laude, 1975); University of California, Los Angeles (M.A., 1978); Boalt Hall School of Law, University of California at Berkeley (J.D., 1981). Author: Note, "Responsibilities under RCRA: Administrative Law Issues," Vol. 9, Ecology Law Quarterly 555, 1981. (Resident, Irvine Office).

**CAROLYN A. MATHEWS,** born New Jersey, July 29, 1936; admitted to bar, 1988, California. *Education:* University of Texas at Austin (B.F.A., 1967) Alpha Lambda Delta; University of West Los Angeles School of Law (J.D., 1988). Recipient: Alfred Gitelson Award for Excellence in Legal Writing; Corpus Juris Secundum Awards; American Jurisprudence Awards in Contracts, Civil and Criminal Procedure and Trusts and Estates. Editor-in-Chief, UWLA Law Review, 1987-1988. Licensed Real Estate Broker: California, 1980; Arizona, 1981. Author: "Exploring the Murky Waters of the Intent of the Insane - Searle v. Allstate," University of West Los Angeles Law Review, Vol. 18. Trustee Member, University of West Los Angeles Academic Standards, Admissions, Library and Scholarship Committee, 1987-1989.

**KEVIN P. MCNAMARA,** born Cincinnati, Ohio, October 16, 1968; admitted to bar, 1995, California and U.S. District Court, Central District of California. *Education:* University of California at Berkeley (B.A., 1992); Pepperdine University (J.D., 1995).

**MARGARET R. MIGLIETTA,** born New Brunswick, New Jersey, February 3, 1958; admitted to bar, 1984, California and U.S. District Court, Central District of California. *Education:* Emory University (B.A., 1980); Loyola Law School, Los Angeles (J.D., 1984). Phi Sigma Tau. (Resident, Irvine Office).

**JULIA A. MOUSER,** born Pasadena, California, April 6, 1959; admitted to bar, 1985, California and U.S. District Court, Central District of California. *Education:* Point Loma College (B.A., magna cum laude, 1981); Southwestern University of the Law (J.D., 1984). Recipient, American Jurisprudence Book Award in Intellectual Property. (Resident, Irvine Office).

**NANCY N. POTTER,** born Seattle, Washington, December 5, 1954; admitted to bar, 1980, California; 1981, U.S. District Court, Central District of California; 1986, U.S. Court of Appeals, Ninth Circuit; 1991, U.S. District Court, Southern District of California. *Education:* Pitzer College (B.A., 1976); Stanford University (J.D., 1979). Judicial Clerk, Hon. F. Douglas McDaniel, California Court of Appeal, 1979-1980.

**ROBERT S. ROBINSON,** born Baltimore, Maryland, November 1, 1962; admitted to bar, 1987, California; 1988, U.S. District Court, Central District of California; 1991, U.S. Court of Appeals, Ninth Circuit. *Education:* University of California at Berkeley (B.A., 1984); University of Southern California (J.D., 1987). Phi Delta Phi. Alumni Scholar. Member: Mortar Board; Hale Moot Court Honors Program. *Member:* Orange County Bar Association; State Bar of California. (Resident, Irvine Office).

**STEPHEN A. SHAPIRO,** born New York, N.Y., August 23, 1965; admitted to bar, 1991, California; U.S. District Court, Southern District of California. *Education:* University of California at Berkeley (B.A., 1987); Hastings College of the Law (J.D., 1991). Finalist, Moot Court Best Brief Competition. (Resident, Irvine Office).

**STEVEN H. SILVERMAN,** born New York, N.Y., July 15, 1953; admitted to bar, 1991, California; 1994, District of Columbia. *Education:* State University of New York Stony Brook (B.A., History, 1975; B.A., Theatre, 1975); Southwestern University (J.D., 1991). Recipient, American Jurisprudence Award for Pre Trial Lawyering Skills.

**MAXIM VAYNEROV,** born Moscow, Russia, January 11, 1969; admitted to bar, 1995, California and U.S. District Court, Central and Southern Districts of California. *Education:* University of California at Los Angeles (B.A., 1991; J.D., 1994). *LANGUAGES:* Russian.

**FRED TIMOTHY WINTERS,** born Burbank, California, September 26, 1950; admitted to bar, 1979, California; 1982, U.S. District Court, Central District of California; 1983, U.S. Court of Appeals, Ninth Circuit; 1988, U.S. District Court, Southern District of California. *Education:* California State University (B.A., magna cum laude, with honors in English, 1974); Loyola Law School (J.D., 1979). (Resident, Irvine Office).

**HALI E. ZIFF,** born Santa Monica, California, June 10, 1959; admitted to bar, 1986, California; 1987, U.S. Court of Appeals, Ninth Circuit and U.S. District Court, Central and Northern Districts of California. *Education:* University of California at Los Angeles; University of California at Santa Barbara (B.A., 1982); Loyola Law School (J.D., 1986). *Member:* Los Angeles County (Member, Sections on: Litigation; Real Property; Business) and American Bar Associations; State Bar of California (Member, Sections on: Business; Real Property). (Resident, Irvine Office).

*(This Listing Continued)*

## BERGER, KAHN, SHAFTON, MOSS, FIGLER, SIMON & GLADSTONE, Los Angeles—Continued

### OF COUNSEL

**PAUL S. BERGER,** born Los Angeles, California, November 6, 1936; admitted to bar, 1964, California. *Education:* University of California at Los Angeles (B.S., 1958; J.D., 1963). [Lieut. (j.g.), U.S.N., 1958-1960]

**CHARLES H. KAHN,** born Appleton, Wisconsin, August 7, 1936; admitted to bar, 1961, Wisconsin; 1962, Illinois; 1964, California; 1965, U.S. Court of Military Appeals and U.S. Supreme Court. *Education:* Cornell University (B.A., 1958); Northwestern University (J.D., 1961). Order of the Coif. Member, Northwestern University Law School Law Review, 1960-1961.

**JAMES B. KRUG,** born Los Angeles, California, January 15, 1953; admitted to bar, 1978, California and U.S. District Court, Central District of California. *Education:* University of California (B.A., 1975), Loyola University of Los Angeles (J.D., with honors, 1978).

**KENJI MACHIDA, (A PROFESSIONAL CORPORATION),** born Tulelake, California, January 1, 1943; admitted to bar, 1969, California, U.S. District Court, Central District of California and U.S. Court of Appeals, 9th Circuit. *Education:* University of California at Los Angeles (B.A., with honors, 1965); Harvard University (J.D., 1968). *Member:* Los Angeles County Bar Association (Board of Trustees, 1980-1982; Judicial Appointments Committee; Judicial Evaluations Committee); Japanese American Bar Association (President, 1980; Board of Governors, 1979-1982); Public Counsel (Board of Directors, 1983-1985); Los Angeles County Bar Foundation (Board of Directors, 1985-1987).

REPRESENTATIVE CLIENTS: Allstate Insurance Co.; Budget Rent-A-Car Corp.; California State Automobile Assn.; The Canada Life Assurance Co. (Real Estate Investments); Century National Insurance; Chubb Group of Insurance Companies; The CIGNA Cos.; City of Redondo Beach; CNA Insurance Co.; C.W. Reese Company; Donnelly Directory; Farmers Insurance Group of Companies; Firemans Fund Insurance Companies; Hartford Insurance Co.; Honda North America, Inc.; Independent Cities and Risk Management Association; Independent Order of Foresters (Real Estate Investments); Insurance Company of the West; Mellon Mortgage (Mortgage Banking); Mutual Life Insurance Co. of New York; National Continental Insurance Co.; Nevada General Insurance Company; Principal Commercial Advisors, Inc. (Real Estate Investments); Progressive Casualty Insurance Co.; Prudential Insurance and Financial Services; Resolution Trust Corp.; State Farm Insurance Companies; Textron Financial Corporation (Lease Financing); Tokio Marine & Fire Insurance Co.; 20th Century Insurance Co.
ENTERTAINMENT CLIENTS: Bonnie Raitt; Budda Heads; Edoya Records; Elton John; Frank Zappa; Jeffrey Osborne; Kenny Rogers; Paul Anka; Rick Trevino; Suzanne Vega; The Nixons; Troubadour Entertainment.
REFERENCE: Western Bank.

---

## BERGER & NORTON

*A LAW CORPORATION*

**LOS ANGELES, CALIFORNIA**

(See Santa Monica)

*Real Property Litigation, Trial and Appellate.*

---

## ROBERT D. BERGMAN

EIGHTH FLOOR
10100 SANTA MONICA BOULEVARD
**LOS ANGELES, CALIFORNIA 90067-4012**
Telephone: 310-557-1888
Fax: 310-557-9888

*Business, Corporate, Real Estate, Estate Planning, Probate and Taxation Law.*

**ROBERT D. BERGMAN,** born Santa Monica, California, March 20, 1956; admitted to bar, 1983, California. *Education:* University of California at Los Angeles (B.A., 1978); Southwestern University (J.D., magna cum laude, 1983); New York University (LL.M., Taxation, 1984). *Member:* Moot Court Honors Program; Southwestern Law Review, 1982-1983. Judicial Extern, Honorable A. Andrew Houk, 1983. *Member:* Beverly Hills, Los Angeles County (Member, Section on: Taxation) and American (Member, Section on Taxation, Committee on Real Estate Tax Problems) Bar Associations.

REFERENCE: Century Bank (West Los Angeles Branch).

---

## BERGMAN & WEDNER, INC.

*Established in 1983*

SUITE 900, 10880 WILSHIRE BOULEVARD
**LOS ANGELES, CALIFORNIA 90024**
Telephone: 310-470-6110
Fax: Available on Request

*Business, Professional Liability, Real Estate, Land Use, Earth Movement, Banking, Securities, Taxation, Condominium, Insurance, Public Entity, Environmental, Computer Litigation, Toxic Tort, Product Liability, Entertainment, Construction, Fraud and Recession Action, Employment and White-Collar Criminal Law and Federal and State Litigation.*

FIRM PROFILE: *Bergman & Wedner, Inc. has solid substantive and litigation experience in the areas of real property, environmental, commercial, banking, antitrust and trade regulation, professional liability, corporate partnership, securities insurance (coverage and defense), and general business law. We have handled such diverse matters as civil and criminal antitrust investigations, business fraud, entertainment disputes, title insurance claims, insurance coverage opinions, employment discrimination, tax and bankruptcy litigation, administrative proceedings, creditor rights and provisional remedies (receiverships, attachments and injunctions). Individuals within the firm are also knowledgeable in estate planning, probate, personal injury and products liability law. Our civil litigation practice extends to all state and federal trial and appellate courts.*

*The firm's clients run the gamut from "Fortune 500" corporations, insurance companies, financial institutions, government agencies and national advertisers to investors, attorneys, accountants, contractors, limited and general partnerships and corporations, and developers.*

**GREGORY M. BERGMAN,** born Los Angeles, California, September 12, 1947; admitted to bar, 1975, California. *Education:* University of California at Los Angeles (B.A., 1970); Southwestern University (J.D., 1975). Note and Comment Editor, Southwestern University Law Review, 1974-1975. Law Clerk Extern, California Court of Appeals, Second Appellate District, 1975. *Member:* Beverly Hills, Los Angeles County and American Bar Associations; State Bar of California; The Association of Trial Lawyers of America; Association of Real Estate Attorneys; Association of Business Trial Attorney, Trial Work and Arbitration. [With USNR, active duty, 1970-1972]. **PRACTICE AREAS:** Business Litigation; Commercial Real Property; Commercial Litigation; Professional Liability Defense; Commercial Insurance; Computer Law; Securities Litigation.

**GREGORY A. WEDNER,** born Los Angeles, California, September 25, 1950; admitted to bar, 1975, California; 1975, U.S. Court of Appeals, Ninth Circuit; 1980, U.S. Supreme Court. *Education:* University of California at Los Angeles (B.A., cum laude, 1972); Southwestern University (J.D., cum laude, 1975). Member, Moot Court Honors Program, 1974-1975. Recipient: American Jurisprudence Awards, 1973, 1974 and 1975; Distinguished Service Award, Southwestern University, 1975. Editor, Southwestern University Law Review, 1974-1975. Author: Note, "A Disappearing Trace: California's Blood Alcohol Search Doctrines," 6 Southwestern University Law Review 640, 1974; "A Compendium of California Statutes of Limitations," Southwestern University Law Review, Special Edition, 1975. Co-Author: "Stated Discretion and Bail Pending Appeal: Judicial Silence May No Longer Be Golden," 8 Southwestern University Law Review 810, 1976. *Member:* Beverly Hills, Los Angeles County, Federal and American (Member, Criminal Justice Section) Bar Associations; State Bar of California.
**PRACTICE AREAS:** Computer Law; Professional Liability Defense; Securities Litigation; Commercial Insurance; Business Litigation; Commercial Real Property; Commercial Litigation.

**MARK E. FINGERMAN,** born Los Angeles, California, April 22, 1954; admitted to bar, 1981, California; 1983, U.S. District Court, Central District of California; 1985, U.S. District Court, Northern District of California. *Education:* University of California, San Diego (B.A., 1977); California Western School of Law (J.D., 1981). Associate/Contributing Lead Articles Editor, California Western International Law Journal, 1980-1981. Author: "Skyjacking and the Bonn Declaration of 1978: Sanctions Applicable to Recalcitrant Nations," 10 California Western International Law Journal 123, 1980. Judge Pro Tem, West Los Angeles Municipal Court, 1983—. *Member:* Beverly Hills and Los Angeles County (Member, Sections on: International Law; Trial Lawyers and Prejudgment Remedies) Bar Associations; State Bar of California. **LANGUAGES:** French. **PRACTICE AREAS:** Earth Movement; Toxic Torts; Construction Liability; Insurance Fraud; Personal Injury Defense; Community Redevelopment.

*(This Listing Continued)*

*ALAN HARVEY MITTELMAN,* born Philadelphia, Pennsylvania, October 20, 1953; admitted to bar, 1982, California and U.S. District Court, Central District of California; 1986, U.S. Court of Appeals, Ninth Circuit and U.S. District Court, Northern and Southern Districts of California. *Education:* Washington University (B.A., 1975); Southwestern University School of Law (J.D., 1981); Temple University (M.B.A., 1982). Law Clerk, Honorable David W. Williams, Senior U.S. District Judge, Central District of California, 1981-1986. *Member:* Los Angeles County Bar Association; State Bar of California. *PRACTICE AREAS:* Civil Litigation in both state and federal courts; Personal Injury Defense; Business Litigation; Insurance Coverage; Insurance Fraud; Commercial Real Property; Construction Liability.

*ROBERT M. MASON III,* born San Francisco, California, June 24, 1955; admitted to bar, 1981, California and U.S. District Court, Northern District of California; 1986, U.S. District Court, Central District of California. *Education:* University of Santa Clara (B.A., 1977); University of California at Davis (J.D., 1980). Neumiller Honors Moot Court Board, 1978-1979. *Member:* Los Angeles County Bar Association; State Bar of California. *PRACTICE AREAS:* Commercial Insurance; Civil Litigation; Civil Appeals.

*KRISTI ANNE SJOHOLM-SIERCHIO,* born Fort Eustis, Virginia, January 4, 1958; admitted to bar, 1987, California, U.S. District Court, Central District of California and U.S. Court of Appeals, Ninth Circuit. *Education:* Hampshire College (B.A., 1978); University of Southern California Law Center (J.D./M.B.T., 1987). Phi Alpha Delta. Recipient, Shattuck Award. Publications Editor, Environmental Law Journal, 1984-1985. *Member:* Los Angeles County Bar Association; State Bar of California (Member, Taxation Section). *PRACTICE AREAS:* Business Litigation; Governmental Law; Contract Litigation; Bankruptcy Litigation.

*KEITH A. ROBINSON,* born Detroit, Michigan, April 3, 1958; admitted to bar, 1986, California, U.S. District Court, Central District of California and U.S. Court of Appeals, Ninth Circuit. *Education:* University of California at Los Angeles; Stanford University (A.B., 1980); University of Southern California (J.D., 1986). Phi Delta Phi. Quarter Finalist, Moot Court Honors Program. Recipient, American Jurisprudence Award in Contracts. Staff Member, Environmental Law Journal, 1984-1985. *Member:* Los Angeles County and Ventura County Bar Associations; State Bar of California. *PRACTICE AREAS:* Business Litigation; Contract Litigation; Real Estate Litigation; Environmental Liability; Federal Taxation.

*JOHN P. DACEY,* born Newark, New Jersey, March 23, 1957; admitted to bar, 1988, California and U.S. District Court, Central District of California. *Education:* North Texas State University; Ramapo College (B.A., 1980); Southwestern University School of Law (J.D., 1988). Recipient: National Legal Studies Award; American Jurisprudence Award in Torts, Labor Law, Community Property and Corporations. Advocate, The Association of Trial Lawyers of America Team Competition, 1988. *Member:* Beverly Hills, Los Angeles County and American Bar Associations; State Bar of California; The Association of Trial Lawyers of America. *PRACTICE AREAS:* Environmental Liability; Commercial Real Property; Business Litigation; Civil Fraud; Construction Liability; Securities Litigation.

---

*JOHN V. TAMBORELLI,* born Providence, Rhode Island, January 29, 1961; admitted to bar, 1988, California. *Education:* Providence College (B.S., 1984); Pepperdine University (J.D., 1987). *Member:* Beverly Hills and Los Angeles County Bar Associations; State Bar of California. *PRACTICE AREAS:* Products Liability Defense; Tort Defense; Real Estate Litigation; Commercial Litigation; Toxic Exposure; Construction Defects; Land Use Law; Contract Dispute Resolution; Premises Liability Defense.

*BLITHE ANN SMITH,* born January 23, 1966; admitted to bar, 1992, California. *Education:* University of Chicago (B.A., with honors, 1987); University of California School of Law (J.D., 1992). Externship, United States Department of State, 1991. *Member:* State Bar of California. *LANGUAGES:* French. *PRACTICE AREAS:* Federal and State Contract Procurement; Contract Litigation; Civil Rights Defense; Business Litigation.

*LISA S. SHUKIAR,* admitted to bar, 1992, California. *Education:* University of California at Los Angeles (B.A., 1989); University of Southern California (J.D., 1992). Editor, Review of Law and Women's Studies, University of Southern California Law Center. *Member:* State Bar of California. *PRACTICE AREAS:* Complex Litigation.

*DAPHNE M. HUMPHREYS,* admitted to bar, 1994, California and U.S. District Court, Central District of California. *Education:* University of Toronto; University of California-San Diego; Southwestern University School of Law (J.D., magna cum laude, 1994). Member, Moot Court Honors Program. Recipient: Best Brief, American Bar Association Regional Moot Court Competition, 1993; Outstanding Woman Legal Graduate Award; American Jurisprudence Award for Torts, Contracts and Civil Pretrial Practice; Exceptional Achievement Award for Intellectual Property. Editor, Southwestern Law Review. *Member:* State Bar of California. *PRACTICE AREAS:* Complex Litigation.

*SUZANNE Z. SHBARO,* born Inglewood, California, April 27, 1966; admitted to bar, 1994, California. *Education:* University of California at Los Angeles (B.A., 1988); Southwestern University School of Law (J.D., 1994). Phi Alpha Theta. Dean's Honor List, University of California at Los Angeles, 1986-1988). Dean's List, Southwestern University School of Law, 1993-1994. Mabel Wilson Richards Scholarship; J. Kramer Scholarship. Recipient: Exceptional Achievement Award, Interviewing, Counseling and Negotiating; American Jurisprudence Award - Legal Writing. *Member:* Women Lawyers Association of Los Angeles. *LANGUAGES:* American Sign Language.

*OF COUNSEL*

*LLOYD A. BERGMAN* (1923-1994).

*JACOB A. WEDNER,* born Pittsburgh, Pennsylvania, August 31, 1919; admitted to bar, 1949, California; 1961, U.S. Supreme Court. *Education:* University of Pittsburgh (B.S., 1941); University of Southern California (J.D., 1949). Phi Eta Sigma. *Member:* State Bar of California; American Bar Association (Member: Public Contracts Section, 1969-1978; Corporation, Banking and Business Law Section; Credit Union Committee, 1975—); Procurement/Legal National Security Industrial Association; Aerospace Industries Association. [U.S.A.F., 1942-1950, 1st Lt.]

*SPECIAL COUNSEL*

*RICHARD V. GODINO,* born Santa Monica, California, August 16, 1929; admitted to bar, 1960, California and U.S. District Court, Northern District of California. *Education:* Stanford University (A.B., 1952; M.B.A., 1954); University of San Francisco (LL.B., 1960). *Member:* State Bar of California. *PRACTICE AREAS:* Commercial Real Property; Public School Law; Public Entity Law.

## KENNETH R. BERMAN

*3315 GLENDALE BOULEVARD, SUITE 1*
**LOS ANGELES, CALIFORNIA 90039**
Telephone: 213-660-8120
Fax: 213-669-1712

*Workers Compensation Applicants, Personal Injury Plaintiff.*

*KENNETH R. BERMAN,* born Los Angeles, California, December 13, 1956; admitted to bar, 1982, California. *Education:* University of California at Los Angeles (B.A., cum laude, 1978); Loyola Law School of Los Angeles (J.D., 1981). *Member:* Los Angeles County Bar Association; State Bar of California; California Applicants Attorneys Association. (Certified Specialist, Workers' Compensation Law, The State Bar of California Board of Legal Specialization). *PRACTICE AREAS:* Workers Compensation Law; Personal Injury Law.

## BERMAN, BERMAN & BERMAN

*Established in 1980*

*11900 WEST OLYMPIC BOULEVARD, 6TH FLOOR*
**LOS ANGELES, CALIFORNIA 90064-1151**
Telephone: 310-447-9000
Fax: 310-447-9011
Email: rberman156@aol.com

*Chicago, Illinois Office:* Berman, Berman & Markey, 30 North LaSalle Street, Suite 1530, 60602. Telephone: 312-201-9191. Fax: 312-201-9195.

*General Insurance Defense and Business Litigation. Professional Liability including Design Professionals, Real Estate Brokers, Appraisers, Lawyers, Insurance Brokers, Psychologists and Accountants. Product Liability, Employment Law, Insurance Coverage and Construction Defects. Monitoring Counsel, Litigation Management, Insurance Regulations and Consulting to the Insurance Industry.*

*FIRM PROFILE: The firm brings together an experienced, seasoned staff. The firm strives to maintain a high caliber of client service, emphasizing a strong sensitivity to containing litigation costs while providing top quality legal service.*

(This Listing Continued)

## BERMAN, BERMAN & BERMAN, Los Angeles—Continued

**RONALD S. BERMAN,** born Los Angeles, California, July 9, 1938; admitted to bar, 1972, California, U.S. District Court, Central, Northern and Eastern Districts of California and U.S. Claims Court. *Education:* University of California at Los Angeles (B.S. in Business Administration, 1960; M.B.A., 1964); Loyola Law School (J.D., 1970). Recipient, American Jurisprudence Award in Evidence. Licensed Real Estate Broker, California, 1961. Co-Author: "Conflict of Interest: The Attorney-Client Joint Business Venture," Lawyers' Professional Liability Update, April, 1985; "Changing From The Inside Out," Business Insurance, November 17, 1986; "Is Litigation Looming In Your Future," Valuation Practice Alert, May, 1987; "Defending Another Attorney," Case & Comment, March/April, 1988; "Mistakes That Don't Have To Happen," Insurance Advocate, April 9, 1988; "Malpractice: An 11-point Checklist to Help Investor Advisors Avoid Claims," Managers Magazine, November, 1988; "Investment Advisor Malpractice-A Bull Market for Plaintiffs," The National Public Accountant, January 1989. Co-Author: "Insurance Producer Liability—In Plain Language,"; "Real Estate Agent & Appraiser Liability—In Plain Language." Member, Board of Directors, Southern California Tennis Association. General Counsel, Professional Liability Underwriting Society. Of Counsel, California Association of Independent Insurance Adjusters. *Member:* Los Angeles County and American (Associate Member, Standing Committee, Lawyers Professional Liability; Member, Sections of: Tort and Insurance Practice; Litigation) Bar Associations; State Bar of California; Association of Southern California Defense Counsel. [Capt., USAR, 1961-1969]

**EVAN A. BERMAN,** born Los Angeles, California, November 8, 1964; admitted to bar, 1990, California; 1991, U.S. District Court, Central District of California. *Education:* University of Washington (B.A., 1987); Pepperdine University, School of Law (J.D., 1990). *Member:* State Bar of California.

**MYRA L. MARKEY,** born Chicago, Illinois, August 2, 1963; admitted to bar, 1987, Illinois; U.S. District Court, Northern District of Illinois (Not admitted in California). *Education:* Northern Illinois University (B.S., 1984); De Paul University (J.D., 1987). Phi Sigma Alpha. Member, Mortar Board. Recipient: American Jurisprudence Award in Torts; De Paul Moot Court Finalist, 1985-1986. *Member:* Chicago (Member, Aviation and Insurance Law Committees), Illinois State and American Bar Associations. (Resident, Chicago, Illinois Office).

**STEPHANIE J. BERMAN,** born Los Angeles, California March 22, 1968; admitted to bar, 1993, California and U.S. District Court, District of California. *Education:* University of California at Los Angeles (B.A., magna cum laude, 1990); Loyola Marymount University (J.D., 1993). Staff Member, Loyola of Los Angeles Entertainment Law Journal, 1991-1992. Chief Articles Editor, Loyola of Los Angeles Entertainment Law Journal, 1992-1993. Author: "View at Your Own Risk: Gang Movies and Spectator Violence," 12 Loy. L.A. Ent. L.J., 477. *Member:* Los Angeles County Bar Association; State Bar of California.

### ASSOCIATES

**MATTHEW S. SHORR,** born Los Angeles, California, July 16, 1953; admitted to bar, 1982, California and U.S. District Court, Central District of California; 1986, U.S. Court of Appeals, Ninth Circuit. *Education:* California State University at Northridge (B.A., 1976); Southwestern University School of Law (J.D., 1980); University of Cambridge (Queens's College) (LL.M., 1985). Member, Legislation Committee, Los Angeles Court of International Commercial Arbitration, 1986.

**MARK LOWARY,** born West Covina, California, February 27, 1966; admitted to bar, 1993, California. *Education:* California State University (B.A., 1989); Southwestern University School of Law (J.D., 1993).

**CHARLES G. WHITEHEAD,** born Las Vegas, Nevada, April 3, 1964; admitted to bar, 1990, California; 1991 District of Columbia; 1993, Arizona. *Education:* Northeastern University (B.S., cum laude, 1987); Pepperdine University (J.D., 1990). Phi Alpha Delta. *Member:* Los Angeles County Bar Association; State Bar of California.

**CHRISTOPHER C. MCNATT, JR.,** born Glendale, California, July 30, 1966; admitted to bar, 1994, California and U.S. District Court, Central District of California; 1995, U.S. District Court, Southern District of California. *Education:* University of California, San Diego (B.A., 1988); University of Denver (J.D., 1994). Author, "The Push for Statutes of Repose in General Aviation," 23 Transp. Law J. 323. *Member:* Transportation Lawyers Association (Chair, Young Lawyers Division, 1996—).

*(This Listing Continued)*

### OF COUNSEL

**PAMELA A. DAVIS,** born Montreal, Canada, June 19, 1960; admitted to bar, 1983, California. *Education:* Vanier College (D.E.C., Mathematics, English, 1979); McGill University (J.D., with distinction, 1982). Author, "Lien Releases: From Certainty to Confusion," California Construction Law Reporter, Vol. 2, McGraw Hill, February 1994. Judge Pro Tem, Los Angeles Municipal Court, 1991-1997. San Bernardino Superior Court Juvenile Hearing Officer, 1996-1997. *Member:* Beverly Hills and Los Angeles County (Member, Federal Courts Committee) Bar Associations; Women Lawyers Association of Los Angeles (Co-Chair, Trial Lawyers Section, 1995-1996); California Women Lawyers. **LANGUAGES:** French and Spanish. **SPECIAL AGENCIES:** Member, Penal Code 987 Panel, Burbank Municipal Court; Director, Westside Village Civic Association; Member, Los Angeles City Attorney's Task Force on Economic Recovery.

**ROBERT C. FISHMAN,** born New York, N. Y., July 1, 1954; admitted to bar, 1979, Massachusetts; 1980, New York and U.S. District Court, District of Massachusetts; 1983, California; 1985, U.S. District Court, Central District of California; 1992, U.S. District Court, Northern District of California; 1994, U.S. District Court, Eastern and Southern Districts of California. *Education:* Vassar College (A.B., 1976); Boston University (J.D., 1979). *Member:* Beverly Hills, Los Angeles County, New York State, Massachusetts and American Bar Associations; State Bar of California. **REPORTED CASES:** Dumas v. Research Testing Labs, Inc. (In re EPI Products USA, Inc.), 162 B.R. 1 (Bankr. C.D. Cal. 1993).

**WILLIAM M. AITKEN,** born Ann Arbor, Michigan, January 21, 1950; admitted to bar, 1978, California. *Education:* University of California at Los Angeles; University of California at Berkeley (A.B., 1971); University of California at Los Angeles (J.D., 1977). Phi Beta Kappa. Member, Board of Editors, University of California at Los Angeles Law Review, 1975-1977. *Member:* Los Angeles County and American Bar Associations; State Bar of California.

---

## BERMAN, BLANCHARD, MAUSNER & RESSER

*A LAW CORPORATION*

Established in 1984

**4727 WILSHIRE BOULEVARD, SUITE 500**
**LOS ANGELES, CALIFORNIA 90010**
Telephone: 213-965-1200
Telecopier: 213-965-1919
Email: BBMR@ix.netcom.com

*General Civil Trial and Appellate Practice in all State and Federal Courts and Administrative Agencies, with emphasis on Litigation in the following areas: Copyright, Trademark, Trade Secrets, Computer Law, Securities, Antitrust, Unfair Competition, Real Estate, Construction, Torts, Insurance, Employment, Probate and General Commercial Litigation.*

**LAURENCE M. BERMAN,** born Denver, Colorado, August 8, 1955; admitted to bar, 1980, California; 1981, U.S. District Court, Central District of California and U.S. Court of Appeals, Ninth Circuit; U.S. Supreme Court. *Education:* University of Wisconsin-Madison (B.A., with honors, 1976); University of California at Los Angeles (J.D., 1980). Managing Editor, UCLA/Alaska Law Review, University of California at Los Angeles, 1979-1980. Judge Pro Tem, Los Angeles Municipal Court. Member, International Trademark Association. *Member:* American Bar Association. **PRACTICE AREAS:** Commercial Litigation; Intellectual Property Litigation; Real Estate Litigation; Insurance Litigation; Telecommunications Law.

**LONNIE C. BLANCHARD, III,** born Three Rivers, Michigan, March 25, 1954; admitted to bar, 1980, California, U.S. District Court, Central District of California, U.S. Court of Appeals, Ninth Circuit and U.S. Tax Court. *Education:* Indiana University, Bloomington (B.S., 1975; M.B.A., 1977) Beta Gamma Sigma; University of California at Los Angeles (J.D., 1980) Order of the Coif. **PRACTICE AREAS:** Commercial Litigation; Real Estate; Real Estate Litigation; Probate Litigation; Construction Litigation; Tort Litigation; Insurance Litigation; Telecommunications Law; Complex Damage Analysis.

**JEFFREY N. MAUSNER,** born Detroit, Michigan, June 6, 1950; admitted to bar, 1977, New York; 1982, District of Columbia; 1986, California and Colorado; U.S. Supreme Court; U.S. Court of Appeals, Second, Third, Fourth, Sixth and Ninth Circuits. *Education:* Brown University

*(This Listing Continued)*

(B.A., 1972); Cornell Law School (J.D., magna cum laude, 1976). Member, Order of the Coif. Editor, Cornell Law Review, 1974-1976. Adjunct Associate Professor of Law, Southwestern University Law School, Intellectual Property Law and Computer Law. Author: "Protecting Your Product from Counterfeiters--What the Legal System Can Do for You," Ceramics Magazine, July 1994; "Protecting Your Product from Counterfeiters," Bobbin Magazine, July 1994; "The Ex Parte Seizure: Your Weapon Against Counterfeiters," The Crafts Report, Vol. 20, no. 221, September 1994; "State Exemptions from Securities Regulations Coextensive with Rule 146," 61 Cornell Law Review 157, republished in 1976 Securities Law Review 785; "Apprehending and Prosecuting Nazi War Criminals in the United States," 15 Nova Law Review 747. Moderator and Speaker at MCLE Seminar: Company Assets, Confidential Information, and The Mobile Employee. Trial Attorney, U.S. Justice Department, Office of Special Investigations, 1979-1985 (prosecution of Nazi war criminals). Recipient: Justice Department Meritorious Award for "Superior Performance of Duties on a Continuous Basis," 1982; Justice Department Exceptional Performance Award, 1982; Justice Department Special Achievement Award, 1984; Justice Department Outstanding Performance Award for, 1983, 1984, 1985. Special Assistant United States Attorney. Member, Panel of Arbitration, American Arbitration Association. **REPORTED CASES:** Tuchman v. Aetna, 44 Cal. App. 4th 1607 (1996); McCalden v. Simon Wiesenthal Center, 955 F.2d 1214 (9th Cir. 1992); McCalden v. Simon Wiesenthal Center, 919 F.2d 538 (9th Cir. 1990); U.S. v. Kowalchuk, 571 F. Supp. 72 (E.D. Pa. 199 3), affen banc, 773 F.2d 488 (3d Cir. 1985); Maikovskis v. I.N.S., 773 F.2d 435 (2d Cir. 1985); U.S v. Sprogis, 763 F.2d 115 (2d Cir. 1985); U.S. v. Linnas, 19 I & N Dec. 302. **PRACTICE AREAS:** Intellectual Property Litigation; Copyright; Trademark; Trade Secrets; Computer Law; Securities; Unfair Competition Law; Travel Law; Antitrust; Counterfeit Products.

**BERNARD M. RESSER,** born Chicago, Illinois, April 28, 1954; admitted to bar, 1980, California. *Education:* University of California, Los Angeles (B.A., cum laude, 1976; J.D., 1979). Trial Attorney, U.S. Department of Justice, Antitrust Division, 1980-1981. Assistant United States Attorney, Central District of California, 1982. Judge Pro Tem, Los Angeles Superior Court, 1990—; Municipal Court, 1986-1989. *Member:* Los Angeles County (Member, Public Affairs Committee, 1981-1982; Antitrust Law Section) and American (Member, Litigation Section) Bar Associations; State Bar of California; Association of Business Trial Lawyers. **PRACTICE AREAS:** Business Litigation; Real Estate Litigation; Insurance Litigation; Creditor's Remedies; Competitive Business Practices.

---

**PAUL A. HOFFMAN,** born Logan, Utah, January 15, 1960; admitted to bar, 1988, Utah; 1990, California. *Education:* Brigham Young University (B.A., cum laude, 1985); J. Reuben Clark Law School (J.D., cum laude, 1988). Member, 1986-1988 and Note and Comment Editor, 1987-1988, Brigham Young University Law Review. Author: Comment, "Standing and Liability of State and Local Government Under the Civil RICO Statute," Brigham Young University Law Review 175, 1989. Clerk to Justice I. Daniel Stewart, Utah Supreme Court, 1988-1989. *Member:* Utah State Bar; State Bar of California. LANGUAGES: Spanish. **REPORTED CASES:** Tuchman v. Aetna, 44 Cal. App. 4th 1607 (1996); LMV Leasing, Inc. v. Conlin, 805 P.2d 189 (Vt. App. 1991). **PRACTICE AREAS:** Appellate Law; Commercial Litigation; Probate Litigation; Landlord/Tenant; Real Estate Litigation; Construction Law; Tort Litigation; Intellectual Property Litigation.

**ERIC LEVINRAD,** born Johannesburg, South Africa, October 11, 1966; admitted to bar, 1993, California. *Education:* University of California at Los Angeles (B.A., 1989); Boalt Hall School of Law, University of California (J.D., 1993). Book Review Editor, Industrial Relations Law Journal. **PRACTICE AREAS:** Commercial Litigation; Intellectual Property Litigation; Trademark; Copyrights; Trade Secrets; Unfair Competition.

**CARY P. OCON,** born Santa Monica, California, August 14, 1961; admitted to bar, 1994, California. *Education:* University of California at Berkeley (B.A, 1987); University of Minnesota Law School (J.D., 1992). LANGUAGES: Spanish. **PRACTICE AREAS:** Construction Litigation; Commercial Litigation.

**LISÉ HAMILTON,** born New York, N.Y., November 4, 1959; admitted to bar, 1993, California. *Education:* Rutgers College (B.A., summa cum laude, 1982); Columbia University (M.A., 1984); Yale University (J.D., 1993). Coker Fellow, Yale Law School. Author: article on Racial Identities, Reconstruction. ed., Randall Kennedy, republished in *PICTURING US: African American Identity in Photography,* ed. Deborah Willis, The New York Press, 1994. Extern to Judge Alex R. Munson, U.S. District Court,

*(This Listing Continued)*

Northern Mariana Islands, 1991. **PRACTICE AREAS:** Commercial Litigation; Intellectual Property Litigation; Corporate; Entertainment.

REPRESENTATIVE CLIENTS: Sears, Roebuck and Co.; Nestle USA, Inc.; Infinite Broadcasting Corp.; Select Restaurants, Inc.; General Media Corp.; Allstate Insurance Co.; Birdy Electronics Co., Ltd.; Rhino Toys Manufacturing, Ltd.; Scioto Ceramic Products, Inc.; Source Services Corp.; Fruit of the Loom, Inc.; Haseko, Inc.; First Alabama Bank; Golden State Health Centers; Watts Health Foundation, Inc.; D/B/A United Health Plan; Teletech Telecommunications, Inc.; Transportation Displays, Inc.; J.J. Newberry Co.; Simon Wiesenthal Center.

---

## MICHAEL A. BERTZ

SUITE 2400, 1801 CENTURY PARK EAST
**LOS ANGELES, CALIFORNIA 90067**
*Telephone: 310-277-2811*
*Fax: 310-277-2914*

*Securities and Corporate Litigation.*

**MICHAEL A. BERTZ,** born July 21, 1941, Alhambra, California; admitted to bar, 1967, New York; 1970, California. *Education:* University of California at Los Angeles (B.S., 1962; M.B.A., 1963); Boalt Hall School of Law, University of California (J.D., 1966); Pepperdine University School of Law for Dispute Resolution (Certified, Mediating the Litigated Case, 1996). Author: "Pursuing a Business Fraud RICO Claim", California Western Law Review, Vol. 21, No 2, 1985; Editorial, RICO Law Reporter, Vol. 2, No. 4, October, 1985; "Security Fraud Time Limit Restricted-Looking For Alternatives," Securities & RICO Update, October, 1991; "Pattern of Racketeering Activity-A Jury Issue: Opposing Views," Beverly Hills Bar Association Journal, Vol. 26, No. 1, Winter, 1992; "Securities Arbitration: A Matter of Fairness," ABTL Report, Vol. XIV, No. 3 May, 1992; "Section 1962 (a) Liability-Injury From Racketeering Acts," L.A. Co. Bar Assn., Lit. Section Newsletter, Vol. 9, No. 1, Summer 1992; "Punitive Damages in Securities Arbitration," Securities & RICO Update, January, 1993; "Liability Under RICO Section 1962 (c): The Supreme Court Adopts The 'Operation or Management' Test," L.A. Co. Bar Assn. Lit. Section Newsletter, Vol 9, No. 4, Spring 1993; "No Economic Motive Required for RICO: Supreme Court Simplifies Proofs for A RICO Claim," Beverly Hills Bar Association Journal, Vol. 28, No. 2, Spring, 1994. Author and Publisher: *Securities & RICO Update, Quarterly.* Legal Assistant, VISTA, Mobilization for Youth, Legal Services Unit New York, New York, 1966-1967. Staff Attorney, Nassau County Law Services Committee, New York, 1967-1969. Trial Attorney, U.S. Securities and Exchange Commission, Los Angeles Regional Office, 1969-1975. Special Attorney, U.S. Department of Justice, Los Angeles Organized Crime and Racketeering Strike Force, 1975. Adjunct Associate Professor, Glendale College of Law, 1971-1977. Member: Panel of Arbitrators, American Arbitration Association, 1976—; Panel of Business Law Arbitrators of the Los Angeles Superior Court, 1980—. Judge Pro Tem, Los Angeles Municipal Court, 1984, 1989—. *Member:* Los Angeles County and Beverly Hills Bar Associations; State Bar of California; Association of Business Trial Lawyers (Board of Governors, 1994—); Los Angeles Complex Litigation Inn of Court (Executive Committee, 1994—).

---

## BEWLEY, LASSLEBEN & MILLER

**LOS ANGELES, CALIFORNIA**

(See Whittier)

*General Civil and Criminal Trial Practice in all State and Federal Courts. Probate, Corporation, Estate Planning and Trust, Federal and State Taxation, Real Estate, Commercial Litigation and Collection, Personal Injury, Products Liability and Federal and State Court Appeals.*

---

## JONATHAN W. BIDDLE

**LOS ANGELES, CALIFORNIA**

(See Beverly Hills)

*General Civil Practice before State and Federal Courts. Labor and Employment Law.*

## BIENSTOCK & CLARK
### LOS ANGELES, CALIFORNIA
(See Santa Monica)

*General Trial and Appellate Practice in all Courts. Antitrust, Civil Rights, Communications and Media, Complex Commercial, Constitutional, Debtor and Creditor Rights, Defamation, Employment, Financial Institutions, Insurance, Intellectual Property, Patent, Personal Injury, Professional Malpractice, Real Estate, and Securities Litigation.*

---

## BIESTY, McCOOL & GARRETTY
### A PROFESSIONAL CORPORATION
Established in 1978

725 SOUTH FIGUEROA STREET, SUITE 2200
### LOS ANGELES, CALIFORNIA 90017
Telephone: 213-617-9193
Facsimile: 213-620-0746

Insurance Defense. Legal, Real Estate, Insurance Agents and Brokers' Errors & Omissions. Construction Defect and Family Law. Governmental Tort Liability. General Civil Litigation, Alternate Dispute Resolution.

FIRM PROFILE: Biesty, McCool & Garretty has been doing business for over eighteen years in the Los Angeles area and all surrounding counties. Given the extensive insurance background of each partner, before starting this practice Biesty, McCool & Garretty are very sensitive to the issues of cost containment and litigation expense management without compromising the quality of the representation to our clients. We have considerable experience in dealing with all areas of insurance defense including construction defect, construction personal injury and property damage liability, products liability, governmental tort liability, auto and truck liability as well as legal, real estate broker and insurance broker errors and omission liability.

**JAMES T. BIESTY,** born New York, New York, February 2, 1940; admitted to bar, 1978, California and U.S. District Court, Central District of California. *Education:* California State University at Los Angeles (B.S., 1972); Southwestern University (J.D., 1977). *Member:* Beverly Hills, Los Angeles County, American and Irish-American Bar Associations; State Bar of California; Southern California Association of Defense County; Defense Research Institute. **PRACTICE AREAS:** Insurance Defense Law; Insurance Coverage; Bad Faith Law; Construction Law; Arbitration; Mediation.

**CLINTON T. MCCOOL,** admitted to bar, 1986, California and U.S. District Court, Central District of California. *Education:* East Stroudsburg State College (B.A.); Southwestern University College of Law (J.D., 1980). *Member:* Los Angeles County Bar Association (Member, Business Litigation Section); State Bar of California; South California Association of Defense Counsel. **PRACTICE AREAS:** Insurance Defense Litigation; Insurance Coverage; Bad Faith Litigation; Errors and Omissions; Contract Litigation; Arbitration; Mediation.

**REETHA HAYNES-GARRETTY,** born Alhambra, California, 1954; admitted to bar, 1986, California and U.S. District Court, Central District of California; 1996, Arizona. *Education:* California State University, Los Angeles (B.A., 1977); Glendale University College of Law (B.S.L., 1980; J.D., 1982). *Member:* Los Angeles County Bar Association; State Bar of California; Southern California Association of Defense Counsel; Los Angeles County Women Lawyer's Association. **PRACTICE AREAS:** Insurance Defense Litigation; Construction Litigation; Business Litigation; Family Law.

---

**DAVID N. BALL,** born Park Ridge, Illinois; February 20, 1962; admitted to bar, 1988, California. *Education:* University of California at San Diego (B.A., 1983); Loyola University of Los Angeles (J.D., 1986). *Member:* Los Angeles County and American (Member, Litigation Section) Bar Associations; State Bar of California. **PRACTICE AREAS:** Insurance Defense Litigation; Construction Litigation; Real Estate; Family Law; Business Litigation; Personal Injury Law.

**MARINA M. MORRISON,** born Tehran, Iran, May 1, 1960; admitted to bar, 1992, California and U.S. District Court, Central District of California. *Education:* University of California at Los Angeles (B.A., Psychology, 1984); Southwestern University School of Law (J.D., 1992). Member, Legal Eagles for Truth, Justice and the American Way. *Member:* Los Angeles County and American Bar Associations; State Bar of California.

*(This Listing Continued)*

---

**BRETT G. HAMPTON,** born Santa Monica, California, May 29, 1963; admitted to bar, 1989, California; 1990, U.S. District Court, Central District of California. *Education:* University of California at Santa Barbara; University of California at Berkeley (B.A., 1983); Pepperdine University (J.D., 1987). Recipient, American Jurisprudence Awards in Constitutional Law and Individual Rights and Trial Advocacy II. *Member:* Los Angeles County and American (Member, Sections on: Litigation; Individual Rights & Responsibilities) Bar Associations; State Bar of California; Association of Southern California Defense Counsel.

REPRESENTATIVE CLIENTS: Allstate Insurance Co.; Carl Warren & Co.; Sutter Insurance Co.; Laidlaw; Golden Eagle Insurance Co.; Biller-Smith Associates, Inc.; Penn-America Insurance Co.; Stevedoring Services of America; Crawford & Co.; Los Angeles County; California Insurance Guarantee Association; Investors Insurance Co.

---

## BIGELOW, MOORE & TYRE
### LOS ANGELES, CALIFORNIA
(See Pasadena)

*Corporate, Tax, General and Business Litigation, Entertainment, Real Estate, Appellate Practice, Health Care, First Amendment, Administrative Law, Probate and Estate Planning.*

---

## BILLET & KAPLAN
A Partnership of Professional Corporations

Established in 1993

SUITE 1700, 1888 CENTURY PARK EAST
### LOS ANGELES, CALIFORNIA 90067-1721
Telephone: 310-551-1700
Fax: 310-277-7062

*General Civil and Commercial Litigation, including Title Insurance Litigation, Financial Institution Litigation, Real Estate Litigation, Insolvency and related Litigation, Wrongful Termination Litigation, Fidelity and Blanket Bond Litigation.*

FIRM PROFILE: Members, principals and associates of the firm have served as lecturers or authors on trial practice, title insurance, banking, bankruptcy, federal and state securities laws, and arbitration matters, and as Judges Pro Tem.

### MEMBER OF FIRM

**TERRY S. KAPLAN, (A PROFESSIONAL CORPORATION),** born New York, N.Y., October 20, 1944; admitted to bar, 1971, California, U.S. District Courts, Northern, Southern, Eastern and Central Districts of California; U.S. court of Appeals, Ninth Circuit. *Education:* University of California at Los Angeles (B.A., with honors, 1966; M.A., 1968); University of Southern California (J.D., 1971). Order of the Coif. Comment Editor, Southern California Law Review, 1970-1971. Lecturer, Seminars on: Loan Documentation, Bank-Operation Problems and Banker's Blanket Bonds, Banking Law Institute, 1977-1983; Lecturer, Title Insurance Matters. Associate Member, California Land Title Association, 1984-1993. *Member:* Los Angeles County Bar Association; The State Bar of California. **PRACTICE AREAS:** Litigation.

**RONALD J. SOKOL, (A PROFESSIONAL CORPORATION),** born Los Angeles, California, February 10, 1950; admitted to bar, 1978, California. *Education:* University of California at Los Angeles (B.A., Philosophy, cum laude, 1971); University of Santa Clara (J.D., magna cum laude, 1977). Recipient, Mary J. Emery Academic Scholarship. Law Clerk to the Honorable Robert Firth, U.S. District Court, Central District of California, 1978-1979. Columnist, The Sacramento Union, "You and the Law, 1981-1982. Instructor and Assistant Professor, American River College, California State University, Sacramento, and California State University, Long Beach, 1981-1987. Legislative Consultant to the Governor, State of California, 1981-1982. Chairperson, State Commission on Voting Machines and Vote Tabulating Devices, 1982. Judge Pro Tem, Municipal Court, 1988—. Formerly Litigation Partner, Katten, Muchen, Zavis & Weitzman. Member, Panel of Arbitrators, American Arbitration Association. *Member:* The State Bar of California.

**GREGORY A. DAWLEY, (A PROFESSIONAL CORPORATION),** born Pasadena, California, August 21, 1954; admitted to bar, 1985, California, U.S. District Court, Northern, Southern and Central Districts of California and U.S. Circuit Court, Ninth Circuit. *Education:* California Polytechnic State University, San Luis Obispo (B.A., English, 1976); Whittier

*(This Listing Continued)*

College School of Law (J.D., magna cum laude, 1985). Recipient, American Jurisprudence Awards in Contracts II, Torts I, Legal Process, Constitutional Law I, Secured Transactions, and Criminal Procedure. *Member:* Los Angeles County Bar Association; The State Bar of California.

### ASSOCIATES

**MICHAEL K. DEWBERRY,** born Memphis, Tennessee, October 29, 1952; admitted to bar, 1990, California. *Education:* Harvard University (A.B., 1978); University of Southern California (J.D., 1981). *Member:* Los Angeles County Bar Association; The State Bar of California. **PRACTICE AREAS:** Litigation.

**PAUL N. GLASSER,** born Los Angeles, California, September 23, 1958; admitted to bar, 1986, California and U.S. District Court, Central District of California. *Education:* University of California at Berkeley (B.A., Journalism, with high honors, 1980; B.A., Poli. Sci, 1980); University of Oregon (J.D., 1985). Associate Editor, University of Oregon Law Review, 1984-1985. *Member:* Los Angeles County Bar Association; State Bar of California. **PRACTICE AREAS:** Civil Litigation.

**JORDAN TRACHTENBERG,** born Boston, Massachusetts, June 1, 1957; admitted to bar, 1984, California. *Education:* Connecticut College (B.A., Government and History, cum laude, 1979); University of California School of Law (J.D., 1984). Recipient, American Jurisprudence Award in Business Associations. Participant, Moot Court Honors Program. Recipient, Earl Cilliam Western States Scholarship. Former Treasurer, Los Angeles Public Defenders Association. Former Member, District Attorney and Public Defenders Collective Bargaining Committee. *Member:* Los Angeles County and American Bar Associations; The State Bar of California; California Public Defenders Association.

**ROGER C. GLIENKE,** born Chicago, Illinois, October 31, 1950; admitted to bar, 1982, Illinois; 1983, California, U.S. Tax Court, U.S. District Court, Central District of California and U.S. Court of Appeals, Ninth Circuit; 1991, U.S. Court of Federal Claims. *Education:* University of Illinois; Columbia College at Chicago (B.A., with honors, 1975); University of Notre Dame School of Law, London, England; De Paul University (J.D., 1982). Member, De Paul Law Review, 1980-1982. Author: "Title VII: New Restrictions on the Disparate Impact Prima Facie Case: E.E.O.C. v. Greyhound Lines, Inc." 30 DePaul L. Rev. 945, 1982. *Member:* Los Angeles County, Bar Association (Member, Litigation Section and Real Property Section) and American Bar Association (Member, Litigation Section); State Bar of California; Association of Business Trial Lawyers. **REPORTED CASES:** Facilities Systems Engineering Corp. v. United States, 25 Cl.Ct. 76 1 (1992); Wilson v. Commissioner of Internal Revenue, 57 T.C.M. (CCH 576 T.C. Memo. 1989-266; Graff v. Commissioner, 52 T.C.M. 9cch0 1025, T.C. Memo. 1986-550; Rowles v. Commissioner, 51 TC.M. (CCH) 27, T.C. MEMO. 1985-266; Gabaldon v. Commissioner, 47 T.C.M. (CCH) 1218, T.C. Memo 1984-107; Africa v. Commissioner, 47 T.C.M. (CCH) 1178, T.C. Memo. 1984-1995; Urban V. Commissioner, 47 T.C.M. (CCH) 1130, T.C. Memo. 1984-1985.

**TODD M. LANDER,** born Kelowna, British Columbia, June 19, 1968; admitted to bar, 1994, California. *Education:* University of British Columbia (B.A., 1990); Whittier College (J.D., cum laude, 1994). Recipient: Dean's Merit Award Scholarship; American Jurisprudence Award.

### OF COUNSEL

**JEROME S. BILLET, (A PROFESSIONAL CORPORATION),** born Washington, D.C., April 5, 1935; admitted to bar, 1963, California, U.S. District Court, Central and Southern Districts of California; 1973, U.S. Court of Appeals, Ninth Circuit; 1975, U.S. District Court, Northern District of California; 1983, U.S. Court of International Trade. *Education:* University of California at Los Angeles (B.A., 1958; J.D., 1962). Member, UCLA Law Review. *Member:* Beverly Hills and Los Angeles County and American (Member: Sections on: Litigation; Antitrust) Bar Associations; State Bar of California; Los Angeles Trial Lawyers Association; Association of Business Trial Lawyers. **PRACTICE AREAS:** Civil Litigation.

**ARTHUR L. ROLSTON, (A PROFESSIONAL LAW CORPORATION),** born Los Angeles, California, May 5, 1942; admitted to bar, 1967, California, U.S. District Court, Northern, Central, Eastern and Southern Districts of California, U.S. District Court, District of Arizona and U.S. Court of Appeals, Ninth Circuit. *Education:* University of Southern California (B.A., 1964); Boalt Hall School of Law, University of California (J.D., 1967). Judge Pro Tem: East Los Angeles Municipal Court, 1973-1974; Los Angeles Municipal Court, 1984. Hearing Officer, Los Angeles Police Commission, 1984-1992. Member, National Panel of Commercial Arbitrators, American Arbitration Association. *Member:* Los Angeles County Bar Association; State Bar of California. **PRACTICE AREAS:** Commercial; Bankruptcy; Equipment Leasing; Business Law; Litigation.

REPRESENTATIVE CLIENTS: California Commerce Bank; Frontier State Bank; Community Construction, Inc.; California Land Title Company of Marin; Continental Lawyers Title Company; Land Title Insurance Company; Lawyers Title Insurance Corporation; Bergen Brunswig Drug Co.; Bell & Howell Acceptance Corp.; Great Western Bank; the Illinois Office of the Special Deputy Receiver; Manhattan Village Estate Homes Association; Los Feliz Estates Association; S.B.c. Ltd., dba Autospecialty; E & E Development and Investment Corp.

---

## BIRD & BIRD

*A LAW CORPORATION*

**LOS ANGELES, CALIFORNIA**

(See Torrance)

*Criminal Trials and Criminal Appeals, White Collar Criminal Defense.*

---

## BIRD, MARELLA, BOXER, WOLPERT & MATZ

*A PROFESSIONAL CORPORATION*

Established in 1981

1875 CENTURY PARK EAST, 23RD FLOOR
**LOS ANGELES, CALIFORNIA 90067-2561**
Telephone: 310-201-2100
Facsimile: 310-201-2110

*Civil and Criminal, Trial and Appellate Litigation.*

*FIRM PROFILE: The firm engages only in litigation, including civil and criminal trials and appeals, arbitrations, mediations and other alternative dispute mechanisms, and administrative proceedings.*

*In our civil practice, we represent plaintiffs and defendants in matters involving business torts, contract disputes, probate litigation, products and environmental liability. Among the active facets of our civil practice is the representation of lawyers and law firms -- and other kinds of partnerships as well -- in a variety of professional matters, such as disputes over partnership rights, dissolutions, fee allocations and claims brought by third parties.*

*Our criminal defense practice, which is concentrated in federal court, is restricted to economic crimes. Our ranks include six former federal prosecutors. We frequently defend corporate officers and directors, accountants, physicians, lawyers and business entities in a broad range of investigations and prosecutions. These cases often involve banks, savings and loan associations, government contractors, and official corruption. We also have conducted internal investigations for corporations that are evaluating their own possible criminal or regulatory exposure.*

**TERRY W. BIRD,** born Los Angeles, California, February 11, 1946; admitted to bar, 1970, California. *Education:* Stanford University (B.A., 1967); University of California at Los Angeles (J.D., 1970). Member, Moot Court. Law Clerk, California Court of Appeals, Second District, 1970-1972. Assistant U.S. Attorney, 1972-1977. Author: "Shooting Holes in The 'Shell' Game with Expert Testimony," Association of Business Trial Lawyers Report, Volume 16, No. 2, February 1994. Co-Author: "Exposing the 'Shell' Game," Environmental Law Reporter, Volume 1993, Issue No. 10, October 1993; "Successfully Coping With the Corporate Criminal Investigation," Corporate Criminal Liability Reporter, Sept., 1986; "Preserving Confidentiality in Corporate Internal Investigations," Corporate Criminal Liability Reporter, Spring, 1987. Co-Chairman, Lawyer Representatives, Ninth Circuit Judicial Conference, Central District of California, 1989-1990. Chairman, Lawyers Representatives, Ninth Circuit Judicial Conference, 1991-1992. Member: Ninth Circuit's Gender Bias Task Force, 1991-1994; Ninth Circuit Judicial Conference Magistrates Advisory Committee, 1988-1991; Ninth Circuit Executive Committee, 1989-1993; ABA White Collar Crime Committee; Chairman, Federal Courts Committee, Los Angeles County Bar Association, 1991-1995. Member, Board of Directors, Association of Business Trial Lawyers, 1991-1993. President, Inns of Court, Complex Litigation, 1993-1994. Member, Central District of California's Attorney Admission Fund Board, 1992-1996. Member, ABA Litigation Sections' Merit Selection of Judges Task Force, 1996-1997. Deputy General Counsel, Hon. Judge William Webster, Special Advisor for the Investigation Into The LAPD's Response To The April 1992 Urban Disorders. Counsel, Christopher Commission Study, Los Angeles Police Department,

*(This Listing Continued)*

**BIRD, MARELLA, BOXER, WOLPERT & MATZ,** A PROFESSIONAL CORPORATION, Los Angeles—Continued

1991. RICO lecturer, Continuing Education of the Bar, 1991. Lecturer, Federal Bar Association, Grand Jury Investigations. Lecturer: White Collar Criminal Law Reporter, Corporate Criminal Investigations; ABA White Collar Crime Committee, "Funding a Defense in the '90's"; CYLA 1993 State Bar Meeting, "The Future of Insurance Coverage for Environmental and Toxic Hazards"; Prentice Hall Law & Business, "Eighth Annual Insurance Litigation Institute," January-February 1994; Association of Business Trial Lawyers, "Changing the Federal Rules, Is The Cure Worse Than The Illness." *Member:* Los Angeles County and American Bar Associations; State Bar of California. Fellow, American College of Trial Lawyers.

**JOEL E. BOXER,** born Chicago, Illinois, July 9, 1944; admitted to bar, 1972, California. *Education:* University of California at Los Angeles (B.A., 1967); Harvard University (J.D., cum laude, 1971). Teaching Fellow and Instructor, Stanford Law School, 1972-1973. Law Clerk, Hon. Stanley A. Weigel, U.S. District Judge, Northern District of California, 1971-1972. Co-Author: "Copyright Infringement of Audio-Visual Works and Characters," 52 U.S.C. Law Review, p. 315, January, 1979; Co-Author: "Major Pitfalls in Drafting Transactional Documents (A Litigator's Prospective)," Beverly Hills Bar Association, 1988, 1990 and 1992 Editions. Judge Pro Tem, Los Angeles and Beverly Hills Municipal Courts, 1976-1988. *Member:* Beverly Hills (Chair, Judge Pro Tem Committee, 1981-1983) and Los Angeles County (Member of Arbitrators Panel Attorney-Clients Fee Disputes, 1987-1993) Bar Associations; The State Bar of California (Member, 1973-1975 and Advisor, 1975-1976, Federal Courts Committee).

**VINCENT J. MARELLA,** born Philadelphia, Pennsylvania, July 6, 1946; admitted to bar, 1972, Pennsylvania; 1973, U.S. Tax Court and California; 1976, U.S. Supreme Court; U.S. District Court, Northern, Southern, Eastern and Central Districts of California. *Education:* Temple University (B.A., 1968; J.D., 1972). Adjunct Professor of Law, Loyola Law School, 1985-1987. Author: "Issues and Strategies in Defending Criminal Environmental Cases," The Defense of Environmental Cases, ABA National Institute on White Collar Crime, March 1991; "The Department of Justice Prosecutive Guidelines in Environmental Cases Involving Voluntary Disclosure—a Leap Forward or a Leap of Faith?" American Criminal Law Review, Vol. 29, 1992; "The Defense of Environmental Cases," ABA National Institute on White Collar Crime, March 1991; "Introduction to Ninth Circuit Review of Criminal Cases," Loyola Law Review, 1976. Co-Author: "Rough Remedial Justice: Implications of *Halper and Austin* in Civil Forfeiture Actions," National Institute on Criminal Tax Fraud and Money Laundering, December 1993; "A Primer on Federal Environmental Crimes," Criminal Law News, Winter 1993; "Successfully Coping With the Corporate Criminal Investigation," Corporate Criminal Liability Reporter, September 1986; "Preserving Confidentiality in Corporate Internal Investigations," Corporate Criminal Liability Reporter, Spring 1987. Contributing Author, West's California Criminal Law, West Publishing Co., 1995. Lecturer: "Defending Environmental Prosecutions," ABA National Institute on White Collar Crime, 1991-1996; NYU Tax Institute, 1988. California Regional Chairman, 1990-1994 and Vice Chairman, 1991-1994, ABA National White Collar Crime Committee. National Chairman, Criminal Justice Section's White Collar Crime Committee, 1994-1996. Member, Federal Appointments Evaluation Committee, Los Angeles County Bar Association, 1989-1992. Deputy General Counsel to Hon. Judge William Webster, Special Advisor for the Investigation into the LAPD's Response To The April 1992 Urban Disorders. Member, Advisory Board, Bureau of National Affairs, (BNA) ACCA Corporate Compliance Manual. Assistant United States Attorney, 1972-1977, Assistant Chief Criminal Division, 1976-1977, Central District of California. Member of Temple Law School Board of Visitors, 1996—. *Member:* Pennsylvania, Federal and American Bar Associations; State Bar of California; National Association of Criminal Defense Lawyers. Fellow, American College of Trial Lawyers (Member: Attorney-Client Relationship Committee, 1996—; Southern California State Committee, 1995—).

**A. HOWARD MATZ,** born Brooklyn, New York, August 3, 1943; admitted to bar, 1970, New York; 1973, California. *Education:* Columbia University (A.B., cum laude, 1965); Harvard University (J.D., 1968). Co-Author: "Obtaining Evidence For Federal Economic Crime Prosecutions," 14 American Criminal Law Review 651, 1977. Author: "Determining the Standard of Proof In Law Suits Brought Under RICO," The National Law Journal, October 1983. Co-Author: "Potential Tort Liability in Business Takeovers," The California Lawyer, September, 1986; "Compensating Non-Expert Witnesses," The Los Angeles Lawyer, March 1989. Law Clerk, Hon. Morris E. Lasker, United States District Court, Southern District of
*(This Listing Continued)*

New York, 1969-1970. Assistant United States Attorney, 1974-1978 and Chief, Special Prosecutions Unit, 1977-1978, Central District of California. Member, Board of Directors, Legal Aid Foundation of Los Angeles, 1990-1991. Board Member and President, 1992-1993, Bet Tzedek Legal Services. Member, Board of Editors of Business Crimes Bulletin. *Member:* Los Angeles County, Beverly Hills, New York State and American Bar Associations; State Bar of California.

**DOROTHY WOLPERT,** born New York, N.Y., December 19, 1934; admitted to bar, 1976, California, U.S. District Court, Northern, Southern, Eastern and Central Districts of California and U.S. Court of Appeals, 9th Circuit. *Education:* City College of the City University of New York and University of Pennsylvania (B.A., 1959); University of California at Los Angeles (J.D., 1976). Phi Beta Kappa. Member, Moot Court. Contributing Author, California Trial Objections, Second Edition, C.E.B., 1984. Judge Pro Tem, Los Angeles Municipal Courts, 1982-1996. Member, Panel of Arbitrators, LASC. *Member:* Beverly Hills and Los Angeles County Bar Associations; The State Bar of California.

**JASON D. KOGAN,** born New Haven, Connecticut, April 7, 1944; admitted to bar, 1969, Virginia; 1970, District of Columbia; 1983, California. *Education:* Pennsylvania State University (B.A., 1966); George Washington University (J.D., 1969). Author: "On Being a Good Expert Witness in a Criminal Case," 23 Journal of Forensic Science 190, 1978; "Reducing the Cost of Responding to a Subpoena Duces Tecum for Business Records," CEB Civil Litigation Reporter, June 1987. Co-Author: "Compensating Non-Expert Witnesses," Los Angeles Lawyer, March, 1989. Law Clerk, Hon. Andrew M. Hood, Chief Judge, District of Columbia Court of Appeals, 1969-1970. Assistant United States Attorney, 1970-1983 and Senior Litigation Counsel, 1981-1983, District of Columbia. Co-Chair, Criminal Law Section, Century City Bar Association, 1995—. *Member:* Los Angeles County Bar Association; District of Columbia Bar; Virginia State Bar; The State Bar of California.

**MARK T. DROOKS,** born New York, N.Y., July 22, 1957; admitted to bar, 1982, District of Columbia; 1986, California. *Education:* Cornell University (B.A., cum laude, 1978); Harvard University (J.D., magna cum laude, 1981). Comments Editor, Harvard Civil Rights-Civil Liberties Law Review, 1980-1981. Author: "Amending The Federal Tort Claims Act," 17 Harvard J. Legis. 357, 1980; "Environmental Liability, Concurrent Causation and Insurance Coverage: Some Practical Experience,: Mealey's Litigation Reports, 12/1/93. Co-Author: "Preserving Confidentiality In Corporate Internal Investigations," Corporate Criminal Liability Reporter, Vol. 1, No. 2, Spring, 1987. Law Clerk to Hon. Pierre N. Leval, United States District Court, Southern District of New York, 1981-1982. Panel of Public Arbitrators, National Association of Securities Dealers. Board Member, Bet Tzedek Legal Services. *Member:* Los Angeles County Bar Association; The District of Columbia Bar; The State Bar of California.

**RONALD J. NESSIM,** born Los Angeles, California, January 23, 1955; admitted to bar, 1980, California. *Education:* Stanford University (A.B., with distinction, 1977); University of Michigan (J.D., cum laude, 1980). Phi Beta Kappa. Member, University of Michigan Journal of Law Reform, 1978-1979. Assistant United States Attorney, Central District of California, 1984-1987. Author: "Parallel Civil and Criminal Litigation," The Los Angeles Lawyer, December 1990; "Conflicts and Confidences, The Defense Viewpoint," ABA Criminal Justice, Spring, 1992; "Joint Defense Privilege and Conflicts of Interest," The Los Angeles Lawyer, May 1992; "Internal Investigations," ABA National Institute on Health Care Fraud, February 1994; "The Glass Slipper," The Los Angeles Lawyer, November, 1994; "Criminal (and Civil) Trademark Infringement: What Statute of Limitation Applies?," Journal of the Patent and Trademark Society, December, 1994. Lecturer, Health Care Fraud, ABA National Institute, 1993-1996. Faculty Member, ABA National Institute on Health Care Fraud, 1993-1997. Steering Committee Member, ABA National Institute on Health Care Fraud, 1995-1997. Counsel to Judge William Webster, Special Advisor for the Investigation into the LAPD's Response To The April 1992 Urban Disorders. National Co-Chairman Ethical Issues Subcommittee, ABA White Collar Crime Committee, 1990-1992. Panel of Public Arbitrators, National Association of Securities Dealers. *Member:* Los Angeles County and American Bar Associations; State Bar of California.

**THOMAS R. FREEMAN,** born Chicago, Illinois, November 11, 1960; admitted to bar, 1987, California. *Education:* Rollins College (B.A., 1983); Northwestern University (J.D., cum laude, 1987). Order of the Coif. Associate Articles Editor, Journal of Criminal Law and Criminology, 1985-1987. Law Clerk to the Honorable Edward Rafeedie, U.S. District Court, Central District of California, 1987-1988. Author, "Pretrial Procedure, Motions and Considerations," Ninth Circuit Trial Practice Guide. *Member:* Los
*(This Listing Continued)*

## PROFESSIONAL BIOGRAPHIES
## CALIFORNIA—LOS ANGELES

Angeles County Bar Association (Member, Appellate Courts Committee); State Bar of California.

**GARY S. LINCENBERG,** born Chicago, Illinois, January 29, 1960; admitted to bar, 1986, California. *Education:* University of Illinois (B.A., summa cum laude, 1982); Harvard University (J.D., 1985). Assistant United States Attorney (Deputy Chief), 1987-1993. Editorial Board, ABA Criminal Justice Magazine. Author: "Critique of the Proposed Federal Sentencing Guidelines for Corporations Convicted of Environmental Crimes," California Environmental Law Reporter, April 1994; "The Hazards of Wasting Time: When Facing Possible Charges for an Environmental Crime, Your First Steps May be Your Most Important Ones," 9 American Bar Association Criminal Justice Magazine, No. 1, Spring 1994; "Recent Developments in Federal Prosecution of Environmental Crimes," Los Angeles Country Bar Environmental Law Section Newsletter, Fall 1993; "Sentencing Environmental Crimes," 4 American Criminal Law Review 29, Summer 1992; "Lowered Intent Requirements in Environmental Crimes Cases," 7 ABA Criminal Justice Magazine 2, Summer 1992. Co-Author: "Issues and Strategies in Defending Criminal Environmental Cases," Third Annual Environmental Litigation Institute, March 1994; "A Primer on Federal Environmental Crimes," 13 Criminal Law News, Winter 1993; "Rough Remedial Justice: Implications of *Halper and Austin* in Civil Forfeiture Actions," National Institute on Criminal Tax Fraud and Money Laundering, December 1993. Lecturer: ABA National White Collar Crimes Conference, 1992 and 1993; Commercial Law Affiliates National Practice Institute, 1993; State Bar of California Environmental Law Institute, 1993 and 1994. Witness: United States Sentencing Commission Hearings on Environmental Guidelines for Organizations, 1993. *Member:* State Bar of California; American Bar Association (Chair, Environmental Crimes Committee).

---

**EFREM M. GRAIL,** born Columbus, Ohio, December 24, 1959; admitted to bar, 1986, California. *Education:* Northwestern University (B.A., 1981); Columbia University (J.D., 1986). Deputy District Attorney, County of Los Angeles, 1989-1996; Special Investigations Division, 1991-1996. Adjunct Professor, Constitutional and Criminal Law, University of La Verne School of Law, 1993—. *Member:* Los Angeles County and American Bar Associations; State Bar of California. *LANGUAGES:* Spanish. *PRACTICE AREAS:* Criminal Law; General Commercial Law; Securities Law; First Amendment Practice.

**KRISTIN L. JAMESON,** born Newport Beach, California, June 25, 1955; admitted to bar, 1980, California and U.S. District Court, Central District of California. *Education:* San Diego State University (B.A., magna cum laude, 1977); University of Southern California (J.D., 1980). *Member:* Los Angeles County Bar Association; State Bar of California.

**JOHN MILTON MCCOY, III,** born Philadelphia, Pennsylvania, September 12, 1968; admitted to bar, 1993, California and U.S. District Court, Central District of California. *Education:* University of California at Berkeley (B.A., with high distinction, 1990); University of California, Boalt Hall School of Law (J.D., 1993). Phi Beta Kappa. Executive Editor, 1991-1992 and Senior Managing Editor, 1992-1993, Industrial Relations Law Journal. Recipient, Wiley W. Manuel Pro Bono Services Award. *Member:* Los Angeles County and American Bar Associations; State Bar of California.

**ELIZABETH A. NEWMAN,** born Los Angeles, California, October 13, 1958; admitted to bar, 1992, California; 1993, U.S. District Court, Central District of California and U.S. Court of Appeals, Ninth Circuit. *Education:* Harvard University (A.B., with honors, 1980); University of Southern California (J.D., 1992). Order of the Coif. Member, 1990-1991 and Articles Editor, 1991-1992, Southern California Law Review. Law Clerk, Hon. Stephen Reinhardt, U.S. Court of Appeals, Ninth Circuit, 1992-1993.

**THOMAS V. REICHERT,** born New Rochelle, New York, September 29, 1964; admitted to bar, 1994, California. *Education:* Georgetown University (B.S.F.S., cum laude, 1986); Harvard University (A.M., 1988); University of Virginia (J.D., 1993). Order of the Coif. Dillard Scholar. Law Clerk, Hon. Sam J. Ervin, Chief Judge, U.S. Court of Appeals, Fourth Circuit, 1993-1994. Executive Editor, Virginia Journal of Social Policy & the Law, 1992-1993.

**EKWAN E. RHOW,** born Reading, Pennsylvania, May 19, 1969; admitted to bar, 1994, California. *Education:* Stanford University (B.A., 1991); Harvard University (J.D., 1994). *Member:* Los Angeles County Bar Association; State Bar of California; Korean American Bar Association.

*(This Listing Continued)*

---

### OF COUNSEL

**LOUISE A. LAMOTHE, (A PROFESSIONAL CORPORATION),** born Manchester, New Hampshire, December 9, 1946; admitted to bar, 1972, California and Kansas. *Education:* Stanford University (B.A., with distinction, 1968; J.D., 1971). Note Editor, Stanford Law Review, 1970-1971. Assistant Professor, 1971-1973 and Associate Professor, 1973-1974, University of Kansas. Faculty Member, National Institute for Trial Advocacy, 1978-1989. Member, Board of Trustees, National Institute for Trial Advocacy, 1991-1996. Member, Board of Trustees, Graduate Theological Union, 1996. Member, Board of Directors, Alliance for Children's Rights, 1993-1996. Member, Board of Directors, Public Counsel, 1980-1983. Member, Board of Visitors, Stanford University School of Law, 1986-1992, Executive Committee, 1989-1991. Lawyer Representative, Ninth Circuit Judicial Conference, 1986-1987; 1993-1995. Member: Editorial Board, Journal of the Ninth Circuit Historical Society; California State Judicial Council, 1990-1992. Member, Board of Directors, Inner City Law Center, 1991-1996. Deputy General Counsel, Independent Commission on the Los Angeles Police Department, 1991. Author/Consultant: (with Hon. William Masterson and Douglas Young), *Business Litigation* (California Civil Practice; Bancroft-Whitney, 1993). *Member:* Los Angeles County (Member, Executive Committee, ADR Section, 1994—) and American (Council Member, Section of Litigation, 1986-1989; Chair, 1992-1993; Member, House of Delegates, 1993—) Bar Associations; State Bar of California (Committee on Women in the Law, Vice Chair, 1986-1987; Chair, 1987-1988); California Women Lawyers; Association of Business Trial Lawyers (Member, Board of Governors, 1982-1984); American Law Institute; Member and Arbitrator, American Arbitration Association, 1993—; National Association of Securities Dealers (NASO), Inc. (Board Member, 1996—).

REFERENCE: Bank of California (Downtown Los Angeles Branch).

---

## MATTHEW B. F. BIREN & ASSOCIATES

*Established in 1977*

**815 MORAGA DRIVE
LOS ANGELES, CALIFORNIA 90049-1633**
Telephone: 310-476-3031; 381-5609
FAX: 310-471-3165
Email: mbfba@primenet.com

*Practice Limited to Personal Injury, Products Liability, Neurolaw, Business Torts and Professional Negligence.*

*FIRM PROFILE: The firm handles a broad spectrum of substantial personal injury cases, including, but not limited to cases involving: general and professional negligence; products liability; premises liability; business torts; toxic exposure; and, insurance bad faith. The firm has developed a particular specialty in handling cases involving considerable technological complexity.*

**MATTHEW B. F. BIREN,** born Los Angeles, California, January 19, 1948; admitted to bar, 1973, California; 1975, U.S. Court of Appeals, Ninth Circuit and U.S. Court of Appeals for the District of Columbia Circuit; 1980, U.S. Supreme Court. *Education:* University of California (B.A., 1970); Loyola University of Los Angeles (J.D., cum laude, 1973). *Member:* Beverly Hills, Santa Monica, Los Angeles County and American Bar Associations; State Bar of California; The Association of Trial Lawyers of America; Trial Lawyers for Public Justice; Consumers Attorneys Association of Los Angeles; Consumer Attorneys of California. *PRACTICE AREAS:* Products Liability; Personal Injury (with Complex Technological Issues); Professional Negligence; Neurolaw; Insurance Bad Faith; Business Torts.

---

**MARC J. KATZMAN,** born Los Angeles, California, May 26, 1953; admitted to bar, 1992, California and U.S. District Court, Central District of California. *Education:* University of California at Los Angeles (B.A., 1976); San Fernando Valley College of Law (J.D., 1979). *Member:* Los Angeles County and American Bar Associations; State Bar of California; The Association of Trial Lawyers of America; Consumer Attorneys Association of Los Angeles; Consumer Attorneys of California; Trial Lawyers for Public Justice.

**DEBRA J. TAUGER,** born San Bernardino, California, August 21, 1957; admitted to bar, 1988, Massachusetts and U.S. District Court, District of Massachusetts; 1989, California and U.S. Court of Appeals, Ninth Circuit; 1990, U.S. District Court, Central District of California. *Education:* University of California at Los Angeles (B.A., 1981); Suffolk University Law School (J.D., 1987). *Member:* Los Angeles County and American Bar Associations; State Bar of California; Women Lawyers Association of Los Angeles.

*(This Listing Continued)*

CAA523B

## MATTHEW B. F. BIREN & ASSOCIATES, Los Angeles—Continued

**EDMONT T. BARRETT,** born 1946; admitted to bar, 1977, California. *Education:* Loyola University of Los Angeles (B.A.; J.D.). *Member:* State Bar of California. *PRACTICE AREAS:* Personal Injury.

REFERENCE: First Los Angeles Bank (Century City, Los Angeles, Branch).

## BISHTON • GUBERNICK

2029 CENTURY PARK EAST, SUITE 3150
**LOS ANGELES, CALIFORNIA 90067**
Telephone: 310-556-1801
Fax: 310-556-1050

*Civil Trial and Appellate Practice in all State and Federal Courts. Real Estate, Business, Bankruptcy, Corporate, Construction Law and Insurance Coverage.*

### MEMBERS OF FIRM

**NORRIS J. BISHTON, JR.,** born Chicago, Illinois, July 3, 1936; admitted to bar, 1960, Illinois and U.S. District Court, Northern District of Illinois 1966, U.S. Tax Court; 1971, California; 1975, U.S. District Court, Central District of California. *Education:* University of Notre Dame (A.B., 1957; J.D., 1959). Associate Articles Editor, Notre Dame Law Review, 1958-1959. *Member:* Chicago and Los Angeles County Bar Associations; State Bar of California; The Association of Trial Lawyers of America. [Captain, U.S. Army, 1959-1960]. *PRACTICE AREAS:* Civil Trial; Appellate; Business; Bankruptcy; Corporate; Construction.

**JEFFREY S. GUBERNICK,** born Brooklyn, New York, July 23, 1958; admitted to bar, 1984, New York and U.S. District Court, Southern District of New York; 1989, California, U.S. District Court, Northern District of California and U.S. Court of Appeals, Ninth Circuit; 1992, U.S. District Court, Eastern District of California. *Education:* Lehigh University (B.A., summa cum laude, 1979); New York University (J.D., 1983). *Member:* New York State and American Bar Associations; State Bar of California. *PRACTICE AREAS:* Civil Trial; Appellate; Business; Bankruptcy; Corporate; Construction; Insurance Coverage.

## BISNO & SAMBERG

**LOS ANGELES, CALIFORNIA**

(See Pasadena)

*Trial, Arbitration, and Appellate Practice. Extensive experience in Receiverships, Foreclosures, Business Law, Insolvency Law, Debtor/Creditor Rights, Bankruptcy, Medical and Legal Malpractice, and Insurance Defense Litigation.*

## BIVONA & COHEN

TWO CENTURY PLAZA
2049 CENTURY PARK EAST
**LOS ANGELES, CALIFORNIA 90067**
Telephone: 310-553-4114
Telex: 691681
Telecopier: (310) 553-2510

*New York, N.Y. Office:* Wall Street Plaza. Telephone: 212-363-3100. Telex: 640179. Cable Address: "Insurlaw" Telecopier: (212) 363-9824.

*Warren, New Jersey Office:* 15 Mountain Boulevard. Telephone: 908-757-7800. Telecopier: 908-757-8039.

*General Defense, Appellate and Trial Practice. Product Liability, Malpractice, Property, Casualty and Surety Insurance Law. Toxic and Hazardous Waste Litigation.*

**LAURENCE A. DORNSTEIN,** born New York, N.Y., June 8, 1939; admitted to bar, 1964, New York; 1972, U.S. District Court, Southern District of New York; 1973, California and U.S. District Court, Central District of California; 1985, U.S. District Court, Eastern District of California. *Education:* Cornell University (B.A., 1960); New York University (LL.B., 1963). Hearing Officer, New York Traffic Violations Bureau, 1970-1972. Judge Pro-Tem, Small Claims (Civil), 1976-1982. *Member:* State Bar of California; New York State Bar Association.

**MARLA M. STEWART,** born Brooklyn, New York, April 25, 1952; admitted to bar, 1979, Ohio; 1980, Michigan; 1983, California. *Education:*
*(This Listing Continued)*

University of Toledo; Pepperdine University (B.A., cum laude, 1974); University of Toledo (J.D., 1978). Phi Kappa Phi. Recipient, American Jurisprudence Book Awards in Secured Transactions and Creditors Rights. *Member:* Orange County (California) and Ohio State (inactive) Bar Associations; State Bar of Michigan; State Bar of California.

**LAURA LYN LIPSCOMB,** born Hollywood, California, February 26, 1962; admitted to bar, 1988, California, U.S. District Court, Central District of California. *Education:* California State University, Northridge (B.A., 1984); Whittier College School of Law (J.D., 1987).

(For complete biographical data on all personnel, see Professional Biographies at New York, New York)

## BLACK COMPEAN HALL & LENNEMAN

Established in 1991
ONE WILSHIRE, SUITE 1000
624 SOUTH GRAND AVENUE
**LOS ANGELES, CALIFORNIA 90017**
Telephone: 213-629-9500
FAX: 213-629-4868
Email: bchl@earthlink.net

*Trial and Appellate Practice in all State and Federal Courts, Concentrating in the areas of Insurance Coverage, Coverage Litigation, Bad Faith Litigation, Insurance Guarantee Association Practice, Reinsurance and Insurance Related Matters.*

*FIRM PROFILE:* Black, Compean, Hall & Lenneman was founded by Robert H. Black, Michael D. Compean, Frederick G. Hall and Annette J. Lenneman. The firm represents numerous insurance companies and an insurance guarantee association, providing both litigation and non-litigation services. The firm continually reviews and analyzes industry and legal publications and opinions relevant to its practice. Consistent with its practice, all partners are members of the Association of Southern California Defense Counsel. Additionally, all attorneys participate in continuing education regarding insurance issues and are members of various practice sections of the bar associations.

### MEMBERS OF FIRM

**ROBERT H. BLACK,** born Torrance, California, June 10, 1941; admitted to bar, 1981, California and U.S. District Court, Central District of California; 1982, U.S. District Court, Eastern District of California; 1987, U.S. District Court, Southern District of California; 1988, U.S. District Court, Northern District of California; 1991, U.S. Court of Appeals, Ninth Circuit. *Education:* Occidental College (B.A., 1964); California State University at Los Angeles (M.A., 1969); Southwestern University (J.D., cum laude, 1980). *Member:* Los Angeles County and American Bar Associations; State Bar of California; Association of Southern California Defense Counsel; Defense Research and Trial Lawyers Association. *PRACTICE AREAS:* Insurance Coverage; Coverage Litigation; Bad Faith Litigation; Insurance Defense; Appellate Practice.

**MICHAEL D. COMPEAN,** born Los Angeles, California, February 4, 1952; admitted to bar, 1986, California; 1987, U.S. District Court, Central District of California; 1990, U.S. District Court, Eastern District of California; 1992, U.S. District Court, Southern District of California. *Education:* University of California at Berkeley; University of California at Los Angeles (B.A., 1981; J.D.,1984). Judicial Extern for Honorable Laughlin E. Waters, U.S. District Court, Central District, 1984. *Member:* Los Angeles County and American (Member, Torts and Insurance Practice Section) Bar Associations; State Bar of California; Association of Southern California Defense Counsel. *REPORTED CASES:* Pruyn vs. Agricultural Ins. Co. (1995), Cal. App. 4th [42 Cal. Rptr. 2d 2985]; Stonewall Ins. Co. vs. City of P.V. Estates (1992) 29 Cal.App.4th 98 (9 Cal.2d 663). *PRACTICE AREAS:* Insurance Coverage; Coverage Litigation; Bad Faith Litigation; Insurer Insolvency; Reinsurance; Insurance Defense; Appellate Practice. *Email:* mdcompean@aol.com

**FREDERICK G. HALL,** born New York, N.Y., August 3, 1962; admitted to bar, 1987, California and U.S. District Court, Central District of California; 1988, U.S. Court of Appeals, Ninth Circuit and U.S. District Court, Northern and Southern Districts of California; 1992, U.S. District Court, Eastern District of California. *Education:* University of Southern California (B.S., 1984); Southwestern University (J.D., 1987). Member, Moot Court Honors Program, 1985-1987. Quarter Finalist Oralist/Writer, 1986 National Moot Court Competition. *Member:* Los Angeles County and American (Member, Litigation Section) Bar Associations; State Bar of California; Association of Southern California Defense Counsel. *REPORTED CASES:* R.J. Reynolds Co. v. Cal. Ins. Guarantee Assn. (1991) 235 Cal-
*(This Listing Continued)*

# PROFESSIONAL BIOGRAPHIES

CALIFORNIA—LOS ANGELES

.App.3d 595 (1 Cal.Rept.2d.405); Cal. Ins. Guarantee Assn. v. Argonaut Ins. Co. (1991) 227 Cal.App.3d 624 (278 Cal.Rptr. 23); Abraugh v. Gillespie (1988) 203 Cal.App.3d 462 (250 Cal.Rptr. 21); Isaacson v. Cal. Ins. Guarantee Association (1988) 44 Cal.3d.775 (244 Cal.Rptr. 655,750 P.2d.297). *PRACTICE AREAS:* Appellate Practice; Insurance Coverage; Coverage Litigation; Insurance Guarantee Association Practice. *Email:* BCHL__Hall@msn.com

**ANNETTE J. LENNEMAN,** born St. Michael, Minnesota, February 10, 1959; admitted to bar, 1988, California; 1989, U.S. District Court, Central, Southern, Northern and Eastern Districts of California and U.S. Court of Appeals, Ninth Circuit; 1990, Minnesota. *Education:* College of St. Benedict (B.A., 1981); University of Minnesota (J.D., 1986). President, Minnesota Justice Foundation, 1985-1986. *Member:* Los Angeles County, Minnesota State and American (Member: Litigation, Law practice Management, Tort and Insurance Law Sections) Bar Associations; State Bar of California; State Bar of Minnesota; Association of Southern California Defense Counsel; Defense Research Institute; California Women Lawyers Association; Los Angeles County Barristers. *PRACTICE AREAS:* Coverage Litigation; Bad Faith Litigation; Insurer Insolvency; Insurance Guarantee Association Practice; Insurance Defense; Appellate Practice.

## ASSOCIATES

**WILLIAM J. LIGHT,** born Miles City, Montana, November 28, 1963; admitted to bar, 1989, California; U.S. District Court, Central District of California; 1990, Colorado and Minnesota; 1991, U.S. District Court, Northern, Central and Southern Districts of California and U.S. Court Appeals, Ninth Circuit; 1992, U.S. District Court, Eastern District of California. *Education:* University of North Dakota (B.A., magna cum laude, 1986); Southwestern University School of Law (J.D., 1988). Recipient: Dean Paul Wildman Scholarship; American Jurisprudence Award in Evidence. *Member:* Colorado, Minnesota State and American Bar Associations; State Bar of California. *PRACTICE AREAS:* Insurance Coverage; Bad Faith Litigation; Insurance Guarantee Association Practice; Insurance Defense; Appellate Practice. *Email:* wmlight@h4h.com

**VICENTE VALENCIA, JR.,** born Los Angeles, California, September 20, 1958; admitted to bar, 1991, California, U.S. Court of Appeals, Ninth Circuit and U.S. District Court, Central, Southern, Northern and Eastern Districts of California. *Education:* Loyola Marymount University (B.A., 1980; M.P.A., 1982, J.D., 1985). California Insurance Guarantee Association Practice. *Member:* Los Angeles County, American and Mexican American Bar Associations. *LANGUAGES:* Spanish. *PRACTICE AREAS:* Insurance Coverage; Coverage Litigation; Bad Faith Litigation.

**MARGIE CASTILLO,** born Colombia, December 22, 1957; admitted to bar, 1994, California and U.S. District Court, Central District of California; 1995, U.S. District Court, Southern District of California. *Education:* St. Johns University (B.S., cum laude, 1987); Hastings College of the Law (J.D., 1994). Associate Executive Editor, Comment Law Journal, 1993-1994. *Member:* Los Angeles County Bar Association; State Bar of California. *LANGUAGES:* Spanish. *PRACTICE AREAS:* Insurance Coverage; Coverage Litigation; Bad Faith Litigation; Appellate Practice.

**LARA MICHELLE BRYA,** born Plainfield, New Jersey, March 23, 1969; admitted to bar, 1995, California and U.S. District Court, Central District of California. *Education:* University of Santa Clara (B.S., 1990); University of Southern California (J.D., 1994). *Member:* Los Angeles County Bar Association; State Bar of California.

**MEREDITH A. CZAPLA,** born Detroit, Michigan December 15, 1970; admitted to bar, 1996, California. *Education:* University of Michigan (B.A., 1991); University of Minnesota Law School (J.D., cum laude, 1995). *Member:* Los Angeles County Bar Association; State Bar of California. *PRACTICE AREAS:* Insurance Coverage; Bad Faith Litigation.

REPRESENTATIVE CLIENTS: Allstate Insurance Co.; American States Insurance Co.; Argonaut Insurance Co.; California Insurance Guarantee Assn.; California State Compensation Insurance Fund; Central Mutual Insurance Co.; Financial Indemnity Company; Liberty Mutual Group; Scottsdale Insurance Company; Superior National Insurance Co.; Yasuda Fire and Marine.

## *BLAKELEY & BRINKMAN*

**333 SOUTH GRAND AVENUE, 37TH FLOOR**
**LOS ANGELES, CALIFORNIA 90071-1599**
Telephone: 213-628-2190
Telecopier: 213-625-1832

*Bankruptcy, Creditors Rights, Commercial Litigation, Business Litigation and Real Estate.*

### MEMBERS OF FIRM

**SCOTT E. BLAKELEY,** born Chehalis, Washington; admitted to bar, 1989, California; U.S. District Court, Central District of California. *Education:* Pepperdine University (B.S., 1982); Loyola University (M.B.A., 1987); Southwestern University (J.D., 1988). Law Clerk to the Hon. John J. Wilson, Bankruptcy Judge, Central District of California, 1989-1990. Author: "Current Developments in Involuntary Bank Petitions," Practising Law Institute, 1993; "Recent Developments Regarding Assignment of Rents, Issues and Profits," Practising Law Institute, 1994; "Creditors' Committees in Chapter 11: Appointment, Duties and Operations," NACM, 1993. Board of Editors, California Bankruptcy Journal. Member, Legislative Subcommittee of Unsecured Trade Creditors Committee, American Bankruptcy Institute.

**DAREN R. BRINKMAN,** born Idaho Falls, Idaho, December 13, 1961; admitted to bar, 1988, Texas; 1992, California. *Education:* Brigham Young University (B.A., magna cum laude, 1985); University of California at Berkeley (J.D., 1988). Hinckley Scholar, 1984-1985. Associate Editor, The International Tax and Business Lawyer, 1987-1988. Author: "The New Value Exception to the Absolute Priority Rule After *Ahlers,* " 106 Banking Law Journal 351 (1989). *Member:* Los Angeles County and American Bar Associations; State Bar of Texas; State Bar of California; Commercial Law League of America. *PRACTICE AREAS:* Bankruptcy; Creditor's Rights.

## *BLAKELY, SOKOLOFF, TAYLOR & ZAFMAN*

A Limited Liability Partnership
*Established in 1975*

**7TH FLOOR, 12400 WILSHIRE BOULEVARD**
**LOS ANGELES, CALIFORNIA 90025**
Telephone: 310-207-3800
Facsimile: 310-820-5988
Email: BSTZ__mail@bstz.com
URL: http://www.bstz.com

*Sunnyvale, California Office:* 1279 Oakmead Parkway. Telephone: 408-720-8598. Facsimile: 408-720-9397.
*Costa Mesa, California Office:* Suite 850, 611 Anton Boulevard. Telephone: 714-557-3800. Facsimile: 714-557-3347.
*Lake Oswego, Oregon Office:* Suite 101, 5285 SW Meadows Road. Telephone: 503-684-6200. Facsimile: 503-684-3245.

*Intellectual Property Law, including Patents, Trademarks, Copyrights, Related Prosecution and Litigation.*

### MEMBERS OF FIRM

**†ROGER W. BLAKELY, JR.,** born Pulaski, New York, August 9, 1935; admitted to bar, 1970, California; registered to practice before U.S. Patent and Trademark Office. *Education:* Cornell University (B.M.E., 1958); University of Southern California (M.S.E.E., 1965); Loyola University of Los Angeles (J.D., 1969). (Resident, Costa Mesa Office).

**†STANLEY W. SOKOLOFF,** born Brooklyn, New York, January 6, 1938; admitted to bar, 1966, Massachusetts; 1969, California; 1982, U.S. Court of Appeals for the Federal Circuit; registered to practice before U.S. Patent and Trademark Office. *Education:* Worcester Polytechnic Institute (B.S.Ch.E., 1959); Northeastern University; Suffolk University (J.D., cum laude, 1966); Georgetown University (M.P.L., 1969). *Member:* Massachusetts Bar Association; State Bar of California.

**†EDWIN H. TAYLOR,** born Paterson, New Jersey, March 9, 1939; admitted to bar, 1967, Texas; 1968, California; 1995, Oregon; registered to practice before U.S. Patent and Trademark Office. *Education:* Newark College of Engineering (B.S., 1960); Columbia University (M.S., 1961); St. Mary's University of San Antonio (J.D., cum laude, 1967). Instructor, Patent Law Practice, Santa Clara University. Member, Santa Clara University High Tech Advisory Board. Lawyer Delegate, 9th Circuit Judicial Confer-

*(This Listing Continued)*

**BLAKELY, SOKOLOFF, TAYLOR & ZAFMAN,** Los Angeles—Continued

ence, 1981-1983. *Member:* State Bar of Texas; State Bar of California; Oregon State Bar. (Resident, Sunnyvale Office).

**†NORMAN ZAFMAN,** born Paterson, New Jersey, October 13, 1934; admitted to bar, 1970, California; registered to practice before U.S. Patent and Trademark Office. *Education:* City College of New York (B.E.E., 1957); University of Southern California (M.S.E.E., 1964); Southwestern University (J.D., cum laude, 1969). Eta Kappa Nu. Co-Author: "The Trademark Law Revision Act of 1988: A New Era," Beverly Hills Bar Association Journal, Winter 1989. Author: "Profile of an Air Pollution Controversy," Journal of the Beverly Hills Bar Association, 1972; articles on the protection of trade secrets (1973) and the patentability of software (1976), Los Angeles Daily Journal. South Coast Air Quality Management District (Alternate Director for Los Angeles County, 1981-1987). Associate Editor, Beverly Hills Association Journal, 1990—. *Member:* Century City (Member, Board of Governors, 1976-1978), Beverly Hills (Member, Board of Governors, 1979-1982; Chair, Committee on Legislation, 1978-1981), Los Angeles County Bar Association; State Bar of California.

**ERIC S. HYMAN,** born Brooklyn, New York, March 5, 1948; admitted to bar, 1979, California; 1980, U.S. District Court, Central District of California; 1984, U.S. District Court, Northern District of California and U.S. Court of Appeals for the Federal Circuit; 1994, U.S. Court of Appeals, Ninth Circuit; registered to practice before U.S. Patent and Trademark Office. *Education:* University of Southern California (B.S.E.E., 1972; M.S.C.Sci., 1975); Western State University (J.D., 1979). *Member:* American Bar Association.

**STEPHEN D. GROSS** (1953-1995).

**GEORGE W HOOVER II,** born Pt. Washington, New York, November 19, 1946; admitted to bar, 1986, California; 1989, U.S. District Court, Central District of California and U.S. Court of Appeals, Ninth Circuit; registered to practice before U.S. Patent and Trademark Office. *Education:* University of California at Berkeley (B.S. in Engineering Physics, 1968); University of California at Los Angeles (M.B.A., 1972); Loyola Law School (J.D. , magna cum laude, 1986). Tau Beta Pi. Recipient, J. Rex Dibble Honor Award. *Member:* American Bar Association.

**LORI N. BOATRIGHT,** born Joplin, Missouri, March 27, 1959; admitted to bar, 1984, Missouri; 1989, California. *Education:* Southwest Missouri State University (B.A., summa cum laude, 1980); University of Missouri at Columbia (J.D., 1984). Member, Order of Barristers. Former, Trademark Examining Attorney, U.S. Patent and Trademark Office. *Member:* State Bar of California; The Missouri Bar; American Bar Association; International Trademark Association.

**DENNIS G. MARTIN,** born San Francisco, California, July 27, 1947; admitted to bar, 1972, California; 1976, U.S. Court of Appeals, Ninth Circuit; 1984, U.S. Court of Appeals for the Federal Circuit and U.S. District Court, Central and Northern Districts of California. *Education:* University of California at Davis (B.A., with highest honors, 1969); Yale University (J.D., 1972). Phi Beta Kappa. Author: "Multiplying Your Success Through Franchising," Inland Business, December, 1984. *Member:* Los Angeles County (Member: Antitrust Law Section; Amicus Briefs Committee) and American (Member, Sections on: Antitrust Law; Patent, Trademark and Copyright Law; Member, Forum Committee on Franchising) Bar Associations; The State Bar of California (Member, Intellectual Property Law Section).

*OF COUNSEL*

**STEPHEN L. KING,** born Omaha, Nebraska, December 15, 1931; admitted to bar, 1962, California; 1963, New York; 1972, Oregon; 1979, U.S. Supreme Court; registered to practice before U.S. Patent and Trademark Office. *Education:* Iowa State University (B.S.E.E., 1957); New York University (J.D., 1961). Tau Beta Pi; Eta Kappa Nu. Member, New York University Law Review, 1958-1961. *Member:* State Bar of California; State Bar of Oregon; American Bar Association.

**RONALD W. REAGIN,** born Independence, Missouri, December 17, 1936; admitted to bar, 1962, District of Columbia; 1967, California; 1979, U.S. Supreme Court; registered to practice before U.S. Patent and Trademark Office. *Education:* University of Missouri (B.S., 1958); George Washington University (LL.B., 1961). Tau Beta Pi; Eta Kappa Nu. *Member:* State Bar of California; The District of Columbia Bar.

*(This Listing Continued)*

CAA526B

**THOMAS M. COESTER,** born Iowa City, Iowa, July 24, 1967; admitted to bar, 1994, California; registered to practice before U.S. Patent and Trademark Office. *Education:* University of Iowa (B.S.E.E., 1991; J.D., with distinction, 1994). Member, Iowa Law Review. Associate Editor, Transnational Law and Contemporary Problems.

**MICHAEL W. HICKS,** born Bristol, Tennessee, April 20, 1962; admitted to bar, 1988, Pennsylvania; 1989, Tennessee; 1996, California. *Education:* University of Tennessee at Knoxville (B.A., with honors, 1984); University of Pittsburgh (J.D., 1987). Former Trademark Examining Attorney, U.S. Patent and Trademark Office. (Also at Sunnyvale Office).

**ERIC HO,** born Long Beach, California, November 2, 1968; admitted to bar, 1994, California; registered to practice before U.S. Patent and Trademark Office. *Education:* University of California at Berkeley (B.S., Electrical Engineering, Computer Science, 1990); University of Southern California (J.D., 1994). Member, Consumer Attorneys Association of Los Angeles. *Member:* Los Angeles County and American (Member: Committee on Intellectual Property Litigation; Subcommittee on Business and Corporate Litigation) Bar Associations; Southern California Chinese Lawyers Association; American Intellectual Property Law Association; Asian Business League.

**W. THOMAS BABBITT,** born July 14, 1961; admitted to bar, 1993, California; registered to practice before U.S. Patent and Trademark Office. *Education:* University of California, Riverside (B.S., Biochemistry, 1986); California State University, Long Beach (B.S., Chemical Engineering, 1987); University of the Pacific, McGeorge School of Law (J.D., 1992). Order of the Coif. Comment Editor, Pacific Law Journal. Law Clerk to the Honorable H. Russel Holland, Chief Judge, U.S. District Court, District of Alaska, 1992-1994.

**KAREN L. FEISTHAMEL,** born Manchester, Connecticut, December 25, 1965; admitted to bar, 1990, Connecticut; 1996, California; registered to practice before U.S. Patent and Trademark Office. *Education:* Brown University (B.Sc., magna cum laude, 1987); Georgetown University (J.D., 1990). Tau Beta Pi. Former Trademark Examining Attorney, U.S. Patent and Trademark Office.

**DINU GRUIA,** born Bucharest, Romania, May 22, 1962; admitted to bar, 1995, California. *Education:* Technion-Israel Institute of Technology, Haifa, Israel (B.S.E.E., 1988); Suffolk University Law School (J.D., cum laude, 1994). Staff Member, 1992-1993 and Technical Editor, 1993-1994, Suffolk University Law Review. Recipient, American Jurisprudence Awards in Equitable Remedies and Trusts. Author: "Patent Law: Restrictions on Use of Purchased Patented Goods Subject to the Rule of Reason -- Mallinckrodt, Inc. v. Medipart, Inc.," 27 Suffolk U.L. Rev. 292, 1993; "Evidence--Confrontation Clause Does Not Include Right to Question Prosecution Witness About Penalty Avoided Through Plea Agreement---Brown v. Powell," 27 Suffolk, U.L. Rev. 1011, 1993.

**ANAND SETHURAMAN,** born Musiri, India, April 24, 1970; admitted to bar, 1996, California. *Education:* Northwestern University (B.S.E.E., 1992); University of Notre Dame (J.D., cum laude, 1995). Managing Editor, Journal of Legislation, 1993-1995.

**GEORGE G.C. TSENG,** born Taipei, Taiwan, June 2, 1969; admitted to bar, 1996, California. *Education:* University of California at Los Angeles (B.S.E.E., 1991); Loyola Marymount University (M.B.A., 1995; J.D., 1995). Recipient, American Jurisprudence Award in Legal Writing.

**FARZAD E. AMINI,** born Columbus, Ohio, February 17, 1966; admitted to bar, 1996, California and U.S. District Court, Central District of California. *Education:* University of Southern California (B.S.E.E., 1988); Loyola Marymount University (J.D., 1996).

†Indicates A Law Corporation.

REPRESENTATIVE CLIENTS: Allfast Fastening Systems; Applied Materials, Inc.; Apple Computer, Inc.; Auto-Shade, Inc.; Bay Networks; California Institute of Technology; Citicorp; Cirrus Logic; Computer Motion, Inc.; Cymer Laser Technologies; Cypress Semiconductor; Dep Corporation; Echelon Corporation; Fred Hayman Beverly Hills, Inc.; Freeman Cosmetic Corporation; Imperial Toy Corporation; Information Storage Devices; Intel Corporation; Landmark Entertainment Group; LTX Corporation; Maxim Integrated Products; McDonnell Douglas Corporation; Mentor Corporation; Mentor Graphics Corporation; Netscape Communications; On Trak Systems, Inc.; Oracle Corporation; Pacific Communication Sciences, Inc.; Pharmatric Corporation; Rambus, Inc.; Ricoh Corporation; Silicon Graphics; Sony Corporation of America; Sterling Software; Stratacom, Inc.; Sun Microsystems, Inc.; Systemix; Tekelec;

*(This Listing Continued)*

Thermal Equipment Corporation; Time Warner Cable; Weider Health & Fitness; Xilinx.

(For complete biographical data on personnel at Sunnyvale and Costa Mesa, California and Lake Oswego, Oregon, see Professional Biographies at those locations)

## BLALOCK & GRAY

*Established in 1983*

**11726 SAN VICENTE BOULEVARD, SUITE 650
LOS ANGELES, CALIFORNIA 90049**

Telephone: 310-447-5665
Fax: 310-820-7143
Email: B&G@BBS.la.com

*Practice Limited to Immigration and Nationality Law.*

**FIRM PROFILE:** Steven Blalock and Humberto Gray are two Los Angeles-based immigration attorneys who have helped bring many successful immigrant stories to America. In addition to the professional business people, Blalock and Gray have helped actors, boxers, photographers, writers, stand-up comedians and chefs acquire legal status in the U.S. Their offices are really America in miniature, a starter melting pot of sorts; England, Norway, Sweden, Paraguay, Ireland, Guatemala, Ecuador, China --- they have represented everything from small ventures to major companies, with clients from all over the world and with a variety of professions in the business of doing business in America, for America!

*MEMBERS OF FIRM*

**HUMBERTO R. GRAY,** born Fairbanks, Alaska, March 24, 1962; admitted to bar, 1988, California and U.S. District Court, District of California; 1991, U.S. Court of Appeals, 9th Circuit. *Education:* Whittier College (B.A., 1984); Whittier School of Law (J.D., 1987). **PRACTICE AREAS:** Immigration and Nationality Law.

**STEVEN W. BLALOCK,** born 1952; admitted to bar, 1977, California and U.S. Court of Appeals, 9th Circuit; 1989, U.S. District Court, Central District of California. *Education:* University of Redlands (B.A., 1974); Loyola University of Los Angeles (J.D., 1977). (Certified Specialist, Immigration and Nationality Law the State Bar of California Board of Legal Specialization). **PRACTICE AREAS:** Immigration and Nationality Law.

*ASSOCIATE*

**CRISTINA E. PEREZ,** born New York, N.Y., October 27, 1968; admitted to bar, 1994, California; 1995, U.S. District Court, Central District of California and U.S. Court of Appeals, Ninth Circuit. *Education:* University of California at Los Angeles (B.A., 1991); Whittier College School of Law (J.D., 1994). Deans List, Whittier College School of Law. **LANGUAGES:** Spanish. **PRACTICE AREAS:** Immigration and Naturalization.

## BLANC WILLIAMS JOHNSTON & KRONSTADT

*A Partnership including Professional Corporations*

*Established in 1980*

**SUITE 1700, 1900 AVENUE OF THE STARS
LOS ANGELES, CALIFORNIA 90067**

Telephone: 310-552-2500
Telecopier: 310-552-1191

*Commercial, Computer and Technology, Proprietary Rights, including Copyright, Trademark, Trade Secret and Patent Law, , Corporate and Securities, Entertainment, Federal and State Taxation, International Business and Taxation and Real Property Law and Employment Law. General Civil and Trial Practice in all State and Federal Courts.*

*MEMBERS OF FIRM*

**RONALD L. BLANC, (P.C.),** born Denver, Colorado, October 20, 1937; admitted to bar, 1962, New York; 1964, California. *Education:* University of Colorado (B.S., 1959); New York University (LL.B., 1962). Order of the Coif. Member, Board of Editors, New York University Law Review, 1961-1962. Law Clerk to Justice Byron R. White, U.S. Supreme Court, 1962-1963. Lecturer, Federal Taxation, University of Southern California Annual Institute on Federal Taxation. Member, Board of Directors, Motion Picture and Television Tax Institute. *Member:* Los Angeles County Bar Association. (Certified Specialist, Taxation Law, The State Bar of California Board of Legal Specialization).

*(This Listing Continued)*

**HARLEY J. WILLIAMS, (P.C.),** born Mount Pleasant, Iowa, June 10, 1950; admitted to bar, 1976, California. *Education:* University of Iowa (B.B.A., with highest distinction, 1972); Yale University (J.D., 1975). Beta Gamma Sigma. Editor, Yale Law Journal, 1974-1975. Author: "The Investment Tax Credit in Connection with Record Masters and Motion Pictures —The Only Game in Town," 52 Southern California Law Review 1121, 1979. Co-Author: "The Impact of the Tax Reform Act of 1976 on Independent Film Production," 1 Review of Taxation of Individuals 314, 1977. *Member:* Beverly Hills, Century City, Los Angeles County and American Bar Associations; The State Bar of California; The Copyright Society of the U.S.A.

**RONALD L. JOHNSTON, (P.C.),** born Topeka, Kansas, February 6, 1948; admitted to bar, 1973, California. *Education:* California State College at Fullerton (B.A., 1970); University of Southern California (J.D., 1973). Order of the Coif; Beta Gamma Sigma. Editor, Southern California Law Review, 1972-1973. Director, Computer Law Association, 1988—. Founder and Chairman, USC Computer Law Institute, 1979—. Co-Chairman, Trial Advocacy Institute-Intellectual Property Litigation, Aspen Publishing Law & Business, Inc. Co-Founder and Editor-in-Chief, The Computer Lawyer, Aspen Publishing Law & Business, 1983—. Board of Editors, The Journal of Proprietary Rights; Board of Editors, The Cyberspace Lawyer. Co-Author: "Trade Secret Protection For Software Generally and In The Mass Market," 3 Computer Law Journal 211, 1982. Author: "Attempted Monopolization Claims in Litigation with Competitors," in Computer Litigation 757, Practicing Law Institute, 1983; "Antitrust Issues: Tying Arrangements, Robinson-Patman Act Considerations and Resale Price Maintenance," in Marketing and Protecting Rights in Computer Software, American Bar Association, 1983; "Avoiding or Resolving the Controversy," in Computer and Data Processing Contracts 197, Law Journal Seminars-Press, 1982; "A Decision-Making Process for the California Coastal Zone," 46 Southern California Law Review 513, 1973; "A Guide for the Proponent and Opponent of Computer-Based Evidence," 1 Computer Law Journal 667, 1979; "Product Bundling Faces Increased Spector of Illegality Under the Antitrust Laws," The Computer Lawyer 1 (Aug. 1984); "The IBM-Fujitsu Arbitration Revisited—A Case Study in Effective ADR," 7 The Computer Lawyer 13 (1990); "A Primer: The Formulation of an Effective Strategy in Software Copyright Litigation," in Mid-Winter Institute, 1992, AIPLA, 1992; "Copyright Protection for Command Driven Interfaces," 8 The Computer Lawyer 1 (June, 1991). "Toward an Effective Strategy in Software Copyright Litigation," 19 Rutgers Computer and Technology Law Journal, 1993; "Trade Secret Protection for Mass Distributed Software", The Computer Lawyer 1 November, 1994. *Member:* State Bar of California; American Bar Association (Member, Litigation Section); Computer Law Association. **REPORTED CASES:** Abdul-Jabbar v. General Motors Corp., 75 F.3d 1391 (9th Cir. 1996); Balzer-Wolf Assoc., Inc. v. Parlex Corp., 753 F.2d 771 (9th Cir. 1985). **PRACTICE AREAS:** Commercial Litigation; Proprietary Rights; Antitrust; Computer Law.

**JOHN A. KRONSTADT,** born Washington, D.C., March 5, 1951; admitted to bar, 1976, California; 1978, District of Columbia. *Education:* Cornell University (B.A., with distinction, 1973); Yale University (J.D., 1976). Law Clerk to Hon. William P. Gray, U.S. District Court, Central District of California, 1976-1977. *Member:* The State Bar of California (Member, Section of Antitrust and Trade Regulation Law); District of Columbia Bar. **PRACTICE AREAS:** Commercial Litigation; Environmental Law; Antitrust and Trade Regulation.

**JAMES R. FARRAND,** born Altadena, California, September 6, 1945; admitted to bar, 1972, California and District of Columbia; 1980, U.S. Supreme Court and U.S. Court of Appeals, 2nd Circuit; registered to practice before U.S. Patent and Trademark Office. *Education:* Pomona College (B.A., 1967); University of Wisconsin (M.S., 1968); Boalt Hall School of Law, University of California (J.D., 1971). Order of the Coif. Member, Editorial Board, California Law Review, 1970-1971. Recipient, Cavenagh Crum Scholarship. Author: "Ancillary Relief in S.E.C. Civil Enforcement Actions," 89 Harvard Law Review 1179-1814, 1976; "Two-Thirds Vote in Bond Elections," 59 California Law Review 140-158, 1971; "Expanded Rights for Economic Strikers," 58 California Law Review 511, 1970. Lecturer: Securities and Exchange Commission, 1980, 1981; Practising Law Institute, 1980; North American Securities Administration Association, 1981; Computer Law Institute, 1988; Los Angeles County Bar Association, 1986, 1992; Beverly Hills Bar Association, 1992-1994; Aspen Publishing Law and Business, 1995; UCLA Extension, 1995. Assistant General Counsel, Securities and Exchange Commission, 1978-1981. *Member:* State Bar of California; District of Columbia Bar; American Bar Association (Member: Section on Corporation, Banking and Business Law; Committee on Federal

*(This Listing Continued)*

CAA527B

**BLANC WILLIAMS JOHNSTON & KRONSTADT**, Los Angeles—Continued

Regulations of Securities). *PRACTICE AREAS:* Securities and Corporate Law; Mergers and Acquisitions; Partnerships; Business Law; Patent Law.

**GARY A. DAVID,** born New York, N.Y., August 4, 1950; admitted to bar, 1977, California. *Education:* University of California, Los Angeles (B.A., 1971; J.D., 1977). Order of the Coif. Member, UCLA Law Review, 1975-1977. Extern to Associate Justice Frank Richardson, California Supreme Court, Spring, 1976. California State Bar Court Referee and Probation Monitor, 1984—. *Member:* The State Bar of California. *PRACTICE AREAS:* Mergers and Acquisitions; Proprietary Rights; Real Estate; Computer Law.

**ALLEN R. GROGAN,** born Fort Belvoir, Virginia, November 4, 1953; admitted to bar, 1979, California. *Education:* Oberlin College (A.B., with honors, 1975); University of Southern California (M.A., 1976; J.D., 1979). Sigma Xi. Member, Southern California Law Review, 1977-1979. Co-Founder and Editor-in-Chief: The Computer Lawyer, Aspen Publishing Law & Business, 1983—; The International Computer Lawyer, Aspen Publishing Law & Business, 1992-1995. Member, Board of Editors, The Cyberspace Lawyer, Glasser Legal Works, 1996—. Vice Chairman, American Bar Association Computer Law Division of the Section of Science and Technology, 1988-1989. Co-editor, Computer Law Annual 1985, Law & Business, Inc./Harcourt Brace Javonovich, 1985. Author: "Licensing for Next Generation New Media Technology", The Computer Lawyer, November, 1993; "Acquiring Content for New Media Works," The Computer Lawyer, January, 1991; "Copyright Considerations in the Use of Computer Software on Local Area Networks and Multi-User Configurations," The Computer Lawyer, August, 1986; "Decompilation and Disassembly: Undoing Software Protection," The Computer Lawyer, February, 1984; "Negotiating and Drafting Service Bureau Contracts," Computer Law Annual 1985; "Statutory Minimum Compensation and the Granting of Injunctive Relief to Enforce Personal Service Contracts in the Entertainment Industries: The Need for Legislative Reform," 52 Southern California Law Review 489, 1979. Co-Author: "Copyright Protection for Command Driven Interfaces," The Computer Lawyer, June 1991; "Outsourcing of Data Processing Operations," The Computer Lawyer, December, 1991; "Computer System Procurement," 30 Emory Law Journal 395, 1981; "Taxation of Computer Hardware and Software," in Computers and the Law: An Introductory Handbook 197, 3d Ed. 1981. *Member:* State Bar of California; Computer Law Association. *PRACTICE AREAS:* Computer and Technology; Proprietary Rights; Licensing; Commercial Transactions.

**RICHARD T. MCCOY III,** born Fort Worth, Texas, February 16, 1955; admitted to bar, 1979, California; 1993, Pennsylvania. *Education:* Michigan State University (B.S., summa cum laude, 1976); Duke University (J.D., 1979); University of Virginia (Ph.D., Theoretical Particle Physics, 1994). Phi Beta Kappa; Order of the Coif. Staff Member, 1977-1978 and Note and Comment Editor, 1978-1979, Duke Law Review. Author: "Unitary Taxation: a Primer for the Expanding Technology Company," The Computer Lawyer, November 1984; "Attracting and Retaining Key Employees in the Computer Industry," The Computer Lawyer, April, 1984, May, 1984; "Involuntary Conversions Under Section 1033: Recent Developments Breathe New Life Into an Old Section," *Major Tax Planning 1990*, U.S.C. Tax Institute, 1990; *Major Tax Planning, 1995*, U.S.C. Tax Institute. Co-Author: "Negative Delta Rho and 4th Generation Bound States," Phys. Rev. D 50, 2082, 1994; "The Antitrust Liability of Professional Associations After Goldfarb: Reformulating the Learned Professions Exemption in the Lower Courts," Duke Law Review 1047, 1977. *Member:* State Bar of California; Pennsylvania Bar Association. *PRACTICE AREAS:* Mergers and Acquisitions; Taxation; Partnerships; Business Law; Proprietary Rights.

**REGINA A. STAGG,** born Tokyo, Japan, July 8, 1956; admitted to bar, 1982, California. *Education:* University of California at Berkeley (A.B., 1978); Boalt Hall School of Law, University of California (J.D., 1981). Phi Beta Kappa; Order of the Coif. Visiting Lecturer, School of Law, University of Warwick, England, 1981-1982. Speaker: American Intellectual Property Law Association Institute on Law of Computer Related Technology, 1992; "Understanding Basic Copyright Laws," Practising Law Institute, 1995. *Member:* Los Angeles County Bar Association; State Bar of California. *REPORTED CASES:* Mitchell v. Superior Court, 37 Cal. 3d 268. *PRACTICE AREAS:* Commercial, Copyright and Proprietary Rights Litigation; Employment and Discrimination Law.

**JOHN C. RAWLS III,** born Shreveport, Louisiana, June 14, 1957; admitted to bar, 1982, California. *Education:* Columbia University (A.B., 1979); University of Texas (J.D., 1982). Author: "Recent Changes in Patent Litigation: A Whole New Ballgame," The Computer Lawyer, January 1996. *Member:* Century City (Member, Board of Governors) and Los Angeles County Bar Associations; State Bar of California; Association of Business Trial Lawyers; Federal Circuit Bar Association. *REPORTED CASES:* Jeff Foxworthy v. Custom Tees, Inc., 879 F. Supp. 1200 (N.D. Ga. 1995). *PRACTICE AREAS:* Proprietary Rights Litigation; Business Litigation. *Email:* bockrawl@aol.com

**SAM C. MANDEL,** born New York, N.Y., July 9, 1961; admitted to bar, 1987, California and U.S. District Court, Central District of California. *Education:* University of California, San Diego (B.A., magna cum laude and high distinction, 1984); Yale University (J.D., 1987). Lecturer, U.S.C. Tax Institute, 1989. *Member:* The State Bar of California; Los Angeles County Bar Association. *PRACTICE AREAS:* Entertainment; New Media Law; Technology; Corporate; Taxation.

---

**SUZANNE V. WILSON,** born Ventura, California, June 15, 1962; admitted to bar, 1991, California and U.S. District Court, Central District of California. *Education:* University of California at Berkeley (B.A., with honors, 1985); Harvard University (J.D., magna cum laude, 1990). Editor, Harvard Human Rights Journal, 1989-1990. Law Clerk to the Honorable Warren J. Ferguson, U.S. Court of Appeals, Ninth Circuit, 1990-1991. Legal Writing Instructor, Harvard Law School, Fall, 1989. *Member:* Los Angeles County Bar Association; Women Lawyers Association of Los Angeles; California Women Lawyers Association. *REPORTED CASES:* Jeff Foxworthy v. Custom Tees, Inc., 879 F. Supp. 1200 (N.D. Ga. 1995). *PRACTICE AREAS:* Commercial Litigation; Proprietary Rights Litigation; Employment Law; Discrimination Law.

**DAWN WEEKES GLENN,** born Los Angeles, California, June 1, 1965; admitted to bar, 1992, California. *Education:* The Colorado College; University of California at Los Angeles; California State University at Northridge (B.A., Psychology, 1987; University of California at Los Angeles J.D., 1991). Order of the Coif. Hortense Fishbaugh Scholar. Paul Hastings, Janofsky & Walker Scholar. Secretary, Black Law Students' Association. Co-Founder, UCLA Women's Law Journal. Teaching Assistant, Torts, UCLA, 1989-1990. Extern, ACLU, Southern California, 1990. *Member:* The State Bar of California. *PRACTICE AREAS:* Entertainment; Corporate; Employment Law.

**CYNTHIA S. ARATO,** born Los Angeles, California, July 30, 1964; admitted to bar, 1991, California. *Education:* University of Pennsylvania (B.A., cum laude and with distinction in International Relations, 1986); Columbia University (J.D., 1991). Harlan Fiske Stone Scholar, 1988-1991. Managing Editor, Columbia and American Journal of Transnational Law, 1990-1991. *Member:* Los Angeles County Bar Association; The State Bar of California. *REPORTED CASES:* Abdul-Jabbar v. General Motors Corp., 75 F.3d 1391 (9th Cir. 1996). *PRACTICE AREAS:* Commercial Litigation; Proprietary Rights Litigation; Employment Law; Discrimination Law.

**GIO HUNT,** born San Francisco, California, August 12, 1966; admitted to bar, 1990, California. *Education:* University of California, Los Angeles (B.A., magna cum laude, 1987); Harvard University (J.D., cum laude, 1990). *LANGUAGES:* Spanish. *PRACTICE AREAS:* Corporate; Taxation; Proprietary Rights Law; Computers.

**JAMES S. BLACKBURN,** born Mountain View, California, June 9, 1969; admitted to bar, 1994, California. *Education:* University of California at Berkeley (B.A., 1990); Boalt Hall, University of California at Berkeley (J.D., 1993). *PRACTICE AREAS:* Commercial Litigation; Proprietary Rights Litigation.

*OF COUNSEL*

**SOL ROSENTHAL,** born Baltimore, Maryland, October 17, 1934; admitted to bar, 1959, Maryland; 1961, California. *Education:* Princeton University (A.B., magna cum laude, 1956); Harvard University (J.D., cum laude, 1959). President, Beverly Hills Barristers, 1968. Member, Panel of Arbitrators, Directors Guild of America and Writers Guild of America, 1976—. President, Beverly Hills Bar Association, 1983. *Member:* Beverly Hills (Member, Board of Governors, 1968-1969; 1972-1974; 1975-1984; Co-Chairman, Entertainment Law Committee, 1971-1979), Los Angeles County (Member, Board of Trustees, 1981-1982) and American (Member, Executive Committee, Motion Picture, Television and Radio Division, Forum Committee on the Entertainment and Sports Industries, 1978-1984) Bar Associations; The State Bar of California; Los Angeles Copyright Society (President, 1973-1974). *PRACTICE AREAS:* Entertainment Law.

**SAMUEL J. FOX,** born Brooklyn, New York, September 8, 1944; admitted to bar, 1970, New York; 1975, U.S. District Court, Eastern and

*(This Listing Continued)*

Southern Districts of New York and U.S. Court of Appeals, Second Circuit; 1977, California; 1980, U.S. District Court, Central District of California. *Education:* Cornell University (B.A., 1966); New York University (J.D., 1969). Author: "Entertainment Industry Contracts - Negotiating and Drafting Guide," Music Volume, Matthew Bender, 1986. *Member:* The State Bar of California; Los Angeles County (Member, Intellectual Property Section) and New York State Bar Associations. *PRACTICE AREAS:* Entertainment; Music Publishing; International Copyright; Television Production; Syndication Licensing.

*MONA D. MILLER,* born Coral Gables, Florida, February 9, 1953; admitted to bar, 1977, California; 1978, U.S. District Court, Central District of California; 1994, U.S. Supreme Court. *Education:* Cornell University (A.B. with distinction, 1973); Stanford University (J.D., 1977). Phi Beta Kappa; Alpha Lamda Delta. Speaker: "Legal Aspects of Negotiable Instruments", Financial Institute of Education Conference, April 1987; "Litigation Awareness", Annual Meeting of California League of Savings and Loan Associations, Spring 1985; Program on Construction Project Breakdowns presented by the Los Angeles County Bar Real Property Section, January 1981. Member of Board, California Attorneys Federal Credit Union, 1982. *Member:* Los Angeles County (Member, Real Property and Commercial Law Sections) and American Bar Associations; Women Lawyers Association of Los Angeles (Member of Board and Chair, Committee to Improve Status of Women, 1995-1996). *LANGUAGES:* French, Russian. *PRACTICE AREAS:* Business Litigation.

REFERENCE: First Los Angeles Bank (Main Office).

## MARTIN H. BLANK, JR.
*11755 WILSHIRE BOULEVARD, SUITE 1400*
**LOS ANGELES, CALIFORNIA 90025-1520**
*Telephone: 310-477-5455*
*Fax: 310-444-9203*
*Email: marty@general.net*

*General Civil Practice. Corporation, Real Property, Business and Estate Planning Law.*

*MARTIN H. BLANK, JR.,* born Los Angeles, California, July 3, 1942; admitted to bar, 1966, California; 1967, U.S. District Court, Central District of California; 1994, U.S. Supreme Court. *Education:* University of California at Berkeley (A.B., 1963); Boalt Hall School of Law, University of California (LL.B., 1966). Phi Delta Phi. *Member:* Beverly Hills and Los Angeles County Bar Associations; The State Bar of California.

## BLEAU, FOX & GOLDBERG
*A PROFESSIONAL LAW CORPORATION*
*3575 CAHUENGA BOULEVARD, WEST, SUITE 580*
**LOS ANGELES, CALIFORNIA 90068**
*Telephone: 213-874-8613*
*Fax: 213-874-1234*

*Litigation in all State and Federal Courts. Complex Tort Liability, Intellectual Property, Contract and Real Estate Litigation, Unfair Competition, Trademark, Trade Dress and Copyright Matters, Royalty Reclamation, High Profile Civil Rights and Discrimination Claims, Personal Injury, Medical and Legal Malpractice and Insurance Bad Faith Claims.*

*THOMAS P. BLEAU,* born Webster, Massachusetts, June 4, 1965; admitted to bar, 1991, California. *Education:* Framingham State College (B.A., 1987); University of LaVerne (J.D., 1990). Recipient: American Jurisprudence Award, Criminal Law, 1990. Law Clerk, 1988-1991 and Associate Attorney, 1991-1994, Aidikoff & Kesluk. Intern, Los Angeles, California District Attorney's Office, 1989. *Member:* Beverly Hills Bar Association; California State Bar; California Association of Trial Lawyers; Consumer Attorneys Association of Los Angeles. *PRACTICE AREAS:* Complex Litigation; Insurance Bad Faith; Medical Malpractice; Legal Malpractice; Business Litigation.

*MARTIN R. FOX,* born Mission Hills, March 29, 1963; admitted to bar, 1991, California. *Education:* College of the Canyons; University of La Verne (J.D., 1990). Recipient: American Jurisprudence Award, Criminal Law. Law Clerk, Simi Valley, California Attorney's Office, 1990. California State Contracting License, 1981. *Member:* Los Angeles Trial Lawyers Association. *PRACTICE AREAS:* Business Litigation; Insurance Bad Faith; Contracts; Employment Law; Personal Injury; Real Estate; Construction Litigation.

*(This Listing Continued)*

*SETH M. GOLDBERG,* born MacDill AFB, Tampa, Florida, March 20, 1964; admitted to bar, 1992, California. *Education:* University of California at Santa Barbara (B.A., History, 1987); University of La Verne (J.D., 1991). Recipient: American Jurisprudence Award, Excellence in Lawyering Skills Practicum. Law Clerk: Law Offices of Kirk G. Downing, 1988-1989; Law Offices of Aidikoff & Kesluk, 1990-1991. *Member:* Beverly Hills and Los Angeles County Bar Associations; Consumer Attorneys Association of Los Angeles. [Capt., U.S. Army National Guard, 1985—]

REPRESENTATIVE CLIENTS: Carpeteria, Inc.; Commercial Account Management, Inc.; American Linen; Abacus Engineering, Inc.; High Desert Adventures, Inc.; Giant Textiles, Inc.; Southern California Glass Corporation; 26 Enterprises, Inc.; M-N-Z Janitorial; Austin Su International; Colony Royal Oaks Homeowners Association; Sunshine Estates Homeowners Association; Beverly-Doheny Homeowners Association; Top Hat Productions; Neil Haislop & Company.

## BLECHER & COLLINS
*A PROFESSIONAL CORPORATION*
*Established in 1971*
*611 WEST SIXTH STREET, 20TH FLOOR*
**LOS ANGELES, CALIFORNIA 90017**
*Telephone: 213-622-4222*
*Telecopier: 213-622-1656*

*Complex Business Litigation in Federal and State Courts. Antitrust, Intellectual Property, Professional Malpractice, Patent and Trademark Infringement, Contract and Fraud Litigation, Sports Law, Trials and Appeals.*

*FIRM PROFILE: Blecher & Collins engages in complex business litigation for both plaintiffs and defendants. Its clients have consisted of a broad spectrum of domestic and international companies.*

*MAXWELL M. BLECHER,* born Chicago, Illinois, May 27, 1933; admitted to bar, 1955, California; 1971, U.S. Supreme Court. *Education:* De Paul University (B.A., 1953); University of Southern California (LL.B., 1955). Author: "An Effective Deterrent to 'Hard Core' Violations of the Antitrust Laws: The Public Agency Treble Damage Suit," UCLA Law Review, Vol. 14, No. 4, May, 1967; "Attempt to Monopolize Under Section 2 of the Sherman Act: Dangerous Probability of Monopolization Within the 'Relevant Market'," George Washington Law Review, Vol. 38, No. 2, December, 1969; "Antitrust in Galbraith's New Industrial State," Antitrust Bulletin, Vol. XIII, Spring, 1968; "Litigation as an Integral Part of a Scheme to Create or Maintain an Illegal Monopoly," Mercer Law Review, Vol. 26, No. 2, Winter, 1975; "Toward More Effective Handling of Complex Antitrust Cases," Utah Law Review, 1980. Member, National Commission for the Review of Antitrust Laws and Procedures, 1978-1979. *Member:* State Bar of California (Member, Sections on: Antitrust; Litigation); Los Angeles County (Member, Antitrust Section), Federal and American (Chairman, Private Antitrust Litigation Committee, 1974-1976 and Member, Council, 1976-1977, Member, Sections on: Antitrust Law; Intellectual Property; Litigation) Bar Associations; Association of Business Trial Lawyers; Chancery Club; American Board of Trial Advocates. Fellow, American College of Trial Lawyers. *PRACTICE AREAS:* Antitrust; Complex Business Litigation; Intellectual Property; Professional Malpractice; Patent Infringement; Trademark Infringement; Contract Litigation; Sports Law.

*HAROLD R. COLLINS, JR.,* born Corpus Christi, Texas, June 3, 1938; admitted to bar, 1965, California. *Education:* San Diego State University (A.B., 1961); University of California, Hastings College of Law (J.D., 1964). Phi Alpha Delta. Publication Editor, Hastings Law Journal, 1963-1964. Law Clerk to Justice James R. Agee, California Court of Appeal, First District, 1964-1966. *Member:* State Bar of California (Member, Sections on: Antitrust; Law Practice Management; Litigation); Los Angeles County (Member, Antitrust Section), Federal and American (Member, Sections on: Antitrust Law; Litigation; Law Practice Management; Judicial Administrative Division; Intellectual Property Law; Science and Technology) Bar Associations; Association of Business Trial Lawyers. *PRACTICE AREAS:* Antitrust; Business Litigation; Intellectual Property; Professional Malpractice; Patent Infringement; Contract Litigation; Fraud and Deceit.

*JOHN E. ANDREWS,* born Washington, D.C., June 14, 1950; admitted to bar, 1982, California; 1986, New York. *Education:* University of New Hampshire (B.A., magna cum laude, 1975); Albany Law School of Union University (J.D., 1982). Managing Editor, Albany Law Review, Vol.. 46, 1981-1982. *Member:* Association of the Bar of the City of New York; Los Angeles County and American (Member, Patent, Trademark and Copyright Law Section) Bar Associations; State Bar of California (Member, Sec-

*(This Listing Continued)*

**BLECHER & COLLINS,** A PROFESSIONAL CORPORATION, Los Angeles—Continued

tions on: Antitrust; Intellectual Property; Litigation). **PRACTICE AREAS:** Antitrust; Intellectual Property; Entertainment Litigation.

**FLORENCE F. CAMERON,** born Hoboken, New Jersey, January 13, 1958; admitted to bar, 1987, New York; 1990, District of Columbia; 1991, California. *Education:* Barnard College (B.A., magna cum laude, 1981); Columbia University (J.D., 1986). Member, Columbia Law Review, 1984-1985; Senior Editor, 1985-1986. Harlan Fiske Stone Scholar. Law Clerk to Hon. Carl McGowan, U.S. Court of Appeals, District of Columbia Circuit, 1986-1987. Author: "Defamation Survivability and the Demise of the Actio Personalis Doctrine," 85 Columbia L. Rev. 1833 (1985). *Member:* Los Angeles County, New York State and American (Member, Antitrust Law Section) Bar Associations; Bar Association of the District of Columbia; State Bar of California (Member, Sections on: Antitrust; Intellectual Property; Litigation). **PRACTICE AREAS:** Antitrust; Business Litigation; Intellectual Property; Business Torts.

**RALPH C. HOFER,** born Toronto, Canada, March 16, 1953; admitted to bar, 1979, California; 1993, U.S. Supreme Court. *Education:* University of Göttingen, Germany; University of California at Los Angeles (B.A., magna cum laude, 1975); University of Southern California (J.D., cum laude, 1978). Phi Beta Kappa; Phi Alpha Delta. Member, Moot Court Honors Program, Moot Court Executive Board, 1977-1978. Assistant U.S. Attorney, Presidential Task Force on Narcotics Enforcement, U.S. Department of Justice, Central District of California, 1983-1986. Judge, Pro Tem Program, Los Angeles County Municipal and Superior Courts, 1987-1992. Antitrust Columnist, Los Angeles Daily Journal, 1988-1992. Adjunct Professor, Antitrust, Loyola Law School, 1989-1997. *Member:* Los Angeles County (Member, Sections on: Antitrust; Chair and Member of Executive Committee, 1995-1996; Intellectual Property; Litigation; Commercial Law; Criminal Justice) and American (Member, Sections on: Antitrust Law; Litigation; Criminal Justice) Bar Associations; State Bar of California (Member, Sections on: Antitrust; Business Law; Criminal Law; Intellectual Property; Litigation). **LANGUAGES:** German and Spanish. **PRACTICE AREAS:** Antitrust; Business Litigation; Intellectual Property.

**WILLIAM C. HSU,** born Monterey, California, December 22, 1955; admitted to bar, 1983, California. *Education:* University of California at Berkeley (B.A., 1979); University of California at Los Angeles (J.D., 1982). *Member:* Los Angeles County Bar Association; State Bar of California. **PRACTICE AREAS:** Antitrust; Intellectual Property.

**JAMES ROBERT NOBLIN,** born Palo Alto, California, March 20, 1959; admitted to bar, 1984, California. *Education:* University of Southern California (B.A., summa cum laude, 1980); Harvard University (J.D., cum laude, 1983). Editor, Harvard Law Review, 1981-1983. Law Clerk to Hon. William A. Norris, U.S. Circuit Court of Appeals, Ninth Circuit, 1983-1984. *Member:* Los Angeles County Bar Association; State Bar of California (Member, Sections on: Antitrust; Intellectual Property; Litigation). **PRACTICE AREAS:** Antitrust; Business Litigation; Intellectual Property.

**DONALD R. PEPPERMAN,** born Burbank, California, August 10, 1957; admitted to bar, 1983, California. *Education:* University of California at Los Angeles; University of Hawaii; California State University at Northridge (B.S., 1979); Whittier College School of Law (J.D., cum laude, 1983). *Member:* Los Angeles County (Member, Antitrust Section) and American (Member, Sections on: Antitrust Law; Litigation; Business Law; Intellectual Property Law) Bar Associations; State Bar of California (Member, Sections on: Antitrust; Intellectual Property; Law Practice Management; Litigation); Association of Business Trial Lawyers. **PRACTICE AREAS:** Antitrust; Intellectual Property.

**ALICIA G. ROSENBERG,** born Montevideo, Uruguay, May 25, 1961; admitted to bar, 1985, California; 1989, U.S. Supreme Court. *Education:* Wellesley College (B.A., 1982); University of California at Los Angeles (J.D., 1985). Phi Beta Kappa. Durant Scholar. Managing Editor, UCLA Law Review, 1984-1985. Author: "Automation and the Work Preservation Doctrine: Accommodating Productivity and Job Security Interests," 32 UCLA Law Review 135, (1984). *Member:* Los Angeles County (Member, Antitrust Law Section) and Federal Bar Associations; State Bar of California (Member, Antitrust Section); International Association of Jewish Lawyers and Jurists. **PRACTICE AREAS:** Antitrust; Intellectual Property.

## LAW OFFICES OF DAVID B. BLOOM

A PROFESSIONAL CORPORATION
Established in 1974

3325 WILSHIRE BOULEVARD, NINTH FLOOR
**LOS ANGELES, CALIFORNIA 90010**
Telephone: 213-938-5248; 384-4088
Telecopier: 213-385-2009

*General Civil Practice, Litigation, Insurance, Personal Injury, Bankruptcy, Creditors Rights, Probate, Real Property, Banking and Entertainment Law.*

**DAVID B. BLOOM,** born Los Angeles, California, February 17, 1949; admitted to bar, 1973, California; 1974, U.S. District Court, Central District of California; 1976, U.S. District Court, Southern District of California. *Education:* University of Southern California (B.A., cum laude, 1970); Loyola University of Los Angeles (J.D., 1973). Phi Alpha Delta. Lecturer, Scalpel & Subpoenas III, Seminar jointly sponsored by the Los Angeles County Medical Association and Los Angeles County Bar Association, February, 1981; "Handling Debt Collection Matters Before and After Judgment," 1982, "Remedies for Breach of Contract," 1985, "Liens on Personal Injury Recoveries," 1985, 1989 and 1993 and "Creditors' Remedies and Debtors' Rights," 1986, all California Continuing Education of the Bar Panels; "Creditors Rights and Protection of Security Interests in Bankruptcy," National Business Institute Panel, 1987. "Collecting Judgements in California," National Business Institute Panel, 1992. *Member:* Los Angeles County and American Bar Associations; State Bar of California; Commercial Law League of America.

---

**STEPHEN S. MONROE, (A PROFESSIONAL CORPORATION),** born San Francisco, California, August 3, 1947; admitted to bar, 1973, California and U.S. District Court, Central District of California; 1976, U.S. Tax Court; 1978, U.S. Supreme Court; 1982, U.S. Court of Appeals, Ninth Circuit. *Education:* Claremont Mens College; University of California at Los Angeles (B.A., Political Science, B.S., Economics, 1969); Loyola University of Los Angeles (J.D., 1973). Member: St. Thomas More Law Honor Society; Loyola University Law Review 1972-1973. Instructor, Torts and Civil Procedure, Mid-Valley College of Law, 1976-1979. *Member:* Los Angeles County Bar Association; State Bar of California. [Capt., USAR, 1969-1977]. **LANGUAGES:** German; Russian. **REPORTED CASES:** Burnett v. Natl. Enq., 144 CA 3d 991; Calder v. Jones Mueller v. Lacera, 8 CA 4th 41.

**RAPHAEL A. ROSEMBLAT,** born Santiago, Chile, March 5, 1958; admitted to bar, 1983, California; 1984, U.S. Court of Appeals, Ninth Circuit; U.S. District Court, Central, Northern, Southern and Eastern Districts of California. *Education:* University of California, Los Angeles (B.A., magna cum laude, 1980); University of San Francisco (J.D., 1983). *Member:* Los Angeles County Bar Association; State Bar of California.

**JAMES E. ADLER,** born Fayetteville, Arkansas, May 27, 1952; admitted to bar, 1977, California; 1982, U.S. District Court, Central District of California; 1985, U.S. Court of Appeals, Ninth Circuit; 1989, U.S. District Court, Eastern, Northern and Southern Districts of California; 1992, U.S. Supreme Court. *Education:* University of Wisconsin; University of California at Los Angeles (B.A., 1974); Loyola University of Los Angeles (J.D., 1977). *Member:* Wilshire and Los Angeles County Bar Associations; State Bar of California.

**BONNI S. MANTOVANI,** born Brooklyn, New York, May 16, 1956; admitted to bar, 1982, California, U.S. Court of Appeals, Ninth Circuit and U.S. District Court, Central District of California; 1983, U.S. Court of Military Appeals and U.S. Court of Appeals, Second Circuit. *Education:* Syracuse University; Adelphi University (B.S., 1976); Southwestern University School of Law (J.D., 1980). *Member:* State Bar of California.

**ROY A. LEVUN,** born Chicago, Illinois, November 19, 1951; admitted to bar, 1980, California; 1982, U.S. District Court, Central District of California; 1984, U.S. District Court, Southern District of California. *Education:* University of Illinois (B.A., 1973); Southwestern University (J.D., 1978). *Member:* Wilshire and Los Angeles County Bar Associations.

**CHERIE S. RAIDY,** born Kansas City, Missouri, June 10, 1956; admitted to bar, 1981, California; 1982, U.S. District Court, Central District of California. *Education:* University of Southern California (B.A., magna cum laude, 1978); Southwestern University School of Law (J.D., 1981). President, Themis Society, Southwestern University School of Law, 1989. Delegate, California State Bar Conference of Delegates, 1986-1989. Speaker: "Loan Documentation Strategies in the '90's-Lessons from the Battle Lines,"

*(This Listing Continued)*

# PROFESSIONAL BIOGRAPHIES

Los Angeles County Bar Association; "Resolving Troubled Real Estate Loans-Foreclosures and other Terminations of the Mortgage," Infocast Banking Seminar. *Member:* Los Angeles County (Member: Executive Committee, Barristers, 1986—; Steering Committee, Real Estate Finance Subcommittee, Real Property Section; Co-Chair, Community Law Week Committee, 1985—) and American (Member, Section of Business Law) Bar Associations; Women Lawyers of Los Angeles.

*JONATHAN UDELL,* born New York, N.Y., August 17, 1944; admitted to bar, 1983, California, U.S. District Court, Central District of California and U.S. Court of Appeals, Ninth Circuit. *Education:* University of California at Berkeley; University of California at Los Angeles (B.A., 1966); California State University at Northridge (M.A., 1969); The Ohio State University (Ph.D., 1974); Loyola University at Los Angeles (J.D., 1982). *Member:* State Bar of California; Consumer Attorney Association of Los Angeles; American Sociological Association.

*SUSAN CAROLE JAY,* born Los Angeles, California, May 12, 1949; admitted to bar, 1985, California and U.S. District Court, Central, Southern and Eastern Districts of California; 1986, U.S. District Court, Northern District of California. *Education:* El Camino College (A.A., 1971); California State University at San Diego (B.A., 1973); University of San Diego (J.D., 1984). Phi Alpha Delta. *Member:* Los Angeles County Bar Association (Member, Commercial and Bankruptcy Section); State Bar of California. *LANGUAGES:* Spanish.

*EDWARD IDELL,* born Brooklyn, New York, May 9, 1955; admitted to bar, 1981, New York and Florida; 1989, California; 1990, U.S. District Court, Central District of California and U.S. Court of Appeals, Ninth Circuit. *Education:* State University of New York at Stony Brook (B.A., 1977); University of Miami (J.D., 1980). Phi Delta Phi. *Member:* Los Angeles County Bar Association (Litigation Section); State Bar of California. *LANGUAGES:* Hebrew.

*SANDRA KAMENIR,* born Chicago, Illinois, February 18, 1949; admitted to bar, 1976, California. *Education:* University of California at Berkeley (B.A., 1971); University of San Fernando Valley College of Law (J.D., 1976). Member, San Fernando Law Review, 1975-1976. *Member:* Los Angeles County Bar Association.

*STEVEN WAYNE LAZARUS,* born Los Angeles, California, December 20, 1960; admitted to bar, 1988, California, U.S. District Court, Northern and Central District of California and U.S. Court of Appeals, Ninth Circuit. *Education:* University of California at Los Angeles (B.A., 1984); Pepperdine University (J.D., 1988). *Member:* State Bar of California.

*ANDREW EDWARD BRISENO,* born Mexicali, Baja California, Mexico, February 16, 1958; admitted to bar, 1983, California and U.S. District Court, Eastern District of California; 1985, U.S. District Court, Northern District of California and U.S. Court of Appeals, Ninth Circuit; 1987, Nevada and U.S. Supreme Court; 1988, U.S. District Court, District of Nevada; 1991, U.S. District Court, Central and Southern Districts of California. *Education:* University of California at Los Angeles (B.A., 1980); University of the Pacific, McGeorge School of Law (J.D., 1983). Phi Alpha Delta. Member, Anthony M. Kennedy American Inns of Court, 1988-1990. Law Clerk to Judge Edward J. Garcia, U.S. District Court, Eastern District of California, 1984-1985. *Member:* State Bar of California; State Bar of Nevada. *LANGUAGES:* Spanish.

*HAROLD C. KLASKIN,* born Los Angeles, California, April 6, 1963; admitted to bar, 1992, California. *Education:* California State Polytechnic University; California State University, Los Angeles; Gemological Institute of America; University of West Los Angeles (B.S., J.D., 1992). *Member:* State Bar of California.

*SHELLEY M. GOULD,* born New York, N.Y., June 7, 1952; admitted to bar, 1976, California; 1978, U.S. Court of Appeals for the District of Columbia; 1979, U.S. District Court, Central District of California. *Education:* State University of New York at Binghamton; University of California at Los Angeles (B.A., cum laude, 1974); Southwestern University (J.D., 1976). *Member:* Beverly Hills (Member, Business Section) and Los Angeles County Bar Associations; State Bar of California (Member, Business Section); Lawyers Club of Los Angeles County.

*PETER O. ISRAEL,* born Los Angeles, California, April 5, 1943; admitted to bar, 1972, California. *Education:* University of California at Berkeley (B.A., 1965); Loyola University of Los Angeles (J.D., 1971). Managing Editor, Loyola Law Review, 1970-1971. Law Clerk for Honorable Otto M. Kaus, Presiding Justice, California Court of Appeal, Second District, Division Five, 1972. Contributing Author: CEB, "California Civil Procedure During Trial," Vol. 1, 1985 and 1986 Supplements. Consulting Editor: Procedure Module, California Civil Practice (Bancroft-Whitney, 1992).

*(This Listing Continued)*

Member, Board of Directors, San Fernando Valley Neighborhood Legal Services, 1989—. Instructor, Southern California Institute of Law, 1992—. *Member:* Los Angeles County (Member, Amicus Briefs Committee, 1976—) and Ventura County Bar Associations; State Bar of California; Ventura County Trial Lawyers Association.

REPRESENTATIVE CLIENTS: Matsushita Electric Corporation of America dba Panasonic; Sony Corporation of America; Rossignol Ski Co., Inc.; Salomon North America, Inc.; Alpine Electric Corporation; Clarion Corporation; Federal Express; Electro Rent Corp.; Nordica, Inc.; Fremont Indemnity Co.; Marathon National Bank; Simi Valley Bank; Western Bank; Preferred Bank; Bank Leumi; ; Central Protective National Insurance; Developers Insurance Co.; East-West Federal Banks; American International Bank; Verdugo Banking Co.
REFERENCE: Verdugo Banking Co., Glendale, CA.

## *BLOOM, HERGOTT, COOK, DIEMER & KLEIN, LLP*

**LOS ANGELES, CALIFORNIA**

(See Beverly Hills)

*Entertainment Law, General Business, Corporate.*

## *BLUM, PROPPER & HARDACRE*

INCORPORATED

Established in 1946

SUITE 905

12100 WILSHIRE BOULEVARD

**LOS ANGELES, CALIFORNIA 90025**

Telephone: 310-826-7900
Fax: 310-826-1480
Email: BPHINC@AOL.COM

*Corporate, Business and Securities Law. Insurance, Negligence and Family Law. Probate, Trusts, Estate Planning and Copyright Law, Business Litigation.*

*GRANT E. PROPPER,* born Los Angeles, California, May 18, 1933; admitted to bar, 1961, California. *Education:* University of California at Los Angeles (B.A., 1957; LL.B., 1960). Editor, University of California at Los Angeles Law Review, 1958-1960. Member, Panel of Arbitrators, American Arbitration Association. Mediator, Los Angeles and Santa Monica Superior Court, Family Law Matters, 1978—. Family Law Editor, California Trial Lawyers Association Forum, 1979. *Member:* Beverly Hills and Los Angeles County Bar Associations; The State Bar of California.

*IVON B. BLUM,* born Los Angeles, California, March 12, 1934; admitted to bar, 1961, California. *Education:* Haileybury Imperial Service College, England and University of California at Los Angeles (A.B., 1957); University of California at Los Angeles (J.D., with honors, 1960). Editor, University of California at Los Angeles Law Review, 1958-1960. Member, Board of Governors, West Valley Y.M.C.A., 1975-1978. Author: "Status of Intra-Corporate Arrangements Under Antitrust Laws," 52 Los Angeles Bar Journal 580, 1977. *Member:* Beverly Hills (Chairman, Membership Committee, 1973-1974) and Los Angeles County (Member, Intellectual Property and Unfair Competition Section) Bar Associations; The State Bar of California.

*DAVID W. HARDACRE,* born Liverpool, England, May 3, 1940; admitted to bar, 1969, California. *Education:* Chapman College (B.A., 1963); Loyola University of Los Angeles (J.D., 1968). Adjunct Professor of Law, Copyright Law, San Fernando School of Law, 1979—. *Member:* Beverly Hills (Chairman, Continuing Education Committee, 1973-1974) and Los Angeles County Bar Associations; The State Bar of California.

---

*EDWIN GRANTLEY HARDACRE,* born Orange, California, September 28, 1962; admitted to bar, 1992, California; 1993, U.S. District Court, Central District of California. *Education:* University of California at Los Angeles (B.A., in English literature, 1987); Whittier College School of Law (J.D., 1991). *Member:* Beverly Hills and Los Angeles County Bar Associations; State Bar of California.

## MERRICK J. BOBB

355 SOUTH GRAND AVENUE, 40TH FLOOR
LOS ANGELES, CALIFORNIA 90071-3101
Telephone: 213-683-8759
Fax: 213-683-0225

*Police and Public Entity Lose Prevention and Risk Management, Business Litigation and Antitrust.*

**MERRICK J. BOBB,** born Denver, Colorado, February 17, 1946; admitted to bar, 1972, California. *Education:* Dartmouth College (B.A., 1968); University of California at Berkeley (J.D., 1971). Associate Editor, California Law Review, 1970-1971. Law Clerk to Judge Irving Hill, U.S. District Court, Central District of California, 1971-1973. Legal Aid Foundation of Los Angeles (Board of Directors, 1983-1991 and Chair, 1989-1990. San Fernando Valley Neighborhood Legal Services (Board of Directors, 1979-1983 and Chair, 1981-1982. Public Counsel, Board of Directors, 1994—). Deputy General Counsel, Christopher Commission on the Los Angeles Police Department, 1991. General Counsel, Kolts Investigation of the Los Angeles County Sheriff's Department, 1992. Special Counsel to the Los Angeles Police Commission, 1995—. Member, Board of Directors, Ketchum Downtown YMCA, 1992—. *Member:* Los Angeles County Bar Association (Member, Board of Trustees, 1993-1995; Pro Bono Council, 1988-1996; Co-Chair, 1992-1993; Chair, 1994-1996; Member, Legal Services for the Poor Committee, 1990-1996; Co-Chair, 1990-1991; Access to Justice Committee, 1996—; Central District Lawyer Representative to U.S. Ninth Circuit Judicial Conference, 1994—). **PRACTICE AREAS:** Law Enforcement; Civil Litigation; Antitrust.

## LAW OFFICES OF CLAUDIA C. BOHORQUEZ

445 SOUTH FIGUEROA STREET, SUITE 2400
LOS ANGELES, CALIFORNIA 90071-1628
Telephone: 213-488-0545
Fax: 213-488-0344

*Commercial Law and Litigation. Bankruptcy, Banking, Corporate Law, Real Estate and International Law.*

**CLAUDIA C. BOHORQUEZ,** born Houston, Texas, December 16, 1965; admitted to bar, 1990, California. *Education:* University of Texas at Austin (B.A., 1987); Georgetown University (J.D., 1990). Executive Editor, Georgetown International Law Review, 1989-1990. Author: Translation, "Citizens of Chanaral v. Codelco-Chile, Salvador Division," Georgetown Intl. Envir. Law Review, 1990. *Member:* Los Angeles County and American Bar Associations; The State Bar of California (Member, Litigation Section). **LANGUAGES:** Spanish; French. **PRACTICE AREAS:** Commercial Law; Banking Law; Business Litigation; Bankruptcy; Corporate and Real Estate; Litigation.

## BOLDRA & KLUEGER

15760 VENTURA BOULEVARD, SUITE 1900
LOS ANGELES, CALIFORNIA 91436
Telephone: 818-716-7710
FAX: 818-716-0042

*Tax Litigation and Controversies, Tax Planning, Estate Tax Planning, Estate Planning.*

### MEMBERS OF FIRM

**ROBERT F. KLUEGER,** born New York, N.Y., October 28, 1945; admitted to bar, 1974, Colorado; 1978, New York; 1980, U.S. Tax Court; 1989, California; 1996, U.S. Supreme Court. *Education:* Boston University and University of Pennsylvania (B.A., 1967); Fordham University (J.D., 1973); University of Denver (LL.M. in Taxation, 1980). Editor, University of Denver Tax Law Journal, 1980. Author: "Tax Aspects of the Purchase and Sale of a Corporate Business," The Colorado Lawyer, May, 1980; "Deductibility of Prepaid Intangible Drilling and Development Costs," Oil and Gas Tax Quarterly, May, 1982; "Analyzing an Oil and Gas Drilling Fund," Oil and Gas Taxes, May, 1984; "The Rabbi Trust: A Unique Way to Defer Compensation," The Colorado Lawyer, April 1987; "Mergers and Acquisitions in Colorado, A Practitioner's Roadmap," The Colorado Lawyer, May, 1987; "Buying and Selling A Business," John Wiley & Sons, 1987; "Mergers and Acquisitions, A Practical Guide," Executive Enterprises Publications, 1989; "The Guide to Asset Protection," John Wiley & Sons, 1996. Instructor, Tax Principles, Research and Writing, Graduate Tax Program, University of Denver, 1980. Adjunct Professor, Corporate Reorganizations, University of Denver Graduate Tax Program, 1988. *Member:* San Fernando Valley (Chair, Tax Section, 1992), Colorado and American Bar Associations; State Bar of California. [LTJG, U.S. Navy, 1967-1970]. (Certified Specialist, Taxation Law The State Bar of California Board of Legal Specialization). **REPORTED CASES:** Brockamp v. United States, 859 F. Supp. 1283 (1994) 67 F.3d 260 (9th Cir., 1995). **PRACTICE AREAS:** Tax Litigation and Controversies; Tax Planning; Estate Tax Planning.

**PATRICIA E. BOLDRA,** born Inglewood, California, January 4, 1945; admitted to bar, 1977, Illinois; 1978, Colorado; 1985, U.S. Tax Court; 1992, California. *Education:* University of Southern California (B.A., 1966; M.S., 1968); Southwestern University School of Law (J.D., 1974). Licensed Real Estate Broker, Colorado, 1978. *Member:* Los Angeles County, Denver, Colorado and American Bar Associations; State Bar of California; Women Lawyers Association of Los Angeles; San Fernando Valley Women Lawyers Association. **PRACTICE AREAS:** Estate Planning; Bankruptcy; Real Estate Law.

REFERENCE: Bank of Granada Hills, Granada Hills, CA.

## BOLTON, DUNN & YATES

LOS ANGELES, CALIFORNIA
(See Santa Monica)

*General Civil and Trial Practice in all State and Federal Courts. Insurance.*

## BONAPARTE & MIYAMOTO

A PROFESSIONAL LAW CORPORATION
Established in 1960
11911 SAN VICENTE BOULEVARD, SUITE 355
LOS ANGELES, CALIFORNIA 90049
Telephone: 310-471-3481
FAX: 310-471-1686
Email: 73344.441@Compuserve.com

Other Los Angeles Office: 919 South Grand Avenue, Suite 208E. Telephone: 213-688-8872. FAX: 213-688-8887.
Newport Beach, California Office: 5030 Campus Drive. Telephone: 714-955-2012. FAX: 714-833-1423.

*Practice limited to Immigration and Nationality Law.*

FIRM PROFILE: *The firm was started in 1930 and has become one of the largest and oldest law firms specializing in immigration law in the United States. The firm has three offices in Southern California. It also has of counsel arrangements with lawyers in San Francisco, Washington, D.C., London, and Hong Kong.*

**RONALD H. BONAPARTE,** born Hollywood, California, April 7, 1935; admitted to bar, 1959, California; 1965, U.S. Supreme Court. *Education:* Pomona College (A.B., 1956); Stanford University (J.D., 1959). Phi Alpha Delta. Lecturer: University of California at Los Angeles School of Law, 1973—; Advanced Professional Program, University of Southern California School of Law, 1974. Southwestern School of Law, 1982-1983. Author: "Rodeno Bill," One Chicano Law Review. Chairman, U.S.C. Law Center, Advanced Professional Program, Immigration Law Institute, The Immigration Act of 1987 and 1990. Member, Immigration and Nationality Law Advisory Commission, California Board of Legal Specialization, 1986-1991. *Member:* Los Angeles County and American (Chairman, Immigration Committee, International Law Section, 1975-1979, 1980-1983) Bar Associations; The State Bar of California; American Immigration Lawyers Association (Chairman, Los Angeles Chapter, 1969-1970 and 1986-1987). (Certified Specialist, Immigration and Nationality Law, The State Bar of California Board of Legal Specialization). **PRACTICE AREAS:** Immigration and Nationality Law.

**LYNN MIYAMOTO,** born Los Angeles, California, May 12, 1960; admitted to bar, 1987, California. *Education:* University of California at Davis (B.A., 1982; J.D., 1986). Phi Delta Phi. *Member:* Los Angeles County (Immigration Section; Public Counsel; Volunteer Mentor Attorney-Immigration) and Japanese-American Bar Associations; State Bar of California (International Law Section); American Immigration Lawyers Association; National Lawyers Guild. (Certified Specialist, Immigration and Na-

*(This Listing Continued)*

tionality Law, The State Bar of California Board of Legal Specialization). *LANGUAGES:* Japanese. *PRACTICE AREAS:* Immigration and Nationality Law.

**THOMAS E. CUMMINGS,** born San Francisco, California, October 5, 1927; admitted to bar, 1957, California; 1962, U.S. Supreme Court. *Education:* University of California at Berkeley; San Jose State College; University of Santa Clara (J.D., 1956). Chief, Immigrant Visa Branch, American Embassy, Buenos Aires, Argentina, 1958-1959. Chief Consular Officer, American Consulate General, Monterey, Mexico. Chief, Visa Section, American Embassy, Tokyo, Japan. Deputy Consul General, American Consulate General, Naples, Italy. Chief, Consular Section, American Embassy, Port-au-Prince, Haiti. Chief American Consulate, Brisbane, Australia. Consul General of the U.S., Palermo, Italy. Chief of Consular Section, American Consulate General, Hong Kong. *Member:* State Bar of California. *LANGUAGES:* Spanish and Italian. *PRACTICE AREAS:* Immigration and Nationality Law.

## BONNE, BRIDGES, MUELLER, O'KEEFE & NICHOLS

PROFESSIONAL CORPORATION

3699 WILSHIRE BOULEVARD, 10TH FLOOR
**LOS ANGELES, CALIFORNIA 90010-2719**
Telephone: 213-480-1900
Fax: 213-738-5888

*Santa Ana, California Office:* 1750 East Fourth Street, Suite 450, P.O. Box 22018, 92702-2018. Telephone: 714-835-1157. Fax: 714-480-2585.
*Santa Barbara, California Office:* 801 Garden Street, Suite 300, 93101-5502. Telephone: 805-965-2992. Fax: 805-962-6509.
*Riverside, California Office:* 3403 Tenth Street, Suite 800, 92501-0749. Telephone: 909-788-1944. Fax: 909-683-7827.
*San Luis Obispo, California Office:* 1060 Palm Street, 93401-3221. Telephone: 805-541-8350. Fax: 805-541-6817.

*General Insurance Defense, Professional Malpractice, Products Liability Claims, Drug and Medical Device Claims, Environmental and Toxic Tort Claims, Insurance and Wrongful Termination, Professional Administrative Hearing Counsel.*

**RIED BRIDGES,** born Kansas City, Missouri, October 20, 1927; admitted to bar, 1954, California. *Education:* University of Southern California (B.S., 1951; J.D., 1954). *Member:* Los Angeles County and American Bar Associations; The State Bar of California; Association of Southern California Defense Counsel; American Board of Trial Advocates (Diplomate). Fellow: American College of Trial Lawyers; American Academy of Forensic Sciences; International Academy of Trial Lawyers.

**KENNETH N. MUELLER,** born Pasadena, California, June 27, 1935; admitted to bar, 1964, California. *Education:* Stanford University (A.B., 1957); Hastings College of Law, University of California (LL.B., 1963). Phi Delta Phi. *Member:* Los Angeles County and American Bar Associations; The State Bar of California; Association of Southern California Defense Counsel; American Board of Trial Advocates. Fellow, American College of Trial Lawyers; International Academy of Trial Lawyers.

**DAVID J. O'KEEFE,** born Los Angeles, California, December 26, 1939; admitted to bar, 1965, California. *Education:* Loyola University of Los Angeles (B.A., 1961); University of California at Los Angeles (LL.B., 1964). Phi Delta Phi. *Member:* Los Angeles County and American Bar Associations; The State Bar of California; Association of Southern California Defense Counsel; American Board of Trial Advocates (President, Los Angeles Chapter, 1987); American Board of Professional Liability Attorneys. Fellow, American College of Trial Lawyers.

**JAMES D. NICHOLS,** born Los Angeles, California, December 20, 1944; admitted to bar, 1976, California; 1981, U.S. Supreme Court. *Education:* University of Hawaii; Abilene Christian University (B.S., 1968); Southwestern University (J.D., 1975). Delta Theta Phi (Vice Dean, 1973; Master of Ritual, 1974). Member, The American Society of Law and Medicine, 1975-1977. Counsel, U.S. Section of the International College of Surgeons, 1981-1993. *Member:* Los Angeles County and American Bar Associations; State Bar of California; Association of Southern California Defense Counsel; American Board of Trial Advocates (Diplomate); Defense Research Institute; Cowboy Lawyers Association, Inc. (Founding Member and President, 1989-1991). Fellow, American College of Trial Lawyers.

*(This Listing Continued)*

**GEORGE E. PETERSON,** born Portland, Oregon, March 12, 1947; admitted to bar, 1972, California. *Education:* Loyola University (B.A., 1969; J.D., 1972). Phi Alpha Delta. Member, Loyola Law Review, 1971-1972. *Member:* Los Angeles County and American Bar Associations; The State Bar of California; Association of Southern California Defense Counsel; American Board of Trial Advocates. [Capt., JAG, USMC, 1973-1977]

**JOEL BRUCE DOUGLAS,** born Los Angeles, California, January 25, 1948; admitted to bar, 1973, California; 1974, U.S. District Court, Central District of California; 1978, U.S. Court of Appeals, Ninth Circuit; 1979, U.S. Supreme Court. *Education:* California State University at Northridge (B.A., magna cum laude, 1970) and East Los Angeles College; Loyola University of Los Angeles School of Law (J.D., 1973). Phi Alpha Delta. Member, St. Thomas Moore Law Honor Society. Associate Editor, Loyola University of Los Angeles Law Review, 1972-1973. Chief Justice, Associated Students California State University at Northridge Constitutional Court, 1967-1970. Adjunct Professor of Law, Pepperdine University School of Law, Malibu, California, 1981-1984. Member, Joint Liaison Sub-Committee of Los Angeles County Medical Association and Los Angeles County Bar Association, 1979-1983. Judge, Pro Tempore, Los Angeles Municipal Court, 1980—. Judge Pro Tempore, Los Angeles Superior Court, 1988—. *Member:* San Fernando Valley, Los Angeles County (Member, Legal-Medical Committee, 1979-1983; Staff Attorney, Medical-Legal Hot Line, 1979-1982) and American (Member, Sections on: Litigation; Tort and Insurance Practice) Bar Associations; The State Bar of California; American Board of Trial Advocates.

**ALEXANDER B. T. COBB,** born Fort Smith, Arkansas, July 19, 1946; admitted to bar, 1972, California; 1973, U.S. District Court, Central District of California; 1978, U.S. District Court, Southern District of California. *Education:* Tulane University (B.A., 1968); Hastings College of Law, University of California (J.D., 1971). Phi Delta Phi. Moot Court Judge, Hastings College of Law. *Member:* Los Angeles County and American Bar Associations; The State Bar of California; Association of Southern California Defense Counsel; American Board of Trial Advocates.

**PETER R. OSINOFF,** born New York, N.Y., May 4, 1952; admitted to bar, 1976, California; 1978, District of Columbia. *Education:* Yale College (B.A., magna cum laude, 1973) Phi Beta Kappa; Stanford University (M.A., 1976); Stanford Law School (J.D., 1976). Law Clerk to the Hon. Sherman G. Finesilver, U.S. District Court for the District of Colorado, 1976-1977. Adjunct Professor of Law, University of West Los Angeles School of Law, 1980-1981. Assistant U.S. Attorney for the Central District of California, 1978-1983. *Member:* Los Angeles County and American Bar Associations; The State Bar of California; Governor, Wilshire Bar Association.

**MARGARET MANTON HOLM,** born San Francisco, California, March 10, 1951; admitted to bar, 1976, California; 1977, U.S. District Court, Central District of California; 1991, U.S. District Court, Southern District of California. *Education:* University of California at San Diego (B.A., 1973); University of Santa Clara (J.D., 1976). Member, Arbitration Panel: Los Angeles Superior Court, 1981—; San Bernardino County Superior Court, 1981—; Orange County Superior Court, 1988—. Judge Pro Tempore, Orange County Superior Court, 1989—. *Member:* Orange County and Los Angeles County Bar Associations; State Bar of California; Association of Southern California Defense Counsel; American Board of Trial Advocates (Advocate). Master, Robert Banyon Inn of Court. (Resident in Santa Ana Office).

**JEFFREY C. MOFFAT,** born Glendale, California, July 27, 1954; admitted to bar, 1981, California; 1982, U.S. District Court, Central District of California and U.S. Court of Appeals, Ninth Circuit; 1987, U.S. Supreme Court. *Education:* Brigham Young University (B.A., 1978; J.D., 1981). Co-Author: "Standards of Care in Emergency Medicine," Little, Brown & Co., 1994. *Member:* Los Angeles County and American Bar Associations; The State Bar of California.

**N. DENISE TAYLOR,** born Indianapolis, Indiana, September 22, 1957; admitted to bar, 1981, California. *Education:* Pacific Union College (B.A., magna cum laude, 1978); Pepperdine University School of Law (J.D., 1981). Member, Pepperdine Law Review, 1979-1981. Author: "California Expands Tort Liability under the Novel 'Market Share' Theory: Sindell v. Abbott Laboratories," Vol. 8, No. 4, Pepperdine Law Review, 1981. *Member:* Los Angeles County and American Bar Associations; The State Bar of California; Association of Southern California Defense Counsel; American Board of Trial Advocates (Associate).

**PATRICIA K. RAMSEY,** born Lincoln, Nebraska, December 21, 1950; admitted to bar, 1979, Nebraska and U.S. District Court, District of Nebraska; 1980, California; 1982, U.S. District Court, Central District of Cali-

*(This Listing Continued)*

## BONNE, BRIDGES, MUELLER, O'KEEFE & NICHOLS, PROFESSIONAL CORPORATION, Los Angeles—Continued

fornia. *Education:* University of Nebraska (B.A., 1973; J.D., 1979). Alpha Lambda Delta. *Member:* Santa Barbara County and Nebraska State Bar Associations; State Bar of California; Association of Southern California Defense Counsel. (Resident in Santa Barbara Office).

**THEODORE H. O'LEARY,** born Braintree, Massachusetts, June 9, 1949; admitted to bar, 1982, California; 1983, U.S. District Court, Central District of California and U.S. Court of Appeals, Ninth Circuit. *Education:* University of Minnesota (B.A., 1971); Southwestern University School of Law (J.D., 1982). *Member:* Los Angeles County and American Bar Associations; The State Bar of California; Association of Southern California Defense Counsel; Defense Research Institute.

**MICHAEL D. LUBRANI,** born Summit, New Jersey, December 26, 1959; admitted to bar, 1984, California and U.S. District Court, Central District of California. *Education:* Rutgers University (B.A., 1981); Pepperdine University (J.D., cum laude, 1984). Member, Pepperdine Law Review, 1982-1984. Pepperdine University Board of Professional Standards, 1982-1984. *Member:* Los Angeles County, Riverside County and American (Member, Law Student Division; 9th Circuit, Lt. Governor, 1983-1984) Bar Associations; The State Bar of California; Association of Southern California Defense Counsel. (Resident in Riverside Office).

**CHRISTOPHER B. MARSHALL,** born Santa Monica, California, November 30, 1951; admitted to bar, 1982, California and U.S. District Court, Central District of California; 1983, U.S. Court of Appeals, Ninth Circuit. *Education:* University of California at Los Angeles (B.A., 1973); Loyola University Law School, Los Angeles (J.D., 1978). *Member:* Los Angeles County and American Bar Associations; The State Bar of California; Association of Southern California Defense Counsel; National Health Lawyers Association; California Society for Healthcare Attorneys. (Resident in Riverside Office).

**THOMAS M. O'NEIL,** born Los Angeles, California, December 22, 1956; admitted to bar, 1982, California; 1983, U.S. Court of Appeals, Ninth Circuit and U.S. District Court, Central District of California. *Education:* California State University at Northridge (B.A., cum laude, 1979); Pepperdine University (J.D., 1982). Phi Delta Phi. Member, Pepperdine Law Review, 1981-1982. Author: "Truman v. Thomas: The Rise of Informed Refusal," Pepperdine Law Review, Vol. 8, No. 4, 1981. *Member:* Los Angeles County and American Bar Associations; The State Bar of California; Association of Southern California Defense Counsel.

**MARK B. CONNELY,** born Lynwood, California, March 11, 1961; admitted to bar, 1986, California; 1987, U.S. District Court, Central District of California, U.S. Court of Appeals, Ninth Circuit and U.S. Supreme Court. *Education:* California Polytechnic State University (B.A., 1983); Loyola University; University of San Diego (J.D., 1986). Panel Attorney, California Appellate Project. Member, U.S. Supreme Court Historical Society. *Member:* San Luis Obispo County and American Bar Associations; The State Bar of California; Association of Southern California Defense Counsel. (Resident in San Luis Obispo Office).

**PETER G. BERTLING,** born Niagara Falls, New York, July 11, 1960; admitted to bar, 1987, California and U.S. District Court, Central District of California. *Education:* Bob Jones University (B.A., 1982; M.A., 1984); California Western School of Law (J.D., 1987). National Trial Competition Championship. American College of Trial Lawyers Best Oralist Award. *Member:* State Bar of California. (Resident in Santa Barbara Office).

**THOMAS R. BRADFORD,** born Providence, Rhode Island, February 5, 1950; admitted to bar, 1983, California and U.S. District Court, Central District of California; 1987, U.S. Court of Appeals, Ninth Circuit and U.S. Supreme Court. *Education:* Villanova University (B.S., 1972; B.A., 1972); George Washington University (M.A., 1975); Southwestern University (J.D., 1982). *Member:* Santa Barbara County and American Bar Associations; State Bar of California; Association of Southern California Defense Counsel; American Society of Law and Medicine; The Association of Trial Lawyers of America; Southern California Association of Healthcare Risk Managers. (Also in Santa Barbara Office).

---

**LOUIS W. PAPPAS,** born Los Angeles, California, March 31, 1957; admitted to bar, 1985, California and U.S. District Court, Central District of California; 1987, U.S. District Court, Northern and Southern Districts of California; 1988, U.S. Court of Appeals, Ninth Circuit; 1991, U.S. District Court, Eastern District of California. *Education:* California State Polytechnic University, Pomona (B.A., 1979); Southwestern University School of Law (J.D., 1982). Recipient, American Jurisprudence Award. *Member:* Los Angeles County and American Bar Associations; State Bar of California; Association of Southern California Defense Counsel.

**YUK KWONG LAW,** born Canton, China, September 22, 1958; admitted to bar, 1985, New York and U.S. District Court, Southern and Eastern Districts of New York; 1988, California; 1990, U.S. District Court, Central, Southern and Northern Districts of California and U.S. Court of Appeals, Ninth Circuit. *Education:* University of Vermont (B.A., 1981); Fordham University (J.D., 1984). Commentary Editor, Fordham International Law Journal, 1983-1984. Author: "Foreign Agents Registration Act: A New Standard For Determining Agency," 6 Fordham International Law Journal, p. 365, 1982-1983. *Member:* Los Angeles, New York State and American Bar Associations; State Bar of California; Southern California Chinese Lawyers Association. **LANGUAGES:** Chinese.

**MARY A. SELIGER,** born Cincinnati, Ohio, September 16, 1944; admitted to bar, 1982, California; 1983, U.S. Federal Court. *Education:* Queen of Angels School of Nursing (R.N. Diploma); California State University, Northridge (B.A., 1978); Loyola Law School (J.D., 1982). Licensed Registered Nurse, California, 1966. *Member:* Los Angeles County and American Bar Associations; State Bar of California; Association of Southern California Defense Counsel.

**THOMAS G. SCULLY,** born Erie, Pennsylvania, June 4, 1958; admitted to bar, 1985, Pennsylvania; 1986, U.S. Court of Military Appeals; 1990, California and U.S. District Court, Northern, Eastern, Central and Southern Districts of California; 1991, District of Columbia, U.S. Court of Appeals, District of Columbia Circuit and U.S. Court of Appeals, Ninth Circuit; 1992, U.S. Supreme Court; 1994, U.S. District Court, Western District of Pennsylvania. *Education:* Allegheny College (B.A., cum laude, 1981); Duquesne University (J.D., 1984). Phi Alpha Delta; Order of the Barristers. *Member:* Los Angeles County and American Bar Associations; State Bar of California; The District of Columbia Bar; Association of Southern California Defense Counsel. [Major, U.S.M.C.R.]. (Resident in Santa Ana Office).

**JANICE B. LEE,** born Chicago, Illinois, December 26, 1946; admitted to bar, 1985, California and U.S. District Court, Central District of California. *Education:* Arizona State University (B.S., 1969); California State University at Dominguez Hills (M.S., 1980); Loyola Marymount University (J.D., 1985). Clinical Laboratory Technologist, California, 1969. *Member:* Los Angeles County and American Bar Associations; State Bar of California; Association of Southern California Defense Counsel.

**MARTHA A. H. BERMAN,** born Denver, Colorado March 10, 1954; admitted to bar, 1980, Colorado and U.S. Court of Appeals, 10th Circuit; 1981, Pennsylvania; 1985, California and U.S. District Court, Central District of California; U.S. Court of Appeals, 11th Circuit. *Education:* Northwestern University (B.A., cum laude, 1976); University of Denver (J.D., 1980). Staff Member, University of Denver Law Journal, 1979-1980. *Member:* Los Angeles County, Colorado, Pennsylvania and American Bar Associations; State Bar of California.

**CARMEN VIGIL,** born Los Angeles, California, June 11, 1944; admitted to bar, 1986, California; 1989, U.S. District Court, Central District of California; U.S. Court of Appeals, 11th Circuit. *Education:* Mt. St. Mary's College (B.S., 1968); University of California at Los Angeles (M.S., 1974); Loyola Law School (J.D., 1985). Licensed Registered Nurse, California, 1968. *Member:* Los Angeles County Bar Association (Member, Bioethics Committee, 1985—); State Bar of California.

**KATHRYN S. PYKE,** born Elgin, Illinois, April 3, 1958; admitted to bar, 1985, Texas; 1990, California; 1991, Arizona. *Education:* University of Illinois (B.A., 1981); South Texas College of Law (J.D., 1985). Kappa Tau Alpha. *Member:* Los Angeles County and American Bar Associations; State Bar of California; State Bar of Arizona; State Bar of Texas.

**ROBERT W. BATES,** born Santa Monica, California, September 26, 1961; admitted to bar, 1986, California; 1987, U.S. Court of Appeals, Ninth Circuit and U.S. District Court, Central, Southern and Northern Districts of California; 1988, U.S. District Court, Eastern District of California. *Education:* University of California at Los Angeles (B.A., 1983); Pepperdine University (J.D., 1986). Phi Alpha Delta. Recipient, American Jurisprudence Award for Real Property II. *Member:* Riverside County, San Bernardino County and American Bar Associations; State Bar of California; Association of Southern California Defense Counsel. (Resident in Riverside Office).

**DOUGLAS C. SMITH,** born Kingston Pennsylvania, March 20, 1960; admitted to bar, 1986, Ohio; 1992, California. *Education:* Kenyon College (B.A., 1983); Capital University (J.D., 1986). Articles Editor, Capital Uni-

*(This Listing Continued)*

versity Law Review, 1985-1986. Recipient, American Jurisprudence Award in Constitutional Law. Member, National Moot Court Team. *Member:* State Bar of California. [Capt., USMCR, 1987-1992]. (Resident in Riverside Office).

**HENRY YEKIKIAN,** born Tehran, Iran, March 27, 1959; admitted to bar, 1986, California; 1987, U.S. District Court, Central District of California and U.S. Court of Appeals, Ninth Circuit; 1991, U.S. Supreme Court; 1994, U.S. District Court, Eastern and Southern Districts of California. *Education:* California State University at Northridge (B.A., 1983); Southwestern University (J.D., 1986). *Member:* Los Angeles County and American Bar Associations; State Bar of California; California Trial Lawyers Association. (Resident in Riverside Office). *LANGUAGES:* Armenian. *REPORTED CASES:* Casella v. Webb, 9th Cir., 1989, 883 F2d 805.

**DONNA BRUCE KOCH,** born Bronx, New York, April 6, 1949; admitted to bar, 1987, California; U.S. District Court, Central District of California; 1994, U.S. Court of Appeals, Ninth Circuit. *Education:* California State University at Los Angeles; University of La Verne (J.D., 1987). Reserve Deputy Coroner, Los Angeles County Department of Medical Examiner-Coroner, 1980-1987. *Member:* Wilshire, Los Angeles County and Federal Bar Associations; State Bar of California; Southern California Defense Counsel.

**JULIANNE M. DEMARCO,** born Newark, New Jersey, November 10, 1956; admitted to bar, 1987, California; U.S. District Court, Central District of California. *Education:* University of North Carolina (B.A., 1978); Southwestern University (J.D., 1987). *Member:* State Bar of California; Association of Southern California Defense Counsel.

**JOHN H. DODD,** born Van Nuys, California, December 21, 1961; admitted to bar, 1988, California, U.S. District Court, Central District of California and U.S. Court of Appeals, Ninth Circuit. *Education:* University of California at Los Angeles (B.A., 1984); Southwestern University (J.D., 1987). Phi Alpha Delta. *Member:* Los Angeles County Bar Association; The State Bar of California; Association of Southern California Defense Counsel.

**KIPPY L. WROTEN,** born Montebello, California, June 9, 1955; admitted to bar, 1988, California. *Education:* California State University at Long Beach (B.A., 1977); Western State University (J.D., 1987). Associate Director and Award Winner, Honors Moot Court. Recipient, American Jurisprudence Award. *Member:* Orange County Bar Association; State Bar of California. (Resident in Santa Ana Office).

**SARA E. HERSH,** born Israel, October 1, 1953; admitted to bar, 1989, California. *Education:* Tufts University (B.S., 1976); California Western School of Law (J.D., 1988). Registered Occupational Therapist, 1976—. *Member:* Los Angeles County Bar Association; State Bar of California.

**HEATHER J. HIGSON,** born Newfoundland, Canada, June 10, 1961; admitted to bar, 1989, California and U.S. District Court, Southern District of California. *Education:* Middlebury College (B.A., 1983); Pepperdine University (J.D., 1989). Recipient: Highest Honors for Senior Thesis, Middlebury College; American Jurisprudence Award, Pepperdine University; First Place Respondent's Brief, Dalsimer Moot Court Competition. *Member:* State Bar of California; Southern California Defense Counsel Association. (Resident in Santa Ana Office).

**BARBARA SPRINGE KILROY,** born Orange, California, September 6, 1958; admitted to bar, 1990, California; 1991, U.S. District Court, Central District of California. *Education:* Orange Coast College; University of Portland (B.S.N., cum laude, 1981); Southwestern University School of Law (J.D., 1989). Recipient, American Jurisprudence Award in Forensic Evidence. Member, Trial Advocacy Team. Registered Nurse: California, 1986—; Oregon, 1981-1986; New Zealand, 1983-1984. *Member:* Santa Barbara County and American Bar Associations; State Bar of California. (Resident in Santa Barbara Office). *LANGUAGES:* Portuguese.

**MARY LAWRENCE TEST,** born Los Angeles, California, May 19, 1942; admitted to bar, 1990, California. *Education:* Smith College (B.A., cum laude, 1964); University of California at Los Angeles (M.A., 1966; Ph.D., 1973); Southwestern University (J.D., 1989). Member Modern Language Association. *Member:* Wilshire Bar Association (Board Member, 1991-1993; State Bar of California; California Women Lawyers; Association of Southern California Defense Counsel. *LANGUAGES:* French.

**GREGORY REYNA BUNCH,** born Wichita, Kansas, June 15, 1952; admitted to bar, 1990, California; 1991, U.S. District Court, Central District of California. *Education:* University of California at Los Angeles (B.S., 1978); California State University at Los Angeles (M.B.A., 1984); Whittier College School of Law (J.D., 1989). *Member:* Los Angeles County and

*(This Listing Continued)*

American Bar Associations; State Bar of California; Mexican-American Bar Association; Association of Southern California Defense Counsel.

**GEORGE E. NOWOTNY, III,** born Fort Worth, Texas, October 21, 1960; admitted to bar, 1987, Arkansas; 1990, California. *Education:* Southern Methodist University (B.A., 1983); University of Arkansas (J.D., 1987); University of Edinburgh, Edinburgh, Scotland (LL.M., 1988). Phi Alpha Delta (Justice, 1987; Vice-Justice, 1986). Recipient, Outstanding Student Bar Association. President of the 10th Circuit by American Bar Association Law Student Division. *Member:* Los Angeles County, Arkansas and American Bar Associations; State Bar of California (Member, Section on: Litigation); Association of Attenders and Alumni of the Hague Academy of International Law; Association of Southern California Defense Counsel. (Resident in Santa Ana Office).

**MARIE E. COLMEY,** born Livingston, Montana, April 26, 1963; admitted to bar, 1989, Oregon; 1993, California. *Education:* Oregon State University (B.S., 1981); Willamette University (J.D., 1989). Phi Delta Phi (Clerk, 1987); Moot Court Board, 1988-1989; Member, The Order of the Barristers. *Member:* Los Angeles County and American (Past Liaison to Judicial Selection, Tenure and Compensation Subcommittee) Bar Associations; Oregon State Bar; Oregon State Bar; State Bar of California; Association of Southern California Defense Counsel.

**GREGORY D. WERRE,** born Yakima, Washington, March 30, 1964; admitted to bar, 1990, California; 1991, U.S. District Court, Central District of California. *Education:* University of Washington (B.A., 1987); Southwestern University School of Law (J.D., 1990). Phi Alpha Delta. Semifinalist-Oralist, Third Place Brief, National Environmental Law Moot Court Competition. *Member:* Los Angeles County and American Bar Associations; State Bar of California; Association of Southern California Defense Counsel.

**BRIAN L. HOFFMAN,** born Encino, California, March 27, 1963; admitted to bar, 1990, California; 1991, U.S. District Court, Central District of California. *Education:* University of California at Davis (B.S., 1986); Southwestern University School of Law (J.D., 1990). Phi Alpha Delta. *Member:* Los Angeles County and American Bar Associations; State Bar of California; Southern California Defense Attorneys; Los Angeles Association Defense Counsel.

**ALISON J. VITACOLONNA,** born Syracuse, New York, October 20, 1954; admitted to bar, 1990, California; 1991, District of Columbia; 1993, U.S. District Court, Central District of California. *Education:* State University of New York at Oswego (B.A., 1976); State University of New York at Buffalo (M.S.W., 1980); Loyola Law School (J.D., 1990). Member, National Association of Social Workers, 1980. Licensed Clinical Social Worker, California, 1990. *Member:* American Bar Association; State Bar of California. (Resident in Santa Ana Office).

**KATHLEEN M. WALKER,** born Hollywood, California, June 22, 1965; admitted to bar, 1991, California and U.S. District Court, Central District of California. *Education:* University of California at Los Angeles (B.S., 1988); Southwestern University School of Law (J.D., cum laude, 1991). Member, Southwestern University Law Review, 1991. *Member:* Los Angeles County and American Bar Associations; State Bar of California.

**JENNIFER L. STURGES,** born Rochester, New York, October 21, 1966; admitted to bar, 1991, California; 1992, U.S. District Court, Central District of California; 1994, U.S. District Court, Eastern District of California. *Education:* University of Colorado at Denver (B.S., 1988); California Western School of Law (J.D., 1991). *Member:* Los Angeles County Bar Association; State Bar of California; Association of Southern California Defense Counsel.

**ANDREW S. LEVEY,** born Detroit, Michigan, June 20, 1966; admitted to bar, 1992, California and U.S. District Court, Central District of California. *Education:* University of California at Berkeley (B.A., 1988); University of the Pacific, McGeorge School of Law (J.D., 1992). Phi Delta Phi. Volunteer Arbitrator, Los Angeles County Superior and Municipal Courts. *Member:* Los Angeles County and American Bar Associations; State Bar of California; Association of Southern California Defense Counsel.

**BRIAN H. CLAUSEN,** born Ojai, California, September 19, 1966; admitted to bar, 1992, California and U.S. District Court, Central District of California. *Education:* University of California at Santa Barbara (B.A., 1989); Pepperdine University (J.D., 1992). *Member:* Santa Barbara County Bar Association; State Bar of California; Association of Southern California Defense Counsel. (Resident in Santa Barbara Office).

**PATRICIA M. EGAN,** born Santa Monica, California, December 28, 1959; admitted to bar, 1992, California and U.S. District Court, Central

*(This Listing Continued)*

**BONNE, BRIDGES, MUELLER, O'KEEFE & NICHOLS,**
*PROFESSIONAL CORPORATION, Los Angeles—Continued*

District of California; 1993, Nevada; 1996, Colorado. *Education:* Loyola Marymount University (B.A., 1986); Gonzaga University School of Law (J.D., cum laude, 1992). Phi Delta Phi. Thomas More Scholar. American Jurisprudence Awards: Legal Research and Writing I, II, III and IV. Associate Editor, Gonzaga Law Review, 1991-1992. President, Moot Court Honors Council, 1991-1992. Student Tutor in Torts. Pupil, Inns of Court. Law Clerk to Hon. Robert E. Rose, Chief Justice, Nevada Supreme Court, 1993. Author: "Supreme Court Signals an End To Discriminatory Use Of Preemptories," 60 Defense Counsel Journal, No. 2 April, 1993. *Member:* Los Angeles County Bar Association (Delegate to State Bar Conference of Delegates, 1995 and 1996); Association of Southern California Defense Counsel; International Association of Defense Counsel; Women Lawyers Association of Los Angeles; Los Angeles County Bar Association Barristers (Member, Executive Committee; Vice-Chair, Bench and Bar Relations; Vice-Chair, Moot Court Committee). Fellow, Los Angeles County Bar Association Foundation of Barristers'.

*RUSSELL M. MORTYN,* born San Francisco, California, September 26, 1963; admitted to bar, 1992, California, U.S. District Court, Northern District of California and U.S. Court of Appeals, Ninth Circuit. *Education:* University of California, Santa Cruz (B.A., 1986); Hastings College of Law (J.D., 1992). Research Attorney, Superior Court, San Diego, 1993-1995. Intern: U.S. Attorney's Office, Southern District of New York, 1991; District Attorney's Office, San Francisco, 1991. Author: "The Rehnquist Court and The New Establishment Clause," 19 Hastings Const. L.Q. 567, 1992.

*ROBERT A. MOSIER,* born Los Angeles, California, July 17, 1963; admitted to bar, 1992, California. *Education:* Thomas Jefferson College of Law (B.A., 1992; J.D., with honors, 1992). Recipient: Moot Court, Best Brief; American Jurisprudence Award, Contracts I and II; Home Federal-San Diego County Bar Association Scholarship. Listed in Who's Who Among American Colleges and Universities. Member, Jefferson Law Review, 1991-1992. Judicial Chair, Student Bar Association. *Member:* Orange County Bar Association; State Bar of California; Orange County Bar Association College of Trial Advocacy; Association of Southern California Defense Counsel. (Resident in Santa Ana Office).

*CYNTHIA M. HERRERA,* born Corona, California, May 8, 1963; admitted to bar, 1993, California and U.S. Court of Appeals, Ninth Circuit. *Education:* California State University (B.A., 1986); Western State University (J.D., 1992). Recipient, American Jurisprudence Awards. Member, Western State Law Review, 1991-1992. *Member:* Riverside County and American Bar Associations; State Bar of California. (Resident in Riverside Office).

*JOHN A. HAUGHTON,* born Pasadena, California, October 28, 1963; admitted to bar, 1993, Pennsylvania, 1994, California. *Education:* University of California, Irvine (B.A., 1988); Whittier College School of Law (J.D., 1991). Phi Alpha Delta. *Member:* State Bar of California; American Bar Association. [Capt., Judge Advocate, USMC, 1992-1996]

*MELANIE C. BUTTS,* born Washington, D.C., September 6, 1967; admitted to bar, 1993, California. *Education:* University of California at Berkeley (B.A., 1989); Southwestern University School of Law (J.D., 1992). *Member:* Los Angeles County Bar Association; State Bar of California. *PRACTICE AREAS:* Medical Malpractice.

*PAUL F. ARENTZ,* born St. Ann's Bay, Jamaica, April 26, 1966; admitted to bar, 1993, California and U.S. District Court, Central District of California. *Education:* University of Arizona (B.A., 1990); California Western School of Law (J.D., cum laude, 1993). Member, Executive Editor, California Western Law Review, 1992-1993. National Appellate Advocacy Competition; American Jurisprudence Awards in Evidence, Legal Skills. Listed in Who's Who Among American Law Students. Extern 4th District Court of Appeals, 1993. Author: "Defining Professional Negligence After Central Pathology Service Medical Clinic vs Superior Court: Should California's Medical Injury Compensation Reform Act Cover Intention Torts?" 30 Cal. W.L. Rev. 221, 1994. *Member:* State Bar of California. *LANGUAGES:* German.

*JEANNETTE LYNNE VAN HORST,* born Los Angeles, California, July 30, 1954; admitted to bar, 1993, California and U.S. District Court, Central District of California. *Education:* California State University, Fresno (B.S., 1976); California State University, Los Angeles (M.S., 1987); Southwestern University School of Law (J.D., 1993). Registered Nurse, California, 1976. *Member:* State Bar of California.

*(This Listing Continued)*

*ROBERT A. MADISON,* born Seville, Spain, October 9, 1963; admitted to bar, 1993, California and U.S. District Court, Central District of California. *Education:* California Polytechnic State University (B.A., 1990); Hastings College of the Law, University of California, San Francisco (J.D., 1993). Associate Editor, Hastings International and Comparative Law Journal, 1992-1993. *Member:* State Bar of California.

*BARBARA KAMENIR FRANKEL,* born Chicago, Illinois, September 16, 1950; admitted to bar, 1993, California. *Education:* University of California (B.S., Physical Therapy, 1971; R.P.T., 1971; M.P.H., 1974); Southwestern University School of Law (J.D., magna cum laude, 1993). Articles Editor, Southwestern Law School Law Review. Author: "The Impact of the Americans With Disabilities Act on Collective Bargaining," Southwestern Law Review, 1992. Registered Physical Therapist, California, 1971. *Member:* State Bar of California; Association of Southern California Defense Counsel; American Physical Therapy Association.

*RAYMOND J. MC MAHON,* born Rapid City, South Dakota, September 22, 1967; admitted to bar, 1993, California, U.S. District Court, Central District of California and U.S. Court of Appeals, Ninth Circuit. *Education:* California State University at Fullerton (B.A., cum laude, 1990); University of California at Los Angeles (J.D., 1993). Beta Gamma Sigma, Golden Key National Honor Society, Levern F. Graves Economics Award. Recipient: American Jurisprudence Award in Torts; Moot Court Honors Program. *Member:* State Bar of California.

*MITZIE L. DOBSON,* born Mason City, Iowa, January 22, 1963; admitted to bar, 1994, California and U.S. District Court, Central District of California. *Education:* University of Kansas (B.S.J., 1985); Loyola Law School (J.D., 1994). Phi Delta Phi. Member, 1992-1993 and Articles Editor, 1993-1994, Loyola Law Review. *Member:* State Bar of California.

*DIANA L. KREINMAN,* born Los Angeles, California, October 20, 1967; admitted to bar, 1994, California and U.S. District Court, Central District of California. *Education:* University of California at Berkeley (B.A., 1989); McGeorge School of Law (J.D., 1994). Finalist, McGeorge Moot Court Program. Finalist, Best Oralist, McGeorge Moot Court Program. *Member:* Beverly Hills and Wilshire Bar Associations; State Bar of California; Association of Southern California Defense Counsel.

*RAYMOND L. BLESSEY,* born New York, N.Y., July 26, 1947; admitted to bar, 1995, California; U.S. District Court, Central District of California and U.S. Court of Appeals, Ninth Circuit. *Education:* University of Southern California (M.S., 1973); Southwestern University School of Law (J.D., 1994). Clinical Assistant Professor, USC Center for Health Professions. *Member:* State Bar of California.

*JO LYNN VALOFF,* born Whittier, California, April 22, 1957; admitted to bar, 1995, California. *Education:* University of Southern California (B.A., magna cum laude, 1979) Phi Beta Kappa; University of San Diego (J.D., 1994). Best Oralist 1994 Alumni Moot Court Tort Competition. *Member:* Orange County and American Bar Associations; State Bar of California; Association of Southern California Defense Counsel. (Resident in Santa Ana Office).

*YOSHIAKI C. KUBOTA,* born Hollywood, California, November 15, 1964; admitted to bar, 1994, California. *Education:* University of California, Riverside (B.A., 1989); Western State University (J.D., 1994). *Member:* State Bar of California. (Resident in Riverside Office).

*KIMBERLY NETTA,* born Wilmington, Delaware, October 14, 1967; admitted to bar, 1995, California. *Education:* California State University (B.A., 1990); Western State University (J.D., 1994). Recipient: American Jurisprudence Awards in Legal Writing and Wills. Associate Editor, Western State University Law Review, 1993-1994. Externship with Justice Henry T. Moore and Presiding Justice David G. Sills of the California Court of Appeals, Fourth District Division Three; Moot Court; 1st Place in Team Competition, 2nd Place Brief. Listed in Who's Who Among Students in American Colleges and Universities. *Member:* State Bar of California. (Resident in Riverside Office).

*HOLLY H. MCGREGOR,* born Pittsburgh, Pennsylvania, March 9, 1961; admitted to bar, 1995, California and U.S. Court of Appeals, 9th Circuit. *Education:* California State University, Fullerton (B.A., 1990); Western State University (J.D., summa cum laude, Valedictorian, 1994). Recipient, American Jurisprudence Awards in Legal Writing I, Torts II, Contracts II, Civil Procedure II, Criminal Law and Property I. Production Editor, Western State Law Review, 1993-1994. Author: Article, "The Drug War: Another Battle Lost," published in Western State University Law Review, Spring, 1994. Listed in Who's Who Among Colleges and Universities, 1995. Extern for Presiding Justice David G. Sills, Fourth District Court of

*(This Listing Continued)*

# PROFESSIONAL BIOGRAPHIES

Appeal, Division Three, 1994. *Member:* State Bar of California. (Resident in Riverside Office). **PRACTICE AREAS:** Medical Malpractice Defense.

**MARK S. SALZ,** born Santa Monica, California, May 3, 1969; admitted to bar, 1995, California and U.S. District Court, Central District of California. *Education:* University of San Diego (B.A., 1991); Pepperdine University (J.D., 1995). *Member:* Los Angeles County and American Bar Associations; State Bar of California. **PRACTICE AREAS:** Medical Malpractice.

**JAMES A. KEENS,** born Montreal, Canada, November 10, 1953; admitted to bar, 1995, California. *Education:* University of California, Los Angeles (B.A., 1975); University of Ottawa, Canada (M.H.A., 1978); California Western School of Law (LL.D., 1995). Member, American College of Healthcare Executives, 1980—. *Member:* State Bar of California. **PRACTICE AREAS:** Medical Malpractice.

**MICHAEL L. BAZZO,** born Chicago, Illinois, August 18, 1956; admitted to bar, 1996, California; U.S. District Court, Central District of California and U.S. Court of Appeals, 9th Circuit. *Education:* Mt. San Antonio Junior College (A.S., 1981); University of California, Los Angeles (B.A., 1984); Western State University (J.D., 1993). Recipient, Director's Scholarship. Member, Christian Legal Society. Certified Radiologic Technician, California, 1981—. Member: California Society of Radiologic Technologists, 1981-1996; American Registry of Radiologic Technologists, 1981-1996. *Member:* State Bar of California; American Bar Association; Orange County Barrister's. (Resident in Riverside Office). **LANGUAGES:** Spanish and Italian. **PRACTICE AREAS:** Medical Malpractice Defense.

**KEVIN A. DUFFIS,** born New York, N.Y., July 19, 1953; admitted to bar, 1996, California. *Education:* University of Southern California (B.A., 1981); Loyola Marymount University (J.D., 1996). Nursing License, California, 1978—. Screen Actors Guild, 1980—. [U.S. Navy, 1972-1976]. **LANGUAGES:** Spanish. **PRACTICE AREAS:** Medical Malpractice; General Civil Litigation.

**MARTA A. ALCUMBRAC,** born Phoenix, Arizona, October 28, 1966; admitted to bar, 1996, California and U.S. District Court, Central District of California. *Education:* Arizona State University (B.S., 1988); Southwestern University School of Law (J.D., 1996). Moot Court Honors Program. Extern for Hon. Judge Arthur Alarcon, Ninth Circuit Court of Appeals. **PRACTICE AREAS:** Medical Malpractice Defense.

**CYNTHIA C. MILLER,** born Arcadia, California, December 20, 1969; admitted to bar, 1996, California. *Education:* University of California, San Diego (B.A., 1992); University of Southern California (J.D., 1996).

**MELANIE M. FRAYER,** born Granada Hills, California, March 12, 1971; admitted to bar, 1996, California. *Education:* Loyola Marymount University (B.A., 1993); Loyola Law School (J.D., 1996). *Member:* Los Angeles County Bar Association. **LANGUAGES:** French.

**NANA NAKANO,** admitted to bar, 1996, California. *Education:* Loyola Marymount University (B.A., 1990); Pepperdine University (J.D., 1996).

### OF COUNSEL

**BRUCE J. BONNE,** born Illinois, February 29, 1928; admitted to bar, 1957, California. *Education:* Augustana College (B.A., 1950); University of California at Los Angeles (J.D., 1956). Phi Alpha Delta. *Member:* Los Angeles County and American Bar Associations; The State Bar of California; American Board of Trial Advocates; Association of Southern California Defense Counsel.

REPRESENTATIVE CLIENTS: Southern California Physicians Insurance Exchange; Doctor's Company; Cooperative of American Physicians; Norcal Mutual Insurance Company; Farmers Insurance Group of Companies; National Chiropractic Mutual Insurance Company; Kaiser Foundation Health Plan; Chubb Group of Companies; The Travelers; APIC Insurance Corporation Limited; Sequoia Insurance Company.

---

## BOOTH, MITCHEL & STRANGE
### 30TH FLOOR-EQUITABLE PLAZA
### 3435 WILSHIRE BOULEVARD
### LOS ANGELES, CALIFORNIA 90010-2050
Telephone: 213-738-0100
Fax: 213-380-3308

*Costa Mesa, California Office:* 3080 Bristol Street, Suite 550. Telephone: 714-641-0217. Fax: 714-957-0411.

*San Diego, California Office:* 550 West "C" Street. Suite 1560. Telephone: 619-238-7620. Fax: 619-238-7625.

*(This Listing Continued)*

---

*General Civil and Commercial Trial Practice in all State and Federal Courts. Construction, Professional Liability, Environmental, Corporation, Real Property, Savings and Loan, Tax, Insurance, Surety, Estate Planning, Trust and Probate Law.*

### MEMBERS OF FIRM

**BATES BOOTH** (1903-1967).

**NORMAN R. WILLIAN** (1917-1968).

**MICHAEL D. KELLOGG** (1949-1996).

**WILLIAM F. RUMMLER,** born Long Beach, California, July 1, 1943; admitted to bar, 1970, California. *Education:* University of Utah (J.D., 1969). *Member:* Los Angeles County and American Bar Associations; State Bar of California; National Health Lawyers Association; Defense Research Institute; Association of Southern California Defense Counsel.

**MICHAEL T. LOWE,** born Salt Lake City, Utah, May 8, 1943; admitted to bar, 1970, Utah; 1971, California. *Education:* University of Utah (B.S., 1967; J.D., 1970). Member, Moot Court Board, 1968-1970. *Member:* Los Angeles County, Orange County and American (Member, Sections of: Litigation; Insurance, Negligence and Compensation Law) Bar Associations; State Bar of California; Utah State Bar; Association of Southern California Defense Counsel; Defense Research Institute. (Resident, Costa Mesa Office).

**JOSEPH A. BURROW,** born Whittier, California, December 31, 1937; admitted to bar, 1973, California. *Education:* University of California at Los Angeles (B.A., 1959); Loyola University of Los Angeles (J.D., 1973). Member, St. Thomas More Law Honor Society. *Member:* Los Angeles County and American Bar Associations; State Bar of California.

**SETH W. WHITAKER,** born Somers, Connecticut, December 7, 1950; admitted to bar, 1978, California. *Education:* Duke University (B.A., 1973); Golden Gate University and Hastings College of Law, University of California (J.D., 1978). *Member:* Los Angeles County and American Bar Associations; State Bar of California.

**WALTER B. HILL, JR.,** born Long Beach, California, June 16, 1943; admitted to bar, 1977, California and U.S. District Court, Central District of California; 1983, U.S. District Court, Southern District of California. *Education:* Occidental College (B.A., 1965); Southwestern University (J.D., 1976). Recipient, American Jurisprudence Award on Civil Procedure. *Member:* Los Angeles County, Orange County and American Bar Associations; State Bar of California; Association of Southern California Defense Counsel. (Resident, Costa Mesa Office). **Email:** 76627,1220@compuserve.com

**ROBERT H. BRIGGS,** born San Francisco, California, June 1, 1949; admitted to bar, 1977, California; 1978, U.S. District Court, Central District of California. *Education:* Brigham Young University (B.A., 1974); Pepperdine University (J.D., 1977). *Member:* Orange County (Member, Sections on: Litigation; Environmental Law), Los Angeles County and American (Member, Sections on: Litigation; Tort and Insurance Practice) Bar Associations; State Bar of California. (Resident, Costa Mesa Office).

**DAVID R. KIPPER,** born Denver, Colorado, January 2, 1952; admitted to bar, 1982, California; 1983, U.S. District Court, Southern, Northern and Central Districts of California, U.S. Court of Appeals, Ninth Circuit and U.S. Supreme Court. *Education:* University of California at San Diego (B.A., 1974); University of San Diego (J.D., cum laude, 1982). Member, San Diego Law Review, 1980-1982. *Member:* Orange County, San Diego and American (Member, Section on Tort and Insurance Practice) Bar Associations; State Bar of California; Defense Research Institute. (Also at Costa Mesa Office).

**MARLA LAMEDMAN KELLEY,** born Bethpage, New York, January 27, 1958; admitted to bar, 1983, California and U.S. District Court, Central District of California. *Education:* University of California at Irvine (B.A., with honors, 1980); Loyola Law School (J.D., 1983). Member, Moot Court. Staff Editor, Entertainment Law Journal, 1982-1983. *Member:* Orange County and American Bar Associations; Association of Southern California Defense Counsel. (Resident, Costa Mesa Office).

**KEVIN K. CALLAHAN,** born Boston, Massachusetts, May 15, 1959; admitted to bar, 1984, California; 1985, U.S. District Court, Central, Southern, Eastern and Northern Districts of California; 1986, U.S. Court of Appeals, Ninth Circuit. *Education:* Brown University (B.A., 1981); University of California at Los Angeles (J.D., 1984). *Member:* Los Angeles County and American Bar Associations; State Bar of California; Southern California Defense Counsel.

*(This Listing Continued)*

## BOOTH, MITCHEL & STRANGE, Los Angeles—Continued

**ROBERT F. KEEHN,** born Kansas City, Missouri, August 6, 1959; admitted to bar, 1984, California and U.S. District Court, Central District of California; 1985, U.S. District Court, Eastern, Northern and Southern Districts of California. *Education:* University of California at Los Angeles (B.A., 1981); University of Southern California (J.D., 1984). *Member:* State Bar of California.

**PAUL R. HOWELL,** born Salt Lake City, Utah, December 22, 1948; admitted to bar, 1977, Washington; 1978, Utah; 1988, California, U.S. District Court, District of Arizona, U.S. Court of Appeals, Ninth, Tenth and The Federal Circuit, U.S. Court of Federal Claims and U.S. Supreme Court. *Education:* University of Utah (B.S., 1972; M.B.A., 1973); University of Puget Sound School of Law (J.D., 1976). Member, Panel of Arbitrators, American Arbitration Association. *Member:* American Bar Association (Member, Sections on: Litigation; Tort and Insurance Practice; Government Contracts; Member, Forum on the Construction Industry). (At Costa Mesa and San Diego Offices).

**CRAIG E. GUENTHER,** born Anaheim, California, August 12, 1960; admitted to bar, 1986, California. *Education:* California State University at Fullerton (B.A., 1983); Loyola University of Los Angeles (J.D., 1986). *Member:* Orange County, Los Angeles County and American (Member, Fidelity and Surety Law Committee, Tort and Insurance Practice Section) Bar Associations. (Resident, Costa Mesa Office).

**DAVID L. HUGHES,** born Spokane, Washington, January 8, 1949; admitted to bar, 1986, Utah; 1987, California. *Education:* Brigham Young University (B.S., 1973); George Washington University; McGeorge School of Law, University of the Pacific (J.D., 1985). Recipient, American Jurisprudence Award for Community Property, 1983. Registered Medical Technologist, 1973-1976. *Member:* Utah State and American (Member: Tort and Insurance Practice Section, 1986—; Forum Committee on the Construction Industry, 1985—) Bar Associations; State Bar of California. [With U.S. Army, 1967-1969]. (Resident, Costa Mesa Office).

**DANIEL M. CROWLEY,** born Trenton, New Jersey, April 29, 1960; admitted to bar, 1987, California. *Education:* University of Santa Clara (B.S., 1982); University of San Diego (J.D., 1987). Mediator, Los Angeles Superior Court, 1996. Settlement Officer, Los Angeles Municipal Court, 1996. *Member:* Los Angeles County Bar Association (Member, Litigation Section); Association of Southern California Defense Counsel.

**STEVEN M. MITCHEL,** born Los Angeles, California, June 10, 1961; admitted to bar, 1987, California, U.S. District Court, Central District of California and U.S. Court of Appeals, Ninth Circuit. *Education:* University of California at Santa Barbara (B.A., 1984); McGeorge School of Law, University of the Pacific (J.D., with distinction, 1987). *Member:* State Bar of California.

**ROBERT C. NIESLEY,** born San Diego, California, October 11, 1962; admitted to bar, 1987, California and U.S. District Court, Central, Northern, Southern and Eastern Districts of California. *Education:* University of San Diego (B.A., 1984; J.D., 1987). Member, San Diego Law Review, 1986-1987. Vice-Chair, University of San Diego Appellate Moot Court Board, 1986-1987. Author: "Dismantling An Asset Protection Plan Using Fraudulent Transfer Laws," presented at the 1996 American Bar Association Annual Meeting; "Where Have All the Assets Gone? Prosecuting Fraudulent Conveyance Claims," presented at the 1995 Western States Surety Conference; "Financing The Principal: Practical Considerations," presented at the 1994 Western States Surety Conference; "The Surety's Compulsory Participation in Arbitration Proceedings," Shepard's California Construction Law Reporter, Vol. 5, No. 5, p. 137, 1995. Contributing Editor, Shepard's California Construction Law Reporter. *Member:* Los Angeles County (Member, Construction Law Section) and American (Member: TIPS; Fidelity and Surety Law Committee; Construction Forum) Bar Associations; The Association of Business Trial Lawyers. *Email:* bmsrcn@earthlink.net

**JAMES G. STANLEY,** born Lakewood, California, March 11, 1962; admitted to bar, 1988, California; 1992, U.S. District Court, Central District of California. *Education:* California State University at Long Beach (B.S.C.E., 1985); McGeorge School of Law, University of the Pacific (J.D., 1988). *Member:* Orange County Bar Association. (Resident, Costa Mesa Office).

*(This Listing Continued)*

CAA538B

## OF COUNSEL

**GEORGE C. MITCHEL,** born Los Angeles, California, December 4, 1927; admitted to bar, 1954, California. *Education:* University of Southern California (B.S., 1950; LL.B., 1953). *Member:* Los Angeles County and American (Member, Tort and Insurance Practice Section) Bar Associations; State Bar of California.

**OWEN W. STRANGE,** born Hollywood, California, May 28, 1928; admitted to bar, 1953, California. *Education:* Occidental College (A.B., 1950); University of Southern California (LL.B., 1953). Phi Delta Phi. *Member:* San Diego County Bar Association (Member, Sections on: Real Property, Probate and Trust Law; Insurance Law); Bar of the Republic of Korea; International Association of Insurance Counsel.

## ASSOCIATES

**JOHN J. ARENS,** born New Port Beach, California, December 7, 1967; admitted to bar, 1995, California. *Education:* University of San Diego (B.A., 1990; J.D., 1995). *Member:* State Bar of California.

**RICHARD W. DAVIS,** born Indio, California, January 18, 1967; admitted to bar, 1992, California and U.S. District Court, Central District of California. *Education:* University of California at Los Angeles (B.A., cum laude, 1989); Pepperdine University School of Law (J.D., 1992). Moot Court Honor Board, 1991-1992; Fall Individual Advocacy Tournament Finalist, 1990; Moot Court Interschool Team Member, 1990-1992; Best Brief, Outstanding Oral Advocate, Finalist Team Member; National Appellate Advocacy Competition; Semifinalist, New York Barristers National Moot Court Competition. *Member:* State Bar of California.

**JAMES A. HOLL, III,** born Philadelphia, Pennsylvania, December 29, 1970; admitted to bar, 1995, California. *Education:* University of California at Los Angeles (B.A., 1991); Pepperdine University (J.D., 1995). *Member:* State Bar of California.

**ROBERT W. HUSTON,** born Pasadena, California, February 9, 1968; admitted to bar, 1993, California and U.S. District Court, Central and Southern Districts of California. *Education:* University of Notre Dame (B.B.A., 1990); University of San Diego (J.D., 1993). Phi Alpha Delta. *Member:* Los Angeles County Bar Association.

**THOMAS T. JOHNSON,** born Glendale, California, November 17, 1961; admitted to bar, 1992, California. *Education:* California State University at Los Angeles (B.A., 1986); Loyola Law School (J.D., 1982). *Member:* State Bar of California.

**CORY J. KING,** born American Fork, Utah, August 3, 1967; admitted to bar, 1995, California and U.S. District Court, Southern, Central, Eastern and Northern Districts of California. *Education:* Brigham Young University (B.A., 1991); University of San Diego (J.D., 1995). Phi Alpha Delta. Member, Order of Barristers. Member: J. Reuben Clark Law Society, 1992-1996; University of San Diego Moot Court Board, 1994-1995. Coach, U.S. National Champion and International Third Place, Jessup International Law Moot Court Team, University of San Diego, 1994-1995. Member, Surety Claims Association of Los Angeles. *Member:* Los Angeles County (Member, Sections on: Litigation; Labor and Employment Law; Business Law; Corporation Law) and American (Member, Tort and Insurance Practice Law Section) Bar Associations; State Bar of California; American Society of International Law. *LANGUAGES:* Korean.

**MICHELLE M. LA MAR,** born Inglewood, California, July 8, 1965; admitted to bar, 1992, California; 1994, U.S. District Court, Central District of California. *Education:* University of California at Los Angeles (B.A., cum laude, 1988); Loyola University of Los Angeles (J.D., 1992). Staff Writer, International and Comparative Law Journal, 1991-1992. *Member:* State Bar of California; Women's Lawyers Association (Member, Litigation Section).

**CHRISTOPHER C. LEWI,** born Santa Monica, California, January 22, 1962; admitted to bar, 1989, California, U.S. Court of Appeals, Ninth Circuit and U.S. District Court, Central District of California. *Education:* University of Montana; University of California at Los Angeles (B.A., 1986); Loyola University of Los Angeles (J.D., 1989). *Member:* Los Angeles County and American Bar Associations; State Bar of California (Member, Litigation Section, 1989-1996).

**CLINTON DAVIS ROBISON,** born Los Angeles, California, September 21, 1964; admitted to bar, 1992, California. *Education:* University of California at Los Angeles (B.A., 1986); Pepperdine University (J.D., 1991). Recipient, American Jurisprudence Awards in Civil Procedure and Agency and Partnership. *Member:* Beverly Hills Bar Association; State Bar of California. *LANGUAGES:* Spanish.

*(This Listing Continued)*

## PROFESSIONAL BIOGRAPHIES

**ROBERT H. SHAFFER, JR.,** born Los Angeles, California; admitted to bar, 1991, California; 1992, U.S. District Court, Northern, Southern, Eastern and Western Districts of California; 1995, Colorado. *Education:* Pepperdine University (B.A., 1988; J.D., 1991). *Member:* Los Angeles County and Colorado Bar Associations.

### RESIDENT ASSOCIATES COSTA MESA OFFICE

**ELIZABETH CURRIN BONN,** born Flagstaff, Arizona, June 25, 1956; admitted to bar, 1984, California; 1985, U.S. District Court, Central and Southern Districts of California. *Education:* University of Arizona (B.S., with distinction, 1978); Pepperdine University (J.D., cum laude, 1984). Member, Los Angeles County Bar Association, 1985-1988. *Member:* Orange County and American Bar Associations; State Bar of California.

**STACIE L. BRANDT,** born Steubenville, Ohio, August 8, 1957; admitted to bar, 1993, California; 1994, U.S. District Court, Central and Southern Districts of California. *Education:* Cornell University (B.S., 1979); University of San Diego (J.D., 1993). Member, San Diego Law Review, 1992-1993. Member: Society of Women Engineers, 1975-1979; Society of Plastic Engineer, 1979-1990. *Member:* State Bar of California.

**DAVID F. MCPHERSON,** born Pomona, California, April 4, 1969; admitted to bar, 1994, California. *Education:* University of Southern California (B.S., 1991); Southwestern University School of Law (J.D., 1994). *Member:* State Bar of California.

**SCOTT S. MIZEN,** born Buffalo, New York, December 31, 1964; admitted to bar, 1990, California. *Education:* University of Illinois at Champaign/Urbana (B.S., 1987); Pepperdine University (J.D., 1990). Phi Alpha Delta. *Member:* Beverly Hills and Orange County Bar Associations; State Bar of California; Southern California Defense Counsel.

**SEAN T. OSBORN,** born Highland Park, Illinois, May 8, 1958; admitted to bar, 1984, California; 1985, U.S. District Court, Central District of California; 1987, U.S. District Court, Northern, Southern and Eastern Districts of California and U.S. Court of Appeals, 9th Circuit; 1988, U.S. Tax Court; 1990, U.S. Supreme Court. *Education:* University of Southern California (B.S., 1980); McGeorge School of the Law, University of the Pacific (J.D., 1984). Member, Moot Court Honors Board, 1983-1984. *Member:* The State Bar of California; American Bar Association; Association of Southern California Defense Counsel.

**LAILA MORCOS SANTANA,** born Hollywood, California, March 27, 1965; admitted to bar, 1991, California; 1994, U.S. District Court, Central District of California. *Education:* Pepperdine University, Seaver College (B.A., 1987); Pepperdine University School of Law (J.D., 1991). Phi Alpha Delta. Orange County Barristers. Member, Arab-American Law Society, 1990-1991. *Member:* Kern County, Orange County and American (Member, Litigation Section) Bar Associations; State Bar of California; California Women Lawyers Association.

### RESIDENT ASSOCIATES SAN DIEGO OFFICE

**DEREK J. EMGE,** born Glendale, California, August 27, 1967; admitted to bar, 1992, California. *Education:* Claremont McKenna College (B.A., 1989); University of San Diego (J.D., 1992). Member, University of San Diego Law Review, 1991-1992. *Member:* San Diego and American Bar Association; State Bar of California; San Diego Defense Lawyers Association.

**ROBERT F. TYSON, JR.,** born Staten Island, New York, April 10, 1964; admitted to bar, 1990, California, U.S. Court of Appeals, Ninth Circuit and U.S. District Court, Southern District of California; 1993, District of Columbia. *Education:* Villanova University (B.S., 1986; J.D., 1989). Omicron Delta Epsilon. President, Barristers Club of San Diego, 1995. *Member:* San Diego County (Member, Committees on: Financial Professional Liaison, 1994-1997; Medical Professional Liaison, 1996) and American Bar Associations; State Bar of California; The District of Columbia Bar; San Diego Defense Lawyers Association.

REPRESENTATIVE CLIENTS: Ahmanson Trust Co.; American Home Assurance Co.; American International Life Assurance Company; CNA; Continental Assurance Co.; Continental Casualty Co.; Firemans Fund American Insurance; Fred S. James & Co.; Globe Life Insurance Co.; Great American Insurance Co.; Greater Los Angeles Visitors and Convention Bureau; Hitachi Maxco, Inc.; Insurance Company of North America; J.C. Penney Life Insurance Co.; Kemper Insurance Cos.; Mutual of Omaha; Mutual of Omaha Insurance Co.; Provident Life and Accident Insurance Co.; Safeco Insurance Company of America; Safeco Title Insurance Co.; Security Title Insurance Co.; Southern Counties Title Insurance Co.; U-Haul Corp; Avco Financial.

## BORTON, PETRINI & CONRON
### 707 WILSHIRE BOULEVARD, SUITE 5100
### LOS ANGELES, CALIFORNIA 90017
Telephone: 213-624-2869
Fax: 213-489-3930
Email: bpcla@bpclaw.com

*Bakersfield, California Office:* The Borton, Petrini & Conron Building, 1600 Truxtun Avenue, P.O. Box 2026. Telephone: 805-322-3051. Fax: 805-322-4628. Email: bpcbak@bpclaw.com.
*San Luis Obispo, California Office:* 1114 Marsh Street. Telephone: 805-541-4340. Fax: 805-541-4558. Email: bpcslo@bpclaw.com.
*Visalia, California Office:* 206 South Mooney Boulevard, P.O. Box 1028. Telephone: 209-627-5600. Fax: 209-627-4309. Email: bpcvis@bpclaw.com.
*Fresno, California Office:* T. W. Patterson Building, 2014 Tulare Street, Suite 830. Telephone: 209-268-0117. Fax: 209-237-7995. Email: bpcfrs@bpclaw.com.
*Sacramento, California Office:* 2233 Watt Avenue, Suite 290. Telephone: 916-484-3555. Fax: 916-484-3550. Email: bpcsac@bpclaw.com.
*Santa Barbara, California Office:* 211 East Victoria Street, Suite D. Telephone: 805-564-2404. Fax: 805-564-2176. Email: bpcsb@bpclaw.com.
*San Diego, California Office:* John Burnham Building, 610 West Ash Street, 9th Floor. Telephone: 619-232-2424. Fax: 619-531-0794. Email: bpcsd@bpclaw.com.
*Newport Beach, California Office:* 4675 MacArthur Court, Suite 1150. Telephone: 714-752-2333. Fax: 714-752-2854. Email: bpcnb@bpclaw.com.
*Modesto, California Office:* The Turner Building, 900 "H" Street, Suite D. Telephone: 209-576-1701. Fax: 209-527-9753. Email: bpcmod@bpclaw.com.
*San Francisco, California Office:* 111 Pine Street, Suite 730. Telephone: 415-981-4415. Fax: 415-391-5538. Email: bpcsf@bpclaw.com.
*Redding, California Office:* 280 Hemsted Drive, Suite 100. Telephone: 916-222-1530. Fax: 916-222-4498. Email: bpcred@bpclaw.com.
*San Bernardino, California Office:* 290 North "D" Street, Suite 500. Telephone: 909-381-0527. Fax: 909-381-0658. Email: bpcsbdo@bpclaw.com.
*San Jose, California Office:* 2 North Second Street. Telephone: 408-298-3997. Fax: 408-298-3365. Email: bpcsj@bpclaw.com.
*Ventura, California Office:* 1000 Hill Road, Suite 310. Telephone: 805-650-9994. Fax: 805-650-7125. Email: bpcvta@bpclaw.com.
*Santa Rosa, California Office:* 50 Santa Rosa Avenue, Suite 300. Telephone: 707-527-9477. Fax: 707-527-9488. Email: bpcsr@bpclaw.com.

*Commercial/Real Estate Litigation, Insurance Law, General Civil Trial and Appellate Practice in State and Federal Courts, Personal Injury and Casualty Defense Litigation, Insurance Bad Faith and Coverage, Labor and Employment, Toxic Torts, Real Estate, Land Use Planning, Zoning, Municipal, Professional Errors and Omissions, Healthcare Provider Malpractice Defense, Products Liability, Oil and Gas, Water, Natural Resources, Environmental, Public Entity, Administrative, Agricultural, Banking, Contracts, Corporations, Partnerships, Taxation, Creditor's Remedies, Bankruptcy, Probate, Estate Planning, Family Law.*

*FIRM PROFILE: Founded by Fred E. Borton in 1899, the firm offers high quality legal services in all of the practice areas described above through its California network of sixteen regional offices. Our mission is to handle each file as if we were the client. We are responsive to the clients' need for communication, cost effectiveness and prompt evaluation.*

### MEMBERS OF FIRM

**ROBERT N. RIDENOUR,** born Gary, Indiana, April 25, 1959; admitted to bar, 1983, California. *Education:* Murray State University (B.S., summa cum laude, 1980); Northwestern University (J.D., 1983). Author, "Legal Malpractice: The Statute of Limitation," *California Defense,* Spring 1994. *Member:* The State Bar of California. **PRACTICE AREAS:** Casualty Litigation; Business Litigation.

**RICHARD M. MACIAS,** born Ventura, California, August 11, 1951; admitted to bar, 1976, California. *Education:* University of California at Berkeley (A.B., 1973); Boalt Hall School of Law, University of California at Berkeley (J.D., 1976). Director, California Rural Legal Assistance. Member: Los Angeles Area Chamber of Commerce; Lincoln Heights Chamber of Commerce; Highland Park Chamber of Commerce; Los Angeles World Affairs Council; Town Hall of Los Angeles. Director, Jenesse Center for Battered Women and Children. *Member:* Beverly Hills, Los Angeles County (Member, Judicial Evaluation Committee) and American (Member,

*(This Listing Continued)*

*BORTON, PETRINI & CONRON, Los Angeles—Continued*

Nominating Committee, 1996—; Standing Committee on Federal Judiciary, 1994—; House of Delegates, 1991—; Sections on Litigation, Tort and Insurance Practice) Bar Associations; State Bar of California (Member, Insurance Law Committee of Business Law Section); Mexican-American Bar Association of Los Angeles County (Member, Board of Trustees, 1990—); La Raza Lawyers Association of California; Hispanic National Bar Association; Association of Southern California Defense Counsel; Defense Research Institute; National Health Lawyers Association; American Society of Law and Medicine; Association of Business Trial Lawyers; Latin Business Association. *PRACTICE AREAS:* Business Litigation; Commercial Litigation; Tort Litigation Defense.

**GEORGE J. HERNANDEZ, JR.,** born El Paso, Texas, January 27, 1955; admitted to bar, 1983, California. *Education:* California State University, Northridge (B.A., 1977); Lewis and Clark Law School (J.D., 1980). Member, Cornelius Honor Society. *Member:* Los Angeles County and American Bar Associations; The State Bar of California. *LANGUAGES:* Spanish, Italian, French and American Sign Language. *PRACTICE AREAS:* Civil Litigation; Construction Litigation; Public Entity Defense; Wrongful Termination.

**STEVEN G. GATLEY,** born Long Beach, California, December 31, 1965; admitted to bar, 1991, California. *Education:* University of California at Santa Barbara (B.A., 1988); Loyola University School of Law (J.D., 1991). Phi Alpha Delta. *Member:* Los Angeles County and American Bar Associations; The State Bar of California; Mexican-American Bar Association; National Hispanic Bar Association.

**ROSEMARIE SUAZO LEWIS,** born Los Angeles, California, December 23, 1963; admitted to bar, 1992, California; U.S. District Court, Central District of California. *Education:* University of Southern California (B.A., 1983); Western State University (J.D., 1991). *Member:* Los Angeles County and Mexican American Bar Associations; State Bar of California; Hispanic National Bar Association; Women Lawyers Association of Los Angeles; USC Commerce Associates. *PRACTICE AREAS:* Insurance; Personal Injury; Construction Defect.

### ASSOCIATES

**DENNIS D. RESH,** born Glendale, California, February 10, 1951; admitted to bar, 1977, California and U.S. District Court, Central, Northern and Southern Districts of California; 1985, U.S. Court of Appeals, Ninth Circuit; 1988, U.S. Supreme Court. *Education:* University of Southern California (A.B., magna cum laude, 1973); Hastings College of the Law, University of California (J.D., 1977). Phi Beta Kappa; Phi Eta Sigma; Phi Alpha Delta. Member, Board of Editors, 1975-1977 and Associate Editor, 1976-1977, Hastings Law Journal. Law Clerk to Justice Raymond L. Sullivan, California Supreme Court, 1976. Judge Pro Tem, Los Angeles Superior Court, 1988—. *Member:* Pasadena (Treasurer, 1982-1983; Delegate, State Bar Conference of Delegates, 1983), Los Angeles County (Delegate, State Bar Conference of Delegates, 1989-1996; Member, Trial Lawyers and Governmental Law Sections) and American (Member: Sections on Litigation, and Tort and Insurance Practice; Forum Committee Construction Industry, 1985—) Bar Associations; State Bar of California; Association of Southern California Defense Counsel. *PRACTICE AREAS:* Construction Litigation; Professional Liability.

**STEVEN P. OWEN,** born Meridian, Mississippi, October 19, 1967; admitted to bar, 1994, California. *Education:* Texas A & M University (B.A., 1990); Whittier College School of Law (J.D., 1994). *Member:* The State Bar of California. *PRACTICE AREAS:* Premises Liability; Personal Injury.

**GUY CHIRINIAN,** born Los Angeles, California, February 9, 1966; admitted to bar, 1992, California. *Education:* University of California, Irvine (B.A., 1988); Southwestern University School of Law (J.D., 1991). *Member:* Los Angeles County Bar Association; State Bar of California. *PRACTICE AREAS:* Personal Injury; Automobile Accidents.

**SHARON P. MCALEENAN,** born Albany, New York, February 21, 1960; admitted to bar, 1987, California. *Education:* Occidental College (B.A., 1982); University of San Diego (J.D., 1985). *Member:* Los Angeles County Bar Association; State Bar of California; Southern California Defense Counsel. *PRACTICE AREAS:* Coverage Analysis; Products Liability; Construction Defect.

(For a Complete Listing of Personnel and Representative Clients, please refer to our Bakersfield listing.)

---

## GARY L. BOSTWICK
### LOS ANGELES, CALIFORNIA
(See Santa Monica)

*General Civil Litigation Practice. Trials and Appeals in all Courts. Libel and Slander, Securities, Corporate, Banking, Insurance, Real Estate and Labor Relations Law.*

---

## BOTTUM & FELITON
*A PROFESSIONAL CORPORATION*

Established in 1981

SUITE 1500, SOUTH TOWER
3200 WILSHIRE BOULEVARD
**LOS ANGELES, CALIFORNIA 90010**
Telephone: 213-487-0402
Fax: 213-386-9803

*San Diego, California Office:* Suite 400 Emerald Plaza, 402 West Broadway. Telephone: 619-595-4857. Fax: 619-595-4863.

*Professional Malpractice Defense. General Civil, Trial and Appellate Practice. Fidelity and Surety. Insurance. Corporations.*

*FIRM PROFILE:* Founded in 1981, Bottum & Feliton is a litigation firm providing representation in the defense of third party lawsuits against insureds, and as coverage and defense counsel for insurance companies and underwriters with respect to first and third party claims and "bad faith" suits.

*The firm specializes in professional liability litigation and acts as defense counsel and insurance coverage counsel in actions involving lawyers, accountants, directors and officers, real estate and insurance agents and brokers, architects and engineers, design professionals, and health care providers, including physicians, hospitals and dentists. Additional areas of expertise include contract surety and fidelity law, financial institutions, environmental law, ERISA, construction law, product liability, moving and storage, automobile liability, security guards and premises liability.*

*With offices in Los Angeles and San Diego, the firm's practice extends throughout California and the Western United States, in both federal and state courts.*

**ROSWELL BOTTUM** (1936-1993).

**JOHN R. FELITON, JR.,** born Syracuse, New York, August 19, 1948; admitted to bar, 1973, California. *Education:* Syracuse University (A.B., 1970); Loyola University of Los Angeles (J.D., 1973). Member and Lecturer, Professional Liability Underwriting Society. Member, Association of Southern California Insurance Professionals. *Member:* Los Angeles County and American (Member, Tort and Insurance Practice Section) Bar Associations; The State Bar of California (Member, Litigation Section); Association of Trial Lawyers of America; Association of Southern California Defense Counsel; Defense Research Institute; Claims Prevention Procedure Council. *PRACTICE AREAS:* Professional Liability; Civil Law; Trial Practice; Appellate Practice; Insurance Law; Corporate Law; Transportation Law.

**ROBERT A. WOOTEN, JR.,** born Santa Maria, California, August 20, 1947; admitted to bar, 1973, California. *Education:* University of California at Santa Barbara (A.B., 1969); University of California at Los Angeles (J.D., 1973; M.B.A., 1978). Production Editor and Contributing Author, UCLA-Alaska Law Review, 1972-1973. Member, Professional Liability Underwriters Society. *Member:* Los Angeles County and American (Vice Chair and Editor of Newsletter, Committee on Professional, Officers' and Directors' Liability, Tort and Insurance Practice Section, 1990-1992) Bar Associations; State Bar of California. *PRACTICE AREAS:* Professional Malpractice Law; Civil Law; Trial Practice; Appellate Practice; Fidelity and Surety Law; Insurance Law; Corporate Law.

**STEVE JOHNSON,** born Lincoln, Nebraska, July 26, 1955; admitted to bar, 1982, California. *Education:* University of Nebraska (B.A., 1977); Loyola Law School, Los Angeles (J.D.,1982). Staff Member, Loyola of Los Angeles Law Review, 1981-1982. Co-Author: "Labor Law in the Ninth Circuit: Recent Developments," 16 Loyola of Los Angeles Law Review 285, 1983. Consultant, "Legal Malpractice," chapter of Bancroft Whitney's California Civil Practice set. *Member:* Los Angeles County and American (Member, Torts and Insurance Practices Section, Forum on the Construction Industry, Fidelity and Surety Subcommittee) Bar Associations; State Bar of California. *PRACTICE AREAS:* Professional Malpractice Law; Civil Law; Trial Practice; Appellate Practice; Fidelity and Surety Law; Insurance Law; Corporate Law.

*(This Listing Continued)*

## PROFESSIONAL BIOGRAPHIES

## CALIFORNIA—LOS ANGELES

**MARK A. OERTEL,** born Whittier, California, November 7, 1958; admitted to bar, 1985, California. *Education:* Brigham Young University (B.S., 1982); Southwestern University (J.D., 1985). Recipient: American Jurisprudence Award in Legal Profession; Exceptional Merit Award in Employment Discrimination Law, 1985. Associate Professor, Southern California College of Law, 1988-1990. *Member:* Los Angeles County, Orange County and American (Member, Tort and Insurance Practice and International Tort and Insurance Practice Sections and Forum on Construction Industry; Fidelity and Surety Subcommittee, Tort and Insurance Practice Section) Bar Associations; State Bar of California (Member, Litigation Section); Association of Southern California Defense Counsel; Los Angeles Surety Claims Association; International Association of Defense Counsel (Fidelity Surety Section); Professional Liability Underwriting Society; National Bond Claims Association. LANGUAGES: German. PRACTICE AREAS: Professional Malpractice Law; Civil Law; Trial Practice; Appellate Practice; Fidelity and Surety Law; Insurance Law; Corporate Law.

**ALEXANDER F. GIOVANNIELLO,** born Sturno, Italy, August 11, 1959; admitted to bar, 1986, California; 1988, New York; U.S. District Court, Central, Southern and Eastern Districts of California. *Education:* Nassau Community College (A.S., with honors, 1977); State University of New York, College of Brockport (B.S., cum laude, 1982); University of San Diego (J.D., 1985). Member: California Dental Association; Professional Liability Underwriters Society. *Member:* Los Angeles County, San Diego, New York State and American Bar Associations; State Bar of California; Association of Southern California Defense Counsel. LANGUAGES: Italian. PRACTICE AREAS: Professional Malpractice Law; Civil Law; Trial Practice; Insurance Law; Corporate Law; Bad Faith; Construction Defects.

---

**KENNETH C. FELDMAN,** born Hollywood, California, June 28, 1962; admitted to bar, 1987, California. *Education:* California State University at Northridge (B.S., Business Administration, Finance Option, 1984); Loyola Law School, Los Angeles (J.D., 1987). Phi Delta Phi; Order of Omega. Member, Scott Moot Court Honors Competition. *Member:* Los Angeles County Bar Association (Member, Bench and Bar Relations Committee); State Bar of California (Member, Litigation Section); Association of Business Trial Lawyers; Association of Southern California Defense Counsel.

**JERRY GARCIA,** born Delano, California, August 18, 1956; admitted to bar, 1987, California. *Education:* Bakersfield College; Long Beach State University (B.A., 1980); University of California at Davis (J.D., 1987). Phi Kappa Phi. Law Clerk, Hon. Edward Garcia, U.S. District Court, Eastern District of California, 1987. *Member:* Los Angeles County and Mexican-American Bar Associations; State Bar of California (Member, Litigation Section). LANGUAGES: Spanish.

**PAUL K. SCHRIEFFER,** born Philadelphia, Pennsylvania, January 30, 1965; admitted to bar, 1990, California. *Education:* University of California at Santa Barbara (B.A., 1987); Southwestern University (J.D., 1990). Capitol Hill Program Scholar. Outstanding Achievement, Legal Writing. Lecturer: Americans with Disabilities Act - How Businesses can Comply with the Reasonable Accommodations Requirement (Phoenix, Arizona, 1992). *Member:* Los Angeles County (Member, Litigation, Business and Corporations Law Sections) and American (Tort and Insurance Practice Section) Bar Associations; State Bar of California; Association of Southern California Defense Counsel.

**SCOTT A. HAMPTON,** born Harbor City, California, August 30, 1964; admitted to bar, 1991, California. *Education:* University of California, Santa Barbara (B.A., 1986); Loyola Law School, Los Angeles (J.D., 1990). Recipient, First American Title Insurance Legal Service Award. Business & Directory Editor, Loyola Entertainment Law Journal, 1989-1990. Chairman, Loyola Environmental Law Society, 1988-1990. Author: "Anatomy of a Suicide - Media Liability for Audience Acts of Violence," 9 Loyola Ent.L.J. 95, 1989. Co-Author: "Recent Developments in Attorney Liability for Countersuits--An Update," C.E.B. Professional Liability Seminar, 1991. Co-Chairman, Southern California Public Interest Environmental Law Conferences, 1990-1991. *Member:* Los Angeles County and American Bar Associations; State Bar of California.

**GREGG S. GARFINKEL,** born Canoga Park, California, August 6, 1965; admitted to bar, 1991, California. *Education:* California State University at Northridge (B.A., Political Science, 1988); University of the Pacific, McGeorge School of Law (J.D., 1991). Wiley H. Manuel Scholarship. *Member:* Los Angeles County Bar Association (Member, Law Students' Support Committee); State Bar of California (Member, Litigation Section); American Bar Association (Member, Tort and Insurance Practice Section).

*(This Listing Continued)*

**BRIAN E. COOPER,** born Torrance, California, August 22, 1965; admitted to bar, 1990, California. *Education:* University of California at Berkeley (B.A., History, 1987); Loyola of Los Angeles (J.D., 1990). Staff Member: Loyola Entertainment Law Journal, 1988-1989. Author: "The Beck Decision, Will it Destroy Entertainment Unions," 1989, Vol. 9. *Member:* Los Angeles County and American Bar Associations; State Bar of California.

**JULIE A. COVELL,** born Long Beach, California, May 18, 1965; admitted to bar, 1991, California. *Education:* California State University, Long Beach (B.A., Political Science, Public Law Option, 1988); Loyola Law School, Los Angeles (J.D., 1991). Moot Court Honors Program. Member, Phillip C. Jessup International Moot Court Competition Team, 1990-1991. *Member:* Los Angeles County (Member, Litigation Section) and American Bar Associations; State Bar of California.

**KARL R. LOUREIRO,** born Valencia, Venezuela, March 4, 1964; admitted to bar, 1992, California. *Education:* California State University at Northridge (B.S., cum laude, Business Administration, Management Option, 1988); Loyola Law School (J.D., 1992). Beta Gamma Sigma. Phi Alpha Delta. Member, Scott Moot Court Honors Competition. *Member:* Los Angeles County Bar Association; State Bar of California. LANGUAGES: Spanish.

**SEAN T. HAMADA,** born Cincinnati, Ohio, September 29, 1966; admitted to bar, 1993, California. *Education:* University of California at Berkeley (B.A., 1988); Southern Methodist University School of Law (J.D., 1993). Phi Delta Phi. *Member:* Los Angeles Bar Association; State Bar of California.

**GARY F. WERNER,** born Cleveland, Ohio, February 22, 1962; admitted to bar, 1994, California. *Education:* University of California at Los Angeles (B.A., summa cum laude, 1991); Loyola Law School (J.D., 1994). Phi Beta Kappa; Phi Delta Phi. *Member:* Los Angeles County Bar Association; State Bar of California.

**VICTOR I. KING,** born Hong Kong, November 12, 1964; admitted to bar, 1991, California, U.S. District Court, Central and Eastern Districts of California and U.S. Court of Appeals, Ninth Circuit. *Education:* University of Chicago (B.A., with honors, 1986; M.A., 1986); University of Michigan (J.D., 1989). Articles Editor, 1988-1989 and Associate Editor, 1987-1988, University of Michigan Journal of International Law. *Member:* Los Angeles County and American Bar Associations; State Bar of California; Southern California Chinese Lawyers Association.

**ANDREA J. LANG,** born Bethlehem, Pennsylvania, July 14, 1962; admitted to bar, 1995, California, U.S. District Court, Central District of California and U.S. Court of Appeals, Ninth Circuit. *Education:* California State University, Northridge (B.A., 1987); Whittier College School of Law (J.D., 1995).

**LINWOOD WARREN, JR.,** born Portsmouth, Virginia, November 3, 1958; admitted to bar, 1989, California; 1993, U.S. District Court, Central District of California and U.S. Court of Appeals, Ninth Circuit. *Education:* Williams College (B.A., 1981); Rensselaer Polytechnic Institute (M.S., 1984); University of Virginia (J.D., 1987). *Member:* Beverly Hills (Member, Legal Technology Committee) and American (Member, Intellectual Property Section) Bar Associations. PRACTICE AREAS: Litigation.

REPRESENTATIVE CLIENTS: Alexander Howden North America; Atlanta International Insurance Co.; CNA Insurance Cos.; Continental Insurance; E&O Professionals; Fireman's Fund Insurance; First Mercury Limited; Forum Insurance Co.; Fremont Indemnity Co.; Frontier Insurance Co.; Generali; Hughes Aircraft Employees Federal Credit Union; Industrial Indemnity; INSCO/DICO; Insurance Company of the West; Lucky Stores, Inc.; Metropolitan Life Insurance Co.; National Union Fire Insurance Co.; New Hampshire Insurance Co.; North American Van Lines; Northwestern National Insurance; Pacific National Insurance Co.; Penn-America Insurance Co.; Reliance Insurance Cos.; Safeco; Sentry Life Insurance; Stewart Smith West, Inc.; The Bekins Co.; The Home Insurance Co.; TIG Insurance Co.; Toplis and Harding, Inc.; Transamerica Insurance Services; Underwriters at Lloyd's, London; UNIRISC; Utica Mutual Insurance Co.; Vasa North Atlantic Casualty Surety Co.; Warner Bros., Inc.; Western Surety Co.; World Savings & Loan; State Farm Insurance Co.

## THOMAS K. BOURKE
*ONE BUNKER HILL, 8TH FLOOR*
*601 WEST FIFTH STREET*
**LOS ANGELES, CALIFORNIA 90071-2094**
*Telephone: 213-623-1092*
*Fax: 213-680-4060*

*Civil Litigation with emphasis on Unfair Competition, Insurance, Sales, Secured Transactions, Collection of Judgements and Securities Litigation.*

*(This Listing Continued)*

THOMAS K. BOURKE, Los Angeles—Continued

**THOMAS K. BOURKE,** born Chicago, Illinois, June 28, 1946; admitted to bar, 1972, New York; 1973, California. *Education:* University of Notre Dame (A.B., magna cum laude, 1968); New York University (J.D., cum laude, 1971). Order of the Coif. Root Tilden Scholar. Author: "The Shape of Things to Come: The Supreme Court's Shaw v. Reno decision calls into question the future of racial gerrymandering," Los Angeles Lawyer, December, 1994; "The Practitioner's Column: Fraud-and-RICO Case Results in Huge Fee Award," Los Angeles Daily Journal, September 19, 1994. Staff Member, Office of Counsel to the Departmental Committees for Court Administration, First and Second Judicial Departments, Appellate Division of the New York State Supreme Court, 1971-1972. Alternate Attorney Representative to the Ninth Circuit Judicial Conference, 1994, 1995. *Member:* Los Angeles County and American Bar Associations; State Bar of California; Association of Business Trial Lawyers; Los Angeles Complex Litigation Inn of Court. *REPORTED CASES:* Layman v. Combs, 994 F.2d 1344 (9th Cir.) cert. denied, 114 S.Ct. 303 (1993); McGonigle v. Combs, 968 F.2d 810, 814-15 (9th Cir.), cert. dismissed, 113 S.Ct. 399 (1992); Schultz v. Hembree, 975 F.2d 572 (9th Cir. 1992).

---

## BOUTWELL, BEHRENDT & ENNOR
### LOS ANGELES, CALIFORNIA

(See Irvine)

*Banking, Finance, Mortgage Banking, Pensions/ERISA, Tax Exempt Entities, Corporate and Municipal Finance Law.*

---

## BOVITZ & SPITZER
Established in 1991
WELLS FARGO CENTER
333 SOUTH GRAND AVENUE, SUITE 2000
LOS ANGELES, CALIFORNIA 90071-1524
Telephone: 213-346-8300
FAX: 213-620-1811
Email: bovitz@mrinter.net

*Bankruptcy and Workouts, Uniform Commercial Code Matters, Related Litigation, Alternative Dispute Resolution and Mediation in Bankruptcy.*

FIRM PROFILE: *The firm represents every major player in California bankruptcy courts. On the debtor side, the firm represents chapter 11 debtors in possession, involuntary petitioning creditors, individuals seeking pre-petition planning and advice, shareholders in companies on the brink, and directors and officers. On the creditor side, the firm represents creditors' committees, individual members of committees, secured creditors, major unsecured creditors, landlords, holders of executory contracts, and holders of equity interests. The firm represents parties seeking to purchase assets from bankruptcy estates. Mr. Bovitz of the firm also serves as an expert witness in malpractice cases which arise from bankruptcy proceedings and as a mediator for resolving bankruptcy disputes.*

### MEMBERS OF THE FIRM

**J. SCOTT BOVITZ,** born Los Angeles, California, June 5, 1955; admitted to bar, 1980, California; 1981, U.S. District Court, Northern, Southern, Eastern and Central Districts of California and U.S. Tax Court; 1986, U.S. Court of Appeals, Ninth Circuit. *Education:* University of California at Santa Barbara (B.A., with high honors, 1977); Loyola Law School, Los Angeles (J.D., 1980); University of San Diego (Diploma in Taxation, 1983). Recipient: American Jurisprudence Award for Bankruptcy; Benno M. Brink Memorial Award for Bankruptcy, Loyola Law School. Adjunct Professor of Law, Bankruptcy Law, Debtor-Creditor Relations and Uniform Commercial Code Transactions, Loyola Law School, Los Angeles, 1982-1987. Speaker on, "What Every Lawyer Need to Know About Bankruptcy," Professional Education Seminar at law firm of Sedgwick, Detert, Moran & Arnold, 1996; Panelist, "Advanced Estate Planning With An Emphasis On Asset Protection Planning," Mainsail Financial Group, 1996; Panelist, Orange County Bankruptcy Forum Special Projects Committee Program on Bankruptcy Litigation: A Workshop in Trial Strategy and Technique, 1995; Panelist, "Bankruptcy Litigation Skills," California State Bar Convention, 1994; Alternative Dispute Resolution in Bankruptcy," American Bankruptcy Institute, Battleground West, 1994; "Latest Weapons For the Battlefield: Current Developments," American Bankruptcy Institute—First Annual Bankruptcy Battleground West, 1993; Speaker on, "The 1994 Amendments to the Bankruptcy Code," Credit Managers Association of California, 1995; Speaker on, "The Intersection of Environmental and Bankruptcy Law," Professional Education Seminar at Demetriou, Del Guercio, Springer & Moyer, 1995; Speaker on, "What Every Accountant Should Know About Bankruptcy," Pasadena Organization of Certified Public Accountants, 1994; Speaker on, "Get Yourself Ready To Be A Bar Certified Bankruptcy Specialist," Los Angeles Bankruptcy Forum 1993; Panelist, California State Bar Convention, 1984, 1986-1989, 1991, 1992, "Recent Developments in Bankruptcy Law"; Speaker on, "Current Issues in Bankruptcy Litigation From The Ninth Circuit Perspective," National Conference of Bankruptcy Judges, Bankruptcy Litigation Subcommittee Meeting, 1991; Speaker on "Loan Workouts and Collections," Bankers' Compliance Group Seminar, 1992; Speaker on, "Real Estate in Bankruptcy," BEST Seminar on residential real estate transactions for attorneys, 1992; Speaker at Professional Education Seminar at accounting firm of Braverman, Codron & Co. on "What Every Accountant Should Know About Bankruptcies," 1992; Speaker at Professional Education Seminar at Law Firm of McClintock, Weston, Benshoof, Rochefort, Rubalcava & MacCuish on "The Conflict Between Environmental and Bankruptcy Laws: The Topic of the 1990's," 1992; Speaker on "Treatment of Secured Claims in Bankruptcy in California," National Business Institute, 1993; Panelist, Infocast Seminars on "Lender Liability," 1990, "Bankruptcy Cases and Lending Institutions," and "Chapter 11," Spring and Fall, 1991; Speaker at South Bay Bar Association on Chapter 7, 1984; Speaker at Business Investigation Services Meeting at Coopers and Lybrand on "Protecting Professional Fees from Recovery by the Bankruptcy Trustee," 1991; Speaker at Professional Education Seminar at Poms, Smith, Lande and Rose Professional Corporation on "The Impact of Bankruptcy on Licensors and Licensees of Intellectual Property," 1991; American Radio Relay League (ARRL) Southwest Division Convention on "Amateur Radio Antennas and the Law," 1988. Producer, writer and moderator of 6-show cable series on legal topics entitled "Lex Loci: The Law of the Land," 1982-1983. Member: American Radio Relay League, Volunteer Legal Counsel Program, 1981—. Director, Los Angeles Bankruptcy Forum, 1994—. Appointed to Inaugural Panel of Mediators, Bankruptcy Mediation Program, United States Bankruptcy Court, Central District of California, 1995—. Committee Member, Central District of California Bankruptcy Bench/Bar Judicial Variance Committee, 1994-1995. *Member:* Los Angeles County and American Bar Associations; State Bar of California; Financial Lawyers Conference, Los Angeles; Commercial Law League of America; Los Angeles Bankruptcy Forum; Orange County Bankruptcy Forum. (Certified Specialist, Personal and Small Business Bankruptcy Law, The State Bar of California Board of Legal Specialization; Board Certified, Business Bankruptcy Law, Commercial Law League of America Academy of Commercial and Bankruptcy Law Specialists; Certified Specialist, Business Bankruptcy Law, American Bankruptcy Board of Certification). (Also Of Counsel to Dixon & Jessup, Ltd., L.L.P.). *PRACTICE AREAS:* Bankruptcy Chapter 11; Bankruptcy Law; Business Reorganization; Secured Transactions Law; Creditor Bankruptcy; Mediation. *Email:* bovitz@mrinter.net

**SUSAN MICHELLE SPITZER,** born Montebello, California, November 17, 1957; admitted to bar, 1982, California; U.S. District Court, Northern, Southern, Eastern and Central Districts of California. *Education:* Loyola Marymount University (B.A., cum laude, 1978); Loyola Law School, Los Angeles (J.D., cum laude, 1982). Member: Pi Gamma Mu Social Science Honor Society; St. Thomas More Law Honor Society; Fr. R.A. Vachon Memorial Scholarship Committee. In-House Counsel and Retail Manager, Bi-Rite Quality Pharmacies, Inc., La Habra, California, 1983-1988. Attorney, Tax Law and Estate Planning, Law Offices of William A. Fazio, Inc., La Habra, California, 1983. *Member:* Los Angeles County Bar Association; State Bar of California; Los Angeles Bankruptcy Forum; Orange County Bankruptcy Forum; Financial Lawyers Conference; American Bankruptcy Institute. (Also Of Counsel to Dixon & Jessup, Ltd., L.L.P.). *PRACTICE AREAS:* Bankruptcy Law; Finance. *Email:* bovitz@mrinter.net

---

## BOWMAN AND BROOKE
### LOS ANGELES, CALIFORNIA

(See Torrance)

*Civil Litigation in all Courts.*

(This Listing Continued)

## SANDOR T. BOXER
SUITE 900
2049 CENTURY PARK EAST
**LOS ANGELES, CALIFORNIA 90067-3111**
Telephone: 310-282-8118
Fax: 310-282-8077
Email: tedb@themall.net

*Commercial, Bankruptcy, Business Law, and Business Litigation.*

**SANDOR T. BOXER,** born Chicago, Illinois, December 23, 1939; admitted to bar, 1965, California. *Education:* University of California, Los Angeles (A.B., 1961; LL.B., 1964). Phi Alpha Delta. Member, University of California, Los Angeles Law Review, 1963-1964. Author: "Default, Civil Procedure Before Trial," Continuing Education of the Bar, Vol. 3, 1990. Lecturer, Continuing Education of the Bar: Fundamentals of Civil Litigation During Trial, 1984-1986; Remedies for Breach of Contract, 1984-1985; Fundamentals of Civil Procedure Before Trial, 1990. "How to Avoid and Survive Attorneys' Fee Disputes", 1993. Law Clerk to Justice Raymond E. Peters, California Supreme Court, 1964-1965. Judge Pro Tem, Los Angeles Municipal Court, 1977-1994; Arbitrator, Superior Court of Los Angeles County, 1979-1994. *Member:* Los Angeles County (Chairman, Arbitration Committee, 1987-1990; Chair, Dispute Resolution Services Operations Committee, 1990-1992) and American (Member, Business Bankruptcy Committee, Corporation, Banking and Business Law Section, 1981— Bar Associations; State Bar of California (Chair, Committee on Mandatory Fee Arbitration, 1992-1993; Assistant Presiding Arbitrator, Mandatory Fee Arbitration Program, 1993—) Association of Business Trial Lawyers.

## JEFFERY P. BOYKIN
4484 WILSHIRE BOULEVARD, SECOND FLOOR
**LOS ANGELES, CALIFORNIA 90010**
Telephone: 213-857-7175
Fax: 213-857-7185

*General Civil Trial in all State and Federal Courts, Personal Injury, Plaintiff and Defense, Criminal Law, Family Law, Commercial Litigation including Collections.*

**JEFFERY P. BOYKIN,** born Panama City, Florida, March 31, 1961; admitted to bar, 1987, California, U.S. District Court, Southern and Northern District of California and U.S. Court of Appeals, Ninth Circuit; 1988, U.S. District Court, Central District of California; 1990, North Carolina. *Education:* University of North Carolina (B.A., with honors, 1983); Pepperdine University (J.D., cum laude, 1987). *Member:* Los Angeles County Bar Association; State Bar of California; North Carolina State Bar.

## BOYLE, OLSON & ROBINSON
**LOS ANGELES, CALIFORNIA**
(See Pasadena)

*General Civil and Trial Practice in all State and Federal Courts. Corporation, Probate, Estate Planning, Family, Construction, State and Federal Tax Law.*

## MARC H. BOZEMAN
SUITE 1600
ONE CENTURY PLAZA
2029 CENTURY PARK EAST
**LOS ANGELES, CALIFORNIA 90067**
Telephone: 310-553-4876
Fax: 310-553-3316
Email: MHB@DC4.HHLAW.COM

*Food, Drug, Biologics, Medical Device and Cosmetic (FDA) Law.*

**MARC H. BOZEMAN,** born Brooklyn, New York, October 9, 1945; admitted to bar, 1972, California. *Education:* University of California (A.B., 1967; M.C.P., 1971); University of California, Boalt Hall School of Law (J.D., 1971); Pepperdine University (M.B.A., 1985). (Counsel, Hogan & Hartson L.L.P., Washington, D.C.). **PRACTICE AREAS:** Food, Drug, Biologics, Medical Device and Cosmetic (FDA) Law.

## BRADY & BERLINER
*Established in 1985*
1875 CENTURY PARK EAST, SUITE 700
**LOS ANGELES, CALIFORNIA 90067**
Telephone: 310-282-6848
Telecopy: 310-282-6841

*Washington, D.C. Office:* 1225 Nineteenth Street, N.W., Suite 800. Telephone: 202-955-6067. Telecopy: 202-822-0109.
*Berkeley, California Office:* 2560 Ninth Street, Suite 316. Telephone: 510-549-6926. Telecopy: 510-649-9793.
*Sacramento, California Office:* 1121 L Street, Suite 606. Telephone: 916-448-7819. Telecopy: 916-448-1140.

*Administrative Law, Commercial Litigation, Appellate Advocacy, Intergovernmental Affairs, Legislative Practice, Health Policy, International Trade, North American Energy Transactions, Oil and Gas Law and Public Utility Law.*

(For Complete Biographical Data on all personnel, see Professional Biographies at Washington, D.C.)

## LAW OFFICES OF DENNIS N. BRAGER
*A PROFESSIONAL CORPORATION*
2029 CENTURY PARK EAST, SUITE 600
**LOS ANGELES, CALIFORNIA 90067**
Telephone: 310-277-1734
Fax: 310-277-6431

*Civil and Criminal Tax Litigation. Federal and State Tax Controversies.*

**DENNIS N. BRAGER,** born New York, N.Y., July 1, 1953; admitted to bar, 1978, California, U.S. Tax Court, U.S. District Court, Central and Northern Districts of California, U.S. Court of Appeals, Ninth Circuit, U.S. Court of Federal Claims, U.S. Supreme Court. *Education:* Pace University (B.B.A., magna cum laude, 1975); New York University (J.D., 1978). Author: "Tax Brakes: The Taxpayer Bill of Rights 2," Los Angeles Lawyer, November 1996; "IRS Guidelines for Installment-Payment Agreements," Los Angeles Lawyer, March 1996; "The Innocent Spouse Defense," Los Angeles Lawyer, December 1995; "The Innocent Spouse Defense," Family Law News, Spring 1993; "Challenging the IRS Requires a Cohesive Strategy," Taxation for Lawyers, July/August, 1991. "The Taxpayer Bill of Rights—A Small Step Toward Reigning in the IRS," Los Angeles Lawyer, May, 1989; "How to Handle Tax Shelter Registration Under the 1984 Tax Reform Act," Journal of Taxation of Investments, Spring, 1985. Lecturer: 1987, California Continuing Education of the Bar, Tax Procedure Institute, "How to Handle Civil and Criminal Controversies with the Internal Revenue Service, Franchise Tax Board and in Court,"; 1986, Golden Gate University, Masters in Taxation Program, "Taxation of Capital Assets,". Senior Trial Attorney, Office of Chief Counsel, Internal Revenue Service, Los Angeles, California, 1978-1984. *Member:* Beverly Hills (Tax Section) and Los Angeles County (Chairman Small Firm and Sole Practitioner Section (1993-1994); Vice-Chairman, Client Relations Committee, 1980-1984; Officer, Tax Section, Tax Compliance Procedure and Litigation Subcommittee, 1990, 1995) Bar Associations. (Certified Specialist, Tax Law, The State Bar of California Board of Legal Specialization).

## BRAGG, SHORT, SEROTA & KULUVA
801 SOUTH FIGUEROA STREET, SUITE 2100
**LOS ANGELES, CALIFORNIA 90017-2575**
Telephone: 213-612-5335
Fax: 213-612-5712

*San Francisco, California Office:* Bragg & Dziesinski, Two Embarcadero Center, Suite 1400. Telephone: 415-954-1850. Fax: 415-434-2179.
*Newport Beach, California Office:* 4695 MacArthur Court, Suite 530. Telephone: 714-442-4800. Fax: 714-442-4816.

*Insurance Defense, Products Liability, Personal Injury, Directors and Officers, and Worker's Compensation.*

**ROBERT A. BRAGG,** born San Francisco, California, November 18, 1951; admitted to bar, 1981, California and U.S. District Court, Northern District of California; 1983, U.S. Court of Appeals, Ninth Circuit; 1986, U.S. District Court, Eastern District of California. *Education:* University of San Francisco (B.A., cum laude, 1974); San Francisco Law School (J.D.,
*(This Listing Continued)*

### BRAGG, SHORT, SEROTA & KULUVA, Los Angeles—Continued

1980). Arbitrator, San Francisco County Superior Court, 1985. *Member:* Bar Association of San Francisco; Contra Costa County, Alameda County, San Mateo County and American Bar Associations; The State Bar of California (Member, Litigation Section); Defense Research Institute; National Institute for Trial Advocacy. *PRACTICE AREAS:* Insurance Defense.

*CAROL D. KULUVA,* born Burbank, California; admitted to bar, 1979, California; 1980, U.S. District Court, Northern, Eastern, Southern and Central Districts of California; 1982, Montana. *Education:* California State University at Northridge (B.A., cum laude, 1976); San Fernando Valley College of Law (J.D., 1979). Member, San Fernando Valley Law Review, 1978-1979. Arbitrator, Special Arbitration Panel, Los Angeles Superior Court, 1993—. Judge Pro Tem, Municipal Court, Los Angeles, 1993—. *Member:* Los Angeles County (Member, Attorneys Errors and Omissions Committee, 1994—; Delegate to State Bar, 1989; Attorney Client Relations Mediator, 1987—) and American (Member, Standing Committee on Professional Liability, 1985—) Bar Associations; State Bar of California (Member, Committee on Professional Liability Insurance, 1991—); State Bar of Montana; Association of Southern California Defense Counsel; California Trial Lawyers Association. *PRACTICE AREAS:* Professional Liability Defense; Directors and Officers Errors and Omissions Law; Product Liability; Personal Injury Defense.

#### ASSOCIATES

*LOUIS E. GOLDBERG,* born Hartford, Connecticut, April 23, 1936; admitted to bar, 1974, California and U.S. District Court, Central and Southern Districts of California; 1974-1982, U.S. Court of Customs and Patent Appeals; 1975, U.S. Court of Appeals, Fifth, Seventh and Ninth Circuits; 1977, U.S. Supreme Court. *Education:* Arizona State University (B.A., 1958); University of Arizona College of Law; South Bay University (J.D., 1973). Phi Alpha Delta. Instructor, Legal Ethics, Criminal Law and Workmen Compensation Under Federal Longshore and Harbor Workers' Act, 1976-1977. Delegate to State Bar, 1978-1979. *Member:* Harbor (Secretary/Treasurer, 1977; Member, Board of Directors, 1977-1978; President, 1978), Ventura, Los Angeles County and American Bar Associations; State Bar of California; American Society of Testing Materials (ASTM); International Association of Defense Counsel (IADC); Association of Southern California Defense Counsel; Defense Research Institute (DRI).

*THOMAS J. MCDERMOTT,* born Topeka, Kansas, December 12, 1956; admitted to bar, 1982, California; 1986, U.S. District Court, Central District of California. *Education:* San Diego State University (B.A., 1979); Loyola University Law School (J.D., 1982). *Member:* State Bar of California.

*ANDREW MANCINI,* born Los Angeles, California, August 8, 1944; admitted to bar, 1987, California and U.S. District Court, Central District of California. *Education:* California State University at Los Angeles (B.A., 1966); University of West Los Angeles (J.D., 1986). *Member:* Los Angeles County Bar Association; State Bar of California.

*GAIL D. RACKLIFFE,* born November 30, 1955; admitted to bar, 1980, California. *Education:* Occidental College (B.A., 1977); Southwestern University (J.D. cum laude, 1980). *Member:* The State Bar of California; California Women Lawyers Association. *PRACTICE AREAS:* Workers Compensation Law.

*JOHN E. BOWER, JR.,* born Hackensack, New Jersey, November 28, 1949; admitted to bar, 1977, California; 1978, U.S. District Court, Central District of California; 1979, U.S. Court of Appeals, Ninth Circuit. *Education:* California State University at Northridge (B.A., 1972); Southwestern University (J.D., 1977). Phi Alpha Delta. *Member:* Los Angeles County and American (Member, Tort and Insurance Practice Section) Bar Associations; State Bar of California. *PRACTICE AREAS:* Insurance Defense.

*AMELIA M. ENG,* born San Francisco, California; admitted to bar, 1978, California. *Education:* California State University of Los Angeles (B.A., 1974); Southwestern University School of Law (J.D., 1977). *Member:* State Bar of California; Southern California Chinese Lawyers Association. (Certified Specialist, Workers' Compensation Law, The State Bar of California Board of Legal Specialization). *PRACTICE AREAS:* Workers Compensation Law.

*ZAHAVA AROESTY STROUD,* born Berkeley, California, December 9, 1958; admitted to bar, 1985, California and U.S. District Court, Central District of California; 1986, U.S. Court of Appeals, Ninth Circuit. *Education:* University of California (B.A., Valedictorian, 1981; J.D., 1985). For-

*(This Listing Continued)*

merly with: Los Angeles County District Attorney's Office, 1986-1989; Morris, Polich & Purdy, 1989-1996. *Member:* Los Angeles County Bar Association; Women Lawyers of Los Angeles. *PRACTICE AREAS:* Insurance Defense Litigation.

#### LEGAL SUPPORT PERSONNEL

**Deborah Butler** (Hearing Representative)

REPRESENTATIVE CLIENT: Chubb Group of Insurance Companies.

---

## BRAND FARRAR DZIUBLA FREILICH & KOLSTAD, LLP

Counsellors at Law

**515 SOUTH FLOWER STREET, SUITE 3500**
**LOS ANGELES, CALIFORNIA 90071-2201**
Telephone: 213-228-0288
Facsimile: 213-426-6222

*Correspondent Offices:* Hong Kong, Shanghai, Beijing, Guangzhou, Xiamen, Shenzhen, Ulaanbaatar, New York and San Francisco.

General Corporate, International Tax, Finance, Real Estate, Public-Private Development, Land Use and Workouts.

FIRM PROFILE: *As veterans of large law and accounting firms, our founding partners established Brand Farrar in response to clients' concerns about the quality of work produced and its costs. The firm's goal is a simple one: to provide quality legal representation at a reasonable cost.*

*Our lawyers are "counsellors" who are knowledgeable and experienced not only about specific legal issues, but also about the broader business context in which our clients must act. Brand Farrar clients work primarily with the lawyer they hired who has the experience they need and who is available when needed.*

*MICHAEL A. BRAND,* born Phoenix, Arizona, August 29, 1952; admitted to bar, 1977, Colorado; 1979, California. *Education:* Indiana University (A.B., 1974); Harvard University (J.D., 1977). Phi Beta Kappa. *Member:* State Bar of California; American Bar Association. (Also Of Counsel to Arnberger, Kim, Buxbaum & Choy, Los Angeles, California). *PRACTICE AREAS:* Real Estate Law; International Law.

*DAVID W. FARRAR,* born Clifton Forge, Virginia, August 25, 1942; admitted to bar, 1973, California. *Education:* University of Virginia (B.A., 1964; J.D., 1973). Law Clerk to Hon. Kelleher, U.S. District Judge, Central District of California, 1973-1974. Los Angeles County Commissioner, 1992—. Vice Chairman, County Economy & Efficiency Commission, 1995—. Chair, County Real Estate Asset Management Task Force, 1994—. Chapter 11 Bankruptcy Trustee, 1992—. *Member:* State Bar of California; Los Angeles County and American Bar Associations; Urban Land Institute. *SPECIAL AGENCIES:* Special Counsel to U.S. District Court in Keith v Volpe with respect to administration of the $500 million Century Freeway Housing Program, 1990—. *PRACTICE AREAS:* Real Estate Development and Finance; Public-Private Development; Real Estate Asset Management; Public Agency Representations; Affordable Housing.

*ROBERT W. DZIUBLA,* born Chicago, Illinois, July 18, 1952; admitted to bar, 1980, Illinois; 1988, California. *Education:* Northwestern University (B.A., 1974; J.D., 1980); University of Chicago (M.A., 1978); University of Washington (LL.M., 1983). 1979 Jessup International Moot Court Competition: World Championship Team; National Championship Team; Best Brief in National Competition. Adjunct Professor, International Finance Law and International Business Transactions, University of Southern California, 1994—. Senior Fulbright Fellow in Japanese Corporate and Securities Law, 1983-1984, Faculty of Law, University of Kyoto. Author: "Hotel Bankruptcies and Restructurings in the 1990s (Part 1) (in Japanese: Iza to iu toki no tame ni)" Vol. 1-4, 60 (Nov. 1992); "Japan's New Tax System," Venture Japan, Vol. 1, No. 3, 56 (1989); "Enforcing Corporate Responsibility: Japanese Corporate Directors' Liability to Third Parties for Failure to Supervise," 18 Law in Japan 55 (1986); "The Impotent Sword of Japanese Justice: the Doctrine of Shobunsei as a Barrier to Administrative Litigation," 18 Cornell International Law Journal 37 (1985); "International Trading Companies: Building on the Japanese Model," 4 Northwestern Journal International Law & Business 422 (1982); "Zenith Radio Corp. v. United States: The Demise of Congressionally Mandated Countervailing Duties," 1 Northwestern Journal International Law and Business 318 (1979). Contributing Author: " U.S. International Trade and Taxation," Perkins, Coie, Stone, Olsen & Williams, (1984); East Asian Affairs Advisor to Senator Paul Simon, 1982, 1988 and Senator Alan Dixon, 1982. *Member:* Illinois State and American Bar Associations; State Bar of California; Financial

*(This Listing Continued)*

Lawyers Conference; International Bankers Association of California; American Chamber of Commerce in Japan. (Also Of Counsel to Arnberger, Kim, Buxbaum & Choy, Los Angeles, California). **LANGUAGES:** Japanese. **PRACTICE AREAS:** Finance; Real Estate; International Trade. **Email:** Dziublar@BrandFarrar.com

**AMY E. FREILICH,** born Suffern, New York, September 15, 1962; admitted to bar, 1987, New York; 1990, California. *Education:* University of Chicago (A.B., with honors, 1983); Harvard University (J.D., cum laude, 1986). Law Clerk to Judge Bowman, U.S. Court of Appeals, Eighth Circuit, 1986-1987. *Member:* Los Angeles County (Member, Real Property Law and Land Use Sections), New York State and American Bar Associations; State Bar of California. **PRACTICE AREAS:** Real Estate Law; Land Use Law; Environmental Quality Act Compliance; Public-Private Development. **Email:** Freilicha@BrandFarrar.com

**CHARLES K. KOLSTAD,** born West Lafayette, Indiana, September 6, 1953; admitted to bar, 1980, New York; 1992, California. *Education:* University of Villanova (B.S., cum laude, 1975); Columbia University (M.B.A., 1978); University of Notre Dame (J.D., 1979). *Member:* State Bar of California; New York State and American Bar Associations. (Also Of Counsel to Arnberger, Kim, Buxbaum & Choy, Los Angeles, California). **PRACTICE AREAS:** Taxation; International Trade and Finance. **Email:** Kolstadc@BrandFarrar.com

**MARGARET G. GRAF,** born March 16, 1943; admitted to bar, 1974, New York; 1987, California. *Education:* Iowa State University (B.S., 1964); Indiana University (M.S., 1966); Cornell University (J.D., 1973), *Member:* The Association of the Bar of the City of New York; American Bar Assn. **PRACTICE AREAS:** Corporate Law; Finance; Securities. **Email:** Grafm@BrandFarrar.com

*OF COUNSEL*

**H. BENNETT ARNBERGER,** born Globe, Arizona, July, 1953; admitted to bar, 1983, California and U.S. District Court, Northern and Central Districts of California. *Education:* University of California at Berkeley (A.B., with honors and distinction, 1977); University of San Francisco (J.D., 1983). Phi Delta Phi. (Also Member, Arnberger, Kim, Buxbaum & Choy, San Francisco, California). **PRACTICE AREAS:** Business and Commercial Transactions; Intellectual Property Transactions; Corporate Law; Employment Law; International Transactions; Insurance; Litigation and Arbitration.

**DAVID C. BUXBAUM,** born New York, N.Y., July, 1933; admitted to bar, 1970, New York and U.S. District Court, Southern, Eastern, Northern and Western Districts of New York; 1971, U.S. Court of Appeals, Second Circuit; 1974, U.S. Supreme Court; 1975, U.S. Court of Appeals, Seventh Circuit and Fourth Circuits; 1978, U.S. Court of Appeals, Eighth Circuit; 1979, U.S. Court of Appeals, First Circuit; 1981, California; 1989, U.S. District Court, Central District of California; 1991, U.S. District Court, Northern District of California and U.S. Court of Appeals, Ninth Circuit. *Education:* New York University (B.A., 1954); University of Michigan (J.D., 1959) concurrent graduate studies, University of Michigan Graduate School; graduate study, Harvard University and University of Washington (M.A., 1963; Ph.D., 1968). (Also of Counsel to: Collier, Shannon, Rill & Scott, Sydney, Australia and Member, Arnberger, Kim, Buxbaum & Choy, Los Angeles, California). **LANGUAGES:** Chinese. **PRACTICE AREAS:** International Law; Complex International Litigation; Complex International Contract; Joint Venture Contract; Investment Law; Trademark, Copyright and Patent Protection and Enforcement; Commodities and Securities.

**SHERRY L. GEYER,** born Los Angeles, California, April 1, 1948; admitted to bar, 1988, California. *Education:* University of California, Los Angeles (B.A., 1971); Loyola Law School, Los Angeles (J.D., 1988). *Member:* State Bar of California; American Bar Association (Former Chair, Meeting Committee, Administrative and Regulatory Practice Law Section). **PRACTICE AREAS:** Real Estate; General Corporate. **Email:** Geyers@BrandFarrar.com

**MANENDER M. GREWAL,** born India, June, 1958; admitted to bar, 1988, England and Wales; 1991, Hong Kong (not admitted in the United States). *Education:* University of London (Bsc., Hons, Biochemistry, 1980) Guildhall University (Common Professional Examination, 1984); College of Law (Law Society Final Examination, 1985); University of London (LL.M., Intellectual Property, 1989). (Also Member, Arnberger, Kim, Buxbaum & Choy, Los Angeles, California). **LANGUAGES:** English, Hindi. **PRACTICE AREAS:** Intellectual Property Licensing; Civil Litigation; Commercial Litigation.

*(This Listing Continued)*

**JULIA MARIE SHYMANSKY,** born Wheeling, West Virginia, May 15, 1962; admitted to bar, 1987, California. *Education:* West Virginia University (B.A., summa cum laude, 1984); Duke Law School (J.D., 1987). Phi Beta Kappa. *Member:* State Bar of California; Women Lawyers of Los Angeles (Delegate for State Bar Convention, 1990). **PRACTICE AREAS:** Commercial Litigation.

**YELENA YERUHIM,** born Leningrad, Russia, November 14, 1966; admitted to bar, 1992, California. *Education:* University of California at Los Angeles (B.A., magna cum laude, 1988); University of Southern California Law Center (J.D., 1991). Phi Beta Kappa; Alpha Lambda Delta; Phi Alpha Delta; Golden Key; Recipient, College Honors, Departmental Honors in Communications. Member, Southern California Law Review, 1989-1991; Editor: Computer Law Journal, 1990-1991; Editor: Major Tax Planning Journal, 1990-1991. *Member:* Beverly Hills, Century City and Los Angeles County Bar Associations; State Bar of California; District of Columbia Bar. **PRACTICE AREAS:** Real Estate Law; Corporate Law.

**NORMAN A. CHERNIN,** born Toronto, Ontario, Canada, June 12, 1946; admitted to bar, 1971, California and U.S. District Court, Central District of California. *Education:* University of California at Los Angeles (B.A., 1967); Loyola University of Los Angeles (J.D., 1970). Member, St. Thomas More Law Honor Society. Author, "Securing Deferred Consideration," 4 Cal. Real Prop. J, 9-11, Summer 1986. *Member:* Los Angeles County and American Bar Associations; State Bar of California. **REPORTED CASES:** People v. Orr (1972) 26 Cal. App.3d 849, 103 Cal. Rptr. 266. **PRACTICE AREAS:** Real Estate; Land Use. **Email:** Yeruhimy@BrandFarrar.com

**JOAN M. MARQUARDT,** born Wichita, Kansas, March 7, 1962; admitted to bar, 1987, California. *Education:* University of Chicago (A.B., with honors, 1984); University of Texas (J.D., with honors, 1987). *Member:* Los Angeles County Bar Association; Women Lawyers of Los Angeles. **PRACTICE AREAS:** Finance; General Corporate; Real Estate. **Email:** Marquardtj@BrandFarrar.com

---

# LISA E. BRANDON

## LOS ANGELES, CALIFORNIA

(See Long Beach)

*Family Practice emphasizing Dissolution, Marital Contracts, Custody Issues, Wills, Trusts and Related Civil Litigation.*

---

# HARLAND W. BRAUN

### PROFESSIONAL CORPORATION

### SUITE 1800, TWO CENTURY PLAZA BUILDING

### 2049 CENTURY PARK EAST

## LOS ANGELES, CALIFORNIA 90067

Telephone: 310-277-4777

*Practice Limited to Criminal Law, State Bar Defense and Medical Board Defense.*

**FIRM PROFILE:** Mr. Braun represented Officer Theodore Briseno, acquitted in the federal Rodney King beating case; In the "Twilight Zone" manslaughter case, represented director John Landis and producer George Folsey; Represented Assembly Whip Gwen Moore in political corruption case in Sacramento; Represented attorney Vincent Bugliosi in perjury case arising out of Charles Manson prosecution; Represented Congresswoman Bobbie Fiedler in bribery case arising out of Republican Senate Primary; Represented physician Robert Nejdl in the "Kaiser Doctors" murder case establishing that a physician can disconnect an I.V. in a comatose patient; Represented Elizabeth Taylor's physician, Michael Gottlieb, in over-prescribing case.

**HARLAND W. BRAUN,** born New York, N.Y., September 21, 1942; admitted to bar, 1967, California and U.S. District Court, Central District of California. *Education:* University of California at Los Angeles (B.A., 1964); University of California School of Law at Los Angeles (J.D., 1967). Member, UCLA Law Review, 1965-1967. Deputy District Attorney, Los Angeles County, 1968-1973. Member, California Council of Criminal Justice, 1973-1975. *Member:* State Bar of California; Criminal Courts Bar Association; California Attorneys for Criminal Justice. **PRACTICE AREAS:** Criminal Law.

REFERENCE: Bank of America (Century City Office).

## BREIDENBACH, BUCKLEY, HUCHTING, HALM & HAMBLET

*A LAW CORPORATION*
Established in 1956

611 WEST SIXTH STREET, THIRTEENTH FLOOR
**LOS ANGELES, CALIFORNIA 90017-3100**
Telephone: 213-624-3431
Fax: 213-488-1493
Email: law@bbhhh.com

*Riverside, California Office:* 3403 Tenth Street, Seventh Floor. Telephone: 909-686-7058.

*Orange County Office:* 1851 East First Street, Ninth Floor, Santa Ana, California. Telephone: 714-564-2515.

*Civil Trial and Appellate Practice. Environmental, Toxic Torts, Products Liability, Professional Liability, Property and Casualty Insurance Coverage and Litigation, Fire Subrogation, Decedent's Estate Litigation and Business, Construction Defect.*

**FRANCIS BREIDENBACH,** born Oakes, North Dakota, May 12, 1930; admitted to bar, 1957, North Dakota; 1963, U.S. Supreme Court; 1965, California. *Education:* University of North Dakota (Ph.B., 1952; J.D., 1957). Phi Alpha Delta. Editor-in-Chief, North Dakota Law Review, 1956-1957. Author: "Will Contests," California Continuing Education of the Bar, 1975. Author: "What Kind of a Lawyer Should Defend Your Company Against Employee Claims," L.A. Business Journal, April 11-17, 1994. Assistant Attorney General, North Dakota, 1957-1960. *Member:* Los Angeles County and American Bar Associations; State Bar Association of North Dakota; State Bar of California (Delegate, Conference of Delegates, 1971-1978); Diplomate, American Board of Trial Advocates; Association of Southern California Defense Counsel (President, 1976-1977); Association of Business Trial Lawyers; Trial Attorneys of America; National Association of Defense Lawyers in Criminal Cases (Director, 1963-1966); Federation of Insurance and Corporate Counsel; Defense Research Institute (Area Chairman, 1983-1984). **PRACTICE AREAS:** Business Litigation; Casualty Insurance; Insurance Defense Appeals; Probate Litigation. **Email:** fbreiden@counsel.com

**HOWARD L. HALM,** born Honolulu, Hawaii, July 17, 1942; admitted to bar, 1969, California. *Education:* University of California at Los Angeles (B.A., 1965); University of San Diego (J.D., 1968). Phi Delta Phi. Notes and Comments Editor, San Diego Law Review, 1967-1968. Deputy Attorney General, California, 1969-1975. *Member:* Los Angeles County (Member: Environmental Law Section; Litigation Section, Executive Committee; Judicial Evaluation Committee, 1986; Chair, 1988) and American (Member: Sections on Litigation and Tort and Insurance Practice; Subcommittees on Environmental Litigation and Toxic Torts, Governmental Law) Bar Associations; State Bar of California (Member: Special Committee on Civil Discovery, 1978-1979; Committee on the Administration of Justice, 1980-1982; Commission on Judicial Nominees Evaluation, 1984); Defense Research Institute and Trial Lawyers Association; Association of Southern California Defense Counsel (Chair, Court Liaison and Benefits Committees, 1986-1988); California Trial Lawyers Association; Japanese American Bar Association (Member, Board of Governors, 1981-1985; President, 1985); Korean American Bar Association (Member, Board of Governors, 1981-1989; President, 1989); Asian Pacific American Legal Center (Member: Advisory Committee, 1985; Board of Directors, 1986-1989; Advisory Committee, 1990—). **PRACTICE AREAS:** Environmental Insurance Defense; Governmental Tort Liability; Municipal Defense; Products Liability Defense. **Email:** law@bbhhh.com

**STEPHEN H. HUCHTING,** born Escondido, California, April 6, 1948; admitted to bar, 1973, California. *Education:* Loyola University of Los Angeles (B.S., cum laude, 1970; J.D., 1973). Alpha Sigma Nu. Student Teaching Fellow, Loyola Law School, Legal Research and Writing, 1972-1973. Member: California Arson Prevention Committee, 1978-1988; California Conference of Arson Investigators, 1979-1989. Legal Counsel, California Arson Prevention Committee, 1986-1988. *Member:* Los Angeles County and American Bar Associations; State Bar of California; Association of Southern California Defense Counsel; Loss Executive Association. **PRACTICE AREAS:** Arson and Insurance Fraud; First Party Property Insurance; Insurance Fraud; Property Insurance Coverage; Property Subrogation. **Email:** law@bbhhh.com

**GARY A. HAMBLET,** born Lincoln, Nebraska, July 17, 1953; admitted to bar, 1979, California and U.S. District Court, Central District of California. *Education:* Stanford University (B.A., with distinction, 1976); Rutgers School of Law (J.D., with honors, 1979). Recipient, American Jurisprudence Awards in Constitutional Law and Civil Procedure, 1979. Articles Editor, Rutgers-Camden Law Journal, 1978-1979. Author: Note, "Deceptive Interrogation Techniques and The Relinquishment of Constitutional Rights," 10 Rutgers-Camden, Law Journal, 109, 1978. *Member:* State Bar of California; Defense Research Institute; Association of Southern California Defense Counsel; American Board of Trial Advocates (Associate). **PRACTICE AREAS:** Business Litigation; Civil Rights Defense; Insurance Bad Faith; Subrogation; Professional Malpractice. **Email:** law@bbhhh.com

**DANIEL J. BUCKLEY,** born Rego Park, New York, February 20, 1955; admitted to bar, 1980, California; 1981, U.S. District Court, Central District of California and U.S. Court of Appeals, Ninth Circuit. *Education:* University of Notre Dame (B.A., with honors, 1977; J.D., 1980). Member, National Moot Court Trial Team. Instructor: Civil Litigation, University of California at Los Angeles, 1985-1987; Civil Litigation and Legal Research, University of California at Irvine, 1985-1988. *Member:* Los Angeles County and American Bar Associations; State Bar of California; Association of Southern California Defense Counsel; Defense Research Institute. **PRACTICE AREAS:** Environmental Law; Government Tort Liability; Insurance Agents and Brokers Errors and Omissions; Casualty Defense; Civil Litigation. **Email:** law@bbhhh.com

**RANDI S. LEWIS,** born Baltimore, Maryland, August 23, 1955; admitted to bar, 1983, California; 1984, U.S. District Court, Central District of California; 1987, District of Columbia. *Education:* University of Maryland (B.A., 1977); George Washington University (J.D., 1983). *Member:* Los Angeles County and American Bar Associations; State Bar of California; California Women Lawyers; Association of Southern California Defense Counsel. **Email:** law@bbhhh.com

**DOUGLAS W. ANDREWS,** born Miami, Florida, August 7, 1958; admitted to bar, 1985, California. *Education:* Brigham Young University (B.A., 1982; M.P.A., 1985; J.D., 1985). *Member:* State Bar of California. **Email:** law@bbhhh.com

**SHARI L. ROSENTHAL,** born New York, New York, November 22, 1960; admitted to bar, 1985, California; 1990, U.S. District Court, Central District of California. *Education:* Syracuse University (B.A., 1982); Southwestern University School of Law (J.D., 1985). Phi Alpha Delta. *Member:* Los Angeles County and American Bar Associations; State Bar of California. **Email:** law@bbhhh.com

**LANCE S. GAMS,** born Chicago, Illinois, February 7, 1961; admitted to bar, 1986, California, U.S. District Court, Central District of California and U.S. Court of Appeals, Ninth Circuit. *Education:* University of Illinois (B.A., 1983); University of Southern California (J.D., 1986). Phi Alpha Delta; Phi Beta Kappa. Member, Moot Court Honors Program; Editor, Moot Court Board. *Member:* Los Angeles County and American Bar Associations; State Bar of California. **Email:** law@bbhhh.com

**EUGENE J. EGAN,** born Seattle, Washington, February 20, 1962; admitted to bar, 1987, California and U.S. District Court, Central District of California. *Education:* University of California at Berkeley (B.A., 1984); Loyola Marymount University (J.D., 1987). *Member:* State Bar of California. **LANGUAGES:** French. **Email:** law@bbhhh.com

**MARK K. KITABAYASHI,** born Los Angeles, California, March 18, 1960; admitted to bar, 1986, California, U.S. District Court, Central District of California and U.S. Court of Appeals, Ninth Circuit. *Education:* College of Idaho; University of California at Los Angeles (B.A., 1983); University of Southern California (J.D., 1986). Phi Alpha Delta. *Member:* State Bar of California; American Bar Association; Japanese-American Bar Association. **Email:** law@bbhhh.com

**RANDI J. THEODOSOPOULOS,** born New York, N.Y., November 9, 1963; admitted to bar, 1988, California, U.S. District Court, Central District of California and U.S. Court of Appeals, Ninth Circuit. *Education:* University of Missouri (B.J., 1985; J.D., 1988); University of Southern California. Phi Alpha Delta. Member, Inn of Court. *Member:* Los Angeles County Bar Association (Member, Litigation Section, Newsletter Editorial Board and Programs Committee); State Bar of California. **Email:** law@bbhhh.com

**M. KENDALL CAUDRY,** born Jacksonville, Florida, September, 1, 1964; admitted to bar, 1989, California, U.S. Court of Appeals, Ninth Circuit and U.S. District Court, Central District of California. *Education:* Loyola Marymount University (B.B.A., magna cum laude, 1986); Loyola Law

*(This Listing Continued)*

School (J.D., 1989). *Member:* State Bar of California; California Young Lawyers Association. *Email:* law@bbhhh.com

**LEON A. VICTOR,** born Los Angeles, California, July 16, 1965; admitted to bar, 1990, California. *Education:* University of California (B.A. in Political Science, 1987); University of San Diego (J.D., 1990). *Member:* Los Angeles County and American Bar Associations; State Bar of California. *Email:* law@bbhhh.com

---

**MICHELE VANRIPER,** born Encino, California, January 7, 1967; admitted to bar, 1991, California. *Education:* University of San Diego (B.A., magna cum laude, 1988); St. Clare's College; Loyola University of Los Angeles (J.D., 1991). Pi Sigma Alpha. *Member:* Los Angeles County and American Bar Associations; State Bar of California. *Email:* law@bbhhh.com

**MONIKA M. ARBOLES,** born Arcadia, California, August 20, 1967; admitted to bar, 1994, California. *Education:* University of California at Los Angeles (B.A., 1989); University of Southern California (J.D., 1993). Hale Moot Court Competition, Quarter Finalist. *Member:* State Bar of California. *LANGUAGES:* Spanish. *Email:* law@bbhhh.com

**MARK W. WATERMAN,** born Fresno, California, December 25, 1967; admitted to bar, 1994, California. *Education:* University of California at Los Angeles (B.S., magna cum laude, Psychology, 1991); University of California at Davis (J.D., 1994). *Email:* law@bbhhh.com

**BRIAN W. RHODES,** born Lakewood, California, July 22, 1966; admitted to bar, 1994, California. *Education:* Brigham Young University (B.S., 1991); Southwestern University School of Law (J.D., 1994). *Member:* State Bar of California. *LANGUAGES:* Spanish. *Email:* law@bbhhh.com

**CHRISTINA O. NYHAN,** born Long Beach, California, January 28, 1967; admitted to bar, 1992, California; 1994, U.S. District Court, District of California. *Education:* University of California, Santa Barbara (B.A., 1988); Pepperdine University (J.D., 1992). *Member:* Los Angeles County Bar Association; State Bar of California; The Association of Trial Lawyers of America; California Trial Lawyers Association; Los Angeles Trial Lawyers Association. *Email:* law@bbhhh.com

**KIMBERLY A. MILLINGTON,** born Pasadena, California, May 24, 1963; admitted to bar, 1993, California and U.S. District Court, Central District of California. *Education:* University of California at Los Angeles (B.A., 1987); Southwestern University School of Law (J.D., 1993). Staff Member and Research Editor, Southwestern University Law Review. Recipient: American Jurisprudence Book Award for Legal Research and Writing, 1989; Exceptional Achievement Award for Community Property, 1992; Exceptional Achievement Award for Entertainment Law, 1993; Dean's Merit Scholarship; Southwestern Affiliates Scholarship Fund. *Member:* Los Angeles County Bar Association; State Bar of California. *LANGUAGES:* French, Spanish and Italian. *Email:* law@bbhhh.com

**PAUL B. HUNDLEY,** born Reno, Nevada, September 19, 1961; admitted to bar, 1994, California. *Education:* San Francisco State University (B.A., 1985); University of California at Davis (J.D., 1994). Phi Delta Phi. *Email:* law@bbhhh.com

**ANGELA T. EDWARDS,** born Los Angeles, California, April 9, 1970; admitted to bar, 1995, California. *Education:* University of Southern California (B.S., Business, 1992); University of California at Los Angeles (J.D., 1995). Phi Delta Phi. Federal Communications and Entertainment Law Journal. Moot Court Honors Program; Board Member, Moot Court. Externed with Federal District Judge Consuela Marshall, Central District of California. *Member:* American Bar Association; Black Women Lawyers. *PRACTICE AREAS:* Environmental; Torts; Insurance; Construction Litigation. *Email:* law@bbhhh.com

**JASON S.J. KIM,** born Seoul, Republic of Korea; admitted to bar, 1992, California and U.S. District Court, District of California; 1995, Maryland. *Education:* University of California at Los Angeles (B.A., 1989; J.D., 1992). *LANGUAGES:* Korean. *PRACTICE AREAS:* Litigation. *Email:* law@bbhhh.com

**MARK E. CLOUSER,** born Harrisburg, Pennsylvania, February 15, 1963; admitted to bar, 1992, California. *Education:* College of William & Mary (B.A., 1986); Southwestern University School of Law (J.D., 1992). Member, Southwestern University Law Review. *Member:* Los Angeles County Bar Association; State Bar of California. *PRACTICE AREAS:* Civil Litigation; Business Transactions. *Email:* law@bbhhh.com

**RICKI J. SHOSS,** born Houston, Texas, August 25, 1966; admitted to bar, 1991, Texas; 1996, California. *Education:* University of Michigan

*(This Listing Continued)*

(B.B.A., 1988); University of Houston (J.D., 1991). Phi Delta Phi. Recipient, Outstanding Legal Research Award, 1988. Staff Member, Houston Journal of International Law, 1991. *Member:* Houston and American Bar Associations; Houston Young Lawyers Association. *PRACTICE AREAS:* General Litigation; Insurance Bad Faith; Construction Defect. *Email:* law@bbhhh.com

**GREGORY M. SINDERBRAND,** born Los Angeles, California, August 11, 1970; admitted to bar, 1995, California and U.S. District Court, Central District of California. *Education:* University of Arizona (B.S., cum laude, 1992); Southwestern University School of Law (J.D., 1995). *Member:* Beverly Hills and Los Angeles County Bar Associations. *PRACTICE AREAS:* Insurance Coverage; Bad Faith Litigation. *Email:* law@bbhhh.com

**MICHAEL P. BRYANT,** born Orange, California, November 16, 1967; admitted to bar, 1994, California. *Education:* University of California at Los Angeles (B.A., 1991); McGeorge School of Law (J.D., with distinction, 1994). Pacific Law Journal, 1992-1993. American Inns of Court, 1996-1997. *Email:* law@bbhhh.com

**AIDE C. ONTIVEROS,** born Los Angeles, California, September 17, 1967; admitted to bar, 1994, California; U.S. District Court, Central District of California and U.S. Court of Appeals, Ninth Circuit. *Education:* University of California at Los Angeles (B.A., 1990; J.D., 1993). *LANGUAGES:* Spanish. *PRACTICE AREAS:* Family Law; Criminal Defense; Insurance Defense. *Email:* law@bbhhh.com

**SUZANNE M. HENDERSON,** born Portland, Oregon, March 18, 1968; admitted to bar, 1993, California and U.S. District Court, Northern District of California; 1994, U.S. District Court, Eastern District of California and U.S. Court of Appeals, Ninth Circuit. *Education:* Santa Clara University (B.S., cum laude, finance, 1990); Institute of European Studies, Vienna, Austria; University of California Boalt Hall School of Law (J.D., 1993). Alpha Sigma Nu; Beta Gamma Sigma. *Member:* State Bar of California (Member, Environmental Law Section, 1993—); American Bar Association (Member, Natural Resources Section, 1993—). *PRACTICE AREAS:* Environmental Litigation; Environmental Compliance. *Email:* law@bbhhh.com

**KENNETH R. PEDROZA,** born Ventura, California, November 7, 1970; admitted to bar, 1996, California. *Education:* Stanford University (B.A., 1993); University of Arizona (J.D., cum laude, 1996). Author: "Cutting Fat or Cutting Corners: Health Care Delivery and Its Respondent Affect on Liability,"38 Ariz. L. Rev. 399. *Email:* law@bbhhh.com

**JENNIFER L. WALSLEBEN,** born Inglewood, California, August 3, 1965; admitted to bar, 1996, California. *Education:* University of Texas at Austin (B.J., 1987); Pepperdine University (J.D., 199 6). Phi Delta Phi; National Merit Scholar; First Place, Law Review Write-On Competition, 1994; Law Review Literary and Citation Editor, Fall 1995, Spring 1996. *Email:* law@bbhhh.com

*OF COUNSEL*

**DONALD A. WAY,** born Cleveland, Ohio, February 1, 1934; admitted to bar, 1965, California; 1983, U.S. Supreme Court. *Education:* University of California at Los Angeles (A.B., 1959); Loyola University of Los Angeles (LL.B., 1965). Phi Beta Kappa. *Member:* National Panel of Arbitrators, American Arbitration Association, 1969—; Panel of Arbitrators, Los Angeles Superior Court, 1974—. *Member:* Los Angeles County and American (Member, Sections on: Litigation; Tort and Insurance Practice) Bar Associations; The State Bar of California (Member, Special Committee on Civil Discovery, 1984-1985); Association of Southern California Defense Counsel (Director, 1979; Secretary-Treasurer, 1982-1983; First Vice President, 1984; President, 1985); National Association of Railroad Trial Counsel; American Board of Trial Advocates; Defense Research Institute. *Email:* law@bbhhh.com

*RETIRED*

**HOWARD D. SWAINSTON,** born Preston, Idaho, December 10, 1926; admitted to bar, 1965, California. *Education:* Utah State University; University of Utah (J.D., 1954). Phi Delta Phi. *Member:* Los Angeles County and American Bar Associations; The State Bar of California; Association of Southern California Defense Counsel. (Retired). *Email:* law@bbhhh.com

REPRESENTATIVE CLIENTS: Astra Pharmaceutical Products, Inc.; Carl Warren & Co.; Century Parking, Inc.; Crawford & Co.; Dresser Industries, Inc.; E&O Professionals; Farmers Insurance Group; General Adjustment Bureau Business Services; Medtronic, Inc.; Metropolitan Transportation Authority; National Car Rental System, Inc.; Rockwell International; Safeco Insurance

*(This Listing Continued)*

CAA547B

**BREIDENBACH, BUCKLEY, HUCHTING, HALM & HAMBLET, A LAW CORPORATION, Los Angeles—** *Continued*

Co.; State Farm Fire & Casualty Co.; Southern Pacific Transportation Co.; The Hartford; Ohio Casualty; The Stanley Works; The Travelers Insurance Companies; United States Gypsum Co.
REFERENCE: 1st Business Banks, Los Angeles, California.

## ROBERT H. BRETZ
*A PROFESSIONAL CORPORATION*
Established in 1977
520 WASHINGTON BOULEVARD, SUITE 428
**LOS ANGELES, CALIFORNIA 90292**
Telephone: 310-578-1957
FAX: 310-578-5443

*Corporate, Corporate Finance and Securities Law. Commercial Litigation.*

**ROBERT H. BRETZ,** born Wichita, Kansas, August 8, 1943; admitted to bar, 1973, California; 1977, U.S. District Court, Central District of California and U.S. Court of Appeals, Ninth Circuit. *Education:* University of Arizona (B.S., 1968; M.B.A., 1971; J.D., with distinction, 1972). Phi Delta Phi (President, 1970-1971); Order of the Coif. Recipient: University of Arizona College of Law Scholarship Award; Pima County Bar Auxiliary Scholarship Award; John S. Sundt Scholarship Award; American Jurisprudence Awards for Criminal Procedure, Evidence, Real Estate Transactions and Securities Regulation. Legal Intern to Dean Burch, Chairman of the Federal Communications Commission, Washington, D.C., 1970. Associate, Gibson, Dunn & Crutcher, 1972-1974. *Member:* Los Angeles County, (Member, Section on Corporation, Banking and Business Law) and American (Member, Section on Corporation, Banking and Business Law) Bar Associations; State Bar of California. **REPORTED CASES:** Stahl v. Gibraltar Financial Corp., 967 F.2d 335 (9th Cir. 1992).

## BRIGHT AND BROWN
**LOS ANGELES, CALIFORNIA**
(See Glendale)

*Business Litigation, Oil, Gas and Energy Law and Environmental Law.*

## BRIGHT & LORIG
*A PROFESSIONAL CORPORATION*
633 WEST FIFTH STREET, SUITE 3330
**LOS ANGELES, CALIFORNIA 90071**
Telephone: 213-627-7774
Telecopier: 213-627-8508

*Patents, Trademarks, Copyright, Antitrust and Unfair Competition Law. Trials.*

**FREDERICK A. LORIG,** born Chicago, Illinois, January 28, 1946; admitted to bar, 1973, California. *Education:* University of California (B.A., with distinction, 1969) Phi Beta Kappa; Harvard University (J.D., 1973). *Member:* Los Angeles County (Member, Litigation and Antitrust Sections) and American (Member, Litigation and Antitrust Sections) Bar Associations; The State Bar of California; Association of Business Trial Lawyers; Los Angeles Intellectual Property Law Association; American Intellectual Property Law Association. **PRACTICE AREAS:** Patent, Trade Secret and Antitrust Litigation.

**PATRICK F. BRIGHT,** born Seattle, Washington, December 4, 1943; admitted to bar, 1969, New York; 1976, California; registered to practice before U.S. Patent and Trademark Office. *Education:* Georgetown University (B.S., 1965); George Washington University (J.D., with honors, 1969); New York University (LL.M., in Taxation, 1972). *Member:* Los Angeles County Bar Association; The State Bar of California; Los Angeles Intellectual Property Law Association (President, 1985); American Intellectual Property Law Association. **PRACTICE AREAS:** Patent, Copyright, Trademark, Trade Secret and Antitrust including Litigation.

*(This Listing Continued)*

**LOIS A. STONE,** born Minneapolis, Minnesota; admitted to bar, 1989, California. *Education:* California State University at Los Angeles (B.S., 1974) Beta Gamma Sigma; Southwestern University School of Law (J.D., 1978). *Member:* Los Angeles County and American Bar Associations; The State Bar of California. **PRACTICE AREAS:** Intellectual Property Law; Litigation.

**SIDFORD LEWIS BROWN,** born Fullerton, California, June 25, 1955; admitted to bar, 1982, California. *Education:* University of California at Berkeley (B.A., 1976); Princeton University (M.S., 1979); University of Southern California (J.D., 1982). Recipient, ABA Section on State and Local Government Law School Achievement Award. *Member:* Los Angeles County and American Bar Associations; State Bar of California; Bar Association of the District of Columbia; American Economics Association. **PRACTICE AREAS:** Intellectual Property Law; Antitrust; Litigation.

**EDWARD C. SCHEWE,** born Peoria, Illinois, June 15, 1957; admitted to bar, 1989, California and U.S. Court of Appeals, Ninth Circuit; 1990, U.S. District Court, Central District of California and U.S. Court of Appeals, Federal Circuit; registered to practice before the U.S. Patent and Trademark Office. *Education:* Arizona State University (B.S., 1980); University of Illinois (M.S., 1982); Pepperdine University (J.D., 1989). Member, Moot Court Honors Board. Professional Engineer, California, 1984. *Member:* Los Angeles County and American Bar Associations; State Bar of California; American Intellectual Property Law Association; Los Angeles Intellectual Property Law Association. **PRACTICE AREAS:** Intellectual Property Law.

**BRUCE R. ZISSER,** born Los Angeles, California, December 8, 1961; admitted to bar, 1995, California. *Education:* University of California at Los Angeles (B.S.E.E., 1985); Loyola Marymount University (J.D., cum laude, 1995). Tau Beta Pi; Eta Kappa Nu; Alpha Sigma Nu; Order of the Coif. *Member:* Los Angeles Intellectual Property Law Association. [Capt., U.S. Air Force, 1985-1990]. **PRACTICE AREAS:** Intellectual Property Law; Litigation.

REFERENCE: Manufacturers Bank (Headquarters Office).

## BROBECK, PHLEGER & HARRISON LLP
*A Partnership including a Professional Corporation*
550 SOUTH HOPE STREET
**LOS ANGELES, CALIFORNIA 90071-2604**
Telephone: 213-489-4060
Facsimile: 213-745-3345
Cable Address: "Brobeck"
Telex: 181164 BPH LSA

*San Francisco, California Office:* Spear Street Tower, One Market. Telephone: 415-442-0900. Facsimile: 415-442-1010.
*Palo Alto, California Office:* Two Embarcadero Place, 2200 Geng Road. Telephone: 415-424-0160. Facsimile: 415-496-2885.
*San Diego, California Office:* 550 West C Street, Suite 1300. Telephone: 619-234-1966. Facsimile: 619-236-1403.
*Orange County, California Office:* 4675 MacArthur Court, Suite 1000, Newport Beach. Telephone: 714-752-7535. Facsimile: 714-752-7522.
*Austin, Texas Office:* Brobeck, Phleger & Harrison LLP, 301 Congress Avenue, Suite 1200. Telephone: 512-477-5495. Facsimile: 512-477-5813.
*Denver, Colorado Office:* Brobeck, Phleger & Harrison LLP, 1125 Seventeenth Street, 25th Floor. Telephone: 303-293-0760. Facsimile: 303-299-8819.
*New York, N.Y. Office:* Brobeck, Phleger & Harrison LLP, 1633 Broadway, 47th Floor. Telephone: 212-581-1600. Facsimile: 212-586-7878.
*Brobeck Hale and Dorr International Office:*
*London, England Office:* Veritas House, 125 Finsbury Pavement, London EC2A 1NQ. Telephone: 44 071 638 6688. Facsimile: 44 071 638 5888.

*General Practice, including Business and Technology, Litigation, Real Estate Litigation, Insurance Coverage Litigation, Securities Litigation, Technology Litigation, Environmental Litigation, Product Liability Litigation, Labor and Employment Law, Financial Services and Insolvency (including Bankruptcy and Loan Workout), Real Estate, and Tax/Estate Planning.*

### MANAGING PARTNER

**THOMAS P. BURKE,** born San Bernardino, California, January 29, 1938; admitted to bar, 1966, California; 1979, District of Columbia. *Education:* Loyola Marymount University (B.S., 1959); University of California at Los Angeles School of Law (J.D., 1965). Phi Delta Phi; Order of the Coif.

*(This Listing Continued)*

Senior Editor, U.C.L.A. Law Review, 1964-1965. Member, 1975—, Chairman, 1989-1992, Committee on Practice and Procedure before the National Labor Relations Board, Section on Labor and Employment Law; Member, Co-Chair, Membership and Finance Committee, Section of Labor and Employment Law, 1992—, American Bar Association. Member, Hearing Subcommittee, Committee of Bar Examiners, 1971-1973; Chairman, Hearing Subcommittee, 1973-1976, State Bar of California. *Member:* American Bar Foundation. *Email:* tburke@brobeck.com

### RESIDENT PARTNERS

**LAURIE A. ALLEN,** born Santa Monica, California, November 11, 1960; admitted to bar, 1989, California; 1990, U.S. Tax Court. *Education:* Edinburgh University, Scotland; University of California at Los Angeles (B.A., 1982); Emory University (J.D., 1988); New York University (LL.M., Taxation, 1989). Order of the Barristers. First Place, Albert R. Mugel National Moot Court Competition. Member, Special Teams, 1987 and Board of Directors, 1988, Emory Moot Court Society. Author: "Biotechnology Investment Strategies in the United States," delivered at the BioEurope '93 Conference, Brussels, Belgium, June 2, 1993. "Changes, Challenges and Strategies in Estate Tax Planning for the 1990's," ISI Investor Guide, 1990. Co-Author: "Rule 701: Securities Act of 1933 Exemption for Issuance Under Compensatory Benefit Plans," Current Developments in Private Financings, PLI, Private Placements, 1992-1993. Member, Taxation Section, State Bar of California. Member: Taxation Section; Committee of U.S. Activities of Foreigners and Tax Treaties, Taxation Section, 1992—, American Bar Association. *Email:* lallen@brobeck.com

**KENNETH R. BENDER,** born Burbank, California, February 1, 1950; admitted to bar, 1975, California. *Education:* Claremont Men's College (B.A., magna cum laude, 1972); Harvard University (J.D., 1975). *Member:* Los Angeles County (Member, Barristers Executive Committee, 1979-1981) and American (Council, Real Property, Probate and Trust Section, 1984-1986) Bar Associations. *PRACTICE AREAS:* Corporate Law; Business Law. *Email:* kbender@brobeck.com

**LINDA J. BOZUNG,** born Pasadena, California, July 17, 1944; admitted to bar, 1978, California. *Education:* Purdue University (B.S., 1969); Suffolk University (J.D., cum laude, 1977); Harvard University (LL.M., 1979). Executive Editor, Law Review, 1977. Professor of Law, Pepperdine University, 1980-1983. Member, Board of Directors, Los Angeles County Bar Foundation; American Bar Association Governing Council, Urban, State and Local Government Law Section, 1989-1991; National Chairman, Land Use Planning and Zoning Committee, 1986-1988; National Co-Chair, Hazardous Waste Subcommittee, 1984-1986; Residential Council Member, Urban Land Institute, 1992—; Chair and Board Member, Weingart Center Association, 1991—; California State Bar Committee on the Environment, 1986-1989; Founding Member, National Association of Home Builders LANDS Program; Board Member, Public Counsel, 1991-1993. *PRACTICE AREAS:* Land Use Law; Zoning, Entitlement and California Quality Act Law. *Email:* lbozung@brobeck.com

**EDMOND R. DAVIS,** born Glendale, California, September 4, 1928; admitted to bar, 1953, California. *Education:* George Pepperdine College; Hastings College of Law, University of California (J.D., 1952). Order of the Coif. Member, Chancery Club. Author: Chapter on Instructions, California Decedent Estate Practice, California Continuing Education of the Bar, 1987. California Chairman, American College of Trust and Estate Counsel, 1981-1986. Member, International Academy of Estate and Trust Law. Chairman, Estate Planning, Trust and Probate Law Section, State Bar of California, 1977-1978. Member, Executive Committee, Probate and Trust Law Section, Los Angeles County Bar Association, 1972-1974 and 1986-1989; Chair, 1974). Recipient, 1991 Arthur K. Marshall Award, Los Angeles County Bar Association. (Certified Specialist, Taxation Law, The State Bar of California Board of Legal Specialization). *PRACTICE AREAS:* Trusts and Estates Law; Planning and Litigation. *Email:* edavis@brobeck.com

**GREGG A. FARLEY,** born Sacramento, California, February 19, 1958; admitted to bar, 1984, California. *Education:* University of California at Berkeley (A.B., summa cum laude, 1981); University of California at Los Angeles (J.D., 1984). Phi Beta Kappa; Order of the Coif. Member and Editor, University of California at Los Angeles Law Review, 1982-1984. Member, "Los Angeles Lawyer" Editorial Board, 1995-1995. Author, "Reservations Needed: Insurers May Recover the Cost of Defense Damage". Author, "Going Private: Citizens Suits on the Public's Behalf". *Email:* gfarley@brobeck.com

**WILLIAM B. FITZGERALD,** born Waterbury, Connecticut, May 4, 1936; admitted to bar, 1961, Connecticut; 1962, U.S. District Court, District of Connecticut; 1971, U.S. Supreme Court; 1985, California, U.S. District Court, Central District of California and U.S. Court of Appeals, Second and Ninth Circuits. *Education:* Yale University (B.A., cum laude, 1958); Harvard University (J.D., 1961), graduate study at College of Europe, Bruges, Belgium (Cert., 1962). Author: "Direct Examination of the Medical Expert," *The Trial Masters* (Prentice Hall, 1984); "Preparing Your Witness," For The Defense (Defense Research Institute, July, 1992); "The Perils of CEO Depositions," National Law Journal (February 6, 1995). Editor, Declaratory Relief Actions Chapter of *California Civil Practice, Torts* (Bancroft-Whitney 1992). Connecticut State Trial Referee, 1984-1985. Rotary International Fellow. Vice-Chairman, Trial Techniques Committee, Torts and Insurance Practice Section, American Bar Association, 1988. *Member:* Connecticut Bar Association (Charter Member, Academy of Continuing Professional Development, 1982; Member: Judiciary Committee, 1982-1985; Judicial Liaison Committee, 1985); Association of Southern California Defense Counsel; Defense Research and Trial Lawyers Association; Connecticut Trial Lawyers Association (President, 1985); American Board of Trial Advocates. Diplomate, National Board of Trial Advocacy. Fellow, American College of Trial Lawyers. *LANGUAGES:* French, Italian. *PRACTICE AREAS:* Litigation; Products Liability Litigation; General Commercial Litigation. *Email:* wfitzgerald@brobeck.com

**DAVID M. HALBREICH,** born New York, N.Y., July 24, 1958; admitted to bar, 1983, District of Columbia; 1988, California. *Education:* State University of New York at Binghamton (B.A., Outstanding Academic Excellence, 1980); George Washington University (J.D., with honors, 1983). Phi Beta Kappa; Pi Sigma Alpha. Founder and Co-Chair, ADR Subcommittee of ABA's Insurance Coverage Committee. Author: Publications: "Coverage for High Tech Product Liabilities," Intellectual Properties; The Recorder, Spring 1995; "Lost But Not Forgotten--Proving Up Missing Coverage," San Diego Business Journal, Dec. 1994; "Paid to Prosecute: Coverage for the Costs of Pressing a Patent Infringement Action," Coverage, Vol. 4, No. 4 and Intellectual Properties; The Recorder, Spring 1994. Contributing Author: "Mandatory Prediscovery Disclosure: A First Look," ABA Section of Litigation; "Does Your Liability Insurance Cover What You Think It Covers," San Jose Business Journal, Oct. 21, 1991; "Getting Reassurance From Your Insurance," California Builder, Feb./Mar. 1992. Presentations: Emerging Issues in Coverage Litigation, Mealey's, February 1996; Issues in Coverage Litigation, Executive Enterprise, December 1995; Hot Topics on California Insurance Law, Executive Enterprises, November 1995; Bad Faith Insurance Litigation, American Conf. Institute, May 1995; ADR for the Insurance Industry, ABA, March 1995; Coverage for Construction Defects, Building Industry Assoc., March 1995; Coverage for Environmental Liabilities under D&O Policies, February 1995; American Society of Corporate Secretaries, January 19, 1995, Fundamentals of Corporate Practice, Directors and Officers Coverage; American Society of Corporate Secretaries, November 16, 1994, Directors and Officers Coverage; Environmental Coverage Litigation Update, October 12, 1994, Sonoma County Bar Association; N.A.S.F.A. Legal Forum, March 18, 1994, New Orleans, Louisiana; The Construction Superconference--The Chaning Construction Industry, November 11 - 12, 1993, San Francisco, California; Laying Evidentiary Foundations, Continuing Education of the Bar, June 1993; The Expected or Intended Clause, February 7, 1992 at PLI's symposium - Insurance, Excess, and Reinsurance Coverage Disputes 1992. Risk and Insurance Management Society, Summer 1992. *PRACTICE AREAS:* Insurance Coverage Law; Antitrust Law; General Commercial Litigation. *Email:* dhalbreich@brobeck.com

**SUSAN B. HALL,** born San Diego, California, August 22, 1951; admitted to bar, 1983, California. *Education:* San Diego State University (B.A., with honors, 1974); University of San Diego (J.D., 1982). Editor-in-Chief, San Diego Law Review, 1981-1982. Law Clerk to the Honorable Ross M. Pyle, U.S. Bankruptcy Court, 1983-1984. *PRACTICE AREAS:* Bankruptcy and Loan Workout Law. *Email:* shall@brobeck.com

**JEFFERY D. HERMANN,** born Bloomington, Indiana, October 11, 1952; admitted to bar, 1977, Hawaii; 1979, California. *Education:* University of Hawaii (B.S.M.E., 1974; J.D., 1977). Law Clerk to the Hon. Martin Pence, Senior Judge, U.S. District Court for the District of Hawaii, 1977-1979. *PRACTICE AREAS:* Bankruptcy Law; Commercial Insolvency Law; Loan Workouts. *Email:* jhermann@brobeck.com

**DAVID M. HIGGINS,** born Albany, California, December 8, 1944; admitted to bar, 1970, California; 1971, New York. *Education:* University of California at Berkeley (A.B., 1966); University of California at Los Angeles (J.D., 1969); New York University (LL.M., in Taxation, 1974). Lecturer, Practising Law Institute, "Recent Developments in the Life Insurance Industry," 1986 and "Fundamental Planning for the Closely-Held Business," 1979-1986. Member, Income Tax Committee, State Bar of California, 1978—. Chair, Committee on Taxation of Insurance Companies, Torts and

*(This Listing Continued)*

**BROBECK, PHLEGER & HARRISON LLP**, Los Angeles—
*Continued*

Insurance Practice Section, American Bar Association, 1992-1993. Chairman, Subcommittee on Personal Injury Damages, Taxation Section, American Bar Association, 1992-1993. Vice-Chair, Committee on Investments and Workouts, Taxation Section, ABA, 1995—. Member, Joint Task Force on Insurance Insolvencies, American Bar Association, 1992—. Treasurer, Personal Injury Compensation Political Action Committee, 1984-1986. Executive Director, The National Structured Settlements Trade Association, 1985-1987. *Member:* New York State Bar Association. **Email:** dhiggins@brobeck.com

**JOHN FRANCIS HILSON**, born Boston, Massachusetts, March 11, 1952; admitted to bar, 1977, Massachusetts and California. *Education:* Boston University (B.A., magna cum laude, 1973); University of Colorado (J.D., 1976). Order of the Coif. Comment Editor, University of Colorado Law Review, 1975-1976. Co-author: "Inter-Creditor Agreements," Asset Based Financing - A Transactional Guide, Matthew Bender & Co., Spring, 1985; "Aircraft Financing," Asset Based Financing - A Transactional Guide, Matthew Bender & Co., Spring, 1985. Law Clerk to Hon. John F. McGrath, Bankruptcy Judge, District of Colorado, 1975. *Member:* Financial Lawyers Conference (Member, Board of Governors, 1982-1987; President, 1987-1988); American College of Commercial Finance Attorneys. **Email:** jhilson@brobeck.com

**DREW JONES**, born Santa Monica, California, July 9, 1953; admitted to bar, 1978, California. *Education:* University of California at Berkeley (A.B., Distinction in General Scholarship with Highest Honors, 1975; J.D., 1978). Phi Beta Kappa. Member, 1976-1978 and Comments Editor, 1977-1978, Ecology Law Quarterly. [With USN, 1980-1981; USNR, 1981—]. **PRACTICE AREAS:** Business Law; Real Property Law; Finance Law; Development Law. **Email:** djones@brobeck.com

**ALBERT R. KAREL**, born Bemidji, Minnesota, November 10, 1942; admitted to bar, 1971, Wisconsin and Illinois; 1981, California. *Education:* University of Wisconsin-Madison (B.B.A., 1964; J.D., 1970). *Member:* Chicago Bar Association; State Bar of Wisconsin. **PRACTICE AREAS:** Insolvency of Banks Law; Financial Institutions Law. **Email:** akarel@brobeck.com

**GEORGE H. LINK**, born Sacramento, California, March 26, 1939; admitted to bar, 1965, California. *Education:* University of California at Berkeley (A.B., cum laude, 1961); Harvard University (LL.B., 1964). Chairman, Pacific Rim Advisory Council, 1991-1994. Member, Board of Directors, 1966-1975, President, 1972-1975, California Alumni Association (Berkeley). Member, Board of Regents of the University of California, 1974-1975. Vice President and Member, Board of Trustees, California Alumni Foundation, 1972-1975. President, Statewide Alumni Association of the University of California, 1974-1975. Chairman, Advisory Committee to the Governor of California on Selection of University Regents, 1975-1976. Member, Board of Directors International House, 1975-1981. Member, Board of Trustees: Regional Vice President, 1987-1993; California Historical Society, 1988-1994. Fellow, American Bar Foundation. (Managing Partner, 1993-1996; Managing Partner Los Angeles Office, 1975-1992). **Email:** glink@brobeck.com

**DEBRA E. POLE**, born Birmingham, Alabama, October 15, 1951; admitted to bar, 1977, Florida and U.S. District Court, Southern District of Florida; 1981, California and U.S. District Court, Central District of California; 1984, U.S. District Court, Southern District of California; 1988, U.S. District Court, Northern and Eastern Districts of California; 1991, U.S. Court of Appeals, Ninth Circuit. *Education:* Dickinson College (B.A., 1973); University of Florida (J.D., 1975). Phi Alpha Delta. Member, John Marshall Bar Association. Member, University of Florida Law Review, 1974-1975. Lecturer, Legal Writing and Research; Appellate Practice, University of Florida, Gainesville, Florida, 1975-1976. Guest Lecturer, Business Law, Jones College, West Palm Beach, Florida, 1977-1979. Lecturer, Defense Research Institute and Continuing Legal Education of the Bar. Assistant State Attorney, West Palm Beach, Florida, 1976-1980. Member, Litigation Section, American Bar Association. Member, Executive Committee, Litigation Section, The State Bar of California, 1991-1993. *Member:* Santa Monica, Langston, Los Angeles County and National; Bar Associations; The Florida Bar; Black Women Lawyers Association; Association of Southern California Defense Counsel; Defense Research Institute (Member, Steering Committee, Drug and Device Section); California Association of Black Lawyers; Federation of Insurance and Corporate Counsel. Fellow, American College of Trial Lawyers. **PRACTICE AREAS:** Products Liability; Medical Devices; Pharmaceutical Litigation. **Email:** dpole@brobeck.com

**TODD B. SEROTA**, born Philadelphia, Pennsylvania, June 25, 1958; admitted to bar, 1983, California; 1984, U.S. Court of Appeals for the Federal Circuit, U.S. District Court, Central, Northern, Southern and Eastern Districts of California and U.S. Court of Appeals, Ninth Circuit; 1992, U.S. District Court, Eastern District of Michigan; registered to practice before U.S. Patent and Trademark Office. *Education:* Massachusetts Institute of Technology (S.B., Chem. Eng., 1980); Dickinson School of Law (J.D., 1983). Member, Marshall Appellate Moot Court Team. *Member:* Century City, Los Angeles County and American Bar Associations; Association of Business Trial Lawyers; American Intellectual Property Law Association; Los Angeles Intellectual Property Law Association; Licensing Executives Society. **PRACTICE AREAS:** Intellectual Property; Litigation; Licensing. **Email:** tserota@brobeck.com

**V. JOSEPH STUBBS**, born Washington, D.C., March 19, 1949; admitted to bar, 1975, Missouri and U.S. Tax Court; 1977, California. *Education:* Montgomery Junior College and Southwest Missouri State University (B.A., 1972); University of Missouri at Kansas City (J.D., 1975). *Member:* The Missouri Bar. **Email:** jstubbs@brobeck.com

**WILLIAM K. SWANK**, born College Station, Texas, February 22, 1951; admitted to bar, 1976, California. *Education:* Pomona College (B.A., magna cum laude, 1973); Stanford University (J.D., 1976). Phi Beta Kappa. Member, Stanford Law Review, 1975-1976. **Email:** wswank@brobeck.com

**JEFFREY S. TURNER**, born Owensboro, Kentucky, October 16, 1955; admitted to bar, 1979, California. *Education:* University of Kentucky (B.A., with highest distinction, 1976); Duke University (J.D., with high distinction, 1979). Phi Beta Kappa; Order of the Coif. Editorial Board, Duke Law Journal, 1978-1979. Regent, American College of Commercial Finance Lawyers, 1995—; Fellow, American College of Commercial Finance Lawyers, 1994—; Advisor of the Business Law Section of the State Bar of California to the Drafting Committee to Revise Article 9 of the Uniform Commercial Code, 1993—; Chair, Secured Lending Subcommittee, Commercial Financial Services Committee, Business Law Section, American Bar Association, 1994—; Advisor, Council of Section Chairs, State Bar of California, 1995-1996; Chair, Council of Section Chairs, State Bar of California, 1994-1995; Vice Chair, Council of Section Chairs, State Bar of California, 1993-1994; Advisor, Business Law Section, State Bar of California, 1993-1994; Chair, Business Law Section, State Bar of California, 1992-1993; Vice Chair, Business Law Section, State Bar of California, 1991-1992; Treasurer, Business Law Section, State Bar of California, 1990-1991; Chair, Uniform Commercial Code Committee, State Bar of California, 1988-1989; Vice Chair, Uniform Commercial Code Committee, State Bar of California, 1987-1988; Delegate to the Conference of Delegates of the State Bar of California, 1992-1994; Advisor, Commercial Law and Bankruptcy Section, Los Angeles County BAr Association, 1996-1997; Chair, Commercial Law and Bankruptcy Section, Los Angeles County Bar Association, 1995-1996; Vice Chair, Commercial Law and Bankruptcy Section, Los Angeles County Bar Association, 1994-1995; Secretary, Commercial Law and Bankruptcy Section, Los Angeles County Bar Association, 1993-1994; Treasurer, Commercial Law and Bankruptcy Section, Los Angeles County Bar Association, 1992-1993; Chair, Commercial Law Committee, Commercial Law and Bankruptcy Section, Los Angeles County Bar Association, 1989-1992; President, Financial Lawyers Conference, 1991-1992; Vice President, Financial Lawyers Conference, 1990-1991; Secretary, Financial Lawyers Conference, 1989-1990. **PRACTICE AREAS:** Commercial Law; Banking Law; Financial Services Law; Loan Restructuring Law; Workouts Law; Bankruptcy Law. **Email:** jturner@brobeck.com

**DANIEL J. TYUKODY**, born Passaic, New Jersey, August 14, 1956; admitted to bar, 1986, California. *Education:* Duke University (B.S., magna cum laude, with distinction, 1978); University of Chicago (J.D., 1985). Associate Editor, University of Chicago Law Review, 1984-1985. Author: Comment, "Good Faith Inquiries Under the Bankruptcy Code," 52 University of Chicago Law Review 795, 1985. Co-Author with H. Saferstein, "Expert Discovery Under the Federal Rules and the California Code of Civil Procedure," The State of the Art Trial, Association of Business Trial Lawyers, 1986. Member: Litigation Section, State Bar of California; Sections of Litigation, Antitrust, American Bar Association. **PRACTICE AREAS:** Litigation; Securities Law; Antitrust Law; Patent Law; Insurance Law. **Email:** dtyukody@brobeck.com

**KENNETH L. WAGGONER**, born Los Angeles, California, May 8, 1948; admitted to bar, 1973, California. *Education:* California State University (B.A., cum laude, 1970; Loyola University (J.D., cum laude, 1973). St. Thomas More Law Honor Society (Member, Executive Board, 1971-1973).

*(This Listing Continued)*

Member, Loyola Law Review, 1971-1973. Teaching Fellow, Legal Research & Writing, Loyola School of Law, 1973. *Member:* Los Angeles County (Secretary-Treasurer, Barristers, 1980; Chairperson, Activities and Services Committee, Barristers, 1980; Vice President, Barristers, 1981-1982) and American (Region 9 Chairman, Disaster Legal Assistance Program, Young Lawyers Division, 1979; Chairman, Committee on Judicial Administration, Young Lawyers Division, 1979-1980; Liaison to the Judicial Administration Division, Young Lawyers Division, 1979-1981; Chairperson, Publicity Committee, Young Lawyers Division, 1980) Bar Associations; The State Bar of California. (Managing Partner, Los Angeles Office, 1993—). *PRACTICE AREAS:* Environmental Law; Petroleum Marketing Litigation; Insurance Coverage Litigation. *Email:* kwaggoner@brobeck.com

**GERARD J. WALSH,** born Brooklyn, New York, July 27, 1953; admitted to bar, 1978, California. *Education:* University of Pennsylvania (B.A., 1975); University of California at Berkeley (J.D., 1978). *PRACTICE AREAS:* Real Estate Law; Banking Law; Financial Services Law. *Email:* gwalsh@brobeck.com

**JOHN J. WASILCZYK,** born Jersey City, New Jersey, June 16, 1949; admitted to bar, 1977, California. *Education:* Monmouth College (B.S., 1971); University of California at Berkeley (M.S., 1973; J.D., 1977). Order of the Coif. Member, 1975-1977 and Articles Editor, 1976-1977, California Law Review. Extern Clerk to the Hon. Donald Wright, Chief Justice, California Supreme Court, 1976. Member: Committee on Trial Attorney Project, Los Angeles County Bar Association, 1979-1980; Section of Natural Resources, Energy and Environmental Law; Labor Law Section, American Bar Association, 1978—. *PRACTICE AREAS:* Environmental Law; Employment Law; Petroleum Marketing Litigation; Insurance Coverage Litigation; General Business Litigation. *Email:* jwasilczyk@brobeck.com

**MICHAEL S. WHALEN,** born Minneapolis, Minnesota, June 14, 1954; admitted to bar, 1979, California. *Education:* California State University, Fullerton (B.A., with high honors, 1976); Boalt Hall School of Law, University of California (J.D., 1979). Order of the Coif; Phi Kappa Phi (Fellow); Beta Gamma Sigma. Associate Editor, 1977-1978 and Publication Editor, 1978-1979, California Law Review. Director, Moot Court Program, 1978-1979. Trustee: John Stauffer Charitable Trust, 1993—. Member: Board of Directors, Constitutional Rights Foundation, 1990-1993; Board of Fellows, Center for Creative Photography, University of Arizona, 1991—; Member: Board of Advisors, Center for Organization and Behavioral Sciences, Claremont Graduate School, 1994—; Board of Directors, Pasadena Child Health Foundation, 1990-1991. Member: Board of Directors, Orthopaedic Hospital Foundation, 1996—. *Member:* Los Angeles County Bar Association (Member, Section on Taxation; Chairman, Vice Chairman & Secretary, Executive Committee, Trusts and Estates Section, 1985-1992). (Board Certified, Estate Planning, Trust and Probate Law, The State Bar of California Board of Legal Specialization). *Email:* mwhalen@brobeck.com

**MICHAEL T. ZARRO,** born Newark, New Jersey, September 30, 1955; admitted to bar, 1983, California. *Education:* University of California at Los Angeles (B.A., cum laude, 1978; J.D., 1983). *PRACTICE AREAS:* General Civil Litigation. *Email:* mzarro@brobeck.com

### OF COUNSEL

**TOM BRADLEY,** born 1917; admitted to bar, 1957, California. *Education:* University of California, Los Angeles; Southwestern University (J.D., 1956). *PRACTICE AREAS:* Corporate Law. *Email:* tbradley@brobeck.com

**CHRIS STEVEN JACOBSEN,** born Burbank, California, June 2, 1957; admitted to bar, 1981, California. *Education:* Loyola Marymount University (B.A., magna cum laude, 1978); University of California at Los Angeles School of Law (J.D., 1981). *PRACTICE AREAS:* General Corporate Law; Financial Services Law. *Email:* cjacobsen@brobeck.com

**EARLE MILLER,** born Los Angeles, California, April 14, 1960; admitted to bar, 1984, California. *Education:* Harvard University (A.B., cum laude, 1981); University of Chicago (J.D., 1984). *PRACTICE AREAS:* Commercial Litigation; Banking Litigation; Employment Law. *Email:* emiller@brobeck.com

**JOHN A. PAYNE, JR.,** born Lakewood, Ohio, May 15, 1948; admitted to bar, 1973, Ohio; 1976, California. *Education:* Baldwin-Wallace College (B.A., cum laude, 1970); University of Michigan (J.D., cum laude, 1973). Staff Editor, University of Michigan Journal of Law Reform, 1972-1973. Co-Author: "Will Contests," CEB, California Decedent Estate Practice Vol. 3, 1987. Member, Executive Committee, Trust and Estate Section, Los Angeles County Bar Association, 1989-1992; Vice Chair, Trust and Estate

*(This Listing Continued)*

Section, 1995-1996. [Lt., JAGC, USNR, 1974-1977]. *PRACTICE AREAS:* Tax. *Email:* jpayne@brobeck.com

**THOMAS H. PETRIDES,** born Hartford, Connecticut, February 2, 1959; admitted to bar, 1984, California, U.S. District Court, Northern, Southern, Eastern and Central Districts of California and U.S. Court of Appeals, Ninth Circuit. *Education:* Boston College (A.B., cum laude, 1981); University of Southern California (J.D., 1984). Member, 1982-1983 and Editor, 1983-1984, Hale Moot Court Honors Program. President, University of Southern California Student Bar Association, 1983-1984. Member, Section of Labor and Employment Law; Committee on the Development of the Law Under the National Labor Relations Act, 1992—, American Bar Association. *Member:* Los Angeles County Bar Association. *PRACTICE AREAS:* Labor and Employment. *Email:* tpetrides@brobeck.com

### RESIDENT ASSOCIATES

**Michael L. Armstrong; David W. Berry; Kara L. Bue; Richard L. Daniels; Paul M. Gleason; Marcia Z. Gordon; John Hameetman; Bruce W. Hepler** (Not admitted in CA); **Bernard C. Jasper; Jamie L. Johnson; Wayne E. Johnson; Brian W. Kasell; Patty H. Le; Howard L. Magee; Christopher J. Menjou; Chaka C. Okadigbo** (admission pending).; **Cynthia M. Patton; Braden W. Penhoet; Howard M. Privette; Douglas C. Rawles; Steven J. Renshaw; Eddie Rodriguez; David L. Schrader; Konrad F. Schreier, III; Jody L. Spiegel; Raymond T. Sung; Edward D. Totino; David R. Venderbush; Daniel I. Villapando; Todd W. Walker; Perrie M. Weiner; Daniel Weisberg; Gerard Wiener** (admission pending).; **Pamela J. Yates; Thomas B. Youth; Gregg Zucker.**

### CONTRACT ATTORNEY

**GARY D. ROTHSTEIN,** born Los Angeles, California, December 28, 1957; admitted to bar, 1989, California. *Education:* San Diego State University (A.B., with honors, with distinction in Psychology, 1979); University of Santa Clara School of Law (J.D., 1983). *PRACTICE AREAS:* Trusts and Estates; Estate Planning; Probate.

All Members and Associates of the Firm are Members of the State Bar of California, American Bar Association and the Los Angeles County Bar Association.
Brobeck, Phleger & Harrison and Brobeck Hale and Dorr International have a joint venture office in London, England.

---

## JONATHAN A. BROD LAW CORPORATION

Established in 1992

*1801 CENTURY PARK EAST, 25TH FLOOR*
**LOS ANGELES, CALIFORNIA 90067**
Telephone: 310-556-2282
Facsimile: 310-556-2024

*Estate Planning, Probate, Wills and Trusts, Tax Planning and Litigation, Pensions, Corporate and General Business.*

*FIRM PROFILE:* Sole practitioner since February 1, 1992. Practiced tax and estate planning since early 1971, starting as a trial lawyer for the I.R.S. and spending 11 years as a shareholder (including managing partner) of Valensi, Rose & Magaram in Los Angeles.

**JONATHAN A. BROD,** born Los Angeles, California, September 19, 1946; admitted to bar, 1971, California. *Education:* Purdue University (B.A., 1967); Cornell University (J.D., 1970). Author: "Tax Planning for Professionals," "Tax Shelters," and "Retirement Plans for the Professional," all chapters of Financial Planning for the Independent Professional, a Wiley— Interscience Publication, 1978; Articles, "Settling the Corporate Debt: Who Gets Taxed?" Los Angeles Lawyer, February, 1979; "Nonsimultaneous Real Estate Exchanges--Important Problems and Pitfalls of Starker," Taxes, The Tax Magazine, June, 1980, reprinted in Beverly Hills Bar Association Journal, Summer, 1980; "Recent Developments in Corporate Liquidations," Major Tax Planning, September, 1980; "Exercise Caution in Forming Sec. 337 Liquidating Trusts," Taxes, The Tax Magazine, January, 1981; "Tax Planning for the Liquidating Corporation That Owes Money To Its Shareholders," Taxation for Accountants, October, 1980 and Taxation for Lawyers, November-December, 1980; "Liquidations Involving Shareholder Creditors--Tax Traps for the Unwary," Journal of Corporate Taxation, December, 1980; "Section 337 Liquidating Trusts Revisited--The IRS Revises Rev. Proc. 79-1," Taxes, The Tax Magazine, May, 1981, reprinted by the National Tax Education Program of the AICPA; "Use of Disclaimers and QTIP Elections to Cure Defective Marital Deduction Provisions," Beverly Hills Bar Association Journal, Fall, 1985. Adjunct Professor of Law, San

*(This Listing Continued)*

### JONATHAN A. BROD LAW CORPORATION, Los Angeles—Continued

Fernando Valley School of Law, 1975-1978. Lecturer, University of Southern California Tax Institute, 1980. Trial Counsel for Tax Court Division, Office of Regional Counsel, Internal Revenue Service, 1970-1975. Founder and Director, Tax Court Pro Se Program, Co-sponsored by Beverly Hills, Los Angeles County and Century City Bar Associations, 1979-1989. *Member:* Beverly Hills (Nominee for the 1986 Ninth Circuit Judicial Conference Pro Bono Service Award; Board of Governors, 1986-1988) and Los Angeles County (Nominee for the 1985 California State Bar Pro Bono Services Award) Bar Associations; The State Bar of California.

---

## ROGER J. BRODERICK
700 SOUTH FLOWER STREET, SUITE 500
LOS ANGELES, CALIFORNIA 90017
Telephone: 213-626-8711

*Insurance Defense.*

**ROGER J. BRODERICK,** born New York, N.Y., January 17, 1933; admitted to bar, 1961, California. *Education:* University of Scranton and University of California at Los Angeles (A.B., 1957); University of California at Los Angeles (LL.B., 1960). Lecturer in Law, La Verne College Law Center, 1973 and 1975. Panelist, "Privileges for the Trial and Business Lawyer," California Continuing Education of the Bar, 1984. *Member:* Los Angeles County, San Bernardino County and American Bar Associations; The State Bar of California; American Board of Trial Advocates (Diplomate).

---

## BRONSON, BRONSON & McKINNON LLP

A Partnership including Professional Corporations
444 SOUTH FLOWER STREET, 24TH FLOOR
LOS ANGELES, CALIFORNIA 90071
Telephone: 213-627-2000
Fax: 213-627-2277

*San Francisco, California Office:* 505 Montgomery Street. Telephone: 415-986-4200.
*San Jose, California Office:* 10 Almaden Boulevard, Suite 600. Telephone: 408-293-0599.

General Civil, Trial and Appellate and General Business Practice. Commercial Law and Secured Transactions, Bankruptcy, Insolvency, Business Reorganization, Real Estate, Federal and State Litigation, Corporate Partnerships, Federal, State and Local Taxation, Financial Institutions, Estate Planning.

### RESIDENT PARTNERS

**ERIC A. AMADOR,** born Boston, Massachusetts, June 26, 1963; admitted to bar, 1989, California. *Education:* University of California at Berkeley (A.B., 1986); University of California at Los Angeles; Hastings College of the Law, University of California (J.D., 1989). California Graduate Fellow. Recipient, American Jurisprudence Award for: Insurance Law; Appellate Process. Production Editor, Hastings Constitutional Law Quarterly. *Email:* EAmador@bronson.com

**DONNA P. ARLOW,** born Toronto, Canada, October 17, 1956; admitted to bar, 1981, California. *Education:* California State University at Long Beach (B.A., 1978); University of San Diego (J.D., 1981). *Member:* Los Angeles County and American (Tort and Insurance Practice Section) Bar Associations; Association of Southern California Defense Counsel. *PRACTICE AREAS:* Insurance Coverage Litigation. *Email:* DArlow@bronson.com

**STEPHEN L. BACKUS,** born New York, N.Y., March 16, 1951; admitted to bar, 1980, California and Texas. *Education:* Colgate University (B.A., 1973); Pepperdine University (J.D., 1980). *Member:* The Defense Research Institute; Building Industry Association of Southern California. *PRACTICE AREAS:* Civil Litigation; Construction and Real Estate Law and Professional Liability. *Email:* SBackus@bronson.com

**CHARLES N. BLAND, JR.,** born Washington, D.C., September 19, 1954; admitted to bar, 1980, California. *Education:* Tufts University (B.A., 1976); Georgetown University (J.D., 1979). Member, Board of Governors, Civil Trial Department, Bureau of National Affairs, 1984. *PRACTICE AREAS:* Employment; Wrongful Termination; Commercial Litigation; Construction Litigation. *Email:* CBland@bronson.com

*(This Listing Continued)*

CAA552B

---

**BRETON AUGUST BOCCHIERI,** born New Jersey, October 14, 1955; admitted to bar, 1985, California; registered to practice before U.S. Patent and Trademark Office. *Education:* Rutgers College, Rutgers University (B.A., 1978); Middlesex County College (A.S.E.E.T., 1982); Franklin Pierce Law Center (J.D., specializing in Intellectual Property Law, 1985). Author: "The Trap of Willful Patent Infringement: A Corporate Dilemma," Idea: The Journal of Law and Technology, Vol. 29, 1988 cited in 5, Chism, A Treatise on the Law of Patentability, Validity and Infringement, 20.30 (4)(b)(v), 1994; "Obtaining Attorney's Fees in Intellectual Property Cases, Rule 11 and other Sanctioning Mechanisms, " Idea: The Journal of Law and Technology, Vol. 33, 1993; "The Reluctant Plaintiff: The Court of Appeals Upholds Stiff Discovery, Sanctions In Refac International, Ltd. v. Hitachi, Ltd. et al.," published in Westlaw Hot Topics, 1990. Co-Author: "Strategic Considerations For A Defendant In A Patent Enforcement Action," published by the Sunnyvale Center For Invention, Innovation and Ideas, January 1996. *Member:* Los Angeles, Century City (Co-Chairman, Patent, Copyrights and Trademark Section) and American (Vice-Chair, Committee on Intellectual Property, Tort and Insurance Section) Bar Associations; State Bar of California (Editor, New Matter, The Official Publication of the Intellectual Property Section); Los Angeles Intellectual Property Law Association; American Business Trial Lawyers Association. *PRACTICE AREAS:* Intellectual Property Litigation emphasis on litigation involving complex technologies. *Email:* BBocchieri@bronson.com

**JOHN D. BOYLE,** born Pasadena, California, January 30, 1957; admitted to bar, 1982, California. *Education:* University of California at Berkeley (B.A., magna cum laude, 1979); Hastings College of Law, University of California at San Francisco (J.D., 1982). *PRACTICE AREAS:* Insurance Bad Faith; Professional Liability; Civil Litigation. *Email:* JBoyle@bronson.com

**THOMAS T. CARPENTER,** born Queens, New York, February 18, 1948; admitted to bar, 1981, California and Colorado; 1983, Alaska. *Education:* United States Naval Academy (B.S., 1970); Golden Gate University School of Law (J.D., 1980). *Member:* Alaska and Colorado Bar Associations; Aviation Insurance Association; Association for Transportation Law, Logistics and Policy. [Major, USMCR, 1970-1980]. *PRACTICE AREAS:* Aviation; Transportation; Product Liability; Civil Litigation. *Email:* TCarpenter@bronson.com

**WILLIAM B. CREIM,** born Seattle, Washington, May 12, 1954; admitted to bar, 1979, California. *Education:* University of California at Los Angeles (B.A., summa cum laude, with highest departmental honors, 1976); University of Southern California (J.D., 1979). Phi Beta Kappa; Order of the Coif; Phi Delta Phi; Pi Gamma Mu. Recipient, American Jurisprudence Award in Constitutional Law. Member, 1977-1979 and Note Editor and Member, Editorial Board, 1978-1979, Southern California Law Review. Author: "The Buckley Amendment and a Student's Right of Access to His Letters of Recommendation," 52 Southern California Law Review, 1979. *Member:* The State Bar of California; Conference of Financial Lawyers; Legion Lex (Member, Board of Directors). *PRACTICE AREAS:* Commercial Law and Secured Transactions; Creditors' Rights, Bankruptcy and Antitrust. *Email:* WCreim@bronson.com

**L. MORRIS DENNIS (A PROFESSIONAL CORPORATION),** born Pomona, California, August 26, 1939; admitted to bar, 1965, California. *Education:* Stanford University (B.A., 1961); University of California at Los Angeles (J.D., 1964); University of Southern California (LL.M., 1969). Assistant Editor, University of Southern California Tax Institute, 1968. *Member:* Beverly Hills and Los Angeles County Bar Associations; State Bar of California (Member, Sections on Business Law; Taxation). *PRACTICE AREAS:* Taxation; Estate Planning; Bankruptcy; Corporations and Partnerships. *Email:* LMDennis@bronson.com

**LUCINDA DENNIS (A PROFESSIONAL CORPORATION),** born Los Angeles, California; admitted to bar, 1966, California. *Education:* University of Colorado (B.A., 1962); University of California at Los Angeles (J.D., 1965). Phi Delta Delta. *Member:* Los Angeles County (Member, Sections on Commercial Law and Bankruptcy) and American (Member, Sections on Corporation, Banking and Business Law) Bar Associations; Bankruptcy Study Group (Member, Executive Board, 1981—); Conference of Financial Lawyers (President, 1980-1981; Member, Board of Governors, 1977—). *PRACTICE AREAS:* Creditors Rights; Bankruptcy; Business Reorganization; Commercial Law; Secured Transactions. *Email:* LDennis@bronson.com

**ELIZABETH A. ERSKINE,** born Hartford, Connecticut, February 26, 1956; admitted to bar, 1986, California. *Education:* Northeastern University (B.S., with high honors, 1979); Boston College (J.D., 1986). *PRAC-*

*(This Listing Continued)*

**TICE AREAS:** Business Litigation; Banking Litigation; Professional Liability Litigation. **Email:** EErskine@bronson.com

**EDWIN W. GREEN,** born Santa Barbara, California, November 27, 1935; admitted to bar, 1960, California. *Education:* University of Southern California (B.S., 1957; LL.B., 1960). Phi Delta Phi. Listed in "The Best Lawyers in America"-Published by Woodward/White, 1987-1993. Founder, National Women's Advocacy Institute, 1989. *Member:* American Board of Trial Advocates; Fellow, American College of Trial Lawyers; Federation of Insurance and Corporate Counsel; International Bar Association. **PRACTICE AREAS:** Jury Trials. **Email:** EGreen@bronson.com

**CLAUDIA L. GREENSPOON,** born Burbank, California, September 30, 1957; admitted to bar, 1983, California. *Education:* University of California at Los Angeles (B.A., cum laude, 1978); Southwestern University (J.D., 1983). Delta Theta Phi. Recipient, American Jurisprudence Award in Constitutional Law. *Member:* Los Angeles County (Member, Section on Real Estate) and American (Member, Section on Litigation) Bar Associations; The State Bar of California (Member, Sections on Real Property Law and Litigation; Financial Lawyers Conference); Women's Lawyer Association. **LANGUAGES:** Hebrew. **PRACTICE AREAS:** Commercial and Business Litigation; Real Estate Brokerage Defense. **Email:** CGreenspoon@bronson.com

**STUART I. KOENIG,** born New York, N.Y., August 23, 1956; admitted to bar, 1982, California. *Education:* University of California at Los Angeles (B.A., 1978); Loyola University of Los Angeles (J.D., 1981). Member, Moot Court Honors Program. *Member:* Los Angeles County (Member, Section on Commercial Law and Bankruptcy) and American (Member, Section on Litigation) Bar Associations. **PRACTICE AREAS:** Federal and State Litigation; Bankruptcy Litigation and Commercial Law. **Email:** SKoenig@bronson.com

**RALPH S. LAMONTAGNE, JR.,** born Boston, Massachusetts, September 2, 1954; admitted to bar, 1979, California. *Education:* University of California at Los Angeles (B.A., cum laude, 1976); Southwestern University (J.D., cum laude, 1979). *Member:* Lawyer-Pilots Bar Association. **PRACTICE AREAS:** Insurance Coverage; Civil Appellate Law. **Email:** RLaMontagne@bronson.com

**RICHARD C. MACIAS,** born Walsenburg, Colorado, May 29, 1950; admitted to bar, 1976, California; 1990, Colorado. *Education:* Pomona College (B.A., 1972); Harvard University (J.D., 1975). Member, Harvard Civil Rights-Civil Liberties Law Review, 1974-1975. Associate Professor, Loyola Law School, 1984-1989: Special Counsel to the City Attorney of Los Angeles, 1978. *Member:* Los Angeles County and American Bar Associations; Federal Courts Bar Association. **PRACTICE AREAS:** Federal and State Litigation; Commercial Law and Bankruptcy. **Email:** RMacias@bronson.com

**DANI H. ROGERS,** born Los Angeles, California, January 22, 1962; admitted to bar, 1987, California. *Education:* University of California at Los Angeles (B.A., 1984); University of San Francisco (J.D., magna cum laude, 1987). Author: Casenote, "Dealing Defective Drugs-Limiting Pharmacist and Manufacturer Liability: Murphy v. E.R. Squibb & Sons, Inc.," 21 U.S.F. Law Review 1973, 1986. Recipient, American Jurisprudence Award in Property. Adjunct Faculty, Trial Practice-Civil, Whittier College of Law, 1993. *Member:* Los Angeles County Bar Association; Women Lawyer's Association of Los Angeles. **LANGUAGES:** Spanish. **PRACTICE AREAS:** Product Liability and Personal Injury Litigation. **Email:** DRogers@bronson.com

**MANUEL SALDAÑA,** born Los Angeles, California, March 9, 1963; admitted to bar, 1988, California. *Education:* Stanford University (A.B., 1985); Hastings College of the Law, University of California (J.D., 1988). Editor, Hastings Law Journal, 1987-1988. Extern, California Supreme Court, Justice John Arguelles. Board Trustee, Mexican-American Bar Association. Member, Latino Who's Who. **LANGUAGES:** Spanish. **PRACTICE AREAS:** Civil Litigation; Product Liability. **Email:** MSaldana@bronson.com

**DAVID M. WALSH,** born Arcadia, California, March 19, 1961; admitted to bar, 1985, California. *Education:* University of California at Los Angeles; University of California at Santa Barbara (B.A., 1982); University of Southern California (J.D., 1985). Law Clerk to the Honorable Howard B. Turrentine, U.S. District Court, Southern District of California, 1988-1989. Editor, Major Tax Planning, 1984-1985. Editor, Computer/Law Journal, 1984-1985. **PRACTICE AREAS:** Commercial and Environmental Litigation; Commercial Law. **Email:** DWalsh@bronson.com

**SHELDON J. WARREN,** born Inglewood, California, March 27, 1948; admitted to bar, 1980, California; 1982, Nebraska. *Education:* University of California at Los Angeles (B.A., 1970); University of San Francisco School of Law (J.D., cum laude, 1980). Adjunct Professor, Whittier College School of Law. Member, American Bar Association Standing Committee on Lawyer Referral and Information Service, 1990-1993. Co-Chair, State Bar of California Standing Committee on Lawyer Referral and Information Services, 1990-1992. *Member:* Los Angeles County Bar Association (Chair, Lawyer Referral and Information Service Advisory Committee, 1985-1987); California Attorneys for Criminal Justice. **PRACTICE AREAS:** Product Liability; Personal Injury. **Email:** SWarren@bronson.com

*OF COUNSEL*

**DAVID L. HORGAN,** born Quincy, Massachusetts, 1956; admitted to bar, 1981, California. *Education:* Waseda University, Tokyo, Japan; University of Southern California (B.A., 1978; J.D., 1981). Member, Hale Moot Court Honors Program. Director, 1987— and President, 1992, California-Taiwan Trade and Investment Council. *Member:* Los Angeles County (Member, Commercial Law and Bankruptcy Section) and American Bar Associations; Financial Lawyers Conference; Korea Society (Director, Executive Committee, 1986—). **LANGUAGES:** Japanese. **PRACTICE AREAS:** International Law; Corporate and Business; Financial Institutions; Bankruptcy. **Email:** DHorgan@bronson.com

**ROBERT WEBER, JR.,** born Los Angeles, California, March 27, 1951; admitted to bar, 1976, California. *Education:* University of Southern California (B.A., magna cum laude, 1973) Phi Beta Kappa; Harvard University (J.D., 1976). *Member:* Los Angeles County (Sections on Real Estate and Commercial Law) and American Bar Associations. **PRACTICE AREAS:** Real Estate Law; Real Estate Finance Law; Corporate Law; Securities Law; Business and Commercial Law. **Email:** RWeber@bronson.com

*RESIDENT ASSOCIATES*

**JANET ANDREA,** born New York, N.Y., October 4, 1960; admitted to bar, 1986, California. *Education:* University of Southern California (B.A., magna cum laude, 1983); Hastings College of the Law, University of California (J.D., 1986). **PRACTICE AREAS:** Civil Litigation; Bad Faith Litigation. **Email:** JAndrea@bronson.com

**RAYMON B. BILBEAUX, III,** born Belvedere, California, March 31, 1959; admitted to bar, 1991, California. *Education:* California State University at Northridge (B.A., 1986); University of Southern California (J.D., 1991). Editor, Computer Law Journal. **Email:** RBilbeaux@bronson.com

**LAURIE K. JONES,** born New Ulm, Minnesota, February 4, 1964; admitted to bar, 1995, California. *Education:* University of Wisconsin-LaCrosse (B.A., with honors, 1986); Southwestern University School of Law (J.D., cum laude, 1995). Member, Southwestern University Law Review, 1993-1994. Listed: Who's Who Among American Law Students, 13th, 14th and 15th eds, 1993-1995. Alternate Oral Finalists: Intramural Moot Court Competition, 1992. Recipient: American Jurisprudence Book Awards: Legal Research and Writing (1992); Criminal Law (1991); West's Corpus Juris Secundum Award: Criminal Law (1991). *Member:* Los Angeles County and American Bar Associations; The State Bar of California; Los Angeles Bankruptcy Forum; California Women Lawyers Association; Lawyers for Human Rights. **PRACTICE AREAS:** Bankruptcy; Creditors' Rights; Commercial Litigation. **Email:** LJones@bronson.com

**LAURIE S. JULIEN,** born Chicago, Illinois, July 22, 1962; admitted to bar, 1988, California. *Education:* University of California at Los Angeles (B.A., cum laude, 1984); Hastings College of the Law, University of California (J.D., 1988). Note Editor and Member, Hastings International and Comparative Law Review, 1987-1988. **PRACTICE AREAS:** Insurance Coverage and Bad Faith; Civil Litigation; Appellate. **Email:** LJulien@bronson.com

**CHARLES E. KORO,** born Boston, Massachusetts, April 21, 1951; admitted to bar, 1992, California. *Education:* University of Massachusetts (B.A., in theater and speech education, cum laude, 1973); Southwestern University (J.D., magna cum laude, 1992). Member, Southwestern University Law Review, Moot Court Honors Program. Recipient: American Jurisprudence Awards in Civil Practice, Criminal Procedure, Criminal Law, Property, Trial Advocacy, Dispute Resolution, Wills and Trusts, Remedies and Uniform Commercial Code. Licensed Real Estate Broker, California, 1988. **Email:** CKoro@bronson.com

**KATHLEEN R. O'LAUGHLIN,** born Niagara Falls, New York, November 23, 1954; admitted to bar, 1982, California. *Education:* University of Notre Dame (B.A., 1976); University of Southern California (M.S.L.S., 1977); Loyola University of Los Angeles (J.D., 1982). Legal Research Instructor and Reference Librarian, Southwestern University School of Law,

*(This Listing Continued)*

### BRONSON, BRONSON & McKINNON LLP, Los Angeles—Continued

Fall, 1979 and 1980. *PRACTICE AREAS:* Business Litigation. *Email:* KOLaughlin@bronson.com

**HAYLEY L. SNEIDERMAN,** born Portsmouth, Virginia, November 19, 1966; admitted to bar, 1994, California. *Education:* University of California, San Diego (B.A., 1989); University of California, Davis (J.D., 1994). Editor, University of California, Davis Law Review. Recipient, American Jurisprudence Award in Civil Procedure. *Email:* HSneiderman@bronson.com

**JOHN F. STEPHENS,** born Philadelphia, Pennsylvania, May 25, 1968; admitted to bar, 1995, California. *Education:* Rutgers University (B.S., with high honors, 1990; J.D., with honors, 1995). Notes and Casenotes Editor, Rutgers Law Journal, 1994-1995. Author: "The Denaturalization and Extradition of Ivan the Terrible," Rutgers Law Journal, Vol. 26, No. 3, Spring, 1995. *Email:* JStephens@bronson.com

**NANCY L. TETREAULT,** born San Pedro, California, December 22, 1955; admitted to bar, 1990, California. *Education:* University of California at Santa Barbara (B.A., 1976); University of California at Berkeley (Teaching Credential, 1978); Loyola Law School (J.D., cum laude, 1990). Order of the Coif. Member, St. Thomas More Law Honor Society. Recipient, American Jurisprudence Awards: Real Property; Trusts and Wills. Staff Member, Loyola Law Review, 1989-1990. Author: "The Death of Comparable Worth: A Critical Analysis of the United States Supreme Court's Decision in *Wards Cove Packing Co. v. Atonio,*" vol. 23, Loyola of Los Angeles Law Review, Issue 3.

**JAMES B. YOBSKI,** born Decatur, Illinois, March 13, 1964; admitted to bar, 1989, Illinois; 1990, Missouri; 1992, California. *Education:* Anderson College (B.A., 1986); Southern Illinois University (J.D., 1989). *Email:* JYobski@bronson.com

#### REGISTERED PATENT AGENT

**DAVID ALEXANDER,** born Miami, Florida. Registered to practice before U.S. Patent and Trademark Office, 1976. *Education:* Massachusetts Institute of Technology (B.S.M.E., 1971). Founding Member, Japan Technology Licensing, Ltd., Tokyo, Japan. [U.S. Navy, 1963-1967]. *PRACTICE AREAS:* Patent Prosecution; Computer Architecture; Software; Semiconductor Fabrication; Lasers; Optics. *Email:* DAlexander@bronson.com

All Attorneys with the Firm are Members of The State Bar of California.

---

## LAW OFFICES OF
## EDYTHE L. BRONSTON
**11377 WEST OLYMPIC BOULEVARD, SUITE 900**
**LOS ANGELES, CALIFORNIA 90064-1683**
Telephone: 310-914-7972
Fax: 310-914-7973

*Bankruptcy, Receivership, Creditors' Rights, Civil Litigation.*

**EDYTHE L. BRONSTON,** born Scranton, Pennsylvania; admitted to bar, 1980, California and U.S. District Court, Central District of California; 1982, U.S. District Court, Southern, Northern and Eastern Districts of California. *Education:* California State University (B.A., summa cum laude, 1977); Loyola University of Los Angeles (J.D., 1980). Author: "Obtaining Appointment of a Receiver and Monitoring the Receivership," CEB Action Guide, 1991, 1993; "The Enforceability of Prepayment Premiums in Bankruptcy Court," 18 California Bankruptcy Journal 54 (1990); "What Elements Constitute an Unsecured Creditor's 'Allowed Claim' in a Section 1111(b)(2) Election?" 17 Calif. Bankruptcy Journal 87 (1989); "Highlights of New Local Bankruptcy Rules," 7 BSGJ 3 (1988); "Ex Parte Procedures in the Central District," 3 BSGJ 7 (1987). Contributing Editor, *California Foreclosure Law and Practice,* Shepards McGraw Hill, 1993; *Provisional Remedies Handbook,* Matthew Bender, 1993, 1994, 1995, 1996. Lecturer: "Emerging Issues in Private and Judicial Foreclosures, Deeds-in-Lieu, and Actions on Guarantees," Continuing Education of the Bar, 1993; "Basic Bankruptcy in California," National Business Institute, Inc., 1992; "Remedies During a Recession: Attachments, Injunctions, Receiverships and the New Lis Pendens Law," Los Angeles County Bar Association, Continuing Legal Education and Trade Show, 1993; "The Benefits of Receivership, or Locking the Barn Door Before the Horse is Stolen," Continuing Education of the Bar, University of California, 1991. Member, Editorial Board, California Bankruptcy Journal, 1986—. Certified Mediator, U.S. Bankruptcy Court, 1995—. Lawyer Representative to 9th circuit Judicial Conference, 1994—. *Member:* Los Angeles County (Member: Executive Committee, Provisional and Post-Judgment Remedies Section, 1985—; Chair, 1987-1988; Executive Committee, Litigation, 1993—) and American (Member, Business Law Section, Subcommittee on Secured Creditors) Bar Associations; State Bar of California (Member, Business Law Section); Women Lawyers Association of Los Angeles; California Women Lawyers; Financial Lawyers Conference; Los Angeles Bankruptcy Forum (Member, Board of Directors, 1987—, President, 1991-1992; California Bankruptcy Forum (Founding Director, 1989—; President, 1991-1992); California Receivers Forum (Founding Director).

*(This Listing Continued)*

---

## RONALD F. BROT
**LOS ANGELES, CALIFORNIA**
(See Woodland Hills)
*Family Law, Related Civil Trial Practice.*

---

## GARY BROWN
**1888 CENTURY PARK EAST, SUITE 1550**
**LOS ANGELES, CALIFORNIA 90067-1706**
Telephone: 310-201-0007
Facsimile: 310-277-2293
Email: browngrp@postoffice.worldnet.att.net

*General Practice.*

**GARY BROWN,** born 1944; admitted to bar, 1972, California. *Education:* University of California (B.S., 1967) University of California, Los Angeles (M.S., M.B.A.,1968) University of California School of Law, Los Angeles (J.D., 1971). (Certified as a Civil Trial Advocate by the National Board of Trial Advocacy). *PRACTICE AREAS:* Litigation (70%); Real Estate (25%).

---

## LAW OFFICE OF
## V. EMILE BROWN
**ONE WILSHIRE BUILDING**
**624 SOUTH GRAND, 29TH FLOOR**
**LOS ANGELES, CALIFORNIA 90017**
Telephone: 213-426-6533
Fax: 213-426-6562

*General Civil Trial, Consumer Protection, specializing in Lemon Law. Real Estate and Business Law.*

**V. EMILE BROWN,** born Brooklyn, New York, July 19, 1959; admitted to bar, 1990, California and U.S. Court of Appeals, 9th Circuit. *Education:* Dartmouth College (B.A., Urban Studies, 1981); University of California School of Law at Los Angeles (M.B.A.; J.D., 1989).

---

## BAIRD A. BROWN
**A PROFESSIONAL CORPORATION**
**1000 WILSHIRE BOULEVARD, SUITE 620**
**LOS ANGELES, CALIFORNIA 90017**
Telephone: 213-688-7795
Fax: 213-688-1080

*Trial and Appellate Practice in State and Federal Courts. Business Law.*

**BAIRD A. BROWN,** born Exeter, New Hampshire, June 18, 1946; admitted to bar, 1973, California; U.S. District Court, Northern, Central, Southern and Eastern Districts of California and U.S. Court of Appeals, Ninth Circuit. *Education:* Northwestern University (B.S., 1968); Stanford University (J.D., 1973). *Member:* Los Angeles County Bar Association; State Bar of California; Association of Business Trial Lawyers; The Association of Trial Lawyers of America.

## JOHN CLARK BROWN, JR.
### LOS ANGELES, CALIFORNIA
(See Inglewood)

*Real Estate, Business and Bankruptcy Litigation and Trial Practice in all Courts.*

---

## BROWN, PISTONE, HURLEY & VAN VLEAR
### A PROFESSIONAL CORPORATION
### LOS ANGELES, CALIFORNIA
(See Irvine)

*Construction, Environmental and Technology Trial Practice, Public Works, Contractor Professional Licensing and Bonding, Mechanics Liens, Insurance Coverage, Malpractice, International Projects, Arbitration, Environmental Law, Air and Water Permits, Trial and Appellate Practice.*

---

## BROWN RAYSMAN MILLSTEIN FELDER & STEINER LLP
### 1925 CENTURY PARK EAST, ELEVENTH FLOOR
### LOS ANGELES, CALIFORNIA 90067
Telephone: 310-789-2100
Fax: 310-789-2129
Email: brownraysman.com

*New York, New York Office:* 120 West Forty-Fifth Street. Telephone: 212-944-1515. Fax: 212-840-2429.

*Hartford, Connecticut Office:* City Place I, 185 Asylum Street, 37th Floor. Telephone: 860-275-6400. Fax: 860-275-6410.

*Newark, New Jersey Office:* One Gateway Center. Telephone: 201-596-1480. Fax: 201-622-3317.

*General Practice. Litigation, Arbitration, Computer, Corporate, Securities, Copyright, High Technology, Bankruptcy, Equipment Leasing, Tax, Patent, Trade Secrets, Insurance and Real Estate Law. Trial and Appellate Practice.*

### MEMBERS OF FIRM

**DAN C. AARDAL,** born Denver, Colorado, September 10, 1947; admitted to bar, 1975, California. *Education:* University of Denver (B.A., 1969; J.D., cum laude, 1975). Order of St. Ives. Managing Editor, University of Denver Law Review. Author: "Does Intellectual Property Trump Real Property," Journal of Property Management, July/August, 1996 at 74; "Protecting Bank Interests on Home, PC Services," American Banker, January 6, 1995 at 4; "Copyright Infringement on the Internet," Los Angeles Daily Journal, December 11, 1995 at 7; "Software License Agreements Need Careful Drafting," Los Angeles Daily Journal, August 14, 1995 at 5; "A Reliable Outsource," Los Angeles Daily Journal, May 11, 1995 at 7; "Bank Investment in Insurance Companies," New York Law Journal, September 15, 1994 at 5; "Retail Securities Activities of U.S. Banking Organizations," PLI Institute of Banking Law and Regulation, 1990 at 699; "Securities Related Activities of Banks and Bank Holding Companies," PLI Institute of Banking and Regulation, 1989 at 757. Chairman, Lawyers Committee, Bank Capital Markets Association, 1988-1989. *Member:* State Bar of California; American Bar Association (Section of Business Law, Banking Committee, 1984—; Committee on the Law of Cyberspace, 1995—; Intellectual Property Section, Special Committee on Software Licensing, 1995—). (Resident). **PRACTICE AREAS:** Computer Law; Banking; Real Estate Finance. *Email:* aardal@attmail.com

**HENRY J. SILBERBERG,** born Paris, Tennessee, January 30, 1944; admitted to bar, 1968, New York; 1976, California. *Education:* City College of New York (B.S., 1965); New York University (J.D., cum laude, 1968). Order of the Coif. Pomeroy Scholar. Member and Editor, New York University Law Review, 1966-1968. Co-Author: "Are The Courts Expanding the Meaning of 'Manipulation' Under the Federal Securities Law?" 11 Securities Regulation Law Journal 265 (1983); "To Arbitrate or Not to Arbitrate," Preventive Law Reporter, December (1983); "'Manipulation'—Should It Be Interpreted to Have a Different Meaning in Tender Offers Than in 10b-5 Cases," 12 Securities Regulation Law Journal 69 (1984); "Eroding Protection of Customer Lists and Customer Information Under the Uniform Trade Secrets Act," 42 Business Lawyer 487 (1987); "Corporate Crime: When to Retain Outside Counsel," 34 The Practical Lawyer, No. 3 (1988). Instructor of Law, U.C.L.A. School of Law, 1969-1970. Law Clerk, Hon. Sterry R. Waterman, United States Court of Appeals for the Second Circuit, 1968-1969. *Member:* New York University School of Law Alumni Board of Class Representatives, 1986—; Board of Directors, Law Alumni Association of New York University School of Law, 1988—; The President's Council, New York University. Settlement Officer, Los Angeles Superior Court, 1989—. Member, Panel of Arbitrators, American Arbitration Association. *Member:* Beverly Hills (Member, Judiciary Committee, 1992-1993), Los Angeles County (Member, Federal Courts Practice Standards Committee, 1982-1983) and American (Member, Litigation Section, Trial Practice, Corporate Counsel and Business Torts Committees, 1989—) Bar Associations; Association of Business Trial Lawyers; Securities Industry Association. **PRACTICE AREAS:** Litigation; Arbitration; Business Divorce. *Email:* hjs@attmail.com

**MAUREEN MCGUIRL,** born Jersey City, New Jersey, February 2, 1950; admitted to bar, 1979, New York; 1982, California. *Education:* Barnard College (B.A., cum laude, 1973); Columbia University (J.D., 1978). Writing and Research Editor, Columbia Journal of Law and Social Problems, 1977-1978. Co-Author: "Antitrust Laws and Trade Regulation," Matthew Bender (2nd Edition). *Member:* Los Angeles County, New York State and American Bar Associations. **REPORTED CASES:** City of Anaheim v. Southern California Edison Co., 1990-2 Trade Cas. (CCH) 69426 (C.D. Cal. 1990), aff'd., 955 F.2d 1373 (9th Cir. 1992); City of Vernon v. Southern California Edison Co., 955 F.2d 1361 (9th Cir.), cert. denied, 121 L.Ed.2d 228 (1992); Eurim-Pharm GmbH v. Pfizer Inc., 593 F. Supp. 1102 (S.D.N.Y. 1984); Ikonen v. Hartz Mountain, 122 F.R.D. 258 (S.D. Cal. 1988); Kuhfeldt v. Liberty Mutual Insurance Co., (E.D. Mich); State Board of Equalization v. Title Insurance Company of Minnesota, 4 Cal. 4th 715 (1992); Whittaker Corporation v. Execuair Corporation, 736 F.2d 1341 (9th Cir. 1984); Execuair Corporation. Whittaker Corporation, 953 F.2d 510 (9th Cir. 1982); 1992 U.S. App. LEXIS 30258 (9th Cir. 1991); In re Execuair, 125 B.R. 600 (Bankr. C.D. Cal. 1991). **PRACTICE AREAS:** Antitrust; Intellectual Property; Business Litigation. *Email:* mmcg@attmail.com

**BENZION J. WESTREICH,** born New York, N.Y., 1952; admitted to bar, 1979, New York; 1988, California. *Education:* City College of the City University of New York (B.A., 1974); Columbia University (J.D., 1978). (Resident). *Email:* bwestreich@attmail.com

### ASSOCIATES

**TIMOTHY J. MARTIN,** born Detroit, Michigan, October 27, 1965; admitted to bar, 1990, California; 1995, U.S. District Court, Central District of California; 1996, U.S. District Court, Southern District of California. *Education:* Georgetown University (A.B., summa cum laude, 1987); University of Michigan (J.D., 1990). Phi Beta Kappa. *Member:* State Bar of California. **LANGUAGES:** French. **PRACTICE AREAS:** Litigation. *Email:* tjm@attmail.com

**RON BURNOVSKI,** born Brooklyn, New York, May 28, 1969; admitted to bar, 1994, California; U.S. District Court, Central District of California and U.S. Court of Appeals, Ninth Circuit. *Education:* State University of New York at Binghamton (B.A., with honors, 1991); University of California at Los Angeles (J.D., 1994). Phi Beta Kappa. Judicial Extern to the Hon. Dickran Tevrizian, U.S. District Court, Central District of California. *Member:* Los Angeles County and American Bar Associations; State Bar of California. (Resident). **PRACTICE AREAS:** Litigation; Insurance Defense; Bad Faith; Product Liability. *Email:* rburnovski@attmail.com

(For complete biographical data on all personnel See Professional Biographies at New York, N.Y.)

---

## BROWN, WINFIELD & CANZONERI
### INCORPORATED
*Established in 1974*
### SUITE 1500 CALIFORNIA PLAZA
### 300 SOUTH GRAND AVENUE
### LOS ANGELES, CALIFORNIA 90071-3125
Telephone: 213-687-2100
Fax: 213-687-2149

*General Civil and Appellate Trial Practice in all State and Federal Courts. Municipal, Administrative, Corporation, Business, Banking, Real Property, Estate Planning, Trust, Probate and Tax Law.*

(This Listing Continued)

**BROWN, WINFIELD & CANZONERI,** INCORPORATED, Los Angeles—Continued

FIRM PROFILE: *Brown, Winfield & Canzoneri, Inc. has a broad-based civil practice, including business, commercial, governmental, real estate, tax, transportation and administrative law, and the litigation related to those areas of law. The firm's client base is both broad based and economically substantial. It includes government entities, New York Stock Exchange and smaller corporations, financial institutions, real estate developers and lenders, individuals, partnerships and trusts.*

**J. KENNETH BROWN,** born Cleveland, Ohio, April 22, 1935; admitted to bar, 1961, Ohio; 1963, California; 1976, U.S. Supreme Court. *Education:* John Carroll University (B.S.S., 1957); Western Reserve University (LL.B., 1961). Phi Delta Phi. City Attorney: Cerritos, 1965—; Bell Gardens, 1965-1969; Lawndale, 1967-1970; Norwalk, 1969-1989; Signal Hill, 1975-1984; La Canada Flintridge, 1976—; San Dimas, 1977—; San Gabriel, 1988-1989. General Counsel: Los Angeles County Housing Authority, 1982—; Long Beach Housing Company, 1992—. Independent Cities Risk Management Authority, 1987. Member, City Attorney's Department, League of California Cities, 1965—. *Member:* Los Angeles County and Ohio State Bar Associations; The State Bar of California. *PRACTICE AREAS:* Redevelopment; Municipal Law; Real Estate.

**THOMAS F. WINFIELD, III,** born New York, N.Y., April 14, 1942; admitted to bar, 1968, California; 1976, U.S. Supreme Court. *Education:* Rutgers University (B.A., 1964); Rutgers University (J.D., 1967). Editor, Rutgers Law Review, 1966-1967. Law Clerk to the Honorable William M. Byrne, U.S. District Court, Los Angeles, 1967-1968. City Attorney, Lawndale, 1970-1983; Palos Verdes Estates, 1992-1993. Agency Counsel, Monterey Park Redevelopment Agency, 1980-1986. *Member:* Los Angeles County (Member, Real Estate and Public Law Sections) and American (Member, Real Estate and Litigation Sections) Bar Associations; The State Bar of California. *PRACTICE AREAS:* Litigation; Real Estate; Environmental; Land Use.

**ANTHONY CANZONERI,** born Los Angeles, California, October 23, 1946; admitted to bar, 1972, California. *Education:* California State College at Fullerton (B.A., 1969); University of California at Los Angeles (J.D., 1972). Lecturer: California Continuing Education of the Bar Programs, Real Property Sales Transactions, 1978; Introduction to Real Property Secured Transactions, 1980; Homeowners Association Counseling and Litigation, 1980 and 1986; Community Redevelopment Agencies Association Program Land Leasing, 1985; U.C.L.A. Extension Program Utilizing the Wealth in California's Public Real Estate, 1986; California Association for Local Economic Development Programs Economic Development and Tax Reform 1986 and Land Leasing, 1987; California Redevelopment Association, Redevelopment Institute, 1991 and 1992; City Attorney and Redevelopment Agency Counsel for City of Monterey Park, 1986—. *Member:* Los Angeles County (Member, Real Estate Section) and American (Member, Sections on: Real Property, Probate and Trust Law; Urban State and Local Government Law; Corporation, Banking and Business Law) Bar Associations; The State Bar of California. *PRACTICE AREAS:* Real Estate; Governmental Law; Finance; Real Estate Development; Environmental; Land Use; Housing Redevelopment.

**VICKI E. LAND,** born Plainfield, New Jersey, September 25, 1940; admitted to bar, 1976, Texas; 1977, District of Columbia; 1979, California. *Education:* University of Houston (B.A., magna cum laude, 1972); University of Texas (J.D., cum laude, 1976). Order of the Coif; Phi Delta Phi. Member, 1974-1976 and Note and Comment Editor, 1975-1976, Texas Law Review. *Member:* Los Angeles County (Member, Section of Trial Lawyers; Environmental Law Section) and American (Member, Section of Litigation) Bar Associations; The District of Columbia Bar; State Bar of Texas; State Bar of California; Women Lawyers Association of Los Angeles (Member, Board of Governors, 1986-1988, 1993-1996; Chair, Trial Lawyers Section, 1987-1988). *PRACTICE AREAS:* Litigation.

**JAMES C. CAMP,** born Greenville, South Carolina, January 7, 1951; admitted to bar, 1976, Georgia; 1977, California and U.S. District Court, Central District of California; 1981, U.S. Tax Court. *Education:* Duke University (A.B., cum laude, 1973); Emory University (J.D., 1976). *Member:* Century City (Chairman, Real Property Committee, 1982-1984), Los Angeles County (Co-Chairman, Lawyers and the Arts Committee, Barristers, 1982-1983; Member, 1985-1988 and Chairman, 1986-1987, Editorial Board, Los Angeles Magazine; Sections of: Real Property; Corporations) and American (Member, Sections of: Real Property, Trust and Probate Law; Corporation, Banking and Business Law; Real Estate Finance Subcommittee; Public/Private Cooperation in Development of Real Estate Subcommittee) Bar Associations; State Bar of California; State Bar of Georgia. *PRACTICE AREAS:* Real Property; Commercial Law; Finance; Corporate.

**STEVEN ABRAM,** born Cincinnati, Ohio, October 10, 1954; admitted to bar, 1980, California. *Education:* University of California at Los Angeles (B.A., magna cum laude, Honors in Economics, 1976; M.A., in Economics, 1980; J.D., 1979). *Member:* Los Angeles County Bar Association; State Bar of California. *PRACTICE AREAS:* Real Property Transactions; Commercial Leasing.

**DENNIS S. ROY,** born Inglewood, California, November 7, 1954; admitted to bar, 1981, California. *Education:* Brown University (A.B., magna cum laude, 1977); University of California at Los Angeles (M.B.A.; J.D., 1981). Order of the Coif. Law Clerk to Justice George E. Lohr, Colorado Supreme Court, Denver, 1981-1982. *Member:* Los Angeles County Bar Association; The State Bar of California. *PRACTICE AREAS:* Real Estate; Redevelopment Law.

**MARK STERES,** born St. Louis, Missouri, May 23, 1959; admitted to bar, 1984, California. *Education:* University of California at Los Angeles (A.B., cum laude, 1981); University of Southern California (J.D., 1984). Participant Hale Moot Court Honors Program. *Member:* Los Angeles County Bar Association; State Bar of California. *PRACTICE AREAS:* Zoning; Municipal Law.

**KATHARINE ARAUJO MILLER,** born Los Angeles, California, June 24, 1955; admitted to bar, 1987, California and U.S. Court of Appeals, Eighth and Ninth Circuits. *Education:* University of Puget Sound (B.S., magna cum laude, 1977); Whittier College School of Law (J.D., summa cum laude, 1986). Phi Kappa Phi. Mortar Board. Editor, Whittier Law Review, 1985-1986. Recipient: American Jurisprudence Awards, Civil Procedure I and II, Constitutional Law II, Remedies, Legal Research and Writing I and II, Legal Process, Professional Responsibility, and Criminal Law. Judicial Clerkship, U.S. Court of Appeals, Eighth Circuit, 1986-1987. *Member:* State Bar of California. *PRACTICE AREAS:* Municipal Law; Civil Litigation.

**CHRISTOPHER NORGAARD,** born Oklahoma City, Oklahoma, October 14, 1948; admitted to bar, 1973, Colorado and U.S. District Court, District of Colorado; 1979, California and U.S. District Court, Northern District of California; 1980, U.S. District Court, Central District of California; 1986, U.S. Court of Appeals, Ninth Circuit; 1991, U.S. District Court, Eastern District of California; 1992, U.S. District Court, Southern District of California. *Education:* Stanford University (A.B., with distinction, 1970); Georgetown University Law Center (J.D., 1973). Author: "Monopolization of Computer Peripheral Equipment: Telex v. I.B.M.," 53 Denver Law Journal 295, 1976. *Member:* Los Angeles County and American (Member, Sections on: Antitrust Law; Litigation) Bar Associations; The State Bar of California. *PRACTICE AREAS:* Litigation.

**C. GEOFFREY MITCHELL,** born Raleigh, North Carolina, May 27, 1953; admitted to bar, 1979, North Carolina and U.S. District Court, Eastern District of North Carolina; 1986, California. *Education:* University of North Carolina (A.B., with honors, 1975; J.D., 1979). Lecturer: Legal Environment of Business; Principles of Real Estate, East Carolina University, 1980-1981. *Member:* Los Angeles County (Member, Section on Real Property Law) and American (Member, Real Property, Probate and Trust Law Sections) Bar Associations; North Carolina State Bar; State Bar of California (Member, Real Property and Business Law Sections). *PRACTICE AREAS:* Real Estate Law; Real Estate Finance; Business Law; Partnership Law.

**SCOTT H. CAMPBELL,** born Palo Alto, California, December 16, 1961; admitted to bar, 1987, California and U.S. District Court, Central District of California; 1988, U.S. Court of Appeals, Ninth Circuit; 1992, U.S. Supreme Court. *Education:* University of California at Berkeley (B.A., 1984); University of California at Los Angeles (J.D., 1987). Phi Beta Kappa. Moot Court Honors Program. *Member:* Los Angeles County (Litigation Section) and American Bar Associations; State Bar of California. *PRACTICE AREAS:* Business Litigation; Municipal Litigation.

**JOSHUA C. GOTTHEIM,** born Evanston, Illinois, May 1, 1963; admitted to bar, 1989, California. *Education:* Yale University (B.A., 1986); Boalt Hall School of Law, University of California (J.D., 1989). Panelist, California Redevelopment Association Financial Reporting Seminar, 1994. *Member:* Los Angeles County Bar Association (Member, Real Property Law Section); State Bar of California. *PRACTICE AREAS:* Real Estate; Land Use; Local Government Law.

**DONALD PAUL RIES,** born Hazleton, Pennsylvania, November 24, 1959; admitted to bar, 1986, Arizona; 1988, California. *Education:* Arizona

*(This Listing Continued)*

State University (B.S., 1981); University of Chicago (J.D., 1985). Beta Gamma Sigma; Phi Kappa Phi; Alpha Lambda Delta. *Member:* State Bar of California; State Bar of Arizona. **PRACTICE AREAS:** Real Estate; Finance.

**MUIRA K. SETHI,** born Los Angeles, California, January 29, 1970; admitted to bar, 1994, California and U.S. District Court, Central, Second and Eastern Districts of California. *Education:* University of California at Los Angeles (B.A., cum laude, 1991); Loyola Law School, Los Angeles (J.D., 1994). Phi Delta Phi. St. Thomas More Law Honor Society. Participant: Scott Moot Court Program, 1993; *Member:* Los Angeles County and American Bar Associations; State Bar of California (Litigation and Real Property Sections). **LANGUAGES:** Spanish and Hindi. **PRACTICE AREAS:** Litigation.

**SETH I. WEISSMAN,** born Van Nuys, California, December 23, 1969; admitted to bar, 1995, California, U.S. District Court, Central District of California and U.S. Court of Appeals, Ninth Circuit. *Education:* University of California at Los Angeles (B.A., magna cum laude, 1992); University of Southern California (J.D., 1995). Phi Beta Kappa; Golden Key; Omicron Delta Epsilon; Phi Eta Sigma. Judicial Extern to the Honorable James M. Ideman, U.S. District Court Judge, Central District of California, 1993. *Member:* Los Angeles County and American (Member, Sections on: Business Law, Taxation, Entertainment and Sports Law) Bar Associations; State Bar of California. **PRACTICE AREAS:** Real Estate; Business; Corporate Law.

**JOHN H. HOLLOWAY,** born Santa Monica, California, February 28, 1966; admitted to bar, 1995, California. *Education:* College of William & Mary (B.A., 1988); Tulane University of Louisiana (J.D., 1995). Phi Delta Phi. Member Moot Court Board. Tulane Journal of International and Comparative Law. Senior Fellow, Tulane University. *Member:* Los Angeles County Bar Association (Member, Litigation Section); State Bar of California.

**RAFAEL E. ALFONZO,** born Brooklyn, New York, November 20, 1972; admitted to bar, 1996, California. *Education:* University of Michigan (B.A., 1972); George Washington University (J.D., 1996). *Member:* Los Angeles County Bar Association; State Bar of California. **LANGUAGES:** Spanish.

**SONYA L. KARPOWICH,** born Santa Monica, California, January 13, 1969; admitted to bar, 1995, California. *Education:* University of Southern California (B.S., cum laude, 1991); Southwestern University School of Law (J.D., magna cum laude, 1995). Beta Gamma Sigma. Associate Editor, Southwestern University Law Review. *Member:* Los Angeles County Bar Association; State Bar of California. **PRACTICE AREAS:** Real Estate Transactions.

REFERENCE: Wells Fargo Bank.

## BROWN & WOOD LLP

10877 WILSHIRE BOULEVARD
**LOS ANGELES, CALIFORNIA 90024**
Telephone: 310-443-0200
Telecopier: 310-208-5740

*New York, New York Office:* One World Trade Center, 10048-0557.
Telephone: 212-839-5300.
*Washington, D.C. Office:* 815 Connecticut Avenue, N.W., Suite 701, 20006-4004.
Telephone: 202-973-0600.
*San Francisco, California Office:* 555 California Street, 94104-1715.
Telephone: 415-772-1200.
*London, England Office:* Blackwell House, Guildhall Yard.
Telephone: 011-44-171-778-1800.
*Hong Kong Office:* 2606 Asia Pacific Finance Tower, Citibank Plaza, 3 Garden Road, Central.
Telephone: 011-852-2509-7888.
*Sao Paulo, Brazil Office:* Rua da Consolacao, 247 - 5° Andar.
Telephone: 011-55-11-256-9785.
*Beijing, China Office:* 2315, China World Tower, 1 Jian Guo Men Wai Avenue.
Telephone: 011-8610-6505-5359; 011-8610-6505-1807.

General Practice.
*(This Listing Continued)*

*PARTNER*
**PAUL C. PRINGLE,** born Summit, New Jersey, May 7, 1943; admitted to bar, 1969, New York; 1972, California. *Education:* Dartmouth College (A.B., 1965); University of Michigan (J.D., 1968). (Also at San Francisco Office.)

(For Complete Biographical Data on all Partners and Associates, see Professional Biographies at New York, New York).

## BROWNE & WOODS LLP
**LOS ANGELES, CALIFORNIA**
(See Beverly Hills)

General Civil Trial and Appellate Practice in all State and Federal Courts with emphasis on Competitive Business Practices, Unfair Competition, Trade Secrets, Business Torts, Defamation, Entertainment Litigation and Insurance Litigation.

## ALEX M. BRUCKER
*A LAW CORPORATION*
Established in 1992

10880 WILSHIRE BOULEVARD, SUITE 2210
**LOS ANGELES, CALIFORNIA 90024**
Telephone: 310-475-7540
Fax: 310-470-4806
URL: http://www.pensionlawyers.com

Taxation, ERISA, Employee Benefits, Qualified Pension and Profit Sharing Plans and Non-qualified Deferred Compensation Plans.

FIRM PROFILE: *The Firm practices exclusively in all tax, ERISA and litigation aspects of the following employee benefit areas: Consultation, design, implementation and termination of pension, profit sharing, 401 (k) and ESOP plans; Consultation, handling negotiating and settling IRS and ERISA qualified plan and employee benefits audits and controversies (including VCR and CAP) with governmental agencies; prohibited transactions problem solving and exemptions and other ERISA fiduciary matters; Consultation and planning for retirement distributions from Qualified Plans and IRAs, division of plan benefits at divorce, negotiation and preparation of QDROs and expert testimony in adversarial marital contests; litigation support and expert testimony in employee benefits tax and ERISA matters; and consultation, design and implementation of non-qualified deferred compensation, cafeteria, fringe benefit and welfare plans.*

**ALEX M. BRUCKER,** born Los Angeles, California, February 13, 1945; admitted to bar, 1974, California. *Education:* California State University at San Diego (B.S., 1967); Whittier College School of Law (J.D., cum laude, 1974). Certified Public Accountant, California, 1970. Member, Editorial Board, Journal of Pension Benefits, 1994. Author: "Small Business Pension Plan IRS Actuarial Audits," 43rd Annual USC Institute on Federal Taxation (Chapter, 9, 1992. "Tax Planning for Qualified Plan Distributions and IRAs," California CPA Foundation for Education and Research, 1986—; " Impact of TEFRA and DEFRA on Required Distributions under Qualified Plans," NYU Institute on Federal Taxation, 1984 Tax Conference Series - Estate Planning, Chapter 9; "Debt-Financed Real Estate Investments and the Qualified Trust," 15 Beverly Hills Bar Association Journal 527, Summer, 1981. Co-Author: Distribution Column in Journal of Pension Benefits (1991); "Estate Planning for Qualified and Non-Qualified Plans," 41st Annual USC Institute on Federal Taxation (Chapter 17, 1989); "Estate Planning for Qualified Plan Benefits After 1986," Estate Planning 1987; "California Taxation of Literary Properties," 2 Comment Law Journal, Winter, 1979-1980. Instructor: California CPA Foundation for Education and Research, 1986—; CPE Tax Planning Taxes, 1988—. Lecturer: Employee Benefits: USC Annual Institute on Federal Taxation New York University Institute on Federal Taxation; Southern California Tax and Estate Planning and Employee Benefits Forums; California Continuing Education of the Bar; California CPA Foundation for Research and Education; Los Angeles County and Beverly Hills Bar Associations; American Society of Pension Actuaries; National Institute of Pension Administrators; Western Pension and Benefit Conference. *Member:* Los Angeles County (Chairperson, Employee Benefits Committee, 1982; Tax Section Executive Committee, 1980-1983), Beverly Hills (Member, Board of Governors, 1985-1987; Co-Chair, Annual Employee Benefits Conference, 1980-1989) and American (Member, Tax Section, Employer Benefits Committee) Bar Associations; State Bar of California (Chair, Employee Benefits Committee); Western Pension
*(This Listing Continued)*

CAA557B

## ALEX M. BRUCKER A LAW CORPORATION, Los Angeles—Continued

and Benefits Conference; California Society of Certified Public Accountants (Member, Planning Committees Various Tax Conferences); American Society of Pension Actuaries (Board of Directors, 1992-1995); National Institute of Pension Administrators; Motion Picture and Television Tax Institute. *PRACTICE AREAS:* Employee Benefits Law.

---

**LINDA RUSSANO MORRA,** born New York, N.Y., January 28, 1952; admitted to bar, 1982, California. *Education:* Hunter College of the City University of New York (B.A., cum laude, 1974); Southwestern University School of Law (J.D., cum laude, 1982). Member, 1979-1980, and Articles Editor, 1980-1981, Southwestern University Law Review. Recipient, American Jurisprudence Awards for Contracts and Real Property. Speaker: 1985 Annual Conference of Current Developments in Taxation, Taxation Section and 1989 Annual Spring Seminar of Estate and Gift Tax Subsection of Los Angeles County Bar Association. Vice Chairperson, 1985-1986; Chairperson, 1986-1987, Employee Benefits Committee, Beverly Hills Bar Association. *Member:* Los Angeles County Bar Association; State Bar of California. *PRACTICE AREAS:* Employee Benefits Law.

**MICHAEL L. COTTER,** born Little Rock, Arkansas, September 13, 1949; admitted to bar, 1975, California. *Education:* Loyola Marymount University (B.A., 1972); Southwestern University School of Law (J.D., 1975). Recipient, American Jurisprudence Award for Conflicts of Law. Instructor, Pension Tax, Los Angeles Employee Plans Division of the Internal Revenue Service, 1987-1989. Lecturer: Pension and Profit Sharing Plans, 1991; California State University, Los Angeles. Lecturer: Internal Revenue Qualified Plans, 1992; Internal Revenue Pension Audits, California State University, Los Angeles, 1993-1995. California Society of Certified Public Accountants, 1992. *Member:* Los Angeles County Bar Association; State Bar of California. *PRACTICE AREAS:* Employee Benefits Law.

**SCOTT E. HILTUNEN,** born L'Anse, Michigan, March 11, 1959; admitted to bar, 1993, California. *Education:* University of Michigan (B.A., 1981); University of Southern California (J.D., 1993). Recipient, American Jurisprudence Awards for Estate Planning and Gifts, Wills and Trusts. Instructor: American Society of Pension Actuaries, Pension Fundamentals, 1988; Statutory and Regulatory Aspects of Qualified Pension Plans, 1989; Advanced Retirement Plan Consulting, 1996. Lecturer: American Society of Pension Actuaries, 1995—; Western Pension and Benefit Conference, 1996. Certified Pension Consultant, American Society of Pension Actuaries, 1989. Co-Author: Distribution Column in Journal of Pension Benefits (1994—). *Member:* Los Angeles County Bar Association; State Bar of California; American Society of Pension Actuaries (Educational and Examination Committee). *PRACTICE AREAS:* Employee Benefits Law.

---

## NORMAN E. BRUNELL
2049 CENTURY PARK EAST, SUITE 1080
**LOS ANGELES, CALIFORNIA 90067-3112**
Telephone: 310-553-0100
Fax: 310-553-1452
Email: nbrunell@netcom.com

*Practice limited to Patent and Trademark Law, specializing in preparation of Domestic and International Patent and Trademark Applications, Novelty, Infringement and Validity Searches, Studies and Opinions and Domestic and International Licensing Business Negotiations.*

FIRM PROFILE: Mr. Brunell's technical expertise includes all aspects of electrical and electronic engineering and high technology devices as well as many aspects of mechanical engineering. He has particular expertise in the following areas: computer hardware and software, integrated circuit fabrication, radio frequency and underwater communications, spread spectrum modulation, seismic exploration, solid state lasers, the internet, automotive products and electronic and mechanical packaging. While working as a computer design engineer at the Foxboro Instrument Co., Mr. Brunell began drafting patent applications for computer hardware and software inventions in 1969. Subsequently, Foxboro Instrument Co. sent Mr. Brunell to law school to develop and manage the company's patent department.

Mr. Brunell has been group patent and licensing counsel and international licensing counsel for Litton Industries; division general and patent counsel for Beckman Industries and patent counsel for the Foxboro Instrument Co.

Mr. Brunell has been listed in the LA Business Journals Top 100 of Who's Who in High Technology.

*(This Listing Continued)*

CAA558B

---

**NORMAN E. BRUNELL,** born Worcester, Massachusetts, April 18, 1946; admitted to bar, 1973, Massachusetts; 1975, California. *Education:* Worcester Polytechnic Institute (B.S.E.E., 1968); Suffolk University (J.D., 1973). National Merit Scholar. Author: "Looming Patent War With Japan," Los Angeles Daily Journal, San Francisco Daily Journal and Japan Law Journal, May 1992; "Patents Provide Us Window Opportunity," Los Angeles Business Journal, September 21, 1992; "A Patent Primer, Removing the Mystery From Product Protection," Los Angeles Daily Journal, April 7, 1995; "Changing Trends in Patent Law," Metropolitan News-Enterprise, September 20, 1995. Co-Author: How To Write A Patent Application, Practicing Law Institute, 1992; Chapter on Intellectual Property Audits in the Legal Audit, published by Clark, Boardman & Callahan, 1996. Adjunct Professor, Southwestern University Law School. Listed Who's Who in High Technology-Top 100, Los Angeles Business Journal, 1995. *Member:* State Bar of California; Los Angeles Intellectual Property Law Association; American Intellectual Property Law Association. *PRACTICE AREAS:* Patent and Trademark Law (Computer and Software).

REPRESENTATIVE CLIENTS: Litton Industries; California Institute of Technology; Jet Propulsion Laboratory (JPL); NASA; Northrop Corp.; Hughes Aircraft Corp.; Hewlett Packard Co.; Applied Materials, Inc.; Western Atlas Int'l., Inc.

---

## BRYAN CAVE LLP

A Partnership including a Professional Corporation

*Established in 1873*

**777 SOUTH FIGUEROA STREET
SUITE 2700
LOS ANGELES, CALIFORNIA 90017-5418**
Telephone: (213) 243-4300
Facsimile: (213) 243-4343
*For attorney e-mails use: First initial, last name, firm name, e.g., rsmith@bryancavellp.com*

*St. Louis, Missouri Office:* One Metropolitan Square, 211 North Broadway, Suite 3600, 63102-2750. Telephone: (314) 259-2000. Facsimile: (314) 259-2020.
*Washington, D.C. Office:* 700 Thirteenth Street, N.W., 20005-3960. Telephone: (202) 508-6000. Facsimile: (202) 508-6200.
*New York, N.Y. Office:* 245 Park Avenue, 10167-0034. Telephone: (212) 692-1800. Facsimile: (212) 692-1900.
*Kansas City, Missouri Office:* 3500 One Kansas City Place, 1200 Main Street, 64141-6914. Telephone: (816) 374-3200. Facsimile: (816) 374-3300.
*Overland Park, Kansas Office:* 7500 College Boulevard, Suite 1100, 66210-4035. Telephone: (913) 338-7700. Facsimile: (913) 338-7777.
*Phoenix, Arizona Office:* 2800 North Central Avenue, Twenty-First Floor, 85004-1098. Telephone: (602) 230-7000. Facsimile: (602) 266-5938.
*Santa Monica, California Office:* 120 Broadway, Suite 500, 90401-2305. Telephone: (310) 576-2100. Facsimile: (310) 576-2200.
*Irvine, California Office:* 18881 Von Karman, Suite 1500, 92715-1500. Telephone: (714) 223-7000. Facsimile: (714) 223-7100.
*London, SW1H 9BU England Office:* 29 Queen Anne's Gate. Telephone: 171-896-1900. Facsimile: 171-896-1919.
*Riyadh 11465 Saudi Arabia Office:* In Cooperation with Kadasah Law Firm, P.O. Box 20883. Telephone: 966-1-474-0888. Facsimile: 966-1-476-2881.
*Kuwait City, Kuwait Office:* Mashora Advocates & Legal Consultants, Sheraton Towers, Second Floor, P.O. Box 5902 Safat, 13060. Telephone: 965-240-4470/240-6000. Facsimile: 965-245-9000.
*Dubai, U.A.E. Office:* Al-Mehairi Legal Consultants - Bryan Cave LLP, Dubai, Holiday Centre, Commercial Tower, Suite 1103, P.O. Box 13677, UAE. Telephone: 971-4-1-314-123. Facsimile: 971-4-318-287.
*Abu Dhabi, U.A.E. Office:* Al-Mehairi Legal Consultants - Bryan Cave LLP, Abu Dhabi, Dhabi Tower, Suite 304, P.O. Box 47645. Telephone: 971-2-260-335. Facsimile: 971-2-260-332.
*Hong Kong Office:* Suite 2106, Lippo Tower, 21/F, Lippo Centre, 89 Queensway. Telephone: 852-2522-2821. Facsimile: 852-2522-3830.
*Shanghai, People's Republic of China Associated Office:* 100 Fu Xing Xi Lu, 3C, 200031. Telephone: 86-21-6466-3845. Facsimile: 86-21-6466-4280.

*Administrative and General Civil Practice. Antitrust, Aviation, Banking, Computer, Corporate Financing, Corporation, Estate Planning, Government Contracts, International, Labor, Probate, Products Liability, Real Estate, Securities, Taxation, Technology, Transportation, Trust and University Law. General Civil Trial and Appellate Practice.*

*(This Listing Continued)*

## PARTNERS

**JOHN W. AMBERG,** born Michigan, 1951; admitted to bar, 1980, Michigan; 1981, Missouri; 1983, California. *Education:* Princeton University (A.B., 1974); University of Michigan (J.D., cum laude, 1979). Author: "Who Is Your Client?" Association of Business Trial Lawyers Report, Vol. XVIII, No. 2, February, 1996. Clerk to Hon. Douglas W. Hillman, U.S. District Court, Western District of Michigan, 1980. Settlement Officer and Member, Council of Dispute Resolution Services. Member, Litigation, Tort and Insurance Practice and Aviation Sections, American Bar Association. *Member:* Los Angeles (Litigation and Alternative Dispute Resolution Sections) and Federal Bar Associations; State Bar of California (Litigation Section); Association of Business Trial Lawyers. **PRACTICE AREAS:** Business and Commercial Litigation; Products Liability Law; Professional Liability Law.

**GERALD E. BOLTZ,** born Ohio, 1931; admitted to bar, 1955, Ohio; 1964, U.S. Supreme Court; 1978, California. *Education:* Ohio Northern University (B.A., 1953; J.D., 1955). Contributing Author: "Securities Law Techniques," Matthew Bender, 1986—. Assistant Attorney General, State of Ohio, 1958. Legal Assistant to SEC Commissioner Daniel J. McCauley, Jr., 1961. Regional Administrator, SEC Fort Worth Regional Office, 1967-1971. Regional Administrator, SEC, Los Angeles Regional Office, 1972-1979. *Member:* Los Angeles County (Chairman, Business and Corporations Section, 1988) and American (Member: Committee on Federal Regulation of Securities, Subcommittee on SEC Enforcement and Litigation Matters) Bar Associations. (Resident, Santa Monica, California Office).

**HOWARD O. BOLTZ, JR.,** born California, 1951; admitted to bar, 1976, California. *Education:* University of California at Berkeley (A.B., 1973); Harvard University (J.D., 1976). Phi Beta Kappa. Adjunct Professor, Southwestern University School of Law, 1984-1990. Editor, Federal Bar Association Journal for the Central District of California, 1984-1991. *Member:* Federal Bar Association (President, Los Angeles Chapter, 1990-1991); Association of Business Trial Lawyers (President, 1987-1988; Member, Board of Governors, 1982-1988, Los Angeles Chapter).

**ROBERT E. BOONE III,** born Alabama, 1962; admitted to bar, 1987, California; 1989, District of Columbia. *Education:* Vanderbilt University (B.E., Civil and Environmental Engineering, cum laude, 1984; J.D., 1987). Chi Epsilon. **PRACTICE AREAS:** Product Liability; Employment and Commercial Litigation.

**RONALD W. BUCKLY,** born Illinois, 1951; admitted to bar, 1978, California. *Education:* University of California at Berkeley (A.B., 1974); Hastings College of Law, University of California (J.D., 1978); New York University (LL.M., 1980). Member, Business Law Section, American Bar Association. *Member:* State Bar of California. (Resident, Santa Monica, California Office).

**WILLIAM I. CHERTOK,** born California, 1937; admitted to bar, 1961, California. *Education:* Stanford University (B.A., 1958; J.D., 1960); University of Southern California (LL.M., 1964). Phi Delta Phi. Member: Litigation Section; Torts and Insurance Defense Section, American Bar Association. *Member:* Los Angeles County (Member: Executive Council, Junior Barristers, 1965-1968; Executive Committee, State Bar Conference, 1972-1975; Judicial Appointments Committee, 1973-1979; Member, 1970-1978 and Vice Chairman, 1972-1975, Legal Ethics Committee; Chairman: Los Angeles County Bar Delegation to State Bar Conference, 1975) and Federal Bar Associations; Association of Business Trial Lawyers. (Resident, Santa Monica, California Office).

**BONITA L. CHURNEY,** born California, 1951; admitted to bar, 1978, California. *Education:* University of California at Berkeley (A.B., with great distinction, 1973); Harvard University (J.D., 1978). Phi Beta Kappa. (Resident, Santa Monica, California Office). **PRACTICE AREAS:** Business and Commercial Litigation; Securities Litigation.

**STEPHEN J. DENSMORE,** born California, 1952; admitted to bar, 1977, California. *Education:* University of Southern California (B.A., 1974); Waseda University, Tokyo, Japan; Loyola University (J.D., 1977). Member, Loyola University of Los Angeles Law Review, 1976-1977. Part-time Faculty Member, Construction Law, California State University at Long Beach, 1983-1986. President, 1993-1994, Los Angeles Chapter of Construction Specifications Institute. Construction Industry Arbitration and Mediation Panel of American Arbitration Association. Member, Large Complex Case Panel, American Arbitration Association. Member, California Council American Institute of Architects, Document Review Task Force, 1987. American Arbitration Association Construction ADR Task Force, 1995. CSI Ad Hoc Committee for Review of AIA 1997 Document Revisions,

*(This Listing Continued)*

1995. (Resident, Santa Monica, California Office). **PRACTICE AREAS:** Construction Law.

**CURT M. DOMBEK,** born Missouri, 1958; admitted to bar, 1983, Missouri; 1984, California; 1995, District of Columbia. *Education:* Harvard University (A.B., magna cum laude with highest honors in Statistics, 1980; J.D., magna cum laude, 1983). Edwards Whitaker Scholar. Editor-in-Chief, Harvard Journal of Law and Public Policy, 1982-1983. Author: "The Twilight Zone of International Arbitration," 21 *Litigation* 42 (1995); "Implications of the Proposed Product Liability Fairness Act for Commercial Space Launches," I.B.A. (1995); "Harmonizing Allocations of Risk for Commercial Space Activities," Inter-Pacific Bar Association (1991). **LANGUAGES:** German. **PRACTICE AREAS:** Litigation; International Arbitration; International Trade Regulation; Aviation and Space Law.

**DAVID I. GINDLER,** born California, 1959; admitted to bar, 1985, California. *Education:* Pomona College (B.A., 1981); University of California at Los Angeles (J.D., 1984). Advocacy Chair, UCLA Moot Court Executive Board. Extern to the Hon. Stephen Reinhardt, U.S. Court of Appeals, Ninth Circuit, 1982. Member, Sections on Labor and Employment Law and Litigation, American Bar Association. *Member:* Los Angeles County Bar Association (Member, Sections on: Labor Law; Litigation); State Bar of California (Member, Sections on: Labor Law; Litigation).

**LAWRENCE H. HELLER,** born Colorado, 1944; admitted to bar, 1969, Colorado; 1971, California; 1975, U.S. District Court, Central District of California; 1979, U.S. Tax Court. *Education:* Colorado University (B.A., 1966; J.D., 1969); New York University (LL.M. in Taxation, 1970). Author: " A Primer of Estate and Gift Tax Issues Involved in Representing Foreign Individuals," 1991-1992, Vol. 3, No. 2, *The California International Tax Practitioner;* "Proposed Regulation Section 26.2663 2 and the Application of the Generation-Skipping Transfer Tax to Transfers by Nonresident Aliens," *International Tax and Business Lawyer,* Volume 12, 1994. Member, Committees: Foreign Activities of U.S. Taxpayers; Estate and Gift Tax, Section of Taxation; Section of International Law and Practice; Chair, International Property, Estate and Trust Law Committee, 1991—, American Bar Association. *Member:* Los Angeles County and International Bar Associations; State Bar of California (Member, Executive Committee, Estate and Gift Tax Subcommittee of Taxation Section; International Law Section). (Certified Specialist, Taxation Law, The State Bar of California Board of Legal Specialization) (Resident, Santa Monica, California Office). **PRACTICE AREAS:** International Estate Planning; Federal Estate and Gift Taxation; Federal Income Tax; Family Wealth Transfer; Limited Liability Companies.

**BRUCE L. ISHIMATSU,** born California, 1952; admitted to bar, 1979, California; U.S. District Court, Central District of California; 1985, U.S. District Court, Northern District of California and U.S. Court of Appeals, 9th Circuit; 1988, U.S. District Court, Southern District of California; 1989, U.S. District Court, Eastern District of California. *Education:* Pomona College (B.A., 1975); Georgetown University Law Center (J.D., 1978). *Member:* Japanese-American Bar Association of the Greater Los Angeles Area (President, 1993); Asian Pacific Bar of California (President, 1996-1997). **PRACTICE AREAS:** Antitrust Law; Dealer and Distributor Termination; Litigation; International.

**NORMAN H. LANE,** born New York, 1940; admitted to bar, 1965, New York; 1971, California. *Education:* Columbia University (A.B., summa cum laude, 1960); Harvard University (J.D., magna cum laude, 1963). Phi Beta Kappa. Staff Editor, Harvard Law Review, 1961-1963. Co-Author: (with H. Zaritsky) "Federal Income Taxation of Estates and Trusts," (1989). Author: California Practice - State and Local Taxation (1988). Professor, University of Southern California Law Center, 1969-1989; Lecturer, 1989—. (Resident, Santa Monica, California Office). **PRACTICE AREAS:** Taxation (Federal, State and Local Estate Planning); Estate Planning.

**THOMAS S. LOO,** born California, 1943; admitted to bar, 1969, California. *Education:* University of Southern California (B.S., magna cum laude, in Accounting, 1965; J.D., 1968). Phi Kappa Phi; Order of the Coif; Beta Gamma Sigma. Associate Editor, Southern California Law Review, 1967-1968. Author: "Lawyers' Use of Financial Statements in Counseling and Litigation," California C.E.B.; 1980; "Acquisitions and Mergers," Practising Law Institute, 1980-1990; "Representing Publicly Traded Corporations," Practising Law Institute, 1987. "Opinions in SEC Transactions 1990-1991," Practising Law Institute, 1990; "Introduction to Securities Law," Practising Law Institute, 1992-1995. Co-Author: "The SEC's New Regulation D," 5 Los Angeles Lawyer, September 1982; "Section 25102(f): California's New Counterpart to Regulation D," 5 Los Angeles Lawyer, October 1982; "The 'Fairness Hearing ' Exemption," 18 Sec. to Comm. Reg. 73,

*(This Listing Continued)*

## BRYAN CAVE LLP, Los Angeles—Continued

March, 1985; "The Regulation D Exemption," Securities Law Techniques, Matthew Bender, 1992-1996. Institute for Corporate Counsel, Board of Governors, 1988-1996. Adjunct Professor of Law, Securities Regulation, University of Southern California Law School, 1972-1993. (Resident, Santa Monica, California Office).

**M. SEAN MCMILLAN, (A PROFESSIONAL CORPORATION),** admitted to bar, 1971, California. *Education:* University of Munich, Munich, West Germany (Diploma, 1963); International School of Copenhagen, Copenhagen, Denmark (Certificate, 1964); University of Southern California (S.B., summa cum laude, 1967) Phi Kappa Phi; Harvard University (J.D., 1970). Note and Comment Editor, Harvard International Law Journal, 1968-1970. Adjunct Professor of Law, Public International Law, Loyola University, 1979-1981. Vice-Chairman, International Law Section, American Bar Association, 1979-1981. (Resident, Santa Monica, California Office). *LANGUAGES:* German. *PRACTICE AREAS:* International Business Transactions; Intellectual Property; Corporate Law.

**AGATHA M. MELAMED,** born Wisconsin, 1947; admitted to bar, 1972, Wisconsin; 1976, California; 1980, U.S. Supreme Court. *Education:* University of Rochester; University of Wisconsin (B.A., with honors, 1969; LL.B., 1972). Legal Writing and Research Teaching Assistant, University of Wisconsin Law School, 1970-1972. *PRACTICE AREAS:* Litigation Products Liability Law; Commercial Litigation; Labor.

**FRANK E. MERIDETH, JR.,** born California, 1944; admitted to bar, 1970, California. *Education:* University of California at Santa Barbara (B.A., 1966); University of California at Los Angeles (J.D., 1969). Order of the Coif. Member and Senior Editor, U.C.L.A. Law Review, 1968-1969. Author: "Tax Shelter Litigation," USC Tax Shelter Institute, 1973; "Litigation Involving Hybrid Securities," 3 Southern California Corporate Law and Finance Institute, 1975. Faculty Member, Los Angeles College of Trial Advocacy, 1980-1981. *Member:* Santa Monica Bar Association (Trustee); Association of Business Trial Lawyers. (Resident, Santa Monica, California Office).

**GRACE N. MITSUHATA,** born California, 1947; admitted to bar, 1975, California. *Education:* International Christian University, Tokyo, Japan and University of California at Los Angeles (B.A, 1969); University of California at Los Angeles (J.D., 1975). (Resident, Santa Monica, California Office).

**JEFFREY W. MOROF,** born Michigan, 1954; admitted to bar, 1979, Missouri; 1982, California. *Education:* University of Michigan (A.B., 1976); Washington University (J.D., 1979). Editor-in-Chief, Washington University Urban Law Annual, 1978-1979. Lecturer, Washington University School of Law, 1980-1981. *PRACTICE AREAS:* Civil Practice; Aviation Law; Products Liability Law.

**ANGELO A. PAPARELLI** (See Irvine, California for Listing).

**JON A. PFEIFFER,** born Nebraska, 1958; admitted to bar, 1983, Colorado; 1984, Nebraska; 1985, California. *Education:* University of Nebraska (B.S., with distinction, 1980); University of Denver (J.D., 1983). (Resident, Santa Monica, California Office). *PRACTICE AREAS:* Civil Litigation.

**CATHERINE F. RATCLIFFE,** born California, 1957; admitted to bar, 1984, Georgia; 1986, California. *Education:* University of California, Los Angeles (B.A., 1979); University of California, Berkeley (Boalt Hall) (J.D., 1983). Phi Beta Kappa. Law Clerk to the Hon. Richard C. Freeman, U.S. District Court, Northern District of Georgia, 1983-1985. (Resident, Santa Monica, California Office). *PRACTICE AREAS:* Corporate; Securities.

**PAMELA M. SODERBECK,** born Iowa, 1953; admitted to bar, 1978, California. *Education:* San Diego State University (A.B., 1975); Harvard University (J.D., 1978). Phi Beta Kappa. (Resident, Santa Monica, California Office). *PRACTICE AREAS:* Corporate and Securities.

**HARRY R. STANG,** born Germany, 1936; admitted to bar, 1963, California. *Education:* Oberlin College (A.B., 1959); Stanford University (LL.B., 1962). *PRACTICE AREAS:* Employment and Labor Relations.

**LYNN K. THOMPSON,** born Minnesota, 1952; admitted to bar, 1977, California. *Education:* Stanford University (A.B., 1974); Hastings College of Law, University of California (J.D., 1977). Member, Hastings Law Journal, 1976-1977. Attorney, National Labor Relations Board, Region 31, Los Angeles, California, 1977-1982. Member, Executive Committee, Labor Law Section, Los Angeles County Bar Association, 1988—; Chair, Labor Relations Section, ABA Construction Law Forum 1991-1992. *PRACTICE AREAS:* Labor and Employment Law.

*(This Listing Continued)*

**ROBERT D. VOGEL,** born Michigan, 1950; admitted to bar, 1974, California, U.S. Court of Appeals, Ninth and Tenth Circuits and U.S. Supreme Court. *Education:* Brigham Young University; University of Loyola at Los Angeles (J.D., with honors, 1974). Member, Loyola Law Review, 1973-1974. Author: Comment: "Attorney's Fees Under the Landrum-Griffin Act: The Need for Union Therapeutics," 7 Loyola L.A.L. Rev. 137 (Fed. 1974); "Recent Decision, Labor Law--Bodle, Fogel, Julber, Reinhardt & Rothschild," 205 N.L.R.B. No. 60 (Oct. 23, 1973), 7 Loyola L.A.L. Rev. 393 (June 1974). *PRACTICE AREAS:* Employment Law; Civil Litigation.

**BARRYE L. WALL,** born Virginia, 1956; admitted to bar, 1982, New York; 1989, California. *Education:* Hampden-Sydney College (B.A., summa cum laude, 1978); University of Virginia (J.D., 1981). Phi Beta Kappa; Order of the Coif. *Member:* New York State Bar Association; State Bar of California. (Resident, Santa Monica, California Office).

### OF COUNSEL

**DONALD K. GARNER,** born California, 1944; admitted to bar, 1971, California. *Education:* University of Southern California (B.S., cum laude, 1966; M.B.A., magna cum laude, 1967; J.D., 1970). Beta Alpha Psi; Beta Gamma Sigma; Order of the Coif; Phi Delta Phi. Member, Skull and Dagger. Member, Southern California Law Review, 1968-1970. Member, Board of Governors, University of Southern California General Alumni Association, 1985-1990. (Resident, Santa Monica, California Office).

**HUGH T. SCOGIN, JR.,** born 1950; admitted to bar, 1983, New York (Not admitted in California). *Education:* College of Charleston (B.A., 1972); University of Chicago (A.M., 1975); Harvard University (J.D., 1982). (Resident, Santa Monica, California Office).

### COUNSEL

**KATHERINE FLEMING ASHTON,** born Michigan, 1959; admitted to bar, 1985, California. *Education:* Stanford University (A.B., with distinction, 1981; J.D., 1985). Phi Beta Kappa; Omicron Delta Epsilon. *Member:* Los Angeles County Bar Association; State Bar of California. (Resident, Santa Monica, California Office).

**ELIZABETH A. KING,** born California, 1957; admitted to bar, 1984, California. *Education:* California State University, Long Beach (B.A., summa cum laude, 1981); University of California at Los Angeles (J.D., 1984). Order of the Coif. (Resident, Santa Monica, California Office). *PRACTICE AREAS:* Corporate; Securities; Business Transactions; Corporate Law.

**KENNETH G. PETRULIS,** born 1945; admitted to bar, 1973, California. *Education:* Illinois Institute of Technology (B.S., 1971); University of Illinois (J.D., 1973). Author: "Joint Tenancy a Mere Form," State Bar of California, Estate Planning, Trust and Probate News. Speaker: State Bar Program on Probate Administration, 1988, 1991, 1993 and 1995. *Member:* Beverly Hills (Member, 1985—; Board of Governors 1991-1995; Chair, 1990-1991 Probate Section; Chair, Resolutions Committee, 1992-1993; Los Angeles County Fee Arbitration Panel, 1983—) Bar Associations. (Resident, Santa Monica, California Office).

### ASSOCIATES

**MICHELLE D. BOYDSTON,** born California, 1966; admitted to bar, 1992, California. *Education:* University of California at Los Angeles (B.A., 1989); Loyola Law School (J.D., 1992). Loyola Law Review, Member, 1990-1991 and Note and Comment Editor, 1991-1992. Author: "Press Censorship and Access Restrictions During the Persian Gulf War: A First Amendment Analysis," 25 Loyola of Los Angeles Law Review 1073, 1992. (Resident, Santa Monica, California Office). *PRACTICE AREAS:* SEC Enforcement; Litigation.

**PAMELA C. CALVET,** born California, 1958; admitted to bar, 1983, California and U.S. Court of Appeals, Ninth Circuit. *Education:* University of Southern California (B.S., 1980; J.D., 1983). *PRACTICE AREAS:* Labor and Employment Law.

**CHRISTOPHER L. DUERINGER,** born Louisiana, 1958; admitted to bar, 1994, California and U.S. District Court, Central District of California. *Education:* Indiana University (B.S., with distinction, 1982); Loyola Law School (J.D., Order of the Coif, 1994). Sayer NcNeil Scholar. Editor, Loyola Law Review. (Resident, Santa Monica, California Office). *PRACTICE AREAS:* Litigation.

**DAVID ERIKSON,** born California, 1963; (admission pending). *Education:* University of California at Los Angeles (B.A., 1987; J.D., 1996).

**THOMAS N. FITZGIBBON,** born Illinois, 1965; admitted to bar, 1993, California; U.S. District Court, Central, Northern, Southern and

*(This Listing Continued)*

Eastern Districts of California; U.S. Court of Appeals, Ninth Circuit. *Education:* Williams College (B.A., 1987); Washington University (J.D., 1993). Managing Editor, Washington University Law Quarterly, 1992-1993. (Resident, Santa Monica, California Office). **PRACTICE AREAS:** Environmental; Litigation.

**ANDREW H. FRIEDMAN,** born Missouri, 1963; admitted to bar, 1990, Missouri; 1991, California; 1992, District of Columbia. *Education:* Vanderbilt University (B.A., cum laude, 1986); Cornell University (J.D., 1989). Member: Moot Court Board, 1988-1989; Cornell Law Review, 1988-1989. Clerk, Hon. John T. Nixon, U.S. District Court, Middle District of Tennessee, 1989-1990. **PRACTICE AREAS:** Labor and Employment Law; Litigation.

**CLAIRE M. GOLDBLOOM,** born District of Columbia, 1966; admitted to bar, 1992, California; 1993, District of Columbia. *Education:* University of Wisconsin (B.A., 1987); University of Southern California (J.D., 1991). Clerk, Honorable Howard D. McKibben, U.S. District Court, 1991-1992. (Resident, Santa Monica, California Office). **LANGUAGES:** French. **PRACTICE AREAS:** Corporate; Securities.

**CATHERINE L. HAIGHT,** born Ohio, 1957; admitted to bar, 1989, California. *Education:* University of California at Berkeley (B.A., cum laude, 1979); Southwestern University (J.D., 1989). Member: Moot Court Honors Program, 1988-1989; Board of Governors, 1988-1989. (Resident, Santa Monica, California Office). **PRACTICE AREAS:** Immigration; International Law.

**LESLIE L. HECHT HELMER,** born Nevada, 1963; admitted to bar, 1990, California. *Education:* Stanford University (B.A., 1985); University of California School of Law (J.D., 1990). **PRACTICE AREAS:** Labor and Employment Law.

**KEVIN A. KYLE,** born Florida, 1968; admitted to bar, 1993, Florida; 1994, California, U.S. District Court, Central District of California and U.S. Tax Court. *Education:* Emory University (B.B.A., with highest distinction, 1990); University of Florida (J.D., with honors, 1993); New York University (LL.M., Taxation, 1994). (Resident, Santa Monica, California Office).

**MAUREEN M. MURANAKA,** born California, 1951; admitted to bar, 1984, California; 1986, Hawaii. *Education:* University of Redlands (A.B., 1973); University of the Pacific, McGeorge School of Law (J.D., with distinction, 1984). Member, Pacific Law Journal, 1982-1983. (Resident, Santa Monica, California Office).

**RICHARD C. OCHOA,** born Illinois, 1960; admitted to bar, 1989, California; 1990, U.S. District Court, Central, Eastern, Northern and Southern Districts of California and U.S. Claims Court; 1991 U.S. Court of Appeals, Ninth Circuit. *Education:* DePaul University (B.S., cum laude, 1982); University of Michigan (J.D., 1987). Blue Key, Order of the Barristers. (Resident, Santa Monica, California Office). **PRACTICE AREAS:** Commercial, Construction and Insurance Coverage Litigation.

**JULIE E. PATTERSON,** born Michigan, 1959; admitted to bar, 1993, California. *Education:* The Ohio State University (B.S., cum laude, 1981); University of Southern California (J.D., 1993). Order of the Coif. Notes Editor, Southern California Law Review. Co-Author: "Labor Law Reform: A Management Perspective," 45 Labor L.J. 565, 1994. **PRACTICE AREAS:** Labor and Employment Law.

**TRACEY A. QUINN,** born New Jersey, 1966; admitted to bar, 1991, California, U.S. District Court, Central District of California and U.S. Court of Appeals, 9th Circuit. *Education:* Vassar College (A.B., with honors, 1988); University of Southern California (J.D., 1991). Member, Hale Moot Court Honors Program. **PRACTICE AREAS:** Labor and Employment Law.

**MICHAEL W. SOUVEROFF,** born California, 1961; admitted to bar, 1986, California. *Education:* Stanford University (A.B., 1983); University of Southern California (J.D., 1986). **PRACTICE AREAS:** Corporate.

**MICHAEL D. STEIN,** born California, 1962; admitted to bar, 1987, California and U.S. District Court, Central District of California; 1989, U.S. District Court, Northern, Southern and Eastern Districts of California and U.S. Court of Appeals, Ninth Circuit. *Education:* University of California at Los Angeles (B.A., magna cum laude, 1983); University of California, Boalt Hall School of Law (J.D., 1987). **PRACTICE AREAS:** General Civil Practice; Contract Law.

**ADAM J. THURSTON,** born California, 1966; admitted to bar, 1992, California. *Education:* Boston University (B.A., magna cum laude, 1988); Vanderbilt University (J.D., 1992).

*(This Listing Continued)*

**CHRISTINE M. TORRE,** born New York, 1958; admitted to bar, 1992, California. *Education:* Smith College (B.A., magna cum laude, 1981); Loyola Law School (J.D., cum laude, 1992). Phi Beta Kappa; Order of the Coif. Law Clerk to the Hon. Ronald S. W. Lew, U.S. District Court, Central District of California, 1992-1993. **PRACTICE AREAS:** Employment; Labor Relations.

**ROBERT E. WYNNER,** born California, 1970; admitted to bar, 1996, California. *Education:* University of California, Irvine (B.A., 1992); Loyola University of Los Angeles (J.D., 1996). Alpha Sigma Nu. Member: Moot Court Honors Board, 1995-1996; Jessup International Law Moot Court Team, 1995-1996; Sayre MacNeil Scholar. (Resident, Santa Monica, California Office).

**KAREN D. YARDLEY,** born Utah, 1958; admitted to bar, 1989, California and U.S. District Court, Southern District of California. *Education:* University of Utah (B.S., 1980; M.S., 1983); Georgetown University (J.D., cum laude, 1989). Co-Author: "Is It Time For A New Client Information Letter," Estate Planning, Trust and Probate Newsletter, Vol. 2, 1991. Member: Beverly Hills Bar Association; State Bar of California. (Resident, Santa Monica, California Office). **PRACTICE AREAS:** Estate Planning Law; Probate Law; Trust Law.

**LESLEY D. YOUNG,** born California, 1970; admitted to bar, 1995, California. *Education:* University of Southern California (B.A., magna cum laude, 1992; J.D., 1995). Phi Beta Kappa.

All Partners and Associates of the Firm are members of the American Bar Association.

REPRESENTATIVE CLIENTS: American Isuzu Motors, Inc.; Blue Cross of California; Canteen Corp.; City of Hope National Medical Center; Community Psychiatric Centers; Conde Nast Publications, Inc.; Hiuka America Corp.; Honda North America, Inc.; Intel Corp.; LaCosta Resort and Spa; Lloyds of London; Maxicare Health Plan; MAXXAM, Inc.; McDonnell Douglas Corp.; Occidental College; Packard Bell; Pasadena Area Community College; Superior Industries International, Inc.; Teledyne, Inc.; The Union Ice Co.; United Foods, Inc.; Watt Industries, Inc.; Yamaha Motor Corporation, U.S.

---

# BUCHALTER, NEMER, FIELDS & YOUNGER

*A PROFESSIONAL CORPORATION*

Established in 1949

24TH FLOOR, 601 SOUTH FIGUEROA STREET
**LOS ANGELES, CALIFORNIA 90017**
Telephone: 213-891-0700
Fax: 213-896-0400
Email: buchalter@earthlink.net
URL: http://www.buchalter.com

*New York, New York Office:* 15th Floor, 605 Third Avenue. Telephone: 212-490-8600. Fax: 212-490-6022.

*San Francisco, California Office:* 29th Floor, 333 Market Street. Telephone: 415-227-0900. Fax: 415-227-0770.

*Newport Beach, California Office:* Suite 1450, 620 Newport Center Drive. Telephone: 714-760-1121. Fax: 714-720-0182.

FIRM PROFILE: *Buchalter, Nemer, Fields & Younger was founded in 1949 by Irwin R. Buchalter, who passed away in 1994, Murray M. Fields, who is still with the firm, and Jerry Nemer, who passed away in 1980. The firm's legal practice encompasses every major area of business law including Commercial, Corporate, Environmental, Banking, Finance, Intellectual Property, Entertainment, Real Property, Probate, Insurance, Securities, Taxation, Labor, Reorganization, Bankruptcy, International Business Law, Alternate Dispute Resolution, and General Civil and Trial Practice in all State and Federal Courts.*

**MURRAY M. FIELDS,** born New York, N.Y., October 11, 1909; admitted to bar, 1935, New York; 1947, California. *Education:* Duke University; Columbia University; New York University (LL.B., 1934). Member, Board of Directors, New York University Law Alumni Association, 1973—. Member, Board of Directors, Ninth Judicial Circuit Historical Society, 1990. Member, National Panel of Arbitrators, American Arbitration Association, 1965—. *Member:* Los Angeles County and American Bar Associations; The State Bar of California; Association of Business Trial Lawyers (Member, Board of Governors, 1973-1978; President, 1977-1978). **PRACTICE AREAS:** Construction; General Business; Legal Malpractice; Real Property. **Email:** mfields.bnfy@mcimail.com

**RICHARD JAY GOLDSTEIN,** born Brooklyn, New York, February 18, 1941; admitted to bar, 1966, California. *Education:* Menlo College and

*(This Listing Continued)*

## BUCHALTER, NEMER, FIELDS & YOUNGER, A PROFESSIONAL CORPORATION, Los Angeles—Continued

Stanford University (B.A., 1962); University of California, Los Angeles (LL.B., 1965). Member, Board of Governors, 1970—; Secretary-Treasurer, 1971-1972; Vice President, 1974-1975; President, 1975-1976, Financial Lawyers Conference. *Member:* Los Angeles County, American (Member: Section of Corporation, Banking and Business Law; Uniform Commercial Code Committee and the Sub-Committees on Secured Transactions and Letters of Credit, 1980—) and International (Member, Section on Business Law, Aeronautical Law, Vice-Chair, 1989-1992, Chair, 1992— and Commercial Banking Committee, 1977—) Bar Associations; The State Bar of California; American Society of Corporate Secretaries (Member, Tender Offer Committee, 1988—); American College of Commercial Finance Attorneys. *PRACTICE AREAS:* Financial Law; Personal Property; Secured Transactions; Workouts. *Email:* rgoldstein.bnfy@mcimail.com

**MICHAEL L. WACHTELL,** born Bronx, New York, 1942; admitted to bar, 1967, Virginia and District of Columbia; 1970, California; 1992, Nevada; registered to practice before U.S. Patent and Trademark Office. *Education:* City College of the City University of New York (B.E.E., 1965); George Washington University (J.D., with honors, 1968). *Member:* Beverly Hills, Century City, Los Angeles County and American Bar Associations; State Bar of California; Virginia State Bar; The District of Columbia Bar; State Bar of Nevada; Nevada Trial Lawyers Association; Los Angeles Business Trial Lawyers Association. *PRACTICE AREAS:* Banking; Commercial Litigation; Patent and Trademark. *Email:* mwachtell.bnfy@mcimail.com

**ROBERT C. COLTON,** born Maywood, California, May 15, 1943; admitted to bar, 1969, California. *Education:* University of Colorado (B.A., 1965); University of California, Los Angeles (J.D., 1968). *Member:* Los Angeles County (Member, Corporation Section) and American (Member: Business Law Section; Committee on Commercial Financial Services; Chairman, Subcommittee on Acquisition Financing, 1982-1986) Bar Associations; State Bar of California (Chairman, Education Committee, Business Law Section, 1985-1986; Member, Executive Committee, Business Law Section, 1986). *PRACTICE AREAS:* Banking; Corporate; Finance. *Email:* rcolton.bnfy@mcimail.com

**GARY A. YORK,** born Glendale, California, August 29, 1943; admitted to bar, 1969, California. *Education:* Pomona College (B.A., 1965); Stanford Law School (LL.B., 1968). Phi Beta Kappa. Member, Board of Editors, Stanford Law Review, 1966-1968. Instructor, University of California, Los Angeles Law School, 1968-1969. *Member:* Los Angeles County (Chairman, Real Estate Finance Subsection, 1994-1996) and American (Chairman, Real Estate Finance Committee, Real Property, Probate and Trust Section, 1987-1989) Bar Associations; State Bar of California; American College of Real Estate Lawyers. *PRACTICE AREAS:* Real Estate. *Email:* gyork.bnfy@mcimail.com

**ARTHUR CHINSKI,** born Lodz, Poland, April 13, 1945; admitted to bar, 1971, California. *Education:* University of California, Los Angeles (B.A., 1967); University of California, Davis (J.D., 1970). Attorney, National Labor Relations Board, Region 21, Los Angeles, 1971-1974. Director and Chairperson, Employment Regulations Program, 1980-1981 and Director, Compensation and Benefits Program, 1980-1981, California Business Law Institute. Director and Chairperson, Human Resources Institute, Institute of Business Law 1984—. *Member:* Los Angeles County (Member, Executive Board, Labor Law Section, 1981-1982; Vice-Chair, Executive Committee, Arbitration Committee, Attorney-Client Relations Office, 1986-1987), American (Member, Labor Relations Law and Litigation Sections) and International (Member, Labour Law Committee, 1977—) Bar Associations; State Bar of California (Member, Labor and Employment Law Section). *PRACTICE AREAS:* Labor and Employment Law (Management); Employment Litigation; Collective Bargaining/Union Organizing; Workplace Safety and Health; Employee Benefits. *Email:* achinski.bnfy@mcimail.com

**JAY R. ZIEGLER,** born Los Angeles, California, March 16, 1947; admitted to bar, 1972, California. *Education:* University of California, Los Angeles (B.A., cum laude, 1969); Boalt Hall School of Law, University of California (J.D., 1972). *Member:* Los Angeles County Bar Association; The State Bar of California; Association of Business Trial Lawyers. *PRACTICE AREAS:* Business Litigation. *Email:* jziegler.bnfy@mcimail.com

**MICHAEL J. CERESETO,** born 1948; admitted to bar, 1973, California. *Education:* University of California, Irvine and University of California at Los Angeles (B.A., 1970); University of California, Los Angeles (J.D., 1973). *Member:* Los Angeles County Bar Association; State Bar of California. *PRACTICE AREAS:* Real Estate Litigation. *Email:* mcereseto.bnfy@mcimail.com

**BERNARD E. LE SAGE,** born Pasadena, California, March 29, 1949; admitted to bar, 1974, California. *Education:* University of Notre Dame (B.A., 1971); Loyola University of Los Angeles (J.D., 1974). President, Los Angeles County Bar Barristers, 1983-1984. *Member:* Los Angeles County (Trustee, 1982-1984) and American Bar Associations; The State Bar of California; Chancery Club. *PRACTICE AREAS:* Business and Financial Institution Litigation. *Email:* blesage.bnfy@mcimail.com

**GREGORY KEEVER,** born San Diego, California, 1949; admitted to bar, 1974, Virginia; 1977, District of Columbia; 1980, California; 1982, Texas. *Education:* University of North Carolina (B.A., with honors, 1971); University of Virginia (J.D., 1974); George Washington University (LL.M., 1977). Phi Beta Kappa. Clerk, U.S. Court of Claims, 1975-1976. [LTJG, U.S.N.R., 1971-1977] *Email:* gkeever.bnfy@mcimail.com

**ROGER D. LOOMIS, JR.,** born Madera, California, 1948; admitted to bar, 1974, California; 1976, New York. *Education:* University of California at Davis (B.A., with highest honors, 1971); Columbia University (J.D., 1974); New York University (LL.M., in Taxation, 1979). Phi Beta Kappa; Phi Kappa Phi. Harlan Fiske Stone Scholar. *Member:* Los Angeles County (Member, Executive Committee, Business and Corporations Law Section, 1992—) and American Bar Associations; State Bar of California. *Email:* rloomis.bnfy@mcimail.com

**PHILIP J. WOLMAN,** born Altadena, California, January 20, 1950; admitted to bar, 1976, California. *Education:* University of California at Berkeley (A.B., 1973); University of California at Los Angeles (J.D., 1976); New York University (LL.M. in Taxation, 1977). *Member:* Beverly Hills (Member, Committee on Taxation), Los Angeles County (Member, Taxation Section) and American (Member: Taxation Section; Committee on Personal Service Organizations) Bar Associations; State Bar of California. (Certified Specialist, Taxation Law, The State Bar of California Board of Legal Specialization). *PRACTICE AREAS:* Taxation (100%). *Email:* pwolman.bnfy@mcimail.com

**KEITH B. BARDELLINI,** born Oakland, California, November 13, 1952; admitted to bar, 1977, California. *Education:* University of California at Berkeley (B.A., 1974); Hastings College of Law, University of California (J.D., 1977). Member, Moot Court Board. Governor's Appointee to Commission on Juvenile Justice and Delinquency Prevention, 1979-1983. *Member:* State Bar of California; American Bar Association (Member, Sections of: Labor Law; Litigation). *REPORTED CASES:* Cole v. Fair Oaks Fire Protection District (1987) 43 Cal 3d 148. *PRACTICE AREAS:* Civil Litigation; Employment Litigation; Labor Law. *Email:* kbardellini.bnfy@mcimail.com

**MARK A. BONENFANT,** born Santa Monica, California, August 28, 1953; admitted to bar, 1978, California and U.S. District Court, Northern District of California. *Education:* California State University, Northridge (B.A., cum laude, 1974); University of San Diego (J.D., cum laude, 1978); Georgetown University (LL.M., Taxation, 1982). *Member:* Los Angeles County (Member, State Securities Regulation Committee, Business Law Section) and American (Member: Corporation, Banking and Business Law Section; Committee on Federal Regulations of Securities) Bar Associations; State Bar of California (Member, Corporations Committee, Business Law Section). *PRACTICE AREAS:* Corporate Securities Mergers and Acquisitions; General Corporate; Venture Capital; General Business. *Email:* mbonenfant.bnfy@mci.mail.com

**DAVID S. KYMAN,** born Mount Vernon, New York, June 8, 1954; admitted to bar, 1979, California and U.S. District Court, Northern, Eastern and Central Districts of California. *Education:* University of California, Los Angeles and Santa Barbara (B.A., 1977); Southwestern University (J.D., 1979). *Member:* Los Angeles County (Member, Business and Corporations Law Section) and American Bar Associations; State Bar of California. *PRACTICE AREAS:* Banking; Corporate; Finance. *Email:* dkyman.bnfy@mcimail.com

**JAMES H. TURKEN,** born New York, N.Y., March 15, 1952; admitted to bar, 1979, California and U.S. District Court, Central District of California. *Education:* University of California at Los Angeles; Loyola University (B.S., 1975); Southwestern University (J.D., cum laude, 1979). Phi Alpha Delta. Member, Southwestern University Law Review, 1978-1979. Author: "Britt v. Superior Court: A U-Turn on the Road to Liberal Discovery V.11 (2)," Southwestern University Law Review, 1979. *Member:* Beverly Hills, Los Angeles County and American Bar Associations. *PRACTICE AREAS:* Civil Litigation. *Email:* jturken.bnfy@mcimail.com

*(This Listing Continued)*

**KEVIN M. BRANDT,** born Cheyenne, Wyoming, July 18, 1953; admitted to bar, 1980, California; 1982, U.S. District Court, Central, Eastern and Southern Districts of California; 1984, U.S. Court of Appeals, Ninth Circuit. *Education:* Georgetown University (A.B., with honors, 1975; J.D., 1979). *Member:* Los Angeles County (Member, Real Property Section) and American (Member, Real Property, Probate and Trust Law Section) Bar Associations; State Bar of California; Financial Lawyers Conference; Mortgage Bankers Association. *PRACTICE AREAS:* Real Estate Development; Real Estate Finance; Real Estate Restructuring; Bankruptcy. *Email:* kbrandt.bnfy@mcimail.com

**JEFFREY S. WRUBLE,** born Detroit, Michigan, 1955; admitted to bar, 1980, California; 1981, U.S. District Court, Central District of California and U.S. Court of Appeals, Ninth Circuit; 1984, U.S. District Court, Northern District of California; 1989, U.S. District Court, Eastern District of California. *Education:* University of California, Berkeley (B.A., 1977); University of San Diego (J.D., cum laude, 1980). Member, Los Angeles Bar Association, Attorneys Errors and Omissions Prevention Committee, 1988—. *Member:* Century City, Beverly Hills and Los Angeles County (Member: Attorney, Client Relations Committee, 1988—; Errors and Omissions Committee, 1988—) Bar Associations; State Bar of California. *PRACTICE AREAS:* Commercial Litigation; Real Estate Litigation; Banking and Bank Operations; Business Litigation. *Email:* jwruble.bnfy@mcimail.com

**RANDYE B. SOREF,** born New York, N.Y., May 11, 1955; admitted to bar, 1981, California; 1987, U.S. Supreme Court; 1989, U.S. District Court, District of Arizona. *Education:* Hofstra University (B.A., 1976); California Western School of Law (J.D., 1980). Head Lead Articles Editor, International Law Journal; Staff Writer, International Law Journal. *Member:* Los Angeles County Bar Association; State Bar of California; Financial Lawyers Conference and Bankruptcy Forum. *PRACTICE AREAS:* Insolvency; Chapter 11; Commercial Litigation. *Email:* rsoref.bnfy@mcimail.com

**PAMELA KOHLMAN WEBSTER,** born San Jose, California, October 30, 1955; admitted to bar, 1982, California, U.S. Court of Appeals, Ninth Circuit and U.S. District Court, Central, Eastern, Northern and Southern Districts of California. *Education:* San Jose State University (B.A., 1978); University of California Law School at Davis (J.D., 1982). *Member:* Board of Governors, Financial Lawyers Conference; Executive Committee, Commercial Law and Bankruptcy Section of the Los Angeles County Bar Association. Director, Los Angeles County Bankruptcy Forum, 1991—. *Member:* Los Angeles County and American (Member, Business Bankruptcy Section) Bar Associations; State Bar of California. *PRACTICE AREAS:* Bankruptcy; Insurance Insolvency. *Email:* pwebster.bnfy@mcimail.com

**MATTHEW W. KAVANAUGH,** born San Francisco, California, March 27, 1957; admitted to bar, 1983, California. *Education:* University of California, Davis (B.A., French and Economics, cum laude, 1979); University of California, Los Angeles (M.B.A., 1983; J.D., 1983). *Member:* Los Angeles County (Vice-Chair, Commercial Law Committee and Bankruptcy Section) and American (Member, Commercial Financial Services Committee) Bar Associations; State Bar of California; Equipment Leasing Association of America (ELA) (Former Member, Lawyers Committee; Member, Transportation Committee, Products Liability Subcommittee and State Government Relations Committee); Western Association of Equipment Lessors (Member, Standards Committee and the Legal Committee); Financial Lawyers Conference. *LANGUAGES:* French. *PRACTICE AREAS:* Commercial Finance; Workouts; Problem Loan Restructuring; Equipment Leasing; Unsecured Lending. *Email:* mkavanaugh.bnfy@mcimail.com

**RICHARD S. ANGEL,** born Los Angeles, California, June 9, 1958; admitted to bar, 1983, California. *Education:* University of California at San Diego (B.S., 1980); University of Birmingham, England; University of Southern California (J.D., 1983). *Member:* Los Angeles County (Member: Real Property Section; Steering Committee, General Real Property Subsection, 1987—) and American (Member, Real Property, Probate and Trust Law Section) Bar Associations; State Bar of California. *PRACTICE AREAS:* Real Estate Development; Acquisition; Sales & Leasing. *Email:* rangel.bnfy@mcimail.com

**BRYAN MASHIAN,** born Tehran, Iran, February 14, 1960; admitted to bar, 1984, California and U.S. District Court, Central District of California. *Education:* University of California, Los Angeles (B.A., 1981; J.D., 1984). *Member:* Beverly Hills and Los Angeles County (Member: Real Property Section; Steering Committee, Commercial Development Subsection) Bar Associations; State Bar of California. *PRACTICE AREAS:* Real Estate Development; Acquisition Sales; Leasing, Exchange & Workouts. *Email:* bmashian.bnfy@mcimail.com

*(This Listing Continued)*

**ROBERT J. DAVIDSON,** born Los Angeles, California, December 6, 1958; admitted to bar, 1985, California. *Education:* University of California, Los Angeles; University of Southern California (B.S., magna cum laude, 1980; M.B.A., 1984; J.D., 1984). *Member:* State Bar of California. *PRACTICE AREAS:* Banking; Corporate; Finance. *Email:* rdavidson.bnfy@mcimail.com

**BERNARD D. BOLLINGER, JR.,** born Duarte, California, June 5, 1961; admitted to bar, 1987, California; 1988, U.S. District Court, Central, Northern and Southern Districts of California. *Education:* Citrus College (A.A., 1982); University of Southern California (B.A., 1984); Loyola Law School, Los Angeles (J.D., 1987). *Member:* State Bar of California; American Bankruptcy Institute; Financial Lawyer's Conference; The Los Angeles Bankruptcy Forum. *PRACTICE AREAS:* Bankruptcy. *Email:* bbollinger.bnfy@mcimail.com

*OF COUNSEL*

**RONALD E. GORDON,** born Chicago, Illinois, December 18, 1932; admitted to bar, 1961, California. *Education:* University of Washington (B.A., 1955); University of California, Berkeley (LL.B., 1960). Past Member, Bankruptcy Committee, Ninth Circuit Judicial Conference, 1976-1977. Lecturer: Continuing Legal Education of the Bar, 1991—. *Member:* Los Angeles County (Past Member: Executive Committee, Commercial Law Section; Federal Practice Committee) and American Bar Associations; The State Bar of California. *PRACTICE AREAS:* Insolvency. *Email:* rgordon.bnfy@mcimail.com

**STUART D. BUCHALTER,** born Los Angeles, California, August 13, 1937; admitted to bar, 1963, California; 1976, District of Columbia. *Education:* University of California, Berkeley (B.A., 1959); Harvard University (LL.B. , 1962). *Member:* Los Angeles County (Chairman, Business and Corporate Law Section, 1973-1974) and American (Member, Federal Regulation of Securities Committee, Section of Corporation, Banking and Business Law, 1974-1983) Bar Associations; The District of Columbia Bar; The State Bar of California. *PRACTICE AREAS:* Banking; Corporate; Finance. *Email:* sbuchalter.bnfy@mcimail.com

**BARRY A. SMITH,** born Waterbury, Connecticut, November 1, 1943; admitted to bar, 1971, California, U.S. District Court, Central, Northern, Eastern & Southern Districts of California and U.S. Supreme Court; 1973, U.S. Tax Court; 1974, U.S. Court of Appeals, Ninth Circuit. *Education:* California State University, Northridge (B.S., 1966); Southwestern University (J.D., 1970). Professor of Law, University of West Los Angeles in Trial Tactics and Litigation Procedure, 1976-1978. *Member:* Beverly Hills (Member, Commercial Law Section), Los Angeles County (Member, Sections on: Commercial Law; Banking; Debt Collection; Litigation) and American Bar Associations; State Bar of California; Los Angeles Trial Lawyers Association; California Trial Lawyers Association; The Association of Trial Lawyers of America; The Association of Business Trial Lawyers of America; Association of Los Angeles Business Trial Lawyers; Financial Lawyers Conference; California Bankers Association; Southern California Mortgage Bankers Association; Western Association of Equipment Lessors; National Vehicle Leasing Association; California Trustees Association. *Email:* bsmith.bnfy@mcimil.com

**GEOFFREY FORSYTHE BOGEAUS,** born Los Angeles, California, June 3, 1941; admitted to bar, 1974, California; 1976, U.S. Court of Appeals, Ninth Circuit; 1988, U.S. District Court, Eastern District of Michigan. *Education:* Yale University (B.A., 1962); University of California, Los Angeles (J.D., 1972). *Member:* The State Bar of California. [With U.S. Coast Guard, 1959-1965]. *PRACTICE AREAS:* Complex Civil Litigation. *Email:* gbogeaus.bnfy@mcimail.com

**SCOTT O. SMITH,** born Altadena, California, March 30, 1948; admitted to bar, 1974, California, U.S. District Court, Central, Northern, Eastern and Southern Districts of California and U.S. Court of Appeals, Ninth Circuit; 1986, U.S. Supreme Court. *Education:* University of Southern California (B.S., cum laude, 1971); Loyola University of Los Angeles (J.D., 1974). Beta Gamma Sigma; Phi Alpha Delta. Judge Pro Tem, Los Angeles Municipal Court, 1982—. Lecturer: Creditors Remedies, Continuing Education of the Bar; The Rutter Group, 1983—. *Member:* Los Angeles County (Member, Commercial Law and Bankruptcy and Provisional and Prejudgment Remedies Sections) and American (Member, Commercial Law and Bankruptcy Litigation Sections) Bar Associations; State Bar of California; Financial Lawyers Conference (Member. Board of Governors, 1983-1985); Bankruptcy Forum; California Bankers Association; Southern California Mortgage Bankers Association; National Vehicle Leasing Association; Western Association of Equipment Lessors; National Association of Bankruptcy Trustees. *PRACTICE AREAS:* Insolvency; Commercial Litigation; Creditor Rights. *Email:* ssmith.bnfy@mcimail.com

*(This Listing Continued)*

**BUCHALTER, NEMER, FIELDS & YOUNGER,** A PROFESSIONAL CORPORATION, Los Angeles—Continued

**HOLLY J. FUJIE,** born Oakland, California, December 5, 1955; admitted to bar, 1978, California and U.S. District Court, Central District of California; 1982, U.S. District Court, Southern District of California; 1983, U.S. District Court, Northern District of California; 1986, U.S. District Court, Eastern District of California and U.S. Court of Appeals, Ninth Circuit. *Education:* University of California, Berkeley (A.B., with greatest distinction, 1975); Boalt Hall School of Law, University of California (J.D., 1978). Judge Pro Tem, Los Angeles Municipal Court, 1985—. *Member:* Los Angeles County and American (Member, Litigation Section) Bar Associations; State Bar of California; Association of Business Trial Lawyers; Japanese American Bar Association; California Women Lawyers Association; Los Angeles Women Lawyers Association. **PRACTICE AREAS:** Civil Litigation; Insurance Coverage Law; Reinsurance Coverage. **Email:** hfujie.bnfy@mcimail.com

**ELIZABETH S. TRUSSELL,** born Stockton, California, June 17, 1946; admitted to bar, 1978, California. *Education:* University of California, Berkeley (A.B., 1968); Loyola Law School of Los Angeles (J.D., 1978). Member, Loyola Law Review, 1977-1978. Co-Author: "Contractual Choice of Law Provisions," *Business Law News* (Fall 1993). *Member:* Los Angeles County (Vice-Chair, Commercial Law and Bankruptcy Section, 1994-1995) and American Bar Associations; Financial Lawyers Conference. **PRACTICE AREAS:** Commercial Law; Finance Law; Secured Transactions Law.

**HARRIET M. WELCH,** born Bayonne, New Jersey, February 4, 1954; admitted to bar, 1978, New Jersey; 1979, New York; 1988, California. *Education:* Loyola University of the South (B.A., 1975); Catholic University (J.D., 1978). Member, Catholic University Law Review, 1977-1978. Moot Court Associate, Original Trials Committee, Catholic University Law School, 1977-1978. *Member:* State Bar of California (Member, Sections on: Corporate and Business Law); Women Lawyers of Los Angeles (Board Member); National Association of Bond Lawyers. **PRACTICE AREAS:** Municipal Finance; Corporate. **Email:** hwelch.bnfy@mcimail.com

**WILLIAM MARK LEVINSON,** born Newport News, Virginia, September 5, 1953; admitted to bar, 1982, New York; 1983, New Jersey; 1987, California. *Education:* Brandeis University (A.B., 1978); Benjamin N. Cardozo School of Law, Yeshiva University (J.D., 1981). Note Editor, Cardozo Arts and Entertainment Law Journal, 1980-1981. *Member:* Los Angeles County and American (Member, Sections on: Business; Real Property Law) Bar Associations; State Bar of California; National and California Associations of Bond Lawyers (Trustee, Counsel Section). **PRACTICE AREAS:** Municipal Bond Financing Law; Corporate Law; Real Estate Law; Securities Law. **Email:** wlevinson.bnfy@mcimail.com

**HARRIET B. ALEXSON,** born Stratford, Connecticut, January 12, 1950; admitted to bar, 1983, California. *Education:* Boston University (B.S., 1974; M.A., 1975); University of Southern California (J.D., 1983). *Member:* Orange County and Los Angeles County Bar Associations; Robert Morris Association. **PRACTICE AREAS:** Corporate and Commercial Matters; Real Estate Law; Healthcare Matters; Software Licensing.

**BARRY F. SOOSMAN,** born Brookline, Massachusetts, January 20, 1960; admitted to bar, 1984, California. *Education:* University of Southern California (B.S., 1981; J.D., 1984). Beta Gamma Sigma. Member, Blackstonian Society. *Member:* State Bar of California. **PRACTICE AREAS:** Real Estate; Bank and Finance.

---

**JANIS S. PENTON,** born Los Angeles, California, October 17, 1954; admitted to bar, 1980, California, U.S. District Court, Central District of California and U.S. Court of Appeals, Ninth Circuit; 1991, Florida. *Education:* University of California, Los Angeles (A.B., cum laude, 1976); University of Southern California (M.B.A., 1980; J.D., 1980). Order of the Coif. Listed in: Who's Who in American Law Sixth Edition. Co-Author: "Uniform Commercial Code Survey: Letters of Credit," The Business Lawyer, August, 1992. Member, U.S. Department of State Advisory Committee on Private International Law, 1989—. *Member:* State Bar of California (Member, Uniform Commercial Code Committee, Business Law Section, 1993—); American Bar Association ( Vice Chairman, Working Group on International Letters of Credit and Bank Guarantees, 1990—).

**JERRY A. HAGER,** born Van Nuys, California, December 17, 1957; admitted to bar, 1982, California; 1983, U.S. District Court, Central, Eastern, Northern and Southern Districts of California; 1986, U.S. Court of Appeals, Ninth Circuit. *Education:* California State University, (B.A., 1979); Pepperdine University School of Law (J.D., 1982). Phi Delta Phi (Clerk, Prosser Inn). Secretary, Moot Court Board, 1981-1982. Recipient: Dean's Scholarship; Am Jur Award in Criminal Proceed. Adjunct Professor, Pepperdine University School of Law, 1993—. *Member:* Los Angeles County and American Bar Associations; State Bar of California; Financial Lawyers Conference; Los Angeles Bankruptcy Forum. **PRACTICE AREAS:** Real Estate Litigation; Bankruptcy; Real Estate Transactions. **Email:** jhager.bnfy@mcimail.com

**JONATHAN D. FINK,** born New York, N.Y., January 11, 1958; admitted to bar, 1983, California; 1984, U.S. District Court, Central District of California and U.S. Court of Appeals, Ninth Circuit. *Education:* University of Pennsylvania (B.A., magna cum laude, 1980); Boston University (J.D., 1983). *Member:* Los Angeles County (Member, Federal Courts Committee) and American Bar Associations. State Bar of California. **PRACTICE AREAS:** Bank and Financial; Commercial; Real Estate; Appeals and Employment Litigation. **Email:** jlink.bnfy@mcimail.com

**JULIE A. GOREN,** born Los Angeles, California, November 22, 1953; admitted to bar, 1987, California; 1989, U.S. District Court, Northern District of Texas. *Education:* University of California at Los Angeles (A.B., cum laude, 1975); Loyola Law School of Los Angeles (J.D., cum laude, 1987). **PRACTICE AREAS:** Insolvency. **Email:** jgoren.bnfy@mcimail.com

**GLENN L. SAVARD,** born Bay Shore, New York, December 27, 1958; admitted to bar, 1987, California, U.S. Court of Appeals, Ninth Circuit and U.S. District Court, Central, Eastern, Northern and Southern Districts of California. *Education:* California State University, San Bernardino (B.A., 1980); Loyola Law School (J.D., 1986). *Member:* Los Angeles County (Member, Litigation Section; Participant in Trial Attorney Project, 1989) and American Bar Associations; State Bar of California. **Email:** gsavard.bnfy@mcimail.com

**PAUL S. ARROW,** born Los Angeles, California, November 3, 1956; admitted to bar, 1988, California and U.S. District Court, Central District of California. *Education:* University of California, Los Angeles (B.A., 1979); Southwestern University (J.D., cum laude, 1988). *Member:* State Bar of California. **PRACTICE AREAS:** Insolvency. **Email:** parrow.bnfy@mcimail.com

**WILLIAM S. BRODY,** born Los Angeles, California, April 15, 1962; admitted to bar, 1988, California, U.S. District Court, Northern District of California and U.S. Court of Appeals, Ninth Circuit; 1989, U.S. District Court, Southern, Central and Eastern Districts of California. *Education:* University of California, Los Angeles (B.A., 1984); University of San Diego (J.D., 1988). Managing Editor, San Diego Law Review, 1987-1988. **PRACTICE AREAS:** Insolvency. **Email:** wbrody.bnfy@mcimail.com

**AMY L. RUBINFELD,** born Peoria, Illinois, May 22, 1964; admitted to bar, 1989, California and U.S. District Court, Central District of California. *Education:* University of San Diego (B.A., 1986); University of Southern California (J.D., 1989). *Member:* Beverly Hills Bar Association; State Bar of California. **PRACTICE AREAS:** Commercial Business Litigation; Banking Law; Financial Institutions; Insurance Coverage; Prejudgment Remedies including Receivership Actions. **Email:** arubinfeld.bnfy@mcimail.com

**DEAN STACKEL,** born Queens, New York, July 9, 1964; admitted to bar, 1989, California. *Education:* New York University (B.S., 1986; J.D., 1989). *Member:* Los Angeles County Bar Association; State Bar of California. **PRACTICE AREAS:** Real Estate Law; Environmental Law. **Email:** dstackel.bnfy@mcimail.com

**ABRAHAM J. COLMAN,** born Suffern, New York, February 6, 1964; admitted to bar, 1989, New York; 1990, California; 1991, U.S. District Court, Central District of California. *Education:* Bernard M. Baruch College of the City University of New York (B.B.A., cum laude, 1985); Fordham University Law School (J.D., 1988). *Member:* Los Angeles County, New York State and American Bar Associations: State Bar of California. **PRACTICE AREAS:** Business Litigation; Creditor's Rights. **Email:** acolman.bnfy@mcimail.com

**MONIKA L. MCCARTHY,** born New York, New York, October 7, 1958; admitted to bar, 1990, California and U.S. District Court, Southern District of California. *Education:* California State University, Northridge (B.A., 1987); Loyola Marymount University (J.D., 1990). Chief Articles Editor, Loyola of Los Angeles Law Review. First Place, National Institute of Trial Advocacy Regional Competition, 1990. *Member:* Association of Business Trial Lawyers; Women Lawyers Association of Los Angeles. **LANGUAGES:** German. **PRACTICE AREAS:** Financial Institution Litigation; Banking; Patent Infringement. **Email:** mmccarthy.bnfy@mcimail.com

*(This Listing Continued)*

**MARY LEPIQUE DICKSON,** born St. Louis, Missouri, April 23, 1960; admitted to bar, 1991, California. *Education:* University of Missouri; Indiana State University (B.S., 1982); St. Louis University; Southwestern University (J.D., 1991). *PRACTICE AREAS:* Real Estate Development; Real Estate Finance. *Email:* mdickson.bnfy@mcimail.com

**SHIRLEY SHEAU-LIH LU,** born Seoul, Korea, August 15, 1966; admitted to bar, 1991, California. *Education:* University of California, Berkeley (B.A., 1988); University of California at Los Angeles (J.D., 1991). *Member:* Los Angeles County and American Bar Associations; Southern California Chinese Lawyers' Association. *LANGUAGES:* Mandarin Chinese and Korean. *PRACTICE AREAS:* Real Estate Transactions; Business. *Email:* slu.bnfy@mcimail.com

**ROBERT A. WILLNER,** born Long Beach, California, June 17, 1956; admitted to bar, 1991, California. *Education:* University of California, Los Angeles (B.A., cum laude, 1978); Loyola Marymount University (J.D., 1991). Order of the Coif. Judicial Extern, Honorable Justice Allen E. Broussard of the California Supreme Court, 1991. *Member:* Los Angeles County (Member, Sections on: Commercial Law and Bankruptcy) and American (Member, Committee on Commercial Financial Services) Bar Associations. *PRACTICE AREAS:* Secured and Unsecured Financing and Lending; General Corporate and Transactional Practice. *Email:* rwillner.bnfy@mcimail.com

**ADAM JOEL BASS,** born Los Angeles, California, September 1, 1965; admitted to bar, 1991, California; 1992, U.S. District Court, Northern District of California and U.S. Court of Appeals, Ninth Circuit. *Education:* University of San Diego (B.A., 1988; J.D., 1991). *Member:* Orange County and American Bar Associations; State Bar of California. *LANGUAGES:* Spanish. *PRACTICE AREAS:* Business Litigation; Real Property Litigation; Commercial Litigation; Loan Workouts. *Email:* abass.bnfy@mcimail.com

**DAVID L. ARONOFF,** born Bridgeport, Connecticut, December 9, 1961; admitted to bar, 1991, California. *Education:* University of Southern California (B.A., 1985); Southwestern University School of Law (J.A., 1990). Best Appellate Brief, Southwestern University School of Law; Moot Court Intramural Competition. *Member:* Beverly Hills, Los Angeles County and American Bar Associations; State Bar of California. *PRACTICE AREAS:* Civil Litigation. *Email:* daronoff.bnfy@mcimail.com

**KIM ALLMAN,** born Brooklyn, New York, September 1, 1964; admitted to bar, 1992, California. *Education:* Bernard M. Baruch College (B.B.A., 1988); University of San Diego (J.D., 1992). Phi Delta Phi. *PRACTICE AREAS:* Financial Institutions Litigation; Business Litigation. *Email:* kallman.bnfy@mcimail.com

**WILLIAM P. FONG,** born Berkeley, California, December 15, 1965; admitted to bar, 1992, California. *Education:* Columbia University (B.A., 1987); University of Southern California (J.D., 1991; M.B.A., 1991). *PRACTICE AREAS:* Bankruptcy. *Email:* wfong.bnfy@mcimail.com

**HELEN GOLDBERGER PALMER,** born St. Paul, Minnesota, October 6, 1966; admitted to bar, 1992, California. *Education:* University of California, Berkeley (B.A., 1989); University of Southern California School of Law (J.D., 1992). Recipient, Regents Scholarships. *LANGUAGES:* Spanish. *PRACTICE AREAS:* Commercial Litigation. *Email:* hpalmer.bnfy@mcimail.com

**BRETT MICHAEL BRODERICK,** born Anchorage, Alaska, July 1, 1966; admitted to bar, 1993, California. *Education:* Northeastern Oklahoma State; California State University, Los Angeles (B.S., magna cum laude, 1989); Southwestern University School of Law (J.D., 1993). Managing Editor, Southwestern University Law Review. Recipient, Am Jur Award, Legal Writing. *Member:* State Bar of California (Member, Business Law Section). *PRACTICE AREAS:* Insolvency. *Email:* bbroderick.bnfy@mcimail.com

**ROBERT ALEXANDER PILMER,** born Annapolis, Maryland, March 22, 1966; admitted to bar, 1993, California. *Education:* Occidental College (A.B., cum laude, 1988); Loyola Marymount University (J.D., cum laude, 1993). Phi Beta Kappa; Order of the Coif. *PRACTICE AREAS:* Financial Institutions Litigation; Real Property Litigation; Business Litigation. *Email:* rpilmer.bnfy@mcimail.com

**KIRK H. SHARPE,** born Southampton, New York, July 16, 1967; admitted to bar, 1993, California. *Education:* University of Oklahoma (B.B.A., 1989); Southwestern University (J.D., 1993). Recipient, American Jurisprudence Book Award, Exceptional Achievement Award and Contracts. Notes and Comments Editor, Southwestern University Law Review. *Member:* Los Angeles County Bar Association; State Bar of California.

*(This Listing Continued)*

*PRACTICE AREAS:* Corporate; Banking; Finance. *Email:* ksharpe.bnfy@mcimail.com

**NICOLAS M. KUBLICKI,** born Los Angeles, California, October 17, 1966; admitted to bar, 1993, California, U.S. District Court, Central District of California and U.S. Court of Appeals, Ninth Circuit; 1994, District of Columbia. *Education:* University of California, Los Angeles (B.A., 1987); Pepperdine University (J.D., 1992); George Washington University (LL.M., 1993). Articles Editor, 1991-1992, Staff Member, 1990-1991, Pepperdine Law Review. First Place, Best Respondent's Brief, Vincent S. Dalsimer Pepperdine Moot Court Competition, 1992. Recipient, American Jurisprudence Award, Administrative Law, 1992. *Member:* Beverly Hills (Member, Sections on: Environmental Law and Real Estate), Los Angeles County (Member, Sections on: Environmental Law and Real Estate) and District of Columbia (Member, Environmental Law Section) Bar Associations; State Bar of California (Member, Sections on: Environmental and Real Property). *PRACTICE AREAS:* Real Estate Finance; Environmental Law. *Email:* nkublicki.bnfy@mcimail.com

**VINCENT I.S. HSIEH,** born Taipei, Taiwan, January 15, 1964; admitted to bar, 1993, New York (Not admitted in California). *Education:* National Taiwan University (LL.B., 1987) Boston University (LL.M., in International Banking, 1992). *Member:* American Bar Association; New York County Lawyers Association. *LANGUAGES:* Mandarin Chinese. *PRACTICE AREAS:* International Transactions; Corporate Practice. *Email:* vhsieh.bnfy@mcimail.com

**SIMONE MARGARET BENNETT,** born Godalming, England; admitted to bar, 1994, California. *Education:* Duke University (B.A., cum laude, 1988); University of California, Los Angeles School of Law (J.D., 1994). Golden Key. Articles Editor, Pacific Basin Law Journal, 1991-1993. Managing Editor, The Docket, University of California School of Law's Newspaper. Extern Clerk, Honorable Judge Richard Goodbois, Jr., U.S. District Court, Central District of California, 1993. *Member:* Los Angeles County and American Bar Associations. *PRACTICE AREAS:* Commercial Litigation; Labor Litigation; Financial Institutions Litigation. *Email:* sbennett.bnfy@mcimail.com

**CHRISTINA M. CARLSON,** born San Diego, California, November 30, 1963; admitted to bar, 1994, California. *Education:* University of California, Los Angeles (B.A., 1987); Loyola Law School of Los Angeles (J.D., 1994). Member, International and Comparative Law Journal. *PRACTICE AREAS:* Bankruptcy Litigation. *Email:* ccarlson.bnfy@mcimail.com

**RACHAEL H. BERMAN,** born Heidelberg, Germany, November 9, 1968; admitted to bar, 1994, California. *Education:* University of California, Los Angeles (B.A., magna cum laude, 1990); Hastings College of the Law, University of California (J.D., 1994). Phi Beta Kappa. *PRACTICE AREAS:* Bankruptcy. *Email:* rberman.bnfy@mcimail.com

**DANIEL JOSEPH KOLODZIEJ,** born Charlottesville, Virginia, May 30, 1969; admitted to bar, 1994, California. *Education:* University of Michigan at Ann Arbor (B.A., 1990); University of California, Los Angeles (J.D., 1993). *Member:* Los Angeles and American County Bar Associations; State Bar of California. *Email:* dkolodziej.bnfy@mcimail.com

**ELIZABETH H. MURPHY,** born Inglewood, California, December 12, 1968; admitted to bar, 1994, California. *Education:* University of California, Santa Barbara (B.A., 1990); University of Southern California (J.D., 1994). Recipient: AmJur Awards, Torts, Civil Procedure and Legal Writing. Member: California Receivership Forum; Women in Public Affairs. *PRACTICE AREAS:* Litigation; Receiverships. *Email:* emurphy.bnfy@mcimail.com

**LANCE R. DIXON,** born Harare, Zimbabwe, July 21, 1970; admitted to bar, 1994, California and barrister to the Supreme Court of South Africa; U.S. District Court, Central District of California. *Education:* University of Cape Town, South Africa (B.A., 1990; LL.B., with honors, 1993). *Member:* Beverly Hills, Century City and Los Angeles County Bar Associations; State Bar of California; Bar of the Supreme Court of South Africa. *PRACTICE AREAS:* Business Law; Commerical Litigation; International Transactions and Litigation.

**ALLAN R. MOUW,** born Johannesburg, South Africa, March 19, 1969; admitted to bar, 1995, California. *Education:* University of California, Los Angeles (B.A., cum laude, 1991); University of Southern California (J.D., 1994). *Member:* State Bar of California. *PRACTICE AREAS:* Corporate; Securities.

**DANIEL C. WONG,** born Hong Kong, October 25, 1963; admitted to bar, 1996, California. *Education:* Thames Valley University, London (LL.B., 1985); Brigham Young University (J.D., 1995). *Member:* Los An-

*(This Listing Continued)*

CALIFORNIA—LOS ANGELES                                                                                           MARTINDALE-HUBBELL LAW DIRECTORY 1997

**BUCHALTER, NEMER, FIELDS & YOUNGER,** A
PROFESSIONAL CORPORATION, Los Angeles—Continued

geles County and American Bar Associations; State Bar of California; Asian Business League. **PRACTICE AREAS:** General Commercial Litigation; Financial Institution and Insolvency Litigation.

REFERENCES: City National Bank; Wells Fargo Bank; Metrobank.

(For complete biographical data on all personnel, see Professional Biographies at New York, New York, Newport Beach an San Francisco)

## *BUCHANAN & KINDEM*

420 BOYD STREET, SUITE 400
**LOS ANGELES, CALIFORNIA 90013**
Telephone: 213-625-2974
Fax: 213-625-2668

*General Civil Trial and Appellate Practice in all State and Federal Courts and Administrative Agencies with emphasis on Litigation. General Business and Commercial Litigation, Securities, Unfair Competition, Real Estate, Construction, Copyright, Trademark, Trade Secrets, Intellectual Property, Computer Law, Tort Litigation, Insurance, Employment Litigation, Probate and Family Law.*

### *MEMBERS OF FIRM*

**BRIAN F. BUCHANAN,** born Boulder, Colorado, January 12, 1952; admitted to bar, 1979, California; 1987, U.S. District Court, Central District of California. *Education:* Claremont Men's College (B.A., magna cum laude, 1974); University of Colorado (J.D., 1978). *Member:* Los Angeles County and Colorado Bar Associations (Member, Sections on: Litigation and Real Property); State Bar of California (Member, Sections on: Litigation and Real Property). **PRACTICE AREAS:** Civil Litigation.

**PETER R. DION-KINDEM,** born Whitefish, Montana, September 5, 1955; admitted to bar, 1980, California; U.S. Supreme Court; U.S. District Court, Central, Northern and Eastern Districts of California; U.S. Court of Appeals, Ninth Circuit. *Education:* St. Olaf College (B.A., magna cum laude, 1977); University of California at Los Angeles (J.D., 1980). **REPORTED CASES:** Epstein v. MCA Inc., 50 F.3d 644 (9th. Cir. 1995); California Air Resources Board v. Hart, 21 Cal.App.4th 289 (1993); McCann v. Welden, 153 Cal.App.3d 814 (1984); Stevens v. Rifkin, 608 F.Supp. 710 (N.D.Cal. 1984). **PRACTICE AREAS:** Securities Litigation; Commercial Litigation; Insurance; Partnership Disputes; Corporate Law; Family Law.

### *OF COUNSEL*

**LAWRENCE W. CHAMBLEE,** born Beacon, New York, September 18, 1942; admitted to bar, 1973, Maryland and District of Columbia; 1974, U.S. Court of Appeals, Eighth and Ninth Circuits; 1976, U.S. Supreme Court and U.S. Court of Appeals, Seventh Circuit; 1978, U.S. Court of Appeals, Fourth, Fifth and Sixth Circuits and U.S. District Court, Eastern District of Virginia; 1985, California and U.S. District Court, Central District of California; 1986, U.S. Court of Appeals, Second Circuit and U.S. District Court, Southern District of New York. *Education:* State University of New York at Albany; University of Maryland (A.B., 1966; J.D., with honors, 1972). Captain, Moot Court Team. Author: "International Legal Assistance in Criminal Cases," ABA National Institute, March, 1984. Instructor, Immigration Law and Procedure, University of Southern California Law Center, Spring, 1986. Trial Attorney, Division of Enforcement, Interstate Commerce Commission, Washington, D.C., 1973-1974. Senior Trial Attorney, Criminal Division, U.S. Department of Justice, 1974-1984. Special Assistant, U.S. Attorney, Eastern District of Virginia, 1978 and Central District of California, 1985-1986. Special Assistant U.S. Attorney, Chief, Immigration Litigation Unit, Southern District of New York, 1986-1987. *Member:* Los Angeles County and American Bar Associations; District of Columbia Bar; State Bar of California. [Petty Officer, 2nd Class, U.S. Navy Seabees, 1966-1968]. **LANGUAGES:** French. **PRACTICE AREAS:** Civil Litigation.

## *BUCKSBAUM & SASAKI*

A PROFESSIONAL CORPORATION
1900 AVENUE OF THE STARS, SUITE 1800
**LOS ANGELES, CALIFORNIA 90067**
Telephone: 310-286-3396

*General Business Litigation, including Real Estate, Business Fraud, Financial Institution, Intellectual Property and Unfair Competition Litigation.*

(This Listing Continued)

**FIRM PROFILE:** *Bucksbaum & Sasaki attorneys were all formerly with Proskauer Rose Goetz & Mendelsohn, Los Angeles. The firm's clients range from large corporations to small businesses and individuals involved in business disputes. The firm is also general counsel for the Coalition of Asian Pacific Entertainers (CAPE). Bucksbaum & Sasaki is certified as a 100 percent woman-owned law firm.*

**DEBORAH S. BUCKSBAUM,** born Pasadena, California, June 15, 1954; admitted to bar, 1983, California; 1984, U.S. District Court, Central District of California. *Education:* University of California at Santa Barbara (B.A., cum laude, 1976); Georgetown University (J.D., 1982). Member, 1980-1981 and White Collar Crime Project Editor, 1981-1982, American Criminal Law Review. Author: "Securities Fraud," 19 American Criminal Law Review 438, 1981. Advisor, Los Angeles Free Clinic Domestic Violence Program, 1987-1990. *Member:* Los Angeles County and American Bar Associations; State Bar of California; Women Lawyers Association of Los Angeles. **PRACTICE AREAS:** Business Litigation; Real Estate Litigation; Intellectual Property Litigation.

**JUDITH M. SASAKI,** born Honolulu, Hawaii, September 15, 1958; admitted to bar, 1985, California. *Education:* Kokusai Kiristokyoo Daigaku, Tokyo, Japan; University of Hawaii (B.A., 1982; J.D., 1985). Phi Delta Phi. Member and Articles Editor, University of Hawaii Law Review, 1984-1985. Judge Pro Tem, Beverly Hills Municipal Court. *Member:* Beverly Hills Bar Association; State Bar of California (Member, Litigation Section); Constitutional Rights Foundation. **PRACTICE AREAS:** Financial Institution Litigation; Real Estate Litigation; Business Litigation.

---

**W. CLARK BROWN,** born Mt. Kisco, New York, March 26 1954; admitted to bar, 1989, California and U.S. District Court, Central District of California. *Education:* Hampshire College (B.A., 1978); University of California at Los Angeles J.D., 1989). Distinguished Advocate, Moot Court Board. *Member:* Los Angeles County Bar Association (Member: Intellectual Property Law Society; Judiciary Committee); State Bar of California. **PRACTICE AREAS:** Business Litigation; Intellectual Property; Unfair Competition; Securities Fraud.

**KATHLEEN M. WOOD,** born Kansas City, Missouri, January 25, 1961; admitted to bar, 1987, New York; 1989, U.S. District Court, Southern and Eastern Districts of New York; 1990, California, U.S. District Court, Central and Southern Districts of California. *Education:* University of Kansas (B.A., 1982); Columbia University (J.D., 1986). *Member:* State Bar of California (Member, Litigation Section). **PRACTICE AREAS:** Intellectual Property; General Corporate Commercial; Securities; Antitrust.

## *BURKE, WILLIAMS & SORENSEN*

A Partnership including a Professional Corporation
611 WEST SIXTH STREET, 25TH FLOOR
**LOS ANGELES, CALIFORNIA 90017**
Telephone: 213-236-0600
Telecopiers: 213-236-2700; 236-2800
Telex: 671-1271
Cable Address: "BWSLA UW"
Email: bws@bwslaw.com
URL: http://www.bwslaw.com

*Orange County Office:* 3200 Park Center Drive, Suite 750, Costa Mesa, California. Telephone: 714-545-5559.
*Ventura County Office:* 2310 Ponderosa Drive, Suite 1, Camarillo, California. Telephone: 805-987-3468.

*General Civil and Trial Practice in all State and Federal Courts. Securities, Corporate, Taxation, Insurance and Commercial Law. Municipal and Public Agency Representation. Local Government Financing, Taxation and Assessments. Community Redevelopment, Eminent Domain, Environmental and Land Use Law. Employee Benefit Plans, Probate and Estate Planning. Health Care, Medical Research, College and University and Non-Profit Organization Law, Employment and Personnel Law. Tort, Workers Compensation and Insurance Defense.*

### *MEMBERS OF FIRM*

**HARRY C. WILLIAMS** (1912-1967).

**ROYAL M. SORENSEN** (1914-1983).

**JAMES T. BRADSHAW, JR.,** born Los Angeles, California, June 12, 1923; admitted to bar, 1949, California. *Education:* George Pepperdine Col-

(This Listing Continued)

lege and University of Redlands; University of Southern California (LL.B., 1949). Phi Alpha Delta. *PRACTICE AREAS:* Corporate Law; Commercial Law; Trade Regulation Law. *Email:* bradshaw@bwslaw.com

**MARTIN L. BURKE,** born Los Angeles, California, September 9, 1936; admitted to bar, 1962, California. *Education:* Loyola University (B.S., 1958; LL.B., 1961). *Member:* American Bar Association (Vice Chairman, ABA Committee on Torts in Non-Profit, Charitable and Religious Organizations, Section of Tort and Insurance Practice); National Association of University Counsel. *PRACTICE AREAS:* Corporate Law; Aviation Law; Education Law. *Email:* burke@bwslaw.com

**CARL K. NEWTON,** born Los Angeles, California, December 24, 1931; admitted to bar, 1963, California. *Education:* University of California at Los Angeles (B.S., 1955); Loyola University of Los Angeles (LL.B., 1962). Phi Delta Phi. Law Clerk, California Court of Appeals, 1962. City Attorney: Manhattan Beach, California, 1968-1994, Azusa, 1976-1982; Downey, 1983-1987; Santa Clarita, 1987—; Bellflower, 1995—. *Member:* Los Angeles County (Chairman, Condemnation Procedures Committee, 1974-1975) and American (Chairman, Committee on Condemnation, 1981-1983) Bar Associations; National Institute of Municipal Law Officers. *PRACTICE AREAS:* Eminent Domain Law; Municipal Law; Litigation. *Email:* newton@bwslaw.com

**J. ROBERT FLANDRICK,** born St. Paul, Minnesota, December 27, 1928; admitted to bar, 1956, California; 1975, U.S. Supreme Court. *Education:* Los Angeles City College and University of Southern California (B.S., 1953); University of Southern California (J.D., 1955). Recipient, Archibald Mayo Criminal Law Scholarship. Lecturer, City Attorneys Continuing Education Program, League of California Cities. Member, Public Safety Committee, League of California Cities. Editor, Municipal Law Handbook, published by The League of California Cities. City Attorney: South El Monte, 1958-1963; Montebello, 1960-1979; Baldwin Park, 1961-1976, 1977-1990; Hidden Hills, 1979-1984; Irwindale, 1964-1969; Whittier, 1969-1989; Bell, 1968-1994; Camarillo, 1990—; Bellflower, 1993-1995. President, City Attorneys Department, League of California Cities, 1985-1986. [USAF-JAG (1st Lt., 1956-1958)]. *PRACTICE AREAS:* Municipal Law; Eminent Domain Law; Redevelopment Law. *Email:* flandrick@bwslaw.com

**EDWARD M. FOX,** born Evanston, Illinois, April 24, 1933; admitted to bar, 1957, Illinois; 1963, California. *Education:* University of Notre Dame (A.B., 1956; LL.B., 1957). President, Notre Dame Student Law Association, 1956-1957. Law Clerk to Chief Judge Luther M. Swygert, U.S. District Court, Northern District of Indiana, 1957-1958. Trial Attorney, Office of Chief Counsel, Internal Revenue Service, Los Angeles, 1959-1966. President, Association of Tax Counsel of Los Angeles, 1990-1994. *Member:* Illinois State Bar Association. (Certified Specialist, Taxation Law, The State Bar of California Board of Legal Specialization). *PRACTICE AREAS:* Taxation Law; Corporate and Business Law; Estate Planning Law; Probate Law. *Email:* fox@bwslaw.com

**DENNIS P. BURKE,** born Los Angeles, California, May 12, 1942; admitted to bar, 1968, California. *Education:* Loyola University (B.A., 1964; J.D., 1967). Member, St. Thomas More Law Honor Society. *Member:* Los Angeles County Bar Association (Member, Sections on: Business and Corporations; Real Property); State Bar of California (Chair, Corporate Division). *PRACTICE AREAS:* Corporate Law; Real Estate Law; Bankruptcy Law. *Email:* dburke@bwslaw.com

**LELAND C. DOLLEY,** born Long Beach, California, June 1, 1935; admitted to bar, 1968, California. *Education:* University of Southern California (A.B., 1964); University of San Diego (J.D., 1967). Phi Delta Phi. Deputy District Attorney, Los Angeles County, 1968-1969. City Attorney, Lomita, California, 1975-1990; Alhambra, 1976-1982, 1984—; Bradbury, 1979-1982; El Segundo, 1982—. General Counsel, Alhambra Redevelopment Agency, 1982—. *Member:* Los Angeles County (Chairman, Governmental Law Section, 1982-1983) and American (Chairman, Airport Law Committee, Section of Urban, State and Local Government Law, 1982-1984; Member of Council, 1984-1985) Bar Associations; City Attorneys Association of Los Angeles County (President, 1985-1986; Co-Chair, Public Law Division). (Resident, Orange County Office). *PRACTICE AREAS:* Municipal Law; Redevelopment Law; Municipal Planning; Municipal Personnel Law; Municipal Labor Law; Municipal Litigation. *Email:* dolley@bwslaw.com

**NEIL F. YEAGER,** born Newark, New Jersey, July 15, 1948; admitted to bar, 1974, California. *Education:* Claremont Men's College (B.A., cum laude, 1970); University of Southern California (J.D., 1974). *PRACTICE AREAS:* Corporate and Corporate Finance Law; Real Estate Law; Securities Law; Commercial Law. *Email:* yeager@bwslaw.com

*(This Listing Continued)*

**BRIAN A. PIERIK,** born Santa Monica, California, December 24, 1949; admitted to bar, 1974, California. *Education:* Loyola University of Los Angeles (B.A., 1971; J.D., 1974). Teaching Fellow, National Moot Court Team. *Member:* Association of Southern California Defense Counsel; Defense Research Institute; American Business Trial Lawyers Association; Ventura County Trial Lawyers Association. (Resident, Ventura County Office). *PRACTICE AREAS:* Litigation; Environmental Law; Insurance Law; Construction Law; Labor Law. *Email:* pierik@bwslaw.com

**CHARLES M. CALDERON,** born Los Angeles, California, March 12, 1950; admitted to bar, 1975, California. *Education:* California State University at Los Angeles (B.A., 1972); University of California at Davis (J.D., 1975). Trustee, Montebello Unified School District Board of Education, 1979-1982. Consultant: California State Department of Health, 1976-1977; Secretary of State, 1977-1979. Deputy City Attorney, Los Angeles City Attorney's Office, 1979-1981. General Counsel, Los Angeles Board of Public Works Commissioners, 1980-1981. Member, California State Assembly, 59th District, 1982-1990. Member, California State Senate, 26th District, 1990—, Chair, Senate Judiciary Committee. *Member:* Los Angeles County Bar Association (Member, Municipal Law Section). *PRACTICE AREAS:* Municipal Law. *Email:* calderon@bwslaw.com

**JERRY M. PATTERSON,** born El Paso, Texas, October 25, 1934; admitted to bar, 1967, California; 1975, U.S. Supreme Court; 1985, District of Columbia, U.S. District Court, District of Columbia and U.S. Court of Appeals, District of Columbia Circuit. *Education:* California State University at Long Beach (B.A., 1960); University of Southern California; University of California at Los Angeles, School of Law (J.D., 1966). Pi Gamma Mu; Phi Delta Phi. Professor, Graduate Center on Public Policy, California State University, Long Beach, 1986. City Attorney, Cypress, 1987-1992; Dana Point, 1989—; Lake Forest, 1991—. City Councilman, 1969-1975 and Mayor, 1973-1974, City of Santa Ana, California. U.S. Congressman, House of Representatives, 1975-1985. [Corpsman, 2nd Class, U.S. Coast Guard, 1953-1957]. (Resident, Orange County Office). *PRACTICE AREAS:* Municipal Law; Planning and Zoning Law. *Email:* patterson@bwslaw.com

**HAROLD A. BRIDGES,** born Oakland, California, July 16, 1955; admitted to bar, 1980, California; 1984, U.S. Tax Court. *Education:* Loyola Marymount University (B.A., magna cum laude, 1977); Loyola University of Los Angeles (J.D., magna cum laude, 1980). Alpha Sigma Nu; Pi Gamma Mu. Recipient, American Jurisprudence Book Award in Corporations, Remedies and Secured Transactions in Personal Property. Member, Loyola of Los Angeles Law Review, 1978-1979. *Member:* State Bar of California (Member, Sections on: Business Law; Labor and Employment Law; Real Property Law. (Chair, Litigation Division). *PRACTICE AREAS:* Litigation; Public Law; Business Law; Employment Litigation; Education Law; Construction Law. *Email:* bridges@bwslaw.com

**CHERYL J. KANE,** born Norwich, England, March 16, 1946; admitted to bar, 1979, California. *Education:* University of California at Riverside (B.A., 1968); University of Washington (M.U.P., 1971); Southwestern University (J.D., 1978). City Attorney: Moorpark, 1984—; Glendora, 1984-1994; Downey, 1994-1996. *PRACTICE AREAS:* Municipal Law; Land Use Law; Environmental Law; Labor Law; Writs and Appeals. *Email:* kane@bwslaw.com

**BARRY S. GLASER,** born Philadelphia, Pennsylvania, September 13, 1947; admitted to bar, 1976, California; 1994, U.S. District Court, District of Hawaii and Central, Northern, Eastern and Southern Districts of California; U.S. Court of Appeals, Ninth Circuit. *Education:* California State University at Northridge (B.A., 1970); University of Copenhagen, Denmark; Southwestern University (J.D., 1976); University Kent, England. Recipient, Bancroft-Whitney Award in Constitutional Law. Associate Professor of Law, Northrop University School of Law, 1976-1977. Contributing Author: "Business Lawyer's Bankruptcy Guide," Guarantees and Letters of Credit, Clark Boardman Callaghan, 1992 edition. Judge-Pro-Tem, Los Angeles Municipal Court, 1982-1989. Serving Judge Pro-Tem, Superior Court of Los Angeles, 1991-1994. *Member:* State Bar of California (Delegate, State Bar Convention, 1981; Speaker, 1989 Convention; Member, Committee on Creditor Debtor Relations, 1988-1991); Los Angeles Bankruptcy Forum; Financial Lawyers Conference; American Bankruptcy Institute. *PRACTICE AREAS:* Bankruptcy; Corporate Reorganization; Creditors Rights; Real Estate and Title Insurance Litigation. *Email:* glaser@bwslaw.com

**B. DEREK STRAATSMA,** born New York, N.Y., December 11, 1955; admitted to bar, 1981, California. *Education:* University of California at Santa Barbara (B.A., 1978); University of West Los Angeles (J.D., 1981). Graduate, Los Angeles Trial Attorney Project, 1984. Recipient, Louis Kel-

*(This Listing Continued)*

**BURKE, WILLIAMS & SORENSEN, Los Angeles—**
*Continued*

ton Award. Assistant City Attorney, Glendora, 1995—. Judge Pro-Tem, Los Angeles Workers' Compensation Board. *Member:* The Association of Southern California Defense Counsel. **PRACTICE AREAS:** Workers Compensation Law; Civil Litigation; Labor Law; Municipal Law. **Email:** straatsma@bwslaw.com

**DON G. KIRCHER,** born Los Angeles, California, June 3, 1933; admitted to bar, 1961, California; 1971, U.S. Supreme Court. *Education:* Occidental College (B.A., 1955); Loyola Marymount University (J.D., 1960). Phi Delta Phi. City Attorney, Port Hueneme, 1989—. City Attorney, Buellton, 1992—. *Member:* Southwestern Legal Foundation (Research Fellow and Member, Executive Committee, International Oil and Gas Center, 1978—). (Resident, Ventura County Office). **PRACTICE AREAS:** Municipal Law; Corporate Law; Natural Resources. **Email:** kircher@bwslaw.com

**MICHELE R. VADON,** born Santa Rosa, California, July 17, 1952; admitted to bar, 1982, California. *Education:* University of California at Los Angeles (A.B., magna cum laude, 1976); Loyola University of Los Angeles (J.D., 1981). City Attorney: City of Lomita, 1994—; City of Bellflower, 1995—. Judge Pro Tem. *Member:* The Association of Southern California Defense Counsel. **PRACTICE AREAS:** Civil Rights Litigation; Municipal Law; Municipal Litigation; Tort Litigation. **Email:** vadon@bwslaw.com

**MARY REDUS GAYLE,** born Harrisburg, Illinois, September 27, 1929; admitted to bar, 1980, California. *Education:* Clarke College (B.A., cum laude, 1951); Immaculate Heart College (M.A., with honors, 1969); Oxford University, Oxford, England; Loyola University of Los Angeles (J.D., 1980). Mayor, Camarillo, California, 1980-1981. Camarillo City Council Member, 1974-1982. Director, 1974-1982 and Chairman, 1978-1980, Camarillo Sanitary District. Director, Ventura County Sanitation District, 1978-1981. Co-City Attorney, Atascadero, California. General Counsel, Ventura County Transportation Commission. City Attorney, Glendora, 1994—. (Resident, Ventura County Office). **Email:** gayle@bwslaw.com

**RUFUS C. YOUNG, JR.,** born Wyandotte, Michigan, November 10, 1940; admitted to bar, 1965, Oregon; 1966, California and U.S. Supreme Court. *Education:* Washington & Lee University; San Diego State (B.A., 1962); University of San Diego School of Law (J.D., 1965); George Washington University (LL.M., 1978). Phi Alpha Delta. Author: "Hazardous Waste & Toxic Substances Laws," "Electromagnetic Fields" and "Endangered Species," in Handling the Land Use Case, Schnidman, Abrams & Delaney, (Clark Boardman Callaghan, 1997); "California Environmental Reporting and Disclosure Requirements," California Real Estate Reporter, June, 1996; "Electromagnetic Fields: Invisible Hazards?" 1994 California Environmental Law Reporter, March, 1994; "Beyond Superfund: Other Federal Hazardous Substance-Related Laws Affecting Land Use," ALI-ABA Land Use Institute 1996; "Electromagnetic Fields and Their Land Use Implications" ALI-ABA Land Use Institute 1996; "Special Report Solid Waste An Obituary For 'Flow Control'," California Environmental Insider (August 15, 1994); "How the Endangered Species Act Affects Land Use," ALI-ABA Course Materials Journal (April 1992); *Management & Control of Growth,* Volume IV, Urban Land Institute, Washington, D.C. (Co-Editor). Senior Deputy City Attorney, City of San Jose, California, 1987-1989. *Member:* Los Angeles County (Member: Environmental Law and Public Law Sections) and San Diego County (Environmental Law/Land Use Section) Bar Associations. [With U.S. Marine Corps., Col., 1965-1987]. **LANGUAGES:** Japanese, Spanish and Vietnamese. **SPECIAL AGENCIES:** E.P.A., California Regional Water Quality Control Boards, California Department of Health Services, California Integrated Waste Management Board, South Coast Air Quality Management District. **PRACTICE AREAS:** Environmental Law; Hazardous Waste and Toxic Substances; Solid Waste Law; Endangered Species; Contaminated Property Cleanup Law; Cost Recovery Litigation. **Email:** ryoung09@counsel.com

**TIMOTHY B. MCOSKER,** born San Pedro, California, June 14, 1962; admitted to bar, 1987, California; 1988, U.S. District Court, Central District of California. *Education:* University of Notre Dame (B.A., cum laude, 1984); University of California at Los Angeles (J.D., 1987). City Attorney, City of Downey, 1994, 1996—. General Counsel, Downey Community Development Commission, 1994, 1996—. City Attorney, City of Lomita, 1992 and 1994. City Attorney, City of Manhattan Beach, 1994; City Attorney and General Counsel to the Long Beach Airport, 1994-1996. *Member:* State Bar of California. **PRACTICE AREAS:** Municipal Law; Redevelopment Law; Planning Law; Airport Law. **Email:** mcosker@bwslaw.com

*(This Listing Continued)*

**THOMAS C. WOOD,** born Minneapolis, Minnesota, January 19, 1940; admitted to bar, 1969, California; 1986, U.S. Supreme Court. *Education:* Glendale College (A.A., 1960); University of California at Berkeley; University of California at Los Angeles (B.A., 1962); Hastings College of the Law, University of California (J.D., 1968). Order of the Coif. Member, Thurston Honor Society. Member, 1966-1968 and Note and Comment Editor, 1967-1968, Hastings Law Journal. Co-Author: *Land Use Initiatives and Referenda in California,* Solano Press, 1990. Assistant City Attorney, 1977-1980 and City Attorney, 1980-1989, City of Costa Mesa. City Attorney: Lake Forest, 1992-1994; Chino Hills, 1992-1995; Manhattan Beach, 1994-1996. President, City Attorneys' Department, League of California Cities, 1987-1988. President, Orange County City Attorneys Association, 1987. [Capt., USMC Reserves, 1962-1969]. (Resident, Orange County Office). **PRACTICE AREAS:** Land Use Law; Governmental Law. **Email:** wood@bwslaw.com

**THOMAS W. ALLEN,** born Pasadena, California, September 11, 1937; admitted to bar, 1970, California. *Education:* California State University at Fullerton (B.A., 1966); Santa Clara University (J.D., 1969). *Member:* Orange County Bar Association; State Bar of California. (Resident, Orange County Office). **PRACTICE AREAS:** Municipal Law. **Email:** allen@bwslaw.com

**STEVEN J. DAWSON,** born Santa Monica, California, December 27, 1959; admitted to bar, 1987, California. *Education:* Stanford University (A.B., 1982); Hastings College of Law, University of California (J.D., 1986). Graduate, Los Angeles Trial Attorney Project, 1989. Member, COMM/ENT, the Hastings Communications and Entertainment Law Journal, 1985. Extern-Clerk to Associate Justice Otto M. Kaus of the California Supreme Court, 1985. *Member:* Los Angeles County (Member, Business and Corporations Law Section and Barristers) and American Bar Associations; State Bar of California (Member, Sections on: Real Property Law; Labor and Employment Law). **LANGUAGES:** French. **PRACTICE AREAS:** Business Litigation; Real Estate/Commercial Law; Labor Law; Trials and Appeals; Commercial Litigation. **Email:** dawson@bwslaw.com

**STEPHEN R. ONSTOT,** born San Francisco, California, May 13, 1959; admitted to bar, 1989, California. *Education:* United States Military Academy; University of California at Davis (B.S., Chem Eng., 1984; B.A., Pol. Sc., 1984); McGeorge School of Law, University of the Pacific (J.D., 1988). Arbitrator, Los Angeles County Superior Court. **PRACTICE AREAS:** Environmental Law; Environmental Litigation; Regulatory Representation. **Email:** onstot@bwslaw.com

**MARK D. HENSLEY,** born Sacramento, California, October 4, 1960; admitted to bar, 1989, California. *Education:* University of California at Los Angeles (A.B., Economics, 1986); Loyola Law School (J.D., 1989). Extern for Judge William J. Rea, U.S. District Court, Central District of California, 1988. City Attorney, Chino Hills, 1995—. Assistant City Attorney: El Segundo, 1995—; Downey, 1993—. **PRACTICE AREAS:** Public Law; Municipal and Business Litigation; Public and Private Employment Law. **Email:** hensley@bwslaw.com

**JOHN J. WELSH,** born Catskill, New York, December 16, 1962; admitted to bar, 1989, New York; 1991, California and U.S. District Court, Central District of California; 1992, District of Columbia. *Education:* University of Notre Dame (B.B.A., 1984); Albany Law School of Union University (J.D., 1988); Indiana University (M.B.A., 1990). *Member:* New York State Bar Association; The District of Columbia Bar. **PRACTICE AREAS:** Education Law; Business Transactions; Corporate Litigation. **Email:** welsh@bwslaw.com

*ASSOCIATES*

**CARLETON H. MORRISON, JR.,** born Honolulu, Hawaii, July 12, 1942; admitted to bar, 1976, Illinois, U.S. District Court, Northern District of Illinois and U.S. Court of Appeals, Seventh Circuit; 1980, U.S. Supreme Court; 1995, California. *Education:* Brigham Young University (B.A., 1966); Loyola University of Chicago (M.A., 1972) DePaul University (J.D., 1976); George Washington University (LL.M., 1980). School Board Trustee, Fallbrook, California, 1992-1994. *Member:* State Bar of California (Sections on: Environmental Law; Public Law); American Bar Association. [Lt. Col. USMC, 1966-1986]. **LANGUAGES:** Spanish. **PRACTICE AREAS:** Environmental Law; Public Law; Government Relations; Legislative Advocacy. **Email:** morrison@bwslaw.com

**JOSEPH P. BUCHMAN,** born Los Angeles, California, July 27, 1963; admitted to bar, 1990, California. *Education:* University of California at Los Angeles (B.A., 1986); Loyola Marymount University (J.D., 1990). Phi Delta Phi. Member, Editorial Staff, Loyola Entertainment Law Journal, 1989-1990. **PRACTICE AREAS:** Bankruptcy/Litigation; Debtor/-

*(This Listing Continued)*

Creditor/Trustee; Creditors' Rights; Real Property Transactions; Litigation; Taxation; Civil Rico; Real Estate. *Email:* jpbuchman@aol.com

**GREGORY T. DION,** born Philadelphia, Pennsylvania, March 22, 1963; admitted to bar, 1990, California. *Education:* University of California at Los Angeles (B.A., 1985); Loyola Marymount University (J.D., 1990). Recipient: American Jurisprudence Award for Civil Procedure and Advanced Trial Advocacy; 1990 Byrne Trial Advocacy Award. *Member:* Los Angeles County Bar Association (Member, Environmental Section). **PRACTICE AREAS:** Civil Litigation; Employment Law; Environmental Law; Land Use Law. *Email:* dion@bwslaw.com

**WILLIAM A. VALLEJOS,** born Virginia Beach, Virginia, January 21, 1958; admitted to bar, 1989, California. *Education:* Pitzer College (B.A., 1980); University of Southern California (M.P.A., 1983) Hispanic Field Services Fellowship; University of California at Los Angeles (J.D., 1987). *Member:* Los Angeles County, American and Mexican American Bar Associations. **PRACTICE AREAS:** Municipal Law; Land Use Law; Police Malpractice Defense. *Email:* vallejos@bwslaw.com

**THOMAS L. ALTMAYER,** born 1966; admitted to bar, 1991, California. *Education:* University of California at Irvine (B.A., 1988); University of Southern California School of Law (J.D., 1991). **PRACTICE AREAS:** Corporate and Municipal Litigation; Environmental Law. *Email:* thomasalt@aol.com

**BILLY D. DUNSMORE,** born Enid, Oklahoma, July 7, 1950; admitted to bar, 1979, Colorado; 1994, California. *Education:* University of Oklahoma (B.S., 1972); University of Denver (J.D., 1979); George Washington University (LL.M. Labor Law, 1987). **PRACTICE AREAS:** Labor Law; Employment Law; Personnel Law. *Email:* dunsmore@bwslaw.com

**GREGORY G. DIAZ,** born Salt Lake City, Utah, February 11, 1962; admitted to bar, 1991, California. *Education:* California State University at Long Beach (B.A., 1984); Consortium of the California State University (M.P.A., 1985); Western State University College of the Law (J.D., 1991). Pi Sigma Alpha. Recipient, John T. Amendt Academic Achievement. Co-Author: "Housing Element Update: Benefits and Risks of Alternative Actions," Orange County Planner, March 1996. Commissioner, Second District, Orange County Citizens Direction Finding Commission, 1981-1982. Assistant City Attorney, Dana Point and Lake Forest. Former Assistant City Attorney for City of Chino Hills and Temecula. Assistant General Counsel, Lake Forest Redevelopment Agency. Registered Federal Lobbyist. (Resident, Orange County Office). **PRACTICE AREAS:** Municipal and Public Law. *Email:* diaz@bwslaw.com

**KENNETH D. ROZELL,** born Asheville, North Carolina, August 30, 1962; admitted to bar, 1991, California; 1992, U.S. District Court, Central District of California and U.S. Court of Appeals, Ninth Circuit. *Education:* Southern Adventist University (B.A., 1984); Loyola Law School (J.D., 1991). Staff Member, Loyola Entertainment Law Journal, 1989-1990. Extern to U.S. District Judge William J. Rea, Central District of California, 1990. Author: Comment, "Missouri Attacks 'Violent' Videos: Are First Amendment Rights in Danger?" 10 Loyola E.L.J. 655, 1990. Assistant City Attorney, Camarillo and Dana Point. Assistant General Counsel: Alhambra Redevelopment Agency; Camarillo Community Development Commission. *Member:* Los Angeles County (Member, Governmental Law Section) and American Bar Associations. **PRACTICE AREAS:** Municipal and Public Law; Land Use; Redevelopment; Litigation. *Email:* rozell@bwslaw.com

**DEANNA L. BALLESTEROS,** born Chicago, Illinois, January 5, 1963; admitted to bar, 1992, California. *Education:* Barnard College (A.B., 1984); Catholic University of America (J.D., 1991). Member: Catholic University of America Law Review. Member, Moot Court Board. **PRACTICE AREAS:** Litigation. *Email:* ballesteros@bwslaw.com

**ELIZABETH M. CALCIANO,** born Santa Cruz, California, May 26, 1966; admitted to bar, 1992, California. *Education:* Bowdoin College (A.B., cum laude, 1988); Hastings College of the Law, University of California (J.D., 1992). Member, Moot Court Board. Co-Author: "Housing Element Update: Benefits and Risks of Alternative Actions," Orange County Planner, March 1996; "United Nations Convention on the Rights of the Child: Will it Help Children in the United States?" Hastings International and Comparative Law Review, Vol. 15, Issue 3, Spring 1992. Assistant City Attorney, City of Chino Hills. Assistant General Counsel, San Gabriel Valley Council of Governments. *Member:* Los Angeles County Bar Association (Barristers Liaison to the Executive Committee of the State and Local Government Law Section; Chair, Barristers Partners to Success Committee). **PRACTICE AREAS:** Public Law; Land Use; Environmental Law; Litigation. *Email:* calciano@netcom.com

*(This Listing Continued)*

**CAROL R. VICTOR,** born Upland, California, December 31, 1965; admitted to bar, 1992, California. *Education:* Georgetown University (B.S., 1988); Hastings College of the Law, University of California (J.D., 1992). California State Senate Fellow, 1988-1989. Member, Hastings International and Comparative Law Review, 1990-1991. **PRACTICE AREAS:** Litigation; Employment Law. *Email:* crv@aol.com

**HEATHER C. BEATTY,** born Long Beach, California, November 23, 1965; admitted to bar, 1992, California. *Education:* University of California at Berkeley (B.A., 1987); Loyola Law School of Los Angeles (J.D., 1992). Phi Delta Phi. Staff Member and Note and Comment Editor, Loyola Entertainment Law Journal, 1990-1992. Author: Note, "Skywalker Records, Inc. v. Navarro: 'Enough Already' to the Obscene Results of Miller v. California," 11 Loy. Ent. L.J. 623 (1991). Extern to Stephen Reinhardt, U.S. Ninth Circuit Court of Appeals, 1990. **PRACTICE AREAS:** Litigation; Employment Law; Labor Relations. *Email:* beatty@bwslaw.com

**ELIZABETH R. FEFFER,** born Fremont, California, September 3, 1968; admitted to bar, 1993, California. *Education:* University of California at Los Angeles (B.A., cum laude, 1990) Regents Scholar; University of Southern California (M.A., 1993; J.D., 1993). Member: Legion Lex Inns of Court; American Inns of Court. **PRACTICE AREAS:** Municipal Litigation. *Email:* feffer@bwslaw.com

**CRAIG S. GUNTHER,** born Reno, Nevada, December 21, 1959; admitted to bar, 1993, California. *Education:* University of California at Los Angeles (B.S.E.E., 1986); University of Southern California (M.S.E.E., 1986); Loyola Law School of Los Angeles (J.D., 1993). **PRACTICE AREAS:** Corporate Law; General Civil Litigation; Environmental Law; Communications. *Email:* gunther@bwslaw.com

**THOMAS P. CARTER,** born Milwaukee, Wisconsin, March 17, 1963; admitted to bar, 1993, California; 1994, U.S. District Court, Central District of California. *Education:* Loyola Marymount University (B.A., 1986; J.D., 1993). **PRACTICE AREAS:** General Civil Litigation. *Email:* carter@bwslaw.com

**SUSAN GEIER MEJIA,** born Jamaica, New York, March 30, 1962; admitted to bar, 1989, California. *Education:* State University of New York at Stony Brook (B.A., 1985); City University of New York at Queens College (J.D., 1988). *Member:* State Bar of California (Workers Compensation Section). **PRACTICE AREAS:** Workers Compensation. *Email:* mejia@bwslaw.com

**ROBERT F. MESSINGER,** born Decatur, Illinois, 1957; admitted to bar, 1994, California; 1995, Colorado. *Education:* The American University (B.A., 1981); University of Southern California (M.P.A., 1987); University of Illinois (J.D., 1994). Member, 1992-1993 and Editor-in-Chief, 1993-1994, Recent Decisions Section, Illinois Bar Journal. Member, 1992-1993 and Associate Editor, 1993-1994, The Elder Law Journal. Assistant City Attorney, Downey, 1996—. Deputy City Attorney, El Segundo, 1996—. **PRACTICE AREAS:** Municipal Law. *Email:* messinger@bwslaw.com

**ANNA PARK KANG,** born Korea, October 8, 1969; admitted to bar, 1994, California. *Education:* University of California at Los Angeles (B.A., summa cum laude, 1991); Hastings College of the Law, University of California (J.D., 1994). Pi Gamma Mu; Phi Delta Phi. Member, UCLA Division of Honors, 1988-1991. Member, Hastings Communication and Entertainment Journal, 1992-1993. Mediator, Asian Pacific American Dispute Resolution Center, 1992. Extern to California Court of Appeal Judge Carl Anderson, 1st District, 1993. **PRACTICE AREAS:** Municipal Law; Bankruptcy Law. *Email:* kang@bwslaw.com

**JOSEPH M. MONTES,** born Alhambra, California, June 15, 1968; admitted to bar, 1994, California. *Education:* Santa Clara University (B.A., magna cum laude, 1990); Loyola Law School (J.D., 1994). Chief Note and Comment Editor, Loy. of L.A. Ent. L.J. 1993-1994. Author: "Celebrity Goodwill: Nailing Jello to the Wall," 13 Loy. of L.A. Ent. L.J. 615. **PRACTICE AREAS:** Municipal Law; Civil Litigation. *Email:* montes@bwslaw.com

**MAJ-LE R. TATE,** born San Francisco, California, September 13, 1970; admitted to bar, 1995, California. *Education:* University of California at Berkeley (B.A., 1992); University of San Diego (J.D., 1995). Co-Author: "Bankers to Battlestations," Business Law Today, Sept/Oct. 1995. **PRACTICE AREAS:** Litigation. *Email:* tate@bwslaw.com

**CHRISTOPHER R. CHELEDEN,** born Glendale, California, January 9, 1968; admitted to bar, 1995, California. *Education:* University of Pennsylvania (A.B., cum laude, 1989); University of California, Los Angeles (Master of Arts, Urban Planning, 1991); University of California, Davis (J.D., 1995). Staff Editor, University of California, Davis Law Review,

*(This Listing Continued)*

## BURKE, WILLIAMS & SORENSEN, Los Angeles—Continued

1994-1995. Certified City Planner, American Institute of Certified Planners, 1991—. **PRACTICE AREAS:** Municipal Law; Environmental Law. **Email:** cheleden@jovanet.com

**TIMOTHY L. DAVIS,** born Los Angeles, California, May 11, 1970; admitted to bar, 1996, California and U.S. District Court, Central District of California. *Education:* Saint Marys College of California (B.A., 1992); McGeorge School of Law, University of the Pacific (J.D., 1995). Recipient, American Jurisprudence Award in Remedies, 1995. **PRACTICE AREAS:** General Civil Litigation. **Email:** davis@bwslaw.com

**BRYAN CAMERON LEROY,** born Newport Beach, California, May 12, 1965; admitted to bar, 1995, California. *Education:* University of California at Los Angeles (B.A., 1988); Hastings College of Law, University of California (J.D., 1995). Staff Editor, Hastings Constitutional Law Quarterly. (Resident, Orange County Office). **PRACTICE AREAS:** Municipal Law. **Email:** leroy@bwslaw.com

**NEDY A. WILLIAMS,** born Angeles City, Philippines, June 13, 1971; admitted to bar, 1996, California. *Education:* California State University at Long Beach (B.A., 1993); University of California, Los Angeles (J.D., 1996). Member, University of California Law Review. **PRACTICE AREAS:** Civil Litigation. **Email:** williams@bwslaw.com

### OF COUNSEL

**MARK C. ALLEN, JR., (PROFESSIONAL CORPORATION),** born Santa Monica, California, September 13, 1922; admitted to bar, 1950, California. *Education:* Louisiana State University, Santa Monica City College and University of Southern California (A.B., 1947); University of Southern California (J.D., 1949). Phi Alpha Delta. Assistant City Attorney, Santa Monica, 1952-1956. City Attorney: Inglewood, 1956-1968; Maywood, 1961; El Segundo, 1967-1983; Palos Verdes Estates, 1967-1990; Lomita, 1974-1975; Moorpark, 1983-1984; Port Hueneme, 1985-1989. *Member:* Los Angeles County Bar Association (Member, Board of Trustees, 1966-1968; President, 1961); The State Bar of California (Member, 1961-1970 and Chairman, 1969-1970, Committee on Administration of Justice; Member, Committee of Bar Examiners, 1981-1985). **PRACTICE AREAS:** Municipal Law. **Email:** mcallen@bwslaw.com

**KATHERINE F. ASCHIERIS,** born Buffalo, New York, July 31, 1956; admitted to bar, 1980, California. *Education:* California State University at Long Beach (B.A., summa cum laude, 1977); Hastings College of the Law, University of California (J.D., 1980). Member, Ball, Hunt Inn of Court. Member, 1994-1998 and President, 1996-1997, Board of Trustees, Long Beach Community College District. **PRACTICE AREAS:** Municipal Prosecution; Municipal Law; Civil Litigation. **Email:** aschieris@bwslaw.com

### RETIRED PARTNER

**MARTIN J. BURKE,** born Winnipeg, Canada, November 24, 1903; admitted to bar, 1927, California. *Education:* Loyola University (Ph.B., 1926; LL.B., 1926). *Member:* Los Angeles County and American Bar Associations; The State Bar of California. (Retired). **PRACTICE AREAS:** Business Law; Reorganizations Law; Commercial Law. **Email:** mjburke@bwslaw.com

REFERENCE: First Interstate Bank, Los Angeles Main Office.

---

## BURKLEY, GREENBERG, FIELDS & WHITCOMBE, L.L.P.
### LOS ANGELES, CALIFORNIA
(See Torrance)

General Civil Trial and Appellate Practice, State and Federal Courts. Business, Real Estate, Intellectual Property, Banking and Business Bankruptcy Law, Tort Defense, Estate and Succession Planning.

---

## BURNS, AMMIRATO, PALUMBO, MILAM & BARONIAN
### A PROFESSIONAL LAW CORPORATION
### LOS ANGELES, CALIFORNIA
(See Pasadena)

General Civil and Trial Practice in all Courts. Insurance Defense, Products Liability, Toxic Torts, Construction Litigation, Medical Malpractice, Personal Injury, Tort, Subrogation and Wrongful Termination.

---

## BURNS & GOLDSTONE, P.C.
### 1900 AVENUE OF THE STARS, SUITE 2700
### LOS ANGELES, CALIFORNIA 90067-4301
Telephone: 310-553-1900
Telecopier: 310-553-4207

General Business, Commercial and Corporate Law. Financial Institutions Law, Public Finance, International Business Transactions. Real Estate, Business and Civil Litigation. Administrative, Trade Association. Fiduciary Law and Public Pension Fund Law.

**DONALD E. BURNS,** born Teaneck, New Jersey, November 3, 1938; admitted to bar, 1965, District of Columbia; 1975, California; U.S. District Court, Central District of California. *Education:* Georgetown University (A.B., 1961); Yale University (LL.B., 1964). Law Clerk for Associate Justice Paul Peek, Supreme Court of California, 1965-1966. Assistant General Counsel, Federal Home Loan Bank Board, 1968-1971. Counsel, Federal Home Loan Mortgage Corporation, 1970-1971. Secretary, Business and Transportation Agency, 1975-1976. President, 1986-1989, California Council for Environmental and Economic Balance. *Member:* State Bar of California. **PRACTICE AREAS:** Financial Institutions; Public Finance; Real Estate.

**HILARY F. GOLDSTONE,** born Los Angeles, California, October 26, 1947; admitted to bar, 1972, California and U.S. District Court, Central District of California; 1974, U.S. Tax Court; 1979, U.S. Court of Appeals, Ninth Circuit. *Education:* Barnard College (B.A., 1968); Stanford University (J.D., 1971). Member, 1969-1970 and Executive Editor, 1970-1971, Stanford Law Review. Law Clerk for Judge William P. Gray, U.S. District Court, 1971-1972. Special Counsel to the Los Angeles City Attorney, 1975-1976. *Member:* State Bar of California. **PRACTICE AREAS:** Business; Civil Litigation; International; Real Estate; Commercial.

REFERENCE: Union Bank.

---

## BURTON & NORRIS
### LOS ANGELES, CALIFORNIA
(See Pasadena)

Trial and Appellate Litigation in all State and Federal Courts including Civil Rights, Commercial, Securities, Intellectual Property, Professional Responsibility and Personal Injury. Medical Malpractice and Criminal Law.

---

## ANDRÉS Z. BUSTAMANTE
### 811 WEST 7TH STREET
### 11TH FLOOR
### LOS ANGELES, CALIFORNIA 90017
Telephone: 213-891-9009
Fax: 213-627-1655

Criminal Law and Deportation Defense including Juvenile and Adult cases in State and Federal Court as well as Immigration Consequences of a Criminal Conviction both Pre and Post Conviction.

**ANDRÉS Z. BUSTAMANTE,** born El Paso, Texas, March 10, 1955; admitted to bar, 1990, California and U.S. District Court, Central District of California; 1991, U.S. District Court, Southern District of California; 1992, U.S. District Court, Northern District of California and U.S. Court of Appeals, 9th Circuit; 1994, U.S. District Court, District of Arizona. *Education:* University of California at Riverside (B.A., 1978); Peoples College of Law (J.D., 1987). *Member:* State Bar of California; California Public Defenders Association; National Association of Criminal Defense Lawyers; California Attorney of Criminal Justice. **LANGUAGES:** Spanish.

## DOUGLAS BUTLER
### LOS ANGELES, CALIFORNIA
(See Torrance)

*Estate Planning, Probate, Trusts, Wills, Taxation and International Estate Planning.*

---

## CADWALADER, WICKERSHAM & TAFT
### 660 SOUTH FIGUEROA STREET
### LOS ANGELES, CALIFORNIA 90017
Telephone: 213-955-4600
Telecopier: 213-955-4666
Email: postmaster@cadwalader.com
URL: http://www.cadwalader.com

*New York, N.Y. Office:* 100 Maiden Lane, 10038. Telephone: 212-504-6000. Cable Address: "LABELLUM". Telex: 12-9146/667465. Telecopier: 212-504-6666.

*Washington, D.C. Office:* 1333 New Hampshire Avenue, N.W., 20036. Telephone: 202-862-2200. TWX: 710-822-1934. Cable Address: "LABELLUM WASHINGTON". Telecopier: 202-862-2400.

*Charlotte, North Carolina Office:* Suite 1510, 201 South College Street. Telephone: 704-348-5100. Fax: 704-348-5200.

*General Practice.*

### MEMBERS OF FIRM

**RICHARD C. FIELD,** born Stanford, California, July 13, 1940; admitted to bar, 1966, California; 1971, U.S. Supreme Court. *Education:* University of California at Riverside (B.A., with honors, 1962); Harvard University (J.D., 1965). Judge Pro Tempore, Los Angeles Municipal Court, 1971-1977. Member, Panel of Commercial Arbitrators, American Arbitration Association. *Member:* Los Angeles County (Member, Trial Lawyers Section) and American (Member, Sections on: Litigation; Torts and Insurance Practice; Member, Products, General Liability and Consumer Law Committee) Bar Associations; State Bar of California (Member, Litigation Section); Association of Business Trial Lawyers (Member, Board of Governors, 1978-1982). *Email:* rfield@cwt.com

**JOSEPH M. MALINOWSKI,** born Detroit, Michigan, September 30, 1947; admitted to bar, 1972, California, U.S. District Court, Central District of California and U.S. Court of Appeals, Ninth Circuit. *Education:* Michigan State University; Wayne State University (B.A., 1969; J.D., magna cum laude, 1972). Member, Wayne State University Law Review, 1970-1971. *Member:* Los Angeles County (Member: Section on Commercial Law and Bankruptcy; Executive Committee, 1983-1986; Commercial Law Subcommittee, 1981-1988) and American (Member: Section on Business Law; Subcommittee on Personal Property Leasing, 1984—; Committee on the Uniform Commercial Code, 1984—; Subcommittee on Aircraft Financing, 1986—; Committee on Commercial Financial Services, 1986—) Bar Associations; State Bar of California. *Email:* joseph@cwt.com

**JOHN E. MCDERMOTT,** born Ravenna, Ohio, October 25, 1946; admitted to bar, 1972, California; U.S. District Court, Central District of California and U.S. Court of Appeals, Ninth Circuit. *Education:* Ohio Wesleyan University (B.A., 1968); Harvard Law School (J.D., 1971). Phi Beta Kappa. Lecturer, University of Southern California Law Center, 1974-1981. *Member:* State Bar of California; American Bar Association. *Email:* john@cwt.com

**ROGER W. ROSENDAHL,** born Bremerton, Washington, June 1, 1943; admitted to bar, 1973, New York; 1975, California. *Education:* University of Southern California (A.B., cum laude, 1965); Cambridge University, England; Georgetown University (J.D., 1969; LL.M., 1971). Managing Editor, Law and Policy in International Business. Schulte Zur Hausen Fellow, International Law Institute, Washington, D.C., 1969-1971. Editor, Current Legal Aspects of Doing Business in the Pacific Basin, American Bar Association, 1987. Member, Panel of Commercial Arbitrators, American Arbitration Association. *Member:* State Bar of California; American Bar Association (Chairman, Asia-Pacific Law Committee, Section of International Law and Practice, 1986-1988). *LANGUAGES:* German. *Email:* rrosenda@cwt.com

**MICHAEL A. SANTORO,** born Los Angeles, California, June 14, 1954; admitted to bar, 1979, California and U.S. District Court, Central District of California. *Education:* University of Southern California (B.S.,
*(This Listing Continued)*

---

magna cum laude, 1976); Loyola University of Los Angeles (J.D., 1979). Member, Loyola International and Comparative Law Journal, 1978-1979. *Member:* Los Angeles County and American Bar Associations; State Bar of California. *Email:* msantoro@cwt.com

### COUNSEL

**ROBERT E. CAMPBELL,** born Harrisburg, Pennsylvania, October 29, 1952; admitted to bar, 1977, District of Columbia; 1990, California; U.S. Supreme Court; U.S. Court of Appeals for the District of Columbia, Fourth, Fifth, Ninth, Eleventh and Federal Circuits; U.S. District Court, Northern, Eastern, Central and Southern Districts of California and District of Columbia. *Education:* Bucknell University (B.A., 1974); Vanderbilt University (J.D., 1977); Georgetown University (LL.M., Labor, 1982). *Member:* Los Angeles County and American Bar Associations; State Bar of California. *Email:* rcampbel@cwt.com

**PHILIP G. GRANT,** born Portland, Oregon, December 1, 1941; admitted to bar, 1983, California and U.S. District Court, Central, Northern, Eastern and Southern Districts of California; 1986, U.S. Court of Appeals, Ninth Circuit. *Education:* Stanford University (B.A., 1964); University of California at Berkeley (B.A., 1964; M.A., 1968; Ph.D., 1973); University of Texas (J.D., 1983). *Member:* State Bar of California. *Email:* pgrant@cwt.com

---

## J. T. CAIRNS & ASSOCIATES
### 200 N. LARCHMONT BOULEVARD
### LOS ANGELES, CALIFORNIA 90004
Telephone: 213-962-5588
Telecopier: 213-463-4412

*Business, Real Estate and Commercial Law, Civil Trial and Transactions. Bankruptcy, Aviation Law, Travel Law, Probate and Estate Planning.*

**J. T. CAIRNS,** born El Paso, Texas, March 24, 1952; admitted to bar, 1977, California; 1978, U.S. District Court, Central District of California and U.S. Court of Appeals, Ninth Circuit; 1987, U.S. Court of Appeals, Fifth Circuit. *Education:* Cornell University (A.B., cum laude, 1974); Pomona College; Hastings College of Law, University of California (J.D., 1977). Phi Delta Phi. Member, 1975-1977 and Associate Editor, 1976-1977, Hastings Law Journal. Author: "Imputed Negligence As A Defense In Wrongful Death Actions," published by California Lawyer, Journal of the State Bar of California, October, 1984. Licensed Pilot, Instrument Rating. Real Estate Brokers Licence, 1979. *Member:* Los Angeles County (Member, Sections on: Litigation; Real Property) and American (Member, Sections on: Litigation; Corporation, Banking and Business Law) Bar Associations; State Bar of California; Aircraft Owners and Pilots Association.

### ASSOCIATES

**DEANN HAMPTON,** born September 17, 1966; admitted to bar, 1994, California. *Education:* University of California at Los Angeles (B.A., 1989); Loyola University of Los Angeles (J.D., 1994). *Member:* Los Angeles County Bar Association; State Bar of California. *PRACTICE AREAS:* Real Estate; Civil Trial.

---

## CAIRNS, DOYLE, LANS, NICHOLAS & SONI
### LOS ANGELES, CALIFORNIA
(See Pasadena)

*General Civil and Trial Practice in all State and Federal Courts. Banking, Bankruptcy, Corporation, Business, Insurance, Negligence, Malpractice, Real Property, Construction, Motor Transport, Employment Law, Fraud and Toxic Torts.*

---

## CALENDO, PUCKETT, SHEEDY & DiCORRADO
### LOS ANGELES, CALIFORNIA
(See Glendale)

*General Practice.*

## JOHN A. CALFAS
A PROFESSIONAL CORPORATION
Established in 1957

11601 WILSHIRE BOULEVARD
SUITE 1920
**LOS ANGELES, CALIFORNIA 90025**
Telephone: 310-477-1920
FAX: 310-477-7132

*Corporation, Securities, Taxation, Estate Planning, Trust and Probate Law.*

**JOHN A. CALFAS,** born Hartford, Connecticut, November 29, 1926; admitted to bar, 1957, California. *Education:* University of California at Los Angeles (B.S., 1951; LL.B., 1956). Phi Alpha Delta. *Member:* Santa Monica Bay District and American Bar Associations; The State Bar of California.

REFERENCES: Bank of America (Wilshire-Westwood Office), Los Angeles.

---

## CALLAHAN, McCUNE & WILLIS
Established in 1975

SUITE 1200, 11755 WILSHIRE BOULEVARD
**LOS ANGELES, CALIFORNIA 90025**
Telephone: 310-312-1860
Fax: 310-477-3481

*Tustin, California Office:* 111 Fashion Lane, 92680. Telephone: 714-730-5700. Fax: 714-730-1642.

*San Diego, California Office:* 402 West Broadway, Suite 800, 92101. Telephone: 619-232-5700. Fax: 619-232-2206.

*Civil, Trial and Appellate Practice. Insurance Defense, Personal Injury, Products and Professional Liability, Property Damage, Construction Law, Litigation, Employment Discrimination, Business Litigation and Medical Malpractice.*

### MEMBERS OF FIRM

**JOHN J. TASKER,** born Chicago, Illinois, March 16, 1953; admitted to bar, 1978, Illinois; 1982, California. *Education:* Valparaiso University (B.S., 1975; J.D., 1978). Delta Theta Phi. *Member:* Orange County (Member, Litigation Section), Illinois State and American (Member, Section of Litigation) Bar Associations; State Bar of California; The Association of Trial Lawyers of America.

**STEVEN A. SIMONS,** born Van Nuys, California, March 19, 1956; admitted to bar, 1987, California and U.S. District Court, Central District of California. *Education:* Los Angeles Mission College (A.A., 1980); California State University at Northridge (B.A., 1984); Southwestern University School of Law (J.D., 1987). *Member:* San Fernando Valley Bar Association (Co-chair, Litigation Section); State Bar of California. [Petty Officer Third Class, U.S. Navy, 1974-1976]

**JOHN A. NOJIMA,** born Evanston, Illinois, June 17, 1965; admitted to bar, 1992, California and U.S. District Court, Central District of California. *Education:* California State University at Dominguez Hills (B.S., summa cum laude, 1987); Loyola Marymount (M.B.A., 1989); Pepperdine University (J.D., 1992). Phi Kappa Phi. NCAA Academic All-American. NCAA Post-Grad Scholar. California Rhodes Scholar. The Outstanding Graduate, 1987. Recipient, National Wood Hayes Scholar Athlete Award. Who's Who in American Colleges and Universities. *Member:* State Bar of California; Southern California Defense Counsel.

**ALLISON L. JONES,** born Andrews, North Carolina, December 29, 1966; admitted to bar, 1992, California. *Education:* University of California (B.A., 1989); Hastings College of Law, University of California (J.D., 1992). *Member:* State Bar of California. **PRACTICE AREAS:** Civil Litigation.

**CHARLES T. BROWN,** born San Gabriel, California, January 1, 1959; admitted to bar, 1989, California and U.S. District Court, Central District of California. *Education:* California State University (B.A., with honors, 1985); Brigham Young University (J.D., 1988). *Member:* Orange County and American Bar Associations; State Bar of California; American Inns of Court.

**PAMELA S. COOKE,** born Harrisburg, Pennsylvania, March 4, 1961; admitted to bar, 1986, California; 1987, U.S. District Court, Central District of California. *Education:* Hofstra University (B.A., cum laude, 1983);

*(This Listing Continued)*

Southwestern University School of Law (J.D., 1986). *Member:* State Bar of California.

**JEREMY L. TISSOT,** born Norwood, Massachusetts, November 26, 1969; admitted to bar, 1994, California. *Education:* University of Massachusetts at Amherst (B.A., Economics/Business, 1994); Pepperdine University (J.D., cum laude, 1994). Phi Delta Phi (Chairman, 1992-1993). Senior Editor, Pepperdine Law Review, 1992-1994. **PRACTICE AREAS:** Insurance Defense; Real Estate Litigation.

### ASSOCIATE

**MICHAEL C. ROGERS,** born Long Beach, California, February 17, 1970; admitted to bar, 1995, California and U.S. District Court, Central and Southern Districts of New York. *Education:* University of San Diego (B.A., 1992; J.D., 1995). University of San Diego Environmental Law Society, 1992-1995. Recipient, James R. Webb Environmental Law Award, 1995. *Member:* Los Angeles County and American Bar Associations. **PRACTICE AREAS:** Civil Litigation; Insurance Defense.

REPRESENTATIVE CLIENTS: Allstate Insurance Company; Associated Claims Enterprises; Aetna Casualty, AIG Specialty; Atlantic Companies; Crum & Forster; Chicago Insurance, CIGNA/ESIS; CNA Insurance; Continental Pro; Design Professional Inc.; Diocese of San Diego; Evanston Insurance Company; Firemans Fund; Gallagher Bassett Services; General Star Management; K&K Insurance; City of Laguna Beach; Lucky Stores; Aetna Insurance; Marie Callender's; Midland Risk Insurance Company; National General Insurance; Pro Claims; Savon; State Farm; Republic Indemnity Company; TIG; Topa Risk Services; The Ordinary Mutual; Tri Star Risk; Universal Underwriters; VASA North Atlantic; Viking Insurance Company; Wawanesa Mutual; Willis Corroon Group.

(For complete biographical info on all personnel, see professional biographies at Tustin, California.)

---

## CALVILLO, STEVAN R.
**LOS ANGELES, CALIFORNIA**
(See Long Beach)

*Business, Real Estate Litigation and Shareholder Litigation.*

---

## CAMERON, MADDEN, PEARLSON, GALE & SELLARS
**LOS ANGELES, CALIFORNIA**
(See Long Beach)

*General Civil Trial and Appellate Practice, State and Federal Courts, Real Estate, Land Use, Environmental, Administrative, Corporate, Partnership, Taxation, Estate Planning, Trust and Employment Law.*

---

## CANTILO, MAISEL & HUBBARD, L.L.P.
A Partnership of Professional Corporations

11500 WEST OLYMPIC BOULEVARD
FOURTH FLOOR
**LOS ANGELES, CALIFORNIA 90064**
Telephone: 310-478-7586
Fax: 310-312-2464

*Austin, Texas Office:* 111 Congress Avenue, Suite 1700. Telephone: 512-478-6000. Fax: 512-404-6550.

*Dallas, Texas Office:* 1717 Main Street, Suite 3200, 75201. Telephone: 214-740-4600. Fax: 214-740-4646.

*Bankruptcy, General Corporate, Health Care Law, Insolvencies, Insurance, Litigation, Mergers and Acquisitions, Real Estate, Workouts and Reorganizations.*

### MEMBERS OF FIRM

**ROBERT W. BIEDERMAN, (P.C.),** born Chicago, Illinois, October 22, 1952; admitted to bar, 1978, Illinois and U.S. District Court, Northern District of Illinois; 1985, Texas; 1986, U.S. District Court, Northern District of Texas; 1989, U.S. District Court, Eastern, Southern and Western Districts of Texas; 1992, Massachusetts; 1995, California and U.S. Court of Appeals, Fifth Circuit. *Education:* Sarah Lawrence College (B.A., 1973); Loyola University (J.D., 1978). Co-Author: "Cases of First Impression: Prosecuting and Defending Against Motions for Temporary Restraining Order," Vol.

*(This Listing Continued)*

70, No. 9 Illinois Bar Journal, May, 1982. Author: "Classification in Single-Asset Bankruptcy Cases: Debtor and Lender Strategies," Vol. 3, No. 6, Real Estate Workouts and Asset Management, December 1994; "Taming the Beast: Creditor Strategies Under Section 105 (a) of the Bankruptcy Code," Bankruptcy Litigation, Vol. 3, No. 4, Fall, 1995. *Member:* Dallas and American Bar Associations; State Bar of Texas; State Bar of California. *PRACTICE AREAS:* Bankruptcy; Insurance Insolvency; Commercial Litigation.

**CHRISTOPHER M. MAISEL, (P.C.),** born Galveston, Texas, November 2, 1951; admitted to bar, 1977, Alaska; 1978, Texas; 1980, U.S. District Court, Western District of Texas; 1981, U.S. District Court, Southern and Northern Districts of Texas; 1988, California; U.S. District Court, Central District of California. *Education:* Texas Arts & Industries University (B.B.A., summa cum laude, 1973); University of Texas (J.D., 1976). Counsel for Liquidation Division, Texas State Board of Insurance, 1978-1982, Deputy Liquidator, 1983-1984. Special Deputy Insurance Commissioner for Executive Life Insurance Company in Rehabilitation/Liquidation, 1993—. Author: "Managing a Large Life Insurer Insolvency - The Executive Life of California Experience," ABA National Institute On Life Insurer Insolvency, June, 1993; "Returning Unearned Premiums," Texas Insurer, March, 1985; "Dissenting Opinion to the Majority Report of the Study Group on Reinsurance Setoff," N.A.I.C. Rehabilitators and Liquidators Task Force, September, 1988. Member, National Association of Insurance Commissioners, Rehabilitators and Liquidators Task Force Working Groups of "Study Group on Reinsurance Setoff," "Relationships Committee," "Other Issues Model Act," 1987, N.A.I.C. Rehabilitators and Liquidators (EX5) Task Force Model Act Issues Working Group. *Member:* Travis County, Alaska State and American (Member, Litigation Section) Bar Associations; State Bar of Texas; State Bar of California. *PRACTICE AREAS:* Insurance Insolvency; Regulatory; Litigation.

### OF COUNSEL

**JEFFREY H. KARLIN, (P.C.),** born New York, New York, January 9, 1955; admitted to bar, 1980, California. *Education:* State University of New York at Stony Brook (B.S., 1975); University of California, Hastings College of the Law (J.D., 1980); Golden Gate University Graduate School of Taxation (LL.M., in Taxation, 1981). Certified Public Accountant, California, 1983. Senior Adjunct Professor of Taxation, Golden Gate University Graduate School of Taxation. Author: "Federal Income Taxation of Real Estate." Co-Author: "Investments By Tax Exempt Entities in U.S. Realty." *Member:* American Bar Association (Member, Sections on: Taxation; Business Law; Real Estate, Probate and Trust Law). *PRACTICE AREAS:* Business Transactions; Tax; Securities; Partnership; Insurance; Corporate; Real Estate Acquisitions.

(For complete biographical data on all personnel, see Professional Biographies at Austin and Dallas, Texas)

---

## CHRISTOPHER D. CARICO

### LOS ANGELES, CALIFORNIA

(See Manhattan Beach)

*Estate Planning, Trust, Probate and Elder Law.*

---

## CARLSMITH BALL WICHMAN CASE & ICHIKI

A Partnership including Law Corporations

Established in 1857

**555 SOUTH FLOWER STREET, 25TH FLOOR**
**LOS ANGELES, CALIFORNIA 90071**
Telephone: 213-955-1200
Cable Address: CWCMI LOSANGELESCALIFORNIA
Fax: 213-623-0032; 213-624-7183

*REVISERS OF THE HAWAII LAW DIGEST FOR THIS DIRECTORY.*

*Honolulu, Hawaii Office:* Suite 2200, Pacific Tower, 1001 Bishop Street. P.O. Box 656. Telephone: 808-523-2500.
*Kapolei, Hawaii Office:* Kapolei Building, Suite 318, 1001 Kamokila Boulevard. Telephone: 808-523-2500.
*Wailuku, Maui Hawaii Office:* One Main Plaza, Suite 400, 2200 Main Street, P.O. Box 1086. Telephone: 808-242-4535.

(This Listing Continued)

*Kailua-Kona, Hawaii Office:* Second Floor, Bank of Hawaii Annex Building, P.O. Box 1720. Telephone: 808-329-6464.
*Hilo, Hawaii Office:* 121 Waianuenue Avenue, P.O. Box 686. Telephone: 808-935-6644.
*Agana, Guam Office:* 4th Floor, Bank of Hawaii Building, P.O. Box BF. Telephone: 671-472-6813.
*Saipan, Commonwealth of the Northern Mariana Islands Office:* Carlsmith Building, Capitol Hill, P.O. Box 5241. Telephone: (011) 670-322-3455.
*Washington, D.C. Office:* 700 14th Street, N.W., 9th Floor. Telephone: 202-508-1025.
*Mexico City, Mexico Office:* Monte Pelvous 111, Piso 1, Col. Lomas de Chapultepec 11000, Mexico, D.F. Telephone: (011-52-5) 520-8514. Fax: (011-52-5) 540-1545.
*Mexico, D.F. Office of Carlsmith Ball Garcia Cacho y Asociados, S.C. (Authorized to practice Mexican Law):* Monte Pelvoux 111, Piso 1, Col. Lomas de Chapultepec, 11000 Mexico, D.F. Telephone: (011-52-5) 520-8514. Fax: (011-52-5) 540-1545.

*Admiralty & Maritime, Administrative, Banking & Finance, Corporate, Environmental, Foreign Investment Interests, Hotel, Resort & Entertainment, Immigration, International, Labor & Employment, Litigation and Dispute Resolution, Public Utilities, Real Property and Land Use, Tax, Trusts, and Comparative Planning.*

FIRM PROFILE: *The law firm of Carlsmith Ball Wichman Case & Ichiki was established in 1857 in Hilo, Hawaii. The firm currently has 115 attorneys in ten offices located throughout Hawaii, in Guam, Saipan, Los Angeles, Washington, D.C. and Mexico City, Mexico.*

*Our firm assists businesses in solving problems or concerns that arise in the course of business operations. The attorneys in this firm concentrate exclusively in business law and have extensive experience with the industries in the Pacific Region. In addition, our Washington, D.C. office provides essential representation when our clients have needs at the federal level. Our clientele includes businesses from the construction, health care, retail, real estate, transportation, maritime, media, agricultural, education, tourism, entertainment, and finance industries, amongst others. Our understanding of the Pacific Region, including extensive foreign language capabilities, allows us to provide you a distinct combination of technical skills and practical experience to serve your legal and business needs.*

*With 140 years of successful practice, we identify and anticipate obstacles to business procedures and solve problems more rapidly than less experienced firms. Our attorneys have long-established working relationships with the regulators in our jurisdictions, making us knowledgeable of the internal, informal administrative practices of government agencies, and the political forces that affect their decision making outcomes. This means more cost-effective representation for our clients.*

*Our goals are to:*

*Assist you in developing a business structure which complements the operational and financial needs of your company.*

*Anticipate business issues which may affect your company and guide you in efficiently resolving any problems or obstacles that arise.*

*Develop options to enable you to avoid or minimize potential problems.*

*Provide a level of client service which will ensure that you return to Carlsmith Ball time and again and recommend our firm to others.*

### MEMBERS OF FIRM

**ANNIE KUN BAKER,** born Romania, August 5, 1947; admitted to bar, 1981, California and U.S. District Court, Central District of California; 1982, U.S. Tax Court. *Education:* University of California at Los Angeles (B.A., summa cum laude, 1969; M.A., 1971; Ph.D., 1979; J.D., 1981). Phi Beta Kappa. Regents Scholar. Chancellors Fellow. *Member:* Los Angeles County Bar Association (Member, International Law Section, Executive Committee, 1982—; First Vice Chair, 1988-1989); State Bar of California. *LANGUAGES:* French, Italian, German and Russian. *PRACTICE AREAS:* Business Law; Corporate Law; Real Estate; International Law. *Email:* AKB@Carlsmith.com

**JOSEPH A. BALL,** born Stuart, Iowa, December 16, 1902; admitted to bar, 1927, California. *Education:* Creighton University (A.B., 1925); University of Southern California (J.D., 1927). Order of the Coif. Member: Advisory Committee on Federal Criminal Rules, 1960-1972; California Law Revision Commission, 1960-1967; Committee to Revise Constitution of California, 1963-1970. Counsel, Warren Commission, 1964. *Member:* Long Beach (President, 1951-1952), Los Angeles County (Member, Board of Trustees, 1945-1946) and American (Chairman, National Conference of Bar Presidents, 1960-1961; State Delegate, 1956-1959; 1963-1965) Bar Associa-

(This Listing Continued)

**CARLSMITH BALL WICHMAN CASE & ICHIKI, Los Angeles—Continued**

tions; The State Bar of California (President, 1956-1957). Fellow, American College of Trial Lawyers (President, 1967-1968). *PRACTICE AREAS:* Litigation. *Email:* JAB@Carlsmith.com

**ROGER B. BAYMILLER,** born Phoenix, Arizona, October 25, 1941; admitted to bar, 1969, California. *Education:* California State University at Long Beach; Arizona State University (B.A., 1963); University of Southern California (J.D., 1968). Phi Kappa Phi. Phi Delta Phi. Order of the Coif. Member of Staff, 1966-1967 and Lead Articles Editor, 1967-1968, Southern California Law Review. *Member:* Los Angeles County and American Bar Associations; The State Bar of California. [1st Lt., U.S. Army, 1963-1965]. *PRACTICE AREAS:* Corporate Finance; Securities; Corporate Formation; Commercial Real Estate Acquisitions; Commercial Real Estate Sales. *Email:* RBB@Carlsmith.com

**NANCY M. BECKNER,** born Carlisle, Pennsylvania, December 22, 1944; admitted to bar, 1979, Hawaii; 1990, California; 1992, District of Columbia (inactive). *Education:* Wilson College and University of Maryland (B.A., with high honors, 1966); Washington College of Law and University of Hawaii (J.D., 1979). Recipient: American Jurisprudence Awards in Labor Law and Criminal Justice; Dean's Award for Scholastic Excellence. *Member:* Los Angeles County Bar Association (Former Chair, Foreign Tax Committee). *PRACTICE AREAS:* International Taxation; International Estate Planning; Corporate and Partnership Tax; Non-Profit Tax Law. *Email:* NMB@Carlsmith.com

**STEPHEN L. BRADFORD,** born Salt Lake City, Utah, November 20, 1958; admitted to bar, 1987, California; 1989, Nevada; 1991, District of Columbia. *Education:* Brigham Young University (B.S., magna cum laude, 1983); University of Virginia (J.D., 1986). *Member:* State Bar of California; State Bar of Nevada; The District of Columbia Bar; American Bar Association (International Law Section); US-Mexico Chamber of Commerce. *LANGUAGES:* Spanish. *PRACTICE AREAS:* Latin America Trade; Corporate Law. *Email:* SLB@Carlsmith.com

**ALBERT H. EBRIGHT,** born Los Angeles, California, June 27, 1933; admitted to bar, 1959, California. *Education:* University of California at Berkeley (A.B., 1955); Loyola University of Los Angeles (LL.B., 1958); University of Southern California (LL.M., 1961); Harvard Law School (LL.M., 1962). *Member:* Los Angeles County Bar Association; State Bar of California. *PRACTICE AREAS:* Commercial Litigation; Commercial Law; Corporate Litigation. *Email:* AHE@Carlsmith.com

**TERRENCE A. EVERETT,** born Glendale, California, February 24, 1953; admitted to bar, 1978, California. *Education:* University of California at Los Angeles (A.B., 1975); Loyola University (J.D., cum laude, 1978). Recipient, American Jurisprudence Award for Corporations. *Member:* Beverly Hills, Los Angeles County and American (Member: Section of Corporation, Banking and Business Law; Section of Real Property Law) Bar Associations; The State Bar of California; American Judicature Society. *PRACTICE AREAS:* Corporate Law; Corporate Organization; Hotel and Resort Development; International Financial Real Estate. *Email:* TAE@Carlsmith.com

**JONATHAN R. HODES,** born Portland, Oregon, February 19, 1945; admitted to bar, 1971, New York; 1974, California. *Education:* Cornell University (A.B., 1966); Rutgers University, Newark (J.D., 1969); New York University. Member, California Corporation Commissioner's Corporate Securities Law Advisory Committee, 1980-1981. Co-Author: "Using the Brady Bond Approach in Mexican Corporate Financing," 2 Mexico Trade and Law Reporter 5 (April 1992). *Member:* The Association of the Bar of the City of New York; Beverly Hills, Los Angeles County and American Bar Associations; State Bar of California. *PRACTICE AREAS:* Maritime Finance; Corporate Law; Contracts; Commercial Law; Corporate Finance. *Email:* JRH@Carlsmith.com

**ROBERT F. KULL,** born Benton Harbor, Michigan, March 9, 1948; admitted to bar, 1976, California and U.S. District Court, Central District of California. *Education:* University of California at Los Angeles (A.B., 1971); Hastings College of Law, University of California (J.D., 1975). *Member:* Los Angeles County and American Bar Associations; State Bar of California. *Email:* RFK@Carlsmith.com

**JOHN R. McDONOUGH,** born St. Paul, Minnesota, May 16, 1919; admitted to bar, 1949, California; 1967, U.S. Supreme Court; U.S. Court of Appeals, Ninth Circuit and U.S. District Courts in California. *Education:* University of Washington; Columbia University (LL.B., 1946). Assistant Professor of Law, Stanford University, 1946-1949. Associate, Brobeck,

*(This Listing Continued)*

Phleger & Harrison, San Francisco, 1949-1952. Professor of Law, Stanford University, 1952-1970. Executive Secretary, 1954-1959, Member, 1960-1967, California Law Revision Commission. Assistant and Associate Deputy Attorney General, U.S. Department of Justice, 1967-1969. *Member:* Los Angeles County and American Bar Associations; State Bar of California. Fellow, American College of Trial Lawyers. [With U.S. Army, 1942-1946]. *PRACTICE AREAS:* Civil Litigation (100%). *Email:* JRM@Carlsmith.com

**RANDOLPH G. MUHLESTEIN,** born Provo, Utah, July 22, 1952; admitted to bar, 1979, California. *Education:* Brigham Young University (B.S., summa cum laude, 1976; J.D., magna cum laude, 1979). Case and Comment Editor, Brigham Young University Law Review. Author: "Government Aid to Church-Related Education: An Alternative Rationale," Brigham Young University L. Rev. 617, 1978. Co-Author: "Perfecting and Protecting Security Interests in Ordinary Goods Moving Across State Lines," 29 The Practical Lawyer, No. 2, 1983. *Member:* State Bar of California. *LANGUAGES:* Spanish. *PRACTICE AREAS:* Latin American Trade (20%); Corporate Law (80%). *Email:* RGM@Carlsmith.com

**JOSEPH D. MULLENDER, JR.,** born Los Angeles, California, May 10, 1927; admitted to bar, 1954, California. *Education:* Occidental College (B.A., 1950); University of Southern California (LL.B., 1953). Order of the Coif. Associate Editor, Southern California Law Review, 1953. Assistant U.S. Attorney, Southern District of California, 1954-1956. *Member:* Los Angeles County, Long Beach, Federal and American Bar Associations; The State Bar of California. *Email:* JM1@Carlsmith.com

**DAVID S. OLSON,** born Brooklyn, New York, July 7, 1961; admitted to bar, 1987, California. *Education:* University of Delaware (B.A., 1983); University of Southern California (J.D., 1986). Order of the Coif; Phi Alpha Delta. Staff Member, 1984-1985 and Notes Editor, 1985-1986, USC Law Review. *Member:* State Bar of California; American Bar Association (Member, Litigation Section). *PRACTICE AREAS:* Corporate Litigation; Business Law; Commercial Law. *Email:* DSO@Carlsmith.com

**JAMES M. POLISH,** born Los Angeles, California, August 20, 1948; admitted to bar, 1973, California. *Education:* University of California at Los Angeles (A.B., in Psychology, magna cum laude, 1970; J.D., 1973). Order of the Coif; Phi Beta Kappa; Pi Gamma Mu. Associate Editor, U.C.-L.A. Law Review, 1972-1973. *Member:* Los Angeles County and American Bar Associations; State Bar of California. *PRACTICE AREAS:* Commercial Litigation; Corporate Litigation; International Commercial Law. *Email:* JMP@Carlsmith.com

**JONATHAN L. SMOLLER,** born Los Angeles, California, October 14, 1961; admitted to bar, 1988, California; 1989, U.S. District Court, Central District of California; 1994, U.S. District Court, District of Hawaii; 1995, U.S. District Court, Northern District of California. *Education:* University of California at Los Angeles (B.A., magna cum laude, 1983; J.D., 1988). Phi Beta Kappa. Managing Editor, UCLA Journal of Environmental Law and Policy, 1987-1988. Teaching Assistant, Legal Research and Writing, University of California at Los Angeles, 1986-1987. *Member:* Los Angeles County Bar Association; State Bar of California. *PRACTICE AREAS:* Commercial Litigation; Corporate Litigation. *Email:* JLS1@Carlsmith.com

**ALLAN EDWARD TEBBETTS,** born Santiago, Chile, February 2, 1940; admitted to bar, 1972, California; 1981, District of Columbia. *Education:* University of Southern California (B.A., 1961); Loyola University of Los Angeles (J.D., 1971). Editor in Chief, Loyola University of Los Angeles Law Review, 1970-1971. Law Clerk to Hon. E. Avery Crary, U.S. District Court for the Central District of California, 1971-1972. *Member:* Long Beach (Member, Board of Governors, 1980-1982, President, 1995), Los Angeles County and American Bar Associations; The State Bar of California; District of Columbia Bar; California Political Attorneys Association (Chairman, 1990-1991). [Lt. Comdr., JAGC, USNR, ret]. *PRACTICE AREAS:* Environmental Law; Commercial Litigation; Corporate Litigation; Government Law; Municipal Law. *Email:* AET@Carlsmith.com

**DONALD C. WILLIAMS,** born Oxnard, California, October 12, 1939; admitted to bar, 1967, Oregon; 1970, American Samoa; 1977, Trust Territory of the Pacific Islands, Hawaii and Guam; 1978, Commonwealth of the Northern Mariana Islands; 1992, California. *Education:* Fresno State University (B.A., 1963); Willamette University (J.D., 1967). Assistant Attorney General, 1970-1971 and Attorney General, 1971-1975, American Samoa. Associate Justice, Trust Territory of the Pacific Islands, 1975-1977. Chairman, Guam Bar Association Ethics Committee, 1990-1992. [U.S. Coast Guard Reserve]. *PRACTICE AREAS:* Commercial Law; Commercial Real Estate Development; Pacific Rim Trade. *Email:* DCW@Carlsmith.com

*(This Listing Continued)*

**DUANE H. ZOBRIST,** born Salt Lake City, Utah, September 11, 1940; admitted to bar, 1969, California. *Education:* University of Utah (A.B., 1965); University of Southern California (J.D., 1968). Phi Delta Phi. Co-author of "Businessman's Legal Guide To Doing Business In The United States". Member, Board of Directors, 1969— and President, 1977-1978, University of Southern California Law Alumni Association. Trustee, Legion Lex, 1981-1984, 1991-1992, Trustee, 1974— and President, 1979-1981, Brazil-California Trade Association. Member, Board of Directors, United States-Mexico Chamber of Commerce, 1981— and President, 1986-1988, 1991-1994, and Chairman, 1994—. Instructor, University of California at Los Angeles, 1993—. *Member:* Los Angeles County and American Bar Associations; State Bar of California. *LANGUAGES:* Spanish, Portuguese. *PRACTICE AREAS:* International Law; Business Law; North American Free Trade Agreement; Commercial Law; Mexico Trade. *Email:* DHZ@Carlsmith.com

### RESIDENT ASSOCIATES

**PETER N. GREENFELD,** born Wilmington, Delaware, October 16, 1963; admitted to bar, 1991, California; 1992, Guam. *Education:* Vassar College (B.A., 1985); University of Pennsylvania (M.G.A., Masters in Government Administration, 1987); Loyola Law School (J.D., 1991). President, St. Thomas More Law Honor Society, 1990-1991. *PRACTICE AREAS:* Business Litigation; Environmental Law. *Email:* PNG@Carlsmith.com

**ANN LUOTTO WOLF,** born Evanston, Illinois, January 30, 1962; admitted to bar, 1988, California. *Education:* Lewis and Clark College (B.A., 1984); Hastings College of Law, University of California (J.D., 1988). Member, Hastings Constitutional Law Quarterly, 1986-1988. *Member:* Los Angeles County and American Bar Associations; State Bar of California. *LANGUAGES:* French and Spanish. *PRACTICE AREAS:* Commercial Litigation; Corporate Litigation; Latin American Trade. *Email:* APL@Carlsmith.com

### RESIDENT OF COUNSEL

**HERBERT G. BAERWITZ,** born New York, N.Y., May 29, 1920; admitted to bar, 1947, California. *Education:* University of California at Los Angeles (B.A., 1940); University of Southern California (LL.B., 1947). *Member:* Beverly Hills and American (Member, Sections of: Corporation, Banking and Business Law; Patent, Trademark and Copyright Law) Bar Associations; The State Bar of California; Los Angeles Copyright Society; American Judicature Society. *PRACTICE AREAS:* Intellectual Property; Entertainment Law; Copyrights; Business Law. *Email:* HGB@Carlsmith.com

**DAGMAR V. HALAMKA,** born Riga Latvia, July 15, 1942; admitted to bar, 1973, California. *Education:* Trenton State College; Loyola School of Law, L.A. (J.D., 1973). International Law Studies, Cambridge Law School, Cambridge. Phi Alpha Delta. Advisor, Blackstonian, 1974—. Recipient, American Jurisprudence Award. Professor of Business Law, University of Southern California, 1973—. *Member:* Los Angeles County Bar Association (Member, Bridging the Gap Committee, 1988-1991; Professional Responsibility Committee); State Bar of California (Business Law Section, Education Committee, 1990— ). Co-Advisor, L.A. Law Club. Master, American Inns of Court. Author of *Joy of Law and More Joy of Law,* West Publishing. *Email:* DVH@Carlsmith.com

**TOM K. HOUSTON,** born St. Louis, Missouri, November 1, 1945; admitted to bar, 1972, California; 1973, District of Columbia. *Education:* Princeton University (A.B., Government, cum laude, 1967); Stanford University (J.D., 1972). Order of the Coif. Law Clerk to Mathew O. Tobriner, Associate Justice, California Supreme Court. Deputy Mayor and Chief of Staff, City of Los Angeles, 1984-1987. President, Los Angeles Environmental Quality Board, 1987-1989. Co-author: "Proposition 65 -- The Safe Drinking Water and Toxic Waste Initiative," 1986. Chairman, California Fair Political Practices Commission (FPPC), 1979-1983. Under Secretary and General Counsel, California State and Consumer Services Agency, 1975-1979. Deputy Secretary, California Agriculture and Services Agency, 1974-1975. Administrator (State Designee), California Occupational Safety and Health Program CAL/OSHA, 1974-1975. Deputy/Assistant General Counsel, Federal Energy Administration (FEA), 1974. *Member:* Los Angeles County Bar Association; State Bar of California; The District of Columbia Bar. *PRACTICE AREAS:* Environmental; Administrative Law; Occupational Safety and Health; Municipal Law. *Email:* TKH@Carlsmith.com

**ROBERT R. THORNTON,** born Lafayette, Indiana, June 25, 1929; admitted to bar, 1957, California; 1961, U.S. Supreme Court; registered to practice before U.S. Patent and Trademark Office. *Education:* Princeton University (B.S.E., 1951); Harvard University (LL.B., 1957). *Member:* Los

*(This Listing Continued)*

Angeles County and American (Member, Sections on: Intellectual Property Law; Litigation) Bar Associations; State Bar of California (Member, Intellectual Property Section). [Office, U.S. Navy, 1951-1954]. *PRACTICE AREAS:* Intellectual Property; Artistic Properties; Literary Properties; Commercial Law. *Email:* RRT@Carlsmith.com

### REVISERS OF THE HAWAII LAW DIGEST FOR THIS DIRECTORY.

(For Complete Personnel and Biographical Data, see Professional Biographies at Honolulu, Hawaii)

---

## JAMES P. CARR
### A PROFESSIONAL CORPORATION
Established in 1989

11755 WILSHIRE BOULEVARD, SUITE 1170
**LOS ANGELES, CALIFORNIA 90025**
Telephone: 310-444-7179
Fax: 310-473-0708

*Trial Practice in all State and Federal Courts. Product Liability, Governmental Liability, Negligence, Professional Malpractice.*

**JAMES P. CARR,** born Cheverly, Maryland, April 13, 1950; admitted to bar, 1976, Maryland; 1977, California and U.S. District Court, Central and Southern Districts of California. *Education:* University of Notre Dame (B.A., with honors, 1972; J.D., 1976); George Washington University. *Member:* Maryland State Bar Association; The State Bar of California; American Board of Trial Advocates; Consumer Attorneys of California; The Association of Trial Lawyers of America; Consumer Attorney Association of Los Angeles.

---

## LAW OFFICES OF
## GERALDINE C. CARTER
Established in 1989

2029 CENTURY PARK EAST, SUITE 600
**LOS ANGELES, CALIFORNIA 90067-3012**
Telephone: 310-551-1714
Telecopier: 310-556-7975

*Business, Corporate, Real Property, with Emphasis in the Areas of Secured and Unsecured Financing. Leasing, Acquisitions, Property Management, Hazardous Materials Compliance and Remediation and International Trade.*

**GERALDINE C. CARTER,** born New Haven, Connecticut, April 4, 1953; admitted to bar, 1983, California. *Education:* University of Connecticut (B.A., 1975; M.B.A., cum laude, 1977); Loyola Law School, Los Angeles (J.D., 1982). Member, American Bankers Association, 1979-1987. Private Pilot, 1970. Real Estate Broker, California, 1988. Commissioner, City of Los Angeles, Rent Stabilization Commission, 1986—. *Member:* Los Angeles County Bar Association (Member, Sections on: Environmental and Business); State Bar of California. *LANGUAGES:* Spanish. *PRACTICE AREAS:* Real Estate; Business and Corporate; Financial Institutions; Environmental.

### OF COUNSEL

**KIRTLEY M. THIESMEYER,** born Appleton, Wisconsin, May 12, 1938; admitted to bar, 1967, California and U.S. District Court, Central District of California; 1968, District of Columbia and U.S. Court of Military Appeals; 1970, U.S. Supreme Court. *Education:* Hanover College (A.B., 1959); University of California at Berkeley (J.D., 1966). Attorney Advisor, United States Comptroller of the Currency, 1966-1969. Mediator, Los Angeles Center for Dispute Resolution. *Member:* Los Angeles and American Bar Associations; State Bar of California; District of Columbia Bar. *LANGUAGES:* French and German. *PRACTICE AREAS:* Banking; International Trade; Commercial Law and Real Estate; General Corporate.

# CASE, KNOWLSON, BURNETT & WRIGHT

A Partnership including Professional Corporations

*Established in 1987*

**SUITE 1700, 2121 AVENUE OF THE STARS
LOS ANGELES, CALIFORNIA 90067**
Telephone: 310-552-2766
Telecopier: 310-552-3229

*Irvine, California Office:* 5 Park Plaza, Suite 800. Telephone: 714-955-1050. Telecopier: 714-851-9112.

General Civil Trial and Appellate Practice in all State and Federal Courts. Corporate, Real Estate, Real Estate Finance, Taxation, Estate Planning, Trusts and Probate Law.

FIRM PROFILE: Case, Knowlson, Mobley, Burnett & Wright, a Partnership including Professional Corporations, is a full-service law firm specializing in real estate, corporate transactions, civil litigation, and taxation, with substantial activity in estate planning and probate and bankruptcy matters. Members of our firm have been practicing law since 1974 with substantial experience at major Los Angeles law firms prior to the formation of the firm in 1986. The firm has 15 attorneys and maintains offices in Los Angeles and Irvine.

**DANIEL A. CASE, (P.C.),** born Los Angeles, California, April 22, 1951; admitted to bar, 1976, California; 1977, U.S. District Court, Central District of California. *Education:* Massachusetts Institute of Technology (B.S., 1973; M.S., 1973); University of California at Berkeley (J.D., 1976). Notes and Comments Editor, Industrial Relations Law Journal, 1975-1976. *Member:* The State Bar of California. **PRACTICE AREAS:** Corporate; Real Estate.

**RICK A. CIGEL,** born Stevens Point, Wisconsin, June 14, 1956; admitted to bar, 1982, California; 1983, U.S Court of Appeals, Ninth Circuit and U.S. District Court, Northern, Southern, Eastern and Central Districts of California. *Education:* University of Malaya, Kuala Lumpur, Malaysia; Jagiellonian University, Krakow, Poland; University of Wisconsin (B.S., with high honors, 1979); Northwestern University (J.D., 1982). *Member:* State Bar of California. **PRACTICE AREAS:** Tax; Estate Planning; Trust; Probate.

**MICHAEL F. WRIGHT,** born Jackson, Mississippi, September 14, 1954; admitted to bar, 1979, California; 1989, U.S. Court of Appeals, Federal Circuit and Ninth Circuit. *Education:* Stanford University (B.A., 1976; J.D., 1979). Phi Beta Kappa. Law Clerk to the Honorable Lawrence T. Lydick, U.S. District Court, Central District of California, 1979-1980. *Member:* State Bar of California.

**PATRICK W. WALSH,** born Brooklyn, New York, June 1, 1949; admitted to bar, 1974, California; 1980, District of Columbia. *Education:* Stanford University (B.A., with distinction, 1971); Boalt Hall School of Law, University of California (J.D., 1974). Associate Editor, 1972-1973 and Research Editor, 1973-1974, California Law Review. *Member:* The State Bar of California; District of Columbia Bar. **PRACTICE AREAS:** Civil Trial; Real Estate; Health.

**RICK AUGUSTINI,** born Berkeley, California, August 30, 1967; admitted to bar, 1992, California, U.S. District Court, Central and Southern Districts of California and U.S. Court of Appeals, Ninth Circuit. *Education:* University of California, Irvine (B.A., 1989); Loyola Law School (J.D., 1992). Member, Loyola Law Review, 1991-1992. *Member:* State Bar of California.

*OF COUNSEL*

**DAVID M. LUBER,** born Los Angeles, California, July 5, 1950; admitted to bar, 1977, California. *Education:* University of California at Los Angeles (B.A., magna cum laude, 1973); Boalt Hall School of Law, University of California (J.D., 1976). Member, Environmental Law Quarterly, 1975-1976. Member, Century City Chamber of Commerce Real Estate Advisory Cabinet. *Member:* Century City, Los Angeles County and American (Member, Sections on: Real Estate; Real Estate Financing) Bar Associations; The State Bar of California. **PRACTICE AREAS:** Real Estate; Real Estate Financing.

**EDWIN I. LASMAN,** born Los Angeles, California, March 5, 1955; admitted to bar, 1982, California; 1983, U.S. District Court, Central District of California and U.S. Court of Appeals, Ninth Circuit; 1987, U.S. District Court, Southern, Northern and Eastern Districts of California. *Education:* University of California at Berkeley (B.A., summa cum laude, 1976); University of California at Los Angeles (M.B.A., 1981; J.D., 1981). Phi Beta Kappa. Member, Moot Court Honors Program. Executive Editor,

*(This Listing Continued)*

University of California at Los Angeles Journal of International Law, 1986-1987. Professor, Corporations, University of West Los Angeles School of Paralegal Studies, 1986. Member, French-American Chamber of Commerce, 1986-1987. *Member:* Los Angeles County and American (Member, Sections on: Business Law; Litigation) Bar Associations; State Bar of California. **LANGUAGES:** French. **PRACTICE AREAS:** Corporate Law; Real Estate; Civil Litigation.

**DANIEL G. JORDAN,** born Los Angeles, California, June 29, 1954; admitted to bar, 1981, California and U.S. District Court, Central District of California. *Education:* University of California at Los Angeles (A.B., 1978); Boalt Hall School of Law, University of California (J.D., 1981). *Member:* Los Angeles County and American Bar Associations; State Bar of California.

---

# DAVID C. CASHION

**LOS ANGELES, CALIFORNIA**

(See Pasadena)

Family, Personal Injury, Business, Probate and Commercial Law. General Civil and Trial Practice.

---

# CATES & HAN

**LOS ANGELES, CALIFORNIA**

(See Irvine)

Business Transactions, Estate Planning, Litigation and Arbitration involving Franchising, Distribution, Unfair Competition, Trade Secrets and Business Torts.

---

# CAYER, KILSTOFTE & CRATON

**LOS ANGELES, CALIFORNIA**

(See Long Beach)

General Business and Civil Trial Practice before all Federal and State Courts. Banking and Bank Litigation, Business Litigation, Corporations, Corporate Securities, Federal and State Taxation, Estate Planning, Probate, Real Property Sales and Financing, Equine Law and Syndication, Family Law, Personal Injury and Workers Compensation Law.

---

# CELEBREZZE & WESLEY

A PROFESSIONAL CORPORATION

**444 SOUTH FLOWER STREET, SUITE 2300
LOS ANGELES, CALIFORNIA 90071**
Telephone: 213-243-1277
Facsimile: 213-243-1286
Email: 7345748@mcimail.com

*San Francisco, California Office:* 655 Montgomery Street, 17th Floor, 94111. Telephone: 415-288-3900. Facsimile: 415-288-3919. Email: 7365740@mcimail.com.

*San Luis Obispo, California Office:* 763 B Foothill Boulevard, Suite 146, 93405. Telephone: 805-927-9700. Facsimile: 805-927-9701. Email: 7305744@mcimail.com.

Insurance Coverage, Insurance Litigation and Business Litigation.

**BRUCE D. CELEBREZZE,** born Lakewood, Ohio, April 10, 1954; admitted to bar, 1979, Ohio; 1982, California and Illinois. *Education:* University of Notre Dame (A.B., with highest honors, 1976); University of Michigan (J.D., 1979). *Member:* Bar Association of San Francisco; American Bar Association; Association of Defense Counsel of Northern California; Federation of Insurance and Corporate Counsel; Defense Research Institute.

**NANCY M. WESLEY,** born Bridgeport, Connecticut, April 8, 1945; admitted to bar, 1989, California. *Education:* Pacific Lutheran University (B.A., 1984); University of San Francisco (J.D., 1987). Executive Editor, University of San Francisco Law Review, 1986-1987. *Member:* San Francisco Chapter of NAIW; San Francisco Insurance Claims Forum.

**KATHERINE CRANSTON POTTER,** born Hollywood, California, June 12, 1964; admitted to bar, 1990, California. *Education:* University of

*(This Listing Continued)*

California at Los Angeles (B.A., 1986); University of Southern California Law Center (J.D., 1990). *Member:* California Women Lawyers (District Governor).

**GRAZIELLA WALSH COGGAN,** born San Francisco, California, November 21, 1958; admitted to bar, 1983, California. *Education:* University of San Francisco (B.A., magna cum laude, 1980); Hastings College of the Law, University of California (J.D., 1983).

**HOWARD S. VALLENS,** born Los Angeles, California, September 13, 1960; admitted to bar, 1986, California. *Education:* Claremont McKenna College (B.A., 1982); McGeorge School of Law, University of the Pacific (J.D., 1985). *Member:* James Madison Honor Society; International Moot Court Honors Board. Outstanding International Law Moot Court Brief. Recipient, Emil Gumpert Trial Advocacy Award. *Member:* San Luis Obispo County and American Bar Associations; Property Loss Research Bureau. **LANGUAGES:** Danish.

**JEFFREY A. MEYERS,** born San Francisco, California, February 7, 1966; admitted to bar, 1994, California. *Education:* University of California, Berkeley (B.A., 1989); University of Southern California (J.D., 1994).

### OF COUNSEL

**SCOTT CONLEY,** born New York, N.Y., November 7, 1923; admitted to bar, 1949, California. *Education:* Yale University (B.A., 1944; LL.B., 1948). President, Federation of Insurance and Corporate Counsel, 1986-1987. *Member:* Bar Association of San Francisco; American Bar Association (Vice Chair, ADR Committee); Federation of Insurance and Corporate Counsel.

**STEVEN X. SCHWENK,** admitted to bar, 1989, California and U.S. District Court, Northern District of California. *Education:* Temple University (B.A., 1986); University of Pennsylvania (J.D., 1989). Judge Pro Tem San Francisco Municipal Court, 1996—.

## CHADBOURNE & PARKE LLP
### 601 SOUTH FIGUEROA STREET
### LOS ANGELES, CALIFORNIA 90017
*Telephone: 213-892-1000*
*Facsimile: 213-622-9865*

*New York, N.Y. Office:* 30 Rockefeller Plaza, 10112. Telephone: 212-408-5100. Facsimile: 212-541-5369.

*Washington, D.C. Office:* 1101 Vermont Avenue, N.W., 20005. Telephone: 202-289-3000. Facsimile: 202-289-3002.

*London, England Office:* 86 Jermyn Street, SW1 6JD. Telephone: 44-171-925-7400. Facsimile: 44-171-839-3393.

*Moscow, Russia Office:* 38 Kosmodamianskaya Naberezhnaya, 113035. Telephone: 7095-974-2424. Facsimile: 7095-974-2425. International satellite lines via U.S.: Telephone: 212-408-1190. Facsimile: 212-408-1199.

*Hong Kong Office:* Suite 3704, Peregrine Tower, Lippo Centre, 89 Queensway. Telephone: 852-2842-5400. Facsimile: 852-2521-7527.

*General Practice.*

### PARTNERS

**RICHARD J. NEY,** born Harrisonburg, Virginia, July 6, 1942; admitted to bar, 1968, District of Columbia; 1974, New York; 1987, California. *Education:* Duke University (B.A., 1964); George Washington University (J.D., with honors, 1967). Order of the Coif. *Member:* Los Angeles County, Federal and American (Member, Section on Public Contract Law) Bar Associations; State Bar of California.

**JONATHAN F. BANK,** born Omaha, Nebraska, May 4, 1943; admitted to bar, 1968, Nebraska; 1969, California; 1982, New York. *Education:* University of Oklahoma (B.B.A., 1965); Creighton University (J.D., 1968). Associate Editor, Creighton University Law Review, 1967-1968. Lecturer: "A Brief Course in Reinsurance," College of Insurance, Western Division and Insurance Educational Association, 1981—; Reinsurance Association of America Claims Seminar, 1983, 1996; Executive Enterprises, Inc. New Developments In Reinsurance, 1983, 1984, 1985, 1986, 1987, 1988, 1989, 1991, 1992; Finance and Insurance Committee of the California Assembly, 1985, 1990; Cayman Islands Captive Insurance Symposium, 1986; Coopers & Lybrand/Hawksmere International Reinsurance Congress, 1989, 1990, 1991, 1992, 1994; DRI Annual Symposium on Excess & Reinsurance, 1990; PLI Insurance, Excess & Reinsurance Coverage Disputes, 1990, 1991, 1993, 1995; Rehabilitators & Liquidators Task Force Workshop, 1991, 1992, 1993; Environmental Claims Managers Seminar, 1991; Institute for International Research, 1991; World Insurance Conference, 1992; Prentice Hall,

*(This Listing Continued)*

1992. Co-Author: Reinsurance Practices," College of Insurance, 1981. Author: "Extra-Contractual Damages Are Analyzed," *National Underwriter,* September 17, 1982; "Reinsurance Intermediaries Write Excess of Limits Clauses into Treaties," *Business Insurance,* October 25, 1982; "A Reinsurer's Exposure for Bad Faith," *Reinsurance,* November 1982; "Never Say Always When Talking About Reinsurance," *Business Insurance,* March 21, 1983; "With Minimal Impact--Hopefully," *Reinsurance,* March 1983; "The Contract v. The Contact," *Reinsurance,* August 1983; "Cut Through Endorsements," *Business Insurance,* October 10, 1983; "The Changing Legal Climate," *Reinsurance,* January 1984; "The Role of Reinsurance," *Business Insurance,* April 16, 1984; "How to Keep One's Distance," *Reinsurance,* June 1984; "It's Not So Easy to Follow-the-Fortunes," *Reinsurance,* August 1984; "The California Reinsurance Bureau," *Reinsurance,* May 1985; "One for the Price of Two," *Best's Review,* June 1985; "Right on Target," *Reinsurance,* August 1985; "The Questionable Benefit of Underlying Re," *RISE Quarterly,* Fall 1985; "By Mutual Consent," *Best's Review,* January 1986; "Umbrella Coverage," *Reinsurance,* March 1986; "Functions of Reinsurance," *Reinsurance,* March 1986; "U.S. Arbitration Update," *Reinsurance,* April 1986; "A Question of Timeliness," *Best's Review,* October 1986; "Reinsurers' Role," *Business Insurance,* November 10, 1986; "A Legal Headache," *Reinsurance,* November 1986; "Shield of Defense," *Reinsurance,* February 1987 (Part One); "Reinsurers Setting Off," *Reinsurance,* March 1987 (Part Two); "Drawing Lots Undermines Arbitration," *Business Insurance,* June 1, 1987; "How It All Started," *Best's Review,* October 1987; "Queen Bee Theory," *Business Insurance,* November 16, 1987; "A Reinsurer's Right of Set-Off In Liquidation Proceedings," *Journal of Insurance Regulation,* December 1987; "Did the Court Get Cold Feet?" *Reinsurance,* September 1988; "Reinsurance Arbitration: A U.S. Perspective," *Journal of Insurance Regulation,* March 1989; "Seeking a Fair Return," *Business Insurance,* June 12, 1989; "The Quest For An Orderly House," *Reinsurance,* July 1989; "Reassuring Rendezvous," *ReActions,* September 1989; "Regulation of Reinsurance Past, Present and Future-The Politics of Insolvency," *Journal of Insurance Regulation,* September 1989; "State of the Law - Reinsurance and Insurer Insolvency," *Law and Practice of Insurance Company Insolvency Revisited,* 1989 (ABA); "'Fraud' in the Context of Reinsurance," *Federation of Insurance & Corporate Counsel,* Winter 1990; "Liquidation Assets," *Reinsurance,* June 1990; "See You in Court!," *Reinsurance,* September 1990; "Judgment Day," *Reinsurance,* October 1990; "Claims Involving Insurer Insolvency," *California Liability Insurance Practice, Claims & Litigation,* October 1990; "Stepping Up Collections," *Best's Review,* December 1990; "Recent Reinsurance Decisions," *Insurance Litigation Reporter,* February 1991; "The Regulation of Reinsurance, " *The State of Insurance Regulation,* May 1991 (ABA); "The Reinsurance of Environmental Claims - Shades of Grey," *Tort & Insurance Law Journal,* Summer 1991; "Late Notice: In Harm's Way," *Reinsurance,* September 1991; "Too Big for Their Boots," *ReActions,* September 1992 (Part One); "Communication Under Wraps," *Best's Review,* September 1992; "An Unequal Footing," *ReActions,* October 1992 (Part Two); "N is for NAIC," *A-Z of Risk,* 1993/94; "Unigard v. North River, A New Mathematical Equation - 'In Addition Thereto'Does Not Giveth, it Taketh Away," *Declarations,* Winter 1993/94. Editorial board for publication, Legal Business in Asia. Contributing Editor, Underwriters Report. President, Conference of Insurance Counsel, Los Angeles, 1980-1981. Member, Board of Directors, Underwriters Reinsurance Corporation, 1994—. *Member:* Los Angeles County, New York State and American (Member, Tort and Insurance Practice Section) Bar Associations; State Bar of California; Defense Research Institute; International Association of Insurance Counsel; National Association of Insurance Commissioners (Member, Reinsurance Advisory Committee, Rehabilitation and Liquidation Task Force, 1982—); The Federation of Regulatory Council, Inc.; Society of Financial Examiners; International Association of Insurance Receivers.

**HARVEY I. SAFERSTEIN,** born Kansas City, Missouri, September 27, 1943; admitted to bar, 1969, District of Columbia; 1971, California. *Education:* University of California at Berkeley (B.A., 1965); Harvard University (LL.B., magna cum laude, 1968). Phi Beta Kappa. Member, Editorial Board, 1966-1967 and Executive Editor, 1967-1968, Harvard Law Review. Author: "The Ascendancy of Business Tort Claims in Antitrust Practice," 59 Antitrust Law Journal 379, 1991; "Nonreviewability: A Functional Analysis of 'Committed to Agency Discretion'," 82 Harvard Law Review 367, December, 1968. Co-Author: "Creative Funding for High Technology Ventures," LA Lawyer, Vol. 11, No. 4, June, 1988. Author: "Professor Phillip E. Areeda, Chronicler for the 'Antitrust Masses'" published in the Spring, 1996 edition of the *ABA Antitrust Magazine* . Author: "An Overview of the Federal and State Law of Price Discrimination" published in 37th Annual Antitrust Law Institute for Practising Law Institute, 1996. Adjunct Professor, Antitrust, Trade Regulation, Consumer Law and Remedies: University of Southern California Law Center, 1976; Southwestern Univer-

*(This Listing Continued)*

## CHADBOURNE & PARKE LLP, Los Angeles—Continued

sity School of Law, 1977-1983. Law Clerk to Judge Bailey Aldrich, U.S. Court of Appeals, First Circuit, 1968-1969. Advisor to Philip Elman, Federal Trade Commissioner, 1969-1970. Regional Director, Federal Trade Commission, Los Angeles Regional Office, 1978-1979. Member, Advisory Committee, 17th Far West Regional Conference on Women and the Law. Member, Central District of California Attorney Admission Fund Board, 1989—. CNN-Financial News Network, Antitrust Correspondent, 1996. *Member:* The District of Columbia Bar; Los Angeles County (Member: Board of Trustees, 1987-1989; Executive Committee, 1977-1983 and Treasurer, 1982, Antitrust Section; Executive Committee, 1980-1983; Secretary, 1986-1987, Chairman, 1987-1989, Law and Technology Section) and American (Member, Federal Trade Commission Committee; Special Coordinating Committee on RICO; Chair, Business Torts and Unfair Competition Committee, 1989-1992, Vice Chairman, Civil Practice and Procedure Committee, 1988-1990, Antitrust Law Section; Section of Litigation) Bar Associations; State Bar of California (Member, Board of Governors, 1989-1992; President, 1992-1993); Association of Business Trial Lawyers (Member, Board of Governors, 1984-1991; Treasurer and Program Chair, 1987-1988; Secretary, 1988-1989; Vice President, 1989-1990; President, 1990-1991); Legal Aid Foundation of Los Angeles (Member, Board of Directors, 1984-1989; President, 1987-1989); Ninth Circuit Judicial Conference (Delegate, 1985-1987; Executive Committee, 1987-1991; Activities Chair, 1989; Program Chair, 1990; Chair, 1991); California Judicial Council (Member, 1993—). Fellow, American Bar Foundation.

**PETER R. CHAFFETZ,** born Chicago, Illinois, May 4, 1952; admitted to bar, 1979, New York and U.S. District Court, Eastern and Southern Districts of New York; 1983, U.S. Supreme Court; 1984, California and U.S. District Court, Central District of California. *Education:* Harvard University (A.B., 1974); University of Chicago (J.D., 1978). *Member:* Association of Business Trial Lawyers.

**JAY R. HENNEBERRY,** born Des Moines, Iowa, January 31, 1955; admitted to bar, 1983, New York; 1988, California. *Education:* Tufts University (B.A., cum laude, 1978); New York University (J.D., 1982). Staff Editor, Journal of International Law and Politics, 1981-1982. *Member:* State Bar of California; American Bar Association (Member, Sections on Litigation and Public Contract Law).

**LINDA DAKIN-GRIMM,** born Fort Wayne, Indiana, June 30, 1960; admitted to bar, 1985, California. *Education:* Yale University (B.A., cum laude, 1982); Harvard Law School (J.D., 1985). Author: Chapter on corporate criminal liability in the treatise Compliance Programs and the Corporate Sentencing Guidelines, published by Clark, Boardman Callaghan (New York); "Homelessness: The Role of The Legal Profession, ABA Family Law Quarterly, Spring, 1987, Edition. co-authored articles: "Mealey's Litigation Reports: Insurance," "Environmental Claims Journal," "California Litigation," "California Management Review," "Corporate Conduct Quarterly" "Reinsurance". Spoken at Forbes Magazine Conference on Latin America Business and Mealey's Insurance Conference.

**KENNETH J. LANGAN,** born New York, N.Y., September 14, 1955; admitted to bar, 1981, New York; 1993, California. *Education:* University of Maryland; Georgetown University (B.S.F.S., with honors, 1977) Phi Beta Kappa; Columbia University (J.D., 1980). Harlan Fiske Stone Scholar. *LANGUAGES:* Spanish.

### RESIDENT COUNSEL

**WILLIAM J. KELLEY, III,** born Sunbury, Pennsylvania, November 20, 1957; admitted to bar, 1985, New York and California. *Education:* University of California at Riverside (B.A., with honors, 1980); Stanford University (J.D., 1984). Member, Moot Court Board. Hilmer Oehlman, Jr. Award. Co-Author: "Spreading the Word: Use of Computer Spreadsheets in the Practice of Law," 4 California Lawyer 57, June 1984. State Bar of California Wiley W. Manuel Award for Pro Bono Legal Services. *Member:* New York State and American Bar Associations; State Bar of California.

(For Biographical Data of other Personnel, see Professional Biographies at New York, N.Y., Washington, D.C., London, England, Moscow, Russia and Hong Kong)

## CHALEFF & ENGLISH
### LOS ANGELES, CALIFORNIA
(See Santa Monica)
*Criminal and Juvenile Law Practice.*

## CHAN LAW GROUP
### A PROFESSIONAL LAW CORPORATION
911 WILSHIRE BOULEVARD, SUITE 2288
P.O. BOX 79159
### LOS ANGELES, CALIFORNIA 90017-3451
Telephone: 213-624-6560
Fax: 213-622-1154
Email: chanlaw@counsel.com
URL: http://CHANLAW.COM

*Patent, Trademark, Copyright, Unfair Competition, Trade Secret, Licensing, Computer, Commercial, Acquisition and Merger, Corporation, International, China Trade and Customs, Export Control, Antitrust, Civil Litigation in all Courts.*

**THOMAS T. CHAN,** born Hong Kong, June 5, 1950; admitted to bar, 1979, Wisconsin; 1983, Minnesota; 1987, California. *Education:* University of Wisconsin-Whitewater (B.A., magna cum laude, 1973); University of Wisconsin-Madison (J.D., 1979). Student Judicial Intern, Wisconsin Supreme Court, 1978. Instructor, CPCU Legal Environment of Insurance, 1980. U.S. Trade Advisor, Industry Sector Advisory Committee, U.S. Commerce and U.S. Trade Representative, 1988-1991. Member, Advisory Board, U.S. SBA-Export Small Business Development Center, 1991-1996. Author, "Computer Pirates Unmasked," The Recorder, April 4, 1988. *Member:* American Bar Association; Export Managers Association of California (Member, Board of Directors, 1990-1992); Computer Law Association. *LANGUAGES:* Chinese. **REPORTED CASES:** Z-Nix v. Microsoft. **PRACTICE AREAS:** Patent, Trademark and Copyrights; Computer Law; International Law.

**RONALD M. ST. MARIE,** born Los Angeles, California, July 5, 1956; admitted to bar, 1981, California; 1982, U.S. District Court, Central and Southern Districts of California; 1983, U.S. District Court, Northern and Eastern Districts of California; 1984, U.S. Court of Appeals, Ninth Circuit; 1992, U.S. Tax Court. *Education:* California State University at Northridge (B.A., magna cum laude, 1978); University of Southern California (J.D., 1981). Member, *Southern California Law Review,* 1979-1981. **REPORTED CASES:** Clamp Mfg. Co., Inc. v. Enco Mfg. Co., 5 U.S.P.Q. 2d 1643 (C.D. Cal. 1987) aff'd 870 F.2d 512 (9th Cir. 1989); Indiana Plumbing Supply v, Standard of Lynn, Inc., 880 F.Supp. 743 (C.D. Cal. 1995); San Francisco Mercantile Co., Inc. v. Beebas Creations, Inc., 704 F.Supp. 1005 (C.D. Cal.1988); Dorman v. DWLC Corp., 35 Cal.App.4th 1808 (2d Dist. 1995). **PRACTICE AREAS:** Business Litigation emphasizing Intellectual Property; Unfair Competition; Trade Secrets.

**RUBY P. SHIMOMURA,** born March 28, 1964; admitted to bar, 1991, California. *Education:* University of Hawaii (B.A., 1987); Loyola Law School (J.D., 1990). Phi Beta Kappa; Phi Eta Sigma; Phi Alpha Delta. *Member:* Los Angeles County and American Bar Associations; State Bar of California; Philippino Bar Association; Association of Southern California Defense Counsel. *LANGUAGES:* Ilocano (Filipino dialect). **PRACTICE AREAS:** General Litigation.

### LEGAL SUPPORT PERSONNEL

**BRYAN J. ARMSTRONG,** born Los Angeles, California, August 11, 1962. *Education:* U.S. Military Academy (B.S., 1984). (Litigation Paralegal).

**TIANHUA GU,** born Shanghai, China, October 1, 1942. *Education:* Shanghai Agriculture University (B.A., 1964). (Patent Paralegal). *LANGUAGES:* Chinese, Japanese.

**CHARLOTTE YU-CHI CHEN,** born Taipei, Taiwan Republic of China, May 24, 1970. *Education:* University of California at Irvine (B.A., 1992). (Paralegal). *LANGUAGES:* Mandarin, Taiwanese. **Email:** PCHENXC0@COUNSEL.COM

# CHAPIN, FLEMING & WINET
SUITE 401, 12121 WILSHIRE BOULEVARD
**LOS ANGELES, CALIFORNIA 90025**
Telephone: 310-826-0133
Fax: 310-207-4236

*San Diego, California Office:* Library, 501 West Broadway, 15th Floor. Telephone: 619-232-4261. Telefax: 619-323-4840.

*Vista, California Office:* 410 South Melrose Drive, Suite 101. Telephone: 619-758-4261. Telefax: 619-758-6420.

*Palm Springs, California Office:* 225 North El Cielo Road, Suite 470. Telephone: 619-416-1400. Telefax: 619-416-1405.

*Insurance Bad Faith and Coverage Practice in Liability, Disability, Life, Property, Health, Accident, Marine, Malpractice, Surety, Aviation, Self-Insurance Law, General Business, Corporate and Real Estate Litigation.*

**CRAIG H. BELL,** born Long Beach, California, November 2, 1953; admitted to bar, 1978, California and U.S. District Court, Central District of California; 1982, U.S. District Court, Eastern and Southern Districts of California and U.S. Court of Appeals, Ninth Circuit. *Education:* University of California at Los Angeles (B.A., magna cum laude, 1975); Loyola University of Los Angeles (J.D., cum laude, 1978). Phi Beta Kappa. *Member:* State Bar of California. **REPORTED CASES:** Warner v. Fire Ins. Exch. (1991) 230 Cal. App.3d 1029; Beaty v. Truck Ins. Exch. (1992) 6 Cal. App 4th 1455. **PRACTICE AREAS:** Civil Appeals; Insurance Coverage; Bad Faith Litigation.

**DAVID H. BUSHNELL,** born Minneapolis, Minnesota, February 22, 1954; admitted to bar, 1991, California; 1992, U.S. District Court, Central District of California. *Education:* Yale University (B.A., cum laude, 1976); University of California at Los Angeles (M.A.,1978; J.D., 1991). Recipient, American Jurisprudence Award-Torts. *Member:* State Bar of California.

**RICHARD D. CARTER,** born San Diego, California, March 14, 1960; admitted to bar, 1986, California; 1987, U.S. District Court, Central and Southern Districts of California. *Education:* San Diego State University (B.A., 1983); McGeorge School of the Law, University of the Pacific (J.D., 1986). *Member:* State Bar of California; American Bar Association; Association of Southern California Defense Counsel.

**GEORGE CHUANG,** born Taipei, Taiwan, March 4, 1960; admitted to bar, 1985, California; 1986, U.S. District Court, Central District of California. *Education:* University of California at Los Angeles (B.A., 1982); University of San Diego (J.D., 1985). Recipient: U.S.D. Academic Achievement Scholarship, 1983-1984. *Member:* State Bar of California.

**ROBERT EHRENREICH,** born Phoenix, Arizona, December 6, 1960; admitted to bar, 1986, California; 1987, Arizona. *Education:* University of Arizona (B.S., 1982); University of the Pacific, McGeorge School of Law (J.D., 1986). *Member:* Los Angeles County and American Bar Associations; State Bar of California; State Bar of Arizona; Association of Southern California Defense Counsel. (Resident).

**HOWARD L. HOFFENBERG,** admitted to bar, 1985, Illinois; 1987, California, U.S. Court of Appeals for the Seventh, Ninth and Federal Circuits and U.S. District Court for the Central, Northern, Eastern and Southern Districts of California and the Northern District of Illinois; 1989, New York; registered to practice before U.S. Patent and Trademark Office. *Education:* University of Illinois (B.S., Biochemistry and Chemistry, 1981); DePaul University (J.D., 1985). Member, DePaul University Law Review. Author: "Practical Pointers in Trying Intellectual Property Cases, *New Matter,* 1991. Member: Judicial Evaluation Committee and Appellate Law Committee of the Los Angeles County Bar Association; Legal Division of the Jewish Federation Counsel of Los Angeles. *Member:* Los Angeles County Bar Association (Member, Appellate Law Committee); American Chemical Society.

**DANA MARIE LAWSON,** born Los Angeles, California, July 19, 1970; admitted to bar, 1996, California. *Education:* University of California, Los Angeles (B.A., 1993); Loyola Law School (J.D., 1996). *Member:* Langston Bar Association; Women Lawyers of Los Angeles. **PRACTICE AREAS:** Insurance Defense.

**JEFFREY J. LEIST,** born St. Joseph, Missouri, April 5, 1956; admitted to bar, 1981, California, U.S. District Court, Central District of California and U.S. Court of Appeals, Ninth Circuit. *Education:* University of California at Los Angeles (B.A., magna cum laude, 1978); University of Southern California (J.D., 1981). Phi Beta Kappa; Phi Alpha Delta. *Member:* Pasadena, Los Angeles County and American (Member, Sections on: Tort and Insurance Practice; Litigation; Corporate, Banking and Business Law) Bar Associations; The State Bar of California; The Association of Trial Lawyers of America.

**TONYA L. MORGAN,** born Alameda, California, March 26, 1959; admitted to bar, 1990, California. *Education:* University of California, Los Angeles (B.A., magna cum laude, with honors, 1987); Loyola Law School (J.D., 1990). *Member:* Los Angeles County Bar Association; State Bar of California; Women Lawyers Association of Los Angeles.

**DAVID A. MYERS,** born Redondo Beach, California, September 21, 1963; admitted to bar, 1989, California and U.S. District Court, Central District of California; 1990, Colorado. *Education:* California State University at Long Beach (B.A., 1985); Loyola Law School (J.D., 1988). Recipient, American Jurisprudence Award, Land Use Controls. *Member:* State Bar of California.

**BRENDA J. PANNELL,** born Limestone, Maine, July 19, 1965; admitted to bar, 1995, California. *Education:* University of California, Los Angeles (B.A., 1988); University of Maryland (J.D., 1992). Phi Delta Phi. *Member:* Los Angeles County and American Bar Associations; State Bar of California; California Young Lawyers Association (Member, Board of Directors, 1996-1999); Black Women Lawyers. **PRACTICE AREAS:** Bad Faith Litigation.

**THOMAS V. PEREA,** born Martinez, California, September 25, 1963; admitted to bar, 1989, California. *Education:* California State University at Hayward (B.A., 1985); Hastings College of the Law, University of California (J.D., 1988). *Member:* Los Angeles County Bar Association; State Bar of California. [U.S.M.C, 1982-1989; 1st Lt.]. **LANGUAGES:** Spanish.

**SPENCER C. SKEEN,** born Riverside, California, 1968; admitted to bar, 1996, California and U.S. District Court, Southern District of California. *Education:* University of California at Davis (B.A., in English, 1992); McGeorge School of Law, University of Pacific (J.D., 1995).

**HOWARD SMITH,** born Far Rockaway, New York, May 5, 1968; admitted to bar, 1993, California, U.S. District Court, Central District of California and U.S. Court of Appeals, Ninth Circuit. *Education:* State University of New York at Buffalo (B.S., 1990); Whittier College (J.D., 1993). **PRACTICE AREAS:** Insurance Litigation; Medical Malpractice; Civil Appeals.

**GRACE I. WANG,** born Lafayette, Indiana, March 5, 1968; admitted to bar, 1993, California and U.S. District Court, Central District of California. *Education:* Exeter University; University of California at Berkeley (B.A., 1990); University of California at Davis (J.D., 1993). Chair, Jessup Moot Court. Recipient, American Jurisprudence Award for Contracts. Author, "The Arctic National Wildlife Refuge: Wildlife Preserve or Oil Reserve?" Environs, Environmental Law and Policy Journal, Volume 16, No. 3, May 1993. *Member:* State Bar of California; Christian Legal Society. **LANGUAGES:** Taiwanese.

*OF COUNSEL*

**ARTHUR D. RUTLEDGE,** born Seattle, Washington, September 23, 1941; admitted to bar, 1969, California; 1972, U.S. Supreme Court. *Education:* University of California at Los Angeles (B.S., Bus. Adm., 1963); California Western University (J.D., 1968). Phi Alpha Delta. Recipient, American Jurisprudence Award in Commercial Trials. Advanced, Ham Radio License, 1974. Senior Trial Lawyer, Los Angeles City Attorney, Tort Liability Section, 1969-1980. Commendation Los Angeles Police Protective League, 1975; Commendation Los Angeles City Fire Department, 1976. *Member:* State Bar of California (Former Member, Committee on Jury Instructions, 1978-1979); American Board of Trial Advocates. **PRACTICE AREAS:** Insurance Defense Law; General Tort Litigation.

**JEFFREY C. STODEL,** born Hollywood, California, October 14, 1947; admitted to bar, 1974, California. *Education:* University of Southern California (B.A., 1969); Loyola University School of Law (J.D., 1974). Associate Editor, Loyola University of Los Angeles Law Review, 1973-1974. *Member:* Los Angeles County Bar Association; State Bar of California.

**IRWIN WALDMAN, (A P.C.),** born Brooklyn, New York, April 13, 1935; admitted to bar, 1959, New York; 1971, California. *Education:* New York University (A.B., 1955); Columbia University (J.D., 1958). Co-author: "The Commercial Laws of the U.S.," *The Digest of Commercial Laws of the World,* Oceana Publications, Inc., 1967. Lecturer: Practicing Law Institute, 1986 and 1987; California Continuing Education of the Bar on Defense of Insurance Companies in Bad Faith Cases, 1985—. *Member:* The State Bar of California; New York State and American (Member, Sec-

*(This Listing Continued)*

### CHAPIN, FLEMING & WINET, Los Angeles—Continued

tions on: Litigation; Torts and Insurance Practice) Bar Associations; Association of Southern California Defense Counsel; Association of Business Trial Lawyers; Defense Research Institute.

A list of Representative Clients available upon request.

---

## CHAPMAN & GLUCKSMAN
### A PROFESSIONAL CORPORATION
### 11900 WEST OLYMPIC BOULEVARD, SUITE 800
### LOS ANGELES, CALIFORNIA 90064-0704
Telephone: 310-207-7722
Facsimile: 310-207-6550

*General Civil Practice in all State and Federal Trial and Appellate Courts. Commercial and Business Litigation and General Insurance Practice, including Products Liability, Professional Liability, Coverage, Construction Litigation, Complex and Multi-District Litigation, Commercial, Wrongful Termination, Corporation, Director and Officer Liability, Association Liability, Toxic and Hazardous Substance, Real Estate and Estate Planning, Excess and Surplus Insurance.*

**RICHARD H. GLUCKSMAN,** born Santa Monica, California, January 29, 1952; admitted to bar, 1977, California and U.S. District Court, Central District of California. *Education:* University of California at Santa Barbara; University of California at Los Angeles (B.S., History, cum laude, 1974); Loyola Marymount University School of Law (J.D., 1977). Co-Author: "A Profile of Liability and Damages For Accountants," 1983; "Guidelines for Risk Management in Today's Litigious Environment," National Public Accountant, June, 1986; "Recent Developments in Corporate Director and Officer Liability and Liability Insurance," Barclays California Law Monthly, October, 1988; "Account Liability For Embezzlement and Ways To Prevent It," The National Public Accountant," August 1989; "A Profile of Wrongful Termination," The Interpreter, December, 1988; "Accountant Beware: Your Client's Employee is Stealing," National Public Accountant, August, 1989; "For Developers, Contractors...Suggestions on Dealing with Claims," Southern California Builder, June, 1990; "Managing Construction Defect Cases," The Construction Lawyer, July 1996. . Law Clerk for Judge Laurence J. Rittenband, Los Angeles Superior Court, 1975-1976. Speaker: Seminar, "Alternative Dispute Resolution - The Answer For the Construction Industry," Judicial Arbitration & Mediation Services, Inc., May, 1991; Seminar, "1991 Professional Liability & Loss Prevention," California State Society of Certified Public Accountants and CAMICO, September, 1991; Area discussion groups to the Los Angeles, Chapter of State Society of Certified Public Accountants, 1990's. Co-Legal Counsel, Academy of Science Fiction, Fantasy and Horror Films, 1983—. *Member:* Santa Monica (Member, Litigation Section), Los Angeles County (Member, Sections on: Trial Lawyers; Business and Corporations Law) and American (Member, Tort Section) Bar Associations; State Bar of California; Business Trial Lawyers; Defense Research Institute; Southern California Defense Counsel. **PRACTICE AREAS:** Professional Malpractice; Construction Law; Business Litigation; Taxes and Hazardous Substance Litigation; Director and Officer Liability Litigation.

**ARTHUR J. CHAPMAN,** born Newark, New Jersey, September 12, 1951; admitted to bar, 1977, California and U.S. District Court, Central District of California. *Education:* Villanova University; University of California at Los Angeles (B.A., Political Science, magna cum laude, 1973); Loyola Marymount University School of Law (J.D., 1977). Co-Author: "Insurer's Duty to Defend," 13, Pacific Law Journal, 889-904, 1982. Fireman's Fund Insurance Company Claims Representative, 1973-1974. *Member:* Los Angeles County, Orange County and American Bar Associations; State Bar of California; Business Trial Lawyers; Southern California Defense Counsel; Defense Research Institute; Community Association Institute. **PRACTICE AREAS:** Business and Commercial Litigation; Products Liability; Negligence; Coverage; Professional Malpractice.

**RANDALL J. DEAN,** born Los Angeles, California, June 17, 1957; admitted to bar, 1983, California and U.S. District Court, Central District of California. *Education:* University of California at Los Angeles (B.A., Pol. Sci., 1979); Loyola Marymount University School of Law (J.D., 1983). Author: "In Defense of Tight Building Syndrome," For The Defense, August, 1991; "In Door Air Quality and the Law," HVAC Product News, April, 1992. Co-author: "Practical Guide for Accountants Concerning Claims, Litigation and Prevention," 1985; "Guidelines for Risk Management in Today's Litigious Environment," National Public Accountant, June, 1986; "For Developers, Contractors... Suggestions on Dealing with Claims," Southern California Builder, July, 1990. *Member:* American Bar Association. **PRACTICE AREAS:** Products Liability; Professional Liability Law; Commercial Law; Business Litigation; Environmental Law; Coverage.

**WENDY M. HOUSMAN,** born Poughkeepsie, New York, July 9, 1958; admitted to bar, 1985, California and U.S. District Court, Northern District of California. *Education:* University of California at Santa Barbara (B.A., Pol. Sci., 1980); Pepperdine University School of Law, Malibu (J.D., 1984). Co-Author: "A Profile of Wrongful Termination," The Interpreter, December, 1988. *Member:* Los Angeles County and American Bar Associations; State Bar of California; The Association of Trial Lawyers of America. **PRACTICE AREAS:** Products Liability Law; Coverage; Commercial and Business Litigation; Labor Law; Construction Litigation; General Negligence; Wrongful Termination.

**JAMES C. EARLE,** born Mount Holly, New Jersey, October 27, 1952; admitted to bar, 1986, California and U.S. District Court, Northern District of California; 1987, U.S. District Court, Central District of California. *Education:* Glassboro State College (B.A., 1978); San Jose State University (M.A., 1981); Golden Gate University (J.D., 1985). Recipient, American Jurisprudence Award. Certified Mediation Training, Pepperdine University. California Construction Contractor License, (B-1) (C-36), 1982. Author: "Recovering Expert Fees, A Closer Look." Construction Surveyor and Soil Analyst, U.S. Army Corps of Engineers, 1970-1973. *Member:* Los Angeles County Bar Association; State Bar of California. **PRACTICE AREAS:** Construction Litigation; Products Liability; Coverage; Business Litigation; Trial; Arbitration; Mediation.

**CRAIG A. ROEB,** born Los Angeles, California, June 30, 1961; admitted to bar, 1987, California; 1988, U.S. District Court, Central District of California. *Education:* University of California at Los Angeles (B.A., Political Science, 1984); Loyola Marymount University School of Law (J.D., 1987). Author: "Recent Developments in Corporate Director and Officer Liability and Liability Insurance," Barclays California Law Monthly, October, 1988; "Accountant Liability For Embezzlement and Ways To Prevent It," The National Public Accountant, August 1989; "Defending Professionals and Avoiding Liability in Business Management Engagements," The Verdict, July 1996. Extern Law Clerk to U.S. District Judge David V. Kenyon, 1985. *Member:* Los Angeles County and American Bar Associations; State Bar of California. **PRACTICE AREAS:** Professional Liability Law; Business and Commercial Litigation; Products Liability Law.

---

**THOMAS L. HALLIWELL,** born Detroit, Michigan, March 5, 1954; admitted to bar, 1986, California; 1987, U.S. District Court, Central and Southern Districts of California and U.S. Court of Appeals, Ninth Circuit. *Education:* University of Redlands (B.S., with distinction, honors, 1981); Loyola Law School of Los Angeles (J.D., 1986). Author: "Defamation and Invasion of Privacy: Piggie Porn in the Fifth Circuit," Loyola Entertainment Law Journal 167, 1986. *Member:* Los Angeles County Bar Association; Association of Southern California Defense Counsel. **PRACTICE AREAS:** Construction Litigation; Products Liability; Professional Liability.

**DOMINIC J. FOTE,** born Miami, Florida, August 22, 1961; admitted to bar, 1987, California. *Education:* Cornell University (B.A., in Government and History, with highest distinction, 1983); Pepperdine University School of Law (J.D., 1986). Associate Editor, Pepperdine Law Review, 1985-1986. Author: "Child Witnesses in Sexual Abuse Proceedings: Their Capabilities, Special Problems, and Proposals for Reform," Pepperdine Law Review, Vol. 13, No. 1, 1985. *Member:* Beverly Hills and Los Angeles County Bar Associations; State Bar of California; The Association of Trial Lawyers of America; Italian-American Lawyers Association. **PRACTICE AREAS:** Insurance Coverage; General Negligence; Products Liability; Construction Litigation; Professional Liability; Commercial Law; Business Litigation; Environmental Law; Toxic and Hazardous Substance Litigation.

**CHRISTOPHER R. KENT,** born Santa Monica, California, April 3, 1954; admitted to bar, 1988, California. *Education:* California State University at Northridge (B.A., summa cum laude, 1978); Humboldt State University (M.S., 1981); Loyola Marymount University School of Law (J.D., 1988). *Member:* Los Angeles County Bar Association; State Bar of California. **PRACTICE AREAS:** General Negligence; Products Liability Law; Environmental Law; Toxic and Hazardous Substance Litigation.

**ANDREW B. COHN,** born Forest Hills, New York, July 11, 1964; admitted to bar, 1990, California and U.S. District Court, Central District of California. *Education:* Université de Grenoble, Grenoble, France, 1984; Boston University (B.A., cum laude, International Relations, 1986); Loyola Marymount University School of Law (J.D., 1990); University of Santa

*(This Listing Continued)*

Monica (M.A., Applied Psychology, 1995). Note and Comment Editor, Loyola of Los Angeles International and Comparative Law Journal, 1989-1990. Los Angeles County District Attorney Clinic, 1990. *Member:* Los Angeles County; State Bar of California. **LANGUAGES:** French. **PRACTICE AREAS:** General Negligence; Construction Litigation; Coverage.

**JEFFREY A. COHEN,** born Los Angeles, California, September 15, 1965; admitted to bar, 1990, California and U.S. District Court, Central District of California. *Education:* Arizona State University (B.S. Business, 1987); Pepperdine University School of Law (J.D., 1990). Member, International Moot Court, Oxford, England. *Member:* Los Angeles County Bar Association (Member, Litigation Section); State Bar of California. **PRACTICE AREAS:** General Negligence; Professional Liability; Commercial and Business Litigation; Construction Litigation; Wood Destroying Organism Litigation.

**GLENN T. BARGER,** born Sacramento, California, April 18, 1966; admitted to bar, 1991, California. *Education:* University of California at Davis (B.A., Economics, 1988); Pepperdine University School of Law (J.D., 1991). Phi Delta Phi. Co-Author: "Tight Building Syndrome—In Defense of HVAC Contractors," HVAC Product News, April 1992; "In Defense of Tight Building Syndrome," For the Defense, August 1991; "Managing Construction Defect Cases," The Construction Lawyer, July 1996. *Member:* Los Angeles County and Orange County Bar Associations; State Bar of California. **PRACTICE AREAS:** General Negligence; Construction Litigation; Product Liability; Environmental Law; Professional Liability.

**CHRISTINE L. VANDERBILT,** born New York, N.Y., January 9, 1953; admitted to bar, 1977, California; 1978, U.S. District Court, Central District of California; 1979, U.S. District Court, Southern District of California. *Education:* Grinnell College (B.A., with honors, 1974); University of Southern California Law Center (J.D., 1977). *Member:* Los Angeles County Bar Association; State Bar of California; Women Lawyers Association of Los Angeles. **PRACTICE AREAS:** Professional Liability; Insurance Coverage Litigation; Business and Commercial Litigation.

**GREGORY SABO,** born Fullerton, California, August 3, 1967; admitted to bar, 1993, California. *Education:* University of California (B.A., English and American Literature, 1989); Loyola Marymount University (J.D., 1993). *Member:* State Bar of California. **PRACTICE AREAS:** Professional Liability; General Negligence; Construction Litigation.

**MICHAEL R. O'NEILL,** born Summit, New Jersey, December 28, 1965; (admission pending).; admitted to bar, 1994, California, U.S. District Court, Central District of California and U.S. Court of Appeals, Ninth Circuit. *Education:* Rutgers University (B.S. with honors, 1990); Pepperdine University (J.D. magna cum laude, 1994). Phi Delta Phi; Beta Gamma Sigma; Alpha Sigma Lambda; Tau Alpha Pi. Articles Editor, Pepperdine Law Review. Author: "Reducing Accounting Malpractice Claims Through Effective Client Screening Techniques," The National Public Accountant, August, 1996; Comment "Government's Denigration of Religion: Is God the Victim of Discrimination in Our Public Schools?" 21 Pepp. L. Rev. 477, 1993; "California Supreme Court Survey," Smith v. Regents of the University of California: Mandatory Student Fees Can Not Be Used to Support Political or Ideological Activities," 21 Pepp. L. Rev. 287, 1993; Co-Author, "Defending Professionals and Avoiding Liability in Business Management Engagements," The Verdict, July, 1996. **PRACTICE AREAS:** Accounting Malpractice; Legal Malpractice; Insurance Coverage; General Civil.

**RITA MONGOVEN MILLER,** born Chicago, Illinois, October 30, 1963; admitted to bar, 1988, California; 1989, U.S. District Court, Central District of California; 1990, U.S. District Court, Eastern District of California. *Education:* Ealing College, London, England; University of Wisconsin-La Crosse (B.S., 1985); Santa Clara University School of Law (J.D., 1988). Phi Alpha Delta. Technical Editor, Santa Clara University Law Review, 1987-1988. Judicial Externship to Judge Spencer Williams, Federal District Court, 1987. Co-Author: "Something More to Discuss With Your Clients," American Industrial Real Estate Association Newsletter, Spring, 1994. *Member:* Los Angeles County and American (Member, Sections on: Litigation; Business Law) Bar Associations; The State Bar of California; Association of Business Trial Lawyers; National Association of Female Executives; California Elected Womens Association for Education and Research. **PRACTICE AREAS:** General Negligence; Products Liability; Insurance Bad Faith.

**TODD M. MOBLEY,** born Norfolk, Nebraska, May 24, 1966; admitted to bar, 1995, California. *Education:* California State University at Sacramento (B.S., cum laude, 1989); Southwestern University School of Law (J.D., 1994). Phi Beta Kappa; Golden Key National Honor Society. Judicial Externship to the Hon. Judge Barry Russell, Federal Bankruptcy Court and to Bankruptcy Appellate Panel, Ninth Circuit, 1994. **PRACTICE**

*(This Listing Continued)*

**AREAS:** Product Liability; Professional Liability; Environmental Law; Construction Litigation; General Negligence.

**D. SCOTT DODD,** born Los Angeles, California, May 9, 1967; admitted to bar, 1994, California and U.S. District Court, Central District of California. *Education:* University of California at San Diego (B.A., Ec., 1989); University of Southern California (J.D., 1993). Phi Alpha Delta. **PRACTICE AREAS:** Construction Defect; Personal Injury; Premises Liability; Insurance Coverage.

**JON A. TURIGLIATTO,** born Lynwood, California, October 14, 1966; admitted to bar, 1993, California and U.S. District Court, Northern District of California; U.S. Court of Appeals, Ninth Circuit; 1996, U.S. District Court, Central District of California. *Education:* University of California at Irvine (B.A., 1989); Southern Methodist University (J.D., 1993). Delta Theta Phi. Vincent S. Dalsimer Moot Court Finalist. Extern to the Honorable A. Andrew Hauk, Senior Judge and Chief Judge Emeritus, U.S. District Court, Central District of California, 1992. *Member:* Beverly Hills, Los Angeles County and American Bar Associations; State Bar of California; The Association of Trial Lawyers of America; Womens Lawyers Association. **PRACTICE AREAS:** General Negligence; Professional Liability; Construction Litigation; Business Litigation; Commercial Litigation; Products Liability.

**KAREN S. DANTO,** born Ann Arbor, Michigan, December 22, 1967; admitted to bar, 1994, California. *Education:* University of California at Davis (B.A., 1991); Pepperdine University (J.D., 1994). Phi Alpha Delta. Vincent S. Dalsimer Moot Court Finalist. *Member:* Beverly Hills and Los Angeles County Bar Associations; State Bar of California; Womens Lawyers Association; The Association of Trial Lawyers of America. **PRACTICE AREAS:** Insurance Defense; General Negligence; Auto Liability; Professional Liability; Construct Defect; Business; Commercial Litigation.

*OF COUNSEL*

**THOMAS J. PABST,** born Los Angeles, California, June 17, 1951; admitted to bar, 1978, California and U.S. District Court, Central District of California; 1979, U.S. Tax Court. *Education:* University of California, Los Angeles (A.B., History, cum laude, 1974); Loyola University School of Law, Los Angeles (J.D., 1978). *Member:* Los Angeles County Bar Association; State Bar of California. **PRACTICE AREAS:** Estate Planning Law; Estate Administration Law; Business; Corporate; Real Estate Law.

REPRESENTATIVE CLIENTS: Allianz Insurance Co.; Allianz Versicherungs, A.G.; California Accountants Mutual Insurance Co.; Chubb Insurance Co.; Clarklift of Los Angeles, Inc.; Explorer Ins. Co.; Frontier Ins. Co.; Great American Insurance Co.; Imperial Casualty & Indemnity Co.; Imperial Premium Financing, Inc.; INA/CIGNA; John Deere Ins. Co.; Insurance Company of the West; Motors Ins. Co.; Neoplan USA Corp.; Pioneer Claims Services, Inc.; Rhulen Ins. Agency; Robert Moreno Ins. Services; Royal Ins. Co.; Sequoia Ins. Co.; Transamerica Premier Ins. Co.; TOPA Insurance Co.; Underwriters Reinsurance Co.; Unigard Insurance Co.; United Pacific Reliance; Maryland Cos.; Liberty Mutual Ins. Co.
REFERENCE: First Professional Bank (Santa Monica, CA).

## CHARLSTON, REVICH & WILLIAMS LLP

Established in 1987

*1840 CENTURY PARK EAST*
*THIRD FLOOR*
**LOS ANGELES, CALIFORNIA 90067-2104**
Telephone: 310-551-7000
Telecopier: 310-203-9321

*General Civil Trial and Appellate Practice before all State and Federal Courts. Insurance Coverage Litigation, Environmental, Toxic Torts and Hazardous Waste Law. Professional Liability, Officer and Director Liability, and Products Liability Coverage and Defense Litigation, Securities and Real Estate Litigation. Tax, Estate Planning and Trusts, and Business Law. Receivership Representation and Workouts and Wrongful Discharge Defense. Employment Law, Criminal Defense, White-Collar Fraud and Intellectual Property.*

*FIRM PROFILE: Charlston, Revich & Williams LLP is a business litigation law firm. The firm has particular expertise in the representation of lawyers, accountants and other professionals, and in the representation of insurance companies in environmental, toxic tort and construction defect actions. The firm represents corporate clients in a variety of complex civil litigation actions. We serve as trial lawyers for business and insurance clients.*

*(This Listing Continued)*

## CHARLSTON, REVICH & WILLIAMS LLP, Los Angeles—Continued

### PARTNERS OF THE FIRM

**JEFFREY A. CHARLSTON,** born Los Angeles, California, January 20, 1950; admitted to bar, 1975, California and U.S. District Court, Central District of California; 1981, U.S. District Court, Northern, Eastern and Southern Districts of California and U.S. Court of Appeals, Ninth Circuit; 1990, U.S. District Court, District of Arizona. *Education:* Pomona College (B.A., magna cum laude, 1971); University of California at Los Angeles (J.D., 1975). Phi Beta Kappa. Member, Moot Court Executive Board, 1974-1975.

**IRA REVICH,** born Detroit, Michigan, February 21, 1949; admitted to bar, 1974, Michigan; 1975, New York and U.S. Tax Court; 1977, California. *Education:* University of Michigan (B.S., 1970); Wayne State University (J.D., 1973); New York University (LL.M., 1974).

**RICHARD D. WILLIAMS,** born Los Angeles, California, August 30, 1946; admitted to bar, 1973, California; 1974, U.S. District Court, Central District of California and U.S. Court of Appeals, Ninth Circuit; 1980, U.S. District Court, Northern District of California. *Education:* Washington State University (B.A., Business Administration, with distinction, 1969); University of California at Los Angeles (J.D., 1973). Beta Gamma Sigma. Board of Editors and Comment Editor, UCLA Law Review, 1972-1973.

**HOWARD N. WOLLITZ,** born Minneapolis, Minnesota, June 14, 1948; admitted to bar, 1973, California; U.S. Supreme Court. *Education:* San Diego State University (B.A., 1970); University of California at Los Angeles (J.D., 1973). Comment Editor, UCLA Law Review, 1972-1973.

**TIMOTHY J. HARRIS,** born Yakima, Washington, February 7, 1953; admitted to bar, 1978, California, U.S. District Court, Central, Northern, Southern and Eastern Districts of California and U.S. District Court, District of Arizona; 1979, U.S. Court of Appeals, Fourth, Sixth and Ninth Circuits. *Education:* University of Washington (B.A., with distinction, 1975); University of California at Los Angeles (J.D., 1978). Articles Editor, UCLA Law Review, 1977-1978.

**EUGENE C. MOSCOVITCH,** born New York, N.Y., December 8, 1946; admitted to bar, 1973, California. *Education:* Whittier College (B.S., with honors, 1968) Omicron Delta Kappa, Pi Sigma Alpha; University of California at Los Angeles (J.D., 1973). Member, Board of Editors, UCLA Law Review, 1972-1973.

**STEPHEN P. SOSKIN,** born Cook County, Illinois, January 10, 1956; admitted to bar, 1981, California; 1982, U.S. District Court, Central District of California and U.S. Claims Court. *Education:* University of Illinois (B.S., Accounting, with high honors, 1978; J.D., with honors, 1981). Member, 1979-1980 and Editor, 1980-1981, University of Illinois Law Review.

**ROBERT W. KEASTER,** born Everett, Washington, January 16, 1959; admitted to bar, 1984, California; 1995, Arizona; 1988, U.S. Tax Court; 1989, U.S. District Court, Central District of California; 1990, U.S. District Court, District of Arizona; 1990, U.S. Court of Appeals, Ninth Circuit; 1991, U.S. District Court, Northern and Southern Districts of California. *Education:* California State University at Northridge (B.A., with honors, 1980); Pepperdine University (J.D., cum laude, 1984); New York University (LL.M., Taxation, 1986).

**RICHARD C. GILLER,** born Omaha, Nebraska, November 20, 1958; admitted to bar, 1985, California. *Education:* College of the Holy Cross (B.A., 1981); King's College, University of Aberdeen; Southwestern University (J.D., cum laude, 1984). Member, Southwestern University Law Review, 1983-1984.

**ROBERT D. HOFFMAN,** born Philadelphia, Pennsylvania, October 28, 1960; admitted to bar, 1986, California; 1989, District of Columbia. *Education:* Colby College (B.A., magna cum laude, 1982); Boston College Law School (J.D., 1985). Phi Beta Kappa.

**KIRK C. CHAMBERLIN,** born Northbrook, Illinois, August 16, 1962; admitted to bar, 1987, California; 1988, U.S. District Court, Central District of California. *Education:* Indiana University (B.A., 1984); University of Iowa (J.D., with distinction, 1987).

### ASSOCIATES

| | |
|---|---|
| Paul D. Albus | Susan L. Germaise |
| John D. Antoni | Lisa M. Hatton |
| David A. Eisenberg | Margret J. Kim |
| Vanci Y. Fuller | David S. Levy |

*(This Listing Continued)*

### ASSOCIATES (Continued)

| | |
|---|---|
| Shervin Mirhashemi | Randolph C. Simpson |
| Robert P. Mitrovich | Wayne C. Smith |
| Elizabeth A. Moussouros | Bruce T. Smyth |
| Robert A. Rosen | Michael K. Staub |
| Guy M. Roy | Patricia I. Taue |
| Stephanie H. Scherby | Christopher R. Wagner |
| | Chad B. Wootton |

## LAW OFFICES OF TOBI J. CHINSKI

1801 CENTURY PARK EAST, SUITE 2500
**LOS ANGELES, CALIFORNIA 90067**
Telephone: 310-286-6767
Fax: 310-286-1633

*Estate Planning, Probate and Trust Law, Charitable Tax Planning.*

**TOBI J. CHINSKI,** born Chicago, Illinois, February 20, 1947; admitted to bar, 1980, California; 1981, U.S. Court of Appeals, Ninth Circuit and U.S. District Courts, Central, Northern and Southern Districts of California. *Education:* University of Illinois (B.A., 1967); University of West Los Angeles (J.D., cum laude, 1980). Member, Moot Court Board of Governors. Recipient: American Jurisprudence Awards in Constitutional Law Corporations and Real Property; West Publishing Co. Hornbook Award. *Member:* Beverly Hills and Los Angeles County (Member, Sections on: Probate and Trust Law; Taxation) Bar Associations; State Bar of California (Member, Probate and Trust Law Section).

## CHOATE AND CHOATE

523 WEST SIXTH STREET, SUITE 541
**LOS ANGELES, CALIFORNIA 90014**
Telephone: 213-623-8136; 623-2297
Telecopier: 213-623-6429

*General Trial Practice. International, Agricultural and Probate Law.*

### MEMBERS OF FIRM

**JOSEPH CHOATE,** born Santa Ana, California, January 14, 1900; admitted to bar, 1927, California; 1934, Massachusetts; 1935, U.S. Supreme Court. *Education:* Pomona College and University of Southern California (B.A., 1925); University of Southern California (LL.B., 1925); Harvard University (LL.M., 1936). Delta Theta Phi. Member, Public Panel, War Labor Board, 1942. *Member:* State Bar of California; International Bar Association; American Society of International Law. **PRACTICE AREAS:** International.

**JOSEPH CHOATE, JR.,** born Los Angeles, California, May 21, 1941; admitted to bar, 1966, California; 1968, U.S. Court of Military Appeals; 1970, U.S. Supreme Court. *Education:* Pomona College (B.A., 1963); University of Southern California (J.D., 1966); Harvard University (LL.M., 1971). Phi Alpha Delta. Instructor, International Law, University of Maryland Far East Division, 1967-1968. *Member:* Los Angeles County (Member, Probate and Trust Section) and International Bar Associations; State Bar of California; Judge Advocates Association. [With JAGC, 1967-1970]. **PRACTICE AREAS:** International; Agricultural.

**ROBERT P. LEWIS, JR.,** born Pasadena, California, December 8, 1944; admitted to bar, 1973, California; 1974, U.S. District Court, Central District of California; 1985, U.S. Court of Appeals, Ninth Circuit and U.S. Army Court of Military Review; 1988, U.S. Supreme Court; 1989, U.S. District Court, Eastern District of California. *Education:* University of Michigan (A.B., 1970); University of Southern California (J.D., 1973). Phi Alpha Delta. *Member:* State Bar of California; American Bar Association. [With USAF, 1964-1968; Lt. Col. JAGC, USAR, Ret.]. **LANGUAGES:** Chinese (Mandarin). **PRACTICE AREAS:** International; Agricultural.

**BRADLEY L. CORNELL,** born Sacramento, California, January 20, 1963; admitted to bar, 1992, California and U.S. District Court, Northern, Southern, Eastern and Central Districts of California. *Education:* Pomona College (B.A., 1985); Loyola Law School (J.D., 1992). *Member:* Los Angeles County Bar Association; State Bar of California. **PRACTICE AREAS:** International; Agricultural.

## DEBORAH CHODOS
12400 WILSHIRE BOULEVARD, SUITE 400
LOS ANGELES, CALIFORNIA 90025-1023
Telephone: 310-207-0569
Fax: 310-207-5313

*General Business Litigation, Real Estate and Construction Litigation, Insurance Bad Faith and Personal Injury Litigation.*

**DEBORAH CHODOS,** born Norman, Oklahoma, March 1, 1953; admitted to bar, 1978, California and Illinois; 1985, U.S. Supreme Court and U.S. District Court, Central District of California. *Education:* University of California at Berkeley (B.A., 1974); University of Southern California (J.D., 1977). Lecturer: Law and Motion Advocacy, CEB/WLALA, 1990, Trial Skills Workshop, CEB, 1993. Chair, Editorial Board, Los Angeles Lawyer Magazine, 1991-1992. *Member:* Los Angeles County Bar Association (Barristers Executive Committee, 1987-1989; Chair, Barristers Artists and the Law Committee, 1985-1986); State Bar of California; Women Lawyers' Association of Los Angeles (Board of Governors, 1984-1993); California Women Lawyers.

---

## CHRISTA & JACKSON
SUITE 1100
1901 AVENUE OF THE STARS
LOS ANGELES, CALIFORNIA 90067-6002
Telephone: 310-282-8040
Fax: 310-282-8421
Email: lchrista@christalaw.com
URL: http://www.Christalaw.com

*Business Litigation Practice on behalf of Domestic and International Clients, in Courts and other Adjudicative Tribunals on Matters Involving General Contract, Securities, Intellectual Property, Real Property and Construction, Travel and Tourism, Business Torts and Related Business Disputes.*

*FIRM PROFILE: Christa & Jackson is a dynamic young business litigation law firm. Its attorneys developed successful practices, most as partners, in leading Los Angeles law firms before forming Christa & Jackson.*

*All Partners have substantial litigation and trial experience. The firm represents a wide range of business clients, many engaged in national and international business transactions and often including out-of-state entities seeking California representation.*

*The firm is dedicated to providing its clients with excellent and innovative representation, leading to outstanding results.*

### MEMBERS OF FIRM

**LAURA KASSNER CHRISTA,** born March 29, 1955; admitted to bar, 1981, California and U.S. District Court, Central, Northern, Southern and Eastern Districts of California. *Education:* Brandeis University (B.A., summa cum laude, 1976); University of Pennsylvania (J.D., 1980). Phi Beta Kappa. Judicial Settlement Officer, Los Angeles County Superior Court, 1992—. Judge Pro Tem, Los Angeles Municipal Court, 1986—, At-Large Appointee, West Hollywood General Plan Advisory Commission, 1985-1987. Pro Bono Attorney, Public Counsel, 1985-1990. *Member:* State Bar of California (Member: Committee on Administration of Justice, 1994—; Litigation and Intellectual Property Sections); Women Lawyers Association of Los Angeles (Member, Board of Governors, 1992—; Co-Chair, Special Events, 1992-1993, Co-Chair, Appointive Office, 1993-1994; Secretary, 1995-1996); Copyright Society. *PRACTICE AREAS:* Litigation. *Email:* lchrista@christalaw.com

**LAURENCE D. JACKSON,** born Clinton, Iowa, April 8, 1955; admitted to bar, 1978, California; 1982, U.S. Tax Court. *Education:* Iowa State University; University of Iowa (B.S., with honors, 1975); University of Chicago (J.D., 1978). Associate Editor, Association of Business Trial Lawyers Report. Author: "Getting Visual Information Before the Jury in the Opening Statement," XV Association of Business Trial Lawyers Rep 9, 1992. Co-author: "Motions in Limine: Getting the Judge's Attention," XIV Association of Business Trial Lawyers Rep 1, 1991; "Turning Your Client's Position Into the Judge's First Impression," California Litigation, Vol. 6, Number 1, Fall 1992. *Member:* Los Angeles County (Member, Litigation Section Executive Committee) and American Bar Associations; Association of Business Trial Lawyers. *PRACTICE AREAS:* Litigation. *Email:* ljackson@christalaw.com

**ANN LOEB,** born Brooklyn, New York, February 27, 1955; admitted to bar, 1979, New York and U.S. District Court, Southern and Eastern Districts of New York; 1982, U.S. Court of Appeals, Second Circuit; 1984, U.S. Supreme Court; 1988, California; U.S. District Court, Central District of California. *Education:* Brooklyn College (B.A., magna cum laude, 1975); Harvard University (J.D., cum laude, 1978). Phi Beta Kappa. *Member:* State Bar of California (Co-Chair, Education Committee, Intellectual Property Section); Association of Business Trial Lawyers; Women Lawyers Association of Los Angeles; Copyright Society. *PRACTICE AREAS:* Litigation; Media; Appeals.

### ASSOCIATES

**CAROL K. SAMEK,** born Bratislava, Slovakia, May 1, 1958; admitted to bar, 1983, California; registered to practice before U.S. Patent and Trademark Office; U.S. District Court, Northern and Southern Districts of California. *Education:* University of California at Los Angeles (B.A., cum laude, 1980); Boalt Hall School of Law, University of California at Berkeley (J.D., 1983). Law Clerk to Justice E. M. Gunderson, Supreme Court of Nevada, 1983-1984. *Member:* Pasadena, Los Angeles County and American Bar Associations; The State Bar of California. *LANGUAGES:* Slovak and Czech. *PRACTICE AREAS:* Business Litigation.

### OF COUNSEL

**ELIZABETH G. CHILTON,** born Philadelphia, Pennsylvania, September 18, 1958; admitted to bar, 1983, California; 1984, U.S. District Court, Central District of California and U.S. Court of Appeals, Ninth Circuit. *Education:* University of California at Santa Barbara; University of California at Los Angeles (B.A., summa cum laude, 1980; J.D., 1983). Phi Beta Kappa; Phi Alpha Delta; Order of the Coif. Distinguished Advocate, UCLA Moot Court Honors Program, 1982. *Member:* The State Bar of California; Women Lawyers Association of Los Angeles. *PRACTICE AREAS:* Business Litigation; Real Estate Litigation; Land Use Litigation; Appellate Work. *Email:* echilton@christalaw.com

---

## JAY D. CHRISTENSEN AND ASSOCIATES
LOS ANGELES, CALIFORNIA
(See Pasadena)

*General Healthcare Law, Managed Healthcare Arrangements, Peer Review Issues, Related Litigation.*

---

## CHRISTENSEN, MILLER, FINK, JACOBS, GLASER, WEIL AND SHAPIRO, LLP
2121 AVENUE OF THE STARS
EIGHTEENTH FLOOR
LOS ANGELES, CALIFORNIA 90067
Telephone: 310-553-3000
Fax: 310-556-2920

San Francisco, California Office: 650 California Street, Suite 2200. 94108. Telephone: 415-288-1377. Fax: 415-362-1021.

*General Civil and Trial Practice in all State and Federal Courts. Corporation, Securities, Banking, Real Estate and General Business Law. International and Entertainment Law. Taxation, Estate Planning, Trust, Probate, Insurance, Environmental Law, Energy Law, Constitutional and Civil Rights, Employment, Copyright and Trademark, Toxic Tort, Government Relations, Regulatory and Administrative Law.*

### MEMBERS OF FIRM

**TERRY N. CHRISTENSEN,** born Los Angeles, California, January 5, 1941; admitted to bar, 1966, California. *Education:* Stanford University (A.B., 1962); University of Southern California (J.D., 1965). Phi Delta Phi; Order of the Coif. Member, Board of Editors, University of Southern California Law Review, 1963-1965. Chairman, City of Los Angeles Risk Management Task Force. *Member:* Beverly Hills, Los Angeles County and American Bar Associations; The State Bar of California. *PRACTICE AREAS:* Corporate; Entertainment; Civil Litigation.

**BARRY E. FINK,** born Bay City, Michigan, November 22, 1938; admitted to bar, 1963, Illinois, California, District of Columbia, U.S. Supreme Court, U.S. Tax Court and U.S. Claims Court. *Education:* University of Illinois; De Paul University (B.S.C., 1960); University of Chicago (J.D., 1963); John Marshall Law School. Phi Delta Phi (President, 1962-1963). Winner, Hinton Moot Court Competition, 1963. Certified Public Accountant, Illinois, 1962. Member of Faculty, John Marshall Law School, 1964-

*(This Listing Continued)*

**CHRISTENSEN, MILLER, FINK, JACOBS, GLASER, WEIL AND SHAPIRO, LLP,** Los Angeles—Continued

1966. Member, President Carter's Tax Advisory Committee. Co-Author: "Advising California Partnerships," Continuing Education of the Bar, 1988. *Member:* The District of Columbia Bar; Los Angeles County, Illinois State and American Bar Associations; The State Bar of California; American Institute of Certified Public Accountants. **PRACTICE AREAS:** Corporation; Taxation; Tax Litigation; Corporate; Business Law; International Law; International Business Transactions.

**GARY N. JACOBS,** born New York, N.Y., July 12, 1945; admitted to bar, 1970, New York; 1972, California. *Education:* Brandeis University (B.A., summa cum laude, 1966); London School of Economics, London, England; Yale University (LL.B., 1969). Phi Beta Kappa; Order of the Coif. Editor, Yale Law Journal, 1967-1969. Author: "Nuclear Britain," III International Relations (London) 61, 1966; "Border Searches and the Fourth Amendment," 77 Yale Law Journal 1007, 1968. Law Clerk to Hon. Wilfred Feinberg, Circuit Judge, U.S. Court of Appeals, Second Circuit, 1969-1970. Visiting Lecturer, UCLA Law School, 1982. *Member:* Beverly Hills, Los Angeles County, New York State and American Bar Associations; The State Bar of California. **PRACTICE AREAS:** Corporate; Securities; General Business Law.

**LOUIS R. MILLER, III,** born Chicago, Illinois, February 3, 1947; admitted to bar, 1972, California. *Education:* University of Denver (B.S.B.A., 1969); University of California at Los Angeles (J.D., 1972). Beta Gamma Sigma; Mu Kappa Tau. Member, Board of Editors, University of California at Los Angeles Law Review, 1971-1972. Law Clerk to Hon. Jesse W. Curtis, Jr., United States District Judge, Central District of California, 1972-1973. *Member:* Los Angeles County and American Bar Associations; State Bar of California. **PRACTICE AREAS:** Trials and Litigation.

**PATRICIA GLASER,** born Charleston, West Virginia, September 15, 1947; admitted to bar, 1973, California. *Education:* The American University (B.A., 1969); Rutgers University (J.D., 1973). Member, Rutgers Law Review, 1973. President, Student Bar Association, 1973. Law Clerk to Hon. David W. Williams, U.S. District Judge, Central District of California, 1972-1973. *Member:* Los Angeles County and American Bar Associations; The State Bar of California. **PRACTICE AREAS:** Civil Litigation; Entertainment.

**ROBERT L. SHAPIRO,** born Plainfield, New Jersey, September 2, 1942; admitted to bar, 1969, California, U.S. District Court, Central, Southern and Northern Districts of California and U.S. Court of Appeals, Ninth Circuit. *Education:* University of California at Los Angeles (B.S., 1965); Loyola University of Los Angeles (J.D., 1968). Winner, Scott Moot Court Competition, 1968. Chief Justice, Moot Court, 1969. Recipient, American Jurisprudence Award. Author: "The Search for Justice: A Defense Attorney," Brief on the O.J. Simpson Case, 1996; "When the Press Calls: A Lawyer's View," California Litigation, Volume 5, Number 1, Fall, 1991. Deputy District Attorney, 1969-1972. Listed in Best Lawyers in America, 1993-1996. *Member:* State Bar of California; American Bar Association; California Trial Lawyers Association; National Association of Criminal Defense Lawyers; California Attorneys for Criminal Justice; Trial Lawyers for Public Justice (Founder). **REPORTED CASES:** Lead Counsel in United States of America v. Samango (607 Fed. 2d 877); People v. Christian Brando; People v. O.J. Simpson. **PRACTICE AREAS:** Criminal Defense; Litigation Law.

**PETER M. WEIL,** born St. Louis, Missouri, January 19, 1948; admitted to bar, 1974, Wisconsin and Illinois; 1977, California. *Education:* University of Wisconsin-Madison (B.A., 1970; J.D., 1974); University of California at Berkeley (M.A., 1971). Member, City of Los Angeles Rent Stabilization Commission, 1986-1990. Vice-President, City of Los Angeles Planning Commission, 1995—. Chairman, City of Los Angeles Board of Zoning Appeals, 1993-1995. *Member:* Beverly Hills, Century City (Member, Board of Governors, 1982-1988; President, 1987-1988), Los Angeles County (Member, Board of Trustees, 1988-1989) and American Bar Associations; The State Bar of California. **PRACTICE AREAS:** Real Estate; Corporate Law.

**JAMES S. SCHREIER,** born Detroit, Michigan, February 27, 1950; admitted to bar, 1975, California and U.S. District Court, Central, Southern and Northern Districts of California. *Education:* University of Michigan (B.A., with high honors, 1971); Yale University (J.D., 1974). Phi Beta Kappa. *Member:* Beverly Hills and Los Angeles County Bar Associations; The State Bar of California. **PRACTICE AREAS:** Civil Litigation.

**JANET S. MCCLOUD,** born Drumright, Oklahoma, May 16, 1947; admitted to bar, 1975, California. *Education:* University of Delaware (B.A., *(This Listing Continued)*

1969); University of Denver (M.A., 1970); Yale University (J.D., 1975). Phi Kappa Phi; Phi Beta Kappa. *Member:* Beverly Hills, Los Angeles County and American Bar Associations; The State Bar of California. **PRACTICE AREAS:** Corporate.

**TERRY D. AVCHEN,** born Perth Amboy, New Jersey, September 9, 1951; admitted to bar, 1977, California. *Education:* University of California at Los Angeles (B.A., 1974; J.D., 1977). Phi Beta Kappa; Pi Gamma Mu. Member, Moot Court. Member, University of California at Los Angeles Law Review, 1975-1976. *Member:* State Bar of California. **PRACTICE AREAS:** Civil Litigation; Environmental Law.

**J. JAY RAKOW,** born New York, N.Y., January 28, 1953; admitted to bar, 1978, New York; 1980, District of Columbia and California. *Education:* New York University (B.A., 1974); Cornell University (J.D., 1977). President, Cornell Law Student Association, 1976-1977. *Member:* Century City (Chairman, Section on Litigation, 1987), Los Angeles County and American Bar Associations; State Bar of California. **PRACTICE AREAS:** Entertainment Law; Litigation.

**ROGER H. HOWARD,** born Los Angeles, California, December 5, 1944; admitted to bar, 1972, California. *Education:* University of California at Los Angeles (B.A., 1966; J.D., 1971). Member, Board of Alumni Trustees, University of California At Los Angeles, 1974-1976. Author: "Commercial Condominiums: Legal Consideration," Beverly Hills Bar Association Journal, Fall 1981. *Member:* Beverly Hills, Los Angeles County and American Bar Associations; State Bar of California. **PRACTICE AREAS:** Real Estate; Business Law.

**ERIC N. LANDAU,** born Fairlawn, New Jersey, May 30, 1957; admitted to bar, 1982, District of Columbia; 1983, Illinois; 1987, New York; 1988, California. *Education:* Hamilton College; Washington University (A.B., Econ and A.B., Biology, cum laude, 1979; J.D., 1982). Phi Beta Kappa. Author: "You Must Remember This—Oral Agreements and the Motion Picture Industry," 25 University of West Los Angeles Law Review 155, 1994; "Restructuring The Corporation - As A Response To A Hostile Takeover Bid," 7th Annual Ray Garrett, Jr. Corporate and Securities Law Institute, April 29-30, 1987. *Member:* Chicago, Beverly Hills, Los Angeles County, New York State and American Bar Associations; State Bar of California. **PRACTICE AREAS:** Civil Litigation; Securities Litigation; Corporate Governance.

**SEAN RILEY,** born Sydney, Australia, November 14, 1957; admitted to bar, 1982, New South Wales, Australia; 1986, California. *Education:* University of Sydney, Australia (B.Ec., 1979; LL.B., 1981). *Member:* Los Angeles County Bar Association; State Bar of California; Australian-American Lawyers Association. **PRACTICE AREAS:** Civil Litigation.

**MARK G. KRUM,** born Des Moines, Iowa, October 31, 1956; admitted to bar, 1983, Illinois and U.S. District Court, Northern District of Illinois; 1989, New York, U.S. District Court, Southern District of New York and U.S. Court of Appeals, Eleventh Circuit; 1990, California and U.S. District Court, Central District of California. *Education:* Wheaton College (B.A., with high honors, 1979); Northwestern University (J.D., 1983). *Member:* Illinois State and New York State Bar Associations; State Bar of California. **PRACTICE AREAS:** Civil Litigation; Securities Litigation; Corporate Governance.

**CLARE BRONOWSKI,** born Cheltenham, England, July 16, 1955; admitted to bar, 1983, California. *Education:* Harvard University (B.A., 1976); University of California at Los Angeles (J.D, 1983). Order of the Coif. Moot Court Honors Program. Extern Clerk, Hon. Harry Pregerson, U.S. Court of Appeals, Ninth Circuit, 1982. Member: Los Angeles Civil Service Commission, 1990-1992; Los Angeles Convention Center Commission, 1992-1994; Los Angeles County Beach Commission, 1996—. *Member:* Los Angeles County and Century City (Member, Board of Governors, 1995—) Bar Associations; State Bar of California. **PRACTICE AREAS:** Real Estate; Land Use; Environmental.

**BRETT J. COHEN,** born Brooklyn, New York, April 15, 1958; admitted to bar, 1985, California; 1986, U.S. District Court, Central District of California. *Education:* Cornell University (B.S., 1979); University of California at Los Angeles (J.D., 1985; M.B.A., 1985). *Member:* Beverly Hills and Los Angeles County Bar Associations; State Bar of California. **PRACTICE AREAS:** Real Estate; Land Use; Environmental.

**STEPHEN N. BESSER,** born St. Paul, Minnesota, March 17, 1936; admitted to bar, 1963, California; 1966, U.S. Supreme Court. *Education:* University of California at Los Angeles (B.A., 1959); Loyola University of Los Angeles (J.D., 1962). *Member:* State Bar of California. (Also at San Francisco Office). **PRACTICE AREAS:** Governmental Relations.

*(This Listing Continued)*

# PROFESSIONAL BIOGRAPHIES — CALIFORNIA—LOS ANGELES

**PETER C. SHERIDAN,** born Woodland Hills, California, October 25, 1960; admitted to bar, 1988, California; U.S. District Court, Central and Southern Districts of California; U.S. Court of Appeals, Ninth Circuit. *Education:* California State University at Northridge (B.A., Speech, 1983; B.A., Pol. Sc., 1983); Willamette University (J.D., cum laude, 1988). Pi Kappa Delta; Order of the Barristers. Recipient, Richard B. Aronstam Scholarship. First Place Moot Court and Brief Writing Competition. First Place, American Bar Association National Mock Trial Intraschool Competition, 1986 and 1987; Staff Member, 1986-1987 and Editor-in-Chief, 1987-1988, Willamette Law Review. Author: "In Defense of Poetic License: Why Created Quotations Deserve Constitutional Protection," Vol. 13, No. 2, Los Angeles Lawyer (April 1990); Article, "Grand Jury Subpoenas to Criminal Defense Attorneys: Massachusetts Restrains the Federal Prosecutor Through an 'Ethical' Rule," 2 Georgetown Journal of Legal Ethics 485 (1988); Note, "The Accession to GATT of the People's Republic of China: New Challenges for the World Trade Regime," 23 Willamette Law Review, (Fall 1987); Note, "Cain v. Rijken: Creation of a Statutory Duty of Care to Protect Others from the Tortious Conduct of Third Persons," 23 Willamette Law Review 493 (1987). Adjunct Professor, Department of Speech Communication: California State University, Northridge, 1984-1985; Willamette University, 1985-1987. *Member:* Los Angeles County (Member, Litigation Section) and American (Member, Litigation Section) Bar Associations; State Bar of California (Member, Litigation Section); Los Angeles Barristers Association. *PRACTICE AREAS:* Civil Litigation.

**CAROLYN COMPARET JORDAN,** born Los Angeles, California, February 18, 1962; admitted to bar, 1986, California. *Education:* University of California at Los Angeles (B.A., 1983; J.D., 1986). Member, Order of the Barristers. Administrative Chair, UCLA Moot Court Honors Program. Recipient, American Jurisprudence Award in Property. Associate Member, Federal Communications Law Journal, 1983-1986. Co-Author: "Techniques for Renegotiating or Terminating A Lease," 22 Real Estate Law Journal 2, Fall, 1993. *Member:* Los Angeles County and American Bar Associations; State Bar of California. *PRACTICE AREAS:* Real Estate; Corporate Law.

**RONALD E. GUTTMAN,** born Bronx, New York, January 17, 1943; admitted to bar, 1970, New York; 1971, U.S. Court of Appeals, Second Circuit and U.S. District Court, Southern and Eastern Districts of New York; 1974, U.S. Supreme Court; 1985, U.S. Court of Appeals, Sixth Circuit; 1986, U.S. Court of Appeals, Fifth Circuit; 1988, Pennsylvania and U.S. District Court, Eastern District of Pennsylvania; 1991, California and U.S. District Court, Central District of California; 1994, U.S. Court of Appeals, Ninth Circuit. *Education:* University of Florida (B.A.E., 1964); Brooklyn Law School (J.D., magna cum laude, 1969). *Member:* Association of the Bar of the City of New York; New York State and American (Chair, Media Law and Defamation Torts Committee, Tort and Insurance Practice Section, 1990-1991; Advisor to Uniform Commissioner's Committee on Uniform Defamation Law, 1988-1992; Co-Chair, Libel Defense Resource Center, Defense Counsel Section, 1987-1989); State Bar of California. *PRACTICE AREAS:* Litigation; Entertainment; Media; Employment.

**DAVID A. GIANNOTTI,** born Rome, New York, May 27, 1947; admitted to bar, 1972, Georgia and Tennessee; 1976, New York; 1981, California. *Education:* Ithaca College (B.A., 1969); Emory University (J.D., 1971). Phi Delta Phi (Vice-Magister, 1969-1970). Member: Moot Court; International Law Moot Court Team. Author: "Handling the EPA Inspection," ALI-ABA Course Material Journal, June, 1983, Revised and Reprinted, ALI-ABA CMJ Manual on Government Relations, 1987; "Advising the Corporate Client on Environmental Compliance," The Lawyer's Brief, Vol. 13, Issue 12, November 1983 and PLI Course Handbook Series No. 129, September, 1983; "The Environmental Assessment Program," The National Law Journal, November, 1983; "Environmental Auditing Programs," Chemical Times and Trends, April, 1985; "Environmental Assessments of Contracts with Consultants," Environmental Auditing Newsletter, March, 1985. Contributing Author: "Law of Environmental Protection," Environmental Law Institute, 1987; "A Practical Guide to Environmental Law," ALI-ABA, 1987. *Member:* Los Angeles County and American Bar Associations; State Bar of Georgia; The State Bar of California (Member, Committee on the Environment, 1984-1987). *PRACTICE AREAS:* Environmental Law.

**NABIL L. ABU-ASSAL,** born Cairo, Egypt, June 1, 1962; admitted to bar, 1988, California; 1989, U.S. District Court, Central, Eastern, Southern and Northern Districts of California. *Education:* Claremont McKenna College (B.A., summa cum laude, 1984); University of Chicago (M.A., 1985); University of California (J.D., 1988). Member, Moot Court Honors Program. Recipient, American Jurisprudence Award, Constitutional Law I. *Member:* Los Angeles County Bar Association; State Bar of California. *LANGUAGES:* Arabic and French. *PRACTICE AREAS:* Civil Litigation.

*(This Listing Continued)*

**MARK L. BLOCK,** born Passaic, New Jersey, August 25, 1959; admitted to bar, 1984, California and U.S. District Court, Central District of California; 1991, U.S. Court of Appeals, Ninth Circuit. *Education:* University of Tennessee at Knoxville (B.A., with highest honors, 1981); Northwestern University School of Law (J.D. cum laude, 1984). Recipient, Best Brief Award in Miner Moot Court Tournament. Member, Editorial Board, Journal of Criminal Law and Criminology, 1982-1984. *Member:* Los Angeles County and American Bar Associations; State Bar of California. *PRACTICE AREAS:* Civil Litigation.

**JEFFREY C. SOZA,** born Castro Valley, California, August 5, 1962; admitted to bar, 1987, California. *Education:* University of Southern California (B.S., magna cum laude, 1984); Hastings College of the Law, University of California (J.D., magna cum laude, 1987). Beta Gamma Sigma; Order of the Coif. Articles Editor, Hastings Law Journal, 1986-1987. *Member:* State Bar of California. *PRACTICE AREAS:* Corporate; Securities Law.

## OF COUNSEL

**STEPHEN D. SILBERT, (A PROFESSIONAL CORPORATION),** born Los Angeles, California, September 4, 1942; admitted to bar, 1968, California. *Education:* Claremont McKenna College (B.A., summa cum laude, 1964); Claremont Graduate School (M.B.E., 1965); University of California at Berkeley (J.D., 1967). Order of the Coif; Pi Mu Epsilon. President, MGM/UA Communications Company, 1985-1988. *Member:* American Bar Association; The State Bar of California. *PRACTICE AREAS:* Corporate; Securities; Transactions.

**CHRISTINE BURDICK-BELL,** born Torrance, California, May 23, 1954; admitted to bar, 1979, California and U.S. District Court, Central District of California. *Education:* University of California at Irvine (B.S. Bio. Sc., magna cum laude and B.A. Ch., magna cum laude, 1976); Stanford University (J.D., 1979). Phi Beta Kappa. *Member:* Century City, Los Angeles County and American Bar Associations; The State Bar of California. *PRACTICE AREAS:* Corporate.

**ALISA J. FREUNDLICH,** born Los Angeles, California, 1960; admitted to bar, 1985, California. *Education:* University of California at Santa Barbara (B.A., with honors, 1982); Loyola University of Los Angeles (J.D., 1985). Member, St. Thomas More Honor Society. Business Editor, Loyola Entertainment Law Journal, 1984-1985. Recipient, American Jurisprudence Award, 1984. "Recent Developments in Prepayment Charges and Default Interest Rates," Presentation to the *Los Angeles County Bar Association*, 1989. "Real Estate Purchase and Sale Transactions," Presentation to University of Southern California MBA program, March 1994; "The Future of the CMBS Market; Legal Implications for Commercial Real Estate Lending and Asset Diversification Strategies," Presentation to the *American Real Estate Society*, April 15, 1994; Panelist: Real Property Purchase and Sale Agreements," California Continuing Education of the Bar, June 29, 1994. Author: "Opportunities for Lenders: How the New Banking Legislation Affects Commercial Mortgage Backed Securities," *The Journal of Commercial Lending*, November 1994; "Retail Mortgage Securitization" part of a Special Monograph edition entitled *Megatrends in Retail Property* published by The American University, Washington, D.C., Fall, 1995. *Member:* Los Angeles County Bar Association (Member, Real Property Section); State Bar of California; Women Lawyers Association of Los Angeles. *PRACTICE AREAS:* Real Estate Finance; Real Estate Development.

**KAREN L. FILIPI,** born Phoenix, Arizona; admitted to bar, 1986, California; 1991, New Jersey and U.S. District Court, Central District of California. *Education:* Arizona State University (B.S., 1980); Whittier College School of Law (J.D., 1986). Recipient, Moot Court Honors Board, Best Brief and Best Overall Competitor, 1986. Deputy District Attorney, Los Angeles County, 1986-1990. *Member:* State Bar of California; New Jersey State Bar Association. *PRACTICE AREAS:* Criminal Defense; Civil Litigation.

**SARA L. CAPLAN,** born Detroit, Michigan, December 25, 1955; admitted to bar, 1983, Michigan; 1990, California, U.S. Court of Appeals, Sixth and Ninth Circuits, U.S. District Court, Central, Southern and Northern Districts of California, U.S. District Court, Eastern District of Michigan and U.S. Tax Court. *Education:* Wayne State University (B.A., with high distinction, 1977; J.D., 1983); University of Michigan (M.S.W, 1978). Phi Beta Kappa; Psi Chi. *Member:* State Bar of California; State Bar of Michigan. *PRACTICE AREAS:* Criminal Defense; Business Litigation; Commercial Litigation; Civil Litigation; Appeals.

**KENNETH G. MCKENNA,** born New York, N.Y., January 11, 1953; admitted to bar, 1985, California; 1987, New York. *Education:* Yale University (A.B., 1975; Ph.D., 1978); University of Chicago (J.D., 1984). Law Clerk to Judge E. Grady Jolly, U.S. Court of Appeals, Fifth Circuit, 1984-

*(This Listing Continued)*

## CHRISTENSEN, MILLER, FINK, JACOBS, GLASER, WEIL AND SHAPIRO, LLP, Los Angeles—Continued

1985. *Member:* State Bar of California. **PRACTICE AREAS:** Corporate Law; Finance Law; Bankruptcy Law.

### ASSOCIATES

**GERARD R. KILROY,** born Long Branch, New Jersey, May 24, 1955; admitted to bar, 1980, California and U.S. District Court, Central District of California. *Education:* University of California at Los Angeles (B.A., 1977); Loyola University of Los Angeles (J.D., with honors, 1980). Member, Scott Moot Court. *Member:* Los Angeles County and American Bar Associations; State Bar of California. **PRACTICE AREAS:** Civil Litigation.

**ALISA M. MORGENTHALER,** born St. Louis, Missouri, June 3, 1960; admitted to bar, 1986, New York; 1988, District of Columbia; 1990, California; 1991, U.S. District Court, Central District of California and U.S. Court of Appeals, Ninth Circuit. *Education:* Southwest Missouri State University (B.A., magna cum laude, 1982); Cornell University (J.D., 1985). Finalist, Cuccia Cup Moot Court Competition. Phi Kappa Phi; Pi Sigma Alpha; Phi Alpha Delta (Vice Justice, 1984-1985). Co-author: with D. Humphrey, D. Mengle and O. Ireland, "Pricing Fedwire Daylight Overdrafts," Federal Reserve Board Press Release, January 13, 1986. Staff Attorney, Board of Governors of the Federal Reserve System, 1985-1986. *Member:* Century City, Beverly Hills, Los Angeles County, Federal and American Bar Associations; State Bar of California; Women Lawyers Association of Los Angeles (Member, Board of Directors, 1995—). **PRACTICE AREAS:** Civil Litigation; Entertainment; Banking Law.

**MARK K. LI,** born Hong Kong, September 15, 1958; admitted to bar, 1986, California; 1989, U.S. Tax Court. *Education:* University of California at Berkeley (B.S., Accounting and Finance, 1980); University of San Francisco (J.D., 1986); New York University (LL.M., Taxation, 1987). Certified Public Accountant, California, 1990. *Member:* Los Angeles County Bar Association (Member, Tax Section); State Bar of California. **PRACTICE AREAS:** Taxation; Estate Planning Law.

**KEVIN J. LEICHTER,** born New York, N.Y., June 23, 1961; admitted to bar, 1991, California, New York, U.S. District Court, Southern, Central, Eastern and Northern Districts of California; 1992, U.S. Court of Appeals, Ninth Circuit and Temporary Emergency Court of Appeals; 1993, U.S. District Court, Eastern District of Wisconsin. *Education:* Skidmore College (B.A., 1983); Columbia University (M.A., 1985); Boston University (J.D., 1988). Law Clerk: Hon. Conrad K. Cyr, U.S. Court of Appeals for the First Circuit, 1989-1990; Hon. D. Brock Hornby, U.S. District Court, District of Maine, 1990. *Member:* Los Angeles County (Member, Committee on Federal Courts), Suffolk County, New York State and American (Member: Committee on Pretrial Procedure and Discovery; Committee on Federal Procedure) Bar Associations; State Bar of California (Member, Committee on Federal Courts). **PRACTICE AREAS:** Civil Litigation; Entertainment Litigation; Bankruptcy Law.

**STEVEN J. AARONOFF,** born New York, N.Y., January 22, 1964; admitted to bar, 1989, Illinois and U.S. District Court, Northern District of Illinois; 1992, California and U.S. District Court, Central, Eastern, Southern and Northern Districts of California. *Education:* Harvard University (A.B., cum laude, 1986); Northwestern University (J.D., 1989). *Member:* Beverly Hills, Los Angeles County, Illinois State and American Bar Associations; State Bar of California. **PRACTICE AREAS:** Litigation.

**ANTHONY J. SARKIS,** born Tehran, Iran, January 22, 1964; admitted to bar, 1990, California; 1991, U.S. District Court, Eastern and Northern Districts of California; 1995, U.S. District Court, Central District of California. *Education:* University of California at Berkeley (B.A., with highest honors, 1986); Boalt Hall School of Law, University of California, Berkeley (J.D., 1989). Phi Beta Kappa. Member, Board of Editors, International Tax and Business Lawyer, 1988. Extern to Honorable David Eagleson, Associate Justice, California Supreme Court, 1988. *Member:* Los Angeles County and American Bar Associations; State Bar of California. **LANGUAGES:** Persian, Assyrian and German. **PRACTICE AREAS:** Civil Litigation; Securities Litigation.

**CYNTHIA M. TAKÁCS,** born Fort Campbell, Kentucky, January 16, 1964; admitted to bar, 1990, California. *Education:* University of Rochester (B.A., cum laude, 1986); University of Southern California (J.D., 1990). Phi Alpha Delta. Editor, Hale Moot Court Honors Program. *Member:* Los Angeles, Beverly Hills and American Bar Associations; State Bar of California. **LANGUAGES:** Hungarian. **PRACTICE AREAS:** Civil Litigation; Intellectual Property; Entertainment.

*(This Listing Continued)*

**RISA B. WINOGRAD,** born Windsor, Ontario, Canada, March 20, 1964; admitted to bar, 1991, California. *Education:* University of California at Los Angeles (B.A., cum laude, 1987); Loyola University of Los Angeles (J.D., 1991). Order of the Coif. Chief Justice, Scott Moot Court Honor's Board. Recipient: American Jurisprudence Awards in Constitutional Law, 1990; Corporations, 1990; Contracts Writing, 1989. Extern to Hon. Dickran Tevrizian, U.S. District Court, Central District of California, 1991. *Member:* Los Angeles County Bar Association; State Bar of California. **PRACTICE AREAS:** Real Estate.

**PETER E. GARRELL,** born Bridgeport, Connecticut, February 3, 1966; admitted to bar, 1991, California and U.S. District Court, Central District of California. *Education:* Clark University (B.A., 1988); University of Bridgeport (J.D., 1991). Associate Editor, Connecticut Probate Law Journal, 1990-1991. Recipient, Class Award, Excellence in Clinical Work. *Member:* Orange County and American Bar Associations; State Bar of California; Southern California Defense Counsel. **PRACTICE AREAS:** Civil Litigation; Liability Defense.

**CHRISTOPHER R. O'BRIEN,** born Boston, Massachusetts, September 4, 1965; admitted to bar, 1991, California. *Education:* The American University (B.A., 1987); University of Southern California (J.D., 1991). *Member:* State Bar of California. **PRACTICE AREAS:** Corporate Law.

**DAVID J. NACHMAN,** born Passaic, New Jersey, March 14, 1968; admitted to bar, 1992, Pennsylvania; 1995, California. *Education:* University of California at Los Angeles (B.A., 1989); University of Pennsylvania (J.D., 1992). Co-Author: "IRS Issues New Foreign Currency Rules," 20 International Tax Journal 1, 1993; "OBRA Scaleback of § 936 Benefits Means Companies Should Consider Their Options," Tax Management International Journal, Dec., 1993. *Member:* State Bar of California. **PRACTICE AREAS:** Tax Law; Corporate Law; Business Law; Real Estate Law.

**ERIC P. EARLY,** born Ann Arbor, Michigan, August 20, 1958; admitted to bar, 1993, California and U.S. District Court, Central District of California; 1994, U.S. District Court, Southern District of California. *Education:* New York University (B.F.A., 1981); Southwestern University School of Law (J.D., 1992). Mobil Student Film Finalist. Listed in, Who's Who Among American Law Students, 1992. Author: "It's a Wonderful Life - Motion Picture Studios Can Regain Control of Their Wayward Classics," 1 UCLA Ent. L. Rev. 139, 1994. *Member:* Los Angeles County Bar Association; State Bar of California; American Business Trial Lawyers Association. **PRACTICE AREAS:** Commercial; Entertainment; Litigation.

**KIMBERLEE A. KONJOYAN,** born Pasadena, California, July 8, 1965; admitted to bar, 1991, California and U.S. District Court, Central District of California; 1992, U.S. District Court, Eastern District of California. *Education:* University of Southern California (B.S., 1987; B.A., 1990); Loyola University of Los Angeles (J.D., 1990). Phi Alpha Delta. *Member:* Los Angeles County and American Bar Associations; State Bar of California; Armenian Bar Association. **LANGUAGES:** Spanish. **PRACTICE AREAS:** Litigation.

**TALIN V. YACOUBIAN,** born Beirut, Lebanon; admitted to bar, 1993, California. *Education:* Pomona College (B.A., Economics, 1990); George Washington University (J.D., 1993). *Member:* Los Angeles County, Beverly Hills and American Bar Associations; State Bar of California. **LANGUAGES:** Armenian; Arabic; French. **PRACTICE AREAS:** Business; Entertainment Litigation.

**ROBERT JAMES SHILLIDAY III,** born Hickory, North Carolina, August 29, 1967; admitted to bar, 1993, California. *Education:* University of Georgia (B.A., 1989); University of Minnesota (J.D., 1993). Staff Member, Minnesota Law Review, 1992-1993. Law Clerk, Hon. Samuel L. Bufford, U.S. Bankruptcy Judge, Central District of California, 1993-1994. *Member:* State Bar of California. **PRACTICE AREAS:** Litigation.

**PAUL R. ROSENBAUM,** born Los Angeles, California, May 5, 1964; admitted to bar, 1993, California. *Education:* University of California at Berkeley (B.S., 1986); University of Southern California (J.D., 1993). Recipient, American Jurisprudence Award, Real Estate Transactions. *Member:* State Bar of California. **PRACTICE AREAS:** Real Estate; Business Law.

**SEONG HWAN KIM,** born Daegu, South Korea, March 1, 1968; admitted to bar, 1993, California. *Education:* University of California, Berkeley, Walter A. Haas School of Business (B.S., 1990); University of California, Los Angeles (J.D., 1993). Brief Writer, 1992 UCLA National Moot Court Team, 1992-1993. Executive Board Member, UCLA Moot Court Honors Program, 1992-1993. Author: "California's Unfair Competition Act: Will It Give Rise to Yet Another "Wave" in Smoking and Health Litigation?" 35 Santa Clara Law Review 193, 1995. Legal Extern, to the Honor-

*(This Listing Continued)*

able Ronald S.W. Lew, U.S. District Court Judge, 1991. Member, Pacific Basin Law Journal, 1991-1993. Legal Counsel, Korean American Garment Industry Association, 1995—. *Member:* State Bar of California. *LANGUAGES:* Korean. *PRACTICE AREAS:* Business Litigation.

**BRIAN CENTER,** born Augusta, Georgia, September 4, 1967; admitted to bar, 1993, California. *Education:* University of Kansas (B.A., 1990); University of California, Los Angeles (J.D., 1993). Phi Beta Kappa. *Member:* State Bar of California. *PRACTICE AREAS:* Business Litigation.

**NICOLAS MORGAN,** born Los Angeles, California, September 1, 1967; admitted to bar, 1993, California. *Education:* University of California, Los Angeles (B.A., 1989); University of California, Davis (J.D., 1993). Editor and Writer, University of California, Davis Law Review, 1992-1993. Author: "Guidelines for Privatization at the State Level," Public Law Journal, Spring, 1995. *Member:* State Bar of California. *PRACTICE AREAS:* Litigation.

**LISA D. SINGER,** born Brooklyn, New York, May 3, 1969; admitted to bar, 1994, California. *Education:* University of Florida (B.S., 1991); University of Pennsylvania (J.D., 1994). Phi Beta Kappa. Editor, University of Pennsylvania Law Review, 1993-1994. *Member:* State Bar of California. *PRACTICE AREAS:* Real Estate Law.

**SOROUSH RICHARD SHEHABI,** born Emporia, Kansas, January 20, 1965; admitted to bar, 1995, California. *Education:* Harvard University (A.B., cum laude Conc., magna thesis, 1988); University of California, Hastings College of the Law (J.D., 1994). Law Clerk, U.S. Department of Justice, Environmental Enforcement Section, 1994-1995. Associate Notes Editor, Hastings Journal of Environmental Law, 1994. Recipient: Harvard Boylston Speaking Competition Award, 1988; Ford Foundation and Harvard Kennedy School of Government International Research Awards, 1987. Finalist, National Debate Championships. Author: "Potential Environmental Liabilities Under CERCLA for Land Trusts and Conservation Easements," Back Forty, May, 1994; "Military Base Closure, Conversion and Cleanup," Public Law Research Institute Journal, July-December, 1994 Ed.; "What Goes Up Must Come Down, The Science, Economics and International Law of Ozone Depletion and Acid Deposition," Harvard Archives, June, 1988. Member, Board of Directors, Harvard Coop., 1987-1988. Financial Analyst, Salomon Brothers, Inc., New York, 1988-1990. *Member:* State Bar of California. *LANGUAGES:* Persian and French. *PRACTICE AREAS:* Environmental Law; Land Use Law; Civil Litigation.

**GARY J. GORHAM,** born Troy, New York, August 10, 1964; admitted to bar, 1994, California and U.S. District Court, Northern District of New York. *Education:* Syracuse University (J.D., magna cum laude, 1993). Member, Order of the Coif. Notes and Comments Editor, Syracuse Law Review, 1993. Law Clerk, Hon. Howard G. Munson, New York, N.Y., 1993-1995. *Member:* State Bar of California. *PRACTICE AREAS:* Litigation.

**MITCHELL M. CHUPACK,** born Los Angeles, California, June 17, 1962; admitted to bar, 1992, California. *Education:* University of California at Los Angeles (A.B., History, 1984); University of California at Berkeley, Boalt Hall School of Law (J.D., 1987). Executive Editor, International Tax and Business Lawyer, 1986-1987. California Real Estate Broker, 1991. *Member:* American Bar Association; Los Angeles Trial Lawyers Association. *LANGUAGES:* Spanish. *PRACTICE AREAS:* Real Estate Law.

**ANGELA BARNES,** born Chicago, Illinois, January 22, 1969; admitted to bar, 1994, Illinois and U.S. District Court, Northern District of Illinois (Not admitted in California). *Education:* Wellesley College (B.A., 1991); Columbia University (J.D., 1994). *Member:* Chicago, Illinois State and American (Member, Business Law Section, 1996) Bar Associations. *PRACTICE AREAS:* Corporate Law.

**AMY LEW POWELL,** born Los Angeles, California, June 29, 1969; admitted to bar, 1994, California and U.S. District Court, Central District of California. *Education:* University of Southern California (B.S., 1991); Southwestern University School of Law (J.D., 1994). Law Clerk to Honorable Dickran T. Gvrizian, U.S. District Court, 1995. *Member:* Los Angeles County and American Bar Associations; State Bar of California. *PRACTICE AREAS:* Litigation.

**ROBERT J. MULLER,** born Rochester, New York, December 6, 1958; admitted to bar, 1995, New York and U.S. District Court, Northern District of New York; 1996, Washington (Not admitted in California). *Education:* State University of New York at Binghamton (B.A., 1985); Oxford University, Oxford, England; University of Toledo (J.D., cum laude, 1994). Order of the Coif. Lead Articles Editor, University of Toledo Law Review, 1994. Law Clerk to Honorable Howard G. Munson, Senior Judge, U.S.

*(This Listing Continued)*

District Court, Northern District of New York, 1994. *Member:* Washington State Bar Association. *PRACTICE AREAS:* Litigation.

**RICHARD D. ROLL,** born Detroit, Michigan, October 20, 1966; admitted to bar, 1995, California and U.S. Court of Appeals, 9th Circuit. *Education:* Stanford University (A.B., 1989); Cornell University (J.D., 1994). *Member:* State Bar of California. *PRACTICE AREAS:* General Civil Litigation.

**JOIE MARIE GALLO,** born New York, N.Y., January 11, 1962; admitted to bar, 1995, California. *Education:* New York University (B.F.A., 1983); Loyola Marymount University (J.D., cum laude, 1995). Member, Order of the Coif. Executive Editor, Loyola Law Review, 1994-1995. Member, St. Thomas More Honor Society, 1994-1995. Recipient, American Jurisprudence Award in Trial Advocacy and Appellate Advocacy. Author: "Kervins v. Hartley: Fear of Aids Begets New 'Implied Exception' to the Theory of Medical Battery," Loyola of Los Angeles Law Review, Volume 28:4. Law Clerk to the Honorable Laughlin E. Waters, U.S. District Court, Central District of California, 1993. *Member:* State Bar of California. *PRACTICE AREAS:* Civil Litigation.

**DAVID N. LAKE,** born New York, N.Y., October 17, 1969; admitted to bar, 1995, California. *Education:* Brandeis University (B.A., 1991); University of San Francisco (J.D., 1995). *Member:* State Bar of California. *PRACTICE AREAS:* Litigation.

**JANE McCLURE,** born Mechanicsburg, Pennsylvania, April 1, 1967; admitted to bar, 1995, California. *Education:* University of Virginia (B.S., 1989); Hastings College of the Law, University of California (J.D., magna cum laude, 1995). Member, Order of the Coif. *Member:* State Bar of California. *PRACTICE AREAS:* Litigation.

**XIANCHUN J. VENDLER,** born Changde P.R., China, April 18, 1963; admitted to bar, 1995, California. *Education:* Beijing University (B.A., 1983); The Chinese Academy of Social Sciences (M.A., 1986); University of Texas, Austin (Ph.D., 1995); Loyola Marymount University (J.D., 1995). Member, St. Thomas More Honor Society, 1993-1995. *Member:* State Bar of California. *LANGUAGES:* Mandarin Chinese. *PRACTICE AREAS:* Corporate Law; Securities Law.

**MICHAEL A. MINDEN,** born Los Angeles, California, December 16, 1968; admitted to bar, 1995, California. *Education:* University of California at Los Angeles (B.A., cum laude, 1991); Loyola Marymount University (J.D., cum laude, 1995). Phi Delta Phi. Member, Order of the Coif. Staff Member, 1993-1994 and Articles Editor, 1994-1995, Loyola of Los Angeles Law Review. Recipient, American Jurisprudence Awards in Legal Writing and Ethics, Counseling and Negotiation. Extern to the Honorable William J. Rea, U.S. District Court, Central District of California, 1995. Member, St. Thomas More Law Honor Society. *Member:* State Bar of California. *PRACTICE AREAS:* Civil Litigation; Entertainment Litigation.

**JOSHUA D. HELDERMAN,** born Livingston, New Jersey, April 28, 1970; admitted to bar, 1995, California. *Education:* Duke University (B.S.B.A., 1992); Northwestern University (J.D., cum laude, 1995). *Member:* State Bar of California. *PRACTICE AREAS:* Litigation.

**SUBODH CHANDRA,** born Oklahoma City, Oklahoma, July 17, 1967; admitted to bar, 1995, New Mexico; 1996, California. *Education:* Stanford University (A.B., with honors and distinction in Sociology and Political Science, 1994); Yale University (J.D., 1994). Phi Beta Kappa; Alpha Kappa Delta. Executive Editor, Yale Law and Policy Review, 1993-1994. John Gardner Fellow, Haas Center for Public Service, Stanford University, 1989-1990. Aide: Ohio Governor Richard F. Celeste, 1990-1991; Oklahoma Governor David Walters, 1991; Texas Governor Ann Richards, 1992; Special Presidential Counsel, American Bar Association, 1994-1995. Outstanding Lawyer, New Mexico Bar Foundation and Albuquerque Bar Association, 1995. Board Member, KUNM Public Radio, Albuquerque, New Mexico, 1995-1996. *Member:* State Bar of New Mexico; State Bar of California; American Bar Association (Member, Sections on: Litigation; Criminal Justice; Member, Planning Board, Access to Justice Committee, Young Lawyers Division). *LANGUAGES:* Hindi. *PRACTICE AREAS:* General Litigation; Entertainment Litigation; Governmental Law; Defense Litigation. *Email:* subodhc@aol.com

**TONIE M. FRANZESE-DAMRON,** born Syracuse, New York, June 13, 1965; admitted to bar, 1996, Michigan and California. *Education:* University of Michigan (A.B., 1987); Detroit College of Law (J.D., 1995). Research Editor, Detroit College of Law Review, 1994-1995. Author: "United States v. James Daniel Good: Asset Forfeiture of Real Property and the 1993 Trilogy of Restraint," 1994, Detroit College of Law Rev., Issue IV. Law Clerk to Hon. Mario G. Recanzone, Third Judicial District, Nevada,

*(This Listing Continued)*

## CHRISTENSEN, MILLER, FINK, JACOBS, GLASER, WEIL AND SHAPIRO, LLP, Los Angeles—Continued

1995. *Member:* State Bar of Michigan; State Bar of California. **PRACTICE AREAS:** Litigation.

**BRENT D. BRADLEY,** born Napa, California, April 8, 1963; admitted to bar, 1996, California. *Education:* University of California, Riverside (B.A., 1992); Loyola Marymount University (J.D., 1996). *Member:* State Bar of California. **PRACTICE AREAS:** Corporate Law; Real Estate Law.

**PAMELA BRIAND,** born Detroit, Michigan; admitted to bar, 1996, California. *Education:* University of Nevada, Las Vegas (B.A., magna cum laude, 1993); New York University (J.D., 1996). *Member:* State Bar of California. **PRACTICE AREAS:** Litigation.

**FIONA A. BROPHY,** born Phoenix, Arizona, February 19, 1969; admitted to bar, 1996, California. *Education:* Georgetown University (B.S., 1991); University of California, Berkeley, Boalt Hall School of Law (J.D., 1996). *Member:* State Bar of California. **PRACTICE AREAS:** Litigation.

**ROBERT J. COMER,** born Libertyville, Illinois, August 1, 1963; admitted to bar, 1996, California. *Education:* California State University, Northridge (B.A., 1991); Loyola Marymount University (J.D., 1996). Member, Moot Court Honors Board. Articles Editor, Loyola University of Los Angeles Law Review, 1995-1996. Fellow, Coro Foundation, 1991-1992. *Member:* State Bar of California. **PRACTICE AREAS:** Real Estate Law; Land Use Law; Environmental Law.

**JULIE GIACOPUZZI,** born Fullerton, California, July 5, 1971; admitted to bar, 1996, California. *Education:* University of California, Los Angeles (B.A., 1993); University of Southern California (J.D., 1996). Member, Moot Court Honors Program, 1995-1996. *Member:* State Bar of California. **PRACTICE AREAS:** Litigation.

**DEBORAH R. GOLDBERG,** born California, January 21, 1968; admitted to bar, 1996, California. *Education:* Bryn Mawr College; Brown University (B.A., 1990); Freie University, Berlin, Germany; University of California, Los Angeles (J.D., 1996). Author: "Developments in German Abortion Law: A U.S. Perspective," 5 UCLA Women's L.J. 531, 1995. *Member:* State Bar of California. **LANGUAGES:** German. **PRACTICE AREAS:** Litigation.

**ADRIENNE W. GOLDSTONE,** born Philadelphia, Pennsylvania, May 12, 1953; admitted to bar, 1987, California. *Education:* University of Chicago (B.A., 1976); University of California at Los Angeles (J.D., 1987). Member, 1985-1986 and Executive, 1986-1987, Board of Editors, UCLA Law Review. *Member:* State Bar of California. **PRACTICE AREAS:** Corporations Law; Securities Law.

**JOHN E. HOFFMAN,** born Montreal, Quebec, Canada, January 21, 1947; admitted to bar, 1972, California, U.S. District Court, Central District of California and U.S. Court of Appeals, Ninth Circuit; 1986, U.S. Tax Court. *Education:* McGill University; University of Southern California (B.S.E.E., 1969; J.D., 1972). Tau Beta Pi; Eta Kappa Nu; Order of the Coif. Member, University of Southern California Law Review, 1970-1972. Member, Editorial Board, Los Angeles Bar Journal, 1974-1976. Author: Chapters, "Consent Judgments," and "Submitted Case," California Civil Procedure Before Trial, Vol. 2, California Continuing Education of the Bar, 1978; "Cross-Complaints," Civil Procedure Before Trial, California Continuing Education of the Bar, 1990. Consultant: "Complaints and Motions," Chapter in California Civil Practice-Procedure, Bancroft-Whitney, 1992; "Limited Partnerships," Chapter in California Civil Practice-Business Litigation, Bancroft-Whitney, 1992. *Member:* Los Angeles County (Member, 1974-1992 and Chairman, 1977-1978, Continuing Education of the Bar Committee) and American (Member, 1981-1987 and Chairman, 1983-1987, Important Developments Subcommittee, Committee on Civil and Criminal Tax Penalties, Tax Section) Bar Associations; Institute of Electrical and Electronic Engineers; Association of Business Trial Lawyers.

**JON M. KONHEIM,** born Santa Monica, California, June 17, 1970; admitted to bar, 1996, California. *Education:* University of Pennsylvania (B.A.B.S., 1993); Loyola Marymount University (J.D., 1996). Law Clerk to the Honorable Lisa Hill Fenning, Central District of California, 1996. *Member:* State Bar of California; American Bar Association. **PRACTICE AREAS:** Real Estate Law; Corporate Law.

**DONALD E. LEONHARDT,** born Los Angeles, California, March 1, 1968; admitted to bar, 1996, California. *Education:* University of California, San Diego (B.A., summa cum laude, 1991); University of California, Hastings College of the Law (J.D., 1996). Phi Alpha Delta. Member, Golden Key National Honor Society. *Member:* State Bar of California. **PRACTICE AREAS:** Litigation.

**D. MICHAEL OBERBECK,** born Evansville, Indiana, July 27, 1971; admitted to bar, 1996, California. *Education:* Purdue University (B.A., 1993); Northwestern University (J.D., 1996). Phi Beta Kappa. *Member:* State Bar of California. **PRACTICE AREAS:** Litigation.

**ERIC MICHAEL SHERMAN,** born Encino, California, August 31, 1971; admitted to bar, 1996, California. *Education:* University of California, Berkeley (B.A., 1993); University of Michigan (J.D., 1996). *Member:* State Bar of California. **LANGUAGES:** Spanish. **PRACTICE AREAS:** Litigation.

**MICHAEL W. WHITAKER,** born Harbor City, California, April 3, 1970; admitted to bar, 1996, California. *Education:* California State University, Fullerton (B.A., 1993); Boalt Hall School of Law, University of California, Berkeley (J.D., 1996). Member, Boalt Hall School of Law, University of California, Berkeley Law Review, 1994-1996. Recipient, American Jurisprudence Award, Constitutional Law, 1995. Teaching Assistant, Research and Writing, Boalt Hall School of Law, University of California, Berkeley, 1995. *Member:* State Bar of California. **PRACTICE AREAS:** Litigation.

**NORMAN Y. WONG,** born Sacramento, California, November 12, 1971; admitted to bar, 1996, California. *Education:* University of California, Berkeley (B.S., 1993); University of California, Los Angeles (J.D., 1996). *Member:* State Bar of California. **PRACTICE AREAS:** Litigation.

---

## CHRISTIE, PARKER & HALE, LLP
### LOS ANGELES, CALIFORNIA
(See Pasadena)

*Patent, Trademark and Copyright Law. Unfair Competition, Trade Secrets, Computer Law, Biotechnology, Licensing, Antitrust and Complex Business Litigation.*

---

## LAW OFFICES
## CHRYSTIE & BERLE
*A PROFESSIONAL CORPORATION*
**SUITE 2200, 1925 CENTURY PARK EAST**
### LOS ANGELES, CALIFORNIA 90067
Telephone: 310-788-7700
Fax: 310-201-0436

*General Civil, Trial and Appellate Practice in all State and Federal Courts. Bankruptcy and Insolvency Law, Entertainment, Commercial, Corporate, Banking, Financial Transactions, Real Estate.*

**STEPHEN CHRYSTIE,** born Albany, New York, September 7, 1936; admitted to bar, 1963, California. *Education:* University of California at Los Angeles (B.A., with honors, 1957); Harvard University (LL.B., cum laude, 1962). Panelist, U.S.C. Entertainment Law Institute, "Rules of the Game/Insolvency Law," 1992. Speaker, Los Angeles Bankruptcy Forum, "Involuntary Petitions: The Damoclean Sword of Bankruptcy," 1991. Co Author: "Insolvency and The Production and The Distribution of Entertainment Products," The Entertainment and Sports Lawyer (ABA, Vol. 6 No. 4, Spring, 1988). Los Angeles City Commissioner, 1974-1978 and President, City Employee's Retirement System, 1975-1977. President, Attorneys Division of the Anti-Defamation League, Los Angeles Chapter, 1983—. *Member:* Los Angeles County (Chairman, Commercial Law and Bankruptcy Section, 1973-1974) and American Bar Associations; The State Bar of California (Chairman, Committee on Relations of Debtor and Creditor, 1972-1973). **PRACTICE AREAS:** Financial Institutions Law; Entertainment Law; Bankruptcy Law.

**ELIHU M. BERLE,** born Brooklyn, New York, August 20, 1943; admitted to bar, 1970, California; 1973, U.S. Court of Appeals, Ninth Circuit and U.S. Supreme Court. *Education:* Brooklyn College of the City University of New York (B.A., cum laude, 1965); University of Pennsylvania (M.B.A., 1966); Columbia University (J.D., 1969). Law Clerk to Justice Aiso, California Court of Appeal, 1969-1970. State Bar Court Referee, 1982-1985. Arbitrator, Los Angeles Superior Court, 1982—. Speaker, Los Angeles Bankruptcy Forum, "Involuntary Petitions: The Damoclean Sword of Bankruptcy," 1991. Co-Chair, American Bar Association Litigation Section Committee on Commercial Banking and Financial Litigation Program

*(This Listing Continued)*

on "Confidentiality Agreements," 1988. California State Bar Litigation Section Panelist: "New Developing Theories of Tort Liability," 1987. California Continuing Education of the Bar Panelist: "Civil Procedure Before Trial," 1988 and 1990; "Preparing a Case For Trial: The Last 100 Days," 1984; "Depositions," 1983; "Handling The Short Non-Jury Trial," 1982. Author: "Applications and Motions," California Civil Appellate Practice (2nd Edition, 1985), California Continuing Education of the Bar; "The Case for the Master Calendar System," ABTL Report, Vol. IV, No. 1. Member, Los Angeles County Board of Supervisors Court Reform Task Force. *Member:* Los Angeles County (Member: Superior Court Committee, 1973-1979; Federal Courts Committee, 1977-1983) and American (Member, Litigation Section, Committee on Commercial Banking and Financial Transaction Litigation) Bar Associations; The State Bar of California (Litigation Section, Treasurer, 1988-1989; Member, Executive Committee, 1987-1990; Delegate, State Bar Conference of Delegates, 1987-1988); Association of Business Trial Lawyers (Member, Board of Governors 1979-1983; President, 1985-1986; Vice President, 1984-1985; Secretary, 1983-1984; Treasurer, 1982-1983). *PRACTICE AREAS:* Business Law; Commercial Litigation; Business Litigation.

**SHERILYN L. WILLIAMS** (1958-1994).

OF COUNSEL

**ARTHUR L. STASHOWER,** born Cleveland, Ohio, April 12, 1930; admitted to bar, 1953, Ohio and Michigan; 1957, California; 1962, U.S. Court of Appeals, Ninth Circuit. *Education:* University of Michigan (A.B., 1951; J.D., with distinction, 1953). Order of the Coif. Member, National Panel of Labor Arbitrators, American Arbitration Association, 1969—. Labor Arbitrator, Federal Mediation and Conciliation Service, 1972—. *Member:* Beverly Hills and American Bar Associations; The State Bar of California; State Bar of Michigan; Los Angeles Copyright Society (Trustee, 1986-1990). *PRACTICE AREAS:* Entertainment Law; Labor Arbitration Law.

## CITRON & DEUTSCH
*A LAW CORPORATION*

SUITE 970, WESTWOOD PLACE
10866 WILSHIRE BOULEVARD
**LOS ANGELES, CALIFORNIA 90024**
Telephone: 310-475-0321
Fax: 310-475-1368
URL: http://www.candlaw.globalcenter.net

*Entrepreneurial Business Law, General Business Law including formation, purchase and sale of businesses, and Wills and Trusts, Estate Planning, Real Estate Transactions and Employment Law.*

**RICHARD K. CITRON,** born Queens, New York, February 9, 1945; admitted to bar, 1970, California. *Education:* University of California at Berkeley (B.S., 1966; M.B.A., 1967); University of California at Los Angeles (J.D., 1970). Moot Court Honors Program, 1968. Assistant Professor of Law at Western State University, 1970-1973. Assistant Professor of Business, Business Law, Marketing and Statistics at California State University at Northridge, 1968-1973. National lecturer on law office technology. *Member:* Los Angeles County Bar Association; State Bar of California.

**DAVID R. DEUTSCH,** born Queens, New York, April 4, 1949; admitted to bar, 1978, California and U.S. District Court, Central District of California; 1979, U.S. District Court, Southern District of California. *Education:* Queens College (B.A., 1971); Temple University (M.A., Psychology, 1974); University of California at Los Angeles (J.D., 1978). Phi Beta Kappa. Extern for the Honorable William P. Gray, Judge, U.S. District Court, Central District of California, 1978. Member, University of California at Los Angeles Law Review, 1977-1978. *Member:* Los Angeles County Bar Association; State Bar of California.

## LAW OFFICES OF JOEL F. CITRON
**LOS ANGELES, CALIFORNIA**

(See Santa Monica)

*Insurance Defense Law, General Civil Trial Practice, Environmental Coverage, Construction Defect, Products Liability, Personal Injury, Business Torts, Professional Negligence and Complex Litigation in all State and Federal Courts.*

## ELFORD H. CLARK
1910 WEST SUNSET BOULEVARD, SUITE 200
**LOS ANGELES, CALIFORNIA 90026**
Telephone: 213-484-1925
Fax: 213-484-4471
Email: mopar__49@ix.netcom.com

*Probate and Estate Planning, Conservatorship, Bus Transactions, Corporations, Non-Profit Organizations.*

**ELFORD H. CLARK,** born Memphis, Tennessee, June 19, 1948; admitted to bar, 1989, California. *Education:* University of Florida (B.A., 1971); Western State University (J.D., cum laude, 1989). Adjunct Professor, Western State University, 1990-1992. *Member:* Los Angeles and American Bar Associations; State Bar of California (Member, Probate and Estate Section); Christian Legal Society. *PRACTICE AREAS:* Probate; Estate Planning; Religious Nonprofit Corporation Law; Personal Injury.

CORPORATE COUNSEL FOR: The International Church of The Foursquare Gospel.

## JAMES DEXTER CLARK
**LOS ANGELES, CALIFORNIA**

(See Pasadena)

*Municipal Law, Eminent Domain, Economic Development and Redevelopment.*

## CLARK & TREVITHICK
*A PROFESSIONAL CORPORATION*

Established in 1977

800 WILSHIRE BOULEVARD, 12TH FLOOR
**LOS ANGELES, CALIFORNIA 90017**
Telephone: 213-629-5700
Telecopier: 213-624-9441

*San Francisco, California Office:* 456 Montgomery Street, 20th Floor.
Telephone: 415-288-6520. Fax: 415-398-2820.

*General Business Practice and Litigation Practice in all State and Federal Courts and Arbitration Tribunals. General Corporate, Corporate Securities and Finance, Mergers and Acquisitions, Venture Capital, Federal, State and Local Taxation, Estate Planning, Trusts and Probate, Partnerships, Real Estate, Real Estate Leasing, Real Estate Finance and Land Use, Pension and Profit Sharing, Antitrust and Trade Regulation Litigation, General Business and Commercial Litigation, Banking, Credit Law, Bankruptcy, Creditors Rights, Collateral Recovery and Financial Institutions Law, Employer-Employee Litigation, Insurance Defense and Personal Injury Litigation, Products Liability Litigation, Real Estate Litigation, Securities Litigation, Unfair Competition and Trade Secrets Litigation; Sports Law.*

*FIRM PROFILE: The firm generally represents small and medium sized businesses, entrepreneurs and other individuals as well as a smaller number of banks and other financial institutions, large corporations and insurers in a broad range of civil contexts, relying on the high level of experience and expertise of its attorneys. The firm was founded with an emphasis on personalized service and close client relationships without the inefficiencies, bureaucracy, attorney turnover and other burdens of large firms. To this end, the firm refrains from employing inexperienced attorneys but does employ full and part-time paralegals.*

**DONALD P. CLARK,** born Los Angeles, California, October 4, 1935; admitted to bar, 1960, California. *Education:* Stanford University (A.B., 1956); University of Southern California (LL.B., 1959). Phi Delta Phi. *Member:* Los Angeles County and American Bar Associations; The State Bar of California. *PRACTICE AREAS:* General Corporate; Corporate Securities and Finance; Mergers and Acquisitions; Venture Capital.

**ALEXANDER C. McGILVRAY, JR.,** born Pasadena, California, February 3, 1949; admitted to bar, 1974, California. *Education:* Stanford University (A.B., 1971); University of California at Los Angeles (J.D., 1974). *Member:* Los Angeles County and American Bar Associations; The State Bar of California (Member, Business Law Section). *PRACTICE AREAS:* General Corporate; Corporate Securities and Finance; Mergers and Acquisitions; Venture Capital.

*(This Listing Continued)*

CAA589B

**CLARK & TREVITHICK, A PROFESSIONAL CORPORATION,**
*Los Angeles—Continued*

**PHILIP W. BARTENETTI,** born Tacoma, Washington, May 26, 1942; admitted to bar, 1971, California. *Education:* University of San Francisco (B.S., 1964); Hastings College of Law, University of California (J.D., 1970). Order of the Coif. Editor, Hastings Law Journal, 1969-1970. President, Hastings College of Law Alumni Association, 1982-1983. *Member:* Los Angeles County (Member, Board of Trustees, 1984-1986) and American Bar Associations; The State Bar of California (Member, Judicial Nominee Evaluation Commission, 1990—; Chair, 1993); Association of Business Trial Lawyers. *PRACTICE AREAS:* General Business Litigation; Commercial Litigation; Insurance Litigation; Securities Litigation; Unfair Competition Litigation; Trade Secrets Litigation.

**KEVIN P. FIORE,** born Los Angeles, California, December 12, 1942; admitted to bar, 1970, California. *Education:* Loyola University of Los Angeles (B.B.A., 1964; J.D., 1969). Phi Alpha Delta. Member, St. Thomas More Law Honor Society. Certified Public Accountant, California, 1967. Member, Board of Governors, Loyola Law School, 1980-1989. *Member:* Los Angeles County Bar Association; State Bar of California; Italian American Lawyers Association. *PRACTICE AREAS:* Real Estate; Real Estate Leasing; Real Estate Finance; Land Use.

**DOLORES CORDELL,** born Los Angeles, California, July 31, 1947; admitted to bar, 1977, California. *Education:* University of California at Berkeley (B.A., 1972); University of Southern California (J.D., 1977). Best Oral Advocate and Best Brief, Hale Moot Court Competition, 1975-1976; Outstanding Oral Advocate, Traynor State Moot Court Competition, 1977. Member, Moot Court Board, 1976-1977. *Member:* Los Angeles County (Chairperson, Prejudgment Remedies Section, 1986-1987) and American Bar Associations; The State Bar of California; Los Angeles Women Lawyers Association. *PRACTICE AREAS:* General Business Litigation; Commercial Litigation; Collections Litigation; Employer-Employee Litigation; Unfair Competition; Trade Secrets Litigation.

**VINCENT TRICARICO,** born New York, N.Y., May 1, 1942; admitted to bar, 1972, New York; 1973, U.S. Court of Appeals, First and Seventh Circuits; 1974, U.S. Court of Appeals for the District of Columbia Circuit; 1977, District of Columbia; 1985, California. *Education:* St. John's University (B.A., 1968); St. John's University School of Law (J.D., 1971). Attorney, General Counsel's Office, Federal Trade Commission, 1971-1973. *Member:* Los Angeles County, New York State and American Bar Associations; The State Bar of California; District of Columbia Bar. [With U.S. Army, 1959-1962]. *PRACTICE AREAS:* General Business Litigation; Commercial Litigation; Antitrust Litigation; Unfair Competition Litigation; Securities Litigation.

**JOHN A. LAPINSKI,** born Rochester, New York, March 4, 1947; admitted to bar, 1976, California; U.S. Supreme Court. *Education:* Pennsylvania State University (B.S., 1969); University of West Los Angeles School of Law (J.D., 1976). Recipient, American Jurisprudence Award in Bankruptcy Law. Author: "Making the Creditor Secure," Los Angeles Lawyer, January, 1981; "The New Rules For Now," Los Angeles Lawyer, February, 1984. Co-Author: "Special Enforcement Remedies: Turnover and Assignment Orders," Beverly Hills Bar Association Journal, September 1987. Member: Section of Commercial Law and Bankruptcy; Bicentennial of the Constitution Committee, Trustee, 1989-1990) Los Angeles County Bar Association. *Member:* Federal (Los Angeles Chapter: President, 1983-1984; National Association, Ninth Circuit, Vice-President, 1985-1989); State Bar of California (Member, Business Law Section, Creditor/Debtor and Bankruptcy Law; Chair, 1983-1984; Member, Federal Courts Committee, 1984-1987); Lawyers Club of Los Angeles County (Member, Board of Governors, 1984-1989; President, 1986-1987); Financial Lawyers Conference; Bankruptcy Study Group. *PRACTICE AREAS:* Banking; Credit Law; Bankruptcy; Creditors Rights; Collateral Recovery; Financial Institutions Law.

**LEONARD BRAZIL,** born Mallow, Ireland, May 6, 1957; admitted to bar, 1982, California. *Education:* University of Southern California (B.S., cum laude, 1979); Loyola Marymount University (J.D., 1982). First Place, Loyola Law School Trial Advocacy Competition, 1982. Representative, National Trial Advocacy Competition, 1982. *Member:* Los Angeles County and American Bar Associations; The State Bar of California; Association of Business Trial Lawyers. *PRACTICE AREAS:* General Business Litigation; Commercial Litigation; Products Liability Litigation; Unfair Competition Law; Trade Secrets Litigation.

**DEAN I. FRIEDMAN,** born Los Angeles, California, January 27, 1950; admitted to bar, 1976, California; 1977, U.S. Tax Court; 1985, U.S. Claims Court. *Education:* University of Southern California (A.B., 1971); Southwestern University (J.D., cum laude, 1974); Georgetown University (LL.M., 1975). Recipient: American Jurisprudence Award; Wall Street Journal Student Achievement Award. Co-Author: "Centralizing the International Operations of Multinationals," 11 San Diego Law Review, 1974. Lecturer: California Continuing Education of the Bar, 1985; Los Angeles County Bar Association, 1986-1992; State Bar of California, 1993. Treasurer and Member, Executive Committee, California Museum Foundation Advisory Board of the California Museum of Science and Industry, 1988-1991. Chairman, Taxation Law Advisory Commission, California Board of Legal Specialization, 1988—. Member, California Board of Legal Specialization, 1991—. *Member:* Los Angeles County (Member, Taxation Section and Member, Pass-Through Entities Committee, Taxation Section, 1990—) and American (Member, Sections on: Taxation; International Law) Bar Associations; The State Bar of California (Member, Section on Taxation). (Certified Specialist, Taxation Law, The State Bar of California Board of Legal Specialization). *PRACTICE AREAS:* Federal, State and Local Taxation; Estate Planning; Trusts and Probate.

**ROBERT F. DEMETER,** born Cleveland, Ohio, September 11, 1948; admitted to bar, 1975, District of Columbia, Ohio and U.S. Tax Court; 1977, California. *Education:* The Ohio State University (B.A., 1971); American University (J.D., 1974); Georgetown University (LL.M. in Taxation, 1976). Editor: American University Law Review, 1973-1974; The Tax Lawyer, 1976. Author: "Lobbying by Section 501 (c) (3) Organizations Under the Tax Reform Act of 1976," 30 Tax Lawyer 214, 1976; "Tax Planning For Commercial and Industrial Condominiums," 15 Beverly Hills Bar Association Journal 639, 1981. Chair, California Board of Legal Specialization, 1990. *Member:* Century City (President, 1985; Member, Board of Governors, 1981-1987) and Los Angeles County (Member, Board of Trustees, 1986-1987; Chairman, Pro Bono Taxpayer Services Committee, 1985-1987) Bar Associations; The State Bar of California. (Certified Specialist, Taxation Law, The State Bar of California Board of Legal Specialization). *PRACTICE AREAS:* Taxation Law; Business Law; Estate Planning Law.

**MICHAEL K. WOFFORD,** born Palo Alto, California, February 25, 1959; admitted to bar, 1986, California; 1987, U.S. District Court, Central District of California. *Education:* University of Southern California (B.S., 1981); Loyola Marymount University (J.D., 1986). Business Editor, Loyola Law School Entertainment Law Journal, 1985-1986. Author: Comment, "Evangelical Broadcasting: FCC Investigation of Use of Donations Does Not Infringe First Amendment Rights," Loyola Law School Entertainment Law Journal, Vol. V 1985. *Member:* Los Angeles County and American Bar Associations; The State Bar of California. *PRACTICE AREAS:* General Corporate; Corporate Securities and Finance; Mergers and Acquisitions.

**LESLIE R. HOROWITZ,** born Los Angeles, California, July 6, 1954; admitted to bar, 1981, California. *Education:* Occidental College (A.B., 1976); Southwestern University School of Law (J.D., 1980). Co-Author: "Special Enforcement Remedies: Turnover and Assignment Orders," Beverly Hills Bar Association Journal, September, 1986. Instructor, Civil Trial Practice, CEB, 1990. Member, Immigration Project, Los Angeles County Bar Association, 1982-1983. *Member:* Federal Bar Association (Member, 1990 Convention Committee; Executive Committee, Bankruptcy); Los Angeles Chapter Board of Directors, 1990—; Treasurer, 1992-1993; Financial Lawyers Conference; Lawyers Club of Los Angeles (Board Member, 1987—; President-Elect, 1990-1991). *PRACTICE AREAS:* Banking; Credit Law; Bankruptcy; Creditors Rights; Collateral Recovery.

**BRENT A. REINKE,** born Orange, California, May 7, 1961; admitted to bar, 1988, California. *Education:* Occidental College (A.B., 1984); Loyola Law School, Los Angeles (J.D., 1988). Omicron Delta Epsilon. Recipient, American Jurisprudence Award. Extern for the Honorable Judge Ideman, U.S. District Court, Central District of California. *Member:* Los Angeles County and American Bar Associations; State Bar of California (Member, Business Law Section); Sports Lawyers Association. *PRACTICE AREAS:* General Corporate; Mergers and Acquisitions; Corporate Securities and Finance.

**ARTURO SANTANA JR.,** born Pt. Hueneme, California, April 7, 1960; admitted to bar, 1987, California. *Education:* University of California at Los Angeles (B.A., 1983; J.D., 1986). *Member:* Los Angeles County Bar Association; State Bar of California. *LANGUAGES:* Spanish. *PRACTICE AREAS:* General Business Litigation; Commercial Litigation; Unfair Competition Litigation; Trade Secrets Litigation; Insurance Defense and Personal Injury Litigation.

**KERRY T. RYAN,** born Fort Wayne, Indiana, September 13, 1959; admitted to bar, 1987, California; 1988, U.S. District Court, Central District of California. *Education:* Indiana University (B.S., 1981); University of

*(This Listing Continued)*

Florida (J.D., 1987). Order of the Coif. Author: "Using the Uniform Commercial Code to Protect the 'Ideas' that Make the Movies," Santa Clara Law Review, Vol. 27, No. 4, 1987. *Member:* Los Angeles County Bar Association (Member, Intellectual Property and Unfair Competition Section); State Bar of California. **PRACTICE AREAS:** General Business Litigation; Commercial Litigation; Unfair Competition Litigation; Trade Secrets Litigation.

**JAMES S. ARICO,** born Los Angeles, California, November 23, 1958; admitted to bar, 1987, California. *Education:* University of Southern California (B.S., 1981); Loyola Marymount University (J.D., 1986). Member, Loyola Marymount Law Review, 1984-1986. Author: "NCAA vs. Board of Regents of the University of Oklahoma: Has the Supreme Court Abrogated the Per Se Rule of Antitrust Analysis?" 19 Loyola Marymount Law Review, No. 2, December 1985, article selected by West Publishing Co. for reproduction in Westlaw Computer Research Service. *Member:* State Bar of California; American Bar Association. **PRACTICE AREAS:** Real Estate; Real Estate Leasing; Sports Law; General Corporate.

*OF COUNSEL*

**JOHN A. TUCKER, JR.,** born Los Angeles, California, May 2, 1932; admitted to bar, 1961, California; 1971, District of Columbia. *Education:* Stanford University (A.B., 1954); University of Denver (J.D., 1959). Phi Delta Phi; Omicron Delta Kappa. Member, Board of Editors, University of Denver Law Review, 1958-1959. *Member:* Los Angeles County and American Bar Associations; District of Columbia Bar; The State Bar of California. (Also practicing individually). **PRACTICE AREAS:** Real Estate Law; Land Use; Estate Planning; Trusts and Probate Law.

**JUDITH ILENE BLOOM,** born Los Angeles, California, December 5, 1950; admitted to bar, 1975, California. *Education:* University of California at Santa Barbara (B.A., cum laude, 1972); Loyola University Law School (J.D., cum laude, 1975); University of California at Los Angeles (M.B.A., 1983). Member, Mortarboard. Note and Comment Editor, Loyola Law Review, 1974-1975. Author: "RICO Damages," Chapter of Damages in Business Litigation, 1990; "Minimizing Bank Liability for Criminal Assaults on Customers," March-April 1988, Banking L. J., 151; "Ethical Dilemmas In Corporate Representation," Los Angeles Lawyer 1987; "Protecting Experts' Reports," Los Angeles Lawyer 1985; "Right to Nonjury Trial for Trust and Probate Issues," Los Angeles Lawyer 1984; "The Work Product Doctrine," Los Angeles Lawyer, 1983; "Los Angeles Superior Court Management Information System," 1983. Member, Board of Governors, 1985— and President, 1990-1991, Loyola Alumni Association. Member, Trial Lawyers Section Executive Committee, 1980—; Treasurer, 1984-1985; Vice Chair, 1985-1986; Chair, 1986-1987; Bicentennial of the Constitution Committee; Co-Chair, 1985-1987; Los Angeles Lawyer, Chair Editorial Board, 1983-1984; Chair, Continuing Education Committee, 1985-1986, Los Angeles County Bar Association. Consultant to Bancroft Whitney's California Civil Practice. *Member:* Association of Business Trial Lawyers (Member, Board of Governors, 1985-1987). **PRACTICE AREAS:** Banking; Bankruptcy; Creditors Rights; Collateral Recovery; Financial Institutions Law.

REFERENCES: Wells Fargo Bank (Los Angeles Main Office); National Bank of California.

## CLARKSON & GORE
### LOS ANGELES, CALIFORNIA
(See Torrance)

*Bankruptcy, Corporate Reorganization, Debtor-Creditor Matters, Civil Litigation, Commercial Law, Corporate Law and Real Estate.*

## RICHARD D. CLEARY
**601 WEST FIFTH STREET, 8TH FLOOR**
**LOS ANGELES, CALIFORNIA 90071-2094**
Telephone: 213-627-0464
Telecopier: 213-627-1964

*Civil Trials and Appeals in all Courts. Business Litigation, Trust and Estate Litigation.*

**RICHARD D. CLEARY,** born Bridgeport, Connecticut, 1952; admitted to bar, 1981, New York; 1989, California. *Education:* Georgetown University (B.S.F.S., 1975; J.D., cum laude, 1980). Member, Georgetown Law Journal, 1978-1980. Judicial Law Clerk, Hon. Murray M. Schwartz, U.S.

*(This Listing Continued)*

District Court, District of Delaware, 1980-1981. *Member:* Los Angeles County and American Bar Associations; Los Angeles Complex Litigation Inn of Court.

## RICHARD R. CLEMENTS
*A PROFESSIONAL CORPORATION*
### LOS ANGELES, CALIFORNIA
(See Los Angeles)

*Bankruptcy, Insolvency Counseling and Commercial Law.*

## CLINNIN & CLINNIN
*A Partnership including a Professional Corporation*
**SUITE 2875**
**333 SOUTH GRAND AVENUE**
### LOS ANGELES, CALIFORNIA 90071
Telephone: 213-895-4343
FAX: 213-895-4423

*General Civil, Trial and Appellate Practice in All State and Federal Courts. Products Liability and Negligence Law. Administrative, Insurance, Corporate and Real Property Law.*

FIRM PROFILE: Clinnin & Clinnin is a service oriented law firm providing experienced individual, partnership and corporate representation.

We are an established civil litigation practice with extensive jury trial, court trial, administrative hearing, arbitration and mediation experience. The members of the firm alo offer qualified representation in transactional matters, including contract negotiation and formation, real estate law, intellectual property protection and regulatory law.

We emphasize cost efficient and effective representation of corporate and individual legal interests.

*MEMBERS OF FIRM*

**ROBERT G. CLINNIN, (A PROFESSIONAL CORPORATION),** born Oak Park, Illinois, November 13, 1923; admitted to bar, 1954, California. *Education:* University of Arizona; Loyola University; Loyola University of Los Angeles (LL.B., 1953). Phi Alpha Delta. Member, 1960-1961 and President, 1961-1962, Board of Governors, Loyola Law School Alumni Association. *Member:* Los Angeles County and American Bar Associations; The State Bar of California. Advocate, American Board of Trial Advocates (President, Los Angeles Chapter, 1982-1983). Fellow, International Academy of Trial Fellow Lawyers. Fellow, American College of Trial Lawyers. **PRACTICE AREAS:** Insurance Defense; Products Liability; Civil Trial Litigation.

**MARK G. CLINNIN,** born Los Angeles, California, July 30, 1955; admitted to bar, 1988, California and U.S. District Court, Central District of California. *Education:* Fort Lewis College; University of Santa Clara (B.A., 1978); Southwestern University School of Law (J.D., 1987). Licensed Private Investigator, 1983. *Member:* Los Angeles County Bar Association; State Bar of California. **PRACTICE AREAS:** Insurance Defense; Consumer Litigation Defense; Products Liability; Civil Trial Litigation.

**JOHN A. CLINNIN,** born Los Angeles, California, November 22, 1959; admitted to bar, 1991, California and U.S. District Court, Central District of California. *Education:* San Diego State University (B.A., 1985); Whittier College School of Law (J.D., 1990). *Member:* Los Angeles County Bar Association; State Bar of California. **PRACTICE AREAS:** Insurance Defense; Consumer Litigation Defense; Products Liability; Civil Trial Litigation.

REPRESENTATIVE CLIENTS: Chrysler Corp.; Alfa Romeo Distributors of North America; Cagiva North American, Inc.; Weber Trucking and Distribution; Van Pool Services, Inc.; Truesdail Laboratories, Inc.; Steve P. Rados Construction; Dana Corp.; Chumo Construction; Gallager Bassett Services; Hartford Insurance Co.; Home Insurance Co.

# CLOPTON, PENNY & BRENNER, A P.C.

1055 WEST SEVENTH STREET, SUITE 3000
**LOS ANGELES, CALIFORNIA 90017-2570**
Telephone: 213-629-6680
Fax: 213-629-6668
Email: steveb@cpandb.com

*Workers Compensation Defense and Subrogation.*

**THEODORE A. PENNY,** born Los Angeles, California, February 3, 1950; admitted to bar, 1974, California. *Education:* University of California at Los Angeles (A.B., cum laude, 1971); University of Southern California (J.D., 1974). Lecturer, UCLA Extension and California Manufacturers Association, 1981—. Member, Technical Advisor: California Manufacturers Association; Workers Compensation Committee, California Chamber of Commerce, 1994. *Member:* Los Angeles County (Member, Executive Board, Workers Compensation Section) and American Bar Associations; State Bar of California. (Certified Specialist, Workers Compensation Law, The State Bar of California Board of Legal Specialization). **PRACTICE AREAS:** Workers Compensation; Defense; Subrogation. *Email:* TedP@CPandB.com

**STEVEN G. BRENNER,** born Chicago, Illinois, August 10, 1949; admitted to bar, 1974, California and U.S. District Court, Central District of California. *Education:* University of California at Los Angeles (A.B., cum laude, 1971); Loyola University School of Law (J.D., 1974). President, UCLA Pre-Law Society, Member, National Law Honor Society. Finalist and Member, Loyola National Moot Court Team. Member, Presiding Judge's Attorney Advisory Committee, 1983-1985. Judge Pro Tem, 1984—. *Member:* State Bar of California; California Workers' Compensation Defense Attorneys Association. **PRACTICE AREAS:** Workers Compensation; Defense; Subrogation. *Email:* SteveB@CPandB.com

**RONALD R. KOLLITZ,** born Chicago, Illinois, February 15, 1950; admitted to bar, 1974, California and U.S. District Court, Central District of California. *Education:* University of California at Los Angeles (B.A., cum laude, 1971; J.D., 1974). Pi Gamma Mu; Psi Chi. Senior Member, UCLA-Alaska Law Review, 1973-1974. Technical Editor, Hampton, "Workers' Compensation Claims-Desk Book 2," (1993). Associate Adjunct Professor of Law, Southwestern University School of Law, 1978-1979. Clinical Assistant Professor of Psychiatry and the Behavioral Sciences, University of Southern California Department of Psychiatry, 1978. Lecturer: USC School of Law, Advanced Professional Program-Workers Compensation, 1982—; "Recent Developments in Workers Compensation Practice," California Continuing Education of the Bar, 1987. Senior Attorney, WCAB Writs, Court of Appeal, State of California, Second Appellate District, 1977-1981. Workers Compensation Judge, 1981-1983 and Presiding Workers Compensation Judge, 1983-1985, State of California, Workers Compensation Appeals Board, Los Angeles District Office. Special Counsel, Workers Compensation Advisory Committee to the California Assembly, 1986. *Member:* Los Angeles County Bar Association (Member, Section on Workers Compensation); The State Bar of California (Member, Sections on Labor Law and Workers Compensation). (Certified Specialist, Workers Compensation Law, The State Bar of California Board of Legal Specialization). **PRACTICE AREAS:** Workers Compensation; Defense; Subrogation. *Email:* RonK@CPandB.com

---

**LOUISE G. MORSE,** born Los Angeles, California, June 16, 1947; admitted to bar, 1974, California. *Education:* California State University, Northridge (B.A., 1970); Southwestern University School of Law (J.D., 1973). (Certified Specialist, Workers Compensation Law, California Board of Legal Specialization). *Email:* LouiseM@CPandB.com

**MARLENE C. TASSONE,** born Youngstown, Ohio, March 24, 1941; admitted to bar, 1975, California; 1976, Texas; 1982, U.S. Supreme Court, U.S. District Court, Southern, Central and Northern Districts of California and U.S. District Court, Western District of Texas. *Education:* California State University at San Diego (A.B., 1963); Southwestern University School of Law (J.D., 1974). *Email:* MarleneT@CPandB.com

**GARY PAUL ANDRÉ,** born Highland Park, Michigan, April 17, 1950; admitted to bar, 1983, California. *Education:* Michigan State University (B.S., 1972); University of San Fernando Valley (J.D., 1979). *Email:* GaryA@CPandB.com

**JAY A. SIEGEL,** born Fort Lauderdale, Florida, June 2, 1951; admitted to bar, 1988, California. *Education:* Florida State University (B.A., 1974); Southwestern University School of Law (J.D., 1985). *Email:* JayS@CPandB.com

*(This Listing Continued)*

**GARY A. KANTER,** born Los Angeles, California, January 18, 1947; admitted to bar, 1972, California. *Education:* University of Arizona (B.A., 1968); Loyola Marymount University (J.D., 1971). *Email:* GaryK@CPandB.com

**ELLIOTT KUSHNER,** born Winnipeg, Canada, July 22, 1950; admitted to bar, 1975, California. *Education:* University of California, Los Angeles (A.B., magna cum laude, 1972); Loyola Marymount University (J.D., 1975). *Email:* ElliotK@CPandB.com

**ANDREW W. BARCLAY,** born Pasadena, California, November 15, 1938; admitted to bar, 1965, California. *Education:* Pasadena City College (A.A., 1958); University of California at Los Angeles (B.A., 1961); Hastings College of Law, University of California (LL.B., 1964). (Certified Specialist, Workers Compensation Law, The State Bar of California Board of Legal Specialization). *Email:* AndyB@CPandB.com

**R. RANDOLPH RECK,** born Burbank, California, April 19, 1953; admitted to bar, 1980, California. *Education:* University of California, Los Angeles (B.S., cum laude, 1975); Southwestern University School of Law (J.D., 1979). *Email:* Randolph@CPandB.com

**PENNY R. HAND,** born Los Angeles, California, September 23, 1941; admitted to bar, 1992, California. *Education:* University of Southern California (B.A., cum laude, 1980); University of West Los Angeles (J.D., 1991). *Email:* PennyH@CPandB.com

**GILBERT KATEN,** born Los Angeles, California, October 26, 1944; admitted to bar, 1970, California, U.S. District Court, Central District of California, U.S. Court of Appeals, Ninth Circuit and U.S. Supreme Court. *Education:* University of California, Los Angeles (B.S., 1966); University of California School of Law, Los Angeles (J.D., 1969). **LANGUAGES:** Spanish, English. *Email:* GilK@CPandB.com

**JAMES C. SPOERI,** born Chicago, Illinois, 1952; admitted to bar, 1977, Illinois; 1990, California. *Education:* Marquette University (B.A., 1974); Loyola University (J.D., 1977). *Email:* James@CPandB.com

**DENNIS N. ROMAN,** born Cleveland, Ohio, 1944; admitted to bar, 1975, California. *Education:* Ohio State University (B.S.); Whittier College of Law (J.D., 1974).

REPRESENTATIVE CLIENTS: The Walt Disney Co.; Southern California Gas Co.; Chevron Corp.; Ralph's Grocery Co.; Weyerhaeuser Co.; Los Angeles Times; Nordstrom, Inc.; Mattel Toys, Inc.; Hughes Aircraft Co.; Lockheed Martin Co,; Northrop Grumman Corp.; Hughes Family Markets; Chicago Bridge & Iron Co.; Atlantic Richfield Co.; Chubb Group of Insurance Cos.; Golden Eagle Insurance Co.; Industrial Indemnity Co.; Cigna.

---

# LAW OFFICES OF JOHNNIE L. COCHRAN, JR.

*A PROFESSIONAL CORPORATION*

Established in 1982

4929 WILSHIRE BOULEVARD, SUITE 1010
**LOS ANGELES, CALIFORNIA 90010**
Telephone: 213-931-6200
Fax: 213-931-9521

*Washington, D.C. Office:* 201 Massachusetts Avenue, N.E. Capitol Hill West Building, 20002. Telephone: 202-547-9225.

*Personal Injury, Entertainment, Sports Law, Civil Litigation, Employment, Criminal and Civil Rights Law, Mass Tort Litigation.*

*FIRM PROFILE: The Law Offices of Johnnie L. Cochran, Jr. has established itself nationwide as a full-service law firm on the cutting-edge of modern day trial practice and technology. The firm has solidified its standing as a bedrock of the legal community via its record-breaking multimillion dollar jury awards in precedent setting police misconduct cases and through its diverse roster of stellar clientele such as Michael Jackson, Aretha Franklin and O.J. Simpson. Founded in 1981, offices are located in both Los Angeles and Washington, D.C. The Cochran firm is composed of seasoned trial and transactional attorneys. The firm provides services in civil rights and personal injury litigation; criminal defense; sports and entertainment as well as negotiating and arbitrating contractual disputes. Cochran Consulting International is the newest division of the Law Offices of Johnnie L. Cochran, Jr. Cochran Consulting specializes in business and governmental affairs and represents large multi-national corporation, as well as small businesses in the United States, South Africa and Europe. Cochran Consulting International facilitates strategic interaction at the local, state, federal, national and international levels.*

*(This Listing Continued)*

**JOHNNIE L. COCHRAN, JR.,** born Shreveport, Louisiana, October 2, 1937; admitted to bar, 1963, California; 1966, U.S. District Court, Western District of Texas; 1968, U.S. Supreme Court. *Education:* University of California at Los Angeles (B.S., 1959); Loyola University (J.D., 1962); University of Southern California. Recipient: Criminal Trial Lawyer of the Year, Los Angles Criminal Courts Bar Association, 1977; Pioneer of Black Legal Leadership Award, Los Angeles Brotherhood Crusade, August 1979; Outstanding Law Enforcement Office of 1979, California Trial Lawyers Association; Trial Lawyer of the Year, Hon. Loren Miller Award, John M Langston Bar Association, 1982-1983; Equal Justice in Law Award, Legal Defense Fund, National Association for the Advancement of Colored People; Distinguished Alumni Award, UCLA Black Alumni Association, March 1988; Alumni Award of Excellence in Professional Achievement, UCLA, June 1988; Outstanding Criminal Defense Attorneys, Southern California, July 1989; Trial Lawyer of the Year, The Los Angeles Trial Lawyers Association, January 1991; Trial Lawyer of the Year Award, Criminal Courts Bar Association, 1977; 1990 Trial Lawyer of the Year; Kappa Alpha Psi, 1991; Civil Rights Lawyer of the Year Award, L.A. Chapter of the NAACP Legal Defense Fund; Presidential Award, L.A. Chapter of the NAACP; Lifetime Achievement Award, Pasadena Branch, NAACP, 1991; Man of the Year, Los Angeles International Airport Kiwanis Club, 1991. Deputy City Attorney, Criminal Division, City of Los Angeles, 1963-1965. Assistant District Attorney of Los Angeles County, 1978-1982. Former Adjunct Professor of Law: Trial Tactics and Techniques, UCLA School of Law and Loyola University, School of Law. Member, Board of Directors: Los Angeles Urban League; Oscar Joel Bryant Foundation; 28th Street Y.M.C.A., L.A. Family Housing Corp.; Los Angeles African American Chamber of Commerce; Airport Commissioners City of Los Angeles; American Civil Liberties Union Foundation of Southern California; Lawyers Mutual Insurance Company. Special Counsel, Chairman of the Rules Committee, Democratic National Convention, June 1984. Special Counsel, Committee on Standard of Official Conduct (Ethics Committee) House of Representatives, 99th Congress. Lawyer Representative, Central District of California, Ninth Circuit Judicial Conference, August 1990. President, Black Business Association of Los Angeles, California, 1989. *Member:* State Bar of California (Co-Chair, Board of Legal Service Corps., 1993); American College of Trial Lawyers. Fellow, American Bar Foundation. *PRACTICE AREAS:* Personal Injury; Entertainment; Sports Law; Professional Liability; Business Litigation; Mass Tort Litigation; Criminal Law; Civil Rights Law.

**CARL E. DOUGLAS,** born New Haven, Connecticut, May 8, 1955; admitted to bar, 1980, California; 1981, U.S. District Court, Central District of California; 1987, U.S. District Court, Southern District of California. *Education:* Northwestern University (B.S., Political Science and Sociology, 1977); University of California, Boalt Hall School of Law (J.D., 1980). Recipient: Loren Miller Lawyer of the Year, 1994. Employment: Federal Communications Commission, Washington, D.C., 1980-1981; Federal Public Defender's Office, Los Angeles, California, 1981-1987. *Member:* Los Angeles County and American Bar Association; State Bar of California; California Association of Black Lawyers; John M. Langston Bar Association (Former Board Member). *PRACTICE AREAS:* Civil Rights Litigation; Personal Injury; Business Litigation; Entertainment Litigation; Criminal Defense; Mass Tort Litigation; Employment Litigation.

**RALPH L. LOTKIN,** born Philadelphia, Pennsylvania, December 15, 1946; admitted to bar, 1971, District of Columbia and U.S. District Court for the District of Columbia. *Education:* Southern Illinois University (B.A., 1968); University of Tennessee at Knoxville (J.D., 1971). *Member:* District of Columbia Bar. (Resident, Washington, D.C. Office). *PRACTICE AREAS:* Ethics; Criminal Defense; Government Relations.

---

**EDDIE J. HARRIS,** born Montgomery, Alabama, October 27, 1939; admitted to bar, 1975, California; U.S. Supreme Court; U.S. District Court, Central and Eastern Districts of California. *Education:* Alabama State University (B.A., 1961); University of California at Los Angeles (M.B.A., Business Administration, 1970; J.D., 1973). *Member:* Los Angeles County Bar Association; State Bar of California; California Association of Black Lawyers; John M. Langston Bar Association. *PRACTICE AREAS:* Personal Injury Law; Criminal Law; Business Litigation.

**ERIC G. FERRER,** born New York, N.Y., February 5, 1956; admitted to bar, 1982, California; 1987, New York. *Education:* State University of New York at Stony Brook (B.A., 1979); Averell Harriman College at S.U.N.Y. (M.S., 1979); University of California at Los Angeles, School of Law (J.D., 1982). *Member:* State Bar of California; Los Angeles Trial Lawyers Association (Member, Board of Governors). *PRACTICE AREAS:* Personal Injury; Police Misconduct; Civil Rights Litigation.

**CAMERON A. STEWART,** born Vancouver, Washington, December 4, 1960; admitted to bar, 1988, California. *Education:* Gonzaga University (B.A., 1983); Pepperdine University (J.D., 1987). *Member:* Los Angeles County Bar Association; State Bar of California. *PRACTICE AREAS:* Personal Injury; Employment Litigation; Civil Rights Litigation.

**SHAWN SNIDER CHAPMAN,** born Los Angeles, California, April 11, 1962; admitted to bar, 1988, California and U.S. District Court, Central District of California. *Education:* University of California at Los Angeles (B.A., 1984); Southwestern University School of Law (J.D., 1988). *Member:* State Bar of California; John M. Langston Bar Association; Black Women Lawyers; California Young Democrats; Consumer Attorneys Association. *PRACTICE AREAS:* Criminal Defense; Personal Injury.

**BRIAN T. DUNN,** born Los Angeles, California, September 25, 1968; admitted to bar, 1995, California and U.S. District Court, Central District of California. *Education:* University of California at Berkeley (B.A., with honors, 1990); University of Michigan Law School (J.D., 1993). *Member:* State Bar of California. *PRACTICE AREAS:* Personal Injury; Police Misconduct; Civil Rights Litigation.

*OF COUNSEL*

**DONALD K. WILSON, JR.,** born Lancaster, Pennsylvania, March 5, 1954; admitted to bar, 1979, California. *Education:* University of Southern California (B.S., 1976); New York Law School (J.D., 1979). Author: "Termination of Copyrights," Los Angeles Daily Journal, 1990. *Member:* State Bar of California. *PRACTICE AREAS:* Entertainment and Sports Law.

**DION-CHERIE RAYMOND,** born Los Angeles, California, September 22, 1962; admitted to bar, 1990, California; 1995, U.S. District Court, Central District of California. *Education:* University of California, Los Angles (B.A., English, 1985); University of California, Hastings College of the Law (J.D., 1989). *Member:* State Bar of California; John M. Langston Bar Association; Black Women Lawyers. *PRACTICE AREAS:* Personal Injury Law; Business Litigation.

REPRESENTATIVE CLIENTS: George Clinton; Council of Black Administrators; Aretha Franklin; Michael Jackson; Chaka Khan; Fred S. Moltrie Accountancy Corp.; James M. Montgomery Consulting Engineers, Inc.; PRWT; Resolution Trust Corp. (RTC); University of Southern California.

---

## STEPHEN E. COCKRIEL

*LOS ANGELES, CALIFORNIA*

(See Long Beach)

*Estate Planning, Probate, Real Estate and Business Law.*

---

## PAUL F. COHEN

4929 WILSHIRE, SUITE 410
*LOS ANGELES, CALIFORNIA 90010*
Telephone: 213-937-7105
Fax: 213-965-9907
Email: paulfred@aol.com

*Business law, Complex and Multi-District Litigation and Probate Law.*

**PAUL F. COHEN,** born Pittsburgh, Pennsylvania, March 14, 1938; admitted to bar, 1964, District of Columbia; 1970, California. *Education:* University of Pennsylvania (B.A., cum laude, 1959); New York University (LL.B., 1963). Member, Moot Court Board. Arbitrator, Los Angeles Superior Court, Business Litigation Panel, 1979—. *Member:* Beverly Hills, Los Angeles County (Member, Board of Trustees, 1989-1991; Member, Superior Courts Committee, 1983-1987; Chair, 1984-1986; Vice Chair, Client Relations Committee, 1985—; Arbitrator, 1979—; Member, Judicial Appointments Committee, 1987-1990; Member, Delegation to State Bar Conference of Delegates, 1976—; Member, Executive Committee, Alternative Dispute Resolutions Section; and American Bar Associations; The State Bar of California; Association of Business Trial Lawyers (Member, Board of Governors, 1979-1981).

## ROBERT M. COHEN

2049 CENTURY PARK EAST, SUITE 2790
**LOS ANGELES, CALIFORNIA 90067**
Telephone: 310-277-1127
Fax: 310-277-6722

*Family Law and Sports Law.*

**ROBERT M. COHEN,** born Westerly, Rhode Island, November 1, 1940; admitted to bar, 1965, Massachusetts; 1966, Rhode Island; 1967, California and U.S. District Court, Central District of California. *Education:* Boston University (A.B., 1962; LL.B., 1965). Recipient: American Jurisprudence Award for Excellence in Equity; William V. Rowe Scholarship; Judge Elmer J. Rathburn Scholarship Award. Instructor, Pepperdine University Law School, 1980-1981. Judge Pro Tem: Beverly Hills Municipal Court, 1976-1978, 1990-1991; Los Angeles Municipal Court, 1980-1981. Family Law Mediator, Los Angeles Superior Court, 1986—. Arbitrator, Los Angeles Superior Court, 1984—. Family Law Mediator, Santa Monica Bar Association, 1990-1991. *Member:* Beverly Hills and Los Angeles County (Member, Executive Committee, Family Law Section, 1987-1991; Participant, Family Law Annual Symposium and Colloquium, 1988) Bar Associations; State Bar of California.

## COHEN, ALEXANDER & CLAYTON

*A PROFESSIONAL CORPORATION*

**LOS ANGELES, CALIFORNIA**
(See Thousand Oaks)

*General Civil Trial Practice. Administrative, Appellate, Arbitration, Business, Condemnation, Corporation, Family Law, Estate Planning, Personal Injury, Probate and Real Estate Development and Zoning.*

## LAW OFFICES OF HILARY HUEBSCH COHEN

*A PROFESSIONAL CORPORATION*

**LOS ANGELES, CALIFORNIA**
(See Torrance)

*Business Law, Health Care.*

## LAW OFFICES OF JEROME S. COHEN

**LOS ANGELES, CALIFORNIA**
(See Long Beach)

*Bankruptcy, Business Reorganization, Commercial Collections, Judgment Enforcement, Insolvency, Creditors' Rights, Domestic and International Commercial Law.*

## COHEN & LORD

*A PROFESSIONAL CORPORATION*

SUITE 200, 4720 LINCOLN BOULEVARD (MARINA DEL REY)
**LOS ANGELES, CALIFORNIA 90292**
Telephone: 310-821-1163
Facsimile: 310-821-7828

**FIRM PROFILE:** Cohen & Lord, A P.C. handles significant business and commercial litigation, emphasizing the areas of construction, wrongful termination, securities, commodities, partnership and unfair competition, and also provides corporate, tax and entertainment representation.

**BRUCE M. COHEN,** born St. John's, Newfoundland, Canada, July 26, 1954; admitted to bar, 1978, California. *Education:* University of California at Berkeley (A.B., with honors, 1975); University of California at Los Angeles (J.D., 1978). Law Clerk to Hon. Otto M. Kaus, retired, Associate Justice Supreme Court (then Presiding Justice, California Court of Appeal, 2nd Appellate District, Division Five, 1978-1980). **PRACTICE AREAS:** Architects and Engineers Representation; Construction Law; Environmental Law; Entertainment Law; General Business Litigation.

*(This Listing Continued)*

**SCOTT R. LORD,** born Oak Park, Illinois, August 31, 1954; admitted to bar, 1979, California. *Education:* University of California at Santa Cruz (B.A., with honors, 1976); Santa Clara University School of Law (J.D., 1979). **REPORTED CASES:** Regional Steel Corp. v. Superior Court (1994) 25 Cal.App.4th 525, 32 Cal.Rptr.2d 417. **PRACTICE AREAS:** Civil Litigation; Construction Law; Representation of Design Professionals; Wrongful Termination; Unfair Competition; Securities Litigation.

---

**ARI J. LAUER,** born Los Angeles, California, May 21, 1965; admitted to bar, 1989, California. *Education:* University of California at Berkeley (A.B., summa cum laude, 1985); Loyola Marymount University (J.D., 1989). St. Thomas More Society. **PRACTICE AREAS:** Construction; Real Estate; Unfair Competition; Wrongful Termination; Securities and Commodities Litigation.

**CYNTHIA R. HODES,** born Toledo, Ohio, June 1, 1951; admitted to bar, 1984, California; 1985, Washington. *Education:* University of Toledo (B.A., 1974); Georgetown University (J.D., 1984). **PRACTICE AREAS:** Business; Wrongful Termination; Unfair Competition; Securities Litigation.

**JEFFREY L. LINDEN,** born Los Angeles, California, November 1, 1942; admitted to bar, 1968, California. *Education:* University of California at Los Angeles (A.B., 1964; J.D., 1967). Phi Delta Phi. Attorney, Securities and Exchange Commission, 1967-1968. Judge Pro Tem, Los Angeles Municipal Court, 1975-1980. Lecturer, Representing Business Buyers and Sellers, California Continuing Education of the Bar, 1976. *Member:* Century City Bar Association (Chairman, Business Organizations Section, 1974-1975; Member, Board of Trustees, 1975-1981; President, 1979). **PRACTICE AREAS:** Business Law; Securities Law; Real Estate Law.

*OF COUNSEL*

**DOUG GUMMERMAN,** born Los Angeles, California, October 18, 1951; admitted to bar, 1982, California. *Education:* University of California, Berkeley (B.A., 1975); Hastings College of Law, University of California (J.D., magna cum laude, 1982). Order of the Coif. Member, Thurston Society. **PRACTICE AREAS:** Corporate Law; Taxation.

## COHEN PRIMIANI & FOSTER

*A PROFESSIONAL CORPORATION*
Established in 1988

2029 CENTURY PARK EAST, SUITE 480
**LOS ANGELES, CALIFORNIA 90067**
Telephone: 310-277-3963
Fax: 310-277-4351

*Federal, State, Local and International Taxation. Entertainment Tax, Tax Litigation and Controversies, Corporate, Real Estate and Partnership Law. Estate Planning, Probate, Trust and General Business Law.*

**MARC S. PRIMIANI,** born San Francisco, California, December 5, 1954; admitted to bar, 1979, California. *Education:* University of Colorado at Boulder (B.A., magna cum laude, 1976); University of Santa Clara (J.D., 1979); New York University (LL.M., in Taxation, 1980). Phi Beta Kappa. Articles Editor, Santa Clara Law Review, 1978-1979. Clerk, California Court of Appeals, 1978. *Member:* Los Angeles County Bar Association; State Bar of California.

**BRADFORD S. COHEN,** born New York, N.Y., May 16, 1953; admitted to bar, 1979, New York; 1983, California. *Education:* Northeastern University (B.S. cum laude, 1976); Hofstra University (J.D., 1979); New York University (LL.M., in Taxation, 1981). Author: "Taxation of Americans Abroad," People & Taxes; Installment Sales Chapter of Commerce Clearing House's Federal Tax Service. *Member:* Century City, Los Angeles County, New York State and American Bar Associations; State Bar of California.

**MICHAEL D. FOSTER,** born Detroit, Michigan, September 27, 1955; admitted to bar, 1981, California; 1983, New York. *Education:* Wayne State University (B.S., 1977; J.D., cum laude, 1980); New York University (LL.M., in Taxation, 1981). Adjunct Professor, University of San Diego School of Law Graduate Tax Program, 1984-1986. *Member:* Los Angeles County, New York State and American Bar Associations; State Bar of California.

**BERNARD OSTER,** born Antwerp, Belgium, November 24, 1946; admitted to bar, 1981, New York and California. *Education:* Brooklyn College of the City University of New York (B.A., 1968); New York University

*(This Listing Continued)*

(M.A., 1971); Brooklyn Law School (J.D., cum laude, 1980). Author: Installment Sales Chapter of Commerce Clearing House's Federal Tax Service; Columnist, "Tax Law," The Los Angeles Daily Journal, 1985—; "Rule 75 and Tax Court Litigation," 21 Trial 77, 1985; "The Taxpayer, The IRS and Requests for Statute Extensions," 91 Case & Comment 63, 1986; "Strategies For Successful IRS Negotiations," 94 Case & Comment 3, 1989; "Reporting Requirements For Cash In Excess of $10,000 Received," 65 Taxes, The Tax Magazine 173, March, 1987; "How to Resolve a Federal Tax Audit," 2 The Practical Lawyer 19, Summer, 1988; "Structuring Structured Settlements," 4 The Practical Tax Lawyer, No. 2 Winter 1990; "The Taxing Question of Punitive Damages Awards," 24 Beverly Hills Bar Association Journal, No. 1 Winter 1990. Attorney, Office of the Chief Counsel, Treasury Department, 1980-1984. *Member:* Century City (Co-Chairperson, Taxation Section), Los Angeles County, New York State and American Bar Associations; State Bar of California.

**SAMUEL ISRAEL,** born Bronx, New York, April 16, 1957; admitted to bar, 1982, California and U.S. District Court, Northern and Central Districts of California; 1984, U.S. Tax Court. *Education:* State University of New York at Binghamton (B.S., accounting, 1978); University of California at Los Angeles (J.D., 1981); New York University School (LL.M., in taxation, 1982). Licensed Real Estate Broker, California, 1985. Member, UCLA Journal of International Law, 1980-1981. Extern, to Hon. Ellsworth Van Graafeiland, U.S. Court of Appeals for the 2nd Circuit, 1980. Lecturer, USC Tax Institute, 1990. *Member:* Beverly Hills Bar Association (Chairman, Taxation Section, 1987-1988; Member, Board of Governors, 1989-1990).

**JEFFREY FORER,** born New York, May 15, 1955; admitted to bar, 1983, California. *Education:* University of California at Los Angeles (B.A., 1977); Southwestern University (J.D., cum laude, 1983); New York University (LL.M., in Taxation, 1984). *Member:* Beverly Hills, Santa Monica, Los Angeles County and American Bar Associations; State Bar of California.

REFERENCE: Western Bank (Los Angeles, Calif.).

---

## LAW OFFICE
## TERRI E. COHN

**1801 CENTURY PARK EAST, 23RD FLOOR**
**LOS ANGELES, CALIFORNIA 90067**
Telephone: 310-553-8333
Fax: 310-553-8337

*Business Transactions, Domestic and International; Telecommunications; Corporate Law; Business Litigation.*

**TERRI E. COHN,** born Chicago, Illinois, January 3, 1961; admitted to bar, 1986, California; 1987, U.S. District Court, Central District of California. *Education:* University of Redlands (B.A., 1983); McGeorge School of the Law, University of the Pacific (J.D., 1986). *Member:* Beverly Hills (Member, Board of Governors, 1992-1996; ; Chairman, Business Law Section, 1990-1992; Chairman, Bylaws Committee; Governing Board, Business Law Section, 1987—; State Bar Delegate, 1989-1994; Chairman, State Bar Delegation, 1993-1994, First Vice-Chair, 1992; Chairman, Resolutions Committee, 1993-1994; Chairman, Business Law School Committee, 1994-1995; Secretary, Long Range Planning Committee, 1989; Bylaws Committee, 1990—), Los Angeles County (Member, State Bar Delegation, 1995—; Business and Corporate Law Section; Director, Barristers, 1989-1992; Chairman, Moot Court Committee, 1989-1991) and American Bar Associations; State Bar of California (Member: Resolutions Committee, Conference of Delegates, 1995—). *LANGUAGES:* French, German and Russian. *PRACTICE AREAS:* Business Law; Transactions (Domestic and International); Telecommunications; Corporate Law; Business Litigation.

---

## COLEMAN & RICHARDS

*A PROFESSIONAL CORPORATION*
*Established in 1971*
**SUITE 810, 1801 AVENUE OF THE STARS (CENTURY CITY)**
**LOS ANGELES, CALIFORNIA 90067**
Telephone: 310-277-2700

*General Civil and Criminal Trial and Appellate Practice in all State and Federal Courts, Mediation and Arbitration.*

FIRM PROFILE: *Coleman & Richards engages exclusively in litigation, civil and criminal. Its civil practice includes the prosecution, defense, arbitration and mediation of contractual disputes, partnership disputes, business torts and*

*(This Listing Continued)*

*the defense of employment discrimination and sexual harassment claims. Its clients include lawyers, law firms and accountants involved in partnership and fee disputes. Its criminal practice emphasizes the defense of economic crimes and environmental prosecutions.*

**RICHARD M. COLEMAN,** born Brooklyn, New York, 1935; admitted to bar, 1960, District of Columbia; 1964, U.S. Supreme Court; 1967, California. *Education:* Georgetown University (A.B., summa cum laude, 1957); Harvard University (J.D., 1960); Georgetown University (LL.M., 1961). Recipient, E. Barrett Prettyman Fellowship in Trial Advocacy, 1960-1961. Special Attorney, U.S. Department of Justice, 1962-1964. Assistant U.S. Attorney, 1961-1962, 1964-1967. Chief, Organized Crime Section, U.S. Attorney's Office, Washington, D.C., 1964-1966. Chief, Special Prosecutions Division, U.S. Attorney's Office, Los Angeles, 1966-1967. Member, Civil Justice Advisory Group, Central District of California, 1990-1994. Member, Executive Council, National Conference of Bar Presidents, 1985-1988. President, National Caucus of Metropolitan Bar Leaders, 1982-1983. *Member:* Century City (President, 1977; Member, Board of Governors, 1973-1985) and Los Angeles County (President, 1981-1982; Member: Board of Trustees, 1978-1982) Bar Associations; The State Bar of California (Member, Judicial Nominees Evaluation Commission, 1986-1989); Los Angeles Trial Lawyers Association; Association of Business Trial Lawyers (Member, Board of Governors, 1976-1978). Fellow, American College of Trial Lawyers.

**LAURIE J. RICHARDS,** born Iowa, 1943; admitted to bar, 1975, California. *Education:* Whittier College of Law (J.D., magna cum laude, 1975). Member, Bureau of Electrical and Appliance Repair Services Advisory Board, California Department of Consumer Affairs, 1978-1985. Chairwoman, Los Angeles County Tax Advisory Committee, Pacific Palisades, 1981. Member, Development Committee, Los Angeles Center for International Commercial Arbitration, 1987. *Member:* Beverly Hills Bar Association (Member, Resolutions Committee and Conference of Delegates, 1981-1982); Association of Business Trial Lawyers; Women Lawyers of Los Angeles (Member, Legislation Committee); California Women Lawyers.

---

## COLEMAN & WRIGHT

**333 SOUTH GRAND AVENUE, SUITE 3950**
**LOS ANGELES, CALIFORNIA 90071**
Telephone: 213-624-4292
Telecopier: 213-624-1354

*Civil Litigation. Torts and Insurance Defense. Products Liability.*

FIRM PROFILE: *We are proud of the rather unique nature of the firm, in that it is female-owned and actively seeks to maintain a racially and culturally diverse staff.*

*The firm is composed of well over fifty percent minority employees.*

*Coleman & Wright actively supports Los Angeles community programs, particularly the efforts of the United Way and the Red Cross. One of the programs we support, the Koko Challenge, directly benefits the surrounding community.*

### MEMBERS OF FIRM

**JOHN M. COLEMAN,** born Carbondale, Pennsylvania, July 16, 1952; admitted to bar, 1978, California and U.S. District Court, Central District of California. *Education:* Georgetown University (B.A., 1974); University of San Fernando Valley (J.D., 1977). Law Clerk, Hon. James J. Walsh, Court of Common Pleas, Scranton, Pennsylvania, 1977-1978. Arbitrator, Los Angeles Superior Court, 1982—. *Member:* Wilshire and Los Angeles County (Member, Trial Lawyer's Division) Bar Associations; State Bar of California; Association of Southern California Defense Counsel. *PRACTICE AREAS:* Civil Litigation; Torts; Insurance Defense; Products Liability.

**PATRICIA E. WRIGHT,** born Carbondale, Pennsylvania, May 4, 1954; admitted to bar, 1985, California. *Education:* Muhlenberg College (B.A., 1976); Simmons College (M.S.L.S., 1977); University of Southern California (J.D., 1984). Phi Sigma Iota. *Member:* Wilshire and Los Angeles County Bar Associations; State Bar of California; Association of Southern California Defense Counsel. *PRACTICE AREAS:* Civil Litigation; Torts; Insurance Defense; Products Liability.

**KENNETH K. TANJI, JR.,** born Sacramento, California, January 31, 1965; admitted to bar, 1992, California. *Education:* University of California at Davis (B.S., 1988); McGeorge School of Law (J.D., 1992). *Member:* State Bar of California. *PRACTICE AREAS:* Civil Litigation; Torts; Insurance Defense; Products Liability.

*(This Listing Continued)*

## COLEMAN & WRIGHT, Los Angeles—Continued

**TRACY KAWANO,** born Torrance, California, May 7, 1964; admitted to bar, 1991, California. *Education:* University of California, Santa Cruz; University of California, Berkeley (B.A., 1986); Loyola University of Los Angeles (J.D., 1989). *Member:* Los Angeles County and American Bar Associations; State Bar of California. *PRACTICE AREAS:* Civil Litigation; Torts; Insurance Defense; Products Liability.

**CHARLES K. COLLINS,** born Harrison, Arkansas, January 23, 1951; admitted to bar, 1981, California; 1982, U.S. District Court, Central District of California; 1985, U.S. District Court, Southern and Eastern Districts of California. *Education:* California State University at Long Beach (B.A., 1978); Loyola University School of Law (J.D., 1981). Commercial Pilot, 1972; Licensed Private Pilot, Instrument and Commercial Ratings, 1973. *Member:* State Bar of California. [CW2, U.S. Army, 1970-1973]. *PRACTICE AREAS:* Personal Injury Law; Business Litigation.

**MATTHEW J. LUCE,** born Edina, Minnesota, August 9, 1968; admitted to bar, 1993, California. *Education:* University of Southern California (B.S., 1990); Loyola University Law School (J.D., 1993). *Member:* Association of Business Trial Lawyers.

**ROBERT F. BEAL,** born Newton, Massachusetts, April 10, 1970; admitted to bar, 1995, California. *Education:* Boston College (B.A., 1992); University of San Diego (J.D., 1995). Chairman, USD Appellate Moot Court Board. Author, "The Vulnerability of the Pacific Rim Orbital Spectrum," 9 NY Int'l L. Rev. 69, 1996. Legal Extern to the Hon. John S. Rhoades, U.S. District Court, Southern District of California. *Member:* Los Angeles County Bar Association. *PRACTICE AREAS:* Civil Litigation; Torts; Insurance Defense; Products Liability.

**ROBERT MONTES, JR.,** born Tijuana, Mexico, November 5, 1965; admitted to bar, 1992, California. *Education:* University of California at Los Angeles (B.A., 1988; J.D., 1991). *Member:* Los Angeles County and Mexican-American Bar Associations. *LANGUAGES:* Spanish.

### OF COUNSEL

**JOHN J. QUINN,** born Volga, Iowa, March 8, 1923; admitted to bar, 1959, District of Columbia; 1960, Montana and U.S. District Court, District of Montana (Not admitted in California). *Education:* Gonzaga University (A.B., 1949); Georgetown University Law Center (LL.B., 1959; J.D., 1967). Member, Board of Personnel Appeals, State of Montana, 1976-1980. *Member:* State Bar of Montana (Chairman, Legal Education and Admission to the Bar Committee, 1974); District of Columbia Bar; American Bar Association. [Specialty Navigator (Air T/SGT., USMC, 1942-1945]

REPRESENTATIVE CLIENTS: Bank of America; E.I. DuPont de Nemours & Co.; Abbott Laboratories; Cosco, Inc.; Admiral Insurance Co.; Scibal Insurance Group; Interseptre Tyres, Inc. (London & Germany); Penn-American Insurance Co.; Kidde, Inc.; County of Los Angeles; Pennsylvania Manufacturers' Association; Virco Mfg. Corp.; Crawford & Co.; Sav-On Drugs, Inc.; Investors Insurance Group; RJR Nabisco; Royal Insurance Group; March Insurance Co. (Hong Kong); Fuwa Trading Corp (Hong Kong); General Star; Kemper Group; The Vons Companies, Inc.; Acceptance Insurance Co.; Graham Miller Group (Hong-Kong & L.A.); Alexsis Risk Management Services, Inc.; The Hanover Insurance Companies; Cathay Pacific Airways; Taiwan Shin Yeh Enterprises Co. (Taiwan); Beaufort Taiwan, Inc (Taiwan); Lee Chi Enterprises (Taiwan); Gallagher Bassett Services, Inc.; TM Claims Service, Inc.

---

## COLLINS, COLLINS, MUIR & TRAVER
### LOS ANGELES, CALIFORNIA
(See Pasadena)

*Casualty, Products Liability, Construction, Malpractice Insurance, Employment Termination, Sexual Abuse and Personal Injury Law. General Trial Practice.*

---

## COLLINS, ROBILLARD & KATZ
### LOS ANGELES, CALIFORNIA
(See Torrance)

*Real Property Transactions and Litigation, Commercial Leasing, Landlord Tenant, Creditor Bankruptcy, Business and Corporate Law, Estate Planning and Probate, Trust Administration and Litigation, General Civil and Trial Practice in State and Federal Courts.*

---

## COMSTOCK & SHARPE, INC.
### LOS ANGELES, CALIFORNIA
(See Culver City)

*Estate Planning and Probate, Family Law, Real Estate and Business, General Civil and Personal Injury and Corporate Law.*

---

## CONDON & FORSYTH
### 1900 AVENUE OF THE STARS
### LOS ANGELES, CALIFORNIA 90067
Telephone: 310-557-2030
Telecopier: 310-557-1299

**New York, N.Y. Office:** 1251 Avenue of the Americas. Telephone: 212-921-5100. Telex: 426978. Telecopier: 212-575-3638

**Washington, D.C. Office:** 1016 Sixteenth Street, N.W. Telephone: 202-289-0500. Telecopier: 202-289-4524.

*Civil and Commercial Litigation, Transactional and Regulatory, Aviation, Business, Employment, Products Liability, Administrative and Insurance Law.*

### RESIDENT PARTNERS

**FRANK A. SILANE,** born Bronx, New York, 1945; admitted to bar, 1974, New York and U.S. District Court, Southern and Eastern Districts of New York and U.S. Court of Appeals, Second and Ninth Circuits; 1979, California and U.S. District Court, Central, Northern and Eastern Districts of California and U.S. District Court, Eastern District of Michigan; 1987, U.S. Supreme Court. *Education:* Fordham University (A.B., 1967; J.D., 1973). *Member:* Los Angeles County, New York State, Federal and American Bar Associations; The State Bar of California. [Lt., U.S. Navy, 1967-1970]

**RODERICK D. MARGO,** born Johannesburg, South Africa, 1950; admitted to bar, 1974, South Africa; 1979, Georgia; 1981, California and U.S. District Court, Northern, Central, Southern and Eastern Districts of California; 1984, U.S. Court of Appeals Ninth Circuit; 1995, District of Columbia. *Education:* Witwatersrand University, Johannesburg (B.Com., 1970; LL.B., cum laude, 1973); Cambridge University, England; McGill University, Canada (Ph.D., 1979). Author: "Aviation Insurance," Butterworths, London, 2nd Ed 1989. Co-Editor: Shawcross and Beaumont "Air Law," 4th Ed, 1996 (rev.). Lecturer in Law: Aviation Law, 1981—, University of California at Los Angeles School of Law. Member, Board of Advisors, Air and Space Law, published by Kluwer & Co., The Netherlands. *Member:* Los Angeles County, Federal and American Bar Associations; The State Bar of California; District of Columbia Bar; State Bar of Georgia. Fellow, Royal Aeronautical Society.

**STEPHEN R. GINGER,** born Los Angeles, California, 1956; admitted to bar, 1982, California and U.S. District Court, Central District of California; 1984, U.S. Court of Appeals, Ninth Circuit; 1987, U.S. Supreme Court. *Education:* California State University, Dominguez Hills (B.A., 1979); Southwestern University (J.D., 1982). Law Clerk to the Honorable Albert Lee Stephens, Jr., U.S. District Court, Central District of California, 1982-1984. Author: "Regulation of Quasi-Foreign Corporations in California: Reflections on Section 2115 After Wilson v. Louisiana-Pacific Resources, Inc.," S.W.U. L. Rev. (1984). Co-Author: "Current Events in Space Litigation," American Bar Association National Institute on Litigation in Aviation (October 1990); "Lost in Space," 13 L.A. Lawyer 26 (February 1991). *Member:* Los Angeles County, Federal and American Bar Associations; The State Bar of California.

**JENNIFER J. JOHNSTON,** born Pomona, California, 1958; admitted to bar, 1986, California; 1987, U.S. District Court, Central, Southern and Northern Districts of California; 1987, U.S. Court of Appeals, Ninth Circuit; 1994, U.S. District Court, Eastern District of California. *Education:* California State Polytechnic University (B.S., magna cum laude, 1980); Loyola Law School (J.D., 1986). *Member:* The State Bar of California; Federal and American Bar Associations.

### RESIDENT ASSOCIATES

**WILLIAM T. MACCARY,** born Montclair, New Jersey, 1964; admitted to bar, 1990, California, U.S. District Court, Northern District of California and U.S. Court of Appeals, 9th Circuit; 1991, U.S. District Court, Eastern District of California; 1992, U.S. District Court, Central District of California. *Education:* Stanford University (A.B., with distinction, 1986);

*(This Listing Continued)*

University of California at Los Angeles School of Law (J.D., 1990). *Member:* The State Bar of California; American Bar Association (Member, Forum Committee on Air and Space Law).

**KEVIN R. SUTHERLAND,** born Torrance, California, 1965; admitted to bar, 1992, California; U.S. District Court, Central, Eastern, Southern and Northern Districts of California and U.S. Court of Appeals, Ninth Circuit; 1995, District of Columbia; U.S. District Court for the District of Columbia. *Education:* University of California (B.A., 1988); Syracuse University (J.D., 1992). Executive Editor, Syracuse Journal of International Law and Commerce, 1991-1992. *Member:* Los Angeles County, Federal and American Bar Associations; The State Bar of California.

**ERIN L. NORDBY,** born Redwood City, California, February 18, 1971; admitted to bar, 1995, California, U.S. District Court, Central, Eastern, Southern and Northern Districts of California and U.S. Court of Appeals, Ninth Circuit. *Education:* University of Southern California (B.A., magna cum laude, 1992; J.D., 1995). *Member:* State Bar of California.

---

## CONKLE & OLESTEN

### LOS ANGELES, CALIFORNIA

(See Santa Monica)

*Arbitration, Mediation and Alternative Dispute Resolution. Litigation in State and Federal Trial and Appellate Courts, including Insurance Policyholder's Rights, Intellectual Property, Business Torts, Trade Regulation, Real Estate Transactions, Employee Relations and Contracts.*

---

## JACK K. CONWAY

### LOS ANGELES, CALIFORNIA

(See San Marino)

*Insurance, Products Liability and Professional Liability Law. Litigation. Family Law, Personal Injury Litigation.*

---

## COOMBER LAW FIRM

601 SOUTH FIGUEROA STREET, 41ST FLOOR
### LOS ANGELES, CALIFORNIA 90017-5704
Telephone: 213-622-2200
Fax: 213-243-0000
Email: scoomber@aol.com

Rancho Santa Fe, California Office: 16909 Via de Santa Fe, Suite 200. P.O. Box 7299, 92067-7299. Telephone: 619-759-3939. Facsimile: 619-759-3930.

*Business Transactions and Business Litigation.*

**SKIP R. COOMBER, III,** born January 7, 1961; admitted to bar, 1990, California. *Education:* University of California at Irvine (B.A., 1984); Loyola Law School (J.D., 1987). President, Associated Students, University of California at Irvine, 1983-1984; President, Student Bar Association, Loyola Law School, 1986-1987. *Member:* Los Angeles County Bar Association. The State Bar of California. **PRACTICE AREAS:** Business Law.

---

## COOPER & HEMAR

### LOS ANGELES, CALIFORNIA

(See Santa Monica)

*Commercial Collections, Creditor Bankruptcy, Equipment Leasing, Banking. Secured Transactions and General Trial Practice.*

---

## LAW OFFICES OF ROBERT L. CORBIN, P.C.

601 WEST FIFTH STREET, 12TH FLOOR
### LOS ANGELES, CALIFORNIA 90071
Telephone: 213-612-0001
Facsimile: 213-612-0061

*Criminal and Civil Litigation in State and Federal Courts and before Administrative Agencies.*

**ROBERT L. CORBIN,** born Brooklyn, N.Y., December 19, 1945; admitted to bar, 1972, New York; 1975, U.S. Court of Appeals, Second Circuit and U.S. District Court, Southern and Eastern Districts of New York; 1977, California; 1978, U.S. Court of Appeals, Ninth Circuit and U.S. District Court, Central District of California; 1990, U.S. District Court, Southern District of California and U.S. District Court, District of Arizona. *Education:* Colgate University (B.A., 1967); Fordham University (J.D., 1971). Deputy Federal Public Defender, Central District of California, 1978-1981. Staff Counsel, Independent Commission on The Los Angeles Police Department, 1991. *Member:* Los Angeles County (Member, White Collar Crime Committee), New York State, Federal and American (Member, White Collar Crime Committee, California Regional Subcommittee) Bar Associations; State Bar of California.

---

**MICHAEL W. FITZGERALD,** born Los Angeles, California, July 11, 1959; admitted to bar, 1987, California, U.S. District Court, Central District of California; 1988, U.S. Court of Appeals, Ninth Circuit; 1992, U.S. District Court, Northern District of California. *Education:* Harvard University (A.B., magna cum laude, 1981); University of California at Berkeley (J.D., 1985). Order of the Coif. Maynard Toll Associate Pro Bono Award Winner, 1994. Law Clerk to the Hon. Irving R. Kaufman, U.S. Court of Appeals, Second Circuit, 1985-1986. Managing Editor, Industrial Relations Law Journal, 1984-1985. Assistant U.S. Attorney, Central District of California, 1988-1991. Member, Advisory Committee on the Office of District Attorney, 1994. Counsel, Special Advisor to the Board of Police Commissioners, 1992. *Member:* Los Angeles County, Federal and American (Member, White Collar Crime Committee, California Regional Subcommittee) Bar Associations. **REPORTED CASES:** United States v. Alvarez-Sanchez, 975 F. 2d 461 (9th Cir. 1991); United States v. Mejia, 953 F.2d 461 (9th Cir. 1991); Doganiere v. United States, 914 F. 2d 165 (9th Cir. 1990); United States v. Affinito, 873 F. 2d 1261 (9th Cir. 1989); United States v. Pace, 709 F Supp. 948 (C.D. Cal. 1989), affirmed, 893 F. 2d 1103 (9th Cir. 1990).

*OF COUNSEL*

**KEVIN F. RUF,** born Wilmington, Delaware, December 7, 1961; admitted to bar, 1988, California. *Education:* University of California at Berkeley (A.B., 1984); University of Michigan Law School (J.D., 1987). **REPORTED CASES:** Teitel v. First Los Angeles Bank, 91 Daily Journal D.A.R., 79 79 (1991).

---

## CORINBLIT & SELTZER

A PROFESSIONAL CORPORATION
SUITE 820 WILSHIRE PARK PLACE
3700 WILSHIRE BOULEVARD
### LOS ANGELES, CALIFORNIA 90010-3085
Telephone: 213-380-4200
Telecopier: 213-385-7503; 385-4560
Email: mseltzer@AOL.com

*General Civil and Trial Practice in all State and Federal Courts. Antitrust, Securities and Corporation Law.*

FIRM PROFILE: *Corinblit & Seltzer, a Professional Corporation, of Los Angeles, California, has concentrated its practice in the prosecution and defense of complex business litigation, with a strong emphasis on antitrust, securities, corporate and financial institution cases, for more than twenty years. The firm has acted as counsel for plaintiffs and defendants in litigation brought in federal and state courts throughout the United States.*

**MARC M. SELTZER,** born Los Angeles, California, April 30, 1947; admitted to bar, 1972, California. *Education:* University of California at Berkeley (A.B., 1969); University of California at Los Angeles (J.D., 1972). Deputy Attorney General, State of California, 1972-1973. *Member:* State Bar of California; Los Angeles County and American (Member, Sections

*(This Listing Continued)*

**CORINBLIT & SELTZER,** A PROFESSIONAL CORPORATION, Los Angeles—Continued

on: Business Law; Antitrust Law; Litigation) Bar Associations; American Law Institute; Selden Society. **REPORTED CASES:** Wool v. Tandem Computers, Inc., 818 F.2d 1433 (9th Cir. 1987); In re ZZZZ Best Securities Litigation, 864 F.Supp. 960 (C.D. Cal. 1994); In re Corrugated Container Antitrust Litigation 752 F.2d 137 (5th Cir.), cert. denied, 473 U.S. 911 (1985); In re Taxable Municipal Bonds Litigation (1994-1995 Transfer Binder) Fed.Sec.L.Rep. (CCH) 98,405 (E.D. La. 1994). **PRACTICE AREAS:** Complex Civil Litigation; Antitrust; Securities.

**CHRISTINA A. SNYDER,** born Los Angeles, California, May 27, 1947; admitted to bar, 1973, California. *Education:* Pomona College (B.A., 1969); Stanford Law School (J.D., 1972). *Member:* Beverly Hills, Los Angeles County and American (Member, Sections on: Antitrust; Business Law; Litigation) Bar Associations; American Law Institute. **REPORTED CASES:** Norman Williams v. Baxter Rice, 458 U.S. 654 (1982); Jedwab v. MGM Grand Hotels, Inc., 509 A.2d 584 (Del. Ch. 1986); Medallion Television Enterprises, Inc. v. SelecTV, 833 F.2d 1360 (9th Cir. 1987); Inforex Corp. v. MGM/UA Entertainment Co., 608 F.Supp. 129 (C.D. Cal. 1984). **PRACTICE AREAS:** Complex Civil Litigation; Antitrust; Securities.

*OF COUNSEL*

**JACK CORINBLIT, A LAW CORPORATION,** born Detroit, Michigan, January 3, 1923; admitted to bar, 1951, California. *Education:* Wayne University; University of Chicago (J.D., 1949). *Member:* Los Angeles County and American (Member, Section on Antitrust Law) Bar Associations; State Bar of California. **REPORTED CASES:** Beacon Theatres, Inc. v. Westover, 359 U.S. 500 (1959); In re Equity Funding Corp. of America Securities Litigation, 438 F.Supp. 1303 (C.D. Cal. 1977). **PRACTICE AREAS:** Complex Civil Litigation; Antitrust; Securities.

**EARL P. WILLENS,** born Stockton, California, January 29, 1935; admitted to bar, 1960, California. *Education:* University of California (A.B., 1956); Boalt Hall Berkeley (LL.B., 1959). Assistant U.S. Attorney, 1960-1961. Member, Board of Regents, University of California, 1976-1977. *Member:* State Bar of California. **PRACTICE AREAS:** Complex Civil Litigation; Antitrust; Securities.

---

**GRETCHEN M. NELSON,** born Corona, California, July 15, 1954; admitted to bar, 1984, California. *Education:* Smith College (B.A., magna cum laude, 1976); Georgetown University (J.D., 1983). *Member:* Los Angeles County and American Bar Associations; State Bar of California. **PRACTICE AREAS:** Complex Civil Litigation; Antitrust; Securities.

**GEORGE A. SHOHET,** born New York, N.Y., February 24, 1960; admitted to bar, 1983, California. *Education:* University of California at Irvine (B.A., with honors, 1980); Loyola Marymount University (J.D., cum laude, 1983). Member: Moot Court; St. Thomas More Society; Loyola Law Review, 1982-1983. Legislative Counsel, Congressman Jerry M. Patterson, 1983-1985. Attorney, Government Accountability Project, Washington D.C., 1985. *Member:* Los Angeles County and American Bar Associations; State Bar of California. **PRACTICE AREAS:** Complex Civil Litigation; Antitrust; Securities.

**MOSES GARCIA,** born Cheyenne, Wyoming, October 25, 1966; admitted to bar, 1994, California. *Education:* University d'Angers, France; University of Wyoming (B.S., with honors, 1990)); University of Notre Dame (J.D., 1993). Member, International Law Society, 1990-1993. *Member:* Los Angeles County Bar Association; State Bar of California; Lawyers for Human Rights. **LANGUAGES:** French, Spanish. **PRACTICE AREAS:** Complex Civil Litigation.

---

## COSKEY & BALDRIDGE

*16TH FLOOR, 1801 CENTURY PARK EAST*
**LOS ANGELES, CALIFORNIA 90067-2317**
Telephone: 310-277-7001
Telecopier: 310-277-9704

*Negotiation, Documentation and Litigation of Commercial Transactions including Lending, Sales, Real Estate, Landlord Tenant, Bankruptcy, Insolvency and Debtor-Creditor Matters.*

*MEMBERS OF FIRM*

**TOBIAS COSKEY** (1896-1974).

*(This Listing Continued)*

**HAL L. COSKEY,** born September 5, 1930; admitted to bar, 1954, California. *Education:* Stanford University (B.A., with distinction, 1952; J.D., 1954). Member, Stanford Law Review, 1953-1954. Author and Lecturer of Debt Collection and Practice for Continuing Education of the Bar, 1976-1980. Judge Pro Tem, Los Angeles Municipal Court, Beverly Hills Municipal Court and Culver City Municipal Court, 1973—. Arbitrator and Mediator, Superior Court of Los Angeles County, 1979—. *Member:* State Bar of California; American Bar Association; Association of Business Trial Lawyers; Commercial Law League of America. **PRACTICE AREAS:** Bankruptcy; Insolvency; Debtor Creditor; Secured Transaction; Landlord and Tenant; Commercial Litigation and Documentation.

**MARY ELLEN BALDRIDGE,** born Wyoming, June 22, 1950; admitted to bar, 1976, California. *Education:* University of Wyoming (B.A., 1972); Columbia University (J.D., 1975). Phi Beta Kappa. *Member:* Los Angeles County and American Bar Associations; Commercial Law League of America; State Bar of California. **PRACTICE AREAS:** Debtor Creditor; Secured Transactions; Landlord and Tenant; Commercial Litigation and Documentation; Bankruptcy; Insolvency.

REFERENCE: Wells Fargo Bank (Century City Branch).

---

## COTCHETT & PITRE

*SUITE 1100, 12100 WILSHIRE BOULEVARD*
**LOS ANGELES, CALIFORNIA 90025**
Telephone: 310-826-4211
Email: CandPLegal@aol.com

*Burlingame, California Office:* San Francisco Airport Office Center, Suite 200, 840 Malcolm Road. Telephone: 415-697-6000.

*Affiliated Office:* Friedlander & Friedlander, P.C., 2018 Clarendon Boulevard, Arlington, Virginia 22201. Telephone: 703-525-6750.

*Practice limited to Tort Law, Environmental, Products Liability, Securities, Antitrust and Commercial Litigation. General Trial and Appellate Practice.*

(For Complete Biographical data on all Partners and Associates, see Burlingame, California Professional Biographies)

---

## COTKIN & COLLINS

A PROFESSIONAL CORPORATION

Established in 1978

*1055 WEST SEVENTH STREET, SUITE 1900*
**LOS ANGELES, CALIFORNIA 90017-2503**
Telephone: 213-688-9350
FAX: 213-688-9351
Email: cotkinla@sprynet.com

*Santa Ana, California Office:* 200 West Santa Ana Boulevard, Suite 800. Telephone: 714-835-2330. FAX: 714-835-2209.

*General Civil and Appellate Practice. Insurance Coverage, Regulatory and Administrative Law and Litigation, Professional and Product Liability Defense, Family Law, Health Law*

FIRM PROFILE: *Cotkin & Collins is a civil litigation firm. With expertise in complex practice areas, the firm has as extensive trial practice in insurance law, bad faith, business law, labor law and professional liability. Cotkin & Collins has a recognized national reputation in insurance coverage litigation, as well as in the representation of professionals.*

*Two offices located in Los Angeles and Santa Ana provide a solid base from which to serve clients. Cotkin & Collins attorneys strive for excellence in client representation by aggressively upholding clients' interests while simultaneously streamlining litigation and controlling costs.*

**RAPHAEL COTKIN,** born New York, N.Y., July 31, 1939; admitted to bar, 1965, California and U.S. District Court, Northern, Central and Southern Districts of California. *Education:* University of California at Los Angeles (B.A., 1960); University of Southern California (J.D., 1964). Panelist and Author: "Brave New World: Today's Extracontractual Liability," American Insurance Association, General Counsel's Symposium, June, 1989. Speaker and Author: "Third Party Claims," Stanford Bar Institute-Bad Faith, March, 1988; Author: "Bad Faith Before *Moredi-Shalal*," Beverly Hills Bar Journal, September, 1988; "Litigating an Insurer's Bad Faith," ABA, Litigation, Summer, 1988. Panelist: CEB Seminars, "Bad Faith Insurance Litigation," and "Insurance Coverage Programs in Motor Vehicle Cases," February, 1983; SCDC Annual Seminar, "Sweaty Palms: Dealing With the Policy Limits Demands," January, 1985; Business Trial Lawyers

*(This Listing Continued)*

Seminar re, "Insurance Coverage and Business Litigation -- 'Where the Dollars Are and How to Get Them2'" February, 1985; CEB Seminar, Second Annual Real Property Practice Institute: Construction Law "Liability Insurance for Defective Work and Property Damage," February, 1985; California Business Law Institute Seminar: "California Environmental Compliance Workshop" "Getting Your Insurance Carrier to Pay the Bills," May, 1985; ABA Seminar, "Coping with the Latest Corporate Insurance Crisis: Are You Covered?" November, 1986; CEB program on Bad Faith Litigation: "Recent Trends and Effective Tactics," March, 1987; PLI Seminar, "Media Insurance: Protecting Against High Judgments, Punitive Damages and Defense Costs," July, 1983; PLI Seminar, Insurance, Excess & Reinsurance Coverage Issues: "Coverage for Punitive Damages Assessed Against an Insured," January, 1986; Southern California Adjusters Association Seminar, "Policy Limits Demands: How to Deal With Them From a Carrier's Standpoint," March, 1986; CPCU Society of Orange County: Panel Discussion of *Cumis,* April, 1986; Title Insurance Underwriters Section of the American Land Title Association Meeting: "Brave New World: Carriers Under a Microscope," September, 1986; General Real Estate Law Subsection of the Real Property Section of the Los Angeles County Bar "Significant Insurance Developments," November, 1986; Public Risk & Insurance Management Association 8th National Conference "Pollution Claims: Who Foots the Bill?" May 1987. Speaker and Author: "PLI Seminar on Professional Liability Insurance for Attorneys, Accountants and Insurance Brokers: Coverage Aspects of Claims against Professional: Plaintiff's Perspective," June 1986. Panelist and Author: Association of Business Trial Lawyers, "The Deepest Pocket Strikes Back: Recent Developments in the Avoidance, Preparation, Settlement and Trial of Bad Faith Insurance Lawsuits," June 1986. Speaker and Author: California Business Law Institute, California Environmental Regulation Conference "Insurance Coverage for Spills - Recent Developments," October 1987; ABA Seminar, Going Bare: A Survival Course for Self-Insureds: "Digging Up Coverage Under Old Insurance Policies: Why, How and What Are the Pitfalls?" March 1987 and November, 1987. Author: "Arguments for A.B. 209 - Attorneys, Professional Responsibility Fund," State Bar of California Reports, July 1977; "The Outlook for Availability of Attorneys Errors and Omissions Coverage," Report of the Seventeenth Annual Seminar, Association of Southern California Defense Counsel, 1978; "Update: Legal Malpractice Insurance," Report of Eighteenth Annual Seminar, Association of Southern California Defense Counsel, 1979; "Rules of Construction Applicable to Insurance Policies: Carriers Duty to Its Insured, General Rules of Policy Construction," PLI, July 1983; "CEB California Automobile Insurance Law Guide," annual Supplements, 1982-1987. Author: TIPS: "Insurance: The Golden Goose for Intellectual Property Disputes?" Winter 1991; Panelist and Author: ABA Seminar: "Walking the Tightrope: Contesting Coverage During the Underlying Case," August 1991; USC Institute for Corporate Counsel: "ABC's of ERISA," March 1992. Speaker: Legal Aid Foundation: "After the Los Angeles Riots," May 1992. Author and Panelist: "Recent Developments in Insurance Law," Lorman Business Center Seminars in Los Angeles and Newport Beach, California, February 1993. Author and Speaker: "Fundamentals of Subrogation and Pursuing These Rights Notwithstanding Coverage Disputes," ABA National Meeting, NYC, August 1993. Co-Author and Speaker: "Insurance Coverage for Unfair Competition," ABA-TIPS Mid-Winter Meeting, Orlando Florida, February 1994. Author and Panelist: PLI Seminar, "Insurance Excess and Reinsurance Coverage Disputes," March 1995. Moderator: ABA-Tips Seminar: "Cutting the Gordian Knot: Mediating the Construction Coverage Dispute," February 1996. Member, Los Angeles Superior Court Arbitration Panel, Judicial Arbitration of Civil Cases, 1978-1982. Member, International Association of Property Insurance Council, 1981—. *Member:* Los Angeles County (Member, Trial Lawyers Section) and American (Member, Tort and Insurance Practice Section; Vice-Chair, Insurance Litigation Section; Chair, Subcommittee on Inland Marine and Trucking Coverage, 1991—; Vice Chairman, Insurance Litigation Section and Tort and Insurance Practice Section, 1990—; Chairman, TIPS Inland Marine Subcommittee, 1992) Bar Associations; The State Bar of California (Member, 1976— and Chairman, 1978-1979, Group Insurance Committee; Member, Client Protection Board, 1977- 1978) Defense Research Institute; Association of Southern California Defense Counsel (Member, Board of Governors, 1976-1978; Chairman, Industry Liaison Committee, 1978); Association of Business Trial Lawyers; International Association of Property Insurance Counsel. **PRACTICE AREAS:** Insurance Coverage Law; Toxic Substances Litigation; Professional Liability Litigation and Coverage.

**JAMES P. COLLINS, JR.** (Resident, Santa Ana Office; For complete biographical data, see professional biographies for Santa Ana).

**STEVEN L. PAINE,** born Camden, New Jersey, May 12, 1948; admitted to bar, 1976, California; 1977, U.S. District Court, Northern, Southern and Central Districts of California and U.S. Court of Appeals, Ninth Circuit. *Education:* Occidental College (B.A., 1970) Honors in Economics; Loyola University School of Law (J.D., 1976). Publications: Co-Author: California Continuing Education of the Bar, "California Automobile Insurance Law Guide," 1988 Supplement; Author: "Sudden and Accidental Pollution," *C&C Legal Update,* Spring 1992; "Workers' Comp Dividend Disputes Multiply as Policyholder Expectations are Disappointed," *C&C Legal Update,* Summer, 1992; "California Adopts Workers' Comp Open Rating," *C&C Legal Update,* Special Issue, August 1993; "Anatomy of a Reinsurance Arbitration," *C&C Legal Update,* Fall 1993; "California Appellate Court Skeptical Regarding Insurance Claim for 'Sudden' Pollution," *C&C Legal Update,* Winter 1995; "Intentional Wrongdoing and the Stipulated Judgment in Insurance Cases," *Recent Developments in Insurance Law* (Lorman Business Center, 1993); "Recent Developments in California Insurance Law: Enforceability of Stipulated Judgments Against Insurance Carriers," *Pepperdine Law Review,* Vol. 22, No. 3 (1995). Lecturer: "Insurance Issues in Automobile Accident Cases," California Continuing Education of the Bar, 1985-1986 (various locations); "Insurance and the Industry: Nuts and Bolts," Risk & Insurance Management Society Annual Conference, Atlanta, 1989; "Rights and Duties of Primary and Excess Carriers," Southern California Defense Counsel, 1989; "Recent Developments in Insurance Law," Lorman Business Center Seminar, Los Angeles and Newport Beach, February 1993. Activities: Arbitrator, Los Angeles Superior Court Judicial Arbitration Program, 1982. Managing Shareholder of the Firm. **PRACTICE AREAS:** Insurance Coverage and Bad Faith Litigation; Reinsurance Disputes; Insurance Regulatory Matters; Professional Liability Litigation.

**WILLIAM D. NAEVE** (Resident, Santa Ana Office; For complete biographical data, see professional biographies for Santa Ana).

**TERRY C. LEUIN,** born Pittsburgh, Pennsylvania, March 6, 1946; admitted to bar, 1982, California, U.S. District Court, Central, Southern and Northern Districts of California and U.S. Court of Appeals, Ninth Circuit. *Education:* University of California at Berkeley (B.A., 1967; Ph.D., 1976); Loyola Marymount University (J.D., cum laude, 1982). Member, St. Thomas More Law Honor Society. Recipient, American Jurisprudence Award in Secured Transactions and Real Property. Contributing Author: *Insurance Handbook for Business Litigators,* 1989. Author: "Maximizing Insurance Coverage and Minimizing Insurance Disputes: An Outline for Developers, Builders and General Contractors," April 1991; "Trigger Date Determined for Insurance Coverage," *Legal Update,* Fall 1988; "Home v. Landmark Rehearing," *Legal Update,* Spring 1989; "Insurance Coverage for Wrongful Termination," Parts I & II, *C&C Legal Update,* Summer 1992. Contributing Author: *Insurance Handbook for Litigators.* Panelist and Contributing Author in "Cutting the Gordian Knot: Mediating the Construction Coverage Dispute," Insurance Coverage Litigation Committee of the Tort and Insurance Practice Section of the American Bar Association, Newport Beach, California, February 1996. *Member:* Beverly Hills and Los Angeles County Bar Associations; State Bar of California (Member, Law Practice Management Section); International Association of Property Counsel. **PRACTICE AREAS:** Insurance Coverage Law; Insurance Bad Faith Litigation.

**ROGER W. SIMPSON,** born Houston, Texas, August 17, 1952; admitted to bar, 1983, California; 1984, U.S. District Court, Central District of California and U.S. Court of Appeals, Ninth Circuit. *Education:* California State University, Humboldt (B.A., magna cum laude, 1975); Western State University College of Law (J.D., magna cum laude, 1983). Recipient: American Jurisprudence Award in Evidence, Torts, Uniform Commercial Code. Author: "Supreme Court to Consider 'Advertising Injury' Coverage for Unfair Competition," *CC&F Legal Update,* Summer, 1991. *Member:* State Bar of California. **PRACTICE AREAS:** Insurance Coverage and Bad Faith Litigation.

**JOAN M. DOLINSKY,** born Princeton, New Jersey, October 19, 1949; admitted to bar, 1976, California; 1977, U.S. District Court, Central District of California; 1987, U.S. District Court, Southern District of California; 1990, U.S. District Court, Eastern District of California. *Education:* Mills College (B.A., 1972); USC Law Center; Villanova University School of Law (J.D., 1976). Author: "Recent Developments in Directors and Officers Liability Insurance," *ABTL Report* August 1990; "Recent Developments in Securities Litigation," *CC&F Legal Update,* Fall 1990; "Recent Developments in Directors and Officers Liability Insurance," and "Trends in Claims Against Corporate Directors and Officers," *ABTL Report,* January 1993 and *C&C Legal Update,* Spring & Summer, 1993; "Obtaining Advancement of Defense Costs in D&O Insurance Policies," *The Risk Management Newsletter,* Volume 14, Issue 4 1993; "Allocation of Loss in Directors and Officers Insurance Policies," *The D&O Book,* February 1994; "D&O Scene after Nordstrom," published by Swett & Crawford, June (1995);

*(This Listing Continued)*

**COTKIN & COLLINS,** A PROFESSIONAL CORPORATION, Los Angeles—Continued

"Nordstrom Court Drives Stake Through Heart of Insurers' Argument For Allocating Loss In D&O Insurance," *The Risk Management Letter,* Vol. 16, Issue 3, 1995 and *Legal Update,* Fall 1995; "Directors and Officers Liability Insurance for Employment-Related Claims," *Legal Update,* Part I Spring-/Summer 1995 and Part II, Fall 1995; "Employment Practices Liability Insurance," *Legal Update,* Fall 1995. Contributing Author: "California and Federal Subsidized Housing Law," *Insurance Handbook for Litigators,* 1989; CEB's *Fundamental of Civil Litigation Before Trial;* "Business Risk Policy Covers Economic Damages," Los Angeles County Bar Association publication, 1978. *Panelist:* Practicing Law Institute Seminar, "D&O Liability Issues," Spring 1994; Plus Day 1994, Professional Liability Underwriters Assoc., PLI Seminar: Employment Law Liability Claims: "What you need to know about Insurance Coverage," June 7, 1995. Seminar Speaker on "Insurance Coverage Law in California" at National Business Institute, Inc., Los Angeles, January 1996. Member, Master Level-Los Angeles Complex Litigation Inns of Court. *Member:* Los Angeles County Bar Association (Vice-Chair, Attorney Client Relations Committee, 1980-1982); State Bar of California; Association of Southern California Defense Counsel; The Association of Trial Lawyers of America. *LANGUAGES:* French. *PRACTICE AREAS:* Insurance Coverage; Insurance Bad Faith Litigation; Complex Business Litigation; Legal Malpractice Defense; Employment Practices Litigation.

**ROBERT G. WILSON,** born Fresno, California, July 19, 1948; admitted to bar, 1974, California; 1975, New York; 1976, District of Columbia; 1978, U.S. Supreme Court. *Education:* University of California at Santa Barbara (B.A., cum laude, 1970); Stanford University (J.D., 1973). Articles Editor, *Stanford Law Review,* 1972-1973. Author: "Settlement of Civil Litigation with the Government," and "Special Ethical Considerations in Federal Government Civil Litigation," in Federal Government Civil Litigation, P.L.I. No. 195, 1982; "Potential Pitfalls in Purchasing a Business," *C & C Legal Update,* Summer 1993. Co-Author: "New Limitations on the Manner of Conducting Depositions," Matthew Bender's *Federal Evidence Practice Guide Reporter,* May 1994. Member, Panel of Arbitrators, Pacific Stock Exchange and National Association of Securities Dealers. *Member:* Los Angeles County and American (Member, Sections on: Antitrust and Litigation) Bar Associations. *PRACTICE AREAS:* Antitrust; Bankruptcy; Business; Commercial and Securities Litigation.

**DAVID A. WINKLE** (Resident, Santa Ana Office; For complete biographical data, see professional biographies for Santa Ana).

**PHILIP S. GUTIERREZ** (Resident, Santa Ana Office; For complete biographical data, see professional biographies for Santa Ana).

**KAREN C. FREITAS,** born Hilo, Hawaii, October 7, 1956; admitted to bar, 1982, California; 1983, U.S. District Court, Central District of California and U.S. Court of Appeals, Ninth Circuit. *Education:* University of Hawaii (B.B.A., 1978); Loyola Law School (J.D., 1982). Author: "The New Mandatory Child Support Guidelines May Significantly Impact Your Existing Child Support," *C&C Legal Update,* Fall 1992. Speaker: Lawyers Mutual Insurance Company Seminar, "Preventing Malpractice in the Specialties," August 1992; "Obtaining the Dissolution of Marriage Judgment - An Overview" - *C&C Legal Update,* Winter 1994. Arbitrator, Los Angeles County Bar Association Dispute Resolution Services. Los Angeles County Bar Association Barristers Domestic Violence Volunteer. *Member:* Pasadena (Founding Chair and Member, Family Law Section), Los Angeles County (Member, Family Law Section) and American (Member, Family Law Section) Bar Associations. (Certified Specialist, Family Law, The State Bar of California Board of Legal Specialization). *PRACTICE AREAS:* Family Law.

**BRIAN R. HILL** (Resident, Santa Ana Office; For complete biographical data, see professional biographies for Santa Ana).

---

**LORI S. BLITSTIEN,** born Chicago, Illinois, October 25, 1949; admitted to bar, 1990, California, U.S. District Court, Central, Eastern and Southern Districts of California and U.S. Court of Appeals, Ninth Circuit. *Education:* University of Illinois (B.S., 1971); National College of Education (M.Ed., 1975); Loyola Law School (J.D., 1990). Kappa Delta Pi. Settlement Referee, North Central District's Court - Ordered Settlement Conference Program; Subcommittee Chair, Local Rules Committee, Los Angeles Chapter, Federal Bar Association. *Member:* State Bar of California (Member, Litigation Section); Los Angeles County, Federal and American Bar Associations. *PRACTICE AREAS:* Insurance Coverage and Bad Faith Litigation; General Civil Litigation; Professional Liability.

**CARRIE F. SMITH,** born Detroit, Michigan, January 22, 1962; admitted to bar, 1990, California, U.S. District Court, Central District of California and U.S. Court of Appeals, Ninth Circuit. *Education:* University of California (B.S., 1984); Whittier College (J.D., 1990). Managing Editor, *Whittier Law Review.* Co-Author: "California Liability Insurance Practice," Claims and Litigation, Chapter 8. *Member:* Orange County (Member, Family Law Section) and American Bar Associations; State Bar of California (Member, Litigation Section). *PRACTICE AREAS:* Family Law; General Business and Civil Litigation; Municipal Liability Defense; Civil Rights Litigation.

**GREGORY A. SARGENTI** (Resident, Santa Ana Office; For complete biographical data, see professional biographies for Santa Ana).

**TERRY L. KESINGER** (Resident, Santa Ana Office; For complete biographical data, see professional biographies for Santa Ana).

**BRADLEY W. JACKS,** born Minneapolis, Minnesota, September 20, 1958; admitted to bar, 1983, Illinois, U.S. Circuit Court of Appeals, Ninth Circuit, U.S. District Court, Northern District of Illinois; 1986, California; U.S. District Court Court, Central District of California. *Education:* University of North Carolina at Chapel Hill (B.A., 1979); University of Minnesota (J.D., 1983). Phi Beta Kappa. Author: "HMO Exposures," Business Insurance Magazine, August, 1983. Appellate Advocacy Instructor, University of Minnesota, 1982-1983. *Member:* Illinois State Bar Association; State Bar of California. *PRACTICE AREAS:* Professional Liability; Personal Injury; Insurance Coverage Litigation; Commercial Litigation.

**SCOTT P. WARD,** born Montebello, California, November 17, 1967; admitted to bar, 1995, California, U.S. District Court, Central District of California and U.S. Court of Appeals, Ninth Circuit. *Education:* University of Washington (B.A., cum laude, 1991); University of California at Los Angeles School of Law (J.D., 1995). Phi Beta Kappa; Beta Gamma Sigma; Golden Key National Honor Society. *Member:* State Bar of California. *PRACTICE AREAS:* General Civil and Business Litigation; Professional Liability Litigation; Insurance Coverage and Defense.

**ELLEN M. TIPPING** (Resident, Santa Ana Office; For complete biographical data, see professional biographies for Santa Ana).

REPRESENTATIVE CLIENTS: Agency Managers, Inc.- Reinsurance Intermediaries; American Healthcare Management; Bank of America; Bergen Brunswig Corp.; Canadian Insurance Co.; Ceradyne, Inc.; Comarco, Inc.; Crum & Forster; Dynatech Corporation; Farmers Insurance Group of Companies; Frawley Corporation; Grubb and Ellis; Hawthorne Community Medical Group; HK Microwave, Inc.; Irish Construction Company; John Hancock Mutual Life Ins. Co.; L.A. Gear.; Larchmont Reinsurance Company, Ltd.; Loral Aerospace Corp.; Manhattan Reinsurance Company; MDM, Inc.; Metropolitan Life Insurance Co.; National Medical Enterprises; Northwestern Mutual Life Insurance Co.; Northwestern National Life Insurance Co.; OrNda Health Corp.; Fremont - Pacific Compensation Insurance Co.; Pacific Mutual Life Insurance Co.; Pacific Telephone Co.; Piiceon; Risk Enterprise Management, Ltd.; Southern California Physicians Council; State of California; Tandem Computers, Inc.; Tandon Corp.; Transport Life Insurance Co.; Universal Health Services, Inc.; Watt Industries, Inc.; Western Design Corp.; Zurich Reinsurance Company.

---

# COUDERT BROTHERS
*1055 WEST SEVENTH STREET, TWENTIETH FLOOR*
**LOS ANGELES, CALIFORNIA 90017**
Telephone: 213-688-9088
Telecopier: 213-689-4467
URL: http://www.coudert.com

*REVISERS OF THE FRANCE LAW DIGEST FOR THIS DIRECTORY.*

*New York, N.Y. 10036-7703:* 1114 Avenue of the Americas.
*Washington, D.C. 20006:* 1627 I Street, N.W.
*San Francisco, California 94111:* 4 Embarcadero Center, Suite 3300.
*San Jose, California 95113:* Suite 1250, Ten Almaden Boulevard.
*Denver, Colorado 80202:* 1999 Broadway, Suite 2235.
*Paris 75008, France:* Coudert Frères, 52 Avenue des Champs-Elysees.
*London, EC4M 7JP, England:* 20 Old Bailey.
*Brussels B-1050, Belgium:* Tour Louise - Box 8, 149 Avenue Louise.
*Berlin 10707, Germany:* Kurfürstendamm 52.
*Beijing, People's Republic of China 100020:* 2708-09 Jing Guang Centre, Hu Jia Lou, Chao Yang Qu.
*Hong Kong:* Nine Queen's Road Central, 25th Floor.
*Singapore 049319:* Tung Centre, #21-00, 20 Collyer Quay.
*Sydney N.S.W. 2000, Australia:* Suite 2202, Colonial Centre, 52 Martin Place.

*(This Listing Continued)*

# PROFESSIONAL BIOGRAPHIES

*Tokyo 107, Japan:* 1355 West Tower, Aoyama Twin Towers, 1-1-1 Minami-Aoyama, Minato-ku.

*Moscow 109004, Russia:* Ul. Nikoloyamskaya 54 (formerly Ulyanovskaya).

*St. Petersburg 191011, Russia:* U1. Italianskaya 5, Office 56/57.

*Bangkok 10500, Thailand:* Bubhajit Building, 20 North Sathorn Road, 10th Floor.

*Ho Chi Minh City, Vietnam:* c/o Saigon Business Centre, 58 Dong Khoi Street, Suite 3B, District 1.

*Hanoi, Vietnam:* 38 Bui Thi Xuan Street, Hai Ba Trung District.

*General Practice.*

## MEMBERS OF FIRM

**RICHARD J. GARZILLI,** born New York City, N.Y., October 31, 1947; admitted to bar, 1973, New York; 1981, California. *Education:* Yale University (B.A., cum laude, 1969); New York University (J.D., 1972). Member and Managing Editor, New York University Law Review, 1971-1972. *Member:* State Bar of California; New York State and American Bar Associations. (Resident). *LANGUAGES:* Spanish, Italian and French.

**DAVID HUEBNER,** born Mahanoy City, Pennsylvania, May 7, 1960; admitted to bar, 1989, California, U.S. District Court, Southern, Central, Eastern and Northern Districts of California and U.S. Court of Appeals, Ninth Circuit; 1990, District of Columbia; 1992, U.S. Court of Appeals for the Federal Circuit and U.S. Court of International Trade. *Education:* Woodrow Wilson School of Public and International Affairs, Princeton University (A.B., summa cum laude, 1982); Yale University (J.D., 1986). Phi Beta Kappa. Henry Luce Fellow, Tokyo, Japan, 1984-1985. Editor-in-Chief, Yale Journal on Regulation, 1985-1986. Visiting Fellow, Center for Law in the Public Interest, Los Angeles, California, 1986-1987. Staff Attorney, Independent Commission on the Los Angeles Police Department, 1991. President, Los Angeles City Quality and Productivity Commission, 1994—. Member, Advisory Panel, Institute for Transnational Arbitration. Member and Arbitrator, British Columbia International Commercial Arbitration Centre; Arbitration and Mediation Institute of Canada. *Member:* Los Angeles County, Federal, American and International Bar Associations; State Bar of California; District of Columbia Bar. *LANGUAGES:* Japanese and German.

**ROBERT R. JESUELE,** born Los Angeles, California, October 27, 1960; admitted to bar, 1986, California. *Education:* Loyola Marymount University (B.A., 1982); Loyola Law School, Los Angeles (J.D., 1986). St. Thomas More Law Honor Society. Managing Editor, Loyola of Los Angeles International and Comparative Law Journal, 1985-1986. Author: "The Development of Japanese Telecommunications Policy and Its Impact on United States Trade," 8 Loyola of Los Angeles International and Comparative Law Journal 95, 1986. *Member:* State Bar of California; American Bar Association.

**RALPH C. NAVARRO,** born Los Angeles, California, February 5, 1949; admitted to bar, 1974, California. *Education:* University of Southern California (A.B., magna cum laude, 1971); Stanford University (J.D., 1974). Phi Beta Kappa; Phi Kappa Phi. Managing Editor, Stanford Journal of International Studies, 1973-1974. Lecturer, University of California Continuing Education of the Bar, 1981, 1983-1986; California Building Industry Foundation, 1996. *Member:* Los Angeles County (Member, Section on Real Estate) and American (Member, Sections on: Real Property, Probate and Trust Law; Business Law) Bar Associations; State Bar of California; Financial Attorneys Conference; American Land Title Association.

**SETH A. RIBNER,** born New York, N.Y., March 23, 1958; admitted to bar, 1984, New York; 1986, U.S. District Court, Southern and Eastern Districts of New York; 1990, U.S. Court of Appeals, Second Circuit; 1995, California; 1996, U.S. District Court, Central District of California and U.S. Court of Appeals, Ninth Circuit. *Education:* University of Pennsylvania (A.B., summa cum laude with distinction, 1979; A.M., 1979); Columbia University (J.D., 1982). Phi Beta Kappa. Harlan Fiske Stone Scholar. Author: "Modern Environmental Insurance Law: "Sudden and Accidental," 63 St. John's L. Rev. 755 (1988). Law Clerk to the Honorable Jerome Farris, U.S. Court of Appeals for the Ninth Circuit, 1982-1983. *Member:* Association of the Bar of the City of New York; American Bar Association.

**RICHARD G. WALLACE,** born Pittsburgh, Pennsylvania, May 26, 1949; admitted to bar, 1978, California. *Education:* Princeton University (A.B., summa cum laude, 1972); Columbia University (J.D., 1977). *Member:* State Bar of California. (Resident). *LANGUAGES:* Japanese.

*(This Listing Continued)*

# CALIFORNIA—LOS ANGELES

## OF COUNSEL

**BRUCE M. BOYD,** born Santa Monica, California, January 12, 1947; admitted to bar, 1973, California and U.S. District Court, Northern District of California. *Education:* University of California at Santa Barbara (B.A., summa cum laude, 1969); Boalt Hall School of Law, University of California (J.D., 1973). Phi Beta Kappa; Pi Sigma Alpha. Associate Editor, Ecology Law Quarterly, 1972-1973. Berkeley Professional Studies Scholar, All-India Law Institute, New Delhi, India, 1971-1972. California Real Estate Broker, 1981. Author: "Film Censorship in India: a Reasonable Restriction on Freedom of Speech and Expression?," 14 Journal of the Indian Law Institute 501 (New Delhi, 1972); Editorial Consultant, Drafting Business Contracts: Principals, Techniques and Forms (Continuing Education of the Bar, 1995 Ed.) Adjunct Instructor, Real Estate and Business Law, College of San Mateo, 1976-1982. Certified Instructor, California Department of Real Estate, Continuing Education Program, 1979-1990. Guest Lecturer, Real Property Management Courses, Golden Gate University, 1986. Research and Teaching Fellow, All-India Law Institute, New Delhi, India, 1971-1972. *Member:* Los Angeles and Orange County Bar Associations; International and Comparative Law Society. *PRACTICE AREAS:* Real Estate; International Business; Corporate.

## RESIDENT ASSOCIATES

Megan M. Bruce  
Sylvia K. Burks  
Lillian Hou  
J. Monica Kim  
Stephen G. Mason  
John Robert Renner  
Glenn W. Trost  
William M. Walker

### REVISERS OF THE FRANCE LAW DIGEST FOR THIS DIRECTORY.

(For biographical data of the New York personnel, see Professional Biographies at New York, N.Y.).

(For biographical data of the Washington personnel, see Professional Biographies at Washington, D.C.).

(For biographical data of San Francisco personnel, see Professional Biographies at San Francisco, California).

(For biographical data of the San Jose personnel, see Professional Biographies at San Jose, California).

(For biographical data of the Brussels personnel, see Professional Biographies at Brussels, Belgium).

(For biographical data of the London personnel, see Professional Biographies at London, England).

(For biographical data of the Paris personnel, see Professional Biographies at Paris, France).

(For biographical data of the Tokyo personnel, see Professional Biographies at Tokyo, Japan).

(For biographical data of the Hong Kong personnel, see Professional Biographies at Hong Kong).

(For biographical data of the Singapore personnel, see Professional Biographies at Singapore).

(For biographical data of the Moscow personnel, see Professional Biographies at Moscow, U.S.S.R.).

(For biographical data of the St. Petersburg personnel, see Professional Biographies at St. Petersburg, Russia).

(For biographical data of the Beijing personnel, see Professional Biographies at Beijing, People's Republic of China).

(For biographical data of the Sydney personnel, see Professional Biographies at Sydney, Australia).

(For biographical data of the Ho Chi Minh City personnel, see Professional Biographies at Ho Chi Minh City, Vietnam).

(For biographical data of the Hanoi personnel, see Professional Biographies at Hanoi, Vietnam).

# COVINGTON & CROWE

## LOS ANGELES, CALIFORNIA

(See Ontario)

*General Civil and Trial Practice. Corporations, Municipal, Real Estate, Estate Planning, Trust, Probate, Family, Labor Law, Criminal Defense, Bankruptcy, Creditor's Rights and Water Rights Law.*

## DAVID J. COWAN
THE WILTERN THEATRE TOWER
3780 WILSHIRE BOULEVARD, SUITE 910
**LOS ANGELES, CALIFORNIA 90010**
Telephone: 213-386-7957
FAX: 213-386-7958

*Business Litigation including Real Estate, Banking, Contracts, Bankruptcy, Insurance, Partnerships, Corporate and Securities Matters.*

**DAVID J. COWAN,** born London, England, June 10, 1963; admitted to bar, 1988, California. *Education:* Columbia University (B.A., 1984); Hastings College of the Law, University of California (J.D., 1988). Senior Member, Comment Law Journal, 1987-1988. Author: Comment, "Salinger v. Random House," 10 Comm/Ent Law Journal, Vol. 3 (1988); Comment, "Munroe v. Daily Herald", 10 Comm/Ent Law Journal, Vol. 4 (1988). Extern to Hon. Lucy Kelly McCabe, San Francisco Superior Court, 1987. Volunteer Settlement Officer, Los Angeles Municipal Court, 1990—. Editorial Board, Los Angeles Lawyer, 1994—. Associate: Rogers & Wells, 1988-1992; Leland, Parachini, et. al., 1992-1994. *Member:* State Bar of California. **REPORTED CASES:** Daniels v. Centennial Group, 16 Cal. App. 4th 467 (1993); Ocean Services Corp. v. Ventura Port District, 15 Cal. App. 4th 1762 (1993); Kim v. Sumitomo Bank, 17 Cal. App. 4th 974 (1993).

---

## COX, CASTLE & NICHOLSON, LLP
A Limited Liability Partnership including Professional Corporations

*28TH FLOOR, TWO CENTURY PLAZA*
*2049 CENTURY PARK EAST*
**LOS ANGELES, CALIFORNIA 90067**
Telephone: 310-277-4222
Fax: 310-277-7889

*Irvine, California Office:* 19800 MacArthur Boulevard, Suite 600. Telephone: 714-476-2111. Fax: 714-476-0256.

*General Civil, Trial and Appellate Practice in all State and Federal Courts. Real Property and Construction Law. Land Use and Environmental Law. Public Bond Financing. International Law. Labor Relations. Receiverships and Creditors Rights. Taxation, Trusts, Estate Planning and Probate Law.*

*FIRM PROFILE: Cox, Castle & Nicholson, LLP was founded over 40 years ago and has consistently focused its practice on the representation of businesses and individuals involved in all aspects of the real estate, construction and financial services industries. With offices in both Los Angeles and Irvine, California, Cox, Castle & Nicholson, LLP is one of the largest firms serving the real estate industry in the United States. The firm provides the breadth and depth of legal services typically required by developers, builders, investors, landlords, tenants, lenders and others who are involved in a wide range of commercial, industrial, residential, hotel and resort projects.*

**GEORGE M. COX** (Retired).

**RICHARD N. CASTLE** (1932-1992).

### RESIDENT PARTNERS

**PHILLIP R. NICHOLSON, (A PROFESSIONAL CORPORATION),** born Ottumwa, Iowa, December 17, 1935; admitted to bar, 1962, California. *Education:* University of Southern California (B.S., 1957; J.D., 1961). Phi Delta Phi; Order of the Coif. Member, Board of Editors, Southern California Law Review, 1959-1961. Member, Board of Councilors, University of Southern California School of Law, 1991-1995. Member, Economic Development Corporation of Los Angeles (Member, Board of Directors, 1984—; Chairman, 1989-1991; Executive Committee Member, 1986—). *Member:* Beverly Hills, Los Angeles County (Member, Executive Committee, Real Property Section, 1969-1990) and American Bar Associations; State Bar of California; Lambda Alpha International; American College of Real Estate Lawyers. **PRACTICE AREAS:** Real Property Law.

**LAWRENCE TEPLIN,** born Chicago, Illinois, October 30, 1936; admitted to bar, 1964, California; 1966, U.S. Supreme Court. *Education:* California State University at Los Angeles (B.A, 1958); University of California at Los Angeles (LL.B., 1964). Lecturer: "Stigma Damages in Environmental Litigation," 27th Annual Litigation Seminar, Appraisal Institute, 1995; "Property Valuation and Environmental Contamination," UCLA, 1995. [Capt., U.S. Marine Corps Reserve, 1958-1961]. **PRACTICE AREAS:** Civil Litigation; Construction Litigation; Real Property Law; Hazardous and Toxic Substances Law.

*(This Listing Continued)*

**RONALD I. SILVERMAN, (A PROFESSIONAL CORPORATION),** born Big Spring, Texas, August 30, 1939; admitted to bar, 1967, California. *Education:* University of California at Los Angeles (B.A., 1961; J.D., 1966). Author: "Supplement, California Real Property Financing," 1990. Editor: *Real Estate Development Principles and Process*, 2nd Edition, ULI, 1995. *Member:* Los Angeles County and American Bar Associations; State Bar of California; Urban Land Institute (Vice-Chair, Development Regulations Council; Membership Chair, L.A. District Council Chair, District Council Executive Committee and Steering Committee). **PRACTICE AREAS:** Real Property Law; Land Use Law; Vested Rights Law; Development Agreements and Real Estate Finance Law.

**MARIO CAMARA,** born Maywood, California, October 20, 1948; admitted to bar, 1973, California. *Education:* University of California at Los Angeles (B.A., cum laude, 1970; J.D., 1973). Pi Sigma Alpha. Member, U.C.L.A. Law Review, 1971-1972. Member, Board of Directors, Legal Aid Foundation of Los Angeles, 1987—; Vice-President, 1994-1995; President, 1995-1996. Member, Board of Governors, California Consortium for Transportation Research and Development, 1994—. Member, Policy Advisory Board, Center for Real Estate and Urban Economics, 1991—. *Member:* Beverly Hills, Los Angeles County and American Bar Associations; State Bar of California. **PRACTICE AREAS:** Real Property Law; Construction Law.

**GEORGE D. CALKINS, II,** born Dayton, Ohio, June 29, 1946; admitted to bar, 1973, California. *Education:* University of California at Los Angeles (B.A., 1968); Loyola University School of Law (J.D., 1973). Co-Author: "Handling Earth Movement After *Garvey:* A Practical Guide to Selecting and Retaining Geotechnical Engineers," CEB Real Property Law Reporter, August, 1989. Panelist, "Settling Real Estate Disputes," Rutter Group, December 1991; "Construction Damages," L.A. County Bar, Winter 1991; "Developer's Opposition to its Lender's Request for a Receiver," L.A. County Bar, Fall 1991; "The Construction Litigation Explosion," So. Cal. Defense Counsel, 1992. Certified Member, American Arbitration Association. Panel of Arbitrators: California Public Works Arbitration Program. **PRACTICE AREAS:** Real Estate and Construction Litigation; Bankruptcy Law; Insurance Law.

**JOHN H. KUHL,** born Santa Monica, California, June 27, 1949; admitted to bar, 1974, California. *Education:* University of California at Davis (B.S., with highest honors, 1971; J.D., 1974). Lecturer: "Significant Legal Issues," Conference on Real Estate Investment Strategies for Pension Funds, 1988; "Due Diligence in Real Estate Investments," Conference on Real Estate Investment Strategies for Pension Funds, 1989; "Decision-Making Process of Commercial Mortgages," National Forum on Real Estate Investment for Pension Funds, 1996. *Member:* Los Angeles County and American Bar Associations; State Bar of California; Pension Real Estate Association; National Association of Public Pension Attorneys. **PRACTICE AREAS:** Real Property Law; Real Estate Acquisitions and Finance.

**ARTHUR O. SPAULDING, JR.** (Irvine Office).

**JEFFREY LAPOTA,** born Los Angeles, California, March 30, 1946; admitted to bar, 1975, California. *Education:* University of California at Los Angeles (B.S., summa cum laude, 1968); Harvard University (J.D., cum laude, 1975). Phi Beta Kappa; Beta Gamma Sigma. *Member:* Beverly Hills, Century City (Co-Chair, Trust and Estates Section, 1995—), Los Angeles County and American (Member, Real Property, Probate and Trust Law Section) Bar Associations; State Bar of California. **PRACTICE AREAS:** Estate Planning Law; Probate Law; Tax Law.

**DAVID A. LEIPZIGER,** born New York, N.Y., July 12, 1937; admitted to bar, 1968, California. *Education:* Harvard University (A.B., cum laude, 1959); Boalt Hall School of Law, University of California (J.D., 1967). Order of the Coif. Articles Editor, California Law Review, 1966-1967. Author: "Deficiency Judgments in California: The Supreme Court Tries Again," 22 U.C.L.A. Law Review 753, 1975; "The Mortgagee's Remedies for Waste," 64 California Law Review 1086, 1976. Acting Professor of Law, 1972-1977 and Adjunct Professor of Law, 1980-1981, University of California at Los Angeles. *Member:* Los Angeles County and American Bar Associations; State Bar of California. **PRACTICE AREAS:** Bankruptcy Law; Creditors Rights Law; Real Property Law; Commercial Law.

**JOHN S. MILLER, JR.,** born Austin, Texas, May 31, 1949; admitted to bar, 1977, California. *Education:* University of California at Davis, University of Nevada at Las Vegas and California State University at Long Beach (B.S., 1974); University of California at Los Angeles (J.D., 1977). Contributing Author: *Employee Benefits Law*, ABA Section of Labor and Employment Law, BNA, 1991. Director: Natl. Coord. Comm. of Multiemployer Plans, 1991—. Commissioner: City of Manhattan Beach, 1992—. **REPORTED CASES:** Concrete Pipe and Products of California v. Construction

*(This Listing Continued)*

Laborers Pension Trust for Southern California —U.S.—, 113 S.Ct. 2264 (1993); *Tippett v. Terich,* 37 Cal. App. 4th 1517 (1995). *PRACTICE AREAS:* Labor Relations Law; Employee Benefits Law; Construction Law.

**KENNETH B. BLEY,** born San Francisco, California, May 1, 1939; admitted to bar, 1974, California and U.S. District Court, Northern District of California; 1975, U.S. District Court, Central District of California; 1976, U.S. District Court, Eastern District of California; 1982, U.S. Court of Federal Claims and U.S. Court of Appeals for the Federal Circuit; 1986, U.S. Supreme Court; 1991, U.S. Court of Appeals, Third Circuit; U.S. Court of Appeals, Ninth Circuit. *Education:* University of California at Berkeley (B.S., 1961; M.S., 1963); University of California at Los Angeles (Ph.D., 1969); Harvard University (J.D., magna cum laude, 1974). *PRACTICE AREAS:* Appellate Litigation; Land Use Litigation; Land Use and Eminent Domain Law.

**IRA J. WALDMAN,** born Brooklyn, New York, May 2, 1951; admitted to bar, 1976, Maine; 1981, California. *Education:* Bates College (B.A., 1973); University of Maine (J.D., cum laude, 1976). Panelist: "Restructuring Real Property Relationships," CEB, 1994; "Loan Document Strategies: Lessons From the Battle Lines," L.A. County Bar Association, 1994; "Lenders & Leases: For Whom the Cash Flows," L.A. County Bar Association, 1995; "Third Party Liability for Real Estate Secured Loan Obligations," Crocker Symposium, 1995; "Guarantor Rights Under Borrower Anti-Deficiency Laws," ABA Convention, 1995; "Lending Risks: California's Changing Orientation," L.A. County Bar, 1995. *Member:* Beverly Hills, Los Angeles County, Maine State and American Bar Associations; State Bar of California. *PRACTICE AREAS:* Real Property Law; Bankruptcy Law; Creditors Rights Law.

**JOHN F. NICHOLSON,** born San Francisco, California, May 5, 1952; admitted to bar, 1979, California. *Education:* University of Illinois (B.A., magna cum laude, 1974); Northwestern University (J.D., 1978). Phi Beta Kappa. Instructor, "Fundamentals of Real Property Practice - Recent Developments in Real Property," Continuing Education of the Bar, University of California, February, 1983, 1984 and 1986. Author: "A Winning Strategy for Condominium Projects," Chicago Title Magazine, 1989; "Franchise Tax Board Audits Country Clubs in Effort to Find 'Discriminatory Practices'," Los Angeles Business Journal, 1989. *Member:* Los Angeles County Bar Association; State Bar of California. *PRACTICE AREAS:* Real Property Law; Land Use Law; Destination Resort and Country Club Law; Subdivisions and Real Estate Finance Law.

**CHARLES E. NONEMAN,** born El Paso, Texas, December 13, 1952; admitted to bar, 1978, California. *Education:* University of California at Los Angeles (B.A., 1975); Hastings College of Law, University of California (J.D., 1978). Phi Beta Kappa; Pi Gamma Mu; Phi Delta Phi; Order of the Coif. Member, Thurston Society. Member, 1976-1977 and Editor, 1977-1978, Hastings Law Journal. Editor, Hastings International and Comparative Law Review, 1976-1977. Law Clerk to Justice Boochever, Alaska Supreme Court, 1978-1979. *Member:* Beverly Hills (Member, Board of Governors, 1986-1988), Los Angeles County and American Bar Associations; State Bar of California; Association of Business Trial Lawyers. *PRACTICE AREAS:* Civil Litigation; Employee Benefits Law; Labor and Employment Law; Construction Law.

**WILLIAM KAMER,** born New York, N.Y., March 30, 1951; admitted to bar, 1978, California. *Education:* George Washington University, Vassar College (A.B., with honors, 1973); Harvard University (Master of City and Regional Planning, 1978); Boston University (J.D., cum laude, 1978). Member, Boston University Law Review, 1976-1978. *Member:* Los Angeles County Bar Association (Member, Real Property Section); State Bar of California (Member, Real Property Section). *PRACTICE AREAS:* Real Property Law.

**MARLENE D. GOODFRIED,** born Windsor, Ontario, Canada, November 2, 1954; admitted to bar, 1979, California. *Education:* University of California at Los Angeles (B.A., summa cum laude, 1976; J.D., 1979). Phi Beta Kappa; The Order of Barristers. Member, Moot Court. *Member:* Century City and Los Angeles County Bar Associations; State Bar of California. *PRACTICE AREAS:* Real Property Law; Commercial Leasing Law.

**BARRY P. JABLON,** born Chicago, Illinois, January 14, 1940; admitted to bar, 1978, California. *Education:* Columbia University (B.A., 1960); University of California at Berkeley (M.A., 1961; Ph.D., 1967); Boalt Hall School of Law, University of California (J.D., 1978). Managing Editor, California Law Review, 1977-1978. Author: "The 'Top 10'," California Real Property Journal, 1990—. Co-Author: "The New Lis Pendens Law," Los Angeles Lawyer, Vol. 19, No. 4, 1996. Lecturer: Real Property Practice Institute (CEB), 1994; Real Property Retreat, State Bar, 1995. *Member:* Los Angeles County Bar Association (Co-Chair, Real Estate Litigation,

*(This Listing Continued)*

1994—). *REPORTED CASES: Laborers Clean-Up Contract Administration Trust Fund v. Uriarte Clean-Up Service, Inc.* , 736 F.2d 516, 9th Cir., 1984; *Mattel, Inc. v. Hyatt* , 664 F.2d 757, 9th Cir., 1981. *PRACTICE AREAS:* Real Property Law; Civil Litigation.

**JEFFREY D. MASTERS,** born Gary, Indiana, June 28, 1954; admitted to bar, 1980, California. *Education:* University of California at Los Angeles (B.A., summa cum laude, 1976; M.B.A., 1980; J.D., 1980). Phi Beta Kappa. Technical Consultant: *Broad Form Property Damage Coverage* (3rd Ed., International Risk Management Institute, 1992); *California Liability Insurance Practice: Claims and Litigation,* (CEB, 1991). Author: "Implementing Effective Record Retention Policies for Developers," *Journal of Construction Accounting and Taxation,* Summer, 1995; "Risk Reduction Strategies for Builders," *Builder's Management Journal,* Fall, 1994. Instructor: "CGL Overview: The Pollution Liability Exclusions," International Risk Management Institute, 1995; "Broad Form Property Damage Coverage for Developers," International Risk Management Institute. *PRACTICE AREAS:* Real Estate and Construction Litigation; Insurance Law.

**ROBERT D. INFELISE,** born Long Beach, California, November 23, 1955; admitted to bar, 1980, California. *Education:* University of California at Berkeley (A.B., summa cum laude, 1977); Boalt Hall School of Law, University of California (J.D., 1980). Phi Beta Kappa. Adjunct Professor, Boalt Hall School of Law, University of California at Berkeley, 1994—. Author: "CGL Policies After *Montrose,*" Real Estate/Environmental Liability News, August 1995. Lecturer: "Overview of California's Proposition 65," Indoor Environment Conference, April 1996; "Changing Face of Environmental Litigation," UC Berkeley, March 1996. *REPORTED CASES:* Resolution Trust Corp. v. Rossmoor Corp., 34 Cal. App. 4th 93 (1995). *PRACTICE AREAS:* Environmental Law; Civil Litigation.

**TAMAR C. STEIN,** born Los Angeles, California, February 25, 1948; admitted to bar, 1977, California; 1978, U.S. District Court, Central District of California; 1980, U.S. Court of Appeals, Ninth Circuit; 1982, U.S. District Court, Northern District of California; 1984, U.S. District Court, Southern and Eastern Districts of California. *Education:* University of California at Berkeley (B.A., 1969); University of California at Los Angeles (J.D., 1977). Order of the Coif. Member, UCLA Law Review, 1976-1977. *Member:* Beverly Hills, Century City and Los Angeles County Bar Associations; State Bar of California. *SPECIAL AGENCIES:* All city councils and planning commissions; California Coastal Commission; California services districts. *PRACTICE AREAS:* Land Use Law; Land Use and Real Estate Litigation; Business Litigation.

**DOUGLAS P. SNYDER,** born Los Angeles, California, November 12, 1954; admitted to bar, 1981, California. *Education:* University of California (B.A., 1976; M.B.A., 1981); University of California School of Law (J.D., 1981). Phi Beta Kappa. *Member:* Los Angeles County Bar Association; State Bar of California. *PRACTICE AREAS:* Real Property Law.

**GARY A. GLICK,** born Teaneck, New Jersey, March 23, 1954; admitted to bar, 1979, California. *Education:* University of Rochester (B.A., cum laude, 1976); Loyola University of Los Angeles (J.D., 1979). Author: "Negotiating the Common Area Expense Provision in a Retail Lease," CEB Real Property Law Reporter, January, 1996; "Exclusive Use Provisions in Retail Leases," CEB Real Property Law Reporter, April, 1995. *Member:* Los Angeles County Bar Association; State Bar of California (Member, Real Property Subsection); International Council of Shopping Centers (Southern California State Director; Southern California Program Committee). *PRACTICE AREAS:* Shopping Center Development; Commercial Leasing.

**LORA LEE MOORE** (Irvine Office).

**LEWIS G. FELDMAN,** born New York, N.Y., February 13, 1956; admitted to bar, 1982, California. *Education:* University of California at Santa Cruz (B.A., with highest honors, 1978); University of California at Davis (J.D., 1982). Member, University of California at Davis Moot Court, 1980-1981. Member and Executive Editor, University of California, Davis Law Review, 1980-1982. *Member:* Beverly Hills, Century City, Los Angeles County and American Bar Associations; State Bar of California; Urban Land Institute; National Association of Bond Lawyers; National Association of Real Estate Investment Trusts. *PRACTICE AREAS:* Public Financing Law; Land Use Law; Real Property Law.

**P. JEROLD WALSH** (Irvine Office).

**MARK P. MCCLANATHAN** (Irvine Office).

**JOHN A. KINCANNON** (Irvine Office).

**STANLEY W. LAMPORT,** born Hollywood, California, January 18, 1957; admitted to bar, 1982, California. *Education:* University of Southern

*(This Listing Continued)*

**COX, CASTLE & NICHOLSON, LLP,** *Los Angeles—Continued*

California (A.B., magna cum laude, 1979); Northwestern University (J.D., 1982). Phi Beta Kappa, Phi Kappa Phi, Blue Key. Order of Troy. Contributing Author: "Attorney Practice and Ethics," in *California Pleading and Practice,* Matthew Bender, 1994. *Member:* Los Angeles County Bar Association (Committee on Professional Responsibility, Chair, 1991-1992); State Bar of California (Member, Standing Committee on Professional Responsibility and Conduct, 1992-1998; Vice-Chair, 1995-1996); National Association of Industrial and Office Properties (Member, Board of Directors). *REPORTED CASES: Thompson v. Allert,* 233 C.A. 3d 1462 (1991). *PRACTICE AREAS:* Civil Litigation; Land Use Law; Legal Ethics; Insurance Law.

**RANDALL W. BLACK,** born Newport Beach, California, July 17, 1960; admitted to bar, 1983, California. *Education:* University of California at Los Angeles (B.A., 1980); University of California, Boalt Hall School of Law at Berkeley (J.D., 1983). Associate Editor, California Law Review, 1981-1982. Co-Author: "The Partnership Vehicle in Retail Joint Ventures," CEB Real Property Law Reporter, January 1992. Moderator: "Disclosure Pitfalls in Real Estate Transactions," Los Angeles County Bar Association, 1995; "The Successful Joint Venture," Pacific Resources Conference, 1992. *Member:* Century City (Co-Chair, Real Property Section, 1993-1995) and Los Angeles County (Steering Committee, Commercial Development Subsection) Bar Associations; State Bar of California. *PRACTICE AREAS:* Corporate Law; Real Property Law.

**PERRY D. MOCCIARO,** born Lynwood, California, June 29, 1950; admitted to bar, 1975, California; 1978, U.S. Supreme Court; 1991, U.S. Tax Court; U.S. Court of Appeals, Ninth Circuit; U.S. District Court, Central, Northern, Southern and Eastern Districts of California. *Education:* University of Southern California (A.B., magna cum laude, Phi Beta Kappa, 1972); Boalt Hall School of Law, University of California at Berkeley (J.D., 1975). Author: "Leasewise: Economic Effects on a Property's Use," Los Angeles Daily Journal, November 2, 1995. Lecturer: "Real Property Remedies," Continuing Education of the Bar, University of California, 1991; "Franchise Dispute Resolution," International Franchising Association, 1987. *Member:* Association of Business Trial Lawyers. *PRACTICE AREAS:* Civil Litigation; Real Property; Franchising Law.

**JESS R. BRESSI** (Irvine Office).

**GREGORY J. KARNS,** born Los Angeles, California, December 26, 1956; admitted to bar, 1983, California. *Education:* University of California at Los Angeles; University of California at Santa Cruz (B.A., with honors, 1980); Loyola University of Los Angeles (J.D., cum laude, 1983). Saint Thomas More Law Honor Society. *Member:* Los Angeles County Bar Association (Member: Real Property Section; Steering Committee); State Bar of California (Member, Real Property Section); Pacific Resources Council. *PRACTICE AREAS:* Real Property Law.

**D. SCOTT TURNER** (Irvine Office).

**SAMUEL H. GRUENBAUM,** born Tel Aviv, Israel, June 26, 1952; admitted to bar, 1978, California; 1980, District of Columbia. *Education:* California State University at Northridge (B.S., 1973); Loyola University of Los Angeles (J.D., 1977); Georgetown University (LL.M., 1980). Certified Public Accountant, California, 1975. Adjunct Professor of Law: Loyola University of Los Angeles, 1980-1985, 1988; University of Miami Law School LL.M. Program, 1995—. Attorney, Division of Enforcement, Securities and Exchange Commission, 1977-1979. *Member:* Los Angeles County Bar Association (Member, Executive Committee, Business and Corporations Law Section; Chair, 1991-1992); State Bar of California; National Association of Real Estate Investment Trusts. *PRACTICE AREAS:* Corporate Law; Securities Law.

**SANDRA C. STEWART,** born Los Angeles, California; admitted to bar, 1984, California. *Education:* University of California at Los Angeles (B.A., 1980); Loyola Law School of Los Angeles (J.D., 1983). Member, Loyola Law Review, 1982-1983. Co-Author: "What *Montrose* Means for Construction Defect and Insurance Litigation," Los Angeles Daily Journal, Oct. 23, 1995. Lecturer: Pacific Cast Builders Conference, "If You Build It, They Will Sue," 1995; BIA, "Construction Defect Litigation Reform," 1996. Home Aid Board Member, Construction Defect Task Force. *Member:* State Bar of California. *PRACTICE AREAS:* Real Estate and Construction Litigation.

**MATHEW A. WYMAN,** born Los Angeles, California, May 18, 1961; admitted to bar, 1986, California. *Education:* Pomona College (B.A., cum laude, 1983); Columbia University (J.D., 1986). Phi Beta Kappa. *Member:*

*(This Listing Continued)*

Beverly Hills, Los Angeles County and American Bar Associations; State Bar of California.

**RANDY P. ORLIK,** born Cincinnati, Ohio, June 15, 1952; admitted to bar, 1979, California and U.S. District Court, Northern District of California; 1982, U.S. Court of Appeals, Ninth Circuit; 1983, U.S. District Court, Central and Southern Districts of California. *Education:* Amherst College (B.A., cum laude, 1974); University of California at Berkeley School of Business (M.B.A., 1979); University of California, Boalt Hall School of Law (J.D., 1979). Order of the Coif. *Member:* State Bar of California; American Bankruptcy Institute; California Bankruptcy Forum; Financial Lawyers Conference. *PRACTICE AREAS:* Bankruptcy; Real Estate Finance; UCC Secured Transactions.

**KENNETH WILLIAMS,** born New York, N.Y., September 9, 1959; admitted to bar, 1985, California; 1986, U.S. District Court, Central District of California. *Education:* University of Virginia (B.A., with high distinction, 1981); Boston University School of Law (J.D., cum laude, 1985). Staff Member, 1983-1984 and Articles Editor, 1984-1985, International Law Journal, Boston University School of Law. *Member:* Los Angeles County and American Bar Associations; State Bar of California. *PRACTICE AREAS:* Construction Law; Real Property Law.

**LAUREL R. BALLARD,** born Los Angeles, California, June 1, 1955; admitted to bar, 1986, California; 1987, U.S. District Court, Southern District of California; 1988, U.S. District Court, Central and Northern Districts of California and U.S. Court of Appeals, Ninth Circuit. *Education:* Pomona College (B.A., 1977); University of Southern California (J.D., 1986). *Member:* Los Angeles County Bar Association State Bar of California (Member, Legislation Committee, Litigation Section); Los Angeles Complex Litigation American Inn of Court; California Women Lawyers. *PRACTICE AREAS:* Real Estate and Business Litigation; Construction Litigation.

**AMY H. WELLS,** born Los Angeles California, January 30, 1957; admitted to bar, 1988, California. *Education:* Occidental College (B.A., cum laude, 1978); University of California at Los Angeles (J.D., 1988). Member: Moot Court; Executive Board of Judges, Moot Court Honors Program. Recipient, American Jurisprudence Award in Corporations and Partnerships. Co-Author: "LLCs and The Institutional Investor," Daily Journal, April, 1996; "Issues in Portfolio Acquisitions and Sales," Institutional Real Estate Letter, February, 1996; "A Review of the Most Significant Legal Developments in 1995," Institutional Real Estate Letter, December, 1995; "Hart-Scott-Rodino Revisited," Institutional Real Estate Letter, July, 1995. *Member:* Los Angeles County Bar Association; State Bar of California. *PRACTICE AREAS:* Real Property Law.

**SCOTT D. BROOKS,** born Orange, New Jersey, October 18, 1963; admitted to bar, 1989, California. *Education:* Cornell University (B.A., cum laude, 1985); Yale University (J.D., 1988). Editor, Yale Law Journal, 1987. Member, International Council of Shopping Centers. *Member:* State Bar of California. *PRACTICE AREAS:* Real Property Law.

**GARY P. DOWNS,** born Berkeley, California, July 31, 1962; admitted to bar, 1988, California. *Education:* DePauw University (B.A., magna cum laude, 1985); University of California, Hastings College of the Law (J.D., 1988). Phi Beta Kappa. Senior Articles Editor, Hastings Constitutional Law Quarterly, 1987-1988. Author: "The California Campaign Spending Limits Act of 1988," Hastings Constitutional Law Quarterly, Volume 15, Number 1; "Building with Tax-Exempt, Low-Interest Rate Bonds," *Urban Land,* May 1994. *Member:* State Bar of California; American Bar Association; National Association of Bond Lawyers. *PRACTICE AREAS:* Public Finance.

**VALERIE L. FLORES,** born Glendale, California, March 6, 1960; admitted to bar, 1988, California and U.S. District Court, Central District of California. *Education:* University of California at Los Angeles (B.A., 1985); Pepperdine University (J.D., 1988). Recipient, American Jurisprudence Awards in Real Property and Professional Responsibility. Member, Pepperdine Moot Court Board and Law Review (published California Survey, Vol. 14, 1987). *Member:* State Bar of California. *PRACTICE AREAS:* Real Estate and Business Litigation.

### RESIDENT OF COUNSEL

**JAMES E. BARNETT,** born Monahans, Texas, January 3, 1942; admitted to bar, 1966, Texas; 1970, U.S. Tax Court and U.S. District Court, Northern District of Texas; 1988, California. *Education:* Southern Methodist University (B.B.A., 1964; LL.B., 1966; LL.M., 1972). Phi Delta Phi. Editor, Journal of Law and Commerce, Southern Methodist University, 1966. Adjunct Professor, Southern Methodist University School of Law, 1977-1978. *Member:* Los Angeles County and American (Member, Taxa-

*(This Listing Continued)*

tion Section) Bar Associations; State Bar of Texas (Council Member, Taxation Section); State Bar of California. [Captain, USMC, 1966-1969]. *PRACTICE AREAS:* Taxation Law.

**EDWARD C. DYGERT,** born Santa Monica, California, December 27, 1946; admitted to bar, 1973, California; 1977, U.S. District Court, Central District of California; 1983, U.S. Court of Appeals, Ninth Circuit; 1985, U.S. Supreme Court. *Education:* California State University, Fullerton (B.A., 1970); University of San Diego (J.D., 1973). *Member:* Los Angeles County Bar Association (Real Property Section; Chair, Land Use Planning Subsection 1990-1995); State Bar of California (Real Property Section, Co-Chair, Zoning and Land Use Subsection, 1995—). *REPORTED CASES: City of Oakland v. Oakland Raiders* (1985), 174 Cal.App.3d 414. *PRACTICE AREAS:* Land Use Law; Eminent Domain Law; Environmental Law.

### RESIDENT ASSOCIATES

Maria Victoria Bernstein; Estelle M. Braaf; Preston W. Brooks; Christine Costa; Kevin J. Crabtree; Susan S. Davis; Sherry M. DuPont; Scott L. Grossfeld; Robert M. Haight, Jr.; John A. Henning, Jr.; Herbert Jay Klein; Mark T. Lammas; Mark Moore; Carlisle G. Packard; Scott Price; Edward F. Quigley, III; Anne-Marie Reader; David S. Rosenberg; John D. Rosenfeld; Stephanie Ann Schroeder; Cynthia K. Simons; Sharon L. Tamiya; Paul J. Titcher; Daniel J. Villalpando; Lisa A. Weinberg; Adam B. Weissburg.

REFERENCE: Bank of America National Trust & Savings Assn. (Beverly Hills Main Branch, Beverly Hills).

---

# COZEN AND O'CONNOR

A PROFESSIONAL CORPORATION

777 TOWER
777 SOUTH FIGUEROA STREET
SUITE 2850
**LOS ANGELES, CALIFORNIA 90017**
Telephone: 213-892-7900
800-563-1027
Fax: 213-892-7999

*Philadelphia, Pennsylvania Office:* 1900 Market Street, 19103. Telephones: 215-665-2000; 800-523-2900; Fax: 215-665-2013.
*Charlotte, North Carolina Office:* One First Union Plaza, 301 South College Street, Suite 2100, 28202. Telephones: 704-376-3400; 800-762-3575. Fax: 704-334-3351.
*Columbia, South Carolina Office:* The Palmetto Center, 1426 Main Street, 29201. Telephones: 803-799-3900; 800-338-1117. Fax: 803-254-7233.
*Dallas, Texas Office:* Suite 4100, NationsBank Plaza, 901 Main Street, 75202. Telephones: 214-761-6700; 800-448-1207. Fax: 214-761-6788.
*New York, N.Y. Office:* 45 Broadway Atrium, 16th Floor, 10006. Telephones: 212-509-9400; 800-437-9400. Fax: 212-509-9492.
*San Diego, California Office:* Suite 1610, 501 West Broadway, 92101. Telephones: 619-234-1700; 800-782-3366. Fax: 619-234-7831.
*Seattle, Washington Office:* Suite 5200, Washington Mutual Tower, 1201 Third Avenue, 98101. Telephones: 206-340-1000; 800-423-1950. Fax: 206-621-8783.
*Westmont, New Jersey Office:* 316 Haddon Avenue, 08108. Telephones: 609-854-4900; 800-523-2900. Fax: 609-854-1782.
*Atlanta, Georgia Office:* Suite 2200, One Peachtree Center, 303 Peachtree Street, N.E., 30308. Telephones: 404-572-2000; 800-890-1393. Fax: 404-572-2199.

*Property Insurance Law; Subrogation and Recovery; Casualty Defense; Insurance Coverage; Arson and Fraud Defense; Environmental and Toxic Tort; Primary/Excess and Re-Insurance Claims and Defense; Professional Liability Defense; Architects and Engineers Errors and Omissions; Agent and Brokers Errors and Omissions Defense; Employment Law; Directors and Officers Errors and Omissions Defense; Business and Commercial Litigation; Securities Litigation; RICO; Trade Secrets and Restrictive Covenants; Copyright Infringement; Construction Litigation; Lender Liability; White Collar Criminal Defense; Environmental; Medicare Fraud and Taxation; Corporate; Real Estate; Taxation; Labor and Employee Relations; Securities; Bankruptcy; Health Care.*

*(This Listing Continued)*

---

### FIRM MEMBERS IN LOS ANGELES

**HUEY P. COTTON,** born Los Angeles California, July 2, 1956; admitted to bar, 1982, Pennsylvania; 1988, California and U.S. District Court, Eastern District of Pennsylvania; U.S. Court of Appeals, Third and Fifth Circuits. *Education:* Amherst College (B.A., cum laude, 1978); Temple University (J.D., 1981). Instructor, Cardoza Law School, Intensive Trial Advocacy Program, January, 1985. *PRACTICE AREAS:* Products Liability Law; Insurance Coverage; Uniform Commercial Code.

**MARK S. ROTH,** born Newark, New Jersey, September 12, 1951; admitted to bar, 1978, California; U.S. District Court, Central District of California; U.S. District Court, Southern District of Texas. *Education:* University of Southern California (B.A. in Social Sciences and Communication, 1973); Southwestern University (J.D., 1977). Note and Comment Editor, Southwestern University Law Review, 1976-1977. Moot Court Member. Recipient, Schweitzer Moot Court Competition Outstanding Brief Award, 1975. Author: "A Willing Substitute-Protecting Subrogation Flights," Los Angeles Daily Journal, November 9, 1995; "Buying the Smoking Gun," Los Angeles Daily Journal, Verdict Settlements, Jan. 19, 1996. *Member:* Los Angeles County, San Fernando Valley and American Bar Associations; State Bar of California. *PRACTICE AREAS:* Subrogation; Products Liability; Negligence; Construction Defects; Trials.

---

**JENNIFER L. LARSON,** born Santa Barbara, California, September 20, 1970; admitted to bar, 1995, California. *Education:* University of California, Irvine (B.A., 1998); Hastings College of the Law, University of California (J.D., 1995).

**COLBERN C. STUART,** born Arkadelphia, Arkansas, March 2, 1968; admitted to bar, 1995, California and U.S. District Court, Southern District of Pennsylvania. *Education:* Southern Methodist University (B.A., 1990); California Western University (J.D., 1995). *PRACTICE AREAS:* Insurance Subrogation; Insurance Coverage-Defense.

REPRESENTATIVE CLIENTS: Available upon request.

---

# RICHARD W. CRAIGO

10580 WILSHIRE BOULEVARD, SUITE 3 S.E.
**LOS ANGELES, CALIFORNIA 90024**
Telephone: 310-470-9647
Fax: 310-470-9687

*Equine/Horse Law, Taxation Law including Federal and State Income Tax Planning and Dispute Resolution and handling State Sales and Use Tax Disputes, General Business.*

**RICHARD W. CRAIGO,** born Hot Springs, Arkansas, April 30, 1934; admitted to bar, 1967, California, U.S. District Court, Central District of California and U.S. Court of Appeals, Ninth Circuit, 1970, U.S. Tax Court. *Education:* University of Arkansas (B.A., 1956); University of Southern California (J.D., 1966). Order of the Coif. Member, University of Southern California Law Review, 1966. Author: "Tax Planning for the Horse Industry," Warren, Gorham & Lamont, 1987, 1990, 1994; "The Tax Aspects of Equine Investments," 1987 Major Tax Planning, U.S.C. Federal Tax Institute Publication; "Sales and Use Tax Planning for the Horse Industry," University of Kentucky Law Review, 1990; and articles regarding taxation in the horse industry in "The Thoroughbred Record," "The Thoroughbred of California," "The Blood Horse," "The Horsemen's Journal," "The Daily Racing Form" and "Thoroughbred Times". Lecturer, Equine Law Matters: American Horse Council, 1989, 1991, 1994, 1995 and 1996; University of Southern California Tax Institute, 1987; University of Kentucky Symposium on Equine Law, 1989, 1990 and 1995; University of Arizona Symposium on Equine Law, 1988. Associate Professor, Taxation and Contracts, Northrop School of Law, Inglewood, California, 1972-1973. President, California Horsemen's Benevolent and Protective Association, 1977-1979. *Member:* State Bar of California; American Bar Association. [First Lt., U.S. Air Force, 1957-1959]. (Certified Specialist, Taxation Law, The State Bar of California Board of Legal Specialization).

REPRESENTATIVE CLIENTS: Joe Allen; Burt Bacharach; Tom Bachman (Pegasus Ranch); Stanley and Rita Bell; Richard Bloch (Piñon Farm); Cardiff Stud Farm; Brandon and Marianne Chase; Richard Eamer; John Forsythe; Ed Friendly; Edward Gaylord; John Gosden; Bart and Ronelle Heller; Gary Jones; Jack Klugman; Rene and Marjorie Lambert; Marvin Malmuth; Ed Nahem; Marshall Naify; Narvick International; Hal Oliver; Allen Paulson (Brookside Farm); Poms, Smith, Lande & Rose; Premier II Harness Racing Association, Inc.; Dion Recachina; Bernard and Gloria Salick (Sandstone); Bill Shoemaker; Ray Stark; Tapmatic Corporation; Thomas Tatham (Oak Cliff Stables); Steve Taub; Team Valor; Ventura Farms; Ron Volkman; Helmuth Von Bluecher, D.V.M.; Charles Whittingham; Martin Wygod (River Edge Farm).

## PAUL N. CRANE

SUITE 900, TWO CENTURY PLAZA
2049 CENTURY PARK EAST
**LOS ANGELES, CALIFORNIA 90067-3111**
Telephone: 310-282-8118
FAX: 310-282-8077

*Real Estate Law. General Business Practice.*

**PAUL N. CRANE,** born Chicago, Illinois, December 5, 1937; admitted to bar, 1963, California. *Education:* University of California at Los Angeles (B.S., 1959); Harvard University (J.D., 1962). Law Clerk to Justice Mathew O. Tobriner, Supreme Court of California, 1963. *Member:* Beverly Hills, Los Angeles County (Vice Chair, Fee Arbitration Committee, 1983-1989; Chair, 1990-1993; Member, Judicial Election Evaluations Committee, 1995—; Professional Responsibility Committee, 1996—) and American Bar Associations; The State Bar of California (Member, 1993-1995; Chair, 1994-1995, Mandatory Fee Arbitration Committee).

REFERENCE: City National Bank.

---

## CRAWFORD & BANGS

**LOS ANGELES, CALIFORNIA**
(See West Covina)

*Construction and Business Law.*

---

## CRAWFORD & REIMANN LLP

15TH FLOOR
11755 WILSHIRE BOULEVARD
**LOS ANGELES, CALIFORNIA 90025**
Telephone: 310-478-7442
Fax: 310-575-4575

*Civil Litigation in all Courts, including Business, Construction, Environmental, Real Estate and Insurance Litigation.*

### MEMBERS OF FIRM

**THOMAS W. CRAWFORD,** born Wichita, Kansas, August 12, 1957; admitted to bar, 1982, California and U.S. District Court, Central District of California; 1984, U.S. Court of Appeals, Ninth Circuit. *Education:* University of California at Santa Barbara (B.A., with high honors, 1979); University of California at Los Angeles (J.D., 1982). *Member:* Los Angeles County (Member, Litigation and Environmental Sections) and American Bar Associations; The State Bar of California. **PRACTICE AREAS:** Business Litigation; Environmental Litigation; Real Estate Litigation; Construction Litigation.

**DAVID W. REIMANN,** born Wiesbaden, Germany, February 6, 1953; admitted to bar, 1982, California; 1983, U.S. District Court, Southern and Central Districts of California; 1989, U.S. Court of Appeals, Ninth Circuit; 1995, U.S. Supreme Court. *Education:* Williams College (B.A., cum laude, 1975); University of California at Los Angeles (J.D., 1982). Phi Beta Kappa; Order of the Coif; Distinguished Advocate. Recipient, Hunter Award. Instructor, Trial Advocacy, Legal Writing and Research, University of California at Los Angeles School of Law, 1985-1987. Volunteer Trial Attorney, Los Angeles County District Attorney's Office, 1986. *Member:* Los Angeles County Bar Association (Member, Litigation Section); The State Bar of California. **PRACTICE AREAS:** Business Litigation; Construction Litigation; Insurance Litigation.

### ASSOCIATE

**ROBERT C. CARTWRIGHT,** born Encino, California, March 17, 1960; admitted to bar, 1989, California, U.S. District Court, Central and Southern Districts of California and U.S. Court of Appeals, Ninth Circuit. *Education:* University of California at Los Angeles (B.A., 1986); Loyola Law School (J.D., 1989). Phi Delta Phi. *Member:* Los Angeles County Bar Association; State Bar of California. **PRACTICE AREAS:** Business Litigation; Environmental Litigation; Construction Litigation; Employment Litigation.

**GLENN D. HAMOVITZ,** born Los Angeles, California, November 8, 1963; admitted to bar, 1988, California; 1992, U.S. District Court, Central

*(This Listing Continued)*

---

District of California; 1995, U.S. District Court, Northern District of California. *Education:* University of California at Los Angeles (B.A., 1985); Loyola University of Los Angeles (J.D., 1988). Phi Eta Sigma. Settlement Officer, Los Angeles County Municipal and Superior Court, 1990—. *Member:* Los Angeles County and American Bar Associations; State Bar of California. **REPORTED CASES:** Fundamental Investment Etc. Realty Fund v. Gradow (1994) 28 Cal. App. 4th 966, 33 Cal. Rptr. 2d 812 (review den.). **PRACTICE AREAS:** Real Estate Litigation; Business Litigation; Construction Litigation.

REFERENCE: Santa Monica Bank, Brentwood Office.

---

## CREUTZ AND CREUTZ

206 BRENTWOOD SQUARE BUILDING
11661 SAN VICENTE BOULEVARD
**LOS ANGELES, CALIFORNIA 90049**
Telephone: 310-826-3545; 213-879-0339

*Estate Planning, Probate, Wills and Trusts. Real Estate Law.*

FIRM PROFILE: The law firm of Creutz and Creutz was founded over 38 years ago and is highly experienced and well recognized for its practice in the areas of estate planning, wills, trusts, probate proceedings, court litigation in connection with will and trust contests, federal and state estate and gift taxes, conservatorships and elder law. The firm lectures regularly to attorneys through the Continuing Education of the State Bar, as well as to the public, in those areas.

**GREGORY M. CREUTZ** (1892-1966).

**MARY G. CREUTZ,** born Inglewood, California, October 28, 1931; admitted to bar, 1955, California and U.S. District Court, Central District of California; 1957, U.S. Court of Appeals, Ninth Circuit. *Education:* Mount St. Mary's College; Loyola University of Los Angeles (LL.B., 1954). Research Attorney, Appellate Department, Superior Court, Los Angeles County, 1955-1957. Assistant U.S. Attorney, 1957-1958. Arbitrator: American Arbitration Association, 1978—; Los Angeles Superior Court, 1980—. Lecturer, Estate Planning, Continuing Education of the Bar (CEB), 1978—. *Member:* Westwood (President, 1982-1983), Los Angeles County and Southwest (President, 1982-1983) Bar Associations; The State Bar of California (Member: Executive Committee, State Bar Conference of Delegates, 1977-1979; Probate and Trust Law Section); Women Lawyers' Bar Association; Lawyers Club of Los Angeles County (President, 1966-1967); International Academy of Estate and Trust Law.

### ASSOCIATE

**REGINE DERRENDINGER,** born Marcillac, France, November 3, 1945; admitted to bar, 1992, California. *Education:* Universite De Toulouse; University of California at Los Angeles; Southwestern University School of Law (J.D., 1991). **LANGUAGES:** French and Spanish.

REFERENCE: Union Bank, Brentwood Branch.

---

## CROSBY, HEAFEY, ROACH & MAY

PROFESSIONAL CORPORATION
*Established in 1900*

700 SOUTH FLOWER STREET, SUITE 2200
**LOS ANGELES, CALIFORNIA 90017**
Telephone: 213-896-8000
FAX: 213-896-8080
URL: http://www.chrm.com

*Oakland, California Office:* 1999 Harrison Street. Telephone: 510-763-2000. FAX: 510-273-8832.
*San Francisco, California Office:* One Market Plaza, Spear Street Tower, Suite 1800. Telephone: 415-543-8700. FAX: 415-391-8269.
*Santa Rosa, California Office:* 1330 N. Dutton. Telephone: 707-523-2433. FAX: 707-546-1360.

*General Civil Practice and Litigation in all State and Federal Courts. Litigation: Product Liability; Pharmaceutical and Medical Device; Insurance Coverage and Claims; Business Litigation; Labor and Employment; Intellectual Property; Environmental/Toxic Tort; Property, Land Use and Condemnation; Construction; Professional Liability; Antitrust; Appellate; Bankruptcy and Creditors' Rights; Media and First Amendment Rights; Health Care. Business: Real Estate; General Corporate and Partnership; Commercial Transactions; Mergers and Acquisitions; Trust and Estate Planning; Tax; Finance and Banking; Securities.*

*(This Listing Continued)*

# PROFESSIONAL BIOGRAPHIES

**TERRY B. BATES,** born Taipei, Taiwan, May 18, 1959; admitted to bar, 1984, California. *Education:* University of California at San Diego (B.A., 1981); Hastings College of Law, University of California (J.D., 1984). Phi Delta Phi. Member, 1982-1983 and Note Editor, 1983-1984, Hastings International and Comparative Law Review. *Member:* Los Angeles County (Member: State Appellate Judicial Evaluation Committee; Appellate Elections Evaluation Committee, 1992—; Delegate to State Bar Conference of Delegates, 1992-1994; Barristers' Executive Committee 1993-1994; Chair, Barristers' Committee in the State Bar 1993-1994; Fee Arbitration Committee, 1994—; Litigation Section) and American Bar Associations; State Bar of California (Special Master, 1991—; Committee on Mandatory Fee Arbitration, 1993-1994); Southern California Chinese Lawyers Association; Coalition of Asian Pacifics in Entertainment. (Resident). *PRACTICE AREAS:* Business Litigation; Insurance; Malpractice. **Email:** tbb@chrm.com

**MICHAEL K. BROWN,** born Woodside, New York, April 13, 1956; admitted to bar, 1982, California. *Education:* Georgetown University (A.B., 1978); University of San Francisco (J.D., 1982). Topics Editor, University of San Francisco Law Review, 1981-1982. Member, Board of Governors, University of San Francisco Law Society, 1989-1991. Board of Counselor's, University of San Francisco School of Law, 1991—. *Member:* Los Angeles County (Member, Litigation, Health Care and Intellectual Property Section) and American Bar Associations; Defense Research Institute (Member, Drug and Medical Device Section); Association of Southern California Defense Counsel; International Trademark Association; Association of Business Trial Lawyers. (Resident). *PRACTICE AREAS:* Civil Litigation; Products Liability; Pharmaceuticals and Medical Device Litigation; Intellectual Property; Business Litigation. **Email:** mkb@chrm.com

**JAMES D. DEROCHE,** born Santa Monica, California, December 6, 1948; admitted to bar, 1976, California. *Education:* Santa Clara University (B.A., 1971); McGeorge School of Law, University of the Pacific (J.D., 1975). *Member:* Los Angeles County and American Bar Associations. (Resident). **Email:** jdd@chrm.com

**LORENZO E. GASPARETTI,** born Beloit, Wisconsin, October 15, 1962; admitted to bar, 1988, California; 1995, District of Columbia. *Education:* University of California at Berkeley (B.A., 1984) Boalt Hall School of Law, University of California at Berkeley (J.D., 1988). *PRACTICE AREAS:* Business Litigation; Product Liability; Legal Malpractice; Insurance. **Email:** leg@chrm.com

**ROY AI-JI GOTO,** born Honolulu, Hawaii, October 25, 1946; admitted to bar, 1977, Hawaii; 1978, California. *Education:* Northwestern University (B.A., 1968); University of Michigan (A.M., 1972); Washington University (J.D., 1976). *Member:* Los Angeles County and American Bar Associations; State Bar of Hawaii; Association of Southern California Defense Counsel. (Resident). *PRACTICE AREAS:* Insurance; Environmental Law; Medical Devices. **Email:** rag@chrm.com

**M. REED HUNTER,** born Salt Lake City, Utah, October 5, 1932; admitted to bar, 1961, Utah; 1969, California. *Education:* Brigham Young University (B.S., 1955); University of Utah (J.D., 1961). Assistant Attorney General, State of Utah, 1961-1968. *Member:* California Academy of Appellate Lawyers (President, 1979-1980). (Resident). *PRACTICE AREAS:* Appellate Expert in Land Use and Condemnation Law. **Email:** mrh@chrm.com

**WILLIAM PAUL KANNOW,** born Santa Monica, California, August 9, 1951; admitted to bar, 1976, California; 1985, U.S. Supreme Court. *Education:* Loyola University of Los Angeles (B.A., summa cum laude, 1973); Loyola University of Los Angeles School of Law (J.D., 1976). Alpha Sigma Nu; National Jesuit Honor Society. Member, American Association for Automotive Medicine. Member, Senior Counsel Panel, California Association for Tort Reform. *Member:* Los Angeles County, Ventura County and American Bar Associations; The Association of Trial Lawyers of America. (Resident). *PRACTICE AREAS:* Product Liability; Professional Negligence; Commercial Litigation. **Email:** wpk@chrm.com

**JAMES C. MARTIN,** born Oakland, California, November 13, 1952; admitted to bar, 1978, California. *Education:* Colorado College (B.A., 1974); Santa Clara University (J.D., summa cum laude, 1978). Phi Beta Kappa; Pi Gamma Mu. Editor-in-Chief, Santa Clara Law Review, 1977-1978. Author, Civil Appellate Practice (Supplement), CEB 1993, 1994, 1995. Co-Author: "California Expert Witness Guide," CEB, 1991 and Supplements, 1992, 1993, 1994; 1995; "California Complex Litigation Manual," (Chapter on Appellate Issues) Buttersworth, 1990. *Member:* Los Angeles County (Appellate Courts Committee), Federal and American (Sections on Tort, Insurance and Litigation) Bar Associations; California Academy of Appellate Lawyers. (Resident). *PRACTICE AREAS:* Appellate; Civil Writs; Post-Trial Motions. **Email:** jcm@chrm.com

**ANNA SEGOBIA MASTERS,** born Riverside, California, February 17, 1959; admitted to bar, 1984, California. *Education:* University of California at Riverside (B.A., 1981); University of California at Los Angeles (J.D., 1984). Chief Editor, State Bar Employment Law Section Quarterly, 1992-1994. (Resident). *PRACTICE AREAS:* Employment Litigation. **Email:** asm@chrm.com

**MARILYN A. MOBERG,** born San Francisco, California, April 29, 1961; admitted to bar, 1986, California. *Education:* University of California at San Diego (B.A., 1983); Santa Clara University (J.D., 1986). Technical Editor, Santa Clara Law Review, 1985-1986. *Member:* Los Angeles County and American (Member, Litigation Section) Bar Associations; California Women Lawyers. (Resident). *PRACTICE AREAS:* Business Litigation; Professional Liability; Insurance; Products Liability. **Email:** mam@chrm.com

**KURT C. PETERSON,** born Salem, New Jersey, March 31, 1953; admitted to bar, 1978, California. *Education:* Stanford University (B.A., 1975); Hastings College of the Law, University of California (J.D., 1978). Law Clerk to The Honorable Robert F. Kane, California Court of Appeals, First Appellate District, 1978. *Member:* Bar Association of San Francisco; Los Angeles, Alameda County, Beverly Hills and American (Litigation Section, Legal Malpractice Subcommittee, Vice Chair, 1989-1993) Bar Associations; Association of Defense Counsel; California Society for Healthcare Attorneys; Association of Business Trial Lawyers. (Resident). *PRACTICE AREAS:* Commercial Litigation with special emphasis on Professional Liability; Securities; Insurance; Entertainment. **Email:** kcp@chrm.com

**RICHARD SALCIDO,** born Los Angeles, California, October 7, 1950; admitted to bar, 1977, California. *Education:* Loyola University of Los Angeles (B.A., 1972); Golden Gate University (J.D., 1977). *Member:* Los Angeles County, La Raza National and American Bar Associations; Mexican American Bar Association of Los Angeles; National Association of Railroad Trial Counsel. (Resident). *PRACTICE AREAS:* Civil Litigation; Products Liability; Pharmaceutical Litigation; Insurance. **Email:** rsx@chrm.com

**LINDA MARGOLIES SALEM,** born Los Angeles, California, July 25, 1959; admitted to bar, 1984, California. *Education:* Pomona College (B.A., 1981); Hastings College of the Law, University of California (J.D., 1984). Member and Substantive Editor, Hastings Constitutional Law Quarterly, 1982-1984. *Member:* Los Angeles County and American (Member, Sections on: Litigation; Antitrust Law) Bar Associations; California Women Lawyers. (Resident). *PRACTICE AREAS:* Business Litigation; Insurance; Intellectual Property. **Email:** ljm@chrm.com

**ROBERT S. SCHULMAN,** born New York, New York, July 9, 1941; admitted to bar, 1967, New Jersey; 1970, U.S. Supreme Court; 1976, California. *Education:* Rutgers University (A.B., 1963; J.D., cum laude, 1966). Phi Delta Phi. Author: "Reinsurance: A Primer for the Practitioner," 3 Los Angeles Lawyer, October 1980; "The Civil and Criminal Liability of Safety Professionals Under OSHA," Monograph, The National Safety Council, 1981. Counsel, Boards of Education and Adjustment, Fairview, New Jersey, 1970-1972. Deputy Attorney General of New Jersey, 1974. Panelist, National Safety Council Congress, 1981. Member, Board of Directors, Deaf West Theatre, 1992—. Member, Panel of Arbitrators, American Arbitration Association. *Member:* Los Angeles County Bar Association; Association of Business Trial Lawyers. (Resident). *PRACTICE AREAS:* Commercial Litigation; Insurance and Reinsurance.

**PHILIP L. SIRACUSE,** born Buffalo, New York, July 8, 1940; admitted to bar, 1967, California. *Education:* University of California at Riverside (B.A., 1963); Loyola University of Los Angeles (J.D., 1966). Phi Delta Phi. Member, St. Thomas More Law Society. *Member:* Los Angeles County Bar Association. (Resident). *PRACTICE AREAS:* General Litigation including Product Liability; Intellectual Property; Commercial and Insurance Litigation. **Email:** pls@chrm.com

---

Colette M. Asel
Lisa M. Baird
L. Amy Blum
Maureen V. Brennan
Ellen R. Brostrom
Amy E. Deutsch
Mallory J. Garner

Scott C. Glovsky
Ginger F. Heyman
Peter J. Kennedy
Janet H. Kwuon
Stacey L. Meltzer
Theodore F. Monroe
Garet D. O'Keefe

*(This Listing Continued)*

CROSBY, HEAFEY, ROACH & MAY, PROFESSIONAL CORPORATION, Los Angeles—Continued

———————(Continued)————————

| | |
|---|---|
| Eric S. Oto | Richard K. Shuter |
| Laura G. Peraino | Kenneth N. Smersfelt |
| Douglas H. Riegelhuth | Matthew A. Smith |
| Thomas P. Seltz | Tamara C. Smith |
| Benjamin G. Shatz | Barry J. Thompson |

OF COUNSEL

**LAUREN T. DIEHL,** born Mt. Kisco, New York, June 2, 1955; admitted to bar, 1983, California. *Education:* Yale University (B.A., cum laude, 1977); Georgetown University (J.D., 1982). *Member:* Los Angeles County (Member: Commercial Law and Bankruptcy Section; Committee on Federal Court Practices and Procedures, Bankruptcy Subsection) and American (Member, Business Law Section, Business Bankruptcy Committee, Subcommittees on Avoiding Powers and Secured Creditors) Bar Associations; State Bar of California (Member, Business Law Section); Financial Lawyers Conference; Los Angeles Bankruptcy Forum. *Email:* ltd@chrm.com

**KRISTIN HUBBARD,** born New Orleans, Louisiana, October 13, 1955; admitted to bar, 1983, California. *Education:* Stanford University (B.A., 1977; M.A., 1978); University of Southern California (J.D., 1983). *Email:* kzh@chrm.com

**NANCY A. NEWHOUSE-PORTER,** born Pasadena, California; admitted to bar, 1978, California. *Education:* University of Southern California (A.B., magna cum laude, 1975); University of California, Los Angeles (J.D., 1978). *PRACTICE AREAS:* Corporate; Entertainment Law. *Email:* nnp@chrm.com

All Members and Associates of the firm are members of The State Bar of California.

REPRESENTATIVE CLIENTS: AirTouch Communications; Allstate Insurance Company; Chevron Corporation; The Coca-Cola Company; Dai-Tokyo Fire & Marine Co., Ltd.; Farmers Insurance Group of Companies; First USA Bank; ITT Hartford; Mills College, Northern Telecom Inc.; Oakland-Alameda County Coliseum, Inc.; Pacific Telesis Group; Pfizer Inc.; Sofamor Danek Group, Inc.; Summit Medical Center; Tele-Communications, Inc.; United States Surgical Corp.; Wells Fargo Bank; Valent USA Inc.; Westinghouse Electric Corporation; WMX Technologies, Inc.; The Yasuda Fire & Marine Insurance Company; Yokohama Tire Corporation.

(For complete biographical data on all personnel at Oakland, San Francisco and Santa Rosa, California, see Professional Biographies at those Locations)

## LAW OFFICES OF DOUGLAS A. CROWDER

*A PROFESSIONAL CORPORATION*

WORLD TRADE CENTER
350 SOUTH FIGUEROA STREET
SUITE 190
**LOS ANGELES, CALIFORNIA 90071**
Telephone: 213-621-2115
Fax: 213-621-2900
Email: DOUG@CROWDER7.COM
URL: http://www.crowder7.com

*Bankruptcy, Family Law.*

**DOUGLAS A. CROWDER,** born Hobbs, New Mexico, April 11, 1953; admitted to bar, 1977, New Mexico; 1980, Washington; 1989, California. *Education:* Coe College (B.A., 1975); University of Iowa (J.D., 1977). *PRACTICE AREAS:* Bankruptcy; Debtor and Creditor; Litigation; Business Law; Family Law.

## CROWE & DAY

LOS ANGELES, CALIFORNIA

(See Santa Monica)

*General Civil Litigation, Toxic Tort and Products Liability, Commercial and Entertainment Litigation.*

## CROWELL & MORING LLP

LOS ANGELES, CALIFORNIA

(See Irvine)

*General Practice.*

## LEONARD G. CRUZ

Established in 1993

12100 WILSHIRE BOULEVARD
15TH FLOOR
**LOS ANGELES, CALIFORNIA 90025-7115**
Telephone: 310-826-9315
Telecopier: 310-207-3230
Email: Lawoff__LeonardCruz@MSN.Com

*Business Litigation Practice. Probate, Unlawful Detainer and Real Estate.*

**LEONARD G. CRUZ,** born Los Angeles, California, November 17, 1959; admitted to bar, 1986, California; 1987, U.S. District Court, Central and Southern Districts of California. *Education:* University of California at Los Angeles (B.A., 1981; J.D., 1985). *Member:* Los Angeles County and Mexican-American Bar Associations; State Bar of California; Latin Business Association.

## LINDA CUKIER

SECOND FLOOR
11377 WEST OLYMPIC BOULEVARD
**LOS ANGELES, CALIFORNIA 90064-1683**
Telephone: 310-312-3229
Fax: 310-268-7972

*Family and Domestic Relations.*

**LINDA CUKIER,** born Los Angeles, California, June 25, 1958; admitted to bar, 1984, California. *Education:* Sarah Lawrence College (B.A., 1979); Loyola University of Los Angeles (J.D., 1983). *Member:* Los Angeles County Bar Association; State Bar of California. (Also of Counsel, Deutsch & Rubin). *LANGUAGES:* French.

## M. NEIL CUMMINGS

1800 AVENUE OF THE STARS, SUITE 1000
**LOS ANGELES, CALIFORNIA 90067-4212**
Telephone: 310-277-7550
FAX: 310-277-7553

*Corporate, Licensing, Banking. Business Litigation in State and Federal Courts.*

**M. NEIL CUMMINGS,** born Honolulu, Hawaii, August 25, 1951; admitted to bar, 1977, California. *Education:* United States Naval Academy and University of California at Berkeley (B.S., 1974); Hastings College of Law, University of California (J.D., 1977). *Member:* Los Angeles County and American Bar Associations; State Bar of California. [With U.S. Navy, 1969-1971]

REPRESENTATIVE CLIENTS: Carroll Shelby Enterprises; Shelby American, Inc.; Thyssen Henschel America, Inc.; Transrapid International; Santa Monica Bank; Park Labrea Apartments; APEX Voice Communications, Inc.; Armour of America, Inc.

## CUMMINS & WHITE, LLP

Limited Liability Partnership, including Professional Corporations

Established in 1962

865 SOUTH FIGUEROA STREET, 24TH FLOOR
**LOS ANGELES, CALIFORNIA 90017**
Telephone: 213-614-1000
Telecopier: 213-614-0500
Email: cwllp@netcom.com
URL: http://www.cwnb@cwoc.usa.com

Orange County Office: 2424 S.E. Bristol Street, Suite 300, P.O. Box 2513, Newport Beach. Telephone: 714-852-1800. Telecopier: 714-852-8510.

*(This Listing Continued)*

# PROFESSIONAL BIOGRAPHIES

CALIFORNIA—LOS ANGELES

*Affiliated Taipei, Taiwan Office:* Chang & Associates, No. 12 Jen-Ai Road, Section 21, Seventh Floor, Taipei, Taiwan, Republic of China. Telephone: (02) 341-4602. Fax: (02) 321-6388.

*Administrative, Appellate, Banking, Bankruptcy, Business Litigation, Business Transactions, Condemnation and Land Use, Construction, Construction Defect, Entertainment, Environmental, Estates and Trusts, Healthcare, Insurance, Intellectual Property, International Law, Maritime, Personal Injury, Products Liability, Professional Liability, Railroad and Transportation, Real Estate, Regulatory Law and Securities.*

*FIRM PROFILE: Cummins & White, LLP is a mid-sized firm that historically has been one of the leading litigation law firms in SOuthern California. The firm was founded in 1962 by Mr. Louis M. Welsh and Mr. Joseph H. Cummins. In 1965 Jim White joined the firm. Historically the firm was rooted in insurance and railroad litigation, by over the years it has expanded into more complex commercial litigation and transactional matters. The firm prides itself on its philosophy of providing clients with quality services and innovative cost reduction options.*

## MEMBERS OF FIRM

**JAMES D. OTTO, (PROFESSIONAL CORPORATION),** born Long Beach, California, June 9, 1949; admitted to bar, 1974, California and U.S. District Court, Central District of California; 1981, U.S. District Court, Southern District of California; 1983, U.S. Court of Appeals, Ninth Circuit; 1990, U.S. District Court, District of Arizona. *Education:* San Diego State University (B.A., summa cum laude, 1971); Northwestern University (J.D., 1974). Phi Kappa Phi; Pi Sigma Alpha; Alpha Mu Gamma. *Member:* Los Angeles County and American Bar Associations; State Bar of California; Defense Research Institute; International Association of Defense Counsel; Legal Malpractice Committee. **PRACTICE AREAS:** Business Litigation; Insurance Coverage Litigation; Professional Errors and Omissions; Reinsurance Law; Environmental Law.

**LARRY M. ARNOLD, (PROFESSIONAL CORPORATION),** born Los Angeles, California, October 22, 1949; admitted to bar, 1974, California, U.S. District Court, Central, Southern and Northern Districts of California, U.S. District Court, District of Arizona; U.S. District Court, Eastern District of Michigan and U.S. Court of Appeals, Ninth Circuit. *Education:* University of Southern California (B.A., 1971); California Western School of Law (J.D., 1974). Phi Delta Phi (Clerk, 1973). *Member:* Orange County and American Bar Associations; State Bar of California; Defense Research Institute. (Resident, Newport Beach Office). **PRACTICE AREAS:** Civil Litigation; Insurance; Real Estate; Environmental; Business Litigation and Transactions.

**FRANCIS X. SARCONE,** born Washington, D.C., February 4, 1947; admitted to bar, 1972, Iowa; 1977, California and U.S. District Court, Central District of California. *Education:* Rockhurst College (A.B., 1969); Loyola University of Chicago Rome Center; Drake University (J.D., 1972). *Member:* State Bar of California; American Bar Association; National Association of Railroad Trial Counsel; Association of Southern California Defense Counsel. **LANGUAGES:** Italian. **PRACTICE AREAS:** Property Coverage; First Party Coverage; Fraud and Errors Investigation; Personal Injury Defense; Bad Faith.

**MARSHALL W. VORKINK,** born Salt Lake City, Utah, October 11, 1927; admitted to bar, 1955, California and U.S. District Court, Central District of California; 1963, U.S. Court of Appeals, Ninth Circuit. *Education:* University of California at Los Angeles (B.A., 1951; J.D., 1954). Phi Delta Phi. *Member:* Los Angeles County and American Bar Associations; State Bar of California; National Association of Railroad Trial Counsel; American Board of Trial Advocates (Advocate). **PRACTICE AREAS:** Personal Injury Litigation Defense; Railroad Law; Complex Fire; Subrogation; Third Party Tortfeasor Litigation.

**ROBERT E. PERKINS,** born Miami Beach, Florida, February 25, 1944; admitted to bar, 1975, California, U.S. District Court, Northern, Eastern, Central and Southern Districts of California and U.S. Court of Appeals, Ninth Circuit. *Education:* Stanford University (B.S., in Electrical Engineering, 1966); Boalt Hall School of Law, University of California (J.D., 1975). Recipient, American Jurisprudence Award, 1975. *Member:* State Bar of California; Association of Business Trial Lawyers. **PRACTICE AREAS:** Insurance Defense Litigation.

**GENE A. WEISBERG,** born Englewood, New Jersey, April 15, 1954; admitted to bar, 1979, California, U.S. District Court, Southern, Central, Northern and Eastern Districts of California, U.S. Court of Appeals, Ninth Circuit and U.S. Supreme Court. *Education:* State University of New York at Binghamton (B.A., with honors, 1976); University of Southern California (J.D., 1979). *Member:* Los Angeles County Bar Association; State Bar of

*(This Listing Continued)*

California; Association of Southern California Defense Counsel. **PRACTICE AREAS:** Insurance Coverage; Business Litigation; Construction; Insurance Fraud; Subrogation.

**DAVID B. SHAPIRO,** born Los Angeles, California, February 18, 1959; admitted to bar, 1982, California; 1983, U.S. District Court, Central District of California; 1988, U.S. District Court, Southern District of California. *Education:* University of California at Los Angeles (B.A., magna cum laude, 1979; J.D., 1982). Phi Beta Kappa. *Member:* State Bar of California; American Bar Association. **PRACTICE AREAS:** Premises Liability; Insurance Defense; Personal Injury.

**JAMES R. WAKEFIELD,** born Las Vegas, Nevada, December 18, 1952; admitted to bar, 1981, California and U.S. District Court, Central District of California; 1983, U.S. Court of Appeals, Ninth Circuit; 1985, U.S. Court of Appeals, Federal Circuit. *Education:* California State University at Fullerton (B.A., 1978); University of the Pacific, McGeorge School of the Law (J.D., 1981). Phi Alpha Delta. Extern Law Clerk for Hon. Edward C. Reed Jr., U.S. District Court, District of Nevada, 1979-1980. Law Clerk for Hon. A. Andrew Hauk, Chief Judge, U.S. District Court, Central District of California, 1981-1982. *Member:* State Bar of California; Association of Southern California Defense Counsel. (Resident, Newport Beach Office). **PRACTICE AREAS:** Construction Law; Insurance Defense.

**CLYDE E. HIRSCHFELD,** born Philadelphia, Pennsylvania, September 9, 1952; admitted to bar, 1981, California, U.S. District Court, Central District of California and U.S. Court of Appeals, Ninth Circuit; 1987, U.S. District Court, Eastern District of California. *Education:* California State University at Fullerton (B.A., 1978); University of California School of Law at Los Angeles (J.D., 1981). *Member:* State Bar of California. [Sgt. USMC, 1970-1974]. **PRACTICE AREAS:** Litigation; Environmental Law; Insurance Coverage and Bad Faith; Utility Ratemaking.

**DANIEL G. BATH,** born Santa Rosa, California, January 23, 1957; admitted to bar, 1985, California; 1986, U.S. District Court, Central District of California and U.S. Court of Appeals, Ninth Circuit; 1987, U.S. District Court, Northern, Southern and Eastern Districts of California. *Education:* University of California at Santa Barbara (B.A., in English Literature, 1981); McGeorge School of Law, University of the Pacific (J.D., 1985). *Member:* Los Angeles County and American Bar Associations; State Bar of California; American Bankruptcy Institute; Alliance for Children's Rights. **PRACTICE AREAS:** Bankruptcy; Commercial Litigation; Debtor-Creditor Disputes; Personal Injury Insurance Coverage and Litigation.

**DAVID LEE CAROLLO,** born Detroit, Michigan, December 16, 1959; admitted to bar, 1986, California and U.S. District Court, Southern District of California; 1987, U.S. District Court, Central and Northern Districts of California; 1988, U.S. Court of Appeals, Ninth Circuit. *Education:* Wayne State University (B.A., 1982); Georgetown University (J.D., 1985). Phi Beta Kappa. *Member:* Orange County and American Bar Associations; State Bar of California. (Resident, Newport Beach Office). **PRACTICE AREAS:** Bad Faith Litigation; Real Estate Litigation; Bankruptcy Adversary Litigation; Business Litigation; Coverage Analysis.

**ROBERT W. BOLLAR,** born Pomona, California, August 23, 1961; admitted to bar, 1986, California; 1987, U.S. District Court, Central District of California. *Education:* University of Southern California (B.A., 1983); McGeorge School of Law, University of the Pacific (J.D., 1986). Phi Alpha Delta. Member, Order of Barristers. Recipient, Corpus Juris Secundum Award. *Member:* Orange County and American Bar Associations; State Bar of California. (Resident, Newport Beach Office). **PRACTICE AREAS:** Insurance Coverage.

**KAREN L. TAILLON,** born Oakland, California, November 2, 1947; admitted to bar, 1983, California and U.S. District Court, Central District of California; 1993, U.S. District Court, Western District of Pennsylvania. *Education:* California State University at Fullerton; Western State University (B.S.L., with high honors, 1981; J.D., magna cum laude, 1982). Charter Member, Women In Commercial Real Estate, Orange County, 1987. *Member:* Orange County and Los Angeles County Bar Associations; State Bar of California; National Health Lawyers Association. (Resident, Newport Beach Office). **PRACTICE AREAS:** Real Estate Law; Hospital and Health Care Law; Commercial Law; Contracts Law; Employment Law.

**MICHAEL T. FOX,** born April 8, 1947; admitted to bar, 1974, California and U.S. District Court, Central District of California; 1975; U.S. Court of Appeals, Ninth Circuit; 1978, U.S. Supreme Court; 1985, Missouri. *Education:* University of California, Los Angeles (B.A., Economics, 1971); University of San Diego School of Law (J.D., cum laude, 1974); Rockhurst College (M.B.A., 1981). *Member:* Defense Research Institute; International

*(This Listing Continued)*

CAA609B

## CUMMINS & WHITE, LLP, Los Angeles—Continued

Association of Defense Counsel. *PRACTICE AREAS:* Personal Injury; Premises Liability.

**ANNABELLE MOORE HARRIS,** born Fullerton, California, March 5, 1961; admitted to bar, 1987, California; 1988, U.S. District Court, Central, Southern and Eastern Districts of California; 1992, U.S. Court of Appeals, Ninth Circuit. *Education:* California State University at Fullerton (B.A., 1985); Salzburg Institute of Legal Studies, Salzburg, Austria (1986); McGeorge School of Law, University of the Pacific (J.D., 1987). Phi Alpha Delta. *Member:* Orange County and American Bar Associations; State Bar of California; Orange County Trial Lawyers Association. (Resident, Newport Beach Office). *LANGUAGES:* American Sign. *PRACTICE AREAS:* Insurance Coverage and Bad Faith.

**SHERRY L. PANTAGES,** born Boston, Massachusetts, January 26, 1964; admitted to bar, 1988, California; 1989, U.S. District Court, Central District of California and U.S. Court of Appeals, Ninth Circuit. *Education:* University of Southern California (B.A., cum laude, 1985); McGeorge School of Law, University of the Pacific (J.D., with great distinction, 1988). Order of Coif. *Member:* Los Angeles County and American Bar Associations; State Bar of California; Barristers; Women Lawyers of Los Angeles. *PRACTICE AREAS:* Environmental Coverage Litigation; Insurance Coverage Law; Bad Faith Litigation; Insurance Defense; Business Litigation.

**LOUIS H. ALTMAN,** born Fort Worth, Texas, May 20, 1953; admitted to bar, 1978, Texas and U.S. Court of Appeals, Fifth Circuit; 1984, U.S. District Court, Northern District of Texas; 1985, U.S. District Court, Western District of Texas; 1993, California. *Education:* University of Texas (B.A., 1974; J.D., 1978). Order of Barristers. *Member:* State Bar of Texas (Member, 1990-1994 and Vice-Chairperson, 1993-1994, District 6 Grievance Committee). (Board Certified, Civil Trial Law, Texas Board of Legal Specialization). *PRACTICE AREAS:* Commercial Litigation; Bankruptcy.

**BLENDA EYVAZZADEH,** born Tehran, Iran, May 19, 1960; admitted to bar, 1985, California. *Education:* University of California at Los Angeles (B.A., 1982); Loyola Marymount University (J.D., 1985). *Member:* State Bar of California; California Trial Lawyers Association. *PRACTICE AREAS:* Personal Injury.

**JOHN E. PEER,** born San Francisco, California, July 17, 1949; admitted to bar, 1980, California. *Education:* Colorado State University (B.A., cum laude, 1971); Northern Illinois University (M.A., 1973); University of San Francisco (J.D., cum laude, 1980). Member: McAuliffe Law Honor Society; University of San Francisco Law Review, 1979-1980. *Member:* Bar Association of San Francisco; State Bar of California.

### OF COUNSEL

**THOMAS W. BURTON,** born 1946; admitted to bar, 1973, California and District of Columbia. *Education:* Claremont McKenna College; University of San Diego. (Resident, Newport Beach Office). *PRACTICE AREAS:* Business Law; Trusts and Estates; Technology and Science; Real Estate; Computers and Software.

**JOSEPH H. CUMMINS,** born Winchester, Indiana, June 19, 1916; admitted to bar, 1940, Illinois; 1941, Colorado; 1946, California; 1972, U.S. Supreme Court, U.S. District Court, Central, Southern, Eastern and Northern Districts of California and U.S. Court of Appeals, Ninth and Seventh Circuits. *Education:* DePauw University (A.B., 1937); Northwestern University (J.D., 1940). Phi Alpha Delta. *Member:* State Bar of California; American Board of Trial Advocates (President, 1970, Los Angeles Chapter; National President, 1972); National Association of Railroad Trial Counsel; Chancery Club-Los Angeles. Fellow, American College of Trial Lawyers (Southern California Chairman, 1980-1981). *PRACTICE AREAS:* Malpractice; Negligence; Products Liability; Arbitration and Mediation; Transportation Law.

**MARSHALL T. HUNT,** born San Francisco, California, April 10, 1920; admitted to bar, 1949, California. *Education:* University of California (B.A., 1942); University of Southern California (LL.B., 1948). Phi Delta Phi. California Trial Lawyer of the Year, 1984. *Member:* Los Angeles County and American Bar Associations; The State Bar of California; The American Board of Trial Advocates (President, Los Angeles Chapter, 1977; National President, 1978-1979); Association of Southern California Defense Counsel; International Association of Insurance Counsel; Defense Research Institute; Association of Insurance Attorneys. Fellow: International Society of Barristers; American College of Trial Lawyers; International Academy of Trial Lawyers. (Resident, Newport Beach Office). *PRACTICE AREAS:* Manufacturers Products Liability; Construction Litigation; Insurance Company Defense; Libel; Professional Errors and Omissions; Medical Negligence.

**JAY F. STOCKER,** born Seattle, Washington, October 12, 1960; admitted to bar, 1987, California. *Education:* University of Washington (B.A., 1984); Pepperdine University (J.D., 1987). *Member:* Orange County and American Bar Associations. (Resident, Newport Beach Office). *PRACTICE AREAS:* Business Law; Real Estate Law.

**ALAN K. STAZER,** born Pittsburgh, Pennsylvania, October 5, 1936; admitted to bar, 1980, California and U.S. District Court, Central District of California. *Education:* University of California at Los Angeles (B.A., 1962); Southwestern University (J.D., 1978). *Member:* State Bar of California; American Bar Association. *PRACTICE AREAS:* Environmental Law.

**WILLIAM BRUCE VOSS,** born Alexandria, Virginia, May 10, 1948; admitted to bar, 1975, California; 1977, U.S. Tax Court; 1979, U.S. Supreme Court, U.S. Court of Appeals, Ninth Circuit, U.S. District Court, Central District of California, U.S. Claims Court and U.S. Court of Customs and Patent Appeals. *Education:* California State University at Fullerton (B.A., 1970); Pepperdine University (J.D., 1974). Real Estate Broker, California, 1980. Judge, Pro Tem Superior Court, 1980. *Member:* Orange County and American Bar Associations; State Bar of California; California Trial Lawyers Association. (Resident, Newport Beach Office). *PRACTICE AREAS:* International Business Law and Disputes.

**JAMES O. WHITE, JR.,** born Salt Lake City, Utah, May 30, 1920; admitted to bar, 1948, California, U.S. District Court, Central, Southern, Eastern and Northern Districts of California and U.S. Court of Appeals, Eighth and Ninth Circuits. *Education:* Stanford University (A.B., 1942; LL.B., 1948). Phi Alpha Delta. *Member:* Los Angeles County (Member, Judicial Qualification Committee, 1976-1981; Chairman, Insurance Committee, 1970-1971) and American Bar Associations; State Bar of California; Association of Southern California Defense Counsel (Director, 1970-1974; President, 1973-1974); American Board of Trial Advocates; American Judicature Society; International Association of Defense Counsel. Fellow, American College of Trial Lawyers.

### ASSOCIATES

**DAVID M. SMITHSON,** born Chicago, Illinois, January 14, 1957; admitted to bar, 1985, California and U.S. District Court, Central District of California; 1987, U.S. District Court, Southern District of California. *Education:* University of Oregon (B.S., 1980); Boston College (J.D., 1984). *Member:* Los Angeles County Bar Association; State Bar of California; Association of Southern California Defense Counsel. *PRACTICE AREAS:* Insurance Coverage; Environmental Defense; Business Litigation.

**LAWRENCE E. JOHNSON,** born Montreal, Quebec, February 1, 1956; admitted to bar, 1984, Quebec; 1995, California. *Education:* McGill University (B.Comm., 1978); University of Montreal (LL.B., 1983); College Jean De Brebeuf (D.E.C., 1975). Recipient: Scarlet Key Award, 1978; Prix Du Barreau De Montreal for Excellence in Commercial Law, 1983. Board of Directors, Orange County Venture Forum. *Member:* Montreal, Quebec and Canadian (Member, Computer and Technology Committee) Bar Associations; American Marketing Association; International Marketing Association. (Resident, Newport Beach Office). *LANGUAGES:* English, French and Spanish. *PRACTICE AREAS:* Corporate Law; Securities Law; Technology Law; International Trade.

**KEVIN ALMETER,** born Stanford, California, January 12, 1962; admitted to bar, 1988, California; 1989, U.S. District Court, Central District of California and U.S. Court of Appeals, Ninth Circuit. *Education:* University of California at Davis (B.A., 1985; J.D., 1988). *Member:* Los Angeles County and American Bar Associations; State Bar of California. *PRACTICE AREAS:* Insurance Defense; Litigation.

**MICHAEL M. BERGFELD,** born St. Louis, Missouri, December 31, 1949; admitted to bar, 1988, California; 1989, U.S. District Court, Central District of California and U.S. Court of Appeals, Ninth Circuit; 1990, U.S. Claims Court; 1992, U.S. District Court, Southern District of California. *Education:* California State University at Fullerton (B.A., 1973; M.A., 1979); Hastings College of Law, University of California (J.D., 1988). *Member:* Los Angeles County and American Bar Associations; State Bar of California; California Lawyers for the Arts; Association of Business Trial Lawyers. *PRACTICE AREAS:* Appellate Law; Litigation.

**HENRY SHYN,** born Seoul, Korea, May 15, 1963; admitted to bar, 1989, California; 1990, U.S. District Court, Central, Eastern, Northern and Southern Districts of California, District of Columbia and U.S. Court of Appeals, Ninth Circuit. *Education:* University of California at Berkeley (B.A., 1985); Boston College (J.D., 1988). Phi Alpha Delta. *Member:* Los

*(This Listing Continued)*

Angeles County and American Bar Associations; State Bar of California. **LANGUAGES:** Korean. **PRACTICE AREAS:** Business Law.

**LAURA N. MACPHERSON,** born Sacramento, California, August 4, 1962; admitted to bar, 1988, California; 1992, U.S. District Court, Central District of California. *Education:* University of San Diego (B.B.A., Business Economics, 1984; J.D., 1988). *Member:* Orange County Bar Association; State Bar of California. (Resident, Newport Beach Office). **PRACTICE AREAS:** Insurance Coverage; Bad Faith Litigation; Civil Litigation.

**BRADLEY V. BLACK,** born Emmetsburg, Iowa, December 14, 1960; admitted to bar, 1986, Iowa; 1987, Missouri and U.S. District Court, Western District of Missouri; 1989, California; 1993, U.S. District Court, Central and Southern Districts of California. *Education:* Iowa State University (B.A., with distinction, 1983); University of Iowa (J.D., with distinction, 1986). Phi Kappa Phi; Pi Sigma Alpha. Recipient, American Jurisprudence Award, Remedies. *Member:* Orange County, Iowa State and American Bar Associations; The Missouri Bar; State Bar of California. (Resident, Newport Beach Office). **PRACTICE AREAS:** Civil Litigation.

**J. THOMAS GILBERT,** born Amarillo, Texas, August 29, 1963; admitted to bar, 1987, Texas; 1988, U.S. District Court, Northern District of Texas; 1989, U.S. District Court, Southern District of Texas; 1991, U.S. Court of Appeals, Fifth Circuit; 1992, U.S. District Court, Western District of Texas; 1996, California and U.S. District Court, Central District of California. *Education:* Baylor University (B.F.A., with honors, 1984); Baylor School of Law (J.D., 1987). Member, Order of Barristers. President, Harvey M. Richey Moot Court Society, 1986-1987. *Member:* State Bar of Texas (Member, Sections on: Litigation; Consumer Law); American Bar Association; Dallas Association of Young Lawyers; Texas Association of Young Lawyers. **PRACTICE AREAS:** Insurance Coverage and Litigation; Products Liability; Medical Malpractice; Commercial Litigation.

**ESTHER P. HOLM,** born Chicago, Illinois, April 2, 1954; admitted to bar, 1989, California, U.S. District Court, Central, Northern, Southern and Eastern Districts of California and U.S. Court of Appeals, Ninth Circuit. *Education:* University of California at Davis (B.A., 1977); Santa Clara University (J.D., 1988). *Member:* Wilshire, Beverly Hills, Los Angeles County and American Bar Associations; State Bar of California. **PRACTICE AREAS:** Insurance Coverage; Insurance Bad Faith; Personal Injury; Insurance Broker Malpractice.

**PATTI L. WHITFIELD,** born Oakland, California, July 18, 1965; admitted to bar, 1991, California. *Education:* University of California at San Diego (B.A., Political Science, 1987); McGeorge School of Law (J.D., with distinction, 1991; LL.M., International Business Transactions, 1993). (Resident, Newport Beach Office). **PRACTICE AREAS:** Business Law; International Business; Securities and Estate Planning.

**JEFFREY DANIEL MANSUKHANI,** born Chicago, Illinois, March 6, 1965; admitted to bar, 1991, California and U.S. District Court, Southern District of California. *Education:* University of San Diego (B.A., cum laude, 1987); Florida State University (J.D., with honors, 1991). Member, Journal of Land Use and Environmental Law. Judicial Externship for Justice Parker Lee McDonald, Florida Supreme Court. (Resident, Newport Beach Office). **PRACTICE AREAS:** Insurance Coverage; Business Litigation; Bad Faith Litigation.

**RANDY A. MOSS,** born Los Angeles, California, June 19, 1966; admitted to bar, 1991, California, U.S. District Court, Northern District of California and U.S. Court of Appeals, Ninth Circuit; 1993, U.S. Court of Appeals for the Federal Circuit and U.S. Court of Federal Claims. *Education:* University of California at Los Angeles (B.A., 1988); Hastings College of the Law, University of California (J.D., 1991). *Member:* State Bar of California (Member, Section on Intellectual Property). **LANGUAGES:** French. **PRACTICE AREAS:** Insurance Defense.

**SUSAN M. OGLESBY,** born Upland, California, March 18, 1966; admitted to bar, 1992, California. *Education:* University of California, San Diego (B.A., 1989); University of San Diego (J.D., cum laude, 1992). (Resident, Newport Beach Office). **PRACTICE AREAS:** Civil Litigation; First Party Insurance Property Coverage; Bad Faith Litigation; Business Litigation.

**MICHAEL A. MCLAIN,** born Panorama City, California, January 29, 1967; admitted to bar, 1992, California. *Education:* Loyola Marymount University (B.A., magna cum laude, 1989); Loyola University at Los Angeles (J.D., 1992). Alpha Sigma Nu; Phi Alpha Theta; Pi Gamma Mu; Order of the Coif. Recipient, American Jurisprudence Award. Judicial Extern for the Honorable Samuel Bufford, U.S. Bankruptcy Court, Central District of California. **PRACTICE AREAS:** Litigation; Insurance Coverage; Bankruptcy.

*(This Listing Continued)*

**HEATHER SKINNER NEVIS,** born Amarillo, Texas, October 5, 1967; admitted to bar, 1992, California; 1993, U.S. District Court, Central District of California. *Education:* University of California at Davis (B.A., 1989); McGeorge School of Law (J.D., with honors, 1992). Phi Delta Phi. Recipient, American Jurisprudence Awards in Corporations and Agency. *Member:* Orange County Bar Association; State Bar of California. (Resident, Newport Beach Office). **PRACTICE AREAS:** Business Litigation; Insurance Defense.

**RONDI JAN WALSH,** born Lakewood, California, February 2, 1965; admitted to bar, 1992, California and U.S. District Court, Eastern Central and Southern Districts of California; 1993, U.S. District Court, Northern District of California and U.S. Court of Appeals, Ninth Circuit. *Education:* University of California, Los Angeles (B.A., 1988); Loyola Law School (J.D., 1991). *Member:* Los Angeles County (Member: Barristers' Homeless Shelter Advocacy Project; Steering Committee; Vice-Chair, Barristers' Law Student Support Committee) and American Bar Associations; State Bar of California (Conference Delegates, Los Angeles County Bar, Delegate). **PRACTICE AREAS:** Coverage Litigation; Bad Faith Litigation.

**PATRICIA M. MICHELENA,** born Los Angeles, California, March 12, 1966; admitted to bar, 1992, California. *Education:* University of California at Los Angeles (B.A., 1988); Loyola Law School of Los Angeles (J.D., 1991). *Member:* Los Angeles Bar Association; State Bar of California; Los Angeles County Barristers. **PRACTICE AREAS:** Insurance Litigation; Insurance Subrogation.

**CHINYE UWECHUE-AKPATI,** born Yaounde, Cameroon, June 27, 1962; admitted to bar, 1986, England and Nigeria; 1993, California and U.S. District Court, Southern, Central, Eastern and Northern Districts of California. *Education:* London School of Economics, London, England (LL.B., with Honors, 1984; LL.M., with Merit, 1989). Life Member, The Honorable Society of the Middle Temple, London. *Member:* State Bar of California; American Bar Association; Womens Lawyers Association of Los Angeles. **PRACTICE AREAS:** Environmental Coverage.

**MONICA J. WALKER,** born Yokohama, Japan, November 7, 1968; admitted to bar, 1993, California. *Education:* University of California, Irvine (B.A., cum laude, 1990); Loyola Law School (J.D., 1993). **LANGUAGES:** Japanese. **PRACTICE AREAS:** Insurance Defense; Litigation; Insurance Coverage; Insurance Bad Faith.

**SABRINA KONG,** born Vietnam, November 9, 1968; admitted to bar, 1993, California; 1994, New York. *Education:* University of Southern California at Los Angeles (B.S., 1989); Southwestern University School of Law (J.D., 1993). *Member:* Beverly Hills and Los Angeles County Bar Associations. **PRACTICE AREAS:** Corporate; Securities; Litigation.

**JOETTE MAREA GONZALEZ,** born Van Nuys, California, March 15, 1960; admitted to bar, 1994, California. *Education:* California State University, Los Angeles (B.S., 1984); McGeorge School of Law (J.D., 1994). Member, National Moot Court Executive Committee, 1993-1994. **PRACTICE AREAS:** Complex Insurance Coverage Litigation; Business Litigation; Insurance Defense.

**IAN C. ULLMAN,** born Newport Beach, California, May 1, 1968; admitted to bar, 1994, California, U.S. District Court, Central District of California and U.S. Court of Appeals, Ninth Circuit; 1995, District of Columbia. *Education:* University of California (B.A., 1990); Loyola Marymount University (J.D., 1994). Extern to Hon. Stephen Reinhardt, U.S. Court of Appeals, Ninth Circuit. **PRACTICE AREAS:** Insurance Coverage; Subrogation.

**D. TODD PARRISH,** born Edinburgh, Scotland, January 9, 1968; admitted to bar, 1994, California and U.S. District Court, Central District of California. *Education:* Abilene Christian University (B.B.A., 1990); Pepperdine University (J.D., 1994). Phi Delta Phi. *Member:* American Bar Association. **PRACTICE AREAS:** Litigation; Insurance Coverage; Bad Faith; Construction Defect.

**ROGER G. HONEY,** born Santa Barbara, California, September 22, 1964; admitted to bar, 1994, California, U.S. District Court, Central District of California and U.S. Court of Appeals, Ninth Circuit. *Education:* San Diego State University (B.A., 1989); University of Southern California (J.D., 1994). *Member:* State Bar of California. **PRACTICE AREAS:** Insurance Coverage; Construction Defect.

**LISA EMILY EISMA,** born Hawthorne, California, October 22, 1969; admitted to bar, 1995, California. *Education:* University of California, Los Angeles (B.A., 1991); University of California, Davis (J.D., 1995). **PRACTICE AREAS:** Insurance Defense Litigation; Subrogation.

*(This Listing Continued)*

CAA611B

CUMMINS & WHITE, LLP, Los Angeles—Continued

REPRESENTATIVE CLIENTS: Alhambra Hospital; American International Group; American States Insurance Group; Atlantic Companies; Baker Ranch Properties; Balboa Life & Casualty Co.; Bank One Management and Consulting; CB Commercial; CNA Insurance Cos.; California FAIR Plan Association; Chief Auto Parts; Chinatown 21st Dynasty Corp.; Chubb Group Insurance Cos.; CIGNA Cos.; Citation Insurance Co.; Deans & Horner; Envision Claims Management Corp.; Government Employees' Insurance Co.; Great American Insurance Co.; International Telecommunications Administration of the Republic of China; Kemper Risk Management; Lifestyle California; Marsh & McLennan Cos.; Maryland Casualty Co.; Mi-Jack Products; Mobil Oil Corp.; Prudential Reinsurance Co.; RLI Insurance Co.; Reliance National Insurance Co.; Sea-Land Services, Inc.; Scott Wetzel Services, Inc.; South Coast Medial Center; Southern Counties Oil Co.; Southland Corporation (7-11); South Pacific Duty Free Shops; State Farm Fire & Casualty Co.; Swett & Crawford; TGI Friday's Inc.; TIG Insurance Group; Texaco, Inc.; Teachers Retirement System of Texas; The Parsons Corp.; Tokio Marine Insurance Co.; Toplis & HArding, Inc.; Union Electric Wire and Cable Co., Ltd.; Wei-Chaun Construction & Development Co.; Wm. H. McGee & Company; Zurich Insurance Co.

---

## DAAR & NEWMAN

PROFESSIONAL CORPORATION

Established in 1956

SUITE 2500
865 SOUTH FIGUEROA STREET
**LOS ANGELES, CALIFORNIA 90017-2567**
Telephone: 213-892-0999
FAX: 213-892-1066

*Insurance, Insurance Coverage, Corporation, Business, Aviation, Antitrust and Securities Law. Litigation and Appellate Practice.*

**DAVID DAAR,** born Chicago, Illinois, May 23, 1931; admitted to bar, 1956, California; 1960, U.S. Tax Court and U.S. Supreme Court. *Education:* Loyola University of Los Angeles (J.D., 1956). Author: "Punitive Damage Avoidance in the Business of Insurance," National Association of Independent Insurers, 1985; "Antitrust Compliance Programs for the Business of Insurance," ABA National Institute, Antitrust and the Business of Insurance, 1985; *Class Actions-Can Business Ever Be The Same,* 1973; "Potential Use of the Class Action in Aircraft Crash Litigation," 1977, published in Rotor and Wing; "Punitive Damage Avoidance-Internal Program," C.P.C.U Journal, 1986; "Aviation Insurance Law (California)," Mathew-Bender & Company, 1987; "Marketing Under the Risk Retention Act, CPCU, 1987; "Daar's Laws of Flying Helicopters," 1993. Member, Advisory Committee to State Superintendent of Public Instruction, 1965. Faculty, First National College of Advocacy-Hastings College of Law, National College of Advocacy, 1971. Lecturer, Trial Tactics in Federal Securities Litigation, Practising Law Institute, 1977. *Member:* State Bar of California (Chairman, State Bar Committee, Federal Courts, 1973); Association of Business Trial Lawyers; Conference of Insurance Counsel.

**MICHAEL R. NEWMAN,** born New York, N.Y., October 2, 1945; admitted to bar, 1971, California; 1978, U.S. Supreme Court; 1979, U.S. Tax Court. *Education:* University of Denver (B.A., 1967); John Marshall Law School/University of Chicago (J.D., 1970). Delta Theta Phi. Judge Pro Tempore, Los Angeles Municipal Court, 1983—. Los Angeles Superior Court, 1985—. Member: Board of Directors, The Athletes Congress of the United States, 1984-1987; Los Angeles Olympic Citizens Advisory Commission, 1980-1984; Governmental Liaison Advisory Commission, 1980-1984; Southern California Committee, 1980-1984, 1984, Olympic Summer Games. Lecturer, Eastern Claims Conference, Eastern Life Claims Conference, 1987; National Health Care Anti-fraud Association, 1986, 1987; American Insurance Association, 1988-1991. *Member:* Los Angeles County (Chairman, Errors and Omissions Committee) and American (Member, Advisory Committee on Multi-District Litigation; Member, Committee on Class Actions and Derivative Suits) Bar Associations; State Bar of California; Association of Business Trial Lawyers (Member, Insurance Committee); Conference of Insurance Counsel.

**JEFFERY J. DAAR,** born Los Angeles, California, October 23, 1957; admitted to bar, 1982, California. *Education:* Claremont Men's College (B.A., 1979); University of California at Davis (J.D., 1982). Member: University of California at Davis Law Review, 1980-1981; Moot Court Board, 1980-1982. Recipient: First Place and Best Brief Award, Moot Court Competition of Intellectual Property Section of Los Angeles County Bar Association, 1981. Judge Pro Tempore, Los Angeles Municipal Court, 1990—.Author: "Licensing and Regulation of Insurance Adjusters," Mathew Bender & Company, 1987; "Overview of AIDS and the Insurance Industry, Insurance Advocate, 1988. *Member:* Los Angeles County and American Bar Associations; State Bar of California; Conference of Insurance Counsel.

*(This Listing Continued)*

American Bar Associations; State Bar of California; Conference of Insurance Counsel.

**MARSHA MCLEAN-UTLEY,** admitted to bar, 1965, California. *Education:* UCLA (A.B., 1961; LL.B., 1964). Order of the Coif. Law Clerk to Chief Justice Roger Traynor and Justice Mathew Tobriner, California Supreme Court, 1964-1965. Lecturer: UCLA/CEB, Estate Planning Institute, "Surcharge Problems of Trustees and Executors," 1983; Civil Litigation, Civil Procedure and Practice. Attorney, Gibson, Dunn & Crutcher, 1964-1988 (emphasis on civil and probate litigation). *Member:* State Bar of California (Member, Board of Governors, 1983-1986); American Bar Association (Delegate, 1987); Ninth Circuit Chairperson, Business Torts Committee, 1975-1976); Association of Business Trial Lawyers (President, 1982-1983); California Women Lawyers; Women Lawyers Association of Los Angeles.

**MICHAEL J. WHITE,** born Newton, Massachusetts, May 25, 1942; admitted to bar, 1985, California; 1986, U.S. District Court, Central District of California; 1989, U.S. District Court, Southern District of California. *Education:* M.I.T. (B.S., 1965); Northwestern Univ. (M.A., 1967; Ph.D., 1974); UCLA (J.D., 1985). Associate Professor, University of Southern California, School of Public Administration, 1975-1987. Hearing Officer, L.A. County Civil Service Commission, 1992—.

### OF COUNSEL

**RODNEY W. LOEB,** born Los Angeles, California, July 29, 1928; admitted to bar, 1953, District of Columbia; 1960, U.S. Supreme Court; 1961, California. *Education:* University of California at Berkeley (A.B., 1949); Harvard University (LL.B., 1952; LL.M., 1957). *Member:* The State Bar of California.

**WILLIAM F. WHITE, JR.,** born Boston, Massachusetts, March 4, 1935; admitted to bar, 1960, Massachusetts; 1976, New York; 1978, California; 1979, U.S. District Court, Central District of California. *Education:* Harvard University (A.B., 1957; LL.B., 1960). Adjunct Professor, University of West Los Angeles Law School, 1986-1987. *Member:* Association of the Bar of the City of New York; Los Angeles County Bar Association; State Bar of California.

**SAMUEL T. REES,** born Kansas City, Missouri, February 9, 1946; admitted to bar, 1973, California; 1974, U.S. District Court, Central District of California; 1975, U.S. Court of Appeals, Ninth Circuit; 1978, U.S. District Court, Southern District of California. *Education:* University of Colorado and University of Southern California (A.B., 1970; J.D., 1973). *Member:* Los Angeles County and American Bar Associations.

### LEGAL SUPPORT PERSONNEL

**JOE A. MORTON,** born Sibley, Iowa, February 18, 1915. State of California Department of Insurance, 36 Years; field examination, 15 years; Conservation and Liquidation Division, 13 years; Deputy Insurance Commissioner; Chief of Conservation and Liquidation Division, Department of Insurance, California, 8 years. (Consultant).

**FRANK E. RAAB,** born Riverside, California, August 4, 1921. *Education:* University of California (Berkeley), B.S., Business Administration. Former President and Chief Executive Officer, Insurance Company of North America. Former Chairman, Allianz Insurance Co. Past National President, Society of Chartered Property and Casualty Underwriters. [U.S. Navy Sea Cadets; Rear Admiral, U.S. Naval Reserve (Retired).]. (Consultant).

REPRESENTATIVE CLIENTS: Admiral Insurance Co.; Allianz Insurance Co.; American Income Life Insurance Co.; American Life and Casualty Insurance Co.; Balboa Insurance Co.; California Casualty Insurance Co.; National Benefit Life Insurance Co.; Capital Life Insurance Co.; Charter National Life; Columbian Mutual Life; Connecticut Mutual Life Insurance Co.; Evanston Insurance Co.; Firemans Fund Insurance Co.; General Accident Insurance Company of America; Great Republic Life Insurance Co.; Guaranty National Insurance Co.; Hill & Knowlton; Imperial Industries; Fred S. James & Co. of Texas; John Adams Life Insurance Co.; Landauer & Associates, Inc.; Life Insurance Company of California; Los Angeles Daily Journal; Market Insurance Corp.; Maryland Casualty Insurance Co.; Massachusetts Indemnity & Life Insurance Co.; Penncorp; Potomac Insurance Co.; Presidential Life Insurance Co.; Security First Group; Shand, Morahan & Co.; Ticor Title Insurance & Trust Co.; Union Fidelity Life; Unity Mutual Life; U.S. Facilities Corp.; United States Fidelity & Guaranty Company; Kemper National Insurance Companies; Lumbermens Mutual Casualty Co.; American Motorists Insurance Company; American Manufacturers Mutual Insurance Company; American Protection Insurance Company; Atlanta Casualty Companies.

## DANIELS, BARATTA & FINE
A Partnership including a Professional Corporation

*Established in 1982*

*1801 CENTURY PARK EAST, 9TH FLOOR*
**LOS ANGELES, CALIFORNIA 90067**
Telephone: 310-556-7900
Telecopier: 310-556-2807

*Bakersfield, California Office:* 5201 California Avenue, Suite 400. Telephone: 805-335-7788. Telecopier: 805-324-3660.

*General Civil Trial and Appellate Practice in all State and Federal Courts. Insurance, Products Liability, Tort, Wrongful Termination and Employment Discrimination, Business, Entertainment, Real Estate and Construction Law, Environmental and Toxic Torts.*

FIRM PROFILE: Daniels, Baratta & Fine was founded in 1982. The firm specializes in civil trial practice in all State and Federal Courts, with emphasis in the areas of Insurance (including defense, coverage and bad faith), business litigation, real estate and construction law (including litigation, commercial leasing and transactional matters), entertainment (including litigation and transactional matters), environmental and toxic torts.

### MEMBERS OF FIRM

**JOHN P. DANIELS, (INC.),** born New York, N.Y., February 5, 1937; admitted to bar, 1964, California. *Education:* Dartmouth College (A.B., 1959); University of Southern California (J.D., 1963). Phi Delta Phi. Editor: *Defense Dialogue,* a Monthly Publication of the Association of Southern California Defense Counsel, 1975-1981. Co-author: "Revised Legal Aspects of Diving Instruction," p. 50, National Association of Underwater Instructors, 1976; *Diary for Federal Civil Litigation in the Wake of the 1993 Amendments to the Federal Rules of Civil Procedure,* Federation of Insurance & Corporate Counsel Quarterly, Volume 45, No. 3, Spring, 1995. Member, Los Angeles Superior Court Arbitration Panel. Chairman, Trial Tactics and Procedures Committee, Federation of Insurance and Corporate Counsel, 1994-1996. *Member:* Los Angeles County and American Bar Associations; State Bar of California; Association of Southern California Defense Counsel; American Board of Trial Advocates (Board of Directors, Los Angeles Chapter, 1985—; President, 1996; Course Director of the Jack Daniels' L.A. ABOTA Trial Academy, 1988—; President, Los Angeles Chapter, 1994); California American Board of Trial Advocates (President, 1995). **PRACTICE AREAS:** Trial Law; Products Liability; Insurance.

**JAMES M. BARATTA,** born Chicago, Illinois, January 19, 1947; admitted to bar, 1972, California. *Education:* University of California at Los Angeles (B.A., cum laude, 1969); Loyola University of Los Angeles (J.D., cum laude, 1972). Pi Gamma Mu. Member, St. Thomas More Honor Society. Comment Editor, Loyola University Law Review, 1971-1972. Associate Editor, *Defense Dialogue,* a Monthly Publication of the Association of Southern California Defense Counsel, 1975-1981. Author: "Reliance v. Emerson," 5 Loyola Law Review, 426. Co-Author: "California Construction Law Manual," 2nd Edition, p. 460, McGraw-Hill Book Co-Shepherds, Inc., 1977; 1979, 1980 and 1981 supplements; "Attorneys Guide to California Construction Contracts and Disputes," California Continuing Education of the Bar, 1979, 1980 and 1981 supplements. Member: Panel of Arbitrators, American Arbitration Association; Los Angeles Superior Court Arbitration Panel. *Member:* Los Angeles County Bar Association; State Bar of California; Association of Southern California Defense Counsel; American Board of Trial Advocates. **PRACTICE AREAS:** Trial Law; Insurance.

**PAUL R. FINE,** born Tucson, Arizona, November 15, 1947; admitted to bar, 1972, California. *Education:* University of California at Los Angeles (B.A., 1969); Loyola University of Los Angeles (J.D., 1972). Associate Editor, *Defense Dialogue,* a Monthly Publication of the Association of Southern California Defense Counsel, 1975-1981. Member: Panel of Arbitrators, American Arbitration Association; State Construction Arbitration Panel; Los Angeles Superior Court Arbitration Panel. *Member:* Los Angeles County Bar Association; State Bar of California; Maritime Law Association of the United States; Association of Southern California Defense Counsel (Member, Board of Directors, 1994—); International Association of Defense Counsel. **PRACTICE AREAS:** Trial Law; Insurance; Business; Real Estate and Construction.

**NATHAN B. HOFFMAN,** born Los Angeles, California, June 2, 1953; admitted to bar, 1979, California. *Education:* University of Southern California (B.A., cum laude, 1975); Loyola University of Los Angeles (J.D., 1979). Member: St. Thomas More Law Society; Moot Court Team. Associate Justice, Scott Moot Court Honors Board, 1978-1979. Staff Member, 1977-1978 and Acquisitions Editor, 1978-1979, Loyola of Los Angeles International and Comparative Law Annual. Member, Panel of Arbitrators, American Arbitration Association and Los Angeles Superior Court. *Member:* Beverly Hills and Los Angeles County Bar Associations; State Bar of California; Association of Southern California Defense Counsel. **PRACTICE AREAS:** Trial Law; Insurance; Construction; Business.

**MARY HULETT,** born Mexico, Missouri, April 9, 1942; admitted to bar, 1977, District of Columbia and Virginia; 1980, California. *Education:* Stanford University (B.A., 1963); George Washington University (J.D., with high honors, 1977). Member, Order of the Coif. Author: "Privacy and the Freedom of Information Act," 27 Administrative Law Review, 275, 1975. Counsel to the Consumer Products Safety Commission, 1977-1980. *Member:* Los Angeles County Bar Association; State Bar of California; District of Columbia Bar; Virginia State Bar; Association of Southern California Defense Counsel (Member, Board of Directors, 1991-1993). **PRACTICE AREAS:** Trial and Appellate Law; Products Liability; Business; Wrongful Termination; Employment Discrimination; Environmental and Toxic Torts.

**MICHAEL B. GEIBEL,** born Pasadena, California, March 28, 1950; admitted to bar, 1981, California. *Education:* University of California at Los Angeles (B.A., 1972); Loyola University of Los Angeles (J.D., cum laude, 1981). Member: St. Thomas More Honor Society; Law Review Staff, Loyola University, 1980-1981. Author: "Absolute Immunity for Attorney Communications Under California Civil Code Section 42(a)," 14 University of West Los Angeles Law Review 35, 1982. *Member:* Los Angeles County Bar Association; State Bar of California; Association of Southern California Defense Counsel. **PRACTICE AREAS:** Trial and Appellate Law; Insurance.

**JAMES I. MONTGOMERY, JR.,** born Louisville, Kentucky, April 18, 1956; admitted to bar, 1981, California. *Education:* Northwestern University (B.A., 1978); University of California at Los Angeles School of Law (J.D., 1981). Member, University of California at Los Angeles Moot Court Honors Program. President, 1978-1979, John M. Langston Bar Association. Listed Strathmore's Who's Who, 1996. *Member:* Los Angeles County Bar Association; State Bar of California; National Bar Association; Association of Southern California Defense Counsel. **PRACTICE AREAS:** Trial Law; Insurance; Products Liability; Workers Compensation.

**LANCE D. ORLOFF,** born Bakersfield, California, January 10, 1959; admitted to bar, 1984, California. *Education:* University of California (A.B., with honors, 1981); Loyola Marymount University (J.D., 1984). Legislative Intern State Senator David Roberti, 1980. University of California Student Lobby, 1979-1981. Extern to Hon. Ronald S.W. Lew. Judge Pro Tem, California Court of Appeals, Los Angeles, 1984. Judge Pro Tem, Los Angeles County Municipal Court. Member, Panel of Arbitrators, Los Angeles County Superior Court. *Member:* Los Angeles County and American Bar Associations; State Bar of California; Los Angeles Chapter, American Board of Trial Advocates Inns of Court; Association of Southern California Defense Counsel. **PRACTICE AREAS:** Trial and Appellate Law; Insurance.

**MARK R. ISRAEL,** born Altoona, Pennsylvania, January 6, 1962; admitted to bar, 1986, California. *Education:* Pennsylvania State University (B.A., with high honors and distinction, 1983); University of California at Los Angeles (J.D., 1986). Phi Beta Kappa. Member, Moot Court Honors Society. *Member:* Los Angeles County and American Bar Associations; State Bar of California; Association of Southern California Defense Counsel. **PRACTICE AREAS:** Trial and Appellate Law; Insurance.

### ASSOCIATES

**ILENE WENDY KURTZMAN,** born Los Angeles, California, September 19, 1958; admitted to bar, 1985, California. *Education:* University of California at Santa Barbara; University of California at Los Angeles (B.A., 1980); University of Southern California (J.D., 1985). *Member:* State Bar of California; Association of Southern California Defense Counsel.

**JANET SACKS,** born Santa Monica, California, October 15, 1963; admitted to bar, 1989, California. *Education:* University of Southern California (B.A., 1985); Loyola Marymount University (J.D., 1989). *Member:* Beverly Hills, Los Angeles County and American Bar Associations; State Bar of California; Association of Southern California Defense Counsel.

**MICHAEL N. SCHONBUCH,** born Dearborn, Michigan, October 30, 1965; admitted to bar, 1990, California. *Education:* State University of New York at Albany (B.A., magna cum laude, 1987); Boston University (J.D., 1990). Phi Alpha Delta. Senatorial Intern, United States Senator Alfonse D'Amato, 1986-1987. *Member:* State Bar of California; Association of Southern California Defense Counsel.

*(This Listing Continued)*

## DANIELS, BARATTA & FINE, Los Angeles—Continued

**SCOTT M. LEAVITT,** born Torrance, California, October 26, 1963; admitted to bar, 1991, California. *Education:* University of California at San Diego (B.A., with honors in political science, 1987); Loyola Marymount University (J.D., 1991). Recipient, American Jurisprudence Award in Torts. *Member:* State Bar of California; Association of Southern California Defense Counsel.

**MICHELLE R. PRESS,** born Natick, Massachusetts, November 3, 1966; admitted to bar, 1992, California. *Education:* Boston University (B.S.B.A., summa cum laude, 1989; J.D., cum laude, 1992). Beta Gamma Sigma. G. Joseph Tauro Scholar. Golden Key. Recipient, School of Management Award for Outstanding Achievement, 1989. *Member:* State Bar of California; Association of Southern California Defense Counsel.

**SCOTT ASHFORD BROOKS,** born Los Angeles, California, February 4, 1964; admitted to bar, 1992, California. *Education:* University of California at Berkeley (B.A., 1987); Loyola Marymount University (J.D., 1992). Phi Delta Phi. Member: Scott Moot Court Honors Board, 1991-1992; Jessup Moot Court Competition Team, 1991-1992. *Member:* State Bar of California.

**CRAIG A. LAIDIG,** born Los Angeles, California, February 2, 1955; admitted to bar, 1992, California. *Education:* University of California at Los Angeles (B.A., 1982; M.S. 1987); Loyola Marymount University (J.D., 1992). Staff Member, 1990-1991 and Chief Note and Comment Editor, 1991-1992, Loyola Law Review. Author: "Lotus Leaves Software Copyright in a Dream State: Defining Protection of the User Interface Following Lotus Development Corp. v. Paperback Software International," 24 Loyola of Los Angeles Law Review 1301, 1991. *Member:* State Bar of California (Member, Intellectual Property Section); Federal Bar Association; Association of Southern California Defense Counsel.

**ROBIN A. WEBB,** born April 8, 1967; admitted to bar, 1992, California. *Education:* University of Southern California (B.A., magna cum laude, 1989; J.D., 1992). Phi Beta Kappa; Phi Kappa Phi. Member, Moot Court Honors Program. *Member:* State Bar of California; Association of Southern California Defense Counsel.

**CRAIG S. MOMITA,** born El Paso, Texas, May 7, 1961; admitted to bar, 1992, California. *Education:* University of California, Los Angeles (B.A., 1986); University of San Francisco (J.D., 1992). *Member:* State Bar of California; Association of Southern California Defense Counsel.

**SPENCER A. SCHNEIDER,** born Encino, California, January 17, 1969; admitted to bar, 1994, California. *Education:* University of California at Los Angeles (B.A., 1991); University of California at Davis (J.D., 1994). *Member:* State Bar of California; Association of Southern California Defense Counsel.

**ANGELO A. DU PLANTIER, III,** born Los Angeles, California, March 20, 1966; admitted to bar, 1992, California. *Education:* University of California at Irvine (B.A., 1988); McGeorge School of Law, University of the Pacific (J.D., 1992). *Member:* State Bar of California; Association of Southern California Defense Counsel.

**LESLIE E. WRIGHT, III.,** born Batavia, New York, December 1, 1962; admitted to bar, 1992, Arizona; 1995, California. *Education:* University of Arizona (B.Arch., 1986; J.D., 1992). Licensed Architect, Arizona, 1989. *Member:* State Bar of California; State Bar of Arizona; Association of Southern California Defense Counsel.

**ERIN B. HALLISSY,** born Los Angeles, California, September 17. 1969; admitted to bar, 1995, California. *Education:* University of San Francisco (B.A., 1991); McGeorge School of Law (J.D., 1994). *Member:* State Bar of California; Association of Southern California Defense Counsel.

**KENA B. CHIN,** born Mountain View, California, September 11, 1967; admitted to bar, 1995, California. *Education:* University of California-Los Angeles (B.A., 1989); Santa Clara University (J.D., 1994). *Member:* State Bar of California; Association of Southern California Defense Counsel.

**DEAN BENGSTON,** born Los Angeles, California, December 22, 1968; admitted to bar, 1995, California. *Education:* University of California at Los Angeles (B.A., 1992); University of California School of Law, Davis (J.D., 1995). Member, Moot Court Board, 1994-1995. *Member:* State Bar of California; Association of Southern California Defense Counsel.

**PETER ANDERS NYQUIST,** born Los Angeles, California, January 23, 1968; admitted to bar, 1995, California. *Education:* University of California at Los Angeles (B.A., 1991); University of California School of Law, Davis (J.D., 1995). Executive Editor and Trial Practice Honors Board,

*(This Listing Continued)*

1994-1995, U.C. Davis Law Review. *Member:* State Bar of California; Association of Southern California Defense Counsel.

**JEANNIE MASSE,** born Los Angeles, California, September 6, 1969; admitted to bar, 1995, California. *Education:* University of California at Los Angeles (B.A., 1992); Loyola Marymount University (J.D., 1995). Phi Delta Phi. Golden Key National Honor Society. St. Thomas More Law Honor Society, 1993—. *Member:* State Bar of California; Association of Southern California Defense Counsel.

**LORI CHOTINER,** born Los Angeles, California, April 1, 1971; admitted to bar, 1996, California. *Education:* California State University, Northridge (B.A., 1993); Loyola Marymount University (J.D., 1996). Golden Key National Honor Society. St. Thomas More Law Honor Society. *Member:* State Bar of California; Association of Southern California Defense Counsel.

**MAUREEN M. MICHAIL,** born Winsor, Canada, August 11, 1971; admitted to bar, 1996, California. *Education:* University of California at Los Angeles (B.A., 1993); Loyola Marymount University (J.D., 1996). *Member:* State Bar of California; Association of Southern California Defense Counsel.

### OF COUNSEL

**TIMOTHY J. HUGHES,** born Altadena, California, March 20, 1951; admitted to bar, 1978, California. *Education:* Loyola University of Los Angeles (B.A., summa cum laude, 1973); Hastings College of Law, University of California (J.D., 1976). Recipient, Ignatian Award and Scholar of the Year. *Member:* Los Angeles County and American (Member, Sections on: Real Property; Business Law) Bar Associations; State Bar of California; Association of Southern California Defense Counsel. **LANGUAGES:** Spanish. **PRACTICE AREAS:** Real Estate; Business Law.

**DREW T. HANKER,** born Newport Beach, California, June 23, 1957; admitted to bar, 1983, California. *Education:* Bucknell University (B.A., with honors, 1980); University of Southern California (J.D., 1983). Phi Delta Phi. Quarter Finalist, Hale Moot Court Competition. Member, Entertainment Law Journal, 1981-1982. *Member:* Los Angeles County and Beverly Hills Bar Associations; State Bar of California; Association of Southern California Defense Counsel. **LANGUAGES:** French. **PRACTICE AREAS:** Trial Law; Hotel and Innkeeper Law; Products Liability; Wrongful Termination; Employment Discrimination.

**MARK A. VEGA,** born Canton, Ohio, September 24, 1963; admitted to bar, 1992, California. *Education:* University of Arizona (B.A., magna cum laude, 1989; J.D., 1992). Phi Beta Kappa. Order of the Barristers. Member, Arizona National Moot Court Team. Recipient: Outstanding Advocate, Joseph S. Jenckes Advocacy Award, 1992; Best Oral Advocate, O'Connor, Cavanaugh Advocacy Award, 1991. Articles Editor, Best Editor, 1991-1992 and Most Helpful Editor, 1991-1992, Arizona Journal of International And Comparative Law. *Member:* Los Angeles County and Beverly Hills (Member, Women in Film, Independent Features Project, West) Bar Associations; State Bar of California. **PRACTICE AREAS:** Entertainment Litigation; Intellectual Property; Media and First Amendment.

REPRESENTATIVE CLIENTS: Arizona Insurance Guarantee Assn.; Back State Door Productions, L.L.C.; Coregis; Gencon; Georgia and Island Insurance Company; Heitman Advisory Corp.; Heitman Properties Ltd.; Hilton Hotels Corp.; Kaiser Permanente; Los Angeles County Metropolitan Transportation Authority (MTA); MCA/Universal City Studios, Inc.; Messiah Productions, L.L.C.; State Farm Fire and Casualty Co.; State Farm Mutual Automobile Insurance Co.; Texaco, Inc.; Trustees of the California State University; TRW Inc.; United Services Automobile Association; U.S. Risk Managers, Inc.; Watkins Associated Industries, Inc.; Wausau-Nationwide Insurance Cos.; Weyerhaeuser Co.

---

# DANNER & CHONOLES, L.L.P.

## LOS ANGELES, CALIFORNIA

(See Long Beach)

*General Civil Trial and Appellate Practice in State and Federal Courts. Products Liability, Premises Liability, Wrongful Termination, Business Litigation.*

## DANNER & MARTYN, LLP
WATT PLAZA-SUITE 1070
1925 CENTURY PARK EAST
**LOS ANGELES, CALIFORNIA 90067-2799**
Telephone: 310-789-3800
Telecopier: 310-789-3814

General Commercial Practice, Bankruptcy, Reorganization and Workouts, Commercial Transactions, Corporations and Business Law, Creditors' Rights, Environmental, Financial Services and Commercial Lending, Litigation and Appellate Practice, Mergers and Acquisitions, Real Estate, White Collar Crime, Zoning, Land Use and Condemnation Law.

**ROBERT C. DANNER,** born Los Angeles, California, 1953; admitted to bar, 1978, California. *Education:* University of Southern California (A.B., cum laude, 1975); Loyola University of Los Angeles (J.D., cum laude, 1978). Member, Loyola University of Los Angeles Law Review, 1976-1977. *Member:* Los Angeles County and American Bar Associations; State Bar of California.

**DANIEL E. MARTYN, JR.,** born New York, N.Y., 1952; admitted to bar, 1979, New York; 1982, Michigan; 1988, California. *Education:* Villanova University; Hofstra University (B.A., 1975); New York Law School (J.D., 1978). *Member:* State Bar of California; State Bar of Michigan; American Bar Association (Member, Commercial Financial Services Committee, Business Law Section); Financial Lawyers Conference.

**DAVID S. POOLE,** born Wilmington, Delaware, April 26, 1955; admitted to bar, 1980, California; 1985, U.S. Court of Claims; 1988, U.S. Supreme Court. *Education:* University of California at Los Angeles (A.B., cum laude, 1977); University of Southern California (J.D., 1980). Phi Eta Sigma; Pi Gamma Mu. Deputy Attorney General, State of California Department of Justice, 1980-1984. *Member:* State Bar of California.

---

**MELANIE J. BINGHAM,** born Hartford, Connecticut, 1965; admitted to bar, 1993, California. *Education:* Amherst College (B.A., 1987); University of California at Los Angeles (J.D., 1992). Consulting Editor, The National Black Law Journal, 1991-1992. Law Clerk, Hon. David W. Williams, U.S. District Court, Central District of California, 1992-1993. *Member:* State Bar of California.

**ADRYANE R. OMENS,** born Encino, California, 1964; admitted to bar, 1990, California and U.S. District Court, Central, Southern, Northern and Eastern Districts of California. *Education:* University of California at Los Angeles (B.A., 1986); Loyola Marymount University (J.D., 1989). *Member:* Los Angeles County and American Bar Associations; State Bar of California.

REPRESENTATIVE CLIENTS: American Magnetics Corp.; Catellus Management Corp.; Comerica Acceptance Corporation; General Motors Corporation; Hughes Aircraft Co.; Hyundai Motors Finance Company; V.W. Credit, Inc.; Argonaut Holding, Inc.; Comerica Bank; General Motor Acceptance Corporation.

## DANNING, GILL, DIAMOND & KOLLITZ, LLP

A Limited Liability Partnership Composed of Professional Corporations
*Established in 1953*

2029 CENTURY PARK EAST, SUITE 1900
**LOS ANGELES, CALIFORNIA 90067-3005**
Telephone: 310-277-0077
Fax: 310-277-5735
Email: dgdk@dgdk.com

Bankruptcy, Business Reorganization, Insolvency, Corporate Dissolutions, Partnership Dissolutions, Commercial Law, Bankruptcy Trusteeships, Federal Receiverships and State Receiverships.

FIRM PROFILE: Danning, Gill, Diamond & Kollitz, LLP, a limited liability partnership composed of professional corporations, is a firm which has specialized in business reorganizations, insolvency, bankruptcy and commercial law since it was founded in 1953. The Firm's attorneys are experienced in representing all major constituencies in the areas of the Firm's practice, including, among others, debtors, bankruptcy trustees, bankruptcy examiners, receivers, assignees for the benefit of creditors, secured creditors, unsecured creditors, creditors' committees, equity security holders' committees, asset purchasers, third party plan proponents and parties to bankruptcy related or commerical
*(This Listing Continued)*

litigation. The Firm includes lawyers who are experienced as Chapter 11 reorganization trustees, Chapter 11 disbursing agents, Chapter 7 liquidating trustees, bankruptcy examiners, Federal and State Court Receivers, as well as experienced support personnel.

The Firm and its members have acted as principal counsel to the Official Creditors' committee in the Maxicare reorganization and as bankruptcy or reorganization trustee in the matters of Oasis Petroleum, Producers Sales Organization and Financial Corporation of America, the parent of American Savings & Loan, each multi-million dollar bankruptcy court operations and/or liquidations. The Firm represents the City of Los Angeles in bankruptcy-related matters.

### MEMBERS OF FIRM

**DAVID A. GILL, (A PROFESSIONAL CORPORATION),** born Chicago, Illinois, November 14, 1936; admitted to bar, 1962, California and U.S. Supreme Court; U.S. Court of Appeals, Ninth Circuit. *Education:* University of California at Los Angeles (B.A., 1958); Stanford University (J.D., 1961). Phi Delta Phi. Author: "Personal Bankruptcy and Wage Earner Plans," University of California—Continuing Education of the Bar, 1971. Co-editor: "Basic Bankruptcy," Matthew Bender, 1992. *Member:* Los Angeles County (Chair, Commercial Law and Bankruptcy Sections, 1984-1985) and American (Member, Consumer Bankruptcy Committee and Business Bankruptcy Committee on Corporation, Banking and Business Law, 1976-1982) Bar Associations; State Bar of California (Member, Committee on Debtor-Creditor Relations and Bankruptcy, 1976-1982); American Bankruptcy Institute; National Association of Bankruptcy Trustees. *Email:* dagill@dgdk.com

**RICHARD K. DIAMOND, (A PROFESSIONAL CORPORATION),** born Los Angeles, California, May 10, 1950; admitted to bar, 1976, California. *Education:* University of California, Berkeley (A.B., 1973); University of California, Los Angeles (J.D., 1976). Phi Beta Kappa; Order of the Coif. *Member:* Los Angeles County (Member, Bankruptcy Committee of Section on Commercial Law and Bankruptcy) and American Bar Associations; State Bar of California (Member, 1988-1991, Chair, 1991, Debtor-Creditor Relations and Bankruptcy Committee); Financial Lawyers Conference; California Bankruptcy Forum; Los Angeles Bankruptcy Forum; National Association of Bankruptcy Trustees. *Email:* rdiamond@dgdk.com

**HOWARD KOLLITZ, (A PROFESSIONAL CORPORATION),** born Chicago, Illinois, January 25, 1948; admitted to bar, 1974, California. *Education:* University of California at Los Angeles (A.B., 1969; J.D., 1973). *Member:* Los Angeles County and American Bar Associations; State Bar of California (Member, Debtor/Creditor Relations and Bankruptcy Committee, 1995—); Financial Lawyers Conference; California Bankruptcy Forum; Los Angeles Bankruptcy Forum. *Email:* hkollitz@dgdk.com

**JOHN J. BINGHAM, JR., (A PROFESSIONAL CORPORATION),** born Ridgecrest, California, July 6, 1946; admitted to bar, 1977, California. *Education:* University of Southern California (B.A., 1968); Southwestern University (J.D., 1977). *Member:* Los Angeles County Bar Association; State Bar of California (Member, Debtor/Creditor Relations and Bankruptcy Committee, 1991-1994); American Bankruptcy Institute; Financial Lawyers Conference; California Bankruptcy Forum; Los Angeles Bankruptcy Forum. [Lieut., USNR, Judge Advocate Corps, 1974-1976; active duty, 1968-1973; Reserve duty, 1974-1976] *Email:* jbingham@dgdk.com

**STEVEN E. SMITH, (A PROFESSIONAL CORPORATION),** born Santa Barbara, California, March 26, 1955; admitted to bar, 1980, California. *Education:* University of Southern California (B.A., 1977); Loyola Marymount University (J.D., 1980). Editor, Loyola Law Review, 1979-1980. Recipient, Bancroft Whitney Award for Secured Transactions in Personal Property. *Member:* Los Angeles County and American Bar Associations; State Bar of California; Financial Lawyers Conference; California Bankruptcy Forum; Los Angeles Bankruptcy Forum (Member, Board of Directors). *Email:* ssmith@dgdk.com

**ERIC P. ISRAEL, (A PROFESSIONAL CORPORATION),** born Los Angeles, California, September 22, 1959; admitted to bar, 1987, California and U.S. District Court, Central District of California. *Education:* University of California at Los Angeles (B.A., 1981); Southwestern University School of Law (J.D., with honors, 1987). Member, Southwestern University Law Review, 1987. Author: "Of Racketeers, Rico, the Enterprise - Pattern Separateness Issue and Chicken Little: What's Really Falling?" 17 Southwestern University Law Review 565, 1987. Mediator on the Panel for the Bankruptcy Courts, Central District of California, 1995—. *Member:* State Bar of California; American Bar Association; Los Angeles Bankruptcy Forum; California Bankruptcy Forum; Financial Lawyers Conference. *Email:* eisrael@dgdk.com

*(This Listing Continued)*

## DANNING, GILL, DIAMOND & KOLLITZ, LLP, Los Angeles—Continued

**DAVID M. POITRAS, (A PROFESSIONAL CORPORATION),** born Dracut, Massachusetts, October 4, 1962; admitted to bar, 1989, Massachusetts, California and U.S. District Court, Central District of California; 1990, U.S. Court of Appeals, Ninth Circuit. *Education:* Suffolk University (B.S.B.A., 1985); Loyola Marymount University (J.D., 1988). Recipient, American Jurisprudence Award in Bankruptcy. Law Clerk to U.S. Bankruptcy Judge, Alan M. Ahart, 1988-1989. *Member:* Beverly Hills, Los Angeles County and Massachusetts Bar Associations; State Bar of California; Financial Lawyers Conference; Los Angeles Bankruptcy Forum; California Bankruptcy Forum. **LANGUAGES:** French. **Email:** dpoitras@dgdk.com

**GEORGE E. SCHULMAN, (A PROFESSIONAL CORPORATION),** born Flushing, New York, 1947; admitted to bar, 1972, New York; 1975, California. *Education:* Queens College (B.A., 1968); New York University (J.D., 1971). Co-Author: "Debtor's Rights and Remedies," Annual Survey of American Law, 1969-1970. Judge Pro-Tem, Los Angeles Municipal Court, 1988—. Judge Pro-Tem Los Angeles Superior Court, 1992—. Trial Attorney, Federal Trade Commission, New York and Los Angeles offices, 1971-1987. *Member:* Los Angeles County (Chair of Executive Committee, Antitrust Section, 1996-1997), New York State and American Bar Associations; State Bar of California. **PRACTICE AREAS:** Litigation; Receivership Law; Bankruptcy Law; Antitrust Law; Trade Regulation Law. **Email:** gschulman@dgdk.com

### ASSOCIATES

**ROBERT A. HESSLING,** born Milwaukee, Wisconsin, July 27, 1955; admitted to bar, 1980, California and Arizona; 1981, U.S. District Court, Central District of California; 1986, U.S. District Court, Southern District of California. *Education:* University of Minnesota; University of Nebraska (B.A., with high distinction, 1977); University of Arizona (J.D., with high distinction, 1980). Phi Beta Kappa; Order of the Coif. Author: "Reaffirmation and Redemption," The Michie Co., June 1994. *Member:* San Diego County and Los Angeles County Bar Associations; State Bar of California; State Bar of Arizona; Financial Lawyers Conference; California Bankruptcy Forum; Los Angeles Bankruptcy Forum. **REPORTED CASES:** In re Rivers, 55 B.R. 699 (Banks, C.D. Cal. 1984); Taxel v. Electronic Sports Research, 111 B.R. 892 (Bank v. S.D. Cal. 1990). **Email:** rhessling@dgdk.com

**KEVIN L. HING,** born San Jose, California, May 8, 1962; admitted to bar, 1988, California, U.S. District Court, Central, Southern and Eastern Districts of California and U.S. Court of Appeals, Ninth Circuit. *Education:* University of California at Los Angeles (B.A., cum laude, 1985); University of Southern California (J.D., 1988). *Member:* Financial Lawyers Conference; The Los Angeles Bankruptcy Forum; California Bankruptcy Forum. *Member:* Los Angeles County and American Bar Associations; State Bar of California. **Email:** khing@dgdk.com

**BARRY LURIE,** born Ashqelon, Israel, September 18, 1963; admitted to bar, 1989, California and U.S. District Court, Southern and Central Districts of California. *Education:* Stanford University (B.A., 1985); University of California at Los Angeles (J.D., 1989; M.B.A., 1989). Moot Court Board of Judges. Recipient, Olin Fellowship Award. *Member:* Los Angeles Bar Association; State Bar of California; Financial Lawyers Conference; Los Angeles Bankruptcy Forum; California Bankruptcy Forum. **LANGUAGES:** French. **Email:** blurie@dgdk.com

**KATHY BAZOIAN PHELPS,** born Los Angeles, California, August 2, 1966; admitted to bar, 1991, California. *Education:* Pomona College (B.A., 1988); University of California at Los Angeles (J.D., 1991). Phi Alpha Delta. *Member:* Beverly Hills, Los Angeles and American Bar Associations; State Bar of California; Financial Lawyers Conference; Los Angeles Bankruptcy Forum; California Bankruptcy Forum. **LANGUAGES:** Mandarin Chinese. **Email:** kphelps@dgdk.com

**DANIEL H. GILL,** born Los Angeles, California, July 3, 1963; admitted to bar, 1991, California, U.S. District Court, Central District of California and U.S. Court of Appeals, Ninth Circuit. *Education:* University of California at Santa Cruz (B.A. with honors, 1985); University of California at Los Angeles (J.D., 1991). Initial Law Clerk, The Honorable Robert W. Alberts, United States Bankruptcy Court, Central District of California, February 1992 to January 1993. Served as a Judicial Extern to the Honorable Harry Pregerson, United States Court of Appeals, for the Ninth Circuit, from January 1990 to May 1990. *Member:* State Bar of California; Los Angeles County and American Bar Associations; Financial Lawyers Conference; Los Angeles Bankruptcy Forum; California Bankruptcy Forum. **Email:** dhgill@dgdk.com

*(This Listing Continued)*

**GLENN C. KELBLE,** born Decatur, Georgia, October 12, 1966; admitted to bar, 1992, California. *Education:* University of California (B.A., magna cum laude, 1988) Phi Beta Kappa; University of California, Los Angeles (J.D., 1992). Phi Alpha Delta. University of California at Los Angeles Journal of Environmental Law and Policy (Member, 1989-1992; Chief Articles Editor, 1991-1992). *Member:* Century City, Los Angeles County and Ventura County Bar Associations; State Bar of California; Ventura County Barristers Association (Member, Executive Board, 1993); Los Angeles Bankruptcy Forum; Financial Lawyers Conference. **PRACTICE AREAS:** Bankruptcy; Litigation. **Email:** gkelble@dgdk.com

**SARAH E. PETTY,** born Albuquerque, New Mexico, September 2, 1969; admitted to bar, 1994, California, U.S. District Court, Central District of California and U.S. Court of Appeals, Ninth Circuit. *Education:* University of California at Irvine (B.A., 1991); University of Southern California (J.D., 1994). Judicial Law Clerk to the Hon. Thomas B. Donovan, Ernest M. Robles, and Erithe A. Smith, U.S. Bankruptcy Court, Central District of California, 1995. *Member:* Century City, Los Angeles County and Orange County Bar Associations; State Bar of California; Orange County Bankruptcy Forum; Los Angeles Bankruptcy Forum; Financial Lawyers Conference. **PRACTICE AREAS:** Bankruptcy; Insolvency. **Email:** spetty@dgdk.com

**ELAN R. SCHWARTZ,** born Royal Oak, Michigan, April 21, 1969; admitted to bar, 1994, California. *Education:* University of Arizona (B.A., 1991); University of the Pacific, McGeorge School of Law (J.D., 1994). Phi Alpha Delta. Moot Court Honors. **PRACTICE AREAS:** Bankruptcy. **Email:** eschwartz@dgdk.com

### OF COUNSEL

**CURTIS B. DANNING, (A PROFESSIONAL CORPORATION),** born Los Angeles, California, December 3, 1920; admitted to bar, 1953, California. *Education:* University of California at Berkeley (A.B., 1942); University of California at Los Angeles (LL.B., 1952). *Member:* Los Angeles County Bar Association; State Bar of California; Financial Lawyers Conference; Los Angeles Bankruptcy Forum; California Bankruptcy Forum; National Association of Bankruptcy Trustees. **Email:** cdanning@dgdk.com

**JAMES J. JOSEPH, (A PROFESSIONAL CORPORATION),** born Orange, California, September 12, 1947; admitted to bar, 1972, California. *Education:* Reed College (B.A., 1969); University of California at Berkeley (J.D., 1972). Phi Beta Kappa. *Member:* Los Angeles County Bar Association; State Bar of California; Financial Lawyers Conference; Los Angeles Bankruptcy Forum; California Bankruptcy Forum. **Email:** jjoseph@dgdk.com

---

## DAPEER, ROSENBLIT & LITVAK, LLP

### LOS ANGELES, CALIFORNIA

(See Beverly Hills)

*Business and Real Estate Litigation, Commercial and Corporate Law, including Creditors Rights Law and Commercial Collections, Professional Liability Litigation, Municipal Law and Land Use Law, Civil Trial Practice.*

---

## DARBY & DARBY

PROFESSIONAL CORPORATION

707 WILSHIRE BOULEVARD
THIRTY SECOND FLOOR
**LOS ANGELES, CALIFORNIA 90017**
Telephone: 213-243-8000
Telecopier: 213-243-8050

*New York, New York Office:* 805 Third Avenue. Telephone: 212-527-7700. Telecopier: 212-753-6237. Telex: 236687.

*Intellectual Property and Technology, including Patent, Trademark, Copyright, Computer, Trade Secrets, Unfair Competition, Licensing and Related Antitrust Law.*

**BYARD G. NILSSON,** born Provo, Utah, September 8, 1925; admitted to bar, 1954, District of Columbia; 1956, California; registered to practice before U.S. Patent and Trademark Office. *Education:* Brigham Young University; University of Utah (B.S.E.E., 1953); George Washington University (J.D., with honors, 1953). Author: "Foreign Sales and Trademark Pitfalls," Los Angeles Bar Bulletin, December, 1972; "A Litigation Settling Experi-

*(This Listing Continued)*

ment," ABA Journal, December, 1979. Co-Author: "Possible Impact of 35 USC 294," New Matter, Publication of State Bar of California, Fall, 1983. *Member:* American Bar Association (Chairman: Protection of Confidential Rights Committee, 1971; Government Relations to Patents Committee, 1972-1973; Patent System Policy Committee, 1975; Patent Law Revision Committee, 1976; Patent Division, 1977; Council Member, 1977-1981; Chairman, Inventors Committee, 1982; Bar Referral Services Committee, 1983-1985); State Bar of California (Member, Executive Committee, Patent, Trademark and Copyright Section, 1982-1984; Delegate, Conference of Delegates, 1983). *REPORTED CASES:* TOHO Co. Ltd. et al v. Sears, Roebuck & Co., 645 F.2d 788 (CA9 1981). *TRANSACTIONS:* First "Minitrial", ABA Journal, Dec. 1979. Early Computer Patents, 3,274,376; 3,212,062. *PRACTICE AREAS:* Patent Law; Trademark Law.

**HAROLD E. WURST,** born Ft. Smith, Arkansas, August 16, 1939; admitted to bar, 1965, District of Columbia; 1972, California; registered to practice before U.S. Patent and Trademark Office. *Education:* University of Notre Dame (B.S.E.E., 1961); Georgetown University (J.D., 1965). Author: "The Patentability of Computer Programs," Los Angeles Bar Bulletin, May 1973; "Getting The Most From Jury Instructions In Patent Cases", Journal Of Proprietary Rights, October, 1991. Judge Pro Tem, Los Angeles Municipal Court, 1987—. Arbitrator, Superior Court, County of Los Angeles, 1993—. *Member:* American Bar Association (Committee Chairman, 1968, 1969); The District of Columbia Bar; State Bar of California. *REPORTED CASES:* Windsurfing International, Inc. v. BIC Leisure Products, Inc., AMF, Inc. and James Drake, Intervenor, 613 F. Supp. 933 (S.D.N.Y 1985); 231 U.S.P.Q. 19 (S.D.N.Y 1986); 782 F.2d 995 (CAFC 1986); cert. den., 477 U.S. 905 (1986); 828 F.2d 755 (CAFC 1987); 687 F.Supp. 134 (S.D.N.Y 1988); Registration Control Systems, Inc. v. Compusystems, Inc., 922 F. 2d 805 (CAFC 1990); Ricon Corp. v. Adaptive Driving Systems, Inc., 229 U.S.P.Q. 731 (C.D.Cal. 1986); Trell v. Marlee Electronics Corp., 5 U.S.P.Q. 2d 1501 (C.D.Cal. 1987); 912 F.2d 1443 (CAFC 1990); Break-Away Tours, Inc. v. British Caledonian Airways, 704 F.Supp. 178 (S.D.Cal. 1988); Winterland Concessions Co., et al v. Sileo, et al, 528 F.Supp. 1201 (N.D.Ill. E.D. 1982); 830 F.2d 195 (CA7 1987); Winterland Concessions Co., et al v. Creative Screen Design, Ltd., et al, 210 U.S.P.Q. 6 (N.D.Ill.E.D. 1980); 214 U.S.P.Q. 188 (N.D.Ill.E.D. 1981); United States Golf Assn. v. St. Andrews Systems, 749 F. 2d 1029 (CA3 1984); Lascano v. State of Arkansas, 669 S.W. 2d 453 (Ark.Sup.Ct.1984). *PRACTICE AREAS:* Litigation.

**ROBERT A. GREEN,** born Los Angeles, California, July 24, 1949; admitted to bar, 1975, California and U.S. Court of Appeals, Ninth Circuit; registered to practice before U.S. Patent and Trademark Office. *Education:* University of California at Los Angeles (B.S. in Engineering, Solid State Electronics, magna cum laude, 1972; J.D., 1975). *Member:* Los Angeles County (Trustee, 1992-1993) and American (Member, Section of Patent, Trademark and Copyright Law) Bar Associations; State Bar of California; Los Angeles Patent Law Association (Director, 1986-1988) Lawyers' Club of Los Angeles County (President, 1990-1991; Governor, 1986—; Treasurer, 1986-1987; Secretary, 1987-1988; Delegate, State Bar Conference, 1985—). *PRACTICE AREAS:* Patent Law; Trademark Law; Copyright Law.

---

**CLARKE A. WIXON,** born Buffalo, New York, December 21, 1968; admitted to bar, 1994, California; U.S. District Court, Central District of California; U.S. Court of Appeals, Ninth Circuit; registered to practice before U.S. Patent and Trademark Office. *Education:* University of California, Irvine (B.S., 1991); University of Southern California (J.D., 1994). Phi Alpha Delta. *Member:* Los Angeles County and American Bar Associations; State Bar of California; Los Angeles Intellectual Property Law Association. *PRACTICE AREAS:* Patent Law; Trademark Law.

**STEPHEN D. BURBACH,** born Hebron, Nebraska, July 9, 1959; admitted to bar, 1994, California; U.S. District Court, Central District of California; U.S. Court of Appeals, Ninth Circuit; registered to practice before U.S. Patent and Trademark Office. *Education:* University of Colorado, Denver (B.S.E.E., 1988); University of California, Los Angeles (J.D., 1994). Managing Editor, UCLA J. Envtl. & Pol'y. *Member:* Los Angeles County Bar Association; State Bar of California; Los Angeles Intellectual Property Law Association. *PRACTICE AREAS:* Patent Law; Trademark Law.

**JOHN E. WURST,** born Alexandria, Virginia, October 14, 1965; admitted to bar, 1994, Nebraska; registered to practice before U.S. Patent and Trademark Office (Not admitted in California). *Education:* University of California at San Diego (B.A. in biochemistry, 1990); Creighton University (J.D., 1994). *Member:* American Bar Association; Los Angeles Intellectual Property Law Association. *PRACTICE AREAS:* Patent Law.

*(This Listing Continued)*

**LANCE M. KREISMAN,** born Tacoma, Washington, December 29, 1964; admitted to bar, 1994, California; registered to practice before U.S. Patent and Trademark Office. *Education:* University of California at Los Angeles (B.S.E.E., 1987); Whittier College School of Law (J.D., 1993). *PRACTICE AREAS:* Patent Prosecution; Patent Litigation; Trademark.

### OF COUNSEL

**WILLIAM P. GREEN, (LAW CORPORATION),** born Jacksonville, Illinois, March 19, 1920; admitted to bar, 1947, Illinois; 1948, California and U.S. District Court, Central District of California; 1970-1982, U.S. Court of Customs and Patent Appeals; 1973, U.S. Supreme Court; 1978, U.S. Court of Appeals, Fifth and Ninth Circuits; 1982, U.S. Court of Appeals for the Federal Circuit; 1986, U.S. District Court, Southern District of Texas; registered to practice before U.S. Patent and Trademark Office. *Education:* Illinois College (B.A., 1941); Northwestern University (J.D., 1947). Phi Beta Kappa; Phi Delta Phi. Member, Board of Editors, Illinois Law Review, 1947. *Member:* Los Angeles County and American (Member, Sections on: Patent, Trademark and Copyright Law; Antitrust Law) Bar Associations; State Bar of California; American Intellectual Property Law Association (Member, Committee on Federal Practice and Procedure, 1973—); Lawyers Club of Los Angeles County (Member of the Board, 1981—; President, 1984-1985); Los Angeles Patent Law Association. [Lieut., USNR, Eng. Off., 1942-1946]. (Also practicing individually at the same address).

### LEGAL SUPPORT PERSONNEL

### PATENT AGENT

**REENA KUYPER,** born New Delhi, India, May 29, 1962. registered to practice before U.S. Patent and Trademark Office. *Education:* California State University, Fullerton (B.S.E.E., 1986).

(For complete biographical data on all personnel, see Professional Biographies at New York, New York)

---

## *DARLING, HALL & RAE*

*Established in 1928*

*777 SOUTH FIGUEROA, 37TH FLOOR*
**LOS ANGELES, CALIFORNIA 90017**
Telephone: 213-627-8104
Fax: 213-627-7795
Email: 71555.1466@Compuserve.com

*Trust, Estate Planning, Probate, Corporation, Business and Real Property. Civil and Trial Practice in all State and Federal Courts.*

### MEMBERS OF FIRM

**HUGH W. DARLING** (1901-1986).

**EDWARD S. SHATTUCK** (1901-1965).

**GEORGE GAYLORD GUTE** (1922-1981).

**DONALD KEITH HALL** (1918-1984).

**MATTHEW S. RAE, JR.,** born Pittsburgh, Pennsylvania, September 12, 1922; admitted to bar, 1948, Maryland; 1951, California and U.S. Court of Appeals, Ninth Circuit; 1954, U.S. District Court, Central District of California; 1967, U.S. Supreme Court. *Education:* Duke University (A.B., 1946; LL.B., 1947); Stanford University. Phi Alpha Delta (Supreme Justice, 1972-1974); Phi Beta Kappa (President, Southern California Association, 1996—); Omicron Delta Kappa; Phi Eta Sigma. Member, Chancery Club (President, 1996—), Breakfast Club (Chairman, 1989-1990). Administrative Assistant to the Dean, Duke University School of Law, 1947-1948. Research Attorney to the Hon. Douglas L. Edmonds, Associate Justice, Supreme Court of California, 1951-1952. Trustee, 1964— and President, 1969-1971, Legion Lex. *Member:* Committee on Legislation, Baltimore Junior Bar Association, 1948-1949; California Commission on Uniform State Laws, 1985—. *Member:* Los Angeles County (Trustee, 1983-1985; Recipient, Shattuck-Price Memorial Award, 1990; Chairman, Probate and Trust Law Committee, 1964-1966; Recipient, Arthur K. Marshall Probate and Trust Award, 1984; Chairman, 1979-1981 and Co-Chairman, 1982-1986, Legislation Committee), South Bay and American Bar Associations; The State Bar of California (Chairman, State Bar Journal Committee, 1970-1971; Chairman, Probate and Trust Law Committee, 1974-1975; Member, Executive Committee, 1977-1983, Chairman, 1977-1989 and Co-Chairman, 1991-1992, Legislation Committee, Estate Planning, Trust and Probate Law Section; Member, Probate Law Consulting Group, California Board of Legal Specialization, 1977-1988; Chairman, Resolutions Committee, 1987 and Member, Executive Committee, 1987-1990, Conference of Delegates);

*(This Listing Continued)*

CAA617B

## DARLING, HALL & RAE, Los Angeles—Continued

Lawyers Club of Los Angeles (Member, Board of Governors, 1981-1987; First Vice President, 1982-1983); International Academy of Estate and Trust Law (Member, Executive Council, 1974-1978); Los Angeles County Bar Foundation (Director, 1987-1993). Fellow, American College of Trust and Estate Counsel. *PRACTICE AREAS:* Estate Planning Law; Trust Law; Probate Law.

**RICHARD L. STACK,** born Los Angeles, California, November 29, 1947; admitted to bar, 1973, California; 1974, U.S. District Court, Central District of California and U.S. Court of Appeals, Ninth Circuit; 1980, U.S. Supreme Court. *Education:* University of California at Los Angeles (B.A., with honors, 1969); Loyola University of Los Angeles (J.D., 1973). Member: St. Thomas More Law Society; Chancery Club. Trustee, Hugh and Hazel Darling Foundation, 1987—. *Member:* Los Angeles County (Member, Executive Committee, Probate and Trust Law Section, 1983-1990; Chairman, 1988-1989; Member, Continuing Education Advisory Board, 1985-1986) and American (Member: Corporation, Banking and Business Law Section; General Practice Section; Real Property, Probate and Trust Law Section) Bar Associations; State Bar of California (Member, Resolutions Committee, Conference of Delegates, 1989-1991); Lawyers Club of Los Angeles County (Member, Board of Governors, 1982-1988). Fellow, American College of Trust and Estate Counsel. *PRACTICE AREAS:* Trusts and Estates; Corporate; Real Property; Non-Profit Organizations.

**EDWIN FRESTON,** born Los Angeles, California, July 12, 1937; admitted to bar, 1963, California; 1973, U.S. Supreme Court. *Education:* University of Southern California (A.B., 1959; J.D., 1962). Phi Alpha Delta. Article Editor, University of Southern California Law Review, 1962. *Member:* Los Angeles County and American Bar Associations; State Bar of California; Chancery Club. *REPORTED CASES:* Cal. 1976. Archibald v. Cinerama Hotels, 126 Cal.Rptr. 811, 15 Cal.3d 853, 544 P.2d 947 Cal. 1965; Powell v. California Dept. of Employment, 45 Cal.Rptr. 136, 403 P.2d 392, 63 Cal.2d 103; Cal.App. 2 Dist. 1993; A Local and Regional Monitor v. City of Los Angeles, 16 Cal.Rptr.2d 358, 12 Cal.App.4th 1773; Cal.App. 2 Dist. 1993; Arcadia Redevelopment Agency v. Ikemoto, 20 Cal.Rptr.2d 112, 16 Cal.App.4th 444; Cal.App. 2 Dist. 1975; Coffee-Rich, Inc. v. Fielder 122 Cal.Rptr. 302, 48 Cal.App.3d 990 Cal.App. 3 Dist. 1974; Archibald v. Cinerama Hotels 117 Cal.Rptr. 843, 43 Cal.App.3d 511 Cal-.App. 1972; Coffee-Rich, Inc. v. Fielder, 104 Cal.Rptr. 252, 27 Cal.App.3d 792, 1972 Trade Cases P 74.186 Cal.App. 1971; Farr v. Superior Court of Los Angeles County, 99 Cal.Rptr. 342, 22 Cal.App.3d 60, 1 Media L. Rep. 2545 Cal.App. 1967; Doctor v. Lakeridge Const. Co., 60 Cal.Rptr. 824, 252 Cal.App.2d 715 C.A.Cal. 1982; Mende v. Dun & Bradstreet, Inc. 670 F.2d 129 C.A.N.M. 1980; Solomon v. Pendaries Properties, Inc. 623 F.2d 602 C.A.Mo. 1976; In re Cessna Distributorship Antitrust Litigation, 532 F.2d 64, 1976-1 Trade Cases P 60,749. *PRACTICE AREAS:* Probate; Trust; Real Property Litigation; Real Property Transactions.

### OF COUNSEL

**JOHN L. FLOWERS,** born San Bernardino, California, March 26, 1941; admitted to bar, 1966, California; 1969, U.S. District Court, Southern District of California; 1970, U.S. District Court, Central District of California; 1979, U.S. Court of Appeals, Ninth Circuit; 1982, U.S. Supreme Court; 1994, Washington. *Education:* University of Redlands; University of Southern California (B.S.L., 1965; J.D., 1966). Phi Delta Phi; Order of the Coif. Recipient, American Jurisprudence Award in Contracts. Member, Editorial Board, Southern California Law Review, 1965-1966. Author: "Federal Rules of Civil Procedure: Attacking the Party Problem," 38 So. Cal. L. Rev. 80, 1965; "Legal Aspects of Direct Mail Fund Raising," Direct Mail Fund Raising Handbook, 1975. Instructor of Business Law, San Bernardino Valley College, 1966-1967. Deputy District Attorney, Napa County, California, 1968-1969. Trial Attorney, U.S. Immigration and Naturalization Service, 1987-1988. *Member:* Pasadena, Los Angeles County and American Bar Associations; State Bar of California. (Also practicing individually at Pasadena). *REPORTED CASES:* Springs Industries, Inc. v. Kris Knit, Inc. (9th Circuit 1989) 880 F.2d 1129. *PRACTICE AREAS:* Civil Litigation; Trust Planning; Business Planning; Estate Planning; Trust and Estate Litigation.

REFERENCE: City National Bank (Pershing Square Office, Los Angeles, California).

---

## LAW OFFICES OF GERALDINE MELE DART

*611 WEST SIXTH STREET, SUITE 2500*
*LOS ANGELES, CALIFORNIA 90071-3102*
Telephone: 213-489-2456
Fax: 213-489-2457

General Civil Practice, Plaintiff's Employment including Wrongful Discharge, Sexual Harassment, Sex, Race, Age, National Origin, Disability, Discrimination, Federal, State and County Employment, Plaintiff's Personal Injury including Vehicular, Premises Liability and Business Litigation.

**GERALDINE MELE DART,** born New Orleans, Louisiana, October 6, 1947; admitted to bar, 1974, California and U.S. District Court, Northern District of California; 1975, U.S. District Court, Southern District of California; 1983, U.S. Court of Appeals, Ninth Circuit. *Education:* Louisiana State University (B.A., 1969); Boston University (J.D., 1974). *Member:* Los Angeles County Bar Association; Women Lawyers Association of Los Angeles.

---

## DAVIDOFF & DAVIDOFF

*LOS ANGELES, CALIFORNIA*
(See Beverly Hills)

General, Civil Trial and Appellate Practice in all State and Federal Courts, Business, Commercial, Estate and Probate Litigation.

---

## LAW OFFICES OF ROXANNE A. DAVIS

*1801 AVENUE OF THE STARS, SUITE 934*
*LOS ANGELES, CALIFORNIA 90067*
Telephone: 310-551-1222
Fax: 310-551-1333

*Labor and Employment*

**ROXANNE A. DAVIS,** born Philadelphia, Pennsylvania, December 18, 1961; admitted to bar, 1987, California, U.S. District Court, Central and Southern District and U.S. Court of Appeals, Ninth Circuit. *Education:* New York University (B.A., with honors, 1981); University of Southern California (M.A. in International Relations, 1986; J.D., 1986). Senior Associate, Jackson, Lewis, Schnitzler & Krupman, 1988-1993. Member, Volunteers in Parole. *Member:* Los Angeles County and American Bar Associations; California Employment Lawyers Association; National Employment Lawyers Association. *LANGUAGES:* Italian.

### ASSOCIATE

**FRANK HAKIM,** born Tehran, Iran, February 15, 1968; admitted to bar, 1994, California, U.S. District Court, Central District of California and U.S. Court of Appeals, Ninth Circuit. *Education:* University of California at Los Angeles (B.S., 1989); Whittier College School of Law (J.D., 1992). Volunteer, Harriett Buhai Center for Family Law. Judicial Externship, Hon. J. Kalin, Department of Fair Employment and Housing. *Member:* Beverly Hills, Los Angeles County, San Fernando Valley and American Bar Associations; California Employment Lawyers Association; Lawyers Club of Los Angeles County; Iranian-American Lawyers Association. *LANGUAGES:* Farsi.

---

## DAVIS & DAVIS, L.L.P.

*1875 CENTURY PARK EAST, SUITE 700*
*LOS ANGELES, CALIFORNIA 90067*
Telephone: 310-229-1200
Fax: 310-229-1205

Bankruptcy, Business Reorganization, Insolvency, Family Law, Commercial Litigation.

### MEMBERS OF FIRM

**BRET J. DAVIS,** born Tokyo, Japan, April 29, 1955; admitted to bar, 1983, New Jersey and U.S. District Court, District of New Jersey; 1991, Connecticut and New York; 1992, California and U.S. District Court, Central District of California; 1993, U.S. District Court, Northern, Eastern and

*(This Listing Continued)*

Southern Districts of California and U.S. Court of Appeals, Ninth Circuit; 1994, Minnesota. *Education:* University of Michigan (A.B., with distinction, 1975); University of Chicago (M.A., 1977); Columbia University School of Law (J.D., 1981). Recipient: Federal Junior Fellowship, Department of Pathology, National Zoological Park, Smithsonian Institution, 1972-1976; Fellowship, International Fellows Program, Columbia University, 1979-1981; Hillman Fund Scholarship, University of Chicago, 1976-1977. Staff Member, Columbia Journal of Environmental Law. Author: "Poland 1976-1977: Implications for Eastern Europe's Future" and "The Crisis of Polish Agriculture," Department of State, U.S.A., 1977; "Nigeria: Survey of Investment Opportunities for U.S. Companies," Department of Commerce, U.S.A., 1979. Member, Rotary International. *Member:* Los Angeles County, New York State, New Jersey State, Connecticut and American (Member, Commercial Law and Bankruptcy Sections) Bar Associations; State Bar of California (Member, Environmental Law Section; Delegate, Conference of Delegates, 1994—); Japan-America Society; American Fertility Society; Los Angeles Bankruptcy Forum; Financial Lawyers' Forum. *LANGUAGES:* French, Japanese. *PRACTICE AREAS:* Bankruptcy; Business Reorganization; Insolvency; Asset Protection; Commercial Litigation.

**DEBORAH NEUFELD DAVIS,** born New York, N.Y., March 19, 1957; admitted to bar, 1985, New Jersey and U.S. District Court, District of New Jersey; 1995, California, U.S. District Court, Central District of California and U.S. Court of Appeals, Ninth Circuit. *Education:* University of Maryland (B.S., with honors, 1978); Brooklyn Law School (J.D., 1981). Recipient, Byrd Prize for Citizenship, 1978. Certified Arbitrator, Los Angeles Center for Dispute Resolution, 1992. *Member:* Beverly Hills, Los Angeles County and New Jersey State Bar Associations; State Bar of California; Japan-America Society; American Fertility Society. *PRACTICE AREAS:* Commercial Litigation; Bankruptcy; Family Law.

## DAVIS & FOX

1901 AVENUE OF THE STARS, SUITE 400
**LOS ANGELES, CALIFORNIA 90067**
Telephone: 310-286-2915
Fax: 310-286-2916

*General Civil Litigation including Business, Real Estate and Entertainment Litigation, Insurance Coverage Disputes, Real Estate Transactions, Business Transactions and Environmental Law.*

### MEMBERS OF FIRM

**CALVIN E. DAVIS,** born Yokosuka, Japan, November 5, 1955; admitted to bar, 1981, California; 1984, U.S. District Court, Central District of California. *Education:* University of California at Los Angeles (B.A., 1977); Loyola Law School (J.D., 1981). Finalist, National Moot Court Competition. Secretary, St. Thomas More Law Honor Society. Editor-in-Chief, International and Comparative Law Journal. Trial Attorney, Civil Division, U.S. Department of Justice, 1981-1984. Judge Pro Tem, Beverly Hills Municipal Court. Member, Board of Directors, Western Center on Law and Poverty, 1986-1991. *PRACTICE AREAS:* Trial Practice in State and Federal Courts; Business Litigation; Real Estate Litigation; Entertainment Litigation.

**STEVEN A. FOX,** born Los Angeles, California, January 16, 1954; admitted to bar, 1985, California and U.S. District Court, Central District of California; 1986, U.S. District Court, Northern District of California and U.S. Court of Appeals, Ninth Circuit. *Education:* California State University (B.A., 1975); Hebrew Union College (M.A., 1978); Northeastern University (J.D., 1985). Author: "A Guide to California Good Faith Settlement Laws," December, 1985. *LANGUAGES:* Hebrew. *PRACTICE AREAS:* Business Litigation; Insurance Coverage Disputes; Real Estate Litigation; Professional Liability.

### ASSOCIATES

**BRIAN ARONSON,** born Port Elizabeth, South Africa, November 22, 1966; admitted to bar, 1991, California. *Education:* American University (B.A., cum laude, 1988); Georgetown University (J.D., cum laude, 1991). *Member:* State Bar of California. *LANGUAGES:* Afrikaans. *PRACTICE AREAS:* Real Estate Law; Environmental Law.

**AMY L. FREISLEBEN,** born Brooklyn, New York, April 27, 1959; admitted to bar, 1985, California and U.S. District Court, Central and Northern Districts of California. *Education:* University of California at Los Angeles (B.A., 1981); Southwestern University School of Law (J.D., 1984). *PRACTICE AREAS:* Business Litigation.

*(This Listing Continued)*

**SUSAN R. PECK,** born Lowell, Massachusetts, July 3, 1958; admitted to bar, 1990, California. *Education:* Wheaton College (A.B., summa cum laude, 1980); University of Southern California (J.D., 1990). Phi Beta Kappa. *LANGUAGES:* Spanish and French. *PRACTICE AREAS:* Business Litigation.

### OF COUNSEL

**HERBERT D. MEYERS,** born Gary, Indiana, July 15, 1952; admitted to bar, 1977, California; 1981, U.S. District Court, Central District of California. *Education:* University of California at Los Angeles (B.A., 1974); University of California School of Law (J.D., 1977). Phi Beta Kappa. *Member:* State Bar of California (Member, Real Estate Section). *LANGUAGES:* Swedish. *PRACTICE AREAS:* Real Estate; Corporate; Environmental.

REPRESENTATIVE CLIENTS: Westmark Realty Advisors L.L.C.; TCW Realty Advisors; American Realty Advisors; Trust Company of the West; California State Teachers' Retirement System; Academy of Television Arts & Sciences; Hope Enterprises, Inc.; Shochiku-Fuji Co., Ltd.; Transmundo Home Video; Desilu, too; Talent Management Enterprises; Pacificare of California, Inc.; Farmers Insurance Group of Companies; Superior National Insurance Company.

## DAVIS WRIGHT TREMAINE LLP

A Partnership including Professional Corporations
SUITE 600, 1000 WILSHIRE BOULEVARD
**LOS ANGELES, CALIFORNIA 90017**
Telephone: 213-633-6800
FAX: 213-633-6899
URL: http://www.dwt.com

*Anchorage, Alaska Office:* Suite 1450, 550 W. Seventh Avenue. 99501. Telephone: 907-257-5300. FAX: 907-257-5399.
*Bellevue, Washington Office:* 1800 Bellevue Place, 10500 NE 8th Street. 98004. Telephone: 206-646-6100. FAX: 206-646-6199.
*Boise, Idaho Office:* Suite 911, 999 Main Street, 83702-9010. Telephone: 208-338-8200. FAX: 208-338-8299.
*Honolulu, Hawaii Office:* 1360 Pauahi Tower, 1001 Bishop Street, 96813. Telephone: 808-538-3360. FAX: 808-526-0101.
*Portland, Oregon Office:* 2300 First Interstate Tower, 1300 SW Fifth Avenue. 97201. Telephone: 503-241-2300. FAX: 503-778-5299.
*Richland, Washington Office:* Suite 3A, 601 Williams Boulevard, 99352. Telephone: 509-946-5369. FAX: 509-946-4211.
*San Francisco, California Office:* One Embarcadero Center, Suite 600, 94111. Telephone: 415-276-6500. FAX: 415-276-6599.
*Seattle, Washington Office:* 2600 Century Square, 1501 Fourth Avenue. 98101. Telephone: 206-622-3150. FAX: 206-628-7040.
*Washington, D.C. Office:* Suite 700, 1155 Connecticut Avenue, N.W., 20036. Telephone: 202-508-6600. FAX: 202-508-6699.
*Shanghai, China Office:* Suite 1008/1009 Jin Jiang Hotel, 59 Mao Ming Road (S), 200020. Telephones: 011-8621-6472-3344; 011-8621-6415-3002. FAX: 011-8621-6415-3003.

*Healthcare, Corporate, Tax, Securities, International, Media and Communications, Litigation.*

FIRM PROFILE: *Since its founding in the early 1900s in Seattle, Washington, Davis Wright Tremaine has continued to grow and change in response to the needs of its clients. Today the firm is organized by practice industry groups, and offers a wide range of legal services to regional, national and international clients through offices in Washington, Oregon, Alaska, Idaho, California, Washington D.C., Hawaii and Shanghai, China. A state-of-the-art communications network provides our clients the benefit of immediate access to shared knowledge, experience and resources of attorneys firm-wide. Dedicated to a tradition of public and professional service, the people of Davis Wright Tremaine are active in professional groups at the national, state and local levels.*

### RESIDENT PARTNERS

**RICHARD D. ELLINGSEN,** born Seattle, Washington, January 5, 1954; admitted to bar, 1979, California. *Education:* University of Washington (B.A., magna cum laude, 1976); Duke University (J.D., with distinction, 1979). Phi Beta Kappa. *Member:* Los Angeles County Bar Association; The State Bar of California; National Health Lawyers Association; American Academy of Healthcare Attorneys; California Society of Healthcare Attorneys.

**ZHI-YING JAMES FANG,** born Shanghai, China, February 19, 1950; admitted to bar, 1984, China; 1991, New York; 1994, California. *Education:* Shanghai Academy of Social Sciences Law Institute (Master of Law, 1982); University of Washington School of Law (LL.M., 1986; Ph.D., 1991). Law Professor, East China Institute of Political Science and Law,

*(This Listing Continued)*

CAA619B

**DAVIS WRIGHT TREMAINE LLP,** Los Angeles—
*Continued*

1982-1985. Visiting Guest Lecturer, University of Washington School of Law and Willamette University College of Law, 1986-1988. Member, Shanghai Lawyers Association, 1984-1991. *Member:* State Bar of California; New York State Bar Association. LANGUAGES: Mandarin Chinese and Shanghai Dialect.

**ANDREW R. HALL,** born New York, N.Y., 1956; admitted to bar, 1986, California; 1987, U.S. District Court, Central District of California. *Education:* University of Pennsylvania (B.A., cum laude, 1979); University of California at Los Angeles (J.D., 1986). LANGUAGES: French. *PRACTICE AREAS:* Litigation.

**CHARLES PEREYRA-SUAREZ,** born Paysandu, Uruguay, September 7, 1947; admitted to bar, 1975, California; 1980, District of Columbia. *Education:* Pacific Union College (B.A., magna cum laude, 1970); Boalt Hall School of Law, University of California at Berkeley (J.D., 1975). Member, Moot Court Board, 1973-1975. Member, Ecology Law Quarterly, 1973-1975. Trial and Appellate Attorney, Civil Rights Division, U.S. Department of Justice, 1976-1979. Assistant U.S. Attorney, Criminal Division, Central District of California, 1979-1982. Adjunct Associate Professor, Trial Advocacy, Southwestern University School of Law, 1990-1993. Deputy General Counsel to Hon. William H. Webster, Special Advisor to the Los Angeles Police Commission, 1992. *Member:* Los Angeles County (Member, Federal Courts Committee; Chair, Criminal Practice Subcommittee, 1991-1993) and American Bar Associations; The State Bar of California (Member, Executive Committee, Criminal Law Section, 1992-1995); The District of Columbia Bar. LANGUAGES: Spanish. *PRACTICE AREAS:* Civil Litigation; White Collar Defense; Health Law; Media and First Amendment.

**KELLI L. SAGER,** born February 11, 1960; admitted to bar, 1985, California. *Education:* University of Southern California; West Georgia College (B.A., cum laude, 1981); University of Utah (J.D., 1985). Order of the Coif. Member, 1983-1985 and Editor-in-Chief, 1984-1985, University of Utah Law Review. *PRACTICE AREAS:* Media Law; Constitutional Law; Civil Appeal; Copyright/Trademark.

**ROBERT A. STEINBERG,** born Brooklyn, New York, November 7, 1952; admitted to bar, 1977, California. *Education:* University of Michigan (A.B., 1974); Duke University (J.D., 1977); New York University (LL.M., in Taxation, 1982). Member, Editorial Board, Duke Law Journal, 1976-1977; Moot Court Board. First Place, Dean's Cup Moot Court Competition. Author: "Defamation, Privacy and the First Amendment," 1976 Duke Law Journal 1016. *Member:* State Bar of California; American Bar Association (Member, Sections on: Taxation; Corporation, Banking and Business Law). *PRACTICE AREAS:* Business Transactions; Taxation; Corporate and Securities Law.

**HENRY J. TASHMAN,** born Bronx, New York, November 8, 1948; admitted to bar, 1974, New York; 1983, California. *Education:* University of Connecticut (B.A., magna cum laude, 1970); Georgetown University (J.D., 1973). Phi Beta Kappa; Phi Kappa Phi. Recipient, ASCAP Copyright Prize. Editor, Law and Policy in International Business, The International Law Journal of the Georgetown University Law Center, 1972-1973. Faculty, "Litigating Copyright and Unfair Competition Cases," Practicing Law Institute, Los Angeles, 1983, 1985, 1988. *PRACTICE AREAS:* Litigation; Copyright; Trademark; Antitrust; Entertainment; Communications.

**MICHAEL JOHN TICHON,** born September 7, 1942; admitted to bar, 1969, Illinois; 1976, California. *Education:* University of Notre Dame (B.A., cum laude, 1964); University of Chicago (J.D., 1969). U.S. Peace Corps Volunteer, Nepal, 1964-1966. *Member:* National Health Lawyers Association (President, 1982-1983); Healthcare Financial Management Association (Board Member, 1986-1991).

*RESIDENT ASSOCIATES*

**KAREN NANCY FREDERIKSEN,** born May 30, 1960; admitted to bar, 1988, California. *Education:* California State University at Northridge (B.A., 1983; B.A., 1986); University of Southern California (J.D., 1988). Winner, USC Moot Court Honors Program. *PRACTICE AREAS:* Media Law; Constitutional Law; Business Litigation.

**MARY H. HAAS,** born October 23, 1965; admitted to bar, 1990, California. *Education:* University of Michigan (B.A., 1987); Catholic University of America (J.D., 1990). Student Editor-in-Chief, Journal of Contemporary Health Law and Policy, 1989-1990. *PRACTICE AREAS:* General Litigation; Real Estate Litigation.

*(This Listing Continued)*

**CAROLE A. KLOVE,** born Los Angeles, California, December 19, 1958; admitted to bar, 1986, California; 1988, District of Columbia; 1989, U.S. Court of Claims. *Education:* Duke University (B.S.N., 1980); Southwestern University School of Law (J.D., 1986). Registered Nurse, California, 1981. *Member:* State Bar of California; The District of Columbia Bar; National Health Lawyers Association; The Association of Trial Lawyers of America; California Trial Lawyers Association; Los Angeles Trial Lawyers Association.

**ELIZABETH STAGGS-WILSON,** born New London, Connecticut, March 3, 1966; admitted to bar, 1991, Illinois; 1996, California. *Education:* Harvard College (B.A., magna cum laude, 1987); Northwestern University (J.D., 1991). *PRACTICE AREAS:* Commercial Litigation; Media Law; Copyright; Employment Law.

**TODD D. THIBODO,** born Holyoke, Massachusetts, November 25, 1963; admitted to bar, 1993, Connecticut; 1994, California. *Education:* San Diego State University (B.A., cum laude, with distinction, in political science, 1990); Cornell University (J.D., 1993). Member, Moot Court Board, 1992-1993. [Sgt. U.S. Army, 1981-1985.]

**STEVEN J. WESTMAN,** born Burbank, California, July 30, 1970; admitted to bar, 1996, California. *Education:* University of California at Los Angeles (B.A., magna cum laude, 1992); University of Michigan (J.D., 1996). Phi Beta Kappa. Member, 1994-1995 and Articles Editor, 1995-1996, Michigan Telecommunications and Technology Law Review. *PRACTICE AREAS:* Media Law; General Civil Litigation.

**SUSAN E. WOGOMAN,** born Oakland, California, May 10, 1950; admitted to bar, 1993, California. *Education:* Brigham Young University (B.A., cum laude, 1972); University of Southern California (J.D., 1993). *Member:* Los Angeles County Bar Association; National Health Lawyers Association; California Society of Healthcare Attorneys. *PRACTICE AREAS:* Health Law.

*OF COUNSEL*

**MARC E. JACOBOWITZ,** born January 17, 1958; admitted to bar, 1982, California. *Education:* State University of New York at Albany (B.S., summa cum laude, 1979); University of California at Los Angeles School of Law (J.D., 1982). Phi Beta Kappa. Member, 1980-1981 and Topics Editor, 1981-1982, UCLA-Alaska Law Review. Judicial Extern to the Honorable Winslow Christian, California Court of Appeal, 1981. *Member:* State Bar of California.

**JAMES R. LAHANA,** born Mexico City, Mexico, December 3, 1951; admitted to bar, 1976, California; 1977, U.S. District Court, Southern District of California; 1978, U.S. District Court, Central District of California and U.S. Court of Appeals, Ninth Circuit; 1980, U.S. Supreme Court. *Education:* University of California at Los Angeles (B.A., cum laude, 1973); Boalt Hall School of Law, University of California (J.D., 1976). *Member:* The State Bar of California. *PRACTICE AREAS:* Health Care; Medical Staff Law.

REPRESENTATIVE CLIENTS: Columbia Pictures; Del Amo Diagnostic Center; Galpin Ford; Merv Griffin Enterprises; HCA Las Encinas Hospital; Hemet Valley Hospital District; Hokkaido Takushoku Bank; Humana, Inc.; Huntington Memorial Hospital; Medical Management Associates; NME Hospital, Inc.; NuMed Hospitals, Inc.; St. Joseph Medical Center; Sony Pictures Entertainment; UCLA Medical Center and Neuropsychiatric Institute; Westside District Hospital.

(For Complete Biographical Data on Personnel at Anchorage, Alaska, San Francisco, California, Washington, D.C., Honolulu, Hawaii, Boise, Idaho, Portland, Oregon, Bellevue, Richland and Seattle Washington and Shanghai, China, see Professional Biographies at those locations)

---

# DEAR & KELLEY

### LOS ANGELES, CALIFORNIA

(See Pasadena)

*Corporate, Commercial, Gaming and Real Estate Transactions, Business Litigation and Bankruptcy.*

## EDWARD J. DEASON
### LOS ANGELES, CALIFORNIA
(See Torrance)
*Practice Limited to Personal Injury Law.*

---

## PATRICK DeCAROLIS, JR.
### A PROFESSIONAL LAW CORPORATION
### 2029 CENTURY PARK EAST, SUITE 2860
### LOS ANGELES, CALIFORNIA 90067
Telephone: 310-552-3312
Telecopier: 310-552-0441

*Practice Limited to Family Law.*

**PATRICK DECAROLIS, JR.,** born Rochester, New York, March 4, 1953; admitted to bar, 1978, California. *Education:* California State University (B.A., 1975); Whittier College (J.D., 1978). *Member:* Los Angeles County (Member, Executive Committee, Family Law Section, 1988—; Secretary, 1994-1995; Vice Chair, 1995-1996; Chair, 1990 Child Custody Colloquium) and Beverly Hills Bar Associations; State Bar of California. (Certified Specialist, Family Law, The State Bar of California Board of Legal Specialization).

---

## DE CASTRO, WEST & CHODOROW, INC.
### Established in 1952
### EIGHTEENTH FLOOR, 10960 WILSHIRE BOULEVARD
### LOS ANGELES, CALIFORNIA 90024-3804
Telephone: 310-478-2541
Telecopier: 310-473-0123
Email: dwandc@aol.com

*General Civil and Business Practice, including Federal, State, Local, and International Taxation, Corporations, Partnerships, Real Estate, Pension Planning and ERISA, Health Care Law, Estate Planning, Trusts and Probates, Civil and Criminal Tax Litigation, Business Trial and Appellate Litigation in State and Federal Courts, including Litigation in Connection with Environmental, Land Use and Toxic Tort Matters, Estate and Trust Disputes, and General Business Litigation.*

*FIRM PROFILE: De Castro, West & Chodorow, Inc. has a large and diversified business and litigation practice rooted in the areas of taxation, real estate, commercial transactions, and trusts and estates. De Castro, West & Chodorow, Inc. is dedicated to traditions of excellence in its work product.*

**HUGO D. DE CASTRO,** born Panama City, Republic of Panama, September 12, 1935; admitted to bar, 1961, California. *Education:* University of California at Los Angeles (B.S., cum laude, 1957; J.D., summa cum laude, 1960). Member, Board of Editors: U.C.L.A. Law Review, 1959-1960; Taxation for Lawyers, 1971-1988. Lecturer: Tax Accounting and C.P.A. Review, Income Tax Aspects of Real Estate Transactions, Seminar in Taxation, University of California at Los Angeles; The 17th Annual Tax Forum, Title Insurance and Trust Company; "Lawyers' Use of Financial Statements, Preparing and Negotiating Commercial Leases," Continuing Education of California Bar; Estate Planning Seminar, University of California at Los Angeles School of Law; "Tax Oriented Investments—Real Estate," ALI-ABA. *Member:* The State Bar of California (Commissioner, California Tax Advisory Commission, 1980-1983). **PRACTICE AREAS:** Business Law; Real Property Law; Taxation Law. **Email:** dwandc@aol.com

**HILTON I. CHODOROW,** born Waco, Texas, December 25, 1935; admitted to bar, 1963, California. *Education:* University of Texas (B.B.A., 1957; LL.B., 1959); University of Southern California (LL.M. in Taxation, 1962). Order of the Coif; Chancellors. Associate Editor, Texas Law Review, 1958-1959. Lecturer: Federal Tax Accounting and Small Business Management Seminars, University of California at Los Angeles; Tax Institutes, University of Southern California School of Law; Entertainment Law Institutes, University of Southern California School of Law. *Member:* Los Angeles County Bar Association; The State Bar of California. **PRACTICE AREAS:** Taxation Law; Business Law; Real Property Law. **Email:** dwandc@aol.com

*(This Listing Continued)*

**JEROME A. RABOW,** born Buffalo, New York, April 2, 1937; admitted to bar, 1961, New York; 1964, California. *Education:* Harvard University (A.B., magna cum laude, 1958; Phi Beta Kappa); Harvard Law School (J.D., cum laude, 1961). Instructor, Probate Administrator Training Course, University of California at Los Angeles, 1971-1976; National College of Probate Judges, 1989. Chairman, University of Southern California Probate and Trust Conference, 1980-1993. Author: "Terminating Life Support - Who Gets to Decide?" National College of Probate Judges, Fall 1989. Co-Author: "Estate Planning: A Client Based Approach," 39th Tax Institute, University of Southern California, 1987. *Member:* American College of Trust and Estate Counsel. **PRACTICE AREAS:** Probate Law; Trusts Law; Estate Planning Law. **Email:** dwandc@aol.com

**NEIL CARREY,** born Bronx, New York, November 19, 1942; admitted to bar, 1968, California. *Education:* Wharton School of the University of Pennsylvania (B.S., 1964); Stanford University (J.D., 1967). Author: "Nonqualified Deferred Compensation Plans: The Wave of the Future," Trust Services of America, Inc. Trust and Tax Forum, 1985. Instructor, Qualified Retirement Plans and Employee Benefits, Program for Paralegal Professionals, University of Southern California Law School, 1977, 1978, 1979, 1980, 1981, 1982, 1983, 1984, 1985, 1986, 1987, 1988 and 1989. Guest Speaker, University of Southern California Dental School, 1988, 1989, 1990, 1991, 1992 , 1993, 1994, 1995 and 1996. Lecturer, Employee Benefits Institute, 1996; "Conflict of Interest in Representing Employee Benefit Plans." *Member:* Los Angeles County and American (Member, Sections on: Taxation; Corporation, Banking and Business Law) Bar Associations; The State Bar of California. **PRACTICE AREAS:** Business Law; Qualified Retirement Plans Law; Retirement Benefits Law; Taxation Law and Health Care Law. **Email:** dwandc@aol.com

**BRUCE S. GLICKFELD,** born New York, N.Y., March 9, 1948; admitted to bar, 1972, California; 1973, U.S. District Court, Central District of California and U.S. Tax Court; 1977, U.S. Court of Claims. *Education:* University of California at Los Angeles (B.A., 1969; J.D., 1972). Order of the Coif. Member, U.C.L.A. Law Review, 1970-1971. **PRACTICE AREAS:** Taxation Law; Real Estate Law; Business Law. **Email:** dwandc@aol.com

**BUDDY EPSTEIN,** born Los Angeles, California, November 21, 1948; admitted to bar, 1974, California, U.S. Tax Court and U.S. Court of Appeals, Ninth Circuit. *Education:* University of California at Los Angeles (B.A., 1971; J.D., 1974). Order of the Coif. Member, University of California at Los Angeles Law Review, 1972-1974. Author: Program Materials and Outline, "Tax Deferred Real Property Exchanges," California Continuing Education of the Bar, 1980-1981, 1987 and 1990; Program Materials, "Financing California Real Property Transactions," California Continuing Education of the Bar, 1982, 1984 and 1986; Program Materials, "Annual Institute on Advanced Tax Planning for Real Property Transactions," California Continuing Education of the Bar, 1988; "Fundamentals of Real Property Transactions," California Continuing Education of the Bar, 1989. Lecturer: "Foreign Investment in United States Real Estate," Beverly Hills Bar Association, The Symposium 1979; "Tax Deferred Real Property Exchanges," California Continuing Education of the Bar, 1981, 1987 and 1990; "Tax Shelter Transactions for the Highly Compensated and Wealthy," New York Law Journal Seminar, 1981; "Financing California Real Property Transactions," California Continuing Education of the Bar, 1982, 1984 and 1986; "The Tax Equity and Fiscal Responsibility Act of 1982," California Continuing Education of the Bar, 1982-1983; "Changing Legal Aspects of Tenant Representation By Brokers," Society of Industrial and Office Realtors National Convention, 1986; "Forecast of Legal Trends Affecting Real Property," Society of Industrial and Office Realtors National Convention, 1988; "Annual Institute on Advanced Tax Planning for Real Property Transactions," California Continuing Education of the Bar, 1988; "Fundamentals of Real Property Transactions," California Continuing Education of the Bar, 1989. *Member:* Beverly Hills, Los Angeles County and American Bar Associations; The State Bar of California. **PRACTICE AREAS:** Real Estate Law; Taxation Law; Business Law. **Email:** dwandc@aol.com

**JAMES A. GINSBURG,** born Rice Lake, Wisconsin, March 24, 1943; admitted to bar, 1969, California. *Education:* University of Minnesota (B.S.B., 1965; J.D., 1968). Member, Minnesota Law Review, 1966-1967. Member, Board of Directors, University of Minnesota Law School, 1990-1995. *Member:* Los Angeles County Bar Association; The State Bar of California. **PRACTICE AREAS:** Real Estate Law; Business Law. **Email:** dwandc@aol.com

**MENASCHE M. NASS,** born Munich, Germany, November 21, 1949; admitted to bar, 1982, California and U.S. Tax Court. *Education:* The Cooper Union (B.S., summa cum laude, 1970); Brown University (Ph.D., 1975); Stanford University (J.D., 1982). Articles Editor, Stanford Journal of Inter-

*(This Listing Continued)*

## DE CASTRO, WEST & CHODOROW, INC., Los Angeles— Continued

national Law, 1981-1982. Co-Author: "Executive Compensation with Real Estate," 38th Tax Institute, University of Southern California School of Law, 1986. Member, American Physical Society. *Member:* Los Angeles County Bar Association; The State Bar of California. *PRACTICE AREAS:* Taxation Law; Business Law.

**DAVID T. STOWELL,** born Columbus, Indiana, June 10, 1955; admitted to bar, 1981, California; 1982, U.S. District Court, Central District of California and U.S. Court of Appeals, Ninth Circuit; 1985, U.S. Supreme Court; 1988, U.S. District Court, Eastern District of California. *Education:* Indiana Central University (B.A., cum laude, 1977); Pepperdine University (J.D., cum laude, 1981). Recipient, American Jurisprudence Awards for Torts, Contracts, Real Property, Civil Procedure, Antitrust and Administrative Law. Editor-in-Chief, Pepperdine University Law Review, 1980-1981. *Member:* Los Angeles County Bar Association; State Bar of California. *Email:* dwandc@aol.com

**DAVID C. RUTH,** born Fresno, California, June 26, 1956; admitted to bar, 1984, California and U.S. Tax Court. *Education:* Claremont McKenna College (B.A., magna cum laude, 1978); Harvard Law School (J.D., 1984). Certified Public Accountant, California, 1981. *Member:* Beverly Hills and Los Angeles County Bar Associations; The State Bar of California; California Institute of Certified Public Accountants. *PRACTICE AREAS:* Taxation Law; Real Estate Law; Business Law. *Email:* dwandc@aol.com

**JONATHAN I. REICH,** born Los Angeles, California, November 6, 1958; admitted to bar, 1984, California; 1985, U.S. District Court, Central and Northern Districts of California and U.S. Court of Appeals, Ninth Circuit; 1996, U.S. Tax Court. *Education:* University of California at Los Angeles (B.A., cum laude, 1979; M.B.A., J.D., 1984). *Member:* Los Angeles County (Litigation and Real Property Sections), Beverly Hills and American Bar Associations; The State Bar of California. *PRACTICE AREAS:* Business; Real Estate; Construction Defect; Corporate and Insurance Coverage Litigation. *Email:* dwandc@aol.com

**SCOTT M. MENDLER,** born Queens, New York, September 11, 1957; admitted to bar, 1982, California; 1983, U.S. Tax Court. *Education:* Queens College of the City University of New York (B.A., summa cum laude in Accounting, 1979); University of California at Los Angeles School of Law (J.D., 1982). Member, University of California at Los Angeles Law Review, 1981-1982. Recipient, New York State Society of Certified Public Accountants Award, January, 1979. Editor, Estate and Gift Taxes Chapter of Rhodes and Langer, "Income Taxation of Foreign Related Transactions," 1990. Co-Author: "Estate Planning for the Foreign Entertainer," Conference on the Business of International Entertainment sponsored by Laventhol & Horwath, Horwath & Horwath International and U.C.L.A. Extension, 1988. Vice Chairman, Tax Section Pro Bono Oversight Committee, 1989-1990. *Member:* Los Angeles County Bar Association (Member, Tax Committee); The State Bar of California. *PRACTICE AREAS:* Taxation Law; Probate Law; Trusts Law; Estate Planning Law. *Email:* dwandc@aol.com

**RICHARD S. ZEILENGA,** born Harvey, Illinois, April 15, 1962; admitted to bar, 1987, California and U.S. District Court, Central District of California. *Education:* Northwestern University (B.S., with distinction, 1984; J.D., 1987). Member, Northwestern University National Moot Court Team #1. *Member:* Los Angeles County Bar Association; The State Bar of California. *PRACTICE AREAS:* Business Litigation; Land Use; CEQA Planning and Litigation; Entitlement Disputes; Environmental/Insurance Coverage Litigation; Subdivision Map Act Litigation; Initiative and Referendum Litigation. *Email:* dwandc@aol.com

**MICHAEL C. COHEN,** born New York, N.Y., October 7, 1955; admitted to bar, 1980, California; 1981, U.S. Tax Court and U.S. District Court, Central District of California; 1985, U.S. Court of Appeals, Ninth Circuit; 1986, U.S. Claims Court. *Education:* Massachusetts Institute of Technology (B.S., 1977); Boalt Hall School of Law, University of California (J.D., 1980). Speaker, "New Tax Procedures and Penalties," California Continuing Education of the Bar, 1991; "Recent Legislative and Case Law Developments Affecting the Entertainment Industry," Los Angeles County Bar, 1994; "New IRS Guidelines for Worker Classification in the Commercial Production Industry," Los Angeles County Bar, 1994; "Current Developments in IRS Audits and Appeals," Tax Executives Institute, 1994; "Market Segment Understandings," ABA Employment Tax Committee, 1995; "Employee/Independent Contractor Issue," UCLA Tax Controversy Institute, 1995; Chair, UCLA Tax Controversy Institute, 1996. Trial Attorney, Office of Chief Counsel, Internal Revenue Service, Los Angeles District Counsel, 1980-1985. *Member:* Los Angeles County Bar Association (Chairman, Tax

*(This Listing Continued)*

Section Procedure and Litigation Committee, 1995-1996); The State Bar of California. *PRACTICE AREAS:* Tax Litigation. *Email:* dwandc@aol.com

**HENRY A. REITZENSTEIN,** born New York, N.Y., July 10, 1956; admitted to bar, 1981, California, U.S. Tax Court. *Education:* University of California at Los Angeles (B.A. Economics, magna cum laude, 1978); Boalt Hall School of Law, University of California (J.D., 1981). Omicron Delta Epsilon; Pi Gamma Mu. *Member:* State Bar of California. *PRACTICE AREAS:* Tax Law; Business Law. *Email:* dwandc@aol.com

**RICHARD D. FURMAN,** born New York, New York, July 14, 1966; admitted to bar, 1991, California; 1992, U.S. Tax Court. *Education:* The Wharton School, University of Pennsylvania (B.S., magna cum laude, 1988); University of California School of Law, Los Angeles (J.D., 1991). *Member:* State Bar of California. *PRACTICE AREAS:* Tax Law; Business Law. *Email:* dwandc@aol.com

**JAMES D. VAUGHN,** born Torrance, California, November 21, 1967; admitted to bar, 1993, California and U.S. District Court, Central District of California. *Education:* Georgetown University (B.S., magna cum laude, 1990); Boalt Hall School of Law, University of California (J.D., 1993). *Member:* Beverly Hills and Los Angeles County Bar Associations. *PRACTICE AREAS:* Business Litigation; Real Estate Litigation. *Email:* dwandc@aol.com

**NEAL B. JANNOL,** born Los Angeles, California, August 23, 1970; admitted to bar, 1995, California. *Education:* University of California at Los Angeles (B.A., magna cum laude, 1992) Phi Beta Kappa; Boalt Hall School of Law, University of California (J.D., 1995). Recipient, American Jurisprudence Award in Contracts, 1992. Extern, Circuit Court Judge Stephen J. Reinhardt, Ninth Circuit Court of Appeals. *LANGUAGES:* Hebrew. *PRACTICE AREAS:* Tax Planning; Estates and Trusts. *Email:* dwandc@aol.com

---

## HAROLD J. DELEVIE

### INCORPORATED

*1875 CENTURY PARK EAST, FIFTEENTH FLOOR*
**LOS ANGELES, CALIFORNIA 90067-2516**
Telephone: 310-277-7490;
Direct Dial: 310-282-9475
Fax: 310-277-8923

*Business Law, Business Transactions, Real Property Law, Estate Planning.*

**HAROLD J. DELEVIE,** born Los Angeles, California, April 24, 1931; admitted to bar, 1957, California and U.S. Tax Court. *Education:* University of California at Los Angeles (A.B., 1953; J.D., 1956). Phi Beta Kappa; Order of the Coif. Member, Board of Editors, *UCLA Law Review,* 1955-1956. Member, UCLA Law Alumni Association. Lecturer: Evolution of A Partnership, 1981; Incorporating A Business, 1982; CPA Partnerships and Professional Corporations, 1982, California Certified Public Accountants Foundation. Member, Board of Directors, 1989—, Secretary, 1992-1994 and Executive Secretary, 1994—, Guardians of Jewish Home for the Aging of Greater Los Angeles. Member, Board of Directors, 1970-1974 and Treasurer, 1972-1973, UCLA Law Alumni Association. President, UCLA Business School Association, 1960-1961. Member, Executive Council, UCLA Alumni Association, 1960-1961. Member, Beverly Hills Estate Planning Council. *Member:* Wilshire (President, 1970-1971), Beverly Hills (Member, Board of Governors, 1993—; Chair, Legislation Committee, 1993-1996; Member, Sections on: Business Law, Real Property Law, Probate and Estate Planning), Los Angeles County and American (Member, Real Property, Probate and Trust Law Section) Bar Associations; State Bar of California (Member of Conference, State Bar Delegates, 1969-1971; Member, 1967-1974 and Chairman, 1969-1970, Local Administrative Committee; Member, Sections on: Business Law, Real Property and Estate Planning). *PRACTICE AREAS:* Business Law; Business Transactions; Real Property Law; Estate Planning.

## DEL, RUBEL, SHAW, MASON & DERIN

*A LAW CORPORATION*

**2029 CENTURY PARK EAST, SUITE 3910**

**LOS ANGELES, CALIFORNIA 90067-3025**

Telephone: 310-772-2000
Telecopier: 310-772-2777

*Entertainment, Television, Motion Picture, Theatre, Corporation, Partnership, Taxation, Real Property Law, Litigation in State and Federal Courts and Arbitration.*

**ERNEST DEL,** born Santa Monica, California, January 16, 1952; admitted to bar, 1976, California and U.S. District Court, Central District of California. *Education:* University of California, Berkeley (A.B., 1973); Stanford University (J.D., 1976). Phi Beta Kappa. *Member:* Los Angeles County Bar Association; State Bar of California. **PRACTICE AREAS:** Entertainment Law; Television Law; Motion Picture Law.

**MICHAEL A. RUBEL,** born Norwalk, Connecticut, May 2, 1949; admitted to bar, 1976, California and U.S. District Court, Central District of California. *Education:* Brown University (A.B., 1971; M.A.T., 1973); University of California at Los Angeles (J.D., 1976). Order of the Coif. Member, UCLA Law Review, 1974-1975. *Member:* Los Angeles County and American Bar Associations; State Bar of California. **PRACTICE AREAS:** Real Estate Law; Partnership Law; Corporation Law.

**NINA L. SHAW,** born New York, N.Y.; admitted to bar, 1981, California. *Education:* Barnard College (B.A., 1976); Columbia University (J.D., 1979). *Member:* Los Angeles County Bar Association; State Bar of California; Black Women Lawyers Association. **PRACTICE AREAS:** Entertainment Law; Television Law; Motion Picture Law; Theater Law.

**GREG DAVID DERIN,** born San Francisco, California, September 30, 1954; admitted to bar, 1979, California; 1980, U.S. District Courts, Central and Northern Districts of California and U.S. Court of Appeals, 9th Circuit; 1983, U.S. District Court, Eastern and Southern Districts of California; 1984, U.S. Supreme Court; 1985, U.S. Court of Appeals, Federal Circuit. *Education:* University of California at Berkeley (A.B., 1976); University of California at Berkeley, Boalt Hall School of Law (J.D., 1979). Phi Beta Kappa. Research and Book Review Editor, California Law Review, 1979. *Member:* Los Angeles County and American (Member, Litigation Section) Bar Associations; State Bar of California. **PRACTICE AREAS:** Civil Litigation; Appellate Litigation; Commercial Law; Intellectual Property Litigation.

**JEAN E. TANAKA,** born Palo Alto, California, July 16, 1958; admitted to bar, 1984, California. *Education:* University of California at Berkeley (B.A., 1980); University of California at Los Angeles (J.D., 1984). Phi Beta Kappa. Regents Scholar. Abstracts Editor, Federal Communications Law Journal, 1983-1984. *Member:* Los Angeles County Bar Association; State Bar of California; Japanese American Bar Association. **PRACTICE AREAS:** Entertainment Law; Television Law; Motion Picture Law.

**JEFFREY D. BLYE,** born Toronto, Ontario, Canada, February 17, 1962; admitted to bar, 1987, California. *Education:* University of California at Los Angeles (B.A., 1984); University of California at Berkeley, Boalt Hall School of Law (J.D., 1987). *Member:* Los Angeles County Bar Association; State Bar of California. **PRACTICE AREAS:** Entertainment Law; Television Law; Motion Picture Law.

**JEFFREY S. FINKELSTEIN,** born Montreal, Canada, October 24, 1957; admitted to bar, 1987, California. *Education:* University of California at Los Angeles (B.A., 1980); Boalt Hall School of Law, University of California at Berkeley (J.D., 1987). Recipient, American Jurisprudence Awards in Agency and Civil Procedure. *Member:* Beverly Hills and Los Angeles County Bar Associations; State Bar of California. **PRACTICE AREAS:** Entertainment Law; Television Law; Motion Picture Law.

**JONATHAN D. MOONVES,** born New York, N.Y., March 29, 1959; admitted to bar, 1985, Georgia; 1991, California. *Education:* University of Virginia (B.A., 1981; J.D., 1985). Member, National Moot Court Team. *Member:* Beverly Hills and Los Angeles County Bar Associations; State Bar of California; State Bar of Georgia (Member, Litigation and Sports and Entertainment Law Sections). **PRACTICE AREAS:** Entertainment Law; Television Law; Motion Picture Law.

*(This Listing Continued)*

**JAY AARON GOLDBERG,** born Brooklyn, New York, June 11, 1949; admitted to bar, 1975, New York; 1977, California. *Education:* Columbia College (B.A., 1970); Harvard University (J.D., 1974). Phi Beta Kappa. Member, Harvard Law Review, 1973-1974. Vice President, Program and Talent Contracts, National Broadcasting Co., New York, N.Y., 1980-1991. *Member:* Los Angeles County and New York State Bar Association; State Bar of California. **PRACTICE AREAS:** Entertainment Law; Television Law; Motion Picture Law.

## DEL TONDO & SHEEHAN

**11355 WEST OLYMPIC BOULEVARD, SUITE 500**

**LOS ANGELES, CALIFORNIA 90064**

Telephone: 310-312-0027
Fax: 310-477-5021

*Complex Litigation, Civil Trials, Insurance Defense, Insurance Coverage, Entertainment Litigation.*

### MEMBERS OF FIRM

**JOSEPH J. SHEEHAN,** born Battle Creek, Michigan, September 7, 1954; admitted to bar, 1981, New York, U.S. District Court, Southern District of New York and U.S. Court of Appeals, Second Circuit; 1984, California; 1985, U.S. Court of Appeals, Ninth Circuit and U.S. District Court, Central District of California. *Education:* University of California at Santa Cruz (A.B., with highest honors, 1975); Yale University (J.D., 1979). Editor, Yale Law Journal, Volumes 87 and 88, 1978-1979. Assistant in Instruction, Yale Law School, 1978-1979. Author: Note, "Judicial Control of Systemic Inadequacies in Federal Administrative Enforcement," 88 Yale Law Journal 407, 1978. Law Clerk to Hon. Louis F. Oberdorfer, U.S. District Court, District of Columbia, 1979-1980. Assistant District Attorney, Manhattan District Attorneys Office, 1980-1984. Arbitrator, Los Angeles Superior Court, 1991-1994. Judge Pro Tem, Los Angeles Municipal Court, 1992-1994. *Member:* Los Angeles County Bar Association ; State Bar of California (Chairperson, 1994—; Member, 1991—, Legislation Committee of Administration of Justice Committee of Litigation Section); Association of Southern California Defense Counsel; Souther California Fraud Investigators Association. **PRACTICE AREAS:** Complex Litigation; Civil Trial; Insurance Defense; Insurance Coverage.

**DOUGLAS J. DEL TONDO,** born Bronx, New York, July 31, 1958; admitted to bar, 1981, California; 1982, U.S. District Court, Central District of California; 1983, U.S. Court of Appeals, Ninth Circuit; 1990, U.S. Supreme Court. *Education:* Fordham University (B.A., 1978); Southwestern University (J.D., cum laude, 1981). Law Clerk to Honorable Arthur L. Alarcon, Ninth Circuit, 1981. Chief Note and Comment Editor, Southwestern University Law Review, 1980-1981. Arbitrator: Los Angeles Superior Court, 1991—; American Arbitration Association, 1992—. *Member:* Los Angeles County Bar Association; State Bar of California; Southern California Fraud Investigators Association; Association of Southern California Defense Counsel; Italian-American Lawyers Association. **LANGUAGES:** Italian and Spanish. **PRACTICE AREAS:** Civil Trial; Complex Litigation; Insurance Defense; Insurance Coverage.

## FRANK DE MARCO, JR.

**LOS ANGELES, CALIFORNIA**

(See South Pasadena)

*General Civil, Trial and Appellate Practice in State and Federal Courts. Corporation, Real Estate, Insurance, Copyright, Trademark and Probate Law.*

# DEMETRIOU, DEL GUERCIO, SPRINGER & MOYER, LLP

*Established in 1947*

**801 SOUTH GRAND AVENUE, 10TH FLOOR**
**LOS ANGELES, CALIFORNIA 90017**

Telephone: 213-624-8407
Telecopy: 213-624-0174
Email: ddsm@juno.com
URL: http://www.ddsm.com

*General Civil Practice and Litigation in all State and Federal Courts. Environmental, Eminent Domain, Energy, Oil and Gas, Business Law and Taxation, Securities Law, Commercial Law, Administrative, Health Care, Estate Planning, Trust and Probate, International Business and Real Estate Law.*

FIRM PROFILE: *The firm's approach to solving business and legal issues has earned it a well-developed reputation for being tough, creative and cost-sensitive in its representation of clients. For almost fifty years, the firm has been dedicated to providing legal services of the highest quality to its clients. This dedication has led to a steadily increasing client base which includes public companies, successful middle market businesses, public agencies, municipalities, trade associations, sole proprietorships, partnerships, entrepreneurs and highly compensated individuals.*

## MEMBERS OF FIRM

**CHRIS G. DEMETRIOU** (1915-1989).

**JEFFREY Z. B. SPRINGER,** born Sacramento, California, September 4, 1953; admitted to bar, 1979, California. *Education:* University of California at Berkeley (A.B., 1974); University of Southern California (J.D., 1979). Phi Alpha Delta. *Member:* Los Angeles County and American (Member, Sections on: Administrative Law; Natural Resources Law) Bar Associations; State Bar of California. **PRACTICE AREAS:** Eminent Domain; Environmental Law; Commercial Law; General Civil Litigation.

**CRAIG A. MOYER,** born Bethlehem, Pennsylvania, October 17, 1955; admitted to bar, 1980, California. *Education:* University of Southern California (B.A., magna cum laude, 1977); University of California at Los Angeles (J.D., 1980). Phi Beta Kappa. Author: *Hazard Communication Handbook, A Right-to-Know Compliance Guide* (Clark Boardman Callaghan, 1993 3d Ed.); *Clean Air Act Handbook, A Practical Guide to Compliance* (Clark Boardman Callaghan, 1993 3d Ed.); "Trends in Arrangements for the Development of Alaskan Petroleum Resources," 12 U.C.L.A.-Alaska Law Review 1-35, 1983; "Coping with a Decrease in Collateral: The Less-Secured Loan in Petroleum Financing," 18 Uniform Commercial Code Law Journal 3-29, 1985. Instructor, Environmental (Protection) Law, Regulatory Framework, University of California at Santa Barbara Extension, 1988—; Hazardous Materials Regulatory Framework, Environmental (Protection) Law, University of California at Los Angeles Extension, 1988—. *Member:* Los Angeles County (Member, Section on Environmental Law; Chairman, Legislative Committee, 1989-1991; Member, Executive Committee, 1989—, Secretary, 1992-1993, Treasurer, 1993—) and American (Member, Section on Natural Resources, Energy and Environmental Law) Bar Associations; State Bar of California. **PRACTICE AREAS:** Environmental Law; Energy Law; Administrative Law.

**ANGELA SHANAHAN,** born Liverpool, England, January 28, 1955; admitted to bar, 1985, California. *Education:* University of Southern California (B.A., cum laude, 1979); Loyola University (J.D., 1984). *Member:* Los Angeles County Bar Association (Member, Sections on: Probate; Taxation); State Bar of California. **PRACTICE AREAS:** Probate; Trust Administration; Estate Planning; Business Transactions.

**STEPHEN A. DEL GUERCIO,** born Los Angeles, California, September 27, 1961; admitted to bar, 1986, California. *Education:* University of Southern California (B.A., magna cum laude, 1983; J.D., 1986). Phi Beta Kappa; Order of the Coif. Staff Member, Southern California Law Review, 1985-1986. Author: "Boot Distributions in Acquisitive Reorganizations: The Wright-Shimberg Controversy," 59 Southern California Law Review 1295, 1986. *Member:* State Bar of California. **PRACTICE AREAS:** Health Care; Business Law.

**MICHAEL A. FRANCIS,** born Granite City, Illinois, February 21, 1956; admitted to bar, 1987, California. *Education:* Southern Illinois University (B.S., 1978; M.S., 1980); Southwestern University School of Law, (J.D., 1986). Author: *Hazard Communication Handbook, A Right-to-Know Compliance Guide,* (Clark Boardman Callaghan, 1994 Ed.); *Clean Air Act Handbook, A Practical Guide to Compliance,* (Clark Boardman Callaghan, 1993 3d Ed.). Instructor, "Hazardous Materials Regulatory Framework,"

*(This Listing Continued)*

"Managing Environmental Compliance," University of California at Los Angeles Extension, 1988—. *Member:* Los Angeles County (Member, Environmental Law Section; Chairman, Hazardous Materials and Water Quality Committee, 1992-1993; Chairman, Air Quality Committee, 1994-1995; Member, Executive Committee, 1992—) and American (Member, Section on National Resources Law) Bar Associations; State Bar of California. **PRACTICE AREAS:** Environmental Law; Business Law.

**REGINA LIUDZIUS COBB,** born Los Angeles, California, October 11, 1959; admitted to bar, 1985, California. *Education:* University of California at Los Angeles (B.A., magna cum laude; J.D., 1985). Member, Board of Editors, UCLA Law Review, 1984-1985. Member, Executive Board of Judges, 1984-1985, Distinguished Advocate and Roscoe Pound Finalist, 1984, Moot Court Honors Program. *Member:* Beverly Hills, Los Angeles County (Member, Section on Litigation) and American (Member, Section on Litigation) Bar Associations; The State Bar of California. **PRACTICE AREAS:** Complex Litigation; General Civil Litigation; Environmental Law.

**LAURIE E. DAVIS,** born Detroit, Michigan, August 15, 1957; admitted to bar, 1982, California, U.S. District Court, Central District of California and U.S. Court of Appeals, Ninth Circuit. *Education:* University of Michigan (B.A., with high distinction, 1979); University of Southern California (J.D., 1982). Phi Alpha Delta. Member, Mortar Board. Supervising Editor, USC Entertainment Law Journal, 1981-1982. *Member:* Los Angeles County Bar Association (Chairperson, Barristers Social Committee, 1985-1987; Member: Barristers-Artists and the Law Committee, 1983-1985; Business and Corporation Law Section, 1983-1990, 1992—); State Bar of California (Member, Business Law Section). **PRACTICE AREAS:** General Business Corporate Law/Transactions; Securities Law/Transactions.

**GREGORY D. TRIMARCHE,** born Oceanside, New York, August 23, 1963; admitted to bar, 1989, California. *Education:* University of Kansas (B.A., 1986; J.D.,1989). Member, 1987-1988 and Note and Comment Editor, 1988-1989, Kansas Law Review. Author: "Brownfields: A Practical Guide to Cleanup, Transfer and Redevelopment of Contaminated Sites," Argent Communications, 1996; "Insurance Coverage for Environmental Cleanups: A Primer for the Land Use Practitioner," California Land Use Law & Policy Reporter, May 1996; "The Law of Environmental Cleanup Cost Recovery: Shooting at a Moving Target," California Environmental Insider, May, 1995. *Member:* Los Angeles County (Member, Environmental Law Section; Vice-Chair, Programs Subsection) and American (Member, Natural Resources, Energy and Environmental Law Section) Bar Associations; State Bar of California (Member: Environmental Law Section; Education Committee; Hazardous Waste Remediation and Regulation Subcommittee). **PRACTICE AREAS:** Environmental Law; Civil Litigation; Insurance Law.

**KAREN McLAURIN CHANG,** born St. Louis, Missouri, October 8, 1961; admitted to bar, 1990, California. *Education:* University of California at Los Angeles (B.A., 1987); University of Southern California (J.D., 1990). Member, Moot Court Honors Program, 1988-1989. City of Los Angeles Community Planning Advisory Committee. *Member:* Los Angeles County (Member, Litigation Section, Condemnation and Land Valuation Committee) and American Bar Associations; State Bar of California; International Right of Way Association. **PRACTICE AREAS:** Environmental Law; Civil Litigation.

**LESLIE M. SMARIO,** born Los Angeles, California, July 5, 1960; admitted to bar, 1985, California. *Education:* Claremont McKenna College (B.A., cum laude, 1982); University of Southern California (J.D., 1985). Phi Alpha Delta. Law Clerk to Hon. Edward Rafeedie, Central District of California, 1985-1986. *Member:* Los Angeles County Bar Association. **PRACTICE AREAS:** General Business Litigation; Complex Civil Litigation; Environmental Law.

**ANDREW J. BRACKER,** born Los Angeles, California, November 25, 1963; admitted to bar, 1991, California. *Education:* University of California at Santa Cruz (B.A., with honors, 1986); Harvard University (J.D., cum laude, 1990). Phi Beta Kappa. *Member:* Los Angeles County (Member, Environmental Law Section) and American (Member, Natural Resources, Energy and Environmental Law Section) Bar Associations; State Bar of California; Hazardous Waste Association of California. **PRACTICE AREAS:** Environmental Law; Civil Litigation.

**KIMBERLY E. LEWAND,** born Los Angeles, California, July 23, 1966; admitted to bar, 1992, California and U.S. District Court, Central District of California; 1994, U.S. Court of Appeals, Ninth Circuit. *Education:* University of California at Los Angeles (B.A., 1988); Pepperdine University (J.D., 1992). Law Clerk to Hon. Thomas F. Crosby, California Court of Appeal, Fourth Appellate District, Division Three. *Member:* Los Angeles

*(This Listing Continued)*

County (Member, Environmental Law Section) and American (Member, Sections on: Natural Resources, Energy and Environmental Law) Bar Associations; State Bar of California (Member, Environmental Law Section).

**JENNIFER T. TAGGART,** born Hammond, Indiana, October 8, 1968; admitted to bar, 1995, California. *Education:* California Polytechnic State University (B.S., Engineering Science, 1990); Southwestern University School of Law (J.D., cum laude, 1995). Member, Order of the Barristers. Moot Court Honors Program, 1992-1995. Environmental Law Forum. Recipient: American Jurisprudence Award - Constitutional Law I, Fall, 1992; Remedies, 1994; Academic Excellence Award - Juvenile Law, 1993; Environmental Law, 1994; Administrative Law, 1995; International Environmental Law, 1995. Rockwell International Environmental Engineer, 1990-1995. Commissioner, Los Angeles City Environmental Affairs Commission. *Member:* Los Angeles County (Member, Environmental Law Section) and American (Member, Sections on, Natural Resources, Energy and Environmental Law) Bar Associations; State Bar of California (Member, Environmental Law Section); Valley Industry and Commerce Association (Chair, Environment and Water Committee, 1991-1996; Chair, Downtown Committee, 1996—; Board of Directors, 1995—); Environmental Law Institute. *PRACTICE AREAS:* Environmental Law. *Email:* jttddsm@aol.com

**ROBERT P. SILVERSTEIN,** born Los Angeles, California, October 24, 1968; admitted to bar, 1996, California and U.S. District Court, Central District of California. *Education:* University of California at Los Angeles (B.A., magna cum laude, 1990); University of California, Hastings College of the Law (J.D., 1996). Phi Beta Kappa. Recipient, American Jurisprudence Award, Legal Writing and Research. Judicial Extern to the Honorable Marvin R. Baxter, Associate Justice, California Supreme Court, 1995. *Member:* State Bar of California. *PRACTICE AREAS:* Eminent Domain; Environmental Law; General Civil Litigation.

*OF COUNSEL*

**RONALD J. DEL GUERCIO,** born Los Angeles, California, January 13, 1931; admitted to bar, 1960, California. *Education:* University of Southern California (A.B., 1957; LL.B., 1959). Phi Delta Phi; Phi Sigma Alpha. Law Clerk to Hon. Peirson M. Hall, Chief Judge U.S. District Court, Southern District of California, 1959-1960. *Member:* Los Angeles County and American Bar Associations; State Bar of California. *PRACTICE AREAS:* Business Law.

**RICHARD A. DEL GUERCIO,** born Los Angeles, California, August 27, 1928; admitted to bar, 1952, California. *Education:* University of California at Los Angeles; Loyola University (LL.B., 1952). Phi Delta Phi. *Member:* Los Angeles County Bar Association; State Bar of California. *PRACTICE AREAS:* Eminent Domain; Civil Litigation.

**JAMES P. DEL GUERCIO,** born Los Angeles, California, January 10, 1933; admitted to bar, 1958, California. *Education:* University of California at Los Angeles (A.B., 1954); Loyola Law School, Los Angeles (LL.B., 1957). Law Clerk to U.S. District Court Judge, Peirson M. Hall. *Member:* Los Angeles County Bar Association; State Bar of California. *PRACTICE AREAS:* Banking Transactions; Compliance; Business Law.

REFERENCE: Bank of America, L.A. Main Office, Los Angeles, Calif.

## DEMPSEY & JOHNSON, P.C.
1925 CENTURY PARK EAST, SUITE 2350
**LOS ANGELES, CALIFORNIA 90067-2724**
Telephone: 310-551-2300
Facsimile: 310-556-2021

*General Civil and Trial Practice in all State and Federal Courts, Real Estate, Corporation, Corporate Securities and Probate.*

FIRM PROFILE: *Dempsey & Johnson, P.C. is a boutique law firm specializing in all areas of business and civil litigation, corporate finance and transactions, and employment law. The firm's transactional practice encompasses all aspects of business law, including corporate, partnership, real estate, landlord-tenant, probate and securities law. The litigation department handles cases in all major categories, including federal and state court matters and appeals accountant liability, bankruptcy, director's and officer's liability, intellectual property, securities law, RICO matters and commercial real estate disputes. The litigation practice has a sub-specialty in the representation of corporations in defense of wrongful termination cases and the representation of officers, directors and accountants in securities fraud cases.*

**MICHAEL D. DEMPSEY,** born Los Angeles, California, March 21, 1943; admitted to bar, 1969, California. *Education:* San Fernando Valley
*(This Listing Continued)*

State College (B.A., magna cum laude, 1965); University of California at Los Angeles (J.D., 1968). Order of the Coif. Member, University of California at Los Angeles Law Review, 1966-1968. *Member:* State Bar of California. *PRACTICE AREAS:* Business Litigation; Securities Fraud; Directors and Officers Liability; Accountant's Liability.

**STEPHEN C. JOHNSON,** born Glenn Cove, New York, May 23, 1961; admitted to bar, 1989, California; U.S. District Court, Central District of California; U.S. Court of Appeals, Ninth Circuit. *Education:* Loyola Marymount University (B.A., cum laude, 1984); University of Southern California (J.D., 1989). Order of the Coif. *Member:* State Bar of California. *PRACTICE AREAS:* Business Litigation; Securities Fraud; Officers and Directors Liability; Accountant's Liability; Employers Discrimination Defense.

---

**ROBERT D. DONALDSON,** born Seattle, Washington, September 25, 1944; admitted to bar, 1973, California; 1974, U.S. District Court, Central District of California, U.S. Court of Appeals, Ninth Circuit and U.S. Court of Appeals for the District of Columbia. *Education:* Yale University (B.A., 1966); Vanderbilt University (J.D., 1973). *Member:* State Bar of California. *PRACTICE AREAS:* Business Litigation; Securities Fraud; Directors and Officers Liability; Accountant's Liability.

**HEATHER M. NOELTE,** born Wheaton, Illinois, July 7, 1964; admitted to bar, 1995, California. *Education:* Brigham Young University (B.A., 1985); Loyola Marymount University (J.D., 1995). Phi Delta Phi. Listed in Who's Who Among American Law Students, 1995. *PRACTICE AREAS:* Business Litigation; Securities Fraud; Officers and Directors Liability; Accountant's Liability; Employer Discrimination Defense.

*OF COUNSEL*

**MICHAEL A. CROSS,** born Los Angeles, California, September 26, 1955; admitted to bar, 1980, California. *Education:* University of California at Los Angeles (B.A., cum laude, 1977); Harvard University (J.D., 1980). Articles Editor, Harvard Civil Rights-Civil Liberties Law Review, 1979-1980. Adjunct Professor, Southwestern University School of Law, 1982-1983. *Member:* Century City, Beverly Hills, Los Angeles County and American Bar Associations; State Bar of California. *PRACTICE AREAS:* Corporate Law; Corporate Securities; Public Offerings; Private Placements; Mergers and Acquisitions.

## DENNEY & OTHS
**LOS ANGELES, CALIFORNIA**
(See Glendale)
*Environmental Law and Litigation.*

## DENNISON, BENNETT & PRESS, LLP
Established in 1981
*WARNER CENTER*
21031 VENTURA BOULEVARD, 12TH FLOOR (WOODLAND HILLS)
**LOS ANGELES, CALIFORNIA 91364**
Telephone: 818-716-7200
Fax: 818-347-5284
Email: DbANDPLAW@aol.com

*General Civil, Trial and Appellate Practice in all State and Federal Courts. Insurance and Tort Defense, Business Litigation, Products Liability, Earth Movement, Construction Defects, Wrongful Termination and Discrimination, Sexual Harassment, and Insurance Coverage and Bad Faith Law.*

*MEMBERS OF FIRM*

**BRUCE B. DENNISON,** born Sacramento, California, November 25, 1947; admitted to bar, 1972, California; 1976, U.S. Supreme Court. *Education:* University of California at Berkeley (B.S. in Accounting, 1969); University of California at Los Angeles (J.D., 1972). Member, Board of Directors, Moot Court Honors Program, 1971-1972. Attorney, Los Angeles Public Defenders Office, 1972-1974. Member, Panel of Arbitrators, American Arbitration Association. Superior Court Settlement Officer, CEB and Insurance Lecturer. *Member:* Association of Southern California Defense Counsel. *PRACTICE AREAS:* Insurance and Tort Defense; Products Lia-
*(This Listing Continued)*

## DENNISON, BENNETT & PRESS, LLP, Los Angeles—Continued

bility; Wrongful Termination and Discrimination; Sexual Harassment; Insurance Coverage and Bad Faith Law; First Party Insurance Claims.

**CHARLES A. BENNETT,** born New York, N.Y., December 20, 1942; admitted to bar, 1974, California. *Education:* University of California at Berkeley (B.S., 1966); Loyola University of Los Angeles (J.D., cum laude, 1974). Registered Civil Engineer, California, 1969. *Member:* Association of Southern California Defense Counsel; American Society of Civil Engineers. **PRACTICE AREAS:** Construction Defect Litigation; Products Liability; Earth Movement and Drainage Litigation; Property Insurance Coverage Issues; Property Damage Litigation.

**STEPHEN M. PRESS,** born Los Angeles, California, March 26, 1944; admitted to bar, 1975, California. *Education:* University of California at Los Angeles (B.S., 1966); Southwestern University School of Law (J.D., 1975). Editor, Southwestern University Law Review, 1974-1975. *Member:* Association of Southern California Defense Counsel. **PRACTICE AREAS:** Insurance and Tort Defense; Business Litigation; Property Disputes; Uninsured Motorist Litigation.

**JAMES H. GOUDGE,** born Los Angeles, California, October 10, 1945; admitted to bar, 1980, California; 1988, U.S. Supreme Court. *Education:* California State University, Northridge (B.A., 1967; M.A., 1974); Loyola Law School (J.D., 1979). *Member:* Los Angeles County and American Bar Associations; Association of Southern California Defense Counsel. **PRACTICE AREAS:** Insurance and Tort Defense; Business Litigation; Products Liability; Wrongful Termination and Discrimination; Sexual Harassment.

**THOMAS A. STEWART,** born California, September 17, 1946; admitted to bar, 1985, California. *Education:* San Diego State University 1968; Western State University (J.D., 1985). *Member:* Los Angeles County Bar Association. **PRACTICE AREAS:** Construction Defect Litigation; Earth Movement Litigation; Products Liability; Business Litigation; Tort Defense.

**LISA G. ROSENWASSER,** born Los Angeles, California, January 3, 1958; admitted to bar, 1985, California. *Education:* University of California at Los Angeles (B.A., 1979); Southwestern University School of Law (J.D., magna cum laude, 1985). Phi Alpha Delta. Member, Southwestern University Law Review, 1984-1985. **PRACTICE AREAS:** Insurance and Tort Defense; Business Litigation; Property Disputes; Uninsured Motorist Litigation.

### ASSOCIATES

**MICHAEL KAPLAN,** born Los Angeles, California, February 24, 1960; admitted to bar, 1986, California. *Education:* University of California at Los Angeles (B.A., 1982); University of California at Davis (J.D., 1985).

**LEONARD P. JANNER,** born Chicago, Illinois, July 5, 1961; admitted to bar, 1989, California. *Education:* University of California, Los Angeles (B.A., 1984); Loyola University of Los Angeles (J.D., 1989).

**SHEILA E. SCHAEFER,** born Dallas, Texas, October 28, 1961; admitted to bar, 1987, Texas; 1988, California. *Education:* Bowdoin College (B.A., 1984); Southern Methodist University (J.D., 1987). [Lt., JAGC, U.S. Navy, 1987-1992]

**ROBERT SCOTT SILVER,** born Aurora, Illinois, April 26, 1966; admitted to bar, 1992, California. *Education:* Brandeis University (B.A., 1988); University of California at Los Angeles (J.D., 1991).

**DEBORAH A. LIEBER,** born Granada Hills, California, June 20, 1964; admitted to bar, 1990, California and U.S. District Court, Central District of California. *Education:* University of California at Los Angeles (B.A., 1986); Southern University School of Law (J.D., 1990).

**TIMOTHY MCWILLIAMS,** born Melrose, Massachusetts, October 29, 1963; admitted to bar, 1993, California. *Education:* Michigan State University (B.A., 1986); Whittier Law School (J.D., 1993).

**PHILLIP M. HAYES,** born Tulsa, Oklahoma, October 16, 1957; admitted to bar, 1991, California. *Education:* University of Notre Dame (B.A, 1980); Southwestern University (J.D., 1991).

**MICHAEL TUDZIN,** born Santa Monica, California, January 2, 1961; admitted to bar, 1993, California; 1994, Arizona; 1995, District of Columbia and Colorado. *Education:* California State University, Northridge (B.S., 1985); Whittier College School of Law (J.D., 1993). *Member:* State Bar of California; State Bar of Arizona; District of Columbia Bar.

*(This Listing Continued)*

REPRESENTATIVE CLIENTS: State Farm Fire and Casualty Co.; Allstate Insurance Co.; Wausau/Nationwide Insurance Co.; ; Harnischfeger Corp.; Fireman's Fund Insurance Co.; State Farm Mutual Automobile Insurance Co.; PPM Cranes, Inc.; Grove North America; Beloit Corporation; Golden Eagle Insurance; Western Mutual Insurance Co.; Farmers Insurance Co.; Fire Insurance Exchange.

---

## DePASQUALE & PAULSON

WORLD TRADE CENTER
350 SOUTH FIGUEROA STREET, SUITE 900
**LOS ANGELES, CALIFORNIA 90071**
Telephone: 213-895-0685
Fax: 213-895-0686

*Santa Ana, California Office:* 4 Hutton Center Drive, Suite 200. Telephone: 714-755-3055. Fax: 714-755-1570.

*General Civil Practice. Corporate, Taxation, Real Estate, Estate Planning, Business Litigation, Bankruptcy, Creditors' Rights and General Business Law.*

### MEMBERS OF FIRM

**DAVID L. DePASQUALE,** born Pireaus, Greece, October 4, 1957; admitted to bar, 1986, California and U.S. District Court, Central District of California; 1986, U,S. Tax Court. *Education:* California State University at Los Angeles (B.A., Political Science, 1981); University of San Diego (J.D., 1985); Boston University (LL.M., Taxation, 1986). Recipient, American Jurisprudence Award in Corporations. Author: "Computer Software Developed in Connection with an R & D Partnership," 5 Boston Univ. Tax Journal (1987). Associate Professor, Simon Greenleaf University School of Law, 1989-1993. *Member:* Pasadena and Los Angeles County Bar Associations. State Bar of California. **PRACTICE AREAS:** Corporate; Real Estate; Business Litigation; Bankruptcy; Creditors' Rights; Estate Planning; Taxation.

(For Complete Biographical Data on all Personnel, see Professional Biographies at Santa Ana, California)

---

## DIXON Q. DERN, P.C.

Established in 1990

SUITE 400
1901 AVENUE OF THE STARS
**LOS ANGELES, CALIFORNIA 90067**
Telephone: 310-557-2244
Fax: 310-557-2224

*Entertainment, Copyright and Communication Law.*

**DIXON Q. DERN,** born Colorado Springs, Colorado, January 29, 1929; admitted to bar, 1954, California, U.S. Court of Appeals, 9th Circuit and U.S. District Court, Northern District of California; 1966, U.S. District Court, Central District of California; 1973, District of Columbia and U.S. Supreme Court. *Education:* Stanford University (A.B., 1950; J.D., 1953). Editor, Stanford Law Review, 1952-1953. *Member:* Beverly Hills (Chair, Entertainment Law Committee, 1969; President, 1979-1980), Los Angeles County (Trustee, 1978-1979) and American (Member: Patent, Trademark and Copyright Law Section; Forum Committee on Entertainment and Sports Industries, 1980—; Forum Committee on Communication Law, 1980—) Bar Associations; State Bar of California (Member, Board of Governors, 1982-1985; Vice President, 1985); The District of Columbia Bar (Inactive); Los Angeles Copyright Society (President, 1972-1973). **LANGUAGES:** German. **PRACTICE AREAS:** Entertainment Law; Copyright Law; Communications Law.

---

**CHRISTINE G. ALBRECHT-BUEHLER,** born Munich, Germany, June 24, 1969; admitted to bar, 1995, California and U.S. District Court, Central District of California. *Education:* Northwestern University (B.A., 1991); Loyola University of School of Law (J.D., 1994). **PRACTICE AREAS:** Entertainment Law.

## DEUTSCH & RUBIN

SECOND FLOOR, WEST TOWER
11377 WEST OLYMPIC BOULEVARD
**LOS ANGELES, CALIFORNIA 90064-1683**
Telephone: 310-312-3222
FAX: 310-312-3205

*Family, Domestic Relations, Matrimonial and Divorce Law.*

### MEMBERS OF FIRM

**MILES J. RUBIN, (A PROFESSIONAL CORPORATION),** born Brooklyn, New York, September 17, 1929; admitted to bar, 1954, New York; 1957, California; 1966, U.S. Supreme Court. *Education:* College of William & Mary (B.A., 1949); Brooklyn Law School (LL.B., 1954). Deputy Attorney General, 1957-1961. Senior Assistant Attorney General, 1965-1970. Certified Family Law Specialist, 1981. *Member:* Beverly Hills (Member, Section on Family Law), Los Angeles County (Member: Section on Family Law; Family Law Mediation Panel, 1984-1990; Special Mediation Program, 1989-1990) and American (Member, Section on Family Law; Panelist, Mid-Year Convention, 1989) Bar Associations; The State Bar of California (Member: Family Law Section; State Bar Certification Exam Writing Committee, 1984-1990; Chairman, 1986-1990). *PRACTICE AREAS:* Family Law; Domestic Relations Law; Matrimonial Law; Divorce Law.

**WENDY A. HERZOG,** born Chicago, Illinois, January 4, 1950; admitted to bar, 1983, California. *Education:* University of Illinois (B.A., with honors, 1972); University of California at Berkeley (Secondary Teaching Credential, 1974); Hastings College of the Law, University of California (J.D., 1983). Member, Moot Court Board. Prize Winner, David E. Snodgrass Moot Court Writing Competition. Extern for the Honorable Allen E. Broussard, Associate Justice, California Supreme Court, 1983. Author: "The Duty of Care of a Spouse Who Manages and Controls Community Property," Beverly Hills Bar Association Journal, August 1990. Program Panelist: Division of Matrimonial Property, Continuing Education, State Bar of California, 1994. *Member:* Beverly Hills and Los Angeles Bar Associations; State Bar of California. *PRACTICE AREAS:* Family Law; Domestic Relations Law; Matrimonial Law; Divorce Law.

**LAURI A. KRITT,** born Los Angeles, California, March 16, 1963; admitted to bar, 1990, California; 1991, U.S. District Court, Central District of California and U.S. Court of Appeals, Ninth Circuit. *Education:* Claremont McKenna College (B.A., 1985); Santa Clara University (J.D., 1990). *Member:* Los Angeles County Bar Association. *PRACTICE AREAS:* Family Law.

### OF COUNSEL

**LINDA CUKIER,** born Los Angeles, California, June 25, 1958; admitted to bar, 1984, California. *Education:* Sarah Lawrence College (B.A., 1979); Loyola University of Los Angeles (J.D., 1983). *Member:* Los Angeles County Bar Association; State Bar of California. (Also Practicing Individually). *LANGUAGES:* French. *PRACTICE AREAS:* Family Law; Domestic Relations Law; Matrimonial Law; Divorce Law.

---

## DEVIRIAN & SHINMOTO

A PROFESSIONAL CORPORATION
WELLESLEY PLAZA, SUITE 215
12304 SANTA MONICA BOULEVARD
**LOS ANGELES, CALIFORNIA 90025**
Telephone: 310-571-1600
Fax: 310-571-1609

*General Practice.*

**DONALD B. DEVIRIAN,** born Los Angeles, California, August 7, 1945; admitted to bar, 1971, California, U.S. District Court, Central and Southern Districts of California and U.S. Court of Appeals, Ninth Circuit; 1976, U.S. Supreme Court. *Education:* University of Redlands (B.A., 1967); University of California at Los Angeles (J.D., 1970). Member, Panel of Arbitrators, American Arbitration Association, 1978—. *Member:* Los Angeles County Bar Association; The State Bar of California. *PRACTICE AREAS:* General Trial Law; Civil Litigation; Construction Law.

**LYNN A. SHINMOTO,** born Gardena, California, September 2, 1955; admitted to bar, 1980, California, U.S. District Court, Central District of California and U.S. Court of Appeals, Ninth Circuit; 1985, U.S. Supreme Court. *Education:* University of Southern California (B.A., magna cum laude, 1977; J.D., 1980). Phi Beta Kappa; Phi Alpha Delta. *Member:* State Bar of California. *PRACTICE AREAS:* General Trial Law; Civil Litigation; Construction Law.

---

**ARMENAK KAVCIOGLU,** born Istanbul, Turkey, January 6, 1969; admitted to bar, 1994, California, U.S. District Court, Central District of California and U.S. Court of Appeals, Ninth Circuit. *Education:* University of California at Los Angeles (B.A., 1991); University of Southern California (J.D., 1994). Member, Major Tax Planning Journal, 1992-1993. Senior Editor, Interdisciplinary Law Journal, 1992-1994. *Member:* State Bar of California. *LANGUAGES:* Armenian, Turkish. *PRACTICE AREAS:* Civil Litigation; Construction Law; Bankruptcy.

---

## DEWEY BALLANTINE

333 SOUTH HOPE STREET
**LOS ANGELES, CALIFORNIA 90071-1406**
Telephone: 213-626-3399
Fax: 213-625-0562

*Other offices:* New York, New York; Washington, D.C.; London, England; Hong Kong; Budapest, Hungary; Prague, Czech Republic; and Warsaw, Poland.

*General Practice.*

### RESIDENT PARTNERS

**ALAN M. ALBRIGHT,** born Los Angeles, California, May 26, 1949; admitted to bar, 1976, California. *Education:* University of California at Los Angeles (B.A., cum laude, 1971; M.B.A., 1973; J.D., 1976). Pi Gamma Mu; Omicron Delta Epsilon; Beta Gamma Sigma; Order of the Coif. Member, U.C.L.A. Law Review, 1974-1976. *Member:* Los Angeles County (Member, Sections on: Business and Corporations Law, Real Property) and American (Member, Business Law Section) Bar Associations; State Bar of California. *PRACTICE AREAS:* Corporate.

**RICHARD J. BURDGE, JR.,** born Long Beach, California, December 4, 1949; admitted to bar, 1979, California. *Education:* Yale University (B.S., 1972); University of California at Los Angeles (J.D., 1979). Order of the Coif. Managing Editor, UCLA Law Review, 1978-1979. *Member:* Los Angeles County (Member, Delegation to the State Bar Conference, 1989; Litigation Section) and American (Member, Sections on: Litigation and Business Law) Bar Associations; State Bar of California; Association of Business Trial Lawyers (Governor, 1989-1991, 1993-1994; Officer, 1995-1996). *PRACTICE AREAS:* Litigation.

**GEORGE T. CAPLAN,** born Cleveland, Ohio, November 23, 1942; admitted to bar, 1969, California and Ohio. *Education:* University of California at Berkeley (A.B., 1965); Columbia University (LL.B., 1968). Law Clerk to Chief Judge Paul C. Weick, U.S. Court of Appeals, Sixth Circuit, 1968-1969. President, Jewish Television Network. President, Jewish Federation Council of Greater Los Angeles, 1988-1990. *Member:* Los Angeles County and American (Member, Section of Litigation) Bar Associations; State Bar of California; Association of Business Trial Lawyers; Computer Law Association. *PRACTICE AREAS:* Litigation.

**KELLY CHARLES CRABB,** born Payson, Utah, November 8, 1946; admitted to bar, 1985, New York; 1991, California. *Education:* Brigham Young University (B.A., 1971; M.P.A., 1973); Columbia University (J.D., 1984). Editor, Columbia Law Review, 1982-1984. Author: "The Reality of Extra Legal Barriers to Mergers and Acquisitions in Japan," 21 Int'l Lawyer 97, Winter 1987. Adjunct, Seminar in Japan Joint Ventures, Columbia Law School, 1989. *PRACTICE AREAS:* Entertainment and Media; Japan Trade.

**LEE SMALLEY EDMON,** born Champaign, Illinois, November 9, 1955; admitted to bar, 1981, California. *Education:* Bob Jones University (B.A., 1977); University of Illinois (J.D., 1981). *Member:* Los Angeles County (Senior Vice President, 1996-1997; Chair, Litigation Section, 1996-1997; Member, Board of Trustees, 1988-1990, 1993-1997; Chair, Lawyer Referral and Information Service Advisory Board, 1991-1994; Chair, Delegation to State Bar Conference of Delegates, 1993; Member, Foundation Board of Directors, 1990-1996; Barristers President, 1989-1990) and American (Member, Board of Directors, American Bar Endowment, 1995-1997; Member, House of Delegates, 1996-1998) Bar Associations; State Bar of California (Member, Committee on the Administration of Justice, 1995-1997); Association of Business Trial Lawyers (Member, Board of Governors, 1992-1994); Women Lawyers Association of Los Angeles (Board of

*(This Listing Continued)*

**DEWEY BALLANTINE,** Los Angeles—Continued

Governors, 1994-1996); Ninth Judicial Circuit Conference (Representative, 1992-1996). *PRACTICE AREAS:* Litigation.

**ROBERT W. FISCHER, JR.,** born Minneapolis, Minnesota, November 5, 1948; admitted to bar, 1973, California. *Education:* Occidental College (B.A., 1970); University of California at Los Angeles (J.D., 1973). Associate Editor, U.C.L.A. Law Review, 1972-1973. *Member:* Los Angeles County and American Bar Associations; State Bar of California. *PRACTICE AREAS:* Litigation.

**DAVID S. MCLEOD,** born Corvallis, Oregon, August 19, 1950; admitted to bar, 1975, California. *Education:* University of Southern California (B.A., magna cum laude, 1972); University of San Francisco (J.D., cum laude, 1975). Phi Beta Kappa. Assistant Editor, University of San Francisco Law Review, 1974-1975. *Member:* Los Angeles County and American Bar Associations; The State Bar of California. *PRACTICE AREAS:* Litigation.

**ROBERT M. SMITH,** born Pasadena, Texas, January 18, 1953; admitted to bar, 1981, New York; 1994, California. *Education:* California State University (B.A., 1977); University of California at Berkeley (J.D., 1980). *PRACTICE AREAS:* Corporate.

**KATHY TESTRAKE WALES,** born Muscatine, Iowa, March 17, 1945; admitted to bar, 1978, California. *Education:* University of Wisconsin (B.S., 1967); University of California at Los Angeles (J.D., 1978). Phi Beta Kappa; Order of the Coif. *Member:* The State Bar of California. *PRACTICE AREAS:* Corporate.

**ALAN WAYTE,** born Huntington Park, California, December 30, 1936; admitted to bar, 1961, California. *Education:* Stanford University (A.B., 1958; J.D., 1960). Phi Delta Phi. Member, Moot Court Board, 1959. Member, Board of Editors, Stanford Law Review, 1959-1960. Member, Chancery Club Member and Chairman, California Continuing Education of the Bar Advisory Committee on Real Property Programs, 1980-1981. Member, Anglo-American Real Property Institute, 1984. *Member:* Los Angeles County (Member, Executive Committee, 1979-1980 and Chairman, 1977-1978, Real Property Section; Chairman, Subsection on Real Estate Financing, 1976-1977) and American Bar Associations; State Bar of California (Member, Executive Committee and Chairman, Real Estate Section, 1981-1982); American College of Mortgage Attorneys, Inc.; American College of Real Estate Lawyers (President, 1994-1995). *PRACTICE AREAS:* Real Estate.

**JEFFREY R. WITHAM,** born Cincinnati, Ohio, January 22, 1959; admitted to bar, 1984, California. *Education:* California State University at Los Angeles (B.A., with high honors, 1981); Boalt Hall School of Law, University of California (J.D., 1984). Phi Kappa Phi. Member, California Law Review, 1982-1983. Lillick McHose & Charles, 1984-1986. *Member:* Los Angeles County and American Bar Associations; State Bar of California. *PRACTICE AREAS:* Litigation.

**ROBERT WOLL,** born Ithaca, New York, November 26, 1956; admitted to bar, 1985, New York; 1995, California. *Education:* Princeton University (A.B., summa cum laude, 1978); Stanford University (J.D., 1984). Note Editor, Stanford Law Review. *PRACTICE AREAS:* Banking Law; Corporate and Securities; International; Financial Transactions; Telecommunications Law.

**DONALD F. WOODS, JR.,** born Rockville Centre, New York, April 13, 1946; admitted to bar, 1972, California. *Education:* Georgetown University (B.S., 1968); Columbia University (J.D., 1971). Member, Board of Editors, Columbia Law Review, 1969-1971. Author: "Jury Selection in Federal Court," Los Angeles County Bar Association, Litigation, Vol. 7, No. 1, Spring, 1990. Member, Panel of Arbitrators, American Arbitration Association. *Member:* Los Angeles County (Member, Litigation and Antitrust Sections) and American (Member, Litigation and Antitrust Sections) Bar Associations; State Bar of California. *PRACTICE AREAS:* Litigation.

COUNSEL

**SCOTTA E. MCFARLAND,** born Borger, Texas, May 12, 1947; admitted to bar, 1980, Texas; 1993, California. *Education:* John Brown University; University of North Texas (B.S.Ed., with honors, 1969); George Washington University; Southern Methodist University (J.D., 1980). *Member:* Dallas (Member, Courthouse Liaison Committee of Bankruptcy Section) and American Bar Associations; State Bar of Texas; State Bar of California.

*(This Listing Continued)*

OF COUNSEL

**JOHN K. VAN DE KAMP,** born Pasadena, California, February 7, 1936; admitted to bar, 1960, California. *Education:* Dartmouth College (B.A., 1956); Stanford University School of Law (J.D., 1959). California Attorney General, 1983-1991. District Attorney, County of Los Angeles, California, 1975-1983. Federal Public Defender, Los Angeles, California, 1971-1975. Director and Deputy Director, Executive Office for United States Attorneys, Washington, D.C., 1967-1969. United States Attorney and Assistant United States Attorney, Los Angeles, California, 1960-1967. *Member:* Los Angeles County and American Bar Associations; Stat e Bar of California; Institute for Corporate Counsel (Member, Advisory Board). *PRACTICE AREAS:* Litigation.

(For Biographical Data of all Partners, Counsel, Of Counsel and Office Addresses, see Professional Biographies at New York, N.Y.)

## DIAMOND & WILSON

**SUITE 300, 12304 SANTA MONICA BOULEVARD**
**LOS ANGELES, CALIFORNIA 90025**
*Telephone: 310-820-7808*
*Fax: 310-826-9658*

*Entertainment, Music, Motion Picture, Television, Copyright and Intellectual Property Law.*

MEMBERS OF FIRM

**STANLEY J. DIAMOND,** born Los Angeles, California, November 27, 1927; admitted to bar, 1953, California; 1971, U.S. Supreme Court. *Education:* University of California at Los Angeles (A.B., 1949); University of Southern California (J.D., 1952). Nu Beta Epsilon. Member, Board of Directors, Los Angeles Suicide Prevention Center, 1971-1979. Member, California Copyright Conference, 1975—. *Member:* Beverly Hills, Los Angeles County and American Bar Associations; State Bar of California; American Judicature Society. *PRACTICE AREAS:* Entertainment Law; Music Recording Law; Motion Picture Law; Television Law.

**JAMES J. WILSON,** born Passaic, New Jersey, October 19, 1946; admitted to bar, 1972, California. *Education:* University of Tennessee (B.S., 1968); Indiana University (J.D., 1971). Order of the Coif; Phi Delta Phi. Note Editor, Indiana Law Journal, 1970-1971. Author: "Use of Tax Benefit Principles to Override Section 337," 45 Indiana Law Journal 413, 1970, reprinted in October, 1970 Issue of The Monthly Digest of Tax Articles. Co-Author: "Centralizing the International Operations of Multinationals," 11 San Diego Law Review, 70, 1973. *Member:* State Bar of California. *PRACTICE AREAS:* Entertainment Law; Music Recording Law; Motion Picture Law; Television Law.

REPRESENTATIVE CLIENTS: David Bowie; Ronnie James Dio; Jose Feliciano; John Fogerty; Buddy Guy; Great White; John Lee Hooker; Immature; John Kay and Steppenwolf; Kingdom Come; Kool and the Gang; Mister Bungle; Eddie Money; Van Morrison; Chuck Norris; Shaquille O'Neal; Lee Oskar; Otis Rush; Joe Satriani; Gene Simmons; Tin Machine; Trauma Records; TN/SM Records, UFO; Gino Vannelli; Ross Vannelli; Joe Louis Walker; Yes.
REFERENCE: City National Bank, Beverly Hills.

## DICKSON, CARLSON & CAMPILLO

**LOS ANGELES, CALIFORNIA**

(See Santa Monica)

*General Civil, Trial and Appellate Practice in all State and Federal Courts. Product Liability, Toxic Torts, Casualty, Commercial and Real Estate Litigation, Insurance Law, Professional Malpractice, Antitrust, Wrongful Termination, Administrative, First Amendment.*

## DIDAK & JACK

*Established in 1994*

**11755 WILSHIRE BOULEVARD, 15TH FLOOR**
**LOS ANGELES, CALIFORNIA 90025**
*Telephone: 310-473-7173*
*Fax: 310-312-1077*

*Insurance Coverage/Bad Faith; Legal Malpractice; Torts/Contract Litigation; Statutory Corporations; Fidelity Insurance; Real Estate. Civil Appeals.*

*(This Listing Continued)*

## PROFESSIONAL BIOGRAPHIES

CALIFORNIA—LOS ANGELES

### MEMBERS OF FIRM

**MARK F. DIDAK,** born Los Angeles, California, March 1, 1957; admitted to bar, 1982, California; U.S. District Court, Central and Southern Districts of California and U.S. Court of Appeals, Ninth Circuit. *Education:* Reed College (B.A., 1978); University of Southern California (J.D., 1982). *Member:* Los Angeles County and American Bar Associations; State Bar of California. **PRACTICE AREAS:** Insurance Coverage and Defense; Bad Faith; Legal Malpractice; Statutory Corporations; Civil Appeals.

**TRAVIS R. JACK,** born Kankakee, Illinois, September 6, 1952; admitted to bar, 1979, California. *Education:* University of California at Berkeley (A.B., 1976); Hastings College of Law, University of California (J.D., 1979). Member, Moot Court Board. Extern, Court of Appeal, Fourth Appellate District, the Honorable Howard Wiener. *Member:* Los Angeles County Bar Association; State Bar of California. **PRACTICE AREAS:** Insurance Coverage and Defense; Bad Faith; Real Estate; Suretyship.

REPRESENTATIVE CLIENTS: Hartford Insurance; Fireman's Fund Insurance; Proactive Management; AIG Risk Management; Argonaut Insurance.

---

## DIXON & JESSUP LTD., L.L.P.
SUITE 2000, WELLS FARGO CENTER
333 SOUTH GRAND AVENUE
LOS ANGELES, CALIFORNIA 90071-1524
Telephone: 213-346-8310
Fax: 213-620-1811

*Omaha, Nebraska Office:* One First National Center, Sixteenth & Dodge Streets, Suite 1800, 68102. Telephone: 402-345-3900. Fax: 402-345-0965 or 402-345-3341.

*Washington, D.C. Office:* 1850 M Street, N.W., Suite 450, 20036. Telephone: 202-452-1034. Fax: 202-452-1822.

*Dallas, Texas Office:* Suite 5500, Fountain Place, 1445 Ross Avenue, 75202-2733. Telephone: 214-754-0155. Fax: 214-754-0704.

*Kuwait City Office:* Al-Hilali Street, Murgab, Al-Burrak Building 2, P.O. Box 22833 SAFAT, 13089. Telephone: 011-965-241-5617. Fax: 011-965-240-7030.

Bankruptcy, Banking, Securities, Corporate, Commercial Finance, International, Real Estate, Insurance Regulation, Legislation, Litigation, and Employment.

**CLIFTON R. JESSUP, JR.,** born Detroit, Michigan, March 12, 1955; admitted to bar, 1979, Nebraska; 1990, Texas (Not admitted in California). *Education:* Oakwood College (B.A., summa cum laude, 1976); University of Michigan Law School (J.D., 1978). *Member:* Nebraska State and American Bar Associations; State Bar of Texas. **PRACTICE AREAS:** Bankruptcy Law; Creditors Rights Law; Corporate Reorganization.

### OF COUNSEL

**J. SCOTT BOVITZ,** born Los Angeles, California, June 5, 1955; admitted to bar, 1980, California; 1981, U.S. District Court, Northern, Southern, Eastern and Central Districts of California and U.S. Tax Court; 1986, U.S. Court of Appeals, Ninth Circuit. *Education:* University of California at Santa Barbara (B.A., with high honors, 1977); Loyola Law School, Los Angeles (J.D., 1980); University of San Diego (Diploma in Taxation, 1983). Recipient: American Jurisprudence Award for Bankruptcy; Benno M. Brink Memorial Award for Bankruptcy, Loyola Law School. Adjunct Professor of Law, Bankruptcy Law, Debtor-Creditor Relations and Uniform Commercial Code Transactions, Loyola Law School, Los Angeles, 1982-1987. Panelist: "Bankruptcy Litigation Skills," California State Bar Convention, 1994; Alternative Dispute Resolution in Bankruptcy," American Bankruptcy Institute, Battleground West, 1994; "Latest Weapons For the Battlefield: Current Developments," American Bankruptcy Institute—First Annual Bankruptcy Battleground West, 1993. Speaker on, "The 1994 Amendments to the Bankruptcy Code," Credit Managers Association of California, 1995; Speaker on, "The Intersection of Environmental and Bankruptcy Law," Professional Education Seminar at Demetriou, Del Guercio, Springer & Moyer, 1995; Speaker on, "What Every Accountant Should Know About Bankruptcy," Pasadena Organization of Certified Public Accountants, 1994; Speaker on, "Get Yourself Ready To Be A Bar Certified Bankruptcy Specialist," Los Angeles Bankruptcy Forum 1993; Frequent Lecturer on Bankruptcy Topics ; Speaker on, "Current Issues in Bankruptcy Litigation From The Ninth Circuit Perspective," National Conference of Bankruptcy Judges, Bankruptcy Litigation Subcommittee Meeting, 1991; Speaker on "Loan Workouts and Collections," Bankers' Compliance Group Seminar, 1992; Speaker on, "Real Estate in Bankruptcy," BEST Seminar on residential real estate transactions for attorneys, 1992; Speaker at Professional Education Seminar at accounting firm of Braverman, Codron & Co. on "What Every Accountant Should Know About Bankruptcies," 1992; Speaker at Professional Education Seminar at Law Firm of McClintock, Weston, Benshoof, Rochefort, Rubalcava & MacCuish on "The Conflict Between Environmental and Bankruptcy Laws: The Topic of the 1990's," 1992; Speaker on "Treatment of Secured Claims in Bankruptcy in California," National Business Institute, 1993; Infocast Seminars on "Lender Liability," 1990, "Bankruptcy Cases and Lending Institutions," and "Chapter 11," Spring and Fall, 1991; South Bay Bar Association on Chapter 7, 1984; Business Investigation Services Meeting at Coopers and Lybrand on "Protecting Professional Fees from Recovery by the Bankruptcy Trustee," 1991; Professional Education Seminar at Poms, Smith, Lande and Rose Professional Corporation on "The Impact of Bankruptcy on Licensors and Licensees of Intellectual Property," 1991; American Radio Relay League (ARRL) Southwest Division Convention on "Amateur Radio Antennas and the Law," 1988. Panelist on "Latest Weapons For The Battlefield: Current Developments," American Bankruptcy Institute—First Annual Bankruptcy Battleground West, 1993. Producer, writer and moderator of 6-show cable series on legal topics entitled "Lex Loci: The Law of the Land," 1982-1983. Chairman: Bankruptcy Rules Subcommittee of Los Angeles Chapter, Federal Rules Committee, Federal Bar Association, 1984-1985. Member: American Radio Relay League, Volunteer Legal Counsel Program, 1981—. Director, Los Angeles Bankruptcy Forum, 1994—. Appointed by Bankruptcy Court to Inaugural Panel of Mediators, Bankruptcy Mediation Program, United States Bankruptcy Court, Central District of California, 1995—. *Member:* Los Angeles County and American Bar Associations; State Bar of California; Financial Lawyers Conference, Los Angeles; Commercial Law League of America; Los Angeles Bankruptcy Forum; Orange County Bankruptcy Forum. (Certified Specialist, Personal and Small Business Bankruptcy Law, The State Bar of California Board of Legal Specialization; Board Certified, Business Bankruptcy Law, Commercial Law League of America Academy of Commercial and Bankruptcy Law Specialists; Board Certified, Business Bankruptcy Law, American Bankruptcy Board of Certification). **PRACTICE AREAS:** Bankruptcy Chapter 11; Bankruptcy Law; Business Reorganization; Secured Transactions Law; Creditor Bankruptcy; Mediation. *Email:* bovitz@ashford.com

**SUSAN MICHELLE SPITZER,** born Montebello, California, November 17, 1957; admitted to bar, 1982, California; U.S. District Court, Northern, Southern, Eastern and Central Districts of California. *Education:* Loyola Marymount University (B.A., cum laude, 1978); Loyola Law School, Los Angeles (J.D., cum laude, 1982). Member: Pi Gamma Mu Social Science Honor Society; St. Thomas More Law Honor Society; Fr. R.A. Vachon Memorial Scholarship Committee. In-House Counsel and Retail Manager, Bi-Rite Quality Pharmacies, Inc., La Habra, California, 1983-1988. Attorney, Tax Law and Estate Planning, Law Offices of William A. Fazio, Inc., La Habra, California, 1983. *Member:* Los Angeles County Bar Association; State Bar of California; Los Angeles Bankruptcy Forum; Orange County Bankruptcy Forum; Financial Lawyers Conference; American Bankruptcy Institute. **PRACTICE AREAS:** Bankruptcy Law; Creditor's Rights. *Email:* bovitz@ashford.com

**NANCY A. CHERNEY,** born San Francisco, California, 1952; admitted to bar, 1977, California; U.S. Court of Appeals, Ninth Circuit; U.S. District Court, Northern District of California. *Education:* Northwestern University; University of California at Berkeley (B.A., with honors, 1973); Golden Gate University (J.D., 1977; L.L.M., Tax, 1982) and Masters in Laws Taxation. Clerk to the Honorable Donald Constine, Superior Court for the City and County of San Francisco, California, 1976. Senior Vice President, General Counsel and Corporate Secretary for Capital Guaranty Corporation, Capital Guaranty Insurance Company and Capital Guaranty Service Corporation, 1986-1995; member of the Board of Directors of Capital Guaranty Insurance Company and Capital Guaranty Service Corporation, 1992-1995; Underwriting Committee Voting member for Capital Guaranty Insurance Company, 1991-1995 and advisory member to the Underwriting Committee, 1986-1990; member of the Senior Management Executive Committee for Capital Guaranty Insurance Company, 1990-1996; General Counsel of USF&G Financial Security Company, 1985-1986; Counsel in the Corporate Section of the General Counsel's Office of Fireman's Fund Insurance Company, 1980-1985; Golden Gate University School of Taxation Teaching Assistant, 1979-1980; Private Practice, 1978-1980; Laventhol and Horwath CPA firm Tax Department, 1977-1978. (Senior Vice President, General Counsel and Corporate Secretary). **PRACTICE AREAS:** Corporate; Municipal Finance. *Email:* ncherney@aol.com

REPRESENTATIVE CLIENTS: Aetna Life Insurance Company; American Airlines; AT&T; Barclays American Business Credit, Inc.; Bombardier Capital, Inc.; C.I.T. Corporation; Capital Guaranty Corporation; Capital Guaranty Insur-

*(This Listing Continued)*

## DIXON & JESSUP LTD., L.L.P., Los Angeles—Continued

ance Company; Chrysler Financial; CIGNA Investments, Inc.; Cinemark; Coldwell Banker/Mark Renner & Associates; Connecticut General Life Insurance Company (a division of CIGNA); Dimatic Die & Tool, Inc.; Douglas County Bank & Trust Co.; FamilyMed, Inc.; Federal Deposit Insurance Corporation (FDIC); First American Bank; First American Savings Co.; First National Bank of Omaha; Gaddis Construction, Inc.; Gallup, Inc.; General Motors Acceptance Corporation; Globe Life & Accident Insurance Co.; Gourmet Popping Corn Company; Home Bank; Hyundai Credit Corp.; MACC Private Equities Inc.; Metropolitan Life Insurance Company; Millard Refrigerated Services, Inc.; MorAmerica Capital Corporation; Mountain Broadcasting; Mutual Life Insurance Company of New York; National Therapeutic Associates, Inc.; Official Creditors' Committee Ancona Bros. Co.; Official Creditors' Committee Lockwood, Inc.; Paccar Financial; Peony Park; Pioneer Hi-Bred International, Inc.; PHI Financial Services, Inc.; Pizza Inn, Inc.; Producers Livestock Marketing Assn.; Producers Livestock Credit Corp.; Prudential Insurance Company of America; Resolution Trust Corporation (RTC); Richman Gordman 1/2 Price Stores, Inc.; Saddleman, Inc.; Sanitary Improvement Districts #23, 114, 206 and 344 of Nebraska; Scoular Grain Company; Sophir Morris Paints; Sperry New Holland; TEK Industries, Inc.; Texas Livestock Marketing Assn.; The Aetna Casualty & Surety Company; The Northwestern Mutual Life Insurance Co.; The Travelers Indemnity Company; TIC/Nebraska Engineering Co.; Trans Texas Amusements, Inc.; Unigard; Vic's Popping Corn Co., Inc.; Wells Fargo Bank; Woodmen of the World Life Insurance Society.

(For Biographical Data on Personnel at Washington, D.C., Omaha, Nebraska, Dallas, Texas and Kuwait, Kuwait, see Professional Biographies at those locations)

---

## DOLAND & GOULD

Established in 1978

10866 WILSHIRE BOULEVARD, SUITE 300
LOS ANGELES, CALIFORNIA 90024
Telephone: 310-478-1000
FAX: 310-446-1363
Email: EUROLEX@AOL.COM

*Domestic and International Business and Real Estate Transactions and Litigation, Insurance and Bankruptcy Law.*

**MICHAEL C. DOLAND,** born New York, N.Y., August 3, 1951; admitted to bar, 1977, California; 1978, District of Columbia. *Education:* Georgetown University (B.A., 1973; J.D., 1977). Author: "Advice to Exporters to the U.S.," I.C.E.-Rome, 1987; "Product Liability Consideration for Exporters to the U.S.," I.C.E-Rome, 1988; "Forms of Payment in International Trade," I.C.E-Rome, 1988. *LANGUAGES:* Italian, French, Spanish.

**HOWARD N. GOULD,** born Omaha, Nebraska, December 27, 1951; admitted to bar, 1977, Nebraska; 1978, California; 1987, U.S. Supreme Court. *Education:* Columbia University (A.B., Physics, 1973); Georgetown University (J.D., 1977). Associate Editor, The Tax Journal, 1977. Real Estate Broker, California, 1981—. *Member:* Beverly Hills and American Bar Associations.

REPRESENTATIVE CLIENTS: Resolution Trust Corporation; Safeco Insurance Co.; Kemper Group; Vuarnet; Credit Lyonnais; Banca Nazionale Del Lavoro.

---

## NORMAN M. DOLIN

Established in 1982

SUITE 2200, 1925 CENTURY PARK EAST (CENTURY CITY)
LOS ANGELES, CALIFORNIA 90067-2723
Telephone: 310-552-9338
Fax: 310-552-1922

*Family Law.*

FIRM PROFILE: *The law offices of Norman M. Dolin exclusively specialize in Family Law and matters related to dissolution of marriage, cohabitation and pre-marital agreements. The firm's clients include prominent persons in entertainment, business and professional executives, sports personalities and their respective spouses. The members of the firm are active participants in continuing legal education symposiums including participation on various panels over the years for the American Academy of Matrimonial Lawyers, the Los Angeles County Bar Association Family Law Section, and the Beverly Hills Bar Association Family Law Section.*

**NORMAN M. DOLIN,** born New York, N.Y., June 10, 1932; admitted to bar, 1960, California. *Education:* University of California at Los Angeles (B.A., 1956); Loyola Law School of Los Angeles (J.D., 1959). Judge Pro Tem, Family Law Department, Los Angeles Superior Court, 1980-1983.

(This Listing Continued)

CAA630B

---

Mediator, Family Law Department, Los Angeles Superior Court, 1980—. *Member:* Beverly Hills (Member, Family Law Section), Los Angeles County (Member, Executive Committee, Family Law Section, 1979-1987 and 1992—) and American (Member, Family Law Section) Bar Associations; State Bar of California. Fellow, American Academy of Matrimonial Lawyers. (Certified Specialist, Family Law, The State Bar of California Board of Legal Specialization). *PRACTICE AREAS:* Family Law.

### ASSOCIATES

**LYNN LANGLEY,** born Newton, Massachusetts, December 13, 1951; admitted to bar, 1986, California, U.S. District Court, Central District of California and U.S. Court of Appeals, Ninth Circuit. *Education:* University of California at Irvine (B.A., magna cum laude, 1982); University of Southern California (J.D., 1985). *Member:* Los Angeles County, Beverly Hills, and American Bar Associations; State Bar of California. *PRACTICE AREAS:* Family Law.

**ANI M. GARIKIAN,** born Los Angeles, California, August 14, 1965; admitted to bar, 1989, California. *Education:* University of California at Los Angeles (B.A., 1986); Loyola Law School (J.D., 1989). *Member:* Los Angeles County, Beverly Hills and American (Member, Section on Family Law) Bar Associations; State Bar of California. *LANGUAGES:* Armenian. *PRACTICE AREAS:* Family Law.

---

## DOLLE AND DOLLE

A PROFESSIONAL CORPORATION

11766 WILSHIRE BOULEVARD, SUITE 1450
LOS ANGELES, CALIFORNIA 90025
Telephone: 310-478-7516
Fax: 310-478-2780

*Condemnation, Inverse Condemnation, Zoning and Land Use.*

FIRM PROFILE: *Hodge L. Dolle, Jr. has been chief trial counsel in major jury trials for owners and governmental bodies for over 30 years. The trials have included all types of commercial and residential properties in California, Texas and Nevada. He has developed a subspecialty involving special properties such as churches, schools and airports. He has also been instrumental in the creation of legislation to benefit his clients. Lawrence H. Thompson has worked closely with Mr. Dolle in the areas of eminent domain, inverse condemnation and land use. Mr. Thompson has obtained successful results in compensation cases involving all types of properties from vacant properties with commercial or residential development potential, to fully developed special use properties such as churches and schools. He also continues to be the firm's specialist on the issue of loss of goodwill and the California Environmental Quality Act. Thomas M. Garcin has participated in and conducted major valuation trials involving commercial properties in Southern California. The properties have included regional shopping centers, auto malls, salvage yards, high schools, colleges, strip malls, airport properties, banks and savings and loans. Additionally, in connection with real property acquisition and valuation projects, he has extensive knowledge of all aspects of personal property valuation.*

**HODGE L. DOLLE, JR.,** born 1934; admitted to bar, 1962, California and U.S. District Court, Central District of California; 1965, U.S. Supreme Court. *Education:* University of Southern California (B.S., 1956; J.D., 1961). Phi Delta Phi (Province President, Province XI, 1968-1975). Director, Legion Lex, 1966-1972; President, 1973-1974. Author: "Impending Condemnation and Stultification of Use," American Bar Association Real Property, Probate and Trust Journal, Vol. 3, No. 1, Spring, 1968; "Inverse Condemnation: The Property Owners Breach of Promise Remedy," Real Estate Review, Fall, 1979. *Member:* Los Angeles County (Member, 1967— and Chairman, 1979-1980, Committee on Condemnation Law) and American (Member: Condemnation Law Committee, Section on Real Property, Probate and Trust Law, 1967—; Chairman, Section of Litigation, 1984-1986; Member, Committee on Condemnation, Zoning and Property Use Litigation, 1979—) Bar Associations; State Bar of California (Member, Committee on Condemnation, 1988-1993). Fellow, American College of Trial Lawyers. *PRACTICE AREAS:* Condemnation Law; Inverse Condemnation Law; Zoning and Land Use Law.

**LAWRENCE H. THOMPSON,** born Palo Alto, California, August 13, 1947; admitted to bar, 1975, California. *Education:* University of California at Davis (B.A., 1969); University of California at Los Angeles (J.D., 1975). *Member:* Los Angeles County and American Bar Associations. *PRACTICE AREAS:* Condemnation Law; Inverse Condemnation Law; Zoning and Land Use Law.

(This Listing Continued)

## PROFESSIONAL BIOGRAPHIES

**THOMAS M. GARCIN,** born Glendale, California, January 21, 1962; admitted to bar, 1988, California. *Education:* University of Southern California (B.S., 1984); Loyola University of Los Angeles (J.D., 1987). Phi Alpha Delta (Vice Justice, 1985-1986). President, Business Law and Litigation Society, 1986-1987. *Member:* Los Angeles County and American (Member, Litigation Section) Bar Associations; State Bar of California. **PRACTICE AREAS:** Condemnation Law; Inverse Condemnation Law; Zoning and Land Use Law.

*OF COUNSEL*

**HODGE L. DOLLE** (1908-1989).

---

## DOLMAN & SAMUELS

A Partnership of Professional Corporations

*Established in 1987*

**SUITE 2300, 1900 AVENUE OF THE STARS**
**LOS ANGELES, CALIFORNIA 90067**
Telephone: 310-201-0777
Telecopier: 310-556-1346

*Corporation, Real Property, Estate Planning, Probate, State and Federal Tax Law. Administrative, Commercial Law.*

**MAURICE H. DOLMAN, (P.C.),** born New York, N.Y., October 15, 1913; admitted to bar, 1954, California. *Education:* University of California at Los Angeles (B.S., 1937); Loyola University of Los Angeles (J.D., 1953). Lecturer, Annual Meeting of American Association of Attorney/CPA's-"Protecting your Assets in a Litigious Society," 1991. *Member:* Beverly Hills, Los Angeles County and American Bar Associations; The State Bar of California; California Association of Attorney-Certified Public Accountants; California Society of Certified Public Accountants. (Certified Specialist, Taxation Law, The State Bar of California Board of Legal Specialization). **PRACTICE AREAS:** Tax Law; Probate Law; Trust Law; Estate Planning.

**S. ZACHARY SAMUELS, (P.C.),** born Los Angeles, California, January 7, 1945; admitted to bar, 1969, California; 1974, U.S. Tax Court. *Education:* University of California at Los Angeles (B.S., 1965; M.B.A., 1966); University of Southern California (J.D., 1969). Certified Public Accountant, California, 1971. Author, "Special Amortization Elections Under the Internal Revenue Code," Prentiss Hall Tax Ideas, 1974. Co-Author: "Explanation of Tax Reform Act of 1976." Los Angeles County Bar Association, 1976; "How to Handle the Deduction for Legal Fees," Prentice Hall Tax Ideas, 1977. Lecturer, California Continuing Education of the Bar, 1993. *Member:* Los Angeles County Bar Association; State Bar of California; California Association of Attorney-Certified Public Accountants. **PRACTICE AREAS:** Tax Law; Probate Law; Trust Law; Estate Planning; Real Estate; Corporate.

REPRESENTATIVE CLIENTS: Paper Coating Co.; Karen Kane, Inc.; Berger Specialty Co.
REFERENCE: 1st Business Bank, Los Angeles.

---

## LAW OFFICES OF
## KAREN PHILLIPS DONAHOE

**12100 WILSHIRE BOULEVARD**
**16TH FLOOR**
**LOS ANGELES, CALIFORNIA 90025**
Telephone: 310-442-1488
Fax: 310-442-1490

*General Civil Litigation in all State and Federal Courts.*

**KAREN PHILLIPS DONAHOE,** born Madison, Tennessee, October 21, 1955; admitted to bar, 1980, California. *Education:* University of California at Santa Barbara (B.A., 1977); Hastings College of Law, University of California (J.D., 1980). **PRACTICE AREAS:** Family Law; Divorce Law; Custody Law; Pre-Nuptial Agreements.

---

## DONAHUE & MESEREAU

A Partnership including a Professional Corporation

*1900 AVENUE OF THE STARS*
**SUITE 2700**
**LOS ANGELES, CALIFORNIA 90067**
Telephone: 310-277-1441
Telecopier: 310-277-2888
Email: SECORPLAW@AWOL.com

*General and International Business and Corporate Matters. Securities Transactions and Regulations. Investment Banking, Venture Capital, Mergers and Acquisitions, Franchising. Securities Litigation and Arbitration. Business Litigation in State and Federal Courts. Criminal Defense (State and Federal).*

**MICHAEL D. DONAHUE,** born Corpus Christi, Texas, April 1, 1944; admitted to bar, 1969, Nebraska; 1970, Colorado; 1972, District of Columbia; 1973, California. *Education:* University of Notre Dame (B.A., 1966); University of Colorado (J.D., 1969). Staff Attorney, U.S. Securities and Exchange Commission, Washington, D.C., 1969-1972; Chief, Branch of Enforcement, U.S. Securities and Exchange Commission, Los Angeles Region, 1973-1976. Chairman, Education Committee, 1984-1985; President-Elect, 1984-1985; President, 1985-1987, Los Angeles Chapter, Real Estate Securities and Syndication Institute. Member, Board of Directors, Los Angeles Chapter, International Association for Financial Planning, 1986-1988. Chairman, UCLA-RESSI Real Estate Syndication Seminar, 1984. Lecturer, Continuing Education of the Bar, 1986. Member, Arbitration Panel, National Association of Securities Dealers, Inc., 1982—. President, California Association for Financial Planning, 1988-1989. Member, Board of Directors, Los Angeles Venture Association, 1992—. Member: National Society of Compliance Professionals. Chairman: The 1994 Investment Capital Conference, The 1995 Investment Capital Conference; The 1996 Investment Capital Conference. *Member:* Los Angeles County (Member, Business Law Section) and American (Member, Business Law Section, International Law and Practice Section) Bar Associations; State Bar of California. **SPECIAL AGENCIES:** United States Securities Exchange Commission; State Securities Administrators; New York Stock Exchange; American Stock Exchange; National Association of Securities Dealers, Inc. **PRACTICE AREAS:** Securities; General Business and Corporate; Investment Banking and Venture Capital; Securities Litigation and Arbitration.

**THOMAS A. MESEREAU, JR. (PROFESSIONAL CORPORATION),** born West Point, New York, July 1, 1950; admitted to bar, 1979, California; 1980, District of Columbia. *Education:* Harvard University (B.A., cum laude, 1973); London School of Economics, London, England (M.Sc., 1975); University of California, Hastings College of the Law (J.D., 1979). Former Member, Inns of Court. Deputy District Attorney, Orange County, California, 1981-1982. Judge Pro-Tem, Beverly Hills Municipal Court, 1990—. *Member:* State Bar of California; Board of Governors, Italian American Lawyers Association; California Attorneys for Criminal Justice. **PRACTICE AREAS:** Complex Civil Litigation; Criminal; Healthcare Law.

**DAVE LENNY,** born St. Louis, Missouri, September 6, 1950; admitted to bar, 1975, District of Columbia, 1984, New York and California; 1985, U.S. District Court, Central District of California; 1990, U.S. Tax Court. *Education:* University of Illinois (B.A., magna cum laude, 1972); Columbia University (J.D., 1975). Author: "The Case for Funding Citizen Participation on the Administrative Process," American Bar Association Administrative Law Review, 1976; "Copyright Problems of a Network/Home Cable Record Selection and Playing System," Rutgers Journal of Computers and the Law, 1975. Staff Attorney, U.S. Department of Agriculture, Washington, D.C., 1977. *Member:* District of Columbia Bar; New York State Bar Association; State Bar of California. **SPECIAL AGENCIES:** United States Department of Agriculture. **REPORTED CASES:** National Union Fire Insurance Company of Pittsburgh v. Stites Professional Law Corporation (Cal. App. 2nd Dist. 1991) 235 Cal. App. 3d 1718 1 Cal. Rptr. 2d 570. **PRACTICE AREAS:** Securities Arbitration and Litigation; Insurance Litigation; Bankruptcy Litigation; Real Estate Litigation; Attorney Malpractice Litigation.

**ASHER M. LEIDS,** born New York, N.Y., November 12, 1961; admitted to bar, 1988, California. *Education:* State University of New York at Binghamton (B.A., with honors, 1983); Georgetown University Law School (J.D., cum laude, 1986). Pi Sigma Alpha. Judicial Law Clerk to The Honorable Joseph J. Farnan, Jr., District of Delaware. Member, Los Angeles Venture Association, 1994—. *Member:* State Bar of California; American Bar Association (Member, Business Law Section). **PRACTICE AREAS:** Securities; Corporate Finance; Investment Banking and Venture Capital; Merg-

*(This Listing Continued)*

DONAHUE & MESEREAU, Los Angeles—Continued

ers and Acquisitions; Franchise Offerings; General and International Business; Corporate Law.

**SUSAN H. TREGUB,** born Washington, D.C., October 17, 1967; admitted to bar, 1993, California. *Education:* University of Southern California (B.A., cum laude, with honors, 1989); Loyola Marymount University (J.D., 1992). *Member:* Los Angeles County Bar Association; State Bar of California. **PRACTICE AREAS:** Securities Arbitration; Business Law; Corporate Law.

## DONFELD, KELLEY & ROLLMAN

A Partnership including a Professional Corporation

*Established in 1985*

**SUITE 1245, 11845 WEST OLYMPIC BOULEVARD
LOS ANGELES, CALIFORNIA 90064**

Telephone: 310-312-8080
Telecopier: 310-312-8014

*Real Estate, Acquisitions, Leasing, Work-outs and Land Use, Partnership Formations, Corporations, Unfair Competition and Trade Regulation, General Business and Business Litigation, Construction and Construction Defect Defense, Employer/Employee Dispute Resolution, Family Law. General Civil Trial and Appellate Practice.*

**JEFFREY E. DONFELD, (A PROFESSIONAL CORPORATION),** born Brooklyn, New York, June 9, 1943; admitted to bar, 1969, California. *Education:* University of California at Los Angeles (A.B., with honors in political science, 1965); Boalt Hall School of Law, University of California (J.D., 1968). Member, Moot Court Board. Staff Assistant to the President of the United States, 1969-1971. Assistant Director, White House Special Action Office for Drug Abuse Prevention, 1971-1973. *Member:* Century City (Member, Real Property Section) and Los Angeles County (Member, Real Property Section) Bar Associations; State Bar of California. **PRACTICE AREAS:** Real Estate Acquisitions; Leasing; Workouts; Land Use; Partnership Formations; Business Acquisitions.

**PAUL M. KELLEY,** born Newark, New Jersey, May 22, 1952; admitted to bar, 1979, California. *Education:* Trinity College (B.A., 1975); McGeorge College of Law, University of the Pacific (J.D., cum laude, 1978). Member, Traynor Society. Recipient, American Jurisprudence Award in Torts. Staff Writer, 1976-1977 and Associate Comment Editor, 1977-1978, Pacific Law Journal. *Member:* Los Angeles County Bar Association; State Bar of California. **PRACTICE AREAS:** Business Litigation; Unfair Competition and Trade Regulation; Real Property Litigation; Construction Defect Defense; Employer/Employee Dispute Resolution.

**FREDRIC A. ROLLMAN,** born Orange, New Jersey, September 12, 1955; admitted to bar, 1980, California. *Education:* Wharton School, University of Pennsylvania (B.S., cum laude, 1977); Duke University (J.D., 1980). Co-Author: "Restrictive Covenants," Acquisitions of Closely-Held Companies, pp. 23-36, 1982. *Member:* Century City and Los Angeles County (Member, Sections on: Business and Corporations Law; Real Estate) Bar Associations; State Bar of California. **PRACTICE AREAS:** Real Estate; General Business Transactions.

---

**AMY SEMMEL,** born Passaic, New Jersey, May 17, 1957; admitted to bar, 1984, California. *Education:* University of Pennsylvania (B.A., 1980); Boalt Hall School of Law, University of California (J.D., 1984). Phi Beta Kappa; Psi Chi. Articles Editor, Ecology Law Quarterly, 1984. Author: "Ruckelshaus v. Sierra Club, A Misinterpretation of the Clean Air Act's Attorneys Fees Provisions," 12 Ecology Law Quarterly 399, 1985. *Member:* Beverly Hills and Los Angeles County Bar Associations; State Bar of California; Women Lawyers Association. **LANGUAGES:** Spanish. **PRACTICE AREAS:** Business Litigation; Employer/Employee Dispute Resolution; Family Law; Real Property Litigation.

REFERENCE: Marathon National Bank.

## DONIGER & FETTER

**606 SOUTH OLIVE STREET, SUITE 530
LOS ANGELES, CALIFORNIA 90014**

Telephone: 213-488-7733
Facsimile: 213-488-7734

*General Civil Trial and Appellate Practice, Entertainment and General Business Litigation.*

### MEMBERS OF FIRM

**THOMAS DONIGER,** born Los Angeles, California, July 29, 1945; admitted to bar, 1977, California. *Education:* University of California at Berkeley; University of California at Los Angeles (B.A., 1972); University of Southern California (J.D., 1977). Order of the Coif. Member, Southern California Law Review, 1976-1977. *Member:* Los Angeles County Bar Association; State Bar of California. **PRACTICE AREAS:** Business Litigation; Entertainment Litigation; Civil Appeals.

**HENRY DAVID FETTER,** born New York, N.Y., July 18, 1949; admitted to bar, 1977, California; 1980, New York. *Education:* Harvard University (A.B., magna cum laude, 1971; J.D., cum laude, 1977); University of California at Berkeley (M.A., 1974). Recipient, National First Prize, Nathan Burkan Memorial Competition, 1977. Author: "Copyright Revision and the Preemption of State 'Misappropriation' Law," 25 Bulletin of the Copyright Society of the U.S.A. 367, June, 1978. *Member:* Los Angeles County Bar Association; State Bar of California. **PRACTICE AREAS:** Business Litigation; Entertainment Litigation; Copyright Law.

## DONNELLY, CLARK, CHASE & SMILAND

**LOS ANGELES, CALIFORNIA**

(See Smiland & Khachigian)

## LAW OFFICES OF JAMES M. DONOVAN

*Established in 1975*

**515 SOUTH FIGUEROA STREET, SUITE 1000
LOS ANGELES, CALIFORNIA 90071-3327**

Telephone: 213-629-4861
Telecopier: 213-689-8784
Email: tdolaw@aol.com

*General Commercial Practice. Business, International Business, Corporate, Securities, Real Estate, Labor, Agricultural, Estate Planning, Trust, Probate, Tax, State and Federal Criminal Trials, Entertainment, Advertising, Publishing and Family Law, Life Insurance, Commercial Casualty Insurance and Business Litigation.*

**JAMES M. DONOVAN,** born Albany, New York, November 6, 1943; admitted to bar, 1969, Florida; 1972, Minnesota; 1975, California; 1985, U.S. District Court, Central District of California. *Education:* Catholic University of America (B.A., 1966); University of Miami (J.D., 1969). Phi Delta Phi. Attorney-Advisor, Division of Corporation Finance, Securities and Exchange Commission, 1969-1972. Co-Author: "Resort Condominiums," P.L.I., 1973; *The Dow Jones-Irwin Handbook for Entertainers and their Professional Advisors,* 1987. *Member:* Los Angeles County, Tulare County, Hennepin County, Minnesota State and American Bar Associations; The Florida Bar; State Bar of California.

### ASSOCIATES

**MARK D. MAISONNEUVE,** born Oklahoma City, Oklahoma, April 28, 1952; admitted to bar, 1984, California; 1985, Colorado and U.S. District Court, Central District of California. *Education:* Colorado School of Mines (B.S., Geo.Eng., 1974); Southwestern University School of Law (J.D., 1982). *Member:* Beverly Hills, Los Angeles County, Colorado and American Bar Associations; State Bar of California.

**MICHAEL J. GLENN,** born Covina, California, November 29, 1954; admitted to bar, 1979, California and U.S. District Court, Central District of California; 1980, U.S. Court of Appeals, Ninth Circuit. *Education:* University of Southern California (B.S., summa cum laude, 1976; J.D., 1979). Phi Beta Kappa; Phi Kappa Phi. Staff Member, 1977-1978 and Executive

*(This Listing Continued)*

Managing Editor, 1978-1979, Southern California Law Review. Judge Pro Tem, Los Angeles Judicial District, 1995—. *Member:* Los Angeles County Bar Association; State Bar of California.

*OF COUNSEL*

**LOUIS LAROSE** (1914-1986).

**ROBERT L. FAIRMAN,** born Kansas City, Missouri, July 9, 1935; admitted to bar, 1963, California; U.S. District Court, Central, Eastern and Southern Districts of California; U.S. Court of Appeals, Ninth Circuit. *Education:* University of Southern California (A.B., 1957; LL.B., 1960). Phi Delta Phi. Deputy City Attorney, City of Los Angeles, 1963-1964. Arbitrator, Los Angeles Superior Court, 1978—. Judge Pro Tem, Los Angeles Municipal Court, 1974—. *Member:* Los Angeles County (Member: Trial Lawyer Section; Family Law Section; Insurance Programs Committee, 1982-1989; Co-Chair, 1983-1989) and American (Member, Sections on: Litigation; Insurance, Negligence and Compensation Law) Bar Associations; The State Bar of California; Conference of Insurance Counsel. (Also Member, Norton & Fairman). *PRACTICE AREAS:* Insurance Law; Litigation.

**EGON DUMLER,** born Berlin, Germany, October 14, 1929; admitted to bar, 1956, New York (Not admitted in California). *Education:* City College of New York (B.S., 1951); New York University School of Law (J.D., cum laude, 1956). Phi Delta Phi. *Member:* The Association of the Bar of the City of New York; New York State and American Bar Associations. (Also Member of Dumler & Giroux, New York). *PRACTICE AREAS:* Entertainment Law; Motion Picture Law; Theater Law; Television Law; Advertising Law; Publishing Law.

**RICHARD S. MISSAN,** born New Haven, Connecticut, October 5, 1933; admitted to bar, 1959, New York; 1979, U.S. District Court, Southern and Eastern Districts of New York (Not admitted in California). *Education:* Yale University (B.A., 1955; J.D., 1958). Revision Author, "Corporations," New York Practice Guide (Business and Commercial) Matthew Bender & Co., 1992—. Special Professor of Law, Hofstra University School of Law, 1988—. Vice President and General Counsel, Avis, Inc., 1987-1988. Member, Panel of Arbitrators, American Arbitration Association. *Member:* The Association of the Bar of the City of New York (Member: Committee on Corrections, 1979—; Committee on Juvenile Justice, 1983-1987; Committee on Atomic Energy, 1968-1971; Committee on Municipal Affairs, 1965-1968; Committee on Housing and Urban Development, 1965-1967); New York State and American Bar Associations. (Also practising individually at New York, New York and Of Counsel to Fieldman Berman & Hay at the same address). *PRACTICE AREAS:* Corporate Law; Securities Law; Litigation; Business Law.

**PETER R. BIERSTEDT,** born Rhinebeck, New York, January 2, 1943; admitted to bar, 1969, New York; 1976, California; 1973, U.S. Supreme Court, U.S. District Court, Southern and Eastern Districts of New York and U.S. Court of Appeals, Second Circuit. *Education:* Columbia University (A.B., 1965; J.D., cum laude, 1969). Guest Lecturer: "MATRIMONIAL LAW," University of California At Riverside, 1977-1978.; "Producing Motion Pictures: Making a Studio Deal," University of Southern California, 1986; "Wide Release of a Studio Motion Picture, Limited Release of an Independent Distributor's Motion Picture and the Acquisition of a Completed Motion Picture by a Distribution Company," University of California at Los Angeles, 1987; "Foreign Sales Agents," Intellectual Property and Unfair Competition Section of the Los Angeles County Bar Associations, 1989. *Member:* New York State Bar Association; State Bar of California; Academy of Motion Picture Arts and Sciences (Executive Branch). *PRACTICE AREAS:* Entertainment Industry Contracts.

**MARTIN HABDANK,** born Schweinfurt, West Germany, September 1, 1928; admitted to bar, 1959, Munich, West Germany (Not admitted in the United States). *Education:* University of Washington (M.Econ., 1959); Universities of Munich and Wurzburg (L.L.B., Dr. Jur., 1949 - 1957). (Also Member of Habdank, Gerhart and Bauman, Rechtsanwalte, Munich, West Germany). *PRACTICE AREAS:* International Business Law.

**GRAHAM L. STERLING, III,** born Los Angeles, California, March 19, 1929; admitted to bar, 1957, California. *Education:* Occidental College (B.A., 1952); Stanford University (J.D., 1956); California State University at San Luis Obispo (M.S., 1977). Member, Chancery Club. Contributing Author: "Federal Securities Acts Amendments of 1964," University of California Continuing Education of the Bar Series. Author: "Study Outline of Securities Acts Amendments of 1964: Self-Regulation and the National Association of Securities Dealers," American Law Institute-American Bar Association. *Member:* Los Angeles County (Member: Real Property Law Committee, 1961-1966; Executive Committee, 1967-1969; Member, 1961-1968 and Chairman, 1964-1966, Committee on Corporations, Business and Corporation Law Section; Alternate Delegate, Conference of State Bar Delegates, 1965), Federal and American (Member: Advisory Committee on Briefing Conference on Security Laws and Regulations, 1964-1965; Committee on Federal Regulation of Securities, 1963-1972) Bar Associations; State Bar of California (Member, Committee on Corporations, 1961-1969); American Law Institute. *PRACTICE AREAS:* Securities Law; Corporate Law.

**CAROL LYNN AKIYAMA,** born Chicago, Illinois, December 5, 1946; admitted to bar, 1973, California; 1974, U.S. District Court, Central District of California. *Education:* University of Southern California (B.A., magna cum laude, Economics, 1968); (J.D., 1971). Phi Beta Kappa; Phi Kappa Phi; Delta Phi Kappa. Listed in: Who's Who in the West; Who's Who in Entertainment and Who's Who of Emerging Leaders in America. Field Attorney, National Labor Relations Board, Region 21, 1971-1975. Attorney, Labor Relations and Legal Affairs, American Broadcasting Company, 1975-1979. Labor Counsel, Edison Company, Southern California, 1980-1981. Assistant General Attorney, CBS Inc., 1981-1982. Senior Vice President, Alliance of Motion Picture and Television Producers, 1982-1988. *Member:* Los Angeles County (Former Chair of Labor Law Section, Member of Executive Committee, Labor Law Section) Bar Association; State Bar of California. *LANGUAGES:* Spanish. *PRACTICE AREAS:* Labor Law; Entertainment Law.

**STEPHEN M. LOSH,** born Detroit, Michigan, May 11, 1939; admitted to bar, 1964, Michigan and U.S. District Court, Eastern and Southern Districts of Michigan; 1985, U.S. Court of Appeals, Sixth Circuit; 1987, California. *Education:* University of Michigan (B.A., 1960; J.D., 1963). Tau Epsilon Rho. Member: Macomb County Bar Association, 1970-1987; Oakland County Bar Association, 1982-1987; The Association of Trial Lawyers of America, 1978-1982. *Member:* Los Angeles County and American Bar Associations; State Bar of California; State Bar of Michigan. *PRACTICE AREAS:* Litigation.

**RICHARD J. KELLUM,** born Los Angeles, California, February 13, 1953; admitted to bar, 1979, California. *Education:* University of Southern California (B.A., 1976); Loyola University of Los Angeles (J.D., 1979). Phi Beta Kappa. Member, Loyola Law Review, 1976-1977. *Member:* Los Angeles County Bar Association; State Bar of California. (Also Associate of Norton & Fairman). *PRACTICE AREAS:* Litigation.

**JOHN S. PRESTON,** born Springfield, Massachusetts, April 16, 1947; admitted to bar, 1972, Wisconsin and U.S. District Court, Western District of Wisconsin; 1978, Washington and U.S. District Court, Southern District of Washington; 1979, California and U.S. District Court, Southern District of California. *Education:* Syracuse University (B.A., 1969); University of Wisconsin (J.D., 1972). Author: "Environmental Impact of All-Terrain Vehicles," Wisconsin Law Review 477, 1974. Lecturer: "Environmental Law," University of Wisconsin Continuing Education of the Bar, 1974-1975. *Member:* The State Bar of California; Washington State Bar Association; State Bar of Wisconsin. *PRACTICE AREAS:* Business Law; International Law.

**WALT D. MAHAFFA,** born New London, Connecticut, October 29, 1954; admitted to bar, 1980, California and U.S. District Court, Central District of California. *Education:* Loyola University of Los Angeles (B.A., 1976); Pepperdine University (J.D., 1979). Phi Alpha Delta. *Member:* Orange County and American Bar Associations; The State Bar of California. (Also Of Counsel to Callahan & Gauntlett, Irvine, California). *PRACTICE AREAS:* Litigation; Business Law; Real Estate Law.

**BABAK SOTOODEH,** born Tehran, Iran, June 16, 1958; admitted to bar, 1984, California; 1985, U.S. District Court, Southern District of California. *Education:* University of Geneva, Switzerland; University of California at Los Angeles; California State University at Fullerton (B.A., Economics, 1981); University of California at Davis (J.D.,1984). Beta Gamma Sigma. *Member:* State Bar of California; American Bar Association. (Also Member of Sotoodeh & Ghiassi, Santa Ana, California). *LANGUAGES:* French and Persian. *PRACTICE AREAS:* Immigration Law.

**RICHARD D. SABA,** born Sarasota, Florida, September 25, 1948; admitted to bar, 1974, Florida; 1978, Colorado (Not admitted in California). *Education:* University of Florida (B.S.B.A., 1970; J.D., 1973). Phi Delta Phi. Chief Deputy District Attorney, Moffat County, Colorado, 1977-1979. *Member:* Sarasota County Bar Association; The Florida Bar (Member, Section on Real Property, Probate and Trust Law). (Also practicing individually, Sarasota, Florida). *PRACTICE AREAS:* Real Estate Law; Litigation; Corporate Law.

*(This Listing Continued)*

## LAW OFFICES OF JAMES M. DONOVAN, Los Angeles—Continued

**HOWARD M. BARTNOF,** born Los Angeles, California, April 9, 1949; admitted to bar, 1975, California and U.S. District Court, Central District of California. *Education:* California State University at Northridge (B.S., 1971); Southwestern University (J.D., 1974). Certified Public Accountant, California, 1976. *Member:* State Bar of California (Member, Estate Planning Trust and Probate Section); California Society of Certified Public Accountants (President, 1981; Board of Directors, 1981-1986); American Institute of Certified Public Accounts. **PRACTICE AREAS:** Probate Law; Estate Planning; Trust Law.

REFERENCE: Bank of California, Los Angeles Main Office.

## DONOVAN LEISURE NEWTON & IRVINE

SUITE 4100, 333 SOUTH GRAND AVENUE
**LOS ANGELES, CALIFORNIA 90071**
Telephone: 213-253-4000
Cable Address: "Donlard, L.A."
Telecopier: 213-617-2368; 213-617-3246

*New York, New York Office:* 30 Rockefeller Plaza. Telephone: 212-632-3000. Cable Address: "Donlard, N.Y." Telecopiers: 212-632-3315; 212-632-3321; 212-632-3322.
*Paris, France Office:* 130, rue du Faubourg Saint-Honoré, 75008 Paris. Telephone: 011-33-01-53-93-77-00. Telecopier: 011-33-01-42-56-08-06.
*Palm Beach, Florida Office:* 450 Royal Palm Way, Suite 450, 33480. Telephone: 561-833-1040. Telecopier: 561-835-8511.

*General Practice.*

### MEMBERS OF FIRM

**MICHAEL C. COHEN,** born St. Louis, Missouri, February 5, 1947; admitted to bar, 1972, California. *Education:* University of California at Los Angeles (B.A., 1969); Loyola University of School of Law of Los Angeles (J.D., magna cum laude, 1972). Alpha Sigma Nu. Note Editor, Loyola University of Los Angeles Law Review, 1971-1972. *Member:* Beverly Hills, Los Angeles and American (Chairman, Project and Corporate Financings and Transactions Subcommittee, Gaming Committee, Business Law Section) Bar Associations; The State Bar of California. *Email:* mccohen@ix.netcom.com

**JAMES B. HICKS,** born Los Angeles, California, March 28, 1959; admitted to bar, 1982, California; 1988, U.S. Supreme Court. *Education:* Yale University (B.A., magna cum laude, 1978; M.A., with honors, 1978); Harvard University (M.B.A., 1982; J.D., cum laude, 1982). Editor, Harvard Law Review, 1980-1982. Selected Publications: "Piercing the Corporate Law Veil: The Alter Ego Doctrine Under Federal Common Law," 95 Harvard Law Review 853 (1982), adopted as Ninth Circuit rule of decision in *Board of Trustees v. Valley Cabinet & Mfg. Co.,* 877 F.2d 769, 774 (9th Cir. 1989); "The Politics of Legal Reform: Egyptian Courts in the Sudan 1821-1854," in N.J. Coulson (ed.), *Studies in Islamic Law* (Cambridge University Press, in press); "Expert Witnesses and Disqualification Motions: The Do's and Don't's," in CEB Civil Litigtion Reporter (October 1996-Co-author). *Member:* Los Angeles County (Member: Moot Court Committee, 1987-1989; Bench-Bar-Media Committee, 1985—) and American (Member: Appellate Committee, 1991—; Labor Law Committee, 1991—; Intellectual Property Committee, 1991—; Business Torts Committee, 1992—) Bar Associations; State Bar of California (Chairman, California Supreme Court Historical Society Subcommittee, 1987-1988; Member, Committee on Appellate Courts, 1994—); Los Angeles Conservancy (Member, Legal Committee, 1992—). **PRACTICE AREAS:** Commercial Litigation; Intellectual Property; Labor; Securities Litigation; Unfair Competition.

**KATHY A. JORRIE,** born Los Angeles, California, December 24, 1959; admitted to bar, 1985, California. *Education:* University of California, Los Angeles (B.A., cum laude, 1982); Hastings College of the Law, University of California (J.D., 1985). Publication: "Expert Witnesses and Disqualification Motions: The Do's and Don't's," in CEB Civil Litigation Reporter (October, 1996-Co-author). *Member:* Los Angeles County and American (Member, Sections on Litigation and Intellectual Property) Bar Associations; State Bar of California.

**HOWARD B. SOLOWAY,** born Washington, D.C., October 8, 1946; admitted to bar, 1972, California; 1976, U.S. Court of Appeals, Ninth Circuit; 1982, U.S. Supreme Court. *Education:* University of California at Berkeley (A.B., 1968); Harvard Law School (J.D., 1971). Law Clerk for U.S. District Court Judge William P. Gray, 1971-1972. *Member:* The State Bar of California.

### RESIDENT ASSOCIATES

**SHOSHANA B. BOTNICK,** born Chicago, Illinois, October 31, 1961; admitted to bar, 1987, Illinois; 1989, California. *Education:* Barnard College (B.A., cum laude, 1983); George Washington University Law Center (J.D., 1986). *Member:* Beverly Hills, Los Angeles County and Illinois State Bar Associations; State Bar of California. **LANGUAGES:** Hebrew. **PRACTICE AREAS:** Corporate; Real Estate.

**CHRISTIE GAUMER,** born Longview, Texas, 1962; admitted to bar, 1990, California; 1991, Texas. *Education:* University of Texas (B.B.A., 1984; J.D., with honors, 1990). Member, Board of Advocates for Outstanding Participation in Moot Court of Mock Trial. **PRACTICE AREAS:** Commercial Litigation; Business Litigation; Trademark and Copyright Law.

**MITHRA SHEYBANI,** born Tehran, Iran, November 20, 1961; admitted to bar, 1988, California. *Education:* Mills College (B.A., 1983); American College in Paris; Loyola Law School (J.D., 1987). Member and Note and Comment Editor, Loyola of Los Angeles International and Comparative Law Journal, 1985-1987. Author: "Cultural Defense: One Person's Culture is Another's Crime," Loyola of Los Angeles International and Comparative Law Journal, Vol. 9, 1987. *Member:* State Bar of California.

### RESIDENT COUNSEL

**NORMAN A. JENKINS, III,** born Philadelphia, Pennsylvania, December 24, 1950; admitted to bar, 1978, New York (Not admitted in California). *Education:* Williams College (B.A., 1973); New York University School of Law (J.D., 1977). Field Attorney, National Labor Relations Board, Region 29, 1977-1982. Labor Relations Counsel, National Football League Management, 1982-1990.

(For Biographical data of all partners, See Professional Biographies at New York, N.Y.).

## LAW OFFICES OF DONOVAN & SAPIENZA

**LOS ANGELES, CALIFORNIA**

(See Santa Monica)

*Products Liability, Insurance Law, Insurance Broker and Agent Errors and Omissions, Alternative Dispute Resolution, Mediation, Tort Defense, Contractor and Construction Litigation, Entertainment Industry Transactions and Dispute Resolution, Real Estate Litigation and Personal Injury Law.*

## DORAIS & WHEAT

A PROFESSIONAL LAW CORPORATION
*Established in 1982*

11726 SAN VICENTE BOULEVARD, SUITE 550
**LOS ANGELES, CALIFORNIA 90049**
Telephone: 310-826-4400
FAX: 310-820-7397

*Insurance Corporate, Business and Regulatory Law. Employee Benefit Law. Litigation. Uniform Commercial Code Transactions.*

**CLAUDE J. DORAIS,** born Edmonton, Alberta, Canada, May 19, 1949; admitted to bar, 1974, California and U.S. District Court, Central District of California; 1977, U.S. District Court, Northern District of California; 1979, U.S. Supreme Court; 1981, U.S. Court of Appeals, Ninth Circuit. *Education:* University of California (A.B., 1971; J.D., 1974). *Member:* Los Angeles County and Beverly Hills Bar Associations; State Bar of California; Conference of Insurance Counsel; Federation of Regulatory Counsel.

**SHELDON R. EMMER,** born Los Angeles, California, July 28, 1952; admitted to bar, 1981, California; U.S. District Court, Central and Southern Districts of California; U.S. Court of Appeals, Ninth Circuit; 1982, U.S. Tax Court; 1989, U.S. Supreme Court; 1990, District of Columbia. *Education:* Claremont McKenna College (B.A., 1974); California State University, Northridge (M.A., 1989); La Verne College of Law (J.D., 1981). Phi Alpha Theta. Author: "Health Care Reform: One Aspect of California's Head Start," VI, 3 Federation of Regulatory Counsel Quarterly Journal of Insurance Law and Regulation 1, 1994; "Age Discrimination in Private Pension Plans," 9 San Fernando Valley Law Review 67, 1981. *Member:* Los

*(This Listing Continued)*

Angeles County Bar Association; State Bar of California; District of Columbia Bar. *PRACTICE AREAS:* Employment Benefits.

**LAWRENCE O. GRAEBER, III,** born San Bernadino, California, March 5, 1944; admitted to bar, 1982, California and U.S. District Court, Central District of California. *Education:* Dartmouth College (A.B., 1966); Loyola University of Los Angeles (J.D., 1981). *Member:* Los Angeles County Bar Association; The State Bar of California; American Bar Association.

**MAUREEN A. GRATTAN,** born Rochester, Minnesota, September 11, 1950; admitted to bar, 1981, California; U.S. District Court, Northern, Eastern, Central and Southern Districts of California. *Education:* University of Santa Clara; University of California at Berkeley (A.B., 1972); University of California at Davis; Hastings College of Law, University of California (J.D., 1981). Writer, 1979-1980 and Review Editor, 1980-1981, Hastings Constitutional Law Quarterly. *Member:* Santa Monica, Los Angeles County, San Mateo County and American Bar Associations; State Bar of California; California Women Lawyers; Women Lawyers Association of Los Angeles; Association of Defense Counsel.

**ERIC ANTHONY JOE,** born Berkeley, California, August 15, 1954; admitted to bar, 1982, California, U.S. Court of Appeals, Ninth Circuit and U.S. District Court, Central District of California; 1983, Arizona; 1989, U.S. District Court, Eastern District of California; U.S. District Court, Southern District of California. *Education:* Arizona State University; University of California at Santa Cruz (B.A., 1977); Loyola University Law School (J.D., 1982). *Member:* Beverly Hills, Los Angeles County (Member, Prejudgment Remedies Subsection) and American (Member, Sections on: General Practice; Litigation) Bar Associations; State Bar of California (Member, Sections on: Real Property; Business Law; Litigation); State Bar of Arizona; Financial Lawyers Conference.

**MARILYN A. MONAHAN,** born Toronto, Ontario, Canada, December 26, 1959; admitted to bar, 1985, California; U.S. Court of Appeals, Ninth Circuit; U.S. District Court, Central, Eastern and Southern Districts of California; U.S. District Court, District of Arizona. *Education:* University of California at Los Angeles (B.A., 1981); Loyola Marymount University (J.D., 1985). Note and Comment Editor, Loyola of Los Angeles International and Comparative Law Journal, 1984-1985. Author: Comment, "Waiver of Rights under the Hague Convention on the Taking of Evidence Abroad in Civil or Commercial Matters," 7 Loyola International and Comparative Law Journal 601, 1984. *Member:* Los Angeles County Bar Association; State Bar of California; Association of Business Trial Lawyers.

**JAMES F. WHEAT** (1938-1985).

## LAW OFFICES OF KEITH W. DOUGLAS

12424 WILSHIRE BOULEVARD, SUITE 900
**LOS ANGELES, CALIFORNIA 90025-1043**
Telephone: 310-207-2727
Fax: 310-442-6400

*Real Property Litigation, including Condemnation, Inverse Condemnation, Land Use, and related Environmental and Civil Rights Litigation.*

*FIRM PROFILE: The Law Offices of Keith W. Douglas represents primarily property owners against government agencies. Clients range from developers and Fortune 500 corporations to small businesses and homeowner groups.*

**KEITH W. DOUGLAS,** born San Diego, California, April 3, 1942; admitted to bar, 1969, California; 1973, U.S. District Court, Central District of California; 1993, U.S. Court of Federal Claims, U.S. Supreme Court and U.S. Court of Appeals, Federal Circuit. *Education:* University of California at Los Angeles (B.A., 1964); California Western University (J.D., 1967). Phi Alpha Delta. Editor, California Western Law Review, 1966-1967. Chairman, Appellate Moot Court, 1967. Participant, National Moot Court Competition. Recipient: American Board of Trial Advocates Distinguished Trial Advocacy Award; American Jurisprudence Award in Torts. Adjunct Professor of Law, University of Maryland, 1970. Deputy City Attorney, City of Los Angeles, 1972-1977. *Member:* Los Angeles County Bar Association (Member, Sections on: Real Property; Trial Lawyers; Condemnation and Land Valuation and Litigation); State Bar of California (Member, Committee on Condemnation and Condemnation Procedure, 1978-1982). [Capt., USAF, 1968-1972]

## LAW OFFICES OF JACK A. DRAPER

2121 AVENUE OF THE STARS, SUITE 1750
**LOS ANGELES, CALIFORNIA 90067**
Telephone: 805-322-7272
FAX: 805-322-9359

*Bakersfield, California Office:* 901 Tower Way, Suite 301. Telephone: 805-322-7272. FAX: 805-322-9359.

*Environmental, Natural Resources, Employment, Real Estate and International Law, Trials in all Courts.*

**JACK ALDEN DRAPER II,** born Albany, Oregon, February 13, 1950; admitted to bar, 1975, California. *Education:* Occidental College (B.A., 1971); University of Southern California (M.S., 1974; J.D., 1974). Phi Alpha Delta. Diplomat, Hastings College of Trial Advocacy. *Member:* Los Angeles County, American and International Bar Associations; State Bar of California; California Independent Petroleum Association. *LANGUAGES:* German, Indonesian, Spanish and Cantonese. *PRACTICE AREAS:* Environmental; Natural Resources; Employment Law; Real Estate; International Law.

## LAW OFFICES OF STEVEN DRAPKIN

11377 WEST OLYMPIC BOULEVARD, SUITE 900
**LOS ANGELES, CALIFORNIA 90064-1683**
Telephone: 310-914-7909
Fax: 310-914-7959

*All aspects of Labor and Employment Law. Exclusively representing Management including Arbitration, Litigation and Appellate Practice.*

**STEVEN DRAPKIN,** admitted to bar, 1976, California. *Education:* University of California at Riverside (B.A., with highest honors, 1972); University of California at Los Angeles School of Law (J.D., 1976). Phi Beta Kappa; Order of the Coif. Law Clerk to Justice Mathew O. Tobriner, California Supreme Court, 1974. *REPORTED CASES:* (Partial Listing) Foley v. Interactive Data, 47 Cal.3d 654 (1988); Newman v. Emerson Radio, 48 Cal.3d 973 (1989); Moore v. Conliffe, 7 Cal.4th 634 (1994); Jennings v. Marralle, 8 Cal.4th 121 (1994); Gantt v. Sentry Insurance Co. 1 Cal.4th 1083 (1992); Rojo v. Kliger, 52 Cal.3d 65 (1990); Silberg v. Anderson, 50 Cal.3d 205 (1990); Wagner v. Glendale Adventist Medical Center, 216 Cal..App.3d 1379 (1989); Howard v. Drapkin, 222 Cal.App.3d 843 (1990); Arriaga v. Loma Linda University, 10 Cal.App.4th 1556 (1992); Livadas v. Bradshaw, 114 S.Ct. 2068 (1994); National Broadcasting Company v. Bradshaw, 70 F.3d 69 (9th Cir. 1995).

**LEE W. RIERSON,** admitted to bar, 1993, California. *Education:* University of California at Los Angeles (B.A., cum laude, 1990); University of California School of Law, Los Angeles (J.D., 1993). Order of the Coif.

## DENNIS R. DUBROW

SUITE 2000, 1925 CENTURY PARK EAST
**LOS ANGELES, CALIFORNIA 90067**
Telephone: 310-277-2236
FAX: 310-556-5653

*Practice Limited to Family Law.*

**DENNIS R. DUBROW,** born Detroit, Michigan, October 22, 1939; admitted to bar, 1965, California and U.S. District Court, Central District of California; 1968, U.S. District Court, Southern District of California. *Education:* University of Michigan (A.B., 1961; LL.B., 1964). Co-Author, "In Re Marriage of Fabian-Reimbursement For Separate Property Contributions To Community Property Acquisitions," Los Angeles Lawyer 35, December, 1986; "A Guide to Community Property," Family Law and Practice, Matthew Bender, 1988. Mediator, Los Angeles Superior Court, 1984—. *Member:* Beverly Hills (Member, Family Law Committee, 1981—) and Los Angeles County (Member, Family Law Committee, 1981—) Bar Associations; State Bar of California. (Certified Specialist, Family Law, The State Bar of California Board of Legal Specialization).

## DUMMIT, FABER & BRIEGLEB

11755 WILSHIRE BOULEVARD, 15TH FLOOR
**LOS ANGELES, CALIFORNIA 90025**
*Telephone: 310-479-0944*
*Fax: 310-312-3836*

*Sacramento, California Office:* 1661 Garden Highway, 95833. Telephone: 916-929-9600. Fax: 916-927-5368.

*San Diego, California Office:* 750 B Street, Suite 1900, 92101. Telephone: 619-231-7738. Fax: 619-231-0886.

*Las Vegas, Nevada Office:* 808 South Seventh Street, 89101. Telephone: 702-471-0090. Fax: 702-386-8626.

Civil Litigation in all State and Federal Courts. Professional Malpractice, Products Liability, Negligence, Insurance Defense, Hospital, Business, Entertainment, Sports and Labor Law.

### MEMBERS OF FIRM

**CRAIG S. DUMMIT,** born Long Beach, California, February 5, 1946; admitted to bar, 1972, California. *Education:* Long Beach State College (B.S., 1968); University of Southern California (J.D., 1971). Phi Delta Phi. Member, University of Southern California Law Review, 1970-1971. Author: "Investigatory Powers of the Grand Jury," California State Bar Journal, May, 1971. Member, Section on Healthcare Law, Los Angeles County Bar Association. *Member:* State Bar of California; American Bar Association (Member, Section on Tort and Insurance Practice; Forum Committees on Entertainment and Sports Law); Association of Southern California Defense Counsel; California Society for Healthcare Attorneys; American Academy of Hospital Attorneys; Sports Lawyers Association, Inc.; Southern California Association of Healthcare Risk Managers.

**CHRISTOPHER J. FABER,** born Sewart AFB, Tennessee, March 27, 1954; admitted to bar, 1981, California. *Education:* Furman University (B.A., 1974); Clemson University (M.B.A., 1977); Pepperdine University (J.D., 1981). Phi Delta Phi. Member, Pepperdine Law Review, 1980-1981. *Member:* State Bar of California; American Bar Association (Member, Section on Labor and Employment Law and Subcommittee on Sports Law); American Academy of Hospital Attorneys. [1st. Lt., USAR, 1974-1976]

**B. JOHN BRIEGLEB,** born Castro Valley, California, August 1, 1955; admitted to bar, 1981, California; 1982, Utah. *Education:* California State University at Hayward (B.A., 1978); Pepperdine University (J.D., cum laude, 1981). *Member:* State Bar of California; Utah State Bar; California Trial Lawyers Association; Capitol City Trial Lawyers Association. (Resident, Sacramento Office).

**SCOTT R. DIAMOND,** born Queens, New York, July 8, 1952; admitted to bar, 1980, California. *Education:* University of Bridgeport (B.S., 1974); Southwestern University (J.D., 1980). *Member:* State Bar of California; American Bar Association; Association of Southern California Defense Counsel.

**ANN L. HOLIDAY,** born San Francisco, California, November 20, 1958; admitted to bar, 1984, California. *Education:* University of California at Irvine (B.A., 1980); Pepperdine University School of Law (J.D., 1983). Alpha Epsilon Delta; Phi Delta Phi. *Member:* The State Bar of California (Member, Labor Law Section); American Bar Association; Association of Southern California Defense Counsel; Women Lawyers Association of Los Angeles.

**WILLIAM R. BOYCE,** born Fairmont, West Virginia, July 9, 1943; admitted to bar, 1982, California. *Education:* California State University at Northridge (B.A., 1970; M.A., 1972); Southwestern University School of Law (J.D., 1980). *Member:* State Bar of California.

**BRUCE S. BAILEY,** born Dayton, Ohio, March 9, 1945; admitted to bar, 1970, Ohio; 1971, U.S. Court of Military Appeals; 1975, U.S. Supreme Court; 1977, California; 1978, U.S. District Court, Central District of Ohio. *Education:* Denison University (B.A., 1967); University of Toledo (J.D., 1970). Instructor, Business Law and Real Estate Law, City College of Chicago, 1974-1975. Appointed to the U.S. Air Force Trial Judiciary, Area Defense Council, 6th Circuit, 1973-1975. *Member:* Ohio State and American Bar Associations; State Bar of California; Association of Southern California Defense Counsel; Defense Research Institute; American Board of Trial Advocates; Reserve Officers Association of the United States (Member, Board of Directors, March Air Force Base Chapter, 1982-1984; Vice President, 1984). [Capt., USAF, Judge Advocate General, 1971-1976; Maj., USAF Reserves, 1976—]. (Resident, San Diego Office).

*(This Listing Continued)*

### ASSOCIATES

**JOHN E. TIEDT,** born Anaheim, July 29, 1961; admitted to bar, 1988, California. *Education:* University of California at Los Angeles (B.A., 1983); Pepperdine University (J.D., 1987). Member, Moot Court Honor Board.

**LAWRENCE A. GREENFIELD,** born Los Angeles, March 2, 1957; admitted to bar, 1985, California. *Education:* California State University, Northridge (B.A., 1981); Southwestern University (J.D., 1984). *Member:* The State Bar of California.

**SCOTT D. BUCHHOLZ,** born New York, N.Y., April 10, 1959; admitted to bar, 1985, New Jersey and Pennsylvania; 1988, District of Columbia; 1989, California; U.S. District Court, District of New Jersey; U.S. District Court, Southern District of California. *Education:* Bucknell University (B.A., 1981); Temple University (M.A., 1985); Rutgers University (J.D., 1984). Author: "Pre-trial Discovery of Peer Review Proceedings," 117 New Jersey Lawyer 26, Fall 1986. Adjunct Instructor, Economics Law, Ocean County College, 1985-1988. Instructor, Business Law, University of Redlands, 1991—. *Member:* New Jersey State (Member, Health Law Committee), Pennsylvania and American Bar Associations; District of Columbia Bar; State Bar of California. New Jersey Hospital Attorneys Association. (Resident, San Diego Office).

**DOUGLAS H. SWOPE,** born Chicago, Illinois, February 5, 1960; admitted to bar, 1988, California; 1991, Hawaii and U.S. District Court, Southern District of California and District of Hawaii. *Education:* University of Oregon (B.S., 1982); Southwestern University School of Law (J.D., 1988). *Member:* Hawaii State Bar Association; State Bar of California; National Eagle Scout Association. (Resident, San Diego Office).

**RANDALL R. MCKINNON,** born Salt Lake City, Utah, February 3, 1953; admitted to bar, 1981, California; 1994, Nevada. *Education:* Brigham Young University (B.S., 1977); Southwestern University (J.D., cum laude, 1980). Member, Southwestern University Law Review, 1979-1980. Recipient, American Jurisprudence Award in Labor Law. *Member:* State Bar of California; State Bar of Nevada. [Officer, U.S. Army Reserve, 1977-1985]. (Sacramento and Las Vegas, Nevada Office).

**RONALD W. AITKEN,** born Whittier, California, February 17, 1959; admitted to bar, 1986, California, U.S. District Court, Northern District of California and U.S. Court of Appeals, Ninth Circuit. *Education:* Hastings College (B.A., 1983); University of San Francisco School of Law (J.D., 1986). Co-Director, Moot Court Board, 1985-1986. *Member:* The State Bar of California; Lawyers Club of San Francisco. (Resident, Sacramento Office).

**PAUL A. BUCKLEY,** born Boston, Massachusetts, September 6, 1963; admitted to bar, 1989, California. *Education:* Tufts University (B.A., 1985); Pepperdine University (J.D., 1989). Best Brief, Vincent S. Dalsmer Moot Court Competition. *Member:* American Bar Association. (Resident, San Diego Office). **LANGUAGES:** French.

**JANET E. TRAPP,** born Indianapolis, Indiana, January 31, 1961; admitted to bar, 1989, California. *Education:* University of California (B.S., 1983); Whittier College School of Law (J.D., 1987). Recipient, American Jurisprudence Award for Legal Research and Writing. *Member:* State Bar of California.

**STEVEN E. KUSHNER,** born Boston, Massachusetts, March 21, 1949; admitted to bar, 1977, California, U.S. District Court, Southern District of California and U.S. Court of Appeals, Ninth Circuit. *Education:* California State University at San Diego (B.A., 1971); California Western School of Law (J.D., 1977). Member, California Western Law Review, 1975-1977. Recipient, American Jurisprudence Award. *Member:* The State Bar of California.

**SUSAN J. VEIS,** born Los Angeles, California, February 18, 1955; admitted to bar, 1988, California; 1989, U.S. District Court, Central District of California. *Education:* University of California at Los Angeles (B.A., cum laude, 1976); Pepperdine University (J.D., 1987). Judicial Extern for Honorable Stephen Reinhardt, U.S. Court of Appeals, Ninth Circuit, 1986. *Member:* State Bar of California.

**B. ELIZABETH GAST,** born Fort Myers, Florida, April 15, 1963; admitted to bar, 1992. *Education:* Pasadena City College; University of Colorado at Colorado Springs (B.A., magna cum laude, 1985); Pepperdine University (J.D., cum laude, 1992). Recipient, American Jurisprudence Award, Constitutional Law. Extern to the Honorable William J. Reg, U.S. District Court, Central District of California. *Member:* State Bar of California. **PRACTICE AREAS:** Civil Litigation.

*(This Listing Continued)*

# PROFESSIONAL BIOGRAPHIES

## CALIFORNIA—LOS ANGELES

**JEFFRY A. MILLER,** born Erie, Pennsylvania, April 6, 1960; admitted to bar, 1986, California and U.S. District Court, Southern District of California; 1987, U.S. Court of Appeals, Ninth Circuit. *Education:* Gannon University (B.A., cum laude, 1982); California Western School of Law (J.D., 1985). *Member:* Foothills, San Diego County (Member, Appellate Court Committee; Civil Rules Subcommittee) and American Bar Associations; State Bar of California; The Association of Trial Lawyers of America; San Diego Trial Lawyers Association; San Diego Defense Lawyers. (Resident, San Diego Office). *REPORTED CASES:* Duncan v. Southwest Airlines, Inc., 833 F2d 1301 (9th Cir. 1987)-published opinion, argued and reversed Decision of U.S. District Court, Southern District of California.

**MICHAEL A. SCHERAGO,** born Hartford, Connecticut, July 24, 1967; admitted to bar, 1993, California. *Education:* George Washington University (B.A., 1990); Loyola Law School, Los Angeles (J.D., 1993). Winner, First Place Brief, Roger J. Traynor California Moot Court Competition. Staff Member, 1991-1992 and Senior Note and Comment Editor, 1992-1993, Loyola of Los Angeles Law Review. Author: Note, "Closing The Door On The Public Forum," 26 Loyola of Los Angeles Law Review 241, 1992. Judicial Extern to The Hon. Samuel L. Bufford, U.S. Bankruptcy Court, Central District of California, 1991. *Member:* State Bar of California.

**K. SUE HUMMEL,** born Berkeley, California, November 14, 1950; admitted to bar, 1993, California. *Education:* University of the Pacific (B.A., cum laude, 1972); National University (M.B.A., 1985); Pepperdine University, Malibu (J.D., summa cum laude, 1993). Member, Pepperdine University Law Review, 1992-1993. *Member:* State Bar of California. (Resident, Sacramento Office).

**LANE E. WEBB,** born Chicago, Illinois, June 1, 1964; admitted to bar, 1989, California and U.S. District Court, Southern District of California. *Education:* DePaul University (B.A., 1986); University of San Diego (J.D., 1989). Phi Alpha Delta. Instructor, Paralegal Program, University of San Diego School of Law, 1991—. *Member:* San Diego County Bar Association; San Diego Defense Lawyers Association. (Resident, San Diego Office).

**CYNTHIA L. PERTILE,** born Orange, California, April 12, 1970; admitted to bar, 1995, California. *Education:* Oklahoma State University (B.A., 1992); Southern Methodist University (J.D., 1995). President, Phi Alpha Delta, 1991-1992. Member, Moot Court Board, 1993-1995; National Health Law Moot Court Team, 1994-1995. Dean's List, Southern Methodist University. Recipient: Board of Advocates Outstanding Service Award, 1995; Organ, Bell & Tucker Advocacy Award Scholarship (Advocates). Chairperson, Board of Advocates Litigation Society, 1994-1995. *Member:* American Bar Association (Member, Litigation Section); Young Lawyers Association.

**STEVEN J. BECHTOLD,** born Cincinnati, Ohio, December 13, 1954; admitted to bar, 1980, Ohio; 1985, California. *Education:* Georgetown University; Xavier University (B.A., 1977); University of Cincinnati (J.D., 1980). Assistant Public Defender, Clermont County, Ohio, 1980-1981. *Member:* Sacramento County Bar Association; The State Bar of California; National Health Lawyers Association; California Society of Healthcare Attorneys. [Lt., JAGC, USN, 1981-1985]. (Resident, Sacramento Office). *PRACTICE AREAS:* Civil Litigation; Health Care Law.

### OF COUNSEL

**RICHARD C. DUPAR,** born Brooklyn, New York, April 8, 1933; admitted to bar, 1960, California and U.S. District Court, Southern District of California; 1967, U.S. Supreme Court. *Education:* University of Southern California (B.S., 1954; J.D., 1959). *Member:* Southern California Chapter of American Academy of Attorney Mediators. *PRACTICE AREAS:* Personal Injury Law; Insurance Law; Civil Trial; Products Liability Law; Medical Malpractice Law.

REPRESENTATIVE CLIENTS: American Building Maintenance, Inc.; Crawford & Co.; The Doctors' Co.; Paracelsus Health Care Corp.; Hospital Underwriters Group; Long Beach Memorial Hospital; Kraco Car Stereos; Tyrolia; AMTECH-Reliable Elevator Co.; State Farm; Columbia/HCA; Tenet Healthcare Corp.; ORNDA; Freemont Indemnity; Truck Insurance Exchange.

## LAW OFFICES OF
## DANIEL V. DuROSS
### LOS ANGELES, CALIFORNIA
(See Manhattan Beach)
*Probate and Estate Planning.*

## DWYER, DALY, BROTZEN & BRUNO, LLP
### 550 SOUTH HOPE STREET, SUITE 1900
### LOS ANGELES, CALIFORNIA 90071
Telephone: 213-627-9300
Email: DB2LAW@ix.netcom.com

*General Civil Litigation and Appellate Practice in all State and Federal Courts, Business Litigation, Aviation, Product Liability, Premises Liability, Construction, Bad Faith, Labor and Employment Law, Professional Negligence, Legal Malpractice, Accountant Malpractice.*

### PARTNERS

**RONALD A. DWYER,** born Los Angeles, California, April 14, 1929; admitted to bar, 1958, California. *Education:* Loyola University of Los Angeles (B.A., 1952; LL.B., 1957). Phi Delta Phi. Deputy City Attorney for City of Los Angeles (1957-1961); Settlement Officer, Los Angeles Superior Court (Member of the Board of Directors, Los Angeles Chapter for American Board of Trial Advocates (1990-1992). *Member:* Los Angeles County Bar Association; The State Bar of California; Association of Southern California Defense Counsel; American Board of Trial Advocates.

**JOHN A. DALY,** born Los Angeles, California, June 16, 1931; admitted to bar, 1957, California. *Education:* University of Santa Clara (B.S., 1953); University of Southern California (LL.B., 1956). Phi Delta Phi. Assistant Los Angeles City Attorney, 1957-1967. Chief Assistant, Los Angeles City Attorney, 1967-1973. *Member:* Los Angeles County and American Bar Associations; State Bar of California (Member, Committee on Maintenance of Professional Competence, 1973); American Board of Trial Advocates (Member: Los Angeles Executive Council, 1974-1976; President, Los Angeles Chapter, 1975; National Executive Council, 1975); National Association of Railroad Trial Counsel.

**PETER P. BROTZEN,** born Berlin, Germany, September 22, 1942; admitted to bar, 1972, California. *Education:* Northrop University (B.S., 1965); University of West Los Angele s School of Law (J.D., 1972). Nu Beta Epsilon. Member, Panel of Arbitrators: American Arbitration Association (Executive Committee, Trial Lawyer Section); Los Angeles County Superior Court. Flight Test Engineer, McDonnell Douglas, 1965-1970. *Member:* Los Angeles County and American Bar Associations; The State Bar of California; National Transportation Safety Board Bar Association; American Board of Trial Advocates; International Society of Air Safety Investigators; American Institute of Aeronautics and Astronautics; Association of Southern California Defense Counsel. *PRACTICE AREAS:* Civil Trials; Aviation; Products Liability; Construction Law; Bad Faith.

**TONI RAE BRUNO,** born South Gate, California, July 7, 1944; admitted to bar, 1970, California. *Education:* California State University at Los Angeles (B.A., 1966); University of Southern California (J.D., 1969). Phi Kappa Phi; Phi Delta Delta. Deputy Attorney General, Department of Justice, State of California, 1970-1973. *Member:* Los Angeles County (Member, Appellate Court Committee, 1978) and American Bar Associations; The State Bar of California; Association of Southern California Defense Counsel (Chair Amicus Curiae Committee, 1989-1991); Women Lawyers' Association of Los Angeles (Member, State Bar Convention Committee, 1976). *SPECIAL AGENCIES:* Los Angeles County Superior Court Panel of Arbitrators and Mediators, 1974—. *REPORTED CASES:* Eisen v. Carlisle & Jacquelin, et al. 417 U.S. 156; Mireles v. Waco 502 U.S. 9; Bermudez v. Municipal Court 1 Cal.4th 855; Secrest Machine Corp. v. Superior Court 33 Cal.3d 664; Purdy v. Pacific Auto Ins. Co. 157 Cal.App.3d 59; Rosenbaum v. Security Bank Corp., 43 Cal.App.4th 1084. *PRACTICE AREAS:* Litigation; Appellate Practice; Construction Law; Contracts; Insurance; Professional Liability.

### ASSOCIATES

**DOUGLAS W. SCHROEDER,** born Orange, California, May 5, 1965; admitted to bar, 1988, California; 1989, U.S. District Court, Central, Southern , Northern and Eastern Districts of California. *Education:* Western State University, Fullerton (J.D., cum laude, 1988). Warren J. Ferguson Honors Moot Court Associate Director, 1988. Associate Editor, Western State University Law Review, 1987-1988. Author: "Adding Insult to Injury: California's Community Property Classification of Personal Injury Damage Awards," Vol. 16, Western State L.Rev., 521 1989. *Member:* Orange County Bar Association (Chair, Aviation Law Section, 1994-1995); The State Bar of California. (Resident). *TRANSACTIONS:* Trial of in Re December 7, 1987, Air Crash Cases. *PRACTICE AREAS:* Tort Defense; Civil Appeals; Products Liability; Insurance Coverage; Construction Litigation. *Email:* DB2law@ix.netcom.com

*(This Listing Continued)*

**DWYER, DALY, BROTZEN & BRUNO, LLP,** Los Angeles—Continued

**GREGORY L. ANDERSON,** born Roseville, California, June 21, 1960; admitted to bar, 1987, California. *Education:* San Jose State University Aeronautics Engineering and Business (B.S., 1984); Southwestern University School of Law Scale Program (J.D., 1987). *Member:* Los Angeles County Bar Association; State Bar of California.

**PATRICIA M. MUÑOZ,** born Stockton, California, May 19, 1960; admitted to bar, 1988, California. *Education:* University of California at Berkeley (B.A., 1982); University of California at Los Angeles School of Law (J.D., 1985). *Member:* Los Angeles County Bar Association; State Bar of California. **PRACTICE AREAS:** Personal Injury Claims.

**DIANE A. SINGLETON,** born Vallejo, California, June 12, 1955; admitted to bar, 1991, California. *Education:* San Jose State University (B.A., with honors, 1977); Pepperdine University (M.B.A., 1985); Western State University (J.D., with scholastic merit, 1991). Editor-in-Chief, Western State Law Review, 1990. Author: "What's Wrong With Drug Testing?" Western State University Law Review, Vol. 17, No. 1. *Member:* Orange County Bar Association (Member, Aviation Section); State Bar of California. **LANGUAGES:** French.

**GREGORY J. SALUTE,** born Los Angeles, California, April 12, 1966; admitted to bar, 1993, California; U.S. District Court, Central District of California. *Education:* University of California, San Diego (B.A., 1989); Southwestern University School of Law (J.D., 1992). *Member:* Los Angeles County Bar Association; State Bar of California. **PRACTICE AREAS:** Insurance Defense.

REPRESENTATIVE CLIENTS: United States Aviation Underwriters, Inc.; Southern California Edison Company; the Southland Corporation; Kemper Insurance Company; American Building Maintenance, Inc.; Lockheed Martin, Inc.; General Dynamics Corporation; Martin Aviation; Piper Aircraft Company; Grumman Corporation; County of Los Angeles; City of Long Beach; City of Torrance; First Interstate Bank; Wells Fargo Bank; Alaska Airlines; American Airlines; American West Airlines; Continental Airlines; Hawaiian Airlines; Trans World Airlines; Delta Airlines; Skywest Airlines; US Air, United Airlines; Hexcel Corporation; Allied Signal Corporation; Denny's Inc.; Sears Roebuck and Company.

---

## EASTON & SCHIFF

A Partnership of Professional Corporations

SUITE 2610 ONE CENTURY PLAZA
2029 CENTURY PARK EAST
**LOS ANGELES, CALIFORNIA 90067**
Telephone: 310-557-2436
FAX: 310-785-0027

*General Civil and Trial Practice in all State and Federal Courts. Corporation, Tax, Business, Real Property, Trust and Probate Law. Estate Planning. Arbitration and Mediation.*

### MEMBERS OF FIRM

**HAROLD EASTON, (P.C.),** born Los Angeles, California, April 11, 1913; admitted to bar, 1937, California; 1943, U.S. Supreme Court. *Education:* University of California at Los Angeles (A.B., 1934); Boalt Hall School of Law, University of California (J.D., 1937). Order of the Coif; Phi Beta Kappa; Pi Sigma Alpha; Pi Kappa Delta; Pi Gamma Mu. Associate Editor, California Law Review, 1935-1937. Chief Counsel, Enforcement Department, Office of Price Administration, Washington, D.C., 1942-1946. Member, National Panel of Arbitrators, American Arbitration Association, 1964—. *Member:* Century City Bar Association; The State Bar of California; American Bar Association.

**MICHAEL J. SCHIFF, (P.C.),** born Detroit, Michigan, November 3, 1938; admitted to bar, 1963, California and Michigan. *Education:* University of Michigan (B.B.A., 1960; J.D., 1962). *Member:* Beverly Hills, Century City and Los Angeles County Bar Associations; State Bar of California.

REFERENCES: Bank of America National Trust & Savings Assn. (Los Angeles Main Office); City National Bank (Century Towers Office).

---

## ECKARDT & KHOURY

Established in 1973

333 SOUTH GRAND AVENUE
SUITE 3700
**LOS ANGELES, CALIFORNIA 90071**
Telephone: 213-626-5061
Cable Address: "Richeck"
Fax: 213-626-3629
ABA/Net: ABA 18857
Email: REckardt95@aol.com

*General Civil and Trial Practice in all State and Federal Courts. Banking, Corporation, Construction, Insurance, Real Property, Estate Planning, Trust, Probate, Corporate Financing and International Business Law.*

*FIRM PROFILE: Organized in 1973, the firm is an established general practice business law firm with areas of emphasis in complex real property litigation and in complex business litigation. The firm was formerly known as Eckardt & Ruonala, and earlier, as Katsky, Ker, Eckardt & Hunt. Commencing in the year 1968, Mr. Eckardt was counsel for Pacific Lighting Corporation (now known as Pacific Enterprises), the holding company for Southern California Gas Company. He later was associated with the law firms of Mitchell & Mitchell, and with Sprague & Clements, before establishing this firm. Mr. Eckardt was the organizing attorney for Unity Savings & Loan Association. In the California Supreme Court, Mr. Eckardt made new law on the subject of extraordinary attorney fees in establishing and defending fee claims in contested probates; Estate of Trynin (1989) 49 Cal. 3d 868; 264 Cal. Rptr. 93; 782 P.2d 232.*

*Mr. Khoury was an attorney for Bank of America, NT&SA, for Lloyds Bank California (now Sanwa Bank California) and was a partner in the law firm of Ivanjack, Lambirth & Aranoff.*

**RICHARD W. ECKARDT,** born Saint Charles, Illinois, March 8, 1938; admitted to bar, 1967, California and U.S. District Court, Northern and Central Districts of California; 1972, U.S. Supreme Court. *Education:* Ohio State University (B.A., 1959); University of Southern California (J.D., 1966). Phi Alpha Delta (Secretary, 1965-1966). Member, Board of Directors, and Co-President, Lambda Alumni Association, University of Southern California, 1993—. Master Bencher, Los Angeles Legion Lex American Inns of Court. Judge Pro Tempore, Los Angeles Municipal Court, 1978-1985. Member, Los Angeles World Affairs Council. *Member:* Los Angeles County (Member: Judicial Evaluation Committee, 1989—; Legal Services for the Poor Committee, 1985-1989; Delegate to State Bar Conference of Delegates, 1983—, Executive Committee, 1987—; Member, Sections of: Business and Corporation Law; Real Property; Taxation; Probate and Trust Law; Law Office Management), Federal and American (Member, Sections of: Real Property, Probate and Trust Law; Corporation, Banking and Business Law; Taxation; Economics of Law Practice) Bar Associations; The State Bar of California; Los Angeles Lawyers for Human Rights (Secretary, 1979-1985; Member, Board of Trustees, 1979-1985); Association of Business Trial Lawyers; American Judicature Society. **PRACTICE AREAS:** Business Litigation; Real Property Title Litigation; Transactions; Estate Planning and Probate.

**ROBERT P. KHOURY,** born Utica, New York, March 18, 1947; admitted to bar, 1974, California; U.S. District Court, Northern, Eastern, Central and Southern Districts of California. *Education:* University of California at Berkeley (A.B., with distinction, 1969); Johns Hopkins University; Hastings College of Law, University of California (J.D., 1974). Phi Beta Kappa. *Member:* Los Angeles County Bar Association; State Bar of California; Los Angeles Lawyers for Human Rights. **LANGUAGES:** German. **PRACTICE AREAS:** Banking; Civil Litigation.

REFERENCES: Allied Record Co.; Apartment Investment Rehabilitation Enterprises of Los Angeles; Aqueonics, Inc.; Bank of America National Trust & Savings Assn. (Los Angeles Main Office); Bradshaw Enterprises, Inc.; Central Plants Inc.; Figueroa Arms Apts., Inc.; Hamilton Gregg Asset Management Corp.; Harvard Village Condominium Owners Assn.; Ho Cheng Chemical & Pharmaceutical Co., Ltd. (Taiwan); Huntington Productions; Martin G. Field, M.D., Inc.; Luis Gonzalez & Associates, Inc.; NALCO Chemical Company; Number One Software, Inc.; Walter Odemer Co., Inc.; P. T. Maruco Farma (Indonesia); Pacific Lighting Corp.; R.L. Smith Company; Sandhill Scientific, Incorporated; Sanwa Bank California; Security Pacific National Bank (Headquarters Trust Dept.); Shel-Lee Productions, Ltd.; Standard Tropic Industries Pte Ltd. (Singapore); Sterling Truck Equipment & Repair, Inc.; Stevens Medi-Unit; TICOR Title Insurance Company of California; Union Bank (Capital Management); Unity Savings and Loan Assn.; C. J. Welch, Inc.; Wells Fargo Bank, N.A. (Los Angeles, Main Office); Woo and Locke, Inc.

## EDWARDS, EDWARDS & ASHTON

*A PROFESSIONAL CORPORATION*

### LOS ANGELES, CALIFORNIA

(See Glendale)

*General Civil and Trial Practice. Wills, Trusts, Probate, Estate Planning, Taxation, Corporations, Business, Commercial, Real Property, Family and Personal Injury Law.*

---

## RICK EDWARDS, INC.

20TH FLOOR, 1925 CENTURY PARK EAST
### LOS ANGELES, CALIFORNIA 90067
*Telephone: 310-277-6464*
*Telecopier: 310-286-9501*

Litigation.

**RICK EDWARDS,** born Altadena, California, May 20, 1947; admitted to bar, 1972, California; 1973, U.S. District Court, Central District of California. *Education:* Stanford University (B.A., with distinction, 1969); University of Southern California (J.D., 1972). Recipient, American Jurisprudence Award. Author: "Professional Incorporation Can Be a Blessing--But it is not Heaven," Orthopedics, March, 1980; "Tax Shelters Help Build Physicians Spendable Income," Orthopedics Today, July-August, 1981. *Member:* Century City and Los Angeles County Bar Associations; State Bar of California.

**ANTHONY C. EDWARDS,** born Pasadena, California, January 25, 1956; admitted to bar, 1982, California and U.S. District Court, Central District of California. *Education:* Stanford University (B.A., 1978); Loyola Law School (J.D., cum laude, 1982). Recipient, American Jurisprudence Award. Former Associate, Sheppard, Mullin, Richter & Hampton. General Counsel, Beech Street, Inc. *Member:* Orange County Bar Association; State Bar of California.

**KEN YUWILER,** born Ann Arbor, Michigan, October 14, 1961; admitted to bar, 1986, California and U.S. District Court, Eastern District of California; 1987, U.S. District Court, Central and Northern Districts of California and U.S. Court of Appeals, Ninth Circuit; 1995, U.S. Supreme Court. *Education:* California State University at Northridge (B.A., 1983); Southwestern University (J.D., 1986). Co-Author: chapter, "The Neurotransmitter Revolution, Serotonin, Social Behavior, and the Law," Southern Illinois University Press, 1994. Landlord Tenant Settlement Officer, Los Angeles County Bar Association Dispute Resolution Services, 1989-1991. Judge Pro Tem, Los Angeles County Municipal Court, 1994—. *Member:* Los Angeles County Bar Association; State Bar of California.

### OF COUNSEL

**WILLIAM R. BISHIN,** born New York, N.Y., September 1, 1939; admitted to bar, 1964, New York; 1965, California; 1978, Washington. *Education:* Columbia University (B.A., cum laude, 1960); Harvard University (LL.B., magna cum laude, 1963). Editor-in-Chief, Columbia Daily Spectator, 1959-1960. Editor, Harvard Law Review, 1961-1963. Author: "The Law Finders: An Essay in Statutory Interpretation," 38 Southern California Law Review (1965) and Legislation (3rd ed., 1973); "Law, Language and Ethics," 39 Southern California Law Review (1965) and California Weekly Law Digest (1965); "Smith's Development of Legal Institutions," 68 Columbia Law Review (1968); "The Court's Constitutional Role," Mass Media and the Supreme Court (2d ed. 1976); "Judicial Review in Democratic Theory," 50 Southern California Law Review (1977); "First Amendments' Exemptions from the Antitrust Laws," Washington State Bar Association Reference Notebook for State Bar Convention, 1979; "Recent Developments in Federal Pre-Trial Discovery," CLE Handbook: Pre-Trial Discovery Practice in Federal Courts (1980). Co-Author: with C.D. Stone, *Law, Language and Ethics*, Foundation Press, 1972. Professor of Law: University of Puget Sound, 1978-1980; University of Southern California Law Center, 1968-1980. Assistant and Associate Professor of Law, 1963-1968, University of Southern California. Visiting Scholar in Philosophy, Columbia University, 1968. President, Federal Bar Association of Western Washington, 1984-1985. *Member:* State Bar of California; Seattle-King County, Washington State, Federal and American Bar Associations. (Also Practicing Individually at Seattle, Washington).

REFERENCE: Union Bank, 445 South Figueroa Street, Los Angeles, California 90071.

---

## THOMAS H. EDWARDS

### LOS ANGELES, CALIFORNIA

(See Pasadena)

*Business, Construction, Employment and Labor Litigation, Antitrust and Trade Regulation, Insurance Law, Trial Practice in all State and Federal Courts.*

---

## EGGER & HALLETT

*PROFESSIONAL LAW CORPORATION*

### LOS ANGELES, CALIFORNIA

(See San Bernardino)

*Workers Compensation Defense and Wills and Probate Law.*

---

## RALPH EHRENPREIS

*A PROFESSIONAL LAW CORPORATION*

SUITE 450, 1801 CENTURY PARK EAST
### LOS ANGELES, CALIFORNIA 90067
*Telephone: 310-553-6600*
*Telefax: 310-553-2616*
*Cable Address: "Immlaw"*

Immigration and Nationality Law.

**RALPH EHRENPREIS,** born Memphis, Tennessee, June 9, 1942; admitted to bar, 1967, California. *Education:* University of Michigan (A.B., 1963); Stanford University School of Law (LL.B., 1967). Author: "Treaty Status: Immigration Law's Overlooked Benefit," 3 Los Angeles Lawyer 34, 1980; "Community Property: Commingled Accounts and the Family-Expense Presumption," 19 Stanford Law Review 661, 1967. Lecturer, University of West Los Angeles School of Law, 1971-1973. Lecturer, Immigration Law Seminar, University of California at Los Angeles, 1976. Speaker, UCLA Entertainment Law Symposium, 1992. *Member:* Beverly Hills (Delegate to State Bar Convention, 1977, 1978, 1980; Member: Board of Governors, 1979-1982; Board of Governors, Barristers, 1977-1979; Future of the Bar Association Committee, 1977, 1979; Chairperson, Membership Committee, 1978), Century City (Member, Board of Governors, 1977-1980; Chairperson, Law Day Committee, 1977) and Los Angeles County (Vice-Chairperson, 1978-1979 and Treasurer, 1977-1978, Immigration Section; Chairperson and Moderator, Third Annual Immigration and Naturalization Symposium of the Bar, 1977; Lecturer, Fourth Annual Immigration and Naturalization Symposium of the Bar, 1978) Bar Associations; State Bar of California; American Immigration Lawyers Association (President, 1980-1981; Vice-President, 1979-1980; Secretary, 1978-1979; Southern California Chapter).

**BERNARD J. LURIE,** born Chicago, Illinois, October 3, 1955; admitted to bar, 1980, California. *Education:* University of California at Los Angeles (B.A., 1976; J.D., 1980). Articles Editor, UCLA Journal of International Law, 1978-1979. Author: "Cameras in Court: Focusing on Constitutional Problems," Hawaii Bar Journal, Summer 1980. *Member:* Los Angeles County (Member, Immigration Section) and American Bar Associations; State Bar of California; American Immigration Lawyers Association.

REPRESENTATIVE IMMIGRATION CLIENTS: American Medical International, Inc.; Borg-Warner Acceptance Corp.; Bunker Hill Associates; City of Hope National Medical Center; Compucorp; Dataproducts Corp.; Elektra/Asylum Records; Filmation Studios; Global Van Lines, Inc.; Harbor-UCLA Medical Center; International Business Machines Corp.; Jeffries Banknote Co.; Kenner Products; Los Angeles Olympic Organizing Committee; Lucasfilm, Ltd.; Metropolitan Theatres Corp.; MTM Enterprises; National Medical Enterprises; The Nippon Credit Bank, Ltd.; Nissan Motor Corp.; The Pacific Stock Exchange Inc.; The Record Plant; Republic Corp.; Security Pacific National Bank; Siemens Corp.; Smith International, Inc.; System Development Corp.; Tandem Productions, Inc.; TEAC Corporation of America; Telecredit, Inc.; Teledyne, Inc.; Union Bank; Veterans Administration Medical Center; Warner Bros. Records, Inc.; Westin International; Whittaker Corp.; Wickes Companies, Inc.; Yamaha International Corp.
REFERENCES: City National Bank (Beverly Hills Office, Beverly Hills, California); Great American Bank (Century City Office, Los Angeles, California).

## FRANCES EHRMANN
SUITE 1800
2049 CENTURY PARK EAST
**LOS ANGELES, CALIFORNIA 90067**
Telephone: 310-553-2049
Fax: 310-553-8820

*Property Insurance and Liability Insurance Coverage, Subrogation, Civil Trial and Appellate Practice.*

**FRANCES EHRMANN,** born Kansas City, Missouri, July 25, 1934; admitted to bar, 1963, California. *Education:* University of California at Los Angeles (B.A., 1954; J.D., 1963). Phi Beta Kappa. *Member:* Los Angeles County and American Bar Associations; State Bar of California; California Women Lawyers. **PRACTICE AREAS:** Property Damage Subrogation; Property and Liability Insurance Coverage; Trial and Appellate Practice.

REPRESENTATIVE CLIENTS: American International Group; Zurich-American Insurance Group; Chubb Group; Farmers Insurance Group.

## HERBERT Z. EHRMANN
1875 CENTURY PARK EAST, 15TH FLOOR
**LOS ANGELES, CALIFORNIA 90067**
Telephone: 310-553-5500
Fax: 310-553-8613

*Civil Litigation, Insurance Coverage, Property and Business Insurance Appraisals, Property and Casualty Insurance Law. Property Damage and Subrogation.*

**HERBERT Z. EHRMANN,** born New York, N.Y., March 28, 1932; admitted to bar, 1955, California. *Education:* University of California at Berkeley and University of California at Los Angeles (B.A., 1952); University of California at Los Angeles (LL.B., 1955). Phi Beta Kappa; Order of the Coif. Associate Editor, U.C.L.A. Law Review, 1954-1955. *Member:* Los Angeles County Bar Association; The State Bar of California.

## LAW OFFICES OF
## IRVING M. EINHORN
11900 OLYMPIC BOULEVARD, SUITE 510
**LOS ANGELES, CALIFORNIA 90064-1151**
Telephone: 310-207-8994
Telecopier: 310-442-7663
Email: irveinhorn@earthlink.net

*Securities Law.*

**IRVING M. EINHORN,** born Philadelphia, Pennsylvania, December 13, 1941; admitted to bar, 1972, Illinois; 1973, Pennsylvania; 1981, District of Columbia; 1988, California. *Education:* Temple University (B.S., 1968); Valparaiso University (J.D., 1972). Attorney, U.S. Securities and Exchange Commission, Chicago Regional Office, 1972-1974; Branch Chief, Enforcement, 1974-1975; Senior Trial Counsel, 1975-1980. Assistant Chief Trial Attorney, U.S. Securities and Exchange Commission, Division of Enforcement Trial Unit, Washington, D.C., 1980-1984. Regional Administrator, Los Angeles Regional Office, U.S. Securities and Exchange Commission, 1984-1989. *Member:* Los Angeles County and American Bar Associations; State Bar of California. **PRACTICE AREAS:** Securities Arbitration; Securities Regulation; Securities Fraud; Regulatory Investigations; Self Regulatory Agency Investigations.

## LAW OFFICES OF
## ROBERT W. EISFELDER, P.C.
Established in 1985
SUITE 400, 11726 SAN VICENTE BOULEVARD
**LOS ANGELES, CALIFORNIA 90049-5047**
Telephone: 310-820-4500

*General Civil and Trial Practice in all State and Federal Courts. Commercial, Insurance, Bad Faith, Personal Injury, Accident and Health Insurance and Family Litigation.*

**ROBERT W. EISFELDER,** born Los Angeles, California, May 16, 1947; admitted to bar, 1972, California. *Education:* University of California
*(This Listing Continued)*

---

at Los Angeles (B.A., cum laude, 1969); Hastings College of Law, University of California (J.D., 1972). *Member:* Beverly Hills (Member, Executive Committee, Family Law Section), Los Angeles County and American Bar Associations; State Bar of California; Los Angeles County Trial Lawyers Association; California Trial Lawyers Association; Los Angeles County Business Trial Lawyers Association. **PRACTICE AREAS:** Commercial Litigation; Insurance Law; Bad Faith Litigation; Family Law.

REFERENCE: Imperial Bank.

## DAVID A. ELDEN
1975 CENTURY PARK EAST, SUITE 2200
**LOS ANGELES, CALIFORNIA 90067**
Telephone: 310-788-7775
Fax: 310-843-9933

*Criminal Law, Federal and State Appellate.*

**DAVID A. ELDEN,** born Chicago, Illinois, April 2, 1942; admitted to bar, 1970, California; U.S. District Court, Central and Southern Districts of California; State Tax Court; U.S. Supreme Court. *Education:* San Diego State University (B.S., 1966); University of San Diego (J.D., 1969). Los Angeles County Deputy Public Defender, 1970-1973. Arbitrator, Los Angeles County Bar Association. Member, Dispute Resolution Services. *Member:* Los Angeles County Bar Association; State Bar of California; Los Angeles Criminal Court Bar Association (President, 1988-1989); National Association of Criminal Attorneys (Member: Strike Force; White Collar Task Force; Environmental Section); Public Defenders Association; California Attorneys for Criminal Justice.

## THE LAW OFFICES OF
## JAMES R. ELIASER
12100 WILSHIRE BOULEVARD, SUITE 1600
**LOS ANGELES, CALIFORNIA 90025**
Telephone: 310-820-7971
Fax: 310-820-7071

*Family Law.*

**JAMES R. ELIASER,** born Los Angeles, California, April 10, 1947; admitted to bar, 1972, California; 1973, U.S. District Court, Central District of California. *Education:* San Diego State University (B.A., 1969); Loyola University of Los Angeles (J.D., 1972). Lecturer: California Trial Lawyers Association, 1981; Los Angeles County Bar Association, 1994, 1995 and 1996; Beverly Hills Bar Association, 1985 and Los Angeles Bankruptcy Forum. Mediator, Los Angeles Superior Court (Family Law). Past Member, Executive Committee of Family Law Section, Los Angeles County Bar Association. *Member:* Beverly Hills (Member, Family Law Section) and Los Angeles County (Member, Family Law Section) Bar Associations; State Bar of California. **PRACTICE AREAS:** Family Law.

REFERENCE: Imperial Bank.

## ELLIOT, LAMB, LEIBL & SNYDER
**LOS ANGELES, CALIFORNIA**
(See Encino)

*Civil Litigation. Insurance Defense and Medical Malpractice Defense.*

## LAW OFFICES OF
## GEORGE H. ELLIS
811 WEST 7TH STREET, SUITE 1220
**LOS ANGELES, CALIFORNIA 90017**
Telephone: 213-622-9001
Fax: 213-622-5949

*General Civil and Trial Practice in all State Courts. Insurance Litigation, Products Liability, Personal Injury, Malpractice and Criminal Law. Appellate Practice.*

**GEORGE H. ELLIS,** born St. Louis, Missouri, July 27, 1938; admitted to bar, 1966, California and U.S. District Court, Central District of Califor-
*(This Listing Continued)*

nia. *Education:* Stanford University (A.B., 1959); Hastings College of Law, University of California (J.D., 1965). Phi Delta Phi. Dean and Professor of Law, California College of Law, 1966-1972. Deputy Public Defender, Los Angeles County, 1968-1971. Candidate for California State Assembly, 1970. Appointed by Governor Reagan to California Assigned Risk Committee, 1971-1973. Member, Board of Directors, Wilshire YMCA, 1971-1974. Judge Pro Tem, Los Angeles Municipal Court, 1974-1976. *Member:* Los Angeles County and American Bar Associations; State Bar of California; Association of Southern California Defense Counsel; American Board of Trial Advocates. [Capt., JAGC, U.S. Army Reserve]

REPRESENTATIVE CLIENTS: Allegiance Insurance; Babcock Ladder Co.; The Black & Decker (U.S.) Inc. Manufacturing Co.; Columbia Ladder Corp.; Foremost Insurance Co.; Fremont Indemnity Co.; Horace Mann Cos.; Howard Manufacturing Co.; Imperial Casualty & Indemnity Co.; Inland Ladder; Ladder Management Services; Liberty Mutual Insurance Co.; Risk Retention Services; Teachers Insurance Co.; Topa Insurance Co.; U.S.A.A.; Western Surety Co.; Milwaukee Electric Tool Corp.

## RONALD D. ELLIS
### LOS ANGELES, CALIFORNIA
(See Torrance)

*Transactional/Commercial Documentation, Personal Injury, Corporate and International Corporate and Consumer and Commercial Collections Law. General Civil Trial Practice.*

## ENGSTROM, LIPSCOMB & LACK
*A PROFESSIONAL CORPORATION*

Established in 1974

16TH FLOOR
10100 SANTA MONICA BOULEVARD
**LOS ANGELES, CALIFORNIA 90067**
Telephone: 310-552-3800
Telecopier: 310-552-9434
URL: http://www.elllaw.com

*General Civil and Trial Practice in all State and Federal Courts. Aviation, Corporation, Domestic and International Insurance, Maritime, Professional Liability, Products Liability and Real Property Law.*

FIRM PROFILE: Founded in 1974, the law firm of Engstrom, Lipscomb & Lack has specialized in a broad range of high profile tort and commercial litigation with an emphasis on disputes involving the environment, entertainment and the insurance industries. Areas of expertise include aviation, construction defect, professional liability, comprehensive liability matters, business litigation concerning the business community's relationship with the insurance industry, public carrier and public entity disputes, environmental and toxic litigation, and insurance matters.

**PAUL W. ENGSTROM,** born Evanston, Illinois, May 19, 1941; admitted to bar, 1966, Illinois, U.S. District Court, Northern District of Illinois and U.S. Court of Appeals, Seventh Circuit; 1974, California, U.S. District Court, Central District of California and U.S. Court of Appeals, Ninth Circuit; 1976, U.S. District Court, Southern District of California. *Education:* Northwestern University (B.A., 1963); DePaul University (J.D., 1966). Editor-in-Chief, DePaul Law Review, 1965-1966. Member, DePaul Moot Court Team. Author: "Conflicts of Law: For the Defendant," American Bar Association Small Aircraft Accident Litigation, Part 1, 1973; "Alternative Wordings to the Present General Aviation Insurance Policies," Journal of Air Law and Commerce, 1977; "Liability of the Fixed Base Operator: The Legal Impact," Association of Independent Aviation Insurers, The Binder, 1978; "The Liability of the Owner and Pilot of General Aviation Aircraft," 1978 and "Punitive Damages in Aviation Litigation: For the Defendant," 1980, New York Law Journal, Aviation Accident Litigation. Lecturer, University of Southern California Institute of Safety and Systems Management, 1980-1981. *Member:* State Bar of California; Federation of Insurance and Corporate Counsel; Association of Southern California Defense Counsel. **PRACTICE AREAS:** Insurance Policy Interpretation; Bad Faith Defense; Environmental Coverage; Construction Litigation; Aviation; Professional Liability; Excess Insurance.

**LEE G. LIPSCOMB,** born Charlotte, North Carolina, July 20, 1939; admitted to bar, 1974, California; 1975, U.S. District Court, Central District of California. *Education:* Southeastern Oklahoma State University (B.A., 1962); Southwestern School of Law (LL.B., 1974). *Member:* American Bar Association; State Bar of California. **PRACTICE AREAS:** Products Liability; Entertainment Insurance; Aviation; Trial Practice.

**WALTER J. LACK,** born Los Angeles, California, January 10, 1948; admitted to bar, 1973, California; 1979, U.S. Court of Appeals, Ninth Circuit; 1981, U.S. Supreme Court. *Education:* Loyola Marymount University (B.A., 1970; J.D., 1973). Author: "The Anatomy of a Federal Employer's Liability Act Case," October, 1972 and "The Availability of Strict Liability in the Excess Judgment Case," Spring, 1973, California Trial Lawyers Journal; "Formulating A Defendant's Discovery Plan in a Mid-Air Collision," Southern Methodist University School of Law, Journal of Air Law and Commerce, Vol. 47, No. 4, 1982. Member, Superior Court Arbitration Panel, 1976—. Arbitrator, Bar Fee Dispute, Los Angeles County, 1979—. Advocate-American Board of Trial Advocates; Board of Directors-Houston Casualty Company, Inc.; Board of Directors, Loyola-Marymount University. Member, Panel of Arbitrators, American Arbitration Association. *Member:* Los Angeles County and American Bar Associations; State Bar of California; The Association of Trial Lawyers of America; California Trial Lawyers Association; Los Angeles Trial Lawyers Association; Lawyer-Pilots Bar Association. **LANGUAGES:** French. **PRACTICE AREAS:** Complex Business Litigation; Insurance Policy Interpretation; Bad Faith; Environmental Coverage; Professional Liability; Aviation; Maritime; Excess Insurance.

**JERRY A. RAMSEY,** born January 9, 1936; admitted to bar, 1965, California. *Education:* California State University at Los Angeles (B.A., 1961); California State University at Los Angeles School of Law (LL.B., 1964); University of California at Los Angeles (J.D., 1964). *Member:* Los Angeles County and American Bar Associations; State Bar of California; Association of Southern California Defense Counsel; Diplomate, American Board of Trial Advocates (Member, Executive Committee); Defense Research Institute; National Association of Railroad Trial Counsel. **PRACTICE AREAS:** Insurance Casualty Defense; Insurance Policy Interpretation; Bad Faith Litigation; Civil Trials.

**STEVEN C. SHUMAN,** born Los Angeles, California, December 11, 1954; admitted to bar, 1978, California and U.S. District Court, Central, Southern, Northern and Eastern Districts of California. *Education:* University of California at Riverside (B.A., with highest honors, 1975); University of California at Davis; University of California at Los Angeles School of Law (J.D., 1978). Phi Alpha Delta. *Member:* State Bar of California. **PRACTICE AREAS:** Jewelers Block Litigation; Insurance Policy Interpretation; Bad Faith Defense; Complex Business Litigation; Professional Liability Claims; First-party Insurance Matters; General Business Matters; Insurance Defense.

**ELIZABETH LANE CROOKE,** born Princeton, New Jersey, June 4, 1952; admitted to bar, 1979, California, U.S. District Court, Eastern and Central Districts of California and U.S. Court of Appeals, Ninth Circuit. *Education:* University of California at Santa Barbara (B.A., 1974); Loyola Marymount University (J.D., cum laude, 1979). *Member:* Los Angeles County and American Bar Associations; State Bar of California. **PRACTICE AREAS:** Insurance Policy Interpretation; Bad Faith Defense; Environmental Coverage; Construction Litigation; Aviation and Governmental Agency Defense; First-party Insurance Matters.

**BRIAN D. DEPEW,** born Santa Monica, California, February 11, 1948; admitted to bar, 1979, California and U.S. District Court, Central District of California; U.S. Court of Appeals, Ninth Circuit. *Education:* California State University at Northridge (B.A., 1976); Southwestern University (J.D., 1979). Delta Theta Phi. *Member:* State Bar of California; California Trial Lawyers Association; The Association of Trial Lawyers of America; California Lawyers for the Arts; American Society of Law and Medicine; American Academy of Hospital Attorneys; National Health Lawyers Association. **PRACTICE AREAS:** Medical Professional Liability; Chiropractic Professional Liability; Products Liability; General Trials.

**JEFFREY T. BOLSON,** born Glendale, California, June 15, 1957; admitted to bar, 1981, California; 1983, U.S. District Court, Central District of California. *Education:* University of Redlands (B.S., 1978); McGeorge School of Law, University of the Pacific (J.D., 1981). Phi Delta Phi; Order of the Coif. Member, Traynor Honor Society. Recipient, American Jurisprudence Award in Criminal Law. Editor: "Significant Developments in Private International Law," Comparative Law Yearbook, 1981. *Member:* American Bar Association; State Bar of California; The Association of Trial Lawyers of America. **PRACTICE AREAS:** Insurance Policy Interpretation; Bad Faith Defense; Entertainment Insurance; Professional Liability; Excess Insurance.

**ALAN B. NISHIMURA,** born Honolulu, Hawaii, September 24, 1946; admitted to bar, 1983, California; 1984, U.S. District Court, Northern,

*(This Listing Continued)*

**ENGSTROM, LIPSCOMB & LACK, A PROFESSIONAL CORPORATION, Los Angeles—Continued**

Eastern, Central and Southern Districts of California and U.S. Court of Appeals, Ninth Circuit. *Education:* Occidental College (B.A., 1968); University of Southern California (M.B.A., 1970); Loyola Marymount University (J.D., 1983). *Member:* Los Angeles County and American Bar Associations; State Bar of California; Los Angeles County Superior Court Arbitration Panel. [1st. Lt., USAF, 1970-1972]. *PRACTICE AREAS:* Governmental Agency Defense; Construction Litigation; Products Liability; General Trials.

*GARY A. PRAGLIN,* born Los Angeles, California, October 7, 1955; admitted to bar, 1981, California and U.S. District Court, Central and Southern Districts of California. *Education:* University of California at Los Angeles (B.A., 1978); Southwestern University (J.D., 1981). *Member:* Los Angeles County Bar Association; State Bar of California. *PRACTICE AREAS:* Products Liability; Professional Liability; General Trials.

*WILLIAM T. CLEMONS III,* born Rochester, New York, April 18, 1941; admitted to bar, 1984, California and U.S. District Court, Central District of California; 1993, North Carolina. *Education:* University of Southern California (B.A. cum laude, 1964); Loyola Marymount University (J.D., 1983). Adjunct Professor, University of Phoenix, Business Law, Mediation and Negotiations. Member, Los Angeles County Sheriffs Department, 1974-1984. *Member:* Los Angeles County Bar Association (Member, Section on Litigation); The State Bar of California. [Captain, USAF, 1964-1970]. *LANGUAGES:* Spanish. *PRACTICE AREAS:* Aviation; Products Liability; Professional Liability; Governmental Agency Defense; General Trials.

*MATTHEW J. SAUNDERS,* born Los Angeles, California, September 18, 1958; admitted to bar, 1985, California and U.S. District Court, Central District of California. *Education:* University of Edinburgh, Scotland; University of California at Santa Barbara (B.A., 1980); Southwestern University (J.D., 1984). *Member:* Los Angeles County Bar Association; State Bar of California. *PRACTICE AREAS:* Governmental Agency Defense; Construction Litigation; General Trials.

*ROBERT J. WOLFE,* born Whittier, California, September 9, 1961; admitted to bar, 1987, California and U.S. District Court, Central District of California. *Education:* California State University at Long Beach (B.S., 1984); Southwestern University (J.D., 1987). Recipient, American Jurisprudence Award in Products Liability. *Member:* Los Angeles County and American Bar Associations; State Bar of California. *PRACTICE AREAS:* Construction Litigation; Real Estate; Title Insurance Matters; Bad Faith; Professional Liability; General Trials.

---

*DANIEL G. WHALEN,* born Concord, Massachusetts, March 7, 1961; admitted to bar, 1986, California; U.S. District Court, Central and Southern Districts of California. *Education:* Claremont McKenna College (B.A., 1983); Loyola Marymount University (J.D., 1986). Phi Alpha Delta. *Member:* Los Angeles County and American (Member, Tort and Insurance Practice Section) Bar Associations; State Bar of California; Association of Southern California Defense Counsel.

*BRIAN J. HEFFERNAN,* born Oceanside, New York, May 8, 1961; admitted to bar, 1987, California; U.S. District Court, Central District of California. *Education:* Loyola Marymount University (B.A., 1984); McGeorge School of Law, University of the Pacific (J.D., 1987). *Member:* Los Angeles County and American Bar Associations; State Bar of California.

*ERIC BERG,* born Los Angeles, California, October 26, 1962; admitted to bar, 1988, California and U.S. District Court, Central District of California. *Education:* University of California at San Diego (B.A., 1984); University of Southern California (J.D., 1987). Phi Delta Phi. *Member:* State Bar of California; American Bar Association.

*KAREN-DENISE LEE,* born Pasadena, California, August 23, 1961; admitted to bar, 1987, California; 1989, U.S. District Court, Central, Eastern and Southern Districts of California; 1996, U.S. Court of Appeals, Ninth Circuit. *Education:* Western Oregon State College (B.S., 1984); Willamette University (J.D., 1987). Phi Alpha Delta (Treasurer, 1985-1987). Member, Moot Court Board. Listed in: Who's Who Among Students in American University and Colleges; American Association of University Women; Who's Who Among American Law Students. *Member:* Orange County, San Joaquin County and American Bar Associations; State Bar of California; Irish American Bar Association.

*(This Listing Continued)*

CAA642B

*ADAM D. MILLER,* born Wilkes Barre, Pennsylvania, June 6, 1958; admitted to bar, 1985, New York and U.S. District Court, Federal and Eastern Districts of New York; 1989, California. *Education:* University of Wisconsin (B.S., 1981); De Paul University (J.D., 1984). Member, DePaul Law Review, 1984. Assistant District Attorney, Kings County District Attorney's Office, Brooklyn, N.Y., 1984-1988. Attorney, U.S. Securities & Exchange Commission, Division of Enforcement, Los Angeles, California, 1988-1990. Associate General Counsel, Directors Guild of America, Inc., Los Angeles, California, 1990-1992. Executive Vice President in charge of Business/Legal Affairs, 21st Century Film, Corp./IDP, Beverly Hills, California, 1993-1994. *Member:* The Association of the Bar of the City of New York; Los Angeles County Bar Association; New York State Bar Association.

*JILL L. FEINBERG,* born New York, April 2, 1963; admitted to bar, 1989, California. *Education:* University of California (B.A., 1985); University of San Francisco (J.D., 1989). *Member:* State Bar of California.

*DAWN M. FLORES-OSTER,* born North Hollywood, California, November 25, 1958; admitted to bar, 1991, California and U.S. District Court, District of California. *Education:* University of California at Los Angeles (B.A., cum laude, 1980); Southwestern University (J.D., 1991). Recipient: California State Scholarship; Mabel Wilson Richards Scholarship; John J. Schumaker Scholarship. Externship: District Attorney's Office; California Court of Appeal. *LANGUAGES:* French, Spanish. *PRACTICE AREAS:* Civil Litigation Defense; Civil Litigation Plaintiff.

*PAUL A. TRAINA,* born Detroit, Michigan, November 16, 1964; admitted to bar, 1991, California. *Education:* Macalester University; University of Minnesota; Pepperdine University School of Law (J.D., 1991). *Member:* State Bar of California; Italian Bar Association.

*CYNTHIA JANE EMRY,* born Vermillion, South Dakota, October 17, 1964; admitted to bar, 1992, California. *Education:* University of California at Los Angeles (B.A., 1986); Pepperdine University School of Law (J.D., cum laude, 1992). Phi Alpha Delta. Literary Editor, Pepperdine Law Review. Author: In re Marriage of Arceneaux, 18 Pepp. L. Rev. 1063 (1991); Pasadena Police Officers Association v. City of Pasadena, 18 Pepp. L. Rev. 1078 (1991); Raven v. Deukmenian, 18 Pepp. L. Rev. 1084 (1991). *Member:* Los Angeles County Bar Association; State Bar of California.

*BRIAN J. LEINBACH,* born Santa Monica, California, September 4, 1966; admitted to bar, 1992, California and U.S. District Court, Central District of California. *Education:* University of Colorado (B.A., Economics, 1988); Pepperdine University, Malibu (J.D., 1992). *Member:* State Bar of California; American Bar Association.

*JOY L. ROBERTSON,* born July 12, 1966; admitted to bar, 1993, California. *Education:* University of California, Santa Barbara (B.A., 1988); Southwestern University School of Law (J.D., 1992). *Member:* State Bar of California.

*JILL P. McDONELL,* born Chippewa Falls, Wisconsin, December 31, 1964; admitted to bar, 1992, California. *Education:* University of California, Irvine (B.A., magna cum laude, 1986); Southwestern University School of Law (J.D., 1992). Phi Beta Kappa. Paul Wildman Scholar, Southwestern University. *Member:* Los Angeles County Bar Association; State Bar of California.

*LAURA M. WATKINS,* born Long Beach, California, January 23, 1968; admitted to bar, 1993, California. *Education:* University of Southern California (B.A., cum laude, 1990); University of San Diego (J.D., 1993). Phi Alpha Delta. *Member:* State Bar of California.

*MARK EVANS MILLARD,* born Boulder, Colorado, February 22, 1960; admitted to bar, 1994, California. *Education:* Pepperdine University (B.S., 1989); Southwestern University School of Law (J.D., 1994);. *Member:* State Bar of California; American Bar Association (Member, Sections on: Torts; Litigation; Entertainment); The Association of Trial Lawyers of America.

*STUART R. FRAENKEL,* born Burbank, California, August 17, 1963; admitted to bar, 1994, California; 1995, U.S. District Court, Central District of California and U.S. Court of Appeals, Ninth Circuit. *Education:* Embry-Riddle Aeronautical University (B.S., 1989); Southwestern University School of Law (J.D., 1994). Phi Delta Phi (President, 1992-1994). Recipient, Balfow Award, 1989. Listed, Who's Who in American Law Schools. President and Founder, Southwestern University Aviation and Space Law Society, 1992-1994. *Member:* Los Angeles County (Member, Litigation Section and Barristers Community Outreach and Children's Rights Committees, 1995) and American (Member, Sections on: Air and Space Law, 1990-1995; Litigation, 1990-1995). [Sgt. USMC, 1983-1988]

*(This Listing Continued)*

**TRACY MICHELLE TUSO,** born Encino, California, August 23, 1969; admitted to bar, 1995, California. *Education:* Loyola Marymount University (B.A., 1991); Southwestern University School of Law (J.D., 1995). *Member:* State Bar of California.

**DAVID M. ROBINSON,** born Bountiful, Utah, December 5, 1967; admitted to bar, 1995, California. *Education:* University of Utah (B.S.B.A., 1990); Pepperdine University (J.D., 1994). Delta Theta Phi. Member, Salt Lake County Board of Realtors, 1988-1990. *Member:* Beverly Hills and American Bar Associations. *LANGUAGES:* Spanish, German.

**KAREN L. HINDIN,** born Los Angeles, California, April 26, 1969; admitted to bar, 1994, California. *Education:* University of California at Los Angeles (B.A., 1991); Santa Clara University (J.D., 1994). Author, "C.C.P.§128.7: The New Sanctions Statute," Advocate, May 1995. *Member:* Century City and Los Angeles County Bar Associations; Women Lawyers Association; Consumer Attorneys Association of Los Angeles.

**TROY H. SLOME,** born Fremont, California, August 23, 1965; admitted to bar, 1995, California; 1996, Colorado. *Education:* University of California at Los Angeles (B.A., 1989); Loyola Law School; McGeorge School of Law, University of the Pacific (J.D., 1994). *Member:* Los Angeles County and American Bar Associations; State Bar of California.

**DANIEL J. PADOVA,** born Philadelphia, Pennsylvania, June 25, 1963; admitted to bar, 1996, California. *Education:* Pepperdine University (B.S.M., 1991); Western State University (J.D., 1995).

**MICHELE HITT,** born Flint, Michigan, December 13, 1970; (admission pending). *Education:* University of California at Los Angeles (B.A., cum laude, 1993); Loyola Marymount University (J.D., 1996). Alpha Lambda Delta; Phi Eta Sigma. *Member:* American Bar Association. *LANGUAGES:* French.

REPRESENTATIVE CLIENTS: Avemco Insurance Co.; Aviation Insurance Services Inc.; Chrysler Insurance Co.; County of Los Angeles; First Mercury Syndicate, Inc.; Granite State Insurance Co.; Great Southwest Fire Insurance Co.; Houston Casualty Insurance Co.; Insurance Company of the State of Pennsylvania; Los Angeles County Transportation Commission; Pacific Indemnity Co.; Reliance Insurance Co.; Sentry Insurance, a Mutual Company; RLI Insurance Co.; Sentry Indemnity Co.; TCO Insurance Services; Underwriters at Lloyds, London; Western Underwriters Insurance Co.
REFERENCE: Comerica Bank.

## EPPORT & RICHMAN

A California General Partnership

*Established in 1957*

SUITE 1450, 10100 SANTA MONICA BOULEVARD
**LOS ANGELES, CALIFORNIA 90067**
Telephone: 310-785-0885
Telecopier: 310-785-0787

*General Civil and Trial Practice in all State and Federal Courts. Banking, Secured Transactions, Corporation, Real Property, Commercial and Bankruptcy Law.*

### MEMBERS OF FIRM

**STEVEN N. RICHMAN,** born Los Angeles, California, April 29, 1956; admitted to bar, 1981, California. *Education:* University of Southern California (B.A., cum laude, 1978); Loyola Law School (J.D., cum laude, 1981). Member: St. Thomas More Law Honor Society; Scott Moot Court Honors Board. Selected to Who's Who in American Law, 1992, 1993. *Member:* State Bar of California; Financial Lawyers Conference; California Bankruptcy Forum.

**MARK ROBBINS,** born Los Angeles, California, May 18, 1961; admitted to bar, 1988, California; 1989, U.S. District Court, Central District of California. *Education:* University of California at Los Angeles (B.A., 1983); Loyola Law School, Los Angeles (J.D., 1988). Pi Sigma Alpha; Phi Delta Phi. Staff Member, Loyola International and Comparative Law Journal, 1988—. *Member:* Beverly Hills and Los Angeles County Bar Associations; State Bar of California. *PRACTICE AREAS:* Commercial Litigation; Bankruptcy; Real Property; Banking Transactions.

**BETH ANN R. YOUNG,** born Santa Monica, California, June 30, 1964; admitted to bar, 1989, California; U.S. Court of Appeals, Ninth Circuit and U.S. District Court, Central District of California. *Education:* University of California at Los Angeles (B.A., 1986); Loyola Law School, Los Angeles (J.D., 1989). Phi Delta Phi. Recipient, American Jurisprudence Award in Contracts. *Member:* Beverly Hills and Los Angeles County Bar Associations; State Bar of California; Financial Lawyers Conference - Los Angeles.

*(This Listing Continued)*

*PRACTICE AREAS:* Commercial Litigation; Bankruptcy; Real Property; Banking Transactions.

### ASSOCIATES

**STEVEN C. HUSKEY,** born Philadelphia, Pennsylvania, December 23, 1964; admitted to bar, 1989, California, U.S. District Court, Central, Northern and Southern Districts of California; U.S. Supreme Court. *Education:* Columbia University (B.A., 1986); London School of Economics, London, England; University of Southern California (J.D., 1989). Secretary, Legal Advisory Committee, Angeles Chapter, Sierra Club, 1991—. *Member:* Los Angeles County Bar Association (Member, Real Property and Environmental Sections); State Bar of California. *PRACTICE AREAS:* Real Property and Banking Transactions; Bankruptcy; Litigation.

**LAURA E. McSWIGGIN,** born Portland, Maine, October 16, 1958; admitted to bar, 1992, California and U.S. District Court, Central District of California. *Education:* California State University at Northridge; University of Southern California (B.A. in Social Science, Communications and Economics, 1988); Loyola Marymount University (J.D., 1992). Phi Delta Phi; Order of the Coif; Moot Court. Recipient, American Jurisprudence Awards in Trial Advocacy and Family Law - Community Property. *Member:* Beverly Hills and Orange County Bar Associations; State Bar of California.

**WENDY K. SHAPNICK,** born Los Angeles, California, March 30, 1967; admitted to bar, 1992, California; 1993, U.S. District Court, Central, Northern and Southern Districts of California. *Education:* University of California at Berkeley (B.A., 1989); Boalt Hall School of Law, University of California (J.D., 1992). Phi Beta Kappa. *Member:* Beverly Hills Bar Association; State Bar of California.

**VICTOR R. BERWIN,** born New York, N.Y., May 3, 1968; admitted to bar, 1993, California, U.S. District Court, Central District of California and U.S. Court of Appeals, Ninth Circuit. *Education:* Duke University (B.A., cum laude, 1990); University of Southern California (J.D., 1993). *Member:* State Bar of California.

**AMIR YARIV,** born Tel-Aviv, Israel, February 17, 1967; admitted to bar, 1994, California. *Education:* University of California at Los Angeles (B.A., cum laude, 1989); Loyola Law School (J.D., 1994). Phi Delta Phi. Recipient of American Jurisprudence Award in Real Estate Transactions. Member, 1992-1993 and Editor, 1993-1994, Loyola of Los Angeles Law Review. Judicial Extern to Hon. Calvin K. Ashland, U.S. Bankruptcy Court, 1993. *Member:* State Bar of California. *LANGUAGES:* Hebrew and Spanish. *PRACTICE AREAS:* Real Property; Contract; Bankruptcy.

**SCOTT H. NOSKIN,** born Chicago, Illinois, October 20, 1966; admitted to bar, 1991, Illinois; 1993, California and U.S. District Court, Central District of California. *Education:* University of Michigan (B.B.A., 1988); Loyola University of Chicago (J.D., 1991). *Member:* Los Angeles County and American Bar Associations; State Bar of California.

**PHILIP H. R. NEVINNY,** born Boston, Massachusetts, May 18, 1964; admitted to bar, 1990, California and U.S. District Court, Southern, Northern and Central Districts of California. *Education:* Columbia University (B.A., 1986); Boston College Law School (J.D., 1990). General Counsel, Endangered Species Zoological Society. *Member:* Beverly Hills and Los Angeles County Bar Associations; State Bar of California. *LANGUAGES:* German, French, Spanish.

**MICHAEL D. SHORE,** born Los Angeles, California, January 18, 1967; admitted to bar, 1993, California; 1994, U.S. District Court, Central District of California and U.S. Court of Appeals, Ninth Circuit. *Education:* University of California, Los Angeles (B.A., 1989); Loyola Law School (J.D., 1993). *Member:* Beverly Hills and Los Angeles County Bar Associations; State Bar of California. *PRACTICE AREAS:* Real Property; Banking; Finance.

**FRANCIS CURTIS HUNG, JR.,** born Los Angeles, California; admitted to bar, 1991, California and U.S. District Court, Northern, Southern, Eastern and Central Districts of California. *Education:* University of Southern California (B.S., 1986); University of California, Davis (J.D., 1991). Phi Delta Phi. Member, Asian Law Students Association, 1988-1991. California Real Estate Brokers License, 1994. *Member:* Beverly Hills and Los Angeles County Bar Associations; State Bar of California (Member, Real Property Section). *PRACTICE AREAS:* Creditors Rights Law; Bankruptcy; Commercial Litigation.

**RENU MAGO SETARO,** born Richmond, Virginia, October 6, 1968; admitted to bar, 1993, California and U.S. District Court, Central and Southern Districts of California; 1995, District of Columbia. *Education:* University of Virginia (B.A., 1990); Boston University (J.D., 1993). *Mem-*

*(This Listing Continued)*

CAA643B

**EPPORT & RICHMAN, Los Angeles—Continued**

ber: Los Angeles County Bar Association; State Bar of California. *LANGUAGES:* French.

**LAWRENCE A. ABELSON,** born Los Angeles, California, June 3, 1967; admitted to bar, 1992, California and U.S. District Court, Central District of California. *Education:* Tufts University (B.A., magna cum laude, 1989); University of California at Los Angeles (J.D., 1992). Phi Beta Kappa; Phi Alpha Delta. Member, Moot Court Honors Program. Member, Federal Communications Law Journal. Recipient, Distinguished Achievement Award in International Relations. *Member:* Los Angeles County (Member, Sections on: Barristers; Commercial Law; Bankruptcy; Litigation; Real Property), Beverly Hills (Member, Sections on: Business Law; Litigation; Real Estate) and American (Member, Sections on: Business Law; Litigation; Tort and Insurance Practice) Bar Associations; State Bar of California (Member, Sections on: Litigation; Real Property Law). *LANGUAGES:* French. *PRACTICE AREAS:* Real Property; Bankruptcy; Commercial Litigation.

**PAUL A. FUHRMAN,** born Chicago, Illinois, May 13, 1969; admitted to bar, 1995, California and U.S. District Court, Central District of California. *Education:* University of California at Los Angeles (B.A., 1991); Loyola Law School (J.D. cum laude, 1995). Member: Order of the Coif; St. Thomas More Law Honor Society. Recipient, American Jurisprudence Awards in Criminal Procedure and Ethics, Counseling and Negotiations. Managing Editor, Loyola of Los Angeles Entertainment Law Journal, 1994-1995. Judicial Extern to the Honorable Geraldine Mund, U.S. Bankruptcy Court, 1993. Author: "United States v. X-Citement Video: The Pariah Opinion," 15 Loy. L.A. Ent. L.J., 85 (1994). *Member:* Los Angeles County Bar Association; State Bar of California. *PRACTICE AREAS:* Real Property; Bankruptcy; Commercial Litigation.

## OF COUNSEL

**VICTOR M. EPPORT, (A LAW CORPORATION),** born Dairen, China, December 10, 1929; admitted to bar, 1953, California. *Education:* University of California at Los Angeles (B.A., 1950; J.D., 1953). Phi Alpha Delta. Member, Panel of Arbitrators, American Arbitration Association. Former Member, Board of Governors, Financial Lawyers Conference, 1980-1983. Chairman, Los Angeles County Anti Pornography Task Force, 1987. President, Los Angeles County Commission on Obscenity and Pornography, 1986-1987. Member, Committee on Administration of Justice of the State Bar. Judge Pro Tem, Los Angeles Municipal Court. Arbitrator, Los Angeles Superior Court. *Member:* Los Angeles County and American (Member, Section of Corporation, Banking and Business Law) Bar Associations; State Bar of California; Association of Business Trial Lawyers.

**LINDA A. NETZER,** born Los Angeles, California, May 6, 1954; admitted to bar, 1980, California, U.S. District Court, Central District of California and U.S. Court of Appeals, Ninth Circuit. *Education:* University of California at Los Angeles (B.A., 1976; J.D., 1980). Phi Beta Kappa. Managing Editor, Federal Communications Law Journal, 1979-1980. *Member:* Beverly Hills and Los Angeles County Bar Associations; State Bar of California.

REPRESENTATIVE CLIENTS: First Federal Bank of California; Toyota of Cerritos; Home Bank; CBA Management; First Regional Bank; Comerica Bank-California (Formerly Bank of Industry); Bank of Los Angeles; Merrill Development Co., Inc.; Bohle Company; Buick Mart; Bank of Westminster; Firstline Mortgage; City National Bank; National Bank of Southern California; AMRESCO; San Paolo Bank; Union Federal Bank; Berkeley Federal Bank.

## EPSTEIN, ADELSON & RUBIN
EAST TOWER
11835 WEST OLYMPIC BOULEVARD, SUITE 1235
**LOS ANGELES, CALIFORNIA 90064**
Telephone: 310-473-6447
Fax: 310-473-3097

*Practice Limited to Criminal Law.*

### MEMBERS OF FIRM

**JAMES M. EPSTEIN,** born Los Angeles, California, June 25, 1940; admitted to bar, 1967, California; 1973, U.S. Supreme Court. *Education:* Stanford University (B.A., 1963); University of California at Los Angeles (J.D., 1966). Recipient, American Jurisprudence Award for Excellence in Evidence and Conflict of Laws. Lecturer, on Voir Dire, California Public Defender Association, Riverside Seminar, 1979 and Los Angeles District Attorneys Seminar. Lecturer, The Department of Public Advocacy, Drunk

*(This Listing Continued)*

Driving Seminar, Lexington, Kentucky. *Member:* State Bar of California; California Attorneys for Criminal Justice. (Certified Specialist, Criminal Law, The State Bar of California Board of Legal Specialization). *PRACTICE AREAS:* Criminal Law.

**MICHAEL ADELSON,** born Detroit, Michigan, September 7, 1941; admitted to bar, 1966, California. *Education:* University of Detroit; Detroit College of Law (J.D., 1965). Recipient, Jerry Giesler Memorial Award, Trial Lawyer of the Year awarded by Criminal Courts Bar Association, 1983. Lecturer: "Argument in a Capital Case, Effective Direct and Cross Exam," Continuing Education of the Bar; "Cross of Police Officers in Driving under the Influence Cases," California Public Defenders Association; "Voire Dire in a Capital Case," California Public Defenders Association; "Cross Exam of Forensic Experts," California Association of Forensic Scientist. *Member:* Los Angeles County Bar Association; State Bar of California (Member, Executive Committee, Criminal Justice Section); Criminal Courts Bar Association; California Public Defender Association; Board of Directors, California Attorneys for Criminal Justice. *PRACTICE AREAS:* Criminal Law.

**ALAN RUBIN,** born Brooklyn, New York, September 25, 1950; admitted to bar, 1976, New York and District of Columbia; 1979, U.S. Supreme Court; 1982, California. *Education:* Johns Hopkins University (B.A., cum laude, 1972); University of Michigan (J.D., cum laude, 1975). Phi Beta Kappa; Phi Delta Phi. *Member:* Los Angeles County, New York State and American Bar Associations; State Bar of California; The District of Columbia Bar. *PRACTICE AREAS:* Criminal Law.

REFERENCE: City National Bank.

## EPSTEIN BECKER & GREEN
SUITE 500, 1875 CENTURY PARK, EAST
**LOS ANGELES, CALIFORNIA 90067**
Telephone: 310-556-8861
Facsimile: 310-553-2165

*San Francisco, California Office:* Two Embarcadero Center, Suite 1650. Telephone: 415-398-3500.
*New York, N.Y. Office:* Epstein Becker & Green, P.C., 250 Park Avenue. Telephone: 212-351-4500.
*Washington, D.C. Office:* Epstein Becker & Green, P.C., 1227 25th Street, N.W., Suite 700. Telephone: 202-861-0900.
*Dallas, Texas Office:* Epstein Becker & Green, P.C., Park Central VII, 12750 Merit Drive, Suite 1320. Telephone: 972-490-3143.
*Stamford, Connecticut Office:* Epstein Becker & Green, P.C., Suite 603, Six Landmark Square. Telephone: 203-348-3737.
*Newark, New Jersey Office:* Epstein Becker & Green, P.C., Seventh Floor, The Legal Center, One Riverfront Plaza. Telephone: 201-642-1900.
*Miami, Florida Office:* Suite 100, 2400 South Dixie Highway. Telephone: 305-856-1100.
*Boston, Massachusetts Office:* Epstein Becker & Green, P.C., 75 State Street. Telephone: 617-342-4000.
*Alexandria, Virginia Office:* Epstein Becker & Green, P.C., Suite 301, 510 King Street. Telephone: 703-684-1204.

*General Practice. Corporation, Securities, Commercial Law and Bankruptcy. Health Care and Hospital Law. Management Labor Relations and Employee Benefits Law. Equal Employment Opportunity and Affirmative Action Law and Practice. Taxation, Insurance, Government Procurement, Municipal Finance, Real Estate, Political Activities, Legislation and Election Law. Arbitration, Administrative Proceedings, State and Federal Civil and Appellate Practice.*

### MEMBERS OF THE FIRM

**DAVID P. BENDER, JR.,** born Los Angeles, California, April 12, 1956; admitted to bar, 1986, California; U.S. District Court, Central District of California; 1989, U.S. District Court, Northern, Eastern and Southern Districts of California. *Education:* University of Notre Dame (B.A., 1978); Southwestern University School of Law (J.D., 1985). Staff Member, 1983-1984 and Production Editor, 1984-1985, Southwestern University Law Review. Trustee, 1979-1987 and President, 1980-1981, 1986-1987, Ventura County Community College District Board of Trustees. *Member:* The State Bar of California.

**THOMAS P. BROWN IV,** born Philadelphia, Pennsylvania, November 6, 1946; admitted to bar, 1975, Georgia, U.S. District Court, Northern District of Georgia and U.S. Court of Appeals, Fifth Circuit; 1981, California and U.S. District Court, Central District of California. *Education:* Temple University (B.A., cum laude, 1971); Vanderbilt University (J.D., 1974).

*(This Listing Continued)*

Trial Attorney: Office of the Solicitor, U.S. Department of Labor, 1976-1979; Equal Employment Opportunity Commission, 1979-1981. *Member:* State Bar of California; State Bar of Georgia.

**B. ALAN DICKSON,** born Vallejo, California, May 24, 1943; admitted to bar, 1969, California and U.S. District Court, Central District of California; 1982, District of Columbia; U.S. Court of Federal Claims; U.S. Court of Military Appeals; U.S. Court of Appeals, Ninth Circuit; U.S. Court of Appeals for the Federal Circuit. *Education:* Yale University (B.A., cum laude, 1965); Harvard University (J.D., 1968); George Washington University (LL.M., summa cum laude, 1972); University of New Mexico (1973-1975). *Member:* Los Angeles County, Federal (Member, Government Contracts Committee) and American (Member, Sections on: Litigation; Public Contract Law) Bar Associations; State Bar of California; The District of Columbia Bar. [Attorney, U.S. Air Force, 1969-1975; Col., Air Force Reserve]

**ROBERT A. DYE,** born Oakland, California, September 11, 1960; admitted to bar, 1986, California; 1987, U.S. District Court, Northern, Eastern and Southern Districts of California and U.S. Court of Appeals, Ninth Circuit; 1988, U.S. District Court, Central District of California; 1993, U.S. District Court, District of Arizona; 1995, U.S. Court of Appeals for the District of Columbia Circuit. *Education:* California State University, Hayward (B.S., with honors, 1982; B.A., 1983); University of the Pacific, McGeorge School of Law (J.D., with great distinction, 1986). Order of the Coif. Co-Author: with James A. Goodman, "'You're Fired': Cross-Examination of a Wrongful Termination Plaintiff," 8 California Litigation, No. 3, Spring 1995. Contributing Author: *California Employment Law*, Merchants & Manufacturers Association, 1990; *California Employment Law*, 3d Ed., The Employers Group, 1996. *Member:* The State Bar of California. *PRACTICE AREAS:* Labor and Employment Law; Litigation.

**CYNTHIA E. GITT,** born York, Pennsylvania, November 14, 1946; admitted to bar, 1971, District of Columbia; 1974, California; 1976, Michigan and U.S. Supreme Court; 1978, Arizona. *Education:* Wheaton College (B.A., 1968); George Washington University (J.D., with high honors, 1971). Order of the Coif. Legislative Assistant, Hon. Bella Abzug, 1971. Trial Attorney, Equal Employment Opportunity Commission, Washington, D.C. and San Francisco, California, 1971-1975. *Member:* Los Angeles County (Member, Sections on: Labor Law; Litigation) and American (Member, Labor and Employment Law Section) Bar Associations; The State Bar of California; The District of Columbia Bar; The Association of Trial Lawyers of America.

**JAMES A. GOODMAN,** born Hollywood, Florida, August 19, 1953; admitted to bar, 1979, California. *Education:* University of Oregon (B.S., 1975); Loyola University of Los Angeles (J.D., 1979). *Member:* Los Angeles County Bar Association; The State Bar of California.

**DAVID JACOBS,** admitted to bar, 1977, New York; 1986, California. *Education:* University of California (B.A., magna cum laude, 1973); Loyola University; New York University (J.D., 1977).

**MARK A. KADZIELSKI,** born Cleveland, Ohio, July 1, 1947; admitted to bar, 1976, California. *Education:* John Carroll University (A.B., magna cum laude, 1968); University of Pennsylvania (J.D., 1976). Member, Advisory Board, Town Hall of California, (West) 1981—. Alpha Sigma Nu; Phi Alpha Theta. Author: "Title IX of the Education Amendments of 1972: Change or Continuity?" 6 Journal of Law and Education 183, 1977; "The Admissibility of Evidence on the Absence of Similar Accidents," 53 Los Angeles Bar Journal 22, July, 1977; "Title IX and Residential Living: An Analysis," 16 NASPA Journal 29, 1978; "Postsecondary Athletics in An Era of Equality: An Appraisal of the Effect of Title IX," 5 Journal of College and University Law 123, 1979; "Legal Approaches to Sex Discrimination in Amateur Athletics: The First Decade," Law and Amateur Sports, Indiana University Press, 1982. Co-Author: with Robert C. Kunda, "The Origins of Modern Dissent: The Unmaking of Judicial Consensus in the 1930's," 15 UWLA Law Rev. 43, 1983. *Member:* Los Angeles County (Delegate, State Bar Convention, 1982-1986; Member, Board of Editors, Los Angeles Lawyer, 1980-1985; Vice-Chair, 1981-1983) and American (Member: Forum Committee on Health Law, 1983—; Section on Litigation) Bar Associations; The State Bar of California (Member, Committee on the History of Law in California, 1978-1982; Chair, 1981-1982; Member: Committee to Confer with California Medical Association, 1982-1986; Section on Litigation); American Academy of Hospital Attorneys; California Society for Healthcare Attorneys; Catholic Health Association of the United States (Member, Legal Services Committee, 1986-1989). *PRACTICE AREAS:* Health and Hospital Law; Medical Staff Law.

**JOHN P. KRAVE,** born Santa Monica, California, November 17, 1952; admitted to bar, 1980, California and U.S. District Court, Central District

*(This Listing Continued)*

of California. *Education:* Loyola University of Los Angeles (B.A., cum laude, 1974); Loyola University (J.D., 1980). Alpha Sigma Nu. *Member:* The State Bar of California; National Health Lawyers Association. [1st. Lt., U.S. Air Force, 1974-1976]. *PRACTICE AREAS:* Corporate Health Care.

**ANGEL MANZANO, JR.,** born New York, N.Y., September 12, 1950; admitted to bar, 1977, California; 1979, U.S. District Court, Central District of California; 1980, U.S. Court of Appeals, 9th Circuit; 1982, U.S. District Court, Eastern and Northern Districts of California; 1986, U.S. District Court, Southern District of California. *Education:* Stanford University (B.A., 1972); Columbia University (J.D., 1976). Charles Evans Hughes Fellow, Columbia Law School, 1974-1976. Attorney, United States Department of Justice, Civil Rights Division, 1977-1979. Senior Attorney, President's Reorganization Project, 1978. *Member:* State Bar of California; American Bar Association (Member, Sections on: Labor and Employment Law; Litigation).

**ALAN E. WALCHER,** born Chicago, Illinois, October 2, 1949; admitted to bar, 1974, Utah, U.S. District Court, District of Utah and U.S. Court of Appeals, Tenth Circuit; 1979, California, U.S. District Court, Central District of California and U.S. Court of Appeals, Ninth Circuit. *Education:* University of Utah (B.S., 1971; Certificate in International Relations, 1971; J.D., 1974). Phi Delta Phi. Member, Bar and Gavel (Vice-President, 1975). Moot Court Honors Board. Teaching Associate, Antitrust Law, University of Utah, 1975. Judge Pro Tem, Los Angeles Municipal Court, 1986. *Member:* Century City, Beverly Hills, Los Angeles County and American (Member, Sections on: Litigation; Public Contract Law) Bar Associations; Utah State Bar; State Bar of California (Member, Business Law Section); Association of Business Trial Lawyers.

## SENIOR ATTORNEYS

**ABBIE P. MALINIAK,** born New York, N.Y., June 11, 1950; admitted to bar, 1982, New Jersey; 1988, California. *Education:* University of California at Los Angeles (B.A., cum laude, 1972); Rutgers University (J.D., 1982). *PRACTICE AREAS:* Health Law.

**ALYCE ANN RUBINFELD,** born Los Angeles, California, October 4, 1955; admitted to bar, 1983, California; U.S. District Court, Central and Southern Districts of California and U.S. Court of Appeals, Ninth Circuit. *Education:* California State University, Northridge (B.A., magna cum laude, 1978); Hastings College of Law, University of California (J.D., 1982). Executive Editor, COMM/ENT Law Journal, 1980-1982. Senior Trial Attorney, Equal Employment Opportunity Commission, 1985-1988. Member, Board of Directors, Pasadena Police Foundation. *Member:* Los Angeles County Bar Association (Member, Labor and Employment Law Section); State Bar of California; California Women Lawyers. *PRACTICE AREAS:* Labor and Employment Law; Litigation.

---

**LESTER F. APONTE,** admitted to bar, 1989, California. *Education:* Haverford College (B.A., 1986); Columbia University (J.D., 1986). *Member:* Puerto Rican Bar Association. *PRACTICE AREAS:* Labor and Employment Law; Litigation.

**JUDITH L. BAXTER,** admitted to bar, 1987, California. *Education:* University of Southern California (B.A., 1984); Ohio State University (J.D., 1987). *PRACTICE AREAS:* Labor and Employment Law; Construction; Litigation.

**I. BENJAMIN BLADY,** admitted to bar, 1992, California. *Education:* University of California at Los Angeles (B.A., 1989); Loyola Marymount University (J.D., 1992). *Member:* Los Angeles County Bar Association (Member, Sections on: Employment Law; Litigation); American Inns of Court. *PRACTICE AREAS:* Labor and Employment Law; Litigation.

**JANA L. DEMEIRE,** admitted to bar, 1975, California. *Education:* Vassar College (B.A., 1980); University of Virginia (J.D., 1984). *PRACTICE AREAS:* Labor and Employment Law; Education Law; Litigation.

**GREGORY S. GLAZER,** admitted to bar, 1994, California. *Education:* University of California, Berkeley (B.A., 1991); University of Southern California (J.D., 1994). *PRACTICE AREAS:* Labor and Employment Law; Litigation.

**JILL H. GORDON,** (admission pending). *Education:* Sarah Lawrence College (A.B., 1991); Washington University (J.D., 1996; M.H.A., 1996). *PRACTICE AREAS:* Health Law.

**PAMELA G. GROSS,** admitted to bar, 1992, California. *Education:* University of Michigan (B.A., with high distinction, 1967); University of California at Los Angeles School of Social Welfare (M.S.W., 1971); (Uni-

*(This Listing Continued)*

CALIFORNIA—LOS ANGELES                     MARTINDALE-HUBBELL LAW DIRECTORY 1997

**EPSTEIN BECKER & GREEN,** *Los Angeles—Continued*

versity of California at Los Angeles (J.D., 1992). Phi Beta Kappa. *PRACTICE AREAS:* Health Law.

**DANIEL J. HAMMOND,** admitted to bar, 1989, California. *Education:* University of Minnesota (B.S., 1983; B.A., 1983; J.D., cum laude, 1989). *PRACTICE AREAS:* Labor and Employment Law; Education Law; Litigation.

**ELONA KOGAN,** admitted to bar, 1994, California. *Education:* Barnard College (B.S., cum laude, 1991); Southwestern University School of Law (J.D., 1994). *PRACTICE AREAS:* Health Law.

**PATRICIA Y. MILLER,** admitted to bar, 1988, California; 1991, Colorado. *Education:* Villanova University (B.S.N., 1974); Southwestern University School of Law (J.D., 1988). *PRACTICE AREAS:* Health Law.

**MARGARET B. REYNOLDS,** admitted to bar, 1990, California. *Education:* University of the Pacific (B.A., 1980); University of Colorado (M.S., 1982); Whittier College School of Law (J.D., magna cum laude, 1990). *Member:* American Academy of Healthcare Attorneys; Women in Health Administration in Southern California; American College of Healthcare Executives. *PRACTICE AREAS:* Health Law.

**RALPH M. SEMIEN,** admitted to bar, 1992, California. *Education:* University of West Los Angeles of Paralegal Studies (B.S., with honors, 1988); Loyola Law School (J.D., 1992). *PRACTICE AREAS:* Labor and Employment Law; Education Law; Litigation.

(For other Personnel and Biographical Data, see Professional Biographies at San Francisco, California, Stamford, Connecticut, Washington, D.C., Miami and Tallahassee, Florida, Boston, Massachusetts, Newark, New Jersey, New York, N.Y., Alexandria, Virginia and Dallas, Texas Offices)

---

## ERICKSEN, ARBUTHNOT, KILDUFF, DAY & LINDSTROM, INC.

*Established in 1950*

**835 WILSHIRE BOULEVARD, SUITE 500
LOS ANGELES, CALIFORNIA 90017-2603**
*Telephone: 213-489-4411
Fax: 213-489-4332*

*Oakland, California Office:* 530 Water Street, Port Building, Suite 720. Telephone: 510-832-7770. Fax: 510-832-0102.
*San Francisco, California Office:* 260 California Street, Suite 1100. Telephone: 415-362-7126. Fax: 415-362-6401.
*Sacramento, California Office:* 100 Howe Avenue, Suite 240N. Telephone: 916-483-5181. Fax: 916-483-7558.
*Fresno, California Office:* 2440 West Shaw Avenue, Suite 101. Telephone: 209-449-2600. Fax: 209-449-2603.
*San Jose, California Office:* 152 North Third Street, Suite 700. Telephone: 408-286-0880. Fax: 408-286-0337.
*Walnut Creek, California Office:* 2700 Ygnacio Valley Road, Suite 280. Telephone: 510-947-1702. Fax: 510-947-4921.
*Riverside, California Office:* 1770 Iowa Avenue, Suite 210. Telephone: 909-682-3246. Fax: 909-682-4013.

*General Civil, Trial and Appellate Practice in all State and Federal Courts. Corporate, Probate and Insurance Law.*

*FIRM PROFILE: Ericksen, Arbuthnot, Kilduff, Day & Lindstrom is a statewide, civil litigation and insurance defense firm founded in 1950. This multiple office approach ensures uniform procedures and capabilities for both out-of-state and California-based clients. Experienced attorneys, backed by a well-trained paralegal staff, handle cases involving liability defense and insurance coverage and general civil litigation.*

**THOMAS J. McDONNELL,** born San Francisco, California, October 29, 1959; admitted to bar, 1986, California; 1987, U.S. District Court, Southern and Central Districts of California. *Education:* University of California at Los Angeles (B.A., 1983); University of Oregon (J.D., 1986). Phi Alpha Delta. *Member:* Santa Monica and Los Angeles County Bar Associations; State Bar of California. *PRACTICE AREAS:* Insurance Defense Litigation; Insurance Coverage.

**MARK L. KIEFER,** born Lynwood, California, June 30, 1959; admitted to bar, 1984, California and U.S. District Court, Northern District of California; 1987, U.S. District Court, Central District of California. *Education:* University of California at Los Angeles (B.A., magna cum laude, 1981); University of Santa Clara (J.D., 1984). *Member:* American Bar Association;

*(This Listing Continued)*

CAA646B

State Bar of California; Association of Southern California Defense Counsel. *PRACTICE AREAS:* Insurance Litigation.

**DEBORAH S. TROPP,** born Santiago, Chile, September 5, 1967; admitted to bar, 1992, California. *Education:* University of California at Los Angeles (B.A., Political Science/Public Law, 1989); McGeorge School of Law, University of the Pacific (J.D., 1992). Recipient, Order of the Barristers Award. *Member:* Los Angles County and American Bar Associations; The State Bar of California. *LANGUAGES:* Spanish. *PRACTICE AREAS:* Insurance Defense; Personal Injury.

**BUD SPENCER,** born Riverside, California, November 25, 1968; admitted to bar, 1994, California and U.S. District Court, Central District of California. *Education:* University of California at Riverside (B.S., 1991); Southwestern University (J.D., 1994). *Member:* State Bar of California. *PRACTICE AREAS:* Insurance Defense Litigation.

(For biographical data on other personnel, see Professional Biographies at other office locations).

---

## ERVIN, COHEN & JESSUP LLP

**LOS ANGELES, CALIFORNIA**

(See Beverly Hills)

*Federal and State Taxation, Business, Corporation, Securities and Real Estate Law. General Business and Commercial Litigation in all State and Federal Trial and Appellate Courts with emphasis on Unfair Competition, Business Torts, Intellectual Property, Trademarks, Trade Secrets and Insurance Coverage and Litigation. Environmental Law. Probate, Estate Planning and Trusts, Insolvency and Creditors' Rights, Health Care and Entertainment Law.*

---

## ESNER HIGA & CHANG

**523 WEST SIXTH STREET
LOS ANGELES, CALIFORNIA 90014**
*Telephone: 213-630-1990
Fax: 213-630-1999*

*San Francisco, California Office:* 625 Market St., 10th Floor. Telephone: 415-882-4056. Fax: 415-495-4566.

*Appellate Practice.*

(For Complete biographical data on all personnel, see Professional Biographies at San Francisco).

---

## EZER, SMENT & WILLIAMSON

**LOS ANGELES, CALIFORNIA**

(See Michael R. Sment, Ventura and Los Angeles)

---

## EZER & WILLIAMSON, LLP

*Established in 1964*

(Formerly Rich & Ezer)

**1888 CENTURY PARK EAST, SUITE 1550**
(CENTURY CITY)
**LOS ANGELES, CALIFORNIA 90067-1706**
*Telephone: 310-277-7747
Telecopier: 310-277-2576*

*General Civil, Trial and Appellate Practice in all State and Federal Courts. Real Estate, Corporate, Partnership Law, Business, Construction, Foreclosures, Probate, Creditors Rights.*

*FIRM PROFILE: The firm was originally established as Rich & Ezer, in 1964. The firm specializes in the representation of entrepreneurs, small and medium-size businesses and partnerships. Representation focuses on complex business, commercial and real estate litigation, real property foreclosures, real property receiverships and other provisional remedies, construction litigation, transactional matters and business formation. Areas in which the firm's clients are involved include real estate investment and syndication, real estate brokerage, construction, manufacturing and sales, insurance, elevator maintenance, manufacturing and installation.*

*(This Listing Continued)*

The firm is dedicated to providing its clients with personalized service and delivering excellent results. The firm prides itself on its ability to recognize practical approaches and implement practical solutions which produce tangible and cost effective results. Quality, creativity, integrity, efficiency and an uncompromising commitment to delivering results for a reasonable fee are the backbone of Ezer & Williamson's approach.

**MITCHEL J. EZER,** born Chicago, Illinois, January 3, 1935; admitted to bar, 1960, California; 1967, U.S. Tax Court; 1970, U.S. Supreme Court. *Education:* Northwestern University (B.S., 1956); Yale University (J.D., 1959). Phi Alpha Delta; Order of the Coif; Beta Gamma Sigma; Beta Alpha Psi. Note and Comment Editor, Yale Law Journal, 1958-1959. Author: Chapters 5-9, *California Commercial Law I* (CEB, 1966); Uniform Commercial Code Bibliography, 1972; "The Impact of the Uniform Commercial Code on the California Law of Sales Warranties," 8 University of California at Los Angeles Law Review 281, 1961; "Serious Tax Traps Exist in Recovery of Wrongfully Withheld Profits," 14 Journal of Taxation 328, 1961; "Requirements and Output Contracts in California Under the Uniform Commercial Code," 1 Loyola Digest 56, 1966; Book Review, "Religion and the Law of Church and State and the Supreme Court," 11 University of California at Los Angeles Law Review 174, 1963; "Intrusion on Solitude," 21 Law in Transition 63, 1961. Associate in Law, University of California at Los Angeles, 1959-1960. Lecturer: Law, Loyola University of Los Angeles, 1964-1967; Secured Transactions, California Judges Association, December 1991. Member: National Panel of Arbitrators American Arbitration Association. *Member:* Beverly Hills Bar Association (Member, Board of Governors, 1979-1981); State Bar of California; American Judicature Society; Scribes. **PRACTICE AREAS:** Real Estate; Foreclosures; Partnership; Business and Probate Litigation.

**RICHARD E. WILLIAMSON,** born Perth Amboy, New Jersey, April 21, 1960; admitted to bar, 1985, California, U.S. District Court, Central District of California and U.S. Court of Appeals, Ninth Circuit. *Education:* Arizona State University (B.S., 1981); McGeorge School of Law, University of the Pacific (J.D., 1985). Real Estate Broker, California, Department of Real Estate, 1990—. Arbitrator, Beverly Hills Bar Association, 1991—. Arbitrator, Los Angeles Superior Court, 1993—. Member: Beverly Hills and Los Angeles County Bar Associations; State Bar of California; Consumer Attorneys Association of Los Angeles; Los Angeles County Barristers (Member, Moot Court Committee). **PRACTICE AREAS:** Partnership; Real Estate; Business; Commercial; Construction Litigation.

### OF COUNSEL

**JOHN CRAMER,** born Los Angeles, California, August 22, 1939; admitted to bar, 1966, California. *Education:* Stanford University (B.S., cum laude, 1961); University of California at Berkeley (J.D., 1965). Tau Beta Pi. Vice President/General Counsel, Easton, Inc., 1989—. *Member:* Los Angeles County and American Bar Associations.

### ASSOCIATES

**FREDERICK D. HALE,** born Hawthorne, California, May 6, 1960; admitted to bar, 1995, California. *Education:* California State University at Chico (B.S., cum laude, 1990); McGeorge School of Law, University of the Pacific (J.D., 1994). Recipient, IOLTA Scholarship, 1993, 1994. Member: Beverly Hills and Los Angeles Bar Associations; State Bar of California (Member, Sections on: Real Estate Law, Business and Litigation). **PRACTICE AREAS:** Construction; Real Estate; Business.

---

## HARRY M. FAIN

### LOS ANGELES, CALIFORNIA

(See Beverly Hills)

*Practice Limited to Family Law.*

---

## FAINSBERT, MASE & SNYDER

A Partnership including Professional Corporations

*Established in 1987*

SUITE 1100, 11835 WEST OLYMPIC BOULEVARD
**LOS ANGELES, CALIFORNIA 90064**
Telephone: 310-473-6400
Telecopier: 310-473-8702

*Real Property, Federal and State Taxation, Business, Corporate, Partnership, Estate Planning, Probate and Entertainment Law. General Civil and Trial Practice in State and Federal Courts, Creditors Rights.*

### MEMBERS OF FIRM

**STEPHEN B. FAINSBERT, (A P.C.),** born New York, N.Y., October 31, 1936; admitted to bar, 1966, California. *Education:* Wharton School; University of Pennsylvania (B.S., 1958); Michigan State University (M.A., 1960); University of California at Los Angeles (J.D., 1966). Phi Alpha Delta. Author: "Secondary Financing by Seller and the Need for Subordination Agreements," California Escrow Association News, March, 1983. Co-author: "Creative Real Estate: Performance Deeds of Trust," California Real Estate Magazine, December, 1981; "Real Property Exchanges," California Continuing Education of the Bar, 1988, 1990 and 1991 Supplements, 2nd Edition, 1994. Lecturer: Tax Deferred Real Property Exchanges, 1979; Real Property Practice, 1980-1986; How to Handle An Escrow, 1985, Financing Real Estate Transactions, 1986 and How to Prevent or Handle Disputes in Real Property Escrows, 1987, California Continuing Education of the Bar; Escrow Closings, California Continuing Education of the Bar Annual Real Estate Institute, 1989, Tenancy in Common Agreements, All-Inclusive Deeds of Trust and Land Contracts, California Continuing Education of the Bar Annual Real Estate Institute, 1990. Consultant to the California Continuing Education of the Bar publication "Real Property Exchanges," 1982, "California Real Property Financing," 1988 and "Mortgage and Deed of Trust Practice," 1990. *Member:* Santa Monica, Los Angeles County (Member, Real Property Section) and American Bar Associations; State Bar of California (Member, Real Property Section). **PRACTICE AREAS:** Real Estate; Real Estate-Commercial Law; Real Estate Finance; Title Insurance Law.

**JOHN A. MASE, (A P.C.),** born Bridgeport, Connecticut, August 11, 1958; admitted to bar, 1983, California; 1984, U.S. District Court, Central District of California and U.S. Tax Court. *Education:* University of Rhode Island (B.S., summa cum laude, 1980); Boston University (J.D., 1983). Beta Alpha Psi; Phi Kappa Phi; Beta Gamma Sigma. Executive Editor, Boston University Law School Commentaries Journal, 1982-1983. Co-Author: "Real Property Exchanges," California Continuing Education of the Bar, 1988, 1990 and 1991 Supplements, 2nd Edition, 1994. Consultant to the California Continuing Education of the Bar publication, "California Mortgage and Deed of Trust Practice," 1989. Lecturer: Tax Deferred Real Property Exchanges, 1991-1994; Low-Income Housing Partnerships, 1992-1994. *Member:* Beverly Hills, Los Angeles County (Member, Tax Section) and American (Member, Section of Taxation) Bar Associations; State Bar of California (Member, Taxation Section). (Certified Specialist, Taxation Law, The State Bar of California Board of Legal Specialization). **PRACTICE AREAS:** Taxation Law; Real Estate; Business Transactions; Corporate Law.

**LAWRENCE A. SNYDER, (A P.C.),** born Los Angeles, California, May 23, 1953; admitted to bar, 1981, California; 1982, U.S. District Court, Central District of California and U.S. Tax Court. *Education:* University of California at Los Angeles (B.A., 1975); Loyola Law School-Los Angeles (J.D., cum laude, 1981). Certified Public Accountant, California, 1977. Co-author: "Real Property Exchanges," California Continuing Education of the Bar, 1988, 1990 and 1991 Supplements, 2nd Edition, 1994. *Member:* Beverly Hills, Los Angeles County and American (Member, Section of Taxation) Bar Associations; State Bar of California; American Institute of Certified Public Accountants; California Society of Certified Public Accountants. (Certified Specialist, Taxation Law, The State Bar of California Board of Legal Specialization). **PRACTICE AREAS:** Taxation Law; Estate Planning; Business Transactions; Real Estate.

**RAYMOND H. AVER,** born Vancouver, British Columbia, Canada, July 11, 1957; admitted to bar, 1983, California; 1984, U.S. District Court, Central District of California and U.S. Court of Appeals, Ninth Circuit; 1985, U.S. District Court, Northern, Eastern and Southern Districts of California. *Education:* University of California at Los Angeles (B.A., cum laude, 1980); Hastings College of the Law, University of California (J.D., 1983). Editor and Co-Author: "Fundamentals of Bankruptcy," Los Angeles

*(This Listing Continued)*

**FAINSBERT, MASE & SNYDER, Los Angeles—Continued**

County Bar Association, 1991-1994. *Member:* Los Angeles County and American Bar Associations; State Bar of California. **PRACTICE AREAS:** Insolvency Law; Real Estate Law; Business Litigation.

*ASSOCIATES*

**COLIN J. TANNER,** born Oyster Bay, New York, July 13, 1965; admitted to bar, 1990, California; 1993, Colorado; U.S. District Court, Northern, Eastern, Central and Southern Districts of California. *Education:* University of California at San Diego (B.A., 1987); Hastings College of Law (J.D., 1990). Phi Alpha Delta (Treasurer, 1989). *Member:* State Bar of California (Member, Litigation Section); American Bar Association. **PRACTICE AREAS:** Commercial Litigation; Real Estate Litigation; Tort Litigation; Insurance Bad Faith Litigation; Products Liability Litigation.

**SARAH K. ANDRUS,** born Harbor City, California, June 7, 1969; admitted to bar, 1994, California. *Education:* University of Michigan (A.B., 1990); Hastings College of the Law (J.D., 1994). Sigma Iota Rho. Author: "The Czech Republic and Slovakia: Foreign Investment in Changing Economies," Hastings International and Comparative Law Review, Spring 1994. *Member:* State Bar of California.

---

## *FAIRBANK & VINCENT*

**11755 WILSHIRE BOULEVARD, SUITE 800**
**LOS ANGELES, CALIFORNIA 90025**
Telephone: 310-996-5520
Fax: 310-996-5530
Email: fairvin@earthlink.net

*General Civil Trial and Appellate Practice in all Courts.*

FIRM PROFILE: *Fairbank & Vincent is a business litigation law firm specializing in civil trial and appellate work. The firm was created by two lawyers from the Los Angeles office of Gibson, Dunn & Crutcher. The firm primarily represents companies, as defendants or plaintiffs, in a wide variety of complex business disputes, including securities and consumer class actions, shareholder derivative actions, employment litigation, competitive business torts, unfair competition, antitrust, breach of contract and fraud cases.*

*MEMBERS OF FIRM*

**ROBERT HAROLD FAIRBANK,** born March 4, 1948; admitted to bar, 1977, California. *Education:* Pomona College, Stanford University (A.B., 1972); University of California at Berkeley (M.L.S., 1973); Boalt Hall School of Law, University of California; New York University (J.D., 1977). Associate Editor, New York University Law Review, 1975-1976. Co-Author: *California Practice Guide Civil Trials and Evidence* (The Rutter Group 1993, updated annually); "Defending Officers, Directors and Majority Shareholders - The Defense Viewpoint," (PLI, 1980). Author, "Effective Pretrial and Trial Motions," (ABTL, 1983). Partner, 1984-1986 and Associate, 1977-1984, Gibson, Dunn & Crutcher. Co-founding Partner, Fairbank & Vincent, 1996. Panelist on Civil Procedure and Trial Practice, ABTL Annual Seminars, 1986, 1994. The Rutter Group Statewide Programs, (1986-1995). Chair, Subcommittee on Civil Trial Rules, Judicial Council of California Advisory Committee on Local Rules, 1989-1991. *Member:* Association of Business Trial Lawyers (Member, Board of Governors, 1983-1985; Treasurer, 1986; Secretary, 1987; Vice President, 1988; President, 1989). **PRACTICE AREAS:** Complex Business Litigation; Securities; Consumer Class Actions; Competitive Business Torts; Director and Officer Liability; Unfair Competition Litigation; Antitrust; Trial Practice. **Email:** fairvin@earthlink.net

**DIRK L. VINCENT,** born March 24, 1967; admitted to bar, 1992, California and Washington. *Education:* Pacific Lutheran University (B.B.A., 1988); Columbia University (J.D., 1991). Stone Scholar. Senior Articles Editor, Columbia Business Law Review. Law Clerk to the Honorable Andrew J. Kleinfeld, U.S. Court of Appeals, Ninth Circuit. Member, Gibson, Dunn & Crutcher, 1992-1996. Co-founding Partner, Fairbank & Vincent, 1996. *Member:* Los Angeles County Bar Association; Association of Business Trial Lawyers. **PRACTICE AREAS:** Complex Business Litigation; Securities; Consumer Class Actions; Competitive Business Torts; Trial Practice. **Email:** fairvin@earthlink.net

CAA648B

---

## *FAIRSHTER & ASSOCIATES*

**LOS ANGELES, CALIFORNIA**
(See Pasadena)

*Corporate, Business, Bankruptcy, Entertainment, Media, International Transactions, Finance and Real Estate Law.*

---

## *FALK & SHARP*

A PROFESSIONAL CORPORATION
Established in 1990

**660 SOUTH FIGUEROA STREET, SUITE 1600**
**LOS ANGELES, CALIFORNIA 90017-3452**
Telephone: 213-622-6868
FAX: 213-622-4486

*General Corporate and Labor.*

**ETHAN J. FALK,** born New York, N.Y., January 22, 1954; admitted to bar, 1979, California. *Education:* State University of New York at Binghamton (B.A., magna cum laude, 1976); University of Michigan (J.D., magna cum laude, 1979). Phi Beta Kappa; Order of the Coif. Author: "Structuring and Negotiating Acquisitions in the United States," NBL Journal, Tokyo, Japan, Sept.-Oct., 1986. *Member:* Los Angeles County (Editor, Business and Corporation Law Section Newsletter, 1988-1990) and American Bar Associations; State Bar of California (Member, Corporations Committee, 1987-1990). **PRACTICE AREAS:** Corporate.

**KEITH A. SHARP,** born Winnipeg, Manitoba, Canada, September 14, 1958; admitted to bar, 1983, California. *Education:* Occidental College (A.B., cum laude, 1980); Loyola Law School (J.D., cum laude, 1983). Phi Beta Kappa; Omicron Delta Epsilon; Phi Alpha Delta. Member, St. Thomas More Law Honor Society. Foreign Attorney, Nagashima & Ohno, Tokyo, Japan, 1986-1987. *Member:* Los Angeles County and American Bar Associations; State Bar of California. **PRACTICE AREAS:** Labor; Corporate.

---

## *FARMER & RIDLEY*

A Partnership including Professional Corporations
Established in 1990

**SUITE 2300**
**444 SOUTH FLOWER STREET**
**LOS ANGELES, CALIFORNIA 90071**
Telephone: 213-626-0291
Fax: 213-687-9807

*Federal and State Taxation, Corporation, Real Property and Land Use. Estate Planning, Probate and Trust Law, Securities, Pension and Profit Sharing. General Civil and Trial Practice in all State and Federal Courts and Administrative Agencies.*

**ROBERT L. FARMER, (A PROFESSIONAL CORPORATION),** born Portland, Oregon, September 29, 1922; admitted to bar, 1949, California. *Education:* University of California at Los Angeles (B.S., 1946); University of Southern California (LL.B., 1949). Order of the Coif; Phi Delta Phi. *Member:* Los Angeles County and American (Member, Section of Taxation) Bar Associations; The State Bar of California; Chancery Club. **PRACTICE AREAS:** Taxation; Estate Planning; Transactional Law.

**TERRY R. FINUCANE, (A PROFESSIONAL CORPORATION),** born Los Angeles, California, March 29, 1946; admitted to bar, 1973, California. *Education:* University of California at Los Angeles (B.A., 1969); Hastings College of Law, University of California (J.D., 1973). *Member:* Los Angeles County and American (Member, Taxation and Corporation, Banking and Business Law Sections) Bar Associations; State Bar of California. **PRACTICE AREAS:** Corporate; Business; Tax; Employee Benefit Law.

**ALLAN J. GRAF,** born Los Angeles, California, August 25, 1946; admitted to bar, 1973, New York and California. *Education:* Johns Hopkins University (B.A., 1969; M.A., 1969); Columbia University (J.D., 1972). Phi Beta Kappa. *Member:* Los Angeles County and American Bar Associations; State Bar of California. **LANGUAGES:** French and Spanish. **PRACTICE AREAS:** Litigation.

*(This Listing Continued)*

**PERRY E. MAGUIRE, (A PROFESSIONAL CORPORATION),** born Fullerton, California, September 26, 1943; admitted to bar, 1971, California. *Education:* University of California at Los Angeles (B.A., 1965; M.A., 1967; J.D., 1970). *Member:* Los Angeles County and American (Member, Taxation, Corporation, Banking and Business Law Section) Bar Associations; The State Bar of California. *PRACTICE AREAS:* Employee Benefit Law.

**JOHN G. POWERS, (A PROFESSIONAL CORPORATION),** born Lompoc, California, January 9, 1957; admitted to bar, 1980, California. *Education:* California State University at San Diego (B.S., 1977); University of Santa Clara (J.D., 1980). Beta Gamma Sigma; Phi Kappa Phi; Pi Sigma Alpha. Associate Editor, Santa Clara Law Review, 1979-1980. Mayor, City of La Habra Heights. *Member:* Los Angeles County, Orange County (Member, Litigation, Real Property and Corporations Sections), San Bernardino County and American Bar Associations; The State Bar of California. *PRACTICE AREAS:* Environmental; Corporate Real Estate; Land Use Law.

**ROBERT W. RIDLEY, (A PROFESSIONAL CORPORATION),** born Los Angeles, California, February 14, 1937; admitted to bar, 1963, California. *Education:* St. John's College; Loyola University of Los Angeles (LL.B., 1962). Phi Alpha Delta. *Member:* Los Angeles County and American (Member, Section of Taxation) Bar Associations; The State Bar of California. *PRACTICE AREAS:* ERISA.

**ROBERT L. WEAVER, (A PROFESSIONAL CORPORATION),** born Fullerton, California, May 30, 1943; admitted to bar, 1969, California. *Education:* Stanford University (A.B., 1965); Columbia University (LL.B., 1968). Phi Delta Phi. *Member:* Los Angeles County and American (Member, Section of Real Property, Probate and Trust Law) Bar Associations; The State Bar of California. *PRACTICE AREAS:* Estate Planning; Probate Law; Taxation.

---

## FAUSTMAN, CARLTON, DiSANTE & FREUDENBERGER LLP

700 SOUTH FLOWER STREET, ELEVENTH FLOOR
LOS ANGELES, CALIFORNIA 90017
Telephone: 213-892-6308

*Irvine, California Office:* 2600 Michelson Drive, Suite 800, 92612.
Telephone: 714-622-1661. Fax: 714-622-1669.
*Sacramento, California Office:* 711 9th Street, Suite 100, 95814. Telephone: 916-443-0999. Fax: 916-442-5140.
*San Francisco, California Office:* 388 Market Street, Suite 400, 94111.
Telephone: 415-296-3813. Fax: 415-296-3814.
*San Diego, California Office:* 8910 University Center Lane, Suite 500, 92122.
Telephone: 619-678-8446. Fax: 619-678-8447.

On behalf of Employers, Employment Discrimination, Wrongful Discharge, Sexual Harassment and ERISA Litigation. Union Organizing Campaigns, Unfair Labor Practice Proceedings, Collective Bargaining Negotiations, Grievance Arbitration and other Labor Proceedings. Trade Secrets and Unfair Competition Litigation. Employee Handbooks and Advice on Personnel Issues.

### MEMBERS OF FIRM

**CHRISTOPHER W. CARLTON,** born Seattle, Washington, November, 18, 1956; admitted to bar, 1983, California. *Education:* Duke University (A.B., magna cum laude, 1979); Cornell University (J.D., 1982). Senior Note Editor, Cornell Law Review, 1981-1982, Member, 1980-1981. Law Clerk to the Honorable Cynthia Holcomb Hall, U.S. District Judge, Central District of California, 1982-1983. *Member:* Los Angeles County and Orange County (Member, Labor and Employment Law Section) Bar Associations; State Bar of California. *PRACTICE AREAS:* Employment Law; Labor Law; Business Litigation.

### ASSOCIATE

**DIANE L. SCHLESINGER,** born Los Angeles, California, March 5, 1963; admitted to bar, 1988, California. *Education:* University of California at Los Angeles (B.A., summa cum laude, 1984); Boalt Hall School of Law, University of California (J.D., 1988). Phi Beta Kappa. Associate Editor, California Law Review, 1987-1988. *Member:* American Bar Association; State Bar of California. *PRACTICE AREAS:* Employment Law; Labor Law; Business Litigation.

(For complete biographical data on all personnel, see Professional Biographies at Irvine).

---

## FEDER & MILLS

A PROFESSIONAL CORPORATION
Established in 1991

1901 AVENUE OF THE STARS, SEVENTH FLOOR
LOS ANGELES, CALIFORNIA 90067
Telephone: 310-201-2075
Facsimile: 310-284-6020; 310-284-6018

Corporate Reorganization, Bankruptcy, Insolvency, Debtor-Creditor Relations, Business and Commercial Law, Arbitration and Mediation.

*FIRM PROFILE:* The firm was founded in 1991, by James J. Feder, formerly chair of the Corporate Bankruptcy and Reorganization practices of Jones, Day, Reavis & Pogue (Los Angeles) and Wyman Bautzer Kuchel & Silbert and John W. Mills III, formerly an associate in the Bankruptcy and Reorganization practices of Wyman Bautzer Kuchel & Silbert and Katten Muchin & Zavis.

The firm engages in the practice of business law and litigation, insolvency, bankruptcy, reorganization, workouts and creditors' remedies. The experience of the firm's members provides the depth of knowledge required in the most complex matters. During their practice, members of the firm have represented all of the various parties to bankruptcy and reorganization cases, including many, varied contested matters, adversary proceedings and litigation in state and federal courts.

*Trustee/Debtor representation:* Members of the firm have been lead counsel to the Chapter X and chapter 11 trustees in THC Financial Corp. (D. Haw. 1977-1989) and Manoa Finance Co. (D. Haw. 1982-1986) and have served as lead counsel for the debtor in the chapter 11 cases of Hamakua Sugar Company, Inc. (D. Haw. 1992-1993); American Continental Corp. (D. Ariz. 1989-1991); and, Gibraltar Financial Corp. (C.D. Cal. 1990). Significant partnership chapter 11 debtor and restructuring representations have included the partnerships which owned and operated the Registry Hotel in Irvine, California; the Ramada Renaissance Hotel in Walnut Creek, California; the St. Claire Hilton in San Jose, California; the Sheraton Sunrise in Sacramento, California; and, the Round Barn Inn in Sonoma, California. The members of the firm have also been lead counsel to several debtor corporations in the Commonwealth of the Northern Mariana Islands (Saipan) regarding a challenge to the constitutionality of land ownership restrictions.

*Creditor/Creditors' Committee Representation:* Members of the firm have represented insurance companies in matters such as director and officer liability issues arising out of failed institutions; contractors bonds related to chapter 11 cases involving defaulted developers; work-outs on office complexes, apartment buildings and hotels; and, positions as either lender or venture capital participant in various chapter 11 cases. Clients have included The Home Insurance Company; Mutual of New York; Industrial Indemnity Company; National Union Fire Insurance Company; Mutual Benefit Life; and, Allstate Insurance Company.

The members of the firm have also represented a number of major banks in connection with various workout and litigation matters including repossession of aircraft; recovery of motion pictures from production companies in chapter 11; debtor in possession financing; workouts of large agricultural loans; and, various real estate restructurings.

During the past several years, members of the firm have represented a number of major creditors and creditors' committees in chapter 11 reorganizations in various jurisdictions. They include: Creditors' Committee of Bajan Resorts, a time share developer (Utah); Equity Committee of Pea Soup Andersens' Partnership, a hotel and restaurant chain (California); Creditors' Committee of the United States Bedding/Southern Cross and Vanvorst Companies, major bedding manufacturers (California); Creditors' Committee of Attorney's Office Management Company (AOMI) ("Fegen Suites"), a professional office space provider (California); Lead lender in the De Laurentis Entertainment chapter 11 reorganization (California); Major Lender in the chapter 11 reorganization of America West Air Lines (Arizona); and Lead Lender in the chapter 11 reorganization of South Pacific Island Airways (American Samoa).

*Appointments As Receiver/Trustee/Examiner:* Mr. Feder has acted as an equity receiver in the United States District Court as well as having been appointed as a reorganization trustee and as an Examiner in operating chapter 11 cases. Receiverships have included various real estate projects.

Mr. Feder has acted as Examiner in several large, complex chapter 11 cases, including the Wickes Companies, Inc. (1982), First Capital Holdings Corp. and its affiliates, First Capital Life (California) and Fidelity Bankers Life (Virginia) and California Target Enterprises (1993).

*Acquisitions:* Members of the firm have represented a number of major parties in mergers and acquisitions of chapter 11 companies including Malibu Grand Prix Corporation; Castle Entertainment, Inc.; and, Foremost. Members of the

*(This Listing Continued)*

**FEDER & MILLS,** A PROFESSIONAL CORPORATION, Los Angeles—Continued

firm also represented a number of major banks in connection with various workout and litigation matters; debtor in possession financing; workouts of large agricultural loans; and, various real estate restructurings.

**JAMES J. FEDER,** born New York, N.Y., January 11, 1943; admitted to bar, 1975, California. *Education:* Notre Dame University; Auburn University; University of California at Los Angeles (B.A., 1965); University of Southern California (M.P.A., 1972; J.D., 1975). Order of the Coif. Editor-in-Chief, Southern California Law Review, 1974-1975. Author: "The Future of Testimonial Immunity in Bankruptcy Proceedings," 48 S. Cal. Law Rev. 92, 1974. Adjunct Professor of Law, Loyola University School of Law, 1979-1983. Judge Pro-tem, Los Angeles Municipal Court, 1980-1987. Member, Bankruptcy Judge Merit Selection Panel, Central District of California, 1984. Member, Panel of Arbitrators, American Arbitration Association, 1970—. Member, Mediation Panel, Bankruptcy Court, Central District of California, 1995—. *Member:* Los Angeles County (Member, Sections on: Commercial Law and Bankruptcy) and American (Member, Sections on: Business Law; Business Bankruptcy Committee; Litigation) Bar Associations; State Bar of California (Member, Debtor/Creditor Relations Committee, Business Law Section); Financial Lawyers Conference; Association of Business Trial Lawyers. *LANGUAGES:* German. *REPORTED CASES:* In re THC Financial Corp., 659 F.2d 951 (9th Cir. 1981) Cert. den. 456 U.S. 977 (1982); Falcon Capital Corporation Shareholders v. Osborne, 679 F.2d 784 (9th Cir. 1982); In re Manoa Finance Co., 853 F.2d 687 (9th Cir. 1988). *TRANSACTIONS:* Examiner, First Capital Holdings Corp., First Capital Life Insurance Group, Inc. and Fidelity Bankers Life Insurance Group Inc., 1991; Examiner, The Wickes Companies, 1982; California Target Enterprises, 1993. Lead Counsel for Chapter X reorganization of THC Financial Corp., 1976 and the Chapter 11 reorganization of American Continental Corp., 1989; Castle Entertainment/Malibu Grand Prix Chapter 11 acquisition, 1984. *PRACTICE AREAS:* Insolvency Law; Commercial Litigation; Appeals.

**JOHN W. MILLS, III,** born Richmond, Virginia, October 4, 1960; admitted to bar, 1990, California. *Education:* Wofford College (B.A., 1982); Emory University School of Law (J.D., 1990). Editor-in-Chief, Emory Bankruptcy Developments Journal, 1989-1990. Vice-Chairman, Beverly Hills Bar Association Journal. *Member:* Beverly Hills (Member, Executive Committee, Bankruptcy Section), Los Angeles County and American (Member, Business Bankruptcy Committee, Business Law Section) Bar Associations; State Bar of California; Los Angeles Bankruptcy Forum; Financial Lawyers Conference. *PRACTICE AREAS:* Insolvency Law; Commercial Litigation; Debtor Creditor Law; Creditors Rights Law.

REPRESENTATIVE CLIENTS: Bank of Hawaii; Gibraltar Financial Corp.; THC Financial Corp.; AOMI Creditor's Committee; Pea Soup Andersen's Equity Committee; Hamakua Sugar Company, Inc.

## FEDERMAN, GRIDLEY & GRADWOHL

A PROFESSIONAL LAW CORPORATION
Established in 1976
SUITE 1060, ONE CENTURY PLAZA
2029 CENTURY PARK EAST (CENTURY CITY)
**LOS ANGELES, CALIFORNIA 90067**
Telephone: 310-552-9181
FAX: 310-552-3121

*San Luis Obispo (Central Coast), California Office:* 992 Monterey Street #D, 93401. Telephone: 805-542-9002. Fax: 805-544-5837.

*Civil Trial and Appellate Practice in all California State and Federal Courts, Insurance and Reinsurance, Excess and Surplus Lines Law, and General Civil Litigation.*

FIRM PROFILE: *Federman, Gridley & Gradwohl was founded by Robert J. Federman in 1976 and has since expanded to 5 partners and several associates. Our litigation oriented practice provides cost effective legal services in our areas of expertise in all California courts. We maintain a central coast office in San Luis Obispo to provide better service to our clients.*

**ROBERT J. FEDERMAN,** born Cleveland, Ohio, August 27, 1931; admitted to bar, 1957, Ohio and U.S. Customs Court; 1975, California; 1977, U.S. Supreme Court. *Education:* Case Western Reserve University (B.A., 1953; J.D., 1956). Harvard Law School, Mediation Workshop Certification, 1993. Author: "Gray Turns To Black," F.I.C.C., Quarterly, Summer, 1985. Member of Panel, American Arbitration Association. Los Angeles Superior Court Arbitrator, 1978—. *Member:* State Bar of California; Ohio State and American (Vice-Chairman, Committee of Excess, Surplus Lines and Reinsurance, 1987-1990 and Chair, Arrangements Committee, Annual Meeting, 1989, Tort and Insurance Practice Section) Bar Associations; Federation of Insurance and Corporate Counsel (President, 1991-1992; Chairman, Industry Cooperation Section, 1987-1990; Chairman, Excess and Surplus Lines, Reinsurance Committee, 1976-1977; Vice President, 1977-1978, 1983-1984; Director, 1984-1989; Secretary/Treasurer, 1990; President-Elect, 1990-1991; President, 1991-1992; Chairman of the Board, 1992-1993); Association of Defense Trial Attorneys; Defense Research Institute (Director, 1991-1994); Lawyers for Civil Justice (Director, 1991-1994). *PRACTICE AREAS:* Complex Litigation; Insurance; Reinsurance; Excess Surplus Lines; Insurance Coverage Law; Arbitration and Mediation.

**BRUCE C. GRIDLEY,** born Evanston, Illinois, September 18, 1947; admitted to bar, 1973, California. *Education:* Grove City College and University of Wisconsin (B.A., 1970); University of Southern California (J.D., 1973). Arbitrator, Los Angeles Bar Association Fee Dispute Panel, 1987-1992. *Member:* Los Angeles County and American Bar Associations; State Bar of California; Association of Southern California Defense Counsel.

**ALAN J. GRADWOHL,** born Los Angeles, California, October 25, 1933; admitted to bar, 1977, California. *Education:* University of California at Berkeley (B.S., 1955; M.S., 1958); Whittier College School of Law (J.D., 1977). Sigma Xi; Alpha Pi Mu. Recipient, American Jurisprudence Award in Civil Procedure, 1976. Registered Professional Engineer, California, 1969. *Member:* The State Bar of California; American Bar Association (Member, Tort and Insurance Practice Section). *PRACTICE AREAS:* Complex Civil Litigation; Insurance Coverage.

**TEMPLE K. HARVEY,** born Richmond, Virginia, April 22, 1951; admitted to bar, 1979, California and U.S. District Court, Central District of California. *Education:* Indiana University (B.A., 1973); Pepperdine University (J.D., 1979). *Member:* State Bar of California.

**MARC R. WARD,** born Los Angeles, California, November 22, 1959; admitted to bar, 1985, California; 1986, U.S. District Court, Central District of California. *Education:* Loyola University of Los Angeles (B.A., cum laude, 1981; J.D., 1984). Pi Gamma Mu. *Member:* San Luis Obispo County Bar Association; State Bar of California. *PRACTICE AREAS:* General Civil Litigation, Property and Casualty Emphasis.

**ROBERT NATION,** born Fort Worth, Texas, July 21, 1953; admitted to bar, 1983, California and U.S. District Court, Central District of California; 1991, U.S. District Court, Northern District of California. *Education:* Baylor University; University of California at Los Angeles (B.A., 1979); University of San Fernando Valley (J.D., cum laude, 1982) Valedictorian. Recipient: Bancroft-Whitney Hornbook Award, 1981-1982 and 1982-1983; American Jurisprudence Awards: Civil Procedure, Conflict of Laws, Criminal Procedure, Corporations, Evidence, Remedies and Commercial Sales. Member, University of San Fernando Valley Law Review. *Member:* State Bar of California. *PRACTICE AREAS:* Complex Litigation; ADR; Insurance Coverage; Architectural; Engineering; Construction; Biochemical; Contract and Casualty Claims.

**R. DEREK CLASSEN,** born Buffalo, New York, September 29, 1967; admitted to bar, 1992, California. *Education:* University of California, Los Angeles (B.A., magna cum laude, 1989); University of San Diego (J.D., cum laude, 1992). Phi Beta Kappa. Member, San Diego Law Review, 1992. Author, Federation of Regulatory Counsel, Inc. Quarterly Newsletter, December 3, 1993, Vol. V, Edition 4.

**DEBRA HARTMAN WARFEL,** born Los Angeles, California, April 4, 1960; admitted to bar, 1985, California. *Education:* University of California at Berkeley (B.A., 1982); Southwestern University (J.D., 1985). *Member:* State Bar of California.

**ROBERT B. KLEPA,** born Los Angeles, California, June 14, 1964; admitted to bar, 1989, California, U.S. Court of Appeals, Ninth Circuit and U.S. District Court, Central District of California. *Education:* University of California at Los Angeles (B.A., 1986); Loyola Marymount University (J.D., 1989). Los Angeles Superior Court/Santa Monica Judge Pro Tem (1996); Central Landlord/Tenant Dispute Mediator (1993). *Member:* Los Angeles County Bar Association (Member, Sub-Committees on Small Claims, 1991-1993; Homeless, 1993—) ; State Bar of California. *PRACTICE AREAS:* Construction Defect; Business Litigation.

**STUART E. SUPOWIT,** born Frackville, Pennsylvania, August 4, 1953; admitted to bar, 1985, California, U.S. District Court, Central, Eastern,

*(This Listing Continued)*

Southern and Northern Districts of California and U.S. Court of Appeals, Ninth Circuit. *Education:* Pennsylvania State University (B.A., 1976); Southwestern University School of Law (J.D., 1984). *Member:* Los Angeles County Bar Association; State Bar of California. **PRACTICE AREAS:** Products Liability; Premises Liability; Business Torts.

REPRESENTATIVE CLIENTS: Allen-Bradley; Alliance Insurance Group; Asea Brown Boveri; Bituminous Insurance Company; Burlington Air Express, Inc.; Century Surety Co.; Crawford & Co.; Federal Home Life Insurance; Greyhound Lines; Horace Mann; Hysen-Johson; National Casualty Co.; Osram-Sylvania, Inc.; Reliance Insurance Co.; Republic Claims; Santa Anita Racetrack; Scottsdale Ins.; Teranova Insurance Co.; Topa Insurance Co.; U-Haul; Underwriters at Lloyds; Vanliner Insurance Co.; Ashland Chemical, Inc.; National Universal Underwriters.
REFERENCE: City National (Century City).

---

# LAW OFFICES OF
# THOMAS J. FEELEY, P.C.

### 700 SOUTH FLOWER STREET, FOURTH FLOOR
### LOS ANGELES, CALIFORNIA 90017

Telephone: 213-236-9670
Facsimile: 213-627-2561

General Civil and Municipal Law.

FIRM PROFILE: *I commenced this practice in 1991 as a Los Angeles-based defense litigation firm, with emphasis on police litigation, focus my practice upon tort defense. For the convenience of clients, I maintain offices in both Los Angeles and Orange Counties. I am prepared to undertake the representation of governmental and private entities, officials, law enforcement officers and administrators in civil, criminal and administrative matters in both State and Federal Courts throughout California. I support affirmative action, not only in hiring and purchasing policies and practices, but also by entering into joint ventures with minority-and women-owned firms.*

**THOMAS J. FEELEY,** born Los Angeles, California, February 10, 1937; admitted to bar, 1969, California. *Education:* Loyola University of Los Angeles (B.S., 1958); Southwestern University (J.D., 1964). Phi Delta Phi. Supervising Special Investigator, California Department of Alcoholic Beverage Control, 1966-1969. Principal Deputy City Attorney, Los Angeles City Attorney's Office, 1969-1973. *Member:* Los Angeles County and American Bar Associations; State Bar of California; Association of Southern California Defense Counsel; Orange County Chiefs of Police and Sheriff's Association. [LCDR, U.S. Coast Guard Reserve, 1960-1967]. **PRACTICE AREAS:** Civil Trial; Municipal Law.

---

**S. PAUL BRUGUERA,** born Pittsburgh, Pennsylvania, May 5, 1956; admitted to bar, 1981, California. *Education:* Claremont Mens College (B.A., 1978); Loyola University of Los Angeles (J.D., 1981). Author: "New Standard for Award of Attorneys' Fees," published in ABA Governmental Liability Committee Newsletter, Winter, 1993. Arbitrator, Los Angeles Superior and Municipal Courts. *Member:* American Bar Association (Vice-Chair of Governmental Liability Committee); The Association of Southern California Defense Counsel. **PRACTICE AREAS:** Eminent Domain; Environmental Law; Civil Rights; Public Law; General Litigation; Arbitration.

### LEGAL SUPPORT PERSONNEL

**DONNA D'AMORE** (Paralegal).

REPRESENTATIVE CLIENTS: State of California; Los Angeles; Long Beach; Glendale; Huntington Beach; Newport Beach; Cypress; Ventura; San Luis Obispo; United States Drug Enforcement Administration (DEA) Agents; Hub Cities Job Training Consortium; Pittsburg, CA.

---

# FEINGOLD & SPIEGEL

### SUITE 175 COMMERCE PLAZA
### 11340 WEST OLYMPIC BOULEVARD
### LOS ANGELES, CALIFORNIA 90064

Telephone: 310-477-7007
Fax: 310-477-7248

General Civil Trial Practice. Real Property, Property Management, Construction Law, Corporate Law, Alternative Dispute Resolution and Commercial Law.

*(This Listing Continued)*

---

### MEMBERS OF FIRM

**KENNETH A. FEINGOLD,** born Los Angeles, California, September 24, 1949; admitted to bar, 1975, California. *Education:* University of California at Santa Cruz (B.A., 1971); University of San Francisco (J.D., magna cum laude, 1975). Phi Delta Phi. *Member:* McAuliffe Law Honor Society. Member, University of San Francisco Law Review, 1974-1975. Legal Extern to Justice Raymond L. Sullivan, California Supreme Court, 1975. Deputy City Attorney, Los Angeles City Attorney's Office, 1975-1976. Member: Board of Trustees, U.C. Santa Cruz Foundation. *Member:* Beverly Hills and Los Angeles County Bar Associations; State Bar of California. **PRACTICE AREAS:** Civil Trial; Real Property Litigation and Transactions; Property Management Law; Construction Law; Alternative Dispute Resolution.

**RONALD L. SPIEGEL,** born Los Angeles, California, September 22, 1958; admitted to bar, 1987, California and U.S. District Court, Central District of California; 1988, U.S. Court of Appeals, Ninth Circuit. *Education:* California State University at Northridge (B.S., 1981); Loyola Law School (J.D., 1986). *Member:* Century City, Beverly Hills and Los Angeles County Bar Associations; The State Bar of California. **PRACTICE AREAS:** Civil Trial; Real Property Litigation; Construction and Tort Litigation.

---

# LAW OFFICES OF
# ROBERT J. FELDHAKE

### LOS ANGELES, CALIFORNIA

(See Costa Mesa)

Litigation, General Business-Corporate Law.

---

# FELDMAN & FELDMAN

### A PROFESSIONAL CORPORATION

### LOS ANGELES, CALIFORNIA

(See Woodland Hills)

General Corporate, Business, Computer, and Real Estate Law, Transactions and Litigation (State and Federal Courts, Provisional Remedies, Trials and Appeals), Probate, Conservatorship, Estate Planning and Dispute Resolution.

---

# FELDMAN & SHAFFERY

### 611 WEST SIXTH STREET, 26TH FLOOR
### LOS ANGELES, CALIFORNIA 90017

Telephone: 213-955-5400
Facsimile: 213-489-3677

Labor and Employment, Environmental, Toxic Torts, General Liability, Products Liability, Aviation and General Civil Litigation in all State and Federal Courts.

### MEMBERS OF FIRM

**CARLA J. FELDMAN,** born Placerville, California, January 22, 1959; admitted to bar, 1985, California. *Education:* University of California at San Diego (B.A., 1981); University of San Diego (J.D., 1985). *Member:* Los Angeles County and American Bar Associations; State Bar of California; California Women Lawyers; Defense Research Institute; Association of Southern California Defense Counsel; Environmental Law Institute. **PRACTICE AREAS:** Environmental Law; Employment Law; Toxic Torts; Products Liability Law.

**JOHN SHAFFERY,** admitted to bar, 1992, California. *Education:* Florida Institute of Technology, School of Aeronautics (B.S., 1982); Southwestern University (J.D., 1991). F.A.A. Licenses: Commercial Pilot, 1980; Aircraft Flight Dispatcher, 1985. *Member:* Los Angeles County Bar Association; State Bar of California; Southern California Defense Counsel; Lawyer Pilots Bar Association. **PRACTICE AREAS:** Environmental Litigation; Groundwater Contamination; Environmental Cleanup; Underground Storage Tanks; Proposition 65; Premises Liability; Products Liability; Chemical Exposure; Sexual Harassment; Personal Injury; Aviation.

*(This Listing Continued)*

FELDMAN & SHAFFERY, Los Angeles—Continued

---

**JILL FASSO,** born Elizabeth, New Jersey, January 22, 1969; admitted to bar, 1995, California. *Education:* Rutgers University (B.A., 1991); Pepperdine University (J.D., 1995). *PRACTICE AREAS:* Labor Law; Environmental Law; General Civil Practice.

---

## FENIGSTEIN & KAUFMAN

A PROFESSIONAL CORPORATION

Established in 1988

(Formerly Chasalow, Fenigstein & Kaufman, Established 1979)

SUITE 2300, 1900 AVENUE OF THE STARS (CENTURY CITY)
LOS ANGELES, CALIFORNIA 90067-4314
Telephone: 310-201-0777
Telecopier: 310-556-1346

*Business Litigation. Corporate, Real Estate, Business, and Commercial Law. Health Care Law. Tax and Estate Planning.*

**S. JACK FENIGSTEIN,** born Santa Monica, California, November 11, 1947; admitted to bar, 1975, California; U.S. District Court, Central District of California. *Education:* University of Rochester (B.A., cum laude, 1969); University of Michigan (J.D., with distinction, 1974). *Member:* Century City, Los Angeles County (Member, Sections on: Business; Real Estate; Taxation) Bar Associations; State Bar of California; National Health Lawyers Association. *PRACTICE AREAS:* Corporate; Real Estate; Business; Health Care and Commercial Law; Estate Planning.

**RON S. KAUFMAN,** born Tiberias, Israel, October 7, 1949; admitted to bar, 1974, California; U.S. District Court, Central District of California; U.S. Court of Appeals, Ninth Circuit. *Education:* University of California at Santa Barbara (B.A., magna cum laude, 1971); Boalt Hall School of Law, University of California at Berkeley (J.D., 1974). *Member:* Century City, Beverly Hills, Los Angeles County (Member, Section on Trial Lawyers) and American (Member, Sections on: General Practice; Litigation) Bar Associations; State Bar of California; Association of Business Trial Lawyers; National Health Lawyers Association. *PRACTICE AREAS:* Business; Health Care; Employment and Real Estate Litigation.

**DAVID F. TILLES,** born Los Angeles, California, November 4, 1955; admitted to bar, 1980, California; U.S. District Court, Central District of California; 1987, U.S. Supreme Court; U.S. Court of Appeals, Ninth Circuit. *Education:* University of California at Los Angeles (B.A., magna cum laude, 1977; J.D., 1980). *Member:* Century City, Los Angeles County and American Bar Associations; State Bar of California; National Health Lawyers Association. *PRACTICE AREAS:* Corporate, Real Estate, Business, and Commercial Law; Business Litigation.

**KARL S. THURMOND,** born Oceanside, California, June 5, 1960; admitted to bar, 1986, California; U.S. District Court, Central District of California. *Education:* Dartmouth College (A.B., 1982); Harvard University (J.D., 1985). Ames Moot Court Prize. Captain Final Round, Ames Moot Court Team. Williston Prize for best overall Contract. Counsel to the Black Business Association of Los Angeles, Inc. West Coast General Counsel to National Black Business Council. General Counsel to Committee to Elect Adam Schiff to Assembly. Panelist, Labor and Employment Law Symposium, State Bar of California Labor and Employment Law Section, Spring 1995. *Member:* Los Angeles County Bar Association; State Bar of California; Dartmouth Lawyers Association; Langston Bar Association. *PRACTICE AREAS:* Business Litigation; Business and Commercial Law.

---

**STEPHANIE G. PEARL,** born Kansas City, Missouri, February 15, 1960; admitted to bar, 1985, California; 1986, U.S. District Court, Central District of California and U.S. Court of Appeals, Ninth Circuit. *Education:* University of California at Los Angeles (B.A., magna cum laude, 1982; J.D., 1985). Phi Beta Kappa. *Member:* Los Angeles County and Century City Bar Associations; State Bar of California. *PRACTICE AREAS:* Business, Employment and Health Care Litigation.

**HENRY LIEN,** born Taipei, Taiwan, April 23, 1970; admitted to bar, 1996, California. *Education:* Brown University (B.A., 1992); University of California Los Angeles (J.D., 1995). Moot Court Honors Program. *PRACTICE AREAS:* Litigation.

*(This Listing Continued)*

**PATRICK J. FARRELL,** born San Bernardino, California, November 17, 1969; admitted to bar, 1996, California. *Education:* University of California-Berkeley (B.A., 1992; J.D., 1995). Phi Beta Kappa. *PRACTICE AREAS:* Business Litigation; General Corporate.

*OF COUNSEL*

**LYNNE DROHLICH KAUFMAN,** born St. Louis, Missouri, April 17, 1949; admitted to bar, 1974, California and U.S. District Court, Central District of California. *Education:* University of California at Berkeley (B.A., 1971; J.D., 1974). Phi Beta Kappa. Former Vice President and Senior Counsel, American Medical International, Inc. *Member:* Los Angeles County (Member, Committee on Medical Staff and Physician Relations); State Bar of California; California Society for Healthcare Attorneys; American Academy of Hospital Attorneys (Member, Committee on Medical Staff and Physician Relations); National Health Lawyers Association. *PRACTICE AREAS:* Health Care and Hospital Law.

**HAROLD J. TOMIN,** born Chicago, Illinois, May 28, 1940; admitted to bar, 1965, California; 1966, Illinois; 1969, U.S. Court of Appeals Ninth Circuit; 1972, U.S. District Court, Central District of California; 1980, U.S. Supreme Court. *Education:* George Washington University (A.B., 1961); Northwestern University (J.D., 1964). *Member:* State Bar of California; American Bar Association. *PRACTICE AREAS:* Complex Business Litigation; Antitrust Counseling and Litigation; Securities Litigation; Employment Litigation.

**ERIC D. BERKOWITZ,** born Detroit, Michigan, November 4, 1958; admitted to bar, 1984, California, U.S. District Court, Northern District of California and U.S. Circuit Court, Ninth Circuit; 1985, U.S. District Court, Central District of California; 1987, U.S. District Court, Southern District of California. *Education:* University of California at Santa Cruz (B.A., with honors, 1981); University of San Francisco (J.D., 1984). Member, University of San Francisco Law Review, 1983-1984. Author: "Low Power Television and the Doctrine of Localism, The Need to Reconcile a Medium with Its Message," University of San Francisco Law Review, Vol. 18, 1984. *Member:* Los Angeles County Bar Association; State Bar of California; National Health Lawyers Association. *PRACTICE AREAS:* Business; Litigation.

**ANTHONY D. DE TORO,** born Jersey City, New Jersey, April 29, 1959; admitted to bar, 1984, California; 1985, U.S. District Court, Central District of California; 1986, U.S. District Court, Northern District of California and U.S. Court of Appeals, Ninth Circuit; 1989, U.S. Supreme Court; 1990, New York. *Education:* New York University (B.A., 1981); University of San Francisco (J.D., 1984). Staff Member, University of San Francisco Law Review, 1983-1984. Co-Author: "Securities Arbitration Special Report," Wiley Law Publishers, 1989; "Tapping Equity Markets for Small Businesses: The SCOR Alternative," 25 Rev. of Sec. and Comm. L. 159 (August 1992); "A Guide to the SEC's Small Business Initiative," 17 Seaton Hall Leg. J. 75 (1993). Author: "Market Manipulation of Penny Stocks," 17 Sec. Reg. L.J. 241 (1989); "Waiver of the Right to Compel Arbitration of Investor-Broker Disputes," 21 Cumb. L. Rev. 615 (1991). Contributor: "Securities Litigation: State and Federal," Program Materials, California Continuing Education of the Bar (1988); *National ADR Handbook*, Lawyers Co-operative Publishing Co., 1994. *Member:* American Bar Association (Member: Section of Business Law; Federal Regulation of Securities Committee). *PRACTICE AREAS:* Business Litigation; Securities Arbitration and Litigation.

---

## FRANKLIN L. FERGUSON, JR.

4929 WILSHIRE BOULEVARD, SUITE 930
LOS ANGELES, CALIFORNIA 90010
Telephone: 213-936-4375
Fax: 213-930-0338
Email: FLFERGUSONJR@IGC.ORG

*Civil Rights, Labor (Plaintiffs - Employment Discrimination), Police Misconduct, Criminal Defense.*

**FRANKLIN L. FERGUSON, JR.,** born New York, N.Y., December 23, 1968; admitted to bar, 1994, California. *Education:* University of Pennsylvania (B.A., with honors, 1990); New York University School of Law (J.D., 1993). Root-Tilden-Snow Public Interest Scholar. Associate Adjunct Professor, Southwestern University School of Law, 1995—. American Civil Liberties Union of Southern California, 1993-1994. *Member:* Los Angeles County Bar Association (Member, Sections on: Civil Rights, Criminal and Labor); State Bar of California.

## MICHAEL S. FIELDS
### LOS ANGELES, CALIFORNIA
(See Beverly Hills)

*Practice limited to Personal Injury Litigation, Professional Malpractice, Product Liability, Vehicular Accidents, Construction Accidents and Insurance Company Bad Faith Actions.*

---

## LAW OFFICE OF
## IRA M. FIERBERG
### LOS ANGELES, CALIFORNIA
(See Manhattan Beach)

*Personal Injury, including Vehicular, Slip and Fall, Major Bodily Injury, Dog Bites, Wrongful Death. General Civil Litigation in all State and Federal Courts, Trial, Business Litigation, Real Property Litigation, Sports Law, Auto Racing Sports Representation.*

---

## FIERSTEIN & STURMAN
### LAW CORPORATION
*Established in 1976*

**1875 CENTURY PARK EAST, FIFTEENTH FLOOR**
**LOS ANGELES, CALIFORNIA 90067**
Telephone: 310-553-5500
Fax: 310-552-3228

*General Civil and Appellate Practice in all State and Federal Courts. Corporate, Tax Planning, Commercial Transactions, Litigation, Wrongful Termination, Securities (NYSE, NASD and SEC), Construction Defect, Environmental, Real Estate, Insolvency, Workout, Estate Planning, Probate and Entertainment Law.*

*FIRM PROFILE: Fierstein & Sturman Law Corporation is recognized for the innovative, aggressive and sophisticated nature of its results-oriented practice. The firm emphasizes personal service, constructive and practical approaches to problem solving and a keen awareness of the need for productivity in the use of lawyer time.*

*The firm's clients have traditionally been entrepreneurs, some of whom have been associated with the firm or its predecessors for more than 25 years. More recently, the firm has been retained by institutional clients to handle significant matters in state and federal courts throughout California and the nation. The Law firm is listed in the Bar Register of Preeminent Lawyers.*

**HERBERT D. STURMAN,** born New York, N.Y., September 22, 1936; admitted to bar, 1961, New York; 1963, California, U.S. District Court, Central District of California and U.S. Court of Appeals, 9th Circuit; 1964, U.S. Tax Court; 1968, U.S. Claims Court; 1975, U.S. Supreme Court. *Education:* Columbia University (A.B., 1957; LL.B., 1961). Harlan Fiske Stone Scholar, 1961. Author: "The Collection Process: Litigative Aspects," Federal Tax Procedure for General Practitioners, publication of the California Continuing Education of the Bar, 1969; "Criminal Tax Investigations," Tax Practice in California, publication of the California Continuing Education of the Bar, 1984. Assistant U.S. Attorney, Central District of California, Tax Division, 1962-1964. *Member:* New York State Bar Association; The State Bar of California. (Certified Specialist, Taxation Law, The State Bar of California Board of Legal Specialization). **PRACTICE AREAS:** Corporate Law; Tax Planning Law; Litigation and Probate Law.

**HARVEY FIERSTEIN** (1923-1984).

**MICHAEL BLUMENFELD,** born San Jose, Costa Rica, November 30, 1948; admitted to bar, 1973, California, U.S. District Court, Central and Northern Districts of California and U.S. Court of Appeals, Ninth and Third Circuits; U.S. Tax Court. *Education:* University of California at Los Angeles (A.B., 1970); Loyola Law School (J.D., 1973). Recipient, American Jurisprudence Award. Editor, Loyola University, Urban Law Reporter, 1971. *Member:* Century City, Los Angeles County and American Bar Associations; The State Bar of California. (Managing Partner). **PRACTICE AREAS:** Business and Commercial Litigation; Real Property Litigation; Federal and State Courts Employment Law; Securities Industry Litigation and Employment Disputes.

**EDWARD C. BROFFMAN,** born Los Angeles, California, May 30, 1948; admitted to bar, 1975, California; 1980, U.S. District Court, Central

*(This Listing Continued)*

and Northern Districts of California and U.S. Court of Appeals, Ninth Circuit. *Education:* University of California at Los Angeles (A.B., magna cum laude, 1970); Loyola Law School (J.D., magna cum laude, 1975). Phi Beta Kappa. *Member:* The State Bar of California. **PRACTICE AREAS:** Business Law; Construction Defect Litigation; Real Property Litigation (Federal and State Courts) Law.

**WILLIAM T. KING,** born Detroit, Michigan, February 3, 1933; admitted to bar, 1958, California and U.S. District Court, Central District of California; 1964, U.S. Supreme Court; 1970, U.S. Tax Court. *Education:* The Principia College (B.A., cum laude, 1954); Harvard University (J.D., 1957). Listed in Who's Who in America, Bicentennial Edition, 1976. President, Board of Traffic Commissioners of Los Angeles, 1973-1975. Member, Board of Commissioners of the Los Angeles Department of Water and Power, 1975-1976. Member, California Advisory Commission to U.S. Commission on Civil Rights, 1969-1970. Research Associate, Institute of Government and Public Affairs U.C.L.A., 1969-1970. Trustee, Constitutional Rights Foundation, 1970—. Counsel: Directors' Guild of America Educational and Benevolent Foundation; Beverly Hills Bar Association; Century City Bar Association. *Member:* Los Angeles County (Member: Executive Committee, Probate and Trust Section, 1966-1971; Family Law Section) and American Bar Associations; The State Bar of California (Member, Family Law Section); California Trial Lawyers Association; Fellow, American College of Probate Counsel. **PRACTICE AREAS:** Estate Planning; Family Law; Business Law.

**RICHARD M. JOHNSON, JR.,** admitted to bar, 1987, California. *Education:* University of Washington (B.A.); Santa Clara University (J.D., 1987). **PRACTICE AREAS:** Real Estate Finance; Insolvency; Workout.

---

**TASHA DIAN LEVINSON,** born San Francisco, California, September 3, 1948; admitted to bar, 1977, California. *Education:* Lincoln University (LL.B., magna cum laude, 1977). *Member:* Los Angeles County Bar Association; State Bar of California. **PRACTICE AREAS:** Estate Planning; Probate.

**BRUCE E. ALTSCHULD,** born Amityville, New York, December 14, 1954; admitted to bar, 1983, California. *Education:* State University at New York (B.A., 1977); Southwestern University School of Law (J.D., 1982). *Member:* The State Bar of California. **PRACTICE AREAS:** Real Estate; Business Law; Litigation.

**LESLIE E. WALLIS,** born Los Angeles, California, February 7, 1958; admitted to bar, 1987, California, U.S. District Court, Central District of California and U.S. Court of Appeals, Ninth Circuit. *Education:* Indiana University (B.S., with high honors, 1980); University of California at Los Angeles (J.D., 1986). Pi Kappa Lambda; Order of the Coif. Member, 1984-1985 and Associate Editor, 1985-1986, UCLA Law Review. Author: Comment, "The Different Art: Choreography and Copyright," 33 U.C.L.A. L. Rev. Issue 5. *Member:* Los Angeles County Bar Association; Women Lawyers of Los Angeles. **LANGUAGES:** German. **PRACTICE AREAS:** Civil Trial; Appellate Practice; Trademark; Copyright.

**LEE A. EDLUND,** born Corvallis, Oregon, December 31, 1968; admitted to bar, 1994, California. *Education:* University of California, Berkeley (A.B., 1991); Boalt Hall School of Law, University of California (J.D., 1994). Phi Beta Kappa. Golden Key Honor Society; Moot Court Award for Excellence in Oral Advocacy. Recipient, American Jurisprudence Award for Contracts. *Member:* Los Angeles County Bar Association. **PRACTICE AREAS:** Real Estate Finance; Insolvency; Workout.

**THOMAS M. FERLAUTO,** born Long Beach, California, July 1, 1966; admitted to bar, 1991, California. *Education:* University of Texas (B.S., 1987; J.D., 1990). **PRACTICE AREAS:** State and Federal Courts Litigation.

**ALLAN S. WILLIAMS,** born Van Nuys, California, November 9, 1969; admitted to bar, 1995, California. *Education:* California State University, Long Beach (B.A., 1992); California Western School of Law (J.D., 1995). Phi Alpha Delta. Recipient: American Jurisprudence Awards in Real Property and Trial Practice. Executive Director, Advocacy Honors Board, California Western School of Law. *Member:* The Association of Trial Lawyers of America. **PRACTICE AREAS:** Business Litigation; Tort Litigation; Trusts and Estates; Construction Defect Litigation.

*(This Listing Continued)*

**FIERSTEIN & STURMAN, LAW CORPORATION, Los Angeles—Continued**

*OF COUNSEL*

**MARVIN JUBAS,** born 1929; admitted to bar, 1955, California; 1983, U.S. Supreme Court. *Education:* University of California at Los Angeles (A.A., 1950; J.D., 1954); University of California at Berkeley (B.S., 1951). *PRACTICE AREAS:* Trademark; Licensing; Copyright; Unfair Competition; Antitrust; Contracts.

---

## LAW OFFICES OF
## RICHARD I. FINE & ASSOCIATES

*A PROFESSIONAL CORPORATION*

Established in 1974

SUITE 1000, 10100 SANTA MONICA BOULEVARD (CENTURY CITY)
**LOS ANGELES, CALIFORNIA 90067-4090**
*Telephone: 310-277-5833*
*Rapifax: 310-277-1543*

*Complex Litigation, Class Action, Taxpayer, Government Misuse of Funds and Unique Cases. General Civil and Trial Practice in all State and Federal Courts. Corporation, Antitrust, International, Trade Regulation, Government, Business Law.*

**RICHARD I. FINE,** born Milwaukee, Wisconsin, January 22, 1940; admitted to bar, 1964, Illinois; 1972, District of Columbia and U.S. Supreme Court; 1973, California. *Education:* University of Wisconsin (B.S., 1961); University of Chicago (J.D., 1964); University of London, London School of Economics and Political Science (Ph.D., International Law, 1967). Certificate-Hague Academy of International Law, 1965, 1966. Certificate of Comparative Law-International University of Comparative Science, Luxembourg, 1966. Diplome d'Etudes Superieure du Droit Compare (Faculte International pour l'Enseignement du Droit Compare), Strasbourg, 1967. Phi Delta Phi. Member, Moot Court Board. Author: "Article 19 of the U.N. Charter: A Catalyst of Thought," Revue de Droit International de Sciences Diplomatiques et Politiques, The International Law Review, No. 1, 1965; "Peace-Keeping Costs and Article 19 of the U.N. Charter: An Invitation to Responsibility," International and Comparative Law Quarterly, April 1966 and Revue de Droit International de Sciences Diplomatiques et Politiques, The International Law Review, No. 1, 1966; "Technical Assistance to International Law, A Reality," International and Comparative Law Quarterly, October 1966; "Procedure Under Articles 85 and 86 of the EEC Treaty as Interpreted by the Commission, The European Court of Justice and the Courts of the Member States," il Diritto Negli Scambi Internazionali, March-June 1966; "The Substance of Articles 85 and 86 as Viewed by the Courts of the Member States: A Case Analysis," il Diritto Negli Scambi Internazionali, Part 1 Sept., 1966, Part II December, 1966; "Comparative Offer and Acceptance in Contracts by Correspondence in German, French, Soviet and Anglo-American Law: The Uniform Law on the Formation of Contracts for the International Sale of Goods, an Advance," il Diritto Negli Scambi Internazionali, March-June 1967; "Extra Territorial Application of Restrictive Trade Practice Legislation: A Restatement of Underlying Conflicts," il Diritto Negli Scambi Internazionali, March-June 1967; "Exclusive Dealing Under the Treaty of Rome," The Journal of Business Law, April 1967; "The Nature of a Restrictive Practice Under Articles 85 and 86 of the Treaty of Rome," Part 1, Journal of Law and Economic Development, Fall 1969, Part II, Journal of International Law Economics, January 1971; "The Control of Restrictive Practices in International Trade—A Viable Proposal," The International Lawyer, June, 1973; "Sovereign Immunity and the Nation State Cartel," Los Angeles Bar Journal, December, 1975. Professor in International, Comparative and EEC Antitrust Law, University of Syracuse Law School Overseas Program, Summer 1970-1972. Trial Attorney, United States Department of Justice, Antitrust Division, Foreign Commerce Section, Special Litigation Section, Cleveland Field Office, 1968-1972. Chief, Antitrust Division, City Attorney's Office, 1973-1974 and Special Counsel, Governmental Efficiency Committee, 1973-1974, City of Los Angeles. Member, BNA Antitrust Advisory Board, 1980—. Co-Chairman, Southern California Chapter, American Friends of the London School of Economics, 1984—. Co-Chairman, 1990—and Board of Directors, 1984—, American Friends of the London School of Economics. Board of Directors, Retinitis Pigmentosa International, 1985-1991. Chairman, London School of Economics, Los Angeles Advisory Committee, 1992—. Member, University of Chicago Law School, Visiting Committee, 1992-1994. Member, Board of Directors, Citizen Is-

*(This Listing Continued)*

land Bridge Company Limited, Lake Havasu, Arizona, 1991—. Participant, White House Conference on NAFTA, Oct. 21, 1993. Honarary Consul General, Kingdom of Norway, 1995—. *Member:* Los Angeles County (Co-Chairman, Antitrust Committee, 1975-1977; Chairman, Antitrust Section, 1977-1978; Member, Executive Committee, International Law Section, 1993—), Illinois State, Federal and American (Member, Section of Antitrust Law; Chairman, Subcommittee on International Antitrust and Trade Regulations, International Law Section, 1972-1977; Vice Chairman, 1975-1977 and Chairman, 1977-1981, Committee on International Economic Organizations) Bar Associations; The State Bar of California (Chairman, Antitrust and Trade Regulation Law Committee, 1978-1981; Chairman, Antitrust Trade Regulation Law Section, 1981-1985); The District of Columbia Bar; American Society of International Law (Life Member; Member of Panel, International Trade Regulations, 1971-1977; Co-Chairman, Committee on Corporate Membership, 1978-1983; Member: Executive Council, 1984-1987; Development Committee 1988; Budget Committee, 1992—; Regional Coordinator for Los Angeles, 1994—; 1995 Annual Program Committee, 1994-1995; Corresponding Editor, International Legal Materials, 1983—); American Foreign Law Association; International Law Association; British Institute of International and Comparative Law; Association of Trial Lawyers of America (Distinguishing Member); California Trial Lawyers Association; Los Angeles World Affairs Council, International Circle.

---

**SUNNY S. HUO,** born Taiwan, April 12, 1970; admitted to bar, 1995, California, U.S. District Court, Central District of California and U.S. Court of Appeals, Ninth Circuit. *Education:* University of California at Los Angeles (B.A., 1992); University of California School of Law, Los Angeles (J.D., 1995). U.C.L.A. Moot Court Honors Program, 1993-1995. Editor-in-Chief, U.C.L.A. Pacific Basin Law Journal, 1994-1995. *Member:* Los Angeles County Bar Association; State Bar of California. *LANGUAGES:* Mandarin Chinese. *PRACTICE AREAS:* Litigation; Antitrust; Government; Business; Class Actions.

**GENALIN Y. SULAT,** born September 2, 1969; admitted to bar, 1996, California, U.S. District Court, Central District of California and U.S. Court of Appeals, Ninth Circuit. *Education:* Rutgers University (B.S.N., 1990; B.A., 1992); University of California, School of Law, Los Angeles (J.D., 1995). Board Member, U.C.L.A. Moot Court Honors Program, 1994-1995. Comments Editor, U.C.L.A. Pacific Basin Law Journal. Registered Nurse, New Jersey, 1990; California, 1992. *Member:* State Bar of California. *LANGUAGES:* Tagalog. *PRACTICE AREAS:* General Litigation; Class Actions; Antitrust; Government.

*LEGAL SUPPORT PERSONNEL*

**MARY BENSON.** *Education:* University of California at Los Angeles (B.A., 1965; Attorney Assistant Program, Certification with honors, 1983). (Senior Paralegal). *LANGUAGES:* Spanish.

---

## FINER, KIM & STEARNS

**LOS ANGELES, CALIFORNIA**

(See Torrance)

*Corporate, Business, Partnership and Real Estate Litigation; Bankruptcy, Commercial Law. Estate Planning and Probate Law. Civil Trial Practice. Environmental Policy and Law, Insurance Coverage.*

---

## FIRESTEIN & FARRUGGIA

SUITE 550, 5900 SEPULVEDA BOULEVARD (VAN NUYS)
**LOS ANGELES, CALIFORNIA 91411**
*Telephone: 818-785-1999*
*Fax: 818-785-8347*

*Subrogation, Premium and Deductible Collections, Insurance, Civil Litigation and Business Litigation.*

*MEMBERS OF FIRM*

**SAMUEL A. FARRUGGIA,** born Chicago, Illinois, May 22, 1945; admitted to bar, 1973, Illinois and U.S. District Court, Northern District of Illinois; 1974, U.S. Court of Appeals, Seventh Circuit; 1984, California and U.S. District Court, Central District of California; 1985, U.S. Court of Appeals, Ninth Circuit. *Education:* University of Illinois (B.A, 1968); De Paul University (J.D., 1973). Author: "Allocation of Defense Costs Between Primary and Excess Carriers," Defense Research Institute (DRI) No I, Vol

*(This Listing Continued)*

1984. Member, Panel of Arbitrators, American Arbitration Association. *Member:* Los Angeles County, Illinois State and American Bar Associations; State Bar of California. **PRACTICE AREAS:** Subrogation; Premium and Deductible Collections; Insurance.

**MARTIN L. FIRESTEIN,** born Los Angeles, California, October 9, 1949; admitted to bar, 1978, California and U.S. District Court, Central District of California; 1979, U.S. Court of Appeals, Ninth Circuit; 1980, U.S. District Court, Northern, Eastern and Southern Districts of California and U.S. Tax Court; 1981, U.S. Supreme Court, U.S. Claims Court, U.S. Court of International Trade, U.S. Court of Customs and Patent Appeals and U.S. Court of Military Appeals. *Education:* California State University at Northridge (B.A., 1973); University of San Fernando Valley (J.D., 1977). Member, University of San Fernando Valley Law Review, 1977. Landlord Settlement Officer, Los Angeles Municipal Court, 1981. Judge Pro-Tem, Los Angeles Municipal Court, 1983—. Member, Panel of Arbitrators, American Arbitration Association. *Member:* San Fernando Valley, Los Angeles County and American Bar Associations; The State Bar of California. [United States Coast Guard Merchant Marine Master/Captain]. **PRACTICE AREAS:** Subrogation; Insurance; Business Litigation. **Email:** martyf@directnet.com

OF COUNSEL

Craig S. Elkin     Toni Lewis
        John S. Levitt

REPRESENTATIVE CLIENTS: Al Marine Agency; Audubon Indemnity; American Home Assurance Co.; American International Adjusting Co.; American International Recovery; American International Surplus Lines Insurance Co.; American International Underwriters Insurance Co.; American Sentinel Insurance Co.; Automotive Rentals, Inc.; Birmingham Fire Insurance Co.; Civil Service Employees Insurance; Colonial Insurance Co.; Commerce and Industry Insurance Co.; Economy Fire & Casualty; Farmers Insurance Exchange; Fire Insurance Exchange; Firemans Fund Insurance; Grange Insurance Association; Granite State Insurance Co.; Insurance Company of the State of Pennsylvania; Integral Insurance Co.; Jefferson Insurance Group; John Deere Transportation Services, Inc.; Kemper Insurance; Lexington Insurance Co.; Liberty Mutual Insurance Co.; Mid-Century Insurance Co.; National Car Rentals Systems, Inc.; National Colonial Insurance Co.; National Union Fire Insurance Co.; New Hampshire Indemnity Co.; Ohio Indemnity Insurance Co.; Reinsurance Company of America; St. Paul Insurance Co.; Scottsdale Insurance; Senneca Insurance Co.; Stonewall Insurance Co.; Transamerica Insurance Company; Truck Insurance Exchange; Valley Insurance Co.; Willis Corroon Insurance Services.

## JAMES Q. FISHER

1801 CENTURY PARK EAST, SUITE 2400
LOS ANGELES, CALIFORNIA 90067-2326
Telephone: 310-556-3300
Facsimile: 310-556-2424

*Estate Planning (Wills and Trusts), Tax Planning, Business Transactions, Real Estate, Corporations and Partnerships.*

**JAMES Q. FISHER,** born Brooklyn, New York, July 25, 1943; admitted to bar, 1968, California; 1974, U.S. Tax Court. *Education:* University of Southern California (A.B., cum laude, 1964; J.D., 1967). *Member:* Beverly Hills (Member, Sections on: Taxation; Estate Planning) and Los Angeles County (Member, Sections on: Taxation; Estate Planning) Bar Associations; State Bar of California. (Certified Specialist, Estate Planning, Trust and Probate Law, The State Bar of California Board of Legal Specialization).

## SCOTT D. FISHER

12424 WILSHIRE BOULEVARD, SUITE 900
LOS ANGELES, CALIFORNIA 90025-1043
Telephone: 310-442-7171
Fax: 310-442-6400

*Real Estate and Business Litigation, Insurance Defense, Employment Law, Discrimination/Civil Rights and Personal Injury Law, Conservatorships, Probate Litigation.*

**SCOTT D. FISHER,** born Los Angeles, California, October 4, 1960; admitted to bar, 1987, California and U.S. District Court, Central District of California; 1989, U.S. Tax Court; 1996, U.S. District Court, Eastern District of California. *Education:* University of Arizona (B.S.B.A., 1982); Arizona State University (J.D., 1985). Recipient, Wiley W. Manuel Award for Pro Bono Legal Services, 1995. Member: Santa Monica Chamber of Com-
*(This Listing Continued)*

merce; Community Business Network. Member and Volunteer Attorney, Bet Tzedek Legal Services. *Member:* Los Angeles County Bar Association; State Bar of California. **LANGUAGES:** Spanish.

## FISHER & PHILLIPS

**LOS ANGELES, CALIFORNIA**

(See Newport Beach)

*Labor Relations, Representing Management -- Employment Discrimination, Wrongful Discharge, Employee Pensions and Benefits, Wage and Hour, Airline and Railway Law, Business Immigration and OSHA.*

## FISHER & PORTER

**LOS ANGELES, CALIFORNIA**

(See Long Beach)

*Admiralty, Aviation, Insurance and General Business Litigation, Transportation Law, Environmental Law.*

## KAREN S. FISHMAN

A LAW CORPORATION
1901 AVENUE OF THE STARS, 7TH FLOOR
LOS ANGELES, CALIFORNIA 90067
Telephone: 310-277-9350
Fax: 310-277-9032

*Complex Business Litigation.*

**KAREN S. FISHMAN,** born New York, N.Y., July 17, 1959; admitted to bar, 1984, Pennsylvania; 1985, District of Columbia and U.S. Claims Court; 1988, California, U.S. District Court, Central District of California and U.S. Court of Appeals for the Federal Circuit; 1992, U.S. District Court, Southern District of California and U.S. Court of Appeals, Ninth Circuit; 1994, U.S. District Court, Northern District of California. *Education:* Cornell University (A.B., magna cum laude, 1981); George Washington University (J.D., 1984). Author Articles: "History of Consumer Law," The Consumer Protection Reporting Service, May 1985; "Truth-in Lending: Enforcement" and "Garnishment," The Consumer Protection Reporting Service, April, 1983. Trial Attorney, U.S. Department of Justice, Civil Division, Commercial Litigation Branch, 1985-1987. Law Clerk to Chief Administrative Judge I.P. Snyder, U.S. Department of Transportation Contract Appeals Board. **REPORTED CASES:** United Technologies Corp. v. United States, 830 F.2d 1121 (Fed. Cir. 1987); Nuclear Research Corp. v. United States, 814 F.2d 647 (Fed. Cir. 1987); Rogers v. Overseas Ed. Ass'n, 814 F.2d 1549 (Fed. Cir. 1987); Dominquez v. Department of Air Force, 803 F.2d 680 (Fed. Cir. 1986); Smith v. United States Postal Service, 789 F.2d 1540 (Fed. Cir. 1986); Sanders-Midwest, Inc. v. United States, 15 Cl. Ct. 345 (1988); Rogers Truck Line v. United States, 14Cl. Ct. 108 (1987); W & J Construction Corp. v. United States, 12 Cl Ct. 507 (1987); MW Kellogg Co./Siciliana Appaliti Construzioni, S.p.A. v. United States, 10 Cl.Ct. 17 (1986); Caddell Construction Co./ISE Construzioni, S.p.A. v. United States, 9 Cl Ct. 610 (1986).

## FITCH, EVEN, TABIN & FLANNERY

**LOS ANGELES, CALIFORNIA**

(See San Diego)

*Intellectual Property and Technology-Related Law including Patents, Trademarks, Trade Secret, Copyrights and Unfair Competition, Antitrust and International Trade Commission Causes and Related Litigation.*

## RICHARD L. FITZER

**LOS ANGELES, CALIFORNIA**

(See Long Beach)

*Entertainment, representing Musicians, Intellectual Property and Criminal Appeals.*

CALIFORNIA—LOS ANGELES                                              MARTINDALE-HUBBELL LAW DIRECTORY 1997

## FLANAGAN, BOOTH, UNGER & MOSES
### LOS ANGELES, CALIFORNIA
(See Glendale)

General Civil and Trial Practice in all Courts. Criminal, Driving While Intoxicated and Personal Injury Law.

## FOGEL, FELDMAN, OSTROV, RINGLER & KLEVENS
### A LAW CORPORATION
### LOS ANGELES, CALIFORNIA
(See Santa Monica)

General Civil and Trial Practice in all State and Federal Courts. Corporation, Government Contract, Labor, Admiralty and Railroad Law.

## JANICE FOGG
*10880 WILSHIRE BOULEVARD, SUITE 2200*
**LOS ANGELES, CALIFORNIA 90024**
*Telephone: 310-446-9773*
*Fax: 310-470-6735*
*Email: JEFogg@AOL.com*

Probate, Estate Planning, Estates, Gift Taxation, Conservatorship, Trusts and Wills.

**JANICE FOGG,** born Montana, May 25, 1948; admitted to bar, 1989, California. *Education:* University of California at Los Angeles (B.A., magna cum laude, 1978; J.D., 1989). Alpha Lambda Delta. *Member:* Beverly Hills (Chair, Probate, Trust and Estate Planning Section, 1996-1997), Los Angeles County and American Bar Associations; State Bar of California. (Certified Specialist, Estate Planning, Trust and Probate Law The State Bar of California Board of Legal Specialization). **PRACTICE AREAS:** Probate; Trust Law; Estate Planning; Wills.

*OF COUNSEL*

**MANYA M. BERTRAM, (MRS.),** born Denver, Colorado; admitted to bar, 1963, California. *Education:* Southwestern University School of Law (J.D., magna cum laude, 1962). Iota Tau Tau Legal Sorority. Past Member: California Commission on Aging; Board of Governors, Whittier College School of Law; Past Trustee, Southwestern University School of Law. Past President, Southwestern University School of Law Alumni Association. Member, Board of Directors of Jewish Family Service of Los Angeles. *Member:* Los Angeles County and American Bar Associations; State Bar of California; Federacion Internacional de Abogadas. **LANGUAGES:** Yiddish. **PRACTICE AREAS:** Wills; Trust Law; Trust Administration. *Email:* 75304.247@CompuServe.com

## FOLEY LARDNER WEISSBURG & ARONSON
*Established in 1842*
*35TH FLOOR, ONE CENTURY PLAZA*
*2029 CENTURY PARK EAST (CENTURY CITY)*
**LOS ANGELES, CALIFORNIA 90067-3021**
*Telephone: 310-277-2223*
*Facsimile: 310-557-8475*

Sacramento, California Office: Suite 1050, 770 L Street. Telephone: 916-443-8005. Facsimile: 916-443-2240.
San Diego, California Office: 402 West Broadway, 23rd. Floor. Telephone: 619-234-6655. Facsimile: 619-234-3510.
San Francisco, California Office: One Maritime Plaza, 6th Floor. Telephone: 415-434-4484. Facsimile: 415-434-4507.

Health Care; Hospitals; Medicare and Medicaid; Litigation; Labor and Employment; Business, Corporate and Commercial Law; Administrative and Legislative Practice before all State and Federal Agencies; Finance; Real Estate; Employee Benefits; Municipal Law.

*(This Listing Continued)*

CAA656B

**ROBERT A. KLEIN,** born Detroit, Michigan, November 17, 1933; admitted to bar, 1959, California and U.S. District Court, Central District of California; 1962, U.S. Court of Appeals, Ninth Circuit; 1969, U.S. District Court, District of Columbia; 1975, U.S. Claims Court; 1978, U.S. Court of Appeals, Fourth Circuit; 1980, U.S. Court of Appeals, District of Columbia Circuit, U.S. Court of Appeals, Fifth and Tenth Circuits; 1981, U.S. Supreme Court. *Education:* University of Michigan (B.A., 1954; M.B.A., 1958; J.D., 1958). Tau Epsilon Rho. Assistant Senior Editor, Michigan Law Review, 1957-1958. *Member:* Los Angeles County Bar Association; American Academy of Healthcare Attorneys; National Health Lawyers Association; Healthcare Financial Management Association. **PRACTICE AREAS:** Health Care; Hospitals; Medicare and Medicaid; Administrative Law.

**PETER ARONSON,** born Vienna, Austria, September 17, 1933; admitted to bar, 1960, California, U.S. District Court, Central and Eastern Districts of California and U.S. Court of Appeals, Ninth Circuit. *Education:* University of Illinois (B.A., cum laude, 1955); University of Southern California (LL.B., 1960). *Member:* Los Angeles County and American Bar Associations. **LANGUAGES:** German. **REPORTED CASES:** Wilson v. Blue Cross, 271 Cal Rptr. 876 (1990). **PRACTICE AREAS:** Commercial Litigation; Administrative Law; Business Torts; Legal Law; Antitrust; Unfair Competition.

**CARL WEISSBURG,** born Braddock, Pennsylvania, December 10, 1930; admitted to bar, 1958, California; 1975, U.S. Claims Court and U.S. Supreme Court. *Education:* University of California at Los Angeles (A.A., 1950; B.A., with honors, 1954); Boalt Hall School of Law, University of California at Berkeley (J.D., 1957). Phi Alpha Delta. Recipient, Award of Merit from the California Association of Hospitals and Health Systems, October 27, 1988. Executive Director, United Hospital Association, 1970—. General Counsel, Federation of American Health Systems, 1970—. *Member:* California Society for Healthcare Attorneys (President, 1985-1986); Healthcare Association of Southern California; Healthcare Financial Management Association. [U.S. Air Force Reserve, 1950-1954]. **PRACTICE AREAS:** Health Care Corporate Law; Health Care Legislation; Integrated Health Care Delivery Systems; Medicare Fraud and Abuse; Administrative Agency Law.

**RICHARD A. BLACKER,** born Hartford, Connecticut, July 10, 1937; admitted to bar, 1972, California. *Education:* Cornell University (B.S., 1960; M.S., 1961); University of California at Los Angeles (J.D., 1972). Phi Alpha Delta. Order of the Coif. Member, UCLA Law Review, 1971-1972. Founding Editor, "Health Care Law Newsletter," published by Matthew Bender & Co., Inc., 1986-1996. *Member:* Beverly Hills Bar Association. **PRACTICE AREAS:** Health Care; Hospitals; Nonprofit Corporations; Business Law.

**MARK S. WINDISCH,** born Los Angeles, California, October 12, 1949; admitted to bar, 1975, California and U.S. District Court, Central District of California; 1977, U.S. District Court, Southern District of California; 1979, U.S. Court of Appeals, Ninth Circuit; 1987, U.S. Supreme Court. *Education:* Duke University (A.B., magna cum laude, 1971); University of California at Los Angeles (J.D., 1975). Pi Sigma Alpha; Order of the Coif. Recipient, High Commendation Award from the Los Angeles County Board of Supervisors, May 26, 1992. General Counsel, California Association of Public Hospitals and Health Systems, 1986—. *Member:* American Academy of Healthcare Attorneys. **PRACTICE AREAS:** Health Care; Hospitals; Administrative Law; State and Federal Legislative Practice; Managed Care.

**J. MARK WAXMAN,** born Denver, Colorado, January 10, 1950; admitted to bar, 1973, California; 1974, U.S. District Court, Central, Southern, Eastern and Northern Districts of California and U.S. Court of Appeals, Ninth Circuit; 1980, U.S. Court of Appeals, Eighth Circuit; 1981, U.S. Supreme Court; 1986, U.S. Claims Court. *Education:* University of California at San Diego (B.A., summa cum laude, 1970); Boalt Hall School of Law, University of California at Berkeley (J.D., 1973). Articles and Book Review Editor, Ecology Law Quarterly, 1972-1973. Assistant U.S. Attorney, Central District of California, 1974-1977. Legal Counsel, California Association of Health Facilities. *Member:* National Health Lawyers Association (Member, Board of Directors, 1986-1992; Chairman, First and Second Symposium on Preferred Provider Organizations, 1983-1984); American Academy of Healthcare Attorneys; American Hospital Association (Member, Adjunct Task Force on Antitrust). (Also at Foley & Lardner, Washington, D.C. Office). **REPORTED CASES:** Summit Health Ltd. v. Pinhas, 111 S.Ct. 1842 (1991). **PRACTICE AREAS:** Health Care; Hospitals; Commercial Litigation; Administrative Law; Antitrust and Trade Regulation; Long Term Care.

*(This Listing Continued)*

**CARL H. HITCHNER,** born Bridgeton, New Jersey, September 23, 1940; admitted to bar, 1973, California, U.S. District Court, Northern District of California and U.S. Court of Appeals, Ninth Circuit. *Education:* Susquehanna University (B.S., 1962); University of Notre Dame (J.D., 1973). Certified Public Accountant, California, 1969. Co-Author: "Integrated Delivery Systems: A Survey of Organizational Models," 29 Wake Forest L. Rev. 273 (1994). *Member:* Bar Association of San Francisco; American Academy of Healthcare Attorneys; National Health Lawyers Association; California Society of Certified Public Accountants; American Institute of Certified Public Accountants; Healthcare Financial Management Association (Member, National Board of Directors, 1988-1990). (Resident at San Francisco Office). **PRACTICE AREAS:** Health Care; Hospitals; Integrated Health Care Delivery Systems; Corporate Law; Health Care Mergers and Acquisitions.

**ROBERT D. SEVELL,** born Los Angeles, California, June 10, 1948; admitted to bar, 1973, California. *Education:* University of California at Los Angeles (B.A., 1970); Loyola Law School, Los Angeles (J.D., 1973). Member, Loyola University Law Review, 1972-1973. Author: "Valuing Physician Practices by the Book: New IRS Text Offers Clues for Exempt Organizations," Inside Health Law, Vol. 1, No. 1, January 1996; "Managing the Due Diligence Process," Inside Health Law, Vol. 1, No. 8, August 1996; "An Integrated Delivery Systems Review: Common Problems to be Addressed," Health Care Law Newsletter, Vol. 10, No. 1, January 1995. *Member:* Los Angeles County and American Bar Associations; American Academy of Healthcare Attorneys. **PRACTICE AREAS:** Business Law; Health Care Finance; Corporate Law.

**RICHARD F. SEIDEN,** born Brooklyn, New York, June 22, 1949; admitted to bar, 1974, California. *Education:* University of Pennsylvania (B.A., magna cum laude, 1971) Phi Beta Kappa; Boalt Hall School of Law, University of California at Berkeley (J.D., 1974). *Member:* Los Angeles County and American Bar Associations; Healthcare Financial Management Association. **PRACTICE AREAS:** Corporate Law; Business Law; Health Care; Hospitals; Financing.

**GREGORY W. McCLUNE,** born Belfast, North Ireland, March 16, 1945; admitted to bar, 1978, California; 1981, U.S. District Court, Northern District of California; 1987, U.S. Supreme Court. *Education:* University of Cape Town, Cape Town, South Africa (B.A., 1965; LL.B., 1968). (Resident at San Francisco Office). **SPECIAL AGENCIES:** National Labor Relations Board; Equal Employment and Opportunity Commission and State Counterparts; Wage and Hour Division and State Counterparts. **REPORTED CASES:** O'Connor Hospital v. Superior Court of Santa Clara County and Cleu, 2 IER Cases (BNA) 1190 (1987). **PRACTICE AREAS:** Labor and Employment; Management Labor Relations; Wrongful Termination; Employment Discrimination; Wage and Hour Law.

**GEORGE L. ROOT, JR.,** born Cleveland, Ohio, November 17, 1947; admitted to bar, 1975, California. *Education:* Syracuse University (B.A., 1969); University of San Diego (J.D., cum laude, 1975). Co-Author: "A Practical Approach to Hospital-Physician Affiliations," Health Care Law Newsletter, Vol. 8, No. 11, October 1993. *Member:* San Diego County Bar Association (Chairman, Mental Health Committee, 1983; Task Force on Children at Risk, 1995); Association of California Hospital Districts (Member, Legislative Committee, 1995); California Society for Healthcare Attorneys; California Association of Hospitals and Health Systems; Healthcare Financial Management Association; National Health Lawyers Association. (Resident at San Diego Office). **PRACTICE AREAS:** Health Care; Hospitals; Mental Health Law; Health Maintenance Organizations; Non-Profit Corporations; Integrated Health Care Delivery Systems.

**JAMES R. KALYVAS,** born Milwaukee, Wisconsin, December 5, 1956; admitted to bar, 1981, California and U.S. District Court, Central and Southern Districts of California. *Education:* Oakland University (B.A., 1977); University of Michigan (J.D., 1981). Author: "Designing an Integrated Information System to Minimize Antitrust Concerns," Inside Health Law, Vol. 1, No. 9, September 1996; "Information Systems Electronic Medical Records: Addressing the Conflict Between Need for Access and Confidentiality Concerns," Inside Health Law, Vol. 1, No. 2, February 1996; "'Debugging' the Information System Contracting Process," Health Systems Review, February 1995; "Effectively Negotiating Integrated Information System Contracts: Parts I and II," Health Care Law Newsletter, Vol. 9, No. 12, December 1994 and Vol. 10, No. 1, January 1995. *Member:* Los Angeles County Bar Association; State Bar of California (Member, Business Law and Litigation Sections); Healthcare Information and Management Systems Society. **PRACTICE AREAS:** Commercial Litigation; Information Systems; Health Care; Hospitals; Real Estate.

*(This Listing Continued)*

**MICHAEL G. McCARTY,** born Carbondale, Pennsylvania, August 4, 1952; admitted to bar, 1983, Wisconsin; 1987, U.S. Court of Appeals, Seventh Circuit; 1989, U.S. Supreme Court; 1991, U.S. Courts of Appeal, Fifth and Ninth Circuits. *Education:* University of Scranton (B.S., 1974; M.A., 1976); Syracuse University (J.D., summa cum laude, 1983). Order of the Coif. Justinian Honor Society. Member, Board of Directors, Wisconsin Correctional Service, 1988-1993, President, 1991-1993. *Member:* Milwaukee and American Bar Associations; State Bar of Wisconsin; Wisconsin Academy of Trial Lawyers. (Resident, San Diego Office). **PRACTICE AREAS:** Litigation.

**RICHARD M. ALBERT,** born Lansing, Michigan, October 3, 1953; admitted to bar, 1979, California. *Education:* University of Michigan (B.B.A., 1975; J.D., 1978). *Member:* Los Angeles County (Member, Labor and Employment Law Section; Forum Committee on Health Care Law, 1978—) and American Bar Associations; Industrial Relations Research Association. **SPECIAL AGENCIES:** National Labor Relations Board; National Mediation Board; Equal Employment Opportunity Commission and State Counterparts; Wage and Hour Division and State Counterparts. **PRACTICE AREAS:** Labor and Employment; Wrongful Termination; Employment Discrimination; Wage and Hour Law; Administrative Law; Health Care; Hospitals.

**RALPH B. KOSTANT,** born Phoenix, Arizona, October 23, 1951; admitted to bar, 1978, California. *Education:* Stanford University (A.B., 1972); Arizona State University (J.D., magna cum laude, 1976). Comment Editor, Arizona State Law Journal, 1975-1976. Contributing Author: The American Law of Mining, 2d. Ed., 1984. Author: The Natural Resources Manual, 1995; "Geothermal Law: The Last and Next 23 Years," 37 Rocky Mountain Mineral Law Institute 2-1, 1991, reprinted in Geothermal Resources Council Bulletin, January 1993, P. 4; "The Status of the Promissory Note Under the Federal Securities Laws," 1975 Arizona State Law Journal 175. *Member:* Los Angeles County (Member: Natural Resources, Energy and Environmental Law; Real Property, Probate and Trust Sections) and American (Member, Real Estate Section) Bar Associations; State Bar of California (Member, Real Property Section). **PRACTICE AREAS:** Real Estate Development; Real Estate Finance; Real Estate Workouts; Real Estate Leasing; Secured Finance; Health Care; Long Term Care; Commercial Leasing; Geothermal Resources; Mining and Minerals; Oil and Gas.

**LAURENCE R. ARNOLD,** born Charleston, West Virginia, January 24, 1952; admitted to bar, 1976, Georgia, U.S. District Court, Northern District of Georgia and U.S. Court of Appeals, Fifth Circuit; 1983, U.S. Court of Appeals, Fourth and Eleventh Circuits; 1987, Virginia; 1988, California, U.S. District Court, Northern District of California and U.S. Court of Appeals, Ninth Circuit; 1990, U.S. Supreme Court; 1992, U.S. Court of Appeals, District of Columbia Circuit. *Education:* University of Virginia (B.A., 1973); Emory University School of Law (J.D., with distinction, 1976). Order of the Coif. Member, Board of Editors, Emory Law Journal, 1975-1976. *Member:* Bar Association of San Francisco; State Bar of California (Member, Labor and Employment Section); American Bar Association (Member, Labor and Employment Law Section). (Resident at San Francisco Office). **SPECIAL AGENCIES:** National Labor Relations Board; National Mediation Board; Equal Employment Opportunity Commission and State Counterparts; Wage and Hour Division and State Counterparts. **PRACTICE AREAS:** Labor and Employment; Employment Discrimination; Collective Bargaining; Labor Arbitration; Administrative Hearings and Appeals; Wage and Hour Law.

**ANITA D. LEE,** born San Mateo, California, April 13, 1957; admitted to bar, 1982, California, U.S. District Court, Eastern, Central and Southern Districts of California and U.S. Court of Appeals, Ninth Circuit. *Education:* Stanford University (A.B., 1979); University of California at Los Angeles (J.D., 1982). Order of the Coif. Law Clerk for the Hon. Joan Dempsey Klein, California Court of Appeals, 1982-1983. Author: "Questions Concerning the Process of Requesting Exceptions from Cost Limits," Health Care Law Newsletter, Vol. 10, No. 10, October, 1995; "Financial Support for Graduate Medical Education Under the Clinton Health Security Act," Health Care Law Newsletter, Vol. 9, No. 4, April 1994; "New Teaching Physician Regulations Require a Physical Presence and More Documentation," Inside Health Law, Vol. 1, No. 7, July 1996. *Member:* Los Angeles County (Member, Health Care Law Section, Executive Committee, 1989-1996) and American (Governing Board, Forum on Health Care law, 1995-1996) Bar Associations; Women Lawyers of Los Angeles. **SPECIAL AGENCIES:** Provider Reimbursement Review Board. **PRACTICE AREAS:** Health Care; Hospitals; Medicare and Medicaid; Administrative Law.

*(This Listing Continued)*

CAA657B

**FOLEY LARDNER WEISSBURG & ARONSON, Los Angeles—Continued**

**SAMUEL F. HOFFMAN,** born San Diego, California, November 21, 1957; admitted to bar, 1982, California. *Education:* San Diego State University (A.B., 1979); Hastings College of Law, University of California (J.D., 1982). Member, National Moot Court Team. Author: Articles in Health Care Law Newsletter: "IRS Focuses on Employment Status of Hospital-Based Physicians," Vol. 10, No. 5, May 1995; "Use of Registry Employees Can Pose Legal Problems," Vol. 9, No. 7, July 1994. Co-Author: "Health Security Act Will Dramatically Alter Employer Health Care Burdens," Health Care Law Newsletter, Vol. 9, No. 1, January 1994. *Member:* San Diego County (Member, Labor and Employment Law Section, Employee Benefits Subcommittee) and American Bar Associations; San Diego Society of Human Resource Managers; Western Pension and Benefits Conference; California Society for Healthcare Attorneys. (Resident at San Diego Office). *PRACTICE AREAS:* Labor and Employment; Employee Benefits.

**SAMUEL H. WEISSBARD,** born Brooklyn, New York, March 3, 1947; admitted to bar, 1970, District of Columbia; 1974, U.S. Supreme Court (Not admitted in California). *Education:* Western Reserve University (B.A., 1967); George Washington University (J.D., with highest honors, 1970). Order of the Coif. Editor-in-Chief, George Washington Law Review, 1969-1970. Member: Georgetown Business and Professional Association (Member, Board of Directors and Executive Committee, Secretary, General Counsel). Georgetown Arts Commission (Member, Board of Directors and Executive Committee, General Counsel); National Learning Center/Capital Childrens' Museum (Member, Board of Directors and Executive Committee; Co-General Counsel). *Member:* The District of Columbia Bar; American Bar Association (Member, Real Property, Probate and Trust Law Section; Forum on Affordable Housing). *PRACTICE AREAS:* Commercial Real Estate; Commercial Leasing; Financial Transactions; Workouts and Creditor's Rights.

**THOMAS L. DRISCOLL,** born Oceanside, New York, August 3, 1949; admitted to bar, 1980, California and U.S. District Court, Central District of California; 1985, U.S. District Court, Northern District of California. *Education:* Catholic University of America (A.B., 1972); Southwestern University (J.D., 1980); New York University (LL.M., in Taxation, 1985). Recipient, American Jurisprudence Award for Administrative Law. Member, Southwestern University Law Review, 1979-1980. Co-Author: "Tax Exemption Criteria for Integrated Delivery Systems," Health Care Law Newsletter, Vol. 8, No. 10, October 1993. Author: "Rural Health Care Under the Health Security Act," Health Care Law Newsletter, Vol. 9, No. 3, March 1994. *Member:* National Health Lawyers Association; Healthcare Financial Management Association (Member, Northern California Chapter; Chair, Committee on Taxation, 1990-1991); National Rural Health Association. (Resident, San Francisco Office). *PRACTICE AREAS:* Tax-Exempt Organizations; Health Care; Managed Care; Integrated Health Care Delivery Systems; Physicians and Physician Group Representation; Hospitals; Health Care Contracts; Corporate.

**JONATHAN M. LINDEKE,** born Pittsburgh, Pennsylvania, November 6, 1948; admitted to bar, 1976, California; 1978, U.S. Court of Appeals, Ninth and District of Columbia Circuits. *Education:* University of California at Los Angeles (B.A., 1970); Boalt Hall School of Law, University of California at Berkeley (J.D., 1976). Editor, Health Care Law Newsletter, Matthew Bender, 1990-1992. Author: Articles in Inside Health Law: "Beware of the Sale of Your PPO Discounts!" Vol. 1, No. 2, February 1996; "States Scramble to Regulate Risk-Bearing Provider Networks," Vol. 2, No. 4, April 1996; "'Gag Rules' Hard to Swallow in Managed Care Contracting," Vol. 1, No. 6, June 1996. *Member:* Bar Association of San Francisco. (Resident at San Francisco Office). *PRACTICE AREAS:* Health Care; Hospitals; Corporate.

**C. DARRYL CORDERO,** born El Paso, Texas, August 2, 1956; admitted to bar, 1983, California; 1984, U.S. District Court, Central District of California; 1987, U.S. District Court, Eastern District of California; 1988, U.S. District Court, Northern District of California; 1989, U.S. Supreme Court and U.S. District Court, Southern District of California; 1990, U.S. Court of Appeals, Ninth Circuit. *Education:* University of Texas (B.A., 1978); Harvard University (J.D., 1981). Law Clerk to the Hon. Harry Lee Hudspeth, U.S. District Court, Western District of Texas, 1981-1982. *Member:* Los Angeles County Bar Association. *PRACTICE AREAS:* Insurance Coverage and Bad Faith; Antitrust; Federal Litigation; Commercial Litigation.

**DENISE R. RODRIGUEZ,** born Detroit, Michigan, April 5, 1951; admitted to bar, 1979, Michigan; 1988, California and U.S. District Court, Central District of California. *Education:* Henry Ford Community College (A.A., 1971); Wayne State University (B.A., with distinction, 1975); University of Michigan (J.D., cum laude, 1979). *Member:* Hispanic National Bar Association; Mexican-American Bar Association; Healthcare Financial Management Association; National Health Lawyers Association. *SPECIAL AGENCIES:* Provider Reimbursement Review Board. *PRACTICE AREAS:* Health Care; Hospitals; Medicare and Medicaid; Administrative Law.

**STEPHEN W. PARRISH,** born Chicago, Illinois, November 14, 1951; admitted to bar, 1976, Colorado and U.S. District Court, District of Colorado; 1978, California and U.S. District Court, Southern District of California; 1980, U.S. District Court, Northern District of California; 1981, U.S. Supreme Court and U.S. Court of Appeals, Ninth Circuit; 1984, U.S. District Court, Central District of California; 1986, U.S. District Court, Eastern District of California. *Education:* The American University (B.A., 1973); University of Denver (J.D., 1975). Co-Author: "An Open Question: Does the Americans with Disabilities Act Apply to Medical Staff Decisions: Part I and II," Health Care Law Newsletter, Vol. 7, No. 11 and 12, November and December, 1992. Author: "'Refusal to Treat' Cases Involving HIV-Infected Persons Under the Americans With Disabilities Act," Health Care Law Newsletter, Vol. 9, No. 11, November 1994; "Federal Support for Application of the Americans with Disabilities Act to Medical Staff Decisions," Health Care Law Newsletter, Vol. 9, No. 4, April 1994. *Member:* Bar Association of San Francisco; Los Angeles County Bar Association; State Bar of California (Member, Labor and Employment Law Section). (Resident at San Francisco Office). *PRACTICE AREAS:* Labor and Employment; Management Labor Relations; Employment Discrimination; Litigation; Government Contracts; Administrative Law.

**R. MICHAEL SCARANO, JR.,** born Englewood, New Jersey, February 11, 1956; admitted to bar, 1984, California. *Education:* University of California at Berkeley (A.B. with academic distinction, 1978); Boalt Hall School of Law, University of California at Berkeley (J.D., 1984). Associate Editor, Ecology Law Quarterly, 1983-1984. *Member:* San Diego County Bar Association; California Society for Healthcare Attorneys; National Health Lawyers Association; Healthcare Financial Management Association. (Resident at San Diego Office). *PRACTICE AREAS:* Health Care; Hospitals; Health Care Mergers and Acquisitions; Managed Care; Integrated Health Care Delivery Systems; Emergency Medical Services; Long Term Care.

**DAVID A. BLUMENTHAL,** born Norfolk, Virginia, February 10, 1945; admitted to bar, 1974, Virginia; 1974-1982, U.S. Court of Customs and Patent Appeals; 1975, U.S. District Court, Eastern District of Virginia; 1978, U.S. Claims Court; 1979, District of Columbia; 1980, U.S. Supreme Court; 1982, U.S. Court of Appeals for the Federal Circuit; registered to practice before U.S. Patent and Trademark Office (Not admitted in California). *Education:* College of William & Mary (B.S., 1966); University of Pennsylvania (Ph.D., 1970); George Washington University (J.D., with honors, 1974). Phi Beta Kappa; Phi Delta Phi; Sigma Pi Sigma. Recipient, Joseph Rossman Memorial Award, 1980-1981. Author: "The Status of Programmable Inventions in the United States," Gewerblicher Rechtsschutz and Urheberrecht International Teil, 1980; "Statutory or Non-Statutory?: An Analysis of the Patentability of Computer Related Inventions," Journal of the Patent Office Society, Vol. 62, No. 8, Aug., 1980; "Supreme Court Sets Guidelines for Patentability of Computer Related Inventions," Journal of the Patent Office Society, February, 1981; "Computer Programs: Recent Developments in U.S. Patent, Copyright and Trade Secret Law," AIPPI Journal, June, 1982; "Software Protection in the United States," NIKKEI Computer, September, 1982; "Lifeforms, Computer Programs, and the Pursuit of a Patent," Technology Review, Feb./March 1983. Lecturer and Chairman, Electronics and Computer Patent and Copyright Practice, Patent Resources Group, Florida and Washington, D.C., 1986—. Lecturer, Patent Bar Review Course, Patent Resources Group, 1987. Adjunct Professor of Law, George Mason University, 1990-1996. Roundtable Member, Patent and Trademark Office, Project XL. *Member:* Virginia State Bar; American Bar Association (Member, Patent, Trademark and Copyright Law Section); American Intellectual Property Law Association; International Patent and Trademark Association; International Federation of Industrial Property Attorneys. (Resident also at Foley & Lardner, Washington, D.C. & Annapolis, Maryland Offices). *PRACTICE AREAS:* Intellectual Property.

**LOWELL C. BROWN,** born Salt Lake City, Utah, October 21, 1954; admitted to bar, 1983, California, U.S. District Court, Central District of California and U.S. Court of Appeals, Ninth Circuit. *Education:* University of Utah (B.A., magna cum laude, 1979; J.D., 1982). Topics Editor, 1981-1982, Utah Law Review. Author: "New 'Mental Models' for Credentialing

*(This Listing Continued)*

and Peer Review," Health Systems Review, May/June 1994; "A Case Study from California - The Sharing of Peer Review Information Between Hospitals and Nonhospital Providers," Topics In Health Information Management, Vol. 14, No. 4, May 1994; "Patient Dumping by Specialized Care Facilities," HealthSpan, Vol. 9, No. 6, June 1991. *Member:* Los Angeles County (Member, Health Law Section, Executive Committee, 1990-1991; Chair, 1993-1994) and American (Member: Forum Committee on Health Law; Litigation Section) Bar Associations; American Academy of Healthcare Attorneys (Member: Committee on Medical Staff and Physician Relations); California Society for Healthcare Attorneys (Member, Board of Directors, 1995—); Healthcare Association of Southern California (Member, Professional Services Committee, 1991—). *LANGUAGES:* Spanish. *SPECIAL AGENCIES:* Division of Health Standards and Quality; Health Care Financing Administration. *REPORTED CASES:* Scripps Memorial Hospital v. Superior Court, 87 Cal.App.4th 1720 (1995); Mir v. Charter Suburban Hospital, 27 Cal. App. 4th 1471 (1994); Bollengier v. Doctors Medical Center, 222 Cal.App. 3d 1115 (1990). *PRACTICE AREAS:* Health Care; Hospitals; Integrated Health Care Delivery; Medical Staff; Health Care Facility Licensing and Regulation; Bioethics.

***GREGORY V. MOSER,*** born Washington, D.C., May 11, 1955; admitted to bar, 1981, California. *Education:* Haverford College (B.A., 1977); Georgetown University (J.D., cum laude, 1981). Member, American Criminal Law Review, 1979-1981. Editor, Georgetown Law Weekly, 1980-1981. *Member:* San Diego County Bar Association; State Bar of California (Member, Public Law Section); Association of California Water Agencies; California Council of School Attorneys. (Resident at San Diego Office). *REPORTED CASES:* City of South El Monte v. Southern California Joint Powers Insurance Authority, 38 Cal.App.4th 1629 (1955); EBMUD v. City of Lafayette 16 Cal. App. 4th 1005 (1993); Ektelon v. City of San Diego, 200 Cal. App. 3d 378, (1988). *PRACTICE AREAS:* Municipal Law; Water Rights; Environmental Law; Insurance; Self-Insurance; School Law.

***ROBERT E. GOLDSTEIN,*** born Hartford, Connecticut, August 6, 1947; admitted to bar, 1973, Connecticut; 1975, Florida; 1981, District of Columbia; 1993, California. *Education:* University of Connecticut (B.A., 1969); Suffolk University Law School (J.D., 1973); University of Miami (LL.M., 1974). Author: "Insurance Plans of Exempt Organizations May Threaten Exemptions," Journal of Taxation, May 1979; "Keogh Plan and IRA Limits Increased," Journal of Taxation, January 1982; "Health Care Legislation Struck Down by Federal Courts," Health Systems Review, Vol. 26, No. 3, (May/June 1993); "Forming and Operating a Nonprofit Entity Under California Law," Journal of Exempt Organizations (January/February 1996). *Member:* American Bar Association (Member, Tax Section). [U.S. Army Reserves, December 1968 - February 1974]. *PRACTICE AREAS:* Employee Benefits; Tax Exempt Organizations; Taxation.

***TAMI S. SMASON,*** born Chicago, Illinois, May 30, 1959; admitted to bar, 1985, California; 1986, U.S. District Court, Central District of California and U.S. Court of Appeals, Ninth Circuit; 1988, U.S. District Court, Southern District of California; 1990, U.S. Supreme Court; 1994, U.S. District Court, Eastern District of California. *Education:* University of California at Berkeley (B.S., with honors, 1981); Boalt Hall School of Law, University of California at Berkeley (J.D., 1985). Judge pro tempore for Municipal Court of California, Los Angeles Judicial District. Volunteered for Los Angeles County Bar Association Domestic Violence Project and Barristers' Disaster Relief Project. Author: "Corporate Compliance Issues," ABA Forum on Health Law: Health Care Fraud and Abuse and the False Claims Act, 1996. Co-Author: "Health Care Executives Risk Criminal Liability for 'See-No-Evil' Mentality," Inside Health Law, Vol. 1, No. 6, June 1996. *Member:* Los Angeles County Bar Association; State Bar of California. *PRACTICE AREAS:* Commercial Litigation; Health Care Litigation; Business Torts.

***LAWRENCE C. CONN,*** born Washington, D.C., May 20, 1959; admitted to bar, 1985, California. *Education:* Princeton University (B.A., summa cum laude, 1981); Phi Beta Kappa; Stanford Law School (J.D., 1984). Law Clerk to the Hon. Lawrence T. Lydick, U.S. District Court, Central District of California, 1984-1986. Principal Author: "Demythologizing Hanlester," Health Systems Review, Vol. 28, No. 4, July/August 1995; "The Stark Regulations," Health Systems Review, Vol. 28, No. 6, November/December 1995; "Fraud and Abuse," California Association of Health Facilities Guidelines Bulletin, February 1993. Co-Author: "Federal Anti-Referral Statute Raises Unanswered Questions, Part I: Group Practice Issues and Part II: Issues Relating to Exceptions," Health Care Law Newsletter, Vol. 9, No. 10, October 1994 and Vol. 9, No. 11, November 1994. *PRACTICE AREAS:* Health Care; Hospitals; Integrated Health Care Delivery Systems; Long Term Care; Business Law.

***MARK T. SCHIEBLE,*** born Ann Arbor, Michigan, April 9, 1951; admitted to bar, 1980, Pennsylvania; 1981, U.S. District Court, Eastern District of Pennsylvania; 1984, California. *Education:* University of California at Berkeley (B.A., with honors, 1975); Temple University (J.D., cum laude, 1980). Associate Editor, Temple Law Quarterly, 1979-1980. Author: "Intermediate Sanctions; Turning the Table," Inside Health Law, Vol. 1, No. 10, October 1996; Articles in Health Care Law Newsletter: "Proposed Regulations to Govern Private Business Use of Tax-Exempt Bond Financed Facilities," Vol. 10, No. 6, June 1995; "New IRS Revenue Procedure Clarifies Tax Classification of Limited Liability Companies," Vol. 10, No. 5, May 1995; "The Hermann Hospital Closing Agreement: Is Informal Guidance Better Than No Guidance at All?." Vol. 10, No. 2, February 1995. *Member:* National Association of Bond Lawyers; Healthcare Financial Management Association (Member, Tax Committee, 1992-1993). (Resident at San Francisco Office). *PRACTICE AREAS:* Taxation; Employee Benefits; Business Law.

***ROBERT C. LEVENTHAL,*** born New York, New York, September 3, 1957; admitted to bar, 1985, California; 1986, U.S. District Court, Central District of California and U.S. Court of Appeals, Ninth Circuit; 1993, U.S. District Court, Southern District of California. *Education:* State University of New York at Binghamton (B.A., 1979); Vanderbilt University (J.D., 1985). Order of the Coif. Member, Vanderbilt Journal of Transactional Law, 1983-1985. Author: "Tort Reform Proposals: A Toolbox for Change," Health Care Law Newsletter, Vol. 9, No. 9, September 1994. Co-Author: "Duty to Preserve Discoverable Material Created by Emergent Technologies," Health Care Law Newsletter, Vol. 9, No. 4, April 1994. *Member:* American Bar Association (Member, Litigation Section). *REPORTED CASES:* Burton v. Security Pacific National Bank, 197 Cal. App. 3d 972 (1988). *PRACTICE AREAS:* Commercial Litigation; Construction Defects; Antitrust; Labor and Employment Litigation.

***LARRY L. MARSHALL,*** born Portsmouth, Virginia, December 29, 1942; admitted to bar, 1968, California. *Education:* University of California at Riverside (B.A., 1964); Boalt Hall School of Law, University of California at Berkeley (J.D., 1967). Phi Delta Phi. Member, Moot Court Board. *Member:* San Diego County Bar Association (Chairman, Section on Eminent Domain, 1976); State Bar of California (Member, Public Law Section); Downtown San Diego Partnership (Vice President); Japanese Friendship Garden Society (President); International Right of Way Association. (Resident at San Diego Office). *PRACTICE AREAS:* Public Agency; Nonprofit and Charitable Organizations; Municipal Law; Eminent Domain.

***CLARE RICHARDSON,*** born Aberdeen, Scotland, July 2, 1962; admitted to bar, 1986, California, U.S. District Court, Central District of California and U.S. Court of Appeals, Ninth Circuit. *Education:* University of Southern California (A.B., magna cum laude, 1981; J.D.,1986). Phi Delta Phi. Co-Author: "Integrated Delivery Systems: A Survey of Organizational Models," 29 Wake Forest L. Rev. 273 (1994); "Contracts" chapter of "Physicians and Facilities Manual," Aspen Publishers, Inc. (1996). *Member:* National Association of Bond Lawyers. *PRACTICE AREAS:* Corporate Law; Finance; Health Care; Hospitals.

***CAROL ISACKSON,*** born Alpena, Michigan, February 5, 1942; admitted to bar, 1983, California; 1985, U.S. District Court, Southern and Central Districts of California. *Education:* University of Michigan (B.A., with distinction, 1964); University of Illinois (M.S.W., with honors, 1966); Chicago Kent College of Law (J.D., with high honors, 1982). Member, Moot Court. Member, Law Review, 1981-1982. Co-Author: "The HIV-Infected Health Care Provider," Health Care Law Newsletter, Vol. 10, No. 1, January 1995. Author: "Futile Treatment: The Need for Legislation and Uniform Policies," Health Care Law Newsletter, Vol. 9, No. 10, October 1994. Co-Author: "Arnett v. Dal Cielo: Peer Review Confidentiality Threatened by Medical Board Investigational Subpoenas, " Health Care Law Newsletter, Vol. 10, No. 11, November, 1995. *Member:* San Diego County Bar Association; San Diego Women in Health Administration; National Health Lawyers Association; Lawyers Club of San Diego; California Society for Healthcare Attorneys. (Resident at San Diego Office). *PRACTICE AREAS:* Medical Staff; Labor and Employment Law; Health Care; Litigation.

***DOROTHY J. STEPHENS,*** born Indiana, Pennsylvania, April 8, 1953; admitted to bar, 1987, California; U.S. Court of Appeals, Ninth Circuit and District of Columbia Circuit; U.S. District Court, Northern and Eastern Districts of California. *Education:* Downstate Medical Center, State University of New York (B.S., cum laude, 1975); New York University (M.A., 1979); Hastings College of the Law, University of California (J.D., 1987). Member, Moot Court Board, 1987. Registered Physical Therapist: New York, 1975; California, 1979. Extern, the Hon. Robert P. Aguilar, United

*(This Listing Continued)*

**FOLEY LARDNER WEISSBURG & ARONSON, Los Angeles**—*Continued*

States District Court, Northern District of California, 1987. Author: Articles in Health Care Law Newsletter, "Supreme Court Strikes Down National Labor Relations Board's Restrictive Definition of Health Care Supervisor," Vol. 9, No. 9, September 1994; "Employee Participation Committees: A Union in Sheep's Clothing?" Vol. 8, No. 8, September 1993. *Member:* Bar Association of San Francisco; State Bar of California (Member, Labor Management Section); American Bar Association (Member, Litigation and Labor Law Sections). (Resident at Sacramento Office). **PRACTICE AREAS:** Labor and Employment; Employee Benefits.

**PAUL GUSTAV NEUMANN,** born Linz, Austria, November 27, 1958; admitted to bar, 1987, California. *Education:* Haverford College (B.A., 1981); University of Virginia (J.D., 1987). Recipient, Taylor Taswell Scholarship. Dillard Teaching Fellow. Author: "Patenting Medical Procedures: Do Financial Incentives to Innovate Really Benefit the Delivery of Health Care?" Inside Health Law, Vol. 1, No. 3, March 1996; "State Legislative Approaches to Regulating the Use of Generic Information," Health Care Law Newsletter, Vol. 10, No. 11, November 1995; "Telemedicine - The Diagnostic Tool of the Future," Health Care Law Newsletter, Vol. 10, No. 8, August 1995. *Member:* American Academy of Health Care Attorneys. (Resident at San Francisco Office). **PRACTICE AREAS:** Health Care; Hospitals; Bioethics.

**CHARLES B. OPPENHEIM,** born New York, N.Y., October 18, 1962; admitted to bar, 1988, California. *Education:* Cornell University (B.A., 1984); Fordham University (J.D., 1988). Member, Fordham Law Review, 1986-1987. Co-Author: "Integrated Delivery Systems: A Survey of Organizational Models," 29 Wake Forest L. Rev. 273, 1994; "Compliance Issues Under the New Fraud and Abuse Rules," 16 Whittier L.Rev. 1085, 1995. *Member:* California Society for Health Care Attorneys; National Health Lawyers Association. **PRACTICE AREAS:** Health Care; Integrated Health Care Delivery Systems; Managed Care; Health Care Fraud.

**JAMES N. GODES,** born St. Paul, Minnesota, October 7, 1962; admitted to bar, 1987, California, U.S. District Court, Central, Southern and Northern Districts of California and U.S. Court of Appeals, Ninth Circuit. *Education:* University of the Pacific (B.A., cum laude, 1984); University of Southern California (J.D., 1987). Phi Delta Phi. Member, Major Tax Planning Journal, Computer Law Journal, 1986-1987. Author: "Developing a New Set of Liability Rules for a New Generation of Technology: Assessing Liability for Computer-Related Injuries in the Health Care Field," USC Computer Law Journal, 1988. *Member:* Los Angeles County Bar Association; State Bar of California (Member, Litigation Section). **SPECIAL AGENCIES:** California State Dept. of Health Services, California Dept. of Social Services, California Medical Review, Inc.; U.S. Health Care Financing Administration; Dept. of Fair Employment and Housing; Equal Employment Opportunity Commission. **PRACTICE AREAS:** Labor and Employment Law; Litigation; Long Term Care; Health Care; Bioethics; Hospitals.

**INGEBORG E. PENNER,** born Hötensleben, Germany, December 2, 1946; admitted to bar, 1986, Pennsylvania; 1989, California, U.S. Court of Appeals, Ninth Circuit and U.S. District Court, Northern District of California. *Education:* Kansas University (B.A., cum laude, 1969); Temple University (M.S.W., 1979; J.D., 1986). Co-Author: "State Legislation Focuses Debate on Costs v. Quality," Inside Health Law, Vol. 1, No. 5, May 1996. Author: Articles in Health Care Law Newsletter: "HCFA Enacts New Enforcement Remedies Covering Nursing Facilities," Vol. 10, No. 4, April 1995; "Joint Commission Completes Transition to Functional Standards," Vol. 10, No. 1, January 1995; "Ninth Circuit Buttresses Peer Review Immunities," Vol. 9, No. 11, November 1994. *Member:* Bar Association of San Francisco; California Society for Health Care Attorneys. (Resident at San Francisco Office). **LANGUAGES:** German. **PRACTICE AREAS:** Medical Staff; Health Care; Provider Operations.

**ROBYN A. MEINHARDT,** born Los Angeles, California, October 23, 1953; admitted to bar, 1984, Colorado; 1985, California and U.S. District Court, Central District of California. *Education:* Southern College (B.S.N., cum laude, 1977); University of San Diego (Diploma, Institute on International and Comparative Law, Guadalajara, Mexico, 1982); University of Colorado, Boulder (J.D., 1984). Casenote and Comment Editor, University of Colorado Law Review, 1983-1984. Author: "Bioethics and the Law: The Case of Helga Wanglie: A Clash at the Bedside-Medically Futile Treatment v. Patient Autonomy," 14 Whittier Law Review 137 (1991); "The Case for Hospital Lawyers on Bioethics Committees," 22 Ethical Currents 4 (Spring 90); "AIDS and Issues of Partner Notification," 4 FOCUS a Guide to Aids

*(This Listing Continued)*

Research and Counseling 1 (Nov. 89); "Defining Hospital Policies for HIV-Infected Health Care Providers," 9 California Health Law News, 56 (Summer 89); "People In The Interest of A.M.D.: Are Parental Rights Terminated Too Easily in Colorado?" U. Colo. L. Rev., Issue 3 (1984). *Member:* Los Angeles County Bar Association (Co-Chair, Bio Ethics Committee, 1990-1992; Co-Chair, Joint Committee on Biomedical Ethics of the Los Angeles County Bar and Medical Association, 1995—); American Academy of Hospital Attorneys; National Health Lawyers Association; California Society for Healthcare Attorneys. **PRACTICE AREAS:** Health Care; Hospitals.

*OF COUNSEL*

**JUDITH E. SOLOMON,** born White Plains, New York, July 26, 1947; admitted to bar, 1978, California. *Education:* University of Pennsylvania (B.A., cum laude, 1968; M.S., Education, 1970) Phi Beta Kappa; University of San Diego (J.D., magna cum laude, 1977). Member, San Diego Law Review, 1976-1977. Recipient: American Jurisprudence Award in nine subjects: West Publishing Company Harnbook Award, 1975-1976. Editor, Health Care Law Newsletter (Matthew Bender & Co., Inc., 1992-1995). Editor, Inside Health Law (Aspen Publishers Inc., 1996—). Co-Author: "Integrated Delivery Systems: A Survey of Organizational Models," 29 Wake Forest L. Rev. 273 (1994); "A Practical Approach to Hospital-Physician Affiliations," Health Care Law Newsletter, Vol. 9, No. 10, October 1993. *Member:* San Diego County Bar Association; Lawyers Club of San Diego; California Society for Healthcare Attorneys. (Resident at San Diego Office). **PRACTICE AREAS:** Business Law; Corporate Law; Health Care; Hospitals; Managed Care; Health Care Finance.

**ROBERT J. ENDERS,** born Milwaukee, Wisconsin, March 21, 1946; admitted to bar, 1975, California and U.S. District Court, Southern and Central Districts of California; 1983, U.S. Supreme Court. *Education:* University of Wisconsin (B.B.A., with honors, 1968) Phi Kappa Phi; California State University at Long Beach (M.B.A., 1973); University of California at Los Angeles (J.D., 1975). Order of the Coif. Distinguished Advocate Award. Professor of Business Law, College of Business Administration, California State Polytechnic University at Pomona, 1982—. Author: "An Introduction to Special Antitrust Issues in Health Care Provider Joint Ventures," 61 Antitrust Law Journal 805 (1993); "Antitrust and Health Care: Reconciling Competing Values-Medical Staff Issues," 6 Whittier Law Review 737, 1984; "Federal Antitrust Issues Involvement in the Denial of Medical Staff Privileges," 17 Loyola University of Chicago Law Journal 331, 1986. *Member:* Los Angeles County (Member, Executive Committee, 1979—, Chairman, 1988-1989, Antitrust Section) and American (Member, Antitrust Section) Bar Associations; The State Bar of California (Member, Executive Committee, Antitrust and Trade Regulation Section, 1982-1984, 1989-1992). [Lieutenant, U.S. Navy, 1968-1972]. **SPECIAL AGENCIES:** Federal Trade Commission. **PRACTICE AREAS:** Antitrust and Trade Regulation; Business Torts; Unfair Competition; Advertising and Marketing.

**MARK E. REAGAN,** born Santa Monica, California, February 5, 1961; admitted to bar, 1989, California and U.S. District Court, Eastern District of California; 1990, U.S. District Court, Central District of California; 1992, U.S. District Court, Northern District of California; 1993, U.S. District Court, Southern District of California. *Education:* Stanford University (B.A., 1983); Loyola Law School, Los Angeles (J.D., 1989). Articles: Health Care Law Newsletter: "HCFA Enacts New Enforcement Remedies Covering Nursing Facilities," Vol. 10, No. 4, April 1995; "Recent State Legislative Approaches to Regulating Utilization Review Reflect URAC National Standards," Vol. 10, No. 3, March 1995. *Member:* State Bar of California; American Bar Association; American College of Medical Quality (Advisory Panel, National Ethics and Policy Committee). (Resident at San Francisco Office). **REPORTED CASES:** Muse v. Charter Hospital of Winston-Salem, Inc., 452 S.E.2d 589 aff'd 464 S.E.2d 44 (1995). **PRACTICE AREAS:** Managed Care; Long Term Care; Health Care Risk Management; Health Care; Hospitals; Health Insurance.

**FREDERICK MARTIN, JR.,** born Washington, D.C., September 13, 1943; admitted to bar, 1968, Oklahoma; 1972, California. *Education:* Yale University (B.A., 1965); Oklahoma University (J.D., 1968). Oklahoma Law Review, 1968. Law Clerk to Judge Wm. B. Enright, U.S. District Court for the Southern District of California, 1972-1973. Assistant Editor, California C.E.B. Business Law Reporter, 1979-1982. Author: "How to Respond to an Auditors' Inquiry Letter," CEB California Business Law Practitioner, Vol. III, No. 3, 1988; "Commercial Leasing Traps," CEB Real Property Law Reporter Vol. 15, No. 7, 1992; "California Upholds Gestational Surrogacy Contract," Health Care Law Newsletter, Vol. 8, No. 11, 1993. *Member:* San Diego County (Member, Dicta Committee, 1981-1985; Real Property Leg-

*(This Listing Continued)*

islation Subcommittee, 1985-1986; Client Relations Committee, 1991) and Oklahoma Bar Associations. [U.S. Navy Reserve, Judge Advocate General Corps, 1968-1972]. (Resident at San Diego Office). **PRACTICE AREAS:** Real Estate.

**MARY K. NORVELL,** born St. Louis, Missouri, November 11, 1950; admitted to bar, 1985, California. *Education:* University of California at Los Angeles (B.A., cum laude, 1977); University of Southern California (J.D., 1984). *Member:* San Diego County Bar Association. (Resident at San Diego Office). **PRACTICE AREAS:** Health Care; Business Organization; Corporate Organization; Corporate Finance; Partnerships; Commercial Contracts; Asset Sales; Tax-Exempt Financing.

**JEFFREY R. BATES,** born Hamilton, Ohio, November 23, 1954; admitted to bar, 1983, District of Columbia; 1989, California. *Education:* The College of Wooster (B.A., 1976); Georgetown University Law Center (J.D., cum laude, 198 3). Editor, Georgetown Law Journal. *Member:* National Health Lawyers Association. **SPECIAL AGENCIES:** Provider Reimbursement Review Board. **PRACTICE AREAS:** Medicare and Medicaid; Health Care; Long Term Care.

**ADAM B. SCHIFF,** born Framingham, Massachusetts, June 22, 1960; admitted to bar, 1986, California, U.S. District Court, Central District of California and U.S. Court of Appeals, Ninth Circuit. *Education:* Stanford University (A.B., with distinction, 1982); Harvard University (J.D., cum laude, 1985). Author: "State Discriminatory Action," Harvard Journal on Legislation (1985). *Member:* State Bar of California (Member, Committee on Environment, 1990-1991); American Bar Association. **PRACTICE AREAS:** Litigation; Fraud and Abuse Compliance Plans.

---

**SHIRLEY J. PAINE,** born Salinas, California, December 16, 1950; admitted to bar, 1990, California, U.S. Court of Appeals, Ninth Circuit and U.S. District Court, Central District of California. *Education:* Stanford University (A.B., 1974); Yale University (P.A., 1977); University of California at Davis (M.H.S., 1979); University of Southern California (J.D., 1990). Staff, Journal of Law and the Environment, 1988-1989. Board of Editors, Computer Law Journal and Major Tax Planning, 1989-1990. Recipient, American Jurisprudence Award, Comparative Constitutional Law, USC Law Center, 1989. Certified Physician Assistant, 1977. Author: "California Peer Reviewers Are Shielded from Paying Physician's Attorneys' Fees," HealthSpan, Vol. 11, No. 10, November 1994; "Physician-Assisted Suicide: Pros and Cons of First Federal Case," Health Span, Vol. 11, No. 7, July/August 1994; "Patient Dumping by Specialized Care Facilities," Health Span, Vol. 9, No. 6, June 1992; "The Patient Self-Determination Act: It's In Effect," Health Systems Review, Vol. 25, No. 1, January/February 1992. *Member:* Los Angeles County (Member, Health Law Section, Bioethics Committee); and American (Member, Forum Committee on Health Law; Litigation Law Section) Bar Associations; American Society of Law, Medicine and Ethics; California Society for Healthcare Attorneys; American Civil Liberties Union; American Academy of Physicians Assistants; California Academy of Physician Assistants. **REPORTED CASES:** Mir v. Charter Suburban Hospital, 27 Cal. App. 4th 1471 (1994); Scripps Memorial Hospital v. Superior Court, 95 Daily Journal 11961, 1995. **PRACTICE AREAS:** Health Care; Bioethics; Medical Staff Credentialing; Peer Review; Health Care Facility Licensing and Regulation; Long Term Care.

**HOWARD W. COHEN,** born Brooklyn, New York, March 24, 1955; admitted to bar, 1985, California, U.S. District Court, Central District of California and U.S. Court of Appeals, Ninth Circuit; 1986, U.S. District Court, Northern and Southern Districts of California; 1993, U.S. District Court, Eastern District of California. *Education:* University of California, Los Angeles (B.A., 1979); University of Michigan (J.D., 1985). Director, Eco-Cities Council, 1992—. Judge pro tempore, Municipal Court of California, Los Angeles Judicial District, 1994—. *Member:* Los Angeles County Bar Association (Member, Fair Judicial Election Practices Committee, 1989—). **PRACTICE AREAS:** Commercial Litigation; Business Torts; Health Care Litigation; Insurance Coverage and Bad Faith Litigation.

**JONATHON E. COHN,** born Sacramento, California, December 5, 1960; admitted to bar, 1988, California and U.S. District Court, Central District of California. *Education:* Pomona College (B.A., cum laude, 1984); University of California at Los Angeles (J.D., 1988). Member, Moot Court Honors Program, 1987. *Member:* Los Angeles Bankruptcy Forum. **PRACTICE AREAS:** Commercial Litigation; Health Care; Bankruptcy; Workers Compensation.

**STEVEN J. SIMERLEIN,** born Milwaukee, Wisconsin, December 4, 1960; admitted to bar, 1991, California. *Education:* Tulane University

*(This Listing Continued)*

(B.A., cum laude, 1983); Loyola Law School, Los Angeles (J.D., 1991). Author: Note, "Summary Exclusion and the Procedural Due Process Rights of Permanent Resident Aliens," 13 Loy. L.A. Int'l & Comp. L.J. 179, (1990). *Member:* San Diego County and American Bar Associations; California Society for Healthcare Attorneys. (Resident at San Diego Office). **LANGUAGES:** Spanish. **PRACTICE AREAS:** Local Government Law; Elder Law; Environmental Law; Health Care; Health Care Fraud.

**AMY B. HAFEY,** born New York, N.Y., May 17, 1967; admitted to bar, 1993, California; 1996, U.S. Court of Appeals, District of Columbia. *Education:* Barnard College (B.A., 1989); University of Southern California (J.D., 1992). *Member:* National Health Lawyers Association. **PRACTICE AREAS:** Health Care; Hospitals; Medicare and Medicaid; Administrative Law.

**DIANE UNG,** born Los Angeles, California, August 3, 1963; admitted to bar, 1993, California. *Education:* Pomona College (B.A., 1985); University of California at Los Angeles (M.S.P.H., 1987); Loyola Law School, Los Angeles (J.D., 1993). Order of the Coif. *Member:* National Health Lawyers Association; Southern California Chinese Lawyers Association. **PRACTICE AREAS:** Hospitals; Health Care Legislation; Medicare and Medicaid.

**CHRISTOPHER E. LOVE,** born Mexico, Missouri, October 6, 1962; admitted to bar, 1992, California. *Education:* University of Missouri (B.J., 1985); University of Minnesota Law School (J.D., magna cum laude, 1992). Note and Comment Editor, University of Minnesota Law Review, 1991-1992. *Member:* Los Angeles County Bar Association (Member, Healthcare Law and Business and Corporate Law Sections); Minnesota State (Member, Health Law and Corporate Sections) and American Bar Associations. **PRACTICE AREAS:** Health Care; Corporate Law.

**TERRI WAGNER CAMMARANO,** born Glendora, California, November 17, 1963; admitted to bar, 1988, California, U.S. Tax Court and U.S. District Court, Central District of California. *Education:* University of California at Fullerton (B.A., with honors, 1985); Loyola Law School, Los Angeles (J.D., 1988). **SPECIAL AGENCIES:** Franchise Tax Board, State Board of Equalization, California Public Utilities Commission, Federal Energy Regulatory Commission. **PRACTICE AREAS:** Health Care; Business Law; Tax Planning; Tax Controversies; Tax Exempt Organizations; Commercial Law; Estate Planning; Adoptions; Utility Regulation; Business Organization; Partnerships; Charitable Giving; Asset Sales; Mergers; Corporate Finance; Tax Exempt Financing.

**LEILA NOURANI,** born Monthey, Switzerland, November 10, 1967; admitted to bar, 1990, England and Wales; 1992, California. *Education:* Joint English and French Law Degree from the University of London, Kings College and the Universite de Paris I, Sorbonne (1989); London School of Law: Prerequisite Course for English Bar (1990). *Member:* Los Angeles County Bar Association. **LANGUAGES:** French and Persian. **PRACTICE AREAS:** Civil and Commercial Litigation; Antitrust.

**KAREN R. WEINSTEIN,** born Los Angeles, California, August 11, 1961; admitted to bar, 1994, California, U.S. District Court, Central District of California and U.S. Court of Appeals, Ninth Circuit. *Education:* University of California at Berkeley (B.A., 1984); University of Southern California (M.P.A., 1989); University of California at Los Angeles (J.D., 1994). **PRACTICE AREAS:** Health Care; Corporate Law; Medical Staff Credentialing; Health Care Facility Regulation.

**LORNA D. HENNINGTON,** born Los Angeles, California, July 8, 1965; admitted to bar, 1994, California, U.S. District Court, Central District of California and U.S. Court of Appeals, Ninth Circuit. *Education:* University of California at Berkeley (B.A., 1988); University of California at Los Angeles (M.S.P.H., 1991); University of Southern California (J.D., 1994). *Member:* Los Angeles County and American Bar Associations; Black Women Lawyers. **PRACTICE AREAS:** Health Care; Hospitals; Medicare and Medicaid; Administrative Law.

**BRAULIO MONTESINO,** born Havana, Cuba, November 22, 1952; admitted to bar, 1994, California. *Education:* California State University at Los Angeles (B.A., 1980); Loyola Law School, Los Angeles (J.D., 1994). Editor, Health Care Law Sourcebook (Matthew Bender). Contributor, Health Systems Review (Federation of American Health Systems). Order of the Coif. Editor in Chief, Loyola Entertainment Law Journal, 1993-1994. American Jurisprudence Awards for Excellence. **PRACTICE AREAS:** Real Property Law; Corporate Law; Health Care Regulation; Integrated Health Care Delivery Systems.

**SHANA T. TOREM,** born Harbor City, California, June 21, 1969; admitted to bar, 1994, California, U.S. District Court, Central, Southern, Northern Eastern and Western Districts of California and U.S. Court of

*(This Listing Continued)*

**FOLEY LARDNER WEISSBURG & ARONSON, Los Angeles—Continued**

Appeals, Ninth Circuit. *Education:* University of California at Los Angeles (B.A., magna cum laude, Phi Beta Kappa, 1991); University of California at Los Angeles (J.D., 1994). **LANGUAGES:** Hebrew. **REPORTED CASES:** Summit Technology, Inc. v. High-Line Medical Instruments Company, Inc. et al., 922 F.Supp. 299 (C.D. Cal. 1996). **PRACTICE AREAS:** Litigation.

**DAVID A. RENAS,** born San Diego, California, November 25, 1964; admitted to bar, 1991, California. *Education:* Stanford University (B.A., 1985); University of California at Davis (J.D., 1991). Certified Public Accountant, California, 1988. *Member:* San Diego County Bar Association; Healthcare Financial Management Association. (Resident at San Diego Office). **PRACTICE AREAS:** Business Law; Corporate Law.

**IOANA PETROU,** born Bologna, Italy, July 28, 1968; admitted to bar, 1994, California, U.S. District Court, Northern District of California and U.S. Court of Appeals, Ninth Circuit. *Education:* University of California at Berkeley (B.A., with highest honors, 1988); Boalt Hall School of Law, University of California at Berkeley (J.D., 1993). Externship with the Hon. Sheila Prell Sonenshine, California Court of Appeals, Fourth Circuit. *Member:* American Bar Association; AIDS Legal Referral Panel. (Resident at San Francisco Office). **LANGUAGES:** Italian. **SPECIAL AGENCIES:** Equal Employment Opportunity Commission; Department of Fair Employment and Housing. **PRACTICE AREAS:** Labor and Employment; Wrongful Termination; Employment Discrimination; Management-Labor Relations; Managed Care; Long Term Care; Health Insurance.

**T. JOSHUA RITZ,** born Haifa, Israel, April 5, 1967; admitted to bar, 1992, New York; 1993, U.S. District Court, Southern District of New York; 1994, California and U.S. District Court, Central and Southern Districts of California. *Education:* University of Southern California (B.A., summa cum laude, 1988) Phi Beta Kappa; Boalt Hall School of Law, University of California at Berkeley (J.D., 1991). *Member:* Los Angeles County Bar Association; New York State Bar Association.

**SHARON M. KOPMAN,** born Encino, California, June 25, 1968; admitted to bar, 1993, California, U.S. District Court, Central District of California and U.S. Court of Appeals, Ninth Circuit. *Education:* University of Pennsylvania (B.A., 1990); Loyola Law School, Los Angeles (J.D., 1992). *Member:* Los Angeles County Bar Association (Member, Barristers Sports Project Committee, 1994—). **LANGUAGES:** Spanish. **PRACTICE AREAS:** Labor and Employment; Litigation; Personal Injury.

**KIMBERLY F. APPLEQUIST,** born Pasadena, California, March 26, 1966; admitted to bar, 1995, California, U.S. District Court, Central District of California and U.S. Court of Appeals, Ninth Circuit. *Education:* University of Utah (B.A., magna cum laude, 1988); University of Southern California (J.D., 1995). Managing Editor, Southern California Interdisciplinary Law Journal, 1994-1995. *Member:* State Bar of California. **PRACTICE AREAS:** Health Care; Hospitals; Corporate Law.

**LYNN R. GOODFELLOW,** born Dowagiac, Michigan, June 19, 1958; admitted to bar, 1994, California. *Education:* Western Michigan University (B.B.A., 1984); California Western School of Law (J.D., 1994); University of San Diego School of Law (LL.M., 1995). *Member:* State Bar of California; American Bar Association. (Resident, San Diego Office). **PRACTICE AREAS:** Labor and Employment; Benefits.

**JAMES D. NGUYEN,** born Saigon, Vietnam, September 20, 1972; admitted to bar, 1995, California, U.S. Court of Appeals, Ninth Circuit and U.S. District Court, Central District of California; 1996, U.S. District Court, Northern, Southern and Eastern Districts of California. *Education:* University of California at Los Angeles (B.A., in Communication Studies, magna cum laude, 1992); University of Southern California (J.D., 1995). Phi Alpha Delta, Chair and Champion, Moot Court Honors Program, USC, National Moot Court Team; Southern California Review of Law and Women's Studies, 1993-1994. Recipient: American Jurisprudence Award in Criminal Law, 1995 Mason C. Brown Award for Excellence in Trial Advocacy. Co-Author: "Health Care Executives Risk Criminal Liability for 'See-No-Evil' Mentality," Inside Health Law, Vol. 1, No. 6, June 1996. *Member:* American Bar Association. **LANGUAGES:** French. **PRACTICE AREAS:** Litigation.

**ANDREW M. AGTAGMA,** born Honolulu, Hawaii, October 5, 1970; admitted to bar, 1995, California; 1996, U.S. District Court, Northern, Southern, Central and Eastern Districts of California. *Education:* University of California at Los Angeles (B.A., magna cum laude, 1992); Phi Beta Kappa; Boalt Hall School of Law, University of California at Berkeley

*(This Listing Continued)*

(J.D., 1995). Articles Editor, California Law Review, 1994-1995. **PRACTICE AREAS:** Litigation.

**JOHN H. DOUGLAS,** born Providence, Rhode Island, December 4, 1961; admitted to bar, 1995, California. *Education:* Harvard University (B.A., 1983); University of California at Berkeley (J.D., 1995). Moot Court Board. Recipient: American Jurisprudence Award in Evidence, Immigration Law; Prosser Award in Income Tax I. Comment: "HIV Disease and Disparate Impact Under the Americans With Disabilities Act: A Federal Prohibition of Discrimination on the Basis of Sexual Orientation?" 16 Berkeley Journal of Employment and Labor Law 288, 1995. First Year Moot Court Instructor, 1994. First Year Moot Court Director, 1994-1995. (Resident, San Francisco Office). **LANGUAGES:** Japanese. **PRACTICE AREAS:** Labor and Employment; Health Care; Disabilities Act.

**MARGARET M. MCCAHILL,** born Monterey, California, April 12, 1972; admitted to bar, 1995, California and U.S. District Court, Southern District of California. *Education:* University of New Mexico (B.A., magna cum laude, 1992) Phi Beta Kappa; University of San Diego (J.D., 1995). University of San Diego School of Law, Member: Moot Court Board, 1994-1995; USD National Moot Court Team, 1994-1995. Recipient: American Jurisprudence Award, Insurance Law. *Member:* San Diego County and American Bar Associations. (Resident, San Diego Office). **LANGUAGES:** Spanish. **PRACTICE AREAS:** Health Care; Medical Staff Issues; Hospitals.

**DAVID T. MORRIS,** born Tallahassee, Florida, December 16, 1966; admitted to bar, 1995, California. *Education:* University of California at Berkeley (B.A., 1990); Boston University School of Law (J.D., concentration in Health Law, 1995). Editor-in-Chief, American Journal of Law and Medicine, 1995. Managing Editor, American Journal of Law and Medicine, 1994. Author: "Cost Containment and Reproductive Authority: Prenatal Genetic Screening and The American Health Surety Act of 1993," 20 American Journal of Law and Medicine 295, 1994. *Member:* American Bar Association (Member, Health Law Forum, 1994—). (Resident, San Francisco Office). **PRACTICE AREAS:** Health Care Mergers and Acquisition; Integrated Health Care Delivery Systems; Health Care Corporate Law; Health Care Fraud; Medical Ethics.

**NATHAN D. SCHMIDT,** born Santa Monica, California, September 22, 1961; admitted to bar, 1994; 1995, U.S. District Court, Eastern District of California, U.S. Court of Appeals, Ninth Circuit. *Education:* University of California at Davis (B.A., 1983); McGeorge School of Law, University of the Pacific (J.D., with great distinction, 1994). Phi Alpha Delta. Order of the Coif. Traynor Honor Society. American Jurisprudence Awards in Civil Procedure, Criminal Law, Legal Research and Writing, Business Associations and Decedent's Estates and Trusts. Member, McGeorge Moot Court Executive Board, 1993-1994. Author: "New OSHA Guidelines Target Workplace Violence in Healthcare Setting," Inside Health Law, Vol. 1, No. 8, August 1996. Fellow, College of Public Interest Law, Pacific Legal Foundation, 1994-1995. *Member:* Sacramento County and American Bar Associations. (Resident, Sacramento Office). **PRACTICE AREAS:** Labor and Employment; Administrative Law; Civil Litigation; Health Care.

**PAULA C. OHLIGER,** born Los Angeles, California, March 2, 1953; admitted to bar, 1992, California. *Education:* University of Puget Sound (B.S., cum laude, 1975); Golden Gate University (J.D., with honors, 1992). *Member:* Queen's Bench; California Women Lawyers Association; Bar Association of San Francisco. (Resident, San Francisco Office). **PRACTICE AREAS:** Health Care Corporate Law; Health Care Regulatory; Managed Care; Integrated Delivery Systems; Medicare Fraud and Abuse; Stark, Speier.

**MICHAEL J. SIERADZKI,** born Oakland, California, July 24, 1964; admitted to bar, 1992, New York; 1995, California. *Education:* Harvard College (A.B., 1986); New York University School of Law (J.D., 1991). Melvin C. Steen Legal Aid Fellowship, 1991-1993. *Member:* Bay Area Lawyers for Individual Freedom; AIDS Legal Referral Panel. (Resident, San Francisco, Office). **LANGUAGES:** Hebrew, Spanish. **PRACTICE AREAS:** Litigation; Labor and Employment.

**LISA GOODWIN MICHAEL,** born Santa Monica, California; admitted to bar, 1991, California. *Education:* University of Southern California (B.A., cum laude, in Honors History and International Relations (1985); Cambridge University, Cambridge, England, 1984; University of Virginia School of Law (J.D., 1991). Phi Beta Kappa; Alpha Lambda Delta. Mortar Board; Blue Key; Skull and Dagger, Order of Laurel; William Minor Lile Moot Court Board. **PRACTICE AREAS:** Civil Litigation; Labor and Employment Law.

*(This Listing Continued)*

**RENÉ BOWSER,** born Edenton, North Carolina, June 16, 1963; admitted to bar, 1994, California. *Education:* University of Maryland, College Park (B.A., high honors, 1985); Northwestern University (M.A., 1987); Stanford Law School (J.D., 1994). *Member:* State Bar of California. (Resident, San Francisco Office). *PRACTICE AREAS:* Labor and Employment; Health Care.

**JEFFREY M. POMERANCE,** born Milwaukee, Wisconsin, March 23, 1961; admitted to bar, 1987, Illinois and U.S. District Court, Northern District of Illinois; 1992, California. *Education:* University of Wisconsin-Madison (B.B.A., Accounting with highest distinction, 1983); University of Michigan Law School (J.D., 1987). Certified Public Accountant, Illinois, 1988. Beta Gamma Sigma National Business Honor Society (President, 1983). Beta Alpha Psi. Contributing Editor, University of Michigan Law Journal of Law Reform (1986-1987). Author: "1987 Amendments to the Delaware Corporation Code," and "Proposed Amendments to the Revised Uniform Limited Partnership Act of Illinois," 33 Corporation and Securities Law Illinois State Bar Association), 1988. *PRACTICE AREAS:* Business Law; Health Care Finance; Mergers and Acquisitions; Corporate Law.

**CHARLES R. ZUBRZYCKI,** born Camden, New Jersey, February 21, 1950; admitted to bar, 1994, California. *Education:* Univ. of Notre Dame (B.A., magna cum laude, 1972); University of California at Berkeley (M.A., 1979); University of Chicago (M.B.A., 1981); Georgetown Law Center (J.D., cum laude, 1994). *Member:* American Inns of Court. *PRACTICE AREAS:* Intellectual Property; Environmental.

**LISA A. PALOMBO,** born Detroit, Michigan, September 15, 1962; admitted to bar, 1990, Illinois; 1993, California. *Education:* Wayne State University (B.A., with honors, 1985); Boston University School of Law (J.D., 1988). Article Editor, Boston University School of Law, International Law Journal, 1987-1988. *LANGUAGES:* Italian. *PRACTICE AREAS:* Business and Commercial Litigation.

**MARK TAE LEE,** born Bangkok, Thailand, July 20, 1970; (admission pending). *Education:* Pomona College (B.A., 1992); University of Minnesota Law School (J.D., cum laude, 1996). *LANGUAGES:* Korean. *PRACTICE AREAS:* Health Care Payments; Hospitals.

**DOAA A. FATHALLAH,** born Cairo, Egypt, December 3, 1970; (admission pending). *Education:* University of Southern California (B.S., 1992; J.D., 1996). Sample Fellow, Norman Topping Scholar, Phi Alpha Delta. *LANGUAGES:* Spanish, Arabic. *PRACTICE AREAS:* Health Care.

**SUSANNA ELIZABETH HATHAWAY,** born Los Angeles, California, June 9, 1964; (admission pending). *Education:* Boston University (B.S., Business, 1986); Johns Hopkins University (B.S., Nursing, 1990); University of Southern California (J.D., 1996). California Licensed Registered Nurse. *PRACTICE AREAS:* Health Care.

**DARON L. TOOCH,** born Johannesburg, South Africa, April 27, 1963; admitted to bar, 1988, California. *Education:* University of California at Los Angeles (B.A., magna cum laude, 1985) Phi Beta Kappa; Harvard University (J.D., 1988). Senior Editor, Journal on Legislation, 1986-1988. Co-Author: "The Defense of Environmental Cases," ABA National Institute on White Collar Crimes, March 1991; "Rough Remedial Justice: Implications of *Halper* and *Austin* in Civil Forfeiture Actions," National Institute on Criminal Tax Fraud and Money Laundering, December 1993.

**CYNTHIA C. BRADFORD,** born Detroit, Michigan, January 15, 1969; (admission pending). *Education:* University of Florida (B.S., with honors, 1991); University of Texas at Austin (M.B.A., 1992); Stanford Law School (J.D., 1996). *Member:* American Bar Association (Health Law and Antitrust Law Sections); National Health Lawyers Association; American College of Legal Medicine. (Resident at San Francisco Office). *PRACTICE AREAS:* Health Care.

**JULIE CHRISTINE ASHBY,** born Anaheim, California, September 29, 1969; admitted to bar, 1995, Texas; 1996, California. *Education:* University of California, Los Angeles (B.A., magna cum laude, 1991); Tulane University School of Law (J.D., cum laude, 1995). Phi Beta Kappa. (Resident at San Diego Office). *PRACTICE AREAS:* Administrative Law; Public Agency.

**MONICA GONZALEZ BRISBANE,** born Pasadena, California, August 14, 1966; admitted to bar, 1991, California. *Education:* University of California at San Diego (B.A., 1988); University of Iowa College of Law (J.D., 1991). President, Iowa Student Bar Association, 1990-1991. Commissioner, Planning Commission of the City of Pasadena, 1993-1994. *Member:* State Bar of California; American Bar Association (Member, Litigation Section). (Resident at Sacramento Office). *LANGUAGES:* Spanish. *PRACTICE AREAS:* Litigation.

*(This Listing Continued)*

**ROBERT J. WENBOURNE,** born San Diego, California, November 23, 1954; admitted to bar, 1987, California. *Education:* University of La Verne (B.A., 1975); Hastings College of the Law, University of California (J.D., 1987). Resident at Sacramento Office). *PRACTICE AREAS:* Labor and Employment.

## *FOLGER LEVIN & KAHN LLP*

*28TH FLOOR, 1900 AVENUE OF THE STARS*
**LOS ANGELES, CALIFORNIA 90067**
*Telephone: 310-556-3700*
*FAX: 310-556-3770*

*San Francisco, California Office:* Embarcadero Center West, 23rd Floor, 275 Battery Street. Telephone: 415-986-2800. FAX: 415-986-2827.

*General Practice.*

(For Personnel and Biographical data, see Professional Biographies, San Francisco, California).

## *FONDA, GARRARD, HILBERMAN & DAVIS*

*A PROFESSIONAL CORPORATION*
*Established in 1979*

*1888 CENTURY PARK EAST, 21ST FLOOR*
**LOS ANGELES, CALIFORNIA 90067**
*Telephone: 310-553-1121*
*FAX: 310-553-4232*

*General Civil, Trial and Appellate Practice. Insurance Defense, Property and Casualty Insurance, Medical Malpractice Defense, Personal Injury and Products Liability Law. Insurance Coverage (Primary, Excess and Reinsurance) and Bad Faith, Insurance Fraud.*

*FIRM PROFILE: Founded in 1979, Fonda, Garrard, Hilberman & Davis specializes in civil litigation, primarily in the defense of personal injury and casualty loss claims. Building upon a foundation of insurance defense litigation, including issues of coverage, bad faith, first and third party casualty losses, Fonda, Garrard, Hilberman & Davis has grown into areas which most recently have stressed the defense of medical malpractice, personal injury, premises liability, construction, and suspected fraudulent casualty claims.*

**DONALD A. GARRARD,** born Bakersfield, California, June 6, 1944; admitted to bar, 1970, California; 1979, U.S. Supreme Court. *Education:* University of California at Los Angeles (A.B., 1966); Loyola University of Los Angeles (J.D., 1969). Los Angeles Superior Court Referee Panelist, 1988—. *Member:* Santa Monica, Los Angeles County and American Bar Associations; The State Bar of California; Association of Southern California Defense Counsel; Defense Research Institute; Southern California Fraud Investigator's Association.

**PETER M. FONDA,** born New York, N.Y., October 6, 1947; admitted to bar, 1973, California; 1979, U.S. Supreme Court; 1989, U.S. Court of Appeals, Ninth Circuit. *Education:* Michigan State University (B.A., 1969); University of California at Los Angeles (J.D., 1973). Phi Beta Kappa; Phi Kappa Phi. *Member:* Santa Monica, Los Angeles County and American Bar Associations; State Bar of California; Association of Southern California Defense Counsel; Defense Research Institute.

**JOE W. HILBERMAN,** born Los Angeles, California, November 16, 1948; admitted to bar, 1973, California; 1974, U.S. District Court, Central District of California; 1989, U.S., Supreme Court; 1993, Colorado. *Education:* University of California at Los Angeles (A.B., 1970; J.D., 1973). Instructor, U.C.L.A. Extension-Attorney Assistant Training Program, 1981-1984. *Member:* Century City, Santa Monica, Los Angeles County (Member, Committees on: Judiciary, 1979-1982; Attorney-Client Relations, 1979-1982; Medical-Legal Hotline, 1979-1981) and American Bar Associations; State Bar of California; Association of Southern California Defense Counsel; American Board of Trial Advocates.

**STEVEN D. DAVIS,** born Hartford, Connecticut, March 14, 1950; admitted to bar, 1979, California. *Education:* University of the South, Sewanee, Tennessee; University of California at Los Angeles (B.A., 1974); Southwestern University (J.D., 1979). Member, California District Attorney's Association, 1980-1983. *Member:* Los Angeles County Bar Association; State Bar of California; Association of Southern California Defense Counsel.

**PATRICK W. MAYER,** born Georgetown, Washington, D.C., February 20, 1959; admitted to bar, 1984, California; 1985, U.S. Federal Court,

*(This Listing Continued)*

FONDA, GARRARD, HILBERMAN & DAVIS, A
PROFESSIONAL CORPORATION, Los Angeles—Continued

Ninth Circuit. *Education:* University of Maryland (B.A., 1981); Pepperdine University (J.D., 1984). *Member:* Beverly Hills and Los Angeles County Bar Associations; State Bar of California. **LANGUAGES:** Spanish. **PRACTICE AREAS:** Medical General Casualty Defense Law.

**GLORIA KURMAN APT,** born Los Angeles, California, May 29, 1954; admitted to bar, 1980, California and U.S. District Court, Central District of California. *Education:* University of California at Los Angeles (B.A., 1975); Whittier College (J.D., 1980). *Member:* Los Angeles County and American Bar Associations; State Bar of California. **LANGUAGES:** Spanish and French. **PRACTICE AREAS:** Medical Malpractice Defense Law.

**DIANE M. DALY,** born Miami, Florida, March 23, 1961; admitted to bar, 1990, California. *Education:* California State University at Northridge (B.A., cum laude, 1986); Loyola Law School (J.D., 1990). Phi Delta Phi; Golden Key National Honor Society. *Member:* State Bar of California; American Bar Association.

**TRACY T. DAVIS,** born Detroit, Michigan, May 10, 1963; admitted to bar, 1989, California. *Education:* Universite Paul Valery, Montpellier, France; University of California at Los Angeles (B.A., 1985); Southwestern University School of Law (J.D., 1988). Recipient, American Jurisprudence Award. *Member:* Los Angeles County and American Bar Associations; State Bar of California; California Women Lawyers; Southern California Fraud Investigators Association. **LANGUAGES:** French and Spanish.

**LAURIE DEYOUNG,** born Philadelphia, Pennsylvania, April 15, 1966; admitted to bar, 1991, California and U.S. District Court, Central District of California. *Education:* New York University (B.A., 1988); Pepperdine University (J.D., cum laude, 1991). Member, Order of the Barristers. Member, Moot Court Honor Board, 1990-1991. *Member:* Los Angeles County and American Bar Associations; State Bar of California; Association of Southern California Defense Counsel.

**THOMAS E. DONAHUE,** born Omaha, Nebraska, January 29, 1961; admitted to bar, 1991, California. *Education:* University of Nebraska, Omaha (B.A., 1985); Southwestern University School of Law (J.D., 1991). Pi Gamma Mu. Member, National Social Science Honor Society, 1984-1985. *Member:* State Bar of California; American Bar Association.

**FREDERICK JAMES,** born Atlanta, Georgia, May 25, 1955; admitted to bar, 1988, California. *Education:* California State University, Dominguez Hills (B.A., magna cum laude, 1983); University of Southern California (J.D., 1986).

**DAVID M. SAMUELS,** born Los Angeles, California, August 15, 1963; admitted to bar, 1991, California. *Education:* Menlo College (A.A., 1984); University of California, Davis (B.A., 1987); Pepperdine University (J.D., 1991). *Member:* Los Angeles County and American Bar Associations; State Bar of California.

REPRESENTATIVE CLIENTS: State Farm Insurance Companies; Allstate Insurance Company; Northbrook Property and Casualty Insurance Company; National Indemnity Company; National Fire and Marine Insurance Company; Farmers Insurance Group; Truck Insurance Exchange; Utica Mutual Insurance Company; Regents of the University of California; Professional Risk Management of California, Inc.; Fireman's Fund Insurance Cos.; MMI Companies, Inc.; Multi Systems Agency, Ltd.; Twentieth Century Insurance Co.; Huntington Memorial Hospital; Columbia Insurance Co.; Home & Auto Insurance Co.
REFERENCE: Sanwa Bank of California (Los Angeles Headquarters Corporate Office).

## FORD & HARRISON
### 333 SOUTH GRAND AVENUE
### SUITE 3680
### LOS ANGELES, CALIFORNIA 90071
Telephone: 213-680-3410
FAX: 213-680-4161

*Atlanta, Georgia Office:* 600 Peachtree at the Circle Building, 1275 Peachtree Street, N.E., 30309. Telephone: 404-888-3800. Fax: 404-888-3863.
*Miami, Florida Office:* Alley and Alley/Ford & Harrison. 516 Ingraham Building, 25 S.E. 2nd Avenue, 33131. Telephone: 305-379-3811. Fax: 305-358-5933.
*Tampa, Florida Office:* Alley and Alley/Ford & Harrison. 205 Brush Street, P.O. Box 1427, 33601. Telephone: 813-229-6481. Fax: 813-223-7029.
*Washington, D.C. Office:* 1920 N Street, N.W., Suite 200, 20036. Telephone: 202-463-6633. Fax: 202-466-5705.

*(This Listing Continued)*

Labor Relations, Equal Employment, Wage and Hour, Airline Labor Law, OSHA, Environmental Law, Commercial Litigation, Employee Benefits and Immigration Law.

FIRM PROFILE: Ford & Harrison represents employers in all areas of labor and employment law including National Labor Relations Act, Railway Labor Act, Title VII (Civil Rights Act of 1964, amended 1991), Americans with Disabilities Act (ADA), Age Discrimination in Employment Act (ADEA), Employee Retirement Income Security Act of 1974 (ERISA), Family Medical Leave Act (FMLA), Occupational Safety and Health Act of 1970 (OSHA) and Fair Labor Standards Act (FLSA). We also represent our clients in grievance and arbitration cases, mediation of contract disputes, union election cases, unfair labor practice proceedings, employment litigation, unfair competition and trade-secret disputes, pension and benefit plan design, environmental law matters and business immigration.

The labor and employment lawyers who founded Ford & Harrison in 1978 did so to ensure that their clients had the best possible legal assistance and representation. On January 1, 1995, we merged with the Atlanta labor and employment firm of Clark, Paul, Hoover & Mallard. In April, 1996, we merged with Alley and Alley, Chartered (Tampa and Miami, Florida) and Joseph Z. Fleming, P.A. (Miami, Florida). These mergers brought together a group of highly experienced labor and employment lawyers whose practices and philosophies strengthened and complemented one another. In Tampa and Miami, the firm is known as Alley and Alley/Ford & Harrison. The combination of these firms and individuals enhances the firm's ability to provide quality legal services nationwide in all areas of labor and employment law, without diminishing its commitment to the individual needs of each client.

### MEMBERS OF FIRM

**MICHAEL L. LOWRY,** born Charleston, South Carolina, July 21, 1943; admitted to bar, 1968, Virginia; 1970, Georgia; 1988, California. *Education:* Duke University (A.B. 1965); Washington & Lee University (J.D., 1968). Phi Delta Phi. Editor, Washington & Lee Law Review, 1967-1968. Author: "Commodities Under The Robinson-Patman Act," 24 Washington & Lee Law Review 309, 1967. *Member:* Atlanta and American Bar Associations; Virginia State Bar; State Bar of Georgia; State Bar of California.

**GLEN H. MERTENS,** born Fresno, California, April 13, 1956; admitted to bar, 1981, California; 1982, U.S. District Court, Northern and Central Districts of California; 1986, U.S. Court of Appeals, Ninth Circuit; 1987, U.S. District Court, Eastern District of California. *Education:* Claremont Men's College (A.B., magna cum laude, 1978); Boalt Hall School of Law, University of California (J.D., 1981). Executive Editor, California Law Review, 1980-1981. *Member:* Los Angeles County Bar Association; State Bar of California.

### ASSOCIATES

**MARAL DONOYAN,** born Beirut, Lebanon, November 26, 1965; admitted to bar, 1990, California. *Education:* University of California at Berkeley (B.A., magna cum laude, 1986); University of California at Los Angeles (J.D., 1990). Member: Phi Beta Kappa; Golden Key Honor Society. Member, 1988-1989, and Associate Editor, 1989-1990, UCLA Law Review. *Member:* Los Angeles County and American Bar Associations; State Bar of California; Armenian Bar Association.

**KARI HAUGEN,** born Astoria, Oregon, June 7, 1959; admitted to bar, 1988, California. *Education:* Whitman College (B.A., 1981); Columbia University (J.D., 1988). Harlan Fiske Stone Scholar. *Member:* Los Angeles County and American Bar Associations; State Bar of California.

REPRESENTATIVE CLIENTS: Argyle Communications, Inc.; Athlete's Foot Group, Inc.; BTR, Inc.; Carrier Corporation; Coats North America; Coca-Cola Enterprises; Columbia/HCA Healthcare Corp.; Continental Airlines, Inc.; Corrections Corporation of America; Delta Air Lines, Inc.; DHL Airways, Inc.; Federal Express Corp.; General Shale Products Corp.; Hendrick Automotive Group; Kay-Bee Toy Stores; Kellogg Company; Landmark Communications, Inc.; LIN Television Corp.; Marshalls, Inc.; The Mead Corporation; Nestle USA, Inc.; Norrell Services, Inc.; Northern Telecom, Inc.; OKI telecom; Quorum Health Group, Inc.; Redman Industries, Inc.; Regional Airline Assn.; Solvay Automotive, Inc.; Southwest Airlines Co.; The Standard Register Co.; The Weather Channel; WorldCorp; WorldSpan; Wyle Laboratories, Inc.

(For Complete Biographical Data on all Personnel, see Professional Biographies at Atlanta, Georgia)

## THE FORD LAW FIRM
12400 WILSHIRE BOULEVARD, SUITE 540
**LOS ANGELES, CALIFORNIA 90025**
Telephone: 310-826-2648
Facsimile: 310-826-2658

*Business Litigation, Trials and Appeals, Insurance Bad Faith Litigation.*

FIRM PROFILE: *The Ford Law Firm is a small but aggressive litigation firm that engages in complex business litigation on behalf of both plaintiffs and defendants, with special emphasis in insurance coverage and bad faith litigation. The named principal is WILLIAM H. FORD, III.*

**WILLIAM H. FORD, III,** born Oklahoma City, Oklahoma, November 9, 1944; admitted to bar, 1971, California and U.S. District Court, Northern, Central, Southern and Eastern Districts of California and U.S. Court of Appeals, Ninth Circuit. *Education:* University of Santa Clara (B.A., 1966); Loyola University of Los Angeles (J.D., 1971). Phi Delta Phi. Member, St. Thomas More Law Honor Society. *Member:* Los Angeles County and American (Business Litigation Section) Bar Associations; State Bar of California. [U.S. Army, Capt., 101st. Airborne, 1967-1968]. **PRACTICE AREAS:** Insurance Coverage; Civil Litigation; Insurance Bad Faith.

### ASSOCIATES

**CLAUDIA J. SERVISS,** born New York, N.Y., September 14, 1947; admitted to bar, 1992, California and U.S. District Court, Central District of California. *Education:* College of New Rochelle (B.A., English Literature, 1969); Western State University College of Law (J.D., summa cum laude, 1992). Editor, Western State University Law Review. Recipient, Ten American Jurisprudence Awards including Best Brief in the Warren J. Ferguson Moot Court Competition. Author: "Lehr v. Robertson's 'Grasp the Opportunity': For California's Natural Fathers, Custody May Be Beyond Their Grasp," 18 W. St. U.L. Rev. 771. *Member:* Beverly Hills and Los Angeles County Bar Associations; State Bar of California (Member, Anti-Trust Section); Women Lawyers Association of Los Angeles.

**GEORGE H. KIM,** born Seoul, South Korea, November 14, 1966; admitted to bar, 1992, California, U.S. District Court, Central District of California and U.S. Court of Appeals, Ninth Circuit. *Education:* University of California at Berkeley (B.A., 1988); University of Southern California Law Center (J.D., 1992). Member, Hale Moot Court Honors Program. *Member:* Los Angeles County Bar Association; State Bar of California.

**MICHAEL D. COLLINS,** born Portsmouth, Virginia, December 24, 1955; admitted to bar, 1993, California, U.S. District Court, Northern, Southern, Eastern and Central Districts of California and U.S. Court of Appeals, Ninth Circuit. *Education:* California State University (B.A., English, with honors, 1989); Loyola Marymount Law School (J.D., 1993). Recipient, American Jurisprudence Awards in Constitutional Law and Ethics, Counseling and Negotiation and Dean Scholar. Research Assistant to Professor on Sylvester, Article Entitled "Impracticability, Mutual Mistake and Related Contractual Basis for Equitable Adjusting the External Debt of Sub-Saharan Africa," published in the Northwestern Journal of International Law and Business (1992). *Member:* Los Angeles County Bar Association; State Bar of California.

**PAUL C. COOK,** born Northridge, California, January 2, 1966; admitted to bar, 1994, California. *Education:* California State University at Northridge (B.A. cum laude, 1991); California Western School of Law (J.D. cum laude, 1994). Phi Delta Phi. Recipient, American Jurisprudence Award in Secured Transactions. Staff Editor, California Western Law Review. Judicial Extern for Justice William Todd, the Court of Appeals, State of California, Fourth District. *Member:* State Bar of California.

## FORD, WALKER, HAGGERTY & BEHAR
**LOS ANGELES, CALIFORNIA**
(See Long Beach)

*Alternative dispute resolution, Appellate practice, Automobile negligence, Bad faith, Casualty defense, Commercial litigation, Construction defect litigation, Dental Malpractice, Declaratory relief, Employment discrimination, Environmental litigation, False arrest, Fire losses, Fraudulent and suspect claims, Homeowners liability, Insurance coverage, Legal malpractice, Malicious prosecution, Mass catastrophe, Municipality defense, Pollution and toxic torts, Premises liability, Product liability, Security related litigation, Sexual harassment claims, Wrongful termination.*

## FORWARD & DIX
*Established in 1992*
2049 CENTURY PARK EAST, SUITE 880
**LOS ANGELES, CALIFORNIA 90067**
Telephone: 310-785-9770
Fax: 310-785-9775

*Bologna, Italy Office:* Studio Legale de Capoa-Guiducci & Associati. Via Albertazzi, 22, 40137. Telephone: (39-51) 346 062/348835. Telecopier: (39-51) 344 125.

*International and United States Business Law, Real Estate and Land Use Law, Entertainment Law.*

**ROBERT H. FORWARD, JR.,** born Orange, California, February 3, 1945; admitted to bar, 1970, California. *Education:* Stanford University (B.A., 1966); Harvard University (J.D., 1969). *Member:* Los Angeles County (Member, Real Property Section) and American (member, International Law Section) Bar Associations; State Bar of California (Member: Real Property Section; Business Section). **LANGUAGES:** French, Italian and Spanish. **PRACTICE AREAS:** Real Estate; Land Use; International Business; Entertainment. *Email:* rforwardjr@aol.com

**SIMON DIX,** born London, England, October 3, 1950; admitted to bar, 1978, England; 1986, California. *Education:* Trinity College, Cambridge (B.A., 1972; M.A., 1975); University of Southern California (M.A., 1983). *Member:* State Bar of California (Member, International Law Section). **LANGUAGES:** Italian and French. **PRACTICE AREAS:** International Business; Business; Entertainment. *Email:* s.dix@globe.it

## FOSS & ROBERTS
**LOS ANGELES, CALIFORNIA**
(See Pasadena)

*Financial Institutions, Creditor Rights, Bankruptcy, Real Estate, Workouts, Insolvency, Commercial Law.*

## FOX & FRUMKIN
11377 WEST OLYMPIC BOULEVARD, SUITE 1000
**LOS ANGELES, CALIFORNIA 90064**
Telephone: 310-235-2414
Fax: 310-235-2479

*General Civil Practice in State and Federal Courts. Trials and Appeals. Business, Construction and Real Estate Litigation.*

### MEMBERS OF FIRM

**RONDA FOX,** born Shreveport, Louisiana, October 28, 1959; admitted to bar, 1987, California. *Education:* University of California at San Diego (B.A., 1980); University of California at Berkeley; University of California at San Diego (Ph.D., 1984); University of California at Davis (J.D., 1987). Associate, Pettit & Martin, 1987-1989. *Member:* State Bar of California; California Appellate Project. **PRACTICE AREAS:** Business; Real Estate Litigation.

**ARTHUR S. FRUMKIN,** born Los Angeles, California, May 21, 1958; admitted to bar, 1985, California. *Education:* University of California at Berkeley (B.A., 1980); Hastings College of the Law, University of California (J.D., 1984). Mediator: Real Estate, Construction and Commercial Litigation. Settlement Officer, Los Angeles County Superior Court. Associate, Lillick & McHose/Pillsbury, Madison & Sutro, 1987-1993. *Member:* State Bar of California; California Appellate Project. **PRACTICE AREAS:** Business; Construction; Real Estate Litigation.

## FOX & SPILLANE, P.C.
10866 WILSHIRE BOULEVARD, SUITE 900
**LOS ANGELES, CALIFORNIA 90024**
Telephone: 310-441-5202
Fax: 310-441-5207

*General Civil Litigation including Entertainment, Intellectual Property, Real Estate, Sports, Partnership and Product Liability Litigation.*

(This Listing Continued)

*FOX & SPILLANE, P.C., Los Angeles—Continued*

**GERARD P. FOX,** born New York, N.Y., October 16, 1960; admitted to bar, 1985, Maryland; 1986, District of Columbia; 1990, California. *Education:* University of Richmond (B.S., 1982); Georgetown University (J.D., magna cum laude, 1985). *Member:* Los Angeles County and American Bar Associations; The Association of Trial Lawyers of America. **PRACTICE AREAS:** Litigation; Intellectual Property; Infringement.

**JAY M. SPILLANE,** born Escondido, California, June 25, 1960; admitted to bar, 1986, California and U.S. District Court, Central District of California; 1987, U.S. District Court, Northern District of California. *Education:* University of California at Los Angeles (B.A., cum laude, 1983); Hastings College of the Law, University of California (J.D., cum laude, 1986). Order of the Coif; Thurston Society; Phi Delta Phi (President, 1985). Recipient, American Jurisprudence Award in Constitutional Law. Editor, Hastings International and Comparative Law Review, 1985-1986. Author: "Terrorists and Special Status: The British Experience in Northern Ireland," 9 Hast. Intl. & Comp. L.R. 481; "Lawsuits over 'Handshake Deals' Are as Old as the Entertainment Industry (and Can Be Easily Avoided)," The Entertainment and Sports Lawyer, Vol. 11, No. 1, Spring 1993. *Member:* Beverly Hills and Los Angeles County Bar Associations; State Bar of California. **PRACTICE AREAS:** Litigation.

---

**CYNTHIA A. VROOM,** born San Jose, California, October 6, 1949; admitted to bar, 1987, California; 1989, U.S. District Court, Central District of California; 1990, U.S. District Court, Northern District of California; 1996, U.S. Court of Appeals, Ninth Circuit. *Education:* San Jose State University (B.A., 1971); University of California at Los Angeles (Ph.D., 1981); Stanford University (J.D., 1987). Recipient, Carl Mason Franklin Prize for outstanding paper on International Law. Author: "Equal Protection Versus the Principle of Equality: American and French Views on Equality," 21 Capital University Law Review 199, 1992. "La Nouvelle Jurisprudence de la peine de mort de la Cour supreme des Etats-Unis," (The New Jurisprudence of the Supreme Court on the Death Penalty, 1989; Revue de science criminelle et de droit penal compare 833; "Constitutional Protection of Individual Liberty in France: the Conseil constitutionnel, Since 1971," Tulane Law Review 265, 1988; "La liberte individuelle au stade de l'enquete de police en France et aux Etats-Unis" (Individual Rights in the Police Investigatory Stage in France and the United States), 1988; Revue de science criminelle et de droit penal compare, 487; "A Case for Judicial Review of Consular Visa Decisions," 22 Stanford Journal of International Law 363, 1986. Visiting Professor, Faculty of Law, University of Aix-Marseille III, Aix-en-Provence, France, 1988-1989. *Member:* Los Angeles County Bar Association; State Bar of California; American and International Bar Associations; French Association of Constitutionalists. **LANGUAGES:** French and Italian. **PRACTICE AREAS:** Litigation; Intellectual Property; Infringement.

---

## FRAGOMEN, DEL REY & BERNSEN, P.C.

11400 WEST OLYMPIC BOULEVARD, SUITE 1050
**LOS ANGELES, CALIFORNIA 90064**
Telephone: 310-473-8700
Facsimile: 310-473-5383
URL: http://www.fragomen.com

*New York, New York Office:* 515 Madison Avenue. Telephone: 212-688-8555. Facsimile: 212-319-5236; 212-758-7215.
*Washington, D.C. Office:* 1212 New York Avenue, N.W., Suite 850. Telephone: 202-223-5515. Facsimile: 202-371-2898.
*Coral Gables, Florida Office:* 890 South Dixie Highway. Telephone: 305-666-4655. Facsimile: 305-666-4467.
*San Francisco, California Office:* 88 Kearny Street, Suite 1300. Telephone: 415-986-1446. Facsimile: 415-986-7964.
*Palo Alto, California Office:* 525 University Avenue, Suite 1450. Telephone: 415-323-7557. Facsimile: 415-323-5030.
*Chicago, Illinois Office:* 300 South Wacker Drive, Suite 2900. Telephone: 312-263-6101. Facsimile: 312-431-0517.
*Stamford, Connecticut Office:* Fragomen Del Rey & Bernsen, 1177 High Ridge Road. Telephone: 203-321-1278. Facsimile: 203-321-1279.
*Short Hills, New Jersey Office:* Fragomen, Del Rey & Bernsen, 51 John F. Kennedy Parkway. Telephone: 201-564-5222. FAX: 201-564-5230.

U.S. and Foreign Immigration and Nationality Law.

*(This Listing Continued)*

---

**PETER H. LOEWY,** born New York, N.Y., October 2, 1955; admitted to bar, 1979, New Jersey; 1980, New York; 1981, Florida; 1984, California. *Education:* City College of the City University of New York (B.A., summa cum laude, 1976); Rutgers University (J.D., 1979). Phi Beta Kappa. Adjunct Professor of Law, Southwestern School of Law, 1989. *Member:* Practising Law Institute (Co-Chair, Annual Immigration Institute, 1993—). (Also at San Francisco and Palo Alto). **LANGUAGES:** French.

**CYNTHIA J. LANGE,** born Berkeley, California, January 5, 1959; admitted to bar, 1986, California and U.S. District Court, Central District of California; 1987, U.S. Court of Appeals, Ninth Circuit. *Education:* Brigham Young University (B.A., 1980), Phi Kappa Phi; Southwestern University (J.D., 1985). Adjunct Professor of Law, Southwestern University, 1988—. *Member:* Beverly Hills (Chairperson, Immigration Law Section, 1994-1995; Member, Board of Governors, 1995—) and Century City (Chairperson, Immigration and Nationality Law Committee, 1989-1994) Bar Associations. **LANGUAGES:** German and Spanish.

---

**TIMOTHY S. BARKER,** born Chicago, Illinois, September 6, 1950; admitted to bar, 1976, California and U.S. District Court, Central and Southern Districts of California; 1977, U.S. Court of Appeals, Ninth Circuit. *Education:* University of California at San Diego (B.S., 1972); University of San Diego School of Law (J.D., 1976). Adjunct Professor of Law, University of San Diego School of Law, 1977-1979. *Member:* Los Angeles County Bar Association (Member, Executive Committee, Immigration Section, 1983-1984); The State Bar of California (Member, Special Needs Committee, 1983-1984).

**SUSAN BIERENBAUM,** born Newark, New Jersey, August 10, 1955; admitted to bar, 1981, New Jersey; 1982, California. *Education:* Rutgers University (B.A., 1977; J.D., 1980). **LANGUAGES:** Spanish.

**MICHAEL H. BOSHNAICK,** born Manhasset, New York, May 1, 1965; admitted to bar, 1993, California and U.S. District Court, Central District of California. *Education:* New York University (B.A., 1987); Southwestern University School of Law (J.D., 1993). **LANGUAGES:** Spanish, French.

**COLLEEN McGRATH DENISON,** born Los Angeles, California, March 10, 1960; admitted to bar, 1990, California. *Education:* University of California at Santa Barbara (B.A., 1982); Loyola Marymount University (J.D., 1990). Member, International & Comparative Law Journal. *Member:* Los Angeles County Bar Association. **LANGUAGES:** Spanish.

**MICHAEL K. MOLITZ,** born Los Angeles, California, November 2, 1965; admitted to bar, 1993, California. *Education:* University of California (B.A., 1987); Loyola University of Los Angeles (J.D., 1992). Member, Moot Court.

(For complete biographical data on Personnel at New York, New York, Washington, D.C., Coral Gables, Florida, San Francisco and Palo Alto, California, Chicago, Illinois, Stamford, Connecticut and Short Hills, New Jersey, see Professional Biographies at those locations)

---

## LAW OFFICES OF
## ARTHUR W. FRANCIS, JR.

A PROFESSIONAL CORPORATION

**LOS ANGELES, CALIFORNIA**

(See Redondo Beach)

*Insurance Defense, ERISA, Coverage and Bad Faith Matters; General Liability; Personal Injury; Casualty; Life, Disability, Health and Accident; Errors and Omissions; Construction Accident; and Workman's Compensation.*

---

## FRANDZEL & SHARE

A LAW CORPORATION

6500 WILSHIRE BOULEVARD
17TH FLOOR
**LOS ANGELES, CALIFORNIA 90048-4920**
Telephone: 213-852-1000
Telecopier: 213-651-2577

*San Francisco, California Office:* 100 Pine Street, 26th Floor. Telephone: 415-788-7400. Telecopier: 415-291-9153.

*(This Listing Continued)*

*Banking, Commercial Creditors Rights and Bankruptcy Law. General Civil, Trial Practice and Real Estate Law.*

**ROBERT D. FRANDZEL** (1942-1996).

**RICHARD HUDSON SHARE,** born Minneapolis, Minnesota, September 6, 1938; admitted to bar, 1964, California and U.S. District Court, Central District of California. *Education:* University of California at Los Angeles (B.S., 1960); University of Southern California (J.D., 1963). Lecturer: Successful Judgment Collections, 1993-1996; How to Get Results in the Collection of Delinquent Debts, 1995-1996, National Business Institute; Development of Cost-Effective Collection Programs and Creditors' Rights, National Business Institute, 1992; Debt Collection and Torts, California Continuing Education of the Bar, 1971. Listed in First edition of *Who's Who in American Law* and All subsequent editions. Member, Lawyers Section, California Bankers Association. Commercial Finance Association, Community Bankers of Southern California, Asian Business League, Beverly Hills Host of All Cities Resource Network Group. Beverly Hills host of Professional Network Group (PNG). Delegate to U.S./China Joint Session on Trade Investment and Economic Law, Beijing, China, 1987. Co-founder, Frandzel & Share, A Law Corporation, and its predecessor. *Member:* Los Angeles Bar Association (Member, Prejudgment Remedies Section); State Bar of California. *Email:* rshare@la.frandzel-share.com

**THOMAS M. ROBINS, III,** born Portland, Oregon, October 29, 1946; admitted to bar, 1972, California. *Education:* University of California at Los Angeles (B.A., 1969); University of Southern California (J.D., 1972). Judge Pro Tem: Los Angeles Municipal Court and Los Angeles Small Claims Court, 1978, 1979, 1980 and 1981. *Member:* Los Angeles County, Beverly Hills and American (Member, Section on Tort and Insurance Practice) Bar Associations; State Bar of California; Los Angeles Trial Lawyers Association; Association of Southern California Defense Counsel; Association of Business Trial Lawyers; American Trial Lawyers Association; American Board of Trial Advocates (Associate Member). *Email:* trobins@la.frandzel-share.com

**JOHN A. GRAHAM,** born Newark, New Jersey, August 1, 1950; admitted to bar, 1976, California. *Education:* Pennsylvania State University (B.A., 1972); University of San Diego (J.D., 1976). Graduate, Pepperdine University School of Law Institute for Dispute Resolution. Judge Pro Tem, Los Angeles Superior Court, 1993-1995. *Member:* Los Angeles County Bar Association (Member: Sections on Commercial Law and Bankruptcy; Bankruptcy Committee, Commercial Law Section); State Bar of California; Los Angeles Bankruptcy Forum (Member, Board of Directors); Financial Lawyers Conference; American Bankruptcy Institute. *PRACTICE AREAS:* Bankruptcy Chapter 11; Bankruptcy Litigation; Bankruptcy Reorganization; Commercial Law; Uniform Commercial Code; Real Estate Secured Transactions; Lender Liability Workouts; Fraudulent Business Schemes; Fraudulent Conveyances. *Email:* jaglaw@attmail.com

**RONALD L. GRUZEN,** born Los Angeles, California, March 19, 1948; admitted to bar, 1973, California. *Education:* University of California at Los Angeles (B.A., 1970); University of Santa Clara (J.D., 1973). Phi Alpha Delta. Instructor, Business Law, Law for California Layperson, Los Angeles Harbor College, 1977-1981. *Member:* Los Angeles County and American Bar Associations; State Bar of California; Los Angeles Trial Lawyers Association; California Trial Lawyers Association. *PRACTICE AREAS:* Business Litigation; Lender Liability Defense; Debt Collection; Creditors' Rights. *Email:* rgruzen@la.frandzel-share.com

**MICHAEL GERARD FLETCHER,** born Salinas, California, April 11, 1951; admitted to bar, 1976, California. *Education:* Stanford University (A.B., with distinction, 1973); University of Southern California (J.D., 1976). *Member:* Los Angeles County Bar Association; State Bar of California; Financial Lawyers Conference; Los Angeles County Bankruptcy Forum. *PRACTICE AREAS:* Commercial Litigation; Bankruptcy; Bankruptcy Litigation; Real Estate; Workout Negotiations and Documentation. *Email:* mfletcher@la.frandzel-share.com

**STEVEN N. BLOOM,** born Los Angeles, California, April 27, 1953; admitted to bar, 1979, California. *Education:* University of Southern California (A.B., magna cum laude, 1976); Loyola University of Los Angeles (J.D., cum laude, 1979). Phi Beta Kappa. Member, St. Thomas More Law Honor Society. Executive Editor, Loyola University of Los Angeles, International & Comparative Law Annual, 1978-1979. *Member:* Los Angeles County (Member, Real Property Section) and American Bar Associations; State Bar of California. *Email:* sbloom@la.frandzel-share.com

**PETER CSATO,** born Oradea, Rumania, May 21, 1951; admitted to bar, 1979, California. *Education:* University of California (B.A., summa cum laude, 1976); Loyola University of Los Angeles (J.D., cum laude, 1979). Phi Beta Kappa. Lecturer, CEB Pre and Post Judgment Remedies, 1985—. *Member:* Los Angeles County Bar Association; State Bar of California. *Email:* pcsato@la.frandzel-share.com

**GARY OWEN CARIS,** born Seattle, Washington, October 19, 1955; admitted to bar, 1979, California; 1980, U.S. District Court, Northern, Eastern, Southern and Central Districts of California 1991, U.S. Court of Appeals, Ninth Circuit. *Education:* California State University at Northridge (B.A., summa cum laude, 1976); University of California at Los Angeles (J.D., 1979). *Member:* Los Angeles County and American Bar Associations; State Bar of California; American Bankruptcy Institute; Financial Lawyers Conference. *Email:* gcaris@la.frandzel-share.com

**DAVID K. GOLDING,** born Los Angeles, California, August 26, 1937; admitted to bar, 1964, California. *Education:* University of California at Los Angeles (B.A., 1958); Boalt Hall School of Law, University of California (J.D., 1963). Phi Alpha Delta. Chairman, Attorneys Committee, California League of Savings Institutions, 1987-1988. General Counsel: Brentwood Savings and Loan Association, 1972-1977; Mercury Savings and Loan Association, 1979-1984. *Member:* Los Angeles County Bar Association (Member, Real Estate and Corporate Sections); State Bar of California. [Lt. jg, U.S. Navy, 1958-1960] *Email:* dgolding@la.frandzel-share.com

**STEPHEN H. MARCUS,** born New York, N.Y., June 30, 1945; admitted to bar, 1971, California. *Education:* Massachusetts Institute of Technology (B.S., 1967); Harvard University (J.D., cum laude, 1970). Tau Beta Pi; Sigma Xi. Editor, Harvard Law Review, 1969-1970. Author: "Equal Protection: The Custody of the Illegitimate Child," Journal of Family, Fall Quarter, 1971; "Obtaining Trial Date and Completing Pretrial Procedure," Ch. 37, California Civil Procedure During Trial, C.E.B., 1982. Co-author, "Court Conferences and Selected Pretrial Motions," Ch. 6, California Civil Procedure During Trial, C.E.B. 1995. President, 1977-1978 and Governor at Large, 1978-1982, M.I.T. Club of Southern California. Judge Pro Tem, Los Angeles Municipal Court, 1978-1982. *Member:* Century City Bar Association (Member, Board of Governors, 1985-1993); State Bar of California. *PRACTICE AREAS:* Business Litigation; Banking and Finance. *Email:* smarcus@la.frandzel-share.com

**LISA A. OGAWA,** born Los Angeles, California, April 15, 1957; admitted to bar, 1982, California, U.S. District Court, Central and Southern Districts of California and U.S. Court of Appeals, Ninth Circuit. *Education:* University of Southern California (B.S., cum laude, 1979; J.D., 1982). *Member:* Los Angeles County and American Bar Associations; State Bar of California; Financial Lawyers Conference. *PRACTICE AREAS:* Loan Restructuring; Loan Workouts; Loans; Secured Transactions; Real Estate Finance. *Email:* logawa@la.frandzel-share.com

**HOWARD S FREDMAN,** born St. Louis, Missouri, February 1, 1944; admitted to bar, 1970, California, U.S. District Court, Northern District of California and U.S. Court of Appeals, Ninth Circuit; 1973, U.S. District Court, Southern District of California; 1975, U.S. District Court, Central District of California; 1985, U.S. Temporary Emergency Court of Appeals. *Education:* Princeton University (A.B., 1966); Columbia University (J.D., cum laude, 1969). Recipient, Moot Court First Year Brief Prize; Finalist, Harlan Stone Moot Court Honors Competition; Representative, Quadrangular, Moot Court Arguments. Speaker, Practicing Law Institute on: Product Liability of Manufacturers, 1982; Depositions, 1986; Negotiation, 1987 and 1988. Law Clerk to Hon. Milton Pollack, U.S. District Judge, Southern District of New York, 1969-1970. *Member:* Los Angeles County (Member, Nominating Committee, 1986; Antitrust Section, Executive Committee, 1983—, Chairman, 1986-1987, First Vice Chair, 1985-1986; Delegate, State Bar Conference of Delegates, 1987 and 1988), Federal and American (Member, Sections on: Antitrust; Litigation) Bar Associations; State Bar of California; Association of Business Trial Lawyers. *PRACTICE AREAS:* Antitrust; Civil Appeals; Lender Liability; Business Torts; Business Litigation; Trademark Infringement; Trade Secrets. *Email:* hfredman@la.frandzel-share.com

**STEPHEN M. SKACEVIC,** born Los Angeles, California, October 8, 1953; admitted to bar, 1980, California. *Education:* University of California at Irvine (B.A., 1975); Pepperdine University (J.D., 1980). *Member:* State Bar of California. *PRACTICE AREAS:* Bankruptcy. *Email:* sskacevic@la.frandzel-share.com

**THOMAS S. ARTHUR,** born San Diego, California, April 27, 1949; admitted to bar, 1976, California. *Education:* University of California at Santa Barbara and California State University at San Diego (B.A., cum laude, 1973); University of San Diego (J.D., 1976). *Member:* Los Angeles County and American Bar Associations; State Bar of California; Financial Lawyers Conference. *Email:* tarthur@la.frandzel-share.com

*(This Listing Continued)*

**FRANDZEL & SHARE,** A LAW CORPORATION, Los Angeles—Continued

**LESLEY ANNE HAWES,** born Hollywood, California, July 7, 1959; admitted to bar, 1984, California, U.S. Court of Appeals, Ninth Circuit and U.S. Supreme Court. *Education:* University of California at Los Angeles; University of Southern California (A.B., 1981; J.D., 1984). Phi Beta Kappa; Phi Kappa Phi; Order of the Coif; Phi Alpha Delta. Recipient, American Jurisprudence Awards in Evidence and Remedies. Author: "Bankruptcy Preference Litigation: ZZZZ Best and Beyond," Los Angeles Lawyer, October, 1992 at 28; "Hazardous Duty: Attorney-Client Privilege Barely Prevents Jailing," The Bankruptcy Strategist, December 1992 at 1. Regular legal columnist for The Leasing and Financial Services Monitor, 1991—. Member: Financial Lawyers Conference; Los Angeles Bankruptcy Forum. *Member:* Los Angeles County Bar Association; State Bar of California. *PRACTICE AREAS:* Creditors' Rights in Insolvency Proceedings and Workouts; Secured Transactions; Bankruptcy. *Email:* lhawes@la.frandzel-share.com

**MARSHALL J. AUGUST,** born Los Angeles, California, August 31, 1957; admitted to bar, 1982, California and U.S. District Court, Northern, Southern, Eastern and Central Districts of California. *Education:* University of California at Los Angeles (B.A., 1979); Southwestern University (J.D., 1982). *Member:* Los Angeles County (Secretary, Executive Committee, Provisional and Post-Judgment Remedies Section, 1988—; Secretary, 1990-1991; Treasurer, 1991-1992; Vice Chair, 1992-1993; Chair, 1993-1994; Member, Editorial Board, Provisional and Post Judgment Section Newsletter, 1989) and American Bar Associations; State Bar of California. *Email:* maugust@la.frandzel-share.com

**LEROY ANDERSON,** born Lexington, Nebraska, May 27, 1949; admitted to bar, 1974, Nebraska and U.S. District Court, District of Nebraska; 1980, U.S. Supreme Court and U.S. Court of Appeals, 8th Circuit; 1987, California; 1988, U.S. District Court, Central, Northern, Eastern and Southern Districts of California and U.S. Court of Appeals, 9th Circuit. *Education:* University of Nebraska-Kearney (B.S., with honorable mention, 1971); University of Nebraska (J.D., 1973). Assistant Editor, Nebraska Law Review, 1972-1973. Author: Casenote, "Security Interest: Grace Period Examined, North Platte State Bank v. Production Credit Association," 52 Nebraska Law Review 421, 1973. Member, Panel of Trustees, U.S. District Court, 1983-1988. Adjunct Professor, Loyola Law School, 1989. Instructor, Real Estate Law, Mid Plains Community College, 1978-1987. Deputy County Attorney, Logan County, Nebraska, 1983-1987. *Member:* Los Angeles County, Nebraska State and American Bar Associations; State Bar of California; American Trial Lawyers Association; Los Angeles Trial Lawyers Association; Financial Lawyers Conference. *PRACTICE AREAS:* Business Litigation; Bankruptcy Litigation; Bankruptcy Reorganization; Creditors' Rights; Secured Leasing; Real Estate Litigation. *Email:* landerson@la.frandzel-share.com

**KENNETH C. BOVARD,** born Mesa, Arizona, November 2, 1947; admitted to bar, 1973, California and U.S. District Court, Southern District of California. *Education:* University of California at Berkeley (B.A., 1969); University of San Diego (J.D., 1973). *Member:* Orange County Bar Association; State Bar of California. *PRACTICE AREAS:* Banking; Financial Practice; Real Estate; Commercial Law. *Email:* kbovard@la.frandzel-share.com

**PATRICIA YAMAMOTO TRENDACOSTA,** born Los Angeles, California, December 31, 1951; admitted to bar, 1986, California. *Education:* University of California, Santa Barbara (B.A., 1974); Loyola Marymount Law School (J.D., 1986). *Member:* California State Bar. *Email:* ptrendacosta@la.frandzel-share.com

**CRAIG A. WELIN,** born Long Beach, California, April 27, 1963; admitted to bar, 1988, California and U.S. District Court, Central, Northern, Southern and Eastern Districts of California. *Education:* University of Southern California (B.S., magna cum laude, 1985; J.D., 1988). Phi Kappa Phi; Beta Gamma Sigma; Golden Key. Hale Moot Court Honors Program. *Member:* Beverly Hills, Los Angeles County and American Bar Associations; State Bar of California. *PRACTICE AREAS:* Bankruptcy; Banks and Banking; Business Law; Commercial Law; Collections; Debtor and Creditor. *Email:* cwelin@la.frandzel-share.com

**JULIA E. SYLVA,** born Los Angeles, California, November 13, 1955; admitted to bar, 1983, California and U.S. District Court, Central District of California. *Education:* California State University at Long Beach (B.A., 1978); Loyola Marymount University (J.D., 1983). Phi Alpha Delta. City Council Member, 1976, Vice-Mayor, 1977 and Mayor, 1978-1980, City of Hawaiian Gardens. City Attorney: City of Bradbury, 1984-1986; City of San Fernando, 1993-1995; City of Hawaiian Gardens, 1996—. Assistant City Attorney and City Prosecutor, City of Duarte, 1983-1987. *Member:* Los Angeles County Bar Association (Member, Government Law Section); State Bar of California (Member, Executive Committee, Public Law Section); Mexican-American Bar Association; California Women Lawyers of Los Angeles; National Women's Political Cause (Founding Member Los Angeles County Chapter); National Association of Bond Lawyers. *LANGUAGES:* Spanish. *PRACTICE AREAS:* Municipal Law; Municipal Finance Law. *Email:* jsylva@la.frandzel-share.com

**HENRY G. WEINSTEIN,** born Los Angeles, California, July 21, 1962; admitted to bar, 1989, California. *Education:* University of California at Los Angeles (B.A., 1985); Loyola of Los Angeles Law School (J.D., 1988). Staff Member, 1986-1987 and Note and Comment Editor, 1987-1988, Loyola of Los Angeles Law Review. Author: "Common-Law Bad Faith in White v. Western Title Insurance Co.; The Duty Continues," 21 Loy. L.A. L. Rev. 399, Nov. 1987. *Member:* State Bar of California. *LANGUAGES:* Spanish. *Email:* hweinstein@la.frandzel-share.com

**ROBB MICHAEL STROM,** born Los Angeles, California, December 1, 1959; admitted to bar, 1985, California. *Education:* University of California at San Diego (B.A., 1982); University of San Diego (J.D., 1985). President, John Muir College. Author, "The Tender Years Presumption: Is it Presumably Unconstitutional?" 21 San Diego Law Review 829 (1984). *Member:* Los Angeles County and American Bar Associations. *LANGUAGES:* Spanish. *PRACTICE AREAS:* Civil Litigation. *Email:* rstrom@la.frandzel-share.com

**SHIRLEY D. RAMIREZ,** admitted to bar, 1991, California. *Education:* Occidental College (B.A., cum laude, 1984); University of California, Los Angeles (M.B.A., 1990; J.D., 1991). Member, Financial Lawyers Conference; Los Angeles Bankruptcy Forum. *Member:* Los Angeles County Bar Association; State Bar of California (Member, Sections on: Business Law, Litigation and Real Property Law). *LANGUAGES:* Spanish. *PRACTICE AREAS:* Bankruptcy; Commercial Litigation. *Email:* sramirez@la.frandzel-share.com

**BRUCE D. POLTROCK,** born Chicago, Illinois; admitted to bar, 1992, California and U.S. District Court, Central District of California. *Education:* University of Southern California (B.S., cum laude, 1989); University of San Francisco (J.D., 1992). Staff Member, University of San Francisco Law Review, 1990-1992. Recipient, American Jurisprudence Award, Legal Research and Writing. *Member:* Los Angeles County and Beverly Hills Bar Associations; State Bar of California. *Email:* bpoltrock@la.frandzel-share.com

**SUZANNE KAHN WYNNE,** born Los Angeles, California, October 18, 1968; admitted to bar, 1993, California. *Education:* University of California, Santa Barbara (B.A., with honors, 1990); Loyola University (J.D., 1993). Order of the Coif; Saint Thomas Moore Society. Recipient, American Jurisprudence Book Award, Appellate Advocacy. *Member:* Los Angeles and Beverly Hills Bar Associations. *PRACTICE AREAS:* Litigation; Commercial Litigation. *Email:* swynne@la.frandzel-share.com

**JUDY MAN-LING LAM,** born San Francisco, California, February 3, 1965; admitted to bar, 1994, California. *Education:* Occidental College (A.B., 1987); Loyola Law School (J.D., 1994). Member, Scott Moot Court Honors Board, 1993-1994. Staff Writer, 1992-1993, Executive Editor, 1993-1994, Loyola of Los Angeles Entertainment Law Journal, 1992-1993. Judicial Extern to the Honorable Geraldine Mund, U.S. Bankruptcy Court, Central District, 1991. Judicial Extern to the Honorable Stephen R. Reinhardt, U.S. Court of Appeals, Ninth Judicial Circuit, 1992. Author, "Banking on A Dream: Protecting International Security Interests in Copyrights -- An International Survey," 13 Loyola of Los Angeles Entertainment Law Journal 319, 1993. *LANGUAGES:* Chinese. *PRACTICE AREAS:* Litigation; Transactional; Banking Law; Commercial Law; Bankruptcy. *Email:* jlam@la.frandzel-share.com

**ROBERT GONZALEZ,** born Hollister, California, August 18, 1965; admitted to bar, 1994, California, U.S. District Court, Northern, Southern, Eastern and Central Districts of California. *Education:* University of Southern California (B.S., 1988); Southwestern University School of Law (J.D., 1993). *Member:* Beverly Hills, Los Angeles County and Mexican-American Bar Associations; State Bar of California. *LANGUAGES:* Spanish. *PRACTICE AREAS:* Creditor's Rights; Bankruptcy. *Email:* rgonzalez@la.frandzel-share.com

**JOON W. SONG,** born Seoul, Korea, June 12, 1967; admitted to bar, 1995, California. *Education:* University of California at Los Angeles (B.A., 1990; J.D., 1995). Managing Editor, U.C.L.A. Asian Pacific Islander Law

*(This Listing Continued)*

Journal, 1993-1994. President, Student Bar Association, University of California at Los Angeles, School of Law, 1994-1995. **LANGUAGES:** Korean. **PRACTICE AREAS:** Commercial Litigation; Municipal Law. **Email:** jsong@la.frandzel-share.com

**AMY JESSICA FRANKEL,** born Alexandria, Virginia, December 14, 1969; admitted to bar, 1994, California. *Education:* University of California, Santa Barbara (B.A., summa cum laude, 1991); Hastings College of the Law, University of California, San Francisco (J.D., 1994). Note Editor, Hastings International & Comparative Law Review. Recipient, American Jurisprudence Award in Legal Writing and Research. **PRACTICE AREAS:** Commercial Litigation; Civil Litigation. **Email:** afrankel@la.frandzel-share.com

REPRESENTATIVE CLIENTS: AMRESCO Management, Inc.; A.T.&T.; Bank Hapoalim B.M.; Bank of America; Bank of Hawaii; Bank of San Francisco; Bankers Mutual; California Commerce Bank; California Federal Bank; Cathay Bank; Charter Pacific Bank; Chemical Bank; City National Bank; Coast Federal Bank; Commercial Center Bank; Community Bank; Countrywide Funding; Deere Credit Services; East-West Federal Bank; 1st Nationwide Bank; Fidelity Federal Bank; First Business Bank; First Charter Bank; First Interstate Bank; First Los Angeles Bank; First Professional Bank; Fullerton Savings and Loan; General American Life Insurance Co.; General Electric Capital Asset Management Corporation; Glendale Federal Bank; Guardian Bank; Hanmi Bank; Heller First Capital Corp.; Imperial Bank; Kawasaki Motors Corp., U.S.A.; Landmark Bank; Manufacturers Bank; Manufacturers Hanover; McDonnell Douglas Finance Corporation; Mercantile National Bank; Mercedes-Benz Credit Corporation; Metrobank; Mortgage and Realty Trust; National Bank of Long Beach; Phoenix Leasing; The Prudential Insurance Company of America; Riverside National Bank; J.E. Robert Company; Sanwa Bank; Scientific Leasing, Inc.; Seafirst Bank; Southern California Savings and Loan; Technology Funding Secured Investors; Tokai Bank; Tokai Credit Corporation; Topa Thrift and Loan; Transamerica Insurance Finance Corp.; Union Bank; U.S. Borax; Virginia National Bank; Wells Fargo Bank; Western Federal Savings; Wilshire State Bank; World Savings.
REFERENCES: Cathay Bank; Community Bank; General Electric Capital Asset Management Corp; Phoenix Leasing; J.E. Robert Company; Sanwa Bank; Tokai Bank.

(For Complete Biographical Data of other Firm Personnel, see Professional Biographies at San Francisco, California)

---

# DEBRA S. FRANK
### A PROFESSIONAL LAW CORPORATION
### TWO CENTURY PLAZA, SUITE 1800
### 2049 CENTURY PARK EAST
### LOS ANGELES, CALIFORNIA 90067-3120
Telephone: 310-277-5121
Fax: 310-277-5932

*Family Law, Divorce Mediation, Civil, Personal Injury and Criminal Litigation.*

**DEBRA SUSAN FRANK,** born 1949; admitted to bar, 1977, California; 1980, District of Columbia. *Education:* Boston University (B.A., with honors, 1970); Carnegie Institute of Technology (M.A., with honors, 1972); Southwestern University School of Law (J.D., 1977). Judge Pro Tempore, 1984-1986. Commissioner, 1982-1983 and Vice Chairperson, 1983, California Law Revision Commission. Member, Family Law Section Minor's Counsel Committee, 1995—. *Member:* Beverly Hills, Century City and Los Angeles County Bar Associations; State Bar of California (Member, Family Law Section, Executive Committee, 1995—; Secretary-Treasurer, 1996-1997; Assistant Editor, Family Law News, 1995—; Liaison to Support Committee South, 1995—; Support Committee South, 1984—, Secretary, 1994—); Criminal Courts Bar Association; Consumer Attorneys of Los Angeles. (Certified Specialist, Family Law, The State Bar of California Board of Legal Specialization).

---

# FRANSCELL, STRICKLAND, ROBERTS & LAWRENCE
### A PROFESSIONAL CORPORATION
### LOS ANGELES, CALIFORNIA
(See Pasadena)

*Police Misconduct Liability Defense, Civil Rights Defense, Employment Defense, Municipal and Administrative Law, General Civil and Criminal Trial and Appellate Practice, Administrative Law and Litigation.*

---

# FREDERICKSON & YOUNG
### SUITE 481, 5757 WILSHIRE BOULEVARD
### LOS ANGELES, CALIFORNIA 90036-3664
Telephone: 213-964-7373
Fax: 213-964-7377
Email: FNYMAN@AOL.com

*Business Litigation, Administrative, Real Property, Construction, Commercial and General Transactional Law. General Civil and Trial Practice in State and Federal Courts.*

FIRM PROFILE: Frederickson & Young is a small but aggressive litigation firm that specializes in complex civil litigation on behalf of both plaintiffs and defendants. Our business transactional practice includes business formations, dissolutions and mergers and acquisitions. Our litigation practice includes employment disputes, real property disputes, will contests, tort actions and partnership litigation. Frederickson & Young handle matters throughout the Southern California area as well as interstate litigation.

## MEMBERS OF FIRM

**DAVID H. FREDERICKSON,** born Salt Lake City, Utah, June 19, 1939; admitted to bar, 1969, California, U.S. Court of Appeals, Ninth Circuit and U.S. District Court, Northern and Eastern Districts of California; 1973, U.S. District Court, Central and Southern Districts of California; 1994, Colorado. *Education:* University of Utah; California State University at San Francisco (B.A., 1965); Boalt Hall School of Law, University of California (J.D., 1968). Phi Alpha Delta. Member, Moot Court Board. *Member:* Los Angeles County (Member, Committee on State Bar; Member, Sections on: Litigation; Antitrust; Prejudgment Remedies) and American (Member, Sections on: Litigation; Antitrust; Real Property; Patent, Trademark and Copyright Law) Bar Associations; State Bar of California; The Association of Trial Lawyers of America; Association of Business Trial Lawyers; California Consumer Lawyers Association. **PRACTICE AREAS:** Business Litigation; Real Estate Litigation; Commercial Litigation; Civil Litigation; Partnership Disputes; Legal Malpractice; Employment Litigation.

**ROBERT E. YOUNG,** born San Francisco, California, August 20, 1947; admitted to bar, 1972, California. *Education:* San Francisco City College and University of California at Berkeley (B.A., 1969); Hastings College of Law, University of California (J.D., 1972); Georgetown University (LL.M. in Federal Taxation, 1975). Phi Beta Kappa. Author: "Section 334(b) (2): The Purchase Requirement," 30 The Tax Lawyer 188, Fall 1976; "The Law of Forceable Entry and Detainer in California," 10 Lincoln Law Review 1, 1977. Law Clerk to Judge Phillip M. Saeta, Los Angeles Superior Court, 1977-1978. Listed Who's Who of California Law, 1995. *Member:* Los Angeles County Bar Association; State Bar of California. **REPORTED CASES:** State of Trynin 49 Cal 3rd 868 1989. **PRACTICE AREAS:** Business Litigation; Conservatorships; Securities Litigation; Civil Litigation; Unlawful Detainers; Real Estate Litigation.

## ASSOCIATES

**BRIAN M. PLESSALA,** born Houston, Texas, November 20, 1962; admitted to bar, 1989, California. *Education:* California State University (B.A., History, 1986); Loyola Law School (J.D., 1989). *Member:* State Bar of California. **PRACTICE AREAS:** Business Litigation; Civil Litigation; Securities; Litigation.

REPRESENTATIVE CLIENTS: Information International, Inc.; Nordoff Investments, Inc.; International Broadcasting, Inc.; Patrick Media Group; Palm Plaza Development; Cobe Laboratories, Inc.; Amusements International; Oxford Group of Companies.

---

# FREEBURG, JUDY & NETTELS
### LOS ANGELES, CALIFORNIA
(See Pasadena)

*General Civil Trial and Appellate Practice. Casualty, Malpractice, Products Liability, Insurance and Environmental Law. Personal Defense.*

CALIFORNIA—LOS ANGELES                    MARTINDALE-HUBBELL LAW DIRECTORY 1997

## FREEMAN, FREEMAN & SMILEY, LLP

A Limited Liability Partnership including Law Corporations

*Established in 1976*

PENTHOUSE, SUITE 1200
3415 SEPULVEDA BOULEVARD
**LOS ANGELES, CALIFORNIA 90034-6060**
*Telephone: 310-398-6227*
*Facsimile: 310-391-4042*

**Irvine, California Office:** 2010 Main Street, Suite 580. Telephone: 714-833-7966. Facsimile: 714-833-9584.

**San Francisco, California Office:** One Market, Steuart Tower, 16th Floor. Telephone: 415-974-1930.

*Estate and Gift Planning, Probate, Real Estate, Corporate, Business Succession Planning, Trial and Appellate Litigation.*

FIRM PROFILE: From its multiple office locations, the firm enjoys a national reputation for its expertise in estate and gift planning, charitable and philanthropic planning, planning for highly compensated individuals, and formation of domestic and international charities and foundations. The firm also engages in a broad-based real estate practice and its real estate clients include several of the country's largest and most successful high-volume retailers and warehouse operators, institutional lenders, and one of the nation's largest regional mall developers. Our Litigation practice includes breach of contract and employment disputes, real property disputes, will contests, tort actions, and partnership litigation. The firm also maintains a diversified Business Transactional practice providing services to clients engaged in all aspects of business activity, including formation, sales and acquisitions, employment matters, and contract negotiations.

**DOUGLAS K. FREEMAN,** admitted to bar, 1971, California, U.S. Supreme Court, U.S. Tax Court, U.S. District Court, 9th Circuit and U.S. Court of Military Appeals. *Education:* Stanford University (A.B., with distinction, 1967); University of California at Los Angeles (J.D., 1970); University of San Diego (LL.M., in Taxation, 1984). Author: "Estate Freezing Techniques: Tools and Techniques," Matthew Bender, 1984. Editor: "Tax Exempt Organizations and Private Foundations Federal Tax Services," Matthew Bender. Co-Author: "How to Live and Die With California Probate," Los Angeles County Bar Association, 1984. Lecturer and Instructor: California Continuing Education of the Bar; NYU Tax Institute; USC Tax Institute; ALI-ABA; International Association of Financial Planners; Million Dollar Roundtable; American Association of Life Underwriters, International Association of Financial Planners; National Committee on Planned Giving; National Society for Fund Raising Executives; Council for the Advancement and Support of Education. Member, Board of Trustees of Foundation for Independent Higher Education. Member, Board of Trustees, Independent Colleges of Northern California, 1989—; Member, Board of Trustees, California Institute of the Arts, 1986—. Founder, National Philanthropy Day. (Certified Specialist, Taxation Law, The State Bar of California Board of Legal Specialization). **PRACTICE AREAS:** Tax; Estate Planning; Exempt Organizations.

**RICHARD D. FREEMAN,** admitted to bar, 1970, California. *Education:* University of California at Berkeley (B.A., 1966); Loyola University (J.D., 1969). Author: "Disability Buy-Sell Problems In The Small Business," California Magazine, 1982; "Business Disability Buy-Out Insurance: An Analysis of Significant Issues and Key Policy Provisions," C.L.U. Journal, 1981. Panelist and Lecturer, "Financial Fitness Update," (regionally syndicated estate and financial planning television program). Lecturer, Estate and Business Planning. Instructor: Institute of Business Law, Pepperdine University School of Business and Management, 1984. **PRACTICE AREAS:** Estate Planning; Business Succession Planning.

**BRUCE M. SMILEY,** admitted to bar, 1974, California. *Education:* University of California at Los Angeles (B.A., 1971); Southwestern University (J.D., 1974). Associate Staff Member, Southwestern University Law Review, 1972-1973. Co-Author: "Assignment and Subletting - The Changing Standards and Practical Solutions," National Mall Monitor, Vol. 15, No. 2, May, 1985. Lecturer and Instructor, Real Estate Law, University of California at Los Angeles, Extension, International Council of Shopping Centers and Georgetown University Law Centers. **PRACTICE AREAS:** Real Property Law; Shopping Center Law.

**GLENN T. SHERMAN,** admitted to bar, 1979, California, U.S. Court of Appeals, Ninth Circuit and U.S. District Court, Central District of California. *Education:* University of California at Los Angeles (B.A., 1976); Southwestern University (J.D., cum laude, 1979). **PRACTICE AREAS:** Commercial Real Estate Transactions; Construction and Franchise Law.

*(This Listing Continued)*

CAA670B

**FRED J. MARCUS,** admitted to bar, 1981, California. *Education:* University of California at Berkeley; Pacific Oaks College (B.A., 1974); Loyola Law School (J.D., 1981); New York University School of Law (LL.M. in Taxation, 1984). Author: "Acquiring and Maintaining Tax-Exempt Status," Federal Tax Service, Matthew Bender, 1988. **PRACTICE AREAS:** Transactional Business; Tax Exempt Organizations; Estate Planning Law.

**LAURENCE L. HUMMER,** admitted to bar, 1980, California; U.S. Court of Appeals, Ninth Circuit; U.S. District Court, Central, Northern and Southern Districts of California; U.S. Court of Federal Claims. *Education:* Stanford University (B.A., with distinction, 1973); University of California at Los Angeles (J.D., 1980). Order of the Coif. Member, UCLA Law Review, 1978-1980. Author: "Managing Multiple Documents in Complex Cases," Los Angeles Lawyer, June 1992. **PRACTICE AREAS:** Civil; Business; Real Estate Litigation.

**BRUCE L. GELB,** admitted to bar, 1978, California, U.S. Court of Appeals, Ninth Circuit and U.S. District Court, Central District of California. *Education:* University of Pittsburgh (B.A., cum laude, 1973); Temple University Law Center (J.D., 1977). Lecturer: Adjunct Professor Business Faculty, El Camino College, Real Estate Law, Real Estate Taxation and Exchanges, 1979-1989. **PRACTICE AREAS:** Real Estate; Business; Civil Litigation.

**JANE PEEBLES,** admitted to bar, 1984, Colorado; 1988, California. *Education:* City College of New York (B.A., cum laude, 1974); M.A., magna cum laude, 1977); New York University School of Law (J.D., 1984). Lecturer: "Life Insurance and Buy-Sell Agreements," Fifteenth Annual Inland Empire Estate Planning Seminar (November 1994): "Uses of Life Insurance in Charitable Giving," Desert Estate Planning Councils (October 1994); "U.S. Estate and Gift Taxation of Aliens," California Society of Certified Public Accountants (August 1994); "The Uses of Tax Consequences of Crummey Powers," Riverside and San Bernardino Estate Planning Councils (March 1994); "Selected Funding Alternatives and Investments in Charitable Remainder Trusts," Desert Estate Planning Councils (March 1994). Co-Author: "Socially Responsible Investment," August 1992; Probate & Property, American Bar Association July/August 1992; "A Primer on United States Taxation of Aliens," Major Tax Planning, University of Southern California Law Center, 1991. Member, Board of Directors, St. Barnabas Senior Services, 1992—. *Member:* Los Angeles County Bar Association (Probate and Trust Section); State Bar of California (Member, Estate Planning, Probate and Trust Law Section, Taxation Section). **PRACTICE AREAS:** Estate Planning (Domestic and International); Charitable Giving.

**RICHARD E. GILBERT,** admitted to bar, 1973, Maryland; 1974, District of Columbia; 1976, U.S. Tax Court and California. *Education:* American University (B.A., 1968; J.D., 1973); New York University (LL.M. in Taxation, 1974). Member, American University Law Review, 1972-1973. Law Clerk, Hon. Judge Cynthia Holcomb Hall, U.S. Tax Court, 1974-1976. Author: "Despite Complexity, Private Foundations Offer Advantages To Donors With Charitable Intentions," July 1985; "How to Use Gifts and Leasebacks As a Tax-Planning Tool," Prentice Hall Tax Ideas, 1982. Lecturer: Division of Business and Industry Services (Continuing Professional Education) California State University, Northridge, 1981—; California Society of CPA's Entertainment Industry Conference, "Estate Planning For Entertainers," 1991; California Society of CPA's Estate Planning Conference, "Private Foundations," "Estate Planning Foundation,"; "Design and Implementation of Charitable Remainder Trusts," 1990, 1991, 1994; "Effective Use of Charitable Partners in Estate Planning," University of Southern California Tax Institute, 1984; "The Dark Side of Life Insurance Trusts," Los Angeles and Warner Center Estate Planning Councils, 1996. Chairman, 1993 and Member, 1990—, Planning Committee, California Society of CPA's Estate Planning Conference. Member, Planning Committee, California Society of CPA's Advanced Estate Planning Institute, 1995. Chairman, 1996 and Member, 1995—, Planning Committee, California Society of CPA's Strategies for High Income Individuals Conference, 1995. **PRACTICE AREAS:** Estate Planning; Tax and Related Business Planning.

### ASSOCIATES

**STEPHEN F. WELTMAN,** admitted to bar, 1967, District of Columbia; 1974, California; 1980, U.S. Tax Court. *Education:* Yale University (A.B., 1963); University of Pennsylvania (LL.B., 1966); Boston University (LL.M., in Taxation, 1967).

**WARREN O. HODGES, JR.,** admitted to bar, 1990, California and U.S. District Court, Southern, Eastern and Central Districts of California. *Education:* Yale University (B.A., 1985); University of Southern California (J.D., 1989).

*(This Listing Continued)*

**KYLE M. ROBERTSON**, admitted to bar, 1988, California. *Education:* Wellesley College (B.A., magna cum laude, 1983); Boston College (J.D., summa cum laude, 1988).

**MARTIN P. HOCHMAN**, admitted to bar, 1993, California and U.S. District Court, Central District of California. *Education:* Bard College (B.A., with honors, 1984); Loyola Law School, Los Angeles (J.D., 1992).

**PAUL J. GOLDMAN**, admitted to bar, 1990, California. *Education:* California State University at Long Beach (B.A., with honors, 1987); University of Southern California Law Center (J.D., 1990).

**GREGORY M. BORDO**, admitted to bar, 1991, California and U.S. District Court, Central District of California. *Education:* University of California at San Diego (B.A., 1987); Loyola Law School Los Angeles (J.D., 1991).

## OF COUNSEL

**PAUL P. DENZER**, admitted to bar, 1981, California. *Education:* Rockhurst College (B.S.B.A., summa cum laude, 1978); University of California at Los Angeles (J.D., 1991). Alpha Gamma Sigma; Alpha Sigma Nu. Member, UCLA - Alaska Law Review, 1980-1981. *Member:* State Bar of California.

**MICHAEL R. MAGASIN**, admitted to bar, 1969, California, U.S. District Court, Central District of California, U.S. Court of Military Appeals and U.S. Supreme Court. *Education:* University of California at Los Angeles (B.A. in History and Political Science, 1965); University of California at Los Angeles (J.D., 1968). Phi Delta Phi. Assistant Professor of Law, United States Academy, West Point, 1970-1973. Associate Professor, Business Law, Pepperdine University, 1985—. Author: "The Dynamics of a State Environmental Law Prosecution," Pacific Southwest Journal, 1984. Judge Pro Tem: Los Angeles Municipal Court, 1983; Culver Judicial District, 1985—. Deputy District Attorney, Los Angeles County, 1973-1981. *Member:* Los Angeles County Bar Association; State Bar of California. [Col. JAGC, USAR]

**BARBARA J. BAILEY**, admitted to bar, 1979, California; 1987, U.S. Tax Court; U.S. District Court, Central and Southern Districts of California. Author: "The New Case Plan in Conservatorships," CEB Probate Trust and Estate Planning Reporter, June 1991. Lecturer: Continuing Education of the Bar; Beverly Hills Bar Association. (Certified Specialist, Probate, Estate Planning and Trust Law, The State Bar of California Board of Legal Specialization). *PRACTICE AREAS:* Probate; Conservatorships; Probate and Trust Litigation.

**STEVEN M. KRAUS**, admitted to bar, 1984, California and U.S. District Court, Central District of California. *Education:* University of California at Los Angeles (B.A., summa cum laude, 1981) Phi Beta Kappa; Boalt Hall School of Law, University of California (J.D., 1984). University of California Regents Scholar. Co-Author: "Life Without Operating Covenants: Minimizing Risks of Major Tenants Going Dark in Retail Projects," C.E.B. Real Property Law Reporter, Vol. XII, No. 7 (Oct. 1989). Formerly employed as Regional Counsel, Western United States for Homart Development Co. *Member:* Los Angeles County Bar Association (Member Real Property Section). *LANGUAGES:* French. *PRACTICE AREAS:* Real Estate Sales and Acquisitions; Development; Leasing and Financing.

**ARTHUR MAZIROW**, admitted to bar, 1959, California. *Education:* University of California at Los Angeles (B.S., 1955; J.D., 1958). Instructor: Real Estate Law, Industrial and Commercial Leases, University of California Extension, 1961-1995. Author: "The Broker as Agent and Fiduciary-Part III: Reducing the Broker's Risk," CEA News (California Escrow Association, January 1990; "Subject to Approval By Board of Directors- What Does It Mean?" CEA News (California Escrow Association), February 1990; "Tenants Have Options in Case of Lessor Default," National Real Estate Investor, April 1990; "Broker's Listings - A Seller's Viewpoint," CEA News (California Escrow Association), June 1990; "Courts Give Brokers Safety Valve," National Real Estate Investor, August 1990; "Title Insurance Provides Fraud Coverage," National Real Estate Investor, October 1990; "Understanding the Americans with Disabilities Act," California Real Estate Magazine of the California Association of Realtors, July/August 1992 (co-author); "Special Report: The Nature and Function of Long Term Ground Leasing," Buchalter, Nemer, Fields & Younger Real Estate Report, September 1993. *Member:* Beverly Hills, Los Angeles County and American Bar Associations; State Bar of California. (Also Practicing Individually). *PRACTICE AREAS:* Real Estate Development; Leases; Sales and Purchases of Real Estate.

**STEVEN L. ZIVEN**, admitted to bar, 1978, Wisconsin and California. *Education:* Wharton School of Finance and Commerce; University of Pennsylvania (B.S., cum laude, 1975); University of Wisconsin-Madison (J.D., 1978). *Member:* Los Angeles County Bar Association; The State Bar of California; The State Bar of Wisconsin. *PRACTICE AREAS:* Corporations Law; Business Transactions; Real Estate Law.

**ERNEST J. SCHAG, JR.**, admitted to bar, 1960, California and New York; U.S. District Court, Northern and Southern Districts of California; U.S. Court of Appeals, Ninth Circuit; U.S. Supreme Court. *Education:* University of Southern California (A.B., 1954; J.D., 1959); New York University (LL.M., in Trade Regulation, 1960). Phi Delta Phi. Winner, Hale Moot Court Competition, 1958. Member, Orange County Estate Planning Council. *Member:* Orange County (Chairman: Probate and Trust Law Committee, 1970-1971; Unauthorized Practice of Law Committee, 1972-1973), Los Angeles County, New York State and American Bar Associations; State Bar of California (Member, Estate Planning, Trust and Probate Law Section). Fellow, American College of Trust and Estate Counsel. (Resident, Irvine Office). *PRACTICE AREAS:* Estate Planning; Charitable Tax Planning and Private Foundations.

**LYNDA S. MOERSCHBAECHER**, born Chicago, Illinois, September 12, 1943; admitted to bar, 1977, California. *Education:* University of Wisconsin (B.A., with honors, 1966); Golden Gate University (J.D., 1977; M.B.A., 1977). Author and Co-Editor: Charitable Gift Planning News and The Practical Gift Planner. Author: "Integrating Planned Giving into the Overall Fund Raising Program," Trusts and Estates, October, 1983; "Long-Awaited Changes in Valuation Tables Cause Doubt-Uncertainty in Tax Planning," Tax Section News, Winter, 1984; "Substantiation of Charitable Deductions: New Appraisal Regulations," Estates, Gifts and Trusts Journal, May/June, 1985; "The New Planned Giving Landscape," CASE Currents, June, 1987; "Ethics in Planned Giving," Fund Raising Management, February 1988. *Member:* Bar Association of San Francisco (Chairman, Probate and Trust Law Section, 1987-1988); State Bar of California; American Bar Association (Member, Exempt Organizations Committee, Tax Section, 1981—); San Francisco Estate Planning Council (Director, 1985-1991; President, 1989-1990). *LANGUAGES:* French. *PRACTICE AREAS:* Charitable Giving; Public Charities (Domestic and International); Corporate Law; Private Foundations; Estate Planning; Trust Administration.

REFERENCE: Union Bank (Beverly Hills, California).

## FREID AND GOLDSMAN

*A PROFESSIONAL LAW CORPORATION*
*2029 CENTURY PARK EAST, SUITE 860*
**LOS ANGELES, CALIFORNIA 90067**
Telephone: 310-552-2700
Telecopier: 310-552-2770

*General Civil and Trial Practice. Family Law.*

**MANLEY FREID**, born Wilmington, Delaware, December 11, 1937; admitted to bar, 1962, California. *Education:* University of Delaware and Temple University (B.S., 1959); University of California at Los Angeles (J.D., 1962). Phi Alpha Delta. Judge Pro Tem, Beverly Hills Small Claims Court, 1968-1973. Consultant for the California Continuing Education of the Bar Publication, "Spousal and Child Support," 1974-1975 and "Domestic Relations Litigation," 1976. Judge Pro Tem: Beverly Hills, Los Angeles and Century City Small Claims Court, 1968—; Beverly Hills Municipal Court, 1974; Los Angeles Municipal Court, 1978-1979. *Member:* Beverly Hills (Member, Family Law Section), Century City (Member, Board of Governors, 1973-1976), Los Angeles County (Member, Executive Committee, Family Law Section, 1975-1982, 1985-1990; Co-Chairman, 1976-1978 and Chairman, 1990, Family Law Annual Symposium; Past Chairman, Executive Committee, Family Law Section, 1991-1992) and American Bar Associations; State Bar of California. (Certified Specialist, Family Law, The State Bar of California Board of Legal Specialization). *PRACTICE AREAS:* Family Law.

**MELVIN S. GOLDSMAN**, born Los Angeles, California, March 25, 1947; admitted to bar, 1975, California. *Education:* University of California at Santa Barbara and University of California at Los Angeles (B.A., 1969); Southwestern University (J.D., 1975). Editorial Assistant, Los Angeles County Bar Association Family Law Symposium, 1976 and 1977. Editor, Beverly Hills Bar Association, Family Law Symposium Book, "Tax Aspects of Dissolution, the Apportionment of Property on Dissolution and Avoiding Malpractice," 14th Annual Symposium. Contributing Author: "Selection, Preparation of, Preparation by and Protection of Expert Witnesses," Twelfth Annual Family Law Symposium, BHBA, Update of Law, 1989-

*(This Listing Continued)*

### FREID AND GOLDSMAN, A PROFESSIONAL LAW CORPORATION, Los Angeles—Continued

1990; "Recent Developments in Family Law" and "Executive Goodwill," LACBA, Family Law Symposium, 1987 and 1990; "Ninth Annual Update of Law," BHBA, 1989; "Tenth Annual Update of Law, BHBA, 1990. Continuing Education of the Bar, "Enforcement of Family Law Orders," 1991. *Member:* Beverly Hills (Member: Family Law Section; Family Law Executive Committee; Chairperson: Family Law Section, 1989-1990; Family Law Symposium, 1989) and Los Angeles County (Member, Family Law Section; Family Law Executive Committee); Bar Associations; State Bar of California. Fellow, American Academy of Matrimonial Lawyers. (Certified Specialist, Family Law, The State Bar of California Board of Legal Specialization). *PRACTICE AREAS:* Family Law.

**GARY J. COHEN,** born Los Angeles, California, October 31, 1949; admitted to bar, 1975, California and U.S. District Court, Central District of California. *Education:* University of California, Los Angeles (A.B., 1971; J.D., 1974). Author: "Jurisdiction in Family Law Matters," Family Law Reference Book, Los Angeles County Bar Association, Family Law Section, 1992. Co-Author: "Post Trial: Rights and Remedies," Symposium Syllabus 13th Annual Symposium, Beverly Hills Bar Association, Family Law Section, 1987. *Member:* Los Angeles County Bar Association; State Bar of California (Member, Family Law Section). *PRACTICE AREAS:* Family Law; Civil Appeals.

**MARCI R. LEVINE,** born Los Angeles, California, December 7, 1962; admitted to bar, 1990, California and U.S. District Court, Central District of California. *Education:* University of California, Los Angeles (B.A., 1986); Southwestern University (J.D., 1990). Recipient, Achievement Award in Writing, Southwestern University. *Member:* Beverly Hills and Los Angeles Bar Associations; State Bar of California. *PRACTICE AREAS:* Family Law.

**JOANNE D. RATINOFF,** born Los Angeles, California, January 7, 1953; admitted to bar, 1978, California; 1979, U.S. District Court, Central District of California; 1981, U.S. District Court, Southern District of California; 1982, U.S. District Court, Northern and Eastern Districts of California; 1990, U.S. Court of Appeals, Ninth Circuit. *Education:* University of California at Berkeley (B.A., 1974); Loyola Law School (J.D., 1978). *Member:* Beverly Hills and Los Angeles County Bar Associations; State Bar of California. *PRACTICE AREAS:* Family Law.

**HEATHER RICKETT GRAHAM,** born Castro Valley, California, December 17, 1965; admitted to bar, 1992, California. *Education:* University of California at Santa Barbara; University of California at Los Angeles (B.A., 1988); Loyola Law School (J.D., 1992). *Member:* Beverly Hills and Los Angeles Bar Associations; State Bar of California. *PRACTICE AREAS:* Family Law.

**LORI A. LOO,** born Burbank, California, June 19, 1964; admitted to bar, 1990, California. *Education:* University of California, at Berkeley (B.A., 1986); University of Southern California (J.D., 1990). *Member:* Beverly Hills, Los Angeles County and American (Family Law Section) Bar Associations; State Bar of California; Southern California Chinese Lawyers Association; Asian Business League. *PRACTICE AREAS:* Family Law.

---

**JANET KAPLAN,** born New York, N.Y., November 23, 1953; admitted to bar, 1994, California and U.S. District Court, Central District of California. *Education:* Cornell University (B.S., 1975); University of Pennsylvania (M.S.W., 1977); Loyola Law School (J.D., 1994). Phi Delta Phi. International Law Journal, Loyola Law School. Externship, Hon. Judge Michael Pirosh, Los Angeles Superior Court, Family Law Department, Spring, 1994. Licensed Clinical Social Worker, California, 1986—. *Member:* Beverly Hills and Los Angeles County Bar Associations; State Bar of California. *PRACTICE AREAS:* Family Law.

**REUEL M. BALUYOT,** born Real, Quezon, Philippines, May 2, 1968; admitted to bar, 1995, California. *Education:* University of the Philippines (B.A., 1987); Southwestern University School of Law (J.D., 1995). Extern, Honorable J. Earl Johnson, California Court of Appeal, District 2, Division 7. *Member:* Beverly Hills, Los Angeles County and American Bar Associations; State Bar of California. *LANGUAGES:* Tagalog. *PRACTICE AREAS:* Family Law.

### FREILICH, HORNBAKER & ROSEN, P.C.
*Established in 1962*

SUITE 1434, 10960 WILSHIRE BOULEVARD
**LOS ANGELES, CALIFORNIA 90024**
Telephone: 310-477-0578
Telex: 298725 Patl Ur
Telecopy: 310-473-9277

Patent, Trademark, Copyright, Unfair Competition and Antitrust Law. Trials in State and Federal Courts.

FIRM PROFILE: The following are the Firm's Reported Cases: R. Josephs Sportswear, Inc. v. Wright's Knitwear Corp., 28 USPQ2d 1799 (C.D. Calif. 1993); Levi Strauss & Co. v. R. Josephs Sportswear, Inc. 28 USPQ2d 1464 (TTAB 1993); DAK Industries v. Daiichi Kosho, 25 USPQ2d 1622 (TTAB 1993); Consumer Direct, Inc. v. McLaughlin, 20 USPQ2d 1949 (N.D. Ohio 1991); Hadady Corporation v. Dean Witter Reynolds, Inc., 739 F. Supp. 1392, 16 USPQ2d 1149 (C.D. Calif. 1990); Henkin v. Letro Products, Inc., 12 USPQ2d 1397 (C.D. Calif. 1989); Yamaha International Corporation v. Hoshino Gakki, Ltd., 840 F.2d 1572, 6 USPQ2d 1001 (CAFC 1988); Cels Enterprises Inc. v. California Ivy Inc., 2 USPQ2d 1440 (C.D. Calif. 1987); Yamaha International Corporation v. Hoshino Gakki Co., Ltd., 231 USPQ 926 (TTAB 1986); Classic Golf Co. v. Karsten Manufacturing Co., et. al., 231 USPQ 884 (N.D. Ill. 1986); McDonnell Douglas Corporation v. National Data Corporation, 228 USPQ 45 (TTAB 1985); Avakoff v. Southern Pacific Company, 765 F.2d 1097, 226 USPQ 435 (Fed. Cir. 1985); Information International v. Itek, 477 F. Supp. 1043, 206 USPQ 88 (D. Mass. 1979); Satco v. Transequip, 415 F. Supp. 221, 193 USPQ 208 (C.D. Calif. 1976), aff'd., 594 F.2d 1318, 202 USPQ 567 (9th Cir. 1979), cert. denied, 444 U.S. 865 (1979); Satco v. Transequip, 191 USPQ 253 (C.D. Calif. 1975); Sidewinder Marine v. Starbuck Kustom Boats, 481 F. Supp. 224, 193 USPQ 776 (D. Colo. 1976), aff'd., 597 F.2d 201, 202 USPQ 356 (10th Cir. 1979); Sidewinder Marine v. Burns, 176 USPQ 499 (C.D. Calif. 1972); Golomb v. Wadsworth, 592 F.2d 1184, 201 USPQ 200 (CCPA 1979); Rheodyne v. Ramin, 201 USPQ 667 (N.D. Calif. 1978); Mailand v. Burkle, 20 Cal. 3d 367, 143 Cal. Rptr. 1, 572 P.2d 1142 (1978); Mailand v. Powerine, 1973 Trade Cases, ¶74,472 (C.D. Calif. 1972); Yamaha v. Stevenson, 196 USPQ 701 (TTAB 1977); Electronic Memories v. Control Data 188 USPQ 449 (N.D. Ill. 1975); Hollowform v. Delma Aeh, 515 F.2d 1174, 185 USPQ 790 (CCPA 1975); Electronic Memories v. Control Data, 188 USPQ 448 (N.D. Ill. 1975); Electronic Memories v. Control Data 184 USPQ 18 (N.D. Ill. 1974); Burgess v. Klingensmith, 487 F.2d 321, 180 USPQ 115 and 547 (9th Cir. 1973); Paul Dodds v. Harry Liss, 383 F.2d 196, 155 USPQ 308 (9th Cir., 1967); Runge v. Lee, 161 USPQ 770 (C.D. Calif. 1969), aff'd., 441 F.2d 579, 169 USPQ 388 (9th Cir. 1971), cert. denied with dissenting opinion by Douglas, 404 U.S. 887, 171 USPQ 322 (1971).

**ARTHUR FREILICH,** born Brooklyn, New York, May 17, 1935; admitted to bar, 1962, California; 1982, U.S. Court of Appeals for the Federal Circuit; registered to practice before U.S. Patent and Trademark Office. *Education:* Rensselaer Polytechnic Institute (B.E.E., 1956); George Washington University (LL.B., 1960). Examiner, U.S. Patent & Trademark Office, 1956-1958. Member, Board of Governors, 1970-1978 and President, 1976-1977, Patent Law Association of Los Angeles. *Member:* State Bar of California; American Bar Association; American Intellectual Property Law Association; Los Angeles Intellectual Property Law Association. *PRACTICE AREAS:* Patent Law; Trademark Law; Licensing Law; Litigation; Technology Business Startups.

**ROBERT D. HORNBAKER,** born Mt. Sterling, Iowa, January 6, 1926; admitted to bar, 1949, Iowa; 1951, New York; 1957, California; 1967, U.S. Supreme Court; 1982, U.S. Court of Appeals for the Federal Circuit; registered to practice before U.S. Patent and Trademark Office. *Education:* Iowa State University (B.S.E.E., with highest scholastic record, 1946); University of Iowa (J.D., with distinction, 1949); Columbia University (LL.M., 1951). Phi Delta Phi; Phi Kappa Phi; Eta Kappa Nu; Pi Mu Epsilon. Cahill, Gordon & Reindel, New York City, 1950-1957. Assistant U.S. Attorney, Central District of California, 1958-1960. *Member:* Iowa State and American Bar Associations; State Bar of California; American Intellectual Property Law Association. [Retired Naval Officer]. *PRACTICE AREAS:* Litigation; Patent Law; Trademark Law; Unfair Competition Law.

**LEON D. ROSEN,** born Chicago, Illinois, April 3, 1937; admitted to bar, 1962, California and U.S. Court of Appeals for the Federal Circuit; registered to practice before U.S. Patent and Trademark Office. *Education:* University of Chicago (B.A., 1955); Illinois Institute of Technology (B.S.M.E., 1958); City College of the City University of New York (B.E.E., 1961); Columbia University (LL.B., 1961). Tau Beta Pi; Pi Tau Sigma; Mensa. *Member:* State Bar of California; American Intellectual Property

*(This Listing Continued)*

Law Association; Los Angeles Intellectual Property Law Association. ***PRACTICE AREAS:*** Patent Law; Trademark Law; Patent Applications; Licensing Law.

**TIMOTHY T. TYSON,** born Charleston, Illinois, March 6, 1943; admitted to bar, 1977, California and Illinois; 1978, U.S. District Court, Central District of California; 1982, U.S. Court of Appeals for the Federal Circuit; 1983, U.S. Court of Appeals, 9th Circuit; registered to practice before U.S. Patent and Trademark Office. *Education:* Vanderbilt University (B.A., 1965); Columbia University (M.B.A., 1967); Southwestern University (J.D., 1976). Mensa. *Member:* State Bar of California; Los Angeles Intellectual Property Law Association. ***PRACTICE AREAS:*** Patent, Trademark and Copyright Law; Trademark Law; Copyright Law; Litigation; Licensing Law.

**LAWRENCE S. COHEN,** born Boston, Massachusetts, April 21, 1939; admitted to bar, 1966, Massachusetts; 1975, Illinois; 1977, California; 1982, U.S. Court of Appeals for the Federal Circuit; 1990, U.S. District Court, Central District of California; registered to practice before the U.S. Patent and Trademark Office. *Education:* Northeastern University (B.S.M.E.-/E.E., 1962); Boston University Law School (J.D., 1965). Managing Editor, Boston University Law Review, 1964-1965; Northeastern University, High Polymor Chemistry and Computer Science, 1972. Author: "Fourth Amendment," Boston University Law Review, 1963. Patent and Licensing Counsel TRW, Inc., 1973-1984. General Counsel, Magnavox Advanced Products and Systems Co., 1984-1989. *Member:* State Bar of California; Illinois State, Massachusetts and American Bar Associations; American Intellectual Property Law Association; Los Angeles Intellectual Property Law Association; Licensing Executives Society. [U.S. Army Intelligence Officer, 1966-1968]. ***PRACTICE AREAS:*** Patent, Trademark and Copyright Law; Unfair Competition Law; Litigation; Licensing Law; Technology Transfer.

**LEE JAY MANDELL,** born September, 18, 1948; admitted to bar, 1991, California and U.S. District Court, Central District of California; registered to practice before U.S. Patent and Trademark Office. *Education:* Rensselaer Polytechnic Institute (B.S.E.E., 1970; M.E.E.E., 1971); Southwestern University School of Law (J.D., 1991). *Member:* State Bar of California; American Bar Association; Los Angeles Intellectual Property Law Association. ***PRACTICE AREAS:*** Patent; Patent Applications.

REFERENCE: Bank of America (Wilshire-Westwood Branch).

## *FREILICH, KAUFMAN, FOX & SOHAGI*

*Established in 1988*

*WILSHIRE LANDMARK*
*SUITE 1230, 11755 WILSHIRE BOULEVARD*
**LOS ANGELES, CALIFORNIA 90025-1518**
*Telephone: 310-444-7805*
*Facsimile: 310-477-7663*

Kansas City, Missouri Office: Freilich, Leitner & Carlisle, 1000 Plaza West, 4600 Madison. Telephone: 816-561-4414. Facsimile: 816-561-7931.

Land Use, Zoning, Environmental, Municipal Finance, State and Local Government Law, Civil Litigation.

### MEMBERS OF FIRM

**BENJAMIN KAUFMAN,** born Pittsburgh, Pennsylvania, October 25, 1955; admitted to bar, 1984, California, U.S. Court of Appeals, Ninth Circuit and U.S. District Court, Central, Eastern, Northern and Southern Districts of California. *Education:* Cornell University (B.S., 1980); University of Southern California (J.D., 1984). Recipient, Edward and Elinor Shattuck Award, 1984. Editor-in-Chief, University of Southern California Journal of Law and the Environment, 1983-1984. Executive Editor of Articles, Computer/Law Journal, 1983-1984. Chairman of Planning Committee, 3rd Annual University of Southern California Environmental Law Symposium, 1983-1984. *Member:* Beverly Hills, Los Angeles County and American Bar Associations; State Bar of California. ***REPORTED CASES:*** Ehrlich v. City of Culver City (1996); Hensler v. City of Glendale (1994) 8 Cal 4th 1, Cert. denied (1995) 115 5 Ct. 1176; Rogers v. Superior Court (City of Burbank) (1993) 19 Cal.App.4th 469; 3570 East Foothill Blvd. v. City of Pasadena (C.D. Calif., 1995) 912 F.Supp. 1257; Tensor Group, Ltd. v. City of Glendale (1993) 14 Cal.App.4th 154; El Dorado Palm Springs, Ltd. v. Rent Review Commission of the City of Palm Springs (1991) 230 Cal.App.3d 355; AIU v. Superior Court (1990) 51 Cal.3d 807.

**DEBORAH J. FOX,** born Kansas City, Missouri, February 2, 1958; admitted to bar, 1983, California; 1986, U.S. District Court, Central, Eastern and Southern Districts of California. *Education:* University of Michigan

*(This Listing Continued)*

(B.A., 1980); University of San Diego (J.D., 1983). *Member:* Los Angeles County (Member, Condemnation and Land Valuation Litigation Committee) and American Bar Associations; State Bar of California. ***REPORTED CASES:*** Santa Fe Realty Corp. v. City of Westminster (C.D. Cal. 1995) 906 F.Supp. 1341; Eldorado Drive v. City of Mesquite (D. Nev. 1994) 863 F.Supp. 1252.

**MARGARET MOORE SOHAGI,** born Palo Alto, California, January 24, 1955; admitted to bar, 1986, California and U.S. District Court, Central and Southern Districts of California; 1987, U.S. Court of Appeals, Ninth Circuit. *Education:* University of California at Los Angeles (B.A., 1977); Loyola Marymount University (J.D., 1986). Co-editor: Continuing Education of The Law; Land Use Forum. *Member:* Los Angeles County Bar Association; State Bar of California.

### ASSOCIATE

**DAWN R. ANDREWS,** born Detroit, Michigan, December 20, 1966; admitted to bar, 1992, California. *Education:* University of Maryland (B.S., 1988); University of California (J.D., 1992). Chair, Moot Court Board. Member, Women's Caucus Admissions Committee. Staff Editor, "Environs." Environmental Law and Policy Journal. *Member:* Los Angeles County and American Bar Associations; The State Bar of California; California Women Lawyers.

### OF COUNSEL

**TERRY P. KAUFMANN MACIAS,** born Los Angeles, California, March 9, 1952; admitted to bar, 1988, California; 1991, U.S. District Court, Central District of California; 1993, U.S. Court of Appeals, Ninth Circuit. *Education:* University of California at Los Angeles (B.A., 1973); California State University at Northridge (1979-1984); Loyola Law School, Los Angeles (J.D., 1988). *Member:* State Bar of California.

REPRESENTATIVE CLIENTS: City of Arcadia, California; Arcadia Redevelopment Agency; City of Bakersfield, California; City of Burbank, California; Burbank Redevelopment Agency; City of Glendale, California; City of Culver City, California; City of Indian Wells, California; City of Long Beach, California; City of Oxnard, California; City of Palo Alto, California; City of Rohnert Park, California; City of Simi Valley, California; City of Stanton, California; City of Pasadena, California; City of Rialto, California; County of San Bernardino, California; City of Mesquite, Nevada; City of Westminster, California.

(For Biographical data on all Personnel, see Professional Biographies at Kansas City, Missouri)

## *FRESHMAN, MARANTZ, ORLANSKI,*
## *COOPER & KLEIN*

*A LAW CORPORATION*

**LOS ANGELES, CALIFORNIA**

(See Beverly Hills)

*General Civil Trial and Appellate Practice. Banking, Corporate, Securities, Commercial, Employment, Real Estate, Real Estate Lending, Sports Law, Taxation and Creditors Rights.*

## *FRIED, BIRD & CRUMPACKER*

*A PROFESSIONAL CORPORATION*

*10100 SANTA MONICA BOULEVARD, SUITE 300*
**LOS ANGELES, CALIFORNIA 90067-6031**
*Telephone: 310-551-7400*
*Facsimile: 310-556-4487*

*Banking, Corporate, Securities, Real Estate, General Civil Litigation and Trial Practice in all State and Federal Courts, Insurance, Bankruptcy and Creditors Rights.*

**JACK FRIED,** born Rome, Italy, February 3, 1949; admitted to bar, 1974, California and U.S. District Court, Central District of California. *Education:* University of California at Los Angeles (A.B., magna cum laude, 1971; J.D., 1974). Phi Beta Kappa; Pi Gamma Mu; Omicron Delta Epsilon. Counsel, California State Banking Department, 1974-1976. *Member:* Los Angeles County and American (Member, Corporation, Banking and Business Law) Bar Associations; State Bar of California; California Bankers Association; Community Bankers of Southern California; Western Independent Bankers. ***PRACTICE AREAS:*** Financial Institutions Law - General Corporate and Regulatory Representation; Mergers and Acquisitions; Bank Applications and Organizations; Corporate Securities.

*(This Listing Continued)*

CAA673B

## FRIED, BIRD & CRUMPACKER, A PROFESSIONAL CORPORATION, Los Angeles—Continued

**BRIAN JAMES BIRD,** born London, England, October 7, 1949; admitted to bar, 1978, California. *Education:* Yale University (B.A., 1971); Loyola University of Los Angeles (J.D., cum laude, 1978). Member, Loyola of Los Angeles Law Review, 1977-1978. *Member:* Los Angeles County and American (Member, Section on Litigation) Bar Associations; State Bar of California; Community Bankers of Southern California; California Bankers Association. *PRACTICE AREAS:* Business Litigation - General Civil and Trial Practice in all State and Federal Courts; Lender Liability; Insurance Coverage; Securities; Bankruptcy; Real Estate; Creditors Rights.

**DAVID W. CRUMPACKER, JR.,** born Woodland, California, November 16, 1955; admitted to bar, 1981, California and U.S. District Court, Central District of California. *Education:* University of Colorado at Boulder (B.A., with distinction, 1978); George Washington University (J.D., with honors, 1981). Phi Beta Kappa. *Member:* Los Angeles County (Member, Real Estate Subsection) and American Bar Associations; State Bar of California (Member, Real Estate Subsection); Building Owners and Managers Association of Greater Los Angeles (Member, BOMA Codes Committee); Community Bankers of Southern California; California Bankers Association. *PRACTICE AREAS:* Real Estate - Leasing and Lease Enforcement; Acquisitions and Dispositions of Real Property; Construction Law; Loan Workout and Debt Restructuring; Real Estate Lending; Partnerships and Joint Ventures; Land Title Insurance.

**NIKKI WOLONTIS,** born Morristown, New Jersey, April 27, 1953; admitted to bar, 1978, California. *Education:* New York University (B.A., magna cum laude, 1974); Stanford University (J.D., 1978). Phi Beta Kappa. Founding Member, Stanford Public Interest Law Foundation. *Member:* Los Angeles County and American Bar Associations; State Bar of California; California Bankers Association; Community Bankers of Southern California. *PRACTICE AREAS:* Financial Institutions Law - General Corporate and Regulatory Representation; Mergers and Acquisitions; Bank Applications and Organizations; Corporate Securities.

**DAVID M. SCHACHTER,** born Brooklyn, New York, October 18, 1959; admitted to bar, 1985, California. *Education:* University of California at San Diego (B.A., cum laude, 1981); University of San Diego (M.B.A., 1985; J.D., cum laude, 1985). Member, San Diego Law Review, 1982-1985. *Member:* State Bar of California; American Bar Association; Western Independent Bankers; Community Bankers of Southern California; California Bankers Association. *PRACTICE AREAS:* Financial Institutions Law - Corporate Securities; General Corporate and Regulatory Representation; Mergers and Acquisitions; Bank Applications and Organizations.

---

**DAVID K. JOHNSON,** born Escondido, California, December 22, 1960; admitted to bar, 1986, California. *Education:* University of California at Los Angeles (B.A., 1983); University of San Diego (J.D., 1986). Recipient, American Jurisprudence Award in Civil Procedure. *Member:* Los Angeles County Bar Association; State Bar of California; Community Bankers of Southern California; California Bankers Association. *PRACTICE AREAS:* Business Litigation - General Civil and Trial Practice in all State and Federal Courts; Lender Liability; Insurance Coverage; Securities; Bankruptcy; Real Estate; Creditors Rights.

REPRESENTATIVE CLIENTS: Banks: Antelope Valley Bank; Bay Cities National Bank; Business Bank of California; Cathay Bank; The Bank of Hollywood; Mid-State Bank; Montecito Bancorp; North County Bank; Bank of the Sierra; Six Rivers National Bank; South Bay Bank; Valencia National Bank; Wilshire State Bank. Real Estate: Dean Witter Realty, Inc.; Connecticut General Life Insurance Company; John Hancock Mutual Life Insurance Company; TA Associates Realty; Equitable Real Estate; National Bank of Canada. Insurance Companies: First State Insurance Co.; New England Insurance Co.
REFERENCES: The Bank of Hollywood; Business Bank of California; North County Bank; South Bay Bank; Valencia National Bank.

## FRIED, FRANK, HARRIS, SHRIVER & JACOBSON

A Partnership including Professional Corporations
**350 SOUTH GRAND AVENUE
THIRTY-SECOND FLOOR
LOS ANGELES, CALIFORNIA 90071**
Telephone: 213-473-2000
Telecopier: 213-473-2222
Email: postmaster@ffhsj.com

*New York, New York Office:* One New York Plaza. Telephone: 212-859-8000. Cable Address: "Steric New York." W.U. Int. Telex: 620223. W.U. Int. Telex: 662119. W.U. Domestic: 128173. Telecopier: 212-859-4000 (Dex) 6200).
*Washington, D.C. Office:* Suite 800, 1001 Pennsylvania Avenue, N.W. Telephone: 202-639-7000.
*London, England Office:* 4 Chiswell Street, London EC1Y 4UP. Telephone: 011-44-171-972-9600. Fax: 011-44-171-972-9602.
*Paris, France Office:* 7, Rue Royale, 75008. Telephone: (+331) 40 17 04 04. Fax (+331) 40 17 08 30.

*General Practice.*

### RESIDENT PARTNERS

**DEBRA J. ALBIN-RILEY,** born Culver City, California, February 26, 1959; admitted to bar, 1983, California. *Education:* University of California at Los Angeles (B.A., cum laude, 1980); University of Southern California (J.D., 1983). *Member:* Los Angeles County (Member, Litigation and Intellectual Property Sections) and American (Member, Litigation Section and Forum on Franchising) Bar Associations; The State Bar of California. *LANGUAGES:* French. *PRACTICE AREAS:* Business Torts; Intellectual Property; Entertainment and Franchise Litigation. *Email:* albinde@ffhsj.com

**STEPHEN D. ALEXANDER,** born St. Paul, Minnesota, February 8, 1949; admitted to bar, 1976, New York; 1989, California. *Education:* Macalester College (B.A., cum laude, 1971); University of Minnesota (J.D., cum laude, 1975). *Member:* The Association of the Bar of the City of New York; Beverly Hills, Los Angeles County, New York State, Federal and American Bar Associations; State Bar of California. *Email:* alexast@ffhsj.com

**JOHN W. CHIERICHELLA,** born New York, N.Y., March 26, 1947; admitted to bar, 1973, New York; 1975, District of Columbia; 1976, U.S. District Court, District of Columbia; 1976, U.S. Claims Court; 1980, U.S. Supreme Court; 1997, California. *Education:* Cornell University (A.B., 1969); Columbia University (J.D., 1972). Phi Eta Sigma. James Kent Scholar; Harlan Fiske Stone Scholar. Member, Columbia University Law Review, 1971-1972. Attorney Advisor to the Secretary, U.S. Air Force General Counsel's Office, 1973-1975. Member, Board of Governors, Board of Contract Appeals Bar Association, 1993. Member, Advisory Board, Federal Contracts Report, 1987-1993. Member, Advisory Board, The Government Contractor, 1993—; Commentator to the Criminal Division Chapter of Prentice Hall's Annotated Edition of Department of Justice Manual. Author: The Buy American Act and the Use of Foreign Sources in Federal Procurements--An Issues Analysis," 9 *Public Contract Law Journal* 73 (December 1977); "New Interim DoD Rules Ease Security-Related Restrictions on Foreign Ownership of U.S Contractors," *Contract Management* (December 1983) (Co-author with Lisa A. Everhart; "Financing Government Contracts," *The Government Contractor Briefing Papers,* No. 86-7 (1986) (Co-author with Lisa A. Everhart, Jeffrey M. Villet and Dale H. Oliver); "Antitrust Considerations Affecting Teaming Agreements," 57 *Antitrust Law Journal* 555 (1988); "Foreign Investment in Defense-Related Companies," 51 *Federal Contracts Report* 837 (BNA, May 8, 1989), reprinted in *Foreign Investments in the U.S. News & Analysis* (London, June 1989) (Co-author with Douglas E. Perry); "IR&D vs. Contract Effort," *Government Contract Cost, Pricing & Accounting Report,* Issue 90-2 (February 1990); "Foreign Selling Costs Under the Cost Principles," *Government Contract Cost, Pricing & Accounting Report,* Issue 90-12 (December 1990) (Co-author with Rosemary Maxwell); "Negotiated Teaming Agreements," *Acquisition Issues,* Volume 1 (June 1991) (Co-author with Douglas E. Perry); "Improving Business Opportunities Through Teaming," *Federal Acquisition Report,* Volume VIII, No. 4 (April 1991) (Co-author with Douglas E. Perry); "Comparative Bid Protest Procedures in International Contracting," *International Quarterly,* Vol. 4, No. 4 (October 1992) (Co-author with Rosemary Maxwell); "Government Procurement Under the North American Free Trade Agreement," 58 *Federal Contracts Report* (BNA, October 26, 1992) (Co-author with

*(This Listing Continued)*

Rosemary Maxwell); "IR&D Redux," *Government Contract Cost, Pricing & Accounting Report,* Issue 93-2 (February 1993) (Co-author with Lynda T. O'Sullivan and Douglas E. Perry); "Mergers and Acquisitions of Government Contractors: Special Considerations and Due Diligence Concerns," *American Bar Association Public Contract Law Journal,* Vol. 23, No. 4, 1994 (Co-author with Douglas E. Perry); "Complying With the New Limits on Personal Compensation Under FY 1995 DOD Contracts," *Government Contract Costs, Pricing & Accounting Report,* Issue 95-1, Jan. 1995 (Co-Author with James M. Weitzel, Jr.). *Member:* American Bar Association; National Contract Management Association. (Also at Washington, D.C. Office). **PRACTICE AREAS:** Government Contracts; Litigation.

**BARBARA A. REEVES,** born Buffalo, New York, March 29, 1949; admitted to bar, 1973, California; 1977, District of Columbia. *Education:* Wellesley College; New College (B.A., 1970); Harvard Law School (J.D., cum laude, 1973). Editor, Harvard Journal on Legislation, 1972-1973. Lecturer on Antitrust Law for Practising Law Institute, California Continuing Legal Education of the Bar and National Judicial College, 1979—. Law Clerk to Judge Alfred T. Goodwin, U.S. Court of Appeals, Ninth Circuit, 1973-1974. Chief, Los Angeles Field Office, 1978-1981, Antitrust Division, U.S. Department of Justice. Chairman, Antitrust Section, 1980-1981, Los Angeles County Bar Association. Trustee, Los Angeles County Bar Association, 1990-1992. Member, Executive Committee, Litigation Section, Los Angeles County Bar Association, 1983-1992; Officer, 1988-1992; Member and Committee Officer, Antitrust Section and Litigation Section, American Bar Association, 1978—. Delegate, Ninth Circuit Judicial Conference, 1986-1990. Member, Board of Directors, Public Counsel, 1988-1992. Member, Board of Directors, Western Center on Law in Poverty. Member, Board of Directors, Los Angeles County Bar Foundation, 1991—. *Email:* reevba@ffhsj.com

**DAVID K. ROBBINS,** born Miami, Florida, April 5, 1957; admitted to bar, 1983, Florida and New York; 1990, California. *Education:* Vassar College (A.B., cum laude, 1978); University of Miami (J.D., cum laude, 1982); New York University (LL.M., Taxation, 1986). *Member:* State Bar of California; The Florida Bar; New York State Bar Association. *Email:* robbida@ffhsj.com

**EDWARD S. ROSENTHAL,** born Washington, D.C., November 1, 1954; admitted to bar, 1981, New York; 1988, California. *Education:* Carleton College (B.A., cum laude, 1976); Columbia University (J.D., 1979). Co-Author: "The Remedial Process in Institutional Reform Litigation," Columbia Law Review, 1978. Law Clerk to Chief Judge Daniel M. Friedman, U.S. Court of Claims, 1979-1980. *Member:* State Bar of California; American Bar Association (Member, Section on Corporation, Banking and Business Law). *Email:* rosened@ffhsj.com

**LOUIS D. VICTORINO,** born Lemoore, California, May 27, 1945; admitted to bar, 1971, California; 1978, District of Columbia. *Education:* Stanford University (B.A., 1967); University of California at Los Angeles (J.D., 1970). Member, Board of Editors, UCLA Law Review, 1969-1970. Author: "Government Failure to Disclose," Government Contract Briefing Papers, No. 92-10, Sept. 1992; "Anti-trust Implications of Defense Industry Combinations," Government Contract Briefing Papers, No. 93-7, June 1993; Multiple Award Task & Delivery Order Contracts, Government Contract Briefing Papers, No. 96-10, Sept. 1996. Member, Legal Remedies Staff, Commission on Government Procurement 1971. Member: Advisory Board, *The Government Contractor,* 1991—; Board of Editors, The Public Contract Law Journal, 1991-1995. *Member:* Federal and American (Member, Public Contract Law Section, 1971—) Bar Associations. (Also at Washington, D.C. Office). *Email:* victolo@ffhsj.com

## RESIDENT ASSOCIATES

**JOEY L. BLANCH,** born Chicago, Illinois, April 3, 1972; admitted to bar, 1996, California. *Education:* Utah State University (B.A., 1993); Harvard University (J.D., 1996). Phi Beta Kappa; Pi Sigma Alpha; Mortar Board. National Merit Scholar. *Email:* blancjo@ffhsj.com

**DAVID R. BOYKO,** born Los Angeles, California, August 27, 1962; admitted to bar, 1995, California. *Education:* Cornell University (B.S.M.E., with distinction, 1984); University of Southern California (M.A., with honors, 1988) University of California at Los Angeles (J.D., 1995). Best Oral Advocate, UCLA Moot Court Honors Program. Recipient, American Jurisprudence Award in Moot Court. Chief Articles Editor, UCLA Pacific Basin Law Journal, 1994-1995. Co-Author: *Unilateral Refusal to License Intellectual Property Rights,* Practicing Law Institute Intellectual Property Antitrust Seminar, July 1996 (with Barbara A. Reeves and Neil Arney); *Seventh Circuit Ruling Mitigates Impact of Kodak, Declines to Find Bundled Products Define Own Market,* Corporate Counsel Weekly, BNA, April 24, 1996 (with Barbara A. Reeves); *Vertical Restrictions,* Practicing Law Institute Advanced Antitrust Seminar, January 1996 (with Barbara A. Reeves, Neil Arney and Donald Baker); *Individual Liability for a Corporation's Environmental Contamination,* Continuing Education of the Bar Program on Hazardous Wastes, September 1994 (with Janice Kamenir-Reznik) *Member:* Los Angeles County and American Bar Associations. [Capt. USAF, 1984-1992] *Email:* boykoda@ffhsj.com

**BRIAN I-AN CHENG,** born Ann Arbor, Michigan, August 13, 1970; admitted to bar, 1996, California and U.S. District Court, Central District of California. *Education:* University of California at Berkeley (B.A., 1993); Harvard Law School (J.D., 1996). Phi Beta Kappa. **LANGUAGES:** Mandarin Chinese. *Email:* chengbr@ffhsj.com

**LAUREN R. FIRESTONE,** born Lancaster, California, April 1, 1959; admitted to bar, 1988, New York; 1993, California. *Education:* Beloit College (B.S., 1980); Rutgers University, Newark (J.D., 1986). *Member:* Los Angeles County, New York State and American Bar Associations; State Bar of California; Women Lawyers Association of Los Angeles. *Email:* firesla@ffhsj.com

**DON A. HERNANDEZ,** born Wichita, Kansas, October 9, 1961; admitted to bar, 1986, California. *Education:* Harvard University (A.B., cum laude, 1983); Stanford University (J.D., 1986). R. Hunter Sumner Trial Advocacy Award. Moot Court Board. Member, Board of Directors, Los Angeles Center for Law and Justice, 1993—. *Member:* Los Angeles County (Litigation Section) and American (Litigation Section) Bar Associations; State Bar of California. *Email:* hernado@ffhsj.com

**JODY RENE KATZ,** born Los Angeles, California, May 22, 1971; admitted to bar, 1996, California. *Education:* University of California at Berkeley (B.A., 1993); University of Southern California (J.D., 1996). *Email:* katzjo@ffhsj.com

**RAY LA SOYA,** born Los Angeles, California, June 2, 1964; admitted to bar, 1992, California and U.S. District Court, Central, Northern and Southern Districts of California. *Education:* Whittier College (B.A., with honors, 1985); Yale Law School (J.D., 1991). Editor, Yale Journal on Regulation, 1989-1991. *Email:* lasoyra@ffhsj.com

**MARIBEL S. MEDINA,** born Michoacan, Mexico, September 1, 1968; admitted to bar, 1996, New York and U.S. District Court, Southern and Eastern Districts of New York (Not admitted in California). *Education:* University of California, Berkley (B.A., 1991); Harvard University (M.P.A., 1994); Boalt Hall School of Law, University of California (J.D., 1995). *Member:* New York State and American Bar Associations; New York County Lawyers Association; National Hispanic Bar Association. *Email:* medinma@ffhsj.com

**DARREL C. MENTHE,** born Hartford, Connecticut, December 5, 1971; admitted to bar, 1996, California. *Education:* University of California, San Diego (B.A., magna cum laude, 1993); Stanford Law School (J.D., 1996). Phi Beta Kappa. Senior Submissions Editor, Stanford Journal of International Law. **LANGUAGES:** Russian, German, Spanish. *Email:* menthda@ffhsj.com

**MALENA R. NEAL,** born Detroit, Michigan, July 13, 1966; admitted to bar, 1991, California. *Education:* Howard University (B.A., 1988; J.D., cum laude, 1991). Member, Howard Law Journal. Recipient: Dean's Award, Government Regulation of Business; American Jurisprudence Awards for Criminal Law and Environmental Law. Merit Scholarship, 1988, 1989, 1990; Earl Warren Legal Training Fellow; Alcoa Foundation Scholarship. Law Clerk to Hon. Consuelo B. Marshall, U.S. District Court, Central District of California, 1992-1993. *Member:* Los Angeles County and American Bar Associations; State Bar of California; Black Women Lawyers.

**WILLIAM A. MOLINSKI,** born Bloomfield, New Jersey, June 15, 1964; admitted to bar, 1989, California; U.S. District Court, Central District of California. *Education:* University of Southern California (A.B., 1986; J.D., with honors, 1989). Member, Moot Court Honors Program. Co-Author: "Competition for Professional Services Contracts," Government Contracting Briefing Papers, No. 94-10 (Sept. 1994). *Member:* Los Angeles County and American (Member, Sections on: Litigation; Intellectual Property; Public Contract Law) Bar Associations; State Bar of California. *Email:* molinwi@ffhsj.com

**KAREN B. SETO,** born New York, N.Y., February 26, 1965; admitted to bar, 1994, California. *Education:* Wharton School, University of Pennsylvania (B.S.Econ., cum laude, 1987); University of California, Los Angeles (J.D., 1994).

**STACY J. WEINSTEIN,** born Bellflower, California, December 5, 1969; admitted to bar, 1994, California. *Education:* University of California at Berkeley (B.A., highest honors, 1991); University of California at Los

*(This Listing Continued)*

CALIFORNIA—LOS ANGELES

**FRIED, FRANK, HARRIS, SHRIVER & JACOBSON,** Los Angeles—Continued

Angeles (J.D., 1994). Phi Beta Kappa. *Member:* Los Angeles County Bar Association; State Bar of California; Women Lawyers Association of Los Angeles. *Email:* weinsst@ffhsj.com

(For Biographical Data of New York, New York, Personnel, see Professional Biographies at New York, New York).
(For Biographical Data of Washington, D.C. Personnel, see Professional Biographies at Washington, D.C.).
(For Biographical Data of London Personnel, see Professional Biographies at London, England).
(For Biographical Data of Paris Personnel, see Professional Biographies at Paris, France).

---

## FRIEDLANDER & WERLIN LLP

11611 SAN VICENTE BOULEVARD, SUITE 615
**LOS ANGELES, CALIFORNIA 90049**
Telephone: 310-820-4778
Fax: 310-820-6588

*Civil Litigation, Business and Commercial Litigation and Transactions, Immigration, Tax, International Business.*

### MEMBERS OF FIRM

**MICHAEL I. FRIEDLANDER,** born Johannesburg, South Africa, August 10, 1948; admitted to bar, 1972, South Africa; 1979, California and U.S. District Court, Central District of California. *Education:* Witwatersrand University (B.A., 1968; LL.B., 1971). *Member:* Beverly Hills, Los Angeles County (Member, Sections on: Business Law; Immigration) and American (Member, International Law and Practice Section) Bar Associations; State Bar of California. *PRACTICE AREAS:* International Business and Licensing Transactions; General Corporate; Business; Commercial Transactions; Business Immigration Matters. *Email:* MFriedlander@aol.com

**LESLIE M. WERLIN,** born Albany, New York, May 12, 1950; admitted to bar, 1975, California and U.S. District Court, Central District of California; 1979, U.S. Court of Appeals, Ninth Circuit. *Education:* University of California at Los Angeles (B.A., 1972; J.D., 1975). Order of the Coif. Member, University of California at Los Angeles Law Review, 1974-1975. Co-Author: "Forum Selection Covenants In American Practice: Bremen in Perspective," Case Western Reserve Journal of International Law, Vol. 11, No. 3, 1979. Law Clerk to Honorable Robert I. Kelleher, U.S. District Judge, Central District of California, 1975-1976. *Member:* Los Angeles County Bar Association; State Bar of California. *PRACTICE AREAS:* Business and Commercial Litigation. *Email:* LWerlin@aol.com

### ASSOCIATES

**LLOYD K. CHAPMAN,** born Livermore, California, February 4, 1960; admitted to bar, 1986, California, U.S. Court of Appeals, Ninth Circuit and U.S. District Court, Central, Southern, Eastern and Northern Districts of California. *Education:* University of California at Los Angeles (B.A., Business/Economics, 1982); University of California at Davis (J.D., 1985). Member: Order of Omega; Moot Court Competition; Moot Court Board; Environmental Law Society. Staff Writer, "Environs", 1983-1984. Co-Author, "Appraiser's Liability for False or Negligently Prepared Appraisal," Appraisal and Mortgage Underwriting Review Journal, Winter 1990. Author, "Potential Tort Liability of an Independent Contractor's Employer," San Fernando Valley Bar Bulletin, May, 1989. Settlement Officer, Los Angeles Superior Court, North Valley Branch. *Member:* Los Angeles County Bar Association (Member: Federal Courts Committee, 1989—; Litigation Section); State Bar of California. *PRACTICE AREAS:* Business and Commercial Litigation; Real Estate Litigation.

**TRACY L. SNEED,** born Honolulu, Hawaii, November 19, 1968; admitted to bar, 1993, Texas; 1994, California. *Education:* University of Virginia (B.A., 1990); University of Texas (J.D., 1993). *PRACTICE AREAS:* Business Transactions.

**VALERIE M. RIERDAN,** born Los Angeles, California, October 19, 1969; admitted to bar, 1995, California. *Education:* Pepperdine University (B.A., 1991; J.D., cum laude, 1995). *Member:* Beverly Hills Bar Association. *PRACTICE AREAS:* Business Transactions.

**PETER K. ZWEIGHAFT,** born Buffalo, New York, July 24, 1970; admitted to bar, 1996, Florida and California. *Education:* Skidmore College (B.A., 1992); University of Miami (J.D., cum laude, 1995). Member, University of Miami Law Review, 1993-1995. *PRACTICE AREAS:* Business Litigation; Commercial Litigation. *Email:* PZweighaft@aol.com

### OF COUNSEL

**JEANINE JACOBS GOLDBERG,** born Philadelphia, Pennsylvania, September 27, 1939; admitted to bar, 1963, Pennsylvania; 1964, District of Columbia; 1966, U.S. Court of Claims; 1967, U.S. Supreme Court; 1970, Connecticut; 1976, Massachusetts; 1978, U.S. Tax Court; 1980, California; 1983, U.S. District Court, Central District of California. *Education:* University of Pennsylvania (B.S., summa cum laude, 1960); Harvard University (LL.B., 1963). Kappa Beta Pi. Secretary-Treasurer of Board, 1988-1989; President of Board, 1989-1990, Beverly Hills Estate Counselors Forum. *Member:* Los Angeles County, Beverly Hills and Century City Bar Associations; State Bar of California (Member, Sections on: Taxation; Estate Planning, Trust and Probate); District of Columbia Bar; National Association of Women Lawyers (Life Member); Women Lawyers Association of Los Angeles; Women Lawyers Association of California. *PRACTICE AREAS:* Tax; Tax Controversy; Estate Planning; Corporate; ERISA; Probate. *Email:* JJGLC@aol.com

REPRESENTATIVE CLIENTS: Breath Asure, Inc.; Breath Asure TV, Inc.; MBNA America Bank; Far East National Bank; Raceco International; Raceco - HSMV Limited Partnership; Metrolight Studios, Inc.; Blue Pacific Flavors and Fragrances, Inc.; The Air Freight Masters (Hong Kong); Air China Cargo; Cross Creek Homeowners Association; Northridge Gardens Homeowners Association; Teacher's PET; Mad Dogg Athletics, Inc.; Wilkes and Associates, Inc.; Teck Medical Purchasing, Inc.; Evriholder Products, Inc.; Imperial Bank; North American Honda.

---

## MICHAEL N. FRIEDMAN

1901 AVENUE OF THE STARS, SUITE 1901
**LOS ANGELES, CALIFORNIA 90067-6020**
Telephone: 310-552-3336
Fax: 310-552-1850

*Toxic Torts and Long-Term Disability Claims for Chemical Injuries.*

**MICHAEL N. FRIEDMAN,** born Chicago, Illinois, April 11, 1959; admitted to bar, 1985, California and U.S. District Court, Southern District of California; 1986, U.S. District Court, Central District of California; 1995, U.S. District Court, Northern District of California; 1996, U.S. Supreme Court. *Education:* University of California at Los Angeles (B.A., 1981); University of Southern California (J.D., 1984). Member, Hale Moot Court Honors Program, Honors Brief, 1983. Editor, Hale Moot Court Honors Program, 1984. *Member:* State Bar of California; Chemical Injury Information Network. *PRACTICE AREAS:* Toxic Exposure Tort Law; ERISA; Land Use Law; Appellate Law; Family Law.

---

## ROBERT P. FRIEDMAN

827 MORAGA DRIVE (BEL AIR)
**LOS ANGELES, CALIFORNIA 90049**
Telephone: 310-471-3413
Facsimile: 310-472-7014

*Real Estate, Corporate and Business Law and Civil Litigation.*

**ROBERT P. FRIEDMAN,** born Los Angeles, California, September 21, 1952; admitted to bar, 1978, California. *Education:* University of California at Berkeley (A.B., with honors, 1975); Georgetown University (J.D., cum laude, 1978). *Member:* Board of Directors, Public Counsel, 1983-1986; Board of Editors, Shopping Center Legal Update, 1983-1988; Board of Editors, Commercial Leasing Law and Strategy, 1988—. *Member:* Century City, Beverly Hills, Los Angeles County and American Bar Associations; State Bar of California. (Also Of Counsel to Peter J. McNulty).

---

## LAW OFFICES OF MICHAEL FRIEDMAN

**LOS ANGELES, CALIFORNIA**

(See Torrance)

*Family Law, Criminal Law, Probate, Personal Injury, Juvenile Law and General Practice.*

## FRYE, ALBERTS & MALCHOW

*Established in 1991*

**1901 AVENUE OF THE STARS, SUITE 390**
**LOS ANGELES, CALIFORNIA 90067**
*Telephone: 310-553-7733*
*FAX: 310-553-7730*

*San Francisco, California Office:* 225 Bush Street, 16th Floor. Telephone: 415-439-8315. Facsimile: 415-439-8317.

*Civil Litigation in all State and Federal Trial and Appellate Courts, including General Commercial and Business, Property, Casualty, Life, Health, Fidelity and Surety Insurance, Bad Faith, ERISA, Employment, Construction, Franchise and Unfair Trade Practices.*

**JOHN N. FRYE,** born Tacoma, Washington, December 8, 1944; admitted to bar, 1970, California; 1973, U.S. District Court, Northern District of California; 1982, U.S. District Court, Eastern District of California; 1983, U.S. Court of Appeals, Ninth Circuit and U.S. Claims Court; 1985, U.S. District Court, Central and Southern Districts of California. *Education:* University of California at Davis (B.A., 1966); Hastings College of Law, University of California (J.D., 1969). *Member:* State Bar of California; Association of Defense Counsel; Defense Research Institute. *PRACTICE AREAS:* Litigation; General Commercial; Business Disputes; Insurance Law; Property and Casualty Insurance; Bad Faith; Employment; Construction; Administrative Matters.

**RONALD K. ALBERTS,** born St. Joseph, Missouri, November 24, 1955; admitted to bar, 1981, California and U.S. District Court, Central District of California; 1982, U.S. District Court, Northern and Eastern Districts of California and U.S. Court of Appeals, Ninth Circuit. *Education:* University of California at Berkeley (B.A., with honors, 1978); University of California School of Law at Davis (J.D., 1981). *Member:* American Bar Association (Member: Sections on Torts and Insurance Practice, Business Law and Litigation; Committees on Fidelity and Surety Law, Health Insurance, Life Insurance and Property Insurance). *LANGUAGES:* French. *PRACTICE AREAS:* Bad Faith Litigation; Insurance Law; Life and Health Insurance Law; ERISA Litigation; Fidelity and Surety Law.

**E. LYNN MALCHOW,** born Oshkosh, Wisconsin, October 16, 1951; admitted to bar, 1979, District of Columbia, U.S. Court of Appeals, for the District of Columbia Circuit and U.S. Claims Court; 1988, California; 1989, U.S. Court of Appeals, Ninth Circuit. *Education:* University of Wisconsin (B.S., 1974; J.D., 1979). *Member:* State Bar of California; District of Columbia Bar. (Resident at San Francisco Office). *PRACTICE AREAS:* Appellate Law.

### ASSOCIATES

**JEFFREY A. KATZ,** born Los Angeles, California, May 24, 1962; admitted to bar, 1988, California; 1989, U.S. District Court, Central District of California. *Education:* University of California at Los Angeles; Yeshiva University (B.A., 1984); Hastings College of Law, University of California (J.D., 1988). First Place, National Appellate Advocacy Competition, California Region. *Member:* Los Angeles County and American Bar Associations; State Bar of California.

**FELICIANO M. (BUD) FERRER,** born Detroit, Michigan, April 28, 1962; admitted to bar, 1988, California; 1989, U.S. District Court, Central District of California and U.S. Court of Appeals, Ninth Circuit. *Education:* University of Michigan (B.S., 1985); University of Southern California (J.D., 1988). Staff Member, 1986-1987, and Articles Editor, 1987-1988, Southern California Law Review. *Member:* Los Angeles County Bar Association; State Bar of California.

**EUGENIE A. GIFFORD,** born San Francisco, California, July 19, 1968; admitted to bar, 1993, California, U.S. District Court, Central District of California and U.S. Court of Appeals, Ninth Circuit. *Education:* Amherst College (B.A., cum laude, 1990); University of California, Los Angeles (J.D., 1993). Editor, University of California Los Angeles Law Review, 1992-1993. Editor-in-Chief, University of California Los Angeles Women's Law Journal. Author, Comment, "Artes Moriendi: Active Euthanasia and the Art of Dying," 40 U.C.L.A. Law Review, 1545 (1993). *PRACTICE AREAS:* Insurance Bad Faith; Insurance Coverage; Insurance Defense.

**TAMAR BLAUFARB,** born Santa Monica, California, December 17, 1968; admitted to bar, 1994, California and U.S. District Court, Central District of California. *Education:* University of California at Santa Cruz (B.A., 1991); Hastings College of the Law, University of California (J.D., 1994). Staff Member, 1992-1993 and Articles Editor, 1993-1994, Hastings

*(This Listing Continued)*

Constitutional Law Quarterly. *Member:* Los Angeles County Bar Association; State Bar of California.

### OF COUNSEL

**GARY A. SCHLESSINGER,** born Oehringer, Germany, April 16, 1931; admitted to bar, 1960, California and U.S. District Court, Southern District of of California. *Education:* College of the City of New York (B.A., 1953); University of California, Boalt Hall (J.D., 1960). Order of the Coif; Phi Alpha Delta. Editor-in-Chief, California Law Review, 1959-1960. Law Clerk to Justice Roger J. Traynor, California Supreme Court, 1960-1961. Author: "California Law on the Duty to Defend," Environmental Claims Journal, Summer Ed., 1992; "The Evolution of the Rule Determining an Insurer's Duty to Defend," Environmental Claims Journal, 1994. Compendium of Bad Faith Law; "What Triggers the Duty to Defend DRI Practice Seminar," 1993. *Member:* Beverly Hills, Los Angeles County and American Bar Associations; The State Bar of California; Defense Research Institute. [U.S. Air Force, 1953-1957]. *PRACTICE AREAS:* Insurance Coverage Law; Litigation; Partnership Dissolutions Law; Legal Malpractice.

**SAMUEL M. ZAIF,** born Germany, March 22, 1948; admitted to bar, 1984, California and U.S. District Court, Central District of California; 1985, U.S. District Court, Northern District of California; 1988, U.S. District Court, Eastern District of California. *Education:* University of California, Los Angeles (B.A., 1969; M.A., 1972); University of Massachusetts (M.A., 1977); University of California, Davis (J.D., 1984). Member, Law Review. Finalist, NAAC Moot Court. *Member:* State Bar of California.

REPRESENTATIVE CLIENTS: Allstate Life Insurance Company; Farmers Insurance Group of Companies; Fidelity and Deposit Company of Maryland; Gulf Insurance Company; Motors Insurance Company; The Prudential Insurance Company of America; Republic Insurance Company; State Farm Mutual Automobile Insurance Company; Surety Life Insurance Company; Walmart Stores, Inc.; Workers' Compensation Insurance Rating Bureau.

## FULBRIGHT & JAWORSKI L.L.P.

*Established in 1919*

**865 SOUTH FIGUEROA STREET**
**29TH FLOOR**
**LOS ANGELES, CALIFORNIA 90017-2571**
*Telephone: 213-892-9200*
*Fax: 213-680-4518*
*Email:* info@fulbright.com
*URL:* http://www.fulbright.com

*Houston, Texas Office:* 1301 McKinney, Suite 5100, 77010. Telephone: 713-651-5151. Fax: 713-651-5246.

*Washington, D.C. Office:* Market Square, 801 Pennsylvania Avenue, N.W., 20004. Telephone: 202-662-0200. Fax: 202-662-4643.

*Austin, Texas Office:* 600 Congress Avenue, Suite 2400, 78701. Telephone: 512-474-5201. Fax: 512-320-4598.

*San Antonio, Texas Office:* 300 Convent Street, Suite 2200, 78205. Telephone: 210-224-5575. Fax: 210-270-7205.

*Dallas, Texas Office:* 2200 Ross Avenue, Suite 2800, 75201. Telephone: 214-855-8000. Fax: 214-855-8200.

*New York, New York Office:* 666 Fifth Avenue, 31st Floor, 10103. Telephone: 212-318-3000. Fax: 212-752-5958

*London, England Office:* 2 St. James's Place, SW1A 1NP. Telephone: 011-44171-629-1207. Fax: 011-44171-493-8259.

*Hong Kong Office:* The Hong Kong Club Building, Nineteenth Floor, 3A Chater Road, Central. Telephone: 011-852-2523-3200. Fax 011-852-2523-3255.

*General Civil Practice. Trial and Appellate Practice, Antitrust and Trade Regulation, Administrative Law, Banking, Bankruptcy, Reorganization and Creditors' Rights, Corporate and Securities, International, Labor and Employment, Probate, Public Utilities, Public Finance, Real Estate, Taxation.*

### MEMBERS OF FIRM

**PAUL S. BLENCOWE,** born Amityville, New York, February 10, 1953; admitted to bar, 1979, Texas (Inactive); 1989, California. *Education:* University of Wisconsin (B.A., with honors, 1975); University of Pennsylvania (M.B.A., 1976); Stanford Law School (J.D., 1979). Phi Beta Kappa. *Member:* American and International Bar Associations; State Bar of California. *PRACTICE AREAS:* Corporate Law; Mergers, Acquisitions and Divestitures; Securities. *Email:* pblencowe@fulbright.com

**TIM C. BRUINSMA,** born Cambridge, Massachusetts, January 21, 1947; admitted to bar, 1974, California. *Education:* Lehigh University; Claremont McKenna College (B.A., 1970); Loyola Law School (J.D.,

*(This Listing Continued)*

**FULBRIGHT & JAWORSKI L.L.P.**, *Los Angeles—Continued*

1973). Member, St. Thomas More Law Honor Society. Los Angeles County Superior Court Special Master, 1984-1985. Director, Los Angeles Center for International Commercial Arbitration, 1986-1993. Advisor, California World Trade Commission, 1987-1992. Director, L.A. International Visitors Council, 1989-1993. Chairman, California-Russia Trade Association, 1988—. Member, U.S. Department of Commerce District Export Council, 1992—. Member, Board of Directors, Los Angeles - St. Petersburg Sister Committee. *PRACTICE AREAS:* Corporate Law; Mergers and Acquisitions; International Law. *Email:* tbruinsma@fulbright.com

**STEPHEN T. COLE,** born Helena, Montana, December 27, 1953; admitted to bar, 1980, New York and U.S. District Court, Southern and Eastern Districts of New York; 1988, California, U.S. District Court, Central and Northern Districts of California and U.S. Court of Appeals, Ninth Circuit. *Education:* Montana State University (B.A., 1976); New York University (J.D., 1979). Phi Kappa Phi; Phi Eta Sigma; Phi Kappa Delta; Advanced Honor Scholarship; Root Tilden Scholar. *Member:* New York State Bar Association; State Bar of California. *PRACTICE AREAS:* Municipal Finance; Finance. *Email:* scole@fulbright.com

**ROBERT E. DARBY,** born Philadelphia, Pennsylvania, December 23, 1947; admitted to bar, 1976, California. *Education:* Rutgers University (A.B., 1970); University of California at Berkeley (J.D., 1976). Phi Beta Kappa. *Member:* Los Angeles County and American Bar Associations; State Bar of California. *PRACTICE AREAS:* Business Law; Bankruptcy; Creditors Rights. *Email:* rdarby@fulbright.com

**ROBERT M. DAWSON,** born New York, N.Y., August 21, 1954; admitted to bar, 1978, California. *Education:* Sorbonne University, Paris, France and University of Santa Clara (B.A., 1975); University of California at Los Angeles (J.D., 1978). Phi Alpha Theta. Staff Research Assistant, California Citizens Commission on Tort Reform, 1976-1977. Member, The Order of Barristers. *Member:* Los Angeles County (Member, Executive Committee, Health Law Section, 1979-1989; Chairman, 1986-1987) and American Bar Associations; State Bar of California. *LANGUAGES:* French. *PRACTICE AREAS:* Business Law; Business Litigation. *Email:* rmdawson@fulbright.com

**DAVID A. EBERSHOFF,** born Milwaukee, Wisconsin, June 17, 1939; admitted to bar, 1966, California and Wisconsin. *Education:* Duke University (B.A., 1961); University of Michigan (J.D., 1965). Phi Delta Phi. Law Clerk to Judge F. Ryan Duffy, 7th Circuit Court of Appeals, 1965-1966. *Member:* State Bar of California; American Bar Association (Member, Committee on Federal Regulation of Securities; Former Member, Editorial Review Board of ABA's Business Lawyer); International Fiscal Association. *PRACTICE AREAS:* Corporate Law; Securities; Utilities; Healthcare. *Email:* debershoff@fulbright.com

**THOMAS A. FREIBERG, JR.,** born Cincinnati, Ohio, April 7, 1937; admitted to bar, 1965, California. *Education:* Yale University (B.A., 1959); University of Southern California (LL.B., 1964). Deputy Attorney General, 1965-1968. Chairman, Los Angeles County Assessor's Task Force on the Implementation of Proposition 13. Counsel to Special Advisor for the Board of Police Commissioners (Webster Commission) 1992. Member, Commercial Panel, American Arbitration Association. *Member:* Los Angeles County (Member, 1965— and Chairperson, 1978-1979 and 1988-1990, Condemnation and Land Valuation Litigation Committee) and American (Chairman, National Institute Subcommittee of the Real Property Litigation Committee, 1981-1984) Bar Associations; State Bar of California; American Board of Trial Advocates. *PRACTICE AREAS:* Eminent Domain; Land Use. *Email:* tfreiberg@fulbright.com

**TIMOTHY R. GREENLEAF,** born Bay City, Michigan, June 18, 1956; admitted to bar, 1981, California. *Education:* University of California at Riverside (A.B., 1978); Loyola Law School (J.D., 1981); New York University (LL.M., Taxation, 1985). *Member:* Los Angeles County and American Bar Associations; State Bar of California. *PRACTICE AREAS:* Taxation; Mergers and Acquisitions. *Email:* tgreenleaf@fulbright.com

**HARRY L. HATHAWAY,** born Pasadena, California, May 8, 1937; admitted to bar, 1963, California. *Education:* University of California at Berkeley (B.S., 1959); University of Southern California (J.D., 1962). Member, Chancery Club. President, Public Counsel, 1984-1985. Vice Chair, U.C. Berkeley Foundation, 1994—. *Member:* Los Angeles County (President, 1989-1990; Member, Board of Trustees, 1984-1990; Delegate to Conference of Delegates, State Bar, 1991) and American (Member, Board of Governors, 1991-1994; Chair, Board Communications Committee, 1993-1994; Chair, Young Lawyers Division, 1972-1973; Council Member, Senior Lawyers Division, 1996—; Member, House of Delegates, 1973-1975; 1984—; Member, Audit Committee, 1996—. Member, Standing Committee on Membership, 1984-1991; Chair, 1989-1990 and Member, Scope and Correlation of Work, 1986-1990 Chair, 1990; President, 1987-1989 and Member, Board of Directors, American Bar Endowment, 1979-1996; Member, Board of Editors, ABA Journal, 1982-1989) Bar Associations; California Barristers Association (Vice President and Member, Executive Council, 1968-1972). Life Fellow, American Bar Foundation; Los Angeles County Bar Foundation (Trustee, 1992—). *PRACTICE AREAS:* Corporate Law; Trusts and Estates. *Email:* hhathaway@fulbright.com

**DONALD L. HUNT,** born Iola, Kansas, March 1, 1949; admitted to bar, 1974, California. *Education:* University of Kansas (B.A., 1971); University of Chicago (J.D., 1974). Phi Beta Kappa; Delta Sigma Rho; Sigma Psi. *Member:* State Bar of California; American Bar Association. *PRACTICE AREAS:* Banks and Banking; Public Finance; Corporate Law. *Email:* dhunt@fulbright.com

**RICHARD L. KORNBLITH,** born Highland Park, Illinois, October 15, 1947; admitted to bar, 1977, Pennsylvania; 1978, District of Columbia and U.S. District Court, Eastern District of Pennsylvania; 1985, Texas; 1995, California. *Education:* Washington University (B.A., magna cum laude, 1969); University of Rochester (Ph.D., 1976); University of Pennsylvania (J.D., 1977). Editor, University of Pennsylvania Law Review, 1975-1977. Instructor, Villanova University (Adjunct in LL.M. Program), 1981-1982. Law Clerk to Honorable Caleb Wright, Federal District Court, Delaware, 1977-1979. *Member:* State Bar of Texas (Member, Committee on Tax Exempt Financing; Chair, 1985-1987); American Bar Association (Member, Section of Taxation: Committee on Tax Exempt Financing; Chair, Subcommittee on Governmental Obligations, 1993—; Committee on Sales, Exchange and Basis; Member, Section of Intellectual Property Law; Chair, Committee on Taxation, 1996—); National Association of Bond Lawyers (Chair, Seminars on Arbitrage and Other Tax Topics, 1992). *PRACTICE AREAS:* Taxation; Finance; Municipal Finance. *Email:* rkornblith@fulbright.com

**COLIN LENNARD,** born Hove, Sussex, England, October 18, 1942; admitted to bar, 1968, California. *Education:* University of California at Los Angeles; Loyola University of Los Angeles (J.D., 1967). Phi Alpha Delta. Co-Author: "Hazardous Waste: The Failure of the California Regulatory Framework," University of Southern California Law Center Journal of Law and the Environment, Vol. 3, 1987; "Public Agencies Meet CERCLA, RCRA and Other Environmental Hazardous," 8 Calif. Real Estate Rptr. 257 (August, 1993). Instructor, Administrative Law, University of Southern California, 1972-1975. Assistant City Attorney, Beverly Hills, 1968-1970. General Counsel, Southern California Association of Governments, 1975—. Member, Toxic Substances Certificate Program, University of California at Los Angeles, 1987-1989. Member, Environmental Policy Committee, League of California Cities, 1989-1990. President, Attorney's Committee of the California Association of Sanitation, 1990. *Member:* Los Angeles County Bar Association (Founding Member, Environmental Law Section, 1985); State Bar of California (Member, Section on Environmental Law). *PRACTICE AREAS:* Land Use; Environmental Law. *Email:* clennard@fulbright.com

**RICHARD R. MAINLAND,** born Glendale, California, March 14, 1939; admitted to bar, 1965, California. *Education:* Stanford University (A.B. with distinction, 1961); Harvard University (LL.B., cum laude, 1964). *Member:* Los Angeles County (Member, Board of Trustees, 1995) and American (Member, Litigation Section; Co-Chair, Committee on Liaison with State and Local Bar Associations, 1993-1995) Bar Associations; The State Bar of California; Association of Business Trial Lawyers (President, 1993). Fellow, American College of Trial Lawyers. *PRACTICE AREAS:* Intellectual Property Litigation; Securities Litigation; Antitrust; Unfair Trade; Alternative Dispute Resolution. *Email:* rmainland@fulbright.com

**PETER H. MASON,** born Los Angeles, CA, 1951; admitted to bar, 1976, California. *Education:* University of California at Berkeley (B.A., 1973); Brown University; Washington College of Law, American University (J.D., 1976). Adjunct Professor, Antitrust, Pepperdine University School of Law, 1986-1987. *Member:* State Bar of California. *PRACTICE AREAS:* Antitrust; Insurance. *Email:* pmason@fulbright.com

**JESSE D. MILLER,** born Chicago, IL, 1930; admitted to bar, 1959, Wisconsin; 1965, California; 1966, U.S. Supreme Court. *Education:* University of California at Los Angeles (B.S., 1956); Harvard University (LL.B., 1959). Beta Gamma Sigma; Phi Beta Kappa. *Member:* Los Angeles County and American (Member, Antitrust Section; Chairman, Subcommittee on Litigation Management Techniques, 1991—; Vice Chair, Corporate Coun-

*(This Listing Continued)*

## PROFESSIONAL BIOGRAPHIES — CALIFORNIA—LOS ANGELES

sel Committee, Litigation Section, 1994—) Bar Associations; The State Bar of California; State Bar of Wisconsin; American Judicature Society. *PRACTICE AREAS:* Antitrust; Securities Litigation; Products Liability; Litigation. *Email:* jmiller@fulbright.com

**JOHN A. O'MALLEY,** born Los Angeles, California, April 11, 1953; admitted to bar, 1981, California. *Education:* Northwestern University; Hampshire College (B.A., 1975); University of California at Berkeley (J.D., 1981). Extern, Hon. Spencer Williams, U.S. District Court, Northern District of California. *Member:* Los Angeles County and American Bar Associations; State Bar of California. *PRACTICE AREAS:* Litigation. *Email:* jo'malley@fulbright.com

**MICHAEL G. SMOOKE,** born Los Angeles, California, October 2, 1945; admitted to bar, 1971, California. *Education:* University of California at Los Angeles (B.A., 1967); Harvard University (J.D., 1970). Phi Beta Kappa; Omicron Delta Epsilon; Pi Gamma Mu. *Member:* Los Angeles County and American Bar Associations; The State Bar of California. *PRACTICE AREAS:* Real Estate; Finance. *Email:* msmooke@fulbright.com

**DOUGLAS W. STERN,** born Long Beach, CA, 1953; admitted to bar, 1978, California. *Education:* University of California at Los Angeles (A.B., 1975; J.D., 1978). *Member:* State Bar of California. *PRACTICE AREAS:* Antitrust; Business Litigation. *Email:* dstern@fulbright.com

### OF COUNSEL

**FRED G. YANNEY,** born Omaha, Nebraska, April 2, 1952; admitted to bar, 1977, Nebraska and U.S. District Court, District of Nebraska; 1988, California. *Education:* University of Nebraska (B.S., 1974; J.D., 1976). Phi Beta Kappa. *Member:* State Bar of California; Nebraska State Bar Association. *PRACTICE AREAS:* Public Finance; Electric Utility Regulation. *Email:* fyanney@fulbright.com

### ASSOCIATES

**CHAD CHASE COOMBS,** born Santa Monica, California, November 4, 1959; admitted to bar, 1991, California. *Education:* California State University at Hayward (B.S., 1982); University of Washington (M.B.A., 1983); University of Southern California (J.D., 1991). *PRACTICE AREAS:* Bankruptcy. *Email:* ccoombs@fulbright.com

**JUDITH A. HOLIBER,** born Washington, D.C., July 13, 1968; admitted to bar, 1995, California. *Education:* Vassar College (B.A., 1990); Georgetown University Law Center (J.D., 1995). *PRACTICE AREAS:* Litigation. *Email:* jholiber@fulbright.com

**LARISSA A.J. KEHOE,** born Nashville, Tennessee, November 28, 1970; admitted to bar, 1995, California. *Education:* Yale University (B.A., 1992); University of San Diego (J.D., 1995). *PRACTICE AREAS:* Litigation. *Email:* lkehoe@fulbright.com

**LISA R. KLEIN,** born San Jose, California, February 11, 1967; admitted to bar, 1992, California. *Education:* University of California at Los Angeles (B.A., 1989); Hastings College of the Law, University of California (J.D., 1992). *PRACTICE AREAS:* Litigation. *Email:* lisa.klein@fulbright.com

**FREDERICK S. KUHLMAN,** born Evanston, Illinois, February 6, 1953; admitted to bar, 1992, California. *Education:* Northern Illinois University (B.A., 1976); University of Southern California (M.A., 1977); Loyola Law School, Los Angeles (J.D., 1992). *PRACTICE AREAS:* Public Finance. *Email:* fkuhlman@fulbright.com

**JOSHUA D. LICHTMAN,** born Lexington, Kentucky, December 17, 1968; admitted to bar, 1995, California. *Education:* Duke University (A.B., cum laude, 1991); University of California, Los Angeles (J.D., 1994). *PRACTICE AREAS:* Litigation. *Email:* jlichtman@fulbright.com

**J. KELLY MOFFAT,** born Los Angeles, California, June 16, 1965; admitted to bar, 1991, California. *Education:* University of California, Berkeley (B.A., 1987); University of California, Hastings College of the Law (J.D., 1991). *PRACTICE AREAS:* Corporate Law; Securities; Public Finance. *Email:* kmoffat@fulbright.com

**HARDY RAY MURPHY,** born Albuquerque, New Mexico, August 26, 1968; admitted to bar, 1996, California, U.S. District Court, Central District of California and U.S. Court of Appeals, Ninth Circuit. *Education:* University of Southern California (B.S., 1991); University of California at Los Angeles (J.D., 1996). *PRACTICE AREAS:* General Litigation. *Email:* hmurphy@fulbright.com

**TODD M. SORRELL,** born Bakersfield, California, January 12, 1969; admitted to bar, 1994, California. *Education:* University of California at Santa Barbara (B.A., magna cum laude, 1991); University of California,
*(This Listing Continued)*

Los Angeles (J.D., 1994). *LANGUAGES:* Spanish. *PRACTICE AREAS:* Litigation. *Email:* tsorrell@fulbright.com

**JARLON TSANG,** born Toronto, Canada; admitted to bar, 1996, California. *Education:* University of California at Berkeley (B.S., 1990); Boston University (M.B.A., 1995; J.D., 1995). *LANGUAGES:* Mandarin Chinese. *PRACTICE AREAS:* Corporate Law; Public Finance. *Email:* jtsang@fulbright.com

**KIMBERLY R. WELLS,** born Los Angeles, California, July 8, 1968; admitted to bar, 1993, California. *Education:* Pomona College (B.A., 1990); University of California at Los Angeles (J.D., 1993). *PRACTICE AREAS:* Litigation. *Email:* kwells@fulbright.com

**BETH MEZOFF WILSON,** born New Rochelle, New York, May 4, 1962; admitted to bar, 1988, California. *Education:* Brown University (A.B., 1984); University of California at Los Angeles (J.D., 1987). *PRACTICE AREAS:* Corporate Law. *Email:* bwilson@fulbright.com

### STAFF ATTORNEYS

**ROBERT M. ARONSON,** born Greenville, South Carolina, February 20, 1953; admitted to bar, 1978, California. *Education:* University of California at Los Angeles (B.A., 1975); Loyola Law School (J.D., 1978). *PRACTICE AREAS:* Litigation; Bankruptcy; Real Estate. *Email:* raronson@fulbright.com

**ROBERT C. BARNES,** born Washington, D.C., December 8, 1954; admitted to bar, 1983, California. *Education:* Brown University (A.B., 1978); University of Pennsylvania (J.D., 1983). *PRACTICE AREAS:* Real Estate. *Email:* rbarnes@fulbright.com

**ANNE K. EDWARDS,** born Hackensack, New Jersey, February 9, 1951; admitted to bar, 1983, California; 1989, U.S. District Court, Central, Northern, Southern and Eastern Districts of California. *Education:* University of Maryland (B.A., 1973); Western State University (J.D., 1983). *PRACTICE AREAS:* Creditors Rights; Litigation. *Email:* aedwards@fulbright.com

**JAMES M. GILBERT,** born Santa Monica, California, July 9, 1964; admitted to bar, 1990, California; 1991, U.S. District Court, Central District of California. *Education:* University of California at Los Angeles (B.A., 1987); Southwestern University School of Law (J.D., 1990). *PRACTICE AREAS:* Real Estate Litigation; Business Litigation; Banks and Banking; Litigation. *Email:* jgilbert@fulbright.com

**ANA M. INGUANZO,** born Miami, Florida, May 29, 1963; admitted to bar, 1989, California. *Education:* University of Southern California (B.A., 1985); University of California, Los Angeles (J.D., 1989). *PRACTICE AREAS:* Litigation. *Email:* ainguanzo@fulbright.com

**PAUL E. LIGUORI,** born Orange, New Jersey, 1962; admitted to bar, 1987, California; 1988, U.S. District Court, Central District of California; 1989, District of Columbia. *Education:* Georgetown University (B.S.B.A., cum laude, 1984; J.D., 1987). *PRACTICE AREAS:* Bankruptcy. *Email:* pliguori@fulbright.com

(For Biographies of Houston, Texas Personnel, see Houston, Texas Professional Biographies).
(For Biographies of Austin, Texas Personnel, see Austin, Texas Professional Biographies).
(For Biographies of San Antonio, Texas Personnel, see San Antonio, Texas Professional Biographies).
(For Biographies of Dallas, Texas Personnel, see Dallas, Texas Professional Biographies).
(For Biographies of New York, New York Personnel, see New York, New York Professional Biographies);
(For Biographies of London, England Personnel, see London, England Professional Biographies).
(For Biographies of Hong Kong Personnel, see Hong Kong Professional Biographies).

---

## FULLER & FULLER
### LOS ANGELES, CALIFORNIA
(See Woodland Hills)

*Wills, Trusts, Probate, Estate Planning, Estate Litigation.*

# FULWIDER PATTON LEE & UTECHT, LLP

*Established in 1938*

**10877 WILSHIRE BOULEVARD
10TH FLOOR
LOS ANGELES, CALIFORNIA 90024**

Telephone: 310-824-5555
FAX: 310-824-9696
Email: fulwidr@primenet.com
Email: fulwidr@aol.com

*Long Beach, California Office:* 200 Oceangate, Suite 1550. Telephone: 310-432-0453. Fax: 310-435-6014. Internet: fulwidrlb@aol.com.

*Patent, Trademark, Copyright and Unfair Competition Law. Litigation.*

**FIRM PROFILE:** Fulwider, Patton, Lee & Utecht, LLP, was founded in 1938 in Los Angeles, California and the Long Beach office was established in 1953. The firm engages in a full service domestic and foreign practice limited to the field of intellectual property, including patents, trademarks, copyrights, trade secrets, unfair competition, licensing and other technology-related matters for individuals and businesses.

## MEMBERS OF FIRM

**ROBERT W. FULWIDER** (1903-1979).

**JOHN M. LEE** (1921-1978).

**WARREN L. PATTON** (1912-1985).

**RICHARD A. BARDIN,** born Oxnard, California, December 14, 1934; admitted to bar, 1965, California; registered to practice before U.S. Patent and Trademark Office. *Education:* University of California at Los Angeles (B.S.M.E., 1957); University of Southern California (J.D., 1965). Order of the Coif. *Member:* American Intellectual Property Law Association. **PRACTICE AREAS:** Patent, Trademark, Copyright and Unfair Competition Law; Litigation.

**GILBERT G. KOVELMAN,** born New York, N.Y., June 2, 1936; admitted to bar, 1960, Virginia, District of Columbia and U.S. Claims Court; 1960-1982, U.S. Court of Customs and Patent Appeals; 1962, California; registered to practice before U.S. Patent and Trademark Office. *Education:* Cooper Union (B.E.E., 1956); George Washington University (J.D., 1960). Examiner, United State Patent and Trademark Office, 1956-1959. *Member:* San Fernando Valley and International Bar Associations; District of Columbia Bar; Virginia State Bar; American Intellectual Property Law Association; Licensing Executive Society; American Institute of Aeronautics and Astronautics; Mensa Society. **PRACTICE AREAS:** Patent, Trademark, Copyright and Unfair Competition Law; Litigation.

**VERN SCHOOLEY,** born Reed City, Michigan, September 26, 1937; admitted to bar, 1967, California; registered to practice before U.S. Patent and Trademark Office. *Education:* Ferris State College and Michigan State University (B.S.M.E., 1961); University of San Diego (J.D., 1966). President, Joseph A. Ball/Clarence S. Hunt Inn of Court, 1991-1992. *Member:* Long Beach Bar Association (Past President); Los Angeles and American Intellectual Property Law Association. (Long Beach Resident Partner). **PRACTICE AREAS:** Patent, Trademark, Copyright and Unfair Competition Law; Litigation.

**JAMES W. PAUL,** born Blairsville, Pennsylvania, August 19, 1938; admitted to bar, 1979, California; registered to practice before U.S. Patent and Trademark Office. *Education:* The Ohio State University (B.S.M.E., 1961); Northrop University (J.D., 1979). *Member:* Federal and International Bar Associations; Los Angeles and American Intellectual Property Law Associations. **PRACTICE AREAS:** Patent, Trademark, Copyright and Unfair Competition Law; Litigation.

**CRAIG B. BAILEY,** born Camden, New Jersey, August 20, 1952; admitted to bar, 1978, District of Columbia; 1979, U.S. Court of Appeals, 4th, 5th, 7th, 8th, 9th 10th and D.C. Circuits, U.S. District Court, District of Columbia and U.S. Tax Court; 1980, U.S. Court of Appeals, 1st Circuit and U.S. Court of Military Appeals; 1982, U.S. Court of Appeals, Federal Circuit; 1984, California, 1985, U.S. Supreme Court; 1986, U.S. District Court, Northern, Eastern, Central and Southern Districts of California; registered to practice before U.S. Patent and Trademark Office. *Education:* Bucknell University (B.A. and B.S.E.E., cum laude, 1975); George Washington University (J.D., with honors, 1978). Tau Beta Pi. Law Clerk and Technical Advisor to Chief Judge Howard T. Markey, U.S. Court of Customs and Patent Appeals, 1978-1980. *Member:* The District of Columbia Bar; Los Angeles and American Intellectual Property Law Associations. **PRAC-**

*(This Listing Continued)*

**TICE AREAS:** Patent, Trademark, Copyright and Unfair Competition Law; Litigation.

**JOHN S. NAGY,** born Chicago, Illinois, July 23, 1951; admitted to bar, 1981, Illinois; 1983, U.S. Court of Appeals for the Federal Circuit; 1987, California; registered to practice before U.S. Patent and Trademark Office. *Education:* Western Michigan University (B.S.I.E., 1974); De Paul University (J.D., 1981). Symposium Issue Editor, DePaul Law Review, 1980-1981. *Member:* Los Angeles Intellectual Property Law Association. **PRACTICE AREAS:** Patent, Trademark, Copyright and Unfair Competition Law; Litigation.

**STEPHEN J. STRAUSS,** born Los Angeles, California, July 24, 1956; admitted to bar, 1983, California; 1984, U.S. Court of Appeals, Ninth and Federal Circuits, U.S. District Court, Central and Southern Districts of California; 1985, District of Columbia; registered to practice before U.S. Patent and Trademark Office. *Education:* American University (B.A., Pol. Sc., 1979; M.A., Pol.Sc., 1980); Temple University; Southwestern University (J.D., 1983). Phi Alpha Delta. Managing Editor, Commentator, 1982-1983. Assistant to Senator Bill Bradley for International and Defense related matters, 1979. Author: "Don't Be Burned By Berne: A Guide to the Changes in the Copyright Laws as a Result of the Berne Convention Implementation Act of 1988," Journal of the Patent and Trademark Office Society, May, 1989; "Beat The Clock: The Effect of Section 412 of the Copyright Act on Post-Infringement Registration," Journal of the Patent and Trademark Office Society, October, 1990; "Don't Be Burned By Berne II: Recent Changes to the Copyright Act Regarding Architectural Works," New Matter, Summer, 1991. Member, Intellectual Property Section, State Bar of California. *Member:* Los Angeles and Long Beach Bar Associations; California Lawyers for the Arts. **PRACTICE AREAS:** Patent, Trademark, Copyright and Unfair Competition Law; Litigation.

**THOMAS H. MAJCHER,** born Elizabeth, New Jersey, September 11, 1957; admitted to bar, 1983, California; U.S. District Court, Central District of California; 1986, U.S. Court of Appeals, Ninth Circuit; 1988, U.S. Court of Appeals, Federal Circuit; registered to practice before U.S. Patent and Trademark Office. *Education:* Stevens Institute of Technology (B.E., Mech. Eng., 1979); Southwestern University (J.D., 1982). **PRACTICE AREAS:** Patent, Trademark, Copyright and Unfair Competition Law; Litigation.

**THOMAS A. RUNK,** born Auburn, New York, November 16, 1948; admitted to bar, 1981, California, U.S. Court of Appeals, Ninth Circuit and U.S. District Court, Central District of California; 1984, U.S. Court of Appeals for the Federal Circuit; 1985, U.S. Supreme Court; registered to practice before U.S. Patent and Trademark Office. *Education:* Lowell Technological Institute (B.S., 1970); Western State University (J.D., 1981). **PRACTICE AREAS:** Patent, Trademark, Copyright and Unfair Competition Law; Litigation.

## ASSOCIATES

**DAVID G. PARKHURST,** born Pasadena, California, April 5, 1947; admitted to bar, 1973, California and U.S. District Court, Central District of California; registered to practice before U.S. Patent and Trademark Office. *Education:* University of California at Los Angeles (B.A., 1969); University of Southern California Law School (J.D., 1973); California State University at Northridge (B.A., Chemistry, 1980). *Member:* Glendale Bar Association. **PRACTICE AREAS:** Patent, Trademark, Copyright and Unfair Competition Law; Litigation.

**PAUL M. STULL,** born Salem, Ohio, September 30, 1952; admitted to bar, 1977, California and U.S. District Court, Central District of California; registered to practice before U.S. Patent and Trademark Office. *Education:* Wittenberg University (B.A., 1974); University of Michigan (J.D., 1977). Phi Delta Phi. *Member:* Long Beach Bar Association. **PRACTICE AREAS:** Patent, Trademark, Copyright and Unfair Competition Law; Litigation.

**GUNTHER D. HANKE,** born Linz, Austria, June 23, 1955; admitted to bar, 1986, California; registered to practice before U.S. Patent and Trademark Office. *Education:* University of Southern California (B.S., cum laude, 1977); University of California at Los Angeles; Southwestern University School of Law (J.D., 1985). Member, Joseph A. Ball/Clarence S. Hunt Inn of Court. *Member:* Long Beach Bar Association; Los Angeles Intellectual Property Law Association; Orange County Patent Law Association. (Long Beach Resident Associate). **LANGUAGES:** German. **PRACTICE AREAS:** Patent, Trademark, Copyright and Unfair Competition Law; Litigation.

**GARY M. ANDERSON,** born Oakland, California, November 13, 1949; admitted to bar, 1981, California, U.S. District Court, Central District of

*(This Listing Continued)*

California; registered to practice before U.S. Patent and Trademark Office. *Education:* University of California at Los Angeles (B.S.M.E., 1972); Southwestern University (J.D., cum laude, 1980). Phi Alpha Delta. Staff Member, 1978-1979 and Managing Editor, 1979-1980, Southwestern University Law Review. Member: American Inns of Court; Joseph A. Ball/Clarence S. Hunt Inn of Court. *Member:* Orange County Bar Association; American Intellectual Property Law Association; Orange County Patent Law Association. (Long Beach Resident Associate). *PRACTICE AREAS:* Patent, Trademark, Copyright and Unfair Competition Law; Litigation.

**RONALD E. PEREZ,** born Milwaukee, Wisconsin, July 16, 1956; admitted to bar, 1990, Wisconsin and California; registered to practice before U.S. Patent and Trademark Office. *Education:* Ohio State University (B.S.Ch. E., 1978); California State Polytechnic University, Pomona (M.B.A., 1987); University of Wisconsin-Madison (J.D., 1990). Business Manager, Wisconsin International Law Journal. *Member:* State Bar of Wisconsin; The Computer Law Association. *PRACTICE AREAS:* Patent, Trademark, Copyright and Unfair Competition Law; Litigation.

**ROBERT L. KOVELMAN,** born Los Angeles, California, March 13, 1963; admitted to bar, 1991, California. *Education:* University of California at Los Angeles (B.A., 1986); Southwestern University School of Law (J.D., 1991). Who's Who Among American Law Students, 1990-1991. Alternate Finalist International Moot Court Oral Competition, 1989. Recipient, American Jurisprudence Book Award (Corporations). *PRACTICE AREAS:* Patent, Trademark, Copyright and Unfair Competition Law; Litigation.

**PAMELA G. MAHER,** born Melrose, Massachusetts, November 30, 1959; admitted to bar, 1992, California. *Education:* Boston University (B.S./B.M.E., 1981); Loyola Marymount University (J.D., 1992). *PRACTICE AREAS:* Intellectual Property Law.

**JOHN V. HANLEY,** born Jersey City, New Jersey, January 4, 1962; admitted to bar, 1992, California; 1993, U.S. District Court, Central District of California; 1994, U.S. District Court, Northern District of California; 1995, U.S. District Court, Southern District of California; registered to practice before U.S. Patent and Trademark Office. *Education:* University of California at San Diego (B.S.M.E., 1985); California State Polytechnic University (M.B.A., 1990); University of San Francisco (J.D., 1992). *Member:* American Intellectual Property Law Association. *PRACTICE AREAS:* Patent; Trademark; Copyright; Unfair Competition; Litigation.

**PAUL T. LAVOIE,** born Scarborough, Ontario, December 15, 1965; admitted to bar, 1994, California; 1995, U.S. District Court, Southern, Northern and Central Districts of California; registered to practice before U.S. Patent and Trademark Office. *Education:* Brigham Young University (B.A., Chemistry, 1989; J.D., M.B.A., 1994). *Member:* Beverly Hills Bar Association; American Inn of Courts. *PRACTICE AREAS:* Patent; Trademark.

**JOHN K. FITZGERALD,** born Evergreen Park, Illinois, August 25, 1950; admitted to bar, 1993, California; registered to practice before U.S. Patent and Trademark Office. *Education:* DePaul University (B.S., 1972); Central Michigan University (M.B.A., 1981); Whittier College School of Law (J.D., 1993). Editor-in-Chief, Whittier Law Review, 1992-1993. Fellow, American Academy of Optometry, 1981—. Member, Association for Research and Vision and Ophthalmology, 1991—. *PRACTICE AREAS:* Patent; Trademark; Copyright.

**JAMES JUO,** born Peekskill, New York, November 10, 1967; admitted to bar, 1993, Virginia; registered to practice before U.S. Patent and Trademark Office (Not admitted in California). *Education:* Clarkson University (B.S.E.E., 1989); George Washington University (J.D., 1993). Patent Examiner, U.S. Patent and Trademark Office, 1989-1990. *Member:* Virginia State Bar. *PRACTICE AREAS:* Intellectual Property.

**RUSSELL C. PANGBORN,** born Long Beach, California, December 21, 1966; admitted to bar, 1994, California; registered to practice before U.S. Patent and Trademark Office. *Education:* Stanford University (B.A., 1989); Hastings College of the Law, University of California (J.D., 1993). *Member:* Long Beach Bar Association. (Long Beach Resident Associate). *PRACTICE AREAS:* Trademark; Copyright; Patent Litigation; Trade Secret.

**RICHARD B. CATES,** born Tacoma, Washington, March 9, 1963; admitted to bar, 1993, California; 1994, U.S. District Court, Central District of California; 1995, Colorado; registered to practice before U.S. Patent and Trademark Office. *Education:* University of Colorado at Boulder (B.S., Aerospace Engineering, 1985); Hastings College of the Law, University of California (J.D., 1992). *PRACTICE AREAS:* Patent; Trademark; Copyright; Litigation.

*(This Listing Continued)*

**DERRICK W. REED,** born Santa Monica, California, October 7, 1969; admitted to bar, 1995, California; registered to practice before U.S. Patent and Trademark Office. *Education:* University of California at San Diego (B.S.E.E., 1992); Loyola University of Los Angeles (J.D., 1995). *Member:* Long Beach Bar Association; American Inns of Court; Long Beach Barristers. (Long Beach Resident Associate). *PRACTICE AREAS:* Patent Prosecution; Patent Litigation; Trademark Law; Unfair Competition Law; Intellectual Property Law.

**PAUL Y. FENG,** born Republic of China, September 24, 1960; admitted to bar, 1990, California, U.S. District Court, Central District of California, U.S. Court of Appeals for the Federal Circuit and U.S. Supreme Court; registered to practice before U.S. Patent and Trademark Office. *Education:* University of Wisconsin-Madison (B.S.M.E., with honor and distinction, 1983); University of Minnesota (J.D., 1989). Tau Beta Pi; Pi Tau Sigma. *Member:* Century City Bar Association; Asian Business Association; Los Angeles Intellectual Property Law Association. *LANGUAGES:* Chinese (Mandarin). *PRACTICE AREAS:* Patent Prosecution; Intellectual Property; Trademark Law.

**JOANNE M. YBABEN,** born Los Angeles, California, June 4, 1966; admitted to bar, 1994, California and U.S. District Court, Southern District of California; registered to practice before U.S. Patent and Trademark Office. *Education:* University of California at San Diego (B.A., 1989); California Western School of Law (J.D., 1994). Adjunct Professor, National University School of Management and Technology, 1995-1996. *Member:* Long Beach Bar Association; Women Lawyers Association; American Inns of Court. (Long Beach Resident Associate).

**SEAN M. CASEY,** born Port Chester, New York; admitted to bar, 1995, California; registered to practice before U.S. Patent and Trademark Office. *Education:* Boston University College of Engineering (B.S.A.E., 1988); Southwestern University School of Law (J.D., 1995). *Member:* Orange County and Long Beach County Bar Associations; Long Beach Barristers; American Inns of Court; American Intellectual Property Association; Patent and Trademark Office Society; Southern California Professional Engineers Association; A.I.A.A.; A.F.C.E.A. (Long Beach Resident Associate). *PRACTICE AREAS:* Patent; Copyright; Trademark Prosecution; Intellectual Property Litigation.

**MURIEL C. HARITCHABALET,** born Pau, Béarn, France, August 9, 1968; admitted to bar, 1994, California and U.S. District Court, Central District of California. *Education:* University of San Francisco (B.A., 1989); Pepperdine University (J.D., 1993). *LANGUAGES:* French and Spanish. *PRACTICE AREAS:* Trademarks.

*OF COUNSEL*

**FRANCIS A. UTECHT,** born Minneapolis, Minnesota, March 6, 1923; admitted to bar, 1952, California; 1958, U.S. Supreme Court; 1960, U.S. Claims Court; 1970-1982, U.S. Court of Customs and Patent Appeals; registered to practice before U.S. Patent and Trademark Office. *Education:* University of Southern California (B.S.M.E., 1947); Southwestern University (J.D., 1951). Chairman, Patent, Trademark and Copyright Section, State Bar of California, 1982-1983. *Member:* Long Beach Bar Association; American Intellectual Property Law Association. (Resident, Of Counsel, Long Beach Office). *PRACTICE AREAS:* Patent, Trademark, Copyright and Unfair Competition Law; Litigation.

**I. MORLEY DRUCKER, (A PROFESSIONAL CORPORATION),** born Winnipeg, Canada, January 4, 1931; admitted to bar, 1959, California. *Education:* Massachusetts Institute of Technology (B.S.Ch.E., 1951); Southwestern University (J.D., 1956). Special Master, U.S. District Court, Central District of California, 1978-1979. *Member:* Beverly Hills Bar Association; American Patent Law Association. *REPORTED CASES:* Oromeccanica, Inc. v. Ottmar Botzenhardt GmbH & Co. KG, 226 USPQ 996 (USDC, D.C. Calif. 1985); MWS Wire Industries, Inc. v. California Fine Wire Industries, Inc., 230 USPQ 873 (Ct of Appeals, 9th Cir. 1986); Cento Group S.p.A. v. OroAmerica, Inc., 822 F. Supp 1058 (USDC, SDNY, 1993). *PRACTICE AREAS:* Patent Law; Trademark Law; Copyright Law; Unfair Competition Law.

**HOWARD N. SOMMERS,** born Newark, New Jersey, November 3, 1942; admitted to bar, 1967, New Jersey; 1969, Florida; 1982, California. *Education:* Case Institute of Technology (B.S.E.E., 1964); New York University (J.D., 1967). Assistant Examiner, U.S. Patent Office, 1964. Law Clerk, New Jersey Attorney General, 1965-1966. Co-Author: "Guide to Federal Discovery Rules," New Jersey State Bar Association Journal, 1971. *Member:* New Jersey State Bar Association (Chairman, Patent Law Section, 1971); Attorneys Society of Bergen County (President, 1975-1977); Los Angeles Patent Law Association; New Jersey Patent Law Association

*(This Listing Continued)*

CALIFORNIA—LOS ANGELES                                    MARTINDALE-HUBBELL LAW DIRECTORY 1997

**FULWIDER PATTON LEE & UTECHT, LLP,** Los Angeles—*Continued*

(President-Elect, 1979-1980). *REPORTED CASES:* Raceway Components, Inc. v. Butler Mfg. Co., F.Supp. 856; 11 USPQ2d 1799 (USDC, SDWVa, 1989) MW; Cento Group, S.p.A. v. OroAmerica, Inc., 822 F.Supp 1058 (USDC, SDNY, 1993). *PRACTICE AREAS:* Patent Law; Trademark Law; Copyright Law; Unfair Competition Law.

All Members and Associates of the Firm are Members of State Bar of California, Los Angeles County and American Bar Associations, Los Angeles Patent Law Association, and American Intellectual Property Law Association.

---

## FUNSTEN & FRANZEN
### LOS ANGELES, CALIFORNIA
(See Beverly Hills)
*Business, Entertainment and Tax Law. Civil Litigation (State and Federal).*

---

## SCOTT S. FURSTMAN
### LOS ANGELES, CALIFORNIA
(See Santa Monica)
*Criminal Trial and Appellate, Asset Forfeiture in State and Federal Courts.*

---

## GABRIEL, HERMAN & PERETZ
*1800 CENTURY PARK EAST, 5TH FLOOR*
### LOS ANGELES, CALIFORNIA 90067-1508
Telephone: 310-286-1300
Fax: 310-286-1331

*Business and Commercial Litigation, Insurance Coverage and Defense, Professional Liability, Business Transactions, Real Estate, Finance and General Business Law.*

### MEMBERS OF FIRM

**ALLAN GABRIEL,** born Brooklyn, New York, May 7, 1947; admitted to bar, 1975, New Jersey; 1977, California; 1978, U.S. Court of Appeals, Ninth and Fifth Circuits and U.S. Supreme Court. *Education:* Queens College of the City University of New York (B.A., 1969); Brooklyn Law School; Rutgers University (J.D., 1975). Co-Author: "Trademarks," Chapter 6, Attorney's Guide to the Law of Competitive Business Practices, California Continuing Education of the Bar, 1981; "Product Counterfeiting--Protection Under the Lanham Act Section 43 (a)," Product Counterfeiting Remedies, Practising Law Institute, 1984; Contributing Editor On Competitive Business Practices, California Business Law Reporter, California Continuing Education of the Bar, 1984. *REPORTED CASES:* Clamp Manufacturing Co. v. Enco Manufacturing Co., 870 F.2d 512 (9th Cir. 1989); American Credit Indemnity v. Sacks, 213 Cal.App.3d 622 (1989); Abba Rubber Co., Inc. v. Seaquist, 235 Cal.App.3d 1 (1991); Berg v. Leason, 32 F.3d 422 (9th Cir. 1995); Taylor Made Golf Company, Inc., v. Trend Precision Golf, Inc., 903 F.Supp. 1506 (M.D. Fla. 1995).

**DEAN B. HERMAN,** born Brooklyn, New York, May 12, 1952; admitted to bar, 1977, California. *Education:* California State University at Fullerton (B.A., with honors, 1974); Loyola Law School (J.D., with honors, 1977); University of California, Berkley, Boalt, (LL.M., 1978). Member, St. Thomas More Law Honor Society. Author: "Supreme Court Limits Claims Against Insurance Companies-Will the Voters Agree," Business and Corporations Law Section Newsletter, Los Angeles County Bar Association 1987. "Senate Bill 241-Insurance Reform in Theory and Practice," The Barristers of the Los Angeles County Bar Association, 1988; "Recent Developments Concerning Attorneys' Liability in Business Transactions," Glendon Tremaine Symposium, Business and Corporations Law Section, Los Angeles County Bar Association, 1990-1991; Conference on Exposure Evaluation: Management of a Business Client's Litigation Portfolio, CLE Approved; Real Estate Practice in the 90's, Real Estate Litigation: Selected Issues, CLE Approved, 1993 Annual Meeting of the State Bar of California. *Member:* American Insurance Attorneys; Defense Research Institute, Inc. *RE-*
*(This Listing Continued)*

CAA682B

*PORTED CASES:* Taub v. First State, 44 Cal.App.4th 811 (1995); Concha v. London, 62 F.3d 1493 (9th Cir. 1995); Trulis v. Barton, 67 F.3d779 (9th Cir. 1995); Trulis v. Burton, 67 F.3d 779 (9th Cir. 1995).

**AVI S. PERETZ,** born Winnipeg, Manitoba, Canada, January 30, 1952; admitted to bar, 1977, California. *Education:* University of California at Los Angeles (B.A., 1973); Loyola Law School (J.D., with honors, 1977). Member, St. Thomas More Law Honor Society. Staff Member, Loyola Law Review, 1976-1977. Speaker, Transactional Real Estate Practice, Loyola Law Symposium. Guest Speaker and Co-Host, Business and the Law, Los Angeles Radio Station, KBLA, 1991. Speaker/Moderator, Real Estate Practice in the 90's, Real Estate Litigation: Selected Issues, CLE Approved, 1993 Annual Meeting of the State Bar of California. *Member:* American Bar Association; Association of Real Estate Attorneys.

**PETER SCHWARTZ,** born New Rochelle, New York, September 24, 1957; admitted to bar, 1983, California and U.S. District Court, Central District of California. *Education:* Leeds University, Leeds, England; University of California at Riverside (B.A., cum laude, 1979); Loyola Law School (J.D., cum laude, 1983). *REPORTED CASES:* Berg v. Leason, 32 F.3d 422 (9th Cir, 1994); Trulis v. Barton, 67 F.3d 779 (9th Cir. 1995); Taub v. First State, 44 Cal.App.4th 811 (1995).

**ALBERT J. TUMPSON,** born Huntington, West Virginia, April 25, 1953; admitted to bar, 1977, Tennessee; 1978, U.S. District Court, Eastern District of Tennessee; 1981, U.S. Court of Appeals, Fifth and Eleventh Circuits; 1984, Florida; 1986, California, U.S. District Court, Northern District of California and U.S. Court of Appeals, Ninth Circuit; 1990, U.S. Supreme Court and U.S. District Court, District of Arizona; 1993, U.S. District Court, Southern and Central Districts of California. *Education:* University of California at Berkeley (B.A., 1974); University of California, Hastings College of the Law (J.D., 1977). Regional Counsel, Federal Deposit Insurance Corporation, 1984-1987. *Member:* Bar Association of San Francisco, Beverly Hills and American (Member, Business Law Section) Bar Associations; Tennessee Bar Association; The Florida Bar. *LANGUAGES:* French. *PRACTICE AREAS:* Banking, Commercial and Real Estate Litigation; Trials and Appeals; Receivership Law; Loan Workouts and Lending Transactions.

**JOHN H. ODENDAHL,** born Silvis, Illinois, November 24, 1961; admitted to bar, 1986, Ohio; 1987, California. *Education:* Western Illinois University (B.A., magna cum laude, 1983); University of Iowa (J.D., with honors, 1986). *REPORTED CASES:* Concha v. London, 62 F.3d 1493 (9th Cir. 1995); Taylor Made Golf Company, Inc. v. Trend Precision Golf, Inc. 903 F.Supp. 1506 (M.D. Fla. 1995).

### ASSOCIATES

**LYNDA M. RILEY,** born Sydney, Australia, January 18, 1957; admitted to bar, 1980, New South Wales, Australia; 1985, High Court of Australia; 1986, California and U.S. District Courts, Central, Southern and Northern Districts of California. *Education:* University of New South Wales, Sydney, Australia (B.A., 1980; LL.B., 1980). Recipient, First Prize, Diploma of General Insurance, Insurance Institute of New South Wales, 1984. Member, Law Society of New South Wales, 1980-1985. *Member:* Australian American Lawyers Association (Founding Member, 1987).

**LINDSAY S. JOHNSON,** born Hamilton, Ontario, Canada, May 14, 1961; admitted to bar, 1986, California. *Education:* University of California at Los Angeles (B.A., 1983); Hastings College of the Law, University of California (J.D., 1986). Phi Alpha Delta; Pi Gamma Mu. *Member:* Los Angeles County and American Bar Associations; State Bar of California; Los Angeles County Barristers.

**KAREN M. COSTELLO,** born Chicago, Illinois, October 26, 1956; admitted to bar, 1984, Illinois; 1993, California. *Education:* University of Wisconsin-Madison (B.A., 1979); Loyola University (J.D., 1984). *PRACTICE AREAS:* Insurance Coverage; Professional Liability; Directors and Officers Liability; Fiduciary Liability; Bad Faith Litigation.

**DEBORAH SCHMIDT,** born Washington, D.C., October 4, 1958; admitted to bar, 1987, Pennsylvania; 1991, California. *Education:* Barnard College (B.A., cum laude, 1981); University of Pennsylvania (M.A., 1982); Benjamin N. Cardozo School of Law, Yeshiva University (J.D., cum laude, 1987). Samuel Belkin Scholar. Member, Cardozo Arts and Entertainment Law Journal, 1985-1987. Author: "Do Cable Operators Want Free Speech or a Free Market? Preferred Communications, Inc. v. City of Los Angeles," 6 Cardozo A & E L.J. 161 (1987). *Member:* Beverly Hills, Los Angeles County and Pennsylvania Bar Associations; State Bar of California. *LANGUAGES:* Hebrew. *PRACTICE AREAS:* Business Transactions; Real Estate; Loan Workouts and Lending Transactions.

*(This Listing Continued)*

**LEONARD R. SCHWIGEN,** born Moline, Illinois, July 16, 1961; admitted to bar, 1993, California. *Education:* Western Illinois University (B.A., 1983); University of Iowa (J.D., 1991). Co-Author: "Real Estate Litigation in the 1990's—Selected Issues," California Real Estate Reporter, Issue No. 10, Oct., 1993. Author: "The Interwit Arbitration Decision: Right or Wrong? Assumption of the Risk in Horseracing," 11th Annual National Equine Law Conference, University of Kentucky College of Law, May 1996; "The Interwit Arbitration Decision: Arbitrator Finds Owner, Trainer and Jockey Financially Liable for Racing Accident," Equine Law & Business Letter, May-June 1996, Vol. 7, No. 3. *Member:* American Bar Association; State Bar of California.

**MATTHEW J. HAFEY,** born Northampton, Massachusetts, October 21, 1964; admitted to bar, 1993, California; 1994, U.S. District Court, Central District of California; 1995, U.S. Court of Appeals, Ninth Circuit. *Education:* Columbia College, Columbia University (A.B., 1987); Loyola Law School (J.D., 1993). Member, Loyola of Los Angeles Law Review, 1991-1992. *Member:* State Bar of California.

## JAN C. GABRIELSON

*A LAW CORPORATION*

1875 CENTURY PARK EAST, SUITE 2150
**LOS ANGELES, CALIFORNIA 90067-2710**
Telephone: 310-785-9731

*Practice Limited to Family Law.*

**JAN C. GABRIELSON,** born San Francisco, California, July 15, 1944; admitted to bar, 1970, California. *Education:* University of California at Los Angeles (A.B., 1966); University of California School of Law (J.D., 1969). Author: "Valuation of Stock in Closely Held Corporations at the Time of Marriage Dissolution," Journal of the American Academy of Matrimonial Lawyers, 1985; "Surviving Your Own Divorce," California Lawyer, June, 1987; Book: "Practical Reflections of a California Divorce Lawyer," 1989. Lecturer: "Celebrity Goodwill and Valuation of Publicity Rights," California Society of Certified Public Accountants Entertainment Industry Conference, June 1990; "Tax Strategies in Divorce," Professional Education Systems, Inc., 1982; "Protecting the Professional in Divorce," Professional Education Systems, Inc., 1983, 1984; "Selected Issues in California Community Property Law," California Continuing Education of the Bar, 1983, 1985, 1990; "Evidentiary Issues and Trial Strategies in Marital Dissolutions," California Continuing Education of the Bar, October-November, 1984. *Member:* Century City (Chair, Family Law Section, 1984-1987; President, 1991) and Los Angeles County (Board of Trustees, 1992-1996; Member, Family Law Section, Executive Committee, 1985-1987) Bar Associations; State Bar of California (Family Law Section, Executive Committee, 1981-1984). Fellow, American Academy of Matrimonial Lawyers (Southern California Chapter; President, 1988-1989). (Certified Specialist, Family Law, The State Bar of California Board of Legal Specialization). *LANGUAGES:* French, Spanish and Italian.

## SCOTT GAILEN, INC.

*A PROFESSIONAL LAW CORPORATION*

SUITE 830
21700 OXNARD STREET, (WOODLAND HILLS)
**LOS ANGELES, CALIFORNIA 91367-3666**
Telephone: 818-715-7070
Fax: 818-715-7076

*Criminal Defense, Family Law, Insurance Defense, Civil Litigation, Personal Injury, Bankruptcy, Debt Consolidation, Entertainment Litigation.*

**SCOTT R. GAILEN,** born Los Angeles, California, September 20, 1954; admitted to bar, 1980, California and U.S. District Court, Central and Southern Districts of California; U.S. Court of Appeals, Seventh and Ninth Circuits; U.S. Court of Appeals for the Federal Circuit; U.S. Tax Court. *Education:* California State University, Northridge (B.A., cum laude, 1977); University of San Fernando (J.D., 1980). *Member:* San Fernando Valley and Los Angeles County Bar Associations; State Bar of California. *LANGUAGES:* Spanish.

## GAIMS, WEIL, WEST & EPSTEIN, LLP

A Partnership including a Professional Corporation

1875 CENTURY PARK EAST, TWELFTH FLOOR
**LOS ANGELES, CALIFORNIA 90067**
Telephone: 310-553-6666
Fax: 310-277-2133
Answer Back: Wild West
Telex: 910678746

*General Civil Trial and Appellate Practice in all State and Federal Courts and Government Agencies. Business Litigation, Insurance Coverage, Professional Liability, Antitrust, White Collar Criminal Defense, and International Law.*

### MEMBERS OF FIRM

**JOHN GAIMS,** born Sterling, Colorado, June 23, 1934; admitted to bar, 1968, California and U.S. District Courts, Central and Northern Districts of California. *Education:* University of California at Berkeley (B.A., 1956); University of California at Los Angeles (M.B.A., 1963); University of Southern California (J.D., 1967). Beta Gamma Sigma; Order of the Coif; Phi Alpha Delta. Recipient: Law Alumni Award; Executive Editor, University of Southern California Law Review, 1966-1967. Professor of Law, Northrop University Law School, 1973-1989; Recipient, Distinguished Professor Award. Judge Pro Tempore of the Los Angeles Municipal Court, 1976-1986. Arbitrator, American Stock Exchange, 1983—. Chairman of the State Bar Administrative Committee No. 45, 1973. *Member:* Beverly Hills Bar Association; State Bar of California.

**BARRY G. WEST,** born New York, N.Y., February 3, 1943; admitted to bar, 1967, New York; 1973, California. *Education:* Queen's College of the City University of New York (B.A., 1963); St. John's University School of Law (LL.B., 1966); Harvard University (LL.M., 1967). Associate Editor, St. John's Law Review, 1964. Arbitrator, Los Angeles County Superior Court, 1979—. *Member:* State Bar of California. *Email:* bgwest@primenet.com

**ALAN JAY WEIL,** born Houston, Texas, October 22, 1948; admitted to bar, 1973, Texas; 1974, California. *Education:* University of Texas (B.A., Plan II, with highest honors, 1970; J.D., with honors, 1973). Phi Beta Kappa. Law Clerk to Judge Homer Thornberry, U.S. Court of Appeals, Fifth Circuit, 1973-1974. Teaching Quizmaster, Legal Research and Writing and Oral Advocacy, University of Texas School of Law, 1972-1973. Assistant U.S. Attorney, Criminal Division, C.D. California, 1978-1981. Arbitrator, American Stock Exchange, 1983—. *Member:* State Bar of Texas; State Bar of California; American Bar Association.

**MARC EPSTEIN, (P.C.),** born Hollywood, California, March 1, 1949; admitted to bar, 1974, California. *Education:* University of California at Los Angeles (B.S., 1971; J.D., 1974). Tau Beta Pi; Order of the Coif. Member, 1972-1973, Articles Editor, 1973-1974, UCLA Law Review. Author, "Civil Responsibility for Corporate Political Expenditures," 20 UCLA Law Review 1327, 1973. Judge Pro Tempore, Los Angeles Municipal Court, 1981—. Committee Member, UCLA Law Annual Fund, 1987—. *Member:* State Bar of California; Association of Business Trial Lawyers.

**STEVEN S. DAVIS,** born Los Angeles, California, September 7, 1952; admitted to bar, 1977, California. *Education:* Dartmouth College (B.A., magna cum laude, 1974) Phi Beta Kappa; University of California at Los Angeles (J.D., 1977). Member, U.C.L.A. Law Review. Co-Author: "Toward the Regulation of Anticompetitive Insurance Mergers," *The Forum*, Section of Insurance, Negligence and Compensation Law, American Bar Association, Vol. XIII, No. 4, Summer, 1978. Extern to the Honorable David W. Williams, U.S. District Court, Central District of California, 1977. *Member:* State Bar of California.

**JEFFREY B. ELLIS,** born Philadelphia, Pennsylvania, April 23, 1953; admitted to bar, 1978, California; 1980, U.S. District Court, Central District of California. *Education:* University of Pennsylvania (B.A., cum laude, 1975); Loyola Law School, Los Angeles (J.D., 1978). Author: "Revisiting the Cumis Rule," California Lawyer, May, 1991; "Updated Approaches to Punitive Damages," California Lawyer, December, 1984. *Member:* Los Angeles County Bar Association; State Bar of California.

**AMY L. RICE,** born Pasadena, California, June 12, 1957; admitted to bar, 1983, California, U.S. District Court, Central, Eastern, Northern and Southern Districts of California and U.S. Court of Appeals, Ninth Circuit. *Education:* American University of Cairo, Cairo, Egypt; University of California at Los Angeles (B.A., cum laude, 1979); University of Southern California (J.D., 1983). Member, Moot Court Honors Program. *Member:* State Bar of California.

*(This Listing Continued)*

## GAIMS, WEIL, WEST & EPSTEIN, LLP, Los Angeles— Continued

**COREY E. KLEIN,** born St. Louis, Missouri, November 20, 1960; admitted to bar, 1987, California; 1988, U.S. District Court, Central District of California and U.S. Court of Appeals, Ninth Circuit. *Education:* University of California at Davis (B.S., with high honors, 1984); University of California at Los Angeles (J.D., 1987). Phi Kappa Phi. Recipient: Citation for Outstanding Performance. Member, UCLA Moot Court Honors Program. *Member:* American Bar Association; State Bar of California; Association of Business Trial Lawyers.

### ASSOCIATES

**PETER L. STEINMAN,** born East Brunswick, New Jersey, January 14, 1963; admitted to bar, 1989, California and U.S. District Court, Central District of California; 1991, District of Columbia. *Education:* University of Maryland (B.S., cum laude, with distinction, 1986); Georgetown University (J.D., cum laude, 1989). Phi Kappa Phi. Vice President, National Political Science Honor Society; John Marshall Pre-Law Honor Society; Political Science Honor Society. Recipient, Distinguished Scholar Award. Senior Staff Member, The Tax Lawyer, 1987-1989. *Member:* State Bar of California; District of Columbia Bar. *Email:* plslaw@loop.com

**SCOTT A. SCHNEIDER,** born Des Moines, Iowa, November 10, 1963; admitted to bar, 1989, California and U.S. District Court, Southern District of California. *Education:* University of Iowa (B.A., 1986; J.D., 1989). Associate Editor, University of Iowa Law Review, 1988-1989. *Member:* State Bar of California.

**ANNETTE E. DAVIS,** born Johannesburg, South Africa, March 11, 1964; admitted to bar, 1990, California; 1991, U.S. District Court, Central District of California. *Education:* University of Texas at Austin (B.A., summa cum laude, 1987; J.D., 1990). Phi Beta Kappa, Phi Kappa Phi. Distinguished Scholar. Recipient: Tom Head Law School Scholarship; National Endowed Presidential Scholarship; Texas Ex-Students' Lifetime Member Scholarship; Liberal Arts Council Scholarship. First Place, Texas State Moot Court Competition, 1990. Regional Semifinalist, ABA Moot Court Competition, 1989. Harvard Journal of Law and Public Policy. *Member:* Los Angeles County and American Bar Associations; State Bar of California; California Women Lawyers. *Email:* aedavis@loop.com

**SYLVIA M. VIRSIK,** born Bratislava, Czechoslovakia, October 3, 1965; admitted to bar, 1992, California. *Education:* University of California at Berkeley (B.A., 1987); University of Southern California (J.D., 1992). Editor, Interdisciplinary Journal.

**JESSICA D. LAZARUS,** born Los Angeles, California, November 16, 1970; admitted to bar, 1995, California, U.S. District Court, Central District of California and U.S. Court of Appeals, Ninth Circuit. *Education:* University of California at Berkeley (B.S., highest honors, 1992); University of California at Los Angeles (J.D., 1995). Phi Beta Kappa. Moot Court Honors Program. Extern to the Honorable William M. Byrne, Jr., U.S. District Judge, Central District of California, 1993. *Member:* State Bar of California.

---

## GALL & GALL
### 37TH FLOOR, 333 SOUTH GRAND AVENUE
### LOS ANGELES, CALIFORNIA 90071-1599
Telephone: 213-628-7269

*Corporation, Real Estate, Trust and Probate Law. Commercial Law and Collections. General Civil and Trial Practice in all State and Federal Courts.*

### MEMBERS OF FIRM

**HERBERT GALL** (1900-1984).

**JOHN U. GALL,** born Los Angeles, California, May 9, 1928; admitted to bar, 1954, California. *Education:* University of Missouri (B.S., 1950); University of Missouri and University of California at Los Angeles (LL.B., 1953). Delta Theta Phi. *Member:* Los Angeles County and American Bar Associations; The State Bar of California.

REFERENCE: Union Bank.

---

## JAMES A. GALLO
### LOS ANGELES, CALIFORNIA
(See Pasadena)

*Civil Litigation in all State and Federal Courts. Real Estate, Criminal Defense and Business Litigation.*

---

## GALTON & HELM
### 500 SOUTH GRAND AVENUE, SUITE 1200
### LOS ANGELES, CALIFORNIA 90071
Telephone: 213-629-8800
Telecopier: 213-629-0037

Palm Desert, California Office: 73-290 El Paseo, Suite 377. Telephone: 619-776-5600. Fax: 619-776-5602.

*Civil Litigation Practice in State and Federal Courts. Insurance Defense. (Life, Accident and Health, Bad Faith Defense, Professional Negligence, Reinsurance Law and ERISA).*

FIRM PROFILE: *The firm of Galton & Helm is engaged in a specialized legal practice involving life, accident and health, and disability insurance law, including the representation of insurers in "bad faith" and ERISA litigation. The firm's practice also includes the representation of insurance brokers and other professionals in professional negligence litigation. All attorneys in the firm are active in professional and civil endeavors related to our clients' interest. The firm of Galton & Helm maintains a commitment to provide the highest quality of legal service to its clients, at rates which are fair. Listed in Best's Directory of Recommended Insurance Attorneys, The Insurance Bar, Hines Insurance Counsel and American Insurance Attorneys.*

### MEMBERS OF FIRM

**STEPHEN H. GALTON,** born Tulare, California, December 23, 1937; admitted to bar, 1970, California. *Education:* University of Southern California (B.A., 1966; J.D., 1969). Author: "Coping with Punitive Damages: A California Perspective," Best's Review, November, 1981. *Member:* Los Angeles County (Member: Board of Trustees, 1987-1989; Trial Lawyers Section; Legislative Activity Committee, 1986-1987; Federal Courts Practices and Procedures Committee, 1986-1987; Superior Courts Committee, 1976-1978 and 1986-1987), Wilshire (President, 1986-1987; Member, Board of Governors, 1979-1989) and American (Member: Sections on Torts and Insurance Practice and Litigation; Committees on Life Insurance and Health Insurance) Bar Associations; State Bar of California (Chairman, Committee on Federal Courts, 1990-1991; Delegate, Conference of Delegates, 1973, 1976-1986); Association of Southern California Defense Counsel; Conference of Insurance Counsel; Defense Research Institute. **PRACTICE AREAS:** Civil Litigation.

**HUGH H. HELM,** born Douglas, Arizona, January 20, 1941; admitted to bar, 1970, California. *Education:* University of Southern California (B.S., 1962; J.D., 1969). Phi Delta Phi; Beta Gamma Sigma; Phi Kappa Phi. President, USC Alumni Association, 1984-1985 and Member, Board of Trustees, 1983-1989, University of Southern California. Chair of the Board, 1990-1992, Member, 1983-1994, Five Acres Boys and Girls Aid Society of Los Angeles. *Member:* Los Angeles County, Wilshire and American (Member, Sections on: Economics of Law; Torts and Insurance Practice; Health Insurance Law) Bar Associations; State Bar of California; Maritime Law Association of the United States; Defense Research Institute; Conference of Insurance Counsel. [Capt., USMC, 1962-1966]. **PRACTICE AREAS:** Civil Litigation.

**MICHAEL F. BELL,** born Little Rock, Arkansas, November 10, 1954; admitted to bar, 1979, California. *Education:* Texas Christian University (B.A., magna cum laude, 1975); Stanford University (J.D., 1979). Phi Beta Kappa. Vice President, Moot Court Board, 1978-1979. Editor and Business Manager, Stanford Journal of International Studies, 1977-1979. *Member:* Los Angeles County Bar Association; State Bar of California; Conference of Insurance Counsel. **PRACTICE AREAS:** Civil Litigation.

**DANIEL W. MAGUIRE,** born New York, N.Y., August 31, 1960; admitted to bar, 1985, California. *Education:* University of Notre Dame (B.A., 1981); Pepperdine University (J.D., cum laude, 1985). Student Director, Clinical Law, National Moot Court Team. *Member:* Wilshire, Los Angeles County (Member, Appellate Courts Committee, 1986—) and American Bar Associations; State Bar of California; Supreme Court of The United States; Los Angeles Public Counsel. (Resident at Palm Desert). **PRACTICE AREAS:** Civil Litigation.

*(This Listing Continued)*

# PROFESSIONAL BIOGRAPHIES

**CALIFORNIA—LOS ANGELES**

**DAVID A. LINGENBRINK,** born Seattle, Washington, June 16, 1962; admitted to bar, 1988, California and U.S. District Court, Central and Eastern Districts of California; 1991, U.S. District Court, Northern and Southern Districts of California. *Education:* University of Washington (B.A., 1985; J.D., 1988). *Member:* Los Angeles County Bar Association; State Bar of California (Member, Litigation Section). **REPORTED CASES:** Shadoan v. Provident Life & Accident Ins. Co., 824 F.Supp. 907 (C.D.CA 1993); Qualls v. Blue Cross, 22 F.3d 839 (9th Cir. 1994); Redlands Community Hosp. v. New England Mutual, 28 Cal.Rptr.2d 582 (1994); Bellisario v. Lone Star Life Ins. Co., 871 F.Supp. 374 (C.D.CA 1994). *PRACTICE AREAS:* Civil Litigation.

## ASSOCIATES

**CHRIS D. OLSEN,** born Ilwaco, Washington, February 9, 1965; admitted to bar, 1990, California, U.S. District Court, Central District of California and U.S. Court of Appeals, Ninth Circuit. *Education:* Cornell University (A.B., 1987); Universidad de Seville, Seville, Spain, 1985-1986; University of Southern California Law Center (J.D., 1990). Member, Moot Court Honors Program, 1988-1989. *Member:* Los Angeles County Bar Association; State Bar of California. *LANGUAGES:* Spanish. *PRACTICE AREAS:* Civil Litigation.

**MELISSA M. COWAN,** born Bellflower, California, November 7, 1970; admitted to bar, 1994, California. *Education:* California State University at Long Beach (B.S., finance, summa cum laude, 1991); University of California at Los Angeles (J.D., 1994). Phi Kappa Phi; Beta Gamma Sigma; Phi Delta Phi. Recipient: Outstanding Senior for Finance, Wall Street Journal Award; Managing Editor and Member, U.C.L.A. Law Review 1992-1994. Author: "Determining Insider Status Under Bankruptcy Code Section 547 (b)(4)(B) when 'I Resign' May Not Be Enough to Terminate Insider Status," 41 UCLA Rev. 1541 (1994). *Member:* State Bar of California. *PRACTICE AREAS:* General Civil Practice; Probate.

**EDITH SANCHEZ SHEA,** born Weehawken, New Jersey, August 3, 1966; admitted to bar, 1991, New Jersey; 1992, New York; 1995, California. *Education:* Cornell University (B.A., 1988); Boston University (J.D., 1991). Editor, Boston International Law Journal, 1991. Trial Attorney, U.S. Department of Justice, New York City, 1992-1994. Associate, Heidell Pittoni Murphy & Bach, New York City, 1991-1992. Summer Associate, Townley & Updike, New York City, 1990. Investigator, Massachusetts Commission Against Discrimination, Boston, Massachusetts, 1989. Summer Assistant, Finance Department, Paine Webber, Inc., 1987-1988. Member, Harriett Bukai Family Law Center, Women in International Trade. *Member:* State Bar of California. *LANGUAGES:* Spanish. *PRACTICE AREAS:* Civil Litigation.

**JOANNA M. EOFF,** born Nevada City, California, November 7, 1968; admitted to bar, 1995, California, U.S. District Court, Central District of California and U.S. Court of Appeals, Ninth Circuit. *Education:* University of California at Los Angeles (B.A., 1991); University of California School of Law (J.D., 1995). Teaching Assistant, Legal Research and Writing, 1993-1994. *Member:* Los Angeles County Bar Association; State Bar of California. *PRACTICE AREAS:* Civil Litigation.

**MICHAEL B. BERNACCHI,** born Oxnard, California, November 25, 1965; admitted to bar, 1992, California. *Education:* University of California at Berkeley (B.A., cum laude, 1988); Loyola University at Los Angeles (J.D., 1992). Note and Comment Editor, Loyola Law Review, 1990-1992. Author: "The Doctrine of Specialty: A More Liberal Exposition of Private Rights," 25 Loyola Law Review 1263. *Member:* State Bar of California. *PRACTICE AREAS:* General Litigation.

**MARK A. RIEKHOF,** born Portland, Oregon, January 24, 1969; admitted to bar, 1994, California. *Education:* University of San Diego (B.A., Business Economics, cum laude, 1991); Santa Clara University (J.D., 1994). Technical Editor, Santa Clara Law Review. Staff Editor, Santa Clara Environmental & International Law Bulletin. Author: "Fraud, Withdrawal & Disclosure: What to Tell The Lawyer Who Steps into My Shoes," 34 Santa Clara Law Review, 1235 (1994). *Member:* State Bar of California. (Resident, Glendale Office).

## LEGAL SUPPORT PERSONNEL

**LANA BANKS,** born Long Beach, California, March 26, 1945. *Education:* University of San Diego (Paralegal Program, 1982-1983). *Member:* San Diego Legal Assistants Association, 1984-1990; South Florida Legal Assistants Association, 1991-1992; National Association of Legal Secretaries, 1984-1992. (Paralegal). *PRACTICE AREAS:* Discovery; Trial Preparation; Legal Research.

*(This Listing Continued)*

**STEPHANIE M. MCCARTHY,** born Cork, Ireland, September 23, 1964. *Education:* National University of Ireland, UCC (BCL, 1990). Solicitor, Law Society of Ireland, 1993 and 1994. (Paralegal). *LANGUAGES:* French. *PRACTICE AREAS:* Discovery; Trial Preparation; Legal Research.

REPRESENTATIVE CLIENTS: A.I.G. Life Insurance Co.; Aetna Life Insurance Co.; Alexander & Alexander; American Home Assurance Co.; American General Group; Amex Life Assurance Co.; Banner Life Insurance Co.; Benefit Trust Life Insurance Co.; Blue Cross of California; Celtic Life Insurance Co.; CIGNA Cos.; Cologne Life Reinsurance Co.; Fidelity Mutual Life Insurance Co.; General American Life Insurance Co.; Great American Reserve Insurance Co.; The Guardian Life Insurance Company of America; Hartford Life and Accident Insurance Co.; Home Insurance Co.; J.C. Penney Life Insurance Co.; Lone Star Life Insurance Co.; Massachusetts Casualty Insurance Co.; MBL Life Assurance Corp.; Provident Life and Accident Insurance Co.; Royal Maccabees Life Insurance Co.; Chubb Sovereign; Sovereign Life Insurance Co.; State Farm Life Insurance Co.; Standard Insurance Co.; Standard Security Life Insurance Company of New York; Transport Life Insurance Co.; United American Insurance Co.; United Insurance Cos.; U.S. Life Insurance Co.

---

## THE LAW OFFICES OF
## MAE R. GALVEZ-LANTION

3250 WILSHIRE BOULEVARD, SUITE 1110
**LOS ANGELES, CALIFORNIA 90010**
Telephone: 213-385-4040
Fax: 213-385-0444
Email: gllaw@worldnetaccess.com

*General Civil Litigation and Appellate Practice in all State and Federal Courts. Business, Corporate, Commercial, Personal Injury, Estate Planning and Trusts.*

**MAE R. GALVEZ-LANTION,** born Quezon City, Philippines, March 29, 1955; admitted to bar, 1979, Philippines; 1990, California. *Education:* University of the Philippines (A.B. cum laude; LL.B. cum laude). *Member:* Los Angeles County Bar Association; Integrated Bar of the Philippines; Asian Law Association; The Association of Trial Lawyers of America. *LANGUAGES:* Filipino. *PRACTICE AREAS:* Business Law; Civil Litigation; Estate Planning and Trusts; Personal Injury.

---

## GANG, TYRE, RAMER & BROWN, INC.

**LOS ANGELES, CALIFORNIA**
(See Beverly Hills)

*Entertainment and Communications Industries Law and Related Services.*

---

## GANSINGER, HINSHAW, BUCKLEY & PADILLA, LLP

Established in 1981

300 SOUTH GRAND AVENUE
SUITE 3850
**LOS ANGELES, CALIFORNIA 90071**
Telephone: 213-229-2500
FAX: 213-625-0755

*General Civil Litigation. Construction, Securities, Insurance Coverage, Unfair Competition and Receivership.*

### MEMBERS OF FIRM

**JAMES M. GANSINGER,** born Pittsburgh, Pennsylvania, December 4, 1945; admitted to bar, 1970, Colorado, U.S. District Court, District of Colorado and U.S. Court of Appeals, Tenth Circuit; 1971, California; 1975, U.S. District Court, Northern, Central and Southern Districts of California and U.S. Court of Appeals, Ninth Circuit; 1976, U.S. Supreme Court. *Education:* Bucknell University (B.A., 1967); Stanford University (J.D., 1970). Member, Stanford Law School Board of Visitors, 1987—. Judge Pro Tem, Los Angeles Municipal Court, 1977—. Arbitrator, National Association of Securities Dealers and New York Stock Exchange, 1987-1995. Member, Panel of Arbitrators, (Civil and Construction), American Arbitration Association. *Member:* Los Angeles County, Colorado and American Bar Associations; The State Bar of California. *PRACTICE AREAS:* Complex Commercial Litigation; Construction; Securities; Trade Regulation.

*(This Listing Continued)*

CAA685B

## GANSINGER, HINSHAW, BUCKLEY & PADILLA, LLP,
*Los Angeles—Continued*

**DAVID C. HINSHAW,** born Columbia, Missouri, April 20, 1950; admitted to bar, 1977, Missouri; 1980, California and U.S. District Court, Central District of California; 1982, U.S. Court of Appeals, Ninth Circuit; 1983, U.S. District Court, Southern and Northern Districts of California. *Education:* University of Missouri (B.A., 1972); Harvard Law School (J.D., 1976). Arbitrator: Los Angeles County Bar Association, 1982—; National Association of Securities Dealers, 1987—. Judge Pro Tem, Los Angeles Municipal Court, 1985—. *Member:* Los Angeles County and American Bar Associations; The Missouri Bar; State Bar of California. **PRACTICE AREAS:** Civil Litigation; Insurance Coverage; Securities.

**BRIAN L. BUCKLEY,** born New Orleans, Louisiana, September 6, 1954; admitted to bar, 1980, New York and U.S. District Court, Southern and Eastern Districts of New York; 1984, California; 1985, U.S. District Court, Central and Southern Districts of California; 1986, U.S. Court of Appeals, Ninth Circuit. *Education:* Dartmouth College (A.B., cum laude, 1976); Marshall-Wythe School of Law at the College of William and Mary (J.D., 1979). Arbitrator, Los Angeles County Bar Association, 1986—. Judge Pro Tem, Los Angeles Municipal Court, 1988—. *Member:* Association of the Bar of the City of New York; Los Angeles County, New York State and American Bar Associations; State Bar of California. **REPORTED CASES:** Securities and Exchange Commission v. American Principals Holding, Inc., 817 F.2d 1349 (9th cir, 1987). **PRACTICE AREAS:** Complex Commercial Litigation; Unfair Competition.

**JOSE L. PADILLA, JR.,** born Santa Monica, California, September 3, 1957; admitted to bar, 1982, California; 1983, U.S. Tax Court, U.S. Court of Appeals, Ninth Circuit and U.S. District Court, Central District of California; 1984, U.S. District Court, Southern District of California. *Education:* University of California at Los Angeles (B.A., 1979); University of Santa Clara (J.D., cum laude, 1982). *Member:* Los Angeles County Bar Association; State Bar of California. **LANGUAGES:** Spanish. **PRACTICE AREAS:** Construction Litigation; Business Litigation; Civil Litigation.

### ASSOCIATES

**T.A. TAURINO,** born Philadelphia, Pennsylvania, November 20, 1959; admitted to bar, 1988, California; 1989, U.S. Court of Appeals, Ninth Circuit. *Education:* Haverford College (B.S., 1985); Stanford University (J.D., 1988). *Member:* Los Angeles County and American Bar Associations. State Bar of California. **PRACTICE AREAS:** Business Litigation; Civil Litigation; Insurance Coverage.

**MICHAEL A. CLOUSER,** born Harrisburg, Pennsylvania, February 15, 1963; admitted to bar, 1989, California and U.S. Court of Appeals, Ninth Circuit; 1994, Pennsylvania. *Education:* College of William & Mary (B.S., Beta Gamma Sigma, Accounting, 1986); University of Miami (J.D., cum laude, 1989). Managing Editor, University of Miami Law Review, 1988-1989. Editor, University of Miami Sports and Entertainment Law Journal, 1989. *Member:* Beverly Hills, Los Angeles County, Pennsylvania and American Bar Associations; State Bar of California; Sports Lawyers Association. **LANGUAGES:** Spanish. **PRACTICE AREAS:** Business Litigation; Civil Litigation.

**MARY MOSS APPLETON,** born Boston, Massachusetts, January 8, 1948; admitted to bar, 1994, California, U.S. District Court, Central District of California and U.S. Court of Appeals, Ninth Circuit. *Education:* California State University at Northridge (B.A., 1983); University of California at Los Angeles (J.D., 1994).

### OF COUNSEL

**BRUCE D. BERLS,** born Glendale, California, November 15, 1954; admitted to bar, 1980, California and U.S. District Court, Central District of California; 1992, U.S. Court of Appeals, Ninth Circuit. *Education:* Claremont McKenna College (B.A., magna cum laude with honors, 1976); University of California at Los Angeles (J.D., 1979). *Member:* Los Angeles County and Sonoma County Bar Associations; State Bar of California. **PRACTICE AREAS:** Civil Litigation; Insurance Coverage; Travel Law. **Email:** bruceb@wco.com

REPRESENTATIVE CLIENTS: N.V. Philips Goleilampenfabrikien; Cardiotronics, Inc.; Magnavox Corp.; Sylvania, Inc.; Zieman Manufacturing Co.; Staff Pro Security, Inc.; Polygram Records, Inc.; Gosnell Builders, Inc.; Pointe Resorts, Inc.; Ashley Orr, Receiver of American Principals Holdings Inc.; Eric Davis; Danny Cox; Darryl Strawberry; Marquis Grissom; Ron Gant; David Justice; Standard Flour Company; Allergan, Inc.; Metzler International Optik, GmBH; Prescott, Ball & Turbin, Inc.; Allied Bakery Equipment Inc.; Kemper Securities Group, Inc.; Mars Sales Co.; 3D Systems, Inc.; Philip Morris, Inc.; California Commerce Casino; A.B.N.T. Group; Intra-American Foundation & Drilling Co.; Charles Pankow Builders, Ltd.

*(This Listing Continued)*

---

## LAW OFFICE OF EMMETT J. GANTZ
### LOS ANGELES, CALIFORNIA
(See Beverly Hills)

*Professional Liability, Products Liability, Medical Malpractice, Insurance Bad Faith, Complex Civil Litigation and Personal Injury. Civil Trial and Appellate Practice.*

---

## GANZ & GORSLINE, A LAW PARTNERSHIP
### 11620 WILSHIRE BOULEVARD, SUITE 340
### LOS ANGELES, CALIFORNIA 90025-1769
Telephone: 310-235-1700
Fax: 310-235-1707
Email: Info@GanzGorsLaw.com
URL: http://www.GanzGorsLaw.com

*Employment Law, Civil Trial, Business Litigation.*

**PHILIP J. GANZ, JR.,** born Chicago, Illinois, June 10, 1948; admitted to bar, 1973, California. *Education:* Michigan State University, Honors College (B.A., with high honors, 1970); University of Michigan (J.D., cum laude, 1973). Phi Eta Sigma. Panel Speaker: "Effective Opening Statements and Closing Arguments," CEB, 1992; "For the Plaintiff: Determining and Proving Damages," NBI, 1993; "Use of Psychiatrists, Psychologists and Other Behavioral Scientists As Experts In Sexual Harassment Cases," Georgetown University Law Center, 13th Annual Employment Law and Litigation Conference, EEO Update, 1995. Member, Panel of Arbitrators Los Angeles County Superior Court, 1982—. Delegate, Los Angeles County Bar Association Delegation, California State Bar Conference of Delegates, 1982-1984. *Member:* Malibu, Los Angeles County and American (Member, Litigation Section) Bar Associations; State Bar of California (Member, Labor and Employment Law Section); Association of Business Trial Lawyers (Member, Committee on Private Judging); The Association of Trial Lawyers of America; Consumer Attorneys of California; Consumer Attorneys Association of Los Angeles. **REPORTED CASES:** Hyatt v. Northrop Corporation, 80 F3d 1425 (9th Cir. 1996). **PRACTICE AREAS:** Civil Trials; Employment Law; Business Litigation.

**LAURIE SUSAN GORSLINE,** born San Bernardino, California, October 22, 1959; admitted to bar, 1986, California; 1987, U.S. District Court, Central District of California and U.S. Court of Appeals, Ninth Circuit. *Education:* University of California at Los Angeles (B.A., 1981); Loyola Law School, Los Angeles (J.D., 1984). Phi Alpha Delta; Phi Sigma Alpha. Staff Attorney to: Hon. Charles Jones, Superior Court Judge, 1985; Hon. Robert H. O'Brien, Superior Court Judge, 1986; Hon. Ricardo Torres, Superior Court Judge, 1987-1988. Supervising Staff Attorney for the Law Departments, Central District, 1988. Speaker: Sexual Harassment In the Workplace, Internal Revenue Service, 1994; Century City Bar Association, 1993; Association of Real Estate Attorneys, 1995. *Member:* Santa Monica, Los Angeles County and American Bar Associations (Member, Labor and Employment Law and Litigation Sections); State Bar of California (Member, Labor and Employment Law Section); California Women Lawyers; Los Angeles County Bar Barristers. **REPORTED CASES:** Hyatt v. Northrop Corporation, 80 F3d 1425 (9th Cir. 1996). **PRACTICE AREAS:** Employment; Civil Litigation.

---

## WILLIAM J. GARGARO, JR.
### A PROFESSIONAL CORPORATION
### SUITE 1800, 2049 CENTURY PARK EAST
### LOS ANGELES, CALIFORNIA 90067
Telephone: 310-552-0633
Fax: 310-552-9760

*Medical Malpractice Law. Federal and State Trial and Appellate Practice.*

**WILLIAM J. GARGARO, JR.,** born Detroit, Michigan, August 9, 1939; admitted to bar, 1965, District of Columbia; 1966, California. *Education:* Georgetown University (A.B., 1961; LL.B., 1964). Author: "Presenting the Medical Evidence: Does Doctor's Failure to Make Timely Cancer Diag-

*(This Listing Continued)*

nosis Constitute Legal Proximate Cause?" a six part article appearing in the October and December, 1977 and February, April, June and August, 1978 issues of TRAUMA, published by Matthew Bender & Company; "Specimen Final Argument," published in Lawyer's Guide to Medical Proof, Vol. 3, pgs. 1900-4 to 1900-106, published by Matthew Bender & Company, 1978; "Contrasting Witness' Own Standards of Practice With Those of Defendant Doctor—Delayed Diagnosis of Breast Cancer," Chapter 7 and "Impeachment of Defendant on Standard of Care—Bias—Delayed Diagnosis of Breast Cancer," Chapter 29, Art of Advocacy, Matthew Bender & Company, 1982; Neonatology for the Clinician, Chapter 41 "What Clinician Should Know About Malpractice Law," published by Appleton & Lange, 1992. Lecturer in Law, Law Center, University of Southern California, 1974-1977. Adjunct Professor of Law, Loyola Marymount University School of Law, 1985-1992. Assistant U.S. Attorney, Southern and Central Districts of California, 1966-1968. Deputy District Attorney, County of Los Angeles, 1969-1973. Chief, District Attorney's Strike Force Investigations, Hospitals, Pharmacies and Clinics, 1972-1973. Member, Liaison Committee, California Medical Association, 1980-1983. *Member:* Century City, Los Angeles County (Member, Special Committee on Public Disorder Intelligence Guidelines, 1975-1980; Member, Medical-Legal Relations Committee 1976-1980; Member, 1976-1983 and Chairman, 1980-1983, County Medical Association Joint Liaison Committee; Member: Designee to County Select Citizens Committee on Life Support Policies, 1978-1981; Bioethics Committee, 1978-1983; Legislative Committee, 1978-1982; Co-Chairman, Subcommittee on Medical-Legal Legislation, 1979-1981), Federal and American (Vice-Chair: Committee on Medicine and Law, Section of Tort and Insurance Practice, 1988-1989; Medical Malpractice Committee, 1988—) Bar Associations; State Bar of California; San Francisco Trial Lawyers Association; California Trial Lawyers Association; The Association of Trial Lawyers of America; American Board of Trial Advocates; District of Columbia Bar. **PRACTICE AREAS:** Medical Malpractice Law; Personal Injury Law.

REFERENCE: Wells Fargo Bank.

## GARRETT & TULLY

A PROFESSIONAL CORPORATION

**LOS ANGELES, CALIFORNIA**

(See Pasadena)

*Business and Real Estate Litigation in all State and Federal Courts.*

## GARTENBERG JAFFE GELFAND & STEIN LLP

*11755 WILSHIRE BOULEVARD, SUITE 1230*
**LOS ANGELES, CALIFORNIA 90025-1518**
Telephone: 310-479-0044
Fax: 310-477-7663

*Securities, Corporate and Litigation in State and Federal Courts.*

**EDWARD GARTENBERG,** born Regensburg, West Germany, June 29, 1949; admitted to bar, 1975, New York, U.S. District Court, Southern and Eastern Districts of New York and U.S. Court of Appeals, Second Circuit; 1980, District of Columbia, U.S. District Court, District of Columbia and Eastern District of Wisconsin and U.S. Court of Appeals, District of Columbia Circuit; 1982, California, U.S. District Court, Central and Northern Districts of California and U.S. Court of Appeals, Ninth Circuit. *Education:* Columbia University (B.A., 1971; J.D., 1974). Associate Editor, Columbia Journal of Law and Social Problems, 1973-1974. Author: "Mandatory Arbitration of Stockbroker-Customer Disputes," Los Angeles Lawyer, December, 1987; "Many Estate Planners are Also Investment Advisers Required to Register with the SEC," Estate Planning, January/February, 1987; "Air Pollution—The Landlords and New York City's New Air Code," 9 Columbia Journal of Law and Social Problems 495, 1973. Staff Attorney, 1976-1979 and Special Counsel, 1979-1981, Division of Enforcement, United States Securities and Exchange Commission, 1976-1981. Special Assistant United States Attorney, United States Attorney's Office for the District of Columbia, 1980-1981. Arbitrator, National Association of Securities Dealers, 1986—. Arbitrator, National Futures Association. *Member:* Westwood (Member, Board of Governors, 1988—; Secretary, 1988-1989; Treasurer, 1989-1990; Vice President, 1990-1991) and American (Member, Federal Regulation of Securities Committee and Subcommittee on Broker-

*(This Listing Continued)*

Dealers Matters) Bar Associations; District of Columbia Bar; State Bar of California. **PRACTICE AREAS:** Civil Litigation; Securities Law.

**SHELDON M. JAFFE,** born Hartford, Connecticut, November 21, 1934; admitted to bar, 1962, Massachusetts; 1964, Connecticut; 1965, California and U.S. District Court, Central District of California; 1971, U.S. Supreme Court; 1976, U.S. Court of Appeals, Seventh Circuit; 1980, U.S. Court of Appeals, Ninth Circuit. *Education:* Yale University (B.A., 1956); Harvard University (LL.B., 1962). Author: *Pitfalls in the Public Sale of Shares Acquired in Mergers,* 1969; "Broker-Dealers and Securities Markets—A Guide to the Regulatory Process," Shepard's, Inc., 1977; "SIPC Insurance," Review of Securities Regulation, December, 1977. Attorney, United States Securities and Exchange Commission, 1962-1963. Arbitrator, National Association of Securities Dealers. Appointed Receiver by Federal and State Courts, 1982—. *Member:* Los Angeles County (Member: Business and Corporations Law Section; Executive Committee, 1969-1982), Massachusetts and American (Member, Subcommittee in Federal Regulation of Securities, Section of Corporation, Banking and Business Law, 1981-1982) Bar Associations; The State Bar of California.

**EDWARD S. GELFAND,** born Chicago, Illinois, February 4, 1948; admitted to bar, 1976, California; 1977, U.S. District Court, Central District of California; 1982, U.S. Court of Appeals, Ninth Circuit and U.S. Supreme Court. *Education:* Roosevelt University (B.S., 1970); University of San Fernando Valley College of Law (J.D., 1976). Chief, Branch of Enforcement and Special Counsel, 1981-1984 and Staff Attorney, 1978-1981, U.S. Securities and Exchange Commission. *Member:* Los Angeles County Bar Association; State Bar of California. **PRACTICE AREAS:** Public and Private Securities Offerings; Securities Arbitration; Broker-Dealer; Investment Adviser Regulation; NASD Arbitration; Business Planning; Business Formation and Structure.

**CRAIG J. STEIN,** born New York, N.Y., March 19, 1952; admitted to bar, 1979, New York and U.S. District Court, Eastern & Southern Districts of New York; 1981, California and U.S. District Court, Central District of California. *Education:* Bryant College (B.S., 1974); Hofstra University (J.D., 1979). *Member:* The State Bar of California. **PRACTICE AREAS:** Business Litigation.

ASSOCIATE

**TORGNY R. NILSSON,** born Göteborg, Sweden, March 22, 1965; admitted to bar, 1992, California. *Education:* University of California at Davis (B.A., 1988); Institute of International & Comparative Law at Magdalen College, Oxford University, Oxford, England (Certificate of Completion, 1990); Santa Clara University (J.D., 1992). Phi Delta Phi (Historian and Charter Member, Field Inn, 1991-1992). Pupil, Santa Clara Inn, America Inns of Court. Recipient, American Jurisprudence Award for Constitutional Law. Technical Editor, Santa Clara Law Review, 1991-1992. Barrister, West Los Angeles Inn, American Inns of Court, 1993—. *Member:* State Bar of California (Member, International Law Section); American Bar Association (Student Representative, 1991-1992); American Branch of the International Law Association. **LANGUAGES:** Swedish and German.

## GARTNER & YOUNG

A PROFESSIONAL CORPORATION

*1925 CENTURY PARK EAST, SUITE 2050*
**LOS ANGELES, CALIFORNIA 90067-2709**
Telephone: 310-556-3576
Fax: 310-556-8459

*Labor Relations, Management, Public and Private Sectors.*

FIRM PROFILE: *Gartner & Young was founded in 1985 by Lawrence J. Gartner and Naomi Young. This Boutique Labor and Employment Law firm exclusively represents private and public sector employers in Labor Relations, Equal Employment Opportunity and Wrongful Discharge Matters. Gartner & Young is a 51% Minority and Female Owned Business Enterprise.*

**NAOMI YOUNG,** born Bronx, New York, August 6, 1950; admitted to bar, 1974, California. *Education:* St. Louis University (B.A., 1971); Santa Clara University (J.D., 1974). Field Attorney, National Labor Relations Board, 1974-1975. Member, California Fair Employment and Housing Commission, 1987-1989. *Member:* Los Angeles County (Member, Executive Committee, Labor and Employment Law Section, 1993—) and American Bar Associations; State Bar of California (Referee: Hearing Department, State Bar Court, 1983-1985; Review Department, State Bar Court, 1986-1988); John M. Langston Bar Association (Member, Board of Directors, 1982-1983); California Association of Black Lawyers (Vice President,

*(This Listing Continued)*

**GARTNER & YOUNG,** A PROFESSIONAL CORPORATION, Los Angeles—Continued

1977); National Bar Association; California Women Lawyers (Member, Board of Governors, 1978); Black Women Lawyers Association of Los Angeles. *PRACTICE AREAS:* Labor and Employment Law.

**LAWRENCE J. GARTNER,** born Brooklyn, New York, September 26, 1945; admitted to bar, 1971, California. *Education:* University of California at Berkeley (B.A., 1967); Harvard University (J.D., 1970). Trial Attorney, U.S. Equal Employment Opportunity Commission, 1970-1976. *Member:* Los Angeles County and American Bar Associations; State Bar of California (Chairperson, Public Employment Committee, Labor Section, 1985-1986). *PRACTICE AREAS:* Labor and Employment Law.

**CHRISTOPHER ADAMS THORN,** born Hammond, Indiana, February 4, 1959; admitted to bar, 1984, California and U.S. District Court, Central District of California; 1988, U.S. Supreme Court; 1990, U.S. District Court, Southern District of California; 1991, U.S. District Court, Eastern and Northern Districts of California. *Education:* University of Wisconsin-Madison (B.B.A., cum laude, 1981); University of Southern California (J.D., 1984). Articles Editor, Southern California Law Review, 1983-1984. Author: "Retribution Exclusive of Deterrence: An Insufficient Justification for Capital Punishment," 57 Southern California Law Review 199, 1983. Co-Author: Chapter 19 Responding to Internal Complaints in B. Lindemann & D. Kadue, Sexual Harassment in Employment Law (BNA 1992—). Member, Board of Directors, International Institute of Los Angeles, 1991—; and Executive Committee, 1992—). *Member:* Los Angeles County (Litigation and Labor Law Sections, 1986—) and American (Labor and Employment Law Section, 1986—) Bar Associations; State Bar of California (Litigation Section, 1985—; Labor and Employment Law Section, 1986—). *PRACTICE AREAS:* Labor and Employment Law.

**KIMBERLY M. TALLEY,** born Columbus, Ohio; admitted to bar, 1990, California; 1994, U.S. District Court, Central, Northern and Southern Districts of California. *Education:* University of South Carolina (B.S., magna cum laude, 1986); Harvard University (J.D., 1989). Phi Beta Kappa. Presidential Scholar Recipient, Earl Warren Scholarship. Member, Black Women Lawyers, 1994—. *Member:* State Bar of California. *PRACTICE AREAS:* Labor and Employment Law.

**JENNIFER L. FUTCH,** born West Monroe, Louisiana, July 1, 1969; admitted to bar, 1994, California; U.S. District Court, Central, Northern, Eastern and Southern Districts of California; U.S. Court of Appeals, Ninth Circuit. *Education:* Louisiana State University (B.A., cum laude, 1991); Pepperdine University School of Law (J.D., cum laude, 1994). Phi Alpha Delta. Member, Pepperdine University School of Law Law Review, 1992-1994. *Member:* Beverly Hills Bar Association; State Bar of California. *PRACTICE AREAS:* Labor and Employment Law.

**JILL HENSON,** born Clovis, New Mexico, January 22, 1972; admitted to bar, 1996, California and U.S. District Court, Central and Southern Districts of California. *Education:* New Mexico State University (B.B.A., 1993); Pepperdine University (J.D., cum laude, 1995). Outstanding Graduate, College of Business Administration, New Mexico State University, 1993. *PRACTICE AREAS:* Labor and Employment Law.

**ANGELA J. REDDOCK,** born Wurzburg, Germany, November 2, 1969; admitted to bar, 1996, California. *Education:* Amherst College (B.A., 1991); University of California School of Law at Los Angeles (J.D., 1995). Special Features Editor, National Black Law Journal, 1993-1995. *Member:* Black Law Students Association of California. *PRACTICE AREAS:* Labor and Employment Law.

**GREGORY P. BRIGHT,** born Los Angeles, California, September 9, 1963; admitted to bar, 1991, California and U.S. District Court, Central District of California; 1993, U.S. District Court, Southern District of California. *Education:* University of Southern California (B.A., 1987); Pepperdine University, School of Law (J.D., 1990). Recipient: American Jurisprudence Awards for Contracts, Torts and Government Contracts; Dean's Merit Scholarship, 1988-1989. Member, National Dean's List, 1989. Author, "Reconciling an Old Dog's New Tricks: The California Supreme Court Remodels Assumption of Risk in Knight and Ford," Beverly Hills Bar Association Journal Vol. 26, No. 4 Fall 1992. Volunteer Arbitrator, Los Angeles Superior Court, 1993-1996. *Member:* Los Angeles County and American Bar Associations; State Bar of California; Barristers. *PRACTICE AREAS:* Labor and Employment Law.

CAA688B

## DONALD J. GARY, JR., P.C.
*445 SOUTH FIGUEROA STREET*
*TWENTY-SIXTH FLOOR*
**LOS ANGELES, CALIFORNIA 90017**
Telephone: 213-439-5385

*Riverside, California Office:* 3700 Sixth Street at Main, Second Floor. P.O. Box 664. 92502-0664. Telephone: 909-786-0100. Facsimile: 909-683-8458.

*Federal and State Taxation, Probate and Estate Planning, General Business, Corporation, Partnerships, Limited Liability Company.*

(For biographical data on all personnel, see Professional Biographies at Riverside, California)

## GASCOU, GEMMILL & THORNTON
*Established in 1980*
*15TH FLOOR 10866 WILSHIRE BOULEVARD*
**LOS ANGELES, CALIFORNIA 90024**
Telephone: 310-470-4226
Fax: 310-470-1360
Email: ggt@leonardo.net

*General Civil, Trial and Appellate Practice in all State and Federal Courts. Fidelity and Surety, Insurance, Corporate, Probate and Escrow Law.*

*FIRM PROFILE: As a medium-sized firm, GASCOU, GEMMILL & THORNTON provides clients with the personal representation of a small firm and the resources of a large firm. The firm originated in the mid 1970's representing clients in fidelity and surety matters. The firm works with clients to resolve matters ranging from small license bonds to large and complicated contract surety defaults helps clients unravel complex fraud cases involving employee dishonesty under financial institution or commercial fidelity packages, expanded into the field of property and casualty coverages.*

*The firm renders coverage advice to clients on issues arising under comprehensive general liability policies, home warranty insurance policies and many other types of policies, investigates and provides opinions concerning issues arising under many types of property and casualty policies. The firm has set up and supervised claims procedures for risk retention groups in the products liability area, provides assistance to clients in avoiding or defending allegations of breach of the covenant of good faith and fair dealing or bad faith.*

**RENÉ J. GASCOU, JR.,** born Compton, California, January 31, 1945; admitted to bar, 1972, California. *Education:* University of Southern California (B.A., cum laude, 1967); Georgetown University (J.D., 1970). Member, Blackstonians. President, Surety Claims Association of Los Angeles, 1983-1984. *Member:* State Bar of California; American Bar Association (Member, Fidelity and Surety Committee, The Forum Committee on the Construction Industry, The Bonding and Insurance Committee, Section of Public Contract Law and the Committee on Law in Public Service); Inter-Pacific Bar Association (Member, Committee on International Construction Projects). *LANGUAGES:* German. *PRACTICE AREAS:* Fidelity Law; Suretyship Law; Construction Law; Trials.

**WILLIAM P. GEMMILL,** born Colorado Springs, Colorado, July 22, 1948; admitted to bar, 1976, California. *Education:* University of California at Santa Barbara (B.A., 1970); Columbia University (J.D., 1975). *Member:* State Bar of California; Los Angeles County (Member, TIPS, Insurance Coverage Section, Fidelity and Surety Section) and American Bar Associations. *LANGUAGES:* French and Japanese. *PRACTICE AREAS:* Trials and Appeals; Insurance Coverage; Defense; Suretyship Law; Fidelity Law; Unfair Competition.

**BRUCE M. THORNTON,** born Tampa, Florida, August 13, 1951; admitted to bar, 1976, California. *Education:* University of Texas (B.A., summa cum laude, 1973); University of California at Los Angeles (J.D., 1976). Phi Beta Kappa; Phi Eta Sigma. Member, Moot Court. Author: "Insurability of Losses Resulting from Liability Under The Federal Securities Laws," 13 Pacific Law Journal 959, 1982. *Member:* Los Angeles County Bar Association; The State Bar of California. *PRACTICE AREAS:* Trials and Appeals; Insurance Coverage; Construction; Fidelity; Suretyship.

**MICHAEL G. EVANS,** born Oak Park, Illinois, October 13, 1954; admitted to bar, 1980, California, U.S. District Court, Southern, Central, Northern and Eastern Districts of California and U.S. Court of Appeals, 9th Circuit; 1981, U.S. Court of Appeals, Federal Circuit; 1984, U.S. Claims Court. *Education:* University of California at Santa Barbara (B.A., magna cum laude, 1977); Loyola University of Los Angeles (J.D., 1980). Phi Alpha Delta. Associate Justice, Scott Moot Court. Competitor, Roger

*(This Listing Continued)*

Traynor Moot Court Competition, 1980. *Member:* Los Angeles County and American Bar Associations; The State Bar of California; Los Angeles Trial Lawyer's Association. *REPORTED CASES:* Escrow Agents Fidelity Corp. v. Superior Court, (1992) 4 Cal. 4th 491. *PRACTICE AREAS:* Fidelity; Commercial Litigation; Real Estate Litigation; Legislation; Creditor Rights.

**RONALD W. HOPKINS,** born Ft. Worth, Texas, January 10, 1954; admitted to bar, 1981, California. *Education:* L'Universita Italiana Per Stranieri, Perugia, Italy; Stanford University (A.B., with distinction, 1977); University of California at Los Angeles (J.D., 1981). Member, Moot Court Honors Program. *Member:* State Bar of California; American Bar Association. *LANGUAGES:* French, Italian, Spanish and German. *PRACTICE AREAS:* Fidelity; Suretyship; Construction Law.

### ASSOCIATES

**CARLOS V. YGUICO,** born Manila, Philippines, February 16, 1962; admitted to bar, 1987, California, U.S. District Court, Central District of California and U.S. Court of Appeals, Ninth Circuit. *Education:* University of California at Los Angeles (B.A., with honors, 1983); University of Southern California (J.D., 1987). Pi Gamma Mu. Staff Editor, 1985-1986 and Managing Editor, 1986-1987, Major Tax Planning and Computer/Law Journal. *Member:* State Bar of California; Philippine American Bar Association of Los Angeles (Treasurer, 1989-1990). [First Lieutenant, U.S. Army Reserve, J.A.G.C., 1996—]. *LANGUAGES:* Filipino. *REPORTED CASES:* FSR Brokerage, Inc. v. Superior Court (1995) 35 Cal. App. 4th 6a, 41 Cal. Rptr. 2d 404. *PRACTICE AREAS:* Trials and Appeals; Insurance Coverage; Construction; Fidelity; Suretyship.

**CAROLYN TAYLOR MCQUEEN,** born Los Angeles, California, February 24, 1963; admitted to bar, 1989, California; 1990, U.S. District Court, Central District of California. *Education:* Spelman College (B.A., cum laude, 1985) Mortar Board; University of California, Hastings College of the Law (J.D., 1988). Co-Author, "Damages Recoverable Under a Performance Bond," presented to American Bar Association Meeting, Forum on the Construction Industry and Fidelity and Surety Law Committee, January 26, 1995. *Member:* Los Angeles County and American Bar Associations; State Bar of California (Member, Litigation Section); National Bar Association. *PRACTICE AREAS:* Fidelity; Suretyship; Construction Law.

**JOHN M. HAMILTON,** born Ridley, Pennsylvania, January 24, 1962; admitted to bar, 1991, California and U.S. District Court, Central District of California. *Education:* Swarthmore College (B.A., 1984); University of Southern California Law Center (J.D., 1991). *Member:* State Bar of California. *PRACTICE AREAS:* Commercial Litigation; Bankruptcy.

**MONA H. YOUNG,** born Los Angeles, California, October 15, 1964; admitted to bar, 1991, California. *Education:* University of Houston (B.S., Political Science, Psychology, magna cum laude, 1988); University of Minnesota (J.D., cum laude, 1991). Member, Mortar Board Honor Society. *Member:* Los Angeles County and American Bar Associations; State Bar of California. *PRACTICE AREAS:* Litigation; Suretyship.

**DEBORAH J. WILSON,** born San Francisco, California, June 21, 1966; admitted to bar, 1991, California; 1992, U.S. District Court, Eastern, Northern, Southern and Central Districts of California and U.S. Court of Appeals, 9th Circuit. *Education:* Pacific Union College (B.S., 1988); University of California School of Law (J.D., 1991). Recipient, Judge M.C. Taft Scholarship. Teaching Assistant, Legal Research and Writing, University of California School of Law, 1989-1990. *Member:* State Bar of California; American Bar Association.

REPRESENTATIVE CLIENTS: Firemans Fund Insurance Co.; American Insurance Co.; Central Mutual Insurance Co.; TIG Insurance Co.; Insurance Company of North America; Escrow Agents Fidelity Corp.; Acceleration National Insurance Co.; United States Fidelity & Guaranty Co.; National Home Insurance Co. (A Risk Retention Group); Home Buyers Warranty Corp.; National Union Fire Insurance Co.

---

## ROBERT A. GASTON
**11755 WILSHIRE BOULEVARD, 15TH FLOOR**
**LOS ANGELES, CALIFORNIA 90025-1506**
Telephone: 310-477-9744
Fax: 310-479-7612

*Family, Domestic Relations, Matrimonial and Divorce Law.*

**ROBERT A. GASTON,** born 1930; admitted to bar, 1958, California. *Education:* University of Alabama (A.B., 1952); University of Virginia (J.D., 1954). Pilots License, Multi-Engine Instrument. Judge Pro Tem, Superior Court. Director, Rotary Club, 1988—. President, 1991, Board of
*(This Listing Continued)*

Directors, 1990—, Association of Certified Family Law Specialists. Commissioner, Los Angeles Convention Center. *Member:* Beverly Hills, Los Angeles and American Bar Associations; State Bar of California. [Capt., U.S. Air Force, 1951-1958]. Certified Specialist, Family Law, The State Bar of California Board of Legal Specialization.

---

## GAUHAN AND KING
**LOS ANGELES, CALIFORNIA**
(See Long Beach)
*Tort Litigation, Personal Injury Law, Insurance Matters.*

---

## GELFAND & GLASER
A Partnership including a Professional Corporation
*Established in 1986*

**SUITE 1000, 11111 SANTA MONICA BOULEVARD**
**LOS ANGELES, CALIFORNIA 90025-3333**
Telephone: 310-477-7446
Facsimile: 310-473-0906

*FIRM PROFILE: Gelfand & Glaser is a general business and corporate law and civil litigation firm providing responsive, personal and quality legal services to a broad based clientele. The firm has developed an emphasis on assisting business clients in securing benefits due under insurance policies.*

**MARVIN GELFAND, (A PROFESSIONAL CORPORATION),** born New York, N.Y., August 20, 1948; admitted to bar, 1972, California, U.S. Court of Appeals, Ninth Circuit and U.S. District Court, Central and Northern Districts of California. *Education:* California State University (B.A., 1969); University of Southern California (J.D., 1972). Member, Los Angeles County Bar Association Judge Pro Tem Program, Los Angeles Municipal Court, 1979—. *Member:* Los Angeles County and American (Member, Sections on: Corporation, Banking and Business Law; Labor and Employment Law; Litigation) Bar Associations; State Bar of California. *PRACTICE AREAS:* Corporate and Business Law and Litigation.

**STEVEN H. GLASER,** born Los Angeles, California, December 30, 1958; admitted to bar, 1985, California, U.S. District Court, Central District of California and U.S. Court of Appeals, Ninth Circuit. *Education:* University of California at Los Angeles (B.A., cum laude, 1981); University of Southern California (J.D., 1985). Member, Hale Moot Court Honors Program. *Member:* State Bar of California. *PRACTICE AREAS:* Business Litigation.

### ASSOCIATES

**JENNIFER B. GOOSENBERG,** born Los Angeles, California, March 18, 1965; admitted to bar, 1989, California and U.S. Court of Appeals, Ninth Circuit; 1990, U.S. District Court, Eastern, Northern, Southern and Central Districts of California. *Education:* Oxford University, Oxford, England; Brandeis University (B.A., cum laude, 1986); University of California at Los Angeles (J.D., 1989). Member, Federal Communications Law Journal, 1987-1989. President, UCLA Entertainment Law Society, 1988-1989. *Member:* Beverly Hills (Member, Entertainment Section), Los Angeles County and American Bar Associations; State Bar of California. *PRACTICE AREAS:* Civil Litigation.

**GRANT A. CARLSON,** born Torrance, California, November 6, 1964; admitted to bar, 1991, California. *Education:* University of California at Santa Barbara (B.A., 1988); Loyola Law School (J.D., 1991). Associate Justice, Scott Moot Court Honors Board, 1990-1991. *Member:* State Bar of California. *PRACTICE AREAS:* Civil Litigation.

**ROBERT D. SENCER,** born Los Angeles, California, November 3, 1961; admitted to bar, 1988, California. *Education:* University of California at Berkeley (B.A., with high honors, 1983); University of Southern California (J.D., 1988); London School of Economics, London, England (LL.M., 1990). *Member:* State Bar of California. *LANGUAGES:* Spanish. *PRACTICE AREAS:* Products Liability Law; Litigation.

REFERENCE: City National Bank, Sunset/Doheny Branch (L.A.).

## PETER A. GELLES
1801 CENTURY PARK EAST
16TH FLOOR
**LOS ANGELES, CALIFORNIA 90067**
Telephone: 310-201-7900
Facsimile: 310-201-4746

*Real Estate, Business and International Law.*

**PETER A. GELLES,** born London, England, June 17, 1944; admitted to bar, 1970, Solicitor of the Supreme Court of England and Wales; 1972, California; 1996, Solicitor, Hong Kong. *Education:* Oxford University (B.A. Hons. Jurisprudence, 1965; M.A., 1970). Recipient: Open Exhibition in Jurisprudence, 1963. Legal Officer, Department of International Labor Standards, International Labor Organization, Geneva, Switzerland, 1965-1967. Author: "Foreign Investment in U.S. Real Estate," Southwestern University Institute, Los Angeles, California, 1975; "Foreign Investment in U.S. Real Estate," American Management Association, Atlanta, Georgia, 1978; "Legal Aspects of Foreign Investment in U.S. Real Estate," California Society of Certified Public Accountants, Los Angeles, California, 1983; "Real Estate Aspects of Mergers and Acquisitions in the U.S.," Chiyoda Kokusai Seminar, Tokyo, Japan, 1987; "Role of U.S. Counsel in Advising U.S. Investors in Foreign Real Estate," American Bar Association, 1991; "Current Perspectives on U.S. Investment in U.K. Property," Property Finance, London, 1991. "Effects of U.S. Product Liability Exposure on International Business Planning for Japanese Companies," Japan Management Association, Tokyo, Japan, 1991; "Practical Business Aspects of U.S. Immigration Planning for Japanese Companies," Chiyoda Kokusai, Tokyo, Japan, 1991; "U.S. Business Planning" in "How to Get a U.S. Visa," Japan Times, Tokyo, Japan, 1993 (3rd Printing). Co-Author: with Sandra S. Ikuta of O'Melveny & Myers, "Can Sellers Protect Themselves from Continuing Environmental Liability?" Los Angeles County Bar Association Real Property Section Newsletter, May/June 1994; "Global U.S. Real Estate Investment," Institutional Real Estate Investor, 1995. *Member:* Los Angeles County (Member, Real Property Section Executive Committee, 1988—; Editor, Real Property Section Newsletter/Review, 1993-1994, and Secretary, 1994-1995; Treasurer, 1995-1996; Vice-Chair, 1996-1997. Member, International Law Section Executive Committee, 1994—; Member, Pacific Rim Committee, 1995—), American (Chair, Committee on International Investment in Real Estate, Real Estate, Probate and Trust Law Section; Chair, Committee on International Real Property Law, Section of International Law and Practice) and International (Member: General Practice and Business Law Sections) Bar Associations; State Bar of California; Asia and Pacific Lawyers Association; The Law Society, London, England; The Law Society, Hong Kong; Arbitrator, Real Estate Mediation and Arbitration, Inc. (Also Consultant to Siao, Wen & Leung, Hong Kong). **PRACTICE AREAS:** U.S. and International Real Estate and Business Transactions.

## EDWARD P. GEORGE, JR., INC.
A PROFESSIONAL CORPORATION
**LOS ANGELES, CALIFORNIA**
(See Long Beach)

*General Civil and Criminal Practice in all Courts. Trials and Appeals, Personal Injury.*

## GERAGOS & GERAGOS
201 N. FIGUEROA STREET
5TH FLOOR
**LOS ANGELES, CALIFORNIA 90012-2628**
Telephone: 213-250-5055
Fax: 213-250-2828

*Criminal Defense and Civil Litigation.*

**PAUL J. GERAGOS,** born Chicago, Illinois, January 23, 1927; admitted to bar, 1957, California and U.S. District Court, Central District of California. *Education:* University of California at Los Angeles (B.A., 1949); University of Southern California (LL.B., 1956). Senior Trial Deputy, Office of District Attorney, Los Angeles County, 1957-1968. Member: Committee on California Jury Instructions, Criminal, 1968—; Criminal Law Advisory Commission, California Board of Legal Specialization, 1975-1981. Member, American College of Trial Lawyers, 1982—. *Member:* Los Angeles County Bar Association (Member, Judiciary Committee, 1979-
*(This Listing Continued)*

1993); State Bar of California (Advisory Commissioner Criminal Law Specialization, 1975-1979). **PRACTICE AREAS:** Criminal Law; Civil Litigation.

**MARK J. GERAGOS,** born Los Angeles, California, October 5, 1957; admitted to bar, 1983, California. *Education:* Haverford College (B.A., 1979); Loyola Marymount University (J.D., 1982). Speaker: "Criminal Enforcement," Political Lawyers Association, 1995; "Criminal Law Bridging The Gap," Los Angeles County Bar Association, 1995. *Member:* Los Angeles County Bar Association (Member, Judicial Appointments Committee; Outstanding Trial Jurist Award Committee, 1992-1993; Judicial Committee, 1994—); State Bar of California. **PRACTICE AREAS:** Criminal Law.

**MATTHEW J. GERAGOS,** born Los Angeles, California, October 20, 1958; admitted to bar, 1991, California. *Education:* Menlo College (A.A., 1978); University of Southern California (B.S., 1980); Southwestern University School of Law (J.D., 1990). *Member:* State Bar of California. **PRACTICE AREAS:** Civil Litigation; Criminal Law; Transactional Law.

*OF COUNSEL*

**SUSAN P. STRICK,** born Chicago, Illinois, September 3, 1954; admitted to bar, 1982, California; 1983, U.S. District Court, Central District of California. *Education:* California State, Sonoma; University of California at Berkeley (B.A., 1977); Southwestern University School of Law (J.D., 1981). *Member:* State Bar of California; Women Lawyers of Los Angeles; California Women Lawyers Association. **PRACTICE AREAS:** Civil Rights; Criminal Defense; Civil Litigation.

## STEPHEN A. GERSHMAN
1901 AVENUE OF THE STARS
SUITE 1800
**LOS ANGELES, CALIFORNIA 90067**
Telephone: 310-553-5465
Fax: 310-553-5430

*Family Law, Civil Litigation.*

**STEPHEN A. GERSHMAN,** born Philadelphia, Pennsylvania, July 14, 1950; admitted to bar, 1976, California. *Education:* Pennsylvania State University (B.A., 1972); Pepperdine University (J.D., 1976). Phi Alpha Delta. *Member:* Los Angeles County Bar Association; State Bar of California. (Certified Specialist, Family Law, The State Bar of California Board of Legal Specialization). **PRACTICE AREAS:** Family Law (90%); Personal Injury (10%).

## GIBBS, GIDEN, LOCHER & ACRET
ONE CENTURY PLAZA, 34TH FLOOR
2029 CENTURY PARK EAST
**LOS ANGELES, CALIFORNIA 90067**
Telephone: 310-552-3400
Facsimile: 310-552-0805

*Construction, Public Contract, Fidelity and Surety, Title Insurance, Commercial, Business Litigation, Real Property, Commercial Leasing and Labor and Employment Law.*

*FIRM PROFILE: Gibbs, Giden, Locher & Acret was founded in 1978. The firm has grown from 2 attorneys in 1978 to its present size of 34 attorneys. The firm practices throughout California and is one of the preeminent construction law, title insurance and commercial litigation firms in the state. Additionally, GGLA represents clients with regard to real property, commercial leasing and labor law matters.*

*In its construction practice, the firm represents owner/developers, public entities, general contractors, subcontractors, material suppliers, and design professionals in all aspects of construction law, including procurement, contract negotiations, litigation, arbitration, mechanic's liens, and claim preparation and defense.*

*In addition to the lawyers in the firm, GGLA has relationships with construction analysts with contracting and architectural backgrounds who assist in the evaluation of construction claims and the preparation of technical data. With the joint efforts of these construction analysts and the attorneys of the firm, GGLA is expert in assisting clients in preparing and/or evaluating construction claims, either before or after litigation has commenced.*

*The commercial law practice primarily pertains to the representation of corporate creditors in debtor/creditor litigation. By its nature, this practice involves the Uniform Commercial Code (primarily Articles 2 and 9),*
*(This Listing Continued)*

provisional remedies, and bankruptcy proceedings.

The title insurance practice involves the representation of major title insurance companies in connection with claims arising out of title insurance policies and matters relating thereto. In its real estate practice, the firm represents owner/developers both with regard to the purchase and sale of property and with regard to commercial leasing matters.

The firm also has a substantial labor, employment and general business practice. Many of the firm's clients who have construction, commercial or real estate needs also rely on the Firm's expertise for their transactional, labor and employment matters.

**KENNETH C. GIBBS,** born Washington, D.C., November 5, 1949; admitted to bar, 1974, California; 1980, District of Columbia. *Education:* University of California at Berkeley (A.B., magna cum laude, 1971); University of California at Los Angeles (J.D., 1974). Phi Beta Kappa. Author: "California Construction Law, 15th Ed." Wiley Law Publications, 1992; "Change Order Claims," Wiley Law Publications, 1994; "Law and Construction Scheduling," Hill International, 1987; "Construction Liabilities," Professional Educations Systems Inc., 1985. Member, State Board of Directors, Associated General Contractors of California, 1989-1991. Member: California Advisory Council to American Arbitration Association re Large Complex Case Program; Panel of Arbitrators and Mediators, American Arbitration Association; State of California, Public Works Arbitration Panel. *Member:* The District of Columbia Bar; Los Angeles County (Member: Real Property Section; Construction Law Subsection) and American (Member, Public Contract Law Section) Bar Associations; State Bar of California. *PRACTICE AREAS:* Construction Law; Business Litigation; Public Contract Law.

**JOSEPH M. GIDEN,** born New York, N.Y., October 26, 1933; admitted to bar, 1959, California. *Education:* Dartmouth College (A.B., cum laude, 1955); Harvard University (LL.B., cum laude, 1958). Phi Beta Kappa. Member, Panel of Arbitrators, American Arbitration Association. *Member:* Los Angeles County and American (Member, Fidelity and Surety Law Committee, Section of Insurance, Negligence and Compensation Law, 1976-1985) Bar Associations; The State Bar of California. *PRACTICE AREAS:* Title Insurance Law; Fidelity and Surety Law; Construction Law.

**WILLIAM D. LOCHER,** born Manhattan, Kansas, September 17, 1954; admitted to bar, 1979, California. *Education:* Arizona State University (B.S., 1976); Pepperdine University (J.D., 1979). *Member:* Los Angeles County and American Bar Associations; State Bar of California. *PRACTICE AREAS:* Business Litigation; Commercial Law; Construction Law.

**GLENN E. TURNER, III,** born Aberdeen, Maryland, April 11, 1953; admitted to bar, 1980, California. *Education:* Arizona State University (B.S., 1975; M.B.A., 1977); Pepperdine University (J.D., 1980). *Member:* Los Angeles County Bar Association; State Bar of California. *PRACTICE AREAS:* Business Litigation; Commercial Law; Construction Law.

**GERALD A. GRIFFIN,** born New York, N.Y., January 7, 1947; admitted to bar, 1977, California; 1981, U.S. Court of Appeals, Ninth Circuit; 1983, U.S. Supreme Court. *Education:* Fordham University; University of California at Irvine (A.B., cum laude, 1972); Pepperdine University (J.D., 1977). *Member:* Los Angeles (Member, Sections on: Labor Law; Labor and Employment Law) and American Bar Associations; State Bar of California (Member, Private Collective Bargaining Committee, 1982). *PRACTICE AREAS:* Business Litigation; Labor Law; Employment Law; Commercial Law.

**ANYA STANLEY,** born Sparta, Wisconsin, September 10, 1949; admitted to bar, 1975, California. *Education:* San Diego State University (B.A., 1972); Syracuse University (J.D., 1975). Phi Alpha Delta. *Member:* Los Angeles Bar Association; State Bar of California; Pasadena Young Lawyers Association (President, 1977-1978). *PRACTICE AREAS:* Title Insurance Law; Real Property Law.

**JAMES D. LIPSCHULTZ,** born Burbank, California, February 25, 1958; admitted to bar, 1982, California. *Education:* University of California at Los Angeles (B.A., 1979); Hastings College of Law, University of California (J.D., 1982). Author and Editor, Hastings Law Journal, 1980-1982. Author: "The Class Action Suit Under the Age Discrimination in Employment Act: Current Status, Controversies and Suggested Resolutions," 32 Hastings Law Journal 1377, 1982. *Member:* Los Angeles County Bar Association; State Bar of California. *PRACTICE AREAS:* Construction Law; Business Litigation; Commercial Law.

**JERIEL C. SMITH,** born Charleston, South Carolina, April 14, 1945; admitted to bar, 1974, California and U.S. District Court, Central District of California; 1978, U.S. Court of Appeals, Ninth Circuit. *Education:* University of California at Los Angeles (B.A., 1968; J.D., 1974). *Member:* Moot Court Honors Program. Traynor Moot Court Competition Winner. Recipient, Distinguished Advocate Award, 1973-1974. Member, U.C.L.A. Law Review, 1972-1974. *Member:* State Bar of California. *PRACTICE AREAS:* Construction Law; Business Litigation.

**THEODORE L. SENET,** born Los Angeles, California, December 27, 1951; admitted to bar, 1978, California; 1979, U.S. District Court, Central District of California and U.S. Court of Appeals, Ninth Circuit. *Education:* University of California at Santa Barbara (B.A., 1975); Loyola University Law School (J.D., 1978). *Member:* Los Angeles County (Member, Sections on: Commercial Law and Real Property; Member, Subsections on: Construction Law and Title Insurance) and American Bar (Member, Tort and Insurance Practice Section and Forum on the Construction Industry) Associations; State Bar of California. *PRACTICE AREAS:* Real Property Law; Insurance Law; Construction Law.

**JAMES L. FERRO,** born New York, N.Y., April 23, 1957; admitted to bar, 1983, California; 1984, U.S. District Court, Central District of California and U.S. Court of Appeals, Ninth Circuit; 1985, U.S. District Court, Northern, Southern and Eastern Districts of California. *Education:* University of South Florida (A.A., 1976); California State University at Northridge (B.S., cum laude, 1980); Loyola Law School, Los Angeles (J.D., 1983). Blue Key; Beta Gamma Sigma; Phi Alpha Delta. Author: Chapter 10, "The Cardinal Change," Construction Change Order Claims, Wiley Law, 1994. *Member:* Los Angeles County (Member, Litigation Section) and American (Member: Forum Committee on the Construction Industry, Litigation, Public Contract, and Tort and Insurance Practice Sections) Bar Associations; State Bar of California. *PRACTICE AREAS:* Construction Law; Fidelity and Surety Law; Business Litigation.

**NORMAN D. BOWLING,** born Sierra Madre, California, December 4, 1960; admitted to bar, 1986, California; 1987, U.S. District Court, Central, Eastern, Northern and Southern Districts of California. *Education:* Claremont Mckenna College (B.A., cum laude, 1983); Loyola Marymount University (J.D., 1986). Member, St. Thomas More Society. *Member:* Beverly Hills, Los Angeles County (Member, Commercial Law and Bankruptcy Section) and American Bar Associations; State Bar of California; Financial Lawyer's Conference-Los Angeles. *PRACTICE AREAS:* Commercial Law; Business Litigation; Construction Law.

**BARBARA R. GADBOIS,** born Peoria, Illinois, March 10, 1960; admitted to bar, 1985, California. *Education:* Northwestern University (B.A., 1982); University of California at Los Angeles (J.D., 1985). *Member:* Los Angeles County and American (Member, Forum Committee on the Construction Industry) Bar Associations; State Bar of California; Association of Business Trial Lawyers. *PRACTICE AREAS:* Construction Law; Public Contracts; Business Litigation.

**JEAN M. BOYLAN,** born Staten Island, New York, July 29, 1961; admitted to bar, 1986, California. *Education:* Loyola Marymount University (B.S., cum laude, 1983); Loyola University Law School (J.D., 1986). Adjunct Business Law Professor, California State University, Northridge. *Member:* Los Angeles County Bar Association (Member: Real Property Section; Trial Lawyers Section); State Bar of California; California Trial Lawyers Association. *PRACTICE AREAS:* Construction Law; Business Litigation; Public Contract Law.

**PETER F. LINDBORG,** born Yuma, Arizona, February 10, 1957; admitted to bar, 1981, New Mexico; 1990, California. *Education:* University of Scranton (B.A., 1978); St. Louis University; University of New Mexico (J.D., 1981). Alpha Sigma Nu; Phi Alpha Theta. Member, National Moot Court Team (Winner Best Brief, Region XI). Member, Natural Resources Journal, 1980-1981. Author: "Is a Winter-Only Drilling Restriction a Suspension of Operations and Productions Under 30 USC 209?" Natural Resources Journal, 1980. Co-Editor: "Retrospect," University of Scranton History Publication, 1977-1978. Member, Board of Directors, Commercial Litigation and Antitrust Section, State Bar of New Mexico, 1987-1990. *Member:* Los Angeles County and American (Member, Forum Committee on the Construction Industry) Bar Associations; State Bar of California; State Bar of New Mexico (Inactive). *PRACTICE AREAS:* Construction Law; Business Litigation; Bankruptcy.

**PEGGY A. GERBER,** born Wallingford, Connecticut, October 24, 1941; admitted to bar, 1981, California and U.S. District Court, Central District of California; 1982, U.S. Court of Appeals, Ninth Circuit; 1987, New York and U.S. District Court, Southern and Eastern Districts of New York. *Education:* University of Maryland (B.S., summa cum laude, 1977); Loyola University of Los Angeles (J.D., 1981). Clerk to Honorable Arthur L. Alarcon, U.S. Court of Appeals, Ninth Circuit, 1982-1983. Lecturer, UCLA and CEB Seminars, Construction and Mechanic's Lien Law, Uni-

*(This Listing Continued)*

## GIBBS, GIDEN, LOCHER & ACRET, Los Angeles—Continued

versity of California at Los Angeles, and San Diego, 1984-1987. Adjunct Professor, New York Law School, 1988-1990. *Member:* Association of the Bar of the City of New York; Los Angeles County, New York State and American Bar Associations; State Bar of California (Member, Sections on: Real Property, Construction). *PRACTICE AREAS:* Construction; Litigation; Real Estate.

**MARY A. SALAMONE,** born Rochester, New York, July 21, 1962; admitted to bar, 1987, California; 1988, U.S. District Court, Eastern, Central, Northern and Southern Districts of California. *Education:* University of Rochester (B.A., magna cum laude, 1984); Cornell University (J.D., 1987). Phi Beta Kappa. Member, Moot Court Board, 1985-1987. *Member:* Beverly Hills, Los Angeles County and American Bar Associations; State Bar of California; Women Lawyers Association. *PRACTICE AREAS:* Commercial Law; Business Litigation; Construction Law.

**RICHARD J. WITTBRODT,** born Flint, Michigan, October 3, 1957; admitted to bar, 1988, California and U.S. District Court, Central District of California. *Education:* University of Michigan (B.B.A., with distinction, 1980); Golden Gate University (M.B.A., 1984); Pepperdine University (J.D., cum laude, 1988). Recipient, American Jurisprudence Awards in Corporations, Creditors Rights and Bankruptcy. Member, 1986-1987, Lead Articles Editor, 1987-1988, Pepperdine University Law Review. Certified Public Accountant: Michigan, 1983; California, 1983. Author: Note, "The Supreme Court Refused to Expand the Right of Privacy to Include Homosexual Sodomy in Bowers v. Hardwick," 14 Pepperdine Law Review 313, 1987. *Member:* State Bar of California; American Institute of Certified Public Accountants. *PRACTICE AREAS:* Real Estate Construction Law; Commercial Law.

**ROBERT E. KENT,** born Los Angeles, California, October 17, 1962; admitted to bar, 1989, California, U.S. District Court, Southern, Northern, Central and Eastern Districts of California and U.S. Court of Appeals, Ninth Circuit. *Education:* Brown University (A.B., 1984); Loyola University of Los Angeles (J.D., 1989). *PRACTICE AREAS:* Business Litigation; Employment Law; Labor Law.

**SHARON E. FOSTER,** born Los Angeles, California, February 22, 1961; admitted to bar, 1988, California and U.S. District Court, Central District of California; 1989, U.S. District Court, Northern District of California and U.S. Court of Appeals, Ninth Circuit; 1990, U.S. District Court, Eastern and Southern Districts of California. *Education:* Pierce Jr. College (A.A., 1980); University of California at Los Angeles (B.A., 1983); Loyola Marymount University (J.D., 1987). Phi Alpha Delta. *Member:* State Bar of California; Los Angeles County and American (Member, Law Student Division, 1984-1987) Bar Associations. *PRACTICE AREAS:* General Business Litigation; Commercial Law.

---

**STEVEN R. CUNEO, JR.,** born Hayward, California, June 15, 1969; admitted to bar, 1994, California, U.S. District Court, Central District of California and U.S. Court of Appeals, Ninth Circuit. *Education:* University of California at Los Angeles (B.A., summa cum laude, 1991); University of California at Los Angeles School of Law (J.D., 1994). Phi Beta Kappa. *Member:* State Bar of California. *PRACTICE AREAS:* Construction Law; Insurance Law; Business Litigation.

**MICHAEL I. GIDEN,** born Santa Monica, California, September 18, 1962; admitted to bar, 1993, California. *Education:* Haverford College (B.A., 1984); Johns Hopkins University (M.A., 1988); George Mason University (J.D., 1992). *Member:* State Bar of California. *PRACTICE AREAS:* Construction Law; Title Insurance.

**BARBARA L. HAMILTON,** born Redding, California, July 2, 1960; admitted to bar, 1992, California. *Education:* University of California at Santa Barbara (B.A., magna cum laude, 1982); University of California School of Law (J.D., 1992). *Member:* Los Angeles County Bar Association; State Bar of California. *PRACTICE AREAS:* Title Insurance; Real Property; Construction Law.

**JOHN F. HEUER,** born New York, N.Y., January 21, 1965; admitted to bar, 1993, California. *Education:* Bucknell University (B.A.P.S., 1987); Southwestern University (J.D., 1993). Associate Member, Associated General Contractors of California, 1995. *Member:* State Bar of California. *PRACTICE AREAS:* Commercial; Construction; Business Litigation.

**MATTHEW P. KANNY,** born Detroit, Michigan, December 7, 1964; admitted to bar, 1993, California. *Education:* University of Michigan (B.S.,

*(This Listing Continued)*

cum laude, 1988); Loyola Law School of Los Angeles (J.D., 1993). *Member:* State Bar of California. *PRACTICE AREAS:* Construction Litigation; Employment Law.

**LARRY T. LASNIK,** born Philadelphia, Pennsylvania, May 16, 1947; admitted to bar, 1974, California and U.S. District Court, Central District of California. *Education:* University of California at Berkeley (B.A., 1971); University of California at Los Angeles (J.D., 1974). *Member:* State Bar of California. *PRACTICE AREAS:* Construction Litigation; Business Litigation; Insurance Defense.

**LEON F. MEAD, II,** born Norwalk, California, February 24, 1962; admitted to bar, 1990, California. *Education:* Life Bible College (A.A., 1985); Azusa Pacific University (B.A., cum laude, 1986); Loyola Law School (J.D., 1990). Phi Alpha Delta. Co-Author: "The New Progress Payment Release Forms: The Cure is Once Again Worse Than the Disease," California Construction Law, Vol. 3, No. 12, P6. 227 (Jan. 1993). Author: "Raiders: $7.2 Million, City of Oakland: O . . . Was That the Final Gun? A Story of Intrigue, Suspense and Questionable Reasoning," 9 Loy. L.A. Ent. L.J. 401 (1989). *Member:* Beverly Hills, Los Angeles County and American Bar Associations; State Bar of California (Member, Litigation Section). *PRACTICE AREAS:* Commercial Litigation; Construction Law.

**DANA M. RUDNICK,** born Chicago, Illinois, May 2, 1969; admitted to bar, 1993, California. *Education:* University of Maryland (B.S., magna cum laude, 1990); University of California at Los Angeles School of Law (J.D., 1993). Phi Kappa Phi; Golden Key. Recipient, Award for Trial Advocacy from American Board of Trial Advocates. Second Place Oral Advocate, Roger Traynor State Moot Court Competition. UCLA Moot Court Honors Program. Board Member, UCLA Moot Court Honors Program. Chief Articles Editor, Federal Communications Law Journal. Teaching Assistant, Legal Research and Writing Program, 1991-1993. *Member:* State Bar of California; American Bar Association (Member, Section on Litigation). *PRACTICE AREAS:* Commercial; Business Law.

**GARY EDWARD SCALABRINI,** born Inglewood, California, March 30, 1961; admitted to bar, 1992, California. *Education:* University of Southern California (B.S., 1987); Hastings College of the Law, University of California (J.D., 1992). *Member:* State Bar of California. *PRACTICE AREAS:* Construction Law; Business Litigation; Labor and Employment Law.

**JILL R. SCHECTER,** born Los Angeles, California, January 14, 1968; admitted to bar, 1993, California. *Education:* University of California at Berkeley (B.A., summa cum laude, 1990); University of California at Los Angeles School of Law (J.D., 1993). Phi Beta Kappa. Member, Moot Court Honors Program. Associate Member, Federal Communications Law Journal. Teaching Assistant, Legal Research and Writing, 1991-1992. Extern to Hon. Arthur L. Alarcon, U.S. Court of Appeals, Ninth Circuit, 1992. *Member:* State Bar of California. *PRACTICE AREAS:* Construction Litigation.

### OF COUNSEL

**JAMES ACRET,** born Minneapolis, Minnesota, December 19, 1930; admitted to bar, 1957, California. *Education:* University of California at Los Angeles (B.A., 1951; LL.B., 1957). Phi Alpha Delta. Member, UCLA Law Review, 1956-1957. Recipient, Los Angeles Chamber of Commerce Construction Industry Lifetime Achievement Award, 1990. Author: *California Construction Law Manual, Contractors Edition,* Shepard's/McGraw-Hill, 1994; *Acret's California Construction Laws Annotated,* Shepard's/McGraw-Hill, 1994; *California Construction Law Digests,* Shepard's/McGraw-Hill, 1994; *California Construction Law Manual,* Shepard's/McGraw-Hill, 4th Edition, 1990; *Attorneys' Guide to California Construction Contracts and Disputes,* Second Edition, California Continuing Education of the Bar, 1990; *Architects and Engineers, Their Professional Responsibilities,* Shepard's/McGraw-Hill, 2nd Edition, 1984; *Construction Arbitration Handbook,* Shepard's/McGraw-Hill, 1985; *Construction Litigation Handbook,* Shepard's/McGraw-Hill, 1986; *Construction Industry Formbook,* 2nd Edition, Shepard's/McGraw-Hill, 1990; *Construction Law Digests,* Shepard's/McGraw-Hill, 1990; *California Construction Law Reporter,* Shepard's/McGraw-Hill, 1991. *Member:* State Bar of California. [Staff Sergeant, U.S. Air Force, 1951-1952]. *PRACTICE AREAS:* Construction Litigation; Construction Arbitration; Insurance Coverage of Construction Claims.

**ALFRED FADEL,** born Los Angeles, California, March 7, 1941; admitted to bar, 1968, California; 1976, U.S. Court of Federal Claims. *Education:* University of Southern California (B.S.); University of San Fernando Valley (J.D.). *Member:* State Bar of California. *PRACTICE AREAS:* Construction Law; Design; Real Estate.

*(This Listing Continued)*

**RONALD S. SOFEN,** born Los Angeles, California, September 11, 1948; admitted to bar, 1974, California. *Education:* University of California, Santa Barbara (B.A., cum laude, 1970); University of California, Los Angeles (J.D., 1974). *Member:* Los Angeles County and San Fernando Valley Bar Associations; State Bar of California. *PRACTICE AREAS:* Construction; Business Litigation.

**JOHN H. STEPHENS,** born New York, N.Y., August 21, 1938; admitted to bar, 1968, California. *Education:* University of Southern California (B.S., 1963; J.D., 1967). Assistant Editor: The Developing Labor Law, Third Edition, Ch.24, The "Hot Cargo" Agreement, American Bar Association Section on Labor an Employment Law. Author: "Multiemployer Defined Contribution Pension Plans - A Collective Bargaining Solution to Employer Withdrawal Liability," International Foundation of Employee Benefit Plans, 1983. *Member:* The State Bar of California (Member, Section on Labor and Employment Law); Associated General Contractors Labor Lawyers Council (Member, Executive Committee, 1984—). *PRACTICE AREAS:* Labor and Employment Law; Employee Benefits Law; Litigation.

**BARRY C. VAUGHAN,** born Chicago, Illinois, May 20, 1950; admitted to bar, 1981, Colorado and U.S. District Court, District of Colorado; 1982, U.S. Court of Appeals, 10th Circuit; 1987, California, U.S. Court of Appeals, 9th Circuit and U.S. District Court, Central District of California. *Education:* University of Colorado (B.A., 1977); University of Chicago (J.D., 1981). Member, University of Chicago Law Review, 1980-1981. *Member:* State Bar of California; American Bar Association (Member, Sections on: Litigation, Natural Resources, Energy and Environmental Law, Construction Industry, Business Law). *PRACTICE AREAS:* Business Litigation; Construction Litigation; Environmental.

REPRESENTATIVE CLIENTS: Arrow Electronics; CalMat Co.; Centex-Golden Construction Co.; Chicago Title Insurance Co.; City of Anaheim; City of Long Beach; City of Pasadena; County of San Bernardino; Exxon Corporation; Familian Corp; General Electric Co.; Home Savings of America; Kaiser Foundation Hospitals; University of Southern California; K-Mart Corp.; Morley Construction; Morrison Knudsen, Inc.; Newberg/Perini Construction; Oltman's Construction; Swinerton & Walberg Co.

---

# GIBSON, DUNN & CRUTCHER LLP
*Established in 1890*

**333 SOUTH GRAND AVENUE**
**LOS ANGELES, CALIFORNIA 90071-3197**
Telephone: 213-229-7000
Telex: 188171 GIBTRASK LSA (TRT), 674930 GIBTRASK LSA (WUT)
Telecopier: 213-229-7520; 213-229-7268
Cable Address: GIBTRASK LOS ANGELES

*Century City, Los Angeles, California Office:* 2029 Century Park East, Suite 4000. Telephone: 310-552-8500. Telecopier: 310-551-8741. Cable Address: GIBTRASKCC LOS ANGELES.

*Irvine, California Office:* 4 Park Plaza, Suites 1400, 1500, 1700 and 1800. Telephone: 714-451-3800. Telecopier: 714-451-4220.

*San Diego, California Office:* 750 B Street, Suite 3300. Telephone: 619-544-8000. Telecopier: 619-544-8190; 619-544-8191.

*San Francisco, California Office:* One Montgomery Street, 26th Floor and 31st Floor. Telephone: 415-393-8200. Telecopier: 415-986-5309.

*Palo Alto, California Office:* 525 University Avenue, Suite 220. Telephone: 415-463-7300. Telecopier: 415-463-7333.

*Denver, Colorado Office:* 1801 California Street, Suite 4100. Telephone: 303-298-5700. Telecopier: 303-296-5310.

*Washington, D.C. Office:* 1050 Connecticut Avenue, N.W. Telephone: 202-955-8500. Telex: 197659 GIBTRASK WSH (TRT), 892501 GIBTRASK WSH (WUT). Telecopier: 202-467-0539. Cable Address: GIBTRASK WASHINGTON DC.

*New York, New York Office:* 200 Park Avenue. Telephone: 212-351-4000. Telecopier: 212-351-4035. Cable Address: GIBTRASK NEWYORK.

*Dallas, Texas Office:* 1717 Main Street, Suite 5400. Telephone: 214-698-3100. Telecopier: 214-698-3400.

*Paris, France Office:* 104 Avenue Raymond Poincare, 75116. Telephone: 011-33-1-45-01-93-83. Telecopier: 011-33-1-45-00-69-59. Cable Address: GIBTRAK PARIS.

*London, England Office:* 30/35 Pall Mall, SW1Y 5LP. Telephone: 011-44-171-925-0440. Telex: 27731 GIBTRK G; 916176 GIBTRK G. Telecopier: 011-44-171-925-2465. Cable Address: GIBTRASK LONDON W1.

*Affiliated Jeddah, Saudi Arabia Office:* Law Office of Abdulaziz Fahad, Sixth Floor, Haji Hussein Alireza Building, Bab Makkah, Post Office Box 16206, Jeddah, 21464. Telephone: 011-966-2-644-2663. Telecopier: 011-966-2-643-5401.

*Affiliated Riyadh, Saudi Arabia Office:* Law Office of Abdulaziz Fahad, Jarir Plaza, 4th Floor, Olaya Street, Post Office Box 15870, Riyadh, 11454. Telephone: 011-966-1-464-8081. Telex: 406176 LAWS SJ. Telecopier: 011-966-1-462-4968.

*Hong Kong Office:* 10th Floor, Two Pacific Place, 88 Queensway. Telephone: 011-852-2526-6816. Telex: 65665 GIBTK HX. Telecopier: 011-852-2845-9144.

*General Civil, Trial and Appellate Practice, State and Federal Courts. Antitrust Law. Specialized Criminal Defense. General Corporation, Securities, Administrative, Labor and Employment, Taxation, Estate Planning, Probate and Trust, International Business, Entertainment, Commercial, Insolvency, Bankruptcy and Reorganization, Natural Resources, Oil and Gas, Environmental Energy, Municipal and Public Utility Law.*

*FIRM PROFILE: Gibson, Dunn & Crutcher LLP, originating in Los Angeles, has been providing legal services to clients since 1890. Today, the firm has grown to one of the largest law firms in the world with approximately 600 active attorneys in 15 offices situated in most of the world's important business centers. The firm has experts in virtually every area of the law, particularly those which relate to commercial transactions and disputes, and has more effective geographical coverage in the United States than any other major firm. The firm's lawyers and staff are dedicated to providing quality service on a timely and cost effective basis.*

*Our Los Angeles office headquartered in downtown Los Angeles is the largest office within the firm. All of the firm's departments are represented, including business and corporate, labor, real estate, litigation and tax and estates. Within these areas, we offer particular experience in insolvency and restructuring, entertainment law, media law, business crimes, environment, financial institutions, government contracts and international transactions and trade.*

*Our trial lawyers handle virtually every type of civil litigation and certain criminal matters. We have tried cases and argued appeals in nearly every federal and state court, and we handle disputes before all types of non-judicial forums and international regulatory institutions.*

*Our real estate practice handles a broad range of sophisticated matters and is well dispersed geographically. We have had a labor practice since the early 1930s, well before other comparable firms. Our lawyers help employers cope with the constantly varying problems created by changing economic forces, new legislative and regulatory demands and individual and class litigation.*

*Our tax practice encompasses effective tax planning and the representation of taxpayers, both individual and corporate, in disputes with the IRS and other domestic and foreign tax collecting agencies. We take pride in our record of negotiating favorable settlements in audit situations.*

*We know that size does not mean excellence; providing quality legal services does. Our lawyers in Los Angeles demonstrate this belief daily in services to our clients.*

*Our Century City office, on the west side of Los Angeles, has 25 lawyers who cover all areas of our practice with particular emphasis on corporate and securities matters, tax and estate planning and entertainment industry practice.*

*Our Irvine office was originally established in 1964 to serve Orange County's growing real estate developments. It now has grown to approximately 75 lawyers involved in most practice areas, representing large businesses as well as emerging and small entrepreneurial companies and individuals. This office offers particular expertise in venture capital financing, mergers and acquisitions and public offerings, antitrust, unfair competition, trade secrets, insolvency, ERISA, real estate development and finance, employment and commercial litigation.*

*The San Diego office was opened in 1976 to serve the needs of our clients in all of the various practice areas engaged in by the firm. The trial lawyers in the office handle all types of business, commercial and employment litigation, with particular emphasis on securities litigation, accountants' malpractice cases and other complex litigation. The office also offers the full range of corporate services, including assistance with securities offerings, mergers and acquisitions, and general business advice.*

*The San Francisco office, with more than 30 lawyers, offers a full range of services with specific expertise in public offerings and securities matters, corporate and business matters, intellectual property (including licensing as well as litigation), acquisitions, antitrust, real estate financing, securities defense litigation, accountants' liability, insolvency and labor.*

*The Palo Alto office emphasizes the representation of high technology clients in the Silicon Valley and throughout the world, serving both established and emerging growth companies as well as venture capital firms. Lawyers in this office provide expertise in intellectual property protection, securities and corporate matters, litigation and labor.*

*(This Listing Continued)*

**GIBSON, DUNN & CRUTCHER LLP,** Los Angeles—
*Continued*

The firm has maintained a full-service office in Denver for over fifteen years. The Denver office was established to serve our national clients in the Rocky Mountain region and to provide counseling to our clients nationwide on natural resources issues. Thirty lawyers currently work out of the Denver office, with experience in all practice areas, emphasizing business litigation in federal and state courts, corporate securities and transactional engagements, real estate, employment law, and environmental and natural resources law.

Denver lawyers handle a variety of litigation in federal and state courts throughout the Rocky Mountain region and western United States. In recent years, cases have involved trial and appellate work concerning securities, antitrust, accounting defense, government contracts, insurance, employment discrimination, employee benefits, intellectual property, bankruptcy, and lender liability issues, as well as disputes concerning contracts, business torts, toxic waste, defamation, products liability, water, oil and gas, and land use issues. The corporate and transactional lawyers in Denver practice primarily in the field of mergers and acquisitions, securities, and real estate law, handling such things as public offerings, secured asset financing, buying, selling and representing closely held businesses, and sizable real estate and natural resources transactions and financings.

Environmental lawyers in the Denver office represent clients in enforcement actions, administrative proceedings, and citizen suits under federal and state law throughout the United States. They represent defendants and some plaintiffs in toxic tort litigation. They also advise clients about a wide variety of compliance matters relating to air quality, water quality, hazardous waste, solid waste, and the mining and oil and gas industries.

Gibson, Dunn & Crutcher's Washington, D.C. office has been serving national, local and international clients since 1977. Approximately 100 lawyers provide a full range of legal services, including general commercial representation and the representation of clients before key federal agencies and federal and state courts.

Many of the practice areas in the Washington, D.C. office are led by lawyers who have previously served at the highest levels of government, including in the Justice Department, State Department, Treasury Department, Labor Department, Securities and Exchange Commission, Overseas Private Investment Corporation, Occupational Safety and Health Administration, Environmental Protection Agency, Federal Communications Commission, Comptroller of the Currency and the U.S. House of Representatives. Some of the more important activities of the Washington, D.C. office practice groups are as follows:

*Supreme Court and Appellate:* Major appellate litigation including over 20 U.S. Supreme Court cases in the last five years.

*Antitrust and Competition Law:* Counseling domestic and international clients on laws of the United States and other countries, including the European Community, regarding competition; representing plaintiffs and defendants in investigations and litigation; advising as to Hart-Scott-Rodino compliance.

*White Collar Crime and Special Investigations:* Representing corporate and individual clients targeted by criminal and civil governmental investigations and representing special committees and acting as special counsel, in all types of corporate internal investigations.

*General Commercial and Class Action Litigation:* Representing clients in all types of commercial litigation, including securities and tort class action cases and patent, trademark and copyright cases brought in federal and state courts throughout the country.

*Securities Law Enforcement:* Representing corporations and individuals before the S.E.C. and related agencies, in processing transactions, obtaining regulatory determinations and defending clients that are subject to enforcement investigations.

*Financial Institutions Regulatory Practice:* Advising banks, thrifts, insurance companies, and securities firms in matters related to federal, state and international regulation and transactions.

*General Corporate, Securities, Bankruptcy and M & A Advice:* Representing national and local clients in corporate transactions including LBOs, IPOs, financings and acquisitions, and executive compensation matters.

*International Business, Trade and Customs Law:* Providing advice regarding international business issues and transactions, including application of the Foreign Corrupt Practices Act and the anti-boycott laws; advising importers and exporters and representing them before government agencies.

*Federal, State and International Tax:* Advising national, local and international clients with respect to corporate, cross border and related tax matters including tax litigation.

*(This Listing Continued)*

*Employee Benefits Law and Other Laws Related to the Workplace:* Includes representing national and local clients in matters involving employee benefits (and related ERISA litigation), claims of discrimination, OHSA and other issues related to the workplace.

*Environmental Law:* Providing advice and representing national and local clients before federal and state courts and agencies with respect to environmental matters, including toxic torts and air and water quality issues.

*Communications Law:* Advising major participants in the communications revolution (manufacturers, FCC licensees, etc.) both nationally and internationally.

*Governmental Contracts Law:* Providing advice and representing national and local clients before federal and state courts and agencies with respect to contracts with government entities.

*Legislative Advocacy:* Ongoing retainer arrangements and specific representations for major clients and trade associations.

With approximately 80 lawyers in the New York office, we have emerged as a major participant in the New York legal community, serving both domestic and foreign corporations and individuals. Our corporate practice focuses on negotiated mergers and acquisitions, public and private financings including bank credits, underwritten debt and equity offerings and complex asset securitization and lease and project financings, and restructurings and insolvency. Litigation strengths include accountants' liability, media/First Amendment law, securities and antitrust issues.

In 1984, Gibson, Dunn & Crutcher opened its office in Dallas with two lawyers. Today, the Dallas office has approximately fifty attorneys, and is rapidly gaining recognition as a major, full service Texas law firm. Our Dallas attorneys are involved in a wide range of practice areas, including: all aspects of commercial litigation; personal injury litigation; general corporate work (including public offerings and mergers and acquisitions); oil and gas; real estate; taxation; bankruptcy; labor and employee benefits.

The Paris office is positioned to serve our clients throughout the growing European market. It is staffed with a majority of European lawyers, with extensive experience in transnational transactions. This office provides both U.S. and non-U.S. clients with legal services in connection with a large variety of corporate operations as well as litigation, including transnational mergers, acquisitions, mining activities and general joint ventures, international financings and international commercial transactions from licensing and distribution to trade dispute matters. It has recently developed very strong securities and insurance practices, on behalf of both U.S. and European clients.

Our London office is positioned to serve our U.S. and other clients throughout the growing European market and to serve our European and Middle Eastern clients throughout the U.S. Indeed, our London office is now among the largest offices of all U.S.-based law firms in the United Kingdom. This office provides both U.S. and non-U.S. clients with a full range of legal services in connection with a variety of corporate operations and transactions, including transnational mergers, acquisitions, and joint ventures, international financings, restructurings and bankruptcies, and international commercial transactions from licensing and distribution to trade dispute matters. In addition to providing significant corporate and tax planning advice required for such transactions, this office also has a well-developed practice advising individuals and families on complex income and estate planning and corporate and investment matters. This office also has substantial expertise in advising clients located in the Middle East and in the developing law of the new free market systems emerging in Central and Eastern Europe.

The Law Office of Abdulaziz H. Fahad is staffed by Saudi Arabian and American lawyers and provides expertise to our clients on a wide range of legal matters, including banking and finance, commercial transactions, companies law matters, Saudi Arabian government contracts, joint ventures, licensing, agencies, taxation, trademarks, and litigation. They also provide "on-the spot" representation of foreign clients seeking to do business in the Middle East and clients resident in the Middle East who invest abroad, particularly in the United States, Europe and Asia. The clients of the office include major international and local companies in the banking, manufacturing and trading sectors.

The Hong Kong office provides advice in connection with a broad range of areas, including financings, acquisitions, international tax planning, international corporate finance and capital markets transactions; trust and estate planning; banking, corporate and commercial investments; international matters; and matters relating to the People's Republic of China, including joint ventures and other investment vehicles for participation in China's growth.

**JAS. A. GIBSON** (1852-1922).

**W. E. DUNN** (1861-1925).

*(This Listing Continued)*

# PROFESSIONAL BIOGRAPHIES

## CALIFORNIA—LOS ANGELES

**ALBERT CRUTCHER** (1860-1931).

### PARTNERS

**NORMAN B. BARKER,** born August 20, 1928; admitted to bar, 1954, California. *Education:* University of California at Los Angeles (B.S., honors, 1948; LL.B., 1953). Order of the Coif. *Member:* Los Angeles County and American Bar Associations. **PRACTICE AREAS:** Federal, State and Local Taxation; International Taxation; Tax Controversies. **Email:** nbarker@gdclaw.com

**ROBERT S. WARREN,** born December 9, 1931; admitted to bar, 1956, California. *Education:* Occidental College; University of Southern California (B.A., 1953; LL.B., 1956). Order of the Coif; Phi Beta Kappa. Associate Editor, Southern California Law Review, 1955-1956. Member, former officer and Shattuck-Price Awardee of the Los Angeles County Bar Association. *Member:* American College of Trial Lawyers (1974); Association of Business Trial Lawyers; Chancery Club. Fellow, American Bar Foundation. **PRACTICE AREAS:** Litigation, including Communications and Securities and Business cases. **Email:** rwarren@gdclaw.com

**RONALD E. GOTHER,** born November 23, 1932; admitted to bar, 1956, Wisconsin; 1961, California. *Education:* University of Wisconsin (1950-1951); Valparaiso University (B.A., 1954; LL.B., 1956); Harvard Law School (LL.M., 1960). *Member:* Los Angeles County (Member, Executive Committee of probate and Trust Law Section, 1973-1976, Chairman, 1975-1976) and American (Member, Council of Real Property, Probate and Trust Law Section, 1981-1987, Officer, 1985-1987) Bar Associations; State Bar of California (Member, Executive Committee of Estate Planning, Probate and Trust Law Section, 1969-1976, Chairman, 1972-1973). Fellow, American College of Trust and Estate Counsel, 1974—, Regent, 1984-1990. Fellow and Life Member, American Bar Foundation, 1977—. Fellow: The International Academy of Estate and Trust Law, 1974—, Member, Executive Council, 1984-1987; UCLA-CEB Estate Planning Institute, Member, Advisory Committee, 1978—, Chairman, 1985-1992. [U.S. Air Force, Judge Advocate Corps, 1956-1959]. **PRACTICE AREAS:** Estate and Personal Planning. **Email:** rgother@gdclaw.com

**STEPHEN E. TALLENT,** born August 10, 1937; admitted to bar, 1963, California; 1981, District of Columbia; 1984, New York. *Education:* Stanford University (A.B., 1959); University of Chicago (J.D., 1962); Awarded LL.D. by Lincoln University, 1991. Order of the Coif. Associate Editor, University of Chicago Law Review, 1961-1962. President, Southern California Chapter, Industrial Relations Research Association, 1975-1976. Co-Chairman, ABA Committee on Equal Employment Opportunity Law, Labor and Employment Law Section, 1977-1980. Chairman, Employment Law Committee, Defense Research Institute, 1982-1985. Chairman, NAM Labor Law Advisory Committee, 1986-1987. Co-Chairman, Membership and Finance Committee, 1985-1987 and Member of the Council, ABA Labor and Employment Section, 1987. Founding Director, American Employment Law Council, 1993. Founding Fellow and President, The College of Labor and Employment Lawyers, Inc., 1995—. (Los Angeles and Washington, D.C. Offices). **PRACTICE AREAS:** Labor; Employee Benefits; Employment and Discrimination Litigation; International Labor Law. **Email:** stallent@gdclaw.com

**ROBERT E. COOPER,** born September 6, 1939; admitted to bar, 1965, California. *Education:* Northwestern University (A.B., 1961); Yale University (LL.B., 1964). Order of the Coif; Phi Beta Kappa. Member, Board of Officers, Yale Law Journal, 1963-1964. Contributing Author: "Antitrust Advisor," Shepards, McGraw Hill, 1971. Member, Board of Directors, National Institute of Transplantation Foundation, 1989. Secretary, Citizens Research Foundation, 1980-1990. *Member:* Los Angeles County and American (Vice-Chairman, Criminal Practice and Procedure Committee, Antitrust Law Section, 1984-1986) Bar Associations; American College of Trial Lawyers. **PRACTICE AREAS:** Antitrust; Business Tort Litigation. **Email:** rcooper@gdclaw.com

**RONALD S. BEARD,** born February 13, 1939; admitted to bar, 1965, California. *Education:* Denison University (B.A., 1961); Yale University (LL.B., 1964). Phi Beta Kappa. **PRACTICE AREAS:** Corporate Law; Mergers, Acquisitions and Divestitures; Securities. **Email:** rbeard@gdclaw.com

**JOHN H. SHARER,** born December 1, 1932; admitted to bar, 1962, California. *Education:* University of California at Los Angeles (B.A., 1958; LL.B., 1961). Order of the Coif. U.C.L.A. Law Review, 1960-1961. *Member:* Los Angeles County and American Bar Associations; International Academy of Trial Lawyers. Fellow, American College of Trial Lawyers. **Email:** jsharer@gdclaw.com

*(This Listing Continued)*

**WESLEY G. HOWELL, JR.,** born December 4, 1937; admitted to bar, 1966, California; 1982, District of Columbia; 1984, New York. *Education:* University of Utah (B.S., E.E., cum laude, 1962); Columbia University (LL.B., magna cum laude, 1965). Member, Board of Editors, Columbia Law Review, 1964-1965. *Member:* The Association of the Bar of the City of New York; Los Angeles County and American Bar Associations; State Bar of California; The District of Columbia Bar. (New York City and Los Angeles, California Offices). **Email:** whowell@gdclaw.com

**JOHN F. OLSON** (Washington, D.C. Office).

**ANDREW E. BOGEN,** born August 23, 1941; admitted to bar, 1967, California. *Education:* Pomona College (B.A., cum laude, 1963); Harvard University (LL.B., cum laude, 1966). *Member:* American Bar Association. **PRACTICE AREAS:** Corporate; Securities. **Email:** abogen@gdclaw.com

**ROBERT K. MONTGOMERY,** born December 22, 1938; admitted to bar, 1965, California. *Education:* Williams College (A.B., cum laude, High Honors, 1961); Duke University (LL.B., 1964). *Member:* Los Angeles County and American Bar Associations. (Century City and Los Angeles Offices). **PRACTICE AREAS:** Business and Corporate Finance; Mergers and Acquisitions. **Email:** rmontgomery@gdclaw.com

**THEODORE B. OLSON** (Washington, D.C. Office).

**JOHN J. SWENSON,** born October 17, 1942; admitted to bar, 1968, California. *Education:* University of Minnesota (B.A., 1964; J.D., magna cum laude, 1967). Fellow, American College of Trial Lawyers. *Member:* Los Angeles County and American Bar Associations. **PRACTICE AREAS:** Bad Faith Defense; Punitive Damage Litigation; Insurance; General Commercial Litigation; Antitrust. **Email:** jswenson@gdclaw.com

**JOHN T. BEHRENDT,** born October 26, 1945; admitted to bar, 1971, California; 1972, Texas; 1989, New York. *Education:* Sterling College (B.A., 1967); University of Minnesota (J.D., cum laude, 1970). Order of the Coif. Member, University of Minnesota Law Review, 1969-1970. *Member:* American Bar Association. (Los Angeles and New York City Offices). **PRACTICE AREAS:** Litigation; Accountant's Liability.

**CHARLES K. MARQUIS,** born September 30, 1942; admitted to bar, 1968, California. *Education:* Georgetown University; Stanford University (B.A., 1964); University of Michigan (J.D., 1967). Associate Editor, Michigan Law Review, 1966-1967. *Member:* Los Angeles County and American Bar Associations; State Bar of California. (New York City and Los Angeles Offices).

**WILLIAM J. KILBERG** (Washington, D.C. Office).

**CHARLES S. BATTLES, JR.,** born June 24, 1934; admitted to bar, 1963, California. *Education:* Princeton University (A.B., summa cum laude, 1956); Yale University (LL.B., cum laude, 1962). Order of the Coif. *Member:* Los Angeles County and American Bar Associations. **PRACTICE AREAS:** Alternative Dispute Resolution; Litigation; Constitutional; Securities. **Email:** cbattles@gdclaw.com

**ROBERT T. GELBER,** born August 19, 1935; admitted to bar, 1961, California; 1970, Conseil Juridique (France). *Education:* California Institute of Technology (B.S., 1957); Harvard University (LL.B., cum laude, 1960). *Member:* State Bar of California. [United States Air Force, officer, 1961-1964 (Judge Advocate General, litigation before U.S. Armed Services Board of Contract Appeals)]. **LANGUAGES:** French. **PRACTICE AREAS:** International and Domestic Arbitration; Negotiation; Corporate and Business Transactions; International Law (Business Transactions). **Email:** rgelber@gdclaw.com

**KENNETH E. RISTAU, JR.** (Irvine Office).

**BRUCE L. GITELSON** (San Francisco and Palo Alto Offices).

**DEAN STERN,** born July 12, 1938; admitted to bar, 1964, California. *Education:* University of California at Los Angeles (B.S., 1960; LL.B., 1963). Order of the Coif. Associate Editor, U.C.L.A. Law Review, 1962-1963. *Member:* Los Angeles County Bar Association. **PRACTICE AREAS:** General Litigation. **Email:** dstern@gdclaw.com

**JACK H. HALGREN,** born March 12, 1940; admitted to bar, 1966, California. *Education:* Wesleyan University (B.A., 1962); Stanford University (J.D., 1965). Recent Developments Editor, Stanford Law Review, 1964-1965. Instructor in Law, University of California at Los Angeles, 1965-1966. *Member:* Los Angeles County and American Bar Associations. **PRACTICE AREAS:** Labor Law; Employment Law; Civil Rights; Housing Discrimination. **Email:** jhalgren@gdclaw.com

**ROY J. SCHMIDT, JR.,** born June 23, 1941; admitted to bar, 1966, California. *Education:* Stanford University (A.B., 1963; J.D., 1966). Order

*(This Listing Continued)*

CAA695B

**GIBSON, DUNN & CRUTCHER LLP,** Los Angeles—
*Continued*

of the Coif. Articles Editor, Stanford Law Review, 1965-1966. Teaching Fellow, Stanford Law School, 1966-1967. *Member:* Beverly Hills (Chairman, Corporation Section, 1975-1977), Century City, Los Angeles County and American Bar Associations; State Bar of California (Member, Corporations Committee, 1996-1999). (Century City Office). *PRACTICE AREAS:* Corporate and Corporate Securities; Mergers and Acquisitions; Real Estate. *Email:* rschmidt@gdclaw.com

**RICHARD G. DUNCAN, JR.** (Irvine Office).

**JOHN A. RUSKEY,** born February 6, 1939; admitted to bar, 1967, California. *Education:* Temple University (B.S., summa cum laude, 1963); New York University (LL.B., cum laude, 1966). Order of the Coif. Member, Board of Editors, Annual Survey of American Law, 1965-1966. *Member:* Los Angeles County Bar Association. *PRACTICE AREAS:* Litigation; Trusts and Estates; Family Law. *Email:* jruskey@gdclaw.com

**FRED F. GREGORY,** born January 7, 1941; admitted to bar, 1966, California. *Education:* Yuba College (A.A., 1960); University of California at Berkeley (A.B., 1962); University of California, Boalt Hall School of Law (LL.B., 1965). President, Boalt Hall Alumni Association, 1984-1985. Vice-Chair, Business Law Section, State Bar of California, 1996-1997. *Member:* Los Angeles County and American Bar Associations. [LCDR, United States Coast Guard, Assistant Legal Officer, Eleventh Coast Guard District, 1965-1968]. *PRACTICE AREAS:* Litigation; Insurance Coverage Disputes; Commercial Contract Disputes; Appellate Practice. *Email:* fgregory@gdclaw.com

**KENNETH W. ANDERSON,** born April 5, 1940; admitted to bar, 1966, California. *Education:* Harvard University (B.A., 1962; LL.B., magna cum laude, 1965). Phi Beta Kappa. Member, Board of Editors, Harvard Law Review, 1963-1965. *Member:* Los Angeles County and American Bar Associations. [Lt., JAG Corps, U.S. Navy, 1966-1969]. *PRACTICE AREAS:* Labor Law Matters; Wrongful Termination Litigation; Title VII and EEO Matters; Collective Bargaining; Labor Arbitration. *Email:* kwanderson@gdclaw.com

**STEPHEN M. BLITZ** (Denver, Colorado Office).

**RALPH C. WINTRODE** (Irvine Office).

**DWIGHT L. NYE** (Dallas, Texas Office).

**JAMES G. PHILLIPP,** born March 3, 1942; admitted to bar, 1967, Michigan; 1969, California. *Education:* College of the Holy Cross (A.B., cum laude, 1963); University of Michigan (J.D., with distinction, 1966). Order of the Coif. Comment, Note and Recent Developments Editor, Michigan Law Review, 1965-1966. *Member:* Los Angeles County and American Bar Associations; State Bar of Michigan. *PRACTICE AREAS:* Federal and State Tax Litigation; Transfer Pricing Issues. *Email:* jphillipp@gdclaw.com

**BLAKE T. FRANKLIN** (New York City and Irvine Offices).

**DAVID A. CATHCART,** born June 1, 1940; admitted to bar, 1968, California. *Education:* Stanford University (A.B., with great distinction, 1961); Harvard University (M.A., 1966; LL.B., cum laude, 1967). Phi Beta Kappa. Editor-in-Chief: "Five Year Supplement to Employment Discrimination Law," American Bar Association/Bureau of National Affairs, 1989; "Employment-at-Will: A 1989 State-By-State Report," National Employment Law Institute, 1989. Founding Chair, The American Employment Law Council, 1993. *Member:* Los Angeles County (Chair, Labor and Employment Law Section, 1991-1992), American (Co-Chair, Employment and Labor Relations Law Committee, Litigation Section, 1985-1988; Management Co-Chair, Equal Employment Opportunity Law Committee, Section of Labor and Employment Law, 1994-1996) and International (Vice-Chair, Labor Committee, Business Law Section, 1987-1990) Bar Associations. *PRACTICE AREAS:* Labor and Employment Law; Litigation; Alternative Dispute Resolution; Administrative Law. *Email:* dcathcart@gdclaw.com

**ROBERT C. BONNER,** born January 29, 1942; admitted to bar, 1966, District of Columbia; 1967, California. *Education:* Maryland University (B.A., magna cum laude, 1963); Georgetown University (J.D., 1966). Law Clerk to the Honorable Albert Lee Stephens, U.S. District Court for the Central District of California, 1966-1967. Assistant U.S. Attorney, Central District of California, 1971-1975. U.S. Attorney, Central District of California, 1984-1989. U.S. District Judge, Central District of California, 1989-1990. Administrator of the United States Drug Enforcement Administration, 1990-1993. Vice Chair, California Commission on Judicial Performance, 1995—. Fellow, American College of Trial Lawyers. President, Federal Bar Association, Los Angeles Chapter, 1982-1983. *Member:* Los Angeles County and American (Co-Chair, Subcommittee on Criminal Antitrust, 1994—) Bar Associations; District of Columbia Bar; State Bar of California. [Lt., JAG Corps, U.S. Navy, 1967-1971]. (Washington, D.C. and Los Angeles, California Offices). *PRACTICE AREAS:* Business Crime Matters; Complex Civil Cases and Implementation of Corporate Compliance Programs. *Email:* rbonner@gdclaw.com

**STEVEN ALAN MEIERS,** born December 22, 1942; admitted to bar, 1969, California. *Education:* University of Southern California (B.A., 1964); New York University (J.D., 1968). Phi Beta Kappa. Articles Editor, *Annual Survey of American Law,* 1967-1968. Author: "Limited Liability Partnerships, The Nightmare of Vicarious Liability Is Over," Metropolitan News - Enterprise, The Legal Community, October 30, 1995; "Significant Amendments to the California Revised Uniform Limited Partnership Act," Vol. 11, No. 1, Business Law News (An Official Publication of the California State Bar Association), Spring 1988. Member, 1984-1987, Chair, 1986-1987, Committee on Partnerships and Member, Executive Committee, 1987-1990, Business Law Section, State Bar of California. *PRACTICE AREAS:* Corporate and Securities Law; General Limited and Limited Liability Partnerships; Mergers and Acquisitions; Consumer Product Safety Act. *Email:* smeiers@gdclaw.com

**ARTHUR L. SHERWOOD,** born January 25, 1943; admitted to bar, 1969, California. *Education:* University of California at Berkeley (B.A., magna cum laude, 1964); University of Chicago (M.S., 1965); Harvard University (J.D., cum laude, 1968). Phi Beta Kappa. Instructor in Law, U.C.-L.A. Law School, 1968-1969. Co-Author: "Civil Procedure Before Trial," 1990 and "Civil Procedure During Trial," 1995 California Continuing Education of the Bar. Judge Pro Tem, Los Angeles Superior and Municipal Courts. *Member:* Los Angeles County and American Bar Associations. *PRACTICE AREAS:* Civil Litigation; Antitrust; Securities; Regulatory Law; Environmental. *Email:* asherwood@gdclaw.com

**JOHN C. WELLS** (Irvine Office).

**JAMES R. MARTIN,** born November 14, 1937; admitted to bar, 1968, Texas; 1969, California. *Education:* Rutgers University (B.A., 1959); University of Houston (J.D., 1968). Editor-in-Chief, Houston Law Review, 1967-1968. Lecturer in Law, University of Houston, 1967-1968. Law Clerk to Hon. John R. Brown, Chief Judge, U.S. Court of Appeals, Fifth Circuit, 1968-1969. Former Chair, American Bar Association, Antitrust Section, State Action Immunity and Noerr-Pennington Committee and Former Vice-Chair Section Intellectual Property Committee. [Captain, United States Air Force, Air Rescue Service]. *PRACTICE AREAS:* Antitrust; Communications; Patent; Litigation. *Email:* jmartin@gdclaw.com

**RICHARD A. STRONG,** born April 16, 1943; admitted to bar, 1969, California. *Education:* University of Utah (B.S., 1965); Harvard University (J.D., 1968). Member, Board of Editors, Harvard Law Review, 1967-1968. *Member:* American Bar Association. *PRACTICE AREAS:* General Corporate; Securities; Mergers and Acquisitions. *Email:* rstrong@gdclaw.com

**RICHARD D. HALL,** born January 22, 1942; admitted to bar, 1970, California. *Education:* University of Maine (B.A., 1964); Harvard University (J.D., 1969). *Member:* American Bar Association. *PRACTICE AREAS:* Professional Liability; Legal Ethics and Professional Responsibility; Litigation; Insurance; Antitrust. *Email:* rdhall@gdclaw.com

**WILLIAM STINEHART, JR.,** born December 15, 1943; admitted to bar, 1970, California. *Education:* Stanford University (B.A., 1966); University of California at Los Angeles (J.D., 1969). Order of the Coif. (Century City Office). *PRACTICE AREAS:* Personal Tax Planning. *Email:* wstinehart@gdclaw.com

**R. RANDALL HUFF,** born October 5, 1940; admitted to bar, 1970, California. *Education:* Brigham Young University (B.A., cum laude, 1966); Duke University (J.D., 1969). Phi Kappa Phi. *Member:* Association of Business Trial Lawyers. *PRACTICE AREAS:* Litigation; Employment Law (Wrongful Discharge); Health Care; Fraud and Deceit; Unfair Competition. *Email:* rhuff@gdclaw.com

**LAWRENCE CALOF** (San Francisco Office).

**JOHN EDD STEPP, JR.,** born August 17, 1943; admitted to bar, 1968, Texas; 1971, California. *Education:* University of Texas (B.B.A., 1965); University of Houston (LL.B., 1968). Editor, Houston Law Review, 1967-1968. Instructor in Research and Writing, University of Houston Law School, 1968. Law Clerk to Hon. Joe Ingraham, U.S. Circuit Judge, Fifth Circuit, 1968-1970. *Member:* Los Angeles County and American (Member, Antitrust Section) Bar Associations; State Bar of Texas. *PRACTICE*

*(This Listing Continued)*

**AREAS:** Antitrust Litigation; Antitrust Counseling; Business Litigation. **Email:** estepp@gdclaw.com

**ROBERT FORGNONE,** born December 4, 1936; admitted to bar, 1970, California. *Education:* California State University at Long Beach; Loyola University of Los Angeles (J.D., 1970). Articles Editor, Loyola Law Review, 1969-1970. Member, Board of Trustees, Loyola Marymount University, 1994. Member, Loyola Marymount University, Board of Regents, 1982-1994 (Chairman, 1990-1992). *Member:* Los Angeles County (Member: Executive Committee, Trial Lawyers Section, 1984-1986; Executive Committee, Delegation State Bar Convention, 1986-1989) and American Bar Associations; Lawyer-Pilots Bar Association. [United States Air Force, 1957-1961]. **PRACTICE AREAS:** General Litigation; Business Law; Products Liability; Aviation Law; Equine Law. **Email:** rforgnone@gdclaw.com

**CHARLES C. IVIE,** born November 28, 1947; admitted to bar, 1971, California. *Education:* Vanderbilt University (B.A., cum laude, 1967); University of Chicago (J.D., 1970). Order of the Coif. **Email:** civie@gdclaw.com

**BRUCE D. MEYER,** born August 31, 1945; admitted to bar, 1971, California. *Education:* University of Illinois (B.A., 1967; J.D., with honors, 1970). Order of the Coif. *Member:* Los Angeles County and American (Chairman, Middle East Law Committee, International Law Section, 1984-1985) Bar Associations. **PRACTICE AREAS:** Mergers and Acquisitions; Corporate and Securities; Banking and Savings and Loan Associations. **Email:** bmeyer@gdclaw.com

**MELDON E. LEVINE,** born June 7, 1943; admitted to bar, 1970, California; 1972, District of Columbia. *Education:* University of California (A.B., 1964); Princeton University (M.P.A., 1966); Harvard University (J.D., 1969). Book Review Editor, Harvard Int'l Law Journal. Member: U.S. Congress, 1983-1993; California Assembly, 1977-1982. *Member:* Los Angeles County Bar Association; District of Columbia Bar. (Los Angeles and Washington, D.C. Offices). **LANGUAGES:** Spanish. **PRACTICE AREAS:** International Transactions and Trade; Federal and State Administrative/Legislative and Governmental Advocacy. **Email:** mlevine@gdclaw.com

**C. RANSOM SAMUELSON II,** born June 12, 1946; admitted to bar, 1971, California; 1982, New York. *Education:* Dartmouth College (A.B., 1967); University of Southern California (J.D., 1970). Comment Editor, Southern California Law Review, 1969-1970. *Member:* The Association of the Bar of the City of New York; Los Angeles County and American Bar Associations. **PRACTICE AREAS:** Real Estate Law. **Email:** samuelson@gdclaw.com

**J. ANTHONY SINCLITICO, III** (San Diego Office).

**PETER J. WALLISON** (Washington, D.C. Office).

**J. MICHAEL BRENNAN** (Irvine Office).

**DON PARRIS,** born July 2, 1944; admitted to bar, 1968, California. *Education:* University of California at Los Angeles (B.S., 1965; J.D., 1968). Order of the Coif. Articles Editor, UCLA Law Review, 1967-1968. Law Clerk to the Honorable Roger J. Traynor, California Supreme Court, 1968-1969. Associate Professor of Law, Haile Selassie I. School of Law, Addis Ababa, Ethiopia, 1969-1970. *Member:* National Lawyer's Guild. (Century City Office). **PRACTICE AREAS:** Entertainment; Intellectual Property; Financing; Mergers and Acquisitions; Computers, Software and Technology. **Email:** dparris@gdclaw.com

**JOSEPH H. PRICE** (Washington, D.C. Office).

**MARC R. ISAACSON,** born May 24, 1945; admitted to bar, 1972, California. *Education:* University of Chicago (B.A., 1965; M.B.A., 1967; J.D., 1971). *Member:* Los Angeles County and American Bar Associations. **PRACTICE AREAS:** Estate Planning; Trust and Estate Administration; Charitable Organizations. **Email:** misaacson@gdclaw.com

**MICHAEL D. RYAN,** born August 31, 1944; admitted to bar, 1972, California. *Education:* University of Washington (B.A., cum laude, 1967); Universität Munchen, Munich, Germany (1968-1969); Harvard University (J.D., 1971). **LANGUAGES:** German. **PRACTICE AREAS:** Labor and Employment Law. **Email:** mryan@gdclaw.com

**JAMES C. OPEL,** born October 7, 1945; admitted to bar, 1971, California. *Education:* Pomona College (B.A., 1967); Boalt Hall School of Law, University of California (J.D., 1970).

**MARTIN CARL WASHTON,** born May 3, 1947; admitted to bar, 1972, New York and California. *Education:* Long Island University (B.A., summa cum laude, 1968); Columbia University (J.D., 1971). Harlan Fiske Stone Scholar. Editor, Columbia Law Review, 1969-1971. Law Clerk to Judge Orrin G. Judd, Federal District Court, Eastern District of New York, 1971-1972. General Counsel and Secretary, Center Theatre Group, Los Angeles Music Center, 1983. *Member:* Los Angeles County and American Bar Associations. **PRACTICE AREAS:** Complex Business Litigation; Federal Securities; Class Action; Financial Institution Litigation. **Email:** mwashton@gdclaw.com

**CANTWELL FAULKNER MUCKENFUSS III** (Washington, D.C. Office).

**SCOTT AUGUST KRUSE,** born July 15, 1947; admitted to bar, 1972, California. *Education:* Princeton University (A.B., magna cum laude, 1969); Harvard University (J.D., 1972). General Counsel, Federal Mediation and Conciliation Service, Washington, D.C., 1977-1979. *Member:* American (Co-Chairman, OFCCP Liaison Committee, 1978-1979) and International Bar Associations. **PRACTICE AREAS:** Labor and Employment Law; Civil Rights; Occupational Safety and Health; Employee Benefits; Transportation. **Email:** skruse@gdclaw.com

**WAYNE W. SMITH,** born June 8, 1942; admitted to bar, 1972, California. *Education:* California State College at Long Beach (B.A., cum laude, 1965); University of California at Los Angeles (J.D., 1972). Order of the Coif. (Los Angeles and Irvine Offices). **PRACTICE AREAS:** Business and Securities Litigation; Entertainment Litigation. **Email:** wsmith@gdclaw.com

**PETER L. BAUMBUSCH** (Washington, D.C. Office).

**RICHARD PAUL LEVY,** born July 17, 1947; admitted to bar, 1972, California. *Education:* University of Wisconsin (B.A., 1969); University of Michigan (J.D., 1972). Member, Journal of Law Reform, 1970-1972. Author: "Litigating Libel and Invasion of Privacy Case," California Continuing Education of the Bar, 1981, 1984. Adjunct Professor, Southwestern School of Law, 1982, 1983, 1985. *Member:* Los Angeles County and American Bar Associations. **PRACTICE AREAS:** Securities Related Litigation; Class Action Defense Litigation; First Amendment Litigation; General Business Litigation; Plaintiffs/Contingent Fee Catastrophic Injury Litigation. **Email:** rplevy@gdclaw.com

**ROBERT D. SACK** (New York City Office).

**DENNIS A. GLADWELL** (Irvine Office).

**S. DAVID BLINN,** born March 7, 1945; admitted to bar, 1970, California. *Education:* Wesleyan University (B.A., 1967); Southern Methodist University (J.D., 1970). Order of the Coif. Member, 1968-1970 and Casenote Editor, 1969-1970, Southwestern Law Journal. (Los Angeles and Irvine Offices). **Email:** dblinn@gdclaw.com

**RONALD S. ORR,** born November 19, 1946; admitted to bar, 1972, California. *Education:* Stanford University (B.S.E.E., 1968); University of Southern California (J.D., 1972; M.B.A., 1987). Order of the Coif; Lambda Sigma. Lecturer: Impact of the New Bankruptcy Act on California Law Practice, Continuing Education of the Bar, 1979, 1980, 1981 and 1983; Bankruptcy Act Amendments of 1984, Arizona Bar Association Legal Education; Litigation and Workouts, Law Journal Press, 1992, 1993; Real Estate Workouts and Bankruptcies, Practice Law Institute, 1992, 1993, 1994; Understanding SOP 90-7, Association of Real Estate Accountants. Member: Board of Trustees, University of Southern California, 1986-1992; Board of Governors and Executive Committee, President, General Alumni Association, University of Southern California, 1984-1989; Board of Directors and Executive Committee, University of Southern California Associates, 1980-1988; Board of Counselors, University of Southern California Law School, 1973-1977; Board of Directors, Legion Lex, University of Southern California, 1975-1979. *Member:* Los Angeles County (Chair, 1979-1980; Member, Executive Committee, Commercial Law and Bankruptcy Section, 1979) and American (Member, Business Bankruptcy Subcommittee, Corporation, Banking and Business Law Section, 1975; Chair, Judicial Appointments Subcommittee, 1981-1986) Bar Associations; State Bar of California (Member: Relations of Debtors and Creditors Committee, 1975-1977; Executive Committee, Business Law Section, 1978-1981; Chair, 1979-1980). **PRACTICE AREAS:** Debtor Creditor Relations; Bankruptcy; Corporate Reorganizations; Nonjudicial Debt Restructuring. **Email:** rorr@gdclaw.com

**JONATHAN M. LANDERS** (San Francisco Office).

**IRWIN F. SENTILLES, III** (Dallas, Texas Office).

**AULANA L. PETERS,** born November 30, 1941; admitted to bar, 1974, California. *Education:* College of New Rochelle (B.A., 1963); University of Southern California (J.D., 1973). Co-Chair, Moot Court Honors Program,

*(This Listing Continued)*

**GIBSON, DUNN & CRUTCHER LLP**, Los Angeles—
*Continued*

1973. Commissioner, U.S. Securities and Exchange Commission, 1984-1988. *Member:* American Bar Association. (Los Angeles and Washington, D.C. Offices). *LANGUAGES:* French; Italian. *PRACTICE AREAS:* Securities Litigation; Securities Law; SEC Regulatory Matters; Accountant's Liability; Commercial Litigation. *Email:* apeters@gdclaw.com

**FRED GILBERT BENNETT,** born May 28, 1946; admitted to bar, 1974, California. *Education:* University of Utah (H.B.A., magna cum laude, 1970); University of California School of Law at Los Angeles (J.D., 1973). Phi Beta Kappa. Managing Editor, UCLA Law Review, 1972-1973. Member, National Committee on Arbitration, U.S. Council for International Business, 1984. Chairman, Western Subcommittee, 1989, U.S. Council for International Business, Committee on Arbitration. Arbitrator, International Chamber of Commerce; Arbitrator and Chairman, Education and Training Committee, American Arbitration Association; Large and Complex Case Program, Advisory Board, Institute for Transnational Arbitration. *Member:* Los Angeles County, American, International and Inter-Pacific Bar Associations. *PRACTICE AREAS:* International and Domestic Arbitration and Dispute Resolution; Technical, Construction and Commercial Litigation and Contract Drafting; Intellectual Property and Patent Litigation; Real Estate Litigation; Corporate and Partnership Dissolutions. *Email:* fbennett@gdclaw.com

**GERARD J. KENNY** (Irvine Office).

**JAMES P. CLARK,** born February 10, 1948; admitted to bar, 1974, New York; 1975, California. *Education:* Georgetown University (A.B., cum laude, 1970); New York University (J.D., 1973). Root-Tilden Scholar. Note and Comment Editor, New York University Law Review, 1972-1973. Co-Editor, Antitrust Laws and Trade Regulation, Desk Edition, 2 Vol., Matthew Bender, 1983-1997. Law Clerk to Hon. John Minor Wisdom, Circuit Judge, U.S. Court of Appeals, 5th Circuit, 1973-1974. Member, 1988-1997 and Vice-Chairman, 1991-1994, Board of Regents, Georgetown University. Deputy General Counsel, Special Advisor to the Los Angeles Police Commission (The Webster Commission), 1992. Member, Board of Directors, 1990-1997, Vice President, 1993-1995 and President, 1995, Bet Tzedek ("The House of Justice") Legal Services. *Member:* Los Angeles County and American Bar Associations. (Century City Office). *PRACTICE AREAS:* Entertainment and Intellectual Property Litigation; Antitrust and Trade Regulation; White Collar Criminal; Complex Civil Litigation and Unfair Competition; Business Torts. *Email:* jclark@gdclaw.com

**JOHN A. HERFORT** (New York City Office).

**LAWRENCE J. HOHLT** (New York City Office).

**JERRY J. STROCHLIC** (New York City Office).

**BENNETT L. SILVERMAN,** born February 4, 1942; admitted to bar, 1972, California. *Education:* University of Southern California (B.S.C.E., 1964); Loyola University of Los Angeles (J.D., cum laude, 1972). *Email:* bsilverman@gdclaw.com

**KIRK A. PATRICK,** born July 25, 1948; admitted to bar, 1974, California. *Education:* Iowa State University (B.S., 1970); University of Minnesota (J.D., magna cum laude, 1974). Order of the Coif. Member, 1972-1974 and Research Editor, 1973-1974, Minnesota Law Review. Contributing Editor, "Antitrust Laws and Trade Regulation," Desk Edition, 2 Volumes, Matthew Bender, 1981. *PRACTICE AREAS:* Litigation; Insurance; Insurance Defense; Securities Litigation; Antitrust and Trade Regulation. *Email:* kpatrick@gdclaw.com

**THOMAS E. HOLLIDAY,** born July 3, 1948; admitted to bar, 1974, California. *Education:* Stanford University (B.A., with distinction, 1971); University of Southern California (J.D., 1974). Phi Beta Kappa; Order of the Coif. Member, 1972-1974 and Executive Editor, 1973-1974, University of Southern California Law Review. Contributing Editor, "Antitrust Laws and Trade Regulations," Desk Edition 2 Volumes, Matthew Bender, 1981. Member, Board of Trustees: Southwest Museum, 1981—, President of Board, 1993-1995. *Member:* American Bar Association; National Association of Criminal Defense Lawyers. Fellow, American College of Trial Lawyers. *PRACTICE AREAS:* White Collar Criminal Defense. *Email:* tholliday@gdclaw.com

**PETER F. ZIEGLER,** born August 31, 1945; admitted to bar, 1974, California. *Education:* Yale University (B.S., 1967); University of Southern California (J.D., 1974). Order of the Coif. Member, 1972-1974 and Note and Article Editor, 1973-1974, University of Southern California Law Review. *Member:* Los Angeles County (Chair, Business and Corporate Law Section, 1990-1991) and American Bar Associations. *PRACTICE AREAS:* Business Practice; Securities Offerings/Public and Private Companies; Mergers and Acquisitions; Finance and General Corporate Matters. *Email:* pziegler@gdclaw.com

**STEPHEN C. JOHNSON** (Dallas, Texas Office).

**CHRISTOPHER H. BUCKLEY, JR.** (Washington, D.C. Office).

**GORDON A. SCHALLER** (Irvine Office).

**DAVID R. JOHNSON** (Washington, D.C. Office).

**DONALD HARRISON** (Washington, D.C. Office).

**DAVID G. PALMER** (Denver, Colorado Office).

**PAMELA A. RAY** (Denver, Colorado Office).

**GAYNELL C. METHVIN** (Dallas, Texas Office).

**RICHARD MICHAEL RUSSO** (Denver, Colorado Office).

**PHILLIP L. BOSL,** born February 27, 1945; admitted to bar, 1975, California. *Education:* University of California at Santa Barbara (B.A., 1968); University of Southern California (J.D., 1975). Order of the Coif. Member, Southern California Law Review, 1973-1975. Co-Chairman, Moot Court Honors Program, University of Southern California, 1974-1975. *Member:* Los Angeles County, Federal and American Bar Associations; Association of Business Trial Lawyers (Member, Board of Governors, 1981-1985); Securities Industry Association (Member, Compliance and Legal Division); National Association of Securities Dealers (Arbitrator); National Futures Association (Arbitrator). Gibson, Dunn & Crutcher, Co-Chair, Securities Litigation Practice Group. [Officer, U.S. Coast Guard, 1969-1972]. *PRACTICE AREAS:* Securities and Business Litigation; Arbitrations and Mediation. *Email:* pbosl@gdclaw.com

**WAYNE A. SCHRADER** (Washington, D.C. Office).

**WILLIAM F. HIGHBERGER,** born May 15, 1950; admitted to bar, 1976, California; 1981, District of Columbia (Inactive); 1984, New York. *Education:* Princeton University (A.B., 1972); Columbia University (J.D., 1975). James Kent Scholar. Notes and Comments Editor, Columbia Law Review, 1974-1975. Author: "Current Evidentiary Issues In Employment Litigation," 22 Employee Relations L. J. 31 (Summer 1996). Law Clerk to Judge William H. Timbers, U.S. Court of Appeals, Second Circuit, 1975-1976. *Member:* American Bar Association (Chair, ERISA Litigation Subcommittee, Committee On Employee Rights and Responsibilities). *LANGUAGES:* French. *SPECIAL AGENCIES:* National Labor Relations Board; Equal Employment Opportunity Commission; Calif. Dept. of Fair Employment & Housing; Calif. Division of Occupational Safety & Health. *PRACTICE AREAS:* Labor and Employment; Employee Benefits; Trade Secrets; Occupational Safety and Health; Alternative Dispute Resolution. *Email:* whighberger@gdclaw.com

**REX S. HEINKE,** born June 9, 1950; admitted to bar, 1975, California. *Education:* University of Witwatersrand, Johannesburg, South Africa (B.A., 1971); Columbia University (J.D., 1975). Kent Scholar. Author: "Media Law," Bureau of National Affairs 1994. Law Clerk for Honorable Frederick J.R. Heebe, U.S. District Court, New Orleans, Louisiana, 1975-1976. Adjunct Professor of Law, Pepperdine University, 1983. Lecturer of Journalism, U.S.C., 1996. Judge Pro Tem, Los Angeles Municipal Court, 1981-1988. Trustee, Los Angeles County Bar Association, 1994-1996. *PRACTICE AREAS:* Media Law; Constitutional Law; Appellate Practice; Copyrights/Trademarks; Entertainment and the Arts. *Email:* rheinke@gdclaw.com

**ROBERT W. LOEWEN** (Irvine Office).

**ANTHONY BONANNO** (London, England Office).

**PETER H. TURZA** (Washington, D.C. Office).

**JONATHAN L. SULDS** (New York City Office).

**CHARLES F. FELDMAN** (New York City Office).

**CONOR D. REILLY** (New York City Office).

**DENNIS B. ARNOLD,** born April 25, 1950; admitted to bar, 1976, California. *Education:* State University of New York at Buffalo (B.A., magna cum laude, 1972); Yale University (J.D., 1975). Phi Beta Kappa. Chairman, Yale Legislative Services, 1974-1975. Assistant-in-Instruction, Yale Law School, 1974-1975. Adjunct Associate Professor of Law, Southwestern University School of Law, 1980-1982. Law Clerk to Hon. Murray M. Schwartz, U.S. District Judge, District of Delaware, 1975-1976. Author: "Creditor's Rights and Partnership Debtors: Selected Issues in Structuring Partnership Debt and an Approach to Workouts," *The Real Estate Partnership in De-*

*(This Listing Continued)*

*fault: Up-Front Protections-Workouts and Bankruptcy* (Practicing Law Institute, 1990); "The U.C.C. Mixed Collateral Statute: Has Paradise Really Been Lost?" 85 *U.C.L.A. L. Rev,* 1 (1988) (with M. Hirsch, E. Rabin, H. Sigman); "Guaranties of Indebtedness Under California Law: Issues in Drafting and Enforcement," 1 *California Real Property Journal* 17, No. 2, 1983; "Anti-Deficiency in the Eighties: The Sanction Aspect; Fair Value and Where the Action Is (And Isn't)," 5 *California Real Property Journal,* No. 2, 1987. Advisor, The American Law Institute (Restatement of The Law, Third, Suretyship and Guaranty, 1991-1995). *Member:* Los Angeles County (Member: Real Property and Commercial Law and Bankruptcy Sections; Executive Committee, Commercial Law and Bankruptcy Section; Executive Committee, Real Property Section, 1987-1990 and 1996—; Executive Committee, Real Property Section, 1987-1992) and American Bar Associations; The State Bar of California (Member: Standing Joint Committee on Anti-Deficiency Laws, 1985-1989; Real Property and Business Law Sections, 1978—); Financial Lawyers Conference (Member, 1979 and Board of Governors, 1986-1989, 1992-1995 and 1996—); American College of Real Estate Lawyers (Member, 1989—); The American Law Institute (Member, 1994—). *PRACTICE AREAS:* Real Estate; Banking; Debt Restructure; Commercial Law and Secured Transactions; Bankruptcy/Reorganization. *Email:* darnold@gdclaw.com

**STEVEN R. FINLEY** (New York City Office).

**JOHN J. A. HOSSENLOPP** (New York City Office).

**MARTIN B. MCNAMARA** (Dallas, Texas Office).

**MICHAEL L. DENGER** (Washington, D.C. Office).

**F. JOSEPH WARIN** (Washington, D.C. Office).

**CHARLES M. SCHWARTZ** (Dallas, Texas Office).

**LAWRENCE J. ULMAN,** born January 25, 1950; admitted to bar, 1975, California. *Education:* University of Southern California (A.B., 1972; J.D., 1975); University of California at Los Angeles (M.B.A., 1980). Recipient, ASCAP Nathan Burkan Memorial Award in Copyright Law, 1975. Adjunct Professor, University of Southern California School of Film and Television, 1995-1997. *PRACTICE AREAS:* Entertainment; Banking; Commercial Law. *Email:* lulman@gdclaw.com

**JANE LINDSEY WINGFIELD,** born November 13, 1944; admitted to bar, 1977, California. *Education:* University of Colorado (B.A., with distinction, 1967); University of Wisconsin (M.A., French, 1968); University of Southern California (J.D., 1976). Phi Beta Kappa; Order of the Coif. Member, 1974-1976 and Notes and Articles Editor, 1975-1976, Southern California Law Review. Adjunct Professor, Real Estate Finance, Loyola Law School, 1984. *LANGUAGES:* French. *PRACTICE AREAS:* Real Estate and Business Transactions. *Email:* jwingfield@gdclaw.com

**ROBERT EVERETT DEAN** (Irvine Office).

**THOMAS D. MAGILL** (Irvine Office).

**GEORGE B. CURTIS** (Denver, Colorado Office).

**WILLIAM D. CLASTER** (Irvine Office).

**JOSEPH P. BUSCH III** (Irvine Office).

**PAMELA LYNN HEMMINGER,** born June 29, 1949; admitted to bar, 1976, California. *Education:* Pomona (B.A., magna cum laude, 1971); Claremont Graduate School; Pepperdine University (J.D., magna cum laude, 1976). Phi Beta Kappa. Member, 1974-1976 and Literary Editor, 1975-1976, Pepperdine Law Review. Appointee to California Comparable Worth Task Force (Gov. George Duekmejian, 1984-1985). Alumnus of the Year, 1996, Pepperdine University School of Law. Contributing Author: *Employment Discrimination Law* (BNA 3rd ed. forthcoming); *Sexual Harassment In Employment Law* (BNA 1992). *Member:* Los Angeles County (Chair, Labor and Employment Law Section, 1996-1997; Member, Executive Committee, Alternative Dispute Resolution Section, 1996-1997) and American Bar Associations; State Bar of California. *PRACTICE AREAS:* Labor and Employment Law; Occupational Safety and Health; Litigation; ERISA. *Email:* phemminger@gdclaw.com

**DONALD E. SLOAN** (San Francisco Office).

**DANIEL Q. CALLISTER** (Washington, D.C. Office).

**FRED L. PILLON** (San Francisco Office).

**DENIS R. SALMON** (Palo Alto Office).

**SCOTT BLAKE HARRIS** (Washington, D.C. Office).

**LARRY C. BOYD** (Irvine Office).

*(This Listing Continued)*

**E. MICHAEL GREANEY** (Irvine, California and New York, N.Y. Offices).

**NANCY P. MCCLELLAND,** born May 22, 1944; admitted to bar, 1977, California. *Education:* California State University at Los Angeles (B.A., 1967); University of Southern California (J.D., 1977). *PRACTICE AREAS:* Labor and Employment Law. *Email:* nmcclelland@gdclaw.com

**MARY LAURA DAVIS,** born February 26, 1938; admitted to bar, 1978, California. *Education:* St. Mary's Junior College (A.A., 1958); Hunter College (B.A., 1973); Emory University School of Law (J.D., 1977). Order of the Coif. Staff Member, 1975-1976 and Executive Articles Editor, 1976-1977, Emory Law Journal. Law Clerk to Chief Judge John R. Brown, U.S. Court of Appeals, Fifth Circuit, 1977-1978. (Century City Office). *PRACTICE AREAS:* Litigation including Medical Malpractice; Products Liability; Personal Injury; Antitrust. *Email:* cdavis@gdclaw.com

**H. RICHARD DALLAS** (New York City Office).

**JOHN D. FOGNANI** (Denver, Colorado Office).

**HOWARD B. ADLER** (Washington, D.C. Office).

**KAREN H. CLARK** (Irvine Office).

**DHIYA EL-SADEN,** born July 31, 1952; admitted to bar, 1977, California. *Education:* University of California at Los Angeles (B.A., summa cum laude, 1974; J.D., 1977). Phi Beta Kappa; Order of the Coif. Member, UCLA Law Review, 1975-1976. *PRACTICE AREAS:* Corporate Finance; Mergers and Acquisitions; Real Estate Investment Trusts; Investment Companies; Financial Institutions. *Email:* delsaden@gdclaw.com

**DEAN J. KITCHENS,** born November 4, 1952; admitted to bar, 1978, California. *Education:* University of California at Berkeley (A.B., 1974); University of California at Los Angeles (J.D., 1978). Order of the Coif. Article Editor, UCLA Law Review, 1977-1978. *PRACTICE AREAS:* Business, Commercial and Insurance Litigation. *Email:* dkitchens@gdclaw.com

**JEFFREY REID HUDSON,** born March 15, 1952; admitted to bar, 1978, California. *Education:* Claremont McKenna College (B.A., summa cum laude, 1974); Harvard University (J.D., cum laude, 1978). *PRACTICE AREAS:* Finance; Banks and Banking; Mergers, Acquisitions and Divestitures; Debtor and Creditor. *Email:* jhudson@gdclaw.com

**CHARLES A. LARSON,** born December 6, 1952; admitted to bar, 1978, California. *Education:* Stanford University (A.B., 1975); Yale University (J.D., 1978). Phi Beta Kappa. Contributing Author: "Drafting California Revocable Living Trusts," California Continuing Education of the Bar, 1994. (Century City Office). *PRACTICE AREAS:* Tax Law; Probate and Estate Planning. *Email:* clarson@gdclaw.com

**MARK W. SHURTLEFF** (Irvine Office).

**CHRISTOPHER J. MARTIN** (San Francisco and Palo Alto Offices).

**LESLEY SARA WOLF,** born January 15, 1953; admitted to bar, 1978, California. *Education:* Sarah Lawrence College (B.A., 1975); University of Virginia (J.D., 1978). *PRACTICE AREAS:* Real Estate Development and Finance (Workouts and Foreclosures included).

**PETER SULLIVAN,** born November 9, 1952; admitted to bar, 1978, New York; 1981, California. *Education:* Columbia College (A.B., 1974); Fordham Law School (J.D., cum laude, 1977). Articles Editor, Fordham Law Review, 1976-1977. Co-Author: with von Kalinowski and McGuirl "Antitrust Laws and Trade Regulation," 2d ed. Matthew Bender; with von Kalinowski and Rose "Pricing Practices," Matthew Bender; with von Kalinowski "Distribution Practices," Matthew Bender. Contributing Editor: "United States Antitrust Law," Recueil Practique du Droit des Affaires (Editions Jupiter, France). Contributing Author (1985-1993): "Business Organizations with Tax Planning," Matthew Bender. Author: "A Guide to Joint Ventures and Other Cooperative Business Endeavors," Antitrust Counseling and Litigation Techniques, Matthew Bender, 1989. General Editor, "Antitrust Report," Matthew Bender, 1993—. Contributing Editor: "Antitrust Laws and Trade Regulation Report," 1984-1992. *Member:* Association of the Bar of the City of New York; State Bar of California (Chair, Intellectual Property Section, Section on Antitrust, 1996-1997); American Bar Association (Member, Section on Antitrust Law). *PRACTICE AREAS:* Antitrust Litigation and Counseling (U.S. and International); Unfair Competition; Intellectual Property; Government Investigations; General Commercial Litigation. *Email:* psullivan@gdclaw.com

**SHARI LEINWAND,** born January 24, 1951; admitted to bar, 1976, California. *Education:* University of California at Berkeley (A.B., 1972); University of Southern California (J.D., 1976). Order of the Coif. Note and Article Editor, Southern California Law Review, 1975-1976. (Century City

*(This Listing Continued)*

**GIBSON, DUNN & CRUTCHER LLP,** Los Angeles—*Continued*

Office). *PRACTICE AREAS:* Estate Planning; Tax; Trusts and Estates; Probate; Charitable Organizations and Planning. *Email:* sleinwand@gdclaw.com

**GARY L. JUSTICE,** born May 22, 1954; admitted to bar, 1979, California. *Education:* University of Cincinnati (B.S., 1976); Duke University (J.D., 1979). Order of the Coif. Member, Editorial Board, Duke Law Journal, 1978-1979. *PRACTICE AREAS:* Insurance "Bad Faith" and Coverage Litigation; Environmental Litigation; Products Liability and Toxic Torts; Commercial Litigation; Common Carrier Liability Law. *Email:* gjustice@gdclaw.com

**JONATHAN K. LAYNE,** born July 16, 1953; admitted to bar, 1979, Georgia and California. *Education:* College of William & Mary (B.A., 1975); Emory University (M.B.A., 1979; J.D., with distinction, 1979). Order of the Coif. Staff Member, 1977-1978 and Managing Editor, 1978-1979, Emory Law Journal. *Member:* Los Angeles County and American Bar Associations. *PRACTICE AREAS:* Corporate Law; Securities; Finance; Mergers, Acquisitions and Divestitures; Business Law. *Email:* jlayne@gdclaw.com

**SCOTT A. FINK** (San Francisco Office).

**WILLIAM D. CONNELL** (San Francisco Office).

**GAIL ELLEN LEES,** born June 13, 1950; admitted to bar, 1979, California. *Education:* Northwestern University (B.S., Journalism, 1971); University of California at Los Angeles (J.D., 1979). Order of the Coif. Editor-in-Chief, UCLA Law Review, 1978-1979. Author: "Jury Selection" in Civil Trial Practice: Strategies and Techniques, PLI, 1986; "Jury Selection" in Winning Strategies and Techniques for Civil Litigators, PLI, 1992. Law Clerk to Honorable Warren J. Ferguson, U.S. District Court and Ninth Circuit Court of Appeals, 1979-1980. Member: Board of Directors, Women Lawyers' Association of Los Angeles, 1993-1994; Board of Governors, Association of Business Trial Lawyers, 1990-1992. *PRACTICE AREAS:* Advertising and Consumer Fraud Litigation; Securities Class Action and Derivative Litigation; Corporate Control; Entertainment Litigation. *Email:* glees@gdclaw.com

**MARJORIE EHRICH LEWIS,** born November 21, 1954; admitted to bar, 1979, California. *Education:* Tufts University (B.A., magna cum laude, 1976); New York University (J.D., 1979). Member, New York University Law Review, 1977-1978. Law Clerk to Honorable Warren J. Ferguson, U.S. Court of Appeals, Ninth Circuit, 1979-1980. *PRACTICE AREAS:* General Business Litigation. *Email:* mlewis@gdclaw.com

**TIMOTHY L. DICKINSON** (Washington, D.C. Office).

**DAVID WEST,** born December 12, 1952; admitted to bar, 1980, New York; 1982, California. *Education:* Lehigh University (B.S., magna cum laude, 1974); Fordham University (J.D., cum laude, 1979). Member, Fordham Law Review, 1977-1979. *Member:* Los Angeles County Bar Association (Member, Tax Section, Employee Benefits Committee; Chairman, 1991-1992). *PRACTICE AREAS:* Employee Benefits; Executive Compensation; Exempt Organizations; Federal and California Political and Election Law. *Email:* dwest@gdclaw.com

**RUSSELL C. HANSEN,** born April 30, 1955; admitted to bar, 1980, Texas; 1981, California. *Education:* Princeton University (A.B., summa cum laude, 1976); Stanford University (M.B.A., 1980; J.D., 1980). Phi Beta Kappa. Articles Editor, Stanford Journal of International Studies, 1979-1980. Chairman, Business Law Section, Beverly Hills Bar Association, 1986-1987. (Century City Office). *PRACTICE AREAS:* Corporate Law; Securities; Mergers, Acquisitions and Divestitures; Finance; Business Law. *Email:* rhansen@gdclaw.com

**WALTER L. SCHINDLER** (Irvine Office).

**WILLIAM EDWARD WEGNER,** born April 2, 1950; admitted to bar, 1980, California. *Education:* University of Santa Clara (B.A., 1973); University of Puget Sound (J.D., magna cum laude, 1980). Recipient, Judge James Lawless Award for highest G.P.A. Member, Section Two Subcommittee, ABA Antitrust Section. *Member:* Association of Business Trial Lawyers (President). [Captain Medical Services Corps, U.S. Army, 1973-1979]. (Los Angeles and Century City Offices). *PRACTICE AREAS:* General Commercial Trial Law; Antitrust Law; Construction Law; Intellectual Property Law; Entertainment Law. *Email:* wwegner@gdclaw.com

**MERYL L. YOUNG** (San Diego Office).

**LARRY L. SIMMS** (Washington, D.C. Office).

*(This Listing Continued)*

**JOHN H. STURC** (Washington, D.C. Office).

**JONATHAN C. DICKEY** (Palo Alto Office).

**SCOTT R. HOYT** (Dallas, Texas Office).

**RHONDA S. WAGNER** (San Diego Office).

**ELIZABETH A. GRIMES,** born March 1, 1954; admitted to bar, 1980, California. *Education:* Holyoke College; Universidad de los Andes; University of Texas (B.A., 1976); Stanford University (J.D., 1980). Phi Beta Kappa. Associate Editor, Stanford Law Review, 1979-1980. *Member:* Los Angeles County and American Bar Associations. *LANGUAGES:* Spanish. *PRACTICE AREAS:* Litigation; Franchises and Franchising; Administrative Law. *Email:* egrimes@gdclaw.com

**PAUL D. INMAN** (Dallas, Texas Office).

**MITCHELL A. KARLAN** (New York City Office).

**THOMAS C. MCGRAW** (Dallas, Texas Office).

**MICHAEL A. BARRETT** (Washington, D.C. Office).

**HATEF BEHNIA,** born May 12, 1953; admitted to bar, 1981, California. *Education:* Reed College (B.A., 1975); Stanford University, Graduate School of Business (M.B.A., 1977); University of Southern California Law Center (J.D., 1981). Order of the Coif. Note and Article Editor, Southern California Law Review, 1979-1981. *Email:* hbehnia@gdclaw.com

**JOEL A. FEUER,** born September 5, 1954; admitted to bar, 1981, California. *Education:* Pomona College (B.A., 1976); University College, Oxford, England (M.A., 1978); University of California, Boalt Hall School of Law (J.D., 1981). Phi Beta Kappa. Supreme Court Editor, California Law Review, 1980-1981. Law Clerk to Honorable Pamela Ann Rymer, U.S. District Judge, Central District of California, 1983-1984. *PRACTICE AREAS:* Securities Litigation; Business Litigation; Real Property Litigation; Professional Liability. *Email:* jfeuer@gdclaw.com

**KENNETH M. DORAN,** born June 10, 1955; admitted to bar, 1981, California. *Education:* Stanford University (A.B., with distinction, 1977); University of Southern California (J.D., 1981). Order of the Coif. Executive Articles Editor, Southern California Law Review, 1979-1981. (Los Angeles and Century City Offices). *PRACTICE AREAS:* Securities; Mergers, Acquisitions and Divestitures; Business Law; Corporate Law; Real Estate. *Email:* kdoran@gdclaw.com

**J. NICHOLSON THOMAS,** born July 20, 1952; admitted to bar, 1978, California. *Education:* University of Arizona (B.S., 1974; J.D., 1977). Certified Public Accountant, California, 1981. *PRACTICE AREAS:* Business Tax; Real Estate. *Email:* nthomas@gdclaw.com

**MICHAEL A. MONAHAN,** born June 20, 1952; admitted to bar, 1979, Massachusetts; 1980, California. *Education:* Loyola University of Los Angeles (B.S., magna cum laude, 1974); University of California, Los Angeles (M.A., 1975); Georgetown University (J.D., cum laude, 1978). Editor, The Georgetown Law Journal, 1976-1978. Co-Editor, California Environmental Law Handbook, 9th edition, Government Institutes 1995. *Member:* Los Angeles County (Past Chair, Environmental Law Section) and American Bar Associations; State Bar of California. *PRACTICE AREAS:* Environmental; Administrative Law; Litigation. *Email:* mmonahan@gdclaw.com

**MICHELE C. COYLE** (Irvine Office).

**SUSAN ERBURU REARDON,** born September 23, 1956; admitted to bar, 1980, California. *Education:* Radcliffe College (A.B., magna cum laude, 1977); Harvard University (J.D., 1980). Phi Beta Kappa. Adjunct Professor, Copyright Law, Southwestern Law School, 1989. *PRACTICE AREAS:* Business Litigation; Media Law; Copyright Litigation; Eminent Domain and Land Use Litigation. *Email:* sreardon@gdclaw.com

**KAREN E. BERTERO,** born March 16, 1957; admitted to bar, 1981, California. *Education:* University of California at Berkeley (A.B., 1978); University of California at Los Angeles (J.D., 1981). Phi Beta Kappa; Order of the Coif. *PRACTICE AREAS:* General Corporate; Securities. *Email:* kbertero@gdclaw.com

**ROBERT C. EAGER** (Washington, D.C. Office).

**RAY T. KHIRALLAH** (Dallas, Texas Office).

**ROBERT L. WEIGEL** (New York City Office).

**MARK E. WEBER,** born July 12, 1956; admitted to bar, 1980, Illinois; 1984, Texas; 1985, California. *Education:* George Washington University (B.A., 1977); University of Illinois (J.D., 1980). *PRACTICE AREAS:* Antitrust Law; Appellate Practice; Litigation. *Email:* mweber@gdclaw.com

*(This Listing Continued)*

**PROFESSIONAL BIOGRAPHIES**   CALIFORNIA—LOS ANGELES

**TODD H. BAKER** (San Francisco Office).

**STEPHEN L. TOLLES,** born September 14, 1946; admitted to bar, 1982, California. *Education:* Princeton University (A.B., magna cum laude, 1968); Boalt Hall School of Law, University of California (J.D., 1982). Order of the Coif. Supreme Court Editor, California Law Review, 1981-1982. *PRACTICE AREAS:* Federal Income Taxation; California Income, Property and Sales Taxation. *Email:* stolles@gdclaw.com

**CHERYL D. JUSTICE,** born October 16, 1945; admitted to bar, 1982, California. *Education:* University of California at Berkeley (B.A., 1967); California State University at Los Angeles (M.A., 1972); Harvard Law School (J.D., cum laude, 1982). Past Chair, California State Bar's Committee on Federal Courts. Member, Board of Directors, California Women's Law Center. *PRACTICE AREAS:* Complex Commercial and Business Litigation; Defense of Federal Securities Class Actions; Professional Malpractice Actions; SEC Investigations. *Email:* cjustice@gdclaw.com

**JEFFREY T. THOMAS** (Irvine Office).

**STEVEN EUGENE SLETTEN,** born November 27, 1957; admitted to bar, 1982, California. *Education:* California State University at Northridge (B.A., summa cum laude, 1979) Phi Kappa Phi; University of California at Los Angeles (J.D., 1982, Order of the Coif). Law Clerk for Honorable Edward Rafeedie, U.S. District Court, Central District of California, 1982-1983. Adjunct Professor of Law, Pepperdine School of Law, 1994. *Member:* Los Angeles County, American and International Bar Associations. *PRACTICE AREAS:* Commercial Litigation with concentration in Antitrust, Entertainment; Insurance/Reinsurance; Alternative Dispute Resolution. *Email:* ssletten@gdclaw.com

**BARUCH A. FELLNER** (Washington, D.C. Office).

**PATRICK W. DENNIS,** born December 12, 1952; admitted to bar, 1982, California. *Education:* University of California, Los Angeles (B.S., Civil Engr., 1976; M.S., Mechanical Engr., 1978; M.B.A., 1982); University of California School of Law at Los Angeles (J.D., 1982). Tau Beta Pi; Phi Beta Kappa. Managing Editor, UCLA Journal of Environmental Law and Policy, 1981-1982. California - Engineer in Training, 1996. Author: "Private Party Cost Recovery," CEB Land Use and Environment Forum, Spring 1994. Chair, Environmental Law Section, Los Angeles County Bar Association, 1990-1991. *SPECIAL AGENCIES:* California Department of Toxic Substances Control, Regional Water Quality Control Boards; United States Environmental Protection Agency; South Coast Air Quality Management District. *PRACTICE AREAS:* Environmental Litigation; Environmental Due Diligence; Environmental Compliance. *Email:* pdennis@gdclaw.com

**CRAIG H. MILLET** (Irvine Office).

**ROBERT BRUCE VERNON** (New York City Office).

**MICHAEL A. ROSENTHAL** (Dallas, Texas Office).

**MITRI J. NAJJAR** (London, England Office).

**JENNIFER BELLAH,** born November 1, 1956; admitted to bar, 1983, California. *Education:* Bryn Mawr College (B.A., magna cum laude, 1978); Sorbonne University, Paris, France; Boalt Hall School of Law, University of California (J.D., 1982). Order of the Coif. Associate Editor, California Law Review, 1981-1982. Law Clerk for the Honorable Mary M. Schroeder, U.S. Court of Appeals, Ninth Circuit, 1982-1983. Gibson, Dunn & Crutcher, Member, Corporate Transactions, International Transactions and Technical Practice Group. *LANGUAGES:* French. *PRACTICE AREAS:* Corporations; Securities; General Corporate; International. *Email:* jbellah@gdclaw.com

**JOEL S. SANDERS** (San Francisco Office).

**PHILLIP HOWARD RUDOLPH** (Washington, D.C. Office).

**RORY MICHAEL HERNANDEZ,** born November 11, 1954; admitted to bar, 1983, California. *Education:* California State University, Los Angeles (B.A., 1978); Southwestern University (J.D., cum laude, 1983). Note and Comment Editor, Southwestern Law Review, 1982-1983. Judicial Extern, Honorable Arthur L. Alarcon, U.S. Court of Appeals, Ninth Circuit, 1983. *Email:* rmhernandez@gdclaw.com

**ARTHUR DAVID PASTERNAK** (Washington, D.C. Office).

**PAUL R. HARTER** (London, England Office).

**TERENCE P. ROSS** (Washington, D.C. Office).

**KATHRYN ANNE COLEMAN** (San Francisco Office).

**JOHN C. MILLIAN** (Washington, D.C. Office).

*(This Listing Continued)*

**BRIAN D. KILB,** born December 20, 1957; admitted to bar, 1983, Massachusetts; 1987, California. *Education:* Cornell University (B.S., with honors, 1980); Harvard Law School (J.D., cum laude, 1983). Managing Editor, Harvard International Law Review. Law Clerk to Justice Warren W. Matthews, Alaska Supreme Court, 1983-1984. Vice-Chair, Uniform Commercial Code Committee, Business Law Section, State Bar of California, 1994-1995. *PRACTICE AREAS:* Banking; Commercial Law; Workouts and Financial Reorganizations. *Email:* bkilb@gdclaw.com

**ROBERT B. KRAKOW** (Dallas, Texas Office).

**THOMAS SATROM,** born August 1, 1953; admitted to bar, 1984, California. *Education:* Williams College (A.B., cum laude, 1975); Indiana University (J.D., magna cum laude, 1983). Order of the Coif. Member, Indiana Law Journal, 1983. *PRACTICE AREAS:* Litigation. *Email:* tsatrom@gdclaw.com

**M. BYRON WILDER** (Dallas, Texas Office).

**ROBERT E. PALMER** (Irvine Office).

**STEVEN P. BUFFONE** (New York City Office).

**MARK S. PÉCHECK,** born December 20, 1958; admitted to bar, 1984, California. *Education:* University of California, Los Angeles (B.A., cum laude, 1979); University of California, Boalt Hall School of Law (J.D., 1984). *PRACTICE AREAS:* Real Estate. *Email:* mpecheck@gdclaw.com

**DANIEL G. SWANSON,** born November 5, 1957; admitted to bar, 1984, California. *Education:* University of California at Berkeley (A.B., with highest honors, 1979); Harvard University (A.M., 1984; J.D., magna cum laude, 1984; Ph.D. in Economics, 1985). Contributing Author, von Kalinowski, *Antitrust Laws and Trade Regulation*, Scher, *Antitrust Adviser* (4th edition) and Cavitch, *Business Organizations*; Member, Board of Editors, Antitrust Report. *Member:* American and International Bar Associations; American Economic Association; American Law and Economics Association. *PRACTICE AREAS:* Antitrust; International Competition Law; Communications/Entertainment; Intellectual Property; Business Litigation. *Email:* dswanson@gdclaw.com

**GREGORY J. KERWIN** (Denver, Colorado Office).

**SCOTT A. EDELMAN,** born March 25, 1959; admitted to bar, 1984, California. *Education:* Stanford University (B.A., with distinction, 1981); University of California, Boalt Hall School of Law (J.D., 1984). Co-Editor-in-Chief, Ecology Law Quarterly, 1983-1984. Law Clerk to Honorable Jesse W. Curtis, U.S. District Court, Central District of California, 1984-1985. (Los Angeles and Century City Offices). *PRACTICE AREAS:* Litigation; Entertainment and the Arts; Intellectual Property; Trade Secrets; Labor and Employment. *Email:* sedelman@gdclaw.com

**DAVID B. PENDARVIS** (San Diego Office).

**DAVID B. ROSENAUER** (New York City Office).

**RAYMOND B. LUDWISZEWSKI** (Washington, D.C. Office).

**AMY R. FORBES,** born June 30, 1959; admitted to bar, 1984, California. *Education:* Princeton University (B.S.E., 1980); University of Southern California (J.D., 1984). Order of the Coif. Luce Scholar, Bangkok, Thailand, 1988-1989. *PRACTICE AREAS:* Real Estate; Land Use Planning. *Email:* aforbes@gdclaw.com

**DAVID I. SCHILLER** (Dallas, Texas Office).

**JOHN R. CREWS** (Dallas, Texas Office).

**KENNETH R. LAMB** (San Francisco Office).

**JOERG H. ESDORN** (New York City Office).

**DANIEL S. FLOYD,** born July 3, 1960; admitted to bar, 1986, California. *Education:* University of California at Los Angeles (B.A., magna cum laude, 1982); Boalt Hall School of Law, University of California (J.D., 1985). Order of the Coif. Managing Editor, Industrial Relations Law Journal, 1984-1985. Law Clerk for Hon. Pamela Ann Rymer, U.S. District Court, Central District of California, 1985-1986. *PRACTICE AREAS:* Litigation. *Email:* dfloyd@gdclaw.com

**WILLIAM R. LINDSAY,** born August 8, 1959; admitted to bar, 1987, California. *Education:* Dartmouth College (B.A., 1981); Boalt Hall School of Law, University of California (J.D., 1985). Order of the Coif. Editor-in-Chief, California Law Review, 1984-1985. Law Clerk: Chief Justice of the United States Wm. H. Rehnquist, Supreme Court of the U.S., Washington D.C., 1986-1987; Honorable Carl McGowan, U.S. Court of Appeals for the District of Columbia Circuit, Washington, D.C., 1985-1986. *PRACTICE*

*(This Listing Continued)*

CAA701B

**GIBSON, DUNN & CRUTCHER LLP, Los Angeles—**
*Continued*

**AREAS:** Real Estate Finance and Acquisition and Disposition. **Email:** wlindsay@gdclaw.com

**CLAY A. HALVORSEN,** born October 14, 1959; admitted to bar, 1985, California. *Education:* California State University at Northridge (B.A., 1982); University of Southern California (J.D., 1985). Order of the Coif. Member, Southern California Law Review, 1984-1985. (Century City Office). **PRACTICE AREAS:** Corporate Law; Securities; Mergers, Acquisitions and Divestitures; Partnerships; Franchises and Franchising. **Email:** chalvorsen@gdclaw.com

**ROBERT FRANCIS SERIO** (New York City Office).

**KIMMARIE SINATRA** (New York City Office).

**STEVEN A. RUBEN,** born June 20, 1960; admitted to bar, 1986, California. *Education:* California State University at Northridge (B.S., 1983); University of California School of Law at Los Angeles (J.D., 1986). Co-Author: *Business Buy-Sell Agreements,* California Continuing Education of the Bar 1993. *Member:* Los Angeles County (Chair, Gift and Estate Tax Committee, 1993-1994; Executive Committee, Trust and Estates Section, 1994; Executive Committee, Taxation Section, 1993-1994) and American (Vice Chair, Legislative Developments Committee, 1994) Bar Associations. **PRACTICE AREAS:** Trusts and Estates. **Email:** sruben@gdclaw.com

**THOMAS R. DENISON** (Denver, Colorado Office).

**PAUL S. ISSLER,** born October 16, 1960; admitted to bar, 1986, California. *Education:* California State University at Northridge (B.S., summa cum laude, 1982); University of Southern California Law Center (J.D., 1986). Order of the Coif. Staff Member, 1984-1985 and Managing Editor, 1985-1986, Southern California Law Review. **PRACTICE AREAS:** Corporate and Partnership Taxation; Tax aspects of Corporate and Partnership Formations; Mergers, Acquisitions, Dispositions; Reorganizations and Financings; Real Estate Investment Trusts; Tax aspects of Bankruptcies and Workouts; Executive Compensation. **Email:** pissler@gdclaw.com

**KAY ELLEN KOCHENDERFER,** born September 27, 1955; admitted to bar, 1986, California. *Education:* University of California at Riverside (B.A., 1978); University of Southern California (M.A., 1983; J.D., 1986). Phi Beta Kappa. Staff Member, 1984-1985 and Executive Notes Editor, 1985-1986, University of Southern California Law Review. **PRACTICE AREAS:** Litigation; Class Actions. **Email:** kkochenderfer@gdclaw.com

**JOSEPH M. SALAMUNOVICH,** born May 23, 1959; admitted to bar, 1986, California. *Education:* Loyola Marymount University (B.A. magna cum laude, 1981; J.D., cum laude, 1986). Externship, Justice Cruz Reynoso, California State Supreme Court, 1985. **PRACTICE AREAS:** Securities; Mergers, Acquisitions and Divestitures; Corporate Law; Contracts; Business Law. **Email:** jsalamunovich@gdclaw.com

**RICHARD J. DOREN,** born July 9, 1960; admitted to bar, 1986, California. *Education:* University of California at Los Angeles (B.A., 1982); University of San Diego (J.D., cum laude, 1986). Editor-in-Chief, San Diego Law Review. **PRACTICE AREAS:** Litigation; Insurance. **Email:** rdoren@gdclaw.com

**JESSE SHARF,** born November 30, 1962; admitted to bar, 1986, California. *Education:* University of Pennsylvania (B.A., 1982); New York University (J.D., 1986). Staff Member, 1984-1985 and Member, Editorial Board, 1985-1986, New York University Law Review. **PRACTICE AREAS:** Real Estate; Finance; Leases and Leasing. **Email:** jsharf@gdclaw.com

**SEAN P. GRIFFITHS** (New York City Office).

**JULIA A. DAHLBERG** (Washington, D.C. Office).

**PATRICIA S. RADEZ** (San Francisco Office).

**TIMOTHY J. HATCH,** born September 3, 1955; admitted to bar, 1983, District of Columbia; 1993, California. *Education:* University of Wisconsin (B.B.A., 1977; J.D., 1980); Georgetown University (M.A., 1984). Assistant to the Army General Counsel, 1980-1984. Managing Editor, Wisconsin Law Review, 1979-1980. **PRACTICE AREAS:** Government Contracts; Litigation; White Collar Crime; Computers and Software. **Email:** thatch@gdclaw.com

**BRADFORD P. WEIRICK,** born September 15, 1960; admitted to bar, 1987, California. *Education:* Dartmouth College (A.B., magna cum laude, 1982) Phi Beta Kappa; Boalt Hall School of Law, University of California (J.D., 1986). Member, Business Law Section, State Bar of California.

**PRACTICE AREAS:** Corporate and Securities Practice, Specializing in Mergers and Acquisitions; High Technology Company Acquisitions and Financings; Public and Private Securities Offerings; Joint Venture Capital Financings. **Email:** bweirick@gdclaw.com

**JAMES P. RICCIARDI** (New York City Office).

**DAVID ALAN BATTAGLIA,** born September 9, 1962; admitted to bar, 1987, California; 1989, District of Columbia. *Education:* Georgetown University (B.A., 1984); Boalt Hall School of Law, University of California (J.D., 1987). Best Brief Award, McBaine Honors Moot Court Competition. Senior Articles Editor, High Technology Law Journal, 1986-1987. **Email:** dbattaglia@gdclaw.com

**THEODORE J. BOUTROUS, JR.** (Washington, D.C. Office).

**BRIAN W. COPPLE** (Irvine Office).

**JAMES EDWARD BASS** (Hong Kong Office).

**KEVIN S. ROSEN,** born July 8, 1962; admitted to bar, 1988, California. *Education:* Dartmouth College (A.B., magna cum laude with honors, 1984); Columbia University (J.D., 1987). Harlan Fiske Stone Scholar. Writing and Research Editor, Columbia Journal of Transnational Law, 1986-1987. Law Clerk to the Honorable William D. Keller, U.S. District Judge, Central District of California, 1987-1988. Chair, Legal Malpractice Defense Practice Group. **PRACTICE AREAS:** Litigation, including Securities; Real Estate; Consumer Lender and Broker Liability; Bad Faith; Unfair Competition. **Email:** krosen@gdclaw.com

**HSIAO-CHIUNG LI** (Hong Kong Office).

**JANET POPOFSKY VANCE** (New York City Office).

**STEVEN MARK SCHULTZ,** born March 7, 1962; admitted to bar, 1987, California. *Education:* University of California at Los Angeles (B.A., summa cum laude, 1984; J.D., 1987). Phi Beta Kappa. Law Clerk to Honorable Stephen V. Wilson, U.S. District Court, Central District of California, 1987-1988. **Email:** sschultz@gdclaw.com

**JUDITH A. LEE** (Washington, D.C. Office).

**A. JAMES ISBESTER** (San Francisco Office).

**BERNARD GRINSPAN** (Paris, France Office).

**JEFFREY M. TRINKLEIN** (Dallas, Texas Office).

**RONALD O. MUELLER** (Washington, D.C. Office).

**TIMOTHY J. KAY** (Irvine Office).

**DOUGLAS R. COX** (Washington, D.C. Office).

**GENIENE B. STILLWELL** (Irvine Office).

**CHAD S. HUMMEL,** born February 25, 1963; admitted to bar, 1988, California. *Education:* Harvard University (B.A., 1985); University of Chicago (J.D., 1988). **PRACTICE AREAS:** White Collar Crime; Litigation; Antitrust and Trade Regulation. **Email:** chummel@gdclaw.com

**STEVEN R. SHOEMATE** (New York City Office).

**GREGORY TOLL DAVIDSON** (San Francisco Office).

**JOHN NOVAK** (New York City Office).

**KIMBERLY S. MCGOVERN** (San Francisco Office).

**SUSAN M. MARCELLA,** admitted to bar, 1988, California. *Education:* Columbia University (B.S.N., 1980); University of Southern California (J.D., 1988). Order of the Coif. Member, Southern California Law Review, 1986-1987. Judicial Clerkship with Honorable Edward Rafeedie, U.S. District Court, Central District of California, 1988-1989. **PRACTICE AREAS:** Litigation; Antitrust and Trade Regulation; Securities; Fraud and Deceit. **Email:** smarcella@gdclaw.com

**THOMAS G. HUNGAR** (Washington, D.C. Office).

**WENDY M. SINGER** (London, England and Paris, France Offices) (European Partner).

*ADVISORY COUNSELS*

**SHERMAN SEYMOUR WELPTON, JR.,** born March 21, 1908; admitted to bar, 1931, Nebraska; 1942, California (Inactive). *Education:* University of Nebraska (J.D., 1931); Awarded LL.D. by Pepperdine University, 1977 and University of Nebraska, 1978. *Member:* Los Angeles County, Nebraska State and American Bar Associations; International Bar Association; American Judicature Society; Chancery Club. Fellow: American College of Trial Lawyers; American Bar Foundation.

*(This Listing Continued)*

**JULIAN O. VON KALINOWSKI,** born May 19, 1916; admitted to bar, 1940, Virginia; 1946, California. *Education:* Mississippi College (B.A., cum laude, 1937); University of Virginia (J.D., 1940) Dean's List. General Editor: "World Law of Competition," Matthew Bender; "Antitrust Counseling and Litigation Techniques," Matthew Bender. General Editor Emeritus, "Antitrust Report," Matthew Bender. Author: "Antitrust Laws and Trade Regulations," 16 Vol. Matthew Bender; "World Law of Competition Overview," Matthew Bender; "Antitrust Laws and Trade Regulation Desk Edition," Matthew Bender. *Member:* Los Angeles County, Virginia and American (Member of Council, 1967-1972 and Chairman, 1972-1973, Section of Antitrust Law) Bar Associations; State Bar of California. Fellow: American College of Trial Lawyers (Chairman, Complex Litigation Committee, 1984-1987); American Bar Foundation. Expert on Mission to UNESCO, to Republic of China, regarding Transfer of Technology, 1983. [Captain, USNR (Retired)]. *PRACTICE AREAS:* Antitrust Law; Business Litigation; Complex Litigation.

**F. DANIEL FROST,** born February 2, 1922; admitted to bar, 1948, Arizona; 1949, California. *Education:* University of California; University of Arizona (J.D., with distinction, 1948; LL.D., (hon.), 1993). Recipient: University of Arizona Centennial Medallion 1989 Alumni Achievement Award; Law School outstanding Graduate Award, 1989; 1986 Dana Latham Memorial Award. Chairman, Management Committee, Gibson, Dunn & Crutcher, 1979-1986. Member, Planning Committee, University of Southern California Tax Institute, 1962-1972. Chairman, Tax Committee, The State Bar of California, 1963-1964. President, Association of Tax Counsel, 1972. Chairman, 1986-1988 and Member, Board of Governors, 1966-1992, The Music Center of Los Angeles County. President and Director, The Music Center Foundation, 1977-1989. Member, Board of Fellows and Vice Chairman, Claremont University Center, 1967-1978. Author of numerous articles published in Stamford Law Review, Arizona Law Review, Journal of Taxation, California Bar Bulletin, ABA Journal, Proceedings of the Patent Society and USC Tax Institute. Lecturer, USC and UCLA Law Schools. *Member:* Los Angeles County (Chairman, Tax Committee, 1961-1962) and American Bar Associations; State Bar of Arizona.

**SHARP WHITMORE** (San Diego Office).

**FRANCIS M. WHEAT,** born February 4, 1921; admitted to bar, 1949, California. *Education:* Pomona College (A.B., 1942); Harvard Law School (LL.B., cum laude, 1948). Phi Beta Kappa. Commissioner, United States Securities and Exchange Commission, 1964-1969. Vice President, Board of Trustees, Pomona College, 1973-1993. Member, Board of Governors, National Association of Securities Dealers, 1973-1976. Member, Legal Advisory Committee, New York Stock Exchange, 1982-1987. *Member:* Los Angeles County (President, 1975-1976) and American Bar Associations; Chancery Club; American Law Institute.

**ARTHUR W. SCHMUTZ,** born August 2, 1921; admitted to bar, 1953, California (Inactive). *Education:* The Johns Hopkins University (A.B., 1949); Harvard Law School (LL.B., cum laude, 1952).

**WILLIAM F. SPALDING,** born January 14, 1919; admitted to bar, 1948, California. *Education:* University of Notre Dame (B.S.C., cum laude, 1941); Harvard Law School (LL.B., cum laude, 1948). *Member:* American Bar Association. [Captain, U.S. Army Air Force]. *PRACTICE AREAS:* Labor and Employment Law; Administrative Law.

**JAMES R. HUTTER,** born March 20, 1924; admitted to bar, 1951, California. *Education:* University of California at Los Angeles (B.S., 1947); Stanford University (J.D., 1950). Member, Executive Committee, Business Law Section, State Bar of California, 1977-1978. Member, Committee on Corporations, State Bar of California, 1973-1978. *Member:* Beverly Hills (Member, Board of Governors, 1968-1970), Los Angeles County and American Bar Associations; American Judicature Society.

**ROBERT D. BURCH,** born January 30, 1928; admitted to bar, 1954, California. *Education:* Virginia Military Institute; University of California at Berkeley (B.S., 1950; LL.B., 1953). Order of the Coif; Phi Beta Kappa. President, Law Trust Insurance Council, 1957-1958. Member, International Academy of Estate and Trust Law, 1975. *Member:* Beverly Hills (Member, Board of Governors, 1968-1970), Los Angeles County and American Bar Associations. (Century City Office). *PRACTICE AREAS:* Trusts and Estates; Tax Law.

**JOHN L. ENDICOTT,** born July 23, 1927; admitted to bar, 1954, California. *Education:* Rutgers University (B.A., 1950); Yale University (LL.B., 1953). Phi Beta Kappa.

**JOHN J. HANSON,** born October 22, 1922; admitted to bar, 1952, New York; 1955, California. *Education:* University of Denver (A.B., 1948); Harvard Law School (LL.B., cum laude, 1951). *Member:* Los Angeles County (Chairman, Antitrust Section, 1978-1979) and American Bar Associations. Fellow, American College of Trial Lawyers. *PRACTICE AREAS:* Antitrust and Trade Regulation.

**JEROME C. BYRNE,** born October 3, 1925; admitted to bar, 1952, California (Inactive). *Education:* Aquinas College (A.B., 1948); Harvard Law School (J.D., magna cum laude, 1951). Special Counsel, Regents of the University of California, 1965. Director, 1966 and President, 1970-1972, Constitutional Rights Foundation. Member, 1967 and President, 1969-1970, Industrial Relations Research Association. Member, Board of Regents, Mount St. Mary's College, 1978—. Trustee, Aquinas College, 1983-1995. Director/Secretary, Kolb Foundation, 1984—. *PRACTICE AREAS:* Labor; Employment; Employee Benefits Law.

**GEORGE W. BERMANT** (Denver, Colorado Office).

**WILLARD Z. CARR, JR.,** born December 18, 1927; admitted to bar, 1951, California. *Education:* Purdue University (B.S., 1948); Indiana University (LL.B., 1950). Member, Board of Editors, 1949-1950 and Editor, 1950, Indiana Law Journal. Member, Academy of Alumni Fellows, Indiana University School of Law. Member, Board of Visitors, Southwestern University Law School, 1981. Trustee, 1973-1993 and Chairman, 1975 and 1987, Pacific Legal Foundation. Chairman, California Chamber of Commerce, 1991. President and Chairman, Los Angeles Area Chamber of Commerce, 1981-1982. Member, California State World Trade Commission, 1991. Founding Director, American Employment Law Council, 1993. Chairman, Labor and Employment Practice Group, The Federalist Society, 1996—. *Member:* Los Angeles County, American and International (Chairman, Labor Law Committee, IBA Business Law Section, 1975-1985; Co-Chair, Committee on Benefits of Unemployed Persons, ABA Labor Law Section, 1986-1992) Bar Associations. Life Fellow, American Bar Foundation. Fellow Emeritus, College of Labor and Employment Lawyers, American Bar Association. *PRACTICE AREAS:* Labor Arbitration; Employment Law including Wrongful Termination; Negotiations; Strikes; Drug and Alcohol Testing; OSHA Matters.

**G. EDWARD FITZGERALD,** born April 20, 1928; admitted to bar, 1953, California (Inactive). *Education:* University of California at Los Angeles (A.B., 1950); Stanford University (LL.B., 1953). Member, Board of Editors, Stanford Law Review, 1952-1953. Fellow, American College of Trial Lawyers.

**RUSSELL L. JOHNSON,** born June 15, 1933; admitted to bar, 1959, California. *Education:* Harvard University (A.B., 1955); Stanford University (LL.B., 1958). Order of the Coif. Note Editor, Stanford Law Review, 1957-1958. Member, 1967-1969, Chairman, 1969-1970, Committee on Corporations, State Bar of California. Member, Board of Governors, American College of Real Estate Lawyers, 1980-1983. *Member:* Los Angeles County (Vice Chairman, 1970-1972 and Chairman, 1972-1973, Real Property Section) and American (Vice Chairman, Committee on Partnerships, Joint Ventures and other Investment Vehicles, Real Property, Probate and Trust Law Section, 1984-1985) Bar Associations; American College of Real Estate Lawyers; Anglo-American Real Property Institute; Chancery Club. *PRACTICE AREAS:* Real Estate; Financing and Leasing. *Email:* rjohnson@gdclaw.com

**THOMAS B. PITCHER** (Irvine Office).

**GEORGE H. WHITNEY,** born March 3, 1914; admitted to bar, 1940, California (Inactive). *Education:* Williams College (A.B., cum laude, 1936); Stanford University (LL.B., 1939). Phi Beta Kappa. *Member:* Los Angeles County and American Bar Associations; Chancery Club (President, 1977-1978). [Lt. Comdr., USNR]. *LANGUAGES:* French. *PRACTICE AREAS:* Corporation Finance; Real Property.

**FRANK L. MALLORY** (Irvine Office).

**JOHN T. PIGOTT,** born January 30, 1920; admitted to bar, 1950, California (Inactive). *Education:* Yale University (B.A., 1942; LL.B., 1949). Managing Editor, Yale Law Journal, 1948-1949. *Member:* Los Angeles County and American Bar Associations; American Judicature Society. Fellow, American College of Trust and Estate Counsel. [Lt. Comdr. USNR (Ret.)]. (Century City Office). *PRACTICE AREAS:* Trusts and Estates; Real Property.

**RAYMOND L. CURRAN,** born May 12, 1922; admitted to bar, 1953, California. *Education:* University of California at Los Angeles (B.S., 1949); University of Michigan (LL.B., 1952). *Member:* Los Angeles County Bar Association.

**DEAN C. DUNLAVEY,** born October 31, 1925; admitted to bar, 1955, California. *Education:* Harvard University (B.S., 1949); Harvard Law School (LL.M., 1956); University of California (Ph.D., 1952; LL.B., 1955).

*(This Listing Continued)*

## GIBSON, DUNN & CRUTCHER LLP, Los Angeles—Continued

Order of the Coif. Editor-in-Chief, California Law Review, 1954-1955. Faculty Fellow, Harvard Law School, 1955-1956. *Member:* State Bar of California. Fellow, American College of Trial Lawyers. [Captain, AUS Infantry, Leyte, P. I., 1943-1946]. **PRACTICE AREAS:** Litigation.

**ROY D. MILLER,** born September 26, 1929; admitted to bar, 1955, California. *Education:* Pomona College (B.A., 1951); Stanford Law School (J.D., 1954). Phi Beta Kappa. *Member:* Los Angeles County and American Bar Associations. **PRACTICE AREAS:** Taxation; Estate Planning; Trust and Estate Administration.

**GUY K. CLAIRE** (Irvine Office).

**HERBERT KRAUS,** born February 6, 1930; admitted to bar, 1955, California. *Education:* Stanford University (A.B., 1952; LL.B., 1955). Order of the Coif. Author: "The California Corporation: Legal Aspects of Organization and Operation," The Bureau of National Affairs, 1982; "Executive Stock Options and Stock Appreciation Rights," Law Journal Seminars-Press, 1994. Co-Author: "Start-up-Companies," Law Journal Seminars-Press, 1985; "Advising California Partnerships," Continuing Education of the Bar, 1988; "Partnership and Joint Venture Agreements," Law Journal Seminars-Press, 1992; "California Partnerships and Proprietorships," Matthew Bender, 1992. *Member:* Los Angeles County (Chairman, 1971-1972, Business and Corporation Law Section) and American Bar Associations; State Bar of California (Chairman, Business Law Section, 1986-1987). **PRACTICE AREAS:** Corporate Law; Securities Law.

**IRWIN F. WOODLAND,** born September 2, 1922; admitted to bar, 1961, California; 1991, Washington. *Education:* Columbia University (A.B., 1948); Ohio State University (J.D., 1959). Editor in Chief, Ohio State Law Journal, 1959. *Member:* Los Angeles County, King County, Washington State, Federal Energy and American Bar Associations; State Bar of California. [Air Force (Army), 1942-1945]. **PRACTICE AREAS:** Antitrust; Securities Litigation; Accountants Liability; Administrative Law.

**JAMES M. MURPHY,** born April 16, 1935; admitted to bar, 1963, California. *Education:* Harvard University (A.B., summa cum laude, 1959; LL.B., magna cum laude, 1962). Phi Beta Kappa. Member, Board of Editors, 1960-1961 and Article Editor, 1961-1962, Harvard Law Review. *Member:* Los Angeles County and American Bar Associations.

**PAUL G. BOWER,** born April 21, 1933; admitted to bar, 1964, California. *Education:* Rice University (B.A., 1955); California Institute of Technology, 1959-1960; Stanford University (LL.B., 1963). Order of the Coif. Associate Comment Editor, Stanford Law Review, 1962-1963. Assistant Director, National Advisory Commission on Civil Disorders, 1967-1968. Special Assistant to the Deputy Attorney General and Consumer Counsel, U.S. Department of Justice, 1968-1969. Director, 1976-1985 and President, 1979-1980, Legal Aid Foundation. Trustee, Sierra Club Legal Defense Fund. Member, Legal Services Trust Fund Commission, 1989-1993, Chair, 1993. Deputy General Counsel, Staff of the Special Advisor to the Los Angeles Police Commission.

**CHARLES R. COLLINS** (San Francisco Office).

**LEO G. ZIFFREN,** born September 27, 1922; admitted to bar, 1950, Iowa; 1952, California. *Education:* University of Iowa (B.A., 1949; J.D., 1950). Member, Board of Editors, Iowa Law Review, 1949-1950. *Member:* Iowa State Bar Association; Los Angeles Copyright Society. (Century City Office). **PRACTICE AREAS:** Copyright/Trademark; Entertainment; General Corporate; Real Estate.

**BRUCE A. TOOR,** born February 27, 1934; admitted to bar, 1967, California. *Education:* University of California at Los Angeles (A.A., 1953; J.D., 1966); University of California at Berkeley (B.A., 1955). Articles Editor, U.C.L.A. Law Review, 1965-1966. *Member:* Los Angeles County Bar Association. **PRACTICE AREAS:** Civil Litigation; Medical Malpractice; Alternative Dispute Resolution.

**LESTER ZIFFREN,** born April 13, 1925; admitted to bar, 1953, California. *Education:* University of California at Los Angeles (B.A., 1949; J.D., 1952). Co-author: "Handling Condemnation Cases," Chapters re Consolidation & Separation of Actions, Interests and Costs, California Continuing Education of the Bar, 1960. Deputy Attorney General, California Department of Justice, 1953-1959. *Member:* Beverly Hills, Los Angeles County and American Bar Associations. (Century City Office). **PRACTICE AREAS:** General Corporate; Real Estate.

**MICHAEL E. ALPERT** (San Diego Office).

*(This Listing Continued)*

### OF COUNSELS

**JOHN A. ARGUELLES** (Irvine Office).

**PETER J. ARTURO,** born November 11, 1940; admitted to bar, 1972, California. *Education:* University of Southern California (B.A., 1967); Southwestern University (J.D., 1971). **PRACTICE AREAS:** Medical Malpractice; Product Liability. *Email:* parturo@gdclaw.com

**KEVIN W. BARRETT** (New York City Office).

**PAUL BLANKENSTEIN** (Washington, D.C. Office).

**SUSAN B. BURR** (Palo Alto Office).

**SHEILA R. CAUDLE,** born February 20, 1950; admitted to bar, 1987, California. *Education:* University of Nevada, Reno (B.A., 1971); Catholic University of America (J.D., 1986). Member, Catholic University, Communications Law Institute. **PRACTICE AREAS:** Litigation; General Practice. *Email:* scaudle@gdclaw.com

**ELLEN J. CURNES** (Dallas, Texas Office).

**MICHAEL J. ELIASBERG,** born December 21, 1945; admitted to bar, 1971, California. *Education:* University of California at Berkeley (A.B., 1967); Harvard University (J.D., cum laude, 1970). (Century City Office). **PRACTICE AREAS:** Entertainment. *Email:* meliasberg@gdclaw.com

**DEBORAH S. FEINERMAN,** born August 10, 1955; admitted to bar, 1980, California. *Education:* University of California at Los Angeles (B.A., cum laude, 1977); Loyola Law School (J.D., cum laude, 1980). Member, St. Thomas More Law Honor Society. (Century City Office). **PRACTICE AREAS:** Entertainment and the Arts; Bankruptcy. *Email:* dfeinerman@gdclaw.com

**CYNTHIA LEAP GOLDMAN** (Denver, Colorado Office).

**MARK A. GRANNIS** (Washington, D.C. Office).

**XUHUA HUANG** (New York City and Hong Kong Offices).

**JOANNE FRANZEL** (New York City Office).

**DAVID W. JACKSON** (Jeddah, Saudi Arabia Office).

**GARY M. JOYE,** born July 11, 1956; admitted to bar, 1982, Missouri; 1985, California. *Education:* University of Missouri (B.A., with distinction, 1978); University of California at Los Angeles (J.D., 1982). UCLA Moot Court Honors Program. Judicial Extern for the Honorable Laughlin Waters, U.S. District Court, Central District of California, 1981. Law Clerk to the Honorable Floyd R. Gibson, U.S. Court of Appeals, Eighth Circuit, 1982-1984. **PRACTICE AREAS:** Litigation. *Email:* gjoye@gdclaw.com

**SUNGYONG KANG,** born April 13, 1948; admitted to bar, 1986, California. *Education:* Simpson College (B.A., magna cum laude, 1974); University of Maryland (M.A., 1977); Georgetown University (J.D., 1986). **LANGUAGES:** Korean. **PRACTICE AREAS:** General Corporate.

**DAVID H. KENNEDY** (Washington, D.C. Office).

**RICHARD G. LYON** (Dallas, Texas Office).

**ROBERT A. MCCONNELL** (Washington, D.C. Office).

**ROBERT E. MELLOR** (San Francisco Office).

**JOHN A. MINTZ** (Washington, D.C. Office).

**NATHAN I. NAHM** (New York City Office).

**JOHN O'HALLORAN,** born May 11, 1957; admitted to bar, 1988, California. *Education:* Newcastle University, England (B.A., 1979); City University of New York Graduate Center (M.A., 1986); New York University (J.D., 1988). (Century City Office). **PRACTICE AREAS:** Probate; Trusts and Estates. *Email:* ohalloran@gdclaw.com

**GONZALO PARDO DE ZELA** (New York City Office).

**MALCOLM R. PFUNDER** (Washington, D.C. Office).

**THOMAS M. PICCONE** (Denver, Colorado Office).

**THERESE D. PRITCHARD** (Washington, D.C. Office).

**AMY G. RUDNICK** (Washington, D.C. Office).

**W. RICHARD SMITH, JR.** (Irvine Office).

**LAWRENCE W. TREECE** (Denver, Colorado Office).

**STEPHANIE TSACOUMIS** (Washington, D.C. Office).

**WILLIAM M. WILTSHIRE** (Washington, D.C. Office).

*(This Listing Continued)*

## PROFESSIONAL BIOGRAPHIES

### SPECIAL COUNSELS

**DEBORAH E. MILLER** (New York City Office).

**JOSIAH O. HATCH III** (Denver, Colorado Office).

**DAVID ANDREW CHEIT** (San Francisco Office).

**DERRY DEAN SPARLIN JR.** (Washington, D.C. Office).

**TERESA JOANNING FARRELL** (Irvine Office).

**APRIL MCGANDY EVANS,** admitted to bar, 1986, California. *Education:* Washington State University (B.A., summa cum laude, 1981); University of California (J.D., 1986; M.B.A., 1986). Order of the Coif. Member, 1983-1984 and Editor, 1984-1985, UCLA Law Review. **PRACTICE AREAS:** Banking; Corporations. **Email:** aevans@gdclaw.com

**MARILYN G. MCDOWELL,** born November 26, 1953; admitted to bar, 1987, California; 1988, Colorado. *Education:* University of Southern California (B.S., 1981); Southwestern University School of Law (J.D., 1986). **PRACTICE AREAS:** Litigation; Antitrust. **Email:** mmcdowell@gdclaw.com

**BRENT M. COHEN** (San Francisco Office).

**DAVID C. MAHAFFEY** (Washington, D.C. Office).

**I. RICHARD LEVY** (Dallas, Texas Office).

**LAURA BEN-PORAT,** born September 19, 1963; admitted to bar, 1988, California. *Education:* University of California at Santa Barbara (B.A., 1985); Loyola Marymount University (J.D., 1988). Order of the Coif. Staff Member, Loyola of Los Angeles Law Review, 1986-1987. (Century City Office). **PRACTICE AREAS:** Entertainment; Intellectual Property. **Email:** lbenporat@gdclaw.com

**THOMAS D. BOYLE** (Dallas, Texas Office).

**STEPHEN H. WILLARD** (Washington, D.C. Office).

**STEVEN JAMES JOHNSON** (San Francisco Office).

**KEVIN R. NOWICKI** (San Diego Office).

**JOHN MASAO IINO,** born April 19, 1962; admitted to bar, 1987, California. *Education:* Pomona College (B.A., 1984); University of Southern California (J.D., 1987). Order of the Coif. Staff Editor, 1985-1986 and Managing Editor, 1986-1987, Southern California Law Review. Law Clerk to Hon. J. Spencer Letts, U.S. District Court, Central District of California, 1987-1988. **LANGUAGES:** Japanese. **PRACTICE AREAS:** International Business; Corporate Law; Corporate Finance. **Email:** jiino@gdclaw.com

**GARY M. ROBERTS,** born September 30, 1962; admitted to bar, 1987, California. *Education:* Princeton University (A.B., cum laude, 1984); Stanford Law School (J.D., 1987). Notes Editor, Stanford Law Review, Member, Stanford Journal of International Law, 1986-1987. Clerk to the Honorable David R. Thompson, Circuit Judge, U.S. Court of Appeals, Ninth Circuit, 1987-1988. **PRACTICE AREAS:** Litigation. **Email:** groberts@gdclaw.com

### ASSOCIATES

**DEBORAH ANN AIWASIAN,** born June 11, 1961; admitted to bar, 1986, California. *Education:* University of Southern California (B.A., 1983; J.D., 1986). Phi Alpha Delta. Hale Moot Court Honors Program (Finalist, 1985; Chairperson, 1985-1986). **PRACTICE AREAS:** Litigation; Insurance. **Email:** daiwasian@gdclaw.com

**ADAM S. BENDELL,** born September 10, 1961; admitted to bar, 1987, California and Hawaii. *Education:* London School of Economics, London, England; Cornell University (B.A., 1983); University of Chicago (J.D., 1986). Executive Editor, University of Chicago Legal Forum, 1985-1986. Associate Editor, University of Chicago Law Review, 1985-1986. Law Clerk, U.S. District Court, Judge Martin Pence, Honolulu, Hawaii, 1986-1987. **PRACTICE AREAS:** Technology; Practice Systems. **Email:** abendell@gdclaw.com

**MARIANNE SHIPP** (Irvine Office).

**MARKUS U. DIETHELM** (New York City Office).

**D. ERIC REMENSPERGER,** born April 11, 1957; admitted to bar, 1985, New York; 1995, California. *Education:* Manhattanville College (B.A., 1981); Brooklyn Law School (J.D., cum laude, 1984). Moot Court Honor Society. Member, Brooklyn Law Review. **PRACTICE AREAS:** Finance; Real Estate; Commercial Real Estate; Partnerships. **Email:** eremensperger@gdclaw.com

*(This Listing Continued)*

**GREGORY L. SURMAN,** born October 15, 1962; admitted to bar, 1987, California. *Education:* University of California, Los Angeles (B.A., 1984); University of California, Boalt Hall School of Law, Berkeley (J.D., 1987). Managing Editor, Industrial Relations Law Journal, 1986-1987. **PRACTICE AREAS:** Corporations; International. **Email:** gsurman@gdclaw.com

**MICHAEL J. KELIHER** (Dallas, Texas Office).

**ALICIA J. BENTLEY,** born August 14, 1963; admitted to bar, 1988, California. *Education:* University of Akron (B.A., summa cum laude, 1985); Ohio State University (J.D., with honors, 1988). Order of the Coif. Managing Editor, The Ohio State Law Journal, 1987-1988. Judicial Extern, The Honorable Alan E. Norris, U.S. Court of Appeals, Sixth Circuit, 1988. **PRACTICE AREAS:** Litigation. **Email:** abentley@gdclaw.com

**LAWRENCE M. ISENBERG,** born February 22, 1958; admitted to bar, 1988, California. *Education:* State University of New York at Potsdam (B.A., 1980); Southwestern University (J.D., 1988). Editor, Southwestern Law Review, 1987-1988. **Email:** lisenberg@gdclaw.com

**MITCHELL STEVEN COHEN,** born August 29, 1958; admitted to bar, 1988, California. *Education:* Occidental College (A.B., 1980); The Fletcher School of Law and Diplomacy (M.A.L.D., 1983); Columbia University (J.D., 1988). Harlan Fiske Stone Scholar, 1987-1988. **PRACTICE AREAS:** Corporate Law; Mergers, Acquisitions and Divestitures. **Email:** mcohen@gdclaw.com

**LIISA ANSELMI STITH** (Irvine Office).

**RIAZ A. KARAMALI** (Palo Alto Office).

**JEFFREY DAVID DINTZER,** born May 19, 1962; admitted to bar, 1988, California. *Education:* University of California at Los Angeles (B.A., 1985); Boston University (J.D., cum laude, 1988). Law Clerk to Honorable Alicemarie H. Stotler, U.S. District Court, Central District of California, 1988-1989. **PRACTICE AREAS:** Environmental Litigation; Environmental Due Diligence; Business Litigation. **Email:** jdintzer@gdclaw.com

**CARL TIMOTHY CROW,** born November 23, 1960; admitted to bar, 1988, California; 1990, Washington. *Education:* Washington State University (B.A., 1984); University of Utah (J.D., 1988). Order of the Coif. Senior Staff Member, University of Utah Law Review, 1987-1988. Law Clerk to the Honorable David A. Ezra, U.S. District Judge, District of Hawaii, 1988-1989. **PRACTICE AREAS:** Federal Income; Taxation. **Email:** ccrow@gdclaw.com

**GREGORY J. CONKLIN** (San Francisco Office).

**PETER C. D'APICE** (Dallas, Texas Office).

**LEONARD H. HERSH** (New York City Office).

**DUNCAN T. O'BRIEN** (New York City Office).

**DEBORAH J. CLARKE,** born March 15, 1963; admitted to bar, 1989, California. *Education:* University of Oklahoma (B.A., cum laude, 1985; J.D., magna cum laude, 1989). Order of the Coif. Chief Article and Book Review Editor, Oklahoma Law Review, 1988-1989. **PRACTICE AREAS:** Labor and Employment Law. **Email:** dclarke@gdclaw.com

**VIVIENNE ANGELA VELLA,** born October 16, 1964; admitted to bar, 1989, California. *Education:* University of California at Los Angeles (B.A., 1985); University of California, Boalt Hall School of Law (J.D., 1989). **PRACTICE AREAS:** Intellectual Property/Media Law. **Email:** vvella@gdclaw.com

**MARGARET B. GRAHAM** (Denver, Colorado Office).

**LAWRENCE S. ACHORN** (San Francisco Office).

**GUNNAR BLAISE GOODING** (Irvine Office).

**CYNTHIA L. SALMEN,** born June 25, 1956; admitted to bar, 1989, California; 1992, Minnesota. *Education:* University of Minnesota (B.A., 1980; J.D. cum laude, 1989). **PRACTICE AREAS:** Antitrust and Trade Regulation; Insurance. **Email:** csalmengdclaw.com

**SCOTT MONRO DREYER,** born April 7, 1964; admitted to bar, 1989, California. *Education:* University of California at Berkeley (A.B., 1986); Boalt Hall School of Law, University of California (J.D., 1989). Phi Beta Kappa. Notes and Comments Editor, High Technology Law Journal, 1987-1988 and Associate Editor, Ecology Law Quarterly, 1988-1989. **PRACTICE AREAS:** Environmental; Insurance. **Email:** sdreyer@gdclaw.com

**ADAM H. OFFENHARTZ** (New York City Office).

*(This Listing Continued)*

**GIBSON, DUNN & CRUTCHER LLP, Los Angeles—** *Continued*

**GARETH T. EVANS,** born July 20, 1961; admitted to bar, 1988, California. *Education:* University of California at Berkeley (B.A., 1983); New York University (J.D., 1988). Chairman, Moot Court Board. Order of the Barristers. Law Clerk, Honorable Gordon Thompson, Jr., United States District Court, Southern District of California, 1988-1990. **PRACTICE AREAS:** Securities Litigation; General Business Litigation; Insurance Coverage and Bad Faith Litigation; Professional Liability. *Email:* gevans@gdclaw.com

**JEFFREY F. WEBB,** born June 14, 1964; admitted to bar, 1990, California. *Education:* Wharton School, University of Pennsylvania (B.S. in Economics, magna cum laude, 1985); University of Virginia (J.D., 1988); London School of Economics, University of London (LL.M., 1989). Notes Editor, Journal of Law and Politics, 1987-1988. Finalist, William Minor Lile Moot Court Competition. Law Clerk, Honorable Robert R. Beezer, United States Court of Appeals for the Ninth Circuit, 1989-1990. **PRACTICE AREAS:** Labor and Employment Law. *Email:* jwebb@gdclaw.com

**RODNEY J. STONE,** born April 8, 1961; admitted to bar, 1988, Illinois; 1989, California. *Education:* Southern Illinois University (B.S., cum laude, 1984); University of Illinois (J.D., magna cum laude, 1988). Order of the Coif. Member, 1986-1987 and Associate Editor, 1987-1988, University of Illinois Law Review. **PRACTICE AREAS:** Antitrust and Trade Regulation; Litigation. *Email:* rstone@gdclaw.com

**DESMOND CUSSEN** (San Francisco Office).

**MARK SNYDERMAN** (Washington, D.C. Office).

**CHRISTOPHER J. BELLINI** (Washington, D.C. Office).

**DAVID W. MAYO** (New York City Office).

**LAWRENCE BYRNE** (New York City Office).

**JANET M. WEISS** (New York City Office).

**WALTER J. SCOTT, JR.** (Dallas, Texas Office).

**MARGARET C. McCULLA** (Washington, D.C. Office).

**DIANA GALE RICHARD** (Washington, D.C. Office).

**LINDA L. CURTIS,** born September 19, 1960; admitted to bar, 1988, California. *Education:* Princeton University (A.B., summa cum laude, 1982); Oxford University (Balliol College), Oxford, U.K. (B.A., 1984); Stanford University (J.D. with distinction, M.B.A., 1987). Phi Beta Kappa. Article Editor, Stanford Law Review, 1986-1987. Law Clerk, Chief Judge Robert F. Peckham, Northern District of California, 1987-1988. **PRACTICE AREAS:** Corporate Finance; Mergers and Acquisitions. *Email:* lcurtis@gdclaw.com

**SEELEY ANN BROOKS,** born March 11, 1964; admitted to bar, 1991, California. *Education:* Harvard University (A.B., 1986); Columbia University (J.D., 1989). Harlan Fiske Stone Scholar. Managing Editor, Columbia Journal of Law and Social Problems. Law Clerk to the Honorable J. Lawrence Irving, Southern District of California, 1989-1990. **PRACTICE AREAS:** Real Estate. *Email:* sbrooks@gdclaw.com

**J. MARK DUNBAR** (San Diego Office).

**MEREDITH C. BRAXTON** (New York City Office).

**STANTON P. EIGENBRODT** (Dallas, Texas Office).

**OSCAR GARZA** (Irvine Office).

**ALAN N. BICK** (Irvine Office).

**JOHN W. FRICKS,** born September 2, 1964; admitted to bar, 1990, California. *Education:* California Polytechnic State University (B.S., 1987); Boston University (J.D., cum laude, 1990). **PRACTICE AREAS:** Litigation; Commercial Real Estate. *Email:* jfricks@gdclaw.com

**JEFFREY T. GILLERAN** (Washington, D.C. Office).

**KIM A. THOMPSON** (San Francisco Office).

**CHERYL WRIGHT OLSEN,** born August 7, 1965; admitted to bar, 1990, California. *Education:* Mount Holyoke College (A.B., cum laude with highest honors in History, 1987); University of Southern California (J.D., 1990). Member, Southern California Law Review, 1988-1990. **PRACTICE AREAS:** Labor. *Email:* colsen@gdclaw.com

**MICHAEL F. FLANAGAN** (Washington, D.C. Office).

**ANDREA E. NEUMAN** (Irvine Office).

*(This Listing Continued)*

**JOHN ANDREW YU-CHENG CHANG,** born June 12, 1965; admitted to bar, 1990, California. *Education:* Princeton University (A.B., 1987); Georgetown University (J.D., 1990).

**CLARK D. STITH** (Irvine Office).

**EUGENE SCALIA** (Washington, D.C. Office).

**ROBERT E. MALCHMAN** (New York City Office).

**HENRY A. THOMPSON** (Jeddah, Riyadh and Washington, D.C. Offices).

**CHRISTOPHER L. THORNE** (Denver, Colorado Office).

**J. FRED NEUMAN** (Irvine Office).

**JERRY S. FOWLER, JR.** (Washington, D.C. Office).

**M. SEAN ROYALL** (Washington, D.C. Office).

**RALPH H. BLAKENEY** (Dallas, Texas Office).

**EBEN PAUL PERISON,** born May 10, 1965; admitted to bar, 1990, California. *Education:* University of California at Irvine (B.A., magna cum laude, 1987); University of California, Hastings College of the Law (J.D., cum laude, 1990). Phi Beta Kappa. Order of the Coif. (Century City Office). **PRACTICE AREAS:** Corporate; Securities. *Email:* eperison@gdclaw.com

**PETER J. BESHAR** (New York City Office).

**RICHARD D. GLUCK** (San Diego Office).

**JEFFREY B. CONNER,** born June 16, 1957; admitted to bar, 1989, Pennsylvania; 1991, Michigan (Not admitted in California). *Education:* University of California at Los Angeles (B.A., 1978); Harvard University (Ph.D., 1980); Harvard Law School (J.D., magna cum laude, 1989). Member, Harvard Law Review, 1987-1989. Law Clerk to Judge A. J. Scirica, U.S. Court of Appeals for the Third Circuit, 1989-1990. **PRACTICE AREAS:** Corporations; Securities. *Email:* jconner@gdclaw.com

**NOËL C. LOHR,** admitted to bar, 1990, California. *Education:* University of Southern California (B.A., summa cum laude, 1987; J.D., 1990). *Email:* nlohr@gdclaw.com

**FRÉDÉRIQUE SAUVAGE,** born November 25, 1965; admitted to bar, 1993, France (Not admitted in United States) (Not admitted in California). *Education:* Panthéon Sorbonne, Paris, France (Maîtrise droit privé, 1988;DESS droit des affaires et fiscalite, 1989); Kings College, London, England (LL.B., 1988). **LANGUAGES:** French and English. **PRACTICE AREAS:** Corporate Law; Commercial Law. *Email:* fsauvage@gdclaw.com

**SCOTT M. KNUTSON** (Irvine Office).

**KARL G. NELSON** (Dallas, Texas Office).

**WILLIAM A. MACARTHUR,** born September 10, 1964; admitted to bar, 1991, California. *Education:* California State University at Northridge (B.A., 1988); Loyola of Los Angeles (J.D., 1991). Order of the Coif. Chief Note and Comment Editor, Loyola Law Review, 1989-1991. *Email:* wmacarthur@gdclaw.com

**JEFFREY H. REEVES** (Irvine Office).

**WILLIAM J. GALLAGHER** (New York City Office).

**MARSHALL R. KING** (New York City Office).

**SCOTT J. CALFAS,** born November 12, 1965; admitted to bar, 1991, California. *Education:* University of California at Los Angeles (B.A., cum laude, 1988); University of Michigan (J.D., cum laude, 1991). *Member:* Los Angeles County and American Bar Associations. *Email:* scalfas@gdclaw.com

**JODI M. NEWBERRY,** born September 29, 1965; admitted to bar, 1991, California. *Education:* University of California at Santa Barbara (B.S., 1987); Loyola Law School of Los Angeles (J.D., 1991). Order of the Coif. **PRACTICE AREAS:** Litigation.

**J. MITCHELL DOLLOFF** (New York City Office).

**MARK R. DUNN** (Dallas, Texas Office).

**KRISTINE D. RISTAINO,** born August 1, 1966; admitted to bar, 1991, California. *Education:* Duke University (A.B., cum laude, 1987); Northwestern University (J.D., 1991). **PRACTICE AREAS:** Real Estate; General Corporate. *Email:* kristaino@gdclaw.com

**MICHAEL S. UDOVIC,** born January 2, 1966; admitted to bar, 1991, California. *Education:* Occidental College (A.B., 1987); Loyola Law School

*(This Listing Continued)*

of Los Angeles (J.D., 1991). Order of the Coif. Articles Editor, Loyola Law Review, 1990-1991. *Email:* mudovic@gdclaw.com

ROBERT H. WRIGHT, born October 4, 1964; admitted to bar, 1991, California. *Education:* University of Virginia (B.A., 1987); Indiana University (J.D., magna cum laude, 1991). Order of the Coif. Member, 1989-1990 and Notes Editor, 1990-1991, Indiana Law Journal. *Email:* rwright@gdclaw.com

LAURA A. ZWICKER, born October 19, 1966; admitted to bar, 1991, California. *Education:* Washington University (B.A., cum laude, 1988); Indiana University (J.D., magna cum laude, 1991). Order of the Coif. Associate, 1989-1990 and Articles Editor, 1990-1991, Indiana Law Journal. *PRACTICE AREAS:* Trusts and Estates; Tax. *Email:* lzwicker@gdclaw.com

JOHN M. WILLIAMS, III (Irvine Office).

GREGG P. GOLDMAN (Irvine Office).

DAVID A. LEVINE (Washington, D.C. Office).

STEVEN K. TALLEY (Denver, Colorado Office).

HOLLY B. WINDHAM (Dallas, Texas Office).

AUDREY S. TRUNDLE (New York City Office).

W. JAMES BIEDERMAN (Washington, D.C. Office).

ANTOINETTE D. PAGLIA, born October 25, 1956; admitted to bar, 1991, California; registered to practice before U.S. Patent and Trademark Office. *Education:* California State University (B.A., 1981; M.S., 1986); Southwestern University School of Law (J.D., magna cum laude, 1991). Member, 1989-1990, Articles Editor, Executive Board, 1990-1991, Southwestern Law Review. Extern, Honorable Robert H. Takasugi, Central District, U.S. District Court, 1991. *PRACTICE AREAS:* Medical Malpractice and Health Law; General Civil Litigation; Intellectual Property; Patent Law. *Email:* apaglia@gdclaw.com

SHAHIN REZAI (Washington, D.C. Office).

PETER M. STONE (Irvine Office).

TRACEY NELSON TIEDMAN (Denver, Colorado Office).

MARK J. PAYNE (Irvine Office).

CHARLES F. KESTER, born February 6, 1965; admitted to bar, 1992, California. *Education:* University of Virginia (B.A., 1987; J.D., 1991). Phi Beta Kappa. Member, 1989-1991 and Executive Editor, 1990-1991, Virginia Law Review. Law Clerk to Hon. Stephen V. Wilson, United States District Judge for the Central District of California, 1991-1992. *PRACTICE AREAS:* Litigation. *Email:* ckester@gdclaw.com

TANYA S. MCVEIGH, born October 7, 1966; admitted to bar, 1992, California. *Education:* University of Southern California (B.A., magna cum laude, 1988); University of California, Hastings College of the Law (J.D., 1991). Law Clerk to Honorable Robert J. Kelleher, U.S. District Court, 1991-1992. *PRACTICE AREAS:* Antitrust; Real Estate Litigation. *Email:* tmcveigh@gdclaw.com

BRIAN L. DUFFY (Denver, Colorado Office).

REBECCA A. WOMELDORF (Washington, D.C. Office).

JAMES C. DOUGHERTY (Washington, D.C. Office).

MARK A. PERRY (Washington, D.C. Office).

MICHELE L. SHELDON (New York City Office).

LEEANNA IZUEL, born February 23, 1967; admitted to bar, 1991, California. *Education:* University of California at Los Angeles (B.A., magna cum laude, 1988); University of California School of Law at Los Angeles (J.D., 1991). Member, 1989-1991 and Editor, 1990-1991, UCLA Law Review. *PRACTICE AREAS:* Securities; Mergers, Acquisitions and Divestitures. *Email:* lizuel@gdclaw.com

PREETA D. BANSAL (New York City Office).

DARA L. FREEDMAN, born October 17, 1966; admitted to bar, 1992, California; 1993, District of Columbia. *Education:* Rice University (B.A., 1988); Emory University (J.D., 1991). Order of the Coif. Articles Editor, Emory Law Journal, 1991. Law Clerk to Senior Judge Kenneth R. Harkins, U.S. Claims Court, 1991-1992. *LANGUAGES:* Spanish. *PRACTICE AREAS:* Taxation. *Email:* dfreedman@gdclaw.com

ALAN R. STRUBLE (Dallas, Texas Office).

*(This Listing Continued)*

JAMES P. FOGELMAN, born October 25, 1967; admitted to bar, 1992, California. *Education:* Wharton School, University of Pennsylvania (B.S., 1989); University of California School of Law (J.D., 1992). *Email:* jfogelman@gdclaw.com

CORI L. MACDONNEIL, born March 28, 1967; admitted to bar, 1992, California. *Education:* University of California (B.A., summa cum laude, 1989); Pepperdine University (J.D., cum laude, 1992). Member, Pepperdine University Law Review. Extern: The Honorable Armand Arabian, California Supreme Court, 1990; United States Securities Exchange Commission, 1992. *LANGUAGES:* Spanish. *PRACTICE AREAS:* Litigation; Health Care Fraud and Abuse. *Email:* cmacdonneil@gdclaw.com

CRAIG V. RICHARDSON (Denver, Colorado Office).

TIMOTHY L. ALGER, born April 23, 1955; admitted to bar, 1992, California. *Education:* Seton Hall University (B.A., magna cum laude, 1977); University of Colorado (M.A., 1978); Loyola Law School (J.D., magna cum laude, 1992). Order of the Coif. Senior Note and Comment Editor, Loyola of Los Angeles Law Review. *PRACTICE AREAS:* Media and Entertainment Litigation; Business Litigation. *Email:* talger@gdclaw.com

STELLA S. LEUNG (Hong Kong and Dallas, Texas Offices).

MICHAEL P. DE SIMONE (New York City Office).

TRYGVE M. THORESEN (Irvine Office).

RICHARD B. LEVY, born November 7, 1968; admitted to bar, 1992, California. *Education:* McGill University (B.A., 1989); New York University (J.D., 1992). Member, 1990-1991 and Senior Staff Editor, 1991-1992, New York University Law Review. *PRACTICE AREAS:* Labor and Employment Law; Entertainment and Sports Law. *Email:* rblevy@gdclaw.com

IGNACIO M. FONCILLAS (New York City Office).

MARYN L. MILLER (Irvine Office).

LESLIE ELLEN MOORE (New York City Office).

PATRICIA E. FOLEY (Denver, Colorado Office).

JODY L. JOHNSON, born May 17, 1966; admitted to bar, 1992, California. *Education:* Oklahoma State University (B.S., 1989); University of California, Boalt Hall School of Law (J.D., 1992). Associate Editor, Ecology Law Quarterly, 1991-1992. *Email:* jjohnson@gdclaw.com

MICHELLE D. LUSTIG (Irvine Office).

WILLIAM L. MENARD (Washington, D.C. Office).

ELISE D. CHARBONNET (New York City Office).

MAYA R. CRONE (Washington, D.C. Office).

SHARYL P. BILAS (Irvine Office).

MICHAEL A. LEVY (San Francisco Office).

CHRIS D. BIONDI (New York City Office).

BRIAN E. CASEY (Denver, Colorado Office).

LAWRENCE J. LA SALA (New York City Office).

MATTHEW BEN HINERFELD (San Francisco Office).

DAVID A. SEGAL (Irvine Office).

ALAN LAWHEAD (San Diego Office).

BOYD M. JOHNSON III (New York City Office).

PETER P. MURPHY (Washington, D.C. Office).

STEVEN N. GOFMAN, born June 15, 1962; admitted to bar, 1992, Illinois; 1996, California. *Education:* Washington University (B.S.B.A., 1984); Columbia University (M.A., 1987); Cornell Law School (J.D., magna cum laude, 1992). Order of the Coif. Editor, Cornell Law Review. *PRACTICE AREAS:* Corporate Law; Securities. *Email:* sgofman@gdclaw.com

H. MARK LYON (Palo Alto Office).

PAUL J. COLLINS (Palo Alto Office).

LINDA GREIF (New York City Office).

TIMOTHY D. BLANTON (Palo Alto Office).

DANIEL W. NELSON (Washington, D.C. Office).

*(This Listing Continued)*

**GIBSON, DUNN & CRUTCHER LLP, Los Angeles—**
*Continued*

**LESLIE Y. KIM,** born July 17, 1964; admitted to bar, 1993, California. *Education:* University of California at Los Angeles (B.A., 1987); Georgetown University (J.D., cum laude, 1993). Member, The Georgetown Law Journal. **PRACTICE AREAS:** Corporate Law; Securities. **Email:** lkim@gdclaw.com

**DEBRA ALLIGOOD WHITE,** born October 5, 1960; admitted to bar, 1993, California. *Education:* Harvard/Radcliffe College (A.B., 1982); University of California School of Law (J.D., 1993). **PRACTICE AREAS:** General Corporate. **Email:** dwhite@gdclaw.com

**JEFFREY A. FIARMAN** (Washington, D.C. Office).

**MONIQUE MICHAL DRAKE** (Denver, Colorado Office).

**T. MICHAEL CRIMMINS** (Denver, Colorado Office).

**TIMOTHY J. HART,** born July 2, 1964; admitted to bar, 1993, California. *Education:* Merrimack College (B.A., 1986); University of San Diego School of Law (J.D., 1993). Member, San Diego Law Review, 1992-1993. **PRACTICE AREAS:** Securities; Mergers and Acquisitions. **Email:** thart@gdclaw.com

**LESLIE R. OLSON** (Irvine Office).

**PETER E. SELEY** (Washington, D.C. Office).

**LISA A. SLEBODA** (New York City Office).

**LINDSEY F. BUSS** (Washington, D.C. Office).

**LISA M. LANDMEIER** (Washington, D.C. Office).

**D. JARRETT ARP** (Washington, D.C. Office).

**LINCOLN D. BANDLOW,** born April 1, 1966; admitted to bar, 1994, California. *Education:* University of California, Los Angeles (B.A., 1990); Boston University School of Law (J.D., magna cum laude, 1993). Editor, American Journal of Law & Medicine, 1992-1993. **PRACTICE AREAS:** Media and Intellectual Property Litigation. **Email:** lbandlow@gdclaw.com

**JEFFREY D. GOLDSTEIN,** born September 20, 1968; admitted to bar, 1993, California. *Education:* University of California at Berkeley (B.A., 1990); Columbia University School of Law (J.D., 1993). Harlan Fiske Stone Scholar. **PRACTICE AREAS:** Corporations. **Email:** jgoldstein@gdclaw.com

**KATHLEEN M. VANDERZIEL,** born December 17, 1964; admitted to bar, 1992, California. *Education:* University of California at Berkeley (B.A., 1987); Boston College (J.D., magna cum laude, 1992). Order of the Coif. Member, Boston College Environmental Affairs Law Review. Law Clerk, Ruggero J. Aldisert, U.S. Senior Circuit Judge, U.S. Court of Appeals, 3rd Circuit. **PRACTICE AREAS:** Labor and Employment. **Email:** kvanderziel@gdclaw.com

**JON G. SHEPHERD** (Dallas, Texas Office).

**JASON C. MURRAY,** born March 27, 1967; admitted to bar, 1994, California. *Education:* University of Nevada, Las Vegas (B.A., 1990); University of Southern California (J.D., 1993). Editor, University of Southern California Law Review, 1991-1993. Clerk to Justice Charles E. Sprinaer, Nevada Supreme Court, 1993-1994. (Los Angeles and Century City Offices). **PRACTICE AREAS:** Entertainment Litigation; General Commercial Litigation. **Email:** jmurray@gdclaw.com

**DONNA M. BIGI** (Irvine Office).

**JONATHAN K. TYCKO** (Washington, D.C. Office).

**KIMBERLY ANN UDOVIC,** born February 23, 1968; admitted to bar, 1993, California. *Education:* University of Pennsylvania (B.S., B.A.S., 1990); University of Chicago (J.D., with honors, 1993). Judicial Clerk, Hon. A. Wallace Tashima, U.S. District Court, Central District of California, 1993-1994. **PRACTICE AREAS:** Litigation; Copyright and Trademark Litigation. **Email:** kudovic@gdclaw.com

**THOMAS S. JONES** (Irvine Office).

**STEPHANIE YOST CAMERON,** born October 21, 1960; admitted to bar, 1994, California. *Education:* University of California (B.A., cum laude, 1984); Southwestern University School of Law (J.D., magna cum laude, 1993). Member, Moot Court, 1992-1993. Member, Southwest Law Review, 1992-1993. Law Clerk, Judge Harry Pregerson, Ninth Circuit Court of Appeals, 1993-1994. **PRACTICE AREAS:** Entertainment and the Arts; Intellectual Property. **Email:** scameron@gdclaw.com

**JONATHAN L. ISRAEL** (New York City Office).

**O. REY RODRIGUEZ** (Dallas, Texas Office).

**JEANETTE M. BAZIS,** born January 29, 1966; admitted to bar, 1993, California; 1994, Minnesota. *Education:* Temple University (B.B.A., 1988); University of Minnesota (J.D., 1992). Order of the Coif. Editor, Journal of Law and Inequality. Clerk, Hon. James M. Rosenbaum, U.S. District Court, Minnesota. (Century City Office). **PRACTICE AREAS:** General Commercial Litigation; Intellectual Property Litigation. **Email:** jbazis@gdclaw.com

**JESSICA BOLGER LEE** (Denver, Colorado Office).

**DEBORAH A. HULSE** (Washington, D.C. Office).

**TORREY A. OLINS** (Irvine Office).

**GEORGIANA G. RODIGER,** born December 22, 1953; admitted to bar, 1980, California. *Education:* Pitzer College (B.A., 1976); Pepperdine Law School (J.D., 1980). Member, Pepperdine Law Review. **PRACTICE AREAS:** Litigation; Bankruptcy. **Email:** crodiger@gdclaw.com

**STEPHEN B. DORROUGH,** born January 2, 1967; admitted to bar, 1994, Washington; 1995, California. *Education:* Brigham Young University (B.A., 1991); East China University of Politics and Law, Shanghai, P.R.C.; University of Hong Kong Faculty of Law, Hong Kong; University of Utah (J.D., 1994). William H. Leary Scholar. **LANGUAGES:** Cantonese, Mandarin. **PRACTICE AREAS:** Corporate Law; Securities. **Email:** sdorrough@gdclaw.com

**CATHERINE HERRIN GORECKI** (Washington, D.C. Office).

**PAUL B. LACKEY** (Dallas, Texas Office).

**CHARLES R. BOGLE** (New York City Office).

**STACY V. BROWN** (New York City Office).

**CORINNE A. FRANZEN,** born October 1, 1966; admitted to bar, 1994, California. *Education:* University of California (B.A., 1988); University of Minnesota (J.D., 1994). Order of the Coif. **PRACTICE AREAS:** Labor and Employment. **Email:** cfranzen@gdclaw.com

**THOMAS G. MACKEY,** born May 9, 1969; admitted to bar, 1994, California. *Education:* California State University at Northridge (B.S., 1991); University of California, Hastings College of the Law (J.D., 1994). Associate Articles Editor, Hastings Law Journal. Member, Thurston Society. **PRACTICE AREAS:** Labor and Employment Law. **Email:** tmackey@gdclaw.com

**FREDERICK A. WALTERS** (New York City Office).

**REBECCA SANHUEZA** (San Francisco Office).

**COSMAS N. LYKOS** (Irvine Office).

**SHELLEY R. MEACHAM,** born June 30, 1954; admitted to bar, 1994, California. *Education:* California State University at Los Angeles (B.A., 1976); Southwestern University (J.D., summa cum laude, 1994). **PRACTICE AREAS:** Legal Ethics and Professional Responsibility; Professional Liability. **Email:** smeacham@gdclaw.com

**WILLIAM M. RUSTUM,** born November 26, 1965; admitted to bar, 1994, California. *Education:* University of Richmond (B.S., 1988); New York University School of Law (J.D., 1994). (Century City Office). **PRACTICE AREAS:** Corporate. **Email:** wrustum@gdclaw.com

**MARY SIKRA THOMAS,** born May 19, 1969; admitted to bar, 1994, California. *Education:* University of Delaware (B.A., magna cum laude, 1991); Harvard Law School (J.D., magna cum laude, 1994). **PRACTICE AREAS:** Litigation; Environmental Law. **Email:** mthomas@gdclaw.com

**MICHELLE M. BRISSETTE** (Denver, Colorado Office).

**LAURA C. ROCHE** (Palo Alto Office).

**MARY K. PORTER** (Denver, Colorado Office).

**BRIAN JAYWOO KIM,** born May 26, 1968; admitted to bar, 1994, California. *Education:* Yale University (B.A., 1990); University of California, Boalt Hall School of Law (J.D., 1994). **LANGUAGES:** Korean. **Email:** bkim@gdclaw.com

**DAVID N. KING,** born March 11, 1967; admitted to bar, 1994, California. *Education:* University of Southern California (A.B., 1988); University of Southern California Law Center (J.D., 1994). Staff Member, Southern California Law Review. **PRACTICE AREAS:** Labor and Employment. **Email:** dnking@gdclaw.com

*(This Listing Continued)*

**LILA E. ROGERS,** born October 10, 1968; admitted to bar, 1994, California. *Education:* Barnard College (B.A., 1991); University of Southern California Law Center (J.D., 1994). Executive Editor, Southern California Law Review. *PRACTICE AREAS:* Real Estate; Finance. *Email:* lrogers@gdclaw.com

**HILARY JOY HATCH,** born November 3, 1969; admitted to bar, 1994, California. *Education:* University of California at Berkeley (B.A., 1991); Loyola Law School (J.D., cum laude, 1994). Order of the Coif. Senior Note and Comment Editor, Loyola of Los Angeles International and Comparative Law Journal, 1992-1994. *PRACTICE AREAS:* Corporate Law; Securities. *Email:* hhatch@gdclaw.com

**MICHAEL L. REED,** born March 27, 1966; admitted to bar, 1994, California. *Education:* University of California at Berkeley (B.A., 1988); University of California School of Law at Los Angeles (J.D., 1994). (Century City Office). *PRACTICE AREAS:* Corporate Law; Securities. *Email:* mreed@gdclaw.com

**LARA M. KRIEGER** (New York City Office).

**ALBERT R. MORALES** (New York City Office).

**THEODORE A. RUSSELL,** born June 5, 1970; admitted to bar, 1994, California. *Education:* Cornell University (B.A., 1991); University of Southern California Law Center (J.D., 1994). Order of the Coif. Executive Notes Editor, Southern California Law Review, 1993-1994. Law Clerk, Honorable John G. Davies, United States District Court for the Central District of California, 1994-1995. *PRACTICE AREAS:* Labor and Employment; Litigation. *Email:* trussell@gdclaw.com

**TODD M. NOONAN** (San Francisco Office).

**TRACEY M. WHITNEY,** born November 25, 1969; admitted to bar, 1994, California. *Education:* Duke University (B.A., 1991); University of Southern California Law Center (J.D., 1994). Order of the Coif. Member: University of Southern California Law Review, 1992-1993; University of Southern California Review of Law and Women's Studies, 1993-1994. *Email:* twhitneygdclaw.com

**CHRISTOPHER D. DUSSEAULT,** born May 6, 1969; admitted to bar, 1995, California. *Education:* Yale University (B.A., summa cum laude, 1991); Duke University School of Law (J.D., with high honors, 1994). Special Projects and Notes Editor, Law and Contemporary Problems, 1993-1994. Law Clerk, The Hon. Robert E. Payne, U.S. District Court, Eastern District of Virginia, 1994-1995. *PRACTICE AREAS:* Litigation; Antitrust and Trade Regulation. *Email:* cdusseault@gdclaw.com

**JEFFREY E. ORAKER** (Denver, Colorado Office).

**SIMONE PROCAS** (New York City Office).

**CHRISTINA L. ROOKE** (San Francisco Office).

**ALEX E. SADLER** (Washington, D.C. Office).

**ADAM E. MUCHNICK** (Irvine Office).

**ELLEN L. FARRELL,** born December 22, 1964; admitted to bar, 1994, California. *Education:* Rice University (B.A., 1987); Loyola University of Los Angeles (J.D., 1994). Order of the Coif. Chief Note and Comment Editor/Executive Board, Loyola of Los Angeles Law Review. Law Clerk, The Honorable Edward Rafeedie, U.S. District Court, Central District of California, 1994-1995. *Email:* efarrell@gdclaw.com

**SUE J. NAM** (New York City Office).

**PAULINE H. YOO** (New York City Office).

**C. GLEN MORRIS** (Dallas, Texas Office).

**SABRINA Y. T. FANG** (Hong Kong Office).

**SEAN E. ANDRUSSIER** (Washington, D.C. Office).

**HELGARD C. WALKER** (Washington, D.C. Office).

**HILLARY S. ZILZ** (New York City Office).

**BRETTE S. SIMON,** born March 28, 1971; admitted to bar, 1994, California; 1996, District of Columbia. *Education:* University of California, San Diego (B.A., magna cum laude, 1991); University of California School of Law, Los Angeles (J.D., 1994). Phi Beta Kappa. Order of the Coif. Editor, UCLA Law Review, 1992-1994. *PRACTICE AREAS:* Corporate Law. *Email:* bsimon@gdclaw.com

**SAHILY H. FELICIANO,** born February 20, 1961; admitted to bar, 1995, California. *Education:* Arizona State University (B.A., 1985); Southwestern University (J.D., magna cum laude, 1994). Staff Member, Southwestern University Law Review, 1993-1994. *LANGUAGES:* Spanish. *Email:* sfeliciano@gdclaw.com

**ROBERT R. STARK, JR.** (Denver, Colorado Office).

**ANDREW H. CAUDAL** (Dallas, Texas Office).

**KELBY D. HAGAR** (Dallas, Texas Office).

**JOHN C. CONWAY,** born July 20, 1956; admitted to bar, 1995, California. *Education:* University of South Dakota (B.S., 1978); University of Southern California (J.D., 1995). Order of the Coif. Member, Southern California Law Review, 1993-1995. *Email:* jconway@gdclaw.com

**ARUN JHA,** born March 24, 1970; admitted to bar, 1995, California. *Education:* Cornell University (A.B., 1992); University of Southern California (J.D., 1995). Member, Southern California Law Review, 1993-1994. *Email:* ajha@gdclaw.com

**MARK N. MAZDA** (Irvine Office).

**NATALIE KAY SIDLES** (Dallas, Texas Office).

**PAUL A. ANDRONICO** (Irvine Office).

**JAMES P. MANISCALCO,** born March 13, 1969; admitted to bar, 1995, California. *Education:* University of California, Berkeley (B.A., 1991); University of Southern California Law Center (J.D., 1995). Order of the Coif. Staff Member, Southern California Law Review, 1994-1995. *Email:* jmaniscalco@gdclaw.com

**MICHAEL E. SANDERS** (Irvine Office).

**TODD D. KANTORCZYK** (Washington, D.C. Office).

**CONNIE J. RAND** (San Diego Office).

**DYLAN K. REMLEY** (New York City Office).

**LISA A. ALFARO** (New York City Office).

**RACHAEL A. SIMONOFF,** born January 23, 1971; admitted to bar, 1996, California. *Education:* University of Chicago (B.A., 1992; M.A., 1992); Columbia University (J.D., 1995). Harlan Fiske Stone Scholar. *LANGUAGES:* French. *Email:* rsimonoff@gdclaw.com

**DOUGLAS C. FREEMAN** (New York City Office).

**SEAN C. CARR** (Washington, D.C. Office).

**JEFF AUGUSTINI** (Irvine Office).

**WENDY A. LUTZKER,** born April 10, 1969; admitted to bar, 1995, California. *Education:* University of Southern California (B.A., 1990; J.D., 1995). Order of the Coif. Member, Southern California Law Review. *Email:* wlutzker@gdclaw.com

**JENNIFER R. POE** (Dallas, Texas Office).

**TIFFANY DOON SILVA,** born August 24, 1966; admitted to bar, 1995, California. *Education:* Stanford University (A.B., 1988); Southwestern University (J.D., 1995). *Email:* tsilva@gdclaw.com

**WALKER J. WALLACE III** (New York City Office).

**DANIEL H. BAREN** (Irvine Office).

**TODD S. COHEN** (New York City Office).

**MICHELE J. HERSCHKOWITZ** (New York City Office).

**LAURIE MCLAUGHLIN** (New York City Office).

**STACY S. SHIBAO** (Washington, D.C. Office).

**SAMUEL G. LIVERSIDGE,** born May 29, 1969; admitted to bar, 1995, California. *Education:* Andrews University (B.A., 1992); Pepperdine University (J.D., 1995). Dean's List. Staff Member, Pepperdine University Law Review, 1993-1995. *Email:* sliversidge@gdclaw.com

**TIMOTHY S. LYKOWSKI,** born July 2, 1970; admitted to bar, 1995, California. *Education:* Northwestern University (B.A., 1992); University of Southern California Law Center (J.D., 1995). Order of the Coif. Editor, USC Law Review, 1994-1995. *Email:* tlykowski@gdclaw.com

**STEWART L. MCDOWELL** (New York City Office).

**HASSAN A. ZAVAREEI** (Washington, D.C. Office).

**JULIE R. ZEBRAK** (Washington, D.C. Office).

**RICHARD F. ROMERO,** born May 16, 1970; admitted to bar, 1995, California. *Education:* Harvard College (B.A., 1992); University of California School of Law at Los Angeles (J.D., 1995). *Email:* rromero@gdclaw.com

*(This Listing Continued)*

## GIBSON, DUNN & CRUTCHER LLP, Los Angeles—Continued

**JOANNE S. FIELD,** born April 20, 1968; admitted to bar, 1995, California. *Education:* Tufts University (B.A., 1990); University of Virginia (J.D., 1995). *Email:* jfield@gdclaw.com

**MICHAEL PIEROVICH,** born May 24, 1967; admitted to bar, 1996, California. *Education:* Georgetown University (B.S.F.S., 1990; M.S.F.S., 1990); Duke University (J.D., 1995). Staff Editor, Law & Contemporary Problems, 1994-1995. *Email:* mpierovich@gdclaw.com

**KEVIN F. MABREY,** born March 15, 1967; admitted to bar, 1996, California. *Education:* Arizona State University (B.S., 1990); Washington University, St. Louis (M.B.A., 1992); University of Southern California (J.D., 1995). *Email:* kmabrey@gdclaw.com

**HOLLI H. PAYNE** (San Diego Office).

**SACHIN D. ADARKAR** (San Francisco Office).

**JAY P. SRINIVASAN,** born May 28, 1969; admitted to bar, 1996, California. *Education:* University of Illinois (B.S., 1991); New York University School of Law (J.D., 1995). Member, Annual Survey of American Law, 1993-1995. **LANGUAGES:** Tamil. *Email:* jsrinivasan@gdclaw.com

**THOMAS R. GREENBERG,** born July 30, 1958; admitted to bar, 1996, California. *Education:* Beloit College (B.A., 1980); American University (J.D., 1995). Winner, First Year Moot Court Competition. Member, American University Law Review, 1993-1995. Editor, Federal Circuit, 1994-1995. *Email:* tgreenberg@gdclaw.com

**ROBERT H. PRITCHARD, JR.** (New York City Office).

**DANIEL N. SHALLMAN,** born July 21, 1970; admitted to bar, 1995, California. *Education:* University of Illinois (B.S., 1992); University of Chicago (J.D., 1995). *Email:* dshallman@gdclaw.com

**KARIN L. WOLFF** (New York City Office).

**GAVIN A. BESKE** (San Francisco Office).

**JEFFREY L. MENGOLI** (San Diego Office).

**S. ELIZABETH FOSTER** (New York City Office).

**MICHAEL D. NEWTON,** born October 25, 1970; admitted to bar, 1996, California. *Education:* Harvard University (A.B., 1992); Harvard Law School (J.D., 1995). Articles Editor, Harvard Law Review, Vol. 108. Clerk to J. Eschbach, U.S. Court of Appeals, Seventh Circuit, 1995-1996. *Email:* dnewton@gdclaw.com

**PHILLIP F. SMITH, JR.** (Denver, Colorado Office).

**JESSE S. FINLAYSON** (Irvine Office).

**ALLISON C. GOODMAN** (Washington, D.C. Office).

**RAYMOND KU** (Washington, D.C. Office).

**LINDA RICHICHI STAHL** (Dallas, Texas Office).

**MICHAEL A. BARMETTLER** (Irvine Office).

**KATE JEFFERY STOIA** (San Francisco Office).

**JILL M. DENNIS** (Washington, D.C. Office).

**COLLEEN R. MCMILLIN** (Dallas, Texas Office).

**SETH M. M. STODDER,** born July 26, 1970; admitted to bar, 1995, California. *Education:* Haverford College (B.A., 1991); University of Southern California (J.D., 1995). Order of the Coif. Executive Articles Editor, Southern California Law Review. Judicial Law Clerk, The Honorable Audrey B. Collins, United States District Court, Central District of California, 1995-1996. *Email:* sstodder@gdclaw.com

**INNA IDELCHIK** (New York City Office).

**ROGER P. CAPRIOTTI,** born September 20, 1970; admitted to bar, 1996, California. *Education:* University of Virginia (B.A., 1992); Harvard Law School (J.D., 1995). 1994 Harvard Ames Moot Court Champions. **LANGUAGES:** Italian. *Email:* rcapriotti@gdclaw.com

**DAISY C. WU,** born May 14, 1974; admitted to bar, 1996, California. *Education:* College of William & Mary (B.A., 1992); University of Virginia Law School (J.D., 1995). Order of the Coif. Clerkship, Chief Judge Jerry Buchmeyer, Northern District of Texas, 1995-1996. **LANGUAGES:** Mandarin Chinese. *Email:* dwu@gdclaw.com

**DANIEL T. PERINI** (Denver, Colorado Office).

*(This Listing Continued)*

**JEAN DE FOREST BILLYOU** (Irvine Office).

**JONATHAN M. FINGERET** (Denver, Colorado Office).

**ABDUL AZIZ I. AL-AJLAN** (Riyadh, Saudi Arabia Office).

**ABDULLAH A. AL HABARDI** (Riyadh, Saudi Arabia Office).

### STAFF ATTORNEYS

**WILLIAM H. BOYLES** (Dallas, Texas Office).

**MARGARET ANN GARNER** (Washington, D.C. Office).

**SALLY NOVAK JANIN** (Washington, D.C. Office).

**BRIAN R. KIRCHOFF** (Irvine Office).

**SHARON W. KOPLAN** (Dallas, Texas Office).

**CHRISTINE NAYLOR,** born May 22, 1965; admitted to bar, 1994, California. *Education:* California State University at Fullerton (B.A., 1987); Southwestern University School of Law (J.D., 1994). *Email:* cnaylor@gdclaw.com

**LINDA NOONAN** (Washington, D.C. Office).

**IRENE M. RAMIREZ** (Dallas, Texas Office).

**ROBERTO REDONDO** (New York City Office).

**RANDY RHODES,** born December 10, 1957; admitted to bar, 1989, California. *Education:* California State University at Northridge (B.A., 1981); University of West Los Angeles (J.D., 1986). **PRACTICE AREAS:** Medical Malpractice Defense; Bad Faith Defense. *Email:* rrhodes@gdclaw.com

**KENNETH A. SCHAGRIN** (Washington, D.C. Office).

**ANNA C. SILVA** (San Francisco Office).

**SYDNEY M. SMITH** (Washington, D.C. Office).

**MARK ONEAL SUTTLE,** born February 27, 1950; admitted to bar, 1990, California. *Education:* University of California at Davis (B.A., with highest honors, 1979); Harvard Law School (J.D., magna cum laude, 1986). Judicial Clerkship, United States Court of Appeals, Ninth Circuit, The Honorable Dorothy W. Nelson, 1987. **PRACTICE AREAS:** Business Litigation. *Email:* msuttle@gdclaw.com

**KATHLEEN G. VAGT** (Washington, D.C. Office).

**MELINDA DALTON WATERMAN** (Irvine Office).

## LAW OFFICES OF RICHARD H. GIBSON

*A PROFESSIONAL CORPORATION*

**WELLS FARGO CENTER**
*333 SOUTH GRAND AVENUE, SUITE 1860*
**LOS ANGELES, CALIFORNIA 90071**
Telephone: 213-617-1185
Facsimile: 213-617-1902

*Bankruptcy, Real Estate, Business Law and Civil Litigation.*

**FIRM PROFILE:** The Law Offices of Richard H. Gibson represents a diverse mixture of business clients. Our institutional clients include Bank of America, N.T.&S.A., First Interstate Bank of California and California Korea Bank. We also represent a number of hotel owners and other small businesses.

**RICHARD H. GIBSON,** born Baltimore, Maryland, January 7, 1958; admitted to bar, 1983, California and U.S. District Court, Northern District of California; 1987, U.S. District Court, Eastern, Southern and Central Districts of California and U.S. Court of Appeals, Ninth Circuit. *Education:* Princeton University; University of California, Santa Cruz (B.A., honors, 1979); University of Santa Clara (J.D., cum laude, 1983). Author: "Loan Workouts After Deprizio: Structuring to Reduce Preference Risk," 18 California Bankruptcy Journal 161 (Spring 1990); "Deprizio v. Established Preference Analysis: Another View on Indirect Preferences," 17 California Bankruptcy Journal (Fall 1989); "Home Court, Outpost Court: Reconciling Bankruptcy Case Control with Venue Flexibility in Proceedings," 62 American Bankruptcy Law Journal 37 (Winter 1988); "The New Law on Rejection of Collective Bargaining Agreements in Chapter 11: An Analysis of 11 U.S.C. Section 1113," 58 American Bankruptcy Law Journal 325 (Fall 1984), reprinted in Corporate Counsel's Annual, Matthew Bender (1985); "Labor Contracts in Chapter 11: Early Case Law Under Section 1113," Norton Bankruptcy Law Adviser, Dec. 1985; "Chapter 11 Is a Two-Edged Sword: Union Options in Corporate Chapter 11 Proceedings," 35 Labor

*(This Listing Continued)*

Law Journal 624 (1984). *Member:* Los Angeles County Bar Association (Member, Commercial Law and Bankruptcy Section); State Bar of California (Member, Section on Business Law); Financial Lawyers Conference; California Bankruptcy Forum. *PRACTICE AREAS:* Banking; Bankruptcy; Real Estate; Corporate Law; Civil Litigation.

## GIBSON AND RIVERA
### LOS ANGELES, CALIFORNIA
(See Pasadena)

*General Business Litigation, including Real Estate, Unfair Business Practices, Employer-Employee Relations, Plaintiff and Defendant Personal Injury, Wrongful Death, Premises Liability Law and Probate Litigation.*

## GIFFORD & DEARING
Established in 1948
SUITE 1222, 700 SOUTH FLOWER STREET
**LOS ANGELES, CALIFORNIA 90017**
Telephone: 213-626-4481
Fax: 213-627-3719

*General Civil and Trial Practice in all State Courts. Corporation, Estate Planning, Trust and Probate Law.*

*FIRM PROFILE: Gifford & Dearing concentrates its work in estate planning, probate and trust and estate administration. In addition, it assists family owned corporations, entertainers, entrepreneurs, trusts and foundations in Southern California with their general legal needs, including commercial transactions, real estate and landlord/tenant, collections and other litigation in state courts. The firm and its predecessors have been located in downtown Los Angeles for over 45 years.*

### MEMBERS OF FIRM

**G. GRANT GIFFORD,** born Los Angeles, California, March 14, 1945; admitted to bar, 1971, California. *Education:* Occidental College (A.B., 1967); University of California at Los Angeles (J.D., 1970). *Member:* The State Bar of California (Member, Estate Planning, Trust and Probate Law Section); American Bar Association. *PRACTICE AREAS:* Trusts; Private Foundations; Real Estate Transactions; Wills; Probate Administration.

**HENRY H. DEARING,** born Boston, Massachusetts, February 10, 1948; admitted to bar, 1974, California. *Education:* Harvard University (A.B., cum laude, 1970); Boston University (J.D., 1974). Real Estate Broker, California, 1976. *Member:* State Bar of California (Member, Business Law Section); American Bar Association (Member, Real Property, Probate and Trust Law Section). *PRACTICE AREAS:* Wills; Trusts; Probate Administration; Litigation.

### ASSOCIATE

**MICHELE L. ABERNATHY,** born Pasadena, California, November 19, 1970; admitted to bar, 1995, California, U.S. District Court, Central District of California and U.S. Court of Appeals, 9th Circuit. *Education:* California State Polytechnic University (B.S., 1992); Pepperdine University (J.D., 1995). Phi Alpha Delta. *Member:* State Bar of California (Member, Real Property Section). *PRACTICE AREAS:* Trusts; Wills; Real Estate Transactions; Conservatorships; Probate Administration; Estate and Gift Tax.

REFERENCE: Bank of America, Los Angeles, California (Head Office, Trust Dept.).

## GILBERT, KELLY, CROWLEY & JENNETT
1200 WILSHIRE BOULEVARD
**LOS ANGELES, CALIFORNIA 90017**
Telephone: 213-580-7000
Fax: 213-580-7100

*Orange County Office:* Suite 310 Nexus Financial Center, 721 South Parker Street, Orange, California. Telephone: 714-541-5000. Fax: 714-541-0670.

*Riverside County Office:* 3801 University Avenue, Suite 700, Riverside, California. Telephone: 909-276-4000. Fax: 909-276-4100.

*San Diego, California Office:* 501 West Broadway, Suite 1260 Koll Center. Telephone: 619-687-3000. Fax: 619-687-3100.

*General Civil and Trial Practice in all State and Federal Courts. Appellate Practice. Corporation and Insurance Law.*

*(This Listing Continued)*

### MEMBERS OF FIRM

**W. I. GILBERT** (1876-1940).

**W. I. GILBERT, JR.** (1906-1972).

**JOHN D. ST. PIERRE** (1930-1981).

**THOMAS J. VIOLA,** born Los Angeles, California, November 12, 1936; admitted to bar, 1962, California. *Education:* Loyola University (B.S., 1958; LL.B., 1961). Phi Delta Phi. *Member:* Los Angeles County and American (Member, Section of, Insurance, Negligence and Compensation Law) Bar Associations; State Bar of California; Association of Southern California Defense Counsel (Director, 1982).

**ROBERT W. RAU,** born Los Angeles, California, February 14, 1936; admitted to bar, 1964, California. *Education:* University of California at Los Angeles (B.A., 1958; LL.B., 1963). Phi Delta Phi. *Member:* Los Angeles County and American Bar Associations; State Bar of California; Association of Southern California Defense Counsel (Member, Board of Directors, 1995; Co-Chairman, Education Seminar, 1985).

**MICHAEL J. MALONEY,** born Los Angeles, California, March 28, 1939; admitted to bar, 1966, California. *Education:* University of Notre Dame and University of Southern California (A.B., 1962); Loyola University of Los Angeles (LL.B., 1965). Phi Alpha Delta. *Member:* Los Angeles County Bar Association; State Bar of California; American Board of Trial Advocates.

**PATRICK A. MESISCA, JR.,** born Bethesda, Maryland, June 6, 1948; admitted to bar, 1973, California. *Education:* University of Southern California (B.A., 1970); Loyola University of Los Angeles (J.D., magna cum laude, 1973). Alpha Sigma Nu. Member, St. Thomas More Law Honor Society. *Member:* Los Angeles and American Bar Associations; State Bar of California; Association of Southern California Defense Counsel.

**CLAYTON E. COOPER,** born Torrance, California, November 8, 1943; admitted to bar, 1970, California. *Education:* University of California at Berkeley (B.A., 1966); Loyola University of Los Angeles (J.D., 1969). *Member:* Los Angeles County and American Bar Associations; State Bar of California; American Board of Trial Advocates; Association of Southern California Defense Counsel. *PRACTICE AREAS:* Insurance Defense; Construction Defect.

**STEPHEN M. MOLONEY,** born Los Angeles, California, July 1, 1949; admitted to bar, 1975, California. *Education:* St. John's Seminary College; University of Santa Clara (B.S., 1971; J.D., 1975). Recipient: DRI (Chicago) Outstanding Service Award (1992); Volunteers in Parole Program (1976-1977). Arbitrator and Mediator: Los Angeles County Superior Court. Author: "Loyalty," For the Defense (1994). Lecturer: Rutter Group; Association of Defense Counsel; Association of Southern California Defense Counsel; Los Angeles County Trial Lawyers Association; California Consumer Association; Los Angeles County Bar Association; California Trial Lawyers Association. Listed in Who's Who (Law), 1994—. *Member:* Los Angeles County (Employment Law and Litigation Sections; Executive Committee on the ADR Section, 1992—) and American (Tort, Insurance and Employment Law) Bar Associations; Defense Research Institute; International Association of Defense Counsel (Vice Chair, Newsletter, Casualty Section, 1993—); Association of Southern California Defense Counsel (President, 1992; Committee Chair, 1982-1984; Member, Board of Directors, 1984-1988; Officer, 1989-1993); American Board of Trial Advocates (Associate, 1989—); American Inns of Court (Los Angeles Chapter, 1990-1994); California Defense Counsel (Member, Board of Directors, 1989-1994); Los Angeles County Superior Court (Bench and Bar Committee, 1989-1991); Association of Defense Trial Attorneys. *PRACTICE AREAS:* Personal Injury Defense; Employment; Construction Defect; Contract and Business Litigation.

**ARTHUR J. MCKEON III,** born Detroit, Michigan, January 3, 1952; admitted to bar, 1978, California. *Education:* Loyola University of Los Angeles (B.A., 1974; J.D., cum laude, 1978). Member, St. Thomas More Law Honor Society. *Member:* Los Angeles County and American Bar Associations; State Bar of California (Employment Law Section); Association of Southern California Defense Counsel; American Business Trial Lawyers Association. *PRACTICE AREAS:* Insurance Defense; Employment Law; Business Litigation.

**JOHN J. RUSSO,** born Chicago, Illinois, November 24, 1952; admitted to bar, 1979, California. *Education:* University of Southern California (B.A., cum laude, 1974); Loyola University of Los Angeles (J.D., 1978). *Member:* Los Angeles County and American Bar Associations; State Bar of California; Association of Southern California Defense Counsel. *PRACTICE AREAS:* Insurance Defense; Estate Planning.

*(This Listing Continued)*

## GILBERT, KELLY, CROWLEY & JENNETT, Los Angeles—Continued

**JON H. TISDALE,** born Pasadena, California, January 8, 1954; admitted to bar, 1980, California. *Education:* California Polytechnic University (B.A., cum laude, 1977); University of Southern California Law Center (J.D., 1980). Phi Alpha Delta. *Member:* Los Angeles County and American Bar Associations; State Bar of California; Association of Southern California Defense Counsel.

**PETER J. GODFREY,** born Los Angeles, California, March 6, 1953; admitted to bar, 1980, California and U.S. District Court, Central District of California. *Education:* St. Mary's College (B.A., 1976); University of Southern California (J.D., 1980). *Member:* Los Angeles County and American (Co-Chairman, Amicus Curiae Committee, 1986-1987) Bar Associations; State Bar of California; Association of Southern California Defense Counsel.

**PAUL A. BIGLEY,** born Pasadena, California, April 24, 1959; admitted to bar, 1985, California; 1986, U.S. District Court, Central District of California and U.S. Court of Appeals, Ninth Circuit. *Education:* University of California at San Diego (B.A., 1981); Loyola Marymount University (J.D., 1984). Arbitrator, Los Angeles County Superior Court. *Member:* Los Angeles County, Federal and American Bar Associations; State Bar of California; Los Angeles Trial Lawyers Association; Association of Southern California Defense Counsel; Southern California Insurance Professionals. *PRACTICE AREAS:* Personal Injury Defense; Premises Liability; Construction Defect; Entertainment Law; Medical Malpractice.

**EUGENE J. LANDAU,** born Cleveland, Ohio, March 27, 1914; admitted to bar, 1937, California; 1968, U.S. Tax Court. *Education:* Pacific Coast University (LL.B., 1936). *Member:* Los Angeles County and American Bar Associations; State Bar of California. Fellow, American College of Trust and Estate Counsel. *PRACTICE AREAS:* Estate Planning and Probate.

**RODNEY L. TERRAZONE,** born Pasadena, California, March 10, 1951; admitted to bar, 1978, California. *Education:* University of Redlands (B.A., 1973); Southwestern University (J.D., 1977). *Member:* Los Angeles and American Bar Associations; State Bar of California; Association of Southern California Defense Counsel.

**RANDALL W. KALER,** born Great Falls, Montana, July 22, 1952; admitted to bar, 1982, California. *Education:* Montana State University (B.S., 1974); Pepperdine University (J.D., 1981). *Member:* Los Angeles County and American Bar Associations; State Bar of California; State Bar of Montana; Association of Southern California Defense Counsel.

**PETER R. NELSON,** born Los Angeles, California, April 14, 1955; admitted to bar, 1984, California, U.S. District Court, Central District of California and U.S. Court of Appeals, Ninth Circuit. *Education:* Loyola Marymount University (B.A., magna cum laude, 1977; J.D., 1983). *Member:* Los Angeles County and American Bar Associations; State Bar of California; Association of Southern California Defense Counse. *PRACTICE AREAS:* Workers' Compensation Law.

**JAMES J. PERKINS,** born Castro Valley, California, May 5, 1956; admitted to bar, 1986, California. *Education:* University of California at Santa Cruz (B.A., 1983); University of Santa Clara (J.D., 1986). *Member:* Los Angeles County and American Bar Associations; State Bar of California; Los Angeles County Trial Lawyers Association.

**MARY-CLAIRE MIRA,** born New Haven, Connecticut; admitted to bar, 1986, California. *Education:* Loyola Marymount University; Southwestern University School of Law (J.D., 1986). *Member:* Los Angeles County and American Bar Associations; State Bar of California; California Women Lawyers Association. *PRACTICE AREAS:* Insurance Defense; Estate Planning.

### OF COUNSEL

**ROGER E. KELLY,** born Winnipeg, Canada, January 23, 1916; admitted to bar, 1939, California. *Education:* Loyola University of Los Angeles (A.B., 1936); Loyola University (LL.B., 1939). Honorary Member, The American Board of Trial Advocates. *Member:* Los Angeles County and American Bar Associations; State Bar of California; Association of Southern California Defense Counsel; International Academy of Trial Lawyers. Fellow, American College of Trial Lawyers.

**JAMES B. CROWLEY,** born Los Angeles, California, March 6, 1930; admitted to bar, 1954, California. *Education:* St. John's University (M.A., 1951); Loyola University of Los Angeles (LL.B., 1954). Phi Delta Phi. *Member:* Los Angeles County Bar Association; State Bar of California; The American Board of Trial Advocates; Association of Southern California Defense Counsel.

**WILLIAM D. JENNETT,** born Stockton, California, September 9, 1930; admitted to bar, 1959, California. *Education:* University of California at Los Angeles; Loyola University (LL.B., 1958). Phi Delta Phi. *Member:* Los Angeles County Bar Association; State Bar of California; Association of Southern California Defense Counsel.

**CLIFFORD H. WOOSLEY,** born Chicago, Illinois, September 20, 1951; admitted to bar, 1979, California. *Education:* University of Southern California; University of Wisconsin-Madison (B.A., 1974); Loyola University of Los Angeles (J.D., cum laude, 1979). Member, National Moot Court. Recipient, American Jurisprudence Award in Insurance Law. *Member:* Los Angeles County and American (Member, Tort and Insurance Practice Section) Bar Associations; State Bar of California; Association of Southern California Defense Counsel.

**LISA A. SATTER,** born Sacramento, California, June 7, 1956; admitted to bar, 1984, California. *Education:* California State University at Sacramento (B.A., 1977); University of Uppsala, Uppsala, Sweden; University of San Diego (J.D., 1983). *Member:* Los Angeles County Bar Association; State Bar of California; Association of Southern California Defense Counsel.

### ASSOCIATES

**SCOTT E. BRAYBROOKE,** born Eglin, A.F.B., Florida, July 31, 1961; admitted to bar, 1987, California and U.S. District Court, Central District of California. *Education:* Franklin & Marshall College (B.A., 1983); University of Southern California (J.D., 1986). Member, Hale Moot Court Honors Program. Arbitrator and Referee: Los Angeles County Superior and Municipal Court. *Member:* Los Angeles County Bar Association; State Bar of California; Association of Southern California Defense Counsel; California Trial Lawyers Association; Association of Trial Lawyers of America. *PRACTICE AREAS:* Insurance Defense; Products Liability.

**FRANK CANNIZZARO,** born Los Angeles, California, April 26, 1964; admitted to bar, 1992, California. *Education:* University of California at Los Angeles (B.A., 1986); Southwestern University (J.D., 1992). *Member:* Los Angeles County and American Bar Associations; State Bar of California. *PRACTICE AREAS:* Workers' Compensation.

**CAROLYN WAGNER CROWLEY,** born Pasadena, California, April 25, 1965; admitted to bar, 1990, California. *Education:* University of California (B.A., 1987); Santa Clara University (J.D., 1990). *Member:* Los Angeles County and Santa Clara County Bar Associations; State Bar of California.

**LEAH D. DAVIS,** born Los Angeles, California, November 9, 1955; admitted to bar, 1992, California. *Education:* California State University (B.A., 1988); University of San Diego (J.D., 1992). Member, Appellate Moot Court Board. *Member:* State Bar of California. *PRACTICE AREAS:* Workers Compensation.

**OWEN E. GIRARD,** born North Platte, Nebraska, July 16, 1965; admitted to bar, 1995, California. *Education:* University of Nebraska at Lincoln (B.A., 1989); Creighton University (J.D., 1995). *Member:* Orange County and American Bar Associations; State Bar of California. *PRACTICE AREAS:* Insurance Defense.

**VANESSA H. HUBERT,** born Evanston, Illinois, April 20, 1959; admitted to bar, 1987, California. *Education:* University of California at Irvine (B.A., 1982); Southwestern University (J.D., 1986). *Member:* Los Angeles County Bar Association; State Bar of California; Association of Southern California Defense Counse.

**THOMAS JOSEPH JENNETT,** born Los Angeles, California, August 3, 1959; admitted to bar, 1991, California. *Education:* University of California at Los Angeles (B.A., 1987); Southwestern University (J.D., 1991). *Member:* Los Angeles County and American Bar Associations; State Bar of California.

**CHERYL HANNAH KARZ,** born Orange County, California, April 11, 1969; admitted to bar, 1995, California. *Education:* University of California at Berkeley (B.A., 1991); Loyola University of Los Angeles (J.D., 1995). Author: "Injustice Revisited: Did Iran The Terrible Get Away Again?" Loyola of Los Angeles International and Comparative Law Journal, Vol. 16, August, 1994.

**FRANCINE B. KELLY,** born New York, N.Y., May 28, 1958; admitted to bar, 1987, California. *Education:* University of Maryland (B.A., 1980; M.Ed., 1982); Loyola Law School (J.D., 1987). *Member:* Los Angeles County and American Bar Associations; State Bar of California.

*(This Listing Continued)*

**CATHERINE LUKEHART,** born Torrance, California, May 15, 1966; admitted to bar, 1991, California. *Education:* University of San Diego (B.A., 1988); Southwestern University (J.D., 1991). *Member:* Los Angeles and American Bar Associations; State Bar Of California.

**SCOTT L. MACDONALD,** born Fullerton, California, April 5, 1967; admitted to bar, 1994, California and U.S. District Court, Central District of California. *Education:* University of California, Los Angeles (B.A., 1990); Southwestern University School of Law (J.D., 1994). *Member:* State Bar of California; American Bar Association; Association of Southern California Defense Counsel. **PRACTICE AREAS:** Insurance Defense.

**RONALD MAWHINNEY,** born Zambia, October 24, 1960; admitted to bar, 1996, California. *Education:* University of Redlands (B.A., 1982); Southwestern University (J.D., 1995). *Member:* State Bar of California.

**MAUREEN O'GRADY NIX,** born Glendale, California, February 2, 1966; admitted to bar, 1991, California. *Education:* University of California at Santa Barbara (B.A., 1988); Southwestern University (J.D., 1991). *Member:* State Bar of California; American Bar Association.

**R. TIMOTHY O'CONNOR,** born Los Angeles, California, August 20, 1962; admitted to bar, 1995, California and U.S. District Court, Central District of California. *Education:* Loyola Marymount University (B.B.A., 1984); Southwestern University (J.D., 1995). Author: "Computer Training for the Law Office," Ventura County Bar Association, Citations, May, 1996; "Weaving Your Web Site on the Net," November, 1996. Member: Software Engineering Institute, 1996; International Council on Systems, 1996. *Member:* Beverly Hills, San Fernando Valley, Los Angeles County and Ventura County (Member, Editorial Board, 1995—) Bar Associations; State Bar of California. **PRACTICE AREAS:** Personal Injury Defense in Vehicular, Premises and Products-Liability arenas.

**GREGORY J. PEDRICK,** born Mission Hills, California, December 12, 1961; admitted to bar, 1993, California. *Education:* California State University, Northridge (B.A., 1987); Loyola University of Los Angeles (J.D., 1992). *Member:* Los Angeles County (Business Law, Probate and Estate Planning Sections); State Bar of California; California Manufacturers Association (Corporate Counsel Steering Committee); Valley Industry and Commerce Association (Education and Tax Committee). **PRACTICE AREAS:** Business Planning; Estate Planning and Probate.

**DEREK A. SIMPSON,** born Pasadena, California, February 24, 1971; admitted to bar, 1996, California and U.S. District Court, Central District of California. *Education:* University of Richmond (B.A., 1993); Southern Methodist University (J.D., 1996). Phi Delta Phi. Recipient, American Jurisprudence Award in Secured Transactions.

**REBECCA J. SMITH,** born Huntington Park, California, July 27, 1958; admitted to bar, 1990, California. *Education:* Cerritos Community College (A.A., 1981); California State University at Long Beach (B.A., 1985); Southwestern University School of Law (J.D., 1990). Recipient, Outstanding Achievement Award-Public International Law. Author: "Navigating the Labyrinth of California Pregnancy Leave," Verdict, 1995. *Member:* Los Angeles County and American Bar Associations; State Bar of California (Labor and Employment Law Section); California Women Lawyers Association.

**TERRY LYNN SMITH,** born Mangum, Oklahoma, May 1, 1952; admitted to bar, 1994, California. *Education:* Ventura College (A.A., 1974); University of Laverne (B.A., 1988); Southwestern University (J.D., 1990). *Member:* State Bar of California; American Bar Association. **PRACTICE AREAS:** Insurance Defense; Workers' Compensation Law.

REPRESENTATIVE CLIENTS: Interinsurance Exchange of the Automobile Club of Southern California; Brown & Williamson Tobacco Co.; Allianz Insurance Co.; Civil Service Employees Insurance Co.; California State Auto Assn.; Avis; County of Los Angeles; National Automobile and Casualty Co.; Allstate Insurance Co.; Colonial Insurance Co.; Protective National Insurance Company of Omaha; Sentry Insurance Co.
REFERENCE: Bank of America National Trust & Savings Assn., Main Branch, Los Angeles, California.

## GILCHRIST & RUTTER
PROFESSIONAL CORPORATION
355 SOUTH GRAND AVENUE, SUITE 4100
**LOS ANGELES, CALIFORNIA 90071**
Telephone: 213-617-8000
Facsimile: 213-346-7973

*Santa Monica, California Office:* 1299 Ocean Avenue, Suite 900. Telephone: 310-393-4000. Facsimile: 310-394-4700.

*(This Listing Continued)*

Real Estate, Business, Corporate, Partnerships, Commercial, Taxation and Environmental Law, Civil, Business, Intellectual Property and Securities Litigation in State and Federal Courts, Debtor/Creditor Rights, Commercial Law and Corporate Reorganization, and Estate Planning.

FIRM PROFILE: Founded in 1983, Gilchrist & Rutter serves clients in a broad range of sophisticated business transactions and commercial litigation. The Firm's real estate practice counsels clients on development, acquisitions and dispositions, financing, leasing, land use, troubled project work-outs, development entitlement issues and environmental matters, involving local and national transactions. The Firm also handles business formations and dissolutions, mergers and acquisitions, and general corporate representation. The Firm's litigation practice includes representation of clients in the following areas of law: insurance, employment, labor relations, bankruptcy, environmental, securities, intellectual property, antitrust and real estate. The Firm's taxation practice counsels clients in all phases of federal, state and local tax matters in connection with the organization, operation, transfer and dissolution of businesses, ownership and development of real estate and tax-deferred exchanges of real property. The Firm also provides estate planning services ranging from the preparation of wills to sophisticated estate plans involving trust and will arrangements, contested estate matters, and representation of trust and estate fiduciaries.

(For Complete Biographical Data on all Personnel, see Professional Biographies at Santa Monica, California)

## GILL AND BALDWIN
**LOS ANGELES, CALIFORNIA**
(See Glendale)

*General Civil and Trial Practice in all State and Federal Courts. Public Contract and Construction Law, Tax and Administrative Law, Estate Planning and Probate.*

## LAW OFFICES OF CAROL L. GILLAM
**LOS ANGELES, CALIFORNIA**
(See Torrance)

*Complex Business Litigation, White Collar Crime, Mergers and Acquisitions, Environmental Law, Administrative Law.*

## GINSBURG, STEPHAN, ORINGHER & RICHMAN, P.C.
10100 SANTA MONICA BOULEVARD
EIGHTH FLOOR
**LOS ANGELES, CALIFORNIA 90067-4012**
Telephone: 310-557-2009
Fax: 310-551-0283

*Costa Mesa, California Office:* 535 Anton Boulevard, Suite 800, 92626-1902. Telephone: 714-241-0420. Fax: 714-241-0622.

*General Civil Practice, General Business Litigation, Health Care Law, Corporate and Business Transactions, Professional Liability Defense, Employment Litigation, Coverage Litigation, Intellectual Property Litigation, White Collar Criminal Defense, Real Estate Litigation, Product Liability, Securities Fraud and RICO Defense, Consumer Credit Litigation, Copyright, Trademark, Antitrust and Unfair Competition Law.*

**WILLIAM H. GINSBURG,** born Philadelphia, Pennsylvania, March 25, 1943; admitted to bar, 1968, California. *Education:* University of California at Berkeley (B.A., 1964); University of Southern California (J.D., 1967).

**GEORGE J. STEPHAN,** born Brooklyn, New York, October 16, 1950; admitted to bar, 1975, California; 1978, U.S. District Court, Central District of California; 1982, U.S. Supreme Court; 1984, U.S. District Court, Southern District of California. *Education:* University of Southern California (B.S., 1972); Southwestern University (J.D., cum laude, 1975). Author: "Court: Physician Can Sue Plaintiff's Attorney," 9 Health Law Vigil No. 10, May, 1986; "Father in Delivery Room Wins Decision That Could Land You in Court," 7 Legal Aspects of Medical Practice No. 7, July, 1979; "An Overview of Domestic Aviation Route Awards," 10 Journal of the Beverly

*(This Listing Continued)*

**GINSBURG, STEPHAN, ORINGHER & RICHMAN, P.C.,**
Los Angeles—Continued

Hills Bar Association, No. 6, Sept.-Oct., 1976. Co-Instructor, Torts, Golden West University School of Law, 1976. Appointed Judge Pro Tem, Municipal Court, Desert Judicial District, 1981-1984, Los Angeles Municipal Court, 1985—, Los Angeles Superior Court, 1987—. *Member:* State Bar of California; California Society For Health Care Attorneys; Association of Real Estate Attorneys.

**HARVEY T. ORINGHER,** born Brooklyn, New York, July 4, 1949; admitted to bar, 1974, New York and U.S. Court of Military Appeals; 1977, U.S. Supreme Court; 1979, California; 1981, U.S. District Court, Central District of California; 1984, U.S. District Court, Southern District of California. *Education:* Hofstra University (B.A., 1970); Brooklyn Law School (J.D., 1973). Special Attorney, Organized Crime and Racketeering Section, U.S. Department of Justice, 1977-1980. *Member:* Los Angeles County and American Bar Associations; State Bar of California. [Capt., U.S. Army, JAG, 1974-1977]

**DAVID S. RICHMAN,** born Phoenixville, Pennsylvania, May 9, 1952; admitted to bar, 1977, Illinois and U.S. District Court, Northern District of Illinois; 1980, California; 1981, U.S. District Court, Central District of California; 1985, U.S. District Court, Southern District of California; 1986, U.S. District Court, Northern and Eastern Districts of California. *Education:* University of Colorado (B.A., with distinction, 1974); University of Chicago (J.D., 1977). Phi Beta Kappa. *Member:* State Bar of California; Illinois State Bar Association.

**MICHAEL C. THORNHILL,** born Columbus, Ohio, February 24, 1951; admitted to bar, 1976, Florida; 1977, U.S. District Court, Middle District of Florida; 1978, California; 1980, U.S. District Court, Central District of California and U.S. Court of Appeals, Ninth Circuit. *Education:* Southern Methodist University; Vassar College (A.B., cum laude, 1973); Boston University (J.D., 1976). *Member:* Los Angeles County Bar Association (Chair, Health Care Law Section, 1988); State Bar of California; Group Health Association of America; California Association of HMOs; National Health Lawyers Association; California Society for the Health Care Attorneys.

---

**NAIDA L. BROWN,** born Portales, New Mexico, July 14, 1956; admitted to bar, 1985, California, U.S. Court of Appeals, Ninth Circuit and U.S . District Court, Central District of California; 1987, U.S. District Court, Eastern District of California. *Education:* University of New Mexico (B.A., magna cum laude, 1980); University of San Diego (J.D., 1985). Member, San Diego Law Review, 1985. *Member:* Beverly Hills and Los Angeles County Bar Associations; State Bar of California.

**CHRISTOPHER M. DANIELS,** born Hammond, Indiana, October 31, 1959; admitted to bar, 1988, Illinois; 1989, U.S. District Court, Northern District of Illinois; 1990, California and U.S. District Court, Central District of California. *Education:* University of Wisconsin-Madison (B.B.A., 1982); University of Texas (J.D., with honors, 1988). Phi Delta Phi; Order of Barristers. Managing Editor, The Review of Litigation, 1987-1988. Certified Public Accountant, Texas, 1984. *Member:* State Bar of California; American Bar Association.

**MYRNA L. D'INCOGNITO,** born Long Beach, California, May 24, 1955; admitted to bar, 1990, California; U.S. Court of Appeals, Ninth Circuit and U.S. District Court, Central District of California. *Education:* California State Polytechnic University (B.A., 1980); Southwestern University School of Law (J.D., 1984). *Member:* Los Angeles County and Beverly Hills Bar Associations; State Bar of California.

**LINDA HATCHER,** born Butler, Pennsylvania, July 10, 1962; admitted to bar, 1994, California. *Education:* Murray State University (B.S. magna cum laude, 1984); Loyola Marymount University (J.D., 1994). Phi Theta Kappa; Gamma Beta Phi; Beta Gamma Sigma; Phi Delta Phi. Recipient, American Jurisprudence Award in Trial Advocacy. *Member:* Los Angels County Bar Association (Member: Business Law Section and Health Law Section); State Bar of California.

**NANCY B. HERSMAN,** born Chatham, Ontario, Canada, October 12, 1954; admitted to bar, 1986, California; 1988, District of Columbia and U.S. Court of Appeals, District of Columbia; 1989, Virginia. *Education:* University of California at Los Angeles (B.A., 1983); Loyola Law School (J.D., cum laude, 1986). Member, 1984-1986, and President, 1985-1986, St. Thomas More Law Honor Society. Note and Comment Editor, Loyola Law Review. Author: "Lynch v. Donnelly: Has the Lemon Test Soured?" 19

*(This Listing Continued)*

Loyola Law Review 133. *Member:* Los Angeles County and American Bar Associations; Virginia State Bar; State Bar of California; District of Columbia Bar.

**DAVID J. MASUTANI,** born Los Angeles, California, December 24, 1965; admitted to bar, 1994, California and U.S. Court of Appeals, Ninth Circuit. *Education:* University of Southern California (B.S. cum laude, 1987; J.D., 1994). Hale Moot Court. *Member:* Japanese American Bar Association; State Bar of California.

**GERALD J. MILLER,** born Los Angeles, California, October 10, 1955; admitted to bar, 1985, California; 1986, U.S. District Court, Central District of California and U.S. Court of Appeals, Ninth Circuit. *Education:* University of California at Los Angeles (B.A., 1977); Eagleton Institute of Politics, Rutgers University (M.A., 1978); University of California, Davis (J.D., 1985). Managing Editor, U.C. Davis Law Review, 1984-1985. Eagleton Fellow, Rutgers University, 1977-1978. Author: "Collective Bargaining vs. the First Amendment Court Ordered Remedies for the Political Use of Mandatory Union Fees," 18 U.C. Davis Law Review 555, 1985. Legal Writing Instructor, Whittier College School of Law, 1988-1992. Legislative Assistant to Congressman Julian C. Dixon, 1979-1982. *Member:* Los Angeles County Bar Association; State Bar of California. **PRACTICE AREAS:** Business Litigation.

**DEAN J. SMITH,** born Canoga Park, California, May 27, 1962; admitted to bar, 1987, California; 1988, U.S. District Court, Central District of California; 1991, U.S. District Court, Southern District of California. *Education:* Loyola Marymount University (B.A., 1984; J.D., 1987). Member, 1985-1986 and Articles Editor, 1986-1987, Loyola of Los Angeles International and Comparative Law Journal. Member, Scott Moot Court Honors Program. *Member:* Los Angeles County and American Bar Associations.

**PETER WEINBERGER,** born Los Angeles, California, November 9, 1961; admitted to bar, 1991, California and U.S. District Court, Central District of California; 1992, U.S. District Court, Northern District of California. *Education:* University of California at Los Angeles (A.B., 1987); Loyola Marymount University (J.D., 1991). Phi Delta Phi. Member, West Hollywood Planning Commission, 1985-1986. *Member:* State Bar of California.

*OF COUNSEL*

**GORDON E. BOSSERMAN,** born Long Beach, California, November 24, 1948; admitted to bar, 1975, California. *Education:* University of California at Los Angeles (B.A., 1971); Loyola University of Los Angeles (J.D., 1975). Member, Board of Governors, Loyola Law School Alumni Association, 1990-1991. *Member:* Los Angeles County (Member, Litigation, Employment and Health Care Sections) and American (Member, Sections on: Litigation; Labor and Employment Law) Bar Associations; State Bar of California.

**ARTHUR R. CHENEN,** born Brooklyn, New York, April 20, 1946; admitted to bar, 1971, California; 1976, U.S. Court of Appeals, Ninth Circuit; 1977, U.S. Claims Court; 1978, U.S. Court of Appeals, Fifth Circuit; 1980, U.S. Supreme Court. *Education:* University of California at Los Angeles (B.A., 1967; J.D., 1970). Order of the Coif. Member, University of California at Los Angeles Law Review, 1969-1970. Editor-in-Chief, Medical Staff Counselor, Matthew Bender, 1987-1993. *Member:* Century City (Treasurer, 1980; Vice President, 1981; President, 1982), Los Angeles County and American Bar Associations; State Bar of California; American Academy of Hospital Attorneys; National Health Lawyers Association; American Society of Law and Medicine. **PRACTICE AREAS:** Health Law; Litigation; Contract Law; Administrative Law.

**RICHARD J. DECKER,** born Manhasset, New York, August 26, 1959; admitted to bar, 1984, New York and Massachusetts; 1985, California and U.S. District Court, Central District of California; 1986, U.S. District Court, Southern District of California. *Education:* Union College (B.A., cum laude, 1981); Boston University (J.D., 1984). *Member:* Beverly Hills and Los Angeles County Bar Associations; The State Bar of California.

**BRUCE E. DIZENFELD,** born Reading, Pennsylvania, June 12, 1953; admitted to bar, 1978, California. *Education:* University of Southern California (B.A., 1975); University of California at Los Angeles (J.D., 1978). Member, Moot Court Executive Board. Executive Editor, U.C.L.A.-Alaska Law Review. Associate Editor, International Law Section Newsletter, State Bar of California, 1994—. Editor-in-Chief, California Health Law News, 1981-1984. Editor, Los Angeles Health Law Update, 1979-1982. Co-Editor and Co-Author: *Handbook of Appellate Advocacy,* West Pub. 2d Ed., 1979. Co-Editor: "Financing Techniques for Small and Emerging Businesses," Business Law Section, State Bar of California, May 1987; "Limited Partnership Syndications: Public and Private Financing Vehicle," Business Law

*(This Listing Continued)*

Section, State Bar of California, May 1984; "Legal Opinions, Due Diligence and the Attorney's Responsibilities in Business Transactions," Business Law Section, State Bar of California, May 1985. Author: "Risk Pools, Technology Consortia, Integrated Health Systems and Other Collaborative Enterprise Forms," Choice of Entity—Well Beyond the Basics, Beverly Hills Bar Association, May 1993; "Unincorporated Associations, Workers' Cooperatives and Co-Ownerships: Another Approach to Doing Business in California," Choice of Entity: Beyond the Basics, Beverly Hills Bar Association, May 1991; "Advertising and the California Medical Professional," 2 Whittier Law Review 61, 1979; "Premium Financing: Insurer Beware," Business Insurance, 1979; "Premium Financing Agencies and the California Laws of Usury," Los Angeles Daily Journal Report No. 79-22, Nov. 16, 1979; "Close Corporations in Alaska," 7 UCLA-Alaska L. Rev. 123, 1978; "Pro-Competition Statutes: An Unbundling of Health Care Services," Modern Healthcare, Nov. 1982; "Product Liability Self Insurance Pools and the Federal Pre-Emption of the State Insurance Law," Business Law News, Vol. 6, No. 1, Fall 1982. Co-Author: "Protecting Your Health Care Client's Intellectual Property Rights," 11 California Health Law News 76, Winter 1991; "No Code Orders: Terminal Illness as a Business Attorney's Dilemma, Business Law News, Vol. 5, No. 2, Winter 1982. *Member:* Los Angeles County Bar Association (Member, Healthcare Law Section, Chairman, 1979-1980); State Bar of California (Member, Business Law Section Not-Profit Corporations and Unincorporated Association Committee, 1991-1993; Committee to Confer with California Medical Association, Chair, Subcommittee on Physician Joint Ventures); California Society of Healthcare Attorneys; Los Angeles Venture Association. **PRACTICE AREAS:** Healthcare; Business Organization; Intellectual Property; Licensing.

**TERRENCE M. KING,** born Inglewood, California, June 29, 1954; admitted to bar, 1983, California and U.S. District Court, Central District of California. *Education:* California State University at Dominguez Hills (B.A., with highest honors, 1978); Loyola University of Los Angeles (J.D., cum laude, 1983). Member, St. Thomas Moore Law Honor Society. Staff Member, 1981-1982 and Editor, 1982-1983, Loyola Law Review. Extern Law Clerk to Hon. William Matthew Byrne, U.S. District Court, Central District of California, 1983. *Member:* Los Angeles County and American Bar Associations; State Bar of California.

### LEGAL SUPPORT PERSONNEL

**MORRIS E. SCHORR,** born New York, N.Y., August 30, 1944. *Education:* State University of New York (B.A., 1966); University of Illinois (M.A., 1974); California State University at Northridge (M.B.A., 1993). Author: "Climbing The Law Firm Ladder," People-To-People, June 1988; "A World of Information at Your Fingertips," Systems & Technology, Winter 1990; "Evaluating the Effectiveness of Yellow Pages Advertising," Law Marketing Exchange, March 1991; "Invasion of The Bios Snatchers," Interchange, July, 1994. Chair, Plaintiff/Contingency Administrators Section, Association of Legal Administrators, 1988. President, San Fernando Valley Chapter, ALA, 1988-1989. President, Los Angeles Chapter, National Law Firm Marketing Association, 1990-1991 and Member at Large, Board of Directors, National Law Firm Marketing Association, 1991-1992. President, Cyber Chapter, ALA, 1994-1996. (Director of Administration).

(For Biographical Data on Personnel at Costa Mesa, see Professional Biographies at Costa Mesa, California)

---

# GIPSON HOFFMAN & PANCIONE

### A PROFESSIONAL CORPORATION
### SUITE 1100, 1901 AVENUE OF THE STARS
### LOS ANGELES, CALIFORNIA 90067-6002
Telephone: 310-556-4660
Telex: 910-490-2531 GHST LAW;
Fax: 310-556-8945, 310-556-4301
Email: mail@ghplaw.com

*Zurich, Switzerland Office:* Zeppelinstrasse 28, CH-8057. Telephone: 011-411-364-2600. Telefax: 011-411-364-2713.

Business, Entertainment and Tax Litigation. Corporate and Banking. Corporate and Securities Matters. Domestic and International Taxation. General Business. Motion Picture Financing and Securities Transactions. Motion Picture, Television and Music Production, Distribution and Talent Representation. Real Estate and Real Estate Securities.

*FIRM PROFILE:* Gipson Hoffman & Pancione is a business law firm. We offer domestic and international clients extensive experience in structuring, negotiating and documenting banking, business, corporate, entertainment and
*(This Listing Continued)*

*real estate transactions and in settling and litigating business and tax disputes. Our experience in finance includes public offerings, private syndications and domestic and international bank credit facilities.*

**MARKUS W. BARMETTLER,** born Lucerne, Switzerland, April 28, 1960; admitted to bar, 1986, Switzerland. *Education:* Bern University (Lic.-Jur., summa cum laude, 1986). (Resident, Zurich, Switzerland Office). **LANGUAGES:** German, French, Spanish, Italian and English.

**LAWRENCE R. BARNETT,** born New York, N.Y., June 6, 1956; admitted to bar, 1983, California and U.S. District Court, Central District of California. *Education:* Stanford University (B.A., with honors, 1978); University of Southern California (M.B.A., 1982; J.D., 1982). *Member:* Los Angeles County Bar Association; State Bar of California.

**JACK BRANDON,** born Glendale, California, November 27, 1954; admitted to bar, 1984, California. *Education:* Lewis and Clark College (B.S., cum laude, 1976); University of California at Los Angeles (M.B.A., 1983; J.D., 1983). Order of the Coif. Recipient, John M. Olin Fellowship. *Member:* Los Angeles County Bar Association (Member, Taxation Section; Entertainment Tax Subsection); State Bar of California. **PRACTICE AREAS:** Domestic and International Tax Law.

**VINCENT H. CHIEFFO,** born New York, N.Y., October 5, 1945; admitted to bar, 1971, California. *Education:* Hamilton College (A.B., 1967); Columbia University School of Law (J.D., magna cum laude, 1970). Staff Member 1968-1969 and Articles Editor, 1969-1970, Columbia Law Review. Law Clerk to Judge Wilfred Feinberg, U.S. Court of Appeals for the Second Circuit, New York, 1970-1971. Author: "Entertainment Law Practice in California," Parts I and II, California Business Law Reporter (CEB), September and November, 1991; "Bette Midler v. Ford Motor Co.: 'To Impersonate Her Voice Is To Pirate Her Identity'" June, 1992; "Descendibility of Publicity, Rights/Flaws in the New State Law," Los Angeles Lawyer; "It's a Crude, Crude World: The Buchwald Case," Montage, April, 1990. Co-Author: "Vanna White and Tom Waits: Recent Court Decisions Expand Rights of Celebrities To Resist Unwanted Commercial Exploitation," California Business Law Reporter (CEB), December, 1992. Lecturer: Independent Feature Project/West (1988 Seminar Series - selected infringement and right of publicity subjects); "Current Issues in Entertainment Law," Intellectual Property Section of the State Bar of California, Los Angeles County, and the Los Angeles Copyright Society, 1989. Lecturer and Member, Planning Committee, 1991, and Co-Chairman, 1992-1993, USC Entertainment Law Institute. Member, California Copyright Conference. *Member:* Beverly Hills, Los Angeles County (Member, Intellectual Property and Unfair Competition Section), American and International Bar Associations; State Bar of California; Los Angeles Copyright Society (Past President); Copyright Society of the U.S.A.

**PETER F. DEL GRECO,** born Brooklyn, New York, March 14, 1955; admitted to bar, 1993, California. *Education:* State University of New York at Binghamton (B.A., 1978); University of California at Los Angeles (J.D., 1992). **PRACTICE AREAS:** Litigation.

**ROBERT E. (REG) GIPSON,** born Boise, Idaho, August 31, 1946; admitted to bar, 1973, California. *Education:* Harvard University (A.B., 1967); Yale University (J.D., 1973). Managing Editor, Yale Law Journal, 1972-1973. Lecturer, University of Southern California Law Center, 1977-1978. *Member:* Los Angeles County and American (Member, Section on Taxation) Bar Associations; State Bar of California. **PRACTICE AREAS:** General Business; General Counsel for Private Companies; Tax Law; Real Estate Law.

**JOHN R. MCHALE,** born Los Angeles, California, May 26, 1960; admitted to bar, 1985, California. *Education:* Stanford University (A.B., with distinction, 1982); University of Chicago (J.D., 1985). **PRACTICE AREAS:** General Business; Corporate and Securities Law; Entertainment Transactions.

**MARA MORNER-RITT,** born Glendale, California, October 12, 1961; admitted to bar, 1988, California. *Education:* University of Southern California (B.A., magna cum laude, with honors, 1983); Boalt Hall School of Law, University of California (J.D., 1987). Phi Beta Kappa. Member, Mortar Board, 1982-1983. Associate Editor, California Law Review, 1986-1987. *Member:* Beverly Hills (Member, Governing Board of the Business Law Section) and Los Angeles County Bar Associations; State Bar of California. **PRACTICE AREAS:** Corporate Law; Securities Law.

**PETER R. PANCIONE,** born Rochester, New York, June 21, 1936; admitted to bar, 1964, New York; 1965, California. *Education:* Niagara University (B.S., 1958); State University of New York at Buffalo (LL.B., 1964). Acting Commissioner of Corporations, State of California, 1979.
*(This Listing Continued)*

**GIPSON HOFFMAN & PANCIONE,** A PROFESSIONAL CORPORATION, Los Angeles—Continued

Lecturer: California Continuing Education of the Bar, California Society of Certified Public Accountants; Practising Law Institute. *Member:* Los Angeles County (Member, Executive Committee, Business and Corporation Law Section, 1976-1984), Beverly Hills (Member, Executive Committee, Corporations and Commercial Law Section, 1980-1983) and American (Member, Committee on Unincorporated Associations and Partnerships, Corporation, Banking and Business Law Section, 1982—) Bar Associations; State Bar of California (Member, Committee on Unincorporated Associations and Partnerships, Business Law Section, 1978-1982, 1989-1992).

**ANN L. PARSONS,** born Palos Verdes Estates, California, August 20, 1965; admitted to bar, 1994, California. *Education:* University of California, Los Angeles (B.A., 1988); University of Chicago (J.D., 1994). *PRACTICE AREAS:* Corporate; General.

**ELLEN J. SHADUR,** born Encino, California, July 15, 1960; admitted to bar, 1986, California and U.S. District Court, Central District of California. *Education:* Wellesley College (B.A., 1982); Phi Beta Kappa; Durrant Scholar; Yale University (J.D., 1985). Phi Beta Kappa. Durant Scholar. Guest Lecturer, University of Nice Law School, 1993. *Member:* The State Bar of California. *LANGUAGES:* French.

**KENNETH I. SIDLE,** born Wooster, Ohio, October 6, 1945; admitted to bar, 1971, California and U.S. District Court, Central District of California; 1975, U.S. Court of Appeals, Ninth Circuit; 1984, U.S. Supreme Court, U.S. Claims Court and U.S. Tax Court; 1985, U.S. District Court, Northern District of California. *Education:* University of California at Riverside (B.A., 1967); Yale University (LL.B., 1970). Phi Beta Kappa. Editor, Yale Law Journal, 1969-1970. Lecturer: "Provisional Remedies: Protecting Your Client Before Judgment," November/December, 1976; "Creating and Implementing A Discovery Plan," June/July, 1975, The California Continuing Education of the Bar; "Evidence and Problems of Proof," UCLA Extension Program, Spring 1974, Fall 1975, Spring 1976, Fall 1976; Spring 1977, Winter 1977, Summer 1978, Fall 1979, Summer 1980, Spring 1981, Fall 1981, Summer 1982; "Entertainment Law Update - 1994," Beverly Hills Bar Association Seminar, January, 1994. *Member:* Beverly Hills, Los Angeles County and American (Member, Sections on: Litigation; Corporation, Banking and Business Law) Bar Associations; State Bar of California; Association of Business Trial Lawyers. *REPORTED CASES:* Fogerty vs. Fantasy, Inc. - U.S. -, 114 S.Ct. 1023 (1994); Fantasy, Inc. vs. John Fogerty, 654 F.Supp. 1129 (N.D. Cal. 1986), 664 F.Supp. 1345 (N.D. Cal. 1987); Goldberg vs. Dolly Parton, Jane Fonda, Tom Hayden, 924 F.2d 1062 (9th Cir., 1991) (Unpublished). *PRACTICE AREAS:* Civil and Business Litigation; Entertainment Law; Copyright Law; Defamation Law.

**MARY K. SOLBERG,** born Indianapolis, Indiana, June 16, 1956; admitted to bar, 1981, California; 1987, Illinois. *Education:* Purdue University (B.S., 1978); University of Chicago (J.D., 1981). *Member:* State Bar of California. *PRACTICE AREAS:* Corporate Securities.

**COREY J. SPIVEY,** born Houston, Texas, January 13, 1969; admitted to bar, 1994, California. *Education:* Rice University (B.A., 1991); Yale University (J.D., 1994). Phi Beta Kappa; Omicron Delta Epsilon. Olin Foundation Fellow. Barrister's Union Semifinalist. Member, Moot Court Board. *Member:* State Bar of California. *PRACTICE AREAS:* Litigation.

**ROBERT H. STEINBERG,** born Omaha, Nebraska, February 19, 1958; admitted to bar, 1983, California; 1984, U.S. District Court, Central District of California. *Education:* Indiana University (B.S., with highest distinction, 1980); University of California at Los Angeles (J.D., 1983). Beta Gamma Sigma. Certified Public Accountant, Illinois, 1982. *Member:* Century City, Los Angeles County and American Bar Associations; State Bar of California. *PRACTICE AREAS:* Secured Lending; Motion Picture Finance; Real Estate; General Business.

*OF COUNSEL*

**JEFFREY M. BOREN,** born Stuttgart, Germany, November 14, 1947; admitted to bar, 1973, California; 1981, U.S. Supreme Court; U.S. Tax Court. *Education:* University of Southern California (B.S., 1969); Loyola University of Los Angeles (J.D., 1973). Co-Author: "Form Your Own REIT," Real Estate Finance Journal, Spring 1994. *Member:* Beverly Hills, Los Angeles County and American Bar Associations; The State Bar of California; American Institute of Certified Public Accountants; American Association of Attorneys-Certified Public Accountants. *PRACTICE AREAS:* Real Estate Law; General Business Law.

*(This Listing Continued)*

**G. RAYMOND F. GROSS,** born Providence, Rhode Island, December 27, 1956; admitted to bar, 1981, California and U.S. District Court, Central District of California; 1982, U.S. District Court, Northern, Eastern and Southern Districts of California; 1986, U.S. Court of Appeals, Ninth Circuit. *Education:* Brown University (A.B., 1978); Columbia University (J.D., 1981). Harlan Fiske Stone Scholar. Associate Editor, Columbia Journal of Environmental Law, 1980-1981. Author: "Combatting the Counterfeiter's Bankruptcy Petition," PLI, 1984. *Member:* Beverly Hills, Century City, Los Angeles County and American Bar Associations; State Bar of California. *TRANSACTIONS:* Acquisition of Ed Sullivan Show library for Sofa Entertainment. Negotiation of Prime Time Entertainment Network License Agreement with Warner Bros. *PRACTICE AREAS:* Entertainment Law; Motion Picture and Television Financing Law.

**JULIA L. ROSS,** born New Brunswick, New Jersey, January 10, 1962; admitted to bar, 1989, California; 1990, U.S. District Court, Central, Northern and Southern Districts of California and U.S. Court of Appeals, Ninth Circuit; 1993, U.S. Supreme Court. *Education:* Hamilton College (B.A., summa cum laude, salutatorian, 1984); Vanderbilt University, France; Harvard University (J.D., magna cum laude, 1988). Phi Beta Kappa; Phi Sigma Iota; Psi Chi; Sigma Xi. Member, HLS Board of Student Advisors, 1986-1988; Legal Methods Instructor, 1986-1988. Law Clerk to Hon. H. Lee Sarokin, U.S. District Court for the District of New Jersey, 1988-1989. Author: "It's a Crude, Crude World: The Buchwald Case," Montage Magazine, April 1990 (co-authored with Vincent H. Chieffo). *Member:* Beverly Hills (Barristers Committee, 1990-1991); Los Angeles and American (Member, Judicial Administrative Division, Federal Courts Committee, 1990-1994) Bar Associations; State Bar of California. *LANGUAGES:* French. *PRACTICE AREAS:* Litigation.

**NORMAN D. SLOAN,** born Los Angeles, California, 1947; admitted to bar, 1973, California, U.S. Supreme Court, U.S. Tax Court, U.S. District Court, Central District of California and U.S. Court of Appeals, Ninth Circuit. *Education:* California State University at Northridge (B.S., 1970); Loyola University of Los Angeles (J.D., 1973). Co-Author: "Form Your Own REIT," Real Estate Finance Journal, Spring 1994. *Member:* Beverly Hills and Los Angeles County Bar Associations; The State Bar of California (Member, Partnerships and Unincorporated Business Organizations Committee, Business Law Section). *PRACTICE AREAS:* Real Property Law; Corporate Law; General Business Law. *Email:* bhlawyer@aol.com

---

# GIRARDI AND KEESE

*Established in 1976*

**1126 WILSHIRE BOULEVARD**
**LOS ANGELES, CALIFORNIA 90017-1904**
*Telephone: 213-977-0211*
*FAX: 213-481-1554*

San Bernardino, California Office: 596 North Arrowhead. Telephone: 714-381-1551. FAX: 714-381-2566.

*General Civil and Trial Practice in all State and Federal Courts. Business Litigation, Entertainment Law, Professional Negligence, Environmental Law, Toxic Torts, Personal Injury, Products Liability, Appellate Practice.*

*MEMBERS OF FIRM*

**THOMAS V. GIRARDI,** born Denver, Colorado, June 3, 1939; admitted to bar, 1965, California. *Education:* Loyola University of Los Angeles (B.S., 1961; LL.B., 1964); New York University (LL.M., 1965; S.J.D., 1965). Listed in First Lawyers of America. Associate Professor, Loyola University Law School, 1976—. *Member:* Los Angeles County, Orange County and American Bar Associations; State Bar of California; American Board of Trial Advocates; California Trial Lawyers Association; Los Angeles Trial Lawyers Association; The Association of Trial Lawyers of America; International Academy of Trial Lawyers; Inner Circle of Advocates. *PRACTICE AREAS:* Professional Liability; Toxic Torts; Business Litigation; Entertainment Law Litigation.

**ROBERT M. KEESE,** born Milwaukee, Wisconsin, March 1, 1943; admitted to bar, 1970, California. *Education:* Loyola University (J.D., 1969). *Member:* Los Angeles County, Orange County and American Bar Associations; State Bar of California; Los Angeles Trial Lawyers Association; California Trial Lawyers Association; The Association of Trial Lawyers of America. *PRACTICE AREAS:* Professional Liability; Toxic Torts.

**JOHN A. GIRARDI,** born Santa Monica, California, February 14, 1947; admitted to bar, 1972, California. *Education:* University of Notre Dame (B.A., 1969); Loyola University of Los Angeles (J.D., 1972). Phi Delta Phi. Member, Los Angeles Superior Court Arbitration Committee.

*(This Listing Continued)*

Judge Pro Tem: Los Angeles Municipal Court; Los Angeles Superior Court. *Member:* Los Angeles County, Orange County and American Bar Associations; State Bar of California; American Board of Trial Advocates; American Board of Professional Liability Attorneys; Los Angeles Trial Lawyers Association; Orange County Trial Lawyers Association; California Trial Lawyers Association; The Association of Trial Lawyers of America. *PRACTICE AREAS:* Civil Trials; Professional Negligence; Government Entity Negligence; Product Liability; Toxic Tort Litigation.

**JAMES B. KROPFF,** born Oxnard, California, June 5, 1954; admitted to bar, 1980, California. *Education:* San Diego State University (A.B., cum laude, 1977); Loyola University of Los Angeles (J.D., 1980). Externship, Hon. Joan Dempsey-Klein, California Court of Appeal, 1979. Clerkship, Hon. Dickran M. Tevrizian, Jr., Los Angeles Superior Court, 1980-1982. *Member:* Los Angeles County Bar Association (Member, Law Office Management Section); State Bar of California; Association of Trial Lawyers of America; California Trial Lawyers Association (Recognition of Experience: Appellate Law and Motion); Los Angeles Trial Lawyers Association. *PRACTICE AREAS:* Appellate Practice.

**ROBERT W. FINNERTY,** born Long Island, New York, August 12, 1955; admitted to bar, 1985, California. *Education:* University of California at Los Angeles (B.A., 1978); Pepperdine University (J.D., 1982). Phi Delta Phi. *Member:* Los Angeles County Bar Association; California Trial Lawyers Association; Los Angeles Trial Lawyers Association; The Association of Trial Lawyers of America. *PRACTICE AREAS:* Civil Litigation; Toxic Torts; General Negligence; Legal Negligence.

**JAMES G. O'CALLAHAN,** born Chicago, Illinois, March 8, 1956; admitted to bar, 1986, California. *Education:* University of Sussex, England; University of California at Santa Cruz (A.B., 1982); University of California at Los Angeles (J.D., 1986). *Member:* Los Angeles County Bar Association; State Bar of California; California Trial Lawyers Association; Los Angeles Trial Lawyers Association; Association of Trial Lawyers of America. *PRACTICE AREAS:* Products Liability; Medical and Professional Negligence; General Negligence; Business Torts.

**V. ANDRE REKTE,** born Long Beach, California, February 2, 1960; admitted to bar, 1987, California. *Education:* California State University, Fullerton (B.A., Biochem, 1983); Pepperdine Law School (J.D., 1986). *Member:* State Bar of California; California Trial Lawyers Association. (Resident, San Bernardino Office). *PRACTICE AREAS:* Professional Liability; Toxic Torts.

**JOHN K. COURTNEY,** born Torrance, California, December 27, 1962; admitted to bar, 1988, California. *Education:* Loyola Marymount University (B.A., cum laude, 1985; J.D., 1988). *Member:* State Bar of California; California Trial Lawyers Association; Los Angeles Trial Lawyers Association; Association of Trial Lawyers of America. *PRACTICE AREAS:* Professional Liability; Toxic Torts.

**AMY FISCH SOLOMON,** born Redwood City, California, January 24, 1960; admitted to bar, 1989, California; U.S. District Court, Central District of California. *Education:* California State University (B.A., cum laude, 1984); Loyola Marymount University (J.D., 1987). *Member:* State Bar of California; California Trial Lawyers Association; Los Angeles Trial Lawyers Association; The Association of Trial Lawyers of America; Los Angeles County Bar Association. *PRACTICE AREAS:* Professional Liability; Toxic Torts.

**THOMAS C. MORGAN,** born Corning, New York, April 21, 1963; admitted to bar, 1991, California. *Education:* University of California at Berkeley (B.A., English and History, 1985); Loyola Marymount University (J.D., 1990). *Member:* State Bar of California. *PRACTICE AREAS:* Personal Injury.

**DAVID N. BIGELOW,** born Alhambra, California, July 9, 1952; admitted to bar, 1995, California. *Education:* Whittier College (B.A., 1976); University of San Diego School of Law (J.D., cum laude, 1995). California State Champion, Roger Traynor Moot Court Competition, 1994; Order of the Barristers, 1995. *Member:* State Bar of California. *PRACTICE AREAS:* Personal Injury; Professional Liability; Toxic Torts.

**CARRIE J. ROGNLIEN,** born Los Angeles, California, December 4, 1966; admitted to bar, 1994, California. *Education:* University of California at Los Angeles (B.S., 1989); Loyola Law School (J.D., 1993). *Member:* State Bar of California; Consumer Attorneys of California; Los Angeles Trial Lawyers Association.

REPRESENTATIVE CLIENTS: 642 Lockheed Employees (Plaintiffs); 432 Plaintiffs in Hanford Nuclear Waste Litigation; Mobil Oil.
REFERENCES: Wells Fargo Bank (Los Angeles Head Office); Bank of Industry.

# GLASS, ALPER, GOLDBERG & COHN

*A LAW CORPORATION*

Established in 1986

**856 SOUTH ROBERTSON BOULEVARD**
**LOS ANGELES, CALIFORNIA 90035-1601**
Telephone: 818-715-7000
Telecopier: 818-715-7025

*Woodland Hills, California Office:* 21700 Oxnard Street, Suite 430.

*Business, Commercial and Insolvency Litigation representing creditors, Banking, Creditors Rights, Equipment and Personal Property Leasing, Secured Transactions and Real Estate Law.*

**RONALD R. COHN,** born Oakland, California, November 8, 1948; admitted to bar, 1974, California. *Education:* University of California at Los Angeles (B.A., cum laude, 1970); McGeorge School of Law, University of the Pacific (J.D., 1974). Phi Delta Phi. Author: "The Mixed Collateral Secured Lessor and the One Form of Action Rule," Wael Newsline, Vol. 13, No. 4 and Vol. 13, No. 5. Speaker, Regulation B. *Member:* Los Angeles County Bar Association; State Bar of California; United Association of Equipment Lessors; Equipment Leasing Association of America. [Sgt., California Air National Guard, 1970-1976]. *PRACTICE AREAS:* Creditors Rights; Commercial Law; Insolvency; Equipment/Personal Property Leasing; Secured Transactions.

**MARSHALL F. GOLDBERG,** born Pittsburgh, Pennsylvania, April 11, 1954; admitted to bar, 1979, California. *Education:* University of California at Los Angeles (B.A., cum laude, 1976); Loyola Marymount University School of Law (J.D., 1979). Author: "Beware of SAMPS," Western Association of Equipment Lessors Newsline, Vol. 12, No. 5; "The CHG Case: The Right to Recover Pre-Petition Payments in Bankruptcy," Journal of Equipment Lease Financing, Vol. 8, No. 2. Speaker, "Prejudgment and Post Judgment Remedies," Beverly Hills Bar Association, "New Uniform Personal Property Leasing Act," "Emerging Lender Theories, Mixed Collateral Problems, and UCC Article 9," Western Association of Equipment Lessors, 1986-1994. Member, Editorial Review Board, Journal of Equipment Lease Financing. *Member:* Los Angeles County Bar Association; State Bar of California; United Association of Equipment Lessors; Equipment Leasing Association of America. *PRACTICE AREAS:* Creditors Rights; Commercial Law; Insolvency; Equipment/Personal Property Leasing; Secured Transactions; Real Property.

**ANDREW K. ALPER,** born Hollywood, California, April 1, 1953; admitted to bar, 1979, California. *Education:* University of California at Santa Barbara (B.A. magna cum laude, 1975); Loyola Marymount University School of Law (J.D., 1979). Author: "Maximizing Recovery Against Security on Lessee's Default," Western Association of Equipment Lessor's Newsline, June 1980, reprinted for the *Monitor,* November, 1980; "In the Aftermath of Puritan Leasing," Wael Newsline, November, 1979; "Assignments Under Commercial Code Section 9206," Wael Newsline, November, 1981. Speaker, "Legal Documentation," "Developments in Product Liability for Equipment Lessors," "Equipment Lease Documentation Issues" and "Mixed Collateral Issues," Western Association of Equipment Lessors, October, 1987. *Member:* Los Angeles County Bar Association (Member: Commercial and Bankruptcy Section; Attachment Section); State Bar of California; United Association of Equipment Lessors; Equipment Leasing Association of America; Financial Lawyers Conference. *PRACTICE AREAS:* Banking Law; Commercial Law; Insolvency; Equipment/Personal Property Leasing; Secured Transactions; Real Estate; Business Litigation.

**STEVEN R. GLASS,** born New York, N. Y., September 7, 1950; admitted to bar, 1975, California. *Education:* University of California at Los Angeles (B.A., 1972); Southwestern University (J.D., 1975). Recipient, American Jurisprudence Book Award for Excellent Achievement in the Study of Business Organizations. Member, Legaline Editor and Chairman, Legal Committee, United Association of Equipment Lessors. *Member:* Los Angeles County Bar Association (Member: Commercial and Bankruptcy Section; Pre-Judgment Remedies Section); State Bar of California; United Association of Equipment Lessors; Financial Lawyers Conference; Equipment Leasing Association of America. *PRACTICE AREAS:* Creditors Rights; Commercial Law; Insolvency; Equipment/Personal Property Leasing; Secured Transactions.

*(This Listing Continued)*

GLASS, ALPER, GOLDBERG & COHN, A LAW
CORPORATION, Los Angeles—Continued

---

JOE R. ABRAMSON, born Los Angeles, California, May 6, 1956; admitted to bar, 1982, California. *Education:* University of California at Los Angeles (B.A., 1979); Loyola Marymount University (J.D., 1982). Member, St. Thomas More Law Honor Society. *Member:* Los Angeles County Bar Association; State Bar of California. **PRACTICE AREAS:** Commercial Law; Construction Litigation; Real Estate Development.

REPRESENTATIVE CLIENTS: Tokai Bank of California; Union Bank of California; China Trust Bank of California; First Central Bank; General Electric Capital Corp.; McDonnell Douglas Finance Corp.; Citicorp North America; Sanwa Business Credit Corporation; ORIX Credit Alliance, Inc.; Tokai Credit Corp.; Heller Financial, Inc.; Finova Capital Corp.; The CIT Group; Associates Commercial Corporation; Eastman Kodak Company; Newcourt Financial USA, Inc.; Phoenixcor, Inc.; Balboa Capital Corp.; Fleet Credit Corporation.

## PAUL R. GLASSMAN, P.C.
11400 WEST OLYMPIC BOULEVARD, 2ND FLOOR
LOS ANGELES, CALIFORNIA 90064
Telephone: 310-312-9505
Fax: 310-312-9507

*Business and Real Estate Bankruptcies, Corporate Reorganizations, Workouts, Debtor-Creditor Matters and Related Litigation.*

FIRM PROFILE: *Mr. Glassman was partner in charge of the Bankruptcy Group at a leading Los Angeles law firm for five years prior to starting his own practice in March of 1995. Mr. Glassman represents a wide variety of clients, including financial institutions, commercial lenders, insurance companies, secured and unsecured creditors, creditors committees, debtors, landlords, individuals, partners, partnerships and entities seeking to acquire distressed companies. He has practiced for the last fifteen years exclusively in the bankruptcy area. Mr. Glassman is currently representing one of the major creditor groups in The Orange County Bankruptcy.*

PAUL R. GLASSMAN, born New York, N.Y., June 17, 1952; admitted to bar, 1977, California; 1978, U.S. District Court, Central District of California; 1981, District of Columbia and U.S. District Court, Eastern District of California; 1982, U.S. District Court, Northern District of California. *Education:* University of Pennsylvania (B.A., magna cum laude, 1974; M.A., Economics, 1974); Stanford University (J.D., 1977). Phi Beta Kappa; Omicron Delta Epsilon. Member, Stanford Law Review, 1976-1977. Law Clerk to Hon. Mariana R. Pfaelzer, U.S. District Court, Central District of California, 1978-1979. Author: "Third Party Injunctions in Partnership Bankruptcy Cases," The Business Lawyer, May, 1994, Vol. 49, No. 3; "Solicitation of Plan Rejections under the Bankruptcy Code," American Bankruptcy Law Journal, Summer, 1988. Co-Author with Bernard Shapiro: "Fraudulent Transfers," Bankruptcy Practice after the 1984 Code Amendments, CEB, 1985, Fundamentals of Bankruptcy, CEB, 1986; "Introduction to Bankruptcy Practice," CEB 1987, 1991 and "Fundamentals of Bankruptcy Practice," 1988 and 1989; "Mandatory Withdrawal of Reference," Norton Bankruptcy Law Adviser, January, 1985. *Member:* Century City (Chair, Committee on Bankruptcy and Creditors Rights, 1983-1989; Member, Board of Governors, 1985-1992; Treasurer, 1986-1987; Secretary, 1987-1988; Vice President, 1988-1989; President-Elect, 1989-1990; President, 1990-1991), Los Angeles County (Member: Board of Trustees, 1991-1992; Vice-Chair, Bankruptcy Committee, 1992—; Chair, Bankruptcy Committee, 1994-1995; Member, Executive Committee of the Commercial Law and Bankruptcy Section, 1992-1996) and American (Member, Section on Business Law) Bar Associations; State Bar of California; Financial Lawyers Conference; Bankruptcy Study Group. **PRACTICE AREAS:** Bankruptcy Law; Insolvency Law; Commercial Law.

REPRESENTATIVE CLIENTS: City of Irvine; Official Subcommittee of Orange County Cities of the Investment Pool Participants' Committee in the Orange County Bankruptcy Case; GE Capital Finance Corp.; GE Capital Small Business Finance Corp.; Insurance Co. of North America; Official Subcommittee of Landlords in The Sizzler Bankruptcy Case.
REFERENCE: First Interstate Bank.

## GOLBERT LEE LLP
601 WEST FIFTH STREET
8TH FLOOR
LOS ANGELES, CALIFORNIA 90071-2094
Telephone: 213-891-9641
Telecopier: 213-623-6130

*General Corporate and Commercial Practice, including International Transactions and Disputes, International Trade, Investment and Taxation, Real Estate Transactions and Litigation, Technology Transfers.*

ALBERT S. GOLBERT, born Colorado, November 26, 1932; admitted to bar, 1957, Colorado; 1958, California; 1964, U.S. Supreme Court; 1970, Michigan. *Education:* University of Southern California (B.S., 1954); University of Denver (LL.B., 1956); University of Michigan (LL.M., 1964); Graduate Institute of International Studies, University of Geneva (D.Sc., Jur. Cand., 1968). Co-Author: " Latin American Laws and Institutions," Praeger, N.Y., 1982; "Problems and Materials on International Trade and Investment," UCLA Press, 1973. Author: International Operations Handbook (Ed.), Fed. Publications, Inc., 1972. Professor of Law, 1970-1976 and Adjunct Professor of Law, 1976—, Southwestern University. Lecturer in law: University of Southern California, 1984—; Whittier Law School, 1991—; Loyola Law School, 1992—. Instructor in Multi-National Enterprises and Law in International Business, University of California at Los Angeles, 1972-1977. Member, Board of Editors, 1975-1976 and Assistant Editor-In-Law, 1976-1983, "The International Lawyer," American Bar Association. Founding Member, International Practice Committee, Section of Business Law, 1986-1987. Founder and Member of the Executive Committee, 1987-1990, Advisor, 1990-1993 and Advisor Emeritus, 1993—, Section of International Law; Member, International Tax Committee and Member, Executive Committee, 1995—, Taxation Section, State Bar of California. Chair, Section of International Law, 1984-1985, Chair, 1988-1989, Foreign Tax Committee and Chair, 1993-1994 Section of Taxation, and Chair, 1992-1993, Pacific Rim Committee, Los Angeles County Bar Association. Founding Member and Vice President, 1986-1988 and Chairman of the Board, 1988—, The Los Angeles Center for International Commercial Arbitration. *Member:* Inter-American and International Bar Associations; American Society of International Law (Co-Chairperson, Membership Committee, 1982-1984). (Certified Specialist, Taxation Law, The State Bar of California Board of Legal Specialization). **LANGUAGES:** French, German and Italian. **PRACTICE AREAS:** International Business; Taxation; Trade; General Business.

SAN SAN LEE, born Taiwan, China, November 8, 1963; admitted to bar, 1988, California. *Education:* Claremont McKenna College (B.A., 1985); University of California at Los Angeles (J.D., 1988). Associate: Coudert Brothers, 1988-1992 (Los Angeles, 1988-1989; Tokyo, 1989-1991; Singapore, 1991-1992); Ku & Fong, Los Angeles, 1992-1993; Nossaman, Guthner, Knox & Elliot, Los Angeles, 1993-1994. Corporate Counsel, Inter-Continental Hotels Corp., Hong Kong, 1995-1996. *Member:* Los Angeles County Bar Association (Secretary and Vice-Chair, Pacific Rim Committee); State Bar of California; Southern California Chinese Lawyers Association. **LANGUAGES:** Mandarin, Japanese. **PRACTICE AREAS:** Real Estate and Corporate.

*OF COUNSEL*

CATHERINE DELARBRE PARKER, born Torigni, France, July 4, 1959; admitted to bar, 1981, France; 1990, California and U.S. District Court, Central District of California; 1991, U.S. District Court, Northern and Southern Districts of California. *Education:* University of Caen (License en Droit, LL.B., 1979); University of Paris, I-Pantheon-Sorbonne (Maîtrise en Droit, LL.M., 1980; M.C.L. in common law, 1 984). *Member:* Los Angeles County Bar Association; State Bar of California. **LANGUAGES:** French and Spanish. **PRACTICE AREAS:** Bankruptcy; Litigation.

## GOLDBERG & SCOTT
1901 AVENUE OF THE STARS, SUITE 1100
LOS ANGELES, CALIFORNIA 90067
Telephone: 310-277-6790
Fax: 310-556-8945

*Commercial, Entertainment and Real Estate Litigation.*
(This Listing Continued)

*FIRM PROFILE: The firm brings large law firm experience to a small firm setting. The firm was formed in 1996 by partners from other prestigious Los Angeles firms. The firm continues to handle sophisticated litigation matters in a variety of industries.*

### MEMBERS OF FIRM

**STEVEN M. GOLDBERG,** born Bronx, New York, February 19, 1954; admitted to bar, 1978, California; 1979, New York. *Education:* Harvard University (A.B., 1975); New York University (J.D., 1978). Member, New York University Law Review, 1976-1977. *Member:* Century City, Los Angeles County and American Bar Associations; State Bar of California; Association of Business Trial Lawyers. *PRACTICE AREAS:* Commercial Litigation; Entertainment Litigation; Real Estate Litigation.

**JEFF E. SCOTT,** born New York, N.Y., November 6, 1961; admitted to bar, 1986, California. *Education:* Wesleyan University (B.A., magna cum laude, 1983); University of Michigan Law School (J.D., cum laude, 1986). Phi Beta Kappa; Phi Delta Phi. *Member:* Los Angeles County Bar Association; State Bar of California. *PRACTICE AREAS:* Commercial Litigation; Entertainment Litigation; Real Estate Litigation.

**MICHELE R. VAN GELDEREN,** born Brooklyn, New York, May 26, 1968; admitted to bar, 1994, California. *Education:* Stanford University (Psychology, 1990); Boalt Hall School of Law (J.D, 1994). Phi Beta Kappa. *Member:* Los Angeles County Bar Association; State Bar of California; Womens Law Association of Los Angeles. *PRACTICE AREAS:* Commercial Litigation; Entertainment Litigation; Real Estate Litigation.

### OF COUNSEL

**DAVID L. BURG,** born Los Angeles, California, September 13, 1957; admitted to bar, 1987, California and U.S. Court of Appeals, Ninth Circuit. *Education:* University of California at Los Angeles (B.A., magna cum laude, 1980); Boalt Hall School of Law, University of California, Berkeley (J.D., 1987). Phi Beta Kappa. Member, University of California Law Review, 1986-1987. *Member:* State Bar of California. (Also Of Counsel to Clifford Hirsch at Walnut Creek). *PRACTICE AREAS:* Commercial Litigation; Entertainment Litigation; Real Estate Litigation.

---

## GOLDFARB, STURMAN & AVERBACH

A Partnership including Professional Corporations

**15760 VENTURA BOULEVARD, 19TH FLOOR**
**LOS ANGELES, CALIFORNIA 91436**
Telephone: 213-872-2204; 818-990-4414

*General Practice. Business, Real Estate, Estate Planning, Probate, Taxation Law, Civil Litigation.*

### MEMBERS OF FIRM

**SAMUEL GOLDFARB** (Retired).

**J. HOWARD STURMAN** (1931-1991).

**MARTIN L. STURMAN, (A PROFESSIONAL CORPORATION),** born Chicago, Illinois, May 12, 1933; admitted to bar, 1958, Illinois; 1962, California. *Education:* Roosevelt University; Loyola University (J.D., 1958). Author: "The Importance of the Family Trust," The Practical Lawyer, Vol. 17, No. 1, January, 1971, republished—Case and Comment, December, 1975; "Adapting the Living Trust to 'Special' Problems in Estate Planning," The Practicing Lawyer, Vol. 18, No. 8, December, 1972, Republished Case and Comment, 1977. President, San Fernando Valley Estate Planning Council, 1983-1984. *Member:* San Fernando Valley (Chairman: Probate Section, 1983-1985, Los Angeles County (Member, Sections on: Trusts and Estates, Taxation) and American Bar Associations; State Bar of California (Member, Section on Taxation). *PRACTICE AREAS:* Taxation Law; Corporate Law; Estate Planning Law.

**ZANE S. AVERBACH, (A PROFESSIONAL CORPORATION),** born Chicago, Illinois, September 1, 1951; admitted to bar, 1977, California and U.S. Tax Court; 1978, U.S. District Court, Central District of California. *Education:* University of California at Los Angeles (B.A., 1973); Loyola School of Law (J.D., 1976); New York University (LL.M., Taxation, 1977). President, San Fernando Valley Estate Planning Council, 1988-1989. *Member:* San Fernando Valley Bar Association (Trustee, 1980-1982); State Bar of California. *PRACTICE AREAS:* Taxation Law; Real Estate Law; Estate Planning Law.

**MARTIN B. SNYDER,** born Los Angeles, California, February 14, 1951; admitted to bar, 1977, California; 1978, U.S. District Court, Southern District of California; 1979, U.S. District Court, Central District of Califor-

*(This Listing Continued)*

nia. *Education:* University of California at Los Angeles (B.A., 1973), Phi Beta Kappa; University of San Diego (J.D., 1977). Judge, Pro Tem, Los Angeles Municipal Court, 1987. *Member:* San Fernando Valley (Chair, Judge Pro Tem Committee, 1987; Chair, Continuing Legal Education Committee, 1990-1991; Chair, Judiciary Committee, 1991-1992; Trustee, 1988-1991; Chair, Business Law Section, 1993-1994) Los Angeles County (Member, Litigation Section) and American Bar Associations; State Bar of California; Los Angeles Trial Lawyers Association. *PRACTICE AREAS:* Civil Litigation; Real Estate Law; Business Litigation.

**MARK J. PHILLIPS,** born Los Angeles, California, July 31, 1954; admitted to bar, 1980, California; 1981, U.S. Tax Court; 1982, U.S. District Court, Central District of California. *Education:* University of California at Los Angeles (B.A., cum laude, 1976; J.D., 1979); New York University (LL.M., Taxation, 1980). Adjunct Professor of Law, University of Laverne, College of Law, 1986-1996. Author: "AB21: New Attorney Conflict Rules Invalidate Transfers and Restrict Compensation," 15 CEB Estate Plan. Rep., October, 1993; "Families in Transition: California Continues to Grapple With the Inheritance Rights of Stepchildren," California State Bar Estate Planning, Trust & Probate News, Spring, 1994. President, San Fernando Valley Estate Planning Council, 1996-1997. *Member:* San Fernando Valley and Los Angeles County (Executive Committee, Trusts and Estates Section) Bar Associations; State Bar of California. (Certified Specialist, Estate Planning, Trust and Probate Law, The State Bar of California Board of Legal Specialization). *PRACTICE AREAS:* Taxation Law; Estate Planning Law; Probate Law.

**STEVEN L. FELDMAN,** born Washington, D.C., February 12, 1949; admitted to bar, 1974, California; U.S. District Court, Central and Eastern Districts of California and U.S. Court of Appeals, Ninth Circuit. *Education:* University of California at Los Angeles (B.A., cum laude, 1971); Loyola Marymount University (J.D., 1974). Pi Gamma Mu. California Real Estate Broker, 1990-1996. *Member:* Beverly Hills Bar Association; State Bar of California; Los Angeles Trial Lawyers Association. *PRACTICE AREAS:* Real Estate Law; Construction Law; Business Litigation; Environmental Law; Administrative Law.

**CYNTHIA LU RUBIN,** born Orange, California, August 25, 1953; admitted to bar, 1985, California and U.S. District Court, Central District of California. *Education:* University of California at Berkeley (B.A., 1975); Loyola Marymount University (J.D., cum laude, 1985). Member, Moot Court. Treasurer, St. Thomas More Law Honor Society, 1984-1985. *Member:* San Fernando Valley and Los Angeles County Bar Associations; State Bar of California. *PRACTICE AREAS:* Real Estate Law; Business Litigation.

### ASSOCIATES

**LES J. WOLIN,** born Rochester, New York, May 13, 1956; admitted to bar, 1985, California. *Education:* Loyola College (B.A., 1977); University of Santa Clara (J.D., 1981); University of San Diego (LL.M. in Taxation, 1990). *Member:* San Fernando Valley Bar Association; State Bar of California. *LANGUAGES:* Hebrew. *PRACTICE AREAS:* Probate Law; Taxation Law; Business Law.

**CHRISTINE E. CEDER,** born Ocean Park, New Jersey, September 30, 1968; admitted to bar, 1994, California. *Education:* San Diego State University (B.S., 1990); Pepperdine University (J.D., 1994); University of Miami School of Law (LL.M., Estate Planning, 1995). Member, San Fernando Valley Estate Planning Council. *Member:* San Fernando Valley Bar Association. *PRACTICE AREAS:* Estate Planning; Transactional.

### OF COUNSEL

**WILLIAM L. WINSLOW,** born Tulsa, Oklahoma, January 21, 1950; admitted to bar, 1974, California. *Education:* University of California at Los Angeles (A.B., cum laude, 1971) University of California School of Law at Los Angeles (J.D., 1974); University of San Diego (LL.M., in Taxation, 1988). Author: "Safeguarding Benefits for the Injured," A Primer on Special Needs Trusts, June, 1996; "New Regulations for Medi-Cal Eligibility," Los Angeles Daily Journal, March 11, 1996. *Member:* Los Angeles County Bar Association (Member: Barristers Executive Committee, 1977-1980; Conference of Delegates Executive Committee, 1972-1981; Delegate, 1982); State Bar of California. *PRACTICE AREAS:* Structured Settlements; Estate Planning; Special Needs Trusts.

## MARTIN F. GOLDMAN
*Established in 1977*

**10880 WILSHIRE BOULEVARD, SUITE 2240
LOS ANGELES, CALIFORNIA 90024-4123**
Telephone: 310-470-8487
FAX: 310-474-0653

*Commercial, Collection and Litigation.*

**MARTIN F. GOLDMAN,** born 1944; admitted to bar, 1970, California. *Education:* California State University (B.S., 1966); Loyola University (J.D., 1969). *Member:* State Bar of California; Commercial Law League of America. (Board Certified, Creditors Rights Specialist, Commercial Law League of America). **PRACTICE AREAS:** Creditor's Rights; Collection; Bankruptcy.

---

## GOLDMAN & GORDON, L.L.P.
*Established in 1977*

**SUITE 1920, 1801 CENTURY PARK EAST
LOS ANGELES, CALIFORNIA 90067**
Telephone: 310-277-7171
FAX: 310-277-1547

*General Civil and Trial Practice in all State and Federal Courts. Commercial, Real Estate, Probate, Corporate, Bankruptcy, Consumer, Fidelity and Surety, Insolvency, Insurance and Subrogation Law.*

FIRM PROFILE: Goldman & Gordon, L.L.P. has over 30 years of legal expertise in their respective areas and continue to maintain a high standard of knowledge and proficiency through substantial ongoing continuing legal education programs provided by various specialized sections of the State Bar of California. The firm employs qualified legal secretaries and other assistant personnel who perform all necessary ancillary functions that are required for the proper and orderly handling of all client matters. Support personnel are familiar with the use of computers in the preparation of cases for trial, and as a direct result, Goldman & Gordon, L.L.P. has successfully litigated a number of major cases involving complex factual and legal issues. The attorneys of Goldman & Gordon, L.L.P. endeavor to evaluate with the client the economics of litigation. We regularly consult with the client to estimate the projected cost of litigation. The firm is listed in the Bar Register of Preeminent Lawyers.

*MEMBERS OF FIRM*

**A. S. GOLDMAN** (1895-1966).

**LEONARD A. GOLDMAN,** born Los Angeles, California, February 24, 1930; admitted to bar, 1956, California and Illinois. *Education:* Stanford University (B.A., 1951; J.D., 1955). *Member:* Los Angeles County, Illinois State, Federal and American Bar Associations; The State Bar of California; American Judicature Society; Lawyers Club of Los Angeles County. **REPORTED CASES:** C.A.Cal. 1974. In re Kanter, 505 F.2d 228; C.A.Cal. 1973. Biggins v. Southwest Bank, 490 F. 2d 1304, 13 UCC Rep.Serv. 928; C.A.9 1973. Veeck v. Commodity Enterprises, Inc. 487 F.2d. 423; C.A.Cal. 1971. Parker v. Williams Const. Co., 443 F.2d 597; C.A.Cal. 1966. A. & E. Plastik Pak Co. v. Bowie, 358 F.2d 148; Bkrptcy.C.D.Cal. 1990. In re David Orgell, Inc. 117 B.R. 574, 20 Bkrptcy.Ct.Dec. 1377, Bkrptcy. L. Rep. P 73,590; Bkrptcy.C.D.Cal. 1990. In re McGoldrick 117 B.R.554, Bkrptcy. L. Rep. P 73,587; Bkrptcy.C.D.Cal. 1987. In re Old Town Historic Bldg., Ltd. 79 B.R. 8; Bkrptcy.Cal., 1980. In re Murrieta Hot Springs 6 B.R. 73; In re Dominguez, 995 F2d 162 (9th Circuit 1993); In re Shaw, 157 BR 151 (Bap-Cal. 1993). **PRACTICE AREAS:** Bankruptcy Law; Civil Litigation Law; Debtor-Creditor Law; Real Estate Finance Law.

**ROBERT P. GORDON,** born Los Angeles, California, January 16, 1935; admitted to bar, 1960, California; 1971, U.S. Supreme Court. *Education:* University of California at Los Angeles (B.S., 1956); University of Colorado at Boulder; University of Southern California (J.D., 1959). Nu Beta Epsilon. Judge Pro Tem, Los Angeles Municipal Court, 1972—. Member, Panel of Arbitrators, American Arbitration Association. Member, Arbitration Panel, Los Angeles Superior Court, 1979—. *Member:* Beverly Hills, Century City, Los Angeles County, Federal and American (Member, Sections on: Litigation; Corporation, Banking and Business Law; Insurance, Negligence and Compensation Law) Bar Associations; State Bar of California; Defense Research Institute, Inc.; Association of Southern California Defense Counsel; Commercial Law League of America; American Bankruptcy Institute; Financial Lawyers Conference. **REPORTED CASES:** Plotsky v. Friedman, in re Jack Friedman, BAP-CAL, 1991 126 BR 63; In Re Daylin, Inc., 9th Circuit, 1979, 596 F2d 853; Ruiz v. Ruiz, 6CA 3d 58, 85 CR 674; Lujan v. Gordan, 70 CA 3d 260, 138 CR 389; Associates Capital Services v. Security Pacific National Bank, 91 CA 3d 819, 154 CR 392; Hachten v. Stewart, 42 CA 3d Supp 1, 116 CR 631; United Savings & Loan Assn. v. Hoffman, 30 CA 3d 306, 106 CR 275. **PRACTICE AREAS:** Bankruptcy Law; Civil Litigation Law; Debtor-Creditor Law; Collections Law; Post-Judgement Law; Appellate Law; Real Estate Law.

*ASSOCIATE*

**MELODY G. ANDERSON,** born Torrance, California, January 7, 1965; admitted to bar, 1994, California, U.S. District Court, Central District of California and U.S. Court of Appeals, Ninth Circuit. *Education:* Southern California University (B.A., 1991; J.D., 1994). Phi Alpha Delta. Recipient: American Jurisprudence Award in Secured Transactions. Judicial Extern, Hon. Robert W. Alberts, U.S. Bankruptcy Judge, Central District of California. *Member:* Los Angeles County (Member, Commercial Law and Bankruptcy Section), Beverly Hills (Member, Bankruptcy Law Section) and American Bar Associations; State Bar of California (Member, Business Law Section). **PRACTICE AREAS:** Bankruptcy Law; Commercial Litigation; Debtor-Creditor Law.

REPRESENTATIVE CLIENTS: American Express Co.; Boston Safe Deposit and Trust Co.; Balboa Insurance Co.; Cash Box Publications, Inc.; U.S. Auto Glass Centers, Inc.; Georgia Pacific Corp.; Cardinal Pacific; American Airlines Federal Credit Union; United Stationers Supply Co.; Citicorp North America, Inc.; Micro United, Inc.; Hughes Communications, Inc.; Anixter, Inc.; Exxon Corp.; Advanstar Communications, Inc.; Gold Graphics; Barakat; Luna Music Corp.; Bodies In Motion; Executive Boxing, Inc.; Bankcard America, Inc.; First National Bank of Commerce Barakat; Capital Metals; Los Angeles Cash Register, Inc.; Prime Textile; Comdata Network; Sportswear International.
REFERENCES: Bank of America, Fourth and Spring Branch, Los Angeles; Bank of America, Wilshire-San Vicente Branch, Beverly Hills.

---

## GOLDMAN & KAGON
*LAW CORPORATION*
*Established in 1947*

**1801 CENTURY PARK EAST, SUITE 2222
LOS ANGELES, CALIFORNIA 90067**
Telephone: 310-552-1707
Telecopier: 310-552-7938

*Corporate, Entertainment, Family Law, Probate, Wills and Trusts, Real Estate, Civil Litigation and General Civil Practice.*

**MARK A. GOLDMAN,** born Los Angeles, California, October 27, 1941; admitted to bar, 1968, California and U.S. District Court, Central District of California. *Education:* University of California at Los Angeles (B.A., 1963); University of California at Los Angeles School of Law (J.D., 1967). Phi Beta Kappa; Order of the Coif. Editor, U.C.L.A. Law Review, 1966-1967. *Member:* State Bar of California. **REPORTED CASES:** Marvin v. Marvin, 122 Cal. App. 3d 871, 176 Cal. Rptr. 555 (1981); Marvin v. Marvin, 18C 3d 660, 134 Cal. Rptr. 815 (1976). **PRACTICE AREAS:** Real Estate; Contracts; General Business. *Email:* markg@goldmankagon.com

**BARRY FELSEN,** born Los Angeles, California, October 19, 1950; admitted to bar, 1976, California and U.S. District Court, Central and Southern Districts of California. *Education:* University of California at Los Angeles (B.A., summa cum laude, 1972); University of California at Los Angeles School of Law (J.D., 1975). Phi Beta Kappa. *Member:* State Bar of California. **PRACTICE AREAS:** Entertainment.

**RICHARD D. GOLDMAN,** born Los Angeles, California, June 27, 1953; admitted to bar, 1978, California. *Education:* University of California at Los Angeles (B.A., summa cum laude, 1975); University of Southern California (J.D., 1978). Phi Beta Kappa. *Member:* State Bar of California. **PRACTICE AREAS:** Entertainment; Real Estate; General Business.

**CHARLES D. MEYER,** born Chicago, Illinois, March 15, 1956; admitted to bar, 1980, California and U.S. District Court, Central District of California; 1989, U.S. District Court, Northern District of California; 1993, U.S. District Court, Eastern District of California. *Education:* University of Michigan (B.A., magna cum laude, 1977); University of California at Los Angeles School of Law (J.D., 1980). *Member:* Century City Bar Association; State Bar of California. **REPORTED CASES:** Marvin v. Marvin, 122 Cal. App. 3d 871, 176 Cal. Rptr. 555 (1981); Watkins v. Watkins, 143 Cal. App. 3d 651, 192 Cal. Rptr. 54 (1983). **PRACTICE AREAS:** Real Estate; Cable Television; Premarital Planning; General Business.

**CHRISTOPHER B. FAGAN,** born Los Angeles, California, May 11, 1952; admitted to bar, 1979, California and U.S. District Court, Northern District of California. *Education:* Pomona College (B.A., magna cum laude, 1974); University of San Francisco (J.D., 1979). Phi Beta Kappa. Author: "Funding & Operating Living Trusts," Planning Opportunities with Living

*(This Listing Continued)*

Trusts in California, NBI 1995. Lecturer, National Business Institute, 1995. *Member:* State Bar of California (Member, Estate Planning, Trust and Probate Section, 1989-1993). **PRACTICE AREAS:** Probate; Trusts; Wills. *Email:* chrisf@goldmankagon.com

**TERRY MC NIFF,** born Rochester, Minnesota, October 12, 1954; admitted to bar, 1983, California, U.S. District Court, Central District of California and U.S. Court of Appeals, Ninth Circuit. *Education:* University of Minnesota (B.S., summa cum laude, 1980); University of California at Los Angeles School of Law (J.D., 1983). Author: "Maximizing Support Results," California State Bar, 1995; Revision to "Family Law Techniques and Trial Tips," article by A. David Kagon, Los Angeles County Bar Association Family Law Section Symposium Reference Book, 1996. Co-author: "Marvin Claims," Los Angeles County Bar Family Law Section Symposium Reference Book, 1995. Lecturer, "Maximizing Support Results," Section Education Institute, California State Bar, 1995. Judge Pro Tem, Los Angeles County Municipal Court, 1995; Arbitrator: Los Angeles County Judicial Arbitration Program, 1993—; Arbitrator, Los Angeles County Fee Arbitration, 1994—. *Member:* Beverly Hills, Los Angeles County and American Bar Associations; State Bar of California (Member: Family Law Section, Support South Committee; Chair-Elect, 1993-1995; Chair, 1995-1997). (Certified Specialist, Family Law, The State Bar of California Board of Specialization). **PRACTICE AREAS:** Family Law; Palimony Defense; Premarital Planning; Civil Litigation. *Email:* terrym@goldmankagon.com

**JARED LASKIN,** born New Brunswick, New Jersey, June 10, 1962; admitted to bar, 1987, California and U.S. District Court, Central District of California. *Education:* Washington University (B.A., 1983); University of California at Los Angeles School of Law (J.D., 1987). Phi Beta Kappa; Order of the Coif. Author: "Just Pals," (Palimony), Los Angeles Lawyer, October, 1994; "Marvin Claims," (Laskin and McNiff) 1995 Family Law Reference Book, 1995, Los Angeles County Bar Association. Arbitrator, Los Angeles County Judicial Arbitration Program, 1993—. *Member:* Los Angeles County Bar Association; State Bar of California. **REPORTED CASES:** Bergen v. Wood, 14 Cal. App. 4th 854, 18 Cal. Rptr. 2d 75 (1993). **PRACTICE AREAS:** Civil Litigation; Palimony Defense; General Business. *Email:* jaredl@goldmankagon.com

**MARCO F. WEISS,** born San Francisco, California, April 9, 1931; admitted to bar, 1957, Missouri; 1961, California; 1991, Consultant in American Law, England. *Education:* University of California at Berkeley (A.B., 1952); Stanford University; University of Chicago (J.D., 1956). Author: "Tax Consequences of Estate Termination," California Continuing Education of the Bar-Tax Highlights, 1962. Law Clerk, Hon. R.M. Duncan, Chief Judge, U.S. District Court, Kansas City, Missouri, 1956-1957. *Member:* The Bar Association of San Francisco; Beverly Hills, Los Angeles County and American (Member: Business Law Section; Committee on Federal Regulation of Securities, 1974-1985; Committee on State Regulation of Securities, 1975-1990) Bar Associations; State Bar of California; Associate, The Law Society, England. **PRACTICE AREAS:** International Transactions; Financing; Banking; Joint Ventures.

**EDMUND S. SCHAFFER,** born Springfield, Massachusetts, April 19, 1945; admitted to bar, 1971, California. *Education:* University of California at Los Angeles (A.B., with highest honors, 1966); Harvard University (J.D., cum laude and M.P.A., 1970). Phi Beta Kappa. Law Clerk to Judge Stanley Barnes, U.S. Court of Appeals for the Ninth Circuit, 1970-1971. Reginald Heber Smith Fellow, San Francisco Neighborhood Legal Assistance Foundation, 1971-1973. Judge Pro Tem: Beverly Hills Municipal Court, 1979—; Santa Monica Municipal Court, 1990—. *Member:* Beverly Hills and Los Angeles County (Member, State and Federal Courts Committees) Bar Associations; State Bar of California; Association of Business Trial Lawyers.

*COUNSEL*

**A. DAVID KAGON,** born Woodridge, New York, August 10, 1918; admitted to bar, 1947, New York; 1948, California. *Education:* Columbia University (B.A., 1941; LL.B., 1947). *Member:* Beverly Hills (Member, Board of Governors; Author, Panelist, Lecturer; Founder and First Chairman of ADR Section), Century City, Los Angeles County and American (Member, Alternative Dispute Resolution Committee) Bar Associations; State Bar of California. **REPORTED CASES:** Marvin v. Marvin, 122 Cal. App. 3d 871, 176 Cal. Rptr. 555 (1981); Marvin v. Marvin, 18 C.3d 660 (1976), 134 Cal. Rptr. 815; Watkins v. Watkins, 143 Cal. App. 3d 651, 192 Cal. Rptr. 54 (1983); Bergen v. Wood, 14 Cal. App. 4th 854, 18 Cal. Rptr. 2d 75 (1993). **PRACTICE AREAS:** Mediation and Arbitration; Family Law; Business Law; Real Property Law.

## KENNETH L. GOLDMAN

PROFESSIONAL CORPORATION

1801 CENTURY PARK EAST, SUITE 2222
LOS ANGELES, CALIFORNIA 90067
Telephone: 310-552-1720
Fax: 312-552-7938

*Probate, Wills and Trusts, Probate Litigation and General Business Law.*

**KENNETH L. GOLDMAN,** born Los Angeles, California, July, 27, 1945; admitted to bar, 1969, California. *Education:* University of California at Los Angeles (B.A., 1966); University of California at Los Angeles School of Law (J.D., 1969). *Member:* State Bar of California. **PRACTICE AREAS:** Probate, Wills and Trusts; Probate Litigation; General Business.

## IRWIN D. GOLDRING

SUITE 2000, 1875 CENTURY PARK EAST
LOS ANGELES, CALIFORNIA 90067
Telephone: 310-201-0304
FAX: 310-277-7994

*Taxation, Estate Planning, Trust and Probate Law.*

**IRWIN D. GOLDRING,** born Los Angeles, California, March 26, 1931; admitted to bar, 1957, California; 1960, U.S. Tax Court. *Education:* University of California at Los Angeles (B.S., 1953; J.D., 1956). Phi Alpha Delta. Certified Public Accountant, California, 1954. *Member:* Beverly Hills (Chairman, Committees on: Tax, 1972-1973; Probate and Trust, 1977-1978; Member, Board of Governors, 1978-1980), Los Angeles County and American Bar Associations; State Bar of California (Chairman: Sub-Committee on Income Taxation of Trusts, 1977-1979; Sub-Committee on Trust Administration, 1980-1981; Committee on Trusts, 1981-1982; Member, 1981-1984, 1987-1989, Reporter, 1984-1987, Advisor, 1985-1987, 1989-1992; Vice-Chair, 1987-1988 and Chair, 1988-1989, Executive Committee, Estate Planning, Trust and Probate Law Section; Member, Public Interest Tax Committee, 1977-1980; Member, Committee on Minimum Continuing Legal Education, 1991-1993; Member, 1994—, and Vice Chair, 1996-1997, Estate Planning, Trust and Probate Law Advisory Commission to Board of Legal Specialization). Fellow, American College of Trust and Estate Counsel. [Capt., USAF, JAGC, 1956-1958]. (Certified Specialist, Taxation Law and Estate Planning, Trust and Probate Law, The State Bar of California Board of Legal Specialization). **PRACTICE AREAS:** Estate Planning; Trust and Probate Law; Taxation Law.

REFERENCE: Western Bank.

## GOLDSMITH & BURNS

A Partnership including a Professional Corporation

18425 BURBANK BOULEVARD, SUITE 708 (TARZANA)
LOS ANGELES, CALIFORNIA 91356-2800
Telephone: 818-708-2585
Telecopier: 818-996-4537

*Retail and Commercial Collection, Insurance Defense, Coverage, Subrogation, Personal Injury, Professional Malpractice, Negligence, Construction Defect Litigation, Probate, Estate Planning, Wills and Trusts, Conservatorship, Elder Law, Business Litigation and Commercial Litigation.*

FIRM PROFILE: *Goldsmith & Burns was Awarded one of the First Contracts by the United States Department of Justice Employing Private Law Firms to Collect Debts due the United States of America.*

**WILLIAM I. GOLDSMITH, (A PROFESSIONAL CORPORATION),** born Los Angeles, California, July 15, 1953; admitted to bar, 1978, California; 1979, U.S. District Court, Central and Southern Districts of California and U.S. Court of Appeals, Ninth Circuit. *Education:* University of California at Los Angeles (B.A., 1975); San Fernando Valley College of Law (J.D., 1978). Instructor, Jurisdictional Problems in Enforcing Sister State Judgments, CLLA, 1987. *Member:* San Fernando Valley and Los Angeles County Bar Associations; State Bar of California; Consumer Attorneys of California; Commercial Law League of America (Chairman, Federal Debt Collection Committee, 1993-1994); National Association of Retail Collection Attorneys (NARCA) (Vice President, 1996-1998). **PRACTICE AREAS:** Commercial Litigation; Major Personal Injury Litigation; Real Estate; Collection.

*(This Listing Continued)*

GOLDSMITH & BURNS, Los Angeles—Continued

**JACK D. HULL,** born Champaign, Illinois, November 2, 1951; admitted to bar, 1980, California, U.S. District Court, Central District of California, U.S. Court of Appeals, Ninth Circuit; U.S. Court of Military Appeals, U.S. Tax Court and U.S. Claims Court. *Education:* University of California at Los Angeles (B.A., 1975); University of San Fernando Valley College of Law (J.D., 1979). Delta Theta Phi. Member, University of San Fernando Valley Law Review, 1978-1979. Arbitrator and Voluntary Settlement Conference Officer, Los Angeles Superior Court, 1988—. *Member:* Los Angeles County and San Fernando Valley Bar Associations; State Bar of California; Association of Southern California Defense Counsel; Defense Research Institute. **PRACTICE AREAS:** Insurance Defense; Insurance Coverage; Professional Malpractice; Arbitration; Construction Defects; Business Law.

### ASSOCIATES

**NANCY SANDBERG RAMIREZ,** born Los Angeles, California, September 27, 1945; admitted to bar, 1987, California; 1993, U.S. District Court, Central District of California. *Education:* Citrus College, Azusa, California (A.A., 1970); Western State University, Fullerton, California (B.S.L., 1986; J.D., 1987). Member, Estate Planning Council, San Fernando Valley. *Member:* Los Angeles County, San Fernando Valley, San Bernardino County (Member, Board of Directors, Western San Bernardino County, 1993-1995) Bar Associations; State Bar of California. **PRACTICE AREAS:** Probate; Guardianship and Conservatorship; Estate Planning; Wills; Trusts and Estates; Elder Law; Business Transactions.

**DAVID M. GONOR,** born Los Angeles, California, June 7, 1967; admitted to bar, 1994, California and U.S. District Court, Central District of California. *Education:* University of California at Santa Barbara (B.A., 1989); Pepperdine University (J.D., 1993). *Member:* Los Angeles County, Ventura County and Beverly Hills Bar Associations; State Bar of California; National Association of Retail Collection Attorneys; Commercial Law League of America. **PRACTICE AREAS:** Commercial Collections; Retail Collections; Creditors Rights; Mechanics Liens; Business Litigation; Creditors Bankruptcy.

REPRESENTATIVE CLIENTS: U.S. Department of Justice; Bank of America; Union Bank of California; MCI; Good Year Tire; Federal Express; Safeco Ins.; Farmers Ins.; Allstate Ins.; General Ins. Co.; Hartford Ins.; Firemans Fund; Catepillar; American Express.

---

## GOLDSTEIN & ASHLEY
**10990 WILSHIRE BOULEVARD, SUITE 940**
**LOS ANGELES, CALIFORNIA 90024**
Telephone: 310-575-6100
Fax: 310-575-6101

**NEAL M. GOLDSTEIN,** born Chicago, Illinois, May 13, 1952; admitted to bar, 1978, California. *Education:* Harvard University (A.B., cum laude, 1974); University of Edinburgh, Edinburgh, Scotland; Hastings College of Law, University of California (J.D., 1978). Managing Editor, Hastings International and Comparative Law Review, 1977-1978. *Member:* Los Angeles County and American (Member, Sections on: Litigation; Patent, Trademark and Copyright Law) Bar Associations; State Bar of California. **PRACTICE AREAS:** Civil Litigation; Entertainment Law; Contract Law; Real and Personal Property Law; Copyright Law.

**STEPHEN D. ASHLEY,** born Chicago, Illinois, February 19, 1947; admitted to bar, 1973, New York; 1975, California. *Education:* Harvard University (B.A., magna cum laude, history, 1969); Yale Law School (J.D., 1973). Yale Law Review, 1972-1973. **PRACTICE AREAS:** Entertainment Law; Non Union Employment; Contract Law; Copyrights; Trademarks.

---

## GOLDSTEIN, KENNEDY & PETITO
**SUITE 1018, 1880 CENTURY PARK EAST (CENTURY CITY)**
**LOS ANGELES, CALIFORNIA 90067**
Telephone: 310-553-4746; 213-879-1401
Fax: 310-282-8070

*Labor and Public Employment Relations Law and Equal Opportunity Law. General Civil, Trial and Appellate Practice in all State and Federal Courts.*

**FIRM PROFILE:** *Goldstein, Kennedy & Petito take pride in giving our clients practical legal counsel on how management can effectively maintain its right to ensure a productive organization through timely and effective decision-making. We take an aggressive approach to solving our clients' sophisticated and unique legal needs. The firm not only meets our clients' current requirements, but also anticipates future situations and develops practical solutions for those as well.*

*Goldstein, Kennedy & Petito stresses efficiency and responsiveness to our clients' needs and the partners are directly involved in the day-to-day counsel and litigation for each client. The firm takes pride in listing in the Bar Register of Preeminent Lawyers.*

**CHARLES H. GOLDSTEIN,** born Newark, New Jersey, October 17, 1939; admitted to bar, 1964, Virginia and California; 1972, U.S. Supreme Court. *Education:* Case Western Reserve University (B.A., 1961); George Washington University (J.D., with honors, 1964). Phi Delta Phi; Omicron Delta Kappa; Phi Sigma Alpha; Phi Alpha Theta; Delta Sigma Rho. Author: "Labor Law Ramifications of Corporate Acquisitions and Mergers," Beverly Hills Bar Journal, 1972; "The Alameda County Social Workers and City of Vallejo Cases—The Implications for Public Employers and Employees," Los Angeles Bar Bulletin, March, 1975; "Police Labor Relations in the 80's: Who Will Control the Decision Making Process-Police Unions or Police Management?" California Law Enforcement, Winter, 1981; "Sexual Harassment Liability and Prevention," California Public Employee Labor Relations Association Newsletter, Issue Seven, Volume Three, March, 1982; "Work Continuation Agreements Offer Cities Help in Keeping the Lid on Construction Cost," Western City, September, 1984. Co-Author: "Should Wrongful Discharge be Applied in the Public Sector?" California Public Employee Relations (CPER) No. 74, September, 1987. Member, Board of Directors, Inter-Community Child Guidance Center, 1966-1968. *Member:* Los Angeles County and American (Member, Labor and Employment Law Section) Bar Associations; State Bar of California; Virginia State Bar. **PRACTICE AREAS:** Labor and Employment; Civil Litigation.

**GREGORY G. KENNEDY,** born Los Angeles, California, January 15, 1953; admitted to bar, 1978, California, U.S. District Court, Central, Northern, Eastern and Southern Districts of California and U.S. Court of Appeals, Ninth Circuit; 1982, U.S. Supreme Court. *Education:* University of California at Los Angeles (B.A., 1974); Loyola University of Los Angeles (J.D., 1977). Co-Author: "Should Wrongful Discharge be Applied in the Public Sector?" California Public Employee Relations (CPER) No. 74, September, 1987. *Member:* Century City, Los Angeles County and American Bar Associations; State Bar of California (Member, Labor and Employment Law Section). **PRACTICE AREAS:** Labor and Employment; Civil Litigation.

**DEBORAH HANNA PETITO,** born Detroit, Michigan, March 5, 1959; admitted to bar, 1985, California, U.S. District Court, Central, Northern and Eastern Districts of California and U.S. Court of Appeals, Ninth Circuit; 1993, U.S. Supreme Court. *Education:* University of California at Los Angeles (B.A., 1981); Pepperdine University School of Law (J.D., 1984). *Member:* Century City, Los Angeles County and American Bar Associations; State Bar of California (Member, Labor and Employment Law Section). **PRACTICE AREAS:** Labor and Employment; Civil Litigation.

---

**LAUREN A. DEAN,** born Tucson, Arizona, September 19, 1968; admitted to bar, 1994, California and U.S. District Court, Eastern and Central Districts of California. *Education:* University of California at Los Angeles (B.A., 1990); University of Arizona College of Law (J.D., 1994). *Member:* Century City and Los Angeles County Bar Associations; State Bar of California. **PRACTICE AREAS:** Labor and Employment; Civil Litigation.

**EDWARD J. GERVIN,** born New York, N.Y., November 26, 1968; admitted to bar, 1995, California and U.S. District Court, Central, Southern, Northern and Eastern Districts of California. *Education:* University of Notre Dame (B.A., 1990); Loyola Law School (J.D., 1994). *Member:* Los Angeles County, Century City, San Fernando Valley and American Bar Associations; State Bar of California. **PRACTICE AREAS:** Labor and Employment; Civil Litigation.

**FRANK A. MAGNANIMO,** born Burbank, California, June 7, 1969; admitted to bar, 1994, California; 1995, U.S. District Court, Central District of California. *Education:* University of Southern California (B.A., 1990); University of Arizona (J.D., 1994). Member, Arizona Journal of International and Italian-American Lawyer's Association, 1995—. **LANGUAGES:** Italian.

### OF COUNSEL

**THOMAS A. FOURNIE,** born Belleville, Illinois, October 18, 1939; admitted to bar, 1970, Colorado; 1972, California; U.S. Court of Appeals, Ninth Circuit; U.S. District Court, Central and Northern Districts of California, U.S. District Court, District of Colorado and U.S. Tax Court; registered to practice before U.S. Patent and Trademark Office. *Education:* Uni-

*(This Listing Continued)*

versity of Illinois (B.S.E.E., with honors, 1962); University of Denver (J.D., with honors, 1970). Member, Order of St. Ives. *Member:* Los Angeles County Bar Association; State Bar of California. [Officer, U.S. Navy, 1962-1966]. **LANGUAGES:** French and Spanish. **PRACTICE AREAS:** Litigation; Real Estate Law; Business and Tort Litigation.

## GOLLUB & GOLSAN

LOS ANGELES, CALIFORNIA

(See Culver City)

*Family and Matrimonial Law.*

## GOLOB, BRAGIN & SASSOE, P.C.

SUITE 1400, 11755 WILSHIRE BOULEVARD
**LOS ANGELES, CALIFORNIA 90025-1520**
Telephone: 310-477-1050
Fax: 310-477-0988

*Business, Real Property, Corporate, Commercial Transactions, Federal and State Securities, Secured Lending, Mergers, Acquisitions, Taxation, Estate Planning, Insolvency, Health Care, Environmental, Franchise and Associated Litigation with these areas of law as well as Entertainment and Probate Litigation.*

**DENNIS E. GOLOB,** born Chicago, Illinois, June 14, 1942; admitted to bar, 1968, California and U.S. District Court, Central and Southern Districts of California. *Education:* University of California at Los Angeles (B.S., 1964); University of Southern California (J.D., 1967). Phi Delta Phi. Moot Court Honors. Member, Board of Bar Governors, University of Southern California Law School, 1966-1967. *Member:* Los Angeles County and American Bar Associations; The State Bar of California. **PRACTICE AREAS:** Business and Contracts Law; Real Property Law; Commercial Transactions Law; Corporate and Business, Commercial and Real Property, Construction and related Litigation.

**RONALD A. BRAGIN,** born Los Angeles, California, June 28, 1950; admitted to bar, 1975, California; 1976, U.S. District Court, Central and Southern Districts of California and U.S. Court of Appeals, Ninth Circuit; 1989, U.S. District Court, Northern District of California. *Education:* University of California at Berkeley (A.B., 1972); University of Southern California (J.D., 1975). Phi Alpha Delta. Hale Moot Court Honors Competition, Second Place, 1974. National Moot Court Competition, First Place and Best Oral Advocate Award, Region 9, 1974-1975. *Member:* Beverly Hills (Member, Board of Governors, Barristers, 1979-1984); Los Angeles County and American (Member, Section on Litigation; Real Property Section; Forum Committee on the Entertainment and Sports Industries, 1979—) Bar Associations; The State Bar of California; American Judicature Society; Association of Business Trial Lawyers. **PRACTICE AREAS:** Real Property Law; Business Litigation; Corporate Law; Probate Litigation.

**ALBERT L. SASSOE, JR.,** born Los Angeles, California, June 8, 1957; admitted to bar, 1982, California and U.S. District Court, Central District of California. *Education:* University of California at Santa Barbara (B.A., Business Economics and Political Science, 1979); Loyola University of Los Angeles (J.D., 1982). *Member:* Los Angeles County Bar Association; State Bar of California (Member, Business Law Section). **PRACTICE AREAS:** Business Litigation; Insurance Coverage Law; Mobile Home Park Litigation.

---

**JASON L. GLOVINSKY,** born Detroit, Michigan, April 3, 1963; admitted to bar, 1989, California; 1991, District of Columbia. *Education:* University of California at Berkeley (A.B., cum laude, 1985); University of California at Los Angeles (J.D., 1988). Participant, UCLA Moot Court Honors Program. *Member:* Los Angeles County Bar Association; State Bar of California; District of Columbia Bar; Los Angeles County Barristers. **PRACTICE AREAS:** Real Estate Law; Business Litigation.

## THE LAW OFFICES OF NED GOOD

LOS ANGELES, CALIFORNIA

(See Pasadena)

*Practice Restricted to Plaintiff Personal Injury, Aviation and Malpractice Law in all State and Federal Courts.*

## EARLE GARY GOODMAN

2934 1/2 BEVERLY GLENN CIRCLE
SUITE 395
**LOS ANGELES, CALIFORNIA 90077**
Telephone: 310-470-9033
Fax: 310-470-3494
Email: 23852@MSN.com

*General Business Transactions, Real Property Sales and Lease Transactions, Construction and Development, Business Transactions and LLC, Corporation and Partnership Formation and Operation.*

**EARLE GARY GOODMAN,** born Los Angeles, California, May 21, 1943; admitted to bar, 1969, California and U.S. District Court, Central District of California; 1972, U.S. District Court, Northern District of California; 1979, U.S. Court of Appeals, 9th Circuit; 1980, U.S. Supreme Court. *Education:* University of California at Los Angeles (B.A., 1961; J.D., 1968). Phi Delta Phi. Deputy District Attorney, Los Angeles County, California, 1969-1970. Member, California Secretary of State's Liaison Committee on Uniform Commercial Code Affairs, 1974-1981. Member, Board of Governors, City of Hope, 1981— and Chair, 1996—. Member, Board of Directors, 1981-1996 and Executive Secretary, 1993-1995, Guardians of Jewish Homes for the Aged of Greater Los Angeles. Chairman, Legal Committee, Homes for Aged, 1983-1986. Member, Los Angeles Olympic Citizens Security Advisory Commission, 1982-1984. *Member:* Los Angeles County (Member, Sections on: Real Estate Law; Business and Corporation Law) and American (Member, Sections on: Corporation, Banking and Business Law; Real Property, Probate and Trust Law) Bar Associations; State Bar of California (Member, Sections on: Real Property Law; Corporation Law).

REPRESENTATIVE CLIENTS: Southridge Developments, Inc.; The Goodman Partnership I; Yankee Development, Inc.; Herman Properties; Conjunctive Points; Samitur Constructs.
REFERENCES: Bank of America, Westwood Village Office.

## GOODSON AND WACHTEL

A PROFESSIONAL CORPORATION

Established in 1973

10940 WILSHIRE BOULEVARD, SUITE 1400
**LOS ANGELES, CALIFORNIA 90024-3941**
Telephone: 310-208-8282
Facsimile: 310-208-8582

*Federal Income, Estate, Gift and International Taxation Law. Estate Planning, Business Transactions, Corporations, Partnerships, Non-Profits, ESOPs, ERISA, Real Estate, Securities, Trusts, Probate and Wills.*

**FIRM PROFILE:** *This firm practices law primarily in domestic and foreign tax planning and tax disputes for individuals, families, partnerships and closely held corporations, including estate planning, business transactions, trusts, wills, probate, ESOPS and retirement plans, civil and criminal tax controversies and securities law.*

**MARVIN GOODSON,** born Sacramento, California, November 6, 1918; admitted to bar, 1951, California; 1952, U.S. Tax Court; 1976, U.S. Supreme Court. *Education:* University of California at Berkeley (B.A., 1941); Loyola University of Los Angeles (J.D., cum laude, 1950). Certified Public Accountant, California, 1954. Lecturer: "Recapitalization as a Corporate Option" and "Alternative Techniques to Freezing Real Estate Values," Freezing Estate Taxes, University of Southern California College of Continuing Education, 1980; "The Process of Recapitalization," Freezing Estate Taxes, Georgetown University Law Center and University of California, Berkeley University Extension, 1981. Author: "Planning with Subchapter S in 1960," *12th Tax Institute,* Major Tax Planning, 1960; "Election to Tax Corporate Income to Shareholders," *11th Tax Institute,* Major Tax Planning; "When is a Payment in Discharge of Parent's Legal Obligation?" *11th Annual Tax Forum,* 1959, reprinted in *99 Trusts and Estates 17,* 1960;

*(This Listing Continued)*

## GOODSON AND WACHTEL, A PROFESSIONAL CORPORATION, Los Angeles—Continued

"Life Insurance Proceeds as Gifts in Contemplation of Death," *15th Annual Tax Forum,* 1963, reprinted in *103 Trusts and Estates 22,* 1965; "Tax Incentives for Natural Resources," *Tax Sheltered Investments,* Practising Law Institute, 1973; New York Law Journal: "Pitfalls in Agro-Business Tax Shelters," *Failing, Ailing and Aging Tax Shelters,* 1975; "Tax Problems and Advantages," *Employee Stock Ownership Trusts,* 1975 and 1976; *Drafting & Amending Defined Contribution Plans,* 1976; "Practical Estate Planning and Drafting of Wills and Trusts under the Tax Reform Act of 1976," *New Estate and Gift Tax Law,* 1977; "Tax Developments and Securities Law Aspects of ESOPS," *Securities Regulation—Corporate and Tax Aspects of Securities Transactions,* The Southwestern Legal Foundation, 1976; "Estate Planning—Where Do ESOTS Fit?" CLU Journal, 1976; California State University at Los Angeles; *4th Annual Institute on Taxation,* 1977; "ESOTS—Accentuating the Positive," *ESOP—Latest Developments and Techniques for Installing and Maintaining an ESOP,* 1977; "Private Medical Research Organizations: Long Term Research Funding Source for Non-Profit Hospitals"; Tax Management Estates, Gifts and Trust Journal, March-April 1995. *Member:* Beverly Hills (Member, Section on Taxation), Los Angeles County and American (Member, Section on Taxation) Bar Associations; State Bar of California (Member, Section on Taxation). (Certified Specialist, Taxation Law, The State Bar of California Board of Legal Specialization). **PRACTICE AREAS:** Tax; Estate Planning; Business Transaction Structuring; Corporate Transactions.

***EDWARD W. WACHTEL,*** born San Bernardino, California, February 10, 1948; admitted to bar, 1973, California; 1974, U.S. Tax Court and U.S. Claims Court. *Education:* University of California at Los Angeles and California State University at San Diego (B.S., in Accounting, 1970); University of San Diego (J.D., cum laude, 1973); New York University (LL.M., in Taxation, 1974). Managing Editor, University of San Diego Law Review, 1973. Law Clerk to Judge William A. Goffe, U.S. Tax Court, 1974-1976. Author/Lecturer: "The Expanded Use of ESOPs and ERTA 81: PAYSOPs, Flexible ERTA LESOPs and Re-emergence of the Prohibited Group String," Twelfth Annual Employee Benefits Institute, Practicing Law Institute, 1982; "The Corporate Recapitalization Process," California State University at Los Angeles, Eleventh Institute of Taxation and Ninth Estate Planning Institute, 1984; "Value Shifting: Maximizing or Avoiding Minority Discounts and the Corporate Recapitalization Process," California State University at Los Angeles, Eighth Annual Estate Planning Institute, 1983; "Updating Qualified Plans after TEFRA," California State University at Los Angeles, Seventh Annual Advanced Institute on Taxation, 1982; "ESOPs and ESOFs: Asset and Stock Acquisition Financing Techniques," California State University at Los Angeles, Eighth Annual Institute on Taxation, 1981; "Alternate Valuation Date for Estates," 61 American Bar Association Journal 1136, 1975; "David Meets Goliath in the Legislative Arena: A Losing Battle for an Equal Charitable Voice?" 9 San Diego Law Review 944, 1972. *Member:* Beverly Hills, Los Angeles County and American (Member, Sections on Taxation and Real Property, Probate and Trust Law, Committee on ERISA, 1985) Bar Associations; State Bar of California. **PRACTICE AREAS:** Tax Planning; Tax Controversies; Estate Planning; ERISA; Business Acquisitions and Dispositions; Corporate and Partnership Transactions.

***DAVID W. RILEY,*** born Los Angeles, California June 30, 1956; admitted to bar, 1982, California. *Education:* University of California at Los Angeles (B.A., magna cum laude, 1978); University of Southern California Law Center (J.D., 1982). Phi Beta Kappa. Certified Public Accountant California, 1985. *Member:* Los Angeles County Bar Association (Member, Section of Taxation); State Bar of California; California Society of Certified Public Accountants. **PRACTICE AREAS:** Tax; Business; Corporate; Partnership; Limited Liability Companies; Trust Transactions; Financial Restructuring; Income Tax Planning.

---

***LAURA K. FARRAND,*** born Nashville, Tennessee, September 26, 1948; admitted to bar, 1976, District of Columbia and U.S. District Court, District of Columbia; 1982, California. *Education:* Pomona College; University of Wisconsin-Madison (B.A., 1969); Georgetown University Law Center (J.D., 1975; Master of Laws in Taxation, 1981). Staff Member, 1973-1974 and Topics Editor, 1974-1975, Georgetown Law Review. Contributing Editor: "Practice under the 1984 California Revised Limited Partnership Act," The Rutter Group, 1984. Lecturer, Tax Aspects, CEB Seminar, "Fundamentals of Organizing and Advising California Businesses," May, 1984. Law Clerk to the Honorable Oliver Gasch, U.S. District Court for the District of Columbia, 1975-1976. *Member:* Beverly Hills, Santa Monica; Los Angeles County and American (Member, Section of Taxation) Bar Associations; The District of Columbia Bar; State Bar of California. **PRACTICE AREAS:** Tax; Estate Planning; Business Transaction.

### OF COUNSEL

***LUIS C. DE CASTRO,*** born Panama City, Republic of Panama, September 10, 1938; admitted to bar, 1965, California; 1979, District of Columbia. *Education:* University of California at Los Angeles (B.S., 1961); University of California School of Law (J.D., 1964). Order of the Coif; Phi Alpha Delta. Member, University of California at Los Angeles Law Review, 1962-1964. Co-author: "Can Buyers Payment of Assumed Debt Destroy Seller's Installment Election? Courts Disagree," The Journal of Taxation, September, 1966. Commissioner, Parks and Recreation, Santa Monica California, 1992-1994. *Member:* The State Bar of California; The District of Columbia Bar; American Bar Association. [With U.S. Army, 1957-1963]. (Also practicing individually at the same address). **LANGUAGES:** Spanish. **PRACTICE AREAS:** Tax Controversy and Litigation; Complex Business Litigation.

***LANCE JON KIMMEL,*** born New York, N.Y., December 7, 1954; admitted to bar, 1979, New York; 1985, California. *Education:* Franklin & Marshall College (A.B., cum laude with honors, 1975); New York University (J.D., 1978). Pi Gamma Mu. *Member:* Los Angeles County and American (Member, Section of Corporation, Banking and Business Law) Bar Associations; State Bar of California; New York State Bar Association. (Also practicing individually at same address).

REFERENCES: Union Bank (Beverly Hills Regional Head Office); Ansbacher Limited (Cayman, B.W.I.).

---

## GORDON, EDELSTEIN, KREPACK, GRANT, FELTON & GOLDSTEIN

A Partnership including a Professional Corporation

SUITE 1800, 3580 WILSHIRE BOULEVARD
**LOS ANGELES, CALIFORNIA 90010**
Telephone: 213-739-7000
Fax: 213-386-1671

*Personal Injury, Workers Compensation, Social Security, Products Liability and Insurance Bad Faith Law, Toxic Tort, Premises Liability, Construction, Wrongful Termination, Sexual Harassment, Professional Negligence.*

**FIRM PROFILE:** *The firm represents workers and individuals who have been seriously injured, both on and off the job. The firm focuses on protecting the legal rights of individuals who have suffered serious or catastrophic injuries resulting from product defects, automobile accidents, unsafe premises, construction accidents and medical and professional malpractice, as well as claims for insurance bad faith and civil rights violations such as discrimination. We also specialize in representing individuals who have been harmed in the workplace as a result of occupational illnesses or injuries, both physical and emotional, including injuries from exposure to toxic materials.*

*During more than 20 years in the practice of law, the firm has successfully represented clients in complex litigation at the local, state, federal and appellate level. In recognition of our dedication to the highest standards of professional excellence and personal ethics, GEKGF&G has been recognized by its peers with the highest rating from the premiere national directory of law firms.*

***ROGER L. GORDON,*** born Santa Monica, California, June 28, 1947; admitted to bar, 1972, California. *Education:* University of California at Los Angeles (B.A., 1969); Loyola University of Los Angeles (J.D., 1972). Speaker: "Recent Developments in Torts," C.E.B., 1993. *Member:* Los Angeles County and American Bar Associations; The State Bar of California; Los Angeles Trial Lawyers Association; California Trial Lawyers Association; The Association of Trial Lawyers of America. **PRACTICE AREAS:** Personal Injury Law; Products Liability Law; Insurance Bad Faith Law.

***MARK EDELSTEIN,*** born Scranton, Pennsylvania, March 5, 1945; admitted to bar, 1969, New Jersey; 1970, California. *Education:* State University of New York (B.A., with highest distinction, 1966); Rutgers University (J.D., 1969). Beta Gamma Sigma. Co-Author: *The California Workers' Compensation Rehabilitation System,* published by McWilliam and Co., 1981. Lecturer, Workers' Compensation Law, California Continuing Education of the Bar, 1981-1985. *Member:* Los Angeles County and American Bar Associations; The State Bar of California; California Applicant's Attorney's Association (President, 1984-1985; Legislative Chairman, 1985-1986); Southern California Applicant's Attorney's Association (President, 1981-

*(This Listing Continued)*

1982). (Certified Specialist, Workers Compensation Law, The State Bar of California Board of Legal Specialization). *PRACTICE AREAS:* Workers Compensation Law; Social Security Law.

**HOWARD D. KREPACK,** born Santa Monica, California, April 30, 1948; admitted to bar, 1974, California. *Education:* University of California at Los Angeles (A.B., 1969); University of California School of Law at Los Angeles (J.D., 1972). Judge Pro Tem, Small Claims Appeals Court, 1989-1990. Member, Panel of Arbitration, Los Angeles Superior Court, 1993. *Member:* Los Angeles County Bar Association; The State Bar of California; American Bar Association; Los Angeles Trial Lawyers Association; California Trial Lawyers Association; The Association of Trial Lawyers of America. *PRACTICE AREAS:* Personal Injury Law; Products Liability Law; Insurance Bad Faith Law; Professional Negligence.

**SHERRY E. GRANT,** born Miami, Florida, November 2, 1948; admitted to bar, 1974, California. *Education:* Boston University (B.A., 1969); Loyola University of Los Angeles (J.D., 1974). Adjunct Professor, Southwestern University School of Law, 1979-1984, 1989-1990. Judge Pro Tem, Workers Compensation Appeals Board, 1983—. *Member:* State Bar of California; American Bar Association; California Applicant's Attorney's Association (Education Chairperson, 1982-1984; Member, Board of Governors, 1982—); Southern California Applicant's Attorneys Association (President, 1986-1987). (Certified Specialist, Workers Compensation Law, The State Bar of California Board of Legal Specialization). *PRACTICE AREAS:* Workers Compensation Law; Social Security Law; Third Party Litigation.

**RICHARD I. FELTON,** born Los Angeles, California, June 27, 1951; admitted to bar, 1976, California. *Education:* University of California at Los Angeles (B.A., 1973); Golden Gate University (J.D., 1976). Adjunct Professor, Southwestern University School of Law, 1984-1987. Judge Pro Tem, Workers' Compensation Appeals Board, 1983—. *Member:* Los Angeles County Bar Association (Chairperson, Workers' Compensation Section, 1990-1991); State Bar of California; California Applicants' Attorneys Association (Board of Governors, 1985—); Southern California Applicants Attorneys Association (President, 1989-1990). (Certified Specialist, Workers Compensation Law, The State Bar of California Board of Legal Specialization). *LANGUAGES:* Spanish. *PRACTICE AREAS:* Workers Compensation Law; Social Security Law.

**IRWIN L. GOLDSTEIN, (A PROFESSIONAL CORPORATION),** born Detroit, Michigan, February 5, 1939; admitted to bar, 1964, California. *Education:* Wayne State University (B.A., 1960); University of Southern California (LL.B., 1963). *PRACTICE AREAS:* Workers Compensation Law; Social Security Law.

**STEVEN J. KLEIFIELD,** born Chicago, Illinois, September 3, 1953; admitted to bar, 1980, California and U.S. District Court, Central District of California; 1989, U.S. Court of Appeals, Ninth Circuit and U.S. District Court, Eastern District of California; 1992, U.S. Supreme Court. *Education:* Washington University (A.B., 1975); George Washington University, National Law Center (J.D., 1979). Phi Beta Kappa. Speaker: "Privileges, Privacy and Confidentiality," CTLA Annual Tahoe Seminar, 1985; "Arbitration Award and Trial De Novo," LATLA Las Vegas Seminar, 1990; "Designating Experts - Avoiding The Traps," LATLA Las Vegas Seminar, 1991; "Choice and Timing of Witness Testimony," LATLA Las Vegas Seminar, 1992; " Discovery Privileges and Protections," LATLA MCLE Fair, 1993; "Appellate Practice and the Pitfalls of Appellate Procedure," LATLA Las Vegas Seminar, 1993; "Depositions of Non-Party Witnesses: Who, When and How," LATLA Discovery Seminar, 1993. Co-Chair: 1991 LATLA Las Vegas Seminar, 1992 LATLA Jury Instruction Seminar, 1993 LATLA Travel Seminar; Moderator: LATLA Annual Seminar for Paralegals and Legal Secretaries, 1989 and 1990. Co-Editor: LATLA Jury Instruction Book, 1992. Author: Techniques to Avoid Removal to Federal Court Based on *Pilot Life* and *Metropolitan Life,"* The Advocate, July-August 1987; " Proving Defendant's Financial Condition in a Punitive Damages Case," The Advocate, November 1993. Arbitrator, Los Angeles Superior Court Arbitration Panel, 1985—. Settlement Officer, Los Angeles Superior, Northwest District, 1992—. *Member:* Los Angeles Trial Lawyers Association (Board of Governors, 1992—); California Trial Lawyers Association; Association of Trial Lawyers of America. *PRACTICE AREAS:* Major Personal Injury Litigation; Insurance Bad Faith; Products Liability; Professional Negligence; Government Liability; Premises Liability.

*ASSOCIATES*

**JOSHUA M. MERLISS,** born Los Angeles, California, May 7, 1951; admitted to bar, 1977, California. *Education:* University of California at Berkeley (B.A., 1973); Loyola University of Los Angeles (J.D., 1976); University of Florida (LL.M., 1983). *Member:* Los Angeles County Bar Association; State Bar of California; Los Angeles Trial Lawyers Association.

*(This Listing Continued)*

*PRACTICE AREAS:* Personal Injury Law; Products Liability Law; Insurance Bad Faith Law.

**DAVID A. GOLDSTEIN,** born Michigan, August 31, 1957; admitted to bar, 1985, California, U.S. District Court, Central, Northern and Southern Districts of California and U.S. Court of Appeals, Ninth Circuit. *Education:* Northridge State University; San Francisco State University; University of West Los Angeles (B.S.L., 1985; J.D., 1985). *Member:* Los Angeles County and American Bar Associations; State Bar of California; California Applicants Attorney Association; Southern California Applicants Attorney Association; Association of Trial Lawyers of America; American Immigration Lawyers Association. *PRACTICE AREAS:* Workers Compensation Law; Social Security Law.

**EUGENIA L. STEELE,** born California, March 30, 1965; admitted to bar, 1990, California; 1991, U.S. District Court, Central District of California. *Education:* Loyola Marymount University (B.A., 1987); Southwestern University School of Law (J.D., 1990). *Member:* Los Angeles County and American (Litigation Section) Bar Associations; Los Angeles Trial Lawyers Association; California Trial Lawyers Association. *PRACTICE AREAS:* Personal Injury Law; Products Liability Law; Insurance Bad Faith Law.

---

## GORRY & MEYER L.L.P.

*2029 CENTURY PARK EAST*
*SUITE 480*
**LOS ANGELES, CALIFORNIA 90067**
*Telephone: 310-277-5967*
*Facsimile: 310-277-1470*
*URL: http://www.gorrymeyer.com*

Business Litigation, Commercial, Corporate, Real Estate and Entertainment.

**TIMOTHY J. GORRY,** born San Jose, California, June 9, 1963; admitted to bar, 1989, California; 1990, U.S. District Court, Central and Northern Districts of California and U.S. Court of Appeals, Ninth Circuit. *Education:* University of California at Los Angeles (B.A., 1986); Hastings College of the Law, University of California (J.D., 1989). *Member:* Los Angeles County and American Bar Associations. *PRACTICE AREAS:* Business; Entertainment; Commercial Litigation.

**DAVID C. MEYER,** born Rochester, New York, May 27, 1962; admitted to bar, 1989, California. *Education:* University of California at Berkeley (B.A., 1984); University of Southern California (J.D., 1988). *Member:* Los Angeles County Bar Association. *PRACTICE AREAS:* Corporate Law; Entertainment and the Arts; Real Property.

*ASSOCIATE*

**BRYAN WILSON JARDINE,** born Columbus, Ohio, May 12, 1962; admitted to bar, 1990, California. *Education:* Georgetown University (B.S., 1984); University of California at Los Angeles (J.D., 1990). *LANGUAGES:* Spanish. *PRACTICE AREAS:* Commercial; Real Estate; Insurance Bad Faith; Entertainment; Construction Litigation.

**FRANK SANDELMANN,** born Offenbach, Germany, September 25, 1964; admitted to bar, 1996, California. *Education:* University of California at Los Angeles (B.A., 1987); Boston University School of Law (J.D., 1996). *Member:* Los Angeles County Bar Association. *LANGUAGES:* German. *PRACTICE AREAS:* Commercial Litigation.

---

## FREDERICK GOTHA

**LOS ANGELES, CALIFORNIA**

(See Pasadena)

Patent, Trademark and Unfair Competition Law.

---

## GOULD-SALTMAN LAW OFFICES, LLP

*4727 WILSHIRE BOULEVARD, SUITE 500*
**LOS ANGELES, CALIFORNIA 90010**
*Telephone: 213-939-8400*
*Fax: 213-939-8405*
*Email: dgsaltman@aol.com*

Family Law, Domestic Partnerships, Mediation and Litigation.

*(This Listing Continued)*

## GOULD-SALTMAN LAW OFFICES, LLP, Los Angeles—Continued

*DIANNA J. GOULD-SALTMAN,* born 1958; admitted to bar, 1985, California; 1986, U.S. District Court, Central District of California and U.S. Court of Appeals, Ninth Circuit. *Education:* University of California, Irvine (B.A., 1979); Southwestern University School of Law (J.D., 1985). Author: "Domestic Partnership Agreements and the Gay or Lesbian Couple," Family Law News and Review, Fall 1990; "Ethical Considerations in Representing Gays and Lesbians in Child Custody Cases," Family Law News, Spring 1993; "In Re Marriage of Burgess - Moving Away With the Children," Solo Newsletter, May 1996. *Member:* Fellow, American Academy of Matrimonial Lawyers. (Certified Specialist, Family Law, The State Bar of California Board of Legal Specialization).

*RICHARD F. GOULD-SALTMAN,* born 1954; admitted to bar, 1978, California; 1980, U.S. District Court, Central District of California. *Education:* Ohio State University (B.A., 1975); University of Southern California (J.D., 1978). Author: "The Changing Role of the Family Law Attorney as Advocate Entrepreneur Party," Family Law News, 1981. Instructor, Fiduciary Duty Legislation in Family Law, State Bar Section Education Institute, Fall 1996. *Member:* State Bar of California (Member, Property and Child Custody Committees, 1992—). (Certified Specialist, Family Law, The State Bar of California Board of Legal Specialization).

---

## STEVEN GOURLEY

11355 WEST OLYMPIC BOULEVARD
SUITE 100
**LOS ANGELES, CALIFORNIA 90064**
Telephone: 310-478-1524
Fax: 310-312-4224

*Business Litigation Securities and Mortgage Lending Law.*

**FIRM PROFILE:** *The firm concentrates in mortgage lending and general business litigation. In addition, the firm practices extensively before the California Department of Corporations and the California Department of Real Estate. The firm prides itself on offering personalized knowledgeable attention to its clients.*

*STEVEN GOURLEY,* born 1949; admitted to bar, 1973, California. *Education:* University of California at Los Angeles (B.A., cum laude, 1970) Phi Beta Kappa; Boalt Hall School of Law, University of California (J.D., 1973). Trial Attorney, United States Securities and Exchange Commission, 1973-1977. Chief Deputy Commissioner of Corporations, State of California, 1980-1983. City Councilman, 1988—, and Mayor, 1990-1991 and 1995-1996, Culver City. Member, 1988—, and Chairman, 1991-1992, Culver City Redevelopment Agency. *Member:* State Bar of California. **LANGUAGES:** Spanish. **PRACTICE AREAS:** Securities Law; Real Estate Lending Law; Mortgage Lending Law.

REPRESENTATIVE CLIENTS: First Alliance Mortgage Company; First National Mortgage Company; Home Budget Loans; EquiCredit Corporation of America (Old Stone Credit Corporation); Royal Thrift & Loan Company.

---

## GRACE, SKOCYPEC, COSGROVE & SCHIRM

A PROFESSIONAL CORPORATION
*Established in 1976*

444 SOUTH FLOWER STREET, SUITE 1100
**LOS ANGELES, CALIFORNIA 90071**
Telephone: 213-487-6660
Fax: 213-487-4896

*San Diego, California Office:* First National Bank Building, 401 West A Street, Suite 1815. Telephone: 619-234-6660. Telecopier: 619-234-2721.

*General Civil Practice in all California and Federal Trial and Appellate Courts. Product Liability, Insurance "Bad Faith", Insurance Coverage, Toxic Tort, Environmental, Labor Relations and Professional Malpractice Law.*

*EUGENE R. GRACE,* born Van Nuys, California, September 24, 1929; admitted to bar, 1962, California; U.S. District Court, Central, Southern, Eastern and Northern Districts of California; U.S. Court of Appeals, Ninth Circuit; U.S. Supreme Court. *Education:* Los Angeles State College of Applied Arts and Sciences (B.S., 1957); Southwestern University, California (J.D., 1961). Arbitrator, Los Angeles Superior Court Arbitration Panel, *(This Listing Continued)*

1976—. *Member:* Glendale and Los Angeles County Bar Associations; The State Bar of California; Product Liability Advisory Council; Defense Research Institute; NTSB Bar Association; Diplomate, American Board of Trial Advocates; Association of Southern California Defense Counsel; Lawyer-Pilot Bar Association. **PRACTICE AREAS:** Product Liability Law; Insurance Coverage Law (including Environmental); Insurance Defense Law; Professional Liability Law; Appellate Law; Professional (legal) Liability Defense.

*RONALD J. SKOCYPEC,* born Elizabeth, New Jersey, November 1, 1946; admitted to bar, 1976, California; U.S. District Court, Central, Southern, Eastern and Northern Districts of California; U.S. Court of Appeals, Ninth Circuit; U.S. Supreme Court. *Education:* Rutgers University (B.S., magna cum laude, 1968); University of California at Berkeley (M.S., 1970); University of California at Los Angeles (J.D., 1976). Tau Beta Pi. Phi Lambda Upsilon. Editor, UCLA-Alaska Law Review, 1975-1976. Professional Chemical Engineer, California, 1977. Author: Comment, "The 1973 IMCO Convention: Tightening the Controls on Operational Oil Pollution From Tankers," 5 UCLA-Alaska Law Review, 1976. *Member:* The State Bar of California; Los Angeles County Bar Association; Wilshire Bar Association; American Institute of Chemical Engineers; Association of Southern California Defense Counsel; Defense Research Institute. **PRACTICE AREAS:** Insurance Coverage and Bad Faith Law (including Environmental); Professional Liability Law; Appellate Law; Insurance Defense Law; Product Liability Law.

*PHILIP R. COSGROVE,* born Somerville, New Jersey, January 18, 1954; admitted to bar, 1980, California; U.S. District Court, Central, Southern, Eastern and Northern Districts of California; U.S. Court of Appeals, Ninth Circuit; U.S. Supreme Court. *Education:* Rutgers University (B.A., 1977); Loyola Marymount University of Los Angeles (J.D., cum laude, 1979). Member, Saint Thomas More Law Society. Staff Member, 1978-1979 and Business and Managing Editor, 1979-1980, Loyola of Los Angeles International and Comparative Law Annual. Arbitrator, Los Angeles Superior Court Arbitration Panel. *Member:* Wilshire (Board of Governors, 1987-1989), Los Angeles County, Federal and American Bar Associations; State Bar of California; Association of Southern California Defense Counsel; Defense Research Institute; Product Liability Advisory Council; Society of Automotive Engineers. **PRACTICE AREAS:** Product Liability Law; Insurance Coverage Law and Bad Faith Law (including Environmental); Insurance Defense Law; Professional Liability Law; Appellate Law.

*BARRY R. SCHIRM,* born Pasadena, California, October 7, 1955; admitted to bar, 1980, California; U.S. District Court, Central, Southern, Eastern and Northern Districts of California; U.S. Court of Appeals, Ninth Circuit; U.S. Supreme Court. *Education:* California State University at Fullerton (B.A., 1977); Southwestern University (J.D., 1980). Delta Theta Phi. *Member:* State Bar of California; Association of Southern California Defense Counsel; Defense Research Institute; Product Liability Advisory Council; Society of Automotive Engineers; Steering Committee-Citizens Against Lawsuit Abuse (CALA). **PRACTICE AREAS:** Product Liability Law; Insurance Coverage Law; Insurance Defense Law; Professional Liability Law; Appellate Law.

*SUSAN TANDY OLSON,* born Lynwood, California, June 12, 1948; admitted to bar, 1983, California; U.S. District Court, Central, Southern, Eastern and Northern Districts of California; U.S. Court of Appeals, Ninth Circuit. *Education:* California State University at Northridge (B.A., 1969; M.A., 1977); University of California at Los Angeles (J.D., 1983). *Member:* Los Angeles County and American Bar Associations; State Bar of California; Defense Research Institute. **PRACTICE AREAS:** Insurance Coverage and Bad Faith Law (including Environmental); Professional Liability; Appellate Law; Insurance; Product Liability Law.

*RALPH J. SCALZO,* born Newton, New Jersey, July 25, 1935; admitted to bar, 1967, California; 1979, U.S. Supreme Court; U.S. Court of Appeals, Ninth Circuit; U.S. Court of Appeals for the District of Columbia Circuit; U.S. District Court, Central, Eastern, Northern and Southern Districts of California. *Education:* Lehigh University (B.S.I.E., 1959; B.A., 1959); University of Southern California (J.D., 1966). Tau Beta Pi; Phi Alpha Delta. Law Lecturer, University of West Los Angeles School of Law, 1968. Board of Trustees, Mayfield Senior School, 1987—. *Member:* Los Angeles County and American (Member, Business Law and Litigation Sections) Bar Associations; The State Bar of California (Member, Section of Labor and Employment Law). **PRACTICE AREAS:** Employment Law; Labor Law; Litigation.

*DANIEL L. GARDNER,* born Long Beach, California, October 15, 1948; admitted to bar, 1974, California; U.S. District Court, Northern, Central and Southern Districts of California; U.S. Court of Appeals, Ninth *(This Listing Continued)*

Circuit. *Education:* University of California at Irvine (B.A., cum laude, 1970); Hastings College of Law, University of California (J.D., 1974). Phi Delta Phi. *Member:* Century City and Los Angeles County Bar Associations; State Bar of California; Defense Research Institute. **PRACTICE AREAS:** Insurance Defense Law (Casualty and First Party); Product Liability Law; Insurance Coverage and Bad Faith Law; Professional Liability Law.

**DONALD D. WILSON,** born Pasadena, California, 1945; admitted to bar, 1971, California; U.S. District Court, Central District of California. *Education:* University of California at Santa Barbara (B.A., 1966); ; University of California at Los Angeles (J.D., 1970). Judge, Pro-Tem, Los Angeles Municipal Court, 1980—. Appointed Arbitrator, Los Angeles Superior Court. Publisher, *The California Legal Update. Member:* Pasadena and Los Angeles County Bar Associations; State Bar of California; Lawyer/Pilots Bar Association; Association of Southern California Defense Counsel; California Trial Lawyers Association. **PRACTICE AREAS:** Automobile and Premises Liability; Complex Litigation; Product Liability; Medical Malpractice; Construction Claims; Architects/Engineers; Toxic Torts.

**DEREK S. WHITEFIELD,** born Wyandotte, Michigan, October 22, 1960; admitted to bar, 1985, Michigan, U.S. District Court, Eastern District of Michigan and U.S. Court of Appeals, Sixth Circuit; 1993, California, U.S. District Court, Central District of California and U.S. Court of Appeals, Ninth Circuit. *Education:* Michigan State University (B.A., 1982) Phi Beta Kappa; Wayne State University (J.D., cum laude, 1985). Member, Detroit Barrister Board of Directors, 1987-1991, Barrister of the Year 1990-1991. Member, Legal Staff, General Motors, Detroit, Michigan, 1988-1993. *Member:* State Bar of Michigan; State Bar of California; American Bar Association. **PRACTICE AREAS:** Product Liability Law; Insurance Coverage Law; Insurance Defence Law; Appellate Law.

**PATRICIA M. COLEMAN,** born Chicago, Illinois, September 11, 1946; admitted to bar, 1982, California, U.S. District Court, Central, Northern, Southern and Eastern Districts of California and U.S. Court of Appeals, Ninth Circuit. *Education:* University of California at Los Angeles (B.A., 1968); Loyola Marymount University (J.D., 1981). Arbitrator, Los Angeles Superior Court. *Member:* Los Angeles County Bar Association; State Bar of California. **PRACTICE AREAS:** Insurance Defense Law; Product Liability Law; Construction Defect Law.

*OF COUNSEL*

**GREG W. MARSH,** born Los Angeles, California, February 26, 1959; admitted to bar, 1981, California, Nevada, U.S. District Court, District of Nevada and U.S. Court of Appeals, Ninth Circuit. *Education:* Loyola Marymount University (B.B.A., cum laude, 1978); Southwestern University School of Law (J.D., 1980). Former Member: Association of Defense Trial Attorneys; National Trial Lawyers Association; National Management Association. Former President, Twain Manor Homeowners Association. Former Partner, Oshins, Gibbons & Marsh. Former Fully Vested Partner, 1983-1992 and Member, Board of Directors, 1991-1992, Beckley, Singleton, DeLanoy & Jemison Chtd., Law Firm, Las Vegas, Nevada. *Member:* Clark County and American Bar Associations; State Bar of California; State Bar of Nevada. (Also Member, Law Offices of Greg W. Marsh, Chartered, Las Vegas, Nevada). **PRACTICE AREAS:** General Civil Litigation Defense; Product Liability Law; Public Utility Defense Litigation; Drug Law; Premises Liability Defense; Medical Malpractice Defense; Insurance Defense; Political Subdivision Defense; Appellate Law.

---

**ROD J. CAPPY,** born Detroit, Michigan, May 20, 1963; admitted to bar, 1988, California; 1993, Nevada; U.S. District Court, Central, Southern, Eastern and Northern Districts of California; U.S. District Court, District of Nevada. *Education:* Florida State University (B.S., cum laude, 1985); Emory University (J.D., 1988). Member, Moot Court Society. *Member:* Los Angeles County Bar Association; State Bar of California. **PRACTICE AREAS:** Product Liability Law; Insurance Defense Law; Appellate Law.

**THOMAS H. HUTCHINSON,** born Greenville, Mississippi, April 1, 1954; admitted to bar, 1986, California; U.S. District Court, Central, Eastern, Northern and Southern Districts of California. *Education:* California State University of Dominguez Hills (B.A., magna cum laude, 1979); Loyola Marymount University (J.D., 1986). *Member:* State Bar of California. **PRACTICE AREAS:** Insurance Defense Law; Product Liability Law.

**JEFFREY A. LEWISTON,** born Ann Arbor, Michigan, June 5, 1959; admitted to bar, 1986, California; 1987, Michigan; U.S. District Court, Central, Southern, Eastern and Northern Districts of California and U.S. Court of Appeals, Ninth Circuit. *Education:* Albion College (B.A., 1981); University of San Diego (J.D., 1985). *Member:* Los Angeles County and American Bar Associations; State Bar of California; State Bar of Michigan; Defense Research Institute. **PRACTICE AREAS:** Insurance Coverage Law; Insurance Defense Law; Product Liability Law; Appellate Law.

**DOMMOND E. LONNIE,** born Los Angeles, California, September 2, 1964; admitted to bar, 1989, California, U.S. Court of Appeals, Ninth Circuit and U.S. District Court, Central District of California. *Education:* University of California at Los Angeles (B.A., 1986; J.D., 1989). *Member:* Wilshire and Los Angeles County Bar Associations; State Bar of California; Defense Research Institute. **PRACTICE AREAS:** Product Liability Law; Insurance Defense Law; Appellate Law.

**DAVID KEITH SCHULTZ,** born Long Beach, California, November 29, 1965; admitted to bar, 1990, California; U.S. District Court, Central, Eastern, Southern and Northern Districts; U.S. Court of Appeals, Ninth Circuit of California. *Education:* University of California at Los Angeles (B.A. in History, 1987); Loyola Law School (J.D. with honors, 1990). Recipient of American Jurisprudence Award in Trial Advocacy. Loyola Academic Scholarship 1988-1989. *Member:* Los Angeles County and American Bar Associations; State Bar of California. **PRACTICE AREAS:** Insurance Defense Law; Product Liability Law; Insurance Coverage Law; Professional Liability Law; Appellate Law.

**LISA M. KRALIK,** born Wahoo, Nebraska, March 10, 1965; admitted to bar, 1990, California; 1991, U.S. District Court, Central, Southern, Eastern and Northern Districts of California and U.S. Court of Appeals, Ninth Circuit. *Education:* Creighton University (B.A., 1987; J.D., 1990). Recipient, American Jurisprudence Awards in Federal Courts and Criminal Law. Creighton Law Review, Jessup International Moot Court Team. Domestic Moot Court Board. Best Oralist, Domestic Moot Court Competition. ABA Appellate Advocacy Team; Regional Champion and National Runner-up, 1990 ABA Appellate Advocacy Competition. *Member:* Los Angeles County and American Bar Associations; State Bar of California. **PRACTICE AREAS:** Appellate Law; Insurance Coverage Law; Insurance Bad Faith.

**SCOTT W. MCEWEN,** born Saskatoon, Saskatchewan, Canada, September 23, 1961; admitted to bar, 1987, California and U.S. District Court, Central District of California; U.S. District Court, Southern District of California. *Education:* Oregon State University (B.S., with honors, 1983); University of London, England; McGeorge School of Law, University of the Pacific (J.D., with honors, 1987). Phi Eta Sigma; Alpha Lambda Delta. Best Brief Finalist, International Moot Court. Member: International Law Society; Traynor Honor Society. *Member:* San Diego County, Los Angeles County and American Bar Associations; State Bar of California. (Resident, San Diego Office). **LANGUAGES:** Spanish. **PRACTICE AREAS:** Real Estate Litigation; Business Litigation; International Law; Product Liability Law.

**RANDY L. REZEN,** born Cooperstown, New York, November 13, 1955; admitted to bar, 1980, California; U.S. District Court, Central District of California; U.S. District Court, Northern District of California. *Education:* State University of New York at Albany (B.A., cum laude, 1977); State University of New York at Buffalo (J.D., 1980). Editor, Buffalo Law Review, 1978-1980. *Member:* Los Angeles County Bar Association (Section: Environmental Law); State Bar of California. **PRACTICE AREAS:** Insurance Coverage; Environmental; Real Estate Litigation.

**TERENCE M. KELLY,** born Washington, 1944; admitted to bar, 1979, California; U.S. District Court, Central District of California. *Education:* University of California at Los Angeles (B.A., 1967); Whittier College School of Law (J.D., 1978). Arbitrator, Pasadena Superior Court. *Member:* Pasadena and Los Angeles County Bar Associations; State Bar of California. **PRACTICE AREAS:** Medical Malpractice; Product Liability; Construction; Environmental; Insurance Defense Law.

**CARL E. LOVELL, III,** born Laramie, Wyoming, August 29, 1967; admitted to bar, 1992, California; U.S. District Court, Central, Northern, Southern and Eastern Districts of California; U.S. Court of Appeals, Ninth Circuit. *Education:* Pomona College (B.A., 1989); McGeorge School of Law, University of the Pacific (J.D., 1992). *Member:* Los Angeles County Bar Association; State Bar of California. **PRACTICE AREAS:** Insurance Defense Law; Product Liability Law; Insurance Bad Faith Law; Labor Law; Appellate Law.

**ROBIN JAMES,** born Hornell, New York, April 13, 1949; admitted to bar, 1990, California. *Education:* University of California at Santa Cruz (B.A., 1971); Loyola Law School (J.D., 1990). Phi Delta Phi; Order of the Coif. Member, St. Thomas More Law Honor Society. Loyola of Los Angeles Law Review Staff Member, 1988-1989 and Note and Comment Editor, 1989-1990. Author: Comment, "Res Judicata: Should California Aban-

*(This Listing Continued)*

## GRACE, SKOCYPEC, COSGROVE & SCHIRM, A PROFESSIONAL CORPORATION, Los Angeles—Continued

don Primary Rights?" 23 Loyola of Los Angeles Law Review 351 1989. *Member:* Los Angeles County and American Bar Associations; State Bar of California; California Women Lawyers. *PRACTICE AREAS:* Insurance Coverage; Insurance Bad Faith; General Litigation.

**ALEX W. CRAIGIE,** born Hollywood, California, September 19, 1966; admitted to bar, 1993, California and U.S. District Court, Central, Northern and Southern Districts of California. *Education:* University of California, San Diego (B.A., honors with high distinction, 1990); Loyola Law School (J.D., 1993). Member, Loyola of Los Angeles Law Review, 1992-1993. Author: "Burial of the Tort: The California Supreme Court's Treatment of Tortious Mishandling of Remains in *Christensen v. Superior Court*," 26 Loyola of Los Angeles Law Review 909. *Member:* Los Angeles County Bar Association (Member, Litigation Section); Association of Southern California Defense Counsel; Defense Research Institute. *PRACTICE AREAS:* Product Liability; Construction Defect Litigation; Insurance Coverage; Insurance Bad Faith.

**KURT A. SCHLICHTER,** born Cincinnati, Ohio, December 24, 1964; admitted to bar, 1994, California. *Education:* University of California, San Diego (B.A., 1987); Loyola University of Los Angeles (J.D., 1994). Author, Comment, 26 Loyola Law Review, 1290 (1993). *Member:* State Bar of California. [U.S. Army, 1987-1991 (Persian Gulf), Capt., Infantry, California Army National Guard, 1992—]. *PRACTICE AREAS:* Products Liability; Consumer Warranty; Insurance; Labor; Business Litigation.

**SUSAN K. ANDERSEN,** born Coon Rapids, Minnesota, June 29, 1965; admitted to bar, 1990, California. *Education:* University of Minnesota, Duluth (B.A., 1987); Hamline University and Southwestern University School of Law (J.D., 1990). *Member:* State Bar of California (Member, Litigation Committee); American Bar Association. *PRACTICE AREAS:* Products Liability Law.

**JOSEPH P. AUGUSTINE,** born Kenmore, New York, March 17, 1966; admitted to bar, 1993, New York; 1994, U.S. District Court, Eastern and Southern Districts of New York; 1996, California, U.S. District Court, Northern, Eastern, Central and Southern Districts of California and U.S. Court of Appeals, Ninth Circuit. *Education:* Syracuse University (B.S., Finance, cum laude, 1988; J.D., cum laude, 1992). Member, Moot Court Board. Member, Justinian Society. Law Clerk to Hon. H.G. Munson, Sr. Justice, U.S. District Court, Northern District of New York, Syracuse, N.Y., 1991. Appointed Assistant Corporation Counsel, Office of the Corporation Counsel, City of New York, 1992-1995. *Member:* New York State and American Bar Associations; State Bar of California. *LANGUAGES:* Spanish. *PRACTICE AREAS:* Insurance Coverage; Environmental; Products Liability; Employment Law; Sexual Harassment; Insurance Defense; General Practice.

**ILYA A. KOSTENBOYM,** born Moscow, Russia, March 5, 1968; admitted to bar, 1994, California and U.S. District Court, Central District of California. *Education:* University of California, Los Angeles (B.A., 1990); Pepperdine University (J.D., 1994). *Member:* State Bar of California. *PRACTICE AREAS:* Insurance Defense Law; Construction Defects Litigation; Personal Injury Defense Law.

REPRESENTATIVE CLIENTS: Acceleration National Insurance Company; Access America; Albertsons, Inc.; Allstate Insurance Company; American Honda Motor Co., Inc.; American Stores Company; Argonaut Insurance Company; Arrow Dynamics, Inc.; Ashland Oil, Inc.; Associated Aviation Underwriters; Atlas Insurance Company; Chrysler Corporation; Continental Insurance; Employers Reinsurance Corporation; Forresters Indemnity Company; General Motors Corporation; Golden Bear Insurance; Harvest States Cooperatives; Honda North America, Inc.; J. B. Hunt; Isuzu Motors America, Inc.; Keiper-Recaro; Liberty Mutual Insurance Company; Lucky Stores, Inc.; Motors Insurance Company; Mr. Coffee; MSI Insurance Company; NAPA; National General Insurance Company; Nissan North America Inc.; Ohio Casualty; Oryx Energy Company; Ott Industries; Ralph's Grocery Company; Reliance Insurance Company; Resolution Trust Corporation; Royal Insurance Company; SDG&E; Sherwood, Division of Harsco Corporation; Smith's Food & Drug Centers, Inc.; Star Insurance; State Farm Fire & Casualty Company; State Farm Mutual Automobile Insurance Company; State of Maryland; Sweetheart; Tecumseh Products Company; Thrifty, Inc.; The Toro Company; TRW, Inc.; Travelers Insurance Company; Web Service Company.

## GRADSTEIN, LUSKIN & VAN DALSEM
12100 WILSHIRE BOULEVARD, SUITE 350
LOS ANGELES, CALIFORNIA 90025
Telephone: 310-571-1700
Fax: 310-571-1717

*Civil, Trial and Appellate Practice, in all State and Federal Courts, Specializing in Entertainment and Business Litigation.*

**HENRY D. GRADSTEIN,** born Flushing, New York, February 6, 1956; admitted to bar, 1979, California; U.S. Court of Appeals, Ninth Circuit; U.S. District Court, Central District of California. *Education:* University of South Florida (B.A., cum laude, 1976); University of Southern California (J.D., 1979). Member, University of Southern California Law Review, 1977-1979. Extern to Justice Arthur Alarcon, California Court of Appeals, Second Appellate District. Winner, Irvine Company Scholarship for Urban Planning and Environmental Law. *Member:* Beverly Hills Bar Association; State Bar of California; California Trial Lawyers Association; The Association of Trial Lawyers of America.

**DONNA LUSKIN GRADSTEIN,** born Baltimore, Maryland, December 18, 1956; admitted to bar, 1980, Florida; 1981, New York; 1988, California and U.S. District Court, Central, Eastern and Northern Districts of California. *Education:* University of Iowa (B.A., cum laude, 1977); University of Baltimore (J.D., 1979). *Member:* The Florida Bar; State Bar of California; American Bar Association.

**BRUCE E. VAN DALSEM,** born Palo Alto, California, March 26, 1961; admitted to bar, 1986, California, U.S. Court of Appeals, Ninth Circuit and U.S. District Court, Eastern District of California; 1988, U.S. District Court, Central and Northern Districts of California. *Education:* Charles E. Dederich School of Law (LL.B., 1986). Author: "Lien Claims in The '90's," LATLA, 1994. Arbitrator, Los Angeles County Superior Court. *Member:* Beverly Hills and Los Angeles County Bar Associations; State Bar of California. **Email:** BruceVD@aol.com

**JOEL M. KOZBERG,** born January 16, 1952; admitted to bar, 1979, California, U.S. Court of Appeals, Ninth Circuit, U.S. District Court, Central, Southern, Northern and Eastern Districts of California. *Education:* University of California at Berkeley (A.B., 1974); University of California at Los Angeles (M.B.A., 1976); University of Southern California (J.D., 1979). Judicial Extern to the Hon. David W. Williams, U.S. District Court, Central District of California, 1978. *Member:* State Bar of California.

**R. DAVID SMITH,** born New York, N.Y., December 16, 1950; admitted to bar, 1979, California. *Education:* University of California at Berkeley (A.B., 1976); University of Southern California (J.D., 1979). Order of the Coif. Member, Southern California Law Review, 1977-1979. Judicial Extern to the Hon. Irving Hill, U.S. District Court, Central District of California, 1978. Author: "Rohauer v. Killiam Shows, Inc. and the Derivative Work Exception to the Termination Right," 52 Southern California Law Review 635, 1979. Member of Faculty, American Film Institute Center for Advanced Film Studies, Los Angeles, 1985-1989. Member, USC Entertainment Law Institute Planning Committee, 1987-1994. *Member:* The State Bar of California.

## GRADY & GRADY
654 NORTH SEPULVEDA BOULEVARD
SUITE TWELVE
LOS ANGELES, CALIFORNIA 90049
Telephone: 310-476-5773
Fax: 310-471-1055

*Corporate Law, Business and Transactional Law, Employment Law, Wrongful Discharge/Discrimination, Real Property Litigation, including Land Use, Property Insurance, Fire Insurance, Homeowners Insurance, Inverse Condemnation, Insurance Bad Faith, Earth Movement and Flood Damage. Trial and Appellate Practice in all State and Federal Courts.*

### MEMBERS OF FIRM

**DEENA FRALEY GRADY,** born Whittier, California, December 17, 1963; admitted to bar, 1991, California. *Education:* University of Southern California (B.A., 1987); Whittier College School of Law (J.D., 1991). *PRACTICE AREAS:* Insurance Bad Faith; Real Estate; Corporate; Fire Insurance; Wrongful Termination.

**SCOTT L. GRADY,** born New York, N.Y., February 3, 1963; admitted to bar, 1991, California. *Education:* State University of New York at Albany (B.A., 1985); New York Law School (J.D., 1989). *Member:* Los An-

*(This Listing Continued)*

geles County Bar Association; State Bar of California. *PRACTICE AREAS:* Insurance Bad Faith; Fire Insurance; Homeowners Insurance; Wrongful Termination; Corporate Law.

---

## BRUCE N. GRAHAM
### 21241 VENTURA BOULEVARD, SUITE 283
### LOS ANGELES, CALIFORNIA 91364
Telephone: 818-347-9146
Fax: 818-347-9147
Email: bgraha00@Counsel.com

*General Civil and Trial Practice with emphasis on Property and Casualty, Insurance Coverage, Bad Faith, Fraud, Subrogation, Health Insurance, Life and Disability Insurance, Surety and Construction Bonds.*

**BRUCE N. GRAHAM,** born Cleveland, Ohio, November 7, 1950; admitted to bar, 1979, California and U.S. District Court, Central District of California; 1981, U.S. District Court, Eastern District of California; 1990, U.S. District Court, Northern and Southern Districts of California and U.S. Court of Appeals, Ninth Circuit. *Education:* The Ohio State University (B.A., 1973); University of Toledo (J.D., 1978). Note and Comment Editor, University of Toledo Law Review, Vols. 8 and 9, 1977-1978. Special Justice, Toledo Law Honor Court, 1972. Author: "Groundwater Liability," 8 Ecology Law Quarterly (Boalt Hall) 131 (1979); "The Thinskull Principle," 15 Loyola Law Review 409 (1982); Note, "Administrative Agency Jurisdiction," 8 University of Toledo Law Review 733 (1978). Judge Pro Tem, Arbitrator and Mediator, Los Angeles Municipal Court, Los Angeles Superior Court. *Member:* San Fernando Valley and Los Angeles County Bar Associations; State Bar of California; Southern California Defense Council; Defense Research Institute.

REPRESENTATIVE CLIENTS: American Express Property & Casualty; AMEX Assurance Co.; Associated Indemnity Co.; Civil Service Employees Insurance Co.; Firemans' Fund Insurance Company of Texas; Firemans' Fund Insurance Co.; I.D.S. Property & Casualty Insurance Co; Stewart Construction.

---

## GRAHAM & JAMES LLP
### 14TH FLOOR, 801 SOUTH FIGUEROA STREET
### LOS ANGELES, CALIFORNIA 90017
Telephone: 213-624-2500
Telex: 4720414 GRJAUI
Telecopier: 213-623-4581
Email: dmiyamoto@gj.com
URL: http://www.gj.com

*Other offices located in:* San Francisco, Orange County, Palo Alto, Sacramento and Fresno, California; Seattle, Washington; Washington, D.C.; New York, New York; Milan, Italy; Beijing, China; Tokyo, Japan; London, England; Dusseldorf, Germany.

*Associated Offices:* Deacons Graham & James, Hong Kong, Sydney, Melbourne, Brisbane, Perth and Canberra, Australia.

*Affiliated Offices:* Deacons Graham & James, Hanoi and Ho Chi Minh City, Vietnam; Taipei, Taiwan and Bangkok, Thailand; In association with Dewi Soeharto & Rekan, Jakarta, Indonesia; Graham & James in affiliation with Taylor Joynson Garrett, London, England, Bucharest, Romania and Brussels, Belgium; Mishare M. Al-Ghazali & Partners, Safat, Kuwait; Law Firm of Salah Al-Hejailan, Jeddah and Riyadh, Saudi Arabia.

*General Practice including Civil Litigation in State and Federal Courts, Corporation, Banking and Financial Services, Commercial, International Business, Tax, Labor, Real Estate, Environmental, Intellectual Property, Bankruptcy, Creditors' Rights, Immigration, ERISA and Employee Benefits.*

**JOHN J. ALLEN,** born Tacoma, Washington, 1948; admitted to bar, 1976, California and U.S. District Court, Eastern and Central Districts of California. *Education:* California State University at Long Beach (B.A., 1970); Loyola University (J.D., 1976). Member, Loyola University Law Review, 1975-1976. [With, U.S. Army 1970-1973]. *PRACTICE AREAS:* Environmental Law. *Email:* jallen@gj.com

**JORGE ARCINIEGA,** born Tijuana, Mexico, 1957; admitted to bar, 1983, California. *Education:* University of California at Los Angeles (B.A., 1979); Harvard University (J.D., 1982). *LANGUAGES:* Spanish. *PRACTICE AREAS:* International Law; Intellectual Property; Business. *Email:* jarciniega@gj.com

**HIDETOSHI ASAKURA,** born Tokyo, Japan, 1943; admitted to bar, 1972, Japan; 1980, California. *Education:* University of Tokyo (B.A., 1967); *(This Listing Continued)*

Institute of Legal Research and Training of the Supreme Court, Tokyo and University of Washington (LL.M., 1979). *PRACTICE AREAS:* International Business Law; Corporate Law; Real Estate (Property) Law; Mergers and Acquisitions. *Email:* hasakura@gj.com

**VINCENT J. BELUSKO,** born Portland, Oregon, 1957; admitted to bar, 1981, California; U.S. District Court, Central, Northern, Southern and Eastern Districts of California; U.S. Court of Appeals, Ninth Circuit; U.S. Supreme Court; U.S. Court of Appeals for the Federal Circuit; registered to practice before U.S. Patent and Trademark Office. *Education:* Washington University (B.S.C.E., 1978); George Washington University (J.D., with honors, 1981). *Member:* Licensing Executives Society. *PRACTICE AREAS:* Intellectual Property Law; Litigation. *Email:* vbelusko@gj.com

**JAMES H. BRODERICK, JR.,** born Boston, Massachusetts, 1952; admitted to bar, 1981, California. *Education:* Harvard College (A.B., magna cum laude, 1974); Harvard University (1978-1979) and Boston University (J.D., 1979). Research Fellow, Faculty of Law, Sophia University, Tokyo, Japan (1979-1980). *PRACTICE AREAS:* Litigation. *Email:* jbroderick@gj.com

**JEFFREY A. CHESTER,** born Philadelphia, Pennsylvania, 1955; admitted to bar, 1981, California. *Education:* Pennsylvania State University (B.A., 1977); University of Pennsylvania (J.D., cum laude, 1981). Order of the Coif. Editor, University of Pennsylvania Law Review, Vols. 128 and 129, 1980-1981. Member, Executive Committee, Business and Corporations Law Section, Los Angeles County Bar Association. *PRACTICE AREAS:* Corporate Financing Law; Securities. *Email:* jchester@gj.com

**HILLEL T. COHN,** born Hartford, Connecticut, 1949; admitted to bar, 1974, Connecticut; 1975, California and U.S. District Court, Central District of California; 1979, U.S. Court of Appeals, Ninth Circuit. *Education:* Tufts University (B.A., summa cum laude, 1971); Harvard University (J.D., 1974). Phi Beta Kappa. Co-Author: "H Share Offerings in Hong Kong and the United States," Euromoney, 1994. U.S. Securities and Exchange Commission, 1974-1981. Law Clerk to Hon. Irving M. Pollack, SEC Commissioner. *Member:* Los Angeles County (Member, Executive Committee, Business and Corporation Law Section) and American (Member: Federal Regulation of Securities Committee, 1983—; Subcommittee on International Securities, 1985—) Bar Associations. *PRACTICE AREAS:* Securities; International Investment. *Email:* hcohn@gj.com

**HENRY S. DAVID,** born Bronx, New York, 1954; admitted to bar, 1979, California; 1981, Florida. *Education:* California Institute of Technology (B.S., with honors, 1976); New York University (J.D., cum laude, 1979). Order of the Coif. Member, 1977-1978 and Editor, 1978-1979, New York University Law Review. Author: "Seller's Performance," Chapter 9, Sales and Leases in California Commercial Law Practice, 1993; "1984 Chapter 538 or Tinkering With the 1983 Attachment and Enforcement of Judgments Law," Newsletter of Prejudgment Remedies Section of the Los Angeles County Bar Association, June, 1985. Member, Los Angeles Chamber of Commerce, 1995—. *Member:* Los Angeles County Bar Association (Chairman, Prejudgment Remedies Section, 1985-1986). *PRACTICE AREAS:* Litigation; Collection Law. *Email:* hdavid@gj.com

**CRAIG J. DE RECAT,** born Ross, California, March 7, 1953; admitted to bar, 1982, California and U.S. District Court, Central District of California; 1989, U.S. District Court Southern District of California. *Education:* University of California at Berkeley (B.A., 1975); Loyola University of Los Angeles (J.D., 1982) Valedictorian. Author: "Environmental Litigation: How to Deal with 'As-Is' Contract Language," ABTL Report, Vol. XV, No. 2, January 1993; "Deposition Tactics & Techniques," State Bar of California Environmental Trial Advocacy Conference, May 1995; "Soil and Groundwater Contamination: Litigation for the 1990's," WIP Seminar, December 1993; "A Short Course in Management Concepts for Environmental Compliance," WIP Seminar, December 1993; "The Environmental Audit: A Management Tool to Minimize Risk of Liability," WIP Seminar, 1992. *Member:* State Bar of California (Member, Environmental Law Section); The Association of Trial Lawyers of America (Member, Environmental Law Section; Products Liability Section). [With USNAR, 1971-1974]. *PRACTICE AREAS:* Environmental Law; Real Property; Toxic Torts. *Email:* cderecat@gj.com

**STEVEN S. DOI,** born California, 1962; admitted to bar, 1987, California; 1994, Japan (as a Gaikokuho Jimu Bengoshi). *Education:* Pomona College (B.A., 1983); University of California, Los Angeles (J.D., 1986). (Also at Tokyo, Japan Office). *PRACTICE AREAS:* International Business Law. *Email:* sdoi@gj.com

**DAVID L. FEHRMAN,** born Annapolis, Maryland, 1952; admitted to bar, 1977, Ohio; 1979, California; registered to practice before U.S. Patent *(This Listing Continued)*

**GRAHAM & JAMES LLP, Los Angeles—Continued**

and Trademark Office. *Education:* Vanderbilt University (B.E.E., magna cum laude, 1974); Washington University (J.D., 1977). Tau Beta Pi; Eta Kappa Nu. *Member:* American Intellectual Property Law Association; Los Angeles County Intellectual Property Law Association. *PRACTICE AREAS:* Intellectual Property Law; Patent Law. *Email:* dfehrman@gj.com

**RODNEY A. FUJII,** born Honolulu, Hawaii, October 8, 1948; admitted to bar, 1975, District of Columbia; 1988, California. *Education:* Loyola University of Los Angeles (B.A., 1970); Washington College of Law, American University (J.D., cum laude, 1974); Georgetown University (LL.M., Taxation Program, 1978). *Member:* The District of Columbia Bar. *PRACTICE AREAS:* Employee Benefit Law; Executive Compensation. *Email:* rfujii@gj.com

**BENJAMIN E. GOLDMAN,** born New York, New York, 1940; admitted to bar, 1968, New York; 1973, District of Columbia; 1986, California; U.S. District Court, Central District of California; U.S. District Court, District of Columbia; U.S. Court of Appeals, District of Columbia, Second, Fourth, Fifth and Ninth Circuits. *Education:* New York University (B.S., 1965); Fordham University (J.D., 1968); Georgetown University (LL.M., 1970). Member, 1966-67 and Research and Writing Editor, 1967-68, Fordham Law Review. Attorney Advisor to Chairman, National Labor Relations Board, 1968-72. Member, Panel of Arbitrators, American Arbitration Association. *Member:* The District of Columbia Bar; Los Angeles County, New York State, Federal and American Bar Associations (Member, Section of Labor and Employment Law); National Health Lawyers Association; American Academy of Hospital Attorneys. *PRACTICE AREAS:* Employment Law; Labor Law. *Email:* bgoldman@gj.com

**RANDOLPH H. GUSTAFSON,** born Chicago, Illinois, 1954; admitted to bar, 1981, California; 1982, U.S. District Court, Central District of California. *Education:* Vanderbilt University (B.A., 1976); University of Chicago (M.B.A., 1981; J.D., 1981). Certified Public Accountant, Illinois, 1981. *Member:* Los Angeles County Bar Association (Member, Real Property Section). *LANGUAGES:* Russian. *PRACTICE AREAS:* Real Property Law; Construction Law. *Email:* rgustafson@gj.com

**YASUHIRO HAGIHARA,** born Kagoshima City, Japan, 1937; admitted to bar, 1971, District of Columbia (Not admitted in California). *Education:* Keio University, Tokyo, Japan (LL.B., 1961); George Washington University (M.L.L., 1968). (Also at Washington, D.C. Office). *PRACTICE AREAS:* International Trade Law; Corporate Law. *Email:* yhagihara@gj.com

**DAVID L. HENTY,** born Camrose, Alberta, Canada, 1954; admitted to bar, 1983, California and U.S. District Court, Central, Northern and Southern Districts of California; registered to practice before U.S. Patent and Trademark Office. *Education:* University of Alberta, Canada (B.Sc., 1975; M.Sc., 1979); University of British Columbia (LL.B., 1981). *Member:* Los Angeles County and American (Member, Patents, Trademarks and Copyrights Section) Bar Associations; American Intellectual Property Law Association; American Physical Society. *PRACTICE AREAS:* Intellectual Property Law; Patent Law. *Email:* dhenty@gj.com

**JOHN C. HOLBERTON,** born Los Angeles, California, 1946; admitted to bar, 1972, Oregon; 1979, California. *Education:* Stanford University (B.A., 1968; M.B.A., 1972; J.D., 1972). Lecturer, School of Public Administration, University of Southern California, 1979-1984; University of California at Los Angeles, Extension, 1979-1985. Attorney-Advisor: Office of the International Tax Counsel, U.S. Treasury Department, 1976-1979; Office of the Chief Counsel, Internal Revenue Service, 1975-1976. *Member:* Los Angeles County and American Bar Associations. *PRACTICE AREAS:* Taxation Law. *Email:* jholberton@gj.com

**J. ERIC ISKEN,** born Allentown, Pennsylvania, 1952; admitted to bar, 1977, California; 1978, U.S. District Court, Central and Southern Districts of California; 1980, U.S. District Court, Northern District of California and U.S. Court of Appeals, Ninth Circuit; 1986, U.S. District Court, Eastern District of California. *Education:* University of California at Santa Cruz (B.A., 1974); Hastings College of Law, University of California (J.D., 1977). Extern to Honorable Raymond L. Sullivan, California Supreme Court, 1976. *Member:* Los Angeles County Bar Association. *PRACTICE AREAS:* Litigation. *Email:* eisken@gj.com

**WILLIAM J. JAMES,** born Hollister, California, 1944; admitted to bar, 1975, California; 1976, U.S. District Court, Central District of California and U.S. Court of Appeals, Ninth Circuit; 1979, U.S. Tax Court; 1992, U.S. District Court, Northern District of California. *Education:* Occidental College (B.A., 1966); Hastings College of the Law, University of California (J.D., 1974); New York University (LL.M., 1975). Senior Adjunct Professor, Graduate Tax Program, Golden Gate University, 1978—. Assistant U.S. Attorney, Central District of California, 1976-1986. *Member:* Los Angeles County and Federal (President, Los Angeles Chapter, 1991-1992) Bar Associations. *PRACTICE AREAS:* Litigation; Taxation Law. *Email:* wjames@gj.com

**CHERYL LEE JOHNSON,** born Burlington, Washington, 1950; admitted to bar, 1975, California. *Education:* Barnard College (B.A., magna cum laude, 1971); Harvard University (Ed.M., 1972); Columbia University (J.D., 1975). Harlan Fiske Stone Scholar. Member, Board of Editors, Columbia Law Review, 1974-1975. Editor and Co-Author: California Antitrust Law, 1992. *Member:* Los Angeles County and American Bar Associations; California Women Lawyers Association; American Business Trial Lawyers. *PRACTICE AREAS:* Litigation; Antitrust; RICO; Banking Law. *Email:* cjohnson@gj.com

**WOLFGANG M. KAU,** born Frauental, Germany, 1950; admitted to bar, 1979, Germany; 1981, California; 1982, U.S. Court of Appeals, Ninth and Eleventh Circuits. *Education:* Stadt. Emil-Fischer Gymnasium, Euskirchen, West Germany (Bacca Laurente, 1969); Rhein. Friedrich Wilhelm University, Bonn, West Germany (J.D., 1975); Southwestern University, Los Angeles. Author: "Venture Capital & Going Public - Unternehmensfinanzierung in den USA", Carl Heymanns Verlag, Cologne, 1984; "Zahlung mit Check," Recht der Internationale Wirtschaft, June, 1989; "Handelsblatt", April, 1984; "Venture Capital in den USA," June, 1984; "U.S. Installment Sales Tax (March 1982); "The U.S. Economic Recovery Tax Act of 1981." Co-Author: "Products Liability in Asset Acquisitions," "Acquisitions of Closely-Held Companies," "Registrierung einer California Corporation. als Gesellschafterin einer deutschen GmbH" Recht der Internationalen Wertschaft Jan. 1991. PLI 1982. *Member:* Los Angeles County, American and International Bar Associations; Düsseldorf Bar Association; German American Lawyers Association. (Also at Dusseldorf, Germany Office). *LANGUAGES:* German. *PRACTICE AREAS:* International Business Law; Corporate Law; Entertainment-Media Law; EU Law. *Email:* wkau@gj.com

**JOON YONG KIM,** born Seoul, Korea, 1954; admitted to bar, 1983, California; 1984, U.S. District Court, Central District of California and U.S. Court of International Trade. *Education:* University of Southern California (A.B., 1976; M.A., 1979); Georgetown University (J.D., 1982). *LANGUAGES:* Korean and Japanese. *PRACTICE AREAS:* International Business Law; Corporate Law. *Email:* jkim@gj.com

**STAN H. KOYANAGI,** born Inglewood, California, 1960; admitted to bar, 1985, California and U.S. District Court, Central District of California. *Education:* University of Southern California (B.S., summa cum laude, 1982); Stanford University (J.D., 1985). Phi Kappa Phi; Beta Gamma Sigma. *Member:* Los Angeles County and American Bar Associations. *PRACTICE AREAS:* Real Estate; Secured Transactions; Corporate Law; International Business Law. *Email:* skoyanagi@gj.com

**KEN M. KUROSU,** born Houston, Texas, 1958; admitted to bar, 1983, California; 1984, U.S. District Court, Central District of California and U.S. Court of Appeals, Ninth Circuit; 1993, Japan (as a Gaikokuho Jimu Bengoshi). *Education:* Stanford University (A.B., with distinction, 1980); University of Washington (J.D., 1983). Phi Beta Kappa. (Also at Tokyo, Japan Office). *LANGUAGES:* Japanese. *PRACTICE AREAS:* International Business Law. *Email:* kkurosu@gj.com

**MICHAEL R. LINDSAY,** born Montpelier, Idaho, 1956; admitted to bar, 1983, California and U.S. District Court, Central District of California; 1984, U.S. Court of Appeals, Ninth Circuit; 1985, U.S. District Court, Northern, Eastern and Southern Districts of California. *Education:* University of Maryland; Brigham Young University (B.A., 1979; J.D., cum laude, 1983). Member, National Moot Court Team. Author: "Defense of Equal Employment Claims," Second Edition, Clark Boardman Callaghan, 1996. *Member:* Los Angeles County and American Bar Associations. *LANGUAGES:* French. *PRACTICE AREAS:* Employment Law; Litigation. *Email:* mlindsay@gj.com

**THOMAS T. LIU,** born Taipei, Taiwan, 1957; admitted to bar, 1984, California, U.S. District Court, Northern District of California, U.S. Court of Appeals, Ninth Circuit and U.S. District Court, Central District of California. *Education:* Stanford University (B.A., 1980); University of Southern California (J.D., 1983). Phi Alpha Delta. Extern for the Honorable Laughlin E. Waters, U.S. District Court, Central District of California, 1981. *Member:* Los Angeles County Bar Association; Japanese-American Bar Associations. *LANGUAGES:* Mandarin and Spanish. *PRACTICE AREAS:* Employment Law; Labor Law. *Email:* tliu@gj.com

*(This Listing Continued)*

**DAVID A. LIVDAHL,** born St. Paul, Minnesota, 1947; admitted to bar, 1977, California and U.S. District Court, Central District of California. *Education:* Macalester College (B.A., cum laude, 1969); Columbia University (M.A., 1975; J.D., 1977). (Also at Beijing, People's Republic of China Office). *LANGUAGES:* Chinese and Japanese. **PRACTICE AREAS:** International Business Law; Corporate Law. *Email:* dlivdahl@gj.com

**JOSEPH T. LYNYAK, III,** born Passaic, New Jersey, September 1, 1951; admitted to bar, 1976, New Jersey; 1977, District of Columbia; 1980, California. *Education:* Saint Peter's College (A.B., 1973); Georgetown University (J.D., 1976). Law Clerk to the Hon. James J. Petrella, Superior Court of New Jersey, 1976-1977. Attorney, Federal Deposit Insurance Corporation, Honors Program in Banking Law, 1977-1979. *Member:* American Bar Association (Member: Banking Committee, 1980—; Financial Institutions Committee, 1994—; Chair, Subcommittee on Receiverships and Conservatorships, 1990-1994; Chair, Task Force on Derivatives, 1994—; Chair, Subcommittee on Retail and Consumer Banking, 1984-1990; Member: Committee on Consumer Financial Services, 1984—; Savings Institutions Committee, 1984—). **PRACTICE AREAS:** Financial Service Law; Regulatory Practice. *Email:* jlynyak@gj.com

**THOMAS J. MASENGA,** born Fort Belvoir, Virginia, 1952; admitted to bar, 1977, California. *Education:* University of Notre Dame (B.A., magna cum laude, 1974); Loyola University of Los Angeles (J.D., cum laude, 1977). Phi Alpha Delta. Member, St. Thomas More Law Honor Society. Member, Loyola of Los Angeles Law Review, 1976-1977. Panelist, CEB Program on Real Property Purchase and Sale Agreements, 1985. *Member:* Los Angeles County and American Bar Associations; Pension Real Estate Association; National Association of Public Pension Attorneys. **PRACTICE AREAS:** Real Estate (Property) Law. *Email:* tmasenga@gj.com

**STUART L. MERKADEAU,** born St. Louis, Missouri, 1961; admitted to bar, 1987, California, U.S. District Court, Central and Northern Districts of California and U.S. Court of Appeals for the Federal Circuit; registered to practice before U.S. Patent and Trademark Office. *Education:* Northwestern University (B.S.I.E., with honors, 1983); University of California at Los Angeles (J.D., 1986). Moot Court Honors Program. Co-Author: "Product Liability of Trademark Licensor," LES Nouvelles, Vol. 21, No. 1, March, 1986. *Member:* Los Angeles County Bar Association; Licensing Executive Society; Los Angeles Intellectual Property Law Association (Member, Board of Directors, 1994-1995). **PRACTICE AREAS:** Intellectual Property Law. *Email:* smerkadeau@gj.com

**DAVID T. MIYAMOTO,** born Gardena, California, 1957; admitted to bar, 1981, California, U.S. District Court, Central and Southern Districts of California and U.S. Court of Appeals, Ninth Circuit. *Education:* University of California at Los Angeles (B.A., magna cum laude, 1978); University of California at Los Angeles School of Law (J.D., 1981). Primary Editor, UCLA-Alaska Law Review, 1980-1981. *Member:* Los Angeles County Bar Association. **PRACTICE AREAS:** Litigation. *Email:* dmiyamoto@gj.com

**JOHN T. NAGAI,** born Hiroshima, Japan, 1958; admitted to bar, 1982, California, U.S. District Court, Central District of California and U.S. Court of Appeals, 9th Circuit; 1983, U.S. Tax Court. *Education:* Stanford University (A.B., with distinction, 1979); Harvard Law School (J.D., 1982). Phi Beta Kappa. *Member:* Los Angeles County Bar Association (Member, Sections on: Business and Corporation Law; Taxation). *LANGUAGES:* Japanese. **PRACTICE AREAS:** Taxation Law; Corporate Law; International Business Law. *Email:* jnagai@gj.com

**STEPHEN T. OWENS,** born San Jose, California, 1948; admitted to bar, 1978, California, U.S. District Court, Central, Southern, Northern and Eastern Districts of California, U.S. District Court, Eastern and Western Districts of Arkansas and U.S. Court of Appeals, Ninth Circuit. *Education:* Université d'Aix-Marseille, Aix-en-Provence, France (Diplôme de Langue et Lettres Francaises, 1973); San Jose State University (B.A., 1974); University of California at Los Angeles (J.D., 1978). Member, UCLA Law Review, 1976-1978. Judge Pro Tem, Municipal Court for Los Angeles County, 1989-1994. Board of Directors of Public Counsel, The Public Interest Law Firm of the Los Angeles and Beverly Hills Bar Associations, 1992-1995. Member, Commission on Judicial Nominees Evaluation, 1996—; Special Master, State Bar of California, 1991—. Recipient, John Minor Wisdom Award for Professionalism and Public Service, American Bar Association, 1993. Co-Recipient, President's Pro Bono Service Award, State Bar of California, 1992. *Member:* Los Angeles County and American Bar Associations. *LANGUAGES:* French and Italian. **PRACTICE AREAS:** Commercial Litigation; Banking Litigation; Arbitration; Alternative Dispute Resolution. *Email:* sowens@gj.com

*(This Listing Continued)*

**DENIS H. OYAKAWA,** born Lahaina, Maui, Hawaii, 1950; admitted to bar, 1974, California. *Education:* University of California at Los Angeles (A.B., 1971); Yale University (J.D., 1974). **PRACTICE AREAS:** International Trade Law; Business Law; Commercial Law. *Email:* doyakawa@gj.com

**CHARLES PATURICK,** born New York, N.Y., 1943; admitted to bar, 1974, California; 1975, District of Columbia. *Education:* New York University (B.A., cum laude, 1963); University of Pennsylvania (M.A., 1965); Stanford Law School (LL.B., 1974). **PRACTICE AREAS:** Corporate Law; Business Law. *Email:* cpaturick@gj.com

**STEVEN G. POLARD,** born New York, N.Y., 1954; admitted to bar, 1979, California and U.S. District Court, Central District of California; 1980, U.S. District Court, Northern District of California; 1982, U.S. District Court, Eastern District of California and U.S. Court of Appeals, Ninth Circuit; 1983, U.S. District Court, Southern District of California; 1984, U.S. Supreme Court; 1984, U.S. Court of Appeals, District of Columbia Circuit. *Education:* University of Kansas (B.S.B., with highest distinction, 1976); Duke University (J.D., 1979). Beta Gamma Sigma; Alpha Kappa Psi. Summerfield Scholar. *Member:* Los Angeles County (Member, Sections on: Bankruptcy; International Law) and American Bar Associations; Bankruptcy Forum; Financial Lawyers' Conference; Foreign Trade Association (Member, Legislative Committee, 1989-1990). **PRACTICE AREAS:** Bankruptcy Law; Aviation Litigation; Business Litigation. *Email:* spolard@gj.com

**PAMELA K. PRICKETT,** born Los Angeles, California, 1954; admitted to bar, 1979, California and U.S. District Court, Central District of California; 1980, U.S. District Court, Northern District of California. *Education:* Stanford University (B.A., with distinction, 1976; J.D., 1979). President, Moot Court, 1978-1979. *Member:* Los Angeles County and American Bar Associations; Women Lawyers Association of Los Angeles. **PRACTICE AREAS:** Real Estate (Property) Law. *Email:* pprickett@gj.com

**DON A. PROUDFOOT, JR.,** born Santa Monica, California, 1937; admitted to bar, 1964, California. *Education:* Stanford University (A.B., 1959; LL.B., 1963). Order of the Coif. Recent Developments Editor, Stanford Law Review, 1962-1963. *Member:* American Bar Association (Member, Sections on: Antitrust Law; Litigation). **PRACTICE AREAS:** Litigation; Appellate Practice. *Email:* dproudfoot@gj.com

**EDWIN B. REESER, III,** born Covina, California, 1951; admitted to bar, 1977, California; 1979, U.S. District Court, Central District of California, U.S. Court of Appeals, Ninth Circuit, U.S. Tax Court and U.S. Claims Court; 1980, U.S. Supreme Court. *Education:* Harvard University (A.B., cum laude, 1973); Columbia University (M.B.A., 1978); Hastings College of Law, University of California (J.D., 1976). Member, Moot Court Board, 1975-1976. *Member:* Los Angeles County and American Bar Associations. **PRACTICE AREAS:** Real Estate (Property) Law. *Email:* ebreeser@gj.com

**JAMES C. ROBERTS,** born Long Beach, California, 1945; admitted to bar, 1972, California. *Education:* Claremont Men's College (B.A., summa cum laude, 1968); Harvard University (J.D., cum laude, 1971). **PRACTICE AREAS:** Employment Law; Labor Law. *Email:* jroberts@gj.com

**WILLIAM J. ROBINSON,** born Santa Barbara, California, 1951; admitted to bar, 1978, California, U.S. District Court, Central District of California, U.S. Court of Appeals, Ninth Circuit; 1978-1982, U.S. Court of Customs and Patent Appeals; 1982, U.S. Court of Appeals for the Federal Circuit; registered to practice before U.S. Patent and Trademark Office. *Education:* University of California at Los Angeles (B.S.E.E., with honors, 1974; M.S.E.E., 1975); Loyola University of Los Angeles (J.D., 1978). Tau Beta Pi. Author: "Most Favored Licensee Clauses," Paper Presented at 1986 Spring Meeting of the Licensing Executive Society; "Insurance Coverage of Intellectual Property Lawsuits," 1992 Proceedings, Institute of Corporate Counsel; earlier version in American Intellectual Property Law Association Quarterly Journal, Vol. 17, No. 2, October, 1989, also in 1989 Entertainment, Publishing and the Arts Handbook, Clark-Boardman Co., Ltd.; earlier version in New Matter, Vol. 13, No. 2, Summer, 1988; "Patent Jury Trials—Avoiding the Mistakes of Your Predecessors," Critical Issues in Patent Litigation, Prentice Hall, 1991 also in 4 Journal of Proprietary Rights No. 1 (Jan. 1992) and 16 New Matters No. 4 (Winter 1991-1992); "Recent Developments in Patent Validity: Is The Pendulum Swinging Back?" Patent Litigation, Practicing Law Institute, 1993. Lecturer, Patent Law, Southwestern University School of Law, 1993-1994. *Member:* Los Angeles County and American Bar Associations; Los Angeles Intellectual Property Law Association (Member, Board of Directors, 1985-1991; President, 1990-1991); Licensing Executives Society (Los Angeles Chairman, 1991—); National Conference of Intellectual Property Law Associations

*(This Listing Continued)*

## GRAHAM & JAMES LLP, Los Angeles—Continued

(Delegate, 1988-1991; Secretary, 1991-92); United States/Japan Patent Liaison Council (Delegate); American Intellectual Property Association. **PRACTICE AREAS:** Intellectual Property Law; Litigation. **Email:** wrobinson@gj.com

**MINDA R. SCHECHTER,** born Brooklyn, New York, 1951; admitted to bar, 1975, California; 1976, Illinois; U.S. District Court, Central District of California; U.S. Court of Appeals, Ninth Circuit; registered to practice before U.S. Patent and Trademark Office. *Education:* Williams College; Smith College (A.B., first group scholar, 1972), Sigma Xi. Recipient: Sloan Foundation Chemistry Fellow; Cartesian Award in Political Philosophy; Stanford University Law School (J.D., 1975). Member, Stanford University Law Review. Editor, Stanford Journal of International Law. Co-Editor and Co-Author treatise, *California Antitrust Law.* Author: "Organizational Instruments for Effectiveness: A Comparative Study with Recommendations to a United Nations Environmental Agency," 8 Stan. J. Int'l L. 123, 1973; "Suboptimization by Rationing," 13 Loy. L.A. Rev. 893, 1980; "Legal Status of Vertical Controls Over Distribution," 1 Institute for Corporate Counsel, 1982; "Are Antitrust Per Se Offenses Per Se Illegal?" 2 Institute for Corporate Counsel, 1983; "Civil Rico—Pitfalls of Pleading," Los Angeles County Bar Association Publication, 1987; "Antitrust Damages," Chapter in *American Business Trial Lawyers* book on Getting to the Bottom Line—Damages Before, During and After Trial, 1987; "Mergers," chapter in the State Bar of California, Antitrust and Trade Regulation Law Section treatise California Antitrust Law, Cheryl L. Johnson, Ed. and Minda R. Schechter, Co-Ed, 1991; "International Joint Ventures," in the State Bar of California Seventh Annual International Law Program, 1995. Instructor and Fellow in Law and Economics, Columbia University School of Law, 1978-1979. Associate Professor, Loyola Law School, 1979-1982. Past Chair and Executive Board, Antitrust and Trade Regulation Section, 1982-1991; Delegate, 1982-1992; Member, Executive Committee, International Law Section, 1995—, State Bar of California. Officer and Board of Governors, Institute for Corporate Counsel, 1982-1983. Member, Joint Advisory Committee, Continuing Education of the Bar (CEB), 1986-1987. *Member:* Los Angeles County (Member, Executive Committee, Antitrust Section, 1982-1991) and American (Member, Sections on: Antitrust; Intellectual Property) Bar Associations. **PRACTICE AREAS:** Antitrust Law; Intellectual Property Law; International Joint Ventures and Distribution Law; Franchise Law. **Email:** mschechter@gj.com

**BRIAN E. SCHIELD,** born Detroit, Michigan, 1954; admitted to bar, 1979, California. *Education:* University of Wisconsin (B.A., cum laude, 1976); Georgia State University; Pepperdine University (J.D., 1979). Phi Alpha Delta. *Member:* Los Angeles County Bar Association (Member, Immigration Section); American Immigration Lawyers Association. **LANGUAGES:** French. **PRACTICE AREAS:** Immigration and Nationality or Naturalization Law. **Email:** bschield@gj.com

**ALLAN A. SHENOI,** born Bombay, India, 1958; admitted to bar, 1982, Texas; 1986, California; U.S. District Court, Southern District of Texas; U.S. District Court, Southern, Central and Eastern Districts of California; U.S. Court of Appeals, Fifth and Ninth Circuits; U.S. Supreme Court. *Education:* University of Bombay, Bombay, India; Georgetown University; Rice University (B.A., cum laude, 1979); University of Texas at Austin (J.D., 1982). *Member:* Texas International Law Journal, 1981-1982. Law Clerk to Leland C. Nielsen, U.S. District Court, San Diego, California, 1982-1984. **PRACTICE AREAS:** Maritime Law and Litigation. **Email:** ashenoi@gj.com

**WAYNE M. SMITH,** born Hamilton, Ontario, Canada, 1959; admitted to bar, 1984, California and U.S. District Court, Central District of California; 1986, U.S. Court of Appeals, Ninth Circuit; 1987, U.S. Court of Appeals, Eleventh Circuit; 1994, U.S. Supreme Court; 1995, U.S. Court of Appeals for the Federal Circuit. *Education:* University of Michigan (B.S.E., cum laude, 1981; J.D., 1984). Alpha Phi Mu. Author: "Going on the Offensive: Countering the Pro-Patent Trend in Patent Litigation," The General Counsel Advisor, Spring 1994; "Collecting Damages for Computer Failures," Computer Word Perspectives, 1989. *Member:* American Intellectual Property Law Association. **PRACTICE AREAS:** Intellectual Property; Patent Law; Commercial Litigation. **Email:** wsmith@gj.com

**BRIAN A. SULLIVAN,** born Landstuhl, Germany, 1953; admitted to bar, 1984, California. *Education:* University of Chicago (B.A., with honors, 1974); Boalt Hall School of Law, University of California (J.D., 1984). Recipient, American Jurisprudence Award. *Member:* Los Angeles County Bar Association. **PRACTICE AREAS:** Securities Law; Corporate Law. **Email:** bsullivan@gj.com

**DERRICK K. TAKEUCHI,** born Stockton, California, 1951; admitted to bar, 1981, California. *Education:* Stanford University (A.B., with honors in Political Science, 1974); Tokyo University, Tokyo, Japan; Georgetown University (J.D., 1979). Research Fellow, Faculty of Law, University of Tokyo, 1974-1976. *Member:* Los Angeles County and American Bar Associations. **LANGUAGES:** Japanese. **PRACTICE AREAS:** International Business Law; Corporate Law. **Email:** dtakeuchi@gj.com

**MARTIN J. TRUPIANO,** born Detroit, Michigan, 1946; admitted to bar, 1971, Michigan; 1976, California. *Education:* University of Michigan (B.A., 1968); Wayne State University (J.D., magna cum laude, 1971). Senior Note and Comment Editor, Wayne Law Review, 1970-1971. **PRACTICE AREAS:** Antitrust Litigation; Trade Regulation Litigation; Commercial Litigation. **Email:** mtrupiano@gj.com

**LES J. WEINSTEIN,** born New York, NY, 1934; admitted to bar, 1959, District of Columbia; 1965, California; registered to practice before U.S. Patent and Trademark Office. *Education:* University of Pennsylvania (B.S.M.E., 1956); George Washington University (J.D., with distinction, 1959; LL.M., 1961). Order of the Coif. Member, Board of Editors, George Washington Law Review, 1958-1959. Author: "The Application of Section 7 of the Clayton Act to Patents," The Patent, Trademark and Copyright Journal of Research and Education. Co-Author: "Going on the Offensive: Countering the Pro-Patent Trend in Patent Litigation," Arthur Anderson, The General Counsel Adviser, Vo. 2, No. 1, Spring 1994. Appointed Attorney General's Honor Program, U.S. Department of Justice, 1959. Trial Attorney, Antitrust Division, U.S. Department of Justice, 1959-1964. **PRACTICE AREAS:** Litigation; Antitrust; Patent, Trademark and Copyright. **Email:** lweinstein@gj.com

**BARRY LEIGH WEISSMAN,** born Los Angeles, California, 1948; admitted to bar, 1973, California; 1976, U.S. Court of Appeals, Ninth Circuit; 1977, U.S. Supreme Court; 1978, District of Columbia; 1992, U.S. Court of Appeals, Second Circuit. *Education:* University of California at Davis (B.A., 1970); University of Santa Clara (J.D., 1973). Author: "Prop 51: Panacea or Pandora's Box—Business Insurance," California Pleading & Practice Manual by Callahan. Judge Pro Tempore, Los Angeles Municipal Court, 1975. Publications: Proposition 51: Panacea or Pandora's Box? National Underwriter-Property & Casualty Insurance Edition, October 1986; California Tort Reform Legislation, Insurance and Reinsurance Law International, December 1988; Disaster Litigation—The American Viewpoint, Hawksmere—International Litigation Practitioners Forum Bulletin, May 1990. Insolvent Insurance Companies' Failed Promises, Knapp, Petersen & Clark Report, May 1990; Personal Injury Litigation in the United States, Hawksmere International Litigation Practitioners Forum Bulletin, September 1990; Late Notice Alone Does Not Allow Reinsurers Opportunity to Deny Coverage, ReActions, 10th Anniversary Issue, March 1991; A Grande Strategy, The Review, Worldwide Reinsurance, May, 1991; Insurer Insolvencies and Rehabilitations: A Reinsurer's Perspective, Federation of Regulatory Counsel, Inc. Quarterly Journal of Insurance Law and Regulation, March 11, 1995; Alternative Dispute Resolution Mechanisms in Reinsurance, Hawksmere—9th International Reinsurance Congress, October 1995; Should Reinsurance Arbitration Decisions Be Confidential? Mealey's Litigation Reports, March 13, 1996. Books: California Pleadings and Practice Forms, (2 vol. set) Callaghan and Company, 1986, supplemented once a year. Member, California State Senate Advisory Committee on Malpractice Insurance. Member, Panel of Arbitrators, American Arbitration Association. *Member:* The District of Columbia Bar; New York State and American Bar Associations. **Email:** bweissman@gj.com

### SPECIAL COUNSEL

**WILLIAM G. ANDERSON,** born Oak Park, Illinois, April 9, 1947; admitted to bar, 1975, Illinois; 1979, California; registered to practice before U.S. Patent and Trademark Office. *Education:* Rose-Hulman Institute of Technology (B.S.M.E., 1969); John Marshall Law School (J.D., 1975). *Member:* American Bar Association; Los Angeles Intellectual Property Law Association (Director, 1981-1988; President, 1986-1987). **PRACTICE AREAS:** Intellectual Property. **Email:** wanderson@gj.com

**EVERITT G. BEERS,** born Wichita, Kansas, 1950; admitted to bar, 1980, California, U.S. District Court, Central District of California and U.S. Court of Appeals, Ninth Circuit; 1981, Alaska and U.S. District Court, District of Alaska; 1985, U.S. District Court, Southern, Eastern and Northern Districts of California. *Education:* University of Alaska (A.A., 1973; Two B.A's, cum laude, 1977); Hastings College of Law, University of California (J.D., 1979); University of Southern California (M.S., Computer Science, 1995). Member, 1978-1979 and Associate Editor, 1979, Hastings Law Journal. Extern, Justice Clinton W. White, Presiding Justice, California Court of Appeal, 1979. Law Clerk, Chief Justice Edmond W. Burke,

*(This Listing Continued)*

Alaska Supreme Court, 1980-1981. *Member:* Los Angeles County and Alaska Bar Associations; State Bar of California. *PRACTICE AREAS:* Civil Litigation; Intellectual Property Law; Computers and Software; Copyrights; Online and Internet Law. *Email:* ebeers@gj.com

**LARRY W. MITCHELL,** born Muncie, Indiana, October 18, 1946; admitted to bar, 1976, California; 1977, U.S. District Court, Central District of California and U.S. Court of Appeals, Ninth Circuit; 1980, U.S. Supreme Court; 1987, U.S. District Court, Eastern, Northern and Southern Districts of California. *Education:* California State University at Northridge (B.A., 1972); Loyola University (J.D., magna cum laude, 1976). Phi Delta Phi; Alpha Sigma Nu. Member, St. Thomas More Law Honor Society. Staff Member, 1974-1975 and Member, Board of Editors, 1975-1976, Loyola Law Review. [E-5 USN, 1968-1971]. *PRACTICE AREAS:* Insurance Coverage Law; Primary and Excess Insurance; Reinsurance; Environmental Insurance; Civil Litigation. *Email:* lmitchell@gj.com

### SENIOR COUNSEL

**DANIEL E. CHAMPION,** born Munising, Michigan, 1958; admitted to bar, 1983, Michigan and U.S. District Court, Western District of Michigan; 1984, California and U.S. District Court, Central District of California; 1987, U.S. District Court, Northern and Eastern Districts of California and Eastern District of Michigan; 1989, U.S. Court of Appeals, Ninth and Sixth Circuits and U.S. District Court, Southern District of California. *Education:* Grand Rapids Junior College (A.A., 1978); Grand Valley State University (B.S., with high honors, 1980); University of Michigan (J.D., 1983). Delta Pi Alpha; Phi Kappa Phi. *Member:* Beverly Hills and Los Angeles County Bar Associations; State Bar of Michigan. *PRACTICE AREAS:* Litigation; Commercial Collection Law; Commercial; Enforcement of Judgements; Prejudgement Remedies. *Email:* dchampion@gj.com

**PATRICK J. FIELDS,** born Santa Maria, California, 1956; admitted to bar, 1982, California. *Education:* University of California at Los Angeles (A.B., summa cum laude, 1979); Harvard University (J.D., 1982). *PRACTICE AREAS:* International Business Law; Banking Law. *Email:* pfields@gj.com

### OF COUNSEL

**DAVID A. HAYDEN,** born Rochester, Minnesota, 1938; admitted to bar, 1964, California. *Education:* University of California at Berkeley (A.B., 1960); Boalt Hall School of Law, University of California (LL.B., 1963). *LANGUAGES:* Japanese, Chinese and German. *PRACTICE AREAS:* International Business Law. *Email:* dhayden@gj.com

**RICHARD P. MANSON,** born Cleveland, Ohio, 1949; admitted to bar, 1981, California. *Education:* Yale University (B.A., cum laude, 1971); Northwestern University (M.A., 1973); Stanford University (J.D., 1981). *Member:* American Bar Association. *LANGUAGES:* French. *PRACTICE AREAS:* Securities Law; Mergers and Acquisitions. *Email:* rmanson@gj.com

**WILLIAM W. WELLS,** born Long Beach, California, 1943; admitted to bar, 1973, California. *Education:* Stanford University (B.S., 1965); Georgetown University; University of Southern California (J.D., 1973). Note and Comment Editor, Southern California Law Review, 1972-1973. Member, Business Law Section, State Bar of California. *Member:* American Bar Association (Member, Section on Corporation, Banking and Business Law). *LANGUAGES:* Korean. *Email:* wwells@gj.com

**ERIC E. YOUNGER,** born San Francisco, California, 1943; admitted to bar, 1969, California. *Education:* University of Southern California (B.A., 1965), Phi Beta Kappa; Harvard Law School (LL.B., 1968). Municipal Court Judge, 1974-1981; Superior Court Judge, 1981-1995. Assignment to California Court of Appeals, 1982. *Member:* American Bar Association; California Judge Association. *LANGUAGES:* Spanish and French. *PRACTICE AREAS:* Alternative Dispute Resolution. *Email:* eyounger@gj.com

### COUNSEL

**MERRILL J. BAUMANN, JR.,** born Boston, Massachusetts, 1959; admitted to bar, 1986, California. *Education:* Dartmouth College (A.B., with distinction, 1981); University of Southern California (J.D., 1985). Topic Editor, Hale Moot Court Honors Program, 1984-1985. *Member:* American Bar Association. *PRACTICE AREAS:* Attorney Ethics; Corporate Law. *Email:* mbaumann@gj.com

*(This Listing Continued)*

### ASSOCIATES

*David B. Abel; Michael B. Annis; Martha L. Applebaum; Alison M. Barbarosh; Brian M. Berliner; Kenneth N. Burraston; Lynn D. Cantor* (Not admitted in CA); *Pei-Wen Chang; JoAn H. Cho; Marcus Delgado; Victor de Gyarfas; Marjorie Turk Desmond; Robert Desmond; Peter R. Duchesneau; Shivbir S. Grewal; Jennifer R. Hasbrouck; Gerard A. Hekker* (Also Consultant to Dewi Soeharto & Rekan, Jakarta, Indonesia); *Jonathan E. Johnson III; Allen Choo Kim; Hyunu Lee; Jeanne M. Malitz; David J. Meyer; Rie Miyake; Hisako Muramatsu; Martin M. Noonen; David K. Ritenour; Bin Xue Sang; Thomas P. Schmidt; Eric Shih; Nao S. Shimato; Kristi Miki Springer; Milo M. Stevanovich; Jennifer M. Tsao; Brian Van Vleck; Kimberly G. Winer; Rami S. Yanni.*

All Members and Associates are Members of the State Bar of California except where otherwise indicated.

---

## GRASSINI, WRINKLE & GALLAGHER

*A LAW CORPORATION*

### LOS ANGELES, CALIFORNIA

(See Woodland Hills)

*Plaintiff, Personal Injury, Negligence, Products Liability, Professional Malpractice and Insurance Litigation.*

---

## JEFFREY L. GRAUBART

*2029 CENTURY PARK EAST, SUITE 2700*
### LOS ANGELES, CALIFORNIA 90067-3041
Telephone: 310-788-2650
Fax: 310-788-2657

*Entertainment Law, International Law, Corporate and Business Law, Civil Litigation, Copyright Infringement, Trademark Infringement, Motion Pictures, Music, Music Publishing, Multimedia, Publishing and Theater Law.*

**JEFFREY L. GRAUBART,** born Chicago, Illinois, August 18, 1940; admitted to bar, 1965, Illinois; 1968, California; 1980, New York, U.S. Court of Appeals, Ninth Circuit. *Education:* University of Illinois (B.S., 1962); Northwestern University (J.D., 1965). Recipient, Deems-Taylor Award from American Society of Composers, Authors and Publishers, 1981. Author: "The Validity of the Publisher-Songwriter Agreement," Beverly Hills Bar Association Journal, Fall, 1986; "Self Publishing and the Songwriter/Music Publisher Agreement," Entertainment Law Reporter, September, 1986; "GATT and U.S. Moral Rights," Copyright World, June/July, 1995; "The Agony and the Ecstasy," Los Angeles Lawyer, April, 1995; "U.S. Moral Rights and the GATT," New York Law Journal, April 14, 1995; "Changes in Canadian Copyright Law," New York Law Journal, April 1, 1988; "U.S. Moral Rights: Fact or Fiction," New York Law Journal, August 7, 1992. Faculty Member: The New School for Social Research, 1983-1985; Golden Gate University, 1977-1978; California State University, 1978. Adjunct Professor, New York University, 1983-1986. Lecturer: UCLA, 1988—; University of Southern California, 1988—. Honorary Life Member and Governor, National Academy of Recording Arts and Sciences. Vice President and Trustee, Society for Preservation for Film Music, 1989—. Director, Jazzmobile, Inc., 1983-1986. *Member:* Beverly Hills (Chair, International Law Section, 1995—), Los Angeles County, Illinois State and American (Chair, Moral Rights Sub-Committee, 1992) Bar Associations; State Bar of California; Los Angeles Copyright Society; Intellectual Property Owners; American Intellectual Property Law Association; American Film Institute; Hollywood Radio and Television Society; Inter-Pacific Bar Association. *REPORTED CASES:* Los Angeles News Service vs. Tullo, 973 F.2d 791 (9th Cir. 1992).

---

## GRAY & HIRREL

### LOS ANGELES, CALIFORNIA

(See Pasadena)

*Probate, Trusts and Taxation.*

## GRAY, YORK, DUFFY & RATTET

15760 VENTURA BOULEVARD, 16TH FLOOR (ENCINO)
**LOS ANGELES, CALIFORNIA 91436**
Telephone: 818-907-4000; 310-553-0445
FAX: 818-783-4551

General Civil Trial and Appellate Practice in all State and Federal Courts. Insurance, Malpractice, Products Liability, Construction, Wrongful Termination, Public Liability and Business Law.

FIRM PROFILE: Gray, York, Duffy & Rattet was formed in 1986 as a business law and civil litigation firm specializing in insurance law. The firm presently is a full service firm handling matters ranging from general tort liability and construction defect litigation to labor and employment law and multiparty complex civil litigation. The firm litigates actions in all State and Federal Courts in California.

### MEMBERS OF FIRM

**GARY S. GRAY,** born Palo Alto, California, November 17, 1946; admitted to bar, 1975, California and U.S. District Court, Central and Southern Districts of California. *Education:* California State University at Northridge (B.S., 1972); Loyola University (J.D., 1975). Judge Pro Tem, Los Angeles Superior Court Arbitrator. *Member:* Century City, Los Angeles, San Fernando Valley and American Bar Associations; State Bar of California; Association of Southern California Defense Counsel; Defense Research Institute; California Trial Lawyers Association. **PRACTICE AREAS:** Insurance Law; Environmental Law; Construction Law; Business Law. **Email:** GGRAY@GYDRLAW.COM

**JAMES R. YORK,** born Saginaw, Michigan, November 28, 1945; admitted to bar, 1978, California and U.S. District Court, Central District of California. *Education:* California State University at Northridge (B.S., 1970); Woodland University, Mid Valley College of Law (J.D., 1978). *Member:* Century City, San Fernando Valley and Los Angeles County Bar Associations; State Bar of California (Member, Litigation Section); Association of Southern California Defense Counsel. **PRACTICE AREAS:** Insurance Law; Workers Compensation; Products Liability; Public Entity Law. **Email:** JYORK@GYDRLAW.COM

**JOHN J. DUFFY,** born Elizabeth, New Jersey, March 7, 1951; admitted to bar, 1980, California and U.S. District Court, Central District of California; 1982, New Jersey and U.S. District Court, District of New Jersey. *Education:* University of Notre Dame (B.A., 1973); Southwestern University (J.D., 1979). Judge Pro Tem, Los Angeles Municipal Superior Court, 1988—. Member, Panel of Arbitrators and Mediators, Los Angeles Superior Court. *Member:* San Fernando Valley and Los Angeles County Bar Associations; State Bar of California; Association of Southern California Defense Counsel; Defense Research Institute. **PRACTICE AREAS:** Insurance Law; Bad Faith; Medical Malpractice; Appellate Practice; Employment Law.

**GARY S. RATTET,** born Burbank, California, January 5, 1953; admitted to bar, 1979, California and U.S. District Court, Central District of California. *Education:* Claremont Men's College (B.S., 1974); Boston College (J.D., 1978). Graduate School, Studies in History, 1974. Member, Panel of Arbitrators, Los Angeles Superior Court. *Member:* Century City, San Fernando Valley, Los Angeles County and American Bar Associations. **PRACTICE AREAS:** Business Law; Labor and Employment Law; Products Liability. **Email:** GRATTAT@DYDRLAW.COM

**ARLENE A. COLMAN,** born Chicago, Illinois, May 16, 1942; admitted to bar, 1981, California and U.S. District Court, Central District of California. *Education:* University of California at Berkeley; San Francisco State University (B.A., 1964); University of San Diego (J.D., 1980). *Member:* San Fernando Valley, Los Angeles County and San Diego County Bar Associations; Association of Southern California Defense Counsel. **PRACTICE AREAS:** Labor and Employment Law; Discrimination Law; Insurance Law; Appellate Practice. **Email:** ACOLMAN@GYDRLAW.COM

**LOUIS A. CAPPADONA,** born Jersey City, New Jersey, July 20, 1939; admitted to bar, 1965, Texas; 1971, Florida and U.S. Supreme Court; 1973, California; 1975, U.S. Court of Appeals, Ninth Circuit; 1976, U.S. District Court, Central District of California; 1978, U.S. District Court, Southern District of California; 1991, U.S. District Court, Northern District of California. *Education:* St. Peter's College (B.S., 1961); St. Mary's University of San Antonio (J.D., 1965). Phi Delta Phi. Author: "Arbitration in Settlement of Jurisdictional Disputes," St. Mary's Law Journal, Vol. 3, No. 1, 1971. Co-Author: "Employment Law Bulletin," 1984—; "Employers' New Duties Under the Warn Act," 9 California Lawyer, No. 1 at P.64, Jan., 1989; "Call up of Employee-Reservists Trigger Employer Obligations," California State Bar Labor and Employment Law Quarterly 5, Winter 1991. Attorney, National Labor Relations Board, Region 22, Newark, New Jersey, 1968-1970. Labor Counsel and Division Counsel, Litton Industries, Inc., Beverly Hills, California, 1970-1976. *Member:* San Fernando Valley, Los Angeles County (Member, Labor Law and Alternative Dispute Resolution Sections) and American (Member, Labor and Employment Law Section) Bar Associations; The State Bar of California (Member, Labor and Employment Law Section); State Bar of Texas (Member, Labor and Employment Law Section). [Capt. U.S. Army JAGC, 1961-1968]. **SPECIAL AGENCIES:** Federal: National Labor Relations Board; U.S. Department of Labor; Equal Employment Opportunity Commission. California: Department of Fair Employment and Housing; Division of Labor Standards Enforcement; Employment Development Department; Workers Compensation Appeals Board (Section .132a claims only); CAL-OSHA. **REPORTED CASES:** Auchmoody v. 911 Emergency Services, Inc., 214 Cal App. 3d 1510; Automated Business Systems v. N.L.R.B., 497 F 2d 262, CA 6; Guidance and Control Systems v. N.L.R.B., 217 N.L.R.B., No. 34, 538 F2 336 (enforcement denied) CA9. **PRACTICE AREAS:** Labor and Employment Law.

**BARRY D. BROWN,** born San Francisco, California, July 14, 1951; admitted to bar, 1977, California, U.S. District Court, Central, Eastern, Northern and Southern Districts of California and U.S. Court of Appeals, Ninth Circuit. *Education:* University of San Francisco (B.A., 1973; J.D., 1977). Judge Pro Tem, San Francisco Municipal Court, 1993—. *Member:* Bar Association of San Francisco (Member, Legal Malpractice Committee, 1993—; Chairman, 1995—); Los Angeles County and American (Member, Torts and Insurance Practice Section; Litigation Section, 1990—) Bar Associations; State Bar of California (Member, Litigation Section, 1990—). **REPORTED CASES:** Gurkewitz v. Hobermann (1982) 137 Cal.App. 3d 328; Stoil v. Superior Court (1992) 9 Cal.App. 4th 1362; Bellows v. Aliquot (1994) 25 Cal.App. 4th 426. **Email:** BBROWN@GYDRLAW.COM

**WILLIAM F. FLAHAVAN,** born San Francisco, California, November 6, 1946; admitted to bar, 1972, California and U.S. District Court, Central and Southern Districts of California. *Education:* St. Mary's College of California (B.A., Economics, 1968); Hastings College of Law, University of California (J.D., 1971). Order of the Coif. Member, 1969-1970 and Note and Comment Editor, 1970-1971, Hastings Law Journal. Member, Thurston Honor Society. Co-Author with Judge William John Rea: "Personal Injury Practice," The Rutter Group, 1984. Author: "Smarter Settlements in L.A. Superior Court," 1981, "90 Days to Trial," 1981 and "120 Days to Go," 1983, The Rutter Group. Lecturer, Civil Litigation, 1990—, Continuing Education of the Bar, Los Angeles County, San Francisco, San Diego County and Orange County Bar Associations. *Member:* Los Angeles County and American Bar Associations; State Bar of California; The Association of Trial Lawyers of America; Association of Southern California Defense Counsel (Co-Chair, Legislation Committee). **PRACTICE AREAS:** Insurance Litigation; Professional Malpractice; Personal Injury.

**JEFFREY S. STERN,** born Winnipeg, Manitoba, Canada, February 1, 1954; admitted to bar, 1981, California and U.S. District Court, Central District of California. *Education:* California State University at Northridge (B.A., cum laude, 1976); Loyola University of Los Angeles (J.D., 1981). *Member:* Los Angeles County and American Bar Associations; State Bar of California; Association of Southern California Defense Counsel. **PRACTICE AREAS:** Civil Litigation; Workers' Compensation. **Email:** JSTERN@GYDRLAW.COM

### ASSOCIATES

**AMALIA L. TAYLOR,** born Los Angeles, California, May 28, 1942; admitted to bar, 1974, California; 1985, U.S. District Court, Central District of California. *Education:* California State University at Los Angeles (B.A., 1970); Loyola University; Boalt Hall School of Law, University of California (J.D., 1973). *Member:* San Fernando Valley and American Bar Associations; Association of Southern California Defense Counsel; Association of Women Lawyers. **PRACTICE AREAS:** Insurance Defense; Construction Law; Product Liability.

**KENNETH A. HEARN,** born Chicago, Illinois, March 22, 1952; admitted to bar, 1979, California; 1987, U.S. District Court, Central District of California. *Education:* University of California at Los Angeles (B.A., 1974); University La Verne College of Law (J.D., 1977). *Member:* San Fernando Valley, Los Angeles County and American Bar Associations. **PRACTICE AREAS:** Insurance Law; Environment Law; Appellate Practice.

**GABRIEL H. WAINFELD,** born Buenos Aires, Argentina, October 26, 1961; admitted to bar, 1988, California; 1989, U.S. District Court, Central District of California. *Education:* University of California at Los Angeles (B.A., 1984); Whittier College School of Law (J.D., 1988). *Member:* San

*(This Listing Continued)*

Fernando Valley Bar Association. **PRACTICE AREAS:** Insurance Defense; Premises Liability.

**JOHN L. BARBER,** born St. Louis, Missouri, August 13, 1967; admitted to bar, 1992, California; U.S. District Court, Central District of California. *Education:* Westminster College (B.A., 1989); Loyola Law School, Los Angeles (J.D., 1992). *Member:* San Fernando Valley and Los Angeles County Bar Associations. **PRACTICE AREAS:** Business Law; Labor and Employment Law. **Email:** JBARBER@GYDRLAW.COM

**MILOSLAV KHADILKAR,** born Prague, Czechoslovakia, May 22, 1964; admitted to bar, 1991, California; U.S. District Court, Central District of California. *Education:* University of California at Santa Barbara (B.S., B.A., B.A., 1987); Pepperdine University (J.D., 1990). Phi Alpha Delta. *Member:* Los Angeles County and San Fernando Valley Bar Associations; State Bar of California. **LANGUAGES:** Czech. **PRACTICE AREAS:** Insurance Defense; Premises Liability; Public Entity.

**MICHAEL S. EISENBAUM,** born Fort Dix, New Jersey, June 30, 1964; admitted to bar, 1990, California and U.S. District Court, Central District of California. *Education:* Colorado State University (B.A., 1987); Pepperdine University (J.D., 1990). *Member:* San Fernando Valley, Los Angeles County and American Bar Associations. **PRACTICE AREAS:** Insurance Defense; Public Entity; Civil Litigation.

**FRANK J. OZELLO, JR.,** born Islip, New York, May 26, 1963; admitted to bar, 1989, New York; 1990, U.S. District Court, Southern District of New York; 1991, California and U.S. District Court, Central District of California; 1992, U.S. District Court, Northern District of California. *Education:* Columbia University (B.A., 1985); St. John's University School of Law (J.D., 1988). Recipient, James McClean Scholarship Award. *Member:* New York State (Insurance, Negligence and Compensation Law Section; New York State Bar Litigation Section); American Bar Association (Member, Tort and Insurance Practice Section; Litigation Section); State Bar of California. **PRACTICE AREAS:** Insurance Coverage; Commercial Litigation; Tort Litigation.

**ERIC J. ERICKSON,** born San Jose, California, December 31, 1953; admitted to bar, 1982 California; 1984, U.S. District Court, Central District of California; 1985, U.S. Court of Appeals, Ninth Circuit. *Education:* University of California, Irvine (B.A., 1976); California Western School of Law (J.D., 1982). *Member:* State Bar of California. **PRACTICE AREAS:** Construction Defects Litigation; Product Liability Litigation; Business Litigation; Personal Injury Litigation.

**BRIDGETT ESQUIBIAS,** born Los Angeles, California, January 21, 1966; admitted to bar, 1995, California; 1996, U.S. District Court, Central District of California. *Education:* University of California at Los Angeles (B.A., 1989); University of San Diego (J.D., 1995). *Member:* Los Angeles County Bar Association; State Bar of California. **PRACTICE AREAS:** Labor and Employment Law; Litigation.

**CAROL G. ARNOLD,** born Tampa, Florida, September 16, 1953; admitted to bar, 1987, California and U.S. District Court, Central District of California. *Education:* University of Virginia (B.A., 1978); Southwestern University School of Law (J.D., 1985). Moot Court Honors Program. Member, Southwestern University Law Review. *Member:* San Fernando and Los Angeles County Bar Associations; State Bar of California; Southern California Defense Counsel. **PRACTICE AREAS:** Insurance Defense; Construction Defect; Premises Liability; Personal Injury Defense; Appellate.

**DAVID G. MARCUS,** born Los Angeles, California, September 2, 1952; admitted to bar, 1980, California and U.S. District Court, Central District of California. *Education:* University of California, Berkeley (A.B., Communication and Public Policy, 1974); Southwestern University (J.D., 1979). Order of the Barristers. Moot Court Board of Governors, 1977-1979, Chairman, 1978-1979. Judge Pro Tem, Los Angeles Municipal Court. *Member:* Los Angeles County and American Bar Associations; State Bar of California (Member, Sections on: Workers' Compensation; Real Estate, Probate and Trust Law; Natural Resources, Energy and Environmental Law; Tort and Insurance Practice; Labor and Employment Law); Association of Southern California Defense Counsel; Law and Science Institute; Association of Business Trial Lawyers.

REPRESENTATIVE CLIENTS: National American Insurance Co.; Universal Underwriters Insurance Co.; Southern California Rapid Transit District; Rapid American Corp.; Sterling Casualty; McCrory Corp.; J. J. Newberry Co.; Price Club; T.G. & Y. Stores; WalMart; Crawford and Company; Carl Warren & Co.; Liberty Mutual Insurance Co.; CIGA; Lexington Insurance Co.; Harbor Insurance Company; Brown and Bitterman, Inc.; Continental Insurance Co.; New Hampshire Insurance Co.; Allstate Insurance Co.; 20th Century Insurance Co.; Lancer Insurance Co.; Zurich Insurance Co.; State Farm Insurance Co.; Oxford Property & Casualty Insurance Co.; Universal Underwriters Insurance Co.; Century National Insurance Co.; National American Insurance Co.; CNA Insurance Co.; Woolworth Corp.; McCrory Corp.; Litton Industries; Taylor Woodrow Homes; Billa Bong; Lawyers Mutual Insurance Co.; Crum & Forester Insurance Co.; Ace Insurance Management Ltd.; L.A. County Metropolitan Transit Authority.
REFERENCE: Marathon National Bank, Los Angeles, California.

## *GREENBERG GLUSKER FIELDS CLAMAN & MACHTINGER LLP*

Established in 1959

21TH FLOOR
1900 AVENUE OF THE STARS (CENTURY CITY)
**LOS ANGELES, CALIFORNIA 90067**
Telephone: 310-553-3610
Fax: 310-553-0687

*General Civil, Trial and Appellate Practice; Alternative Dispute Resolution; Real Estate; Corporate and Business; Securities; Entertainment; Communications and Publishing; Intellectual Property; International, Federal and State Taxation; Estate Planning and Probate; Labor and Employee Relations; Bankruptcy; Corporate Reorganizations and Financial Institutions; Environmental.*

FIRM PROFILE: *The firm was founded in 1959 by three lawyers, Arthur Greenberg, Philip Glusker and Irving Hill, who was appointed a judge of the United States District Court in 1961. The firm has grown to over 90 lawyers, serving a diverse client base of entrepreneurs, closely held businesses and major corporations throughout the United States. Recognized as one of the leading midsized law firms in California, the firm maintains close working relations with clients, providing them with a full range of legal services.*

### MEMBERS OF FIRM

**ARTHUR N. GREENBERG,** born Detroit, Michigan, October 4, 1927; admitted to bar, 1953, California; U.S. District Court, Central District of California; U.S. Court of Appeals, Ninth Circuit; U.S. Supreme Court. *Education:* Stanford University and University of California at Los Angeles (A.B., 1949); University of California at Los Angeles (LL.B., 1952). Order of the Coif; Phi Beta Kappa. Selected as UCLA School of Law Alumnus of the Year, 1978. President, Legal Aid Foundation of Los Angeles, 1991-1992. *Member:* Beverly Hills, Los Angeles County and American Bar Associations; The State Bar of California. **PRACTICE AREAS:** Litigation; Alternative Dispute Resolution; Business Litigation; Corporate and Business.

**PHILIP GLUSKER,** born Chicago, Illinois, January 25, 1924; admitted to bar, 1951, California. *Education:* University of Wisconsin, Stanford University and University of California at Los Angeles (B.A., 1947); Yale Law School (LL.B., 1950). Phi Beta Kappa; Order of the Coif. *Member:* Los Angeles County and American Bar Associations; The State Bar of California. **PRACTICE AREAS:** Real Estate; ADR; Transaction; Litigation.

**SIDNEY J. MACHTINGER,** born Poland, April 23, 1922; admitted to bar, 1950, Illinois; 1954, U.S. Supreme Court; 1955, California. *Education:* Northwestern University (B.S., 1947; J.D., 1950). Order of the Coif. Member, Board of Editors, Northwestern University Law Review, 1948-1950. Attorney, Dept. of Justice, Washington, D.C., 1950-1952; Chief Counsel's Office, Internal Revenue Service, Washington, D.C. and Los Angeles, Calif., 1952-1957. *Member:* Beverly Hills, Los Angeles County and American Bar Associations; The State Bar of California; The State Bar of Illinois. (Certified Specialist, Taxation Law, The State Bar of California Board of Legal Specialization). **PRACTICE AREAS:** Federal and State Taxation; Tax Litigation; Estate Planning.

**STEPHEN CLAMAN,** born Los Angeles, California, September 19, 1932; admitted to bar, 1960, California and U.S. District Court, Southern District of California. *Education:* University of California at Los Angeles (A.B., 1954; LL.B., 1959). Phi Beta Kappa; Order of the Coif. Member, Board of Editors, University of California at Los Angeles Law Review, 1958-1959. *Member:* Los Angeles County Bar Association; The State Bar of California. **PRACTICE AREAS:** Real Estate; Corporate; Business.

**BERTRAM FIELDS,** born Los Angeles, California, March 31, 1929; admitted to bar, 1953, California; 1983, New York; U.S. District Court, Central District of California and District of Hawaii; U.S. Court of Appeals, Ninth Circuit; U.S. Supreme Court. *Education:* University of California at Los Angeles (B.A., 1949); Harvard Law School (LL.B., magna cum laude, 1952). Member, Board of Editors, Harvard Law Review, 1950-1952. *Member:* Beverly Hills, Los Angeles County and American Bar Associations; The State Bar of California. [With Judge Advocate General's Depart-

*(This Listing Continued)*

## GREENBERG GLUSKER FIELDS CLAMAN & MACHTINGER LLP, Los Angeles—Continued

ment, U.S. Air Force, 1953-1955]. *PRACTICE AREAS:* Communications; Entertainment; Commercial Transactions and Litigation.

**HARVEY R. FRIEDMAN,** born Hartford, Connecticut, June 2, 1938; admitted to bar, 1964, California. *Education:* Harvard University (B.A., 1960); University of Michigan (J.D., 1963). Assistant Editor, Michigan Law Review, 1962-1963. Senior Judge, Moot Court Honors Program, 1961-1963. *Member:* The State Bar of California. *PRACTICE AREAS:* Business Litigation; Real Estate Litigation.

**BERNARD SHEARER,** born Winnipeg, Manitoba, Canada, January 17, 1935; admitted to bar, 1960, California. *Education:* University of California at Los Angeles (B.A., 1956); Harvard Law School (LL.B., magna cum laude, 1959). Member, Board of Editors, Harvard Law Review, 1957-1959. Law Clerk to Justices Roger J. Traynor and Homer R. Spence, Supreme Court of California, 1959-1960. Member, Los Angeles Copyright Society. *Member:* Los Angeles County, Beverly Hills and American Bar Associations; The State Bar of California. *PRACTICE AREAS:* Corporate; Business.

**JON J. GALLO,** born Santa Monica, California, April 19, 1942; admitted to bar, 1968, California. *Education:* Occidental College (B.A., 1964); University of California at Los Angeles (J.D., 1967). Phi Alpha Delta; Order of the Coif. Member, Board of Editors, U.C.L.A. Law Review, 1965-1967. Chair, UCLA Estate Planning Institute. *Member:* Beverly Hills (President, Barristers' Section, 1973-1974), Los Angeles County and American (Co-Chair, Life Insurance Committee, Real Property, Probate and Trust Law Section) Bar Associations. The State Bar of California (Director, California Barrister's Association, 1971-1974; Vice President, 1974); International Academy of Estate and Trust Law (Academician). Fellow, American College of Trust and Estate Counsel. (Certified Specialist in Probate, Estate Planning and Trust Law, California Board of Legal Specialization). *PRACTICE AREAS:* Estate Planning.

**PAULA J. PETERS,** born Sioux City, Iowa, September 5, 1937; admitted to bar, 1968, California. *Education:* University of California at Los Angeles (B.A., 1963); Boalt Hall School of Law, University of California (J.D., 1967). *Member:* Beverly Hills, Los Angeles County and American Bar Associations; The State Bar of California. *PRACTICE AREAS:* Securities; Corporate; Corporate Reorganization.

**MICHAEL K. COLLINS,** born Sikeston, Missouri, February 13, 1943; admitted to bar, 1970, California, U.S. District Court, Central, Southern and Northern Districts of California and U.S. Court of Appeals, Ninth Circuit. *Education:* Washington University in St. Louis (A.B., 1965; J.D., 1969). Order of the Coif. Editor-in-Chief, Washington University Law Quarterly, 1968-1969. Member, Wilshire Country CLub. *Member:* Century City and Los Angeles County (Member, Executive Committee, Real Property Section, 1981-1983) Bar Associations; The State Bar of California; Association of Business Trial Lawyers. *PRACTICE AREAS:* Civil Appeals; Business; Real Estate and Attorney Malpractice Litigation.

**JOHN L. CHILD,** born Boise, Idaho, November 8, 1935; admitted to bar, 1963, Idaho; 1967, California. *Education:* University of Idaho (B.A., 1961; LL.B., 1963). *Member:* Los Angeles County Bar Association; Idaho State Bar; The State Bar of California. *PRACTICE AREAS:* Real Estate Transactions.

**C. BRUCE LEVINE,** born Liberty, New York, August 20, 1945; admitted to bar, 1971, California. *Education:* Stanford University and University of California at Los Angeles (B.A., magna cum laude, 1967); Harvard University (J.D., cum laude, 1971). Phi Beta Kappa; Pi Gamma Mu. Editor, Harvard Law Review, 1970-1971. *Member:* Beverly Hills (Chairman, Taxation Committee, 1977-1978) and Los Angeles County (Chairman, Income Tax Committee, Tax Section, 1979-1980) Bar Associations; The State Bar of California. *PRACTICE AREAS:* Tax; Estate Planning; Business; Corporate.

**MICHAEL A. GREENE,** born Los Angeles, California, January 27, 1945; admitted to bar, 1971, California. *Education:* University of California at Berkeley (A.B., 1966; M.Crim., 1972); University of Southern California (J.D., 1970). Recipient of American Board of Trial Advocates Award, 1970. Articles Editor, Southern California Law Review, 1969-1970. *Member:* Los Angeles County Bar Association; The State Bar of California; Association of Business Trial Lawyers. *PRACTICE AREAS:* Litigation.

**JOSEPH M. CAHN,** born Washington, D.C., December 30, 1931; admitted to bar, 1973, California. *Education:* Massachusetts Institute of Technology (B.S., 1954; M.S., 1954); Loyola University of Los Angeles (J.D., summa cum laude, 1973). Tau Beta Pi; Eta Kappa Nu; Sigma XI; Phi Alpha Delta. Member. St. Thomas More Society. Recipient, J. Rex Dibble Scholarship Award. Associate Editor, Loyola of Los Angeles Law Review, 1972-1973. *Member:* Beverly Hills, Century City (Member, Board of Governors, 1978-1979) and Los Angeles County Bar Associations; The State Bar of California. *PRACTICE AREAS:* Litigation; Real Estate; Technology. *Email:* jmc20@aol.com

**GARRETT L. HANKEN,** born Fairbanks, Alaska, January 10, 1948; admitted to bar, 1973, California. *Education:* University of Redlands (A.B., summa cum laude, 1970); Stanford University (J.D., 1973). Omicron Delta Kappa; Order of the Coif. Senior Note Editor, Stanford Law Review, 1972-1973. Member, Moot Court Board, 1972-1973. Law Clerk to the Honorable Shirley M. Hufstedler, U.S. Court of Appeals, Ninth Circuit, 1973-1974. *Member:* Los Angeles County and American Bar Associations; The State Bar of California. *PRACTICE AREAS:* General Civil Trial and Appellate Practice.

**NORMAN H. LEVINE,** born Cleveland, Ohio, August 12, 1949; admitted to bar, 1974, California. *Education:* University of Pennsylvania (B.A., 1971; M.A., 1971); Stanford University (J.D., 1974). Law Clerk to the Hon. William B. Enright, U.S. District Court, Southern District of California, 1974-1975. *Member:* Beverly Hills Bar Association; The State Bar of California. *PRACTICE AREAS:* Litigation.

**WILLIAM A. HALAMA,** born Chicago, Illinois, November 7, 1940; admitted to bar, 1967, California; 1994, Wyoming. *Education:* Grinnell College (B.A., 1962); University of Chicago (J.D., 1965); University of Southern California. Instructor of Law, University of Southern California Law School, 1966 and 1969. Title Insurance and Trust Company Foundation Fellow, University of Southern California, 1965-1966. *Member:* Century City (Member, Board of Governors, 1985-1991; Co-Chair, Real Property Section, 1986-1987), Los Angeles County and American Bar Associations; The State Bar of California; Wyoming State Bar. *PRACTICE AREAS:* Real Estate; Real Estate Litigation.

**JAMES E. HORNSTEIN,** born Baltimore, Maryland, August 18, 1950; admitted to bar, 1975, California. *Education:* University of North Carolina (B.A., summa cum laude, 1972); Yale University School of Law (J.D., 1975). Phi Beta Kappa. Member, Order of the Grail. Law Extern to the Honorable Robert Zampano, U.S. District Court, District of Connecticut, 1975. *Member:* Beverly Hills and American Bar Associations; The State Bar of California. *PRACTICE AREAS:* Entertainment Litigation; Labor Litigation; Intellectual Property Litigation; General Business Litigation. *Email:* jhornste@consel.com

**ROBERT S. CHAPMAN,** born Los Angeles, California, July 31, 1951; admitted to bar, 1976, California. *Education:* University of California at Berkeley (A.B., 1973); University of California at Davis (J.D., 1976). Phi Beta Kappa. Winner of Moot Court Competition, 1973-1974. Member, Moot Court Board, 1974-1975. Editor, University of California at Davis Law Review, 1975-1976. Co-Author: "Illegal Aliens and Enforcement: Present Practices and Proposed Legislation," Vol. 8, University of California at Davis Law Review, 1975. Member, Board of Directors of Public Counsel. *Member:* The State Bar of California. *PRACTICE AREAS:* Entertainment Litigation; Defamation; General Business Litigation.

**ROBERT F. MARSHALL,** born Bombay, India, May 17, 1948; admitted to bar, 1973, California. *Education:* University of California at Santa Barbara (B.A., cum laude, 1970); University of California at Los Angeles (J.D., 1973). Phi Delta Phi. Associate Editor, U.C.L.A Law Review, 1972-1973. *Member:* Beverly Hills, Los Angeles County and American Bar Associations; State Bar of California. *PRACTICE AREAS:* Entertainment; Communications; Litigation.

**ROBERT E. BENNETT, JR.,** born Pittsburgh, Pennsylvania, February 28, 1944; admitted to bar, 1970, California. *Education:* University of North Carolina (B.A., 1966); Duke University (J.D., 1969). Member, Editorial Staff, Duke Law Journal, 1967-1969. Author: "Growing Uncomfortable with 'Comfort': An Analysis of Death Tax Law and 'Comfort' as a Standard for Invasion of Trust Corpus," Vol. 53, No. 6, December, 1977, The Los Angeles Bar Journal. Co-Author: "Partnership Interests and Living Trusts," The Los Angeles Lawyer, Vol. 6, No. 11, February, 1984. *Member:* Los Angeles County (Member, Executive Committee, Trusts and Estates Section, 1992—; Member, Executive Committee, Taxation Section, 1978-1985, Treasurer, 1980-1981, Secretary, 1981-1982, Vice-Chair, 1982-1983, Chair Elect, 1983-1984, Chair, 1984-1985; Chair, Death and Gift Taxation Committee, 1979-1980; Chair, Fiduciary Income Taxation Subcommittee, 1975-1977) and American Bar Associations; The State Bar of California.

*(This Listing Continued)*

Fellow, American College of Trust and Estate Counsel. **PRACTICE AREAS:** Probate, Estate Planning and Trust Law.

**MARC S. COHEN,** born Brooklyn, New York, August 24, 1950; admitted to bar, 1974, Ohio; 1975, California. *Education:* Cornell University (B.A., 1971); New York University (J.D., 1974). Order of the Coif. Law Clerk to Judge Robert L. Carter, U.S. District Court, Southern District of New York, 1974-1975. Associate Editor, New York University Law Review, 1973-1974. Author: "Caveat Creditor: The Consumer Debtor Under the Bankruptcy Code," 58 North Carolina Law Review 681, April 1980. Lecturer, "Fundamentals of Bankruptcy," CEB, Spring, 1984, 1986; "Selected Issues in Bankruptcy Practices", CEB, 1991. Lecturer and Author: UCLA Business Bankruptcy Institute, 1993-1994; "Rights of Creditors," UCLA-CEB Estate Planning Institute, May, 1984. Member, Board of Governors, Financial Lawyers Conference, 1987-1990. Lawyer Representative, Ninth Circuit Judicial Conference, 1994-1997. *Member:* Century City (Member, Bankruptcy and Creditors Rights Committee, 1984), Los Angeles County (Vice-Chair, 1988-1989 and Chair, 1989-1990, Executive Committee, Commercial Law and Bankruptcy Section; Chair, Bankruptcy Committee, 1986-1988; Chair, U.S. Trustee Liaison Sub-Committee, 1984-1986) and American (Member, Business Bankruptcy Committee, Chapter 11 Sub-Committee, 1983, Subcommittee on Professional Ethics in Bankruptcy Cases) Bar Associations; The State Bar of California (Delegate, 1989-1990; Member, Debtor/Creditor Relations and Bankruptcy Committee, 1990-1992). Fellow, American College of Bankruptcy. **PRACTICE AREAS:** Corporate Reorganization; Bankruptcy.

**CHARLES N. SHEPHARD,** born Los Angeles, California, December 24, 1951; admitted to bar, 1977, California. *Education:* University of California at Los Angeles (B.A., 1974; J.D., 1977). Phi Beta Kappa; Order of the Coif. Member, U.C.L.A. Law Review, 1976-1977. *Member:* The State Bar of California. **PRACTICE AREAS:** Litigation.

**DENNIS B. ELLMAN,** born Brooklyn, New York, June 13, 1951; admitted to bar, 1977, New York; 1981, California. *Education:* Boston University (B.A., magna cum laude, 1973); New York University (J.D., 1976). Psi Chi. Editor, Warren's Forms Chapters on Real Property Purchase and Sale Agreements and Leases. Faculty, California Continuing Education of the Bar; Instructor, CEB Real Property Law Section Ninth Real Property Institute. *Member:* Los Angeles County Bar Association; The State Bar of California. **PRACTICE AREAS:** Real Estate.

**GARY L. KAPLAN,** born Los Angeles, California, June 9, 1949; admitted to bar, 1976, California. *Education:* Occidental College (A.B., magna cum laude, 1971); Harvard Graduate School of Arts and Sciences (M.A., Regional Studies-East Asia, 1976); Harvard Law School (J.D., 1976). Phi Beta Kappa. Thomas J. Watson Fellow, 1971-1972. Danforth Graduate Fellow, 1972-1976. Instructor: California State University at Los Angeles, Fifth Annual Institute on Taxation, 1978; University of Southern California, 38th, 41st and 45th Annual Institutes on Federal Taxation, 1986, 1989 and 1993. *Member:* Los Angeles County Bar Association (Member, Taxation Section; Chairman, Real Estate Tax Committee, 1992-1993) State Bar of California. **PRACTICE AREAS:** Taxation; General Business.

**ROBERT W. BARNES,** born Tulsa, Oklahoma, September 13, 1953; admitted to bar, 1980, California; 1981, U.S. District Court, Central District of California and U.S. Court of Appeals, Ninth Circuit. *Education:* University of Michigan and Pitzer College (B.A., 1976); University of California at Los Angeles (J.D., 1980). Order of the Barristers. Distinguished Advocate, 1979, Chief Justice, 1979-1980, UCLA Moot Court Honors Program. Judge Pro Tem, Los Angeles Municipal Court, Small Claims Division, 1986-1988. *Member:* Los Angeles County (Barristers, Board of Trustees, 1986-1987; Co-Chair, Large Firm Study Group, 1985-1987; Member, Labor Law Section) and American (Member, Litigation Section) Bar Associations; The State Bar of California (Member, Sections on: Litigation, Labor and Employment Law). **PRACTICE AREAS:** General Civil Litigation; Alternative Dispute Resolution; Labor Law; Employment Law.

**LAWRENCE Y. ISER,** born Washington, D.C., June 28, 1955; admitted to bar, 1980, California. *Education:* University of Michigan (B.A., with distinction, 1976); Hastings College of Law, University of California (J.D., 1980). Order of the Coif. Member, Thurston Society. Associate Editor, Hastings Law Journal, 1979-1980. *Member:* Century City, Los Angeles County (Member, Intellectual Property and Entertainment Law Section; Litigation Section) and American (Member, Intellectual Property Law, Entertainment and Sports Industry; Litigation Section) Bar Associations. **PRACTICE AREAS:** Entertainment Litigation; Intellectual Property Law and Litigation; Real Estate Litigation; Business Litigation. *Email:* lyial lar@aol.com

*(This Listing Continued)*

**E. BARRY HALDEMAN,** born Orange, California, September 28, 1944; admitted to bar, 1970, California. *Education:* University of California at Los Angeles (A.B., 1966); University of Miami; University of California at Los Angeles (J.D., 1969). Phi Delta Phi. Elected to University of Miami Law Review, 1967. Founding Member and Member of Advisory Committee, UCLA Entertainment Symposium; Coordinator of Symposium, 1977-1979. *Member:* Beverly Hills, Los Angeles County and American Bar Associations; The State Bar of California; Los Angeles Copyright Society. **PRACTICE AREAS:** Entertainment. *Email:* ehaldcma@counsel.com

**MARK STANKEVICH,** born Trenton, New Jersey, December 20, 1953; admitted to bar, 1980, California. *Education:* Lafayette College (B.A., magna cum laude, 1975); Boalt Hall School of Law, University of California, Berkeley (J.D., 1980). Phi Beta Kappa. Trustee, Los Angeles Copyright Society. Author, "Negotiating Talent Deals for Independent Films," Entertainment Law & FInance, Vol. X1, Nos. 7 & 8, 1995. *Member:* Beverly Hills (Member, Sections on: Entertainment Law and Patent, Trademark, Copyright), Century City, Los Angeles County (Member, Sections on: Intellectual Property and Entertainment Law) and American (Member, Intellectual Property Law Section; Forum Sections on Communications Law and Entertainment Sports Law) Bar Associations; The State Bar of California (Member, Intellectual Property Law Section). **PRACTICE AREAS:** Entertainment Law; Intellectual Property. *Email:* mas475@primenet.com

**MARTIN H. WEBSTER,** born New York, N.Y., September 20, 1917; admitted to bar, 1941, California. *Education:* California Institute of Technology (B.S., 1937); Harvard Law School (LL.B., 1940). President, Los Angeles County Bar Foundation, 1979-1981. Member, Executive Committee of The California State Bar Conference, 1973-1976. Chairman, Board of Advisors, University of California at Los Angeles Medical Center, 1986-1990. *Member:* Beverly Hills (Chairman, Committee on Taxation, 1962-1964; Member, Board of Governors, 1964-1967, 1969-1973; Vice-President, 1969; President 1970-1971), Los Angeles County (Chairman, Committee on Taxation, 1958-1959; Member, Board of Trustees, 1972-1973) and American (Member, House of Delegates, 1975-1980) Bar Associations; The State Bar of California (Member: Committee on Taxation, 1964-1967, 1967-1970); American Judicature Society. Fellow: American Bar Foundation (Patron); American College of Trust and Estate Counsel. **PRACTICE AREAS:** Tax; Corporate; Estate Planning.

**MICHAEL V. BALES,** born Weed, California, December 19, 1955; admitted to bar, 1981, California. *Education:* University of California at Davis (A.B., with honors, 1978; J.D., 1981). *Member:* Beverly Hills, Los Angeles County and American Bar Associations; The State Bar of California. **PRACTICE AREAS:** Corporate; Business; Entertainment.

**HENRY D. FINKELSTEIN,** born New York, N.Y., July 8, 1955; admitted to bar, 1981, California. *Education:* Colgate University (A.B., 1977); Washington University (J.D., 1981). Member, 1979-1980 and Senior Editor, 1980-1981, Washington University Law Quarterly. *Member:* The State Bar of California. **PRACTICE AREAS:** Real Estate.

**DIANE J. CRUMPACKER,** born New York, N.Y., December 13, 1955; admitted to bar, 1982, California. *Education:* University of California at Los Angeles (B.A., 1977; J.D., 1981). Member, Moot Court Honors Program. Contributing Editor, CEB California Business Law Reporter, November, 1982-July, 1983. *Member:* State Bar of California (Member, Law Office Management Section); American Bar Association (Member, Labor and Employment Law Section). **PRACTICE AREAS:** Labor Law; Employment Law; Employment Litigation.

**JEAN MORRIS,** born Providence, Rhode Island, July 25, 1954; admitted to bar, 1979, California, U.S. District Court, Central, Northern, Southern and Eastern Districts of California and U.S. Court of Appeals, Ninth Circuit. *Education:* Providence College (B.A., magna cum laude, 1976); Boston University (J.D., 1979). Annual Speaker, CEB, Recent Developments in Bankruptcy Law. *Member:* Century City (Member, Board of Directors) and Los Angeles County Bar Associations; State Bar of California (Member, Uniform Commercial Code Subcommittee); Financial Lawyers Conference. **PRACTICE AREAS:** Bankruptcy/Commercial Law.

**ELIZABETH WATSON,** born Lakewood, Ohio, July 20, 1955; admitted to bar, 1981, California. *Education:* Northwestern University (B.S.J., 1977); University of Southern California (J.D., 1981). *Member:* State Bar of California. **PRACTICE AREAS:** Real Estate.

**JILL A. COSSMAN,** born Brooklyn, New York, September 30, 1946; admitted to bar, 1983, California. *Education:* Connecticut College (B.A., cum laude, 1968); University of Southern California (J.D., 1983). *Member:* The State Bar of California. **PRACTICE AREAS:** Corporate; Business.

*(This Listing Continued)*

## GREENBERG GLUSKER FIELDS CLAMAN & MACHTINGER LLP, Los Angeles—Continued

**PETER J. NIEMIEC,** born Yonkers, New York, March 9, 1951; admitted to bar, 1976, California; 1982, District of Columbia; 1983, Indiana. *Education:* Columbia College (B.A., 1973); New York University (J.D., 1976). Associate Editor, Annual Survey of American Law, 1975-1976. Adjunct Professor of Law, Indiana University School of Law, Indianapolis, 1984. Deputy Attorney General, State of Indiana, 1983-1986. Author: "LUST Cleanups: Can You Make the Former Owner Pay?" Toxics Law Reporter, Vol. 5, No. 48, 1991; "Asbestos and CERCLA: Liability Lingers for Sellers," Toxics Law Reporter, Vol. 9 No. 2, 1994. Member: Committee on Review and Evaluation of the Army Chemical Stock Pile Disposal Program, National Research Council 1992-1998; Steering Committee, Environmental Auditing Forum, 1991-1994. *Member:* State Bar of California; District of Columbia Bar; Los Angeles County and American (Section of Natural Resources, Energy and Environmental Law; Vice Chair, Special Committee on Toxic and Environmental Torts, 1992-1994) Bar Associations. *PRACTICE AREAS:* Environmental Law.

**ROGER L. FUNK,** born Wauseon, Ohio, January 26, 1940; admitted to bar, 1983, California and U.S. District Court, Central District of California; 1985, U.S. Court of Appeals, Ninth Circuit; 1987, U.S. Supreme Court; 1989, U.S. District Court, Northern District of California; 1993, U.S. District Court, Southern District of California. *Education:* Huntington College (A.B., 1962); Northwestern University (Ph.D., 1969); University of California at Los Angeles (J.D., 1983). Order of the Coif. Associate Editor, U.C.-L.A. Law Review, 1982-1983. Author: "National Security Controls on the Dissemination of Privately Generated Scientific Information," U.C.L.A. Law Review, Vol. 30, No. 2, 1982. Law Clerk to the Hon. Malcolm M. Lucas, U.S. District Judge, Associate Justice, Supreme Court of California, 1983-1984. *Member:* Los Angeles County and American Bar Associations; State Bar of California. *PRACTICE AREAS:* Litigation. *Email:* rfunk000@reach.com

**RICHARD A. KALE,** born Brooklyn, New York, January 29, 1955; admitted to bar, 1980, California. *Education:* University of California, Los Angeles; University of California, Berkeley (A.B., 1976); Yale Law School (J.D., 1980). Phi Beta Kappa. Adjunct Professor, Loyola Law School, Real Property Secured Transactions. *Member:* Los Angeles County Bar Association (Member, Real Property Section); The State Bar of California. *PRACTICE AREAS:* Real Estate Law.

**DEBBY R. ZURZOLO,** born Los Angeles, California, December 18, 1956; admitted to bar, 1982, California. *Education:* University of California at Los Angeles (B.A., summa cum laude, 1979; J.D., 1982). Phi Beta Kappa, Order of the Coif. Member, University of California at Los Angeles Law Review, 1981-1982. *Member:* State Bar of California; Los Angeles County (Member, Real Property Law Section) and American Bar Associations. *PRACTICE AREAS:* Real Estate.

**ARNOLD D. KAHN,** born Salt Lake City, Utah, January 28, 1939; admitted to bar, 1965, California. *Education:* University of California, Los Angeles (A.B., 1961); University of California, Berkeley (LL.B., 1964). Order of the Coif; Phi Beta Kappa. Member, Board of Editors, California Law Review, 1963-1964. Author, "Family Security Through Estate Planning" 2nd Edition, (McGraw-Hill, 1983). *Member:* Planning Committee, U.S.C. Probate and Trust Conference (1975—); Los Angeles County and Beverly Hills (Chairman, Probate and Trust Committee, 1973) Bar Associations; The State Bar of California; International Academy of Estate and Trust Law; American Legal Council of Trust and Estate Counsel. (Certified Specialist, Probate, Estate Planning and Trust Law, The State Bar of California Board of Legal Specialization). *PRACTICE AREAS:* Estate Planning; Probate and Trust Law.

**MARK A. GOCHMAN,** born Skokie, Illinois, July 1, 1960; admitted to bar, 1986, California and U.S. District Court, Central District of California. *Education:* University of California at San Diego (B.A., 1982); University of California at Los Angeles (J.D., 1986). Recipient, American Jurisprudence Awards in Torts and Evidence. *Member:* Beverly Hills, Los Angeles County and American Bar Associations; State Bar of California. *PRACTICE AREAS:* Entertainment; Intellectual Property.

**EVE H. WAGNER,** born Los Angeles, California, January 10, 1960; admitted to bar, 1986, California; 1987, U.S. District Court, Central District of California. *Education:* University of West Los Angeles (B.S., with honors, 1982); University of Southern California (J.D., 1986). Order of the Coif. Recipient, American Jurisprudence Award in Constitutional Law. Member, University of Southern California Law Review, 1985-1986. Author: "Heckling: A Protected Right or Disorderly Conduct?" 60 Southern California Law Review 215, 1986; Law Clerk to the Hon. William P. Gray, U.S. District Court, 1986-1987. *Member:* Los Angeles County and American Bar Associations; State Bar of California. *PRACTICE AREAS:* Entertainment Litigation; Employment Litigation; Business Litigation.

**GERALD L. SAUER,** born Los Angeles, California, October 19, 1957; admitted to bar, 1984, California. *Education:* University of California at Los Angeles (B.A., 1979); Hastings College of Law, University of California (J.D., 1983). Writer, 1981-1982 and Case/Comment Editor, 1982-1983, Hastings Constitutional Law Quarterly. *Member:* Los Angeles County and American Bar Associations; State Bar of California. *PRACTICE AREAS:* Business Litigation; Real Estate Litigation; Labor Law; Entertainment Litigation.

**NANCY A. BERTRANDO,** born Los Angeles, California, January 26, 1957; admitted to bar, 1985, California and U.S. Court of Appeals, Ninth Circuit; U.S. District Court, Central District of California. *Education:* San Diego State University (B.A., with high honors, 1979); University of Southern California (J.D., 1985). *Member:* Beverly Hills, Los Angeles County and American Bar Associations; State Bar of California. *PRACTICE AREAS:* Employment Law.

**BONNIE E. ESKENAZI,** born Queens, New York, September 16, 1960; admitted to bar, 1985, California, U.S. District Court, Northern District of California and U.S. Court of Appeals, Ninth Circuit; 1986, U.S. District Court, Central District of California. *Education:* University of Virginia (B.A., with highest distinction, 1982); Stanford University (J.D., 1985). Phi Beta Kappa. Law Clerk to Hon. Donald B. King, California Court of Appeals, 1985-1986. *Member:* Los Angeles County (Member, Superior Courts Subcommittee), Century City and American Bar Associations; State Bar of California. *PRACTICE AREAS:* Litigation.

**GLENN A. DRYFOOS,** born Orange, New Jersey, May 30, 1961; admitted to bar, 1987, California, U.S. District Court, Central, Southern, Eastern and Northern Districts of California and U.S. Court of Appeals, Ninth Circuit. *Education:* Princeton University (A.B., cum laude, 1983); New York University (J.D., 1987). *Member:* Los Angeles County Bar Association; State Bar of California. *PRACTICE AREAS:* Bankruptcy; Corporate Reorganization; Business. *Email:* gdryfoos@counsel.com

**RICHARD E. POSELL,** born Los Angeles, California, June 27, 1941; admitted to bar, 1966, California; 1971, U.S. Tax Court and U.S. Claims Court; 1973, U.S. Supreme Court. *Education:* University of California at Los Angeles (B.A., 1962); Boalt Hall School of Law, University of California (J.D., 1965). Author: "Practical Advice Concerning The Business and Legal Aspects of Video Taping Live Musical Performances," 2 Loyola Entertainment Law Journal 35, 1982. Speaker, "Franchisors' Liability For Franchisees' Acts," Continuing Education of the Bar, October, 1986. Law Clerk to Presiding Judge, Lester William Roth, California Court of Appeals, Second District, 1965-1966. *Member:* Century City and Los Angeles County Bar Associations; State Bar of California (Member, Forum Committee on Franchising, 1984—); Association of Independent Commercial Producers. *PRACTICE AREAS:* Entertainment; Litigation; Intellectual Property.

**JEFFREY SPITZ,** born Freeport, New York, January 25, 1956; admitted to bar, 1985, California and U.S. District Court, Eastern and Central Districts of California. *Education:* University of Pennsylvania (B.A., 1975); Rutgers University Graduate School of Education (M.Ed., 1979) Kappa Delta Pi; University of California at Davis (J.D., 1985). Order of the Coif. Judge Pro Tem, Los Angeles County Municipal Court. Arbitrator, Los Angeles County Superior and Municipal Courts. *Member:* Los Angeles County and American Bar Associations; State Bar of California. *PRACTICE AREAS:* Entertainment Litigation; Intellectual Property Litigation; Real Estate Litigation; Bankruptcy Litigation; General Business Litigation.

**STEVEN J. LURIE,** born Los Angeles, California, August 15, 1962; admitted to bar, 1988, California; 1989, U.S. District Court, Central District of California. *Education:* University of California at Berkeley (B.S., with high honors, 1984); Boalt Hall School of Law, University of California (J.D., 1988). Order of the Coif; Phi Beta Kappa; Beta Gamma Sigma. Member, Moot Court Board. Moot Court Board Award for Best Oral Argument. Recipient, American Jurisprudence Award in Corporations, 1987; Wiley W. Manuel Pro Bono Legal Services Award, 1992. Author: "Application of California Code of Civil Procedure Section 580d to a Guaranty Secured by Real Property," 28 California Western Law Review 51, 1991. *Member:* Beverly Hills (Consultant, *Drafting Business Contracts: Principles, Techniques and Forms*, California Continuing Education of the Bar, December 1994; Chairman, Real Estate Section, 1994-1995; Vice Chairman, Real Estate Section, 1993), Los Angeles County and American Bar Associations;

*(This Listing Continued)*

State Bar of California. *PRACTICE AREAS:* Real Estate; Corporate; Business.

**BRIAN L. EDWARDS,** born San Leandro, California, March 20, 1963; admitted to bar, 1989, California, U.S. District Court, Central, Northern, Eastern and Southern Districts of California and U.S. Court of Appeals, Ninth Circuit. *Education:* University of Texas at Austin (B.J., 1986; J.D., with honors 1988). Phi Delta Phi. *Member:* Beverly Hills and Los Angeles County Bar Associations; State Bar of California.

**STANLEY W. LEVY,** born Chicago, Illinois, December 12, 1941; admitted to bar, 1966, California and U.S. District Court, Southern and Central Districts of California; 1970, U.S. Supreme Court and U.S. Court of Appeals, Ninth and Tenth Circuits. *Education:* University of California at Los Angeles (A.B., 1962; J.D., 1965). Adjunct Professor of Law: Loyola University School of Law, Los Angeles, California, 1969-1974; John F. Kennedy School of Law, Orinda, California, 1969-1974. Executive Director: Western Center on Law and Poverty, 1970; Public Counsel, Beverly Hills Bar Association Law Foundation, 1971-1974. Director of Training, Los Angeles City Attorney's Office, 1974-1976. Sole Practitioner, 1976-1983. Partner, Weinberg Zipser Arbiter & Heller, 1984-1990. Of Counsel, Stein & Kahan, 1990-1991. *Member:* State Bar of California. (Also General Counsel to Guess?, Inc., Los Angeles, CA). *PRACTICE AREAS:* Intellectual Property Litigation; Business Litigation; Licensing; Labor and Employment; Business Transactions.

**MICHAEL K. GRACE,** born Mt. Pleasant, Michigan, February 14, 1959; admitted to bar, 1986, California and U.S. District Court, Central District of California. *Education:* Michigan State University (B.A., 1981); University of Michigan (J.D., 1986). Phi Beta Kappa. National Merit Scholar, Rotary International Foundation Scholar. *PRACTICE AREAS:* Intellectual Property; Business.

## ASSOCIATES

**LEE A. DRESIE,** born Portland, Oregon, March 24, 1957; admitted to bar, 1982, California, U.S. District Court, Central District of California and U.S. Court of Appeals, Ninth Circuit. *Education:* Haverford College (B.A., 1978); University of California at Los Angeles (J.D., 1982). *Member:* Los Angeles County Bar Association; State Bar of California; National Association of Basketball Coaches. *PRACTICE AREAS:* Litigation.

**NANCY C. HSIEH,** born Santa Monica, California, July 31, 1962; admitted to bar, 1986, California and U.S. District Court, Central, District of California; 1990, U.S. District Court, Northern, Southern and Eastern Districts of California. *Education:* Yale University (B.A., cum laude, 1982); Boalt Hall School of Law, University of California (J.D., 1986). *Member:* Century City, Los Angeles County and American Bar Associations; State Bar of California; Financial Lawyers Conference. *PRACTICE AREAS:* Bankruptcy.

**NANETTE LYNN KLEIN,** born West Covina, California, March 24, 1963; admitted to bar, 1989, California. *Education:* University of California at Santa Barbara (B.A., summa cum laude, 1985); University of California, Hastings College of the Law (J.D., 1989). Member, COMM/ENT, Hastings Journal of Communications and Entertainment Law, 1987-1988. *Member:* Beverly Hills, Century City, Los Angeles County and American Bar Associations; State Bar of California. *PRACTICE AREAS:* Entertainment Law.

**DAVID R. MERSTEN,** born Tel Aviv, Israel, April 22, 1965; admitted to bar, 1990, California. *Education:* University of California at Los Angeles (B.A., magna cum laude, 1987); Hastings College of the Law, University of California (J.D., 1990). Order of the Coif. Member, Thurston Society. *Member:* State Bar of California. *PRACTICE AREAS:* Civil Litigation.

**PATRICIA A. MILLETT,** born Providence, Rhode Island, December 20, 1965; admitted to bar, 1990, California; 1992, District of Columbia. *Education:* Virginia Polytechnic Institute and State University (B.S. in Business, magna cum laude, 1987); University of Virginia (J.D., 1990). *Member:* Los Angeles County Bar Association; District of Columbia Bar; State Bar of California. *PRACTICE AREAS:* General Commercial Litigation.

**ELISABETH A. BASINI,** born Brooklyn, New York, 1966; admitted to bar, 1991, California. *Education:* State University of New York at Albany (B.A., summa cum laude, 1988) Phi Beta Kappa; University of Rochester; University of California at Los Angeles (J.D., 1991). *PRACTICE AREAS:* Litigation.

**JEFFREY A. KRIEGER,** born Providence, Rhode Island, February 28, 1964; admitted to bar, 1991, California. *Education:* Swarthmore College (B.A., 1986); University of California School of Law, Davis (J.D., 1991).

*(This Listing Continued)*

Recipient, American Jurisprudence Award in Legal Writing. *PRACTICE AREAS:* Corporate Reorganization; Bankruptcy; Creditors Rights.

**CARLA M. ROBERTS,** born Los Angeles, California, July 12, 1964; admitted to bar, 1991, California. *Education:* University of Southern California (A.B., magna cum laude, 1985); Waseda University (1983-1984); Yale Law School (J.D., 1991). Phi Beta Kappa; Phi Kappa Phi. Author, Note, "Worthy of Rejection: Copyright as Community Property," 100 Yale L. J., 1053, 1991. *Member:* Beverly Hills and Century City Bar Associations; State Bar of California. *PRACTICE AREAS:* Entertainment.

**EDWARD N. SABIN,** born Los Angeles, California, 1966; admitted to bar, 1991, California. *Education:* University of California at Los Angeles (B.A., 1988; J.D., 1991). *PRACTICE AREAS:* Litigation.

**MICHAEL W. SCHOLTZ,** born Torrance, California, November 6, 1964; admitted to bar, 1992, California and U.S. District Court, Central District of California; 1993, U.S. District Court, Eastern District of California; 1994, U.S. District Court, Northern and Southern Districts of California. *Education:* University of Southern California (B.A., summa cum laude, 1985); University of California at Los Angeles (M.A., 1987); Boalt Hall School of Law, University of California (J.D., 1992). Phi Beta Kappa; Phi Kappa Phi. *Member:* Los Angeles County Bar Association. *PRACTICE AREAS:* Bankruptcy; Commercial Law. *Email:* mschol000@counsel.com

**JOAN E. SMILES,** born New York, N.Y.; admitted to bar, 1992, California. *Education:* Vassar College (B.A., cum laude, 1965); Stanford University (M.A., 1967; Ph.D., 1976); Fulbright Graduate Fellow, Stanford University; University of Southern California (J.D., 1992). Order of the Coif. Senior Staff, Review of Law and Women's Studies. *PRACTICE AREAS:* Employment Law.

**MARK S. WEINSTOCK,** born Los Angeles, California, July 22, 1966; admitted to bar, 1992, California. *Education:* University of California at Santa Barbara (B.A., summa cum laude, 1988); Northwestern University (J.D., 1992). Recipient, Thomas More Storke Award, University of California, Santa Barbara, 1988. Author: "Cruzan and the Right to Die: The Need for Modified Surrogate Decision-Making," 6 American Journal of Family Law, 77, Summer 1992. *Member:* Beverly Hills and Los Angeles County Bar Associations. *PRACTICE AREAS:* Real Estate.

**KEVIN L. JAMES,** born August 6, 1963; admitted to bar, 1988, California. *Education:* University of Oklahoma (B.A., 1985); University of Houston College of Law (J.D., 1988). Phi Delta Phi. Member, Executive Board of Editors, Alumni Developments Editor, Houston Law Review, 1986-1988. Assistant U.S. Attorney, 1990-1993. *Member:* State Bar of California. *PRACTICE AREAS:* Litigation; Entertainment Litigation; Communications Litigation. *Email:* kjla1@aol.com

**SHERI E. PORATH,** born Albuquerque, New Mexico, February 3, 1965; admitted to bar, 1993, California and U.S. District Court, Central District of California. *Education:* University of California, Berkeley (B.A., cum laude, 1987); University of Southern California (J.D., 1992). Law Clerk to the Hon. George P. Kazen, U.S. District Court, 1992-1993. Author, "Engendering Social Security Disability Determination: The Path of A Woman Claimant," 68 Tulane Law Review, June 1994. Member, Ninth Circuit Task Force on Gender Bias in the Federal Courts, 1992. *PRACTICE AREAS:* Litigation.

**STEPHANIE H. GOLD,** born Salt Lake City, Utah, July 4, 1968; admitted to bar, 1993, California and U.S. District Court, Central District of California. *Education:* Yale University (B.A., summa cum laude, 1990); Boalt Hall School of Law, University of California, Berkeley (J.D., 1993). Recipient, American Jurisprudence Award, Education and the Law. Law Clerk, Hon. Mariana R. Pfaelzer, U.S. District Court, Central District of California; *Member:* Beverly Hills and Los Angeles County Bar Associations; State Bar of California. *PRACTICE AREAS:* Litigation.

**MATTHEW M. JOHNSON,** born New Brunswick, New Jersey, April 19, 1968; admitted to bar, 1993, California. *Education:* Rutgers University (B.A., 1990); New York University (J.D., 1993). *PRACTICE AREAS:* Transactional Entertainment.

**WENDY M. MESNICK,** born Encino, California, October 19, 1967; admitted to bar, 1993, California. *Education:* University of California, Los Angeles (B.A., with honors, 1990); University of California at Davis (J.D., 1993). Order of the Coif. Senior Research Editor, University of California at Davis Law Review. *PRACTICE AREAS:* Litigation.

**STEPHEN S. SMITH,** born Gainesville, Florida, April 29, 1969; admitted to bar, 1993, California. *Education:* Trinity University; Rice University (B.A., 1990); University of Texas (J.D., with honors, 1993). Member, American Journal of Criminal Law. Author, "Justice Douglas and the

*(This Listing Continued)*

## GREENBERG GLUSKER FIELDS CLAMAN & MACHTINGER LLP, Los Angeles—Continued

Death Penalty: A Demanding View of Due Process," 20 *American Journal of Criminal Law* Fall 1992, pg. 3 135-161. **PRACTICE AREAS:** Litigation; Entertainment.

**MARC M. STERN,** born North Hollywood, California, August 6, 1959; admitted to bar, 1986, California and U.S. District Court, Central District of California. *Education:* Stanford University (B.S., 1981); University of Southern California (J.D., 1986). Phi Alpha Delta. Staff Member, 1984-1985, and Publications Editor, 1985-1986, University of Southern California Law Review. Adjunct Professor, Golden Gate University, School of Accounting and Taxation, Los Angeles Campus (Income Taxation of Estates, Trusts and beneficiaries), 1993—. *Member:* Los Angeles County (Member, Executive Committee, Probate and Trust Law Section, 1991-1994) and American Bar Associations; State Bar of California (Chair, Estate Planning and Probate Subcommittee of CEB Joint Advisory Committee to the State Bar, 1995—; CYLA Board of Directors, District 7 Representative, 1991-1994; Treasurer, 1992-1993; Third Vice President, 1993-1994). **PRACTICE AREAS:** Estate Planning; Probate; Trust Administration.

**CURTIS P. HOLDSWORTH,** born New York, N.Y., January 16, 1967; admitted to bar, 1994, California. *Education:* University of California at Los Angeles (B.A., 1990); University of Southern California (J.D., 1994). Editor, Hale Moot Court Honors Program. **PRACTICE AREAS:** Litigation.

**KAREN E. POINTER,** born Los Angeles, California, August 5, 1963; admitted to bar, 1994, California; U.S. District Court, Central District of California and U.S. Court of Appeals, Ninth Circuit. *Education:* Loyola Marymount University (B.S., 1984); University of California at Los Angeles (J.D., 1994). Recipient, American Jurisprudence Award, Contracts, Civil Pro. and Legal Research and Waiting. Editor-In-Chief, National Black Law Journal. *Member:* Los Angeles County Bar Association; State Bar of California. **PRACTICE AREAS:** Employment Law and Litigation.

**PAUL A. BLECHNER,** born Tulsa, Oklahoma, May 21, 1966; admitted to bar, 1992, California. *Education:* Occidental College (A.B., cum laude, 1988); New York University (J.D., cum laude, 1991). Phi Beta Kappa. Senior Articles Editor, Annual Survey of American Law, 1990-1991. Law Clerk to Hon. Gordon Thompson, Jr., U.S. District Court, Southern District of California, 1991-1993. *Member:* State Bar of California; American Bar Association. **PRACTICE AREAS:** Litigation.

**STEPHEN P. CLARK,** born Memphis, Tennessee, January 21, 1968; admitted to bar, 1995, California and U.S. District Court, Central District of California; 1996, U.S. District Court, Eastern and Southern Districts of California. *Education:* Wake Forest University (B.A., cum laude, 1990); Hastings College of the Law, University of California (J.D., cum laude, 1995). Member: Thurston Society; Moot Court Board. Senior Articles Editor, Hastings Law Journal. Recipient, American Jurisprudence Awards for Legal Writing and Moot Court. Extern Clerk, Hon. Fern M. Smith, U.S. District Court, Northern District of California, 1995. Author, "Main Line v. Basinger and the Mixed Motive Manager: Reexamining the Agent's Privilege to Induce Breach of Contract," 46 Hastings Law Journal 609, 1995. *Member:* State Bar of California. **PRACTICE AREAS:** Litigation.

**NATHANAEL M. COUSINS,** born Palo Alto, California, February 21, 1970; admitted to bar, 1995, California; 1996, U.S. District Court, Central and Eastern Districts of California. *Education:* Stanford University (B.A., 1992); Hastings College of the Law, University of California (J.D., cum laude, 1995). Order of the Coif. Note Editor, Hastings Constitutional Law Quarterly. Law Clerk, Hon. F. A. Little, Jr., U.S. District Court, Western District of Louisiana, 1996-1997. *Member:* Los Angeles County Bar Association; State Bar of California. **PRACTICE AREAS:** Litigation. **Email:** ncousins@counsel.com

**PATRICK P. DE GRAVELLES,** born Tracy, California, January 23, 1965; admitted to bar, 1995, California, U.S. District Court, Central District of California and U.S. Court of Appeals, Ninth Circuit. *Education:* Georgetown University (B.S.F.S., magna cum laude, 1987); University of California School of the Law (J.D., 1995). Phi Beta Kappa. **PRACTICE AREAS:** Litigation.

**KRISTEN L. JACOBSMEYER,** born Santa Monica, California, July 30, 1969; admitted to bar, 1995, California and U.S. District Court, Central District of California; 1996, U.S. District Court, Southern District of California. *Education:* University of California, Berkeley (B.A., 1991); University of California School of Law, Los Angeles (J.D., 1995). **PRACTICE AREAS:** Litigation.

*(This Listing Continued)*

**BARRY D. KELLMAN,** born Baltimore, Maryland, June 15, 1953; admitted to bar, 1995, California, U.S. District Court, Central District of California and U.S. Court of Appeals, Ninth Circuit. *Education:* University of California, Los Angeles (B.A., summa cum laude, 1991); University of California School of the Law, Los Angeles (J.D., 1995). Moot Court Distinguished Advocate. *Member:* State Bar of California. **PRACTICE AREAS:** Litigation.

**KELLY L. SATHER,** born Santa Monica, California, August 31, 1969; admitted to bar, 1995, California. *Education:* Princeton University (A.B., 1991); Duke University (J.D., 1995). Editor in Chief, Duke Journal of Gender Law and Policy, 1994-1995. **PRACTICE AREAS:** Transactional Entertainment.

**BRADLEY SMALL,** born Detroit, Michigan, September 22, 1968; admitted to bar, 1994, California; 1995, Florida. *Education:* Brown University (B.A., Economics, 1991); University of California at Los Angeles (J.D., 1994). Member, Moot Court Honors Board. Florida Sports Agent License, 1994. *Member:* Los Angeles County Bar Association; State Bar of California (Member, Sections on: Sports Law and Commerical Law); Sports Lawyers Association; Entertainment Law Association. **PRACTICE AREAS:** Banking; Sports and Entertainment.

**DOUGLAS G. CROWELL,** born Berkeley, California, May 12, 1962; admitted to bar, 1995, California. *Education:* University of California, Los Angeles (B.S., 1984); Notre Dame School of Law (J.D., magna cum laude, 1995). Phi Eta Sigma. International Negotiation Honors, American Bar Association. *Member:* State Bar of California.

**GREGORY J. SATER,** born Los Angeles, California, December 9, 1966; admitted to bar, 1992, California. *Education:* Stanford University (B.A., with distinction, 1988); Harvard Law School (J.D., cum laude, 1991). **PRACTICE AREAS:** Business Litigation; Intellectual Property Litigation; Entertainment Litigation; Copyright Law; Trademark Law.

REFERENCE: Wells Fargo Bank, 1801 Century Park East, Los Angeles, CA 90067.

---

# GARY S. GREENE

*Established in 1975*

**157 SOUTH FAIRFAX AVENUE**
SECOND FLOOR

**LOS ANGELES, CALIFORNIA 90036-2106**
*Telephone: 213-525-1800*
*Fax: 213-525-1300*

Business, Real Property, Personal Injury, Probate and Creditors Rights Law. General Civil and Trial Practice in State and Federal Courts.

**GARY S. GREENE,** born Los Angeles, California, November 11, 1949; admitted to bar, 1975, California; 1976, U.S. District Court, Central District of California; U.S. Court of Appeals, Ninth Circuit; 1978, U.S. Tax Court; 1980, U.S. Supreme Court. *Education:* U.C.L.A. (B.A., summa cum laude, 1971); Loyola University (J.D., 1975). Phi Beta Kappa; Phi Eta Sigma (President, 1968-1971); Pi Sigma Alpha; Pi Gamma Mu; Phi Alpha Delta. Member: Blue Key; St. Thomas More Law Honor Society. President, UCLA Political Science Honor Society, 1970-1971. Law Clerk, Los Angeles County District Attorney, 1973-1974. Concertmaster, Jr. Philharmonic Orchestra of California, 1963—. Lecturer and Author, Continuing Legal Education, Inc., 1980; Princess Cruises, 1995—. Mediator, Los Angeles County Superior Court, 1981-1984. Judge Pro Tem: Los Angeles Superior Court, 1990—; Los Angeles and Beverly Hills Small Claims and Municipal Courts, 1981—; Traffic Court, 1981-1986. Member, Board of Directors of The Cultural Commission, 1981-1982. *Member:* Beverly Hills (Co-Chairman, Barristers Speakers Bureau, 1979-1980) and Los Angeles County (Arbitrator, 1981-1985) Bar Associations; State Bar of California.

COUNSEL FOR: K-G Properties.

## GREENE, BROILLET, TAYLOR, WHEELER, & PANISH
### LOS ANGELES, CALIFORNIA
(See Santa Monica)

General Civil and Trial Practice in all State and Federal Courts. Personal Injury, Insurance, Products Liability, Malpractice, Negligence and Sex Discrimination.

---

## GREENWALD, HOFFMAN & MEYER
### LOS ANGELES, CALIFORNIA
(See Glendale)

General Civil Trial and Appellate Practice. Probate, Trust, Estate Planning, Real Property, Environmental, Condominium, Corporation, Banking, Business and Family Law.

---

## GREINES, MARTIN, STEIN & RICHLAND
### LOS ANGELES, CALIFORNIA
(See Beverly Hills)

Appellate, Law and Motion and Related Practice in State and Federal Courts.

---

## RICHARD T. GRIFFIN
BRADBURY BUILDING, SUITE 225
304 SOUTH BROADWAY
### LOS ANGELES, CALIFORNIA 90013
Telephone: 213-628-5595
Fax: 213-628-8470

Immigration and Nationality. Trial and Appellate Practice in all State and Federal Courts.

**RICHARD T. GRIFFIN,** born Omaha, Nebraska, August 3, 1931; admitted to bar, 1958, California; 1975, U.S. Supreme Court. *Education:* Loyola University of Los Angeles (B.S., 1954); University of California School of Law (J.D., 1957). *Member:* Pasadena Bar Association; State Bar of California; American Immigration Lawyers Association.

---

## RICHARD L. GRIMWADE
333 SOUTH GRAND AVENUE
SUITE 3700
### LOS ANGELES, CALIFORNIA 90071-1599
Telephone: 213-346-9370
Fax: 213-625-1832

Newport Beach Office: 4400 MacArthur Boulevard, 7th Floor. Telephone: 714-752-7551. Fax: 714-752-0288.

Civil Litigation including Wrongful Termination, Business, Related Litigation, Professional Liability, Real Estate and Insurance Bad Faith.

**RICHARD L. GRIMWADE,** born Chicago, Illinois, April 26, 1945; admitted to bar, 1971, Wisconsin; 1972, New York; 1978, Illinois; 1981, California. *Education:* Lawrence University (B.A., 1967); University of Wisconsin (J.D., cum laude, 1971). Order of the Coif. Member, University of Wisconsin Law Review, 1969-1971. Recipient, American Jurisprudence Awards in Evidence, Legislation and Accounting and Law. Member, Toastmasters, CTM. Director, 1992-1994 and Secretary, 1994-1995, Rotary Club of Los Angeles. Ketchum Downtown YMCA Board of Managers, 1990—. Formerly Associated with Davis, Polk & Wardwell, New York, New York. *Member:* Los Angeles County, New York State and Illinois State Bar Associations; State Bar of California; State Bar of Wisconsin.

---

## GRONEMEIER & BARKER
### LOS ANGELES, CALIFORNIA
(See Pasadena)

Commercial, Business, Labor, Land Use, Civil Rights and Public Law. Litigation.

---

## FRED J. GROSSBLATT
1900 AVENUE OF THE STARS
SEVENTEENTH FLOOR
### LOS ANGELES, CALIFORNIA 90067-4403
Telephone: 310-552-2002
Facsimile: 310-552-2324
E-Mail: fredjg@primenet.com

Commercial, Collection, Creditors Rights and Business Litigation.

**FRED J. GROSSBLATT,** born Los Angeles, California, 1953; admitted to bar, 1978, California. *Education:* University of California at Los Angeles (B.A., 1975); Southwestern University School of Law (J.D., 1978). Author, "Successful Judgment Collections in California," National Business Institute Panel, 1996. *Member:* State Bar of California; Commercial Law League of America.

---

## HARVEY M. GROSSMAN
P.O. BOX 36E19
### LOS ANGELES, CALIFORNIA 90036-1419
Telephone: 213-957-1236

Civil Appellate Practice in all State and Federal Courts.

**HARVEY M. GROSSMAN,** born Pittsburgh, Pennsylvania, July 19, 1929; admitted to bar, 1956, California; 1960, U.S. Supreme Court. *Education:* University of California at Los Angeles (A.B., 1951; LL.B., 1954). Order of the Coif. Editor-in-Chief, U.C.L.A. Law Review, 1953-1954. Law Clerk, Hon. Justice William O. Douglas, U.S. Supreme Court, 1954. Author: "Appellant's Opening and Reply Briefs," California Civil Appellate Practice, 3rd Edition (Cont. Ed. Bar, 1996), §12 pp. 633-704. Co-author: "California Pleading," 1981; "California Pretrial and Settlement Procedures," 1963; "California Discovery Practice," 1972. *Member:* Los Angeles County and American Bar Associations; State Bar of California; California Academy of Appellate Lawyers.

REFERENCE: City National Bank (Fairfax Office, Los Angeles, California).

---

## ROBERT JAY GROSSMAN
1801 CENTURY PARK EAST, 24TH FLOOR
### LOS ANGELES, CALIFORNIA 90067
Telephone: 310-282-8330
Fax: 310-282-8454
Email: RJG__LAW@CompuServe.com

Real Estate, Corporate, Finance, Tax, Contract and Transactional Law, Formation of Developmental Entities.

FIRM PROFILE: Mr. Grossman represents clients in sophisticated transactions such as corporate or real estate acquisitions, dispositions and financings, all with particular sensitivity to tax issues.

**ROBERT JAY GROSSMAN,** born Milwaukee, Wisconsin, October 8, 1949; admitted to bar, 1978, California; 1980, U.S. District Court, Central District of California. *Education:* University of Wisconsin-Madison (B.B.A., with honors in Accounting, 1972); University of California at Los Angeles (J.D., 1978). Certified Public Accountant, California, 1975. *Member:* State Bar of California. **PRACTICE AREAS:** Real Estate; Tax; Corporate Law.

## GROSSMAN, GRANT & CRAMER

### LOS ANGELES, CALIFORNIA

(See Santa Monica)

*General Civil Practice, Real Estate, Corporate and Business, Estate Planning and Probate.*

---

## GROTTA, GLASSMAN & HOFFMAN

*A PROFESSIONAL CORPORATION*

TWO CENTURY PLAZA
2049 CENTURY PARK EAST, SUITE 1800
**LOS ANGELES, CALIFORNIA 90067**
*Telephone: 310-556-8786*

*Roseland, New Jersey Office:* 75 Livingston Avenue, 07068. Telephone: 201-992-4800. Telecopier: 201-992-9125.

*New York, N.Y. Office:* 125 West 55th Street, 10019. Telephone: 212-315-3510. Telecopier: 212-315-3992.

*Practice Limited exclusively to the representation of management in all facets of labor and employment law: Employment Discrimination, Wrongful Discharge, ERISA and other employment related litigation, in state and federal courts and before federal and state administrative agencies nationwide; Union Organizing Campaigns; Negotiations; Arbitrations; Wage and Hour; OSHA; Immigration; Public Sector Labor Relations; Affirmative Actions Plans; Employee Benefits and Pension Law.*

*Harold E. Grotta*
(Not admitted in CA)

*Jerold E. Glassman*
(Not admitted in CA)

*Harold L. Hoffman*
(Not admitted in CA)

*Marvin M. Goldstein*
(Not admitted in CA)

*Stephen A. Ploscowe*
(Not admitted in CA)

*Desmond Massey*
(Not admitted in CA)

*Theodore M. Eisenberg*
(Not admitted in CA)

*Joseph J. Malcolm*
(Not admitted in CA)

*M. Joan Foster*
(Not admitted in CA)

*Richard J. Delello*
(Not admitted in CA)

*Michael Barabander*
(Not admitted in CA)

*Stanley L. Goodman*
(Not admitted in CA)

*Jed L. Marcus*
(Not admitted in CA)

*Ilene Lainer*
(Not admitted in CA)

*Jedd Mendelson*
(Not admitted in CA)

*David W. Garland*
(Not admitted in CA)

### OF COUNSEL

**Kenneth J. McCulloch** (Not admitted in CA)

LABOR AND EMPLOYMENT COUNSEL FOR: A-P-A Transport Corp.; Atlantic City Showboat Casino, Hotel and Bowling Center; Automatic Data Processing, Inc.; Bally's Casino Hotels (Atlantic City and Nevada); Block Drug Co., Inc.; CIBA-GEIGY Corp.; Citibank, N.A.; Cornell University; Corporate Express of the East; Culligan Water Company; Dannon Company, Inc.; De-Camp Bus Lines; Drake Bakeries, Inc.; Faber-Castell Corp.; Farmland Dairies, Inc.; Foley Incorporated; The Grand Union Company; The Great Atlantic & Pacific Tea Company ("A&P"); The Hartz Mountain Corp.; Jersey City Medical Center; Kmart Corp.; K. Hovnanian Companies; Lenox, Inc.; Marriott Corp.; Matsushita Electric Corp.; Medco Containment Services, Inc.; Nabisco Brands, Inc.; New England Motor Freight, Inc.; New Jersey Office Supply Inc.; New Jersey Wine & Spirit Wholesalers Assn.; Newark Beth Israel Medical Center; The New York Times; Okonite Co.; The Perrier Group; Princeton University; Prudential Securities Inc.; R.H. Macy & Co.; Seton Co.; Six Flags Great Adventure; St. Michael's Medical Center; Supermarkets General Corp.; The State of New Jersey; Township of Maplewood; Trump Plaza Hotel and Casino; Twin County Grocers, Inc.; U.S. JVC Corp.

(For complete biographical data on all personnel, see Professional Biographies at Roseland, New Jersey)

---

## GRUNFELD, DESIDERIO, LEBOWITZ & SILVERMAN LLP

A Partnership

SUITE 5555, 707 WILSHIRE BOULEVARD
**LOS ANGELES, CALIFORNIA 90017**
*Telephone: 213-624-1970*
*Telecopy: 213-624-1678*

*New York, N.Y. Office:* 33rd Floor, 245 Park Avenue. Telephone: 212-557-4000. Fax: 212-557-4415.

*Washington, D.C. Office:* Suite 680, 1500 K Street N.W. Telephone: 202-783-6881. Telecopy: 202-783-0405.

*Boston, Massachusetts Office:* Grunfeld, Desiderio, Lebowitz, Silverman & Wright, Old City Hall, 45 School Street, 2nd Floor. Telephone: 617-742-8550. Telecopy: 617-523-9429.

*Atlanta, Georgia Office:* Suite 4860, One Atlantic Center, 1201 West Peachtree Street, N.E. Telephone: 404-874-3882. Telecopy: 408-874-6895.

*Houston, Texas Office:* 1100 Louisiana, Suite 1275. Telephone: 713-650-6590. Fax: 713-650-6591.

*Customs and International Trade Law, Trade Regulations and Administrative Law. Trials and Appeals.*

### RESIDENT PARTNER

**BARRY E. POWELL,** born Glendale, California, March 1, 1948; admitted to bar, 1987, California; 1990, U.S. District Court, Central District of California. *Education:* California State University, Northridge (B.A., magna cum laude, 1970); U.S. Customs Service Academy (Advanced Import Specialist Training Certificate, 1986); Loyola Law School (J.D., cum laude, 1987). Member, St. Thomas More Law Honor Society. Recipient, American Jurisprudence Award in Civil Procedure. Member, 1985-1986, Editor, 1986-1987, Loyola of Los Angeles International and Comparative Law Journal. Author: "An Explanation of the Term "Ornamented" As Used in the Tariff Schedules of the United States," Loyola of Los Angeles International and Comparative Law Journal, Vol. 9, No. 1, 1986-1987. Senior Import Specialist, U.S. Customs Service, 1971-1987. Licensed Customs Broker, 1993. Member, Foreign Trade Association of Southern California, 1994-1995. *Member:* Los Angeles County (Chairman, Customs Committee, 1990-1992; Member, Executive Committee, International Law Section, 1993-1995) and American Bar Associations; State Bar of California (Member, Board of Directors). **PRACTICE AREAS:** Customs Law.

(For complete biographical data on all personnel, see Professional Biographies at New York, New York)

---

## JULIUS S. GRUSH

2121 AVENUE OF THE STARS, 22ND FLOOR
**LOS ANGELES, CALIFORNIA 90067**
*Telephone: 310-785-1111*
*Fax: 310-785-0720*
*Email: juglaws1@aol.com*

*General Practice.*

**JULIUS S. GRUSH,** born Los Angeles, California, December 4, 1937; admitted to bar, 1965, California. *Education:* University of California at Los Angeles (B.S., 1960); Hastings College of Law, University of California and Southwestern University (LL.B., 1964). Phi Alpha Delta. Deputy City Attorney, Los Angeles, 1965-1967. Judge Pro Tem for Los Angeles Municipal Court. Instructor for Barbri "Essay Advantage"; Beverly Hills Bar, Co-Chair of Torts, State Bar Delegate. *Member:* Beverly Hills, Los Angeles and American Bar Associations; State Bar of California. **PRACTICE AREAS:** Construction/Mechanic's Lien Litigation; Personal Injury Litigation; Business Litigation.

---

## GUMPORT, REITMAN & MONTGOMERY

550 SOUTH HOPE STREET, SUITE 825
**LOS ANGELES, CALIFORNIA 90071-2627**
*Telephone: 213-452-4900*
*Fax: 213-623-3302*

*Commercial Litigation, Bankruptcy, Mediation, Receiverships, Real Estate and General Corporate.*

FIRM PROFILE: *Gumport, Reitman & Montgomery has substantial experience in bankruptcy, insolvency and receivership-related litigation, and in asset location and recovery litigation. For more than a decade, its members have*

(This Listing Continued)

engaged in complex domestic and foreign fraud and related litigation on behalf of major creditors and bankruptcy trustees. Members of the firm have been called upon to locate and assist in recovering concealed assets throughout the United States and in foreign jurisdictions, including Canada, South America, the Cayman Islands, England, Ireland, the Channel Islands, France, Belgium, The Netherlands, Germany, Thailand, Hong Kong, and The People's Republic of China.

### MEMBERS OF FIRM

**LEONARD L. GUMPORT,** born New York, N.Y., July 16, 1950; admitted to bar, 1978, New York; 1979, California; 1980, U.S. Supreme Court, U.S. Court of Appeals, Ninth Circuit, U.S. District Court, Central, Northern, Southern and Eastern Districts of California and District of Columbia. *Education:* Yale University (B.A., summa cum laude, 1972); Columbia University (J.D., 1977). Phi Beta Kappa. Harlan Fiske Stone Scholar. Author: "The Bankruptcy Examiner," 20 Cal. Bankr. J. 71 (1992). Law Clerk to U.S. District Judge Gus J. Solomon, 1977-1979. Mediator, United States Bankruptcy Court, Central District of California. *Member:* Los Angeles County Bar Association; State Bar of California. **PRACTICE AREAS:** Business and Bankruptcy Litigation; Receiverships.

**JOHN P. REITMAN,** born Detroit, Michigan, 1945; admitted to bar, 1978, California; U.S. Court of Appeals, Ninth Circuit and U.S. District Court, Central, Eastern and Southern Districts of California. *Education:* California State University at Northridge (B.A., 1974); Loyola University of Los Angeles (J.D., cum laude, 1977). Member, Loyola University of Los Angeles Law Review, 1975-1976. Panel of Arbitrators, Pacific Stock Exchange, 1986—. Arbitrator, Los Angeles County Superior Court. Mediator, United States Bankruptcy Court, Central District of California. Judge Pro Tem, Culver City Municipal Court. *Member:* Los Angeles County Bar Association (Bankruptcy, Business Law and Litigation Sections); American Bankruptcy Institute. **PRACTICE AREAS:** Bankruptcy; Business and Commercial Law; Construction Law; Real Estate and Business Litigation; Litigation.

**SUSAN I. MONTGOMERY,** born Los Angeles, California, February 9, 1958; admitted to bar, 1985, California, U.S. District Court, Central, Southern and Eastern Districts of California and U.S. Court of Appeals, Ninth Circuit. *Education:* University of California at Los Angeles (B.S., 1978); University of Southern California (J.D., 1985). Order of the Coif. Recipient: American Board of Trial Advocates Award, 1985; American Jurisprudence Award in Trial Advocacy and Business Organization. *Member:* Los Angeles County and American Bar Associations; The State Bar of California. **PRACTICE AREAS:** Bankruptcy; Commercial and Business Litigation.

## JAY JORDAN GUSTIN AND ASSOCIATES

Established in 1974

SUITE 1240
1901 AVENUE OF THE STARS (CENTURY CITY)
**LOS ANGELES, CALIFORNIA 90067**
Telephone: 310-552-2403; 271-1147
FAX: 310-553-9259

*Commercial Practice. Bankruptcy, Insolvency, Debtor-Creditor Relationship, Corporations, Real Estate, UCC.*

**JAY JORDAN GUSTIN,** born New York, N.Y., May 16, 1924; admitted to bar, 1974, California and U.S. District Court, Central District of California; 1980, U.S. Supreme Court; 1981, U.S. District Court, Northern District of California. *Education:* University of Minnesota; University of San Fernando Valley, (B.A., 1971; J.D., 1973). Editor-in-Chief, University of San Fernando Valley Law Review, 1972-1973. Author: "Law Whose Time Has Come," Los Angeles County Bar Journal, 1978. Lecturer: "Bulk Transfers," 1985 and "Bankruptcy Preferences," 1986-1987, Commercial Law League; "Group Legal Services," Los Angeles County Bar Association, 1977 and State Bar of California, 1978-1982. *Member:* Beverly Hills, Los Angeles County (Chairman, Group Legal Services Committee, 1978-1982; Member, Bankruptcy Section) and American Bar Associations; State Bar of California (Member, Legal Services Section); Commercial Law League of America (Treasurer, 1984; Secretary, 1985; Vice Chair, 1986; Chairman: Western Region, 1987-1988; Site Committee, 1985-1987; National Resolutions Committee, 1987; Executive Council, Bankruptcy and Insolvency Section, 1986-1989; Vice Chairman, National Nominating Council, 1987; Member, Board of Governors, 1989-1992; Executive Council, Creditor's Rights Section, 1992; Co-Chair, Laws and Legislation Committee, Creditor's Rights Section, 1996-1997; Certified Specialist, Creditor's Rights) ;

*(This Listing Continued)*

Commercial Law League of America (Member of Board); Academy for Certifying Creditor's Rights and Bankruptcy Specialists. [2nd. Lt. USAFR, 1943-1950]. **PRACTICE AREAS:** Creditor's Rights; Bankruptcy; Sales Representative Affairs; Shopping Center Leasing; Business; Commercial Law.

### OF COUNSEL

**DAVID A. SCHECHET,** born Flint, Michigan, October 6, 1960; admitted to bar, 1986, California. *Education:* University of California at Los Angeles (B.A., summa cum laude, 1982; J.D., 1986). Pi Gamma Mu; Phi Beta Kappa; Order of the Coif. Recipient, American Jurisprudence Award in Civil Procedure. John M. Olin Fellow in Law and Economics. *Member:* Beverly Hills, Los Angeles County and American Bar Associations. (Also practising individually at same address).

### ASSOCIATES

**MICHAEL LIBRATY,** admitted to bar, 1992, California. *Education:* University of California at Los Angeles (B.A., cum laude, 1989); University of California at Davis (J.D., 1992). Recipient: American Jurisprudence Award in Business Organizations I. *Member:* Beverly Hills Bar Association; State Bar of California. **PRACTICE AREAS:** Commercial and Business Law.

REPRESENTATIVE CLIENTS: Western Shoe Associates; Western Shoe Retailers Association; Graphic Artists Guild; Pacific Coast Travelers; Textile Association of Los Angeles (TALA); American Airlines; Giftware Association of Los Angeles; Ferunion Trade Association of Hungary.
REFERENCE: Union Bank, Century City Branch.

## GUZIK & ASSOCIATES

1800 CENTURY PARK EAST
FIFTH FLOOR
**LOS ANGELES, CALIFORNIA 90067**
Telephone: 310-788-8600
Telecopier: 310-788-2835

*Business, Corporate, Securities, Transactional, Corporate Litigation.*

**SAMUEL S. GUZIK,** born New York, N.Y., October 2, 1952; admitted to bar, 1979, New York; 1981, California. *Education:* Cornell University (B.S., 1974); Stanford University (J.D., 1978). *Member:* Los Angeles County, New York State and American Bar Associations.

## WILLIAM W. HAEFLIGER

**LOS ANGELES, CALIFORNIA**

(See Pasadena)

*Intellectual Property, Patent, Trademark, Copyright and Unfair Competition Law.*

## HAGENBAUGH & MURPHY

**LOS ANGELES, CALIFORNIA**

(See Glendale)

*General Civil and Trial Practice in all State and Federal Courts. Insurance, Casualty, Life, Health, Accident and Disability Insurance, Malpractice, Surety and Aviation Law, Employment Law, Business Litigation (including Commercial and Advertising Disputes) and Workers Compensation Subrogation.*

## HAHN & HAHN

**LOS ANGELES, CALIFORNIA**

(See Pasadena)

*General Civil and Trial and Appellate Practice in Federal and State Courts, Corporation, Real Estate, Estate Planning, Probate, Family, Federal and State Tax Law, Employment Law.*

# CALIFORNIA—LOS ANGELES

## HAIGHT, BROWN & BONESTEEL
LOS ANGELES, CALIFORNIA
(See Santa Monica)

*General Civil and Trial Practice in all State and Federal Courts. Corporation, Tax, Real Estate, International, Franchise, Probate and Labor Law.*

---

## HALL DICKLER KENT FRIEDMAN & WOOD LLP

A Partnership including Professional Corporations

2029 CENTURY PARK EAST
SUITE 3760
**LOS ANGELES, CALIFORNIA 90067**
Telephone: 310-203-8410
Telecopier: 310-203-8559

REVISERS OF THE ROMANIA DIGEST FOR THIS DIRECTORY

*New York, N.Y. Office:* 27th Floor, 909 Third Avenue. Telephone: 212-339-5400. Telecopier: 212-935-3121. Telex: 239857 GONY UR. Cable Address: "Halcasro".

*White Plains, New York Office:* 11 Martine Avenue. Telephone: 914-428-3232.

*Bucharest, Romania Office:* Hall, Dickler (Romania), SRL. World Trade Center, Boulevard Expozitiei, Nr. 2, Suite 225, 78334 Bucharest, Romania. Telephone: (+401) 222-8888. Fax: (+401) 223-4444.

*General Corporate, Securities, Taxation, International, Real Estate, Estate Planning, Probate, Copyright, Advertising, Marketing, Unfair Competition, Radio, Television (CATV), Entertainment, Trade Regulation, Literary Property, Computer Law, Matrimonial and Federal and State Litigation.*

### MEMBERS OF FIRM

**FREDRIC W. ANSIS,** born Brooklyn, New York, August 12, 1941; admitted to bar, 1969, New York and U.S. District Court, Eastern District of New York; 1975, California. *Education:* Bucknell University (B.A., 1963); Fordham University (LL.B., 1966). Member, California Copyright Conference, 1976-1996. Member, Los Angeles Copyright Society, 1995. Member, Board of Directors, Minority Advertising Training Association, 1991. Member, NARAS, California. *Member:* Beverly Hills (Member, Entertainment Law Committee, 1976-1984), Los Angeles County and New York State Bar Associations; State Bar of California. [Capt., U.S. Army Signal Corps, 1966-1968]. (Resident). **PRACTICE AREAS:** Entertainment Law; Intellectual Property Law; Advertising Law.

**DOUGLAS J. WOOD,** born Fort Belvoir, Virginia, August 14, 1950; admitted to bar, 1976, New Jersey and U.S. District Court, District of New Jersey; 1977, New York and U.S. District Court, Southern and Eastern Districts of New York; 1982, U.S. Court of Appeals, Fifth Circuit and U.S. Supreme Court (Not admitted in California). *Education:* University of Rhode Island (B.A., 1972); Franklin Pierce Law Center (J.D., 1976); New York University (LL.M. in Trade Regulation, 1977). Phi Alpha Delta. Author: "Please be Advised: The Legal Reference Guide for the Advertising Executive," (Association of National Advertisers, Inc., 1995). Contributing author: "Business Organizations with Tax Planning, Chapter on Deceptive Advertising," (Matthew Bender & Co., 1996). Co-author: with Felix H. Kent, *Legal Problems In Advertising*, Matthew Bender & Co., 1996. Columnist on Advertising Law, Retail Advertising Digest, 1988-1996. Assistant Editor, IDEA, Law Review, Volume 18, No. 1, 1976. Author: "New Hampshire's Evolving Conflict of Laws Doctrine," 17 N.H.B.J. 43, 1975: "Commentary on the Law-Science Relationship in the Admissibility of Scientific Evidence," 18 IDEA 5, 1976. Columnist, "Advertising Law," National Law Journal. Adjunct Faculty, Legal Business Problems and Solutions in Advertising, UCLA, 1990-1991. President and Member, Board of Directors: Touchdown Club of America, Inc., 1989—; The Natural Guard, 1990—. Director, Romanian American Chamber of Commerce, 1991—; Member, National Panel of Arbitrators, American Arbitration Association. (Also at New York City and Bucharest, Romania Offices). **PRACTICE AREAS:** Advertising Law; Media and Entertainment Law; Marketing Law; International Law; Trade Regulation Law.

**CHRISTOPHER P. O'CONNELL,** born Honolulu, Hawaii, March 15, 1946; admitted to bar, 1973, New York and U.S. District Court, Eastern and Southern Districts of New York; 1996, California. *Education:* Institut d'Etudes Europeennes, Paris, France; College of the Holy Cross (A.B.,

*(This Listing Continued)*

1967); Columbia University (J.D., 1972). Harlan Fiske Stone Scholar, Columbia University. Trustee, Board of Education, Upper Saddle River, New Jersey, 1988-1991. *Member:* American Bar Association. **LANGUAGES:** French. **PRACTICE AREAS:** Corporate Law; Securities Law.

### ASSOCIATES

**ALAN H. FELDSTEIN,** born San Francisco, California, September 3, 1955; admitted to bar, 1984, California, U.S. District Court, Central, Southern and Eastern Districts of California and U.S. Court of Appeals, Ninth Circuit. *Education:* University of California at Los Angeles (B.A., 1977); Southwestern University (J.D., 1984). Member, Moot Court Board of Governors. Co-author: "Negotiation for Celebrity Talent," Response TV Magazine August/September, 1992. Contributing Writer, Response TV Magazine. *Member:* Beverly Hills and Los Angeles County Bar Associations; State Bar of California.

**SALLY KOENIG,** born Chicago, Illinois, June 4, 1961; admitted to bar, 1992, California. *Education:* Boston University (B.A., 1983); Pepperdine University School of Business and Management (M.B.A., 1989); Southwestern University (J.D., 1992). Phi Alpha Delta. *Member:* Los Angeles County Bar Association (Member, Executive Committee, Intellectual Property and Entertainment Law Section, 1994—). (Resident). **PRACTICE AREAS:** Entertainment Law; Licensing; Advertising Law.

REVISERS OF THE ROMANIA DIGEST FOR THIS DIRECTORY

(For Personnel and Biographical Data on all Personnel, see New York City Professional Biographies)

---

## JASON PAUL HALPERN

A PROFESSIONAL CORPORATION
10880 WILSHIRE BOULEVARD
SUITE 1800
**LOS ANGELES, CALIFORNIA 90024-4174**
Telephone: 310-478-2722
Facsimile: 310-470-7003

*Personal Injury, Wrongful Death, Wrongful Termination, Employee Discrimination and Harassment, Medical and Professional Malpractice, Business Litigation and Transactional Law Domestically and Internationally including Contract Preparation and Negotiation, including Severance Packages.*

**JASON P. HALPERN,** born 1944; admitted to bar, 1971, California. *Education:* Brooklyn College of the City University of New York (B.A., 1967); University of Toledo (J.D., 1970). Phi Alpha Delta. Past Settlement Officer, Los Angeles County Bar Association - Dispute Resolution Services (JASOP). Settlement Officer, Los Angeles County Superior Court Crash Settlement Conference Program. Acting Arbitrator, Los Angeles Superior Court Arbitration Program. *Member:* State Bar of California; Consumer Attorneys Association of Los Angeles. **LANGUAGES:** French.

---

## HALSTEAD, BAKER & OLSON
LOS ANGELES, CALIFORNIA
(See Baker, Olson, LeCroy & Danielian, A Law Corporation, Glendale)

---

## HAMBURG, HANOVER, EDWARDS & MARTIN

Established in 1995

2029 CENTURY PARK EAST
SUITE 1640
**LOS ANGELES, CALIFORNIA 90067-3086**
Telephone: 310-552-9292
Fax: 310-552-9291
Email: HHEMLaw@Aol.com

*General Civil Practice in all State and Federal Courts. General Real Estate, Corporate, Employment, Business, Construction, Entertainment, Taxation, Immigration, Environmental, Zoning, Insurance and Insurance Defense, Administrative, Tradenames and Trademarks Infringement, and Copyright Enforcement.*

*(This Listing Continued)*

CAA744B

FIRM PROFILE: Hamburg, Hanover, Edwards & Martin was founded in 1995. We are a full-Service law firm with an active litigation practice in all state and federal courts. We represent both plaintiffs and defendants, businesses and individuals, in a wide variety of civil cases, with an emphasis on complex business-related litigation, such as matters related to breach of contract, business torts, warranty and products-liability claims, securities law, employment disputes, insurance disputes, and all real estate related matters.

Hamburg, Hanover, Edwards & Martin also provides to businesses, their owners and management, substantially all the legal services they require, including the organization of business enterprises, financing and planning, litigation prevention and risk management, products-distribution questions, employment matters, and other business-related activities. We also represent owners, developers, and tenants of commercial and industrial real estate. We provide all services related to tax planning and tax disputes. We also have lawyers with substantial experience in environmental matters and immigration law.

Hamburg, Hanover, Edwards & Martin's clients seek business solutions to their business problems, which arise in an increasingly complex legal environment. We take pride in providing our clients with individual service, intended to produce as efficient a solution to the problem as circumstances will permit, at fair price. Prevention of litigation and containment of legal costs in the event of litigation are our principal concerns for our clients. recognizing that we cannot succeed unless we assist our clients to succeed in their own business.

### MEMBERS OF FIRM

**SIDNEY A. HAMBURG,** born Memphis, Tennessee, February 2, 1952; admitted to bar, 1977, California; 1978, U.S. District Court, Central District of California and U.S. Court of Appeals, Ninth Circuit. *Education:* University of California at Los Angeles; University of San Fernando Valley (J.D., 1977). Member, University of California Law Review. *Member:* Century City, Los Angeles County Bar Association; State Bar of California. **PRACTICE AREAS:** Real Estate Law; General Business Law; State and Federal Court Receiver.

**JOHN D. HANOVER,** born Memphis, Tennessee, June 17, 1961; admitted to bar, 1986, Tennessee; 1989, California. *Education:* Tufts University (B.A., summa cum laude, 1983); Hebrew University of Jerusalem, Jerusalem, Israel; Vanderbilt University (J.D., 1986). Phi Beta Kappa. Moot Court Problem Board Editor. Graduate of National Institute of Trial Advocacy Northwest Regional on "Basic Trial Advocacy" and Program on "Expert Witness and Special Deposition Skills". *Member:* Beverly Hills, Century City, Los Angeles County, Tennessee and American Bar Associations; State Bar of California; Association of Business Trial Lawyers. **LANGUAGES:** French and Hebrew. **REPORTED CASES:** T&R Painting Construction, Inc. v. St. Paul Fire & Marine Insurance Co., (2nd Dist., Div. 2 1994) 23 Cal. App. 4th 738. **PRACTICE AREAS:** Complex Business Litigation; Real Estate Litigation; Construction Litigation; Insurance Litigation; Employment Litigation; Entertainment Litigation.

**BARRY G. EDWARDS,** born Chicago, Illinois, December 9, 1960; admitted to bar, 1986, California and U.S. District Court, Central and Southern Districts of California. *Education:* Indiana University (B.S., 1983); Loyola Marymount University (J.D., 1986). Phi Eta Sigma; Beta Alpha Psi. *Member:* Beverly Hills, Century City and Los Angeles County Bar Associations; State Bar of California. **PRACTICE AREAS:** Taxation Law; Real Estate Law; General Business Law.

**GREGG A. MARTIN,** born Los Angeles, California, April 28, 1962; admitted to bar, 1988, California and U.S. District Court, Central and Southern Districts of California. *Education:* University of California at Los Angeles (B.A., 1984); Loyola University of Los Angeles Law School (J.D., 1987). Phi Delta Phi. Member: Scott Moot Court National Team; Scott Moot Court Honors Board. Judicial Clerk for the Honorable William A. Holohan, Supreme Court of Arizona, 1987-1988. Member, Los Angeles Complex Litigation Inn of Court. *Member:* Beverly Hills, Century City, Culver/Marina, Los Angeles County and American Bar Associations; State Bar of California. **PRACTICE AREAS:** Real Estate Litigation; Business Litigation; Construction Law; Insurance Law; Employment Law; Securities Litigation.

**MEREDITH L. CALIMAN,** born Los Angeles, California, July 16, 1960; admitted to bar, 1987, California, U.S. District Court, Central and Southern Districts of California and U.S. Court of Appeals, Ninth Circuit. *Education:* Princeton University (A.B., 1982); University of California at Los Angeles School of Law (J.D., 1985). Law Clerk to the Honorable Earl B. Gilliam, U.S. District Court, Southern District of California, 1985-1986. Judge Pro-Tem, Los Angeles Municipal Court, 1995—. *Member:* State Bar of California; American Bar Association. **PRACTICE AREAS:** Civil Litigation.

*(This Listing Continued)*

REPRESENTATIVE CLIENTS: Academy Records; American International, Inc.; Cal-American Companies; SanMar Studios; Celembest International Management, Inc.; Cora Corporation; Duncan-Williams, Inc.; Home Shopping Network, Inc.; Key Media, Inc.; La Mancha Development Co.; Lee Canter & Associates; Mike Green Fire Equipment; Ocean Towers Housing Corporation; Piper Industries, Inc.; Synchronics, Inc.; T&R Painting, Inc.; Tavera Music; The Commodre Club; Toibb Enterprises, Inc.; UBC Brokerage, Inc.; Vanguard Plastics Industries; Visiting Nurse Home Pharmacy; Volwood Corporation.

## HAMILTON & CUMARE

### LOS ANGELES, CALIFORNIA

(See Pasadena)

*Employment Discrimination, Trade Secrets, Traditional Labor Law and Client Counseling (Management), Age Discrimination, Civil Rights Defense, Americans with Disabilities Act, Wrongful Termination Defense, Sexual Harassment, Affirmative Action, Collective Bargaining, Employer Rights, Employment Contracts, Labor Relations, Personnel Policies, Title VII Discrimination, Wage and Hour Law and Whistleblower Litigation.*

## HAMMOND, ZUETEL & CAHILL

### LOS ANGELES, CALIFORNIA

(See Pasadena)

*General Civil and Trial Practice. Medical Malpractice, Personal Injury.*

## A. RAYMOND HAMRICK, III

### A LAW CORPORATION
SUITE 2055
10 UNIVERSAL CITY PLAZA (UNIVERSAL CITY)
**LOS ANGELES, CALIFORNIA 91608**
Telephone: 818-763-5292
Fax: 818-763-2308

*Insurance Coverage, including Casualty, Property, Construction Defect and Environmental Claims, Insurance Defense, Bad Faith Litigation, Alternative Dispute Resolution, Civil Litigation, Construction Defect Litigation, Business Litigation, General Liability Litigation, Business Law.*

FIRM PROFILE: A. Raymond Hamrick, III, a Law Corporation is an insurance and civil litigation firm originally formed in 1986. The firm brings specialized and general legal services to a broad spectrum of insurance and business clientele. The firm is dedicated to a service-oriented, cost efficient practice with particular expertise in effective alternative dispute resolution. In addition, the firm has been retained by insurance industry clients to act as monitoring counsel with respect to complex construction defect claims and civil litigation matters.

**A. RAYMOND HAMRICK, III,** born Dallas, Texas, September 8, 1953; admitted to bar, 1980, California; 1981, U.S. Court of Appeals, Ninth Circuit and U.S. District Court for the Northern, Eastern, Central and Southern Districts of California. *Education:* San Diego State University (A.B., magna cum laude, 1976); University of Santa Clara (J.D., 1980). Phi Beta Kappa; Phi Kappa Phi; Phi Eta Sigma. Research Editor, Santa Clara Law Review, 1979-1980. Extern Clerk to Honorable Joseph T. Sneed, U.S. Court of Appeals, Ninth Circuit, Summer, 1979. Judicial Settlement Officer Program, Los Angeles Central, Glendale. *Member:* Los Angeles County and American Bar Associations; State Bar of California; Los Angeles Trial Lawyers Association. **PRACTICE AREAS:** Insurance Coverage; Insurance Defense; Civil Litigation; Bad Faith Litigation; Business Law.

**DAVID L. EVANS,** born Newport Beach, California, January 13, 1965; admitted to bar, 1991, California. *Education:* Colorado College (B.A., 1987); Loyola Law School, Los Angeles (J.D., 1991). Member: Loyola Law School National Moot Court Team, 1990-1991; Scott Moot Court Honors Board. Recipient, American Jurisprudence Award for Appellate Advocacy and Trial Advocacy. **LANGUAGES:** German. **PRACTICE AREAS:** Litigation; Insurance Defense; Bad Faith Litigation; Entertainment Litigation.

**BRADLEY O. FIELD,** born North Hollywood, California, June 20, 1966; admitted to bar, 1993, California. *Education:* University of California at Berkeley (B.A., 1988); Loyola Law School (J.D., 1993). Senior Note and

*(This Listing Continued)*

## A. RAYMOND HAMRICK, III A LAW CORPORATION, Los Angeles—Continued

Comment Editor, International & Comparative Law Journal. Author, "Improving International Evidence Gathering Methods: Piercing Bank Secrecy Laws from Switzerland to the Caribbean and Beyond," 15 Loy. L.A. IN & Comp. L.J. 691 (1993). **PRACTICE AREAS:** Insurance Coverage; Insurance Defense; Bad Faith Litigation; Entertainment Litigation.

**RAYMOND C. DION,** born Valley Forge, Pennsylvania, November 8, 1955; admitted to bar, 1988, California; 1989, U.S. District Court, Central District of California. *Education:* California State University at Northridge (B.A., 1984); University of Maryland; Loyola Marymount University (J.D., 1988). Recipient, American Jurisprudence Award in Business and Tax Planning. *Member:* Conejo Valley, Los Angeles County and American Bar Associations; State Bar of California. **PRACTICE AREAS:** Insurance Coverage; Insurance Defense; Civil Litigation; Bad Faith Litigation; Wrongful Termination and Employment Litigation; Directors and Officers Liability Litigation.

**DAVID A. TABB,** born Miami Beach, Florida, August 22, 1967; admitted to bar, 1993, California and U.S. District Court, Central District of California; 1996, Florida. *Education:* University of California at Los Angeles (B.A., 1989); University of Florida (J.D., 1992). Recipient, American Jurisprudence Award for Constitutional Law. *Member:* Los Angeles County and American Bar Associations; Association of Southern California Defense Counsel.

**JILL ANNE HILLMAN,** born Redbank, New Jersey, February 25, 1960; admitted to bar, 1993, Florida; 1994, California. *Education:* Florida International University (B.B.A., 1984); St. Thomas University School of Law (J.D., 1993). *Member:* The Florida Bar; State Bar of California.

**PHILIP D. CAPUTO,** born Silver Springs, Maryland, November 10, 1969; admitted to bar, 1996, California. *Education:* The College of Wooster (B.A., 1991); Widener University School of Law (J.D., 1995).

REPRESENTATIVE CLIENTS: Aerotrace Hydraulics, Inc.; Alexander Howden Construction, Inc.; Angermann, Inc.; Argonaut Insurance Co.; Assicurazioni Generali S.p.a. Insurance Co.; Commercial Union Assurance Co., P.L.C.; E & O Hörtnagel; Elmon Enterprises International; Ferro Insurance Agency, Inc.; Great Lakes Assurance Co., P.L.C.; Hitachi Cable Limited; Homestead Insurance Co.; Indemnity Marine Assurance Co., Ltd.; MBL, Inc.; McLarens Toplis North America, Inc.; Mobil Oil Corporation; North American Speciality Insurance Co.; Ocean Marine Insurance Co., Ltd.; Parsons Constructors, Inc.; Ralph M. Parsons, Co.; Thomas Howell Group; Schwartzhaupt, Inc.; Schwarzkopf, Inc.; Summitt Risk; United National Insurance Co.; United States Can Co.; VKW USA, Inc.; Wausau Insurance Co.; Ward - THG.

## HANCOCK ROTHERT & BUNSHOFT LLP

17TH FLOOR, 515 SOUTH FIGUEROA STREET
LOS ANGELES, CALIFORNIA 90071-3334
Telephone: 213-623-7777
Telecopy: 213-623-5405

*San Francisco, California Office:* 10th Floor, Four Embarcadero Center, 94111-4168. Telephone: 415-981-5550. Telex: 470369. Telecopy: 415-955-2599.

*Tahoe City, California Office:* Lighthouse Center, 850 North Lake Boulevard, Suite 15, P.O. Box 7199, 96145-7199. Telephone: 916-583-7767. Telecopy: 916-581-3215.

*London Office:* Forum House, 15/18 Lime Street, Sixth Floor, London EC3M 7AP, England. Telephone: 071-220-7567. Telecopy: 071-220-7609.

*Associated Office:* Staiger, Schwald & Sauter. Genferstrasse 24, 8002 Zurich, Switzerland. Telephone: 01-282-8686. Telecopy: 01-282-8787. Telex: 813-273-GND.

*General Civil and Trial Practice in all State and Federal Courts. Corporation, Business, Insurance, Admiralty, Probate, Tax and International Law.*

### MEMBERS OF FIRM

**PATRICK A. CATHCART,** born Palo Alto, California, September 28, 1945; admitted to bar, 1975, California. *Education:* Stanford University (A.B., 1968); Hastings College of Law, University of California (J.D., 1975). Editor-in-Chief, Hastings Constitutional Law Quarterly, 1974-1975. Instructor, Hastings College of Law, University of California, 1975-1977. Research Assistant to Hon. Arthur J. Goldberg, Former Associate Justice, U.S. Supreme Court, 1974-1975. Law Clerk to Judge Spencer Williams, Northern District of California, 1975-1977. *Member:* Bar Association of San Francisco; Los Angeles County Bar Association; State Bar of California (Member, Committee on Federal Courts, 1978-1981, 1989-1991); International Bar Association (Chairman, Committee 13); London International Court of Arbitration (Charter Member); Association of Business Trial Lawyers. **Email:** pcathcart@hrblaw.com

**PATRICIA SHULER SCHIMBOR,** born Ames, Iowa, November 26, 1949; admitted to bar, 1976, California. *Education:* University of California at Santa Cruz (A.B., 1971); University of California at Davis (J.D., 1976). Order of the Coif. Editor, University of California at Davis Law Review, 1976. Extern, Hon. Anthony M. Kennedy, Judge of U.S. Court of Appeals, Ninth Circuit, 1976. Author and Panelist, California Continuing Education of the Bar, 1986-1992. Adjunct Professor of Law, University of San Francisco Law School, 1988. *Member:* Bar Association of San Francisco; The State Bar of California (Member, Committee on Professional Responsibility and Conduct, 1986-1989); American Bar Association.

**EARL J. IMHOFF, JR.,** born Chicago, Illinois, August 2, 1950; admitted to bar, 1979, Wisconsin; 1980, California. *Education:* University of Notre Dame (A.B., 1972); University of Southern California, (M.A., 1977); University of Wisconsin (J.D., 1979). Phi Alpha Delta. *Member:* Los Angeles County and American Bar Associations; State Bar of California; State Bar of Wisconsin; Maritime Law Association of the United States. [Lt., U.S. Navy, 1972-1977] **Email:** ejimhoff@hrblaw.com

**DEBORAH PITTS,** born San Diego, California, February 12, 1954; admitted to bar, 1979, California; 1980, New York. *Education:* University of California at Los Angeles (B.A., 1975; M.B.A., 1979); University of California School of Law (J.D., 1979). Lecturer and Author: "Royal Globe Actions: The Present Confused State of The Law," Practicing Law Institute, 1988; "Overview of Environmental Insurance Coverage: Historical and Current Hot Topics," Executive Enterprises, 1989, 1990, 1991; "Relationship Between First and Third Party Insurers," American Bar Association National Institute Program on Coverage Disputes in Catastrophic Events; Co-Author: American Manual for Complex Insurance Coverage Litigation. *Member:* State Bar of California (Member, Program Committee, Litigation Section); New York State and American (Member, Sections on: Litigation; International Law; Torts and Insurance Practice; Chairman, 1988 and Senior Vice-Chairman, 1989, Commercial Torts Committee) Bar Associations; Association of Business Trial Lawyers; Defense Research and Trial Lawyers Association; Practicing Law Institute; Conference of Insurance Counsel. **Email:** dapitts@hrblaw.com

**VITO C. PERAINO,** born Detroit, Michigan, March 24, 1956; admitted to bar, 1981, Ohio; 1984, California. *Education:* Wayne State University (B.A., 1977); University of Michigan (J.D., 1981). Phi Beta Kappa. Author: "The Shell Oil Coverage Litigation: A Study in Complex Trial Management," Inside Litigation, March, 1988; "Impact of the Savings and Loan Crisis on Insurance Coverage Litigation," PLI, 1991. Lecturer: PLI Environmental Coverage Claim Litigation, 1990, 1991, 1992; PLI Directors and Officers Insurance, PLI, 1991; ; Environmental Coverage Litigation, Executive Enterprises, Inc., 1990-1996; Fulcrum, "Recovering Manufactured Gas Plant Clean-up Costs," 1996; "Legal Strategies in Hazardous Waste Insurance Coverage Litigation," University of California at Santa Barbara, 1992. *Member:* Bar Association of San Francisco; Los Angeles County, Ohio State and American Bar Associations; State Bar of California. **Email:** vperaino@hrblaw.com

**YVETTE D. ROLAND,** born Los Angeles, California, May 30, 1951; admitted to bar, 1985, California. *Education:* University of California, Riverside (B.A., with honors, 1973); Stanford University (M.A., 1974); University of California, Los Angeles (J.D., 1984). *Member:* State Bar of California; Black Women Lawyers Association. **Email:** ydroland@hrblaw.com

**MARC J. DEREWETZKY,** born New York, N.Y., June 30, 1956; admitted to bar, 1987, California. *Education:* Hamilton College; State University of New York at Binghamton (B.A., with honors, 1980); Hastings College of Law, University of California, San Francisco (J.D., 1987). *Member:* Los Angeles County Bar Association; State Bar of California. **Email:** mjderewetzky@hrblaw.com

**ROBERT V. RICHTER,** born Pasadena, California, August 4, 1959; admitted to bar, 1987, California. *Education:* University of Southern California (B.S., 1981); Loyola Law School (J.D., 1986). *Member:* San Fernando Valley Bar Association; State Bar of California. **Email:** rvrichter@hrblaw.com

### SENIOR COUNSEL

**ALBERT I. MOON, JR.,** born Tucson, Arizona, January 25, 1931; admitted to bar, 1962, California and U.S. District Court, Central District of California; 1965, U.S. Court of Appeals, Ninth Circuit; 1968, U.S. Supreme Court; 1971, Hawaii and U.S. District Court, District of Hawaii; 1975, Trust Territory of the Pacific. *Education:* Carnegie Mellon University (B.S., 1952); University of California School of Law (J.D., 1961). Pi Tau Sigma;

*(This Listing Continued)*

Phi Alpha Delta. Author: "A Look at Airspace Sovereignty," 29 Journal of Air Law and Commerce, 328 (1963). Instructor: Hawaii Pacific College, Honolulu, 1978-1980; University of Phoenix, 1993—. Member, Panel of Arbitrators, American Arbitration Association. Listed Arbitrator, Library of Congress, Copyright Arbitration Royalty Panels. *Member:* State Bar of California; Hawaii State, American and International Bar Associations; American Inns of Court (Trustee, 1985—). *Email:* aimoon@hrblaw.com

### ASSOCIATES

**LINDA B. CARR,** born Seattle, Washington, September 14, 1950; admitted to bar, 1988, California. *Education:* St. Marys College (B.A., 1973); Southwestern University School of Law (J.D., 1988). Phi Alpha Delta. *Member:* State Bar of California. *Email:* lbcarr@hrblaw.com

**WILLIAM K. ENGER,** born Covina, California, February 27, 1963; admitted to bar, 1989, California. *Education:* University of California at Berkeley (B.A., with honors, 1985); University of California at Los Angeles (J.D., 1989). *Member:* State Bar of California (Member, International Law Section); American Bar Association. *Email:* wkenger@hrblaw.com

**MARK A. ROBBINS,** born Ann Arbor, Michigan, June 7, 1959; admitted to bar, 1989, California; 1991, District of Columbia. *Education:* George Washington University (B.A., 1981; J.D., 1988). Deputy Associate Director of Presidential Personnel, The White House, Washington, D.C., 1984-1988. Republican Nominee for U.S. House of Representatives 29th Congressional District of California, 1992. *Member:* Los Angeles County and American Bar Associations. *Email:* marobbins@hrblaw.com

**JENNIFER A. VANE,** born Westport, Connecticut, May 17, 1965; admitted to bar, 1990, California. *Education:* University of Notre Dame (B.A., 1987); University of Southern California (J.D., 1990). *Member:* Los Angeles County and American Bar Associations; State Bar of California. *Email:* javane@hrblaw.com

**PATRICIO T.D. BARRERA,** born Falfurrias, Texas, September 12, 1964; admitted to bar, 1990, California. *Education:* Southwest Texas State University (B.B.A., 1987); University of Texas (J.D., 1990). Phi Alpha Delta. Member, Legal Research Board, University of Texas, 1988-1990. *Member:* State Bar of California; Association of Southern California Defense Counsel; Defense Research Institute; Latino Lawyers Association. **LANGUAGES:** Spanish. *Email:* ptbarrera@hrblaw.com

**VIPAL J. PATEL,** born London, England, July 6, 1967; admitted to bar, 1991, California; 1992, U.S. District Court, Southern and Central Districts of California and U.S. Court of Appeal, Ninth Circuit. *Education:* Kent State University (B.S., 1988); George Washington University (J.D., 1991). *Member:* Los Angeles County and American (Member, Tort & Insurance Practice Section) Bar Associations; State Bar of California. *Email:* vjpatel@hrblaw.com

**DOMINIQUE R. SHELTON,** born Los Angeles, California, March 8, 1967; admitted to bar, 1991, California; 1992, U.S. District Court, Central District of California. *Education:* Brown University (B.A., French Civilization and International Relations, 1988); Georgetown University (J.D., 1991). Notes Editor, Georgetown Journal of Legal Ethics, 1990-1991. *Member:* Los Angeles County, American and National Bar Associations; Black Women Lawyers Association of Los Angeles, Inc. (Officer and Board of Directors); Women Lawyers Association of Los Angeles; California Women Lawyers. **LANGUAGES:** French. *Email:* drshelton@hrblaw.com

**R. CHRISTOPHER RHODY,** born Walnut Creek, California, November 22, 1966; admitted to bar, 1992, California and U.S. District Court, Northern and Central Districts of California. *Education:* Georgetown University (B.A., 1989); University of San Francisco School of Law (J.D., 1992). Recipient, American Jurisprudence Award in Legal Research and Writing. Judicial Extern, Honorable Lloyd King, Chief Judge, U.S. Bankruptcy Court, Northern District of California, 1991. *Member:* Bar Association of San Francisco; State Bar of California. *Email:* rcrhody@hrblaw.com

**LAURA A. PACE,** born Van Nuys, California, July 8, 1967; admitted to bar, 1992, California. *Education:* University of California, Los Angeles (B.A., 1989); Loyola University of Los Angeles (J.D., 1992). Recipient, American Jurisprudence Award, Contracts. *Member:* Los Angeles County Bar Association; Women Lawyers of Los Angeles. *Email:* lapace@hrblaw.com

**MELISSA M. HARNETT,** born Austin, Texas, January 19, 1966; admitted to bar, 1993, California. *Education:* University of California at Los Angeles (B.A., with honors, 1989); University of Southern California (J.D., 1992). *Member:* Los Angeles County Bar Association; State Bar of California. **LANGUAGES:** German. *Email:* mmharnett@hrblaw.com

*(This Listing Continued)*

**FRANK A. YOKOYAMA,** born Fort Benning, Georgia, November 2, 1968; admitted to bar, 1994, California and U.S. District Court, Central District of California. *Education:* University of California at Berkeley (B.S., with honors, 1989); Harvard University (J.D., 1993). Phi Beta Kappa. *Member:* State Bar of California. *Email:* fayokoyama@hrblaw.com

**JENNIFER D. MCKEE,** born New York, N.Y., June 12, 1967; admitted to bar, 1993, California. *Education:* Pomona College (B.A., 1989); Hastings College of the Law, University of California, San Francisco (J.D., 1993). Member, Moot Court Board, 1992-1993. *Member:* State Bar of California. **LANGUAGES:** Russian. **PRACTICE AREAS:** Insurance Coverage. *Email:* jdmckee@hrblaw.com

**JOHN E. BREEN,** born Los Angeles, California, November 12, 1962; admitted to bar, 1994, California. *Education:* Santa Clara University (B.S., 1985); Loyola University of Los Angeles Law School (J.D., 1994). *Member:* State Bar of California. *Email:* jebreen@hrblaw.com

**DANIEL W. NUGENT,** born Chico, California, February 21, 1968; admitted to bar, 1994, California. *Education:* Occidental College (B.A., 1990); University of San Francisco, McLaren School of Business (M.B.A., 1994); University of San Francisco (J.D., 1994). Beta Gamma Sigma; Omicron Delta Epsilon. McLaren Research Fellow. Author: "Patenting Living Matter in the European Community," Fordham Intl. Law Journal, Vol. 17, 1993-1994; "International Intellectual Property Protections for Living Matter," Case Western Reserve Journal of Intl. Law, Vol. 27, Winter 1995. *Member:* State Bar of California. *Email:* dwnugent@hrblaw.com

**B. OTIS FELDER,** born Pontiac, Michigan, July 9, 1967; admitted to bar, 1994, Washington; 1995, California. *Education:* University of Michigan (A.B., 1989); University of San Diego (M.A., 1991); University of San Francisco (J.D., 1994). Editor-in-Chief, U.S.F. Maritime Law Journal, 1993-1994. Member, Board of Advisors, U.S.F. Maritime Law Journal, 1994—. *Member:* Washington State Bar Association; State Bar of California; Maritime Law Association of the United States; Longshore Claims Association.

**PETER T. IMHOF,** born Los Angeles, California, December 22, 1969; admitted to bar, 1995, California. *Education:* Princeton University (A.B., cum laude, 1991); Boalt Hall School of Law, University of California at Berkeley (M.C.P., 1995; J.D., 1995). Phi Beta Kappa. Member, American Planning Association, 1993—. *Member:* State Bar of California. **LANGUAGES:** German, French. *Email:* ptimhof@hrblaw.com

**STEVEN C. URIBE,** born Pasadena, California, December 11, 1967; admitted to bar, 1995, California. *Education:* Pitzer College (B.A., 1990); Columbia University (J.D., 1995). *Member:* State Bar of California. *Email:* scuribe@hrblaw.com

**CHRISTOPHER J. KEENE,** born White Plains, New York, June 9, 1970; admitted to bar, 1996, California. *Education:* University of California at Los Angeles (B.A., 1992); Vanderbilt University (J.D., 1996). *Member:* State Bar of California. *Email:* cjkeene@hrblaw.com

(For complete biographical data on all Personnel, see Professional Biographies at San Francisco).

# HANDLER & SCHRAGE

### LOS ANGELES, CALIFORNIA

(See Santa Monica)

*General Business Practice. Business, Corporation, Real Property, Commercial and Apparel Law, Business and Commercial Litigation.*

# MARC B. HANKIN

11355 WEST OLYMPIC BOULEVARD
SUITE 100
### LOS ANGELES, CALIFORNIA 90064-1614
Telephone: 310-996-2699
FAX: 310-996-2695
Email: Marc__B__Hankin@postoffice.worldnet.att.net

*Conservatorships, Elder Law, Estate Planning and Probate with an emphasis on Probate, Trust and Elder Abuse Litigation.*

**MARC B. HANKIN,** born New Haven, Connecticut, 1950; admitted to bar, 1980, California. *Education:* San Francisco State University (B.A., 1976); Loyola Law School of Los Angeles (J.D., 1980); New York University School of Law (LL.M. in Taxation, 1982). Legislation Drafted: 1984,

*(This Listing Continued)*

**MARC B. HANKIN, Los Angeles—Continued**

California Welfare and Institutions Code Section 14006.2 preventing nursing home Medicaid impoverishment of spouse, The Elder Abuse and Dependent Adult Civil Protection Act, The Due Process in Competence Determinations Act. Author: CEB Chapter on Elder Abuse Remedies in Litigation, drafting book on California Elder Law. Adjunct Professor, Loyola Law School of Los Angeles, 1994. Monthly Columnist on Elder Law in the Daily Journal. *Member:* Los Angeles County Bar Association (Member, Executive Committee of the Estates and Trusts Section); State Bar of California (Member, Executive Committee, Estate Planning Trust and Probate Section; Co-Chair, Elder Law Sub Committee). **LANGUAGES:** French.

---

# HANNA AND MORTON

A Partnership including Professional Corporations

*Established in 1915*

SEVENTEENTH FLOOR, WILSHIRE-GRAND BUILDING
600 WILSHIRE BOULEVARD
**LOS ANGELES, CALIFORNIA 90017**
Telephone: 213-628-7131
Facsimile: 213-623-3379

*Trial and General Business Practice. Civil Trial and Appellate Practice. General Business and Corporate Law. Legal and Tax Aspects of Asset Management. Private Foundations and other Charitable and Non-Profit Organizations. Antitrust. Securities. Insurance. Taxation, Employment Law. Real Property. Probate. Trust and Estate Planning Law. Agricultural Law. Natural Resources Law including Energy, Oil and Gas, Environmental, Hazardous Waste, Air Resources and Water Law.*

### MEMBERS OF FIRM

**BYRON C. HANNA** (1887-1951).

**HAROLD C. MORTON** (1895-1978).

**JOHN H. BLAKE** (1916-1971).

**EDWARD S. RENWICK, (A PROFESSIONAL CORPORATION),** born Los Angeles, California, May 10, 1934; admitted to bar, 1959, California and U.S. District Court, Central District of California; 1963, U.S. Court of Appeals, 9th Circuit; 1973, U.S. District Court, Southern District of California; 1977, U.S. District Court, Northern District of California; 1981, U.S. District Court, Eastern District of California; 1985, U.S. Supreme Court. *Education:* Stanford University (A.B., 1956; LL.B., 1958). Phi Delta Phi. Member, Board of Visitors, Stanford Law School, 1967-1969. Member, California Delegation, Legal Committee, Interstate Oil Compact Commission, 1984—. *Member:* Los Angeles County (Chairman, Natural Resources Law Section, 1974-1975) and American (Member, Sections on: Litigation, Antitrust Law; Natural Resources, Energy and Environmental Law; Business Law; Chairman, Section on Natural Resources, Energy and Environmental Law, 1987-1988) Bar Associations; The State Bar of California; Association of Attorney-Mediators; Chancery Club—Los Angeles. Fellow: American College of Trial Lawyers. **PRACTICE AREAS:** Civil Trial and Appellate; Alternative Dispute Resolution; Natural Resources; Environmental Law; General Practice.

**JAMES P. LOWER,** born Los Angeles, California, March 4, 1943; admitted to bar, 1969, California and U.S. District Court, Central District of California; 1982, U.S. District Court, Northern and Eastern Districts of California. *Education:* Claremont McKenna College (A.B., 1965); Loyola University of Los Angeles (J.D., 1968). Phi Delta Phi. Member, Board of Visitors, Loyola Law School, 1983. Member, Legislation and Regulation Committee, Southern California Association of Philanthropy. *Member:* Los Angeles County (Member, Judiciary Committee) and American (Member, Sections on: Antitrust Law; Real Property, Probate and Trust Law; Corporation, Banking and Business Law; General Practice) Bar Associations; The State Bar of California. **PRACTICE AREAS:** Business and Corporate Practice; Civil Trial; Non-Profit and Private Foundations Representation.

**ROBERT M. NEWELL, JR.,** born Bethesda, Maryland, March 24, 1944; admitted to bar, 1970, California. *Education:* Stanford University (A.B., 1966; J.D., 1969). Los Angeles County Deputy District Attorney, 1970-1973. Assistant United States Attorney, Central District of California, 1973-1979, Assistant Division Chief, 1977-1979. Recipient, Special Achievement Award for Sustained Superior Performance Duty. *Member:* Los Angeles County, Federal and American Bar Associations; State Bar of California; Association of Business Trial Lawyers. **PRACTICE AREAS:** Civil Trial; White Collar Criminal Defense; Environmental Law; General Practice.

**JAMES P. MODISETTE,** born Pasadena, California, March 17, 1944; admitted to bar, 1970, California. *Education:* Dartmouth College (B.A., 1966); Hastings College of the Law, University of California (J.D., 1969). Phi Delta Phi. *Member:* Los Angeles County Bar Association (Delegate to State Bar Conference of Delegates, 1974-1976; 1978-1979 ); The State Bar of California; Chancery Club - Los Angeles. **PRACTICE AREAS:** Real Estate; Civil Trial; Probate; Estate Planning; Corporate; Business Transactions; General Practice.

**MICHAEL I. BLAYLOCK,** born Bell, California, July 30, 1942; admitted to bar, 1967, California. *Education:* Occidental College (A.B., 1964); University of Southern California (J.D., 1967). Phi Delta Phi. Author: "Related Party Installment Sales-Income, Gift and Estate Tax Issues," New York University Institute on Federal Taxation, 1983 Tax Conference Series. *Member:* Los Angeles County (Chairman, Delegation to State Bar Conference, 1979; Member: Executive Committee, Business and Corporations Section, 1974-1982; Executive Committee, Probate and Trust Section, 1980-1983) and American (Member: Real Estate Tax Problems Committee, Taxation Section, 1981—; Partnership Tax Matters Committee, Real Property, Probate and Trust Law Section, 1988—) Bar Associations; State Bar of California (Member, 1979-1982 and Vice Chairman, 1982, Executive Committee, Conference of Delegates; Member, Taxation Law Advisory Commission, 1995—). (Certified Specialist, Taxation Law, The State Bar of California Board of Legal Specialization). **PRACTICE AREAS:** Taxation; Estate Planning; General Practice.

**DAVID A. OSSENTJUK,** born Morris, Illinois, February 3, 1961; admitted to bar, 1987, California; 1989, U.S. District Court, Central, Eastern, Northern and Southern Districts of California; 1990, U.S. Court of Appeals, 9th Circuit. *Education:* Claremont McKenna College (B.A., cum laude, 1983); University of California at Los Angeles (J.D., 1987). *Member:* Beverly Hills, Los Angeles County (Member, Sections on: Litigation and Environmental Law) and American (Member, Sections on: Natural Resources, Energy and Environmental Law; Vice-Chair, Energy and Natural Resources Litigation Committee; Vice Chair, Networking Programs Committee; Member, Environmental Litigation Committee Section on Litigation) Bar Associations; State Bar of California (Member, Sections on: Litigation; Environmental Law and Business Litigation); Association of Business Trial Lawyers. **PRACTICE AREAS:** Natural Resources; Civil Trial; Environmental Law; General Practice.

**JUDITH A. LOWER,** born Los Angeles, California, April 19, 1941; admitted to bar, 1985, California and U.S. District Court, Central District of California. *Education:* Stanford University (A.B., 1963); Loyola Law School (J.D., 1984). *Member:* Los Angeles County (Member, Real Property, Government and Environmental Law Sections) and American (Member: Urban, State and Local Government Law Section, Forum on Affordable Housing and Community Development Law, Real Property, Probate and Trust Law Sections) Bar Associations; State Bar of California (Member: Real Property (Member of Steering Committee of Affordable Housing Subsection) and Environmental Law Sections). **PRACTICE AREAS:** Real Estate Law.

**JOHN A. BELCHER,** born La Canada, California, March 3, 1956; admitted to bar, 1981, California. *Education:* University of California at Berkeley (A.B., summa cum laude, 1978); Boalt Hall School of Law, University of California (J.D., 1981). Phi Beta Kappa. Recipient: Edward Kraft Memorial Scholarship; Harry Wollenberg Prize; Medalle Voltaire; Alexander Meicklejohn Award. Extern Clerk, Hon. Cecil F. Poole, Ninth Circuit Court of Appeals, 1980. Deputy District Attorney, Contra Costa County, 1981-1983. Superior Court Trial Deputy, 1982-1983. Chairman, Citizens Advisory Committee on Redevelopment, City of La Canada Flintridge, 1988-1989. *Member:* Los Angeles County and American Bar Associations; State Bar of California. **PRACTICE AREAS:** Insurance Coverage; Litigation; Appellate Practice.

### OF COUNSEL

**WILLIAM N. GREENE,** born Fort Towson, Oklahoma, April 21, 1918; admitted to bar, 1941, Oklahoma; 1948, California. *Education:* University of Oklahoma (LL.B., 1941); University of Michigan (LL.M., 1947). County Attorney, Choctaw County, Oklahoma, 1947. *Member:* Los Angeles County and American (Member, Taxation Section) Bar Associations; The State Bar of California. **PRACTICE AREAS:** Taxation; Real Estate; Probate; Estate Planning; Trusts.

**MILO V. OLSON,** born Dundurn, Saskatchewan, Canada, March 26, 1907; admitted to bar, 1931, California; 1956, U.S. Supreme Court; U.S.

*(This Listing Continued)*

Court of Appeals, 2nd, 8th and 9th Circuits; U.S. District Court, Central, Northern, Southern and Eastern Districts of California, District of Montana, Northern District of Texas and Southern District of New York. *Education:* University of California at Los Angeles (A.B., 1928); University of Southern California (J.D., 1931). Phi Delta Phi. Member, 1950, President, 1975-1976, Chancery Club. Special Assistant to the United States Attorney General, 1955-1959. Member, Board of Trustees, 1959-1963; Treasurer, 1963; Secretary, 1964; President, 1967, University of Southern California Law Alumni Association. Special Master, U.S. District Court, Central District of California, 1981—. *Member:* Los Angeles County (Member, Board of Trustees, 1964-1966; Vice Chairman, 1967-1968; Chairman, 1968-1969, Trial Lawyers Section) and American Bar Associations; The State Bar of California. [Commander, U.S. Naval Reserve, 1942-1945]. **PRACTICE AREAS:** General Practice; Taxation; Real Estate; Natural Resources; Civil Trial; Environmental Law; Probate; Estate Planning.

**DAVID A. THOMAS,** born Hawthorne, California, February 14, 1922; admitted to bar, 1949, California and U.S. Court of Appeals, Ninth Circuit. *Education:* Occidental College (B.A., 1943); Harvard University (LL.B., magna cum laude, 1948). Phi Beta Kappa. Author: Class Action Manual of the Superior Court of Los Angeles County, Los Angles Superior Court, 1973, Revised, 1980. Instructor, La Verne Law School, 1972-1975. Judge, Superior Court, Los Angeles County, 1970-1988. *Member:* State Bar of California. [Lieut, U.S. Navy, 1943-1946]

### ASSOCIATES

**THOMAS N. CAMPBELL,** born Santa Monica, California, March 20, 1954; admitted to bar, 1989, Texas; 1989, California. *Education:* University de Grenoble, France; University of Southern California (B.A., 1985); South Texas College of Law (J.D., 1988). Phi Delta Phi; Order of the Lytae. Recipient, American Jurisprudence Award in Administration of Estates. *Member:* Los Angeles County Bar Association; State Bar of Texas (Inactive); State Bar of California. **LANGUAGES:** French. **PRACTICE AREAS:** General Practice; Civil Trial.

**ROBERT J. ROCHE,** born Newport Beach, California, November 17, 1964; admitted to bar, 1991, California, U.S. District Court, Southern, Eastern, Northern and Central Districts of California and U.S. Court of Appeals Ninth Circuit. *Education:* University of California, Santa Barbara (B.A., Economics, 1987); University of California at Los Angeles (J.D., 1991). Phi Alpha Delta. Author: "Refugee Redefined: An Inquiry Into Mexican Legal Standards Relating to Asylum and Non-Refoulment," 12 Chicano-Latin Law Review, UCLA School of Law 36 (Sp. 1992); "Disqualification - A Trap for the Unwary," Vol. XVII, No. 1 (September 1994). Arbitrator, Los Angeles County Superior Court. *Member:* Los Angeles County and American Bar Associations; State Bar of California; Mexican-American Bar Association. **LANGUAGES:** Spanish. **PRACTICE AREAS:** Natural Resources; Environmental Law; Oil and Gas.

**MICHAEL P. WIPPLER,** born Honolulu, Hawaii, January 24, 1964; admitted to bar, 1991, California; 1992, U.S. District Court, Central, Southern, Northern and Eastern Districts of California and U.S. Court of Appeals, 9th Circuit. *Education:* University of California, San Diego (B.A., 1986); University of California , Hastings College of Law (J.D., 1991). Note Development Editor, Hastings Communications and Entertainment Law Journal, Volume 13, 1990-1991. Arbitrator, Los Angeles County Superior Court. *Member:* Los Angeles County and American Bar Associations. [U.S. Naval Reserve, 1985-1990; California Army National Guard, 1990- 1992]. **PRACTICE AREAS:** Real Estate; Civil Trial; General Practice.

**DANIEL Y. ZOHAR,** born Syosset, New York, May 16, 1968; admitted to bar, 1993, Florida and U.S. District Court, Middle District of Florida; 1995, California, U.S. District Court, Central District of California and U.S. Court of Appeals, Ninth Circuit. *Education:* Duke University (B.A., 1990); University of California at Los Angeles (J.D., 1993). Phi Delta Phi. Member: UCLA Moot Court Honors Program; UCLA Moot Court Executive Board. *Member:* Los Angeles County Bar Association; The Florida Bar; State Bar of California; Association of Business Trial Lawyers. **PRACTICE AREAS:** Civil Trial; General Practice.

REPRESENTATIVE CLIENTS: Atlantic Richfield Co.; Unocal; W.M. Keck Trust; W.M. Keck Foundation; Carrier Corporation; Witco Corporation; Shell Oil Co.; Association of Talent Agents (trade association of talent agents); Texaco, Inc.; Air Liquide America Corp.; Mobil Corporation; Koll Management Services; Anderson Lithograph Co.; Browning-Ferris Industries; Lexicon School of Languages; Comedy III Productions, Inc.; AlliedSignal, Inc.
REFERENCE: First Interstate Bank (Wilshire & Hope Office).

## HANSEN, JACOBSON, TELLER & HOBERMAN
### LOS ANGELES, CALIFORNIA
(See Beverly Hills)

*Entertainment, Motion Pictures, Television, Music and Copyright Law.*

## LES GLENN HARDIE
### LOS ANGELES, CALIFORNIA
(See Santa Monica)

*Family Law and Business Litigation.*

## RICHARD C. HARDING
### LOS ANGELES, CALIFORNIA
(See Pasadena)

*General Civil Practice in State and Federal Courts. Appeals and Business Transactional Law, Personal Injury Law.*

## YALE M. HARLOW
### 777 SOUTH FIGUERORA STREET, SUITE 3700
### LOS ANGELES, CALIFORNIA 90017
Telephone: 213-236-3860
Fax: 213-236-3861
Email: AW357@LAFN.ORG

*Bankruptcy, Commercial Litigation and Collections.*

FIRM PROFILE: The Law Office of Yale M. Harlow represents debtors, creditors, commercial credit and collection matters as well as out of state corporations and Chapter 7 and 11 cases. Mr. Harlow practices throughout California, including Los Angeles, Orange and Ventura Counties and throughout the San Francisco Bay Area. The Law Office of Yale M. Harlow is an efficient, cost effective law firm specializing in bankruptcy, commercial litigation and collections.

**YALE M. HARLOW,** born Sioux City, Iowa, October 7, 1938; admitted to bar, 1966, California and U.S. District Court, Central, Eastern and Southern Districts of California; 1981, U.S. Court of Appeals, Ninth Circuit. *Education:* University of California at Los Angeles; San Fernando Valley State College (B.S., 1962); Hastings College of Law, University of California (J.D., 1965). Member, Moot Court Board. First Place Winner, David E. Snodgrass Moot Court Competition. Author: "New Laws Relating to Dischargeability," Century City Bar Journal, Vol. 2, No. 1, 1971. Co-head Bankruptcy Department, Bank of America Legal Department, 1966-1970. *Member:* Beverly Hills, Los Angeles County (Member, Commercial Law and Bankruptcy Section) and Federal Bar Associations; State Bar of California; Bankruptcy Study Group; Association of Business Trial Lawyers; Financial Lawyers Conference. [With California National Guard, 1959-1965]

## HARNEY LAW OFFICES
### A LEGAL CORPORATION
### SUITE 1300 FIGUEROA PLAZA
### 201 NORTH FIGUEROA STREET
### LOS ANGELES, CALIFORNIA 90012-2636
Telephone: 213-482-0881
Fax: 213-250-4042

*Negligence and Complex Personal Injury Law. Trials and Appeals. Medical Legal, Products Liability, Railroad and Aviation Law.*

**DAVID M. HARNEY,** born Marysville, California, June 30, 1924; admitted to bar, 1949, California. *Education:* Loyola University; Arizona State University; Southwestern Louisiana University; University of Southern California (J.D., 1948). Cited in The Best Lawyers in America, 1991-
*(This Listing Continued)*

**HARNEY LAW OFFICES** A LEGAL CORPORATION, Los Angeles—Continued

1992. Member, University of Southern California Law Review, 1948. Author, Medical Malpractice, published by Allen Smith Co., 1973, 2nd Edition, Michie Co., 1987. *Member:* Los Angeles and American Bar Associations; State Bar of California; American Board of Trial Advocates (Vice-President, 1980-1981; President, 1982, Los Angeles Chapter; Trial Lawyer of the Year, 1971); International Academy of Trial Lawyers (Secretary-Treasurer, 1980-1981; President-Elect, 1982; President, 1983); The Inner Circle of Advocates. *PRACTICE AREAS:* Civil Trial; Product Liability Law; Medical Malpractice Law; Aviation Law.

**DAVID T. HARNEY,** born Pasadena, California, March 30, 1954; admitted to bar, 1989, California, U.S. District Court, Central District of California and U.S. Court of Appeals, Ninth Circuit. *Education:* University of California at Santa Cruz (B.A., 1977); University of West Los Angeles (J.D., 1989). *Member:* Los Angeles County and American Bar Associations; State Bar of California; Los Angeles County Bar Association; California Trial Lawyers Association; The Association of Trial Lawyers of America. *PRACTICE AREAS:* Civil Trial; Products Liability Law; Medical Malpractice Law; Aviation Law; Professional Liability Law.

**JULIE A. HARNEY,** born Los Angeles, California, March 18, 1961; admitted to bar, 1988, California and U.S. Court of Appeals, Ninth Circuit. *Education:* University of California at Los Angeles (B.A., in English, 1983); University of West Los Angeles (J.D., 1987). Recipient, American Jurisprudence Award, Constitutional Law. *Member:* Los Angeles County and American Bar Associations; State Bar of California; Los Angeles Trial Lawyers Association; California Trial Lawyers Association; The Association of Trial Lawyers of America. *PRACTICE AREAS:* Civil Trial; Products Liability Law; Medical Malpractice Law.

**ANDREW J. NOCAS,** born Los Angeles, California, February 4, 1941; admitted to bar, 1965, California; 1983, U.S. Supreme Court. *Education:* Stanford University (B.S., Physics, 1962; J.D., 1964). Author: "ADR: A Primer on Alternative Dispute Resolution Techniques," California Law Business, January 28, 1991, p. 18; "Arbitration of Medical Malpractice Claims", The Forum, Fall 1977, Vol. 13, No. 1; "Insurance and The War in the Gulf", The Brief, Summer 1991, P. 10; Chapter on Structured Settlements in Treatise entitled Medical and Hospital Negligence, Published by Callaghan & Company, 1988; Chapter on Blood Transfusions in text entitled Medical-Legal Aspects of Obstetrics and Gynecology, to be published; "Your Partner's Keeper: The Perils of Law Firm Partnership," Litigation Section Newsletter, Los Angeles County Bar Association, Vol. 8, No. 2, Fall 1991. Arbitrator, American Arbitration Association, 1979—. Voluntary Referee, State Bar Court, 1980-1984. Voluntary Settlement Officer, Los Angeles Superior Court. *Member:* Pasadena, Los Angeles County (Trustee, 1990-1992, Chair, Litigation Section, 1989-1990; President, Inn of Court, 1993-1994; Chair, Law Office Management Section, 1980-1982; Chair, Lawyers' Errors & Omissions Prevention Committee, 1987-1990; Chair, Ad Hoc Committee on Private Judging; Vice-Chair, State Courts Committee, 1991-1992; Special Committee on ABA Evaluation of Professional Standards, 1980-1985; Legislative Activities Committee, 1982-1984; Dispute Resolution Services Operating Committee, 1989-1993; AB 3820 Committee, 1989—) and American (Chair, TIPS Arbitration Committee, 1980-1981; Chair, TIPS Law in the Public Service Committee, 1992-1993) Bar Associations; State Bar of California (Member, Resolutions Committee, 1983-1985; Calendar Coordination Committee, 1988-1991, 1991-1992; Delegate to the State Bar Conference of Delegates, 1971-1992); The Association of Trial Lawyers of America; Los Angeles County Bar Foundation (Director). Fellow, American Bar Foundation. *PRACTICE AREAS:* Civil Litigation.

**VINCENT MCGOWAN,** born Sligo, Ireland, October 16, 1966; admitted to bar, 1990, California, U.S. District Court, Central, Southern, Northern and Eastern Districts of California and U.S. Court of Appeals, Ninth Circuit. *Education:* University College, Dublin Ireland (B.C.L., 1987). The Honorable Society of King's Inn (Barrister at Law, 1989). *Member:* State Bar of California. *PRACTICE AREAS:* Civil Trial; Medical Malpractice Law.

**THOMAS A. SCHULTZ,** born Long Beach, California, November 29, 1965; admitted to bar, 1990, California and U.S. District Court, Central and Southern Districts of California. *Education:* University of California at Los Angeles (B.A, 1987); Loyola University (J.D., with honors, 1990). Recipient, American Jurisprudence Award in Advanced Development of Tort

*(This Listing Continued)*

Law. *Member:* California Trial Lawyers Association; Los Angeles Trial Lawyers Association. *PRACTICE AREAS:* Civil Trial; Products Liability Law; Medical Malpractice Law.

REFERENCE: Bank of America.

# HARRINGTON, FOXX, DUBROW & CANTER
*THIRTIETH FLOOR, 611 WEST SIXTH*
**LOS ANGELES, CALIFORNIA 90017**
*Telephone: 213-489-3222*
*Facsimile: 213-623-7929*

*Orange, California Office:* Suite 1020, 1100 Town and Country Road. Telephone: 714-973-4595. Facsimile: 714-973-7923.

*San Diego, California Office:* Suite 1150, 401 West A Street. Telephone: 619-233-5553. Fax: 619-233-0005.

*San Francisco, California Office:* 444 Market Street, Suite 3050. Telephone: 415-288-6600. Facsimile: 415-288-6618.

*General Civil and Trial Practice in all State and Federal Courts and before Federal and State Administrative Agencies. Real Estate, Corporation, Business, Estate Planning, Trust, Probate, Medical, Products Liability, Health and Insurance Law.*

## MEMBERS OF FIRM

**RICHARD HUNT SAMPSON** (1901-1952).

**LOWELL L. DRYDEN** (1909-1967).

**ROBERT S. HARRINGTON** (1913-1983).

**BRIAN L. GOLLER** (1954-1992).

**RICHARD A. FOXX** (Retired).

**ELI B. DUBROW,** born Des Moines, Iowa, November 23, 1935; admitted to bar, 1961, California. *Education:* University of California at Los Angeles (B.S., 1957); Boalt Hall, University of California (LL.B., 1960). Beta Gamma Sigma. *Member:* Los Angeles County and American Bar Associations; The State Bar of California. *PRACTICE AREAS:* Real Estate Law; Probate and Trusts Law; Estate Planning Law; Business Law.

**DAVID H. CANTER,** born Plainfield, New Jersey, June 4, 1937; admitted to bar, 1965, California. *Education:* Purdue University (B.S., 1959); University of Southern California (J.D., 1964). Phi Alpha Delta. Member, Board of Editors, University of Southern California Law Review, 1963-1964. *Member:* Los Angeles County Bar Association (Member, Trial Lawyers Section); The State Bar of California; Association of Southern California Defense Counsel; Defense Research Institute; American Society of Agricultural Engineers. *PRACTICE AREAS:* Products Liability Law; Toxic Torts Law; Medical Malpractice Law.

**LOWELL M. RAMSEYER,** born Elkton, Michigan, March 25, 1933; admitted to bar, 1965, California; 1975, U.S. Supreme Court. *Education:* Glendale College (A.A., 1959); University of Southern California (B.S., 1961; J.D., 1964). Phi Sigma Alpha; Blue Key; Phi Delta Phi. Member, Blackstonian Law Society. President, University of Southern California School of Public Administration, 1960. University of Southern California School of Public Administration Student of the Year, 1961. Member, Panel of Arbitrators, American Arbitration Association. *Member:* Los Angeles County (Member, Trial Lawyers Section) and American Bar Associations; The State Bar of California; Association of Southern California Defense Counsel. *PRACTICE AREAS:* Professional Negligence Law (Medical Malpractice Law); Personal Injury Defense Law; Products Liability Law.

**LAWRENCE A. BUSH,** born Houston, Texas, April 10, 1931; admitted to bar, 1960, California. *Education:* University of California at Berkeley (B.S. Electrical Engineering, 1953); University of California at Los Angeles (J.D., 1960). Phi Alpha Delta. *Member:* Los Angeles County Bar Association; The State Bar of California; California Trial Lawyers Association; Christian Legal Society. [Commander, USNR, Retired]. *PRACTICE AREAS:* Products Liability Law; Personal Injury Defense Law.

**DALE B. GOLDFARB,** born Cleveland, Ohio, May 23, 1950; admitted to bar, 1975, California. *Education:* University of California at Berkeley (A.B., 1971); Loyola University of Los Angeles (J.D., magna cum laude, 1975). Alpha Sigma Nu. Member, St. Thomas More Law Honor Society. Member, Loyola University Law Review, 1973. Real Estate Agent, California, 1973. Assistant Professor, Drug Abuse and Civil Service Law, California State University at Long Beach, 1977. Member, Commercial Panel, American Arbitration Association. *Member:* The State Bar of California;

*(This Listing Continued)*

Lawyers Club of Los Angeles; Association of Southern California Defense Counsel. **PRACTICE AREAS:** Business and Commercial Litigation; Insurance Coverage; Employment Law; Appellate Practice.

**CRAIG F. SEARS,** born Indianapolis, Indiana, February 6, 1949; admitted to bar, 1975, California. *Education:* Purdue University (B.S., 1971); University of Southern California (J.D., 1975). Tau Beta Pi; Pi Tau Sigma. *Member:* Los Angeles County and American Bar Associations; State Bar of California; Association of Southern California Defense Counsel; American Society of Agricultural Engineers. **PRACTICE AREAS:** Personal Injury Defense Law; Products Liability Law; Construction Defects Law; Professional Negligence Law.

**MARTIN C. KRISTAL,** born Boston, Massachusetts, March 25, 1953; admitted to bar, 1977, California. *Education:* University of California at Los Angeles (B.A., summa cum laude, 1974; J.D., 1977). Phi Beta Kappa. *Member:* Los Angeles County (Member, Probate, Trust and Real Property Sections) and American Bar Associations; State Bar of California; Association of Business Trial Lawyers. **PRACTICE AREAS:** Real Estate Law; Probate and Trusts Law; Estate Planning Law; General Business Law.

**EDWARD R. LEONARD,** born San Diego, California, January 13, 1953; admitted to bar, 1978, California. *Education:* San Diego State University (B.A., cum laude, 1974); University of San Diego (J.D., 1978). *Member:* The State Bar of California; American Bar Association; Association of Southern California Defense Counsel. **PRACTICE AREAS:** Personal Injury Defense Law; Product Liability Law; Professional Negligence Law; Construction Defects Law.

**MARK A. JUHAS,** born Colorado Springs, Colorado, November 2, 1954; admitted to bar, 1979, California. *Education:* Colorado College (B.S., 1976); University of Puget Sound (J.D., cum laude, 1979). Associate Editor, University of Puget Sound Law Review, 1978-1979. *Member:* The State Bar of California; American Bar Association. **PRACTICE AREAS:** Product Liability Law; Personal Injury Defense Law.

**MARK W. FLORY,** born Los Angeles, California, September 24, 1954; admitted to bar, 1980, California. *Education:* University of California at Los Angeles (B.A., cum laude, 1976; J.D., 1979). Phi Eta Sigma. Distinguished Advocate, University of California at Los Angeles, Moot Court Honors Program, 1978-1979. *Member:* State Bar of California; American Bar Association. **REPORTED CASES:** D'Hondt v. Regents of the University of California (1984) 153 Cal. App. 3d 723. Williams v. Transport Indemnity Co. (1984) 157 Cal. App. 3d 953. Mann v. Cracchiolo (1985) 38 Cal. 3d 18. Insurance Company of the State of Pennsylvania v. Associated International Insurance Co. 922 F. 2d 516 (9th Cir. 1990). Span v. Associated International Insurance Co. (1991) 227 Cal. App. 3d 463. **PRACTICE AREAS:** Insurance Coverage Law; Commercial Litigation; Appellate Practice.

**WILLIAM P. FINNEY,** born Milwaukee, Wisconsin, June 27, 1947; admitted to bar, 1980, Wisconsin; 1981, California. *Education:* University of Wisconsin-Milwaukee (B.A., 1969); University of Wisconsin-Madison (M.A., 1979); University of Wisconsin Law School (J.D., 1980). *Member:* State Bar of California; State Bar of Wisconsin; American Bar Association. **PRACTICE AREAS:** Toxic Torts Law; Personal Injury Defense Law; Construction Defects Law.

**THOMAS E. LOTZ,** born Chicago, Illinois, December 4, 1954; admitted to bar, 1981, California. *Education:* University of California at San Diego (B.A., 1977); California Western School of Law (J.D., 1979). Member: California Western Law Review, 1979-1980; Order of the Barristers. Member, Advocacy Honors, Board, Regional Champion and National Quarterfinalist in the National Trial Competition, 1981. National Moot Court Competition Team, 1980. Donald Wright Moot Court Competition Team, 1980. Intellectual Property Moot Court Team, 1979. *Member:* State Bar of California. (Resident, San Diego Office). **PRACTICE AREAS:** Medical Malpractice Law; Products Liability Law; Personal Injury Defense Law; Toxic Torts Law.

**THOMAS O. RUSSELL, III,** born December 16, 1950; admitted to bar, 1983, California. *Education:* University of California at Los Angeles (B.A., magna cum laude, 1973); Loyola Law School of Los Angeles (J.D., 1977). *Member:* Los Angeles County and American Bar Associations; The State Bar of California; Association of Southern California Defense Counsel. **PRACTICE AREAS:** Personal Injury Defense Law; Construction Defect Law; Products Liability Law.

**HENRY A. WIRTA, JR.,** born Sacramento, California, May 29, 1955; admitted to bar, 1983, California and U.S. District Court, Southern District of California; 1984, U.S. District Court, Central District of California. *Education:* University of Southern California (B.A., cum laude, 1977); California State University at San Diego (J.D., cum laude, 1983). Member, Order of the Barrister. Chairman, University of San Diego School of Law, Moot Court Board, 1982-1983. Instructor Moot Court, University of San Diego School of Law, 1983. *Member:* The State Bar of California. **PRACTICE AREAS:** Personal Injury Defense; Products Liability Law; General Civil Litigation Defense.

**MICHAEL F. CRESSEY,** born San Diego, California, March 7, 1955; admitted to bar, 1984, California. *Education:* Humboldt State University (B.S.,1979); California Western University School of Law (J.D., 1984). Member, Order of the Barristers. Regional Champion 1984 National Trial Competition. Regional Quarterfinalist, 1983 and 1984 National Moot Court Competition. *Member:* State Bar of California; American Bar Association; San Diego Trial Lawyers Association. (Resident, San Diego Office). **PRACTICE AREAS:** Construction Defects Law; Products Liability Law; Professional Negligence Law; Personal Injury Defense Law.

**NANCY J. MINDEL,** born Indianapolis, Indiana, February 25, 1961; admitted to bar, 1987, California, U.S. District Court, Central District of California and U.S. Court of Appeals, Ninth Circuit. *Education:* University of Southern California (B.S., magna cum laude, 1983; J.D., 1986). Phi Kappa Phi; Beta Gamma Sigma; Phi Alpha Delta. *Member:* Los Angeles County and American Bar Associations; State Bar of California. **REPORTED CASES:** Span, Inc. v Associated International Insurance Co. 227 Cal. App. 3d 463 (1991). **PRACTICE AREAS:** Insurance Coverage Law; Appellate Law.

**GARY G. DYE,** born Roosevelt, Utah, October 23, 1957; admitted to bar, 1986, California and U.S. District Court, Southern District of California; 1987, Utah and U.S. District Court, District of Utah. *Education:* Utah State University (B.S., with honors, 1983); University of San Diego (J.D., 1986). *Member:* Salt Lake County, Los Angeles County and American Bar Associations; State Bar of California; The Association of Trial Lawyers of America.

**BETH ISAACS GOLUB,** born St. Paul, Minnesota, May 10, 1960; admitted to bar, 1986, California. *Education:* University of Minnesota (B.A., magna cum laude, 1982); University of San Diego (J.D., 1985). Donald Wright Moot Court Competition; Jack Levitt Law and Motion Moot Court Competition. *Member:* San Diego County Bar Association; State Bar of California. (Resident, San Diego Office). **PRACTICE AREAS:** Personal Injury Law; Construction Defect Law; Medical Malpractice Law; Products Liability Law.

**JOHN C. DEWELL,** born Santa Monica, California, June 14, 1962; admitted to bar, 1988, California. *Education:* University of California at Los Angeles (B.A., magna cum laude, 1984); University of Southern California (J.D., 1988). Phi Beta Kappa. *Member:* Los Angeles County and American Bar Associations; State Bar of California; Association of Southern California Defense Counsel.

*ASSOCIATES*

**ALAN M SCHNITZER,** born Los Angeles, California, September 30, 1959; admitted to bar, 1987, California. *Education:* Santa Barbara Community College (A.A., 1980); University of California at Los Angeles (B.A., 1982); Southwestern University School of Law; Loyola Marymount University (J.D., 1986). Member, St. Thomas More Law Honor Society. *Member:* Los Angeles County, Orange County and American Bar Associations; State Bar of California. **LANGUAGES:** French and German. **PRACTICE AREAS:** Litigation; Products Liability Law; Medical Malpractice Law.

**MARGUERITE COYNE HILL,** born Chicago, Illinois, November 28, 1960; admitted to bar, 1985, California. *Education:* Southern Illinois University (B.S., 1982); Loyola Law School at Los Angeles (J.D., 1985). Member, Loyola International Law Journal, 1984-1985. *Member:* State Bar of California; American Bar Association; Los Angeles Trial Lawyers Association; California Trial Lawyers Association.

**PETER A. SCHNEIDER,** born New York, N.Y., June 14, 1959; admitted to bar, 1984, California, U.S. District Court, Central District of California and U.S. Court of Appeals, Ninth Circuit; 1992, U.S. District Court, Southern District of California and U.S. Supreme Court. *Education:* University of California at Riverside (B.A., 1981); University of San Diego (J.D., 1984). Phi Alpha Delta. Author: Opinions: "Burgess v. Superior Court (1992) 2 Cal 4th 1062, 9 Cal Rptr. 2nd 615; Coon vs Nicola (1993) 17 Cal App. 4th 1225. Torts Instructor, First Year Instructional Program, University of San Diego School of Law, 1983-1984. *Member:* Orange County Bar Association; The State Bar of California; Association of Southern California Defense Counsel. (Resident, Orange Office).

*(This Listing Continued)*

**HARRINGTON, FOXX, DUBROW & CANTER,** Los Angeles—Continued

**JEFFREY S. DOGGETT,** born Dallas, Texas, June 14, 1962; admitted to bar, 1990, California and U.S. District Court, Southern District of California. *Education:* Colorado State University (B.A., 1984; M.A., 1986); University of San Diego (J.D., 1989). Member, Moot Court Board, University of San Diego; Order of the Barristers. *Member:* San Diego and Los Angeles County Bar Associations; State Bar of California; San Diego Defense Lawyers Association. (Resident, San Diego Office). *PRACTICE AREAS:* Personal Injury Law; Medical Malpractice Law; Products Liability Law.

**MARK S. SALZBERG,** born Bronx, New York, March 27, 1963; admitted to bar, 1990, California; 1991, U.S. District Court, Central District of California. *Education:* Cornell University (B.S., 1984); University of San Diego (J.D., 1990). *Member:* Los Angeles County and American Bar Associations; State Bar of California. (Resident, San Francisco Office).

**PAMELA HARRINGTON MUNRO,** born Pasadena, California, July 28, 1966; admitted to bar, 1991, California. *Education:* University of California at Los Angeles (B.S., 1988); Loyola Marymount University (J.D., 1991). *Member:* State Bar of California; American Bar Association.

**EDWARD W. LUKAS, JR.,** born Lakewood, California, June 14, 1963; admitted to bar, 1991, California. *Education:* University of Colorado; California State University at Long Beach (B.S., 1986); University of San Diego (J.D., 1991). *Member:* State Bar of California; American Bar Association.

**K. ERIN LENNEMANN,** born Inglewood, California, January 28, 1964; admitted to bar, 1991, California. *Education:* University of Southern California; California State University at Long Beach (B.A., 1988); Loyola Law School (J.D., 1991).

**ELIZABETH J. MILLER,** born Glen Ellen, Illinois, January 14, 1966; admitted to bar, 1991, California; 1992, U.S. District Court, Central, Southern, and Northern Districts of California. *Education:* University of California, Los Angeles (B.A., 1988); Loyola Law School (J.D.,1991). Staff Member, 1990, Articles Editor, 1991, International and Comparative Law Journal. *Member:* State Bar of California.

**ANGELA LUI WALSH,** born Los Angeles, California, November 26, 1967; admitted to bar, 1993, California. *Education:* University of California at Los Angeles (B.A., cum laude, 1989); Boalt Hall School of Law, University of California (J.D., 1993). *Member:* Beverly Hills, Los Angeles County and American Bar Associations; State Bar of California; Southern California Chinese Lawyers Association. *LANGUAGES:* Mandarin and Cantonese Chinese, Spanish.

**DAVID R. CATALINO,** born Buffalo, New York, February 28, 1961; admitted to bar, 1989, California, U.S. District Court, Southern, Eastern and Central Districts of California. *Education:* Rochester Institute of Technology (B.S., 1983); University of San Diego (J.D., 1988). Phi Alpha Delta. Member: Appellate Moot Court Board; Order of Barristers. *Member:* San Diego and American Bar Associations; State Bar of California; San Diego Defense Lawyers. (Resident, San Diego Office). *PRACTICE AREAS:* Personal Injury Defense; Medical Malpractice Defense; Product Liability Defense; Construction Defect Defense.

**STEPHEN L. SMITH,** born Phoenix, Arizona, December 19, 1962; admitted to bar, 1991, California and U.S. District Court, Central and Southern Districts of California. *Education:* University of San Diego (B.A., with honors, 1985); Oxford University, Oxford, England; University of San Diego (J.D., 1991). President, Student Bar Association, University of San Diego, 1990-1991. Recipient: American Jurisprudence Award; University of San Diego Law Alumni Award. Author: "California Coastal Commission," California Regulatory Law Reporter, Winter, 1989, Spring, Summer and Fall, 1990. *Member:* San Diego, Orange County and American Bar Associations; State Bar of California. (Resident, San Diego Office). *PRACTICE AREAS:* Medical Malpractice; Public Entity; General Civil Litigation.

**MARK W. EISENBERG,** born New York, N.Y., March 22, 1965; admitted to bar, 1992, California; 1993, U.S. District Court, Northern and Central Districts of California. *Education:* State University of New York at Albany (B.A., 1987); California Western School of Law (J.D., 1992). *Member:* State Bar of California. (Resident, Orange Office). *PRACTICE AREAS:* Civil Litigation.

**BRAD M. ELDER,** born Fullerton, California, May 9, 1967; admitted to bar, 1994, California. *Education:* California State University at Fullerton (B.A., 1990); Western State University (J.D., 1994). Recipient, American Jurisprudence Award in Professional Responsibility. *Member:* State Bar of California. *PRACTICE AREAS:* Civil Defense Litigation.

**MICHAEL W. JACOBS,** born San Diego, California, July 14, 1967; admitted to bar, 1994, California. *Education:* San Diego State University (B.S., 1989); University of San Diego (J.D., 1994). (Resident, San Diego Office). *PRACTICE AREAS:* General Liability; Medical Malpractice; Products Liability; Collections.

**KIMBERLEE S. STUBBS,** born Salt Lake City, Utah, November 4, 1963; admitted to bar, 1988, California. *Education:* University of California at Santa Barbara (B.A., 1985); University of San Diego School of Law (J.D., 1988). (Resident, San Diego Office). *PRACTICE AREAS:* Medical Malpractice Defense; General Liability Defense.

**ERIK GUNDERSON,** born Nuremberg, West Germany, September 23, 1970; admitted to bar, 1994, California. *Education:* University of California at Santa Barbara (B.A., 1991); Loyola Law School, Los Angeles (J.D., 1994). Recipient, American Jurisprudence Award in Trial Advocacy. Member, Federalist Society, Loyola of Los Angeles, 1993-1994. Author: "Every Little Thing I Do (Incurs Legal Liability): Unauthorized Use of Popular Music in Presidential Campaigns," 14 Loy. L.A. Ent. L.J. 137 (1993). *PRACTICE AREAS:* Personal Injury Litigation; Business Litigation.

**DONALD G. FURNESS,** born Buffalo, New York, December 30, 1961; admitted to bar, 1992, California and U.S. District Court, Central District of California. *Education:* Bennington College (B.A., 1984); Northwestern University (M.A., 1985); University of Southern California (J.D., 1991). *Member:* Los Angeles County Bar Association; State Bar of California (Member, Litigation and International Sections). *LANGUAGES:* German; French. *PRACTICE AREAS:* Banking; Business Litigation.

**KELLY A. WARD,** born Los Angeles, California, August 15, 1962; admitted to bar, 1990, California and U.S. District Court, Central District of California. *Education:* University of California at Santa Barbara (B.A., 1985); Southwestern University (J.D., 1989). *Member:* Los Angeles County and American Bar Associations. *PRACTICE AREAS:* Civil Litigation.

**ESTHER GONZALEZ,** born Los Angeles, California December 31, 1966; admitted to bar, 1993, California. *Education:* University of California, Los Angeles (B.A., 1990); Loyola Law School (J.D., 1993). *Member:* State Bar of California. *LANGUAGES:* Spanish.

**MARK W. NORMAN,** born San Jose, California, October 10, 1962; admitted to bar, 1990, California; U.S. District Court, Southern District of California. *Education:* University of California at Los Angeles (B.A., 1986); Institute of International and Comparative Law, Paris, France (Diploma, 1988); University of San Diego (J.D., 1990). Phi Alpha Delta. *Member:* State Bar of California. *PRACTICE AREAS:* Construction Litigation.

**ANN MICHAEL,** born Bartlesville, Oklahoma, April 3, 1960; admitted to bar, 1992, Oklahoma; 1993, Illinois; 1994, California. *Education:* University of Oklahoma (B.B.A., 1982); Oklahoma City University (J.D., 1992). Phi Delta Phi. Recipient, American Jurisprudence Awards in Administrative Law, Agency and Partnerships, Corporations and Wills and Estates I. *Member:* Oklahoma and Illinois State Bar Associations; State Bar of California. *PRACTICE AREAS:* Civil Litigation; Construction Defect.

**TIMOTHY P. CHANG,** born New York, N.Y., March 16, 1965; admitted to bar, 1992, California and U.S. District Court, Central and Eastern Districts of California. *Education:* University of California, Berkeley (B.S., 1987); McGeorge School of Law, University of the Pacific (J.D., 1992). Phi Delta Phi. *Member:* State Bar of California; Southern California Chinese Lawyers Association; Japanese American Bar Association. *LANGUAGES:* Japanese. *PRACTICE AREAS:* Coverage Litigation; Construction Defect; General Liability.

**KIRK J. RETZ,** born Bakersfield, California, August 7, 1962; admitted to bar, 1994, California. *Education:* California State University at Northridge (B.S., 1989); Loyola Law School, Los Angeles (J.D., 1993). *Member:* Los Angeles County Bar Association; State Bar of California. *PRACTICE AREAS:* Construction Litigation; Products Liability; Medical Malpractice; General Litigation.

**DANIEL E. KENNEY,** born San Diego, California, January 20, 1967; admitted to bar, 1994, California, U.S. District Court, Central District of California and U.S. Court of Appeals, 9th Circuit. *Education:* Pitzer College (B.A., 1989); Southwestern University School of Law (J.D., 1993). Delta Theta Phi. Member, Honors Moot Court. Recipient, American Jurisprudence Awards in Torts and Constitutional Law. Note and Comment Editor, Southwestern University Law Review. *Member:* State Bar of California; Federal Bar Association. *PRACTICE AREAS:* Products Liability; General Liability; Medical Malpractice; Civil Rights.

*(This Listing Continued)*

**MARK A. GOLDSTEIN,** born Gwinn, Michigan, August 14, 1964; admitted to bar, 1994, California. *Education:* Columbia University (B.A., 1986); University of Southern California (M.S., Computer Science, 1988); Southwestern University School of Law (J.D., 1993). *Member:* State Bar of California; Computer Law Association. *PRACTICE AREAS:* Insurance Coverage; Reinsurance Litigation; Insurance Bad Faith Litigation; Civil Defense Litigation; Trademark and Copyright.

**J. JASON HILL,** born Eldorado, Illinois, November 28, 1969; admitted to bar, 1995, California. *Education:* University of Illinois at (B.A., 1992); California Western School of Law (J.D., 1995). Phi Delta Phi. Member, California Western Law Review/International Law Journal. Recipient, American Jurisprudence Awards in Legal Analysis, Academic Achievement and Law and Economics. Author: "Deciphering a Legal Enigma: Encrytion Standards and Data Security," Vol. 5 Telecom News, 1994. *Member:* Federal Communications and American (Member, Communications and Utilities Section) Bar Associations. (Resident, San Diego Office).

REPRESENTATIVE CLIENTS: *Insurance:* Associated International Insurance Co.; The Canada Life Assurance Co.; Canadian Insurance Company of California; CIGNA; Clarendon Insurance Co.; Commercial Underwriters Insurance Co.; Commerical Union Insurance Companies; Crum and Forster; John Deere Insurance Co.; Discovery Re; Dorsey, Nevin & Associates; Employers Self Insurance Service; ESIS International; Farm Bureau Insurance Group; Farmers Insurance Group; Gerling-Konzern; John Hancock Property and Casualty Co.; Gerald J. Sullivan & Associates; Harco Insurance Co.; Industrial Indemnity Insurance Co.; Insurance Company of North America; Liberty Mutual Insurance Co.; Metropolitan Property & Liability Insurance Co.; MMI (Multi-Systems Agency); Pharmacists Mutual Companies; The Robert Plan; Royal Insurance Co; State Farm Fire and Casualty Co.; State Farm Insurance Companies; TCO Insurance Services; Topa Insurance Co.; Transamerica Insurance; Truck Insurance Exchange; Unigard Mutual Insurance Co.; United Companies Life Insurance Co.; The Yasuda Claims Services, Inc.; The Yasuda Fire and Marine Insurance Co. *Health:* Children's Hospital and Health Center of Los Angeles; Children's Hospital of Orange County; Daniel Freeman Hospital; Gallatin Medical Clinic; Health West Inc.; Henry Mayo Memorial Hospital; Huntington Memorial Hospital; Scripps Memorial Hospital; Sharp Cabrillo Hospital; Sharp Healthcare; Sharp Memorial Hospital; St. Mary's Desert Valley Hospital; United Western Medical Centers; Victor Valley Community Hospital. *Manufacturing:* Alamo Group; AGIE USA, Inc.; AGIE Losonne; Altec, Inc.; Applied Power Inc.; B & M Machine Works, Inc.; Butler Manufacturing Co.; Cannon Equipment Co.; Cincinnati Milacron Inc.; Clark Equipment Co.; Cummins Engine Company, Inc.; Cummins West, Inc.; Deere & Co.; ELOX Corporation; Ford Motor Co.; Freightliner Corporation; Fuji Seiko Co., Ltd.; Fuji Seisakusho Co., Ltd.; Gametime, Inc.; Harsco; H.C. Muddox Company; IMI Group, Inc.; Iowa Industrial Hydraulics, Inc.; Iwatani International Corporation; Jaguar; Kartridg Pak, Inc.; Kelley Company, Inc.; Kerr Manufacturing Co.; Mack Trucks, Inc.; The Melroe Company; Mitsubishi Electric Corp.; Navistar International Transportation Corp.; Nissan Motor Corporation U.S.A.; Plasti-Kote, Inc.; The Raymond Corporation; Rexworks Inc.; Savage Arms, Inc.; Sturm Ruger & Company, Inc.; Sybron; Taylor Machine Works, Inc.; Toyota Motor Sales, U.S.A., Inc.; TRW Inc.; Van Dorn Company; VME Americas, Inc.; Waltersheid; Wheeler Manufacturing Company; Yale Security Inc.; Zimmer, Inc. *Business:* Angeles Metal Systems; Bank of America; Brownline, Inc.; Calgary Flames; City of Coronado; Dart Industries Inc.; Fedco, Inc.; Federal Deposit Insurance Corp.; Hussman Refrigeration Co.; Kraft General Foods Inc.; Nestle USA, Inc.; The Newhall Land and Farming Co.; Nissan Motor Acceptance Corp.; Oscar Mayer Corp.; Phillip Morris Companies Inc.; Premark International, Inc.; Resolution Trust Corp.; Santa Monica College District; Schneider National, Inc.; Sears Roebuck & Company; Vanencia Company.

## HARRIS • GINSBERG, LLP
11755 WILSHIRE BOULEVARD, SUITE 1650
**LOS ANGELES, CALIFORNIA 90025**
Telephone: 310-444-6333
Fax: 310-444-6330

*Specializing in all aspects of Dissolution of Marriage, Custody and Visitation, Paternity Issues, Adoption and Pre-Nuptial and Post-Nuptial Agreements.*

FIRM PROFILE: Harris Ginsberg is a newly formed law firm. Both lawyers are certified specialists in family law. The firm believes in hands on service, a one on one client relationship with their clients. Both lawyers were partners of Trope & Trope and Ms. Harris is a former partner of Sheppard, Mullin, Richter & Hampton from 1980 to 1991. With large law firm experience, the firm is able to provide top experience and results at lower fees. Ms. Harris is a Fellow, American Academy of Matrimonial Lawyers from 1990 to present.

### MEMBERS OF FIRM

**SUZANNE HARRIS,** born Rockford, Illinois, December 17, 1940; admitted to bar, 1977, California; 1980, U.S. District Court, Central District of California. *Education:* California State University (B.A., 1973); University of California at Los Angeles (J.D., 1977). Member, Judicial Council's Family Law Advisory Committee to Chief Justice of California, 1987-1990. *Member:* Los Angeles County (Member, Family Law Section Executive Committee, 1980—; Chair, 1989-1990) and American (Member, Section of Family Law; Chair, Scope and Correlation Committee, 1994-1995; Chair,

*(This Listing Continued)*

Committee on Marital Property, 1990-1992) Bar Associations; State Bar of California; Association of Business Trial Lawyers. Fellow, American Academy of Matrimonial Lawyers. (Certified Specialist, Family Law, The State Bar of California Board of Legal Specialization). *PRACTICE AREAS:* Family Law.

**LARRY A. GINSBERG,** born Madison, Wisconsin, June 21, 1959; admitted to bar, 1986, California; 1987, U.S. District Court, Central District of California. *Education:* University of Wisconsin (B.A., 1982); Pepperdine University (J.D., 1986). Board of Directors, Harriet Buhai Center For Family Law, 1993—. *Member:* Beverly Hills (Member, Family Law Section, Executive Committee, 1993—) and Los Angeles County (Member, Family Law Section) Bar Associations; State Bar of California. *PRACTICE AREAS:* Family Law.

## LAW OFFICES OF
## RAND F. HARRIS
A PROFESSIONAL CORPORATION
RIVERSIDE LAW BUILDING
12650 RIVERSIDE DRIVE, SUITE 205
**LOS ANGELES, CALIFORNIA 91607-3492**
Telephone: 818-755-4848
Facsimile: 818-760-2583

*Family Law, Criminal Law, Personal Injury, Workers Compensation Defense, Business and Real Estate.*

**RAND F. HARRIS,** born Los Angeles, California, August 15, 1945; admitted to bar, 1970, California. *Education:* University of California at Berkeley (A.B., 1966); University of California, Hastings College of the Law (J.D., 1969). *Member:* Beverly Hills, San Fernando Valley (Member, Family Law Section) and Los Angeles County (Member, Family Law Section) Bar Associations; State Bar of California (Member, Family Law Section). (Certified Specialist, Family Law, The State Bar of California Board of Legal Specialization). *PRACTICE AREAS:* Family Law; Criminal Law; Workers Compensation Defense; Personal Injury.

## HART & WATTERS
A PROFESSIONAL LAW CORPORATION
12400 WILSHIRE BOULEVARD, SUITE 450
**LOS ANGELES, CALIFORNIA 90025-1061**
Telephone: 310-826-5202
FAX: 310-442-0181

*Civil Litigation Trial and Appellate Practice in all State and Federal Courts. Negligence, Business, Corporate, Insurance and Real Estate Law and Litigation. Probate, Trust and Estate Planning.*

**CHARLES R. HART, JR.,** born Los Angeles, California, April 21, 1939; admitted to bar, 1965, California; 1971, U.S. Supreme Court; U.S. District Court, Central, Northern and Southern Districts of California. *Education:* University of California at Los Angeles (B.S., 1961); Hastings College of Law, University of California (LL.B., 1964); New York University (LL.M., 1970). *Member:* Santa Monica (Member, Board of Trustees, 1970, 1975 and 1976), Los Angeles County and American Bar Associations; State Bar of California. *PRACTICE AREAS:* Corporate Law; Business Law; Real Estate Law; Estate Planning; Tax Law.

**THOMAS L. WATTERS,** born Oklahoma City, Oklahoma, July 12, 1947; admitted to bar, 1975, Ohio; 1977, California; 1980, U.S. District Court, Central District of California; 1981, U.S. Court of Appeals, Ninth Circuit; 1982, U.S. District Court, Southern District of California; 1985, U.S. Court of Appeals, Tenth Circuit. *Education:* Purdue University (B.S. in Industrial Engineering, with honors, 1969); Salmon P. Chase College of Law (J.D., 1975). Member, Order of Curia. *Member:* Los Angeles County, Santa Monica (Member, Board of Trustees, 1989-1992) and American Bar Associations; State Bar of California. *REPORTED CASES:* Trope v. Katz 11 Cal. 4th 274, 45 Cal. Rptr. 2d 241 (S. Ct. In Bank 1995). *PRACTICE AREAS:* Trial and Appellate Practice; Business Litigation; Real Estate Litigation; Civil Litigation; Insurance Defense and Coverage.

**KEITH A. LOVENDOSKY,** born Detroit, Michigan, May 8, 1955; admitted to bar, 1980, California; 1981, U.S. District Court, Central District of California. *Education:* University of Miami (B.A., magna cum laude, 1977); University of California at Los Angeles (J.D., 1980). Author: "Price

*(This Listing Continued)*

CAA753B

**HART & WATTERS, A PROFESSIONAL LAW CORPORATION**, Los Angeles—Continued

Discrimination Involving an Ultimate Consumer," Journal of the Corporate Counsel Section of the State Bar of Texas, January, 1980. President, Santa Monica Lions Club, 1989-1990. Member, Santa Monica College Advisory Board. *Member:* Santa Monica and Los Angeles County Bar Associations; State Bar of California. *PRACTICE AREAS:* Civil Litigation; Insurance Law; Corporate Litigation; Real Estate Litigation; Personal Injury Law.

---

**BRET R. CARTER,** born Muscatine, Iowa, October 8, 1959; admitted to bar, 1987, California; U.S. District Court, Central District of California; 1988, U.S. District Court, Northern District of California; 1992, U.S. District Court, Eastern District of California; 1993, U.S. Court of Appeals, Ninth Circuit. *Education:* Iowa State University (B.S., 1982); Pepperdine University (J.D., 1987). Order of Barristers. *Member:* State Bar of California. *REPORTED CASES:* Clavell vs. North Coast 232 Cal. App. 3d 328 (1991). *PRACTICE AREAS:* Civil Litigation; Insurance Litigation; Real Estate Litigation; Business Litigation; Corporate Litigation.

REFERENCE: Santa Monica Bank.

---

## HARTMAN AND ASSOCIATES
### 12401 WILSHIRE BOULEVARD, SECOND FLOOR
### LOS ANGELES, CALIFORNIA 90025-1015
Telephone: 310-207-9100
Fax: 310-207-5101

*Business, Real Property, Commercial, Corporate, Securities, Housing and Urban Development, Partnership and Limited Liability Company Law.*

**ROGER C. HARTMAN,** born San Francisco, California, September 29, 1942; admitted to bar, 1969, California, New York, U.S. District Court, Northern District of California and U.S. Court of Appeals, Ninth Circuit. *Education:* University of California at Riverside (B.A., 1964); University of California, Hastings College of Law (J.D., 1968). Member, Thurston Society. *Member:* Beverly Hills, Los Angeles County and American (Chairman, Committee on Governmentally Assisted Programs for Real Estate, Section of Real Property, Probate and Trust Law, 1987-1989; Member, Special Committee on Housing and Urban Development Law, 1987-1992; Governing Committee Member-at-Large and Conferences Chair, 1993-1995, Chair-Elect, 1995-1996, Forum Committee on Affordable Housing and Community Development Law) Bar Associations; The State Bar of California. *Email:* rhartman@aol.com

### ASSOCIATES

**DOUGLAS J. WORKMAN,** born Queens, New York, June 17, 1958; admitted to bar, 1983, California; 1984, U.S. District Court, Central District of California and U.S. Tax Court. *Education:* University of Virginia (B.S., with distinction, 1980); Northwestern University (J.D., 1983). Beta Gamma Sigma; Beta Alpha Psi. Book Review Editor, Journal of Criminal Law and Criminology, 1982-1983. Author: "The Use of Offshore Tax Havens for the Purpose of Criminally Evading Income Taxes," 73 Journal of Criminal Law and Criminology 678, 1982. *Member:* American Bar Association (State Regulation of Securities; Subcommittee on Partnership and REIT Products). *TRANSACTIONS:* Real Estate Acquisitions, Dispositions, Financing, Leasing, Public Land Private Offerings of Securities, Partnership and Limited Liability Company Agreements General Corporate. *PRACTICE AREAS:* Corporate and Real Estate Law.

---

## LAW OFFICES OF
## SHARON LYBECK HARTMANN
### 5757 WILSHIRE BOULEVARD, SUITE 560
### LOS ANGELES, CALIFORNIA 90036
Telephone: 213-965-5600
Facsimile: 213-965-5613
Email: Lybeck@aol.com

*Boutique practice in the monitoring of Civil Rights Consent Decrees and Injunctions; Civil Rights Litigation.*

*FIRM PROFILE:* Started in 1991 by Sharon Lybeck Hartmann, this firm is the only one in the United States which specializes in the independent monitoring and enforcement of consent decrees and injunctions, reporting to the courts, the Department of Justice and to independent counsel. Our principal area of concentration lies in civil rights. As part of our monitoring, we also do civil rights training and testing in both housing and public accommodations contexts. We also do civil rights litigation and general civil litigation as well as alternate dispute resolution in a number of formats. Among those represented or monitored by this firm are Fortune 500 corporations, regional companies and individuals. Members of the firm are strikingly diverse and are involved in, and encouraged to participate in, a wide variety of professional associations and community affairs.

**SHARON LYBECK HARTMANN,** born Glendale, California, July 26, 1939; admitted to bar, 1979, California. *Education:* University of California at Los Angeles (A.B., with honors, 1960); University of California at Berkeley (Boalt Hall) (J.D., 1979). Member, Moot Court Board, 1977-1979. Editor in Chief, Industrial Relations Law Journal, 1978-1979. Co-Director, Boalt Hall Legal Research and Writing Program, 1979-1980. Law Clerk to Judge James Fitzgerald, U.S. District Court, District of Alaska, 1980-1982. Law Clerk to Judge Warren Ferguson, U.S. Court of Appeals, 9th Circuit, 1982-1983. Recipient, Maynard Toll Pro-Bono Associate Award of the Legal Aid Foundation of Los Angeles, 1986. Vice-President, Board of Directors of Western Law Center for Disability Rights, 1986-1993. President, Board of Directors, Centro Latino Educacion Popular, 1990—. Member, Board of Directors, Inner City Law Center, 1991—. Pro-Bono work for ACLU of Southern California, NAACP and Western Law Center for Disability Rights. Founder, California Women's Law Center. *Member:* Los Angeles County Bar Association; State Bar of California; California Women Lawyers; Women Lawyers Association of Los Angeles. *PRACTICE AREAS:* Civil Rights Monitoring of Consent Decrees; Civil Rights Litigation; Bankruptcy Litigation; Civil Litigation.

**ELIZABETH GUILLÉN,** born Clark AFB, Philippine Islands, December 5, 1953; admitted to bar, 1988, California. *Education:* Metropolitan State College (B.A., 1983); University of Denver (J.D., 1986). Recipient, Legal Services Achievement Award of State Bar of California, 1995. Staff Member, Mexican American Legal Defense & Education Fund, 1988-1995. *PRACTICE AREAS:* Civil Rights; Civil Rights Monitoring; Immigration; Education.

**LISA ANN HOLLINGWORTH,** born Lynwood, California, May 18, 1954; admitted to bar, 1985, California, U.S. District Court, Central and Southern Districts of California and U.S. Court of Appeals, Ninth Circuit. *Education:* California State University, Long Beach (B.S., cum laude, 1976); Loyola Marymount University (J.D., 1984). Special Agent, U.S. Department of State, Foreign Services 1976-1981. Judge Pro Tem, Orange County, California. *Member:* State Bar of California; American Bar Association. (Also Member, Spaltro & Lamhofer, Long Beach). *REPORTED CASES:* Santa Monica Hospital Medical Center v. Superior Court (1988), 203 Cal. App. 3rd 1026. *PRACTICE AREAS:* Civil Rights; Insurance Defense; Premises Liability; Products Liability; Insurance Fraud Defense.

**SUSAN M. WOOLLEY,** born Torrance, California, May 27, 1959; admitted to bar, 1990, California. *Education:* Stanford University (A.B., 1982; J.D., 1988); University of Wisconsin (M.A., 1985). Phi Beta Kappa. Law Clerk to the Hon. Judith N. Keep, U.S. District Court for the Southern District of California, 1988-1989. The Immigrant Legal Resource Center. Aids Project Los Angeles. *LANGUAGES:* Spanish. *PRACTICE AREAS:* Civil Rights; Litigation; Immigration and Naturalization.

### ASSOCIATES

**MARCELLA A. BELL,** born Inglewood, California, April 26, 1966; admitted to bar, 1994, California. *Education:* Loyola Marymount University (B.A., 1989); University of West Los Angeles School of Law (J.D., 1993). Moot Court of Governors. *Member:* State Bar of California. *LANGUAGES:* Italian, Spanish. *PRACTICE AREAS:* Civil Rights.

**BARBARA E. DALTON,** admitted to bar, 1995, California. *Education:* University of California at Berkeley (B.A., 1982); Loyola University of Los Angeles (J.D., 1994). Member of Board, Institute of Cultural Inquiry. *Member:* Women's Lawyers Association of Los Angeles. *PRACTICE AREAS:* Civil Rights.

**MAURICE P. DESTOUET,** born 1948; admitted to bar, 1978, California. *Education:* Stanford University (B.A.); University of Southern California (J.D., 1973). *Member:* Los Angeles County Bar Association (Chair, Subcommittee on Diversity on the Bench; Committee on Minority Representation in the Legal Profession; Joint Task Force on Diversity in the Legal Profession); Lawyers for Human Rights (The Lesbian and Gay Bar Association) (Member, Board of Governors; Co-Chair, People of Colour Committee; Delegate to Multi-Cultural Bar Alliance; Delegate, State Bar of California Minority Bar Leaders Summit Conference); Women Lawyers Association of Los Angeles (Member, Board of Governors; Co-Chair, Ap-

*(This Listing Continued)*

pointive Office Committee; 1996 Installation Dinner Committee); Multi-Cultural Bar Alliance (Member: Board of Governors; Joint Task Force on HIV Legal Services; Advisory Council, Legal Corps of Los Angeles).

MONA HATHOUT, admitted to bar, 1993, California; 1994, U.S. District Court, Central District of California. *Education:* University of California at Los Angeles (B.A., 1986); Loyola University of Los Angeles (J.D., 1993). Member, Board of Directors, Muslim Public Affairs Council. Western Law Center for Disability Rights. *PRACTICE AREAS:* Civil Rights; Corporate Law.

LEIGH M. LEONARD, born Stoughton, Wisconsin, December 14, 1959; admitted to bar, 1990, California. *Education:* Cornell University (B.S., 1982); University of Texas (M.S., 1984); University of California at Los Angeles (J.D., 1990). Order of the Coif. Member, Lawyers for Human Rights. Member, Lamba Legal Defense and Education Fund. *Member:* State Bar of California (Member, Sections on: Labor and Employment); Los Angeles County Gay and Lesbian Bar Association; American Civil Liberties Union (ACLU). *PRACTICE AREAS:* Civil Rights; Employee Benefits.

WILLIAM M. LITT, born New York, N.Y., January 24, 1967; admitted to bar, 1993, California, U.S. District Court, Central District of California and U.S. Court of Appeals, Ninth Circuit. *Education:* Cornell University (B.A., with distinction, 1990); University of California at Los Angeles (J.D., 1993). Author: "Sexual Harassment Hits Home," Recent Development, 2 UCLA Women's Law Journal, (1992). *Member:* Los Angeles County and American Bar Associations. *PRACTICE AREAS:* Civil Rights; Public Interest Law.

DOREENA WONG, born San Francisco, California, December 2, 1951; admitted to bar, 1988, California; 1994, U.S. Supreme Court. *Education:* University of California at Santa Cruz (B.A., 1974); New York University School of Law (J.D., 1987). Symposium Editor, Review of Law & Social Change. Licensed in, Radiologic Technology, California, 1977—. Member, Lambda Legal Defense and Education Fund. Board Member, National Center for Lesbian Rights, 1991-1993. *Member:* State Bar of California (Member, Human Rights Committee); Asia American Bar Association of the Greater San Francisco Bay Area (Member, Services Section, 1991-1996); Lawyers for Human Rights (Board Member, 1994-1996). *PRACTICE AREAS:* Civil Rights; Constitutional Law.

---

## HAUSMANN & SHRENGER, LLP

333 SOUTH GRAND AVENUE, THIRTY-THIRD FLOOR
**LOS ANGELES, CALIFORNIA 90071-1504**
Telephone: 213-625-8886
Facsimile: 213-625-1388

*General Civil Litigation in State and Federal Courts with emphasis on Real Estate, Commercial Law and International Law emphasizing Greater China.*

EDWIN D. HAUSMANN, born Evanston, Illinois, July 14, 1941; admitted to bar, 1972, California and U.S. District Court, Central and Southern Districts of California; 1980, U.S. Court of Appeals, Ninth Circuit. *Education:* Northwestern University (B.S., 1963); University of California at Berkeley (M.S., 1965); Boalt Hall School of Law; University of California (J.D., 1972). Associate Editor, Ecology Law Quarterly, 1971-1972. Tau Beta Pi. Registered Professional Engineer in Chemical Engineering, California, 1969. Trial Attorney, Antitrust Division, U.S. Department of Justice, 1972-1977. Arbitrator, Los Angeles County Superior Court, 1981—. Judge Pro Tem, Los Angeles Municipal Court, 1981—. *Member:* Beverly Hills, Los Angeles County and American Bar Associations; The State Bar of California; Association of Business Trial Lawyers. *REPORTED CASES:* G.E. Hetrick & Assoc. v. Summit Const. 11 Cal App. 4th 318, 13 Cal Rptr. 2nd 803 (1992); U.S. v. Hughes Tool Co. 415 F. Supp. 637 (C.D. Cal, 1976).

JUSTIN J. SHRENGER, born Little Rock, Arkansas, 1963; admitted to bar, 1990, California and U.S. District Court, Central District of California; 1991, U.S. District Court, Southern District of California; 1995, U.S. Court of Appeals, Ninth Circuit. *Education:* University of California at Riverside; University of California at Berkeley (B.S., Chem., 1985); University of San Francisco; Columbia University (J.D., 1990). Author: "Checklist for Doing Business in China," L.A. County Bar MCLE Publication, 1992. Editor, 1988-1989, Business Editor, 1989-1990, *Journal of Chinese Law*. Member, McAuliffe Honor Society. Harlan Fiske Stone Scholar. Member, Los Angeles County Bar, Pacific Rim Committee. Volunteer Attorney,

*(This Listing Continued)*

---

Asian Pacific Legal Center. *LANGUAGES:* Chinese (Mandarin). *REPORTED CASES:* Cal. Cosmetology Coalition v. Riley, Secy. of Ed., 871 F.Supp. 1263 ((C.D.Cal. 1994).

---

## HAWKINS, DELAFIELD & WOOD

FIRST INTERSTATE WORLD CENTER
633 WEST FIFTH STREET
SUITE 3550
**LOS ANGELES, CALIFORNIA 90071**
Telephone: 213-236-9050
Fax: 213-236-9060

*New York, N.Y. Office:* 67 Wall Street. Telephone: 212-820-9300. Cable Address: "Hawkdel, New York". Telecopier: 212-514-8425.
*Hartford, Connecticut Office:* City Place. Telephone: 203-275-6260.
*Newark, New Jersey Office:* One Gateway Center. Telephone: 201-642-8584.
*Washington, D.C. Office:* 1015 15th Street, N.W., Suite 930. Telephone: 202-682-1480.

*Municipal Law, Municipal Finance, Redevelopment, Real Estate, Civil and Business Litigation, Corporate, Finance and Eminent Domain Law.*

### MEMBERS OF FIRM

ARTO C. BECKER, born Queens, New York, September 4, 1955; admitted to bar, 1981, New York; 1989, California. *Education:* Columbia University (A.B., 1977); Fordham University (J.D., 1980). Editor-in-Chief, Fordham Urban Law Journal. *Member:* New York State and American Bar Associations; State Bar of California.

KEVIN M. CIVALE, born New York, N.Y., June 26, 1959; admitted to bar, 1985, New York; 1992, California. *Education:* Boston College (B.A., cum laude, 1981); Fordham University (J.D., 1984). *Member:* New York State Bar Association; State Bar of California.

(For complete biographical data on all Members and Of Counsel, see Professional Biographies at New York, New York)

---

## HAWKINS, SCHNABEL, LINDAHL & BECK

Established in 1986

660 SOUTH FIGUEROA STREET, SUITE 1500
**LOS ANGELES, CALIFORNIA 90017**
Telephone: 213-488-3900
Telecopier: 213-486-9883
Email: 102175.3573@compuserve.com

*General Civil and Trial Practice in all State and Federal Courts. Products Liability, Professional Liability, Business Litigation, Environmental Law, Insurance Law and Bad Faith Litigation, Maritime Law and Employment Discharge Litigation.*

### MEMBERS OF FIRM

ROGER E. HAWKINS, born St. Paul, Minnesota, January 12, 1940; admitted to bar, 1970, California. *Education:* California State College at Los Angeles (B.S., 1963); University of California at Los Angeles (J.D., 1969). Recipient, American Jurisprudence Awards in Evidence, Control of Crime and Justice and the Legal Profession. Arbitrator, Los Angeles County Superior Court Arbitration Program, 1979—. Settlement Officer, Los Angeles Superior Court Special Settlement Program, 1979—. *Member:* Los Angeles County and American (Member, Admiralty and Maritime Law Committee and Workers Compensation and Employers Liability Law Committee, Tort and Insurance Practice Section) Bar Associations; State Bar of California (Member, Environmental Law Section); Maritime Law Association of the United States (Proctor in Admiralty and Member, Committee on Stevedoring and Terminal Operators); International Association of Defense Counsel; Association of Southern California Defense Counsel; Defense Research Institute.

LAURENCE H. SCHNABEL, born Los Angeles, California, November 24, 1941; admitted to bar, 1968, California. *Education:* Stanford University (A.B., 1963); University of California at Los Angeles (J.D., 1967). Phi Delta Phi. Deputy District Attorney, Los Angeles County, 1968-1970. Arbitrator: Los Angeles County Superior Court Arbitration Program, 1979—; Los Angeles Superior Court Special Settlement Program, 1988—. Faculty, National Institute of Trial Advocacy. *Member:* American Bar Association (Vice-Chairman, Professional Officers' and Directors' Liability Law, Division of Torts and Insurance Practice Section, 1981-1982); American Board of Trial Advocates; Defense Research Institute; International Association of Defense Counsel. [Cmdr., JAGC, USNR-R, ret.]

*(This Listing Continued)*

**HAWKINS, SCHNABEL, LINDAHL & BECK, Los Angeles—Continued**

**GEORGE M. LINDAHL,** born San Francisco, California, February 22, 1949; admitted to bar, 1974, California. *Education:* University of California at Berkeley (A.B., 1971); Hastings College of Law, University of California (J.D., 1974). Member, Thurston Society. Author: "Liability of Attorneys," California Torts, Chapter 32, Matthew Bender & Co., 1985; "Attorney Professional Liability", California Forms of Pleading & Practice, Matthew Bender & Co., 1994. Settlement Officer, Los Angeles Superior Court Special Settlement Program, 1985—. *Member:* Association of Southern California Defense Counsel (Co-Chairman, Industry Liaison Committee, 1993); American Judicature Society; Defense Research Institute; International Association of Defense Counsel; American Board of Trial Advocates.

**KELLEY K. BECK,** born Salt Lake City, Utah, May 2, 1955; admitted to bar, 1979, California. *Education:* University of Utah (B.S., magna cum laude, 1976); University of Texas (J.D., 1979). Phi Delta Phi. Member: Order of the Barristers; National Moot Court Teams, 1977 and 1978; National Championship Team of Patent Law Competition, 1979; Board of Advocates. Commended, International Academy of Trial Lawyers. *Member:* American Bar Association (Member, Tort and Insurance Practice Section); The Conference of Insurance Counsel.

**JON P. KARDASSAKIS,** born Marysville, California, November 10, 1954; admitted to bar, 1979, California. *Education:* University of California at Davis (B.S., 1976; J.D., 1979). Recipient, American Jurisprudence Awards, Contracts and Marital Property. Arbitrator, Los Angeles County Superior Court Arbitration Program. *Member:* Association of Southern California Defense Counsel.

**WILLIAM E. KEITEL,** born Orange, New Jersey, August 31, 1954; admitted to bar, 1981, California. *Education:* George Washington University (B.A., Pol. Sc., with distinction, 1976); L.B.J. School of Public Affairs (M.P.A., 1981); University of Texas (J.D., 1981). Phi Eta Sigma; Phi Sigma Alpha. Member, The Review of Litigation, Board of Advocates and Legal Research Board, University of Texas, 1979-1981. *Member:* State Bar of California.

**RENA DENTON STONE,** born Los Angeles, California, June 1, 1955; admitted to bar, 1984, California. *Education:* University of California at Los Angeles (B.A., 1977); University of Southern California (J.D., 1984). *Member:* State Bar of California.

**TIMOTHY A. GONZALES,** born Bellingham, Washington, August 7, 1959; admitted to bar, 1984, California and Washington. *Education:* University of Washington (B.A., 1981); University of Michigan (J.D., 1984). *Member:* State Bar of California; Washington State Bar Association.

**R. TIMOTHY STONE,** born Ft. Worth, Texas, August 3, 1961; admitted to bar, 1986, California. *Education:* University of Miami (B.B.A., magna cum laude, 1983); Georgetown University Law Center (J.D., cum laude, 1986). Recipient, American Jurisprudence Award. Arbitrator, Los Angeles County Superior and Municipal Courts Arbitration Program. *Member:* State Bar of California (Member, Litigation Section); Association of Southern California Defense Counsel.

**RICHARD C. WESTON,** born Spangler, Pennsylvania, September 3, 1960; admitted to bar, 1986, California. *Education:* Pennsylvania State University (B.A., 1982) University of California at Los Angeles (J.D., 1985). *Member:* State Bar of California.

**RAM F. COGAN,** born Tel-Aviv, Israel, September 21, 1961; admitted to bar, 1987, California. *Education:* University of California at Berkeley (B.A., magna cum laude, 1984) Phi Beta Kappa; University of California at Los Angeles (J.D., 1987). Articles Editor, U.C.L.A. Environmental Law Journal. *Member:* Los Angeles County and American Bar Associations; State Bar of California.

**RANDY M. MCELVAIN,** born Burbank, California, June 13, 1963; admitted to bar, 1988, California. *Education:* Pepperdine University (B.A., cum laude, 1985) Omicron Delta Epsilon; University of California, Hastings College of Law, San Francisco, CA (J.D., 1988). Articles Editor, Hastings Constitutional Law Quarterly, 1987-1988. *Member:* State Bar of California.

*(This Listing Continued)*

**KURT G. GRESENZ,** born New York, N.Y., May 31, 1964; admitted to bar, 1989, California, U.S. Court of Appeals, Ninth Circuit and U.S. District Court, Central and Southern Districts of California. *Education:* Duke University (B.A., 1986); University of Texas at Austin (J.D., 1989). *Member:* State Bar of California.

**DAVID C. MOORE,** born Des Moines, Iowa, April 23, 1966; admitted to bar, 1991, California; 1992, U.S. District Court, Central and Southern Districts of California. *Education:* Dana College (B.A., summa cum laude, 1988); University of Texas (J.D., 1991). Member, 1989-1991 and Notes Editor, 1990-1991, The Review of Litigation; Author: "Invoking The Inherent Powers Doctrine To Compel Representation of Indigent Civil Litigants In Federal Court," The Review of Litigation, Vol. 10, No. 3, Summer 1991. *Member:* State Bar of California.

**WENDY ANNE SCHOLL,** born Los Angeles, California, December 28, 1967; admitted to bar, 1992, California. *Education:* University of California at Los Angeles (B.A., cum laude, 1989); Loyola Marymount University (J.D., 1992). Executive Editor, Loyola of Los Angeles International and Comparative Law Journal, 1991-1992. *Member:* State Bar of California.

**ROBERT J. PRATA,** born West Covina, California, May 29, 1965; admitted to bar, 1992, California. *Education:* University of California at Berkeley, (B.A., with honors, 1989); Santa Clara University (J.D., 1992). *Member:* State Bar of California.

**TODD A. DALEY,** born Princeton, New Jersey, November 2, 1967; admitted to bar, 1993, California. *Education:* University of California at Davis (B.A., 1990); University of California, Hastings College of Law (J.D., 1993). Extern to the Honorable J.P. Vukasin, Jr., U.S. District Judge, Northern District of California, 1992-1993. *Member:* State Bar of California; Maritime Law Association of the United States.

**LAURA E. HOGAN,** born Los Angeles, California, July 9, 1967; admitted to bar, 1993, California. *Education:* University of California at Los Angeles (B.A., 1989); University of California, Hastings College of Law (J.D., 1993). *Member:* State Bar of California.

**TODD B. ALLEN,** born Los Angeles, California, April 19, 1969; admitted to bar, 1995, California. *Education:* University of California at Berkeley (B.A., magna cum laude, 1991); University of California School of Law at Los Angeles (J.D., 1995). Distinguished Advocate, U.C.L.A. Moot Court Competition. *Member:* State Bar of California.

**JULIE A. MOTE,** born Seoul, Korea, September 8, 1965; admitted to bar, 1995, California. *Education:* Towson State University (B.S., cum laude, 1987); Hastings College of the Law, University of California (J.D., 1995). Staff Member, 1993-1994 and Articles Editor, 1994-1995, Hastings Law Journal. Recipient, American Jurisprudence Award in Torts. Extern to the California Supreme Court, Civil Staff, 1995. *Member:* State Bar of California.

**JILL N. BANT,** born Philadelphia, Pennsylvania, January 16, 1968; admitted to bar, 1995, California. *Education:* University of Wisconsin - Madison (B.A., with honors, 1990); University of Southern California (J.D., 1995). Staff Member, Southern California Review of Law & Women's Studies, 1993-1995. *Member:* State Bar of California.

**BRIAN J. GLADSTONE,** born Philadelphia, Pennsylvania, February 19, 1963; admitted to bar, 1993, California. *Education:* New York University (B.F.A., 1985); Georgetown University Law Center (J.D., 1993). University Honors Scholar. Recipient, Founders Day Award. Co-Author: "The Occurrence Problem-Distinguishing the 'Occurrence' Triggering Insurance Coverage from the 'Occurrence' Limiting an Insurer's Liability," Verdict, Fourth Quarter, 1994. *Member:* State Bar of California.

**SHAWN E. COWLES,** born Santa Maria, California, January 3, 1967; admitted to bar, 1993, California. *Education:* Pepperdine University (B.A., magna cum laude, 1989); University of Virginia (J.D., 1992). *Member:* State Bar of California.

REPRESENTATIVE CLIENTS: Abbott Laboratories; American International Group; Avis, Inc.; Brown & Root, Inc.; California Insurance Guarantee Assn.; CNA Insurance; Dunbar Armored, Inc.; Estee Lauder; Fireman's Fund Insurance Co.; Golden Eagle Insurance Co.; Grand Laboratories, Inc.; Great American Insurance Companies; Guardian Life Insurance Company of America; Harris Corporation; Highlands Insurance Co.; Kay-Bee Toy Stores; Lancer Claims Service, Inc.; Marshalls; Melville Corporation; Nationwide Insurance Group; Nestle USA, Inc.; Otis Engineering Corporation; Shaklee Corporation; The Sherwin-Williams Co.; The Travelers Insurance Group; Unocal Corporation; Waste Management, Inc.; Wausau Insurance Company; Wilson House of Swede.

## JOHN GARDNER HAYES
A PROFESSIONAL CORPORATION

Established in 1976

SUITE 600, 11400 WEST OLYMPIC BOULEVARD
**LOS ANGELES, CALIFORNIA 90064**
Telephone: 310-478-4711
Fax: 310-575-4171

*Civil Trials, Insurance Defense, Personal Injury Litigation, Product Liability, Medical and Professional Malpractice, Bad Faith and Casualty Insurance Law, Employment Law, Discrimination.*

**JOHN GARDNER HAYES,** born Los Angeles, California, September 21, 1941; admitted to bar, 1968, California. *Education:* University of California at Los Angeles (B.A., 1964; J.D., 1967). Phi Delta Phi. *Member:* Los Angeles County Bar Association; State Bar of California.

---

**J. WALTER GUSSNER,** born Montreal, Canada, May 5, 1952; admitted to bar, 1979, California. *Education:* University of California at Los Angeles (B.A., 1974); Loyola University (J.D., 1978). *Member:* Beverly Hills, Los Angeles County and American Bar Associations; State Bar of California.

REPRESENTATIVE CLIENTS: A List of Clients Furnished Upon Request.

## STEVEN HECHT

1901 AVENUE OF THE STARS
SUITE 1600
**LOS ANGELES, CALIFORNIA 90067-6017**
Telephone: 310-286-3044
Fax: 310-286-2644

*Business Law, Corporations, Limited Liability Companies, Partnerships, Finance, Investment, Mergers and Acquisitions and International Business Transactions.*

*FIRM PROFILE: Mr. Hecht specializes in transactional business matters for domestic and foreign clients. He has practiced for 20 years, mostly with large multi-office and national firms until starting his own practice in May, 1993.*

*Mr. Hecht has worked with Western and Central European clients and also with Japanese companies. He has lived and attended school in Italy and is a member of the Advisory Council of the Bologna Center of Johns Hopkins University.*

*Mr. Hecht has extensive experience with business formations, acquisitions and divestitures, private placement and public offerings, financing and investment matters, restructurings and reorganizations, and licensing transactions. He advises on business start-ups, including the use of limited liability companies, directors' responsibilities and investor rights.*

*Firms refer matters to Mr. Hecht when a multi-party transaction may require separate representation, when a conflict arises or when a matter cannot be cost-effectively handled by them. Practicing on his own with reduced overhead enables Mr. Hecht to keep his fees as low as possible while providing high quality services based on 20 years of experience.*

*Mr. Hecht is active in Bar Association matters. He is Chair of the International Law Section of the Los Angeles County Bar Association. He devotes considerable time to work for Johns Hopkins University from which he holds a Masters Degree in International Relations with specialization in international economics. He is a Director of the Scott Newman Center which organizes and sponsors national programs focusing on drug prevention through education.*

**STEVEN HECHT,** born Los Angeles, California, July 19, 1948; admitted to bar, 1975, California. *Education:* Occidental College (B.A., magna cum laude, 1970); Johns Hopkins University School of Advanced International Studies (M.A., with highest honors, 1972); University of California at Los Angeles (J.D., 1975). Phi Beta Kappa. Immediate Past Vice-President, Johns Hopkins University National Alumni Council. Member, Advisory Council of The Bologna Center of Johns Hopkins University. Member, The Los Angeles Committee on Foreign Relations. *Member:* Los Angeles County (Immediate Past Chair, International Law Section; Member, Sections on: Corporate and Business Law; Intellectual Property and Entertainment Law) and American (Member, Sections on: Business Law; International Law) Bar Associations; State Bar of California. *PRACTICE AREAS:* International Business; Limited Liability Companies; Corporate Organization; Business Formation; Closely Held Corporations.

*(This Listing Continued)*

## HECHT & RISKIN

1925 CENTURY PARK EAST
SUITE 2000
**LOS ANGELES, CALIFORNIA 90067**
Telephone: 310-277-2236
Facsimile: 310-556-5653

*General Civil and Trial Practice in all State and Federal Courts. Real Property, Corporation, Securities, Franchise, Estate Planning, Trust and Probate Law. International and Taxation Law.*

**IRA D. RISKIN,** born Brooklyn, New York, May 24, 1933; admitted to bar, 1962, California; U.S. Court of Appeals, Ninth Circuit. *Education:* University of California at Los Angeles (B.A., 1955; LL.B., 1961). Order of the Coif; Phi Alpha Delta. Member, University of California at Los Angeles Law Review, 1960-1961. Author, "The Duty of a Securities Broker to Deliver Share Certificates on Demand," Los Angeles Bar Bulletin, July, 1970. Member, Panel of Arbitrators, American Arbitration Association. *Member:* Century City (Member, Board of Governors, 1974-1977), Los Angeles County and American Bar Associations; The State Bar of California; The Association of Trial Lawyers of America; American Judicature Society. [Lt. Jg., USN, 1955-1958]. *PRACTICE AREAS:* Civil Trial; Trial Practice; Civil Appeals; Real Estate; Business Law.

OF COUNSEL

**MERVYN L. HECHT,** born Freeport, Illinois, April 24, 1938; admitted to bar, 1964, California. *Education:* University of California at Los Angeles (B.A., 1960); Sorbonne, Paris, France; Harvard University Law School (J.D., 1963). *LANGUAGES:* French.

## HECKER & HARRIMAN

2029 CENTURY PARK EAST, 16TH FLOOR
**LOS ANGELES, CALIFORNIA 90067**
Telephone: 310-286-0377
Facsimile: 310-286-0488; 310-785-0016
Telex: 6503743401

*Intellectual Property Law including Patent, Trademark, Copyright, Computer Law, Unfair Competition, and Trade Secret. Technology Licensing and Litigation in Federal and State Courts and the International Trade Commission.*

**GARY A. HECKER,** born Newark, New Jersey, March 8, 1955; admitted to bar, 1981, California. *Education:* University of Rhode Island (B.S.M.E., 1977); University of San Diego (J.D., 1981). Pi Tau Sigma. Member, San Diego Law Review, 1979-1981. Author: Comment, "Ocean Thermal Energy Conversion on the High Seas: Toward an International Regulatory Regime," San Diego Law Review, Vol. 18:2, 1981; "Import Controls and Copyright Enforcement," U.S.C. Computer Law Institute, 1985. Lecturer: Copyrights for Producers, Show Biz Expo, Los Angeles, 1987; 11th Annual U.S.C Computer Law Institute, 1990; Software Publisher Association, 1989-1990. Moderator, Hastings College of Law, High Technology Law Symposium, 1991. Advisor, Hastings College of Law Journal, 1990-1992. Senior Articles Editor, Century City Bar Association Journal, 1982. Technical Advisor, U.S. House of Representatives Subcommittee on Oversight and Investigations, Committee on Energy and Commerce, Investigation on Unfair Foreign Trade Practices, 1988. Judicial Intern, California Court of Appeals, 4th District, 1981. Co-Chairman, Computer Law Task Force, International Anticounterfeiting Coalition, 1983—. Plaintiff Co-Counsel, "In re Certain Personal Computers," 224 USPQ 270 (USITC 1984). *Member:* American Bar Association (Member, Section of Patent, Trademark and Copyright Law); State Bar of California; The Association of Trial Lawyers of America; American Society of Mechanical Engineers. *PRACTICE AREAS:* Patent, Trademark and Copyright; Intellectual Property; Computer Law; Unfair Competition.

**J. D. HARRIMAN II,** born Massillon, Ohio, January 26, 1957; admitted to bar, 1984, California, U.S. District Court, Central District of California and U.S. Court of Appeals, Ninth Circuit; registered to practice before U.S. Patent and Trademark Office. *Education:* Ohio State University (B.S.E., 1979); University of Southern California (J.D., 1984). Phi Alpha Delta. Co-Author: "International Enforcement of U.S. Copyrighted Software and Mask Work Registrations," San Francisco Barrister, Sept., 1985.

*(This Listing Continued)*

## HECKER & HARRIMAN, Los Angeles—Continued

*Member:* State Bar of California. **PRACTICE AREAS:** Patent and Trademark; Intellectual Property; Computer Law; Unfair Competition.

### ASSOCIATES

**FRANK M. WEYER,** born San Francisco, California, March 17, 1957; admitted to bar, 1987, California; 1988, New York; registered to practice before U.S. Patent and Trademark Office. *Education:* Stevens Institute of Technology (B.Mech.E., 1979); California Institute of Technology (M.Eng., 1980); University of California at Berkeley, Boalt Hall (J.D., 1986). Coordinator, Rural Technology Unit of the U.S. Peace Corps, 1980-1992. Legislative Intern for the Sciences and Technology Committee for the U.S. House of Representatives. *Member:* State Bar of California.

**ELIZABETH E. BLAKEY,** born Washington, D.C., December 28, 1961; admitted to bar, 1988, California; 1989, U.S. District Court, Central District of California and U.S. Court of Appeals, Ninth Circuit. *Education:* University of Notre Dame (B.A., 1983); Loyola Law School (J.D., 1988). Recipient, First Place Award Indiana Collegiate Press Association, 1982. Casenote Editor, Loyola Entertainment Law Journal, 1987-1988. William Rains Legal Scholar, 1986-1987. Author: Note, "Criminal Copyright Infringement: Music Pirates Don't Sing the 'Jailhouse Rock 'Even When They Steal from the King," 7 Loy. L.A. Ent. L.J. 417, 1987. Teaching Assistant, Evidence, Loyola Law School, 1987-1988. *Member:* Beverly Hills and American Bar Associations; State Bar of California.

**CAROLE A. QUINN,** born Orange, New Jersey, August 11, 1955; admitted to bar, 1991, California, U.S. District Court, for the Central District of California and U.S. Court of Appeals, for the Ninth Circuit. *Education:* Ohio State University (B.A., 1977; J.D., 1991); California State University (M.S., 1981). *Member:* State Bar of California.

**ROSS D. SNYDER,** born Aberdeen Proving Grounds, Maryland, September 10, 1966; admitted to bar, 1992, California. *Education:* Massachusetts Institute of Technology (B.S.E.E., 1989); University of Southern California (J.D., 1992). *Member:* State Bar of California.

**MICHAEL FARJAMI,** born Tehran, Iran, October 12, 1960; (admission pending). *Education:* University of California at Los Angeles (B.S.E.E., magna cum laude, 1983; M.S.E.E., 1985); Loyola Law School (J.D., 1993). Member, Loyola Entertainment Law Journal, 1993. Author: "Protectable Trade Dress Without Secondary Meaning - On Second Thought," Loyola Entertainment Law Journal, Vol. 13, No. 2, pp. 381-411 (1993). **LANGUAGES:** Persian.

**RANDALL J. BLUESTONE,** born Rochester, New York, July 30, 1968; admitted to bar, 1995, California, U.S. District Court, Central District of California and U.S. Court of Appeals, Ninth Circuit. *Education:* University of California at San Diego (B.S., Physics, 1990); University of California School of Law, Los Angeles (J.D., 1995). *Member:* American Bar Association (Member, Intellectual Property Section); State Bar of California; American Intellectual Property Law Association.

REPRESENTATIVE CLIENTS: ADP; Alesis Corporation; Altamira Software, Inc.; AND Communications; Brier Technology; Diamond Sports Co.; Digital Research, Inc.; Dole Fresh Vegetables Company; Intelligent Systems; Kraft Systems, Inc.; Maxtor Corporation; Next, Inc.; Novell, Inc.; Oracle Corporation; Pacific Data Products; Pixar; Quarterdeck Office Systems; Ross Stores, Inc.; Samsung Semiconductor, Inc.; Silicon General, Inc.; Slate Corporation; Synapse Technologies, Inc.; TDK/Silicon Systems; Vicom Systems, Inc.

---

## HEDGES & CALDWELL

### A PROFESSIONAL CORPORATION

**606 SOUTH OLIVE STREET, SUITE 500**
**LOS ANGELES, CALIFORNIA 90014**
Telephone: 213-629-9040
Telecopier: 213-629-9022

General Civil and Criminal Trial and Appellate Practice in all State and Federal Courts and Administrative Agencies.

*FIRM PROFILE: Hedges & Caldwell, a law firm in downtown Los Angeles, specializes in complex litigation. We offer our clients sophisticated, creative and vigorous representation, combining the skills of a large firm with the responsiveness of a small firm. Our lawyers are experienced negotiators and trial lawyers, and have handled cases in state and federal trial and appellate courts in California and elsewhere. Our lawyers graduated at or near the top of their law school classes, and most served as law clerks in federal trial or appellate courts. Our clients include Fortune 500 companies; small closely-held businesses; major studios, artists and production companies; cities, counties and state and local agencies; and individuals and community groups.*

**CHRISTOPHER G. CALDWELL,** born Kansas City, Missouri, November 23, 1957; admitted to bar, 1982, California and U.S. District Court, Central District of California; 1984, U.S. Court of Appeals, Sixth Circuit; 1985, U.S. Court of Appeals, Tenth Circuit; 1986, U.S. Court of Appeals, First Circuit; 1987, U.S. District Court, Western District of Texas; 1988, U.S. Court of Appeals, Fifth and Ninth Circuits and U.S. District Court, Southern District of California; 1989, U.S. District Court, Eastern District of California; 1990, U.S. Supreme Court. *Education:* University of Kansas (B.A., with highest distinction and honors, 1979); Harvard University (J.D., cum laude, 1982). Phi Beta Kappa. Law Clerk to Hon. A. Wallace Tashima, U.S. District Court, Central District of California, 1982-1983. Editor, ABA Complex Crimes Journal, 1993. Trial Attorney, United States Department of Justice, Criminal Division, Public Integrity Section, 1983-1986. *Member:* State Bar of California; Los Angeles County and American Bar Associations; California Attorneys for Criminal Justice.

**GEORGE R. HEDGES,** born Philadelphia, Pennsylvania, February 26, 1952; admitted to bar, 1978, California and U.S. District Court, Central District of California; 1980, U.S. Court of Appeals, Ninth Circuit and U.S. District Court, Southern District of California; 1990, U.S. District Court, Eastern District of California; 1993, U.S. Supreme Court. *Education:* University of Pennsylvania (B.A., 1974, M.A., 1975); University of Southern California (J.D., 1978). Member, Southern California Law Review, 1977-1978. Phi Alpha Delta. Law Clerk to Hon. Lawrence T. Lydick, U.S. District Court, Central District of California, 1978-1979. Member, Board of Directors, Mental Health Advocacy Services, 1983—. Director, The Ubar/-Transarabia Expedition, 1986-1992. *Member:* State Bar of California; Los Angeles County and American Bar Associations.

**H. JAY KALLMAN,** born New York, N.Y., September 26, 1952; admitted to bar, 1991, California; 1992, U.S. District Court, Central District of California; 1995, U.S. Court of Appeals, Ninth Circuit. *Education:* McGill University (B.A., with honors, 1975); University of Wisconsin at Madison (M.S., 1978; Ph.D., Psychology, 1980); Stanford Law School (J.D., 1991). Order of the Coif. Associate Editor, Stanford Law Review, 1990-1991. Law Clerk to Hon. Mariana R. Pfaelzer, U.S. District Court, Central District of California, 1991-1992. Professor of Psychology, State University of New York at Albany, 1980-1988. *Member:* Los Angeles County (Member, Litigation Section) and Federal Bar Associations; State Bar of California.

**MICHAEL R. LESLIE,** born Erie, Pennsylvania, September 30, 1957; admitted to bar, 1986, California and U.S. District Court, Central District of California; 1987, U.S. Court of Appeals, Ninth Circuit; 1993, U.S. District Court, Eastern District of California. *Education:* Dartmouth College (B.A., summa cum laude, 1980) Phi Beta Kappa. Rufus Choate Scholar; Stanford Law School (J.D., 1985). Law Clerk to Hon. A. Wallace Tashima, U.S. District Court, Central District of California, 1985-1986. *Member:* State Bar of California; Los Angeles County and American Bar Associations. **LANGUAGES:** Spanish.

**JOAN MACK,** born Oak Park, Illinois, April 24, 1953; admitted to bar, 1995, California; 1996, U.S. District Court, Central District of California. *Education:* Stanford University (B.A., with honors, 1974); Loyola Marymount University (J.D., magna cum laude, 1995). Alpha Sigma Nu. Order of the Coif. Fritz B. Burns Scholar, 1992-1995. Articles Editor, Loyola of Los Angeles Law Review, 1994-1995. Law Clerk to Hon. Lourdes G. Baird, U.S. District Court, Central District of California, 1995-1996. *Member:* State Bar of California.

**SHERRYL ELISE MICHAELSON,** born North Chicago, Illinois, August 23, 1952; admitted to bar, 1985, New York, U.S. Court of Appeals, Second Circuit and U.S. District Court, Southern and Eastern Districts of New York; 1987, U.S. Court of Appeals, Third Circuit; 1988, California, U.S. Court of Appeals, Ninth Circuit and U.S. District Court, Central, Northern and Eastern Districts of California. *Education:* University of Texas at Austin (B.A., with honors and special honors in economics, 1975); Denver Theological Seminary (M. Div. with honors; Honors Fellow, Historical and Ethical Theology, 1977); New York University (J.D., 1983). Order of the Coif; Order of Barristers. Note and Comment Editor, New York University Law Review. Recipient: Frank Sommers Memorial Award; National Moot Court Award. Root Tilden Scholar. Law Clerk, to Hon. David L. Bazelon, U.S. Court of Appeals, District of Columbia Circuit, 1983-1984. Adjunct Professor of Law: New York University School of Law, 1987-1988; Southwestern School of Law, 1990-1993. Faculty Member: National Institute of Trial Advocacy, 1994-1995; Attorney General's Advocacy Institute, 1991-1994; California Judges Association/The Rutter Group, Courtroom Evidence, 1993; American Bar Association, Practicing

*(This Listing Continued)*

Law Institute, Bureau of National Affairs Law Education continuing legal education institutes on health care and insurance fraud, 1992-1994. Assistant U.S. Attorney, United States Attorney's Office, Central District of California, Major Frauds Section, 1989-1995. Health Care and Insurance Fraud Coordinator, 1990-1995. Recipient: Attorney General's John Marshall Award for Excellence in Litigation; U.S. Department of Justice Special Achievement Award and Meritorious Special Award; Chief Postal Inspector's Award, 1994. Volunteer Attorney, American Civil Liberties Union, Lambda Legal Defense and Education Fund. *Member:* Los Angeles County and American Bar Associations; State Bar of California; Women Lawyers of Los Angeles; Lawyers for Human Rights. Fellow, Hays Civil Liberties.

MARY NEWCOMBE, born Chapel Hill, North Carolina, July 19, 1955; admitted to bar, 1985, California, U.S. District Court, Central District of California and U.S. Court of Appeals, Ninth and Tenth Circuits; 1992, U.S. Supreme Court. *Education:* Swarthmore College; University of North Carolina (B.A., 1976); University of California at Los Angeles School of Law (J.D., 1984). Order of the Coif. Member, U.C.L.A. Law Review, 1982-1984. Law Clerk to Hon. Stephanie K. Seymour, U.S. Court of Appeals, Tenth Circuit, 1984-1985. Cooperating Attorney, ACLU Foundation of Southern California, 1986; Lambda Legal Defense and Education, 1988—. *Member:* Los Angeles County Bar Association; State Bar of California; Lawyers for Human Rights.

DAVID PETTIT, born Santa Monica, California, December 7, 1950; admitted to bar, 1975, California and U.S. District Court, Central District of California; 1979, U.S. Court of Appeals, Ninth Circuit and U.S. Claims Court; 1985, U.S. District Court, Southern District of California; 1990, U.S. District Court, Eastern District of California; 1991, U.S. Supreme Court. *Education:* University of California at Berkeley; University of California at Los Angeles (B.A., 1972; J.D., 1975). Lecturer, UCLA School of Law, 1976-1979. Panelist, California Continuing Education of the Bar, Representing Residential Landlords and Tenants, 1979, 1982. Faculty Member, National Institute of Trial Advocacy Training, 1990. Judge Pro Tem: Los Angeles Superior Court, 1989, 1992, 1993—; Los Angeles Municipal Court, 1983, 1984, 1988. Member, Board of Directors: San Fernando Valley Neighborhood Legal Services, Inc., 1989-1994; Community Corporation of Santa Monica, 1991—; Santa Monica Youth Athletic Foundation, 1995—. *Member:* Los Angeles County Bar Association; State Bar of California.

*OF COUNSEL*

RALPH H. NUTTER, born Norwood, Massachusetts, September 4, 1920; admitted to bar, 1948, Massachusetts; 1949, California. *Education:* Syracuse University; Harvard University (A.B., 1948; LL.B., 1948). Law Clerk, U.S. District Court, Eastern District of New York, 1948. Contributing Author, California Trial Objection, Second Edition, C.E.B., 1984. Attorney and Hearing Officer, National Labor Relations Board, 1948-1959. Municipal Court Judge, 1959-1961. Superior Court Judge, 1961-1969. Presiding Judge Law Department, 1965-1966. Justice ProTem, California Court of Appeal, 1968. Retired Judge sitting by appointment, Los Angeles County Superior Court, 1991-1993. *Member:* Los Angeles County Bar Association; The State Bar of California; American College of Trial Lawyers.

JAN B. NORMAN, born Burlington, Iowa, October 11, 1950; admitted to bar, 1984, California, U.S. District Court, Central District of California and U.S. Court of Appeals, Ninth Circuit; 1985, U.S. District Court, Eastern District of California; 1986, U.S. District Court, District of Colorado and U.S. Court of Appeals, Tenth Circuit; 1987, U.S. District Court, Southern District of California. *Education:* University of California at Los Angeles (B.A., magna cum laude, 1975; M.A., 1978); University of Southern California (J.D., 1984). Notes Editor, USC Law Review. Adjunct Professor, University of Southern California Law School, 1995—. *Member:* Los Angeles County Bar Association; State Bar of California. Fellow, Chancellor's Intern.

## HEENAN BLAIKIE
### LOS ANGELES, CALIFORNIA
(See Beverly Hills)

*U.S. and International Entertainment, Corporate, General Business, Commercial, Litigation, Intellectual Property, Securities, Banking and Finance, Tax, Estate Planning and Real Estate.*

## HEITING & IRWIN
### LOS ANGELES, CALIFORNIA
(See Riverside)

*Civil Trial Practice, Personal Injury, Wrongful Death, Medical Malpractice, Professional Liability, Workers Compensation, Conservatorship and Guardianships, Business, Corporate, Family Law, Dispute Resolution.*

## HELLER & EDWARDS
### LOS ANGELES, CALIFORNIA
(See Beverly Hills)

*General Civil Trial and Appellate Practice in All State and Federal Courts.*

## HELLER EHRMAN WHITE & McAULIFFE
A Partnership including Professional Corporations
*Established in 1890*

**601 S. FIGUEROA STREET**
**LOS ANGELES, CALIFORNIA 90017-5758**
Telephone: 213-689-0200
Facsimile: 213-614-1868
URL: http://www.hewm.com

*San Francisco, California Office:* 333 Bush Street. Telephone: 415-772-6000. Facsimile: 415-772-6268. Cable Address "Helpow". Telex: 340-895; 184-996.
*Palo Alto, California Office:* 525 University Avenue, Suite 1100. Telephone: 415-324-7000. Facsimile: 415-324-0638.
*Seattle, Washington Office:* 6100 Columbia Center, 701 Fifth Avenue. Telephone: 206-447-0900. Facsimile: 206-447-0849.
*Portland, Oregon Office:* 200 S.W. Market Street, Suite 1750. Telephone: 503-227-7400. Facsimile: 503-241-0950.
*Anchorage, Alaska Office:* 1900 Bank of America Center, 550 West 7th Avenue. Telephone: 907-277-1900. Facsimile: 907-277-1920.
*Tacoma, Washington Office:* 1400 First Interstate Plaza, 1201 Pacific Avenue. Telephone: 206-572-6666. Facsimile: 206-572-6743.
*Washington, D.C. Office:* 815 Connecticut Ave., N.W., Suite 200. Telephone: 202-785-4747. Facsimile: 202-785-8877.
*Hong Kong Office:* 1902A, 19/F, Peregrine Tower, Lippo Centre, 89 Queensway, Hong Kong. Telephone: (011) 852-2526-6381. Facsimile: (011) 852-2810-6242.
*Singapore Office:* 50 Raffles Place, 17-04 Shell Tower. Telephone: (011) 65 538-1756. Facsimile: (011) 65 538-1537.

*General Practice.*

*MEMBERS OF FIRM*

††WAYNE S. BRAVEMAN, born New York, N.Y., February 5, 1953; admitted to bar, 1980, California. *Education:* Drew University (B.A., 1975); Harvard University (J.D., 1978). Harvard Law Review, 1976-1978. Law Clerk to Hon. Jack B. Weinstein, Chief Judge, U.S. District Court, Eastern District of New York, 1978-1979. Member, Advisory Committee on Rules of Practice and Internal Operating Procedures for the U.S. Court of Appeals, Ninth Circuit. **PRACTICE AREAS:** Appellate and Complex Civil Litigation. **Email:** wbraveman@hewm.com

††NEAL H. BROCKMEYER, born Glendale, California, April 11, 1938; admitted to bar, 1964, California. *Education:* Stanford University (A.B., cum laude, 1960); University of California (J.D., 1963). Order of the Coif. Managing Editor, California Law Review, 1962-1963. Co-Author: Financing California Businesses, Continuing Education of the Bar, rev. 1995; "Two-Step Acquisitions-Freezing Out Minority Shareholders" and "Products Liability in Asset Acquisitions," Business Acquisitions, Second Edition, Practising Law Institute, 1981 and Supplement. Member, 1977-1979, Chair, 1978-1979, Committee on Corporations and Member, 1979-1982, Executive Committee, Business Law Section, State Bar of California. Member, Executive Committee, 1973-1983, Chair, 1981-1982, Business and Corporations Law Section, Los Angeles County Bar Association. Member, Committee on Federal Regulation of Securities, Committee on Negotiated Acquisitions and Committee on Law Firms (Chair, Subcommittee on Quality Control, 1989-1994), Section of Business Law, American Bar Associa-

*(This Listing Continued)*

## HELLER EHRMAN WHITE & McAULIFFE, Los Angeles—Continued

tion. *PRACTICE AREAS:* Corporate Finance; Mergers and Acquisitions; Securities Law; Corporate Law. *Email:* nbrockmeyer@hewm.com

††*NANCY SHER COHEN,* born Kansas City, Missouri, September 29, 1951; admitted to bar, 1978, California. *Education:* University of Texas at Austin (B.A., 1973); Loyola Law School at Los Angeles (J.D., 1978). Staff Member, Loyola Law Review, 1977-1978. (Office Managing Partner). *PRACTICE AREAS:* Products Liability and Insurance Coverage Litigation. *Email:* ncohen@hewm.com

††*RAYMOND C. FISHER,* born Oakland, California, July 12, 1939; admitted to bar, 1967, California. *Education:* University of California at Santa Barbara (B.A., 1961); Stanford University (LL.B., 1966). Order of the Coif. Stanford Law Review, 1965-1966. Law Clerk to: Hon. J. Skelly Wright, U.S. Court of Appeals, D.C. Circuit, 1966-1967; Hon. William J. Brennan, Jr., U.S. Supreme Court, 1967-1968. Commissioner, Los Angeles Police Commission Board of Directors, Constitutional Rights Foundation, 1977—. Lawyer Representatives, Ninth Circuit Judicial Conference, 1986-1991. Executive Board, Federal Bar Association, Central District. Fellow: American Law Institute; American Bar Foundation. *PRACTICE AREAS:* Antitrust; Financial Institutions; Securities Litigation; Intellectual Property. *Email:* rfisher@hewm.com

††*PAUL H. GREINER,* born Fullerton, California, September 17, 1958; admitted to bar, 1985, California. *Education:* California State University, Fullerton (B.A., 1982); Loyola Law School of Los Angeles (J.D., 1985). Author: Case Note: "NFL's Home Game Blackout Exemption," 4 Loyola of Los Angeles Entertainment Law Journal 209, 1984; Case Note: "NFL's Membership Admissions Procedure," 4 Loyola of Los Angeles Entertainment Law Journal 243, 1984. *PRACTICE AREAS:* General Corporate; Securities and Venture Capital Transactions; Mergers and Acquisitions; Export Regulation and Corporate Investigations. *Email:* pgreiner@hewm.com

††*ROBERT B. HUBBELL,* born Los Angeles, California, April 26, 1956; admitted to bar, 1981, California. *Education:* Loyola Marymount University (B.A., 1978); Loyola University of Los Angeles (J.D., 1981). Loyola Law Review, 1980-1981. Law Clerk to the Hon. Stephen S. Reinhardt, U.S. Court of Appeals, Ninth Circuit. Author: "Neutral Principles Approach to Intra-Church Property Disputes," 13 Loyola of Los Angeles Law Review 109-32. Temporary Judge, Los Angeles Municipal Court, 1995. Courthouse Volunteer, LACBA Domestic Violence Clinic, 1995. Member, Association of Business Trial Lawyers Federal Courts Committee. *PRACTICE AREAS:* Professional Liability and Insurance Coverage Litigation. *Email:* rhubbell@hewm.com

††*JOAN K. IRION,* born Galveston, Texas, September 22, 1953; admitted to bar, 1979, California; 1988, District of Columbia. *Education:* University of California at Davis (B.A., 1974; J.D., 1979); California State University at San Diego (M.P.A., 1976). U.C. Davis Law Review, 1977-1979. *PRACTICE AREAS:* State and Local Taxation; Federal and State Tax Controversy. *Email:* jirion@hewm.com

††*JEFFERY W. JOHNSON,* born Cincinnati, Ohio, July 19, 1962; admitted to bar, 1988, California. *Education:* Butler University (B.A., magna cum laude, 1984); Indiana University (J.D., cum laude, 1987). Member, Indiana Law Review, 1985-1987. Member, Environmental Law Institute. *Email:* jjohnson@hewm.com

††*GARY W. MAEDER,* born Los Angeles, California, December 21, 1949; admitted to bar, 1975, California. *Education:* University of California at Los Angeles (B.A., summa cum laude, 1971; J.D., 1975). Phi Beta Kappa; Order of the Coif. Comment Editor, University of California at Los Angeles Law Review, 1974-1975. Author: "Right of Access to the Broadcast Media for Paid Editorial Advertising-A Plea to Congress," 22 University of California at Los Angeles Law Review 258, 1974. Member, Taxation Section and State and Local Tax Committee Chair, Los Angeles County Bar Association. *Member:* Christian Legal Society (Secretary, 1989-1992). *PRACTICE AREAS:* Federal Income and State and Local Taxation. *Email:* gmaeder@hewm.com

††*STEPHEN E. NEWTON,* born Akron, Ohio, June 11, 1942; admitted to bar, 1968, California. *Education:* Cornell University (A.B., 1964); University of California, Hastings College of the Law (J.D., 1967). Order of the Coif. Member, Thurston Society. Editor-in-Chief, The Hastings Law Journal, 1966-1967. Co-Author: "Financing California Businesses," California Continuing Education of the Bar, 1978, 1980, 1982, 1983, 1985, 1986 and 1988, Supplements. *PRACTICE AREAS:* Corporate Finance; Corporate Law; Mergers and Acquisitions; Securities Law; Banking. *Email:* snewton@hewm.com

††*RONALD C. PETERSON,* born St. Petersburg, Florida, September 10, 1945; admitted to bar, 1972, California. *Education:* University of California at Santa Barbara (B.A., 1967); Yale University (M.A., 1971; J.D., 1971). Member, Litigation and International Law Sections, American Bar Associations. *PRACTICE AREAS:* Complex Civil Litigation. *Email:* rpeterson@hewm.com

††*JON L. REWINSKI,* born New Haven, Connecticut, October 15, 1959; admitted to bar, 1984, California. *Education:* Yale University (B.A., magna cum laude, 1981); New York University School of Law (J.D., 1984). *LANGUAGES:* German. *PRACTICE AREAS:* Litigation; Appellate Practice; Securities Litigation; Securities Arbitration; Regulatory Investigations and Proceedings. *Email:* jrewinski@hewm.com

*DEBORAH CRANDALL SAXE,* born Lima, Ohio, July 23, 1949; admitted to bar, 1978, California; 1979, District of Columbia. *Education:* Pennsylvania State University (B.A., 1971); University of California, Los Angeles (M.A., 1973; J.D., 1978). Phi Beta Kappa. *Email:* dsaxe@hewm.com

††*A. TIMOTHY SCOTT,* born Natchez, Mississippi, February 16, 1952; admitted to bar, 1977, California. *Education:* Stanford University (A.B., 1974; J.D., 1977). Order of the Coif. Member, 1975-1977 and Note Editor, 1976-1977, Stanford Law Review. Author: "The Tax Treatment of the Cost of Terminating a Lease," 30 Stanford Law Review 241, 1977. Co-Author: "The Passive Loss Rules: Guidance from the First Set of Regulations," 41 Major Tax Planning 19-1 (1989); "Impact of the Passive Activity Rules on Real Estate," 40 Major Tax Planning 20-1 (1988). Member, Executive Committee and Chair Real Estate Tax Committee, Los Angeles County Bar Association, 1989-1991. *PRACTICE AREAS:* State and Federal Income Taxation. *Email:* tscott@hewm.com

††*CARLOS SOLIS,* born Managua, Nicaragua, May 15, 1945; admitted to bar, 1970, California; 1973, U.S. Supreme Court. *Education:* University of San Francisco (A.B., 1967; J.D., 1969). Phi Delta Phi (Recipient of Province Award: Graduate of the Year, 1969); Alpha Sigma Nu; Pi Sigma Alpha. Member, McAuliffe Law Honor Society. Author: "Sports Spectators--The Uncompensated Injury Victims," 2 University of San Francisco Law Review 114, 1967; "Coordinated Bargaining— The Unions' Attempt to Answer a Need," 3 University of San Francisco Law Review 353, 1969; "Statute of Limitations in Legal Malpractice Cases: The California Supreme Court Establishes New Guidelines," 7 University of San Francisco Law Review 85, 1972. Associate Editor, University of San Francisco Law Review, 1968-1969. *PRACTICE AREAS:* Complex Litigation; Creditor Bankruptcy Law; Real Estate Litigation; Creditors Rights; Intellectual Property Litigation. *Email:* csolis@hewm.com

††*G. THOMAS STROMBERG, JR.,* born San Francisco, California, February 23, 1955; admitted to bar, 1982, Illinois; 1986, California. *Education:* Harvard University (B.A., 1979); University of Utah (J.D., 1982). *PRACTICE AREAS:* International, Corporate and Project Finance. *Email:* tstromberg@hewm.com

††*STEVEN R. TEKOSKY,* born New York, N.Y., March 2, 1954; admitted to bar, 1982, California. *Education:* University of California at Berkeley (A.B., 1977); Southwestern University College of Law (J.D., 1981). *PRACTICE AREAS:* Environmental Litigation and Regulation. *Email:* stekosky@hewm.com

††*STEPHEN A. TUGGY,* born Manila, Philippines, October 13, 1959; admitted to bar, 1985, California. *Education:* Wheaton College (B.A., 1982); University of California at Los Angeles (J.D., 1985). Order of the Coif. U.C.L.A. Law Review, 1982-1984. John M. Olin Fellowship. *PRACTICE AREAS:* Complex Commercial Litigation. *Email:* stuggy@hewm.com

††*STEVEN O. WEISE,* born Los Angeles, California, November 1, 1949; admitted to bar, 1974, California. *Education:* Yale University (B.A., 1971); Boalt Hall School of Law, University of California (J.D., 1974). Director, House Ear Institute, 1975-1981. Author: "U.C.C. Article 9-Personal Property Secured Transactions," 45 The Business Lawyer, August, 1990; "Commercial Law—1986, 1987 and 1988, Legislation and Other Recent Developments of Interest to California Lawyers," Business Law Section of the State Bar of California; "1986, 1987 and 1988 Commercial Law Developments" Financial Lawyers Conference, ABA Commercial Financial Service Committee; "Payment-in-Full Checks," California Business Law Reporter 193, April, 1984; "The Partnership Agreement: Protection for Troubled Times," 6 Los Angeles Lawyer 34, April, 1983. Contributing Editor (Contracts), California Business Law Reporter, 1984—. Lecturer, Busi-

*(This Listing Continued)*

ness and Commercial Law, American Bar Association, 1988, 1989; Legal Opinions in the 80's, Practicing Law Institute, 1985, 1986; Opinion Letters of Counsel; ABA National Institute, The Standardization of Opinion Letters, State Bar of California, 1989-1990, California Continuing Education of the Bar, 1981-1988, Recent Developments in Business Law. *Member:* Beverly Hills Bar Association; Financial Lawyers Conference (Member, Board of Governors, 1989—). *PRACTICE AREAS:* Corporate Transactions and Work-Outs. *Email:* sweise@hewm.com

## SPECIAL COUNSEL

**LINDA DAVES BARKER,** born Los Angeles, California, September 3, 1955; admitted to bar, 1983, California. *Education:* University of Southern California (B.S., 1977); Loyola Law School (J.D., 1982). *Email:* lbarker@hewm.com

**DALE S. FISCHER,** born East Orange, New Jersey, October 17, 1951; admitted to bar, 1980, California, U.S. Supreme Court, U.S. Court of Appeals, Ninth Circuit and U.S. District Court, District of California. *Education:* Dickinson College and University of South Florida (B.A., 1977); Harvard Law School (J.D., 1980). Notes and Comments Editor, Harvard Women's Law Journal, 1978-1979. Faculty: National Institute of Trial Advocacy (Depositions and Trial Advocacy Courses). Moderator and Panel Member: How to Win Your Case with Depositions (1993). Judge Pro Tem, Los Angeles Municipal Court. Member, Panel of Arbitrators, American Arbitration Association. Pro Bono City Attorney, 1991. Member, Litigation Section, American Bar Association. *Member:* Federal Bar Association (Member, Litigation and Labor Sections). *REPORTED CASES:* Mirkin v. Wasserman, 5 Cal. 4th 1082 (1993); Texas Commerce Bank v. Garamendi, 11 Cal. App. 4th 460 (1992). *PRACTICE AREAS:* Civil Practice; Complex Litigation; Probate and Trust Litigation; ERISA Litigation; Employment Litigation. *Email:* dfischer@hewm.com

**CAROL A. PFAFFMANN,** born Detroit, Michigan, December 29, 1958; admitted to bar, 1984, California. *Education:* Miami University (B.A., magna cum laude, 1981); Cornell Law School (J.D., 1984). Phi Beta Kappa. *PRACTICE AREAS:* Acquisitions, Divestitures and Mergers; Securities Law; Corporate Law. *Email:* cpfaffmann@hewm.com

**DANIEL K. SLAUGHTER,** born Charleston, West Virginia, July 4, 1961; admitted to bar, 1988, California. *Education:* Cornell University (B.A., 1983); University of California at Los Angeles (J.D., 1988). *Email:* dslaughter@hewm.com

## OF COUNSEL

**JOSEPH W. BURDETT,** born Peoria, Illinois, October 23, 1936; admitted to bar, 1966, California. *Education:* Bradley University (B.S., 1957); University of Utah (M.S., 1962); Stanford University (J.D., 1965). Member, 1963-1964 and Board of Revisors, 1964-1965, Stanford Law Review. Author: "Foglesong's Section 482 Approach May Threaten Closely-Held Personal Service Corporations," Journal of Taxation, December 1980; "Tax Deferral-Installment Sales Revision Act of 1980," California Certified Public Accountants Foundation, June 1981; "Choosing the Correct Entity for Motion Picture and Television Production and Distribution," 1995 Entertainment Tax and Financing Institute. *Member:* Beverly Hills Bar Association; California Society of CPA's. *PRACTICE AREAS:* Federal and State Income Taxation; Tax Controversies. *Email:* jburdett@hewm.com

**JAMES H. KINDEL, JR.,** born Los Angeles, California, November 8, 1913; admitted to bar, 1941, California. *Education:* University of California at Los Angeles (A.B., 1934); Loyola University (LL.B., 1940). Phi Delta Phi. Member, Chancery Club. Certified Public Accountant, California, 1942. Former Chairman, Committee on Taxation, Los Angeles County Bar Association. Former Chairman, Committee of Taxation and Committee on Economics of Law Practice, State Bar of California. Lecturer, USC Tax Institute. Recipient, Dana Latham Award, 1983, Los Angeles County Bar Tax Section. *Member:* Orange County Bar Association. *PRACTICE AREAS:* Taxation; Trusts; Estate Planning. *Email:* jkindel@hewm.com

**GAVIN MILLER,** born New York, N.Y., March 8, 1926; admitted to bar, 1955, New York; 1962, California. *Education:* Harvard University (A.B., 1950); Harvard Law School (LL.B., 1953). Phi Beta Kappa. Editor, Harvard Law Review, 1951-1953. *Email:* gmiller@hewm.com

## ASSOCIATES

**K. TOMOKO AOYAMA,** born Tokyo, Japan, February 23, 1964; admitted to bar, 1993, California; U.S. District Court, Central District of California. *Education:* Wellesley College (B.A., cum laude, 1985); Boston College Law School (J.D., 1992). Member, Business Law and International Law and Practice Sections, American Bar Associations. *LANGUAGES:* Japanese. *Email:* taoyama@hewm.com

*(This Listing Continued)*

**ALEXANDER G. ARATO,** born Beverly Hills, California, July 12, 1963; admitted to bar, 1989, California and U.S. District Court, Central and Northern, Districts of California; 1990, U.S. District Court, Eastern and Southern Districts of California and U.S. Court of Appeals, 9th Circuit. *Education:* University of California, Berkeley (B.A., 1985); Benjamin N. Cardozo School of Law (J.D., magna cum laude, 1989). Member, Cardozo Law Review, 1987-1988. Member, Education Committee, Los Angeles County Bar Association, 1989-1994. *Member:* Financial Lawyers Conference. *Email:* aarato@hewm.com

**L. ANTHONY BEALL,** born Orange, California, January 24, 1961; admitted to bar, 1987, California. *Education:* University of California at Los Angeles (B.A., 1983); Loyola Law School (J.D., 1987). *Email:* abeall@hewm.com

**JILL I. BROWN,** born Minneapolis, Minnesota, November 13, 1965; admitted to bar, 1992, California. *Education:* Harvard University (A.B., 1987); University of California at Los Angeles (J.D., 1991). Member, University of California at Los Angeles Law Review, 1989-1991. Author: "Defining 'Reasonable' Police Conduct: Graham v. Connor and Excessive Force During Arrest," 38 UCLA L. Rev. 1257, June, 1991. *Email:* jbrown@hewm.com

**WILLIAM NATHAN CANBY,** born Tacoma, Washington, August 3, 1957; admitted to bar, 1996, California. *Education:* Yale University (B.A., 1979; J.D., 1996); University of California at Los Angeles (M.F.A., 1990). Member, Yale Journal of Law & Humanities, 1993-1996. *Email:* wcanby@hewm.com

**DAVID M. CHERNEK,** born Springfield, Ohio, June 26, 1963; admitted to bar, 1990, California. *Education:* University of California at Los Angeles (B.A., 1985); Boston College (J.D., 1990). *Email:* dchernek@hewm.com

**KENNETH L. CHERNOF,** born Los Angeles, California, July 29, 1967; admitted to bar, 1991, California; 1992, District of Columbia. *Education:* Harvard College (A.B., cum laude, 1988); Georgetown University Law Center (J.D., magna cum laude, 1991). Order of the Coif. Member, American Criminal Law Review. Judicial Intern, Honorable Harry T. Edwards, U.S. Court of Appeals for the District of Columbia Circuit, 1990-1991. *Email:* kchernof@hewm.com

**CHRISTA L. CRAWFORD,** born Kansas City, Missouri, September 19, 1969; admitted to bar, 1994, Kentucky (Not admitted in California). *Education:* Claremont McKenna College (B.A., cum laude, 1991); Harvard Law School (J.D., 1994). *Email:* ccrawford@hewm.com

**STEVEN M. FRIEDMAN,** born Los Angeles, California, January 22, 1963; admitted to bar, 1988, California; 1989, U.S. District Court, Central District of California; 1990, U.S. Court of Appeals, Ninth Circuit. *Education:* University of California at San Diego (B.A., 1985); University of California, Hastings College of the Law (J.D., 1988). Member, 1986-1987 and Note and Comment Editor, 1987-1988, Hastings Constitutional Law Quarterly. *Email:* sfriedman@hewm.com

**M. ART GAMBILL,** born Knoxville, Tennessee, October 8, 1967; admitted to bar, 1996, California. *Education:* Yale University (B.A., cum laude, 1990); University of California School of Law, Los Angeles (J.D., 1996). *Email:* agambill@hewm.com

**SETH D. HILTON,** born San Luis Obispo, California, November 16, 1968; admitted to bar, 1996, California and U.S. District Court, Central District of California. *Education:* Harvard College (A.B., cum laude, 1992); University of California School of Law, Davis (J.D., 1995). Order of the Coif. Senior Articles Editor, UC Davis Law Review, 1994-1995. Author: "Restraints on Homosexual Rights Legislation: Is there a Fundamental Right to Participate in the Political Process?" 28 U.C. Davis Law Review 445 (1995); "American Conceptions of the Middle East and Islam," 1 U.C. Davis Journal of International Law and Policy 355 (1995). Law Clerk to the Honorable David V. Kenyon, 1995-1996. *Email:* shilton@hewm.com

**ROGER W. JANEWAY,** born Newport, Rhode Island, January 17, 1960; admitted to bar, 1995, California. *Education:* Yale University (B.A., 1982); University of California, Los Angeles (M.A., Linguistics, 1989); University of California School of Law, Los Angeles (J.D., 1994). Order of the Coif. Articles Editor, UCLA Law Review, 1993-1994. Law Clerk to Hon. Charles A. Legge, U.S. District Court, Northern District of California. Member, Lawyers for Human Rights, 1992—. *Email:* rjaneway@hewm.com

**HEATHER A. MACTAVISH,** born Redondo Beach, California, May 28, 1970; admitted to bar, 1995, California. *Education:* California Polytechnic State University (B.A., 1992); University of California School of Law (J.D., 1995). Order of the Coif. *Email:* hmactavish@hewm.com

*(This Listing Continued)*

CAA761B

## HELLER EHRMAN WHITE & McAULIFFE, Los Angeles—Continued

**PATRICIA A. MCBRIDE,** born Abington, Pennsylvania, December 5, 1963; admitted to bar, 1990, California. *Education:* Tufts University (B.A., 1986); University of Chicago (J.D., 1990). University of Chicago Legal Forum, 1988-1989. *Email:* pmcbride@hewm.com

**ROBERT OLIVER,** born Los Angeles, California, December 23, 1966; admitted to bar, 1995, California. *Education:* Whittier College (B.A., 1990); Loyola of Los Angeles Law School (J.D., 1995). Order of the Coif. St. Thomas More Honor Society. Member, Loyola of Los Angeles Law Review, 1993-1995. Extern to the Honorable Stephen Reinhardt, Ninth Circuit Court of Appeals. *Member:* Hispanic National Bar Association; Mexican-American Bar Association. *Email:* roliver@hewm.com

**ANN I. PARK,** born Hazleton, Pennsylvania, August 25, 1963; admitted to bar, 1987, California. *Education:* Harvard University (A.B., 1984); University of California at Los Angeles (J.D., 1987). Member, 1985-1986 and Managing Editor, 1986-1987, UCLA Law Review, 1985-1987. Author: "Human Rights and Basic Needs: Using International Norms to Inform Constitutional Interpretation," 34 U.C.L.A. Law Review 1195 (1985). *Email:* apark@hewm.com

**PAUL W. POAREO,** born San Pedro, California, June 16, 1950; admitted to bar, 1991, California. *Education:* California State University, Dominguez Hills (B.A., 1974); University of California at Los Angeles (M.B.A., 1977; J.D., 1991). *Email:* ppoareo@hewm.com

**RHONDA M. REAVES,** born Los Angeles, California, October 20, 1963; admitted to bar, 1992, California. *Education:* Yale University (B.A., 1985); Stanford Law School (J.D., 1991). Clerk to the Hon. James Ware, U.S. District Court, Northern District of California, 1991-1992. *Email:* rreaves@hewm.com

**THOMAS E. REIBER,** born Cincinnati, Ohio, September 16, 1967; admitted to bar, 1992, California. *Education:* University of Virginia (B.A., 1989); University of California, Boalt Hall School of Law (J.D., 1992). Phi Beta Kappa. Order of the Coif. Law Clerk to the Hon. Alicemarie H. Stotler, U.S. District Court for the Central District of California, 1992-1993. *Email:* treiber@hewm.com

**JEFFREY A. RICHMOND,** born Winchester, Massachusetts, March 23, 1962; admitted to bar, 1991, California. *Education:* Harvard University (A.B., 1984); University of California at Los Angeles (J.D., 1991). Member, University of California at Los Angeles Law Review, 1989-1991. *Email:* jrichmond@hewm.com

**REYNOLD L. SIEMENS,** born Winnipeg, Manitoba, Canada, June 11, 1962; admitted to bar, 1995, California. *Education:* University of Oxford (B.Phil., 1985; D.Phil., 1990); Harvard Law School (J.D., 1995). President, Harvard Environmental Law Society, 1994-1995. Editor, Environmental Justice: The New Wave. Author: "Proceedings of the Twenty-Fifth Anniversary Conference of the Harvard Environmental Law Society," Virginia Environmental Law Journal, 1995. *Email:* rsiemens@hewm.com

**EDWARD J. SLIZEWSKI,** born Chicago, Illinois, June 18, 1962; admitted to bar, 1992, California. *Education:* University of Chicago (A.B., with honors, 1985); Columbia University (M.A., 1985); University of California School of Law, Los Angeles (J.D., 1992). Order of the Coif. *Email:* eslizewski@hewm.com

**DEANNA M. WILCOX,** born Salt Lake City, Utah, May 9, 1961; admitted to bar, 1994, California. *Education:* Loma Linda University (B.A., 1983); University of Chicago (J.D., 1994). *Email:* dwilcox@hewm.com

††Lawyer who is a stockholder and an employee of a professional corporation which is a member of the firm

Unless otherwise stated all members and associates resident in Los Angeles are members of the State Bar of California, the Los Angeles County Bar Association and the American Bar Association.

(For complete biographical data on Anchorage, Alaska, Palo Alto, California, San Francisco, California, Washington, D.C., Portland, Oregon, Seattle, Washington, Tacoma, Washington, Hong Kong and Singapore office personnel, see Professional Biographies at each of those cities)

---

## HELMS, HANRAHAN & MYERS
### LOS ANGELES, CALIFORNIA
(See Arcadia)

*General Civil and Trial Practice in all State and Federal Courts. Corporations, Estate Planning, Probate, Personal Injury, Negligence and Family Law.*

---

## HEMAR, ROUSSO & GARWACKI
### LOS ANGELES, CALIFORNIA
(See Encino)

*Commercial Litigation, Creditors Rights, Banking, Equipment Leasing, Bankruptcy and Secured Transactions.*

---

## HEMER, BARKUS & CLARK
### LOS ANGELES, CALIFORNIA
(See Glendale)

*Civil Trial and Appellate Practice. Medical and Legal Professional Liability, Products Liability, Negligence and Insurance Law.*

---

## HENDERSON, WOHLGEMUTH & BOHL
A PROFESSIONAL CORPORATION
### LOS ANGELES, CALIFORNIA
(See Ventura)

*General Civil and Trial Practice. Insurance, Personal Injury, Insurance Defense, Products Liability, Admiralty, Environmental, Construction, Negligence and Malpractice Law.*

---

## HENNELLY & GROSSFELD
17383 WEST SUNSET BOULEVARD, SUITE 420
### LOS ANGELES, CALIFORNIA 90272
Telephone: 310-573-7800
Fax: 310-573-7806
Email: 104066.3016@compuserve.com

Sacramento, California Office: 3600 American River Drive, Suite 205, 95864. Telephone: 916-488-1000.

*General Civil Trial Practice in all State and Federal Courts and Administrative Agencies, Antitrust, Aviation, Bankruptcy, Business, Commercial, Corporate, Employment Counselling and Litigation, Environmental, Insurance, Intellectual Property, Negligence, Personal Injury, Product Liability, Professional Malpractice, Real Estate, Trade Regulation, Trade Secrets, Unfair Competition.*

**JOHN J. HENNELLY, JR.,** born Missouri, 1943; admitted to bar, 1970, Missouri; 1988, California. *Education:* St. Louis University (A.B., 1967; J.D., cum laude, 1970); Harvard University (LL.M., 1972). Alpha Sigma Nu; Pi Sigma Alpha. Editor-in-Chief, St. Louis University Law Journal, 1969-1970. *Member:* Los Angeles County and American Bar Associations; State Bar of California; The Missouri Bar; Product Liability Advisory Council, Inc.; Defense Research Institute. Fellow, American College of Trial Lawyers. **PRACTICE AREAS:** Litigation; Products Liability.

**KENNETH B. GROSSFELD,** born California, 1958; admitted to bar, 1983, California and U.S. District Court, Central District of California; U.S. Court of Appeals, Ninth Circuit. *Education:* University of California at Los Angeles (B.A., 1980); Loyola University of Los Angeles (J.D., cum laude, 1983). *Member:* St. Thomas More Honor Society; Traynor Law Honor Society. Delegate, State Bar Conference of Delegates, 1986—. Member, Loyola University of Los Angeles Law Review, 1982-1983. *Member:* Sacramento County and Federal Bar Associations; American Intellectual Property Law Association. Fellow: Sacramento Law Foundation (President, 1995). (Resident, Sacramento, California Office). **PRACTICE AREAS:** Real Estate Law; Intellectual Property Law; Business and Products Liability Litigation.

*(This Listing Continued)*

# PROFESSIONAL BIOGRAPHIES

**SUSAN J. WILLIAMS,** born Los Angeles, California, April 7, 1952; admitted to bar, 1978, California and U.S. District Court, Central, Northern, Southern and Eastern Districts of California. *Education:* Princeton University (B.A., summa cum laude, 1974); Stanford University (M.A., 1976); Harvard Law School (J.D., 1978). Phi Beta Kappa. Senior Editor, Harvard Civil Rights-Civil Liberties Law Review, 1977-1978. *Member:* State Bar of California. *LANGUAGES:* Spanish. *PRACTICE AREAS:* Litigation.

**JAMES D. DEMET,** born New York, N.Y., June 19, 1962; admitted to bar, 1987, Florida; 1988, U.S. District Court, Southern District of Florida including Trial Bar; 1994, California and U.S. District Court, Central, Eastern and Southern Districts of California. *Education:* Vanderbilt University (B.A., 1984); University of Miami (J.D., cum laude, 1987). Order of the Coif. Board Member, University of Miami Law Review, 1985-1987. *Member:* Los Angeles County, Santa Monica and American Bar Associations; State Bar of California; The Florida Bar. *PRACTICE AREAS:* Business Litigation; Products Liability.

## ASSOCIATES

**BRIAN M. ENGLUND,** born Zeeland, Michigan, July 17, 1951; admitted to bar, 1976, California and U.S. District Court, Northern, Eastern, Central and Southern Districts of California; U.S. Court of Appeals, Ninth Circuit; U.S. Supreme Court. *Education:* University of California at Davis (B.A., 1973); Hastings College of the Law, University of California (J.D., 1976). Phi Beta Kappa; Order of the Coif. Member, Thurston Society. Author: "Oral Employment Contracts and Equitable Estoppel: The Real Estate Broker As Victim," 26 Hastings Law Journal, 1503, 1975. *Member:* Sacramento County and Federal Bar Associations; State Bar of California. (Resident, Sacramento, California Office). *PRACTICE AREAS:* Business and Securities Litigation.

**VICTORIA J. HENNELLY,** born Orange, California, May 9, 1957; admitted to bar, 1983, California; 1985, Missouri. *Education:* University of Southern California (B.A., summa cum laude, 1980; J.D., 1983). Phi Beta Kappa. *Member:* Los Angeles County and American Bar Associations; State Bar of California; The Missouri Bar. *PRACTICE AREAS:* Litigation.

**MICHAEL G. KING,** born New York, New York, October 25, 1963; admitted to bar, 1989, California; 1990, U.S. district Court, Central District of California; 1994, U.S. District Court, Southern District of California. *Education:* Boston College (B.A., 1985); Boalt Hall (J.D., 1989). Phi Beta Kappa. *Member:* Los Angeles County Bar Association; State Bar of California. *PRACTICE AREAS:* Business Litigation; Products Liability.

**KAREN L. ATKINSON,** born Decatur, Georgia, December 5, 1968; admitted to bar, 1996, California. *Education:* Kent State University (B.B.A., 1990); University of San Diego (J.D., 1995; M.B.A., 1996). *Member:* State Bar of California; American Bar Association. *PRACTICE AREAS:* Business Litigation; Products Liability. *Email:* 104066.3016@compuserve.com

REPRESENTATIVE CLIENTS: A.B. Chance Co.; Advantage Concepts, Inc.; Amador Home Health Agency; Ardrox, Inc.; Belgravia Capitol Corporation; California Distributors Association; Capitol Benefit Group, Inc.; Capitol Cigar & Candy; Crosspoint Leasing & Financial Services, Inc.; Daewoo International (America) Corporation; Derby Cycle Corporation d/b/a/ Raleigh U.S.A.,; Diplomat Tours; Earthgrains Company; Electrologists Association of California; Emerson Electric Company; Fisher Controls, International, Inc.; Genoyer Group, Inc.; Geotech Environmental; Kearney-National, Inc.; Legacy Travel & Tours, Inc.; Lloyds of London; Lull Industries; McClatchy Insurance; McCuen & Steele; Mark III Management Company; Morgan Stanley Real Estate Fund, II, LLP; Naber Technical Enterprises; National School Reporting Services; Northern California Fertility Center, Inc.; Oilfield Management, Inc.; Preventative Dental Care Centers; Prime Pump Corporation; Pulsedata International, Ltd.; Residential Growth Fund, LLC; River City Travel; Royal Construction Company; Sacramento Investment Company, Inc.; Schepps Communications, Inc.; Schultz Investment Company; Sears Roebuck & Co.; Sikorslky Aircraft; Steele Enterprises, Inc.; Sterling Contractors; Todd Uniforms, Inc.; United Van Lines, Inc.; VALAIR; Weatherford International, Inc.; Whirlpool Corp.

---

## HENNIGAN, MERCER & BENNETT

601 SOUTH FIGUEROA STREET, SUITE 3300
**LOS ANGELES, CALIFORNIA 90017**
Telephone: 213-694-1200
Fax: 213-694-1234
Email: Silverm@hmb.com

*Commercial and Complex Litigation; Corporate Reorganization, Insolvency, and Bankruptcy Law and Related Litigation; Antitrust Litigation; and Securities Litigation.*

(This Listing Continued)

---

**J. MICHAEL HENNIGAN,** born Tucson, Arizona, November 2, 1943; admitted to bar, 1970, Arizona; 1972, U.S. District Court, District of Arizona and U.S. Court of Appeals, 9th Circuit; 1974, California and U.S. District Court, Northern, Eastern and Southern Districts of California; 1976, U.S. District Court, Central District of California; 1978, U.S. Supreme Court; 1993, Temporary Emergency Court of Appeals and U.S. Court of Appeals for the Federal Circuit. *Education:* University of Arizona (B.A., 1966; J.D., with distinction, 1970). Blue Key (President, 1964-1965); Order of the Coif. Recipient: Charles L. Strauss Award, 1969; Ralph W. Aigler Award, 1970; Prentice-Hall Tax Award, 1970; American Jurisprudence Awards for Corporations, Criminal Procedure, Federal Jurisdiction, Property, Securities Regulation and Torts. Note and Comment Editor, Arizona Law Review, 1969-1970. Author: "The Essence of Standing: The Basis of a Constitutional Right to be Heard," 10 Arizona Law Review 438, 1969; "In Defense of the Conscientious Objector: The Constitutional Right to a Trial de Novo," 11 Arizona Law Review, 249, 1969. Co-Author: American Bar Association Section of Antitrust Law, Monograph 3, "Expediting Pre Trials and Trials of Antitrust Cases," 1979. Lecturer in Research and Writing, University of Arizona College of Law, 1973. Trial Attorney, Antitrust Division, United States Department of Justice, 1970-1972. Member, Board of Visitors, University of Arizona College of Law, 1976-1979, 1990—. Member, Board of Directors, University of Arizona Law College Association, 1983-1985. Member, Board of Editors, "Class Action Reports," 1981-1990. Lawyer Representative, Ninth Circuit Judicial Conference, 1993—. *Member:* Los Angeles County (Member, Executive Committee, Litigation Section) and American (Member: Sections on: Antitrust Law; Litigation) Bar Associations; State Bar of Arizona; The State Bar of California; American Board of Trial Advocates; American Law Institute. *PRACTICE AREAS:* Antitrust; Commercial; Complex Litigation; Litigation; Insurance Coverage; Securities Litigation. *Email:* HenniganJ@hmb.com

**JAMES W. MERCER,** born Pontiac, Michigan, January 27, 1945; admitted to bar, 1971, California; 1974, U.S. District Court, Central District of California. *Education:* University of Michigan (A.B., 1967); University of Chicago (J.D., 1971). Order of the Coif. Visiting Associate Professor of Law, Corporations and Planning for the Business Client, Arizona State University College of Law, 1977. Adjunct Professor, Securities Regulation, Southwestern School of Law, 1979-1981. Staff Attorney, 1974-1976 and Special Counsel, 1976-1979, Securities and Exchange Commission, Los Angeles Regional Office. *Member:* Los Angeles County (Member, Section on Business, Banking and Corporation Law) and American (Member: Corporation, Banking and Business Law; Securities Litigation Committee, Subcommittee on Self-Regulatory Organization, Litigation Section) Bar Associations; The State Bar of California. *Email:* MercerJ@hmb.com

**BRUCE BENNETT,** born Brooklyn, New York, October 3, 1958; admitted to bar, 1982, California. *Education:* Brown University (Sc.B., magna cum laude, 1979); Harvard University (J.D., cum laude, 1982). Commissioner, Personal and Small Business Bankruptcy Law Advisory Commission of The California Board of Legal Specialization, 1993-1995. *Member:* Los Angeles County (Member, Sections on: Commercial Law and Bankruptcy; Business and Corporations) and American (Member, Section on Business Law) Bar Associations; The State Bar of California (Member, Business Law Section); International Bar Association (Member, Section on Business Law, Committee J: Insolvency and Creditors' Rights); Financial Lawyers Conference. *TRANSACTIONS:* Counsel for the County of Orange chapter 9 debt adjustment case; Reorganization counsel for debtors in Federated Stores, Inc., chapter 11 reorganization; Storage Technology Corporation, chapter 11 reorganization; First Capital Holdings corporation, chapter 11 reorganization; Ticor, chapter 11 reorganization; Angeles Corporation, chapter 11 reorganization; Attorney for equity holders in Olympia and York Developments Limited. Attorney for Amoco Canada Petroleum Company Limited in acquisition of Dome Petroleum Limited. *PRACTICE AREAS:* Bankruptcy; Insolvency; Corporate Reorganization; Commercial Litigation. *Email:* BennettB@hmb.com

**JOHN L. AMSDEN,** born Miles City, Montana, May 10, 1961; admitted to bar, 1988, California; 1989, U.S. District Court, Central District of California. *Education:* Montana State University (B.S., 1984); Georgetown University (J.D., 1988). Administrative Editor, Georgetown Law Journal, 1987-1988. *Member:* State Bar of California. *Email:* AmsdenJ@hmb.com

**C. DANA HOBART,** born Los Angeles, California, May 6, 1960; admitted to bar, 1986, California, U.S. District Court, Central District of California and U.S. Court of Appeals, Ninth Circuit. *Education:* University of Southern California (B.A., 1983; J.D., 1986). Phi Delta Phi. Finalist, 1984-1985 and Topic Editor, 1985-1986, Hale Moot Court Honors Program, 1985-1986. *Member:* Los Angeles County and American Bar Associations. *Email:* HobartC@hmb.com

(This Listing Continued)

## HENNIGAN, MERCER & BENNETT, Los Angeles—Continued

**JEANNE E. IRVING,** born Brighton, Massachusetts, August 26, 1953; admitted to bar, 1978, California and U.S. District Court, Central District of California; 1980, U.S. Court of Appeals, Ninth Circuit; 1981, U.S. District Court, Northern District of California; 1982, U.S. District Court, Southern District of California; U.S. District Court, Eastern District of California. *Education:* Boston College (B.A., summa cum laude, 1975, Phi Beta Kappa); Harvard University (J.D., 1978). Co-Author: "Collateral Estoppel," Securities Law Techniques, 1985. *Member:* Los Angeles County Bar Association; State Bar of California; Women Lawyers Association of Los Angeles. **PRACTICE AREAS:** Securities Litigation; Complex Litigation; Accountants' Liability Litigation. **Email:** IrvingJ@hmb.com

**PAMALA J. KING,** born Oxnard, California, July 11, 1956; admitted to bar, 1986, California, U.S. District Court, Central District of California; U.S. District Court, District of Arizona and U.S. Court of Appeals, Ninth Circuit. *Education:* University of California, Los Angeles (B.A., 1983); University of Southern California (J.D., 1986). Registered Nurse (Inactive), California, 1979. *Member:* Los Angeles County Bar Association; State Bar of California; California Women Lawyers. **Email:** KingP@hmb.com

**LAURA LINDGREN,** born Evanston, Illinois, November 8, 1951; admitted to bar, 1978, California, U.S. District Court, Northern, Central and Eastern Districts of California and U.S. Court of Appeals, Ninth Circuit. *Education:* Miami University; Northern Illinois University (B.A., cum laude, 1974); University of California at Los Angeles (J.D., 1978). Order of the Coif. Member, UCLA Law Review, 1977-1978. *Member:* Los Angeles County Bar Association (Member, Litigation Section); The State Bar of California. **Email:** LindgrenL@hmb.com

**BRUCE R. MACLEOD,** born St. Louis, Missouri, January 27, 1948; admitted to bar, 1973, California and U.S. District Court, Central and Northern Districts of California. *Education:* University of Missouri (B.S., 1970); University of Chicago (J.D., cum laude, 1973). Order of the Coif. *Member:* Los Angeles County and American (Member, Litigation Section) Bar Associations; State Bar of California; San Francisco Association of Business Trial Lawyers. **PRACTICE AREAS:** Securities; ERISA; Shareholders; Commercial Litigation. **Email:** MacleodB@hmb.com

**ELIZABETH D. MANN,** born Washington, D.C., January 4, 1957; admitted to bar, 1982, California; 1985, U.S. Court of Appeals, Ninth Circuit; 1987, U.S. District Court, Northern, Southern and Central Districts of California. *Education:* Pomona College (B.A., cum laude, 1979); University of California at Los Angeles (J.D., 1982). Phi Beta Kappa. Extern Law Clerk to Hon. A. Andrew Hank, 1981. *Member:* Los Angeles County Bar Association; State Bar of California (Member, Committee on Administration of Justice). **PRACTICE AREAS:** Commercial; International; Securities. **Email:** MannE@hmb.com

**ROBERT L. PALMER,** born Bryn Mawr, Pennsylvania, August 15, 1946; admitted to bar, 1972, District of Columbia; 1976, Arizona; 1996, California. *Education:* Georgetown University (B.A., 1968); Columbia University (J.D., 1971). Notes and Comments Editor, Columbia Law Review, 1970-1971. Law Clerk to Judge Harold Leventhal, U.S. Court of Appeals, District of Columbia Circuit, 1971-1972. Associate Editor, *Litigation,* Journal of the Section of Litigation, American Bar Association, 1979-1982. Assistant Special Prosecutor, Watergate Special Prosecution Force, U.S. Justice Department, 1973-1974. Member, 1988—, and President, 1990-1992, Board of Directors, Arizona Center for Law in the Public Interest. Adjunct Professor of Law, University of Arizona, 1983. *Member:* Los Angeles County and American Bar Associations; State Bar of California; State Bar of Arizona; District of Columbia Bar. **PRACTICE AREAS:** Antitrust Law; Complex Litigation; False Claims Act; Securities Litigation. **Email:** PalmerR@hmb.com

**LAUREN A. SMITH,** born Rockledge, Florida, September 27, 1955; admitted to bar, 1980, California. *Education:* University of California at Santa Barbara (B.A., with high honors, 1977); Boalt Hall School of Law, University of California (J.D., 1980). *Member:* State Bar of California. **Email:** SmithL@hmb.com

**PETER J. MOST,** born New York, N.Y., August 23, 1964; admitted to bar, 1989, California, U.S. District Court, Central District of California and U.S. Court of Appeals, Ninth Circuit; 1991, U.S. District Court, Northern District of Illinois. *Education:* University of California at Santa Barbara (B.A., magna cum laude, 1986); George Washington University (J.D., 1989). Editor-in-Chief, Consumer Protection Reporting Service. Author: "Chapter 12: The Family Farmer Bankruptcy Act," Consumer Protection Reporting Service, October, 1988. Co-Author: "Remedies for Frivolous Litigation: Malicious Prosecution, Abuse of Process and Sanctions," Corporate Analyst, August, 1990. Judge Pro Tem, Los Angeles Judicial District, 1996—. *Member:* Los Angeles County and American Bar Associations. **PRACTICE AREAS:** Antitrust; Litigation; Securities Litigation. **Email:** MostP@hmb.com

**LEE W. POTTS,** admitted to bar, 1986, California and U.S. District Court, Central District of California; 1987, U.S. Court of Appeals, Ninth Circuit; 1990, U.S. District Court, Eastern District of California; 1994, U.S. District Court, Southern and Northern Districts of California. *Education:* San Jose State University (B.A., 1972; M.A., 1974); University of California at Davis (Ph.D., 1978); Hastings College of the Law, University of California (J.D., 1986). Articles Editor, Hastings Constitutional Law Quarterly, 1985-1986. Author: "Responsible Police Administration: Issues and Approaches," University of Alabama Press, 1983; "Equal Employment Opportunity and Female Employment in Police Agencies," 11 Journal of Criminal Justice 505, 1983; "The Police and Determinants of Rape Prosecution: Decision Making in a Nearly Decomposable System," 6 Police Studies: The International Review of Police Development 37, 1983; Female Professionals in Corrections: Equal Employment Opportunity Issues," 47 Federal Probation 37, 1983; "Criminal Liability, Public Policy and the Principle of Legality in the Republic of South Africa," 73 Journal of Criminal Law and Criminology 1061, 1982; "Law as a Tool of Social Engineering," 5 B.C. International and Comparative Law Review 1, 1982; Equal Employment Opportunity and Female Criminal Justice Employment," 4 Police Studies: The International Review of Police Development 9, 1981; "Common Law and the Legal Fiction of the Citizen Policeman," 13 Anglo-American Law Review 53, 1984; "Custodial Detention and Regime Maintenance in the Republic of South Africa," 10 Journal on Criminal and Civil Confinement 301, 1984. Director of Criminal Justice Program, University of Mississippi, 1978-1983. *Member:* State Bar of California. **PRACTICE AREAS:** Commercial Litigation; Civil Rights; Defamation; First Amendment Litigation. **Email:** PottsL@hmb.com

### ASSOCIATES

**NICHOLE M. AUDEN,** born Riverside, California, July 2, 1970; admitted to bar, 1995, California. *Education:* Santa Clara University (B.A., magna cum laude, 1991); University of California School of Law, Davis (J.D., 1995). Phi Delta Phi, Order of the Coif. Recipient: American Jurisprudence Awards in Criminal Procedure, Civil Rights and Evidence. Executive Editor, U.C. Davis Law Review, 1994-1995. **PRACTICE AREAS:** Complex Business Litigation. **Email:** AudenN@hmb.com

**JACQUELINE BENDY,** born Tokyo, Japan, October 9, 1966; admitted to bar, 1994, Illinois; 1995, California and U.S. District Court, Central and Northern Districts of California. *Education:* Georgetown University (B.A., 1988); Northwestern University (M.S., 1990); Boalt Hall School of Law, University of California (J.D., 1994). *Member:* Women Lawyers Association of Los Angeles. **Email:** BendyJ@hmb.com

**MARY H. CHU,** born Rome, Italy, August 26, 1965; admitted to bar, 1991, California. *Education:* University of California at Los Angeles (B.A., 1987; J.D., 1991). Roscoe Pound Moot Court Competition Finalist. UCLA Representative, Roger Traynor Moot Court Competition. *Member:* Los Angeles County and American Bar Associations; Southern California Chinese Lawyers Association (Member, Board of Governors, 1993—; Secretary, 1994-1995; Executive Vice President, 1995-1996). **LANGUAGES:** Mandarin Chinese. **PRACTICE AREAS:** Litigation; Bankruptcy. **Email:** ChuM@hmb.com

**A. ANN HERED,** born Seattle, Washington, February 16, 1970; admitted to bar, 1994, New York; 1995, Colorado; 1996, California. *Education:* Rice University (B.A., 1990); Cornell Law School (J.D., cum laude, 1993); New York University School of Law (LL.M., Trade Regulation, 1994). Managing Editor, Cornell Journal of Law and Public Policy, 1992-1993. **PRACTICE AREAS:** Intellectual Property; Litigation. **Email:** HeredA@hmb.com

**GREGORY K. JONES,** born Torrance, California, December 2, 1970; admitted to bar, 1995, California, U.S. District Court, Central District of California and U.S. Court of Appeals, Ninth Circuit. *Education:* University of California at Los Angeles (B.A., magna cum laude, 1992); University of California School of Law, Los Angeles (J.D., 1995). Phi Beta Kappa. Managing Editor, UCLA Law Review. Author: "The Classification and Cram Down Controversy," 42 UCLA Law Review 623, (1994). **PRACTICE AREAS:** Bankruptcy Law; Commercial Law. **Email:** JonesG@hmb.com

**ELLEN M. KEANE,** born New York, N.Y., June 5, 1968; admitted to bar, 1993, California. *Education:* Loyola Marymount University (B.A.,

*(This Listing Continued)*

1990); Loyola Law School (J.D., 1993). Law Clerk to Judge James H. Ideman, U.S. District Court, Central District of California, 1994-1995. *Member:* State Bar of California.

**LINDA A. KONTOS,** born Chicago, Illinois, March 1, 1969; admitted to bar, 1994, Illinois; 1996, California. *Education:* University of Illinois (B.A., 1991); George Washington University (J.D., 1994). *Member:* Illinois State and American Bar Associations. **PRACTICE AREAS:** Commercial Litigation. *Email:* KontosL@hmb.com

**JENNIFER SULLA,** born Norwalk, Connecticut, August 15, 1960; admitted to bar, 1994, California; 1995, U.S. District Court, Central District of California. *Education:* Boston College (B.A., 1982); Brown University (M.S., Mathematics, 1986); University of Virginia (J.D., 1994). *Member:* State Bar of California. **PRACTICE AREAS:** Litigation. *Email:* SullaJ@hmb.com

**MICHAEL SWARTZ,** born Cincinnati, Ohio, September 23, 1966; admitted to bar, 1992, California; 1995, District of Columbia. *Education:* Yale University (B.A., 1988; M.A., 1988; J.D., 1992). Phi Beta Kappa. Law Clerk to Judge Stephen V. Wilson, U.S. District Court, Central District of California, 1993-1994. *Member:* State Bar of California; District of Columbia Bar. *Email:* SwartzM@hmb.com

**SHAWNA L. BALLARD,** born Loveland, Colorado, February 22, 1965; admitted to bar, 1991, California; 1992, U.S. Court of Appeals, 7th Circuit; 1993, U.S. District Court, Central District of California; 1995, U.S. District Court, District of Arizona; 1996, U.S. District Court, Southern District of California. *Education:* Arizona State University (B.S., cum laude, 1988); University of Arizona (J.D., summa cum laude, 1991). Order of the Coif. Order of the Barristers. Member, National Moot Court Team. Recipient, Outstanding Senior Award, University of Arizona. Articles Editor, Arizona Law Review, 1990-1991. Law Clerk for the Honorable Harlington Wood, Jr., United States Court of Appeals for the Seventh Circuit, 1991-1992. *Member:* Orange County Bar Association. **PRACTICE AREAS:** Commercial Law.

**CLAUDIA SCHWEIKERT,** born Bryan, Texas, October 26, 1971; admitted to bar, 1995, California. *Education:* Duke University (A.B., 1992); Stanford University (J.D., 1995). *Member:* American Bar Association. **LANGUAGES:** Spanish and French. **PRACTICE AREAS:** Litigation.

**DAVID H. MARTIN,** born Detroit, Michigan, October 1, 1967; admitted to bar, 1992, Illinois; 1994, District of Columbia; 1997, California. *Education:* University of Illinois at Urbana-Champaign (A.B., with highest university honors, 1989); Harvard University (J.D., 1992). Editor, Journal of Law and Public Policy. Instructor, Legal Research and Writing, 1991-1992.

*OF COUNSEL*

**ANTHONY CASTANARES,** born Los Angeles, California, June 26, 1943; admitted to bar, 1971, California. *Education:* University of California at Santa Barbara (B.A., with honors, 1965); University of California at Davis (M.A., 1967); New York University (J.D., 1970). Pi Sigma Alpha. Root-Tilden Scholar. Member, New York University Law Review, 1968-1970. Author: "Foreclosures in Bankruptcy: Are They Fraudulent Conveyances?" 21 Idaho L. Rev. 517, 1985; Comment, "Rowland v. Christian," 44 New York University Law Review 426. Adjunct Professor of Law, Loyola University School of Law, 1976-1983. Faculty Member: Complex Litigation in the Context of the Bankruptcy Laws, Practising Law Institute, 1984; Modern Real Estate Transactions, ALI-ABA, 1978, 1980, 1982, 1986. *Member:* Los Angeles County (Member: Executive Committee, 1979-1981 and Secretary, 1980-1981, Section on Commercial Law and Bankruptcy; Executive Committee, Barristers, 1973-1974; Executive Committee, Los Angeles Delegation to State Bar Conference of Delegates, 1980-1983) and American Bar Associations; The State Bar of California (Member, Committee on Disadvantaged Persons and the Law, 1973-1976; Chairperson, Committee on Human Rights, 1976-1977; Member, Committee on Law School Education, 1977-1979). **LANGUAGES:** Spanish. **PRACTICE AREAS:** Complex Business Litigation. *Email:* CastanaresA@hmb.com

# DANIEL B. HERBERT & ASSOCIATES
*TWENTY FIFTH FLOOR*
*1801 CENTURY PARK EAST (CENTURY CITY)*
*LOS ANGELES, CALIFORNIA 90067*
*Telephone: 310-843-0210*
*Facsimile: 310-201-0143*

*General Civil and Trial Practice, State and Federal Courts. Business, Real Estate, Securities and Entertainment Litigation. Bankruptcy, Reorganization and Commercial Litigation Law. Probate and Conservatorship Estates.*

**FIRM PROFILE:** The firm employs highly skilled and effective professionals with expertise in most areas of civil litigation and bankruptcy practice, representing both plaintiffs and defendants, businesses and individuals, in substantial disputes involving sophisticated and complex legal issues.

**DANIEL B. HERBERT,** born Chicago, Illinois, February 26, 1963; admitted to bar, 1990, California, U.S. District Court, Central District of California and U.S. Court of Appeals, Ninth Circuit; 1994, Illinois; 1996, U.S. District Court, Eastern District of California. *Education:* Eastern Illinois University (B.A., 1986); Whittier College School of Law (J.D., cum laude, 1990). Member: Law Review; International Law Society. Recipient, American Jurisprudence Awards for Civil Procedure I & II, Legal Skills I & II and Legal Process. *Member:* Century City, Santa Monica (Member, Bankruptcy, Business, and Real Property Panels), Los Angeles County (Member: Commercial Law and Bankruptcy Section; Panels on: Bankruptcy and Insolvency, Business, Real Property, and Wills, Trusts and Estates; Disaster Relief Committee) and American (Member, Business Law Section: Bankruptcy Litigation and Taxation and Federal Claims Subcommittees, Business Bankruptcy Committee; Closely Held Business Entities and Securities Regulations Subcommittees, Small Business Committee) Bar Associations; State Bar of California; Illinois State Bar Association (Member, Sections on: Civil Practice and Procedure; Commercial; Banking and Bankruptcy; Corporate; Securities and Business; Real Estate; Trusts and Estates).

# DANIEL M. HERSCHER
*10100 SANTA MONICA BOULEVARD, SUITE 250*
*LOS ANGELES, CALIFORNIA 90067*
*Telephone: 310-556-0833*
*Fax: 310-788-2814*

*Real Estate and Business Law.*

**DANIEL M. HERSCHER,** born Philadelphia, Pennsylvania, July 13, 1927; admitted to bar, 1955, California; 1973, U.S. Supreme Court. *Education:* University of California at Los Angeles (B.S., 1952); University of Southern California (J.D., 1955). Order of the Coif; Nu Beta Epsilon. Member, University of Southern California Law Review, 1954-1955. *Member:* Beverly Hills and American Bar Associations; State Bar of California. (Also Of Counsel, David A. Lapin, A Professional Corporation). **LANGUAGES:** Spanish. **REPORTED CASES:** First Western Bank and Trust Company, a California Corporation, v. Bookasta, 73 Cal.Rptr, 657, 267 Cal.App.2d 910, 5 UCC Rep.Serv. 1181; Feary v. Aaron Burglar Alarm, Inc., 108 Cal.Rptr. 242, 32 Cal.App. 3d 553, 12 UCC Rep. Serv. 881; Acosta v. County of Los Angeles, 363, P.2d 473, 14 Cal.Rptr. 433, 56 Cal.2d 208, 88 A.L.R.2d 1417; Peskin v. Herron, 26 CalRptr. 821, 210 Cal.App.2d 482.

# HERZFELD & RUBIN
*1925 CENTURY PARK EAST*
*LOS ANGELES, CALIFORNIA 90067*
*Telephone: 310-553-0451*
*Telefax: 310-553-0648*

*Orange County, California Office:* Herzfeld & Rubin, 625 The City Drive, Fourth Floor, Orange. Telephone: 714-750-0901. Telefax: 714-750-4708.
*Affiliated Offices:*
*New York, N.Y.:* Herzfeld & Rubin, P.C., 40 Wall Street. Telephone: 212-344-5500. Telefax: 212-344-3333.
*Miami, Florida:* Herzfeld & Rubin, 801 Brickell Avenue, Suite 1501. Telephone: 305-381-7999. Telefax: 305-381-8203.
*Ft. Lauderdale, Florida:* Herzfeld & Rubin, Gulf Atlantic Center, 1901 West Cypress Creek Road, Suite 400. Telephone: 954-772-3599. Telefax: 954-772-2469.
*Orlando, Florida:* DeCiccio, Herzfeld & Rubin, 20 North Orange Avenue, Suite 807. Telephone: 407-841-6391. Telefax: 407-648-0494.

*(This Listing Continued)*

## HERZFELD & RUBIN, Los Angeles—Continued

*Tampa, Florida:* Barr, Murman, Tonelli, Herzfeld & Rubin, Enterprise Plaza, Suite 901, 201 East Kennedy Boulevard. Telephone: 813-223-3951. Telefax: 813-229-2254.

*Jacksonville, Florida:* Bullock, Childs, Pendley, Reed, Herzfeld & Rubin, 233 East Bay Street, Suite 711. Telephone: 904-354-0286. Telefax: 904-354-2778.

*Newark, New Jersey:* Chase Kurshan Suhr Herzfeld & Rubin, The Legal Center, Suite 500, One Riverfront Plaza. Telephone: 201-596-9484. Telefax: 201-596-0762.

*Howell, New Jersey:* Chase Kurshan Suhr Herzfeld & Rubin, 405 Candlewood Commons, Building 4. Telephone: 908-901-2929. Telefax: 908-901-9438.

*Bucharest, Romania:* Herzfeld & Rubin (Romania) S.R.L., 62 Stada Dionisie Lupu, Sector 1. Telephone: 40-1-22.333.58. Telefax: 40-1-22.333.77.

*Düsseldorf, Germany:* Couvenstrasse 2, 40211. Telephone: (49) 211 36 35 35. Telefax: (49) 211 36 35 37.

*General Practice.* Corporation, Antitrust, Administrative, International, Products and Professional Liability, Insurance, Trademark, Copyright and Unfair Competition, Probate, Real Estate, Taxation, Business and Commercial Law. Trials and Appeals.

### RESIDENT PARTNERS

**RICHARD L. ACKERMAN,** born Los Angeles, California, August 31, 1945; admitted to bar, 1972, California, U.S. District Court, Central District of California and U.S. Court of Appeals, Ninth Circuit; 1976, U.S. Supreme Court; 1977, U.S. District Court, Southern District of California; 1982, U.S. District Court, Northern District of California. *Education:* University of California at Los Angeles (B.S., 1968; J.D., 1971). Beta Gamma Sigma. Member of Staff, Glendale College of Law, 1972-1973. *Member:* Los Angeles, Beverly Hills and American Bar Associations; State Bar of California; The Defense Research Institute. **PRACTICE AREAS:** Product Liability; Insurance; Insurance Defense Law; Litigation.

**MARTIN S. FRIEDLANDER,** born New York, N.Y., March 15, 1938; admitted to bar, 1963, New York; 1965, California, U.S. Court of Appeals, Ninth Circuit and U.S. District Courts, Northern, Central and Southern Districts of California. *Education:* City College of the City University of New York (B.B.A., 1959); Northwestern University (J.D., 1962). Member, Northwestern University Law Review, 1960. *Member:* Los Angeles County and American Bar Associations; State Bar of California; The Association of Trial Lawyers of America; California Trial Lawyers Association. **PRACTICE AREAS:** Business; Partnership; Real Estate; Construction and Mechanics Lien Law; Litigation.

**SEYMOUR KAGAN,** born New York, N.Y., July 27, 1930; admitted to bar, 1956, New York; 1958, U.S. District Courts, Southern and Eastern Districts of New York; 1969, U.S. Supreme Court, U.S. Court of Military Appeals and U.S. Claims Court; 1970, California, U.S. Court of Appeals, Ninth Circuit, and U.S. District Court, Central District of California; 1981, U.S. District Courts, Eastern, Northern and Southern Districts of California; 1992, U.S. Court of Appeals, First Circuit. *Education:* Brooklyn College of the City University of New York (B.A., 1953); Brooklyn Law School (J.D., 1956). *Member:* Los Angeles County (Member, Sections on: Real Property Law; Business and Corporate Law), New York State and American (Member, Section on Business Law) Bar Associations; State Bar of California (Member, Section on Business Law); Defense Research Institute. **PRACTICE AREAS:** Business; Environmental; Toxic Torts; Insurance Law; Litigation.

**NICHOLAS BROWNING, III,** born Great Falls, Montana, November 17, 1946; admitted to bar, 1975, California, Montana and U.S. District Court, District of Montana; 1979, U.S. Supreme Court, U.S. Court of Appeals, Ninth Circuit and U.S. District Courts, Central, Northern and Southern Districts of California; 1981, U.S. District Court, Eastern District of California. *Education:* University of Montana (B.S., 1968); Southwestern University (J.D., 1975). Deputy County Attorney, Cascade County, Montana, 1978. *Member:* Los Angeles County and American Bar Associations; State Bar of California; State Bar of Montana. **PRACTICE AREAS:** Business and Litigation Law; Federal Practice.

**CRAIG L. WINTERMAN,** born Denver, Colorado, October 29, 1950; admitted to bar, 1977, California and U.S. District Court, Central District of California; 1980, U.S. Supreme Court, U.S. Court of Appeals, Ninth Circuit, and U.S. District Court, Southern and Northern Districts of California. *Education:* University of Oregon (B.S., 1973); Southwestern University (J.D., 1976). *Member:* State Bar of California; American Bar Association; Association of Southern California Defense Counsel; Association for Advancement of Automotive Medicine. **PRACTICE AREAS:** Product Liability Law; Trial Practice.

**MICHAEL A. ZUK,** born Los Angeles, California, July 2, 1952; admitted to bar, 1978, California; 1979, U.S. District Court, Central District of California; 1980, U.S. Court of Appeals, Ninth Circuit, and U.S. District Courts, Southern and Northern Districts of California. *Education:* Glendale College (A.A., 1973); California State University at Northridge (B.A., 1975); Southwestern University (J.D., 1978). Delta Theta Phi. Member, Board of Governors, Southwestern University Moot Court, 1977-1978. National Member, The Order of Barristers, 1978. Lecturer and Author: "Vaccines in Litigation," presented at Immunizations at the Crossroads Symposium, American Academy of Pediatrics, Spring, 1987. *Member:* Century City, Los Angeles County and American (Member, Committee on Professional Liability) Bar Associations; State Bar of California; Association of Southern California Defense Counsel. **PRACTICE AREAS:** Medical Malpractice; Product Liability Law; Trial Practice.

**RICHARD W. GREENBAUM,** born Brooklyn, New York, April 20, 1954; admitted to bar, 1980, California and U.S. District Court, Central District of California; 1981, U.S. Court of Appeals, Ninth Circuit, and U.S. District Court, Northern District of California. *Education:* University of Cincinnati (B.B.A., 1975); California State University at Long Beach; Pepperdine University (J.D., cum laude, 1980). *Member:* Los Angeles County and American Bar Associations; State Bar of California. **PRACTICE AREAS:** Litigation; Product Liability; Insurance Defense Law.

### RESIDENT ASSOCIATES

**GARY S. YATES,** born Los Angeles, California, August 22, 1954; admitted to bar, 1979, California; 1980, U.S. Court of Appeals, Ninth Circuit, and U.S. District Courts, Northern, Southern and Central Districts of California. *Education:* University of California at Los Angeles (B.A., 1976); Loyola University of Los Angeles (J.D., 1979). Phi Beta Kappa. *Member:* Los Angeles County and American Bar Associations; State Bar of California.

**ROY D. GOLDSTEIN,** born New York, N.Y., January 6, 1955; admitted to bar, 1980, California and U.S. District Court, Central District of California. *Education:* State University of New York at Stony Brook (B.A., 1976); Loyola University of Los Angeles (J.D., 1980). *Member:* Century City and Los Angeles County Bar Associations; State Bar of California.

**TIMOTHY B. FITZHUGH,** born Pasadena, California, March 7, 1953; admitted to bar, 1978, California, U.S. Court of Appeals, Ninth Circuit, and U.S. District Court, Central District of California. *Education:* Mt. San Antonio Community College (A.A., 1973); University of California at Los Angeles (B.A.,1975); Southwestern University (J.D., 1978). Phi Delta Phi; Theta Delta Chi. *Member:* Los Angeles County Bar Association; State Bar of California; Association of Southern California Defense Counsel.

**ALAN I. KAPLAN,** born New York, N.Y., August 6, 1950; admitted to bar, 1979, California and U.S. District Court, Central District of California; 1982, U.S. Tax Court; 1984, U.S. District Court, Northern District of California; 1996, U.S. Court of Appeals, Ninth Circuit. *Education:* Cornell University (B.A., 1972); Loyola University of Los Angeles (J.D., 1979). Lecturer and Author: "Dual Relationships-Protecting the Psychologist," California State Psychologist, Dec., 1988; "The Malpractice Insurance Crisis," presented at California State Psychological Convention, winter, 1987. Member, Arbitration Panel, Los Angeles County Superior Court. *Member:* Los Angeles County and American Bar Associations; State Bar of California.

**MARY A. KIKER,** born San Rafael, California, May 30, 1948; admitted to bar, 1976, Texas; 1981, U.S. Court of Appeals, Fifth and Eighth Circuits; 1985, U.S. District Court, Western District of Texas; 1988, California; and U.S. District Court, Central District of California; 1993, U.S. Court of Appeals, Ninth Circuit; 1996, U.S. District Court, Northern and Eastern Districts of California. *Education:* Southwest Texas State University (B.A., summa cum laude, 1970; M.A., 1972); University of Texas (J.D., 1976). Member, Hildebrand Moot Court Board. Instructor, Legal Issues in Debate and Oral Advocacy and Legal Issues in Bioethics, Louisiana State University at New Orleans, 1976-1980. Staff Counsel, U.S. Court of Appeals, Fifth Circuit, Office of Staff Counsel, 1981-1985. Law Clerk to the Honorable Henry A. Politz, U.S. Court of Appeals, Fifth Circuit, 1985-1986. *Member:* Los Angeles County, Federal and American Bar Associations; State Bar of California; State Bar of Texas; American Society of Law and Medicine. **LANGUAGES:** French.

**STEVEN I. SMITH,** born Los Angeles, California, May 27, 1954; admitted to bar, 1980, California, U.S. Court of Appeals, Ninth Circuit, and

*(This Listing Continued)*

U.S. District Court, Central District of California; 1991, U.S. District Court, Northern District of California. *Education:* University of California at Los Angeles (B.A., 1976); Southwestern University (J.D., 1979). Judge Pro Term, Los Angeles Municipal Court, 1985—. *Member:* Los Angeles County (Member, Attorney-Client Relations Committee), Beverly Hills and American Bar Associations; State Bar of California.

**MATTHEW H. KAGAN,** born New York, N.Y., April 17, 1962; admitted to bar, 1989, California and U.S. District Court, Northern District of California; 1990, U.S. District Court, Central District of California. *Education:* Chapman College (B.S., 1984); University of Santa Clara (J.D., 1988). *Member:* Los Angeles County and American Bar Associations; State Bar of California.

**NAPOLEON G. TERCERO, III,** born Nicaragua, September 19, 1951; admitted to bar, 1989, California; 1996, U.S. District Court, Central and Southern Districts of California. *Education:* University of California at Los Angeles (B.A., 1977); University of La Verne (J.D., 1988). *Member:* Los Angeles County and American Bar Associations; State Bar of California; Defense Research Institute; The Association of Trial Lawyers of America. **LANGUAGES:** Spanish, Italian, French and Russian.

**SUHASINI S. SAWKAR,** born Bombay, India, February 17, 1954; admitted to bar, 1987, California; 1988, U.S. District Court, Central District of California. *Education:* Elphinstone College, University of Bombay (B.A., 1974); University of LaVerne (J.D., 1987). Member, University of LaVerne Law Review, 1986-1987. Author: "Illegitimate Children Are Entitled To Know Both Parents," Journal of Juvenile Law, Vol. #9; "Termination of Parental Duty of Support," Journal of Juvenile Law, Vol. #9. *Member:* State Bar of California.

**ANTHONY C. GROSSMAN,** born Los Angeles, California, August 16, 1966; admitted to bar, 1994, California and U.S. District Court, Central District of California. *Education:* Trinity College (B.A., 1988); Southwestern University (J.D., 1994). *Member:* Los Angeles County and American Bar Associations; State Bar of California.

**SHIRLEY A. BAKER,** born Indianapolis, Indiana, July 7, 1952; admitted to bar, 1992, California and U.S. District Court, Central District of California. *Education:* California State University, Fullerton (B.A., 1987); Western State University (J.D., 1991). *Member:* Orange County Bar Association; State Bar of California.

## ROBERT P. HESS, P.C.
445 SOUTH FIGUEROA STREET
SUITE 3040
LOS ANGELES, CALIFORNIA 90071
Telephone: 213-312-9495
Fax: 213-312-9499

*Tax and Estate Planning. Business Planning.*

**ROBERT P. HESS,** born Evanston, Illinois, May 1, 1942; admitted to bar, 1967, California. *Education:* Lehigh University (B.A., 1964); Stanford University (J.D., 1967). Author: "Desk Book For Setting Up a Closely-Held Corporation," Institute for Business Planning, 1979, Second Edition, 1985, Third Edition, 1987. *Member:* Los Angeles County and American Bar Associations; State Bar of California.

## HEWITT & PROUT
A Partnership including a Professional Corporation
4605 LANKERSHIM BOULEVARD, SUITE 540 (NORTH HOLLYWOOD)
LOS ANGELES, CALIFORNIA 91602
Telephone: 818-509-0311
Fax: 818-509-0402

Sacramento, California Office: 980 Ninth Street, Suite 1750, 95814.
Telephone: 916-443-4849. Fax: 916-325-2322.

*Professional Malpractice, Medical, Dental, Real Estate, Architectural, Engineering, Legal and Accounting, Motor Sports Litigation, Products Liability, Negligence, Insurance Defense Coverage, Hospital, Business and Environmental Law.*

FIRM PROFILE: *Our litigation philosophy emphasizes resourceful and aggressive handling, adapted to the particulars of each case. Our handling objectives are: (1) early evaluation with regular reporting; (2) defense development; (3) restriction of our adversary's contentions; (4) pretrial extrication and (5) settlement/trial. We have a statewide law practice with offices centrally located in Northern and Southern California. We have a familiarity with and a reputation in the various county Superior Courts throughout the State.*

### MEMBERS OF FIRM

**STEPHEN L. HEWITT, (A PROFESSIONAL CORPORATION),** born Shreveport, Louisiana, October 25, 1953; admitted to bar, 1982, California. *Education:* University of California at Santa Barbara (B.A., 1978); California Western School of Law (J.D., 1981). Phi Alpha Delta. *Member:* Los Angeles County and American Bar Associations; State Bar of California; Association of Southern California Defense Counsel. **PRACTICE AREAS:** Insurance Defense; Architects and Engineers; Medical Malpractice; Dental Malpractice; Professional Malpractice.

**R. MAC PROUT,** born Torrance, California, September 11, 1956; admitted to bar, 1981, California. *Education:* Pepperdine University (A.B., cum laude, 1978; J.D., with honors, 1981). Recipient, American Jurisprudence Award for Torts. *Member:* Los Angeles County and Sacramento County Bar Associations; State Bar of California; Association of Southern California Defense Counsel; Sacramento County Health Law Association. (Resident, Sacramento Office). **PRACTICE AREAS:** Insurance Defense (Architects and Engineers); Medical Malpractice; Dental Malpractice; Professional Malpractice.

### ASSOCIATES

**ERICA S. AROUESTY,** born Boston, Massachusetts, March 16, 1957; admitted to bar, 1990, California and U.S. District Court, Central District of California; 1991, U.S. District Court, Eastern District of California. *Education:* Pitzer College (B.A., 1979); Loyola Marymount University (J.D., 1990). Phi Delta Phi. Recipient, American Jurisprudence Award in Conflict of Laws. *Member:* Los Angeles County Bar Association; State Bar of California (Member, Real Property and Environment Sections). **PRACTICE AREAS:** Medical and Dental Malpractice Defense; Insurance Coverage Disputes; Professional Negligence Defense.

**LAURA L. HORTON,** born Des Moines, Iowa, March 2, 1957; admitted to bar, 1992, California and U.S. District Court, Central District of California. *Education:* Arizona State University (B.S., Finance, 1987); Pepperdine University School of Law (J.D., 1991). *Member:* Los Angeles County and American Bar Associations; State Bar of California. **PRACTICE AREAS:** Professional Malpractice; Sport and Leisure Liability; Insurance Coverage; General Civil.

**DANIEL A. ROZANSKY,** born Los Angeles, California, December 29, 1965; admitted to bar, 1992, California. *Education:* University of California at San Diego (B.A., 1988); Loyola Marymount University (J.D., 1992). *Member:* State Bar of California. **PRACTICE AREAS:** Insurance Defense; General Liability; Medical and Dental Malpractice.

**KEITH M. STAUB,** born New York, N.Y., March 3, 1956; admitted to bar, 1988, California and U.S. District Court, Central and Southern Districts of California. *Education:* University of Buffalo (B.S., 1978); University of San Diego (J.D., 1987). *Member:* Los Angeles County and American Bar Associations; State Bar of California. **PRACTICE AREAS:** Medical and Dental Malpractice; Professional Negligence; Insurance Defense.

**SAMUEL M. HUESTIS,** born Ventura, California, October 4, 1954; admitted to bar, 1984, California and U.S. District Court, Cental District of California; 1987, U.S. Court of Appeals, Ninth Circuit; 1991, Washington. *Education:* Biola University; Western State University (B.S.L., 1981; J.D., 1983). *Member:* Ventura County, Spokane County, Santa Barbara County, Washington State and American Bar Associations; State Bar of California.

**JOHN C. NOTTI,** born Los Angeles, California, December 13, 1949; admitted to bar, 1983, California, U.S. Court of Appeals, Ninth Circuit and U.S. District Court, Central and Eastern Districts of California. *Education:* California State University at Northridge (B.A., 1977); University of La Verne, College of Law (J.D., 1982). *Member:* Los Angeles County and American Bar Associations; State Bar of California; Association of Southern California Defense Counsel; Italian-American Lawyers Association. [With U.S. Army-Vietnam, 1970-1972]

**JERRY R. SPARKS,** born Ludington, Michigan, April 3, 1968; admitted to bar, 1993, California. *Education:* Michigan State University (B.A., 1990); Loyola Marymount University (J.D., 1992). Phi Delta Phi. Finalist, Phillip C. Jessup Southwest Regional Moot Court.

**PAUL A. CARRON,** born Detroit, Michigan, June 21, 1960; admitted to bar, 1986, California; 1987, U.S. District Court, Central District of California; 1994, U.S. District Court, Southern District of California. *Education:* University of Notre Dame (B.B.A., with honors, 1982); University of Mich-

*(This Listing Continued)*

**HEWITT & PROUT, Los Angeles—**Continued

igan (J.D., 1985). University of Notre Dame Scholar. *Member:* Los Angeles County Bar Association; State Bar of California (Member, Business and Environmental Law Sections). **PRACTICE AREAS:** Civil Litigation in States and Federal Courts.

**ANTHONY V. SEFERIAN,** born Torrance, California, January 11, 1964; admitted to bar, 1989, California. *Education:* University of Pennsylvania (B.A., 1986); California State University at Los Angeles (J.D., 1989). Member, Journal of Law and The Environment. *Member:* State Bar of California; Los Angeles Trial Lawyers Association.

(For Complete Biographical data on all Sacramento Members and Associates, see Professional Biographies at Sacramento, California)

## GEORGE W. HIGHTOWER
2040 AVENUE OF THE STARS, SUITE 400
**LOS ANGELES, CALIFORNIA 90056**
Telephone: 310-556-1407
Fax: 310-670-6731

*Probate, Wills and Trusts including Related Real Estate Matters.*

**GEORGE W. HIGHTOWER,** born Texas, April 9, 1939; admitted to bar, 1975, California. *Education:* University of Southern California (B.S.E.E., 1964; M.S., 1969); University of West Los Angeles (J.D., 1975). Member, Technical Staff/Manufacturer Representative, Hughes Aircraft Company, Aerospace Division, 1968-1972. *Member:* Beverly Hills, Langston and Los Angeles County Bar Associations; State Bar of California.
**LANGUAGES:** German.

## JOHN S. HILBERT
Established in 1990
11755 WILSHIRE BOULEVARD, 15TH FLOOR
**LOS ANGELES, CALIFORNIA 90025**
Telephone: 310-479-0944
Fax: 310-312-3836
Email: 103061.1712@Compuserve.com

*Probate and General Civil Litigation.*

**JOHN S. HILBERT,** born Lawton, Oklahoma, June 26, 1958; admitted to bar, 1985, Louisiana; 1987, California. *Education:* Louisiana State University (B.A., 1980; J.D., 1985). *Member:* Louisiana State Bar Association; State Bar of California; Court Reporters Board of California.

## C. DICKINSON HILL
12400 WILSHIRE BOULEVARD, SUITE 700
**LOS ANGELES, CALIFORNIA 90025-1026**
Telephone: 310-207-1115
Fax: 310-820-5988

*Business Law. Business, Commercial and Intellectual Property Transactions. State and Federal Tax. Mergers, Acquisitions and Divestitures.*

**C. DICKINSON HILL,** born Baltimore, Maryland, December 9, 1944; admitted to bar, 1976, California; 1984, U.S. Tax Court. *Education:* Stevens Institute of Technology (B.E., 1967); University of San Fernando Valley (J.D., 1976). *Member:* Beverly Hills Bar Association (Member, Sections on Business and Taxation; Chair, Blue Car Project Committee, 1992-1994; Co-Chair, Public Education Division, 1994-1995); State Bar of California (Member, Sections on Business, Taxation and International Law).

## HILL, FARRER & BURRILL LLP
A Limited Liability Partnership including Professional Corporations
35TH FLOOR, UNION BANK SQUARE
445 SOUTH FIGUEROA STREET
**LOS ANGELES, CALIFORNIA 90071**
Telephone: 213-620-0460
Fax: 213-624-4840

*General Civil and Trial Practice in all State and Federal Courts. Corporation, Securities, Antitrust, Real Estate (Finance Development and Environmental), Eminent Domain, Taxation, Bankruptcy and Creditors Rights, Labor Relations and Employment Law, Probate, Trust, Oil and Gas, Insurance, Government Contract and Administrative Law.*

**FIRM PROFILE:** *Hill, Farrer & Burrill LLP, located in downtown Los Angeles, is one of California's oldest and most respected law firms. Today, Hill, Farrer & Burrill LLP represents an array of clients, ranging from Fortune 500 companies to individuals, with a special emphasis on small and mid-sized companies, and companies with small or mid-sized internal legal departments. The clients are served by legal specialists organized into five major practice areas: Litigation, Labor and Employment, Corporate and Business, Real Estate and Tax. Hill, Farrer & Burrill LLP's knowledgeable and experienced litigators have represented clients in courts throughout the U.S. including the federal district courts, and state trial courts. Several are licensed to practice in other states and in federal courts when representing clients in those jurisdictions. Hill, Farrer & Burrill LLP's tax law specialists represent clients in tax litigation, including appellate work, and in administrative proceedings before the Internal Revenue Service and state and local taxing agencies. Hill, Farrer & Burrill LLP's Corporate and Business Department provides full transactional representation for a variety of clients, including individual entrepreneurs, venture capital firms, investment banks, publicly-traded corporations and privately-held companies of every size. We offer particular expertise on the legal concerns of small and mid-sized California corporations. Our real estate specialists are well recognized for their work representing institutional lenders and other creditors in "workouts" of troubled real estate projects and transactions. Our real estate attorneys work closely with our bankruptcy and creditor's rights attorneys to handle issues such as foreclosure transactions, structuring "deed in lieu of foreclosure" transactions, and restructuring secured financings in default. Hill, Farrar & Burrill LLP also boasts considerable expertise in the growing and complex legal field surrounding environmental and toxic waste issues.*

**WILLIAM M. FARRER** (1894-1971).

**ALFRED J. HILL** (1881-1953).

**STANLEY S. BURRILL** (1902-1957).

### MEMBERS OF FIRM

**LEON S. ANGVIRE, (P.C.),** born Spokane, Washington, December 12, 1928; admitted to bar, 1955, California. *Education:* University of California at Los Angeles (A.A., 1950; B.S., with honors, 1951; LL.B., 1954). Phi Delta Phi. Lecturer on Taxation, School of Law and Lecturer, Institute on Federal Taxation, University of Southern California, 1956. Member, Taxation Section, Los Angeles County Bar Association. *Member:* American Bar Association (Member, Section on Taxation). **PRACTICE AREAS:** Federal Taxation; State Taxation; Corporate Tax Planning; Closely Held Corporations; Probate Administration.

**STANLEY E. TOBIN, (P.C.),** born Boston, Massachusetts, September 13, 1930; admitted to bar, 1959, California; 1963, U.S. Supreme Court. *Education:* Harvard University (B.A., 1953); Yale University (LL.B., 1958). Book Review Editor, Yale Law Journal, 1956-1958. Teaching Fellow, 1958-1959 and Lecturer in Law, Labor Law, 1975-1976, Stanford Law School. Consultant, California Law Revision Commission re Eminent Domain, 1959. *Member:* American Bar Association. **PRACTICE AREAS:** Labor (Management) Law.

**JACK R. WHITE, (P.C.),** born Lincoln, Nebraska, October 12, 1936; admitted to bar, 1962, California. *Education:* University of Southern California (A.B., 1958; LL.B., 1961). Phi Alpha Delta; Order of the Coif. Member, Board of Editors, University of Southern California Law Review, 1960-1961. *Member:* American Bar Association. **PRACTICE AREAS:** Business and Tax Litigation; Appellate Practice.

**KYLE D. BROWN, (P.C.),** born Miles City, Montana, March 20, 1940; admitted to bar, 1965, California; 1988, Wisconsin. *Education:* University of Southern California (B.A., 1961; LL.B., 1964). Phi Beta Kappa; Phi Kappa Phi; Phi Delta Phi; Phi Sigma Alpha; Blackstonian. Member, University of Southern California Law Review, 1961-1963. Lecturer, American Management Association, 1975—. *Member:* American Bar Association (Member, Committee on the Development of Equal Opportunity, Labor Relations Law Section, 1973—). **PRACTICE AREAS:** Employment Law; Labor Law; Equal Opportunity Law (Management).

**WILLIAM M. BITTING, (P.C.),** born Santa Monica, California, April 17, 1939; admitted to bar, 1966, California. *Education:* University of California at Los Angeles (A.B., 1961; J.D., 1965). Fellow, American College of Trial Lawyers.

**STUART H. YOUNG, JR., (P.C.),** born Fort Worth, Texas, December 14, 1943; admitted to bar, 1968, California. *Education:* Claremont Men's College (B.A., cum laude, 1965); Stanford University (LL.B., 1968). Field

*(This Listing Continued)*

Attorney, National Labor Relations Board, 1968-1971. *Member:* American Bar Association. *PRACTICE AREAS:* Labor Law; Employee Benefit Law; Employment Discrimination Law; Wrongful Discharge Law; Trust Law.

**STEVEN W. BACON, (P.C.),** born Boston, Massachusetts, December 1, 1948; admitted to bar, 1974, California; 1982, U.S. Supreme Court. *Education:* Princeton University (A.B., cum laude, 1970); Stanford University (J.D., 1973). *Member:* Los Angeles County (Member, Superior Courts Committee, 1984-1989 and Amicus Briefs Committee, 1989—; Chair, Amicus Briefs Committee, 1993—) and American (Member, Litigation and Natural Resources Sections) Bar Associations; State Bar of California (Member: Litigation and Real Property Sections; Executive Committee, Real Property Section, 1994—; Co-Chair, Natural Resources Subsection, Real Property Section, 1991-1994).

**WM. HAROLD BORTHWICK, (P.C.),** born Los Angeles, California, May 24, 1948; admitted to bar, 1974, California. *Education:* University of California at Berkeley (A.B., 1971); University of California at Los Angeles (J.D., 1974). *PRACTICE AREAS:* Commercial Real Estate Finance; Commercial Real Estate Foreclosures; Commercial Real Estate Sales; Commercial Real Estate Acquisitions; Estate Planning.

**ARTHUR B. COOK, II, (P.C.),** born New York, N.Y., November 3, 1948; admitted to bar, 1975, California. *Education:* Stanford University (B.A., 1971); University of Southern California (M.B.A., 1975; J.D., 1975). Member, Panel of Construction Industry Arbitrators, American Arbitration Association. Volunteer Arbitrator, Judicial Arbitration Program, Los Angeles County Superior Court. Volunteer Arbitrator of Attorney-Client Fee Disputes, Los Angeles County Bar Association, Los Angeles County Superior Court. *Member:* Los Angeles, American (Member, Sections on: Litigation and Natural Resources, Energy and Environmental Law) and Federal Bar Associations; Defense Research Institute; Association of Business Trial Lawyers.; Western Agricultural Chemical Association (Affiliate Member); Pest Control Operators of California (Affiliate Member); Western Crop Protection Association (Affiliate Member). *REPORTED CASES:* Surfside Colony, Ltd. v. California Coastal Commission, (1991) 226 Cal. App 3d 1260, 277 Cal. Rptr. 371.

**JAMES G. JOHNSON, (P.C.),** born Santa Monica, California, March 22, 1949; admitted to bar, 1974, California and U.S. District Court, Central District of California; 1975, U.S. District Court, Northern and Southern Districts of California; 1977, U.S. Court of Appeals, Ninth Circuit; 1978, U.S. Supreme Court; 1983, U.S. Court of Appeals for the District of Columbia Circuit; 1993, U.S. Court of Appeals, Eleventh Circuit. *Education:* University of California at Los Angeles (A.B., 1971); California Western University Law School (J.D., 1974); Georgetown University (LL.M., 1975). Phi Delta Phi. Author: "Employment Contracts: How to Prepare Them," Chapter 12, *The Employee Termination Handbook*, John Wiley & Sons, 1986; "Selecting the Forum," Chapter 6, Advising California Employers, C.E.B. California Continuing Education of the Bar, 1981; "Albemarle Paper Company v. Moody: The Aftermath of Griggs and the Death of Employee Testing," 27 Hastings Law Journal 1239, 1976. Los Angeles County Bar Delegate, California State Bar, 1979. Judge Pro Tem, Pasadena Municipal Court, 1994—. Member, Executive Committee, 1983— and Chairman, Seminar Committee, 1985-1987, Labor and Employment Law Section, Continuing Legal Education Planning Committee and Alcohol and Drug Abuse Advisory Committee, 1989-1992, Los Angeles County Bar Association. Vice-Chair, Program Committee, State Bar Labor and Employment Law Section, State Bar of California, 1984-1985. *SPECIAL AGENCIES:* National Labor Relations Board; EEOC; Department of Fair Employment and Housing; Division of Labor Standards Enforcement; U.S. Department of Labor; OSHA. *PRACTICE AREAS:* Labor Management Law; Employer-Employee Relations; Employee Drug Testing; Employment Discrimination Law; Wrongful Discharge Law; Civil Rights Actions; Litigation.

**GEORGE KOIDE, (P.C.),** born Chicago, Illinois, February 25, 1945; admitted to bar, 1977, California. *Education:* University of California at Los Angeles (A.B., 1970; M.B.A., 1971); Southwestern University (J.D., 1977). *PRACTICE AREAS:* Estate Planning Law; Business Planning Law; Taxation Law.

**JONATHAN M. BRANDLER, (P.C.),** born Los Angeles, California, January 8, 1946; admitted to bar, 1971, California. *Education:* University of California at Berkeley (A.B., 1967); University of Southern California (J.D., 1970). Lecturer: "California and Federal Wage and Hour Laws," 1981-1992; "Employee Health and Safety," 1993, Religion Discrimination Accommodating Beliefs and Practices, Institute of Business Law. Member, Labor Law Section, Los Angeles County Bar Association and State Bar of California. *Member:* Los Angeles County (Member, Labor Law Section) and American (Member, Section on Labor and Employment Law) Bar Associa-
*(This Listing Continued)*

tions. *SPECIAL AGENCIES:* National Labor Relations Board; Department of Labor; Equal Employment Opportunity Commission; California Department of Fair Employment and Housing; California Labor Commissioner; California Occupational Safety and Health Administration. *PRACTICE AREAS:* Labor Relations (Management); Employment Discrimination; Wrongful Discharge; Wage and Hour; Safety and Health.

**SCOTT L. GILMORE,** born Inglewood, California, August 21, 1953; admitted to bar, 1978, California. *Education:* University of Southern California (B.S., magna cum laude, 1975; M.B.A., 1978; J.D., 1978). Judge Pro Tempore: Los Angeles Municipal Court, 1988—; Los Angeles Superior Court, 1989—. *Member:* American Bar Association. *PRACTICE AREAS:* Business Litigation; Real Estate Litigation; Construction Litigation.

**KEVIN H. BROGAN,** born Pasadena, California, November 7, 1953; admitted to bar, 1979, California and U.S. District Court, Central District of California; 1980, U.S. District Court, Eastern District of California; 1981, U.S. District Court, Southern and Northern Districts of California and U.S. Court of Appeals, Ninth Circuit; 1988, Wisconsin, U.S. District Court, Eastern District of Wisconsin and U.S. Court of Appeals, Seventh Circuit; 1990, U.S. Court of Federal Claims and U.S. Supreme Court. *Education:* University of California at Berkeley (B.S., 1976); Hastings College of Law, University of California (J.D., 1979). Extern/Law Clerk for Hon. Oliver Seth, Chief Judge of U.S. Court of Appeals, Tenth Circuit, 1979. Member, Trial Attorney Project Committee, 1984-1985, Judicial Evaluation Committee, 1988-1992, Vice-Chair, 1989-1992, and Condemnation and Land Valuation Committee, 1989—, Chairman, 1992—, Los Angeles County Bar Association. Member, Real Property Section, Co-Chairman, Inverse Condemnation and Eminent Domain Subsection, 1995—, State Bar of California. Judge Pro Tempore: Los Angeles Municipal Court, 1986-1988; Los Angeles Superior Court, 1989—. *Member:* Federal and American (Member, Litigation Section and Real Property, Probate and Trust Law Section Condemnation Committee) Bar Associations; Association of Business Trial Lawyers; National Association of Railroad Trial Counsel. *REPORTED CASES:* City of Vista v. Fiedler (1996 Cal. 4th; 96 Daily Journal D.A.R. 8977; Los Angeles Unified School Dist. v. Trump Wilshire Assoc. (1996) 42 Cal. App. 4th 1982; Pincus v. Pabst Brewing Co. (1990) 893 F2d 1544; S.C.R.T.D. v. Bolen (1992) 1 Cal. 4th 654 ; Myers v. Atchison, Topeka (1990) 224 Cal. App. 3d 752; State of Calif. v. Union Pacific et al (1985) 179 CA. 3d 307. *PRACTICE AREAS:* Business and Real Estate Litigation; Eminent Domain; Inverse Condemnation.

**JAMES A. BOWLES, (P.C.),** born Indianapolis, Indiana, January 2, 1954; admitted to bar, 1979, California, U.S. District Court, Central District of California and U.S. Court of Appeals, Ninth Circuit; 1982, U.S. Court of Appeals, for the District of Columbia Circuit and U.S. District Court, Southern District of California; 1983, U.S. Supreme Court; 1987, U.S. District Court, Eastern District of California; 1988, Wisconsin, U.S. Court of Appeals, Seventh Circuit and U.S. District Court, Eastern District of Wisconsin. *Education:* Indiana University (A.B., summa cum laude, 1976); Georgetown University (J.D., cum laude, 1979). Phi Beta Kappa. Author: "Defining the Scope of Bargaining for Teacher Negotiations: A Study of Judicial Approaches," The CCH Labor Law Journal, October, 1978. *Member:* American Bar Association. *LANGUAGES:* Spanish. *SPECIAL AGENCIES:* National Labor Relations Board, Equal Employment Opportunity Commission, California Department of Fair Employment and Housing, California Occupational Safety and Health Appeals Board, California Agricultural Labor Relations Board. *REPORTED CASES:* Wholesale and Retail Food Distribution Local 63 v. Santa Fe Terminal Services, Inc., 836 F.Supp. 326 (C.D. Cal. 1993); Graefenhain v. Pabst Brewing Co., 870 F.2d 1198 (7th Cir., 1989); Cardinal Distributing Co. v. ALRB, 159 Cal.App. 3d 758 (1984); Southern California Pipe Trades Trust Funds v. Franchise Tax Board, 909 F.2d 1266 (9th Cir. 1990). USCP-Wesco v. NLRB, 827 F.2d 581 (9th Cir. 1987). *PRACTICE AREAS:* Labor and Employment Law.

**NEIL D. MARTIN,** born Los Angeles, California, October 5, 1955; admitted to bar, 1980, California. *Education:* California State University at Chico (B.A., 1977); University of Southern California (J.D., 1980). Phi Alpha Delta. *Member:* American Bar Association (Member, Intellectual Property Law Section). *PRACTICE AREAS:* Trade Secret; Copyright and Trademark Litigation; Unfair Competition; General Civil Litigation in State and Federal Courts.

**MICHAEL J. DiBIASE,** born Los Angeles, California, September 23, 1953; admitted to bar, 1979, California. *Education:* University of California at Los Angeles (B.A., 1975; J.D., 1979). Order of the Coif. *PRACTICE AREAS:* Securities Law; Corporate Finance Law; Mergers & Acquisitions Law; Corporate Governance Law; Partnership Law.
*(This Listing Continued)*

*HILL, FARRER & BURRILL LLP, Los Angeles—
Continued*

**ALFRED M. CLARK, III,** born Youngstown, Ohio, July 30, 1954; admitted to bar, 1981, California. *Education:* Stanford University (A.B., 1976); Loyola Law School, Los Angeles (J.D., 1981). Staff Member, Loyola Law Review, 1979-1980. Author: "Federal Housing Programs: Is Subsidized Low-Income Housing An Idea Whose Time Has Passed?" 13 Calif. Real Prop. Law J. 37, 1995. *Member:* American Bar Association. **PRACTICE AREAS:** Real Estate Finance Law; General Real Estate Law; Creditors' Rights.

**DANIEL J. MCCARTHY,** born Detroit, Michigan, September 2, 1957; admitted to bar, 1981, California. *Education:* Harvard University (A.B., cum laude, 1978); University of Michigan (J.D., 1981). Author: "Housing Courts Bibliography," 17 Urban Law Annual 371, 1979. Member, Commercial Law and Bankruptcy Sections, Los Angeles County Bar Association. *Member:* American Bar Association. **REPORTED CASES:** Old Town Historic Building, Ltd., 79 Bankr. 8 (Bankr. C.D. Cal. 1987); Howes, 89 Bankr. 77 (9th Cir. BAP 1988). **PRACTICE AREAS:** Creditor's Rights Law; Bankruptcy Law; Business Litigation.

**RONALD W. NOVOTNY, (P.C.),** born San Diego, California, June 16, 1956; admitted to bar, 1981, California. *Education:* University of California at Berkeley (B.A., 1978); Hastings College of Law, University of California (J.D., 1981). Tony Patino Fellow, Hastings College of Law, 1981. Member, Labor and Employment Law Section, State Bar of California. **SPECIAL AGENCIES:** National Labor Relations Board. **REPORTED CASES:** Southern California Chapter ABC JAC v. State of California (1995) 4 Cal. 4th 422; General Truck Drivers Local 315 v. N.L.R.B, 20 F.3d 1017 (9th Cir. 1994); Inter-Modal Rail Employees Assoc. v. Santa Fe Railway, 80 F.3d 348 (9th Cir. 1996). **PRACTICE AREAS:** Labor and Employment Law; Apprenticeship Law; ERISA Litigation.

**DAVID E. PARRY,** born Knoxville, Tennessee, September 3, 1934; admitted to bar, 1969, California and U.S. District Court, Central District of California; 1972, U.S. Court of Appeals, Ninth Circuit; 1984, U.S. District Court, Northern District of California. *Education:* Berea College (B.A., 1956); Fletcher School of Law and Diplomacy (M.A., 1957); Southwestern University (J.D., 1968). Member, Arcadia, CA, City Council and Redevelopment Agency, 1976-1980. Mayor, City of Arcadia, CA, 1978-1979. *Member:* Foothill Bar Association (President, 1986-1987); National Association of Railroad Trial Counsel (Member, Executive Committee, Pacific Region, 1987—). [Special Agent, U.S. Army Counter Intelligence Corps, 1957-1960]. **PRACTICE AREAS:** Railroad Law; Personal Injury Law; Business Litigation; Medical Malpractice Defense Law; Property Damage Law.

**BENJAMIN B. SALVATY,** born Chicago, Illinois, December 22, 1940; admitted to bar, 1966, California, U.S. District Court, Central District of California, U.S. Court of Appeals, Ninth Circuit and U.S. Tax Court; 1973, U.S. Supreme Court; 1981, U.S. District Court, Northern, Eastern and Southern Districts of California. *Education:* University of Notre Dame (B.B.A., 1962); University of Southern California (J.D., 1965). Phi Delta Phi. Historian, Beatty Inn, 1964-1965. Recipient, American Jurisprudence Award, Bills and Notes. Author: "Eminent Domain Mock Trial," International Right of Way Association, 1987. Judge Pro Tempore, Alhambra Municipal Court, 1978-1981. Member, 1987-1988; Vice-Chairman, 1986-1987; Chairman, 1987-1988, State Bar of California Committee on Condemnation. Member, Los Angeles County Bar Association Committee on Condemnation and Land Valuation Litigation, 1982—. *Member:* Pasadena and American (Member, Sections on: Litigation, 1980—; Urban, State and Local Government Law, Committee on Condemnation, Committee on Zoning and Planning, 1975—) Bar Associations; Irish American Bar Association (President, 1994; Vice President, 1993; Member, Board of Directors, 1985—); Italian American Lawyers Association; State Trial Attorneys Association (President, 1975-1980); American Judicature Society. **REPORTED CASES:** Centerview/Glen Avalon Homeowners Association v. Volpe (C.D. Cal., 1976) 424 F. Supp. 626; Atchison, Topeka and Santa Fe Ry. Co. v. Stockton Port District (1983) 140 CA 3d 111, 189 Cal.Rptr. 208; People v. Home Trust Investment Co. (1970) 8 CA3d 1022, 87 Cal.Rptr. 722; Litigation: Represented one of the California Highway Patrol officers in the Rodney King case. **TRANSACTIONS:** Represented Santa Fe Railway Company in the sale of its First Street Yard to the Metro Rail for its maintenance yard, involving a total consideration of $43,000,000.00. **PRACTICE AREAS:** Eminent Domain; Inverse Condemnation; Land Use; Environmental; Defense of Police Officers in Civil Rights Cases.

**DEAN E. DENNIS,** born Los Angeles, California, September 6, 1958; admitted to bar, 1983, California. *Education:* Princeton University (A.B.,

*(This Listing Continued)*

1980); University of Southern California (J.D., 1983). Recipient, ABA Section of Urban, State and Local Government Law Prize. Member, Appellate Courts Committee, condemnation and Land Valuation Committee, Los Angeles County Bar Association. **SPECIAL AGENCIES:** Planning and Zoning Commissions, Coastal Commission. **REPORTED CASES:** Southern California Rapid Transit Dist. v. Bolen (1992) 1 Cal. 4th 654; City of Manhattan Beach v. Superior Court (1996) 13 Cal. 4th 232; City of Vista v. Fielder, California Supreme Court No. S046856 (decision pending); Los Angeles Unified School District v. Trump Wilshire Associates (1996) 42 Cal. App. 4th 1682; Kalmanovitz v. Bitting (1996) 43 Cal. App. 4th 311; Friends of La Vina v. County of Los Angeles (1991) 232 Cal. App. 3d. 1446; Thomas v. County of Los Angeles (1991) 232 Cal. App. 3d 1446; Smith v. County of Los Angeles (1989) 211 Cal. App. 3d 188; Surfside Colony Ltd. v. Cal. Coastal Comm. (1991) 226 Cal. App. 3d 1260. **PRACTICE AREAS:** Appeals; Land Use Law; Zoning Law; Eminent Domain Law.

**THOMAS F. REED,** born Orange, California, March 9, 1955; admitted to bar, 1980, California. *Education:* University of Southern California (A.B., 1977; J.D., 1980).

**SUZANNE J. HOLLAND,** born Pennsylvania, 1946; admitted to bar, 1981, California, U.S. District Court, Southern, Northern and Central Districts of California and U.S. Court of Appeals, Ninth Circuit. *Education:* University of Pittsburgh (B.A., magna cum laude, 1967); Loyola Law School, Los Angeles (J.D., 1980). Recipient, Loyola Law School Award for Academic Achievement. Law Clerk to Hon. Joseph R. Reichmann and Hon. James J. Penne, U.S. District Court.

**WILLIAM A. WHITE,** born Atlanta, Georgia, August 20, 1960; admitted to bar, 1985, California, U.S. District Court, Central District of California and U.S. Court of Appeals, Ninth Circuit; 1986, U.S. District Court, Southern and Northern Districts of California; 1987, U.S. District Court, Eastern District of California and U.S. Court of Appeals, Second Circuit; 1989, U.S. District Court, Eastern District of Wisconsin and U.S. Court of Appeals, Seventh Circuit; 1990, U.S. District Court, Western District of Wisconsin; 1993, U.S. Tax Court; 1994, U.S. Court of Appeals, Fifth Circuit; 1995, U.S. Court of International Trade. *Education:* Cornell University (B.S., 1982); University of Southern California (J.D., 1985). Co-Winner, Best Brief Award, Hale Moot Court Competition. **REPORTED CASES:** Best Brands Beverage, Inc. v. Falstaff Brewing Corp., 842 F.2d 578 (2d Cir. 1987). **PRACTICE AREAS:** Business Litigation; Antitrust; Insurance Coverage Disputes; Land Use and Condemnation Law.

**R. CURTIS BALLANTYNE,** born Dallas, Texas, May 27, 1946; admitted to bar, 1973, California and U.S. District Court, Central District of California; 1974, Utah and U.S. District Court, District of Utah. *Education:* University of California at Los Angeles (B.A., 1970); University of Utah (J.D., 1973). **LANGUAGES:** French. **PRACTICE AREAS:** Public Utilities Commission Law.

**JAMES R. EVANS, JR.,** born Los Angeles, November 15, 1959; admitted to bar, 1985, California, U.S. District Court, Central, Northern and Southern Districts of California and U.S. Court of Appeals, Ninth Circuit; U.S. District Court, Southern District of Texas. *Education:* University of Southern California (B.S., 1981); Boalt Hall School of Law, University of California, Berkeley (J.D., 1985). Barrister, Los Angeles County Bar Association. Special Master, State Bar of California. Lecturer, CLE Legal Ethics. *Member:* American Bar Association. **LANGUAGES:** Spanish. **PRACTICE AREAS:** Surety Law and Litigation; Business Litigation; Plaintiff's Tort Litigation (Insurance Bad Faith, Personal Injury, Medical Malpractice).

**G. CRESSWELL TEMPLETON III,** born Indianapolis, Indiana, March 26, 1959; admitted to bar, 1985, Texas; 1986, U.S. Court of Appeals, Fifth Circuit and U.S. District Court, Southern District of Texas; 1988, California, U.S. Court of Appeals, Ninth Circuit and U.S. District Court, Central District of California. *Education:* University of Southern California (A.B., cum laude, 1981; J.D., 1985). *Member:* State Bar of California; State Bar of Texas; California State Courts Committee. **PRACTICE AREAS:** Trade Secret Litigation; Construction Law; ERISA Litigation; Entertainment Law.

**CURTIS A. WESTFALL,** born Anaheim, California, April 20, 1960; admitted to bar, 1987, California and U.S. District Court, Central District of California; 1993, U.S. District Court, Southern District of California. *Education:* University of Southern California (A.B., 1983); University of San Diego (J.D., 1986). Officer, Appellate Moot Court Board, 1985-1986. Certified Los Angeles Municipal Court Settlement Officer. **PRACTICE AREAS:** Commercial Litigation; Creditors' Rights Litigation; Plaintiffs Personal Injury Practice.

*(This Listing Continued)*

# PROFESSIONAL BIOGRAPHIES — CALIFORNIA—LOS ANGELES

**JENNIFER COOK LEWIS,** born Honolulu, Hawaii, October 27, 1959; admitted to bar, 1986, California; 1987, U.S. District Court, Central District of California. *Education:* University of Colorado (B.S., 1981); University of Denver (J.D., 1985). Delta Theta Phi. Staff Member, Denver University Law Review, 1984-1985. Author: "Habeas Corpus Section, Eleventh Annual Tenth Circuit Survey," 60 Denver University Law Review, 241, 1985. *LANGUAGES:* French. *PRACTICE AREAS:* Business Litigation; Real Property Litigation; Eminent Domain; Prejudgement Remedies; Enforcement of Judgments.

**MICHAEL S. TURNER,** born Los Angeles, California, September 21, 1961; admitted to bar, 1987, California. *Education:* University of California at Los Angeles (B.A., 1984); Loyola Marymount University (J.D., 1987). Editor, Loyola of Los Angeles Law Review, 1986-1987. Judicial Extern to the Honorable William D. Keller, District Judge, U.S. District Court, Central District of California, 1985. *PRACTICE AREAS:* Litigation; Mechanics Lien Law; Construction Law; Construction Litigation; Representation of Pest Control Operators.

**MICHELLE A. MEGHROUNI,** born Pasadena, California, May 15, 1961; admitted to bar, 1987, California. *Education:* University of California at Berkeley (B.A., 1983); University of San Francisco (J.D., 1987). Associate Editor, California Real Property Journal; Managing Editor, University of San Francisco Law Review, 1986-1987. Author: "1985 Survey of Nonprofit Case Law," 20 University of San Francisco Law Review 949, 1986. *PRACTICE AREAS:* Real Estate Finance; General Real Estate Law; Creditors' Rights.

**JENNIFER L. PANCAKE,** born Encino, California, January 8, 1962; admitted to bar, 1988, California and U.S. District Court, Central District of California. *Education:* University of the Redlands (B.A., 1984); Loyola of Los Angeles Law School (J.D., 1988). Member, St. Thomas More Law Honor Society. Recipient, American Jurisprudence Award in Civil Procedure. Managing Editor, Loyola Law Review, 1987-1988. Extern to Hon. William Matthew Byrne, Jr., U.S. District Court, Central District of California, 1988. Member, Committee on Condemnation and Land Valuation, Los Angeles County Bar Association. *PRACTICE AREAS:* Eminent Domain Law; Real Property and Land Use Litigation.

**BARRY VAN SICKLE,** born Mankato, Minnesota, July 24, 1951; admitted to bar, 1978, Minnesota; 1981, California. *Education:* Mankato State University (B.S., 1974); William Mitchell College of Law (J.D., 1978). *PRACTICE AREAS:* FELA; Railroad Accidents and Injuries; Commercial Litigation; Contract Litigation; Professional Liability.

## OF COUNSEL

**EDWIN H. FRANZEN, (P.C.),** born Kane County, Illinois, March 27, 1927; admitted to bar, 1955, California. *Education:* University of Illinois (B.S., 1949); Loyola University (LL.B., 1954). Phi Delta Phi. *Member:* American Bar Association.

**DARLENE FISCHER PHILLIPS, (P.C.),** born Los Angeles, California, December 3, 1940; admitted to bar, 1978, California. *Education:* University of Southern California (B.A., 1965; J.D., 1978); University of California at Los Angeles (M.A., 1972). Phi Alpha Delta. Hale Moot Court Honors Program, Honors in Written Advocacy. Member, Real Property Law Section, CEQA Task Force, State Bar of California. *Member:* American Bar Association (Member, Section on Real Property, Probate and Trust Law, Committee on Land Use Regulation and Committee on Dispute Resolution. *SPECIAL AGENCIES:* Planning, zoning, and environmental boards and committees, California Coastal Commission; planning commissions, city councils and boards of supervisors for local public agencies; school boards and school district personnel commissions. *REPORTED CASES:* T.M. Smith v. County of Los Angeles (1994) 24 Cal.App.4th 990; J.L. Thomas v. County of Los Angeles (1991) 232 Cal.App.3d 916; Friends of La Vina v. County of Los Angeles (1991) 232 Cal.App.3d 1446; William S. Hart Union High School District v. County of Los Angeles (1991) 226 Cal.App.3d 1612; Personnel Commission of the Lynwood Unified School District v. Board of Trustees (1990) 223 Cal.App.3d 1463; First English Evangelical Lutheran Church v. County of Los Angeles (1989) 210 Cal.App.3d 1353, reh. den. and open. mod, review den.; cert. den. U.S., 110 S.Ct. 866, 107 L.Ed.2d 950; Smith v. County of Los Angeles (1989) 211 Cal.App.3d 188; Best Brands Beverage, Inc., v. Falstaff Brewing Corporation (2d Cir. 1987) 842 F.2d 578; First English Evangelical Lutheran Church v. County of Los Angeles (1987) 482 U.S. 304, 107 S.Ct. 2378, 96 L.Ed.2d 250 (on brief); Roberts v. Gulf Oil Corporation (1983) 147 Cal.App.3d 770 (on behalf of Amici Curiae County of Los Angeles); Pineda v. Los Angeles Turf Club (1980) 112 Cal.App.3d 53. *PRACTICE AREAS:* Land Use Litigation; Environmental Litigation; Representation of School District Personnel Commissions.

*(This Listing Continued)*

## RETIRED

**CARL M. GOULD**
**VINCENT C. PAGE**
**WILLIAM C. FARRER, (P.C.)**

## ASSOCIATES

**IAN M. GREEN,** born Los Angeles, California, December 5, 1963; admitted to bar, 1989, California and U.S. District Court, Central and Northern Districts of California. *Education:* University of California at Santa Barbara (B.A., with honors, 1986); University of California, Hastings College of Law (J.D., 1989). Phi Beta Kappa; Phi Alpha Delta. Extern/Law Clerk to the Hon. John P. Vukasin, Jr., U.S. District Court, Northern District of California, 1989. *PRACTICE AREAS:* Business Litigation.

**BYRON T. BALL,** born Newport Beach, California, December 6, 1964; admitted to bar, 1990, California. *Education:* Vanderbilt University (B.A., History, 1987); Pepperdine University (J.D., 1990). Phi Alpha Delta (President). *Member:* Los Angeles County Bar Association; State Bar of California. *PRACTICE AREAS:* Civil Litigation.

**DEAN A. REEVES,** born Santa Maria, California, June 20, 1961; admitted to bar, 1990, California, U.S. District Court, Eastern and Central Districts of California and U.S. Court of Appeals, Ninth Circuit; 1991, U.S. District Court, Southern and Northern Districts of California. *Education:* California State University, Northridge (B.A., cum laude, 1987);University of Southern California (J.D., 1990). Phi Alpha Delta. Staff Member, Computer Law Journal, University of Southern California, 1988-1989; Staff Member, Major Tax Planning, University of Southern California, 1988-1989. Judicial Extern, Judge David V. Kenyon, U.S. District Court, Central District, of California, 1989. *PRACTICE AREAS:* General Civil and Business Litigation.

**PAUL M. PORTER,** born Northridge, California, December 6, 1963; admitted to bar, 1991, California. *Education:* Loyola Marymount University (B.A., 1986); Loyola Law School (J.D., 1991). *PRACTICE AREAS:* Business Litigation; Eminent Domain Litigation.

**LESLIE G. VAN ZYL,** born Los Angeles, California, October 28, 1961; admitted to bar, 1991, California and U.S. District Court, Central, Southern and Northern Districts of California. *Education:* California Polytechnic State University (B.A., 1985); University of California, Hastings College of the Law (J.D., 1991). Articles Editor, Hastings International and Comparative Law Review. *Member:* National Association of Railroad Trial Counsel; Conference of Freight Counsel; Los Angeles Trial Lawyers Association; Women Lawyers Association of Los Angeles. *PRACTICE AREAS:* Federal Employers Liability Act Defense; Rail Freight Damage/Loss Defense; Business Litigation.

**ARNOLD D. WOO,** born Huntington Park, California, September 9, 1958; admitted to bar, 1992, California, U.S. District Court, Northern, Eastern, Southern and Central Districts of California and U.S. Court of Appeals, Ninth Circuit; 1994, U.S. Court of Federal Claims. *Education:* University of Southern California (A.B., magna cum laude, 1985; J.D., 1992). Phi Beta Kappa; Phi Kappa Phi; Blackstonian. Recipient: Norma Zarky Memorial Award for excellence in the field of entertainment law; American Jurisprudence Awards in The Role of the Lawyer; Professional Responsibility, Gifts, Wills and Trusts. Member, Los Angeles County Bar Association Barristers Community Law Week Committee, 1993-1995. Member, 1994—and Vice-Chair, 1994-1995 and Chair, 1995—, Parks and Recreation Commission, City of Torrance, CA. *Member:* South Bay Bar Association. *PRACTICE AREAS:* Civil Litigation; Business Litigation.

**KAREN S. SEIGEL,** born Roanoke, Virginia, September 14, 1954; admitted to bar, 1992, California, U.S. District Court, Central District of California and U.S. Court of Appeals, Ninth Circuit. *Education:* University of California at Los Angeles (B.A., magna cum laude, 1989); Loyola Law School, Los Angeles (J.D., 1992). Member, National Trial Advocacy Team. Recipient: American Jurisprudence Awards, Trial Advocacy, Trusts and Wills; American Board of Trial Advocates Award, 1990. Extern, Los Angeles District Attorney, Compton, California, 1991. *Member:* American Bar Association (Member, Sections on: Litigation and Employment Law); Los Angeles Complex Litigation Inn of Court. *PRACTICE AREAS:* Business Litigation; Labor and Employment Law (Management); Wrongful Discharge and Discrimination Litigation.

**STACEY A. SULLIVAN,** born Honolulu, Hawaii, May 7, 1968; admitted to bar, 1996, California. *Education:* University of California at Los Angeles (B.A., magna cum laude, 1990); Hastings College of the Law, University of California (J.D., magna cum laude, 1996). Phi Beta Kappa; Order of

*(This Listing Continued)*

## HILL, FARRER & BURRILL LLP, Los Angeles—Continued

the Coif; Thurston Society. Certified Public Accountant, California, 1992—. *Member:* California Society of Certified Public Accountants; American Association of Attorney Certified Public Accountants.

All partners and associates are members of the State Bar of California and Los Angeles County Bar Association.

---

## JOHN HILL & ASSOCIATES
### LOS ANGELES, CALIFORNIA
(See Torrance)

General Civil Litigation. Insurance Defense, Products Liability, Toxic Torts, Environmental, Medical Malpractice, Government Liability, Warranty Action, Real Estate, Corporate and Construction Law, Wills and Trusts, Banking.

---

## HILLSINGER AND COSTANZO
PROFESSIONAL CORPORATION
*Established in 1973*

**12TH FLOOR, 3055 WILSHIRE BOULEVARD**
**LOS ANGELES, CALIFORNIA 90010-1161**
Telephone: 213-388-9441
Cable Address: "Hilcolaw" Los Angeles, CA.
Telecopier: 213-388-1592

Mailing Address: P.O. Box 60858 Terminal Annex, 90060-0858

*Orange, California Office:* 701 South Parker Street, Suite 6000. Telephone: 714-542-6241. Telecopier: 714-667-6806.
*Santa Barbara, California Office:* 220 East Figueroa Street. Telephone: 805-966-3986. Telecopier: 805-965-3798.
*Rancho Cucamonga, California Office:* 10737 Laurel Street, Suite 110 - Main Floor. Telephone: 909-483-6200. Telecopier: 909-483-6277.

*General Civil and Appellate Trial Practice in all State and Federal Courts. Insurance, Corporation, Products Liability and Malpractice Law.*

**JOHN J. COSTANZO** (1924-1985).

**GEORGE R. HILLSINGER,** born Brooklyn, New York, June 4, 1926; admitted to bar, 1952, California; 1964, U.S. Supreme Court. *Education:* Pasadena College; Los Angeles State College; Southwestern University (LL.B., 1950). *Member:* Los Angeles County and American Bar Associations; The State Bar of California (Member, Board of Governors, 1972-1975; Vice-President, 1974-1975); Lawyers Club; Association of Southern California Defense Counsel; American Board of Trial Advocates (President, 1961); Lawyer-Pilots Bar Association. Fellow, American College of Trial Lawyers.

**DARRELL A. FORGEY,** born Los Angeles, California, July 3, 1947; admitted to bar, 1973, California. *Education:* San Fernando Valley State College (B.A., 1969); Loyola University of Los Angeles (J.D., 1973). Blue Key; Pi Sigma Alpha; Phi Alpha Delta. *Member:* Los Angeles County and American Bar Associations; The State Bar of California; Association of Southern California Defense Counsel; American Board of Trial Advocates; Lawyer-Pilots Bar Association; Defense Research Institute; Medi-Legal Committee.

**CAROL A. SALMACIA,** born Seattle, Washington, August 6, 1945; admitted to bar, 1976, California; 1979, U.S. Court of International Trade; 1980, U.S. District Court, Central District of California. *Education:* Occidental College (B.A., 1967); Glendale University (J.D., 1976). Lecturer, Rutter Group and Continuing Education of The Bar. *Member:* Los Angeles County, Long Beach, Orange County and American Bar Associations; The State Bar of California; Association of Southern California Defense Counsel; American Board of Trial Advocates. (Resident, Orange Office).

**JEAN STONE,** born Los Angeles, California, November 10, 1934; admitted to bar, 1977, California. *Education:* University of Southern California; University of San Fernando Valley (J.D., cum laude, 1977). Member, Board of Editors, University of San Fernando Valley Law Review, 1976-1977. *Member:* Los Angeles County, Wilshire and American Bar Associations; The State Bar of California; Association of Southern California Defense Counsel; American Society for Law and Medicine; Defense Research

*(This Listing Continued)*

---

Institute; American Academy of Hospital Attorneys; National Health Lawyers Association.

**THOMAS C. HURRELL,** born Rochester, New York, March 12, 1960; admitted to bar, 1985, California, U.S. District Court, Central District of California; 1986, U.S. Court of Appeals, Ninth Circuit. *Education:* University of California at San Diego (B.A., 1982); Case Western Reserve University School of Law (J.D., 1985). *Member:* Los Angeles County and American Bar Associations; The State Bar of California; Association of Southern California Defense Counsel; American Board of Trial Advocates.

**ROBERT S. RUFFALO,** born Glendale, California, July 5, 1953; admitted to bar, 1980, California; 1981, U.S. District Court, Central District of California; 1983, U.S. District Court, Southern District of California; 1985, U.S. Court of Appeals, Ninth Circuit; 1987, U.S. Supreme Court. *Education:* University of California at Riverside; University of California at Los Angeles (B.A., cum laude, 1975); Southwestern University (J.D., 1979). *Member:* Los Angeles County, Wilshire and American Bar Associations; The State Bar of California; Association of Southern California Defense Counsel.

**DONALD G. FORGEY,** born Los Angeles, California, September 25, 1950; admitted to bar, 1979, California; 1980, South Dakota and U.S. District Court, District of South Dakota; 1981, U.S. District Court, Central District of California; 1983, U.S. District Court, Southern District of California. *Education:* California State University at Northridge (B.A., cum laude, 1972); Southwestern University (J.D., 1977). Blue Key; Phi Alpha Delta. Member, Oglala Sioux Tribal Bar Association, 1979-1981. *Member:* Los Angeles County, Wilshire (Member, Board of Governors, 1983-1987) and American Bar Associations; The State Bar of California; The State Bar of South Dakota.

**MICHAEL C. KELLAR,** born New York, N.Y., March 24, 1952; admitted to bar, 1978, California and U.S. District Court, Central District of California. *Education:* California Lutheran College (B.A., magna cum laude, 1974); University of California at Los Angeles (J.D., 1977). Professor of Constitutional Law, California Lutheran College, 1979-1980. *Member:* Los Angeles County and American Bar Associations; The State Bar of California; National Bar Association; Association of Southern California Defense Counsel. (Also in Rancho Cucamonga Office).

**LINDA STAR,** born Los Angeles, California, November 24, 1953; admitted to bar, 1980, California; 1981, U.S. District Court, Central District of California and U.S. Court of Appeals, Ninth Circuit. *Education:* University of California at Los Angeles (B.A., cum laude, 1975); University of Southern California (M.P.A., 1977); Southwestern University (J.D., 1980). Pi Alpha Delta. *Member:* Los Angeles County Bar Association; The State Bar of California; Association of Southern California Defense Counsel.

**GREGORY G. LYNCH,** born Los Angeles, California, October 21, 1959; admitted to bar, 1985, California; U.S. District Court, Central District of California. *Education:* California Polytechnic University (B.S., with honors, 1980); Universite de Paris, Sorbonne, France; University of Santa Clara (J.D., 1985). *Member:* State Bar of California; American Bar Association; Association of Southern California Defense Counsel. *LANGUAGES:* French, Spanish and Italian.

**SEANA B. THOMAS,** born Providence, Rhode Island, March 6, 1956; admitted to bar, 1988, California; 1989, U.S. District Court, Central District of California and U.S. Court of Appeals, Ninth Circuit. *Education:* Santa Barbara City College; University of California at Santa Barbara; Santa Barbara College of Law (J.D., magna cum laude, 1988). *Member:* Santa Barbara County and American Bar Associations; The State Bar of California; Barristers Club of Santa Barbara; Association of Southern California Defense Counsel; Santa Barbara Women Lawyers. (Resident, Santa Barbara Office).

---

**LISA MARTINELLI,** born Oakland, California, December 15, 1958; admitted to bar, 1983, California; 1986, U.S. District Court, Central District of California. *Education:* University of New Mexico (B.A., 1980); Southwestern University School of Law (J.D., 1983). *Member:* Los Angeles County Bar Association; The State Bar of California.

**MICHAEL J. ELSBERRY,** born Boone, Iowa, January 31, 1959; admitted to bar, 1986, California and U.S. District Court, Central District of California; 1989, U.S. District Court, Eastern, Southern and Northern Districts of California, U.S. Court of Appeals, Ninth Circuit and U.S. Supreme Court. *Education:* Drake University (B.S.B.A., 1981); Western State University (J.D., 1985). *Member:* Orange County and American (Member: Tort and Insurance Section; Products Liability Section) Bar Associations; State

*(This Listing Continued)*

Bar of California; Association of Southern California Defense Counsel (Committee Chairman, 1990—); American Inns of Court. (Resident, Orange Office).

**WONKOO CHANG,** born Seoul, Korea, October 7, 1964; admitted to bar, 1990, California and U.S. District Court, Central District of California. *Education:* University of California, Los Angeles (B.A., cum laude, 1987; J.D., 1990). *Member:* State Bar of California; Korean American Bar Association (Asian Concerns Committee). **LANGUAGES:** Korean.

**LISA M. AGRUSA,** born Arcadia, California, December 14, 1964; admitted to bar, 1990, California; 1991, U.S. District Court, Central District of California. *Education:* University of California at Los Angeles (B.A., 1987); Loyola University of Los Angeles (J.D., 1990). *Member:* Orange County and American Bar Associations. (Resident, Orange Office).

**TYRONE I. TOCZAUER,** born Vancouver, British Columbia, Canada, January 12, 1959; admitted to bar, 1986, California, U.S. District Court, Northern, Central, Eastern and Southern Districts of California and U.S. Court of Appeals, Ninth Circuit. *Education:* California State University at Northridge (B.A., 1982) University of LaVerne (J.D., 1985). *Member:* American Bar Association. **LANGUAGES:** Hungarian.

**LISA D. COLLINSON,** born Vancouver, British Columbia, February 22, 1966; admitted to bar, 1995, California. *Education:* University of California, Los Angeles (B.A., 1989); Southwestern University (J.D., 1994). Member, Association of Southern California Defense Counsel.

**LAURA M. BOOTH,** born Los Angeles, California, December 30, 1970; admitted to bar, 1995, California. *Education:* Arizona State University (B.S., 1992); University of San Diego (J.D., 1995). *Member:* Orange County Bar Association; State Bar of California; Association of Southern California Defense Counsel. (Resident, Orange Office).

**ROBERT T. COLCLOUGH, III,** born Long Beach, California, December 12, 1968; admitted to bar, 1995, California. *Education:* Boston College (B.A., 1991); Whittier Law School (J.D., 1995). *Member:* State Bar of California; Association of Southern California Defense Counsel.

**VALERIE D. ROJAS,** born Fontana, California, October 9, 1970; admitted to bar, 1995, California. *Education:* California State University (B.A., 1992); Southwestern Law School (J.D., 1995).

**ADA RUD PENTZ,** born Riga, Latvia, July 9, 1969; admitted to bar, 1995, California. *Education:* University of California, Los Angeles (B.A., 1991); Loyola Marymount University (J.D., 1994).

**ILONA GORDON,** admitted to bar, 1995, California. *Education:* University of California, Los Angeles (B.A., 1992); Southwestern University Law School (J.D., 1995).

*OF COUNSEL*

**WILLIAM S. HART,** born Pittsburgh, Pennsylvania, September 29, 1942; admitted to bar, 1972, California; 1976, U.S. District Court, Central District of California; 1980, U.S. Court of Appeals, Ninth Circuit; 1982, U.S. Supreme Court and U.S. District Court, Northern District of California; 1989, U.S. District Court, Eastern District of California. *Education:* Massachusetts Institute of Technology (S.B., 1964); Princeton University (S.M., 1966); University of London (Certificate of Law, 1970); Loyola University (J.D., 1972). Adjunct Professor of Law, Loyola University, 1984-1985. *Member:* The State Bar of California; American Bar Association; The Association of Trial Lawyers of America; California Trial Lawyers Association; Association for the Advancement of Automotive Medicine.

**EDWARD A. DEBUYS,** born Denver, Colorado, September 18, 1925; admitted to bar, 1954, California. *Education:* Loyola University of Los Angeles (B.B.A., 1949; LL.B., 1954). Phi Alpha Delta. *Member:* Los Angeles County, San Fernando Valley and American Bar Associations; State Bar of California; Association of Southern California Defense Counsel; Defense Research Institute; American Board of Trial Advocates. (Resident, Orange Office).

**FRANCOIS R. FAVRE,** born France, August 2, 1943; admitted to bar, 1972, California; 1976, U.S. Supreme Court. *Education:* Lycee de Nice, France (M.B.H., 1961); Fine Arts School, Toulon, France (B.A., 1964); Van Norman University (J.D., cum laude, 1972). Awarded LL.D., by Los Angeles State College, 1974. Professor of Law, Van Norman University, 1972-1977. Legal Advisor and Board Member, International Institute of Los Angeles, 1975-1977. Assistant Dean, Van Norman University, 1976-1977. *Member:* Los Angeles County Bar Association (Member: Immigration Committee, 1974-1977; International Law Section); The State Bar of California; Foreign Law Association of Southern California.

*(This Listing Continued)*

**STEVEN H. GURNEE,** born Palo Alto, California, January 16, 1949; admitted to bar, 1975, California and U.S. District Court, Northern District of California; 1977, U.S. District Court, Eastern District of California. *Education:* University of California at Santa Barbara, Institute of American Universities, Aix-en-Provence, France and University of California at San Diego (B.A., 1971); Hastings College of the Law, University of California (J.D., 1975). Member, Hastings Moot Court Board, 1974-1975. Assistant Editor, Hastings Constitutional Law Quarterly, 1973-1974. *Member:* Sacramento County Bar Association; The State Bar of California; Association of Defense Counsel of Northern California (Secretary-Treasurer, 1995-1996; Member, Board of Directors, 1989-1995); California Defense Counsel (Member, Board of Directors, 1994—0; Defense Research Institute; American Board of Trial Advocates; Association of Attorney Mediators, Sacramento Valley Chapter. (Also practicing individually in Sacramento, California).

**WALLACE C. REED,** born Los Angeles, California, December 11, 1927; admitted to bar, 1955, California and U.S. District Court, Southern District of California. *Education:* University of Southern California (A.B., 1951; J.D., 1955). Phi Delta Phi. Lecturer: Los Angeles County Medical Association, 1965; Medilegal Institute, 1975. Faculty, Los Angeles College Trial Advocacy, 1981. Settlement Officer, Los Angeles County Superior Court, 1984. Judge Pro Tem, Los Angeles County Municipal Court, 1996. Member, California Medico Legal Committee. *Member:* Los Angeles County and American Bar Associations; State Bar of California; Association of Southern California Defense Counsel; American Society of Law and Medicine; Defense Research Institute; International Association of Defense Counsel; American Association of Attorney Mediators. Fellow, American College of Trial Lawyers. **PRACTICE AREAS:** Professional Liability; Medical Malpractice; Legal Malpractice; Arbitration - Medication.

**ROXANNA HUDDLESTON,** born Snyder, Texas, July 29, 1956; admitted to bar, 1981, Texas; 1988, California. *Education:* Southern Methodist University (B.A.S., 1978; J.D., 1981). Phi Delta Phi. Instructor, Civil Litigation, El Centro Community College, Dallas, Texas, 1985-1988. Research Attorney, 1985-1988 and Briefing Attorney, 1981-1982, Court of Appeals, Fifth District of Texas. *Member:* Los Angeles County Bar Association (Member, Appellate Courts Committee, 1995—; Appellate Elections Committee, 1995—). **PRACTICE AREAS:** Motions; Appeals.

REPRESENTATIVE CLIENTS: Abex Corp.; Acceptance Risk Managers; Admiral Insurance Company; Allied Signal, Inc.; Allstate; AMVAC Chemical Corp.; Associated Aviation Underwriters; Cabot Safety Corp.; Campagnolo, S.R.L.; Carl Warren & Co.; Caronia Corporation; Continental Insurance Company; Continental Insurance Health Care; Crawford & Co.; Country Wide Services Corporation; The Doctors' Co.; Eisenhower Medical Center; Epic Healthcare Group, Inc.; Esis, Inc. (A CIGNA Co.); Farmers Insurance Group; FHP, Inc.; The Hartford Insurance Group; HCM Claim Management Corp.; Health Cal; Healthtrust, Inc.; Hertz Claims Management Corp.; Hughes Aircraft Company; Humana, Inc.; Hyundai Motor America; Interinsurance Exchange of the Automobile Club of Southern California; Interstate National Corp.; Investors Insurance Group; Los Angeles County Metropolitan Transit Authority; Mercury Insurance Group; National American Insurance; Norcal Mutual Insurance Company; Northwest Airlines; Orinda Healthcorp; Pacific National Insurance Company; Physicians & Surgeons Underwriters Corp.; Pioneer Life Insurance Company of Illinois; PPG Industries, Inc.; Professional Underwriters Liability Insurance Company; Risk Administration & Management; Ryder Truck Rental, Inc.; Scottsdale Insurance Company; Southern California Physicians Insurance Exchange; Southwest Airlines; State Farm Insurance Co.; St. Johns Hospital; Summit Health, Ltd.; TFS Risk Services; Toplis & Harding; Toyota Motor Sales USA; Trans World Airlines; Twentieth Century Insurance Co.; United Airlines; US Air; The Vons Companies; Washington Insurance Guaranty Association.

# ROBERT M. HIMROD

*Established in 1947*

*1055 WILSHIRE BOULEVARD, SUITE 1890*
**LOS ANGELES, CALIFORNIA 90017**
Telephone: 213-250-5722
Fax: 213-250-1894
Email: trhimrod@aol.com

*Probate, Estate Planning, State and Federal Tax, Non-Profit Organizations, Charitable Trusts and Foundations, Corporation and Real Property Law. General Civil Practice.*

**ROBERT M. HIMROD,** born Los Angeles, California, July 2, 1918; admitted to bar, 1947, California. *Education:* Pomona College (B.A., 1940); Yale University and Loyola University of Los Angeles (LL.B., 1947). Phi Delta Phi. *Member:* Los Angeles County (Member, Committee on Continuing Education of the Bar, 1956-1957) and American (Member, Sections on: Taxation; Economics of Law Practice; Real Property, Probate and Trust

*(This Listing Continued)*

### ROBERT M. HIMROD, Los Angeles—Continued

Law) Bar Associations; The State Bar of California. *PRACTICE AREAS:* Estate Planning; Probate and Trusts; Estate Tax; Real Estate.

#### ASSOCIATES

**THOMAS E. HIMROD,** born Los Angeles, California, August 7, 1950; admitted to bar, 1976, California; 1979, Guam. *Education:* Pomona College (B.A., 1972); Georgetown University (J.D., 1975). *Member:* Los Angeles County, Guam, Hawaii State and American Bar Associations; State Bar of California (Member, Sections on: Taxation; Probate; Member, Tax Exempt Organizations Committee). *PRACTICE AREAS:* Charitable Trusts and Foundations; Non-Profit Organizations; Estate Planning; Probate.

REPRESENTATIVE CLIENTS: La Mirada Water Co.; Precision Coil Spring Co., Inc.; George's Pipe & Supply Co.; Zobelein Co.
REFERENCES: Wells Fargo Bank (Wilshire and Lucas Branch).

---

## HINOJOSA & KHOUGAZ

Established in 1991

SUITE 1000, 11111 SANTA MONICA BOULEVARD
**LOS ANGELES, CALIFORNIA 90025-3344**
Telephone: 310-473-7000
Facsimile: 310-473-0906

*Probate Litigation, Estate Administration and Planning, General Business and Corporate Law. Business and Real Estate Litigation.*

**LYNARD C. HINOJOSA,** born Houston, Texas, May 3, 1942; admitted to bar, 1968, California; U.S. District Court, Central District of California and U.S. Court of Appeals, Ninth Circuit; 1976, U.S. Supreme Court. *Education:* Yale University (B.A., 1964); University of California at Los Angeles (J.D., 1967). Author: "The Great Record Ripoff: Penal Sanctions and State Civil Remedies," University of West Los Angeles Law Review, Vol. VII, 1975. Lecturer, Probate Administration, University of West Los Angeles Law School, 1976. *Member:* Beverly Hills, Los Angeles County (Member, Probate Section) and American (Member, Corporation, Banking and Business Law Section; Real Property, Probate and Trust Section) Bar Associations. *PRACTICE AREAS:* Probate Law and Litigation.

**GREGORY J. KHOUGAZ,** born Washington, D.C., November 22, 1956; admitted to bar, 1983, California. *Education:* University of California at Los Angeles (B.A., 1979); Loyola Marymount University (J.D., 1982). *Member:* The State Bar of California; Los Angeles Trial Lawyers Association. *PRACTICE AREAS:* Commercial Litigation; Real Estate Litigation; Probate Litigation; Labor Litigation.

#### ASSOCIATES

**SUSAN JABKOWSKI,** born Los Angeles, California, September 13, 1950; admitted to bar, 1975, California. *Education:* University of California at Los Angeles (B.A., 1972); Southwestern University (J.D., 1975). *Member:* San Fernando Valley (Member, Probate Section) Beverly Hills (Member, Probate Section) and Los Angeles County Bar (Member, Probate Section) Associations; San Fernando Valley Criminal Bar Association (Member, Board of Trustees, 1976-1981; Vice-President, 1981). *PRACTICE AREAS:* Probate; Conservatorship; Guardianship.

#### OF COUNSEL

**SEYMOUR S. GOLDBERG,** born 1930; admitted to bar, 1957, California. *Education:* University of California at Los Angeles (B.A., 1952); University of California School of Law (J.D., 1957). *PRACTICE AREAS:* Real Estate Law.

REFERENCES: City National Bank (Sunset-Doheny Branch); Manufacturers Bank (Beverly Hills Branch).

---

## THE LAW OFFICES OF
## ROBERT F. HINTON

ONE CENTURY PLAZA, SUITE 2600
2029 CENTURY PARK EAST
**LOS ANGELES, CALIFORNIA 90067-2081**
Telephone: 310-552-3670
Telecopier: 310-201-4776

*Business Litigation, Entertainment Litigation, Attorney Malpractice, Medical Malpractice, Professional Negligence Litigation, Real Estate Litigation, Insurance Law and Construction Litigation.*

(This Listing Continued)

---

**ROBERT F. HINTON,** born Karlsruhe, Germany, April 30, 1955; admitted to bar, 1981, California; 1982, U.S. District Court, Northern and Central Districts of California. *Education:* Princeton University (A.B., summa cum laude, 1977); Harvard University (J.D., 1980). *Member:* Beverly Hills, Los Angeles County and American Bar Associations; State Bar of California; The Association of Trial Lawyers of America.

---

## JOEL G. HIRSCH

10100 SANTA MONICA BOULEVARD
SUITE 300
**LOS ANGELES, CALIFORNIA 90067**
Telephone: 310-552-6080
Telecopier: 310-552-7917

*General Business, Real Estate and Corporate Law.*

**JOEL G. HIRSCH,** born Oakland, California, July 8, 1951; admitted to bar, 1976, California. *Education:* University of California at Los Angeles (A.B., summa cum laude, 1973), Phi Beta Kappa; Boalt Hall School of Law, University of California (J.D., 1976). Note and Comment Editor, California Law Review; Co-Authored the following: "Regression Analysis of the Effects of Habitability Laws Upon Rent: An Empirical Observation on the Ackerman-Komisar Debate," 63 California Law Review 1098, (1975), [reviewed at 89 Harvard Law Review 1815, (1976)]; "Sidestepping the Starker Decision to Save the Two-Party Tax-Free Exchange," 48 Journal of Taxation 328, (1978); "Property Taxation and Exclusionary Zoning: The Unique-Ubiquitous Resource Distinction," 6 Southern California Law Review 1671, "The Changing Landlord-Tenant Relationship in California: An Economic Analysis of the Swinging Pendulum," 14 Southwestern Law Review, (1983); ["Portions Reprinted in Property: An Introduction to the Concept and the Institution," by Charles Donahue, Jr., Thomas E. Kauper and Peter W. Martin]; "Legal - Economic Analysis of Rent Controls in a Mobile Home Context: Placement Value and Vacancy Decontrol," 35 University of California at Los Angeles Law Review 399 (1988); [Multiple Citations in Yee v. City of Escondido, United States Supreme Court Reports, 118 L. ed. 2d 153 - 173 (1992)]; Authored: Chapter 4 E, Boilerplate Lease Provisions, Treatise on Commercial Real Estate Leasing and Practice (Matthew Bender & Co. Inc., 1993). *Member:* State Bar of California.

---

## GERT K. HIRSCHBERG

10390 WILSHIRE BOULEVARD, SUITE 1610
**LOS ANGELES, CALIFORNIA 90024-6431**
Telephone: 310-276-5302
Fax: 310-276-4878

*State Bar Disciplinary Defense of Attorneys.*

**GERT K. HIRSCHBERG,** born Berlin, Germany, August 21, 1926; admitted to bar, 1951, California. *Education:* University of Southern California (B.A., 1948); Southwestern University (J.D., cum laude, 1950). Adjunct Professor, 1965-1970 and Professor, 1965-1980, Torts, Procedure, Equity, Trial Practice and Products Liability, Southwestern University School of Law. Professor: University of West Los Angeles, West Los Angeles College of Law, 1980-1986; LaVerne University School of Law, 1986—. Judge Pro Tem, Municipal Court, Los Angeles Judicial District, 1966-1968. Referee, Juvenile Court, Los Angeles Superior Court, 1972-1975. Arbitrator, Los Angeles Superior Court, 1979—. *Member:* State Bar of California (Member: Committee on Juvenile Justice, 1974-1977; Committee of Bar Examiners, Torts Development Team, 1974-1977; Disciplinary Board, 1976-1978; Presiding Disciplinary Referee for State Bar Disciplinary Board and State Bar Court, 1978-1980; Member, Board of Governors, State Bar of California, 1980-1983; Vice-President, State Bar of California, 1982-1983; Appointed to the Judicial Council of the State of California for the term commencing, 1984-1986); The Association of Trial Lawyers of America; American Board of Trial Advocates (Advocate). [With U.S. Army, 1945-1946]. *PRACTICE AREAS:* Civil Trial; Products Liability Law; Medical Malpractice Law; Professional Malpractice.

## LAW OFFICES OF
## RALPH F. HIRSCHMANN

**777 SOUTH FIGUEROA STREET, SUITE 3612**
**LOS ANGELES, CALIFORNIA 90017**
Telephone: 213-891-1700
Telecopy: 213-891-1556

*Business Litigation. Criminal Law.*

**RALPH F. HIRSCHMANN,** born Plainfield, New Jersey, November 10, 1953; admitted to bar, 1978, California; 1985, U.S. District Court, Central District of California and U.S. Court of Appeals, Ninth Circuit. *Education:* Princeton University (A.B., magna cum laude, 1975); Yale University (J.D., 1978). Phi Beta Kappa. Adjunct Professor, Trial Advocacy, University of Southern California Law Center, 1987-1989. Assistant U.S. Attorney, Criminal Division, Central District of California, 1984-1987, Political Corruption and Government Frauds Unit, 1986-1987. Judge Pro Tem, Los Angeles County Superior Court, 1989. *Member:* State Bar of California (Member, Litigation Section, Federal Courts Committee); Los Angeles County (Mediator, Dispute Resolution Services, Attorney-Client Relations Program, 1988-1989) and American (Member, Regional Subcommittee, White Collar Crime Committee) Bar Associations. **PRACTICE AREAS:** Business Litigation; Criminal Law.

*ASSOCIATES*

**JEFFREY P. SIEGEL,** born New York, N.Y., June 16, 1965; admitted to bar, 1993, New York and California; 1994, U.S. District Court, Central District of California. *Education:* Tufts University (B.A., 1987); Benjamin N. Cardozo School of Law (J.D., 1992). *Member:* Los Angeles County Bar Association (Member, Litigation, Entertainment and Commercial Law Sections); State Bar of California (Member, Litigation Section). **PRACTICE AREAS:** Business Litigation; Criminal Law.

**SHARON A. LIGORSKY,** born Farmington Hills, Michigan, July 6, 1970; admitted to bar, 1995, California and U.S. District Court, Central District of California; 1996, Arizona. *Education:* Tufts University (B.A., 1992); Loyola Law School of Los Angeles (J.D., 1995). Note and Comment Editor, Loyola of Los Angeles Law Review, 1994-1995. Author: "Williams v. Garcetti: Constitutional Defects in California's 'Gang-Parent 'Liability Statute," 28 Loy. L.A. L. Rev. 447, November 1994. *Member:* Los Angeles County Bar Association; State Bar of California; State Bar of Arizona; Women's Law Association of Los Angeles.

---

## HIRSON WEXLER PERL & STARK

*A PROFESSIONAL CORPORATION*

**6310 SAN VICENTE BOULEVARD, SUITE 415**
**LOS ANGELES, CALIFORNIA 90048**
Telephone: 213-936-0200
Fax: 213-936-4488
Email: 73411.37@compuserve.com
URL: http://www.immig.com

*Irvine, California Office:* Jamboree Center, One Park Plaza, Suite 950. Telephone: 714-251-8844. Fax: 714-251-1545. E-Mail: immigration_law@msn.com. Web-Site: http://www.immig.com.
*San Diego, California Office:* 4275 Executive Square, Suite 800, 92037. Telephone: 619-452-5700. Fax: 619-452-1911. E-Mail: hkps@immiglaw.com. Web-Site: http://www.immig.com.
*Phoenix, Arizona Office:* 3443 North Central Avenue, Suite 706, 85012. Telephone: 602-266-4700. Fax: 602-265-8108. E-Mail: 73344.21@compuserve.com. Web-Site: http://www.immig.com.
*Dallas, Texas Office:* Heritage Square Tower II, 7th Floor, 5001 L.B.J. Freeway, 75244. Telephone: 214-991-7400. Fax: 214-991-1501. E-Mail: hkps@immig-law.com. Web-Site: http://www.immig.com

*Immigration and International Law Firm.*

(For Complete Biographical Data on All Personnel, see Professional Biographies at Irvine, California).

## PAUL M. HITTELMAN

**1925 CENTURY PARK EAST, SUITE 2200**
**LOS ANGELES, CALIFORNIA 90067**
Telephone: 310-788-7730
Fax: 310-203-8195

*Litigation Practice including Business, Real Property, Intellectual Property, Medical-Legal Matters.*

**PAUL M. HITTELMAN,** born Los Angeles, California, July 7, 1938; admitted to bar, 1963, California. *Education:* University of California at Los Angeles (B.A., 1959); Harvard University (LL.B., 1962). California Continuing Education of the Bar Panelist: "Depositions," 1983; "Using Demonstrative and Documentary Evidence Effectively," 1984-1985; "Attorneys' Fees and Attorneys' Fee Agreements," 1985; "Preparing for, Taking and Using Depositions," 1986. Judge Pro Tempore, Los Angeles Superior Court, 1986—. Member, Panel of Arbitrators, American Arbitration Association. *Member:* Los Angeles County Bar Association; State Bar of California.

---

## HOAG & OVERHOLT

*Established in 1980*

**SUITE 1902 WILSHIRE FINANCIAL TOWER**
**3600 WILSHIRE BOULEVARD**
**LOS ANGELES, CALIFORNIA 90010**
Telephone: 213-386-7848
Fax: 213-386-0194

*Newport Beach, California Office:* 5030 Campus Drive. Telephone: 714-955-2260.

*Probate and Trust Law. Federal and State Taxation. Corporation. General Civil Practice.*

*MEMBERS OF FIRM*

**E. LLEWELLYN OVERHOLT** (1897-1978).

**HALLACK W. HOAG,** born Newton, Kansas, December 5, 1905; admitted to bar, 1932, California. *Education:* University of Paris, 1926; University of Montpellier (Diploma, 1927); Indiana University (A.B., 1928); Yale University Law School (LL.B., 1931). Phi Delta Phi. Trustee, Los Angeles Bar Association, 1938-1940. President, 1951-1956; Member, Board of Directors, 1937-1972, Legal Aid Foundation. *Member:* Los Angeles County Bar Association; The State Bar of California. **PRACTICE AREAS:** Probate; Trust Law; Tax.

**DAVID G. OVERHOLT,** born Los Angeles, California, January 25, 1935; admitted to bar, 1961, California. *Education:* Yale University (B.A., 1956); Stanford University (J.D., 1959). Phi Alpha Delta. Member, Board of Managers, Hollywood Wilshire Y.M.C.A., 1967—. Director, Hollywood Presbyterian Medical Center Foundation, 1979—. Member, Board of Directors, Goodwill Industries of Southern California, 1976-1988. Member, Board of Directors and Trustee, McKinley Home for Boys Foundation, 1978-1988. *Member:* Wilshire, Los Angeles County and American Bar Associations; The State Bar of California; Lawyers Club of Los Angeles; American Judicature Society. [With U.S. Air Force, 1959-1965]. **PRACTICE AREAS:** Probate; Trust Administration; Tax.

*ASSOCIATES*

**CARL L. McGINNIS,** born Los Angeles, California, April 24, 1920; admitted to bar, 1982, California. *Education:* Massachusetts Institute of Technology (B.S., 1942); University of California at Berkeley (Ph.D., 1952); University of Southern California (J.D., 1980). Phi Alpha Delta. Member, Board of Directors and Trustee, McKinley Home for Boys Foundation, 1988—. Director, McKinley Home for Boys, 1988—. *Member:* Wilshire, Los Angeles County and American Bar Associations; The State Bar of California; American Physical Society. **PRACTICE AREAS:** Probate; Tax.

REFERENCE: Bank of America (Harvard & Wilshire Branch).

---

## HOCHMAN, SALKIN AND DeROY

*A PROFESSIONAL CORPORATION*

**LOS ANGELES, CALIFORNIA**

(See Beverly Hills)

*Federal and State Taxation and Corporation Law. Civil and Criminal Tax Litigation and Tax Controversies, Probate, Civil Forfeitures.*

## RICHARD E. HODGE, INC.

*LOS ANGELES, CALIFORNIA*

(See Santa Monica)

*General Civil, Trial and Appellate Practice in all State and Federal Courts. Corporation, Antitrust, Real Property, Entertainment, Estate Planning, Trust, Tax and Probate Law.*

---

## AGGIE R. HOFFMAN

Established in 1976

6300 WILSHIRE BOULEVARD, SUITE 1560
*LOS ANGELES, CALIFORNIA 90048*
Telephone: 213-655-0123
Fax: 213-655-3345

*Immigration and Nationality Law, with emphasis on Business Related Immigration of Professionals, Executives, Extraordinary Aliens and U.S. National Interest Cases.*

**AGGIE R. HOFFMAN,** born Czechoslovakia, May 16, 1946; admitted to bar, 1976, California; 1977, U.S. District Court, Central District of California; 1982, U.S. Supreme Court. *Education:* University of Akron (B.A., 1968); La Verne University (J.D., 1976). Who's Who Among Outstanding Americans, 1995. Past Vice-President and Former Member, Board of Directors of the British American Chamber of Commerce, Los Angeles, 1989-1992. Los Angeles County Bar Association, Attorney-Client Relations, Arbitrator, 1979-1984. *Member:* American Immigration Lawyer's Association (President, Southern California Chapter, 1983-1984; Chair, National Committee for Specialization in Immigration Law, 1985). (Certified Specialist, Immigration and Nationality Law, The State Bar of California Board of Legal Specialization). **LANGUAGES:** Spanish, Russian, Hungarian and Hebrew. **PRACTICE AREAS:** Immigration and Nationality Law.

---

## LAW OFFICES OF
## EDWARD A. HOFFMAN

11620 WILSHIRE BOULEVARD, SUITE 340
*LOS ANGELES, CALIFORNIA 90025*
Telephone: 310-575-3540
Fax: 310-575-6107
Email: eah@hoffmanlaw.com
URL: http://www.hoffmanlaw.com

*General Civil Litigation, Business Litigation and Appellate Practice in all State and Federal Courts.*

**EDWARD A. HOFFMAN,** born New York, N.Y., September 13, 1965; admitted to bar, 1993, California, U.S. District Court, Central District of California and U.S. Court of Appeals, Ninth Circuit; 1994, U.S. District Court, Eastern, Northern and Southern Districts of California. *Education:* Columbia University (B.A., 1987); Harvard University (Graduate Studies in Government, 1988-1990); University of Southern California (J.D., 1993);. Phi Alpha Delta. Executive Articles Editor, 1992-1993 and Staff, 1991-1992, Southern California Interdisciplinary Law Journal and Major Tax Planning Journal. Recipient: Dorothy W. Nelson Justice Award; Edward and Eleanor Shattack Award. Intern, Hon. Alfred T. Goodwin, U.S. Court of Appeals, Ninth Circuit, 1993-1994. Member, Law and Society Association, 1992-1995. Institute of Electrical and Electronics Engineers, 1985-1990; American Association for Advancement of Science, 1988-1989. New York Academy of Science, 1988—. *Member:* State Bar of California; Los Angeles County (Member, Appellate Courts Committee, 1996—) and American Bar Associations. **PRACTICE AREAS:** Litigation; Appellate Practice.

---

## NANCY RUTH HOFFMAN

10880 WILSHIRE BOULEVARD, SUITE 2200
*LOS ANGELES, CALIFORNIA 90024*
Telephone: 310-441-0664
Fax: 310-441-1153

*Practice Limited to Family Law.*

**NANCY RUTH HOFFMAN,** born Kansas City, Missouri, October 22, 1941; admitted to bar, 1977, California. *Education:* Northwestern University (B.M., 1963; M.M., 1964); University of Southern California (J.D., 1977). Phi Alpha Delta (President, Ross Chapter, 1976-1977). Lecturer: ABA Annual Convention "How to Avoid Alimony" August, 1992; California Society of CPAs, Education Division "Recent Developments in Child and Spousal Support", December, 1992. Examiner, State Bar Court; Liaison, California Board of Governors Adjudication and Discipline Committee, 1980-1983. Chair, State Bar Board of Governors Subcommittee on Client Security Fund, 1980-1983. Judge Pro Tempore for Los Angeles Superior Court, West District. Committee Member and Participant in Los Angeles County Bar Association Child Custody Colloquium, February, 1992. *Member:* Beverly Hills (Member, Section on Family Law), Los Angeles County (Member: Section on Family Law; Committee on Legal Specialization, 1980; Panelist, Family Law Symposium and Editor for Syllabus, 1991; Family Law Section Executive Committee, 1992-1998) and American (Member, Section on Family Law; Member, Support Committee) Bar Associations; The State Bar of California (Member: Section on Family Law; Board of Legal Specialization, 1981-1986); California Young Lawyers Association (Member, Board of Directors, 1980-1983; Vice President, 1982-1983). (Certified Specialist, Family Law, The State Bar of California Board of Legal Specialization).

---

## NORMAN J. HOFFMAN, INC.

*A PROFESSIONAL CORPORATION*

PENTHOUSE SUITE A
16133 VENTURA BOULEVARD
*LOS ANGELES, CALIFORNIA 91436*
Telephone: 818-986-8080
Fax: 818-379-4017

*Automobile Law, Tax Law, Estate Planning, Wills, Trusts, Real Estate and Probate.*

**NORMAN J. HOFFMAN,** born Rochester, New York, December 26, 1940; admitted to bar, 1966, New York and U.S. Claims Court; 1973, California; 1974, U.S. Supreme Court; 1975, U.S. Tax Court and U.S. District Court, Central District of California; 1981, U.S. Court of Appeals, Ninth Circuit. *Education:* St. John Fisher College (B.B.A., 1962); Syracuse University (LL.B., magna cum laude, 1966); Georgetown University (LL.M. in Taxation, 1970). Phi Alpha Delta; Order of the Coif. Note Editor, Syracuse Law Review, 1965-1966. *Member:* Los Angeles County (Member, Sections on: Taxation; Probate and Trust Law) and American (Member, Sections on: Taxation; Real Property, Probate and Trust Law) Bar Associations; The State Bar of California. [With U.S. Marine Corp, 1962-1970]. (Certified Specialist, Taxation Law, The State Bar of California Board of Legal Specialization).

---

## HOFFMAN, SABBAN & WATENMAKER

*A PROFESSIONAL CORPORATION*

Established in 1981

10880 WILSHIRE BOULEVARD, SUITE 2200
*LOS ANGELES, CALIFORNIA 90024*
Telephone: 310-470-6010
Fax: 310-470-6735

*Estate Planning, Trust and Estate Administration, Taxation.*

**FIRM PROFILE:** *The Firm practices exclusively in the following areas: Estate planning and trust and estate administration, including wills, living trusts, irrevocable trusts, charitable remainder and charitable lead trusts, insurance trusts, asset protection planning, international estate planning, conservatorships, probate and post-mortem trust administration and dispute resolution. Tax Planning and civil tax controversies, including international, United States and California taxation; corporate, partnership and individual income taxation, sales, use and property taxation, tax-exempt organizations and charitable planning.*

(This Listing Continued)

**PAUL GORDON HOFFMAN,** born Los Angeles, California, October 29, 1950; admitted to bar, 1976, California. *Education:* University of California at Berkeley (B.S., 1972; M.B.A., 1973); University of California at Los Angeles (J.D., 1976). Beta Gamma Sigma; Beta Alpha Psi. Comment Editor, UCLA Law Review, 1975-1976. Author: "Limits on Retroactive Decision Making by the Internal Revenue Service: Redefining Abuse of Discretion Under Section 7805 (b)," 23 UCLA Law Review 529; "Should You Make Gifts Before Year-End? The Effect of the Tax Reform Act of 1976," 52 Los Angeles Bar Journal 226; "Salary-Continuation Plans Can Be Estate Tax Free But May Run Into Gift Tax Problems," 9 Taxation For Lawyers 376; "Estate Planning for Non-Qualified Plan Benefits," 24 University of Miami Institute on Estate Planning ¶1200, 1990; "Current Developments Affecting Trusts and Estates," 51 New York University on Federal Taxation S1, 1993. Co-Author: "Planning An Estate in Light of Recent Changes in Tax and Copyright Laws," 5 Estate Planning 90; "Estate Planning for Individuals in the Entertainment Industry," Southern California Tax Institute 875, 1979; "Income Taxation of Estates and Trusts," CEB, 1980; "Estate Planning for Clients with Special Assets," Estate Planning, 1980; "The Marital Deduction: Beyond the Basics," 35 Major Tax Planning, 1983; "Estate Planning for Qualified Plan Benefits After 1984," Estate Planning 1985; "Estate Planning - A Client Based Approach," 39 Major Tax Planning, 1987; "Estate Planning for Qualified Plan Benefits After 1986," Estate Planning 1987. Contributing Author: "International Estate Planning," Matthew Bender, 1992. Instructor: University of Southern California Law Center Advanced Professional Program, 1976-1979; UCLA School of Law, 1981-1991. Member: Board of Directors, The Samuel Goldwyn Company; Planning Committee, UCLA/CEB Estate Planning Institute, 1980—; Board of Directors, Motion Picture and Television Tax Institute, 1980—. Member, Planning Committee, USC Probate and Trust Conference, 1984—. *Member:* Beverly Hills (Chairman, Tax Committee, 1980-1981), Los Angeles County and American Bar Associations; State Bar of California. Fellow, American College of Trust and Estate Counsel. *PRACTICE AREAS:* Taxation Law; Estate Planning Law.

**NINA MADDEN SABBAN,** born London, Ontario, Canada, February 11, 1944; admitted to bar, 1978, California. *Education:* University of California at Los Angeles (A.B., 1965); Loyola Marymount University (J.D., 1978). Recipient, American Jurisprudence Award for Estate Planning, 1978. Co-Author: "Husband and Wife Property: Who Owns What?" The California Society of Certified Public Accountants, 1980; "California's Community Property Laws: Planning for a Move to California," Trusts & Estates, June, 1982. Lecturer: Probate Administration, Estate Taxation and Estate Planning, California Continuing Education of the Bar, 1981—; Practical Law Courses, 1980, Beverly Hills Bar Association, 1981—; UCLA Graduate School of Management, 1982—; UCLA Law School, 1980—; UCLA/CEB Estate Planning Institute, 1984; 1984 Retirement Planning Conference; USC Probate and Trust Conference, 1985. Member, C.P.A. Foundation Planning Committee, 1984—. Consultant: California Trust Administration, 1986; California Will Drafting Practice, 1988, 1990; New York University Institute on Federal Taxation, 1988. Member: Board of Governors, City of Hope, 1993—; Chair, Planned Giving Committee, Western Region, Board of Directors of the American Technion Society, 1993—. *Member:* Beverly Hills and Los Angeles County (Member, Executive Committee of Probate and Trust Section, 1982-1984; Chairman, Estate Tax Subcommittee, 1987, 1988) Bar Associations; State Bar of California. Fellow, American College of Trust and Estate Counsel. *PRACTICE AREAS:* Estate Planning Law; Probate Law; Trust Law.

**ALAN S. WATENMAKER,** born Los Angeles, California, April 5, 1946; admitted to bar, 1972, California. *Education:* University of California at Los Angeles (B.S., magna cum laude, 1968; M.S., 1969); Boalt Hall School of Law, University of California at Berkeley (J.D., 1972). Order of the Coif; Phi Beta Kappa; Beta Gamma Sigma. Author: "Supplement to California Decedent Estate Practice 1 & 2," 1994. Co-Author: "Post-Mortem Tax Planning Checklist," Twentieth Annual USC Probate and Trust Conference, 1994; "Death of a Spouse 'Now What Do I Do...?' Selected Tax Issues for the Surviving Spouse," Forty-Seventh Annual Institute on Federal Taxation, USC Tax Institute 1995. Contributing Author: *California Decedent Estate Practice 3,* California Continuing Education of the Bar. Member, Planning Committee, USC Probate and Trust Conference, 1981—. *Member:* Beverly Hills and Los Angeles County (Member, Executive Committee, Probate and Trust Law Section, 1982-1985, 1989-1992) Bar Associations; State Bar of California. Fellow, American College of Trust and Estate Counsel. (Certified Specialist, Estate Planning, Trust and Probate Law, The State Bar of California Board of Legal Specialization). *PRACTICE AREAS:* Estate Planning Law; Probate Law; Trust Law.

*(This Listing Continued)*

**JONATHAN C. LURIE,** born November 9, 1953; admitted to bar, 1979, South Africa; 1986, California. *Education:* Witwatersrand University, Johannesburg (B.A., 1974; L.L.B., 1976; H.Dip. Tax, 1980). Chairperson, Law Students Council, 1976. Contributing Author: *Will Drafting 3,* California Continuing Education of the Bar, 1992. Lecturer: UCLA, 1990—; California Society of CPA's Access Programs, 1992-1993; California Continuing Education of the Bar, 1991; State Bar of California, Tax Section, 1991—; Los Angeles County Bar Association, 1991—. Instructor: Whittier Law School, 1989; University of West Los Angeles, 1987-1995. *Member:* Beverly Hills (Member, Board of Governors, 1991—; Chairperson, Blue Car Project, 1991-1992) and Los Angeles County (Secretary, 1993-1994, Vice Chair, 1994-1995, Chairperson, 1995-1996, Estate and Gift Tax Section) Bar Associations; State Bar of California; Fellow, American College of Trust and Estate Counsel. *PRACTICE AREAS:* Estate Planning Law; Probate Law; Trust Law; International Estate Planning.

**MARY K. RAMSDEN,** born Oakland, California, May 19, 1949; admitted to bar, 1981, California; 1982, U.S. Tax Court and U.S. District Court, Central District of California. *Education:* University of California at Los Angeles (A.B., 1971); Loyola University of Los Angeles (J.D., 1981). Phi Alpha Delta. Member, International Law Journal, 1980-1981. Author: "Formula Clauses in Marital Deduction Planning," Spring 1993 Estate Planning, Trust & Probate News, State Bar of California-Estate Planning, Trust and Probate Law Section. Lecturer: Fundamentals of Estate Planning, 1989, Drafting Wills and Estate Planning Documents, 1990, Estate Planning & Administration Practice: 9th Annual Recent Developments Program, 1994, California Continuing Education of the Bar. *Member:* Beverly Hills Bar Association; State Bar of California. (Certified Specialist, Estate Planning, Trust and Probate Law, The State Bar of California Board of Legal Specialization). *PRACTICE AREAS:* Estate Planning Law; Probate Law; Trust Law.

**LORETTA SICILIANO,** born Washington, D.C., January 10, 1949; admitted to bar, 1977, California and U.S. District Court, Northern District of California; 1986, U.S. Tax Court and U.S. District Court, Central District of California. *Education:* University of California, Santa Cruz; Stanford University (B.A., 1971); Hastings College of the Law, University of California (J.D., 1977); Golden Gate University (L.L.M., Tax, with great distinction, 1982). *Member:* Los Angeles County (Member, Tax Section; Tax Procedure Subcommittee; Tax Compliance Procedure and Litigation Subcommittee Task Force) Bar Association; State Bar of California (Member, Taxation Section); Women Lawyers Association of Los Angeles (Chair: Tax Procedures Subcommittee, 1990-1991; Board of Directors, 1990-1991). *PRACTICE AREAS:* Taxation Law.

**LINDA J. RETZ,** born Sacramento, California, April 15, 1953; admitted to bar, 1993, California. *Education:* University of West Los Angeles (B.S., 1977); Southwestern University School of Law; Loyola Law School (J.D., 1993). Author: "Death, Divorce and Exclusions," Los Angeles Lawyer, July-August, 1995. Co-Author: with John R. Cohan, "Section 6166: Supplemental Estate Tax Returns," 10 Probate Notes 178 (Amer. College of Probate Counsel No. 3, 1984). Instructor: "Wills, Trusts & Estate Planning," (1982-1986), University of West Los Angeles School of Paralegal Studies. Panelist for Continuing Education of the Bar, "Mathematics of Estate Planning" (1982). Consultant for California Continuing Education of the Bar on Volume 3 of *California Decedent Estate Practice* (1987). *Member:* Los Angeles County Bar Association; State Bar of California. *PRACTICE AREAS:* Estate Planning Law; Probate Law; Trust Law.

**HENRY J. MORAVEC, III,** born Chicago, Illinois, February 7, 1960; admitted to bar, 1990, California. *Education:* California State University at Long Beach (B.A., 1983); Loyola University of Los Angeles (J.D., cum laude, 1990). Order of the Coif. Member, Scott Moot Court Honor's Board, 1989-1990. Senior Note and Comment Editor, Loyola International and Corporative Law Journal, 1989-1990. Lecturer: "Unrelated Business Taxable Income and You," Los Angeles County Bar Association, Tax Section, March 1995. *Member:* Los Angeles County and American Bar Associations; State Bar of California (Member, Taxation Section). *PRACTICE AREAS:* Estate Planning Law; Probate Law; Tax-Exempt Organizations; Charitable Planning.

*OF COUNSEL*

**KENNETH S. WOLF,** born Cincinnati, Ohio, August 12, 1943; admitted to bar, 1969, California. *Education:* University of Cincinnati (B.A., 1965); Harvard University (J.D., 1968). Chairman, University of Southern California Probate and Trust Conference, 1993—. *Member:* State Bar of California. Fellow, American College of Trust and Estate Counsel. (Certi-

*(This Listing Continued)*

**HOFFMAN, SABBAN & WATENMAKER,** A PROFESSIONAL CORPORATION, Los Angeles—Continued

fied Specialist, Estate Planning, Trust and Probate Law, The State Bar of California Board of Legal Specialization). *PRACTICE AREAS:* Estate Planning Law; Probate Law; Trusts Law; Beneficiary Rights Disputes.

## JAMES W. E. HOFFMANN

SUITE 225, 15821 VENTURA BOULEVARD
**LOS ANGELES, CALIFORNIA 91436-2938**
Telephone: 818-905-6924
Telecopier: 818-907-6709

*Denver, Colorado Office:* 1700 Broadway, Suite 910. Telephone: 303-831-7610. Fax: 303-831-7650.

*Professional Malpractice, Bad Faith, Insurance Coverage, Product Liability, Insurance Defense, General Civil Litigation.*

**JAMES W. E. HOFFMANN,** born Syracuse, New York, June 30, 1951; admitted to bar, 1980, California and U.S. Court of Military Appeals; U.S. Claims Court; U.S. District Court, Central and Southern Districts of California; U.S. Court of Appeals, 9th Circuit; U.S. Supreme Court; 1994, Colorado and U.S. District Court, District of Colorado. *Education:* C.W. Post College and Colorado State University (B.A., 1974); University of San Fernando College of Law (J.D., 1979). Lecturer: Trial Techniques, University of Southern California, 1986—; Los Angeles Trial Lawyers Association, 1986—. Judge Pro Tem and ADR Volunteer, Los Angeles Municipal Court, 1986-1989. *Member:* Los Angeles County (Arbitrator, Attorney-Client Relations Committee, 1984-1989; Performed pro bono work, 1984-1989) Colorado and American Bar Associations; The State Bar of California. (Also Of Counsel to Fields & Fields).

### ASSOCIATES

**TRACY A. NAEGELE,** born Highland Park, Illinois, February 20, 1954; admitted to bar, 1985, California, U.S. District Court, Central and Southern Districts of California, U.S. Court of Appeals, Ninth Circuit and U.S. Supreme Court. *Education:* Carleton College (A.B., 1976); University of Southern California (J.D., 1984). Phi Alpha Delta (Justice, 1983-1984). Judge Pro Tem, Los Angeles Municipal Court, 1988—. Arbitrator, Los Angeles County Superior Court. *Member:* Los Angeles County and American Bar Associations; State Bar of California.

### OF COUNSEL

**HOWARD M. FIELDS,** born Chicago, Illinois, October 30, 1951; admitted to bar, 1976, California, U.S. Court of Appeals, Ninth Circuit and U.S. Supreme Court. *Education:* University of California at Berkeley (B.A., 1973); Southwestern University School of Law (J.D., 1976). Investigative Referee, 1981—, Probation Monitor, 1984—, Hearing Officer, 1981-1989 and Mandatory Settlement Conference Judge, 1987-1988, State Bar Courts, State Bar of California. Judge Pro Tempore, Los Angeles Municipal Court, 1985-1989. Arbitrator, Los Angeles County Superior Court and Los Angeles County Bar Association. Member, Panel of Arbitrators, American Arbitration Association. Member, Board of Directors, President, Calabasas Hills Community Association. *Member:* Los Angeles County and American (Member, Sections on: Litigation; Torts and Insurance Practice Law) Bar Associations; State Bar of California; Defense Research Institute; Association of Southern California Defense Counsel. (Also Member, Fields & Fields).

## HOLLEY & GALEN

Established in 1942

800 SOUTH FIGUEROA, SUITE 1100
**LOS ANGELES, CALIFORNIA 90017**
Telephone: 213-629-1880
Fax: 213-895-0363

*Taxation (Federal and State), Business, Estate Planning, Probate, Antitrust, Corporate, Real Property and Commercial Law. Trial and Appellate Practice.*

### MEMBERS OF FIRM

**CLYDE E. HOLLEY** (1891-1980).

**ALBERT J. GALEN** (Retired).

**W. MICHAEL JOHNSON,** born Los Angeles, California, July 18, 1942; admitted to bar, 1968, California; 1975, U.S. Supreme Court. *Educa-*

*(This Listing Continued)*

*tion:* University of California at Los Angeles (A.B., 1964); University of Southern California (M.Bus.Tax., 1980); University of California School of Law (J.D., 1967). Instructor, Income Tax, School of Accounting, University of Southern California, 1983-1984. Author: "Federal Tax Reporting and Payment Requirements," California Closely Held Corporations, Matthew Bender, 1987. Councilman, City of San Marino, 1988-1992. *Member:* Los Angeles County and American Bar Associations; The State Bar of California. (Certified Specialist, Taxation Law, California Board of Legal Specialization). *PRACTICE AREAS:* Taxation.

**A. STEVEN BROWN,** born Omaha, Nebraska, June 1, 1951; admitted to bar, 1977, California; 1980, U.S. Tax Court. *Education:* University of Notre Dame (B.A., 1973); Loyola University of Los Angeles (J.D., 1977). *Member:* Los Angeles County and American (Member, Taxation, Real Property, Probate and Trust Law Sections) Bar Associations; The State Bar of California.

### ASSOCIATES

**DEBRA BURCHARD COFFEEN,** born Encino, California, January 24, 1963; admitted to bar, 1990, California. *Education:* University of California at Los Angeles (B.A., 1986); Loyola Marymount University (J.D., 1990). Phi Alpha Delta. Co-Chair, Loyola Law School Environmental Law Society, 1989-1990. *Member:* Los Angeles and American Bar Associations; State Bar of California. *PRACTICE AREAS:* Environmental; Property Tax.

**CHARLES A. JORDAN,** born Los Angeles, California, September 7, 1945; admitted to bar, 1977, California; 1978, U.S. District Court, Central District of California. *Education:* California Polytechnic State University (B.S., 1967); Western State University (J.D., 1976). Real Estate Broker, California, 1980. *Member:* Los Angeles County (Member, Business Litigation and Real Estate Sections) and American Bar Associations; State Bar of California; Mensa Society. [Lieut., U.S. Army, active duty, 1968-1970; Captain, U.S. Army, Inactive Reserve, 1970-1972]. *PRACTICE AREAS:* Business Law (Transactional and Litigation); Real Estate Litigation Law.

## HOLLINS & RICE

A PROFESSIONAL CORPORATION

Established in 1987

1925 CENTURY PARK EAST, SUITE 920
**LOS ANGELES, CALIFORNIA 90067**
Telephone: 310-553-3510

*San Diego, California Office:* 402 West Broadway, Fourth Floor. Telephone: 619-232-0222.

*Professional Liability, Medical Malpractice, Legal Malpractice, Insurance Coverage and Bad Faith, Personal Injury, Products Liability and Toxic Tort Law. General Civil, Trial and Appellate Practice in all State and Federal Courts.*

*FIRM PROFILE:* Hollins & Rice was founded in 1987 by Byron S. Hollins and Andrea Lynn Rice. The firm emphasizes legal malpractice and other professional liability defense, as well as insurance coverage analysis and litigation. The firm serves all of Southern California, from San Diego County in the south to San Luis Obispo County in the north. It is the firm's philosophy that the client's interest is paramount. The firm reinforces its commitment to keeping both its members and its clients abreast of current developments in the law through its weekly newsletter, the "Liability Update."

**BYRON S. HOLLINS,** born Brooklyn, New York, February 16, 1950; admitted to bar, 1984, California, U.S. District Court, Central and Southern Districts of California and U.S. Court of Appeals, Ninth Circuit; 1988, U.S. Supreme Court. *Education:* University of Missouri (B.S., 1972); Mid-Valley College of Law (J.D., 1978). Member, Professional Liability Underwriting Society, 1991—. *Member:* Los Angeles County (Member, Group Insurance Committee, 1992—; Chair, 1996—) and American (Member, Section on Lawyers Professional Liability, 1984—); Bar Associations; State Bar of California; California Trial Lawyers Association; Association of Southern California Defense Counsel. *PRACTICE AREAS:* Legal Malpractice; Legal Malpractice Defense; Coverage Defense; Insurance Defense; Medical Malpractice.

**ANDREA LYNN RICE,** born Los Angeles, California, June 22, 1947; admitted to bar, 1980, California; 1981, U.S. District Court, Central, Northern and Southern Districts of California and U.S. Court of Appeals, Ninth Circuit; 1984, U.S. Supreme Court. *Education:* University of California at Los Angeles (A.B., 1968; M.Ed., 1974); Loyola University of Los

*(This Listing Continued)*

Angeles (J.D., 1980). Recipient, American Jurisprudence Award in Bills and Notes. Los Angeles County Bar Association Family Law Scholarship, 1980. Member, Professional Liability Underwriting Society, 1991—. *Member:* Los Angeles County and American (Member, Section on Lawyers Professional Liability) Bar Associations; The State Bar of California; Association of Southern California Defense Counsel. **PRACTICE AREAS:** Legal Malpractice Defense; Legal Malpractice; Insurance Coverage/Bad Faith; Real Estate/Brokers and Agents Errors & Omissions; Insurance Brokers and Agents Errors and Omissions.

---

**KIM A. HAYASHI,** born San Francisco, California, October 27, 1956; admitted to bar, 1981, California; 1982, U.S. District Court, Central District of California and U.S. Court of Appeals, Ninth Circuit. *Education:* University of Southern California (A.B., with high honors, 1978; J.D., 1981). Phi Beta Kappa. *Member:* State Bar of California.

**ADAM L. JOHNSON,** born Newport Beach, California, September 5, 1967; admitted to bar, 1993, California. *Education:* Pomona College (B.A., 1989); Pepperdine University (J.D., cum laude, 1993). Associate Editor, Pepperdine Law Review, 1992-1994. **LANGUAGES:** German.

### LEGAL SUPPORT PERSONNEL

**TERESA ORTEGA,** born Anaheim, California, December 30, 1969. *Education:* University of Southern California (B.A., 1992). IBM Scholar Athlete, 1991. Marks Foundation Scholar, 1992. NSCA Athlete of the Year, 1992. (Paralegal). **LANGUAGES:** Spanish.

REPRESENTATIVE CLIENTS: Safeco Insurance Cos.; Utica Mutual Insurance Cos.; Lawyers Mutual Insurance Cos.; Texas Lawyers Insurance Exchange; Minnesota Lawyers Mutual Insurance Co.; United Healthcare Corp.; State Farm Fire and Casualty Co.; Professional Prototype; Northland Insurance Companies; Vasa-North Atlantic; American Claims Management, Inc.
REFERENCE: Union Bank.

---

## HONG & CHANG

*Established in 1981*

SUITE 1010
800 WEST SIXTH STREET
**LOS ANGELES, CALIFORNIA 90017**
Telephone: 213-629-5611
Telecopier: 213-629-1170

*Seoul, Korea Associated Office:* Kim & Chang, Seyang Building, 223, Naeja-Dong, Chongro-Ku, Seoul, Korea. Telephone:(+82 2) 737-4455. Telecopier: (+82 2) 737-9091-3. E-Mail: lawkim@soback.kornet.nm.kr; Web Site Address: http://www.kimchang.com

*Commercial, Banking, Corporate, Real Property, Business Trials and Litigation, Bankruptcy.*

FIRM PROFILE: Hong & Chang is a Korean-American law firm located in downtown Los Angeles, which since its founding in 1981, has been composed of the attorneys and staff capable of meeting the dual-language business, bank and litigation needs of its diverse domestic and Korea-based corporate business clientele.

**SEBONG HONG,** born Seoul, Korea, January 1, 1949; admitted to bar, 1978, District of Columbia; 1981, New York; 1982, California and U.S. District Court, Central District of California. *Education:* College of Law, Seoul National University (B.Jur., 1971); American University (B.A., 1975; J.D., 1978); Hague Academy of International Law (Certificate of Attendance, 1980). Kim & Chang, Seoul, Korea, 1978-1980. *Member:* Los Angeles County Bar Associations; The District of Columbia Bar; State Bar of California. **LANGUAGES:** Korean. **PRACTICE AREAS:** Corporate and Commercial Transactions; Banking and Finance; Real Estate Transactions.

**RICHARD W. SWARTZ,** born Los Angeles, California, May 26, 1950; admitted to bar, 1976, California and U.S. District Court, Central District of California; 1986, U.S. District Court, Southern District of California. *Education:* University of California at Los Angeles (B.A., 1972); Southwestern University (J.D., 1975). Member, Southwestern University Law Review, 1974-1975. Co-Recipient, Institute for Human Studies Fellowship, Southwestern University. *Member:* State Bar of California; American Bar Association; Association of Business Trial Lawyers. **PRACTICE AREAS:** Business Trials; Litigation.

**RICK D. NAVARRETTE,** born Tucson, Arizona, November 9, 1960; admitted to bar, 1986, California and U.S. District Court, Central District of California. *Education:* University of Arizona (B.A., cum laude, 1982); University of California at Los Angeles (J.D., 1985). *Member:* Los Angeles

*(This Listing Continued)*

---

County Bar Association (Member, Litigation and Bankruptcy Sections); Mexican-American Bar Association. **PRACTICE AREAS:** Business Trials and Litigation; Bankruptcy; Commercial Law.

**HENRY GWEON,** born Seoul, Korea, September 12, 1964; admitted to bar, 1991, California. *Education:* University of California at Berkeley (B.A., 1987); Georgetown University Law Center (J.D., 1991). **LANGUAGES:** English and Korean. **PRACTICE AREAS:** Business Litigation; Corporate Law; Commercial Law; Banking; Finance; Real Estate.

---

## HONN & SECOF

*Established in 1982*

510 WEST SIXTH STREET, SUITE 910
**LOS ANGELES, CALIFORNIA 90014-1310**
Telephone: 213-629-3900
Telecopier: 213-624-5362

*General Civil and Trial Practice. Business, Commercial and Insolvency Law and Banking, Corporate, Probate and Real Estate Law, Entertainment Law, Tort and Insurance Law.*

FIRM PROFILE: Honn & Secof is a small law firm, dedicated to close contact with its clients and committed to professional service. We take pride in preserving the one-to-one client contact so often missing in larger firms. The firm began in 1982 and its client base has consistently grown in both size and diversity. We provide high quality legal services, while continuing to support the profession through charitable and pro bono publico activities. In addition to the legal work conducted by the attorneys in the firm, each contributes a substantial portion of his or her time in volunteer work in the community.

Honn & Secof has a general practice history, with a recognition of the need to focus our attention in certain areas. Honn & Secof meets a broad spectrum of the needs of its clients, which include businesses in the real estate, insurance, entertainment and consulting areas.

**RICHARD A. HONN,** born Oxnard, California, June 23, 1952; admitted to bar, 1979, California and U.S. District Court, Central District of California; 1988, U.S. Supreme Court. *Education:* University of California, Santa Barbara (B.A., magna cum laude, 1974); University of California, Los Angeles (M.P.A., 1975); Loyola Law School (J.D., 1978). Associate Professor of Clinical Business Law, University of Southern California, 1980—. Member, Board of Directors, 1990-1994, President, 1992-1994, and Board of Governors, 1995—, California Special Olympics. *Member:* Los Angeles County Bar Association (Member: Sections on: Real Property; Commercial Law and Bankruptcy; Ad Hoc Committee on Private Judging, 1990-1991; Chair, 1990-1991; Ad Hoc Committee on Jury Reform, 1993; Ad Hoc Committee on the Economics of the Practice of Law; Legal Services for the Poor Advisory Committee, 1989—; Lawyer Referral and Information Service Advisory Committee, 1985—; Chair, 1987-1989; Volunteers in Parole Advisory Committee, 1980—; Chair, 1983-1985); State Bar of California. **PRACTICE AREAS:** Litigation; Business Law; Real Property; Insurance Law.

**HOWARD S. SECOF,** born New York, N.Y., August 23, 1953; admitted to bar, 1978, California; 1979, U.S. District Court, Central District of California; 1980; U.S. Court of Appeals, Ninth Circuit; 1988, U.S. Supreme Court; 1991, U.S. District Court, District of Arizona. *Education:* University of California, Los Angeles (B.A., cum laude, 1975); Loyola Law School (J.D., 1978). Judge Pro Tempore, Los Angeles Municipal Court, 1988—. Member, Board of Directors, 1992—, President, 1995—, UCLA Jewish Alumni. Member, UCLA Hillel Advisory Council, 1995—. Member, Diversity Committee, UCLA Alumni Association, 1993-1995. *Member:* Los Angeles County Bar Association (Member: Sections on: Commercial Law and Bankruptcy; Real Property; Litigation; Lawyer Referral and Information Service Advisory Committee, 1985—; Chair, 1989-1991); State Bar of California. **PRACTICE AREAS:** Litigation; Torts; Business Law; Real Property; Entertainment Law.

### ASSOCIATES

**WAYNE T. KASAI,** born Los Angeles, California, November 22, 1955; admitted to bar, 1989, California and U.S. Court of Appeals, Ninth Circuit; 1992, U.S. District Court, Central District of California. *Education:* University of Southern California (B.S., cum laude, 1977); University of California at Davis (J.D., 1989). *Member:* Los Angeles County Bar Association; State Bar of California (Member, Estate Planning, Trust and Probate Section). **PRACTICE AREAS:** Litigation; Business Law; Real Property; Probate; Trusts; Estate Planning.

REFERENCE: Wells Fargo Bank.

## HOOD, WETZLER & REED
### LOS ANGELES, CALIFORNIA
(See Huntington Beach)

*Civil Practice and Appellate practice including Real Property, Financial Institutions, Banking, Mortgage Lending, Title Insurance, Insurance Defense and Coverage, Transactional Matters, Commercial Litigation, Creditors' Rights, Bankruptcy, General Corporate, Probate.*

---

## HOOPER, LUNDY & BOOKMAN, INC.
Established in 1987
**WATT PLAZA, SUITE 1600
1875 CENTURY PARK EAST
LOS ANGELES, CALIFORNIA 90067-2517**
Telephone: 310-551-8111
Telecopier: 310-551-8181

*Healthcare and Hospital Law (General Business Matters, Joint Ventures, Managed Care, Health Care Financing, Third-Party Payment Programs, Medical Staff, Licensing and Certification Issues, Administrative Law and Regulatory Litigation).*

**ROBERT W. LUNDY, JR.,** born San Mateo, California, August 12, 1950; admitted to bar, 1975, California. *Education:* Yale University (B.A., cum laude, with high honors, 1972); University of California at Los Angeles (J.D., 1975). Recipient, Distinguished Advocate Award. *Member:* Los Angeles County Bar Association (Vice Chairperson, Health Law Section, 1980-1981; Chairperson, 1981-1982); The State Bar of California; California Society for Healthcare Attorneys (Member, Board of Directors, 1995—); National Health Lawyers Association. *PRACTICE AREAS:* Healthcare Law; Hospital Law.

**PATRIC HOOPER,** born Altoona, Pennsylvania, December 22, 1948; admitted to bar, 1973, California; U.S. Supreme Court; U.S. Court of Appeals, 5th, 6th, 7th, 8th, 9th, 10th and Federal Circuits. *Education:* University of California at Los Angeles (A.B., 1970); University of San Diego (J.D., 1973). Deputy Attorney General, 1974-1976. *Member:* Los Angeles County and American Bar Associations; The State Bar of California; National Health Lawyers Association; National Association of Private Psychiatric Hospitals; Healthcare Financial Management Association; American Academy of Healthcare Attorneys. *PRACTICE AREAS:* Healthcare Law; Hospital Law.

**LLOYD A. BOOKMAN,** born Amityville, New York, March 8, 1954; admitted to bar, 1979, California. *Education:* University of California at Los Angeles (B.S., cum laude, 1976; J.D., 1979). Member, The Order of the Coif. *Member:* Los Angeles County Bar Association; State Bar of California; Healthcare Financial Management Association. *PRACTICE AREAS:* Healthcare Law; Hospital Law.

**W. BRADLEY TULLY,** born Lexington, Kentucky, September 12, 1957; admitted to bar, 1982, California. *Education:* University of California at Irvine (B.S., 1979; B.A., cum laude, 1979); University of California School of Law at Los Angeles (J.D., 1982). Member, UCLA Law Review, 1980-1982. Judicial Extern Clerk to Mathew O. Tobriner, California State Supreme Court, 1981. *Member:* Los Angeles County Bar Association (Member, Health Law Section, Executive Committee, Treasurer, 1988-1989; Secretary, 1989-1990); State Bar of California. *PRACTICE AREAS:* Healthcare Law; Hospital Law.

**JOHN R. HELLOW,** born Grosse Pointe City, Michigan, January 2, 1956; admitted to bar, 1982, California. *Education:* Oakland University (B.A., 1977); St. Louis University (M.H.A., 1981; J.D., cum laude, 1981). Editor, St. Louis University Health Law Review, 1979-1980. *Member:* State Bar of California; American Bar Association; National Health Lawyers Association; Hospital Financial Management Association. *SPECIAL AGENCIES:* Provider Reimbursement Review Board; Health Care Financing Administration; California Department of Health Services, Office of Administrative Appeals. *PRACTICE AREAS:* Healthcare Government Payment Disputes; Administrative Litigation; Government Contract Disputes; Federal Block Grant Funding.

**ANGELA A. MICKELSON,** born Chico, California, August 9, 1953; admitted to bar, 1981, California. *Education:* University of California at Los Angeles (B.A., cum laude, 1976; J.D., 1981). *Member:* Century City, Los Angeles County and American Bar Associations; State Bar of California; Group Health Association of America; National Health Lawyers Association; Women in Health Administration; California Association of Health Maintenance Organizations. *PRACTICE AREAS:* Hospital Law; Healthcare Law.

**LAURENCE D. GETZOFF,** born Los Angeles, California, January 20, 1957; admitted to bar, 1982, California. *Education:* Stanford University (A.B., with honors, 1978); George Washington University (J.D., 1982). *Member:* Los Angeles County Bar Association; California Society of Health Care Attorneys; National Health Lawyers Association. *SPECIAL AGENCIES:* Medical Board of California; Provider Reimbursement Review Board; California Department of Health Services - Office of Administrative Appeals. *REPORTED CASES:* Mir vs. Little Company of Mary Hospital; Silverman vs. St. Rose Hospital. *PRACTICE AREAS:* Health Care Law (General); Medical Staff Relations Law; Reimbursement Law.

**JAY N. HARTZ,** born Pittsburgh, Pennsylvania, February 21, 1948; admitted to bar, 1973, California. *Education:* Duke University (B.A., 1970); University of Chicago (J.D., 1973). *Member:* Los Angeles County Bar Association (Co-Chair, Joint Committee on Bioethics, Los Angeles County Medical Association, 1986-1989); State Bar of California; American Society of Law and Medicine; Society for Bioethics Consultation; International Bioethics Institute. *SPECIAL AGENCIES:* Medical Board of California; California State Department of Health Services. *PRACTICE AREAS:* Commercial Litigation; Health and Hospital Law; Bioethics Law.

**BYRON J. GROSS,** born Philadelphia, Pennsylvania, November 13, 1948; admitted to bar, 1977, California. *Education:* Yale University (B.A., 1970); Boalt Hall School of Law, University of California (J.D., 1977). *Member:* State Bar of California. *PRACTICE AREAS:* Health Care Law.

**DAVID P. HENNINGER,** born Williamsport, Pennsylvania, November 18, 1950; admitted to bar, 1983, Maryland; 1991, California. *Education:* Bucknell University (B.A., 1972); University of Maryland (M.A., 1977); George Washington University (J.D., with honors, 1983). Phi Kappa Phi. Health Law Instructor, California State University at Northridge, 1990—. *Member:* Maryland State Bar Association; State Bar of California; National Health Lawyers Association. *PRACTICE AREAS:* Health Care Law.

**TODD E. SWANSON,** born Minneapolis, Minnesota, November 7, 1958; admitted to bar, 1985, California. *Education:* University of Minnesota (B.A., Chem, 1982); University of Southern California (J.D., 1985). Phi Alpha Delta. Author: "Legal Considerations Related to the Purchase of An Accounting Practice," Chapter, course book for California Society of Certified Public Accountants, 1989. *Member:* Los Angeles County (Member, Sections on: Health Care Law and Business Law) and American Bar Associations; State Bar of California. *PRACTICE AREAS:* Health Care Law; Hospital Law.

---

**GINA REESE,** born Dodge City, Kansas, November 11, 1955; admitted to bar, 1992, California. *Education:* California State University, Los Angeles (B.A., magna cum laude, 1984); Whittier College School of Law (J.D., magna cum laude, 1991). Registered Nurse, 1976—. Author: "The Drama of Third-Party Payor Tort Liability for Cost Containment Decisions: A Critical Review," 12 Whittier Law Rev 591, 1991. *Member:* National Health Law Association. *LANGUAGES:* Spanish. *PRACTICE AREAS:* Health Care Law.

**JONATHAN P. NEUSTADTER,** born Bethpage, New York, February 2, 1969; admitted to bar, 1994, California. *Education:* University of Virginia (B.A., 1991); London School of Economics; University of California at Los Angeles (J.D., 1994). Recipient, American Jurisprudence Award for Constitutional Criminal Procedure. Judicial Extern to Richard A. Gadbois, U.S. District Court, Central District of California. *Member:* Los Angeles County Bar Association; State Bar of California. *PRACTICE AREAS:* Health Care Law.

**KENNETH J. CARL,** born Chicago, Illinois, 1960; admitted to bar, 1985, Illinois; 1986, California. *Education:* University of Chicago (A.B., with honors, 1982; A.M., 1982); Harvard University (J.D., 1985). Phi Beta Kappa. *PRACTICE AREAS:* Corporate Law; Healthcare.

**JULIA SCHOLLENBERGER,** born California, May 19, 1957; admitted to bar, 1987, California. *Education:* California State University at Northridge (B.A., 1979; M.A., 1981); University of California at Los Angeles (J.D., 1986). Licensed Speech Pathologist, California, 1982. *Member:* State Bar of California. *PRACTICE AREAS:* Health Care Law.

**THOMAS B. CROKE IV,** born Santa Barbara, California, December 8, 1965; admitted to bar, 1991, California. *Education:* University of California at San Diego (B.A., 1988); University of Southern California (J.D., 1991).

*(This Listing Continued)*

*Member:* State Bar of California; American Bar Association. *PRACTICE AREAS:* Commercial Litigation; Products Liability.

**MICHELE MELDEN,** born Omaha, Nebraska, December 15, 1960; admitted to bar, 1988, New York; 1989, California. *Education:* Wellesley College (B.A., 1984); Harvard University (J.D., cum laude, 1988). Phi Beta Kappa. *Member:* State Bar of California. *PRACTICE AREAS:* Health Care Law.

**MARK JEFFRY DICKS,** born Fort Belvoir, Virginia, June 20, 1956; admitted to bar, 1986, California. *Education:* University of Missouri (B.A., cum laude, 1978); University of California at Santa Cruz (M.A., 1980; Ph.D., 1985); University of California at Los Angeles (J.D., 1986). Phi Beta Kappa. *Member:* Los Angeles County Bar Association; State Bar of California. *LANGUAGES:* French. *PRACTICE AREAS:* Health Care; Business Law.

**SALVATORE A. ZOIDA,** born Brooklyn, New York, May 25, 1966; admitted to bar, 1992, California. *Education:* Columbia University (B.A., magna cum laude, Shapiro Scholar, 1988); Georgetown University Law Center (J.D., 1991). Member, International Environmental Law Journal. *Member:* State Bar of California. *LANGUAGES:* Italian. *PRACTICE AREAS:* Health Care Litigation.

**KEVIN A. CORBETT,** born Potsdam, New York, July 8, 1969; admitted to bar, 1995, California. *Education:* University of Pennsylvania (B.A., 1991); Tulane University of Louisiana (J.D., 1995). *PRACTICE AREAS:* Health Care Law; Corporation Law.

**BETTY J. LEVINE,** born Newark, New Jersey, March 27, 1947; admitted to bar, 1982, California and U.S. District Court, Central District of California. *Education:* University of California at Los Angeles (B.A., magna cum laude, 1979); Loyola Marymount University (J.D., 1982). Pi Gamma Mu. Dean's List, UCLA, 1976-1979; Dean's List, Loyola University Law School, 1981, 1982. Member, Loyola University Law Review, 1981-1982. *Member:* Los Angeles County and American Bar Associations; State Bar of California; Los Angeles Trial Lawyers Association. *PRACTICE AREAS:* Health Care; Litigation.

**WILLIAM A. LARKIN,** born Exeter, New Hampshire, December 3, 1964; admitted to bar, 1991, California. *Education:* Dartmouth College (B.A., 1987); University of California, Los Angeles (J.D., 1991); Loyola University of Chicago School of Law, Institute for Health Law (L.LM ,in health Law, 1996). *LANGUAGES:* French.

REPRESENTATIVE CLIENTS: Tenet Healthcare Corp.; Kaiser Foundation Health Plan; City of Hope National Medical Center; Columbia/HCA; Physicians and Surgeons Laboratories, Inc.; Rothman Chafetz Medical Group; Community Psychiatric Centers; Beach Cities Health District; Vista Health Plans.
REFERENCE: City National Bank.

---

## HORGAN, ROSEN, BECKHAM & COREN

A Partnership including Professional Corporations
21700 OXNARD STREET, SUITE 1400 (WOODLAND HILLS)
**LOS ANGELES, CALIFORNIA 91365-4335**
Telephone: 818-340-6100; 310-552-2010; 619-295-3160
Fax: 818-340-6190

Administrative, Banking, Bankruptcy, Civil and Commercial Litigation in all State and Federal Courts. Corporate, Corporate Securities and Finance. Creditors' Rights, Labor, Real Estate and Secured Transactions.

FIRM PROFILE: *The firm specializes in representing financial institutions, businesses and individuals in a wide range of regulatory, commercial and civil contexts, relying on the high level of expertise of its attorneys and an emphasis on personalized service.*

### MEMBERS OF FIRM

**S. ALAN ROSEN, (A PROFESSIONAL CORPORATION),** born Los Angeles, California, May 7, 1948; admitted to bar, 1974, California. *Education:* University of California at Los Angeles (B.A., summa cum laude, 1970; J.D., 1974). Phi Beta Kappa; Pi Gamma Mu; Omicron Delta Epsilon; Order of the Coif. Staff Member, 1972-1973 and Associate Editor, UCLA Law Review, 1973-1974. Author: "Corporate Tax Deductions for Non-Business Assets: A Proposal," 21 UCLA Law Review 1611, 1974. Law Clerk to Chief Justice Donald Wright, California Supreme Court, 1974-1975. *Member:* Los Angeles County and San Diego County Bar Associations; State Bar of California. *PRACTICE AREAS:* Administration; Banking; Corporate; Corporate Securities and Finance.

*(This Listing Continued)*

**ROBERT P. BECKHAM,** born Los Angeles, California, March 7, 1948; admitted to bar, 1973, California. *Education:* University of California at Santa Barbara (B.A., 1970); University of San Francisco (J.D., 1973). *Member:* State Bar of California (Member, Litigation and Labor Sections). *PRACTICE AREAS:* Commercial Litigation; Employee Relations.

**ARTHUR A. COREN,** born Philadelphia, Pennsylvania, March 5, 1955; admitted to bar, 1979, Pennsylvania; 1980, California. *Education:* Temple University (B.A., summa cum laude, 1976); Temple University School of Law (J.D., 1979). Phi Beta Kappa; Tau Epsilon Rho. Presidential Scholar. Law Clerk to Chief Justice Robert N.C. Nix, Jr., Supreme Court of the Commonwealth of Pennsylvania, 1979-1980. *Member:* Pennsylvania and American Bar Associations; State Bar of California. *PRACTICE AREAS:* Banking; Corporate and Corporate Securities.

**GARY M. HORGAN,** born San Francisco, California, December 22, 1947; admitted to bar, 1974, California. *Education:* University of Santa Clara (B.A., 1970); University of California at Los Angeles (J.D., 1974). California Bankers Association panelist, "Equal Credit Opportunity Act and Regulation B," 1976. Extension Faculty, University of California at Los Angeles, Graduate School of Management, "Consumer Law and Banking," 1978-1984. *Member:* The State Bar of California. *PRACTICE AREAS:* Administrative; Banking; Finance; Secured Transactions; Corporate.

**ALAN M. MIRMAN,** born Riverside, California, March 10, 1951; admitted to bar, 1975, California. *Education:* University of California at Los Angeles (B.A., 1972; J.D., 1975). Chief Justice, Moot Court. Contributing Editor, "Provisional Remedies", Matthew Bender California Practice Handbook (1993). Panelist: Pre-Judgment Remedies, 1988; Enforcing Judgments and Debts, Rutter Group, 1989; Attachment, Execution and Other Creditor Remedies-Impact of Bankruptcy, Rutter Group, 1991; Remedies During a Recession, Los Angeles County Bar Association, 1993; Member, 1993-1996, Secretary, 1994-1995, Board of Directors, UCLA Law Alumni Association. *Member:* Los Angeles County Bar Association (Chair, Executive Committee, Pre-Judgment Remedies Section, 1990-1991; Delegate, Conference of Delegates, 1991); State Bar of California (Member: Debtor/Creditor Relations and Bankruptcy Committee, 1983-1986 and 1987-1990); California Receivers Forum (Board of Directors); Financial Lawyers Conference; Association of Business Trial Lawyers. *PRACTICE AREAS:* Business, Banking and Real Property Litigation; Secured Transactions; Bankruptcy.

**MEL ARANOFF, (P.C.),** born Shenandoah, Pennsylvania, June 11, 1950; admitted to bar, 1975, California; U.S. District Court, Northern, Central, Southern and Eastern Districts of California. *Education:* Yeshiva University; University of California at Los Angeles (B.A., cum laude, 1972; J.D., 1975). Author: "Involuntary Bankruptcy: A Default Remedy for Lessors," Vol. 14, No. 5, WAEL Newsline, 1988; "Insolvency Amendment to Ex Parte Issuance of Writs of Attachment," Vol. 5, No. 1 and "Recent Case Developments," Vol. 5, No. 2, LACBA Prejudgment Remedies Section Newsletter, 1989; "How Much is Too Much? or Lender Liability for Overattachment," Vol. 8, No. 2, LACBA Provisional & Post-Judgment Remedies Section Newsletter, 1992. Co-Author: with Thomas E. McCurnin, "Claim and Delivery of Leased Equipment," WAEL Newsline, August 1992. Consultant: Bancroft-Whitney's California Civil Practice, "Business Litigation," 1993. Lecturer, Los Angeles County Bar Association's 1993 Continuing Legal Education Convention and Trade Show, "Remedies During a Recession, Attachment, Injunctions, Receiverships & the New Lis Pendens Law." *Member:* Los Angeles County (Member, Provisional and Post-Judgment Remedies Executive Committee and Chair, 1995-1996) and American Bar Associations; State Bar of California; Western Association of Equipment Lessors (Member, Legal Committee). *LANGUAGES:* Hebrew. *PRACTICE AREAS:* Complex Commercial Litigation; Bankruptcy; Creditors' Rights; Real Estate Receiverships; Loan Work-Outs; Equipment Leasing.

**MICHAEL E. BUBMAN,** born Los Angeles, California, November 6, 1962; admitted to bar, 1989, California and U.S. District Court, Central, Northern, Eastern and Southern Districts of California. *Education:* University of California at Berkeley (B.A., 1984); Loyola Law School (J.D., 1988). Member, Loyola Law School National Moot Court Honors Team. Extern to Judge Stephen A. Reinhardt, Circuit Judge of the Ninth Circuit Court of Appeals, 1988. *Member:* Los Angeles County Bar Association; State Bar of California. *PRACTICE AREAS:* Business; Banking; Real Property Litigation.

**GILLIAN E. FRIEDMAN,** born Palo Alto, California, May 31, 1967; admitted to bar, 1993, California, U.S. District Court, Central District of California; 1994, U.S. District Court, Eastern and Northern Districts of California. *Education:* University of California at Irvine (B.A., 1989);

*(This Listing Continued)*

**HORGAN, ROSEN, BECKHAM & COREN,** Los Angeles—Continued

Southwestern University School of Law (J.D., 1993). Member, Barristers, Commercial Law and Bankruptcy Forum, 1993—. Financial Lawyers Conference, Bankruptcy Forum, 1993—. *PRACTICE AREAS:* Business Law; Commercial Litigation; Bankruptcy.

## *GERSON S. HORN*
*11835 WEST OLYMPIC BOULEVARD, SUITE 1235*
*LOS ANGELES, CALIFORNIA 90064*
*Telephone: 310-231-3419*
*Fax: 310-231-3422*

*Federal and State Criminal Law.*

**GERSON S. HORN,** born Chicago, Illinois, December 9, 1939; admitted to bar, 1967, California. *Education:* California State University, Los Angeles (B.A., 1964); University of California at Los Angeles (J.D., 1967). Recipient: President's Award, 1994; CACJ, for outstanding contribution to the protection of constitutional rights and civil liberties; Los Angeles County Criminal Court's Bar Association Lifetime Achievement Award, 1996. Co-Founder, California Attorneys for Criminal Justice. *Member:* State Bar of California; National Association of Criminal Defense Lawyers; California Attorneys for Criminal Justice; Los Angeles County Criminal Bar Association. (Certified Specialist, Criminal Law, The State Bar of California Board of Legal Specialization). *REPORTED CASES:* Avital v. Superior Ct. 1114 Cal App. 3rd 297; IN RE: Letters Rogatory From the Tokyo District Prosecutor's Office 16 Fed. 3 1016; Tomlin v. Myers 30 Fed.3rd 1235; U.S. v. Isgrow 974 Fed.2d 1091; U.S. v. $277,000 and One 1986 Dodge Ram Charger 69 Fed.3d 1491. *PRACTICE AREAS:* Criminal Law.

## *HORNBERGER & CRISWELL*
*444 SOUTH FLOWER, 31ST FLOOR*
*LOS ANGELES, CALIFORNIA 90071*
*Telephone: 213-488-1655*
*Facsimile: 213-488-1255*
*Email: kbranch0@counsel.com*

*General Civil Trial, Litigation and Appellate Practice in State and Federal Courts, Negligence, Products Liability, Labor and Employment, Insurance Coverage and Bad Faith, Construction Defect, Premises Liability, Commercial, and Environmental Law, Inverse Condemnation, Eminent Domain.*

*FIRM PROFILE:* Hornberger & Criswell's civil litigation and trial practice includes general liability, insurance defense, construction and environmental services, with an emphasis on complex cases and trial work in the California federal and state courts. Our national and local clients include insurance carriers, brokers and agents; contractors and developers; large and small retailers; motor carriers; petroleum operators; elevator and escalator manufacturers and chemical, manufacturing and other corporations.

*We are well staffed and experienced in cases such as construction defect, construction contract disputes, medical and dental malpractice, intellectual property, premises and products liability, employment termination, motor carrier and auto accident litigation, insurance bad faith and coverage, special investigations litigation, inverse condemnation, eminent domain and environmental law services including pollution and toxic torts litigation.*

*Hornberger & Criswell was founded in 1991, upon the dissolution of Shield & Smith. All the partners and most of the associates of Hornberger & Criswell worked together in the same specialized areas of law, for many of the same clients, at the predecessor firm.*

### *MEMBERS OF FIRM*

**NICHOLAS W. HORNBERGER,** born Berkeley, California, January 20, 1946; admitted to bar, 1972, California. *Education:* University of California at Berkeley (B.S., Chemistry, 1968); University of San Francisco (J.D., 1972). Member, McAuliffe Law Honor Society. Member, University of San Francisco Law Review, 1970-1972. *Member:* Los Angeles County and American Bar Associations; State Bar of California; Association of Southern California Defense Counsel; American Board of Trial Advocates; Federation of Insurance and Corporate Counsel; Products Liability Advisory Council. *PRACTICE AREAS:* Insurance Bad Faith; Eminent Domain; Environmental; Employment Termination; Products Liability; Commercial Litigation.

*(This Listing Continued)*

**LESLIE E. CRISWELL,** born Denver, Colorado, August 29, 1950; admitted to bar, 1980, California. *Education:* University of California at Santa Barbara (B.A., 1972); Southwestern University (J.D., 1980). *Member:* State Bar of California; American Bar Association; California Trial Lawyers Association (Member, Litigation Section); Women Lawyers Association of Los Angeles; Association of Southern California Defense Counsel; American Board of Trial Advocates. *PRACTICE AREAS:* Insurance Defense Law; Trial Practice; Products Liability Law; Premises Liability Law; Employment Discrimination.

**ANN M. GHAZARIANS,** born Boston, Massachusetts, September 9, 1960; admitted to bar, 1985, California and U.S. District Court, Central, Southern and Eastern Districts of California. *Education:* University of California at San Diego (B.A., 1982); Southwestern University (J.D., magna cum laude, 1985). Chief Production Editor, Southwestern University Law Review, 1983-1985. Author: Comment, "The Impact of Collateral Estoppel on Postjudgment Settlements," Southwestern University Law Review, Vol. 5:2 p343, 1985. *Member:* Los Angles County and American Bar Associations; State Bar of California; Federal Bar Association; Association of Southern California Defense Counsel; California Women Lawyers; Defense Research Institute. *REPORTED CASES:* A-Mark Finance v. Pacific Indemnity Corp. (1995) 34 Cal. App. 4th 1179. *PRACTICE AREAS:* General Liability; Civil Litigation; Bad Faith; Insurance Coverage; Broker-Agent Liability; Commercial Business Litigation; Insurance Defense; Trial Practice; Insurance Fraud.

**MICHAEL A. BREWER,** born Fullerton, California, June 13, 1957; admitted to bar, 1985, California. *Education:* California State University at Fullerton (B.A., 1982); Whittier Law School (J.D., cum laude, 1985. Los Angeles Superior Court Arbitrator. *Member:* Beverly Hills and Los Angeles County Bar Associations; State Bar of California; Association of Southern California Defense Counsel. *PRACTICE AREAS:* Products Liability; Personal Injury; Construction Defect; Premises Liability; Trial Practice.

**SCOTT ALAN FREEDMAN,** born Lancaster, Pennsylvania, August 11, 1961; admitted to bar, 1987, California and U.S. District Court, Central District of California. *Education:* Georgetown University (B.A., 1983); Pepperdine University (J.D., 1986). Pi Sigma Alpha. Member, Moot Court Board. *Member:* Los Angeles County Bar Association; State Bar of California; American Board of Trial Advocates. *PRACTICE AREAS:* Civil Litigation; Employment Law; Products Liability; Premises Liability; Negligence; Insurance Defense.

### *ASSOCIATES*

**MARLIN E. HOWES,** born Inglewood, California, July 31, 1958; admitted to bar, 1988, California. *Education:* Calvin College; California State University at Fullerton (B.A., 1985); University of San Diego (J.D., 1988). *Member:* State Bar of California. *PRACTICE AREAS:* Insurance Fraud; Environmental Law; Toxic Tort Law; Products Liability; Premises Liability.

**CHRISTOPHER T. OLSEN,** born Los Angeles, California, April 1, 1964; admitted to bar, 1989, California; U.S. Supreme Court; U.S. District Court, Central District of California; U.S. Claims Court. *Education:* Elon College (B.A., cum laude, 1986); Pepperdine University School of Law (J.D., cum laude, 1989). Omicron Delta Kappa. Best Oral Advocate, ABA's National Appellate Advocacy Competition. Member, Pepperdine University Law Review, 1987-1989. Co-Chairman, Honor Board. Vice Chairman, Moot Court Board. *Member:* State Bar of California. *PRACTICE AREAS:* Civil Litigation; Construction Defect; Commercial Law; Personal Injury; Premises Liability.

**SCOTT B. CLOUD,** born Appleton, Wisconsin, March 12, 1963; admitted to bar, 1989, California and U.S. District Court, Central District of California. *Education:* Pepperdine University (B.A., 1985; J.D., 1989). Finalist, ABA National Moot Court Competition. Vice-Chairman, Moot Court Honor Board, 1989. *Member:* Los Angeles County and American Bar Associations; State Bar of California; Association of Southern California Defense Counsel. *PRACTICE AREAS:* Products Liability; Premises Liability; Commercial Disputes; Construction Defect.

**JAMES M. SLOMINSKI,** born Buffalo, New York, October 20, 1960; admitted to bar, 1993, California and Florida; 1994, Massachusetts and U.S. District Court, Central District of California; 1995, U.S. Patent and Trademark Office. *Education:* University of Nebraska (B.S.C.E., 1982); San Diego State University (M.S.A.E., 1990); Arizona State University (J.D., 1992). *PRACTICE AREAS:* Intellectual Property; General Civil Litigation; Products Liability; Construction Defect; Negligence; Premises Liability; Eminent Domain.

*(This Listing Continued)*

# PROFESSIONAL BIOGRAPHIES

# CALIFORNIA—LOS ANGELES

**MICHAEL C. DENLINGER,** born Lancaster, Pennsylvania, September 6, 1956; admitted to bar, 1987, California. *Education:* Biola College (B.A., magna cum laude, 1979); Southwestern University (J.D., 1987). *Member:* State Bar of California; American Bar Association.

**GAYLE L. ESKRIDGE,** born Leavenworth, Kansas, November 11, 1959; admitted to bar, 1988, California. *Education:* University of Missouri at Kansas City (B.A., 1982); National University (J.D., 1988). Recipient, F. Lee Bailey Moot Court Award. *Member:* Los Angeles County (Member, State Courts Committee), San Diego County (Editor, Dicta, 1990-1993; Chair, Civil Litigation Section, 1990-1992) and American Bar Associations; State Bar of California.

## OF COUNSEL

**DAVID E. BOWER,** born Lockport, New York, October 8, 1951; admitted to bar, 1982, New York and U.S. District Court, Western District of New York; 1985, California, U.S. District Court, Central District of California and U.S. Court of Appeals, Ninth Circuit. *Education:* State University of New York at Buffalo (B.A., 1978); Southwestern University (J.D., 1981). *Member:* Los Angeles County Bar Association; State Bar of California (Member, Business Law Section); Associated Builders and Contractors. **PRACTICE AREAS:** Business Law; Litigation; Commercial Law; Construction Law.

**WILLIAM P. DRISCOLL,** born Altadena, California, 1951; admitted to bar, 1978, California, U.S. District Court, Central District of California and U.S. Court of Appeals, Ninth Circuit; 1980, U.S. District Court, Eastern District of California. *Education:* University of Southern California (B.S., 1974); Southwestern University (J.D., 1977). Assistant District Attorney, Tulare County, California, 1979-1981. Associate Professor, Criminal Justice Department, College of the Sequoias, Visalia, California, 1980-1981. *Member:* State Bar of California. (Also Member of Driscoll & Driscoll, Pasadena). **PRACTICE AREAS:** Eminent Domain; Municipal Law; Government; Real Estate.

REPRESENTATIVE CLIENTS: Johnson Controls; Pacific Theatres, Inc.; Metropolitan Theatres; Sanwa Bank; Black Equities; Norm's Restaurant; Lawry's Restaurant; Forest City Enterprises; U.S. Elevator; United Technologies; Travelers Insurance; Tipton & Co.; Sinclair Paint Co.; Otis Elevator Co.; The May Department Stores Co.; Orion Group; Loctite Corp.; Keller Construction Co., Ltd.; J.C. Penney Co., Inc.; Illinois Tool Works; Insilco Corp.; Home Depot; Home Base; Great Western Bank; General Elevator Co.; Rotary Lift; Customized Transportation, Inc.; Hemco Industries; MSA International; I.S.S.; Geo. M. Martin Co.; Fireman's Fund Insurance Co.; Dover Elevator; City of Newport Beach; County of Orange; City of Costa Mesa; CIGNA; Chubb Group of Insurance Companies; CenterMark Properties; Brent Chemical; Best Buy Co., Inc.; Automobile Club of Southern California.

## *EDWARD J. HOROWITZ*

*A PROFESSIONAL CORPORATION*

Established in 1978

SUITE 1015, 11661 SAN VICENTE BOULEVARD
**LOS ANGELES, CALIFORNIA 90049**
Telephone: 310-826-6619
Fax: 310-826-8242
Email: Horowitz@appellatelaw.com

Appellate Practice, Civil and Criminal.

FIRM PROFILE: Sole practice, emphasizing major civil and criminal appeals in state and federal courts, generally in association with referring firms. Mr. Horowitz has been lead counsel on over 380 appellate cases, including approximately 60 reported state and federal decisions.

**EDWARD J. HOROWITZ,** born Milwaukee, Wisconsin, February 13, 1942; admitted to bar, 1967, California; 1971, U.S. Supreme Court. *Education:* University of California at Los Angeles (A.B., summa cum laude, 1963); Harvard University (J.D., 1966). Phi Beta Kappa. Pi Sigma Alpha. Author: "Appellate Practice Handbook," Butterworth, 1982; "Excluding the Exclusionary Rule— Can There Be An Effective Alternative?", 47 Los Angeles Bar Journal 91, 1972; "Practitioner's Guide to California Habeas Corpus," 8 Journal of Beverly Hills Bar Association, No. 3, pg. 10, 1974; "Reflections on Gun Control," 52 Los Angeles Bar Journal 208, 1976; "The Proposed Panel to Resolve Intercircuit Conflicts: A Brief View From the Litigants Perspective," Hastings Constitutional Law Quarterly, Vol. 11, No. 3, Spring, 1984. Co-Author: "Protecting the Record on Appeal," 13 Los Angeles Lawyer, No. 6 p. 40, August-September 1990. Professor of Evidence, University of San Fernando Valley School of Law, 1967-1970. Senior Attorney, California Court of Appeal, Second Appellate District, 1972-1976. Mediator, California Court of Appeal Settlement Panel, 1989—.

*(This Listing Continued)*

Hearing Officer, Southern California Psychiatric Society, 1990—. Member, Panel of Arbitrators and Panel of Mediators, American Arbitration Association, 1980-1994. *Member:* Los Angeles County Bar Association (Chair, Appellate Courts Committee, 1981-1982); State Bar of California; California Academy of Appellate Lawyers (President, 1982-1983); Criminal Courts Bar Association (Member, Board of Directors, 1977-1987; President, 1987; Chief Justice's Committee to Evaluate the California Appellate Projects, 1992-1993); California Appellate Indigent Defense Oversight Advisory Committee (Member, 1994-1995). (Certified Specialist, Appellate Law, The State Bar of California Board of Legal Specialization).

REFERENCE: Union Bank (Brentwood Branch).

## *HORVITZ & LEVY*

A Partnership including Professional Corporations

Established in 1973

18TH FLOOR, 15760 VENTURA BOULEVARD (ENCINO)
**LOS ANGELES, CALIFORNIA 91436**
Telephone: 818-995-0800; 213-872-0802
FAX: 818-995-3157

*All Civil Appeals and Related Appellate Practice, including Trial Consultations, with Emphasis in the Areas of Business Law, Commercial Law, Contracts, Health Care, Hospitals, Insurance and Insurance Defense (including Coverage and Bad Faith), Legal Ethics and Professional Responsibility, Legal and Medical Malpractice, Negligence, Personal Injury, Products Liability, Professional Liability, and Torts.*

*FIRM PROFILE:* Started in 1957 by Ellis Horvitz, Horvitz & Levy is the largest firm in California specializing in civil appellate litigation. The firm appears regularly in the California and federal courts as lead counsel or amicus curiae on behalf of insurance carriers, the health care community, manufacturers and other business organizations, public entities, and business and professional trade associations. Since 1981, it has briefed at least 60 civil cases in the California Supreme Court as lead counsel or as amicus curiae, more than any other private law firm in California. The firm consults with clients and trial counsel in evaluating cases for appeal and in assisting trial counsel to present and preserve issues for appeal. The firm also provides its clients with analyses of new legislation, important court decisions and other matters affecting their interests.

*Representative cases in the California Supreme Court which Horvitz & Levy has briefed and argued as lead counsel or amicus curiae since 1981:* Arnett v. Dal Cielo (1996) Cal.4th; San Diego Gas & Electric Co. v. Superior Court (Covalt) (1996) 13 Cal.4th 893; Lisa M. v. Henry Mayo Newhall Memorial Hospital (1995) 12 Cal.4th 291; Freeman & Mills Incorporated v. Belcher Oil Company (1995) 11 Cal.4th 85; Waller v. Truck Insurance Exchange (1995) 11 Cal.4th 1; College Hospital, Inc. v. Superior Court (Crowell) (1994) 8 Cal.4th 704; Western Steamship Lines, Inc. v. San Pedro Peninsula Hospital (1994) 8 Cal.4th 100; Alexander v. Superior Court (Sheikh Saheb) 5 Cal.4th 1218; Arato v. Avedon (1993) 5 Cal.4th 1172; Horace Mann Ins. Co. v. Barbara B. (1993) 4 Cal.4th 1076; Bank of the West v. Superior Court (Industrial Indemnity Co.) 2 Cal.4th 1254; Laird v. Blacker (1992) 2 Cal.4th 606; State Farm Fire & Casualty Co. v. Von Der Lieth (1991) 54 Cal.3d 1123; Woods v. Young (1991) 53 Cal.3d 315; Gourley v. State Farm Mutual Auto. Ins. Co. (1991) 53 Cal.3d 121; J.C. Penney Casualty Ins. Co. v. M.K. (1991) 52 Cal.3d 1009; Moore v. Regents of University of California (1990) 51 Cal.3d 120; California Assn. of Psychology Providers v. Rank (1990) 51 Cal.3d 1; Phillips v. Desert Hospital District (1989) 49 Cal.3d 699; Thing v. La Chusa (1989) 48 Cal.3d 644; Garvey v. State Farm Fire & Casualty Co. (1989) 48 Cal.3d 395; Keller v. State Bar (1989) 47 Cal.3d 1152; Belair v. Riverside County Flood Control Dist. (1988) 47 Cal.3d 550; Moradi-Shalal v. Fireman's Fund Ins. Companies (1988) 46 Cal.3d 287; Shamblin v. Brattain (1988) 44 Cal.3d 474; Hernandez v. County of Los Angeles (1986) 42 Cal.3d 1020; West Covina Hospital v. Superior Court (Tyus) (1986) 41 Cal.3d 846; Coleman v. Gulf Ins. Group (1986) 41 Cal.3d 782; Waters v. Bourhis (1985) 40 Cal.3d 424; Leoni v. State Bar (1985) 39 Cal.3d 609; Mann v. Cracchiolo (1985) 38 Cal.3d 18; Garcia v. Truck Insurance Exchange (1984) 36 Cal.3d 426; Carson Mobilehome Park Owners' Assn. v. City of Carson (1983) 35 Cal.3d 184; Shepard & Morgan v. Lee & Daniel, Inc. (1982) 31 Cal.3d 256; Farmers Ins. Exchange v. Cocking (1981) 29 Cal.3d 383, as well as four cases upholding the constitutionality of the California Medical Injury Compensation Reform Act of 1975: Fein v. Permanente Medical Group (1985) 38 Cal.3d 137; Barme v. Wood (1984) 37 Cal.3d 174; Roa v. Lodi Medical Group, Inc. (1985) 37 Cal.3d 920; and American Bank & Trust Co. v. Community Hospital (1984) 36 Cal.3d 359.

*(This Listing Continued)*

CAA783B

## HORVITZ & LEVY, Los Angeles—Continued

**ELLIS J. HORVITZ, (A P.C.),** born Cleveland, Ohio, April 27, 1928; admitted to bar, 1951, California; 1961, U.S. Court of Appeals, 9th Circuit; 1962, U.S. Supreme Court. *Education:* Western Reserve University; University of Chicago (A.B., 1947); Stanford University (B.A., 1949; J.D., 1951). Phi Alpha Delta. Member, Stanford Law Review, 1949-1951. Judicial Clerkship: Research Attorney to Chief Justice Phil S. Gibson, California Supreme Court, 1951-1953. Attorney (1953-1955) and Legal Counsel (1957-1962), U.S. Atomic Energy Commission. Lecturer in Law on Appellate Practice, University of Southern California, School of Law, 1961-1967 and 1974-1989. Co-Author: *California Practice Guide: Civil Appeals & Writs,* The Rutter Group (1989); "An Analysis of Recent Supreme Court Developments in Tort and Insurance Law: The Common Law Tradition," 26 Loy. L.A. L. Rev. 1145 (1993); "A Personal Note," (In Memorium of Chief Justice Phil S. Gibson) 72 Cal. L. Rev. 503 (1984); "Protecting Your Record on Appeal," 4 Litig. 34 (1978); "Justice Tobriner's Tort Decisions: A Reaffirmation of the Common Law Process," 29 Hastings L. J. 167 (1977); "Handling Defense Appeals in Light of Expanding Concepts of Liability," For the Defense, September (1975); "Respondent's Brief," California Civil Appellate Practice, Second Edition (Cont. Ed. Bar, 1985) §13 pp. 401-416; "Some Basics of Brief Writing," Efficient Appellate Practice (Cont. Ed. Bar, 1977); "Appeals and Writs in Family Law Cases," Los Angeles Superior Court Family Law Symposium, 1973-1978. Member: American Academy of Appellate Lawyers (Chairperson, Committee on Specialization, 1993), California Academy of Appellate Lawyers (Secretary, 1972-1974, Vice President, 1975-1976, and President, 1976-1977); California Judicial Council Appellate Standing Advisory Committee, 1996; Appellate Law Advisory Commission, Board of Legal Specialization of the State Bar of California, 1994—; Committee on Standard Civil Jury Instructions, The Los Angeles Superior Court, 1991—; California Judicial Council Advisory Committee for Proposition 32, 1984; California Judicial Council Advisory Committee for Implementation of Proposition 32, 1985; California Judicial Council Advisory Committee on Partial Publication of Appellate Opinions, 1980-1983; California Judicial Council Advisory Committee for an Effective Publication Rule, 1979-1980. *Member:* Beverly Hills, Los Angeles County, Federal and American (Member, Appellate Practice Committee; Tort and Insurance Practice Section; Subcommittee for Ninth Circuit, 1975-1977) Bar Associations; State Bar Committee for Legal Aid, 1963-1969; State Bar Committee on Appellate Courts, 1972-1976); Association of Southern California Defense Counsel; Federation of Insurance and Corporate Counsel.

**BARRY R. LEVY, (A P.C.),** born Brooklyn, New York, May 22, 1943; admitted to bar, 1972, California; 1979, U.S. Court of Appeals, Ninth Circuit; 1982, U.S. Supreme Court; 1988, U.S. Court of Appeals, Second Circuit. *Education:* Hunter College and California State University at Northridge (A.B., 1965); Loyola Marymount University Los Angeles, California (J.D., 1972). Teaching Fellow, Legal Writing, Loyola University of Los Angeles, 1970-1971. Adjunct Associate Professor, Whittier College School of Law, 1977. Deputy District Attorney, Los Angeles District Attorney's Office, 1972-1977. Member, Board of Governors, Loyola Law School Alumni Association, 1987-1989. *Member:* Los Angeles County, Federal and American (Member: Section of Tort and Insurance Practice; Appellate Advocacy Committee) Bar Associations; American Academy of Appellate Lawyers; California Academy of Appellate Lawyers (Secretary-Treasurer, 1994-1995; Second Vice-President, 1995-1996; First Vice-President, 1996-1997); Federation of Insurance and Corporate Counsel; Association of Southern California Defense Counsel; Conference of Insurance Counsel; American Judicature Society.

**PETER ABRAHAMS,** born York, England, January 9, 1945; admitted to bar, 1970, California; 1973, U.S. Supreme Court. *Education:* University of California at Los Angeles (B.A., 1966); Loyola Marymount University Los Angeles, California (J.D., 1969). Member, Loyola Law Review, 1968-1969. Judicial Clerkship: Associate Justice Clarke E. Stephens, California Court of Appeal, Second District, Division Five, 1969-1970. Author: Comment, 2 Loy. L.A. L. Rev. 105 (1969); "Dismissal," California Civil Procedure Before Trial, Volume 2, California Continuing Education of the Bar (1978); 1978-1985 supplements to California Civil Procedure Before Trial, Vol. One, California Continuing Education of the Bar. Co-author: "The General Verdict Rule: Appellate Trap or Opportunity?," 16 CEB Civ LR 93 (Mar. 1994). Lecturer: "Appellate Review Before Judgment," California Continuing Education of the Bar, 1982; "Recent Developments in Civil Procedure," California Continuing Education of the Bar, 1984; "Handling Civil Writs,"California Continuing Education of the Bar, 1985; "Recent Developments in Torts," California Continuing Education of the Bar, 1992-1996. *Member:* Los Angeles County Bar Association; American Academy of Appellate Lawyers; California Academy of Appellate Lawyers; Association of Southern California Defense Counsel (Member, Board of Directors, 1990-1991; Co-Chairman, Amicus Curiae Committee, 1988-1992). (Certified Specialist, Appellate Law, The State Bar of California Board of Legal Specialization).

**DAVID M. AXELRAD,** born Salt Lake City, Utah, March 5, 1950; admitted to bar, 1977, California and U.S. Court of Appeals, Ninth Circuit; 1983, U.S. Supreme Court; 1987, U.S. Court of Appeals, Tenth Circuit. *Education:* Stanford University (B.A., with distinction, 1972); Hastings College of Law, University of California (J.D., 1977). Member, 1975-1976 and Note and Comment Editor, 1976-1977, Hastings Law Journal. Adjunct Professor of Law, University of La Verne College of Law at San Fernando Valley, 1988-1990. Author: "Staying Enforcement During Appeal," Chapter 6, Civil Appellate Practice (Cont. Ed. Bar 1996); "Staying Power," Los Angeles Lawyer, Vol. 18, No. 8, p.33 (Nov. 1995). Member, Santa Clara County Advisory Commission on Consumer Affairs, 1976-1977. Staff Attorney: United States Court of Appeals, Ninth Circuit, 1977-1978; Federal Trade Commission, 1978-1980. Assistant to Director, Bureau of Consumer Protection, Federal Trade Commission, 1981. *Member:* Los Angeles County and American Bar Associations; California Academy of Appellate Lawyers; American Academy of Appellate Lawyers. (Certified Specialist, Appellate Law, The State Bar of California Board of Legal Specialization).

**FREDERIC D. COHEN,** born New York, N.Y., September 3, 1948; admitted to bar, 1973, California; 1975, U.S. Court of Appeals, District of Columbia Circuit and U.S. Court of Appeals, Fourth Circuit; 1977, U.S. Court of Appeals, Ninth Circuit; 1980, U.S. Supreme Court. *Education:* Harvey Mudd College (B.S., 1970); University of Southern California (J.D., 1973). Member, Southern California Law Review, 1972-1973. Judicial Clerkship: Justice Robert S. Thompson, California Court of Appeal, 1973-1974. Author: "Selecting the Proper Court," Chapter 4, California Civil Writ Practice (Cont. Ed. Bar 1996); "A Guideline for Equalizing Investment Opportunity: Avoiding the Pitfalls of Selective Disclosure," 46 S. Cal. L. Rev. 139 (1972). Attorney, United States Department of Justice, Civil Division, Appellate Section, 1974-1981. *Member:* Los Angeles County Bar Association (Member, Appellate Courts Committee, 1985—); California Academy of Appellate Lawyers. *LANGUAGES:* German.

**S. THOMAS TODD,** born Frankfurt, Germany, May 26, 1950; admitted to bar, 1975, California; 1979, U.S. Court of Appeals, Ninth Circuit; 1980, U.S. Supreme Court. *Education:* University of California at Irvine (B.A., magna cum laude, 1971); Stanford University (J.D., 1975). Order of the Coif. Member, Stanford Law Review, 1973-1975. Deputy and Assistant City Attorney, Los Angeles, 1975-1981. *Member:* Los Angeles County Bar Association; California Academy of Appellate Lawyers; California Medical-Legal Committee; Lawyers for Human Rights, The Lesbian and Gay Bar Association of Los Angeles.

**DAVID S. ETTINGER,** born New York, N.Y., February 10, 1956; admitted to bar, 1980, California; 1982, U.S. Court of Appeals, Ninth Circuit; 1987, U.S. Court of Appeals, Second Circuit; 1990, U.S. Supreme Court. *Education:* Franklin & Marshall College (B.A., honors in Government, 1977); Loyola Marymount University Los Angeles, California (J.D., cum laude, 1980). Member, St. Thomas More Law Honor Society. Recipient, 1993 Hall of Fame Award, The Harriet Buhai Center for Family Law. Member, Loyola Law Review, 1978-1979. Judicial Clerkship: Research Attorney to Presiding Justice Margaret J. Morris, California Court of Appeal, Fourth District, Division Two, 1980-1982. Author: "The History of School Desegregation in the Ninth Circuit," 12 Loy. L.A. L. Rev. 481 (1979); "Discovery Immunities for Hospital Staff Review Committees: Is There Protection for Information Submitted to, As Well as Documents Prepared by, the Committees?," Professional, Officers' and Directors' Liability Law Newsletter (ABA Tort and Insurance Practice Section), Fall 1992, at 17; "Are Applications for Staff Privileges Discoverable?," Medical Malpractice Law & Strategy, Oct. 1992, at 1; "Guarding Hospital Committee Members' Identities," Medical Malpractice Law & Strategy, March 1993, at 3. *Member:* Los Angeles County (Member: Appellate Courts Committee (Vice-Chair, 1993-1995; Chair, 1995—); Appellate Election Evaluation Committee, 1990—(Chair, 1994-1995); Conference of Delegates, 1986-1990), Ventura County and American Bar Associations; Women Lawyers Association of Los Angeles; California Academy of Appellate Lawyers.

**DANIEL J. GONZALEZ,** born Baltimore, Maryland, June 21, 1950; admitted to bar, 1977, California and U.S. Court of Appeals, Fourth Circuit; 1979, U.S. Court of Appeals, Ninth Circuit; 1990, U.S. Supreme Court. *Education:* Georgetown University (B.S., magna cum laude, 1973); Stanford University (J.D., 1976). Order of the Coif. Member, Stanford Law Review, 1975-1976. Judicial Clerkship: Hon. Joseph H. Young, U.S. District Judge, District of Maryland, 1976-1977. Author: "Open Season on

*(This Listing Continued)*

Containers in Cars," Los Angeles Lawyer, Vol. 6, No. 8 (1983). Deputy City Attorney, Los Angeles, 1977-1978. Assistant U.S. Attorney, Central District of California, 1979-1984. *Member:* American Bar Association.

**MITCHELL C. TILNER,** born Los Angeles, California, July 14, 1953; admitted to bar, 1980, California; 1987, U.S. Court of Appeals, Ninth Circuit; 1989, U.S. Supreme Court. *Education:* Stanford University; Yale University (B.A., 1975); Loyola Marymount University Los Angeles, California (J.D., magna cum laude, 1979); Columbia University (LL.M., 1985). Member, St. Thomas More Law Honor Society. Staff Member, 1977-1978 and Chief Ninth Circuit Editor, 1978-1979, Loyola Law Review. Recipient, American Jurisprudence Prizes in Criminal Procedure and Trusts & Wills. Judicial Clerkship: Hon. Arthur L. Alarcon, U.S. Court of Appeals, Ninth Circuit, 1987-1988. Author: "Ideological Exclusion of Aliens: The Evolution of a Policy," 2 Geo. Imm. L. J. 1 (1987); "Government Compulsion of Corporate Speech: Legitimate Regulation or First Amendment Violation?" 27 Santa Clara L. Rev. 485 (1987). Co-Author: "The Call of Duty," Los Angeles Lawyer, Vol. 18, No. 11, p.28 (Feb. 1996); "Insurance Coverage for Wilful Acts," Los Angeles Lawyer, Vol. 14, No. 6, p.43 (Sept. 1991). Visiting Professor of Law, 1987 and Adjunct Professor of Law, 1988-1990, Loyola Law School. Teaching Fellow, 1985-1987 and Lecturer in Law, 1986, National Law Center, George Washington University. *Member:* Los Angeles County (Member, Appellate Courts Committee), Federal and American (Member, Tort and Insurance Practice Section, Appellate Advocacy Committee) Bar Associations; California Academy of Appellate Lawyers; Scribes - The American Society of Writers on Legal Subjects.

**CHRISTINA J. IMRE,** born Gary, Indiana, October 25, 1950; admitted to bar, 1980, California; 1982, U.S. Court of Appeals, Ninth Circuit. *Education:* Mt. St. Mary's College (B.A., summa cum laude, 1972); University of Notre Dame (M.A., 1974); Loyola Marymount University Los Angeles, California (J.D., cum laude, 1980). Member, St. Thomas More Law Honor Society. Editor-in-Chief, Loyola of Los Angeles International and Comparative Law Journal, 1979-1980. Author: "The World of the Appellate Courts," "The Post - Trial Phase," Chapters 1 and 2, Civil Appellate Practice (Cont. Ed. Bar 1996); " Hiring Independent Counsel," The Recorder (June 20, 1988); "Punitive Damages After Bankers Life v. Crenshaw," For The Defense (Sept., 1988); "The Punitive Remedy: Statutory and Judicial Reforms," California Litigation (May, 1988); "The Battle Over The Right To Sue An Insurance Company," Los Angeles Daily Journal (Nov. 18, 1988); "Proposition 103 and Its Impact on California Insurance Law," Los Angeles Daily Journal (Dec. 16, 1988). Lecturer: Rutter Group "Bad Faith" Seminars, 1988; Defense Research Institute Insurance Coverage and Practice Seminars, 1988. Chair, Joint Advisory Committee, Continuing Education of the Bar, State Bar of California, 1996; Board of Governors, Continuing Education of the Bar. . *Member:* Los Angeles County and American (Member, Tort and Insurance Practice Section, Appellate Advisory Committee) Bar Associations; Association of Southern California Defense Counsel; Defense Research Institute (Member, Insurance Law Committee); Scribes - The American Society of Writers on Legal Subjects.

**LISA PERROCHET,** born Los Angeles, California, October 10, 1962; admitted to bar, 1987, California; 1993, U.S. Court of Appeals, Ninth Circuit. *Education:* University of California, Los Angeles (B.A., magna cum laude, 1984); Loyola Marymount University Los Angeles, California (J.D., cum laude, 1987). Phi Beta Kappa; Alpha Sigma Nu. Recipient, American Jurisprudence Awards in Property and Future Interests. Member, St. Thomas More Law Honor Society. Staff Writer, Loyola Law Review, 1985-1986. Editor, Entertainment Law Journal, 1986-1987. Author: "Writ Intake Procedures," Chapter 2, California Civil Writ Practice (Cont. Ed. Bar 1996). Co-Author: "Lost Chance Recovery and the Folly of Expanding Medical Malpractice Liability," 27 Tort & Ins. L.J. 615 (1992); "What a Difference a Day Makes: Age Presumptions and the Standard of Care Required of Minors," 24 Pac. L.J. 1323 (April 1993). *Member:* Los Angeles County and Federal Bar Associations. *Email:* LPerrochet@Counsel.Com

**STEPHEN E. NORRIS,** born Beardstown, Illinois, November 17, 1957; admitted to bar, 1982, California 1987, U .S. Court of Appeals, Second Circuit; 1988, U.S. Court of Appeals, Ninth Circuit. *Education:* Princeton University (A.B., cum laude, 1979); University of San Francisco (J.D., 1982). Recipient, American Jurisprudence Award, Security Interests in Personal Property. Member, University of San Francisco Law Review, 1981-1982. Judicial Clerkship: Hon. Joseph A. Rattigan, California Court of Appeal, 1983-1984.

**SANDRA J. SMITH,** born Omaha, Nebraska, March 16, 1959; admitted to bar, 1987, California; 1988, U.S. Court of Appeals, Ninth Circuit; 1993, U.S. Supreme Court. *Education:* Stanford University; Wesleyan University (B.A., 1981); University of California, Los Angeles (J.D., 1987).

*(This Listing Continued)*

Order of the Barristers. Member, UCLA National Moot Court Team (First Place, Western Regional Division). Best Brief Award and Roscoe Pound Finalist, UCLA Moot Court Honors Program. Executive Editor, Federal Communications Law Journal, 1986-1987. Judicial Clerkship: Hon. Harry Pregerson, U.S. Court of Appeals, Ninth Circuit, 1987-1988. Co-Author: "Lost Chance Recovery and the Folly of Expanding Medical Malpractice Liability," 27 Tort & In. L.J. 615 (1992). Author: "Responsive Pleadings," Chapter 7, California Civil Writ Practice (Cont. Ed. Bar 1996). Member, Joint Advisory Committee, Continuing Education of the Bar, State Bar of California. *Member:* Los Angeles County and American Bar Associations; Women Lawyers Association of Los Angeles.

**JOHN A. TAYLOR, JR.,** born Cincinnati, Ohio, May 13, 1958; admitted to bar, 1987, California and Utah; 1993, U.S. Court of Appeals, Ninth Circuit. *Education:* Brigham Young University (B.A., summa cum laude, 1982); Harvard University (J.D., magna cum laude, 1985). National Merit Scholar. Hinckley Scholar. Recipient, Phi Kappa Phi Graduate Fellowship. Recipient, 1994 Outstanding Young Lawyer Award, J. Reuben Clark Law Society, Los Angeles Chapter. Judicial Clerkship: Hon. Patrick E. Higginbotham, U.S. Court of Appeals for the Fifth Circuit, 1985-1986. Author: "The Sinking of Seaman's," Verdict, p.16 (4th Qtr. 1995). Co-author: "The General Verdict Rule: Appellate Trap or Opportunity?" 16 CEB Civ LR 93 (Mar. 1994). *Member:* Los Angeles County and Federal Bar Associations; Association of Business Trial Lawyers; American Judicature Society.

---

**MARY F. DANT,** born Los Angeles, California, January 12, 1960; admitted to bar, 1989, California and U.S. Court of Appeals, Ninth Circuit. *Education:* University of California, Los Angeles (B.A., 1982); Columbia University (J .D., 1989). Stone Scholar. Member, 1987-1988 and Articles Editor, 1988-1989, Columbia Journal of Law and Social Problems. *Member:* Los Angeles County and American Bar Associations.

**ARI R. KLEIMAN,** born Los Angeles, California, June 10, 1958; admitted to bar, 1991, California; 1993, U.S. Court of Appeals, Ninth Circuit. *Education:* The Hebrew University of Jerusalem (B.A., cum laude, 1984); University of Southern California (J.D., 1990). Co-Author: "Clarifying the Blockbuster Tort and Insurance Cases," Res Ipsa, p.13 (June 14, 1995). Member, Executive Committee, Legion Lex Inn of Court. *Member:* Los Angeles County Bar Association. *LANGUAGES:* Hebrew.

**LISA R. JASKOL,** born New Rochelle, New York, August 31, 1959; admitted to bar, 1988, California; 1989, U.S. Court of Appeals, Ninth Circuit. *Education:* Bryn Mawr College (A.B., magna cum laude, 1981); University of Chicago (M.A., 1985); Yale University (J.D., 1988). National Science Foundation Fellowship. University of Chicago Humanities Fellowship. Editor, Yale Law Journal, 1988. Judicial Clerkship: Hon. Harry Pregerson, Ninth Circuit Court of Appeals, 1988-1989. *Member:* American and Federal Bar Associations; State Bar of California (Legislation Committee, Litigation Section).

**JULIE L. WOODS,** born Springfield, Missouri, August 13, 1964; admitted to bar, 1989, California and U.S. Court of Appeals, Ninth Circuit. *Education:* University of Missouri (B.S.B.A., summa cum laude, 1986); Harvard University (J.D., cum laude, 1989). Author: "Review of Writ Decisions," Chapter 11, California Civil Writ Practice (Cont. Ed. Bar 1996). Co-Author: "Breach of Contract Damages," Damages In Business Litigation, Rutter Group (1990).

**HOLLY R. PAUL,** born Columbus, Ohio, January 30, 1959; admitted to bar, 1992, California; 1993, U.S. Court of Appeals, Ninth Circuit. *Education:* California State University, Northridge (B.A., summa cum laude, 1980); University of California, Los Angeles (J.D., 1991). Order of the Coif. Order of the Barristers. Executive Board of Judges, UCLA Moot Court, 1990-1991. Recipient: American Jurisprudence Award in Moot Court; UCLA Alumni Association Award. Outstanding Graduate, 1991. Judicial Clerkship: Hon. Harry Pregerson, U.S. Court of Appeals, Ninth Circuit, 1991-1992. Member: Federal Bar Association; California Women Lawyers Association; UCLA Law School Alumni Association (Board of Directors); Foundation for the Junior Blind (Board of Directors); American Blind Lawyers Association.

**H. THOMAS WATSON,** born Savannah, Georgia, May 5, 1960; admitted to bar, 1992, California; 1993, U.S. Court of Appeals, Ninth Circuit. *Education:* University of Idaho (B.S., summa cum laude, 1982); Pepperdine University (M.B.A., 1988); University of California, Los Angeles (J.D., 1992). Order of the Coif. Recipient, American Jurisprudence Award in Evidence. UCLA Journal of Environmental Law & Policy (Business Editor). Member: UCLA Environmental Law Society, 1989-1992; Society of Petro-

*(This Listing Continued)*

## HORVITZ & LEVY, Los Angeles—Continued

leum Engineers, 1982-1988; American Institute of Chemical Engineers, 1982-1984; National Association of Corrosion Engineers, 1988-1991.

**ANDREA M. GAUTHIER,** born Beverly, Massachusetts, December 4, 1965; admitted to bar, 1992, California; 1993, U.S. Court of Appeals, Ninth and Tenth Circuits. *Education:* Harvard University (A.B., summa cum laude, 1987; J.D., magna cum laude, 1990). Phi Beta Kappa. Board of Student Advisors. Elizabeth Cary Agassiz Scholar. Recipient: Palfrey Exhibition Prize; Department of Psychology Faculty Prize; Detur Prize; John Harvard Scholarship. Judicial Clerkship: Hon. A. Wallace Tashima, U.S. District Court, Central District of California, 1990-1991. *Member:* Los Angeles County Bar Association.

**ELIZABETH SKORCZ ANTHONY,** born Milwaukee, Wisconsin, January 4, 1964; admitted to bar, 1992, California. *Education:* Williams College (B.A., cum laude, 1986); University of California, Los Angeles (J.D., 1991). Editor in Chief, UCLA Law Review, 1990-1991. Judicial Clerkship: Hon. J. Spencer Letts, U.S. District Court, Central District of California, 1991-1992. Author: "RICO Forfeiture: Secured Lenders Beware," 37 UCLA L. Rev. 1199 (1990). Co-author: "The Tortification of Contract Law: An Experiment Destined to Fail," Legal Backgrounder, Vol. 11, No. 13 (Washington Legal Foundation 1996).

**CHRISTINE A. PAGAC,** born Detroit, Michigan, June 7, 1967; admitted to bar, 1991, Illinois; 1992, U.S. Court of Appeals, Sixth and Tenth Circuits; 1995, California; 1996, U.S. Court of Appeals, Ninth Circuit. *Education:* University of Michigan (B.A., magna cum laude, 1988; J.D., cum laude, 1991). Note Editor, Michigan Law Review, 1990-1991. Order of the Coif. Judicial Clerkship: Hon. Albert J. Engel, U.S. Court of Appeals, Sixth Circuit, 1991-1992. *Member:* Los Angeles County and American Bar Associations; Women Lawyers Association of Los Angeles.

**JUDITH E. GORDON,** born Los Angeles, California, May 20, 1969; admitted to bar, 1993, California, U.S. Court of Appeals, Ninth Circuit. *Education:* University of California, Los Angeles (B.A., magna cum laude, 1990; J.D., 1993). Phi Beta Kappa. Managing Editor, UCLA Women's Law Journal, 1992-1993. Judicial Clerk to the Hon. Melvin Brunetti, U.S. Court of Appeals, Ninth Circuit, 1993-1994.

**PATRICIA LOFTON,** born Philadelphia, Pennsylvania, May 3, 1947; admitted to bar, 1991, California; 1992, District of Columbia and U.S. Court of Appeals, Ninth Circuit. *Education:* California State University at Northridge (B.A., 1988); Pepperdine University (J.D., magna cum laude, 1991). Recipient: Westlaw Publishing Award for Outstanding Scholastic Achievement; Sorenson Award for Excellence in Legal Writing, American Jurisprudence Award. Notes and Comments Editor, Pepperdine University Law Review, 1990-1991. Judicial Clerkship: Hon. Thomas G. Nelson, U.S. Court of Appeals, Ninth Circuit, 1991-1993. Author: "Texas v. Johnson: The Constitutional Protection of Flag Desecration," 17 Pepperdine L. Rev. 757 (1990).

**L. RACHEL LERMAN HELYAR,** born Rochester, New York, January 21, 1960; admitted to bar, 1995, Idaho; U.S. Court of Appeals, Ninth Circuit (Not admitted in California). *Education:* Yale University (B.A., with honors, 1980); Syracuse University (M.A., Religion, 1986; M.F.A., Painting, 1985); Boalt Hall School of Law, University of California at Berkeley (J.D., 1992). Recipient, American Jurisprudence Award in Jurisprudence, Schurman Scholarship for International and Comparative Law, Universität Heidelberg, 1992. Articles Editor, Berkeley Women's Law Journal, 1989-1991. Judicial Clerkship: Hon. Thomas G. Nelson, U.S. Court of Appeals, Ninth Circuit, 1994-1996. Author: "'Let Order Reign': The Judge as Oracle in Antebellum America," Law, Judges & the State (Max Planck Institute, Frankfurt, Germany, 1996).

### OF COUNSEL

**JON B. EISENBERG,** born Los Angeles, California, July 22, 1953; admitted to bar, 1979, California; U.S. Court of Appeals, Ninth Circuit. *Education:* University of California, Irvine (B.A., 1974); Hastings College of the Law (J.D., 1979). Order of the Coif. Member, Thurston Society. Associate Editor, Hastings Law Journal, 1978-1979. Co-Author: California Practice Guide: Civil Appeals and Writs (The Rutter Group, 1989). Editor-in-Chief: California Practice Guide: Civil Procedure Bulletin (The Rutter Group, 1991-1993). Author: "Legal Research," The Courts and The News Media (Calif. Judges Assoc., 1993); Action Guide: Handling Civil Appeals, First Edition (Cont. Ed. Bar, 1985); "Remittitur," California Civil Appellate Practice, Second Edition (Cont. Ed. Bar, 1985); California Civil Appellate Practice (Cont. Ed. Bar, 1966, 1981-1984 supp.); "Sanctions on Appeal: A Survey and a Proposal for Computation Guidelines," 20 U.S.F.L. Rev. 13

*(This Listing Continued)*

(1985); "Lugosi v. Universal Pictures: Descent of the Right of Publicity," 28 Hastings L.J. 751 (1978). Contributing Editor (appellate practice), Civil Litigation Reporter (Cont. Ed. Bar, 1983-1989). Judicial Staff Attorney, California Court of Appeal, First Appellate District, Division Four, 1979-1980. Judicial Staff Attorney, California Court of Appeal, First Appellate District, Division Five, 1982-1996. *Member:* Alameda County Bar Association (Member: Board of Directors, 1995-1996).

REFERENCE: Bank of California (Los Angeles, California Office).

---

## WILLARD D. HORWICH

Established in 1959

1875 CENTURY PARK EAST, SUITE 2150
**LOS ANGELES, CALIFORNIA 90067**
Telephone: 310-556-3378
FAX: 310-286-0865

*Federal and State Taxation. Probate Law and Bankruptcy Tax Litigation.*

**WILLARD D. HORWICH,** born Chicago, Illinois, January 1, 1929; admitted to bar, 1959, California. *Education:* University of California at Los Angeles (B.S., 1950; J.D., 1958). Certified Public Accountant, California, 1953. Author: "Lawyers' and Accountants' Guide to Purchase and Sale of a Small Business," Prentice Hall/Warren, Gorham & Lamont, 1989; "Tax Issues in Bankruptcy," Business Legal Reports, Inc., 1994. Adjunct Professor of Law, Golden Gate University. *Member:* Beverly Hills, Los Angeles County and American (Member, Sections on: Litigation; Taxation) Bar Associations; State Bar of California (Member, Sections on: Tax Law and Probate Law).

---

## PHILIP J. HOSKINS

10940 WILSHIRE BOULEVARD, SUITE 1400
**LOS ANGELES, CALIFORNIA 90024**
Telephone: 310-209-8080
Fax: 310-208-8582
Email: philip_hoskins@msn.com
URL: http://ntnet.com/pjhbase.htm

*Civil Trial and Appellate Practice in State and Federal Courts, Family Law, Probate and Estate Planning.*

FIRM PROFILE: *I have served the community in the practice of law for over 30 years. In that time I have worked for the U.S. Department of Justice, managed the largest multiple-office law firm in California and handled delicate and difficult legal matters for thousands of clients. I have taught law school and other attorneys, written books and lead workshops on many topics. My personal philosophy is that an attorney should serve his client and the community.*

**PHILIP J. HOSKINS,** born Milwaukee, Wisconsin, October 11, 1938; admitted to bar, 1965, California; 1966, District of Columbia and U.S. District Court, Central District Court; 1988, U.S. Tax Court. *Education:* University of California at Los Angeles (B.A., 1961; LL.B., 1964). Instructor, Golden Gate University School of Law, 1968-1969. *Member:* Los Angeles County Bar Association (Member, Family Law Section); State Bar of California; Lawyers for Human Rights.

---

## HOSP, GILBERT & ASSOCIATES

A LAW CORPORATION

**LOS ANGELES, CALIFORNIA**

(See Pasadena)

*General Civil and Trial Practice in all State and Federal Courts. Banking, Commercial Creditors Rights and Bankruptcy Law, Corporation, Business, Insurance Defense, Automobile Liability, Bad Faith, Construction, Earth Movement, Environmental, ERISA Litigation, Equal Opportunity Law, Insurance Coverage, Insurance Fraud, Premises Liability, Product Liability, Professional Liability, Real Property, Landlord-Tenant Relations, Unlawful Detainer, Subrogation, Wrongful Termination.*

## HOUCK & BALISOK

1925 CENTURY PARK EAST, SUITE 2000
LOS ANGELES, CALIFORNIA 90067-2721
Telephone: 310-277-2236
Telecopier: 310-556-5653

*Civil Litigation including Business, Elder Abuse, Nursing Home Malpractice.*

### MEMBERS OF FIRM

**ALDEN F. HOUCK** (1917-1988).

**RUSSELL S. BALISOK,** born Los Angeles, California, April 25, 1946; admitted to bar, 1975, California; 1976, U.S. District Court, Central District of California. *Education:* California State University at Los Angeles; Troy State University; California State University at Northridge; Southwestern University (J.D., 1975). Member, Moot Court Honors Program. Instructor, Legal Research and Writing Skills, Southwestern University, 1975-1976. Author, "Actions Against Skilled Nursing Facilities," California Elder Law, An Advocate's Guide, CEB, 1993; "Medical Malpractice Actions for the Elderly go Ballistic while Plaintiff's Bar Bemoans Micra," Forum Magazine, Jan.-Feb. 1994. *Member:* Los Angeles County Bar Association (Member, Barristers Subcommittee on Legal Problems of the Elderly, 1981-1983); State Bar of California (Member, Subcommittee on Legal Problems of the Elderly, 1982-1983); The Association of Trial Lawyers of America. [Captain, U.S. Army, Infantry-Aviation, 1966-1971]

## HOULÉ & SEDIN

800 WILSHIRE BOULEVARD, SUITE 1450
LOS ANGELES, CALIFORNIA 90017
Telephone: 213-624-4779
Fax: 213-624-5843

*Public Entity Defense, Insurance Defense and Personal Injury Litigation.*

### MEMBERS OF FIRM

**GREGORY HOULÉ,** born Los Angeles, California, June 12, 1948; admitted to bar, 1974, California. *Education:* University of California at Los Angeles (B.A., summa cum laude, 1970); Boalt Hall School of Law, University of California (J.D., 1974). Phi Beta Kappa. Editor, Ecology Law Quarterly, Boalt Hall School of Law, 1972-1974. Judge Pro Tem, Pasadena Municipal Court, 1982—. Arbitrator, Los Angeles Superior Courts, 1982—. *Member:* Los Angeles County and American Bar Associations; State Bar of California; American Board of Trial Advocates; Association of Southern California Defense Counsel. *PRACTICE AREAS:* Public Entity Defense; Insurance Defense; Personal Injury Litigation.

**TAMMY L. SEDIN,** born Whittier, California, April 28, 1958; admitted to bar, 1986, California. *Education:* University of Southern California (B.A., magna cum laude, 1980); Hastings College of Law, University of California (J.D., 1985). *Member:* Los Angeles County and American Bar Associations; State Bar of California; Association of Business Trial Lawyers. *PRACTICE AREAS:* Public Entity Defense; Insurance Defense; Personal Injury Litigation.

### ASSOCIATES

**RICHARD HOULÉ,** born Los Angeles, California, August 28, 1953; admitted to bar, 1992, California. *Education:* University of California, Los Angeles (B.A., 1976); South Western Universit y (J.D., 1992). *Member:* Los Angeles County Bar Association; State Bar of California.

## HOWARTH & SMITH

*Established in 1985*

SUITE 2900, 700 SOUTH FLOWER STREET
LOS ANGELES, CALIFORNIA 90017
Telephone: 213-955-9400
Fax: 213-622-0791

*General Civil Practice. Litigation in all Courts.*

### MEMBERS OF FIRM

**DON HOWARTH,** born Providence, Rhode Island, March 9, 1946; admitted to bar, 1972, California; 1973, U.S. Court of Appeals, Ninth Circuit and U.S. District Court, Central, Southern and Northern Districts of California; 1979, U.S. Supreme Court. *Education:* Harvard University (B.A., magna cum laude, 1968; J.D., cum laude, 1972); Kennedy School of Government, Harvard University (M.P.P., 1972). Member, Harvard Board of Student Advisors, 1969-1972. Law Clerk to Hon. Shirley M. Hufstedler, U.S. Court of Appeals, Ninth Circuit, 1972-1973. Fellow, American College of Trial Lawyers. Visiting Lecturer, Law Faculty, Oxford University, 1994. Adjunct Professor of Law, Pepperdine University School of Law, 1980-1996. Associate, 1973-1979 and Partner, 1979-1985, Gibson, Dunn & Crutcher. Member, Committee on Antitrust Civil Jury Instructions (A.B.A. Handbook, 1985 revision). Author: *Case Assessment and Evaluation*, Callaghan Publishing Company, 1989 (with Suzelle M. Smith); *Using Economic Experts in Toxic Tort Litigation*, A.T.L.A., 1985 (with Suzelle M. Smith); *Shareholders' Rights and Remedies -- Defense Strategy and Tactics*, C.L.E., 1981; *How to Interview the Client*, American Bar Association, 1983 (with Thrace Hetrick); *Students' Rights to Organize and Meet for Religious Purposes in the University Context*, Valparaiso University Law Review, 1981 (with William D. Connell). *Member:* Los Angeles County and American (Member, Sections on: Litigation; Antitrust Law) Bar Associations; State Bar of California. *PRACTICE AREAS:* Trial Practice; Antitrust Law; Products Liability Law.

**SUZELLE M. SMITH,** born Birmingham, Alabama, December 1, 1953; admitted to bar, 1983, District of Columbia; 1984, California, U.S. District Court, Central, Southern and Northern Districts of California and U.S. Court of Appeals, Ninth Circuit; 1985, Washington. *Education:* Boston University (B.A., summa cum laude, 1975); Oxford University, England (B.Phil, summa cum laude, 1977); University of Virginia School of Law (J.D., 1983). Order of the Coif. Legislative Assistant to United States Senator Howell Heflin, 1979-1980. Associate, Gibson, Dunn & Crutcher, 1983-1985. Member, Board of Experts, Lawyer's Alert, Trial Practice and Procedure Expert, 1990. Adjunct Professor of Law, Pepperdine University School of Law, 1988—. Faculty Visitor, Oxford University, 1996, 1993-1994. Author: Case Assessment and Evaluation, (with Don Howarth), Callaghan Publishing Company, 1989; Using Economic Experts in Toxic Tort Litigation, (with Don Howarth), A,T.L.A., 1985; Rules Governing Demonstrative Evidence At Trial: A Practitioners Guide, (with Don Howarth and Mary LaCesa), Western State University Law Review, 1992; Landlord's Liability for Criminal Acts by Third Parties--A New Test, (with George T. Kliavkoff), Commercial Property Leasing Law and Strategy, 1994; Partnership Divorces: Principles and Pitfalls in Partnership Law, (with Don Howarth), Los Angeles Lawyer, 1994. President, L.A. West Inns of Court; Past Member, Board of Trustees, Episcopal Divinity School, Cambridge, Massachusetts; Board of Trustees, University of Virginia School of Law. *Member:* Los Angeles County (Member, Federal Courts Committee, Appellate Subcommittee Chairperson); Washington State and American (Member, Sections on: Litigation, Toxic Torts) Bar Associations; District of Columbia Bar; State Bar of California (Member, Continuing Education of the Bar Committee); The Association of Trial Lawyers of America; Association of Business Trial Lawyers; California Trial Lawyers Association; Defense Research Institute; Christian Legal Society; The Oxford Society. *PRACTICE AREAS:* Trial Practice; Commercial Litigation; Complex and Multi-District Litigation; Products Liability Law; Appellate Practice.

**DAVID K. RINGWOOD,** born Glens Falls, New York, November 14, 1951; admitted to bar, 1984, California and U.S. District Court, Central and Southern Districts of California; 1989, U.S. District Court, District of Arizona. *Education:* Colgate University (B.A., 1975); Southwestern University School of Law (J.D., magna cum laude, 1984). Member, 1981-1983 and Board of Governors, 1982-1983, Southwestern Moot Court Honors Program. Extern, Hon. Cynthia H. Hall, U.S. District Court, Central District of California, 1983. Adjunct Professor of Trial Advocacy and Products Liability, Southwestern University School of Law. Associate, Gibson, Dunn & Crutcher, 1984-1985. *Member:* Los Angeles County and American Bar Associations; State Bar of California; Association of Business Trial Lawyers; Defense Research Institute; Association of Southern California Defense Counsel. *PRACTICE AREAS:* Trial Practice; Complex and Multi-District Litigation; Products Liability Law; Business Litigation; Professional Liability.

**KENNETH S. TUNE,** born Oakland, California, October 19, 1945; admitted to bar, 1972, California; 1973, U.S. District Court, Central District of California; 1976, U.S. District Court, Eastern District of California; 1994, U.S. District Court, Southern District of California. *Education:* University of California at Berkeley (A.B., 1966); Harvard University (J.D., cum laude, 1972). Member, Board of Student Advisors, 1971-1972. Member, Sacramento County Employees' Retirement Board, 1984-1987. *Member:* State Bar of California. [First Lieut., U.S. Army, 1966-1969]. *PRACTICE AREAS:* Appellate Practice; Complex Litigation.

**BRIAN D. BUBB,** born Baltimore, Maryland, June 22, 1962; admitted to bar, 1988, California. *Education:* Albright College (B.S., 1985); Pepperdine University (J.D., 1988). Recipient, American Jurisprudence Awards in

*(This Listing Continued)*

## HOWARTH & SMITH, Los Angeles—Continued

Civil Procedure and Contracts. Member, Pepperdine University Law Review, 1986-1988. *Member:* Los Angeles County and American Bar Associations; State Bar of California; Association of Trial Lawyers of America; L. A. West Inns of Court.

---

**MARCUS J. BERGER,** born Chicago, Illinois, June 28, 1947; admitted to bar, 1989, California, U.S. District Court, Central District of California and U.S. Court of Appeals, Ninth Circuit. *Education:* Northeastern Illinois University (B.A., 1971); University of Chicago (M.A., 1973); Northwestern University (D.M., 1984); Southwestern University (J.D., cum laude, 1989). Note and Comment Editor, Southwestern University Law Review, 1988-1989. Author: "The Requirements for Impeachment of the President," 18 Sw.U.L. Rev. 373 (1990). *Member:* State Bar of California. **REPORTED CASES:** Freeman v. Hale, 30 Cal. App. 4th 1388, 36 Cal. Rptr. 2d 418 (1994); Barrus v. Sylvania, 55 F.3d 468 (9th Cir. 1995).

**PATRICIA LEE-GULLEY,** born Pasadena, California, January 25, 1953; admitted to bar, 1989, California; 1990, U.S. District Court, Central, Northern, Southern and Eastern Districts of California and U.S. Court of Appeals, Ninth Circuit; 1995, U.S. Supreme Court. *Education:* University of Southern California (B.A., magna cum laude, 1974); East Carolina University (M.B.A., 1981); Western State University (J.D., 1988). Beta Gamma Sigma. Recipient: American Jurisprudence Awards, Professional Responsibility and Evidence I; J. Brower Achievement Award. Moot Court Advocate. President, Asian-American Law Students Association. Who's Who Among Students in American Universities & Colleges (1989). Certified in Production and Inventory Management (CPIM). Who's Who in the West (1989-1990). Member, American Production and Inventory Control Society, 1982-1986. *Member:* Orange County, Los Angeles County, Federal and American Bar Associations; State Bar of California; Los Angeles Consumers Attorneys Association; Orange County Patent Law Association. **PRACTICE AREAS:** Civil Litigation Law.

**THOMAS F. VANDENBURG,** born Fairfax, Virginia, October 27, 1966; admitted to bar, 1992, California; 1993, U.S. District Court, Central District of California; 1994, U.S. District Court, Southern District of California. *Education:* University of Virginia (B.A., 1989; J.D., 1992). *Member:* Los Angeles County and American (Member: Tort and Insurance Practice Section; Chair, TIPS Sports Law Committee; Litigation Section; Forum Committee on the Entertainment and Sports Industries) Bar Associations.

**GREGORY S. TAMKIN,** born Philadelphia, Pennsylvania, November 13, 1969; admitted to bar, 1994, California. *Education:* Dartmouth College (B.A., cum laude, 1991); University of Virginia (J.D., 1994). Phi Delta Phi (Treasurer, 1991-1994). Research and Projects Editor, Journal of Law and Politics, 1994. **LANGUAGES:** Spanish.

**KATY JACOBS,** born Santa Barbara, California, April 2, 1965; admitted to bar, 1994, California; 1995, U.S. District Court, Southern District of California; 1996, U.S. District Court, District of Arizona. *Education:* Humboldt State University (B.A., 1989); Santa Barbara State College (J.D., 1994). Recipient, American Jurisprudence Awards, Torts and Criminal Law, Santa Barbara College of Law. President, Student Bar Association, Santa Barbara College of Law, 1992-1993. *Member:* Federal Bar Association (Member, Indian Law Section). **PRACTICE AREAS:** Trial Practice; Complex and Multi District Litigation; Products Liability; Federal Indian Law; Tribal Law; Radiation Exposure Litigation.

**SHEILA M. BRADLEY,** born Covina, California, January 25, 1970; admitted to bar, 1995, California. *Education:* University of California at Berkeley (A.B., with highest honors, 1992); Harvard University (J.D., cum laude, 1995). Phi Beta Kappa. Executive Editor, Harvard Civil Rights-Civil Liberties Law Review, 1994-1995.

**JULIA S. SWANSON,** born Tavistock, Devon, United Kingdom, April 1, 1946; admitted to bar, 1992, New York; 1993, California and U.S. District Court, Central District of California. *Education:* Aston University (B.S., cum laude, 1968); New York Law School (J.D., cum laude, 1990). **LANGUAGES:** Japanese.

**KIMBERLY L. HONUS,** born Santa Monica, California; admitted to bar, 1995, California. *Education:* University of Arizona (B.A., 1992); Pepperdine University (J.D., 1995). **PRACTICE AREAS:** Litigation; Products Liability.

**RANDALL BOESE,** born San Diego, California, August 27, 1967; admitted to bar, 1995, California. *Education:* University of California at Los Angeles (B.A., magna cum laude, 1992); Southwestern University School of

*(This Listing Continued)*

---

Law (J.D., summa cum laude, 1995). Recipient, American Jurisprudence Awards, Civil Procedure, Torts, White Collar Crime, Computer Law and Estate Planning and Drafting. Lead Articles Editor, Southwestern Law Review, 1993-1995. *Member:* Beverly Hills and American Bar Associations.

---

## HOWREY & SIMON
SUITE 1400, 550 SOUTH HOPE STREET
**LOS ANGELES, CALIFORNIA 90071-2604**
*Telephone: 213-892-1800*
*Fax: 213-892-2300*

*Washington, D.C. Office:* 1299 Pennsylvania Avenue, N.W., 20004-2402. Telephone: 202-783-0800. Fax: 202-383-6610.

*Menlo Park, California Office:* 301 Ravenswood Avenue, 94025. Telephone: 415-463-8100. Fax: 415-463-8400.

*General and Trial Practice including Antitrust, Commercial Litigation, Corporate and Transactional, Environmental, Government Contracts, Insurance Coverage, Intellectual Property, International Trade, Products Liability, Securities Litigation, Supreme Court and Appellate and White Collar Criminal Defense.*

### MEMBERS OF FIRM

**CHRISTOPHER A. BARNES,** born Kingston, Jamaica, December 3, 1962; admitted to bar, 1987, Pennsylvania; 1990, California; 1992, District of Columbia. *Education:* University of Pennsylvania (B.A., 1984); University of Virginia (J.D., 1987). Author: "New Improved Awards Without Discussions or Foreign Competition," Volume 20, Number 4, Public Contract Law Journal, Summer 1991. *Member:* Philadelphia, Pennsylvania and American Bar Associations. **PRACTICE AREAS:** Government Contract Law. *Email:* barnesc@howrey.com

**GEORGE W. BUEHLER,** born San Pedro, California, August 21, 1948; admitted to bar, 1974, California and U.S. District Court, Southern District of California; 1990, U.S. District Court, District of Arizona. *Education:* Occidental College (B.A., 1970); Fuller Theological Seminary (M.A., 1989); University of Southern California (J.D., 1974). Law Clerk, California Court of Appeal, 4th District, 1974-1975. Deputy Attorney General, Special Operations Division, California Attorney General's Office, 1975-1977. *Member:* State Bar of California; American Bar Association. **PRACTICE AREAS:** Complex Commercial and Business Litigation; Directors and Officers Liability; White Collar Criminal Defense. *Email:* buehlerg@howrey.com

**R. DAVID CARLTON,** born New York, N.Y., April 6, 1949; admitted to bar, 1974, Virginia; 1983, California. *Education:* Washington & Lee University (B.A., 1971; J.D., 1974); Georgetown University Law Center. Senior Editor, Washington & Lee Law Review, 1973-1974. Trial Attorney, Contract Appeals Division, U.S. Army Legal Services Agency, 1977-1981. Senior Attorney, 1981-1988 and Group Counsel, 1988-1989, Ford Aerospace Corporation. Associate General Counsel, 1989-1991 and General Counsel, 1991-1992, Douglas Aircraft Company, McDonnell Douglas Corporation. *Member:* Virginia State Bar; State Bar of California; American Bar Association (Member, Public Contract Law Section). [Lt. Col., U.S. Army Reserve]. **PRACTICE AREAS:** Government Contract Law. *Email:* carltonr@howrey.com

**JOANNE E. CARUSO,** born Phoenix, Arizona, November 2, 1960; admitted to bar, 1986, Connecticut; 1987, District of Columbia; 1996, California. *Education:* Boston College (B.A., magna cum laude, 1982; J.D., cum laude, 1986). Alpha Sigma Nu. *Member:* The District of Columbia Bar; American Bar Association. **PRACTICE AREAS:** Antitrust Law; Complex Litigation; Litigation. *Email:* carusoj@howrey.com

**DAVID G. MEYER,** born Kadina A.F.B., Okinawa, Japan, July 3, 1957; admitted to bar, 1984, California; 1985, U.S. District Court, Central District of California; U.S. Court of Appeals, Ninth Circuit. *Education:* Stanford University (B.A., 1979); University of California at Los Angeles (J.D., 1984). Staff Member, University of California at Los Angeles Law Review, 1983-1984. *Member:* State Bar of California. **PRACTICE AREAS:** White Collar Criminal Defense; Commercial Litigation. *Email:* meyerd@howrey.com

**GLENN E. MONROE,** born Ohio, 1945; admitted to bar, 1974, Ohio; 1975, U.S. Court of Military Appeals; 1978, U.S. Supreme Court; 1979, U.S. Tax Court; 1982, District of Columbia and U.S. Court of Appeals, District of Columbia; 1983, U.S. Claims Court; 1988, Arizona (Not admitted in California). *Education:* La Sorbonne, Paris, France; Muskingum College (B.A., 1967); The Ohio State University (J.D., cum laude, 1974); University of Virginia (LL.M., 1979). (Also at St. Louis, Missouri Office).

*(This Listing Continued)*

**PRACTICE AREAS:** Civil Litigation; Government Contract Law. **Email:** monroeg@howrey.com

**THOMAS J. NOLAN,** born New York, N.Y., August 22, 1948; admitted to bar, 1975, California; U.S. District Court, Central and Southern Districts of California and U.S. Court of Appeals, Ninth Circuit. *Education:* Loyola University of Los Angeles (B.B.A., 1971; J.D., 1975). Member, Loyola University School of Law, Law Review, 1974, Assistant U.S. Attorney, 1976-1979, Chief, Fraud and Special Prosecutions Unit, 1978-1979 for the Central District of California. *Member:* State Bar of California; American Bar Association. **PRACTICE AREAS:** White Collar Criminal Defense; Complex Litigation; Directors and Officers Liability; Litigation. **Email:** nolant@howrey.com

**RICHARD S. ODOM,** born Galveston, Texas, August 10, 1944; admitted to bar, 1970, California and U.S. Court of Appeals, 9th Circuit; 1985, U.S. Court of Appeals, 5th Circuit; 1991, U.S. Supreme Court. *Education:* Stanford University (B.S., 1966; J.D., 1969). Editor, 1967-1968; Managing Editor, 1968-1969, Stanford Law Review. Author: "Alternatives to the Present Check Collection System," Volume 20, Stanford Law Review. [Capt. U.S. Army, 1970-1971]. **PRACTICE AREAS:** Complex Commercial Litigation; Products Liability. **Email:** odomr@howrey.com

**CHARLES H. SAMEL,** born Newark, New Jersey, April 17, 1961; admitted to bar, 1985, Maryland; 1986, District of Columbia, U.S. District Court, District of Maryland and U.S. Court of Federal Claims; 1989, U.S. Court of Appeals, Ninth Circuit; 1992, U.S. District Court, District of Columbia and U.S. Court of Appeals, Fourth Circuit; 1996, California. *Education:* University of Maryland (B.A., magna cum laude, 1982); Georgetown University (J.D., cum laude, 1985). Phi Beta Kappa. Member, 1983-1984 and Executive Editor, 1984-1985, The Tax Lawyer. Co-Author: "Peoples Security Life Insurance v. Monumental Insurance: A Study on Customer and Employee Raiding and the Law of Unfair Competition," Commercial Damages, March 1995; "Strategies for Settling Environmental Toxic Tort and Other Complex Insurance Coverage Cases," Legal Times, June, 1995. *Member:* District of Columbia Bar; State Bar of California; Maryland State and American Bar Associations. **PRACTICE AREAS:** Complex Litigation; Construction Litigation; Environmental Law; Insurance Coverage. **Email:** samelc@howrey.com

**ELIZABETH M. WEAVER,** admitted to bar, 1981, Florida; 1986, California. *Education:* Duke University (A.B., 1977; J.D., 1980). Angier B. Duke Scholar. *Member:* The Florida Bar; State Bar of California; American Bar Association; Florida Association of Women Lawyers. **PRACTICE AREAS:** Environmental Law. **Email:** weavere@howrey.com

## OF COUNSEL

**NANCY L. BOUGHTON,** born Danbury, Connecticut, August 15, 1961; admitted to bar, 1987, Maryland (Not admitted in California). *Education:* American University (B.A., cum laude, honors with high distinction, International Affairs, 1983); Georgetown University Law Center (J.D., 1986);. Member, American Criminal Law Review, 1984-1986. *Member:* Maryland State and American Bar Associations. **PRACTICE AREAS:** Government Contract Law; Export International Law; Litigation. **Email:** boughtonn@howrey.com

## RESIDENT ASSOCIATES

**JOHN F. BRIGDEN,** born Milwaukee, Wisconsin, November 15, 1964; admitted to bar, 1991, Virginia; 1993, California and District of Columbia. *Education:* Purdue University (B.S.E.E., with highest distinction, 1988); Georgetown University (J.D., magna cum laude, 1991). Order of the Coif; Tau Beta Pi; Phi Eta Sigma; Phi Kappa Phi. Editor, Purdue Engineering Magazine. Editor, American Criminal Law Review. Author: "Justice Souter's Impact on the Supreme Court's Criminal Procedure Jurisprudence," Amer. Crim. L. Rev., November, 1991; "From Shrink Wrap to Negotiated End User Software Licenses Agreement—A Practical Prospective," Prac. L. Inst., 1989. *Member:* Virginia State Bar; State Bar of California; American Bar Association; Virginia Trial Lawyers Association; American Intellectual Property Law Association. [ROTC, U.S. Army, 1983-1985]. **PRACTICE AREAS:** Commercial Litigation; Intellectual Property Litigation. **Email:** brigdenj@howrey.com

**ELIZABETH A. CARROLL,** born San Diego, California, August 16, 1964; admitted to bar, 1992, California; U.S. District Court, Central District of California; U.S. Court of Appeals, Ninth Circuit. *Education:* University of California at Davis (B.A., with highest honors, 1986); Boalt Hall School of Law, University of California (J.D., 1992). *Member:* American Bar Association. **PRACTICE AREAS:** Commercial Litigation. **Email:** carrolll@howrey.com

**KATHRYN M. CONWAY,** born Boston, Massachusetts, September 26, 1962; admitted to bar, 1990, California; 1993, District of Columbia. *Education:* Smith College (B.A., 1984); Georgetown University Law Center (J.D., 1990). Associate Editor, Law and Policy in International Business. Author: "The ECU: Prospects for a Monetary Union in the European Economic Community," Volume 21, Law and Policy in International Business, 1989. **PRACTICE AREAS:** Commercial Litigation. **Email:** conwayk@howrey.com

**MARY A. DENISE,** born Asheville, North Carolina, May 23, 1961; admitted to bar, 1989, District of Columbia; 1996, California. *Education:* George Washington University (B.A., 1986); University of Florida (J.D., with honors, 1989). *Member:* American Bar Association; The District of Columbia Bar (Member, Public Contracts Section). **PRACTICE AREAS:** Government Contracts Law. **Email:** denisem@howrey.com

**DONNA DRAKE,** born California, May 29, 1965; admitted to bar, 1993, California. *Education:* California State University at Long Beach (B.S., 1989); Loyola Law School, Los Angeles (J.D., 1993). **PRACTICE AREAS:** Government Contracts; General Litigation. **Email:** draked@howrey.com

**NOAH T. FOGELSON,** born New York, January 31, 1970; admitted to bar, 1995, California, U.S. District Court, Central District of California and U.S. Court of Appeals, Ninth Circuit. *Education:* Stanford University (B.A., with distinction, 1992); Boalt Hall School of Law, University of California (J.D., 1995). Member, Moot Court Board. Director, Appellate Advocacy Program. **Email:** fogelsonn@howrey.com

**DALE J. GIALI,** born Fullerton, California, March 23, 1965; admitted to bar, 1990, California; 1991, U.S. District Court, Southern, Central, Eastern and Northern Districts of California and U.S. Court of Appeals, Ninth Circuit; 1993, District of Columbia and U.S. District Court, District of Arizona; 1996, U.S. District Court, Northern District of Texas. *Education:* University of California, Los Angeles (B.A., 1987); University of San Diego (J.D., cum laude, 1990). Member, Appellate Moot Court Board. Member, San Diego Law Review. **Email:** gialid@howrey.com

**ANN E. GRANT,** born Anaheim, California, July 23, 1962; admitted to bar, 1991, California. *Education:* Brigham Young University (B.A., 1984); University of San Diego (J.D., cum laude, 1991). Member, San Diego Law Review. **PRACTICE AREAS:** Complex Litigation; White Collar Criminal Defense. **Email:** granta@howrey.com

**STEVEN C. HELLER,** born Modesto, California, September 1, 1959; admitted to bar, 1995, California. *Education:* University of California, Los Angeles (B.A., 1992; J.D., 1995). Phi Beta Kappa. **Email:** hellers@howrey.com

**ROBERT B. HUMPHREYS,** born Cleveland, Ohio, January 22, 1968; admitted to bar, 1993, California; 1994, U.S. District Court, Central and Eastern Districts of California and U.S. Court of Appeals, Ninth Circuit. *Education:* University of Colorado (B.A., summa cum laude, 1990); Georgetown University Law Center (J.D., magna cum laude, 1993). Order of the Coif. Articles Editor, American Criminal Law Review. Author: "In Search of the Reliable Co-Conspirator," 30 Am. Crim. L. Rev. 337 (1993). **PRACTICE AREAS:** White Collar Criminal Defense; Complex Civil Litigation. **Email:** humphreysr@howrey.com

**BENNET G. KELLEY,** born Providence, Rhode Island, May 4, 1963; admitted to bar, 1990, Maryland and District of Columbia; 1995, California. *Education:* The American University (B.S., 1984); Georgetown University Law Center (J.D., magna cum laude, 1990). Order of Coif. Member, American Criminal Law Review, 1988-1989. Co-Author: "The NCAA In Court: An Outline of Cases Involving the NCAA and Its Rules and Regulations, 19 College L. Dig. 1989. Co-founder, Democratic National Committee Saxophone Club. Delegate, German Ministry of Defense's Multiplikatoren Conference for Young Leaders, 1994. *Member:* The District of Columbia Bar; American Bar Association. **PRACTICE AREAS:** Complex Litigation; Insurance Coverage. **Email:** kelleyb@howrey.com

**BRIAN SUNG YUN KIM,** born Seoul, Korea, October 13, 1966; admitted to bar, 1996, California. *Education:* Stanford University (B.S., 1989); Harvard Law School (J.D., 1996). Phi Beta Kappa; Tau Beta Pi. **LANGUAGES:** Korean. **PRACTICE AREAS:** Intellectual Property.

**JOANNE LICHTMAN,** born Rochester, New York, April 13, 1962; admitted to bar, 1988, California and U.S. District Court, Central District of California; 1989, District of Columbia; 1992, U.S. District Court, Northern District of California. *Education:* University of Vermont (B.A., magna cum laude, 1984); Harvard Law School (J.D., cum laude, 1988). Phi Beta Kappa. *Member:* Los Angeles County and American Bar Associations; The

*(This Listing Continued)*

## HOWREY & SIMON, Los Angeles—Continued

District of Columbia Bar. **PRACTICE AREAS:** Environmental Law. **Email:** lichtmanj@howrey.com

**CHRISTOPHER A. MATHEWS,** born Sonoma, California, December 29, 1962; admitted to bar, 1989, California and U.S. District Court, Central, Eastern, Northern and Southern Districts of California; registered to practice before the U.S. Patent and Trademark Office. *Education:* University of California at Berkeley (B.S., in E.E. and Comp. Sci., magna cum laude, 1985); Stanford University (J.D., 1989). Tau Beta Pi. R. Hunter Summers Trial Practice Award Winner. *Member:* Los Angeles County, Federal, Federal Circuit and American Bar Associations; State Bar of California. **PRACTICE AREAS:** Intellectual Property; Commercial Litigation; Antitrust.

**CATHERINE MOORE,** born Evanston, Illinois, October 3, 1969; admitted to bar, 1994, California. *Education:* Williams College (B.A., 1991); Stanford University (J.D., 1994). Associate Editor, Stanford Law Review. **Email:** moorec@howrey.com

**CHERYL O'CONNOR MURPHY,** born New Bern, North Carolina, May 30, 1968; admitted to bar, 1994, California; U.S. District Court, Central District of California; U.S. Court of Appeals, Ninth Circuit. *Education:* University of California at Los Angeles (B.A., 1991); University of Southern California (J.D., 1994). Best Brief, 1992-1993 and Topic Editor, 1993-1994, U.S.C. Hale Moot Court Honors Competition. *Member:* Los Angeles County and American Bar Associations; State Bar of California. **Email:** murphyc@howrey.com

**GEORGIA P. SAVIOLA,** born Alexandria, Virginia, February 25, 1959; admitted to bar, 1990, California. *Education:* Bowdoin College; Duke University (B.A., cum laude, 1983); University of Virginia (J.D., 1990). **LANGUAGES:** Greek. **PRACTICE AREAS:** White Collar Criminal Defense; Commercial Litigation. **Email:** saviolag@howrey.com

**JOHN S. SCHUSTER,** born Garden Grove, California, October 2, 1964; admitted to bar, 1989, California, U.S. District Court, Northern, Southern Eastern and Central Districts of California and U.S. Court of Appeals, Ninth Circuit. *Education:* University of California at Berkeley (A.B., 1986); Hastings College of the Law, University of California (J.D., magna cum laude, 1989). Order of the Coif; Thurston Society. Member, Hastings Law Journal. Author: Note, "Precertification Settlement of Class Actions: Will California Follow the Federal Lead?" 40 Hastings L.J. 863 (1989). *Member:* State Bar of California; American Bar Association (Member, Litigation Section). **PRACTICE AREAS:** White Collar Criminal Defense; Commercial Litigation. **Email:** schusterj@howrey.com

**PHILIP C. TENCER,** born La Jolla, California, January 26, 1967; admitted to bar, 1994, California. *Education:* University of California at San Diego (B.A., 1990); Boalt Hall School of Law, University of California (J.D., 1994). Articles Editor, California Law Review, 1993-1994. Extern Law Clerk, Hon. Edward J. Garcia, U.S. District Court, Eastern District of California, 1992-1993. *Member:* Los Angeles County and American Bar Associations. **Email:** tencerp@howrey.com

**PETER S. VEREGGE,** born Fullerton, California, September 16, 1958; admitted to bar, 1991, California; 1992, U.S. District Court, Central and Northern Districts of California. *Education:* University of California at Santa Barbara (B.A., 1984); Loyola Marymount University (J.D., 1991). Phi Delta Phi (Vice Magistrate, 1990-1991). Traynor Moot Court Team (Best Brief Award). *Member:* Los Angeles County Bar Association (Member, Environmental Section); State Bar of California (Member, Environmental Section). **PRACTICE AREAS:** Environmental. **Email:** vereggep@howrey.com

**ANDREW E. ZIRKELBACH,** born Erie, Pennsylvania, 1959; admitted to bar, 1991, California. *Education:* Texas A & M University (B.S., 1981); Virginia Polytechnic and State University (M.S., 1982); Georgetown University (J.D., 1990). **PRACTICE AREAS:** Government Contract Law. **Email:** zirkelbacha@howrey.com

## HUANG & MITCHELL
### A PROFESSIONAL LAW CORPORATION
*Established in 1979*

3250 WILSHIRE BOULEVARD
SUITE 1600
**LOS ANGELES, CALIFORNIA 90010**
Telephone: 213-251-8199
Fax: 213-251-8188

*Commercial and Business Arbitration, Litigation, Mediation and Transactions; General Corporate Practice and International Arbitration.*

FIRM PROFILE: Huang & Mitchell, APLC, formerly Huang & Baner, APLC and Weiss & Huang, was founded in 1979 by Patrick K. Huang. The firm's practice is primarily directed to commercial and business dispute resolution, including mediation, arbitration and litigation of commercial, business, corporate, partnership, real estate, construction, contract and other business disputes before State and Federal Courts, the American Arbitration Association and the International Chamber of Commerce, Court of Arbitration (France). The firm is also experienced in domestic and international commercial and business transactions, business entities formation and appellate practice (state and federal).

**PATRICK K. HUANG,** born Nanjing, China, January 21, 1948; admitted to bar, 1975, California; 1976, U.S. District Court, Central District of California; 1977, U.S. Court of Appeals, Ninth Circuit; 1979, U.S. Supreme Court; 1984, U.S. District Court, District of Hawaii. *Education:* University of California at Santa Barbara (B.A., 1971); University of West Los Angeles (J.D., 1975). Recipient, American Jurisprudence Award in Remedies. Author: "Future Interests," AB Press, California, 1976. *Member:* State Bar of California; American and International (Member, London, England Section) Bar Associations. **LANGUAGES:** Cantonese Chinese. **PRACTICE AREAS:** Commercial Litigation; Arbitration; Mediation and Dispute Resolution in State and Federal Court; AAA and International Chamber of Commerce, Court of Arbitration, Paris, France; Commercial Transactions; General Corporate and Partnership Transactions and Disputes; Construction; Real Estate Law.

**JUDITH M. MITCHELL,** born South Bend, Indiana, July 28, 1941; admitted to bar, 1977, California; 1980, U.S. District Court, Central District of California; 1981, U.S. Court of Appeals, Ninth Circuit and U.S. Supreme Court. *Education:* Purdue University (B.A., cum laude, 1963); University of Freiburg, Germany and University of California at Los Angeles (M.A., 1967); Loyola University of Los Angeles (J.D., 1977). *Member:* Los Angeles County (Member, Committees on: Appellate Courts, 1979-1983; Legislation, 1978-1979; Member, Litigation Section), American and International (Member, London England Section) Bar Associations; State Bar of California; South Bay Women Lawyers Association (Recording Secretary); California Women Lawyers; German-American Chamber of Commerce. **LANGUAGES:** German. **REPORTED CASES:** Aroney vs. California Horse Racing Board (1983) 145 Cal.App.3d 928; Valdez vs. Cory (1983) 140 Cal.App.3d 116; Jabola vs. Pasadena Redevelopment Agency (1981) 125 Cal.App.3d 931; Bunker vs. City of Glendale (1980) 111 Cal.App.3d 325. **PRACTICE AREAS:** Commercial Litigation; Arbitration; Appellate and Writ Practice; Litigation with Government Agencies.

*OF COUNSEL*

**STEPHEN S. DUPLANTIS,** born Lafayette, Louisiana, April 11, 1967; admitted to bar, 1992, California and U.S. District Court, Central District of California. *Education:* Louisiana State University and A. and M. College (B.G.S., 1989); Pepperdine University (J.D., 1992). Phi Alpha Delta; Member, Moot Court Board. *Member:* State Bar of California. **PRACTICE AREAS:** Litigation; Tort Law; Appellate Practice.

Languages: English, Cantonese Chinese, and German.

REFERENCES: Union Bank, Beverly Hills; First Interstate Bank, Catalina Branch.

PROFESSIONAL BIOGRAPHIES

CALIFORNIA—LOS ANGELES

## SHARON COVERLY HUGHES

12100 WILSHIRE BOULEVARD, SUITE 945
**LOS ANGELES, CALIFORNIA 90025**
Telephone: 310-442-7622
FAX: 310-442-9923

*Business, Commercial and Bankruptcy Law.*

**SHARON COVERLY HUGHES,** born Michigan, August 13, 1951; admitted to bar, 1986, California. *Education:* Central Michigan University; California State University at Los Angeles (B.A., 1976); Whittier College School of Law (J.D., 1985). Phi Alpha Delta. President, Student Bar Association, Whittier Law School, 1984-1985. Member, Board of Directors, Whittier Law School Alumni Association, 1988-1991. *Member:* Los Angeles County (Member, Commercial Law and Bankruptcy Section; Delegate, State Bar Convention of Delegates, 1989-1991) and American Bar Associations; State Bar of California.

---

## HUGHES HUBBARD & REED LLP

350 SOUTH GRAND AVENUE, SUITE 3600
**LOS ANGELES, CALIFORNIA 90071-3442**
Telephone: 213-613-2800
Telecopier: 213-613-2950

*New York, New York Office:* One Battery Park Plaza, 10004. Telephone: 212-837-6000. Telex: 427120. Telecopier: 212-422-4726.
*Miami, Florida Office:* 201 South Biscayne Boulevard, Suite 2500, 33131-4332. Telephone: 305-358-1666. Fax: 305-371-8759. Telex: 518785.
*Paris, France Office:* 47, Avenue Georges Mandel, 75116. Telephone: 33 (0)1 44 05 80 00. Telecopier: 33 (0)1 45 53 15 04.
*Washington, D.C. Office:* 1300 I Street, N.W., Suite 900 West, 20005. Telephone: 202-408-3600. Telex: 89-2674. Telecopier: 202-408-3636.

*General Practice.*

### RESIDENT PARTNERS

**CHARLES AVRITH,** born Montreal, Canada, June 2, 1956; admitted to bar, 1980, California. *Education:* Brandeis University (B.A., 1977); Stanford University (J.D., 1980). Phi Bata Kappa. *PRACTICE AREAS:* Litigation.

**WILLIAM T. BISSET,** born Andover, Massachusetts, April 30, 1947; admitted to bar, 1973, New York; 1974, California. *Education:* University of Rochester (B.S., 1969); University of Michigan (J.D., cum laude, 1972). Member, Board of Directors, Center for International Commercial Arbitration in Los Angeles, 1986—. Member, Panel of Commercial Arbitrators, American Arbitration Association. *PRACTICE AREAS:* Litigation.

**JOHN A. BLUE,** born Cumberland, Maryland, June 18, 1943; admitted to bar, 1973, New York; 1974, California; 1978, U.S. Supreme Court. *Education:* Carnegie Institute of Technology (B.S., in Chem. Eng., 1965); Harvard University (J.D., 1972). *Member:* Los Angeles County and American Bar Associations; State Bar of California. *PRACTICE AREAS:* Business Torts; Accountants Liability; Securities Arbitration; Securities Litigation.

**RICHARD S. FRIEDMAN,** born Milwaukee, Wisconsin, April 19, 1944; admitted to bar, 1968, Illinois; 1970, California. *Education:* University of Illinois (B.A., 1965; J.D., 1968). Pi Sigma Alpha; Phi Delta Phi. Editor, Codification of Illinois Drainage Laws, 1968. Licensed Real Estate Broker, California, 1975. Lecturer, International Council of Shopping Centers Law Conference, 1988—. Chairman, Los Angeles Community Service Committee, 1975-1976. *PRACTICE AREAS:* Real Estate Law.

**GEORGE A. FURST,** born Chicago, Illinois, July 7, 1946; admitted to bar, 1972, California. *Education:* University of California at Los Angeles (B.A., magna cum laude, 1967); Yale University (M.A., 1969); Harvard University (J.D., cum laude, 1972). Phi Beta Kappa. Author, "Compulsion by a Foreign Government as a Defense in Private Antitrust Actions," 8 Harvard Legal Commentary 26, 1971. *PRACTICE AREAS:* Real Estate.

**RITA M. HAEUSLER,** born Los Angeles, California, May 8, 1958; admitted to bar, 1983, California; 1984, U.S. District Court, Central District of California. *Education:* Universidad de Salamanca, Spain; University of California at Los Angeles (B.A., cum laude, with honors, 1980; J.D., 1983). Pi Gamma Mu; Pi Sigma Alpha. *Member:* State Bar of California (Member, Intellectual Property Section; Trademark Standing Committee); American Bar Association (Member, Committee on International Copyright Treaties and Laws). *PRACTICE AREAS:* Intellectual Property and Entertainment Litigation; Representation of Receivers.

*(This Listing Continued)*

**RICHARD J. KAPLAN,** born Los Angeles, California, July 20, 1948; admitted to bar, 1973, California; 1975, New York. *Education:* University of California at Berkeley (B.A., 1970); University of California at Los Angeles (J.D., 1973). Associate Editor, U.C.L.A. Law Review, 1972-1973. *PRACTICE AREAS:* Federal and State Taxation.

**PETER M. LANGENBERG,** born St. Louis, Missouri, September 16, 1945; admitted to bar, 1977, California. *Education:* Princeton University (A.B., summa cum laude, 1972); Hastings College of Law, University of California (J.D., 1976). *LANGUAGES:* Japanese. *PRACTICE AREAS:* International; Intellectual Property; General Commercial; Corporate.

**THEODORE H. LATTY,** born Boston, Massachusetts, July 16, 1954; admitted to bar, 1973, California; 1984, New York. *Education:* Tufts University (B.S., 1967); Columbia University (M.B.A., 1969); Fordham University (J.D., 1973). Member, 1971-1973 and Editor-in-Chief, 1972-1973, Fordham Law Review. *PRACTICE AREAS:* Corporate Law; Securities Law; Sports Law.

**CHARLES D. SCHOOR,** born Pottsville, Pennsylvania, January 18, 1947; admitted to bar, 1975, California; 1980, U.S. Supreme Court. *Education:* University of Pennsylvania (B.S., Civil Engineering, 1968); University of California at Los Angeles (M.S., Computer Science, 1970); University of Southern California (J.D., 1975). Author: "Class Actions—The Right to Solicit," 16 Santa Clara Law Review 215, 1976. Deputy Chief Counsel, Pacific District Office of Special Counsel, U.S. Department of Energy, 1977-1981. *Member:* Los Angeles County Bar Association; State Bar of California. *PRACTICE AREAS:* Bankruptcy; Receiverships; Real Property and Business Litigation.

**DANIEL H. SLATE,** born Los Angeles, California, September 20, 1952; admitted to bar, 1977, California; 1978, U.S. District Court, Central District of California; 1981, U.S. Court of Appeals, Ninth Circuit. *Education:* University of Redlands (B.A., with distinction, 1974); University of California at Los Angeles (J.D., 1977). Lecturer, State Bar Continuing Education of the Bar on Introduction to Bankruptcy Practice, Handling A Chapter 11 Reorganization, and Bankruptcy Reorganizations (Chapter 11s), 1984-1994; Association of Insolvency Accountants, Ninth Annual Reorganization and Bankruptcy Conference, 1993, Lecturer on Retention of Professionals and Compensation Issues Workshop Leader, Second Annual UCLA School of Law Business Bankruptcy Institute, 1994. *Member:* Los Angeles County and American Bar Associations; The State Bar of California (Member, Business Law Section). *PRACTICE AREAS:* Bankruptcy; Out of Court Debt Restructuring; Workouts.

**MARK R. MOSKOWITZ,** born Brooklyn, New York, August 17, 1946; admitted to bar, 1972, California. *Education:* Brandeis University (B.A., magna cum laude, 1968); Harvard University (J.D., magna cum laude, 1971). Editor, Harvard Law Review, Vols. 83 and 84. Author: "Corporate Stock Repurchases under the Securities Exchange Act of 1934," Nebraska Law Review, Vol. 51, #2, Winter, 1971. Instructor, Corporate Securities, University of Southern California School of Law, 1974-1976. *PRACTICE AREAS:* Corporate Law; Securities Law; Gaming.

**JOHN R. ZEBROWSKI,** born Southampton, New York, January 31, 1953; admitted to bar, 1980, New York and U.S. District Court, Southern and Eastern Districts of New York; 1985, California and U.S. District Court, Central and Northern Districts of California; 1986, U.S. District Court, Southern and Eastern Districts of California and U.S. Court of Appeals, Ninth Circuit. *Education:* State University of New York at Stony Brook (B.A., 1975); Hofstra University (J.D., with distinction, 1979); New York University School of Law. Pi Sigma Alpha. Recipient, American Jurisprudence Awards for Criminal Procedure and Criminal Law. Law Clerk, U.S. District Court, Southern District of New York, 1979-1981. *Member:* The Association of the Bar of the City of New York; Los Angeles County, New York County (Member, Civil Rights Committee, 1982-1983) and American (Member: Natural Resources Law; Committee on Solid and Hazardous Waste, 1991-1992) Bar Associations; The State Bar of California (California EPA Permit Reform Task Force, 1993); National Association of Criminal Defense Lawyers (Environmental Crimes Committee, 1993). *PRACTICE AREAS:* Environmental.

### SPECIAL COUNSEL

**ANDREA H. BRICKER,** born Los Angeles, California, September 7, 1952; admitted to bar, 1977, California. *Education:* University of California at Berkeley (B.A., 1974); University of California at Los Angeles (J.D., 1977). *PRACTICE AREAS:* Corporate Law; Securities Law.

**RANDY B. HOLMAN,** born Schenectady, New York, November 16, 1955; admitted to bar, 1982, California. *Education:* Brigham Young University (B.A., 1979); Boalt Hall School of Law, University of California (J.D.,

*(This Listing Continued)*

CAA791B

## HUGHES HUBBARD & REED LLP, Los Angeles—Continued

1982). Note and Comment Editor, California Law Review, 1981-1982. Law Clerk to Hon. Monroe G. McKay, 10th Circuit Court of Appeals, 1982-1983.

### OF COUNSEL

**HOWARD F. HART,** born Syracuse, New York, September 5, 1947; admitted to bar, 1973, New York; 1982, California. *Education:* Cornell University (A.B., 1969); Harvard University (J.D., cum laude, 1972). Co-author: "Merger Agreements in Takeover Contests," 17 Review of Securities Regulation 779, 1984. *Member:* The Association of the Bar of the City of New York; Los Angeles County (Member, Subcommittee on Federal Regulation of Securities) and American (Member, Section on Corporation, Banking and Business Law) Bar Associations; State Bar of California. *PRACTICE AREAS:* Real Estate Law; Corporate Law; Securities Law; Administrative Law.

(For complete biographical data on all partners, see Professional Biographies at New York, New York).

---

## HUNT, ORTMANN, BLASCO, PALFFY & ROSSELL, INC.

### LOS ANGELES, CALIFORNIA

(See Pasadena)

Construction, Real Estate, Business and Commercial Litigation, Real Estate Finance, Estate Planning, Corporate, Environmental and Business Law.

---

## MICHAEL HUREY

*11679 MONTANA AVENUE, SUITE 10*
**LOS ANGELES, CALIFORNIA 90049**
Telephone: 310-471-3273
Fax: 310-471-5898

Intellectual Property Law, Patent, Trademark, Copyright and related Litigation.

**MICHAEL HUREY,** born Heidelberg, Germany, April 13, 1962; admitted to bar, 1988, California, U.S. District Court, Northern, Central and Southern Districts of California, U.S. Court of Appeals, Ninth and Federal Circuits; registered to practice before U.S. Patent and Trademark Office. *Education:* California State Polytechnic University (B.S., 1985); Loyola Law School (J.D., 1988). Sigma Gamma Tau. Recipient, American Jurisprudence Award in Conflict of Laws, Securities Regulation. Member, Loyola of Los Angeles Entertainment Law Journal, 1986-1987. *Member:* State Bar of California.

---

## HURON, ZIEVE & KIERSTEAD LLP

*1901 AVENUE OF THE STARS*
*EIGHTEENTH FLOOR*
**LOS ANGELES, CALIFORNIA 90067**
Telephone: 310-284-3400
Fax: 310-772-0037

*Portland, Oregon Office:* 1001 S.W. Fifth Avenue, Suite 1100, 97204. Telephone: 503-294-7075.

Real Estate, Representation of Financial Institutions, Bankruptcy, Insurance Bad Faith Litigation, Business Litigation and Commercial Litigaton in State and Federal Courts.

### MEMBERS OF FIRM

**LES ZIEVE,** born Detroit, Michigan, February 21, 1960; admitted to bar, 1986, California and U.S. District Court, Central, Eastern, Southern and Northern Districts of California. *Education:* University of Southern California (B.A., magna cum laude, 1982); Hastings College of the Law, University of California (J.D., 1985). Member, Moot Court Competition. *Member:* Los Angeles County Bar Association; State Bar of California; Los Angeles County Bankruptcy Forum; Orange County Bankruptcy Forum; California Trustee's Association. *PRACTICE AREAS:* Bankruptcy; Creditors Rights; Foreclosure and Real Estate Litigation.

*(This Listing Continued)*

---

**JEFFREY G. HURON,** admitted to bar, 1988, California. *Education:* Marquette University (B.A., 1985); McGeorge School of Law (J.D., 1988). Phi Alpha Theta; Pi Sigma Alpha. Note Editor, Pacific Law Journal, 1987-1988. Legal Writing Instructor, McGeorge School of Law, 1987-1988. Author: Comment, "Section 16 of The Clayton Act: Divestiture, An Intended Type of Injunctive Relief," 19 Pacific Law Journal 143, 1987. *Member:* Beverly Hills, Los Angeles County and American Bar Associations; State Bar of California. *PRACTICE AREAS:* Business; Real Estate; Lender Liability; Commercial Litigation.

---

## IBOLD & ANDERSON

*A PROFESSIONAL CORPORATION*
*PARAMOUNT PLAZA, 16TH FLOOR*
*3580 WILSHIRE BOULEVARD*
**LOS ANGELES, CALIFORNIA 90010**
Telephone: 213-380-7330
Fax: 213-380-5788

*General Civil, Criminal and Trial Practice in all State and Federal Courts. Insurance, Workers Compensation, Corporation, Commercial, Real Property, Personal Injury, Family, Trust and Probate Law.*

*FIRM PROFILE: Ibold & Anderson is a general practice law firm, representing individuals and businesses in a broad range of areas. The firm's practice covers all of California in State Municipal and Superior Court, Federal Court, Appellate Courts, Supreme Court, and State and Federal Agencies.*

*From counseling the Fresno farmer who wishes to ensure that his land will remain in the family, to advising a San Diego company as to how to comply with the Americans with Disabilities Act, Ibold & Anderson remains committed to California's people and its business community.*

**CHARLES R. IBOLD, JR.,** born Cincinnati, Ohio, June 18, 1935; admitted to bar, 1965, California. *Education:* Xavier University; Loyola University of Los Angeles (LL.B., 1964). Phi Alpha Delta. Member, Panel of Arbitrators, American Arbitration Association. Arbitrator, Los Angeles Superior Court Special Arbitration Panel. Member, California Insurance Commissioner's Workers' Compensation Task Force. Member, Fraud and Waste Subcommittee. *Member:* Wilshire and Los Angeles County Bar Associations (Chairman, Worker's Compensation Section, 1974-1975); State Bar of California; Worker's Compensation Insurance Attorneys Association (President, 1973-1974); Association of Southern California Defense Counsel.

**LESLIE G. ANDERSON,** born Jackson, Michigan, July 18, 1935; admitted to bar, 1965, California. *Education:* University of Illinois (B.S., 1957); Hastings College of Law, University of California (J.D., 1964). Phi Alpha Delta. Member, Panel of Arbitrators, American Arbitration Association. *Member:* Wilshire and Los Angeles County (Member, Worker's Compensation Section) Bar Associations; State Bar of California; Worker's Compensation Insurance Attorneys Association.

**MICHAEL I. DOUGLAS,** born Evansville, Indiana, May 13, 1952; admitted to bar, 1978, California and U.S. District Court, Central District of California. *Education:* University of California at Los Angeles (B.A., cum laude, 1974); Loyola University of Los Angeles (J.D., 1978). Judge Pro Tempore, Worker's Compensation Appeals Board. *Member:* Wilshire and Los Angeles County Bar Associations; State Bar of California.

**MARLA KELLY,** born Pocatello, Idaho, December 1, 1946; admitted to bar, 1982, California; 1983, U.S. District Court, Central District of California and U.S. Court of Appeals, Ninth Circuit; 1986 U.S. Supreme Court. *Education:* California State University at Los Angeles (B.S., 1977); Glendale University (J.D., 1981). Member, Glendale Law Review, 1980-1981. *Member:* Wilshire Bar Association; State Bar of California.

**MICHAEL J. GAREY,** born San Antonio, Texas, November 15, 1956; admitted to bar, 1981, California and U.S. District Court, Central District of California, U.S. Court of Appeals, Ninth Circuit; 1992, U.S. District Court, Eastern District of California. *Education:* California State University at Long Beach (B.A., Pol. Science, 1978); Southwestern University (J.D., 1980). Phi Sigma Alpha. Instructor, Law, Lifetime Community College. *Member:* Wilshire, Orange County, Los Angeles County and American Bar Associations; State Bar of California.

**AURORA VASQUEZ,** born Los Angeles, California, October 4, 1961; admitted to bar, 1988, California. *Education:* Loyola Marymount University (B.A., 1983); Western State University (J.D., 1987). *Member:* Wilshire (Member, Board of Governors, 1993-1994) and American Bar Associa-

*(This Listing Continued)*

tions; State Bar of California; Mexican-American Bar Association; Workers' Compensation Defense Association. *LANGUAGES:* Spanish.

**ANN THERESE CANFIELD,** born Phoenixville, Pennsylvania, July 23, 1957; admitted to bar, 1982, California. *Education:* Loyola Marymount University (B.A., magna cum laude, 1978); Loyola Law School (J.D., 1982). Alpha Sigma Nu; Phi Alpha Delta. *Member:* Wilshire (Member, Board of Governors, 1993-1994), Los Angeles County and American Bar Associations; State Bar of California.

**JAMES M. IBOLD,** born Los Angeles, California, January 13, 1964; admitted to bar, 1992, California. *Education:* California State University, Fullerton (B.A., Finance, with high honors, 1986); Georgetown University Law Center (J.D., cum laude, 1991). Phi Kappa Phi. Recipient, American Jurisprudence Award in Evidence. *Member:* Wilshire Bar Association; State Bar of California.

**ROBERT E. ROBINSON,** born Los Angeles, California, December 20, 1967; admitted to bar, 1992, California. *Education:* Loyola Marymount University (B.A., cum laude, 1989; J.D., 1992). Recipient: Presidential Scholar Award; Jesuit Community Scholar Award.

**JEFFREY HAMMILL,** born San Gabriel, California, November 18, 1966; admitted to bar, 1992, California. *Education:* Occidental College (A.B., 1989); Whittier College School of Law (J.D., summa cum laude, 1992). Member, Whittier College Law Review.

**WILLIAM A. HINZ,** born St. Charles, Illinois, May 4, 1949; admitted to bar, 1981, California; 1982, U.S. Court of Appeals, Ninth Circuit and U.S. District Court, Central District of California; 1985, U.S. Supreme Court. *Education:* Adams State College (B.A., 1972); Western State University (J.D., 1980). President, 1986-1987 and Member, Board of Directors, 1984-1988, La Habra City School District. *Member:* North Orange County (Member, Board of Directors, 1989-1994) and Wilshire Bar Associations; State Bar of California.

**DARRYL N. PURKS,** born North Miami, Florida, December 19, 1962; admitted to bar, 1994, California. *Education:* University of California at Los Angeles (B.A., economics, 1984); California Western School of Law (J.D., 1994). *Member:* State Bar of California.

*OF COUNSEL*

**E. BRUCE THOMPSON,** born Seattle, Washington, June 26, 1945; admitted to bar, 1974, California. *Education:* University of Southern California and Arizona State University (B.A., 1970); University of Southern California (J.D., 1974). Judge Pro Tempore, Los Angeles Municipal Court. *Member:* Wilshire and Los Angeles County Bar Associations; State Bar of California; Association of Southern California Defense Counsel.

REFERENCE: National Bank of California.

## STANLEY C. IMERMAN
*1901 AVENUE OF THE STARS, SUITE 1100*
**LOS ANGELES, CALIFORNIA 90067**
Telephone: 310-553-5572
Fax: 310-277-7947

*Corporations, Partnerships, Real Estate, Estate Planning, Probate and Business and Civil Litigation in all Federal and State Courts.*

**STANLEY C. IMERMAN,** born Los Angeles, California, October 2, 1939; admitted to bar, 1966, California and U.S. District Court, Central District of California; 1985, U.S. Tax Court. *Education:* University of Michigan and Stanford University (B.A., 1962; LL.B., 1965). Judge Pro Tem, Los Angeles Municipal Court, 1980-1982. *Member:* Century City and Los Angeles County Bar Associations; State Bar of California; Association of Business Trial Lawyers. *PRACTICE AREAS:* General Civil Practice; Business; Commercial Litigation; Business Transactions.

## JEFFREY C. INGBER
*1801 CENTURY PARK EAST, SUITE 2400*
**LOS ANGELES, CALIFORNIA 90067**
Telephone: 310-552-1047

*Entertainment Law.*

FIRM PROFILE: *Mr. Ingber has specialized in entertainment law, including music, television and motion pictures, since 1973, representing a diverse high-profile clientele including Neil Diamond, Linda Ronstadt, Natalie Cole and numerous producers, production and publishing companies.*

(This Listing Continued)

**JEFFREY C. INGBER,** born New York, N.Y., July 17, 1944; admitted to bar, 1970, New York; 1975, California. *Education:* Lehigh University (B.A., magna cum laude, 1966); Yale University (LL.B., 1969). Member, Panel of Arbitrators, American Arbitration Association. *Member:* The Association of the Bar of the City of New York; Beverly Hills, Los Angeles County, New York State and American Bar Associations; State Bar of California. *PRACTICE AREAS:* Entertainment Law.

## SAMUEL D. INGHAM, III
**LOS ANGELES, CALIFORNIA**
(See Beverly Hills)

*Estate Planning, Trusts, Probate, Guardianship and Conservatorship, Oil and Gas and Real Estate Law.*

## INGLIS, LEDBETTER & GOWER
Established in 1982
*500 SOUTH GRAND AVENUE, 18TH FLOOR*
**LOS ANGELES, CALIFORNIA 90071-2612**
Telephone: 213-627-6800
Facsimile: 213-622-2857

*General Business and Commercial Law, Civil Trial and Appellate Practice, Insurance Defense, Probate and Estate Planning, Tax Law.*

FIRM PROFILE: *Inglis, Ledbetter & Gower was founded in 1982 to continue the business, tax and general litigation practice of its partners. The firm's attorneys have extensive experience in the creation and operation of business entities, tax and estate planning, mergers and acquisitions, and litigation in all courts. The firm serves as corporate counsel to numerous enterprises and is engaged in civil trial and appellate practice, focusing on business litigation, and the defense of personal injury and bad faith cases, and insurance coverage issues. The general business practice includes the formation and dissolution of corporate, limited liability companies and partnership entities, lending transactions, sale and acquisition of businesses, general contract matters and tax and estate planning.*

*MEMBERS OF FIRM*

**MICHAEL K. INGLIS,** born Bronxville, New York, August 28, 1940; admitted to bar, 1967, California. *Education:* University of California at Berkeley (A.B. in Economics, 1962); University of California at Los Angeles (LL.B., 1966). Phi Delta Phi. Member, Moot Court Honors Program, 1966-1967. *Member:* Los Angeles County and American Bar Associations; The State Bar of California. *PRACTICE AREAS:* Mergers and Acquisitions Law; Corporate Law.

**STEVEN K. LEDBETTER,** born Whittier, California, February 7, 1947; admitted to bar, 1975, California. *Education:* University of Southern California (B.S. in Accounting, 1969); Southwestern University (J.D., 1975). Revenue Agent and Appellate Conference, Office of the Regional Commissioner, Internal Revenue Service, 1969-1976. *Member:* Los Angeles County Bar Association; State Bar of California. *PRACTICE AREAS:* Tax Law; Corporate Law.

**RICHARD S. GOWER,** born Chicago, Illinois, March 14, 1947; admitted to bar, 1973, California. *Education:* Northern Illinois University (B.S., 1969); California State University at Los Angeles; Loyola University (J.D., 1973). *Member:* Los Angeles County Bar Association; State Bar of California; Association of Southern California Defense Counsel; Defense Research Institute. *PRACTICE AREAS:* Insurance Defense.

**RICHARD G. RITCHIE,** born Torrance, California, September 12, 1940; admitted to bar, 1972, California. *Education:* California State College (B.A., 1968); University of California at Los Angeles (J.D., 1971). Member, University of California at Los Angeles Law Review, 1971. *Member:* Los Angeles County and American Bar Associations; The State Bar of California; Southern California Defense Counsel. *PRACTICE AREAS:* Business Litigation; Insurance Coverage; Arbitration; Mediation.

**GREGORY H. GOCKE,** born Los Angeles, California, August 27, 1946; admitted to bar, 1974, California. *Education:* University of Southern California (B.S., 1969); Loyola University of Los Angeles (J.D., 1973). *Member:* Los Angeles County Bar Association; State Bar of California; Association of Southern California Defense Counsel; Defense Research Institute. *PRACTICE AREAS:* Insurance Defense.

(This Listing Continued)

## INGLIS, LEDBETTER & GOWER, Los Angeles—Continued

**JOHN E. HOPE,** born San Francisco, California, April 7, 1954; admitted to bar, 1981, Washington and California. *Education:* University of Washington (B.A., 1976); University of San Diego School of Law (J.D., cum laude, 1981). Member: Moot Court Honors Program, 1980-1981; National Order of the Barristers, 1981. *Member:* Los Angeles County, Washington State and American Bar Associations; The State Bar of California. **PRACTICE AREAS:** Business Litigation.

### ASSOCIATES

**TIMOTHY E. KEARNS,** born Sacramento, California, March 22, 1961; admitted to bar, 1989, California. *Education:* California State University at Sacramento (B.A., Econ., 1984; B.A., English, 1984); Loyola Law School, Los Angeles (J.D., 1989). Staff Member, Loyola Law Review, 1988-1989. *Member:* Los Angeles County and American Bar Associations; State Bar of California. **PRACTICE AREAS:** Insurance Defense.

**JAMES W. HOLCHIN,** born Los Angeles, California, August 7, 1964; admitted to bar, 1992, California and U.S. Court of Appeals, Ninth Circuit. *Education:* University of California (B.A., English, 1986; B.A., Economics, 1986); Loyola Law School, Los Angeles (J.D., 1992). Member, St. Thomas Moore Honor Society. Staff, 1990-1991; Articles Editor, 1991-1992, International & Comparative Law Journal, Loyola University of Los Angeles. *Member:* State Bar of California. **PRACTICE AREAS:** Insurance Defense.

**NANCY B. GONZALEZ,** born Havana, Cuba, June 16, 1966; admitted to bar, 1993, California and U.S. Court of Appeals, Ninth Circuit. *Education:* Loyola Marymount University; University of California at Los Angeles (B.A., 1989; J.D., cum laude, 1993). Member Moot Court. *Member:* Los Angeles County (Member, Domestic Violence Project Committee and Senior Citizens Outreach Committee), Cuban American and Hispanic National Bar Associations; Women Lawyers Association of Los Angeles. **LANGUAGES:** Spanish. **PRACTICE AREAS:** Insurance Defense.

### LEGAL SUPPORT PERSONNEL

**KEVIN WATKINS,** born Santa Monica, California, August 25, 1957. *Education:* Waterson College (Certificate of Paralegal).

REPRESENTATIVE CLIENTS: Bio-Diagnostics Laboratories, Inc.; Brehm Communications, Inc.; California Commerce Club; Chubb Group of Insurance Companies; Eddings Brothers, Inc.; Global Manufacturers Corp.; Inter-Insurance Exchange of the Automobile Club of Southern California; K & K Office Furniture; National Cold Storage, Inc.; Presto Food Products, Inc.; Cecil Saydah Company; Transaction Solutions, Inc.; Woodland Farms, Inc.

---

## INMAN, STEINBERG, NYE & STONE, APC
### LOS ANGELES, CALIFORNIA
(See Beverly Hills)

*General Business Law with an emphasis on Business, Real Estate and Securities Litigation in Federal and State Courts, Immigration Law, Estate Planning, Trust Administration, Probate and Corporate Law.*

---

## IRELL & MANELLA LLP

A Law Partnership including Professional Corporations

*Established in 1941*

**SUITE 900, 1800 AVENUE OF THE STARS (CENTURY CITY)**
**LOS ANGELES, CALIFORNIA 90067-4276**

Telephone: 310-277-1010
Cable Address: "Irella LSA"
Telecopier: 310-203-7199
URL: http://www.irell.com

Downtown Los Angeles Office: Suite 3300, 333 South Hope Street, 90071-3042. Telephone: 213-620-1555. Telecopier: 213-229-0515.
Newport Beach, California Office: Suite 500, 840 Newport Center Drive, 92660-6324. Telephone: 714-760-0991. Telecopier: 714-760-5200.

*General Civil Practice and Litigation in all State and Federal Courts and Arbitration Tribunals, Administrative, Antitrust, Aviation, Computer, Corporate, Corporate Securities and Finance, Mergers and Acquisitions, Election and Redistricting, Entertainment, Estate Planning, Trusts and Probate, Federal, State and Local Taxation, First Amendment and Media, International Business and Taxation, Insolvency, Bankruptcy, Reorganization and Creditors Rights, Insurance, Labor Relations, Wrongful Termination and Discrimination, Pension and Profit Sharing, Real Estate, Real Estate Finance, Banking and Secured Transactions Law. Patent, Trademark and Copyright Law. Intellectual Property and Trade Secrets. High Technology Litigation, including Intellectual Property, Trade Secrets and Unfair Competition Litigation. Selected Criminal Defense.*

### MEMBERS OF FIRM

**EUGENE M. BERGER** (1892-1944).

**ALLAN J. ABSHEZ,** born Buffalo, New York, October 5, 1956; admitted to bar, 1984, California. *Education:* University of California at Berkeley (A.B., summa cum laude, 1978); Boalt Hall School of Law, University of California (J.D., 1984). Phi Beta Kappa. Recipient: Boalt Hall and American Jurisprudence Award, Constitution Law. Judicial Extern, Associate Justice Allen Broussard, California Supreme Court, 1983-1984.

**JAMES N. ADLER, (P.C.),** born Kansas City, Missouri, February 12, 1936; admitted to bar, 1961, Missouri; 1966, California. *Education:* Princeton University (B.S.E., 1958); University of Michigan (J.D., 1961). Phi Beta Kappa; Order of the Coif; Barristers; Phi Delta Phi. Editor-in-Chief, Michigan Law Review, 1960-1961. Law Clerk to Justice Charles E. Whittaker and Chief Justice Earl Warren, U.S. Supreme Court, 1961-1962. Special Assistant to Solicitor, U.S. Department of Labor, 1962-1963; Member of Staff, President's Appalachian Regional Commission, 1963-1964. Director (Acting), Men's Urban Centers, Job Corps, U.S. Office of Economic Opportunity, 1964-1965; Member, Board of Directors of the Office of Compliance, 1995—; Chair, Los Angeles County Public Social Services Commission, 1992—. *Member:* Los Angeles County (Chair, Labor Law Section, 1989-1990) and American (Management Co-Chair, Subcommittee on Legislation, Committee on Employee Rights and Responsibilities, Section of Labor and Employment Law, 1988-1991) Bar Associations; State Bar of California; Industrial Relations Research Association, Los Angeles Chapter (President, 1994).

**SCOTT D. BASKIN, (P.C.),** born New York, N.Y., October 24, 1953; admitted to bar, 1978, California. *Education:* Stanford University (B.A., 1975); Yale University (J.D., 1978). Editor, Yale Law Journal, 1977-1978. Author: "Let the Buyer Beware: the Pre-Sale Examination Strategy," Computer Litigation Journal, 1995; Practicalities of Using Experts in Civil Litigation, 1990; "The Use of Experts in Civil Actions," Preparing and Examining Expert Witnesses in Civil Litigation, 1987; "The Use of Experts in Non-Medical Malpractice Actions," Non-Medical Professional Malpractice, 1985. Co-author: "The Internal Corporate Investigation: Ad Hoc 'Search and Destroy' or Routine Record Retention Programs," The Internal Corporate Investigation 209, 1980. Assistant in Instruction, Constitutional Law, Yale Law School, 1977-1978. Law Clerk to Hon. Herbert Y.C. Choy, U.S. Court of Appeals, Ninth Circuit, 1978-1979. *Member:* State Bar of California; American Bar Association. (Resident at Newport Beach).

**CARY J. A. BERGER,** born Cincinnati, Ohio, September 22, 1963; admitted to bar, 1989, California. *Education:* Columbia University (B.A., 1985); Stanford University (J.D., 1989). Assistant Managing Editor, Stanford Law Review, 1988-1989. Editorial Board, Los Angeles Lawyer. *Member:* State Bar of California; American Bar Association; Financial Lawyers Conference. (Downtown Los Angeles Office). **LANGUAGES:** Italian. **Email:** cberger@irell.com

**RICHARD L. BERNACCHI, (P.C.),** born Los Angeles, California, December 15, 1938; admitted to bar, 1965, California. *Education:* University of Santa Clara (B.Sc., 1961); University of Southern California (LL.B., 1964). Beta Gamma Sigma; Order of the Coif. Editor-in-Chief, Southern California Law Review, 1963-1964. Co-author: "Bernacchi on Computer Law: A Guide to the Legal and Management Aspects of Computer Technology," Little Brown & Co., 1986; "Data Processing Contracts and the Law," Little Brown & Co., 1974; "Acquiring Software Companies," 1992 Nordic Yearbook of Law and Informatics; "Distribution of Computer Software in Non-U.S. Countries: Five Important Concerns," 1987 Licensing Law Handbook, D.C. Toedt ed., 1987; "A Structured Approach to Analyzing the Substantial Similarity of Computer Software in Copyright Infringement Cases," 20 Ariz. State Law Journal 625, Fall, 1988; "Computer System Procurement," 30 Emory Law Journal 395, Spring, 1981; "The Leasing of Hardware" and "Taxation of Computer Hardware and Software," Computers and the Law, 3d Edition, Section of Science and Technology, American Bar Association, R. Bigelow ed., 1981. Member: Advisory Board, Arizona Law and Technology Institute, 1982-1986; Planning Committee, U.S.C. Computer Law Institute, 1980—; Advisory Board, Computer and Technology Law Journal, University of Santa Clara Law School, 1984-1990. Member, Board of Editors, Computer Law Strategist, 1986-1993. *Member:* Century City, Los Angeles County and American Bar Associations; State Bar of California; Computer Law Association (Member,

*(This Listing Continued)*

Board of Advisors, 1986—; Director, 1973-1986; President, 1981-1983); International Bar Association (Co-Chairman, Committee R of Section on Business Law, 1994—; Vice Chairman, 1991-1994). *Email:* dbernacchi@irell.com

**SHERI A. BLUEBOND,** born Los Angeles, California, May 15, 1961; admitted to bar, 1985, California. *Education:* University of California at Los Angeles (B.A., summa cum laude, 1982; J.D., 1985). Phi Beta Kappa; Alpha Lambda Delta; Order of the Coif. UCLA Law Review. Recipient, American Jurisprudence Awards in Labor Law, Commercial Law, Conflicts of Law, Remedies and Wills and Trusts; BNA Law Student Award; Hornbook Award. Mediator, Bankruptcy Mediation Program, U.S. Bankruptcy Court, Central District of California. Author: "What Every Real Estate Lawyer Should Know About the 1994 Amendments to the Bankruptcy Code," Practical Real Estate Lawyer (July, 1995); "Assessing the Usefulness of a Chapter 11 Filing," Business Workouts Manual (Supp. 1995); "The Supreme Court Extends Availability of Affirmative Defense to Long-Term Debt," L.A. Bus. J. (Spring 1992); "The Downside Of Taking an Insider's Guaranty," L.A. Bus. J. (Spring 1992); "Decisions on Limitations Period Could Spell Trouble for Debtors in Possession," 3 Bankr. L. Rev. 59 (Fall 1991). Lecturer: Practising Law Institute, American Bar Association, California Continuing Education of the Bar, California CPA Education Foundation, State Bar of California, Los Angeles County Bar Association, Beverly Hills Bar Association, Financial Lawyers Conference. Member, Board of Trustees, Jewish Big Brothers/Camp Max Straus. *Member:* Los Angeles County Bar Association (Bankruptcy Committee and Executive Committee, Commercial Law and Bankruptcy Section); State Bar of California; Los Angeles Bankruptcy Forum (Board of Governors); Financial Lawyers Conference (Board of Governors). (Downtown Los Angeles Office). *Email:* sbluebond@irell.com

**RICHARD H. BOROW, (P.C.),** born New York, N.Y., June 19, 1935; admitted to bar, 1959, New York; 1966, California; 1985, Maine. *Education:* Hunter College (A.B., with honors, 1956); Columbia University (LL.B., 1959). Member, Board of Editors, Columbia Law Review, 1958-1959. Assistant to the Special Master (Hon. Simon H. Rifkind), Arizona v. California et al, 1959-1960. Adjunct Professor of Law, Litigation and Trial Techniques, UCLA Law School, 1971-1983. Member of the ad hoc Committee to Study the Evaluation of Lawyers, 1979-1984, of the Ninth Circuit Judicial Conference. *Member:* Board of Directors, Public Advocates, Inc., 1983-1993; Board of Editors, Federal Litigation Guide, Mathew Bender, 1985—; Board of Trustees and Executive Committee, Washington Institute For Near East Policy, 1987—. Alternative Dispute Resolution Panelist, Center for Public Resources, Inc., 1988—. Civil Justice Advisory Group (Biden Bill), Central District of California, 1991-1993. *Member:* Los Angeles County (Member, 1977-1993 and Chair, 1983-1984, Judiciary Committee; Member, Judicial Appointments Committee, 1990-1992); New York State, Maine State and American (Member, Committee on Corporate Counsel, Section of Litigation) Bar Associations; State Bar of California; The Association of the Bar of the City of New York; American Judicature Society; Association of Business Trial Lawyers (Member, Board of Governors, 1977-1979). *Email:* rborow@irell.com

**DERRICK O. BOSTON,** born Georgetown, Guyana, May 31, 1964; admitted to bar, 1990, California. *Education:* Harvard University (B.A., magna cum laude, 1984; J.D., 1987). Editor, Harvard Law Review, 1985-1987. Law Clerk to the Honorable John T. Noonan, Jr., U.S. Court of Appeals, Ninth Circuit, 1988-1989. Alternate Member, Board of Directors, L.A. County Metropolitan Transportation Authority, 1993. Special Assistant, Office of the Mayor of the City of Los Angeles, 1992. Legal counsel, Independent Commission on the Los Angeles Police Department (The Christopher Commission), 1991. Author, Case Comment, "Leading Cases-Review Barred By State Procedural Default," 100 Harv. L. Rev. 240 (1986). Co-Author: "Overview of SEC Initiatives and Agenda Outline of Regulation S," published in connection with Prentice-Hall Acquisitions and Takeovers Seminar, 1990. *Member:* State Bar of California. **LANGUAGES:** French.

**CHRISTINE W. S. BYRD,** born Oakland, California, April 11, 1951; admitted to bar, 1976, California. *Education:* Stanford University (B.A., 1972); University of Virginia (J.D., 1975). Law Clerk to Judge William P. Gray, U.S. District Court, Central District of California, 1975-1976. Assistant U.S. Attorney, Central District of California, U.S. Attorney's Office, 1982-1987.

**FRANK A. CAPUT,** born Los Angeles, California, August 22, 1940; admitted to bar, 1966, California. *Education:* University of Southern California (B.S. cum laude, 1962); Harvard University (LL.B., 1965). *Member:*
*(This Listing Continued)*

Los Angeles County and American Bar Associations; State Bar of California. (Resident at Newport Beach).

**LOUIS M. CASTRUCCIO, (P.C.),** born Pasadena, California, July 24, 1938; admitted to bar, 1965, California. *Education:* Santa Clara University (A.B., 1960); University of Southern California (LL.B., 1964); Harvard University (LL.M., 1966). Order of the Coif. Managing Editor, Southern California Law Review, 1963-1964. Author: "Becoming More Inevitable? Death and Taxes...and Taxes," Vol. 17, UCLA Law Review, p. 459, 1970. Author or co-author: "Developments in Federal Securities Regulation," 1975, 1976, 1977, 1978, 1982 and 1983; The Business Lawyer; Vol. 31 (July 1976); Vol. 32 (July 1977); Vol. 33 (April 1978); Vol. 34 (April 1979); Vol. 38 (May and August 1983); and Vol. 39 (May 1984) and Vol. 40 (November 1984). *Member:* Board of Regents, Santa Clara University, 1979-1986; Board of Trustees, Santa Clara University, 1986—; Board of Visitors, Santa Clara University School of Law, 1980-1994. *Member:* Los Angeles County (Chairperson, Election Laws Committee, 1975-1977; Vice Chairperson, 1977-1978 and Chairperson, 1978-1979, Business and Corporations Law Section) and American (Chairperson, 1981-1982 and Co-Chairperson, 1983-1985, Subcommittee on Annual Review of Federal Securities Regulation) Bar Associations; State Bar of California.

**DANIEL G. CHRISTOPHER,** born Wilmington, Delaware, June 9, 1964; admitted to bar, 1989, California. *Education:* Villanova University (B.E.E., 1986); Columbia University (J.D., 1989). Stone Scholar. *Member:* State Bar of California; American Bar Association.

**MORGAN CHU,** born New York, New York, December 27, 1950; admitted to bar, 1976, California. *Education:* University of California at Los Angeles (A.B., 1971; M.A., 1972; Ph.D., 1973); Yale University (M.S.L., 1974); Harvard Law School (J.D., magna cum laude, 1976). Clerk, Hon. Charles M. Merrill, U.S. Court of Appeals, Ninth Circuit, 1976-1977. Adjunct Professor of Law, University of California at Los Angeles Law School, 1979-1982. Judge Pro Tem, Los Angeles Municipal Court, 1983-1986. Named as one of the Top 10 Litigators in the Nation by National Law Journal, 1995. Named Executive of the Year-Law by The Los Angeles Business Journal, 1994. Selected as one of the Country's 100 Most Influential Lawyers by National Law Journal, 1994. Chosen by the California Lawyer as one of the top intellectual property lawyers in a survey of clients and lawyers, and as a member of its Dream Team law firm, 1992. Significant Achievement Award for Excellence and Innovation in Alternative Dispute Resolution (ADR) from Center for Public Resources, 1987. Member, Board of Directors, Public Counsel, 1993—. *Member:* Los Angeles County (Member, Judiciary Committee, 1983—), American (Member: Litigation Section; Chairperson, High Technology, Intellectual Property and Patent Trials of Trial Practice Committee, 1986-1990; Vice Chairman, Substantive Committee, Litigation Section, 1990-1991; Associate Editor, Litigation News, 1981-1984) and Federal Circuit Bar Associations; State Bar of California; Los Angeles Intellectual Property Law Association (Member, Board of Directors, 1991-1993).

**RICHARD DE BODO,** born New York, N.Y., July 19, 1956; admitted to bar, 1986, Pennsylvania; 1987, California. *Education:* Harvard University (B.A., 1978; J.D., 1983). Instructor: National Institute of Trial Advocacy, 1988—; Hastings Center for Trial and Appellate Advocacy, 1989—. Law Clerk to: The Honorable James M. Fitzgerald, U.S. District Court, District of Alaska, 1983-1984; The Honorable Betty B. Fletcher, U.S. Court of Appeals for the Ninth Circuit, 1984-1985. *Member:* State Bar of California; Pennsylvania Bar Association.

**DAVID A. DULL,** born Roanoke, Virginia, January 7, 1949; admitted to bar, 1982, California. *Education:* Yale University (B.A., summa cum laude, 1971; J.D., 1982); Oxford University. Phi Beta Kappa. Woodrow Wilson Fellow. Assistant to President, United Nations Association of the U.S.A., New York City, 1977-1980. *Member:* Bar Association of San Francisco; Santa Clara County and American (Member: Section of Business Law; Section of Taxation; Section of International Law and Practice; Section of Science and Technology) Bar Associations; State Bar of California; American Society of International Law; Computer Law Association. *Email:* ddull@irell.com

**JAMES F. ELLIOTT,** born Ames, Iowa, June 2, 1953; admitted to bar, 1980, Arizona; 1981, California; 1982, U.S. Court of Appeals, Ninth Circuit; 1988, U.S. Supreme Court; U.S. District Court, Central, Eastern, Northern and Southern Districts. *Education:* Columbia University; University of Arizona (B.A., 1976; J.D., 1980). Phi Beta Kappa; Phi Beta Phi; Order of the Coif. Member, 1977-1979 and Articles Editor, 1979-1980, Arizona Law Review. Law Clerk to Judge Thomas Tang, U.S. Court of Appeals, Ninth Circuit, 1980-1981. Contributing Editor: "California Practice Handbook: Employment Discrimination," Matthew Bender, October,
*(This Listing Continued)*

**IRELL & MANELLA LLP, Los Angeles—Continued**

1992. Author: "Beyond McKennon v. Nashville Banner Publishing Co.: Using The After-Acquired Evidence Doctrine to Bar Discrimination Claims"; "The After-Acquired Evidence Doctrine: Is There Life After McKennon?", California Employment Law Reporter, Matthew Bender, May, 1995; "Nuts & Bolts of Drafting Executive Employment Agreements and Independent Contractor Agreements," presented by the Los Angeles County Bar Association Labor and Employment Law Section, 1993; "Defense Strategy in the First Ninety Days of a Wrongful Termination Case," Second Annual Prentice-Hall Law and Business Labor and Employment Law Seminar, February, 1993 and Business Law, Inc. in Fall 1993; "California Wrongful Termination and Discrimination Update - 1990 Developments," published by USC Law Center Institute for Corporate Counsel, 1991. Co-Author: "Public Policy Wrongful Termination Actions," Los Angeles Lawyer, October, 1992; "Assessing the Impact of Shoemaker v. Myers and Rojo v. Kliger," by 12th Annual Los Angeles County Bar Labor and Employment Law Symposium, 1992. Chairperson, 16th Annual Los Angeles County Labor and Employment Law Symposium. Moderator and Panelist: 12th-15th Annual Los Angeles County Labor and Employment Law Symposiums, 1992-1995. Panelist, "The After-Acquired Evidence Doctrine Still Lives," Los Angeles County Bar Association Labor and Employment Law Section, May 1995. Faculty Member, National Institute for Trial Advocacy, 1989—. Member, Trial Attorney Project, Los Angeles City Attorney's Office, 1989. *Member:* Los Angeles County Bar Association (Member, Executive Committee, Labor Law Section, 1990—); State Bar of Arizona; State Bar of California; Association of Business Trial Lawyers.

**MICHAEL G. ERMER,** born St. Louis, Missouri, May 20, 1958; admitted to bar, 1983, California. *Education:* Washington University (A.B., with honors, 1979); Harvard University (J.D., cum laude, 1983). Legal Methods Instructor, Harvard Law School, 1982. *Member:* Orange County and American (Member, Sections of Litigation, Tort and Insurance Practice, and National Resources, Energy and Environmental Law) Bar Associations; State Bar of California. (Resident at Newport Beach).

**DORETTE S. FEIT,** born Baltimore, Maryland, September 20, 1954; admitted to bar, 1979, California. *Education:* University of Maryland (B.A., summa cum laude, 1976); University of California at Berkeley (J.D., 1979). Phi Beta Kappa; Phi Kappa Phi. Associate Editor, California Law Review, 1977-1978. *Member:* State Bar of California; American Bar Association (Member, Section of Litigation).

**JOHN C. FOSSUM, (P.C.),** born Minneapolis, Minnesota, May 20, 1941; admitted to bar, 1967, California. *Education:* University of California at Berkeley (B.A., 1963; LL.B., 1966). Order of the Coif. Book Review Editor, California Law Review, 1965-1966. *Member:* State Bar of California. (Resident at Newport Beach).

**ELLIOT G. FREIER,** born Huntington, New York, April 2, 1961; admitted to bar, 1986, California. *Education:* University of Virginia (B.A., 1983); Yale University (J.D., 1986). Phi Beta Kappa. Contributing Author: "Collier on Bankruptcy Taxation". Co-Author: "Preservation and Use of Net Operating Losses and other Tax Attributes in a Consolidated Return Context," 41 Major Tax Planning ¶500 (1989). Board of Editors: The M & A Tax Report (1992-1995). *Member:* State Bar of California; American Bar Association (Chairman, Subcommittee on Affiliation and Control, 1990-1991, Chairman, Subcommittee on Consolidated Returns, 1991-1995, Vice Chairman, 1995-1996, Chairman, 1996—, Committee on Affiliated and Related Corporations, Taxation Section). *Email:* efreier@irell.com

**PAUL N. FRIMMER, (P.C.),** born New York, N.Y., June 8, 1945; admitted to bar, 1970, New York; 1972, California. *Education:* Queens College (B.A., 1966); Fordham University (J.D., cum laude, 1969). National Trustee, Leukemia Society of America, 1979—. Trustee, Los Angeles Children's Museum, 1980-1985. *Member:* State Bar of California. Fellow, International Academy of Probate and Trust Law. Fellow, American College of Trust and Estate Counsel.

**GARY N. FRISCHLING,** born Santa Monica, California, February 9, 1962; admitted to bar, 1987, California. *Education:* University of California at Berkeley (B.S.E.E.C.S., magna cum laude, 1984); University of California at Los Angeles (J.D., 1987). Phi Beta Kappa; Tau Beta Pi; Eta Kappa Nu; Order of the Coif; UCLA National Moot Court Team. *Member:* Los Angeles County (Member, Intellectual Property and Unfair Competition Section) and American (Member, Sections on: Patent, Trademark and Copyright Law; Litigation) Bar Associations; State Bar of California (Member, Intellectual Property Practice Section).

*(This Listing Continued)*

**ROY S. GEIGER,** born Culver City, California, June 8, 1950; admitted to bar, 1979, California. *Education:* University of California at Los Angeles (B.A., 1972); University of California at Berkeley (J.D., 1979). Phi Beta Kappa. Associate Editor, California Real Property Journal, 1990-1993. Co-Author: "Lenders and Leases," 7 California Real Property Journal 17, Fall, 1989. Author: "Dover Mobile Estates v. Fiber Form Products Inc.: The Subordinate Tenant Walks and the Court Enforces an Automatic Subordination Provision in a Lease," 8 California Real Property Journal 30, Fall, 1990; AB 1735: "The Remediation of Hazardous Lending," 10 California Real Property Journal 25, Summer 1992. Co-Chair, Joint Committee on Legal Opinions in California Real Property Transactions. *Member:* Los Angeles County and American (Member, Business Law Section and Property and Probate Section) Bar Associations; State Bar of California (Member, Real Estate Section-Executive Committee, 1990-1994). (Downtown Los Angeles Office).

**MARTIN N. GELFAND,** born Chicago, Illinois, December 10, 1941; admitted to bar, 1965, Illinois; 1968, California. *Education:* University of Illinois; DePaul University (LL.B., 1965); Stanford University (LL.M., 1966). Member, DePaul University Law Review, 1964-1965. Assistant U.S. Attorney, Tax Division, Central District of California, 1970-1972. Lawyer Representative to the Ninth Circuit Judicial Conference from the Central District of California, 1990-1992. *Member:* State Bar of California. [Judge Advocate, USAF, 1966-1970]

**ANDRA BARMASH GREENE,** born Chicago, Illinois, March 11, 1957; admitted to bar, 1981, District of Columbia; 1986, California. *Education:* Brown University (B.A., magna cum laude, 1978); Harvard University (J.D., 1981); Georgetown University. Phi Beta Kappa. Law Clerk to Judge Catherine B. Kelly, D.C. Court of Appeals, 1981-1982. Author: "Everybody's Doing It-But Who Should Be? Standing to Make a Disqualification Motion Based on an Attorney's Representation of a Client with Interests Adverse to Those of a Former Client," 6 University of Puget Sound Law Review 205, Spring, 1983. Co-Editor: "The Woman Advocate: Excelling in the 90's" (1995). *Member:* State Bar of California; The District of Columbia Bar; Orange County (Member, Judicial Nominations Committee) and American (Member, Section on Litigation; Chair, Committee on Program Evaluation and Utilization, 1992-1995; Co-Chair, 1993 Conference on the Woman Advocate) Bar Associations; Orange County Women Lawyers Association. (Resident at Newport Beach).

**PETER J. GREGORA,** born Syracuse, New York, May 25, 1946; admitted to bar, 1971, California. *Education:* University of Redlands (B.A., 1967); Yale University (J.D., 1970). Member, Board of Editors, Yale Law Journal, 1968-1970. *Member:* The State Bar of California; American Bar Association.

**ANDREW W. GROSS,** born Los Angeles, California, March 29, 1961; admitted to bar, 1990, California. *Education:* University of California at Berkeley (A.B., with highest distinction, 1983); Boalt Hall School of Law, University of California (J.D., 1988). Phi Beta Kappa; Omicron Delta Epsilon; Order of the Coif. Law Clerk to the Honorable Stephen Reinhardt, U.S. Court of Appeals, Ninth Circuit, 1988-1989. *Member:* State Bar of California. *Email:* agross@irell.com

**THEODORE E. GUTH,** born Fort Richardson, Alaska, August 22, 1954; admitted to bar, 1978, California. *Education:* University of Notre Dame (B.S., summa cum laude, 1975); Yale University (J.D., 1978). Phi Beta Kappa. Full Time Adjunct Professor, UCLA School of Law, 1981-1983. President, Dabney/Resnick, Inc., 1993-1995. Co-Author: "Drafting Agreements for the Sale of Businesses," California CEB, 1989. *Member:* State Bar of California; American Bar Association.

**KENNETH R. HEITZ,** born Santa Maria, California, June 25, 1947; admitted to bar, 1972, California. *Education:* University of California at Los Angeles (B.A., cum laude, 1969); Harvard University (J.D., cum laude, 1972). Phi Beta Kappa. Deputy General Counsel, The Webster Commission, 1992. *Member:* The State Bar of California; American Bar Association (Member, Sections on: Corporation, Banking and Business Law; Litigation).

**CATHERINE H. HELM,** born West Berlin, Germany, February 9, 1959; admitted to bar, 1983, District of Columbia; 1985, California. *Education:* Harvard University (A.B., magna cum laude, 1980; J.D., cum laude, 1983). Phi Beta Kappa. Author: "The Practicality of Increasing the Use of NLRA Section 10(j) Injunctions," 7 Industrial Relations Law Journal 599 (1985); Chapter 20, "Life As A Mom Who Works Part-Time," in The Woman Advocate (J.M. Snyder and A.B. Greene, eds., 1995). Law Clerk, Hon. James A. Belson, District of Columbia Court of Appeals, 1983-1984. Adjunct Professor, Loyola Law School of Los Angeles, 1992. *Member:*

*(This Listing Continued)*

Century City, Los Angeles County and American Bar Associations; State Bar of California; Industrial Relations Research Association.

**BRIAN J. HENNIGAN,** born Chicago, Illinois, January 14, 1952; admitted to bar, 1976, Illinois; 1979, California. *Education:* Northwestern University (B.A., cum laude, 1972); University of Virginia; Northwestern University (J.D., cum laude, 1976). Chairman, Moot Court Competition, 1976. Assistant U.S. Attorney and Deputy Chief, Government Fraud Section, Central District of California, 1983-1989. *Member:* State Bar of California; Illinois State Bar Association. (Downtown Los Angeles Office).

**LOUIS A. HUSKINS, (P.C.),** born Flushing, New York, October 29, 1943; admitted to bar, 1968, Illinois; 1970, California. *Education:* Trinity College, Connecticut (B.A., cum laude, 1965); University of Chicago (J.D., cum laude, 1968). Phi Beta Kappa; Order of the Coif. Member, Board of Editors, University of Chicago Law Review, 1966-1968. Assistant Professor of Law, University of Nebraska College of Law, 1968-1970. *Member:* State Bar of California.

**MILTON B. HYMAN, (P.C.),** born Los Angeles, California, November 19, 1941; admitted to bar, 1967, California. *Education:* University of California at Los Angeles (B.A., 1963); Harvard University (J.D., magna cum laude, 1966). Phi Beta Kappa. Member, Board of Editors, Harvard Law Review, 1964-1966. Sheldon Traveling Fellow, Harvard University, 1966-1967. Co-Author: Collier on Bankruptcy Taxation, Matthew Bender & Co., Inc. (1992). Assistant to the General Counsel, Office of the Secretary of the Army, 1967-1970. *Member:* State Bar of California; American Bar Association (Chairman, Committee on Affiliated and Related Corporations, Taxation Section, 1981-1983; Chairman, Subcommittee on Affiliated Group Acquisitions, Corporate Tax Committee, Taxation Section, 1988-1995); American Law Institute (Member, Tax Advisory Group, Federal Income Project, 1976—).

**EDEBEATU C. IBEKWE,** born Onitsha, Nigeria, March 25, 1954; admitted to bar, 1983, California. *Education:* Miami University (A.B., 1976); University of Santa Clara (M.B.A., 1979); University of California at Los Angeles (J.D., 1983); The Nigerian Law School (B.L., 1984). *Member:* Los Angeles County Bar Association; State Bar of California; The Nigerian Bar. (Downtown Los Angeles Office). *Email:* eibekwe@irell.com

**ANTHONY T. ILER,** born Santa Monica, California, March 18, 1960; admitted to bar, 1986, California. *Education:* Claremont Men's College (B.A., summa cum laude, 1982); University of California at Berkeley (J.D., 1986). Order of the Coif. Member, University of California Law Review, 1985-1986. Co-Author: "Negotiating an Acquisition," 16th Annual Securities Regulation Institute, 1988 and "Insider Trading Under Section 16 of the Securities Exchange Act," Matthew Bender & Co. Securities Regulation (1991). *Member:* State Bar of California; American Bar Association. (Downtown Los Angeles Office).

**THOMAS W. JOHNSON, JR.,** born Indianapolis, Indiana, October 18, 1941; admitted to bar, 1969, Indiana; 1970, California. *Education:* Indiana University (B.S., 1963; J.D., summa cum laude, 1969). Editor-in-Chief, Indiana Legal Forum, 1967-1968. Law Clerk to Chief Justice Donald H. Hunter, Indiana Supreme Court, 1968-1969. Co-Author: "California Practice Guide: Insurance Litigation" (The Rutter Group, 1995); "California Liability Insurance Practice: Claims & Litigation" (California Continuing Education of the Bar, 1992). *Member:* Orange County (Member, Insurance Law Section) and American (Chair, Insurance Coverage Litigation Committee of the Tort and Insurance Practice Section, 1995-1996) Bar Associations; State Bar of California (Member, Business Law Section; Member, 1978-1980 and Chairman, 1979-1980, Committee on Group Insurance Programs). (Resident at Newport Beach).

**SANDRA GERSON KANENGISER,** born New York, N.Y., December 23, 1955; admitted to bar, 1984, California. *Education:* University of California at San Diego (B.A., summa cum laude, 1977); Hebrew University; University of Southern California (J.D., 1984). Member, Southern California Law Review, 1982-1983. *Member:* State Bar of California; American Bar Association.

**EDMUND M. KAUFMAN, (P.C.),** born Cleveland, Ohio, March 23, 1930; admitted to bar, 1960, California. *Education:* University of California at Los Angeles (B.S., 1956); Columbia University (LL.B., 1959). Phi Beta Kappa. Member, Board of Editors, Columbia Law Review, 1958-1959. Lecturer, University of Southern California Graduate School of Law, 1961-1963. Member, Board of Directors and Executive Committee, Los Angeles Music Center Opera, 1986—. *Member:* State Bar of California. (Downtown Los Angeles Office).

**KYLE S. KAWAKAMI,** born New York, N.Y., November 7, 1959; admitted to bar, 1986, California and U.S. Tax Court. *Education:* University of California at San Diego (B.A., magna cum laude, 1981); Stanford University (J.D., with distinction, 1986). Extern to the Honorable William A. Norris, United States Court of Appeal for the Ninth Circuit, 1985. Law Clerk to the Honorable Richard A. Gadbois, Jr., United States District Court, Central District of California, 1986-1987. *Member:* State Bar of California. (Resident at Newport Beach).

**J. CHRISTOPHER KENNEDY,** born Boston, Massachusetts, July 12, 1950; admitted to bar, 1976, California. *Education:* Harvard University (B.A., 1972); University of Virginia (J.D., 1976). Order of the Coif. Member, Editorial Board, Virginia Law Review, 1974-1976. *Member:* Los Angeles County and American Bar Associations; State Bar of California. (Downtown Los Angeles Office).

**BRUCE D. KUYPER,** born Culver City, California, May 3, 1963; admitted to bar, 1989, California; 1990, U.S. Court of Appeals, Federal Circuit; registered to practice before U.S. Patent and Trademark Office. *Education:* University of California at Berkeley (B.S.E.E.C.S., with honors, 1986); University of California (J.D., 1989). Tau Beta Pi; Eta Kappa Nu. Member, 1987-1988 and Associate Editor, 1988-1989, UCLA Law Review; Moot Court Participant. *Member:* Los Angeles County (Member, Intellectual Property and Unfair Competition Section) and American (Member, Sections on: Litigation; Patent, Trademark and Copyright Law) Bar Associations; State Bar of California (Member, Sections on: Intellectual Property; Litigation); Institute of Electrical and Electronics Engineers; American Intellectual Property Law Association; Los Angeles Intellectual Property Law Association.

**HENRY LESSER,** born London, England, February 28, 1947; admitted to bar, 1969, England and Wales; 1977, New York; 1984, California. *Education:* Cambridge University, Cambridge, England (B.A., Hons., 1968; M.A., 1972); Harvard University (LL.M., 1973). Recipient, Harkness Fellowship of the Commonwealth Fund of New York, 1971. Editor-in-Chief, "The Corporate Governance Advisor". Co-Author: "Takeover Defense," (with Fleischer and Sussman), 1990. *Member:* The Association of the Bar of the City of New York; Los Angeles County (Member, Business and Corporation Law Section Executive Committee, 1991—), New York State, American and International Bar Associations; State Bar of California (Member: Business Law Section Executive Committee, 1991-1994, Vice Chair-Legislation, 1993-1994; Secretary, 1992-1993; Chair, Corporations Committee, 1990-1991); New York County Lawyers Association. (Downtown Los Angeles Office).

**JOAN L. LESSER, (P.C.),** born Los Angeles, California, April 12, 1947; admitted to bar, 1973, California. *Education:* Brandeis University (B.A., 1969); University of Southern California (J.D., 1973). Order of the Coif. Executive Editor, University of Southern California Law Review, 1972-1973. Planning Committee, CEB Annual Real Property Institute. *Member:* Beverly Hills, Los Angeles County and American Bar Associations; State Bar of California. *Email:* jlesser@irell.com

**RONALD M. LOEB, (P.C.),** born Denver, Colorado, September 24, 1932; admitted to bar, 1960, California. *Education:* University of California at Los Angeles (A.B., 1954); Harvard University (LL.B., 1959). Phi Beta Kappa. Member, Board of Editors, Harvard Law Review, 1957-1959. Co-Editor, Duties and Responsibilities of Outside Directors. Member, Advisory Board, University of California, San Diego, Securities Regulation Institute. Member, Harvard Law School Association. Former Member, Legal Advisory Board, National Association of Securities Dealers. Member, Board of Directors, Mattel, Inc. Trustee, Crossroads School of Arts and Sciences, Santa Monica, California, 1987—. Founding Trustee and Counsel to the Board of Directors, World Business Academy, 1991—. *Member:* Beverly Hills, Los Angeles County (Corporate Law Committee, 1986—) and American Bar Associations; State Bar of California. *Email:* rloeb@irell.com

**STEVEN A. MARENBERG,** born New York, N.Y., June 19, 1955; admitted to bar, 1981, Illinois and California. *Education:* Wesleyan University (B.A., magna cum laude, 1977); University of Chicago (J.D., 1980). Law Clerk, Judge James B. Moran, U.S. District Court, Northern District of Illinois, 1980-1981. *Member:* Los Angeles County (Member, Sections on: Litigation; Antitrust) and American (Member, Sections on: Litigation; Intellectual Property Law; Antitrust; Subcommittee on Business Torts and Unfair Competition) Bar Associations; State Bar of California; Association of Business Trial Lawyers (Board of Governors, 1991—); Alliance for Children's Rights (Board of Directors, 1995—). *Email:* smarenberg@irell.com

**C. KEVIN McGEEHAN,** born Silver Springs, Maryland, November 4, 1951; admitted to bar, 1978, California. *Education:* Yale University (B.A., summa cum laude, 1973; J.D., 1976). Phi Beta Kappa. *Member:* State Bar of California.

*(This Listing Continued)*

## IRELL & MANELLA LLP, Los Angeles—Continued

**RICHARD J. MCNEIL,** born Los Angeles, California, September 24, 1959; admitted to bar, 1984, California. *Education:* Yale University (B.A., 1981); Boalt Hall School of Law, University of California, Berkeley (J.D., 1984). Member, California Law Review, 1982-1984. Author: "Proposition 65, Asbestos and the Real Estate Industry," 6 California Real Property Journal 29, (Spring, 1988). Speeches: California Environmental Trial Academy, San Diego, California, May31-June 2, 1996 (Co-Chair); "Swimming Toward A Safe Harbor,": EPA's Lender Liability Rule, State Bar Of California Environmental Subsection Of The Real Property Section, San Diego, California, November 13, 1993; "Environmental Regulations And Financing Transactions: Their Impact On Lenders, Borrowers And Regulators: EPA's Lender Liability Rule," State Bar Of California Environmental Subsection Of The Real Property Section, Irvine, California, June 4, 1993; "Environmental Concerns In Real Estate Transactions: The Developer's Perspective," CEB Presentation, Los Angeles, California, October 31, 1992; "Requirements For Publicly Owned Treatment Works," Executive Enterprises Water Quality Regulation Course, San Francisco, California, May 15, 1990; "Current Developments In Environmental Law," Environmental And Energy Council, Orange County Chamber of Commerce, Santa Ana, California, May 11, 1989; "Asbestos Abatement," Hazardous Materials and Water Pollution Subcommittee of the Environmental Law Section of the Los Angeles County Bar Association, Los Angeles, California, April 14, 1988; "Environmental Issues For Lenders," Pension and Real Estate Advisors Winter Meeting, Los Angeles, California, February 11, 1988. Law Clerk, Chief Judge Aubrey E. Robinson, U.S. District Court, District of Columbia, 1984-1985. *Member:* Orange County (Member, Environmental Law Section) and American (Member, Section of Natural Resources, Energy and Environmental Law) Bar Associations; State Bar of California (Member, Executive Committee, Environmental Law Section). (Resident at Newport Beach).

**ASHOK W. MUKHEY,** born Hamilton, Bermuda, April 1, 1959; admitted to bar, 1984, California. *Education:* University of California at Los Angeles (A.B., summa cum laude, 1981); Harvard University (J.D., 1984). Phi Beta Kappa. *Member:* State Bar of California.

**LAYN R. PHILLIPS,** born Oklahoma City, Oklahoma, January 2, 1952; admitted to bar, 1977, Oklahoma; 1978, District of Columbia; 1981, California. *Education:* University of Tulsa (B.S., Economics, 1974; J.D., 1977); Georgetown University Law School (1978-1979). Recipient: Wall Street Journal Award for Outstanding Economics Graduate, 1974; Robert Butler Award for Outstanding Legal Writing, 1977. Managing Editor, Georgetown University Law Journal, 1978-1979. Trial Attorney, Federal Trade Commission, 1977-1980. Assistant United States Attorney, Central District of California, 1980-1983; United States Attorney, Northern District of Oklahoma, 1984-1987; United States District Judge, Western District of Oklahoma, 1987-1991; Named, United States Junior Chamber of Commerce, One of Ten Outstanding Young Americans, 1989. *Member:* Oklahoma and American (Member: Committee on Environmental Litigation; Committee on White Collar Crime) Bar Associations; The District of Columbia Bar; State Bar of California; State Bar of Texas; American Inn of Court XXIV (President, 1989-1990); American Inn of Court CV (President, 1990-1991); Orange County Federal Bar Association (Board of Directors, 1995-1996). (Resident at Newport Beach).

**ANTHONY W. PIEROTTI,** born Hawthorne, California, December 20, 1960; admitted to bar, 1987, California; 1988, U.S. Tax Court. *Education:* California State University at Long Beach (B.S., 1984); University of California at Davis (J.D., 1987). Order of the Coif; Phi Kappa Phi; Beta Gamma Sigma. Editor, University of California at Davis Law Review, 1986-1987. *Member:* State Bar of California. (Resident at Newport Beach).

**S. THOMAS POLLACK,** born Brooklyn, New York, October 6, 1943; admitted to bar, 1970, California; 1981, New York. *Education:* Brown University (A.B., 1965); New York University (J.D., 1968). Order of the Coif. Article and Book Review Editor, New York University Law Review, 1966-1968. Adjunct Professor, Federal Criminal Trial Practice, Loyola University School of Law, 1973-1976. Acting Federal Public Defender, Los Angeles, 1975-1976. *Member:* State Bar of California; American Bar Association (Co-Chairperson, Western Region Committee on Complex Crimes Litigation, Section of Litigation, 1986-1987; White Collar Crime Committee, 1991—).

**JOEL RABINOVITZ, (P.C.),** born New York, N.Y., June 6, 1939; admitted to bar, 1963, New York; 1981, California. *Education:* Cornell University (A.B., 1960); Harvard University (LL.B., magna cum laude, 1963). Author: "Treaty-Trends - Recent Treaties and the Proposed New United States Model," International Law Institute, State Bar of Texas, 1981. "Sum and Substance of the Law-Federal Estate and Gift Tax," Creative Education Services, 1976, Third Edition, 1979; "Nuts and Bolts in the Ivory Tower," 24 UCLA L. Rev. 742, 1977; "Effect of Prior Year's Transactions on Federal Income Tax Consequences of Current Receipts and Payments," 28 Tax. L. Rev. 85, 1972; "Negotiation and Drafting in a Substantive Course in Acquisitions and Mergers," 23 J. Leg. Ed. 470, 1971; "Non-Liquidating Distributions in Kind: Effect of Recognition of Gain on Earnings and Profits," 17 UCLA L. Rev. 408, 1969; "Allocating Boot in Section 351 Exchanges," 24 Tax. L. Rev. 337, 1969. Co-Author with A. Shashy: "Properties of Property: Indigestion From Corn Products," 27 U. Fla. L. Rev. 964, 1975. Professor of Law, University of California, Los Angeles, 1968-1979. Deputy International Tax Counsel, U.S. Treasury, 1979-1981. *Member:* State Bar of California; New York State Bar Association.

**SUSAN SAKAI,** born Honolulu, Hawaii, February 28, 1960; admitted to bar, 1986, Hawaii and California. *Education:* University of Santa Clara (B.S.C., 1982); University of California at Los Angeles (J.D., 1985). Phi Beta Kappa; Beta Gamma Sigma. Author: "Community Right-to-Know Handbook-A Guide to Compliance with the Emergency Planning and Community Right-to-Know Act," Clark Boardman Co., Ltd., 1988. Law Clerk, Hon. Herbert Y.C. Choy, U.S. Court of Appeals, Ninth Circuit, 1985-1986. *Member:* State Bar of California (Member, Real Property Section; Chair, Environmental Subsection); Hawaii State Bar Association.

**LOIS J. SCALI,** born Brooklyn, New York, July 8, 1948; admitted to bar, 1986, California. *Education:* Brooklyn College (B.A., magna cum laude, 1970); University of California at Los Angeles (J.D., 1986). Phi Beta Kappa; Order of the Coif. Recipient, Distinguished Scholar Award. Member, 1984-1985 and Chief Article Editor, 1985-1986, UCLA Law Review. Author: "Prediction-Making in the Supreme Court: The Granting of Stays by Individual Justices," 32 UCLA Law Review 1020, 1985. Law Clerk to Hon. Dorothy W. Nelson, Ninth Circuit Court of Appeals, 1986-1987. *Member:* State Bar of California. *LANGUAGES:* Italian.

**ALVIN G. SEGEL,** born Boston, Massachusetts, November 27, 1945; admitted to bar, 1971, California. *Education:* Boston University (B.A., cum laude, 1967); Columbia University (J.D., cum laude, 1970). Note and Comments Editor, Columbia Law Review, 1969-1970. *Member:* State Bar of California; American Bar Association.

**MARVIN S. SHAPIRO, (P.C.),** born New York, N.Y., October 26, 1936; admitted to bar, 1959, District of Columbia; 1962, California. *Education:* Columbia University (A.B., 1957; LL.B., 1959). Articles Editor, Columbia Law Review, 1958-1959. Trial Attorney, Appellate Section, Civil Division, U.S. Department of Justice, 1959-1961. *Member:* Beverly Hills (Member, Board of Governors, 1969-1973; President, Barristers, 1970), Los Angeles County and American Bar Associations; State Bar of California. *Email:* mshapiro@irell.com

**RICHARD M. SHERMAN, JR.,(P.C.),** born Denver, Colorado, June 20, 1947; admitted to bar, 1974, U.S. District Court, Central District of California; 1975, California; 1983, U.S. District Court, Southern District of California; 1985, U.S. District Court, Eastern District of California; 1987, U.S. Supreme Court and U.S. Court of Appeals, Ninth Circuit. *Education:* Claremont Men's College (B.A., cum laude, 1969); Occidental College (M.A., 1971); University of California at Berkeley (J.D., 1974). Exec. V.P. and General Counsel, The William Lyon Companies, 1989-1994. Co-author: "A Summary of American Airport Access Law," 1985 and "A Survey of Recent Development in United States Aviation Law," 1986, each presented to the International Bar Association. Member, Panel of Arbitrators, American Arbitration Association. *Member:* Orange County, Federal (Founding Member, Orange County Chapter), American (Member: Section of Litigation; Forum Committee on Air and Space Law) and International (Member, Section on Business Law, Committee on Aeronautical Law) Bar Associations; State Bar of California. (Resident at Newport Beach).

**HENRY SHIELDS, JR., (P.C.),** born Chicago, Illinois, July 2, 1945; admitted to bar, 1974, California. *Education:* University of Illinois and Southern Illinois University (B.S., 1968); University of California at Berkeley (J.D., 1974). Associate Editor, California Law Review, 1972-1974. Teaching Associate in International Law, Boalt Hall School of Law, University of California, 1973-1974. Lawyer Representative, 1988-1991, Member of Executive Committee, 1990-1994, Chair of Executive Committee, 1993-1994, Ninth Circuit Judicial Conference. Member, Ninth Circuit Gender Bias Task Force, 1990-1994. Ex officio member, Ninth Circuit Task Force on Racial, Religious and Ethnic Fairness, 1995—. *Member:* Los Angeles County and American (Member, Section of Litigation) Bar Associations; State Bar of California; NAACP Legal Defense Fund; California Association of Black Lawyers.

*(This Listing Continued)*

***DAVID SIEGEL,*** born Los Angeles, California, March 3, 1956; admitted to bar, 1981, California. *Education:* University of Florida (B.A., with high honors, 1977); University of California (J.D., Valedictorian, 1981). Member: Order of the Coif; Thurston Legal Honor Society. Articles Editor, Hastings Law Journal, 1980-1981. Frequent Panelist and Chairman of Practising Law Institute on Securities Litigation; Prentice-Hall Conference on Stockholders' Class and Derivative Actions, 1990; Practising Law Institute on Bank and Thrift Litigation in the 1990s, 1991. Judicial Extern to Justice Wiley Manuel, California Supreme Court, 1981. 1996 California State Senate Blue Ribbon Task Force on Shareholder Litigation. *Member:* State Bar of California (Member, Sections on Litigation; Corporate Law); American Bar Association (Member, Sections on Litigation; Corporate Law).

***STEVEN P. SIM,*** born Indianapolis, Indiana, December 20, 1951; admitted to bar, 1976, California. *Education:* Indiana University (A.B., with highest distinction, 1973); Stanford University (J.D., 1976). Phi Beta Kappa. *Member:* Los Angeles County Bar Association (Member, Real Property Section); State Bar of California (Member, Real Property Law Section).

***STEVEN L. SLOCA,*** born Plainfield, New Jersey, December 18, 1944; admitted to bar, 1970, California. *Education:* Dartmouth College (B.A., summa cum laude, 1966); Yale University (LL.B., 1969). Phi Beta Kappa; Order of the Coif. Member, Board of Editors, Yale Law Journal, 1967-1969. Instructor, Trial Advocacy, Yale Law School, 1968-1969. Author: "ADR In Landlord-Tenant Cases," The Practical Lawyer, January, 1994. *Member:* Beverly Hills (Member: ADR Committee; Coordinator for Settlement Program) and American (Member: Committee on Condemnation, Zoning and Property Use; Litigation Section; Real Property, Probate and Trust Law Section; Litigation and Dispute Resolution Committee) Bar Associations; State Bar of California (Member: Litigation Section; Real Property Section); The Association of Business Trial Lawyers. [Captain, U.S. Army, 1970-1971.]

***GREGORY R. SMITH,*** born Chicago, Illinois, January 9, 1944; admitted to bar, 1969, California. *Education:* Claremont Men's College (B.A., summa cum laude, 1965); London School of Economics (M.S., 1969); Harvard University (J.D., magna cum laude, 1968). Phi Alpha Delta. Member, Board of Editors, Harvard Law Review, 1966-1968. Visiting Professor, University of Kansas School of Law, 1975. Member, Ninth Circuit Ad Hoc Appellate Advocacy Committee. *Member:* State Bar of California.

***HOWARD J. STEINBERG,*** born Springfield, Massachusetts, December 18, 1954; admitted to bar, 1979, California. *Education:* University of Massachusetts (B.A., 1976); Boston College (J.D., 1979). Phi Beta Kappa. Phi Beta Kappa; Phi Kappa Phi. Staff Writer and Editor, Uniform Commercial Code Reporter Digest, 1977-1979. Author: "Bankruptcy Litigation," Lawyers Cooperative Publishing Company/Bancroft Whitney, 1989. Author: Answers, "Counterclaims and Affirmative Defenses--Secured Creditors and Lessors Under the Bankruptcy Reform Act," 1980, Practising Law Institute; "Land Development, Default, Rescue and Bankruptcy," 1980 California Business Law Institute; "Bankruptcy Appeals," 1984 CEB Civil Litigation Reporter; "Bankruptcy Litigation: Obtaining Injunctive Relief," 1985 CEB Civil Litigation Reporter; "Automatic Stay Litigation," 1985 CEB Civil Litigation Reporter; "Recovering Attorneys' Fees in Automatic Stay Litigation," 1985 CEB Civil Litigation Reporter; "Finality Issues in Bankruptcy Appeals," 1986 CEB Civil Litigation Reporter; "The Effect on Pending Litigation of a Party's Bankruptcy Filling," 1987 CEB Civil Litigation Reporter; " Overview of The Amendments to the Rules of Bankruptcy Procedure," 1987 CEB Civil Litigation Reporter; The Awarding of Sanctions in Bankruptcy Cases," 1990 CEB Civil Litigation Reporter. Contributing Editor, Civil Litigation Reporter, California Continuing Education of the Bar, 1984—. Lecturer: "Bankruptcy Litigation," PES, Inc.; "Post Trial Practice," Law Seminars, Inc.; "Lender Liability Considerations for the Construction Lender," 1989 Learning Tree; Chairman, "California Bankruptcy Litigation Conference," 1990 Learning Tree. Judge Pro Tempore, Los Angeles Municipal Court, 1987-1988. *Member:* Century City Bar Association (Member, Litigation Section); State Bar of California. (Downtown Los Angeles Office.)

***JONATHAN H. STEINBERG,*** born Frederiksberg, Denmark, September 19, 1952; admitted to bar, 1981, California. *Education:* University of California at Berkeley (A.B., with honors, 1976); Universite d'Aix-Marseille, Aix-en-Provence, France; University of California at Los Angeles (J.D., 1980). Member of Staff, 1978-1979 and Note and Comment Editor, 1979-1980, UCLA Law Review. Member, Board of Editors, Federal Communications Law Journal, 1978. Extern Law Clerk to Judge Abner J. Mikva, U.S. Court of Appeals for the District of Columbia Circuit, 1980. Co-author with D. Lowenstein: "The Quest for Legislative Districting in the Public Interest: Elusive or Illusory?" 33 UCLA Law Review 1 (1985). *Member:* State Bar of California; American Bar Association.

***ROBERT STEINBERG,*** born Philadelphia, Pennsylvania, April 4, 1960; admitted to bar, 1986, California; registered to practice before U.S. Patent and Trademark Office. *Education:* University of Pennsylvania, Moore School of Engineering (B.S.S.E., magna cum laude, 1982); Wharton School of Business (B.S. Econ., cum laude, 1982); Georgetown University Law School (J.D., 1986). Tau Beta Pi; Eta Kappa Nu; Phi Eta Sigma. Coach and Member, Judge Rich Moot Court Competition. Recipient: ASCAP Award; Hugo Otto Wolf Memorial Prize for Engin. Associate Editor, Georgetown Journal of Law and Technology, 1986. Legal Intern to the Honorable Jean Galloway Bissell, Court of Appeals for the Federal Circuit, 1985-1996. Author: "NEC v. Intel: The Battle Over Copyright Protection for Microcode," Jurimetrics, Vol. 27, No. 2, Winter, 1987; "Copyright Issues Involving Microcode," New Matter, Vol. 13, No. 1, Spring, 1988; "Microcode Draws the Line on Idea and Expression," International Computer Law Advisor, Vol. 2, No. 1, 1988; "Microcode - Idea or Expression?" Computer Law Journal, Vol. 9, No. 1, Winter, 1989. Co-Author to Chapter 3 of "Bernacchi on Computer Law," Little Brown & Co., 1989; "Managing Intellectual Property: The Steps a Business Can Take to Recognize and Safeguard Its Inventions and Effectively Exploit Its Patents in a Global Market," presented to Committee R of the International Bar Association 24th Biennial Conference, Cannes, France, September, 1992; "CD-ROM Developers Face Licensing Hurdles," with Alan Sege, The National Law Journal, February 20, 1995; "The Multimedia Cookbook," Entertainment Law & Finance; "Internet Icons: Trademark Iconoclasm," The Journal of Proprietary Rights. Speaker: International Conference on Computer and Law, February, 1988. Authored Stac Electronics patent, which he helped to successfully litigate against Microsoft. *Member:* State Bar of California.

***STEVEN E. THOMAS,*** born Miami, Florida, January 23, 1960; admitted to bar, 1987, California and U.S. District Court, Central District of California; 1992, U.S. Supreme Court and U.S. District Court, District of Arizona. *Education:* University of Florida (B.A., 1982); Yale University (J.D., 1985). Book Review Editor, Yale Law and Policy Review, 1983-1985. Law Clerk to the Honorable John A. MacKenzie, Chief Judge, U.S. District Court, Eastern District of Virginia, 1985-1986. *Member:* State Bar of California; Bar of the Supreme Court of the United States.

***RONALD B. TISCHLER, (P.C.),*** born Atlantic City, New Jersey, August 27, 1944; admitted to bar, 1969, California. *Education:* Dickinson College (B.A., summa cum laude, 1966); Harvard University (J.D., cum laude, 1969). Phi Beta Kappa. Co-author: "Developments in Federal Securities Regulation—1975," 31 The Business Lawyer 1885, July, 1976. *Member:* State Bar of California.

***BRUCE A. WESSEL,*** born New Haven, Connecticut, January 24, 1956; admitted to bar, 1984, California. *Education:* Trinity College (B.A., 1977); Occidental College (M.A., Urban Studies, 1984); Yale University (J.D., 1984). Phi Beta Kappa. Law Clerk to the Honorable Edward Rafeedie, U.S. District Court, Central District of California, 1984-1986. *Member:* State Bar of California; American Bar Association.

***ALEXANDER F. WILES,*** born Los Angeles, California, January 19, 1952; admitted to bar, 1977, California and District of Columbia. *Education:* University of California at Berkeley (A.B., 1973; J.D., 1976). *Member:* The District of Columbia Bar; State Bar of California; American Bar Association (Member, Litigation, Antitrust Sections).

***RICHARD C. WIRTHLIN,*** born Boston, Massachusetts, January 23, 1963; admitted to bar, 1988, California. *Education:* Brigham Young University (B.A., summa cum laude, 1984); University of Chicago (M.B.A., 1988; J.D., cum laude, 1988). Beta Gamma Sigma; Order of the Coif. Olin Fellowship in Law and Economics, 1987-1988. Member, University of Chicago Law Review, 1985-1986. *Member:* State Bar of California. (Downtown Los Angeles Office.)

***WERNER F. WOLFEN, (P.C.),*** born Berlin, Germany, May 15, 1930; admitted to bar, 1953, California. *Education:* University of California at Berkeley (B.S., 1950; J.D., 1953). Phi Beta Kappa; Order of the Coif. Article and Book Review Editor, California Law Review, 1952-1953. Lecturer, University of Southern California Graduate School of Law, 1958-1961. Member, Board of Trustees of U.C.L.A. Foundation, 1987—. *Member:* Beverly Hills (President, Junior Bar Section, 1961) and American Bar Associations; State Bar of California.

***ROB C. ZEITINGER,*** born St. Louis, Missouri, June 4, 1957; admitted to bar, 1986, California. *Education:* Cornell University; University of Virginia (B.S., with highest distinction, 1979); Yale University (J.D., 1985).

*(This Listing Continued)*

**IRELL & MANELLA LLP, Los Angeles—Continued**

Eta Kappa Nu; Tau Beta Pi. Editor, Yale Law Journal, 1983-1984. Law Clerk to the Hon. Morey L. Sear, U.S. District Judge, Eastern District of Louisiana, 1984-1985. *Member:* Los Angeles County Bar Association; State Bar of California. *Email:* rzeitinger@irell.com

**EDWARD ZELDOW,** born New York, N.Y.; admitted to bar, 1988, California. *Education:* Berklee College of Music (B.M., magna cum laude, 1981); Boalt Hall School of Law, University of California (J.D., 1988). Instructor, Legal Research and Writing, University of California at Berkeley, 1987. *Member:* State Bar of California.

*OF COUNSEL*

**CHARLES A. COLLIER, JR.,** born Columbus, Ohio, April 18, 1930; admitted to bar, 1955, Ohio; 1960, California. *Education:* Harvard University (A.B., magna cum laude, 1952; LL.B., 1955). Law Clerk, Hon. Ernest Tolin, 1959 and Benjamin Harrison, 1959-1960, U.S. District Court, Central District of California. Advisor, Restatement of Property Donative Transfers, 1990—. *Member:* Beverly Hills, Los Angeles County (Recipient, Arthur K. Marshall Award, Probate and Trust Law Section, 1989) and American (Council Member, Real Property, Probate and Trust Law Section, 1989-1993; Member, Budget and Finance Comm., 1990-1992; Member, Committee on Committees, 1992-1993; Chairman, Committee on Formation, Administration and Distribution of Trusts, 1982-1986; Liaison, National Conference of Commissioners of Uniform State Law, Drafting Committee on Statutory Rule Against Perpetuities, 1985-1986; Member, Task Force on Changing Role of Probate Lawyer, 1985-1987; Chairman, Task Force on Fiduciary Litigation, 1986-1989; Member, Conference of Lawyers and Corporate Fiduciaries, 1989-1992) Bar Associations; The State Bar of California (Member, Trust and Probate Law Committee, 1975-1977; Member, Executive Committee, Estate Planning, Trust and Probate Law Section, 1977-1982; Vice-Chairman, 1979-1980; Chairman, 1980-1981; Advisor, 1982-1985); International Academy of Estate and Trust Law. Fellow: American College of Trust and Estate Counsel (Member, State Laws Committee, 1983-1989; Chairman, 1986-1989, Member, Office Management Committee, 1986-1987, ACTEC Member, Joint Editorial Board, Uniform Probate Code, National Conference of Commissioners on Uniform State Laws, 1988—; Chairman, Expanded Practice Committee, 1989-1992; Member, Executive Committee, 1989—; Treasurer, 1992-1993, Secretary, 1993-1994, Vice President, 1994-1995, Chair, Program Committee, 1994-1995, President-Elect, 1995-1996, President, 1996-1997). Fellow, American Bar Foundation.

**JOHN J. COST, (P.C.),** born Bath, Maine, October 24, 1934; admitted to bar, 1964, California. *Education:* Bowdoin College, Brunswick, Maine and University of Maine (B.A., 1960); Harvard University (LL.B., cum laude, 1963). Phi Beta Kappa; Phi Kappa Phi. *Member:* State Bar of California. (Downtown Los Angeles Office).

**LAWRENCE E. IRELL,** born Boston, Massachusetts, March 23, 1912; admitted to bar, 1936, California. *Education:* University of California at Los Angeles (B.A., 1932); University of Southern California (LL.B., 1935); Harvard University (LL.M., 1936). Order of the Coif. Member, Board of Editors, Southern California Law Review, 1933-1935. Lecturer, University of Southern California Graduate School of Law, 1951-1954. Trustee, 1967—, Chairman, 1975-1978, President, 1971-1975, General Counsel, 1967-1971, Chairman, Grants and Allocations Committee, 1978-1985, UCLA Foundation. Member, 1990—, Founder Chair, 1990-1992, UCLA Board of Visitors. *Member:* Beverly Hills (Chairman, Taxation Committee, 1954-1960; Member, Board of Governors, 1961-1972; President, 1968-1969), Los Angeles County (Member, Board of Trustees, 1971-1972) and American Bar Associations; State Bar of California (Member, Resolutions Committee Conference of Delegates, 1967; Delegate, Annual Conference State Bar Delegates, 1960, 1962-1968, 1970-1972, 1974).

**THOMAS A. KIRSCHBAUM,** born Middletown, Connecticut, October 8, 1952; admitted to bar, 1977, California; 1982, U.S. Tax Court. *Education:* Amherst College (B.A., magna cum laude, 1974); University of California at Los Angeles (J.D., 1977). Member, University of California at Los Angeles Law Review, 1975-1977. Member, UCLA Moot Court Honors Program, 1975-1976. Lecturer: "Designing Qualified Plans In The Light of The Tax Reform Act of 1986," University of Southern California Institute on Federal Taxation, 1987; Fourth Annual Business Law Institute, "Cafeteria Plans/Salary Reduction Plans," California Continuing Education of the Bar, 1985. Co-Author: "Pension Planning Under The Brave New Act," 1988, 40 University of Southern California Tax Institute 700; "Minimizing Taxes on Excess Retirement Distributions and Accumulations," 41 Taxation for Accountants 312 (1988); "Foreign Personal Holding Companies," 103-2d T.M., 1978 reissued as 922 T.M., 1991; "Tax Considerations," Ch. 7, California Condominium and Planned Development Practice, California Continuing Education of the Bar, 1984. Author: "Investment of Pension Plan Assets: Selected Unrelated Business Taxable Income and Prohibited Transaction Issues," 1992, 44 University of Southern California Tax Institute 900.

**ARTHUR MANELLA, (P.C.),** born Toronto, Canada, August 7, 1917; admitted to bar, 1941, California. *Education:* University of Southern California (B.S. in B.A., 1939; LL.B., 1941); Harvard University (LL.M., 1942). Order of the Coif. Editor-in-Chief, Southern California Law Review, 1940-1941. Lecturer, University of Southern California Graduate School of Law, 1951-1955. Member, Planning Committee, University of Southern California Tax Institute, 1948-1969. *Member:* Beverly Hills, Los Angeles County and American Bar Associations; State Bar of California (Taxation Advisory Commission, 1971-1977); American Law Institute (Member, Tax Advisory Group, 1954-1959).

**DAVID NIMMER,** born Los Angeles, California, January 14, 1955; admitted to bar, 1980, California. *Education:* Stanford University (A.B., 1977); Yale University (J.D., 1980). Phi Beta Kappa. Editor, Yale Law Journal, 1979-1980. Author: Nimmer on Copyright, 1985—; "The End of Copyright," 48 Vanderbilt L. Rev 1385 (1995); "United States," in Nimmer & Geller, International Copyright Law and Practice; "Nation, Duration, Violation, Harmonization: An International Copyright Proposal for the United States," 55 Law & Contemp. Probs. 211 (1992); "Refracting the Window's Light: Stewart v. Abend in Myth and in Fact," 39 Journal of the Copyright Society of the USA 18 (1991); "The Impact of Berne on United States Copyright Law," 8 Cardozo Arts & Entertainment Law Journal 27, 1989; "Le Droit D'Auteur en Droit American," Droit des Affaires, 1989; "Copyright Ownership by the Marital Community: Evaluating Worth," 36 U.C.L.A.L. Rev. 383 (1988); "Arbitration and No-Contest Clauses in Copyright Contracts," 9 Entertainment Law Reporter, No. 9, 1988; "Criminal Copyright and Trademark Law: The Importance of Criminal Sanctions to Civil Practitioners," 9 Entertainment Law Reporter, No. 1, 1987; "Criminal Copyright and Criminal Contempt," The Law of Gray and Counterfeit Goods, P.L.I., 1987; "A Structured Approach to Analyzing the Substantial Similarity of Computer Software in Copyright Infringement Cases," 20 Arizona State Law Journal 625, 1988 (with Richard L. Bernacchi and Gary N. Frischling); "Cases and Materials on Copyright and Other Aspects of Entertainment Litigation Including Unfair Competition, Defamation, Privacy," Fourth Edition (with Melville B. Nimmer, Paul Marcus and David A. Myers). Managing Editor, The Multimedia Law Reporter, 1995—. Law Clerk to Hon. Warren Ferguson, Ninth Circuit Court of Appeals, 1980-1981. Assistant U.S. Attorney, Central District of California, 1983-1987. *Member:* State Bar of California; American Bar Association (Chairman, Committee on Intellectual Properties Litigation, Section of Litigation, 1989-1992). *LANGUAGES:* French and Italian. *Email:* dnimmer@irell.com

**ALVARO PASCOTTO,** born Rome, Italy, March 8, 1949; admitted to bar, 1976, Italy; 1987, California, U.S. District Court, Central District of California and U.S. Court of Appeals, Ninth Circuit. *Education:* Le Roche College, Crans, Switzerland (Ginnasio, 1964); Liceo Mameli, Rome, Italy (B.A., 1967); University of Rome (J.D., 1973). Commendatore al Merito delle Republica, 1989. Member, Italy-America Chamber of Commerce, Inc., 1987. *Member:* Los Angeles County and American Bar Associations; State Bar of California; National Italian American Bar Association; Italian-American Lawyers Association. (Also Member, Pascotto & Gallavotti). *LANGUAGES:* English, French, Spanish and Italian. *Email:* apascotto@irell.com

**STEVEN H. SHIFFRIN,** born Los Angeles, California, May 3, 1941; admitted to bar, 1975, California. *Education:* Loyola University of Los Angeles (B.A., 1963); California State University at Northridge (M.A., 1964); Loyola University of Los Angeles (J.D., summa cum laude, 1975). Editor-in-Chief, Loyola of Los Angeles Law Review, 1973-1974. Visiting Professor of Law: Boston University School of Law, 1982-1983; University of Michigan School of Law, 1984; Harvard Law School, 1986-1987. Professor of Law: University of California at Los Angeles, 1977-1987; Cornell University, 1987—. Co-Author: with Choper, "The First Amendment," 1991; with Lockhart, Kamisar and Choper, "Constitutional Law," West Publishing Co., 7th edition, 1991, 6th edition, 1986. Author: "The First Amendment, Democracy and Romance," Harvard University Press, 1990; "Liberalism, Radicalism and Legal Scholarship," 30 UCLA Law Review 1103, 1983; "The First Amendment and Economic Regulation: Away from a General Theory of the First Amendment," 78 Northwestern University Law Review 1212, 1983; Book Review, "Government Speech and the Falsification of Consent," 96 Harvard Law Review 1745, 1983; "Government Speech," 27

*(This Listing Continued)*

UCLA Law Review 565, 1980; "Defamatory Non-Media Speech and First Amendment Methodology," 25 UCLA Law Review 915, 1978. Law Clerk to Hon. Warren J. Ferguson, U.S. District Judge, Central District of California, 1975-1976. *Member:* State Bar of California.

**ROBERT W. STEDMAN, (P.C.),** born Sturgeon Bay, Wisconsin, April 22, 1938; admitted to bar, 1967, California. *Education:* University of Wisconsin (B.B.A., 1960); University of California at Berkeley (LL.B., 1966). Order of the Coif; Beta Gamma Sigma. Article Editor, California Law Review, 1965-1966. *Member:* State Bar of California; American Bar Association. (Resident at Newport Beach).

**LAWRENCE M. STONE, (P.C.),** born Malden, Massachusetts, March 25, 1931; admitted to bar, 1956, Massachusetts; 1958, California. *Education:* Harvard University (A.B., 1953); Harvard Law School (LL.B., 1956). Phi Beta Kappa. Member, Board of Editors, Harvard Law Review, 1955-1956. Fulbright Scholar Awardee. Co-author with B.I. Bittker, Wm. Klein and J. Bankman, "Federal Income Taxation," Little Brown & Co., 1990. Co-author with Doernberg, Abrams and Bittker, " Federal Income Taxation of Corporations and Partnerships," Little Brown & Co., 1987. Professor of Law, University of California at Berkeley, 1966-1979. Visiting Professor of Law: Yale Law School, 1969-1970; Hebrew University of Jerusalem, 1973-1974; University of Southern California, 1983. Staff Member, Federal Income, Gift & Estate Tax Project, American Law Institute, 1956-1957. Tax Legislative Counsel, U.S. Treasury Department, 1964-1966. International Tax Coordinator, U.S. Treasury Department, 1961-1962. *Member:* Advisory Group to Commissioner of Internal Revenue, 1973-1974; United States Tax Court Nominating Commission, 1978-1980; Advisory Board, Little Brown Tax Practice Series. Recipient, Dana Latham Award of Los Angeles County Bar Association, 1995. *Member:* State Bar of California; American Bar Association (Member, Section of Taxation, Committee on Standards of Tax Practice, Committee on Appointments to the Tax Court); American Law Institute (Member, Tax Advisory Group, 1967—). (Certified Specialist, Taxation Law, The State Bar of California Board of Legal Specialization).

**WILLIAM D. WARREN,** born Mt. Vernon, Illinois, November 13, 1924; admitted to bar, 1950, Illinois (Not admitted in California). *Education:* University of Illinois (B.A., 1948; J.D., 1950); Yale University (J.S.D., 1957). Member, Law Faculty, 1959—, Dean, 1975-1982 and Connell Professor, Emeritus, 1994, University of California at Los Angeles School of Law. Scott Professor of Law, Stanford University 1972-1975. Legislative Consultant to the California Assembly Concerning Enactment of the California Commercial Code, 1961-1965. Co-Reporter: Uniform Consumer Credit Code, 1964-1974; American Law Institute-National Conference of Commissioners on Uniform State Laws UCC Current Payments Project, 1985-1990. Co-Author: *Cases and Materials on Debtor-Creditor Law,* 2d ed. Foundation Press, 1981; *Commercial Law,* Foundation Press, 1992 (3d ed.); *Commercial Paper,* Foundation Press, 1992; *Secured Transactions in Personal Property,* Foundation Press, 1992; *California Cases on Security Transactions in Land,* 4th ed. West Publishing Co., 1991; *Bankruptcy,* Foundation Press, 1985 (4th ed. 1995). *Member:* National Bankruptcy Conference.

## ASSOCIATES

**JEFFREY L. ARRINGTON,** born Twin Falls, Idaho, January 20, 1960; admitted to bar, 1989, California. *Education:* University of Utah (B.S., 1985); Loyola Law School, Los Angeles (J.D., 1988). Editor-in-Chief, Loyola of Los Angeles Law Review, 1987-1988. Recipient, American Jurisprudence Award in Torts and Constitutional Law. Author: "California Civil Code Section 47(3): Should There Be a Public Interest Privilege in California?" Vol. 20, Loyola of Los Angeles Law Review. *Member:* State Bar of California.

**SPENCER E. BENDELL,** admitted to bar, 1995, California. *Education:* Cornell University (B.A., magna cum laude, 1992); Harvard Law School (J.D., magna cum laude, 1995). Phi Beta Kappa. *Email:* sbendell@irell.com

**RICHARD M. BIRNHOLZ,** born Livingston, New Jersey, July 26, 1965; admitted to bar, 1990, California; 1992, U.S. District Court, Central, Northern, Eastern and Southern Districts of California, U.S. Court of Appeals, Ninth Circuit. *Education:* Stanford University (B.A., with distinction, 1987); University of California at Los Angeles (J.D., 1990). Order of the Coif. Editorial Board, UCLA Law Review, 1989-1990. Law Clerk to the Hon. Pamela Ann Rymer, U.S. Court of Appeals for the Ninth Circuit, 1990-1991; Extern to the Hon. Ruth Bader Ginsburg, U.S. Court of Appeals for the D.C. Circuit, 1989. Author: Comment, "The Validity and Propriety of Contingent Fee Controls," 37 UCLA L. Rev. 949 (1990). *Member:* State Bar of California.

*(This Listing Continued)*

**ELLIOT N. BROWN,** born Cleveland, Ohio; admitted to bar, 1990, California; 1991, U.S. District Court, Central, Northern, Southern and Eastern Districts of California and U.S. Court of Appeals, Ninth and Federal Circuits. *Education:* Harvard College (A.B., cum laude, 1985); Princeton University (M.A., 1987); Harvard Law School (J.D., magna cum laude, 1990). Phi Beta Kappa. Editor, Harvard Law Review. Law Clerk to the Honorable Pierre N. Leval, U.S. District Court, Southern District of New York, 1991-1992. *Email:* ebrown@irell.com

**ANDRÉ J. BRUNEL,** born Fairfield, California, March 22, 1963; admitted to bar, 1990, California. *Education:* Georgetown University (B.A., magna cum laude, 1985); L.B.J. School of Public Affairs at the University of Texas (M.P.A., with highest honors, 1990); The University of Texas School of Law (J.D., with honors, 1990); Queen Mary & Westfield College, University of London (LL.M., with honors, 1991). Fulbright Scholar; Phi Beta Kappa; Order of the Coif. Author: "Internet Icons: Trademark Iconoclasm," 7:12 The Journal of Proprietary Rights 2 (December 1995); "A Checklist of Trademark Considerations for Multimedia Start-ups," 1:7 The Multimedia Law Report 1 (May 1995); "Billions Registered, But No Rules: The Scope of Trademark Protection for Internet Domain Names," 7:3 The Journal of Proprietary Rights 2 (March 1995); "Post-Altai Computer Copyright and Trade Secret Decisions," 11:1 The Computer Lawyer 1 (Jan. 1994); "Continuum Multimedia: Examining the Fine Print/Possible Contract Pitfalls," Photo District News, Sept. 1993, at 30; "The Shape of Things To Come: Trademark Protection For Computers," 9:12 The Computer Lawyer 1 (Dec. 1992); "The Shape of Things to Come: Design-Patent Protection for Computers," 9:11 The Computer Lawyer 1 (Nov. 1992); "Restructuring the Judicial Evaluation of Employed Inventors' Rights in the High-Technology Industry," 35:2 Saint Louis University Law Journal 399 (1991); "A Proposal to Adopt UNCITRAL's Model Law on International Commercial Arbitration as Federal Law," 25:1 Texas International Law Journal 43 (1990); "Pennsylvania," Chapter 8 of Promoting High-Technology Industry: Initiatives and Policies for State Governments, Jurgen Schmandt and Robert Wilson, eds, Westview Press, Boulder, CO (1987). *Member:* State Bar of California. *LANGUAGES:* German. *Email:* abrunel@irell.com

**ELIZABETH A. CAMACHO,** born San Jose, California, January 18, 1967; admitted to bar, 1994, California. *Education:* Oberlin College (B.A., 1989); Boalt Hall, University of California, Berkeley (J.D., 1994).

**NANCY J. COHEN,** born Los Angeles, California, September 10, 1967; admitted to bar, 1993, California. *Education:* Stanford University (B.A., with distinction, 1989); University of California-Los Angeles (J.D., 1993). Order of the Coif. Editor, UCLA Journal of Environmental Law & Policy. Author, "Emissions Trading and Air Toxics Emissions Reclaim and Toxics Regulation in the South Coast Air Basin," UCLA Journal of Environmental Law & Policy, Volume 11, Number 2, 1993. Law Clerk to Judge Harry Pregerson, U.S. Court of Appeals, Ninth Circuit, 1993-1994. *LANGUAGES:* Spanish.

**LEIGH TAYLOR COMBS,** born Whittier, California, May 2, 1972; admitted to bar, 1994, California. *Education:* California State University, Los Angeles (B.A., 1990); University of Southern California (J.D., 1994). Golden Key Honor Society; Phi Kappa Phi Honor Society. National Dean's List. Honors Program Graduate. Honors at Entrance. CSULA Early Entrance Program. Delta Zeta Scholarship. Delta Zeta Highest Junior GPA. (Resident at Newport Beach).

**GRAHAM L. W. DAY,** born St. Louis, Missouri, August 12, 1971; admitted to bar, 1996, California. *Education:* Saint Louis University (B.A., summa cum laude, 1993); University of Pennsylvania (J.D., cum laude, 1996). Phi Beta Kappa. Recipient, George Schectman Prize. *Member:* State Bar of California. *Email:* gday@irell.com

**JERALD B. DOTSON,** born Atlanta, Georgia, February 2, 1967; admitted to bar, 1994, California, U.S. District Court, Central District of California and U.S. Court of Appeals, Ninth Circuit. *Education:* Georgia Institute of Technology (B.S., 1989); University of California, Los Angeles (J.D., 1994). Editor, UCLA Law Review, 1993-1994. Member, UCLA Entertainment Law Review, 1993-1994. *Member:* State Bar of California.

**CHARLES E. ELDER,** born Columbia University (B.A., 1993); University of Chicago (J.D., cum laude, 1996). Phi Beta Kappa. Law Review. *Email:* celder@irell.com

**SCOTT M. EPSTEIN,** born Chicago, Illinois, November 13, 1962; admitted to bar, 1990, California. *Education:* University of California at Los Angeles (B.A., summa cum laude, 1984); Stanford Law School (J.D., with distinction, 1990). Phi Beta Kappa. *Member:* Century City Bar Association (Co-Chair, Taxation Section, 1995—); State Bar of California.

*(This Listing Continued)*

**IRELL & MANELLA LLP, Los Angeles—Continued**

**MARC A. FENSTER,** born Dallas, Texas, April 5, 1969; admitted to bar, 1995, California. *Education:* University of California, San Diego (B.S., 1991; M.S., Bio-engineering, 1992); University of California, Los Angeles (J.D., 1995). Member, Moot Court, 1993-1995. UCLA State Moot Court Team, 1995. *Email:* mfenster@irell.com

**KEVIN L. FINCH,** born Santa Monica, California, February 19, 1963; admitted to bar, 1992, California. *Education:* University of California, Los Angeles (B.S.E., magna cum laude, 1984; M.S. E.E., 1988; J.D., 1992). Phi Beta Kappa; Tau Beta Pi; Eta Kappa Nu; Order of the Coif. *Member:* State Bar of California.

**ROBERT J. FLACHS,** born Encino, California, March 4, 1971; admitted to bar, 1996, California. *Education:* University of California, Los Angeles (B.A., summa cum laude, 1993); Harvard Law School (J.D., cum laude, 1996). Phi Beta Kappa. *Email:* rflachs@irell.com

**JOSEPH M. FREEMAN,** born Los Angeles, California, October 28, 1964; admitted to bar, 1993, California. *Education:* Harvard College (A.B., 1987); Boalt Hall School of Law, University of California-Berkeley (J.D., 1993).

**MELISSA R. GLEIBERMAN,** born Lancaster, Pennsylvania, May 29, 1968; admitted to bar, 1994, California. *Education:* University of Pennsylvania (B.A., 1990); Stanford University (J.D., 1993). Phi Beta Kappa; Order of the Coif. Executive Editor, Stanford Law Review, 1992-1993. Author, 45 Stan. L. Rev. 2037. Law Clerk, Hon. Pamela Ann Rymer, U.S. Court of Appeals, Ninth Circuit, 1993-1994. *LANGUAGES:* French.

**DARREN J. GOLD,** born London, England, January 17, 1970; admitted to bar, 1995, California. *Education:* University of California, Los Angeles (B.A., cum laude, division of honors, 1992); University of Michigan (J.D., magna cum laude, 1995). Order of the Coif. Associate Editor, University of Michigan Law Review. Author, "Supplemental Jurisdiction Over Claims By Plaintiffs In Diversity Cases: Making Sense Of 28 U.S.C. §1367(b)," 93 Michigan Law Review 2133, 1995.

**PERRY M. GOLDBERG,** born New York, N.Y., April 30, 1969; admitted to bar, 1993, California and U.S. District Court, Central District of California; 1994, U.S. District Court, Northern District of California and U.S. Court of Appeals for the Federal Circuit. *Education:* University of Pennsylvania (B.S., summa cum laude, 1990); Harvard University (J.D., cum laude, 1993). Beta Gamma Sigma. Co-author, with Morgan Chu: "Special Verdicts, Special Tactics," for the ABA, Section of Intellectual Property Law's 1995 Spring CLE Program; "Protecting U.S. Companies Against Illegal Imports: An Overview," for PLI's 1994 Global Trademark & Copyright Seminar. Author: *Mergers and the Federal Antitrust Laws:* A Research Guide for Practitioners, (William S. Hein Co. 1992). *Email:* pgoldberg@irell.com

**PHILIP J. GRAVES,** born Cleveland, Ohio, October 1, 1961; admitted to bar, 1991, California, Alaska and U.S. District Court, District of Alaska; 1992, Washington and U.S. Court of Appeals, Ninth Circuit. *Education:* Whitman College; University of Washington (B.A., 1987); Columbia University (J.D., 1990). Harlan Fiske Stone Scholar. Writing and Research Editor, Columbia Business Law Review, 1989-1990. Law Clerk to the Honorable Andrew J. Kleinfeld, U.S. District Court, District of Alaska, 1990-1991; Law Clerk to the Honorable Andrew J. Kleinfeld, U.S. Court of Appeals, Ninth Circuit, 1991-1992. Author: Note, "Sympathy Strikes, Coterminous Interpretation, and the Clear and Unmistakable Waiver Standard: Unweaving the Tangled Web," 1988 Colum. Bus. L. R. 793 (1989). *Member:* Alaska and Washington State Bar Associations; State Bar of California. *Email:* pgraves@irell.com

**MICHAEL GRIZZI,** born Chicago, Illinois, November 14, 1964; admitted to bar, 1996, California. *Education:* Northwestern University (B.S., Speech, 1986); University of California, Los Angeles (J.D., 1995). Order of the Coif. Editor, UCLA Law Review. Author: "Compelled Antiviral Treatment of HIV Positive Pregnant Women," UCLA Women's Law Journal, Vol. 5, No. 2 (Spring 1995). *Member:* Beverly Hills and Los Angeles County Bar Associations. (Downtown Los Angeles Office). *Email:* mgrizzi@irell.com

**CRAIG A. GROSSMAN,** born Pomona, California, April 12, 1969; admitted to bar, 1994, California and U.S. Court of Appeals, Ninth Circuit. *Education:* Stanford University (B.A., University Distinction, History departmental honors, 1991; M.A., 1991); Harvard University (J.D., magna cum laude, 1994). Phi Beta Kappa. Jordan Scholar. Recipient, Golden Medal in Humanities. Law Clerk to Judge Alfred T. Goodwin, U.S. Court of Appeals, Ninth Circuit.

**BENJAMIN HATTENBACH,** born Santa Monica, California, March 14, 1970; admitted to bar, 1996, California and U.S. District Court, Central District of California. *Education:* Harvey Mudd College (B.S., 1992; M.E., 1993); University of California, Boalt Hall School of Law (J.D., 1996). Order of the Coif. Recipient, American Jurisprudence Awards: Patent Law; Administrative Law; Contracts; Criminal Law; Property. Articles Editor, 1994-1995 and Executive Editor, 1995-1996, Berkeley Technology Law Journal. Author, "GATT TRIPS and the Small American Inventor," 10 Intellectual Property Journal 61, 1995. *Email:* bhattenbach@irell.com

**STEPHANIE KAUFMAN HERNAND,** born Charleston, South Carolina, April 18, 1966; admitted to bar, 1992, California. *Education:* University of Pennsylvania (B.A.,B.S.E., cum laude, 1988); Georgetown University (J.D., cum laude, 1992). Co-Author: "US Intellectual Property Guidelines: Changes in Enforcement Policy and Jurisdiction," 73 Patent World 38 (June/July 1995); "Federal Antitrust and Related Issues in Dealer Terminations and Refusals to Deal," 876 PLI Corp. Law & Prac. 751 (1995); "An Overview and Update of the Federal and State Law of Price Discrimination," 891 PLI Corp. Law & Prac. 255 (1995). Author: "The Speech/Conduct Distinction and First Amendment Protection of Begging in Subways," 79 Geo. L. J. 1830 (1991). *Member:* State Bar of California.

**JOHN W. HOLCOMB,** born Olean, New York, January 27, 1963; admitted to bar, 1993, Illinois; 1994, Pennsylvania and California. *Education:* Massachusetts Institute of Technology (S.B., 1984); Harvard University (J.D., cum laude, 1993). (Downtown Los Angeles Office).

**STEVEN W. HOPKINS,** born Redlands, California, July 11, 1967; admitted to bar, 1996, California. *Education:* University of Utah (B.S., 1990); University of Chicago (J.D./M.B.A., 1995). Comment Editor, University of Chicago Law Review. Author: "Is God a Preferred Creditor Tithing as an Avoidable Transfer in Chapter 7 Bankruptcies," 62 Chicago Law Review 1139, Summer 1995. (Resident at Newport Beach). *LANGUAGES:* Japanese. *Email:* shopkins@irell.com

**PATRICK O. HUNNIUS,** born St. Louis, Missouri, August 5, 1969; admitted to bar, 1994, California. *Education:* University of Texas, Austin (B.A., 1991; J.D., with honors, 1994). Notes Editor, Texas Law Review, 1993-1994.

**PETER M. JUZWIAK,** born Gainesville, Florida, February 8, 1961; admitted to bar, 1991, California and U.S. District Court, Central District of California and U.S. Court of Appeals, Ninth Circuit. *Education:* University of South Florida (B.A., magna cum laude, 1982; M.A., 1984); University of Southern California (J.D., 1991). Order of the Coif. Member and Editor-in-Chief, University of Southern California Law Review. Law Clerk to the Hon. Harry L. Hupp, U.S. District Court, Central District of California, 1991-1992. (Downtown Los Angeles Office).

**JONATHAN S. KAGAN,** born Washington, D.C., August 24, 1968; admitted to bar, 1993, California. *Education:* The Wharton School, University of Pennsylvania (B.S., cum laude, 1990); University of California at Los Angeles (J.D., 1993). Order of the Coif. Author: "Towards a Uniform Application of Punishment: Using the Federal Sentencing Guidelines as a Model for Punitive Damage Reform," UCLA Law Review, Volume 40, Number 3. *Email:* jkagan@irell.com

**GREGORY B. KLEIN,** born New York, August 21, 1971; admitted to bar, 1996, California. *Education:* University of Pennsylvania (B.A., B.S., 1993); UCLA (J.D., 1996). American Jurisprudence Award. UCLA Law Review.

**MICHAEL KRAKOVSKY,** born Brooklyn, New York, October 12, 1969; admitted to bar, 1995, California. *Education:* University of Michigan (B.S.E.E., cum laude, 1991); Columbia University (J.D., 1995). Stone Scholar. Patent Examiner, 1991-1992.

**BRIAN D. LEDAHL,** born Sacramento, California, September 12, 1971; admitted to bar, 1996, California. *Education:* Columbia College (B.A., 1993); Columbia Law School (J.D., 1996). *Email:* bledahl@irell.com

**RICHARD UNG-JIN LEE,** born San Francisco, California, June 9, 1964; admitted to bar, 1990, New York; 1992, California. *Education:* Yale College (B.A., 1986); Columbia University (J.D., 1989). *Member:* New York State Bar Association; State Bar of California. (Downtown Los Angeles Office).

**DANIEL P. LEFLER,** born Kansas City, Missouri, November 16, 1965; admitted to bar, 1990, California. *Education:* University of California, Los Angeles (B.A., magna cum laude, 1987); University of Chicago (J.D., with

*(This Listing Continued)*

honors, 1990). Phi Beta Kappa. Bradley Law and Government Fellow, 1988-1989.

**FRANCINE J. LIPMAN,** born St. Louis, Missouri, March 6, 1959; admitted to bar, 1994, California. *Education:* University of California-Santa Barbara (B.A., 1981); University of California-Davis (J.D., 1993); San Diego State University (M.B.A., 1989); New York University School of Law (LL.M. in Taxation, 1994). Beta Gamma Sigma; Order of the Coif. National Association of Women Lawyers Outstanding Woman Law Graduate, U. C. Davis, 1993. Recipient, Tax Law Review Scholarship. Member, 1991-1992, and Editor-in-Chief, 1992-1993, U.C. Davis Law Review. Graduate Editor, Tax Law Review, 1993-1994. Co-Author: "Will the Final Regulations Under IRC Section 469 (c) (7) Renew Taxpayer Interest in Real Estate?" Real Estate Law Journal, Fall 1996; "Will Changes to the Passive Income Rules Renew Interest in Real Estate?" Journal of Property Management, May/June 1996; "Passive Loss Rules for Real Estate Professionals," Los Angeles Lawyer, January 1996. Author: "Improving the Principal Residence Disaster Relief Provisions," Tax Notes, February 6, 1995. Co-Author: "The Earned Income Tax Credit: Too Difficult for the Targeted Taxpayers?" Tax Notes, November 9, 1992; "Recent Proposals to Redesign the EITC: A Reply to an Economist's Response," Tax Notes, February 28, 1994. (Resident at Newport Beach).

**JOSEPH M. LIPNER,** born Spring Valley, New York, July 25, 1964; admitted to bar, 1990, Massachusetts and New York; 1991, California; 1992, U.S. District Court, Central District of California. *Education:* Yeshiva University (B.A., magna cum laude, 1985); Harvard University (J.D., magna cum laude, 1988). Law Clerk, Hon. Ruth F. Abrams, Supreme Judicial Court of Massachusetts, 1988-1989. Author: "Imposing Federal Business on Officers of the States: What the Tenth Amendment Might Mean," 57 George Washington Law Review 907, 1989. *LANGUAGES:* Hebrew.

**WEN LIU,** born Hong Kong, July 27, 1958; admitted to bar, 1987, California and U.S. District Court, Central District of California; registered to practice before U.S. Patent and Trademark Office. *Education:* California Institute of Technology (B.S. and M.S., with honors, 1980, Tau Beta Pi); Massachusetts Institute of Technology (S.M., 1982); UCLA Law School (J.D., 1986). Judicial Extern, 1985. *Member:* State Bar of California (Intellectual Property Section). *LANGUAGES:* Chinese (Mandarin and Cantonese).

**MICHAEL S. LOWE,** born Queens, New York, July 16, 1968; admitted to bar, 1994, California and U.S. District Court, Central District of California. *Education:* Wesleyan University (B.A., 1990); New York University (J.D., magna cum laude, 1993). Order of the Coif. Law Clerk to Honorable Robert J. Kelleher, U.S. District Court, Central District of California.

**SAMUEL KAI LU,** born Dallas, Texas, April 20, 1969; admitted to bar, 1994, California; 1995, New York. *Education:* Stanford University (B.A.B.S., 1991); Columbia University (J.D., 1994). Stone Scholar. *PRACTICE AREAS:* Intellectual Property Litigation. *Email:* slu@irell.com

**MARC S. MAISTER,** born Johannesburg, South Africa, December 1, 1964; admitted to bar, 1991, California and U.S. District Court, Central District of California; 1995, U.S. Supreme Court. *Education:* University of Witwatersrand, Johannesburg, South Africa (B.Comm., 1987); Boalt Hall, University of California at Berkeley (J.D., 1991). Order of the Coif. Author: "Trigger of Coverage--A Contract Approach," published by the American Bar Association in "The Brief," Spring 1996, Vol. 25, No. 3 and at Mealey's Emerging Insurance Battles Conference, February, 1996. *Member:* Orange County (Member and Vice Chairperson, Insurance Law Section) and American (Tort and Insurance Practice Section) Bar Associations. (Resident at Newport Beach). *LANGUAGES:* English and Afrikaans.

**BENJAMIN R. MARTIN,** born California, July 26, 1971; admitted to bar, 1996, California. *Education:* University of Southern California (B.A., 1993); University of Virginia (J.D., 1996). Phi Beta Kappa; Order of the Coif. Dillard Fellow. Member, Law Review.

**JENNIFER E. MEIER,** born Kansas City, Missouri, January 14, 1972; admitted to bar, 1996, California. *Education:* University of Kansas (B.S., cum laude, 1993); University of California, Los Angeles (J.D., 1996). Order of the Coif. Recipient, American Jurisprudence Award, Constitutional Law. Chief Justice, Moot Court Honors Program. *Email:* jmeier@irell.com

**ROMAN MELNIK,** born Minsk, Belarus, October 8, 1968; admitted to bar, 1995, California, U.S. District Court, Central District of California and U.S. Court of Appeals, Ninth Circuit. *Education:* Harvard University (A.B., magna cum laude, 1989); University of California at Berkeley (M.S., Chemistry, 1990); Columbia University (J.D., 1994). Harlan Fiske Stone Scholar, 1991-1994. Staff, 1992-1993 and Senior Editor, 1993-1994, Columbia Law Review. Law Clerk to the Hon. Phyllis A. Kravitch, U.S. Court of Appeals, Eleventh Circuit, 1994-1995. Teaching Assistant, Civil Procedure, Columbia Law School, 1993. *LANGUAGES:* Russian, Belorussian.

**PHILIP H. MILLER,** born Rutland, Vermont, June 27, 1954; admitted to bar, 1994, New York and California. *Education:* University of Vermont (B.S., summa cum laude, 1976); Harvard University (Ed.M., 1980); Fordham University (J.D., magna cum laude, 1993). Order of the Coif. Notes and Articles Editor, Fordham Law Review. Author: Note, "New Technology, Old Problem: Determining the First Amendment Status of Electronic Information Systems," Fordham Law Review, April 1993; Note, "Life After Feist: Facts, the First Amendment, and the Copyright Status of Automated Databases," Fordham Law Review, December, 1992; *Media Law for Producers,* Focal Press, 1990. *Member:* Los Angeles County and New York State Bar Associations; State Bar of California (Intellectual Property Section).

**HARRY A. MITTLEMAN,** born Los Angeles, California, July 28, 1969; admitted to bar, 1994, California. *Education:* Princeton University (A.B., summa cum laude, 1991); Harvard University (J.D., magna cum laude, 1994). Law Clerk to Hon. Alfred T. Goodwin, Ninth Circuit, 1994-1995.

**JOANNA MOORE,** born Burbank, California, November 29, 1967; admitted to bar, 1993, California. *Education:* University of California at Los Angeles (B.A., 1989); Loyola Law School (J.D., 1993). Order of the Coif. Member, St. Thomas More Society. Judicial Extern to Hon. Arthur L. Alarcon, U.S. Court of Appeals, Ninth Circuit. Executive Editor, Loyola of Los Angeles Law Review. *Member:* State Bar of California.

**DAVID Z. MOSS,** born Los Angeles, California, November 30, 1969; admitted to bar, 1995, California. *Education:* University of California, Berkeley (A.B., 1991); Boalt Hall School of Law, University of California, Berkeley (J.D., 1994). Order of the Coif. Executive Editor, Ecology Law Quarterly, 1993-1994. Law Clerk for Hon. Stephen V. Wilson, United States District Court, Central District of California, 1994-1995.

**MAURINE M. MURTAGH,** born Atlanta, Georgia, May 27, 1946; admitted to bar, 1996, California. *Education:* Georgetown University (B.S.B.A., summa cum laude, 1968); University of Texas at Austin (M.B.A., 1971); Columbia University (M.Phil., 1982); Duke University (J.D., magna cum laude, 1995). Beta Gamma Sigma; Phi Kappa Phi. Dean's Award for Academic Excellence, University of Texas at Austin. Bidlake Writing Award. Duke Law Journal. *LANGUAGES:* Spanish. *Email:* mmurtagh@irell.com

**JOHN M. NAKASHIMA,** born Los Angeles, California, September 10, 1954; admitted to bar, 1987, California. *Education:* California State University at Long Beach (B.A., with high distinction, 1976; B.S., with distinction, 1978; M.B.A., 1983); University of Southern California (J.D., 1987). *Member:* State Bar of California; American Bar Association. (Resident at Newport Beach).

**BEN D. ORLANSKI,** born Santa Monica, California, December 25, 1967; admitted to bar, 1995, California. *Education:* Swarthmore College (B.A., with high honors, 1990); University of California, Los Angeles (J.D., 1995). Phi Beta Kappa; Order of the Coif. Chief Comments Editor, Volume 42, UCLA Law Review. Author, "Whose Representations Are These Anyway?: Attorney Prospectus Liability After Central Bank," 42 UCLA L. Rev. 885; Co-author, "Taking Central Bank of Denver Seriously," in *Class and Derivative Litigation in the Reform Era* 1109 (Glasser Legal Works, 1996). (Downtown Los Angeles Office).

**ELIZABETH K. PENFIL,** born Silver Spring, Maryland, July 14, 1966; admitted to bar, 1995, California. *Education:* Wellesley College (A.B., Art History and Architectural History, 1987); University of Southern California (J.D., 1995). Order of the Coif. Southern California Law Review. Southern California Review of Law and Women's Studies. University of Southern California Law Center, Lawyering Skills Instructor, 1994-1995. (Resident at Newport Beach).

**DAVID J. RICHTER,** born Brooklyn, New York, January 26, 1968; admitted to bar, 1992, California. *Education:* Cornell University (B.A., 1989); Yale University (J.D., 1992). Phi Beta Kappa. Degree Marshal. Senior Editor, Yale Law Journal, 1991-1992. Finalist, Yale Moot Court, 1991. Best Oralist, Best Team, Sutherland Cup Inter-Law School Moot Court, 1992. Law Clerk to Judge Alfred T. Goodwin, U.S. Court of Appeals, 1992-1993. Visiting Professor, China University of Politics & Law, 1994-1995. *Member:* State Bar of California. *Email:* drichter@irell.com

**FLAVIO ROSE,** born Santiago, Chile, June 20, 1955; admitted to bar, 1995, California. *Education:* University of Santiago, Santiago, Chile (1972); Massachusetts Institute of Technology (S.M., 1982); University of Califor-

*(This Listing Continued)*

**IRELL & MANELLA LLP, Los Angeles—Continued**

nia, Berkeley (J.D., 1994). Member, 1992-1993 and Note and Comment Editor, 1993-1994, California Law Review. Law Clerk to U.S. District Judge Irma E. Gonzalez, Southern District of California, 1994-1995. Author, "Related Contracts and Personal Jurisdiction," 82 California Law Review 1545, 1994. *LANGUAGES:* Spanish.

**DAVID J. ROSMANN,** born Fort Dodge, Iowa, February 15, 1958; admitted to bar, 1996, California and U.S. District Court, Central District of California. *Education:* Iowa State University (B.S.E.Sc., 1981); University of Southern California (M.S.E.E., 1990); Loyola Law School (J.D., 1996). Order of the Coif; Phi Delta Phi; St. Thomas More Honor Society. Sayre Macneil Scholar. Faculty Academic Scholar. Moot Court Honors Board. *Email:* drosmann@irell.com

**KATHRYN SCHAEFER,** born Los Angeles, California, March 1, 1969; admitted to bar, 1995, California. *Education:* Georgetown University (B.S.F.S., cum laude, 1991); University of Chicago (J.D., with honors, 1994). Member, Law Review. Judicial Clerk to Honorable Harold H. Greene, 1994-1995.

**DAVID A. SCHWARZ,** born Washington, D.C., April 19, 1960; admitted to bar, 1992, California and U.S. District Court, Central, Northern and Southern Districts of California. *Education:* Columbia University (B.A., 1983); Duke University (J.D., with high honors, 1988). Order of the Coif. Articles Editor, Duke Law Journal, 1987-1988. Recipient, James S. Bidlake Award for Research and Writing. Judicial Clerk to the Hon. Alex Kozinski, U.S. Court of Appeals, Ninth Circuit, 1988-1989. Special Assistant to the U.S. Permanent Representative to the European Office of the United Nations and other International Organizations, 1989-1991. Member, U.S. Delegation to the United Nations Commission on Human Rights, 1990-1991. Co-Author: "Attorney Due Diligence Obligations to Clients After FDIC v. O'Melveny & Myers," Practising Law Institute (1993); "26 U.S.C. §7212(a): Testing the Criminal Boundaries of 'Corrupt Endeavors' to Impede the Due Administration of the Tax Laws," American Bar Association (1994); "The U.N.'s Human Rights Failure," Wall Street Journal (Europe) (Feb. 25-26, 1994); "Taking Central Bank of Denver Seriously," in Solovy et al., *Class and Derivative Litigation in the Reform Era* (Glasser 1996). *Member:* State Bar of California. *LANGUAGES:* French.

**ALAN D. SEGE,** born Washington, D.C., December 23, 1966; admitted to bar, 1995, California. *Education:* Oberlin College (B.A., with honors, 1989); Georgetown University (J.D., cum laude, 1994). Editor, Georgetown Law Journal, 1993-1994. Georgetown University Federal Appellate Litigation Clinic, 1993-1994. *LANGUAGES:* Hebrew.

**LAURA A. SEIGLE,** born Ann Arbor, Michigan, January 22, 1967; admitted to bar, 1994, California. *Education:* Harvard University (A.B., 1989); Yale University (J.D., 1993). Law Clerk, Hon. Diarmuid O'Scannlain, U.S. Court of Appeals for the Ninth Circuit, 1993-1994.

**JEFFREY N. SHAPIRO,** born New York, N.Y., September 24, 1970; admitted to bar, 1996, California. *Education:* University of California at Berkeley (A.B., with highest honors, 1991); University of Chicago (J.D., with high honors, 1995). Phi Beta Kappa; Order of the Coif. Executive Editor, Law Review. Author, "Attorney Liability Under RICO Section 1962(c) after Reves v. Ernst & Young," 61 University of Chicago Law Review 1153, 1994. *Email:* jshapiro@irell.com

**GAIL J. STANDISH,** born Boston, Massachusetts, September 28, 1963; admitted to bar, 1993, California. *Education:* Massachusetts Institute of Technology (S.B., 1985; S.M., 1990); University of California, Los Angeles (J.D., 1993). Tau Beta Pi; Sigma Gamma Tau; Sigma Xi; Order of the Coif. Recipient, American Jurisprudence Award, Evidence. Member, 1991-1992 and Articles Editor, 1992-1993, U.C.L.A. Law Review. Law Clerk to Hon. William J. Rea, U.S. District Court Judge, Central District of California, 1993-1994. *Member:* State Bar of California (Intellectual Property Section). [U.S. Air Force, 1985-1988; Capt., U.S. Air Force Reserves, 1988-1993]

**ETHAN G. STONE,** born Berkeley, California, May 13, 1968; admitted to bar, 1996, California. *Education:* Harvard College (A.B., 1991); Columbia University (J.D., 1995). Kent Scholar. Author, "Must We Teach Abstinence? Pensions' Relationship Investment And The Lessons Of Fiduciary Duty," 94 Columbia Law Review 2222, 1994. Law Clerk to the Hon. Alex Kozinski, U.S. Court of Appeals, Ninth Circuit, 1995-1996. *LANGUAGES:* Hebrew. *Email:* estone@irell.com

**DOUGLAS K. SUGIMOTO,** born Sacramento, California, September 9, 1971; admitted to bar, 1996, California. *Education:* University of Califor-
*(This Listing Continued)*

nia at Berkeley (B.S., with high honors, 1993); Harvard Law School (J.D., cum laude, 1996). Beta Gamma Sigma. *Email:* dsugimoto@irell.com

**MARY-CHRISTINE (M.C.) SUNGAILA,** born Mountain View, California, December 1, 1967; admitted to bar, 1991, California, U.S. District Court, Central District of California and U.S. Court of Appeals, Ninth Circuit; 1995, U.S. Supreme Court and U.S. District Court, Southern District of California. *Education:* Stanford University (B.A., with distinction and honors in Humanities, 1988); University of California at Los Angeles, (J.D., 1991). Recipient: Stanford University Undergraduate Research Grant, 1987-1988; American Jurisprudence Award in Torts; UCLA University Fellowship for Academic Excellence, 1989-1990 and 1990-1991. Member, Moot Court Honors Program, 1989-1990. Publications: Bibliography, *The Woman Advocate: Excelling in the 90's,* (Prentice Hall Law & Business, 1995); "Taking the Gendered Realities of Female Offenders into Account: Downward Departures for Coercion and Duress," 8 Fed. Sent. R. 1 (1995). Extern to the Honorable Dorothy W. Nelson, U.S. Court of Appeals, Ninth Circuit. Law Clerk to the Honorable Alicemarie H. Stotler, U.S. District Court, Central District of California, 1991-1992. Law Clerk to the Honorable Ferdinand F. Fernandez, U.S. Court of Appeals, Ninth Circuit, 1993-1994. *Member:* Orange County (Member, Gender Equity Committee) and American (Newsletter Editor, The Woman Advocate Committee of the Section of Litigation, 1996—) Bar Associations; State Bar of California (Member, Litigation Section, Technology Committee, 1992-1994); Orange County Women Lawyers. (Resident at Newport Beach).

**SANA SWE,** born Rangoon, Burma, December 29, 1964; admitted to bar, 1994, California. *Education:* Occidental College (B.A., honors in political science, 1991); Loyola Law School (J.D., cum laude, 1994). Order of the Coif. Sayre Macrell Scholar. Staff Member, Loyola of Los Angeles Law Review.

**CRAIG VARNEN,** born Los Angeles, California, August 9, 1968; admitted to bar, 1994, California. *Education:* University of California, San Diego (B.A., summa cum laude, 1990) Phi Beta Kappa; Boalt Hall School of Law, University of California, Berkeley (J.D., 1993). Order of the Coif. Editor, California Law Review, 1991-1993. Law Clerk to Judge Cynthia Holcomb Hall, Ninth Circuit Court of Appeals, 1993-1994. *Member:* State Bar of California.

**ERIC A. WEBBER,** born Indianapolis, Indiana, November 9, 1957; admitted to bar, 1988, California and U.S. District Court, Central District of California. *Education:* Indiana University (B.Sc., 1979; M.B.A., 1980); London School of Economics, London, England (M.Sc., 1982, Marshall Scholar); University of Chicago (J.D., 1987). Articles Editor, The University of Chicago Law Review. Law Clerk to Hon. John Minor Wisdom, U.S. Court of Appeals for the Fifth Circuit, New Orleans, Louisiana, 1987-1988. *Member:* Los Angeles County Bar Association (Chair, Commercial Law Committee; Editor, Commercial Law and Bankruptcy Newsletter); State Bar of California (Business Law Section); Financial Lawyers Conference. (Downtown Los Angeles Office).

**TONI WEINSTEIN,** born Syracuse, New York, November 18, 1956; admitted to bar, 1991, California. *Education:* Syracuse University (B.S., 1978); Cornell University (M.B.A., 1980); University of Southern California (J.D., 1991).

**JESSICA WEISEL,** born Los Angeles, California, May 17, 1970; admitted to bar, 1994, California. *Education:* Grinnell College (B.A., 1991); Yale University (J.D., 1994). Phi Beta Kappa. Coker Fellowship, Yale Law School, 1993-1994.

**IAN C. WIENER,** born New York, N.Y., July 27, 1961; admitted to bar, 1992, California. *Education:* Dartmouth College (A.B., cum laude, 1983); Georgetown University (J.D., magna cum laude, 1992). Order of the Coif. Member, 1990-1992 and Articles Editor, 1991-1992, Georgetown Law Journal. Olin Fellowship in Law and Economics, 1991-1992. Author: "Running Rampant: The Imposition of Sanctions and the Use of Force Against Fleeing Criminal Suspects," 80 Georgetown Law Journal 2175 (1992). *Member:* State Bar of California.

**WENDY A. WOLF,** born Los Angeles, California, July 3, 1960; admitted to bar, 1986, California. *Education:* University of California at San Diego (B.A., with high distinction, cum laude, 1982); Yale Law School (J.D., 1985). Phi Beta Kappa. Senior Editor, Yale Law Journal, 1984-1985. Author: "Sex Discrimination in Pension Plans: The Incomplete Relief," 9 Harvard Women's Law Journal, 1986. *Member:* Los Angeles County and American Bar Associations; State Bar of California; Industrial Relations Research Association.

**CHRISTOPHER F. WONG,** born Torrance, California, March 24, 1964; admitted to bar, 1989, California. *Education:* University of California
*(This Listing Continued)*

## PROFESSIONAL BIOGRAPHIES

### CALIFORNIA—LOS ANGELES

at Berkeley (A.B., with high honors, 1986); Yale Law School (J.D., 1989). Phi Beta Kappa. *Member:* State Bar of California.

**JULIETTE YOUNGBLOOD,** born Lake Charles, Louisiana, September 19, 1963; admitted to bar, 1990, California. *Education:* Fitchburg State College (B.A., English, summa cum laude, 1984; B.S., Communications, summa cum laude, 1984); University of Virginia (M.A., English, 1985); Loyola Law School (J.D., cum laude, 1990). Order of the Coif; Alpha Sigma Nu. *Member:* State Bar of California. *Email:* jyoungblood@irell.com

## IRSFELD, IRSFELD & YOUNGER LLP
### LOS ANGELES, CALIFORNIA
(See Glendale)

General Civil, Business and Real Estate Litigation and Arbitration in all State and Federal Courts. Corporations, Securities, Commercial, Municipal, Estate Planning, Real Property, Personal Injury Litigation, Taxation, Probate, Eminent Domain, Construction Law, Bankruptcy (Creditor) and Debt Collection.

## MICHAEL W. IRVING
### 1801 CENTURY PARK EAST, SUITE 2500
### LOS ANGELES, CALIFORNIA 90067
Telephone: 310-284-3420
Fax: 310-277-1278

Business Litigation, Appellate Law, Contracts, Collections, Enforcement of Judgements.

**MICHAEL W. IRVING,** born Los Angeles, California, September 30, 1959; admitted to bar, 1992, California. *Education:* University of California at Los Angeles (B.A., 1985); Loyola Marymount University (J.D., 1991). *Member:* Los Angeles County and American Bar Associations; State Bar of California. *PRACTICE AREAS:* Copyright Law (35%); Appellate Practice (30%); Guardianship Law (20%); Collections (15%).

## IRWIN & REILY
### SUITE 2040, 911 WILSHIRE BOULEVARD
### LOS ANGELES, CALIFORNIA 90017
Telephone: 213-624-3671
Fax: 213-688-7489

Aviation, Products Liability, General Civil and Trial Practice.

**JAMES A. IRWIN,** born Los Angeles, California, April 2, 1933; admitted to bar, 1963, California. *Education:* University of California at Berkeley (A.B., 1958); Boalt Hall School of Law, University of California (LL.B., 1962). Phi Delta Phi. Member, Chancery Club, 1971. *Member:* Los Angeles County and American (Member: Aviation Subcommittee, 1977—; Negligence Section) Bar Associations; State Bar of California. *PRACTICE AREAS:* Aviation; Products Liability; General Civil Practice; Trial Practice.

**DAVID H. REILY,** born Charleston, West Virginia, June 6, 1950; admitted to bar, 1981, California. *Education:* The Ohio State University; University of Maryland, Rota, Spain (B.A., magna cum laude, 1977); University of Southern California (J.D., 1981). Member, State Moot Court Competition, Santa Clara, California, 1980. Editor, Hale Moot Court Executive Board. Arbitrator, Los Angeles Superior Court, 1987—. *Member:* State Bar of California. [With U.S. Navy, 1969-1978]. *PRACTICE AREAS:* Aviation; Products Liability; General Civil Practice; Trial Practice.

**JANINE K. JEFFERY,** born Rome, New York, July 10, 1959; admitted to bar, 1983, California. *Education:* University of California at San Diego; University of California at Irvine (B.A., 1980); University of Southern California (J.D., 1983). Order of the Coif. Hale Moot Court Competitor. *PRACTICE AREAS:* Aviation; Products Liability; General Civil Practice; Trial Practice.

### ASSOCIATES

**PAUL R. AYERS,** born Los Angeles, California, December 16, 1951; admitted to bar, 1991, California, U.S. Court of Appeals, Ninth Circuit and U.S. District Court, Central and Southern Districts of California. *Education:* University of California at Berkeley (B.A., 1977); Whittier College (J.D., summa laude, 1991). Recipient: American Jurisprudence Awards in Civil Procedure, Property, Constitution Law, Professional Responsibility,

*(This Listing Continued)*

Pre-Trial Litigation, Commercial Transactions, Wills and Trusts, Corporations; ABA Award for Excellence in Local Government Law. *Member:* State Bar of California. *PRACTICE AREAS:* Aviation; Products Liability; General Civil Practice; Trial Practice.

## SANDRA McMAHAN IRWIN
### LOS ANGELES, CALIFORNIA
(See Pasadena)

Corporate, General Business and Real Estate Law, Litigation, Estate Planning, Probate including Surrogates Court Practice and Other Law of Reproduction.

## ISAACMAN, KAUFMAN & PAINTER
### LOS ANGELES, CALIFORNIA
(See Beverly Hills)

Civil Litigation, Entertainment Tax, Employment and Business Litigation. Business and Real Estate Transactions. Intellectual Property Matters.

## RUSSELL IUNGERICH
### A PROFESSIONAL LAW CORPORATION
### 3580 WILSHIRE BOULEVARD, SUITE 1920
### LOS ANGELES, CALIFORNIA 90010
Telephone: 213-382-8600
Fax: 213-382-5057
Email: riplc@ix.netcom.com

Appellate Practice. Civil and Criminal Trial Practice in all State and Federal Courts. Administrative, Constitutional and Criminal Law. International Practice.

*FIRM PROFILE:* 70% of practice involves physicians, psychiatrists, psychologists and other health care professionals in license discipline defense, hospital privilege and peer review, criminal defense and related civil and administrative matters; 30% Business and other Litigation.

**RUSSELL IUNGERICH,** born Philadelphia, Pennsylvania, August 12, 1942; admitted to bar, 1969, California, U.S. District Court, Central District of California and U.S. Court of Appeals, Ninth Circuit; 1970, U.S. District Court, Northern District of California; 1972, U.S. Supreme Court; 1977, U.S. District Court, Southern and Eastern Districts of California. *Education:* Claremont Men's College, California (B.A., 1963); School of Law, Boalt Hall, University of California (J.D., 1968). Adjunct Professor of Law, Loyola School of Law, Los Angeles, 1974-1978. Deputy Attorney General, State of California, 1969-1978. President, California Academy of Attorneys for Health Care Professionals, 1994—. *Member:* Los Angeles County (Trustee, 1981-1983; Chairperson, Committees on: Appellate Courts, 1977-1979; Federal Courts and Practice, 1979-1980) and American (Member, Litigation Section and Forum Committee on Health Law) Bar Associations; California Academy of Appellate Lawyers. [Capt., U.S. Army, Intelligence, 1963-1969]. *PRACTICE AREAS:* Administrative Law; Appellate Practice; Civil Trial; White Collar Criminal Defense; International Extradition; Physicians Licensing.

**PAUL SPACKMAN,** born New Rochelle, New York, September 20, 1948; admitted to bar, 1990, California, U.S. District Court, Central District of California and U.S. Court of Appeals, Ninth Circuit. *Education:* San Diego State University (B.A. 1973, M.A. 1974); Loyola Law School, Los Angeles, (J.D. 1990). *Member:* Los Angeles County and American Bar Associations. *REPORTED CASES:* Silva v. Superior Court, (1993) 14 Cal.App. 4th 562. *PRACTICE AREAS:* Administrative Law; Civil Trial; Physicians Licensing.

## IVANJACK & LAMBIRTH

A Partnership including Professional Corporations

Established in 1972

12301 WILSHIRE BOULEVARD, SUITE 600
**LOS ANGELES, CALIFORNIA 90025-1000**
Telephone: 310-820-7211
Telecopier: 310-820-0687
Email: ivanjack@AOL.com

*Irvine, California Office:* 5 Park Plaza, Suite 800. 92614. Telephone: 714-475-4477. Telecopier: 714-475-4475.

General Civil Trial and Appellate Practice in all State and Federal Courts, Commercial, Banking and Financial Institutions, Real Estate, Secured Transactions, Equipment Leasing, Creditors' Rights and Bankruptcy, Transactional Documentation, Operational and Regulatory Compliance Advice, Business and Construction.

FIRM PROFILE: *The firm specializes in representing financial institutions, finance lessors and other corporate clients in every major area of commercial law. The firm offers extensive experience in litigating commercial disputes as well as in structuring and negotiating banking, business and real estate workouts. Although the firm has been historically identified with lending institutions, its clients are engaged in many types of commercial businesses and ventures.*

**LARRY G. IVANJACK, (P.C.),** born Chicago, Illinois, September 6, 1949; admitted to bar, 1975, California; U.S. District Court, Central, Southern and Northern Districts of California. *Education:* University of California at Los Angeles (B.A., 1971; J.D., 1975); Southwestern University. *Member:* Los Angeles County and American Bar Associations; State Bar of California. **REPORTED CASES:** Bank of America National Trust and Savings Association v. Sanati, 11 Cal.App.4th 1079 (1992).

**TIMOTHY A. LAMBIRTH, (P.C.),** born Orange, California, January 5, 1953; admitted to bar, 1978, California; U.S. District Court, Central, Southern, Northern and Eastern Districts of California; 1984, District of Columbia; 1985, Maryland. *Education:* University of California at Riverside (B.A., with honors, 1974); Whittier College School of Law (J.D., cum laude, 1978). Member, Whittier Law Review, 1977-1978. Author: "Costs—Attorney's Fees—Implications of California's Adoption of the Private Attorney General Theory and the Impact of California Code of Civil Procedure Section 1021.5," Vol. 1, No. 2, Whittier Law Review, 1979; "Lenders as Landlords," Los Angeles Lawyer, October, 1983. Speaker: Los Angeles Trial Lawyers Association 11th Annual Convention, "Humanizing and Handling Suits for the Institutional Plaintiff," 1993. *Member:* Los Angeles County and American Bar Associations; State Bar of California, Maryland State and The District of Columbia Bar; The Association of Trial Lawyers of America; Association of Business Trial Lawyers; Italian American Lawyers Association (Member, Past Treasurer and Board of Governors).

**THOMAS E. SHUCK, (P.C.),** born Omaha, Nebraska, October 12, 1953; admitted to bar, 1979, Ohio; 1984, California; U.S. District Court, Eastern, Western, Northern, Southern and Central Districts of California; U.S. District Court, Northern District of Ohio. *Education:* Miami University (A.B., 1976); Cleveland State University (J.D., 1979). Speaker: "Debt Equity Issues in Leveraged Lease Transactions," Equipment Leasing Association Legal Forum, 1996. *Member:* Los Angeles County and American Bar Associations; State Bar of California; Equipment Leasing Association; Financial Lawyers Conference; National Association of Securities Dealers Public Arbitrator. **REPORTED CASES:** In Re Kruger, 77 B.R. 785 (Bankr. C.D.Cal. 1987). **PRACTICE AREAS:** Bankruptcy; Equipment Leasing; Business Litigation; Construction Litigation.

**KATHRYN B. MILSTEAD,** born White Plains, New York, June 1, 1959; admitted to bar, 1985, California, U.S. District Court, Central, Southern and Eastern Districts of California and U.S. Court of Appeals, Ninth Circuit. *Education:* University of New Mexico (B.A., 1980); Southwestern University (J.D., 1985). *Member:* Los Angeles County Bar Association (Member, Real Estate Section); State Bar of California; Financial Lawyers Conference; Womens Lawyers Association of Los Angeles. **PRACTICE AREAS:** Real Estate; Commercial Litigation.

---

**JOSEPH H. LOWTHER,** born Detroit, Michigan, May 14, 1961; admitted to bar, 1987, California; 1988, U.S. District Court, Central and Southern Districts of California. *Education:* Fort Lewis College; University of Southern California (B.S., 1983); Whittier College School of Law (J.D./M.B.A., 1987). Judge Pro Tempore, Los Angeles Municipal Court, *(This Listing Continued)*

1993—. Member of Board of Directors, Legal Corps of Los Angeles. *Member:* Los Angeles County Bar Association; State Bar of California (Provisional and Post Judgment Remedies Section). **LANGUAGES:** German. **PRACTICE AREAS:** Business Torts; Complex Litigation; Contract Law; Financial Institutions; Real Estate; Fraud; Bankruptcy.

**ELISE A. ROSS,** born Brooklyn, New York, September 11, 1957; admitted to bar, 1984, California. *Education:* University of California at Los Angeles (B.A., summa cum laude, 1979); University of California at Davis (J.D., 1984). Phi Beta Kappa. Speaker: CBA Bank Counsel Seminar; CBA Regulatory Compliance Conference; CATL Regulatory Compliance Conference; Inland Empire Bankers Network; Western Association of Equipment Leasors Conference. *Member:* State Bar of California. **LANGUAGES:** Spanish and French. **REPORTED CASES:** Bank of America National Trust and Savings Association v. Sanati, 11 Cal. App. 4th 1079 (1992). **PRACTICE AREAS:** Regulatory Compliance; Operations and Transactional Advice to Financial Institutions.

**GARY TOKUMORI,** born Los Angeles, California, July 2, 1962; admitted to bar, 1990, California; 1991, U.S. District Court, Central and Southern Districts of California; 1992, U.S. District Court, Northern and Eastern Districts of California. *Education:* University of California at Los Angeles (B.A., cum laude, 1985); Loyola Law School, Los Angeles (J.D., 1990). Staff Writer and Note and Comment Editor, International and Comparative Law Journal, 1988-1990. Extern to the Honorable Stephen V. Wilson, U.S. District Court, Central District of California, 1988. *Member:* Los Angeles County and American Bar Associations; State Bar of California. **PRACTICE AREAS:** Business Litigation; Commercial Litigation; Bankruptcy.

**MARY G. LEE,** born Jacksonville, Florida, February 16, 1966; admitted to bar, 1994, California; 1996, U.S. District Court, Central, Eastern, Southern and Northern Districts of California. *Education:* Catholic University of America (B.A., cum laude, 1989); Washington College of Law of the American University (J.D,, 1993). Judicial Extern to the Honorable Eric Bruggink, U.S. Court of Federal Claims. *Member:* State Bar of California. **PRACTICE AREAS:** Bankruptcy; Commercial Litigation; Business Litigation; Real Estate.

### OF COUNSEL

**ROBERT F. NICHOLS, JR.,** born Oak Park, Illinois, July 17, 1927; admitted to bar, 1966, California and U.S. District Court, Central, Southern, Eastern and Northern Districts. *Education:* St. John's College (B.A., 1949); Loyola University of Los Angeles (LL.B., 1965). *Member:* Orange County Bar Association; The State Bar of California. (Also Member, Nichols & Andrews, Irvine). **PRACTICE AREAS:** Commercial Banking Law; Business Law; Real Estate Law; Corporate Law; Creditor's Rights; Appeals.

**CAMILLA N. ANDREWS,** born Los Angeles, California, March 14, 1958; admitted to bar, 1986, California; 1987, U.S. District Court, Central District of California and U.S. District Court, Southern, Eastern and Northern Districts of California. *Education:* University of Santa Clara (B.A., 1980); Loyola Marymount University (J.D., 1986). Member, Board of directors, French American Chamber of Commerce. *Member:* Los Angeles County and Orange County (Financial Institutions, Commercial Law and Bankruptcy, Creditors Rights, Real Estate and Business Litigation Sections) Bar Associations; State Bar of California; Financial Women International; National Association of Women Lawyers. (Also Member, Nichols & Andrews, Irvine). **LANGUAGES:** French. **PRACTICE AREAS:** Commercial Litigation; Creditors' Rights; Contract Disputes; Financial Institution Litigation; Creditor Bankruptcy; Judicial and Nonjudicial Foreclosures; Collections; Business Litigation; Appellate Practice; Real Estate; Wrongful Termination; Sexual Harassment; Personal Injury.

REPRESENTATIVE CLIENTS: Bank of America; Citibank N.A.; Union Bank of California, N.A.; Sanwa Bank California; Great Western Bank; Imperial Bank; First Republic Thrift and Loan; General Electric Capital Corp.; Fleet Credit Corp.; Western Bank; Siemens Credit Corp.; International Bank of California; Center Capital Corp.; Linotype-Hell Co.; Mercedes-Benz Credit Corp.; American Honda Finance Corp.; Don Kott Auto Center; Aggreko, Inc.; AAF-McQuay, Inc.; Chase Manhattan Bank; Citizens Business Bank; Downey National Bank; National Bank of Southern California; The Money Store; One Central Bank; Sunwest Bank; Lee Servicing Co.; Wendover Funding; National Enterprises, Inc.; First Bank and Trust; El Dorado Bank.

PROFESSIONAL BIOGRAPHIES

CALIFORNIA—LOS ANGELES

## MARK A. IVENER
*A LAW CORPORATION*

Established in 1975

11601 WILSHIRE BOULEVARD, SUITE 1430
**LOS ANGELES, CALIFORNIA 90025**
Telephone: 310-477-3000
Fax: 310-477-2652
Email: mark@ivener.com
URL: http://www.ilw.com/ivener

*Canadian Associate Office:* 1300-808 Nelson Street, Vancouver, British Columbia V6Z 2H2. Telephone: 604-688-0558. FAX: 604-685-8972.

*Japanese Associate Office:* 13th Floor Urbannet Otemachi Building, 2-2-2 Otemachi, Chiyoda-Ku, Tokyo 100, Japan. Telephone: 813-3231-8888. Fax: 813-3231-8881.

*Practice Limited to Immigration and Nationality Law including Entertainment Related Matters.*

*FIRM PROFILE:* The staff of Mark A. Ivener have the following language capabilities: Japanese, Spanish, Chinese, Farsi, French and Armenian.

**MARK A. IVENER,** born Sioux City, Iowa, May 2, 1942; admitted to bar, 1968, California. *Education:* University of Illinois (B.A., 1964); University of California at Los Angeles (J.D., 1967). Author: "Handbook of Immigration Law," Volumes I & II, 1980, 2nd Edition, 1982, 3rd Edition, 1986; "Doing Business in The U.S.A. Under Free Trade," 1st Edition, 1989, 2nd Edition, 1990; "Get The Right Visa," 1992; "Get the Right Visa Under NAFTA," 1994; "A Complete Guide to Getting an American Visa" Japanese language Edition, 1993, Second Edition, 1994; "Have You Thought About Immigrating To The U.S.?" Spanish language Edition, 1995. Founding Member, IMMLAW, The National Consortium of Immigration Law Firms.

---

## IVERSON, YOAKUM, PAPIANO & HATCH
ONE WILSHIRE BUILDING
27TH FLOOR 624 SOUTH GRAND AVENUE
**LOS ANGELES, CALIFORNIA 90017**
Telephone: 213-624-7444
Telecopier: 213 629-4563

*General Civil Trial and Appellate Practice in State and Federal Courts including Corporation and Securities Law. Antitrust, Administrative, Insurance and Product Liability Law, Labor, Real Property, Entertainment, Commercial Tax and Municipal Law. Estate Planning, Probate and Trust Law, Wrongful Termination, Employment Discrimination and Construction Litigation.*

**PAUL E. IVERSON** (1907-1975).

**FRANK B. YOAKUM, JR.** (1906-1991).

### MEMBERS OF FIRM

**NEIL PAPIANO,** born Salt Lake City, Utah, November 25, 1934; admitted to bar, 1961, California. *Education:* Stanford University (B.A.; M.A., 1957); Vanderbilt University (LL.B., 1961). Phi Delta Phi. *Member:* Los Angeles County and American Bar Associations; State Bar of California. *PRACTICE AREAS:* Civil Litigation and Appellate Practice; Entertainment Law; Libel and Defamation Litigation; Corporation and Securities Law.

**DENNIS A. PAGE,** born Glendale, California, July 22, 1940; admitted to bar, 1965, California. *Education:* Pomona College (B.A., 1961); University of California at Los Angeles (LL.B., 1964). *Member:* Los Angeles County and American Bar Associations; State Bar of California. [Capt., USAR, 1964-1966]. *PRACTICE AREAS:* Probate; Estate Planning; Unitary Tax; Tax Litigation.

**PATRICK M. MC ADAM,** born Los Angeles, California, January 24, 1946; admitted to bar, 1971, California; 1979, U.S. Supreme Court and U.S. Claims Court; 1987, U.S. Tax Court. *Education:* Loyola University of Los Angeles (B.B.A., 1967); Loyola University of Los Angeles (J.D., 1970). *Member:* Los Angeles County Bar Association; State Bar of California; Association of Business Trial Lawyers. *PRACTICE AREAS:* Civil Litigation and Appellate Practice; Corporation and Securities Law.

**ARNOLD D. LARSON,** born Santa Monica, California, July 22, 1951; admitted to bar, 1977, California; 1988, U.S. Claims Court. *Education:* University of California at Los Angeles (B.A., 1974); Southwestern University (J.D., 1977). *Member:* Los Angeles County Bar Association; State Bar of

*(This Listing Continued)*

California. *PRACTICE AREAS:* Civil Litigation and Appellate Practice; Products Liability; Wrongful Termination and Employment Discrimination; Libel and Defamation; General Business and Commercial Litigation.

**JOHN M. GARRICK,** born Washington, D.C., December 6, 1956; admitted to bar, 1983, California. *Education:* University of California at Los Angeles (B.A., 1979); University of Utah (J.D., 1982). *Member:* Los Angeles County Bar Association; State Bar of California. *PRACTICE AREAS:* Civil Litigation and Appellate Practice; Products Liability; Unitary Tax and Tax Litigation; Antitrust; Libel and Defamation.

### ASSOCIATES

**DOUGLAS C. PEASE,** born Los Angeles, California, August 7, 1951; admitted to bar, 1981, California. *Education:* University of Minnesota; University of California at Los Angeles (B.A., 1973); University of San Diego (J.D., 1980). *Member:* State Bar of California. [With U.S. Navy, 1973-1977; Lieutenant Commander, USNR, 1977-1983]. *PRACTICE AREAS:* Civil Litigation.

**ANDREW K. DOTY,** born Rochester, New York, July 21, 1962; admitted to bar, 1988, California. *Education:* Northwestern University (B.A., 1984); University of California at Los Angeles (J.D., 1987). *Member:* State Bar of California. *PRACTICE AREAS:* Employment Law; Civil Litigation.

**MELISSA A. IMMEL,** born Vandenberg AFB, California, November 15, 1963; admitted to bar, 1988, California. *Education:* University of California at Santa Barbara (B.A., cum laude, 1985); Loyola Law School, Los Angeles (J.D., 1988). Recipient, American Jurisprudence Award for Evidence. *Member:* Los Angeles County Bar Association; State Bar of California. *PRACTICE AREAS:* Products Liability; Employment Law; Civil Litigation; Appellate Practice.

**MARY P. LIGHTFOOT,** born Sun Valley, Idaho, August 21, 1959; admitted to bar, 1988, California. *Education:* University of California at Davis (B.A., 1981); University of California Hastings College of Law (J.D., 1988). Finalist, David E. Snodgrass Moot Court Competition. *Member:* State Bar of California. *PRACTICE AREAS:* Employment Law; Civil Litigation; Products Liability.

**BARBARA LEE BERKOWITZ,** born Downey, California, March 12, 1961; admitted to bar, 1989, California. *Education:* Claremont McKenna College; Boston University (B.A., 1983); McGeorge School of Law, University of the Pacific (J.D., 1987). *Member:* Los Angeles County Bar Association; State Bar of California. *PRACTICE AREAS:* Entertainment Law; Defamation and Privacy Litigation; Civil Litigation and Appellate Practice.

**MARK PEARSON,** born Alhambra, California, March 2, 1957; admitted to bar, 1991, California. *Education:* Waseda University, Tokyo, Japan; California State University, Los Angeles (B.A., 1984); Brigham Young University (J.D., 1990). Managing Editor, Brigham Young University International and Comparative Law Annual, 1989-1990. Certified Public Accountant, California, 1990. Author: "Using Legislation to Open Japan's Financial Markets: An Analysis of the Trade Bills Primary Dealer Provision," Brigham Young University Law Review, Volume 1989, No. 2. *Member:* State Bar of California. *LANGUAGES:* Japanese and Mandarin Chinese. *PRACTICE AREAS:* Civil Litigation; Business Law.

**FREDERICK BREVARD HAYES,** born Spartanburg, South Carolina, September 21, 1961; admitted to bar, 1993, California. *Education:* Vanderbilt University (B.S., 1984); Whittier College School of Law (J.D., 1992). Editor, Whittier College School of Law, Law Review, 1991. *Member:* Los Angeles County and American Bar Associations. *PRACTICE AREAS:* Civil Litigation.

**GIOIA M. FASI,** born Honolulu, Hawaii, September 12, 1963; admitted to bar, 1994, California. *Education:* Boston University (B.A., 1986); Santa Clara University (J.D., 1994). *Member:* State Bar of California. *LANGUAGES:* Italian. *PRACTICE AREAS:* Civil Litigation.

**DENISE RENEE BYRNES,** born Bronxville, New York, April 30, 1968; admitted to bar, 1996, California, U.S. District Court, Central District of California and U.S. Court of Appeals, Ninth Circuit. *Education:* University of California at Santa Barbara (B.A., 1991); Southwestern University School of Law (J.D., 1996). *Member:* Los Angeles County and American Bar Associations. *LANGUAGES:* German. *PRACTICE AREAS:* Civil Litigation; Appellate Practice.

*(This Listing Continued)*

### IVERSON, YOAKUM, PAPIANO & HATCH, Los Angeles—Continued

#### OF COUNSEL

**R. NOEL HATCH,** born Los Angeles, California, January 31, 1932; admitted to bar, 1960, California; 1980, U.S. Supreme Court. *Education:* University of California at Los Angeles (A.B., 1956); Stanford University (LL.B., 1959). Pi Sigma Alpha. Member: Chancery Club; Board of Education, Pasadena, California, 1983-1989. *Member:* Los Angeles County and American Bar Associations; State Bar of California. **PRACTICE AREAS:** Civil Litigation and Appellate Practice; Wrongful Termination and Employment Discrimination; Labor; Real Property.

REPRESENTATIVE CLIENTS: California Thoroughbred Breeders Assn.; Bridgestone/Firestone, Inc.; Dow Corning Corporation; International Paper; Fortifiber Corp.; Transit Mixed Concrete Co.; Freddie Mac; King Nutronics, Inc.; Lockheed-Martin Corp.; The Nederlander Organization; Ogden Corporation; Northrop Corp.; U.S. Steel; Navistar, Inc.; MAXXAM, Inc.; J H Bachmann; Pfizer, Inc.; Los Angeles Community Redevelopment; City of Los Angeles Fire & Police Pension System; Specialty Laboratories; L.A. Supply, Label House; AMPCO System Parking; General Mills; Liberty Mutual Insurance; Merchantile National Bank; Teledyne Corp.
REFERENCE: Bank of America (Los Angeles Head Office).

---

## IVES, KIRWAN & DIBBLE

*A PROFESSIONAL CORPORATION*

Established in 1939

THE BILTMORE COURT, FOURTH FLOOR
520 SOUTH GRAND AVENUE
**LOS ANGELES, CALIFORNIA 90071**
Telephone: 213-627-0113
FAX: 213-627-1545

*Ventura-Santa Barbara Office:* 5210 Carpinteria Avenue, P.O. Box 360, Carpinteria, California. Telephone: 805-684-7641. FAX: 805-684-9649.

*Orange-San Diego County Office:* 101 Pacifica, Suite 250, Irvine, California. Telephone: 714-450-8900. FAX: 714-450-8908.

*San Bernardino-Riverside Office:* 777 Tahquitz Way, Suite 23, Palm Springs, California. Telephone: 619-778-2611. FAX: 619-778-2612.

FIRM PROFILE: *Ives, Kirwan & Dibble specializes in general civil litigation in both State and Federal Courts. For many years we have practiced in the traditional area of general liability defense, including but not limited to products liability, premises liability, professional liability, auto liability, truckers liability, cargo loss and damage, fire loss and damage, construction defect litigation, general negligence, international torts, insurance coverage (primary, excess, and reinsurance), and workers' compensation. In more recent years, our practice has grown in several developing areas such as business torts, directors' and officers' errors and omissions, trademark and copyright infringement, business transactional work and litigation, wrongful termination, legal malpractice, child abuse, insurance bad faith, toxic torts, environmental pollution litigation, Americans with Disabilities Act claims, and municipal liability and Federal civil rights litigation.*

**EUGENE S. IVES** (1903-1972).

**DARWIN L. DIBBLE** (1923-1990).

**MARTIN J. KIRWAN** (Retired from Firm).

**THOMAS P. MINEHAN,** born Los Angeles, California, December 12, 1944; admitted to bar, 1975, California and U.S. District Court, Central District of California. *Education:* University of Santa Clara (B.A., 1966); Southwestern University (J.D., 1975). *Member:* Santa Barbara County, Los Angeles County and American Bar Associations; The State Bar of California; Association of Southern California Defense Counsel. (Resident, Ventura-Santa Barbara Office).

**JAMES M. MCFAUL,** born Los Angeles, California, August 5, 1951; admitted to bar, 1978, California; U.S. District Court, Central District of California and U.S. Supreme Court. *Education:* University of California at Los Angeles (B.A., 1973); Loyola University of Los Angeles (J.D., 1978). *Member:* Santa Barbara County Bar Association; The State Bar of California; Association of Southern California Defense Counsel. (Resident, Ventura-Santa Barbara Office).

**STEPHEN A. BOST,** born Hampton, Virginia, April 16, 1955; admitted to bar, 1981, California and U.S. District Court, Central District of California; 1988, U.S. Court of Appeals, Ninth Circuit; 1989, U.S. Supreme Court. *Education:* Christopher Newport College of the College of William & Mary (B.S., 1977); Southwestern University (J.D., 1980). Delta Theta Phi. *Member:* Los Angeles County and American Bar Associations; State Bar of California; Association of Southern California Defense Counsel. (Also at San Bernardino-Riverside Office).

**JERRY E. MCLINN,** born 1939; admitted to bar, 1977, California; U.S. District Court, Central District of California. *Education:* The Ohio State University (B.S.E.E., 1961); University of California at Santa Barbara (M.S.E.E., 1968); California Western School of Law (J.D., 1977). Member, Santa Barbara Barrister Club. *Member:* Santa Barbara County Bar Association; State Bar of California; Association of Southern California Defense Counsel. (Resident, Ventura-Santa Barbara Office).

**ROGER ERIK MARKEN,** born Seattle, Washington, December 27, 1944; admitted to bar, 1972, California, U.S. District Court, Central District of California, U.S. District Court, Northern District of California and U.S. Court of Appeals, Ninth Circuit. *Education:* University of Washington (B.S., 1967); Southwestern University (J.D., 1972). *Member:* State Bar of California; American Bar Association; Association of Interstate Commerce Commission Practitioners. (Also at Orange County Office).

**CHARLES R. DIAZ,** born Los Angeles, California, November 24, 1953; admitted to bar, 1981, California, U.S. District Court, Central District of California and U.S. Court of Appeals, Ninth Circuit. *Education:* Pitzer College (B.A., 1975); University of Southern California (J.D., 1979). *Member:* Los Angeles County, Orange County and American (Member, Litigation Section) Bar Associations; State Bar of California; Association of Southern California Defense Counsel; Defense Research Institute.

**STEVEN B. KOTULAK,** born Philadelphia, Pennsylvania, February 21, 1959; admitted to bar, 1985, California, U.S. District Court, Central District of California and U.S. Court of Appeals, Ninth Circuit. *Education:* Lafayette College; Trenton State College (B.S., 1981); Southwestern University (J.D., 1985). *Member:* Los Angeles County and American Bar Associations; State Bar of California; The Association of Trial Lawyers of America; California Trial Lawyers Association. (Also at San Bernardino-Riverside Valley Office).

**NEIL D. JOSEPH,** born London, England, October 15, 1957; admitted to bar, 1985, California, U.S. District Court, Central District of California and U.S. Court of Appeals, Ninth Circuit. *Education:* Simon Fraser University (B.A., 1981); Southwestern University School of Law (J.D., 1984). *Member:* Los Angeles County and American Bar Associations; State Bar of California.

**JOSEPH M. WALSH, JR.,** born Washington, D.C., March 25, 1953; admitted to bar, 1982, California; 1983, Maryland, U.S. District Court, Central District of California and U.S. Court of Appeals, Ninth Circuit. *Education:* St. Bonaventure University (B.A., 1976); Loyola Marymount University (J.D., 1982). *Member:* State Bar of California; Maryland State and American Bar Associations.

**KEITH M. SHISHIDO,** born Chicago, Illinois, May 18, 1960; admitted to bar, 1986, California, U.S. District Court, Central District of California and U.S. Court of Appeals, Ninth Circuit. *Education:* University of California at Los Angeles (B.A., 1982); Loyola Marymount University (J.D., 1986). *Member:* Los Angeles County and American Bar Associations; State Bar of California.

**CHRISTOPHER GRIVAKES,** born Montreal, Canada, April 23, 1961; admitted to bar, 1987, California, U.S. District Court, Central District of California and U.S. Court of Appeals, Ninth Circuit. *Education:* Middlebury College (B.A., 1983); University of San Francisco (J.D., 1986). *Member:* State Bar of California; American Bar Association.

**STEVEN S. MARKEN,** born Torrance, California, May 6, 1965; admitted to bar, 1991, California and U.S. District Court, Central District of California. *Education:* Arizona State University (B.S., 1987); Southwestern University of Law at Los Angeles (J.D., 1991). *Member:* Orange County and American Bar Associations; State Bar of California. (Resident, Orange County Office).

**JASMIN A. VELARDE,** born Manila, Philippines, October 26, 1968; admitted to bar, 1993, California. *Education:* University of California, Berkeley (B.A., 1990); American University, Washington College of Law (J.D., cum laude, 1993). *Member:* Los Angeles County Bar Association (Member, Homeless Shelter Project); State Bar of California.

MAJOR INSURANCE COMPANY CLIENTS: Acceptance Insurance Companies; Allianz Insurance Company; Allianz Underwriters Insurance Company; American International Group, Inc.; American Mutual Insurance Company; American Sentinel Ins.; American States Insurance Company; Amica Mutual Insurance Company; The Canadian Insurance Company of California; Citation Insurance Group; The Chubb Group of Insurance Companies; California Insurance Guaranty Association; First State Insurance Company; Government

*(This Listing Continued)*

Employees Insurance Company; Harbor Insurance Company; The Hartford Specialty Company; Home & Automobile Insurance Company; Houston General Insurance Company; Industrial Fire & Casualty; Industrial Indemnity Company; Industrial Underwriters, Inc.; Jefferson Insurance Group; Monticello Insurance Co.; National Indemnity Company; National Union Fire Insurance Company; Planet Insurance Company; Preferred Risk Mutual Insurance Company; Prudential-LMI Mutual Insurance Company; Reliance Insurance Company; Safeco Insurance Company; Stonewall Insurance Company; Tokio Marine & Fire Insurance Company; Transport Insurance Company; Union Bankers Insurance Company; Utica Mutual Insurance Company; Westchester Specialty Group.

## IWASAKI & SHEFFIELD

A PROFESSIONAL ASSOCIATION

Not a Partnership

FOURTH FLOOR
420 BOYD STREET
LOS ANGELES, CALIFORNIA 90013
Telephone: 213-626-6462
Telecopier: 213-626-8203

*International, Corporate, Immigration Business and Real Estate Law. Personal Injury, Probate, Estate Planning and Entertainment Law. General Civil and Trial Practice in all State and Federal Courts.*

**ROBERT Y. IWASAKI,** born Davis, California, August 16, 1922; admitted to bar, 1952, Illinois; 1955, California and U.S. District Court, Southern District of California. *Education:* Case Western Reserve University (B.A., 1947); John Marshall Law School (J.D., 1952). *Member:* Los Angeles County and American Bar Associations; State Bar of California. **LANGUAGES:** Japanese. **PRACTICE AREAS:** General Practice; International Business.

**CHANEY M. SHEFFIELD,** born Van Nuys, California, February 24, 1951; admitted to bar, 1976, California; 1977, U.S. District Court, Central District of California; 1978, U.S. Tax Court. *Education:* University of California at Los Angeles (B.A., cum laude, 1972); California Western University (J.D., 1976). Phi Alpha Delta. *Member:* Los Angeles County and American (Member, Sections on: Tort and Insurance Practice; Taxation) Bar Associations; State Bar of California. **PRACTICE AREAS:** General Practice; Business; Real Estate; Entertainment; Personal Injury.

**KOICHI M. YANAGIZAWA,** born Kagoshima, Japan, October 8, 1946; admitted to bar, 1979, California; 1982, U.S. District Court, Central District of California and U.S. Court of Appeals, Ninth Circuit. *Education:* San Diego State University (B.A., 1975); California Western School of Law (J.D., 1978). *Member:* State Bar of California; American Bar Association; Japanese-American Bar Association. **LANGUAGES:** Japanese. **PRACTICE AREAS:** Immigration; General Practice.

**JOHN F. BUTCHER,** born Tachikawa, Japan, July 27, 1949; admitted to bar, 1983, California, U.S. District Court, Central District of California and U.S. Court of Appeals, Ninth Circuit. *Education:* Hobart College (B.A., 1971); John Marshall Law School (J.D., 1983). Associate Justice, Moot Court Executive Board. Member, Gavel Society. *Member:* Los Angeles County Bar Association; State Bar of California; Lawyer's Club of Los Angeles County. **PRACTICE AREAS:** Real Estate; General Practice; Family Law.

REPRESENTATIVE CLIENTS: Nissan Motor Corp. (U.S.A.); Dentsu Incorporated (Los Angeles); Japan Travel Bureau International Inc.; Makita U.S.A., Inc.; Kyowa Bank of California; Takisawa Machine Tool U.S.A., Corp.; Fuji Television Network, Inc.; Kawasaki Steel America, Inc.; Mitsubishi Trust and Banking Corporation (Los Angeles Agency).
REFERENCE: Kyowa Bank of California.

## JACKSON & LEWIS

Established in 1988

11400 WEST OLYMPIC BOULEVARD, SUITE 600
LOS ANGELES, CALIFORNIA 90064
Telephone: 310-473-3100
Fax: 310-473-1720

*General Civil Litigation in State and Federal Courts, Trials and Appeals, Employment (wrongful termination, discrimination and harassment based on sex, ethnicity, age and disability), Environmental Law, including hazardous wastes and property damage claims, Professional Liability and Toxic Torts, Litigation including multi party "mega litigation," Personal Injury, Products Liability, Eminent Domain and Inverse Condemnation, Real Property Litigation.*

(This Listing Continued)

*FIRM PROFILE: Jackson & Lewis is a minority controlled firm founded in 1988 by Samuel Jackson, a graduate of Columbia University School of Law. The firm has two partners and four associates and serves both a national and local client base in state and federal courts throughout Southern California. Several of the firm's attorneys have advanced degrees in fields which include psychology, architecture and urban planning, social work and political science. They have also practiced with large law firms and with the California State Court of Appeal. The firm's attorneys teach, as well as participate in continuing education of the bar seminars and are active in a broad range of professional and civic organizations. Several of the firm's attorneys have published articles or appeared in reported cases.*

### MEMBERS OF FIRM

**SAMUEL G. JACKSON, JR.,** born Brooklyn, New York, June 7, 1944; admitted to bar, 1970, California and U.S. District Court, Central District of California; 1974, U.S. Court of Appeals, Ninth Circuit; 1980, U.S. Supreme Court. *Education:* Amherst College (B.A., 1966); Columbia University (J.D., 1969). Recipient: John Woodruff Simpson Fellowship; Reginald Heber Smith Fellowship. Vice President, California Young Lawyers Association, 1977-1978. Member, California Commission on Judicial Evaluation, 1979. Lawyer-Delegate, Ninth Circuit Judicial Conference, 1980-1983, 1985-1987. Member: Disciplinary Committee, U.S. District Court, Central District of California, 1983-1990; U.S. Magistrate Judges Merit Selection Panel, 1993-1994; Steering Committee of California Minority Counsel Program, 1994—; Board of Directors of Starlight Foundation, International, 1995—. L.A. County Bar Judiciary Committee. Member, Employment Law Panel, American Arbitration Association, 1994—. *Member:* Los Angeles County, Langston, National and American Bar Associations; State Bar of California. **PRACTICE AREAS:** Employment Law; Discrimination; Sexual Harassment; Products Liability; Environmental Law; Hazardous Wastes and Property Damage Claims.

**JAMES W. LEWIS,** born Denver, Colorado, November 26, 1953; admitted to bar, 1989, California, U.S. District Court, Central and Southern Districts of California and U.S. Court of Appeals, Ninth Circuit. *Education:* Colorado College (B.A., Chemistry, 1974); University of California (M.A., Ph.D., Physiological Psychology, 1982; J.D., 1989). Recipient: American Jurisprudence Award for Criminal Justice; Burton Marks Scholarship for Outstanding Performance in Advanced Criminal Law; Gingerelli Award for Distinguished Thesis (UCLA); Cattell Distinguished Thesis Award from NY Academy of Sciences; NIDA Research Fellowship. Author: "Pre-Menstrual Syndrome as Criminal Defense," *Archives of Sexual Behavior.* Lecturer, in Psychology, UCLA, 1985-1989. Continuing Education of the Bar presentation, "Effective Opening Statements and Closing Arguments." and "Sexual Harassment and Employment Discrimination." *Member:* State Bar of California. **PRACTICE AREAS:** Environmental Law; Toxic Exposure; Employment Law; Civil Rights.

**JOANN ELLEN VICTOR,** born Los Angeles, California, November 22, 1947; admitted to bar, 1985, California and U.S. District Court, Central and Southern Districts of California; U.S. Court of Appeals, Ninth Circuit. *Education:* University of California at Los Angeles (B.A., 1969; M.A., 1971; M.A., 1984); University of California School of Law (J.D., 1984). Recipient, American Jurisprudence Award in Torts. Lecturer in Political Science, California State University, Long Beach, 1974-1992, 1994—. Staff Member, UCLA Law Review, 1981-1983. Senior Law Clerk to Presiding Justice Robert Feinerman and Associate Justice Joyce Kennard, California Court of Appeal, Second District. Adjunct Associate Professor of Law, Southwestern School of Law, 1986-1988. *Member:* State Bar of California. **PRACTICE AREAS:** Directors and Officers Liability; Employment Law; Civil Appeals.

**JULIE YEH,** born Taipei, Taiwan, September 3, 1963; admitted to bar, 1993, California. *Education:* Wellesley College (B.A., 1985); Columbia University (M.S.W., 1988); University of California at Los Angeles (J.D., 1993). *Member:* State Bar of California. **LANGUAGES:** Chinese (Mandarin). **PRACTICE AREAS:** Employment; Underground Storage Tank Litigation.

### OF COUNSEL

**DAVID S. CUNNINGHAM, III,** born Riverside, California, January 26, 1955; admitted to bar, 1981, New York; 1983, California and U.S. District Court, Central District of California. *Education:* University of Southern California (B.A., summa cum laude, 1977); New York University (J.D., 1980). Phi Beta Kappa. Recipient, Root Tilden Scholarship. Adjunct Professor, Trial Advocacy and Banking, Loyola Law School, 1987-1991. Judicial Clerk to the Hon. Terry J. Hatter, Jr., U.S. District Court, Central District of California, 1982-1983. Director, Los Angeles Urban League, 1987-1992. Director of Los Angeles Business Council, 1991-1995. *Member:*

(This Listing Continued)

### JACKSON & LEWIS, Los Angeles—Continued

Los Angeles County and Federal Bar Associations; State Bar of California. **LANGUAGES:** Spanish. **PRACTICE AREAS:** Eminent Domain; Inverse Condemnation; Construction; Real Estate Litigation Redevelopment Law.

> REPRESENTATIVE CLIENTS: Monsanto Chemical; Chevron U.S.A.; Borden; Toyota Motor Credit; Chrysler Corporation; The Quaker Oats Company; Motorola, Inc.; Federal Home Loan Mortgage Corporation; Wells Fargo Bank; Bank of America; Bank of the West; Resolution Trust Corp.; AT&T; Coca-Cola; Federal Deposit Insurance Corp.; Hartford Insurance; State Farm Insurance; Prudential Insurance; Metropolitan Life Insurance; Harleysville Insurance; Bausch & Lomb.

---

## JACKSON, LEWIS, SCHNITZLER & KRUPMAN

*1888 CENTURY PARK EAST*
*SUITE 1600*
**LOS ANGELES, CALIFORNIA 90067**
*Telephone: 310-203-0200*
*Facsimile: 310-203-0391*

*Other offices located in:* Atlanta, Georgia; Boston, Massachusetts; Chicago, Illinois; Dallas, Texas; Greenville, South Carolina; Hartford, Connecticut; Larkspur, California; Miami, Florida; Morristown, New Jersey; New York, New York; Orlando, Florida; Pittsburgh, Pennsylvania; San Francisco, California; Stamford, Connecticut; Washington, D.C.; White Plains, New York; Woodbury, New York.

*Labor Relations, Employment Discrimination, Wrongful Discharge and Other Employment-Related Litigation, Employee Benefits and Pension Law, Wage and Hour, OSHA, Immigration Law, Public Sector and State Labor Relations Law On Behalf of Management.*

### MEMBERS OF FIRM

**DAVID S. ALLEN,** born Los Angeles, California, April 5, 1955; admitted to bar, 1981, California; U.S. District Court, Southern, Central and Northern Districts of California. *Education:* University of California at Davis (A.B., with honors, 1977; J.D., 1981). Presenter: CEB Programs 1995, "Strategies for Preventing Workplace Violence and Harassment." *Member:* State Bar of California (Member, Section on Labor and Employment Law).

**MARK R. ATTWOOD,** born Glendale, California, June 9, 1959; admitted to bar, 1986, California. *Education:* University of Utah College of Business (B.S., magna cum laude, 1981); University of Utah College of Law (J.D., 1985). William H. Leary Scholar. Editor-in-Chief, Utah Journal of Contemporary Law, 1985. *Member:* Los Angeles County and American (Member, Litigation Section) Bar Associations; The State Bar of California.

**G. HARRISON DARBY,** born New York, N.Y., January 24, 1942; admitted to bar, 1967, New York (Not admitted in California). *Education:* Muhlenberg College (B.A., 1963); Brooklyn Law School (LL.B., 1967). Phi Alpha Theta; Phi Sigma Iota. *Member:* New York State and American (Member, Section of Labor and Employment Law) Bar Associations.

**ROBERT J. GIOVANNETTI,** born Albany, New York, October 3, 1946; admitted to bar, 1972, New York; 1981, California; U.S. District Court, Southern District of New York and Central District of California; U.S. Court of Appeals, Ninth Circuit. *Education:* Union College (B.A., cum laude, 1968); Columbia University School of Law (J.D., 1971). Contributing Author: "Winning NLRB Elections," 3rd ed. 1991, Executive Enterprise. PLI. *Member:* New York State and American Bar Associations; State Bar of California.

**LAWRENCE H. STONE,** born Worcester, Massachusetts, October 16, 1958; admitted to bar, 1986, New York, New Jersey and U.S. District Court, Southern and Eastern Districts of New York and U.S. District Court, District of New Jersey; 1990, California. *Education:* Brandeis University (B.A., cum laude, 1980); Brown University (M.A., 1981); Benjamin N. Cardozo School of Law, Yeshiva University (J.D., 1985). *Member:* New York State and American Bar Associations; State Bar of California.

### OF COUNSEL

**EMILY R. BOYLE,** admitted to bar, 1980, California, State and Federal Courts and U.S. Supreme Court. *Education:* Univ. of California at Los Angeles (B.A., 1977); Southwestern Univ. (J.D., cum laude, 1980). *Member:* State Bar of California.

*(This Listing Continued)*

CAA810B

---

**DAVID G. FREEDMAN,** born Los Angeles, California, December 9, 1952; admitted to bar, 1978, California. *Education:* University of California at Berkeley (B.A., 1974); Loyola Law School (J.D., 1978).

### ASSOCIATES

**ELIZABETH PLATTE JOHNSON,** admitted to bar, 1983, South Carolina; 1984, New York; 1985, California. *Education:* University of South Carolina (B.A., 1980; J.D., 1982). *Member:* South Carolina Bar; New York State Bar Association; State Bar of California.

**FRANK M. LIBERATORE,** born Chicago, Illinois, September 26, 1959; admitted to bar, 1985, California and U.S. District Court, Central District of California; 1986, U.S. District Court, Northern, Southern and Eastern Districts of California and U.S. Court of Appeals, Ninth Circuit. *Education:* University of Southern California (B.A., 1982; J.D., 1985). Phi Delta Phi. *Member:* State Bar of California. **PRACTICE AREAS:** Business Litigation; Employment Law.

**ANNE-MARIE P. PIIBE,** born Oxnard, California, February 18, 1964; admitted to bar, 1990, California; 1991, U.S. District Court, Central District of California and U.S. Court of Appeals, Ninth Circuit. *Education:* Univ. of California at Los Angeles (B.A., 1986); Loyola Law School (J.D., 1989).

**MARISA S. RATINOFF,** admitted to bar, 1991, California. *Education:* Cambridge University, Cambridge, England; University of California at Berkeley (B.A., 1987); University of California, Hastings College of the Law (J.D., 1991). *Member:* State Bar of California.

**ANDREW L. WEISS,** born Yonkers, New York, August 28, 1956; admitted to bar, 1991, New Jersey; 1992, New York and California. *Education:* State University of New York at Buffalo (B.S./M.B.A., 1980); Pace University (J.D., 1991). **Email:** FMUS09A@PRODIGY.COM

**C. CRAIG WOO,** admitted to bar, 1987, California. *Education:* University of California at Los Angeles (B.A., 1983); University of the Pacific, McGeorge School of Law (J.D., 1986). *Member:* State Bar of California.

---

## NORMAN D. JAMES

**LOS ANGELES, CALIFORNIA**

(See Hermosa Beach)

*Civil Trials and Appellate Practice in all State and Federal Courts, Business Litigation and Federal Criminal Law.*

---

## HENRY N. JANNOL

*A PROFESSIONAL CORPORATION*
*1875 CENTURY PARK EAST, SUITE 1400*
**LOS ANGELES, CALIFORNIA 90067**
*Telephone: 310-552-7500*
*Telecopier: 310-552-7552*
*Email: hnj@la.saic.com*

*Business Litigation and Real Estate Litigation.*

**HENRY N. JANNOL,** born Inglewood, California, December 2, 1950; admitted to bar, 1975, California, U.S. District Court, Central, Southern and Northern Districts of California, U.S. Court of Appeals, Ninth Circuit and U.S. Court of Appeals, Federal Circuit. *Education:* University of California at Los Angeles (A.B., 1972); Southwestern University School of Law (J.D., 1975). Fee Disputes Arbitrator, Los Angeles County Bar Association, 1980-1996. *Member:* Beverly Hills, Los Angeles County and American Bar Associations; The Association of Trial Lawyers of America. **PRACTICE AREAS:** Commercial Litigation; Real Estate; Probate Litigation; Commercial Formation.

A List of Representative Clients will be furnished upon request.

## JEFFER, MANGELS, BUTLER & MARMARO LLP

A Limited Liability Partnership including Professional Corporations

*2121 AVENUE OF THE STARS, TENTH FLOOR*
**LOS ANGELES, CALIFORNIA 90067**
Telephone: 310-203-8080
FAX: 310-203-0567
*Internet Address: attorney's 3 initials@jmbm.com (unless otherwise indicated)*
URL: http://www.jmbm.com

*San Francisco, California Office:* One Sansome Street, Twelfth Floor. Telephone: 415-398-8080. FAX: 415-398-5584. Internet Address: attorney's initials @ jmbm.com.

General Civil Practice and Litigation in all State and Federal Courts. Corporate, Tax, Real Estate, Entertainment, Labor and Employment, Insolvency and Creditors' Rights, Antitrust, Environmental, Administrative, Corporate, Securities, Financial Institutions (including Banking, Savings and Loans), Fidelity and Surety, Insurance, Syndications, International, Oil and Gas, Apparel Industry, Health Care, Estate Planning, Probate/Trusts, Employee Benefits, Land Use, Hospitality Industry, Trademark, Intellectual Property, Patent, Copyright, Music and Music Publishing, Advertising, Sports, Technology. Member of INTERLAW, an international association of independent law firms in major world centers.

### MEMBERS OF FIRM

**BRUCE P. JEFFER (P.C.),** born New York, N.Y., May 13, 1942; admitted to bar, 1967, California; 1968, New York; 1969, Florida. *Education:* Yale University; University of California, Los Angeles (B.A., summa cum laude, 1964); Harvard University (J.D., cum laude, 1967). Phi Beta Kappa. *Member:* Los Angeles County, New York State and American (Real Property, Probate and Trust Law Section) Bar Associations. *LANGUAGES:* Spanish. *PRACTICE AREAS:* Corporate; General Business; Syndication; Securities.

**ROBERT E. MANGELS (P.C.),** born Washington, D.C., March 14, 1943; admitted to bar, 1970, Virginia; 1971, California. *Education:* Pennsylvania State University (B.A., 1965); George Washington University (J.D., cum laude, 1970). Order of the Coif. Adjunct Professor, Remedies and Civil Procedure, Southwestern School of Law, 1979-1982. Member, Business Law Arbitration Panel, Los Angeles Superior Court. *Member:* Los Angeles County and American (Sections on: Litigation; Corporation, Banking and Business Law; Judicial Evaluation Committee, 1981-1985) Bar Associations; Virginia State Bar; Association of Business Trial Lawyers (Board of Governors, 1984-1987). *PRACTICE AREAS:* Civil Litigation; Trials.

**JAMES R. BUTLER, JR. (P.C.),** born Cleveland, Ohio, May 29, 1946; admitted to bar, 1969, California; 1975, U.S. Supreme Court; 1977, U.S. Tax Court. *Education:* University of California at Berkeley (B.A., magna cum laude, 1966); Boalt Hall School of Law, University of California (J.D., 1969), Order of the Coif; Phi Beta Kappa; Pi Sigma Alpha. Editor, California Law Review, 1968-1969. *PRACTICE AREAS:* Hospitality Industry; Real Estate Workouts; Banking and Corporate Finance.

**MARC MARMARO, (P.C.),** born Bronx, N.Y., February 27, 1948; admitted to bar, 1973, New York; 1979, California. *Education:* George Washington University (B.A., 1969); New York University (J.D., cum laude, 1972). Order of the Coif. Research Editor, New York University Law Review, 1971-1972. Author: "Representing Witnesses Before a Federal Grand Jury," PLI, 1982. Law Clerk to Judge John J. Gibbons, U.S. Court of Appeals, Third Circuit, 1972-1973. Assistant U.S. Attorney, Southern District of New York, 1975-1978. Member, Board of Trustees, Practising Law Institute, 1995—. *Member:* The Association of the Bar of the City of New York; Los Angeles County (Committee on Federal Practice, 1980-1984), New York State and American (Litigation Section) Bar Associations; Association of Business Trial Lawyers (Committee on Superior Court, 1993; Board of Governors, 1986-1988). *PRACTICE AREAS:* Business Litigation. *Email:* mm@jmbm.com

**SUSAN ALLISON,** born Evanston, Illinois, April 21, 1953; admitted to bar, 1980, New York; 1988, California. *Education:* Stanford University (B.A., 1975); Hastings College of Law, University of California (J.D., 1979). Member, Hastings Constitutional Law Quarterly, 1978-1979. *Member:* The Association of the Bar of the City of New York; New York State Bar Association. *PRACTICE AREAS:* Civil Litigation. *Email:* sja@jmbm.com

**SIMON ARON,** born Los Angeles, California, September 18, 1954; admitted to bar, 1983, California and U.S. District Court, Central, Eastern, Southern and Northern Districts of California; U.S. Court of Appeals, Ninth Circuit. *Education:* University of California at Los Angeles (B.A., 1979); Southwestern University (J.D., cum laude, 1982). *Member:* Beverly Hills (Chair, Member, Executive Committee, Bankruptcy Section), Los Angeles County (Member, Bankruptcy Committee of Bankruptcy and Commercial Law Section) and American Bar Associations; Financial Lawyers Conference. *PRACTICE AREAS:* Bankruptcy; Creditors' Rights; Financial Restructurings. *Email:* sxa@jmbm.com

**JOEL I. BENNETT, (P.C.),** born New York, N.Y., February 16, 1955; admitted to bar, 1982, New York; 1983, Florida, California and U.S. District Court, Central District of California. *Education:* Columbia University (B.A., 1977; M.S., 1978); University of Michigan (J.D., 1981). Associate Editor, 1979-1980 and Article and Administrative Editor, 1980-1981, Michigan Law Review. Law Clerk to Hon. J.O. Eaton, Chief Judge, U.S. District Court, Southern District of Florida, 1981-1983. *Member:* Los Angeles County, New York State and American Bar Associations. *PRACTICE AREAS:* General Corporate; Securities.

**P. PETER BENUDIZ, (P.C.),** born Casablanca, Morocco, September 17, 1961; admitted to bar, 1987, California. *Education:* University of California at Berkeley (A.B., 1984); Harvard University (J.D., 1987). Harvard Government Teaching Fellow. Presenter or Moderator: Programs on Renegotiating Management Agreements, Receiverships and Bankruptcies, Purchase Sale, Workouts and Deeds-in-Lieu of Foreclosures, JMBM Hospitality Industry Forum, 1993—; "What Every Real Property Lawyer Should Know About the Auction Process," Los Angeles County Bar Association, 1993; "A Practical Approach to Workouts, Deeds-in-Lieu and Foreclosures," Beverly Hills Bar Association, 1993. Co-author: "The *Western Security* Case: The Next Inevitable Step in California's Antideficiency Scheme," The Real Estate Finance Journal, Winter 1994. *Member:* Los Angeles County Bar Association. *PRACTICE AREAS:* Hospitality Industry; Real Estate Workouts, Finance, Acquisitions/Sale.

**JOEL J. BERMAN, (P.C.),** born Los Angeles, California, December 3, 1954; admitted to bar, 1979, California. *Education:* Harvard University (A.B., cum laude, 1976; J.D., 1979). Co-Author: "Basic Rules for Loan Workouts," 2 Banking Law Report 53, 1985. Author: "Sentencing Reform of S. 1437: Will Guidelines Work?" 17 Harvard Journal on Legislation 98, 1980. *Member:* Los Angeles County and American (Business Law Section) Bar Associations. *PRACTICE AREAS:* Commercial; Real Estate; Corporate; Insolvency and Creditors' Rights.

**ROD S. BERMAN,** born Brooklyn, New York, 1955; admitted to bar, 1982, California; registered to practice before U.S. Patent and Trademark Office. *Education:* University of California, Los Angeles (B.S., 1977); Indiana University (M.S., 1979) Ph.d Candidate; Loyola University School of Law (J.D., cum laude, 1982). Loyola of Los Angeles Law Review, 1981-1982. Author: "Trade Names and Trademarks in Bankruptcy," Rod S. Berman et al. Proceedings, ABA Section of Business Law, Fall Meeting, Business Bankruptcy Committee (1995); "Patent practitioners--don't let GATT get you," R. Berman et al. *Managing Intellectual Property,* March 1995, pp. 20-25; "U.S. and Foreign Trademark Basics," Parker & Barrow Law Publications, Third Edition (1996); "Trademarks in the Personal Care Industry Company," *Soap Cosmetics Chemical Specialties,* December 1992; "The Interfacing Between Industry and Market Share: Patents," 35(5) San Fernando Valley Bar Bulletin 8 (1992); "Kinetics and Mechanism of Oxygen Atom Transfer Mediated by Nickel (O) Complexes," 19 Inorganic Chemistry 248, 1980. Testified before the California Senate Judiciary Committee re Senate Bill 254, Sacramento 1993. *Member:* INTA. *Email:* rxb@jmbm.com

**HERBERT A. BERNHARD, (P.C.),** born Jersey City, New Jersey, September 24, 1927; admitted to bar, 1958, California and U.S. District Court, Central District of California; 1959, U.S. Court of Appeals, Ninth Circuit; 1963-1974, U.S. District Court, Northern, Eastern and Southern Districts of California; 1965, U.S. Supreme Court; 1966, U.S. Claims Court; 1968, U.S. Tax Court; 1979, U.S. Customs Court; 1980, U.S. Court of International Trade; 1982, Temporary Emergency Court of Appeals of the United States. *Education:* Mexico City College; New Jersey Institute of Technology (B.S.E.E., 1949); Columbia University (M.A., 1950); University of Michigan (J.D., with distinction, 1957). Order of the Coif. Assistant Editor, Michigan Law Review, Henry M. Bates Memorial Award. Author: "Restraints on Alienation," 57 Michigan Law Review 1173-1188, 1959. Chairman, Advisory Board, Skirball Museum, 1976-1990. Member, Board of Overseers, Hebrew Union College, 1976—. Referee, Arbitrator and Judge Pro Tem various courts, 1985—. Trustee, Jewish Publication Society, 1986-1995. [U.S. Army Air Corps, 1946-1947]. *PRACTICE AREAS:* Business Litigation; Appeals.

*(This Listing Continued)*

**JEFFER, MANGELS, BUTLER & MARMARO LLP,** Los Angeles—Continued

**ROBERT E. BRAUN, (P.C.),** born Fort Leonard Wood, Missouri, March 14, 1957; admitted to bar, 1981, California; 1982, U.S. District Court, Central District of California. *Education:* University of California at Berkeley (A.B., with highest honors, 1978); University of California at Los Angeles School of Law (J.D., 1981). Phi Alpha Delta; National Order of Barristers. Member, Executive Board, Moot Court Honors Program, 1980-1981. Author: "Documenting Corporate Joint Ventures," California Business Law Practitioner, Fall 1993. *Member:* Los Angeles County (Chairman, Financial Institutions Subcommittee, 1989-1991; Business and Corporations Section Executive Committee, 1989—; First Vice Chair, 1996-1997) and American (Corporation, Banking and Business Law Section) Bar Associations. **PRACTICE AREAS:** Corporate; Securities; Banking.

**PATRICIA S. BRODY** (San Francisco Office).

**RICHARD M. BROWN,** born Chicago, Illinois, November 16, 1942; admitted to bar, 1968, California, U.S. District Court, Central District of California and U.S. Court of Military Appeals. *Education:* University of California at Los Angeles (A.B., 1964; J.D., 1967). Phi Delta Phi. Author: "Making Sports Programming Work," Broadcasting, July 20, 1987; "How to go to College and Obtain a Sports Broadcast License," Television/Radio Age, August 3, 1987; "Air Rights," American School and University, December 1987; "Managers' Corner," Electronic Media, July 31, 1989. President and CEO, California Angels. *Member:* Los Angeles County and American Bar Associations; Federal Communications Bar Association; Academy of Television Arts and Sciences; Sport Lawyers Association. [Captain, US Army JAGC, 1968-1971]. **PRACTICE AREAS:** Sports and Broadcasting.

**BARRY L. BURTEN,** born New York, N.Y., August 3, 1948; admitted to bar, 1974, New York; 1984, California. *Education:* Colgate University (B.A., magna cum laude, 1970), Phi Beta Kappa; Harvard Law School (J.D., 1973). *Member:* Los Angeles County and American Bar Associations. **PRACTICE AREAS:** Corporate; Securities; Bankruptcy.

**WILLIAM F. CAPPS, (P.C.),** born Whittier, California, February 24, 1947; admitted to bar, 1973, California; 1975, U.S. Tax Court. *Education:* Whittier College (B.A., with high honors, 1968); Boalt Hall School of Law, University of California (J.D., 1973). Recipient, American Jurisprudence Award in Conflict of Laws. Note and Comment Editor, California Law Review, 1972-1973. Licensed Real Estate Broker, California, 1982. Author: "Joint Venturing With Your Hospital," Digest of the American Professional Practice Association, April 1987; "Computers Can Cut Legal Costs," Los Angeles Business Journal, May 13, 1991; "Buying or Selling the Parking Company: A Primer," National Parking (published by National Parking Association), September 1992. Co-Author: "The Saudi Arabian Legal-Medical Committee," Middle East Executive Reports, May 1983. Panelist: "Doing Business in Saudi Arabia and The Gulf," Arabico Seminars, 1982. *Member:* Los Angeles County and American Bar Associations. **PRACTICE AREAS:** Corporate; Securities; Real Estate.

**JOEL A. CASSEL, (P.C.),** born Waterbury, Connecticut, February 4, 1940; admitted to bar, 1966, Connecticut; 1969, New York; 1976, California. *Education:* Brown University (B.A., 1962); New York University (LL.B., 1965; LL.M., 1972). Legal Advisor, Office of the President, Government of Malawi, Africa, 1966-1968. *Member:* Century City (Chairman, International Law Section, 1979-1980) and Los Angeles County (Member, Real Estate Subsection) Bar Associations. **PRACTICE AREAS:** Real Estate; General Business; Secured Financing Transactions.

**JOEL DAVID DEUTSCH, (P.C.),** born Los Angeles, California, September 21, 1953; admitted to bar, 1982, California. *Education:* Claremont McKenna College (B.A., summa cum laude, 1977); Stanford University (J.D., 1981). *Member:* Los Angeles County and American (Litigation Section) Bar Associations. **PRACTICE AREAS:** Land Use; Eminent Domain; Business; Real Estate; Commercial Litigation.

**RANDALL G. DICK** (San Francisco Office).

**JOSEPH A. EISENBERG, (P.C.),** born Garmisch, Germany, September 2, 1946; admitted to bar, 1972, California; U.S. District Court, Central District of California and U.S. Court of Appeals, Ninth Circuit. *Education:* University of California at Berkeley (B.A., 1968); Boalt Hall School of Law, University of California (J.D., 1972). Lecturer: Rutter Group/ Orange County and Los Angeles County Bar Association, 1984, "Straight Bankruptcy"; Rutter Group/Los Angeles County Bar Association, 1985, "Bankruptcy: Pre-Petition Planning and Exemptions"; USC Computer Law Institute, 1985, "The Insolvency Laws and the Computer Industry"; UCLA Extension, 1985, "The Music Industry and Bankruptcy"; USC Real Estate Tax and Accounting Conference, November, 1992, "Asset Protection Strategies, 1992"; PESI Seminar 1993, "Ninth Circuit Bankruptcy Symposium." *Member:* Los Angeles County (Judicial Appointments Committee) and American Bar Association; Financial Lawyers Conference; Los Angeles Bankruptcy Forum. **PRACTICE AREAS:** Insolvency.

**KEITH D. ELKINS,** born Los Angeles, California, August 23, 1962; admitted to bar, 1987, California. *Education:* University of California, Los Angeles (B.A., 1984); Hastings College of Law, University of California (J.D., 1987). *Member:* Los Angeles County Bar Association (Real Estate Section). **PRACTICE AREAS:** Real Estate.

**NEIL C. ERICKSON,** born Salt Lake City, Utah, December 1, 1955; admitted to bar, 1983, California. *Education:* Stanford University (B.A., 1978); Hastings College of Law, University of California (J.D., 1982). *Member:* Los Angeles County and American Bar Associations; Association of Business Trial Lawyers. **PRACTICE AREAS:** General Business Litigation; Real Estate; Banking and Securities Litigation.

**LOUISE ANN FERNANDEZ,** born Visalia, California, September 14, 1953; admitted to bar, 1979, California. *Education:* Stanford University (B.A., 1975); George Washington University (J.D., 1978). Field Attorney, National Labor Relations Board, Region 21, 1979-1980. *Member:* Los Angeles County and American (Member, Labor and Employment Law Section) Bar Associations; State Bar of California (Chairperson, Equal Employment Affirmative Action Committee, 1985-1986; Member, Executive Committee, 1986—, Labor and Employment Law Section). **PRACTICE AREAS:** Labor and Employment; Litigation.

**MARTA M. FERNANDEZ,** born Santa Monica, California, February 26, 1960; admitted to bar, 1985, California, U.S. District Court, Central, Southern and Northern Districts of California and U.S. Court of Appeals, Ninth Circuit. *Education:* Loyola Marymount University (B.A., magna cum laude, 1982); University of Southern California Law Center (J.D., with honors, 1985). Member, Personnel and Industrial Relations Association, District 5, 1989—. Counsel, Foundation for the Economic Development of Central American Women. Advisory Counsel, Los Angeles Archdiocese Catholic Commission. *Member:* Los Angeles County (Member, Labor and Employment Law Section) and American Bar Associations. **LANGUAGES:** Spanish. **PRACTICE AREAS:** Labor and Employment; Health and Hospital.

**NICHOLAS S. FREUD** (San Francisco Office).

**DAVID F. GANTZ,** born Los Angeles, California, October 9, 1953; admitted to bar, 1980, California. *Education:* California State University, Fullerton (B.A., cum laude, 1977); Boalt Hall School of Law, University of California at Berkeley (J.D., 1980). Instructor, Financial Aspects of Real Estate Acquisition and Development, UCLA Extension, University of California at Los Angeles, 1986-1993. Speaker, "Current Issues in Leasing," California Society of Certified Public Accountants, 1993. Member, Pacific Southwest Regional Board, Anti-Defamation League, 1994-1995. *Member:* Century City and Los Angeles County Bar Associations; State Bar of California (Real Property Law Section). **PRACTICE AREAS:** General Real Estate; Real Estate Leasing; Construction Development; Acquisition and Financing.

**FREDERICK W. GARTSIDE,** born Neuilly-sur Seine, France, November 2, 1962; admitted to bar, 1987, California. *Education:* Occidental College (B.A., with distinction, 1984); University of Southern California (J.D., 1987). Member and Editor, Moot Court Honors Program. Co-author: "Operating Problems of California Corporations," 1989 Supplement, Continuing Education of the Bar. *Member:* Los Angeles County and American Bar Associations. **PRACTICE AREAS:** Corporate.

**ELIZABETH BARROWMAN GIBSON,** born Chicago, Illinois, September 26, 1964; admitted to bar, 1988, California. *Education:* University of Illinois (B.A., magna cum laude, 1985); University of Michigan (J.D., 1988). Phi Beta Kappa. Author: "The Recovery of Shipwrecks in International Waters: A Multilateral Solution," 8 Mich. Y.B. Intl. Legal Studies 231, 1987; "Recent Misinterpretations of the Avoidable Consequences Rule: The 'Duty' to Mitigate and other Fictions," 16 Harv. J.L. Pub. Pol'y 411, 1993. *Member:* Beverly Hills (Section on Patents, Trademarks and Copyrights) and American (Section on Intellectual Property) Bar Associations; International Trademark Association; Women Lawyers Association. **PRACTICE AREAS:** Business Litigation; Intellectual Property.

**MICHAEL A. GOLD,** born Binghamton, New York, December 6, 1949; admitted to bar, 1979, California; 1980, U.S. District Court, Central District of California; 1984, U.S. Court of Appeals, Ninth Circuit. *Education:* University of Connecticut (B.A., with honors, 1971); Southwestern Univer-

*(This Listing Continued)*

sity (J.D., cum laude, 1979). Member, Moot Court Honor Society. First Place, Southwestern University Law School Intramural Moot Court Competition and Western Region, Giles Sutherland Rich Patent Moot Court Competition. Author: "Reversal of Fortune: Fraudulent Transfers and Business Combinations," Los Angeles County Bar Association, 1994. *Member:* Los Angeles County and American (Litigation and Business Sections) Bar Associations; State Bar of California (Litigation and Business Law Sections); Association of Business Trial Lawyers. *LANGUAGES:* French. *PRACTICE AREAS:* Complex Business, Partnership, Real Estate and Bankruptcy Litigation.

**STEPHEN R. GOLDSTEIN,** born Los Angeles, California, February 8, 1944; admitted to bar, 1969, California. *Education:* University of California at Los Angeles (B.S., with highest honors, 1965); Cornell University (J.D., 1968). Beta Gamma Sigma. Certified Public Accountant, California, 1971. *Member:* Los Angeles County (Tax Section) and American (Taxation Section) Bar Associations; California Society of Certified Public Accountants; American Institute of Certified Public Accountants. *PRACTICE AREAS:* Corporate, Real Estate and International Taxation; Taxation of Entertainers and Entertainment Companies.

**ROBERT H. GOON,** born Birmingham, Alabama, November 3, 1940; admitted to bar, 1966, California. *Education:* University of California, Los Angeles (B.A., 1962; J.D., 1965). Phi Delta Phi. Member, University of California, Los Angeles Law Review, 1964-1965. *Member:* Los Angeles County and American Bar Associations. *PRACTICE AREAS:* Corporate Mergers and Acquisitions; Financing and Securities Transactions.

**PAUL R. HAMILTON,** born Los Angeles, California, October 21, 1934; admitted to bar, 1966, California; U.S. Supreme Court; U.S. Court of Federal Claims; U.S. Court of Appeals, Ninth Circuit; U.S. District Court, Northern, Central and Southern Districts of California, Southern District of Florida and Southern District of Nevada. *Education:* University of Southern California (B.S., 1956); Southwestern University (LL.B., 1966). Lecturer: Lusk Center for Real Estate Development and School of Urban Planning and Development, University of Southern California, 1990-1995; Pacific Coast Builders Conference, 1985. Member: Board of Directors of Orange County Marine Institute; Executive Committee, Lusk Center for Real Estate Development, University of Southern California. *Member:* Los Angeles County, Orange County, South Bay, Santa Barbara and Federal Bar Associations; California Trial Lawyers Association; Building Industry Association; Condemnation Attorneys' Group; National Association of Home Builders; Urban Land Institute. *REPORTED CASES:* Orange Productions Credit Association vs. Frontline Ventures Ltd., 801 F.2d 1581 (1986); Long Beach Equities vs. County of Ventura, 231 Cal.App.3d 1016 (1991); Southwest Diversified Inc. vs. City of Brisbane, 229 Cal.App.3d 1548 (1991); Westlake North Homeowners Association vs. City of Thousand Oaks, 915 F.2d 1301 (9th Circuit 1990); Lacher vs. Superior Court, 230 Cal.App.3d 1038 (1991); Friends of La Vina vs. Southwest Diversified Inc., 232 Cal.App.3d 1446 (1991). *PRACTICE AREAS:* Land Use Law and Entitlement Litigation; Real Estate Litigation; Construction Defect Litigation; Appellate Matters. *Email:* ph@jmbm.com

**MARK H. HESS,** born New York, N.Y., October 21, 1956; admitted to bar, 1980, California. *Education:* Bernard M. Baruch College of the City University of New York (B.B.A., summa cum laude, 1976); Columbia University (J.D., 1980). Beta Gamma Sigma; Beta Alpha Psi. Administrative Editor, Columbia Human Rights Law Review, 1979-1980. Harlan Fiske Stone Scholar. Certified Public Accountant, New York, 1980. Author: "Loanouts and Guilds: Maximizing Entertainer Pensions," Los Angeles Lawyer Magazine, April 1996; "Pension Plan Investment in Real Estate," Major Tax Planning, USC Tax Institute, 1994; "Life After a Death Sentence: Retirement Plans for the 1990s," Major Tax Planning, USC Tax Institute, 1990. President, West Coast Region, Union of Orthodox Jewish Congregations of America, 1990—. *Member:* Los Angeles County and American Bar Associations. *PRACTICE AREAS:* Pensions; Employee Benefits; Taxation; Exempt Organizations; Estate Planning.

**CATHERINE DEBONO HOLMES,** born Stockton, California, March 29, 1953; admitted to bar, 1977, California. *Education:* University of California at Berkeley (B.A., 1974); Boalt Hall School of Law, University of California (J.D., 1977). Phi Beta Kappa. Editor, California Law Review, 1976-1977. Member, Business Law Section, State Bar of California. *PRACTICE AREAS:* Corporate, Partnership and Securities; Mortgage Banking. *Email:* cjd@jmbm.com

**STEVEN J. INSEL,** born Brooklyn, New York, July 21, 1954; admitted to bar, 1979, California; 1981, Pennsylvania. *Education:* Cornell University (B.S., 1976), Phi Kappa Phi; University of Pennsylvania (J.D., 1979). Order

*(This Listing Continued)*

of the Coif. Editor, Law Review, 1978, 1979. *PRACTICE AREAS:* Broker-Dealer; Investment Adviser; Corporate Securities.

**PATRICK W. JORDAN** (San Francisco Office).

**SCOTT M. KALT,** born Detroit, Michigan, July 13, 1963; admitted to bar, 1988, California. *Education:* University of Michigan (B.A., with highest distinction, 1984; J.D., cum laude, 1987). Author: "What Every Retail Landlord Should Know About Negotiating Go-Dark Clauses and Dealing with a Tenant's Breach of Such Clause," 1996. *Member:* Los Angeles County and American Bar Associations. *PRACTICE AREAS:* Real Estate; Acquisitions and Dispositions; Finance; Leasing.

**BURTON A. MITCHELL, (P.C.),** born Brooklyn, New York, December 20, 1953; admitted to bar, 1978, California; 1979, U.S. Tax Court; 1980, U.S. Court of Appeals, Ninth Circuit. *Education:* Bernard M. Baruch College of the City University of New York (B.B.A., summa cum laude, 1974); Georgetown University (J.D., 1977); New York University (LL.M. in Taxation, 1978). Certified Public Accountant, Maryland, 1975. Co-Author: "Like-Kind Exchanges of Personal Property: A Practical Tour of Uncharted Territory," Taxes Magazine, February 1994. Author: "Is There Incorporation After TEFRA?" Beverly Hills Bar Association Journal, Spring 1984. "Interest-Free-Loans: Opportunities For Tax Planning," American Bar Association Journal, April 1979; "Tax Planning for a Condominium or Cooperative Conversion," The Practical Accountant, September 1980. (Certified Specialist, Taxation Law, The State Bar of California Board of Legal Specialization). *PRACTICE AREAS:* Taxation; Estate Planning; Closely-held Entities..

**ALLEN S. RESNICK,** born Los Angeles, California, April 14, 1947; admitted to bar, 1984, California. *Education:* University of California at Berkeley (B.A., 1969); McGill University (M.B.A., 1980); University of Southern California (J.D., 1984). Order of the Coif. Managing Editor, Southern California Law Review, 1983-1984. Chairman, California Senate Advisory Commission on Canada-California Trade Relations, 1989-1991. President, Canada California Chamber of Commerce, 1992-1993. *PRACTICE AREAS:* Corporate, International.

**JEFFREY L. REUBEN, (P.C.),** born Elmhurst, Illinois, July 15, 1960; admitted to bar, 1985, California; 1986, U.S. District Court, Central District of California; 1994, U.S. Tax Court. *Education:* Phillips Academy of Andover; Wesleyan University (B.A., high honors, 1982); Phi Beta Kappa; University of Chicago (J.D., 1985). Part-time Lecturer, University of Southern California School of Accounting, 1990-1992. Lecturer, Beverly Hills Bar Association, Real Estate Section: "The New IRC 1031 Regulations," 1990; "Tax Planning in Real Estate Workouts and Foreclosures," 1991; "Real Estate Loan Workouts," 1993; "1031 Exchanges-Selected Topics," 1994. Author: "Buying Real Estate From Non-U.S. Residents," Los Angeles Lawyer, December, 1989. *Member:* Century City (Co-Chair, Tax Section, 1995—) and American Bar Associations. *PRACTICE AREAS:* Federal and State Taxation.

**JULIA J. RIDER (P.C.),** admitted to bar, 1975, California. *Education:* University of California at Berkeley (A.B., 1969); University of California at Los Angeles (J.D., 1975). Phi Beta Kappa. Member, Mortar Board. Article Editor, UCLA Law Review, 1974-1975. Author: "Dissolution under the California Corporations Code: A Remedy for Minority Shareholders," UCLA Law Review, February 1975; "Lodging & the Law: They've Got the Power, You've Got the Liability," Hotel and Resort Industry, August 1993; "The Insurance Audit: Preventive Maintenance for Client and Counsel," The Interlawyer, January-February 1993. *Member:* Los Angeles County and American (Litigation Section) Bar Associations; Association of Business Trial Lawyers. *PRACTICE AREAS:* General Civil Litigation; Professional Liability; Complex Tort Litigation; Insurance-Related Matters.

**JEFFREY K. RIFFER,** born Gary, Indiana, September 8, 1953; admitted to bar, 1978, Indiana; 1979, California. *Education:* Indiana University (B.S., magna cum laude, 1975; J.D., magna cum laude, 1978). Order of the Coif; Beta Gamma Sigma. Managing Editor, Indiana Law Journal, 1977-1978. Author: "Sports and Recreational Injuries," Shephard's/McGraw Hill, 1985, with 1995 supplement; "An Overview of Sex Discrimination in Amateur Athletics," 6 COMM/ENT 621, 1984; "Recent Misinterpretations of the Avoidable Consequences Rule: The 'Duty' to Mitigate and Other Fictions," 16 Harv. J.L. & Pub. Pol'y 411, 1993. Adjunct Professor of Law, Pepperdine University School of Law, 1981-1991. Law Clerk to Hon. William E. Steckler, Chief Federal Judge, Southern District of Indiana, 1978-1979. *PRACTICE AREAS:* Antitrust; Defamation; Copyright; Trademark; Unfair Competition; Business Litigation.

**RICHARD A. ROGAN** (San Francisco Office).

*(This Listing Continued)*

**JEFFER, MANGELS, BUTLER & MARMARO LLP,** Los Angeles—Continued

**MARK M. ROSENTHAL,** born Norwalk, Connecticut, September 13, 1948; admitted to bar, 1973, New Jersey; 1979, California. *Education:* Wesleyan University (B.A., 1970); University of Michigan Law School (J.D., cum laude, 1973). Associate Editor, University of Michigan Law Review, 1972-1973. Author: "When Your Client's Business Deal Goes Sour," ABA Journal, Vol. 71, June, 1985; "Tactics to Employ When a Lawsuit Looms," Harvard Business Review, Vol. 84, No. 4, July-August, 1984; "The Winning Introduction," 10 Litigation 39, 1984; "Invoking Private Judge Dispute Resolution," California Lawyer, 25, 1984; "How to Get What You Paid For," pamphlet published by the Michigan Bar Association, 1973; Note, "Legal Knowledge of Michigan Citizens," 71 Michigan Law Review 1463, 1973. *Member:* Los Angeles County and American (Litigation Section) Bar Associations. *PRACTICE AREAS:* Business; Sports, Copyright, Trademark and Entertainment Litigation.

**ROBIN M. SCHACHTER, (P.C.),** born Lancaster, Pennsylvania, September 2, 1952; admitted to bar, 1977, District of Columbia; 1981, U.S. Supreme Court; 1990, California. *Education:* American University (B.A., 1974); Catholic University (J.D., 1977); Georgetown University (LL.M., Taxation, 1981). American Jurisprudence Award in Federal Practice and Procedure. Author: "An Analysis of the New Simplified Employee Pension Plan Alternative," 50 Journal of Taxation 322, June, 1979; "Pension Plans Can't Rely on Gender-Based Distinctions," VI Legal Times No. 11, p. 10, August 15, 1983; "Structuring Compensation in the New Environment: New Approaches to Executive Compensation," 3 The Computer Lawyer No. 7, p. 11, July, 1986; "Demystifying the 15% Excise Tax on Excess Distributions," Tax Management Compensation Planning Journal No. 3 p. 47, March 3, 1989. *Member:* Los Angeles County Bar Association (Chair, Employee Benefits Subcommittee, Section of Taxation, 1993-1994). *PRACTICE AREAS:* Employee Benefits; Taxation.

**GARY C. SHEPPARD** (San Francisco Office).

**MICHAEL S. SHERMAN, (P.C.),** born Brooklyn, New York, February 1, 1946; admitted to bar, 1971, California. *Education:* University of California at Los Angeles (A.B., cum laude, 1967); Boalt Hall School of Law, University of California (J.D., 1970). Order of the Coif. Associate in Law, Boalt Hall School of Law, University of California at Berkeley, 1971-1972. Co-Chair, UCLA Entertainment Symposium, 1990-1995. *Member:* Los Angeles County and American Bar Associations; Los Angeles Copyright Society. *PRACTICE AREAS:* Entertainment; General Business; Advertising; Intellectual Property.

**JEFFREY W. SHOPOFF** (San Francisco Office).

**MARK R. SIEKE, (P.C.),** born Manhasset, New York, June 29, 1957; admitted to bar, 1984, California and U.S. District Court, Central District of California; 1986, U.S. Tax Court. *Education:* University of California at Los Angeles (B.A., summa cum laude, 1979); Boalt Hall School of Law, University of California (J.D., 1984). Phi Beta Kappa. Current Developments Editor, International Tax and Business Lawyer, 1983-1984. Certified Public Accountant, California, 1981. Speaker: "What Every Accountant Should Know About Estate Planning for the $1 Million Estate," California Society of Certified Public Accountants, Estate Planning Technical Committee, 1993; "The '93 Tax Act: In Plain English," Beverly Hills Bar Association, 1993. *Member:* Beverly Hills (Chair, Taxation Section, 1993-1994) and Los Angeles County Bar Associations; California Society of Certified Public Accountants. *PRACTICE AREAS:* International and Domestic Taxation; Estate and Trust Administration; Business Transactions.

**WILLIAM S. SOLARI III** (San Francisco Office).

**JEFFREY E. STEINER, (P.C.),** born Brooklyn, New York, January 8, 1950; admitted to bar, 1975, Pennsylvania; 1977, California. *Education:* Yale University (B.S., cum laude, 1972); University of Pennsylvania (J.D., magna cum laude, 1975). Order of the Coif. Associate Editor, 1973-1974, and Research Editor, 1974-1975, University of Pennsylvania Law Review. Law Clerk to the Hon. Edward R. Becker, U.S. District Court, Eastern District of Pennsylvania, 1975-1976. *Member:* Los Angeles County Bar Association (Real Estate Section); State Bar of California (Real Estate Section). *PRACTICE AREAS:* General Real Estate; Commercial Leasing; Real Estate Lending and Loan Workouts; Real Estate Joint Ventures. *Email:* js@jmbm.com

**JEFFREY E. SULTAN (P.C.),** born New York, N.Y., October 25, 1948; admitted to bar, 1973, California. *Education:* University of California, Los Angeles (B.A., 1970; J.D., 1973). Order of the Coif. *Member:* State Bar of California (Partnerships and Unincorporated Business Organizations Committee of the Business Law Section); American Bar Association (Sections on Natural Resources Law and Corporation, Banking and Business Law; Subcommittee on State Regulation of Securities). *PRACTICE AREAS:* Corporate; Securities; Partnerships; Oil and Gas; Nonprofit Religious Corporations.

**PAUL L. WARNER** (San Francisco Office).

**WILLIAM M. WEINTRAUB, (P.C.),** born Brooklyn, New York, July 13, 1952; admitted to bar, 1978, Pennsylvania; 1980, California; 1981, U.S. Tax Court, U.S. District Court, Central District of California and U.S. Court of Appeals, Ninth Circuit. *Education:* Wharton School of Business, University of Pennsylvania (B.S., 1974); Rutgers University (J.D., 1977). Beta Alpha Psi. Co-Author: "Deductions and Allocations for Real Estate Investment Partnerships Under TRA 1984," Major Tax Planning, USC Tax Institute, 1985. Author: "Recovery of Attorneys Fees in Tax Litigation," Los Angeles Lawyer, July/August, 1987. *Member:* Los Angeles County and American Bar Associations. *PRACTICE AREAS:* Civil Tax Litigation; Partnership and Individual Taxation; Real Estate Transactions.

**BARRY M. WEISZ,** born Los Angeles, California, November 16, 1953; admitted to bar, 1978, California. *Education:* University of California at Los Angeles (A.B., 1975; J.D., 1978). Member, Moot Court Honor Society, 1976-1978. Lecturer, Business Law, West Coast University, 1990-1991. Judge Pro Tem, Los Angeles Superior Court, 1985—. *Member:* Beverly Hills, Los Angeles County and American Bar Associations; State Bar of California. *PRACTICE AREAS:* Corporate; Real Estate; Creditor's Rights.

**DENNIS J. WHITE** (San Francisco Office).

**HERBERT N. WOLFE, (P.C.),** born Chicago, Illinois, August 21, 1939; admitted to bar, 1965, California. *Education:* University of Illinois; California State University at Northridge (B.A., 1961); Boalt Hall School of Law, University of California (J.D., 1964). *Member:* Los Angeles County and Federal Bar Associations; American Judicature Society. *PRACTICE AREAS:* Business Law and Litigation.

## OF COUNSEL

**NEIL O. ANDRUS** (San Francisco Office).

**ADRIENNE M. COFFIN,** born New York, N.Y., November 15, 1954; admitted to bar, 1982, New York; 1983, U.S. District Court, Southern and Eastern Districts of New York; 1990, California; 1991, U.S. District Court, Central District of California; 1992, U.S. District Court, Southern and Eastern Districts of California; 1994, U.S. District Court, Northern District of California. *Education:* St. Mary's College (B.A., 1976); Notre Dame Law School (J.D., 1981). Editor, Journal of Legislation, 1979-1981. *Member:* New York State and American Bar Associations; Los Angeles Bankruptcy Forum; Financial Lawyers Conference; The American Bankruptcy Institute; Women Lawyers Association of Los Angeles (Delegate, State Bar of California Convention, 1993-1995); California Women Lawyers. *PRACTICE AREAS:* Insolvency; Creditors Rights, including Cross-Border Insolvencies with Japan and other Countries; Real Estate; Banking; Finance. *Email:* ac@jmbm.com

**RONALD P. GIVNER,** born Cleveland, Ohio, February 9, 1945; admitted to bar, 1971, California. *Education:* University of California at Los Angeles (B.A., 1966; J.D., 1970). Order of the Coif; Phi Delta Phi. Production Editor, UCLA Law Review, 1968-1969. Author, "ESOPS and the Federal Securities Law," 31 The Business Lawyer, 1976. Clerk, Chief Justice Donald Wright, California Supreme Court, 1970-1971. *PRACTICE AREAS:* Federal and State Securities; General Corporate; Mergers and Acquisitions.

**MAXWELL E. GREENBERG,** born Los Angeles, California, March 11, 1922; admitted to bar, 1950, California and U.S. District Court, Central District of California; 1959, Illinois; 1962, U.S. Supreme Court. *Education:* University of California at Los Angeles (A.B., cum laude, 1941); Harvard University (LL.B., magna cum laude, 1949). Phi Beta Kappa; Pi Gamma Mu; Pi Sigma Alpha. Editor, Harvard Law Review, 1948-1949. Adjunct Professor of Law, University of California at Los Angeles School of Law, 1972-1974. Research Attorney to Justice Roger Traynor, California Supreme Court, 1949-1950. Member, National Panel of Arbitration, American Arbitration Association, 1962—. National Chairman, Anti-Defamation League of B'nai B'rith, 1978-1982, Honorary Chairman, 1982—. Vice President, Police Commission of City of Los Angeles, 1980-1984. Chairman, California State Advisory Committee to the United States Civil Rights Commission, 1985-1989. *PRACTICE AREAS:* Estate Planning and Probate; Corporate; Real Estate Transactions.

**ANDREW R. HUNTER,** born Santa Rosa, California, February 25, 1961; admitted to bar, 1986, California. *Education:* University of California

*(This Listing Continued)*

at Los Angeles (B.A., magna cum laude, 1983); University of San Francisco (J.D., magna cum laude, 1986). Phi Beta Kappa. Member, McAuliffe Honor Society. Member, University of San Francisco Law Review, 1984-1985. *Member:* Los Angeles County (Barristers) and American (Litigation Section) Bar Associations. **PRACTICE AREAS:** Business; Construction and Real Estate Litigation.

**DAVID R. KALIFON,** born New York, New York, February 18, 1946; admitted to bar, 1988, California; 1989, U.S. District Court, Central, Northern, Eastern, Southern Districts of California; U.S. Court of Appeals, Ninth Circuit; 1991, District of Columbia. *Education:* Rutgers University (B.A., 1967); Cornell Medical College (M.D., 1971); University of California at Los Angeles (J.D., 1988). Phi Beta Kappa; Alpha Omega Alpha. UCLA Law Review, 1987-1988. Medical Doctor, California. Internship and residency, Internal Medicine, UCLA Hospital, 1971-1973. Resident, Emergency Medicine, USC, 1973-1975. Staff Member, Valley Presbyterian Hospital, Van Nuys, 1975-1990. Examiner, American Board of Emergency Medicine, 1983-1992; Diplomate, 1980—. General Counsel, American College of Emergency Physicians, California State Chapter, 1989—. Fellow: American College of Emergency Physicians; College of Legal Medicine. **PRACTICE AREAS:** Health; Professional Licensing; Contracts; Privileges; Peer Review; Administrative; Health Care Professionals Representation.

**TIMOTHY LAPPEN,** born Los Angeles, California, December 26, 1947; admitted to bar, 1975, California, U.S. District Court, Northern District of California and U.S. Court of Appeals, Ninth Circuit. *Education:* Claremont Men's College; University of California at Berkeley (A.B., 1972); University of California at Los Angeles (J.D., 1975). Member, 1989-1995 and President, 1993, Board of Trustees, UCLA Law School Alumni Association. D.A.R.E. California Executive Committee (1993-1995). President, Lappen Realty and Investment Corporation, 1987—. Member, 1988-1996, and President, 1992-1994, Board of Directors, Los Angeles Regional Food Bank. Los Angeles County District Attorney's Executive Advisory Council, 1992—. Los Angeles World Affairs Council, 1992-1995. Director, Dee Construction Company, 1979—. President and Director, Santa Monica Protective Association, 1981-1990. *Member:* Century City, Los Angeles County and American Bar Associations; California Lexington Group. **PRACTICE AREAS:** General Business; Real Estate; Corporate. **Email:** tl@jmbm.com

**JENNIFER L. LONG,** born New Brunswick, New Jersey, June 28, 1959; admitted to bar, 1987, California and U.S. District Court, Central District of California; 1988, U.S. Tax Court. *Education:* Harvard College (A.B., cum laude, 1981); Boalt Hall School of Law, University of California (J.D., 1987). Co-Author: *Loanouts and Guilds: Maximizing Entertainer Pensions,* Los Angeles Lawyer Magazine, April 1996 issue. *Member:* Beverly Hills (Taxation Section) and Los Angeles County (Taxation Section) Bar Associations; State Bar of California (Taxation Section). **PRACTICE AREAS:** Federal, State and Local Taxation.

**JEFFREY I. MARGOLIS** (San Francisco Office).

**JOHN E. MASON,** born Los Angeles, California, December 6, 1946; admitted to bar, 1972, California; 1988, Nevada; 1995, Tennessee. *Education:* University of California at Los Angeles (B.A., 1968); Boalt Hall School of Law, University of California (J.D., 1971). Order of the Coif. Managing Editor, California Law Review, 1970-1971. Chairman, Moot Court Board, 1970-1971. Associate Editor, Ecology Law Quarterly, 1969-1971. Vice President, Music Industry Chapter, City of Hope, 1982-1986. National Trustee and Member, Executive Committee, National Foundation for Ileitis and Colitis, 1982-1988. Director, LIVE Entertainment, Inc., 1988-1990; Director, Heftel Broadcasting, Inc., 1992. Chairman, Nevada Republican Party, 1995—. Chairman, Nevada Film Commission, 1996—. *Member:* Tennessee Bar Association; State Bar of Nevada. (Also practicing in Zephyr Cove, Nevada and Nashville, Tennessee). **PRACTICE AREAS:** Entertainment; Copyright; Motion Picture; Television; Music; Literary Property; Unfair Competition; Corporate Law.

**MYRON MEYERS (P.C.),** born Chicago, Illinois, October 23, 1928; admitted to bar, 1955, California. *Education:* University of California at Los Angeles (B.S., with honors, 1951; J.D., 1954). Beta Gamma Sigma. Author: "Foreign Investment in U.S. Real Estate," 1 Vol., Dow-Jones-Irwin, 1981; "Chapter on Foreign Investment in Real Estate With Guide For the Foreign Investor," Dow-Jones-Irwin, 1984. Instructor, UCLA Real Estate Acquisition and Finance, and Securitization of Real Estate, 1965—. Panel of Arbitrators, American Arbitration Association; Attorneys Committee, Building Industry Association. *Member:* Beverly Hills, Century City and Los Angeles County (Real Property Section) Bar Associations; Association of Real Estate Attorneys. **PRACTICE AREAS:** Real Estate Acquisition and Finance; Loan Documentation and Workouts; Joint Ventures;

*(This Listing Continued)*

Foreign Investment in U.S.; Arbitration of Real Estate and Construction Disputes. **Email:** mnm@jmbm.com

**FRED SELAN,** born Chicago, Illinois, May 19, 1939; admitted to bar, 1966, California, U.S. Tax Court and U.S. Court of Appeals, Ninth Circuit; 1969, U.S. Supreme Court. *Education:* University of Southern California (B.A., 1962); University of California at Los Angeles (J.D., 1965). Moot Court Honors Program, 1962-1964. Assistant Dean of Students, UCLA, 1965-1966. *Member:* Los Angeles County Bar Association. **PRACTICE AREAS:** General Business; Real Estate and Taxation; Start-up Companies, Finance and Operations. **Email:** fs@jmbm.com

**DAVID P. WAITE, (P.C.),** born Fort Worth, Texas, October 7, 1960; admitted to bar, 1987, California, U.S. Court of Appeals, Ninth Circuit and U.S. District Court, Northern District of California; 1988, U.S. District Court, Eastern and Central Districts of California. *Education:* University of Wisconsin-Madison; New York University (B.A., 1983); Georgetown University (J.D., 1986). Member, 1984-1986 and Associate Editor, 1985-1986, The Tax Lawyer. Author: "Going Around in CERCLA," American City & County, August 1993. *Member:* Los Angeles County and American Bar Associations. **PRACTICE AREAS:** Environmental; Litigation; Real Estate Transactional.

## ASSOCIATES

**GISELLE M. BARTH,** born Berkeley, California, July 25, 1970; (admission pending). *Education:* University of California at San Diego (B.A., 1992); University of California at Los Angeles (J.D., 1996). Order of the Coif. **PRACTICE AREAS:** Corporate.

**ALLISON H. BINDER,** born Brooklyn, New York, October 4, 1971; (admission pending). *Education:* Cornell University (B.A., 1993); Stanford Law School (J.D., 1996). Phi Beta Kappa. **PRACTICE AREAS:** Corporate.

**BRAD J. BRIGANTE,** born Honolulu, Hawaii, December 12, 1966; admitted to bar, 1996, California. *Education:* California Polytechnic State University (B.S., cum laude, 1990); Tulane University (J.D., cum laude, 1995); New York University (LL.M. in Taxation, 1996). Member, NYU Tax Law Review, 1995. Certified Public Accountant, California, 1992. **PRACTICE AREAS:** Federal and State Taxation.

**R. SCOTT BRINK,** born Omaha, Nebraska, 1963; admitted to bar, 1988, California; 1989, U.S. District Court, Central and Northern Districts of California and U.S. Court of Appeals, Ninth Circuit. *Education:* Hastings College (B.A., 1985); University of Nebraska (J.D., 1988). Allen Moot Court Board, National Moot Court Team. Member, Order of the Barristers. Recipient, Lewis F. Powell, Jr. and Thomas Stinson Allen Awards for Appellate Advocacy and Kenneth L. Noah Award for Appellate Brief Writing. *Member:* Los Angeles County (Sections on Labor Law and Litigation) and American Bar Associations. **PRACTICE AREAS:** Labor and Employment Law.

**ADRIANNE J. BROWNSTEIN,** born New York, N.Y., April 4, 1966; admitted to bar, 1990, California. *Education:* University of Florida (B.A., with highest honors, 1986), Phi Beta Kappa, Golden Key; University of Virginia (J.D., 1990). **PRACTICE AREAS:** Commercial and Business Litigation.

**GREGORY S. CAVALLO** (San Francisco Office).

**EVAN Y. CHUCK,** born Hong Kong, British Crown Colony, July 24, 1968; admitted to bar, 1993, Virginia; 1994, Court of International Trade (Not admitted in California). *Education:* The Johns Hopkins University (B.A., with honors, 1989) Thomas J. Watson Foundation Fellow; George Washington University National Law Center (J.D., 1993) Dean's Fellow. Member, Executive Committee, Johns Hopkins University Alumni Association (D.C. Chapter), 1993-1996. *Member:* Virginia State Bar (International Section); American Bar Association (Sections on: International Trade; Business Law; Entertainment and Sports Law Forum). **LANGUAGES:** Chinese, French. **PRACTICE AREAS:** Corporate Securities; International Business; International Trade; Representation before U.S. Government and Agencies.

**MICHAEL G. DWYER,** born Brooklyn, New York, August 17, 1961; admitted to bar, 1986, New York; 1989, District of Columbia; 1995, California. *Education:* University of Virginia (B.A., with distinction, 1983); St. John's University (J.D., 1986). *Member:* Los Angeles County and American Bar Associations. [Captain, JAGC, US Army, 1987-1991]. **LANGUAGES:** Spanish. **PRACTICE AREAS:** Labor and Employment.

**JOHN M. FUJII,** born Yuba City, California, September 20, 1966; admitted to bar, 1994, California. *Education:* University of California at Davis

*(This Listing Continued)*

**JEFFER, MANGELS, BUTLER & MARMARO LLP,** Los Angeles—Continued

(B.S., with high honors, 1989); Boalt Hall School of Law, University of California at Berkeley (J.D., 1994). *Member:* Los Angeles County Bar Association (Member, Environmental Law Section); Japanese American Bar Association. **PRACTICE AREAS:** Environmental Law; General Business Litigation. *Email:* jzf@jmbm.com

**ALFRED M. GARCIA,** born Miami, Florida, April 5, 1965; admitted to bar, 1989, California. *Education:* University of Florida (B.S.B.A., with honors, 1986); Harvard University (J.D., cum laude, 1989). Supreme Court Editor, Harvard Law Review, 1987-1988. *Member:* Los Angeles County and American Bar Associations. **LANGUAGES:** Spanish. **PRACTICE AREAS:** Federal, State, Local and International Taxation.

**MICHAEL M. GERARDI,** born Maywood, California, February 16, 1959; admitted to bar, 1988, Georgia and Virginia; 1989, U.S. District Court Eastern District of Virginia; 1991, U.S. Court of Appeals, Federal Circuit; 1992, Florida; 1994, California; registered to practice before U.S. Patent and Trademark Office. *Education:* Massachusetts Institute of Technology (S.B., 1981); University of Georgia ( J.D., cum laude, 1988). Phi Delta Phi. Member, Managing Board, Georgia Journal of International and Comparative Law, 1987-1988. Co-Author: "Patent practitioners—don't let GATT get you," Managing Intellectual Property, March 1995; "The Burroughs Decision: Conception of Invention in Pharmaceutical Applications," Patent World, March 1995. *Member:* Beverly Hills Bar Association; Italian American Bar Association. **PRACTICE AREAS:** Patent Law.

**STANLEY M. GIBSON,** born Redwood City, California, October 5, 1966; admitted to bar, 1992, California. *Education:* University of California at Berkeley (B.A., 1988); Duke University (M.A., 1991; J.D., 1991). Executive Editor, Duke Law Journal, 1990-1991. Clerk, Hon. Deanell Tacha, U.S. Court of Appeals, Tenth Circuit. **PRACTICE AREAS:** Litigation.

**MICHAEL D. GOOD,** born Mt. Lebanon, Pennsylvania, February 21, 1965; admitted to bar, 1995, California and U.S. District Court, Central, Northern, Eastern and Southern Districts of California. *Education:* University of Pennsylvania (B.A., 1987); Pepperdine University (J.D., 1994). Judicial Law Clerk, Hon. Mitchel R. Goldberg, U.S. Bankruptcy Court, Central District of California. *Member:* Los Angeles County and American Bar Associations. [Lieutenant, U.S. Navy, 1987-1991]. **PRACTICE AREAS:** Insolvency; Creditors Rights.

**SCOTT I. GREENFIELD,** born Los Angeles, California, November 6, 1968; admitted to bar, 1993, California and U.S. District Court, Central District of California. *Education:* University of California, Santa Barbara (B.A., with honors, 1990); Loyola Law School, Los Angeles (J.D., cum laude, 1993). Order of the Coif. Best Oralist, Scott Moot Court Competition. Member, National Moot Court Team, Moot Court Honors Board. Extern, Hon. James M. Ideman, U.S. District Court, Central District. *Member:* Los Angeles County Bar Association. **PRACTICE AREAS:** General Business; Real Estate Litigation.

**BRIAN M. GROSSMAN,** born Newark, New Jersey, September 25, 1968; admitted to bar, 1993, California, U.S. District Court, Central District of California and U.S. Court of Appeals, Ninth Circuit. *Education:* University of Pennsylvania (B.A., cum laude, 1990); University of California, Los Angeles (J.D., 1993). Co-Chief Justice, Moot Court Program. President, Federalist Society, UCLA Law, 1992-1993. **PRACTICE AREAS:** Commercial Litigation.

**LYNNE MARIE HOOK,** born Chicago, Illinois, August 20, 1969; admitted to bar, 1993, California; U.S. District Court, Central District of California. *Education:* University of Southern California (B.A., cum laude, 1990); University of Notre Dame (J.D., 1993). Thomas J. White Scholar. Staff Member, Notre Dame Journal of Law, Ethics & Public Policy, 1991-1993. Author: "Substance Abuse Within the Legal Profession: A Symptom of a Greater Malaise," Notre Dame Journal of Law, Ethics & Public Policy, Vol. 7, No. 1, 1993. Law Clerk: U.S. Attorney, Central District of California, Los Angeles, California, 1991; U.S. Attorney, Northern District of Indiana, South Bend, Indiana, 1991. *Member:* Los Angeles County Bar Association. **PRACTICE AREAS:** Labor and Employment Law.

**SUSAN C. V. JONES,** born Birmingham, England, July 22, 1963; admitted to bar, 1990, California. *Education:* University of Michigan (B.A, with high honors, 1984); Harvard University (J.D., cum laude, 1990). **PRACTICE AREAS:** General Litigation. *Email:* scj@jmbm.com

**VICTORIA S. KAUFMAN,** born Indianapolis, Indiana, March 11, 1964; admitted to bar, 1989, California and U.S. District Court, Southern, Northern, Central and Eastern Districts of California. *Education:* Bryn Mawr College (B.A., magna cum laude, 1986); Harvard University (J.D., 1989). Member, Harvard International Law Journal, 1986-1989. *Member:* American Bar Association; American Bankruptcy Institute; Financial Lawyers Conference. **PRACTICE AREAS:** Bankruptcy; Corporate Insolvency.

**STEVEN M. KORBIN,** born Los Angeles, California, January 26, 1966; admitted to bar, 1995, California. *Education:* University of California, Santa Barbara (B.A., magna cum laude, 1989) Phi Beta Kappa; Columbia University (M.A., 1991); Loyola University, Los Angeles (J.D., 1995). St. Thomas More Honor Society. Recipient, American Jurisprudence Award in Trusts and Wills. **PRACTICE AREAS:** Real Estate. *Email:* sxk@jmbm.com

**JOHN G. LITTELL,** born Washington, D.C., January 30, 1965; admitted to bar, 1991, New York; 1993, District of Columbia; 1994, California. *Education:* University of Virginia (B.S., with distinction, 1987; J.D., 1990). Phi Delta Phi. *Member:* Los Angeles County Bar Association. **PRACTICE AREAS:** Corporate; Mergers and Acquisitions; Banking; Securities; Sports and Entertainment.

**KENNETH W. MULLER** (San Francisco Office).

**MIKE D. NEUE,** born Seattle, Washington, January 5, 1969; admitted to bar, 1995, California, U.S. District Court, Central District of California and U.S. Court of Appeals, Ninth Circuit. *Education:* University of Oregon (B.S., 1991); University of Southern California (J.D., 1995). Law Clerk to the Honorable Samuel L. Bufford, Central District of California, 1995-1996. **PRACTICE AREAS:** Insolvency Law.

**BRADFORD K. NEWMAN** (San Francisco Office).

**STEVEN PLOTKIN,** born Los Angeles, California, October 21, 1960; admitted to bar, 1986, California; 1987, U.S. District Court, Central District of California and U.S. Court of Appeals, Ninth Circuit. *Education:* University of California at Los Angeles (B.A., 1982; J.D., 1986). Phi Beta Kappa; Order of the Barristers. **PRACTICE AREAS:** Trademark; Licensing; Copyright; Business Law. *Email:* stp@jmbm.com

**LINDA A. SAMPSON,** born Evergreen Park, Illinois, November 13, 1968; admitted to bar, 1993, California. *Education:* Loyola Marymount University (B.A., cum laude, 1990); Pepperdine University School of Law (J.D., cum laude, 1993). *Member:* Los Angeles and Orange County Bar Associations. **PRACTICE AREAS:** Land Use Entitlement Law; Business Litigation; Real Estate Litigation; Construction Defect Litigation.

**DAN P. SEDOR,** born Santa Monica, California, August 3, 1960; admitted to bar, 1988, California and U.S. District Court, Central, Southern and Northern Districts of California. *Education:* University of California at Los Angeles (B.A., 1982); Loyola Marymount University (J.D., magna cum laude, 1988). Order of the Coif. Staff Member, Loyola of Los Angeles Law Review, 1986-1987. Author: "Commodity Futures Trading Commission v. Schor: Article III Finds a Home on the Slippery Slope," 21 Loy. L.A. L.Rev. 707, 1988. Assistant Editor: "Damages in Business Litigation," ABTL/Rutter Group, 1990. *Member:* Los Angeles County Bar Association. **PRACTICE AREAS:** General Business and Securities Litigation.

**MARIA SENDRA,** born Derby, Connecticut, October 3, 1961; admitted to bar, 1992, California and U.S. District Court, Central District of California. *Education:* Yale University (B.A., magna cum laude, 1983); Indiana University at Bloomington (M.A., with distinction, 1988); Boalt Hall School of Law, University of California at Berkeley (J.D., 1991). Award for Excellence in Written Advocacy. Associate Editor, Ecology Law Quarterly, 1989-1990. Contributing Member, International Tax and Business Lawyer, 1991. Author: "Strategic Alliances in the Global Market of the 1990s: A Comparative Study of the Relationship Between Innovation and the Patent and Antitrust Mechanisms of the U.S. and the E.E.C.," International Tax and Business Lawyer, Vol. 9, No. 2, Winter 1992. Co-Author: "Documenting Corporate Joint Ventures," California Business Law Practitioner, Vol. VIII, No. 4, Fall 1993. *Member:* State Bar of California (Business Section). **LANGUAGES:** Spanish, French and Valenciano. **PRACTICE AREAS:** Corporate; Securities. *Email:* mps@jmbm.com

**ROBERT STEINBERG,** born New York, N.Y., July 4, 1964; admitted to bar, 1989, California and U.S. District Court, Central District of California. *Education:* Harvard University (B.A., magna cum laude, 1986); Harvard Law School (J.D., 1989). *Member:* Los Angeles County and Beverly Hills Bar Associations. **PRACTICE AREAS:** Securities; Corporate Finance; Mergers and Acquisitions; General Corporate. *Email:* rs@jmbm.com

**ELIZABETH A. STONE,** born Santa Monica, California, September 13, 1963; admitted to bar, 1988, California and U.S. District Court, South-

*(This Listing Continued)*

ern District of California. *Education:* University of California at Santa Barbara (B.A., 1985); McGeorge School of Law (J.D., valedictorian, 1988). Order of the Coif. *Member:* Los Angeles County and American Bar Associations. *LANGUAGES:* Japanese, Spanish. *PRACTICE AREAS:* Real Estate; Corporations; Civil Litigation.

**KATHRYN ELLEN SUAREZ,** born Los Angeles, California, June 5, 1968; admitted to bar, 1994, California. *Education:* University of California at Berkeley (B.A., with honors, 1990); Boalt Hall School of Law, University of California (J.D., 1994). Member, California Law Review. Author: "Teenage Dating Violence: The Need for Expanded Awareness and Legislation," 82 Calif. L. Rev. 423 (1994). *PRACTICE AREAS:* Business and Labor Litigation.

**LAZARUS N. SUN,** born Manila, Philippines, October 8, 1960; admitted to bar, 1987, New York; 1996, California. *Education:* Columbia College (B.A., 1981); Case Western Reserve University (J.D., 1986). Co-Author: "Synthetic Gics and Bics," 1992 & 1993 Pension Plan Investments, PLI. *Member:* American Bar Association. *LANGUAGES:* Mandarin Chinese. *PRACTICE AREAS:* Employee Benefits.

**ALEX O. TAMIN,** born Baltimore, Maryland, September 19, 1970; admitted to bar, 1995, California. *Education:* John Hopkins University (B.A., 1992); University of California, Los Angeles (J.D., 1995). Member, UCLA National Moot Court Team. Editor, UCLA Entertainment Law Review, 1993-1995. *PRACTICE AREAS:* Litigation.

**ELAINE M. TAUBENFELD,** born Great Barrington, Massachusetts, June 28, 1955; admitted to bar, 1992, California. *Education:* Iowa State University (B.S., 1984); University of California at Los Angeles (M.S., 1988); Boalt Hall School of Law, University of California (J.D., 1992). Phi Beta Kappa; Phi Kappa Phi. Member, 1990-1992 and Executive Editor, 1991-1992, California Law Review. *Member:* Los Angeles County (Taxation and Trusts and Estates Section) and American (Sections on Real Property, Probate and Trust Law and Taxation) Bar Associations. *PRACTICE AREAS:* Estate Planning; Taxation.

**DEBORAH J. TIBBETTS,** born Queens, New York, January 28, 1966; admitted to bar, 1993, California. *Education:* Western Connecticut State University (B.S., magna cum laude, 1990); Columbia University School of Law (J.D., 1993). Harlan Fiske Stone Scholar. Editor, Columbia Law Review, 1991-1993. *PRACTICE AREAS:* Labor and Employment.

**REBECCA L. TORREY,** born Vienna, Austria, August 24, 1961; admitted to bar, 1991, California, U.S. Court of Appeals, Ninth Circuit, and U.S. District Court, Central District of California. *Education:* Emporia State University (B.A., 1982); University of Kansas (M.A., 1988); Duke Law School (J.D., 1990; L.L.M., 1990). Member, 1988-1990, and Executive Editor, 1989-1990, Duke Law Journal. Clerk, Hon. Deanell Tacha, U.S. Court of Appeals, Tenth Circuit. Author: "First Amendment Claims Against Public Broadcasters: Testing the Public's Right to a Balanced Presentation," 1989 D.L.J. 1386. *Member:* American Bar Association. *PRACTICE AREAS:* Labor and Employment Litigation.

**STEVEN M. WEISS,** born Brooklyn, New York, September 15, 1961; admitted to bar, 1990, California, U.S. District Court, Central District of California and U.S. Court of Appeals, Federal Circuit; 1994, registered to practice before the U.S. Patent and Trademark Office. *Education:* University of California at Los Angeles (B.S., 1984); University of California at San Diego (M.S., 1986); University of Southern California (J.D., 1990). *Member:* American Bar Association (Member, Patent, Trademark and Copyright Section, 1990-1996). *PRACTICE AREAS:* Patent Law; Trademark; Trade Secrets; Antitrust.

**JAMES P. WILLIAMS,** born Camden, New Jersey, November 27, 1952; admitted to bar, 1989, New York; 1992, U.S. District Court, Western District of New York; 1995, California and U.S. District Court, Central District of California. *Education:* Rutgers University (B.A., 1974; M.F.A., 1977; J.D., 1988). *PRACTICE AREAS:* Trademark and Unfair Competition; Copyright; Advertising. *Email:* jpw@jmbm.com

**ISAAC H. WINER** (San Francisco Office).

**STEPHEN N. YANG** (San Francisco Office).

Unless otherwise indicated all Members of the Firm, Of Counsel and Associates are Members of The State Bar of California.

## JOHN A. JOANNES
*A PROFESSIONAL CORPORATION*
11911 SAN VICENTE BOULEVARD
SUITE 375
**LOS ANGELES, CALIFORNIA 90049**
*Telephone:* 310-440-4240
*Facsimile:* 310-471-2862
*Email:* jjoannespc@aol.com
*URL:* http://www.primenet.com/~joannes/

*Practice limited to Immigration and Nationality Law.*

**JOHN A. JOANNES,** born Monterey Park, California, July 29, 1934; admitted to bar, 1965, California; 1974, U.S. Supreme Court. *Education:* Occidental College (A.B., 1956); University of Southern California School of Public Administration (M.S. in P.A., 1961); University of Southern California (J.D., 1962). Phi Alpha Delta. Law Clerk to: Judge Stanley N. Barnes, U.S. Court of Appeals, Ninth Circuit, 1963; Judge E. Avery Crary, U.S. District Court, Central District of California, 1964-1965. Staff Counsel, McCone Commission (Governor's Commission on Los Angeles Riots), 1965-1966. Co-Author: "The Immigration Reform and Control Act Handbook," Parker and Son Publications, Inc., 1987. Lecturer: Immigration and Nationality Law Seminar, California Continuing Education of the Bar (CEB), 1987, and Immigration Law Institute, University of Southern California Law Center, 1991. *Member:* Los Angeles County Bar Association (Chair: Immigration Section, 1980-1981; International Law Section, 1983-1984; Immigration Legal Assistance Project Committee, 1987-1996); State Bar of California; American Bar Association (Chair, Immigration, Naturalization and Aliens Committee, Section of Administrative Law and Regulatory Practice, 1988-1990); American Immigration Lawyers Association (Chairperson, Southern California Chapter, 1974-1976; Member, Board of Governors, 1983-1984). (Certified Specialist, Immigration and Nationality Law, The State Bar of California Board of Legal Specialization).

*OF COUNSEL*

**STEPHEN L. TELLER,** born Los Angeles, California, August 14, 1950; admitted to bar, 1975, California; 1976, U.S. District Court, Central District of California; 1978, U.S. Court of Appeals, Ninth Circuit. *Education:* University of California at Los Angeles (A.B., Pol. Sci., 1972); University of California at Davis (J.D., 1975). Pi Gamma Mu; Phi Eta Sigma; Phi Delta Phi. Project Director, Los Angeles County Bar Association's Immigration Legal Assistance Project, 1979-1980. Member, Board of Directors of U.S. Pacific Council, 1982-1988. *Member:* Los Angeles County Bar Association (Member, Immigration Law Section, 1977-1993; Section Second Vice-Chair, 1981-1982; Section First Vice-Chair, 1982-1983; Member, Section Executive Committee, 1980-1985; Immigration Legal Assistance Project's Oversight Committee, 1984-1988); American Immigration Lawyers Association (AILA).

## JOHNSEN, MANFREDI & THORPE
*A PROFESSIONAL CORPORATION*
**LOS ANGELES, CALIFORNIA**
(See Perkins Coie)

## THE LAW OFFICES OF RAYMOND PAUL JOHNSON
SUITE 1150
10990 WILSHIRE BOULEVARD (WESTWOOD)
**LOS ANGELES, CALIFORNIA 90024**
*Telephone:* 310-246-9300
*Fax:* 310-312-1551

*Aviation Law, Products Liability, Contract Actions, Technology-Related Litigation, Wrongful Termination, Entertainment Industry Disputes, Civil Trial Practice.*

*FIRM PROFILE:* Established in 1992 to litigate and join with other law firms nationwide in the prosecution of complex matters related to engineering and technology including major products liability, aviation and toxic trauma cases.

*(This Listing Continued)*

# CALIFORNIA—LOS ANGELES

## THE LAW OFFICES OF RAYMOND PAUL JOHNSON, Los Angeles—Continued

**RAYMOND PAUL JOHNSON,** born Jersey City, New Jersey, July 19, 1947; admitted to bar, 1983, California; 1984, U.S. District Court, Central and Southern Districts of California and U.S. Court of Appeals, Ninth Circuit; U.S. Supreme Court. *Education:* New York University (B.S., Engineering, 1969); Air Force Institute of Technology (M.S., Engineering, 1975); The College of William and Mary (J.D., 1983). Commercial Pilot, FAA, 1971. Registrant Professional Engineer, Ohio, 1975. Author: *Defective Product: Evidence to Verdict,* a Michie Butterworth Publication, 1995; Articles, "21st Century Demonstrative Evidence-Today," Published in the Proceedings of the 1996 ATLA National Convention, July 1996; "Products Liability: Hot Topics," *California Forum,* November 1995; "Cross-Examining Adverse Experts," *The Advocate,* October 1995; "Closing Is As Closing Does," *California Forum,* August 1995; "Federal Preemption," *The Advocate,* January 1995; "Unstable Vehicles--Unsafe at Any Speed," *L.A. Trial Lawyer Magazine,* June 1993; "Short on Safety: How Auto Designs Cause Needless Harm," *National Trial Lawyer Magazine,* November 1992; "In Search of the Right Experts," *Trial Magazine,* February 1992; "Beyond the Sale: The Duty to Warn," *L.A. Trial Lawyer Magazine,* May 1991; "The Trial Lawyer As Private Attorney General: Defense Contractor Fraud," *The Advocate,* May 1990. Member: Los Angeles County and American Bar Associations; State Bar of California; Association of Trial Lawyers of America (Sustaining Member; Chairman, Products Liability Section, 1994-1995); Attorneys Information Exchange Group; Consumer Attorneys of California; Consumer Attorneys Association of Los Angeles (Member, Board of Governors); Lawyer-Pilots Bar Association; American Institute of Aeronautics and Astronautics. [U.S.A.F. Pilot/Aerospace Engineer, Space Shuttle Program, 1969-1979]

## JOHNSON, CEBULA & RYGH
### LOS ANGELES, CALIFORNIA
(See Long Beach)

*Automobile Negligence, Insurance Defense, Bad Faith, Complex Litigation, Construction Defect Litigation, Fraudulent and Suspect Claims, Insurance Coverage, Municipality Defense, Premise Liability, Product Liability, Medical Malpractice, Wrongful Termination.*

## JOHNSON, POULSON, COONS & SLATER
Established in 1966
10880 WILSHIRE BOULEVARD, SUITE 1800
**LOS ANGELES, CALIFORNIA 90024**
Telephone: 310-475-0611
Telecopier: 310-475-0143

*Corporation, Real Property, General Business. Family Law, Estate Planning, Probate, Civil Trial Practice in all State and Federal Courts.*

**FIRM PROFILE:** Johnson, Poulson, Coons & Slater, a professional corporation has been engaged in the practice of law in Los Angeles since 1966. The firm provides legal services in the areas of business organization, contract preparation, real estate transactions, civil litigation, family law, estate planning, probate and family law and probate mediation.

The firm specializes in the growth and development of the young, growing and aggressive entrepreneurial company.

The firm strives to provide sound, timely advice and properly drafted agreements, which are the best protection against costly, stressful litigation.

### MEMBERS OF FIRM

**JONATHAN E. JOHNSON,** born Whittier, California, May 1, 1936; admitted to bar, 1964, California; 1972, U.S. Supreme Court. *Education:* Cornell University (B.Ch.E., 1959; M.B.A., 1960); George Washington University (J.D., with honors, 1963). Order of the Coif; Phi Delta Phi. Associate Editor for Case Notes, George Washington Law Review, 1962-1963. Author: Case Note, 30 George Washington Law Review 523, 1962. Co-Author: "Yours, Mine and Ours: Carving Up the Property Pie," Los Angeles Lawyer, Nov., 1983. President, Cornell Club of Southern California, 1966-1968. *Member:* Beverly Hills (Member, Executive Committee, Family Law Section, 1978-1982; 1986-1988; 1993—) and Los Angeles County (Member, Family Law Section) Bar Associations; State Bar of California (Member, Legislation Standing Committee, Family Law Section, 1978-1988; Chairman, 1979-1980); American Academy of Matrimonial Lawyers. (Certified Specialist, Family Law, The State Bar of California Board of Legal Specialization). **PRACTICE AREAS:** Family Law; Litigation; Estate Planning; Probate.

**LYNN O. POULSON, (MR.),** born Provo, Utah, January 27, 1938; admitted to bar, 1967, California; 1972, U.S. Supreme Court; 1990, U.S. Court of Appeals, Ninth Circuit. *Education:* Brigham Young University (B.S., 1963); Columbia University (M.B.A., 1966; J.D., 1966). Thomas G. Shearman National Scholar. Member, Brigham Young University Law School Board of Visitors, 1979-1981. *Member:* Los Angeles County and American Bar Associations; State Bar of California. **PRACTICE AREAS:** Litigation; Corporate Law; Business; Real Estate.

**MICHAEL H. COONS,** born Montebello, California, February 3, 1962; admitted to bar, 1989, California. *Education:* Brigham Young University (B.S., cum laude, 1986; J.D., cum laude, 1989). Member, 1987-1989 and Note and Comment Editor, 1988-1989, Brigham Young University Law Review. Author: "Case Note, Brigham Young University Law Review, 429, 1988. *Member:* Beverly Hills, Los Angeles County and American Bar Associations; State Bar of California. **LANGUAGES:** Spanish. **PRACTICE AREAS:** Business Law; Estate Planning; Probate Law; Real Estate; Personal Injury.

### OF COUNSEL

**MARTIN R. SLATER,** born Lynwood, California, March 31, 1955; admitted to bar, 1982, California and U.S. District Court, Central District of California; 1986, U.S. Supreme Court. *Education:* California State University at Long Beach (B.S., with highest honors, 1979); Brigham Young University (J.D., magna cum laude, 1982). Order of the Coif. J. Reuben Clark Scholar. Co-Author: "Advising Closely Held Corporations," Summary of Utah Corporate Law, Brigham Young University Journal of Legal Studies, 1982. Adjunct Professor of Law, Pepperdine University, 1985. *Member:* Los Angeles County Bar Association; State Bar of California. **LANGUAGES:** Thai. **PRACTICE AREAS:** Corporate Law; Real Estate Transactions; Estate Planning.

## LAW OFFICES OF STEPHEN L. JONES
445 SOUTH FIGUEROA, SUITE 2600
**LOS ANGELES, CALIFORNIA 90071**
Telephone: 213-612-7701
Fax: 213-612-7702
Email: shibumi@loop.com

*Real Estate and Land Use Litigation, General Civil Litigation, Business Litigation, Commercial Litigation and Appellate Practice.*

**STEPHEN L. JONES,** born Austin, Texas, September 26, 1942; admitted to bar, 1976, California and U.S. District Court, Central District of California ; U.S Court of Appeals, 9th Circuit; U.S. Tax Court; 1983, U.S. Supreme Court. *Education:* University of Texas (B.A., 1964); University of Wisconsin-Madison (Ph.D., 1967); University of Michigan (J.D., cum laude, 1976). Phi Beta Kappa. Articles Editor, University of Michigan Journal of Law Reform, 1975-1976. Member, Institute for Advance Study, Princeton, New Jersey, 1967-1996. Teaching Position, University of Massachusetts, Mathematics, 1969-1973. Member, Rotary Club, 1996—. Associate, Latham & Watkins, 1976-1983; Of Counsel, Pillsbury Madison & Sutro, (1988-1992). *Member:* Los Angeles County and American Bar Associations; The State Bar of California (Member Sections on: Real Estate and Litigation). **SPECIAL AGENCIES:** Local Agencies: Planning Commissions, Zoning Administration, City Council, Mediation Dispute Resolution (1992). **REPORTED CASES:** City of West Hollywood v. Beverly Towers, Inc. 52Cal 3rd 1184, 1991; V.D. Registry, Inc. v. State of California 34Cal App 4th 107, 1995;Korean American Legal Foundation v. City of Los Angeles 23Cal App 4th 376, 1994; Baker v. City of Santa Monica 181Cal App 3rd 972, 1986. **PRACTICE AREAS:** Real Estate and Land Use Litigation; General Civil Litigation; Business Litigation; Commercial Litigation; Appellate Practice.

*(This Listing Continued)*

## JONES, BELL, SIMPSON, ABBOTT & FLEMING

*601 SOUTH FIGUEROA STREET, TWENTY-SEVENTH FLOOR*
*LOS ANGELES, CALIFORNIA 90017-5759*
Telephone: 213-485-1555
Telecopier: 213-689-1004
Email: jonesbel@ix.netcom.com

General Civil, Trial and Appellate Practice in all State and Federal Courts. Antitrust, Arbitration, Franchise, Probate, Real Estate and Securities Law.

**FIRM PROFILE:** Jones, Bell, Simpson, Abbott & Fleming is engaged in a sophisticated civil litigation business practice. The firm, located in the downtown Los Angeles financial district, is the successor to a firm that originated in Los Angeles during the early 1900's. The firm has broad trial and appellate practice experience before both Federal and State Courts in areas including securities litigation, real estate disputes, business and partnership dissolutions, contract actions and a variety of business torts. The firm handles matters from trial through appeal. The firm's corporate practice includes business planning advice to its clients including the formation, maintenance and representation of various business entities including corporations and partnerships.

### MEMBERS OF FIRM

**MAURICE JONES, JR.** (1902-1987).

**EUGENE W. BELL** (1926-1996).

**C. EDWARD SIMPSON,** born Los Angeles, California, November 19, 1937; admitted to bar, 1964, California; 1964, U.S. District Court, Central District of California; 1972, U.S. Court of Appeals, Ninth Circuit; 1978, U.S. Supreme Court. *Education:* Vanderbilt University (B.A., 1960); Southern Methodist University and University of Southern California (LL.B., 1963). Phi Alpha Delta. Law Clerk to Honorable Peirson M. Hall, U.S. District Judge, Central District of California, 1964-1965. Faculty, University of San Fernando Valley College of Law, 1964-1971. Judge Pro Tem, Los Angeles Municipal Court. Arbitrator: American Arbitration Association; National Association of Securities Dealers, Inc. *Member:* Los Angeles County and American (Member, Litigation Section; Member, National Conference of Lawyers and Life Insurance Companies, 1974-1980) Bar Associations; The State Bar of California (Member, State Bar Court, 1981-1989); Association of Business Trial Lawyers. **PRACTICE AREAS:** Securities Litigation; Class Actions; Trial Practice.

**MICHAEL J. ABBOTT,** born Madison, Wisconsin, July 26, 1944; admitted to bar, 1972, California; 1973, U.S. District Court, Central District of California; 1974, U.S. Court of Appeals, Ninth Circuit; 1976, U.S. Supreme Court. *Education:* Stanford University (B.A., 1966); University of California at Los Angeles (J.D., 1972). Arbitrator, National Association of Securities Dealers, Inc., 1986—. Arbitrator, National Future's Association, 1989—. Judicial Arbitrator, Los Angeles Superior Court. *Member:* Los Angeles County and American Bar Associations; The State Bar of California; The Association of Business Trial Lawyers; Securities Industry Association (Member, Legal and Compliance Division). **PRACTICE AREAS:** Business Law; Securities Litigation.

**G. THOMAS FLEMING III,** born Oak Park, Illinois, July 13, 1951; admitted to bar, 1976, California; 1977, U.S. District Court, Central District of California; 1978, U.S. Court of Appeals, Ninth Circuit; 1981, U.S. Supreme Court; 1984, U.S. District Court, Eastern District of California; 1986, U.S. District Court, Southern District of California; 1987, U.S. District Court, Northern District of California. *Education:* University of Southern California (B.A., cum laude, 1973); Hastings College of Law, University of California (J.D., 1976). Judge Pro Tem, Los Angeles Municipal Court, 1982—. Arbitrator, National Association of Securities Dealers, 1986—. Arbitrator, National Future's Association, 1989—. *Member:* The State Bar of California. **PRACTICE AREAS:** Litigation; Arbitration; Real Estate; Regulatory Matters.

**KEVIN K. FITZGERALD,** born Emporia, Kansas, May 9, 1956; admitted to bar, 1981, California; 1982, U.S. District Court, Central District of California; 1983, U.S. Court of Appeals, Ninth Circuit; 1984, U.S. Supreme Court. *Education:* Allegheny College (B.A., cum laude, 1978); Duke University (J.D., 1981). Staff Member, 1979-1980 and Editorial Board Member, 1980-1981, Duke Law Journal. *Member:* Los Angeles County Bar Association; State Bar of California. **PRACTICE AREAS:** Litigation; Broker-Dealer Regulation; Class Actions.

**CRAIG R. BOCKMAN,** born Woodstock, Illinois, January 9, 1958; admitted to bar, 1982, California, U.S. District Court, Central, Southern, Eastern and Northern Districts of California and U.S. Court of Appeals,

*(This Listing Continued)*

Second, Ninth, Tenth and District of Columbia Circuits; 1988, U.S. Supreme Court. *Education:* University of California at Los Angeles (B.A., 1979); Loyola University of Los Angeles (J.D., 1982). Recipient, American Jurisprudence Award in Insurance Law. Author: "Business Torts: The (Correct) Statute of Limitations for Breach of Fiduciary Duty Under California Law," 16 Cal. Bus. Law News 9, Winter 1994. Judge Pro Tem, Los Angeles Municipal Court, 1988—. Arbitrator, National Futures Association, 1990—. *Member:* Los Angeles County (Panel Member, Arbitration Committee, 1986—) and American Bar Associations; State Bar of California (Member, Sections on Tax; Real Property and Business). **PRACTICE AREAS:** Litigation; Real Estate; Appellate Practice.

**FREDRICK A. RAFEEDIE,** born Santa Monica, California, September 28, 1962; admitted to bar, 1988, California, U.S. District Court, Northern, Southern, Eastern and Central Districts of California and U.S. Court of Appeals, Ninth Circuit. *Education:* University of Pennsylvania (B.A., 1984); Santa Monica College; University of Southern California (J.D., 1988). *Member:* Los Angeles County and American Bar Associations; State Bar of California. **PRACTICE AREAS:** Securities; Business Litigation; Real Estate; Appellate Practice.

**TRENTON J. HILL,** born Salem, Oregon, February 26, 1963; admitted to bar, 1989, California, U.S. District Court, Central, Southern, Northern and Eastern Districts of California and U.S. Court of Appeals, Ninth Circuit. *Education:* Pomona College (B.A., 1985); University of Southern California (J.D., 1989). Arbitrator, National Futures Association. *Member:* Los Angeles County and American Bar Associations; State Bar of California. **PRACTICE AREAS:** Business; Real Estate.

### OF COUNSEL

**RICHARD F. MILLER,** born Los Angeles, California, May 9, 1937; admitted to bar, 1964, California; 1969, U.S. Supreme Court. *Education:* Stanford University (A.B., with distinction, 1959; LL.B., 1963). Phi Delta Phi; Phi Beta Kappa. *Member:* Pasadena, Los Angeles County (Member, Trust and Probate Law Section) and American (Member, Real Property, Probate and Trust Law Section) Bar Associations; The State Bar of California (Member, Probate and Estate Planning Section). (Also Practices Individually in Pasadena; Certified Specialist, Estate Planning, Trust and Probate Law, The State Bar of California Board of Legal Specialization). **PRACTICE AREAS:** Probate Law; Estate Planning.

### ASSOCIATES

**DIANE A. IRVIN,** born Los Angeles, California, November 9, 1964; admitted to bar, 1990, California and U.S. District Court, Central District of California; 1991, District of Columbia. *Education:* University of California at Los Angeles (B.A., 1987); Pepperdine University (J.D., 1990). Recipient, American Jurisprudence Award in Securities Regulation. *Member:* Los Angeles County and American Bar Associations; State Bar of California.

**MICHAEL A. AMIRI,** born Santa Monica, California, September 1, 1967; admitted to bar, 1994, California; 1995, U.S. District Court, Central and Northern Districts of California; 1995, U.S. Court of Appeals, Ninth Circuit. *Education:* University of California-San Diego (B.A., 1990); University of California-San Francisco, Hastings College of the Law (J.D., 1994). *Member:* Los Angeles County (Member, Litigation Section) and American Bar Associations; State Bar of California; The Association of Business Trial Lawyers.

**ALAN S. PETLAK,** born Los Angeles, California, September 14, 1970; admitted to bar, 1995, California; U.S. District Court, Central and Northern Districts of California. *Education:* University of California, San Diego (B.S., political science, 1992); University of Southern California (J.D., 1995). *Member:* Los Angeles County (Member, Litigation Section) and American Bar Associations; State Bar of California.

**BRIAN G. ARNOLD,** born Arcadia, California, February 2, 1970; admitted to bar, 1996, California. *Education:* Pomona College (B.A., 1990); Claremont Graduate School (M.A., 1992); Loyola Law School (J.D., 1996). Loyola of Los Angeles, Law Review, Staff Member, 1994-1995, Technical Editor, 1995-1996. *Member:* Los Angeles County and American Bar Associations; State Bar of California. **PRACTICE AREAS:** Business Law; Securities Litigation.

REPRESENTATIVE CLIENTS: Dean Witter Reynolds Inc.; Merrill Lynch, Pierce, Fenner & Smith, Inc.; Titan/Value Equities Group, Inc.; Black & Decker, Inc.; Sutro & Co., Inc.; Price Pfister, Inc.; PaineWebber Incorporated; Emhart Glass Machinery (U.S.) Inc.; Securities Investors Protection Corporation; Kennedy, Cabot & Co., Inc.; Great Western Bank; Great Western Financial Securities; Charles Schwab & Co., Inc.; Kwikset Corporation; Spelman & Co., Inc.; Sentra Securities Corp.; The Seeley Company; The California Association of Independent Broker Dealers, Inc.
REFERENCE: Sanwa Bank, California.

# JONES, DAY, REAVIS & POGUE

**555 WEST FIFTH STREET**
**SUITE 4600**
**LOS ANGELES, CALIFORNIA 90013-1025**
Telephone: 213-489-3939
Telex: 181439 UD
Telecopier: 213-243-2539

*In Irvine, California:* 2603 Main Street, Suite 900. Telephone: 714-851-3939. Telex: 194911 Lawyers LSA. Telecopier: 714-553-7539.

*In Atlanta, Georgia:* 3500 One Peachtree Center, 303 Peachtree Street, N.E. Telephone: 404-521-3939. Cable Address: "Attorneys Atlanta". Telex: 54-2711. Telecopier: 404-581-8330.

*In Brussels, Belgium:* Avenue Louise 480, 7th Floor, B-1050 Brussels. Telephone: 32-2-645-14-11. Telecopier: 32-2-645-14-45.

*In Chicago, Illinois:* 77 West Wacker. Telephone: 312-782-3939. Telecopier: 312-782-8585.

*In Cleveland, Ohio:* North Point, 901 Lakeside Avenue. Telephone: 216-586-3939. Cable Address: "Attorneys Cleveland." Telex: 980389. Telecopier: 216-579-0212.

*In Columbus, Ohio:* 1900 Huntington Center. Telephone: 614-469-3939. Cable Address: "Attorneys Columbus." Telecopier: 614-461-4198.

*In Dallas, Texas:* 2300 Trammell Crow Center, 2001 Ross Avenue. Telephone: 214-220-3939. Cable Address: "Attorneys Dallas." Telex: 730852. Telecopier: 214-969-5100.

*In Frankfurt, Germany:* Triton Haus, Bockenheimer Landstrasse 42, 60323 Frankfurt am Main. Telephone: 49-69-9726-3939. Telecopier: 49-69-9726-3993.

*In Geneva, Switzerland:* 20, rue de Candolle. Telephone: 41-22-320-2339. Telecopier: 41-22-320-1232.

*In Hong Kong:* 29th Floor, Entertainment Building, 30 Queen's Road Central. Telephone: 852-2526-6895. Telecopier: 852-2868-5871.

*In London England:* Bucklersbury House, 3 Queen Victoria Street. Telephone: 44-171-236-3939. Telecopier: 44-171-236-1113.

*In New Delhi, India:* Pathak & Associates, 13th Floor, Dr. Gopal Das Bhaven, 28 Barakhamba Road. Telephone: 91-11-373-8793. Telecopier: 91-11-335-3761.

*In New York, New York:* 599 Lexington Avenue. Telephone: 212-326-3939. Cable Address: "JONESDAY NEWYORK." Telex: 237013 JDRP UR. Telecopier: 212-755-7306.

*In Paris, France:* 62, rue du Faubourg Saint-Honore. Telephone: 33-1-44-71-3939. Telex: 290156 Surgoe. Telecopier: 33-1-49-24-0471.

*In Pittsburgh, Pennsylvania:* 500 Grant Street, 31st Floor. Telephone: 412-391-3939. Cable Address: "Attorneys Pittsburgh". Telecopier: 412-394-7959.

*In Riyadh, Saudi Arabia:* The International Law Firm, Sulaymaniyah Center, Tahlia Street, P.O. Box 22166. Telephone: (966-1) 462-8866. Telecopier: (966-1) 462-9001.

*In Taipei, Taiwan:* 8th Floor, 2 Tun Hwa South Road, Section 2. Telephone: (886-2) 704-6808. Telecopier: (886-2) 704-6791.

*In Tokyo, Japan:* Toranomon MT Building, 4th Floor, 10-3, Toranomon 3-Chome, Minato-ku, Tokyo 105, Japan. Telephone: 81-3-3433-3939. Telecopier: 81-3-5401-2725.

*In Washington, D.C.:* Metropolitan Square, 1450 G Street, N.W. Telephone: 202-879-3939. Cable Address: "Attorneys Washington." Telex: 89-2410 ATTORNEYS WASH. Telecopier: 202-737-2832.

*General Practice.*

## MEMBERS OF FIRM IN LOS ANGELES

**BERTRAM R. ZWEIG,** born Pittsburgh, Pennsylvania, June 3, 1934; admitted to bar, 1962, Ohio; 1973, California. *Education:* University of Pennsylvania (A.B., 1956); Columbia University (LL.B., 1962). *Email:* brzweig@jonesday.com

**JAMES F. CHILDS, JR.,** born Buffalo, New York, January 6, 1940; admitted to bar, 1965, California. *Education:* University of Southern California (B.S., 1961); Harvard University (J.D., 1964). Lecturer on Tax Law, University of Southern California, 1969-1986. Chairperson, Section of Taxation, The State Bar of California, 1978-1979. (Certified Specialist, Taxation Law, The State Bar of California Board of Legal Specialization). *Email:* jchilds@jonesday.com

**RONALD S. RIZZO,** born Kenosha, Wisconsin, July 15, 1941; admitted to bar, 1965, Wisconsin; 1967, California. *Education:* St. Norbert College (B.S., 1963); Georgetown University (LL.B., 1965; LL.M., 1966). Co-Chair, Employee Benefits Committee, Section of Taxation, The State Bar of California, 1979-1981. Chair, Employee Benefits Committee, Tax Section, American Bar Association, 1988-1989. Fellow, American College of Tax Counsel. (Also at Chicago, Illinois Office). *Email:* rsrizzo@jonesday.com

**WILLIAM G. WILSON,** born Port Arthur, Texas, July 2, 1941; admitted to bar, 1965 Texas; 1974, California. *Education:* University of Texas (B.B.A., 1963; LL.B., 1965). *Email:* wgwilson@jonesday.com

**ROSS E. STROMBERG,** born Arcata, California, May 5, 1940; admitted to bar, 1966, California. *Education:* Humboldt State University (A.B., 1962); University of California, Berkeley (Boalt Hall) (J.D., 1965). *Email:* restromberg@jonesday.com

**GERALD W. PALMER,** born Cincinnati, Ohio, September 13, 1940; admitted to bar, 1968, Ohio; 1974, California. *Education:* The Ohio State University (B.A., 1962); University of Virginia (LL.B., 1968). Order of the Coif. *Email:* gpalmer@jonesday.com

**VICTOR G. SAVIKAS,** born Pittsburgh, Pennsylvania, March 13, 1941; admitted to bar, 1968, Illinois; 1974, District of Columbia; 1990, California. *Education:* De Paul University (B.A., 1967; J.D., 1968). Instructor in Law, De Paul University, 1976-1978. Member, Special Commission on the Administration of Justice in Cook County, Illinois, 1985. Fellow, American College of Trial Lawyers. *Email:* vgsavikas@jonesday.com

**GERRY D. OSTERLAND,** born Freiburg, Germany, January 10, 1944; admitted to bar, 1969, Missouri; 1971, Illinois; 1981, Texas (Not admitted in California). *Education:* Southern Illinois University (B.A., 1968); University of Missouri (J.D., 1969). *Email:* gdosterland@jonesday.com

**ELWOOD LUI,** born Los Angeles, California, February 4, 1941; admitted to bar, 1970, California; 1990, District of Columbia. *Education:* University of California, Los Angeles (B.S., 1962; M.B.A., 1964; J.D., 1969). Deputy Attorney General, State of California, 1969-1971. Judge, Municipal Court, Los Angeles, Judicial District, 1975-1979. Superior Court, County of Los Angeles, 1980-1981. Associate Justice, California Court of Appeals, Second Appellate District, 1981-1987. President, California Judges Association, 1986-1987. Member, of the Judicial Council of California, 1983-1987. Adjunct Professor of Law, University of Southern California, 1977-1987, Loyola Law School, Los Angeles, 1984. Certified Public Accountant, California, 1964. *Email:* elui@jonesday.com

**ROBERT DEAN AVERY,** born Youngstown, Ohio, April 23, 1944; admitted to bar, 1971, Ohio; 1973, California. *Education:* Northwestern University (B.A., 1966); Columbia University (J.D., 1969). Law Clerk to Judge Anderson, U.S. Court of Appeals, Second Circuit, 1969-1970. *Email:* rdavery@jonesday.com

**DONALD D. GRALNEK,** born Chicago, Illinois, July 24, 1945; admitted to bar, 1971, California. *Education:* Stanford University (B.A., 1967); University of California, Berkeley (M.A., 1971); University of California, Berkeley (Boalt Hall) (J.D., 1970). Committee Consultant, California State Assembly, California Legislature, 1972-1974. *Email:* ddgralnek@jonesday.com

**JAMES L. BAUMOEL,** born Cleveland, Ohio, March 18, 1946; admitted to bar, 1973, Ohio; 1981, Texas; 1996, California. *Education:* Miami University (B.S., 1968); University of Michigan (J.D., 1973). *Email:* jlbaumoel@jonesday.com

**FREDERICK L. MCKNIGHT,** born Kansas City, Missouri, November 28, 1947; admitted to bar, 1973, California; 1974, New York. *Education:* Princeton University (A.B., 1969); University of California, Berkeley (Boalt Hall) (J.D., 1972). Fellow, American College of Trial Lawyers. *Email:* fmcknight@jonesday.com

**DEAN B. ALLISON,** born New York, New York, October 19, 1948; admitted to bar, 1974, New York; 1978, California. *Education:* Brown University (B.A., 1970); New York University (J.D., 1973). Order of the Coif. Assistant U.S. Attorney, Chief, Special Prosecutions Unit, Central District of California, 1976-1982. *Email:* dallison@jonesday.com

**NORMAN A. PEDERSEN,** born Modesto, California, December 29, 1946; admitted to bar, 1975, California; 1976, District of Columbia. *Education:* University of California, Berkeley (B.A., 1970; M.A., 1972); University of California, Los Angeles (LL.B., 1975). Trial Attorney, Federal Power Commission, 1975-1979. Legal Assistant to Commissioner, Federal Energy Regulatory Commission, 1977-1979. Chair, Natural Gas Marketing and Transportation Committee, Section on Natural Resources, Energy and Environmental Law, American Bar Association, 1990-1991. *Email:* napedersen@jonesday.com

*(This Listing Continued)*

**DAVID S. BOYCE,** born Medina, New York, November 6, 1949; admitted to bar, 1978, District of Columbia and Florida; 1979, California. *Education:* Cornell University (A.B., 1971); University of Utah (M.B.A., 1973); University of Florida (J.D., 1977); Georgetown University (LL.M., 1979). Order of the Coif. Attorney Advisor to Judge Dawson, Jr., U.S. Tax Court, 1977 -1979. Adjunct Professor of Law, University of San Diego, 1980-1984. (Certified Specialist, Taxation Law, The State Bar of California Board of Legal Specialization). **Email:** dsboyce@jonesday.com

**ANDREW J. DEMETRIOU,** born Los Angeles, California, November 7, 1954; admitted to bar, 1979, California. *Education:* University of California, Los Angeles (A.B., 1976); University of California, Berkeley (Boalt Hall) (J.D., 1979). Phi Beta Kappa; Order of the Coif. **Email:** ajdemetriou@jonesday.com

**THOMAS R. MUELLER,** born Flagstaff, Arizona, March 19, 1956; admitted to bar, 1979, Ohio; 1983, Arizona; 1984, California. *Education:* Case Western Reserve University (B.A., 1976; J.D., 1979). Phi Beta Kappa; Order of the Coif. **Email:** trmueller@jonesday.com

**THOMAS M. MCMAHON,** born Boston, Massachusetts, June 21, 1957; admitted to bar, 1982, California. *Education:* Boston College (B.A., 1979); University of California, Los Angeles (J.D., 1982). **Email:** tmmcmahon@jonesday.com

**ERIC V. ROWEN,** born Los Angeles, California, March 24, 1957; admitted to bar, 1982, California. *Education:* University of California, Irvine (B.A., 1979); Loyola Law School, Los Angeles (J.D., 1982). **Email:** evrowen@jonesday.com

**LOUIS L. TOUTON,** born Fresno, California, October 27, 1955; admitted to bar, 1982, Arizona, California and Washington; 1992, Texas; registered to practice before U.S. Patent and Trademark Office. *Education:* Massachusetts Institute of Technology (S.B.E.E., 1977; S.B.M.E., 1977); Columbia University (J.D., 1980). Law Clerk to Judge Farris, U. S. Court of Appeals, Ninth Circuit, 1980-1981. **Email:** lltouton@jonesday.com

**DANIEL J. MCLOON,** born Warrenton, Virginia, June 21, 1956; admitted to bar, 1983, California. *Education:* Claremont McKenna College (B.A., 1978); University of California, Los Angeles (J.D., 1983). Order of the Coif. Certified Public Accountant, California, 1980. **Email:** djmcloon@jonesday.com

**SCOTT D. BERTZYK,** born Berlin, Wisconsin, August 8, 1959; admitted to bar, 1984, California. *Education:* University of Wisconsin (B.B.A., 1981); University of Texas (J.D., 1984). Order of the Coif. **Email:** sdbertzyk@jonesday.com

**SARAH HECK GRIFFIN,** born Los Angeles, California, November 29, 1954; admitted to bar, 1984, Colorado; 1987, California. *Education:* University of Southern California (B.A., 1976); University of Colorado (J.D., 1984). Phi Beta Kappa; Order of the Coif. Law Clerk: to Justice Neighbors, Colorado Supreme Court, 1984-1985; to Judge Moore, U.S. Court of Appeals, Tenth Circuit, 1985-1986. **Email:** sgriffin@jonesday.com

**JEFFREY A. LEVEE,** born Chicago, Illinois, December 3, 1959; admitted to bar, 1984, Illinois; 1986, California. *Education:* Duke University (B.A., 1981); Northwestern University (J.D., 1984). **Email:** jlevee@jonesday.com

**LESTER O. BROWN,** born New York, New York, February 29, 1952; admitted to bar, 1985, Maryland; 1988, Connecticut; 1991, New York; 1992, California. *Education:* Cornell University (B.A., 1974); Georgetown University (J.D., 1983). **Email:** lobrown@jonesday.com

**KEVIN G. MCBRIDE,** born Chicago, Illinois, September 1, 1954; admitted to bar, 1985, Illinois; registered to practice before U.S. Patent and Trademark Office (Not admitted in California). *Education:* University of Notre Dame (B.S., 1976); University of California, Davis (M.S., 1978); Northwestern University (J.D., 1985). Tau Beta Pi. **Email:** kgmcbride@jonesday.com

**DAVID J. DIMEGLIO,** born San Pedro, California, March 19, 1962; admitted to bar, 1987, California. *Education:* University of California, Los Angeles (B.A., 1984); Stanford University (J.D., 1987). **Email:** djdimeglio@jonesday.com

**DANIEL D. MCMILLAN,** born Los Angeles, California, January 22, 1961; admitted to bar, 1988, California. *Education:* Loyola Marymount University (B.S., 1983); Loyola Law School, Los Angeles (J.D., 1987). Law Clerk to Chief Judge Clark, Federal Court of Appeals, Fifth Circuit, 1987-1988. **Email:** ddmcmillan@jonesday.com

*(This Listing Continued)*

## OF COUNSEL

**RICHARD H. KOPPES,** born Norfolk, Virginia, August 20, 1946; admitted to bar, 1971, California. *Education:* Loyola Marymount University (B.A., 1968); University of California, Los Angeles (J.D., 1971). General Counsel, 1986-1996 and Deputy Executive Officer, 1994-1996, California Public Employees Retirement System. Lecturer, Stanford University, 1996—. **Email:** rkoppes@jonesday.com

**DAVID C. ZUCKER,** born St. Louis, Missouri, July 29, 1946; admitted to bar, 1971, Missouri; 1989, California. *Education:* University of Missouri (B.A., 1968; J.D., 1971). Prosecutor, 1971-1973; Trial Attorney and Team Chief, Office of Chief Trial Attorney, 1974-1977, 1982-1986; Assistant Chief Counsel, Computer Systems Command, 1977; International Logistics Counsel, Contract Law Division and Deputy Chief, Administrative Law Division, Headquarters, Europe, 1978-1981; Litigation Attorney, Office of the Judge Advocate General, 1982; Professor of Government Contract Law and Chairman, Contract Law Department, The Judge Advocate General's School, 1986-1988; U.S. Army. **Email:** davidczucker@jonesday.com

**RICHARD J. FRICK,** born Charleston, West Virginia, September 5, 1947; admitted to bar, 1972, California. *Education:* University of California, Santa Barbara (B.A., 1968); University of Chicago (J.D., 1971). Phi Beta Kappa. **Email:** rfrick@jonesday.com

**PATRICIA A. VAN DYKE,** born Perth Amboy, New Jersey, June 17, 1958; admitted to bar, 1983, Missouri; 1984, Illinois; 1986, District of Columbia; 1991, New York; 1992, California. *Education:* Pennsylvania State University (B.S., 1979); Washington University (J.D., 1983). **Email:** pavandyke@jonesday.com

## SENIOR ATTORNEY

**DOUGLAS F. LANDRUM,** born Atlanta, Georgia, May 27, 1949; admitted to bar, 1974, California. *Education:* University of Florida (B.S.B.A., 1971); University of California, Hastings College of the Law (J.D., 1974); New York University (LL.M., 1979). Lecturer, The School of Taxation, Golden Gate University, 1986-1988. **Email:** dlandrum@jonesday.com

**LYNN LEVERSEN KAMBE,** born Elmhurst, Illinois, January 30, 1946; admitted to bar, 1981, California. *Education:* University of Santa Clara (B.A., 1966); Loyola Law School, Los Angeles (J.D., 1981); New York University (LL.M., 1982). **Email:** lkambe@jonesday.com

## ASSOCIATES

**MARSHA E. DURKO,** born Oxnard, California, January 31, 1955; admitted to bar, 1980, California. *Education:* University of California, Riverside (B.S., 1977); University of California, Los Angeles (J.D., 1980). Phi Beta Kappa. Lecturer in Law, University of California, Los Angeles, 1981-1982. **Email:** mdurko@jonesday.com

**PETER G. MCALLEN,** born Evanston, Illinois, November 24, 1950; admitted to bar, 1982, California; 1983, Illinois. *Education:* Princeton University (A.B., 1972); University of California, Los Angeles (C .Phil., 1977; J.D., 1981). Order of the Coif. Law Clerk to Judge Ferguson, U.S. Court of Appeals, Ninth Circuit, 1981-1982. Assistant Professor of Law, Southern Illinois University, 1984-1989. Visiting Associate Professor of Law, Southwestern University School of Law, 1988-1989. **Email:** pmcallen@jonesday.com

**THOMAS BOTZ,** born Bonn, Germany, November 2, 1956; admitted to bar, 1983, British Columbia and California. *Education:* University of British Columbia (B.Com., 1980; LL.B., 1981). **Email:** tbotz@jonesday.com

**MARY J. GARNETT,** born Orange, California, August 11, 1962; admitted to bar, 1987, California. *Education:* Loyola Marymount University (B.A., 1984); University of California, Hastings College of the Law (J.D., 1987). **Email:** mgarnett@jonesday.com

**CRAIG S. GATARZ,** born New Brunswick, New Jersey, January 20, 1962; admitted to bar, 1987, New Jersey; 1988, New York (Not admitted in California). *Education:* Boston College (B.A., 1984); University of Virginia (J.D., 1987). Phi Beta Kappa. **Email:** csgatarz@jonesday.com

**ROBERT M. GILCHREST,** born North Tarrytown, New York, October 3, 1961; admitted to bar, 1987, California. *Education:* Hampshire College (B.A., 1983); Northwestern University (J.D., 1986). **Email:** rmgilchrest@jonesday.com

**KEVIN A. DORSE,** born Miami, Florida, June 14, 1961; admitted to bar, 1988, Florida; 1990, California. *Education:* Brown University (A.B., 1983); University of Miami (J.D., 1987). Phi Beta Kappa; Order of the Coif. Law Clerk: to Judge Aronovitz, U.S. District Court, Southern District of

*(This Listing Continued)*

**JONES, DAY, REAVIS & POGUE, Los Angeles—***Continued*

Florida, 1987-1988; to Judge Hall, U.S. Court of Appeals, Ninth Circuit, 1988-1989. **Email:** kdorse@jonesday.com

**CATHERINE A. EHRGOTT,** born Torrance, California, December 22, 1962; admitted to bar, 1988, California. *Education:* University of Southern California (B.S., 1984); Loyola Law School, Los Angeles (J.D., 1988). **Email:** cehrgott@jonesday.com

**KATHERINE M. ELWOOD,** born Peoria, Illinois, July 19, 1962; admitted to bar, 1988, California; 1994, Georgia. *Education:* Stanford University (A.B., 1985; M.A., 1985); Harvard University (J.D., 1988). Phi Beta Kappa. **Email:** kelwood@jonesday.com

**KEVIN R. LUSSIER,** born Whittier, California, February 29, 1964; admitted to bar, 1989, California. *Education:* California State University, Fullerton (B.A., 1986); University of California, Davis (J.D., 1989). **Email:** krlussier@jonesday.com

**JEFFREY A. MILLER,** born Philadelphia, Pennsylvania, September 19, 1963; admitted to bar, 1989, California; 1990, New York. *Education:* Temple University (B.A., 1986); New York University (J.D., 1989). **Email:** jamiller@jonesday.com

**KENNETH A. REMSON,** born New York, New York, June 1, 1956; admitted to bar, 1989, Hawaii; 1991, California. *Education:* Stanford University (A.B., 1979); Columbia University (M.S., 1982); Duke University (J.D., 1989). Law Clerk to Judge Kleinfeld, U.S. District Court, District of Alaska, 1989-1990. Deputy Attorney General, Department of the Attorney General, State of Hawaii, 1995-1996. **Email:** karemson@jonesday.com

**BRUCE J. SHIH,** born Cebu City, Philippines, September 23, 1962; admitted to bar, 1989, California. *Education:* Washington University (A.B., 1983); University of California, Los Angeles (M.P.H., 1985; M.B.A., 1989; J.D., 1989). **Email:** bshih@jonesday.com

**PHILIP E. COOK,** born Emporia, Kansas, October 12, 1955; admitted to bar, 1990, California. *Education:* Pacific Christian College (B.A., 1979); University of California, Los Angeles (J.D., 1990). Law Clerk to Judge Marshall, U.S. District Court, Central District of California, 1991-1992. Adjunct Professor of Law, Pepperdine University, 1994-1996. **Email:** pcook@jonesday.com

**JANE M. NOWOTNY,** born Louisville, Kentucky, May 11, 1960; admitted to bar, 1990, California. *Education:* University of California, Los Angeles (B.A., 1982); University of Tulsa (J.D., 1990). **Email:** jnowotny@jonesday.com

**RICKY L. SHACKELFORD,** born Wichita, Kansas, October 24, 1963; admitted to bar, 1990, California. *Education:* Harvard University (B.A., 1986); Arizona State University (J.D., 1990). **Email:** rlshackelford@jonesday.com

**VALERIE A. BROWN,** born New York, New York, January 24, 1967; admitted to bar, 1991, California. *Education:* University of California, Berkeley (B.A., 1988); Loyola Law School, Los Angeles (J.D., 1991). Order of the Coif. **Email:** vabrown@jonesday.com

**MARY K. HARTIGAN,** born Chicago, Illinois, June 14, 1962; admitted to bar, 1991, California; 1992, Illinois. *Education:* Georgetown University (B.S., 1984); University of Notre Dame (J.D., 1991). **Email:** mhartigan@jonesday.com

**MARK M. KASSABIAN,** born Pasadena, California, January 31, 1965; admitted to bar, 1991, California. *Education:* Dartmouth College (A.B., 1987); University of Southern California (M.A., 1988); University of California, Berkeley (Boalt Hall) (J.D., 1991). **Email:** mmkassabian@jonesday.com

**STANLEY C. MORRIS,** born Washington, D.C., December 7, 1963; admitted to bar, 1991, New York; 1996, California. *Education:* University of North Carolina at Chapel Hill (B.S., 1986); Washington & Lee University (J.D., 1990). Staff Attorney, U.S. Securities and Exchange Commission, 1992-1996. **Email:** smorris@jonesday.com

**MARIA K. NELSON,** born Minneapolis, Minnesota, November 26, 1959; admitted to bar, 1991, California. *Education:* Wesleyan University (B.A., 1981); University of San Diego (J.D., 1991). **Email:** mknelson@jonesday.com

**GARY W. NUGENT,** born Shreveport, Louisiana, June 20, 1966; admitted to bar, 1991, California. *Education:* Southern Methodist University (B.B.A., 1988); Northwestern University (J.D., 1991). **Email:** gnugent@jonesday.com

**WENDY L. THOMAS,** born Jeannette, Pennsylvania, March 28, 1963; admitted to bar, 1991, California; 1993, District of Columbia. *Education:* College of William & Mary (B.A., 1985; J.D., 1991). Law Clerk to Chief Judge Loren A. Smith, U.S. Claims Court, 1991-1992. **Email:** wlthomas@jonesday.com

**EUGENE Y. T. WON,** born Honolulu, Hawaii, August 19, 1944; admitted to bar, 1991, California. *Education:* University of Michigan (B.A., 1966; M.A., 1973; Ph.D., 1978); University of California, Los Angeles (J.D., 1991). Phi Beta Kappa. **Email:** ewon@jonesday.com

**B. MARIA DENNIS,** born Manchester, Connecticut, February 8, 1966; admitted to bar, 1992, California. *Education:* Yale University (B.A., 1988); Georgetown University (J.D., 1991). **Email:** mdennis@jonesday.com

**MIWON YI,** born Seoul, South Korea, September 2, 1965; admitted to bar, 1992, California; 1994, District of Columbia. *Education:* University of Virginia (B.A., 1988; J.D., 1991). Phi Beta Kappa. **Email:** myi@jonesday.com

**SHARON L. FARIS,** born Berkeley, California, September 13, 1962; admitted to bar, 1993, California. *Education:* University of California, Berkeley (B.A., 1984); Santa Monica College (A.A., 1988); Loyola Law School, Los Angeles (J.D., 1993). Order of the Coif. **Email:** sfaris@jonesday.com

**JEFFREY S. KOENIG,** born Chicago, Illinois, October 19, 1955; admitted to bar, 1993, California. *Education:* University of California, Los Angeles (B.A., 1978); Talbot Theological Seminary (Master of Divinity, 1984); Biola University (Master of Theology, 1984); University of Southern California (J.D., 1993). Order of the Coif. **Email:** jskoenig@jonesday.com

**SUSANNE L. MELINE,** born Newport Beach, California, August 15, 1967; admitted to bar, 1993, California. *Education:* University of California, Los Angeles (B.A., 1989); University of California, Hastings College of the Law (J.D., 1993). Law Clerk: to Judge Greenwald, U.S. Bankruptcy Court, Central District of California, 1993-1994; to Judge Tevrizian, U.S. District Court, Central District of California, 1994-1995. **Email:** smeline@jonesday.com

**ELIZABETH G. MORENO,** born Los Angeles, California, May 7, 1965; admitted to bar, 1993, California. *Education:* University of California, Berkeley (A.B., 1988); Harvard University (J.D., 1993). **Email:** emoreno@jonesday.com

**SOPHIA FRIEDMAN ROSLIN,** born New York, New York, April 16, 1967; admitted to bar, 1993, California. *Education:* University of Pennsylvania (B.A., 1989); Northwestern University (J.D., 1993). **Email:** sroslin@jonesday.com

**ALONZO B. WICKERS, IV,** born Sacramento, California, January 7, 1968; admitted to bar, 1993, California. *Education:* Harvard University (A.B., 1989); University of California, Berkeley (Boalt Hall) (J.D., 1993). **Email:** awickers@jonesday.com

**JINSHU ZHANG,** born Chengdu, China, July 11, 1959; admitted to bar, 1993, California. *Education:* Beijing University (B.A., 1982); Chinese Academy of Social Sciences (1984-1986); University of Hawaii (M.A., 1989); University of California, Los Angeles (M.A., 1990); University of California, Berkeley (Boalt Hall) (J.D., 1993). **Email:** jzhang@jonesday.com

**DAVID B. FISCHER,** born Brooklyn, New York, October 26, 1953; admitted to bar, 1994, California. *Education:* Columbia University (B.A., 1976); Yeshiva University (M.A., 1983); University of California, Los Angeles (J.D., 1993). Law Clerk to Judge Boggs, U.S. Court of Appeals, Sixth Circuit, 1993-1994. **Email:** dbfischer@jonesday.com

**ERIN E. NOLAN,** born Arlington Heights, Illinois, April 20, 1969; admitted to bar, 1994, California. *Education:* Villanova University (B.A., 1991); McGeorge School of Law (J.D., 1994). **Email:** enolan@jonesday.com

**KIRSTIN D. POIRIER-WHITLEY,** born New Haven, Connecticut, October 20, 1968; admitted to bar, 1994, California. *Education:* University of California, Los Angeles (B.A., 1991; J.D., 1994). Phi Beta Kappa; Order of the Coif. **Email:** kpoirierwhitley@jonesday.com

**KAREN R. THORLAND,** born Oakland, California, February 20, 1968; admitted to bar, 1994, California. *Education:* University of California, Santa Barbara (B.A., 1990); University of California, Los Angeles (J.D., 1994). **Email:** karenrthorland@jonesday.com

**JACQUELINE M. AGUILERA,** born Ontario, Canada, October 12, 1966; admitted to bar, 1995, New York; 1996, California. *Education:* Uni-

*(This Listing Continued)*

versity of California, Los Angeles (B.S., 1988); Fordham University (J.D., 1994). Order of the Coif. *Email:* jmaguilera@jonesday.com

**KATHRYN BLAGDEN,** born Oakland, California, March 25, 1971; admitted to bar, 1995, California. *Education:* Stanford University (A.B., 1992); University of California, Davis (J.D., 1995). Order of the Coif. *Email:* kblagden@jonesday.com

**AMY R. BROWNSTEIN,** born Philadelphia, Pennsylvania, October 21, 1970; admitted to bar, 1995, California. *Education:* Tufts University (B.A., 1992); Loyola Law School, Los Angeles (J.D., 1995). Order of the Coif. *Email:* abrownstein@jonesday.com

**KATARZYNA A. BUCHEN,** born Lodz, Poland, November 2, 1966; admitted to bar, 1995, New York (Not admitted in California). *Education:* Mount Holyoke College (B.A., 1989); Columbia University (J.D., 1994). *Email:* kbuchen@jonesday.com

**MARC D. FIELD,** born Willingboro, New Jersey, December 31, 1967; admitted to bar, 1995, California. *Education:* Tufts University (B.A., 1990); University of Virginia (J.D., 1995). Phi Beta Kappa. *Email:* mfield@jonesday.com

**JOCELYN M. GUTIÉRREZ,** born Ravenna, Ohio, July 29, 1969; admitted to bar, 1995, California. *Education:* Harvard University (A.B., 1992); University of California, Berkeley (Boalt Hall) (J.D., 1995). *Email:* jgutierr@jonesday.com

**C. MEGAN LAURANCE,** born Lawrence, Kansas, December 14, 1969; admitted to bar, 1995, California. *Education:* University of Southern California (B.A., 1992); Georgetown University (J.D., 1995). *Email:* mlaurance@jonesday.com

**VICK K. MANSOURIAN,** born Beirut, Lebanon, June 20, 1970; admitted to bar, 1995, California. *Education:* California State University, Northridge (B.S., 1992); Loyola Law School, Los Angeles (J.D., 1995). *Email:* vkmansourian@jonesday.com

**ASHLEY S.H. SIM,** born Seoul, Korea, April 5, 1970; admitted to bar, 1995, California. *Education:* Stanford University (A.B., 1992); Harvard University (J.D., 1995). Phi Beta Kappa. *Email:* asim@jonesday.com

**SUSANNE E. STAMEY,** born Los Alamos, New Mexico, August 1, 1966; admitted to bar, 1995, California. *Education:* Claremont McKenna College (B.A., 1988); University of Southern California (M.A., 1990); Loyola Law School, Los Angeles (J.D., 1995). Order of the Coif. *Email:* sstamey@jonesday.com

**ALLAN Z. LITOVSKY,** born Kiev, Ukraine, August 23, 1958; admitted to bar, 1996, California; registered to practice before U.S. Patent and Trademark Office. *Education:* Moscow State University (B.S., 1980; Ph.D., 1987); Arizona State University (J.D., 1995). *Email:* alitovsky@jonesday.com

**ERIN L. BURKE,** born Pittsburgh, Pennsylvania, October 12, 1970; (admission pending). *Education:* California Polytechnic State University (B.S., 1993); University of California, Davis (J.D., 1996). *Email:* eburke@jonesday.com

**EUGENIA L. CASTRUCCIO,** born Burbank, California, October 24, 1970; admitted to bar, 1996, California. *Education:* College of the Holy Cross (B.A., 1992); University of Chicago (J.D., 1996). Phi Beta Kappa. *Email:* gcastruc@jonesday.com

**JACQUELINE A. BRUCE CHINERY,** born Accra, Ghana, November 9, 1967; (admission pending). *Education:* University of Pennsylvania (B.A., 1989); Georgetown University (J.D., 1996). *Email:* jbrucekonuah@jonesday.com

**VINCE L. FARHAT,** born Santa Monica, California, June 15, 1966; admitted to bar, 1996, California. *Education:* American University (B.A., 1987); Pepperdine University (M.B.A., 1991); Loyola Law School, Los Angeles (J.D., 1996). *Email:* vfarhat@jonesday.com

**C. STEVE HAGEMEISTER,** born Fort Bragg, North Carolina, September 26, 1968; admitted to bar, 1996, California. *Education:* California State University, Fullerton (B.A., 1993); University of San Diego (M.B.A., J.D. 1996). *Email:* shagemei@jonesday.com

**GREGORY S.G. KLATT,** born Riverside, California, June 30, 1967; admitted to bar, 1996, California. *Education:* University of San Francisco (B.A., 1989); University of California, Berkeley (Boalt Hall) (J.D., 1996). *Email:* gklatt@jonesday.com

*(This Listing Continued)*

**ANN-MARIE NICCOLAI,** born Bainbridge, Maryland, June 24, 1967; (admission pending). *Education:* Stanford University (B.A., 1989); University of Notre Dame (J.D., 1996). *Email:* amniccolai@jonesday.com

**TRISTAN B.L. SIEGEL,** born Buffalo, New York, April 4, 1966; admitted to bar, 1996, California. *Education:* Niagara University (B.A., 1987); Defense Intelligence College (M.S.S.I., 1992); University of Virginia (J.D., 1996). *Email:* tsiegel@jonesday.com

---

# JONES, KAUFMAN & ACKERMAN LLP

Established in 1987
**10960 WILSHIRE BOULEVARD, SUITE 1225**
**LOS ANGELES, CALIFORNIA 90024**
Telephone: 310-477-8575
Fax: 310-477-8768

Real Estate, Corporation, Finance, Secured Creditor Litigation, Estate Planning and Federal and State Taxation.

FIRM PROFILE: *Jones Kaufman & Ackerman provides a full range of business real estate and tax law services to financial institutions, business and individual clients; The firm has substantial experience in all aspects of real estate transactions and emphasizes financing, purchases and sales, leasing, tax deferred exchanges, land subdivision, commercial and residential development and environmental issues. Our practice also encompasses the formation, operation, restructuring, dissolution, acquisition and disposition of all manner of business entities.*

*The firm's representation of a broad range of business real estate clientele enables it to fully identify and address all issues involved in any business or real property transaction. At the same time, its narrow concentration on transactional and related litigation support matters enables the firm to maintain the highest quality and sophistication in connection with its services and workproduct. Accordingly, it is our goal to provide each client with expert legal services comparable in quality and scope to those provided by business real estate departments within the largest law firms but at a cost and on a personal relationship basis available only in a small firm environment.*

**DONALD H. JONES,** born Los Angeles, California, March 11, 1947; admitted to bar, 1972, California. *Education:* University of Southern California (B.S., 1968); University of California at Los Angeles (J.D., 1971). Senior Editor, U.C.L.A.-Alaska Law Review, 1970-1971. *Member:* Beverly Hills (Member, Real Estate Committee; Secretary-Treasurer, Committee on Taxation, 1972-1973; Chairman, Probate and Trusts Committee, 1979-1980), Los Angeles County and American (Member, Section on Real Property, Probate and Trust Law) Bar Associations; The State Bar of California (Member: Real Property Law and Committee on Taxation). **PRACTICE AREAS:** Real Estate; Corporate; Taxation; Estate Planning.

**PAUL W. KAUFMAN,** born Washington, D.C., May 2, 1957; admitted to bar, 1981, California. *Education:* University of Southern California (A.B., summa cum laude, 1978); Boalt Hall School of Law, University of California (J.D., 1981). Phi Beta Kappa. *Member:* Los Angeles County (Member, Real Property Section) and American (Member, Taxation Section) Bar Associations; State Bar of California (Member, Real Property Law Section). **PRACTICE AREAS:** Real Estate; Taxation; Corporate.

**MICHAEL S. ACKERMAN,** born Chicago, Illinois, April 24, 1957; admitted to bar, 1982, California; 1983, Illinois. *Education:* University of Illinois at Chicago (B.S., summa cum laude, 1979); University of Illinois, Champaign-Urbana (J.D., summa cum laude, 1982). Order of the Coif; Beta Gamma Sigma; Phi Kappa Phi. Member, 1980-1981 and Notes and Comments Editor, 1981-1982, University of Illinois Law Review. Certified Public Accountant, Illinois, 1978. Author: "California's Diminishing Usury Law," California Lawyer, July, 1984; "ERISA: Preemption of State Health Care Laws and Worker Well-Being," University of Illinois Law Review 825, 1981. *Member:* Los Angeles County, Illinois State and American Bar Associations; State Bar of California. **PRACTICE AREAS:** Real Estate; Secured Lending; Corporate.

**MARC H. CORMAN,** born Syracuse, New York, August 8, 1957; admitted to bar, 1982, California; 1983, U.S. District Court, Central, Southern, Northern and Eastern Districts of California. *Education:* University of Southern California (B.A., summa cum laude, 1979); University of California School of Law, Los Angeles (J.D., 1982). Phi Beta Kappa. *Member:* Los Angeles County (Member, Business and Corporate Section) and American (Member: Real Estate Section; Business Law) Bar Associations; State Bar of California. **PRACTICE AREAS:** Real Estate Transactions and Litigation; Secured Lending; Bankruptcy.

*(This Listing Continued)*

CAA823B

**JONES, KAUFMAN & ACKERMAN LLP,** Los Angeles—
*Continued*

**ELLEN ROTH NAGLER,** born Westport, Connecticut, April 16, 1960; admitted to bar, 1986, California and U.S. District Court, Central District of California; 1988, U.S. Court of Appeals, Ninth Circuit. *Education:* University of California at Santa Barbara (B.A., with high honors, 1982); University of Southern California (J.D., 1985). Staff Member, Major Tax Planning and Computer/Law Journal, 1983-1984. Author: "In the Public Interest: An Argument Calling for an Amendment to the Federal Communications Act Requiring More Public Service Announcements in the Broadcast Media," 6 Computer Law Journal 223, 1985. *Member:* Los Angeles County and American Bar Associations; State Bar of California. **PRACTICE AREAS:** Real Estate; Corporate.

REPRESENTATIVE CLIENTS: Weyerhaeuser Mortgage Company (and various affiliates including Weyerhaeuser Financial Investments, Inc., Weyerhaeuser Realty Investors and Weyerhaeuser Venture Company); Metropolitan Life Insurance Company; Highland Federal Bank; MIP Properties, Inc.; Gentra Capital Corporation (formerly Pacific First Bank); Banc One Management and Consulting Corporation; RTC Mortgage Trust 1993-N1; Lehman Brothers; Insignia Financial Group; Imperial Thrift & Loan Association; The Richland Group; Seoul Bank of California; IHOP, Inc.; SunLife Insurance Company of America; Countrywide Funding Corporation; L.J. Melody & Company of California.

---

## JONES, MAHONEY, BRAYTON & SOLL

### LOS ANGELES, CALIFORNIA

(See Claremont)

*General Civil and Trial Practice in State and Federal Courts. Business, Construction, Corporation, Insurance, Civil Litigation, Estate Planning, Probate, Taxation, Real Property and Family Law.*

---

## JAMES V. JORDAN

### 12100 WILSHIRE BOULEVARD
### 15TH FLOOR
### LOS ANGELES, CALIFORNIA 90025

Telephone: 310-826-2255
FAX: 310-207-3230
Email: JORDAN@SJAW.COM

*Franchise, Intellectual Property, Labor, Insurance, Business, Real Estate, Corporate, Tort, Administrative Law and Litigation and Appellate Practice in all State and Federal Courts before Municipal Administrative and Regulatory Boards, Agencies and Elected Councils, Banking and Finance.*

**JAMES V. JORDAN,** born New York, N.Y., July 24, 1949; admitted to bar, 1975, California and U. S. District Court, Central, Southern and Eastern Districts of California; 1976, U.S. Court of Appeals, Ninth Circuit; 1981, U.S. Supreme Court; 1995, U.S. District Court, Northern District of California. *Education:* University of California at Los Angeles (B.A., cum laude, 1971; J.D., 1974). Recipient, Psychology Distinguished Public Service Award, Inland Southern California Psychological Association, 1981. Panelist: Franchise Law Committee, California State Bar Convention, 1992. Author: "An Overview of the Parameters of Litigation Concerning a Franchisee/Franchisor Dispute: What the Litigator Must Be Familiar With and What He/She Should Expect." International Franchise Association Legal Symposium, 1994. Co-Author: papers entitled: "What You Need To Know About Franchise Litigation"; presenter of paper entitled "The Perils of Franchisor Control of Real Estate," American Bar Association Forum on Franchising, 1994. Member, Los Angeles County Superior Court Arbitration Panel, 1988-1991. Member, American Bar Association Commercial Arbitration Panel, 1990—. *Member:* Los Angeles County and American (Member, Forum Committee on Franchising, 1985—) Bar Associations; State Bar of California. **REPORTED CASES:** Cislaw v. 7-Eleven (1992) 4 Cal. App. 4th 1284; CIM v. United States, 641 F 2d 1441 (9th Cir. 1980); The Southland Corporation v. Emerald Oil, 789 F 2d 1441 (9th Cir. 1986). **PRACTICE AREAS:** Securities; Franchise; Intellectual Property; Business; Commercial; Real Estate; Products Liability; Administrative Law; Litigation and Appellate Practice.

### ASSOCIATE

**LEOPOLDO A. BAUTISTA,** born Los Angeles, California, December 11, 1962; admitted to bar, 1990, California; 1992, U.S. District Court, Central District of California; 1993, U.S. District Court, Eastern District of California. *Education:* Stanford University (B.A., 1985); Boalt Hall School
*(This Listing Continued)*

of Law, University of California (J.D., 1990). Managing Editor, La Raza Law Journal, 1988-1989. *Member:* Los Angeles County and Mexican American Bar Associations; Latin Business Association. **LANGUAGES:** Spanish. **PRACTICE AREAS:** Business Litigation; Intellectual Property Law and Litigation; Franchise Law and Litigation; Trademarks; Premises Liability Defense.

---

## SANFORD JOSSEN

Established in 1982

### EIGHTH FLOOR
### 1840 CENTURY PARK EAST
### LOS ANGELES, CALIFORNIA 90067-2101

Telephone: 310-201-0755; 201-0910
Telecopier: 310-553-2033

*Business Litigation of all types including: Corporate Dissolution, Entertainment (all Media), International Freight, Real Estate, Bad Faith Insurance, Personal Injury including Motor Vehicle, Slips, Trips and Falls, Medical Malpractice, Dental Malpractice. Also extensive Arbitration/Mediation experience.*

*FIRM PROFILE: We're a small, full service firm with emphasis on litigation and an enlightened attitude toward the economics of litigation and dispute resolution. We offer personal service and sensitivity to client needs and billing concerns.*

**SANFORD JOSSEN,** born New York, N.Y., January 6, 1951; admitted to bar, 1982, California and U.S. Tax Court; U.S. Court of Appeals, Ninth Circuit; U.S. Supreme Court. *Education:* Southampton College, Long Island University (B.A., English, 1974); University of San Diego (J.D., 1980). Author: "Incorporating the Stars," Volume 4, Number 5, Los Angeles Lawyer, 16 (July/August 1981); "Fiduciary Aspect of the Personal Manager's Relationship with a Performing Artist," 167 Cal.Rptr. 33 (supp.) [Pocket Part] Number 4 (1980); Article of Special Interest reprinted in 11 Performing Arts Review, Journal of Law, Arts and Management 108 (1981). Panel of Editors, Los Angeles Lawyer, 1985-1986. Los Angeles Municipal Court Judge Pro Tem, Beverly Hills and Santa Monica, 1989—. Certified Arbitrator, Los Angeles Superior Court, 1987—. Certified Mediator, Beverly Hills Bar Association, 1989—. Arbitrator, American Arbitration Association, 1985—. *Member:* Beverly Hills (Member: Attorney/Client Relation Committee; Artists and the Law Committee) and Los Angeles County (Attorney/Client Relation Committee) Bar Associations. **PRACTICE AREAS:** Personal Injury; Business Litigation; Real Estate; Insurance Law.

---

## KAJAN MATHER AND BARISH

A PROFESSIONAL CORPORATION

### LOS ANGELES, CALIFORNIA

(See Beverly Hills)

*Civil and Criminal Tax Controversy and Tax Litigation.*

---

## MICHAEL A. KALE

Established in 1978

### SUITE 1225, 10960 WILSHIRE BOULEVARD
### LOS ANGELES, CALIFORNIA 90024-3715

Telephone: 310-473-3133
FAX: 310-477-6778

*Insurance Defense as related to Real Estate and Business Litigation, Construction Defect, Title Insurance Defense in all State and Federal Courts. Banking, Financial Institutions and Business Litigation.*

*FIRM PROFILE: Michael A. Kale, Professional Corporation has been established since 1978 and is located in West Los Angeles. Mr. Kale has acted as cumis counsel since 1986 to American States, Wausau Insurance, Employers Casualty, American Auto Association (AAA) of Southern California. Mr. Kale acts as a litigator for banks as related to REO property and is approved counsel for Great Western Bank. Michael A. Kale is actively pursuing the role of a panel attorney for insurance companies throughout California.*

**MICHAEL A. KALE,** born 1952; admitted to bar, 1978, California; 1979, U.?S. District Court, Central District of California. *Education:* San Diego State University (B.A.); Pepperdine University (J.D.). *Member:* Los
*(This Listing Continued)*

# PROFESSIONAL BIOGRAPHIES

## CALIFORNIA—LOS ANGELES

Angeles County and West Los Angeles County Bar Associations. *PRACTICE AREAS:* Real Estate; Business Litigation.

REPRESENTATIVE CLIENTS: Chicago Title Insurance; California Land Title Insurance; Gibraltar Savings & Loan.
APPROVED COUNSEL FOR: Great Western Bank.

---

## *KALISCH, COTUGNO & RUST*

### LOS ANGELES, CALIFORNIA

(See Beverly Hills)

*General Civil Trial and Appellate Practice in State and Federal Courts, including Business, Real Property, Banking, Insurance, Title Insurance, Entertainment, Commercial, Corporate, Transactional and Personal Injury Litigation.*

---

## *LAW OFFICES OF THOMAS KALLAY*

Established in 1994

### 445 SOUTH FIGUEROA STREET
### 27TH FLOOR
### LOS ANGELES, CALIFORNIA 90071-1603

Telephone: 213-612-7717
Facsimile: 213-426-2181

*Appellate Practice in State and Federal Courts.*

**THOMAS KALLAY,** born Budapest, Hungary, July 14, 1937; admitted to bar, 1963, California and U.S. District Court, Central District of California; 1989, U.S. Ninth Circuit Court of Appeals; U.S. Supreme Court. *Education:* University of California at Los Angeles (A.B., 1958; J.D., 1962); University of Heidelberg, West Germany. Phi Beta Kappa. Fulbright Fellowship. Author: "United States Warships in Foreign Ports and Visit to a Foreign Port - The Warship's Crew Ashore," XXI The JAG Journal 105 and 145, 1967; "Faith Without Illusion: The petition for a Writ of Error Coram Nobis," 47 Los Angeles Bar Bulletin 21, 1971; "The Dismissal of Frivolous Appeals by the California Courts of Appeal," 54 California State Bar Journal 92, 1979; "A Reappraisal of General and Limited Jurisdiction in California," 8 Pepperdine Law Review 1, 1980; Book Review, "Law Clerks and the Judicial Process," 28 UCLA Law Review 605, 1981; "A Study in Rulemaking by Decision: California Courts Adopt Federal Rule 54(b)," 13 Southwestern University Law Review 87, 1982; "A Modest Proposal Concerning Plaintiffs, Additional Defendants and the Five Year Rule," 17 Beverly Hills Bar Association Journal 254, 1983; "Of General Jurisdiction and Other Deceits," No. 84-20 The Los Angeles Daily Journal Report, 1984; "Motions for Reconsideration," The Daily Journal, 1989; "When Does Notice of an Order Constitute Service?" The Daily Journal, 1989. Professor of Law, 1977-1988 and Associate Dean, 1985-1986, Southwestern University School of Law. Deputy Attorney General, State of California, 1967-1970. Senior Research Attorney, California Court of Appeal, 1970-1972, 1976-1977. Public Member, State of California New Motor Vehicle Board, 1973-1974, 1975-1976. Member, National Highway Safety Commission, 1983-1986. Executive Director, California Appellate Project, Los Angeles, 1986-1988. *Member:* Los Angeles County Bar Association (Member: Appellate Courts Committee; Committee on State Appellate Judicial Appointments); State Bar of California; California Academy of Appellate Lawyers. [With USN, 1963-1967; Lieutenant Commander, JAGC, USNR]. **LANGUAGES:** German and Hungarian. *REPORTED CASES:* Scofield v. Critical Air Medicine, Inc. (1996) 45 Cal. App. 4th 990; Photias v. Doertler (1996) 45 Cal. App. 4th 1014; Nguyen v. Los Angeles County Harbor/UCLA Medical Center (1995) 40 Cal. App. 4th 1433; International Engine Parts v. Fedderson (1995) 9 Cal.4th 606; Schultz v. Harney (1994) 27 Cal.App.4th 1611; Hull v. Central Pathology Services (1994) 25 Cal.App.4th 1195; Krieger v. Superior Court (1993) 17 Cal.2d Rptr. 627; Jacoves v. United Merchandising Corporation (1992) 9 Cal. App. 4th 88; Kuhns v. State of California (1992) 8 Cal. App. 4th 982; Nguyen v. County of Los Angeles (1992) 8 Cal App. 4th 729; Central Pathology Service Medical Clinic v. Superior Court (Hull)(1992) 3 Cal. 4th 181; Austin v. McNamara (9th Cir. 1992) 979 F.2d 728 (C.D. Cal. 1990) 731 F. Supp. 934; Fry v. Block (1991) 1 Cal. Rptr. 2d 166; Hegyes v. Unjian Enterprises (1991) 234 Cal. App. 4th 1103; Munro v. Regents of the University of California (1989) 215 Cal. App. 3d 977; Rombalski v. City of Laguna Beach (1989) 213 Cal. App. 3d 842; Nissan v. Motor Corp. in U.S.A. v. Superior Court (Meier) (1989) 212 Cal.App. 2d 980; Fineberg v. Harney & Moore (1989) 201 Cal. App. 3d 1049; Kearns v. Superior Court (1988) 204 Cal..App. 1325; Baker v. Birnbaum (1988) 202 Cal. App. 3d 288; People v. Moore (1985) 166 Cal. App. 3d 540; People v. Allen (1985) 165 Cal. App. 3d 616; People v. Jacobs (1984) 157 Cal. App. 3d 797; People v. Soto (1984) 157 Cal. App. 3d 694; People v. Frausto (1982) 135 Cal. App. 3d 129; Pating v. Board of Medical Quality Assurance (1982) 130 Cal. App. 3d 608; People v. Peggese (1980) 102 Cal. App. 3d 415; People v. Patino (1979) 95 Cal. App. 3d 11; People v. Cornejo (1979) 92 Cal. App. 3d 637; Belli v. State Bar of California (1974) 10 Cal. 3d 824 (with Herman F. Selvin); People v. Brown (1973) 35 Cal. App. 3d 317; In re Brown (1973) 9 Cal. 3d 679; People v. Coleman (1971) 4 Cal. 3d 436; People v. Morrison (1971) 4 Cal. 3d 442; People v. Floyd (1970) 1 Cal. 3d 694; People v. Bandhauer (1970) 1 Cal. 3d. 609; People v. Washington (1969) 71 Cal. 2d 1170; People v. Edwards (1969) 71 Cal. 2d 1096; People v. Ireland (1969) 70 Cal.2d 522; People v. Brown (1973) 35 Cal.App.3d 317; People. v. Starr (1970) 11 Cal..Ap.3d 574; People v. Pearce (1970) 6 Cal.App.3d 364; People v. Johnson (1970) 5 Cal.App.3d 844; People v. Perales (1970) 4 Cal.App.3d 773; People v. Dominguez (1869) 2 Cal.App.ed 1071; People v. Helfend (1969) 1 Cal.App.3d 873; People v. Ballard (1969) 1 Cal.App.3d 292; People v. Gonzales (1969) 275 Cal.App.2d 741; People v. Lamica (1969) 274 Cal.App.2d 640; People v. Bailey (1969) 269 Cal.App.2d 568; People v. Rusling (1969) 268 Cal.App.2d 930; People v. Glass (1968) 266 Cal.App.2d 222; People v. Davis (1968) 265 Cal.App.2d 341; People v. Villareal (1968) 262 Cal..App.2d 438. *PRACTICE AREAS:* Appellate Practice; Civil Trial.

---

## *KAMINE, STEINER & UNGERER*

Established in 1976

### SUITE 250 WORLD TRADE CENTER
### 350 S. FIGUEROA STREET
### LOS ANGELES, CALIFORNIA 90071

Telephone: 213-972-0119

*Construction Industry Litigation, Business Litigation.*

**BERNARD S. KAMINE,** born Oklahoma City, Oklahoma, December 5, 1943; admitted to bar, 1969, California. *Education:* University of Denver (B.A., 1965); Harvard University (J.D., 1968). Co-Author: "Chapter 22. Construction Contracts," California Forms of Jury Instructions, Matthew Bender, 1985. Judge Pro Tem, Municipal Court, 1974—. Board of Directors, Engineering Contractors' Association, 1985—. Board of Directors, Los Angeles District Associated General Contractors, 1995—. Panel of Arbitrators, American Arbitration Association, 1978—, and California Public Works Contract Arbitration Committee, 1990—. *Member:* Los Angeles County (Chair, Construction Law Subsection, 1981-1983) Bar Association; State Bar of California. *PRACTICE AREAS:* Construction.

**PHYLLIS UNGERER,** born New York, N.Y., October 11, 1946; admitted to bar, 1973, California. *Education:* Goucher College (B.A., cum laude, 1968); Hastings College of the Law, University of California (J.D., 1972). Phi Beta Kappa. Chair, Legal Advisory Committee, Associated General Contractors of California, 1987-1988. Judge Pro Tem, Municipal Court, 1988—. *Member:* State Bar of California. *REPORTED CASES:* Wang v. Division of Labor (1990) 219 CA3d 1152. *PRACTICE AREAS:* Construction.

### ASSOCIATES

**MAURYA HOGAN,** born Camp Chaffee, Arkansas, March 19, 1954; admitted to bar, 1987, California. *Education:* University of California at Los Angeles (B.A., 1983); Boalt Hall School of Law, University of California (J.D., 1987). Law Clerk, Los Angeles Superior Court, 1987-1991. *Member:* State Bar of California.

**KEVIN COLLINS,** born Manila, Philippines, April 12, 1963; admitted to bar, 1993, California. *Education:* Pitzer College (B.A., 1981); University of California, Graduate School of Architecture and Urban Planning (M.A., 1989); Loyola Law School (J.D., 1993). *Member:* State Bar of California.

### OF COUNSEL

**MATT STEINER,** born Chicago, Illinois, June 17, 1955; admitted to bar, 1981, California. *Education:* University of California at Los Angeles (B.A., 1978); Loyola University of Los Angeles (J.D., 1981). Judge Pro Tem, Municipal Court, 1990—; Superior Court, 1989—. Panel of Arbitrators, American Arbitration Association, 1990—. *Member:* Los Angeles County (Chair, Construction Law Subsection, 1990-1992) Bar Association; State Bar of California. *PRACTICE AREAS:* Construction.

**LYNN E. HALL,** born Spanish Fork, Utah, March 14, 1946; admitted to bar, 1972, California. *Education:* Stanford University (B.A., with distinction, 1968); Yale Law School (J.D., 1972). Lecturer, California Continuing Education of the Bar, 1978, and California Institute for Trial Advocacy,

*(This Listing Continued)*

KAMINE, STEINER & UNGERER, Los Angeles—
Continued

1979. *Member:* Los Angeles County Bar Association (Chair, Experimental Court Subcommittee, 1977-1980); State Bar of California.
REPRESENTATIVE CLIENTS: Engineering Contractors' Association; City of Rancho Cucamonga, California; Valverde Construction, Inc.

## KANANACK, MURGATROYD, BAUM & HEDLUND

*A PROFESSIONAL CORPORATION*

**LOS ANGELES, CALIFORNIA**

(See Baum, Hedlund, Aristei, Guilford & Downey)

## KANE, BALLMER & BERKMAN

*A LAW CORPORATION*
Established in 1963
515 SOUTH FIGUEROA STREET
SUITE 1850
**LOS ANGELES, CALIFORNIA 90071**
Telephone: 213-617-0480
Telecopier: 213-625-0931

*Housing and Urban Development, Redevelopment, Municipal, Land Use, Real Estate, Eminent Domain, Environmental, Hazardous Waste and Local and State Government Law. Litigation in all Courts.*

FIRM PROFILE: *Kane, Ballmer & Berkman was founded in 1963 by Eugene B. Jacobs. The firm since its inception has specialized in providing legal services to redevelopment agencies, development commissions, and other public entities within and outside the State of California, primarily in the field of redevelopment. The firm also represents cities as contract city attorney and special counsel. In addition the firm provides legal services in related substantive fields such as housing and urban development, land use, general real estate, eminent domain, environmental, hazardous waste, general municipal and trial and appellate litigation related to these subjects.*

*The firm has expertise in financial matters important to public entities and especially to the implementation of redevelopment plans, including the property tax system; the conceptual and practical aspects of tax increment financing and the sharing of property tax by law or agreement among public entities; the methods of obtaining developer advances and payments for redevelopment purposes; bond or other financial alternatives available for capital outlays; and real estate debt and equity financing and security.*

*The firm's litigation practice is designed to coordinate directly with and facilitate the activities of our clients. In eminent domain matters, for example, the firm is able to bring its expertise in the redevelopment process to bear on the right to take and valuation issues peculiar in redevelopment projects. The same is true for validation, environmental and other such cases.*

**MURRAY O. KANE,** born Middlesex County, England, July 14, 1946; admitted to bar, 1971, California. *Education:* University of California at Los Angeles (A.B., 1967; J.D., 1970). Phi Alpha Delta. City Prosecutor, Acting City Attorney and Assistant City Attorney, City of Culver City, 1971-1973. *Member:* The State Bar of California. *TRANSACTIONS:* Fox Hills Mall, Culver City; Santa Monica Place, Santa Monica; Museum of Contemporary Art, Los Angeles; Watts Shopping Center, Los Angeles; Los Angeles Central Library restoration and expansion; Los Angeles Produce Mart; Whittier Earthquake Recovery Redevelopment Project; Riverside Raceway mixed use development, Moreno Valley; Central Business District Redevelopment Plan, Los Angeles. *PRACTICE AREAS:* Redevelopment Law; Public Finance Law; Affordable Housing Law.

**BRUCE D. BALLMER,** born Los Angeles, California, April 29, 1942; admitted to bar, 1974, California. *Education:* University of California at Berkeley (A.B., 1964); University of Southern California (M.S., in City and Regional Planning, 1969); Harvard University (J.D., 1974). Phi Beta Kappa. *Member:* Los Angeles County and American (Member, Section on Local Government Law) Bar Associations; The State Bar of California. *TRANSACTIONS:* In San Diego: Horton Plaza Retail/Entertainment Center, Koll Center, America Plaza, Meridian, Santa Fe Depot Property, Emerald-Shapery Center, Lyceum Theaters, Gateway Center Industrial Parks. In Santa Clara: Great America Theme Park, Bella Vista Residential

*(This Listing Continued)*

Development, Convention Center/Hotel/High Tech Trade Center Complex. *PRACTICE AREAS:* Redevelopment Law; Housing Law; Land Use Law.

**GLENN F. WASSERMAN,** born New York, N.Y., January 4, 1949; admitted to bar, 1975, California; 1981, New York. *Education:* University of Connecticut (B.A., with honors, 1970); University of California at Los Angeles (J.D., 1975). Honors Program for Law Graduates. Co-Author: League of California Cities: The California Municipal Law Handbook - Redevelopment Law, 1994. U.S. Department of Transportation, Office of Secretary of Transportation, Washington, D.C., 1975-1982. Urban Mass Transportation Administration, Office of Chief Counsel, Washington, D.C. and UMTA Regional Counsel, New York (Region II). *Member:* Los Angeles County (Member, Real Property Section), American (Forum on Affordable Housing and Community Development) and New York State Bar Associations; State Bar of California. *SPECIAL AGENCIES:* Special Counsel to City of Carlsbad; Special Counsel to the Housing Authority of the City of Glendale; Special Counsel to the Redevelopment Agency of the Cities of Los Angeles, San Diego, Redondo Beach, Carlsbad, Santa Ana, Santa Clara, Palmdale, Orange, Pasadena and Santa Clara. *REPORTED CASES:* Norfolk Development & Housing Authority v. Chesapeake & Potomac Telephone, 464 U.S. 30, 78 L.Ed.2d 29 (1983) (Amicus brief-relocation); Westport Taxi Service v. Adams, 571 F2d 697 (2d Cir. 1978) (challenge to federal grant project); United Handicapped Federation v. Andre, 558 F.2d 413 (8th Cir. 1977) (challenge to federal grant project); Leary v. Crapsey, 566 F.Supp. 863 (2d Cir. 1977) (challenge to federal grant project); Vanko v. Finley, 440 F.Supp. 656 (N.D. Ohio, 1977) (challenge to federal grant project). *TRANSACTIONS:* Grand Central Square Mixed Use Project (Los Angeles), Horton Plaza-4th Avenue Apartments (San Diego); Villa Santiago Affordable Housing Development (Orange); Baldwin Hills Crenshaw Shopping Center (Los Angeles); Convention Center Expansion (Los Angeles); Japanese American National Museum (Los Angeles); Union Rescue Mission Relocation and Ronald Reagan State Office Building Joint Powers Authority Project (Los Angeles) and LEGO Development Agreement (Carlsbad). *PRACTICE AREAS:* Redevelopment; Affordable Housing; Land Use; Public Financing Law.

**R. BRUCE TEPPER, JR.,** born Long Branch, New Jersey, April 1, 1949; admitted to bar, 1976, Missouri; 1977, California; 1978, Illinois. *Education:* Dartmouth College (A.B., 1971); St. Louis University (M.A., 1976; J.D., cum laude, 1976). Staff Member and Assistant Lead Articles Editor, 1975-1976, St. Louis University Law Journal. Author: "Regional Approach to Urban Problems," 3 Symposium 12, 1974; "Lead Paint Poisoning: The Response in Litigation," 19 St. Louis University Law Journal 244, 1975; "Eighth Circuit Review," 19 St. Louis University Law Journal 574, 1975; "Redevelopment Plan Adoption," The California Municipal Law Handbook, 1993. Judge Pro Tempore, Los Angeles County Municipal Court, 1981-1995. *Member:* Los Angeles County (Member, Board of Editors, Los Angeles Lawyer; Committee on Eminent Domain; Committee on Judicial Evaluation and Selection), Illinois State and American (Member, Local Government Law Section) Bar Associations; The Missouri Bar; State Bar of California (Member, Real Property Law Section; Grader, Committee of Bar Examiners, 1979-1983); The Missouri Bar; The Association of Business Trial Lawyers. *REPORTED CASES:* Dusek v. Anaheim Redevelopment Agency, 173 Cal. App. 3d 1029 (1985) (CEQA); Redevelopment Agency of Burbank v. Gilmore, 38 Cal. 3d 790 (1985) (amicus-eminent domain-interest on deposits); Creighton v. Revitsky, 171 Cal. App. 3d 1225 (1985) (elections); Kane v. Hidden Hills, 179 Cal. App. 3d 899 (1986) (exhaustion of administrative remedies); Community Redevelopment Agency v. Bloodgood, 182 Cal. App. 3d 342 (1986) (tax increment allocation of penalties and interest); Anaheim Redevelopment Agency v. Dusek, 193 Cal. App. 3d 249 (1987) (amicus-eminent domain-right to take); Emmington v. Solano County, 195 Cal. App. 3d 491 (1987) (redevelopment plan invalidation); Redevelopment Agency of Riverside County v. Superior Court, 228 Cal. App. 3d 1487 (1991) (exhaustion of administrative remedies); Morgan v. Community Redevelopment Agency, 231 Cal. App. 3d 243 (1991) (redevelopment plan validation); Lippman v. City of Los Angeles, 234 Cal. App. 3d 1630 (1991) (Project Area Committee); A.L.A.R.M. v. City of Los Angeles, 12 Cal. App. 4th 1773 (1993) (environmental & general plan challenge); Gemtel Corp. v. Community Redevelopment Agency, 23 Fed. 3d 1542 (9th Cir. 1994) (civil rights); Lancaster Redevelopment Agency v. Dibley 20 Cal. App. 4th, 656 (1995) (use of low/moderate housing funds); Castaic Lake Water Agency v. City of Santa. Clara, 41 Cal.App. 4th 257 (1995) (use of emergency exemptions from CEQA). *TRANSACTIONS:* Earthquake Emergency Redevelopment Plans Adopted by the City of Las Angeles. *PRACTICE AREAS:* Litigation; Land Use Law; Environmental Law; Eminent Domain Law.

*(This Listing Continued)*

**JOSEPH W. PANNONE,** born Providence, Rhode Island, March 23, 1954; admitted to bar, 1980, California. *Education:* University of California at Irvine; Golden West College; Loyola Marymount University (B.A., 1976; J.D., 1980). City Attorney, Assistant City Attorney and Deputy City Attorney, Culver City, 1980-1991. Member, Editorial Board for League of California Cities, Municipal Law Handbook, 1989-1994 (Co-author Police Power Chapter). Member, City Attorney's Department of League of California Cities, 1980—. Member, U.S. Supreme Court Historical Society. *Member:* Los Angeles County Bar Association; State Bar of California; National Italian American Lawyers Association; City Attorneys Association of Los Angeles County. *SPECIAL AGENCIES:* Special Counsel to City of Banning, City of Culver City, City of Glendale, City of Hawthorne, City of Pasadena. *REPORTED CASES:* Ehrlich v. City of Culver City, 12 Cal.4th 854 (1996) (challenge to land use approval exactions). *TRANSACTIONS:* Redevelopment Plan Adoptions/Amendments for the Cities of Banning, Glendale and Hawthorne; Sony Pictures Entertainment Developer Agreement for the City of Culver City. *PRACTICE AREAS:* Municipal Law; Land Use Law; Redevelopment Law.

**ROYCE K. JONES,** born Dayton, Ohio, November 9, 1955; admitted to bar, 1982, California. *Education:* University of Southern California (A.B., 1978; J.D., 1982). Member, Board of Trustees, IDMR. Advisory Board Member-USC Minority Real Estate Program. *Member:* Los Angeles County (Member, Sections on: Real Estate; Taxation; Corporations) and American Bar Associations; State Bar of California; National Bar Association. *SPECIAL AGENCIES:* Counsel for Community Redevelopment Agency of the City of Los Angeles, San Diego Redevelopment Agency, Los Angeles County Community Development Commission, San Diego Redevelopment Agency, Lynwood Redevelopment Agency, Federal Deposit Insurance Corporation and Resolution Trust Corporation. *REPORTED CASES:* Centenial Estates v. Griffin Homes (Real Estate litigation); San Diego Redevelopment Agency v. San Diego Gas & Electric (Eminent Domain litigation); Lynwood Redevelopment Agency v. Lucky Stores (Eminent Domain litigation); Bank of America National Trust v. Nu-Med La Mirada (Judicial Foreclosure/Receivership Action); J.E. Roberts Company, Inc. v. DeVere A. Anderson (Receivership - Surety Bond Litigation). *TRANSACTIONS:* Broadway Spring Street Plaza, Chinatown Mall, San Diego College of Retail, Price Club, Chinese Mission (San Diego), Gateway Center East Industrial Park, Gateway Medical Center, Southcrest Plaza, Lynwood Plaza, KV Mart Stores, Mercado Housing Project, Kilgore Manor, Villa Malaga Housing Project, Habitat for Humanities, Brush Research Development, Central Imperial Redevelopment Plan Amendments, East Rancho Dominguez Plan Amendment. *PRACTICE AREAS:* Redevelopment; Municipal; Land Use; Eminent Domain; Affordable Housing Law.

**STEPHANIE R. SCHER,** born Los Angeles, California, March 26, 1948; admitted to bar, 1976, California. *Education:* University of California at Los Angeles (B.A., summa cum laude, 1971); California Polytechnic State University; University of California School of Law (J.D., 1976). City Attorney, Palos Verdes Estates, 1993—. Editorial Board for League of California Cities Municipal Law Handbook, (Co-author: Municipal Finance Chapter). *Member:* State Bar of California; City Attorney Association of Los Angeles County (President, 1993); California Women Lawyers Association. *SPECIAL AGENCIES:* Special Counsel to City of Bell Gardens, West San Gabriel Valley Consortium. *PRACTICE AREAS:* Municipal Law; Land Use Law; Redevelopment Law; Election Law.

---

**JUNE AILIN,** born Washington, D.C., July 19, 1955; admitted to bar, 1983, California. *Education:* University of Maryland (B.A., 1976; M.L.S. 1977); University of Texas (J.D., 1983). *Member:* Los Angeles County Bar Association; State Bar of California. *PRACTICE AREAS:* Real Property Law; Eminent Domain Litigation.

**MARC J. MANASON,** born Detroit, Michigan, October 19, 1959; admitted to bar, 1984, California. *Education:* University of Michigan (B.A., with distinction, 1981); Boalt Hall School of Law, University of California (J.D., 1984). Author, "Legal and Public Policy Justifications for Common Provisions in Redevelopment Agreements," California Land Use Law and Policy Reporter, Spring 1992. *Member:* Los Angeles County Bar Association; State Bar of California. *PRACTICE AREAS:* Redevelopment; Housing Law; Real Estate Law; Land Use Law; Environmental Law; Litigation.

**MICHAEL J. KARGER,** born New York, N.Y., November 16, 1948; admitted to bar, 1975, California; 1980, New York. *Education:* Harpur College - State University of New York at Binghamton (B.A., 1969); State University of New York at Buffalo (J.D., 1974). Author: "Ex-Parte Communications in Quasi-Judicial Administrative Proceedings," National Institute of
*(This Listing Continued)*

Municipal Law Officers (NIMLO) Annual Meeting, 1989. City Attorney, Gardena, California, 1982-1995. Assistant City Attorney, Gardena, California, 1977-1982. Deputy City Attorney, Santa Ana, California, 1975-1977. *Member:* South Bay, Los Angeles County New York State and American Bar Associations; National Institute of Municipal Law Officers (California State Chair, 1993-1995); City Attorneys Association of Los Angeles County (President, 1988-1989); League of California Cities City Attorney's (Legislative Committee, 1986-1988; Chair, 1988; Legal Advocacy Committee, 1990-1992; Public Safety Committee, 1983-1995). *PRACTICE AREAS:* Municipal Law.

**SONIA J. RANSOM,** born New York, N.Y., December 16, 1952; admitted to bar, 1992, California. *Education:* University of California at Los Angeles (B.A., 1988); Loyola Law School (J.D., 1992). *Member:* Los Angeles County Bar Association; State Bar of California (Member, Real Property Law Section); Commercial Real Estate Women-Los Angeles (Member, Board of Directors). *PRACTICE AREAS:* Real Estate; Redevelopment Law; Administrative Law.

GENERAL COUNSEL FOR: Culver City Redevelopment Agency.
SPECIAL COUNSEL FOR REDEVELOPMENT: Cities of: Bakersfield, Banning, Carlsbad, Glendale, Grover Beach, Hawthorne, Huntington Beach, Los Angeles, Lompoc, Lynwood, Moreno Valley, Oceanside, Palmdale, Rancho Mirage, Redondo Beach, San Diego, San Jose, Santa Ana, Santa Clara, Santa Monica, Vernon and Whittier.
CITY ATTORNEY: City of Palos Verdes Estates.
SPECIAL COUNSEL FOR CITIES: Arcadia, Azusa, Bell Gardens, Carlsbad, Culver City, Glendale, Huntington Beach, Inglewood, Oxnard and Palmdale.

---

## KANE & O'BRIEN

*A PROFESSIONAL LAW CORPORATION*

11766 WILSHIRE BOULEVARD, SUITE 1580
**LOS ANGELES, CALIFORNIA 90025**
*Telephone: 310-575-1199*
*Fax: 310-575-1979*

*Civil Litigation and Trial Practice.*

**KEVIN P. KANE,** born Floral Park, New York, March 24, 1946; admitted to bar, 1971, California and U.S. District Court, Central District of California; 1974, U.S. District Court Northern District of California; 1975, U.S. District Court, Southern District of California; 1976, U.S. Court of Appeals, Ninth Circuit and U.S. Supreme Court. *Education:* Providence College (B.A., summa cum laude, 1967); Harvard Law School (J.D., 1970). Delta Epsilon Sigma. Deputy Chief Counsel, President's Commission on the Accident at Three-Mile Island, 1979. Arbitrator, Los Angeles Superior Court, 1983—; Settlement Conference Officer, Los Angeles Superior Court, 1986—; Judge Pro Tem, Los Angeles Municipal Courts, 1987—. *Member:* Los Angeles County and American (Member, Sections on: Antitrust Law; Litigation) Bar Associations; The State Bar of California; American Judicature Society. *PRACTICE AREAS:* Business Litigation; Antitrust Law; Unfair Competition Law; Labor Law; Insurance Law.

**MARK A. O'BRIEN,** born Philadelphia, Pennsylvania, October 1, 1955; admitted to bar, 1983, Massachusetts; 1987, California, U.S. District Court, Central District of California and U.S. Supreme Court; 1989, U.S. Court of Appeals, Ninth Circuit. *Education:* University of Oregon (B.A., with honors, 1980); Boston University (J.D., 1983). Phi Beta Kappa. *Member:* Roppongi and Los Angeles County Bar Associations; The State Bar of California; Japanese American Bar Association; Korean American Bar Association,. *LANGUAGES:* French and Japanese. *PRACTICE AREAS:* Civil Litigation; International Law.

---

## KARNO, SCHWARTZ, FRIEDMAN, SHAFRON & WARREN

**LOS ANGELES, CALIFORNIA**

(See Encino)

*Real Estate, Tax, Corporate, Business, ERISA, Estate Planning and Probate Law. Litigation.*

## KARNS & KARABIAN

SUITE 530 OMNI CENTRE
900 WILSHIRE BOULEVARD
**LOS ANGELES, CALIFORNIA 90017**
Telephone: 213-680-9522
FAX: 213-627-3602

*General Civil Practice including Administrative, Corporate/Business, Education, Public and Private Sector, Labor and Employment Law, Litigation, Taxation, Real Property, Trusts and Probate Law. Government and International Business.*

### MEMBERS OF FIRM

**JOHN KARNS,** born Ronan, Montana, February 21, 1938; admitted to bar, 1964, California and U.S. District Court, Central District of California. *Education:* University of Southern California (B.S., 1960; J.D., 1963). Phi Delta Phi. Instructor, Business Law, Woodbury College, Los Angeles, 1964-1965. *Member:* Los Angeles County Bar Association; State Bar of California. **PRACTICE AREAS:** Administrative Law; Corporate Law; Business Law; Litigation; Real Property; Labor and Employment.

**WALTER J. KARABIAN,** born Fresno, California, March 14, 1938; admitted to bar, 1964, California and U.S. District Court, Central District of California. *Education:* University of Southern California (B.A., 1960; M.S., 1964; J.D., 1963). Phi Alpha Theta; Phi Delta Phi; Blue Key. Member, Blackstonians. Author: "The Equal Rights Amendment: The Contribution of Our Generation of Americans," 1 Pepperdine Law Review 327, 1974; "Legal Services for the Poor: Some Political Observations," 6 University of San Francisco Law Review 253, 1972; "Record of Arrest: The Indelible Stain," 3 Pacific Law Journal 133, 1970; "California's Prison System: We Must Bring it Back into the Twentieth Century," 1 The Black Law Journal 133, 1971; "The Case Against Wiretapping," 1 Pacific Law Journal 133, 1970; "California's Implied Consent Statute: An Examination and Evaluation," 1 Loyola University Law Review 23, 1968. Member, California Assembly, 1966; 1968; 1970; 1972. *Member:* Los Angeles County Bar Association; State Bar of California. **PRACTICE AREAS:** Administrative Law; Taxation; Education Law; Corporate Law; Business Law; Government; International Law; Business Law; Trust Probate.

### ASSOCIATES

**JEFF C. MARDEROSIAN,** born Pasadena, California, June 18, 1954; admitted to bar, 1979, California and U.S. District Court, Central District of California. *Education:* California State University at Northridge (B.A., 1976); California Western School of Law (J.D., cum laude, 1979). Member, 1977-1979 and Research Editor, 1978-1979, California Western Law Review. Author: "The Property Rights of Unmarried Cohabitants-A Proposal," 14 California Western Law Review 485, 1979. *Member:* Los Angeles County Bar Association (Member: Appellate Courts Committee, 1983—; Real Property Section); State Bar of California. **PRACTICE AREAS:** Administrative Law; Education Law; Real Property; Labor Law.

**DAVID E. KENNEY,** born Los Angeles, California, June 11, 1953; admitted to bar, 1984, California; U.S. District Court, Central District of California and U.S. Court of Appeals, Ninth Circuit. *Education:* University of Southern California (B.A., 1979); Pepperdine University (J.D., 1982). President, Christian Legal Society, Pepperdine University, 1981-1982. Senior Consultant, California Legislature, Assembly Subcommittee on Sports and Entertainment, 1985-1986. *Member:* Los Angeles Bar Association; State Bar of California. **PRACTICE AREAS:** Administrative Law; Taxation; Litigation; Government Law; Education Law.

**JEFF A. HARRISON,** born San Gabriel, California, July 22, 1965; admitted to bar, 1990, California; U.S. District Court, Central District of California and U.S. Court of Appeals, Ninth Circuit. *Education:* California State University at Long Beach (B.S., 1987); University of Southern California (J.D., 1990). Participant, Hale Moot Court Honors Program. *Member:* Los Angeles County Bar Association; The State Bar of California. **PRACTICE AREAS:** Administrative Law; Corporate Law; Business Law; Litigation; Trust Probate; Real Property; Labor and Employment.

---

## KARPMAN & ASSOCIATES

12100 WILSHIRE BOULEVARD, SUITE 1600
**LOS ANGELES, CALIFORNIA 90025**
Telephone: 310-447-6110

*Attorney Professional Responsibility and Competence, Attorney Discipline and Legal Ethics, Admissions and Reinstatements, Conflict of Interest and Fiduciary Obligations of Lawyers.*

*(This Listing Continued)*

---

**DIANE L. KARPMAN,** born Quincy, Illinois, January 12, 1948; admitted to bar, 1975, California and U.S. District Court, Central District of California; 1995, U.S. Supreme Court. *Education:* Los Angeles City College; University of California at Los Angeles (B.A., 1970); Western State University College of Law, Fullerton (J.D., 1974). Delta Theta Phi. Recipient: Marks Scholarship; American Jurisprudence Award in Contracts; Hayens Foundation Scholarship. Assistant Dean, University of West Los Angeles College of Law, 1982-1984. Faculty, Western State University College of Law, Fullerton, 1975-1980. Bank of America Woman of the Year, 1968. State Bar Court Referee, 1982-1990. *Member:* Beverly Hills, Los Angeles County and American Bar Associations; State Bar of California.

### ASSOCIATE

**JUDITH FOURNIER GERMAN,** admitted to bar, 1993, California. *Education:* University of California at Los Angeles (B.A.); Loyola Law School (J.D., 1993). Member, Scott Moot Court, 1993. Member, Loyola of Los Angeles Entertainment Law Journal, 1992-1993. *Member:* Beverly Hills (Member, Barristers Board of Governors, 1995-1997) Santa Monica, Los Angeles County (Member, Evaluation of Professional Standards Committee and California State Bar Liaison Committee) and American Bar Associations.

### OF COUNSEL

**DANIEL L. ROTHMAN,** born Milwaukee, Wisconsin, April 19, 1925; admitted to bar, 1951, California, U.S. District Court, Central District of California and U.S. Court of Appeals, Ninth Circuit. *Education:* Loyola University of Los Angeles and Southwestern University (LL.B., cum laude, 1950). Hearing Referee, California State Bar Court, 1982-1990. Member, National Panel, American Arbitration Association. Appointed Judge Pro Tem of State Bar Court, 1990-1995. *Member:* Los Angeles County Bar Association (Chairman, Superior Courts Committee, 1975-1977; Vice Chairman, Judiciary Committee, 1977-1979; 1981-1982, Trial Lawyers Section); State Bar of California.

---

## GAIL D. KASS

**LOS ANGELES, CALIFORNIA**

(See Beverly Hills)
*Estate Planning, Probate, Trust Law and Taxation Law.*

---

## KATTEN MUCHIN & ZAVIS

A Partnership including Professional Corporations

Katten Muchin & Zavis Established in 1974

1999 AVENUE OF THE STARS, SUITE 1400
**LOS ANGELES, CALIFORNIA 90067-6042**
Telephone: 310-788-4400
Telecopier: 310-788-4471

*Chicago, Illinois Office:* 525 West Monroe Street, Suite 1600. Telephone: 312-902-5200. Telecopier: 312-902-1061. Telex: 298264 ATLAW UR.
*Irvine, California Office:* Two Park Plaza, Suite 800. Telephone: 714-263-3500. Telecopier: 714-263-3533.
*New York, New York Office:* 40 Broad Street, Suite 2000. Telephone: 212-612-9500. Telecopier: 212-425-0266.
*Washington, D.C. Office:* 1025 Thomas Jefferson Street, N.W., East Lobby, Suite 700. Telephone: 202-625-3500. Telecopier: 202-298-7570. Telex: 211195 KMZ UR.

*Antitrust and Trade Regulation, Aviation, Banking and Commercial Finance, Bankruptcy and Reorganization, Commodities, Futures and Derivatives, Constitutional Law, Corporate, Corporate Insurance, Creditor's Rights, Customs, Employee Benefits and Executive Compensation, Entertainment, Environmental, Equipment and Facility Leasing, Estate Planning and Probate, Financial Services, Golf Course, Resort and Hotel Acquisition and Development, Governmental Affairs, Health Care, Insurance and Reinsurance, Intellectual Property, International Trade, International Business Transactions and Global Capital Markets, Investment Adviser and Investment Company Regulation, Joint Ventures, Labor and Employment Law, Litigation and Trial Practice, Mergers and Acquisitions, Municipal Law, Municipal Finance and Public Authority Financing Law, Partnerships, Product Liability, Product Manufacturing and Marketing, Professional Malpractice, Project Develop-*

*(This Listing Continued)*

ment and Finance, Real Estate, Real Estate Finance, Real Estate Taxation, Retail Leasing and Shopping Center Development, Securities, Securitization and Structured Finance, Sports, Stadium Financing, Syndications, Taxation-Federal and International, Technology and Computer Law, Thrift Institutions, Variable Insurance Products, Venture Capital, White Collar Civil and Criminal Litigation.

*MEMBERS OF FIRM*

**JAMES K. BAER,** born Los Angeles, California, September 5, 1958; admitted to bar, 1983, California. *Education:* University of California at Santa Barbara (B.A., 1980); Loyola Marymount University (J.D., 1983). *Member:* State Bar of California. **PRACTICE AREAS:** Mergers and Acquisitions; Corporate Securities/Venture Capital.

**KATHRYN A. BALLSUN,** born Los Angeles, California, May 8, 1946; admitted to bar, 1976, California, U.S. Court of Appeals, 9th Circuit; 1995, U.S. Tax Court. *Education:* University of Southern California (B.A., 1968; M.A., 1969); Loyola Law School, Los Angeles (J.D., 1976). Member: Planning Committee of the USC Probate and Trust Conference; UCLA-CEB Estate Planning Institute. *Member:* Beverly Hills Bar Association (President, 1989-1990); State Bar of California (Executive Committee of the Estate Planning, Trust and Probate Law Section, Chair of the "Truth Squad", 1986-1992); California Association of Local Bars (President, 1990-1992). Fellow, American College of Trust and Estate Council. **PRACTICE AREAS:** Estate Planning; Post Death Administration (Probate and Revocable Trust); Individual Tax Planning.

**DAVID M. BASS,** born Los Angeles, California, December 10, 1958; admitted to bar, 1984, California, U.S. District Court, Central District of California and U.S. Court of Appeals, Ninth Circuit. *Education:* University of California at Berkeley (A.B., 1981); University of Southern California (J.D., 1984). *Member:* Century City and American Bar Associations; State Bar of California. **PRACTICE AREAS:** Litigation.

**KENT S. BEYER,** born Santa Monica, California, March 12, 1950; admitted to bar, 1982, California and U.S. District Court, Central District of California. *Education:* University of Virginia (B.A., 1971); University of California at Los Angeles (J.D., 1982). *Member:* Los Angeles County and American Bar Associations; State Bar of California. **PRACTICE AREAS:** Real Estate Law; Finance Law.

**KENNETH L. BLOCK,** born Chicago, Illinois, May 29, 1953; admitted to bar, 1982, Illinois and U.S. District Court, Northern District of Illinois; 1992, California and U.S. District Court, Central and Southern Districts of California. *Education:* Elmhurst College (B.A., 1976); Northwestern University (M.A., 1978); Loyola University of Chicago (J.D., 1982). *Member:* State Bar of California. **PRACTICE AREAS:** Banking.

**MARSHA A. BOYSAW,** born Dallas, Texas, October 29, 1961; admitted to bar, 1987, California, U.S. District Court, Central District of California and U.S. Court of Appeals, Ninth Circuit. *Education:* University of Texas (B.A., 1983); University of Texas (J.D., 1987). *Member:* State Bar of California; Financial Lawyers Association. **PRACTICE AREAS:** Finance and Reorganization.

**JOHN J. CHUNG,** born Seoul, Republic of Korea, July 29, 1960; admitted to bar, 1985, Massachusetts; 1987, California. *Education:* Washington University (B.A., summa cum laude, 1982); Harvard University (J.D., cum laude, 1985). **PRACTICE AREAS:** Commercial Litigation.

**STEVE COCHRAN,** born Los Angeles, California, March 18, 1957; admitted to bar, 1982, California; 1983, U.S. District Court, Central District of California; 1986, U.S. Court of Appeals, Ninth Circuit; 1991, U.S. District Court, Eastern District of California. *Education:* University of California at Santa Cruz (B.A., 1979); Boalt Hall School of Law, University of California at Berkeley (J.D., 1982). **PRACTICE AREAS:** Federal and State Criminal Litigation.

**CRAIG D. CROCKWELL,** born Portland, Oregon, April 26, 1943; admitted to bar, 1969, California. *Education:* Stanford University (B.A., 1965); University of California at Los Angeles (J.D., 1968). *Member:* Los Angeles County and American Bar Associations; State Bar of California. **PRACTICE AREAS:** Real Estate Law.

**ALAN D. CROLL,** born Detroit, Michigan, May 27, 1939; admitted to bar, 1965, California and Michigan. *Education:* Harvard College (A.B., cum laude, 1961); University of Michigan (LL.B., 1964). *Member:* Beverly Hills and Los Angeles County Bar Associations; State Bar of California; State Bar of Michigan. **PRACTICE AREAS:** Litigation.

**RICHARD F. DAVIS, (P.C.),** born December 25, 1945; admitted to bar, 1971, California; 1973, U.S. Tax Court; 1975, U.S. Supreme Court; 1981,

*(This Listing Continued)*

District of Columbia. *Education:* University of California at Los Angeles (A.B., 1967; J.D., 1970). *Member:* Urban Land Institute; American Resort Development Association; International Council of Shopping Centers. **PRACTICE AREAS:** Real Estate and International Law.

**MICHELE M. DESOER,** born Oakland, California, September 4, 1960; admitted to bar, 1985, California. *Education:* University of California at Berkeley (B.S., 1981); University of San Francisco; University of California, Boalt Hall School of Law (J.D., 1985). Order of the Coif. Member, McAuliffe Law Honor Society. Associate Editor, 1983-1984 and Current Developments Editor, 1984-1985, International Tax and Business Lawyer. *Member:* State Bar of California; American Bar Association. **LANGUAGES:** French. **PRACTICE AREAS:** Litigation; Entertainment; Employment.

**ROBERT T. FLICK,** born Buffalo, New York, January 21, 1953; admitted to bar, 1978, California. *Education:* Northern Illinois University (B.S., cum laude, 1975); Stanford University (J.D., 1978). Phi Eta Sigma. *Member:* State Bar of California; American Bar Association (Real Property, Probate and Trust Law); International Council of Shopping Centers. **LANGUAGES:** French. **PRACTICE AREAS:** Real Estate Law.

**ALLAN B. GOLDMAN,** born Auburn, New York, January 1, 1937; admitted to bar, 1964, California; 1977, District of Columbia. *Education:* Harvard College (A.B., magna cum laude, 1958); Harvard University (J.D., 1963). Who's Who in America. *Member:* State Bar of California; The District of Columbia Bar. **PRACTICE AREAS:** Litigation; Mass Torts; Class Actions; Insurance Coverage; Real Estate.

**ROBERT D. GOLDSCHEIN,** born Los Angeles, California, September 28, 1954; admitted to bar, 1980, California, U.S. District Court, Central, Eastern, Northern and Southern Districts of California. *Education:* University of California at Berkeley (B.A., 1977); University of California at Los Angeles (J.D., 1980). **PRACTICE AREAS:** Commercial Finance; Trade Finance; Reorganization and Insolvency.

**ANGEL GOMEZ, III,** admitted to bar, 1977, California; 1985, U.S. Court of Appeals, Ninth Circuit; 1988, U.S. Supreme Court. *Education:* University of California at Berkeley (A.B., 1973); Harvard Law School (J.D., 1976). Management Co-Author, "California Employment Litigation," 1994. *Member:* Los Angeles County Bar Association (Member, Executive Committee, Labor and Employment Law Section, 1987—). **PRACTICE AREAS:** Employment and Labor Law; ERISA.

**KATHERINE E. GOODMAN,** born Los Angeles, California, June 1, 1963; admitted to bar, 1986, California. *Education:* Harvard University (A.B., cum laude, 1983); University of Chicago (J.D., with honors, 1986). *Member:* State Bar of California. **PRACTICE AREAS:** Entertainment Law.

**LESLIE R. KARP,** born Chicago, Illinois, April 29, 1963; admitted to bar, 1988, Illinois (Not admitted in California). *Education:* University of Wisconsin (B.B.A., 1985); IIT Chicago-Kent College of Law (J.D., 1988). *Member:* Chicago Bar Association. **PRACTICE AREAS:** Tax and Estate Planning.

**VALERIE E. KINCAID,** born Los Angeles, California, March 16, 1961; admitted to bar, 1986, California and U.S. District Court, Central District of California. *Education:* University of California at Los Angeles (B.A. summa cum laude, 1982; J.D., 1985). **PRACTICE AREAS:** Civil Litigation; Entertainment Litigation.

**HOWARD P. KING** (June 19, 1945-December 25, 1993).

**THOMAS J. LEANSE,** born Los Angeles, California, February 21, 1954; admitted to bar, 1978, California; 1979, Illinois; 1982, U.S. Supreme Court. *Education:* University of California at San Diego (B.A., 1975); University of San Diego (J.D., 1978). Assistant State's Attorney, Cook County, Illinois, 1979-1981. General Counsel, United States Ski Association and United States Ski Team, 1985-1994. **PRACTICE AREAS:** Real Estate; Bankruptcy; Commercial and Business Litigation.

**THOMAS S. MAHR,** born Reedsburg, Wisconsin, June 23, 1954; admitted to bar, 1981, California and U.S. District Court, Central District of California; 1990, U.S. District Court, Northern District of California; 1991, U.S. court of Appeals, Ninth Circuit; 1994, U.S. District Court, Southern District of California. *Education:* University of Miami (B.M., magna cum laude, 1978; J.D., cum laude, 1981). Member, University of Miami Law Review, 1979-1981. *Member:* Orange County, Los Angeles County and American Bar Associations; State Bar of California. **PRACTICE AREAS:** Business, Entertainment and Commercial Litigation.

**ZIA F. MODABBER,** born Los Angeles, California, January 9, 1962; admitted to bar, 1988, California and U.S. District Court, Central District

*(This Listing Continued)*

## KATTEN MUCHIN & ZAVIS, Los Angeles—Continued

of California. *Education:* University of California at Berkeley (B.A., 1983); Loyola Law School, Los Angeles (J.D., 1988). Member, St. Thomas More Law Honor Society. *Member:* State Bar of California. **PRACTICE AREAS:** Entertainment and General Business Litigation.

**STEPHEN F. MOELLER,** born Covington, Kentucky, December 22, 1945; admitted to bar, 1973, California; 1977, U.S. District Court, Central District of California. *Education:* University of Illinois (B.A., magna cum laude, 1967); Harvard University (M.A., 1972; J.D., cum laude, 1971). Phi Beta Kappa; Pi Sigma Alpha. Deputy Public Defender, Los Angeles County, 1974-1982. *Member:* Century City and Los Angeles County Bar Associations; State Bar of California. **PRACTICE AREAS:** Entertainment Litigation; Business Litigation; General Business; Entertainment.

**DANIEL M. PELLICCIONI, (P.C.),** born Chicago, Illinois, May 28, 1946; admitted to bar, 1975, Illinois; 1991, California. *Education:* University of Michigan-Dearborn (A.B., with high distinction, 1972); University of Detroit (J.D., cum laude, 1975). Chairman of Chicago Bar Association Committee on Bankruptcies and Reorganization, 1985-1986. **PRACTICE AREAS:** Bankruptcy Law; Finance and Reorganization Law.

**STUART M. RICHTER,** born Bethlehem, Pennsylvania, July 17, 1961; admitted to bar, 1986, California and U.S. District Court, Central and Southern Districts of California. *Education:* University of Virginia (B.S., 1983); Pepperdine University (J.D., magna cum laude, 1986). *Member:* Orange County and Los Angeles County Bar Associations; State Bar of California. **PRACTICE AREAS:** Litigation.

**CHARLES M. STERN,** born Denver, Colorado, March 21, 1943; admitted to bar, 1969, California. *Education:* Harvard University (A.B., magna cum laude, 1965; LL.B., 1968). Phi Beta Kappa. Teaching Fellow, Case Western Reserve Law School, 1969-1970. *Member:* Los Angeles County Bar Association; State Bar of California. Fellow, American College of Trial Lawyers. **PRACTICE AREAS:** Business Litigation.

**GAIL MIGDAL TITLE,** born Waldenburg, Germany, May 31, 1946; admitted to bar, 1971, California. *Education:* Wellesley College (A.B., 1967); Boalt Hall School of Law, University of California at Berkeley (J.D., 1970). Adjunct Professor of Law, Federal Criminal Procedure, Loyola University School of Law, 1975-1976. Guest Speaker at various studios "The Pay or Play Clause" and "The Implications of *Buchwald v. Paramount* on Net Profit Definition." *Member:* Beverly Hills, Los Angeles County (Member, Barrister's Executive Committee, 1972-1974); Delegate, State Bar Conference of Delegates, 1974-1976; 1988-1989) and American (Member, Litigation Section and Forum Committee on Entertainment) Bar Associations; The State Bar of California (Member, Standing Committee on Public Interest Law, 1976—); Association of Business Trial Lawyers. **LANGUAGES:** French. **PRACTICE AREAS:** Entertainment Litigation; Intellectual Property; General Commercial Litigation; Business Crimes.

**JOEL R. WEINER,** born Chicago, Illinois, December 19, 1962; admitted to bar, 1988, California; 1989, Hawaii. *Education:* University of California at Santa Barbara (B.A., 1985); University of California at Berkeley, Boalt Hall School of Law (J.D., 1988). *Member:* Los Angeles County and Hawaii State Bar Associations; State Bar of California. **PRACTICE AREAS:** Litigation.

### ASSOCIATES

*Jeffrey I. Abrams; Todd T. Alberstone; Julie R. Benjamin* (Not admitted in CA); *Julia W. Brand; Alexandra J. Brew; Dustin K. Finer; Deborah L. Fink; Stacey K. Fishman; Deborah Giss; Jeremy J. F. Gray; Jon S. Grizel; Andrew J. Hackbert; Carolyn A. Hampton; Shauna D. Jackson; David P. Kaplan; Stacey D. McKee Knight; Stacey R. Konkoff; George Mastras, Jr.; Sherylle Mills; Randee Schuster Motzkin; Nayssan L. Parandeh; James B. Pickell; Janette M. Redd; Jamie Rudman; Paul Schiada; E. Randol Schoenberg; Immanuel I. Spira; Mary Taten; Cheryl L. Van Steenwyk; Raymond Wu; Juan E. Zuniga.*

## MICHELLE KATZ
Established in 1983

**1925 CENTURY PARK EAST, SUITE 2000**
**LOS ANGELES, CALIFORNIA 90067-2721**
Telephone: 310-277-2236
Facsimile: 310-277-7065; 310-556-5653

*Family Law Mediation.*

**MICHELLE KATZ,** born Los Angeles, California, May 26, 1941; admitted to bar, 1978, California and U.S. District Court, Central District of California. *Education:* University of California at Berkeley; Cornell University (B.A., 1964; M.Ed., 1965); Mid-Valley College of Law (J.D., 1977). Mediator, Family Law Mediation Program, Los Angeles Superior Court. *Member:* Beverly Hills (Member: Executive Committee, A.D.R. Section, 1994—; Executive Committee, Family Law Section, 1987—) and Los Angeles County Bar Associations; State Bar of California (Member, Executive Committee, Family Law Section, 1990-1994); Women Lawyers Association of Los Angeles (Member, Board of Governors, 1983-1990). (Certified Specialist, Family Law, The State Bar of California Board of Legal Specialization). **PRACTICE AREAS:** Family Law Mediation.

## KATZ & ASSOCIATES
Established in 1990

**EIGHTEENTH FLOOR**
**2049 CENTURY PARK EAST (CENTURY CITY)**
**LOS ANGELES, CALIFORNIA 90067**
Telephone: 310-203-0701; 281-7380
Fax: 310-203-0312

*White Collar Criminal Defense and Appellate Practice in all State and Federal Courts; Health Claims Defense; Bankruptcy Fraud Defense; Environmental Law. Rights of Financial Institutions and Investors.*

**DAVID A. KATZ,** born Orlando, Florida, August 20, 1952; admitted to bar, 1982, District of Columbia, 1983, California, U.S. District Court, Central District of California and U.S. Court of Appeals, Ninth Circuit. *Education:* University of California at Berkeley (B.A., summa cum laude, 1976, Phi Beta Kappa); Boalt Hall School of Law (J.D., 1980). Member, 1978-1980 and Note and Comment Editor, 1979-1980, California Law Review. Author: "Foreign Affairs Cases: The Need for a Mandatory Certification Procedure," 68 California Law Review 1186, 1980. Co-Authored, Book Review, 68 California Law Review 565, 1980. Adjunct Professor of Law: Whittier College School of Law, 1985-1990. Law Clerk: Chief Judge John Garrett Penn, U.S. District Court for the District of Columbia, 1980-1981; Office of the Solicitor General of the United States, Department of Justice, Summer 1980. Assistant U.S. Attorney, Criminal Division, 1983-1990 and Major Frauds Section, 1986-1990. Chief Postal Inspector's Special Award Winner, 1987 (selected the Outstanding Prosecutor in the United States); Nominee, Department of Justice Special Commendation Award, 1989 (one of 32 nationwide). Coordinator, Southern California Fraud Task Force, 1988-1989. Panelist: Federal Sentencing Guidelines, CEB; Federal Sentencing Guidelines, ALI/ABA, 1989. Expert Witness on Commodities, Investment and Telemarketing Fraud, U.S. House of Representatives, Sub-Committee on Commerce, Consumer and Monetary Affairs, 1990. **LANGUAGES:** Spanish. **REPORTED CASES:** U.S. v. Sterner, 23 F.3d 250 (9th Cir. 1994); U.S. v. Mett, 65 F.3d 1531 (9th Cir. 1995); U.S. v. U.S. District Court, 717 F.2d 478; U.S. v. McCollum, 802 F.2d 344; U.S. v. Fields, 783 F.2d 1382; U.S. v. French, 787 F.2d 1381; U.S. v. Houser, 804 F.2d 565. **PRACTICE AREAS:** White Collar Criminal Defense Law; Health Claims Law; Commodities and Securities Fraud Defense Law; Banking and Savings and Loan Fraud Law.

**JOHN P. DWYER,** born Battle Creek, Michigan, December 5, 1951; admitted to bar, 1981, District of Columbia; 1982, California. *Education:* DePauw University (B.S., with high distinction in chemistry and mathematics, 1973) Phi Beta Kappa; California Institute of Technology (Ph.D., in chemical physics, 1978); Boalt Hall, (J.D., 1980). Order of the Coif; Jamison Award for Advocacy and Scholarship. Member, 1978-1980 and Editor-in-Chief, 1979-1980, Ecology Law Quarterly. Law Clerk to: Justice Sandra Day O'Connor, U.S. Supreme Court, 1981 Term (1981-1982); Judge Harry T. Edwards, U.S. Court of Appeals, District of Columbia Circuit, 1980-1981. Staff Attorney, Washington, D.C. Public Defender Services, 1982-1984. Chairman, State Bar Committee on the Environment, 1989-1990. Member, Technical Advisory Committee on Legal Issues, Governor's Task

*(This Listing Continued)*

Force on Toxics, Waste and Technology, 1986. *PRACTICE AREAS:* Environmental Law; Appellate Practice.

### ASSOCIATES

**LINDA L. KACHEL,** born Whitewater, Wisconsin, December 10, 1954; admitted to bar, 1988, California, U.S. Court of Appeals, Ninth Circuit; 1989, Wisconsin; 1990, U.S. District Court, Central District of California. *Education:* Northwestern University (B.S., Speech, 1975); University of Wisconsin-Madison (M.B.A., 1980); University of Southern California at Los Angeles (J.D., 1985).

All attorneys are members of the California State Bar and the American Bar Association.

## KATZ, GOLDEN & FISHMAN, LLP

10850 WILSHIRE BOULEVARD
SUITE 600
**LOS ANGELES, CALIFORNIA 90024**
Telephone: 310-470-7777
Facsimile: 310-470-7481

*FIRM PROFILE: A law firm offering a full service entertainment and corporate practice, with expertise in motion picture and television transactions, new technologies, book and multimedia publishing, intellectual property, film financing, corporate sponsorship and securities, real estate, tax and estate planning.*

### PARTNERS

**JOEL L. FISHMAN,** born Los Angeles, California, October 12, 1947; admitted to bar, 1977, California; 1979, District of Columbia. *Education:* University of California at Berkeley (A.B., 1969); University of Southern California (J.D., 1976). Phi Beta Kappa. Administrative Assistant to United States Congressman Thomas M. Rees, 1970-1974. Member, L.A. 2000 Committee. *Member:* Los Angeles County and American Bar Associations; The State Bar of California; District of Columbia Bar. *PRACTICE AREAS:* Business Law; Real Estate Law. *Email:* jlf@kgf-law.com

**DIANE A. GOLDEN,** born Bronx, New York, December 2, 1956; admitted to bar, 1983, California. *Education:* Tufts University (B.A., magna cum laude, 1978); New York University School of Law (J.D., cum laude, 1983). Order of the Coif. Author: "Rights of the Handicapped," 3 Annual Survey of American Law 555, 1982. *Member:* Academy of Television Arts and Sciences; Women in Film. *Member:* Los Angeles County Bar Association; The State Bar of California. *PRACTICE AREAS:* Entertainment Law; Motion Pictures and Television; Multimedia Law. *Email:* dag@kgf-law.com

**STEVEN KATZ,** born Brooklyn, New York, January 7, 1949; admitted to bar, 1974, California. *Education:* Hamilton College (A.B., 1970); Harvard University (J.D., cum laude, 1973). Phi Beta Kappa. Charles Dana Scholar. Author: "Production Insurance and Completion Guarantees," Producing For Motion Pictures and Television: A Practical Guide to Legal Issues, a publication of the Los Angeles County Bar Association Intellectual Property and Unfair Competition Section, 1983. *Member:* Los Angeles County Bar Association (Member, 1981-1990 and Chair, 1988-1989, Executive Committee, Intellectual Property and Unfair Competition Section); State Bar of California. *PRACTICE AREAS:* Entertainment Law; Motion Pictures and Television. *Email:* sbk@kgf-law.com

**MARY E. SULLIVAN,** born Havre de Grace, Maryland, November, 25, 1962; admitted to bar, 1987, California; 1988, U.S. District Court, Central District of California. *Education:* Loyola College, Baltimore, Maryland (B.S., summa cum laude, 1984); Georgetown University (J.D., 1987). Member, 1985-1987 and End notes Editor, 1986-1987, Journal of Law and Technology, Computer Law Society. *Member:* Century City Bar Association; The State Bar of California. *PRACTICE AREAS:* Entertainment Law; Motion Picture Finance; Corporate Law. *Email:* mes@kgf-law.com

### OF COUNSEL

**CHARLES D. SILVERBERG, (A PROFESSIONAL CORPORATION),** born Buffalo, New York, April 14, 1932; admitted to bar, 1956, California. *Education:* Stanford University (A.B., 1953; J.D., 1955). Author: "Industry Litigation: Some 1957 Cases of Interest to the Motion Picture and Television Industries," Film Daily Yearbook, 1958; "Percentage Arrangements in Motion Picture and Television Productions," Entertainment Law Institute, 1971; 1981; "The Negotiation of Employment Agreements for Theatrical and Television Motion Pictures," UCLA Entertainment Symposium, 1982. Chairman, Stanford Law School Board of Visitors, 1984-1985. Lecturer: Georgetown University Law Center, 1984-1986; Stanford Law School, 1993-1996. Member, National Panel, American Arbitration Association, 1965—. *Member:* Beverly Hills, Los Angeles County (Delegate, Conference of State Bar Delegates, 1960-1961, 1964-1967, Alternate, 1962-1963) and American (Chairman, Sub Committee Audio Visual Cassettes, 1971-1973) Bar Associations; The State Bar of California; Los Angeles Copyright Society (Trustee, 1969-1976; President, 1975); Copyright Society of the U.S.A. (Trustee, 1986-1987). [Capt., JAGC, U.S. Army Reserve, active duty, 1955-1957]. *PRACTICE AREAS:* Entertainment Law; Motion Pictures and Television. *Email:* cds@kgf-law.com

**PAUL L. MIGDAL,** born Chicago, Illinois, April 15, 1936; admitted to bar, 1962, California. *Education:* De Paul University (B.Sc., 1958); University of California at Los Angeles (J.D., 1962). Member, UCLA, Law Review, 1961-1962. *Member:* Beverly Hills, Los Angeles County and American Bar Associations; The State Bar of California. *PRACTICE AREAS:* Entertainment Law; Motion Pictures and Television. *Email:* plm@kgf-law.com

**PATRICIA A. MCVERRY,** born Phoenix, Arizona, July 11, 1953; admitted to bar, 1979, California; U.S. District Court, Eastern District of California. *Education:* University of California at Berkeley (A.B., 1975); McGeorge School of Law, University of the Pacific (J.D., with great distinction, 1979); New York University (LL.M., Taxation, 1984). Recipient, American Jurisprudence Awards in Torts and Family Law. Associate Editor, Pacific Law Journal, 1978-1979. Adjunct Professor, University of San Diego School of Law, 1986-1988. Adjunct Professor, University of Southern California School of Accounting, 1991—. *Member:* Beverly Hill and Los Angeles County Bar Associations; State Bar of California. *PRACTICE AREAS:* Taxation; Estate Planning; Estate and Trust Administration. *Email:* pmcv@kgf-law.com

**JENNIFER JUSTMAN,** born Los Angeles, California, April 13, 1960; admitted to bar, 1986, California. *Education:* Stanford University (B.A., 1982; M.A., 1983); University of California School of Law at Los Angeles (J.D., 1986). *Member:* The State Bar of California. *PRACTICE AREAS:* Entertainment Law; Motion Pictures and Television; Multimedia Law. *Email:* jj@kgf-law.com

**JEFFREY BRAUER,** born Jersey City, New Jersey, March 16, 1955; admitted to bar, 1984, New York; 1989, California. *Education:* Tufts University (B.A., magna cum laude, 1977); New York University School of Law (J.D., 1983). Member, Review of Law and Social Change, 1981-1982. Massachusetts Executive Office of Energy Resources, 1977-1980. *Member:* State Bar of California; New York State Bar Association. (Senior Vice President, Business and Legal Affairs). *Email:* jmb@kgf-law.com

## KATZ, HOYT, SEIGEL & KAPOR LLP

A Partnership including a Professional Corporation
*Established in 1927*

SUITE 820, 11111 SANTA MONICA BOULEVARD
**LOS ANGELES, CALIFORNIA 90025-3342**
Telephone: 310-473-1300
Telecopier: 310-473-7138

*Commercial, Bankruptcy, Business, Real Estate, Trademark, Copyright, Unfair Competition, Probate, General Civil, Trial and Appellate Practice in all State and Federal Courts.*

*FIRM PROFILE: The partners and associates of Katz, Hoyt, Seigel & Kapor are all members of the State Bar of California and maintain active membership in numerous local and specialized bar associations. Clients of the firm include commercial factors, consumer goods manufacturers, real estate developers, banks and other financial institutions, retailers, franchisors, franchisees, leasing companies, business brokers, entrepreneurs and numerous other business entities located throughout the world.*

*The attorneys in the firm have had a substantial amount of business experience, independent from the practice of law, which enables the firm to provide to its clients an exceptional degree of practicality in the firm's approach to the resolution of business problems and disputes. The firm has developed a reputation for excellence in the area of business planning and preventive law, to enable its clients to avoid the high cost of business litigation. The attorneys in the firm regularly participate in programs of legal education, both as participants and as lecturers, panelists and instructors.*

*In recruiting new associates for the firm, emphasis is placed upon selecting attorneys who have not only achieved academic excellence, but who have also had substantial exposure to the everyday problems of operating a business. Thus, whether it be in a corporate board room or in a courtroom, the attorneys of the*

*(This Listing Continued)*

**KATZ, HOYT, SEIGEL & KAPOR LLP**, Los Angeles— Continued

*firm are able to recognize and act upon the realities of business problems with a special attitude that is unique and innovative.*

### MEMBERS OF FIRM

**CHARLES J. KATZ** (1905-1983).

**LOUIS C. HOYT** (1905-1994).

**BENJAMIN S. SEIGEL, (P.C.),** born Kansas City, Missouri, January 19, 1936; admitted to bar, 1974, California and U.S. District Court, Central District of California; 1983, U.S. Claims Court; 1984, U.S. Tax Court; 1985, District of Columbia. *Education:* University of Missouri (B.S., 1958); University of West Los Angeles (J.D., cum laude, 1974). Adjunct Instructor in Bankruptcy, University of West Los Angeles, School of Paralegal Studies, 1981-1984. Judge Pro Tem, Los Angeles County Municipal Court, Small Claims Division, 1980-1983. Member, Board of Directors, 1983— and President, 1988, Los Angeles Bankruptcy Forum. Founding President, California Bankruptcy Forum. Bankruptcy Court Mediator, 1995—. *Member:* Beverly Hills, Los Angeles County and American (Member, Secured Creditors Sub-Committee of Business Bankruptcy Committee, 1985—) Bar Associations; State Bar of California (Member, Section on Business and Commercial Law); District of Columbia Bar; Financial Lawyers Conference; Commercial Law League of America. **REPORTED CASES:** In Re Confections by Sandra, Inc. 83 BR 729; In Re: Tr-3 Industries 41 BR 128. **PRACTICE AREAS:** Corporate Reorganizations; Debtor/Creditor Rights; Chapter 11 Representations; Bankruptcy; Business Reorganization.

**JEFFREY H. KAPOR,** born New York, October 15, 1953; admitted to bar, 1978, California, U.S. District Court, Central District of California and U.S. Tax Court; 1983, U.S. Claims Court. *Education:* University of California at Los Angeles (B.A., 1975); Southwestern University (J.D., 1978). Delta Theta Phi; The Order of Barristers; Moot Court. Member, Southwestern Law Review, 1977-1978. Judge Pro Tem, Los Angeles Municipal Court, 1984. *Member:* Los Angeles County and American (Member, Trademark Committee, 1985—) Bar Associations; State Bar of California (Member, Section of Business and Commercial Law); Financial Lawyers Conference; Commercial Law League of America. **PRACTICE AREAS:** Mergers and Acquisitions; Corporate Business Law; Commercial Law; Debtor/Creditor Relations; Financial and Business Planning; Copyright and Trademark.

**SCOTT H. JACOBS,** born New York, N.Y., October 31, 1948; admitted to bar, 1978, California. *Education:* Hofstra University (B.A., in Philosophy, 1970); Southwestern University (J.D., 1978). Staff Member, 1977 and Executive Note and Comment Editor, 1978, Southwestern University Law Review. Author: "United States v. Wilson: An Expansive Approach to the Power of the Federal Courts to Punish Contempts Under Rule 42 (a) of the Federal Rules of Criminal Procedure," Southwestern University Law Review, Vol. 9, No. 3. *Member:* Los Angeles County and American Bar Associations; State Bar of California; Financial Lawyers Conference. **REPORTED CASES:** Datatronic Systems Corp. v. Speron, Inc. 176 Cal. App. 3d 1168 (1986). **PRACTICE AREAS:** Business Litigation; Bankruptcy; Debtor/Creditor Relations; Labor Law.

**ALAN JAY COHEN,** born New Haven, Connecticut, August 21, 1951; admitted to bar, 1978, Illinois; 1982, California; U.S. District Court, Northern District of Illinois, U.S. District Court, Central District of California and U.S. Court of Appeals, Ninth Circuit; U.S. District Court, Southern District of California. *Education:* Clark University (B.A., 1973); University of Exeter, England; John Marshall Law School at Chicago, Illinois (J.D., 1977). Member, Los Angeles Bankruptcy Forum. *Member:* Los Angeles County Bar Association; State Bar of California; State Bar of Illinois; Financial Lawyers Conference. **LANGUAGES:** French. **PRACTICE AREAS:** Business Litigation; Prejudgment Remedies; Debtor/Creditor Relations; Personal Property Leasing.

**WILLIAM SCHOENHOLZ,** born Los Angeles, California, August 10, 1955; admitted to bar, 1981, California. *Education:* University of California at Santa Barbara (B.A., with high honors, 1977); University of Southern California (J.D., 1981). Phi Alpha Delta. Recipient, American Jurisprudence Award in Remedies. Co-Author: "Default Remedies of Secured Creditors," 5 National Law Journal 15, Sept., 1983; "Federal Tax Lien Impact of Secured Lenders," 6 National Law Journal 15, Nov., 1983; "Foreclosure and Repossession in California," National Business Institute, Inc., copyright, 1991. *Member:* Los Angeles County Bar Association. **PRACTICE AREAS:** Real Estate; Commercial; Secured Transactions; Corporate.

*(This Listing Continued)*

**JACK R. LENACK,** born Los Angeles, California, August 15, 1956; admitted to bar, 1985, California and U.S. District Court, Central District of California. *Education:* University of California at Los Angeles (B.A., 1978); Southwestern University School of Law (J.D., 1984). *Member:* Los Angeles County Bar Association; State Bar of California. **PRACTICE AREAS:** Corporate Law; Real Estate Law; Commercial Law.

**RUSSELL L. ALLYN,** born Los Angeles, California, March 27, 1964; admitted to bar, 1989, California. *Education:* University of California at San Diego (B.A., 1986); Hastings College of the Law, University of California (J.D., 1989). Recipient, American Jurisprudence Award, Commercial Paper, 1988. **REPORTED CASES:** In re Kingsley, Jennison McNulty & Morse, Inc., Adm. Prac. File No. 3-7446; Securities and Exchange Commission, Initial Decision, Release No. 24, 1991 SEC LEXIS 2587, November 14, 1991. **PRACTICE AREAS:** Business Litigation.

**DOUGLAS M. LIPSTONE,** born Los Angeles, California, January 29, 1963; admitted to bar, 1989, California and U.S. District Court, Central District of California. *Education:* University of California (B.S., 1985); University of California at Los Angeles (J.D., 1988). *Member:* Beverly Hills, Century City, Los Angeles County and American (Member, Sections on International Business and Patent, Trademark and Copyright) Bar Associations; State Bar of California (Member, Sections on Business and Intellectual Property). **PRACTICE AREAS:** Transactional and Intellectual Property.

**MOIRA DOHERTY,** born Winnipeg, Manitoba, Canada, May 1, 1963; admitted to bar, 1990, Pennsylvania; 1993, California. *Education:* Clark University (B.A., 1985); American University, Washington College of Law (J.D., 1990). Editor: California Bankruptcy Journal; Federal Bar Association Newsletter, Los Angeles Chapter. Law Clerk: Hon. Kathleen T. Lax, U.S. Bankruptcy Court, Central District, 1992-1993; Hon. Bruce R. Geernaert, California Superior Court, 1991; Law Clerk Extern to the Hon. Arthur L. Shipe, Administrative Law Judge, Commodity Futures Trading Commission, 1990. Author, "Section 552 - Postpetition Effect of Security Interest," in *Annual Survey of Bankruptcy Law*, 473, William L. Norton, Jr. ed 1993. Instructor, Legal Research and Writing, Civil Procedure and Bankruptcy, Paralegal Studies Program, Catherine College. *Member:* Los Angeles County, Federal and American (Member, Subcommittee on Commercial Law and Bankruptcy Judges) Bar Associations; State Bar of California; Association of Law Clerks to Bankruptcy Judges; Los Angeles Bankruptcy Forum; Financial Lawyers Conference; Association of Business Trial Lawyers; Women Lawyers Association of Los Angeles. **PRACTICE AREAS:** Civil Litigation; Bankruptcy; Debtor/Creditor Relations; Business Law.

**MARLA MILNER,** born Los Angeles, California, September 26, 1967; admitted to bar, 1995, California. *Education:* University of Southern California (B.S., 1990; J.D., 1994). *Member:* State Bar of California. **PRACTICE AREAS:** Corporate.

---

# LAW OFFICES OF
# IRA BENJAMIN KATZ

*A PROFESSIONAL CORPORATION*

**1901 AVENUE OF THE STARS, 20TH FLOOR**
**LOS ANGELES, CALIFORNIA 90067**
Telephone: 310-282-8580
Fax: 310-282-8149

*Bankruptcy, Business, Commercial, Real Estate and Civil Litigation.*

**IRA BENJAMIN KATZ,** admitted to bar, 1978, California; U.S. Supreme Court, U.S. Court of Appeals, Ninth Circuit; U.S. District Court, Central, Eastern, Northern and Southern Districts of California. *Education:* University of California at Los Angeles (B.A., magna cum laude, 1974; Phi Beta Kappa; Pi Gamma Mu); Boalt Hall, University of California at Berkeley (J.D., 1977). Member: Moot Court Board; Ecology Law Quarterly. *Member:* Los Angeles County Bar Association (Member, Commercial Law and Bankruptcy Section); California Bankruptcy Forum.

## LAW OFFICES OF
## BARRY B. KAUFMAN
*2121 AVENUE OF THE STARS, SUITE 1700*
**LOS ANGELES, CALIFORNIA 90067**
Telephone: 310-557-0404
Telecopier: 310-557-1010

*Labor and Employment Law. General Civil Practice.*

**BARRY B. KAUFMAN,** born Los Angeles, California, July 14, 1958; admitted to bar, 1983, California. *Education:* University of California at Los Angeles (B.A., magna cum laude, 1980); University of Southern California (J.D., 1983). Member, Southern California Law Review, 1981-1983. Associate Editor, Computer Law Journal, 1982-1983. Articles Editor, University of Southern California Tax Institute, Major Tax Planning, 1982-1983. Author: "Preferential Hiring Policies For Older Workers Under the Age Discrimination in Employment Act," 56 Southern California Law Review 825, 1983. Former Associations: Proskauer Rose Goetz & Mendelsohn, 1985-1990; Kadison, Pfaelzer, Woodard, Quinn & Rossi, 1983-1985.

---

## WARREN W. KAUFMAN, INC.
*12650 RIVERSIDE DRIVE*
**LOS ANGELES, CALIFORNIA 91607**
Telephone: 818-755-4848
Fax: 818-508-0181

*Government Contracts, Insurance, Product Liability Defense, Commercial Litigation, Construction.*

**WARREN W. KAUFMAN,** born Elizabeth, New Jersey, December 31, 1937; admitted to bar, 1964, California; 1968, U.S. Court of Military Appeals; 1969, U.S. Supreme Court; 1970, U.S. Claims Court. *Education:* University of California at Los Angeles (A.B., 1960); Boalt Hall School of Law, University of California at Berkeley (J.D., 1963); George Washington University (LL.M. in Government Procurement Law, 1971). Phi Delta Phi. Trial Attorney, Contract Appeals Division, Department of the Army, 1969-1972. *Member:* Los Angeles County, Federal and American (Member, Public Contract Law Section) Bar Associations; State Bar of California. (Also Of Counsel to Plotkin, Marutani & Kyriacou, A.P.C.). **SPECIAL AGENCIES:** Armed Services Board of Contract Appeals. **PRACTICE AREAS:** Government Contract Law; Insurance Law; Product Liability Defense; Commercial Litigation; Construction Litigation.

---

## KAUFMAN & YOUNG
*A PROFESSIONAL CORPORATION*
**LOS ANGELES, CALIFORNIA**
(See Beverly Hills)
*Family Law and Trial Practice in all State and Federal Courts.*

---

## MILES L. KAVALLER
*A PROFESSIONAL LAW CORPORATION*
**LOS ANGELES, CALIFORNIA**
(See Beverly Hills)
*General Civil and Trial Practice in all Courts. Transporation Law.*

---

## RICHARD T. KAYAIAN
*A PROFESSIONAL CORPORATION*
*444 SOUTH FLOWER, SUITE 2030*
**LOS ANGELES, CALIFORNIA 90071-2955**
Telephone: 213-627-1450
FAX: 213-627-9858

*General Business, Corporation and Probate Law. Litigation.*

**RICHARD T. KAYAIAN,** born Binghamton, New York, February 23, 1939; admitted to bar, 1965, California. *Education:* Los Angeles City College (A.A., 1959); University of Southern California (B.A., 1961; LL.B., 1964). Beta Gamma Sigma. *Member:* Los Angeles County and American Bar Associations; The State Bar of California.

REFERENCE: Sanwa Bank (Los Angeles Main Office).

---

## KAYE, ROSE & PARTNERS
A Law Partnership
*1801 CENTURY PARK EAST, #1250*
**LOS ANGELES, CALIFORNIA 90067-2302**
Telephone: 310-277-1200
Fax: 310-277-1220
Telex: 371-7740
Email: krpla@aol.com

*San Diego, California Office:* 1230 Columbia Street, Suite 1000. Telephone: 619-232-6555. Fax: 619-232-6577.
*San Francisco, California Office:* 55 Francisco Street, Suite 610. Telephone: 414-433-6555. Fax: 415-433-6577.
*Miami, Florida Office:* One Biscayne Tower, 2 South Biscayne Boulevard, Suite 3750. Telephone: 305-358-6555. Fax: 305-374-9077.

*Maritime Law, Insurance Defense, General Civil Litigation, Customs and Trade Law, Entertainment, Medical Malpractice, Pollution, Legislative Affairs and Product Liability. Civil Trial and Appellate Practice in State and Federal Courts. Admiralty, Maritime, Marine Oil Spill, Construction, Insurance, Surety, Corporate, Product Liability and Business Litigation.*

**LAWRENCE W. KAYE,** admitted to bar, 1979, California and U.S. District Court, Southern District of California; 1984, U.S. Court of Appeals, Ninth Circuit; 1991, U.S. District Court, Central, Northern and Eastern Districts of California; 1992, U.S. District Court, District of Arizona; 1993, U.S. Supreme Court. *Education:* University of Hartford (B.A., summa cum laude, 1976); University of San Diego (J.D., cum laude, 1978). Alpha Chi Honor Society. Recipient: Copley Press Award. Member, San Diego Law Review, 1977-1978. Author: "The Innocent Passage of Warships through Foreign Territorial Seas," 15 San Diego Law Rev. (1976). Law Clerk to Hon. Howard B. Turrentine, U.S. District Court, Southern District of California, 1979-1980. Chairman: Port of San Diego Cruise Ship Advisory Committee, 1990—; Long Range Planning Committee, San Diego Cruise Consortium, 1987-1990. *Member:* Maritime Law Association of the United States. (Also at San Diego). **REPORTED CASES:** Saroza v. Royal Caribbean Corp., 1992 A.M.C. 428 (C.D. Cal. 1991); aff'd 996 F.2d 1227 (9th Cir. 1993); Vander Lind v. The Atchison, Topeka and Santa Fe Railway System, 146 Cal.App. 3D 358, 194 Cal. Rptr. 209; Osborn v. Princess Tours, 1996 AMC 1481, 1995 AMC 2119 (S.D. Tex. 1995); Berman v. Royal Cruise Line, 1995 AMC 1926 (CA 1995); Hayman v. Sitmar, 18 Cal. Rptr. 2d 412 (1993).

**BRADLEY M. ROSE,** admitted to bar, 1985, Oklahoma; 1986, California; 1987, U.S. District Court, Central and Northern Districts of California. *Education:* University of Oklahoma (B.A., 1982; J.D., 1985). Recipient, Eugene Koontz Oxford Scholarship. Oxford Fellow. *Member:* Maritime Law Association of the United States. (Resident). **REPORTED CASES:** Trinidad Corp. v. S/S KEIYOH MARU, 845 P.2d 818 (9th Cir, 1988).

**ANTHONY J. PASSANTE, JR.,** admitted to bar, 1980, California. *Education:* University of California (B.A., 1976); University of San Diego (J.D., 1980). Member, Appellate Moot Court Board, 1979-1980. Member, Law Review, University of San Diego School of Law, Spring 1980. (Also at San Diego).

### ASSOCIATES

**ANITA M. EILERT,** admitted to bar, 1987, California. *Education:* San Diego State University (B.A., 1980); Western State University (J.D., 1986). (Also at San Diego).

**ELSA WARD ARATA,** admitted to bar, 1992, Louisiana; 1994, California. *Education:* Loyola University (B.A., cum laude, 1989; J.D. 1992). (Resident).

**MARVA JO WYATT,** admitted to bar, 1987, Louisiana and U.S. District Court, Western District of Louisiana; 1995, California. *Education:* Tulane University of Louisiana (B.A., magna cum laude, 1983; J.D., 1985; L.L.M. in admiralty, with distinction, 1991). (Resident).

*(This Listing Continued)*

KAYE, ROSE & PARTNERS, Los Angeles—Continued

REPRESENTATIVE CLIENTS: Assuranceforeningen SKULD; Carnival Cruise Lines; Kloster Cruise Ltd; Princess Cruises, Inc.; Regency Cruises, Inc.; Royal Caribbean Cruises Ltd.; Royal Cruise Line; Sea-Land Service, Inc.; The Steamship Mutual Underwriting Association (Bermuda) Ltd.; The United Kingdom Mutual Steam Ship Assurance Association (Bermuda) Ltd; Zim American-Israeli Shipping Company; Seabourn Cruise Lines.

# KAYE, SCHOLER, FIERMAN, HAYS & HANDLER, LLP

A New York Limited Liability Partnership
*1999 AVENUE OF THE STARS, SUITE 1600*
**LOS ANGELES, CALIFORNIA 90067-6048**
Telephone: 310-788-1000
Facsimile: 310-788-1200

*New York, N.Y.:* 425 Park Avenue, 10022-3598. Telephone: 212-836-8000. Telex: 234860 KAY UR. Facsimile: 212-836-8689.

*Washington, D.C.:* McPherson Building, 901 Fifteenth Street, N.W., Suite 1100, 20005-2327. Telephone: 202-682-3500. Facsimile: 202-682-3580.

*Hong Kong:* 9 Queen Road Centre, 18th Floor. Telephone: 852-28458989. Facsimile: 852-28453682; 2389.

FIRM PROFILE: *Kaye, Scholer, Fierman, Hays & Handler, LLP is a full service United States based international law firm representing public and private companies, governmental entities, financial institutions and other organizations in matters across the country and around the world. The Firm's Los Angeles-based attorneys offer a wide range of experience serving clients throughout North America, as well as Europe and the Pacific Rim, in the areas of litigation, corporate and finance, bankruptcy and corporate reorganization, entertainment, intellectual property, real estate, and public law.*

*MEMBERS OF FIRM*

**GARY APFEL,** admitted to bar, 1977, New York and U.S. District Court, Southern and Eastern Districts of New York; 1988, California, U.S. District Court, District of California and U.S. Court of Appeals, Ninth Circuit. *Education:* New York University (A.B., magna cum laude, 1973); Columbia University (J.D., 1976). Phi Beta Kappa. Kent Scholar. Harlan Fiske Stone Scholar. Member, Joseph H. Park History Honors Society. Editor, Columbia Journal of Transnational Law, 1975-1976. *Member:* Los Angeles County, New York State and American Bar Associations; State Bar of California (Member: Corporations Committee, Business Law Section). **PRACTICE AREAS:** Contract Law; Corporate Law; Private Placements; Project Finance; Public Offerings; Securities Law; Stock and Asset Acquisitions.

**ATON ARBISSER,** admitted to bar, 1984, New York; 1990, California. *Education:* Princeton University (A.B., 1978); University of California at Berkeley (M.A., 1982); Boalt Hall School of Law, University of California (J.D., 1982). *Member:* State Bar of California; American Bar Association. **PRACTICE AREAS:** Administrative Law Litigation; Antitrust Law; False Advertising Litigation; Trademark Litigation; Unfair Competition Claims.

**ROBERT BARNES,** admitted to bar, 1985, California, U.S. District Court, Northern, Southern, Central and Eastern Districts of California and U.S. Court of Appeals, Ninth Circuit. *Education:* Wadham College, Oxford University, England (B.A., 1974; M.A., 1976); University of California School of Law (J.D., 1985). Order of the Coif. Editor, UCLA Law Review. Law Clerk, Hon. Harry Pregerson, U.S. Court of Appeals for the Ninth Circuit, 1985-1986. *Member:* State Bar of California. **PRACTICE AREAS:** Litigation; Entertainment.

**T. BRENT COSTELLO,** admitted to bar, 1978, New York (Not admitted in California). *Education:* Yale University (B.A., 1974); Georgetown University (J.D., 1977). **PRACTICE AREAS:** Corporate Finance.

**BARRY L. DASTIN,** admitted to bar, 1979, New York; 1985, California. *Education:* Yale University (B.A., 1975); Harvard University (J.D., 1978). *Member:* The State Bar of California; American Bar Association. **PRACTICE AREAS:** Corporate Law; Securities Law; Mergers and Acquisitions; Banking and Financing.

**MICHAEL D. FERNHOFF,** admitted to bar, 1978, California; 1979, U.S. District Court, Central District of California, U.S. Tax Court and U.S. Court of Appeals, Ninth Circuit. *Education:* University of Wisconsin (B.B.A., Accounting and Finance, with distinction, 1975); University of California at Los Angeles (J.D., 1978); New York University (LL.M., Taxation, 1979). Member, New York Law Review, 1978-1979. **PRACTICE**

*(This Listing Continued)*

CAA834B

**AREAS:** Corporate, Partnership, Individual and International Taxation; Mergers and Acquisitions; Corporate Law; International Business Law; Partnership Law.

**KENNETH A. FREELING,** admitted to bar, 1982, District of Columbia; 1983, U.S. Court of Appeals, Fourth Circuit and U.S. District Court, District of Maryland; 1985, New York and U.S. District Court, Southern and Eastern Districts of New York; 1990, California and U.S. District Court, Central and Northern Districts of California. *Education:* Georgetown University (A.B., magna cum laude, 1979; J.D., 1982). Phi Beta Kappa. Member, Editorial Board, Law and Policy in International Business, 1981-1982. Law Clerk, The Honorable R. Dorsey Watkins, U.S. District Court, District of Maryland, 1982-1984. *Member:* The Association of the Bar of the City of New York; The District of Columbia Bar; American Bar Association.

**JEFFREY S. GORDON,** admitted to bar, 1977, California. *Education:* Golden Gate University (B.A., summa cum laude, 1974); University of California at Davis (J.D., 1977). Order of the Coif; Phi Kappa Phi. Member, Moot Court Board, 1976-1977. Law Clerk to Hon. Robert M. Takasugi, U.S. District Court, Central District of California, 1977-1978. Author: "RICO in Banks and Savings and Loan Failures" and "Strategies For The Plaintiff and Defendant," Sixth Annual RICO Litigation Update, Prentice Hall, 1990; "Me a Racketeer? Tell me it ain't so!" Town Hall of California Reporter, November, 1986. Treasurer, Member of Steering Committee, Independent Citizens Committee to Keep Politics Out of the Courts, 1986-1987. Member, Board of Governors, Pasadena Branch, Los Angeles Urban League, 1981-1986. *Member:* Los Angeles County (Member, Correctional Facilities Grievance Resolution Committee, 1981-1982) and American Bar Associations; State Bar of California; National Association of Criminal Defense Lawyers. **PRACTICE AREAS:** Complex Civil Litigation; Securities Law; Contract Law; Entertainment Law; Environmental Law; Internal Corporate Investigations; Litigation; Real Estate.

**CHANNING D. JOHNSON,** admitted to bar, 1978, California and U.S. District Court, Central District of California. *Education:* Stanford University (B.A., 1972); Harvard University (J.D., 1975). Member, Pasadena Planning Commission, 1982-1986. *Member:* State Bar of California.

**BARRY H. LAWRENCE,** admitted to bar, 1967, California. *Education:* University of California at Los Angeles (B.S., 1963); University of California School of Law (J.D., 1966). Phi Delta Phi. Author: "Who Stole My Brokers Commission," California Real Estate Magazine, February, 1976; "Liability of Brokers and Escrow Agents Using a Contract of Sale Form," California Escrow Association News, March 1975. Professor of Law, 1967-1969 and Assistant Dean, 1969 California College of Law. Deputy Attorney General, State of California, 1967-1968. Member, Committee to Update Plan for Professional Development of Real Estate Industry in California, 1978. Member, California Corporations Commission on Escrow Law, 1981-1983. Court Appointed Receiver for Real Estate Entities, National Television Real Estate Analyst, Financial News Network, 1982. Legal Counsel, California Escrow Association, 1978-1983. Legislative Counsel, Homebuilders Council, 1982. Panelist/Moderator, Real Estate Update, Continuing Education of the Bar Real Estate Programs, University of California at Berkeley, 1985—. *Member:* Los Angeles County Bar Association (Member, Executive Committee, Real Estate Section, 1987); State Bar of California. **PRACTICE AREAS:** Business Law; Real Estate; Securities; Real Estate Development and Finance.

**RONALD L. LEIBOW,** admitted to bar, 1966, California and U.S. District Court, Central District of California; 1972, U.S. District Court, Northern District of California; 1978, U.S. District Court, Southern District of California; 1979, U.S. District Court, Eastern District of California. *Education:* University of California at Los Angeles; California State University, at Northridge (A.B., 1962); University of California School of Law (J.D., 1965). Phi Alpha Delta (Justice 1964-1965). Author: Articles on Municipal Law, 31 Municipal Law Journal, No. 6, 1966 and 32 Municipal Law Journal, No. 6, 1967. Assistant Professor, Legal Aspects of Urban Planning California State University, Northridge, 1971-1972. Member, California Governor's Committee on Children and Youth, 1961-1965. *Member:* Beverly Hills, Los Angeles County (Member, Commercial Law and Bankruptcy Section) and American (Member, Business Bankruptcy Committee, Section of Corporation, Banking and Business Law) Bar Associations; State Bar of California; Financial Lawyers Conference. **PRACTICE AREAS:** Insolvency; Bankruptcy; Corporate Reorganization; Debt Restructure; Workouts.

**HUSHMAND SOHAILI,** admitted to bar, 1979, California. *Education:* University of Southern Illinois (B.A., 1975); University of Southern California (J.D., 1979). Phi Alpha Delta; Order of the Coif. *Member:* Los Angeles

*(This Listing Continued)*

County Bar Association; State Bar of California. *PRACTICE AREAS:* Acquisitions; Joint Ventures; Real Estate; Real Estate Finance; Sales; Syndications; Transactional Law.

**WILLIAM E. THOMSON, JR.,** admitted to bar, 1963, Virginia; 1964, Ohio; 1967-1982, U.S. Court of Customs and Patent Appeals; 1970, California, U.S. District Court, Central District of California and U.S. Court of Appeals, Ninth Circuit; 1981, U.S. Supreme Court; 1982, U.S. Court of Appeals for the Federal Circuit. *Education:* Bucknell University (B.S., in Ch.E., 1957); Georgetown University (J.D., 1963). Adjunct Professor, Church, State and Law, Fuller Theological Seminary, 1977—. Member, City Council, Pasadena, 1981—. Mayor, Pasadena, California, 1988-1990. *Member:* Los Angeles County and American Bar Associations; The State Bar of California; Los Angeles Intellectual Property Law Association; American Intellectual Property Law Association; Association of Business Trial Lawyers.

## SPECIAL COUNSEL

**CRUZ REYNOSO,** admitted to bar, 1959, California and U.S. Court of Appeals, Ninth Circuit; 1968, U.S. Supreme Court; U.S. District Court, Southern, Central and Eastern Districts of California. *Education:* Fullerton Junior College (A.A., 1951); Pomona College (B.A., 1953); George Washington University; University of California at Berkeley (LL.B., 1958); National Autonomous University of Mexico. Alpha Gamma Sigma; Phi Alpha Delta. Professor of Law: University of New Mexico School of Law, 1972-1976; University of California at Los Angeles School of Law, 1991—. Assistant Executive Officer, California Fair Employment Commission, 1965-1966. Staff Secretary to California Governor Edmund G. Brown, 1966. Associate General Counsel, Equal Opportunity Commission, 1967-1968. Associate Justice: Court of Appeals, 1976-1982; California Supreme Court, 1982-1987. *Member:* Los Angeles, Sacramento County and American (Council Member, Section on Legal Education and Admission to the Bar, 1977-1980; Council Member and Officer, Section on Individual Rights and Responsibilities, 1973-1983; Chair of Section, 1981-1982) Bar Associations; State Bar of California; La Raza Lawyers Association; California Judges Association; California Academy of Appellate Lawyers. [U.S. Army, Special Agent, Counter Intelligence Corps, 1953-1955]. *LANGUAGES:* Spanish.

## COUNSEL

**SUSAN A. GRODE,** admitted to bar, 1977, California. *Education:* Cornell University (B.F.A., 1964); University of Southern California (J.D., 1977). Phi Kappa Phi; Alpha Alpha Gamma. Author: "Visual Artist Manual," Doubleday, 1985. *Member:* Beverly Hills (Member, Board of Governors, 1980-1984), Los Angeles County and American (Member: Forum Committee on the Entertainment and Sports Industries; Copyright, Patent and Trademark Committee) Bar Associations; State Bar of California President, California Women's Law Center, 1989-1992. Languages: Spanish and Italian. *PRACTICE AREAS:* Entertainment Law; Intellectual Property Law; Multimedia Law; Publishing Law; Licensing; Merchandising Law.

**PETER L. HAVILAND,** admitted to bar, 1989, California. *Education:* Harvard University (A.B., cum laude, 1977); Stanford University (J.D., 1989). Associate Editor, Stanford Law Review. Foreign Language Area Studies Fellow (Portuguese/Brazilian Law). Clerk, Hon. Warren Ferguson, U.S. Court of Appeals, Ninth Circuit, 1989-1990. Member, John Langston Bar Association; Black Entertainment Sports Lawyers Association. *LANGUAGES:* Portuguese, Spanish. *PRACTICE AREAS:* Civil and Criminal Trials; CERCLA/Superfund; Copyright and Trademark; Insurance Recovery; Entertainment (Record, Film, TV).

**SHERI JEFFREY,** admitted to bar, 1985, California and U.S. Tax Court. *Education:* Loyola Marymount University (B.S. cum laude, 1982; J.D., 1985); New York University (LL.M., 1986). Beta Gamma Sigma. Author: "Pre-Residency Tax Planning for the Foreign Entertainer, Athlete and Other Talent," Entertainment Law Journal, Volume 12, Issue 2, 1992. Co-Author: "Structuring the Multimedia Deal: Legal Issues-Licensing in the Multimedia Arena (Part 2)," Entertainment Law Review, Volume 4, Issue 1, 1993; "Structuring the Multimedia Deal: Legal Issues (Part 1)," Entertainment Law Review, Volume 3, Issue 6, 1992; "Film Financing: The Completion Guaranty Aspect," Entertainment Law Review, Volume 3, Issue 3, 1992. Speaker: "Is the Entertainment Industry on the IRS Hit List," Los Angeles County Bar Association, Entertainment Tax Committee, December, 1992; "Money Behind the Deal: Finance, Accounting and Tax Aspects of Film Production and Distribution," Los Angeles County Bar Association, Entertainment Tax Committee and The Beverly Hills Bar Association, Entertainment Law Section, May, 1992; "Taxation of Foreign and U.S. Artists, Entertainers and Athletes," Los Angeles County Bar Association Entertainment Tax Committee and International Tax Committee; Bankrupt

*(This Listing Continued)*

Producers and Distributors: Planning to Protect the Licensor, Artist or Profit Participant," California Society Certified Public Accountants, April, 1992. *Member:* Beverly Hills (Member, Entertainment Law and Taxation Sections), Los Angeles County (Member, Intellectual Property and Taxation Sections) and American (Member, Entertainment and Sports, International and Taxation Sections) Bar Associations; State Bar of California (Member, Intellectual Property and Taxation Sections). *PRACTICE AREAS:* Entertainment; Tax.

**ANTHONY R. SALANDRA,** admitted to bar, 1980, California; 1982, New Jersey. *Education:* Muhlenberg College (A.B., 1977); Pepperdine University (J.D., cum laude, 1980); New York University (LL.M. in Taxation, 1982). Editor, Pepperdine Law Review, 1979-1980. Author: "Syndications Under the Internal Revenue Code of 1986," University of Southern California Tax Institute-Major Planning, 1987. *Member:* Los Angeles County and New Jersey State Bar Associations; State Bar of California. *PRACTICE AREAS:* Real Estate.

**M. KENNETH SUDDLESON,** admitted to bar, 1969, California. *Education:* University of California at Los Angeles (A.B., 1964); University of Santa Clara and University of California at Los Angeles (J.D., 1968). *Member:* The State Bar of California; Los Angeles Copyright Society. *PRACTICE AREAS:* Entertainment Law.

## ASSOCIATES

**IVY KAGAN BIERMAN,** admitted to bar, 1985, California. *Education:* Duke University (B.A., magna cum laude, 1980); Northwestern University (J.D., cum laude, 1984). *Member:* Century City Bar Association (Chairs, Entertainment and Labor Sections, 1990-1995); State Bar of California. *PRACTICE AREAS:* Entertainment; Employment and Labor.

**RUSS ALAN CASHDAN,** admitted to bar, 1990, California. *Education:* State University of New York at Albany (B.A., 1985); University of Southern California (J.D., 1990). *PRACTICE AREAS:* Corporate (Finance, Mergers and Acquisitions General); Entertainment.

**BRIAN T. CORRIGAN,** admitted to bar, 1989, California, U.S. District Court and U.S. Bankruptcy Court, Northern, Central and Southern Districts of California and U.S. Court of Appeals, Ninth Circuit. *Education:* Loyola Marymount University (B.S., Accounting, 1983); Southwestern University School of Law (J.D., magna cum laude, 1989). Recipient: American Jurisprudence Award in Bankruptcy, Remedies, Introduction to Income Taxation-I, Exceptional Achievement Award in Estate Planning and Drafting. Certified Public Accountant, California, 1985. *Member:* State Bar of California. *PRACTICE AREAS:* Bankruptcy; Corporate Reorganization; Debt Restructure; Workouts.

**ALAN L. FRIEL,** admitted to bar, 1992, Pennsylvania; 1993, California; 1994, U.S. District Court, Central District of California and U.S. Court of Appeals, Ninth Circuit. *Education:* New York University; Georgia State University (B.S., 1988); Northeastern University (J.D., 1991). Recipient: Phil Peters Memorial Scholarship; President Ronald W. Reagan National Leadership Award; U.S. Justice Department Honors Internship (D.E.A.), 1986-1988; Judicial Extern to Chief Judge, Joseph Tauro, U.S.D.C. for Dist. of Massachusetts, 1990; Judicial Clerk, Hon. Robert Coats, Alaska Court of Appeals, 1991-1992. American Civil Liberties Union Legal Fellow, 1992-1994. Member, Board of Directors, AIDS Project, Los Angeles, 1995—. *Member:* ACLU Foundation (Board of Directors, 1994—). *PRACTICE AREAS:* Commercial and Entertainment Litigation and Transactions.

**BRIAN M. HOYE,** admitted to bar, 1988, California. *Education:* University of California at Berkeley (A.B., 1985); University of Southern California (J.D., 1988). Editor, Computer Law/Tax Journal, 1986-1988. *PRACTICE AREAS:* Corporate Finance; Mergers and Acquisitions.

**LILLIE HSU,** admitted to bar, 1992, California. *Education:* Harvard College (A.B., 1986); Stanford Law School (J.D., with distinction, 1991). Associate Editor, Stanford Law Review. Law Clerk, Judge Warren T. Ferguson, U.S. Court of Appeals, Ninth Circuit, 1991-1992. Law Clerk, Judge Mariana R. Pfaelzer, U.S. District Court, Central District of California, 1992-1993. *Member:* State Bar of California; American Bar Association.

**LIZA ILONA KARSAI,** admitted to bar, 1993, California. *Education:* University of California at Los Angeles (B.A., 1988); Pepperdine University (J.D., summa cum laude, 1993). Recipient: American Jurisprudence Award: Legal Research and Writing II, Torts II, Constitutional Law II (Federal/State Powers), Conflict of Laws, Appellate Advocacy. Member, Pepperdine Law Review, 1991-1993. Member, Executive Board, Pepperdine Moot Court Board, 1992-1993. Briefwriter, Regional Finalist Team, National

*(This Listing Continued)*

CAA835B

## KAYE, SCHOLER, FIERMAN, HAYS & HANDLER, LLP,
Los Angeles—Continued

Moot Court Competition. Odell McConnell Scholar, 1991-1992. **PRACTICE AREAS:** Litigation.

**RONALD E. LEVINSON,** admitted to bar, 1983, California. *Education:* Cornell University (A.B., cum laude, 1980); UCLA School of Law (J.D., 1983). Recipient, American Jurisprudence Award in Real Property Secured Transactions. Comments Editor, Federal Communications Law Journal, 1982-1983. *Member:* State Bar of California. **PRACTICE AREAS:** Real Estate; Business Transactions.

**GINA LIMANDRI,** admitted to bar, 1990, California and U.S. District Court, Central District of California; 1992, U.S. District Court, Southern District of California. *Education:* University of California at San Diego (B.A., 1986); Hastings College of Law, University of California (J.D., 1989). Order of the Coif; Phi Alpha Delta; Thurston Society. Author: "Realism and Reasonableness in Statutory Interpretation," Hastings Law Journal, 1989. **LANGUAGES:** Spanish, Italian. **PRACTICE AREAS:** Litigation.

**MITCHELL J. STEINBERGER,** admitted to bar, 1993, California and U.S. District Court, Northern and Central Districts of California. *Education:* Stanford University (A.B., with honors and distinction, 1989); University of California at Boalt Hall (J.D., 1993); Harvard Law School (Exchange Student, 1992-1993). Phi Beta Kappa. Recipient: American Jurisprudence Award in Entertainment Law. Member, California Law Review, 1991-1993. Senior Editor, Harvard Journal of Law and Public Policy, 1992-1993. *Member:* Beverly Hills Bar Association. **LANGUAGES:** German. **PRACTICE AREAS:** Litigation.

**BONNIE STYLIDES,** admitted to bar, 1994, California. *Education:* Tufts University (B.A., 1982); Stanford Law School (J.D., 1994).

**RHONDA RENEE TROTTER,** admitted to bar, 1993, California. *Education:* Stanford University (B.A., 1989); University of California at Berkeley (J.D., 1993). Winner: McBaine Moot Court Honors Program, 1993; Stephen Finney Jamison Award, 1993. Senior Articles Editor, California Law Review. Moot Court Board, 1992-1993. *Member:* American and National Bar Associations. **PRACTICE AREAS:** Litigation; Entertainment Transactions.

**KYM R. WULFE,** admitted to bar, 1993, California. *Education:* Georgetown University (B.A., 1989); University of Southern California (J.D., 1993). Order of the Coif. Member, Southern California Law Review, 1992-1993. **PRACTICE AREAS:** Entertainment Transactional.

**JOHN A. ZECCA,** admitted to bar, 1993, California; 1995, District of Columbia. *Education:* Cornell University (B.S., 1989); Hastings College of Law, University of California (J.D., 1993). Clerk to the Hon. John H. Pratt, U.S. District Court, District of Columbia, 1993-1995. *Member:* American Bar Association (International Law Section). **PRACTICE AREAS:** Securities Law; Corporate Law.

REFERENCE: Security Pacific Bank (6th and Flower Office).

(For complete biographical data on all Partners, see Professional Biographies at New York, New York)

---

## LEWIS B. KEAN
SUITE 808, 3440 WILSHIRE BOULEVARD
**LOS ANGELES, CALIFORNIA 90010**
Telephone: 213-388-9341
Fax: 213-388-9344

*Civil and Trial Practice. Corporation, Securities, Antitrust Law and Bankruptcy.*

**LEWIS B. KEAN,** born Evanston, Illinois, July 15, 1917; admitted to bar, 1942, California; 1957, U.S. Supreme Court. *Education:* University of California at Berkeley (A.B., 1939); Boalt Hall, University of California (LL.B., 1942). Phi Delta Phi. *Member:* Los Angeles County, Long Beach and American (Member: Corporation, Banking and Business Law Section; International Law Section) Bar Associations; State Bar of California.

REFERENCE: Bank of America, Main Office and Wilshire-Mariposa Office.

---

## KEARNEY, BISTLINE & COHOON
A LAW CORPORATION
SUITE 3265
300 S. GRAND
**LOS ANGELES, CALIFORNIA 90074**
Telephone: 213-617-9209
Fax: 213-617-9325

*General Practice.*

**JAMES B. COHOON,** born Ft. Lauderdale, Florida, February 1, 1953; admitted to bar, 1980, California, U.S. District Court, Central District of California and U.S. Court of Appeals, Ninth Circuit; 1983, Washington; 1993, Colorado. *Education:* Washington State University (B.S., cum laude, 1976); University of San Diego School of Law (J.D., cum laude, 1980). Recipient, American Jurisprudence Award in Conflicts of Law. Phi Alpha Delta. Associate Editor, San Diego Law Review, 1980. Editor, "Mealy's Toxic Torts Litigation Reports," 1992—. Author: "Piercing the Doctrine of Corporate Hospital Liability," 17 San Diego Law Review 383, 1979; "Defeating Proximate Causation in Failure-to-Warn Cases," For the Defense 25, Oct. 1986; "Indoor Air Pollution: A Primer for Defense Counsel," For the Defense 12, August 1989; "Indoor Air Pollution: What Are the Risks? To Whom? Who is Potentially Liable? Theories of Recovery and Defenses," DRI Annual Symposium on Environmental Hazardous Waste and Toxic Tort Litigation, 1991. *Member:* State Bar of California; Washington State, Colorado and American Bar Associations; Defense Research Institute; Association of Southern California Defense Counsel (Committee Chairman, 1985-1986).

**GREGORY D. BISTLINE,** born Pocatello, Idaho, June 15, 1951; admitted to bar, 1976, California. *Education:* California State University at Los Angeles (B.A., 1973); Loyola University of Los Angeles (J.D., magna cum laude, 1976). Associate Editor, Loyola of Los Angeles Law Review, 1975-1976. Author: "Standing: Exclusionary Zoning and the Right to Travel," Loyola of Los Angeles Law Review, 1975. *Member:* Los Angeles County Bar Association; State Bar of California; Association of Southern California Defense Counsel (Board of Directors, 1988-1989).

**THOMAS A. KEARNEY,** born Yonkers, New York, June 22, 1952; admitted to bar, 1979, California. *Education:* University of California at Berkeley (B.A., 1974); Loyola University of Los Angeles (J.D., 1979). *Member:* State Bar of California; Association of Southern Defense Counsel.

**LARRY J. KENT,** born Guam, August 17, 1961; admitted to bar, 1986, California; U.S. District Court, Central District of California. *Education:* University of California at Berkeley (B.A., with honors, 1983); Loyola Law School (J.D., 1986). *Member:* State Bar of California; American Bar Association.

**PAUL ALVAREZ,** born Havana, Cuba, March 8, 1958; admitted to bar, 1984, California; 1985, U.S. District Court, Central District of California; 1986, U.S. District Court, Northern and Southern Districts of California. *Education:* University of California at Davis (B.A., 1981); Loyola Law School (J.D., 1984). Member, Loyola of Los Angeles Law Review, 1982-1983. Recipient, American Jurisprudence Award in Landlord-Tenant Law. Author: "The Sixth Amendment Right to Present a Defense," 16 Loyola Los Angeles Law Review 887, 1983; "Investigative Stops," 16 Loyola of Los Angeles Law Review 820, 1983. Arbitrator, Los Angeles Superior Court. *Member:* Los Angeles County (Member, Errors and Omissions Prevention Committee), Orange County (Member, Tort and Insurance Practice Section) and American Bar Associations; State Bar of California; Association of Southern California Defense Counsel. **LANGUAGES:** Spanish.

**TED H. LUYMES,** born Los Angeles, California, May 5, 1964; admitted to bar, 1990, California; 1992, Utah. *Education:* Brigham Young University (B.A., 1987; J.D., 1990). Phi Delta Phi. *Member:* State Bar of California; Utah State Bar; American Bar Association. **LANGUAGES:** Spanish.

**GREGORY A. DILTS,** born Jamestown, New York, October 23, 1964; admitted to bar, 1993, California. *Education:* Jamestown Community College (A.A., 1984); University of North Carolina, Charlotte (B.S., 1986); Pepperdine University (J.D., 1993).

## GARY W. KEARNEY
### LOS ANGELES, CALIFORNIA
(See Pasadena)
*Family Law, Dissolutions, Adoptions and Custody.*

---

## KEGEL, TOBIN & TRUCE
A PROFESSIONAL CORPORATION
Established in 1966
3580 WILSHIRE BOULEVARD, 10TH FLOOR
P.O. BOX 76907
**LOS ANGELES, CALIFORNIA 90076-0907**
Telephone: 213-380-3880
Fax: 213-383-8346
Email: comp-law@ktt.com

*Ventura, California Office:* 5450 Ralston Street, Suite 204, P.O. Box 7779. Telephone: 805-644-2216. Facsimile: 805-644-8625.

*Rancho Cucamonga, California Office:* 10737 Laurel Street, #240, P.O. Box 3329. Telephone: 909-466-5555. Facsimile: 909-466-5562.

*San Diego, California Office:* 2535 Kettner Boulevard, Suite 2A1. Telephone: 619-696-0906.

*Long Beach, California Office:* 330 Golden Shore Drive, Suite 150. Telephone: 310-437-1108. Facsimile: 310-437-3742.

*Van Nuys, California Office:* 14545 Friar Street, Suite 104. Telephone: 818-947-0300. Facsimile: 818-947-0303.

*Workers Compensation, Longshore and Harborworkers', Public Employment, Retirement Law. Insurance Law, Third Party Subrogation.*

**ROBERT A. KEGEL,** born Chicago, Illinois, September 1, 1927; admitted to bar, 1953, California. *Education:* University of California at Los Angeles (B.S., 1949); University of Southern California (LL.B., 1952). *Member:* Los Angeles County and American Bar Associations; State Bar of California. (Certified Specialist, Workers Compensation Law, The State Bar of California Board of Legal Specialization) (Also at San Diego and Long Beach).

**JOHN J. TOBIN,** born Omaha, Nebraska, October 10, 1935; admitted to bar, 1969, California. *Education:* Creighton University, University of Nebraska and Van Norman University (B.A., 1968); Van Norman University (J.D., 1968). *Member:* Los Angeles County Bar Association; State Bar of California. (Certified Specialist, Workers Compensation Law, The State Bar of California Board of Legal Specialization) (Also at Rancho Cucamonga).

**ROBERT R. WILLS,** born Minneapolis, Minnesota, April 25, 1929; admitted to bar, 1957, California. *Education:* University of California at Los Angeles (B.A., 1953); LL.B., 1956). *Member:* Los Angeles County Bar Association; State Bar of California. (Certified Specialist, Workers Compensation Law, The State Bar of California Board of Legal Specialization) (Resident at Van Nuys).

**W. JOSEPH TRUCE,** born Seattle, Washington, September 18, 1943; admitted to bar, 1971, California. *Education:* University of Washington (B.A., 1960); Golden Gate College (J.D., 1970). Member, Panel of Arbitrators, American Arbitration Association. *Member:* Los Angeles County Bar Association; State Bar of California; Lawyers Club of Los Angeles County; Los Angeles Trial Lawyers Association. (Certified Specialist, Workers Compensation Law, The State Bar of California Board of Legal Specialization) (Also at Long Beach).

**E. CHARLES MAKI,** born Glen Dale, West Virginia, March 18, 1943; admitted to bar, 1972, California. *Education:* Loyola University of Los Angeles and California State University at Northridge (B.A., 1967); University of San Fernando Valley (J.D., cum laude, 1971). *Member:* State Bar of California. (Certified Specialist, Workers Compensation Law, The State Bar of California Board of Legal Specialization) (Resident at Ventura).

**MICHAEL A. INGLER,** born Los Angeles, California, November 3, 1946; admitted to bar, 1975, California; 1979, U.S. Supreme Court. *Education:* California State University at Northridge (B.A., 1968); University of San Fernando Valley (J.D., 1975). *Member:* Los Angeles County Bar Association (Member: Barristers Section; New Projects Committee, 1978; Public Education Committee, 1978); State Bar of California; The Association of Trial Lawyers of America. [With U.S. Army Reserves, 1968-1974]. (Resident at Long Beach).

**NANCY J. HANKINSON,** born Chicago, Illinois, November 10, 1949; admitted to bar, 1979, California. *Education:* Valparaiso University and California State University at Los Angeles (B.A., 1971); Southwestern University (J.D., 1978). *Member:* Los Angeles County and American Bar Associations; State Bar of California. (Resident at Ventura).

**JON E. VON LEDEN,** born Evanston, Illinois, December 2, 1949; admitted to bar, 1979, California; 1980, U.S. District Court, Central District of California; 1981, U.S. District Court, Southern District of California. *Education:* California State University at Northridge (B.A., 1976); Southwestern University (J.D., 1979). *Member:* Los Angeles County and American Bar Associations; State Bar of California; The Association of Trial Lawyers of America; Association of Southern California Defense Counsel.

**THEODORE C. HANF,** born Los Angeles, California, December 3, 1950; admitted to bar, 1975, California and U.S. District Court, Central District of California. *Education:* John Hopkins University (B.A., 1971); Loyola University, Los Angeles (J.D., 1975). *Member:* State Bar of California. (Certified Specialist, Workers Compensation Law, The State Bar of California Board of Legal Specialization) (Resident at Van Nuys).

**JOSEPH D. KIEFFER,** born New York, N.Y., April 15, 1949; admitted to bar, 1977, California. *Education:* University of California at Los Angeles; University of California at Santa Barbara (B.A., 1971); American University (J.D., 1976). Member, American University Law Review, 1975-1976. Law Clerk to Judge Lehmen Aarens, U.S. Tax Court. *Member:* Los Angeles County Bar Association; State Bar of California.

**PREETI G. SHAH,** born Bombay, India, May 1, 1958; admitted to bar, 1988, California. *Education:* Sydenham College of Commerce, Bombay, India (B.Com., 1979); Government Law College, Bombay, India (LL.B., 1983). *Member:* San Fernando Valley and Los Angeles County Bar Associations; State Bar of California.

**HUMBERTO GONZALEZ,** born San Bernardino, California, December 22, 1952; admitted to bar, 1980, California. *Education:* University of California at Riverside (B.S., 1974); University of San Diego (J.D., 1977). Sigma Delta Pi. *Member:* State Bar of California.

**TIMOTHY D. SANFORD-WACHTEL,** born Glendale, California, November 29, 1948; admitted to bar, 1978, California; 1979, U.S. Tax Court. *Education:* California State University at Fullerton (B.S., 1972); Western State University (J.D., 1976). *Member:* State Bar of California. (Rancho Cucamonga and San Diego Offices).

**DEBBIE KAYE,** born Los Angeles, California, April 11, 1958; admitted to bar, 1985, California. *Education:* Vassar College (B.A., 1979); Pepperdine University (J.D., 1984). Phi Delta Phi. *Member:* State Bar of California.

---

**PAUL M. RYAN, JR.,** born Elmira, New York, June 13, 1949; admitted to bar, 1986, California. *Education:* University of Virginia (B.A., 1971); University of West Los Angeles (J.D., 1986). Recipient, American Jurisprudence Award for Excellence in Contracts, Corporations, Criminal Law, Criminal Procedure and Evidence. *Member:* Los Angeles County Bar Association; State Bar of California; Workers' Compensation Defense Attorneys Association.

**STEVEN M. GREEN,** born Los Angeles, California, March 17, 1961; admitted to bar, 1985, Oregon; 1986, California; 1987, U.S. District Court, Southern District of California. *Education:* University of Chicago (A.B., 1982); University of Oregon (J.D., 1985). *Member:* State Bar of California.

**D'ARCY T. SWARTZ,** born Toronto, Ontario, Canada, July 1, 1961; admitted to bar, 1987, California and U.S. District Court, Southern District of California. *Education:* University of California at San Diego (B.A., 1984); University of San Diego (J.D., 1987). Recipient: Williams, Brundage Zellman Award for Excellence in Labor Law; American Jurisprudence Awards in Labor Law. *Member:* State Bar of California; California Workers Compensation Defense Attorneys Association. (Resident at Long Beach).

**SANDRA L. ADAMS,** born San Pedro, California; admitted to bar, 1989, California and U.S. Court of Appeals, Ninth Circuit; 1990, U.S. District Court, Southern District of California. *Education:* Los Angeles Harbor College (A.A., 1973); University of Southern California (B.S., 1976); Loyola University (J.D., 1980). *Member:* State Bar of California (Member, Workers' Compensation Section); American Bar Association. (Resident at Long Beach).

*(This Listing Continued)*

### KEGEL, TOBIN & TRUCE, A PROFESSIONAL CORPORATION, Los Angeles—Continued

**DANIEL A. DOBRIN,** born Dallas, Texas, September 22, 1952; admitted to bar, 1976, California. *Education:* University of California at Santa Cruz (A.B., with honors, 1973); University of California at Los Angeles School of Law (J.D., 1976). *Member:* Los Angeles County Bar Association; State Bar of California; California Attorneys for Criminal Justice; California Appellate Lawyers. (Resident at Rancho Cucamonga).

**JEFFREY E. WEISS,** born New York, N.Y., January 7, 1963; admitted to bar, 1989, California, U.S. Court of Appeals, Ninth Circuit and U.S. District Court, Northern, Central and Southern Districts of California. *Education:* Bernard M. Baruch College of the City University of New York (B.B.A., cum laude, 1985); Benjamin N. Cardozo School of Law (J.D., 1988). Member, Moot Court Board. *Member:* Los Angeles County and American Bar Associations; State Bar of California. **LANGUAGES:** Yiddish.

**KELLY M. HARDY,** born Arcadia, California, April 11, 1962; admitted to bar, 1992, California. *Education:* California State University (B.A., 1987); Western State University (J.D., 1991). *Member:* State Bar of California. (Resident at Long Beach).

**ANJU KHURANA,** born Youngstown, Ohio, November 22, 1967; admitted to bar, 1992, California. *Education:* Carnegie Mellon University (B.A., 1989); Southwestern University School of Law (J.D., 1992). Recipient, Los Angeles Board of Trial Advocates Award. Bar Exam Grader, Legal Education Conference Center, 1992—. *Member:* Beverly Hills Bar Association; State Bar of California; Workers Compensation Defense Attorneys Association. **LANGUAGES:** Hindi, French.

REPRESENTATIVE CLIENTS: Fireman's Fund Insurance Co.; Auto Club of Southern California; City of Pasadena; City of Inglewood; County of San Luis Obispo; Holly Sugar Corp.; County of Orange; City of Santa Ana; City of Anaheim; Ralph's Grocery Co.; County of Los Angeles; City of Newport Beach; Self Insurers Service; Sedgwick James; North American Claims Management; Crawford & Co.; City of Beverly Hills; Gallagher Bassett & Co.; U.S. Steel Corp.; American International Group Co.; Central Mutual Insurance Co.; Insurance Company of North America; Los Angeles County Metropolitan Transit Authority; Allied Signal Corp./Garrett Corp.; Colen & Lee; ComCo Management, Inc.; Home Insurance; American Home Assurance; Applied Risk Management; Los Angeles Unified School District; Marriott Corp.; Gates, McDonald & Co.; HCM (Hertz Claims Mgmt.); The Travelers Insurance Co.; Allied Industries; Associated Claims Management; Kemper Group; Southern California Risk Management Associates; Tokio Marine & Fire Unihealth America; General Adjustment Bureau; Transamerica Insurance; American Hardware Mutual; California Fairs Insurance Authority; Helmsman Management Services, Inc.
REFERENCE: American West Bank, Encino.

---

## KEHR, CROOK, TOVMASSIAN & FOX

A PROFESSIONAL CORPORATION
**11755 WILSHIRE BOULEVARD, SUITE 1400**
**LOS ANGELES, CALIFORNIA 90025**
Telephone: 310-479-4994
Fax: 310-479-4855
Email: KCTFox@aol.com

*General Business, Corporate and Partnership Law, Real Estate Law, Condominium Law, Entertainment Law, Professional Liability and Ethics and General Civil Litigation and Appeals.*

**ROBERT L. KEHR,** born Los Angeles, California, May 1, 1944; admitted to bar, 1970, California. *Education:* Cornell University (B.A., 1966); Columbia University (J.D., 1969). Author: "The Changing View of Lease Assignments," Real Estate Review, Vol. 11 No. 2 p. 54, 1981; "Lease Assignments: The Landlord's Consent," 55 California State Bar Journal 108, 1980; "The Application of Green v. Superior Court to Non-Residential Realty," 1 Los Angeles Lawyer 30, 1979. Arbitrator, Los Angeles County Bar Attorneys Fee Arbitration Committee, 1980—. Judge Pro Tem, Los Angeles Municipal Court, 1979-1985. Consultant, Matthew Bender & Co. for California Forms of Pleading and Practice Volume on Attorney Practices and Ethics. *Member:* Los Angeles County Bar Association (Chair, 1986-1987 and Member, 1981—, Professional Responsibility and Ethics Committee; Member, Evaluation of Professional Standards Committee, 1988—); State Bar of California (Member, Standing Committee on Professional Responsibility and Conduct, 1996—).

**GEORGE D. CROOK,** born Bell, California, February 2, 1942; admitted to bar, 1974, California and U.S. District Court, Central District of California; 1978, U.S. Court of Appeals, Ninth Circuit; 1983, U.S. District

*(This Listing Continued)*

Court, Southern District of California. *Education:* St. John's College (B.A., 1964); Loyola University of Los Angeles (J.D., cum laude, 1974). Member, St. Thomas More Honor Society. Member, 1972-1973 and Managing Editor, 1973-1974, Loyola Law Review. Law Clerk, Chief Judge Hon. Albert Lee Stephens, Jr., U.S. District Court, Central District of California, 1974-1975. Author: "You May Kill But You Must Promise Not to Use Discretion," 6 Loyola Law Review, 1974. Clinical Professor of Law, Loyola University of Los Angeles School of Law, 1977-1979. Member, El Rancho Unified School District Board of Trustees, 1977-1986. *Member:* State Bar of California. **LANGUAGES:** Spanish. **PRACTICE AREAS:** Real Estate; Business Litigation.

**DAVID M. FOX,** born San Bernardino, California, November 8, 1960; admitted to bar, 1986, California; 1987, U.S. District Court, Central District of California and U.S. Court of Appeals, Ninth Circuit. *Education:* University of California (B.A., Economics, 1982); Western State University (J.D., 1985). Recipient, American Jurisprudence Awards, Torts, Evidence. California Certified Clerk, Orange County District Attorney's Office. Member, Association Internationale Des Jeunes Avocats. *Member:* Los Angeles County (Member, Sections on: Entertainment and Real Estate) and Beverly Hills (Member, Sections on: Entertainment and Real Estate) Bar Associations; The Association of Trial Lawyers of America; California Lawyers for the Arts. **PRACTICE AREAS:** Entertainment Law; Real Estate; Business Law.

**HENRY TOVMASSIAN,** born Erevan, Armenia, September 13, 1962; admitted to bar, 1989, California and U.S. District Court, Central District of California. *Education:* New York University (B.A., 1985); University of California at Los Angeles (J.D., 1988). Managing Editor, 1986-1987 and Editor-in-Chief, 1987-1988, UCLA Docket. Member, UCLA Moot Court Honor Society, 1986-1988. *Member:* Los Angeles County Bar Association; State Bar of California; The Association of Trial Lawyers of America. **LANGUAGES:** Armenian. **PRACTICE AREAS:** Real Estate; Corporate Litigation; Business Litigation; Civil Litigation.

**SAMANTHA E. BLAKE,** born Tacoma, Washington, May 4, 1965; admitted to bar, 1993, California. *Education:* University of Washington, (B.A., with honors, 1987); Loyola Law School (J.D., 1993). Golden Key Honor Society. Member, Complex Litigation Inns of Court. *Member:* Los Angeles County Bar Association; State Bar of California. **LANGUAGES:** French. **PRACTICE AREAS:** Real Estate; Corporate Litigation; Business Litigation; Civil Litigation.

---

## KELLEY DRYE & WARREN LLP

A Partnership including Professional Associations
**515 SOUTH FLOWER STREET**
**LOS ANGELES, CALIFORNIA 90071**
Telephone: 213-689-1300
Fax: (213) 688-8150
Email: info@kelleydrye.com
URL: http://www.kelleydrye.com

*New York, N.Y. Office:* 101 Park Avenue. Telephone: 212-808-7800. Telex: 12369. Fax: (212) 808-7897.
*Stamford, Connecticut Office:* Two Stamford Plaza, 281 Tresser Boulevard. Telephone: 203-324-1400. Fax: (203) 327-2669; (203) 964-3188.
*Washington, D.C. Office:* 1200 19th Street, N.W., Suite 500. Telephone: 202-955-9600. Fax: (202) 955-9792.
*Miami, Florida Office:* 201 South Biscayne Boulevard, 2400 Miami Center. Telephone: 305-372-2400. Fax: (305) 372-2490.
*Parsippany, New Jersey Office:* 5 Sylvan Way. Telephone: 201-539-0099. Fax: (201) 539-3167.
*Chicago, Illinois Office:* 303 West Madison Street, Suite 1400. Telephone: 312-346-6350. Fax: (312) 346-8982.
*Brussels, Belgium Office:* 106 Avenue Louise, 1050. Telephone: (011) (32) (2) 646-1110. Fax: (011) (32) (2) 640-0589.
*Hong Kong Office:* 509-10 Peregrine Tower, Lippo Centre, 89 Queensway. Telephone: (011) (85) (2) 2869-0821. Fax: (011) (85) (2) 2869-0049.
*New Delhi, India Affiliated Office:* Swarup & Co., J.K. Building, 6th Floor, Vipps Centre, 2 Masjid Moth, Greater Kailash II, 110 048. Telephone: (011) (91) (11) 646-6314. Fax: (011) (91) (11) 642-8939.

*General Practice.*

**PAUL L. BRESSAN,** born Rockville Centre, New York, 1947; admitted to bar, 1976, New York; 1987, California; U.S. Supreme Court; U.S. Court of Appeals, First, Second, Fourth, Seventh, Ninth and Eleventh Circuits; U.S. District Court, Northern, Southern and Eastern Districts of New

*(This Listing Continued)*

York; U.S. District Court, Northern, Eastern and Central Districts of California. *Education:* Fordham College (B.A., cum laude, 1969); Columbia University (J.D., Harlan Fiske Stone Scholar, 1975). Phi Beta Kappa. Author: "U.S. Litigation—A Guide for Asian Corporations," Labor and Employment Law Section of the publication. *Member:* Los Angeles County and American Bar Association; State Bar of California. *REPORTED CASES:* Lead counsel for company on appeal in Fortino, et al. v. Quasar Company, 950 F.2d 389 (7th Cir. 1991). *PRACTICE AREAS:* Employment Discrimination Law; Management Labor Relations; Wrongful Discharge. *Email:* pbressan@kelleydrye.com

**PATRICK DEL DUCA,** born Carlisle, Pennsylvania, August 21, 1957; admitted to bar, 1983, Pennsylvania and U.S. Court of Appeals, Ninth Circuit; 1984, District of Columbia; 1986, California. *Education:* Harvard University (B.A., magna cum laude, 1978; J.D., 1983); Université de Lyon (D.E.A., 1979); European University Institute (Ph.D., 1985); Università di Bologna (dott. di giur., 1987). Fulbright Fellow, 1981-1982. Rotary Fellow, 1978-1979. PPG National Merit Scholar, 1976. Author: "Why Project Finance Can Make Sense," CCM (The American Lawyer's Corporate Counsel Magazine, February 1996; "Thoughts On Focusing the Judgment Of An Environmental Expert," The Metropolitan Corporate Counsel, December 1995; "The Environmental Consultant's Opinion Letter," 20 Environmental Law Reporter 10184, 1990; "La disciplina statunitense sull'ammissione in borsa di valori mobiliari," 88 Rivista di diritto commerciale 603, 1990; "United States, French and Italian Air Pollution Control: Central and Local Relations as a Structural Determinant of Policy," 10 Loyola of Los Angeles International and Comparative Law Journal 497, 1988; "Uniform Law, Federated Jurisdictions and an Example from U.S. and EEC Securities Regulation," International Uniform Law in Practice 470, UNIDROIT, 1988; "Les exigences d'organisation pour le contrôle de la pollution de l'air: les experiences italienne, française, americaine, et communautaire," 15 Droit et ville 118, 1983; "The Clean Air Act: A Realistic Assessment of Cost-Effectiveness," 5 Harvard Environmental Law Review 183, 1981. Co-Author: with Antonio La Pergola, "Community Law, International Law and the Italian Constitution," 79 American Journal of International Law 598, 1985; with Louis Del Duca, "Italy: Commercial, Business and Trade Laws," Oceana, 1983, Supp. 1986; with Dan Mansueto, "Indirect Source Controls: An Intersection of Air Quality Management and Land Use Regulation," 24 Loyola of Los Angeles Law Review 1129, 1991; With Remi Turcon, "An Overview of United States Environmental Law," In *Foreign Direct Investments In The United States: Legal Aspects For Foreign Investors* 269 (Sweet & Maxwell, 1993); with Louis Del Duca, "The Italian Legal System: Adapting to the Needs of a Dynamic Society," 4 National Italian American Bar Association Law Journal (1995); with Yves Miedzianogora and Francisco J. Aparicio, "Columbia's Electricity Law," Issue VIII, Project Finance Monthly 15, 1995; with Eugene E. Mulhern and Francisco J. Aparicio, "Telecommunications in Mexico: Recent Developments," Issue X, Project Finance Monthly 1995; with Richard R. Lury and Hiroshi Sarumida," Recent Changes in Japanese Law Seek Expansion of Private Power Generation," Project Finance Monthly, February 1996. Associate Editor, "European Legal Integration in Light of the U.S. Federal Experience: Environmental Law," by Richard Stewart and Eckard Rehbinder (DeGruyter, 1985). Co-Editor, with Louis Del Duca, 1991, 1993 and 1995 Commercial Law Annual: Callaghan, 1991, 1993 and 1995. Translator, European Community Law by Paolo Mengozzi (Graham & Trotman, 1993). Law Clerk to: Justice Antonio La Pergola, Corte Costituzionale, 1984-1985; Honorable Alfred T. Goodwin, U.S. Court of Appeals for the Ninth Circuit, 1983-1984. Lecturer in European Community Law, UCLA Law School. *LANGUAGES:* French, Italian and Spanish. *PRACTICE AREAS:* Environmental and International Law; Project Finance. *Email:* pdelduca@kelleydrye.com

**RONALD D. HUSDON,** born Vancouver, British Columbia, 1953; called to bar, 1981, British Columbia; admitted to bar, 1985, California. *Education:* University of British Columbia (B.Comm., 1979; LL.B., 1980); McGeorge School of Law, University of the Pacific (LL.M., 1985). *Member:* State Bar of California; Law Society of British Columbia. *PRACTICE AREAS:* Commercial Law; Joint Ventures; Mergers and Acquisitions. *Email:* rhusdon@kelleydrye.com

**WILLIAM H. KIEKHOFER, III,** born Madison, Wisconsin, 1952; admitted to bar, 1980, California. *Education:* University of Wisconsin, Madison (B.A., with distinction, 1976); University of Southern California (J.D., 1980). *PRACTICE AREAS:* Bankruptcy Law; Loan Workouts. *Email:* wkiekhofer@kelleydrye.com

**THERESA A. KRISTOVICH,** born Los Angeles, California; admitted to bar, 1975, California. *Education:* Stanford University (B.A., with honors, 1972); University of California, Berkeley (J.D., 1975); Oxford University, Oxford, England (Diploma in Law, 1977). Assistant Professor: Constitutional Law, Occidental College, 1981, 1982; Civil Procedure, University of Southern California School of Judicial Administration, 1984-1987. Member: Board of Visitors, Southwestern Law School, 1988—; Federal Indigent Defense Panel, 1988—. Lecturer, California Civil Procedure, The Rutter Group Continuing Legal Education Seminars, 1986—, The Continuing Education of the Bar, 1989-1992. Extern-Clerk to the Hon. Donald R. Wright, Chief Justice of California Supreme Court, 1974; Law Clerk to the Hon. Marshall M. McComb, California Supreme Court, 1975-1976. Assistant U.S. Attorney, Central District of California, 1977-1981. *Member:* Los Angeles County (Member: Federal Courts Committee) and American Bar Associations; The State Bar of California; Women Lawyers' Association of Los Angeles. *PRACTICE AREAS:* Business Litigation; Employment Disputes; Professional Negligence; White Collar Fraud. *Email:* tkristovich@kelleydrye.com

**MICHAEL LUBLINSKI,** born Eskilstuna, Sweden, 1951; admitted to bar, 1976, New York; 1978-1982, U.S. Court of Customs and Patent Appeals; 1980, California; 1981, U.S. Court of International Trade; 1982, U.S. Court of Appeals for the Federal Circuit. *Education:* City College of the City University of New York (B.A., magna cum laude, 1972); Georgetown University Law Center (J.D., 1975). Order of the Coif. Phi Beta Kappa. *Member:* State Bar of California; New York State Bar Association. *PRACTICE AREAS:* Intellectual Property Law; Customs and International Trade Law; Corporate Law. *Email:* mlublinski@kelleydrye.com

**JUN MORI,** born San Francisco, California, 1929; admitted to bar, 1959, California; 1970, U.S. Court of International Trade; 1971, U.S. Supreme Court; 1979, District of Columbia. *Education:* University of California at Los Angeles (A.B., 1955); Waseda University, Tokyo, Japan (LL.B., 1951); University of Southern California (J.D., 1958). *PRACTICE AREAS:* Corporate. *Email:* jmori@kelleydrye.com

**KENNETH A. O'BRIEN, JR.,** born Corpus Christi, Texas, 1956; admitted to bar, 1981, New York; 1982, New Jersey; 1992, California. *Education:* Yale University (B.A., 1977); Columbia University (J.D., 1980). *PRACTICE AREAS:* Litigation. *Email:* kobrien@kelleydrye.com

**JAMES D. PRENDERGAST,** born Alameda, California, 1943; admitted to bar, 1974, California and U.S. District Court, Central District of California; 1978, U.S. Supreme Court. *Education:* University of California at Berkeley (A.B., 1965; M.B.A., 1967); Hastings College of Law, University of California (J.D., 1974). Order of the Coif. Member, Editorial Board, Hastings Law Journal, 1973-1974. Author: Note, "Cognovit Revisited," Vol. 24 Hastings Law Review, 1973; "The Use of Data Processing in Litigation," Loyola Law Review, Vol. 10, March, 1977; "Federal Control of Tender Offers," The Review of Securities Regulation, Vol. 10, May, 1977; "Discretionary Trading Accounts," 12 The Review of Securities Regulations 823, December 19, 1979; "Leap Back to Perfection—A Naked Assignment Work?" Uniform Commercial Code Law Journal, ET 371, Spring 1995. Co-author: "Automated Litigation Support Systems for Evidentiary Management," 11 Toledo Law Journal 255, Winter 1980; "Defining a 'Security' After the Forman Decision," 11 Pacific Law Journal 213, January 1980; "Securities Maze Awaits Resort Time-Sharing Offerings," 10 Real Estate Review 59, Spring 1980; "Discretionary Trading Accounts-Revisited," 16 The Review of Securities Regulations 854, September, 14, 1983; "Loan Participations: Are They Securities?," in the Banker's Guide to Multi-Bank Credits & Loan Participations, Chapter VIII, (Executive Enterprise Publications Co., Inc., 1989); "Whether the Pledge of Capital Stock in a Commercial Transaction is the Purchase or Sale of a Security Under Federal Securities Law?" 95 Commercial Law Journal 435, Winter 1990; "Applying Federal Securities Law to the Trading of Bankruptcy Claims," Bankruptcy Law Review, Winter 1992 at 9; "Cross-Boarder Lending Transactions," The Secured Lender, January-February 1994, at 24; "The Stuff at the End of the Loan Agreement," The Secured Lender, July/August 1994, at 34; "Leap Back to Perfection—Will a Naked Assignment Work?" 27 Uniform Commercial Code Law Journal, Spring 1995; "Use of Attorneys in Commercial Finance Transactions—Or Misuse?" The Secured Lender, May/June 1995, at 26; "Portfolio Review—Do it Now!" The Secured Lender, March/April 1996, at 14. *Member:* State Bar of California (Member, Business Law Section, UCC Committee, 1994-1997; Co-Vice-Chair, UCC Committee, 1995-1996). *PRACTICE AREAS:* Commercial Law; Debtor-Creditor Law; Corporate Law. *Email:* jprendergast@kelleydrye.com

**THEODORE J. ROPER,** born Misawa, Japan, 1951; admitted to bar, 1981, California. *Education:* California State University at San Jose (B.A., 1973; M.A., 1975); Golden Gate University (J.D., 1979). *LANGUAGES:* Japanese. *PRACTICE AREAS:* Corporate; International Transactional Law; Mergers and Acquisitions. *Email:* troper@kelleydrye.com

*(This Listing Continued)*

**KELLEY DRYE & WARREN LLP**, Los Angeles—
*Continued*

**MARSHALL C. STODDARD, JR.,** born Rochester, New York, 1951; admitted to bar, 1976, Connecticut and U.S. District Court, District of Connecticut; 1981, California, U.S. District Court, Central District of California and U.S. Court of Appeals, Ninth Circuit. *Education:* Hobart College (B.A., 1973); Western England College School of Law (J.D., 1976). Author: Articles, "Financing Leveraged Buyouts— The Risk Grows," California Banker, Fall, 1987. Co-author: "Advanced Chapter 11 Bankruptcy Practice," Professional Education Systems, Inc., 1987; "Lender Liability, Theory and Practice," Professional Education Systems, Inc., 1988. (Chairman, Financial Institutions Practice Group). *PRACTICE AREAS:* Commercial Law; Banking Law; Bankruptcy Law. *Email:* mstoddard@kelleydrye.com

**SHIGERU WATANABE,** born Amache, Colorado, 1944; admitted to bar, 1972, California. *Education:* University of California at Los Angeles (B.A., 1968); Loyola University (J.D., 1971). *PRACTICE AREAS:* Litigation. *Email:* swatanabe@kelleydrye.com

---

**ALLISON-CLAIRE ACKER,** born San Gabriel, California, 1961; admitted to bar, 1988, California and U.S. District Court, Central District of California. *Education:* University of California at Los Angeles (B.A., cum laude, 1983); University of California at Los Angeles School of Law (J.D., 1988). *PRACTICE AREAS:* Business Immigration. *Email:* aacker@kelleydrye.com

**FRANCISCO JAVIER APARICIO,** born Guantánamo, Cuba, 1959; admitted to bar, 1987, California. *Education:* University of Southern California (A.B., magna cum laude, 1983); University of California at Los Angeles School of Law (J.D., 1987). *PRACTICE AREAS:* Project Finance; Real Estate; Political Law. *Email:* faparicio@kelleydrye.com

**ANTHONY R. CALLOBRE,** born Miami, Florida, 1960; admitted to bar, 1985, Massachusetts; 1986, California. *Education:* Brown University (A.B., 1982); Boston University (J.D., 1985; LL.M., Banking Law, 1986). *PRACTICE AREAS:* Commercial Finance; Loan Restructurings and Workouts. *Email:* acallobre@kelleydrye.com

**DON S. LEMMER,** born Fort Campbell, Kentucky, 1951; admitted to bar, 1981, Georgia; 1989, California; U.S. District Court, Northern District of Georgia and U.S. District Court, Central, Eastern and Northern Districts of California; U.S. Court of Appeals, Third, Fourth, Seventh, Ninth and Eleventh Circuits. *Education:* Berry College (B.A., magna cum laude, 1973); University of Michigan School of Law; University of Georgia School of Law (J.D., cum laude, 1981). *Email:* dlemmer@kelleydrye.com

**CHRISTINA LYCOYANNIS,** born Flushing, N.Y., September 20, 1964; admitted to bar, 1989, New York (Not admitted in California). *Education:* University of Pennsylvania (B.A., 1985); New York University (J.D., 1988). Articles Editor, Annual Survey of American Law, 1987-1988. *Member:* New York State and American Bar Associations. *Email:* clycoyannis@kelleydrye.com

**AKIKO NAKATANI,** born Tokyo, Japan, January 30, 1969; admitted to bar, 1994, California and U.S. District Court, Central District of California. *Education:* Mills College (B.A., 1991); Cornell University (J.D., 1994). *PRACTICE AREAS:* Corporate; International, Asia. *Email:* anakatani@kelleydrye.com

**CYNTHIA S. PAPSDORF,** born New York, N.Y., March 14, 1957; admitted to bar, 1985, New York, New Jersey and U.S. District Court, District of New Jersey; 1988, U.S. District Court, Southern District of New York; 1990, U.S. Court of Appeals, Third Circuit; 1991, California and U.S. District Court, Central District of California; 1992, U.S. District Court, Northern District of California; 1995, U.S. Court of Appeals, Ninth Circuit. *Education:* Stockton State College (B.A., 1981); New York Law School (J.D., magna cum laude, 1984). *Email:* cpapsdorf@kelleydrye.com

**SHARI L. PRUSSIN,** born Stamford, Connecticut, 1967; admitted to bar, 1993, New York (Not admitted in California). *Education:* Cornell University (B.S., 1989); University of Pennsylvania (J.D., 1992). *Email:* sprussin@kelleydrye.com

**KATHERINE M. WINDLER,** born Denver, Colorado, 1963; admitted to bar, 1992, California, U.S. District Court, Central District of California and U.S. Court of Appeal, Ninth Circuit; 1995, Colorado. *Education:* University of Colorado (B.A., 1986); University of California at Los Angeles School of Law (J.D., 1991). *PRACTICE AREAS:* Bankruptcy; Commercial Litigation. *Email:* kwindler@kelleydrye.com

**REBECCA J. WINTHROP,** born Greenwich, Connecticut, 1959; admitted to bar, 1984, California and U.S. District Court, Central, Northern, Southern and Eastern, Districts of California. *Education:* University of Southern California (B.A., magna cum laude, 1981); Loyola Law School (J.D., 1984). *Email:* rwinthrop@kelleydrye.com

**JULIA ZALBA,** born Wasco, California, 1968; admitted to bar, 1993, California. *Education:* University of California at Santa Barbara (B.A., summa cum laude, 1990); University of California at Los Angeles School of Law (J.D., 1993). *Email:* jzalba@kelleydrye.com

(For Biographical data on all Personnel, see Professional Biographies at New York, N.Y.)

---

# KELLY, BAUERSFELD, LOWRY & KELLEY

## LOS ANGELES, CALIFORNIA

(See Woodland Hills)

*Patent, Trademark, Copyright and Unfair Competition. Trials and Appeals.*

---

# KELLY & LYTTON

1900 AVENUE OF THE STARS
SUITE 1450
**LOS ANGELES, CALIFORNIA 90067**
Telephone: 310-277-5333
Facsimile: 310-277-5953

*Administrative, Real Estate, Transactional, Entertainment, Business Law, Election Law, Family Law and Civil Litigation.*

FIRM PROFILE: Kelly & Lytton is a law firm with offices in Los Angeles and Washington, D.C.,

*Although the firm has a general business practice, it has developed a unique specialty in assisting clients from all over the world in dealing with the federal government and with local and state governments throughout the United States, particularly in California. The firm has substantial experience representing clients before the legislative bodies of local and state governments (with the exception of the California State Legislature) as well as the Congress of the United States. The firm also has significant experience representing clients before local, state, and federal government agencies, commissions and other regulatory authorities. Senior lawyers in all of the firm's offices have spent substantial portions of their careers in public service, thus facilitating the creation of these specialized practice areas.*

*The firm's general business practice emphasizes transportation and environmental matters. The firm represents clients faced with the full range of environmental problems, including land use and compliance with state and federal environmental laws. The firm's transportation practice involves all aspects of mass transit, including representing clients engaged in construction of the Los Angeles County metro-rail system, and clients engaged in school and commuter bus transit; the firm also acts as general counsel to a California transit industry trade organization.*

*The firm's litigation practice includes representation of clients before all state and federal courts as well as administrative agencies. Litigation areas of expertise include general business, insurance defense, environmental, unfair competition, real estate, representation of individuals and institutions in lender liability matters, and white collar criminal defense.*

*The firm's real estate practice covers all services required by sophisticated investors, developers, and financial institutions. The firm has developed a substantial reputation in land use and environmental law as a result of representing clients in some of the most complex land use transactions in California.*

*Clients of the firm include international airlines, major national and regional real estate owners and developers, sports facilities managers and developers, international transit, transportation engineering and construction companies, national environmental firms, financial institutions, local and state Governments, and one foreign country.*

*The firm places a premium on the academic honors and the outstanding record of public service of its attorneys. We believe we offer excellence to a unique client base.*

*(This Listing Continued)*

## MEMBERS OF FIRM

**PETER D. KELLY,** born Pasadena, California, July 30, 1948; admitted to bar, 1977, California; 1979, District of Columbia. *Education:* California State University at Fullerton (B.A., 1972); Southwestern University (J.D., 1976). Lead Articles Editor, Southwestern University Law Review, 1976. Author: "Reform of the Delegate Selection Process to Democratic National Conventions: 1964 to the Present," 7 Southwestern University Law Review 273, 1975. California Democratic Party: State Chairman, 1983-1985 and 1987-1989; Southern California Chairman, 1981-1983 and 1985-1987. Finance Chairman: Richard Katz for Mayor of Los Angeles, 1992-1993; Tom Bradley for Mayor of Los Angeles, 1980-1981; Carter/Mondale California Presidential Campaign, 1979-1980. Member, Democratic National Committee, 1983-1985 and 1987-1989. Member, Board of Directors, Los Angeles Central City Association, 1982—. Lecturer, Los Angeles County Bar Association Corporate Section for State and Federal Election Law, 1979. Member, Los Angeles County Probation Commission, 1976-1977. Member, Los Angeles City Attorney's Airport Advisory Committee, 1973. Associate and Partner, Manatt, Phelps, Rothenberg & Tunney, 1976-1983. Director, State Street Bank of California, a subsidiary of the State Street Bank of Boston, 1985-1989. *Member:* District of Columbia, Century City, Los Angeles County and American Bar Associations. **PRACTICE AREAS:** Administrative Law; Real Estate; Land Use.

**SHELDON H. LYTTON,** born Chicago, Illinois, September 20, 1942; admitted to bar, 1973, California. *Education:* Northwestern University (B.S., 1963); University of California at Los Angeles (J.D., 1973). Selected, National Moot Court Team, Roscoe Pound National Moot Court Competition, 1973. Editor-in-Chief, UCLA Law Review, 1973. Author: Comment, "Taxability of the Widow's Allowance," 19 UCLA Law Review 361, 1972. Special Assistant Attorney General, California Department of Justice, 1978-1979. Chief of Staff, Office of the Lieutenant Governor, State of California, 1979-1980. Executive Director and Commissioner, California Commission on Citizen Participation in Government, Office of the Governor, 1980-1982. General Counsel, President Ford Committee (California), 1975-1976. Deputy Director, Younger for Governor Committee, 1973-1974. California Regan-Bush Committee, 1980. Associate, O'Melveny & Meyers; Partner, Finley, Kumble, Wagner, Heine, Underberg, Manley & Casey, 1980-1984. *Member:* Los Angeles County Bar Association; State Bar of California.

**MARSHALL G. MINTZ,** born Detroit, Michigan, May 28, 1947; admitted to bar, 1972, California. *Education:* University of California at Los Angeles (B.A., 1968; J.D., 1971). Member, U.C.L.A. —Alaska Law Review, 1970-1971. Moderator and Panelist: "Privileges for the Trial and Business Lawyer," California Continuing Education of the Bar, May-June 1983; "Depositions," California Continuing Education of the Bar, September-October 1983. Panelist, "Compelling Opposing and Enforcing Discovery in State Court," California Continuing Education of the Bar, March 1985; "Sharpening Your Law and Motion Advocacy Skills," California Continuing Education of the Bar, October 1988; "Sharpening Your Written and Oral Advocacy Skills," California Continuing Education of the Bar, August 1980. Law Clerk to Appellate Department, Los Angeles County Superior Court, 1971-1972. Arbitrator, Los Angeles County Bar Association Arbitration and Client Relations Committee, 1978-1990. Member: Los Angeles County Superior Court Arbitration Administrative Committee, 1979; Los Angeles Superior Court, 1984 Olympics Special Settlement Panel. *Member:* Los Angeles County and American Bar Associations; State Bar of California; Association of Business Trial Lawyers (Member, Board of Governors, 1976-1977; Program Chairman, 1976). **PRACTICE AREAS:** Securities Law; Business Law; Real Estate Litigation.

**BRUCE P. VANN,** born Omaha, Nebraska, 1955; admitted to bar, 1980, California. *Education:* Washington University (A.B., summa cum laude, 1977); Duke University (J.D., 1980). Phi Beta Kappa. Chancellor's Honorary Scholar. Staff and Editorial Board Member, Duke Law Journal, 1979-1980. Lecturer: Independent Feature Project/West, 1988. *Member:* Los Angeles County and American Bar Associations; State Bar of California. **PRACTICE AREAS:** Corporate Law; Securities Offerings; Secured Lending.

**JAMES D. ROBINSON,** born Long Island, New York, July 26, 1959; admitted to bar, 1984, California; 1985, U.S. District Court, Central District of California and U.S. Tax Court. *Education:* Villanova University (B.S., cum laude, 1981); University of San Diego (J.D., cum laude, 1984; LL.M. in Taxation, summa cum laude, 1987). Associate, Morris and Spencer, 1984-1990. *Member:* Los Angeles County Bar Association (Member, Sections on: Real Estate; Taxation); State Bar of California (Member, Real Property Section). **PRACTICE AREAS:** Administrative Law; Business; Real Estate.

## OF COUNSEL

**MARILYN BARRETT,** born Hoisington, Kansas, August 23, 1952; admitted to bar, 1978, California; 1979, District of Columbia and U.S. Tax Court. *Education:* University of Kansas (B.S., with highest distinction, 1973); University of California at Los Angeles (J.D., 1977). Beta Gamma Sigma. Associate Editor, University of California at Los Angeles Law Review, 1976-1977. Certified Public Accountant, Maryland, 1978. Author: "Stock Options: Court Rules That Employees Must Pay Ordinary Income Tax When Their Options Were Sold As Part Of Company's Acquisition," CEB California Business Law Reporter, January 1996; "Loan Out Corporations: Ninth Circuit Rides To The Rescue As The IRS Continues Its Assault On Loan-Out Corporations," CEB California Business Law Reporter, November 1995; "U.S. Supreme Court Holds That ADEA Damages Are Taxable, But Its Decision Creates New Uncertainty," CEB California Business Law Reporter, September 1995; "When Is The Sale Of A Business Subject to Sales Tax Like an Over-the-Counter Retail Sale? In California, Most of the Time," CEB California Business Law Reporter, June 1995; "Ninth Circuit Disallows Corporation's Deduction of Interest Accrued on Deferred Compensation," CEB California Business Law Reporter, March, 1995; "The Not-So-Friendly Skies For Victims of Age Discrimination: The IRS Attacks Exclusion of ADEA Damages," CEB California Business Law Reporter, January, 1995; "Has The Insanity Stopped? IRS Partially Reserves Punitive Policy Denying Deductibility of Clean-up Costs-But Questions Remain," California Environmental Law Reporter, July, 1994; "Tax Issues Concerning Independent Contractors and Loan-Out Corporations," Tax Management Compensation Planning Journal, (In Two Parts), September 3, 1993 and October 1, 1993; "Is the Loan-Out Corporation Dead or Alive? Is the Independent Contractor an Endangered Species?" distributed by the Los Angeles County Bar Association Taxation Section (1992); "Rust vs. Sullivan: New Limits on Choice Imposed by the Supreme Court," Westside Woman, July 17, 1991; "Claim of Right: A Tax Doctrine Unjustly Applied to Accrued Income Subject to Litigation," 24 University of California at Los Angeles Law Review, 877, 1977; "The Recently Proposed Regulations under I.R.C. §704 (b); A Brief Review," 9 Tax Section News, No. 3, Spring, 1983. Co-Author: "Independent Contractors, Employees, the Entertainment Industry and the IRS: Tax Administration Problem Heads for Hollywood," The ABA Entertainment and Sports Lawyer, Fall, 1993; "Proposal On The Taxation of Escrow and Settlement Funds Under I.R.C. §468 B (g), Tax Notes Today, June 13, 1991; "Section 482 and Non-recognition Transfers," Tax Notes, December 1989. Contributing Editor (Taxation), CEB California Business Law Reporter. *Member:* Los Angeles County (Member, Taxation, Business and Corporations Law Sections; Chair-Elect, Taxation Section, 1996-1997; Member At Large, Executive Committee of Taxation Section, 1992-1993; Chair, Entertainment Tax Committee, 1991-1992; Chair, Ad Hoc Disaster Recovery Tax Relief Committee, 1992-1993) and American (Member, Committee on Affiliated and Related Corporations, 1981-1992; Chair, Subcommittee on Intercompany Allocations, 1989-1990) Bar Associations; State Bar of California (Chair, Taxation Section, 1996-1997, Member, 1992—, Executive Committee of Taxation Section); District of Columbia Bar; American Institute of Certified Public Accountants (Member, Tax Section). (Also Practicing Individually). **PRACTICE AREAS:** Business Law; State and Federal Tax Law.

**MICHAEL I. SIDLEY,** born Los Angeles, California, July 23, 1961; admitted to bar, 1988, California; 1990, U.S. District Court, Central District of California. *Education:* University of California at Berkeley (A.B., 1983); University of the Pacific, McGeorge School of Law (J.D., with distinction, 1988). Order of the Coif. President, National Moot Court Program. Los Angeles Count Deputy Public Defender, 1989-1990. Private practice 1990—. Member: National Campaign Staff; Mondale for President, Mondale-Ferraro; National Campaign Staff, Dukakis for President, Dukakis-Bentsen. *Member:* Beverly Hills Bar Association; National Association of Criminal Defense Lawyers; California Attorneys for Criminal Justice; Criminal Courts Bar Association. (Also Practicing Individually).

# KENDIG & ROSS

*1875 CENTURY PARK EAST, SUITE 2150*
**LOS ANGELES, CALIFORNIA 90067**
Telephone: 310-556-8100
Fax: 310-556-8140

*Business Litigation and Employment/Labor Law.*
(This Listing Continued)

## KENDIG & ROSS, Los Angeles—Continued

FIRM PROFILE: The focus of practice at Kendig & Ross is on civil litigation, employment and labor services to businesses, individuals and other law firms. The firm's senior attorneys all have substantial experience as partners with larger firms. Kendig & Ross prides itself on offering "big firm" experience, while being able to provide the service and efficiencies of a smaller firm.

The firm's attorneys have experience in all aspects of litigation, arbitrations and administrative proceedings, including substantial experience in successfully trying cases.

Kendig & Ross also offers employment and labor advice and representation including preventative advice on employment decisions, drafting of employee handbooks and related materials, discrimination, ADA, and wrongful termination litigation, and representation in administrative proceedings including EEOC, DFEH, DOL and Wage and Hour proceedings.

### MEMBERS OF FIRM

**DENNIS A. KENDIG,** born Dayton, Ohio, December 27, 1946; admitted to bar, 1974, Connecticut and New York; 1975, California. *Education:* DePauw University (B.A., 1969); Yale University (J.D., 1973). Phi Beta Kappa. Author: "Discrimination Against Women in Home Mortgage Financing," 3 Yale Review of Law and Social Action 166, 1973; Article, "Procedures for Management of Non-routine Cases," 3 Hofstra Law Review 701, 1975. Judge Pro Tem, Los Angeles Municipal Court, 1989-1991. *Member:* Beverly Hills and Los Angeles County Bar Associations; The State Bar of California. **PRACTICE AREAS:** Business Litigation; Securities Litigation; Franchise Litigation.

**BRADLEY D. ROSS,** born Los Angeles, California, October 14, 1956; admitted to bar, 1981, California. *Education:* University of California at Los Angeles (B.A., cum laude, 1978); Loyola University of Los Angeles (J.D., 1981). Pi Gamma Mu. Chief Ninth Circuit Editor, Loyola of Los Angeles Law Review, 1980-1981. Recipient: National Trial Advocacy Competition Finalist, 1981. E. Thomas Memorial Scholarship Award; Western State Scholarship Award. Co-Author: "Recent Ninth Circuit Developments in Securities Law," 13 Loyola of Los Angeles Law Review 985, Sept., 1980. Judge Pro Tem, Beverly Hills Municipal Court, 1987-1991. *Member:* Beverly Hills, Los Angeles County (Member, Trial Lawyers Section) and American Bar Associations; State Bar of California (Member, Labor and Employment Section); Association of Business Trial Lawyers. **PRACTICE AREAS:** Employment/Labor Law; Business Litigation; Real Estate Litigation.

### ASSOCIATE

**JEFFREY W. COWAN,** born New York, N.Y., January 3, 1964; admitted to bar, 1991, California; 1993, District of Columbia. *Education:* Cornell University (B.A., History, cum laude, 1986); University of California at Los Angeles (J.D., 1991). Member, Moot Court Honors Program, 1989-1990. Recipient, New York Times Guild Merit Scholarship. 9th Circuit Reporter, ABA Employment and Labor Law Section. *Member:* Los Angeles County Bar Association; The State Bar of California. **PRACTICE AREAS:** Business Litigation.

REPRESENTATIVE CLIENTS: Public Storage, Inc.; Carpeteria, Inc.; Aetna Life Insurance Co.; Bienvenidos Children's Center, Inc.; Desert Valley Medical Group; Dacor; Westrec Properties, Inc.; Covina Valley Community Hospital; Sizzler, Inc.; Harbor Distributing Co.; CSX InterModal, Inc.; Joseph T. Ryerson & Son; Normandie Club Casino.

---

## ELWOOD S. KENDRICK, INC.
### 29TH FLOOR, 555 SOUTH FLOWER STREET
### LOS ANGELES, CALIFORNIA 90071-2498
Telephone: 213-622-6030
Fax: 213-688-7564

*Complex Business Litigation. Class Actions.*

**ELWOOD S. KENDRICK,** born April 15, 1912; admitted to bar, 1937, Illinois; 1947, California and U.S. Supreme Court; registered to practice before U.S. Patent and Trademark Office. *Education:* North Dakota State University (B.S., 1933); University of Illinois (J.D., 1937). Phi Alpha Delta. Special Attorney, Antitrust Division, U.S. Department of Justice, 1942-1943. Lawyer Delegate, 1962-1976, Special Guest, 1986, 1987, 1988, 1990, 1993 and 1994 Ninth Circuit Judicial Conference. Director, Ninth Circuit Historical Society, 1986—; Director, Ninth Circuit Pasadena Courthouse Fund, 1987—. Member, Board of Visitors, University of Illinois College of

*(This Listing Continued)*

---

Law, 1989-1991. *Member:* Los Angeles County and American Bar Associations; The State Bar of California.

REFERENCE: The Bank of California, Los Angeles Main Office, Los Angeles, Ca. (BANCAL).

---

## KENOFF & MACHTINGER
### 1999 AVENUE OF THE STARS, SUITE 1250
### LOS ANGELES, CALIFORNIA 90067
Telephone: 310-552-0808
Fax: 310-277-0653

*Entertainment (motion pictures, television and music), Civil Litigation (business and entertainment), Real Estate, Corporate, Banking, Tax.*

**JAY S. KENOFF,** born Los Angeles, California, April 29, 1946; admitted to bar, 1970, District of Columbia; 1971, California; 1973, U.S. Court of Military Appeals; 1974, U.S. Court of Appeals, 9th Circuit; 1975, U.S. District Court, Central and Southern Districts of California. *Education:* University of California at Los Angeles (A.B., magna cum laude, 1967); University of Southern California (M.S., 1974); Harvard University (J.D., 1970). Phi Beta Kappa. Author: "Motion Pictures," Entertainment Industry Contracts: Negotiating and Drafting Guide, Vol. I, Matthew Bender, 1986. Professor of Law, Northrop University School of Law, 1978-1984. Judge Pro Tempore, Los Angeles Municipal Court, 1984—. *Member:* State Bar of California; District of Columbia Bar. [CDR., JAGC, USNR; active duty, 1970-1974]. **PRACTICE AREAS:** Entertainment; Real Estate; Business.

**LEONARD S. MACHTINGER,** born New York, N.Y., December 8, 1941; admitted to bar, 1965, New York; 1966, District of Columbia; 1975, California. *Education:* City College of the City University of New York (B.A., 1962); Harvard Law School (LL.B., 1965); Georgetown University Law Center (LL.M., 1967). Phi Beta Kappa. *Member:* Los Angeles County Bar Association (Member: Public Affairs Committee, 1976-1978; Superior Courts Committee, 1986-1988); The State Bar of California; The District of Columbia Bar. **PRACTICE AREAS:** Civil Litigation (business and entertainment).

### ASSOCIATE

**THOMAS S. RUBIN,** born Somerset, New Jersey, March 11, 1968; admitted to bar, 1995, California; 1996, New Jersey. *Education:* Harvard University (A.B., 1990); University of California School of Law, Los Angeles (J.D., 1995). **PRACTICE AREAS:** Entertainment Law; Litigation.

**COURTNEY F. LEE,** born Atlanta, Georgia, October 25, 1968; admitted to bar, 1996, California. *Education:* Bard College (B.A., 1990); University of California School of Law, Los Angeles (J.D., 1994). **PRACTICE AREAS:** Entertainment Transactions.

### OF COUNSEL

**WILLIAM J. IMMERMAN,** born New York, N.Y., December 29, 1937; admitted to bar, 1964, California. *Education:* University of Wisconsin (B.S., 1959); Stanford Law School (J.D., 1963). Phi Delta Phi. President: Salem Productions, Inc.; Sedric Productions, Inc.; Distribution Expense Company; Immkirk Financial Corporation. *Member:* Los Angeles County Bar Association; State Bar of California; Academy of Motion Pictures Arts and Sciences. **PRACTICE AREAS:** Entertainment Law.

**ROBERT O. KAPLAN,** born Los Angeles, California, July 25, 1941; admitted to bar, 1966, California. *Education:* Dartmouth College (A.B., 1963); Boalt Hall School of Law, University of California (J.D., 1966). Member, Board of Trustees and Chairman of Southern California Regional Board, Outward Bound. *Member:* Beverly Hills Bar Association; State Bar of California. **PRACTICE AREAS:** Entertainment Law.

**LAWRENCE E. MAY,** born New York, N.Y., August 7, 1947; admitted to bar, 1973, California and New York. *Education:* University of California at Los Angeles (B.A., 1969; J.D., 1972). University of California at Los Angeles Law Review, 1970-1971. National Conference of Bar Presidents, 1987—; Public Counsel (Board of Directors, 1989—); Boy Scouts of America (Advisory Board Los Angeles Council, 1985—); Los Angeles Jewish Journal (Editorial Advisory Board, 1985-1991); Member Executive Committee, Pacific Southwest Region Anti-Defamation League ,1985—. *Member:* Beverly Hills (President, 1988-1989, President-Elect, 1987-1988; Vice President, 1986-1987; Secretary, 1985-1986; Treasurer, 1984-1985; Member, Board of Governors, 1981-1990; Chairman, Business Law Section, 1984-1985) and Los Angeles County (Member, Board of Trustees 1987-1988) Bar Associations; State Bar of California (Member, Sections on Real Property Law and Business Law; Delegate, State Bar Conference of Dele-

*(This Listing Continued)*

gates, 1983-1989; Member, District 7, Conference of Delegates Executive Committee Nominating Committee, 1989). *PRACTICE AREAS:* Corporate Law; Real Estate; Estate Planning; Business Planning Law.

## KERN, STREETER & GONZALEZ

601 WEST 5TH STREET, SUITE 1100
**LOS ANGELES, CALIFORNIA 90071**
Telephone: 213-629-8100
Facsimile: 213-627-8765

*Product Liability, Medical and Dental Malpractice, Construction Defect, Premises Liability, Defamation, Employment Law, Insurance Law, and Brokerage Negligence, General Civil Trial and Appellate Practice in all State and Federal Courts.*

FIRM PROFILE: *Kern, Streeter & Gonzalez is a distinctive trial firm with an extensive background in general tort law, specializing in products liability, premises liability, and medical malpractice. Product litigation has included automobiles, motorcycles, off-road vehicles, power saws, bicycles, lawn mowers, exercise equipment, industrial machinery, and chemicals in both commercial and consumer settings. Premises cases range from construction defects and slip and falls to cases alleging inadequate security, including sexual assault and wrongful death allegations. The representation of health care practitioners includes the defense of physicians, hospitals and convalescent homes, dentists, Health Maintenance Organizations (HMOs), and pharmaceutical manufacturers.*

*The goal of Kern, Streeter & Gonzalez is to resolve cases promptly with minimum legal expense while achieving the best possible results.*

### MEMBERS OF FIRM

**RENÉ J. KERN, JR.,** born Brooklyn, New York, May 2, 1947; admitted to bar, 1981, California and U.S. District Court, Central District of California; 1982, U.S. District Court, Southern District of California and U.S. Court of Appeals, Ninth Circuit. *Education:* University of Northern Colorado (B.S., 1970); Western State University College of Law (J.D., 1977). Member, Moot Court Competition. *Member:* Los Angeles County and American Bar Associations; State Bar of California; American Board of Trial Advocates; The Association of Trial Lawyers of America; American Business and Insurance Attorneys; Trial Attorneys of America; California Trial Lawyers Association; U.S. Chapter of AIDA; Defense Research Institute; Association of Southern California Defense Counsel. *PRACTICE AREAS:* Product Liability; Premises Liability; Medical and Dental Malpractice; Employment Discrimination; General Negligence; Insurance Litigation.

**JOHN W. STREETER,** born Staten Island, New York, August 27, 1952; admitted to bar, 1979, California. *Education:* Washington State University (B.A., 1974); Gonzaga University and Loyola University of Los Angeles (J.D., 1978). Pi Sigma Alpha. *Member:* Los Angeles County and American Bar Associations; The State Bar of California; Association of Southern California Defense Counsel; Defense Research Institute; American Board of Trial Advocates. *PRACTICE AREAS:* Construction Defects.

**MICHAEL D. GONZALEZ,** born Glendale, California, March 30, 1958; admitted to bar, 1984, California; 1985, U.S. District Court, Central District of California and U.S. Court of Appeals, Ninth Circuit. *Education:* California State University at Northridge (B.A., 1981); Southwestern University (J.D., 1984). Recipient: American Jurisprudence Awards in Business Organizations; Fulbright and Jaworski Trial Advocacy Competition Award. *Member:* The State Bar of California; American Bar Association; Association of Southern California Defense Counsel. *PRACTICE AREAS:* Medical Malpractice.

### ASSOCIATES

**TINA L. GENTILE,** born Seattle, Washington, August 1, 1957; admitted to bar, 1988, California, U.S. District Court, Central District of California and U.S. Court of Appeals, Ninth Circuit. *Education:* San Jose State University (B.A., summa cum laude, 1980); University of California at Los Angeles (J.D., 1988). Recipient, Hewlett Packard Political Science Scholarship. *Member:* Los Angeles County and American Bar Associations; State Bar of California; California Trial Lawyers Association; The Association of Trial Lawyers of America; Defense Research Institute. *PRACTICE AREAS:* Premises Liability; Products Liability; General Negligence; Defamation; Contract.

**CLAUDIA T. BEIGHTOL,** born Los Angeles, California, September 3, 1965; admitted to bar, 1992, California and U.S. District Court, Central District of California. *Education:* University of California at Los Angeles

*(This Listing Continued)*

(B.A., 1989); Loyola Law School, Los Angeles (J.D., 1992). Phi Alpha Delta. *Member:* Los Angeles County and American Bar Associations; State Bar of California. *PRACTICE AREAS:* Premises Liability; Products Liability; Medical Malpractice; Defamation; Wrongful Termination; Employment Discrimination.

**ANGELA J. ARMITAGE,** born Calgary, Alberta, Canada, August 2, 1968; admitted to bar, 1994, California. *Education:* University of California at Los Angeles (B.A., psychology, 1990); Loyola University of Los Angeles (J.D., 1994). Phi Delta Phi. *Member:* State Bar of California. *PRACTICE AREAS:* Employment Discrimination; Medical Malpractice; Products Liability.

**CHRISTINA L. YOUNG,** born Kansas City, Missouri, December 10, 1968; admitted to bar, 1994, California; 1995, Pennsylvania. *Education:* Duke University (B.A., 1991); Loyola University of Los Angeles (J.D., 1994). Editor, International Law Journal, Loyola University of Los Angeles, 1993-1994. *Member:* State Bar of California. *PRACTICE AREAS:* Premises Liability; Medical Malpractice; Products Liability; Defamation; Contracts.

REPRESENTATIVE CLIENTS: Bridgestone/Firestone, Inc.; Crawford & Company; CTL Environmental Services, Inc.; Dean Witter Reynolds, Inc.; Farmers Insurance Group; Fremont Indemnity; The Hahn Company; Hamada of America; Hasbro, Inc.; Honda Motor Co., Ltd.; Lee & Associates; Merrill Lynch; Nissan Fire & Marine Insurance Co., Ltd; Norcal Mutual Insurance Co.; Scottsdale Insurance Co.; Service Management Systems, Inc.; Summit Health, Ltd.; TIG Insurance Co.; TM Claims Service, Inc.; Toplis & Harding; Tristar Claims Management; United States Fidelity and Guaranty Co.

## KERN & WOOLEY

Established in 1971

SUITE 1150, 10900 WILSHIRE BOULEVARD
**LOS ANGELES, CALIFORNIA 90024**
Telephone: 310-824-1777
Fax: 310-824-0892

*Irving, Texas Office:* Suite 1700 The Central Tower at Williams Square, 5215 North O'Connor Road. Telephone: 214-869-3311. Fax: 214-869-2433.

*Mesa, Arizona Office:* Suite 10550 Financial Plaza, 1201 South Alma School Road; Telephone: 602-834-8811. Fax: 602-834-3433.

*Aviation and Casualty Insurance Law. Products Liability Law; Business Litigation.*

**ROBERT M. KERN,** admitted to bar, 1971, California and U.S. Supreme Court. *Education:* Loyola University of Los Angeles (J.D., 1970).

**M. EUGENE WOOLEY,** admitted to bar, 1965, California; 1971, U.S. Supreme Court. *Education:* University of Southern California (B.A., 1960; J.D., 1964).

**WILLIAM V. O'CONNOR,** admitted to bar, 1973, California. *Education:* U.S. Naval Academy (B.S., 1964); Loyola University of Los Angeles (J.D., 1973).

**GEORGE STEVEN MCCALL,** admitted to bar, 1977, Texas; 1978, U.S. District Court, Northern District of Texas; 1979, U.S. Court of Appeals, Fifth Circuit. *Education:* Baylor University (J.D., 1978). (Resident, Irving, Texas Office).

**DOUGLAS J. PAHL,** admitted to bar, 1978, California and U.S. Supreme Court. *Education:* Duke University (A.B., 1975); Southern Methodist University (J.D., 1978).

**JOHN W. SHAW,** admitted to bar, 1978, California and U.S. Supreme Court. *Education:* California State University at Long Beach (B.A., summa cum laude, 1975); Loyola University of Los Angeles (J.D., 1978).

**MICHAEL J. TERHAR,** admitted to bar, 1979, California; 1983, U.S. Supreme Court. *Education:* California State University at Northridge; University of Washington (B.S., 1975); Loyola University of Los Angeles (J.D., 1979).

**ROBERT L. GREER,** admitted to bar, 1978, Arizona and New Mexico;. *Education:* University of Arizona; Northern Arizona University (B.S., magna cum laude, 1974); University of Arizona (J.D., 1978). (Resident, Mesa, Arizona Office). *LANGUAGES:* Cantonese.

**G. DON SWAIM,** admitted to bar, 1983, Texas. *Education:* University of Redlands; Abilene Christian University (B.A., cum laude, 1980); Baylor University (J.D., 1982). (Resident, Irving, Texas Office).

*(This Listing Continued)*

KERN & WOOLEY, Los Angeles—Continued

**PETER T. KIRCHEN,** admitted to bar, 1976, California. *Education:* Loyola Marymount University (B.S., 1968); Whittier College School of Law (J.D., 1975).

**JONATHAN S. MORSE,** admitted to bar, 1977, California; 1982, Washington. *Education:* Princeton University (B.S.E., with honors, 1966); University of Michigan (J.D., cum laude, 1976).

**STEPHEN G. GOOD,** admitted to bar, 1983, Texas. *Education:* St. Olaf College (B.A., cum laude, 1972); Northwestern University (M.S., 1973); Southern Methodist University (J.D., 1983). (Resident, Irving, Texas Office). **LANGUAGES:** French.

**RAND DUNN CARSTENS,** admitted to bar, 1986, California. *Education:* Fort Lewis College (B.A., cum laude, 1982); Southwestern University (J.D., 1986).

**JOHN H. ISHIKAWA,** admitted to bar, 1983, Arizona. *Education:* Arizona State University (B.S., cum laude, 1980; J.D., 1983). (Resident, Mesa, Arizona Office).

**ANTHONY G. MARRIOTT,** admitted to bar, 1974, As a Solicitor of the Supreme Court of England and Wales; 1990, California. *Education:* Sheffield College of Technology; Sheffield University and Guildford College of Law, England (J.D., Evaluation, 1974).

**JUSTO M. JUSTO,** admitted to bar, 1992, California. *Education:* St. Louis University, Baguio City, Philippines (B.S., 1979); Maryhill Seminary School of Theology; San Beda College of Law (LL.B., 1986).

**JOHN M. SCHUTZA,** admitted to bar, 1990, Texas. *Education:* Southern Methodist University (B.A., magna cum laude, 1987); Texas Tech University (J.D., 1990). (Resident, Irving, Texas Office).

**ELLEN GREER,** admitted to bar, 1993, Texas. *Education:* Austin College (B.A., 1982); Southern Methodist University (M.A., 1987; J.D., 1993).

REPRESENTATIVE CLIENTS: Aetna Life and Casualty; Airclaims, Inc.; American Home Assurance Co.; Avemco Insurance; Chubb/Pacific Indemnity Insurance Group; E.H. Crump of California; International Underwriters Aviation, Inc.; Marsh & McLennan, Inc.; Southern Marine and Aviation Underwriters, Inc.; Underwriters at Lloyds; W. Brown & Associates, Inc.; American Eagle Insurance Co.; American General Aircraft Corp.; Parker Hannifin Corp.; Northrop Corp.

---

## LAW OFFICES OF
## LANCE N. KERR

8833 SUNSET BOULEVARD, SUITE 200
**LOS ANGELES, CALIFORNIA 90069**
Telephone: 310-659-2929
Fax: 310-289-5240

*Civil Litigation, Corporate and Business, Real Estate, Commercial.*

**LANCE N. KERR,** born Los Angeles, California, October 12, 1948; admitted to bar, 1977, California; 1982, U.S. District Court, Central District of California. *Education:* University of California, Los Angeles (B.A., 1966); Loyola University of Los Angeles (J.D., 1976). *Member:* State Bar of California.

---

## KERRY, GARCIA & LEWIS

### LOS ANGELES, CALIFORNIA

(See Long Beach)

*Civil Trial and Appellate Practice emphasizing Defense and Plaintiff Personal Injury, Premises Liability, Products Liability, Professional Negligence, Construction, Aviation, Insurance, Business Litigation and Transaction matters, Commercial, Corporate and Real Estate Transactions, Alternative Dispute Resolution.*

CAA844B

---

## KESSLER & KESSLER
*A LAW CORPORATION*
Established in 1987

2029 CENTURY PARK EAST, SUITE 1520
**LOS ANGELES, CALIFORNIA 90067**
Telephone: 310-552-9800
Fax: 310-552-0442
Email: skiplaw@ix.netcom.com

*Taxation, Corporate, Real Estate, Commercial Litigation, Bankruptcy and General Business Litigation, Estate Planning.*

**WARREN J. KESSLER,** born Rochester, New York, April 22, 1945; admitted to bar, 1973, Illinois; 1974, U.S. Tax Court; 1977, California. *Education:* Cornell University (A.B., 1967); University of Michigan (J.D., cum laude, 1973). Co-Author: "Sidestepping the Impact of *Starker* to Save the Two-Party Tax-Free Exchange," 48 Journal of Taxation 328, June 1978. Instructor: "Tax-Deferred Real Property Exchanges," CEB University of California, April-May, 1981; "The 33rd Annual Institute on Federal Taxation," University of Southern California, 1981; "Straddling the Fence Between Debt and Equity-Tax Considerations of Alternative Financing Techniques," Third Annual Colorado Springs Tax Institute, September, 1982; "Real Estate as an Investment," Thirty-Fifth Annual Institute on Federal Taxation, University of Southern California, January, 1983; "Resuscitating Ailing Partnerships," Fourth Annual Institute on Advanced Tax Planning for Real Property Transactions, California Continuing Education of the Bar, June, 1985; "Refinancing Real Estate," Thirty-Ninth Annual Institute on Federal Taxation, University of Southern California, January, 1987; "Dealing With Distressed Real Estate Projects," Forty-Second Annual Institute on Federal Taxation, University of Southern California, January 1990. Member, International Council of Shopping Centers, 1993—. Member, Cornell University Real Estate Council. *Member:* State Bar of California and American Bar Association. **PRACTICE AREAS:** Taxation Law; Corporate Law; Real Estate Law; Partnership Law; Estate Planning; Limited Liability Company Law.

**JOAN B. KESSLER,** born Pittsburgh, Pennsylvania, July 18, 1945; admitted to bar, 1987, California. *Education:* University of Michigan (B.A., 1967; Ph.D., 1973); University of California at Los Angeles (M.A., 1969); Loyola Law School (J.D., 1986). Recipient, University of Michigan Rackham Prize. Fellowship, Chief Articles Editor, Loyola Law School, International & Comparative Law Journal. Author: Note, "An Empirical Study of Six and Twelve-member Jury Decision-making Processes," 6U. of Mich. J. L. Ref. 712, (1973) (Cited In) Colgrove v. Battin 413 U.S. 149, 159 (1973); Georgia v. Ballew 435 U.S. 223, 238, 242 (1978). The Social Psychology of Jury Deliberation, in R. J. Simon (Ed.), "The Jury System in America, A Critical Overview," Beverly Hills: Sage Publications (1975). Kessler, Karnes & Follert, "The Effect of Juror Sex on the Decision-making of Student and Actual Jurors in a Simulated Civil Case," Speech Communications Association convention Paper, Houston (1975). Co-Author: Kulka & Kessler, "Is Justice Really Blind? - The Influence of Litigant Physical Attractiveness on Juridical Judgement," 8 Journal of Applied Social Psychology, 366 (1978). Kessler, "Use of Videotape for the Expert Witness," 28 Journal of the American Academy of Forensic Science (April, 1983). Co-Author: "Legalese v. Plain English: An Empirical Study of Persuasion and Credibility in Appellate Brief Writing," Loyola of Los Angeles Law Review, 1987, reprinted in Japanese in Vol. 63m Hoha Kenkyu (Journal of Law Politics and Sociology). Author: "The Lawyer's Intercultural Communication Problems with Clients from Diverse Cultures," Northwestern Journal of International Law and Business 64 (Spring, 1988). Author: "Are Lender Liability Actions Alive and Well?" Western Independent Bankers Newsline (October, 1989). Member, Organization of Women Executives. *Member:* State Bar of California; American Bar Association. **PRACTICE AREAS:** Commercial Litigation; Bankruptcy Law; Business Litigation.

**LISA C. ALEXANDER,** born Seattle, Washington, September 9, 1958; admitted to bar, 1986, California. *Education:* University of California at Los Angeles (B.A., 1981); University of Southern California (J.D., 1985). Member: Honors Competition, 1983-1984; Honors Program Executive Board, 1984-1985, Hale Moot Court. Real Estate Brokers License, California, 1992. *Member:* Beverly Hills (Member: Real Estate Section; Probate, Trust and Estates Section Executive Board, 1991-1992; Chair, Probate, Trust and Estates Section Legislative Committee, 1990-1991) and Los Angeles County (Member, Real Property Section) Bar Associations; State Bar of California; California Trustees Association (Member: Board of Direc-

*(This Listing Continued)*

tors, Los Angeles Chapter, 1993-1996; 2nd Vice President, 1995-1996). *PRACTICE AREAS:* Estate Planning; Corporate Law; Real Estate Law; Partnership Law; Limited Liability Company Law.

## PAUL T. KESTENBAUM

2029 CENTURY PARK EAST
SUITE 480
**LOS ANGELES, CALIFORNIA 90067**
Telephone: 310-277-9402
Facsimile: 310-277-4351
Email: ptk@westworld.com

*Federal and State Tax Planning for Individuals and Business Entities. Estate Planning, General Business, Corporate and Real Estate Transactions.*

**PAUL T. KESTENBAUM,** born Schenectady, New York, February 22, 1957; admitted to bar, 1984, New York, Florida and U.S. Tax Court; 1986, California. *Education:* State University of New York at Albany (B.S., magna cum laude, 1978); University of Miami (J.D., cum laude, 1983); New York University (LL.M., 1988). Editor, University of Miami Law Review, 1992-1993. Author: "The Tax Benefit Rule: Recovery Re-evaluated," 36 University of Miami Law Review 533, 1982; "The State Taxation of Pension Income Act of 1995," Los Angeles Lawyer, July-August, 1996. Lecturer, Limited Liability Companies, Continuing Education of the Bar of California, 1995. Certified Public Accountant, Florida, 1980. *Member:* New York State Bar Association; State Bar of California; The Florida Bar.

## JOHN A. KHOURY

10880 WILSHIRE BOULEVARD, SUITE 1050
**LOS ANGELES, CALIFORNIA 90024**
Telephone: 310-475-3772
Fax: 310-470-8590

*Aviation and International Law, Litigation and Entertainment Law.*

**JOHN A. KHOURY,** born 1943; admitted to bar, 1986, California and U.S. District Court, Central District of California; 1987, U.S. Court of Appeals, Ninth Circuit; 1996, U.S. Supreme Court. *Education:* American University of Beirut; California State University at Fullerton (B.A., 1983); Southwestern University School of Law (J.D., 1986). Judge Pro Tem, Los Angeles Municipal Court and Los Angeles Superior Court. *Member:* Beverly Hills, Los Angeles County, Federal and American Bar Associations; The Association of Trial Lawyers of America. *LANGUAGES:* French and Arabic.

## BITA M. KIAIE

10877 WILSHIRE BOULEVARD, SUITE 1401
**LOS ANGELES, CALIFORNIA 90024-4341**
Telephone: 310-443-3229
Fax: 310-443-3233

*Medical Malpractice, Personal Injury.*

**BITA M. KIAIE,** born Tehran, January 6, 1964; admitted to bar, 1989, California. *Education:* University of Southern California (B.A., 1985); Southwestern University (J.D., 1988). *Member:* Beverly Hills, Los Angeles County and American Bar Associations; State Bar of California.

## KIMBALL, TIREY & ST. JOHN

**LOS ANGELES, CALIFORNIA**

(See Newport Beach)

*Residential and Commercial Landlord/Tenant Law, Collections, Real Estate, Business, Banking and Finance Litigation.*

## KIMBALL & WEINER LLP

555 SOUTH FLOWER STREET, SUITE 4540
**LOS ANGELES, CALIFORNIA 90071**
Telephone: 213-538-3800
Fax: 213-538-3810

*General Corporate and Commercial Practice, including Computer Software, Systems and Services, Real Estate Transactions, Corporate Finance and Securities, Mergers and Acquisitions and International Transactions.*

**GEORGE KIMBALL,** born San Diego, California, June 2, 1952; admitted to bar, 1978, California; 1987, U.S. Supreme Court. *Education:* University of California at Los Angeles (A.B., summa cum laude, 1973); University of London, London, England (B.A., 1975); University of Michigan (J.D., cum laude, 1978). Phi Beta Kappa. Senior Editor, Michigan Law Review, 1977-1978. First Place, Henry M. Campbell Moot Court Competition, University of Michigan Law School, 1977. Co-Author: "Preventing Wrongful Payment of Guaranty Letters of Credit--Lessons from Iran," 39 Business Lawyer 417, 1984. Founding Member, Director and Treasurer, Center for International Commercial Arbitration, Los Angeles. *Member:* Los Angeles County (Vice-Chairman, 1993-1994, Pacific Rim Committee; Member, Sections on: Intellectual Property; Real Property; Chairman, 1989-1990, International Law Section) and American (Member, Sections on: International Law; Business Law) Bar Associations; State Bar of California ( Member, Sections on: International Law, Advisor, Executive Committee, 1992-1994; Real Property). *LANGUAGES:* French. *PRACTICE AREAS:* Computer Software, Systems and Services; International Business; Real Property; General Business.

**MATTHEW F. MACCOBY,** born Berkeley, California, June 20, 1960; admitted to bar, 1988, California; 1991, District of Columbia. *Education:* Yale University (B.A. magna cum laude, 1982; J.D., 1988). Semi-Finalist, Yale Moot Court of Appeals. Student Notes Editor, Yale Journal of International Law, 1987-1988. Member, Los Angeles County Bar Association Professional Responsibility and Ethics Committee, 1989-1994. *LANGUAGES:* French and Russian. *PRACTICE AREAS:* General Business; Mergers and Acquisitions; Computer Software, Systems and Services; Real Property.

**JEFFREY M. WEINER,** born Brooklyn, New York, July 26, 1951; admitted to bar, 1976, New York; 1979, California. *Education:* University of California at Los Angeles (B.A., cum laude, 1972); New York University (J.D., 1975). Staff Member, 1973-1974 and Articles Editor, 1974-1975, New York University Law Review. Co-author: "An Investment Decision Analysis of Cash Tender Offer Disclosure," Tender Offer Symposium-Part 2, 23 New York Law School Law Review 553, 1978. *Member:* The State Bar of California (Member, Education Committee, Business Law Section, 1990-1993; Board of Editors, 1990-1992, California Business Law News); American Bar Association (Member: Committee on Federal Regulation of Securities, 1980—; Subcommittee on Employee Benefits and Executive Compensation, 1982—; Section on Corporation, Banking and Business Law). *PRACTICE AREAS:* General Business; Securities; Mergers and Acquisitions.

## LANCE JON KIMMEL

SUITE 1400, 10940 WILSHIRE BOULEVARD
**LOS ANGELES, CALIFORNIA 90024**
Telephone: 310-208-0775
Telecopier: 310-208-8582

*Corporate, Securities, Business Transactions, Mergers and Acquisitions and Finance Law.*

**LANCE JON KIMMEL,** born New York, N.Y., December 7, 1954; admitted to bar, 1979, New York; 1985, California. *Education:* Franklin & Marshall College (A.B., cum laude with honors, 1975); New York University (J.D., 1978). Pi Gamma Mu. *Member:* Los Angeles County, New York State and American (Member, Section of Corporation, Banking and Business Law) Bar Associations; State Bar of California. (Also Of Counsel to Goodson and Wachtel, A Professional Corporation).

REFERENCE: Bank of America.

## KING, PURTICH, HOLMES, PATERNO & BERLINER, LLP

2121 AVENUE OF THE STARS, TWENTY SECOND FLOOR
**LOS ANGELES, CALIFORNIA 90067**
Telephone: 310-282-8989
Facsimile: 310-282-8903

*Real Estate, Financial Institutions, Insolvency, Music, Media and Intellectual Property Law, General Corporate and Corporate Finance Matters, Insurance Bad Faith Litigation and Business Litigation in State and Federal Courts.*

**HOWARD E. KING,** admitted to bar, 1977, California. *Education:* University of California at Los Angeles (B.A., 1974; J.D., 1977). Chief Justice, Moot Court Honors Program. Licensed Real Estate Broker, California, 1979. *Member:* Financial Lawyers Conference; National Order of Barristers; Urban Land Institute; International Council of Shopping Centers; Business Property Council. **PRACTICE AREAS:** Real Estate; Finance; Business; Entertainment.

**RICHARD R. PURTICH,** admitted to bar, 1977, California. *Education:* University of California at Berkeley (B.A., 1973); University of California at Los Angeles (J.D., 1977). Editor, University of California at Los Angeles Law Review, 1977. *Member:* California Trial Lawyers Association; The Association of Trial Lawyers of America. **PRACTICE AREAS:** Business and Real Estate Litigation; Insurance Bad Faith; Unfair Insurance Practices.

**KEITH T. HOLMES,** admitted to bar, 1977, California. *Education:* Northwestern University (B.A., 1974); University of Pennsylvania (J.D., 1977). Editor, University of Pennsylvania Law Review, 1976-1977. **PRACTICE AREAS:** Real Estate Law; Business Law; Banking.

**PETER T. PATERNO,** admitted to bar, 1976, California. *Education:* Harvey Mudd College (B.S., with distinction, 1972); University of Hawaii (M.A., 1973); University of California at Los Angeles (J.D., 1976). *Member:* State Bar of California.

**JILL H. BERLINER,** admitted to bar, 1984, California, U.S. District Court, Central District of California and U.S. Court of Appeals, Ninth Circuit. *Education:* University of California at Santa Cruz (B.A. with honors in history, 1979); University of Southern California (J.D., 1984). Member and Editor, University of Southern California Law Review, 1982-1984. Instructor, Legal Writing, University of Southern California, 1982-1983. **LANGUAGES:** French and Spanish. **PRACTICE AREAS:** Music Law; General Entertainment Law.

### OF COUNSEL

**DAVID M. CORWIN,** admitted to bar, 1988, New York; 1990, California; 1992, Massachusetts. *Education:* Columbia University (B.A., 1983); Georgetown University (J.D., 1987). Clerk to Hon. Edward J. Garcia, U.S. District Court, Eastern District of California, 1988-1989. **PRACTICE AREAS:** Litigation.

---

**GREGORY A. THOMSON,** born Brooklyn, New York, September 9, 1963; admitted to bar, 1990, California. *Education:* Yale University (B.A., 1985; J.D., 1989).

**TRACY E. LOOMIS,** admitted to bar, 1990, California. *Education:* University of California at Los Angeles (B.A., 1987); University of Michigan (J.D., 1990).

**LISA E. SOCRANSKY,** admitted to bar, 1991, California, U.S. Court of Appeals, Ninth Circuit and U.S. District Court, Central District of California. *Education:* University of California at Berkeley (B.A., 1987); Loyola Law School (J.D., 1991). St. Thomas More Law Honor Society. Member, Loyola of Los Angeles Entertainment Law Journal, 1990. Author: Developments in the Law; Title Protection, Loyola of Los Angeles Entertainment Law Journal, 10 Loy. L.A. Ent. L.J. 467 (1990). **LANGUAGES:** French.

**LESLIE E. FRANK,** admitted to bar, 1992, California. *Education:* Carnegie-Mellon University (B.A., with honors, 1987); University of California School of Law, Davis (J.D., 1992). Editor, "Environs" Environmental Law Journal.

REPRESENTATIVE CLIENTS: Fullerton Savings and Loan Association; Malaga Bank; Mitsubishi International Corporation; Hemet Federal Savings & Loan; Western Realty Investments.
REFERENCE: Pacific National Bank.

CAA846B

## STEPHEN SCOTT KING

A PROFESSIONAL CORPORATION

**LOS ANGELES, CALIFORNIA**
(See Santa Monica)

*Plaintiff Legal Malpractice, Personal Injury Law, Family, General Civil and Trial Practice.*

## KING, WEISER, EDELMAN & BAZAR

A LAW CORPORATION
Established in 1969

SUITE 900, TWO CENTURY PLAZA
2049 CENTURY PARK EAST
**LOS ANGELES, CALIFORNIA 90067**
Telephone: 310-553-1600
Panafax: 310-556-5687

*General Civil, Trial and Appellate Practice in all State and Federal Courts. Corporation and General Business Law. Corporate Financing, State and Federal Taxation, Health Care, Pension and Employee Benefit, Estate Planning, Trust and Probate Law, Limited Liability Companies, Real Property, Construction and Redevelopment Law. Public/Private Partnerships.*

**DONALD L. KING,** born Elyria, Ohio, June 21, 1930; admitted to bar, 1957, California; 1971, U.S. Supreme Court. *Education:* University of California at Berkeley (A.B., 1952); Boalt Hall School of Law, University of California (LL.B., 1957). Member, Board of Editors, California Law Review, 1956-1957. *Member:* Los Angeles County and American Bar Associations; State Bar of California. [With U.S. Army, 1952-1954]. **PRACTICE AREAS:** Estate Planning; Gift Estate Tax; Real Estate Tax; Health Care; Pension and Employee Benefits.

**HERBERT M. WEISER,** born Chicago, Illinois, June 6, 1931; admitted to bar, 1955, Colorado; 1957, California; 1973, U.S. Tax Court. *Education:* University of Colorado; University of Denver (B.S.L., 1953); University of Denver (J.D., 1954). Member, University of Denver Law Review, 1953-1954. Law Clerk to Colorado Supreme Court, 1954. Author: "The Public/-Private Partnership: Public Financing of Real Property Development," 1984 and "Development Agreements/Vesting Tentative Maps," 1986, California Continuing Education of the Bar. Adjunct Professor, Civil Procedure and Contracts, Western State University College of Law, 1970-1980. Assistant U.S. Attorney, Los Angeles, 1957-1959. *Member:* Los Angeles County and Federal Bar Associations; State Bar of California.

**GERALD M. BAZAR,** born Providence, Rhode Island, July 19, 1935; admitted to bar, 1959, California; 1987, U.S. Tax Court. *Education:* University of California at Los Angeles (B.A., 1955); University of California School of Law (J.D., 1958). Editor, University of California at Los Angeles Law Review, 1957-1958. *Member:* Beverly Hills (Member, Sections on: Business Law, Real Estate, Law Practice Management and Real Estate Law Committee) and Los Angeles County (Member, Real Property Section) Bar Associations; State Bar of California (Member, Sections on: Business Law and Real Property). **PRACTICE AREAS:** Business Law; Real Property.

**MARC PAUL JACOBS,** born Los Angeles, California, June 9, 1948; admitted to bar, 1973, California; 1974, U.S. Tax Court. *Education:* California State University at Northridge (B.S., 1970); Loyola University of Los Angeles and University of Southern California (J.D., 1973). Author: "A-B Partnerships and Qualified Plans - the Perfect Marriage," 37th Annual Trust and Tax Forum, Trust Services of America, 1985. *Member:* State Bar of California.

### OF COUNSEL

**JERRY EDELMAN,** born Chicago, Illinois, July 16, 1929; admitted to bar, 1957, California and U.S. District Court, Central District of California; 1988, U.S. Tax Court. *Education:* Carleton College; University of California at Los Angeles (B.S., 1950; J.D., 1956). Nu Beta Epsilon (Vice President, 1955). *Member:* Los Angeles County (Member, Litigation Section) and American (Member, Sections on: Business Law; Law Practice Management; Real Property, Probate and Trust Law; Litigation) Bar Associations; State Bar of California (Member, Sections on: Business Law; Real Property Law; Civil Litigation); The Association of Trial Lawyers of America; California Trial Lawyers Association; American Judicature Society; Association of

*(This Listing Continued)*

# PROFESSIONAL BIOGRAPHIES

## CALIFORNIA—LOS ANGELES

Business Trial Lawyers. [With U.S. Army Audit Agency, 1950-1952]. *PRACTICE AREAS:* Real Estate; Business Litigation.

**HERBERT L. WEINBERG,** born Brooklyn, N.Y., March 17, 1933; admitted to bar, 1981, California. *Education:* University of California at Los Angeles; University of California at Berkeley; University of Southern University (Pharm. D., 1956 ); University of West Los Angeles (J.D., 1981). Rho Chi. Member: Beverly Hills Traffic and Parking Commission, 1981-1982; California Pharmacists Association, 1960; American Pharmaceutical Association, 1976. President, Temple Emanuel of Beverly Hills, 1973-1974. *Member:* Los Angeles County Bar Association; State Bar of California. *PRACTICE AREAS:* Business Law; Transactional Law; Pharmacy Law.

---

**MICHAEL B. ALLDERDICE,** born Chicago, Illinois, June 12, 1948; admitted to bar, 1974, Tennessee; 1975, District of Columbia; 1979, California. *Education:* Washington & Lee University (B.S., 1970); George Washington University (J.D., with honors, 1974). Washington Scholar. *Member:* Beverly Hills, Los Angeles County (Member, Real Property Law Section) and American (Member, Corporation, Banking and Business Law Section) Bar Associations; State Bar of California (Member, Real Property Law Section). *PRACTICE AREAS:* Business; Real Estate and Land Use; Housing; Economic Development; Redevelopment.

**PATRICIA N. CHOCK,** born Los Angeles, California, January 7, 1952; admitted to bar, 1987, California, U.S. District Court, Central District of California and U.S. Court of Appeals, Ninth Circuit. *Education:* University of California at Santa Barbara (B.A., 1973; Ph.D., 1979); University of Southern California (J.D., 1987). Kappa Delta Pi. Editor-in-Chief, Major Tax Planning and Computer Law Journal, 1986-1987. Author: "The Use of Computers in Sexual Exploitation of Children and Child Pornography," 7 Computer/Law Journal 383, 1987. *Member:* Beverly Hills, Los Angeles County and American Bar Associations; State Bar of California. *PRACTICE AREAS:* Business; Real Estate; Estate Planning.

**DONALD A. GRALLA,** born Los Angeles, California, April 12, 1933; admitted to bar, 1959, California; 1970 U.S. Supreme Court. *Education:* University of California at Los Angeles (B.S., 1955; LL.B., 1958). *Member:* Los Angeles County Bar Association; State Bar of California. *PRACTICE AREAS:* Civil Litigation; Real Estate; Business Transactions.

**CHRISTINE S. UPTON,** born Pasadena, California, June 3, 1945; admitted to bar, 1980, California. *Education:* University of California at Los Angeles (B.A., 1966); Southwestern School of Law (J.D., summa cum laude, 1980). *Member:* Los Angeles County Bar Association (Member, Sections on: Real Property and Prejudgment Remedies); State Bar of California (Member, Litigation Section). *PRACTICE AREAS:* Civil Trials; Real Estate.

REPRESENTATIVE CLIENTS: Acme Escrow Inc.; Barstow Redevelopment Agency; Asea Brown Boveri; California Mortgage Brokers Institute; California State University, Northridge; Chrysler Corporation; Commerce Redevelopment Agency; Eastern Mortgage Co.; Escrow Center Inc.; Escrow Exchange, Inc.; Glendale Redevelopment Agency; Daniel Horwitz Company, Inc.; Home Budget Loans; Hotel Nikko of Beverly Hills; Leading Jewelers Guild; Long Beach Redevelopment Agency; John Mucci & Associates; Ontario Redevelopment Agency; Pasadena Community Development Commission; Pioneer Magnetics; San Pablo Redevelopment Agency; Santa Barbara Redevelopment Agency; Victorville Redevelopment Agency; City of Victorville; West Covina Redevelopment Agency; Wolff/Sesnon/Buttery Development Co.; Department of Radiology, University Southern California School of Medicine; Department of Radiology and Department of Pathology, Los Robles Medical Center; Department of Radiology, Northridge Hospital Center.
REFERENCES: First Interstate Bank (Century City Office); Santa Monica Bank.

---

## KING & WILLIAMS

*A LAW CORPORATION*

Established in 1975

**10100 SANTA MONICA BOULEVARD, EIGHTH FLOOR**
**LOS ANGELES, CALIFORNIA 90067-4012**
Telephone: 310-553-1101
Telecopier: 310-277-4069

*Civil Trial, Alternative Dispute Resolution and Appellate Practice. Business Litigation, Professional Liability, Real Property, Products Liability, Personal Injury and Insurance Law.*

**MICHAEL P. KING,** born Los Angeles, California, July 10, 1943; admitted to bar, 1969, California, U.S. District Court, Central District of California, U.S. Supreme Court and U.S. Court of Appeals, Ninth Circuit. *Education:* University of California at Los Angeles (B.A., 1965); Loyola

*(This Listing Continued)*

University of Los Angeles (J.D., 1968). Deputy District Attorney, Los Angeles, 1969. Appointed Judge Pro Tem, Los Angeles Municipal Court, 1977—. Member, Panel of Arbitrators of the Los Angeles Superior Court, 1980—. Member, Los Angeles Olympic Citizens Advisory Commission to the Los Angeles Olympic Organizing Committee, 1981—. Member of Panel, American Arbitration Association. Panel of Mediators for the Los Angeles Superior Court, 1994—. *Member:* Los Angeles County (Member, Professional Liability Insurance Committee, 1989-1992) Bar Association; State Bar of California.

**RALPH O. WILLIAMS III,** born Needham, Massachusetts, March 24, 1945; admitted to bar, 1972, California, U.S. District Court, Central, Eastern, Southern and Northern Districts of California, U.S. Court of Appeals, Ninth Circuit and U.S. Supreme Court. *Education:* Glendale University (B.S., 1970; J.D., 1972). Judge Pro Tem, Los Angeles Municipal Court, 1977—. Settlement Officer, Los Angeles County Superior Court, 1985—. Mediator and Arbitrator, American Arbitration Association, 1978—. *Member:* Los Angeles County (Member: Dispute Resolution Section, 1985—) and American Bar Associations; State Bar of California.

**WILLIAM K. HANAGAMI,** born Los Angeles, California, October 27, 1956; admitted to bar, 1985, California; 1986, U.S. District Court, Central District of California and U.S. Court of Appeals, Ninth Circuit; 1992, U.S. Supreme Court; 1993, U.S. District Court, Northern, Eastern and Southern Districts of California. *Education:* University of California at Los Angeles (B.A., 1979); University of California at Irvine (M.B.A., 1981); Loyola Law School (J.D., 1985). Member, Panel of Arbitrators, Los Angeles Superior Court, 1993—. *Member:* Los Angeles County and American Bar Associations; State Bar of California.

Representative Clients available upon request.

---

## KINKLE, RODIGER AND SPRIGGS

*PROFESSIONAL CORPORATION*

**600 NORTH GRAND AVENUE**
**LOS ANGELES, CALIFORNIA 90012**
Telephone: 213-629-1261
Fax: 213-629-8382

*Santa Ana, California Office:* 837 North Ross Street. Telephone: 714-835-9011. Fax: 714-667-7806.
*Riverside, California Office:* 3333 14th Street. Telephone: 909-683-2410; 800-235-2039. Fax: 909-683-7759.
*San Diego, California Office:* Suite 900 Driver Insurance Center, 1620 Fifth Avenue, P.O. Box 127900. Telephone: 619-233-4566. Fax: 619-233-8554.
*Santa Barbara, California Office:* 125 East De La Guerra Street. Telephone: 805-966-4700. Fax: 805-966-4120.

*General Trial Practice. Negligence, Malpractice, Products Liability, Construction and Insurance Law.*

**WILLIAM B. RODIGER,** born Eau Claire, Wisconsin, August 8, 1924; admitted to bar, 1951, California. *Education:* University of Wisconsin (Ph.B., 1945); Harvard University (LL.B., 1949). *Member:* The State Bar of California; American Bar Association; American Board of Trial Advocates. (Managing Attorney at Santa Ana Office).

**EVERETT L. SPRIGGS,** born Safford, Arizona, July 30, 1930; admitted to bar, 1960, California. *Education:* Arizona State University (B.S., 1955); University of Arizona (J.D., 1958). Deputy City Attorney, City of Los Angeles, 1960. *Member:* Los Angeles County Bar Association; The State Bar of California; American Board of Trial Advocates. (Managing Attorney at Riverside Office).

**JOHN V. HAGER,** born Elkhart, Indiana, January 7, 1949; admitted to bar, 1974, California. *Education:* University of Southern California (A.B., magna cum laude, 1971; J.D., 1974). Phi Beta Kappa; Phi Kappa Phi. *Member:* Los Angeles County Bar Association; State Bar of California. (Managing Attorney at Santa Barbara Office).

**THOMAS J. DOWLING,** born Kilkenny, Ireland, April 17, 1940; admitted to bar, 1972, California. *Education:* Loyola University of Los Angeles (B.A., 1969); University of Southern California (J.D., 1972). Phi Alpha Delta. Settlement Conference Referee and Arbitrator, 1988—, Los Angeles County Superior Court. *Member:* Los Angeles County, Ventura County and Federal Bar Associations; State Bar of California; American Board of Trial Advocates; Association of Southern California Defense Counsel. (Managing Attorney).

*(This Listing Continued)*

CAA847B

**KINKLE, RODIGER AND SPRIGGS,** PROFESSIONAL CORPORATION, Los Angeles—Continued

**GUILLERMO W. SCHNAIDER,** born Mexico City, Mexico, December 8, 1944; admitted to bar, 1970, California. *Education:* Loyola University of Los Angeles (B.A., 1966; J.D., 1969). Executive Editor, Loyola Law Review, 1968-1969. *Member:* Los Angeles County Bar Association; State Bar of California.

**DANIEL S. ALDERMAN,** born New Haven, Connecticut, July 22, 1961; admitted to bar, 1986, California. *Education:* University of California at San Diego (B.A., 1983); Dartmouth College; McGeorge School of Law, University of California (J.D., 1986). *Member:* State Bar of California.

**STEPHEN J. CHIASSON,** born Boston, Massachusetts, December 7, 1958; admitted to bar, 1988, California. *Education:* Bentley College (B.S., 1981); University of San Diego (J.D., 1988). *Member:* State Bar of California.

**EMILY E. KORDYBAN,** born Buffalo, New York, March 16, 1965; admitted to bar, 1989, California. *Education:* University of Detroit (B.M.E., 1986); Pepperdine University, School of Law (J.D., 1989). *Member:* State Bar of California; American Bar Association.

**JAMES A. STATHAS,** born Milwaukee, Wisconsin, October 17, 1966; admitted to bar, 1992, California. *Education:* University of Wisconsin, Madison (B.A., 1988); City of London Polytechnic; University of Notre Dame (J.D., 1992); Concannon Program of International Law. *Member:* National Order of Omega Honorary Society; International Law Society; International Moot Court.

**LISA JACOBS,** born Los Angeles, California, May 22, 1965; admitted to bar, 1990, California. *Education:* University of Michigan (B.A., 1987); Loyola University of Los Angeles (J.D., 1990).

**HOWARD GROSS,** born Johannesburg, South Africa, July 2, 1962; admitted to bar, 1995, California. *Education:* University of California, San Diego (B.A., 1983); San Diego State University (M.B.A., 1989); Loyola Marymount University (J.D., 1994). *Member:* Los Angeles County, Beverly Hills, Santa Monica and San Fernando Valley Bar Associations.

(For complete biographical data on personnel at Santa Ana, Riverside, San Diego and Santa Barbara, California, see Professional Biographies at those locations)

---

## RICHARD P. KINNAN

12424 WILSHIRE BOULEVARD, NINTH FLOOR
**LOS ANGELES, CALIFORNIA 90025-1043**
Telephone: 310-820-5570
Facsimile: 310-820-6800

*Civil Trial and Appellate Practice, Business and Casualty Law.*

**RICHARD P. KINNAN,** born Denver, Colorado, April 29, 1960; admitted to bar, 1986, California and U.S. District Court, Central District of California. *Education:* Ohio Wesleyan University (B.A., summa cum laude, 1982); Loyola Marymount University (J.D., 1985). Phi Beta Kappa. Arbitrator, Los Angeles County Superior Court. Associate, Bodkin, McCarthy, Sargent & Smith, 1986-1996. *Member:* Los Angeles County Bar Association; The State Bar of California.

---

## KINSELLA, BOESCH, FUJIKAWA & TOWLE

A Partnership including Professional Corporations
*1901 AVENUE OF THE STARS, SEVENTH FLOOR*
**LOS ANGELES, CALIFORNIA 90067**
Telephone: 310-201-2000
Fax: 310-284-6018

*General Civil Litigation, Corporation, Securities, Creditors Rights, Communication and Media, Real Estate, Finance, Commercial, Secured Transactions and Entertainment Law.*

### MEMBERS OF FIRM

†**DALE F. KINSELLA, (PROFESSIONAL CORPORATION),** born Santa Monica, California, October 19, 1948; admitted to bar, 1974, California; 1975; U.S. District Court, Central District of California; 1983, U.S. District Court, Southern District of California and U.S. Court of Appeals, Ninth Circuit. *Education:* University of California at Santa Barbara (B.A., with high honors, 1970); University of California at Los Angeles (J.D.,
*(This Listing Continued)*

1974). Editor-in-Chief, University of California at Los Angeles Law Review, 1973-1974. Author: "The Antitrust and Labor Law Implications of Private Physician Unions," 20 University of California at Los Angeles Law Review 983, 1972. *Member:* Los Angeles County Bar Association; State Bar of California.

†**PHILIP W. BOESCH, JR., (PROFESSIONAL CORPORATION),** born Washington, D.C., September 12, 1949; admitted to bar, 1974, California; 1976, U.S. District Court, Central District of California and U.S. Court of Appeals, Ninth Circuit; 1983, U.S. Supreme Court; 1985, U.S. District Court, Northern District of California. *Education:* Brown University (A.B., cum laude, 1971); Duke University (J.D., with distinction, 1974). Note and Comment Editor, Duke Law Journal, 1973-1974. Author: "The Reasonable Basis Test in Advertising," Duke Law Journal, 1974. *Member:* Los Angeles County Bar Association; State Bar of California. **PRACTICE AREAS:** Litigation; Communications Law.

†**RONALD K. FUJIKAWA, (PROFESSIONAL CORPORATION),** born Springfield, Missouri, April 6, 1948; admitted to bar, 1973, California and U.S. District Court, Central District of California; 1980, U.S. Tax Court. *Education:* Stanford University (A.B., with distinction, 1970; J.D., 1973). Member: Stanford University Board of Athletics, 1979-1982; Board of Visitors, Stanford Law School, 1983-1985. *Member:* Los Angeles County and American (Member, Section on: Corporation, Banking and Business Law) Bar Associations; State Bar of California.

†**EDMUND J. TOWLE, III, (PROFESSIONAL CORPORATION),** born Ithaca, New York, May 31, 1948; admitted to bar, 1974, California, New York and U.S. District Court, Central District of California; 1980, U.S. Court of Appeals, Ninth Circuit. *Education:* Georgetown University (A.B., 1970); Columbia University (J.D., 1973). Harlan Fiske Stone Scholar, 1970-1971. Managing Editor, Columbia Law Review, 1972-1973. Law Clerk to The Honorable Warren J. Ferguson, U.S. District Court, Central District of California, 1973-1974. *Member:* Los Angeles County Bar Association; State Bar of California.

**MICHAEL C. DENISON,** born Burbank, California, May 6, 1947; admitted to bar, 1974, California and U.S. District Court, Central District of California; 1976, U.S. Court of Appeals, Ninth Circuit. *Education:* University of California at Los Angeles (A.B., 1969); Loyola University of Los Angeles (J.D., 1974). Chief Note Editor, Loyola Law Review, 1973-1974. St. Thomas More Law Honor Society. Law Clerk to The Honorable Manuel L. Real, U.S. District Court, Central District of California, 1974-1975. Assistant United States Attorney, Criminal Division, Central District of California, 1976-1979. *Member:* Los Angeles County Bar Association; State Bar of California; Defense Research Institute. **PRACTICE AREAS:** Civil Litigation; Directors and Officers Liability Insurance Law.

†**MARK F. KATZ, (PROFESSIONAL CORPORATION),** born Jersey City, New Jersey, January 31, 1947; admitted to bar, 1972, New Jersey and U.S. Court of Appeals, Third Circuit; 1974, New York; 1976, California. *Education:* Princeton University (A.B., 1968); University of Michigan (J.D., cum laude, 1971). Law Clerk to Honorable James A. Rosen, Judge of the U.S. Court of Appeals for the Third Circuit, 1971-1972. Associate, White & Chase, New York, New York, 1972-1974. Executive Vice President, 1982-1983, Vice President, 1983-1984 and Director, 1980—, French-American Chamber of Commerce in Los Angeles. Legal Secretary, 1979-1985, and Director, 1978-1985, Friends of Soochow University, Taiwan. Member: United States of America-Republic of China Economic Council, 1978—. *Member:* Los Angeles County (Member, Sections on: International Law; Corporations; Commercial Law; Real Estate) and American (Member, Section on Corporation, Banking and Business Law) Bar Associations; State Bar of California. **LANGUAGES:** French, German and Mandarin Chinese.

**MARK K. BROWN,** born Los Angeles, California, July 26, 1954; admitted to bar, 1979, California. *Education:* Stanford University (B.A., with distinction, 1976); Boalt Hall School of Law, University of California (J.D., 1979). Associate Editor, California Law Review, 1978-1979. Author: "Tracing the Community Interest in Pension Rights Altered By Spousal Election," California Law Review, Vol. 67, No. 4, July, 1979. *Member:* Los Angeles County and American Bar Associations; State Bar of California; Association of Business Trial Lawyers. **PRACTICE AREAS:** Business Litigation; Real Estate; UCC; Bankruptcy Law.

**MICHAEL J. KUMP,** born Northfield, Minnesota, June 5, 1952; admitted to bar, 1981, California; 1982, U.S. Court of Appeals, Ninth Circuit, U.S. District Court, Central District of California and U.S. Tax Court, 1984, U.S. District Court, Northern and Southern Districts of California. *Education:* Grinnell College (B.A., with honors, 1974); University of Michigan (M.A., 1976; Ph.D. in Philosophy, 1979; J.D., cum laude, 1981). Phi Beta Kappa. Staff Member, 1979-1980 and Executive Articles Editor, 1980-
*(This Listing Continued)*

1981. University of Michigan Journal of Law Reform. Co-Author: "Attempted Monopolization Claims in Litigation with Competitors," Computer Litigation 757, Practising Law Institute, 1983; "Antitrust Issues: Tying Arrangements, Robinson-Patman Act Considerations and Resale Price Maintenance," Marketing and Protecting Rights in Computer Software, American Bar Association, 1983; "The Broader Meanings of Apple v. Franklin in the Development of Compatible Operating Systems and in Determining Standards for Injunctive Relief," 1 The Computer Lawyer 15, 1984. Author: "A Model for Determining Publication Requirements of Section 522 (A) (i) of the Administrative Procedure Act," 13 University of Michigan Journal of Law Reform 515, 1980; "Litigation Between Competitors: Antitrust and Tort Liability for Sham Litigation," 7 The Computer Lawyer 9, 1984. *Member:* State Bar of California.

**MICHAEL HOWALD,** born Butte, Montana, November 12, 1956; admitted to bar, 1982, California; 1983, U.S. District Court, Central and Southern Districts of California. *Education:* Northwestern University; Stanford University (B.A., 1979; J.D., 1982). Phi Beta Kappa. Articles Editor, Stanford Law Review, 1981-1982. *Member:* Los Angeles County Bar Association; State Bar of California.

**JACK G. CAIRL, JR.,** born Lansing, Michigan, June 10, 1955; admitted to bar, 1982, California; 1983 U.S. District Court, Central District of California. *Education:* Yale University (B.A., cum laude, 1977); University of California at Los Angeles (J.D., 1982). Order of the Coif. Extern, Honorable William A. Norris, U.S. Court of Appeals for the Ninth Circuit, 1981. Law Clerk, U.S. District Judge, Honorable David W. Williams, Central District of California, 1982-1983. *Member:* Century City Bar Association; State Bar of California.

**DAVID ANDREW PASH,** born Minneapolis, Minnesota, January 20, 1958; admitted to bar, 1982, California; 1984, U.S. District Court, Central District of California; 1988, U.S. Court of Appeals, Ninth Circuit and U.S. District Court, Eastern District of California. *Education:* Harvard University (A.B., cum laude, 1979); University of California at Berkeley (M.P.P., 1983); Boalt Hall School of Law, University of California (J.D., 1983). Member, 1981-1983 and Research and Topics Editor, 1982-1983, California Law Review. Law Clerk to Honorable Collins J. Seitz, U.S. Court of Appeals, Third Circuit, 1983-1984. *Member:* State Bar of California.

**CATHLEEN COLLINS,** born Hartford, Connecticut, January 11, 1947; admitted to bar, 1984, California and U.S. Court of Appeals, Ninth Circuit; 1985, U.S. District Court, Central and Northern Districts of California. *Education:* Manhattanville College (B.A., 1969); New York University (J.D., 1984). Staff Member, Annual Survey of American Law, 1982-1983. Author: Note, "Consumer Credit," Annual Survey of American Law, Vol. 2, 1983. *Member:* Los Angeles County and American Bar Associations; State Bar of California.

**CHARLES G. SMITH,** born San Francisco, California, March 31, 1960; admitted to bar, 1984, California; 1985, U.S. District Court, Northern, Southern, Eastern and Central Districts of California and U.S. Court of Appeals, Ninth Circuit. *Education:* Stanford University (A.B., 1981); Loyola University of Los Angeles (J.D., 1984). Recipient, William P. Hogoboom Award in Juvenile Justice Clinic. Member, St. Thomas More Law Honor Society. Member, 1982-1983 and Board of Editors, 1983-1984, Loyola Law Review. Part-time faculty member, U.S.C. Institute of Safety and Systems Management, 1988—. Judge Pro Tem, Superior Court, 1994—. *Member:* Los Angeles County Bar Associations; State Bar of California. **LANGUAGES:** French. **PRACTICE AREAS:** Civil Litigation; Directors and Officers Liability; Insurance Law.

**GREGORY J. ALDISERT,** born Pittsburgh, Pennsylvania, February 5, 1959; admitted to bar, 1984, California, District of Columbia, U.S. District Court, Central District of California and U.S. Court of Appeals, Third and Ninth Circuit. *Education:* Massachusetts Institute of Technology (B.S., 1981); Boalt Hall School of Law, University of California (J.D., 1984). Phi Beta Kappa. Member, Moot Court Board, Boalt Hall School of Law. *Member:* Los Angeles County Bar Association; State Bar of California. **PRACTICE AREAS:** Entertainment Law; Commercial Litigation.

**JOSEPH P. BARTLETT,** born Los Angeles, California, May 8, 1958; admitted to bar, 1985, California. *Education:* University of Santa Cruz; University of California at Berkeley (A.B., 1980); Hastings College of the Law, University of California (J.D., magna cum laude, 1985). Member: Order of the Coif; Thurston Society. *Member:* Los Angeles County and American Bar Associations; State Bar of California. **PRACTICE AREAS:** Corporate Financing Law; Securities Law; Corporate Law; Business Law.

*(This Listing Continued)*

## ASSOCIATES

**ALAN R. KOSSOFF,** born Bronx, New York, April 2, 1965; admitted to bar, 1990, California; 1991, U.S. District Court, Central, Northern, Southern and Eastern Districts and U.S. Court of Appeals, Ninth Circuit. *Education:* Duke University (B.A., cum laude, 1987); University of California at Los Angeles School of Law. *Member:* Los Angeles County and American Bar Associations. **PRACTICE AREAS:** Litigation.

**MICHELLE BEN-YEHUDA,** born Israel, January 6, 1964; admitted to bar, 1991, California. *Education:* University of California, Los Angeles (B.A., summa cum laude, 1986); Stanford University (J.D., with distinction, 1991). Phi Beta Kappa. *Member:* Beverly Hills and Los Angeles County (Litigation Section) Bar Associations; State Bar of California. **LANGUAGES:** Hebrew. **PRACTICE AREAS:** Litigation.

**BRUCE I. BOLKIN,** born New York, New York, July 17, 1963; admitted to bar, 1992, California. *Education:* Georgetown University (B.S., cum laude, 1985); New York University (J.D., 1992). Recipient, Chairperson's Award, N.Y.U. Moot Court. Member, Moot Court Board, N.Y.U. School of Law. Certified Public Accountant, New York, 1987 (Inactive). **PRACTICE AREAS:** Business Litigation; Entertainment Litigation.

**HELENE E. PRETSKY,** born Los Angeles, California, November 26, 1963; admitted to bar, 1987, California and U.S. District Court, Central and Southern Districts of California. *Education:* University of California at Los Angeles (B.A., magna cum laude, 1984; J.D., 1987). Phi Beta Kappa. Member, University of California at Los Angeles Law Review, 1985-1987. *Member:* Los Angeles County and American Bar Associations; State Bar of California. **PRACTICE AREAS:** Corporate Law; Business Law; Intellectual Property Law.

**SUZANNE M. MADISON,** born Long Beach, California, September 23, 1965; admitted to bar, 1992, California; 1993, U.S. District Court, Central District of California and U.S. Court of Appeals, Ninth Circuit. *Education:* Loyola Marymount University (B.A., magna cum laude, 1989); University of California at Los Angeles (J.D., 1992). Recipient, American Jurisprudence Award in Professional Responsibility, 1992. Member, Moot Court Honors Program, 1990-1991. Editor, Recent Developments, UCLA Women's Law Journal, 1991-1992. *Member:* State Bar of California; American Bar Association. **REPORTED CASES:** Johnson v. Calvert, 5 Cal. 4th 84 (1993).

**JILL ROSENTHAL,** born Chicago, Illinois, February 1, 1963; admitted to bar, 1991, California. *Education:* University of California at Berkeley (B.A., cum laude, 1985); Georgetown University (J.D., 1991). Phi Beta Kappa. *Member:* State Bar of California. **PRACTICE AREAS:** Litigation.

**DAVID P. SHEBBY,** born Inglewood, California, March 20, 1968; admitted to bar, 1994, California and U.S. District Court, Central District of California. *Education:* University of California at Berkeley (B.A., 1990); Stanford University (J.D., 1993). *Member:* State Bar of California; Mexican American Bar Association. **PRACTICE AREAS:** Litigation; Employment; Entertainment.

**GEORGE T. KLIAVKOFF,** born New York, N.Y., April 11, 1967; admitted to bar, 1993, California and U.S. District Court, Central District of California; 1994, U.S. Court of Appeals, Ninth Circuit and U.S. District Court Southern and Northern Districts of California. *Education:* Boston University, College of Communications (B.S., 1989); University of Virginia (J.D., 1993). Author: Landlord's Liability for Criminal Acts by Third Parties--A New Test," with Suzelle M. Smith, Esq., *Commercial Property Leasing Law and Strategy,* May 1994; "Controlling Damages in The Adult Wrongful Death Case," with Suzelle M. Smith, Esq., Defense Research Institute Damages Seminar, March 1994; "Controlling The Vicarious Liability of Hotel and Motel Franchisors," *The Cornell HRA Quarterly,* Vol. 35, No. 1, 1994. Associate, Howarth & Smith, Los Angeles, 1993-1996. *Member:* Los Angeles County and American Bar Associations; State Bar of California; Defense Research Institute; West Los Angeles Inns of Court. **PRACTICE AREAS:** Litigation.

**MONICA Y. HARRIS,** born Los Angeles, California, July 6, 1966; admitted to bar, 1992, California. *Education:* Princeton University (A.B., 1988); Harvard Law School (J.D., 1991). Editor, Harvard Law Review, 1989-1991. Author: "Cleaning Up The Debris After Fleet Factors: Lender Liability and Cercla's Security Interest Exemption," April 1991. *Member:* State Bar of California. **PRACTICE AREAS:** Intellectual Property; Legal Malpractice.

**JOSHUA A. MEYER,** born O'Fallon, Illinois, August 5, 1969; admitted to bar, 1995, California; U.S. District Court, Central District of California; U.S. Court of Appeals, Ninth Circuit. *Education:* University of California

*(This Listing Continued)*

CAA849B

**KINSELLA, BOESCH, FUJIKAWA & TOWLE,** Los Angeles—Continued

at Santa Cruz (B.A., with honors, departmental honors in sociology, 1991); University of Copenhagen, Denmark; University of California at Los Angeles (J.D., 1995). Phi Beta Kappa. Distinguished Advocate. Member, UCLA Moot Court Honors Program, 1993-1994. Briefwriter, UCLA National Moot Court Team, 1994-1995. *Member:* State Bar of California. **LANGUAGES:** Danish. **PRACTICE AREAS:** Litigation.

*OF COUNSEL*

**LEONARD M TAVERA,** born Los Angeles, California, February 27, 1960; admitted to bar, 1986, California and U.S. District Court, Northern and Central Districts of California; 1991, U.S. District Court, District of Arizona. *Education:* Yale University (B.A., 1981); University of California, Los Angeles (J.D., 1984). *Member:* State Bar of California. **PRACTICE AREAS:** Product Liability; Commercial Litigation; Personal Injury; Transactional.

**CATHERINE H. COLEMAN,** born Denver, Colorado, July 10, 1953; admitted to bar, 1979, California; 1980, U.S. District Court, District of Maryland and U.S. Court of Appeals, Fourth Circuit; 1982, District of Columbia and U.S. District Court, District of Columbia and U.S. Court of Appeals, Ninth Circuit; 1984, U.S. District Court, Central District of California; U.S. District Court, Northern and Eastern Districts of California; U.S. District Court, District of Arizona. *Education:* Stanford University (A.B., with distinction, 1975); Harvard University (J.D., 1979). Phi Beta Kappa. Senior Comments Editor, Harvard Civil Rights-Civil Liberties Law Review, 1978-1979. Author: "Re-Emergence of A Controversy: Enforcing Acreage Limitation," 2 Harvard Environmental Law Review, 1977. Law Clerk to the Honorable Herbert F. Murray, U.S. District Court, District of Maryland, 1979-1980. *Member:* State Bar of California. **LANGUAGES:** French and German.

†Denotes a lawyer who is the sole employee of A Professional Corporation which is a member of the firm

## LAW OFFICES OF
## C. WILLIAM KIRCHER, JR.
*A PROFESSIONAL CORPORATION*
**LOS ANGELES, CALIFORNIA**

(See Irvine)

*Civil Business, Commercial and Securities Litigation in Federal and State Courts.*

## KIRKLAND & ELLIS

A Partnership including Professional Corporations

*300 SOUTH GRAND AVENUE, SUITE 3000*
**LOS ANGELES, CALIFORNIA 90071**
Telephone: 213-680-8400
Facsimile: 213-626-0010

*Washington, D.C. Office:* 655 Fifteenth Street, N.W. Telephone: 202-879-5000. Facsimile: (202)-879-5200.

*Chicago, Illinois Office:* 200 East Randolph Drive. Telephone: 312-861-2000. Telex: 25-4361.

*New York, New York Office:* Citicorp Center, 153 East 53rd Street. Telephone: 212-446-4800. Facsimile: (212)-446-4900.

*London England Office:* 199 Bishopsgate, London EC2M 3TY England. Telephone: 171 814 6682. Facsimile: 171 814 6622.

*General Practice.*

*MEMBERS OF FIRM*

**APRIL L. AMMETER,** born Cedar Rapids, Iowa, April 16, 1963; admitted to bar, 1988, Arizona; 1991, California. *Education:* University of Iowa (B.A., 1985; J.D., 1988). **PRACTICE AREAS:** Litigation. **Email:** april_ammeter@kirkland.com

**MICHAEL E. BAUMANN,** born Washington, D.C., April 26, 1954; admitted to bar, 1979, District of Columbia; 1990, California. *Education:* Princeton University (A.B., 1976); College of William & Mary (J.D., 1979). Law Clerk, U.S. Court of Appeals, District of Columbia Circuit, 1979-

*(This Listing Continued)*

1980. **PRACTICE AREAS:** Litigation. **Email:** michael_baumann@kirkland.com

**MARY BLODGETT,** born Decorah, Iowa, March 14, 1962; admitted to bar, 1988, Colorado; 1990, California. *Education:* University of Iowa (B.A., 1984; J.D., 1988). **PRACTICE AREAS:** Litigation. **Email:** mary_blodgett@kirkland.com

**MARTIN R. BOLES,** born West Point, New York, March 6, 1958; admitted to bar, 1986, California; 1988, District of Columbia. *Education:* Dartmouth College (B.A., 1980); Stanford Business School (M.B.A., 1986); Stanford Law School (J.D., 1986). Law Clerk to Hon. Stanley A. Weigel, U.S. District Court, Northern District of California, 1986-1987. **PRACTICE AREAS:** Litigation. **Email:** martin_boles@kirkland.com

**JEFFREY S. DAVIDSON,** born East Chicago, Indiana, November 5, 1947; admitted to bar, 1973, Illinois and Indiana; 1980, District of Columbia; 1989, California. *Education:* Wabash College (A.B., 1970); Columbia University (B.S., 1970); Indiana University (J.D., 1973). **PRACTICE AREAS:** Litigation. **Email:** jeffrey_davidson@kirkland.com

**JAN LAWRENCE HANDZLIK,** born New York, N.Y., September 21, 1945; admitted to bar, 1971, California. *Education:* University of Southern California (B.A., 1967); University of California at Los Angeles (J.D., 1970). Law Clerk to the Hon. Francis C. Whelan, U.S. District Court, Central District of California, 1970-1971. Assistant U.S. Attorney, Criminal Division, 1971-1976 and Fraud and Special Prosecutions Unit, 1974-1976, Central District of California. Lawyer Representative, Ninth Circuit Judicial Conference, 1983-1985. Counsel, Independent Christopher Commission study of the Los Angeles Police Department, 1991. Deputy General Counsel to Hon. William H. Webster, Special Advisor to the Los Angeles Police Commission for the investigation into LAPD's response to urban disorders, 1992. Member, District Attorney's Advisory Committee, 1994. Member, Editorial Advisory Board, DOJ Alert, 1994—. *Member:* Los Angeles County (Member, Committees on Federal Courts, 1988—; Chair, Criminal Practice Subcommittee, 1989-1990; Federal Appointments Evaluation, 1989-1993; White Collar Crime, 1991—; Member, Executive Committee, 1991—), Federal and American (Member, Sections on: Criminal Justice; Member, White Collar Crime Committee, Co-Chair, Securities Fraud Subcommittee, 1994—, Vice Chair, California Regional White Collar Crime Committee, 1992-1996; Chairman, 1996—; Litigation; Member, Criminal Litigation Committee, 1989—) Bar Associations; State Bar of California. **PRACTICE AREAS:** Litigation; White Collar Criminal Defense. **Email:** jan_handzlik@kirkland.com

**ERIC C. LIEBELER,** born Townshend, Vermont, May 11, 1963; admitted to bar, 1990, California. *Education:* Massachusetts Institute of Technology (B.S., 1986); Duke University (J.D., 1989). Law Clerk to the Honorable J.L. Edmondson, United States Court of Appeals, 11th Circuit, 1989-1990. **PRACTICE AREAS:** Litigation. **Email:** eric_liebeler@kirkland.com

**ALEXANDER F. MACKINNON,** born St. Johns, Michigan, August 14, 1955; admitted to bar, 1982, Illinois; 1990, California. *Education:* Albion College; University of Michigan (B.S.C.E., 1977; J.D., 1981). Law Clerk to the Honorable Albert J. Engel, U.S. Court of Appeals, 6th Circuit, 1981-1982. **PRACTICE AREAS:** Litigation; Intellectual Property Law. **Email:** alexander_mackinnon@kirkland.com

**TONY L. RICHARDSON,** born Charleston, South Carolina, November 20, 1955; admitted to bar, 1986, California. *Education:* Harvard College (B.A., 1979); Columbia University; Stanford University (J.D., 1984). Law Clerk to Hon. David W. Williams, U.S. District Court, Central District of California, 1984-1985. **PRACTICE AREAS:** Litigation. **Email:** tony_richardson@kirkland.com

**PHILIP C. SWAIN,** born Akron, Ohio, December 10, 1957; admitted to bar, 1984, Illinois; 1985, Massachusetts; 1988, District of Columbia; 1990, California; registered to practice before U.S. Patent and Trademark Office. *Education:* Tufts University (B.A./B.S.M.E., 1981); Northwestern University (J.D., 1984). Law Clerk to the Hon. Giles S. Rich, U.S. Court of Appeals for the Federal Circuit, 1985-1986. **PRACTICE AREAS:** Litigation; Intellectual Property Law. **Email:** philip_swain@kirkland.com

**JOHN A. ZACKRISON,** born Salt Lake City, Utah, June 23, 1952; admitted to bar, 1979, District of Columbia; 1985, Maryland; 1990, California. *Education:* Brigham Young University (B.A., 1975); Harvard University (J.D., 1979). **PRACTICE AREAS:** Environmental Litigation and Counseling. **Email:** john_zackrison@kirkland.com

*(This Listing Continued)*

## ASSOCIATES

**STEVEN E. BLEDSOE,** born Los Angeles, California, March 21, 1961; admitted to bar, 1992, California. *Education:* California State University, Long Beach (B.A., 1987); Brigham Young University (J.D., 1991). *PRACTICE AREAS:* Litigation. *Email:* steven_bledsoe@kirkland.com

**C. ROBERT BOLDT,** born Los Angeles, California, January 6, 1966; admitted to bar, 1995, California. *Education:* University of California, San Diego (B.A., 1989); University of Notre Dame (J.D., 1995). *PRACTICE AREAS:* Litigation. *Email:* robert_boldt@kirkland.com

**BOAZ M. BRICKMAN,** born Richmond, Virginia, May 25, 1966; admitted to bar, 1992, California. *Education:* University of Toronto (B.A. Sc., 1989); University of California at Los Angeles School of Law (J.D., 1992). *PRACTICE AREAS:* Litigation; Intellectual Property Law. *Email:* boaz_brickman@kirkland.com

**DAMIAN D. CAPOZZOLA,** born Santa Monica, California, February 8, 1971; admitted to bar, 1996, California. *Education:* University of California, Santa Barbara (B.A., 1993); University of Virginia (J.D., 1996). *PRACTICE AREAS:* Litigation.

**DEAN M. FINK,** born Phoenix, Arizona, April 7, 1968; admitted to bar, 1993, Arizona and U.S. District Court, District of Arizona (Not admitted in California). *Education:* University of Arizona (B.A., summa cum laude, 1990); Columbia University (J.D., 1993). Phi Beta Kappa; Phi Kappa Phi. Member, Columbia Journal of Law and Social Problems. *Member:* State Bar of Arizona. *PRACTICE AREAS:* Litigation; Construction Law; Government Contract Law; Public Contract Law. *Email:* dean_fink@kirkland.com

**JOSEPH M. GRAHAM JR.,** born Brockton, Massachusetts, July 12, 1968; admitted to bar, 1993, California. *Education:* University of Dallas (B.A., 1990); University of Chicago (J.D., 1993). *PRACTICE AREAS:* Litigation. *Email:* joseph_graham@kirkland.com

**HAIMANOT HABTU,** born Addis Ababa, Ethiopia, May 25, 1965; admitted to bar, 1996, California. *Education:* University of Eastern Africa (B.B.A., 1986); Southwestern University School of Law (J.D., 1996). *LANGUAGES:* Amharic.

**SHANNON M. HANSEN,** born Pittsburgh, Pennsylvania, May 27, 1965; admitted to bar, 1994, California. *Education:* Carnegie Mellon University (B.S.Ch.E., 1987); Stanford University (J.D., 1994). *PRACTICE AREAS:* Litigation; Intellectual Property. *Email:* shannon_hansen@kirkland.com

**VIDDELL L. HEARD JR.,** born Sacramento, California, March 26, 1968; admitted to bar, 1994, California. *Education:* University of California at Davis (B.A., 1991); University of California at Los Angeles (J.D., 1994). *PRACTICE AREAS:* Litigation. *Email:* lee_heard@kirkland.com

**CHRISTOPHER J. HECK,** born Pittsburgh, Pennsylvania, January 5, 1968; admitted to bar, 1994, California. *Education:* Columbia University (A.B., 1990); Duke University (J.D., 1994). *PRACTICE AREAS:* Litigation. *Email:* christopher_heck@kirkland.com

**THOMAS G. HELLER,** born Grand Rapids, Michigan, August 31, 1967; admitted to bar, 1992, California. *Education:* University of Michigan (A.B., 1989); University of California at Los Angeles School of Law (J.D., 1992). *PRACTICE AREAS:* Litigation. *Email:* thomas_heller@kirkland.com

**CATHERINE C. HWANG,** born Knoxville, Tennessee; admitted to bar, 1995, California. *Education:* University of California, Berkeley (B.A., 1990); Columbia University (J.D., 1993). Law Clerk to Honorable Robert E. Coyle, U.S. District Court, Eastern District of California. *PRACTICE AREAS:* Litigation; Intellectual Property. *Email:* catherine_hwang@kirkland.com

**MELISSA D. INGALLS,** born Van Nuys, California, September 17, 1968; admitted to bar, 1994, California. *Education:* University of Pennsylvania (B.A., 1990); DePaul University (J.D., 1994). *PRACTICE AREAS:* Litigation. *Email:* melissa_ingalls@kirkland.com

**ANNA KOGAN,** born Odessa, Ukraine, March 25, 1971; admitted to bar, 1994, California. *Education:* Stanford University (B.A., 1990); Northwestern University (J.D., 1994). *LANGUAGES:* Russian. *PRACTICE AREAS:* Litigation; Intellectual Property Law. *Email:* anna_kogan@kirkland.com

**ERIC R. LAMISON,** born Akron, Ohio, August 3, 1970; admitted to bar, 1995, California. *Education:* Michigan State University (B.S., 1992);

*(This Listing Continued)*

University of Michigan (J.D., 1995). *PRACTICE AREAS:* Litigation. *Email:* eric_lamison@kirkland.com

**KEVIN P. LATEK,** born Park Ridge, Illinois, July 31, 1970; admitted to bar, 1996, California. *Education:* Georgetown University (B.S.B.A., 1992); University of Virginia (J.D., 1996). *PRACTICE AREAS:* Litigation.

**SALLY S. LIU,** born Taipei, Taiwan, April 22, 1969; admitted to bar, 1995, California. *Education:* University of California, Los Angeles (B.A., 1990); Boalt Hall School of Law, University of California, Berkeley (J.D., 1995). *PRACTICE AREAS:* Litigation. *Email:* sally_liu@kirkland.com

**MICHAEL S. MCCAULEY,** born Joliet, Illinois, March 22, 1971; admitted to bar, 1996, California. *Education:* College of St. Francis (B.A., 1993); University of Notre Dame (J.D., 1996). *PRACTICE AREAS:* Litigation.

**M. SCOTT MCCOY,** born Pittsburgh, Pennsylvania, August 20, 1965; admitted to bar, 1991, Arizona (Not admitted in California). *Education:* University of Southern California (B.S., 1987); University of Arizona (J.D., 1990). Judicial Clerk to the Honorable James Moeller, Arizona Supreme Court, 1990-1991. *PRACTICE AREAS:* Litigation. *Email:* scott_mccoy@kirkland.com

**SYDNE SQUIRE MICHEL,** born Modesto, California; admitted to bar, 1995, California. *Education:* University of California, Los Angeles (B.A., 1980); Loyola Law School (J.D., 1995). *PRACTICE AREAS:* Litigation; White Collar Criminal Defense. *Email:* sydne_squire@kirkland.com

**CHARLES ISAAC NEWTON,** born Abington, Pennsylvania, September 21, 1966; admitted to bar, 1995, California. *Education:* Brown University (B.A., 1989); University of California, Los Angeles (J.D., 1995). *PRACTICE AREAS:* Litigation. *Email:* charles_newton@kirkland.com

**ANDREW E. PARIS,** born Topeka, Kansas, May 2, 1967; admitted to bar, 1992, California. *Education:* Washington University (A.B., 1989); Stanford University (J.D., 1992). *PRACTICE AREAS:* Litigation. *Email:* andrew_paris@kirkland.com

**EPHRAIM STARR,** born Denver, Colorado, February 6, 1971; admitted to bar, 1996, California. *Education:* Amherst College (B.A., 1993); Duke University School of Law (J.D., 1996). *LANGUAGES:* Russian. *PRACTICE AREAS:* Intellectual Property Litigation; Litigation.

**SUZANNE E. TRACY,** born Columbus, Ohio, July 4, 1958; admitted to bar, 1989, California. *Education:* Baylor University (B.A., 1980); Southern Methodist University (J.D., 1988). *PRACTICE AREAS:* Litigation; Real Estate; Arbitration. *Email:* suzanne_tracy@kirkland.com

(For Biographical Data on Chicago, Illinois, Washington, D.C., New York, N.Y. and London, England, see Professional Biographies at those points Respectively).

---

# KIRSCH & MITCHELL

*Established in 1988*

**2029 CENTURY PARK EAST, SUITE 2750**
**LOS ANGELES, CALIFORNIA 90067**
*Telephone: 310-785-1200*
*Facsimile: 310-286-9573*

*General Civil Practice. Civil Litigation, Copyright, Trademark and Intellectual Property, Real Estate, Corporation, Publishing. Administrative Law, Insurance Defense.*

## MEMBERS OF FIRM

**JONATHAN L. KIRSCH,** born Los Angeles, California, December 19, 1949; admitted to bar, 1976, California. *Education:* University of California, Santa Cruz (B.A., with College Honors and Honors in History, 1971); Loyola Marymount University (J.D., cum laude, 1976). Teaching Fellow, Legal Communications, Loyola Law School, 1975-1976. Instructor in Writing, UCLA Extension, 1976—. Author: "Kids Allowed," California Lawyer, November 1983; "Access to Courts," California Lawyer, September, 1984; "War on Lawyers?" California Lawyer, March, 1985; "Malpractice Insurance Crisis," California Lawyer, July, 1985; "Which Courthouse? What Advantage?", California Lawyer, May, 1986; "Prop. 51 Shakes the House of Torts," California Lawyer, June, 1986; "Legal Eagles," California Business, November, 1988; "Look What They've Done to My Songs: Midler v. Ford Motor Co.," California Lawyer, July, 1989; "Lonesome Dove and the Electronic Rights Revolution in Publishing," Los Angeles Lawyers, June 1990; "Buchwald v. Paramount: Beyond the Hype," Los Angeles Lawyer, April 1991; "Vanity of Vanities: 'Subsidy' Publishing After Stellema," Loyola of

*(This Listing Continued)*

## KIRSCH & MITCHELL, Los Angeles—Continued

Los Angeles Entertainment Law Journal, Vol. 12, Issue 2, 1992; "Ethics in Entertainment Law," Los Angeles Lawyer, April 1993; *Kirsch's Handbook of Publishing Law*, Acrobat Books, 1994; *Kirsch's Publishing Law Update*, Acrobat Books, 1995—. *Member:* Los Angeles Bar Association (Intellectual Property Section); State Bar of California (Intellectual Property Section); Los Angeles Copyright Society (Member, Board of Trustees); California Lawyers for the Arts; PEN Center USA West. PRACTICE AREAS: Copyrights; Trademarks; Publishing; Intellectual Property; Entertainment Law; Administrative Law; Civil Litigation.

DENNIS MITCHELL, born Los Angeles, California, August, 13, 1956; admitted to bar, 1984, California; 1985, U.S. District Court, Central District of California. *Education:* Stanford University (B.A., Poli. Sci., 1979); University of California Graduate School of Management (M.B.A., 1984); University of California School of Law (J.D., 1984). Law Clerk to the Honorable David V. Kenyon, U.S. District Court, Central District of California, 1984-1986. *Member:* Los Angeles County Bar Association; State Bar of California. PRACTICE AREAS: Civil Litigation; Business Law; Real Estate Law.

### ASSOCIATES

JOYCE I. CRAIG, born Los Angeles, California; admitted to bar, 1984, California; 1985, U.S. District Court, Central District of California. *Education:* University of California at Berkeley (A.B., with great distinction, Phi Beta Kappa, Mortar Board, 1975); University of California at Los Angeles School of Law (J.D., 1984). *Member:* State Bar of California.

LAWRENCE J. ZERNER, born Los Angeles, California, September 29, 1963; admitted to bar, 1991, California; 1992, U.S. District Court, Central District of California. *Education:* California State University at Northridge (B.A., Theater Arts, 1985); Loyola University at Los Angeles (J.D., 1991). St. Thomas More Law Honors Society. *Member:* Los Angeles Bar Association.

### OF COUNSEL

TED F. GERDES, born Glen Ridge, New Jersey, October 27, 1952; admitted to bar, 1981, California; 1984, U.S. District Court, Central District of California; 1988, U.S. Court of Appeals, Ninth Circuit. *Education:* State University of New York at Oswego (B.A. Music, 1974); California Western School of Law (J.D., 1980). Author, "Special Problems of Docudramas: No Short Cuts in the Clearance Process," Vol. 13, No. 2, Los Angeles Lawyers, April, 1990; "The Legal Do's and Don'ts of Producing for Interactive Technology," Billboard, August 7, 1993. Associate Editor, California Western School of Law International Law Journal, 1979-1980. Member, Editorial Board, Los Angeles Lawyer (Special Editor, Entertainment Law, Chair, 1989-1990). *Member:* Los Angeles County Bar Association (Chair, Intellectual Property and Entertainment Law Sections, 1991-1992); State Bar of California; Los Angeles Copyright Society; California Copyright Conference; National Academy of Recording Arts. PRACTICE AREAS: Entertainment Law; Intellectual Property Law; Media Counselling Law; Litigation.

REPRESENTATIVE CLIENTS: Aetna Life Insurance Company; Publishers Marketing Assn.; Han-Jin Productions, Inc.; Los Angeles Jewish Publications, Inc.; Mitchell J. Hamilburg Agency; Pan-Asia Video Corp.; Paramount Pictures Corp.; Professional Drivers Associations; Impact Publishers; Slawson Communications; Fisher Books; ZM Productions, Inc; Communications and Entertainment Group; Agency Rent-a-Car, Inc.; Univisa, Inc.; Gamma Audio & Video, Inc.; Asia View, Inc.; Sopha Medical Systems, Inc.; Self Realization Fellowship; Park Avenue Publishing; Buzz Magazine; Rider Circulation Services; Poly-Gram Filmed Entertainment Distribution, Inc.; Solus/SunAmerica Realty Partners.

---

## KIRSHMAN & HARRIS
### A PROFESSIONAL CORPORATION
**11500 WEST OLYMPIC BOULEVARD, SUITE 605**
**LOS ANGELES, CALIFORNIA 90064**
Telephone: 310-312-4544
Telecopier: 310-312-4539

*Las Vegas, Nevada Office:* Kirshman, Harris & Cooper, A Professional Corporation, 411 E. Bonneville Avenue, Suite 300. Telephone: 702-384-3877. Telecopier: 702-384-7057.

*General Civil and Trial Practice in all State and Federal Courts. Employment Relations Law Representing Management. Corporation and Corporate Securities Law.*

*(This Listing Continued)*

CAA852B

---

NORMAN H. KIRSHMAN, born New York, N.Y., November 17, 1930; admitted to bar, 1958, New York; 1965, California; 1972, U.S. Supreme Court; 1986, Nevada. *Education:* Columbia University (B.S., 1955); Cornell University (J.D., 1958). Phi Alpha Delta. Author: "Withdrawal from Multi-Employer Bargaining," Los Angeles County Bar Journal, 1971; "The Strategy of Corporate Proxy Contests, An Overview," Los Angeles County Bar Journal, 1973; "Striker Replacements: The Law, The Myths, The Realities, Nevada Lawyer, 1995. Co-Author: "A Primer for Representing Management Before the National Labor Relations Board," California State Bar, Business Law News, 1981. Contributing Editor, "The Developing Labor Law, 1983. Lecturer and Author, "Internal Investigations, Avoiding Common Mistakes," Council on Education in Management, Personal Law Update, 1995. Lecturer, "Wrongful Discharge, Defendants' Perspective," Nevada State Bar Continuing Legal Education, 1989, 1990. Attorney, National Labor Relations Board, 1964-1965. Commercial Arbitrator, American Arbitration Association, 1976—. *Member:* Los Angeles County, Clark County and American (Member, Sections on: Litigation; Labor and Employment Law) Bar Associations. [U.S. Army, JAGC, 1959-1963]

MICHAEL S. HARRIS, born Los Angeles, California, January 25, 1946; admitted to bar, 1977, California; 1980, U.S. Claims Court; 1987, Nevada. *Education:* University of California at Los Angeles (B.A., 1967); Loyola University of Los Angeles (J.D., 1977). *Member:* Los Angeles County Bar Association; State Bar of California; State Bar of Nevada. PRACTICE AREAS: Corporate; Securities Law; Business Law; Civil Litigation; Estate Planning.

WILLIAM E. COOPER, born Stockton, California, September 18, 1949; admitted to bar, 1980, Nevada (Not admitted in California). *Education:* University of Nevada (B.A., 1976); California Western School of Law (J.D., cum laude, 1980). District Attorney, Churchill County, Nevada, 1982-1984. Chief Prosecutor, Nevada Attorney General's Office, 1984-1987. Special Trial Attorney, U.S. Department of Justice, Organized Crime and Racketeering Section, 1987-1989. Assistant U.S. Attorney, District of Nevada, Organized Crime Drug Enforcement Task Force, 1989. *Member:* State Bar of Nevada. PRACTICE AREAS: Civil Litigation; White Collar Crime Law.

GARY G. BRANTON, born Sacramento, California, September 25, 1944; admitted to bar, 1992, Nevada; 1993, California. *Education:* California State University (B.S., 1972); Syracuse University (MBA, 1974); McGeorge School of Law (J.D., 1992). Beta Gamma Sigma. Recipient, Outstanding Student Advocate, Trial Advocacy Award, 1992; American Jurisprudence Awards for Family Law, Sentencing and Post Conviction Remedies, 1992. [USAF, 1965-1969]. PRACTICE AREAS: Personnel; Labor Relations (Management) Law.

REPRESENTATIVE CLIENTS: Allen Drilling; American Pacific Corporation; Arizona Charlie's; Associated General Contractors Las Vegas Chapter; Bell Trans; Bob Allyn Masonry; Bourbon Street Hotel & Casino; Caesars Palace Hotel & Casino; Century Shower Door Co., Inc.; CER Corporation; Collegiate Stores Cooperative, Inc.; Contractors Wardrobe, Inc.; Debbie Reynolds Hotel; Fluor-Daniel; George F. Kalb Construction Company; Gibson Tile & Marble; Grove, Inc.; Highway Rentals, Inc.; Hospitality Network; International Game Technology (IGT); J.A. Tiberti Construction Company, Inc.; J.E. Merit; Jake's Crane & Rigging; James Hardie Gypsum; Kalb Construction; King 8 Hotel & Casino; LA. Yuma Freight Lines; Las Vegas Sun; Longley Construction; Lucky 7 Limousine; Marnell Masonry; Martin-Harris Construction; Max Riggs Construction; Mechanical Contractors Association; MJ Dean Construction; MS Concrete Co.; Nevada Ready Mix; Olson Glass; Pasco Demolition; Pioneer Hotel, Laughlin, Nevada; Prime Cable; Printronix, Inc.; Promod, Inc.; Quality Mechanical, Inc.; RollCut, Inc.; San Gabriel Valley Tribune, Inc.; Santa Fe Hotel & Casino; Silver State Disposal Service, Inc.; Sodak Gaming, Inc.; Southern Nevada Air Conditioning and Sheet Metal Contractors Association; Tab Contractors, Inc.; Western Cab; Whittlesea Blue Cab Co.; WMK Transit Mix.

---

## KIRTLAND & PACKARD LLP
*1900 AVENUE OF THE STARS*
*TWENTY-FIFTH*
*AND*
*TWENTY-SIXTH FLOORS*
**LOS ANGELES, CALIFORNIA 90067**
Telephone: 310-552-9700
Fax: 310-552-0957

*Orange County Office:* 18101 Von Karman Avenue, Nineteenth Floor, Irvine, California. Telephone: 714-263-9700. Fax: 714-263-9090.

*Architects and Engineers, ADR, Aviation and Aerospace, Business and Tax Planning and Litigation, Construction, Employment and Labor Law, Environmental and Toxic Tort, Estate Planning, Food Service and Hospitality, General Liability and Casualty, Health Care Providers Liability, Insurance, Medi-*

*(This Listing Continued)*

ation, Professional Liability, Product Liability, Real Estate, Risk Management and Loss Prevention and SIU.

## MEMBERS OF FIRM

**HAROLD J. HUNTER, JR.,** born Los Angeles, California, February 14, 1933; admitted to bar, 1961, California. *Education:* Stanford University (B.A., 1955; J.D., 1960). Diplomate, American Board of Trial Advocates, 1969— (President, Los Angeles Chapter, 1989-1990). Fellow: International Academy of Trial Lawyers, 1983— (Member, Board of Directors, 1989-1994); American College of Trial Lawyers, 1985—. Member, California Medical-Legal Committee (President, 1988-1989). *Member:* Los Angeles County and American Bar Associations; State Bar of California; Association of Southern California Defense Counsel.

**JACQUES E. SOIRET,** born Chicago, Illinois, September 19, 1942; admitted to bar, 1968, California; and U.S. District Court, Central District of California; 1970, U.S. Court of Appeals, Ninth Circuit 1973, U.S. Supreme Court; 1984, High Court for the United States Trust Territory of the Pacific Islands. *Education:* Loyola University of Los Angeles (B.A., 1964); University of Southern California (J.D., 1967). Phi Delta Phi. Author: "Manufacturers Right to Limit Its Liability to an Airline or Other Contractual Equal," The Forum, Volume X, page 561, November 1974; "Civil Litigation Techniques," paper presented to the CEB Symposium, Los Angeles, California, 1981; "The Use of Experts in Aviation Accident Investigation and Litigation," paper presented to the Southern Methodist University Air Law Symposium, Dallas, Texas, 1981; "Effective Use of Expert Witnesses," paper presented to the CEB Symposium, Los Angeles, California, 1982. Contributing Author: "The Trial of a Product Liability Case," Matthew Bender, 1982; "Using Demonstrative Evidence in Civil Trials," paper presented to the Practicing Law Institute, San Francisco, California, 1982; "Claims by Aircraft Owners and Operators Against Manufacturers" and "Recent Developments Under the Warsaw Convention" papers presented to the International Aviation Air Law Symposium, Marco Island, Florida, 1983; "Courtroom Conduct: Tactics and Ethics," paper presented to the CEB Symposium, Santa Barbara, California, 1983; "The Freedom of Information Act: A Variable Alternative to the Federal Rules?" paper presented to the American Bar Association, National Institute on Litigation in Aviation, Washington, D.C., 1985 (reprinted in the Trial Lawyer's Guide, Volume 29, No. 4). Author: "Jury Selection in Aviation Cases," paper presented to the 20th Annual Southern Methodist University Air Law Symposium, Dallas, Texas, 1986; "Civil Jury Selection," paper presented to the Trial Practice Symposium, San Francisco, California, 1986; Participant in the NBC Today Show on "Aviation Safety," 1987; "Personal Injury Defense Techniques," Matthew Bender, 1987 (with Mark A. Dombroff); "Defense Psychology - *The Handling of A Product Liability Case*," presented to the 7th Annual Southern Methodist University Air Law Symposium on Product Liability, Houston, Texas, 1986; "Winning before the Race Starts," paper presented to the CEB Trial Practice Institute, San Francisco, California, 1988; "Courtroom Conduct: Strategy, Tactics and Common Sense," paper presented to the CEB Symposium, Palm Springs, 1991; "Effective Jury Voir Dire," paper presented to the CEB Symposium, Los Angeles, California, 1991; "Trial Tactics for the Defense," presentation given to the American Bar Association National Institute on Aviation Litigation, Washington, D.C., 1991; "The Uncertainties of Aviation Litigation: or What Are Those Lawyers Doing With Our Money?" presentation given to the Asia-Pacific Insurance Conference, Bangkok, Thailand, 1991; "Update on Choice of Forum: Have U.S. Courts Closed the Gates?" paper presented to the Emery-Riddle Aeronautical University Fifth Annual Aviation Law Symposium, Sarasota, Florida, 1992; "Foreign Defendants in U.S. Courts: Issues of Jurisdiction, Venue, Service of Process and Discovery," paper presented to the American Bar Association Aviation and Space Law Symposium, San Francisco, California, 1992; "The Problems Faced by Foreign Aviation Manufacturers in Defending Product Liability Claims in the United States" and "Punitive Damages--Dinosaur or Lingering Threat?" presentation given to the Seventh International Aviation Seminar, Mauna Lana, Hawaii, 1993; American Bar Association 1994 Annual Meeting, New Orleans, Louisiana - Moderator for Trial Program, "The Crash of Flight 052: *The Trial That Never Was*"; "How Master Trial Attorneys, Barristers, Advocates, and Scottish Solicitors Try Cases," American Bar Association London Trial Advocacy Program, London, England, 1995; "The New Era of Product Liability Law--a Step Forward or a Step Backward? General Aviation Revitalization Act, Pending Federal Product Liability Legislation, Proposed Restatement (Third) of Torts, and Problems Associated With Cross-Border Discovery," Eighth International Aviation Law and Insurance Seminar, London, England, 1995; "Effective Jury Voir Dire by Defense Counsel in a Product Liability Case," American Bar Association Aviation and Space Law Program, Orlando, Florida, 1996; Participant in: NBC Television Program, "Aircraft

*(This Listing Continued)*

Parts - How Safe?"; ABC Television Program, "The Danger in Counterfeit Aircraft Parts," 1985. Contributor: "Disaster Dollars," The Wall Street Journal, July 11, 1980. Instructor, University of Southern California Aerospace Institute, 1971-1986. Lecturer: Panels in Civil Litigation, Continuing Education of the Bar, Southern California, 1980-1986; Southern Methodist University Products Liability Institute, Dallas, Texas, 1982. *Member:* Los Angeles County and American (Member, Sections on: Tort and Insurance Law, Vice-Chair, Aviation and Space Law Committee, 1996-1997; Aviation Litigation Subcommittee, 1971, Manufacturers Liability Subcommittee, 1971) Bar Associations; State Bar of California; Lawyer-Pilots Bar Association; Association of California Defense Counsel.

**MICHAEL L. KELLY,** born John Day, Oregon, September 21, 1953; admitted to bar, 1978, California; 1984, U.S. Trust Territory for the Pacific Islands; 1987, Colorado and U.S. Supreme Court. *Education:* Seattle University (B.A., 1975); University of Idaho (J.D., 1978). Member, 1976-1977, Board of Editors, 1977-1978 and Comments Editor, 1977-1978, Idaho Law Review. Author: "Negotiation of a Sharing Agreement Between an Operator and a Manufacturer," Sixth National Institute on Litigation in Aviation, American Bar Association, May 1987; "Determining Who Was Pilot in Command," Litigation News, March 1991; "Hope on the Horizon That General Aviation Sales Will Take Flight with Product Liability Reform," Aviation Journal of the American Bar Association, Volume II, Number I, 1992. Settlement Officer, Los Angeles County Superior Court, 1988—. *Member:* Los Angeles County, Colorado and American (Vice Chairperson, Committee on Aviation Litigation, 1990-1992; Member, Sections of: Tort and Insurance Practice; Science and Technology) Bar Associations; State Bar of California; Association of Southern California Defense Counsel; Lawyer-Pilots Bar Association. *Email:* MLKELLY.K&P@MCIMAIL.COM

**JOSEPH E. GREGORICH,** born Joliet, Illinois, January 21, 1938; admitted to bar, 1972, California. *Education:* St. Joseph's College (B.A., 1959); University of Illinois, Urbana-Champaign (B.S.E.E., 1960); University of Southern California (M.S.E.E., 1965); Loyola Marymount University, Los Angeles (J.D., 1971). Member, St. Thomas More Honor Society. *Member:* Los Angeles County and American Bar Associations; State Bar of California.

**ROBERT A. MUHLBACH,** born Los Angeles, California, April 13, 1946; admitted to bar, 1976, California. *Education:* University of California, Berkeley (B.S., Mechanical Engineering, 1967); California State University, Long Beach (M.S., Mechanical Engineering, 1969); University of Southern California (M.P.A., 1978); University of California, Hastings College of the Law (J.D., 1976). Member, Hastings Constitutional Law Quarterly, 1975-1976. Public Defender, Los Angeles County, 1977-1979. *Member:* State Bar of California; American Bar Association; International Association of Defense Counsel; American Board of Trial Advocates; American Institute of Aeronautics and Astronautics; Lawyer-Pilots Bar Association; Association of Southern California Defense Counsel. [Capt., Pilot, USAF, 1969-1973]

**MARK P. POLIQUIN** (Resident Partner, Irvine Office).

**ROBERT M. CHURELLA,** born Baltimore, Maryland, May 23, 1949; admitted to bar, 1977, California; 1983, U.S. Supreme Court. *Education:* Massachusetts Institute of Technology (B.S., Aeronautics and Astronautics, 1972; M.S., Aeronautics and Astronautics, 1973); University of Southern California (J.D., 1976). Member, Southern California Law Review, 1974-1976. Author: "Claims by Aircraft Owners and Operators Against Manufacturers" and "Recent Developments Under the Warsaw Convention" (with Jacques E. Soiret), International Aviation Air Law Symposium, Marco Island, Florida 1983 (reprinted by Lloyds of London Law Press). *Member:* Los Angeles County and American (Member, Sections on: Torts and Insurance Practice; Litigation; Forum Committee on Air and Space Law) Bar Associations; State Bar of California (Member, Litigation Section); Association of Business Trial Lawyers; Defense Research Institute; American Association for the Advancement of Science; American Institute of Aeronautics and Astronautics. *Email:* RMCHURELLA@AOL.COM

**SCOTT M. SCHUTZ,** born Aberdeen, South Dakota, July 24, 1959; admitted to bar, 1986, California. *Education:* University of South Dakota; University of Utah (B.S., cum laude, 1982; J.D., 1985). Phi Kappa Phi. Law Clerk to the Honorable David B. Dee, Utah District Court, 1983-1984. *Member:* Los Angeles County and American (Member: Litigation Section; Forum Committee on Air and Space Law) Bar Associations; State Bar of California (Member, Litigation Section); Association of Southern California Defense Counsel.

**JOHN M. GOODSPEED** (Resident Partner, Irvine Office).

*(This Listing Continued)*

## KIRTLAND & PACKARD LLP, Los Angeles—Continued

**STEVEN M. MASLAUSKI,** born Cincinnati, Ohio, October 9, 1959; admitted to bar, 1985, California. *Education:* Northwestern University (B.A., 1981); Pepperdine University (J.D., 1984). Phi Delta Phi. *Member:* State Bar of California; American Bar Association (Member, Litigation Section); Association of Southern California Defense Counsel; Defense Research Institute.

**JOHN M. CARON,** born South Bend, Indiana, July 18, 1963; admitted to bar, 1987, California and U.S. District Court, Central District of California. *Education:* Indiana University (B.S.,1984); Southwestern University School of Law, S.C.A.L.E. Program (J.D., 1987). Member, Southwestern Law Review, 1986-1987. *Member:* Los Angeles County Bar Association; California Young Lawyers Association; South Bay Lawyers Association.

**JEFFREY M. ANIELSKI** (Resident Partner, Irvine Office).

**TERRENCE J. SCHAFER,** born Los Angeles, California, April 9, 1965; admitted to bar, 1990, California; 1991, U.S. District Court, Northern and Central Districts of California; 1992, U.S. District Court, District of Arizona and U.S. Court of Appeals, Ninth Circuit. *Education:* Loyola Marymount University (B.A., 1987); Loyola Law School (J.D., 1990). Phi Alpha Delta. Adjunct Lecturer, Loyola Law School Trial Advocacy Program, 1991—. Co-Author with Jacques Soiret: "Choice of Forum: Have United State Courts Closed the Door?" Embry-Riddle Aeronautical University Annual Aviation Law Symposium, 1991. Author: "Complying with the Corporate Criminal Liability Act," California Lawyer Magazine, May, 1992. Co-Author with Jacques Soiret: "Foreign Defendants in U.S. Courts: Issues of Jurisdiction, Venue, Service of Process and Discovery," Air and Space Law Symposium, American Bar Association, San Francisco, 1992. Author: "Altering Your Practice to Avoid Being Named as a Defendant in a Medical Malpractice Action," International College of Surgeons, Update on the Management of Back Pain & Back Injury, 1993. *Member:* Los Angeles County and American Bar Associations; State Bar of California.

### OF COUNSEL

**ROBERT C. PACKARD,** born Los Angeles, California, September 21, 1919; admitted to bar, 1948, California. *Education:* University of Southern California (B.S., 1941; J.D., 1947). Phi Delta Phi. Diplomate, American Board of Trial Advocates, 1962—. Fellow, American College of Trial Lawyers, 1969—. Member, California Medical-Legal Committee, 1962—. *Member:* Los Angeles County and American (Member, Insurance, Negligence and Compensation Law Section) Bar Associations; State Bar of California; International Association of Defense Counsel; American Judicature Society; Association of Southern California Defense Counsel; International Society of Barristers; Lawyer-Pilots Bar Association; Trial Attorneys of America.

**ROBERT V. BEAUDRY,** born Montreal, Quebec, Canada, December 30, 1946; admitted to bar, 1974, California, U.S. District Court, Central District of California and U.S. Tax Court. *Education:* University of California, Los Angeles (B.A., 1969); Southwestern University (J.D., 1974); New York University (LL.M., Taxation, 1980). Professor of Law, Southwestern University, School of Law: Individual (Federal) Income Tax I; Individual (Federal) Income Tax II; Estate and Gift Taxation; Estate Planning and Drafting; Tax Shelter seminar; Federal Corporate Taxation; Federal Partnership Taxation; Foreign Taxation; Wills and Trusts; Corporations; Partnerships; Business Organizations; Advanced Family Law; Lawyer Process; Trial Practice, 1977-1992. Public Speaking: "Asset Protection and Planning for the Professional," Santa Monica Bar Association, 1993; "Tax, Estate and Asset Preservation Planning for the 90s," Reno, Nevada, 1992; "Estate Planning as a Career," State University of New York, Albany, New York, 1990; "Practice Standards Applicable to the Tax Practitioner," Ohio State University, Columbus, Ohio, 1989; "Tax Planning for the Medical Professional," Los Angeles and San Diego, California, 1989; "Alternative Methods of Compensating the Non-owner Employee," Practicing Law Institute, New York and San Francisco 1987; "Tax Planning for Corporate Liquidations after the 1986 Tax Reform Act," Practicing Law Institute, New York and San Francisco, 1987. Author: "Compensating the Nonshareholder Executive," Practicing Law Institute, 1987; "Corporation Liquidations," Practicing Law Institute, 1987; "The Flat Rate of Tax: Is It a Viable Solution to the Crisis Facing the Internal Revenue Code?" 9.2 Oklahoma City University Law Review, 219 (1984); "Freezing the Value of Real Estate Partnership Interests That Have a Negative Capital Account," Southwestern University Law Review, 1983; "Museum Trusteeships," Book Review, 1982. *Member:* Los Angeles County (Member, Estate Planning, Trust and Probate Section) and American Bar Associations; State Bar of California; Los Angeles County Trial Lawyers Association. [U.S. Air Force, 1970-1975, Sgt. (E-5)]

*(This Listing Continued)*

### ASSOCIATES

James T. La Chance
Gillian N. Pluma
Robert W. Skripko, Jr.
  (Resident, Irvine Office)
William S. Edic
Michelle M. Moyer
Robin S. Bentler
Alice C. Longoria
David S. Brown
C. Christopher Mulder
  (Resident, Irvine Office)
J. Conrad Schroeder

Curtis C. Holmes II
  (Resident, Irvine Office)
Joseph Stephen McMillen
  (Resident, Irvine Office)
Joseph Geri
Timothy D. Otte
  (Resident, Irvine Office)
Layne M. Bukovskis
  (Resident, Irvine Office)
Paul R. Cotter
  (Resident, Irvine Office)
Ronald J. Thommarson
  (Resident, Irvine Office)

---

## MANUEL S. KLAUSNER

ONE BUNKER HILL, EIGHTH FLOOR
601 WEST FIFTH STREET
**LOS ANGELES, CALIFORNIA 90071**
Telephone: 213-680-9940
Fax: 213-680-4060
Email: mklaus@aol.com

*General Civil Trial and Appellate Practice in all State and Federal Courts. Business Litigation, Complex Litigation, Constitutional Litigation, Intellectual Property, Securities and Class Actions.*

**MANUEL S. KLAUSNER,** born New York, N.Y., August 14, 1939; admitted to bar, 1963, California and New York. *Education:* University of California at Los Angeles (A.B., with honors, 1959); New York University (LL.B., 1962; LL.M., 1963); University of Copenhagen, Denmark. Associate Managing Editor, New York University Law Review, 1961-1962. Root-Tilden Scholar. Recipient of 1982 Lawyer-of-the-Year Award from Constitutional Rights Foundation and Los Angeles County Bar Association. Ford Foundation Fellow in Comparative Law, New York University, 1962-1963. Legal Research in Denmark under Combined Ford Foundation, Fulbright and Danish Government Grants, 1963-1964. Teaching Fellow and Instructor, University of Chicago Law School, 1964-1965. Editor, 1971-1978, Senior Editor, 1978-1989 and Founding Editor, 1989—, *Reason.* Interview, "The ACLU v. The Boy Scouts," California Political Review, p. 20, Winter 1992. Author: "The First Amendment and Commercial Speech," 11 George Mason L. Rev. 83 (1988). Participant, "Symposium on the First Amendment and Securities Regulation," 20 Connecticut L. Rev. 383 (1988). Chairman, Libertarian Law Council, 1974—. Trustee, The Reason Foundation, 1978—. Member: Executive Committee, Association of Libertarian Lawyers, 1975-1979; Board of Advisors, National Taxpayers Legal Fund, Inc., 1979—; Panel of Business Law Arbitrators, Los Angeles Superior Court, 1980—. Member, National Advisory Board, Landmark Legal Foundation's Center for Civil Rights, 1988—. Director, Institute for Justice, 1991—. Director, Choice in Education League, 1991-1995. *Member:* Los Angeles County, New York State and American Bar Associations; State Bar of California; Association of Business Trial Lawyers. **REPORTED CASES:** Crawford v. Honig, 37 F.3d 485 (9th Cir. 1994); Choice-in-Education League v Los Angeles Unified School Dist., 17 Cal. App. 4th 415 (1993); Amp Inc. v. Lantrans, Inc., 19 U.S.P.Q. 2d 1929 (C.D. Cal. 1991); Plasticolor Molded Products v. Ford Motor Co, 713 F. Supp. 1329 (C.D. Cal. 1989); Hernandez v. Six Flags Magic Mountain, Inc, 688 F. Supp 560 (C.D. Cal. 1988); Reader's Digest Ass'n, Inc. v. Conservative Digest, Inc, 821 F.2d 800 (D.C. Cir. 1987); Steinberg v. Amplica, Inc., 42 Cal. 3d 1198 (1986); Schwartz v. Harp, 108 F.R.D. 279 (C.D. Cal. 1985); Coalition for Student Action v. City of Fullerton, 153 Cal. App. 3d 1194 (1984); Scope Industries v. Skadden, Arps, Slate, Meagher & Flom, 576 F. Supp 373 (C.D. Cal. 1983); In re Cement Antitrust Litigation, 673 F.2d 1020 (9th Cir. 1982); Jutkowitz v. Bourns, Inc., 118 Cal. App. 3d 102 (1981); Nichols v. Canoga Industries, 83 Cal. App. 3d 956 (1978). **PRACTICE AREAS:** Complex Litigation; Class Actions; Intellectual Property Law; Securities and Constitutional Litigation.

## MARK ALLEN KLEIMAN
### LOS ANGELES, CALIFORNIA
(See Santa Monica)

*False Claims Act (Qui Tam) Litigation, Wrongful Termination, Civil Rights, Professional Malpractice.*

---

## ALAN M. KLEIN
Established in 1980
### 5757 WEST CENTURY BOULEVARD
### SUITE 880
### LOS ANGELES, CALIFORNIA 90045-6407
Telephone: 310-649-3141
Telecopier: 310-649-4349

*Business Litigation in State and Federal Courts. Unfair Competition, Trademark and Copyright Litigation, Business Torts, Real Property, Equine, Employment, Transportation and Insurance Law.*

**ALAN M. KLEIN,** born Brooklyn, New York, April 14, 1947; admitted to bar, 1980, California, U.S. District Court, Central District of California and U.S. Court of Appeals, Ninth Circuit; 1983, U.S. District Court, Southern and Northern Districts of California. *Education:* University of Toledo (B.B.A., 1969); Whittier College (J.D., 1980). *Member:* Los Angeles County Bar Association; State Bar of California. **PRACTICE AREAS:** General Business Litigation; Real Estate Litigation; Construction Litigation; Transportation (Air and Ocean Cargo); Trademark Litigation; Unfair Competition (10%, 10).

### ASSOCIATES
**LAURA J. BARNS,** born Casa Grande, Arizona, March 31, 1955; admitted to bar, 1980, California; 1981, U.S. District Court, Central District of California and U.S. Court of Appeals, Ninth Circuit; 1990, U.S. District Court, Northern, Southern and Eastern Districts of California. *Education:* University of California at Berkeley (A.B., 1977); Southwestern University (J.D., 1980). Phi Beta Kappa. Recipient, American Jurisprudence Awards in: Contracts; Family Law. *Member:* Orange County, Los Angeles County (Member, Antitrust Law Section) and American (Member, Sections on: Antitrust Law; Litigation) Bar Associations; State Bar of California (Member, Antitrust Law Section). **PRACTICE AREAS:** Business Litigation; Antitrust; Lemon Law; Copyright and Trademark; Employment.

REPRESENTATIVE CLIENTS: Concord Express; Morrison Express; K.B. Construction Co.; Polar Air Cargo.
REFERENCE: City National Bank.

---

## HOWARD S. KLEIN
### 11845 WEST OLYMPIC BOULEVARD, SUITE 1075
### LOS ANGELES, CALIFORNIA 90064
Telephone: 310-312-8182

*Contested Trusts and Estates, Conservatorships, Estate Planning and Family Law.*

**HOWARD S. KLEIN,** born Chicago, Illinois, May 21, 1937; admitted to bar, 1963, California. *Education:* University of California at Los Angeles (B.A., summa cum laude, 1958; J.D., 1961). Phi Beta Kappa; Phi Alpha Delta (President, McKenna Chapter, 1960-1961). Trust Administrator, United California Bank, 1962-1963. Author: "When Probate Meets Family Law: Close Encounters in the Twilight Zone - A Consideration of Probate and Family Law Crossover Issues at Death and on Incapacity," California Continuing Education of the Bar Estate Planning and Family Law Practice: Perspectives on the Crossover Issues, 1995; "Before You File That Family Law Petition, Think Estate Planning!" Los Angeles County Bar Association and Los Angeles Superior Court 28th Annual Family Law Symposium, 1996; "Practical Mediation Tips for Attorneys," Los Angeles County Bar Association Trusts and Estates Section, 1996. Assistant Counsel, Bank of America, 1963-1967. Instructor: California College of Law, 1965-1966; California Certified Public Accountants Foundation for Education and Research, 1973-1975. President, District Four, B'nai B'rith, 1980-1981. Member, Board of Governors, B'nai B'rith International, 1979-1982. Panelist, California Continuing Education of the Bar on Probate/Family Law Crossover Issues. Testified as Expert Witness on Standard of Care in California Probate Administration. *Member:* Beverly Hills (Chair, Probate, Trust and Estate Planning Section, 1986-1987; Member, Family Law Sec-
*(This Listing Continued)*

---

tion) and Los Angeles County (Member: Executive Committee and Committee on Probate Mediation, Trusts and Estates Section; Family Law Section) Bar Associations; State Bar of California (Member, Family Law Section). (Certified Specialist, Estate Planning, Trust and Probate Law, The State Bar of California Board of Legal Specialization). **PRACTICE AREAS:** Contested Trusts and Estates (40%); Conservatorships (20%); Family Law (20%); Estate Planning (20%).

---

## KLEIN & MARTIN
### 2029 CENTURY PARK EAST, SUITE 2550
### LOS ANGELES, CALIFORNIA 90067
Telephone: 310-201-2581
Fax: 310-201-0108

*Corporate, Securities, Intellectual Property, Computer Law, Start-Up Companies and Venture Capital, Mergers and Acquisitions, Private Placements, Healthcare Transactions, Financing, Commercial and International Transactions.*

*FIRM PROFILE: Our practice focuses on assisting companies and individuals with establishing, operating, financing and recognizing value from their businesses. We regularly advise clients on corporate and securities law, start-up company and venture capital issues, mergers and acquisitions, intellectual property law, general commercial law, financing, joint ventures, distribution and licensing matters and international business affairs. We work with clients in a broad range of industries, including high technology, healthcare, telecommunications, medical devices, computer hardware and software, manufacturing, biotechnology, financial services and consulting, retailing and consumer goods, publishing and entertainment.*

**ERIC A. KLEIN,** born New York, New York, July 3, 1959; admitted to bar, 1986, California and U.S. District Court, Northern District of California. *Education:* Princeton University (A.B., magna cum laude, Certificate in Russian Studies, 1981); Boston University School of Law (J.D., 1985). Executive Committee Member, CalTech/MIT Enterprise Forum, 1992-1995. Chair, San Francisco Barristers Soviet Law Committee, 1991. Co-Author, "The Subjective Element of Infringement-Advice for the Counselor and Litigator," Intellectual Property Section of the State Bar of California. Seminar, "Crossing the Line: Competing Without Infringing the Rights of Others," 1991. *Member:* State Bar of California (Member, Sections on: Business Law; Intellectual Property; International Law); American Bar Association (Member, Sections on: Business Law; International Law; Patent, Trademark and Copyright Law; Science and Technology; Member, Young Lawyers Division, Patent, Trademark and Intellectual Property Committee; Member, Committee on Soviet and East European Law).

**CLARA RUYAN MARTIN,** born Seattle, Washington, February 3, 1964; admitted to bar, 1989, California and U.S. District Court, Southern District of California. *Education:* University of California at Berkeley (B.A., high honors, 1985); University of Michigan Law School (J.D., 1989). Speaker: "Computer Law and the Internet," Computer Law Conference, 1996; "Software Licensing," Computer Law Conference 1994; "Licensing Technology," Legal Issues for High Tech Companies Conference 1994. *Member:* State Bar of California (Member, Sections on: Business Law, Real Property Law); American Bar Association (Member, Sections on: Business Law and Real Property Law).

### ASSOCIATES
**BARRY S. BABOK,** born Miami, Florida, July 30, 1957; admitted to bar, 1987, Illinois; 1993, California. *Education:* University of Michigan (B.A., 1979); Chicago-Kent College of Law (J.D., 1987; LL.M., 1993). *Member:* Los Angeles County Bar Association; State Bar of California.

**JENNY CHYI CHING CHEN,** born Taipei, Taiwan, September 2, 1971; admitted to bar, 1996, California. *Education:* Stanford University (B.A., 1993; M.A., 1993); New York University (J.D., 1996). **LANGUAGES:** Spanish, French, Mandarin.

**SAMUEL R. SPIRA,** born Los Angeles, California, August 5, 1964; admitted to bar, 1994, California. *Education:* University of California at Berkeley (B.A., 1987); University of Western Los Angeles (J.D., 1994). Recipient, American Jurisprudence Award in Corporate Law. *Member:* Los Angeles County Bar Association.

## KLEIN & ROSENBAUM

**LOS ANGELES, CALIFORNIA**

(See Glendale)

*Practice emphasizing: Representing Management and Plaintiffs in Labor and Employment Law including appearances before State and Federal Agencies and Courts.*

## JOEL W. H. KLEINBERG

A PROFESSIONAL CORPORATION

SUITE 2420, ONE WILSHIRE BOULEVARD
**LOS ANGELES, CALIFORNIA 90017-3325**
Telephone: 213-624-1990
Fax: 213-488-9890

*Plaintiffs Trial Practice. Professional Malpractice, Legal Malpractice, Medical Malpractice, Products Liability and Personal Injury Law. Tort Law, Contingent Fee Business Litigation.*

**JOEL W. H. KLEINBERG,** born Madison, Wisconsin, April 8, 1943; admitted to bar, 1968, District of Columbia, U.S. Court of Appeals, Ninth Circuit, District of Columbia Circuit, U.S. District Court, District of Columbia and U.S. District Court, Central District of California; 1975, U.S. Supreme Court. *Education:* Yale University (B.A., 1964; J.D., 1967). Recipient: Weyland Prize for Litigation. Member, Executive Committee, Yale School Association, 1990-1993. Adjunct Professor of Law, Torts, 1971-1977 and Products Liability, 1978-1979; Professional Responsibility, 1979-1980, University of La Verne Law Center. Lecturer, California Continuing Education of the Bar: Fundamentals of Personal Injury Practice, 1979-1988, Products Liability, Pleading, Practice and Proof, 1980; Handling Motor Vehicle Accident Cases, 1983; "Preparing a Case for Trial," 1986; "Recent Developments in Torts Practice," 1988—; "Joint and Several Liability," 1993; "Gathering and Proving Medical Evidence, 1995. Contributor: "Belli, Modern Trials," 2nd Ed., West Publishing Co., 1982; "Stein, Closing Argument," Callaghan & Co., Supp., 1984; "Dynamic Jury Arguments," California Trial Lawyers Association, Vol. IV, 1983. Consultant: Bancroft-Whitney, *California Civil Practice,* Torts Module; CEB, *California Tort Damages;* CEB, *Fee Agreement Forms Manual;* CEB, *California Tort Guide* (3rd Edition); The Rutter Group, *California Practice Guide—Personal Injury Law.* Arbitrator, Los Angeles County Superior Court Arbitration Panel, 1976-1981. Member, ABOTA. *Member:* Los Angeles County Bar Association (Member, 1973—and Chairman, 1978-1980, Medical-Legal Relations Committee; Member, Judiciary Committee, 1976—; Litigation Section, Executive Committee, 1986—); The State Bar of California (Delegate, 1973 and 1975; Member, Committee to Meet with the California Medical Association, 1975-1980, Chairman, 1978-1979); The Association of Trial Lawyers of America ( President, Civil Justice Foundation, 1995-1996; Member, Board of Governors, 1985-1991; Faculty, "Basic Course in Trial Advocacy," 1987); Association of Business Trial Lawyers; California Trial Lawyers Association (Recognition of Experience Certificate as Experienced Trial Lawyer, in Professional Negligence, in Products Liability and General Personal Injury, 1979—; Member, Board of Governors, 1981-1982, 1984-1985, 1990-1991); American Burn Association (Special Member, 1978—); International Society for Burn Injuries; American Spinal Injury Association; International Medical Society of Paraplegia. Member, State of California Injury Control Advisory Task Force (1990—).

## KLEINBERG LOPEZ LANGE BRISBIN & CUDDY

Established in 1992

2049 CENTURY PARK EAST, SUITE 3180
**LOS ANGELES, CALIFORNIA 90067**
Telephone: 310-286-9696
Fax: 310-277-7145

Sherman Oaks, California Office: 15250 Ventura Boulevard, Penthouse 1220. 91403-3201. Telephone: 818-995-5500. Fax: 818-995-5511.

*Entertainment Industry Transactions including Motion Picture, Television, Music, Amusement/Leisure Parks and Attractions. Intellectual Property Matters.*

*(This Listing Continued)*

CAA856B

**KENNETH KLEINBERG,** born Ohio, May 2, 1942; admitted to bar, 1968, California and District of Columbia. *Education:* University of California at Los Angeles (B.A., with honors, 1964; J.D., 1967). Co-author with Franklin Tom and Michael S. Josephson: *Handbook of Appellate Advocacy: A Guide to Brief Writing and Oral Proficiency for Beginning Appellate Counsel,* 1967. Faculty, American Film Institute Center for Advanced Film Studies, Los Angeles, (1984-1986). Member and Associate Judge, U.C.L.A. Moot Court Honors Program, 1965-1967. Co-Author: "Syllabus, Legal Aspects of the Entertainment Industry," University of Southern California Entertainment Law Institute, 1976 and 1977. General Attorney, Broadcast Bureau, Federal Communications Commission, Washington, D.C., 1967-1969. Member: Board of Directors and Co-Chairman, American Cinematheque, Los Angeles, 1984-1986. Associate, 1969-1974 and Partner, 1974-1985, Chairperson of the Motion Picture/Television Department, also Member of Management Committee, 1979-1985, Mitchell, Silberberg & Knupp, Los Angeles. Executive Vice President/Member of Board of Directors, United Artists Corporation, 1985-1986. President/Chief Operating Officer/Director, Weintraub Entertainment Group, Inc., Los Angeles, California, 1986-1991. *Member:* Beverly Hills (Co-Chairman, Entertainment Law Committee, 1979-1982), Los Angeles County and American (Member: Section on Patent, Trademark and Copyright Law; Forum Committee, Entertainment and Sports Industries, 1979—) Bar Associations; The State Bar of California; The District of Columbia Bar; Los Angeles Copyright Society (Member, Board of Trustees, 1976-1981). **PRACTICE AREAS:** Entertainment Law; Copyright Law.

**PETER M. LOPEZ,** born San Francisco, California, June 7, 1949; admitted to bar, 1974, California. *Education:* University of California at Los Angeles (B.S., 1971; J.D., 1974). *Member:* Beverly Hills and American Bar Associations; State Bar of California (Member, Special Committee on Human Rights); Mexican-American Bar Association. (Resident, Sherman Oaks Office). **PRACTICE AREAS:** Entertainment Law.

**ROBERT M. LANGE,** born Detroit, Michigan, July 23, 1953; admitted to bar, 1980, California. *Education:* Wayne State University (B.S., Bus. Adm., with high distinction, 1977); University of Michigan (J.D., magna cum laude, 1980). *Member:* Beverly Hills and Los Angeles County (Member, Entertainment Section) Bar Associations; State Bar of California. **PRACTICE AREAS:** Entertainment Law; Copyright Law.

**SCOTT T. BRISBIN,** born Madison, Wisconsin, December 1, 1954; admitted to bar, 1981, California. *Education:* University of California at Los Angeles (B.A., summa cum laude, 1978); Georgetown University Law Center (J.D., 1981). Phi Beta Kappa; Omicron Delta Epsilon. Editor, Georgetown Law Journal, 1980-1981. *Member:* State Bar of California. (Resident, Sherman Oaks Office). **PRACTICE AREAS:** Entertainment Law; Copyright Law.

**CHRISTINE S. CUDDY,** born Bethesda, Maryland, February 14, 1950; admitted to bar, 1974, California. *Education:* Harvard University (B.A., summa cum laude, 1971); Stanford University (J.D., 1974). Phi Beta Kappa. *Member:* Beverly Hills Bar Association; State Bar of California; Los Angeles Copyright Society. **LANGUAGES:** Spanish. **PRACTICE AREAS:** Entertainment Law; Copyright Law.

**SCOTT EDEL,** born New York, N.Y., December 29, 1959; admitted to bar, 1987, California. *Education:* Bucknell University (B.S., 1982); Institute of European Studies, Paris, France; University of Southern California (J.D., 1986). Executive Articles Editor: Computer/Law Journal; Major Tax Planning Journal, 1985-1986. *Member:* Beverly Hills Bar Association. **PRACTICE AREAS:** Entertainment Law.

### ASSOCIATES

**DARREN J. LEWIS,** born Brooklyn, New York, June 14, 1965; admitted to bar, 1990, California. *Education:* Boston University (B.S., 1987); University of California School of Law, Los Angeles (J.D., 1990). (Resident, Sherman Oaks Office). **PRACTICE AREAS:** Music Recording Law.

**MARK L. KOVINSKY,** born Detroit, Michigan, 1965; admitted to bar, 1990, California. *Education:* University of Michigan (B.A., 1987); University of California at Los Angeles (J.D., 1990). *Member:* State Bar of California; American Bar Association (Member, Forum on the Entertainment and Sports Industries). (Resident, Sherman Oaks Office). **PRACTICE AREAS:** Entertainment Transactions.

## KNAPP, MARSH, JONES & DORAN

*Established in 1945*

*SUITE 1400, MANULIFE PLAZA*
*515 SOUTH FIGUEROA STREET*
**LOS ANGELES, CALIFORNIA 90071-3329**
Telephone: 213-627-8471
Telecopier: 213-627-7897

*General Civil Practice in State and Federal Courts. Trial and Appellate Practice. Corporation, Estate Planning and Probate. Real Estate, Eminent Domain, Construction, Environmental, Public Utility, Transportation and Administrative Law. Public Entity, Securities, Taxation and Computer Law.*

FIRM PROFILE: Knapp, Marsh, Jones & Doran was founded in 1945 by Hugh Gordon and Wyman C. Knapp and under various prior names has practiced law continuously in Los Angeles for over 50 years. The firm serves a diverse clientele and offers a wide spectrum of legal services designed to suit the needs of individuals, corporations, public agencies and non-profit organizations. Taking advantage of specializations and close cooperation among its attorneys, the firm provides the highest quality legal services in an efficient and professional manner.

### MEMBERS OF FIRM

**B. RICHARD MARSH,** born Los Angeles, California, November 10, 1927; admitted to bar, 1953, California; 1975, U.S. Supreme Court. *Education:* University of California at Los Angeles (A.B., 1949); University of Southern California (J.D., 1952). Phi Delta Phi. *Member:* Los Angeles County and American Bar Associations; State Bar of California. **PRACTICE AREAS:** Public Entity Law; Administrative Law.

**THOMAS A. DORAN,** born Los Angeles, California, November 20, 1939; admitted to bar, 1968, California; 1975, U.S. Supreme Court. *Education:* University of California at Los Angeles (B.S., 1963); Loyola University of Los Angeles (J.D., 1967). *Member:* Los Angeles County and American Bar Associations; State Bar of California; Association of Business Trial Lawyers. **PRACTICE AREAS:** Public Entity Law; Business Litigation; Workers Compensation Law; Construction Law.

**JAMES G. JONES,** born Monterey Park, California, June 28, 1943; admitted to bar, 1969, California; 1975, U.S. Supreme Court; U.S. District Court, Central and Northern Districts of California, U.S. Court of Appeals, Ninth Circuit and U.S. Tax Court. *Education:* Occidental College (A.B., 1965); Hastings College of Law, University of California (J.D., 1968). Jamison Foundation Scholar. Member, Hastings Law Journal, 1966-1968. *Member:* Los Angeles County and American (Member, Sections on: Taxation; Corporation, Banking and Business Law; Real Property, Probate and Trust Law) Bar Associations; State Bar of California. **PRACTICE AREAS:** Business Law; Real Property Law; Business Civil Litigation; Transactional Tax Law.

**DANIEL V. HYDE,** born Fresno, California, May 15, 1947; admitted to bar, 1974, California; U.S. District Court, Central and Northern Districts of California; U.S. Court of Appeals, Ninth Circuit. *Education:* University of Oregon (B.A., 1970); Hastings College of Law, University of California (J.D., 1974). *Member:* Los Angeles County (Member, Environmental and Governmental Law Sections) and American (Member, Litigation Section) Bar Associations; State Bar of California (Member, Environmental Law Section); Association of Business Trial Lawyers. **LANGUAGES:** German. **PRACTICE AREAS:** Trials and Appeals; Construction Law; Environmental Law; Public Entity Law.

**GARY H. GIESLER,** born Compton, California, October 15, 1941; admitted to bar, 1967, California; U.S. District Court, Central, Southern and Northern Districts of California and U.S. Court of Appeals, Ninth Circuit. *Education:* University of California at Los Angeles (B.A. 1964); University of Southern California (J.D., 1967). Assistant U.S. Attorney, 1970-1972. *Member:* Los Angeles County, Federal and American Bar Associations; State Bar of California. [Capt., U.S. Army, 1968-1970]. **PRACTICE AREAS:** Real Property Law; Business Law; Litigation.

**WESLEY G. BEVERLIN,** born Los Angeles, California, April 12, 1952; admitted to bar, 1977, California; 1978, U.S. District Court, Central District of California and U.S. Court of Appeals, 9th Circuit; 1983, U.S. Court of Appeals, 8th Circuit; 1984, U.S. Supreme Court; 1994, U.S. Court of Appeals, Third Circuit. *Education:* University of Southern California (B.A., cum laude, 1974); Loyola University of Los Angeles (J.D., 1977). *Member:* Los Angeles County and American Bar Associations; State Bar of California; Association of Business Trial Lawyers; Transportation Lawyers Association. **SPECIAL AGENCIES:** Interstate Commerce Commission; California Public Utilities Commission. **REPORTED CASES:** Blackburn Truck Lines Inc. v. Francis 723 F.2d 730; U.S. v. Montrose Chemical Corp., 827 F.Supp. 1453; County Sanitation Dist. v. Watson Land Co., 17 Cal.App. 4th 1268; 22 Cal Rptr. 2d 117. **PRACTICE AREAS:** Trials and Appeals; Public Entity Law; Eminent Domain Law; Transportation Law; Public Utility Law; Business Law.

**PATRICIA M. SCHNEGG,** born Pasadena, California, November 6, 1952; admitted to bar, 1977, California; 1984, U.S. Supreme Court; U.S. Court of Appeals, Ninth Circuit and U.S. Tax Court. *Education:* Loyola University of Los Angeles (B.A., summa cum laude, 1974; J.D., 1977). Alpha Sigma Nu; Phi Alpha Delta. Member, St. Thomas More Law Honor Society. Certified Financial Planner. *Member:* Los Angeles County (Member, Board of Trustees, 1992-1993) and American (Member, Standing Committee on Legal Assistants, 1986-1989) Bar Associations; State Bar of California; Transportation Lawyers Association (Vice-President, Los Angeles City Airport Commission, 1993-1997); Women Lawyers Association of Los Angeles (President, 1992-1993; President-Elect, 1990-1991; First Vice President, 1989-1990; Secretary, 1988-1989; Treasurer, 1987-1988; Co-Chair, Committee on the Status of Women Lawyers, 1982-1984; Chair: Lawyer Referral Service, 1984-1985; Special Events Committee, 1985-1986; Appointive Office Committee, 1986-1987; President, Women Lawyers Public Action Grant Foundation, 1985-1986). **SPECIAL AGENCIES:** Interstate Commerce Commission; California Public Utilities Commission. **PRACTICE AREAS:** Litigation; Financial and Estate Planning Law; Business Law; Employment Law; Transportation Law; Public Entity Law.

**JANETTE SARMIENTO KNOWLTON,** born Miami, Florida, January 12, 1960; admitted to bar, 1986, California; 1987, U.S. District Court, Central District of California and U.S. Court of Appeals, 9th Circuit. *Education:* University of Florida (A.A., 1980); University of Southern California (B.A., 1982); Loyola Marymount University (J.D., 1986). Board of Directors and Quality Assurance Board, Harriet Buhai Center for Family Law, 1987-1988. *Member:* Los Angeles County and American (Member, Litigation and Environmental Law and Business Litigation Sections) Bar Associations; State Bar of California; Women Lawyers Association of Los Angeles (Board of Governors, 1988-1989; First Recipient, Public Action Grant, 1985; Committee Member, Public Action Grant Foundation, 1986-1988; Chair, Publicity Committee, 1988-1989; Harriet Buhai Family Law Center Volunteer Attorney, 1984-1989). **PRACTICE AREAS:** Litigation; Public Entity Law; Environmental Law.

### ASSOCIATES

**EILEEN M. WHALEN,** born Paterson, New Jersey, March 3, 1964; admitted to bar, 1989, California, U.S. District Court, Central District of California and U.S. Court of Appeals, Ninth Circuit. *Education:* Duke University (A.B., 1986); University of Southern California (J.D., 1989). Phi Alpha Delta. *Member:* Los Angeles County and American Bar Associations; Women Lawyers Association of Los Angeles (Member, Board of Governors; Co-Chair, Bulletin Committee, 1992-1993). *Member:* State Bar of California. **PRACTICE AREAS:** General Business Litigation.

**PAUL J. BECK,** born Pasadena, California, December 31, 1959; admitted to bar, 1984, California; 1987, U.S. District Court, Central District of California. *Education:* Claremont Men's College (B.A., 1981); University of California, Berkeley (J.D., 1984). Recipient, American Jurisprudence Award. *Member:* Los Angeles County Bar Association; State Bar of California. **PRACTICE AREAS:** Construction Law; Government Contracts Law; Litigation; Public Entity Law.

**ALEXANDER SHIPMAN,** born Los Angeles, California, April 23, 1958; admitted to bar, 1987, California and U.S. District Court, Central District of California. *Education:* University of California at Berkeley (A.B., with honors, 1978); University of Southern California (M.B.A., 1980); Loyola Law School of Los Angeles (J.D., cum laude, 1987). Order of the Coif. Certified Public Accountant, California, 1983. *Member:* Los Angeles County Bar Association. **PRACTICE AREAS:** Corporate; Securities; Real Property; Environmental and Tax Law.

**SCOTT M. OLKEN,** born Chicago, Illinois, April 19, 1965; admitted to bar, 1990, California. *Education:* University of California at Los Angeles (B.A., magna cum laude, 1987) College Honors; Northwestern University School of Law (J.D., 1990). Phi Beta Kappa. Alumni Scholar. *Member:* Los Angeles County and American (Member, Sections on: Business Law; Real Property, Probate and Trust Law) Bar Associations; State Bar of California. **PRACTICE AREAS:** Business Acquisitions; Real Estate; Probate; Estate Planning.

**MARIO A. PICHARDO,** born McAlester, Oklahoma, September 8, 1958; admitted to bar, 1992, New York and Connecticut; 1994, California. *Education:* Columbia University (B.A., 1987; J.D., 1991). Foreign Associ-

*(This Listing Continued)*

KNAPP, MARSH, JONES & DORAN, Los Angeles—
Continued

ate, Showa Law Office, 1991-1993. *Member:* American Bar Association. *LANGUAGES:* French, Spanish and Japanese. *PRACTICE AREAS:* Commercial Litigation; Corporate.

**WENDY W. HUANG,** born Taipei, Taiwan, August 3, 1966; admitted to bar, 1993, California; 1994, New York and District of Columbia. *Education:* Cornell University (B.A., 1988); Boston University (J.D., 1992). Recipient, Westinghouse Science Talent Scholarship. Author: "Belonging To America," Commentaries Law Journal, Fall, 1989. Member, Screen Actors Guild Legislative Committee. Taipei-Los Angeles Sister-City Committee: Chair, Legal Exchange Committee, 1995. Member: SCCLA Board of Governors, 1993; OCA Board of Governors, 1994. *LANGUAGES:* Mandarin Chinese and French. *PRACTICE AREAS:* Business Litigation; Public Agency Law.

## KNAPP, PETERSEN & CLARKE

A PROFESSIONAL CORPORATION

**LOS ANGELES, CALIFORNIA**

(See Glendale)

*General Civil, Trial and Appellate Practice in all State and Federal Courts, Arbitration Tribunals and Administrative Agencies. General Insurance, Professional Liability, Product Liability, Environmental, Corporate and General Business, State, Federal and Local Taxation, Real Estate, Escrow Errors and Omissions Defense, Construction and Land Use, Construction Defect Litigation, Estate Planning, Probate, Labor and Employment, Administrative and Regulatory Insurance Law and Title Banking.*

## KNEE & MASON

A Partnership
Established in 1992

SUITE 2050, 2049 CENTURY PARK EAST
**LOS ANGELES, CALIFORNIA 90067**
Telephone: 310-551-0909
Fax: 310-552-9818
Email: kmfirm@aol.com

*Employment Discrimination, Sexual Harassment and Wrongful Termination Defense, Management Labor Relations, Public Employment Relations, Wage and Hour Law, Employment Contracts, Occupational Safety and Health, Employee Benefits, State and Federal Litigation and Appellate Practice.*

FIRM PROFILE: Knee & Mason represents private and public employers in all aspects of employment law and labor relations.

### MEMBERS OF FIRM

**HOWARD M. KNEE,** born Los Angeles, California, November 29, 1947; admitted to bar, 1973, California; 1978, U.S. Supreme Court; U.S. Court of Appeals, Ninth Circuit; U.S. District Court, Central District of California. *Education:* University of California at Los Angeles (B.A., 1969); University of California School of Law at Los Angeles (J.D., 1972). Pi Sigma Alpha. Legislative Assistant to Hon. James C. Corman, 1974. Co-author with Kenneth M. Schwartz: "Labor Unions and the Antitrust Laws," Strikes, Stoppages and Boycotts, 1977, Walter B. Connolly, Jr., Chairman, Practising Law Institute, 1977. Lecturer, Institute of Business Law, 1993—. Intern, Equal Employment Opportunity Commission and Center for Law and Social Policy, 1971. *Member:* Los Angeles County (Member, Labor Law Section) and American Bar Associations; The State Bar of California. *PRACTICE AREAS:* Employment Litigation; Employment Discrimination; Labor Strikes; Collective Bargaining; Sexual Harassment; Wrongful Termination Defense.

**BELLE C. MASON,** born Boston, Massachusetts, November 25, 1939; admitted to bar, 1979, California. *Education:* University of California at Berkeley and Los Angeles (B.A., 1963); Whittier College School of Law (J.D., 1978). Member, Whittier College Law Review, 1977-1978. Co-Author: "Report on Making Legal Services Available to Middle Income Consumers," State Bar of California, 1978. Founder and Director, Vista Del Mar Girls' School, Los Angeles, 1970-1971. Founder and Co-Director, Wildwood School, Los Angeles, 1971-1973. *Member:* Los Angeles County (Member: Labor Law Section; Executive Committee) and American Bar Associations; State Bar of California; Women Lawyers Association of Los Angeles. *PRACTICE AREAS:* Sexual Harassment; Wrongful Termination Defense; Employment Discrimination; Employment Litigation; Wage and Hour Law; Personnel Policies.

**GREGORY N. KARASIK,** born Los Angeles, California, September 16, 1959; admitted to bar, 1984, California; 1985, U.S. District Court, Central District of California; 1986, U.S. Court of Appeals, Ninth Circuit; 1987, U.S. District Court, Northern, Southern and Eastern Districts of California. *Education:* University of California at Los Angeles (B.A., magna cum laude, 1981); Stanford University (J.D., 1984). *Member:* Century City and Los Angeles County (Member, Labor Law Section) Bar Associations; State Bar of California. *LANGUAGES:* Spanish. *PRACTICE AREAS:* Wrongful Termination Defense; Sexual Harassment; Employment Discrimination; Management Labor Relations; Wage and Hour Law; Personnel Policies.

**MELANIE C. ROSS,** born Bay Shore, New York, August 2, 1965; admitted to bar, 1990, California. *Education:* Emory University (B.A., 1987); University of Southern California (J.D., 1990). Phi Beta Kappa. Phi Sigma Tau. Notes Editor, Southern California Law Review, 1989-1990. Parliamentary Intern to Simon Hughs, 1985. Legislative Intern to Representative Tom Downey. *Member:* Los Angeles County (Member, Labor Law Section) and American Bar Associations; State Bar of California. *PRACTICE AREAS:* Employment Litigation; Employment Discrimination; Wrongful Termination Defense; Sexual Harassment; Labor Arbitration; Wage and Hour Law; Personnel Policies.

**LORA SILVERMAN,** born Los Angeles, California, March 30, 1964; admitted to bar, 1991, California. *Education:* Massachusetts Institute of Technology (S.B., 1985); Loyola Law School (J.D., 1991). Order of the Coif. Chief Articles Editor, Loyola of Los Angeles Law Review, 1990-1991. Recipient, American Jurisprudence Award in Constitutional Law. Member, St. Thomas More Honor Society, 1989-1991. Author: "Unnatural Selection: A Legal Analysis of the Impact of Standardized Testing on Higher Education Resource Allocation," Loyola of Los Angeles Law Review, Vol. 23, Issue 4, 1990. Tutorial Instructor in Constitutional Law, 1990-1991. Judicial Extern to the Hon. Edward Rafeedie, U.S. District Court, Jan. - May, 1991. *Member:* Los Angeles County Bar Association (Member, Labor Law Section); State Bar of California. *PRACTICE AREAS:* Employment Discrimination; Wrongful Termination Defense; Sexual Harassment; Personnel Policies; Employment Contracts; Wage and Hour Law; Employee Discipline.

**STEPHEN M. BENARDO,** born Los Angeles, California, September 19, 1962; admitted to bar, 1992, California. *Education:* University of Minnesota (B.A., 1985); University of California at Los Angeles (J.D., 1991). Member, UCLA Law Review. *Member:* Los Angeles County Bar Association (Member, Labor Law Section); State Bar of California. *LANGUAGES:* Spanish. *PRACTICE AREAS:* Wrongful Termination Defense; Employment Discrimination; Sexual Harassment; Occupational Safety and Health; Occupational Injury.

**LISA G. SHERMAN,** born New York, N.Y., June 9, 1968; admitted to bar, 1993, Nevada; 1995, California. *Education:* University of Rochester (B.A., cum laude, 1990); Washington University School of Law (J.D., 1993). Recipient, American Jurisprudence Award in Trial Advocacy, 1993. Author: "Exempt or Not Exempt Under the Administrative Exemption of the Fair Labor Standards Act - That Is The Question," 11 The Labor Lawyer 209 (1995); "The New Legal Challenge to Employee Participation," 45 Labor Law Journal 1 (1994); "Sexually Provocative Dress Code May Result in Liability," Nevada Labor Letter, Vol. II, No. 5, May 1994; "Managing Leaves of Absence and Controlling Fraud," Personnel Law Update Seminar, Spring 1994; "Fraternization and Dating Policies: May Employers Regulate Matters of the Heart?" 8 Personnel Law Update 12 (1993). *Member:* Los Angeles County (Member, Labor Law Section) and American Bar Associations; State Bar of Nevada; Nevada Inns of Court. *PRACTICE AREAS:* Employment Discrimination; Wrongful Termination Defense; Sexual Harassment; Personnel Policies; Employment Contracts; Wage and Hour Law; Employee Discipline.

### OF COUNSEL

**TED R. HUEBNER,** born Portage, Wisconsin, February 6, 1950; admitted to bar, 1975, California; 1976, U.S. District Court, Central and Southern Districts of California; 1979, U.S. District Court, Eastern District of California and U.S. Court of Appeals, 9th Circuit. *Education:* University of Minnesota (B.S. with high distinction, 1972); University of California School of Law at Los Angeles (J.D., 1975). Beta Gama Sigma. *Member:* Los Angeles County Bar Association (Member, Labor and Employment Law Section). *PRACTICE AREAS:* Labor and Employment; Wrongful Termination; Employment Litigation; Employment Discrimination.

*(This Listing Continued)*

**HEATHER A. LINDQUIST,** born Montreal, Canada, April 15, 1950; admitted to bar, 1981, California. *Education:* California State University, Northridge (B.A., 1972); Southwestern University (J.D., magna cum laude, 1980). Member, Southwestern University Law Review, 1979-1980. Recipient, American Jurisprudence Awards in Administrative Law, Antitrust and Secured Real Estate. Law Clerk to the Hon. Clarke E. Stephens, California Court of Appeal, 1979. Instructor, Loyola Marymount University Center for Industrial Relations, 1989—. Settlement Officer, LASC Joint Association Settlement Office Prague, 1990. *Member:* Los Angeles County (Member, Labor Law Section and Section on Trial Lawyers, Committee on Legislative Review, 1985—) and American (Member, Labor and Employment Law Section) Bar Associations; The State Bar of California (Member, Labor and Employment Law Section). *PRACTICE AREAS:* Employment Law; Labor Law; Discrimination; Sexual Harassment; Wrongful Termination; Family Medical Leave Act; Americans with Disabilities Act; Workers Compensation.

## *KNOBBE, MARTENS, OLSON & BEAR, LLP*
### LOS ANGELES, CALIFORNIA
(See Newport Beach)

*Intellectual Property Law including Patent, Trademark, Copyright, Unfair Competition, Trade Secret, Licensing, Computer Law, Antitrust Law, and related litigation.*

## *KNOPFLER & ROBERTSON*
### A PROFESSIONAL LAW CORPORATION
Established in 1987

SUITE 500
21650 OXNARD STREET (WOODLAND HILLS)
LOS ANGELES, CALIFORNIA 91367
Telephone: 818-227-0770; 213-624-1111
Telefax: 818-227-0777

*General Civil Litigation in all State and Federal Courts with Special Emphasis on Construction, Insurance, Corporate, Real Estate and Business Law.*

*FIRM PROFILE: Knopfler & Robertson is primarily a civil litigation firm that practices in all courts in the State and specializes in construction litigation and related insurance matters. The firm and its members have experience and expertise in all phases of construction law, including complex multi-party construction defect litigation, oil and energy claims; toxic tort litigation, products liability, insurance coverage, business litigation and jobsite accident litigation. The firm also handles disputes involving both private and public works projects, including construction contracts, claims for delay damages and change orders, mechanic's liens and stop notices, surety bond claims, mediation, arbitration and litigation. In addition to litigation, the firm possesses broad based expertise in transactional matters encompassing all aspects of real estate and corporate finance, real estate development, transaction structuring and corporate law.*

**GEORGE KNOPFLER,** born Cluj, Romania, January 21, 1955; admitted to bar, 1980, California and U.S. District Court, Central, Northern, Eastern and Southern Districts of California. *Education:* Hamilton College; Connecticut College (B.A., magna cum laude, 1977); University of Santa Clara (J.D., 1980). Lecturer, "The Practical Effects of the Cumis Doctrine," Annual Meeting of the National Association of Risk Managers, 1986. Law Clerk, Judge William A. Ingram, U.S. District Court, Northern District of California, 1980. *Member:* Los Angeles County and American Bar Associations; State Bar of California; Association of Southern California Defense Counsel; Associated General Contractors of California (Member, Insurance and Bonds Committee). *PRACTICE AREAS:* Insurance Law; Construction Law.

**ALEXANDER ROBERTSON, IV,** born Los Angeles, California, December 27, 1959; admitted to bar, 1986, California and U.S. District Court, Central District of California; 1987, U.S. Claims Court; 1988, U.S. Court of Appeals, Ninth Circuit; 1989, U.S. District Court, Central, Northern, Southern and Eastern Districts of California. *Education:* Pepperdine University (B.S., 1982; J.D., 1986). Member, Moot Court Honor Board. Co-Author, "Manual on Multi-Party Construction Defect Litigation," Los Angeles Superior Court. Lecturer, San Fernando Valley Bar Association, Construction Defect Litigation for Business Lawyers, 1989. Lecturer, Community Association Institute, Construction Defects, 1992-1993; "Construction Defects: Liabilities of Associations, Directors and Officers," June 1991; "Construction Defects: Associations and Members Get Only One Bite At

*(This Listing Continued)*

the Apple," September 1991; "Construction Defects: Reaching Beyond The Corporate Grave To Sue Dissolved Corporations," December 1990; "Construction Defects: Understanding Statutes of Limitations," November 1991; "Expert Witnesses Should be Selected by Attorneys," February 1992; Lecturer, Fourth Annual West Coast Casualty Construction Defects Seminar, 1996; "Lawyers Don't Always Mean Lawsuits," Condo Management Magazine, April 1992; "Keeping the Faith At Settlement Conferences: 'Good Faith' Negotiations Defined," Los Angeles Lawyer Magazine, November 1990; "Why So Many Construction Defects," Focus Magazine, Greater Los Angeles Chapter, Community Assoc. Institute, Sept./Oct. 1995. Member: Cowboy Lawyers Association, 1990—; Building Industry Association, 1990-1993 (Member, Legal Advisory Committee); Associated General Contractors of San Diego, Legal Committee, 1990-1991. Listed: Who's Who in American Law; Who's Who In the West; Who's Who in California. President, Board of Directors, Calabasas Hills Community Association, 1988-1989, Secretary, 1989-1990. Vice-President, Board of Directors, Calabasas Park Homeowners Association, 1991-1992. Member, Board of Directors, Calabasas Park Homeowners Association, 1990-1991. Associate Member, The Beavers, 1980—. Member, Pepperdine University Alumni Board, 1988-1990. Co-Captain, Mounted Search and Rescue Team, City of Agoura Hills; Member, Urban Search and Rescue Team, City of Agoura Hills; Assistant Director, Disaster Response Team, City of Agoura Hills, 1994-1995. Certified Heavy Rescue Specialist, State of California Fire Marshall; Certified Hazardous Waste and Emergency Response. Arbitrator, National Panel of Arbitrators, American Arbitration Association. Member, Steering Committee, Ad Hoc Committee on Multi-Party Construction Defect Litigation, Los Angeles Superior Court. *Member:* Beverly Hills, Los Angeles County and American (Member, Forum Committee on the Construction Industry) Bar Associations; State Bar of California; Associated General Contractors of California (Member, Underground Contractors Committee, 1987-1990). *PRACTICE AREAS:* Construction Law; Construction Defect Litigation; Real Estate Litigation.

**DEBORAH BROOM,** born Victorville, California, June 27, 1957; admitted to bar, 1987, California, U.S. District Court, Central, Northern, Southern and Eastern Districts of California and U.S. Court of Appeals, Ninth Circuit; 1996, Nevada. *Education:* California State University, San Bernardino (B.A., with honors, 1979); Pepperdine University School of Law (J.D., cum laude, 1987). Recipient, American Jurisprudence Award in Corporations. Legal Extern, Judge Stephen Reinhardt, U.S. Court of Appeals, Ninth Circuit, 1986. *Member:* Los Angeles County and American Bar Associations; State Bar of California. *PRACTICE AREAS:* Insurance Law; Environmental Law; Construction Law.

**RICHARD A. CAPELLA,** born Petaluma, California, March 4, 1957; admitted to bar, 1987, California, U.S. District Court, Central, Northern, Eastern and Southern Districts of California and U.S. Court of Appeals, Ninth Circuit. *Education:* California State University, San Francisco (B.A., cum laude, 1980); San Fernando Valley College of Law (J.D., 1986). Listed, Who's Who Among Rising Young Americans. *Member:* Los Angeles County and American Bar Associations; State Bar of California. *PRACTICE AREAS:* Insurance Law; Construction Surety and Bonds; Business Litigation; Construction Defect Litigation.

**EDWARD D. VAISBORT,** born Los Angeles, California, November 30, 1964; admitted to bar, 1988, California, U.S. District Court, Central, Southern, Eastern and Northern Districts of California and U.S. Court of Appeals, Ninth Circuit; 1996, Nevada. *Education:* California State University at Northridge (B.S., with honors, 1985); Hastings College of the Law, University of California, San Francisco (J.D., 1988). Phi Delta Phi. Moot Court. *Member:* Beverly Hills, Los Angeles County and American Bar Associations; State Bar of California. *LANGUAGES:* Spanish. *PRACTICE AREAS:* Business Litigation; Real Estate Litigation and Transactions; Environmental law; Construction Litigation; Insurance Law.

**JONATHAN S. VICK,** born Memphis, Tennessee, May 7, 1960; admitted to bar, 1987, California; 1988, U.S. District Court, Central, Southern, Northern and Eastern Districts of California and U.S. Court of Appeals, Ninth Circuit. *Education:* Pepperdine University (B.A., with honors, 1982; J.D., 1986). Speaker, "OSHA Compliance Update in California," National Business Institute, Inc. Seminar. Certified in "Hazardous Waste-Operations and Emergency Response Standards." *Member:* Los Angeles County Bar Association; State Bar of California. *PRACTICE AREAS:* Construction Law; Wage and Hour Law; Occupational Safety and Health Law; Oil and Gas Litigation.

*(This Listing Continued)*

**KNOPFLER & ROBERTSON,** A PROFESSIONAL LAW CORPORATION, Los Angeles—Continued

OF COUNSEL

**JAMES H. PATTON, JR.,** born Nashville, Tennessee, July 8, 1936; admitted to bar, 1968, California and U.S. District Court, Central District of California; 1971, U.S. Court of Appeals, Ninth Circuit; U.S. Supreme Court. *Education:* University of Southern California (B.S., 1962); Loyola University (J.D., 1967). Registered and Certified, Engineering Geologist. Member, Association of Engineering Geologists, 1978—. *Member:* State Bar of California. [Comm., U.S. Naval Reserves]. **PRACTICE AREAS:** Construction Law; Professional Malpractice Defense.

**ARLEN ROSS GUNNER,** born Brooklyn, New York, February 20, 1949; admitted to bar, 1974, New York; 1981, California. *Education:* University of Pittsburgh (B.A., 1970); St. John's University (J.D., 1973). *Member:* Association of the Bar of the City of New York; Beverly Hills, Century City and Los Angeles County Bar Associations; State Bar of California. **PRACTICE AREAS:** Real Estate Development Law; Real Estate and Corporate Finance Law; Tax Exempt Bond Financing Law; Joint Venture and Partnership Law; Commercial and Business Law.

**SCOTT C. HAITH,** born Los Angeles, California, September 11, 1946; admitted to bar, 1976, California. *Education:* California State University at Long Beach (B.S., 1972); Western State University (J.D., 1976). *Member:* State Bar of California. **PRACTICE AREAS:** General Civil and Trial Practice; Insurance Law; Products Liability; Insurance Bad Faith.

---

**KEVIN MATTHEW DAVIS,** born Key West, Florida, June 3, 1958; admitted to bar, 1989, California and U.S. District Court, Central, Northern, Eastern and Southern Districts of California and U.S. Court of Appeals, Ninth Circuit. *Education:* Arizona State University (B.S., 1981); Pepperdine University (J.D., 1988). Phi Alpha Delta. *Member:* Los Angeles County and American Bar Associations; State Bar of California. **PRACTICE AREAS:** Construction Litigation; Business Litigation; Products Liability Law.

**RICHARD P. RILEY,** born Los Angeles, California, January 3, 1963; admitted to bar, 1990, California; U.S. District Court, Central, Southern, Eastern and Northern Districts of California and U.S. Court of Appeals, Ninth Circuit. *Education:* University of California at Los Angeles (B.A., in Political Science, 1984); Southwestern University (J.D., cum laude, 1990). Recipient, American Jurisprudence Awards in Torts, Property and Secured Transactions. *Member:* Los Angeles County and American Bar Associations; State Bar of California. **PRACTICE AREAS:** Construction Defect Litigation; General Tort Litigation; Employment Law.

**CHRISTINA S. ROBERTSON,** born Santa Monica, California, December 20, 1963; admitted to bar, 1992, California and U.S. District Court, Central, Northern, Southern and Eastern Districts of California. *Education:* University of California (B.A., 1986); Loyola Law School (J.D., 1991). Certified Heavy Rescue Specialist, State of California Fire Marshall. Lecturer, "Avoiding Construction Defects Lawsuits," 1996 Malibu Contractors Association. Member, Urban Search and Rescue Team, City of Agoura Hills. Co-Captain, Mounted Search and Rescue Team, City of Agoura Hills. *Member:* State Bar of California. **PRACTICE AREAS:** Construction Defect Litigation; General Tort Litigation.

**JANICE M. MICHAELS,** born Brooklyn, New York, October 21, 1963; admitted to bar, 1990, California; 1991, Connecticut and New York; 1996, Nevada. *Education:* University of California at Los Angeles (B.A., 1986); Pepperdine University (J.D., 1989). Moot Court Honor Board. *Member:* State Bar of California; New York, Connecticut and American Bar Associations. **PRACTICE AREAS:** Construction Defect Litigation; Insurance Coverage; Business Litigation.

**WILLIAM G. KELSBERG,** born Boston, Massachusetts, August 15, 1962; admitted to bar, 1989, California and U.S. Court of Appeals, Eleventh Circuit; 1990, U.S. Court of Appeals, Ninth Circuit. *Education:* University of British Columbia (B.A., 1984); Whittier College School of Law (J.D., 1988);. Lecturer: Second Annual West Coast Casualty Construction Defects Seminar, 1994; Third Annual West Coast Casualty Construction Defects Seminar, 1995. *Member:* Orange County Bar Association; State Bar of California. **PRACTICE AREAS:** Construction Defect Litigation; Personal Injury Defense.

**ERNESTO F. ALDOVER,** born Manila, Philippines, December 28, 1965; admitted to bar, 1991, California; 1993, U.S. District Court, Central, Northern and Southern Districts of California and U.S. Court of Appeals, Ninth Circuit; 1996, Nevada. *Education:* University of California, Berkeley (B.A., 1988); Santa Clara University (J.D., 1991). Board of Editors, Santa Clara University Law Review, 1990-1991. *Member:* Santa Clara and San Mateo County Bar Associations; The Barristers; State Bar of California. **PRACTICE AREAS:** Construction Defect Litigation; Personal Injury; Insurance Coverage.

**JEANINE M. ST. PIERRE-KUMAR,** born Pittsfield, Massachusetts, June 29, 1964; admitted to bar, 1990, California; 1991, U.S. District Court, Central District of California, U.S. Court of Appeals for the Ninth Circuit, U.S. District Court for the Eastern and Northern Districts of California; 1992, U.S. District Court Southern District of California. *Education:* Pepperdine University (B.A., 1986; J.D., 1990). Phi Delta Phi. *Member:* Los Angeles County; State Bar of California; American Bar Association (Member, Litigation, Labor and Employment Sections); California Young Lawyers Association; Barristers Bench and Bar Relations Committee, 1993—; Barristers Domestic Violence Committee, 1993—. **PRACTICE AREAS:** Construction Litigation; Wrongful Termination Litigation.

**TERRI EILEEN HILLIARD,** born Los Angeles, California, September 26, 1960; admitted to bar, 1989, California and U.S. District Court, Central District of California. *Education:* University of California at Santa Barbara (B.A., 1982); Loyola Marymount University (J.D., 1989). Phi Alpha Delta. Author: Loyola Law School Entertainment Law Journal 9 Loy.L-.A.Ent.L.J. No. 1, 43 (1989). *Member:* Los Angeles County and American Bar Associations; State Bar of California. **REPORTED CASES:** Howard v. Superior Court (1992) 2 Cal.App. 4th 745. **PRACTICE AREAS:** Business/Commercial Litigation; Construction Litigation; Securities Litigation; Insurance Coverage.

**JAMES M. PAZOS,** born San Jose, California, June 27, 1963; admitted to bar, 1992, California. *Education:* University of California at Santa Cruz (B.A., 1989); University of California at Los Angeles (J.D., 1992). Moot Court Board. Legal Extern to Judge William A. Ingrim, U.S. District Court, Northern District of California; Legal Extern, U.S. Department of Justice. *Member:* State Bar of California. **PRACTICE AREAS:** Construction Law; Insurance Coverage.

**LISA BONDY DUNN,** born Burbank, California, September 13, 1968; admitted to bar, 1993, California, U.S. District Court, Central, Southern, Eastern and Northern Districts of California and U.S. Court of Appeals, Ninth Circuit. *Education:* University of California at Los Angeles (B.A., 1990); Loyola University (J.D., 1993). **PRACTICE AREAS:** Construction Law; Insurance Law; Personal Injury Defense.

**BRIAN I. GLICKER,** born Cardiff, Wales, Britain, July 12, 1958; admitted to bar, 1992, California. *Education:* University of Judaism (B.A., 1989); University of California at Hastings (J.D., 1992). Instructor, Comparison of Jewish and American Law, University of Judaism, 1994-1995. *Member:* Contra Costa, Los Angeles County and American Bar Associations; State Bar of California; The Barristers; Community Associations Institute. *LANGUAGES:* Hebrew. **PRACTICE AREAS:** Construction Defect Litigation; Personal Injury Litigation; Environmental Litigation; Business Litigation; Employment and Labor Litigation.

**COLIN E. BARR,** born Minneapolis, Minnesota, August 11, 1966; admitted to bar, 1991, Ohio; 1993, California. *Education:* Denison University (B.A., 1988); Case Western Reserve University (J.D., 1991). Phi Delta Phi. *Member:* Cleveland and Ohio Bar Associations; State Bar of California. **PRACTICE AREAS:** Construction Defect Litigation; Suretyship.

**CYNTHIA COULTER MULVIHILL,** born Chicago, Illinois, October 31, 1964; admitted to bar, 1994, California. *Education:* Chaminade University (B.A., 1987); Western State University (J.D., 1994). Delta Theta Phi. Recipient, American Jurisprudence Award in Constitutional Law and Professional Responsibility. *Member:* State Bar of California. [With U.S. Army, 1982-1986]. **PRACTICE AREAS:** Construction Litigation; Personal Injury Defense.

**CHRISTOPHER J. BAGNASCHI,** born Los Angeles, California, November 10, 1964; admitted to bar, 1991, California and U.S. District Court, Central District of California; 1995, U.S. District Court, Northern and Southern Districts of California. *Education:* California State University at Fullerton (B.A., 1987; M.A., 1988); Southwestern University School of Law (J.D., 1991). *Member:* State Bar of California; Italian-American Bar Association; Association of Southern California Defense Attorneys. **PRACTICE AREAS:** Construction Litigation; Insurance; Environmental; Products Liability; Business Litigation.

**CHERYL A. KIRKPATRICK,** born Trenton, New Jersey, June 28, 1964; admitted to bar, 1990, California and U.S. District Court, Central and Southern Districts of California. *Education:* Loyola Marymount Uni-

*(This Listing Continued)*

# PROFESSIONAL BIOGRAPHIES

versity (B.A., 1986); Southwestern University School of Law (J.D., 1990). Recipient, American Jurisprudence Book Award in Torts. Note and Comment Editor, Southwestern University Law Review, 1989-1990. Extern to the Hon. Arthur Alarcon, U.S. Court of Appeals, Ninth Circuit, 1990. *Member:* South Bay and American Bar Associations; State Bar of California; California Women Lawyers; South Bay Women Lawyers. **PRACTICE AREAS:** Personal Injury; Construction Defect.

**PETER C. BROWN,** born Orange, New Jersey, September 27, 1961; admitted to bar, 1995, California; 1996, Nevada. *Education:* University of California at Davis (B.A., 1984); University of California at San Diego (M.F.A., 1987); Pepperdine University (J.D., 1995). First Place, Individual Advocacy Tournament, Pepperdine University, 1995; First Place, Southern California Defense Attorney Trial Tournaments, 1994. *Member:* Los Angeles County and American Bar Associations; State Bar of California. **PRACTICE AREAS:** Civil Litigation; Construction Defect; Real Property; Personal Injury.

---

## LAW OFFICE OF
## SCOTT P. KOEPKE

*Established in 1992*

ONE BUNKER HILL, 8TH FLOOR
601 WEST FIFTH STREET
**LOS ANGELES, CALIFORNIA 90071-2094**
Telephone: 213-623-7820
Fax: 213-680-4060

*General Business and Unfair Competition Litigation in all State and Federal Courts. Employment, Construction and Real Property Litigation, Dispute Resolution, and Trials.*

**SCOTT P. KOEPKE,** born Utica, New York, February 5, 1959; admitted to bar, 1985, California. *Education:* University of Michigan (B.G.S., with distinction, 1981) James B. Angell Scholar; University of Southern California (J.D., 1984). Member, Hale Honors Moot Court Program. Legislative Intern to Senator Carl Levin, U.S. Senate, 1980. Judicial Extern to Hon. Richard A. Gadbois, Jr., U.S. District Judge, Central District of California, 1984. Los Angeles Barristers' Domestic Violence Program Advisor, 1988. *Member:* Los Angeles County Bar Association; State Bar of California (Member, Litigation Section); Association of Business Trial Lawyers.

---

## KOHRS, FISKE & STEUR

**LOS ANGELES, CALIFORNIA**

(See Santa Monica)

*Insurance Defense, Public Entity Defense, Employment Law, Product Liability Defense, Wrongful Termination and Civil Rights Defense, Professional Malpractice Defense, Insurance Coverage and Appeals in all State and Federal Courts.*

---

## KOLETSKY, MANCINI & FELDMAN

CENTRAL PLAZA, EIGHTH FLOOR
3460 WILSHIRE BOULEVARD
**LOS ANGELES, CALIFORNIA 90010-2228**
Telephone: 213-427-2350
Fax: 213-427-2366

*Insurance Defense, General Civil Litigation.*

**FIRM PROFILE:** Koletsky, Mancini & Feldman was founded in 1987 by Roy A. Koletsky and Stephen C. Mancini and was for many years known as Koletsky & Mancini. In 1993, Marc S. Feldman joined the firm as a partner establishing Koletsky, Mancini & Feldman. The firm handles a broad spectrum of civil defense litigation which includes construction defect defense litigation, general tort defense litigation, wrongful termination defense litigation, sexual harassment defense litigation, toxic tort defense litigation, products liability defense litigation, and various real estate and business disputes. The firm encourages continuing professional development and all partners and associates participate in continuing legal education seminars, professional association activities and civic Affairs.

*(This Listing Continued)*

---

# CALIFORNIA—LOS ANGELES

### MEMBERS OF FIRM

**MARC S. FELDMAN,** born Brooklyn, New York, June 11, 1958; admitted to bar, 1983, California and U.S. District Court, Central District of California. *Education:* University of Florida (B.S., 1979); Southwestern University School of Law (J.D., 1982). Instructor, Catherine College, 1988-1992. Patterson, Ritner, Lockwood, Zanghi & Gartner, 1986-1993 (Partner, 1991-1993). *Member:* Los Angeles County Bar Association; State Bar of California. **PRACTICE AREAS:** Construction Defect Defense Litigation; General Liability Defense Litigation; Toxic Tort Defense Litigation; Product Liability Defense Litigation.

**ROY A. KOLETSKY,** born New York, N.Y., March 1, 1957; admitted to bar, 1982, California; 1983, U.S. District Court, Central District of California; 1984, U.S. District Court, Eastern District of California; 1987, U.S. District Court, Northern District of California. *Education:* Occidental College (B.A., 1979); Southwestern University School of Law (J.D., 1982). Member, Southwestern University Law Review, 1981-1982. Judge Pro Tempore, Beverly Hills Municipal Court, 1989-1993. *Member:* Los Angeles County and American Bar Associations; Southern California Defense Association; Los Angeles Trial Lawyers Association. **PRACTICE AREAS:** Insurance Defense Litigation; Real Estate Litigation; Business Litigation.

**STEPHEN C. MANCINI,** born Washington, D.C., March 21, 1957; admitted to bar, 1986, California; 1987, U.S. District Court, Central District of California. *Education:* Occidental College (B.A., 1980); University of LaVerne School of Law (J.D., 1984). Delta Theta Phi. Staff Member, 1982-1983 and Business Editor, 1983-1984, Law Review. Moot Court Honors. Author, "Criminal Law and Procedure," Charleston Publishing, Inc., 1993. Associate Professor, Merit College, 1992-1995. Judge Pro Tempore, Los Angeles Municipal Court, West Los Angeles, 1989-1992. Los Angeles Public Defenders Office, 1986-1987. *Member:* San Fernando Valley, Los Angeles County and American Bar Associations; State Bar of California. **PRACTICE AREAS:** General Liability Defense Litigation; Construction Defect Defense Litigation; Wrongful Termination Defense Litigation; Sexual Harassment Defense Litigation; Toxic Tort Litigation; Product Liability Defense Litigation.

**CAROLINE L. DASOVICH,** born Chicago, Illinois, September 6, 1959; admitted to bar, 1988, California; 1989, U.S. District Court, Central and Southern Districts of California; 1991, Colorado. *Education:* Western State College of Colorado (B.A., 1979); California Western School of Law (J.D., 1987). Recipient, American Jurisprudence Award - Products Liability. *Member:* Los Angeles County, Colorado and American Bar Associations; State Bar of California; Los Angeles County Defense Lawyers. **LANGUAGES:** Spanish. **PRACTICE AREAS:** Insurance Defense Litigation; Construction Defect Litigation; General Liability Defense Litigation; Premises Liability.

**ANDREW M. MORROW III,** born Hollywood, California, August 15, 1962; admitted to bar, 1987, California and U.S. District Court, Central, Southern and Northern Districts of California. *Education:* Universidad de Madrid, Spain; (Certificate in International Relations, 1981); University of Southern California (B.S., 1983); Boston University (J.D., 1986); Harvard University (A.M., Government, 1987). Panelist: Los Angeles Supreme Court Judge Pro Tem; California Appellate Project. *Member:* Los Angeles County Bar Association. **PRACTICE AREAS:** Construction Defect Defense Litigation; General Liability Defense Litigation.

### ASSOCIATES

**STEVEN R. BARTELL,** born Lubbock, Texas, May 1, 1953; admitted to bar, 1988, California; 1990, Texas, U.S. District Court, Northern District of Texas, U.S. Court of Appeals, Ninth Circuit, and U.S. District Court, Southern, Western, Eastern and Northern Districts of California; 1991 Washington, District of Columbia, U.S. Court of Appeals, Fifth Circuit and U.S. District Court, Eastern and Western Districts of Texas. *Education:* Texas Tech University (B.A., 1974); Brigham Young University (J.D., 1987). Phi Delta Phi. Judge Pro Tempore, Los Angeles Municipal Court, 1994-1996. Arbitrator, Los Angeles Superior and Municipal Courts. *Member:* Los Angeles County and American Bar Associations. **LANGUAGES:** Spanish, German. **PRACTICE AREAS:** Construction Defect Litigation; Litigation; Insurance; Business; Corporate.

**WILLIAM J. BECKER, JR.,** born Sherman, Texas, March 19, 1954; admitted to bar, 1988, California and U.S. District Court, Southern and Central Districts of California. *Education:* University of Nevada at Las Vegas (B.A., 1976; M.A., 1980); University of San Diego (J.D., 1986). Member, Appellate Moot Court Board, 1985-1986. *Member, Beverly Hills Bar Association;* State Bar of California. **REPORTED CASES:** Kuperstein v. Superior Court, (1988) 204 Cal. App.3d 598; Allstate v. Interbank Finan-

*(This Listing Continued)*

CAA861B

**KOLETSKY, MANCINI & FELDMAN,** Los Angeles—
*Continued*

cial Services (1989) 215 Cal. App.3d 825. *PRACTICE AREAS:* Construction Defect Defense; General Liability Defense. *Email:* IRITEGUD@aol.com

**ROBERT T. BERGSTEN,** born Long Beach, California, January 12, 1968; admitted to bar, 1993, California, U.S. District Court, Central District of California and U.S. Court of Appeals, Ninth Circuit. *Education:* Boston University (B.A., 1990); Pepperdine University (J.D., 1993). Phi Alpha Delta. Mediator, Los Angeles Superior Court, 1993—. *Member:* Los Angeles County and American Bar Associations; State Bar of California; Association of Southern California Defense Counsel. *LANGUAGES:* Spanish. *PRACTICE AREAS:* General Liability; Product Liability; Construction Defect; Insurance Coverage.

**KEMBLE CHEN,** born Beijing, China, January 4, 1970; admitted to bar, 1994, California and U.S. District Court, Central District of California. *Education:* University of California at Riverside (B.S., 1991); Loyola Law School (J.D., 1994). Recipient, Faculty Opportunity Scholarship, Loyola Law School. *Member:* Los Angeles County Bar Association; State Bar of California. *LANGUAGES:* Mandarin Chinese. *PRACTICE AREAS:* General Liability; Construction Defect; Immigration; Contracts; Criminal.

**LESLIE M. B. COLE,** born Los Angeles, California, May 22, 1959; admitted to bar, 1988, California and U.S. District Court, Central District of California. *Education:* University of California at Los Angeles; Brandeis University (B.A., cum laude, 1980); San Francisco Law School (J.D., 1986). Delta Theta Phi. *Member:* Los Angeles County Bar Association. *LANGUAGES:* French, German, Spanish. *PRACTICE AREAS:* Construction Defect Litigation; General Liability Litigation; Insurance Fraud Litigation.

**PATRICK A. CONNOLLY, III,** born New York, N.Y., September 10, 1967; admitted to bar, 1994, California. *Education:* George Washington University (B.A., 1989); Whittier College School of Law (J.D., 1994). Recipient, Dean's Merit Scholarship. Member, Whittier Law Review; Whittier International Law Society. *Member:* Los Angeles County and American Bar Associations. *PRACTICE AREAS:* Construction Defect Insurance Defense.

**RISA C. DAUER,** born Queens, New York, January 20, 1968; admitted to bar, 1993, New Jersey and New York; 1994, California. *Education:* University of Michigan (B.A., 1989); Brooklyn Law School (J.D., 1992). Richardson Scholar. *Member:* Beverly Hills and New York State Bar Associations. *PRACTICE AREAS:* Construction Defect; General Liability; Insurance Coverage.

**NANCY J. DUESBERG,** born West Hills, California, March 6, 1967; admitted to bar, 1994, California and U.S. District Court, Central District of California. *Education:* California State University at Northridge (B.S., 1989); Pepperdine University (J.D., 1994). Phi Alpha Delta. Recipient, Dean's Merit Scholarship. *Member:* Beverly Hills and Los Angeles County Bar Associations. *PRACTICE AREAS:* Construction Defect.

**VICTORIA L. ERSOFF,** born Detroit, Michigan, October 14, 1966; admitted to bar, 1992, California. *Education:* Arizona State University (B.S., 1989); Whittier College School of Law (J.D.,1992). Phi Alpha Delta. Member, Moot Court Honors Board. *Member:* Beverly Hills, Los Angeles County and American Bar Associations. *PRACTICE AREAS:* Construction Defect Defense; General Liability Defense; Toxic Tort Defense.

**SHARON G. FRIEDMAN,** born Montreal, Quebec, Canada, August 5, 1965; admitted to bar, 1993, California; 1994, U.S. District Court, Central District of California. *Education:* University of California, Los Angeles (B.S., 1987); Loyola University Law School (J.D., 1993). *Member:* American Bar Association. *PRACTICE AREAS:* Construction Defect Defense; General Liability Defense.

**STACEY R. FRIEDMAN,** born Culver City, California, February 6, 1970; admitted to bar, 1994, California and U.S. District Court, Central District of California; 1995, U.S. District Court, Southern District of California. *Education:* California State University at Northridge (B.A., 1991); Whittier College School of Law (J.D., 1994). *PRACTICE AREAS:* Construction Defect Defense Litigation; General Liability Defense Litigation.

**RANDALL K. L. KAM,** born Honolulu, Hawaii, February 10, 1961; admitted to bar, 1991, California. *Education:* University of Southern California (B.S., 1984); Southwestern University School of Law (J.D., 1991). *Member:* Los Angeles County Bar Association. *PRACTICE AREAS:* General Liability Defense Litigation.

*(This Listing Continued)*

**CHRISTIAN F. LAMOND,** born Newport, Rhode Island, October 4, 1966; admitted to bar, 1994, California. *Education:* Villanova University (B.A., 1987); Whittier College School of Law (J.D., 1994). *PRACTICE AREAS:* Construction Defect Defense Litigation.

**KIM A. NEISTADT,** born New York, N.Y., August 14, 1958; admitted to bar, 1989, California; 1990, U.S. District Court, Central District of California. *Education:* University of California at Los Angeles (B.A., 1981); McGeorge School of Law, University of the Pacific (J.D., 1989). Best Brief Finalist, Moot Court Competition. *Member:* Los Angeles County Bar Association; State Bar of California. *PRACTICE AREAS:* General Liability Defense Litigation; Wrongful Termination Defense Litigation; Sexual Harassment Defense Litigation.

**PETER KEITH PRITCHARD,** born Redwood City, California, April 16, 1964; admitted to bar, 1990, California and U.S. District Court, Central District of California. *Education:* University of California at Irvine (B.A., 1986); Santa Clara University J.D., 1989). *Member:* Los Angeles County Bar Association. *PRACTICE AREAS:* Construction Defect Insurance Defense.

**IRA L. SISKIND,** born Los Angeles, California, September 19, 1955; admitted to bar, 1990, California and U.S. District Court, Central District of California. *Education:* University of California at Los Angeles (B.A., 1978); Northrop University (J.D., 1989). *Member:* State Bar of California. *PRACTICE AREAS:* Construction Defect; General Liability.

**BRIAN P. SMITH,** born Buffalo, New York, September 2, 1965; admitted to bar, 1995, California. *Education:* University of Southern California (B.M., 1987); Southwestern University School of Law (J.D., 1995). *Member:* American Bar Association. *LANGUAGES:* Spanish. *PRACTICE AREAS:* Construction Defect; General Liability.

**JEFFERY E. STOCKLEY,** born Los Gatos, California, June 9, 1968; admitted to bar, 1993, California. *Education:* University of Southern California (B.A., 1990); Loyola Marymount University (J.D., 1993). *PRACTICE AREAS:* Construction Defect Defense; General Liability Defense.

**THOMAS N. THRASHER, JR.,** born Orange, California, March 16, 1967; admitted to bar, 1995, California. *Education:* University of California at Los Angeles (B.A., History, 1990); Western State University (J.D., 1994). Phi Kappa Sigma. Recipient, American Jurisprudence Award, Torts II. Robert H. Banyard Inn of Court. *Member:* Orange County Bar Association; Orange County Barristers. *PRACTICE AREAS:* Construction Defect Litigation; General Civil Litigation.

**TIMOTHY N. THOMPSON,** born San Diego, California, January 24, 1951; admitted to bar, 1991, California and U.S. Court of Appeals, Ninth Circuit. *Education:* University of Washington (B.B.A., 1977); Whittier College School of Law (J.D., 1991). Phi Alpha Delta. Member, ASTM D-10 Packaging Committee, Institute of Packaging Professionals, 1981-1991. *Member:* State Bar of California. *PRACTICE AREAS:* Construction Litigation.

**JOHN C. VOLZ,** born Sacramento, California, September 13, 1962; admitted to bar, 1989, California. *Education:* Moorpark College (A.S., 1983); San Diego State University (B.S., 1986); Whittier College School of Law (J.D., 1989). Recipient, American Jurisprudence Award in Evidence. *Member:* State Bar of California. *PRACTICE AREAS:* Construction Defect; Product Liability; Personal Injury.

**ERIC P. WEISS,** born Washington, D.C., April 18, 1964; admitted to bar, 1992, California, U.S. District Court, Central District of California. *Education:* University of Delaware (B.A.A.S., 1986); Whittier College School of Law (J.D., magna cum laude, 1992). Lead Articles Editor, Whittier Law Review, 1991-1992. Recipient, American Jurisprudence Award. *Member:* Los Angeles County and American Bar Associations; State Bar of California. *PRACTICE AREAS:* Insurance Defense; Automobile Fraud Defense; Landlord-Tenant.

**L. SCOTT WERTLIEB,** born Washington, D.C., December 30, 1968; admitted to bar, 1995, California; 1996, District of Columbia. *Education:* University of Wisconsin - Madison (B.A., 1990); Whittier College School of Law (J.D., 1994). *Member:* Los Angeles County Bar Association. *PRACTICE AREAS:* Construction Defect; General Liability; Insurance.

## KOLLENDER & SARGOY
### LOS ANGELES, CALIFORNIA
(See Santa Monica)

Civil, Business, Probate and Tax Litigation, IRS Dispute Resolution, Employment Counseling and Litigation, Corporate, Family, Personal Injury, White Collar Criminal Defense, Estate and Business Planning.

---

## KOLOD & WAGER
### LOS ANGELES, CALIFORNIA
(See Encino)

General Civil, Trial and Appellate Practice in State and Federal Court, emphasizing Insurance Coverage and Bad Faith, Construction Defect and Real Property, Professional Liability, General Tort Liability Defense, Products Liability and Environmental Impairment.

---

## RAYMOND KIRK KOLTER
SUITE 900, GATEWAY LOS ANGELES
12424 WILSHIRE BOULEVARD
**LOS ANGELES, CALIFORNIA 90025-1043**
Telephone: 310-826-6077
Fax: 310-442-6400

Civil and Business Litigation, including Family, Divorce, Domestic Relations, Plaintiffs Personal Injury, Products Liability, Premises Liability and Bankruptcy Practice. General Civil and Trial Practice in all Courts.

FIRM PROFILE: Mr. Kolter has saved his corporate clients millions of dollars and has recovered hundreds of thousands of dollars through trial and settlements. His cases have been noted in Time Magazine, April 20, 1987; Los Angeles Times, April 9, 1987; New York Times, April 11, 1987 and the Los Angeles Daily Journal, April 1, 1994. His most recognized case (Falcon vs. Worlds of Wonder, Inc.) helped lead to national legislation setting industry safety standards.

**RAYMOND KIRK KOLTER**, born Wichita Falls, Texas, November 6, 1962; admitted to bar, 1991, California and U.S. District Court, District of California; U.S. Court of Appeals, 9th Circuit. *Education:* Midwestern State University (B.A., 1986); St. Mary's University; Pepperdine University (J.D., 1989). Phi Sigma Alpha; Alpha Phi Sigma. Litigation Associate: Schell & Delamer, 1991-1993; Murchison & Cumming, 1993-1994. *Member:* State Bar of California, Los Angeles County and American Bar Associations. Los Angeles Trial Lawyers Association; California Trial Lawyers Association. (Also Of Counsel to John K. Pierson.)

### OF COUNSEL

**JOHN K. PIERSON**, born Redondo Beach, California, December 7, 1963; admitted to bar, 1990, California, U.S. District Court, Northern, Eastern, Southern and Central Districts of California, U.S Court of Appeals, 9th Circuit and U.S. Bankruptcy Court, Central and Southern Districts of California; 1992, Minnesota. *Education:* Cambridge University; St. Olaf College (B.A., 1986); Pepperdine University (J.D., 1989). *Member:* Los Angeles County, Hennepin County and Minnesota State Bar Associations; State Bar of California; California Trial Lawyers Association; Consumer Attorneys Association of Los Angeles. (Also practicing individually).

REPRESENTATIVE CLIENTS: Nissan Financial Ltd.; Law Line, Inc.; Medriatic, Inc.; Cornerstone Development, Inc.; Landshape, Inc.; Certified Property Inspections; Coastal Instrumentation and Telemetry; Pacific Metallurgical Co.; Pro-Sheetmetal, Inc.

---

## KOLTS AND NAWA
### LOS ANGELES, CALIFORNIA
(See Pasadena)

Products Liability, Wrongful Termination, Medical Device Defense, Probate Law and Business Litigation, Construction Litigation, ERISA Litigation and General Civil Litigation.

---

## KONOWIECKI & RANK
A Partnership including a Professional Corporation
Established in 1976
FIRST INTERSTATE WORLD CENTER
633 WEST 5TH STREET, SUITE 3500
**LOS ANGELES, CALIFORNIA 90071-2007**
Telephone: 213-229-0990
Telefax: 213-229-0992

Health Care Law. Mergers and Acquisitions. Corporate, Securities, Real Estate and Environmental Law. General Business and Civil Litigation.

FIRM PROFILE: Konowiecki & Rank (K & R) was founded in 1976 as a law firm dedicated to the provision of legal services to health care organizations. Since that time, K & R has expanded its health care expertise with an emphasis on issues and transactions concerning physicians, hospitals, and managed care organizations, and has developed expertise in a variety of business, corporate, real estate and transactional matters and in litigation.

**PETER C. RANK**, born Berkeley, California, April 18, 1938; admitted to bar, 1963, California. *Education:* Stanford University (B.A., 1960); University of California Boalt School of Law (J.D., 1963). Deputy District Attorney, Contra Costa County, California, 1963-1970. Director, under Ronald Reagan, California Employment Development Department, 1974. Member, National Transition Team for the United States Department of Health and Human Services, 1980 and Director, under George Deukmejian, California Department of Health Services, 1983-1985. *Member:* State Bar of California. **PRACTICE AREAS:** Health Care Law; General Business; Government; Corporate; Environmental Law.

**JOSEPH S. KONOWIECKI**, born Albany, New York, May 17, 1953; admitted to bar, 1978, California; 1993, District of Columbia. *Education:* University of California at Los Angeles (B.A. in Political Science, magna cum laude, 1975); University of California Hastings College of Law (J.D., 1978). Editor, Hastings Communications and Entertainment Law Journal, 1977-1978. Author: "How to Immigrate to The United States: A Practical Guide for the attorney," University of San Diego Law review, Volume 14.1. *Member:* Los Angeles County and American Bar Associations; State Bar of California; District of Columbia. **PRACTICE AREAS:** Health Care Law; Mergers and Acquisitions; Corporate; Partnership and Securities; General Business; Real Estate Law.

**MICHAEL C. FOSTER**, born Burbank, California, March 10, 1955; admitted to bar, 1982, California. *Education:* California State University (B.S. in Molecular Biology, magna cum laude, 1978); Loyola University of Los Angeles Law School (J.D., 1982). Recipient, Honorary Scholarship Certificate, 1981-1982. Member, Loyola Law Review, 1981-1982. Author: "Labor Law in the Ninth Circuit: Recent Developments," 16 Loy. Law Review 185, 1982. *Member:* State Bar of California; American Bar Association; National Health Lawyers Association. **PRACTICE AREAS:** Health Care Law; Mergers and Acquisitions; Corporate; Partnership; Securities Law; General Business.

**JON N. MANZANARES**, born Sherman Oaks, California, November 1, 1957; admitted to bar, 1982, California. *Education:* University of California at Los Angeles (B.A. in Economics, magna cum laude, 1979), Regents Scholar; University of Southern California (J.D., 1982). Finalist, Hale Moot Court Honors Competition, 1980-1981. Winner of Judge E. Avery Crary Moot Court Award, 1980-1981. Chairman, Hale Moot Court Executive Board, 1982. *Member:* Los Angeles County and American Bar Associations; State Bar of California. **PRACTICE AREAS:** General Business; Litigation.

**KEVIN B. KROEKER**, born Hillsboro, Kansas, April 18, 1959; admitted to bar, 1986, California. *Education:* University of Oklahoma (B.A. in Political Science, 1981); University of California School of Law at Davis, (J.D., 1986). *Member:* State Bar of California; National Health Lawyers Association. **PRACTICE AREAS:** Health Care Law; General Business; Administrative.

**PETER ROAN**, born Iowa City, Iowa, December 7, 1959; admitted to bar, 1985, Wisconsin and Iowa; 1988, California. *Education:* University of Iowa (B.B.A. in Economics, 1982); Marquette University (J.D., 1985). *Member:* State Bar of California; State Bar of Wisconsin. **PRACTICE AREAS:** Litigation and Environmental Law.

**PETER R. MASON**, born Boston, Massachusetts, May 22, 1959; admitted to bar, 1986, Massachusetts; 1987, California. *Education:* Harvard University (B.A. in Government, cum laude, 1981); Boston University (J.D.,

*(This Listing Continued)*

### KONOWIECKI & RANK, Los Angeles—Continued

1986). *Member:* Massachusetts Bar Association; State Bar of California. *PRACTICE AREAS:* Health Care; Corporate; General Business.

**DENISE E. HANNA,** born Harrisburg, Pennsylvania, May 26, 1961; admitted to bar, 1987, California. *Education:* The University of Chicago (B.A. in Behavioral Sciences, with honors, 1983); Stanford Law School (J.D., 1986). *Member:* State Bar of California; National Bar Association; Black Women Lawyers of Los Angeles. *PRACTICE AREAS:* Corporate; Mergers and Acquisitions; General Business; Health Care.

#### ASSOCIATES

**CYNTHIA J. BILLEY,** born Los Angeles, California, April 27, 1962; admitted to bar, 1991, California. *Education:* University of California at Los Angeles (B.A. in Political Science, magna cum laude, 1984); University of California, Boalt Hall School of Law (J.D., 1991). Phi Beta Kappa. *Member:* State Bar of California. *PRACTICE AREAS:* General Business; Health Care Law; Corporate.

**EDNA M. CHISM,** born Philadelphia, Pennsylvania, March 5, 1960; admitted to bar, 1987, California. *Education:* Beaver College (B.A., magna cum laude, 1981); New York University (J.D., 1987). Phi Alpha Delta. *Member:* State Bar of California. American Bar Association. *PRACTICE AREAS:* General Business; Corporate; Securities Law.

**RONAN COHEN,** admitted to bar, 1993, California. *Education:* University of California at San Diego (B.A. in Economics and B.A. in Cognitive Psychology cum laude, 1988); Boston University School of Law (J.D. cum Laude, 1993). Recipient, American Jurisprudence Awards in Family Law and Civil Procedure. Paul J. Liacos Scholar and Edward F. Hennessey Scholar. *Member:* State Bar of California. *PRACTICE AREAS:* General Business; Health Care.

**ROSA KWON EASTON,** born Seoul Korea, 1964; admitted to bar, 1994, California. *Education:* Smith College (B.A., 1986); Columbia University (M.I.A., 1990); Boston College Law School (J.D., 1994). Member, Boston College International and Comparative Law Review, 1991-1992. Recipient, Japan Foundation Fellowship, Inter-University Center for Japanese Language Studies, Yokohama, Japan, 1992-1993. Author: "Equal Employment Opportunities for Women in the European Community, Boston College International and Comparative Law Review," 1993. Extern to Hon Cynthia Holcomb Hall, U.S. Court of Appeals, Ninth Circuit, 1994. *Member:* State Bar of California; Korean Bar Association. *LANGUAGES:* Korean and Japanese. *PRACTICE AREAS:* Business Litigation; Employment Litigation.

**ROBERT C. HAYDEN,** born Altadena, California, April 8, 1953; admitted to bar, 1978, California, U.S. Court of Appeals, Ninth Circuit and U.S. District Court, Central, Southern, Northern and Eastern Districts of California. *Education:* Stanford University (B.S., 1975); Boalt Hall School of Law, University of California (J.D., 1978). *PRACTICE AREAS:* Labor and Employment Law; Employment Litigation; General Business Litigation.

**PHILLIP R. MALTIN,** born Los Angeles, California, August 4, 1959; admitted to bar, 1991, California and U.S. District Cort, Central District of California. *Education:* California State University at Chico (B.A. in Philosophy, 1984); Hebrew University, Jerusalem, Israel (B.A., 1985; toward M.A., 1985); De Paul University (J.D., 1990). Senior Editor, Journal of Health and Hospital Law. Recipient, First Place Brief, Phillip Jessup International Moot Court Competition. President, Student Bar Association. President, Decalogue Society of Jewish Attorneys/Law Students, De Paul Chapter. *LANGUAGES:* Hebrew. *PRACTICE AREAS:* ERISA; Employment Litigation; Business Litigation.

**SCOTT J. MOORE,** born North Hollywood, California, November 7, 1962; admitted to bar, 1987, California. *Education:* Loyola Marymount University (B.S., 1984); University of Southern California (M.B.T., 1987); University of Southern California (J.D., 1987). Member, Hale Moot Court Honors Program, 1985-1986. Recipient, American Jurisprudence Award. *Member:* State Bar of California. *PRACTICE AREAS:* General Business; Corporate; Real Estate.

**JOHN A. MUELLER,** born Santa Monica, California, February 27, 1966; admitted to bar, 1991, California. *Education:* University of California at Los Angeles (B.A. in English, 1988); University of Michigan (J.D., 1991). *Member:* Los Angeles County and American Bar Associations; State Bar of California. *PRACTICE AREAS:* General Business; Corporate; Health Care.

*(This Listing Continued)*

**LESLIE OVERFELT,** born Kansas City, Missouri, April 11, 1955; admitted to bar, 1989, California. *Education:* Brown University (B.A., 1977); University of Missouri (M.A., 1984); University of California at Los Angeles (J.D. 1989). Recipient, Graduate Fellowship, Florence-Virginia K. Wilson Scholarship. *Member:* State Bar of California. *PRACTICE AREAS:* Health Care; General Business.

**CATHERINE M. POLISOTO,** born Buffalo, New York, April 23, 1966; admitted to bar, 1991, California; 1992, U.S. District Court, Central District of California. *Education:* Cornell University (B.S. magna cum laude, 1988); University of California at Los Angeles (J.D., 1991). Moot Court Honors Program Participant, 1989. Teaching Assistant, Legal Research and Writing, 1989-1990. *Member:* Los Angeles County and American Bar Associations; State Bar of California; California Women Lawyers. *PRACTICE AREAS:* Corporate; Health Care.

**HAROLD C. POPE,** born Long Beach, California, September 28, 1941; admitted to bar, 1975, Oregon, U.S. Court of Appeals, Ninth Circuit and U.S. District Court, Southern District of Oregon; 1982, California and U.S. District Court, Southern District of California. *Education:* California State University at Long Beach (B.A., cum laude, 1963); Cornell University (M.A., 1969); University of Notre Dame (J.D., magna cum laude, 1975). Phi Kappa Phi. Executive Notes Editor and Member, Editorial Board, Notre Dame Lawyer, 1974-1975. Law Clerk to Hon. John Kilkenny, Ninth Circuit Court of Appeals, 1975-1976. *Member:* The State Bar of California; National Health Lawyers Association. *PRACTICE AREAS:* Health Care Law; Corporate Law; Real Estate Law.

#### LEGAL SUPPORT PERSONNEL

**CURTIS J. BERGERON,** born Houma, Louisiana, January 3, 1955. *Education:* Loyola University (B.M., 1978). Member, Association of Legal Administrators, Los Angeles Chapter, Small Firm Section. (Office Administrator).

REPRESENTATIVE CLIENTS: PacifiCare Health Systems, Inc.; UniHealth America; Columbia General Life Insurance Co.; Santa Clarita Health Care Assoc.; College Health Enterprises; Granada Hills Community Hospital; Redlands Community Hospital; Bay Shores Medical Group.
REFERENCE: Bank of America.

---

## KOPPLE & KLINGER

A Law Partnership including a Professional Corporation

*2029 CENTURY PARK EAST, SUITE 1040*
**LOS ANGELES, CALIFORNIA 90067**
*Telephone: 310-553-1444*
*Facsimile: 310-553-7335*

*Federal and State Taxation, Estate Planning, Trust and Probate Law, Employee Benefits, Business Law.*

#### MEMBERS OF FIRM

**ROBERT C. KOPPLE, (P.C.),** born Chicago, Illinois, March 15, 1944; admitted to bar, 1968, Illinois; 1969, California. *Education:* De Paul University (B.A., 1965; J.D., 1967); New York University (LL.M. in Taxation, 1968). Associate Editor, De Paul Law Review, 1967. Lecturer on Tax Law, University of Southern California School of Law, 1973-1984. Member, Taxation Advisory Commission to the California Board of Legal Specialization, 1977-1981. Member, Planning Committee of the Annual Institute of Federal Taxation of the University of Southern California, 1980—. *Member:* Beverly Hills (Chairman, Tax Committee, 1973-1974; Member, Board of Governors, 1975-1978), Los Angeles County (Chairman: Income Tax Committee, 1973-1974; Tax Section, 1978-1979), Illinois State and American Bar Associations; The State Bar of California (Chairman, Tax Section, 1975-1976).

**LESLIE S. KLINGER,** born Chicago, Illinois, May 2, 1946; admitted to bar, 1971, California; 1972, U.S. Tax Court; 1973, U.S. Claims Court. *Education:* University of California at Berkeley (A.B., 1967); Boalt Hall School of Law, University of California (J.D., 1971). Order of the Coif. Note and Comment Editor, California Law Review, 1968-1970. Chairman: UCLA Entertainment Tax Institute, 1988 and 1989; Estate and Financial Planning for the Closely Held Business, Practising Law Institute, 1977-1987. Vice President, Motion Picture and Television Tax Institute. Member, Advisory Board of Editors, Entertainment Law Reporter, 1979—. *Member:* Beverly Hills (Chairman, Tax Committee, 1975-1976; Member, Board of Governors, The Barristers, 1974-1976), Los Angeles County and American (Member: Section of Taxation; Committee on Corporate Stockholders Relationships, 1974-1975) Bar Associations; The State Bar of California

*(This Listing Continued)*

(Member, Tax Section); American Arbitration Association (Arbitrator, 1992—). *Email:* LKlinger@ix.netcom.com

*OF COUNSEL*

**RICHARD P. AYLES,** born Elgin, Illinois, December 14, 1951; admitted to bar, 1980, Florida and New York; 1985, California. *Education:* State University of New York at Binghamton (B.A., 1974); University of Miami School of Law (J.D., cum laude, 1979). Associate Editor-in-Chief, University of Miami Law Review, 1978-1979. Bar and Gavel Honorary Society. *Member:* American Bar Association (Member, Sections on Business Law; International Law and Practice; Real Property, Probate and Trust Law); The Florida Bar (Member, Sections on Corporation, Banking and Business Law; International Law; Real Property, Probate and Trust Law; Tax Law); State Bar of California (Member, Sections on Business Law; International Law; Real Property Law). *PRACTICE AREAS:* International Business Law; Business Law; Corporate Law; Real Property Law.

*ASSOCIATES*

**DOUGLAS W. SCHWARTZ,** born St. Louis, Missouri, September 6, 1960; admitted to bar, 1985, California; 1986, U.S. District Court, Central District of California; 1990, U.S. Tax Court. *Education:* Princeton University (A.B., summa cum laude, 1982); Stanford University (J.D., 1985). Phi Beta Kappa. Law Clerk to Hon. Pamela A. Rymer, Central District of California, 1985-1986. *Member:* Los Angeles County and American Bar Associations; State Bar of California; (Member, Sections on Taxation and Trust and Estate).

**JEFFREY A. KAYE,** born Newark, New Jersey, October 16, 1966; admitted to bar, 1991, California. *Education:* Yeshiva University (B.A., summa cum laude, 1988); University of Pennsylvania (J.D., magna cum laude, 1991). Order of the Coif. *Member:* State Bar of California (Member, Sections on: Business Law; Real Property Law). *LANGUAGES:* Hebrew.

**RICHARD A. MARSHALL,** born London, England, August 7, 1967; admitted to bar, 1996, California. *Education:* University of Southern California (A.B., magna cum laude, 1989; J.D., 1993); New York University School of Law (LL.M., 1994). Phi Beta Kappa.

## LAW OFFICES OF
## DEBRA L. KORDUNER

*Established in 1990*

*1801 CENTURY PARK EAST, 24TH FLOOR*
**LOS ANGELES, CALIFORNIA 90067-2326**
*Telephone: 310-277-3685*
*Fax: 310-277-5471*

*Business and Real Estate Litigation.*

**FIRM PROFILE:** Ms. Korduner handles all areas of business and real estate litigation, both in state and federal court, from "pre-litigation" resolution through trial and appeal. She also handles general business and real estate matters. Ms. Korduner works efficiently and effectively to provide her clients with high quality work at reasonable cost.

**DEBRA L. KORDUNER,** born Encino, California, October 5, 1955; admitted to bar, 1982, California. *Education:* University of California at Los Angeles (B.A., magna cum laude, 1976); Loyola Law School (J.D., 1982). Pi Gamma Mu; Pi Sigma Alpha. Recipient, American Jurisprudence Award in Torts. Member, 1980-1981 and Editor, 1981-1982, Loyola Law Review. Judge Pro Tem, Los Angeles Municipal Court, 1990—. Member, Inn of Court, 1996—. *Member:* Los Angeles County Bar Association (Member, Attorney-Client Relations Committee); State Bar of California. *PRACTICE AREAS:* Commercial Litigation; Civil Trial; Real Estate; Business Law.

## KORSHAK, KRACOFF, KONG & SUGANO

*11111 SANTA MONICA BOULEVARD*
*SUITE 910*
**LOS ANGELES, CALIFORNIA 90025**
*Telephone: 310-996-2340*
*Fax: 310-996-2334*

*Sacramento, California Office:* 25th & "J" Streets Building, 2430 "J" Street. Telephone: 916-441-6255. Fax: 916-448-8435.
*Chicago, Illinois Office:* 70 West Madison Street, Suite 525. Telephone: 312-346-2700. Fax: 312-346-2710.

*(This Listing Continued)*

*Labor and Employment Relations, Public Employment Relations, Equal Opportunity Law and Civil Litigation.*

**STUART R. KORSHAK,** born Chicago, Illinois, March 6, 1947; admitted to bar, 1976, California; 1977, U.S. District Court, Central District of California; 1981, U.S. Supreme Court; 1984, U.S. District Court, Southern District of California. *Education:* Yale University (B.A., magna cum laude, 1969); University of California at Davis (J.D., 1975). Author: Negotiating Trust in the San Francisco Hotel Industry, California Management Review, Vol. 38, No. 1, 1995; "Arbitrating the Termination of a Union Activist," Personnel Journal, January 1982. *Member:* Los Angeles County and American Bar Associations (Member, Section on Labor Law); The State Bar of California (Member, Section on Labor Law). *PRACTICE AREAS:* Labor and Employment; Equal Opportunity Law; Civil Litigation.

**RICHARD J. KRACOFF,** born Boston, Massachusetts, November 12, 1959; admitted to bar, 1984, California; 1985, U.S. District Court, Central and Southern Districts of California; 1988, U.S. District Court, Eastern District of California; 1990, U.S. Court of Appeals, Ninth Circuit; 1993, U.S. District Court, Northern District of California. *Education:* Dartmouth College (A.B., magna cum laude, 1981); Stanford University (J.D., 1984). Phi Beta Kappa. *Member:* Century City, Los Angeles County and American (Member, Section on Labor Law) Bar Associations; State Bar of California (Member, Section on Labor Law). *PRACTICE AREAS:* Labor and Employment; Public Employment; Equal Opportunity Law; Civil Litigation.

**CLEMENT J. KONG,** born San Jose, California, March 28, 1950; admitted to bar, 1976, California. *Education:* University of California at Berkeley (B.A., with distinction, 1972); University of California at Davis (J.D., 1975). Author: Report on Environmental Assessment of Pesticide Regulatory Programs, California Dept. of Food & Agriculture, Sept. 1978, Chapter 6 "Current Regulatory System," and Chapter 7 "Permits". *Member:* Sacramento County and Asian (Board of Directors, 1981-1982) Bar Associations; State Bar of California; Capitol City Trial Lawyers Association. (Resident, Sacramento Office). *LANGUAGES:* Chinese (Cantonese). *REPORTED CASES:* Neary vs. Regents of the University of California, et al; Kam Ho Eng vs. Bordens. *PRACTICE AREAS:* Corporate and Business Law (50%); Labor Law (25%); Civil Litigation (25%).

**TAKASHI ("T.R.") SUGANO,** born Newell, California, August 2, 1945; admitted to bar, 1972, California and U.S. District Court, Eastern District of California. *Education:* University of California (B.A., with distinction, 1967; M.A., 1968); Boalt Hall School of Law, University of California at Berkeley (J.D., 1972). Pro Tem Referee for Sacramento County Juvenile Court, 1986-1991. Pro Tem Settlement Conference Judge for Sacramento County Superior Court, 1988-1991. *Member:* Sacramento County and Asian (Member, Board of Directors, 1986-1987) Bar Associations; State Bar of California. (Resident, Sacramento Office). *LANGUAGES:* Japanese. *REPORTED CASES:* Wafer vs. Brown; Lim vs. Matranga. *PRACTICE AREAS:* Labor and Employment Law; Equal Opportunity Law; Public Employment Law; Civil Litigation.

**ANNE SIX KNIGHT,** born Lawrence, Kansas, April 11, 1959; admitted to bar, 1989, Illinois and U.S. District Court, Northern District of Illinois (Not admitted in California). *Education:* Grinnell College (B.A., 1981); University of Exeter, Exeter, England; University of Georgia School of Law (J.D., 1988). *Member:* Chicago, Illinois State and American (Member, Employment Law Section) Bar Associations. (Resident, Chicago, Illinois Office). *PRACTICE AREAS:* Employment Discrimination; Labor Law; Civil Litigation.

**MICHAEL W. SCHOENLEBER,** born Orange, California, January 7, 1949; admitted to bar, 1980, California; 1981, U.S. District Court, Eastern District of California; 1985, U.S. District Court, Northern District of California and U.S. Court of Appeals, Ninth Circuit. *Education:* Stanford University (B.A., 1972); University of California at Los Angeles (J.D., 1979). Co-Author, "Riparian Rights to Salinity Control," 19 Pacific Law J., 1143-1164 (1988). *Member:* Sacramento County (Member, Voluntary Legal Services Program) and American Bar Associations; American Immigration Lawyers Association. (Certified Specialist, Immigration and Nationality Law, California Board of Legal Specialization). *LANGUAGES:* Spanish. *PRACTICE AREAS:* Immigration and Naturalization.

**LAUREN E. ZAX,** born Highland Park, Illinois, May 3, 1967; admitted to bar, 1994, Illinois and California. *Education:* Tufts University (B.A., magna cum laude, 1989); University of Michigan (J.D., 1993). *Member:* Los Angeles County and American Bar Associations; State Bar of California (Member, Section on Labor Law). *PRACTICE AREAS:* Labor and Em-

*(This Listing Continued)*

**KORSHAK, KRACOFF, KONG & SUGANO, Los Angeles—Continued**

ployment Law; Equal Opportunity Law; Public Employment Law; Civil Litigation.

*OF COUNSEL*

**MAMORU SAKUMA,** born Oroville, California, August 4, 1918; admitted to bar, 1950, California and U.S. District Court, Northern and Eastern Districts of California; 1956, U.S. Supreme Court. *Education:* University of California, Berkley (A.B., 1940); Hastings College of the Law, University of California (LL.B., 1949). Adjunct Professor, University of Northern California Law School, 1989-1990. CEB Lecturer. Judge, Sacramento Municipal Court, 1964-1966; Sacramento Superior Court, 1966-1985. Judge Pro Tem, District Court of Appeals, Third District. Judicial Arbitration & Mediation Services, Inc. *Member:* Sacramento County Bar Association; Asian Bar Association of Sacramento (President, 1985-1986); State Bar of California. (Resident, Sacramento Office). **LANGUAGES:** Japanese. **REPORTED CASES:** Dorosan vs. Haslett Warehouse Co., a Corporation, et al. (165 CA2d599, 332 P2d 422); Minehart vs. Southern Pacific Company, a Corporation (136 CA2d486, 288 P2d 999); Atchison et al. vs. McGee (141 CA2d 515, 296 P2d 860); Aranda vs. Southern Pacific Company, a Corporation (351 U.S. 493, 100L Ed 1357, 76 S Ct 952). Authored Case: People vs. Finney (110 CA3d 705; 168 Cal.Rptr. 80). **PRACTICE AREAS:** Labor and Employment Law; Equal Opportunity Law; Public Employment Law; Civil Litigation.

**RAY W. FREDERICK,** born Arkadelphia, Arkansas, January 27, 1922; admitted to bar, 1949, Ohio; 1970, Illinois and U.S. District Court, Northern District of Illinois (Not admitted in California). *Education:* University of Cincinnati (B.B.A, 1947; LL.B., 1949). *Member:* Chicago, Illinois State and American (Member, Committee on Labor Arbitration and Collective Bargaining) Bar Associations. (Resident, Chicago, Illinois Office). **PRACTICE AREAS:** Labor and Employment Law; Public Employment Law; Equal Opportunity Law; Civil Litigation.

REPRESENTATIVE CLIENTS: Allied Communications, Inc.; Borenstein & Associates Builders Co.; CalFarm Insurance Co.; De Anza Properties; Fairmont Hotels of San Francisco, Chicago, San Jose, New Orleans and Dallas; Fujiki Transportation & Stevedoring Co.; Ltd.; Ironwood Resorts, Hawaii; International Film Guarantors, Inc.; Los Angeles Dodgers, Inc.; Near North Insurance Brokerage, Inc.; Pacific Gas & Electric Company; Resolution Trust Corporation; San Francisco Hotels Multiemployer Group; Shoei Food Corporation; Southern Wine & Spirits of Nevada; Southern Wine & Spirits of America, Inc. The John Stewart Company; Union Bank; Suburban Ford; Young's Market Co.; Zenith Insurance Co.

## KOSLOV & MEDLEN

30141 AGOURA ROAD, SUITE 200
**LOS ANGELES, CALIFORNIA 91301-4334**
Telephone: 818-597-9996
FAX: 818-597-8848

*Insurance, Real Estate and Construction Law, Personal Injury, Products Liability, Insurance Brokerage. Trials.*

*MEMBERS OF FIRM*

**JOHN KOSLOV,** born Malibu, California, November 5, 1933; admitted to bar, 1972, California; 1974, U.S. District Court, Southern and Central Districts of California. *Education:* University of Southern California (B.A., 1955); Southwestern University (J.D., magna cum laude, 1972). *Member:* Los Angeles County and American Bar Associations; State Bar of California; Lawyers Club of Los Angeles County; Association of Southern California Defense Counsel; Defense Research Institute. [Capt. USNR, Retired]. **REPORTED CASES:** Marsk v. Tilley Steel, 26 C3d. 486; Pacific Estates v. Sup. Ct. 13 CA 4th, 561; So. Calif. White Trucks v. Terezinski 190 CA3d 1393; Knox v. Streatfield, 79 CA3d 565. **PRACTICE AREAS:** Insurance Law; Products Liability Law; Real Estate Law; Construction Law; Personal Injury.

**WILLIAM P. MEDLEN,** born Hermiston, Oregon, May 20, 1959; admitted to bar, 1993, California. *Education:* Oregon State University (B.S., 1983); Loyola Law School, Los Angeles (J.D., 1993). *Member:* Ventura County Bar Association; State Bar of California. **PRACTICE AREAS:** Civil Litigation; Construction Law; Insurance Law.

*(This Listing Continued)*

*ASSOCIATE*

**SABRINA SIMMONS-BRILL,** born Woodland Hills, California, September 5, 1963; admitted to bar, 1992, California. *Education:* University of California at Santa Barbara (B.A., 1989); Whittier College School of Law (J.D., 1992). *Member:* Los Angeles County and Ventura County Bar Associations. **PRACTICE AREAS:** Civil Litigation; Insurance Litigation.

REPRESENTATIVE CLIENTS: Transamerica; Topa Insurance C.; Superior National Insurance co.

## LAW OFFICES OF
## M. SUE KRAFFT
**LOS ANGELES, CALIFORNIA**
(See Covina)

*Probate Law, Conservatorship/Guardianship Law, Estate Planning, Real Estate Law, Corporate Law.*

## KRAKOW & KAPLAN

Established in 1993
1801 CENTURY PARK EAST, SUITE 1520
**LOS ANGELES, CALIFORNIA 90067-2302**
Telephone: 310-229-0900
Fax: 310-229-0912

*Civil Trials and Appeals. Wrongful Termination, Civil and Constitutional Rights, Sexual Harassment, Privacy and Free Expression, Government and Business Misconduct, Insurance Bad Faith, ERISA, Union Representation.*

**MARVIN E. KRAKOW,** born Pittsburgh, Pennsylvania, November 22, 1948; admitted to bar, 1974, Massachusetts; 1975, U.S. District Court, District of Massachusetts; 1978, California; 1979, U.S. District Court, Central District of California and U.S. Court of Appeals, Ninth Circuit; 1984, U.S. District Court, Southern District of California. *Education:* Yale College (B.A., cum laude, 1970); Yale Law School (J.D., 1974). Author: "Attack on Civil Rights" Los Angeles Daily Journal, July 6, 1993, p.6; "Evaluating a Wrongful Firing Case," Los Angeles Trial Lawyers Association Advocate, March 1990, P.5; "One Year After 'Foley,' Where Do Things Stand?" Los Angeles Daily Journal, Monday, December 11, 1989, p.6; "Should the Courts Give Tort Relief if Your Boss is Unfair?" Los Angeles Daily Journal, Friday, September 15, 1989, P.6.; "Stress Management and The Trial Lawyer: Rules From Mother's Knee," LATLA Advocate, March 1985, p.5; "Bleeding the Poor Again," Clearinghouse Review, January 1981, p.1031; "Standards of Practice: A Systematic Approach to Quality Legal Services," Clearinghouse Review, December 1979, p.647; "Defending an Eviction from Private Housing," In: Counseling Low and Moderate Income Clients, Massachusetts Continuing Legal Education-New England Law Institute, Inc. Clinical Instructor, Boston University School of Law, 1976-1978. Member: Board of Directors, 1982-1985 and Executive Committee, 1983-1985, American Civil Liberties Union of Southern California. Director of Litigation, Legal Aid Foundation of Long Beach, 1978-1981. *Member:* Los Angeles County Bar Association (Bar Joint Association Settlement Officer Program); State Bar of California (Committee on the Administration of Justice, 1984-1985); California Employment Lawyers Association; National Employee Lawyers Association; Los Angeles Association of Consumer Attorneys; California Association of Consumer Attorneys; The Association of Trial Lawyers of America. **REPORTED CASES:** Loder v. City of Glendale, 216 Cal. App. 777 (1989); Montecini v. I.N.S., 915 F.2d 518 (9th Cir. 1990); Funk v. Sperry Corp., 842 F.2d 1129 (9th Cir. 1990); Khalsa v. Weinberger, 787 F.2d 1288 (9th Cir. 1985); Knight v. Hallsthammar, 29 Cal. 3d 46 (1981) (amicus); Highland Plastics v. Enders, 109 Cal. App. Supp. 3d 1 (1980). **PRACTICE AREAS:** Wrongful Termination; Employment Discrimination; Civil and Constitutional Rights; Privacy and Free Expression; Government Misconduct; Business Misconduct; Insurance Bad Faith.

**STEVEN J. KAPLAN,** born Los Angeles, California, June 29, 1953; admitted to bar, 1978, California and U.S. District Court, Northern District of California; 1980, U.S. District Court, Central District of California; 1986, U.S. District Court, Southern District of California; 1994, U.S. District Court, Eastern District of California. *Education:* Hebrew University, Jerusalem, Israel; University of California at Berkeley (A.B., 1974); Boalt Hall School of Law, University of California (J.D., 1978). Editor, Industrial Relations Law Journal, 1977-1978. Author: "Statutory Protection Against Wrongful Termination," The Employee Termination Handbook, Wiley In-

*(This Listing Continued)*

terscience, 1986; "The Protection of Employee Privacy," The Employee Termination Handbook, Wiley Interscience, 1986; "John Deklewa & Sons: The Great Leap Backward," 6 California Labor & Employment Law Quarterly 9, 1987; "Injunctions," Chapter 39, California Civil Procedure Before Trial, Continuing Education of the Bar, 1990; "Industrial Dystopia - Richard Vigilante, Strike," (book review) 9 California Labor and Employment Law Quarterly 3, Summer 1995. *Member:* Los Angeles County (Member, Labor and Employment Law Section) and American (Contributor to Report of Subcommittee on Union Administration and Procedure, Labor and Employment Law Section, 1985-1988) Bar Associations; State Bar of California (Chair, Committee on Pension and Other Trust Fund Benefits, Labor and Employment Law Section, 1987-1988); California Employment Lawyers Association; National Employment Lawyers Association. **SPECIAL AGENCIES:** Pacific Southwest Region, American Jewish Congress (Past President); Los Angeles Jewish Community Relations Committee. **REPORTED CASES:** Litton v. N.L.R.B., 501-U.S.-190, 111 S. Ct. 2215, 115 L.Ed.2d 177 (1991) (Brief only); Screen Extras Guild, Inc. v. Superior Court, 51 Cal.3d 1017 (1990); Graphic Communications Union v. GCLU-Employer Retirement Benefit Plan, 917 F.2d 1184 (9th Cir 1990); Foley v. Interactive Data Corporation, 47 Cal.3d 654 (1988); Carpenters Southern California Administrative Corp. v. El Capitan Development Co., 53 Cal.3d 1041 (1991) (Amicus Curiae); United Food and Commercial Workers Union v. Food Employers Council, 827 F.2d 519 (9th Cir. 1987). **PRACTICE AREAS:** Labor and Employment; Employee Benefits.

---

## KRAMER & GOLDWASSER

Established in 1991

5670 WILSHIRE BOULEVARD
SUITE 2420
LOS ANGELES, CALIFORNIA 90036
Telephone: 213-964-7100
FACSIMILE: 213-964-7107

*General Business and Real Estate Transactions, Estate Planning and Probate, Entertainment and Visual Arts Law.*

**STEPHEN W. KRAMER,** born Los Angeles, California, November 25, 1948; admitted to bar, 1976, California. *Education:* American College in Paris (A.A., 1968); University of Southern California (A.B., magna cum laude, 1970); University of California at Los Angeles (J.D., 1974). *Member:* Beverly Hills and Los Angeles County Bar Associations; State Bar of California; California Lawyers for the Arts. **PRACTICE AREAS:** Estates Law; Trusts Law; General Business Law; Fine Arts Law.

**CHARLES A. GOLDWASSER,** born 1950; admitted to bar, 1974, California. *Education:* Franklin & Marshall College (A.B.); University of California School of Law (J.D.). *Member:* State Bar of California. **PRACTICE AREAS:** Public Employment Law; Administration Law; Employment Discrimination Law.

**JEFFREY M. PUGH,** born Pasadena, California, August 21, 1961; admitted to bar, 1987, California. *Education:* University of Southern California (B.A., 1983); Hastings College of Law, University of California (J.D., 1987). *Member:* Beverly Hills and Los Angeles County Bar Associations; State Bar of California. **PRACTICE AREAS:** Corporate Law; Art Law; Entertainment.

**COREY W. GLAVE,** born Van Nuys, California, May 31, 1965; admitted to bar, 1993, California. *Education:* California Polytechnic State University (B.A., 1989); Southwestern University School of Law (J.D., 1992). *Member:* Los Angeles County Bar Association; State Bar of California. **PRACTICE AREAS:** Labor-Employment; Public Employment; Administration Law; Litigation; Employment Discrimination Law; Sports Law.

---

## KRAMER & KRAMER

LOS ANGELES, CALIFORNIA

(See Santa Monica)

*Defense of Civil Litigation Including Premises Liability, Automobile Related Cases, Suspect Claims, Products Liability, Construction Defects and Accidents, Medical and Dental Malpractice and Insurance Related Litigation.*

---

## LAW OFFICES OF ELLIOTT N. KRAMSKY

LOS ANGELES, CALIFORNIA

(See Woodland Hills)

*Patent, Trademark and Copyright Law.*

---

## KREGER & STEIN

A Partnership

3518 CAHUENGA BOULEVARD WEST, SUITE 213
LOS ANGELES, CALIFORNIA 90068
Telephone: 213-876-8118
Fax: 213-876-5612

*General Civil Litigation in all State and Federal Courts, Entertainment, Intellectual Property, Insurance Coverage and Bad Faith, Real Estate, Business, Commercial Litigation, Personal Injury.*

### MEMBERS OF FIRM

**WAYNE S. KREGER,** born Miami, Florida, March 22, 1966; admitted to bar, 1991, California and U.S. District Court, Central and Eastern Districts of California. *Education:* Boston University (B.A., 1988); Pepperdine University School of Law (J.D., 1991). Recipient: Margaret Martin Brock Scholarship. *Member:* Los Angeles County and American Bar Associations; State Bar of California; District of Columbia Bar. **LANGUAGES:** Spanish.

**MITCHELL REED STEIN,** born Los Angeles, California, June 6, 1966; admitted to bar, 1991, California. *Education:* University of Southern California (B.A., 1988); Pepperdine University (J.D., 1991). **PRACTICE AREAS:** General Practice; Entertainment and the Arts.

---

## DONALD A. KRENTZMAN

2049 CENTURY PARK EAST, SUITE 1200
LOS ANGELES, CALIFORNIA 90067-9777
Telephone: 310-277-6520

*Estate Planning, Corporate Planning, Tax Planning, Tax Controversies, Limited Partnerships.*

**DONALD A. KRENTZMAN,** born Culver City, California, February 12, 1950; admitted to bar, 1975, Colorado and U.S. District Court, District of Colorado; 1976, California; 1977, U.S. District Court, Central District of California; 1978, U.S. Tax Court. *Education:* University of California at Los Angeles (B.A., cum laude, 1972); University of Denver (J.D., 1974); New York University (LL.M., in Taxation, 1976). *Member:* State Bar of California (Member, Sections on: Taxation, Business Law, Trusts, Probate and Estate Planning).

---

## KU, FONG, LARSEN & CHEN, LLP

Established in 1981

523 WEST SIXTH STREET, SUITE 528
LOS ANGELES, CALIFORNIA 90014
Telephone: 213-488-1400
Telecopier: 213-236-9235

*Corporate, Business, Real Estate, International, Insurance, Copyright, Trademark, Unfair Competition and Business Litigation Law. General Civil and Trial Practice in all State and Federal Courts.*

### MEMBERS OF FIRM

**H. G. ROBERT FONG,** born Los Angeles, California, July 13, 1946; admitted to bar, 1972, California; 1973, U.S. District Court, Central District of California and U.S. Court of Military Appeals; 1976, U.S. District Court, Southern District of California and U.S. Court of Appeals, Ninth Circuit; 1982, U.S. Tax Court; 1987, U.S. District Court, Northern District of California; 1988, U.S. Supreme Court; 1989, U.S. Court of Appeals for the Federal Circuit. *Education:* University of California at Los Angeles (B.S., Psychology, 1968); Loyola University of Los Angeles (J.D., 1972). Phi Alpha Delta. *Member:* Los Angeles County and American Bar Associations; State Bar of California; Association of Business Trial Lawyers; Southern California Chinese Lawyers Association. [First Lieut., USAFR, 1972-

*(This Listing Continued)*

**KU, FONG, LARSEN & CHEN, LLP, Los Angeles—**
*Continued*

1974]. *PRACTICE AREAS:* Civil Trial; Litigation; Intellectual Property Law.

**PAUL A. LARSEN,** born San Jose, California, June 18, 1963; admitted to bar, 1988, California, U.S. District Court, Northern District of California and U.S. Court of Appeals, 9th Circuit; 1990, U.S. District Court, Central District of California; 1991, U.S. District Court, Southern District of California. *Education:* University of California at Berkeley (A.B., cum laude with high distinction in Economics, 1984); University of California at Los Angeles (M.A., in Economics, 1986; J.D., 1988). Omicron Delta Epsilon. Recipient, American Jurisprudence Award in Evidence. *Member:* Los Angeles County and American Bar Associations; State Bar of California. *PRACTICE AREAS:* Litigation; Intellectual Property; Business Law.

**FRANK W. CHEN,** born Taipei, Taiwan, November 11, 1963; admitted to bar, 1988, California; 1989, U.S. District Court, Central District of California; 1990, U.S. Court of Appeals, Ninth Circuit; U.S. District Court, Northern District of California; 1995, U.S. District Court, Southern District of California. *Education:* Stanford University (A.B., in Economics, 1985); University of California at Los Angeles School of Law (J.D., 1988). Omicron Delta Epsilon. Member, University of California at Los Angeles Moot Court Honors Program, 1986-1987. Member, University of California at Los Angeles Pacific Basin Law Journal, 1986-1988. *Member:* Los Angeles County and American Bar Associations; State Bar of California; Southern California Chinese Lawyers Association (Member, Board of Governors, 1995—). *LANGUAGES:* Chinese (Mandarin and Taiwanese). *PRACTICE AREAS:* Civil Trial; Litigation; Real Estate Law; Business Law.

### OF COUNSEL

**EDWARD Y. KU,** born Chungking, China, April 11, 1942; admitted to bar, 1973, California and Taiwan. *Education:* National Taiwan University (B.A., in Law, 1965); Washington University, St. Louis, Missouri (J.D., 1970). Delta Theta Phi. Founding Director, First Public Savings Bank, Los Angeles. *Member:* American Bar Association; State Bar of California; Southern California Chinese Lawyers Association (President, 1982-1983); Republic of China Bar Association. *LANGUAGES:* Chinese (Mandarin). *PRACTICE AREAS:* International Law; Corporate; Business; Real Estate; Banking; Immigration.

### ASSOCIATES

**JACK S. YEH,** born Taichung, Taiwan, June 25, 1969; admitted to bar, 1994, California; 1995, U.S. District Court, Central, Northern and Southern Districts of California. *Education:* University of California at San Diego (B.A., cum laude, with distinction in Political Science, minor in Law and Society, 1990); University of San Diego School of Law (J.D., 1994). National Team Member, Appellate Moot Court Board, 1993-1994. Semifinalist: Alumni Moot Court Tort Competition, 1992; Constitutional Law Moot Court Competition, 1993. Judicial Intern to the Hon. Jonathan S. Rhoades, United States District Court for the Southern District of California, 1993-1994. *Member:* Los Angeles County and American Bar Associations; State Bar of California; Southern California Chinese Lawyers Association. *LANGUAGES:* Chinese (Mandarin). *PRACTICE AREAS:* Civil Trial; Litigation.

**VICTOR S. SZE,** born Taipei, Taiwan, July 17, 1967; admitted to bar, 1995, California. *Education:* University of California at Los Angeles (B.A., 1990); Loyola Law School (J.D., 1995). Phi Delta Phi. Member, Loyola Law Review. Author, "A Tale of Three Strikes," 28 Loy. LA Law Review 1047 (1995). *Member:* Los Angeles County and American Bar Associations. *LANGUAGES:* Chinese (Mandarin). *PRACTICE AREAS:* Business; Corporate.

## KUDO & DANIELS, LLP

12400 WILSHIRE BOULEVARD, SUITE 400
LOS ANGELES, CALIFORNIA 90025-1023
Telephone: 310-442-7900
Facsimile: 310-442-7999

*Real Estate, Business and Personal Injury Litigation; Commercial Collections in Federal and State Courts, Product Liability; Legal, Accountancy, Medical, Dental and Realtor Malpractice. Business, Corporate, Securities and Transactional Law. Arbitration and Mediation Services.*

(This Listing Continued)

**RICHARD K. KUDO,** born Fujisawa, Japan, April 16, 1951; admitted to bar, 1978, California. *Education:* University of California at Los Angeles (B.A., 1974); Hastings College of the Law, University of California (J.D., 1978). Phi Delta Phi. Attorney, Federal Trade Commission, 1978-1981. *Member:* Santa Monica Bar Association; State Bar of California. *PRACTICE AREAS:* Commercial Collections in Federal and State Courts; Real Estate; Business; Transactional Law; Personal Injury Litigation.

**PAULA A. DANIELS,** born Honolulu, Hawaii, July 5, 1955; admitted to bar, 1981, California, U.S. District Court, Central District of California and U.S. Court of Appeals, Ninth Circuit. *Education:* University of Southern California (B.A., cum laude, 1977); Southwestern University (J.D., 1980). Member, State Bar Committee on the Administration of Justice, 1990-1993 term. Member, Los Angeles ADR Quality Control Subcommittee, 1995—. Arbitrator and Mediator, Santa Monica Superior Court. *Member:* Santa Monica and Los Angeles County Bar Associations; State Bar of California; Association of Southern California Defense Counsel; Southern California Mediation Association. *REPORTED CASES:* Danielson v. ITT Industrial Credit Co. (1988) 199 Cal. App. 3d 645, 245 Cal. Rptr. 126. *PRACTICE AREAS:* Products Liability; Medical, Dental, Legal, Accountant and Realtor Malpractice; Construction Accidents.

## KUSSMAN & WHITEHILL

A Partnership including a Professional Corporation
SUITE 1470, 10866 WILSHIRE BOULEVARD
LOS ANGELES, CALIFORNIA 90024
Telephone: 310-474-4411
Fax: 310-474-6530

*Medical Malpractice, Insurance Bad Faith, Personal Injury, Products Liability and Professional Liability.*

**RUSSELL S. KUSSMAN, (A PROFESSIONAL CORPORATION),** born Schenectady, New York, January 2, 1949; admitted to bar, 1981, California, U.S. District Court, Central District of California and U.S. Court of Appeals, Ninth Circuit. *Education:* Boston University (B.A., 1972; M.D., 1972); Boalt Hall School of Law, University of California (J.D., 1981). Diplomat, American Board of Internal Medicine, 1976. Contributing Editor, Journal of Legal Medicine, 1978-1981. Director, Home Care Service, 1978-1980, University of California, San Francisco, Medical Center. Physician's and Surgeon's License, California, 1975—. Author: "Legal Responsibilities of Independent Nurse-Practitioners," New England Journal of Medicine, Vol. 299, 1978; "Informed Consent-New Rulings, New Concepts, New Terms," Legal Aspects of Medical Practice, October, 1981; "Trial of Medical Malpractice," Los Angeles Times Guest Opinion Section, April 14, 1985; "Guidelines for Attorneys Fees after Waters v. Bourhis," CEB California Litigation Reporter (1986); "Malpractice Cap: Victim Bashing," Los Angeles Times Op-Ed Editorial, Oct. 4, 1987; "The President's Health Security Plan and The Tort System," LATLA Advocate, April, 1994; "Products Liability in Medical Device Cases," CTLA Forum, May 1995; "Obstetrics and The Law," LATLA Medical Malpractice Guide. Co-Author: "Wrongful Life and Birth," CEB California Tort Damages (1988). *Member:* Los Angeles County (Member, Court Improvements Committee, 1987—) and American Bar Associations; State Bar of California; Los Angeles Trial Lawyers Association (Member, Board of Governors, 1993-1994); California Trial Lawyers Association (Member, Board of Governors, 1987-1989); The Association of Trial Lawyers of America; American Board of Trial Advocate - ABOTA (Associate, 1992—); Los Angeles County Medical Association. *PRACTICE AREAS:* Medical Malpractice; Products Liability Law; Professional Liability; Personal Injury.

**MICHAEL H. WHITEHILL,** born Oakland, California, February 20, 1956; admitted to bar, 1981, California, U.S. District Court, Central District of California, U.S. Court of Appeals, Ninth Circuit and U.S. Supreme Court. *Education:* University of California at Berkeley (A.B., with honors, 1978); Boalt Hall School of Law, University of California (J.D., 1981). Associate Editor, California Law Review, 1979-1981. Author: "Punitive Damages for Nondeliberate Torts-The Drunk Driving Context," 68 California Law Review 911, 1980; "The Application of Insurance Bad Faith In First Party and Surety Bond Cases," Forum, May, 1986; "Damages in Employment Contract Cases," Trial, July, 1988; "The Constitutionality of California's Punitive Damage Scheme," Advocate, Sept. 1993; "Undocumented, Non-English Speaking Clients: Common Evidentiary Problems," Advocate, Vol., 1993; "Chasing Corporate Culprits in Insurance Bad Faith Cases," Advocate, July, 1995. *Member:* State Bar of California; American Bar Association; The Association of Trial Lawyers of America; Consumer Attorneys of California; Consumer Attorneys Association of Los Angeles. *PRAC-*

(This Listing Continued)

PROFESSIONAL BIOGRAPHIES — CALIFORNIA—LOS ANGELES

*TICE AREAS:* Insurance Bad Faith Law; Personal Injury; Products Liability Law; Medical Malpractice.

---

**STEVEN G. MEHTA,** born London, England, December 15, 1967; admitted to bar, 1992, California and U.S. District Court, Central District of California. *Education:* California State University, Northridge (B.A., magna cum laude, 1989); McGeorge School of Law, University of the Pacific (J.D., 1992). Order of the Coif. Professor, California State University, Northridge, 1994. Co-Author: "Products Liability in Medical Device Cases, Can David Beat Goliath?" Forum, May, 1995. *Member:* San Fernando Valley (Chair, San Fernando Valley Association, Barristers, 1995-1996;1996-1997) and Los Angeles County Bar Associations; Consumer Attorneys Association of Los Angeles. *REPORTED CASES:* Fraker v. Sentry Life Insurance Co., 19 Cal.App. 4th 276 (1993). *PRACTICE AREAS:* Insurance Bad Faith Litigation; Products Liability; Medical Malpractice.

## LADAS & PARRY

5670 WILSHIRE BOULEVARD
**LOS ANGELES, CALIFORNIA 90036**
Telephone: 213-934-2300
Telex: 240423
Cable Address: "Lawlan LSA"
Telecopier: 213-934-0202
URL: http://www.ladas.com

*New York, New York Office:* 26 West 61st Street. Telephone: 212-708-1800. Telex: 233288. Telecopy: 212-246-8959. Cable Address: "Lawlan New York".

*Chicago, Illinois Office:* 224 South Michigan Avenue. Telephone: 312-427-1300. Telex: 203649. Telecopy: 312-427-6663; 312-427-6668. Cable Address: "Lawlan Chicago".

*London, England Office:* High Holborn House, 52-54 High Holborn, WC1V 6RR. Telephone: 44-71-242-5566. Telex: 262433 MONREF G. Telecopy: 44-71-405-1908 (Groups 2 & 3). Cable Address: "Lawlan London W.C.1".

*Munich, Germany Office:* Altheimer Eck 2, D-80331 Munich. Telephone: (089) 269077. Fax: (089) 269040. Cable Address: "Lawlan Munich".

Patent, Trademark, Copyright, Unfair Competition, Licensing, Entertainment and Litigation.

### MEMBERS OF FIRM

**RICHARD P. BERG,** born Los Angeles, California, May 25, 1945; admitted to bar, 1976, California and Texas; registered to practice before U.S. Patent and Trademark Office and Canadian Patent Office. *Education:* University of Southern California (B.S.E.E., 1967); University of San Diego (J.D., cum laude, 1975).

**HENRY KLEIN,** born New York, N.Y., October 6, 1949; admitted to bar, 1975, California; 1976-1982, U.S. Court of Customs and Patent Appeals; 1985, U.S. Court of Appeals for the Federal Circuit. *Education:* State University of New York at Albany (B.A., 1971); Texas Tech University; University of San Diego (J.D., 1975).

**COLIN P. ABRAHAMS,** born Johannesburg, South Africa, February 13, 1952; admitted to bar, 1982 South Africa; 1984, California; registered to practice before U.S. Patent and Trademark Office. *Education:* University of Witwatersrand, Johannesburg (B.Sc., 1973; LL.B., 1976).

**MAVIS S. GALLENSON,** born Salt Lake City, Utah, November 19, 1951; admitted to bar, 1979, California; registered to practice before U.S. Patent and Trademark Office. *Education:* University of Utah (B.S., cum laude, 1975; J.D., 1978); University of California at San Diego.

**FRANCIE R. GOROWITZ,** born New York, N.Y., March 29, 1955; admitted to bar, 1981, New York; 1986, California. *Education:* State University of New York at Cortland (B.A., magna cum laude, 1977); Albany Law School of Union University (J.D., 1980).

### ASSOCIATES

**IRIS SMITH-HESS,** born Toronto, Canada; admitted to bar, 1982, California. *Education:* California State University at Fresno; University of West Los Angeles (J.D., 1982).

**RICHARD J. PACIULAN,** born Lynn, Massachusetts, June 2, 1947; admitted to bar, 1977, Massachusetts; registered to practice before U.S. Patent and Trademark Office (Not admitted in California). *Education:* Northeastern University (B.S.E.E., 1969); Suffolk University (J.D., 1974). Tau Beta Pi; Eta Kappa Nu.

**JOHN PALMER,** admitted to bar, 1990, California; registered to practice before U.S. Patent and Trademark Office. *Education:* Yale University (B.A., 1982); University of Virginia (J.D., 1990).

### OF COUNSEL

**IRA M. SIEGEL,** born Bronx, New York, October 16, 1949; admitted to bar, 1977, California; registered to practice before U.S. Patent and Trademark Office; 1984, U.S. Court of Appeals for the Ninth Circuit; 1985, U.S. Court of Appeals for the Federal Circuit; 1987, U.S. Supreme Court. *Education:* City College of the City University of New York (B.E.E.E., 1972); University of Miami (J.D., 1977).

**KAM C. LOUIE,** born Hong Kong, October 18, 1950; admitted to bar, 1979, California. *Education:* University of California at Los Angeles (B.A., 1973); University of California School of Law (J.D., 1979).

### LEGAL SUPPORT PERSONNEL

**DON A. HOLLINGSWORTH,** born Decatur, Illinois, September 17, 1934; registered to practice before U.S. Patent and Trademark Office. *Education:* University of Illinois (B.S.E.E., 1961; M.S.E.E., 1962); San Fernando College of Law (J.D., 1973). (Patent Agent).

(For biographical data of the New York personnel, see Professional Biographies at New York, N.Y.)
(For biographical data of the Chicago personnel, see Professional Biographies at Chicago, Illinois)
(For biographical data of the London personnel, see Professional Biographies at London, England)
(For biographical data of the Munich personnel, see Professional Biographies at Munich, Germany)

---

## LA FOLLETTE, JOHNSON, DE HAAS, FESLER & AMES

A PROFESSIONAL CORPORATION
Established in 1965

865 SOUTH FIGUEROA STREET, SUITE 3100
**LOS ANGELES, CALIFORNIA 90017-5443**
Telephone: 213-426-3600
Fax: 213-426-3650

*San Francisco, California Office:* 50 California Street, Suite 3350. Telephone: 415-433-7610. Telecopier: 415-392-7541.

*Santa Ana, California Office:* 2677 North Main Street, Suite 901. Telephone: 714-558-7008. Telecopier: 714-972-0379.

*Riverside, California Office:* 3403 Tenth Street, Suite 820. Telephone: 714-275-9192. Fax: 714-275-9249.

Civil Litigation, Employment Law, Medical Malpractice, Professional Liability, Insurance Defense Coverage and Bad Faith, Construction Law and Product Liability.

FIRM PROFILE: La Follette, Johnson, De Haas, Fesler & Ames recently celebrated its 30th year of dedicated legal service to the insurance industry, medical and professional community. Founded in 1965, the firm has grown steadily over the last quarter century to a position of leadership and innovation in the industry. With over 70 attorneys and an entire complement of highly qualified support personnel, the firm fully staffs offices in Los Angeles, Orange County, the Inland Empire and San Francisco. The firm is thus positioned to serve clients' needs throughout the State of California.

**JOHN T. LA FOLLETTE** (1922-1990).

**DAREN T. JOHNSON,** born Salina, Kansas, July 30, 1928; admitted to bar, 1953, California; U.S. District Court, Central District of California; U.S. Supreme Court. *Education:* University of California at Los Angeles (B.A., 1950; J.D., 1953). Judge Pro Tempore, Los Angeles Superior Court, 1962-1963. *Member:* Los Angeles County and American Bar Associations; The State Bar of California; Association of Southern California Defense Counsel; American Board of Trial Advocates (Diplomate); Federation of Insurance and Corporate Counsel. Fellow: International Society of Barristers; American College of Trial Lawyers. (Also at San Francisco and Santa Ana Offices). *PRACTICE AREAS:* Bad Faith and General Liability Litigation; Insurance Law; Tort Law; Corporate Law.

**LOUIS H. DE HAAS,** born East Cleveland, Ohio, May 1, 1941; admitted to bar, 1967, California and U.S. District Court, Central District of California. *Education:* University of Southern California (B.A., 1963); Hastings College of Law, University of California (LL.B., 1966). Phi Delta Phi. Arbitrator and Member of Settlement Panel, Los Angeles County Superior

*(This Listing Continued)*

**LA FOLLETTE, JOHNSON, DE HAAS, FESLER & AMES,**
*A PROFESSIONAL CORPORATION, Los Angeles—Continued*

Court. Editor, Medio-Legal Digest, 1991. *Member:* Los Angeles County Bar Association (Member, Bench and Bar Committee); State Bar of California; Association of Southern California Defense Counsel (Member, Board of Directors); Defense Research Institute; American Board of Trial Advocates (Advocate; Member, Board of Directors). *REPORTED CASES:* Atienza v. Tamb MD., 194 Ca 3rd 388; Bolanos v. Khalatian MD., 91 Daily Journal D.A.R. 8439; The L.A. Free Press Juc. v. The City of Los Angeles 9 Ca 3rd 448; Willie Leonard v. City of Los Angeles 31 Ca 3rd 473; The City of Los Angeles v. Superior Court of the State of California 176 Ca 3rd 856. *PRACTICE AREAS:* Medical Malpractice Litigation; Wrongful Termination Litigation.

**DONALD C. FESLER,** born Santa Maria, California, November 4, 1948; admitted to bar, 1973, California. *Education:* University of California at Santa Barbara (B.S., 1970); University of California at Los Angeles, Law School (J.D., 1973). Phi Beta Kappa. *Member:* Los Angeles County and American Bar Associations; State Bar of California; American Board of Trial Advocates; Association of Southern California Defense Counsel; Defense Research Institute. *PRACTICE AREAS:* Medical Malpractice; General Litigation.

**DENNIS K. AMES,** born Wichita, Kansas, July 31, 1953; admitted to bar, 1978, California. *Education:* University of California at Los Angeles (A.B., magna cum laude, 1975); Loyola University of Los Angeles (J.D., cum laude, 1978). Lecturer, Physician, Hospital Risk Management and Insurance Coverage (Managing Director, Orange County Office 1991—). Member, St. Thomas More Law Honor Society. *Member:* Orange County and Los Angeles County Bar Associations; State Bar of California; Association of Southern California Defense Counsel. (Manager/Shareholder, Santa Ana Office). *PRACTICE AREAS:* Medical Malpractice; Insurance Law; Commercial Law; Products Liability.

**ALFRED W. GERISCH, JR.,** born Los Angeles, California, July 18, 1948; admitted to bar, 1973, California. *Education:* University of Southern California (B.S., 1970); Loyola University of Los Angeles (J.D., 1973). Managing Editor, Loyola Consumer Protection Journal, 1973. *Member:* Los Angeles County Bar Association; State Bar of California; Association of Southern California Defense Counsel. *PRACTICE AREAS:* General Litigation.

**BRIAN W. BIRNIE,** born Los Angeles, California, November 9, 1952; admitted to bar, 1979, California. *Education:* Occidental College (B.A., 1974); Whittier College (J.D., cum laude, 1979). Recipient, American Jurisprudence Award. Member, Whittier Law Review, 1978-1979. *Member:* State Bar of California; American College of Legal Medicine; National Health Lawyers Association (Arbitrator/Mediator); Association of Southern California Defense Counsel. *PRACTICE AREAS:* Medical Malpractice Litigation.

**PETER J. ZOMBER,** born New York, N.Y., November 30, 1951; admitted to bar, 1980, California. *Education:* University of Southern California (B.A., 1974); Villanova University (J.D., 1979). *Member:* Los Angeles County and American Bar Associations; State Bar of California; Association of Southern California Defense Counsel; American Board of Trial Advocates; Defense Research Institute. *PRACTICE AREAS:* General Liability; Medical Malpractice; Products Liability; Construction Litigation.

**ROBERT E. KELLY, JR.,** born St. Louis, Missouri, January 15, 1941; admitted to bar, 1973, New York; 1976, California. *Education:* St. Louis University (B.S., 1962); New York University (J.D., 1972). *Member:* The State Bar of California; New York State and American Bar Associations. *PRACTICE AREAS:* Products Liability; Environmental Law.

**G. KELLEY REID, JR.,** born Cedar Rapids, Iowa, October 19, 1941; admitted to bar, 1968, Florida; 1973, California. *Education:* University of Iowa and Florida State University (B.A., 1964); University of Florida (J.D., 1968). Arbitrator, San Francisco Superior Court, 1976—. Councilman, Ross Town Council, 1990—. Mayor, Ross Town Council, 1992-1993. *Member:* Bar Association of San Francisco; State Bar of California; The Florida Bar; American Bar Association; California Trial Lawyers Association; The Association of Trial Lawyers of America; Northern California Association of Defense Counsel; San Francisco Trial Lawyers Association; Defense Research Institute; National Football League Players Association (Contract Advisor, 1991—). (Resident, San Francisco Office). *REPORTED CASES:* William Kilpatrick v. Holiday Inn, et al. (1991) 226 Cal. App. 3rd 855. *PRACTICE AREAS:* General Liability Defense.

*(This Listing Continued)*

CAA870B

**DENNIS J. SINCLITICO,** born St. Louis, Missouri, January 9, 1947; admitted to bar, 1971, Wisconsin; 1972, California and U.S. District Court, Central and Southern Districts of California. *Education:* University of San Diego (B.A., 1968); University of Wisconsin (J.D., cum laude, 1971). Phi Alpha Delta. Arbitrator, Los Angeles County Superior Court, Special Arbitration Plan, 1975—. *Member:* State Bar of Wisconsin; State Bar of California; American Board of Trial Advocates (Member, National Executive Committee, 1979—; Editor-in-Chief, "The Newsletter," 1979—; Treasurer, Membership Chairman, 1989-1992; President, L.A. Chapter, 1993; Chairman, California, 1994); Association of Southern California Defense Counsel (Program Chairman, 1980-1981; Member, Board of Directors, 1980—). *PRACTICE AREAS:* Medical Malpractice.

**CHRISTOPHER C. CANNON,** born New Orleans, Louisiana, July 9, 1957; admitted to bar, 1982, California. *Education:* University of California at Los Angeles (B.A., 1979); University of Southern California (J.D., 1982). *Member:* State Bar of California; Association of Southern California Defense Counsel. (Resident, Santa Ana Office). *PRACTICE AREAS:* Medical Malpractice.

**DOROTHY B. REYES,** born Lecompte, Louisiana, September 24, 1952; admitted to bar, 1982, California. *Education:* Grambling University (B.S., 1973); Loyola University of Los Angeles (J.D., 1981). *Member:* Los Angeles County and American Bar Associations; State Bar of California; Association of Southern California Defense Counsel; Black Women Lawyers Association. *PRACTICE AREAS:* Bad Faith; General Liability.

**STEVEN R. ODELL,** born Los Angeles, California, January 26, 1951; admitted to bar, 1980, California. *Education:* California State University at Long Beach (B.A., 1973); Western State University (J.D., 1979). *Member:* Orange County and American Bar Associations; State Bar of California; Orange County Trial Lawyers Association; Association of Southern California Defense Counsel. (Santa Ana and Riverside Offices). *PRACTICE AREAS:* General Liability; Medical Malpractice; Trucking and Products Liability; Construction Defects.

**CHRISTOPHER L. THOMAS,** born Carbondale, Illinois, December 5, 1954; admitted to bar, 1982, California and Indiana. *Education:* Southern Illinois University (B.S., 1977); Western State University (J.D., 1982). Nu Beta Epsilon. Recipient, American Jurisprudence Award in Family Law. *Member:* Indiana State Bar Association; The State Bar of California; Southern California Defense Counsel; American Board of Trial Advocates. (Santa Ana and Riverside Offices). *PRACTICE AREAS:* Personal Injury Litigation; Insurance Litigation; Governmental Tort Litigation.

**ROBERT K. WARFORD,** born Altadena, California, July 18, 1946; admitted to bar, 1977, California and U.S. District Court, Central District of California. *Education:* University of California at Riverside (B.A., 1967; M.A., 1969); University of La Verne (J.D., summa cum laude, 1977). Managing Editor, Journal of Juvenile Law, 1976-1977. Adjunct Professor of Law, University of LaVerne School of Law, La Verne, California, 1981. *Member:* State Bar of California; American Board of Trial Advocates. Manager/Shareholder, Riverside Office. (Resident, Riverside Office). *PRACTICE AREAS:* Medical Malpractice.

**JOHN L. SUPPLE,** born Oak Park, Illinois, April 11, 1953; admitted to bar, 1980, California. *Education:* University of California at Irvine (B.A., 1977); Pepperdine University (J.D., 1980). Publications Editor, Pepperdine Law Journal, 1979-1980. Member, California Medical Legal Committee, 1991—. *Member:* State Bar of California; Association of Northern California Defense Counsel; Association of Southern California Defense Counsel; Defense Research Institute. Manager/Shareholder, San Francisco Office. (Resident, San Francisco Office). *REPORTED CASES:* Richard H. v. Larry D., 198 Cal App 3rd 591 (1988); Perkins v. Howard, 232 Cal App 3rd 708 (1991). *PRACTICE AREAS:* Medical Malpractice; Product Liability; Toxic Tort.

**VINCENT D. LAPOINTE,** born Grosse Pointe, Michigan, August 21, 1953; admitted to bar, 1982, California. *Education:* Oakland University (B.A., cum laude, 1975); Southwestern University (J.D., 1981). *Member:* Los Angeles County Bar Association; State Bar of California. *PRACTICE AREAS:* General Liability; Public Entities; Medical Malpractice.

**STEVEN J. JOFFE,** born Chicago, Illinois, March 13, 1957; admitted to bar, 1983, California. *Education:* University of Minnesota (B.A. in Political Science, with honors, 1979); Western State University (J.D., 1982). Nu Beta Epsilon. Member, Criminal Justice Journal Law Review, 1981-1982. *Member:* San Diego County, Riverside County and Los Angeles County Bar Associations; The State Bar of California; Association of Southern California Defense Counsel. *PRACTICE AREAS:* Bad Faith; General Liability.

*(This Listing Continued)*

**MARK M. STEWART,** born St. Louis, Missouri, August 19, 1953; admitted to bar, 1981, Missouri; 1982, Illinois; 1984, California. *Education:* Emerson College (B.S., cum laude, 1977); St. Louis University (J.D., cum laude, 1981). Gold Key; Delta Theta Phi. Member, St. Louis University Law Journal, 1979-1981. *Member:* The Missouri Bar; State Bar of California; Association of Southern California Defense Counsel. *PRACTICE AREAS:* Medical Malpractice.

**BRADLEY J. MCGIRR,** born Los Angeles, California, July 28, 1956; admitted to bar, 1986, California and U.S. District Court, Central District of California. *Education:* Cypress College (A.A., 1980); California State University at Fullerton (B.A., 1982); Western State University College of Law (J.D., 1985). Recipient, American Jurisprudence Award. Member, Editorial Board, Western State University Law Review, 1984-1985. *Member:* Orange County, Los Angeles County and American Bar Associations; State Bar of California; Association of Southern California Defense Counsel. (Resident, Santa Ana Office). *REPORTED CASES:* Westhart v. Mule, 213 Cal. App 3d 542, 261 Cal. Rept. 640 (1989). *PRACTICE AREAS:* Medical Malpractice; Personal Injury; Insurance Bad Faith; Health Insurance Industry.

**SYDNEY LA BRANCHE MERRITT,** born New Orleans, Louisiana; admitted to bar, 1985, California. *Education:* University of Southern California (B.S., 1965); University of LaVerne (J.D., 1983). Moot Court Honors. Chief Justice, Moot Court. *Member:* Los Angeles County Bar Association; State Bar of California; Association of Southern California Defense Counsel; Langston Bar Association. *LANGUAGES:* Spanish. *PRACTICE AREAS:* Medical Malpractice.

**MARK S. RADER,** born Columbus, Ohio, April 15, 1944; admitted to bar, 1975, California and U.S. District Court, Central District of California; 1981, U.S. Court of Appeals, Ninth Circuit; 1990, U.S. District Court, Eastern District of California. *Education:* Williams College; University of California at Irvine (B.S., 1972); University of Southern California (J.D., 1975). *Member:* American Association for the Advancement of Science; American Board of Trial Advocates (Associate). [1st Lt., USMC, 1966-1970]. (Resident, Riverside Office). *PRACTICE AREAS:* Medical Malpractice Defense; Wrongful Termination Defense.

**MICHAEL R. PACKER,** born Los Angeles, California, October 20, 1951; admitted to bar, 1976, California; 1978, U.S. Court of Appeals, Ninth Circuit. *Education:* University of California at Los Angeles (B.A., 1973); Pepperdine University (J.D., 1976). Member, National Moot Court Team. Member, Moot Court Honor Board, 1975-1976. Judge Pro Tem, Orange County Superior Court, 1982—. Member, Southern California Defense Panel, 1987—. Arbitrator, Orange County Superior Court Personal Injury Panel, 1981—. *Member:* Orange County and American Bar Associations; State Bar of California; Orange County Trial Lawyers Association; Defense Research Institute; Association of Southern California Defense Counsel; American Board of Trial Advocates; Orange County Medical Association (Member, Liaison Committee). (Resident, Santa Ana Office). *PRACTICE AREAS:* Medical Malpractice Defense.

---

**PETER R. BING,** born Berwyn, Illinois, August 13, 1954; admitted to bar, 1979, California. *Education:* Northwestern University (B.A., 1976); University of Southern California (J.D., 1979). *Member:* Los Angeles County and American Bar Associations; State Bar of California; Association of Southern California Defense Counsel. *PRACTICE AREAS:* Product Liability; General Liability; Construction Defect.

**LARRY P. NATHENSON,** born Los Angeles, California, February 10, 1958; admitted to bar, 1982, California and U.S. District Court, Central District of California; 1985, U.S. Court of Appeals, Ninth Circuit. *Education:* Occidental College (A.B., 1979); University of California at Los Angeles (J.D., 1982). Member: Order of the Coif; Moot Court Honors Program. *Member:* Los Angeles County Bar Association; State Bar of California. *PRACTICE AREAS:* Insurance Coverage; Bad Faith Litigation.

**DONALD R. BECK,** born Salida, Colorado, November 15, 1940; admitted to bar, 1971, California. *Education:* California State University at Northridge (B.A., 1965); Southwestern University (J.D., 1971). Arbitrator, Orange County, California. *Member:* Los Angeles County, Orange County and American Bar Associations; The State Bar of California; American Board of Trial Advocates (Advocate). (Resident, Santa Ana Office). *PRACTICE AREAS:* General Liability.

**DAVID J. OZERAN,** born Chicago, Illinois, June 10, 1962; admitted to bar, 1988, California. *Education:* University of California at Los Angeles (B.A., cum laude, 1984); University of California at Davis (J.D., 1988). Phi
*(This Listing Continued)*

Delta Phi. Arbitrator, Los Angeles County Superior Court. *Member:* State Bar of California. *PRACTICE AREAS:* General Liability; Medical Malpractice.

**MARK B. GUTERMAN,** born Los Angeles, California, September 4, 1962; admitted to bar, 1988, California and U.S. District Court, Central District of California. *Education:* San Diego State University (B.A., 1984); Pepperdine University (J.D., 1988). *Member:* Los Angeles County Bar Association; State Bar of California. *PRACTICE AREAS:* Medical Malpractice.

**TERRY A. WOODWARD,** born Alameda, California, May 14, 1961; admitted to bar, 1989, California; 1991, U.S. District Court, Central District of California and U.S. Court of Appeals, Ninth Circuit. *Education:* Scripps College (B.A., 1983); Loyola Law School, Los Angeles (J.D., 1987). Recipient, American Jurisprudence Award in Trial Advocacy. Who's Who Among American College and Universities, 1983; Who's Who Among Rising Young Americans, 1992. *Member:* Los Angeles County and American Bar Associations; State Bar of California; Association of Southern California Defense Counsel. (Resident, Santa Ana Office). *LANGUAGES:* French. *PRACTICE AREAS:* Medical Malpractice.

**STEPHEN C. DREHER,** born Ann Arbor, Michigan, February 23, 1951; admitted to bar, 1987, California. *Education:* University of California at Los Angeles (B.S.N., 1976); Western State School of Law (J.D., 1986). Registered Nurse, California, 1976. *Member:* Orange County and American Bar Associations; State Bar of California. (Resident, Santa Ana Office). *PRACTICE AREAS:* Medical Malpractice.

**TATIANA M. SCHULTZ,** born Washington, D.C., June 8, 1965; admitted to bar, 1989, California. *Education:* University of Southern California (B.A., Political Science, 1986); Pepperdine University (J.D., 1989). Recipient, American Jurisprudence Award, Trial Practice, 1989. *Member:* Los Angeles County Bar Association; State Bar of California; Association of Southern California Defense Counsel; Association of Northern California Defense Counsel. (Resident, San Francisco Office). *PRACTICE AREAS:* General Liability; Medical Malpractice.

**PETER E. THEOPHILOS,** born New York, N.Y., July 22, 1948; admitted to bar, 1989, California and U.S. District Court, Northern District of California. *Education:* Hellenic University, Holy Cross Seminary; San Francisco Law School (J.D., 1989). Delta Theta Phi. Contributing Editor, "Has Mandatory Continuing Legal Education for California Attorneys Come of Age," San Francisco Law School Legal Commentary, 1988-1989. *Member:* State Bar of California; American Bar Association; Hellenic Law Society; Association of Defense Counsel of Northern California. (Resident, San Francisco Office). *LANGUAGES:* Greek and French. *REPORTED CASES:* Kilpatrick v. Superior Court, (1991) 226 Cal. App. 3d. 855; 177 Cal Rept. 230; Perkins v. Timothy Howard (1991) 232 Cal. App. 3d 708; 229 Cal. Rept. 764. *PRACTICE AREAS:* Medical Malpractice; Products Liability; General Civil Litigation.

**DEBORAH A. COWLEY,** born New York, N.Y., May 13, 1963; admitted to bar, 1989, California. *Education:* Niagara University (B.A., 1985); Whittier School of Law (J.D., 1988). Member, Women Executives of America, 1990. *Member:* Beverly Hills, Los Angeles County and American (Member, Sections on: Entertainment and Sports, 1987-1988; Family Law, 1987-1988) Bar Associations; Association of Southern California Defense Counsel; State Bar of California. *PRACTICE AREAS:* Medical Malpractice.

**KENT T. BRANDMEYER,** born Santa Monica, California, June 10, 1963; admitted to bar, 1989, California, U.S. District Court, Central District of California and U.S. Court of Appeals, 9th Circuit. *Education:* Loyola Marymount University (B.A., 1985; J.D., 1988). Judicial Extern to the Honorable James M. Ideman, U.S. District Court Judge. *Member:* Los Angeles County Bar Association; State Bar of California. *PRACTICE AREAS:* Medical Malpractice.

**GARRY O. MOSES,** born Denver, Colorado, January 8, 1955; admitted to bar, 1989, California. *Education:* University of Southern California (B.A., 1977); Antelope Valley College (A.S.N., 1982); Southwestern University (J.D., 1988). *Member:* State Bar of California. *PRACTICE AREAS:* Medical Malpractice.

**JEFFERY R. ERICKSON,** born Ottawa, Ontario, Canada, August 22, 1961; admitted to bar, 1988, California. *Education:* Brigham Young University (B.A., 1985); Southwestern University (J.D., 1988). Listed Who's Who of Young Lawyers of America. Ecclesiastical Representative, France, Paris Mission; Church of Jesus Christ of Latter Day Saints. *Member:* State Bar of California. (Resident, Riverside Office). *LANGUAGES:* French. *PRACTICE AREAS:* Medical Malpractice.
*(This Listing Continued)*

## LA FOLLETTE, JOHNSON, DE HAAS, FESLER & AMES,
*A PROFESSIONAL CORPORATION, Los Angeles—Continued*

**MICHAEL J. O'CONNOR,** born Niagara Falls, New York, September 22, 1953; admitted to bar, 1979, California and U.S. District Court, Central District of California. *Education:* University of Notre Dame (A.B., 1975); Duke University (J.D., 1978). *Member:* Los Angeles County and American Bar Associations; State Bar of California; Association of Southern California Defense Counsel. *PRACTICE AREAS:* General Liability; Medical Malpractice.

**ELIZABETH ANNE SCHERER,** born Charleston, South Carolina, August 29, 1955; admitted to bar, 1986, California; 1987, U.S. Court of Appeals, Ninth Circuit and U.S. District Court, Central District of California. *Education:* Santa Ana College (A.A., 1982); Western State University (B.S.L., 1984; J.D., 1985). Western State University Law Review, 1984-1985. Author: Case Comment, "Bartling v. Superior Court," 12 W. St. U.L. Rev., 1985. *Member:* Orange County and American Bar Associations; State Bar of California. (Resident, Santa Ana Office). *PRACTICE AREAS:* General Liability; Medical Malpractice.

**HUGH R. BURNS,** born Beaumont, Texas, 1962; admitted to bar, 1990, California and U.S. District Court, Central District of California. *Education:* Brigham Young University (B.A., 1987); Southwestern University School of Law (J.D., 1990). Member, Southwestern University School of Law, Law Review. Extern, Honorable Judge Ronald S. Lew, U.S. District Court, 1989. *Member:* State Bar of California; Association of Southern California Defense Counsel. *LANGUAGES:* Spanish. *PRACTICE AREAS:* General Liability; Medical Malpractice.

**STEPHEN K. HIURA,** born Inglewood, California, September 14, 1962; admitted to bar, 1990, California. *Education:* California State University at Los Angeles (B.S., 1986); Southwestern University School of Law (J.D., 1990). Delta Theta Phi. *Member:* Los Angeles County Bar Association; State Bar of California; Japanese-American Bar Association. *PRACTICE AREAS:* General Liability; Medical Malpractice.

**JAMES G. WOLD,** born Redmond, Washington, August 16, 1965; admitted to bar, 1990, California; 1991, U.S. District Court, Central District of California. *Education:* University of Southern California (B.A., 1987); Pepperdine University (J.D., 1990). *Member:* State Bar of California; Association of Southern California Defense Counsel. *PRACTICE AREAS:* Medical Malpractice; General Liability.

**EILEEN S. LEMMON,** born Pittsburgh, Pennsylvania, June 19, 1941; admitted to bar, 1988, California; 1989, U.S. District Court, Southern District of California. *Education:* Duquesne University (B.S., 1963); Loma Linda University (M.S., 1978); Loyola Law School (J.D., 1987). Member, Scott Moot Court Honors Board. Registered Nurse, California, 1963—. Listed, 1993 Who's Who In American Nursing. *Member:* San Bernardino County Bar Association (Member, Medical-Legal Committee); State Bar of California; Defense Research Institute; American Association of Nurse Attorneys; California Nurses Association. (Resident, Riverside Office). *PRACTICE AREAS:* Medical Malpractice.

**DAVID M. WRIGHT,** born Los Angeles, California, March 14, 1958; admitted to bar, 1986, California and U.S. District Court, Central District of California. *Education:* California Polytechnic State University (B.A., 1981); Southwestern University School of Law (J.D., 1986). Recipient, American Jurisprudence Award in Civil Procedure. Oralist, Moot Court Honors Board. *Member:* State Bar of California; Association of Southern California Defense Counsel. *PRACTICE AREAS:* Medical Malpractice.

**LARRY E. WHITE,** born Pasadena, California, May 16, 1956; admitted to bar, 1984, California; 1985, U.S. District Court, Central District of California. *Education:* Citrus Community College (A.A., 1976); California State University at Fullerton (B.A., 1978); University of LaVerne (J.D., 1984). *Member:* Riverside County and Los Angeles County Bar Associations; The State Bar of California; Riverside Barristers; Association of Southern California Defense Counsel. (Resident, Riverside Office). *PRACTICE AREAS:* Personal Injury Defense Law; Medical Malpractice Law.

**MICHELLE McCOY WOLFE,** born Ventura, California, March 19, 1964; admitted to bar, 1991, California. *Education:* University of California at Santa Barbara (B.A., Classics, 1987); Southwestern University School of Law (J.D., 1991). Phi Alpha Delta. Recipient, American Jurisprudence Award for Forensic Evidence. *Member:* State Bar of California; Association of Southern California Defense Counsel; Women Lawyers Association of Los Angeles; California Lawyers for the Arts. *PRACTICE AREAS:* General Liability; Medical Malpractice.

**WILLIAM T. GRAY,** born Fort Kit Carson, Colorado, October 1, 1956; admitted to bar, 1989, California; 1992, U.S. District Court, Central District of California and U.S. Court of Military Appeals; 1993, U.S. Supreme Court. *Education:* Saddleback College (A.A., 1985); University of Puget Sound; Western State University (B.S., 1986; J.D., 1987). *Member:* Orange County, San Diego County and American Bar Associations. [With USAF, 1974-1975; USMC, 1977; USAFR, 1975-1977]. (Resident, Santa Ana Office). *PRACTICE AREAS:* General Liability.

**DANIEL D. SORENSON,** born Seattle, Washington, September 6, 1963; admitted to bar, 1990, California. *Education:* Brigham Young University (B.S., 1987; J.D., 1990). Phi Delta Phi. *Member:* Los Angeles County Bar Association; State Bar of California; Association of Southern California Defense Counsel. (Resident, Riverside Office). *LANGUAGES:* Portuguese. *PRACTICE AREAS:* Civil Litigation.

**JOANNE ROSENDIN,** born San Jose, California, February 15, 1956; admitted to bar, 1985, California. *Education:* University of California at Davis (B.A., 1978); University of San Francisco (J.D., 1985). Recipient, National Moot Court Award, Best Oral Advocate, 1985. *Member:* Bar Association of San Francisco; State Bar of California; American Bar Association; Lawyers Club of San Francisco. (Resident, San Francisco Office). *PRACTICE AREAS:* General Liability.

**HENRY P. CANVEL,** born Los Angeles, California, October 25, 1960; admitted to bar, 1989, California. *Education:* University of California at Berkeley (B.S., summa cum laude, 1984); University of California at Hastings (J.D., 1988). *Member:* State Bar of California. (Resident, San Francisco Office). *LANGUAGES:* Spanish and French. *PRACTICE AREAS:* General Liability.

**JAY B. LAKE,** born Los Angeles, California, May 24, 1960; admitted to bar, 1988, California. *Education:* Santa Monica College (A.A., 1980); University of California at Los Angeles (B.A., 1982); Loyola Law School at Los Angeles (J.D., 1986). Author: "Copyright Protection of Video Games: Pac-Man and Galaxian Granted Extended Play," 5 Loy. Ent. L.J. 143 (1985); " A Joint Venture: Be Careful - You May Have Created One," 6 Loy. Ent. L.J. 191 (1986). *Member:* Langston and Los Angeles County Bar Associations; State Bar of California; Southern California Defense Counsel; Black Women Lawyers Association. *PRACTICE AREAS:* Medical Malpractice Defense.

**ERIN L. MUELLENBERG,** born Whittier, California, January 6, 1954; admitted to bar, 1989, California. *Education:* Western State University (B.S.L., 1988; J.D., with honors, 1988). Member, Western State University Law Review, 1987-1988. *Member:* Los Angeles County Bar Association; State Bar of California; National Health Lawyers Association. (Resident, Riverside Office). *PRACTICE AREAS:* Medical Malpractice; Health Care; External Peer Review.

**PHYLLIS M. WINSTON,** born New York, N.Y., July 13, 1949; admitted to bar, 1987, New York; 1992, California and U.S. District Court, Central District of California. *Education:* Kings County Hospital Center School of Nursing (R.N., 1970); St. Francis College (B.S., 1984); St. John's University (J.D., 1987). Registered Nurse: New York, 1970; California, 1992. *Member:* New York State Bar Association; State Bar of California; California Trial Lawyers Association; Los Angeles Trial Lawyers Association. (Resident, Riverside Office). *PRACTICE AREAS:* Medical Malpractice Defense.

**JOHN CALFEE MULVANA,** born Bakersfield, California, July 25, 1952; admitted to bar, 1980, California; 1981, U.S. District Court, Central District of California; 1986, U.S. District Court, Southern District of California. *Education:* University of California at Davis (A.B., 1975); Western State University (J.D., with honors, 1980). Recipient, American Jurisprudence Award. Member, Editorial Board, Western State Law Review, 1978-1980. Author: "Comatose Conservatee-Restrictions of Legal Capacity-Substance or Procedure," Western State University Law Review, 1980. Arbitrator, Orange County Superior Court Arbitration Panel, 1986—. *Member:* Orange County Bar Association; State Bar of California. (Resident, Santa Ana Office). *PRACTICE AREAS:* Professional Negligence - Medical Malpractice.

**DAVID L. BELL,** born Ponca City, Oklahoma, April 25, 1953; admitted to bar, 1990, California; 1991, U.S. District Court, Central District of California and U.S. Court of Appeals, Ninth Circuit; 1993, U.S. District Court, Eastern District of California. *Education:* University of Oklahoma (B.S., Architecture, 1977); Southwestern University (J.D., 1990). Associate Editor, Adelphi Law Journal, 1989-1990. Copyright Holder of "Brief-It; Legal Studies Software," Copyright 1992. *Member:* State Bar of California.

*(This Listing Continued)*

**BRIAN T. CHU,** born Los Angeles, California, September 3, 1962; admitted to bar, 1992, California. *Education:* University of California (B.A., 1985); University of San Diego (J.D., 1992). Phi Delta Phi. Senior Editor, J. Contemp. Legal Issues, 1991-1992. Secretary, International Law Society, 1990-1992. Author: Note, "The United States and UNCLOS III in the New Decade: Is it Time for a Compromise?" 4 J. Contemp. Legal Issues, 253. Judicial Extern, California Supreme Court, September, 1992-December, 1992. *Member:* State Bar of California. (Resident, Santa Ana Office). ***PRACTICE AREAS:*** General Liability.

**JOHN HAMMOND,** born Grand Rapids, Michigan, October 6, 1955; admitted to bar, 1992, California. *Education:* Oakland University (B.A., 1976); Loyola University (J.D., 1992). *Member:* State Bar of California. ***PRACTICE AREAS:*** Medical Malpractice.

**DAVID PEIM,** born Brooklyn, New York, November 25, 1957; admitted to bar, 1993, California. *Education:* State University of New York at New Paltz (B.A., 1980); University of Southern California (Ph.D., 1986); Loyola Law School (J.D., 1993). Order of the Coif. Managing Editor, 1992-1993 and Staff Member, 1991-1992, Entertainment Law Journal. *Member:* State Bar of California; California Defense Counsel. ***PRACTICE AREAS:*** General Liability; Banking Law; Product Liability.

**DANIEL V. KOHLS,** born Yreka, California, March 31, 1968; admitted to bar, 1993, California. *Education:* Brown University; University of California at Berkeley (A.B., 1990); University of the Pacific, McGeorge School of Law (J.D., 1993). *Member:* State Bar of California. (Resident, San Francisco Office). ***PRACTICE AREAS:*** Insurance Defense.

**JOEL E. D. ODOU,** born Montebello, California, February 24, 1967; admitted to bar, 1993, California. *Education:* University of Southern California (B.A., 1990); Whittier Law School (J.D., 1993). Solicitations Editor, Whittier Law Review. Chapter Vice President, The Association of Trial Lawyers of America. *Member:* State Bar of California. ***PRACTICE AREAS:*** Insurance Defense Litigation.

**HENRY M. SU,** born Taipei, Taiwan, November 15, 1969; admitted to bar, 1994, California. *Education:* University of California at Davis (B.A., 1992); Southwestern University School of Law (J.D., 1994). *Member:* State Bar of California. *LANGUAGES:* Chinese. ***PRACTICE AREAS:*** Construction Liability.

**RICHARD K. KAY,** born Los Angeles, California, June 28, 1965; admitted to bar, 1992, California, U.S. District Court, Central District of California and U.S. Court of Appeals, Ninth Circuit; 1995 Colorado. *Education:* University of California at Los Angeles (B.A., magna cum laude, 1989); University of Southern California Law Center (J.D., 1992). Senior Articles Editor, Interdisciplinary Journal and Computer Law Journal. *Member:* State Bar of California. ***PRACTICE AREAS:*** Medical Malpractice.

**ANNETTE A. PELTON,** born Covina, California, January 26, 1966; admitted to bar, 1993, California. *Education:* University of Southern California (B.A., 1988); Southwestern University (J.D., 1992). *Member:* State Bar of California. ***PRACTICE AREAS:*** Litigation.

**BRAD D. CITRON,** born Peoria, Illinois, November 28, 1956; admitted to bar, 1985, California and U.S. District Court, Central District of California; 1987, U.S. District Court, Northern and Southern Districts of California and U.S. Court of Appeals, Ninth Circuit. *Education:* Florida State University (B.S., 1978); Western State University (J.D., 1982). Nu Beta Epsilon. *Member:* Los Angeles County and American Bar Associations; State Bar of California. ***PRACTICE AREAS:*** General Liability.

**CAREN R. WEAKLEY,** born Philadelphia, Pennsylvania, September 18, 1968; admitted to bar, 1993, California. *Education:* University of California at Los Angeles (B.A., 1990); Loyola Law School (J.D., 1993). St. Thomas Moore Law Honor Society. Member, Entertainment Law Journal. *Member:* State Bar of California; Association of Southern California Defense Counsel. ***PRACTICE AREAS:*** Medical Malpractice.

**KEVIN J. PRICE,** born Pasadena, California, November 26, 1969; admitted to bar, 1995, California. *Education:* Loyola Marymount University (B.A., 1992); Loyola Law School (J.D., 1995). *Member:* State Bar of California. ***PRACTICE AREAS:*** Insurance Defense; General Product Liability.

**AREZOU KHONSARI,** born St. Louis, Missouri, July 20, 1967; admitted to bar, 1995, California. *Education:* Scripps College (B.A., 1988); University of Southern California (M.A., 1991); Whittier College School of Law (J.D., 1995). *Member:* State Bar of California. *LANGUAGES:* Persian, French. ***PRACTICE AREAS:*** Medical Malpractice; General Liability.

*(This Listing Continued)*

**JOHN BEALL,** born Orange, California, November 24, 1964; admitted to bar, 1995, California. *Education:* University of California, Los Angeles (B.A., 1987); McGeorge School of Law (J.D., 1995). *Member:* State Bar of California. (Resident, Santa Ana Office). ***PRACTICE AREAS:*** Medical Malpractice Defense.

**WALTER H. KUBELUN,** born Oakland, California, March 9, 1963; admitted to bar, 1991, California. *Education:* California State University, Northridge (B.A., magna cum laude, 1985); University of San Diego (J.D., 1991). Beta Gamma Sigma. Recipient, American Jurisprudence Award, Wills and Trusts. *Member:* State Bar of California; Southern California Defense Counsel. ***PRACTICE AREAS:*** Medical Malpractice Litigation; Insurance Defense.

**THOMAS S. ALCH,** born Minneapolis, Minnesota, January 9, 1963; admitted to bar, 1988, California; 1991, U.S. District Court, Central and Southern Districts of California and U.S. Court of Appeals, Ninth Circuit. *Education:* University of California at Los Angeles (B.A., 1985); Loyola University School of Law (J.D., 1988). *Member:* State Bar of California; American Bar Association; Association of Southern California Defense Counsel.

**E. CHRISTINE VARTANIAN,** born San Francisco, California, August 14, 1970; admitted to bar, 1996, California. *Education:* University of California (B.S. in Civil Engineering, 1992); Western State University (LL.B., 1995). *Member:* Orange County Bar Association; State Bar of California; Orange County Barristers. (Resident, Santa Ana Office).

**KRISTI A. SCHIFRIN,** born Los Angeles, California, November 3, 1969; admitted to bar, 1996, California. *Education:* University of California, Santa Barbara (B.A., 1991); University of California, Hastings College of the Law (J.D., 1996). Phi Alpha Delta. *Member:* State Bar of California. (Resident, San Francisco Office).

**MARY KATHERINE DOHERTY,** born Washington, D.C., July 7, 1958; admitted to bar, 1989, California and U.S. District Court, Central District of California. *Education:* University of California at Los Angeles (B.A., 1980); Loyola Law School, Los Angeles (J.D., 1989). *Member:* State Bar of California. ***PRACTICE AREAS:*** Medical Malpractice.

REPRESENTATIVE CLIENTS: Ohio Casualty Insurance Co.; AETNA Casualty Insurance Co.; Twentieth Century Insurance Co.; Kaiser Foundation Health Plan; Cooperative of America Physicians (CAP); Crawford & Company; Interinsurance Exchange of Automobile Club of Southern California.
REFERENCES: Union Bank (4th & Figueroa Branch, Los Angeles); California Federal Savings and Loan (Vermont & Beverly Branch, Los Angeles).

## LAGERLOF, SENECAL, BRADLEY & SWIFT, LLP

### LOS ANGELES, CALIFORNIA

(See Pasadena)

*General Civil, Trial and Appellate Practice in all State and Federal Courts and Administrative Agencies. Corporation, Antitrust, Labor, Tax, Real Estate, Probate, Trust, Estate Planning, Water, Natural Resources, and Municipal Law.*

## LAMB & BAUTE

601 SOUTH FIGUEROA STREET, SUITE 4100
### LOS ANGELES, CALIFORNIA 90017
Telephone: 213-630-5000
Fax: 213-683-1225

*General Practice.*

FIRM PROFILE: *The Firm handles a wide range of transactional matters, commercial litigation and trial work for corporate and entrepreneurial clients in the following areas: General Corporate, Labor and Employment Litigation, Antitrust, Intellectual Property, Real Property, Oil & Gas, Workouts, Reorganizations and Creditor Rights, Partnership and Corporate Litigation, Entertainment and General Contract and Tort Litigation, including Trials, Arbitrations and Appellate Litigation in all State and Federal Courts.*

*Lamb & Baute is a full service law firm committed to creative and cost-effective solutions to legal problems. Its attorneys developed their trial and transactional skills at major law firms, but strongly preferred the atmosphere, freedom and flexibility inherent in owning a smaller law firm.*

**MARK D. BAUTE,** born Seattle, Washington, July, 18, 1961; admitted to bar, 1986, California. *Education:* University of Washington (B.A., cum

*(This Listing Continued)*

*LAMB & BAUTE, Los Angeles—Continued*

laude, 1983); University of California at Los Angeles (J.D., 1986). Olin Fellow in Law and Economics. Member, Los Angeles County District Attorney Trial Attorney Program. *Member:* State Bar of California (Member, Sections on: Antitrust; Labor & Employment; Litigation); Los Angeles County (Member, Sections on: Antitrust; Litigation) and American (Member, Sections on: Antitrust Law; Litigation; Entertainment and Sports Industries Forum) Bar Associations; Association of Trial Lawyers of America. *PRACTICE AREAS:* Complex Business Litigation; Labor; Employment; Real Estate; Antitrust; Trade Secrets; Unfair Competition.

**DAVID P. CROCHETIERE,** born Quebec City, Quebec, Canada, March 22, 1958; admitted to bar, 1984, California. *Education:* McGill University (B.A., First Class Honors, 1980); University of Michigan (J.D., cum laude, 1984). *Member:* Los Angeles County (Member, Intellectual Property Law Section) and American Bar Associations; State Bar of California. *PRACTICE AREAS:* Business Litigation; Copyright, Trademark and Unfair Competition; Real Estate; Appellate; Entertainment Law.

**KEVIN J. LAMB,** born Detroit, Michigan, December 2, 1960; admitted to bar, 1986, California. *Education:* University of Michigan (B.A., with honors, 1983; J.D., cum laude, 1986). *Member:* Los Angeles County and American Bar Associations; State Bar of California. *PRACTICE AREAS:* Real Property Law; Oil and Gas; Work-Outs; Reorganizations.

**KARL J. LOTT,** born Landour, India, October 11, 1960; admitted to bar, 1990, California. *Education:* College of William & Mary (B.A., 1982); Columbia University (M.I.A., 1984); University of California, Los Angeles (J.D., 1990). *Member:* Los Angeles County and American Bar Associations; State Bar of California. *PRACTICE AREAS:* Real Property Law; Entertainment Law.

**DALE M. STRUMAN,** born Los Angeles, California, February 10, 1954; admitted to bar, 1989, California, U.S. Court of Appeals, Ninth Circuit and U.S. District Court, Central and Southern Districts of California. *Education:* University of California, Los Angeles; California State University of San Diego (B.A., 1975; Teaching Credential, 1976); Southwestern University (J.D., 1989). Exceptional Achievement Award, Legal Writing. *Member:* Los Angeles County and American Bar Associations; State Bar of California.

## LANE POWELL SPEARS LUBERSKY LLP

A Partnership including Professional Corporations

**333 SOUTH HOPE STREET, SUITE 2400**
**LOS ANGELES, CALIFORNIA 90071**

Telephone: 213-680-1010
FAX: 213-680-1784

*Other Offices at:* Seattle, Washington; Portland, Oregon; Anchorage, Alaska; San Francisco, California; Olympia and Mount Vernon, Washington; Fairbanks, Alaska; London, England.

*Admiralty, Alternative Dispute Resolution, Antitrust, Appellate Practice, Aviation, Banking and Financial Institutions, Bankruptcy and Reorganizations, Construction, Employment Law, Corporate Finance, Emerging Companies, Employee Benefits, Environmental, Forest Products and Natural Resources, Hospital and Healthcare, Immigration, Insurance, Intellectual Property and Computer Law, International Transactions, Litigation, Public Finance, Real Estate and Land Use, Retailing, Securities, Taxation, Toxic Torts, Transportation, Trusts and Estates, White Collar Criminal Law.*

### MEMBERS OF FIRM

**ALLAN M. BOWER,** born Oak Park, Illinois, May 21, 1936; admitted to bar, 1969, California, U.S. Supreme Court and U.S. Tax Court; 1979, U.S. Claims Court. *Education:* Vanderbilt University; State University of Iowa (B.S., 1962); University of Miami (J.D., 1968). *Member:* Santa Monica Municipal Court Judge Pro Tem Panel, 1979-1980; Panel of Arbitrators, American Arbitration Association. *Member:* California Trial Lawyers Association; The Association of Trial Lawyers of America; American Judicature Society; Lawyer Pilots Bar Association. *PRACTICE AREAS:* Aviation Law; Product Liability Law; Medical Malpractice; Insurance; Toxic Torts.

**EDITH N. DINNEEN,** born Springfield, Massachusetts, January 15, 1948; admitted to bar, 1974, New York; 1975, U.S. Court of Appeals, Second Circuit; 1979, U.S. Supreme Court; 1988, Florida; 1989, California, U.S. Court of Appeals, Ninth Circuit. *Education:* Smith College (A.B., 1969); Boston College (J.D., 1973). Member, 1971-1972 and Articles Editor, 1972-1973, Boston College Law Review. *PRACTICE AREAS:* Employment Law, Litigation and Communications Law.

**JOHN J. GEARY, JR.,** born Syracuse, New York, December 31, 1942; admitted to bar, 1974, California; 1976, U.S. Tax Court; 1978, U.S. Supreme Court. *Education:* University of Denver (B.A., 1968); University of Washington; Southwestern University (J.D., 1974). *Member:* American Board of Trial Advocates. *PRACTICE AREAS:* Litigation; Toxic Torts; Products Liability; Personal Injury; Construction Defects; Maritime.

**KATHRYN R. JANSSEN,** born Portland, Oregon, August 26, 1953; admitted to bar, 1981, Oregon; 1991, California. *Education:* Stanford University (B.A., 1975); Lewis & Clark/Northwestern School of Law (J.D., 1981). Member, Moot Court Board, 1980-1981. *Member:* Oregon Association of Defense Counsel; Association of Southern California Defense Counsel. *PRACTICE AREAS:* Products Liability Law; Employment Law; Toxic Tort Law.

**LAURENCE F. JANSSEN,** born San Francisco, California, January 14, 1943; admitted to bar, 1967, Oregon; U.S. Court of Appeals, Ninth Circuit; 1990, California. *Education:* Dartmouth College and University of Oregon (B.S., 1965); University of Oregon (J.D., 1967). Phi Delta Phi. Member, Board of Editors, Oregon Law Review, 1966-1967. *PRACTICE AREAS:* Litigation; Toxic Torts; Products Liability.

**RUTH D. KAHN,** born Chicago, Illinois, May 6, 1960; admitted to bar, 1985, California; 1989, District of Columbia and Hawaii. *Education:* University of Colorado (B.S., 1982); Case Western Reserve University (J.D., 1985). Chair, Childrens Rights Committee; Member, Litigation Section; Court Rule and Procedures Committee, Member, Barristers Executive Committee. *PRACTICE AREAS:* Civil Litigation, Toxic Torts, Products Liability.

**MATTHEW P. KESNER,** born Sewickley, Pennsylvania, October 17, 1960; admitted to bar, 1985, California; U.S. Court of Appeals, Ninth Circuit. *Education:* San Diego State University (B.S., 1980); University of San Diego School of Law (J.D., 1985). *Member:* Federal Bar Association (Member, Section of Litigation Committee on Insurance Coverage Litigation); Lawyer-Pilots Bar Association. *PRACTICE AREAS:* Insurance Coverage; Aviation Law; Product Liability Law.

**GEORGE J. KOELZER,** born Orange, New Jersey, 1938. admitted to bar, 1964, New Jersey; 1968, U.S. Supreme Court and U.S. Court of Appeals, Third Circuit; 1973, U.S. Tax Court; 1976, U.S. Court of Appeals, Second Circuit; 1977, U.S. Court of Appeals for the District of Columbia Circuit; 1978, District of Columbia and U.S. Court of Appeals, Fourth Circuit; 1980, New York; 1983, U.S. Court of Appeals, Fifth Circuit; 1993, California, U.S. Court of Appeals, Ninth Circuit, U.S. District Court, Northern, Central, Eastern and Southern Districts of California and U.S. Court of Appeals, Sixth Circuit. *Education:* Rutgers University (A.B., 1962; J.D., 1964). Assistant U.S. Attorney, District of New Jersey, 1966-1971. Adjunct Professor, Seton Hall University Law School, 1989-1992. Associate Editor, American Maritime Cases, 1985-1992. Delegate, Judicial Conference of the United States Court of Appeals for the Second Circuit, 1987, 1988, 1989. Permanent Member, Judicial Conference of the U.S. Court of Appeals for the Third Circuit, 1971—. Member, 1985-1988, Vice-Chairman, 1986 and Chairman, 1987, Lawyers Advisory Committee, U.S. Court of Appeals for the Third Circuit. Member, Lawyers Advisory Committee, 1984-1990 and District Court Ethics Committee, 1984-1990, U.S. District Court, District of New Jersey. Associate Editor, American Maritime Cases, 1985-1992. Adjunct Professor, Seton Hall University School of Law, 1989-1992. *Member:* American Bar Association (Member, Section of Litigation Council, 1985-1988; Division Director, 1982-1985, 1989-1990; Chairman, Admiralty and Maritime Litigation Committee, 1978-1992, 1990-1991; Liaison, ABA Standing Committee on Lawyer Competence, 1986—); The Maritime Law Association of the United States (Vice Chairman, 1991-1994; Chairman, 1994—, Committee on Maritime Fraud and Crime); Federal Bar Council; Defense Research Association (Chairman, 1982-1985, Admiralty Law Committee). Fellow, American Bar Foundation. *PRACTICE AREAS:* Admiralty; Insurance; Federal Trial and Appellate Practice. *Email:* koelzerg@lanepowell.com

**LAWRENCE P. RIFF,** born Cleveland, Ohio, October 31, 1955; admitted to bar, 1982, California; 1985, Oregon; 1987, Washington. *Education:* University of Michigan (B.A., high honors and highest distinction in History, 1978); University of Oregon (J.D., 1982). Associate Editor, Oregon Litigation Journal, 1989-1990. *Member:* National Association of Railroad Trial Counsel (Member, National Executive Committee); Association of Transportationers. *PRACTICE AREAS:* Chemical Products Liability; Railroad, Trucking and Transportation Law; Commercial Litigation; Insurance Defense.

*(This Listing Continued)*

**RUSSELL W. ROTEN,** born Warrensville, North Carolina, May 10, 1949; admitted to bar, 1977, North Carolina; 1990, Washington; 1991, District of Columbia; 1994, California and U.S. Court of Appeals, Ninth Circuit. *Education:* University of North Carolina (B.A., 1973; J.D., 1977). *PRACTICE AREAS:* International Practice; Business Law; Corporate Law; Commercial Litigation.

**CAROLYN J. SHIELDS,** born Erie, Pennsylvania, August 30, 1945; admitted to bar, 1983, New York; 1994, California. *Education:* Indiana University; University of Connecticut (J.D., 1981); Tulane University (LL.M., Admiralty, 1991). Recipient, American Jurisprudence Award in Constitutional Law. Editor-in-Chief, University of Connecticut Law Review, 1979. Clerk, Supreme Court of the State of Connecticut, 1981-1982. Visiting Assistant Professor: Indiana University School of Law, 1985-1986; Chase College of Law, 1986-1987. Associate, Maritime Law Association. *PRACTICE AREAS:* Maritime Law; Civil Litigation; Insurance; Products Liability. *Email:* shieldsc@lanepowell.com

**SIMON D. WRIGHT,** born Middlesbrough, England, March 9, 1964; admitted to bar, 1988, England and Wales as Solicitor; 1993, California. *Education:* University of Newcastle-Upon-Tyne, England (LL.B., with honors, 1985); College of Law, Lancaster Gate, London, England (Solicitors Finals, 1986). *PRACTICE AREAS:* Insurance Coverage; Insurance Defense; Maritime Law.

**ROBERT J. ZAPF,** born Rochester, New York, August 14, 1950; admitted to bar, 1976, New York and U.S. Court of Appeals, Second Circuit; 1981, U.S. Court of Appeals, Fifth Circuit; 1995, New Jersey and U.S. Court of International Trade (Not admitted in California). *Education:* Boston College (B.A., magna cum laude, 1972; J.D., 1975). Member, U.S. Delegation to IMO/UNCTAD Joint Intergovernmental Group of Experts on Maritime Liens and Mortgage and Related Subjects, Seventh Session on International Convention on Arrest of Sea-Going Ships, 1994. Member, U.S. Delegation to IMO/UNCTAD Joint Intergovernmental Group of Exports on Maritime Lines and Mortgages and Related Subjects, Eighth Session, 1995. *Member:* American Bar Association (Member, Sections on: International Law and Practice; Litigation (Chair, Admiralty and Maritime Litigation Committee, 1991-1994); Maritime Law Association of the United States (Member: Marine Finance Committee, Insolvency and Vessel Foreclosure Subcommittee, Practice and Procedure Committee; Chair, Practice and Procedure Committee, 1995—; Chair, Joint Ad Hoc Committee on OPA 1990 and Concursus, 1994). *PRACTICE AREAS:* Admiralty and Maritime; International Commercial Law; Commercial Litigation and Arbitration.

## ASSOCIATES

**DANIEL R. BLAKEY,** born York, Pennsylvania, February 5, 1960; admitted to bar, 1989, California and U.S. Court of Appeals, Ninth Circuit. *Education:* Williams College (B.A., 1982); Hastings College of the Law, University of California (J.D., 1989). Articles Editor, Comm/Ent, Hastings Journal of Communications and Entertainment Law, 1988-1989. *PRACTICE AREAS:* Toxic Tort Litigation; Products Liability; General Litigation.

**CELESTE V. DE PETRIS,** born Las Vegas, Nevada, September 23, 1966; admitted to bar, 1993, California. *Education:* Cleveland State University (B.A., 1989); Southwestern University (J.D., 1993). Recipient: American Jurisprudence Award in Legal Writing. Moot Court. Member, Southwestern University Law Review, 1992-1993.

**JOSHUA S. FORCE,** born Indianapolis, Indiana, February 15, 1966; admitted to bar, 1991, Texas and U.S. Court of Appeals, Fifth Circuit; 1992, Louisiana; 1995, California, U.S. Supreme Court and U.S. Court of Appeals, Ninth Circuit. *Education:* Haverford College (B.A., 1988); Harvard University (J.D., 1991). Phi Beta Kappa. Harvard International Law Journal, 1989-1991 (Recent Developments Editor, 1990-1991). Law Clerk, U.S. Court of Appeals, Fifth Circuit, 1991-1992. *Member:* Maritime Law Association of the United States. *PRACTICE AREAS:* Admiralty and Maritime Law; Insurance Law. *Email:* forcej@lanepowell.com

**ROBERT M. HUPE,** born Pomona, California, February 4, 1964; admitted to bar, 1989, California and U.S. Court of Appeals, Ninth Circuit; 1995, U.S. Supreme Court. *Education:* University of California at Los Angeles (B.S.A.E., cum laude, 1986); University of Virginia (J.D., 1989). Tau Beta Pi. *PRACTICE AREAS:* General Litigation; Toxic Torts; Products Liability.

**KENNETH W. LORD,** born Greenwich, Connecticut, December 3, 1965; admitted to bar, 1995, New York (Not admitted in California). *Education:* Bowdoin College (B.A., cum laude, 1989); Tulane University of

*(This Listing Continued)*

Louisiana (J.D., 1994). *PRACTICE AREAS:* Maritime Law; Insurance Coverage; Fidelity and Surety Bonds; Commercial Litigation.

**JO-ANN HORN MAYNARD,** born Long Branch, New Jersey, December 2, 1949; admitted to bar, 1974, New Jersey; 1975, Florida; 1979, U.S. Court of Appeals, Second, Fifth, Sixth, Seventh and Ninth Circuits; 1980, U.S. Court of Appeals, Fourth, Eighth and District of Columbia Circuits; 1982, U.S. Supreme Court; 1983, U.S. Court of Appeals, Tenth and Eleventh Circuits; 1987, California. *Education:* University of Rhode Island; George Washington University (B.B.A., 1971); University of Miami (J.D., 1974). Phi Delta Phi (Secretary, 1973-1974). Law Clerk, U.S. District Court of New Jersey, 1974-1975.

**MICHAEL M. MURATA,** born Lihue, Hawaii, January 10, 1961; admitted to bar, 1990, California. *Education:* Yale University (B.A., cum laude, 1983); New York University (J.D., 1990). *Member:* Japanese American Bar Association.

**CONSTANCE E. NORTON,** born Oakland, California, September 29, 1961; admitted to bar, 1990, California; 1992, District of Columbia; 1993, U.S. Court of Appeals, Ninth Circuit. *Education:* University of California at Los Angeles (B.A., 1983); Golden Gate University (J.D., with highest honors, 1989). Associate Editor, Golden Gate Law Review, 1989. *Member:* California Women Lawyers; Women Lawyers Association of Los Angeles. *PRACTICE AREAS:* Litigation.

**JAY E. SMITH,** born Columbus, Ohio, August 16, 1965; admitted to bar, 1992, California. *Education:* Bowling Green State University (B.S.B.A., cum laude, 1987); University of Southern California, Los Angeles (J.D., 1992). Member, Hale Moot Court Honors Program. *Member:* Los Angeles County Bar Association (Member, Litigation Section). *PRACTICE AREAS:* Litigation.

**LISA STEVENS,** born Los Angeles, California, October 7, 1968; admitted to bar, 1994, California. *Education:* Furman University (B.A., 1990); University of Southern California (J.D., 1993); Georgetown University Law Center (LL.M., in Advocacy, 1995). Georgetown University Law Center Graduate Fellow, 1993-1995.

**CYNTHIA T. SOLDWEDEL,** born Long Beach, California, September 24, 1963; admitted to bar, 1989, California. *Education:* Long Beach City College (A.A., 1983); University of California at Los Angeles (B.A., summa cum laude, 1986); Boalt Hall School of Law, University of California at Berkeley (J.D. 1989). Phi Beta Kappa; Moot Court Board. Recipient, Prosser Prize in American Legal History. *Member:* Los Angeles County Bar Association (Member, Litigation and Labor Sections). *PRACTICE AREAS:* Employment Law; Education Law.

**THOMAS H. VAN HORN,** born Oklahoma City, Oklahoma, August 26, 1963; admitted to bar, 1989, Texas; 1990, U.S. Court of Military Appeals (Not admitted in California). *Education:* University of North Texas (B.A., 1986); St. Mary's University of San Antonio (J.D., 1989); Tulane University (LL.M., in Admiralty Law With Distinction, 1995). Editor, Tulane Maritime Law Journal. Recipient: Navy Commendation Medal for Meritorious Professional Achievement form 1991-1994; Navy Achievement Medal for Meritorious Professional Achievement form 1990-1991. [U.S. Naval Reserve, JAGC, 1989—.]. *PRACTICE AREAS:* Litigation.

**PHILIP YOUNG,** born Vienna, Austria, August 30, 1967; admitted to bar, 1991, California. *Education:* University of Notre Dame (B.A., 1988); University of Minnesota (J.D., cum laude, 1991). Recipient, Law Student Achievement Award. Member, Los Angeles County Barristers. *PRACTICE AREAS:* Labor and Employment; Toxic Torts.

REPRESENTATIVE CLIENTS: Aetna Life Insurance Co.; Afognak Native Corp.; A.H. Lundberg Associates, Inc.; AIG Aviation, Inc.; American President Lines, Ltd.; AMOCO Corp.; Amtrak; Ashland Chemical; Associated Aviation Underwriters; Assurance Foreningen Skuld; AT & T; BP America; Broadmark Capital Corp.; Burns Bros., Inc.; The Callison Partnership, Ltd.; Capital Consultants Inc.; Cavenham Forest Industries; Chevron U.S.A. Inc.; CNA Insurance Co.; Confederation Life Insurance Co.; Coffee Bean International, Inc.; Connaught Laboratories, Inc.; Consolidated Freightways; Continental National American Group; Dean Witter Reynolds Inc.; Deep Sea Fisheries, Inc.; Diversified Marime; The Dow Chemical Co.; Dow Corning Corp.; Edmark Corp.; Epson Inc.; Exxon U.S.A.; Fred Hutchinson Cancer Research Center; Fred Meyer, Inc.; General Electric Capital Corp.; General Motors Corp.; Georgia-Pacific Corp.; Great West Casualty Corp.; Great Western Chemical Co.; GTE Mobilnet Inc.; Hampton Affiliates; The Hartford Insurance Group; Hoffman Construction; The Home Depot; The Hillhaven Corp.; Intel; Itogumi Construction Co., Ltd.; James River Corp.; Key Bank; Lexington Insurance Co.; Liberty Mutual Insurance Group; Lincoln National Life Insurance Co.; Litton Industries; Lloyds of London; Louisiana-Pacific Corp.; The Manufacturers Life Insurance Co.; Mitsui & Co., Ltd.; Norm Thompson Outfitters, Inc.; Northwest Natural Gas Co.; Nordstrom, Inc.; Pacific Coast Association of Pulp and Paper Manufacturers; Paine Webber Inc.; Pendleton Woolen Mills; Portland Brewing Co.; Prudential Insurance Company of America; Prudential Securities; Qual-Med Inc.; Roseberg Forest Resources; Royal Insurance Co.; Sears, Roebuck and

*(This Listing Continued)*

CALIFORNIA—LOS ANGELES

**LANE POWELL SPEARS LUBERSKY LLP,** Los Angeles—
*Continued*

Co.; Sequent Computers, Inc.; Shearson Lehman Brothers; Simpson Investment Company; Southern Pacific Transportation Co.; The Stanley Works; Texaco, Inc.; Times Mirror; The Toronto-Dominion Bank; Tri-county Metropolitan Transportation District; Trident Seafood Co.; Union Pacific Railroad Co.; United Parcel Service; Unocal Corp.; Washington State Physicians Insurance Assn.; Wells Fargo Bank; W.R. Grace & Co.; Weyerhaeuser Co.

(For complete biographical data on personnel at Anchorage, Fairbanks, Alaska, San Francisco, Portland, Oregon, Mt. Vernon, Olympia and Seattle, Washington and London, England, see Professional Biographies at those locations)

---

## LANG, TURLEY, NEVERS & PALAZZO

*A PROFESSIONAL LAW CORPORATION*

**LOS ANGELES, CALIFORNIA**

(See Westlake Village)

*General Corporate, Corporate Securities, Litigation, Franchise, Tax, Real Estate, Entertainment Law, Estate Planning and Probate.*

---

## LANGBERG, COHN & DROOZ

A Partnership including a Professional Corporation

**12100 WILSHIRE BOULEVARD
SUITE 1650
LOS ANGELES, CALIFORNIA 90025**
Telephone: 310-979-3200
Telecopier: 310-979-3220

*Libel and Slander, Entertainment Litigation, Intellectual Property Litigation, General Business Litigation, Real Estate Litigation.*

**BARRY B. LANGBERG, (A PROFESSIONAL CORPORATION),** born Baltimore, Maryland, November 24, 1942; admitted to bar, 1971, California and U.S. District Court, Central District of California; 1974, U.S. Supreme Court; 1976, U.S. Tax Court. *Education:* University of San Francisco (J.D., 1968). Professor of Law, Mid-Valley College of Law, 1971-1978. Professor of Law, Southwestern University School of Law, 1996. Judge Pro Tempore, Los Angeles Municipal Court. Author: "Valerie Harper vs. Lorimar: Entertainment Industry Customs on Trial," Los Angeles Lawyer, April, 1989. *Member:* State Bar of California; American Bar Association; The Association of Trial Lawyers of America. **REPORTED CASES:** Carol Burnett vs. National Enquirer, 144 Cal. App. 3d 991, 193 Cal. Rptr. 206 (1983). **PRACTICE AREAS:** Entertainment and the Arts; Litigation; Libel, Slander and Defamation.

**EILEEN M. COHN,** born New York, November, 20, 1953; admitted to bar, 1987, California and U.S. District Court, Central District of California. *Education:* Rutgers University (B.A., highest honors, 1975); University of California at Berkeley (M.A., 1980); Loyola Law School (J.D., 1986). Member, Scott Moot Court Honors Board. Extern Clerk to the Honorable Stephen Reinhardt, U.S. Court of Appeals, Ninth Circuit. Special Advisor to a Commissioner, Energy Commission, State of California, 1979-1981. Special Assistant to the Secretary of the Business and Transportation Agency, State of California, 1977-1979. *Member:* Los Angeles County and American Bar Associations; State Bar of California; Women Lawyers Association of Los Angeles. **PRACTICE AREAS:** General Business Litigation; Complex Business Litigation; Entertainment and the Arts; Government Regulations.

**DEBORAH DROOZ,** born Los Angeles, California, July 27, 1956; admitted to bar, 1986, California. *Education:* University of California at Los Angeles; Southwestern University (J.D., 1986). Recipient, American Jurisprudence Award in Remedies and in Constitutional Law. *Member:* State Bar of California. **REPORTED CASES:** Dangerfield v. Star 7 F. 3d 856 (1993). **PRACTICE AREAS:** Intellectual Property; Libel, Slander and Defamation; Litigation; Appellate Practice; Entertainment and the Arts.

**BETH F. DUMAS,** born Van Nuys, California, December 17, 1964; admitted to bar, 1990, California and U.S. District Court, Central District of California. *Education:* University of California at Los Angeles (B.A., cum laude, 1987); Hastings College of Law, University of California (J.D., 1990). Recipient: UCLA Chancellors Scholarship; American Jurisprudence Award for Legal Writing and Research. Executive Articles Editor, COMM/ENT, Hastings Communication and Entertainment Law Journal, 1989-

*(This Listing Continued)*

1990. Author: "The Functionality Doctrine in Trade Dress and Copyright Infringement Actions: A Call for Clarification," COMM/ENT, Hastings Communications and Entertainment Law Journal, Vol. 12:3. Member, Hollywood Women's Political Committee. *Member:* Beverly Hills (Member, Executive Committee and Entertainment Section) and Los Angeles County Bar Associations; State Bar of California; California Women Lawyers Association. **PRACTICE AREAS:** Litigation; Libel, Slander and Defamation; Intellectual Property; Wrongful Termination.

**MITCHELL J. LANGBERG,** born San Francisco, California, April 27, 1968; admitted to bar, 1994, California, U.S. District Court, Central District of California and U.S. Court of Appeals, Ninth Circuit. *Education:* University of the Pacific (B.S., 1990); University of Southern California (J.D., 1994). Finalist, 1992-1993 and Editor, 1993-1994, Hale Honors Moot Court Program.

**MARY L. MUIR,** born Long Beach, California, February 15, 1955; admitted to bar, 1980, California. *Education:* University of California at Berkeley (B.S., 1977); University of California at Los Angeles (J.D., 1980). Beta Alpha Psi. *Member:* The State Bar of California; American Bar Association. **PRACTICE AREAS:** Estate Planning; Probate; Corporate Law; Taxation.

**BRIAN A. MURPHY,** born Hinsdale, Illinois, November 22, 1964; admitted to bar, 1995, California, U.S. District Court, Central District of California and U.S. Court of Appeals, Ninth Circuit. *Education:* DePaul University (B.S., 1987); University of Southern California (J.D., 1995).

*OF COUNSEL*

**PETER C. RICHARDS, (A PROFESSIONAL CORPORATION),** born Bryn Mawr, Pennsylvania, October 9, 1952; admitted to bar, 1978, Pennsylvania; 1979, New York; 1982, California. *Education:* Albright College (B.A., cum laude, 1975); Temple University (J.D., cum laude, 1978); New York University (LL.M., 1980). **PRACTICE AREAS:** Entertainment Law; Taxation.

**GILBERT GAYNOR,** born San Francisco, California, October 4, 1952; admitted to bar, 1982, California, U.S. District Court, Central District of California and U.S. Court of Appeals, Ninth Circuit; 1985, U.S. District Court, Northern District of California; 1995, U.S. Supreme Court. *Education:* Whittier College School of Law (J.D., 1982); Harvard University (LL.M., 1989). Recipient: American Jurisprudence Awards in Constitutional Law I, Constitutional Law II, Conflict of Laws and Evidence; Corpus Juris Secundum Award, 1982; Harvard Law School Graduate Fellowship, 1988-1989. Executive Editor, Whittier Law Review, 1981-1982. Law Clerk, Hon. Margaret J. Morris, Presiding Justice, California Court of Appeals, Fourth District, 1982-1983. Author: "Executive Action Against AIDS: A Proposal for Federal Regulation Under Existing Law," 49 Ohio State., L.J. 999 (1989); "Administrative Agency Choice of Adjudication," 13 Golden Gate. U.L.Rev.1 (1983); note, "Preventing Corruption in the Electoral Process," 3 Whittier L.Rev.431 (1981). Senior Attorney, staff of Hon. Joyce L. Kennard, California Supreme Court, San Francisco, CA, May, 1990—June, 1994. Staff Attorney, ACLU Foundation of Southern California, Los Angeles, CA, 1983-1985. *Member:* State Bar of California; Queens Bench Bar Association of San Francisco (Member, Amicus Curiae Committee). **REPORTED CASES:** Feminist Women's Health Center v. Philibosian, 157 Cal.App.3d 1076 (1984), stay denied, 469 U.S. 1303 (mem.opn. of Rehnquist, J.), cert. denied, 470 U.S. 1052 (1984); Pines v. Tomson, 160 Cal.App.3d. 370 (1984); Martin v. International Olympic Committee, 740 F.2d 670 (9th Cir. 1984); Alamo Foundation v. Donovan, 471 U.S. 290 (1985); Gay Rights Coalition v. Georgetown University, 536 A.2d.1 (D.C.App. 1987); Church of the Soldiers of the Cross v. City of Riverside, 886 F.Supp 721 (C.D. Cal. 1995). **PRACTICE AREAS:** Appellate Practice; Civil Litigation.

**POLIN COHANNE,** born Drexel Hill, Pennsylvania, April 1, 1950; admitted to bar, 1975, Pennsylvania; 1977, California. *Education:* Pennsylvania State University (B.A., summa cum laude, 1972); Villanova University (J.D., 1975). Phi Beta Kappa. *Member:* State Bar of California. [Capt., USMC, 1975-1978]. **PRACTICE AREAS:** Entertainment.

**MILTON SEGAL,** born Philadelphia, Pennsylvania, September 10, 1927; admitted to bar, 1954, California. *Education:* University of California at Los Angeles (B.A., 1950); University of Southern California (J.D., 1953). *Member:* State Bar of California.

*LEGAL SUPPORT PERSONNEL*

*(This Listing Continued)*

# PROFESSIONAL BIOGRAPHIES

## PARALEGALS

**PATRICIA ANN ESSIG,** born Dallas, Texas, March 23, 1939. *Education:* Loyola Marymount University (B.A., 1984); University of West Los Angeles; School of Paralegal Studies (Litigation Certificate, with honors, 1985; Real Estate Certificate, with honors, 1987). Member: University of West Los Angeles Alumni Association, 1985-1994; Los Angeles Paralegal Association, 1985-1994.

**JEANNE A. LOGÉ,** born Los Angeles, California, August 19, 1951. *Education:* Pacific Legal Arts, 1981. Recipient, National Legal Assistant Certificate (CLA), 1990. *Member:* National Association of Legal Assistants (NALA).

All paralegals are members of the Los Angeles Paralegals Association.

---

## STUART W. LAPP
### 700 SOUTH FLOWER STREET, SUITE 1100
### LOS ANGELES, CALIFORNIA 90017
Telephone: 213-627-7760
Fax: 213-627-3750

*General Civil and Trial Practice. Corporation, Insurance, Probate, Trusts, Life Insurance, Mortgage and Real Estate Law.*

**STUART W. LAPP,** born Los Angeles, California, March 17, 1930; admitted to bar, 1957, California. *Education:* University of Southern California (A.B., cum laude, 1951); University of California at Berkeley (LL.B., 1956). Phi Beta Kappa. *Member:* State Bar of California.

REFERENCE: Security Pacific National Bank (Wilshire Grand Office).

---

## LASCHER & LASCHER
### A PROFESSIONAL CORPORATION
### LOS ANGELES, CALIFORNIA
(See Ventura)

*Civil and Criminal Appellate Practice, Litigation, German Law, Alternative Dispute Resolution.*

---

## LASKIN & GRAHAM
### LOS ANGELES, CALIFORNIA
(See Glendale)

*General Civil and Trial Practice in all State and Federal Courts, Eminent Domain, Municipal Law, Environmental Law, Real Property Damage, Employment Law, Construction Law, Land Use, Insurance Law, Professional Liability, Banking, Leasing, Bankruptcy, Financial Institutions Law, Commercial Documentation, Business Law and Litigation.*

---

## LATHAM & WATKINS
### 633 WEST FIFTH STREET, SUITE 4000
### LOS ANGELES, CALIFORNIA 90071
Telephone: 213-485-1234
Telecopier: 213-891-8763
TWX: 910-321-3733
Cable Address: "Lathwat"
URL: http://www.lw.com

*Costa Mesa, California Office:* Suite 2000, 650 Town Center Drive. Telephone: 714-540-1235.
*San Diego, California Office:* Suite 2100, 701 B Street. Telephone: 619-236-1234.
*San Francisco, California Office:* 505 Montgomery Street, Suite 1990. Telephone: 415-391-0600.
*Washington, D.C. Office:* Suite 1300, 1001 Pennsylvania Avenue, N.W. Telephone: 202-637-2200.
*Chicago, Illinois Office:* Suite 5800 Sears Tower. Telephone: 312-876-7700.
*Newark, New Jersey Office:* One Newark Center. Telephone: 201-639-1234. Fax: 201-639-7298.
*New York, N.Y. Office:* Suite 1000, 885 Third Avenue. Telephone: 212-906-1200.
*London, England Office:* One Angel Court, EC2R 7HJ. Telephone: +-44-171-374 4444. Telecopier: +-44-171-374 4460.
(This Listing Continued)

*Moscow, Russia Office:* Suite C200, 113/1 Leninsky Prospeckt, 117198. Telephone: +-7 503 956-5555. Fax: +-7 503 956-5556.
*Hong Kong Office:* 11th Floor Central Building, Number One Pedder Street, Central Hong Kong. Telephone: 011-852-2841-7779. Fax: 011-852-2841-7749.
*Tokyo, Japan Office:* Infini Akasaka, 8-7-15 Akasaka, Minato-Ku, Tokyo 107, Japan. Telephone: 011 81 3 3423-3970. Fax: 011 81 3 3423-3971.

*General Practice.*

### MEMBERS OF FIRM

**PAUL R. WATKINS** (1899-1973).

**DANA LATHAM** (1898-1974).

**IRA M. PRICE, II** (1919-1968).

**PHILIP F. BELLEVILLE,** born Flint, Michigan, April 24, 1934; admitted to bar, 1961, California. *Education:* University of Michigan (B.A., in Econ., with high distinction and honors, 1956; J.D., 1960). Order of the Coif; Phi Beta Kappa; Phi Kappa Phi; Alpha Kappa Psi. Assistant Editor, University of Michigan Law Review, 1959-1960. Member, Sections on: Antitrust, Trade Regulation Law and Business Law, State Bar of California. *Member:* Los Angeles County (Member, Business Trial Lawyers Section) and American (Member, Sections on: Antitrust Law and Criminal Justice) Bar Associations; Association of Business Trial Lawyers.

**IRVING SALEM** (New York City Office).

**WILLIAM R. NICHOLAS,** born Pontiac, Michigan, June 19, 1934; admitted to bar, 1963, California. *Education:* University of Idaho (B.S., 1956); University of Michigan (J.D., 1962). Order of the Coif. Associate Editor, Michigan Law Review, 1961-1962. *Member:* Los Angeles County Bar Association.

**JOHN P. MCLOUGHLIN,** born Knoxville, Tennessee, June 20, 1936; admitted to bar, 1963, California. *Education:* John Carroll University (B.S.S., magna cum laude, 1958); Harvard University (LL.B., cum laude, 1962). *Member:* Los Angeles County Bar Association.

**ALAN I. ROTHENBERG,** born Detroit, Michigan, April 10, 1939; admitted to bar, 1964, California. *Education:* University of Michigan (B.A., 1960; J.D., with distinction, 1963). Order of the Coif. Member, Barristers. Assistant Editor, Michigan Law Review, 1962-1963. Clarence M. Burton Scholar, University of Michigan Law School, 1962-1963. Member, Board of Directors, 1982— and President, 1987-1989, Constitutional Rights Foundation. Member, Board of Directors, Public Counsel, 1990-1993. Board of Directors, Los Angeles County Bar Foundation, 1990-1993. Member, State of California Judicial Council, 1990-1993. Member, Executive Board, 1979-1992, President, 1989-1992 and Chair, 1992—, Fraternity of Friends of the Music Center. Chairman Emeriti, Board of Governors, Los Angeles Music Center, 1992-1993. Member, Board of Governors: National Basketball Association, 1971-1979, 1982-1990; North American Soccer League, 1977-1980. Commissioner, Soccer, Olympic Games, 1984. Chairman, World Cup USA '94 Organization Committee, 1990—. President, United States Soccer Federation, 1990—. Chairman, Major League Soccer. President, Los Angeles Clippers Basketball Team, 1982-1989. Member, Board of Governors, 1986-1990 and President, 1989-1990, State Bar of California. *Member:* Beverly Hills, Century City (Member, Board of Governors, 1979-1993; President, 1986), Los Angeles County and American (Chairman, Committee on Entertainment, Sports and Media Litigation, Litigation Section, 1981; Member, Executive Committee, Forum on Entertainment and Sports Law, 1980—; Chairman, Sports Division, 1986-1993) Bar Associations.

**FRANCIS K. DECKER, JR.** (New York City Office).

**DAVID H. VENA,** born Los Angeles, California, December 21, 1938; admitted to bar, 1965, California. *Education:* University of California, Los Angeles (A.B., 1961); Harvard University (LL.B., cum laude, 1964). Trustee, Los Angeles County Bar Foundation, 1988-1994. *Member:* Los Angeles County Bar Association; National Health Lawyers Association; American Academy of Hospital Attorneys.

**DONALD P. NEWELL** (San Diego Office).

**JOSEPH A. WHEELOCK JR.** (Costa Mesa Office).

**KENNETH CONBOY** (New York City Office).

**J. THOMAS ROSCH** (San Francisco Office).

**KENNETH M. POOVEY** (San Francisco Office).

**JOHN J. KIRBY, JR.** (New York City Office).

**TAKASHI MATSUMOTO** (Tokyo, Japan Office).

(This Listing Continued)

## LATHAM & WATKINS, Los Angeles—Continued

**ROBERT E. CURRIE** (Costa Mesa Office).

**MICHAEL J. SHOCKRO,** born Laconia, New Hampshire, November 21, 1942; admitted to bar, 1967, California. *Education:* Stanford University (B.A., with distinction, 1964); Columbia University (LL.B., magna cum laude, 1967). Editor, Columbia Law Review, 1966-1967. *Member:* Los Angeles County and American (Member, Sections of: Antitrust Law; Corporation, Banking and Business Law) Bar Associations.

**JOHN R. LIGHT,** born Kansas City, Missouri, February 13, 1941; admitted to bar, 1968, California. *Education:* University of Kansas (B.A., 1963; J.D., with highest distinction, 1967). Phi Beta Kappa; Order of the Coif. Editor-in-Chief, University of Kansas Law Review, 1966-1967. Instructor, University of Michigan Law School, 1967-1968. *Member:* Los Angeles County and American (Member, Section of Antitrust Law and Chairman, Sherman Act Committee, 1984-1985; Member, Section of Corporation, Banking and Business Law) Bar Associations.

**JAMES G. HUNTER, JR.** (Chicago, Illinois Office).

**JOHN P. LYNCH** (Chicago, Illinois Office).

**THOMAS W. DOBSON,** born San Francisco, California, August 17, 1942; admitted to bar, 1967, California. *Education:* Loyola University, Los Angeles (B.A., cum laude, 1964); University of Southern California (J.D., 1967). Order of the Coif. Editor-in-Chief, Southern California Law Review, 1966-1967. Law Clerk to Justice Raymond E. Peters, Supreme Court of California, 1967-1968. *Member:* Los Angeles County and American Bar Associations.

**BRUCE R. LEDERMAN,** born New York, N.Y., October 12, 1942; admitted to bar, 1968, California. *Education:* University of Pennsylvania (B.S., cum laude, 1964); London School of Economics, London, England; Harvard University (LL.B., cum laude, 1967). Beta Gamma Sigma. Law Clerk to Judge Irving Hill, U.S. District Court, Central District of California, 1967-1968. *Member:* Los Angles County Bar Association.

**THOMAS G. BOST,** born Oklahoma City, Oklahoma, July 13, 1942; admitted to bar, 1967, Tennessee; 1969, California. *Education:* Abilene Christian University (B.S., summa cum laude, 1964); Vanderbilt University (J.D., 1967). Order of the Coif, Phi Alpha Delta, Blue Key, Alpha Chi. Note Editor, Vanderbilt Law Review, 1966-1967. Founders Medalist, Vanderbilt University School of Law, 1967. Assistant Professor of Law, Vanderbilt University School of Law, 1967-1968. *Member:* Los Angeles County (Chairperson, 1981-1982, Section of Taxation) and American (Chairperson, Standards of Tax Practice Committee, Section of Taxation, 1988-1990) Bar Associations.

**SELVYN SEIDEL** (New York City Office).

**ALAN W. PETTIS** (Costa Mesa Office).

**GEORGE VRADENBURG III,** born Kinston, North Carolina, March 14, 1943; admitted to bar, 1968, New York; 1995, California. *Education:* Oberlin College (A.B., magna cum laude, highest honors in Economics, 1964); Harvard University (LL.B., cum laude, 1967). Phi Beta Kappa. *Member:* American Bar Association. [Lt. U.S. Navy, 1967-1969 (Ret.)].
**PRACTICE AREAS:** Entertainment; Sports; Media; Communications.

**JOSEPH I. BENTLEY** (Costa Mesa Office).

**FREDRIC J. ZEPP** (San Francisco Office).

**GARY OLSON,** born Harper, Kansas, June 30, 1943; admitted to bar, 1969, California. *Education:* Kansas State College (B.S., 1965); University of Kansas (J.D., 1968). Order of the Coif; Omicron Delta Kappa. Editor-in-Chief, University of Kansas Law Review, 1967-1968. Member, 1981-1984 and Vice Chairperson, 1984, Committee on Corporations, Business Law Section, State Bar of California. *Member:* Los Angeles County (Member, Executive Committee, Business and Corporation Law Section, 1984-1992) and American (Member, Federal Regulation of Securities Committee, Subcommittee on Registration Statements, 1933 Act, 1984—) Bar Associations.

**GEORGE A. RICE** (Chicago, Illinois Office).

**THOMAS L. PATTEN** (Washington, D.C. Office).

**RANDALL C. BASSETT,** born Los Angeles, California, January 22, 1945; admitted to bar, 1970, California; 1985, New York. *Education:* University of California at Los Angeles and University of California at Berkeley (A.B., 1966); Harvard University (J.D., cum laude, 1969).

*(This Listing Continued)*

**A. VICTOR ANTOLA,** born Los Angeles, California, March 18, 1945; admitted to bar, 1970, California. *Education:* University of California at Berkeley (A.B., 1967); University of Michigan (J.D., magna cum laude, 1969). Phi Beta Kappa; Order of the Coif. Associate Editor, University of Michigan Law Review, 1968-1969. Law Clerk to Hon. A. Andrew Hauk, U.S. District Court, Central District of California, 1969-1970. *Member:* Los Angeles County and American Bar Associations.

**JAMES W. DANIELS** (Costa Mesa Office).

**ERNEST J. GETTO,** born DuBois, Pennsylvania, May 24, 1944; admitted to bar, 1970, New York; 1973, California. *Education:* Cornell University (B.A., 1966); Vanderbilt University (J.D., 1969). Author: "Recent Developments in Environmental and Toxic Tort Liability," USC Corporate Institute, 1992; "The Admissibility of Epidemiological Evidence in Toxic Tort Litigation," Industrial Epidemiology Forum, 1991; "Notes on Nuisance: A Framework for Understanding Nuisance Law in a Modern Industrial Setting," Toxic Law Reporter, January 1991; "Expert Witnesses in Chemical Exposure Litigation," in Preparing a Toxic Tort Case for Trial, Practising Law Institute, 1991; "Recent Developments in Toxic Tort Litigations," Environmental Insurance Law Institute, March, 1989; "The Artification of Science: The Problem of Unscientific 'Scientific' Evidence," Environmental Law Reporter, July, 1993; "Potter v. Firestone Tire and Rubber Co.'—Fear Alone is Not Enough," Toxics Law Reporter, March 9, 1994; "Medical Monitoring Claims in Environmental Class Actions," Toxics Law Reporter, March 8, 1995; "Report of the Federal Procedure Committee of the Section of Litigation of the American Bar Association on the Civil Justice Reform Act and the 1993 Discovery Amendments," American Bar Association, Committee on Pretrial Practice and Discovery Newsletter, March 1996. Deputy General Counsel, Independent Commission of the Los Angeles Police Department, 1991—. *Member:* Los Angeles County and American (Chairman, Federal Procedure Committee; Member, Committees on Securities Litigation and Environmental Litigation, Section of Litigation, 1980—) Bar Associations; Association of Business Trial Lawyers (Board of Governors, 1989—).

**PHILIP E. COVIELLO** (New York City Office).

**HENDRIK DE JONG,** born Rotterdam, The Netherlands, February 15, 1946; admitted to bar, 1969, Minnesota; 1983, Wisconsin; 1985, California. *Education:* University of Chicago (A.B., with honors, 1966; J.D., with honors, 1969). Phi Beta Kappa. Order of the Coif. Member, University of Chicago Law Review, 1968-1969. Associate Professor of Law, University of Idaho, 1972-1974. *Member:* American Bar Association (Member, Uniform Commercial Code Committee).

**ROGER M. ZAITZEFF** (New York City Office).

**BARRY A. SANDERS,** born Philadelphia, Pennsylvania, July 29, 1945; admitted to bar, 1971, California; 1985, District of Columbia. *Education:* University of Pennsylvania (A.B., cum laude, 1967); Yale University (LL.B., 1970). Editor, Yale Law Journal, 1968-1970. President, Center for International Commercial Arbitration, 1986-1990. Co-Chair, Rebuild L.A., 1992-1994. Chair, R.L.A. Community Lending Corp., 1993-1994. Secretary: Board of Directors, Los Angeles Library Foundation, 1995—; Amateur Athletic Foundation of Los Angeles, 1985-1989. Chair, Legal Committee, Progress L.A., 1994—; Co-Chair, Workforce L.A., 1995—. Member: Advisory Council of Asia/Pacific Center for Resolution of International Trade Disputes, 1985—. Member, Board of Directors, Legal Aid Foundation of Los Angeles, 1991-1994. Chairman, International Law Section, State Bar of California, 1987-1988. *Member:* Los Angeles County (Chairman, International Law Section, 1986-1987) and American (Member, Section on: International Law) Bar Associations; American Society of International Law; International Bar Association.

**MORRIS A. THURSTON** (Costa Mesa Office).

**PETER H. BENZIAN** (San Diego Office).

**DAVID V. LEE,** born Jamestown, North Dakota, October 29, 1943; admitted to bar, 1971, California. *Education:* North Dakota State University (B.S., 1966); University of Minnesota (J.D., 1970). Order of the Coif. Notes and Comments Editor, Minnesota Law Review, 1969-1970. *Member:* Los Angeles County Bar Association.

**MICHAEL S. LUREY,** born Chicago, Illinois, August 31, 1946; admitted to bar, 1971, California. *Education:* Northwestern University (B.S., with distinction, 1967); Harvard University (J.D., cum laude, 1970). Tau Beta Pi; Pi Mu Epsilon. Author: "Selected Current Developments in Bankruptcy," American Bankruptcy Institute, Course on Second Annual Bankruptcy Battleground, West Publishing, 1994; "Plan Confirmation—Consensual v. Cramdown," Corporate Recovery Conference, 1993; "Developments in Con-

*(This Listing Continued)*

firmation Standards for Chapter 11 Plans" and "Issues in Trading Claims in Chapter 11 Cases," Practising Law Institute, Course on Current Developments in Bankruptcy and Reorganization, 1991; "Restructuring Real Estate Secured Debt in Chapter 11," Los Angeles County Bar Association Symposium, 1990; "Trading Claims," Practicing Law Institute Course on Current Developments in Bankruptcy and Reorganization, 1989; "The Battles for Confirmation of Chapter 11 Plans," Practising Law Institute Advanced Bankruptcy Workshop, Case Studies in Handling Chapter 11 Problems, 1988-1990; "Confirmation of Plans of Reorganization Under Chapter 11," Practising Law Institute, Course on Lending Transactions and the Bankruptcy Reform Act of 1978, 1979-1987; "Impacts of the Bankruptcy Code on Unsecured Term Lending Transactions," Practising Law Institute Course on The Bankruptcy Reform Act for Bank Counsel, 1981-1987. Co-Author: "Collier Lending Institutions and the Bankruptcy Code," published by Matthew Bender, 1985—, Annual Updates, 1986—. Member: American College of Bankruptcy, 1994—; Board of Governors, 1979-1982, 1985— and President, 1988-1989, Financial Lawyers Conference. Director, American Bankruptcy Institute, 1982-1988. *Member:* Los Angeles County (Chairman, Executive Committee, Section on Commercial Law and Bankruptcy, 1981-1982) and American (Member, Committee on Business Bankruptcy, Section on Corporation, Banking and Business Law, 1975—) Bar Associations. **PRACTICE AREAS:** Insolvency; Business Debtors (50%); Creditors (50%).

**MCGEE GRIGSBY** (Washington, D.C. Office).

**ROBERT J. ROSENBERG** (New York City Office).

**PAUL H. DAWES** (San Francisco Office).

**CHRISTOPHER L. KAUFMAN** (San Francisco Office).

**HUGH STEVEN WILSON** (San Diego Office).

**ERIC L. BERNTHAL** (Washington, D.C. Office).

**WILLIAM C. KELLY, JR.** (Washington, D.C. Office).

**WILLIAM C. BOTTGER, JR.,** born Roanoke, Virginia, October 18, 1941; admitted to bar, 1972, California. *Education:* Dartmouth College (A.B., 1966); University of Virginia (J.D., 1971). Order of the Coif. Notes and Decisions Editor, Virginia Law Review, 1970-1971. *Member:* Los Angeles County (Member, Labor Law Section) and American (Member, Sections on: Labor Relations Law; Litigation) Bar Associations. [1st Lt., U.S. Army, 1962-1964]

**LAURENCE H. LEVINE** (Chicago, Illinois Office).

**JOHN F. WALKER, JR.,** born Bronx, New York, March 2, 1942; admitted to bar, 1972, California. *Education:* University of Notre Dame (B.S., 1963); University of North Carolina; Harvard University (J.D., 1971). Law Clerk. *Member:* Los Angeles County Bar Association. [Capt., U.S. Marine Corps, 1965-1968]

**ROBERT A. LONG,** born Martinsville, Indiana, December 26, 1945; admitted to bar, 1972, California. *Education:* Indiana University (A.B., 1968; J.D., summa cum laude, 1971). Order of the Coif. *Member:* Los Angeles County and American (Member, Litigation and Public Contract Law Sections) Bar Associations.

**WILLIAM J. GIBBONS** (Chicago, Illinois Office).

**GARY M. EPSTEIN** (Washington, D.C. Office).

**ROGER H. KIMMEL** (New York City Office).

**JOB TAYLOR, III** (New York City Office).

**JEFFREY T. PERO** (Costa Mesa Office).

**BETTY-JANE KIRWAN,** born Long Island, N.Y., February 4, 1947; admitted to bar, 1972, California; 1984, U.S. Supreme Court. *Education:* University of Pennsylvania; University of California, Berkeley (A.B., 1968); Boalt Hall School of Law, University of California (J.D., 1971). Law Clerk, Francis C. Whelan, U.S. District Court, 1971-1972. *Member:* Los Angeles County and American (Chair, Environmental Controls Committee, Corporations Section and Member of the Council, 1987-1994; Standing Committee on Environmental Law) Bar Associations.

**WILLIAM J. MEESKE,** born Detroit, Michigan, April 12, 1947; admitted to bar, 1972, California. *Education:* University of Michigan (B.A., 1969; J.D., magna cum laude, 1972). Order of the Coif. Associate Editor, Michigan Law Review, 1971-1972. *Member:* Los Angeles County Bar Association. **PRACTICE AREAS:** Securities; Antitrust; Commercial Litigation.

**JOHN J. CLAIR, JR.,** born Trenton, New Jersey, May 26, 1946; admitted to bar, 1973, California. *Education:* Brown University (A.B., 1968); *(This Listing Continued)*

University of Pennsylvania (J.D., 1972). Order of the Coif. Member, 1970-1971 and Comment Editor, 1971-1972, University of Pennsylvania Law Review. *Member:* Los Angeles County Bar Association.

**STEPHEN S. BOWEN** (Chicago, Illinois Office).

**ERICA H. STEINBERGER** (New York City Office).

**ROBERT A. GREENSPON** (New York City Office).

**GENE A. LUCERO,** born San Diego, California, December 10, 1947; admitted to bar, 1973, Colorado, U.S. District Court, District of Colorado and U.S. Court of Appeals, Tenth Circuit; 1974, California; 1990, District of Columbia; 1992, U.S. Court of Appeals, District of Columbia Circuit and U.S. District Court, Central District of California; 1993, U.S. Supreme Court. *Education:* Stanford University (B.A., cum laude, 1970); University of California, Boalt Hall School of Law (J.D., 1972). Author: "Son of Superfund: Can the Program Meet Expectations," 5:1 *The Environmental Forum* March/April, 1988. Co-author: "Recent Regulatory Developments Affecting Medical Waste Management and Disposal," Health Law Series, 1990 Health Law Handbook, Clark Boardman Company, Ltd.; "Superfund Handbook," September 1989, Third Edition, ENSR/Sidley & Austin; "Managing a Superfund Case," Corporate Counsel's Guide to Environmental Law, Business Law, Inc., 1989; "Public Law, Private Policeman: Revitalizing Private Regulation Through Pollution Liability Insurance Requirements," Environmental Claims Journal, Vol. 1, No. 3, Spring, 1989. Director, Office of Waste Programs Enforcement, 1982-1988; Deputy Director, Office of Emergency and Remedial Response, U.S. Environmental Protection Agency, Washington, D.C., 1982. Deputy Regional Administrator, U.S. Environmental Protection Agency, Region VIII, Denver, Colorado, 1980-1982. Deputy Director, Office of Compliance, Action/Peace Corps, 1978-1980. Assistant Attorney General, Litigation Section, Office of the Attorney General, Colorado, 1975-1978. **LANGUAGES:** Spanish.

**RICHARD L. CHADAKOFF** (New York City Office).

**BRUCE A. TESTER** (Costa Mesa Office).

**BARBARA A. CAULFIELD** (San Francisco Office).

**DONALD P. BAKER,** born Los Angeles, California, October 27, 1947; admitted to bar, 1973, California. *Education:* University of Redlands (B.A., 1970); University of California at Los Angeles (J.D., 1973). Order of the Coif. Associate Editor, U.C.L.A. Law Review, 1972-1973. *Member:* Los Angeles County (President, 1986-1987; President-Elect, 1985-1986; Senior Vice President, 1984-1985; Vice President, 1983-1984; Trustee, 1978-1982) and American (Director, Young Lawyers Division, 1982-1983) Bar Associations; The State Bar of California (Member, Commission on Evaluation of Judicial Nominees, 1981-1982); Los Angeles County Bar Barristers (Secretary-Treasurer, 1976-1977; Vice-President, 1977-1978; President Elect, 1978-1979; President, 1979-1980); Los Angeles County Bar Foundation (Secretary, 1983-1984; Director, 1994—); Western Justice Center Foundation (President, 1995—). Fellow, American Bar Foundation.

**JAMES A. CHERNEY** (Chicago, Illinois Office).

**PAUL I. MEYER** (San Diego Office).

**ROBERT M. SUSSMAN** (Washington, D.C. Office).

**JAMES V. KEARNEY** (New York City Office).

**GEOFFREY K. HURLEY** (New York City Office).

**THOMAS L. PFISTER,** born New York, N.Y., March 29, 1948; admitted to bar, 1974, California. *Education:* Stanford University (A.B., with great distinction, 1970); Harvard University (J.D., 1974). Phi Beta Kappa. Law Clerk to Judge William Matthew Byrne, Jr., U.S. District Court, Central District of California, 1974-1975.

**ALAN B. CLARK,** born Anniston, Alabama, October 14, 1946; admitted to bar, 1975, California. *Education:* University of Alabama (B.S., 1968); University of Virginia (J.D., 1974); Cambridge University, Cambridge, England (Diploma in Comparative Legal Studies, 1975). American Board of Trial Advocates, Master, Complex Litigation Inn of Court; Judge Pro Tem. *Member:* Los Angeles County (Member, Entertainment and Intellectual Property Law Section) and American (Member, Litigation and Antitrust Sections) Bar Associations. [Capt., U.S. Army, 1968-1971]

**DALE K. NEAL,** born Danville, Illinois, April 28, 1948; admitted to bar, 1974, California. *Education:* Harvard University (B.A., 1970); Stanford University (J.D., 1974; M.B.A., 1974). *Member:* Los Angeles County Bar Association (Member, Real Property Section).

**DONALD L. SCHWARTZ** (Chicago Office).

**DAVID L. MULLIKEN** (San Diego Office).

*(This Listing Continued)*

**LATHAM & WATKINS, Los Angeles—Continued**

**ROBERT K. BREAK** (Costa Mesa Office).

**JOEL E. KRISCHER,** born Chicago, Illinois, May 30, 1951; admitted to bar, 1975, California. *Education:* University of Illinois (B.A., magna cum laude, 1972); University of Michigan (J.D., cum laude, 1975). Phi Beta Kappa; Phi Kappa Phi. Note Editor, Michigan Law Review, 1974-1975. *Member:* Los Angeles County Bar Association (Member, Labor Law Section).

**JAMES D. C. BARRALL,** born Ray, Arizona, April 22, 1950; admitted to bar, 1975, California; 1976, U.S. Tax Court. *Education:* University of California at Davis (A.B., 1972); University of California at Los Angeles (J.D., 1975). Member, U.C.L.A. Law Review, 1973-1975. Author: "Planning for Incorporated Partners, Captive Loan-Out Corporations and Other Personal Service Corporations After TEFRA," 1984, University of Southern California Tax Institute, 5-1; "Securing Nonqualified Deferred Compensation Arrangements with 'Rabbi' Trusts and Escrows," California Business Law Reporter, 1986; "The Over-Funded Pension Plan: A Hidden Asset in the Sale of a Business," California Business Law Practitioner, Spring, 1986; "Pension Plans and the Tax Reform Act of 1986," California Business Law Reporter, January, 1987; "The Current Status of the Los Angeles Actuarial Assumption Cases," The Pension Actuary, March, 1987. Contributing Editor on Taxation, California Business Law Reporter, 1983-1986. Contributing Editor on Employee Benefits and Executive Compensation, California Business Law Reporter, 1986-1989. Member, Executive Committee, Taxation Section, 1982-1987; Chair, Education Committee, Taxation Section, 1982-1983; Editor, Tax Section News, 1982-1983, 1984-1985; Chair, Taxation Section, 1985-1986, State Bar of California. *Member:* Beverly Hills (Chairman: Taxation Committee, 1978-1979; Sponsored Retirement Plans, 1979-1986; Co-Chairman, Employee Benefits Committee, 1980-1982; Treasurer, 1980-1981; Member, Board of Governors, 1981-1983; Delegate, State Bar Conference of Delegates, 1980-1981), Los Angeles County (Member: Taxation Section and Employee Benefits Committee, 1975—; Executive Committee, Taxation Section, 1983—) and American (Member, Employee Benefits Committee, Taxation Section, 1982—) Bar Associations.

**RONALD W. HANSON** (Chicago, Illinois Office).

**LEONARD A. ZAX** (Washington, D.C. Office).

**JOHN J. LYONS,** born Orange, New Jersey, March 5, 1951; admitted to bar, 1976, California. *Education:* Dartmouth College (A.B., 1973); University of California at Berkeley (J.D., 1976). Phi Beta Kappa. *Member:* Los Angeles County Bar Association.

**JOHN J. HUBER** (Washington, D.C. Office).

**W. HARRISON WELLFORD** (Washington, D.C. Office).

**WALTER P. LOUGHLIN** (New York City Office).

**MILES N. RUTHBERG,** born Washington, D.C., November 7, 1952; admitted to bar, 1979, District of Columbia and California. *Education:* Yale University (B.A., summa cum laude, 1973); Harvard University (J.D., magna cum laude, 1976). Phi Beta Kappa. Member and Developments Editor, Harvard Law Review, 1974-1976. Author: "Expert Opinion: Counsel or Conspirator?" debate with Professor Blakey re RICO liability following Reves v. Ernst & Young, California Lawyer, June 1993; "Federal Class Actions," presented at University of Houston Law Center and University of California at Davis School of Law seminar, July 1993; "Conflicts of Interest in the Modern Law Firm," ABA monograph, August 1993. Law Clerk to: Judge Carl McGowan, U.S. Court of Appeals, District of Columbia Circuit, 1976-1977; Justice Thurgood Marshall, U.S. Supreme Court, 1977-1978. *Member:* Los Angeles County and American Bar Associations; District of Columbia Bar; Association of Business Trial Lawyers (Member, Board of Governors, 1993—). *PRACTICE AREAS:* Professional Liability and Securities Litigation; Class Actions; Complex Litigation.

**JON D. ANDERSON** (Costa Mesa Office).

**JOHN B. SHERRELL,** born Indianapolis, Indiana, January 27, 1951; admitted to bar, 1977, California. *Education:* Yale University (B.A., 1973); University of Michigan (J.D., cum laude, 1977). Co-Chair, State Bar of California Real Estate Finance Subsection, 1990-1992. *Member:* Los Angeles County Bar Association (Member, Real Property Section).

**CARL E. WITSCHY** (Chicago, Illinois Office).

**ROBERT M. DELL** (San Francisco Office).

**MARY B. RUHL,** born Baltimore, Maryland, March 24, 1948; admitted to bar, 1977, Wisconsin and California. *Education:* Wilson College (B.A., *(This Listing Continued)*

magna cum laude, 1971); University of Wisconsin (M.A., 1973; J.D., magna cum laude, 1977). Phi Beta Kappa; Order of the Coif. *Member:* The State Bar of Wisconsin. *LANGUAGES:* Swedish. *PRACTICE AREAS:* Finance Transactions.

**PATRICK T. SEAVER** (Costa Mesa Office).

**THOMAS G. GALLATIN, JR.** (New York City Office).

**VICTORIA E. MARMORSTEIN,** born Miami Beach, Florida, September 22, 1953; admitted to bar, 1977, District of Columbia; 1980, New York; 1989, California. *Education:* University of Oklahoma (B.A., 1973); American University (J.D., 1976); University of Virginia (LL.M., 1978). Phi Beta Kappa. Editor, Virginia Journal of International Law, 1977-1978. Author: "Responding To The Call For Order in International Finance: Cooperation Between the International Monetary Fund and Commercial Banks," Virginia Journal of International Law, 1978; "World Bank Power to Consider Human Rights Factors in Loan Decisions," The Journal of International Law and Economics, 1978. Co-Author: "Review of Foreign Bank Initiatives Taken by Federal Reserve Board in Recent Months," BNA's Banking Report, February 1995. Lecturer: PLI program on International Commercial Agreements in L.A. *Member:* District of Columbia Bar; New York State Bar Association; State Bar of California (Member, Financial Institutions Committee). Member, Financial Lawyers Conference. *LANGUAGES:* Spanish.

**PETER A. WALD** (San Francisco Office).

**GARY L. DICKSON,** born Bend, Oregon, October 15, 1949; admitted to bar, 1978, California. *Education:* University of Oregon (B.S., 1975; J.D., 1977). Phi Beta Kappa; Order of the Coif. *Member:* Los Angeles County and American (Member, Commercial Financial Services Committee, 1983—, Committee on Legal Opinions, 1989—, Business Law Section) Bar Associations. [With U.S. Navy, 1969-1973]

**SCOTT N. WOLFE** (San Diego Office).

**GREGORY P. LINDSTROM** (Costa Mesa Office).

**JOSEPH J. WHEELER** (San Diego Office).

**MAUREEN E. MAHONEY** (Washington, D.C. Office).

**DAVID J. HAYES** (Washington, D.C. Office).

**BRUCE P. HOWARD** (Costa Mesa Office).

**MICHAEL CHERTOFF** (Newark, New Jersey, New York City and Washington, D.C. Offices).

**JON D. DEMOREST** (San Diego Office).

**VIRGINIA SOLLENBERGER GROGAN,** born Pasadena, California, November 19, 1951; admitted to bar, 1979, California. *Education:* Occidental College (B.A., magna cum laude, 1973); University of Southern California (J.D., 1979). Phi Beta Kappa; Phi Alpha Delta. Staff Member, University of Southern California Law Review, 1978-1979. *Member:* Los Angeles County Bar Association.

**KELLEY MICHAEL GALE** (San Diego Office).

**KAREN SMITH BRYAN,** born Hawkinsville, Georgia, July 4, 1950; admitted to bar, 1979. *Education:* Bryn Mawr College (A.B., cum laude, with special honors in Psychology, 1972); University of California at Los Angeles (M.A., 1973); University of Southern California (J.D., 1979). Order of the Coif. Member, University of Southern California Law Review, 1977-1979. Member, Planning Committee USC Tax Institute. *Member:* Los Angeles County (Member, Taxation Section) and American (Member: Corporate Tax Committee; Committee on Individual Investments and Workouts) Bar Associations.

**DEANNE P. GEORGE** (San Diego Office).

**EDWARD SONNENSCHEIN, JR.,** born Highland Park, Illinois, June 3, 1954; admitted to bar, 1979, Illinois; 1980, District of Columbia; 1984, California. *Education:* Harvard University (A.B., cum laude, 1976; J.D., cum laude, 1979).

**MILTON A. MILLER,** born Los Angeles, California, January 15, 1954; admitted to bar, 1979, California. *Education:* Stanford University (A.B., with distinction and with honors in Economics, 1976); Harvard University (J.D., cum laude, 1979). Phi Beta Kappa. Member, Board of Editors, 1977-1979 and Articles Editor, 1978-1979, Harvard Law Review. Author: "The Collateral Estoppel Effect of Prior State Court Findings in Cases Within Exclusive Federal Jurisdiction," 91 Harvard Law Review 1281, 1978. Contributing Author: "Attorney Ethics," California Practice Handbook, 1993; "Attorney Practice and Ethics," California Forms of Pleading and Practice, *(This Listing Continued)*

Matthew Bender, 1994. Law Clerk to U.S. Supreme Court Justice Anthony M. Kennedy, 1979-1980. Member, Standing Committee on Professional Responsibility and Conduct, State Bar of California. *Member:* Los Angeles County Bar Association (Chairman: Professional Responsibility and Ethics Committee).

**MARTIN N. FLICS** (New York City Office).

**PAUL R. DEMURO,** born Aberdeen, Maryland, March 21, 1954; admitted to bar, 1979, Maryland; 1980, District of Columbia; 1982, California. *Education:* University of Maryland (B.A., summa cum laude, 1976); Washington University (J.D., 1979); University of California, Berkeley (M.B.A., 1986). Phi Delta Phi. Article and Book Review Editor, Washington University Law Quarterly, 1978-1979. Author with L. Kalm: "Hospital Contracting with PPOs," The New Healthcare Market, 1985; "Joint Ventures for Mobile Equipment Reduce Hospital Costs," Healthcare Financial Management, April 1989; "Implications of Hospital Transfers to Related Corporations and Joint Ventures," Trustee, October 1989; "Medicare Funded Depreciation - A Plan for Hospitals," HealthSpan, February 1990; "How to Negotiate a Medi-Cal Inpatient Contract," California Hospitals, Sept./Oct. 1991; Author with G. Margolis, "Crisis Management Can Leave Residual Effects," Healthcare Financial Management, October 1991; Author with J. Little, "Know Your Investigator - The Basics of How to Handle a Medicare or Medicaid Audit, Review or Investigation," Homecare, November 1991; "Seeking a Safe Harbor," Legal Times—Special Report on Health Law, November 16, 1992 also reprinted as "A Complex Cure for Health Care Deals," The Recorder, December 4, 1992. Author with J. Roth, "Fraud and Abuse Compliance Programs: Their Time Has Come," Healthcare Financial Management, March 1993; "Struggle for Control," Los Angeles County Medical Association Physician Magazine, Volume 123, Number 20, December 13, 1993; "Capital Finance," Chapter 29, National Healthcare Lawyers Association, Health Law Practice Guide, 1993. Editor and Contributing Author: *Integrated Delivery Systems*, Topics in Health Care Financing issue, 1994; "Antitrust and Integrated Delivery System Models—An Overview," Health Care Reform and Antitrust, Practicing Law Institute, 1994; "Integrated Delivery Systems," Health Care Law and Health Reform, Practicing Law Institute, 1994; "Provider Alliances: Key to Health Care Reform," Healthcare Financial Management, January 1994; "Ten Steps for Integrated Delivery Systems to Maintain Exempt Status," Healthcare and Taxation: Tax Exempt Integration, Compliance and Financing, Vol. 1, No. 1, October 1994; "Practice Integration for the Delivery of Oncology Services," Oncology Reimbursement: Practice Oriented Solutions, Volume I, Issue V, October 1994; "Integrated Delivery System Vehicles—Health Care Law of the 1990s," in CCM: The American Lawyers's Corporate Counsel Magazine, Winter 1994; "How to Manage the Transition to Capitation," Managing Integration and Operations, February 1995; *The Financial Managers Guide to Managed Care and Integrated Delivery Systems*, Irwin, 1995; with T. Rieger, "Pediatric Integrated Delivery Systems: A Market Perspective," Capitation Contracts, A Guide to Negotiating Successful Agreements, June 1995; "Paying Specialists and Subspecialists on a Capitated Basis," Healthcare Financial Management, July 1995; "The Effect of Integration on Debt Arrangements," Northern California Edge, August-/September 1995; "Market Dynamics Spawn Merger Mania in Health Care Industry," California Business, March 4, 1996; "Recent Mergers and Acquisitions in Health Care," Health Care M&A: Commercialization of the Medical Industry, Practicing Law Institute, 1996; "Corporate Structure and Tax Issues in M&A," Health Care M&A: Commercialization of the Medical Industry, Practicing Law Institute, 1996; "Providers as Insurers," Law and Practice of Insurance Regulation of Health Care Arrangements, 1996; with M. Unsuh, *Health Care Mergers and Acquisitions: The Transactional Perspective*, The Bureau of National Affairs, Inc., 1996. Certified Public Accountant, Maryland, 1981. Certified Managed Care Professional, 1995. Certified Manager of Patients Accounts, 1990. Member, Editorial Board: Managed Care Manual, Aspen, 1994—; Healthcare Business & Legal Strategies, Atlantic Information Systems, 1996—. Member, Advisory Board, School of Health, California State University, Dominquez Hills, 1992—. *Member:* Los Angeles County (Member, Section on Healthcare Law) and American (Member, Section on Antitrust and Forum on Health Law) Bar Associations; American Academy of Healthcare Attorneys; National Health Lawyers Association; American Institute of Certified Public Accountants; Medical Group Management Association; The IPA Association of America (Member, Legal Steering Committee, 1996—); Healthcare Financial Management Association (Member, Board of Directors, Northern California Chapter, 1990-1993; Member, Principles and Practices Board, 1992-1995 and Vice Chairperson, 1993-1995; Member, National Board of Directors, 1995—; Member, Executive Committee, 1996—); Healthcare Financial Management Association Education Foundation (Member, Board of Directors, 1996-1997); Accountant 52 Club. Charter Member, Managed Care Forum (Board Liaison, 1995-1997). Fellow, Healthcare Financial Management Association, 1989. (Also at San Francisco Office).
*PRACTICE AREAS:* Healthcare Law; Business Law; Administrative Law.

**ROBERT A. WATERMAN** (San Francisco Office).

**SHELLEY B. O'NEILL** (New York City Office).

**TERRENCE J. CONNOLLY** (New York City Office).

**JAMES F. ROGERS** (Washington, D.C. Office).

**GEORGE J. MIHLSTEN,** born September 17, 1953; admitted to bar, 1980, California. *Education:* University of Southern California (B.S., summa cum laude, 1977; M.B.A., 1980; J.D., 1980). Order of the Coif; Beta Gamma Sigma. Member, Southern California Law Review, 1978-1980.

**PETER L. WINIK** (Washington, D.C. Office).

**RUSSELL F. SAUER, JR.,** born March 9, 1955; admitted to bar, 1980, California. *Education:* Northwestern University (B.A., with highest distinction, 1977); Stanford University (J.D., 1980). Phi Beta Kappa. Graduate, Sports Law Institute. Member, Labor Law Section, State Bar of California. *Member:* Los Angeles County and American (Member, Sports Forum) Bar Associations; California Trial Lawyers Association; Association of Trial Lawyers of America (Member, Litigation Section); Sports Lawyers Association.

**STEVEN DELLA ROCCA** (New York City Office).

**JED W. BRICKNER** (New York City Office).

**ELIZABETH A. BLENDELL,** born Albany, New York, October 11, 1950; admitted to bar, 1980, California. *Education:* Mount Holyoke College (B.A., with distinction, 1972); Boston College (J.D., magna cum laude, 1980). Order of the Coif.

**KEVIN A. RUSSELL** (Chicago, Illinois Office).

**MARC W. RAPPEL,** born Springfield, Illinois, May 1, 1956; admitted to bar, 1981, California. *Education:* Southern Methodist University (B.A.S., summa cum laude, 1977); University of Chicago (J.D., 1980). Phi Beta Kappa.

**MARY K. WESTBROOK** (Costa Mesa Office).

**MARK S. PULLIAM** (San Diego Office).

**ROBERT A. WYMAN, JR.,** born Claremont, New Hampshire, May 25, 1954; admitted to bar, 1980, California. *Education:* Princeton University (A.B., cum laude, 1976); University of Virginia (J.D., 1980). Articles Editor, Virginia Journal of International Law, 1979-1980. Law Clerk to Judge Robert J. Kelleher, U.S. District Court, Central District of California, 1980-1981. Author: Matthew Bender, *Environmental Law Practice Guide*, (Lead Author, "Air Pollution" Chapter). Co-Author: Matthew Bender, *California Environmental Law*, (Chapter on Cleanup of Hazardous Waste and Hazardous Waste Transportation Chapters). Director, West Coast Section, Air Pollution Control Association, 1988-1898. Member, EPA Clean Air Act Advisory Committee, 1991—. *Member:* American Bar Association (Vice Chairman, Committee on Air Quality, 1982-1990, 1991— and Member, Committee on Solid and Hazardous Waste, 1982—, Natural Resources Section).

**ROGER S. GOLDMAN** (Washington, D.C. Office).

**BRUCE E. ROSENBLUM** (Washington, D.C. Office).

**BRIAN G. CARTWRIGHT,** born Seattle, Washington, May 29, 1947; admitted to bar, 1980, District of Columbia; 1984, California. *Education:* Yale University (B.S., 1967); University of Chicago (Ph.D., 1971); Harvard University (J.D., magna cum laude, 1980). President, Harvard Law Review, 1979-1980. Law Clerk to: Judge Malcolm R. Wilkey, U.S. Court of Appeals, District of Columbia Circuit, 1980-1981; Associate Justice Sandra Day O'Connor, U.S. Supreme Court, 1981-1982.

**CHARLES STEPHEN TREAT** (San Francisco Office).

**MARC D. BASSEWITZ** (Chicago, Illinois Office).

**KEVIN M. MURPHY** (Chicago, Illinois Office).

**BRYANT B. EDWARDS,** born Provo, Utah, December 12, 1954; admitted to bar, 1981, California. *Education:* Brigham Young University (B.A., summa cum laude, 1978); University of Chicago (J.D., 1981). Author: "Mandatory Class Action Lawsuits as a Restructuring Technique," 19 Pepperdine L. Rev. 875 (1992); "Modifying Debt Securities: The Search for the Elusive 'New Security'Doctrine," 47 Bus. Law. 571 (1992); "Restructuring High-Yield Securities Through Prepackaged Bankruptcies," 5 Insights 3-10 (May 1991). *Member:* Los Angeles County Bar Association.

*(This Listing Continued)*

LATHAM & WATKINS, Los Angeles—Continued

**CHRISTOPHER W. GARRETT** (San Diego Office).

**EVERETT C. JOHNSON, JR.** (Washington, D.C. Office).

**PAUL D. TOSETTI,** born Pana, Illinois, September 29, 1954; admitted to bar, 1982, District of Columbia and California. *Education:* Harvard University (B.A., cum laude, 1976; J.D., cum laude, 1981); Oxford, Magdalen College, Oxford University, England (M.A., First Class Honors, 1979). Member, 1979-1981 and Supreme Court Editor, 1980-1981, Harvard Law Review. Law Clerk to Judge Edward Allen Tamm, Circuit Judge, U.S. Court of Appeals for the District of Columbia Circuit and Chief Judge, Temporary Emergency Court of Appeals, 1981-1982. Member, Editorial Board, *The Corporate Governance Advisor* (Prentice Hall).

**WILLIAM K. RAWSON** (Washington, D.C. Office).

**MARK W. SMITH** (San Francisco Office).

**DAVID R. HAZELTON** (Washington, D.C. Office).

**G. ANDREW LUNDBERG,** born Seattle, Washington, August 6, 1957; admitted to bar, 1983, California; 1985, District of Columbia. *Education:* Stanford University (A.B., with distinction, 1978); Harvard University (J.D., cum laude, 1981). Editor, Harvard Law Review, 1979-1981. Law Clerk to Judge George E. MacKinnon, U.S. Court of Appeals, District of Columbia Circuit, 1981-1982.

**MARK E. NEWELL** (Washington, D.C. Office).

**JOHN D. SHYER** (New York City Office).

**JOSHUA STEIN** (New York City Office).

**JOHN C. HART** (New York City Office).

**EDWARD J. SHAPIRO** (Washington, D.C. Office).

**SAMUEL A. FISHMAN** (New York City Office).

**TOMOAKI IKENAGA** (New York City Office).

**DAVID C. BOATWRIGHT** (San Diego Office).

**MARK A. HARRIS** (Chicago, Illinois Office).

**MARK A. STEGEMOELLER** (Chicago, Illinois Office).

**ROBERT P. DAHLQUIST** (San Diego Office).

**ROBERT D. CROCKETT,** born Boulder, Colorado, November 29, 1954; admitted to bar, 1982, California. *Education:* Brigham Young University (B.S., cum laude, 1978; J.D., magna cum laude, 1982). Order of the Coif. J. Reuben Clark Scholar. Editorial Associate, B.Y.U. Law Review, 1981-1982. Editorial Board Member, The Los Angeles Lawyer, 1986-1990.

**DAVID J. McLEAN,** born Passaic, New Jersey, December 31, 1955; admitted to bar, 1982, California and U.S. District Court, Central District of California; 1983, U.S. District Court, Northern District of California; 1991, U.S. Court of Appeals, District of Columbia; 1992, District of Columbia, U.S. Supreme Court and U.S. District Court, Southern, Eastern and Western Districts of California. *Education:* Washington & Lee University (B.A., summa cum laude, 1978); University of Edinburgh, Edinburgh, Scotland, 1979; Georgetown University Law Center (J.D., magna cum laude, 1982). Phi Beta Kappa. Editor, Georgetown Law Journal, 1981-1982. Author: "Westinghouse and the Limited Waiver Rule," Los Angeles Lawyer, October 1992; "ADR In Employment Law," 1996. *Member:* Los Angeles County Bar Association (Member, Committees on Alternative Dispute Resolution, Federal Courts and Antitrust Sections); District of Columbia Bar; CPR Institute for Dispute Resolution; Association of Business Trial Lawyers (Member, Committee on Private Judging).

**THOMAS C. SADLER,** born Long Beach, California, March 30, 1954; admitted to bar, 1982, California. *Education:* Stanford University (A.B., with distinction, 1976); Fletcher School of Law and Diplomacy; Tufts University; University of California School of Law, Los Angeles (J.D., 1982).

**RICHARD A. LEVY** (Chicago, Illinois Office).

**JAMES E. BRANDT** (New York City Office).

**SHARON Y. BOWEN** (New York City Office).

**JOHN L. SACHS** (Washington, D.C. Office).

**JERRY R. PETERS** (San Francisco Office).

**KENNETH A. WOLFSON** (Costa Mesa Office).

*(This Listing Continued)*

CAA882B

**PAMELA S. PALMER,** born Orange, California, December 7, 1957; admitted to bar, 1982, California. *Education:* University of California at Irvine (B.A., with honors, 1978); University of Southern California (J.D., 1982). Order of the Coif. Southern California Law Review, 1981-1982. Law Clerk to the Hon. Walter Ely, Ninth Circuit Court of Appeals, 1982-1983. *PRACTICE AREAS:* Professional Liability and Securities Litigation.

**KARL S. LYTZ** (San Francisco Office).

**WILLIAM H. VOGE** (New York City Office).

**NANCY SCHEURWATER HUNTER** (Chicago, Illinois Office).

**URSULA H. HYMAN,** born Redlands, California, September 10, 1951; admitted to bar, 1983, California. *Education:* Immaculate Heart College (B.A., 1973); Loyola Marymount University (M.Ed., 1978); University of Southern California (J.D., 1983). Order of the Coif. Staff Member, Computer Law Journal, 1981-1982. Author: "The Family Educational Rights and Privacy Act of 1974 and The College Records System of the Future," College and University Student Records: A Legal Compendium, June 1989; "Mello-Roos for Revenue; Past-13 Lifeline Pulls its Weight," 19 Real Estate Journal, No. 3, Oct. 15, 1990; "Orange County Should End Its Ambivalence Toward COP Financings," Bond Buyer, Vol. 313, No. 29687, July 10, 1995. *Member:* Los Angeles and American Bar Associations; National Association of Bond Lawyers; California Bond Lawyers Association; California Women Lawyers Association. *PRACTICE AREAS:* Public Finance; FEMA; Public Entity/District Workouts.

**MARTHA BARNHART JORDAN,** born Omaha, Nebraska, September 25, 1954; admitted to bar, 1983, California. *Education:* Pennsylvania State University (B.S., 1976); University of Cincinnati (M.B.A., 1978); Boalt Hall, University of California, Berkeley (J.D., 1983).

**THOMAS A. EDWARDS** (San Diego Office).

**DAVID BOOTH ROGERS,** born New Haven, Connecticut, September 4, 1958; admitted to bar, 1983, California. *Education:* Stanford University (A.B., with distinction, 1980; J.D., 1983).

**JOHN D. WATSON, JR.** (Washington, D.C. Office).

**RICHARD A. CONN, JR.** (Washington, D.C. Office).

**DAVID S. FOSTER** (Chicago, Illinois Office).

**BENNETT J. MURPHY,** born Glen Cove, New York, April 29, 1957; admitted to bar, 1984, New York; 1994, California. *Education:* Amherst College (B.A., magna cum laude, 1978), Phi Beta Kappa; Harvard University (M.P.P., J.D., cum laude, 1983). *Member:* The Association of the Bar of the City of New York; American Bar Association; American Bankruptcy Institute; Financial Lawyers Conference. *PRACTICE AREAS:* Bankruptcy; Creditors Rights.

**ERIC A. STERN** (Washington, D.C. Office).

**LORI E. SIMON** (Chicago, Illinois Office).

**NANCY L. SCHIMMEL** (Chicago, Illinois Office).

**J. DOUGLAS BACON** (Chicago, Illinois Office).

**CARY K. HYDEN** (Costa Mesa Office).

**PETER W. DEVEREAUX,** born Mt. Kisco, New York, February 15, 1954; admitted to bar, 1985, California. *Education:* Virginia Polytechnic Institute and State University (B.S., 1977); Yale University (J.D., 1983). Editor, Yale Law Journal, 1982-1983. Law Clerk to Hon. Norma L. Shapiro, U.S. District Court, Eastern District of Pennsylvania, 1983-1984. *PRACTICE AREAS:* Professional Liability, Securities, Financial Institutions and other Business Litigation.

**MARK A. FLAGEL,** born Los Angeles, California, September 18, 1958; admitted to bar, 1983, California. *Education:* University of California at Los Angeles (B.A., magna cum laude, 1980); University of California at Berkeley (J.D., 1983). Order of the Coif. *Member:* Los Angeles County and American Bar Associations; State Bar of California. *PRACTICE AREAS:* Intellectual Property; Litigation.

**BRUCE P. SHEPHERD** (San Diego Office).

**EDITH R. PEREZ,** born Acambay, Mexico, August 30, 1954; admitted to bar, 1982, California. *Education:* University of California at Davis (B.A., with honors, 1976); Boalt Hall School of Law (J.D., 1980). Phi Beta Kappa; Phi Kappa Phi. Associate Editor, California Law Review, 1978-1980. Extern Law Clerk to the Honorable Spencer Williams, U.S. District Court, Northern District of California, 1980. Vice President, Board of Recreation and Parks Commissioners, City of Los Angeles, 1994-1995. Member, Board

*(This Listing Continued)*

of Police Commissioners, 1995-1999. *Member:* Los Angeles County and American Bar Associations. *LANGUAGES:* Spanish.

**DAVID W. BARBY** (Costa Mesa Office).

**JULI WILSON MARSHALL** (Chicago, Illinois Office).

**ROBERT G. GOLDMAN** (Chicago, Illinois Office).

**MICHAEL J. BRODY,** born Ottumwa, Iowa, March 13, 1959; admitted to bar, 1984, California. *Education:* University of Iowa (B.B.A., with distinction, 1981; J.D., with high distinction, 1984). Phi Eta Sigma; Beta Gamma Sigma; Beta Alpha Psi; Order of the Coif. Hancher Medallion. Moot Court Board. Certified Public Accountant, Iowa, 1981. *Member:* Los Angeles County Bar Association (Member, Taxation Section).

**MARY ELLEN KANOFF,** born Pasadena, California, December 4, 1956; admitted to bar, 1984, California. *Education:* University of California at Berkeley (A.B., magna cum laude, 1978); Pontificia Universidad Catolica, Lima, Peru; Boalt Hall School of Law, University of California (J.D., 1984). Phi Beta Kappa. Associate Editor, California Law Review, 1982-1984. Extern Law Clerk, Justice Otto Kaus, California Supreme Court, 1983.

**PETER F. KERMAN** (San Francisco Office).

**KIRK A. DAVENPORT** (New York City Office).

**LUCINDA STARRETT,** born Washington, D.C., June 21, 1957; admitted to bar, 1986, California. *Education:* Princeton University (A.B., magna cum laude, 1979); University of Nigeria, Nsukka, Nigeria (visiting student, 1980-1981); University of Pennsylvania (J.D., cum laude, 1984). Fulbright Scholar. Chief Comment Editor, Journal of Capital Markets and Securities Regulation, 1983. Law Clerk to Judge Dorothy W. Nelson, U.S. Court of Appeals, Ninth Circuit, 1984-1985. Chair, Land Use Group of Latham & Watkins. Vice Chair, Valley Industry and Commerce Association. Chair, Government Relations Committee and Member, Executive Committee, Central City Association of Los Angeles. *Member:* American Bar Association. *LANGUAGES:* French.

**SCOTT R. HABER** (San Francisco Office).

**KRISTINE L. WILKES** (San Diego Office).

**JOEL H. MACK** (San Diego Office).

**RAYMOND YUNG LIN** (New York City Office).

**ROBERT J. GUNTHER, JR.** (New York City Office).

**GEOFFREY S. BERMAN** (New York City Office).

**JOSEPH D. SULLIVAN** (Washington, D.C. Office).

**RICHARD S. ZBUR,** born Albuquerque, New Mexico, March 2, 1957; admitted to bar, 1985, California. *Education:* Yale University (B.A., summa cum laude, 1979); Harvard University (J.D., 1983). Phi Beta Kappa. Book Review Editor, Harvard Journal on Legislation, 1982-1983.

**DOUGLAS A. FREEDMAN** (Chicago, Illinois Office).

**JOHN M. JAMESON,** born Worcester, Massachusetts, December 6, 1958; admitted to bar, 1985, California. *Education:* Cornell University (B.A., 1980); University of California at Los Angeles (J.D., 1985). Recipient, American Jurisprudence Award in Contracts. Member, UCLA Law Review, 1983-1985. *Member:* Los Angeles County and American Bar Associations.

**JOHN M. NEWELL,** born Berkeley, California, February 6, 1960; admitted to bar, 1985, California. *Education:* Stanford University (A.B., 1982); University of Michigan (J.D., magna cum laude, 1985). Order of the Coif. Associate Note Editor, Michigan Law Review. Author: "ERISA Retirement Plans in Individual Bankruptcy," University of Michigan Journal of Law Reform 183, Vol. 19, Fall, 1985.

**LINDA S. SCHURMAN** (Chicago, Illinois Office).

**GLENDA SANDERS** (Costa Mesa Office).

**PETER J. WILSON** (Costa Mesa Office).

**LAURENCE J. STEIN** (Chicago, Illinois Office).

**JOSEPH BLUM** (London, England Office).

**PATRICIA TIMKO SINCLAIR,** born Meadowbrook, Pennsylvania, May 29, 1960; admitted to bar, 1986, California. *Education:* University of North Carolina at Chapel Hill (B.A., 1982); Harvard University Law School (J.D., magna cum laude, 1985). Phi Beta Kappa; John Motley Morehead Scholar. Articles Editor, Harvard Journal on Legislation, 1984-

*(This Listing Continued)*

1985. Judicial Clerk to the Hon. Sam J. Ervin, III, U.S. Court of Appeals, Fourth Circuit, 1985-1986.

**KIRK A. WILKINSON,** born Lansing, Michigan, May 10, 1959; admitted to bar, 1985, Illinois; 1987, California. *Education:* Miami University (B.A., 1981); Indiana University (J.D., 1984). Order of the Coif. Member, Indiana University Law Journal, 1983-1984. Judicial Clerk to Judge Cynthia Holcomb Hall, Ninth Circuit Court of Appeals, 1984-1986. *PRACTICE AREAS:* Environmental Litigation.

**ALLEN D. HAYNIE** (San Diego Office).

**REBA W. THOMAS,** born Troy, Alabama, August 31, 1946; admitted to bar, 1985, California. *Education:* Stanford University (B.A., 1967); University of California at Los Angeles (J.D., 1985). Phi Beta Kappa. Law Clerk to Hon. David V. Kenyon, 1985-1986 and Hon. Harry L. Hupp, 1986, U.S. District Court, Central District of California.

**KEVIN C. BLAUCH** (New York City Office).

**DAVID A. HAHN** (San Diego Office).

**RICHARD L. WIRTHLIN** (Moscow, Russia Office).

**LINDA M. INSCOE** (San Francisco Office).

**JAMES F. RITTER** (Washington, D.C. Office).

**DAVID A. GORDON** (New York City Office).

**ROBERT A. KOENIG,** born Los Angeles, California, June 15, 1962; admitted to bar, 1986, California. *Education:* Stanford University (A.B., 1983; J.D., 1986). Phi Beta Kappa. Note Editor, Stanford Law Review, 1985-1986. Author: "Personal Jurisdiction and the Corporate Employee: Minimum Contacts Meet the Fiduciary Shield," 38 Stan. L. Rev. 813, 1986. *Member:* Los Angeles County Bar Association.

**PAMELA BROWN KELLY,** born Royal Oak, Michigan, January 29, 1959; admitted to bar, 1986, California. *Education:* University of Virginia (B.A., 1981); University of California at Los Angeles (J.D., 1986).

**DENNIS B. NORDSTROM** (London, England Office).

**PAUL A. GALLEBERG,** born Dearborn, Michigan, June 15, 1960; admitted to bar, 1986, California. *Education:* University of Michigan (A.B., 1983); Harvard University (J.D., cum laude, 1986). Phi Beta Kappa. *Member:* Los Angeles County and American Bar Associations. *PRACTICE AREAS:* Communications Law; Corporate Law.

**KEVIN CHARLES BOYLE** (Washington, D.C. Office).

**GLEN B. COLLYER,** born Farmington, New Mexico, July 19, 1958; admitted to bar, 1987, California. *Education:* Brigham Young University (B.S., 1982; M.B.A., 1986; J.D., 1986). Order of the Coif. Member, 1984-1986 and Lead Articles Editor, 1985-1986, Brigham Young Law Review. Author: Comment, "You Mean I Could've Saved the Farm?" An Examination of the Notice Requirements or Lack Thereof, of 7 U.S.C. § 1981a, 1985 L. Rev. 159. Judicial Clerk for the Honorable Judge Monroe G. McKay, 1986-1987.

**RICHARD W. RAUSHENBUSH** (San Francisco Office).

**WILLIAM J. CERNIUS** (Costa Mesa Office).

**DAVID K. RATHGEBER** (Chicago, Illinois Office).

**JOHN H. KENNEY** (San Francisco Office).

**DAVID T. I. VONG** (Hong Kong Office).

**ANDREW D. SINGER** (San Diego Office).

**MICHAEL BRUCE ABELSON,** born Rochester, New York, January 16, 1963; admitted to bar, 1987, California. *Education:* Occidental College (B.A., summa cum laude, 1984); University of Sussex, Brighton, England; New York University (J.D., 1987). Phi Beta Kappa. Member, Editorial Staff, 1985-1986 and Note and Comment Editor, New York University Law Review, 1986-1987. Author: "Prior to Appeal: Crafting Successful Post-Trial Motions," Los Angeles Daily Journal, June 13, 1995 at 7. *Member:* Los Angeles County, American and Federal Bar Associations.

**JULIA A. HATCHER** (Washington, D.C. Office).

**JOSEPH A. BEVASH** (Hong Kong Office).

**SAMUEL R. WEINER** (San Francisco Office).

**DENA L. BLOOM,** born San Diego, California, January 12, 1962; admitted to bar, 1987, California. *Education:* University of California at Los Angeles (B.A., magna cum laude, 1984); Hastings College of Law, University of California (J.D., magna cum laude, 1987). Order of the Coif. Mem-

*(This Listing Continued)*

**LATHAM & WATKINS, Los Angeles—Continued**

ber, Thurston Society. Member, 1985-1986 and Editor-in-Chief, 1986-1987, Hastings International and Comparative Law Journal.

**CYNTHIA H. CWIK** (San Diego Office).

**PHILIP J. PERZEK** (Chicago, Illinois Office).

**CAROLYNE R. HATHAWAY** (Washington, D.C. Office).

**CARY R. PERLMAN** (Chicago, Illinois Office).

**MICHAEL SCOTT FEELEY,** born Okinawa, December 19, 1961; admitted to bar, 1988, California; 1989, District of Columbia. *Education:* Dartmouth College (A.B., summa cum laude, 1983); The Gregorian University; Harvard Law School (J.D., cum laude, 1987); Oxford University (M.St., in Theology, 1988). Phi Beta Kappa. Rufus Choate Scholar. Daniel Webster Scholar. Recipient, Wiley W. Manuel Pro Bono Award, 1992. Adjunct Professor: Environmental Law, Southwestern University, 1991-1994; Environmental Law, University of Southern California, 1994—. Author: "State Aid to Sectarian Schools in the United States and Israel: A Comparative Historical Analysis," in *International Perspectives on Church and State* (1993); "W(h)ither Goes the EC Directive on Civil Liability for Waste," 15 B.C. Int'l. & Comp. L.R. 241 (1992); "Environmental Considerations of the Emerging U.S.-Mexican Free Trade Agreement," 2 Duke J. of Comp. & Int'l L. (1992); "Green Law Making: A Primer on the European Community's Environmental Legislative Process," 24 Vanderbilt J. of Transactional L. 653 (1991); "Reclaiming the Beautiful Island: Taiwan's Emerging Environmental Regulation," 27 San Diego Law Review 907, 1990; "Toward the Cathedral: Ancient Sanctuary Re-presented in the American Context," 27 San Diego L. Rev. 3, 1990; "The Dissent of Theology: A Legal Analysis of the Curran Case," 15 Hastings Const. L.Q. 7, Fall, 1987. *Member:* Los Angeles County (Chair, International Environmental Subsection, 1991-1993; Environmental Law Section; Executive Committee; International Law Section), American (Member, Sections on: Business Law; Natural Resources) and Inter-Pacific Bar Associations; Air and Hazardous Waste Management Association. *LANGUAGES:* Italian and Spanish.

**JOHN P. JANKA** (Washington, D.C. Office).

**STEVEN M. BAUER** (San Francisco Office).

**LINDA SCHILLING** (Costa Mesa Office).

**BRIAN C. KRISBERG** (New York City Office).

**MICHAEL K. HERTZ** (New York City Office).

**JOSEPH B. FARRELL** (Costa Mesa Office).

**R. RONALD HOPKINSON** (New York City Office).

**SCOTT O. BOWIE,** born Cincinnati, Ohio, October 7, 1960; admitted to bar, 1988, California. *Education:* Occidental College (A.B., cum laude, with highest honors, 1984); London School of Economics and Political Science, London, England; University of California at Los Angeles (J.D., 1988). *Member:* Los Angeles County and American Bar Associations. *LANGUAGES:* French.

**DAVID L. SHAPIRO** (Chicago, Illinois Office).

**TRACY K. EDMONSON** (San Francisco Office).

**DAVID S. RAAB** (Washington, D.C. Office).

**ANTHONY J. RICHMOND,** born San Francisco, California, December 5, 1959; admitted to bar, 1988, California. *Education:* University of California at Berkeley (B.S., 1982); Boalt Hall School of Law, University of California (J.D., 1988). Phi Beta Kappa; Beta Gamma Sigma; Order of the Coif. Certified Public Accountant, California, 1985. *Member:* American Bar Association (Member, Section of Business Law).

**MARK S. MESTER** (Chicago, Illinois Office).

**MICHAEL G. ROMEY,** born Dayton, Ohio, September 9, 1962; admitted to bar, 1988, California. *Education:* Columbia University (B.A., 1985); Boalt Hall School of Law (J.D., 1988). Law Clerk to the Honorable J. Lawrence Irving, U.S. District Court, Southern District of California, 1988-1989. *Member:* Los Angeles County and American Bar Associations. *PRACTICE AREAS:* Environmental Litigation.

**JEFFREY R. HOLMSTEAD** (Washington, D.C. Office).

**SCOTT P. KLEIN,** born New York, N.Y., July 5, 1962; admitted to bar, 1988, California. *Education:* Colgate University (B.A., 1984); Stanford Law School (J.D., with distinction, 1988). Phi Beta Kappa; Order of the Coif.

**SOSI BIRICIK KLIJIAN** (San Diego Office).

*(This Listing Continued)*

**TIMOTHY B. HARDWICKE** (Chicago, Illinois Office).

**ROBERT A. KLYMAN,** born Detroit, Michigan, July 25, 1964; admitted to bar, 1989, California. *Education:* University of Michigan (B.A., with highest distinction, 1986; J.D., cum laude, 1989). Phi Beta Kappa; Otto Graf Scholar; Angell Scholar. Co-Author: "The Revlon Duty As Cause To Terminate Exclusivity: A New Strategy For Effecting Corporate Change in Chapter 11," 4 The Journal of Bankruptcy Law and Practice 621, September/October 1995; "Wading 'Upstream' In Leveraged Transactions: Traditional Guarantees v. 'Net Worth' Guarantees," 46 Business Lawyer 39, 1991. Panelist and Speaker: "Competing Plans of Reorganization," Financial Lawyers Conference, January 1995, Orange County Bankruptcy Forum, April 1995 and Turnaround Management Association, June 1995; "Prepackaged Plans of Reorganization," Financial Lawyers Conference, October 1995. *Member:* Los Angeles County (Member, Subcommittee on Bankruptcy) and American Bar Associations.

**IAN B. BLUMENSTEIN** (New York City Office).

**BARRY J. SHOTTS** (San Diego Office).

**SUSAN S. AZAD,** born Portland, Oregon, May 21, 1962; admitted to bar, 1989, California. *Education:* Oregon State University (B.S., General Science, with highest honors, 1984); University of California at Los Angeles (J.D., 1989). Order of the Coif. Editor, University of California Law Review, 1988-1989. *Member:* Los Angeles and American Bar Associations; California Women Lawyers Association. *PRACTICE AREAS:* Civil Litigation.

**A. BRENT TRUITT** (New York City Office).

**TIMOTHY P. CRUDO** (San Francisco Office).

**GAY L. BRONSON** (New York City Office).

**MICHAEL J. CARROLL,** born Traverse City, Michigan, June 12, 1963; admitted to bar, 1990, California. *Education:* University of Michigan (B.A., 1986; J.D., 1989). Co-Author: "Environmental Law Practice Guide," Matthew Bender & Co., Inc. *Member:* Los Angeles County and American Bar Associations.

**HYUN PARK** (Hong Kong Office).

**MARY ROSE ALEXANDER** (Chicago, Illinois Office).

**J. DREW PAGE** (San Diego Office).

**ROBERT M. HOWARD** (San Diego Office).

**SUSAN PAULSRUD WELCH,** born Vermillion, South Dakota, May 9, 1964; admitted to bar, 1990, California. *Education:* Butler University (B.S., summa cum laude with highest honors in Economics & Business Administration, 1986); University of Chicago (J.D., with honors, 1989). Symposium Editor, University of Chicago Legal Forum, 1989. Clerk to the Honorable W. Eugene Davis, U.S. Court of Appeals for the Fifth Circuit, 1989-1990. *Member:* Los Angeles County and American Bar Associations; California Women Lawyers Association.

**NICHOLAS W. ALLARD** (Washington, D.C. Office).

**JAMES I. HISIGER** (New York City Office).

**RUSSELL HAYMAN,** born Durham, North Carolina, March 19, 1958; admitted to bar, 1983, California and District of Columbia. *Education:* Duke University (B.A., 1979); Yale University (J.D., 1982). Articles Editor, Yale Law Journal, 1981-1982. Author: "Affirmative Action and Electoral Reform," 90 Yale L.J. 1811 (1981); "The Goods or Realty Exemption to Premerger Notification under the Hart-Scott-Rodino Antitrust Improvements Act," 17 U. San Francisco L. Rev. 477 (1983). Assistant U.S. Attorney, Criminal Division, Los Angeles, California, 1983-1990. Executive Assistant to the Administrator, U.S. Drug Enforcement Administration, 1990-1993. *Member:* State Bar of California (Member, Sections on: Antitrust and Trade Regulation Law; Criminal Law; District of Columbia Bar; American Bar Association (Member, Criminal Justice Section).

**DAVID MILES** (London, England Office).

**MARK D. GERSTEIN** (Chicago Office).

*OF COUNSEL*

**JOHN S. WELCH,** born Jerome, Idaho, August 9, 1920; admitted to bar, 1949, California. *Education:* Utah State University (B.S., 1941, Valedictorian); Harvard Law School (LL.B., cum laude, 1948). Phi Kappa Phi. President, Western Pension Conference, Los Angeles Chapter, 1966. *Member:* Los Angeles County and American Bar Associations; Chancery Club

*(This Listing Continued)*

(President, 1980-1981); Los Angeles County Bar Foundation (President, 1981-1982). [Major, U.S. Army, Anti-Aircraft Artillery, 1941-1946]

**CLINTON R. STEVENSON,** born Columbus, Ohio, December 1, 1923; admitted to bar, 1951, California. *Education:* Ohio Wesleyan University (B.A., summa cum laude, 1947); Harvard University (LL.B., cum laude, 1950). Phi Beta Kappa; Pi Sigma Alpha; Omicron Delta Kappa. *Member:* Los Angeles County and American Bar Associations. [LTJG, U.S. Navy, 1942-1946]

**H. RANDALL STOKE,** born Champaign, Illinois, December 14, 1928; admitted to bar, 1955, California. *Education:* University of California at Berkeley (B.S., 1950); University of California (J.D., 1955). Phi Delta Phi. *Member:* Los Angeles County Bar Association (Member, Board of Trustees, 1964-1965).

**RICHARD CARVER,** born Los Angeles, California, July 27, 1933; admitted to bar, 1958, California. *Education:* Stanford University (A.B., 1955; J.D., 1957). Phi Delta Phi; Phi Beta Kappa. Member, Board of Editors, Stanford Law Review, 1956-1957. *Member:* Los Angeles County Bar Association.

**JOHN R. STAHR** (Costa Mesa Office).

**ALAN N. HALKETT,** born Chungking, China, October 5, 1931; admitted to bar, 1962, California. *Education:* University of California at Los Angeles (B.S., 1953; LL.B., 1961). Phi Delta Phi; Order of the Coif. Member, U.C.L.A. Law Review, 1959-1961. *Member:* Los Angeles County Bar Association; Chancery Club. Fellow, American College of Trial Lawyers.

**ROBERT B. WESSLING,** born Chicago, Illinois, October 8, 1937; admitted to bar, 1963, California. *Education:* DePauw University (A.B., 1959); University of Michigan (J.D., with distinction, 1962). Order of the Coif; Phi Beta Kappa; Phi Eta Sigma; Phi Delta Phi; Delta Sigma Rho. Assistant Editor, Michigan Law Review, 1961-1962. Member, Board of Governors, 1971— and President, 1976-1977, Financial Lawyers Conference. *Member:* Los Angeles County Bar Association.

**PHILIP L. REYNOLDS,** born Glendale, California, November 28, 1936; admitted to bar, 1966, California. *Education:* California Institute of Technology (B.S., 1958; M.S., 1959); Harvard University (LL.B., cum laude, 1965).

**WARREN B. ELTERMAN** (New York City Office).

**DAVID A. YORK** (San Francisco Office).

**FREDERICK M. DANZIGER** (New York City Office).

**BETH R. NECKMAN** (New York City Office).

**PATRICK W. DUVAL** (New York City Office).

**REGINA M. SCHLATTER** (Costa Mesa Office).

**JEFFREY S. HABER,** born Chicago, Illinois, September 18, 1962; admitted to bar, 1987, California. *Education:* Yale University (B.A., magna cum laude, 1984; J.D., 1987). *Member:* Los Angeles County and American Bar Associations.

**MICHAEL P. VANDENBERGH** (Washington, D.C. Office).

**ANDREA L. MERSEL** (Costa Mesa Office).

**JOHN P. COFFEY** (New York City Office).

**AUSTIN H. PECK, JR.,** born Pomona, California, December 25, 1913; admitted to bar, 1938, California. *Education:* Stanford University (A.B., with distinction, 1935; J.D., 1938). Phi Delta Phi. Member, Chancery Club. Deputy Commissioner of Corporations, State of California, 1939-1941. Member, Commissioner of Internal Revenue's Advisory Group, 1973-1974. Chairman, Tax Committee, 1967-1968, State Bar of California. *Member:* Los Angeles County and American (Member of Council, Section of Taxation, 1958-1961) Bar Associations; State Bar of California.

**SCOTT R. SMITH** (New York City Office).

**GERALD J. LEWIS** (San Diego Office).

**MARK S. FOWLER** (Washington, D.C. Office).

**STEPHEN M. BURGIN,** born Cincinnati, Ohio, December 10, 1943; admitted to bar, 1970, California. *Education:* University of California at Los Angeles (A.B., with honors, 1966; J.D., 1969). Order of the Coif. Note and Comment Editor, U.C.L.A. Law Review, 1968-1969. *Member:* Los Angeles County and American Bar Associations. **PRACTICE AREAS:** Trusts and Estates.

*(This Listing Continued)*

**DAVID E. NOVITSKI,** born Joliet, Illinois, May 21, 1947; admitted to bar, 1973, New York; 1986, California. *Education:* Northwestern University (B.S.M.E., 1969; J.D., 1972). *Member:* Los Angeles and American Bar Associations.

**DAVID W. FLEMING,** born Davenport, Iowa, September 20, 1934; admitted to bar, 1960, California and U.S. District Court, Southern and Central Districts of California; 1963, U.S. Supreme Court and U.S. Court of Military Appeals; 1970, U.S. Court of Appeals, Ninth Circuit. *Education:* Augustana College (B.A., 1956); University of California at Los Angeles (J.D., 1959). Phi Beta Kappa. Chairman, Valley Presbyterian Hospital, 1988—. President, Los Angeles City Board of Fire Commissioners, 1995—. Chairman, Economic Alliance of the San Fernando Valley, 1996—. Chairman, Los Angeles County Blue Ribbon Children's Services Planning Committee, 1990. Director, Los Angeles 2000 Partnership, 1989-1994. Advisory Director, Automobile Club of Southern California, 1990—. CEO and Vice Chair, 1989—, Technology Foundation of Motion Picture-Television Industry. Vice Chair, Los Angeles County Children's Planning Council, 1990—. Director, LEARN, 1993—. Chairman, Valley Industry and Commerce Association (VICA), 1988-1990. Member, Los Angeles Olympic Organizing Committee, 1979-1985. Los Angeles County Commissioner, 1970-1973. Recipient: The Fernando Award, 1991; The Tree of Life Award, Jewish National Fund, 1991; The Anti-Defamation League Community Award, 1995. Member, National Panel of Arbitrators, American Arbitration Association, 1962—. Member, Los Angeles County's Superior Court Site Selection Committee, 1989—. *Member:* Los Angeles County (Member, Judicial Procedures Commission, 1970-1973), San Fernando Valley and American Bar Associations; State Bar of California; American Judicature Society; American College of Mortgage Attorneys. (Also practicing individually, Universal City).

**THOMAS B. TRIMBLE** (Washington, D.C. Office).

**GORDON SIMONDS** (San Francisco Office).

**DAVID M. LEIVE** (Washington, D.C. Office).

**DESIREE ICAZA KELLOGG** (San Diego Office).

**JEAN M. DONNELLY** (Costa Mesa Office).

**YANLEI WU** (Washington, D.C. Office).

**HERVÉ GOURAIGE** (Newark, New Jersey and New York City Offices).

**RICHARD B. ULMER JR.** (San Francisco Office).

**DANIEL K. SETTELMAYER,** born Whittier, California, February 15, 1961; admitted to bar, 1987, California. *Education:* University of Southern California (A.B., 1983); Santa Clara University (J.D., 1987); New York University (LL.M., 1991).

**DEAN G. DUNLAVEY** (Costa Mesa Office).

**JAMES O. COPLEY** (New York City Office).

**GREGORY K. MILLER** (San Francisco Office).

**JONATHAN S. BERCK** (London Office).

**KENNETH R. WHITING, JR.** (San Francisco Office).

**BRUCE J. PRAGER** (New York City Office).

**BERNARD C. BYRNES** (New York City Office).

**LEV S. SIMKIN** (Moscow, Russia Office).

**LOUISE ZEITZEW** (New York City Office).

**CHRISTOPHER R. PLAUT** (New York City Office).

**JIYEON LEE LIM** (New York City Office).

*ASSOCIATES*

**CHRISTOPHER D. LUEKING** (Chicago, Illinois Office).

**CARLOS ALVAREZ** (New York City Office).

**ADELE K. CARDOZA** (Costa Mesa Office).

**ELISSA GANBARG BENUDIS** (New York City Office).

**GAIL A. MATTHEWS** (New York City Office).

**JEFFREY T. WALD** (New York City Office).

**MARK D. BECKETT** (New York City Office).

**MARC J. VEILLEUX** (New York City Office).

**KATHERINE A. LAUER** (San Diego Office).

*(This Listing Continued)*

*LATHAM & WATKINS, Los Angeles—Continued*

**MARLA S. BECKER** (New York City Office).

**J. WESLEY SKOW** (San Francisco Office).

**GREGORY A. EZRING** (New York City Office).

**KIMBERLY M. MCCORMICK** (San Diego Office).

**AMOS M. LEVY,** born Princeton, New Jersey, March 30, 1962; admitted to bar, 1988, New York (Not admitted in California). *Education:* Harvard College (A.B., magna cum laude, 1984); New York University School of Law (J.D., 1988). *Member:* Los Angeles County Bar Association (Member, Corporate Securities Law and Regulation Committee).

**JEFFREY G. MORAN** (Chicago, Illinois Office).

**JOHN T. BRENNAN** (New York City Office).

**PATRICK J. CARTY** (New York City Office).

**JEFFREY M. GOODMAN** (New York City Office).

**ELISABETH L. GOOT** (New York City Office).

**DEAN T. JANIS** (San Diego Office).

**DAVID C. MECKLER** (Costa Mesa Office).

**JENNIFER C. ARCHIE** (Washington, D.C. Office).

**MARK I. MICHIGAN** (New York City Office).

**E. WILLIAM CATTAN, JR.** (New York City Office).

**KENNETH M. FITZGERALD** (San Diego Office).

**DORN G. BISHOP** (San Diego Office).

**KIM NATALIE ALICIA BORAS** (New York City Office).

**L. SUSAN MCGINNIS,** born Hollywood, California, January 16, 1956; admitted to bar, 1990, California. *Education:* University of California at Los Angeles (A.B., 1978); University of Southern California (A.M., 1986; J.D., 1990). Staff Member, 1988-1989 and Publication Editor, 1989-1990, Southern California Law Review. Instructor, Legal Writing, University of Southern California, 1989-1990. *Member:* Los Angeles County and American Bar Associations; National Health Lawyers Association; Healthcare Financial Management Association; Women in Health Administration.

**MARIAN A. HARVEY,** born Inglewood, California, April 30, 1959; admitted to bar, 1990, California. *Education:* Georgetown University; University of California at San Diego (B.A., 1981); University of San Diego (J.D., magna cum laude, 1990). Member, Association of Environmental Professionals, 1983-1996. Author: "Allegheny-Pittsburgh Coal v. Co. Comr. of Webster Co.: Equal Protection and Property Taxation, A New Challenge to Proposition 13?" 26 San Diego Law Review 1173 (1989). *Member:* Los Angeles County and American Bar Associations. *PRACTICE AREAS:* Environmental; Land Use.

**STEVEN ATLEE,** born Redlands, California, May 3, 1965; admitted to bar, 1990, California. *Education:* Yale University (B.A., summa cum laude, distinction in Economics and Political Science, 1987); University of Southern California Law Center (J.D., 1990). Order of the Coif. Member, Southern California Law Review, 1988-1990. Legal Writing Instructor, University of Southern California Law Center, 1989-1990.

**JAMES L. ARNONE,** born California, January 16, 1965; admitted to bar, 1990, California. *Education:* University of California, Los Angeles (B.A., 1987); Harvard University (J.D., cum laude, 1990). *Member:* Los Angeles County (Chair, Environmental Law Section, Legislative Review Committee; Member, Executive Committee, Environmental Law Section) and American (Member, Litigation and Real Property Sections) Bar Associations.

**JEFF D. WESSELKAMPER** (San Francisco Office).

**MARCUS A. MCDANIEL,** born Dayton, Ohio, April 18, 1964; admitted to bar, 1990, California. *Education:* Wheaton College (B.A., with honors, 1986); Harvard University (J.D., cum laude, 1990). *Member:* Los Angeles County and American Bar Associations.

**DANIEL T. LENNON** (Washington, D.C. Office).

**ANYA GOLDIN** (Moscow, Russia Office).

**EVA HERBST DAVIS,** born Washington, D.C., April 13, 1965; admitted to bar, 1990, California; 1991, District of Columbia. *Education:* Duke University (A.B., summa cum laude, 1987); Harvard University (J.D., cum

*(This Listing Continued)*

laude, 1990). Phi Beta Kappa. *PRACTICE AREAS:* Corporate; Securities; Corporate Finance; Mergers and Acquisitions.

**DAVID C. FLATTUM** (Costa Mesa Office).

**GREGORY N. PIMSTONE,** born Cape Town, South Africa, December 4, 1964; admitted to bar, 1990, California. *Education:* University of California at Berkeley (A.B., with honors, 1987); Boalt Hall School of Law (J.D., 1990). *Member:* Los Angeles County and American Bar Associations; State Bar of California (Member, Litigation Section).

**STEVEN J. LEVINE** (San Diego Office).

**WAYNE S. FLICK,** born Italy, December 11, 1963; admitted to bar, 1990, California; U.S. Supreme Court. *Education:* Cornell University (B.S., 1985); Boston University (J.D., cum laude, 1990). G. Joseph Tauro Scholar, 1988; Paul J. Liacos Scholar, 1989; Edward Hennesey Scholar, 1990. Lecturer, "The First Amendment and the Fourth Estate," Boston University School of Communications Masters Program, 1989-1990. *Member:* Los Angeles County (Member: Litigation and Employment Law Sections) and American (Member, Litigation Section) Bar Associations. *PRACTICE AREAS:* Employment Law.

**MAUREEN SMITH** (New York City Office).

**PETER M. GILHULY,** born Stamford, Connecticut, August 20, 1961; admitted to bar, 1990, California. *Education:* Wesleyan University (B.A., with honors, 1983); Harvard Law School (J.D., cum laude, 1990). Volunteer, U.S. Peace Corps, Volunteer, Nepal, 1983-1986. Co-Author: "W(h)ither Goes the EC Directive on Civil Liability for Waste," 15 B.C. Int'l & Comp. L.R. 241 (1992); "Green Law-Making: A Primer on the European Community's Environmental Legislation Process," 24 Vanderbilt J. of Transnational L. 653 (1991). Member: Advisory Board of Directors, Pacific Gemini Partners, L.L.C., 1995—; Board of Directors, Public Counsel, 1994—; L.A. County Barrister Executive Committee, 1994-1995; Holiday Wish Committee. *Member:* Los Angeles County and American Bar Associations. *LANGUAGES:* Nepali. *TRANSACTIONS:* Chapter 11 Debtor Representations: Wherehouse Entertainment, Inc.; Acme Holdings, Inc. (Prepackaged Bankruptcy); Cherokee, Inc.; First Executive Corporation. *PRACTICE AREAS:* Bankruptcy (80%); Corporate (20%).

**CYNTHIA A. ROTELL,** born Michigan, January 29, 1960; admitted to bar, 1990, California. *Education:* Barnard College (B.A., cum laude, 1982); Yale Law School, 1989-1990; Brooklyn Law School (J.D., summa cum laude, 1990).

**MARK BRUCE ABBOTT,** born Wigston, England, August 20, 1964; admitted to bar, 1989, California. *Education:* Georgetown University (B.S.F.S., 1986); Boalt Hall School of Law, University of California (J.D., 1989). Managing Editor, University of California Law Review, 1988-1989.

**PETER HUSTON** (San Francisco Office).

**ANDREW MARC PALEY,** born Manhasset, New York, October 7, 1965; admitted to bar, 1990, California. *Education:* Yale University (B.A., cum laude, 1987); Stanford University (J.D., 1990). Articles Editor, Stanford Journal of International Law and Stanford Environmental Law Journal, 1987-1990.

**GREGORY M. PETTIGREW,** born Lafayette, Indiana, July 25, 1964; admitted to bar, 1990, California. *Education:* University of Michigan (B.A., with highest distinction, 1986); Northwestern University (J.D., magna cum laude, 1990). Phi Beta Kappa; Order of the Coif.

**ANN K. O'BRIEN,** born St. Louis, Missouri, January 30, 1964; admitted to bar, 1990, California. *Education:* University of Arizona (B.A., magna cum laude, 1986; J.D., magna cum laude, 1990). Phi Beta Kappa; Order of the Coif. Author: "Limited Recovery Rule as a Dam: Preventing a Flood of Litigation for Negligent Infliction of Pure Economic Loss," 31 Ariz. L. Rev. 959, 1989.

**DONNA J. WILLIAMS** (San Diego Office).

**WILLIAM J. CALDARELLI** (San Diego Office).

**JON L. PRAED** (Washington, D.C. Office).

**DAVID F. RANDELL** (Chicago, Illinois Office).

**JAMES H. BARKER, III** (Washington, D.C. Office).

**CURTIS P. LU** (Washington, D.C. Office).

**JENNIFER UPHAM SAUNDERS,** born Laguna Beach, California, July 30, 1960; admitted to bar, 1990, California. *Education:* University of California at Santa Cruz (B.A., with honors, 1982); Birmingham University, U.K.; University of California, Boalt Hall School of Law (J.D., 1990).

*(This Listing Continued)*

# PROFESSIONAL BIOGRAPHIES — CALIFORNIA—LOS ANGELES

Member, U.S. Peace Corps, Sri Lanka, 1983-1986. Senior Executive Editor, California Law Review, 1989-1990. Clerk to the Honorable D. Lowell Jensen, U.S. District Court for the Northern District of California, 1990-1991. Member, Editorial Board, San Francisco Barrister Law Journal, 1991. Member, Los Angeles Barristers Bench and Bar Relations Committee, 1992-1993. *Member:* Los Angeles County and American Bar Associations. **PRACTICE AREAS:** Finance.

**TERESA D. BAER** (Washington, D.C. Office).

**JEFFREY H. KOPPELE** (New York City Office).

**DAVID L. SCHWARTZ** (Washington, D.C. Office).

**S. H. SPENCER COMPTON** (New York City Office).

**DAVID A. BARRETT** (Washington, D.C. Office).

**JOHN R. TINKHAM** (Chicago, Illinois Office).

**REBECCA D. ROBERTS,** born Los Angeles, California, March 28, 1964; admitted to bar, 1992, Pennsylvania (Not admitted in California). *Education:* Stanford University (B.A., 1986); Georgetown University (J.D., 1991). Member, Georgetown University National Law Alumni Board. *Member:* National Health Lawyers Association. **PRACTICE AREAS:** Health Care Law.

**SCOTT R. MCCAW** (New York City Office).

**REGINA L. SCINTA** (New York City Office).

**ANDREW D. RICHMAN** (New York City Office).

**JAMES S. BLANK** (New York City Office).

**CORINNE M. PLUMMER** (London, England Office).

**HOWARD A. MATALON** (Newark, New Jersey Office).

**KATHRYN SHAW COLLINS** (Chicago, Illinois Office).

**JOSEPH M. KRONSNOBLE** (Chicago, Illinois Office).

**DIANA L. DAY** (San Diego Office).

**R. BRIAN TIMMONS** (Costa Mesa Office).

**ORA T. FRUEHAUF** (San Francisco Office).

**DAVID JUDSON BARRETT** (San Diego Office).

**ELLEN L. MARKS** (Chicago, Illinois Office).

**SCOTT C. HERLIHY** (Washington, D.C. Office).

**ROBIN D. DAL SOGLIO,** born Missoula, Montana, October 3, 1964; admitted to bar, 1991, California. *Education:* California State University, Northridge (B.S., 1988); University of Southern California (J.D., 1991). Member, University of Southern California Computer/Tax Law Journals. *Member:* American Bar Association; Women Lawyers' Association of Los Angeles. **PRACTICE AREAS:** Employment Litigation.

**SCOTT B. GARNER** (Costa Mesa Office).

**JAMES P. BEAUBIEN,** born Flint, Michigan, June 14, 1963; admitted to bar, 1991, California. *Education:* Princeton University (A.B., cum laude, 1986); University of California School of Law (J.D., 1991).

**PHILIP J. PERRY** (Washington, D.C. Office).

**RICHARD M. TROBMAN** (New York City Office).

**LISA A. VON ESCHEN,** born New York, N.Y., November 29, 1964; admitted to bar, 1991, California. *Education:* College of William and Mary (B.A., with honors in English, 1986); New York University (J.D., 1991). Phi Beta Kappa.

**JAMES R. BARRETT** (Washington, D.C. Office).

**MICHAEL W. STURROCK,** born Van Nuys, California, August 20, 1965; admitted to bar, 1991, California. *Education:* University of Southern California (B.S., cum laude, 1987); Georgetown University (J.D., cum laude, 1991). **PRACTICE AREAS:** Corporate.

**KIMBERLY L. WILKINSON** (San Francisco Office).

**ROBIN M. HULSHIZER** (Chicago Office).

**AMY G. NEFOUSE** (San Diego Office).

**DEBORAH A. BIGBEE,** born Santa Fe, New Mexico, April 7, 1966; admitted to bar, 1992, California, U.S. District Court, Central and Northern Districts of California and U.S. Court of Appeals, Ninth Circuit. *Education:* University of Arizona (B.S., cum laude, 1988); University of California, Hastings College of the Law (J.D., magna cum laude, 1991). Beta Gamma Sigma. Order of the Coif. Recipient, Golden Eagle Scholar Award, Academic All American. Associate Editor, 1990-1991 and Member, 1989-1991, The Hastings Law Journal. Clerk to the Honorable David R. Thompson, U.S. Court of Appeals for the Ninth Circuit, 1991-1992. *Member:* American Bar Association.

**BRUCE D. GELLMAN** (San Francisco Office).

**PAUL J. HUNT** (Washington, D.C. Office).

**ANTHONY I. FENWICK** (San Francisco Office).

**MARIA P. HOYE,** born Havana, Cuba, October 26, 1966; admitted to bar, 1991, California. *Education:* California State University at Northridge (B.S., 1988); University of California at Los Angeles School of Law (J.D., 1991). **LANGUAGES:** Spanish. **PRACTICE AREAS:** Environmental.

**KATHLEEN M. O'PREY TRUMAN,** born Chicopee Falls, Massachusetts, August 6, 1966; admitted to bar, 1992, California, U.S. District Court, Central District of California and U.S. Court of Appeals, 9th Circuit. *Education:* University of California at Los Angeles (B.A., cum laude, 1988); University of California, Hastings College of the Law (J.D., magna cum laude, 1991). Phi Delta Phi. Clerk to the Honorable Cynthia Holcomb Hall, U.S. Court of Appeals, 9th Circuit, 1992. *Member:* American Bar Association; Women Lawyers Association of Los Angeles; Town Hall Associates.

**VIVIAN CLARA STRACHE** (Washington, D.C. Office).

**CHRISTOPHER J. PETERS** (Chicago, Illinois Office).

**MELISSA A. ROPER** (New York City Office).

**GWYN GOODSON TIMMS** (San Diego Office).

**CHARLES W. COX, II** (Costa Mesa Office).

**DAVID T. KRASKA** (San Francisco Office).

**MARCI L. SMITH,** born Craig, Colorado, September 27, 1965; admitted to bar, 1992, California. *Education:* Brigham Young University (B.A., cum laude, 1988; J.D., magna cum laude, 1991). Order of the Coif. Articles Editor, Brigham Young University Law Review. *Member:* Los Angeles County Bar Association.

**ANNETTE L. HAYES** (Washington, D.C. Office).

**SCOTT C. LEWIS,** born Los Angeles, California, June 10, 1965; admitted to bar, 1991, California. *Education:* University of California at Berkeley (B.A., with honors); University of Michigan (J.D., cum laude, 1991). *Member:* Los Angeles County Bar Association. **PRACTICE AREAS:** Corporate Securities; Mergers and Acquisitions.

**WHITNEY E. PETERSON** (San Diego Office).

**CHARLES K. RUCK** (Costa Mesa Office).

**JULIAN Y. KIM** (Washington, D.C. Office).

**MICHAEL J. GUZMAN** (Washington, D.C. Office).

**KIMBERLY AROUH** (San Diego Office).

**KENNETH A. SCHUHMACHER** (London, England Office).

**PAUL N. SINGARELLA** (Costa Mesa Office).

**MAUREEN A. RILEY** (New York City Office).

**GREG S. SLATER** (Washington, D.C. Office).

**MAUREEN C. SHAY** (New York City Office).

**PETER J. FALCONER** (Chicago, Illinois Office).

**DENNIS M. WALSH** (New York City Office).

**CHRISTOPHER HARRISON** (London, England Office).

**TRACY M. PRESTON** (San Francisco Office).

**STEPHEN K. PHILLIPS** (San Francisco Office).

**JAMES W. BAKER** (San Diego Office).

**J. SCOTT HODGKINS,** born Encino, California, October 31, 1960; admitted to bar, 1992, California. *Education:* University of Southern California (B.S., cum laude, 1982; M.B.T., 1991; J.D., 1992). Beta Alpha Psi; Beta Gamma Sigma; Order of the Coif. **PRACTICE AREAS:** Corporate; Securities.

**DAVID A. NELSON** (Chicago, Illinois Office).

**MICHAEL S. WROBLEWSKI** (Washington, D.C. Office).

**HUGH L. BURNS** (New York City Office).

*(This Listing Continued)*

**LATHAM & WATKINS, Los Angeles—Continued**

**DAVID M. HERNAND,** born Los Angeles, California, December 15, 1966; admitted to bar, 1992, California. *Education:* University of California, Los Angeles (B.A., cum laude, 1989); Georgetown University (J.D., cum laude, 1992). Notes Editor, The Georgetown University Law Journal, 1991-1992.

**MICHAEL A. BELL** (Washington, D.C. Office).

**DEAN M. KATO,** born Los Angeles, California, May 27, 1965; admitted to bar, 1992, California. *Education:* Oxford University, Oxford, England; Columbia University (B.A., 1987); University of California, Boalt Hall School of Law (J.D., 1991). Fulbright Fellow to Japan, Tokyo University Faculty of Law, 1991-1992. Associate Editor, California Law Review. **LANGUAGES:** Japanese.

**CRAIG M. GARNER** (San Diego Office).

**MINH N. VU** (Washington, D.C. Office).

**ERIC A. GAYNOR,** born Los Angeles, California, November 4, 1966; admitted to bar, 1993, California. *Education:* University of California at Los Angeles (B.A., 1989); University of Southern California Law Center (J.D., 1993). Notes Editor, Southern California Law Review, 1992-1993. Order of the Coif. **PRACTICE AREAS:** Corporate.

**ANDREW HAN,** born Cleveland, Ohio, October 29, 1968; admitted to bar, 1993, California; 1994, Illinois. *Education:* Columbia University (B.A., cum laude, 1990); University of Chicago (J.D., 1993). **PRACTICE AREAS:** Corporate.

**AMY N. KEROES,** born San Francisco, California, September 24, 1968; admitted to bar, 1993, California. *Education:* Northwestern University (B.A., with honors, 1990); University of California School of Law (J.D., 1993). Co-Author: "Elements of the Crime and Sufficiency of the Evidence," in *California Crimes and Defenses* (West Publishing, 1996).

**TERI L. WITTEMAN,** born San Pablo, California, May 29, 1968; admitted to bar, 1993, California. *Education:* University of California at Berkeley (B.A., with honors and distinction, 1990); University of California School of Law, Los Angeles (J.D., 1993). Order of the Coif. Co-Author: "Stormy Weather Looms Ahead," International Tax Review (February, 1994).

**LINDA HARRISON EDWARDS,** born Houston, Texas, September 27, 1966; admitted to bar, 1993, California. *Education:* Trinity University (B.A., 1988); University of Texas (J.D., with honors, 1993). **LANGUAGES:** Spanish. **PRACTICE AREAS:** Corporate.

**SIMON J. DICKENS** (Chicago, Illinois Office).

**DANIEL J. O'SHEA,** (admission pending). (New York City Office).

**MARC D. JAFFE** (New York City Office).

**DANIEL J. ROSS** (New York City Office).

**PETER M. LABONSKI** (New York City Office).

**MICHÈLE O. PENZER** (New York City Office).

**ROBERT F. KENNEDY** (New York City Office).

**KENNETH D. CREWS** (Chicago, Illinois Office).

**GARY R. IGNATIN,** born Philadelphia, Pennsylvania, June 11, 1968; admitted to bar, 1993, California. *Education:* Princeton University (B.S.E., cum laude, 1990); University of Pennsylvania (J.D., 1993). Order of the Coif. Recipient, Nathan Burke Memorial Prize for Copyrights, 1993. Editor, University of Pennsylvania Law Review, 1991-1993. Author: "Let the Hackers Hack: Allowing the Reverse Engineering of Copyrighted Computer Programs to Achieve Compatibility," 140 U. Pa. L. Rev. 1999 (1992).

**JEFFREY L. KATEMAN,** born Boston, Massachusetts, November 23, 1966; admitted to bar, 1993, New York; 1994, California. *Education:* Columbia College (A.B., 1989); Columbia Law School (J.D., 1992). Harlan Fiske Stone Scholar.

**JOSEPH A. SULLIVAN** (Chicago, Illinois Office).

**ANAT HAKIM** (New York City Office).

**MICHELLE M. CARROLL,** born Fontana, California, November 19, 1968; admitted to bar, 1993, California. *Education:* Claremont McKenna College (B.A., magna cum laude, 1990); University of California, Boalt Hall School of Law (J.D., 1993); University of Warwick, Coventry, England. Phi Beta Kappa. *Member:* American Bar Association.

**ERIC J. CUSTER,** born Lawton, Oklahoma, August 24, 1968; admitted to bar, 1993, California. *Education:* Kansas State University (B.A., summa cum laude, 1990); University of Texas (J.D., with honors, 1993). Phi Beta Kappa; Phi Kappa Phi. Member, *The Review of Litigation,* 1991-1992.

**BRIAN H. LEVEY,** born Los Angeles, California, September 13, 1967; admitted to bar, 1993, California. *Education:* Stanford University (A.B., with distinction and departmental honors, 1989; J.D., 1993). Associate Editor, Stanford Law Review. Recipient, Anna Laura Meyers Award for Distinguished Honors Thesis in Economics. Co-Author: "Elements of the Crime and Sufficiency of the Evidence," in *California Crimes and Defenses* (West Publishing, 1996).

**STUART L. LEVITON,** born Tulsa, Oklahoma, May 3, 1966; admitted to bar, 1993, California. *Education:* The Wharton School, University of Pennsylvania (B.S., 1987); University of Texas (J.D., with honors, 1993). Order of the Coif. Member, 1991-1992 and Notes Editor, 1992-1993, Texas Law Review. Author: "Is Anyone Listening to Our Students? A Plea for Respect and Inclusion," 21 Fla. St. U. L. Rev. 35, 1993; "The Fourth Amendment in Texas Public High Schools: Friend or Foe? A Question of Perspective," State Bar (Texas) Section Report: Juvenile Law, Dec. 1992, pg. 5. *Member:* American Bar Association.

**SUSAN M. MARSCH,** born Detroit, Michigan, April 18, 1956; admitted to bar, 1993, California. *Education:* University of Michigan (B.B.A., 1978; J.D., with honors, 1993). Certified Public Accountant, Michigan, 1987. *Member:* American Bar Association.

**PARRIS J. SANZ,** born San Francisco, California, August 9, 1968; admitted to bar, 1993, California. *Education:* University of California at Berkeley (A.B., with high honors, 1990); Harvard Law School (J.D., 1993). Phi Beta Kappa. **PRACTICE AREAS:** Taxation.

**JOHN B. DUER** (New York City Office).

**C. CHAD JOHNSON** (New York City Office).

**LEE D. HWANG,** born Seattle, Washington, May 16, 1969; admitted to bar, 1993, California; 1994, District of Columbia. *Education:* Dartmouth College (A.B., 1989); Harvard Law School (J.D., 1992). Phi Beta Kappa. Member, Harvard Law Review.

**DARCI A. LANPHERE,** born Bethesda, Maryland, May 20, 1968; admitted to bar, 1993, California. *Education:* Brown University (A.B., 1990); University of California, Boalt Hall School of Law (J.D., 1993).

**ANDREA S. MATIAUDA** (Costa Mesa Office).

**DANIEL A. THOMSON** (Costa Mesa Office).

**PILAR S. PARDUCCI,** born Buffalo, New York, November 18, 1966; admitted to bar, 1993, California. *Education:* University of California at Los Angeles (B.A., cum laude, 1990); Cornell University (J.D., 1993). Editor, Cornell Law Review.

**BRUCE R. LEDESMA** (San Francisco Office).

**MARY E. BRITTON** (Washington, D.C. Office).

**STEVEN D. MCKENNEY,** born Seattle, Washington, August 12, 1965; admitted to bar, 1993, California; U.S. District Court, Central District of California. *Education:* University of California at Los Angeles (B.A., Economics/Business, summa cum laude, 1988); Harvard University (J.D., cum laude, 1993). Phi Beta Kappa. Economics Department Outstanding Scholar. **PRACTICE AREAS:** International Joint Venture (80%); Corporate (20%).

**DAVID L. KUIPER** (Costa Mesa Office).

**KENNETH G. SCHULER** (Chicago, Illinois Office).

**DANIEL SCOTT SCHECTER,** born Dayton, Ohio, July 25, 1966; admitted to bar, 1993, California; 1994, U.S. District Court, Central District of California and U.S. Court of Appeals, Ninth Circuit. *Education:* University of California, Berkeley (B.A., 1989); University of Southern California Law Center (J.D., 1993). Order of the Coif. Articles Editor, 1992-1993 and Staff Member, 1991-1992, Southern California Law Review. Author: "Consequential Damage Limitations And Cross-Subsidization: An Independent Approach to U.C.C. Section 2-719," 66 Southern California Law Review 1273 (1993). Legal Writing Instructor, University of Southern California Law Center, 1992-1993. Law Clerk to The Honorable Irving Hill, U.S. District Court, Central District of California, 1993-1994.

**SUSAN P. FLATTUM,** born Fullerton, California, April 29, 1968; admitted to bar, 1993, California. *Education:* University of Southern California (B.S., 1990); Georgetown University (J.D., 1993).

*(This Listing Continued)*

**DANIEL W. BURKE** (Costa Mesa Office).

**MICHAEL J. MALECEK** (San Francisco Office).

**WILLIAM C. TAYLER** (San Diego Office).

**LAURA GABRIEL** (San Francisco Office).

**DARIUS OGLOZA,** (admission pending). (San Francisco Office).

**SYLVIA A. STEIN** (Chicago, Illinois Office).

**JOHN H. GOMEZ,** born Portsmouth, Virginia, May 10, 1965; admitted to bar, 1993, California. *Education:* University of San Diego (B.B.A., 1989); Yale University (J.D., 1993). Law Clerk, Judge Marilyn L. Huff, United States District Court, Southern District of California, 1993-1994. **LANGUAGES:** Spanish.

**WILLIAM A. VOXMAN** (Washington, D.C. Office).

**NAOMI H. KOBAYASHI,** born Houston, Texas, April 3, 1968; admitted to bar, 1994, California. *Education:* Columbia College (B.A., summa cum laude, 1990); Yale Law School (J.D., 1993). Phi Beta Kappa. Law Clerk, Chief Judge William Matthew Byrne, Jr., U.S. District Court, Central District of California, 1993-1994.

**JERIANNE E. MANCINI** (New York City Office).

**ANTON LEOF** (San Francisco Office).

**RANDALL D. ROTH** (New York City Office).

**MICHAEL A. BOND** (New York City Office).

**DAVID N. FONG** (New York City Office).

**GARY A. KASHAR,** born New York, N.Y., October 26, 1967; admitted to bar, 1993, California. *Education:* University of Texas School of Business (B.B.A., 1990; M.P.A., 1990); University of Texas School of Law (J.D., 1992). **PRACTICE AREAS:** Corporate.

**MICHAEL D. SMITH** (Chicago, Illinois Office).

**DEIDRE L. SCHNEIDER** (San Diego Office).

**JILL H. SILFEN,** born Far Rockaway, New York, November 25, 1966; admitted to bar, 1991, California. *Education:* State University of New York at Albany (B.A., 1988); University of Southern California (J.D., 1991).

**ALICE S. FISHER** (Washington, D.C. Office).

**NEIL CUMMINGS** (New York City Office).

**JULIA E. PARRY** (San Diego Office).

**DAWN D. SCHILLER** (Chicago, Illinois Office).

**MARSHA Y. REEVES** (Washington, D.C. Office).

**RICHARD S. DAVIS,** born Hartford, Connecticut; admitted to bar, 1994, California. *Education:* University of Pennsylvania; University of Southern California (J.D., 1994).

**TED FIKRE,** born Addis Ababa, Ethiopia, July 19, 1967; admitted to bar, 1994, California. *Education:* Princeton University (A.B., magna cum laude, 1989); Stanford Law School (J.D., with distinction, 1994).

**FRANCIS Y. PARK,** born Seoul, South Korea, October 10, 1968; admitted to bar, 1994, California. *Education:* University of California, Berkeley (B.A., 1991); Columbia University (J.D., 1994). Phi Beta Kappa. Harlan Fiske Stone Scholar.

**ERIC A. RICHARDSON** (New York City Office).

**STEVEN H. SCHULMAN** (Washington, D.C. Office).

**CLAUDIA M. O'BRIEN** (Washington, D.C. Office).

**IAN H. FISHER** (Chicago, Illinois Office).

**GREGORY O. LUNT,** born Salt Lake City, Utah, May 6, 1967; admitted to bar, 1994, California. *Education:* University of Utah (B.A., cum laude, 1991); Columbia University (J.D., 1994). Phi Beta Kappa; Phi Kappa Phi; Kappa Tau Alpha. Harlan Fiske Stone Scholar. Author: "Graduation and the GATT: The Problem of NICs," Columbia Journal of Transnational Law (1994). **LANGUAGES:** Korean.

**DANIEL L. MARTENS,** born Des Moines, Iowa, September 4, 1968; admitted to bar, 1994, California. *Education:* University of Iowa (B.A., with honors and distinction, 1991; J.D., with special honors and high distinction, 1994). Phi Beta Kappa. **PRACTICE AREAS:** Employment Litigation (75%); Litigation (25%).

**CHRISTINE LEGRAND LEHMAN** (San Francisco Office).

*(This Listing Continued)*

**JAMES R. DUTRO** (San Francisco Office).

**CAROLYN R. WORSLEY** (New York City Office).

**ASSAF J. HENIG,** born Kefar Saba, Israel, August 25, 1968; admitted to bar, 1994, California. *Education:* Princeton University (A.B., 1990); University of California School of Law (J.D., 1994). Articles Editor, UCLA Law Review.

**ROBERT S. MICHITARIAN** (San Francisco Office).

**MATTHEW W. WALCH** (Chicago, Illinois Office).

**JENS H. HILLEN,** born Oakland, California, April 17, 1966; admitted to bar, 1994, California. *Education:* University of California at Berkeley (B.S.M.E., 1989); University of Southern California (J.D., 1994). Executive Editor, Southern California Law Review, Volume 67. Author: "The Court of Appeals for the Federal Circuit: Independent Review of Patent Decisions and the Constitutional Facts Doctrine," 67 S. Cal. L. Rev. 187 (1993).

**KATHLEEN KILOURIE,** born Long Beach, California, September 25, 1966; admitted to bar, 1994, California. *Education:* University of Southern California (B.S., 1988; J.D., 1994). Staff Member, Executive Editor, Southern California Law Review. Co-Author: with Brian G. Cartwright and John J. Huber, "Current Developments in Interaction," Prentice Hall Law & Business 16th Annual Institute.

**MICHAEL G. MISHIK,** born Brooklyn, New York, August 28, 1964; admitted to bar, 1994, California. *Education:* United States Naval Academy (B.S., with merit, 1986); University of California School of Law (J.D., 1994). Pi Sigma Alpha. Member, National Moot Court Team. [With U.S. Marine Corps, 1986-1991]

**MARY C. TESH,** born Seattle, Washington, October 29, 1966; admitted to bar, 1994, California. *Education:* Vassar College (B.A., 1989). Phi Beta Kappa.

**DOMINIC K.L. YOONG,** born Singapore, Singapore, August 23, 1967; admitted to bar, 1994, California. *Education:* Pomona College (B.A., cum laude, 1988); University College, Oxford University; Cornell Law School (J.D., magna cum laude, 1994). Phi Delta Phi. Mortar Board. Pomona Scholar. Order of the Coif. Editor, Cornell Law Review. Recipient, American Jurisprudence Awards: Torts; Legal Writing; Commercial Law. [Singapore Armed Forces, 22nd Battalion Singapore Artillery, 1988-1991, Operations Officer, LTA]

**TAD J. FREESE** (San Francisco Office).

**SONY BEN-MOSHE** (San Diego Office).

**MICHELLE DUNCAN BERGMAN** (New York City Office).

**JOANN LAURENTINO** (New York City Office).

**DENISE R. BEN-ATTAR** (New York City Office).

**CAROLE FERGUSON JOHNSON** (New York City Office).

**ROSE GREENBERG** (New York City Office).

**THEODORE K. SMITH** (Moscow, Russia Office).

**ROLAND S. YOUNG** (New York City Office).

**CHRISTIAN B. MCGRATH** (Chicago, Illinois Office).

**LYNNE S. HOFFENBERG** (Chicago, Illinois Office).

**ANDREW B. MUNRO,** born New York, N.Y., August 9, 1968; admitted to bar, 1994, California. *Education:* University of California, Los Angeles (B.A., summa cum laude, 1991); Harvard University (J.D., 1994). Phi Beta Kappa. Submissions Editor, Harvard International Law Journal. **PRACTICE AREAS:** Corporate; Telecommunications; Healthcare.

**LAURA I. BUSHNELL** (Costa Mesa Office).

**R. SCOTT SHEAN** (Costa Mesa Office).

**MALU S. MERCADO** (San Francisco Office).

**DONALD A. FISHMAN** (Washington, D.C. Office).

**OSWALD B. COUSINS, II** (San Francisco Office).

**HYEN-AE JANE SUNG** (San Francisco Office).

**LAUREN E. PASSMORE** (New York City Office).

**IAN A. GERARD** (New York City Office).

**MIRIAM T. JONA** (Chicago, Illinois Office).

**MICHAEL R. ETZIONI,** born New York, N.Y., October 27, 1967; admitted to bar, 1994, California. *Education:* University of Michigan (B.A.,

*(This Listing Continued)*

## LATHAM & WATKINS, Los Angeles—Continued

1989); Harvard University (M.P.P., 1991); University of Michigan (J.D., cum laude, 1994). Note Editor, Michigan Law Review.

**VINCENT H. HERRON,** born Santa Monica, California; admitted to bar, 1994, California. *Education:* University of California, Los Angeles (B.A., 1990); University of Southern California Law Center (J.D., 1994). Order of the Coif. Phi Delta Phi. Recipient, UCLA Alumni Association Award for Academic Excellence, 1989. Author: "Increasing the Speech," 67 U.S.C. Law Review 503.

**BLAIR G. CONNELLY,** born New York, N.Y., October 21, 1969; admitted to bar, 1994, California. *Education:* Georgetown University (A.B., magna cum laude, 1991; J.D., cum laude, 1994). Psi Chi. Recipient, Stephen F. McNamee Ethics Award.

**MARK A. FINKELSTEIN** (Costa Mesa Office).

**DEBRA N. MICHELSON** (New York City Office).

**MARY A. DONOVAN** (Costa Mesa Office).

**LINO J. LAURO** (Chicago, Illinois Office).

**WAYNE G. NITTI,** born Santa Monica, California, August 30, 1968; admitted to bar, 1994, California. *Education:* University of California, Los Angeles (B.A., summa cum laude, 1991); Harvard University (J.D., cum laude, 1994). Senior Editor, Harvard Journal of Law & Public Policy. **PRACTICE AREAS:** Litigation.

**DAVID O. KAHN,** born Los Angeles, California, January 24, 1960; admitted to bar, 1994, California. *Education:* California State University, Northridge (B.S., summa cum laude, 1991); Harvard Law School (J.D., cum laude, 1994). **LANGUAGES:** French.

**CAROL M. MAUCH,** born Teaneck, New Jersey, February 27, 1969; admitted to bar, 1994, California. *Education:* Wesleyan University (B.A., 1990); New York University School of Law (J.D., cum laude, 1994). **LANGUAGES:** French. **PRACTICE AREAS:** Health Care Transactional; Corporate.

**JOHN G. HOLLAND** (Washington, D.C. Office).

**KYLE W. HOFFMAN** (San Diego Office).

**DAVID PITMAN** (Costa Mesa Office).

**KEVIN T. KERNS** (Chicago, Illinois Office).

**ROBERT E. BURWELL** (San Diego Office).

**SANDRA A. MUHLENBECK** (Chicago, Illinois Office).

**PATRICK GIBBS** (Chicago, Illinois Office).

**LANE H. BLUMENFELD** (Washington, D.C. Office).

**JACKLYN KAY BARTLETT** (New York City Office).

**SCOTT R. RABER** (New York City Office).

**DAVID S. DANTZIC** (Washington, D.C. Office).

**WILL B. FITTON** (San Francisco Office).

**ELENA C. NORMAN** (New York City Office).

**MATTHEW D. MOREN** (New York City Office).

**KATHARINE M. ALBRIGHT,** born Mineola, New York, March 5, 1967; admitted to bar, 1994, California; 1995, District of Columbia, U.S. District Court, District of Maryland and U.S. Court of Appeals, Fourth Circuit. *Education:* Williams College (B.A., with honors, 1989); Georgetown University (J.D., cum laude, 1994).

**RICHARD D. STRULSON,** born Abington, Pennsylvania, March 24, 1968; admitted to bar, 1995, California and U.S. District Court, Central District of California. *Education:* University of Virginia (B.A., 1990); Duke University (M.B.A., 1994; J.D., 1994). Senior Editor, Law and Contemporary Problems, 1991-1994. Recipient, American Jurisprudence Award, Property. Law Clerk, Chief Justice E. Norman Veasey, Delaware Supreme Court, 1994-1995.

**JOHN W. CREIGHTON, III** (Washington, D.C. Office).

**CRAIG D. SOLAR** (New York City Office).

**JOSEPH M. YAFFE** (Costa Mesa Office).

**JARED W. JOHNSON** (Washington, D.C. Office).

**SCOTT B. COOPER** (Costa Mesa Office).

*(This Listing Continued)*

CAA890B

**DAVID L. LONDON** (Washington, D.C. Office).

**EVA IZSAK-NIIMURA** (New York City Office).

**DON ROBERT SPELLMANN** (New York City Office).

**GRACE WON,** born Pasadena, California, November 24, 1967; admitted to bar, 1995, California. *Education:* Harvard University (B.A., 1989); Georgetown University (J.D., 1994).

**JEFFREY A. BRANDON** (New York City Office).

**ROBERT BRAUMULLER** (Washington, D.C. Office).

**MONICA YUNG-MIN KIM,** born Seoul, Korea, June 27, 1969; admitted to bar, 1995, California. *Education:* University of California, Los Angeles (B.A., 1992); Yale University (J.D., 1995). Phi Beta Kappa. Member, Yale University Law Journal.

**LESLIE A. PEREIRA,** born Detroit, Michigan, September 30, 1967; admitted to bar, 1995, California. *Education:* University of Michigan (B.A., 1990; M.A., 1992; J.D., cum laude, 1995).

**DAVID A. KASS** (Washington, D.C. Office).

**KATHERINE M. ROLLINS** (Washington, D.C. Office).

**MICHELE T. BLAY** (Chicago, Illinois Office).

**SARAH M. EKDAHL** (Chicago, Illinois Office).

**EDWIN M. COLLINS,** born Bangkok, Thailand, April 28, 1968; (admission pending). *Education:* California State University, Chico (B.S., 1992); University of Pennsylvania (J.D., 1995). Recipient, American Jurisprudence Award, Contracts. Holland & Hart Scholar.

**AUDREY LEE,** born New York, N.Y., November 3, 1970; admitted to bar, 1995, California. *Education:* University of California, Los Angeles (B.A., magna cum laude, 1992); University of Chicago (J.D., 1995). **LANGUAGES:** Mandarin Chinese. **PRACTICE AREAS:** Corporate; Securities; Intellectual Property.

**JACQUES YOUSSEFMIR,** born Tehran, Iran, July 13, 1971; admitted to bar, 1995, California. *Education:* Arizona State University (B.A., summa cum laude, 1992); Harvard University (J.D., cum laude, 1995). Phi Beta Kappa. **LANGUAGES:** Farsi.

**RONIT D. EARLEY** (Costa Mesa Office).

**MARK W. SENECA** (Costa Mesa Office).

**BRADLEY E. KOTLER** (Chicago, Illinois Office).

**LENORA SMITH** (Chicago, Illinois Office).

**DANIEL P. DILLON** (San Diego Office).

**BARBARA L. CAMMARATA** (San Diego Office).

**JOHN C. MARCHESE** (Washington, D.C. Office).

**LYNLEY A. OGILVIE** (Washington, D.C. Office).

**THOMAS R. PAPPAS** (New York City Office).

**J. ERIK SANDSTEDT** (New York City Office).

**SHANE M. SPRADLIN** (New York City Office).

**VIRGINIA C. EDWARDS** (San Francisco Office).

**ROWLAND I. CHENG,** born Seattle, Washington, March 6, 1968; admitted to bar, 1995, California. *Education:* Boston University (B.A., magna cum laude, 1990); Harvard University (J.D., cum laude, 1995). Phi Beta Kappa. **LANGUAGES:** Mandarin Chinese.

**MICHAEL J. LAWRENCE,** born Los Angeles, California, March 8, 1970; admitted to bar, 1995, California. *Education:* University of California, Los Angeles (B.A., summa cum laude, 1992); University of Sussex, Brighton, England; Georgetown University Law Center (J.D., cum laude, 1995). Phi Beta Kappa.

**JACKLYN J. PARK,** born Kwangju, South Korea, June 30, 1970; admitted to bar, 1995, California. *Education:* University of California, Berkeley (B.A., with highest honors, 1992); Harvard University (J.D., cum laude, 1995). Phi Beta Kappa; Prytannaen; Golden Key. Member, Harvard Journal on Legislation, 1993-1995. **LANGUAGES:** Korean.

**SALLY SHEKOU,** born Tehran, Iran, August 1, 1970; admitted to bar, 1995, California. *Education:* University of California (B.A., with highest honors, 1992); University of California, Boalt Hall School of Law (J.D., 1995). Phi Beta Kappa. **LANGUAGES:** Farsi, Spanish and Italian.

**STEPHEN F. CASE** (San Diego Office).

*(This Listing Continued)*

**DIANA L. STRAUSS** (San Diego Office).

**FRED B. JACOBSEN** (Chicago, Illinois Office).

**CLIFFORD MENTRUP** (Chicago, Illinois Office).

**PETER J. MILLONES, JR.** (New York City Office).

**MARK D. SPOTO** (Washington, D.C. Office).

**SUSAN FINCH MOORE** (Washington, D.C. Office).

**DAVID E. ROSS** (Washington, D.C. Office).

**PATRICK J. DEVINE** (Washington, D.C. Office).

**DANIEL S. DUANE** (New York City Office).

**GEORGE FAN,** (admission pending). (New York City Office).

**DANIEL MCCRAY** (New York City Office).

**MALGORZATA BULA,** (admission pending). (New York City Office).

**MELISSA R. TRIEDMAN,** (admission pending). (New York City Office).

**JENNIFER R. FONNER** (San Francisco Office).

**DEBORAH C. LAMBE,** born Geneva, Switzerland, November 14, 1960; admitted to bar, 1995, California. *Education:* University of California, Berkeley (A.B., 1983); University of California, Los Angeles (M.A., 1990); University of California, Boalt Hall School of Law (J.D., 1995).

**HOLLY M. HOLT** (San Diego Office).

**M. MICHELLE ALVAREZ,** born Tegucigalpa, Honduras; admitted to bar, 1995, California. *Education:* Bryn Mawr College (B.A., 1987); Stanford University (J.D., 1995). Executive Editor, Stanford Law Review, 1993-1995. **LANGUAGES:** Spanish.

**WILLIAM C. DAVISSON, III,** born Long Beach, California, May 27, 1970; admitted to bar, 1995, California. *Education:* University of California (A.B., with high honors, 1992); New York University (J.D., 1995). Phi Beta Kappa.

**ROBERT M. O'SHEA,** born Melrose, Massachusetts, May 27, 1969; admitted to bar, 1995, California. *Education:* University of Richmond (B.A., 1991); Boston College (J.D., magna cum laude, 1995).

**HOYT SZE,** born Boston, Massachusetts, August 18, 1970; admitted to bar, 1995, California. *Education:* University of California, Berkeley (B.A., with distinction, 1992); Cornell University (J.D., cum laude, 1995). **LANGUAGES:** Chinese and Spanish.

**DAVID M. TAUB,** born New York, N.Y., January 15, 1969; admitted to bar, 1995, California. *Education:* Duke University (B.A., 1991); University of California, Los Angeles (J.D., 1995).

**VIVIAN W. YANG,** born Taipei, Taiwan, June 10, 1967; admitted to bar, 1995, California. *Education:* Pennsylvania State University (B.S., with distinction, 1989); Georgetown University (J.D., cum laude, 1995). Beta Gamma Sigma; University Scholar; Golden Key. Certified Public Accountant, California, 1991. **LANGUAGES:** Chinese (Mandarin).

**STEFANIE B. ISSER** (New York City Office).

**CHRIS BURT,** born Long Branch, New Jersey, April 28, 1970; admitted to bar, 1995, California. *Education:* University of Chicago (A.B., 1992; J.D., 1995).

**JAMIE L. WINE** (Costa Mesa Office).

**MARTIN A. SABARSKY,** born Silver Spring, Maryland, November 5, 1970; admitted to bar, 1995, California. *Education:* Brown University (A.B., magna cum laude, 1992); Harvard University (J.D., magna cum laude, 1995). Phi Beta Kappa. **LANGUAGES:** Spanish. **PRACTICE AREAS:** Tax; Corporate.

**STEPHEN R. TETRO, II** (Chicago, Illinois Office).

**JOHN D. WHIPPLE** (San Francisco Office).

**KAREN E. HUMPHREYS** (San Francisco Office).

**SANGYEUP LEE** (New York City Office).

**DONNA HERZING** (New York City Office).

**JAMES JOY,** (admission pending). (New York City Office).

**ISAMU PAUL WATSON,** (admission pending). (New York City Office).

*(This Listing Continued)*

**STEPHEN D. BLEVIT,** born Skokie, Illinois, September 11, 1970; admitted to bar, 1995, California. *Education:* DePaul University (B.S., summa cum laude, 1992); University of Southern California (J.D., 1995). Phi Alpha Delta; Order of the Coif. Certified Public Accountant, Illinois, 1992. **PRACTICE AREAS:** Finance; Real Estate.

**JOSHUA R. FRIEMAN,** born Los Angeles, California, July 19, 1970; admitted to bar, 1995, California. *Education:* University of California, Berkeley (A.B., with highest honors, 1992); Harvard University (J.D., cum laude, 1995). Phi Beta Kappa. Member, Mortar Board.

**MICHAEL D. LEWIS,** born Louisville, Kentucky, September 30, 1968; admitted to bar, 1995, California. *Education:* Graceland College (B.A., magna cum laude, 1990); Harvard University; University of California, Boalt Hall School of Law (J.D., 1995). Member, California Law Review. *Member:* Beverly Hills Bar Association (Member, Entertainment Law Section); Los Angeles Lesbian and Gay Bar Association (Member, Lawyers for Human Rights, 1993—).

**KELLY J. SOSNOW,** born Philadelphia, Pennsylvania, December 3, 1970; admitted to bar, 1995, California. *Education:* University of Pennsylvania (B.A., magna cum laude, 1992); Harvard University (J.D., cum laude, 1995). Staff Editor, Harvard Environmental Law Review, 1994-1995. Author: "Recent Development, Insurance Industry Misrepresentation and the Pollution Exclusion Clause—Morton International, Inc. v. General Accident Insurance Company of America," Vol. 18, Harvard Environmental Law Review, 1994.

**CHERYL MILLER COE** (Washington, D.C. Office).

**ERIC WHITAKER** (San Francisco Office).

**JACQUES B. MCCHESNEY,** (admission pending). (New York City Office).

**CATHERINE S. BRIDGE,** born Los Angeles, California, September 21, 1969; admitted to bar, 1995, California. *Education:* University of California, Berkeley (B.A., 1991); Boston University (J.D., magna cum laude, 1995). **LANGUAGES:** Spanish.

**JOHN M. KURIYAMA,** born Honolulu, Hawaii, November 10, 1965; admitted to bar, 1992, Hawaii; 1995, California. *Education:* University of Hawaii (B.B.A., 1988); Stanford University (J.D., 1992). **LANGUAGES:** Japanese.

**ELLEN C. WAGGONER,** born Reading, Pennsylvania, December 17, 1967; admitted to bar, 1995, California. *Education:* Stanford University (A.B., with distinction and honors, 1990); Harvard University (J.D., cum laude, 1995).

**ERIC MILLER,** (admission pending). (New York City Office).

**SARAH K. FREEMAN** (San Diego Office).

**THOMAS M. REITER** (Moscow Office).

**DENNIS D. LAMONT,** (admission pending). (New York City Office).

**DAVID E. CHRISTENSEN,** born Chicago, Illinois, November 18, 1969; admitted to bar, 1996, California and U.S. District Court, Central District of California. *Education:* Cornell University (B.A., 1992); University of California at Los Angeles (J.D., 1995). Fulbright Fellow. **LANGUAGES:** Italian.

**STEPHEN J. NEWMAN,** born New York, N.Y., June 20, 1970; admitted to bar, 1996, California and U.S. Court of Appeals, Fourth Circuit. *Education:* Harvard University (A.B., magna cum laude, 1992); University of Chicago (J.D., with honors, 1995). Member, University of Chicago Law Review, 1993-1995. Author: "Kill The Mere Color Rule: Equal Protection For Color Under The Lanham Act," University of Chicago Law Review, Fall 1994. Law Clerk to Judge M. Blane Michael, U.S. Court of Appeals, Fourth Circuit 1995-1996.

**SUSAN E. MCNEIL** (Washington, D.C. Office).

**JAMES R. HANNA** (Washington, D.C. Office).

**MARTHA ANN MAZZONE** (Washington, D.C. Office).

**CARTER H. STRICKLAND, JR.** (New York City Office).

**MARIA E. PLATSIS** (Washington, D.C. Office).

**STEPHANIE SWITZER BRULE** (San Francisco Office).

**CHRISTOPHER L. ELWELL,** born Indiana, Pennsylvania, November 3, 1966; admitted to bar, 1996, California. *Education:* Georgetown University (B.S.F.S., 1989); Oxford University (M.A., 1992; B.C.L., 1993); Stanford University (J.D., 1995). Rhodes Scholar. Clerk to the Hon. Cynthia

*(This Listing Continued)*

**LATHAM & WATKINS, Los Angeles—Continued**

Holcolm Hall, U.S. Court of Appeals, Ninth Circuit. **LANGUAGES:** French.

**T. EDWARD SMITH,** born Lebanon, Tennessee, January 29, 1970; admitted to bar, 1996, California. *Education:* Yale University (B.A., 1992); Duke University (J.D., cum laude, 1995).

**STEVEN J. OLSON,** born Washington, D.C., February 9, 1968; admitted to bar, 1996, California. *Education:* Stanford University (B.A., 1990); University of Michigan (J.D., 1995).

**LAUREN G. KRASNOW** (New York City Office).

**BRADD L. WILLIAMSON** (New York City Office).

**MARILYN M. SINGLETON** (San Francisco Office).

**MICHAEL VELTHOEN,** (admission pending). (San Francisco Office).

**CHRISTOPHER R. HARRIS,** (admission pending). (New York City Office).

**MARA I. KAPELOVITZ** (San Francisco Office).

**SANJAY BHANDARI** (San Francisco Office).

**MAURINE J. NEIBERG** (Chicago, Illinois Office).

**ERIC A. ROSAND** (Washington, D.C. Office).

**CHUNLIN LEONHARD** (Chicago Office).

**ALAN S. ADLER,** born Brookline, Massachusetts, August 4, 1967; admitted to bar, 1996, California. *Education:* Colby College (B.A., 1985); Boston University (J.D., 1996).

**RANDY R. MERRITT,** born Greenville, Michigan, October 26, 1957; admitted to bar, 1996, California. *Education:* Grand Rapids Baptist College (B.A., 1980); University of Iowa (J.D., 1996). Order of the Coif.

**BRIAN E. CROMER** (San Diego Office).

**LOUIS G. ALONSO** (San Diego Office).

**JACK A. GUGGENHEIM,** (admission pending). (New York City Office).

**MONICA K. THURMOND,** (admission pending). (New York City Office).

**MARIA LOPOTUKHIN,** (admission pending). (New York City Office).

**JOHN C. TANG,** (admission pending). (New York City Office).

**PAUL R. COHEN,** (admission pending). (New York City Office).

**JASON A. HOCHBERG,** (admission pending). (New York City Office).

**MEERA JOSHI CATTAFESTA** (New York City Office).

**STEPHANIE H. KNUTSON** (Costa Mesa Office).

**GREGORY M. SAYLIN** (Costa Mesa Office).

**HEIDI E. KLEIN** (Washington, D.C. Office).

**MONIQUE VALBUENA PERTCHIK** (Washington, D.C. Office).

**DIANA S. DOYLE** (Chicago Office).

**MATTHEW FRADIN** (Chicago Office).

**KATHARINE P. MOIR** (Chicago Office).

**GUY GIBERSON** (New York City Office).

**RACHELLE REINHARDT,** (admission pending). (New York City Office).

**JENA KIRSCH** (San Diego Office).

**JILL M. HOULAHAN** (San Diego Office).

**BRETT ROSENBLATT** (San Diego Office).

**DAVID A. BECKER** (Washington, D.C. Office).

**CHRIS CARR** (Washington, D.C. Office).

**NANDAN M. JOSHI** (Washington, D.C. Office).

**JOSEPH M. BOYLE** (Washington, D.C. Office).

**ALYSSA R. HARVEY** (Washington, D.C. Office).

**PAUL M. WINTERS** (Washington, D.C. Office).

**ARTHUR S. LANDERHOLM** (Washington, D.C. Office).

*(This Listing Continued)*

**ELIZABETH T. CARLSON** (Washington, D.C. Office).

**JOCELYN M. SEITZMAN** (Washington, D.C. Office).

**MEREDITH A. BERLIN** (Chicago Office).

**KATHARINE A. WOLANYK** (Chicago Office).

**ADEL F. BEBAWY,** born Cairo, Egypt, April 11, 1967; admitted to bar, 1996, California. *Education:* University of Chicago (B.A., 1989); University of Pennsylvania (J.D., 1996).

**CONNIE C. CHEN,** born Kaohsiung, Taiwan, R.O.C., March 3, 1971; admitted to bar, 1996, California. *Education:* Princeton University (A.B., magna cum laude, 1993); Harvard University (J.D., 1996). Phi Beta Kappa. Co-Author: "A Fresh Look at the Arbitration or Litigation Dilemma," International Commercial Litigation, September 1995. **LANGUAGES:** Madanrin and Taiwanese.

**SCOTT GLUCK,** born Elmira, New York, April 9, 1970; admitted to bar, 1996, California. *Education:* University of California, Berkeley (B.A., 1992); Columbia University (J.D., 1996). Harlan Fiske Stone Scholar.

**ERIC M. LANYARD,** born Edison, New Jersey, April 22, 1971; admitted to bar, 1996, California. *Education:* Brandeis University (B.A., summa cum laude, 1993); Harvard University (J.D., cum laude, 1996).

**JASON T. MILLER,** born Indianapolis, Indiana, September 27, 1971; admitted to bar, 1996, California. *Education:* Indiana University (B.S., 1993); University of California, Los Angeles (J.D., 1996). Co-Author: with Edith R. Perez, "Removing Barriers," Supplement to California Real Estate Journal, Los Angeles Daily Journal and San Francisco Daily Journal, April 1996.

**JONN R. BEESON** (Costa Mesa Office).

**JULIE VIGIL KING** (Costa Mesa Office).

**STEPHEN J. VENUTO** (Costa Mesa Office).

**ERIC L. CZECH** (New York City Office).

**MARK FELDMAN,** (admission pending). (New York City Office).

**M. CHRISTOPHER HALL** (New York City Office).

**PERRY J. HINDIN** (New York City Office).

**ANNA C. LINCOLN** (New York City Office).

**MICHAEL S. WINDERMAN** (New York City Office).

**KEVIN C. MAY** (Chicago Office).

**STEVEN J. NOVATNEY** (Chicago Office).

**MICAELA H. MARTÍN** (San Francisco Office).

**JENNIFER L. JOHNSON,** (admission pending). (New York City Office).

**KAREN A. MERKLE** (New York City Office).

**MICHELE M. PYLE,** (admission pending). (New York City Office).

**JUDY D. STRATTON** (New York City Office).

**DEREK D. DUNDAS,** born Inglewood, California, November 4, 1969; admitted to bar, 1996, California. *Education:* University of California, Los Angeles (B.A., 1993); Georgetown University Law Center (J.D., 1996).

**ANGELEE FOX,** born Dallas, Texas, June 29, 1968; admitted to bar, 1996, California. *Education:* Southwest Texas State University (B.B.A., 1990); University of Southern California (J.D., 1996). Order of the Coif.

**JEFFREY B. GREENBERG,** born Los Angeles, California, March 13, 1971; admitted to bar, 1996, California. *Education:* University of Southern California (B.A., 1993); Northwestern University (J.D., 1996).

**DANIEL W. S. LAWRENCE,** born Honolulu, Hawaii, January 23, 1968; admitted to bar, 1996, California. *Education:* Santa Clara University (B.S.E.E., 1990); Northwestern University (J.D., cum laude, 1996). Tau Beta Pi.

**SUSAN E. LECKRONE,** born Terre Haute, Indiana, December 28, 1969; admitted to bar, 1996, California. *Education:* Stanford University (B.A., 1992); Indiana University, Bloomington (J.D., magna cum laude, 1996). Order of the Coif. Member, Indiana Law Journal, 1994-1996. Author: "Turning Back the Clock: The Unfunded Mandates Reform Act of 1995 and Its Effective Repeal of Environmental Legislation," Indiana Law Journal, Spring 1996.

*(This Listing Continued)*

**PROFESSIONAL BIOGRAPHIES**  CALIFORNIA—LOS ANGELES

**DEBORAH T. LEE,** born Brooklyn, New York, September 29, 1969; admitted to bar, 1996, California. *Education:* University of Pennsylvania (B.S., 1991); University of California, Los Angeles (J.D., 1996). Phi Alpha Delta; Order of the Coif. Certified Public Accountant, 1993. *LANGUAGES:* Chinese.

**LISA S. PRANGE,** born Los Angeles, California, September 17, 1970; admitted to bar, 1996, California. *Education:* University of California, Los Angeles (B.A., magna cum laude, 1993); Cornell University (J.D., magna cum laude, 1996). Phi Beta Kappa; Order of the Coif. Managing Editor, Cornell Law Review.

**NADIA A. SHABAIK,** born Los Angeles, California, April 10, 1971; admitted to bar, 1996, California and U.S. District Court, Central District of California. *Education:* University of California, Los Angeles (B.A., 1993; J.D., 1996). Phi Beta Kappa; Order of Omega; Order of the Coif.

**MARY J. YOO,** born Inch'on, Korea, November 18, 1969; admitted to bar, 1996, California. *Education:* Radcliffe College, Harvard University (B.A., with honors, 1992); University of Chicago (J.D., with honors, 1996). Phi Beta Kappa. *LANGUAGES:* Korean.

**JEANNETTE M. HILL-YONIS,** born Portsmouth, Virginia; admitted to bar, 1996, California. *Education:* University of Southern California (B.A./B.S., magna cum laude, 1987); New York University (J.D., 1996). Phi Beta Kappa.

**STACEY STERNBERG,** born Philadelphia, Pennsylvania, November 9, 1971; admitted to bar, 1996, California. *Education:* University of California, Los Angeles (B.A., cum laude, 1993); University of Michigan (J.D., magna cum laude, 1996). Phi Beta Kappa.

**AMOS E. HARTSTON,** born Fontana, California, November 5, 1971; admitted to bar, 1996, California. *Education:* University of California (B.A., with honors, 1993); Georgetown University Law Center (J.D., magna cum laude, 1996). Order of the Coif.

**LOREN M. MONTGOMERY,** admitted to bar, 1996, California. *Education:* Princeton University (B.A., 1991); Duke University (J.D., cum laude, 1996).

**EYAL GAMLIEL,** born Haifa, Israel, October 21, 1970; admitted to bar, 1996, California. *Education:* University of California (B.A., 1992); University of Southern California (J.D., 1996). Order of the Coif. Member, University of Southern California Law Review. *LANGUAGES:* Hebrew and Spanish.

**JULIE VAUGHAN** (London, England Office).

**DRU GREENHALGH** (San Diego Office).

**MELINDA A. PFEIFFER** (San Francisco Office).

**SCOTT K. MILSTEN** (San Francisco Office).

**DANA N. LINKER** (San Francisco Office).

**RANDALL K. H. CHING** (San Francisco Office).

**CLAY SHEVLIN** (Costa Mesa Office).

**CATHERINE LAMB** (San Francisco Office).

**DAVID B. ALLEN** (Costa Mesa Office).

**SHARADCHANDRA A. SAMY** (New York City Office).

**MATTHEW J. ROSSMAN** (New York City Office).

**ALEXANDER S. PESIC** (San Francisco Office).

**DAVID A. LEVITT** (New York City Office).

**LISA K. EASTWOOD** (New York City Office).

**THERESA J. MCPHERSON** (San Francisco Office).

**KENNETH R. MORRIS** (San Francisco Office).

**DMITRI A. KOUNITSA** (Moscow, Russian Office).

**IVAN A. SMOLIN** (Moscow, Russia Office).

**LISA BINDER,** born Frankfurt, Germany, September 22, 1967; admitted to bar, 1994, California. *Education:* Harvard University (A.B., 1989; J.D., 1994); University of California at Berkeley (M.A., 1991). Phi Beta Kappa. Author, 18 Harvard Women's Law Journal 265-299. *LANGUAGES:* German, Latin, Greek, Spanish and Classical Arabic.

Unless otherwise indicated all Members and Associates of the Firm are Members of the State Bar of California.

*(This Listing Continued)*

(For biographical data on Costa Mesa, California, San Diego, California, San Francisco, California, Washington, D.C., Chicago, Illinois, Newark, New Jersey, New York, New York, London, England, Moscow, Russia, Hong Kong and Tokyo, Japan personnel, see Professional Biographies at each of those cities)

---

## LA TORRACA AND GOETTSCH

### LOS ANGELES, CALIFORNIA

(See Long Beach)

*General Civil Litigation including Insurance Coverage, Insurance Bad Faith, Insurance Defense, Insurance Fraud, Toxic Tort Law, Personal Injury, Products Liability, Malpractice, Commercial Litigation, Defamation, Unfair Competition, Real Property Litigation, Construction Defects Litigation, Complex Litigation and Civil Appeals. Trial Practice in all State and Federal Court.*

---

## DANIEL S. LATTER

*2029 CENTURY PARK EAST*
*SUITE 480*
### LOS ANGELES, CALIFORNIA 90067
Telephone: 310-277-1358
Fax: 310-277-4351

*General Business Law and Transactions, Trademarks and Real Estate Law.*

**DANIEL S. LATTER,** born Chicago, Illinois, June 5, 1956; admitted to bar, 1981, California; 1988. U.S. District Court, Northern and Central Districts of California. *Education:* University of Illinois at Champaign-Urbana (B.A., with distinction, 1978); George Washington University (J.D., with honors, 1981). Associate Editor, Journal of International Law and Economics, 1979-1981. Author: Note, "The Extraterritorial Application of the Federal Securities Laws: The Need for Reassessment," 14 Journal of International Law and Economics 529, 1980. *Member:* Los Angeles County (Member, Business and Corporations and Real Property Sections) and American (Member, Business Law Section) Bar Associations; State Bar of California (Member, Business Law Section). *LANGUAGES:* French.

---

## JOSÉ Y. LAUCHENGCO, JR.

*3545 WILSHIRE BOULEVARD, SUITE 247*
### LOS ANGELES, CALIFORNIA 90010
Telephone: 213-380-9897

*Personal Injury and Criminal Practice. Trials in State and Federal Courts.*

**JOSÉ Y. LAUCHENGCO, JR.,** born Manila, Philippines, December 6, 1936; admitted to bar, 1972, California, U.S. District Court, Central District of California and U.S. Court of Appeals, Ninth Circuit; 1975, U.S. Supreme Court. *Education:* University of the Philippines, Quezon City, Philippines (A.B., 1959); University of Southern California (M.B.A., 1964); Loyola University of Los Angeles (J.D., 1971). Member, St. Thomas More Law Honor Society. Recipient, City of Los Angeles Human Relations Commission, for Outstanding Volunteer Services, 1984. Member, Commission on Judicial Procedures, Los Angeles County, 1979. Chairman, Kagitingan ng Lahi, a Bi-partisan Filipino-American Southern California Political Action Group, 1978. Counsel, Philippine Presidential Commission on Good Government, Los Angeles, 1986. *Member:* Los Angeles County Bar Association; State Bar of California (Member, Human Rights Committee, 1977-1980); Los Angeles Trial Lawyers Association; The Association of Trial Lawyers of America; California Trial Lawyers Association; California Attorneys for Criminal Justice; Criminal Courts Bar Association; California Public Defenders Association. [Lt., Philippine Army, 1960-1962]. *LANGUAGES:* Pilipino and Spanish.

### OF COUNSEL

**PAUL J. ESTUAR,** admitted to bar, 1993, California. *Education:* Columbia University (A.B., 1990); Loyola Marymount University (J.D., 1993). Recipient, Deans Service Award. *Member:* Los Angeles County Bar Association; Philippine-American Bar Association (Secretary, 1995; President, 1997); The Association of Trial Lawyers of America. *LANGUAGES:* Tagalog.

CAA893B

## LAVELY & SINGER
PROFESSIONAL CORPORATION
2049 CENTURY PARK EAST, SUITE 2400
**LOS ANGELES, CALIFORNIA 90067**
Telephone: 310-556-3501
Telecopier: 310-556-3615
Telex: 4995300 BURX LSA

*Business Litigation, Contracts, Business Torts, Intellectual Property, Libel, Entertainment.*

**JOHN H. LAVELY, JR.,** born Framingham, Massachusetts, December 14, 1943; admitted to bar, 1970, Pennsylvania and New York; 1971, Pennsylvania Supreme Court and U.S. District Court, Southern District of New York; 1972, California, U.S. District Court, Central District of California and U.S. Court of Appeals, Ninth Circuit; 1995, U.S. Supreme Court. *Education:* Yale University (B.A., cum laude, 1965); University of Pennsylvania (LL.B., 1969). *Member:* Beverly Hills, Century City and Los Angeles County Bar Associations; State Bar of California. **SPECIAL AGENCIES:** California Labor Commissioner. **REPORTED CASES:** Richard Pryor, et al v. David McCoy Franklin, California Department of Industrial Relations, Division of Labor Standards Enforcement, Labor Commissioner, Case No. TAC 17 MP114; Bo Derek v. Karen Callan, California Department of Industrial Relations, Division of Labor Standards Enforcement, Labor Commissioner, Case No. TAC 18-80 SFMP 82-80; Selleck vs. Globe International, Inc., 166 Cal.App.3d 1123, 212 Cal.Rptr. 1123 (1985) (Rev. Denied); LaCienega Music Co. v. ZZ Top, 53 F. 3d 950 (9th Cir 1995), cert denied 116 S. Ct. 331 (1995); Gould v. Maryland Sound Industries, Inc., (1995) 31 Cal.App. 4th 1137, 37 Cal.Rptr. 2d 718 (Rev. denied). **PRACTICE AREAS:** Entertainment Litigation; Business Litigation; Right of Publicity and Privacy Law; Libel Law; Copyright Law.

**MARTIN D. SINGER,** born Brooklyn, New York, April 25, 1952; admitted to bar, 1977, California; 1978, U.S. District Court, Central District of California; 1990, U.S. Court of Appeals, Ninth Circuit. *Education:* City College of New York (B.A., 1974); Brooklyn Law School (J.D., 1977). Phi Beta Kappa; Pi Sigma Alpha. Author: "Regulation of Talent Agents," 1983 Entertainment Publishing and the Arts Handbook. *Member:* Beverly Hills, Century City and Los Angeles County Bar Associations; State Bar of California. **SPECIAL AGENCIES:** California Labor Commissioner. **REPORTED CASES:** Harris v. EMI Television Programs, 102 Cal.App.3d 214, 162 Cal.Rptr. 357 (1980); Page v. Something Wierd Video, 908 E. Supp. 714 (C.D. Cal. 1995). **PRACTICE AREAS:** Entertainment Litigation; Business Litigation; Right of Publicity and Privacy Law; Libel Law; Copyright Law.

**MICHAEL J. PLONSKER,** born Chicago, Illinois, May 27, 1956; admitted to bar, 1981, California and U.S. District Court, Central, Eastern and Southern Districts of California; 1982, Illinois; 1987, U.S. Court of Appeals, Eleventh Circuit; 1993, U.S. Court of Appeals, Ninth Circuit; 1994, U.S. Supreme Court. *Education:* Emory University; University of Michigan (B.B.A., in Accounting, 1978); University of Illinois (J.D., 1981). Beta Alpha Psi. Harno Scholar. *Member:* Century City and Los Angeles County Bar Associations; State Bar of California. **REPORTED CASES:** Wood Newton v. Harry Thomason, et al., 22 F.3d 1455 (9th Cir. 1994). **PRACTICE AREAS:** Entertainment Litigation; Business Litigation; Right of Publicity and Privacy Law; Libel Law; Copyright Law.

**BRIAN G. WOLF,** born Saginaw, Michigan, April 10, 1957; admitted to bar, 1985, Texas and U.S. District Court, Southern and Eastern Districts of Texas; 1988, California; 1989, U.S. District Court, Central District of California. *Education:* University of Michigan (B.A., 1979); University of Houston (J.D., 1984). *Member:* Century City, Beverly Hills and Los Angeles County Bar Associations (Member, Section on: Entertainment Law, Litigation, Intellectual Property); State Bar of Texas; State Bar of California; The Association of Trial Lawyers of America; California Trial Lawyers Association. **PRACTICE AREAS:** General Civil and Business Litigation; Entertainment Litigation.

**LYNDA B. GOLDMAN,** born Minneapolis, Minnesota, September 1, 1960; admitted to bar, 1985, California; 1986, U.S. Court of Appeals, Ninth Circuit and U.S. District Court, Central District of California. *Education:* University of California at Berkeley (A.B., 1982); Loyola University of Los Angeles (J.D., 1985). Staff Member, 1983-1984 and Business Editor, 1984-1985, Loyola Entertainment Law Journal. Author, "Cable T.V. Industry Challenges Royalty Rate Structure," 4 Loyola Entertainment Law Journal 360. Externship with Judge William J. Lasarow, Presiding Judge of U.S. Bankruptcy Court, Central District of California, 1983. *Member:* Beverly

*(This Listing Continued)*

Hills (Member, Sections on: Entertainment Law; Litigation), Los Angeles County (Member, Sections on: Intellectual Property; Entertainment; Litigation) and American (Member, Sections on: Intellectual Property and Litigation) Bar Associations; State Bar of California (Member, Litigation Section). **REPORTED CASES:** Prieto v. State Farm Fire & Casualty Company, Cal.App. 3d 1188, 275 Cal.Rptr 362 (1990). **PRACTICE AREAS:** Entertainment Litigation; Defamation; Business Litigation.

**THERESA J. MACELLARO,** born Bronx, N.Y., August 23, 1962; admitted to bar, 1988, New York and U.S. Court of Appeals, Federal Circuit; 1989, U.S. District Court, Southern and Eastern Districts of New York; 1990, California and U.S. Court of Appeals, Fifth Circuit; 1991, U.S. District Court, Central, Eastern and Southern Districts of California and U.S. Court of Appeals, Ninth Circuit. *Education:* London School of Economics and Political Science, London, England; Smith College (B.A., 1984); New York University (J.D., 1987). Phi Beta Kappa. Recipient, American Jurisprudence Award. Editor, "Animal Law Report," American Bar Association publication, 1989-1991. Board of Directors: Public Counsel, 1992-1993; American Judicature Society, 1991-1993. Staff Attorney, Rutgers Law School, 1989. Member, Advisory Committee, LA Zoo, 1993—. *Member:* Beverly Hills (Board of Directors, Entertainment Committee, 1994—), Los Angeles County (Barrister, Executive Committee, 1991-1993; Founder and Chairperson, Animal Rights Committee, 1991—) and American Bar Associations (Chairperson, Animal Protection Committee, 1989-1991). **REPORTED CASES:** ASPCA v. Board of Trustees, 147 Misc. 2d 847, 556 N.Y.S. 2d 447 (S.Ct. 1990). **PRACTICE AREAS:** Entertainment Litigation; Sexual Harassment Litigation; Animal Rights Litigation; SLAPP Suit Expertise; Business Litigation.

**DAVID M. CORDREY,** born London, England, April 29, 1964; admitted to bar, 1988, California; 1989, U.S. District Court, Central District of California and U.S. Court of Appeals, Ninth Circuit. *Education:* University of California (B.A., 1985); Loyola Marymount University Law School (J.D., 1988). Editor, Loyola Entertainment Law Journal, 1987-1988. Author: "Copyright Infringement: When is a Swimsuit not a Swimsuit?" Loyola Entertainment Law Journal, Vol. 7, 1987, No 2, Pages 453-463. President-/Co-Founder, Loyola Entertainment Law Society. *Member:* Beverly Hills and Los Angeles County Bar Associations; State Bar of California; Los Angeles Trial Lawyers Association. **PRACTICE AREAS:** Entertainment Litigation; Business Litigation.

**MAX J. SPRECHER,** born Los Angeles, California, November 13, 1963; admitted to bar, 1993, California. *Education:* University of California (B.A., 1985); Southwestern University School of Law (J.D., 1993). Research Editor, Southwestern University Law Review, 1992-1993. *Member:* Beverly Hills and Los Angeles County Bar Associations; State Bar of California. **REPORTED CASES:** Page v. Something Weird Video, 908 E. Supp. 714 (C.D. Cal. 1995). **PRACTICE AREAS:** Business and Entertainment Litigation; Right of Publicity; Privacy; Defamation; Copyright.

**EUGENE P. SANDS,** born New York, N.Y., March 26, 1953; admitted to bar, 1994, California. *Education:* St. Johns College (B.A., 1983); Loyola Marymount University (J.D., 1993). **PRACTICE AREAS:** Litigation.

REFERENCES: First Los Angeles Bank.

## LAWLER, BONHAM & WALSH
**LOS ANGELES, CALIFORNIA**
(See Oxnard)

*General Civil Trial Practice in all State and Federal Courts. Municipal and School Representation. Personnel, Community Redevelopment, Land Use, Environmental and Toxic Tort Law. Products Liability, Casualty (Defense), General Insurance, Civil Rights, Security Law, Police Defense, Premises Liability and Commercial Transactions.*

## LAWRENCE & HARDING
A PROFESSIONAL CORPORATION
**LOS ANGELES, CALIFORNIA**
(See Santa Monica)

*Real Estate, Land Use, Civil Litigation, Corporate, Partnership and General Business.*

# LeBOEUF, LAMB, GREENE & MacRAE L.L.P.

A Limited Liability Partnership including Professional Corporations
Formerly LeBoeuf, Lamb, Leiby & MacRae

**725 SOUTH FIGUEROA STREET, SUITE 3600**
**LOS ANGELES, CALIFORNIA 90017-5436**
Telephone: 213-955-7300
Facsimile: 213-955-7399
Telex: 678982

*Eastern United States:*
*New York, N.Y. Office:* 125 West 55th Street. Telephone: 212-424-8000. Facsimile: 212-424-8500. Telex: 156363 or 423416.
*Washington, D.C. Office:* 1875 Connecticut Avenue, N.W. Telephone: 202-986-8000. Facsimile: 202-986-8102. Telex: 440274.
*Albany, New York Office:* One Commerce Plaza, Suite 2020, 99 Washington Avenue. Telephone: 518-465-1500. Facsimile: 518-465-1585.
*Boston, Massachusetts Office:* 260 Franklin Street. Telephone: 617-439-9500. Facsimile: 617-439-0341; 439-0342.
*Harrisburg, Pennsylvania Office:* 200 North Third Street, Suite 300, P.O. Box 12105. Telephone: 717-232-8199. Facsimile: 717-232-8720.
*Pittsburgh, Pennsylvania Office:* 601 Grant Street. Telephone: 412-594-2300. Facsimile: 412-594-5237.
*Hartford, Connecticut Office:* Goodwin Square, 225 Asylum Street, 13th Floor. Telephone: 860-293-3500. Facsimile: 860-293-3555.
*Newark, New Jersey Office:* The Legal Center, One Riverfront Plaza. Telephone: 201-643-8000. Facsimile: 201-643-6111.

*Western United States:*
*Salt Lake City, Utah Office:* 1000 Kearns Building, 136 South Main Street. Telephone: 801-320-6700. Facsimile: 801-359-8256.
*San Francisco, California Office:* One Embarcadero Center, Suite 400. Telephone: 415-951-1100. Facsimile: 415-951-1180; 951-1881. Telex: 470167.
*Denver, Colorado Office:* 633 17th Street, Suite 2800. Telephone: 303-291-2600. Facsimile: 303-297-0422.
*Portland, Oregon Office:* KOIN Center, Suite 1600, 222 S.W. Columbia. Telephone: 503-294-3095. Fax: 503-294-3895.

*Southern United States:*
*Jacksonville, Florida Office:* 50 N. Laura Street, Suite 2800. Telephone: 904-354-8000. Facsimile: 904-353-1673.

*European Offices:*
*Brussels, Belgium Office:* Avenue des Arts, 19H, 1000 Brussels, Belgium. Telephone: 001-32-2-227-0900. Facsimile: 011-32-2-227-0909.
*London, England Office:* One Mincining Lane, 6th Floor, London EC3R 7AA England. Telephone: 011-44-171-459-5000. Facsimile: 011-44-171-459-5099.
*Moscow, Russian Federation Office:* Nikitsky Pereulok, 5 (formerly Ulitsa Belinskogo) 103009, Moscow, Russian Federation. Telephone: 011-7-503-956-3935. Facsimile: 011-7-503-956-3936.
*Almaty, Kazakhstan Office:* Ulitsa Zheltoksana, 83 480091 Almaty, Republic of Kazakhstan. Telephone: 011-7-3272-50-7575. Facsimile: 011-7-3272-50-7576.

*General Practice including Corporate Finance, Defense of Government Fraud Investigations, Energy, Environmental, Insolvency, Insurance, Public Utilities, Public Finance, Real Estate, Securities Litigation, Taxation, Trade Associations.*

## PARTNERS

**JEAN M. COSTANZA,** born 1948; admitted to bar, 1981, California. *Education:* Pasadena City College (A.A., with honors, 1978); University of Southern California (J.D., 1981). Order of the Coif; Phi Alpha Delta. Executive Managing Editor, Southern California Law Review, 1980-1981. Recipient, American Jurisprudence Book Awards in Constitutional Law, Gifts, Wills and Trusts, Civil Procedure and Criminal Law and Procedure. Law Clerk to Judge Arthur L. Alarcon, U.S. Court of Appeals, Ninth Circuit, 1981. *Member:* National Association of Bond Lawyers; California Association of Water Agencies. **PRACTICE AREAS:** Municipal; Corporate.

**JOHN W. COTTON,** born 1947; admitted to bar, 1972, California; 1977, District of Columbia. *Education:* University of Santa Clara (B.A., 1969); Hastings College of Law, University of California (J.D., 1972); National Institute for Trial Advocacy Advanced Program, Boulder, Colorado (1981). Lecturer, U.S. Department of Justice, Attorney General's Advocacy Institute, Washington, D.C., 1981-1984. Senior Trial Attorney, U.S. Securi-

*(This Listing Continued)*

ties and Exchange Commission, 1975-1977. Deputy Director, Division of Enforcement, Commodity Futures Trading Commission, 1980-1984. **PRACTICE AREAS:** Litigation; Securities Regulation.

**SHIRLEY E. CURFMAN,** born 1948; admitted to bar, 1979, California; 1994, Colorado. *Education:* Azusa Pacific University (B.A., magna cum laude, 1970); University of California at Los Angeles (J.D., 1979). Alpha Chi; Phi Alpha Delta. Order of Barristers. Executive Member, Moot Court Board. **PRACTICE AREAS:** Corporate; Real Estate; Bankruptcy.

**HELEN L. DUNCAN,** born 1952; admitted to bar, 1981, California. *Education:* Indiana University (B.A., 1974); Southwestern University (J.D., 1981). Trial Attorney, U.S. Department of Justice Tax Division, 1981-1986. Judge Pro Tem, 1988-1991. Master of the Bench LA Complex Litigation Inn of Court, 1993-1995 and President-Elect, 1994-1995. **PRACTICE AREAS:** Litigation; Tax.

**DEAN HANSELL,** admitted to bar, 1977, Illinois; 1980, California. *Education:* Denison University (B.A., cum laude, 1974); Northwestern University (J.D., 1977). Phi Beta Kappa; Omicron Delta Kappa. Author: Book Chapter, "Undertaking and Managing Discovery in a CERCLA Case," Environmental Litigation, ALI-ABA, 1990; "Managing Discovery in a CERCLA Case," The Practical Litigator, ALI-ABA, 1991; "Hazardous and Solid Waste Minimization: Legal Issues," Hazardous and Solid Waste Minimization, Government Institutes, 1986 and 1990; "Lender and Fiduciary Liability Under CERCLA and Other Environmental Laws," Practising Law Institute, 1991. Lecturer: Illinois Institute on Continuing Legal Education, 1977-1979 and 1992; ALI-ABA, 1990; Government Institutes, 1986 and 1990; Practicing Law Institute, 1979. Adjunct Associate Professor, Southwestern University Law School, 1982-1986. Assistant Attorney General, State of Illinois, 1977-1980. Attorney, Federal Trade Commission, 1980-1983. Judge Pro Tem: Municipal Court of Los Angeles County, 1987—; Superior Court of Los Angeles County, 1989—. Member, Advisory Board, National Institute of Citizen Education in the Law, 1987-1994. Member, Illinois Solar Resources Advisory Panel, 1978-1980. Editorial Advisory Board, Los Angeles Lawyers Magazine, 1995—. *Member:* Los Angeles County (Chair, Antitrust Section, 1989-1990) and American (Torts and Insurance Practice Section, 1994—) Bar Associations. **PRACTICE AREAS:** Litigation; Insurance; Environmental.

**HARUMI HATA,** born 1960; admitted to bar, 1986, California. *Education:* Loyola Marymount University (B.A., 1982); Loyola University School of Law ( J.D., 1985). *Member:* Los Angeles County Bar Association; State Bar of California; Women Lawyers Association of Los Angeles. **PRACTICE AREAS:** Corporate; International; Real Estate.

**RICHARD R. TERZIAN,** born 1934; admitted to bar, 1960, California. *Education:* Dartmouth College (A.B., 1956); University of Southern California (LL.B., 1959). Phi Alpha Delta. City Attorney, Rolling Hills Estates, Calif., 1968—. Member, Commission on California Government Organization and Economy (Little Hoover Commission), 1986—. *Member:* Los Angeles County and American (Member, Section on Local Government Law) Bar Associations; The State Bar of California (Member: Disciplinary Board, 1976-1978; Judicial Nominees Evaluation Commission, 1985-1988). **PRACTICE AREAS:** Litigation.

**LISALEE ANNE WELLS,** born 1948; admitted to bar, 1975, California. *Education:* Wellesley College (B.A., with honors, 1970); Stanford Law School (J.D., 1975). Member, Board of Editors, Stanford Law Review, 1973-1975. Recipient, Duniway Scholarship, Stanford Law School, 1972-1973. Author: "Subdivision Land Dedication Requirements," 27 Stanford Law Review 419, 1975. Special Counsel to the Secretary of the Navy, 1977-1978. *Member:* California Association of Bond Lawyers (Member, Board of Directors, 1994—). [U.S. Navy and Reserve, JAGC, 1970—; Capt.]. **PRACTICE AREAS:** Public Finance.

## ASSOCIATES

*Jerrold E. Abeles; Vincent J. Davitt; Alexander H. Fukui; Aaron C. Gundzik; Jared M. Katz; Richard P. Lopez* (admission pending).; *R. Diane McKain; Stephen P. Pfahler; Kristin Pelletier; Allyson S. Taketa; Robert J. Tyson* (admission pending)..

## OF COUNSEL

**STEVEN A. BROILES,** born 1940; admitted to bar, 1966, California. *Education:* University of Redlands (B.A., cum laude, Economics, 1962); University of California at Berkeley (J.D., 1965). Author: "Keeping Secrets," 6 Los Angeles Lawyer, No. 4, June, 1983. Co-Author: "The Pollution Exclusion: Implementing the Social Policy of Preventing Pollution Through the Insurance Policy," 19 Loyola of Los Angeles Law Review 1251, 1986. Author: "Health Risk Assessments: A Critical Scientific Technique," Los

*(This Listing Continued)*

**LeBOEUF, LAMB, GREENE & MacRAE L.L.P.,** Los Angeles—Continued

Angeles Lawyer, 1994. Deputy County Counsel, County of Riverside, 1966-1978. District Counsel, South Coast Air Quality Management District, 1978-1980. *Member:* Riverside County, Los Angeles County and American (Member, Sections on: Administrative Law; Economics of Law Practice; Natural Resources Law) Bar Associations; The State Bar of California; Air and Waste Management Association. *PRACTICE AREAS:* Environmental.

**EDWARD O. HUNTER,** born 1947; admitted to bar, 1974, Michigan; 1975, U.S. Tax Court; 1984, California. *Education:* University of Utah (B.A., 1971); George Washington University (J.D., with honors, 1974). Recipient, Distinguished Advocate Award, 1972. Author: "Service of American Judicial Process on Japanese Nationals in Japan," International Litigation Quarterly, Vol. 5, No. 1, March 1989. *PRACTICE AREAS:* Litigation; Product Liability.

**ROBERT M. JOHNSON,** born 1957; admitted to bar, 1984, Missouri; 1985, Illinois; 1989, California. *Education:* Hamilton College (B.A., 1979); Oxford University, England (M.Phil., 1981); University of Virginia (J.D., 1984). *PRACTICE AREAS:* Real Estate.

**CHARLES F. TIMMS, JR.,** born 1948; admitted to bar, 1977, California. *Education:* Pomona College (B.A., cum laude, 1969); University of Michigan (J.D., 1977). Phi Beta Kappa. Co-Author, *California Spill Reporting Manual*, Government Institutes, 1996. Author: "Buying and Selling the Right to Pollute," Los Angeles Lawyer, Vol. 15, No. 4, June 1992. *PRACTICE AREAS:* Environmental.

(Biographical data on all Members of the Firm, Counsel, Of Counsel and Special Counsel in Washington, D.C., New York, New York, Albany, New York, Boston, Massachusetts, Harrisburg, Pennsylvania, Hartford, Connecticut, Newark, New Jersey, Portland, Oregon, Salt Lake City, Utah, Los Angeles, California, San Francisco, California, Jacksonville, Florida, Pittsburgh, Pennsylvania, Denver, Colorado, London, England, Brussels, Belgium, Almaty, Kazakhstan and Moscow, Russian Federation are listed in the respective Biographical Sections)

---

## LEBOVITS & DAVID
*A PROFESSIONAL CORPORATION*
Established in 1983
SUITE 3100, TWO CENTURY PLAZA
2049 CENTURY PARK EAST
**LOS ANGELES, CALIFORNIA 90067**
Telephone: 310-277-0200
Fax: 310-552-1028

*Product Liability, Professional Negligence, Aviation Law, Insurance Bad Faith, Personal Injury and Business Litigation.*

FIRM PROFILE: *Lebovits & David was founded in 1983 by Moses Lebovits and Deborah A. David, former classmates and 1975 graduates of the University of California at Los Angeles School of Law. Prior to forming Lebovits and David, Mr. Lebovits had eight years experience in plaintiffs' personal injury, and Ms. David had eight years experience in insurance defense with Bronson, Bronson & McKinnon, a large California firm. Lebovits & David offers a range of general civil and trial services emphasizing aviation, personal injury, professional negligence, products liability, insurance bad faith, employment termination and discrimination, and business tort litigation. The firm requires participation in continuing legal education, and both Mr. Lebovits and Ms. David regularly speak at and write for continuing legal education programs. The law firm is listed in the Bar Register of Preeminent Lawyers.*

**MOSES LEBOVITS,** born Munich, Germany, March 30, 1951; admitted to bar, 1975, California. *Education:* University of California at Los Angeles (B.A., cum laude, 1972; J.D., 1975). Member: Moot Court Executive Board of Judges, 1974-1975; 1st Place Southern California Moot Court Tournament, 1975. Adjunct Professor, Aviation Law, Southwestern University School of Law, 1981-1983. Arbitrator, Superior Court, County of Los Angeles, 1979—. Member, Special Panel for Referrals for Special Litigation Needs of Dependent Children of the Superior Court, Los Angeles County, Juvenile Department, 1980—. Member, Arbitration Panel, Reynolds Aluminum Torrance Can Plant (Labor Disputes), 1981—. *Member:* Los Angeles County (Member, Federal Courts and Practices Committee, 1982-1984; Delegate, 1982) and American Bar Associations; State Bar of California (Member, Conference of Delegates, 1982); Consumer Attorneys Association of Los Angeles (Member, Board of Governors, 1982-1985); Consumer Attorneys of California (Member Board of Governors, 1995—); National Order of Barristers. *REPORTED CASES:* Flood v. Wyeth, 183 Cal. App. 3d 1272, 228 Cal. Rptr. 700 (1986); Touri v. Walker - Verdict/Judgment - $7.5 Million; Rose v. Volkswagen - Verdict/Judgment - $3.5 Million ; Charlesworth v. USA, 840 F. Supp. 1484 (D. Utah 1994) - Verdict/Judgment - $1,128,000; Salazar v. Foroughe - Verdict/Judgment - $2.2 Million. *PRACTICE AREAS:* Product Liability; Professional Negligence; Aviation Law; Insurance Bad Faith; Personal Injury.

**DEBORAH A. DAVID,** born Los Angeles, California, November 22, 1950; admitted to bar, 1975, California. *Education:* Scripps College (B.A., 1972); L'Institut d' Etudes Politiques de Paris, Paris, France; University of California at Los Angeles (J.D., 1975). Member, Moot Court Honors Program. Extern to Chief Justice Donald Wright, California Supreme Court, 1974. Co-Author: "Liability of Fixed Based Operators and Airport Owners," published by New York Law Journal for its 1979 Symposium on Aviation Law. Author: "Legal Malpractice Claims: Plaintiff's Viewpoint," Prosecuting and Defending Major Insurance Claims, John Wiley & Sons, 1989. Arbitrator, Los Angeles County Superior Courts, 1981-1987. Judge Pro Tem, Los Angeles County Municipal Courts, 1988—. Member, Board of Trustees, Scripps College, 1990—. Member, Board of Directors, UCLA Law Alumni Association, 1994—. *Member:* Los Angeles County (Member, Executive Committee Litigation Section) and American Bar Associations; State Bar of California; The Association of Trial Lawyers of America; Consumer Attorneys Association of Los Angeles (Member, Board of Governors, 1990—; President-Elect); Consumer Attorneys of California (Member, Board of Governors, 1996—); Association of Business Trial Lawyers (Member of the Board). *LANGUAGES:* French. *REPORTED CASES:* Rose v. Volkswagen - verdict - judgment - $3.5 Million; Leal v. Golden - Verdict/Judgment - $14.9 Million; Goodstein v. Superior Court. *PRACTICE AREAS:* Products Liability; Professional Negligence; Aviation Law; Insurance Bad Faith; Personal Injury.

*OF COUNSEL*

**JOSEPH J. M. LANGE,** born San Diego, California, June 30, 1961; admitted to bar, 1987, California. *Education:* University of California at Los Angeles (B.A., cum laude, 1983); Loyola University of Los Angeles (J.D., 1986). Phi Eta Sigma; Phi Alpha Delta. Law Clerk to Hon. Florence Bernstein, Appellate Department of the Superior Court, 1984. Law Clerk to the United States Justice Department, United States Trustee in Bankruptcy, 1985. *Member:* Los Angeles County and American Bar Associations; State Bar of California; The Association of Trial Lawyers of America; Consumer Attorneys of California; Consumer Attorneys Association of Los Angeles. *REPORTED CASES:* Villa Pacific Building Company v. Superior Court, 223 Cal. App. 328 (1991). *PRACTICE AREAS:* Products Liability; Professional Negligence; Aviation Law; Insurance Bad Faith; Personal Injury; Business Litigation; Health Care.

REFERENCE: Imperial Bank (Main Office - Beverly Hills).

---

## CAROL A. LEBOW
1999 AVENUE OF THE STARS, 27TH FLOOR
**LOS ANGELES, CALIFORNIA 90067**
Telephone: 310-286-1999
Facsimile: 310-551-0027

*Corporate, Real Estate, Partnership and Transactional Business Law. Federal, State, Local and International Taxation. Tax Litigation and Controversies.*

**CAROL A. LEBOW,** born Los Angeles, California, October 18, 1950; admitted to bar, 1975, California; 1978, U.S. Tax Court. *Education:* University of California at Los Angeles (B.A., with honors in Political Science, 1971); Vanderbilt University (J.D., 1975); New York University (LL.M., in Taxation, 1977). *Member:* Beverly Hills (Chairperson, Women and the Law Committee, 1978-1980; Member, Board of Governors, 1981-1983) and Los Angeles County Bar Associations; The State Bar of California.

---

## ALTON LEIB
1801 CENTURY PARK EAST, SUITE 2500
**LOS ANGELES, CALIFORNIA 90067-2326**
Telephone: 310-286-0880
Fax: 310-286-1633
*Business Litigation.*

**ALTON LEIB,** born Detroit, Michigan, August 31, 1932; admitted to bar, 1959, California. *Education:* University of California at Los Angeles

*(This Listing Continued)*

(B.A., 1953); Boalt Hall School of Law, University of California at Los Angeles (J.D., 1958). Phi Alpha Delta. *Member:* Beverly Hills and Century City Bar Associations; State Bar of California; Los Angeles Trial Lawyers Association; California Trial Lawyers Association.

Languages: Italian and French.

REPRESENTATIVE CLIENTS: Ideal Textile Co. Inc.; Cal-Pacific Dyeing and Finishing; Fabric Enterprises, Ltd.; Silver Textile, Inc.; Westex Mills, Inc.; City Dyeing & Finishing Co.; Emday Fabrics, Inc.; Systems Tax Service, Inc.; Fisher & Gentile, Ltd.; Express Air Cargo Inc.; Apia-Pago Express; I.I.F., Inc.
REFERENCES: First Regional Bank (Century City).

---

## LELAND, PARACHINI, STEINBERG, FLINN, MATZGER & MELNICK, L.L.P.

500 SOUTH GRAND AVENUE, SUITE 1100
LOS ANGELES, CALIFORNIA 90071
Telephone: 213-623-7505
Fax: 213-623-7595

*San Francisco, California Office:* 27th Floor, 333 Market Street. Telephone: 415-957-1800. Fax: 415-974-1520.

*General Civil and Trial Practice in all State and Federal Courts. Corporation, Business, Banking, Bankruptcy, Employment, Tax, Estate Planning, Probate, Trust, Family and Real Estate Law.*

### RESIDENT PARTNERS

**RICHARD FANNAN,** born Los Angeles, California, April 27, 1947; admitted to bar, 1977, California. *Education:* University of California at Los Angeles; University of California at Berkeley (B.A., 1968); Boalt Hall School of Law, University of California (J.D., 1977). Order of the Coif. Articles Editor, California Law Review, 1976-1977. Author: Note, "Setback for the 'Newer' Equal Protection," 65 California Law Review 493, 1977. *PRACTICE AREAS:* Business Litigation.

**VICKI L. FREIMANN,** born Los Angeles, California, July 18, 1946; admitted to bar, 1981, California and U.S. District Court, Central, Southern, Northern and Eastern Districts of California. *Education:* University of California at Irvine (B.A., cum laude, 1971); Western State University (J.D., cum laude, 1980). Member, Western State University Law Review, 1979-1980. Member, Executive Committee, Pre-Judgment Remedies Committee, Los Angeles County Bar Association. *Member:* Financial Lawyers Conference. *PRACTICE AREAS:* Banking; Business Litigation; Creditors' Remedies.

**KENNETH MILLER,** born Manhattan, New York, December 19, 1960; admitted to bar, 1986, California and the U.S. District Court, Central, Southern, Northern and Eastern Districts of California. *Education:* University of California at San Diego (B.S., 1983); Loyola Marymount University (J.D., 1986). Participant, Loyola Moot Court Program. *Member:* Los Angeles Bankruptcy Forum. *PRACTICE AREAS:* Creditor's Remedies, Bankruptcy; Business Litigation.

### RESIDENT ASSOCIATES

**DAWN M. COULSON,** born Meadville, Pennsylvania, September 12, 1960; admitted to bar, 1990, Colorado; 1991, California. *Education:* University of Texas (B.A., B.B.A., 1982); University of Denver College of Law (J.D., 1990). *Member:* The Los Angeles Bankruptcy Forum; The Financial Lawyers Conference. *LANGUAGES:* Japanese and Spanish. *PRACTICE AREAS:* Banking; Business; Employment; Bankruptcy Litigation.

**THOMAS A. VIDANO,** born New York, N.Y., December 11, 1962; admitted to bar, 1992, California and U.S. District Court, Central District of California. *Education:* Stanford University (A.B., with distinction, 1985); University of California at Los Angeles (J.D., 1991). Participant, UCLA Moot Court Honors Program. *Member:* State Bar of California; Financial Lawyers Conference. *LANGUAGES:* German. *PRACTICE AREAS:* Business Litigation; Bankruptcy.

### OF COUNSEL

**C. TIMOTHY O'MALLEY,** born Pasadena, California, August 9, 1955; admitted to bar, 1979, California and U.S. District Court, Central, Northern, Southern and Eastern Districts of California. *Education:* University of California at Davis (B.A., 1976); University of Southern California (J.D., 1979). *PRACTICE AREAS:* Financial Institutions; Creditor Bankruptcy; Business Litigation.

All Attorneys in the firm are members of the State Bar of California.

(For Biographical data on persons resident in San Francisco, see Professional Biographies at San Francisco)

---

## BOYD S. LEMON

12304 SANTA MONICA BOULEVARD, SUITE 221
LOS ANGELES, CALIFORNIA 90025
Telephone: 310-979-4848
Fax: 310-979-4840

*Paso Robles, California Office:* 1111 Riverside Avenue, Suite 504, 93446. Telephone: 805-239-4184. Facsimile: 805-239-1049.

*Expert Witness in Legal Malpractice Matters. General Civil and Trial Practice.*

**BOYD S. LEMON,** born Monterey Park, California, October 7, 1940; admitted to bar, 1966, California and U.S. District Court, Central District of California; 1980, U.S. Court of Appeals, Ninth Circuit and U.S. Supreme Court. *Education:* University of Southern California (A.B., magna cum laude, 1962; J.D., 1965). Phi Alpha Delta; Order of the Coif. Note and Comment Editor, Southern California Law Review, 1964-1965. Teaching Credential, California, 1976. Author: "How to Avoid Legal Malpractice," L.A. Lawyer, February 1992; Note, "Timely Objections before Congressional Committees," 37 Southern California Law Review 342, 1964; Note, "People v. Randazzo: A Private Silver Platter Doctrine," 37 Southern California Law Review, 1964. Lecturer, Continuing Education of the Bar, 1975—. Instructor, California Law, El Camino Community College, 1976-1977. Judge Pro Tem, Beverly Hills Municipal Court. Arbitrator, Los Angeles Superior Court, Arbitrator, State Bar of California (Attorney Fee Disputes). *Member:* Los Angeles County Bar Association (Member, Attorney Errors and Omissions Committee, 1966—); State Bar of California (Member, State Bar Disciplinary Committee, 1971-1972); Legal Malpractice Bar Association. *PRACTICE AREAS:* Litigation; Business Litigation; Legal Malpractice; Ethics; Real Estate Litigation.

### ASSOCIATES

**C. KELLY McCOURT,** born Marin County, California, December 4, 1961; admitted to bar, 1986, California. *Education:* University of California at Berkeley (A.B., 1983); Hastings College of the Law, University of California (J.D., 1986). Phi Delta Phi. *Member:* State Bar of California. *PRACTICE AREAS:* Legal Malpractice; Commercial Litigation; Insurance Litigation.

**ERIC E. BRONSON,** born Marshall, Michigan, July 17, 1958; admitted to bar, 1983, California; 1984, U.S. District Court, Central District of California and U.S. Court of Appeals, Ninth Circuit; 1989, U.S. District Court, Northern District of California. *Education:* Michigan State University (B.A., Pol. Sc. with high honors, 1980); University of Michigan (J.D., 1983). *Member:* State Bar of California.

---

## JAMES M. LEONARD

SUITE 645, 11845 WEST OLYMPIC BOULEVARD
LOS ANGELES, CALIFORNIA 90064
Telephone: 310-312-8660
Fax: 310-312-8024

*General Business Practice and Entertainment Law.*

**JAMES M. LEONARD,** born Los Angeles, California, December 13, 1946; admitted to bar, 1971, California. *Education:* University of California at Berkeley (B.A., 1967); University of California at Los Angeles (J.D., 1970). Order of the Coif; Phi Alpha Delta. Law Clerk to the Hon. Ralph M. Holman, Associate Justice of the Supreme Court of Oregon, 1970-1971. Judge Pro Tem, Beverly Hills Municipal Court, 1976-1981. Judge Pro Tem, Los Angeles Municipal Court, 1979-1983. Arbitrator: American Arbitration Association; Los Angeles Superior Court; Santa Monica Municipal Court and Los Angeles County and Beverly Hills Bar, Fee Arbitration Committees, 1979—. *Member:* The State Bar of California.

REPRESENTATIVE CLIENTS: Farrell/Minoff Productions; Bob Kane Productions, Inc.; Amalgamated Dynamics, Inc.; Holmes Body Shop, Inc.; Burco Enterprises, Inc. (Restaurants); Raymond Wagner Productions, Inc.; ATM Global; P M Entertainment Group, Inc.; Animated Engineering, Inc.

CAA897B

## LEONARD, DICKER & SCHREIBER

**LOS ANGELES, CALIFORNIA**

(See Beverly Hills)

*Business and Real Estate Litigation, Entertainment Litigation, Estate and Trust Litigation Bankruptcy Litigation and Appellate Practice in State and Federal Courts, Real Estate, Entertainment, Commercial, Corporate, Estate Planning and Family Law.*

---

## LAWRENCE E. LEONE

Established in 1977

**12100 WILSHIRE BOULEVARD
FIFTEENTH FLOOR
LOS ANGELES, CALIFORNIA 90025**
Telephone: 310-207-1231
Fax: 310-207-5800

*Family Law.*

**LAWRENCE E. LEONE,** born Bakersfield, California, July 25, 1951; admitted to bar, 1977, California. *Education:* University of California at Los Angeles (A.B., magna cum laude, 1973); Loyola University of Los Angeles (J.D., 1977). Political Science Honors Society. Chancellor's Marshall. Moot Court Honors Program. Honors Board Side Justice. Author: "Spreadsheets in a Modern Family Law Practice" American Bar Association, October 1994; "Complex Litigation - Strategies, New Technologies and Presentation Techniques" December 1994; "Trial Preparation and Presentation in the Computer Age" Norton Baja Seminar, October 1994; "Using Computers in a Modern Family Law Practice" 1994 LACB Family Law Symposium; "Computer Utilization in Family Law" The State Bar of California Section Education Institute, November 1993; "Effective Use of Evidence - Family Law Applications" 1993 CLE Convention; "Determining Available Income For Support - Unreported Or Hidden Income Issues," 1992 BHBA Family Law Symposium; "Jurisdiction and Venue" 1991 LACB Family Law Symposium; "Statement of Decision And Post Trial Issues," with Judge James G. Kolts, 1989 & 1990 LACB Family Law Symposium; "Foreign Judgements" with Commissioner Hugh Macbeth, 1984, 1985, 1987 & 1988, LACB Family Law Symposium; "Post Trial: Rights and Remedies" B.H.B.A. Fam. L. Symp. 1987 (Editor and Contributor); "The Expert Witness: Family Law" B.H.B.A. Symp. 1986 (Editor and Contributor); "Possession, Sale and Distribution of the Marital Home" with E. Poll, Matthew Bender, 1985; "California Discovery Practice: Family Law Applications", B.H.B.A. Fam. L. Symp. 1984; "Valuation: Forensic Applications" 1984 Valuation Conference, Cal. C.P.A. Foundation; "Evidentiary Consideration in Family Law Litigation" with M. Raeder B.H.B.A. Fam. L. Symp. 1983. Editor: "LACB Family Law Symposium", 1992, 1993, 1994; "Child Custody Compendium", 1994 LACB; "Annual Family Law Institute - Ethics" University of Southern California, 1993 & 1994. Written Materials Editor: "Beverly Hills Bar Family Law Symposium", 1983, 1984, 1986, 1987. Instructor: Apportionment & Other Accounting Issues, LACB Symposium, 1994; The Family Law Trial, University of West Los Angeles School of law, April 1994; Emerging Technologies - Family Law Applications, LACB CLE Program, July 1993; Presenting Evidence in the Family Law Trial - Examining Experts, LACB CLE Program, 1993; Child Support and Support Issues, 1989-1992; Valuation: Forensic Applications, Cal. C.P.A. Foundation, Los Angeles and San Francisco; Offering and Cross Examining Experts, Beverly Hill Bar Symposium; Hot Tips From The Experts, Beverly Hills Bar Association. Judge Pro Tem, Los Angeles Superior Court, Santa Monica Superior Court, 1993-1994. Family Law Mediator, Los Angeles Central, Van Nuys and Santa Monica, 1985-1994. Attorney, Trope and Trope, Los Angeles, California, 1980-1990. *Member:* Beverly Hills (Member, Executive Committee, Family Law Section, 1983-1994) and Los Angeles County (Member, Family Law Section, 1977-1994, Executive Committee, 1994—; Arbitrator, 1980-1994) Bar Associations; State Bar of California (Member, Family Law Section). (Certified Specialist, Family Law, The State Bar of California Board of Legal Specialization).

---

## LEOPOLD, PETRICH & SMITH

*A PROFESSIONAL CORPORATION*

(Formerly Youngman, Hungate & Leopold)

**SUITE 3110, 2049 CENTURY PARK EAST (CENTURY CITY)
LOS ANGELES, CALIFORNIA 90067**
Telephone: 310-277-3333
Telecopier: 310-277-7444

*General Civil and Trial and Appellate Practice in all State and Federal Courts. Motion Picture, Television, Copyright, Trademark, Libel and Slander and Unfair Competition Law.*

**FIRM PROFILE:** *Leopold, Petrich & Smith are a Professional Law Corporation. The firm believes that the client comes first. The law firm serves clients all over the world, at present, its clients are in Germany, England and France. The firm is listed in the Bar Register of Preeminent Lawyers.*

**GORDON E. YOUNGMAN** (1903-1983).

**A. FREDRIC LEOPOLD,** born New York, N.Y., November 10, 1919; admitted to bar, 1948, New York; 1951, California. *Education:* Dartmouth College (A.B., 1941); Columbia University (J.D., 1948). Phi Beta Kappa. Harlan Fiske Stone Scholar. Member, Board of Editors, Columbia Law Review, 1948. Author: "Errors and Omissions Insurance," International Media Law. Member, Beverly Hills City Council, 1966-1972. Mayor, 1967-1968; 1971-1972. *Member:* Beverly Hills, Los Angeles County and New York State Bar Associations; The State Bar of California; Los Angeles Copyright Society (President, 1983). **PRACTICE AREAS:** Copyright; Trademark; Entertainment; Insurance; Errors and Omissions.

**LOUIS P. PETRICH,** born Duluth, Minnesota, August 13, 1940; admitted to bar, 1966, California. *Education:* University of California at Los Angeles (A.B., 1962; LL.B., 1965). Order of the Coif. Managing Editor, University of California at Los Angeles Law Review, 1964-1965. Author: Chapter on Trial Techniques in Jury and Bench Trials of Copyright Cases, *Intellectual Property Counseling and Litigation,* Matthew Bender. Lecturer, Litigating Copyright, Trademark and Unfair Competition Cases, PLI, 1984—. *Member:* Los Angeles County and American Bar Associations; The State Bar of California; Los Angeles Copyright Society (Member, Board of Trustees, 1980-1982; President, 1987-1988). **PRACTICE AREAS:** Entertainment; Civil Litigation; Copyright and Trademark; Libel and Slander; Unfair Competition.

**JOEL McCABE SMITH,** born Greeley, Colorado, August 20, 1945; admitted to bar, 1972, California. *Education:* University of California at Los Angeles (B.A., 1968; J.D., 1971). Member, University of California at Los Angeles Law Review, 1969-1971. *Member:* The State Bar of California. **PRACTICE AREAS:** Entertainment; Civil Litigation; Copyright and Trademark; Libel and Slander; Unfair Competition.

**EDWARD A. RUTTENBERG,** born Norwalk, Connecticut, June 28, 1950; admitted to bar, 1975, California. *Education:* Yale University (B.A., 1972); Harvard University (J.D., 1975). *Member:* Los Angeles County Bar Association; The State Bar of California. **PRACTICE AREAS:** Entertainment; Civil Litigation; Copyright and Trademark; Libel and Slander; Unfair Competition.

**VINCENT COX,** born New York, N.Y., February 11, 1952; admitted to bar, 1976, California. *Education:* New College (B.A., 1973); State University of New York at Buffalo (J.D., 1976). Research Editor, Buffalo Law Review, 1975-1976. Author: "New York State Unfair Competition Law: A Survey and Analysis," Vol. 25, Buffalo Law Review, 1975. *Member:* Century City, Los Angeles County and American Bar Associations; State Bar of California; Los Angeles Copyright Society (Member, Board of Trustees). **PRACTICE AREAS:** Entertainment; Civil Litigation; Copyright and Trademark; Libel and Slander; Unfair Competition.

**DONALD R. GORDON,** born Glen Ridge, New Jersey, October 9, 1954; admitted to bar, 1979, California. *Education:* Lafayette College (A.B., magna cum laude, 1976); University of Durham, Durham, England; University of Chicago (J.D., 1979). Phi Beta Kappa; Phi Delta Phi. Member, University of Chicago Law Review, 1977-1979. *Member:* Los Angeles County and American Bar Associations; State Bar of California. **PRACTICE AREAS:** Entertainment; Civil Litigation; Copyright and Trademark; Libel and Slander; Unfair Competition.

**WALTER R. SADLER,** born Detroit, Michigan, November 19, 1956; admitted to bar, 1983, California. *Education:* University of California at Santa Barbara (B.A., with honors, 1979); University of California at Davis (J.D., 1982). Phi Delta Phi. Member, 1980-1981 and Editor, 1981-1982,

*(This Listing Continued)*

University of California at Davis Law Review. First Place Prize in 1982 U.C. Davis American Society of Composers, Authors and Publishers Nathan Burkan Memorial Copyright Competition. Author: "Free Lance Artists, Works for Hire and the Copyright Act of 1976," 15 U.C. Davis Law Review 703, 1982; "Copyright Ownership in Commissioned Artworks--A Copyright, Who Dunnit," 16 Intellectual Property Law Review, 1984. *Member:* Century City (Member, Entertainment Law Section), Beverly Hills, Los Angeles County (Member, Intellectual Property and Trial Lawyers Section) and American (Member, Patent, Trademark an Copyright Section) Bar Associations; State Bar of California; Los Angeles Copyright Society; California Trial Lawyers Association; Los Angeles Trial Lawyers Association. **PRACTICE AREAS:** Entertainment; Civil Litigation; Copyright and Trademark; Libel and Slander; Unfair Competition.

**DANIEL M. MAYEDA,** born Tokyo, Japan, December 21, 1957; admitted to bar, 1983, California and District of Columbia. *Education:* University of California at Los Angeles (B.A., magna cum laude, 1979); University of California at Los Angeles School of Law (J.D., 1982). Member, 1980-1982 and Chief Articles Editor, 1981-1982, Federal Communications Law Journal. Author: "High Potential in Low Power: A Model for an Efficient Low Power Television Service," 33 Federal Communications Law Journal 419, 1981. Co-Author: "Copyright Fair Use, The First Amendment and New Communications Technologies: The Impact of Betamax," 38 Federal Communications Law Journal 59, 1986. Policy Analyst, U. S. House of Representatives Subcommittee on Telecommunications, Consumer Protection and Finance, 1981-1982. *Member:* Los Angeles County Bar Association; The District of Columbia Bar; State Bar of California; American Bar Association (Member: Forum Committee on Communications Law; Litigation Section); Federal Communications Bar Association. **PRACTICE AREAS:** Entertainment; Civil Litigation; Copyright and Trademark; Libel and Slander; Unfair Competition.

### OF COUNSEL

**RICHARD HUNGATE,** born Cheney, Washington, January 20, 1909; admitted to bar, 1938, California. *Education:* University of Washington (A.B., 1930); Stanford University (A.M., 1931; LL.B., 1937). Delta Theta Phi; Order of the Coif. *Member:* Beverly Hills and Los Angeles County Bar Associations; The State Bar of California. **PRACTICE AREAS:** Entertainment; Civil Litigation; Copyright and Trademark; Libel and Slander; Unfair Competition.

---

**PAUL M. KREKORIAN,** born Los Angeles, California, March 24, 1960; admitted to bar, 1984, California. *Education:* University of Southern California (A.B., cum laude, 1981); Boalt Hall School of Law, University of California at Berkeley (J.D., 1984). Pi Sigma Alpha; Alpha Lambda Delta. Member, Board of Trustees, Los Angeles County Law Library, 1994—. Member: Los Angeles County Democratic Central Committee, 1980-1982; California State Democratic Central Committee, 1985-1987, 1989-1991, 1994—. *Member:* Los Angeles County (Member: Delegation to State Bar Conference of Delegates, 1993—; Litigation Section Legislative Review Committee, 1990—; Litigation Section Newsletter Editorial Board, 1990-1994), Beverly Hills and American Bar Associations; The State Bar of California (Member, Litigation Section Committee on Administration of Justice, 1991-1994). **PRACTICE AREAS:** Entertainment; Employment; Civil Litigation; Copyright and Trademark; Libel and Slander; Unfair Competition.

**DAVID ARONOFF,** born New York, N.Y., July 17, 1960; admitted to bar, 1986, California. *Education:* University of California at Los Angeles (B.A., 1982); Hastings College of the Law, University of California (J.D., cum laude, 1986). Member, Thurston Honor Society. Articles Editor, 1985-1986 and Member, 1984-1985, Hastings Constitutional Law Quarterly. *Member:* Los Angeles County and American Bar Associations; State Bar of California. **PRACTICE AREAS:** Entertainment; Civil Litigation; Copyright and Trademark; Libel and Slander; Unfair Competition.

**GARY M. GROSSENBACHER,** born San Antonio, Texas, August 13, 1962; admitted to bar, 1988, California. *Education:* University of Texas, Austin (B.A., 1984; J.D., with honors, 1987). **PRACTICE AREAS:** Civil Litigation; Entertainment Law; Media Law; Copyrights and Idea Submissions; Contract Disputes; Guild Agreements; Trademark Infringement and Counterfeiting; Unfair Competition and Defamation.

**ROBERT S. GUTIERREZ,** born Pomona, California, August 10, 1962; admitted to bar, 1989, California; 1990, U.S. Court of Appeals, Ninth Circuit. *Education:* Harvard University (B.A., cum laude, 1984); Stanford Law School (J.D., 1989). Associate Managing Editor, Stanford Law Review, 1988-1989. *Member:* Beverly Hills and Los Angeles County Bar Associa-

*(This Listing Continued)*

tions; State Bar of California. **PRACTICE AREAS:** Entertainment; Civil Litigation; Copyright and Trademark; Libel and Slander; Unfair Competition.

REPRESENTATIVE CLIENTS: Aon Entertainment Ltd.; Chubb/Pacific Indemnity Insurance Group; CNA Insurance Companies; Dove Audio, Inc.; The Gordy Company; Guess?, Inc.; Harper Collins Publishers, Inc.; Jobete Music Co., Inc.; K-III Communications Corp.; MCA Inc.; Media/Professional Insurance, Inc.; Metro-Goldwyn-Mayer, Inc.; Jess S. Morgan & Co., Inc.; News America Publishing, Inc.; Southern Star Productions, Inc.; Tribune Co.; Twentieth Century Fox Film Corp.; Underwriters at Lloyd's; Universal City Studios, Inc.

---

## LESANSKY & ASSOCIATES
*1875 CENTURY PARK EAST, SUITE 700*
**LOS ANGELES, CALIFORNIA 90067**
*Telephone: 310-226-2400*
*Fax: 310-226-2401*
*Email: lesans@ibm.net*

*Unfair Competition, Securities Litigation, Aviation and Aerospace Law and Litigation, Construction Defect Litigation, Intellectual Property, Professional Liability, Insurance Coverage, Probate Litigation, Directors and Officers, Errors and Omissions Litigation and General Commercial Law.*

**STUART K. LESANSKY,** born Brooklyn, New York, April 6, 1952; admitted to bar, 1979, New York, U.S. Court of Appeals, Second Circuit and District of Columbia Circuit and U.S. District Court, Southern and Eastern Districts of New York; 1985, California, U.S. District Court, Northern District of California, U.S. Court of Appeals, Ninth Circuit; 1986, U.S. District Court, Central District of California; 1988, U.S. District Court, Southern District of California. *Education:* State University of New York at Stony Brook (B.A., 1973); Brooklyn Law School (J.D., 1978). Member, Order of the Barristers. Co-Chairman, Moot Court Honor Society, 1977-1978. Moderator: "Resolving Disputes in the 90's Through Alternative Dispute Resolution," Judicial Arbitration and Mediation Services, Inc., Century City Bar Association, 1992; with Judge Robert M. Mallano, "Extension of the Fast Track Rule and the Demise of the Master Calendar Changes in Superior Court," Century City Bar Association, 1993; "Litigation Support Technology?" Century City Bar Association, 1993; "Legal Malpractice in the 90's and the Rules of Professional Conduct," and "One Year Later: Report from Presiding Judge of the Superior Court for Los Angeles County After Implementation of the Individual Calendaring System and Fast Tract for All Cases," Century Bar Association, 1994; with Judge Irving M. Shimer, "Beverly Hills Branch of the Los Angeles Superior Court, West District," Century City Bar Association, 1994. Moderator and Panelist: with Chief Judge Manuel L. Real, "Recent Changes and Trends in Federal Civil Procedure," Century City Bar Association, 1993; "Symposium on Shareholder Litigation," Century City Bar Association, 1993; "Comment or No Comment," Press Seminar, Century City Bar Association, 1993; "What Duties Do Professionals Representing the Syndicator or Promoter Owe to Limited Partners/Investors?" Century City Bar Association, 1994; "Are You My Client? Are You My Lawyer? When Does the Attorney-Client Relationship Begin and When Does it End?" Century City Bar Association, 1995; "Managing the Stress of Litigation: Prevention, Detection Treatment and Ethical Considerations of Substance Abuse," Century City Bar Association, 1995; "Anatomy of a Bad Faith Case," Century City Bar Association, 1995; "Modern Mediation Techniques for Business Litigators," Century City Bar Association, 1995. Author: "Judicial Profile: Hon. Manuel L. Real," Century City Lawyer, August, 1993. *Member:* Association of the Bar of the City of New York (Member, 1983—, Secretary, 1983-1985, Civil Rights Committee); Century City (Secretary, 1996; Member, Board of Governors, 1990—; Chair, Business Litigation Section, 1991—), Beverly Hills, (Member, Litigation Section, 1985—), Los Angeles County (Member, Litigation Section) and American (Member, Sections on: Antitrust, 1974—; Litigation) Bar Associations; State Bar of California. **PRACTICE AREAS:** Unfair Competition; Securities Litigation; Aviation; Aerospace Law; Litigation; Construction Defect Litigation; Intellectual Property; Professional Liability; Insurance Coverage; Probate Litigation; Directors and Officers; Errors and Omissions Litigation; General Commercial Law.

### ASSOCIATES

**STEVEN L. WEINBERG,** born Los Angeles, California, July 18, 1963; admitted to bar, 1992, California. *Education:* University of California at Los Angeles (B.A., magna cum laude, 1988); Loyola Law School (J.D., 1991). Recipient, American Jurisprudence Awards: Criminal Procedure; Property. *Member:* State Bar of California (Member, Intellectual Property Section); American Bar Association (Member, Patent, Trademark and

*(This Listing Continued)*

**LESANSKY & ASSOCIATES,** Los Angeles—Continued

Copyright Section). **PRACTICE AREAS:** Civil Defense; Professional Liability; Intellectual Property; Computer Law.

**CHRISTINE M. MACFARLANE,** born LaGrange, Illinois, March 23, 1964; admitted to bar, 1990, California and U.S. District Court, Central and Southern Districts of California. *Education:* Indiana University (B.A., 1986); Indiana University School of Law (J.D., 1989). Delta Theta Phi. Staff Member, Indiana Law Journal, 1987-1989. *Member:* Century City, Los Angeles County and American Bar Associations; State Bar of California; California Trial Lawyers Association; Women Lawyers Association of Los Angeles. **LANGUAGES:** Italian. **PRACTICE AREAS:** Aviation Law; Products Liability Law.

## LAW OFFICES OF
## PETER J. LESSER

1801 CENTURY PARK EAST, SUITE 2500
LOS ANGELES, CALIFORNIA 90067
Telephone: 310-552-0599
Fax: 310-552-0596
Email: PETELESSER@AOL.COM

*Civil Litigation; Business Counseling and Litigation; Entertainment Transactions and Litigation; Probate and Estate Litigation; Criminal Defense.*

**PETER J. LESSER,** born New York, N.Y., September 10, 1957; admitted to bar, 1984, Virginia; 1985, District of Columbia; 1989, California. *Education:* Oberlin College (B.A., 1979); London School of Economics and Political Science (M.Sc., 1980); University of Virginia (J.D., 1984). Recipient: American Society of International Law, Deak Award For Best Article in USA; UVA Dillard Award For Best Law Review Note at UVA. Senior Editor, Virginia Journal of International Law, 1984. Author: "Superseding Statutory Law by Sole Executive Agreement," 23 Virginia Journal of International Law 671, 1983; Chapter, "The Legal System of Hong Kong," 2 Modern Legal Systems Cyclopedia, 1984. Litigation Attorney: Mitchell Silberberg & Knupp, Los Angeles, 1988-1993; Kelley, Drye & Warren, District of Columbia, 1986-1988; Donovan, Leisure, Newton & Irvine, District of Columbia, 1984-1986. Pro Bono Prosecutor, Los Angeles City Attorney's Office, 1992. *Member:* District of Columbia Bar; Virginia State Bar; State Bar of California; American Bar Association. (Also Of Counsel to Wickens & Lebow, Washington, D.C.).

### OF COUNSEL

**STEVEN M. RICH,** born Philadelphia, Pennsylvania, April 19, 1964; admitted to bar, 1990, California and U.S. District Court, Central District of California. *Education:* University of California at Berkeley (B.S. in Chemistry, 1987); Boalt Hall School of Law, University of California, Berkeley (J.D., 1990). Litigation Attorney, Mitchell, Silberberg & Knupp, Los Angeles, 1990-1995. Vice President and Corporate Counsel, Focus Media, Inc., Santa Monica, 1995-1996. *Member:* American Bar Association (Member, Litigation Section); State Bar of California (Member, Litigation Section). **PRACTICE AREAS:** Litigation.

## LEVENE, NEALE & BENDER L.L.P.

1801 AVENUE OF THE STARS, SUITE 1120
LOS ANGELES, CALIFORNIA 90067
Telephone: 310-229-1234
Fax: 310-229-1244
Email: (attorneys initials)@LNBLAW.COM

*Practice Limited to Bankruptcy Law, Insolvency Law and Business Reorganization.*

**FIRM PROFILE:** Levene, Neale & Bender L.L.P. ("LNB") is a boutique law firm specializing exclusively in matters of bankruptcy, insolvency, and business reorganization, and is comprised of aggressive, yet practical, lawyers who are able to approach legal problems creatively and efficiently, bringing to bear years of experience in handling complex and difficult cases. LNB believes that common sense is often the best indicator of the most efficient and effective solution to a problem, and LNB's lawyers always remain focused upon the ultimate goal of the client in an effort to avoid "winning the battle but losing the war." LNB regularly associates as counsel with many of Los Angeles' leading law firms, and is often called upon to advise other law firms regarding issues within the area of LNB's expertise. In this regard, LNB often serves as the "lawyers' lawyer." LNB has enjoyed great success in converting an impossible problem

*(This Listing Continued)*

into merely a difficult problem which is resolved through hard work, skill and creativity. The law firm is listed in the Bar Register of Preeminent Lawyers.

**DAVID W. LEVENE,** born New York, N.Y., March 24, 1945; admitted to bar, 1974, California, U.S. District Court, Central District of California and U.S. Court of Appeals, Ninth Circuit. *Education:* University of Southern California (B.S., cum laude, 1967; M.B.A., 1968); Loyola University of Los Angeles (J.D., magna cum laude, 1974). Alpha Sigma Nu. Member, St. Thomas More Law Honor Society, 1973, 1974. Recipient: American Jurisprudence Award, 1972; American Law Book Company Award, 1972, 1974; West Publishing Company Award, 1973, 1974; Bancroft-Whitney Award, 1974. Listed Who's Who in Law, Los Angeles Business Journal, February 27, 1995 and February 19, 1996. Guest Lecturer: "Loan Workouts, LBOs and Bankruptcy," Frost & Sullivan, Inc., 1989; "Loan Workout, Restructure and Bankruptcy," The Banking Law Institute, 1989; "Chapter 11," Drexel Burnham Lambert, Inc., 1989; "Fraudulent Conveyances," Financial Lawyers Conference, 1990; "Out of Court Reorganizations," Los Angeles Bankruptcy Forum, 1990; "Restructuring Financially Troubled Businesses," Orange County Bankruptcy Forum, 1991; "Consignment Issues in Bankruptcy," Jewelers Board of Trade, 1992; "Case Study on Representation of Debtor in Out of Court Workout and Chapter 11," Turnaround Management Association, Fall 1992; "Bankruptcy Opportunities," Young Presidents' Organization, 1993, Mergers and Finance Seminar; "Gaining Confidence from Lenders and Creditors," Turnaround Management Association (Washington, D.C.), Fall, 1993; "Valuation Issues in Bankruptcy," Association of Insolvency Accountants, 1994; "The Real Estate Business Plan-Strategic Considerations," The Counselors of Real Estate, 1994 Convention. *Member:* Beverly Hills (Chairman, Bankruptcy Section, 1988, 1989), Los Angeles County (Member: Executive Committee, Commercial Law and Bankruptcy Section, 1982-1987; Bankruptcy Subcommittee, 1981-1987), Federal and American Bar Associations; State Bar of California; Financial Lawyers Conference; American Bankruptcy Institute. **PRACTICE AREAS:** Bankruptcy.

**DAVID L. NEALE,** born Brooklyn, New York, November 20, 1962; admitted to bar, 1988, New York and U.S. District Court, Southern and Eastern Districts of New York; 1989, California, U.S. Court of Appeals, Ninth Circuit and U.S. District Court, Northern, Eastern, Central and Southern Districts of California. *Education:* Princeton University (B.A., summa cum laude, 1984); Columbia University (J.D., 1987). Author: "Bankruptcy and Contractual Relations in the Entertainment Industry--An Overview," 1990 Entertainment Publishing and the Arts Handbook; "A Survey of Recent Bankruptcy Decisions Impacting Upon the Entertainment Industry," Entertainment Publishing & the Arts Handbook, 1992-1993. *Member:* Beverly Hills, Century City, New York County and American Bar Associations; The Association of the Bar of The City of New York; The Association of Trial Lawyers of America; Financial Lawyers Conference. **LANGUAGES:** Chinese (Mandarin); Spanish. **REPORTED CASES:** In re Oak Creek Energy Farms, Ltd., 107 B.R. 266 (Bkrptcy. E.D. Cal. 1989); Energrey Enterprises, Inc. v. Oak Creek Energy Systems, Inc., 119 B.R. 739 (E.D. Cal. 1990); In re Qintex Entertainment, Inc., 950 F.2d 1492 (9th. Cir. 1991); In re Oak Creek Energy Farms, Ltd., 99 B.R. 36 (Bkrptcy. E.D. Cal. 1989). **PRACTICE AREAS:** Bankruptcy. **Email:** DLN@LNBLAW.COM

**RON BENDER,** born Los Angeles, California, July 22, 1964; admitted to bar, 1989, California; U.S. District Court, Central, Eastern, Northern and Southern Districts of California and U.S. Court of Appeals, Ninth Circuit. *Education:* Wharton School of Finance, University of Pennsylvania (B.S., summa cum laude, 1986); Stanford University School of Law (J.D., 1989). Co-author of article on "Setoff," Norton Bankruptcy Seminar, §553 Bankruptcy Code, 1989. Co-author of Article on "Bankruptcy Ethics, Bankruptcy Judges Conference, 1989. Extern for the Hon. Lloyd King, U.S. Bankruptcy Court, Northern District of California. *Member:* Beverly Hills, Century City and Los Angeles County Bar Associations; Financial Lawyers Conference; Los Angeles Bankruptcy Forum. **PRACTICE AREAS:** Bankruptcy.

### ASSOCIATE

**CRAIG M. RANKIN,** born Milwaukee, Wisconsin, September 15, 1965; admitted to bar, 1991, Wisconsin; 1993, California. *Education:* University of Wisconsin (B.S., 1988); Marquette University (J.D., cum laude, 1991). Member, National Moot Court Team. Law Clerk to the Honorable James R. Grube, U.S. Bankruptcy Judge, Northern District of California, 1991-1992. **PRACTICE AREAS:** Bankruptcy.

**NELLWYN VOORHIES,** born Lafayette, Louisiana, January 24, 1968; admitted to bar, 1993, California. *Education:* Georgetown University (B.A., cum laude, 1989); University of California, Boalt Hall School of Law (J.D.,

*(This Listing Continued)*

1993). Extern to Honorable Leslie Tchaikovsky, U.S. Bankruptcy Judge, Northern District of California, 1992. *PRACTICE AREAS:* Bankruptcy.

**MONICA Y. KIM,** born Daejon, South Korea, June 4, 1970; admitted to bar, 1995, California. *Education:* University of California at Berkeley (B.A., 1991); University of California, Hastings College of the Law (J.D., 1995). Law Clerk to the Honorable Jane Dickson McKeag, U.S. Bankruptcy Judge, Eastern District of California, 1995-1996. *PRACTICE AREAS:* Bankruptcy.

REFERENCE: 1st Business Bank.

---

## LEVIN & FREEDMAN, LLP
### LOS ANGELES, CALIFORNIA
(See Santa Monica)

*Real Property, Probate, Trust, Estate Planning, Corporation, Partnership, Health Care, Land Use and Construction Law. General Civil Practice.*

---

## ARTHUR S. LEVINE
### A PROFESSIONAL CORPORATION
### 10390 SANTA MONICA BOULEVARD, 4TH FLOOR
### LOS ANGELES, CALIFORNIA 90025-5058
Telephone: 310-557-1700
Fax: 310-557-0019

*Business and Corporate Transactions, Real Estate and Estate Planning.*

**ARTHUR S. LEVINE,** born Los Angeles, California, March 26, 1942; admitted to bar, 1967, California. *Education:* University of California at Berkeley (B.A., 1963); University of California at Los Angeles (J.D., 1966). *Member:* State Bar of California. (Certified Specialist, Estate Planning, Trust and Probate Law, The State Bar of California Board of Legal Specialization).

---

## LEVINE & ASSOCIATES
*Established in 1990*
### SUITE 710
### 2049 CENTURY PARK EAST
### LOS ANGELES, CALIFORNIA 90067
Telephone: 310-553-8400
Fax: 310-553-8455

*Seattle, Washington Office:* 999 Third Avenue, Suite 3210, 98104. Telephone: 206-626-5310. Fax: 206-626-5313.

*General Business and Civil Trial and Appellate Practice in all State and Federal Courts. Complex Business Litigation, Corporation and Partnership Law, Real Estate, Contract and Business Law, Secured Transactions, International Law, Casino and Gaming Law, Intellectual Property, Advertising, Entertainment, Commercial and Indian Law.*

**JEROME L. LEVINE,** born Los Angeles, California, July 20, 1940; admitted to bar, 1966, California and U.S. District Court, Central District of California; 1985, U.S. Court of Appeals, Ninth Circuit; 1986, U.S. Supreme Court; 1988, U.S. District Court, Eastern District of California; 1989, U.S. Court of Appeals for the Federal Circuit. *Education:* University of Southern California; San Francisco State University (A.B., 1962); Hastings College of Law, University of California (J.D., 1965). Lecturer in Law: University of Southern California Law Center, 1970; Loyola University School of Law, 1971. Member, Board of Directors, 1988-1992 and Co-Chairman, Law and Legislative Committee, 1992—, National Indian Gaming Association. Member, Editorial Board, Indian Gaming Magazine, 1990—. *Member:* Beverly Hills (Member: Corporations and Commercial Law Committee, 1977—; Entertainment Law Committee, 1977—), Los Angeles County (Member, Antitrust Section), American (Member, Sections on: Corporation, Banking and Business Law; Litigation; Patent, Trademark and Copyright Law; Member, Forum Committee on the Entertainment and Sports Industries, 1979) and Federal (Member, Indian Law Section) Bar Associations; State Bar of California; International Association of Gaming Attorneys. *PRACTICE AREAS:* Contract and Business Law; Licensing and Regulation; Litigation; Casino and Gaming Law; Indian Law; Indian Economic Development on Indian Reservations.

*(This Listing Continued)*

---

### ASSOCIATES

**MARY L. PREVOST,** admitted to bar, 1982, Washington and U.S. District Court, Western District of Washington; 1988, U.S. Supreme Court; 1995, U.S. District Court, Eastern District of Washington. *Education:* Evergreen State College (B.A., 1979); University of Puget Sound School of Law (J.D., 1982). Assistant Director, Washington State Gambling Commission, 1991-1993. Executive Director, Conference of Western Attorneys General, 1988-1991. *Member:* Washington State, Federal and American Bar Associations; Government Lawyers Bar Association (President, 1986-1989); Washington Women Lawyers. (Resident, Seattle, Washington Office). *PRACTICE AREAS:* Contract and Business Law; Administrative Law; Indian Law; Gaming Law; Licensing and Regulation.

**ERIN M. COPELAND,** born Plainfield, New Jersey, March 10, 1961; admitted to bar, 1987, California and U.S. District Court, Central District of California; 1990, District of Columbia. *Education:* Boston College (B.A., cum laude, 1983); George Washington University National Law Center (J.D., 1987). *Member:* Los Angeles County Bar Association; State Bar of California; District of Columbia Bar; Women Lawyers Association of Los Angeles. *PRACTICE AREAS:* Litigation; Real Estate; Gaming Law; Licensing and Regulation; Indian Law.

**FRANK R. LAWRENCE,** admitted to bar, 1989, California and U.S. District Court, Eastern District of California; U.S. Court of Appeals, Ninth Circuit; 1995, U.S. Supreme Court. *Education:* University of California at Santa Cruz (B.A., cum laude, 1985); Hastings College of the Law, University of California (J.D., magna cum laude, 1989). Order of the Coif. Articles Editor: Hastings Law Journal; Hastings International and Comparative Law Review. Author: "The Nuremberg Principles," 40 Hast., L.J. 397, 1989. Law Clerk, U.S. District Court, 1989-1991. *Member:* Thurston Society. *PRACTICE AREAS:* Civil Litigation; Appellate Litigation; Administrative Law; Indian Law; Gaming Law.

### OF COUNSEL

**ALLAN ALBALA,** admitted to bar, 1959, California and U.S. District Court, Central District of California; U.S. Court of Appeals, Ninth Circuit; U.S. Supreme Court. *Education:* University of California at Los Angeles (B.S., 1956); Harvard University (J.D., cum laude, 1959). Guest Speaker, Extension Seminars on Shopping Center Development, UCLA. Member, International Council of Shopping Centers. Arbitrator, Los Angeles County Bar Association. *Member:* Los Angeles County Bar Association (Member, Sections on: Real Property; Commercial Law); State Bar of California. *PRACTICE AREAS:* Real Estate; Shopping Center Leasing and Development; Business Law; Contract Law; Corporations and Partnerships.

---

## JOEL LEVINE
### A PROFESSIONAL CORPORATION
### 16000 VENTURA BOULEVARD, SUITE 500 (ENCINO)
### LOS ANGELES, CALIFORNIA 91436
Telephone: 818-995-6052
Fax: 818-955-0407

*General Civil, Criminal and Appellate Practice in all State and Federal Courts. Corporate, Criminal and Commercial.*

**JOEL LEVINE,** born New York, N.Y., March 30, 1945; admitted to bar, 1970, District of Columbia and Virginia; 1972, California, U.S. District Court, Central District of California and U.S. Court of Appeals, Ninth Circuit; 1983, U.S. Supreme Court. *Education:* Brooklyn College (B.A., 1965); Case Western Reserve University (J.D., 1968). Attorney, U.S. Attorneys' Office, Criminal Division, U.S. Department of Justice, 1971-1977. *Member:* Los Angeles County, Federal and American Bar Associations; State Bar of California. [Major, U.S. Marine Corps., 1968-1971]. *REPORTED CASES:* United States v. Miller, 874 F.2d 1255 (9th Cir. 1989); United States v. Gouveia, 704 F.2d 1116 (9th Cir. 1983); United States v. Gouveia, 467 U.S. 180. *PRACTICE AREAS:* White Collar Criminal Defense; General Criminal Defense; Business Civil Litigation.

---

**ANDREA TRUPIN LEVINE,** born New York, N.Y., June 16, 1949; admitted to bar, 1974, California; 1975, U.S. District Court, Central District of California. *Education:* University of Maryland (B.A., cum laude, 1970); University of Southern California (J.D., 1974). Member, John Marshall Honor Society. *Member:* Los Angeles County Bar Association; State Bar of California. *LANGUAGES:* French. *REPORTED CASES:* United

*(This Listing Continued)*

## CALIFORNIA—LOS ANGELES

**JOEL LEVINE A PROFESSIONAL CORPORATION, Los Angeles—Continued**

States v. Miller, 874 F.2d 1255 (9th Cir. 1989); United States v. Gouveia, 704 F.2d 1116 (9th Cir. 1983); United States v. Gouveia, 467 U.S. 180. *PRACTICE AREAS:* White Collar Criminal Defense; General Criminal Defense; Business Civil Litigation.

---

### MARK L. LEVINSON
**1900 AVENUE OF THE STARS, SUITE 1700**
**LOS ANGELES, CALIFORNIA 90067**
*Telephone: 310-277-3799*

*Music Law, Motion Pictures Law, Television Law, Copyright Law and General Entertainment Law.*

**MARK L. LEVINSON,** born New York, N.Y., August 12, 1940; admitted to bar, 1966, New York; 1971, California. *Education:* Brooklyn College (A.B., 1962); New York University (J.D., 1965). Trustee, Los Angeles Copyright Society, 1989-1992. Vice-President and General Counsel, United Artists Music and Records Group, Inc. 1970-1978. Vice-President, Business Affairs, E.M.I. Records, 1978-1983. President, Picture Music International, 1983-1986. Judge Pro Temp, Municipal Court, Beverly Hills, California, 1990—. Member: Academy of Recording Arts and Sciences; Academy of Television Arts and Sciences; California Copyright Conference; Los Angeles Copyright Society. *Member:* Beverly Hills, Los Angeles County, New York State and American (Member, Patents, Trademark and Copyright Law Section; Forum Committee on Sports and Entertainment Law) Bar Associations; State Bar of California.

---

### LEVINSON & KAPLAN
**LOS ANGELES, CALIFORNIA**
(See Encino)

*Business Litigation, Real Estate Litigation, Employment Law and General Business Transactions.*

---

### LEVINSON, LIEBERMAN & MAAS
**A PROFESSIONAL CORPORATION**
**LOS ANGELES, CALIFORNIA**
(See Beverly Hills)

*General Real Estate and Commercial Practice. Civil Litigation.*

---

### LEVINSON, MILLER, JACOBS & PHILLIPS
**A PROFESSIONAL CORPORATION**
**SUITE 2000**
**1875 CENTURY PARK EAST**
**LOS ANGELES, CALIFORNIA 90067-2534**
*Telephone: 310-557-2455*
*Cable Address: "Levrom"*
*Facsimile: 310-282-0472*

*Real Estate, Corporation, Taxation, Estate Planning, Probate, Family and Tort Law. General Civil and Trial Practice in all State and Federal Courts.*

FIRM PROFILE: *Levinson, Miller, Jacobs & Phillips has a diversified litigation and transactional law practice, with special emphasis in Real Estate, Landlord-Tenant, Taxation, Probate, Estates & Trusts, Family Law, Partnership, Corporate, Commercial, Civil & Construction Law. The firm has extensive experience in all aspects of civil litigation and family law. The firm emphasizes and strives for productive and efficient attorney client relationships with its broad based clientele.*

**PAUL LEVINSON,** born Philadelphia, Pennsylvania, March 8, 1931; admitted to bar, 1957, California. *Education:* University of California at Los Angeles (B.S., 1953; J.D., 1956). Phi Alpha Delta. Member, U.C.L.A. Law Review, 1954-1955. *Member:* Beverly Hills, Los Angeles County (Member, Sections on: Taxation; Real Estate) and American Bar Associations; State Bar of California; American Association of Attorney-Certified

*(This Listing Continued)*

CAA902B

---

## MARTINDALE-HUBBELL LAW DIRECTORY 1997

Public Accountants. [With U.S. Air Force, 1956-1958]. (Certified Specialist, Taxation Law, The State Bar of California Board of Legal Specialization). *PRACTICE AREAS:* Taxation Law; Real Estate.

**GARY S. JACOBS,** born Los Angeles, California, June 2, 1935; admitted to bar, 1961, California. *Education:* University of California at Berkeley (B.S., 1957); University of California at Los Angeles (J.D., 1960). *Member:* Beverly Hills and Los Angeles County Bar Associations; State Bar of California. (Certified Specialist, Family Law, The State Bar of California Board of Legal Specialization). *PRACTICE AREAS:* Family Law.

**STANTON LEE PHILLIPS,** born Chicago, Illinois, August 10, 1944; admitted to bar, 1970, California. *Education:* California State University at Northridge (B.A., 1966); Loyola University of Los Angeles (J.D., 1969). Phi Alpha Delta. Deputy District Attorney, Los Angeles County, 1970-1971. Arbitrator, Los Angeles County Superior Court, 1979—. Judge Pro Tem, Beverly Hills and Los Angeles Municipal Courts, 1979-1984. *Member:* Beverly Hills, Los Angeles County and American Bar Associations; State Bar of California; Association of Business Trial Lawyers. *PRACTICE AREAS:* Civil Litigation.

**SAMUEL M. ROBIN,** born Pittsburgh, Pennsylvania, March 15, 1945; admitted to bar, 1971, California. *Education:* University of California at Los Angeles (B.A., 1967; J.D., 1970). Pi Sigma Alpha. *Member:* Beverly Hills and Los Angeles County Bar Associations; State Bar of California. *PRACTICE AREAS:* Civil Litigation; Employment Law.

---

**SHARON JILL SANDLER,** born Johannesburg, South Africa, September 26, 1962; admitted to bar, 1090, California and U.S. District Court, Central District of California; U.S. Court of Appeals, Ninth Circuit. *Education:* University of the Witwatersrand, South Africa (B.Com., 1983); University of Southern California Law Center (J.D., 1990). *Member:* Beverly Hills (Member, Family Law Section) and Los Angeles County (Member, Family Law Section) Bar Associations; State Bar of California (Member, Family Law Section); Women Lawyers Association of Los Angeles (Member, Family Law Section; Pro-Choice Committee, 1991—). *LANGUAGES:* Afrikaans. *PRACTICE AREAS:* Domestic Relation and Family Law.

**J. BENNETT FRIEDMAN,** born Harvey, Illinois, January 11, 1962; admitted to bar, 1988, Illinois; 1990, California. *Education:* University of Illinois (B.A., 1984); Loyola Marymount University (J.D., 1987). Editor, Loyola Entertainment Law Journal. *Member:* Beverly Hills, Los Angeles County and South Bay Bar Associations; State Bar of California. *LANGUAGES:* French. *PRACTICE AREAS:* Bankruptcy; Business Litigation.

**FERN S. NISEN,** born Little Neck, New York, May 16, 1958; admitted to bar, 1992, California and U.S. District Court, Central District of California. *Education:* Cornell University (B.S., 1979); University of California at Los Angeles (M.A., 1981); Loyola Law School, Los Angeles (J.D., 1992). *Member:* Beverly Hills and Los Angeles County Bar Associations; State Bar of California. *PRACTICE AREAS:* Civil Litigation.

**ERIN L. PROUTY,** born Chicago, Illinois, June 14, 1960; admitted to bar, 1985, California; 1986, U.S. District Court, Central District of California; 1987, U.S. Tax Court. *Education:* University of Southern California (B.A., 1980); University of San Diego (J.D., 1985); Boston University, School of Law (LL.M., Taxation, 1986). Phi Alpha Delta. Note Editor, Boston University Journal of Tax Law, 1985-1986. Author: "Withholding Regulations under the Foreign Investment in Real Property Tax Act, as amended," 5 Boston University Journal of Tax Law, 1986. Member, Board of Directors, Beach Cities Symphony Association. *Member:* Los Angeles County Bar Association; State Bar of California.

### OF COUNSEL

**MILTON LOUIS MILLER,** born Los Angeles, California, February 5, 1932; admitted to bar, 1956, California. *Education:* University of California at Los Angeles (B.A., 1953; J.D., 1956). Phi Alpha Delta. *Member:* Beverly Hills and Los Angeles County Bar Associations; State Bar of California.

**STEPHEN I. HALPER,** born St. Paul, Minnesota, January 31, 1952; admitted to bar, 1977, Minnesota; 1980, California. *Education:* Washington University (B.A., summa cum laude, 1974); University of Minnesota (J.D., cum laude, 1977). Phi Beta Kappa. *Member:* Los Angeles County Bar Association; State Bar of California (Member, Partnerships and Unincorporated Business Organizations Committee).

REFERENCES: First Charter Bank; Wells Fargo Trust (Trust Dept., Southern California Headquarters).

## RICHARD A. LEVY
10940 WILSHIRE BOULEVARD, SUITE 1400
LOS ANGELES, CALIFORNIA 90024
Telephone: 310-446-5377
Fax: 310-446-5379

*Business Litigation emphasizing Trademark and Copyright Infringement.*

**RICHARD A. LEVY,** born Los Angeles, California, October 16, 1956; admitted to bar, 1986, California. *Education:* St. John's College (B.A., 1978); London School of Economics, London, England (M.Sc., Econ., 1980); University of Chicago (M.B.A., with honors, 1981); University of Michigan (J.D., magna cum laude, 1986). Order of the Coif. Associate Editor, Michigan Law Review, 1984-1985. Author: "Representing the Innocent Copyright Infringer After Seizure," New York State Bar Journal, November, 1991, at 42; "How to Round up Third-Party Defendants in Trademark and Copyright Infringement Cases," The Practical Litigator, September, 1991, at 53; "Defending Against Contempt for Violation of a Preliminary Injunction in State Court," 25 Beverly Hills Bar Association Journal 203, Fall, 1991. Judge Pro Tem, Los Angeles Municipal Court, 1993—. *Member:* State Bar of California.

---

## LEVY, SMALL & LALLAS
A Partnership of Professional Corporations
*Established in 1975*
815 MORAGA DRIVE
LOS ANGELES, CALIFORNIA 90049-1633
Telephone: 310-471-3000
Telecopier: 310-471-7990

*Commercial and Secured Transactions Law, General Civil, Trial and Appellate Litigation. Banking, Corporate and Real Estate Law.*

FIRM PROFILE: *Levy, Small & Lallas is a nine-lawyer firm located in Los Angeles, California, and established in April 1975.*

*Our firm represents a wide range of business enterprises, including financial institutions, manufacturers, retailers, distributors, developers and entrepreneurs.*

*Our business litigation practice covers a broad spectrum of business disputes, including enforcement of contracts, suits against debtors and guarantors, bankruptcy litigation, lender liability claims, securities fraud actions, copyright infringement, judicial and non-judicial foreclosure actions, priority of lien litigation, unfair competition, partnership and corporation dissolutions, and business torts.*

*Our transactional work is also broadly based. For commercial lenders, this work includes accounts receivable and inventory financing, factoring, equipment financing and leasing, participations, intercreditor agreements, leveraged buyouts, acquisition financing, real estate loans, construction loans, Chapter 11 financing, loans secured by letters of credit, unsecured term loans and other commercial lending transactions. For other clients, the transactional work includes purchase and sale agreements, distributorship agreements, sales of stock, partnership agreements, and corporation or partnership formation.*

**CHARLES M. LEVY, (P.C.),** born Aberdeen, South Dakota, July 13, 1937; admitted to bar, 1962, California. *Education:* Northwestern University (B.S.L., 1959; J.D., 1961). Associate Editor, Northwestern University Law Review, 1960-1961. Co-Author, "Checklist For Secured Commercial Loans," Financial Lawyers Conference, 1979. Associate in Law, University of California at Los Angeles School of Law, 1961-1962. Lecturer, Continuing Education of the Bar, Uniform Commercial Code Secured Transactions, 1973. Member, Board of Governors, Financial Lawyers Conference, 1975-1978. *Member:* Beverly Hills, Los Angeles County and American Bar Associations; State Bar of California. *PRACTICE AREAS:* Commercial Law; Loan Documentation; Enforcement and Workouts.

**STEVEN G. SMALL, (P.C.),** born Detroit, Michigan, August 13, 1947; admitted to bar, 1972, California. *Education:* Harvard College (B.A., cum laude, 1969); Harvard University (J.D., cum laude, 1972). Author: "Coming Changes in Division 9 of the California Commercial Code," 51 Los Angeles Bar Journal 272, 1975; "Secured Lender's Checklist," Financial Lawyers Conference, 1990-1994. Lecturer, Commercial Law Practice, Continuing Education of the Bar, 1982. *Member:* Los Angeles County (Member, Section on Commercial and Bankruptcy Law) and American (Member, Committee on Commercial Financial Services, Subcommittees on Documentation, Acquisition Financing and Inventory and Receivable Financing and Factoring, 1983— ) Bar Associations; State Bar of California; Financial

*(This Listing Continued)*

Lawyers Conference (Member, Board of Governors, 1983-1986; 1989-1992; 1994-1997). *PRACTICE AREAS:* Secured Transactions; Commercial Law; General Business Law.

**TOM LALLAS, (P.C.),** born Bellingham, Washington, January 5, 1951; admitted to bar, 1975, California; 1990, U.S. Supreme Court. *Education:* Stanford University (B.A., cum laude, 1972; J.D., 1975). Phi Beta Kappa. Member, Moot Court Board. Marion Rice Kirkwood Moot Court Champion, 1974. Member, Board of Editors, Stanford Law Review, 1975. Co-Author: "Subdivision Land Dedication; Objectives and Objections," 27 Stanford Law Review 419, 1975. *Member:* Los Angeles County (Member, Prejudgment Remedies Section) and American (Member, Litigation Section) Bar Associations; State Bar of California; The Association of Trial Lawyers of America; Financial Lawyers Conference; California Bankruptcy Forum. *PRACTICE AREAS:* Commercial, Bankruptcy and Real Estate Litigation and Transactions.

**LEO D. PLOTKIN, (P.C.),** born New York, N.Y., May 26, 1956; admitted to bar, 1981, California. *Education:* State University of New York at Binghamton (B.A., 1978); Boalt Hall School of Law, University of California (J.D., 1981). Phi Beta Kappa. Law Clerk to the Honorable Lawrence T. Lydick, U.S. District Court, Central District of California, 1981-1983. *Member:* Los Angeles County and American Bar Associations; State Bar of California. *PRACTICE AREAS:* Creditors Rights Law; Real Estate Litigation; Copyright Litigation; Business and Commercial Litigation.

**WALTER R. MITCHELL,** born New York, N.Y., December 16, 1955; admitted to bar, 1986, California; 1987, New York. *Education:* State University of New York at Albany (B.A., summa cum laude, 1977); University of California, Berkeley (M.A., 1978); University of California, Los Angeles (J.D., 1986). Phi Beta Kappa. Member, UCLA Law Review, 1985-1986. *Member:* State Bar of California. *PRACTICE AREAS:* Commercial Finance; Secured Transactions; General Business Law.

---

**MARK D. HURWITZ,** born Los Angeles, California, March 16, 1967; admitted to bar, 1990, California. *Education:* University of California Los Angeles (B.S., summa cum laude, 1987); University of California Los Angeles School of Law (J.D., 1990). Phi Beta Kappa. Editor, UCLA Law Review, 1989-1990. *Member:* Los Angeles County and American Bar Associations; State Bar of California. *PRACTICE AREAS:* Business and Commercial Litigation.

**THEODORE A. COHEN,** born Los Angeles, California, May 12, 1965; admitted to bar, 1990, California. *Education:* University of California at Los Angeles (B.A., cum laude, 1987); University of California, Davis School of Law (J.D., 1990). Law Clerk to the Honorable Edward C. Reed, Jr., U.S. District Court, District of Nevada, 1990-1992. Executive Editor, Davis Law Review, 1989-1990. Author: "When Should Religious Leaders Face Liability for Defamation?," 33 Journal of Church & State 681, Autumn 1991. *Member:* Los Angeles County and American Bar Associations; State Bar of California. *PRACTICE AREAS:* Commercial Litigation; Bankruptcy.

**ANGEL F. CASTILLO,** born Houston, Texas, August 13, 1964; admitted to bar, 1989, California. *Education:* Stanford University (A.B., 1986; J.D., 1989). *Member:* Los Angeles County and American Bar Associations; State Bar of California; Financial Lawyers Conference. *PRACTICE AREAS:* Commercial Finance; Secured Transactions.

**MICHAEL MERGENTHALER,** born Los Angeles, California, June 3, 1960; admitted to bar, 1987, California. *Education:* University of California at Los Angeles (B.A., magna cum laude, 1982); Harvard Law School, J.D., 1986). Phi Beta Kappa. *Member:* State Bar of California; American Bar Association; Association of Commercial Finance Attorneys. *PRACTICE AREAS:* Commercial Finance; Secured Transactions.

REPRESENTATIVE CLIENTS: Transamerica Commercial Finance Corporation; The Hong Kong and Shanghai Banking Corp.; Congress Financial Corp.; Republic Factors Corp.; CIT Group; Silicon Valley Bank; Congress Talcott Corporation; Greyrock Business Credit; Finova Capital Corporation; AT&T Commercial Finance Corporation; Deutsche Financial Services, Inc.

# LEWIS, D'AMATO, BRISBOIS & BISGAARD

A Partnership including Professional Corporations

SUITE 1200
221 NORTH FIGUEROA STREET
**LOS ANGELES, CALIFORNIA 90012**
Telephone: 213-250-1800
Telex: 194508
Facsimile: 213-250-7900

Lewis, D'Amato, Brisbois & Bisgaard California Offices:
*Costa Mesa Office:* 650 Town Center, Suite 1400, Costa Mesa, California, 92626. Telephone: 714-545-9200. Facsimile: 714-850-1030.
*Sacramento Office:* 2500 Venture Oaks Way, Sacramento, California 95833. Telephone: 916-564-5400. Facsimile: 916-564-5444.
*San Bernardino Office:* 650 East Hospitality Lane, Suite 600, San Bernardino, California 92408. Telephone: 909-387-1130. Facsimile: 909-387-1138.
*San Diego Office:* 550 West C Street, Suite 800, San Diego California 92101. Telephone: 619-233-1006. Facsimile: 619-233-8627.
*San Francisco Office:* 601 California Street, Suite 1900, San Francisco, California 94108. Telephone: 415-362-2580. Facsimile: 415-434-0882.
Affiliated Offices:
*Jakarta, Indonesia Affiliated Office:* Mulya Lubis and Partners, Wisma Bank Dharmala, 16th Floor, Jendral, Sudirman, Kav. 28, Jakarta 12920, Indonesia. Telephone: (62)(21) 521-1931/521-1932. Facsimile: (62)(21) 521-1930.
*Bangkok, Thailand Affiliated Office:* Kanung & Partners Law Offices, Raintree Office Garden, 272 Japanese School Lane, Rama IX Road, Bangkok 10310, Thailand. Telephone: (662) 319-7571/319-7574. Facsimile: (662) 319-6372.

*General Practice.*

FIRM PROFILE: *Founded in 1979, the Firm has over 185 lawyers specializing in the following areas: Antitrust and Trade Regulation; Compensation and Benefits; Corporate, Corporate Finance and Securities, Domestic Private Finance, Financial Institutions, International Private Finance, and Mergers and Acquisitions; Environmental; Individual Clients, Trusts, Estates, and Probate; General Insurance, Professional Liability, Products Liability and Securities Class Actions; International Trade, Government Relations and Business Law; Oil and Gas; Real Estate; Litigation, including Complex Business Litigation; Employment and Labor Law; State and Federal Tax; Intellectual Property; Public Entity Defense; Community Redevelopment Law, and Aircraft and Equipment Leasing.*

## MEMBERS OF FIRM

**ROBERT F. LEWIS, (P.C.),** born Los Angeles, California, October 14, 1936; admitted to bar, 1962, California. *Education:* University of California at Los Angeles (B.A., 1958; J.D., 1961). Phi Delta Phi. Co-Author: "Advising and Defending Corporate Officers and Directors Under the New General Corporation Law," CEB, 1977; "Liability Insurance Coverage Under the Securities Laws," USC Law Center 4th Annual Corporate Law & Finance Institute, 1976. Lawyer Delegate to the Ninth Circuit Judicial Counsel, 1990-1991. *Member:* State Bar of California (Delegate: State Bar, 1973-1978 and State Bar Conference of Delegates, 1975-1977; Member, Committees on: Delegation Executive, 1975-1977; Resolutions, 1976-1978); Maritime Law Association of the United States; American Board of Trial Advocates; International Association of Insurance Counsel; Southern California Defense Counsel.

**CHRISTOPHER P. BISGAARD, (P.C.),** born Los Angeles, California, July 11, 1947; admitted to bar, 1972, California. *Education:* University of Southern California (B.A., cum laude, 1969); University of California at Los Angeles (J.D., 1972). Comment Editor, University of California at Los Angeles Law Review, 1971-1972. Author: "Expanding the Impact of State Court Class Action Adjudications to Provide an Effective Forum for Consumers," 18 UCLA Law Review 1002, 1971. Member, Judicial Evaluation Committee, 1985-1986 and Subcommittee Chair, 1987-1988, Los Angeles County Bar Association.

**ROY M. BRISBOIS, (P.C.),** born Santa Monica, California, October 6, 1947; admitted to bar, 1972, California. *Education:* University of California at Santa Barbara (B.A., cum laude, 1969); University of California at Los Angeles (J.D., 1972). Chief Comment Editor, University of California at Los Angeles Law Review, 1971-1972. Author: "California Products Liability Law & Practices," (West Publishing, 1985). Co-Author: "Guide to Product Liability," (Bureau of National Affairs, 1987). Co-Author and Lecturer: "First Annual Trial Practice Institute, Product Liability," (CEB, 1986); "Sec-

*(This Listing Continued)*

ond Annual Trial Practice Institute, Modern Trial Techniques," (CEB, 1987). Author: "Trumpets in the Corridors of Bureaucracy: A Coming Right to Appointed Counsel in Administrative Adjudicative Proceedings," 18 UCLA Law Review 758, 1971. *Member:* State Bar of California; American Bar Associations; Defense Research Institute.

**R. GAYLORD SMITH** (Resident, San Diego Office).

**DAVID E. REYNOLDS, (P.C.),** born Decatur, Illinois, March 25, 1948; admitted to bar, 1976, California. *Education:* California State University at Northridge (B.A., magna cum laude, 1973); University of California at Los Angeles (J.D., 1976). Member, UCLA Law Review, 1974-1975. Author: "Effect of Defendant Attractiveness, Age, and Injury on Severity of Sentence Given by Simulated Jurors," 96 The Journal of Social Psychology 149, 1975.

**DUANE C. MUSFELT** (Resident, San Francisco Office).

**BARRY G. KAIMAN, (P.C.),** born Omaha, Nebraska, December 15, 1949; admitted to bar, 1975, New York 1977, California. *Education:* Rutgers University (B.A., cum laude, 1972); University of Nebraska (J.D., 1975). Delta Theta Phi. Co-Author: "Courts in the Business of Insurance Claims Made and Reported Policies," 57 Defense Counsel Journal, 32, 1990; "Confidentiality and Privileges Considerations In Voluntary Mediation of Civil Disputes," International Association of Defense Counsel Publications, 1992. Author: "An Historical and Legal Analysis of the Proposed Trademark Registration Treaty," 1980 Symposium, Trademarks Expanding Areas for the 1980, Los Angeles County Bar Association. *Member:* New York State Bar Association; International Association of Defense Counsel (Chairman, Professional Errors and Omissions Committee, 1991—); Association of Southern California Defense Counsel; Defense Research Institute; American Intellectual Property Law Association (Member, Board of Directors, 1993—).

**RAUL L. MARTINEZ, (P.C.),** born Mexico City, Mexico, May 25, 1951; admitted to bar, 1976, California. *Education:* Massachusetts Institute of Technology (B.S., magna cum laude, 1973); Stanford University (J.D., 1976). Note Editor, Stanford Law Review, 1976. Member, Committee on Professional Responsibility and Conduct, 1983—; Vice Chair, 1984-1985; Chair, 1985-1986, State Bar of California.

**STEVEN MARK LEVY,** born Providence, Rhode Island, December 29, 1952; admitted to bar, 1977, Oregon; 1979, California. *Education:* Claremont Men's College (B.A., magna cum laude, 1974); Boalt Hall School of Law, University of California at Berkeley (J.D., 1977). Author: "Liability of The Art Expert for Professional Malpractice," 1991 Wisconsin Law Review 595, 1991. Judge Pro Tempore, Municipal Court of California, Los Angeles Judicial District, 1988—. **LANGUAGES:** French.

**B. CASEY YIM, (P.C.),** born Honolulu, Hawaii, 1948; admitted to bar, 1975, Ohio; 1982, California. *Education:* California State University at San Diego (A.B., 1970); Cleveland State University (J.D., cum laude, 1975). Recipient: C.J.S. Award, 1973; American Jurisprudence Book Award; W.E. Baldwin Award, 1975. Editor-in-Chief, Cleveland State Law Review, 1974-1975. Co-Author: Comment, "United States v. Robinson," 23 Cleveland State Law Review, 135, 1974. *Member:* Cleveland, Ohio State Bar Associations.

**ALAN E. GREENBERG** (Resident, San Diego Office).

**MARY G. WHITAKER, (P.C.),** born Pittsburgh, Pennsylvania, September 20, 1947; admitted to bar, 1978, California. *Education:* Carleton College (B.A., magna cum laude, 1969); Stanford University (M.S., 1971; J.D., 1978). Phi Beta Kappa; Pi Mu Epsilon. Member, Stanford Law Review, 1977-1978.

**SCOTT LICHTIG,** born Los Angeles, California, February 26, 1953; admitted to bar, 1978, California. *Education:* Claremont Men's College (B.A., summa cum laude, 1975); Boalt Hall School of Law, University of California (J.D., 1978).

**DONALD A. RUSTON** (Resident, Costa Mesa Office).

**JAMES D. FRASER,** born Whittier, California, October 22, 1949; admitted to bar, 1975, California. *Education:* University of California at Berkeley (B.A., 1972); University of California at Los Angeles (J.D., 1975). Author: "Developments in Hazardous Materials Law," Exerts From 1989 Conference of Environmental Professionals. Judge Pro Tem, Los Angeles Municipal Court, 1989.

**DAVID B. PAYNTER** (Resident, San Francisco Office).

**DENNIS R. KASPER,** born Glendale, California, October 5, 1948; admitted to bar, 1974, California. *Education:* Whitworth College and United

*(This Listing Continued)*

States International University (B.A., 1971); California Western School of Law, United States International University (J.D., 1974). Phi Alpha Delta. Member, Board of Editors, California Western International Law Journal, 1973-1974. *Member:* Armenian and American Bar Associations; Christian Legal Society.

**ERNEST SLOME** (Resident, San Diego Office).

**KEITH D. TAYLOR** (Resident, Costa Mesa Office).

**DOUGLAS R. REYNOLDS** (Resident, San Diego Office).

**MARILYN R. MORIARTY** (Resident, San Diego Office).

**JEFFREY B. BARTON** (Resident, San Diego Office).

**ROBERT K. WREDE,** born Astoria, New York, August 19, 1939; admitted to bar, 1970, California and U.S. District Court, Central District of California; 1972, U.S. Court of Appeals, 9th Circuit; 1973, U.S. District Court, Northern District of California; 1983, U.S. Supreme Court and U.S. Court of Appeals, 5th Circuit; 1989, U.S. District Court, Southern District of California. *Education:* Cornell University (B.A., 1966; J.D., 1969). *REPORTED CASES:* Purex/PJG -419 F. Supp 931; 596 F2d 881; 664 F 2d 1105; Masterson v Onion, 485 F 2d 252; API v EPA 661 F 2d 340; Rockwell v Evans 801 F 2d 400; USA v Escamilla 975 F 2d 568; CEC v BPA 831 F 2d 1467. *PRACTICE AREAS:* Commercial Disputes; Entertainment; Antitrust; Professional Liability; Products Liability; Environmental.

**TIMOTHY R. GRAVES,** born Concord, North Carolina, August 22, 1960; admitted to bar, 1985, California. *Education:* University of North Carolina (B.S., cum laude, 1982; J.D., 1985). Editor, North Carolina Journal of International Law and Commercial Regulation, 1984-1985.

**PETER L. GARCHIE** (Resident, San Diego Office).

**STEVEN R. LEWIS,** born Inglewood, California, December 15, 1961; admitted to bar, 1987, California. *Education:* University of California at Los Angeles (B.A., 1984); Pepperdine University (J.D., 1987).

**DAVID N. MAKOUS,** born Camp LeJeune, North Carolina, November 9, 1951; admitted to bar, 1978, California and U.S. District Court, Central District of California; 1979, registered to practice before U. S. Patent and Trademark Office; 1983, U.S. Court of Appeals, Ninth Circuit; 1985, U.S. Court of Appeals, Eighth Circuit; 1993, U.S. Court of Appeals, Fifth Circuit; 1994, U.S. Court of Appeals, Federal Circuit. *Education:* Duke University (B.S., 1973); University of Pittsburgh (J.D., 1978). Co-Author: *Attorney's Guide to Trade Secrets,* 2d ed., CEB (1996); "Patent Damages for the Profits of the Infringer After Patent Expiration: Accelerated Re-Entry Damages," *New Matter,* June 1996, republished in *Journal of Proprietary Rights,* Sept. 1996; "Drafting Grant Clauses for Agreements Involving Intellectual Property," *California Business Law Practitioner,* Winter, 1996; "Recent Court Decisions Place Limits on Software Copyright Protection," *Transnational Bulletin,* Jan. 1993; "Untying the Knot of Intellectual Property Licensing, (Part II)," *Transnational Bulletin,* July 1993. Lecturer: Los Angeles County Bar Association, Public Orientation Programs, 1980-1983; American Bar Association, 1978—, Section on International Design Protection, 1984-1986, Section of Intellectual Property Orientation, 1991-1993; Anti-Counterfeiting Coalition, 1981-1984; Congressional Lobbying on Lanham Act, 1983; Lecturer, Chinese Government on U.S. Intellectual Property Law, 1992-1994; Lecturer, Licensing, State Bar of California, Intellectual Property Section; Lecturer, Otis School of Design. Chairman, Community Development Advisory Board, City of El Monte, California, 1979-1981. *Member:* Century City Bar Association (Chairman, 1986-1987; Member, Tort Litigation Section); Intellectual Trademark Association (Member: U.S. Legislation Subcommittee, 1994—; International Trademark Subcommittee, 1989-1990; Publications Subcommittee, 1992-1993); Licensing Executive Society; Los Angeles Intellectual Property Law Association; American Intellectual Property Lawyers Association.

**RANDALL L. MASON** (Resident, San Diego Office).

**ERIC C. CASTRO,** born San Fernando, California, September 18, 1953; admitted to bar, 1979, Hawaii; 1980, California; 1981, District of Columbia. *Education:* Yale University (B.A., 1975); University of Southern California (J.D., 1979). Order of the Coif; Phi Kappa Phi; Phi Alpha Delta. Member, University of Southern California Law Review, 1978-1979. Recipient: American Jurisprudence Awards in Torts, 1976, Community Property, 1978, Civil Procedure and International Law, 1979, and Carl Mason Franklin Prize (International Law), 1979. Law Clerk to Hon. Herbert Y.C. Choy, U.S. Court of Appeals, Ninth Circuit, Honolulu, Hawaii, 1979-1980. *Member:* Hawaii State and American Bar Associations; District of Columbia Bar.

*(This Listing Continued)*

**LAWRENCE N. HALPERIN,** born Chicago, Illinois, March 22, 1950; admitted to bar, 1976, Illinois; 1981, California. *Education:* Harvard University (A.B., cum laude, 1972); University of Michigan (M.P.P., 1975; J.D., 1976). *Member:* Illinois State Bar Association.

**JEFFREY R. KURTOCK, (P.C.)** (Resident, San Francisco Office).

**GARY M. LAPE** (Resident, Costa Mesa Office).

**SHAWN K. DEASY** (Resident, San Diego Office).

**THOMAS RITTENBURG,** born Lynwood, California, November 22, 1953; admitted to bar, 1978, Tennessee; 1983, California. *Education:* Washington & Lee University (B.A., with honors, magna cum laude, 1975); University of Tennessee (J.D., 1978). Phi Alpha Delta. *Member:* Tennessee Bar Association. [Capt., U.S. Army, JAGC, 1978-1982]

**BARTLEY L. BECKER,** born San Francisco, California, June 5, 1947; admitted to bar, 1976, California. *Education:* University of California at Berkeley (B.A., 1969); University of California at Los Angeles (M.A., 1971); Loyola University of Los Angeles (J.D., 1976). Phi Beta Kappa.

**LANCE A. SELFRIDGE,** born Van Nuys, California, June 28, 1956; admitted to bar, 1981, California. *Education:* University of California at Los Angeles (B.A., summa cum laude, 1978; J.D., 1981). Phi Beta Kappa; Phi Eta Sigma; Alpha Kappa Delta. Staff Member, UCLA Law Review, 1979-1980.

**SHARON S. CHANDLER** (Resident, San Francisco Office).

**NANCY E. ZELTZER** (Resident, Costa Mesa Office).

**JOHN H. SHIMADA,** born Fresno, California, December 1, 1957; admitted to bar, 1982, California. *Education:* California State University at Fresno (B.S., magna cum laude, 1979); University of Pennsylvania (J.D., 1982). *Member:* Japanese-American Bar Association.

**GARY L. EFFRON,** born San Diego, California, November 17, 1942; admitted to bar, 1968, California. *Education:* University of California at Los Angeles (B.S., 1964); Hastings College of Law, University of California (J.D., 1967). Licensed Real Estate Broker, California, 1980. Instructor in Criminal Procedure, Conflict of Laws and Remedies, South Bay University College of Law, Carson, California, 1973-1975. Author: "Avoiding Liability Under the New Real Estate Disclosure Laws," California Real Estate Magazine, Volume 67, No. 4, May, 1987. Judge Pro Tem, Los Angeles Municipal Court, 1978-1981. Delegate, State Bar Convention, 1979 and 1980.

**KENNETH T. KREEBLE** (Resident, San Bernardino Office).

**JOSEPH K. HEGEDUS,** born Bordeaux, France, November 24, 1950; admitted to bar, 1975, Pennsylvania; 1976, U.S. District Court, Eastern District of Pennsylvania; 1979, U.S. Court of Appeals for the District of Columbia Circuit and U.S. District Court, Middle District of Pennsylvania; 1980, California and U.S. Court of Appeals, Third Circuit; 1981, New York; 1982, U.S. Court of Appeals, Ninth Circuit and U.S. District Court, Central and Northern Districts of California; 1983, U.S. District Court, Eastern and Southern Districts of New York and U.S. Tax Court. *Education:* Cornell University (B.S., 1972); Temple University (J.D., 1975). Deputy Attorney General, Pennsylvania Department of Justice, 1978-1980. Assistant Attorney General, Pennsylvania Insurance Department, 1976-1978. Honorary Assistant Attorney General, State of Alabama, 1985—. *Member:* Los Angeles County, Pennsylvania, New York State and American (Member, Sections on: Tort and Insurance Practice; Litigation; Corporation, Banking and Business Law) Bar Associations; State Bar of California; The Association of Trial Lawyers of America; Conference of Insurance Counsel; Cornell Society of Engineers.

**JUDITH A. ZIPKIN,** born Akron, Ohio, July 14, 1954; admitted to bar, 1985, California. *Education:* University of Michigan (B.A., cum laude, 1976; M.H.S.A, 1978); Loyola University Law School (J.D., 1984).

**GORDON J. CALHOUN,** born Pittsburgh, Pennsylvania, September 3, 1953; admitted to bar, 1978, California, U.S. District Court, Northern, Eastern, Central and Southern Districts of California and U.S. Court of Appeals, Ninth Circuit. *Education:* Johns Hopkins University (B.A., 1975); Stanford University (J.D., 1978). Phi Beta Kappa; Omicron Delta Kappa; Pi Sigma Alpha. Recipient, Julius Turner Prize.

**RICHARD B. WOLF,** born Fort Worth, Texas, June 1, 1944; admitted to bar, 1970, California and U.S. District Court, Central District of California; 1971, U.S. Court of Appeals, Ninth Circuit; 1985, U.S. Supreme Court. *Education:* University of California at Berkeley (A.B., 1966); University of California at Los Angeles (J.D., 1969). Law Clerk to Hon. Otto M. Kaus, Presiding Justice, Court of Appeals of California, Second Appellate District, Division Five, 1969-1970. Speaker: American Insurance Association,

*(This Listing Continued)*

CAA905B

## LEWIS, D'AMATO, BRISBOIS & BISGAARD, Los Angeles—Continued

Property Claims Services Committee, October, 1983; "Coverage Problems Under the California All-Risk Property Policy Involving Contractor and Municipal Negligence," "Bad Faith: a Two-Way Street," California Association of Independent Insurance Adjusters, February, 1984; "Life After Cumis," Orange County Claims Managers, February, 1985; "Cumis Revisited," Los Angeles County Bar Association Title Insurance Subsection of the Real Property Section. Panelist and Co-Author: "California Title Insurance," (Los Angeles, Orange and San Diego Counties) Professional Education Systems, Inc., March, 1989.

**PAUL Y. LEE,** born Seoul, Korea, April 11, 1953; admitted to bar, 1980, Illinois; 1985, California. *Education:* Washington University (A.B., cum laude, 1976); University of Pennsylvania (J.D., 1979). Pi Sigma Alpha.

**DAVID E. LONG,** born Rochester New York, October 7, 1958; admitted to bar, 1983, California; 1984, U.S. District Court, Central District of California. *Education:* University of Pennsylvania (BA., 1979); State University of New York at Buffalo (J.D., 1983). Note and Comment Editor, Buffalo Law Review, 1982-1983. Author: Note, "The Constitutional Rights of Students at Center Stage: Freedom of Speech in School-Sponsored Plays," 31 Buffalo Law Review, 547, 1983.

**ROGER S. RAPHAEL** (Resident, San Francisco Office).

**CATHEY A. STRICKER,** born Canton, Ohio, September 17, 1957; admitted to bar, 1985, California. *Education:* Mount Union College (B.A., magna cum laude, 1980); University of North Carolina (J.D., 1985). Editor, North Carolina Journal of International Law and Commercial Regulation. Certified Public Accountant, Ohio, 1982.

**THOMAS L. VAZAKAS** (Resident, San Diego Office).

**ELISE D. KLEIN,** born Los Angeles, California, September 23, 1959; admitted to bar, 1983, California and U.S. District Court, Northern, Eastern and Central Districts of California. *Education:* Pomona College (B.A., 1980); Hastings College of the Law, University of California (J.D., 1983). Phi Alpha Delta.

**JOSEPH C. OWENS**

**WILLIAM JOHN REA, JR.,** born Los Angeles, California, November 30, 1953; admitted to bar, 1978, California, U.S. District Court, Central and Southern Districts of California and U.S. Court of Appeals, Ninth Circuit. *Education:* University of California at Los Angeles (B.A., 1975; J.D., 1978); University of Oxford, St. Edmund Hall (M.A., 1977). Judicial Extern, Chief Justice Edward Pringle, Colorado Supreme Court. *Member:* Los Angeles County Bar Association (Mediator Attorney, Client Relations Committee); Southern California Defense Counsel; Defense Research Institute; American Inns of Court. **PRACTICE AREAS:** Civil Litigation; Errors and Omissions Defense; Insurance Coverage; Bad Faith Defense.

**LEE A. WOOD** (Resident, Costa Mesa Office).

**DENNIS G. SELEY** (Resident, Sacramento Office).

**JANA I. LUBERT,** born Brooklyn, New York, August 6, 1963; admitted to bar, 1988, California. *Education:* University of California at Los Angeles (B.A., 1985); Loyola Law School, Los Angeles (J.D., 1988).

**JUDITH M. TISHKOFF,** born Los Angeles, California, October 25, 1957; admitted to bar, 1988, California. *Education:* University of California at Los Angeles; California State University (B.S.N., 1980); University of Southern California (J.D., 1988).

**THOMAS M. DIACHENKO** (Resident, San Diego Office).

**R. ANTHONY MOYA** (Resident, San Diego Office).

**THOMAS E. FRANCIS** (Resident, Costa Mesa Office).

**SUSAN E. LEONARD** (Resident, San Diego Office).

**H. GILBERT JONES** (Resident, Costa Mesa Office).

**HOWARD G. RATH, JR., (P.C.),** born Los Angeles, California, September 2, 1931; admitted to bar, 1959, California. *Education:* University of California at Berkeley (B.S., 1953); University of Southern California (J.D., 1958). Phi Beta Kappa; Order of the Coif; Phi Delta Phi. *Member:* Los Angeles County (Member, Executive Committee, Section on Taxation, 1965-1970) Bar Associations. (Certified Specialist, Taxation Law, The State Bar of California Board of Legal Specialization).

**FRANKIE FOOK-LUN LEUNG,** born Guangzhou, China, October 20, 1949; admitted to bar, 1977, England and Wales; 1978, Hong Kong; 1983, Victoria, Australia; 1987, California. *Education:* Hong Kong University (B.A., 1972); Birmingham University, England (M.Sc., 1974); Oxford University, England (B.A., Jurisprudence, 1976; M.A., 1981); College of Law, London, England (Barrister) 1977. Visiting Scholar, Harvard Law School, 1983. Appointed Lecturer of Law, Stanford Law School, 1995—. Author: Chapter on Hong Kong. In World Law of Competition, J. von Kalinowski Ed. Matthew Bender: New York, 1987; The Commercial Laws of Hong Kong. In Digests of the Commercial Laws of the World, L. Nelson Ed., Oceana New York, 1992. Adjunct Professor: Loyola Law School, 1988—; Pepperdine University School of Law , 1988. Lecturer, Hong Kong University Law Faculty, 1985-1986. Member, Board of Advisors, Hong Kong Project, Hoover Institution, Stanford University, 1990. Director, Center for International Commercial Arbitration, California, 1988—. Member, Executive Committee, International Section, State Bar of California (1989-1992). **LANGUAGES:** French, Japanese (reading), Chinese (Mandarin & Cantonese).

**MICHAEL W. CONNALLY** (Resident, Costa Mesa Office).

**ANNIE VERDRIES** (Resident, Costa Mesa Office).

**STEPHEN T. WAIMEY,** born Mineola, New York, April 19, 1948; admitted to bar, 1976, New York; 1979, California. *Education:* University of the South (B.A., 1968); New York University (J.D., 1975). Sustaining Member, Product Liability Advisory Council, 1987—. *Member:* Los Angeles County, New York State and American Bar Associations; State Bar of California; Society of Automotive Engineers. **PRACTICE AREAS:** Litigation; Commercial; Product Liability.

**MERCEDES CRUZ,** born San Pedro, California, February 25, 1959; admitted to bar, 1985, California. *Education:* California State University at Long Beach (B.A., summa cum laude, 1981); Boalt Hall School of Law, University of California (J.D., 1985). Phi Kappa Phi. Associate Editor, International Tax and Business Law Journal. *Member:* State Bar of California; American Bar Association. **PRACTICE AREAS:** Litigation; Product Liability; Intellectual Property; Labor Law.

**ARMEN HAIRAPETIAN,** born Montebello, California, October 11, 1961; admitted to bar, 1986, California. *Education:* University of California at Los Angeles (B.A., magna cum laude, 1983); University of Southern California (J.D., 1986). Order of the Coif. Recipient, American Jurisprudence Awards in Civil Procedure and Labor Law. Staff Member and Articles Editor, University of Southern California Law Review, 1984-1986. *Member:* Los Angeles County and American Bar Associations; State Bar of California. **PRACTICE AREAS:** Product Liability and Reinsurance Litigation.

**CLAUDIA J. ROBINSON** (Resident, Sacramento Office).

**LEON M. COOPER,** born Los Angeles, California, July 24, 1924; admitted to bar, 1949, Massachusetts; 1950, California and U.S. District Court, Southern District of California; 1956, U.S. Court of Appeals, Ninth Circuit; 1957, U.S. Supreme Court. *Education:* University of California at Los Angeles (A.B., 1944), Phi Beta Kappa; Harvard University (J.D., 1949); University of Southern California (LL.M., 1965). Author: "Limited Application of Property Concepts in the Law of Television," Federal Communications Bar Journal, 1949—; "Commercial Code and the California Law of Chattel Security," 1954 and "Constructive Bargaining to Prevent Labor Disputes," 1964, Southern California Law Review. Member, 1965-1967 and Chairman, 1966-1967, Alcoholic Beverage Control Appeals Board, State of California. *Member:* Los Angeles County, Massachusetts and American (Member, Sections on: Corporation, Banking and Business Law; Administrative Law and Labor Relations Law) Bar Associations; The State Bar of California. [Lt. Comdr., U.S.N.R., Ret.]. **PRACTICE AREAS:** Corporate Law; Corporate Securities; Public Offerings; Private Placements; Mergers and Acquisitions.

**JAMES G. BOHM** (Resident, Costa Mesa Office).

**GEORGE A. BOLAND** (Resident, San Bernardino Office).

**JOAN L. DANIELSEN** (Resident, San Diego Office).

**RICHARD L. ANTOGNINI** (Resident, Sacramento Office).

**LAURA S. INLOW,** born Miami, Florida, March 22, 1962; admitted to bar, 1987, California and U.S. District Court, Central District of California; 1989, District of Columbia. *Education:* University of Virginia (B.A., 1984; J.D., 1987). Phi Delta Phi. *Member:* District of Columbia.

*(This Listing Continued)*

# PROFESSIONAL BIOGRAPHIES

## CALIFORNIA—LOS ANGELES

**DOUGLAS R. IRVINE,** born Cambridge, Massachusetts, November 19, 1960; admitted to bar, 1985, California; 1986, U.S. District Court, Central District of California and U.S. Court of Appeals, Ninth Circuit; 1987, U.S. District Court, Eastern, Northern and Southern Districts of California. *Education:* Pomona College (B.A., 1982); University of Santa Clara (J.D., 1985). Phi Alpha Delta.

**SCOTT W. MONSON** (Resident, Costa Mesa Office).

**MICHAEL C. OLSON** (Resident, Costa Mesa Office).

**JAMES J. WALLACE** (Resident, San Diego Office).

**TIMOTHY J. WATSON,** born Sonora, California, July 27, 1960; admitted to bar, 1987, California and U.S. District Court, Central District of California. *Education:* California Lutheran College (B.A., 1984); Pepperdine University (J.D., 1987).

**LOUIS ROBERT DE STEFANO,** born New York, N. Y., January 31, 1947; admitted to bar, 1976, California. *Education:* St. John's University (B.S., 1968); University of Southern California (J.D., 1973).

**DAVID M. REEDER,** born Cedar Rapids, Iowa, June, 28, 1950; admitted to bar, 1988, California and U.S. District Court, Central, Southern and Eastern Districts of California. *Education:* Morningside College (B.A., 1972); Drake University (J.D., with honors, 1987). Member, Drake University Law Review, 1986-1987. Author: "The Administrative Priority in Bankruptcy - A Survey," 36 Drake Law Review 135, (1987); "The Sinking of American Mariner," 6 Bankruptcy Study Group Journal 5 (March, 1988). *Member:* Los Angeles County (Executive Committee, Bankruptcy and Commercial Law Section; Chair, Individual Bankruptcy Sub Committee) and American Bar Associations; American Bankruptcy Institute; Financial Lawyers Conference; Los Angeles Bankruptcy Forum. **PRACTICE AREAS:** Bankruptcy Law; Debtor Creditor Law; Commercial Law.

**PETER F. HARRIS,** born Youngstown, Ohio, February 15, 1950; admitted to bar, 1981, Ohio; 1989, California. *Education:* Youngstown State University (B.S., with honors, 1976); Akron University Law School (J.D., 1981).

**JOHN F. DAVIS** (Resident, Sacramento Office).

**DAVID E. ISENBERG** (Resident, Costa Mesa Office).

**RUSSELL J. CALLISON** (Resident, Sacramento Office).

**PAUL N. PHILLIPS** (Resident, Sacramento Office).

**BRAD D. KRASNOFF** (Resident, Costa Mesa Office).

**PENNY PAXTON,** born Greenville, Pennsylvania; admitted to bar, 1978, Pennsylvania and U.S. District Court, Western District of Pennsylvania; 1983, U.S. Court of Appeals, Third Circuit; 1991, California. *Education:* Grove City College (B.A., 1967); University of Pittsburgh (M.A., 1969); Duquesne University (J.D., 1978). **PRACTICE AREAS:** Workers Compensation; Employment Law.

**RAUL B. GARCIA** (Resident, Costa Mesa Office).

**MICHAEL J. LANCASTER** (Resident, Costa Mesa Office).

**BRUCE LEGERNES** (Resident, San Francisco Office).

**BRUCE L. SHAFFER** (Resident, Sacramento Office).

**GREGORY P. MATZEN** (Resident, Sacramento Office).

**JOSEPH ARIAS** (Resident, San Bernardino Office).

**RICHARD W. BANE** (Resident, San Bernardino Office).

**ROGER L. BELLOWS** (Resident, San Bernardino Office).

**HENRY W. CROWLE** (Resident, Sacramento Office).

**CHARLES S. HAUGHEY, JR.** (Resident, San Diego Office).

**JANELLE F. GARCHIE** (Resident, San Diego Office).

**ROBERT V. CLOSSON** (Resident, San Diego Office).

**THOMAS M. CORRELL** (Resident, San Diego Office).

**KENNETH E. GOATES** (Resident, San Diego Office).

**HOWARD A. SLAVIN,** born Cleveland, Ohio, December 21, 1941; admitted to bar, 1967, California. *Education:* University of Southern California (B.S., 1963); California College of Law (J.D., 1967). Recipient, American Jurisprudence Award, Evidence, 1966. Instructor: Creditors Rights, Future Interests, 1968-1969; Creditors Rights, Domestic Relations, 1969-1970, California College of Law. Professor, Torts, California College of Law, 1970-1976. Selected as One of America's "Outstanding Educator, 1972," Arbitrator, Los Angeles County Superior Court Special Arbitration Program. Member, National Panel of Arbitrators, American Arbitration Association. Judge Pro Tem, Municipal Court of Los Angeles County, 1978—. Member, Los Angeles Superior Court Civil Trials Manuals Committee. Holder of Private Pilot Certificate with Instrument Rating. Panel Member, California Continuing Education of the Bar, Programs on "Proving Mental and Emotional Damages," 1982 and 1986; "Gathering and Proving Medical Evidence in Personal Injury Cases," 1983 and "Civil Procedure During Trial," 1985, 1987, 1989 and 1991; "Preparing and Examining Expert Witnesses in Civil Litigation," 1988; "Calculating and Proving Damages in Personal Injury and Wrongful Death Cases," 1984 and 1987. Panel Member, Los Angeles Trial Lawyers Association, Programs on "Cross-Examination of Plaintiff's Orthopaedic Surgeon," 1972; "Cross-Examination of Plaintiff's Economist," 1984; "Commercial and Residential Landlord Liability," Las Vegas, Nevada, 1986; "Litigation: Finding and Preparing the Expert Witness," 1988. Panel Member, Association of Southern California Defense Counsel, Programs on: "Voir Dire," 1983; "Medical Malpractice," 1984. Speaker: Medical-Legal Aspects of Intraocular Lenses, "Implant-77," Anaheim, California, 1977; Medical-Legal Aspects of Retrolental Fibroplasia-Dallas Ophthalmology Symposium, Dallas, Texas, 1980; Medical-Legal Aspects of Pneumatic Retinopexy, San Diego, California, 1988; Medical-Legal Problems in Ophthalmology, Royal Hawaiian Eye Foundation, Kona, Hawaii, 1991. Member, California Medical-Legal Committee. *Member:* Los Angeles County and American Bar Associations; State Bar of California; Association of Southern California Defense Counsel; California Trial Lawyers Association; American Board of Trial Advocates; Lawyer-Pilots Bar Association. **PRACTICE AREAS:** Trials and Appeals Emphasizing Defense of Physicians; Health Care Providers in Malpractice Matters.

**EDWARD F. MORRISON, JR.,** born New York, N.Y., July 23, 1962; admitted to bar, 1987, Virginia; 1988, New York; 1990, California. *Education:* Vanderbilt University (B.A., cum laude, 1984; J.D., 1987). Member, Vanderbilt International Law Society, 1985-1987 (President, 1986-1987). *Member:* Beverly Hills, Los Angeles County and American Bar Associations; State Bar of California. **PRACTICE AREAS:** General; Civil; Construction; Errors and Omissions Litigation.

**JACK D. TOMLINSON** (Resident, San Francisco Office).

**KENNETH D. HUSTON** (Resident, San Diego Office).

**GERALD R JUDSON,** born Franklin, Pennsylvania, January 18, 1944; admitted to bar, 1981, California. *Education:* University of California at Los Angeles (B.A., 1974); Southwestern University (J.D., 1981). Member, Moot Court Honors Program. Note and Comment Editor, Southwestern University Law Review, 1980-1981.

### ASSOCIATES

**KELLY D. AKINS,** born Lubbock, Texas, January 19, 1962; admitted to bar, 1988, California. *Education:* Trinity University (B.A., 1984); University of Texas, Austin (J.D., 1988).

**SARIRA D. ALEXANDER,** born Tehran, June 4, 1962; admitted to bar, 1994, California. *Education:* University of California at Los Angeles (B.A. Eng. Lit., 1990); Hastings College of Law (J.D., 1993). Phi Delta Phi. *Member:* Los Angeles County and American Bar Associations; International Trademark Association; Robert A. Banyard Inn of Court; International Association of Young Lawyers. **LANGUAGES:** Farsi and French. **PRACTICE AREAS:** Intellectual Property; International Law.

**NORMAN E. ALLEN** (Resident, San Francisco Office).

**LEE M. AMIDON** (Resident, San Bernardino Office).

**PAUL ELLIS BARON** (Resident, San Francisco Office).

**MARK A. BIRMINGHAM** (Resident, San Diego Office).

**LESLIE S. BOWEN** (Resident, Costa Mesa Office).

**LARRY J. BROCK,** born Washington, Iowa, July 8, 1965; admitted to bar, 1990, California. *Education:* Drake University (B.S., Political Science and Sociology, magna cum laude, 1987); Pepperdine University (J.D., cum laude, 1990). Phi Beta Kappa; Phi Eta Sigma; Alpha Lambda Delta; Phi Mu Alpha. *Member:* Los Angeles County and American Bar Associations; State Bar of California.

**JOSEPH C. CAMPO,** born White Plains, New York, October 20, 1965; admitted to bar, 1990, California. *Education:* Fordham University (B.A., 1987); New York University (J.D., 1990).

**CINDY MERTEN CARDULLO** (Resident, Sacramento Office).

*(This Listing Continued)*

CAA907B

**LEWIS, D'AMATO, BRISBOIS & BISGAARD,** Los Angeles—Continued

**JOHN S. CHRISTOPHER,** born Uniontown, Pennsylvania, August 19, 1946; admitted to bar, 1983, California and U.S. District Court, Northern District of California; 1987, California and U.S. Court of Appeals, Ninth Circuit; registered to practice before U.S. Patent and Trademark Office. *Education:* University of Colorado at Boulder (B.S.E.E., 1973) University of Santa Clara (J.D., 1982).

**G. RUSSELL CLARK** Resident, San Diego Office).

**DAVID S. COHN** (Resident, San Bernardino Office).

**LORI CREASEY** (Resident, Costa Mesa Office).

**TROY A. EDWARDS** (Resident, Costa Mesa Office).

**LAWRENCE A. EUGENIO,** born Manila, Philippines, July 8, 1969; admitted to bar, 1995, California. *Education:* St. John's University (B.A., 1991); University of California at Los Angeles (J.D., 1994). Phi Alpha Delta. [First Lieut., USAR, 1991—]

**KAREN A. FELD** (Resident, San Bernardino Office).

**TINA FISHER,** born Fayetteville, North Carolina, July 9, 1960; admitted to bar, 1991, California; U.S. District Court, Central, Northern and Southern Districts of California and U.S. Court of Appeals, Ninth Circuit. *Education:* Southwest Missouri State University (B.S., cum laude, 1982); University of North Carolina at Chapel Hill (J.D., 1990). *Member:* Black Women Lawyers Association; Barristers.

**KELLY M. FLANAGAN** (Resident, Costa Mesa Office).

**JAMES E. FRIEDHOFER** (Resident, San Diego Office).

**J. ALBERT GARCIA** (Resident, San Diego Office).

**ROBERT H. GARNETT,** born Morristown, New Jersey, August 24, 1966; admitted to bar, 1992, California. *Education:* University of Texas, Austin (B.B.A., 1988; J.D., 1991).

**CHRISTOPHER R. GREEN,** born Minneapolis, Minnesota, August 3, 1965; admitted to bar, 1990, California. *Education:* University of Minnesota (B.A., magna cum laude, 1987; J.D., 1990).

**ALLISON A. GREENE** (Resident, Costa Mesa Office).

**CHRISTOPHER J. GREENLEAF,** born Upper Darby, Pennsylvania, December 28, 1964; admitted to bar, 1994, California. *Education:* University of California, Los Angeles (B.A., magna cum laude, 1990); University of Southern California (J.D., 1993). Member, Southern California Law Review.

**PATRICK P. GUNN,** born Urbana, Illinois, May 26, 1968; admitted to bar, 1994, California. *Education:* University of Colorado (B.A., 1990); Boston University (J.D., 1994). Phi Beta Kappa; Sigma Iota Rho. *LANGUAGES:* Russian and Slovak. *PRACTICE AREAS:* Litigation; International Business Law.

**JAY D. HARKER** (Resident, Costa Mesa Office).

**HEATHER ANNE HENDERSON** (Resident, Costa Mesa Office).

**PAULA F. HENRY** (Resident, Costa Mesa Office).

**HELEN E. HESSE** (Resident, Costa Mesa Office).

**MADONNA L. HULTMAN** (Resident, Costa Mesa Office).

**CHARLES J. HYLAND** (Resident, Costa Mesa Office).

**APRIL M. JOHNSON** (Resident, San Diego Office).

**RAIMO H. KAASIK,** born New York, N.Y., April 30, 1963; admitted to bar, 1989, California and U.S. District Court, Southern District of California; 1991, District of Columbia. *Education:* University of Texas (B.B.A., cum laude, 1985; J.D., 1989). *Member:* The District of Columbia Bar.

**LAURA B. KALISER,** born Shaker Heights, Ohio, October 14, 1966; admitted to bar, 1992, California. *Education:* University of Michigan (B.S., 1988); Whittier College School of Law (J.D., 1991). *Member:* Women Lawyers Association of Los Angeles (Member, Business Law Section).

**JONATHON KAPLAN,** born Ohio, November 18, 1965; admitted to bar, 1990, California; 1992, District of Columbia. *Education:* Emory University (B.A., Russian and Soviet and Eastern European Studies, 1987); Duke University School of Law (J.D., 1990; LL.M., Foreign and International Law, 1990).

**JENIFER L. KIENLE** (Resident, San Diego Office).

*(This Listing Continued)*

**CATHERINE J. KIM** (Resident, Costa Mesa Office).

**HARRY T. KOZAK** (Resident, Costa Mesa Office).

**JACQUELINE S. LASCALA** (Resident, San Diego Office).

**SHARON M. LAWRENCE** (Resident, San Diego Office).

**VALERIE L. LEATHERWOOD,** born Baltimore, Maryland, March 20, 1963; admitted to bar, 1991, California. *Education:* Villa Julie College (A.A., 1984); University of Baltimore (B.A., 1987); Loyola Law School (J.D., 1991). Staff Member, Loyola Law Review, 1990-1991.

**DOUGLAS W. LEWIS** (Resident, San Diego Office).

**JUDITH A. LEWIS** (Resident, San Diego Office).

**JOAN CREIGH. LITTLE** (Resident, San Diego Office).

**MICHAEL S. LITTLE,** born Long Beach, California, January 23, 1970; admitted to bar, 1996, California. *Education:* University of California at Berkeley (B.A., 1992); Boston College (J.D., 1995). Member, Jessup International Moot Court Team, 1995. Articles Editor, Boston College Third World Law Journal, 1994-1995. Author: "A Citizen's Guide to Attacking Mortgage Discrimination: The Lack of Judicial Relief," 15 Boston College Third World Law Journal, 1995. *Member:* State Bar of California. *PRACTICE AREAS:* Insurance Fraud Law.

**CHRISTOPHER D. LOCKWOOD** (Resident, San Bernardino Office).

**DENNIS J. MAHONEY** (Resident, San Bernardino Office).

**GREGORY P. MARTIN,** born Albany, New York, December 3,1951; admitted to bar, 1988, California. *Education:* Colgate University (B.A., 1973); Rutgers University (M.S., 1977); Northrop University School of Law (J.D., 1988). Delta Theta Phi. First Place, 1987 Moot Court Competition. Certified Industrial Hygienist (C.I.H.) California, 1982.

**JAMES P. MAYO** (Resident, Sacramento Office).

**JOHN H. MCCARDLE** (Resident, Sacramento Office).

**STEVEN E. MEYER,** born Palo Alto, California, March 2, 1961; admitted to bar, 1989, California; 1990, U.S. District Court, Central District of California and U.S. Court of Appeals, Ninth Circuit. *Education:* University of California at Los Angeles (B.A.B.S., 1984); Santa Clara University (J.D., cum laude, 1989). *Member:* Los Angeles County Bar Association; State Bar of California. *PRACTICE AREAS:* Civil Litigation; Real Estate; Bankruptcy Litigation.

**GAIL F. MONTGOMERY** (Resident, San Bernardino Office).

**RAFFI A. NAHABEDIAN,** born Los Angeles, California, October 12, 1965; admitted to bar, 1995, California. *Education:* California State University, Northridge (B.S., 1989); Pepperdine University School of Law (J.D., 1994). Judicial Extern to the Hon. Dickran Tevrizian, U.S. District Judge, 1992-1993. *Member:* Los Angeles County and American Bar Associations; State Bar of California.

**PAUL F. O'BRIEN** (Resident, San Diego Office).

**TERRELL A. QUEALY** (Resident, San Diego Office).

**CATHERINE J. QUINN,** born Los Angeles, California, December 7, 1965; admitted to bar, 1995, California. *Education:* California State University (B.S., 1992); Southwestern University School of Law (J.D., 1995). *Member:* State Bar of California.

**LISA K. ROBERTS** (Resident, San Diego Office).

**JAMES F. B. SAWYER,** born Holyoke, Massachusetts, November 22, 1955; admitted to bar, 1990, California and U.S. District Court, Southern District of California. *Education:* University of Massachusetts at Amherst (B.A., 1977); University of San Diego (J.D., 1990). Phi Alpha Delta. Los Angeles Superior Court Arbitrator, 1996—. *Member:* Los Angeles County and American Bar Associations; State Bar of California.

**LARRY R. SCHMADEKA,** born Taipei, Taiwan (ROC), September 8, 1965; admitted to bar, 1992, California, U.S. District Court, Central District of California and U.S. Court of Appeals, Ninth Circuit. *Education:* Claremont-McKenna College (B.A., with honors, 1989); Southwestern University School of Law (J.D., magna cum laude, 1992). Member, Southwestern University Law Review, 1990-1991. Recipient: American Jurisprudence Awards in Torts I, Torts II, Property II, Constitutional Law I and Remedies. *Member:* Lawyers Club of Los Angeles.

**ROBERT M. SHANNON** (Resident, Sacramento Office).

**CHRISTINA M. SLATTON,** born Milton, Florida, March 27, 1962; admitted to bar, 1989, California. *Education:* University of West Florida

*(This Listing Continued)*

## PROFESSIONAL BIOGRAPHIES

(B.A .,1985); Emory University; Pepperdine University (J.D., 1988). Phi Alpha Delta. *Member:* American Bar Association.

**CHRISTINE GRAVES THOENE** (Resident, San Diego Office).

**KAREN E. VAUGHEY,** born Oakland, California, September 9, 1966; admitted to bar, 1995, California. *Education:* Stanford University (B.A., 1988); Loyola Law School (J.D., 1995). *Member:* Los Angeles County Bar Association. *LANGUAGES:* French.

**JULIE A. VELTKAMP,** born Bozeman, Montana, January 18, 1964; admitted to bar, 1991, California. *Education:* Valparaiso University (B.A., 1986); Pepperdine University (J.D., 1991). *Member:* Los Angeles County Bar Association; State Bar of California.

**JAMIE E. WALTERS,** born Fayetteville, Arkansas, October 16, 1964; admitted to bar, 1990, California. *Education:* University of California at Los Angeles (B.A., 1986); University of Missouri (J.D., 1989). Author: "Federalism in Transition: The Emergence of New State and Local Strategies in the Face of the Vanishing Fourth Amendment," 20 Urban Law 863 (1988); Case Digest: "Schultz v. Frisby," 19 Urb.Law. 752 (1987). *Member:* Los Angeles County Bar Association; State Bar of California.

**KENNETH D. WATNICK,** born New York, N.Y., September 11, 1965; admitted to bar, 1990, California. *Education:* Cornell University (B.S., 1987); Duke University School of Law (J.D., 1990).

**SUSAN WEST,** born Whittier, California, September 10, 1962; admitted to bar, 1993, California; 1994, U.S. District Court, Central District of California; 1995, U.S. District Court, Southern District of California. *Education:* University of California, Santa Barbara (B.A., English, 1984); Loyola Marymount University (J.D., 1993). Vice President, Loyola Law School, Women's Law Association, 1992-1993. *Member:* Orange County and American Bar Associations; State Bar of California; Orange County Women Bankruptcy Lawyers. *PRACTICE AREAS:* Surety Law; Construction Litigation; Bankruptcy Creditors Rights.

**CARY L. WOOD,** born Lansing, Michigan, July 4, 1959; admitted to bar, 1990, California. *Education:* Michigan State University (B.A., 1987); University of San Diego (J.D., 1989). *Member:* Los Angeles County and American Bar Associations; State Bar of California.

**BETH E. YOFFIE,** born Pasadena, California, December 13, 1960; admitted to bar, 1985, California. *Education:* University of California at Berkeley (A.B. in English 1982); Hastings College of Law (J.D., 1985).

**JOHN YONG-JIN YOON,** born Los Angeles, California, July 28, 1961; admitted to bar, 1987, California and U.S. District Court, Central District of California. *Education:* Harvard College (A.B., magna cum laude, 1984); University of California at Los Angeles (J.D., 1987). Staff Member, UCLA Federal Communications Law Journal, 1986-1987. *LANGUAGES:* Korean, Japanese and Spanish.

(For Complete Biographical data on Personnel in Costa Mesa, San Diego, San Francisco, San Bernardino and Sacramento, California Offices, see Professional Biographies at those Cities)

## LAW OFFICES OF DAVID LEWIS

*A PROFESSIONAL CORPORATION*

*11400 WEST OLYMPIC BOULEVARD*
*NINTH FLOOR*
**LOS ANGELES, CALIFORNIA 90064**
Telephone: 310-575-0049
Fax: 310-444-9842
Email: lewislaw@ix.netcom.com

*Real Estate Transactional, Securities, Corporate, Business, Civil Trial.*

**DAVID J. LEWIS,** born London, England, November 4, 1953; admitted to bar, 1976, England and Wales; 1978, California. *Education:* University of Bristol, Bristol, England (LL.B., 1975); College of Law, London, England (Barrister-at-Law, 1976). Recipient, Duke of Edinburgh Scholarship, 1976. Author: "Checklist for Lease Negotiation," Volume 2, Number 1, The Journal of Real Estate Development 32-36 Summer, 1986; "How to Structure a Joint Venture," Estates Gazette (U.K.) April 2, 1988; "Negotiation Practice and Procedure," The Worldwide (Asia) March, 1991; "How to Structure a Joint Venture," Estates Gazette (U.K.) April 2, 1988; "Negotiation Practice and Procedure." The Worldwide (Asia) March, 1991. Member, Honourable Society of the Inner Temple, London, England. *Member:* State Bar of California.

## LEWITT, HACKMAN, HOEFFLIN, SHAPIRO, MARSHALL & HARLAN

*A LAW CORPORATION*
**LOS ANGELES, CALIFORNIA**
(See Encino)

*Business, Corporate, Partnership and Securities Law including Syndications, Mergers and Acquisitions and Public Offerings. Real Estate, Taxation, Commercial Finance, Family Law, Estate Planning, Probate, Personal Injury and Insurance Regulatory Law and related Civil Litigation and Administrative Law. Health Care and Hospital Law.*

## LICHTER, GROSSMAN, NICHOLS & ADLER, INC.

Established in 1992

*9200 SUNSET BOULEVARD, SUITE 530*
**LOS ANGELES, CALIFORNIA 90069**
Telephone: 310-205-6999
Fax: 310-205-6990
Email: lgninc@sure.net

*Practice Limited to Entertainment Law.*

**PETER GROSSMAN,** born New York, N.Y., October 6, 1947; admitted to bar, 1974, California. *Education:* Harvard University (A.B., cum laude, 1969); Boalt Hall School of Law, University of California (J.D., 1973). Order of the Coif. Member, Board of Editors, California Law Review, 1971-1973. Author: Case Note, 61 California Law Review 451, 1973. Clerk to Chief Judge Martin Pence, U.S. District Court, District of Hawaii, 1973-1974. *Member:* Beverly Hills and Los Angeles County Bar Associations; The State Bar of California. *PRACTICE AREAS:* Entertainment Law.

**LINDA LICHTER,** born Milwaukee, Wisconsin, February 12, 1951; admitted to bar, 1976, California. *Education:* University of California at Berkeley (A.B., with great distinction, 1973); Boalt Hall School of Law, University of California (J.D., 1976). Phi Beta Kappa. Member, Moot Court Board. Member: Advisory Board, Independent Feature Project West, 1985-1995; Executive Board, College of Letters & Science, University of California, Berkeley, 1993-1994. *Member:* Los Angeles County Bar Association; State Bar of California. *PRACTICE AREAS:* Entertainment Law.

**PETER NICHOLS,** born New York, N.Y., September 14, 1956; admitted to bar, 1981, California; 1984, U.S. Court of Appeals, Ninth Circuit; 1985, U.S. Supreme Court. *Education:* Northwestern University and London School of Economics and Political Science, London, England (B.Sc., with distinction; 1978); Northwestern University (M.A., 1978); Stanford University (J.D., 1981). Senior Editor, Stanford Journal of International Law, 1981. Contributor, Litigating Copyright, Trademark and Unfair Competition Cases, Practising Law Institute, 1983. *Member:* Los Angeles County Bar Association; The State Bar of California. *PRACTICE AREAS:* Entertainment Law.

**MICHAEL I. ADLER,** born San Francisco, California, May 10, 1949; admitted to bar, 1977, California. *Education:* University of California at Los Angeles (B.A., summa cum laude, Political Science, 1971; J.D., 1976) Columbia University (M.A., 1973). Phi Beta Kappa; Phi Eta Sigma. Woodrow Wilson Fellowship, 1972, Columbia University Presidential Fellow, 1973. Member, UCLA First Place Team, Southern California Moot Court Tournament, 1975. Extern to Justice Matthew O. Tobriner, California Supreme Court, 1975. Law Clerk to Judge William B. Enright, U.S. District Court, Southern District of California, 1976-1977. Member, UCLA Entertainment Law Symposium Committee, 1979—. Instructor and Co-Editor, "Entertainment Industry Collective Bargaining Units and Their Agreements" UCLA Extension, 1980. *Member:* Beverly Hills, Los Angeles County and American Bar Associations; State Bar of California. *PRACTICE AREAS:* Entertainment Law; Corporate Law.

**CARLOS K. GOODMAN,** born Detroit, Michigan, September 14, 1962; admitted to bar, 1989, California; 1991, U.S. District Court, Central District of California. *Education:* Brown University (B.A., 1984); University of California at Los Angeles (J.D., 1988). Order of the Coif. Editor, UCLA Law Review, 1987-1988. *Member:* Los Angeles County Bar Association; State Bar of California. *PRACTICE AREAS:* Entertainment Law.

*(This Listing Continued)*

CAA909B

## LICHTER, GROSSMAN, NICHOLS & ADLER, INC., Los Angeles—Continued

**JAMES J. KERSHAW, III,** born Johnson City, California, August 11, 1967; admitted to bar, 1993, California. *Education:* Dartmouth College (B.A., 1989); University of Jordan at Amman (1989-1990); Stanford University (J.D., 1993). Phi Beta Kappa. Fulbright Scholar - Jordan, 1989-1990. *Member:* Beverly Hills and Los Angeles County Bar Associations; State Bar of California. **PRACTICE AREAS:** Entertainment; Copyright.

**PATRICIA L. LAUCELLA,** born Jackson Heights, New York, October 11, 1962; admitted to bar, 1993, New York and California. *Education:* New York University (B.S., summa cum laude, 1987); Harvard Law School (J.D., cum laude, 1992). Certified Public Accountant, New York, 1989. *Member:* State Bar of California; American Bar Association. **PRACTICE AREAS:** Entertainment Law.

**CYNTHIA FARRELLY GESNER,** born Cumberland, Rhode Island, July 19, 1962; admitted to bar, 1989, California; 1992, Massachusetts. *Education:* Tufts University (B.A., 1984); Boston University School of Law (J.D., 1988). Moot Court Society. Entertainment Law Society. Trial Advocacy Program. *Member:* Beverly Hills, Los Angeles County and American Bar Associations; State Bar of California. **LANGUAGES:** French. **PRACTICE AREAS:** Entertainment Law.

### LEGAL SUPPORT PERSONNEL

**ANN L. DUVAL,** born Elkhart, Indiana, August 24, 1953. *Education:* California State University at Northridge (B.A., 1978). **PRACTICE AREAS:** Entertainment Law.

**JEFF SPRINGER,** born Houston, Texas, October 9, 1970. *Education:* Stanford University (B.A., 1993).

---

## LAWRENCE F. LIEBENBAUM
11766 WILSHIRE BOULEVARD, SUITE 700
**LOS ANGELES, CALIFORNIA 90025-6538**
Telephone: 310-471-0043
Fax: 310-445-2191

*Immigration and Naturalization Law.*

**LAWRENCE F. LIEBENBAUM,** born Los Angeles, California, December 26, 1935; admitted to bar, 1970, California and U.S. District Court, Central District of California; 1978, U.S. Court of Appeals, Ninth Circuit; 1980, U.S. Court of International Trade; U.S. Tax Court. *Education:* California State University at Los Angeles (B.A., 1957); Loyola University of Los Angeles (J.D., 1969). Author: "Deportation and Exclusion Consequences Arising Out of Criminal Acts and Convictions," Immigration Law Syllabus, Los Angeles County Bar Association, June, 1979; "Access to Uncompensated Health Care Services for Illegal Aliens," Proceedings of the Select Commission on Immigration and Refugee Policy, Committees on the Judiciary, House of Representatives and United States Senate, October, 1980. *Member:* Los Angeles County Bar Association (Member: Immigration Law Section; Executive Committee, 1976—, Section Chairman, 1978-1979 and 1986-1987; Los Angeles County Delegation to State Bar Conference, 1979—, Executive Committee, 1982-1984 and 1992-1994; Chairman, Committee on Rights of Aliens, 1979-1980; Member: Executive Committee, Immigration Legal Assistance Project, 1980—; Judicial Evaluation Committee, 1989—); State Bar of California; American Immigration Lawyers Association. (Certified Specialist, Immigration and Nationality Law, The State Bar of California Board of Legal Specialization).

REFERENCE: City National Bank, (Wilshire-Westwood Branch)

---

## LIEBMAN & REINER
A PROFESSIONAL LAW CORPORATION
3255 WILSHIRE BOULEVARD
12TH FLOOR
**LOS ANGELES, CALIFORNIA 90010**
Telephone: 213-387-0777
Fax: 213-383-6754

*San Francisco, California Office:* 100 First Street, Suite 2250. Telephone: 415-227-0777. Fax: 415-227-0537.

*(This Listing Continued)*

*Roseville, California Office:* 3017 Douglas Boulevard, Suite 300. Telephone: 916-852-0777. Fax: 916-852-8077.
*San Diego, California Office:* 225 Broadway, Suite 1500. Telephone: 619-232-0777. Fax: 619-238-5442.
*San Jose, California Office:* 95 South Market Street, Suite 300. Telephone: 408-993-0777. Fax: 408-993-0789.

*General Liability, Defense, Products Liability, Workers Compensation Defense, Insurance and Subrogation Law, Insurance Coverage and Bad Faith, Professional Liability. Trial Practice. Appellate Practice. Environmental and Industrial Disease Law.*

*FIRM PROFILE: Liebman & Reiner is a prominent California defense Firm, serving the insurance industry, self insureds, public entities and the business community. With offices in 5 cities, the firm is able to respond to the needs of our clients throughout the State of California.*

**STUART J. LIEBMAN,** born Brooklyn, New York, March 25, 1945; admitted to bar, 1971, California and U.S. District Court, Central District of California. *Education:* University of California at Los Angeles (B.A., 1967); Loyola University of Los Angeles (J.D., 1970). **PRACTICE AREAS:** Personal Injury Defense Law; Insurance Law.

**JOHN REINER,** born Glendale, California, June 3, 1947; admitted to bar, 1975, California; 1976, U.S. District Court, Central District of California and U.S. Court of Appeals, Ninth Circuit; 1996, U.S. District Court, District of Arizona. *Education:* University of California at Los Angeles (B.A., 1971); Southwestern University (J.D., 1974). (Member of California Trial Lawyers Association, with recognized experience in the field of Trial Lawyer). **PRACTICE AREAS:** Personal Injury Defense Law; Insurance Law; Trial Practice.

**LANE QUIGLEY,** born Los Angeles, California, July 12, 1949; admitted to bar, 1974, California and U.S. District Court, Central District of California. *Education:* California State University at Northridge (B.S., 1971); Loyola University of Los Angeles (J.D., 1974). Judge Pro Tem, Los Angeles Municipal Court, 1981. Arbitrator, Los Angeles Superior Court, 1982—. **PRACTICE AREAS:** Personal Injury Defense Law; Insurance Law; Trial Practice.

**JAMES M. O'BRIEN** (Resident, Roseville Office).

**JOHN F. DISTEL** (Resident, San Diego Office).

**CHAD H. PFEIFER** (Resident, San Francisco Office).

**JACK L. SHEPPARD,** born Kalamazoo, Michigan, March 25, 1949; admitted to bar, 1980, California. *Education:* University of California at Los Angeles (B.A., 1976); University of West Los Angeles (J.D., 1980). **PRACTICE AREAS:** Personal Injury Defense Law; Insurance Law; Subrogation Law; Trial Practice.

**SOLOMON SOULEMA,** born Salonika, Greece, May 24, 1950; admitted to bar, 1975, California; 1981, U.S. District Court, Central District of California. *Education:* California State University at Northridge (B.A., 1972); University of San Fernando Valley School of Law (J.D., 1975). **LANGUAGES:** Spanish and Greek. **PRACTICE AREAS:** Workers Compensation Defense Law.

**JAMES J. RIJ** (Resident, San Diego Office).

**TROY D. WIGGINS** (Resident, San Francisco Office).

**MARIJO KUPERMAN** (Certified Specialist, Workers Compensation Law, The State Bar of California Board of Legal Specialization) (Resident, San Diego Office).

---

**PETER A. KARLIN,** born June 26, 1957; admitted to bar, 1984, California and New York. *Education:* California State University at Northridge (B.A., 1980); California Western School of Law (J.D., 1983).

**JOHN W. EVANS,** born July 26, 1955; admitted to bar, 1981, California, U.S. District Court, Central District of California and U.S. Court of Appeals, Ninth Circuit; U.S. Supreme Court. *Education:* University of California at Los Angeles (B.A., 1978); Southwestern University School of Law (J.D., 1981).

**CRAIG D. NELSON,** born January 29, 1954; admitted to bar, 1979, Illinois and California; 1980, U.S. District Court, Central District of California; 1983, U.S. District Court, Southern District of California. *Education:* University of Wisconsin-Madison (B.A., 1976); Washington University (J.D., 1978).

*(This Listing Continued)*

**ARTHUR G. LESMEZ,** born July 26, 1959; admitted to bar, 1985, California and U.S. District Court, Southern District of California; 1986, U.S. District Court, Central District of California. *Education:* Syracuse University (B.A., 1981); California Western School of Law (J.D., 1984).

**RUSSELL M. RUBIN,** born September 6, 1958; admitted to bar, 1986, California and U.S. District Court, Central and Southern Districts of California. *Education:* University of California at Santa Barbara (B.A., 1980); Southwestern University School of Law (J.D., 1984).

**MICHAEL P. HOLLOMON, JR.,** born November 11, 1962; admitted to bar, 1989, California; 1992, U.S. District Court, Central District of California. *Education:* El Camino College (A.A., 1983); University of West Los Angeles (J.D., 1988).

**MAUREEN McCOOL,** born Norfolk, Virginia, October 10, 1958; admitted to bar, 1990, California; 1991, U.S. District Court, Central District of California. *Education:* Loyola Marymount University (B.S., 1980; J.D., 1990); California State University, Dominguez Hills (M.B.A., 1986).

**LESLIE J. ENG,** born Los Angeles, California, July 29, 1957; admitted to bar, 1986, California and U.S. District Court, Central District of California and U.S. Court of Appeals, Ninth Circuit. *Education:* University of California at Los Angeles (B.A., 1979); Loyola Law School of Los Angeles (J.D., 1986).

**BRYAN REINER,** born Glendale, California, August 24, 1966; admitted to bar, 1994, California. *Education:* University of Southern California (B.A., 1988); University of La Verne Law School (J.D., 1994). *PRACTICE AREAS:* Liability; Workmans' Compensation.

REPRESENTATIVE CLIENTS: Hertz Rent-A-Car; Los Angeles County Metropolitan Transportation Authority; Enterprise Rent-A-Car; Cigna Insurance; Transamerica Insurance Co.; Crawford & Co.; Hyatt Hotels; Keenan & Associates; Alexsis Risk Management Services; Circle K Corp.; Financial Indemnity Insurance Co.; G.A.B.; City of San Fernando; Motors Insurance Co.; Workmen's Auto Insurance Co.; Reliance National Insurance Co.; City of Los Angeles/Department of Airports; University of California; Yasuda Insurance Co.; Zurich American Insurance Group; CNA Insurance Co.; Gallagher Bassett Services; Travelers Insurance Co.; Nissan North America; CSX Intermodal, Inc.; International Service Systems, Inc.; Greyhound Lines, Inc.; Chubb Insurance Co.; Home Depot, Inc.; Wells Fargo Bank; Discovery Zone; Raley's Supermarkets; Burger King; Orchard Supply Hardware; C.R. England Trucking; Hanson Industries; Christian Brothers.

---

## *LIM, RUGER & KIM, LLP*

Established in 1986

ARCO CENTER, SUITE 2800
1055 WEST 7TH STREET
**LOS ANGELES, CALIFORNIA 90017**
*Telephone: 213-955-9500*
*Telecopier: 213-955-9511*

*Corporate, Real Estate, International, Bankruptcy, Business and Commercial Litigation, Tort Litigation, and Appellate.*

### MEMBERS OF FIRM

**CHRISTOPHER KIM,** born Los Angeles, California, August 13, 1952; admitted to bar, 1978, California; 1980, U.S. District Court, Central District of California; 1987, U.S. Court of Appeals, Ninth Circuit; 1990, U.S. District Court, Southern and Eastern Districts of California. *Education:* University of California at Berkeley (B.A., with honorary distinction, 1974); University of California at Los Angeles School of Law (J.D., 1978). Co-Author: "Land Development and Environmental Control in the California Supreme Court: The Deferential, the Preservationist and the Preservationist-Erratic Eras," 27 U.C.L.A. Law Review 889, 1980. Public Member, California State Board of Registration for Geologist and Geophysicists, 1983-1986. Member, California Judicial Council Advisory Committee on Racial and Ethnic Bias. *Member:* Los Angeles County (Member, Pacific Rim Committee, 1990-1991) and American Bar Associations; State Bar of California; Korean-American Bar Association (President, 1990). *PRACTICE AREAS:* Civil and Business Litigation.

**RICHARD M. RUGER,** born Seoul, Republic of Korea, June 5, 1955; admitted to bar, 1980, California; 1981, U.S. District Court, Central District of California. *Education:* Loyola University of Los Angeles (B.S., with honorary distinction; B.A., with distinction, 1976); University of Pennsylvania (J.D., with honorary distinction, 1980). *Member:* Los Angeles County Bar Association, Pacific Rim Committee (International Section); Korean American Bar Association of Southern California (Member, Board of Governors); State Bar of California. *LANGUAGES:* Korean. *PRACTICE AREAS:* Corporate; International; Real Estate.

*(This Listing Continued)*

**JOHN S. C. LIM,** born Seoul, Republic of Korea, September 22, 1957; admitted to bar, 1982, California; 1983, U.S. District Court, Central District of California; 1987, U.S. Court of Appeals, Ninth Circuit. *Education:* California State University at Northridge (B.S., 1979); Hastings College of the Law, University of California (J.D., 1982). Teaching Assistant, Contracts, Hastings College of the Law, University of California, 1981-1982. *Member:* Los Angeles County (Real Property Section) and American Bar Associations; State Bar of California; Korean American Bar Association of Southern California (President, 1992; Board of Governor, 1993). *LANGUAGES:* Korean. *PRACTICE AREAS:* Real Estate; Corporate; Bankruptcy.

### OF COUNSEL

**FRANKLIN MICHAELS, JR.,** born Bridgeport, Connecticut, April 28, 1953; admitted to bar, 1982, California and U.S. Court of Appeals, Ninth Circuit. *Education:* University of Pennsylvania; University of Minnesota (B.S., 1979); University of Southern California (J.D., 1982). Law Clerk, Hon. Peter M. Elliott, U.S. Bankruptcy Judge and Judge, Ninth Circuit Bankruptcy Appellate Panel, 1982-1983. *Member:* State Bar of California; American Bar Association (Member, Business Bankruptcy Committee, Section of Business Law); American Bankruptcy Institute; Financial Lawyers Conference. (Board Certified in Business Bankruptcy Law, by the American Bankruptcy Board of Certification). *PRACTICE AREAS:* Bankruptcy; Bankruptcy and Insolvency Law.

### ASSOCIATES

**PIO S. KIM,** born Seoul, Korea, April 5, 1964; admitted to bar, 1991, California. *Education:* University of California, Los Angeles (B.A., 1987; J.D., 1991). Board Member, University of California Moot Court Honors Program Staff, Pacific Basin Law Journal. Extern, American Civil Liberties Union. *Member:* Los Angeles County Bar Association; State Bar of California; Korean American Bar Association (Member, Board of Governor; Chair Community Service) Chair, Asian Concerns Committee, 1993. *LANGUAGES:* Korean. *PRACTICE AREAS:* Civil Litigation.

**HENRY M. LEE,** born Seoul, Korea, May 14, 1966; admitted to bar, 1991, California and U.S. District Court, Central District of California. *Education:* Occidental College (B.A., 1988); University of California at Los Angeles (J.D., 1991). Omicron Delta Epsilon. Extern, Hon. Robert M. Takasugi, U.S. District Court, Central District. Member, University of California Moot Court Honors Program; Staff, Pacific Basin Law Journal. *Member:* Los Angeles County Bar Association; State Bar of California. *PRACTICE AREAS:* Civil Litigation.

**RICHARD D. HENICK,** born Jacksonville, North Carolina, July 26, 1966; admitted to bar, 1991, Pennsylvania, New Jersey, U.S. District Court, Eastern District of Pennsylvania and U.S. District Court, District of New Jersey ; 1992, California and U.S. District Court, Central District of California. *Education:* University of California, Berkeley (B.A., 1988); Temple University (J.D., cum laude, 1991). Recipient: Catherine Donahue Memorial Award; American Jurisprudence Award for Civil Procedure. Notes and Comments Editor: Temple Environmental & Technological Law Journal, 1990-1991. Author: "Rails to Trails: Everyone Benefits, Don't They?" 10 Temple Envtl. & Tech. Law Journal 75, (1991). *Member:* Los Angeles County and American Bar Associations; State Bar of California (Member, Business Law Section). *PRACTICE AREAS:* Real Estate; General Corporate; Bankruptcy.

**A. (JOHN) F. AMER,** born Cairo, Egypt, April 6, 1967; admitted to bar, 1994, California and U.S. District Court, Central District of California. *Education:* University of California at Los Angeles (B.A., 1990); Loyola University of Los Angles (J.D., 1994). Extern, Hon. Aurelio Munoz, Los Angeles Superior Court, Central District, 1993-1994. Omicron Delta Epsilon. Phi Delta Phi. Author: "Play It Again Sam: New York's Renewed Effort To Enact A 'Son Of Sam' Law That Passes Constitutional Muster," 14 Loyola Entertainment Law Journal 115 (1993). *Member:* Los Angeles County and American Bar Associations; State Bar of California (Member, Litigation Section). *PRACTICE AREAS:* Civil Litigation.

**CHRISTINE M. CHANG,** born Los Angeles, California, December 26, 1970; admitted to bar, 1996, California. *Education:* University of California, Los Angeles (B.A., with honorary distinction, 1993); University of California, Hastings College of Law (J.D., 1996). Phi Beta Kappa; Staff, Hastings Communication and Entertainment Law Journal. Internship, State of California, Department of Justice, The Office of the Attorney General; Externship, Honorable Ming W. Chin, California Supreme Court and California Court of Appeals (First District, Division 3), 1996. *Member:* State Bar of California. *PRACTICE AREAS:* Civil Litigation.

*(This Listing Continued)*

*LIM, RUGER & KIM, LLP, Los Angeles—Continued*

REPRESENTATIVE CLIENTS: Federal Deposit Insurance Corporation; Nike, Inc.; PFS, Inc. (Pepsico, Inc); Fashion 21, Inc.; Frontier Food Warehouse; Koreatown Plaza; Ko-Amex General Wholesale, Inc.; San Pedro Wholesale Mart; Shin Hwa Korea; U.S. Dyeing & Finishing, Inc.

## ERIC NELSON LINDQUIST

**445 SOUTH FIGUEROA STREET, SUITE 2600
LOS ANGELES, CALIFORNIA 90071**
Telephone: 213-612-7790
Fax: 213-612-7792

*Civil Litigation in all State and Federal Courts, Business, Transactions, Real Estate, Tax, Probate and Estate Planning, Commercial Litigation.*

**ERIC NELSON LINDQUIST,** born Los Angeles, California, May 9, 1936; admitted to bar, 1967, California. *Education:* University of Paris; Occidental College (B.A., 1959); University of Southern California (J.D., 1967). *Member:* State Bar of California. **PRACTICE AREAS:** Corporation Law; Business Law; Taxation Law.

## LINER, YANKELEVITZ & SUNSHINE LLP

**11620 WILSHIRE BOULEVARD, SUITE 400
LOS ANGELES, CALIFORNIA 90025**
Telephone: 310-478-3869
Fax: 310-445-3377

*General Civil and Trial Practice in all State and Federal Courts, Real Estate, Corporate, Taxation, Estate Planning and Probate.*

FIRM PROFILE: *Liner & Yankelevitz LLP is a law firm specializing in all areas of business and civil litigation, landlord-tenant, corporate finance and transactions and real estate law. The firm's litigation department handles cases in both Federal and State Court involving general commercial disputes, real estate, securities, administrative proceedings, bankruptcy, intellectual property, environmental, ERISA, labor and appeals. The firm's transactional practice encompasses all aspects of business law, including corporate, partnership, taxation, probate, estates and trusts, securities law and real estate including commercial and retail leasing.*

### PARTNERS

**STEVEN B. YANKELEVITZ,** born Brooklyn, New York, March 11, 1952; admitted to bar, 1980, California; 1981, U.S. Tax Court. *Education:* Long Island University (B.S., 1973); Pepperdine University (J.D., 1977). *Member:* Beverly Hills (Member, Sections on: Corporate; Business; Real Estate) and Los Angeles County (Member, Sections on: Corporate; Business; Real Estate) Bar Associations; State Bar of California. **PRACTICE AREAS:** Corporate; Partnership; Limited Liability Companies; Business Law; Securities Law; Taxation Law; Real Estate.

**RANDALL J. SUNSHINE,** born Oceanside, New York, November 22, 1955; admitted to bar, 1986, New York, U.S. District Court, Southern and Eastern Districts of New York and U.S. Court of Appeals, Tenth Circuit; 1988, California; 1989, U.S. District Court, Central, Southern, Northern and Eastern Districts of California, U.S. Court of Appeals, Ninth Circuit; 1990, U.S. Supreme Court. *Education:* Brown University (B.A., 1977); London School of Economics and Political Science (1975-1976); Fordham University (J.D., 1985). Staff Member, Fordham Law Review, 1984-1985. *Member:* Los Angeles County (Public Counsel Program, 1988—) and American Bar Associations; State Bar of California (Delegate, Conference of Delegates, 1990-1995). **PRACTICE AREAS:** Business; Civil Litigation.

**STUART A. LINER,** born San Bernardino, California, March 26, 1962; admitted to bar, 1988, California, U.S. District Court, Central District of California and U.S. Court of Appeals, Ninth Circuit. *Education:* San Diego State University (B.A., 1984); Loyola University of Los Angeles (J.D., 1987). *Member:* Beverly Hills and Los Angeles County Bar Associations; State Bar of California. **PRACTICE AREAS:** Business Civil Litigation; Commercial Real Estate; Creditors' Rights; Insolvency; Construction; Inverse Condemnation.

### ASSOCIATES

**G. FRANK GLABACH,** born Detroit, Michigan, February 20, 1955; admitted to bar, 1981, Michigan; 1985, California and New York. *Education:* Kalamazoo College (B.A., 1977); Wayne State University (J.D., 1981); New York University (LL.M., Tax, 1984). *Member:* Los Angeles County and New York State Bar Associations; State Bar of California; State Bar of

*(This Listing Continued)*

Michigan. (Certified Specialist, Taxation Law, Estate Planning, Trust and Probate Law The State Bar of California Board of Legal Specialization). **PRACTICE AREAS:** Taxation Law; Business Law; Securities Law; Corporate Law; Partnership Law; Trusts; Estate Planning and Probate.

**DAVID M. COHEN,** born Plainview, New York, November 20, 1966; admitted to bar, 1992, California. *Education:* Wharton School of Finance and Commerce; University of Pennsylvania (B.S., Economics, 1988); University of California at Los Angeles (J.D., 1992). *Member:* Los Angeles County Bar Association. **PRACTICE AREAS:** Business Civil Litigation.

**NEIL F. RADICK,** born New York, N.Y., January 3, 1967; admitted to bar, 1993, California, U.S. District Court, Central District of California and U.S. Court of Appeals, Ninth Circuit. *Education:* Northwestern University (B.A., 1988); Loyola University; University of Southern California (J.D., 1993). **PRACTICE AREAS:** Financial Services; Insolvency.

**PETER J. PITCHESS, II,** born Pasadena, California, January 6, 1967; admitted to bar, 1993, California, U.S. District Court, Central District of California and U.S. Court of Appeals, Ninth Circuit; 1995, District of Columbia. *Education:* University of Southern California (B.S.B.A., Finance, 1989); Loyola University of Los Angeles (J.D., 1993). *Member:* Beverly Hills and Los Angeles County Bar Associations; State Bar of California; District of Columbia Bar. **PRACTICE AREAS:** Commercial; Business Litigation.

## LINZER & ASSOCIATES

**12100 WILSHIRE BOULEVARD, 15TH FLOOR
LOS ANGELES, CALIFORNIA 90025**
Telephone: 310-826-2627
Fax: 310-820-3687

*General Corporate, Business, Partnership, Intellectual Property, Trademarks, Copyrights, Entertainment, Franchise, Distribution, Internet, New Media and Multimedia, and Commercial Litigation.*

**KENNETH A. LINZER,** born Champaign, Illinois, August 10, 1950; admitted to bar, 1985, California. *Education:* Tufts University (B.S., cum laude, 1972); University of San Diego (J.D., magna cum laude, 1985). Lead Articles Editor, San Diego Law Review, 1984-1985. Co-Editor, "Licensing and Litigation in the Multimedia Age," Los Angeles County Bar IPELS Symposium Syllabus, 1995. Co-Author: "Franchise Law: Practice and Forms," International Franchise Association, 1992; "Franchise Protection: Laws Against Termination and the Establishment of Additional Franchises," American Bar Association, Antitrust Section Monograph, 1990. Formerly associated with Paul, Hastings, Janofsky & Walker, 1985-1992. Judge Pro Tempore, Los Angeles and Beverly Hills Municipal Courts. *Member:* Beverly Hills (Sections: Business Law; Entertainment Law and Litigation) and Los Angeles County (Executive Committee, Intellectual Property and Entertainment Law) Bar Associations.

## LITTLER, MENDELSON, FASTIFF, TICHY & MATHIASON

*A PROFESSIONAL CORPORATION*

Established in 1942

**2049 CENTURY PARK EAST, SUITE 500
LOS ANGELES, CALIFORNIA 90067**
Telephone: 310-553-0308
Facsimile: 310-553-5583
URL: http://www.littler.com

*Offices located in:* California -- Bakersfield, Fresno, Long Beach, Menlo Park, Oakland, Sacramento, San Diego, San Francisco, San Jose, Santa Maria, Santa Rosa and Stockton; Denver, Colorado; Washington, D.C.; Atlanta, Georgia; Baltimore, Maryland; Reno and Las Vegas, Nevada (a partnership with the Law Offices of Hicks & Walt); Morristown, New Jersey; New York, New York; and Dallas and Houston, Texas.

FIRM PROFILE: *Littler, Mendelson, Fastiff, Tichy & Mathiason is the largest law firm in the United States engaged exclusively in the practice of employment and labor law. The firm has over 250 attorneys in 23 offices nationwide who represent and advise management in all the major sub-specialities of employment and labor law including: wage and hour law; NLRB cases and collective bargaining; workers' compensation; sex, race, and age discrimination; wrongful termination; unemployment benefits; workplace violence; substance*

*(This Listing Continued)*

*abuse; employee privacy rights; occupational safety and health; the ADA; ERISA, employee benefits, tax issues; and immigration.*

**ROBERT F. MILLMAN,** born Milwaukee, Wisconsin, November 2, 1949; admitted to bar, 1974, California; 1991, District of Columbia. *Education:* University of Wisconsin (B.A., with honors, 1971); Cornell University (J.D., 1974). Phi Beta Kappa. Co-Author: "At Will Termination in California," Federal Publications, 1982. "Arbitration, An Alternative to Litigation," Federal Publications, 1981.

**MARK W. ROBBINS,** born Springfield, Massachusetts, December 3, 1951; admitted to bar, 1977, Massachusetts; 1980, District of Columbia; 1981, California. *Education:* University of Rochester (B.A., with distinction, 1973); Boston College (J.D., cum laude, 1976).

**GORDON A. LETTER,** born Washington, D.C., February 8, 1952; admitted to bar, 1979, California. *Education:* University of California at Los Angeles (B.A., 1974); Hastings College of the Law, University of California (J.D., 1977).

**DIANE L. KIMBERLIN,** born Pasadena, California, May 25, 1952; admitted to bar, 1976, California. *Education:* University of Santa Barbara (B.A., magna cum laude, 1973); University of California at Los Angeles (J.D., 1976).

**ROBERT W. FEINSTEIN,** born Brooklyn, New York, October 30, 1950; admitted to bar, 1976, Pennsylvania; 1978, New Jersey; 1979, California. *Education:* University of Rochester (B.A., with distinction, 1972); Washington University (M.S.W., 1975; J.D., 1975).

**RONALD J. COOKE,** born Philadelphia, Pennsylvania, May 19, 1947; admitted to bar, 1972, California. *Education:* University of California at Los Angeles (A.B., 1969); Villanova University (J.D., 1972).

**ENRIQUE L. MUÑOZ,** born San Diego, California, August 23, 1952; admitted to bar, 1978, California. *Education:* San Diego State University (B.A., 1974); University of San Diego (J.D., 1977).

**W. JOSEPH STRAPP,** born Urbana, Ohio, October 24, 1948; admitted to bar, 1973, Ohio; 1986, California. *Education:* The Ohio State University (B.A., 1970; J.D., 1973).

**SHIRLEY D. DEUTSCH,** born Los Angeles, California, July 6, 1952; admitted to bar, 1977, California. *Education:* University of California at Los Angeles (B.A., summa cum laude, 1974); Stanford University (J.D., 1977). Phi Beta Kappa. *LANGUAGES:* French.

**JAFFE D. DICKERSON,** born Washington, D.C., October 24, 1950; admitted to bar, 1977, California. *Education:* College of the Holy Cross (B.A., 1972); Boston College (J.D., 1975).

**LAWRENCE J. SONG,** born Monterey, California, November 7, 1952; admitted to bar, 1977, Virginia; 1988, California. *Education:* Purdue University (B.A., 1974); Catholic University of America (J.D., 1977).

**LESTER L. JONES,** born Detroit, Michigan, August 16, 1950; admitted to bar, 1986, California. *Education:* University of Wisconsin (B.A., 1973; M.S., magna cum laude, 1979); McGeorge School of Law, University of the Pacific (J.D., 1984).

**CONNIE L. MICHAELS,** born Los Angeles, California, July 19, 1961; admitted to bar, 1987, California; 1989, District of Columbia. *Education:* University of California at Berkeley (B.A., with distinction, 1983); Annenberg School of Communications (M.A., 1986); University of Southern California (J.D., 1986).

**ALLISON R. MICHAEL,** born Inglewood, California, December 3, 1960; admitted to bar, 1987, California; 1990, District of Columbia. *Education:* University of California at Berkeley (A.B., summa cum laude, 1983; Phi Beta Kappa]); Harvard Law School; University of California at Los Angeles (J.D., 1987). *LANGUAGES:* Spanish.

---

**RUTH BENSON,** admitted to bar, 1977, California. *Education:* Elmira College (A.B., summa cum laude, 1959); Yale University (Ph.D., 1969); University of California at Los Angeles (J.D., 1977). Phi Beta Kappa.

**J. KEVIN LILLY,** born July 17, 1955; admitted to bar, 1985, California. *Education:* California State University at Northridge (B.M., 1977; M.A., 1979); Loyola Marymount University (J.D., 1985).

**ROBERT H. TAYLOR,** born Yonkers, New York, May 12, 1964; admitted to bar, 1992, California; 1993, U.S. District Court, Central District of California. *Education:* Princeton University (A.B., 1986); University of California at Los Angeles (J.D., 1992).

*(This Listing Continued)*

**ROBERT S. BLUMBERG,** born New York, N.Y., March 1, 1967; admitted to bar, 1992, California; 1993, U.S. District Court, Central District of California. *Education:* University of California at Los Angeles (B.S., cum laude, with highest honors, 1989); New York University (J.D., 1992).

**JODI L. KRUGER,** born Philadelphia, Pennsylvania, May 31, 1968; admitted to bar, 1993, California and U.S. District Court, Northern District of California. *Education:* Cornell University (B.A., 1990; J.D., 1993).

**SHELDON DAVID KASDAN,** born Los Angeles, California, April 5, 1967; admitted to bar, 1992, California and U.S. District Court, Central District of California. *Education:* University of California at Los Angeles (B.A., cum laude, 1989); Loyola Marymount University (J.D., 1992).

**KEITH A. JACOBY,** born Brooklyn, New York, October 20, 1965; admitted to bar, 1990, California. *Education:* Cornell University (B.A., cum laude, 1987); University of California, Los Angeles School of Law (J.D., 1990).

**LORI B. REBER,** born Thousand Oaks, California, September 3, 1970; admitted to bar, 1995, California. *Education:* California State University (B.A., 1992); Pepperdine University (J.D., 1995).

**JACK S. BAILEY,** born Atlantic City, New Jersey, February 10, 1968; admitted to bar, 1993, California. *Education:* Georgetown University (B.S.F.S., 1990); University of Michigan (J.D., 1993).

**GORDON F. PEERY,** born Salt Lake City, Utah, April 23, 1967; admitted to bar, 1996, California. *Education:* University of Southern California (B.A., 1991); Vanderbilt University (J.D., 1995). *LANGUAGES:* Japanese.

**MEGHAN A. WHITE,** born Los Angeles, California, September 2, 1965; admitted to bar, 1991, California. *Education:* University of Southern California (B.S., 1987); Loyola Marymount University (J.D., 1991).

**KAREN LYNN SCARBOROUGH STANITZ,** born Dallas, Texas, November 18, 1967; admitted to bar, 1992, Hawaii and U.S. District Court, District of Hawaii (Not admitted in California). *Education:* University of Hawaii (B.A., with distinction, 1989); William S. Richardson School of Law (J.D., 1992). *PRACTICE AREAS:* Litigation.

(For biographical data on personnel at other locations, see Professional Biographies at those cities).

---

## RONALD A. LITZ & ASSOCIATES

*1901 AVENUE OF THE STARS*
*18TH FLOOR*
**LOS ANGELES, CALIFORNIA 90067**
*Telephone: 310-201-0100*
*Fax: 310-201-0226*

*Civil Litigation, Family Law, General Business Law, Entertainment Law.*

**RONALD A. LITZ,** born New York, N.Y., November 27, 1941; admitted to bar, 1966, California and U.S. District Court, Southern, Central and Northern Districts of California. *Education:* Syracuse University (B.A., 1963); New York University (J.D., 1965). Guest Lecturer, University of Southern California Law School and UCLA, 1976-77. Judge Pro Tem, Beverly Hills Municipal Court, 1980-1981 and Los Angeles Municipal Court, 1989. *Member:* Beverly Hills (Member, Board of Governors, 1973-1975, 1977-1978; Barristers President, 1976-1977; Chairman, Judiciary Litigation Committee, 1976-1977; Program Chairman, 1980-1981; Chairman, Committee to Preserve the Judiciary, 1984-1986) and Los Angeles County Bar Associations; State Bar of California. *REPORTED CASES:* Worton v. Worton, 234 Cal.App.3d 1638 (1991); Wright v. Johnston, 206 Cal.App. 3d 333 (1988).

### ASSOCIATES

**JENNIFER A. LITZ,** born Los Angeles, California, October 31, 1967; admitted to bar, 1992, California and U.S. District Court, Central and Southern Districts of California. *Education:* San Diego State University (B.A., with distinction, 1989); University of San Diego School of Law (J.D., 1992). Phi Delta Phi. *Member:* Beverly Hills (Barrister Board of Governors, 1993—, Treasurer, 1995-1996; Co-Chair, AIDS Project) and Los Angeles County Bar Associations; State Bar of California.

## CARLOS A. LLOREDA

*Established in 1980*

**4727 WILSHIRE BOULEVARD, SUITE 402**
**LOS ANGELES, CALIFORNIA 90010**
*Telephone: 213-965-0365; 965-0366*
*Facsimile: 213-965-0483*

*General Civil Litigation, Attorney Fees Disputes and Personal Injury (Plaintiff and Defendant).*

FIRM PROFILE: *The Law Office of Carlos A. Lloreda, Jr. emphasizes the representation of institutional and individual clients in the defense of civil litigation matters as well as the representation of select plaintiffs in civil litigation cases. Mr. Lloreda avails himself to the representation of matters pertinent to attorney fees disputes and attorney conduct and also serves as an expert witness in litigation relative to issues pertinent to attorney fees.*

**CARLOS A. LLOREDA,** born Los Angeles, California, March 27, 1947; admitted to bar, 1979, California, U.S. District Court, Central District of California and U.S. Court of Appeals, Ninth Circuit. *Education:* University of Southern California (B.A., Pol. Science, 1970; Masters Public Administration, 1974); Santa Clara University (J.D., 1977). Author, "Ethical Considerations Pertinent to Attorney Client Fee Arrangements," Continuing Education of the Bar, April 1993, October, 1994. Principal Author, State Bar of California Formal Ethics Opinion, Formal Opinion No. 1986-1990. Consultant, Civil Procedure During Trial, Second Edition, Continuing Education of the Bar (C.E.B.) 1995. Lecturer, "How to Avoid and Survive Attorneys' Fee Disputes," Continuing Education of the Bar, 1993-1995. Participant, Pro Bono Program as sponsored jointly by Public Counsel and Los Angeles County Bar Association, 1981-1983. *Member:* Los Angeles County Bar Association (Member, Attorney-Client Relations Committee, 1982-1984; Fee Arbitrator, Attorney-Client Fee Disputes, 1983-1990); State Bar of California (Member, Standing Committee on Professional Responsibility and Conduct, 1984-1987). LANGUAGES: Spanish. PRACTICE AREAS: Civil Litigation; Attorney Fee Disputes; Attorney Conduct; Personal Injury (Plaintiff and Defendant).

---

**JAMES R. BALESH,** born Los Angeles, California, December 17, 1967; admitted to bar, 1994, California. *Education:* University of Notre Dame (B.A., 1989); Santa Clara University (J.D., 1993). Phi Alpha Delta. Recipient, Community Service Award, Santa Clara University, 1993. Member, Santa Clara University Moot Court Board, 1993. Editor, Santa Clara University Computer & High Technology Law Journal, 1992-1993. *Member:* Beverly Hills (Member, Committee for the Arts, 1994—), Los Angeles County (Member, Barristers Artists and the Law Committee and Sports Project Committee) and American Bar Associations. PRACTICE AREAS: Civil Litigation; Personal Injury (Plaintiff and Defendant); Business Transactions.

REPRESENTATIVE CLIENTS: The Hughes Aircraft Co.; The Travelers; Raleigh Enterprises; University of Southern California.

## CHARLES LOCKO

*Established in 1988*

**SUITE 2610, 2029 CENTURY PARK EAST**
**LOS ANGELES, CALIFORNIA 90067-3012**
*Telephone: 310-286-9908*
*Telecopier: 310-785-0027*

*Commercial Real Estate Law, Hotel, Multi-Family Residential and Shopping Center Law (Development, Financing, Acquisition and Management). Hazardous Materials Law (Compliance and Remediation).*

**CHARLES LOCKO,** born New York, N.Y., September 27, 1951; admitted to bar, 1980, California; U.S. District Court, Central District of California; U.S. Court of Appeals, Ninth Circuit. *Education:* University of California at Los Angeles (B.A., 1974); University of Southern California (J.D., 1980). *Member:* Beverly Hills, Los Angeles County and American Bar Associations; State Bar of California. PRACTICE AREAS: Real Estate Law.

REPRESENTATIVE CLIENTS: The Edward Thomas Companies; Shutters on the Beach; Centrepointe Apartments; Haight Properties, Inc.; Kemper Construction Company.

## LORRAINE L. LODER

*Established in 1987*

**601 WEST FIFTH STREET**
**SUITE 1200**
**LOS ANGELES, CALIFORNIA 90071**
*Telephone: 213-623-8774*
*Fax: 213-623-1409*

*General Business Practice, Corporate, Business Transactions, Business and Bankruptcy Litigation.*

**LORRAINE L. LODER,** born Glendale, California, November 22, 1952; admitted to bar, 1977, California; 1985, U.S. Supreme Court. *Education:* University of Southern California (B.A., 1974; J.D., 1977). Staff Member and Note and Article Editor, Southern California Law Review, 1975-1977. Author: "The Treatment of Liens in Bankruptcy," CAOC (California Association of Consumer Attorneys), April 1996; "Sexual Harassment Policy For Legal Employers," Los Angeles Lawyer, May 1994. Co-Author: with Kathleen March "Punitive Damages," Chapter, California Tort Damages (C.E.B., 1988). Adjunct Professor, Loyola Law School, 1987-1988. *Member:* Los Angeles County (Chair, Individual Rights Section, 1992-1994; Business Section; Board of Trustees, 1988-1989) and Federal (Member, Board of Governors, Los Angeles Chapter, 1992—) Bar Associations; State Bar of California (Member, Business Section; Los Angeles Bankruptcy Forum); Women Lawyers Association of Los Angeles (President, 1988-1989; Member, Board of Governors, 1981-1991); California Women Lawyers (Treasurer, 1995-1996; Secretary, 1992-1993; Member, Board of Governors, 1991-1993; 1995-1997).

## LOEB & LOEB LLP

A Limited Liability Partnership including Professional Corporations
*Established in 1909*

**SUITE 1800, 1000 WILSHIRE BOULEVARD**
**LOS ANGELES, CALIFORNIA 90017-2475**
*Telephone: 213-688-3400*
*Facsimile: 213-688-3460; 688-3461; 688-3462*

*Century City, California Office:* Suite 2200, 10100 Santa Monica Boulevard, Los Angeles, 90067-4164. Telephone: 310-282-2000. Facsimile: 310-282-2191; 282-2192.
*New York, N.Y. Office:* 345 Park Avenue, 10154-0037. Telephone: 212-407-4000. Facsimile: 212-407-4990.
*Washington, D.C. Office:* Suite 601, 2100 M Street N.W., 20037-1207. Telephone: 202-223-5700. Facsimile: 202-223-5704.
*Nashville, Tennessee Office:* 45 Music Square West, 37203-3205. Telephone: 615-749-8300; Facsimile: 615-749-8305.
*Rome, Italy Office:* Piazza Digione 1, 00197. Telephone: 011-396-808-8456. Facsimile: 011-396-808-8288.

*General Civil Practice.*

FIRM PROFILE: *Loeb & Loeb LLP is a full-service law firm representing organizations and individuals in the business community. The firm was established in Los Angeles in 1909 and now maintains offices in the Central Business District and Century City areas of Los Angeles, in New York City, in Washington, D.C., in Nashville, Tennessee and in Rome, Italy. Although the firm has been identified historically with both the entertainment industry and institutional lending, its client base throughout its history has encompassed individuals and entities engaged in most types of domestic and international businesses and professions. Its principal practice areas include civil litigation in all federal and state courts, patent, trademark, copyright and unfair competition law, general corporate and corporate securities law, banking, insurance company, pension fund and other institutional lending, real estate law, real estate financing, real estate securities, leveraged leasing, asset securitization, franchising, entertainment law (including motion pictures, television, sports, music and dramatic and literary arts), advertising, communication, health care, international, federal, state and local taxation, estate planning, pension and employee benefits, bankruptcy, insolvency and workout matters, environmental law, labor and employment, white collar criminal investigation and corporate counseling and probate and trust law.*

### MEMBERS OF FIRM

**JOSEPH P. LOEB** (1883-1974).

**EDWIN J. LOEB** (1886-1970).

**MORTIMER H. HESS** (1889-1968).

*(This Listing Continued)*

# PROFESSIONAL BIOGRAPHIES

## CALIFORNIA—LOS ANGELES

**PHILLIP E. ADLER, (A P.C.),** born Los Angeles, California, November 4, 1942; admitted to bar, 1967, California. *Education:* University of California at Berkeley (A.B., 1964); Boalt Hall School of Law, University of California (J.D., 1967). *Member:* The State Bar of California. **PRACTICE AREAS:** Corporate Law; Intellectual Property.

**CHRISTOPHER K. AIDUN,** born Syracuse, New York, September 28, 1955; admitted to bar, 1981, New York. *Education:* State University of New York at Albany (B.A., summa cum laude, 1977); New York University (J.D., 1980). Phi Beta Kappa. Root-Tilden Scholar. Recipient, Edmond Cahn Law Review Award. Note and Comment Editor, New York University Law Review, 1979-1980. Author: "A Primer on Asset Securitization," Journal of Commercial Lending, September 1995. Co-Author: "Capital for Middle Market Companies," Business Credit, September 1995; "Legal Considerations Affecting Foreign Bank Acquisitions of United States Banks," 1 Connecticut Journal of International Law 5, 1985-1986. Law Clerk to Honorable Barrington D. Parker, U.S. District Court for the District of Columbia, 1980-1981. (New York City Office). **PRACTICE AREAS:** Corporate; Securities; Financing.

**KENNETH B. ANDERSON,** born Neptune, New Jersey, September 18, 1955; admitted to bar, 1983, New York, New Jersey and U.S. District Court, District of New Jersey. *Education:* Rutgers University (B.A., with honors, 1979; J.D., 1982). Research Editor, Rutgers Computer and Technology Law Journal, 1981-1982. Lecturer: "Record Deal Basics Workshop," New Music Seminar, New York, N.Y., September 1985; "Sampling-Litigation and Settlements," New Music Seminar, New York, July, 1988; "Sampling Solutions," New Music Seminars, New York, July 1990; "Record Deal Symposium: Mock Negotiations," New Music Seminar, New York, July 1991; "Record Contracts," FAE Entertainment and Sports Conference, New York, N.Y., May 1993. "Identity Crisis: A Vision for the Right of Publicity in the Year 2020," VLA 25th Anniversary Program, New York, N.Y., 1995. *Member:* New Jersey State (Member: Patent, Trademark and Copyright Law Section, 1983—; Entertainment and Arts Law Committee, 1986—) and American (Member, Forum Committee on the Entertainment and Sports Industries, 1983—) Bar Associations. (New York City Office). **PRACTICE AREAS:** Entertainment Law.

**JOHN ARAO,** born Illinois, August 25, 1951; admitted to bar, 1981, California; 1982, U.S. Tax Court. *Education:* Harvard University (A.B., 1973); Yale University (J.D., 1981). **PRACTICE AREAS:** Taxation.

**ROGER M. ARAR,** born New York, N.Y., June 25, 1955; admitted to bar, 1983, New York; 1985, California. *Education:* Hebrew University, Jerusalem, Israel; Yale University (B.A., magna cum laude, 1977); Columbia University (J.D., 1982). Harlan Fiske Stone Scholar. Articles Editor, Columbia Law Review, 1981-1982. Teaching Fellow, Civil Procedure and Property, Columbia Law School, 1981-1982. *Member:* State Bar of California. (Century City Office). **LANGUAGES:** French. **PRACTICE AREAS:** Entertainment Law.

**DONALD L. B. BARAF,** born New York, N.Y., June 12, 1941; admitted to bar, 1966, New York; 1968, California. *Education:* Princeton University (A.B., 1962); Harvard University (LL.B., 1965); New York University (LL.M., 1966). Instructor of Law, Legal Research, Brief Writing, Brooklyn Law School, 1966-1967. *Member:* The Association of the Bar of the City of New York; The State Bar of California. (New York City Office). **LANGUAGES:** Spanish. **PRACTICE AREAS:** Entertainment Law.

**ROBERT S. BARRY, JR.,** born Los Angeles, California, August 13, 1949; admitted to bar, 1976, California. *Education:* University of California at Los Angeles (B.A., cum laude, 1972); University of San Diego (J.D., 1975); New York University (LL.M. in Taxation, 1976). Research Editor, San Diego Law Review, 1975-1976. *Member:* The State Bar of California. **PRACTICE AREAS:** Corporate Law.

**HAROLD A. BARZA,** born Montreal, Canada, July 28, 1952; admitted to bar, 1977, New York; 1978, California. *Education:* Boston University (A.B., 1973); Columbia University (J.D., 1976). James Kent Scholar, 1974-1976. Harlan Fiske Stone Scholar, 1973-1974. Member, Board of Editors, Columbia Law Review, 1975-1976. Law Clerk to Hon. Milton Pollack, U.S. District Judge, Southern District of New York, 1976-1977. Adjunct Professor, Mass Communications Law, Southwestern University School of Law, 1979-1982. Judge Pro Tem, Los Angeles Municipal Court, 1985—. *Member:* Los Angeles County (Member, Sections on: Trial Lawyers; Antitrust) and American (Member, Committee on Antitrust Litigation, Section on Litigation, 1982—) Bar Associations; The State Bar of California. **LANGUAGES:** French. **PRACTICE AREAS:** Litigation.

**MICHAEL D. BECK,** born Brooklyn, New York, March 2, 1955; admitted to bar, 1981, New York. *Education:* Columbia University (B.A., *(This Listing Continued)*

cum laude, 1977; LL.B., 1980). (New York City Office). **PRACTICE AREAS:** Real Estate Law.

**CAROL LAURENE BELFIELD,** born Burbank, California, January 9, 1955; admitted to bar, 1981, California. *Education:* University of California at Irvine (A.B., cum laude, 1977); University of California at Los Angeles (J.D., 1981). Member, 1979-1980 and Comment Editor, 1980-1981, University of California at Los Angeles Law Review. *Member:* Los Angeles County Bar Association; The State Bar of California. **LANGUAGES:** French. **PRACTICE AREAS:** Litigation.

**KENNETH R. BENBASSAT,** born Los Angeles, California, February 3, 1947; admitted to bar, 1972, California. *Education:* University of California at Berkeley (A.B., 1968); Harvard Law School (J.D., cum laude, 1971). Phi Beta Kappa. *Member:* Los Angeles County and American Bar Associations; State Bar of California. **PRACTICE AREAS:** Corporate; Securities; Commercial; International.

**MARIBETH A. BORTHWICK,** born Los Angeles, California, June 22, 1951; admitted to bar, 1976, California. *Education:* University of Southern California (B.A., summa cum laude, 1973); University of California at Los Angeles (J.D., 1976). Phi Beta Kappa; Order of the Barristers. *Member:* Los Angeles County Bar Association; The State Bar of California. (Century City Office). **PRACTICE AREAS:** Real Estate Law; Banking Law; Workout Law.

**DAVID H. CARLIN,** born New York, N.Y., March 18, 1943; admitted to bar, 1967, New York. *Education:* Columbia University (A.B., 1964); New York University (J.D., 1967). (New York City Office). **PRACTICE AREAS:** Advertising Law; Corporate Law.

**MARC CHAMLIN,** born Philadelphia, Pennsylvania, June 30, 1955; admitted to bar, 1981, New York. *Education:* Princeton University (A.B., magna cum laude, 1977); New York University School of Law (J.D., 1980). Research Editor, Annual Survey of American Law, 1979-1980. *Member:* American Bar Association. (New York City Office). **PRACTICE AREAS:** Entertainment Law.

**ALEX CHARTOVE,** born Mount Kisco, New York, January 21, 1954; admitted to bar, 1980, California; 1984, New York; 1986, District of Columbia; registered to practice before U.S. Patent and Trademark Office. *Education:* Brandeis University (B.A., magna cum laude, 1976); Massachusetts Institute of Technology; Duke University (J.D., 1980). Author: "Patent Law Developments in the Federal Circuit," PLI Annually, 1994—. (Washington, D.C. Office). **PRACTICE AREAS:** Trademark; Patent; Copyright.

**ANDREW S. CLARE, (A P.C.),** born Los Angeles, California, September 21, 1945; admitted to bar, 1972, California. *Education:* University of California at Berkeley (B.A., 1967; J.D., 1971). *Member:* The State Bar of California. **PRACTICE AREAS:** Insolvency Law; Workout Law.

**RICHARD J. CODDING,** born Valley City, North Dakota, November 10, 1944; admitted to bar, 1970, New York and U.S. District Court, Eastern and Southern Districts of New York; 1977, U.S. Court of Appeals, Tenth Circuit; 1979, U.S. Court of Appeals, First Circuit; 1980, U.S. Court of Appeals, Second Circuit; 1987, California and U.S. District Court, Central District of California; 1988, U.S. Court of Appeals for the Federal Circuit; 1992, U.S. District Court, Northern District of California; 1995, U.S. District Court, Eastern District of Wisconsin. *Education:* Georgia Institute of Technology (B.E.E., with highest honors, 1966); Massachusetts Institute of Technology (M.S.E.E., 1966); Harvard University (J.D., 1969). Tau Beta Pi; Phi Kappa Phi; Phi Eta Sigma; Eta Kappa Nu. *Member:* The State Bar of California; Los Angeles Patent Law Association. (Century City Office). **PRACTICE AREAS:** Patent; Trademark; Copyright; Litigation.

**KENNETH R. COSTELLO,** born Teaneck, New Jersey, July 12, 1953; admitted to bar, 1978, California. *Education:* Loyola University of Los Angeles (B.A., 1974); University of Santa Clara (J.D., magna cum laude, 1978). Member, Board of Editors, Santa Clara Law Review, 1977-1978. Publications: *Franchising Law: Practice and Forms,* a 3-volume book published by Matthew Bender & Co., 1992 (Co-Author); "Applicability of the Federal Trade Commission Rule to International Transactions: Part 2" *Franchise Law Journal,* Volume 15, No. 3, Spring 1996, American Bar Association (Co-Author ); "Acquiring Master Franchise Rights From a U.S. Franchisor Part Two: Negotiating the Master Franchise Agreement," *World Franchise and Business Report,* First Quarter 1996; "Applicability of the Federal Trade Commission Rule to International Transactions," *Franchise Law Journal,* Volume 15, No. 1, Fall 1995, American Bar Association (Co-Author); "Acquiring Master Franchise Rights From a U.S. Franchisor: Part 1: How to Conduct a Due Diligence Investigation," *World Franchise and Business Report,* Fall 1995; "The Use of Intellectual Property Law to Protect *(This Listing Continued)*

## LOEB & LOEB LLP, Los Angeles—Continued

Franchisors' Rights" *Journal of International Franchising and Distribution Law,* Vol. 9, No. 3, Tolley's (Co-Author); "Emerging Technology Issues," *Comments before the 28th Annual Legal Symposium of the International Franchise Association,* Washington D.C., May 1995 (Co-Author); "International Lawyers Say Self-Regulation Not the Answer," *CCH Global Franchising Alert,* Vol. 1, No. 11, November 1994, Commerce Clearing House; "Government Regulation or Self-Regulation: Which is the Answer for International Franchising," *Comments before the 38th Congress of the Union Internationale des Avocats* (Co-Author), Marrakesh, Morocco, October 28-30, 1994; "Advertising by the Franchise System," *12th Annual A.B.A. Forum on Franchising,* October 17, 1991 (Co-Author). *Member:* The State Bar of California (Member: Intellectual Property Section; Business Law Section; Franchise Legislation Committee, 1988-1991); American Bar Association (Member, Intellectual Property Section; Forum Committee on Franchising, 1983—; Antitrust Committee, Sub-committee on Franchising). **PRACTICE AREAS:** Franchise Law; Trademark; Corporate Law; Intellectual Property Law.

**TERENCE F. CUFF,** born Quantico, Virginia, October 1, 1949; admitted to bar, 1977, California. *Education:* University of California at Santa Cruz (A.B., 1974); University of Southern California (J.D., 1977); New York University (LL.M. in Taxation, 1979). Order of the Coif. Member of Staff, Southern California Law Review, 1975-1977. Lecturer: University of Southern California School of Business Administration, Partnership Taxation and Taxation of Corporate Reorganizations, 1982—; New York University Corporate Tax Planning Conference, 1985; California Continuing Education of the Bar, 1983—; ALI/ABA, 1986—; Practising Law Institute, 1986—; California CPA Foundation, 1986—; Prentice Hall Law and Business, 1987. *Member:* Los Angeles County and American (Member, Section on Taxation) Bar Associations; The State Bar of California. [Capt., USMCR]. **PRACTICE AREAS:** Taxation.

**JOHN J. DELLAVERSON,** born New Castle, Pennsylvania, July 5, 1946; admitted to bar, 1978, New York; 1980, California. *Education:* University of Pittsburgh (B.S., 1968); Cornell University; Fordham University School of Law (J.D., 1977). *Member:* National Labor Relations Board, Region 2, New York, N.Y., 1977-1979; Region 32, Oakland, California, 1979. *Member:* The State Bar of California (Member, Labor Relations Law Section); American Bar Association (Member, Labor and Employment Law Section). (Century City Office). **LANGUAGES:** Italian. **PRACTICE AREAS:** Labor Law; Entertainment Law.

**LORENZO DE SANCTIS,** born Rome, Italy, June 4, 1947; admitted to bar, 1975, Rome, Italy; 1982 Albo Degli Avvocati of Rome (Not admitted in the United States). *Education:* University of Rome (Dr. in Jurisprudence, 1970; European Studies, 1970-1972). *Member:* American Film Market Association; Italian Association of European Council of Jurists. [With Italian Air Force, 1970-1972]. (Rome, Italy Office). **LANGUAGES:** English, French and Italian. **PRACTICE AREAS:** Litigation.

**DAVID B. EIZENMAN,** born New York, N.Y., December 17, 1942; admitted to bar, 1965, New York; 1971, U.S. District Court, Southern and Eastern Districts of New York; 1972, U.S. Supreme Court; 1975, U.S. Court of Appeals, Second Circuit; 1979, U.S. Claims Court; 1985, U.S. District Court, Northern District of New York; 1991, U.S. District Court, Western District of New York. *Education:* Queens College of the City University of New York (B.A., 1963); New York University (J.D., 1965). Member, Commercial Arbitration Practice Committee, American Arbitration Association. *Member:* New York State Bar Association (Member, Executive Committee, Commercial and Federal Litigation Section). (New York City Office). **PRACTICE AREAS:** Commercial Litigation.

**FRANK E. FEDER, (A P.C.),** born El Paso, Texas, November 9, 1928; admitted to bar, 1955, California; 1988, New York. *Education:* Yale University (B.A., 1949); Harvard University (LL.B., 1954). *Member:* Los Angeles County and American Bar Associations; The State Bar of California. (Century City and New York Offices). **PRACTICE AREAS:** Real Estate Law; Banking Law.

**MARTIN D. FERN,** born New York, N.Y., January 28, 1943; admitted to bar, 1967, New York; 1972, California. *Education:* City College of the City University of New York (B.A., 1964); New York University School of Law (J.D., 1967). Recipient, American Jurisprudence Awards for Excellence in Contract, Corporations and Administrative Law. Author: "Establishing and Operating Under a Franchise Relationship," Matthew Bender and Company, 1987; "Warrens Forms of Agreements - Fern's Desk Edition," Matthew Bender and Company, 1989; "Warrens Forms of Agreement," Matthew Bender and Company, 1990. Co-Author: "Franchising Law: Practice and Forms," Matthew Bender and Company, 1992. ABA Advisor, National Conference of Commissioners on Uniform State Laws, Drafting Committee of Uniform Franchise and Business Opportunity Act, 1985-1986. *Member:* Franchise Legislation Committee, 1982-1988; Business Law Section, State Bar of California. General Counsel, Corporate Secretary, MGM International, Inc., 1967-1974. *Member:* Century City, Los Angeles County and American (Member: Forum Committee on Franchising, 1978—; Franchising Subcommittee of the Small Business Committee, Section of Corporation, Banking and Business Law, 1978—; Chairman, 1979-1986; Committee on Technology and Intellectual Property) Bar Associations. **PRACTICE AREAS:** Corporate Law; Franchising Law; Intellectual Property Law.

**DAVID L. FICKSMAN,** born Brookline, Massachusetts, October 16, 1944; admitted to bar, 1970, New York; 1973, California. *Education:* Tufts University (A.B., cum laude, 1966); New York University (J.D., 1969; LL.M., 1972). Adjunct Professor of Law, Antitrust, University of San Fernando Valley College of Law, 1975. *Member:* Los Angeles County (Member, Sections on: Antitrust Law; Business and Corporations Law) and American (Member, Sections on: Antitrust Law; Corporation, Banking and Business Law; International Law) Bar Associations; State Bar of California. **PRACTICE AREAS:** Corporate Law.

**EVAN FINKEL,** born 1956; admitted to bar, 1981, California, Supreme Court of California and U.S. District Court, Central, Southern, and Northern District District of California; 1986, U.S. Court of Appeals for the Federal Circuit; 1987, U.S. Court of Appeals, Ninth Circuit; 1988, U.S. Supreme Court. *Education:* State University of New York at Binghamton (B.S., in Mathematics and Comp. Sci., 1978); Hastings College of Law, University of California (J.D., 1981). Phi Beta Kappa. Member: Order of the Coif; Thurston Society. Author: "Computer Software Copyrights and Patents," Santa Clara High Technology Law Journal, Fall, 1991; "Copyright Protection for Computer Software in the Nineties," Santa Clara Computer and High Technology Law Journal, Volume 7, Number 2 (December 1991); Update to: "Copyright Protection for Computer Software in the Nineties," Santa Clara Computer and High Technology Law Journal, Volume 8, Number 1 (May 1992); "What Remains of the Laches and Estoppel Defenses After Aukerman?" Santa Clara Computer and High Technology Law Journal, Volume 9, Number 1 (March 1993); "Intellectual Property Issues Facing Japanese Companies Acquiring American Businesses, International Legal Strategy (a Japanese Publication), Vol. II-9 (September 15, 1993); "Means-Plus-Function Claims in Light of Donaldson and Other Recent Case Developments," IP Quarterly of Intellectual Property (a Japanese Publication), Vol. 21 (April 30, 1994) and Santa Clara Computer and High Technology Law Journal, Volume 10, Number 2 (November 1994); "Gilbert P. Hyatt: The Man Who Could Have Been The Microprocessor King," International Legal Strategy (a Japanese Publication), a 3-part article appearing in Vol. V-1 (January 15, 1996), Vol. V-2 (February 15, 1996) and Vol. V-3 (March 15, 1996). *Member:* Beverly Hills, Los Angeles County and American Bar Associations; State Bar of California. (Century City Office). **PRACTICE AREAS:** Trademark; Patent; Copyright; Trade Secret and Unfair Competition; Computer and Multimedia Law.

**JAY M. FINKELSTEIN,** born 1937; admitted to bar, 1964, District of Columbia; 1966, U.S. Court of Appeals for the District of Columbia Circuit; 1967-1982, U.S. Court of Customs and Patent Appeals; 1970, U.S. Supreme Court; 1982, U.S. Court of Appeals for the Federal Circuit; registered to practice before U.S. Patent and Trademark Office. *Education:* Drexel University (B.S.E.E., 1959); George Washington University (J.D., with honors, 1963). Phi Alpha Delta; Tau Beta Pi; Eta Kappa Nu. Patent Examiner, U.S. Patent Office, 1959-1961. *Member:* The District of Columbia Bar; American Intellectual Property Law Association. (Washington, D.C. Office). **PRACTICE AREAS:** Trademark; Patent; Copyright.

**DAVID C. FISCHER,** born Columbia, South Carolina, October 10, 1952; admitted to bar, 1978, Michigan; 1980, New York. *Education:* Vanderbilt University (B.A., cum laude, 1975); College of William & Mary (J.D., 1978). Staff Member, 1976-1978 and Notes and Comments Editor, 1977-1978, William & Mary Law Review. Author: "Workouts of LBO's: The Secured Lender's Perspective," 5 Comm. Lending R. 19, 1990. *Member:* The Association of the Bar of the City of New York (Member, Committee on Drugs and the Law); State Bar of Michigan. (New York City Office). **PRACTICE AREAS:** Corporate Law; Securities Law. **Email:** 71732.3220@compuserv.com.

**JOHN T. FRANKENHEIMER, (A P.C.),** born Stockton, California, June 28, 1946; admitted to bar, 1973, California; 1994, Tennessee. *Education:* Claremont Men's College (B.A., 1968); University of California at Los Angeles (J.D., 1973). *Member:* Beverly Hills, Century City and American

*(This Listing Continued)*

Bar Associations; The State Bar of California. (Century City Office). *PRACTICE AREAS:* Entertainment Industry Law.

**KENNETH D. FREEMAN,** born Oceanside, New York, November 24, 1955; admitted to bar, 1981, New York. *Education:* Alfred University (B.A., 1977); Fordham University (J.D., 1980). (New York City Office). *PRACTICE AREAS:* Real Estate Finance and Restructurings; Real Estate Leasing and Conveyancing.

**JAMES D. FRIEDMAN,** born Philadelphia, Pennsylvania, January 19, 1953; admitted to bar, 1979, California. *Education:* University of Pennsylvania (B.S. in Economics, summa cum laude, 1975; M.S. in Accounting, 1975); University of California at Los Angeles (J.D., 1979). Certified Public Accountant, Pennsylvania, 1977. Judicial Clerk for Hon. Robert O. Staniforth, Justice of California Court of Appeal, Fourth District, Division 1, 1978. *Member:* Los Angeles County Bar Association (Member, Real Property and Business Law Sections); The State Bar of California (Member, Sections on: Real Property Law; Business Law). *PRACTICE AREAS:* Real Estate Law.

**ANDREW S. GARB, (A P.C.),** born Los Angeles, California, September 23, 1942; admitted to bar, 1968, California; 1987, New York. *Education:* University of California at Santa Barbara and University of California at Los Angeles (A.B., with honors, 1964); Harvard University (LL.B., 1967); Yale University and University of Southern California (LL.M., 1968). Co-Author: Marshall and Garb, "California Probate Procedure," 5th Ed., 1989. *Member:* Los Angeles County Bar Association (Chair, Executive Committee, Trusts and Estates Section); The State Bar of California (Member, Executive Committee, Estate Planning, Trust and Probate Law Section). Fellow, American College of Trust and Estate Counsel. *PRACTICE AREAS:* Trusts and Estates Law and Related Litigation.

**DAVID W. GRACE,** born Bethesda, Maryland, July 3, 1954; admitted to bar, 1982, California and Florida; 1983, U.S. Court of Appeals, Ninth Circuit and U.S. District Court, Central, Eastern, Northern and Southern Districts of California; 1986, U.S. Supreme Court; 1990, U.S. Court of Appeals for the Federal Circuit. *Education:* George Mason University (B.S., with highest distinction, 1978); University of Virginia School of Law (J.D.,1981). Judicial Clerk, Hon. Daniel T.K. Hurley, Florida Fourth District Court of Appeal, 1981-1982. *Member:* Beverly Hills and Los Angeles County Bar Associations; The State Bar of California; International Trademark Association (Publishing Boards Committee); Los Angeles Copyright Society. *PRACTICE AREAS:* Trademark; Copyright; Intellectual Property Litigation.

**FRED B. GRIFFIN,** born Wadesboro, North Carolina, February 16, 1946; admitted to bar, 1975, California. *Education:* Duke University; University of California at Berkeley (B.A., 1972); University of Southern California (J.D., 1975); University of Michigan (M.P.P., 1979). Phi Beta Kappa. *Member:* Los Angeles County Bar Association (Member: Labor and Employment Law Section; Workers Compensation Section); State Bar of California. [1st. Lt., U.S. Army, 1967-1970]. *PRACTICE AREAS:* Employment Law.

**PHILIP J. GROSZ,** born Oshkosh, Wisconsin, February 1, 1952; admitted to bar, 1977, California. *Education:* University of Wisconsin-Madison (B.A., with honors, 1973); Yale University (J.D., 1977). Phi Beta Kappa. *Member:* The State Bar of California. (Century City Office) *PRACTICE AREAS:* Entertainment Law.

**LAWRENCE B. GUTCHO,** born Bronx, New York, September 20, 1957; admitted to bar, 1982, Colorado; 1987, California; 1990, Arizona. *Education:* Yale University (B.A., with highest honors, 1979); Harvard University (J.D., 1982). *Member:* State Bar of California; Colorado Bar Association; State Bar of Arizona. *PRACTICE AREAS:* Insolvency; Workout; Creditors Rights.

**JOSEPH P. HEFFERNAN, (A P.C.),** born Brooklyn, New York, April 22, 1936; admitted to bar, 1968, New York; 1973, California. *Education:* St. John's University (B.A., 1963; LL.B., 1967). *Member:* New York State Bar Association; The State Bar of California. *PRACTICE AREAS:* Real Estate Law; Finance.

**IRV HEPNER,** born Tel-Aviv, Israel, May 17, 1950; admitted to bar, 1980, New York. *Education:* Yale College (B.A., 1973); Benjamin N. Cardozo School of Law (J.D., magna cum laude, 1979). Member, Cardozo Law Review, 1978-1979. Author: Note, "Deterring 'Surface-Bargaining:' Employer Uncertainty and the Duty to Bargain in Good Faith," 2 Cardozo Law Review 127, Fall 1980. *Member:* American Bar Association (Member, Sections on: Real Property, Probate and Trust Law; Corporation, Banking and Business Law). (New York City Office). *PRACTICE AREAS:* Real Estate; Real Estate Finance; Real Estate Securities; Leveraged Leasing.

*(This Listing Continued)*

**JOYCE S. JUN,** born Tokyo, Japan, December 14, 1963; admitted to bar, 1990, California. *Education:* Westmont College-Santa Barbara; University of California at Los Angeles (B.A., 1986; J.D., 1989). *Member:* Los Angeles Bar Association; State Bar of California; Korean-American Bar Association; Japanese Bar Association. (Century City Office). *LANGUAGES:* Korean and Japanese. *PRACTICE AREAS:* Entertainment Law; International Transactions.

**LANCE N. JURICH,** born Edina, Minnesota, June 12, 1962; admitted to bar, 1987, California. *Education:* Arizona State University (B.S., 1984); Boston University School of Law (J.D., 1987). Jessup International Moot Court Competition, 1986. *Member:* State Bar of California. *PRACTICE AREAS:* Insolvency and Workout.

**MICHAEL BRYCE KINNEY,** born Forest Hills, New York, February 25, 1957; admitted to bar, 1984, New York. *Education:* State University of New York at Buffalo (B.A., 1979); Washington College of Law (J.D., 1982). (New York City Office). *PRACTICE AREAS:* Real Estate.

**WILLIAM K. KONRAD,** born 1952; admitted to bar, 1977, Illinois; 1980, California; registered to practice before U.S. Patent and Trademark Office. *Education:* University of Illinois (B.S., 1974; J.D., 1977). Phi Kappa Phi; Tau Beta Pi; Eta Kappa Nu. *Member:* State Bar of California. (Century City Office). *PRACTICE AREAS:* Trademark; Patent; Copyright.

**RICHARD W. KOPENHEFER,** born San Bernardino, California, October 3, 1954; admitted to bar, 1978, Ohio; 1985, California. *Education:* Duke University (B.A., magna cum laude, 1975); University of Cincinnati (J.D., 1978). Field Attorney, National Labor Relations Board, Region 9, Cincinnati, Ohio , 1978-1984; Region 31, Los Angeles, California, 1984-1985. *Member:* Los Angeles County (Member, Labor and Employment Section) and American (Member, Labor and Employment Law Section) Bar Associations; State Bar of California. (Century City Office). *PRACTICE AREAS:* Labor Law.

**MARY D. LANE,** born New York, N.Y., July 13, 1950; admitted to bar, 1976, California. *Education:* Barnard College (B.A., magna cum laude, with honors in Psychology, 1971, Phi Beta Kappa); University of California at Los Angeles (J.D., 1976). Order of the Coif. Article Editor, U.C.L.A. Law Review, 1975-1976. *Member:* Los Angeles County and American (Member, Sections on: Business Law; Commercial Law; Intellectual Property; Litigation; Real Estate) Bar Associations; The State Bar of California; Financial Lawyers Conference. *PRACTICE AREAS:* Insolvency and Workouts; Entertainment; Real Estate.

**JOHN F. LANG,** born New York, N.Y., February 26, 1943; admitted to bar, 1970, New York, U.S. District Court, Southern, Eastern, Western and Northern Districts of New York, U.S. Court of Appeals, Second Circuit; 1984, U.S. Tax Court and U.S. Court of International Trade. *Education:* City College of the City University of New York (B.A., 1964); Fordham University (J.D., 1967). New York County District Attorney's Office, Deputy Chief of Frauds Bureau, 1970-1977. New York State Attorney General's Office, Chief Assistant to Special Prosecutor, 1977-1980. *Member:* The Association of the Bar of the City of New York; New York State (Member, Sections on: Commercial Law; Federal Litigation; Member, Complex Criminal Litigation) and American (Member; Section on Taxation, Committee on Civil and Criminal Tax Penalties; Section on Litigation, Complex Crimes Litigation Committee) Bar Associations. [With U.S. Marine Corps, 1967-1969]. (New York City Office). *PRACTICE AREAS:* Litigation; White Collar Criminal Defense; Corporate Counseling.

**MICHAEL LANGS,** born Newport, Rhode Island, May 25, 1940; admitted to bar, 1968, California. *Education:* University of Southern California (B.A., 1963); California Western University (J.D., 1967). Note and Comment Editor, California Western Law Review, 1966-1967. Law Clerk to Judge Albert Lee Stephens, Jr., U.S. District Court, Central District of California, 1967-1968. Deputy, Los Angeles County Counsel, 1968-1970. *Member:* Los Angeles County and American Bar Associations; The State Bar of California. *PRACTICE AREAS:* Structured Finance; Land Use; Workout and Development Law.

**JEROME L. LEVINE,** born Akron, Ohio, April 27, 1950; admitted to bar, 1975, New York; 1978, U.S. Tax Court. *Education:* University of Pennsylvania (B.S., 1971); New York University (J.D., 1974; LL.M., in Taxation, 1978). *Member:* The Association of the Bar of the City of New York (Member, Committee on Hess Memorial Lecture, 1991—; Member, Committee on Trusts, Estates and Surrogates, 1995—); New York State (Member, Trusts and Estates Section: Executive Committee, 1990—; Chairman, Committee on Charitable Organizations, 1990-1993; Vice Chairman, Committee on Practice and Ethics, 1993—) and American (Member, Real Property, Probate and Trust Law Section: Estate Planning and Drafting-

*(This Listing Continued)*

*LOEB & LOEB LLP, Los Angeles—Continued*

Charitable Giving Committee, 1993—) Bar Associations; Estate Planning Council of New York City. (New York City Office). *PRACTICE AREAS:* Estate Planning; Trusts Law; Estates Law.

**ANDREW E. LIPPMANN,** born New Hyde Park, New York, November 28, 1958; admitted to bar, 1984, New York. *Education:* State University of New York at Stony Brook (B.A., cum laude, 1980); University of Pennsylvania (J.D., 1983). Phi Delta Phi. *Member:* New York State and American (Member, Real Property Law Section) Bar Associations; New York County Lawyers Association. (New York City Office). *PRACTICE AREAS:* Real Estate Law.

**DON F. LIVORNESE,** born Nogales, Arizona, September 1, 1960; admitted to bar, 1986, California; 1989, District of Columbia; registered to practice before U.S. Patent and Trademark Office. *Education:* University of Colorado (B.S.M.E., 1982); George Washington University (J.D., with honors, 1986). *Member:* Century City and Los Angeles County Bar Associations; State Bar of California; The District of Columbia Bar. (Century City Office). *PRACTICE AREAS:* Patent; Trademark; Copyright; Intellectual Property Litigation; Antitrust; Civil Litigation.

**JEFFREY M. LOEB,** born Los Angeles, California, October 27, 1956; admitted to bar, 1981, California, U.S. District Court, Central, Southern, Northern and Eastern Districts of California; 1982, U.S. Court of Appeals, Ninth Circuit; 1985, U.S. Tax Court; 1987, U.S. Supreme Court. *Education:* University of California at Los Angeles and University of California, Santa Barbara (B.A., with honors, 1978); Hastings College of the Law, University of California (J.D., 1981). Member, Editorial Board, Hastings COMM-/ENT Law Journal, 1980. Author: "Unapparent Heirs," Los Angeles Lawyer (June, 1994); "Advising Corporate Fiduciaries Facing Potential Liability for Environmental Contamination," Los Angeles County Bar Association Annual Probate Symposium (April 1995); "Probate and Trust Administration Issues Created by a Recessionary Economy," 1993 Probate Symposium, Los Angeles County Bar Association. Deputy District Attorney, Los Angeles County, 1983-1985. *Member:* Los Angeles County Bar Association (Member, Sections on: Trial Lawyers; Trusts and Estate); State Bar of California. *PRACTICE AREAS:* Trusts Law; Estates Law and Related Litigation.

**STUART LUBITZ,** born Brooklyn, New York, December 17, 1934; admitted to bar, 1961, Florida and Michigan; 1964, California, U.S. Court of Appeals, Ninth Circuit and U.S. District Court, Northern District of California; 1965, U.S. District Court, Central District of California; 1978, U.S. District Court, Southern District of California; 1981, U.S. Court of Customs and Patent Appeals and U.S. Court of International Trade; 1982, U.S. Court of Appeals for the Federal Circuit; registered to practice before U.S. Patent and Trademark Office. *Education:* University of Florida (B.E.E., with high honors, 1957; B.M.E., with high honors, 1958); University of Florida; George Washington University (LL.B., wit h honors, 1961). Phi Eta Sigma; Sigma Tau; Phi Kappa Phi; Order of the Coif. Member, Board of Editors, George Washington Law Review, 1960-1961. Author: "Federal Courts-Venue-Transfer of Action To Another District," George Washington Law Review, March, 1961; "Repair and Reconstruction," George Washington Law Review, June, 1961; "Patent Jury Trials," Intellectual Property Journal of Japan. (1990). Adjunct Professor, Patent Law, Loyola University Law School, 1967-1981. Lecturer, Unfair Competition and ITC Proceedings, ALI and Los Angeles County Bar Association; Keidanreh (Japanese Association of Economic Organizations) and Intellectual Property Association of Japan, 1977-1988; American Conference Institute "Jury Trials in Patent and Other High Tech Litigation," 1995. *Member:* Los Angeles County and American Bar Associations; State Bar of California; American Intellectual Property Law Association. (Century City Office). *PRACTICE AREAS:* Trademark; Patent; Copyright.

**GARY D. MANN,** born 1950; admitted to bar, 1980, Indiana; 1982, Texas, U.S. Court of Appeals, Fifth and Federal Circuits and U.S. District Court, Northern District of Texas; 1992, California; registered to practice before U.S. Patent and Trademark Office. *Education:* United States Naval Academy (B.S., Physics, 1972); Graduate, U.S. Naval Nuclear Power School, 1973; Indiana University (J.D., cum laude, 1980). National Team Member, Moot Court Society. Associate Editor, Indiana Law Review, 1979-1980. *Member:* State Bar of Texas; The State Bar of California; American Bar Association. [Lieut., U.S. Navy, 1972-1977]. (Century City Office). *PRACTICE AREAS:* Patent; Trademark; Copyright; Litigation.

**WILLIAM J. MARLOW,** born Woodmere, N.Y., February 14, 1926; admitted to bar, 1953, New York. *Education:* Syracuse University (B.S., magna cum laude, 1949); Columbia University (J.D., 1952). Beta Gamma Sigma. Second District Legislative Chairman and Member, Legal Affairs Committee, American Advertising Federation. Member, Legal Affairs Committee, American Association of Advertising Agencies. Member, Legal Affairs Committee, Advertising Club of New York. *Member:* The Association of the Bar of the City of New York. (New York City Office). *PRACTICE AREAS:* Advertising Law; Corporate Law.

**MICHAEL A. MAYERSON,** born Dayton, Ohio, July 31, 1956; admitted to bar, 1981, California. *Education:* University of Pennsylvania (B.S., magna cum laude, 1978); Columbia University (J.D., 1981). Beta Gamma Sigma. Harlan Fiske Stone Scholar. *Member:* The State Bar of California. (Century City Office). *PRACTICE AREAS:* Entertainment Law.

**MALISSA HATHAWAY MCKEITH,** born Los Angeles, California, October 16, 1959; admitted to bar, 1983, California and U.S. District Court, Central District of California; 1987, U.S. Court of Appeals, Ninth Circuit. *Education:* University of California at Los Angeles (B.A., 1981); University of San Francisco School of Law (J.D., with honors, 1983); University of California, Riverside (Certificate, Hazardous Waste Management, 1991). Member, University of San Francisco Law Review, 1981-1983. Law Clerk to: Justice Harry Low, California Court of Appeal, 1982; Justice Stanley Mosk, California Supreme Court, 1983; Judge John L. Cole, Los Angeles Superior Court, 1983-1984. Vice President, Los Angeles Junior Chamber of Commerce, 1990-1991. Trustee, Los Angeles County Bar Association, 1992—. Member, Governors Committee on Military Base Reuse, 1993—. *Member:* State Bar of California (Member: Board of Governors, 1994—, Committee on Public Affairs, 1988-1991; Judicial Appointments Committee, 1987-1990; Vice-Chair, Judicial Evaluation Committee, 1989-1990; Member, Environmental Law Section); Women Lawyers Association of Los Angeles (Member, Board of Directors, 1989-1990); Foundation for Employment and Disability (Member, Board of Directors, 1990—). *PRACTICE AREAS:* Environmental Law.

**ROBERT A. MEYER,** born Brooklyn, New York, April 15, 1950; admitted to bar, 1975, California. *Education:* American University School of International Service (B.A., cum laude, 1972); Georgetown University (J.D., 1975). Editor, The American Criminal Law Review, 1974-1975. *Member:* Los Angeles County Bar Association; The State Bar of California; Association of Business Trial Lawyers (Member, Board of Governors, 1986-1988). *PRACTICE AREAS:* Litigation.

**STEPHEN R. MICK,** born Santa Clara, California, January 1, 1963; admitted to bar, 1987, California; 1988, U.S. District Court, Central District of California; 1989, U.S. District Court, Northern District of California; 1993, U.S. Court of Appeals, Fourth and Federal Circuits and U.S. District Court, Southern District of California; 1994, U.S. District Court, District of Arizona; registered to practice before U.S. Patent and Trademark Office. *Education:* Rensselaer Polytechnic Institute (B.S., magna cum laude, 1984); University of Pennsylvania (J.D., magna cum laude, 1987). Order of the Coif. Author: "Applying the Merger Doctrine to the Copyright of Computer Software," 37 ASCAP Copyright Law Symposium No. 173 (1990). *Member:* State Bar of California. *PRACTICE AREAS:* Intellectual Property; Litigation.

**CHARLES H. MILLER,** born Southampton, New York, January 25, 1928; admitted to bar, 1952, New York; 1954, Republic of Korea; 1958, U.S. District Court, Southern and Eastern Districts of New York and U.S. Court of Appeals, Second Circuit; 1969, U.S. Supreme Court; 1972, U.S. Court of Appeals, Third Circuit; 1973, U.S. Court of Appeals, Seventh Circuit. *Education:* Syracuse University (B.A., 1949); Columbia University (LL.B., 1952). Author: "Special Damage Considerations in Class Action Situations," Antitrust Law Journal, Summer, 1980. Section Leader, 1976-1979; Faculty and Program Co-Chairman, 1978-1980, The Trial of an Antitrust Case, Columbia Law School Continuing Legal Education Program. Assistant Counsel, Waterfront Commission of New York Harbor, 1954-1956. Assistant U.S. Attorney, Southern District of New York, 1956-1958. Certified as Arbitrator and Early Neutral Evaluator, Eastern District of New York and as Mediator, Southern District of New York. *Member:* The Association of the Bar of the City of New York (Member, Committee on Trade Regulation, 1978-1981); New York State (Chairman, Federal Courts Committee, 1976-1979; Member, Finance Committee, 1979-1982) and American (Member, Litigation Section and Private Antitrust Litigation Committee) Bar Associations; Federal Bar Council. Fellow, American Bar Foundation. (New York City Office). *PRACTICE AREAS:* Litigation.

**MALCOLM L. MIMMS, JR.,** born Nashville, Tennessee, April 2, 1953; admitted to bar, 1978, Tennessee. *Education:* Rhodes College (B.A., with distinction, 1975); Vanderbilt University (J.D., 1978). Order of the Coif. Author: "Reversion and Derivative Works Under the Copyright Acts of 1909 and 1976," 25 New York Law School Law Review 595, 1980. Ad-

*(This Listing Continued)*

junct Professor, Entertainment Law, Belmont College, 1987-1988. *Member:* Tennessee (Chairman, Copyright, Entertainment, Sport and Literary Property Law Section, 1985-1986) and American (Member, Forum Committee on Entertainment and Sports Industries) Bar Associations. (Nashville, Tennessee Office). *PRACTICE AREAS:* Entertainment Law; Copyright and Trademark Law.

**DOUGLAS E. MIRELL,** born Los Angeles, California, July 1, 1956; admitted to bar, 1980, California. *Education:* Claremont Men's College (B.A., cum laude, 1977); University of California at Davis (J.D., 1980). Topical Volume Editor, University of California at Davis Law Review, 1979-1980. Extern Clerk, Hon. Coleman A. Blease, Associate Justice, California Court of Appeal, Third Appellate District, 1980. Adjunct Professor of Law, Constitutional Law II (First Amendment), University of Southern California Law Center, Spring 1996. Author: "Can O.J. Simpson Profit From the Sale of His Book?" Entertainment Law Reporter, Vol. 16, No. 8, Jan. 1995; "The Latest Threat to Free Speech: California's Proposed Bar Rules," Communications Lawyer, Summer 1995; "The Trial of the Century': Some Implications for the Next Millennium," Entertainment, Publishing and the Arts Handbook, 1995-1996 Edition. *Member:* Los Angeles County (Member, 1982—; Chair, 1984-1985 and Continuing Legal Education Articles Coordinator, 1983-1984, Los Angeles Lawyer Editorial Board; Member: Individual Rights Section Executive Committee, 1985—; Bench Bar Media Committee, 1980—) and American (Member: Individual Rights and Responsibilities Section; Litigation Section; Forum Committee on Communications Law; Section of Intellectual Property Law; Forum on Franchising) Bar Associations; The State Bar of California (Member: Litigation Section; Intellectual Property Section); Association of Business Trial Lawyers. *PRACTICE AREAS:* Litigation; Constitutional and Civil Rights Law; Media Law; Entertainment; Intellectual Property and Franchising Litigation; Appellate Practice. *Email:* dmirelln@reach.com

**DANIEL G. MURPHY,** born Chicago, Illinois, May 22, 1952; admitted to bar, 1983, New York; 1989, California. *Education:* Shimer College (B.A., 1975); Western Washington University (M.A., 1978); Vermont Law (J.D., 1981). Head Notes Editor, Vermont Law Review, 1979-1981. *Member:* The Association of the Bar of the City of New York; Los Angeles County and American Bar Associations; State Bar of California. *PRACTICE AREAS:* Litigation.

**ANTHONY MURRAY,** born Los Angeles, California, April 25, 1937; admitted to bar, 1965, California. *Education:* California State University, Los Angeles; Pasadena City College; Loyola University School of Law (J.D., 1964). Alpha Sigma Nu; Phi Alpha Delta. Recipient, 1982 Distinguished Achievement Award by Alumni Association, Loyola Law School. Associate Professor in Constitutional Law, Los Angeles State College, 1968. Adjunct Professor, Civil Trial Advocacy, Loyola Law School, 1979-1986. Member, California Judicial Council, 1983-1985. *Member:* Los Angeles County and American Bar Associations; The State Bar of California (President, 1982-1983; Member, Board of Governors, 1980-1983; Chair, Executive Committee, Criminal Law Section, 1978-1979; Member: Commission on Judicial Nominees Evaluations, 1978-1979; Disciplinary Board, 1975-1978; Member and Chair, Local Administrative Committee No. 36, 1970-1973). Fellow: American College of Trial Lawyers (Chair, State Committee, 1994); Member, Board of Regents, 1995—); American Bar Foundation. *PRACTICE AREAS:* Civil, Criminal and Commercial Litigation.

**DAVID C. NELSON,** born Glendale, California, December 25, 1959; admitted to bar, 1986, California; 1987, U.S. District Court, Central District of California. *Education:* Pacific Union College (B.S., 1982); Georgetown University (J.D., 1986). *Member:* Los Angeles County Bar Association (Member, Probate and Trust Section); The State Bar of California. *PRACTICE AREAS:* Trusts and Estates Law and Related Litigation.

**SUSAN V. NOONOO,** born Philadelphia, Pennsylvania, November 10, 1949; admitted to bar, 1975, Pennsylvania; 1982, California. *Education:* Bucknell University (B.A., 1971); Temple University School of Law (J.D., 1975). *Member:* Beverly Hills, Los Angeles County, Pennsylvania State and American Bar Associations; State Bar of California. *PRACTICE AREAS:* Real Estate Law; Workout Law.

**DIANE B. PAUL,** born Minneapolis, Minnesota, December 21, 1947; admitted to bar, 1982, California. *Education:* Rice University (B.A., 1970); University of Southern California (J.D., 1982). Member, 1980-1981 and Editor-in-Chief, 1981-1982, Southern California Law Review. Clerk, Honorable Dorothy Nelson, U.S. Court of Appeals, Ninth Circuit, 1982-1983. *Member:* State Bar of California; American Bar Association (Member, Litigation Section, 1988-1992). *PRACTICE AREAS:* Litigation; Bankruptcy.

**ALDEN G. PEARCE, (A P.C.),** born East Orange, New Jersey, September 11, 1924; admitted to bar, 1950, California. *Education:* University of
*(This Listing Continued)*

California at Los Angeles (A.B., 1946); Duke University (LL.B., 1949). Phi Delta Phi. *Member:* Los Angeles County and American Bar Associations; The State Bar of California; Chancery Club. *PRACTICE AREAS:* Corporate Law.

**ROBERT L. PELZ,** born New York, N.Y., November 18, 1918; admitted to bar, 1942, New York. *Education:* Columbia University (B.A., 1939; LL.B., 1942). Phi Beta Kappa. Editor, Columbia Law Review, 1940-1942. Member of Staff, War Crimes Trials, Manila, 1945-1946. Treasurer, 1980-1981, Chairman, Board of Trustees, 1981-1983, Vice President, 1983-1986, American Jewish Committee. Trustee, Federation of Jewish Philanthropies of New York, 1967-1986. Chairman, Board of Directors, FOJP Service Corporation, 1985-1992. Chairman, Commentary Magazine, 1992—. *Member:* The Association of the Bar of the City of New York; New York State and American Bar Associations. (New York City Office). *PRACTICE AREAS:* Corporate Law.

**MARTIN R. POLLNER,** born New York, N.Y., December 17, 1934; admitted to bar, 1960, New York; 1965, U.S. District Court, Eastern and Southern Districts of New York; 1972, District of Columbia; 1973, U.S. Court of International Trade; 1976, U.S. Tax Court; 1977, Florida. *Education:* City College of the City University of New York (A.B., 1957); Brooklyn Law School (LL.B., 1960). Member, Brooklyn Law Review, 1959-1960. Author: "Attorney General Robert F. Kennedy's Program to Combat Organized Crime," B'klyn. Law Review, 1963. Attorney, Office of Deputy Attorney General, U.S. Department of Justice, 1960-1962. Assistant U.S. Attorney, Eastern District of New York, 1963-1966. Director, Office of Law Enforcement, U.S. Treasury Department, 1970-1973. Deputy Assistant Secretary of the Treasury, 1972-1973. U.S. Representative, International Narcotics Control Board of United Nations, 1973-1976. *Member:* The Association of the Bar of the City of New York; American Bar Association (Special Assistant to Chairman, Criminal Law Section, 1969-1970); The Florida Bar; New York State District Attorneys' Association; National District Attorney's Association. (New York City Office). *PRACTICE AREAS:* Litigation; White Collar Criminal Defense; Corporate Counseling.

**GUENDALINA PONTI,** born Rome, Italy, December 5, 1948; admitted to bar, 1979, Rome, Italy; 1985, Albo Degli Avvocati of Rome (Not admitted in the United States). *Education:* University of Rome (Dr. of Jurisprudence, magna cum laude, 1972). Guest Professor, "Commercial Navigation Law," University of Rome, 1972-1975. *Member:* American Film Market Association; Italian Association of European Council Jurists. (Rome, Italy Office). *LANGUAGES:* English, French and Italian. *PRACTICE AREAS:* Corporate Law; Entertainment Law.

**SHIRLEY M. PRICE,** born Frankfurt, Germany, November 8, 1946; admitted to bar, 1983, California. *Education:* University of California at Santa Barbara (B.A., with high honors, 1968); University of Southern California (J.D., 1983). Phi Beta Kappa. Member, Southern California Law Review, 1981-1983. Editor-in-Chief: Computer Law Journal, 1982-1983; Major Tax Planning, 1982-1983. Author: "Pros and Cons of Appellate Settlement Conferences," Los Angeles Lawyer, June, 1984. Judicial Extern Clerk, Justice Earl Johnson, Jr., California Court of Appeal, Second Appellate District, 1983. *Member:* Los Angeles County Bar Association; State Bar of California; Women Lawyers Association of Los Angeles. *LANGUAGES:* French and Russian. *PRACTICE AREAS:* Corporate; Banking; Finance Law.

**ROBERT S. REICH,** born New York, N.Y., August 14, 1945; admitted to bar, 1971, New York. *Education:* University of Pennsylvania (B.S., 1967); New York University (J.D., 1970). Member, Order of the Coif. Editor, New York University Law Review, 1969-1970. *Member:* American Bar Association. (New York City Office). *PRACTICE AREAS:* Sports and Sponsorship Law; Entertainment Law.

**VICTOR A. RODGERS,** born 1958; admitted to bar, 1981, California; 1982, U.S. District Court, Central District of California; 1983, U.S. District Court, Northern District of California. *Education:* University of Southern California (B.S., 1978); Boalt Hall School of Law, University of California (J.D., 1981). *Member:* Los Angeles County Bar Association; State Bar of California. *PRACTICE AREAS:* Trademark; Patent; Copyright.

**THOMAS E. ROHLF, (A P.C.),** born Oakland, California, January 10, 1946; admitted to bar, 1971, California. *Education:* Stanford University (A.B., 1967; J.D., 1970). *Member:* Los Angeles County and American Bar Associations; The State Bar of California. *PRACTICE AREAS:* Corporate Law.

**ANDREW M. ROSS,** born Freeport, New York, May 28, 1955; admitted to bar, 1981, New York and U.S. District Court, Southern District of New York; 1982, California. *Education:* State University of New York at
*(This Listing Continued)*

## LOEB & LOEB LLP, Los Angeles—Continued

Albany (B.A., summa cum laude, 1977); Stanford University (J.D., 1980). Phi Beta Kappa. Associate Editor, Stanford Law Review, 1979-1980. *Member:* New York State Bar Association. (New York City Office). *PRACTICE AREAS:* Corporate Law; Securities Law.

**JONATHAN P. ROTH,** born 1962; admitted to bar, 1988, California. *Education:* University of California at Los Angeles (B.A.); Loyola University of Los Angeles (J.D., 1988).

**STANFORD K. RUBIN, (A P.C.),** born Chicago, Illinois, March 20, 1937; admitted to bar, 1962, California. *Education:* University of Illinois (B.A., 1958); Stanford University (LL.B., 1961). National Chairman, The Arthritis Foundation, 1984-1986. *Member:* Los Angeles County and American Bar Associations; The State Bar of California. (Century City Office). *PRACTICE AREAS:* Trusts and Estates.

**STEPHEN L. SALTZMAN,** born New York, N.Y., May 25, 1960; admitted to bar, 1986, California and U.S. District Court, Central District of California. *Education:* Georgetown University (B.S., magna cum laude, 1982); Columbia University (J.D., 1986). Phi Beta Kappa; Sigma Delta Phi. Harlan Fiske Stone Scholar. Recipient, E.B. Convers Prize. Administrative Editor, Journal of Law and Social Problems, 1985-1986. Law Clerk to the Hon. Harry L. Hupp, U.S. District Court, Central District of California, 1986-1987. *Member:* State Bar of California; American Bar Association (Member, Sections on: International Law and Practice; Corporation, Banking and Business Law). (Century City Office). *LANGUAGES:* German and Spanish.

**FREDRIC M. SANDERS,** born New York, N.Y., January 10, 1941; admitted to bar, 1965, New York. *Education:* Queens College of the City University of New York (B.A., 1961); Harvard University (LL.B., 1964). Phi Beta Kappa. *Member:* The Association of the Bar of the City of New York; New York State Bar Association (Member, Committee on Taxation, 1972—). (New York City Office). *PRACTICE AREAS:* Taxation.

**DAVID M. SATNICK,** born Hicksville, New York, October 31, 1953; admitted to bar, 1979, New York; 1991, U.S. District Court, Southern and Eastern Districts of New York; 1992, U.S. Tax Court and U.S. Court of International Trade. *Education:* University of Colorado (B.A., 1975); Hofstra University (J.D., with honors, 1978); New York University. Contracts Law Fellow, Hofstra University School of Law, 1977. Assistant District Attorney, New York County District Attorney's Office, 1978-1981. *Member:* The Association of the Bar of the City of New York; American Bar Association. (New York City Office). *PRACTICE AREAS:* Litigation; Workout/Insolvency; Entertainment.

**DAVID S. SCHAEFER,** born Brooklyn, New York, November 27, 1955; admitted to bar, 1982, New York. *Education:* Massachusetts Institute of Technology (B.S., 1978); New York University (J.D., 1981). *Member:* New York State and American Bar Associations. (New York City Office). *PRACTICE AREAS:* Banking; Securities; Finance.

**P. GREGORY SCHWED,** born New York, N.Y., February 24, 1952; admitted to bar, 1977, New York; U.S. Court of Appeals, Second Circuit; U.S. District Court, Southern, Eastern, Western and Northern Districts of New York. *Education:* Princeton University (B.A., summa cum laude, 1973); Columbia University (J.D., 1976). Phi Beta Kappa. Harlan Fiske Stone Scholar. Co-author: "Creditors Rights Handbook," Clark Boardman Co., 2nd. Ed., 1982. *Member:* The Association of the Bar of the City of New York; New York State Bar Association. (New York City Office). *PRACTICE AREAS:* Bankruptcy and Creditors' Rights; General Commercial Litigation.

**PAUL A. SCZUDLO,** born Fairbanks, Alaska, March 5, 1955; admitted to bar, 1980, California; 1982, U.S. Tax Court; 1990, U.S. District Court, Central District of California. *Education:* Yale University (B.A., cum laude, 1977); Harvard University (1979-1980); Boalt Hall School of Law, University of California (J.D., 1980). *Member:* Los Angeles County (Vice Chair, 1995—, Section on Taxation, Chair, 1992-1993; Member, Foreign Tax Committee), American (Member, Sections on Taxation; International Law) and International (Member, Business Law Section) Bar Associations; The State Bar of California (Member, Sections on: Taxation; International Law; Chair, International Tax Committee). *PRACTICE AREAS:* Taxation; International Law.

**PETER S. SELVIN,** born Los Angeles, California, December 1, 1953; admitted to bar, 1980, California. *Education:* University of California at San Diego (B.A., with highest honors, 1975); University of Stirling, Scotland and University of Chicago (M.A., 1976); University of California at

*(This Listing Continued)*

CAA920B

Los Angeles (J.D., 1980). Extern Law Clerk to Hon. Otto M. Kaus, Presiding Justice, California Court of Appeals, Second District, Division 5, 1979. Panelist: "Legal Liability of Executives and Their Corporations," The Directors' Roundtable (September 1994); "Preparing and Examining Expert Witnesses in Civil Litigation," Continuing Education of the Bar (September-October 1994); Publications: "An Overview of Lender Liability Litigation," International Commercial Litigation, December, 1995; "Local Franchise Regulation and Investment in the U.S.," International Financial Law Review, September, 1995; "California Court Holds That Travelers Insurance Acted Within Its Rights Under Construction Loan Assessment," Lender Liability Law Report, Vol. 7, No. 9 (Nov., 1993); "The Strange Case of Alienage Jurisdiction," Beverly Hills Bar Journal, Vol. 27, No. 4 (Fall 1993); "Kim v. Sumitomo Bank: More Solace for California's Construction Lenders," California Civil Litigation Reporter, Vol. 15, No. 7 (November 1993); "The Enforceability of Agreements to Settle Litigation: C.C.P. §664.6 Revisited," C.E.B. Civil Litigation Reporter, Vol. 14, No. 1 (February 1992); "Landlord Tort Liability for Criminal Attacks on Tenants: Developments Since Kline," 9 Real Estate Law Journal 311, 1981. *Member:* Los Angeles County and American Bar Associations; The State Bar of California (Member, Committee on Administration of Justice, 1992-1993; Co-Chair, Litigation Section Committee on Technology, 1992-1993). *PRACTICE AREAS:* Litigation.

**DAVID B. SHONTZ,** born Sacramento, California, January 9, 1956; admitted to bar, 1984, California; 1986, New York; U.S. Court of Appeals, Second Circuit; U.S. District Court, Southern and Eastern Districts of New York. *Education:* University of California at Berkeley (B.A., 1981); Hastings College of the Law (J.D., magna cum laude, 1984). Order of the Coif. Editor, Hastings Law Journal, 1983-1984. Author: "Foreign Owners' Rights are Restored by GATT to Public Domain Works," National Law Journal, Feb 20, 1995. Extern Law Clerk to the Hon. Joseph Grodin, Associate Justice, California Supreme Court, 1983. Law Clerk to the Hon. George C. Pratt, U.S. Court of Appeals, Second Circuit, 1984-1986. *Member:* New York State Bar Association; State Bar of California. (New York City Office). *PRACTICE AREAS:* Litigation; Commercial; Intellectual Property; Employment.

**CLARK B. SIEGEL,** born Tehran, Iran, February 7, 1958; admitted to bar, 1984, California. *Education:* Stanford University (A.B., with distinction, 1980); University of Chicago (J.D., with highest honors, 1984). Phi Beta Kappa; Order of the Coif. Member, University of Chicago Law Review, 1983-1984. *Member:* State Bar of California. (Century City Office). *LANGUAGES:* French and Spanish. *PRACTICE AREAS:* Entertainment Law; Banking Law; Corporate Law; Creditors Rights; Interactive and Multi-Media Technology.

**DAVID M. SIMON,** born 1957; admitted to bar, 1982, California and U.S. District Court, Central and Northern Districts of California; 1987, U.S. Court of Appeals for the Eighth and Federal Circuits; 1994, U.S. District Court, Southern District of California; registered to practice before U.S. Patent and Trademark Office. *Education:* Massachusetts Institute of Technology (S.B., 1979); Georgetown University (J.D., cum laude, 1982). Sigma Xi. Author: "FTC V. SGPM: Extraterritorial Service of Administrative Subpoenas," 13 Law and Policy in International Business 847, 1981. *Member:* State Bar of California. (Century City Office). *PRACTICE AREAS:* Trademark; Patent; Copyright; Intellectual Property.

**MICHAEL F. SITZER,** born London, England, August 2, 1957; admitted to bar, 1982, California. *Education:* Stanford University (B.A., 1978); University of Southern California (J.D., 1981). First Place, 1981 Nathan Burkan Copyright Competition. Notes and Articles Editor, Southern California Law Review, 1980-1981. *Member:* Los Angeles County Bar Association (Membership Chairperson, Prejudgment Remedies Section Executive Committee, 1986-1987); State Bar of California (Member, Pre-Judgement Remedies Section). *LANGUAGES:* German. *PRACTICE AREAS:* Insolvency Law; Creditors Rights.

**LEE N. STEINER,** born Newark, New Jersey, November 10, 1922; admitted to bar, 1950, New York. *Education:* Lafayette College (A.B., 1944); University of Pennsylvania (LL.B., 1949). Tau Kappa Alpha. Trustee, Carnegie Hall Cousteau Society, 1971. Special Counsel to United Nations on Film, 1976. Member, Order of Merit, Republic of Italy. *Member:* The Association of the Bar of the City of New York; American Bar Association (Member, Committee on Entertainment and Sports). (New York City Office). *PRACTICE AREAS:* Entertainment Law.

**REBEL R. STEINER, JR.,** born Birmingham, Alabama, August 2, 1960; admitted to bar, 1986, California. *Education:* University of Alabama (B.A., cum laude, 1982); Yale Law School (J.D., 1985). Phi Beta Kappa; Omicron Delta Kappa. Member: Jasons; Mortar Board. *Member:* Century

*(This Listing Continued)*

City Bar Association; State Bar of California. (Century City Office). *PRACTICE AREAS:* Entertainment Law.

**BRUCE M. STIGLITZ, (A P.C.),** born Detroit, Michigan, April 25, 1935; admitted to bar, 1963, New York; 1964, California. *Education:* University of Michigan (B.B.A., 1957; J.D., 1960); Harvard University (LL.M., 1961). Editor, Michigan Law Review, 1959-1960. Co-author: "Taxation of the Motion Picture Industry," BNA Tax Management, Inc., 1978. Lecturer: University of Southern California Law Center, 1981; UCLA Entertainment Tax Institute. *Member:* The State Bar of California. (Certified Specialist, Taxation Law, The State Bar of California Board of Legal Specialization). *PRACTICE AREAS:* Taxation of Entertainment Industry; International Taxation; Estate Planning.

**RICHARD P. STREICHER,** born New York, N.Y., July 10, 1931; admitted to bar, 1955, New York. *Education:* New York University (B.S., 1952); Columbia University (LL.B., 1955). Editor, Columbia Law Review, 1954-1955. Contributing Editor and Author: "Raising Capital-An Introduction to the Securities Law for Non-Public Companies," The New York Corporate Handbook, New York State Bar Association, 1983. *Member:* The Association of the Bar of the City of New York (Member, Committee on Corporation Law, 1971-1974); New York State and American Bar Associations. (New York City Office). *PRACTICE AREAS:* Corporate Law; Securities Law.

**JAMES D. TAYLOR,** born 1957; admitted to bar, 1988, New York. *Education:* University of Illinois (B.S.); Brooklyn Law School (J.D., 1988). (New York City Office). *PRACTICE AREAS:* Entertainment.

**RAYMOND W. THOMAS,** born Pasadena, California, July 17, 1950; admitted to bar, 1976, California. *Education:* University of California at Santa Barbara (B.A., magna cum laude, 1972); Yale Law School (J.D., 1976). *Member:* Los Angeles County (Member, Labor Law Section) and American (Member, Labor and Employment Law Section) Bar Associations; State Bar of California. (Century City Office). *PRACTICE AREAS:* Labor and Employment Law.

**ROBERT N. TREIMAN,** born Los Angeles, California, June 11, 1962; admitted to bar, 1988, California and U.S. District Court, Central District of California. *Education:* Williams College (B.A., cum laude, 1984); University of California at Los Angeles (J.D., 1987). Order of the Coif. Editor, UCLA Law Review, 1986-1987. Author: Comment, "Inter-lawyer Communication and the Prevention of Client Fraud: A Look Back at O.P.M.," 34 UCLA Law Review 925, 1987. Law Clerk to Judge Wm. Mathew Byrne, Central District of California, 1987-1988. *Member:* State Bar of California.

**WILLIAM P. WASSERMAN, (A P.C.),** born Los Angeles, California, September 13, 1945; admitted to bar, 1971, California and U.S. Tax Court. *Education:* University of California at Berkeley (B.A., 1967); Hastings College of Law, University of California (J.D., 1970). Order of the Coif; Phi Alpha Delta. Member, Editorial Board, Hastings Law Journal, 1969-1970. Member, Editorial Board, Warren, Gorham & Lamont's "Federal Tax Annual on Real Estate," 1981-1983. Member, Editorial Advisory Board, BNA Tax Management, Inc., 1984—. Member, Editorial Advisory Board, Thompson Publishing Group's "Real Estate Taxation," 1984-1989. Member, Planning Committee, California Continuing Education of the Bar's "Annual Institute on Advanced Tax Planning for Real Property Transactions," 1981—. Lecturer: New York University's "40th Annual Institute on Federal Taxation," 1981; University of Southern California Law Center, "35th Annual Tax Institute," 1983; The 21st and 23rd Annual Southern Federal Tax Institute, 1986, 1988; University of Chicago Law School's, "40th Annual Federal Tax Conference," 1987. *Member:* Los Angeles County and American (Chairman, Real Estate Tax Problems Committee, Section of Taxation, 1985-1987) Bar Associations; The State Bar of California. Fellow, American College of Tax Counsel. (Certified Specialist, Taxation Law, The State Bar of California Board of Legal Specialization). *PRACTICE AREAS:* Taxation.

**RONALD WEINSTEIN, (A P.C.),** born Vilna, Poland, June 4, 1945; admitted to bar, 1970, Michigan; 1972, California. *Education:* Princeton University (A.B., cum laude, 1966); Yale University (LL.B., 1969). *Member:* Los Angeles County Bar Association; The State Bar of California. *PRACTICE AREAS:* Insolvency Law; Workout Law; Real Estate Law.

**BRUCE J. WEXLER,** born New York, N.Y., February 15, 1955; admitted to bar, 1980, Florida and New York. *Education:* Syracuse University (B.A., magna cum laude, 1975); St. John's University (J.D., 1979); New York University (LL.M., Taxation, 1982). *Member:* New York State and American Bar Associations; The Florida Bar. (New York City Office). *PRACTICE AREAS:* Trusts and Estates; Tax; Corporate.

*(This Listing Continued)*

**REBECCA E. WHITE,** born Newark, New Jersey, September 14, 1965; admitted to bar, 1988, New Jersey and U.S. District Court, District of New Jersey; 1989, New York and U.S. District Court, Southern and Eastern Districts of New York. *Education:* Hull College; New York University; Benjamin N. Cardoza School of Law, Yeshiva University (J.D., 1988). *Member:* New York County and American Bar Associations; New York Women's Bar Association (Member, Committees on: Litigation; Battered Women's Committees). (New York City Office). *LANGUAGES:* French. *PRACTICE AREAS:* Commercial Litigation; White Collar Criminal Defense Law.

**ALAN W. WILKEN,** born Tacoma, Washington, September 18, 1947; admitted to bar, 1974, Alaska; 1975, California. *Education:* Amherst College (A.B., 1969); University of California at Los Angeles (J.D., 1973). Managing Editor, UCLA-Alaska Law Review, 1973. *Member:* Los Angeles County and Alaska Bar Associations; The State Bar of California. *PRACTICE AREAS:* Litigation.

**ROGER R. WISE,** born Decatur, Illinois, 1956; admitted to bar, 1984, Illinois and U.S. District Court, Northern District of Illinois; 1987, California; U.S. District Courts, Central, Eastern and Northern Districts of California; U.S. Court of Appeals, for the Federal Circuit; registered to practice before U.S. Patent and Trademark Office. *Education:* University of Illinois (B.S.E.E., 1978); The John Marshall Law School (J.D., with distinction, 1984). *Member:* State Bar of California; American Intellectual Property Law Association. (Century City Office). *PRACTICE AREAS:* Trademark; Patent; Copyright.

**SUSAN A. WOLF,** born St. Louis, Missouri, September 15, 1956; admitted to bar, 1981, California. *Education:* University of Michigan (B.G.S., 1978; J.D., 1981). *Member:* Los Angeles County Bar Association; The State Bar of California (Member, Business Law Section). *PRACTICE AREAS:* Corporate, Banking and Finance Law.

**WILLIAM S. WOODS, II,** born Lynwood, California, March 29, 1955; admitted to bar, 1980, California; 1981, U.S. Tax Court; 1983, U.S. Claims Court, U.S. District Court, Central District of California and U.S. Court of Appeals, Ninth Circuit. *Education:* Claremont McKenna College (B.A., 1977); University of California at Los Angeles (J.D., 1980); New York University (LL.M., in Taxation, 1982). *Member:* Beverly Hills (Member, Taxation Section), Los Angeles County (Member, Executive Committee, Taxation Section, 1983-1985, 1986-1989; Chair, Income Tax Committee, 1987-1988; Chair, Pass-Through Entities Committee, 1988-1989) and American (Member, Taxation Section) Bar Associations; State Bar of California (Chair, Pass-Through Entities Committee, Taxation Section, 1990-1992). *PRACTICE AREAS:* Taxation.

**RICHARD H. ZAITLEN,** born 1946; admitted to bar, 1973, District of Columbia; 1974, California and U.S. Court of International Trade; 1974-1982, U.S. Court of Customs and Patent Appeals; registered to practice before U.S. Patent and Trademark Office. *Education:* Purdue University (B.S.Ch.E., 1969); George Washington University (J.D., with honors, 1973). Examiner, U.S. Patent Office, 1969-1974. Co-Author: "Preliminary Injunctive Relief in Patent Cases," Los Angeles Lawyer, October 1990. *Member:* Beverly Hills and Los Angeles County (President, Intellectual Property Committee, 1984—) Bar Associations; State Bar of California; The District of Columbia Bar; American Intellectual Property Law Association; United States Trademark Association. (Century City Office). *PRACTICE AREAS:* Trademark; Patent; Copyright.

**MICHAEL P. ZWEIG,** born New York, N.Y., June 5, 1952; admitted to bar, 1978, New York. *Education:* Cornell University (A.B., 1974); New York University (J.D., 1977). Member, Annual Survey of American Law, 1976-1977. Special Counsel, New York State Assembly Committee on Environmental Conservation and Task Force on Toxic Substances, 1980-1981. Editor of "Legal Perspectives" in the Delaney Report. *Member:* The Association of the Bar of the City of New York (Member, Environmental Law Committee, 1982-1984); New York County Lawyers Association. (New York City Office). *PRACTICE AREAS:* Commercial and Intellectual Property Litigation; Employment Law.

*OF COUNSEL*

**HAROLD D. BERKOWITZ, (A P.C.),** born New York, N.Y., February 9, 1918; admitted to bar, 1942, New York; 1944, California. *Education:* College of the City of New York (B.S., 1938); New York University (LL.B., 1942). *Member:* Beverly Hills, Los Angeles County, Hollywood and American Bar Associations; The State Bar of California; Los Angeles Copyright Society. (Century City Office). *PRACTICE AREAS:* Entertainment Law.

**JAMES R. BIRNBERG,** born New York, N.Y., January 15, 1939; admitted to bar, 1966, California; 1973, U.S. Supreme Court. *Education:* Po-

*(This Listing Continued)*

*LOEB & LOEB LLP, Los Angeles—Continued*

mona College (B.A., magna cum laude, 1961); Stanford University (A.M., 1962); University of California at Berkeley (J.D., 1965). Phi Beta Kappa. Recipient: Woodrow Wilson Fellowship, 1961-1962; V. Judson Klein Award. Assistant Inheritance Tax Attorney, 1966-1980. *Member:* Los Angeles County Bar Association (Member: Sections on Taxation and Probate, 1968—; Committee on Legislative Monitoring, 1982-1990; Executive Committee, 1982—; Bioethics Committee, 1985-1988); The State Bar of California (Member, Sections on: Taxation; Estate Planning, Trust and Probate; Vice Chairman, Death and Gift Tax Committee, 1979-1980; Member: Executive Committee, Tax Section, 1979-1983; Executive Committee, Estate Planning, Trust and Probate Section, 1991—). Fellow, American College of Trust and Estate Counsel. *PRACTICE AREAS:* Trusts and Estates.

**MORTON R. FIELD,** born 1923; admitted to bar, 1949, Illinois; 1951, California; 1957, District of Columbia and U.S. Supreme Court. *Education:* University of Illinois (B.A., 1946); De Paul University (LL.B., 1948). Nu Beta Epsilon. Attorney-Advisor, Securities and Exchange Commission, 1948-1952. *Member:* Los Angeles County, Illinois State, Federal and American Bar Associations; State Bar of California; District of Columbia Bar.

**HARRY FIRST,** born Philadelphia, Pennsylvania, January 17, 1945; admitted to bar, 1969, Pennsylvania; 1979, New York. *Education:* University of Pennsylvania (B.A., 1966; J.D., 1969). Phi Beta Kappa; Order of the Coif. Author: "Business Crime," Cases and Materials, 1990. Co-author: with L. Schwartz & J. Flynn: "Free Enterprise and Economic Organization: Antitrust," 1983; "Free Enterprise and Economic Organization: Government Regulation," Foundation Press, 1985. Professor of Law, New York University School of Law, 1976—. Visiting Professor, Sophia University Faculty of Law, Tokyo, Japan, 1983-1984. *Member:* The Association of the Bar of the City of New York. (New York City Office). *PRACTICE AREAS:* Antitrust Law; White Collar Crime Law.

**HOWARD I. FRIEDMAN, (A P.C.),** born Chicago, Illinois, April 21, 1928; admitted to bar, 1952, Oklahoma; 1955, California. *Education:* University of Oklahoma (B.A., 1948); University of Chicago (M.A., 1949); Yale University (LL.B., 1952). Note Editor, Yale Law Journal, 1951-1952. Teaching Fellow, Stanford University Law School, 1954. Deputy Attorney General, State of California, 1955-1957. Chairman, Board of Overseers, California School of Hebrew Union College, 1976-1981. President, American Jewish Committee, 1983-1986. Vice Chairman, Board of Governors, Hebrew Union College, 1978—. *Member:* Los Angeles County and American Bar Associations; The State Bar of California. Fellow, American College of Trial Lawyers. *PRACTICE AREAS:* Litigation; Arbitration; Mediation.

**MARVIN GREENE, (A P.C.),** born San Francisco, California, June 23, 1924; admitted to bar, 1951, California. *Education:* Stanford University (B.A., 1947); University of San Francisco (J.D., 1951). Phi Alpha Delta. Associate Reporter, Securities Acts Amendments of 1964, American Law Institute, 1964. Member, Board of Counsellors, University of San Francisco Law School, 1978-1994. Member, Corporate and Securities Law Advisory Committee, Practicing Law Institute. Arbitrator, National Association of Securities Dealers, Inc., 1972—. *Member:* Los Angeles County (Chairman, Business and Corporations Law Section, 1969-1971; service recognized by creation of "Annual Marvin Greene Distinguished Service Award," 1993) and American (Member, Committee on Federal Regulation of Securities Section of Corporation, Banking and Business Law, 1964-1994) Bar Associations; The State Bar of California. [Major, USAR]. *PRACTICE AREAS:* Corporate Law; Securities Law; Arbitration.

**ABRAHAM S. GUTERMAN,** born Scranton, Pennsylvania, August 10, 1912; admitted to bar, 1937, New York. *Education:* Yeshiva College (A.B., 1933); Harvard Law School (LL.B., 1936). Awarded Doctor of Humane Letters (Hon.) by Yeshiva University, 1982. Member, Scott Law Club. Editor, Harvard Law Review, 1935-1936. Member of Faculty, New York University Institute on Federal Taxation, 1944—. Member, Board of Trustees, Yeshiva University, 1971. Member of Board of Trustees, Benjamin N. Cardozo Law School, 1976. *Member:* The Association of the Bar of the City of New York; New York State and American Bar Associations; New York County Lawyers Association (Member, Committee on Taxation, 1949-1955). (New York City Office). *PRACTICE AREAS:* Taxation.

**ROBERT A. HOLTZMAN, (A P.C.),** born Los Angeles, California, July 17, 1929; admitted to bar, 1955, California. *Education:* University of California at Los Angeles (A.B., 1951); University of Southern California (LL.B., 1954). Order of the Coif. Associate Editor, Southern California Law Review, 1953-1954. Member, Panel of Arbitrators, 1971—, Panel of Mediators, 1992— and Panelist, Large Complex Case Program, 1993—,

*(This Listing Continued)*

American Arbitration Association. *Member:* Los Angeles County and American (Member, Section on Dispute Resolution; Vice-Chair, Committee on Arbitration) Bar Associations; The State Bar of California (Chairman, Committee on Administration of Justice, 1980-1981). *PRACTICE AREAS:* Litigation; Arbitration; Mediation.

**HAROLD I. KAHEN,** born Chicago, Illinois, August 14, 1918; admitted to bar, 1940, Illinois; 1947, New York. *Education:* University of Chicago (A.B., 1938; J.D., cum laude, 1940). Phi Beta Kappa; Order of the Coif. Member, Board of Editors, University of Chicago Law Review, 1939-1940. Member, Legal Staff SEC, 1941-1946. Associate Counsel, N.Y Superintendent of Insurance, 1955 Welfare Fund Inquiry. Special Professor, Hofstra University Law School, 1971-1972. *Member:* The Association of the Bar of the City of New York (Member: Committee on Law Reform, 1955-1958; Special Committee on Securities Regulation, 1962-1966); New York State (Member, Committee on Corporations, 1976-1984) and American Bar Associations. (New York City Office). *LANGUAGES:* Hebrew. *PRACTICE AREAS:* Corporate Law; Securities Law; Financial Law.

**GERALD D. KLEINMAN, (A P.C.),** born St. Paul, Minnesota, December 2, 1933; admitted to bar, 1959, California. *Education:* Dartmouth College (A.B., 1955); Harvard University (LL.B., 1958). *Member:* The State Bar of California. (Century City Office). *PRACTICE AREAS:* Real Estate Law.

**JAY ADAMS KNIGHT,** born Los Angeles, California, November 19, 1945; admitted to bar, 1972, California. *Education:* University of Heidelberg, Heidelberg, Germany; Claremont McKenna College (B.A., 1967); Hastings College of Law, University of California (J.D., 1971). Phi Beta Alpha. Lecturer, Business Law, California State Polytechnic University, 1974. *Member:* The State Bar of California; American Bar Association. *PRACTICE AREAS:* Employee Benefit Plans.

**SAUL N. RITTENBERG, (A P.C.),** born Chicago, Illinois, August 4, 1912; admitted to bar, 1935, California; 1943, U.S. Supreme Court. *Education:* University of California at Los Angeles (A.B., 1932); Northwestern University (J.D., 1935). Phi Beta Kappa; Order of the Coif. Member, Board of Councilors, University of Southern California Law Center, 1972-1984. *Member:* Beverly Hills and American (Member, Section of Patent, Trademark and Copyright Law; Chairman, 1965-1966, 1972-1973, Co-Chairman, 1966-1971, Section Committee 302, International Copyright Treaties and Laws) Bar Associations; The State Bar of California; Los Angeles Copyright Society; Copyright Society of U.S.A. (Century City Office). *PRACTICE AREAS:* Entertainment Law.

**ALFRED I. ROTHMAN, (A P.C.),** born Radom, Poland, May 11, 1917; admitted to bar, 1941, New York; 1947, California. *Education:* University of Michigan (A.B., 1939; J.D., 1941). Order of the Coif. Member, Board of Editors, Michigan Law Review, 1939-1941. *Member:* Los Angeles County and American Bar Associations; The State Bar of California. Fellow, American College of Trial Lawyers. *PRACTICE AREAS:* Litigation; Arbitration and Mediation.

**ARTHUR A. SEGALL,** born New York, N.Y., September 29, 1905; admitted to bar, 1930, New York. *Education:* Dartmouth College; University of Michigan (LL.B., 1928). Assistant Corporation Counsel in Charge of Division of Taxes, Law Department, City of New York, 1939-1943. Special Deputy Commissioner of Investigation, City of New York, 1944. *Member:* The Association of the Bar of the City of New York; New York County Lawyers Association. (New York City Office). *PRACTICE AREAS:* Estate Administration.

**ALAN D. SHULMAN,** born Chicago, Illinois, September 12, 1930; admitted to bar, 1953, Illinois; 1962, California. *Education:* Northwestern University (B.S., 1951; J.D., 1953); University of Southern California (LL.M., 1961). Tau Epsilon Rho. Comment Editor, Northwestern University Law Review, 1952-1953. *Member:* Beverly Hills and Los Angeles County Bar Associations; The State Bar of California (Member, Estate Planning, Trust and Probate Section); American Institute of Certified Public Accountants; California Society of Certified Public Accountants. [United States Army, 1954-1956]. (Century City Office). *PRACTICE AREAS:* Probate; Estate Planning; Individual Taxation.

**BERNARD M. SILBERT,** born Los Angeles, California, August 10, 1914; admitted to bar, 1938, California and U.S. District Court, Southern District of California. *Education:* University of California at Los Angeles and University of Southern California (B.A., 1935); University of Southern California (J.D., 1938). Member, Community Services Resource Corporation, 1985-1991. Member, District Securities Advisory Commission, 1987-1991. *Member:* Beverly Hills, Century City and Los Angeles County Bar

*(This Listing Continued)*

## PROFESSIONAL BIOGRAPHIES

Associations; The State Bar of California. (Century City Office). *PRACTICE AREAS:* Probate and Trust Administration; Trusts and Estates.

**HARVEY L. SILBERT,** born Milwaukee, Wisconsin, June 10, 1912; admitted to bar, 1936, California. *Education:* Southwestern University (J.D., 1935). Awarded Doctor Philosophiae, Hebrew University, 1981. Sigma Tau. *Member:* Beverly Hills and Los Angeles County Bar Associations; The State Bar of California. (Century City Office). *PRACTICE AREAS:* Trusts and Estates.

**MYRON L. SLOBODIEN, (A P.C.),** born Los Angeles, California, April 19, 1923; admitted to bar, 1950, California. *Education:* University of California at Los Angeles (B.S., 1943); University of Southern California (LL.B., 1949). *Member:* The State Bar of California; American Bar Association; Los Angeles Copyright Society (President, 1972-1973). (Century City Office). *PRACTICE AREAS:* Entertainment Law.

**JOHN S. WARREN, (A P.C.),** born Minneapolis, Minnesota, April 29, 1922; admitted to bar, 1951, California. *Education:* University of Minnesota (B.S.L., 1943); Hastings College of Law, University of California (LL.B., 1950). Adjunct Professor of Law in State and Local Taxes, Loyola University School of Law, 1975-1988. *Member:* Los Angeles County (Recipient, Dana Latham Memorial Award, 1988) and American (Chairman, Committee on State and Local Taxes, Taxation Section, 1981-1983) Bar Associations; The State Bar of California. *PRACTICE AREAS:* Taxation.

### SENIOR COUNSEL

Miriam J. Golbert
(Century City Office)
Adrienne Halpern
(New York City Office)
Louis A. Mok
(Century City Office)

Laurie S. Ruckel
(New York City Office)
John P. Scherlacher
(Century City Office)

### ASSOCIATES

Paula G. Atkinson
Curtis W. Bajak
(Century City Office)
Jeremy W. Barber
(Century City Office)
Roberta S. Bell
(New York City Office)
Michele E. Beuerlein
Elana C. Bloom
(New York City Office)
Stephen Bongini
(Century City Office)
Marguerite L. Bui
Matthew Clark Bures
David A. Byrnes
(Century City Office)
Steve S. Chahine
Ying Chen (Century City Office)
Paula K. Colbath
(New York City Office)
Marco D. Costales
Marita T. Covarrubias
(Century City Office)
Anne P. Donovan
(New York City Office)
Brant H. Dveirin
Linda F. Edell
(Nashville, Tennessee Office)
Philippe O. Erwin
(Century City Office)
Jay Fenster
(New York City Office)
David A. Fleissig
(New York City Office)
Kenneth R. Florin
(New York City Office)
Richard J. Frey
(Century City Office)
Bruce Friedman

Daniel J. Friedman
Randall Collins Furlong
(Century City Office)
Raul Carl Galaz
(Century City Office)
Helen Gavaris
(New York City Office)
James P. Goodkind
(Century City Office)
Karen A. Greenstein
(New York City Office)
Kurtiss Lee Grossman
James R. Guerette
(New York City Office)
Karen Nielsen Higgins
Jonathan Y. Kang
(Century City Office)
David D. Kim
(New York City Office)
John W. Kittleson
Amir I. Kornblum
(New York City Office)
Paul H. Kovelman
(Century City Office)
Robert B. Lachenauer
(New York City Office)
Lynda C. Loigman
(New York Office)
Nina B. Luban
David L. Lubitz
Linda McCauley Mack
(Century City Office)
David Alan Makman
(Century City Office)
Sonya Makunga
Jonathan S. Marshall
(Century City Office)
Denise Marie McIntosh
(Century City Office)

*(This Listing Continued)*

### ASSOCIATES (Continued)

Sharon S. Mequet
Beth R. Meyers
(New York City Office)
Paul G. Nagy
(Century City Office)
Lloyd Charles Nathan
(Century City Office)
Theotis F. Oliphant
Giovanni A. Pedde
(Rome, Italy Office)
Chris P. Perque
(Century City Office)
Harry S. Prawer
(New York City Office)
Ted Rittmaster
(Century City Office)
Allison Klayman Rosenthal
(New York City Office)
Michael E. Ross
Glen A. Rothstein
Michelle Oyler Saifer
(New York City Office)
Deborah L. Saltzman
(New York City Office)
Jay D. Sanders
Roni Schneider
(New York City Office)
Scott I. Schneider
(New York City Office)
Rachel Schwartz
(New York City Office)
Terri J. Seligman
(New York City Office)

Edward H. Shapiro
(Nashville, Tennessee Office)
Riccardo Siciliani
(Rome, Italy Office)
Brian R. Socolow
(New York City Office)
Adam F. Streisand
Gerald J. Strenio
Claudia M. Taylor
(New York City Office)
Arya Towfighi
(Century City Office)
David W. Victor
(Century City Office)
Joseph F. von Sauers
(Century City Office)
Courtney I. Williams
(New York City Office)
Susan Z. Williams
(Century City Office)
Weining Yang
(Century City Office)
Wendy W. Yang
(Century City Office)
Richard Kon Yoon
Maria L. Zanfini
(New York City Office)
Andrew D. Zuckerman
(New York City Office)
Richard S. Zuniga
(Century City Office)

---

## DOUGLAS W. LOFGREN

ONE BUNKER HILL
12TH FLOOR
601 WEST FIFTH STREET
**LOS ANGELES, CALIFORNIA 90071**
Telephone: 213-623-8874
FAX: 213-623-9085

*Civil and Criminal Litigation in State and Federal Courts, with Emphasis on Real Estate, Business, and Insurance Litigation and White Collar Criminal Defense.*

**DOUGLAS W. LOFGREN,** born Long Beach, California, May 21, 1946; admitted to bar, 1972, California, U.S. District Court, Central District of California and U.S. Court of Military Appeals; 1976, U.S. Court of Appeals, Ninth Circuit. *Education:* Harvard University (A.B., cum laude, 1968); University of Southern California (J.D., 1971). Member, U.S.C. Law Review, 1969-1971. Assistant U.S. Attorney, 1975-1982 and Head, Labor Corruption Unit, 1977-1978, Criminal Division, Central District of California. Counsel, 1982-1986, Senior Counsel, 1987-1990, and Assistant Vice President, 1985-1990, Coldwell Banker Commercial Group, Inc. *Member:* Los Angeles County and American Bar Associations; State Bar of California; Association of Business Trial Lawyers. [Pros. and Def. Coun., 1972-1975 and Sr. Trial Atty., 1974-1975, U.S. Army JAGC Corps]

---

## LONG & LEVIT LLP

A Limited Liability Partnership including a Professional Corporation

601 S. FIGUEROA, 25TH FLOOR
**LOS ANGELES, CALIFORNIA 90071**
Telephone: 213-356-5900
Facsimile: 213-613-0664

*San Francisco, California Office:* 101 California Street, Suite 2300. Telephone: 415-397-2222. Telex: 340924 HOME OFC SFO-LONG & LEVIT. Facsimile: 415-397-6392.

*Insurance Litigation (Environmental, Property, Casualty, Marine), Professional Liability, Products Liability, Toxic Torts, Securities and Commodities Litigation, Real Estate, Admiralty, Government, Entertainment and Election Law. General Civil Trial and Appellate Practice.*

*(This Listing Continued)*

## LONG & LEVIT LLP, Los Angeles—Continued

### RESIDENT PARTNERS

**RANDALL A. MILLER,** born Amsterdam, New York, June 1, 1958; admitted to bar, 1984, California and U.S. District Court, Northern, Central and Southern Districts of California. *Education:* State University of New York at Brockport (B.S., 1980); University of California at Davis; McGeorge School of Law, University of the Pacific (J.D., 1984). Legislative Review Staff Writer, 1982, Comment Staff Writer, 1982-1983, Board of Editors, Associate Comment Editor, 1983-1984, Pacific Law Journal. *Member:* Bar Association of San Francisco; Los Angeles County and American (Member, Sections on: Tort and Insurance Practice; Litigation) Bar Associations; State Bar of California.

**GRETCHEN S. CARNER,** born Berkeley, California, August 2, 1961; admitted to bar, 1987, California and U.S. District Court, Central, Southern and Eastern Districts of California; U.S. Court of Appeals, Ninth Circuit. *Education:* University of California at Berkeley (A.B., 1983); University of San Francisco (J.D., 1987). *Member:* Los Angeles County and American Bar Associations; State Bar of California.

**CYRIL E. "TED" ARMBRISTER, JR.,** born Englewood, New Jersey, September 26, 1940; admitted to bar, 1968, California. *Education:* Pomona College (B.A.), 1962; University of California at Los Angeles; Southwestern University. Phi Delta Phi (Pound Inn). *Member:* Santa Monica, Los Angeles County and American Bar Associations; State Bar of California; Association of Southern California Defense Counsel; American Board of Trial Advocates; Association of Defense Trial Attorneys. (Also Member, Morgan & Armbrister, Santa Monica).

### RESIDENT ASSOCIATES

| | |
|---|---|
| B. Gerard Cordelli | David M. Morrow |
| Patricia M. De La Peña | Susan Andrews O'Neal |
| J. Andrew Douglas | JoLynn M. Pollard |
| Jeffrey A. Evans | Roni Reed |
| Douglas H. Galt | Stephen E. Ronk |
| Christina Katris-Michael | Valerie J. Wiles |

(For complete biographical data on San Francisco, California personnel, see Professional Biographies at San Francisco, California)

---

## LAW OFFICES OF
## RICHARD P. LONGAKER II
### LOS ANGELES, CALIFORNIA

(See Santa Monica)

*General Civil and Trial Practice. Business, Litigation, Insurance and Corporate Law.*

---

## LORD, BISSELL & BROOK
### 300 SOUTH GRAND AVENUE
### LOS ANGELES, CALIFORNIA 90071-3200
Telephone: 213-485-1500
Telecopy: 213-485-1200
Telex: 18-1135

*Chicago, Illinois Office:* Suites 2600-3600 Harris Bank Building, 115 South LaSalle Street, 60603. Telephone: 312-443-0700. Telecopy: 312-443-0570. Cable Address: "Lowirco". Telex: 25-0336.

*Atlanta, Georgia Office:* One Atlantic Center, 1201 West Peachtree Street, N.W., Suite 3700, 30309. Telephone: 404-870-4600. Telecopy: 404-872-5547.

*Rockford, Illinois Office:* 120 West State Street, Suite 200, 61101. Telephone: 815-963-8050.

*General Practice.*

### RESIDENT PARTNERS

**CHARLES A. ADAMEK,** born Chicago, Illinois, December 24, 1944; admitted to bar, 1969, Illinois and U.S. District Court, Northern District of Illinois; 1972, U.S. Court of Appeals, 7th Circuit; 1978, California. *Education:* University of Michigan (A.B., 1966; J.D., 1969). Administrative Editor, Michigan Journal of Law Reform, 1968-1969. Law Clerk to Hon. Julius J. Hoffman, U.S. District Court, Northern District of Illinois, 1969-1971. Faculty Member, ABA National Insurance Institute, 1986. *Member:* Los Angeles County, Illinois State and American Bar Associations; State Bar of California; National Association of Railroad Trial Counsel. **PRACTICE AREAS:** Insurance Coverage Law; Professional Liability Law; Railroad Tort Defense Law.

**GAIL M. BAEV,** born Chicago, Illinois, August 3, 1953; admitted to bar, 1981, California and U.S. District Court, Central District of California; 1983, U.S. Court of Appeals, Ninth Circuit; 1985, U.S. District Court, Eastern and Northern Districts of California; 1986, U.S. District Court, Southern District of California. *Education:* Knox College (B.A., 1974); Loyola University (J.D., cum laude, 1981). Member, Loyola Law Journal. *Member:* Los Angeles County and American Bar Associations; State Bar of California. **LANGUAGES:** Spanish and French. **PRACTICE AREAS:** Insurance Coverage Litigation; Tort Litigation; Business Litigation.

**C. GUERRY COLLINS,** admitted to bar, 1984, California; U.S. District Court, Central, Northern and Southern Districts of California U.S. Court of. *Education:* Yale University (B.A., 1966); University of Southern California (J.D., 1984). *Member:* State Bar of California.

**CHARLES L. CROUCH, III,** born Baltimore, Maryland, October 16, 1952; admitted to bar, 1978, California and U.S. District Court, Central District of California; 1980, U.S. District Court, Eastern District of California. *Education:* Claremont Mens College (B.A., cum laude, 1974); Claremont Graduate School (M.A., 1975); Loyola Law School, Los Angeles (J.D., cum laude, 1978). Editor-in-Chief, Loyola of Los Angeles Law Review, 1977-1978. Member: Loyola of Los Angeles Law Review, 1976-1977; St. Thomas More Law Honor Society, 1977-1978. Author: "The Extension of Products Liability to Corporate Asset Transferees," 10 Loyola Law Review 584, 1977. President, The Conference of Insurance Counsel, 1996. *Member:* Los Angeles County and American (Member, Sections on: Tort and Insurance Practice; Public Regulation of Insurance Law Committee; Forum on Health Law; Business Law and Antitrust Law) Bar Associations; State Bar of California (Member, Business Law Section; Insurance Law Committee, 1996—). **PRACTICE AREAS:** Corporate Law; Insurance Regulatory Law.

**DAVID F. HAUGE,** born Fort Dodge, Iowa, October 15, 1943; admitted to bar, 1974, Oklahoma; 1977, Illinois; 1987, California; U.S. District Court, Southern District of California; U.S. Supreme Court. *Education:* San Diego State University (B.A., 1969); University of Tulsa (J.D., 1973). Member, California Conference of Insurance Counsel. Member, Fed. of Regulatory Counsel. Associate, Society of Financial Examiners. Associate, NAPSLO. *Member:* Illinois State and Oklahoma Bar Associations.

**JEFFREY S. KRAVITZ,** born Newark, New Jersey, August 3, 1950; admitted to bar, 1975, California. *Education:* University of California at Los Angeles (B.A., cum laude, 1972); Loyola University (J.D., 1975). Phi Alpha Delta; First Place Loyola Moot Court Competition; Captain Moot Court Team. St. Thomas More Society. Editor, Loyola University Law Review, 1974-1975. Note and Comment Editor, Law Review Board, 1974-1975. Author: "Adverse Possession of Abandoned Urban Housing," Loyola Law Review, 1974. *Member:* Los Angeles County Bar Association (Member, Litigation Section); National Association of Railroad Trial Counsel; Association of Southern California Defense Counsel; Association of Business Trial Lawyers. **PRACTICE AREAS:** Professional Malpractice; Railroad Law; Business Litigation.

**RUDOLF H. SCHROETER,** born Los Angeles, California, April 12, 1932; admitted to bar, 1964, California. *Education:* Los Angeles City College and University of California at Los Angeles; Southwestern University (J.D., 1964). *Member:* Los Angeles County Bar Association; The State Bar of California; Association of Business Trial Lawyers. **PRACTICE AREAS:** Product Liability Litigation; Toxic Tort Litigation; Insurance Coverage Litigation; General Litigation.

**KEITH G. WILEMAN,** born Santa Cruz, California, April 4, 1958; admitted to bar, 1983, California; 1984, U.S. District Court, Central District of California and U.S. Court of Appeals, Ninth Circuit; 1992, U.S. District Court, Southern District of California. *Education:* Georgetown University (B.S.F.S., International Economics, cum laude, 1980); New York University; University of Southern California (J.D., 1983). *Member:* State Bar of California; National Association of Railroad Trial Counsel. **PRACTICE AREAS:** Products Liability Defense; Railroad Liability Defense; Insurance Coverage; Architect Liability Defense; Business Litigation.

### OF COUNSEL

**MARGUERITE L. BROWN,** born Portland, Oregon, March 7, 1957; admitted to bar, 1983, California. *Education:* California State University (B.A., 1979); Willamette University (J.D., 1982). Phi Beta Kappa; Phi Kappa Phi; Omicron Delta Epsilon. Co-author: with M. J. Leahy, "Asbestos Coverage Wars Continue: Report From the Front," Defense Counsel

*(This Listing Continued)*

Journal, October 1, 1992; with M. J. Leahy, "Insurance Coverage for Property Damage Claims," Sixth Annual Insurance Litigation Institute, January 1, 1992; M J. Leahy, "Insurance Coverage Issues Relating to Construction Litigation," Association of Southern California Defense Counsel, January 1, 1991.

### RESIDENT ASSOCIATES

Brenda Adams Bissett
Jacqueline C. Brown
John D. Buchanan
Stephen L. Cope
Stephanie Elizabeth Deaner (admission pending).
Charissa Dorian
Franklin T. Dunn
Mark Scott Fall
Cynthia M. Frey
John M. Hochhausler
Barbara J. Klass
Jacqueline Redin Klein
LouCinda Laughlin
Jeri Rouse Looney
George D. Lozano
Mitchell J. Popham
Karen A. Soomekh
Anthony F. Witteman

---

## ALVIN N. LOSKAMP

### A LAW CORPORATION

### LOS ANGELES, CALIFORNIA

(See Burbank)

*Estate Planning, Revocable Living Trusts, Wills, Probate, Asset Protection, Business Entities, Business Trusts, and Corporate Law.*

---

## LAW OFFICE
## MICHAEL A. LOTMAN

### A PROFESSIONAL CORPORATION

THIRD FLOOR
10100 SANTA MONICA BOULEVARD
**LOS ANGELES, CALIFORNIA 90067**
Telephone: 310-286-6626
Fax: 310-286-2966

*General Civil and Commercial Litigation, Title Insurance, Financial Institutions, Real Estate, Fidelity and Blanket Bond, Securities and Entertainment Litigation.*

**MICHAEL A. LOTMAN,** born Chicago, Illinois, June 9, 1946; admitted to bar, 1974, California; 1976, New York. *Education:* University of Pacific (B.A., with honors, 1968); University of California, Hastings College of Law (J.D., 1973); London School of Economics and Political Science (LL.M., 1974). Order of the Coif. Member, Thurston Honor Society. Associate Editor, Hastings Law Journal, 1972-1973. Author: "Court-Ordered Contraception in California," 23 Hastings Law Journal 1505, 1972. Fellow, Institute of Advanced Legal Studies, London, 1973-1974. *Member:* Los Angeles County and American (Member, Sections on: Litigation; Tort and Insurance Practice) Bar Associations; The State Bar of California; The American Arbitration Association.

### OF COUNSEL

**ALAN J. DIAMOND,** born Newark, New Jersey, March, 26, 1948; admitted to bar, 1974, California. *Education:* New York University (B.F.A., 1971); George Washington University (J.D., 1974); Cambridge University (LL.M., 1984; Ph.D., 1992);. Managing Editor, George Washington University Law Review, 1973-1974. Author: "Declassification of Sensitive Information: Comment on Executive Order 11652," 41 George Washington L. Rev. 1052 (1973). Editor and Contributor, "The Victorian Achievement of Sir Henry Maine," 1991. Adjunct Professor, University of Southern California Law School, 1982-1985. *Member:* State Bar of California.

---

## LAW OFFICES OF RICHARD A. LOVE

Established in 1982

11601 WILSHIRE BOULEVARD, SUITE 2000
**LOS ANGELES, CALIFORNIA 90025**
Telephone: 310-477-2070
Fax: 310-477-3922

*Civil Trial and Appellate Practice in all State and Federal Courts. Discrimination and Employment, Business and Commercial Law, Securities, Product Liability, Negligence, and Insurance Bad Faith.*

*(This Listing Continued)*

---

**RICHARD A. LOVE,** born Cedar Rapids, Iowa, March 5, 1947; admitted to bar, 1974, California and U.S. District Court, Central District of California; 1981, U.S. Court of Appeals, Ninth Circuit; 1986, U.S. Court of Appeals, Tenth Circuit. *Education:* University of California at Los Angeles (B.A., in Economics, 1969); Loyola University at Los Angeles (J.D., cum laude, 1974). Member, St. Thomas More Law Honor Society. Recipient, Benno M. Brink Memorial Award in Bankruptcy. Law Clerk to Associate Justice Macklin Fleming, California State Court of Appeals, 1978. *Member:* Los Angeles County Bar Association (Member, Section of Trial Lawyers); State Bar of California.

### ASSOCIATES

**BETH A. SHENFELD,** born Fresno, California, March 13, 1959; admitted to bar, 1984, California and U.S. District Court, Central District of California. *Education:* Brandeis University (B.A., magna cum laude, 1981); University of California at Los Angeles (J.D., 1984). Order of the Coif. Member, Moot Court Honors Program. Scholarship Recipient, Los Angeles County Bar Association, Family Law Section, 1983. *Member:* Los Angeles County Bar Association; State Bar of California.

**ANNE MCWILLIAMS,** born Coatbridge, Scotland, January 30, 1959; admitted to bar, 1987, California, U.S. District Court, Central, Northern and Southern Districts of California and U.S. Court of Appeals, Ninth Circuit. *Education:* University of Southern California (B.S., cum laude, 1982); Hastings College of the Law, University of California (J.D., 1986). Law Clerk, Judges William L. Bettinelli and Laurence K. Sawyer, Sonoma County Superior Court, 1986-1987. Extern to Judge William A. Newsom, California Court of Appeal, First Appellate District, 1986. *Member:* Los Angeles County Bar Association; State Bar of California; Women Lawyers of Los Angeles.

**EILEEN SPADONI,** born Utica, New York, December 12, 1959; admitted to bar, 1987, California and U.S. District Court, Central District of California. *Education:* University of Madrid, Spain; University of California at Irvine (B.A., Spanish, 1982; B.A., magna cum laude, French, 1983); University of California at Los Angeles (J.D., 1987). Phi Beta Kappa. Certified Administrative Hearing Interpreter, State of California, 1984—. Pacific Coast Counsel on Latin American Studies, 1983—. *Member:* Los Angeles County Bar Association; State Bar of California. *LANGUAGES:* Spanish, French.

**NEIL J. SHEFF,** born Los Angeles, California, May 27, 1961; admitted to bar, 1989, California; 1990, U.S. District Court, Central District of California. *Education:* University of California at Los Angeles (B.A., 1983); Hebrew University of Jerusalem, Jerusalem, Israel; Loyola Marymount University (J.D., 1989). Recipient, Alumni Association Award, 1989. Founder/Editor, English Language Student Newspaper, 1980. Founder and President, Loyola Jewish Law Students Association, 1986-1988. *Member:* Los Angeles County and American Bar Associations; State Bar of California. *LANGUAGES:* Spanish, Hebrew.

**MARCY A. PETTITT,** born Whittier, California, March 12, 1962; admitted to bar, 1988, California. *Education:* University of Houston (B.S., 1985); Pepperdine University (J.D., 1988). *PRACTICE AREAS:* Personal Injury Law.

---

## LOVICH & PENN

777 SOUTH FIGUEROA, SUITE 1507
**LOS ANGELES, CALIFORNIA 90017**
Telephone: 213-689-3625
Fax: 213-689-3653

*Products Liability, Professional Liability, Premises Liability, Medical Malpractice, Construction Liability, Workers' Compensation and Auto.*

### STAFF COUNSEL
### AMERICAN INTERNATIONAL COMPANIES

### MANAGING ATTORNEY

**RICHARD A. LOVICH,** born Los Angeles, California, October 3, 1957; admitted to bar, 1984, California and U.S. District Court, Central District of California. *Education:* California State University, Northridge (B.A., 1980); Loyola University (J.D., 1983). *Member:* Los Angeles County Bar Association; State Bar of California; Association of Southern California Defense Counsel.

*(This Listing Continued)*

## LOVICH & PENN, Los Angeles—Continued

### SUPERVISING ATTORNEY

**FRANCIS P. LICATA,** born Montebello, California, June 4, 1951; admitted to bar, 1976, California; 1978, U.S. District Court, Central District of California and U.S. Court of Appeals, 9th Circuit. *Education:* University of California, Irvine (B.A., 1973); Pepperdine University (J.D., 1976). *Member:* State Bar of California.

### SENIOR TRIAL ATTORNEYS

**TIMOTHY W. KAFTEN,** born Walnut Creek, California, December 13, 1959; admitted to bar, 1990, California; 1994, U.S. District Court, Central District of California. *Education:* University of California, Santa Barbara (B.A., 1986); Southwestern University (J.D., 1990). *Member:* State Bar of California; Van Nuy's Workers' Compensation Appeals Board; Agora Hills Workers' Compensation Appeals Board.

**RONALD A. MOSHER,** born Auburn, New York, August 19, 1946; admitted to bar, 1973, California; 1974, U.S. District Court, Central District of California. *Education:* University of Missouri (B.S., 1968); John F. Kennedy University (J.D., 1973).

---

## LOVRETOVICH & KAREN

### LOS ANGELES, CALIFORNIA

(See Woodland Hills)

*A Trial Practice with emphasis in Business, Insurance and Personal Injury Litigation, General Business, Commercial and Insurance Law.*

---

## STEVEN T. LOWE

*Established in 1991*

**12424 WILSHIRE BOULEVARD, SUITE 900**
**LOS ANGELES, CALIFORNIA 90025**
Telephone: 310-447-1727
Fax: 310-447-6485

*Entertainment, Business, Corporate, Intellectual Property, Trademark, Copyright and Real Estate Litigation, Defamation, Investment Fraud.*

**STEVEN T. LOWE,** born Brooklyn, New York, July 28, 1958; admitted to bar, 1984, New York; 1985, California; 1986, U.S. District Court, Southern District of New York and Central District of California; 1989, U.S. Court of Appeals, Ninth Circuit. *Education:* Vanderbilt University (B.S., 1980); University of Connecticut (J.D., 1984). Recipient, Nathan Burkan Memorial Award in Copyright Law, 1982. *Member:* Los Angeles County and Beverly Hills Bar Associations; State Bar of California; California Lawyers for the Arts.

REPRESENTATIVE CLIENTS: A List of Clients Furnished Upon Request.

---

## ROBERT J. LOWE

*A LAW CORPORATION*

**2049 CENTURY PARK EAST**
**SUITE 900**
**LOS ANGELES, CALIFORNIA 90067**
Telephone: 310-551-6979
Fax: 310-551-6980
Email: ERISALAW@AOL.COM

*Employee Benefits and Executive Compensation.*

**ROBERT J. LOWE,** born Forest Hills, New York, October 19, 1954; admitted to bar, 1978, California and U.S. District Court, Central District of California; 1979, U.S. Court of Appeals, Ninth Circuit and U.S. Tax Court. *Education:* State University of New York at Binghamton (B.A., 1975); Boalt Hall School of Law, University of California (J.D., 1978). Phi Beta Kappa. Author: "New Opportunities for Rollovers of Distributions from Qualified Plans," 52 Journal of Taxation 82, 1980; "Reassessing Medical Reimbursement Plans After Changes in the Law and Regulations," 54 Journal of Taxation 30, January, 1981; "Treatment of Educational Benefit Plan Contribution after the Greensboro Decision," 58 Journal of Taxation 330, June, 1983; "When Will the Disability Exclusion Apply to Plan Distributions," 62 Journal of Taxation 342, 1985; "Estate Planning For Business Interests," Estate Planning Practice, CEB, 1987; "Incentive Stock Options," Bender's Federal Tax Service, 1989. Adjunct Professor of Law, University of San Diego Law School Graduate Program in Taxation, 1983-1988. *Member:* Los Angeles County and American Bar Associations; State Bar of California. (Certified Specialist, Taxation Law, The State Bar of California Board of Legal Specialization).

*(This Listing Continued)*

---

## LUCE, FORWARD, HAMILTON & SCRIPPS LLP

A Partnership including Professional Corporations
*Established in 1873*

**777 SOUTH FIGUEROA, SUITE 3600**
**LOS ANGELES, CALIFORNIA 90017**
Telephone: 213-892-4992
Fax: 213-892-7731
URL: http://www.luce.com

*San Diego, California Office:* 600 West Broadway, Suite 2600, 92101. Telephone: 619-236-1414. Fax: 619-232-8311.
*La Jolla, California Office:* 4275 Executive Square, Suite 800, 92037. Telephone: 619-535-2639. Fax: 619-453-2812.
*San Francisco, California Office:* 100 Bush Street, 20th Floor, 94104. Telephone: 415-395-7900. Fax: 415-395-7949.
*New York, N.Y. Office:* Citicorp Center, 153 East 53rd Street, 26th Floor, 10022. Telephone: 212-754-1414. Fax: 212-644-9727.
*Chicago, Illinois Office:* 180 North La Salle Street, Suite 1125, 60601. Telephone: 312-641-0580. Fax: 312-641-0380.

*General Civil Practice and Litigation in all State and Federal Courts. Antitrust, Banking, Bankruptcy, Business, Commercial, Copyright, Corporate Finance, Corporations, Energy and Resource, Environmental, Estate Planning, Family, Fidelity and Surety, First Amendment, Foreign Investment, Health Care Organizations, Immigration and Naturalization, Insurance and Reinsurance, Intellectual Property, International Financial Transactions, Labor, Land Use, Mergers and Acquisitions, Municipal Finance, Partnership, Patent, Pension and Profit-Sharing, Probate, Probate Litigation, Product Liability and Warranty, Professional Responsibility, Public Utility, Real Property, Securities, Taxation, Trademark, Trust and Venture Financing Law, Water Law.*

### RESIDENT PARTNERS

**REX HEESEMAN,** born Chicago, Illinois, November 11, 1942; admitted to bar, 1968, California. *Education:* Claremont McKenna College (B.A., magna cum laude, 1964); Stanford University (J.D., 1967). Recipient, Ford Foundation Fellowship, Costa Rica, 1969-1970. Author: "Insurance Litigation," California Practice Guide, The Rutter Group, 1995; "Insurance Litigation," California Judges Association/The Rutter Group, 1989, 1990, 1994; "Good Faith Duties and Tort Remedies in Lender Liability Litigation," 15 W. St. U. L.Rev. 617, 1988; "The Special Relationship Requirement for Bad Faith Liability," Los Angeles Lawyer, Dec. 1987. Assistant U.S. Attorney, Central District of California, 1971-1974. Member, Board of Trustees, Claremont McKenna College, 1981-1982, 1987-1990. Member, Board of Editors, the Business Torts Reporter, 1988—. Columnist, Los Angeles Daily Journal, "Commercial Torts." Chair, C.D.Cal. Lawyer Representatives to the 1994 Ninth Circuit Judicial Conference. Chair, Los Angeles Delegation to the 1988 State Bar Convention. Lecturer for ABA, California CEB and The Rutter Group programs. Vice Chair, Executive Committee, State Bar of California, 1990-1991. *Member:* Los Angeles County (Chair, Judicial Resources Committee, 1992—, Chair, Judicial Appointments Committee, 1989-1991 and Chair, Litigation Section, 1990-1991) and American Bar Associations; Chancery Club. [Capt., U.S. Army, 1967-1969]. **PRACTICE AREAS:** Commercial Torts; Insurance Coverage Law. *Email:* rheesema@luce.com

**JAMES E. FITZGERALD,** born Roslyn, New York, November 14, 1954; admitted to bar, 1980, New York, U.S. Court of Appeals, Second Circuit and U.S. District Court, Southern and Eastern Districts of New York; 1983, California and U.S. District Court, Southern, Eastern and Central Districts of California. *Education:* Georgetown University (B.S.B.A., 1976); Fordham Law School (J.D., 1979). *Member:* Los Angeles County (Member, Sections on: Litigation; Insurance), New York State and American (Member, Sections on: Litigation; Tort and Insurance Practice) Bar Associations; State Bar of California. **PRACTICE AREAS:** Insurance and Reinsurance; Professional Liability; Business Litigation. *Email:* jfitzger@luce.com

*(This Listing Continued)*

## PROFESSIONAL BIOGRAPHIES

**ANDREW J. WAXLER,** born Los Angeles, California, September 11, 1958; admitted to bar, 1984, California and U.S. District Court, Central District of California; 1986, U.S. Court of Appeals, Ninth Circuit. *Education:* University of California at Los Angeles (B.A., 1980); Florida State University at St. Edmund Hall, Oxford, England; Loyola Law School of Los Angeles (J.D., 1983). *Member:* Los Angeles County and American (Member, Tort and Insurance Practice Section) Bar Associations; State Bar of California. *PRACTICE AREAS:* Insurance Coverage; Professional Liability. *Email:* awaxler@luce.com

**DANIEL I. SIMON,** born Chicago, Illinois, March 13, 1940; admitted to bar, 1968, California and U.S. District Court, Central and Northern Districts of California. *Education:* California State University at Northridge (B.A., 1962); University of California School of Law (J.D., 1965). Phi Alpha Delta. Author: "Capital Uses of Insurance & Reinsurance in the Privatization Process," presented at the Pacific Rim Advisory Council Conference, Jakarta, Indonesia, April 1996; "The Emergence of the British Virgin Islands as an International Financial Center," Global Reinsurance Magazine, March 1996; "The Use and Abuse of Lawyers," Global Reinsurance Magazine, December 1995; "Have I Got A Deal For You," Global Reinsurance Magazine, June 1995; "A California Movement," Global Risk Manager, April 1995; "24 Hour Coverage," Global Risk Managers Magazine, March 1995; "Captives Are For Brokers Too," Global Reinsurance Magazine, November 1994; "Road to Recovery," Reinsurance Magazine, Vol. 23, No. 8, November 1992. Editor, International Insurance Law, 1982—. Contributing Editor, Insurance and Reinsurance Law International, 1883-1989. Chairman, UCLA Insurance Law Institute, 1977—. *Member:* Beverly Hills, Los Angeles County, Santa Barbara County and American Bar Associations; State Bar of California; British Insurance Law Association; Cowboy Lawyers Association. *PRACTICE AREAS:* Captive Insurance; Business Insurance; Reinsurance; Insurance Products; Reinsurance Arbitration; Business Reinsurance. *Email:* dsimon@luce.com

### ASSOCIATES

**TERYL MURABAYASHI,** born Honolulu, Hawaii, September 16, 1962; admitted to bar, 1990, California and U.S. District Court, Southern, Eastern, Northern and Central Districts of California. *Education:* Creighton University (B.S.B.A., cum laude, 1984); University of California, Hastings College of Law (J.D., 1990). Beta Alpha Psi. Member, Hastings Constitutional Law Quarterly. Certified Public Accountant, Nebraska, 1985. *Member:* American Bar Association. (Resident). *PRACTICE AREAS:* Commercial Litigation; Bankruptcy; Secured Creditor Representation. *Email:* tmurabay@luce.com

**CHRISTINA BULL ARNDT,** born Carmichael, California, July 3, 1967; admitted to bar, 1994, California. *Education:* Mount Holyoke College (B.A., cum laude, 1989); University of California, Los Angeles (J.D., 1994). Editor-in-Chief, UCLA Womens Law Journal. Copyright Editor, UCLA Law Review. *Member:* Los Angeles County Bar Association; Women Lawyers Association of Los Angeles. (Resident). *PRACTICE AREAS:* Insurance; Reinsurance; Litigation. *Email:* carndt@luce.com

**MATTHEW C. ELSTEIN,** born Los Angeles, California, May 25, 1970; admitted to bar, 1994, California; 1995, U.S. District Court, Southern and Northern Districts of California and U.S. Court of Appeals, Ninth Circuit. *Education:* University of California, Berkeley (B.A., summa cum laude, 1991); Georgetown University (J.D., cum laude, 1994). Phi Beta Kappa. *Member:* Los Angeles County and American Bar Associations; California Young Lawyers Association. (Resident). *PRACTICE AREAS:* Insurance; Reinsurance; Business Litigation. *Email:* melstein@luce.com

**ERIC TODD JORGENSEN,** born Montebello, California, December 9, 1965; admitted to bar, 1994, California. *Education:* University of California, Los Angeles (B.A., 1988); Hastings College of the Law, University of California (J.D., 1994). *Member:* Los Angeles County Bar Association. (Resident). *PRACTICE AREAS:* Insurance; Reinsurance; Litigation. *Email:* ejorgens@luce.com

**GREG R GROENEVELD,** born Denison, Iowa, November 27, 1963; admitted to bar, 1993, California. *Education:* Southern Methodist University (B.B.A., cum laude, 1986); Harvard University (M.P.P., 1988); Columbia University (J.D., 1993). Harlan Fiske Stone Scholar. *Member:* Los Angeles County Bar Association. (Resident). *PRACTICE AREAS:* Insurance; Reinsurance; Labor. *Email:* ggroenev@luce.com

**GREGORY H. KING,** born Santa Clara, California, February 6, 1966; admitted to bar, 1993, Utah; 1994, California. *Education:* Brigham Young University (B.A., cum laude, 1990; J.D., cum laude, 1993). Senior Editor, Brigham Young University Law Review, 1992-1993. (Resident). *PRAC-*

*(This Listing Continued)*

*TICE AREAS:* Insurance Coverage; Business Litigation; Construction. *Email:* gking@luce.com

**DAVID N. RUBEN,** born Burbank, California, August 30, 1965; admitted to bar, 1991, California and U.S. District Court, Eastern and Southern Districts of California. *Education:* University of California at Los Angeles (B.A., 1988); Southwestern University (J.D., 1991). American Jurisprudence Award. Law Review Candidate, 1989-1990. Moot Court Honors Presidential Candidate, 1989-1990. *Member:* Century City, Los Angeles County and American Bar Associations; State Bar of California (Environmental Law Section, 1993-1994). (Resident). *PRACTICE AREAS:* Product Litigation; Warranty. *Email:* druben@luce.com

(For complete Biographical Data on all Personnel, see Professional Biographies at San Diego).

---

## ALBERT C. LUM
### LOS ANGELES, CALIFORNIA

(See South Pasadena)

*General and Civil Trial Practice in all State and Federal Courts. Business, Real Estate, International, Immigration, Trusts and Taxation, Appellate and Trademark.*

---

## LUND LAW CORPORATION
### 1901 AVENUE OF THE STARS, TWENTIETH FLOOR
### LOS ANGELES, CALIFORNIA 90067
Telephone: 310-286-7485
Fax: 310-286-7486
Email: XLNT706@aol.com

*Estate Planning, Probate and Trust Law.*

**ERIC JAMES LUND,** born Los Angeles, California, March 30, 1959; admitted to bar, 1983, California; 1984, U.S. District Court, Central District of California, U.S. Court of Appeals, Ninth Circuit and U.S. Supreme Court. *Education:* Stanford University (B.A., 1979); University of Southern California (J.D., 1983; M.B.A., 1983). Author: "Estate Planning for the Non-Professional," Beverly Hills Adult School, 1990; "Substance Abuse Among Attorneys and Their Clients," Southern California Tax and Estate Planning Forum, September 1995 and September 1996. Co-Author: with Gerald E. Lunn, Jr. "Income, Estate and Gift Tax Consequences of Transfers Between Unmarried Partners" Century City Family Law Council, 1994. Director of an Advisory Board, 1991-1995 and Member of Chairman's Council, 1994 —, Betty Ford Center at Eisenhower. Member, Alumni Board, Buckley Schools. Member, Development Committee, Neighborhood Youth Association, 1996. Director, Spinal Cord Injury Network International, 1988—. *Member:* Los Angeles County Bar Association; State Bar of California. (Also Member Lund & Lund at Beverly Hills). *LANGUAGES:* French and Farsi. *PRACTICE AREAS:* Estate Planning; Trust and Probate Law.

### OF COUNSEL

**THEODORE V. KREPS,** born Palo Alto, California, January 23, 1957; admitted to bar, 1989, California, 1990, U.S. District Court, Central District of California; 1991 U.S. District Court, Northern, Southern and Eastern Districts of California, District of Arizona and U.S. Court of Appeals, Ninth Circuit. *Education:* American University (B.A., 1985); Southwestern University (J.D., 1989). Delta Theta Phi (Dean, 1988-1989); Member, Moot Court Honors Program. Chief Note and Comment Editor, Southwestern University Law Review, 1987-1989. *PRACTICE AREAS:* Business; Commercial; General Civil Litigation.

---

## GERALD E. LUNN, JR., P.C.
Established in 1989

### 1901 AVENUE OF THE STARS, TWENTIETH FLOOR
### LOS ANGELES, CALIFORNIA 90067
Telephone: 310-277-6264; Mobile: 310-713-0504
Facsimile: 310-277-6271
Email: GLUNN@ix.netcom.com

*Estate and Tax Planning with Emphasis in Prenuptial Agreements and Marital Contracts.*

*(This Listing Continued)*

### GERALD E. LUNN, JR., P.C., Los Angeles—Continued

**GERALD E. LUNN, JR.,** born Memphis, Tennessee, August 23, 1954; admitted to bar, 1980, California; 1981, U.S. Tax Court. *Education:* Emory University (B.A., summa cum laude, 1976); Harvard University (J.D., cum laude, 1980). Phi Beta Kappa. Co-Author: "Recent Developments In Entertainment Taxation," 1983 and 1984 Entertainment, Publishing And The Arts Handbook, Clark Boardman Company, Ltd. *Member:* Beverly Hills, Century City, Los Angeles County and American (Member: Taxation Section; Marital Deduction Subcommittee, Real Property, Probate and Trust Law Section) Bar Associations; State Bar of California. (Certified Specialist, Probate, Estate Planning and Trust Law, The State Bar of California Board of Legal Specialization).

---

## LURVEY & SHAPIRO

*Established in 1984*

FOX PLAZA
2121 AVENUE OF THE STARS, SUITE 1550 (CENTURY CITY)
**LOS ANGELES, CALIFORNIA 90067**
*Telephone: 310-203-0711*
*Fax: 310-203-0610*

*Family Law, Business and Civil Litigation in all State and Federal Courts.*

**FIRM PROFILE:** Lurvey & Shapiro was founded in 1984 by experienced civil litigators to address the fact that Family Law has become one of the most intricate and demanding areas of the law. The firm serves as a specialized boutique to provide intensive, personalized service in Family Law matters involving complex issues of finance, property and custody. In its appellate work, the firm's reported decisions include: Vincent B. v. Joan R., 126 Cal. App. 3d 619 (1981); In re Marriages: Brockman, 194 Cal. App. 3d 1035 (1987); Hubner 205 Cal. App. 3d 660 (1988); Micalizio, 199 Cal. App. 3d 662 (1988) and Caballero, 27 Cal. App. 4th 1139 (1994). The firm's clients include leading members of the entertainment and business communities.

### MEMBERS OF FIRM

**IRA H. LURVEY,** born Chicago, Illinois, April 6, 1935; admitted to bar, 1965, California; 1966, Nevada. *Education:* University of Illinois (B.S., 1956); Northwestern University (M.S., 1961); Boalt Hall School of Law; University of California at Berkeley (J.D., 1965). Editor, Community Property Journal, 1979-1981. Law Clerk to Supreme Court of Nevada, 1965-1966. Fellow, American Academy of Matrimonial Lawyers, 1979—(President, Southern California Chapter, 1991-1992; Member, National Board of Governors, 1992-1994). Author: "Good Will on Marital Dissolution," California State Bar Journal, January, 1977; "Negotiation and Settlement in Family Law," Los Angeles County Bar Syllabus, annual update, 1982—; Annual C.E.B. booklet on "Recent Developments in Family Law," 1983—. Editorial Consultant, Columnist, California Family Law Monthly, 1984—. Primary Editorial Consultant, California Family Law 2d, Treatise, Matthew-Bender, 1994—. Member: State Bar Commission on Family Law Specialization, 1980-1983; California Supreme Court Chief Justice's Commission on Weighted Caseload, 1980. Lecturer, Author, on Commercial Litigation and Family Law, California Continuing Education of the Bar, 1970—. *Member:* Beverly Hills (Chair, Family Law Section, 1976-1977), Los Angeles County (Chair, Family Law Section, 1981-1982) and American (Chair, National Family Law Section, 1996-1997; Member, Governing Council, 1986—; Chair, Continuing Legal Education, 1983-1985; Chair, Committee on Support, 1986-1987; Chair, Task Force on Policy and Issues, 1986—; Member, Board of Editors, "The Advocate" Magazine, 1984—) Bar Associations; State Bar of California (Chair, Family Law Section, 1986-1987; Member, Executive Committee, 1981-1988; Editor/Columnist, Family Law News, 1981—); State Bar of Nevada. (Certified Specialist, Family Law, The State Bar of California Board of Legal Specialization). **PRACTICE AREAS:** Family Law.

**JUDITH SALKOW SHAPIRO,** born Los Angeles, California, August 30, 1938; admitted to bar, 1976, California. *Education:* University of California at Los Angeles (B.A., 1959; M.Ed., 1971); University of California at Los Angeles School of Law (J.D., 1976). Member, U.C.L.A. Law Review, 1975-1976. Author: "Antenuptial Agreements and California Law," Journal of the Beverly Hills Bar Association, September-October, 1975; "Orders to Show Cause for Modification," Los Angeles County Bar Family Law Reference Book, 1985-1996; "Whole-ly Imprecise in California," ABA Family Advocate, Fall, 1986. Editor, Family Law News and Review, Los Angeles County Bar Association, 1984-1987. Lecturer, Family Law, California Continuing Education of the Bar, 1983—. Panelist, Family Law Symposium, Los Angeles County Bar Association, 1993. Panelist, U.S.C. Law School,

*(This Listing Continued)*

---

Family Law Institute, 1996. Member, Board of Directors, 1985-1991 and Advisory Board, 1992—, Harriet Buhai Center for Family Law. *Member:* Beverly Hills (Delegate to State Bar Convention, 1981-1992); Los Angeles County (Chair, Family Law Section, 1990-1991; Member, Executive Committee, 1981-1992) and American Bar Associations; State Bar of California; Women Lawyers Association of Los Angeles (Member, Board of Governors, 1978-1981; First Vice-President, 1980-1981); California Women Lawyers (Member, Board of Governors, 1980-1981). **PRACTICE AREAS:** Family Law.

REFERENCE: City National Bank (Beverly Hills Main Office).

---

## ROBERT L. LUTY

*A PROFESSIONAL CORPORATION*

Established in 1984

SUITE 303, 11661 SAN VICENTE BOULEVARD
**LOS ANGELES, CALIFORNIA 90049**
*Telephone: 310-207-4342*
*Fax: 310-207-5035*

*Personal Injury, Insurance Bad Faith, Products Liability, Medical and Legal Malpractice and General Liability.*

**ROBERT L. LUTY,** born Los Angeles, California, March 12, 1948; admitted to bar, 1973, California; U.S. District Court, Central and Northern Districts of California. *Education:* Duke University (B.A., 1970); Loyola University of Los Angeles (J.D., 1973). Phi Delta Phi. Member, Los Angeles Superior Court Judicial Settlement Officer Program. 1987—. Judge Pro Tem, Santa Monica Municipal Court, 1987—. *Member:* Santa Monica, Los Angeles County and American Bar Associations; State Bar of California; California Trial Lawyers Association; The Association of Trial Lawyers of America; American Board of Trial Advocates (Associate); Cowboy Lawyers Association (Charter Member, Sargent at Arms, 1989-1992; Vice President, 1993; President, 1994-1995; Board of Directors, 1989—).

REFERENCE: Brentwood Savings Bank (Brentwood Branch).

---

## LYNBERG & WATKINS

*A PROFESSIONAL CORPORATION*

SIXTEENTH FLOOR INTERNATIONAL TOWER PLAZA
888 SOUTH FIGUEROA STREET
**LOS ANGELES, CALIFORNIA 90017-2516**
*Telephone: 213-624-8700*
*Fax: 213-892-2763*

Santa Ana, California Office: Suite 101, 2020 E. 1st Street. Telephone: 714-973-1220. Fax: 714-973-1002.

*General Insurance Practice in all California and Federal Trial and Appellate Courts, including Defense of Bad Faith, Insurance Coverage, Excess Liability, Aviation, Product Liability, Casualty and Professional Liability Claims. Defense of Municipalities and Businesses. Environmental and Toxic Coverage and Defense Litigation.*

**CHARLES A. LYNBERG,** born Sioux City, Iowa, August 7, 1929; admitted to bar, 1957, Iowa; 1960, California, U.S. District Court, Central District of California and U.S. Court of Appeals, Ninth Circuit; 1966, U.S. Supreme Court. *Education:* University of Idaho and State University of Iowa (B.A., 1955); State University of Iowa (J.D., 1957). Delta Theta Phi. *Member:* Los Angeles County, Wilshire, Iowa State (Inactive Member) and Federal Bar Associations; State Bar of California; Association of Southern California Defense Counsel (Vice President, 1977-1978; President, 1978-1979); American Board of Trial Advocates (Diplomate: Board of Directors, 1976-1978; National Executive Committee, 1975—; Vice President, 1982-1983; President, 1983-1984); Defense Research and Trial Lawyers Association; International Association of Insurance Counsel (State Area Chairman, 1984-1985).

**JUDITH GOLD,** born Los Angeles, California, January 22, 1938; admitted to bar, 1974, California. *Education:* Whittier College School of Law (J.D., 1974). Recipient, Outstanding Student Scholarship, 1973. *Member:* Los Angeles County and American Bar Associations; State Bar of California; Association of Southern California Defense Counsel; Defense Research and Trial Lawyers Association (Member, Board of Directors, 1980-1982).

**NORMAN J. WATKINS,** born Williamsport, Pennsylvania, April 18, 1945; admitted to bar, 1971, Pennsylvania; 1975, U.S. Supreme Court;

*(This Listing Continued)*

1979, California. *Education:* Texas Christian University and Lycoming College (B.A., 1967); University of Pittsburgh (J.D., 1971). Author: "Kremens vs. Bartley: The Case for the State," 27 Hospital and Community Psychiatry, 706, October, 1976. Deputy Attorney General, Pennsylvania, 1973-1979. Chief, Major Civil Litigation Division, 1978-1979. American Board of Trial Advocates (Advocate). *Member:* State Bar of California; Federal and American Bar Associations; Association of Southern California Defense Counsel; International Association of Defense Counsel; Defense Research and Trial Lawyers Association.

**R. JEFF CARLISLE,** born Santa Monica, California, May 20, 1951; admitted to bar, 1977, California. *Education:* University of California at Berkeley (B.A., 1973); University of Southern California (J.D., 1977). *Member:* State Bar of California; Association of Southern California Defense Counsel; Defense Research and Trial Lawyers Association.

**DANA J. MCCUNE,** born Long Beach, California, June 17, 1953; admitted to bar, 1978, California. *Education:* University of California at Los Angeles (B.A., magna cum laude, 1975); Loyola University of Los Angeles (J.D., 1978). Phi Beta Kappa; Pi Gamma Mu. Recipient: Wilshire Bar Association Scholar. *Member:* State Bar of California; American Bar Association; Association of Southern California Defense Counsel.

**MICHAEL J. LARIN,** born New York, N.Y., December 8, 1950; admitted to bar, 1977, California and U.S. District Court, Central District of California. *Education:* Syracuse University (B.A., 1973); Southwestern University (J.D., 1977). *Member:* Los Angeles County Bar Association; State Bar of California; Association of Southern California Defense Counsel.

**RANDALL J. PETERS,** born Freeport, New York, July 30, 1957; admitted to bar, 1982, California and U.S. District Court, Central District of California; 1983, U.S. District Court, Northern District of California. *Education:* University of California at Los Angeles (B.A., 1979); Southwestern University School of Law (J.D., 1982). *Member:* State Bar of California; Association of Southern California Defense Counsel.

††**RIC C. OTTAIANO,** born Hoboken, New Jersey, May 29, 1956; admitted to bar, 1982, California; 1983, U.S. District Court, Central and Northern Districts of California. *Education:* Rutgers University (B.A., cum laude, 1978); McGeorge School of Law, University of the Pacific (J.D., 1982). Phi Delta Phi. Member, Pacific Law Journal National Moot Court Honors Board. *Member:* Los Angeles County and American Bar Associations; State Bar of California; Association of Southern California Defense Counsel.

**DANA A. FOX,** born Norwalk, Connecticut, June 1, 1960; admitted to bar, 1985, California and U.S. District Court, Central District of California. *Education:* University of Connecticut; California State University of Los Angeles (B.A., 1982); McGeorge School of the Law, University of the Pacific (J.D., with distinction, 1985). Member, Traynor Honor Society. Assistant Editor, Pacific Law Journal, 1984-1985. Author: "Regulating the Professional Sports Agent: Is California in the Right Ballpark," 15 Pacific Law Journal 1231, 1984. *Member:* Los Angeles County and American Bar Associations; State Bar of California.

**STEPHEN M. HARBER,** born Lawton, Oklahoma, November 3, 1959; admitted to bar, 1985, California and U.S. District Court, Central District of California. *Education:* University of Southern California (B.S., 1981); McGeorge School of the Law, University of the Pacific (J.D., with honors, 1985). Phi Alpha Delta. National Moot Court Semifinalist. Author, "Withholding Food and Water from a Patient-Should it Be Condoned in California?" 16 Pacific Law Journal 877. *Member:* State Bar of California; Association of Southern California Defense Counsel.

**RUTH SEGAL,** born Los Angeles, California, September 22, 1960; admitted to bar, 1986, California. *Education:* University of California at Los Angeles (B.A., 1982); Southwestern University School of Law (J.D., 1986). Editor, Southwestern University Law Review, 1985-1986. Recipient, American Jurisprudence Award in Torts. *Member:* State Bar of California.

**CATHERINE L. FERRO,** born Queens, New York, April 1, 1961; admitted to bar, 1987, California. *Education:* California State University at Northridge (B.A., magna cum laude, 1983); Loyola Marymount University (J.D., 1986). Blue Key; Psi Chi. Research Assistant to Dean Arthur Frakt, Loyola Law School, 1984. Federal Judicial Extern to the Honorable James M. Ideman, Federal District Court, 1985-1986. *Member:* Los Angeles County and American Bar Associations; State Bar of California; Association of Southern California Defense Counsel.

**HELLER-ANN C. HANCOCK,** born Philadelphia, Pennsylvania, July 29, 1959; admitted to bar, 1984, California; 1985, District of Columbia; 1988, U.S. Supreme Court. *Education:* University of Maryland (B.S., 1979);

*(This Listing Continued)*

Pepperdine University (J.D., 1984). Author: "AIDS: A Tragedy Not a Handicap," ABA Journal, February, 1987. *Member:* State Bar of California; District of Columbia Bar; American Bar Association.

**LOUIS E. MARINO, JR.,** born Los Angeles, California, December 12, 1960; admitted to bar, 1987, California. *Education:* University of Southern California (B.S., 1983); Southwestern University (J.D., 1987). *Member:* Los Angeles County Bar Association (Member, Litigation Section); State Bar of California; Association of Southern California Defense Counsel.

**DOUGLAS G. MACKAY,** born Whittier, California, December 11, 1961; admitted to bar, 1987, California; 1988, U.S. District Court, Central District of California. *Education:* University of California at Los Angeles (B.S., 1984); Southwestern University (J.D., 1987). Member, Moot Court. *Member:* Western San Bernardino County Bar Association; State Bar of California.

---

**CHRISTINE H. GOSNEY,** born Los Angeles, California, February 1, 1951; admitted to bar, 1983, California; 1990, U.S. District Court, Central District of California. *Education:* University of California at Irvine (B.A., 1979); Western State University-College of Law (J.D., cum laude, 1982). Member, Law Review, Western State University College of Law, 1981-1982. Recipient, American Jurisprudence Awards. *Member:* State Bar of California.

††**WILLIAM F. BERNARD,** born New Brunswick, New Jersey, November 7, 1951; admitted to bar, 1988, California. *Education:* California State University at Long Beach (B.A., 1978); Western State University (J.D., 1987). *Member:* Orange County Bar Association; State Bar of California; Association of Southern California Defense Counsel.

**MICHAEL A. CARTELLI,** born Los Angeles, California, October 8, 1954; admitted to bar, 1979, California; 1980, U.S. District Court, Central District of California; 1990, Washington; 1992, U.S. District Court, District of North Dakota. *Education:* Loyola University of Los Angeles (B.A., 1976; J.D., 1979). *Member:* Washington State Bar Association; State Bar Association of North Dakota; State Bar of California; Association of Southern California Defense Counsel. **PRACTICE AREAS:** Insurance Litigation; Injury Litigation.

**PAMELA H. ROTH,** born Garden City, New York, February 21, 1961; admitted to bar, 1986, California; 1985, District of Columbia; 1987, U.S. Court of Military Appeals. *Education:* Lehigh University (B.A., 1981); George Washington University (J.D., 1984). *Member:* State Bar of California; The District of Columbia Bar. [Capt., U.S. Air Force, 1986-1991]

**CLAUDIA H. HANZLICK,** born Bogota, Colombia, May 12, 1963; admitted to bar, 1990, California. *Education:* Miami Dade Community College (A.A., 1983); Eastern Kentucky University (B.A., 1985); Ohio State University (J.D., 1989). Phi Alpha Delta. *Member:* State Bar of California; American Bar Association. **LANGUAGES:** Spanish.

**THOMAS G. OESTERREICH,** born Lynwood, California, February 5, 1961; admitted to bar, 1986, California; 1987, U.S. District Court, Central District of California. *Education:* Loyola Marymount University (B.B.A., 1983); University of Houston (J.D., 1986). Phi Delta Phi. *Member:* State Bar of California; Association of Southern California Defense Counsel. **PRACTICE AREAS:** Insurance Litigation and Coverage.

**PEGGY KOLKEY,** born New York, N.Y., February 6, 1951; admitted to bar, 1990, California and U.S. District Court, Central District of California. *Education:* California State University (B.A., 1972); Loyola Law School (J.D., 1990). Phi Delta Phi. *Member:* State Bar of California; American Bar Association. **PRACTICE AREAS:** Insurance Defense Law.

**WENDY E. SCHULTZ,** born Los Angeles, California, October 5, 1963; admitted to bar, 1990, California. *Education:* Pomona College (B.A., 1985); Loyola Law School (J.D., 1990). Southern California Defense Counsel. *Member:* Los Angeles County and American Bar Associations; State Bar of California.

**JASON M. BOOTH,** born Boston, Massachusetts, November 12, 1961; admitted to bar, 1989, California, U.S. District Court, Central District of California and U.S. Court of Appeals, Ninth Circuit. *Education:* University of California at Los Angeles (B.A., cum laude, 1985); Southwestern University of Law (J.D., cum laude, 1989). Editor-in-Chief, Southwestern University Law Review, 1988-1989. Author: "Hustler v. Falwell: Intentional Infliction of Emotional Distress and the First Amendment," 17 S.W.U.L. Rev. 441 (1990). *Member:* Los Angeles County Bar Association (Member, Litigation Subsection). *Member:* State Bar of California.

*(This Listing Continued)*

**LYNBERG & WATKINS, A PROFESSIONAL CORPORATION,**
Los Angeles—Continued

**JEROME P. DOCTORS,** born Cleveland, Ohio, November 8, 1963; admitted to bar, 1989, California; 1990, Nevada. *Education:* University of California (B.A., 1986); Southwestern University School of Law (J.D., 1989). *Member:* Los Angeles County, San Fernando Valley and American Bar Associations; State Bar of California; State Bar of Nevada. *REPORTED CASES:* Sargoy v. Resolution Trust Corporation, et al. 10 Cal. Rptr. 2d 889 (Cal. App. 2 Dist. 1992). *PRACTICE AREAS:* Probate Law; Civil Litigation.

**GUY N. WEBSTER,** born Birmingham, England, June 17, 1962; admitted to bar, 1989, California and U.S. District Court, Central District of California; 1996, U.S. Court of Appeals, Ninth Circuit. *Education:* Orange Coast College; University of California at Irvine; Western State University (B.S., 1985; J.D., 1987). Recipient, American Jurisprudence Book Award for Wills. *Member:* Orange County and American Bar Associations; State Bar of California. *REPORTED CASES:* People v. Mark Edwin Taylor (1992) 6 Cal. App. 4th 1084. *PRACTICE AREAS:* Insurance.

**JAMIE L. VELS,** born Los Angeles, California, April 16, 1965; admitted to bar, 1991, California; 1992, U.S. District Court, Northern, Eastern and Southern Districts of California. *Education:* University of California at San Diego (B.A., 1987); Loyola Marymount University (J.D., 1991). Member, Entertainment Law Journal, Loyola Marymount University, 1990-1991. *Member:* State Bar of California. *LANGUAGES:* Spanish. *PRACTICE AREAS:* Insurance Coverage; Insurance Defense (Bad Faith).

**DAVID K. MORRISON,** born Evanston, Illinois, June 6, 1957; admitted to bar, 1991, California; 1992, U.S. District Court, Central District of California. *Education:* Pomona College (B.A., 1979); Claremont Graduate School (M.A., 1982); Southwestern University, (J.D., 1991). Member: Mortar Board. SBA Negotiating Competition. *Member:* State Bar of California. *PRACTICE AREAS:* Insurance Defense.

**TIMOTHY F. RIVERS,** born Los Angeles, California, January 1, 1965; admitted to bar, 1990, California and U.S. District Court, Southern District of California. *Education:* University of California, San Diego (B.A., 1987); University of San Diego School of Law (J.D., 1990). *Member:* State Bar of California. *PRACTICE AREAS:* Insurance Defense; Construction Defect; Insurance Coverage.

**BARRY L. BOOKBINDER,** born Encino, California, August 6, 1963; admitted to bar, 1990, California and U.S. District Court, Central, Northern, Eastern and Southern Districts of California. *Education:* University of California at Los Angeles (B.A., English, 1986); Loyola Law School (J.D., 1990). Phi Delta Phi. *Member:* Los Angeles County and American Bar Associations; State Bar of California. *PRACTICE AREAS:* Litigation.

**TODD J. WENZEL,** born Santa Monica, California, June 1, 1966; admitted to bar, 1992, California and U.S. District Court, Central District of California. *Education:* University of California at Los Angeles (B.A., 1988); Southwestern University (J.D., 1991). *Member:* Los Angeles County and American Bar Associations; State Bar of California. *PRACTICE AREAS:* Insurance Coverage Defense; Insurance Defense; Products Liability Defense.

**MARK F. GAMBOA,** born Los Angeles, California, June 12, 1962; admitted to bar, 1993, California, U.S. District Court, Central District of California and U.S. Court of Appeals, Ninth Circuit. *Education:* California State University at Los Angeles (B.A., 1989); University of Southern California (J.D., 1993). Phi Alpha Delta. *Member:* State Bar of California. *PRACTICE AREAS:* Environmental Coverage; Toxic Tort.

**NICHOLAS R. ANDREA,** born Rochester, New York, July 15, 1968; admitted to bar, 1993, California and U.S. District Court, Central District of California. *Education:* College Misericordia (B.A., summa cum laude, 1990); Pepperdine University (J.D., cum laude, 1993). Author: "Continuous Trigger, Exposure, Manifestation: The Insurance Coverage Quagmire," Pepperdine Law Review, Fall, 1994. *Member:* State Bar of California. *PRACTICE AREAS:* Environmental Insurance Coverage; Toxic Tort.

**DINA M. DE LAURENTIS,** born Chicago, Illinois, March 12, 1967; admitted to bar, 1993, California. *Education:* Marquette University (B.A., 1989); Southwestern University School of Law (J.D., cum laude, 1993). Recipient, American Jurisprudence Award. *Member:* Los Angeles County and Los Angeles County International Bar Associations; State Bar of California; Southern Defense Counsel. *LANGUAGES:* French.

**ANTONIA M. CHAN,** born Kowloon, Hong Kong, March 18, 1967; admitted to bar, 1993, California. *Education:* University of California at Berkeley (B.A.); Loyola Marymount University (J.D., 1993). *Member:* State Bar of California. *LANGUAGES:* Cantonese.

**CHARLES C. MCKENNA,** born West Covina, California, June 5, 1967; admitted to bar, 1993, California; 1995, U.S. District Court, Central District of California. *Education:* University of California at Los Angeles (B.A., 1989); Loyola Marymount University (J.D., 1993). *Member:* State Bar of California. *PRACTICE AREAS:* Governmental Entity Defense; General Liability Defense.

**BRIAN C. PLANTE,** born Woonsocket, Rhode Island, September 28, 1969; admitted to bar, 1994, California and U.S. District Court, Central District of California. *Education:* University of Rhode Island (B.S., 1991); Pepperdine University (J.D., magna cum laude, 1994). Member, Pepperdine Law Review, 1992-1994. *Member:* State Bar of California. *PRACTICE AREAS:* Insurance Coverage Litigation; General Civil Defense.

**††MARY E. LYNCH,** born Rochester, New York, June 1, 1966; admitted to bar, 1994, California and U.S. District Court, Central District of California. *Education:* California State University at Fullerton (B.A., 1988); Southwestern University School of Law (J.D., cum laude, 1994). Recipient, American Jurisprudence Awards in Corporations, Evidence and Community Property. Note and Comment Editor, Southwestern Journal of Law and Trade in the Americas, 1993-1994. Author: "Two-Tier Methodology for Administrative Review of Anti-Dumping Duty Orders," Southwestern Journal of Law and Trade in the Americas, Vol. 1, No. 7. Extern to Hon. Justice Sheila Prell Sonenshine, Fourth Appellate District, Division Three, 1993. *Member:* State Bar of California; Orange County Barristers.

**DENAH H. YOSHIYAMA,** born Los Angeles, California, March 7, 1968; admitted to bar, 1994, California; 1995, U.S. District Court, Eastern and Central Districts of California. *Education:* University of California at Santa Barbara (B.A., 1990); Southwestern University (J.D., 1994). Law Clerk, U.S. Bankruptcy Court, Eastern District of California, 1994-1995. *Member:* Orange County Bar Association; State Bar of California.

**MICHAEL T. TAUREK,** born San Bernardino, California, April 8, 1968; admitted to bar, 1994, California. *Education:* University of California at Santa Barbara (B.A., with honors, 1991); Pepperdine University (J.D., 1994). Phi Delta Phi. Member, Pepperdine Law Review. *Member:* Los Angeles County and American Bar Associations; State Bar of California.

**KATHY M. GANDARA,** born New York, N.Y., October 24, 1960; admitted to bar, 1995, California and U.S. District Court, Central District of California. *Education:* Rio Hondo College (A.S., 1984); University of La Verne College of Law (J.D., 1995). Delta Theta Phi. Recipient, American Jurisprudence Award in Appellate Advocacy. *Member:* State Bar of California. *PRACTICE AREAS:* Civil Litigation.

**MARK A. HOOPER,** born Los Angeles, California, May 7, 1965; admitted to bar, 1994, California. *Education:* Brigham Young University (B.S., 1988); Pepperdine University (J.D., 1994);. President, Criminal Law Society, 1992-1994. *Member:* Orange County Bar Association; State Bar of California. *PRACTICE AREAS:* Insurance Defense; Bad Faith Litigation.

**MICHAEL J. PEPEK,** born Beaufort, South Carolina, October 7, 1969; admitted to bar, 1995, California. *Education:* University of California at San Diego (B.A., 1991); McGeorge School of Law, University of the Pacific (J.D., with distinction, 1995). Member, Justice Traynor Society. Author: "TXO v. Alliance: Due Process Limits and Introducing a Defendant's Wealth When Determining Punitive Damage Awards," 25 Prac. Law.J. 1191, 1994; "Review of Selected 1995 California Legislation," 25 Prac. Law.J. 368, 1994. *Member:* State Bar of California.

**HEATHER C. JELENSKY,** born Fullerton, California, May 29, 1971; admitted to bar, 1995, California and U.S. District Court, Central District of California. *Education:* University of California at Santa Barbara (B.A., 1992); Pepperdine University (J.D., 1995). *Member:* State Bar of California. *PRACTICE AREAS:* Insurance Coverage and Defense; General Defense; Litigation; Products Liability.

**LISA M. BAKER,** born Fullerton, California, December 18, 1969; admitted to bar, 1995, California. *Education:* University of Southern California (B.A., magna cum laude, 1992); Southwestern University School of Law (J.D., magna cum laude, 1995). Phi Beta Kappa; Phi Kappa Phi. Moot Court Honors Program. Board Member, National Corporate and Securities Law Competitions. Recipient, American Jurisprudence Award in Remedies. *Member:* State Bar of California; American Bar Association. *PRACTICE AREAS:* Business Litigation; Insurance Coverage.

**ALAN AGHABEGIAN,** born Tehran, Iran, July 8, 1968; admitted to bar, 1995, California. *Education:* California State University (B.A., 1991); Pepperdine University (J.D., 1995). Treasurer, Armenian Legal Society,

*(This Listing Continued)*

1993-1994. Member, International Law Society, 1993-1994. *Member:* State Bar of California. *LANGUAGES:* French, Armenian, Persian. *PRACTICE AREAS:* Insurance Defense.

**KARA J. PETRECCIA,** born Montreal, Canada, September 17, 1970; admitted to bar, 1995, California. *Education:* California State University (B.B.A., 1991); Southwestern University School of Law (J.D., 1995). Member, Moot Court Honors Program. Member, Asian Pacific Law Society, 1992-1995. *Member:* State Bar of California.

**TODD HARRISON STITT,** born Whittier, California, January 21, 1969; admitted to bar, 1995, California. *Education:* University of California at Irvine (B.A., 1992); Southwestern University School of Law (J.D., 1995). *Member:* State Bar of California. *PRACTICE AREAS:* Insurance Coverage.

**ALEX H. CHERIN,** born Long Beach, California, November 16, 1970; admitted to bar, 1996, California. *Education:* University of Michigan (B.A., 1992); Loyola Law School of Los Angeles (J.D., 1995). Member, International Law Society. *Member:* Long Beach Bar Association; State Bar of California; Ball-Hunt Inn of Court. *LANGUAGES:* Japanese. *PRACTICE AREAS:* Government Entity Litigation.

*OF COUNSEL*

**MARTIN D. KAPLAN,** born New York, N.Y., December 18, 1930; admitted to bar, 1979, California and U.S. District Court, Central and Southern Districts of California. *Education:* University of California at Los Angeles (A.A., 1950); University of Southern California (Pharm.D., 1954); University of West Los Angeles (J.D., 1979). President, Santa Monica Bay Area Pharmaceutical Association, 1961. *Member:* Los Angeles County and American Bar Associations; State Bar of California; Los Angeles Trial Lawyers Association; American Pharmaceutical Association; California Pharmaceutical Association; Association of Southern California Defense Counsel.

††Santa Ana Office

REPRESENTATIVE CLIENTS: American International Group of Companies (AIG); Alliance of Schools for Cooperative Insurance Program (ASCIP); Atlantic-Richfield Company (ARCO); Boise-Cascade Corporation; Carl Warren & Company; City of Culver City, CA; City of El Monte, CA; City of Huntington Park, CA; County of Orange, CA; Firemans' Fund Insurance Company; GAB Business Services; GAB Home Depot; Keenan & Associates; Lindsey Morden Claim Services; Litton Industries; Ralphs Grocery Company; Rowland Unified School District; YMCA of Metropolitan Los Angeles.

# LYNCH ROWIN NOVACK BURNBAUM & CRYSTAL, P.C.

22ND FLOOR, 2121 AVENUE OF THE STARS
LOS ANGELES, CALIFORNIA 90067
Telephone: 310-557-8422
Telex: 181 149 WEST LSA

*New York, New York Office:* 300 East 42nd Street. Telephone: 212-682-4001. Telex: 220 883 TA UR. Telecopier: 212-986-2907.

General Practice. Litigation, Corporate and Commercial, Products Liability, Environmental, Financing and Banking, Real Estate, Securities, Trusts and Estates, Trademark, Copyright, Art Business, International Transactions and Computer Law.

(For Complete Biographical Data, See Professional Biographies at New York, New York)

# LYON & LYON LLP

A Limited Liability Partnership including Professional Corporations

*Established in 1911*

FIRST INTERSTATE WORLD CENTER
47TH FLOOR, 633 WEST FIFTH STREET
LOS ANGELES, CALIFORNIA 90071-2066
Telephone: 213-489-1600
Fax: 213-955-0440
Email: lyon@lyonlyon.com
URL: http://www.lyonlyon.com

*Costa Mesa, California Office:* Suite 1200, 3200 Park Center Drive. Telephone: 714-751-6606. Fax: 714-751-8209.

*San Jose, California Office:* Suite 1150, 303 Almaden Boulevard. Telephone: 408-993-1555. Fax: 408-287-2664.

(This Listing Continued)

*La Jolla, California Office:* Suite 660, 4250 Executive Square. Telephone: 619-552-8400. Fax: 619-552-0159.

Intellectual Property Law including Patent, Trademark, Copyright, Trade Regulation, Unfair Competition and Antitrust Law. Litigation.

FIRM PROFILE: Lyon & Lyon, one of the largest intellectual property firms in the country and the preeminent patent litigation firm in the western United States, has approximately 90 lawyers in four offices across California.

Lyon & Lyon offers a comprehensive program of intellectual property management, including: PATENT PORTFOLIO DEVELOPMENT-devising a patent strategy, auditing the client's internal invention-disclosure and filing-decision policies, securing effective patent claims, prosecuting patent reexamination and reissue proceedings where appropriate; TRADE SECRET PROTECTION- drafting confidentiality agreements, designing client internal procedures and protocols, counseling about special problems of hiring technically-experienced employees who have worked for competitors of the client; COPYRIGHT PROTECTION-registration filing, appropriate notice marking and infringement monitoring, for works as diverse as shop drawings, jewelry designs, client-internal technical literature, screenplays and computer programs; MASK WORK FILINGS-to achieve copyright-like protection for microchip designs; TRADEMARK MANAGEMENT-evaluating marks for selection, prosecuting trademark applications, reviewing packaging and advertising for proper trademark usage, monitoring adverse trademark filings, prosecuting opposition and cancellation proceedings; TRANSACTIONAL WORK-licensing of patents, trademarks, copyright, trade secrets and know-how, antitrust counseling concerning licensing and franchising matters, evaluating patent portfolios for business acquisitions, startups and capitalizations, counseling on infringement avoidance; GLOBAL INTELLECTUAL PROPERTY STRATEGY AND IMPLEMENTATION-via Lyon & Lyon's longstanding affiliation with law firms in every industrialized nation in the world; and ENFORCEMENT OF RIGHTS-litigation of patent, trademark, copyright, trade secret, unfair competition, anti-counterfeiting, franchise, licensing and related antitrust causes in the courts, unfair import proceedings before the U.S. International Trade Commission, interference and cancellation proceedings in the U.S. Patent and Trademark Office.

*MEMBERS OF FIRM*

**ROLAND N. SMOOT,** born New London, Connecticut, September 21, 1925; admitted to bar, 1955, Virginia and California; 1978, U.S. Supreme Court; registered to practice before the U.S. Patent and Trademark Office. *Education:* California Institute of Technology (B.S., 1950); Georgetown University (J.D., 1955). *Member:* Los Angeles County and American Bar Associations; American Intellectual Property Law Association; Los Angeles Intellectual Property Law Association. *PRACTICE AREAS:* Patent, Trademark, Trade Regulation, Unfair Competition; Intellectual Property.

**CONRAD R. SOLUM, JR.,** born Los Angeles, California, March 5, 1935; admitted to bar, 1960, California, U.S. Court of Appeals, Federal and Ninth Circuits and U.S. District Court, Central, Southern and Northern Districts of California; registered to practice before the U.S. Patent and Trademark Office. *Education:* University of Southern California (B.E.-Mech., 1956; LL.B., 1959). Member, 1957-1959 and Associate Editor, 1958-1959, Southern California Law Review. Member: Committee on Intellectual Properties Litigation, 1967—; Patent, Trademark and Copyright Sections, The State Bar of California. *Member:* Los Angeles County and American (Member, Patent, Trademark and Copyright Sections) Bar Associations; Los Angeles Intellectual Property Law Association (Member, Board of Directors, 1963-1965). [1st Lt., U.S. Army Reserve, JAGC, 1963-1965]. *PRACTICE AREAS:* Patent, Trademark, Copyright, Unfair Competition; Intellectual Property.

**JAMES W. GERIAK,** (A PROFESSIONAL CORPORATION) (Costa Mesa Office).

**ROBERT M. TAYLOR, JR.** (Costa Mesa Office).

**SAMUEL B. STONE,** (A PROFESSIONAL CORPORATION) (Costa Mesa Office).

**DOUGLAS E. OLSON,** (A PROFESSIONAL CORPORATION) (La Jolla Office).

**ROBERT E. LYON,** (A PROFESSIONAL CORPORATION), born Los Angeles, California, August 26, 1936; admitted to bar, 1964, California and U.S. District Court, Central, Eastern and Northern Districts of California; 1972, U.S. Court of Appeals, Ninth Circuit; 1984, U.S. Court of Appeals for the Federal Circuit; registered to practice before the U.S. Patent and Trademark Office. *Education:* University of Southern California (B.S. in E.E., 1960; J.D., 1963). *Member:* Los Angeles County, Orange County and American Bar Associations; Los Angeles Intellectual Property Law

(This Listing Continued)

**LYON & LYON LLP**, *Los Angeles—Continued*

Association. **PRACTICE AREAS:** Patent, Trademark, Copyright, Unfair Competition; Intellectual Property. **Email:** rlyon@lyonlyon.com

**ROBERT C. WEISS, (A PROFESSIONAL CORPORATION),** born Los Angeles, California, May 20, 1940; admitted to bar, 1967, California; registered to practice before the U.S. Patent and Trademark Office. *Education:* University of California at Berkeley (B.S.M.E., 1963); University of Southern California (J.D., 1966). Phi Delta Phi. *Member:* Los Angeles County and American Bar Associations; Los Angeles Intellectual Property Law Association; American Intellectual Property Law Association. **PRACTICE AREAS:** Patent, Trademark, Copyright, Trade Regulation; Unfair Competition, Antitrust, Litigation; Intellectual Property.

**RICHARD E. LYON, JR., (A PROFESSIONAL CORPORATION),** born Boston, Massachusetts, October 17, 1943; admitted to bar, 1970, California; registered to practice before the U.S. Patent and Trademark Office. *Education:* Stanford University (B.S., 1966); University of Utah (J.D., 1969). Phi Alpha Delta. *Member:* Los Angeles County and American Bar Associations; Los Angeles Intellectual Property Law Association. **PRACTICE AREAS:** Patent, Trademark, Unfair Competition; Licensing of Intellectual Property; Intellectual Property.

**JOHN D. MCCONAGHY, (A PROFESSIONAL CORPORATION),** born Fresno, California, December 20, 1943; admitted to bar, 1972, California; registered to practice before the U.S. Patent and Trademark Office. *Education:* University of Southern California (B.S.M.E., 1966; M.S.M.E., 1968); University of California at Los Angeles (J.D., 1971). Tau Beta Pi; Pi Tau Sigma. *Member:* Los Angeles County and American Bar Associations; Los Angeles Intellectual Property Law Association. **PRACTICE AREAS:** Patent, Trademark; Intellectual Property. **Email:** lyon@lyonlyon.com

**WILLIAM C. STEFFIN, (A PROFESSIONAL CORPORATION),** born Shawano, Wisconsin, July 17, 1945; admitted to bar, 1972, California; 1984, U.S. Court of Appeals for the Federal Circuit; registered to practice before the U.S. Patent and Trademark Office. *Education:* University of Wisconsin (B.S., in Chem. Engr., 1967); Hastings College of Law, University of California (LL.B., 1972). Phi Delta Phi. Member, Thurston Society. Member, Hastings Law Journal, 1970-1971, 1971-1972. *Member:* Los Angeles County (Chair, Intellectual Property Section, 1980-1981) and American Bar Associations; American Intellectual Property Law Association; U.S. Trademark Association; Los Angeles Intellectual Property Law Association (Chair Elect, Torts and Insurance Practice, Intellectual Property Subcommittee). **PRACTICE AREAS:** Patent, Trademark, Copyright, Unfair Competition; Intellectual Property. **Email:** steffin@lyonlyon.com

**COE A. BLOOMBERG, (A PROFESSIONAL CORPORATION),** born Laurel, Maryland, October 6, 1943; admitted to bar, 1972, California; 1973, U.S. Court of Customs and Patent Appeals; 1974, New York; 1982, U.S. Court of Appeals for the Federal Circuit; registered to practice before the U.S. Patent and Trademark Office. *Education:* Georgia Institute of Technology (B.M.E., 1966); Loyola University of Los Angeles (J.D., with special recognition, 1972). Phi Alpha Delta. Member, St. Thomas More Law Honor Society. Member, 1970-1972 and Associate Editor, 1971, Loyola University of Los Angeles Law Review. *Member:* Los Angeles County and American Bar Associations; American Intellectual Property Law Association; Los Angeles Intellectual Property Law Association. **PRACTICE AREAS:** Intellectual Property.

**J. DONALD MCCARTHY, (A PROFESSIONAL CORPORATION),** born Syracuse, New York, July 7, 1942; admitted to bar, 1968, Massachusetts and U.S. Court of Appeals, First Circuit; 1971, Pennsylvania and U.S. Court of Appeals, Third Circuit; 1976, California and U.S. Court of Appeals, Ninth Circuit; 1977, U.S. Court of Appeals, Fourth Circuit; 1978, U.S. Court of Appeals, Tenth Circuit; 1981, U.S. Court of Appeals, Sixth Circuit; 1982, U.S. Court of Appeals for the Federal Circuit; 1986, U.S. Supreme Court; registered to practice before the U.S. Patent and Trademark Office. *Education:* Cornell University (B.M.E., 1965); Harvard University (J.D., 1968). *Member:* Los Angeles County and American (Member, Sections on: Antitrust Law; Litigation and Intellectual Property) Bar Associations; American Patent Law Association; Los Angeles Intellectual Property Law Association. **PRACTICE AREAS:** Patent, Trademark, Copyright, Trade Regulation; Unfair Competition, Antitrust, Intellectual Property.

**ARNOLD SKLAR,** born Los Angeles, California, April 7, 1946; admitted to bar, 1972, California and U.S. District Court, Central District of California. *Education:* University of California at Los Angeles (B.A., 1968); University of Southern California (J.D., 1971). *Member:* Los Angeles

*(This Listing Continued)*

County Bar Association. **PRACTICE AREAS:** Antitrust, Franchise, Licensing; Intellectual Property.

**JOHN M. BENASSI** (La Jolla Office).

**JAMES H. SHALEK,** born Boston, Massachusetts, October 14, 1953; admitted to bar, 1978, California; 1979, U.S. District Court, Central District of California; 1982, U.S. District Court, Northern and Southern Districts of California and U.S. Court of Appeals for the Ninth and Federal Circuits; registered to practice before the U.S. Patent and Trademark Office. *Education:* University of Pennsylvania (B.A., magna cum laude, 1975); Boston University (J.D., cum laude, 1978). *Member:* Los Angeles County and American Bar Associations; American Intellectual Property Law Association; Los Angeles Intellectual Property Law Association. **PRACTICE AREAS:** Patent, Trademark, Copyright; Intellectual Property.

**ALLAN W. JANSEN** (Costa Mesa Office).

**ROBERT W. DICKERSON,** born Oakdale, California, September 12, 1950; admitted to bar, 1979, California; 1980, U.S. District Court, Central District of California; U.S. Court of Appeals, Sixth and Ninth Circuits; 1981, U.S. Court of Appeals, Tenth Circuit; 1982, U.S. District Court, Eastern District of California; 1983, U.S. Court of Appeals for the Federal Circuit; 1984, U.S. Claims Court; 1984, U.S. District Court, Northern District of California; registered to practice before the U.S. Patent and Trademark Office. *Education:* University of California at Berkeley (B.S., Industrial Engineering and Operations Research, 1973); Southwestern University (J.D., cum laude, 1979). Phi Alpha Delta. Member, The Order of Barristers. Member: Moot Court Honors Program; First Place, Giles Sutherland Rich Patent Law Moot Court Competition, West Coast Regional Finals; Southwestern Law Review, 1978-1979. *Member:* Los Angeles County and American Bar Associations; Los Angeles Intellectual Property Law Association; American Intellectual Property Law Association. **PRACTICE AREAS:** Intellectual Property. **Email:** rdickers@lyonlyon.com

**ROY L. ANDERSON,** born Hinsdale, Illinois, October 31, 1957; admitted to bar, 1982, California; registered to practice before the U.S. Patent and Trademark Office. *Education:* University of Illinois; Illinois Wesleyan University (B.A., Chemistry, 1979); George Washington University (J.D., with honors, 1982). Phi Delta Phi. *Member:* Los Angeles County and American Bar Associations; Los Angeles Intellectual Property Law Association; American Intellectual Property Law Association. **PRACTICE AREAS:** Litigation; Patent, Trademark, Unfair Competition, Antitrust; Intellectual Property.

**DAVID B. MURPHY** (Costa Mesa Office).

**JAMES C. BROOKS,** born Montgomery, Alabama, January 22, 1948; admitted to bar, 1979, District of Columbia; 1987, California; registered to practice before the U.S. Patent and Trademark Office. *Education:* University of Washington (B.S., in Aeronautics and Astronautics, 1970); Hunter College of the City University of New York; Georgetown University (J.D., 1979). *Member:* The District of Columbia Bar; American Bar Association (Member, Sections on: Antitrust Law; Litigation; Patent, Trademark and Copyright Law); American Intellectual Property Law Association. **PRACTICE AREAS:** Patent, Trademark, Copyright, Unfair Competition, Trade Secret; Intellectual Property.

**JEFFREY M. OLSON,** born Rockford, Illinois, November 9, 1955; admitted to bar, 1982, California and U.S. District Court, Central District of California; 1984, U.S. Court of Appeals for the Federal Circuit; registered to practice before the U.S. Patent and Trademark Office. *Education:* University of Illinois (B.S., 1977); University of Michigan (J.D., 1981). *Member:* Los Angeles County and American Bar Associations; American Intellectual Property Law Association; Los Angeles Intellectual Property Law Association. **PRACTICE AREAS:** Intellectual Property.

**STEVEN D. HEMMINGER** (San Jose Office).

**JERROLD B. REILLY,** born Albany, New York, August 30, 1947; admitted to bar, 1976, New York; 1978, U.S. District Court, Western District of New York; 1979, U.S. Court of Appeals, Second Circuit; 1984, California; registered to practice before the U.S. Patent and Trademark Office. *Education:* Boston College (B.S., 1969); Syracuse University (J.D., cum laude, 1975); New York University (LL.M., in Trade Regulation, 1984). Member, Justinian Society. Notes and Comments Editor, Syracuse Law Review, 1974-1975. Law Clerk, New York Supreme Court, Appellate Division, 4th Department, 1975-1977. *Member:* Los Angeles County, New York State and American (Member, Sections on: Patent, Trademark and Copyright Law; Antitrust Law) Bar Associations; The Copyright Society of the U.S.A.; America Intellectual Property Law Association. **PRACTICE AREAS:** Intellectual Property.

*(This Listing Continued)*

**PAUL H. MEIER,** born Camden, New Jersey, August 16, 1957; admitted to bar, 1984, California; 1985, U.S. District Court, Central District of California; registered to practice before the U.S. Patent and Trademark Office. *Education:* University of California at Los Angeles (B.S., cum laude, 1979); Boalt Hall School of Law, University of California (J.D., 1984). Regents Fellow. *Member:* Los Angeles County and American Bar Associations; American Intellectual Property Law Association. *PRACTICE AREAS:* Intellectual Property.

**JOHN A. RAFTER, JR.,** born Washington, D.C., December 4, 1956; admitted to bar, 1986, California; 1987, U.S. District Court, Central District of California; U.S. Court of Appeals for the Federal Circuit; registered to practice before the U.S. Patent and Trademark Office. *Education:* University of Notre Dame (B.S., 1979); Loyola Marymount University (J.D., 1986). Pi Tau Sigma. *Member:* American Bar Association; Los Angeles Intellectual Property Law Association. *PRACTICE AREAS:* Patent; Intellectual Property. *Email:* jrafter@lyonlyon.com

**KENNETH H. OHRINER,** born New York, N.Y., January 14, 1956; admitted to bar, 1987, California; 1988, New York; registered to practice before the U.S. Patent and Trademark Office. *Education:* State University of New York at Stony Brook (B.E.M.E., 1978); St. John's University (J.D., 1986). *Member:* Los Angeles County and American Bar Associations. *PRACTICE AREAS:* Intellectual Property. *Email:* kohriner@lyonlyon.com

**MARY S. CONSALVI** (La Jolla Office).

**LOIS M. KWASIGROCH,** admitted to bar, 1987, California; 1988, U.S. Court of Appeals, Ninth Circuit and U.S. District Court, Central, Southern and Northern Districts of California; U.S. Court of Appeals for the Federal Circuit; registered to practice before the U.S. Patent and Trademark Office. *Education:* San Francisco State University (B.A., 1976); Loyola Marymount University (J.D., 1987). *Member:* Los Angeles County and American Bar Associations; American Society of Clinical Pathologists. *PRACTICE AREAS:* Intellectual Property.

**LAWRENCE R. LAPORTE,** born Tampa, Florida, July 16, 1961; admitted to bar, 1987, California and U.S. District Court, Central District of California; registered to practice before the U.S. Patent and Trademark Office. *Education:* University of Minnesota (B.S., Mech Eng., 1984; J.D., cum laude, 1987). *PRACTICE AREAS:* Complex and Technical Litigation including Patent, Trademark, Copyright; Unfair Competition; Intellectual Property.

**ROBERT C. LAURENSON** (La Jolla Office).

**CAROL A. SCHNEIDER,** born Los Angeles, California, October 20, 1951; admitted to bar, 1988, California, U.S. District Court, Central, Eastern and Northern Districts of California and U.S. Court of Appeals, Ninth and Federal Circuits; registered to practice before the U.S. Patent and Trademark Office. *Education:* University of California at Los Angeles (B.A., 1973); University of Southern California (Ph.D., 1980; Cellular and Molecular Biology, J.D., 1988). Order of the Coif. Adjunct Professor of Patent Law, University of Southern California School of Law, 1996—. *Member:* Los Angeles County and American Bar Associations; American Intellectual Property Law Association; American Association for the Advancement of Science. *PRACTICE AREAS:* Patent; Intellectual Property.

## ASSOCIATES

**HOPE E. MELVILLE,** born Clintonville, Wisconsin, October 29, 1951; admitted to bar, 1989, California, U.S. District Court, Central District of California and U.S. Court of Appeals, Ninth Circuit; 1990, U.S. District Court, Northern District of California; registered to practice before the U.S. Patent and Trademark Office. *Education:* University of Wisconsin (B.S., Med. Tech., cum laude, 1973); Purdue University (B.S., Chem.E., 1977); University of Southern California (J.D., 1989). Extern for U.S. District Judge David V. Kenyon. *Member:* American Bar Association; American Institute of Chemical Engineers. *PRACTICE AREAS:* Patent, Trademark, Copyright, Unfair Competition; Intellectual Property.

**MICHAEL J. WISE,** born Inglewood, California, September 23, 1961; admitted to bar, 1989, California U.S. District Court, Central and Northern Districts of California and U.S. Court of Appeals, Ninth and Federal Circuits; registered to practice before the U.S. Patent and Trademark Office. *Education:* Bates College; University of California at Los Angeles (B.S., Biology, 1985); Loyola Marymount University (J.D., cum laude, 1989). Order of the Coif. *Member,* Thomas More Honors Society. Member, National Moot Court Team. Finalist, Loyola Scott Moot Court Competition. Recipient, American Jurisprudence Awards in: First Amendment Survey; Ethics Counseling and Negotiations. Extern for Ninth Circuit Court of Appeals, Judge Stephen Reinhardt. *Member:* Los Angeles County and American Bar Associations; American Intellectual Property Lawyers Association; Los Angeles Patent Lawyers Association. *PRACTICE AREAS:* Patent, Trademark, Copyright, Unfair Competition; Antitrust; Intellectual Property.

**KURT T. MULVILLE** (Costa Mesa Office).

**THEODORE S. MACEIKO,** born West Islip, New York, July 6, 1962; admitted to bar, 1990, California and U.S. District Court, Central District of California; registered to practice before the U.S. Patent and Trademark Office. *Education:* Clarkson University (B.S.M.E., 1984); Loyola Marymount University (J.D., 1990). *PRACTICE AREAS:* Patent, Trademark, Unfair Competition, Antitrust; Intellectual Property.

**RICHARD WARBURG** (La Jolla Office).

**JAMES P. BROGAN** (Costa Mesa Office).

**JEFFREY D. TEKANIC,** born Euclid, Ohio, July 26, 1966; admitted to bar, 1991, California; registered to practice before the U.S. Patent and Trademark Office. *Education:* California Institute of Technology (B.S., with honors, 1988); University of Chicago (J.D., 1991). *PRACTICE AREAS:* Patent, Trademark, Trade Regulation; Unfair Competition, Antitrust; Intellectual Property.

**CORRINE M. FREEMAN** (Costa Mesa Office).

**DAVID A. RANDALL,** born Santa Maria, California, August 29, 1963; admitted to bar, 1991, California; registered to practice before the U.S. Patent and Trademark Office. *Education:* University of Arizona (B.S., cum laude, 1985); Arizona State University (J.D., cum laude, 1991). Phi Delta Phi. Pedrick Scholar. Recipient, Daniel C. Jackling Award. *PRACTICE AREAS:* Patent, Trademark, Copyright, Unfair Competition; Intellectual Property.

**CHRISTOPHER A. VANDERLAAN,** born Redondo Beach, California, January 13, 1965; admitted to bar, 1991, California; registered to practice before the U.S. Patent and Trademark office. *Education:* University of California at Berkeley (B.S. in Electrical Engineering/Computer Science, 1987); University of California, Hastings College of Law (J.D., magna cum laude, 1991). Regents Scholar. Alumni Scholar. Order of the Coif. Thurston Society. Extern for California Court of Appeals, Justice Perley. *Member:* Los Angeles County and American Bar Associations. *PRACTICE AREAS:* Intellectual Property.

**BRUCE G. CHAPMAN,** born Williamsport, Pennsylvania, February 26, 1960; admitted to bar, 1987, Pennsylvania; 1990, District of Columbia; 1993, California; registered to practice before the U.S. Patent and Trademark Office. *Education:* University of Detroit (B.M.E., magna cum laude, 1983); George Washington University (J.D., with honors, 1987). Tau Beta Pi. *Member:* The District of Columbia Bar; American Bar Association. *PRACTICE AREAS:* Intellectual Property.

**DAVID T. BURSE** (San Jose Office).

**CHARLES R. BALGENORTH,** born Detroit, Michigan, May 18, 1962; admitted to bar, 1992, California; 1993, U.S. District Court, Central District of California; 1995, U.S. Court of Appeals, Ninth Circuit; registered to practice before the U.S. Patent and Trademark Office. *Education:* Wayne State University (B.S.E.E., 1984); University of Michigan (M.B.A., 1992; J.D., 1992). Tau Beta Pi; Eta Kappa Nu. Member, 1988-1992 and Treasurer, 1990-1991, University of Michigan Intellectual Property Students Association. Licensed Real Estate Salesperson, Michigan, 1987-1990. Founder, Professional Computer Systems, Inc. *Member:* Los Angeles County and American Bar Associations; Engineering Society of Detroit; Institute of Electrical and Electronics Engineers. *PRACTICE AREAS:* Intellectual Property.

**WAYNE B. BROWN** (La Jolla Office).

**JEFFREY A. MILLER** (San Jose Office).

**ARMAND F. AYAZI,** born December 1, 1960; admitted to bar, 1992, California and U.S. District Court, Central District of California. *Education:* University of California at Los Angeles (B.S., summa cum laude, 1982; M.S., with highest honors, 1987); Loyola Law School of Los Angeles (J.D., summa cum laude, 1992). Member, Phi Alpha Delta, Alpha Sigma Nu and St. Thomas More Law Honor Society. Order of the Coif. Fritz B. Burns Scholar. Recipient: William Tell Aggeler, J. Rex Dibble and Graduate Study Awards. Member, Loyola of Los Angeles Law Review, 1990-1991. Law Clerk, The Honorable William D. Keller, U.S. District Court, Central District of California, 1992-1993. *Member:* Los Angeles County and American Bar Associations; The Federal Circuit Bar; Los Angeles and American

*(This Listing Continued)*

## LYON & LYON LLP, Los Angeles—Continued

Intellectual Property Law Associations; American Society of Mechanical Engineers. *PRACTICE AREAS:* Patent, Trademark, Copyright, Unfair Competition; Antitrust, Civil Litigation; Business Transaction; Intellectual Property.

**JESSICA R. WOLFF** (La Jolla Office).

**MARK J. CARLOZZI** (Costa Mesa Office).

**SHELDON O. HEBER** (La Jolla Office).

**JEFFREY WILLIAM GUISE** (La Jolla Office).

**CHARLES S. BERKMAN** (La Jolla Office).

**SHERYL RUBINSTEIN SILVERSTEIN** (La Jolla Office).

**DAVID E. WANG,** born Camden, New Jersey, September 22, 1964; admitted to bar, 1993, California, U.S. District Court, Central District of California and U.S. Court of Appeals, Ninth Circuit; registered to practice before the U.S. Patent and Trademark Office. *Education:* University of Southern California (B.S.E.E, 1987; M.S.E.E., 1990; J.D., 1993); University of California at Berkeley. Eta Kappa Phi, Tau Beta Pi. Recipient: Xerox Scholarship; Powell Foundation Scholarship; Alumni Scholar; USC Law Legion Lex Merit Scholarship; American Jurisprudence Awards: Contracts, Property, Real Estate Transactions. Member: Southern California Interdisciplinary Law Journal; Major Tax Planning Law Journal. Judicial Extern to the Honorable Edward Rafeedie, U.S. District Court. *Member:* Los Angeles County and American (Member, Intellectual Property Section) Bar Associations; Patent Bar Association (Member, Sections on: Intellectual Property; Litigation); Intellectual Property Law Society; Los Angeles Intellectual Property Law Association; National Association of Realtors; California Association of Realtors. *LANGUAGES:* German and Chinese. *PRACTICE AREAS:* Patent, Trademark, Copyright, Unfair Competition, Antitrust; Intellectual Property.

**ANTHONY C. CHEN** (La Jolla Office).

**KENNETH S. ROBERTS** (Costa Mesa Office).

**BRENT D. SOKOL,** born Pontiac, Michigan, October 15, 1964; admitted to bar, 1993, California; registered to practice before the U.S. Patent and Trademark Office. *Education:* Northwestern University (B.S., Biomedical Engineering, 1987); Boston University (J.D., cum laude, 1993). Tau Beta Pi. Recipient: G. Joseph Tauro Scholar Award; American Jurisprudence Award in Torts. *PRACTICE AREAS:* Patent, Trademark, Copyright, Antitrust; Trade Secret, Unfair Competition; Intellectual Property.

**CLARKE W. NEUMANN, JR.** (La Jolla Office).

**JOHN C. KAPPOS** (Costa Mesa Office).

**THOMAS J. BRINDISI,** born Baltimore, Maryland, November 25, 1969; admitted to bar, 1995, California; 1996, U.S. District Court, Central District of California; registered to practice before the U.S. Patent and Trademark Office. *Education:* Carnegie Mellon University (B.S., Ch. E./Biomed. E., 1991); University of Baltimore (J.D., cum laude, 1994). Recipient: Wlodzimierz M. Kozak Best Physiologist Award (Neurophysiology). Intellectual Property Law Journal: Staff Member, 1992; Comments and Notes Editor, 1993; Editor-in-Chief, 1993-1994. University of Baltimore Law Review: Staff Member, 1993; Associate Comment Editor, 1993-1994. Author: Note: "Right to Die--Court Requires Clear and Convincing Evidence of Persistent Vegetative Patient's Intent to Terminate Life-Sustaining Procedures; Health Care Decisions Act of 1993 Casts New Light on Outcome," 23 U. Balt. L.Rev. 619 (1994). Co-Author: "Dealing with the Willfulness Issue, Including Bifurcation Motion Practice," Patent Litigation 1996, II:151 (PLI). *Member:* American Bar Association (Member, Section Intellectual Property Law); American Intellectual Property Law Association. *PRACTICE AREAS:* Intellectual Property.

**RICHARD C. HSU,** born San Mateo, California, March 31, 1967; admitted to bar, 1994, California. *Education:* California Institute of Technology (B.S., with honors, EE 1989); Tau Beta Pi, Eta Kappa Nu; Columbia University School of Law (J.D., 1994). Author: "Need Money for Research? Try Investing," NY Times, September 29, 1996 at F12; "From the Research Laboratories the next Bill Gates is Born," International Legal Strategy, V-8 (1996); "What Every Electrical Engineer Should Know about Patents," The Bridge of Eta Kappa Nu, 92:3 (1996); "What Every Biomed Start-Up Should Know about Patents," Biomedical Synergies, I:4 (1996); "The Essentials of Patent Law," Journal of the Assoc. of Energy Engineers, 93:3 (1996). Director, Technology Transfer Roundtable. Member: Executive Committee for the Caltech-MIT Enterprise Forum; Advisory Board for Pasadena Biomedical Committee; Southern California Biomedical Council. *Member:* Los Angeles County and American Bar Associations; American Intellectual Property Law Association; Los Angeles Intellectual Property Law Association; Institute of Electrical and Electronics Engineers (IEEE). *PRACTICE AREAS:* Intellectual Property.

**CATHERINE JOYCE,** born Minneapolis, Minnesota, October 10, 1958; admitted to bar, 1994, California. *Education:* Carleton College (B.A., cum laude, 1980); University of Minnesota (Ph.D., in Genetics, 1990); The George Washington University (J.D., with honors, 1994). *PRACTICE AREAS:* Patent; Trademark.

**CHARLES CALVIN FOWLER** (Costa Mesa Office).

**LISA WARD KARMELICH,** born London, England, May 19, 1970; admitted to bar, 1994, California. *Education:* California State Polytechnic University (B.S.E.E., 1990); University of California at Irvine; Loyola Law School (J.D., 1994). Phi Delta Phi. Recipient: American Jurisprudence Award in Civil Procedure and Legal Writing. St. Thomas More Law Honor Society, 1992-1994. Executive Editor, International Law Journal, 1993-1994. Extern for U.S. District Judge John Davies, 1993. President, I.E.E.E., 1989-1990. *Member:* American Bar Association (Member, Sections on: Patent, Trademark and Copyright; Science and Technology). *PRACTICE AREAS:* Patent, Trademark, Copyright; Intellectual Property.

**VICKI GEE NORTON** (La Jolla Office).

**JONATHAN T. LOSK,** born Minneapolis, Minnesota, April 19, 1958; admitted to bar, 1994, California; registered to practice before the U.S. Patent and Trademark Office. *Education:* University of California (B.A., 1982); University of California (M.S.E.E., 1990); Loyola Law School (J.D., 1994). *Member:* Los Angeles County and American Bar Associations; National Association of Recording Arts and Sciences. *PRACTICE AREAS:* Patent, Trademark, Contract and Unfair Competition; Intellectual Property.

**TIMOTHY J. LITHGOW** (La Jolla Office).

**MICHAEL A. TOMASULO,** born New York, N.Y. November 12, 1968; admitted to bar, 1995, California, U.S. District Court, Central District of California and U.S. Court of Appeals, Ninth Circuit. *Education:* University of California, Berkeley (B.S., Chemical Engineering, 1990); The University of Southern California (J.D., 1994). Order of the Coif. Member, University of Southern California Law Review; Senior Editor, University of Southern California Interdisciplinary Law Journal. Author: "Two Wrongs Don't Make a Right: The Trial of Alvarez-Maehain," 67 S. Cal. L. Rev. 475 (1994). Law Clerk, Chief Judge Juan R. Torruella, United States Court of Appeals for the First Circuit, 1994-1995, San Juan, PR. *LANGUAGES:* Spanish. *PRACTICE AREAS:* Intellectual Property.

**THOMAS R. ROUSE,** born Cambridge, Massachusetts, January 21, 1963; admitted to bar, 1995, California. *Education:* University of California, Los Angeles (B.S. in Electrical Engineering, 1986; M.B.A., 1992); Loyola Law School (J.D., 1995). Loyola of Los Angeles Law Review Staff Member; Loyola of Los Angeles Law Review Articles Editor; St. Thomas More Law Honor Society Member. Author: "The Preclusive Effect of ITC Patent Fact Findings on Federal District Courts: A New Twist on In re Convertible Rowing Exerciser Patent Litigation," 27 Loy. L.A. L. Rev. 1417 (1994). *Member:* American Bar Association (Member, Patent, Trademark and Copyright Law Section); American Intellectual Property Law Association; Institute of Electrical and Electronics Engineers. *LANGUAGES:* French, Spanish. *PRACTICE AREAS:* Patent; Trademark; Copyright; Trade Secret; Unfair Competition; Antitrust; Intellectual Property.

**EDWARD M. JORDAN,** born Whittier, California, October 20, 1966; admitted to bar, 1995, California. *Education:* University of California, Berkeley (B.S. in Mechanical Engineering, 1988); Loyola Law School (J.D., cum laude, 1995). Order of the Coif. Sayre MacNeil Scholar, St. Thomas More Law Honor Society. *PRACTICE AREAS:* Patent; Trademark; Copyright; Unfair Competition; Antitrust; Intellectual Property.

**CHARLES A. KERTELL,** born Salt Lake City, Utah, April 24, 1970; admitted to bar, 1995, California; U.S. District Court, Central District of California. *Education:* Cornell University (B.S., Chemical Engineering, with distinction, 1992; J.D., cum laude, 1995). Note Editor, Cornell International Law Journal. *PRACTICE AREAS:* Patent, Trademark, Copyright, Antitrust and Unfair Competition; Intellectual Property.

**JAMES K. SAKAGUCHI** (Costa Mesa Office).

**GARY H. SILVERSTEIN** (La Jolla Office).

**AMY STARK HELLENKAMP** (La Jolla Office).

*(This Listing Continued)*

## PROFESSIONAL BIOGRAPHIES

**CALIFORNIA—LOS ANGELES**

**RICHARD H. PAGLIERY,** born Havana, Cuba, November 18, 1961; admitted to bar, 1996, California. *Education:* California State University, Long Beach (M.S., 1989); University of Florida (J.D., 1996). *LANGUAGES:* Spanish. *PRACTICE AREAS:* Intellectual Property.

**WILLIAM J. KOLEGRAFF** (La Jolla Office).

**ANDREI IANCU,** born Bucharest, Romania, April 2, 1968; admitted to bar, 1996, California. *Education:* University of California at Los Angeles (B.S.A.E., 1989; M.S.M.E., 1990); University of California at Los Angeles School of Law (J.D., 1996). Order of the Coif. Recipient: American Jurisprudence Awards; Melville B. Nimmer Copyright Award; Hughes Aircraft Co. Malcolm R. Currie Innovation Award. Professional Engineer, 1992. Author: "A Two-Track Approach To The Doctrine of Equivalents in Patent Law," Jurimetrics, Spring 1995. *LANGUAGES:* Romanian. *PRACTICE AREAS:* Patents; Trademarks; Copyrights; Intellectual Property.

**JONATHAN HALLMAN** (La Jolla Office).

**LYNN Y. MCKERNAN** (San Jose Office).

**MICHAEL BOLAN** (San Jose Office).

**FARSHAD FARJAMI,** born Tehran, Iran, August 18, 1964; admitted to bar, 1996, California. *Education:* University of California at Los Angeles (B.S., 1987); Loyola Marymount University (J.D., magna cum laude, 1996). Phi Delta Phi; Order of the Coif. St. Thomas More Law Honor Society. Sayre Macneil Scholar. Recipient, Seven American Jurisprudence Awards. Author: "A Step Toward Harmonization of the U.S. and Japanese Patent Laws: Compulsory Patent Licensing," Spring 1996. *LANGUAGES:* Persian. *PRACTICE AREAS:* Patents; Trademarks; Copyrights; Intellectual Property.

**DMITRY MILIKOVSY** (San Jose Office).

**GREGORY R. STEPHENSON,** born Ann Arbor, Michigan, March 15, 1964; admitted to bar, 1996, California. *Education:* University of Michigan (B.S.M.E., 1988); Boston University (J.D., 1996). *Member:* American Intellectual Property Law Association. *PRACTICE AREAS:* Intellectual Property.

**HOWARD N. WISNIA** (La Jolla Office).

**MARY AGNES TUCK,** born Burlingame, California, January 11, 1971; admitted to bar, 1996, California. *Education:* University of California at Los Angeles (B.A., 1993); University of California School of Law (J.D., 1996). *PRACTICE AREAS:* Intellectual Property.

**ARLYN ALONZO,** born Taipei, Taiwan, January 18, 1962; admitted to bar, 1996, California. *Education:* University of Southern California (B.S.A.E., 1984; M.S.E.E., 1990); Loyola Marymount University (J.D., 1996). Order of the Coif. Sayre Macneil Scholar. Recipient, American Jurisprudence Awards for Criminal Law, Trust and Wills and Remedies. *LANGUAGES:* Taiwanese, Mandarin, Tagalog. *PRACTICE AREAS:* Patents; Trademarks; Copyrights; Intellectual Property.

**NEAL MATTHEW COHEN** (Costa Mesa Office).

### OF COUNSEL

**BRADFORD J. DUFT** (La Jolla Office).

**SUZANNE L. BIGGS** (La Jolla Office).

**F.T. ALEXANDRA MAHANEY** (La Jolla Office).

**STEPHEN S. KORNICZKY** (La Jolla Office).

(Unless otherwise indicted All Members and Associates of the Firm are Members of the State Bar of California)

(For biographical data on Costa Mesa, California, San Jose, California, La Jolla, California, see Professional Biographies at each of those cities)

---

## MacARTHUR, URIBE, HICKS & MIMS
### 626 WILSHIRE BOULEVARD, SUITE 800
### LOS ANGELES, CALIFORNIA 90017-2900
Telephone: 213-538-1370
Fax: 213-538-1375

Other Los Angeles Office: 10940 Wilshire Boulevard, Suite 1600. Telephone: 310-442-4855. Fax: 310-442-4858.

*General Civil, Trial and Appellate Practice in all Courts. Business Litigation, Arbitration, Real Estate, Corporation and General Business Law, State, Local, Federal and International Tax Planning, Tax Compliance, Tax Litigation, Estate Planning.*

*(This Listing Continued)*

### MEMBERS OF FIRM

**FREDERICK E. MACARTHUR,** born Alpena, Michigan, January 9, 1924; admitted to bar, 1952, California. *Education:* University of Michigan (B.S.E., 1948; J.D., 1951). *Member:* Los Angeles County and American Bar Associations; State Bar of California.

**J. A. URIBE,** born Bogota, Colombia, September 1, 1942; admitted to bar, 1967, California. *Education:* Columbia University (A.B., 1964); Hastings College of Law, University of California (J.D., 1967). *Member:* Los Angeles County and American Bar Associations; State Bar of California.

**L. WESTCOTT HICKS, JR.,** born Corpus Christi, Texas, March 3, 1945; admitted to bar, 1970, Illinois; 1973, California, U.S. District Court, Central District of California and U.S. Tax Court. *Education:* Northwestern University (B.A., 1967); University of Illinois-Champaign (J.D., 1970); New York University (LL.M., in Taxation, 1971). Instructor: Taxation, University of Southern California, 1974-1975; Taxation, Golden Gate University, 1976-1977. *Member:* Los Angeles County and American (Member, Taxation Section) Bar Associations; State Bar of California (Member, Sections on: Taxation and Estate Planning). *PRACTICE AREAS:* State, Local, Federal and International Tax Planning; Tax Compliance; Tax Controversies; Estate Planning.

**STEWART S. MIMS,** born New York, N.Y., October 4, 1947; admitted to bar, 1973, California; 1974, U.S. District Court, Central District of California; 1975, U.S. District Court, Northern District of California. *Education:* Claremont McKenna College (B.S., 1969); Hastings College of the Law, University of California (J.D., 1972). Thurston Society. Order of the Coif. Note and Comment Editor, Hasting Law Journal, 1972. Author: "Retroactive Application of the National Environmental Policy Act of 1969," Hastings Law Journal, March, 1971. President, Wilshire Estate Planning Council, 1987. Member, Panel of Arbitrators, American Arbitration Association. *Member:* Los Angeles County Bar Association; State Bar of California; Inns of Court. *PRACTICE AREAS:* Business Litigation; Professional Liability Litigation; Arbitration; Corporate Dissolutions; Partnership Dissolutions.

**STEPHEN L. KAPLAN,** born Los Angeles, California, September 17, 1960; admitted to bar, 1986, California. *Education:* Claremont Men's College (B.A., 1982); Loyola Marymount University (J.D., 1986). *Member:* Los Angeles County and American Bar Associations; State Bar of California.

REFERENCE: Wells Fargo Bank (Office, 707 Wilshire Boulevard).

---

## MACKLIN TATRO
### 1875 CENTURY PARK EAST, SUITE 1220
### LOS ANGELES, CALIFORNIA 90067
Telephone: 310-229-2490
Fax: 310-229-2491

*Complex Business Litigation including Environmental and Insurance Coverage Litigation, Real Estate, Construction Litigation, Antitrust, Accountants' Liability and Securities Fraud.*

FIRM PROFILE: *We have litigated in state and federal courts throughout California and in a number of other jurisdictions across the country. Our clients include Fortune 100 manufacturing companies, major financial services companies, a Big Six accounting firm, solid waste management companies, and major real estate developers. We have litigated all types of complex business cases, from environmental cleanup actions and antitrust cases, to contract disputes, real estate cases, insurance coverage actions, construction defect cases, securities fraud actions, and accountants' liability cases.*

### MEMBERS OF FIRM

**RENÉ P. TATRO,** born Moundridge, Kansas, July 2, 1953; admitted to bar, 1977, California and U.S. District Court, Northern District of California; 1981, U.S. Court of International Trade. *Education:* Kansas State University (B.S., magna cum laude, 1974); Harvard University (J.D., cum laude, 1977). Previous Employment: Associate, 1977-1983 and Member, 1984-1995, Heller Ehrman White & McAuliffe. *Member:* State Bar of California; American Bar Association. *PRACTICE AREAS:* Complex Commercial Litigation; Environmental; Insurance Coverage.

**MERYL MACKLIN,** born Hartford, Connecticut, November 17, 1958; admitted to bar, 1984, California and U.S. District Court, Northern District of California; 1985, U.S. Court of Appeals, Ninth and Eleventh Circuits and U.S. District Court, Central and Southern Districts of California. *Education:* Yale University (B.A., magna cum laude, 1980); University of California at Berkeley (J.D., 1984). Phi Beta Kappa. Member: California Law Review, 1982-1984. Previous Employment: Associate, 1984-1990 and

*(This Listing Continued)*

### MACKLIN TATRO, Los Angeles—Continued

Member, 1991-1995, Heller Ehrman White & McAuliffe. *Member:* State Bar of California (Member, Executive Committee, Litigation Section, 1993-1996). *PRACTICE AREAS:* Complex Business Litigation; Antitrust; Accountants Liability.

**CRAIG S. BLOOMGARDEN,** born New York, N.Y., March 15, 1958; admitted to bar, 1983, California. *Education:* University of Virginia (B.A., in Economics, summa cum laude, 1980); Harvard University (J.D., cum laude, 1983). Phi Beta Kappa. Law Clerk to Hon. Mariana R. Pfaelzer, U.S. District Court, Central District of California, 1983-1984. Author: "How Has California Handled Toxic Torts?," Toxic Torts Practice Guide, McGraw - Hill/Shepards, 1992. Previous Employment, Associate: Sidley & Austin, 1984-1990; Associate and Member, Heller Ehrman White & McAuliffe, 1990-1995. *Member:* State Bar of California. *PRACTICE AREAS:* Environmental Litigation; Insurance Coverage Litigation.

#### ASSOCIATE

**JULIET A. MARKOWITZ,** born New York, N.Y., January 19, 1966; admitted to bar, 1993, California. *Education:* Brandeis University (B.A., summa cum laude, 1987); Stanford University (J.D., 1992). Phi Beta Kappa. Note Editor, Stanford Law Review, 1990-1992. Article Editor, Stanford Environmental Law Journal. Previous Employment: Associate, Heller Ehrman White & McAuliffe, 1992-1995. *Member:* State Bar of California. *PRACTICE AREAS:* Complex Business Litigation.

---

## GERALD C. MACRAE

1840 CENTURY PARK EAST, SUITE 800
LOS ANGELES, CALIFORNIA 90067-2109
Telephone: 310-553-6370
Fax: 310-553-4432

*Civil Trial Practice in State and Federal Courts. Business Tort Litigation, False Claims Act Prosecution, Personal Injury, Professional Malpractice, Products Liability.*

**GERALD C. MACRAE,** born Calgary, Alberta, Canada, August 10, 1956; admitted to bar, 1987, California and U.S. District Court, Central District of California; 1996, U.S. District Court, Eastern District of California. *Education:* University of Alberta, Edmonton, Alberta (B.A., with distinction, 1983); Southwestern University School of Law (J.D., 1987). Phi Alpha Delta. Board of Directors, Southwestern University Themis Society, 1991—. Author: "Setting Up Shop," The New Lawyer Forum, Supplement to Trial, ATLA, Spring, 1994. *Member:* Los Angeles County (Member, Sections on: Litigation; Provisional and Post-Judgment Remedies; Small Firm and Sole Practitioner. Member and Executive Committee, 1994—; Lawyers Using Computers; Law Office Management; Trial Practice Inn of Court) and American (Member, Sections on: Litigation; Torts and Insurance; Law Practice Management) Bar Associations; State Bar of California (Member, Sections on: Litigation, Law Practice Management); Los Angeles County Bar Association Barristers (Member, Education Committee, 1989-1993; Co-Chair, 1992-1993; Strategic Planning Committee, 1992-1993; Executive Committee, 1991-1993); Consumer Attorneys Association of Los Angeles; Association of Business Trial Lawyers; Consumer Attorneys of California; The Association of Trial Lawyers of America (Member, Sections on: Small Office Practice; Motor Vehicle Collision; Highway and Premises Liability; Products Liability).

---

## MADDEN, JONES, COLE & JOHNSON

A PROFESSIONAL CORPORATION

LOS ANGELES, CALIFORNIA

(See Long Beach)

*Civil Litigation, Business, Corporate, Healthcare, Construction, Personal Injury, Real Estate, Tax and Estate Planning Matters.*

---

## MAGAÑA, CATHCART & McCARTHY

A Partnership including Professional Corporations
*Established in 1946*

SUITE 810 GATEWAY WEST BUILDING
1801 AVENUE OF THE STARS (CENTURY CITY)
LOS ANGELES, CALIFORNIA 90067-5899
Telephone: 310-553-6630; 213-879-2531
Fax: 310-785-9143

*Practice limited to Trials in all State and Federal Courts. Negligence Law. Appellate Practice. Aviation, Malpractice, Railroad, Products and Admiralty.*

*FIRM PROFILE: The firm was founded by Raoul D. Magaña, now retired, in 1946. Mr. Magaña quickly became known as one of the most outstanding trial lawyers in medical/legal matters in the United States. The firm has grown to its present size and specializes in the representation of the victims of accidents, including legal and medical malpractice. Daniel C. Cathcart joined the firm in 1957 and founded and developed the Aviation Accident Litigation department of the office. A substantial portion of the firm's work is in the representation of the victims of aviation accidents, including general aviation, common carrier accidents and products liability. The firm handles matters arising throughout the world when jurisdiction can be maintained within the United States.*

**BRIAN R. MAGAÑA, (PROFESSIONAL CORPORATION),** born Los Angeles, California, October 19, 1948; admitted to bar, 1973, California. *Education:* University of California at Los Angeles (A.B., 1970); University of Washington (J.D., 1973). *Member:* Los Angeles County, American and Mexican-American Bar Associations; State Bar of California; The Association of Trial Lawyers of America; California Trial Lawyers Association; Los Angeles Trial Lawyers Association;. *LANGUAGES:* Spanish. *PRACTICE AREAS:* Automobile Product Law; Construction Accidents; FELA; Medical Malpractice Law; Railroad Personal Injury.

**PETER T. CATHCART, (PROFESSIONAL CORPORATION),** born Santa Monica, California, August 30, 1955; admitted to bar, 1980, California; 1981, U.S. District Court, Central District of California and U.S. Court of Appeals, Ninth Circuit; 1990, U.S. District Court, Eastern District of California. *Education:* University of Southern California (B.S., 1977); Loyola University of Los Angeles (J.D., 1980). *Member:* Los Angeles County Bar Association; State Bar of California; Los Angeles Trial Lawyer's Association; The Association of Trial Lawyers of America; California Trial Lawyers Association (Member, Board of Governors, 1990). *PRACTICE AREAS:* Airplane Crash Litigation; Aviation Law; Bad Faith Law; Personal Injury Law; Products Liability Law.

**WILLIAM H. WIMSATT, (PROFESSIONAL CORPORATION),** born Evansville, Indiana, September 21, 1943; admitted to bar, 1975, California; 1976, U.S. District Court, Central District of California; 1988, U.S. Court of Appeals, Ninth Circuit; 1990, U.S. District Court, Southern District of California and U.S. District Court, District of Arizona. *Education:* St. Louis University (B.A., 1965); Boston University (M.S.B.A., cum laude, 1972); Loyola University of Los Angeles (J.D., 1975). Instructor, Aviation Law and Member, Aviation Administrative Advisory Committee, California State University, Los Angeles, 1980-1985. *Member:* San Fernando Valley Bar Association; State Bar of California; California Trial Lawyers Association; Los Angeles Trial Lawyers Association; Lawyer-Pilots Bar Association (Regional Vice-President, 1990-1994); American Board of Trial Advocates (Associate, 1991). [Capt., U.S. Army, 1966-1972]. *PRACTICE AREAS:* Airplane Crash Litigation; Aviation Law; Defective Products; Medical Malpractice Law; Products Liability Law.

---

**RICHARD L. BISETTI,** born Santa Monica, California, January 11, 1948; admitted to bar, 1975, California. *Education:* University of Southern California (B.A., 1970); University of West Los Angeles (J.D., 1975). *Member:* State Bar of California; California Trial Lawyers Association; Italian American Lawyers Association. *PRACTICE AREAS:* Automobile Product Liability; Construction Accident; Premises Liability Law; Products Liability Law; Wrongful Death Law.

**DEBORAH MITZENMACHER,** born New York City, New York, September 8, 1950; admitted to bar, 1981, California, U.S. District Court, Central District of California and U.S. Court of Appeals, Third, Ninth and Tenth Circuits and U.S. Supreme Court. *Education:* Brandeis University (B.A., cum laude, 1971; M.A., 1972); University of California at Los Angeles (M.S., 1975); University of California at Los Angeles (J.D., 1981). *Member:* State Bar of California; American Bar Association; California

*(This Listing Continued)*

Women Lawyers. **PRACTICE AREAS:** Trial Court and Appellate Litigation; Aircraft Accidents; Products Liability; Negligence; Wrongful Death.

**KATHLEEN A. MCCARTHY,** born Long Beach, California, September 27, 1963; admitted to bar, 1992, California. *Education:* University of California at Los Angeles (B.A., 1985); Southwestern University School of Law (J.D., 1992). *Member:* Los Angeles County Bar Association; State Bar of California; Los Angeles Trial Lawyers Association; Women Lawyers Association of Los Angeles; Irish American Bar. **PRACTICE AREAS:** Sexual Harassment and Discrimination; Personal Injury; Products Liability; Wrongful Death.

**DANIEL A. CRIBBS,** born Palm Springs, California, February 19, 1969; admitted to bar, 1994, California. *Education:* University of California at Irvine (B.A., 1991); Whittier College School of Law (J.D., 1994). Phi Delta Phi. Member, Lawyers Club of Los Angeles. *Member:* Century City, San Fernando Valley, Los Angeles County and American Bar Associations; Los Angeles Trial Lawyers Association. **PRACTICE AREAS:** Personal Injury Law; Aviation Law; Products Liability; Wrongful Death.

### OF COUNSEL

**DANIEL C. CATHCART, (PROFESSIONAL CORPORATION),** born Los Angeles, California, October 30, 1932; admitted to bar, 1957, California and U.S. District Court, Northern District of California; 1972, U.S. District Court, Central District of California and Northern District of Texas and U.S. Court of Appeals, Fifth Circuit; 1974, U.S. Supreme Court; 1975, U.S. District Court, Eastern District of Wisconsin and U.S. Court of Appeals, Tenth Circuit; 1982, U.S. Court of Appeals, Third Circuit; 1983, U.S. Court of Appeals, Sixth Circuit. *Education:* California Institute of Technology; University of Southern California (LL.B., 1957). Phi Alpha Delta. Author: Aviation Litigation Techniques, published by Michie Company, Charlottesville, Virginia. *Member:* State Bar of California; Los Angeles Trial Lawyers Association; Lawyer-Pilots Bar Association; The Association of Trial Lawyers of America; Plaintiffs Trial Lawyers Association of Los Angeles; International Academy of Trial Lawyers; American College of Trial Lawyers; California Trial Lawyers Association; Inner Circle of Advocates (President, 1991-1993). **PRACTICE AREAS:** Airplane Crash Litigation; Aviation Law; Personal Injury Law; Products Liability Law; Wrongful Death Law.

### RETIRED

**RAOUL D. MAGAÑA,** born Coyoacan, Mexico, September 21, 1911; admitted to bar, 1936, California. *Education:* University of California (LL.B., 1935). Phi Beta Kappa. *Member:* Los Angeles County, American and Inter-American Bar Associations; State Bar of California; American Judicature Society. Fellow: American College of Trial Lawyers; International Academy of Trial Lawyers (Former President).

**JAMES J. MCCARTHY,** born Meriden, Connecticut, March 25, 1928; admitted to bar, 1962, California. *Education:* Loyola University (Ph.B., 1950); Loyola University of Los Angeles (LL.B., 1961). Alpha Sigma Nu; Phi Alpha Delta. Instructor, Loyola University School of Law, 1964—. *Member:* Los Angeles County (Chairman, Judicial Evaluation Committee, 1982-1983) and American Bar Associations; State Bar of California; American Board of Trial Advocates (Secretary, 1970-1974 and Member, 1970-1974, National Executive Committee); The Association of Trial Lawyers of America; American College of Trial Lawyers. [1st Lt., USAF, Strategic Air Command, 1951-1955]. **PRACTICE AREAS:** Airplane Crash Litigation; Aviation Law; Motor Vehicle Litigation; Products Liability Law.

REFERENCE: First Los Angeles Bank (1950 Avenue of the Stars, Los Angeles (Century City), California).

---

## MAGASINN & MAGASINN

### A LAW CORPORATION

### LOS ANGELES, CALIFORNIA

(See Marina Del Rey)

*Specializing in Taxation, Estate Planning, Probate, Trusts, Charitable Organizations, Real Estate, Business, Corporate and Partnership Law and Business Secession Planning.*

## MAGUIRE & ORBACH

### LAW CORPORATION

### SUITE 300, 10866 WILSHIRE BOULEVARD
### LOS ANGELES, CALIFORNIA 90024-4311
Telephone: 310-470-2929
Fax: 310-474-4710

*Construction Law, Real Estate and Insurance. Civil Trial and Appellate Practice in State and Federal Courts.*

**EVERETT W. MAGUIRE,** born San Bernardino, California, January 2, 1928; admitted to bar, 1958, California; 1975, U.S. Supreme Court. *Education:* University of California at Berkeley (B.S., 1950); University of California at Los Angeles (J.D., 1957). Registered Civil Engineer, California, 1955. Contributing Consultant and Lecturer, California CEB, "California Mechanic's Liens and Other Remedies," 1988, 1995; "Basic Techniques of Public Contract Practice," 1977. Attorney, State Department of Public Works, 1958-1965. Member, Board of Contributing Editors, Shepards "California Construction Law Reporter," 1991—. American Arbitration Association and State Arbitrator. **PRACTICE AREAS:** Construction Law.

**DAVID M. ORBACH,** born Berkeley, California, July 13, 1958; admitted to bar, 1983, California. *Education:* University of California at Berkeley (B.A., 1980); Loyola University of Los Angeles (J.D., 1983). Author: "Recovery of Payments to Unlicensed Contractors: The Shape of Things to Come," California Construction Law Reporter, Shepard, October, 1992; "Undisclosed Rebates Between Contractors," California Construction Law Reporter, Shepard, November, 1992; "Strict Compliance Damages: Beyond Cost to Repair/Diminution in Value," California Construction Law Reporter, August 1993; "A Day in the Life of the Legislative Process," California Construction Law Reporter, Shepard, January, 1994; "A Survival Guide to A Client's Home Construction Project," California Construction Law Reporter, Shepard, June, 1994; "Contractual Limitation of Liability: Recent Trends," Construction Law Reporter, Shepard, June, 1995. Director, Southern California Chapter of Construction Management Association of America, 1990-1993). Regional General Counsel, Roofing Consultants Institute, 1992—. American Arbitration Association Arbitrator, 1995—. **PRACTICE AREAS:** Construction Law; Business Litigation.

**JEFFREY D. PEARLMAN,** born Norfolk, Virginia, November 2, 1960; admitted to bar, 1986, California; 1988, District of Columbia. *Education:* George Washington University (B.A., with distinction, 1982; J.D., 1985). **PRACTICE AREAS:** Construction Law; Public Contracts; Business Litigation.

**DAVID M. HUFF,** born Bloomington, Illinois, February 20, 1967; admitted to bar, 1992, California. *Education:* University of California at Santa Barbara (B.A., with honors, 1989); Loyola Marymount University (J.D., 1992). Member, Roofing Consultants Institute. **PRACTICE AREAS:** Construction Law; Business Litigation; Technology Litigation.

**MICHAEL D. GERMAIN,** born Whittier, California, April 17, 1965; admitted to bar, 1991, California; 1994, Colorado. *Education:* Colorado State University; San Diego State University (B.A., with distinction, 1988); Pepperdine University (J.D., 1991). *Member:* State Bar of California. **PRACTICE AREAS:** Construction Law; Surety Law; Business Litigation.

All Attorneys are Members of the Los Angeles County, California and American Bar Associations.

## MAHONEY, COPPENRATH, JAFFE & PEARSON LLP

A Partnership including Professional Corporations

*Established in 1985*

### 2049 CENTURY PARK EAST, SUITE 2480
### LOS ANGELES, CALIFORNIA 90067-3283
Telephone: 310-557-1919
Telecopier: 310-277-6536

*General Civil, Trial and Appellate Practice. Commercial, Real Property, Insurance, Corporate, Probate, Trust, Estate Planning and Litigation, Admiralty, Marine and Inland Marine Insurance Law. Federal, State and Local Taxation, Guardianships and Conservatorships.*

FIRM PROFILE: Our attorneys have more than a decade of legal experience and three of us have been practicing together for over 15 years. Civil litigation has always been a mainstay of our practice, we value long-term relationships with our clients. Our belief and experience is that such mutually beneficial

*(This Listing Continued)*

## MAHONEY, COPPENRATH, JAFFE & PEARSON LLP, Los Angeles—Continued

*relationships are created through a combination of client involvement, quality professional service and results.*

*We keep our clients informed on the status of their pending matters through an ongoing dialogue which includes the prompt return of phone calls and candid response to each inquiry. Our clients can expect an ongoing exchange concerning the available legal options and the prospective cost of client-selected legal services. We encourage our clients to participate regularly in the decision-making process to determine whether a case should be settled or aggressively prosecuted or defended after a thorough review of options, risks and estimated costs. We constantly strive to pursue and achieve our clients' goals with energy, creativity and cost effectiveness.*

### MEMBERS OF FIRM

**JAMES E. MAHONEY, (P.C.),** born Schenectady, New York, July 16, 1940; admitted to bar, 1967, California. *Education:* California State College at Long Beach (A.B., 1963); Hastings College of the Law, University of California (LL.B., 1966). Associate Editor, Hastings Law Review, 1965-1966. Member: Panel of Arbitrators, Mandatory Arbitration Program, Los Angeles Superior Court, 1982—; Panel of Judges Pro Tem, Los Angeles Superior Court, 1982. Member, Board of Directors, University of California, Hastings College of the Law, 1985—; Chair, 1989-1991. *Member:* Los Angeles County (Member, Judicial Evaluation Committee, 1978-1984; Chairperson: Continuing Education of the Bar Committee, 1972-1974; Youth Education Committee, 1974-1976; Lawyer Referral Service Committee, 1978-1980) and American Bar Associations; State Bar of California; Maritime Law Association of the United States; Association of Business Trial Lawyers. **PRACTICE AREAS:** Real Estate; Business; Corporate; Commercial Litigation; Estate Planning.

**WALTER G. COPPENRATH, JR., (P.C.),** born Clinton, Massachusetts, June 19, 1946; admitted to bar, 1978, California. *Education:* University of Santa Clara (B.A., 1968); Loyola University, Rome, Italy; University of California, Los Angeles School of Law (J.D., 1978). Member, Moot Court Honors Program. United States Peace Corps Volunteer, Sierra Leone, West Africa, 1968-1970. Visiting Course Instructor, Maritime Law, Marine Insurance and Contracts for International Sale of Goods, International Development Law Institute, Rome, Italy, 1984, 1988, 1993 and Kaunas, Lithuania, November 1993. Panel of Judges Pro Tem, Los Angeles Superior Court, 1987, 1989—. Panel of Arbitrators, Los Angeles Superior Court, 1993—. *Member:* Los Angeles County and American Bar Associations; State Bar of California; Maritime Law Association of the United States (Member Comite, Maritime International Committee); Association of Business Trial Lawyers. **PRACTICE AREAS:** Business; Real Estate; Maritime; Insurance; Construction Litigation.

**HOWARD M. JAFFE, (P.C.),** born Philadelphia, Pennsylvania, February 25, 1936; admitted to bar, 1961, New Jersey; 1963, New York; 1965, U.S. Supreme Court; 1972, California. *Education:* University of Pennsylvania (B.S., 1958; LL.B., cum laude, 1961); New York University (LL.M., in Taxation, 1969). Order of the Coif. Case Editor, University of Pennsylvania Law Review, 1959-1961. Law Secretary to Chief Justice Joseph Weintraub, Supreme Court of New Jersey, 1961-1962. Panel of Judges Pro Tem, Los Angeles Superior Court, 1988—. *Member:* Los Angeles County (Panel of Arbitrators, Fee Arbitration Program, 1990—; Member, Committee on Evaluation of Professional Standards, 1991—) and American Bar Associations; State Bar of California; Association of Business Trial Lawyers; American Arbitration Association. **PRACTICE AREAS:** Business, Professional and Employment Litigation; Business Transactions and Entities; Probate.

**RONALD C. PEARSON,** born Kansas City, Missouri, June 8, 1957; admitted to bar, 1984, California. *Education:* Pacific Union College (B.S., 1980); University of San Diego (J.D., 1984); Georgetown University Law Center (M.L.T., 1985). Law Clerk, Honors Program, Department of Justice, Tax Division, 1985. *Member:* State Bar of California (Member, Estate and Gift Tax Committee, 1991—; Chair-Elect, 1993); Los Angeles County (Member, Executive Committee, Trusts and Estates Section, 1991—) and American (Member, Real Property, Probate and Trust Law Section) Bar Associations.

**DARYL G. PARKER,** born San Antonio, Texas, June 17, 1944; admitted to bar, 1970, California. *Education:* Rice University; Stanford University (A.B., with distinction, 1966); Stanford University (J.D., 1969). Phi Beta Kappa. Author: "War Risks Annotation to Marine P&I Policy Annotations," Admiralty and Maritime Law Committee, Section on Tort and Insurance Practice, American Bar Association, 1981. *Member:* Los Angeles County and American (Member, Law, Science and Technology) Bar Associations; State Bar of California; Maritime Law Association of the United States (Member, Committee on Marine Insurance, General Average and Salvage). **PRACTICE AREAS:** Real Estate, Insurance, Business and Maritime Litigation and Transactions.

**CHARLES L. GROTTS,** born Hillsboro, Illinois, May 28, 1948; admitted to bar, 1974, Illinois; 1979, California. *Education:* Washington University (B.A., 1970); University of Illinois at Urbana (J.D., 1974). Phi Beta Kappa; Order of the Coif. Member, Supreme Court Historical Society. *Member:* Illinois State Bar Association; State Bar of California. **PRACTICE AREAS:** Business; Real Estate; Probate Litigation.

**ARTHUR L. MARTIN,** born Richmond, Virginia, May 8, 1942; admitted to bar, 1973, California; 1977, U.S. Supreme Court; registered to practice before U.S. Patent and Trademark Office. *Education:* Cornell University and Polytechnic Institute of Brooklyn (B.S.Ch.E., 1965; M.S.Ch.E., 1967); University of San Francisco School of Law (J.D., 1973). Tau Beta Pi; Omega Chi Epsilon; Sigma Xi. Member, McAuliffe Law Honor Society. Member, 1971-1973 and Assistant Topics Editor, 1972-1973, University of San Francisco Law Review. *Member:* State Bar of California; American Institute of Chemical Engineers. **PRACTICE AREAS:** Business Litigation.

### OF COUNSEL

**GERALD LEE TAHAJIAN,** born Los Angeles, California, February 28, 1941; admitted to bar, 1970, California. *Education:* California State University at Fresno (B.S., 1963); University of San Francisco (J.D., 1969). Blue Key; Pi Gamma Mu; Phi Delta Phi. Certified Public Accountant, California, 1968. Fresno City Council, 1985. President, Fresno County and City Chamber of Commerce, 1984. Chairman, Fresno County Economic Development Corporation, 1989. *Member:* Fresno County (Member, Estate, Probate and Trust Section) and American (Member, Sections on: Real Property, Probate and Trust Law; Economics of Law Practice; Member, Committees on: Estate and Gift Taxes, 1980—, Memberships, 1980—, Agriculture, 1980, Section on Taxation) Bar Associations; State Bar of California (Member, Sections on: Economics of Law Practice; Family Law; Business Law; Estate Planning, Probate and Trust Law; Member, Tax Committee, 1980—); California Society of Certified Public Accountants (Member, Government Relations Committee, 1980—); American Society of Certified Public Accountants. (Also practicing individually, Fresno, California; Also Of Counsel, McVey & Kim, Los Angeles and Anaheim, California). **PRACTICE AREAS:** Estate Planning and Probate.

REFERENCE: First Professional Bank, Santa Monica, California.

---

## LISA L. MAKI
### 815 MORAGA DRIVE
### LOS ANGELES, CALIFORNIA 90049-1633
Telephone: 310-440-5575
Facsimile: 310-440-5576

*Labor and Employment Law, including Plaintiff's Employment, Discrimination, Sexual Harassment, Disability Discrimination and Age Discrimination, Property Damage, Inverse Condemnation.*

**LISA L. MAKI,** born Omaha, Nebraska, February 15, 1965; admitted to bar, 1992, California. *Education:* Loyola Marymount (B.A., English; B.A., Political Science, 1988); Pepperdine University (J.D., 1991). *Member:* Beverly Hills, Los Angeles County and American Bar Associations; State Bar of California; Consumer Attorneys of Los Angeles; Womens' Lawyers Association; National Employment Lawyers Association; California Employment Lawyers Association. **REPORTED CASES:** Fennessy v. Southwest Airlines, (1996) 91 F.3d 1359. **PRACTICE AREAS:** Civil Practice; Civil Litigation.

---

## ROGER L. MALKUS
### LOS ANGELES, CALIFORNIA

(See Torrance)

*Practice Limited to Family Law.*

## PROFESSIONAL BIOGRAPHIES
## CALIFORNIA—LOS ANGELES

### DANIEL C. MALLERY
1875 CENTURY PARK EAST, SUITE 700
**LOS ANGELES, CALIFORNIA 90067**
*Telephone: 310-551-5252*
*Fax: 310-551-5251*
*Email: DCM100@concentric.net*

*Intellectual Property, Patent, Trademark, Copyright and Unfair Competition.*

**DANIEL C. MALLERY,** born Denver, Colorado, March 19, 1960; admitted to bar, 1991, Pennsylvania; 1992, California; registered to practice before U.S. Patent and Trademark Office. *Education:* University of California at Los Angeles (B.S., 1982); California State University at Northridge (M.S., 1983); George Washington University (J.D., 1990). Co-Author: "Complex Polynomial Phase Integration," IEEE Transactions on Antennas and Propagation, Vol AP-33, No. 7, July 1985. *Member:* State Bar of California; American Intellectual Property Law Association.

### MANATT, PHELPS & PHILLIPS, LLP
*A Limited Liability Partnership*
*Established in 1965*
TRIDENT CENTER, EAST TOWER
11355 WEST OLYMPIC BOULEVARD
**LOS ANGELES, CALIFORNIA 90064**
*Telephone: 310-312-4000*
*Fax: 310-312-4224*
*Telex: 21-5653*
*Email: mpp@manatt.com*

*Washington, D.C. Office:* 1500 M Street, N.W., Suite 700. Telephone: 202-463-4300. Fax: 202-463-4394.

*Nashville, Tennessee Office:* 1233 17th Avenue South. Telephone: 615-327-2600. Fax: 615-327-2044.

*General Civil and Trial Practice in all Courts. Banking and Financial Services; Bankruptcy and Creditors' Rights; Corporate Finance and Securities; Election and Campaign; Entertainment; Environmental; Estate Planning, Executive Compensation and Employee Benefits; Family; Fashion Industry; Federal, State and Local Government; Government Contracts; Healthcare; High Technology; Insurance; Intellectual Property; International Trade and Customs; Labor and Employment; Land Use; Legislative and Administrative; Motion Picture and Television; Music; New Media; Real Estate; Sports; Tax; White-Collar Criminal Defense.*

**FIRM PROFILE:** Manatt, Phelps & Phillips, LLP was founded in 1965 by Charles T. Manatt and Thomas D. Phelps. Today, with approximately 160 attorneys in Los Angeles, Nashville and Washington, D.C., Manatt, Phelps & Phillips, LLP is recognized as one of the most influential law firms in the United States, and is particularly distinguished for its financial services, health, entertainment and government practice groups.

#### MEMBERS OF FIRM

**CHARLES T. MANATT,** (P.C.), born Chicago, Illinois, June 9, 1936; admitted to bar, 1962, California; 1967, U.S. Supreme Court; 1985, District of Columbia. *Education:* Iowa State University (B.S., 1958); George Washington University (J.D., 1962). Chairman, International Foundation for Electoral Systems. Chairman, Greater Washington Board of Trade's International Business Council. Served as Chairman of Democratic National Committee and Co-Chairman of the 1992 Clinton/Gore campaign. (Also at Washington, D.C. Office). **PRACTICE AREAS:** Government. **Email:** cmanatt@manatt.com

**THOMAS D. PHELPS,** (P.C.), born Sigourney, Iowa, October 10, 1936; admitted to bar, 1963, Iowa; 1964, California; 1979, U.S. Supreme Court. *Education:* Iowa State University (B.S., 1959); George Washington University (J.D., 1963). Member, Board of Editors, George Washington Law Review, 1961-1962. President, American Law Student Association, 1961-1962. Director: Tokai Bank of California, 1974-1992; Community Reinvestment Institute, 1989—. Chairman, 25th Anniversary Goodwill Mission to Nagoya, Japan, Los Angeles-Nagoya Sister City Affiliation, 1984. *Member:* California Bankers Association (Member, Federal Government Relations Committee); Western Independent Bankers Association; Japan America Society of Southern California. **PRACTICE AREAS:** Corporate Securities; Financial Services. **Email:** tphelps@manatt.com

**L. LEE PHILLIPS,** (P.C.), born New York, N.Y., August 16, 1937; admitted to bar, 1959, District of Columbia; 1960, New York; 1964, California. *Education:* Cornell University (A.B., 1957; J.D., with distinction,

*(This Listing Continued)*

1959). Order of the Coif; Phi Kappa Phi. Note Editor, Cornell Law Quarterly, 1957-1959. Trial Attorney, Department of Justice, Tax Division, 1959-1963. Recording Artist Director of the Board of Directors of the Alliance of Artists and Record Companies (AARC). Member, Board of Directors of "Rock the Vote" Action Project, 1994—. Vice President of Executive Board of Directors of the Fraternity of Friends of the Music Center, 1994—. *Member:* The District of Columbia Bar; New York State Bar Association. **PRACTICE AREAS:** Entertainment (Music) Law. **Email:** lphillips@manatt.com

**RONALD S. BARAK,** born Los Angeles, California, June 7, 1943; admitted to bar, 1969, California. *Education:* University of Southern California (B.S., 1964; J.D., 1968). Order of the Coif. Associate Editor, University of Southern California Law Review, 1967-1968. Author: *Foreign Investment in U.S. Real Estate,* Harcourt Brace Jovanovich, 1981, republished in Japanese, Press Aid Center, Inc., 1983. **PRACTICE AREAS:** Real Estate; Leasing; Lease Audits; Finance. **Email:** rbarak@manatt.com

**GORDON M. BAVA,** (P.C.), born Stockton, California, February 12, 1948; admitted to bar, 1974, California. *Education:* Georgetown University School of Foreign Service (B.S.F.S., magna cum laude, 1970); University of Southern California (J.D., 1974). Member, 1972-1973 and Executive Editor of Student Notes, 1973-1974, Southern California Law Review. Phi Beta Kappa. Member, Board of Directors, Public Counsel. *Member:* Los Angeles County and American Bar Associations. **PRACTICE AREAS:** Corporate Law; Securities Law; Financial Institutions Law; Mergers and Acquisitions. **Email:** gbava@manatt.com

**IRWIN P. ALTSCHULER** (Resident, Washington, D.C. Office). **PRACTICE AREAS:** International Trade. **Email:** ialtschuler@manatt.com

**DAVID R. AMERINE** (Resident, Washington, D.C. Office). **PRACTICE AREAS:** International Trade and Customs. **Email:** damerine@manatt.com

**GEORGE M. BELFIELD,** born Philadelphia, Pennsylvania, October 30, 1954; admitted to bar, 1981, California. *Education:* Lehigh University (B.S., 1976); University of Southern California (J.D., 1981). **PRACTICE AREAS:** Litigation. **Email:** gbelfield@manatt.com

**GEOFFREY A. BERKIN,** born Chicago, Illinois, July 26, 1951; admitted to bar, 1983, California and U.S. District Court, Central District of California; 1984, U.S. Court of Appeals, Ninth Circuit; 1989, U.S. Supreme Court. *Education:* University of California at Los Angeles (A.B., 1974); University of California at Los Angeles School of Law (J.D., 1983). Editor-in-Chief, 1982-1983, Federal Communications Law Journal. Author: "Publication of Entertainment Software," (Ch.116) and "Distribution of Entertainment Software," (Ch.117) in Entertainment Industry Contracts (Matthew Bender). Instructor, U.C.L.A. Extension, 1996—. *Member:* State Bar of California; Computer Law Association; Los Angeles Copyright Society; California Copyright Conference. **PRACTICE AREAS:** Intellectual Property Law; Computer and Multimedia Law; Entertainment Law. **Email:** gberkin@manatt.com

**ELLEN BERKOWITZ,** born Los Angeles, California, July 12, 1957; admitted to bar, 1989, California and U.S. Court of Appeals, Ninth Circuit. *Education:* Brandeis University (B.A., cum laude, 1977); Loyola University of Los Angeles (J.D., magna cum laude, 1989). Order of the Coif; Alpha Sigma Nu; St. Thomas More Society. Fritz Burns Scholar. Chosen, Outstanding Woman Law Graduate, by National Association of Women Lawyers. Production Editor, Loyola University of Los Angeles Law Review, 1989. Counsel, Independent Commission of the Los Angeles Police Department, Board of Directors, Century City Chamber of Commerce. Board of Governors, Century City Bar Association. *Member:* Los Angeles County (Fair Judicial Election Practice Committee) and American Bar Associations. **PRACTICE AREAS:** Administrative Law; Land Use; Government Practice. **Email:** eberkowitz@manatt.com

**DONNA R. BLACK,** born Yuma, Arizona, September 13, 1947; admitted to bar, 1975, California and U.S. District Court, Central District of California; 1978, U.S. Court of Appeals, Eighth Circuit; 1979, District of Columbia and U.S. Court of Appeals, District of Columbia Circuit; 1983, U.S. Court of Appeals, Ninth Circuit; 1987, U.S. District Court, Northern District of California; 1989, U.S. District Court, Eastern District of California; 1995, U.S. Supreme Court. *Education:* University of Arizona (B.A., 1969); University of California, Los Angeles (J.D., 1975). Phi Beta Kappa. Section Officers Conference Advisory Board, Board of Directors, U.C.L.A. Law Alumni Association. *Member:* Los Angeles County (Environmental Section) and American (Chair, Section of Natural Resources, Energy and Environmental Law) Bar Associations. **PRACTICE AREAS:** Environmental Law; Land Use; Administrative Law. **Email:** dblack@manatt.com

*(This Listing Continued)*

CAA939B

CALIFORNIA—LOS ANGELES                                MARTINDALE-HUBBELL LAW DIRECTORY 1997

**MANATT, PHELPS & PHILLIPS, LLP,** Los Angeles—
  Continued

**ROBERT A. BLAIR, (P.C.)** (Also Of Counsel to Arnold, Grobmyer & Haley, A Professional Association, Little Rock, Arkansas) (Resident, Washington, D.C. Office). *PRACTICE AREAS:* Government; Legislative; Transportation; Corporate; Business. *Email:* rblair@manatt.com

**LAWRENCE J. BLAKE,** born New York, N.Y., November 28, 1950; admitted to bar, 1976, California and U.S. District Court, Central District of California. *Education:* Le Moyne College (B.A., magna cum laude, 1972); Harvard University (J.D., 1976). Author: "Analysis of a Recording Contract" and "Merchandising in the Music Industry," The Musician's Business and Legal Guide, (Prentice Hall), 1991, 1996. Lecturer, "Understanding Contracts in the Music Industry," U.C.L.A. Extension, 1993, 1994; "Merchandising," 1996 U.S.C. Entertainment Law Institute Member, Board of Governors, Barristers, 1979-1984; President, 1983-1984. *Member:* Beverly Hills (Co-Chairperson, Committee for the Arts, 1979-1984; Member, Board of Governors, Barristers, 1979-1984; President, 1983-1984), Century City and Los Angeles County Bar Associations. *PRACTICE AREAS:* Music. *Email:* lblake@manatt.com

**T. HALE BOGGS,** born Washington, D.C., November 1, 1961; admitted to bar, 1986, California. *Education:* Stanford University (B.A., 1983); University of California at Los Angeles (J.D., 1986). Member, University of California at Los Angeles Law Review, 1984-1986. Extern, Hon. Richard Gadbois, United States District Court, Central District of California, 1985. Speaker/Author: "Indemnification Agreements and Golden Parachutes," Bankgroup of California, June, 1995; "Regulation O Update," California League of Savings Institutions, June, 1993; "International Banking and Regulation K," Bankgroup of California, June, 1992; "An Overview of the FDIC Improvement Act of 1991," California League of Savings Institutions, February, 1992; "Financial Institution Directors: Mitigating Risks of Liability in Shareholder Actions," (Co-author) Banking Law Journal, July/August 1992; "Golden Parachutes and Indemnification Payments," Bankers' Bulletin, January, 1992; "Legal Developments Relevant for Commercial Banks and Their Holding Companies," (Co-author) State Bar of California Business Law Section Annual Review of Recent Developments and Legislation of Interest to California Business Lawyers, July, 1990. Member, California State Bar Financial Institutions Committee, 1993-1995; American Bar Association Banking Law Committee, 1995—. *Member:* Century City and American Bar Associations. *PRACTICE AREAS:* Banking Law; Corporate and Securities Law. *Email:* hboggs@manatt.com

**DIANA K. BROWN,** born Minneapolis, Minnesota, August 14, 1963; admitted to bar, 1988, California. *Education:* Barnard College, Columbia University (B.A., 1985); University of Michigan (J.D., 1988). Notes Editor, 1987-1988, Editor, 1986-1987, Michigan Yearbook of International Legal Studies. *PRACTICE AREAS:* Health Law. *Email:* dkbrown@manatt.com

**RICHARD A. BROWN,** born Lindsay, California, December 5, 1943; admitted to bar, 1972, California; 1973, District of Columbia; 1985, Florida. *Education:* California State University at Los Angeles (B.S., 1969); University of California at Los Angeles (J.D., 1972). Order of the Coif. Article and Comment Editor, UCLA Law Review, 1971-1972. Law Clerk to Judge George R. Gallagher, District of Columbia Court of Appeals, 1972-1973. *PRACTICE AREAS:* Insurance Regulation; Insurance Legislation; Insurance Transactions; Corporate-Level Insurance Litigation Reinsurance. *Email:* rbrown@manatt.com

**WILLIAM S. BRUNSTEN, (P.C.),** born Los Angeles, California, April 6, 1947; admitted to bar, 1974, California. *Education:* University of California at Berkeley (B.A., with honors, 1970); University of California at Los Angeles (J.D., 1974). *Member:* Beverly Hills and Los Angeles County Bar Associations. *PRACTICE AREAS:* Financial Services; Real Estate. *Email:* wbrunsten@manatt.com

**ALAN M. BRUNSWICK,** born Springfield, Massachusetts, April 2, 1947; admitted to bar, 1972, California. *Education:* University of Florida (B.A., 1968); Georgetown University (J.D., 1971). *Member:* Beverly Hills (Member, Section on Labor Law, Chair, 1988-1990; Member, Section on Entertainment Law), Los Angeles County (Member, Labor Law Section) and American (Member, Forum Committee on Entertainment and Sports Law, 1977—; Section on Labor Law) Bar Associations; State Bar of California (Member, Section on Labor and Employment Law). *PRACTICE AREAS:* Labor and Employment; Motion Pictures and Television. *Email:* abrunswick@manatt.com

*(This Listing Continued)*

CAA940B

**JACK W. BUECHNER** (Resident, Washington, D.C. Office). *PRACTICE AREAS:* Government; Health; Intellectual Property. *Email:* jbuechner@manatt.com

**CARA R. BURNS,** born New York, N.Y., September 28, 1963; admitted to bar, 1988, California; 1989, U.S. District Court, Southern, Northern, Central and Eastern Districts of California; U.S. District Court, Southern District of Texas; U.S. District Court, District of Hawaii; U.S. District Court, District of Arizona; U.S. District Court, Eastern District of Michigan; U.S. Court of Appeals, Ninth and Fifth Circuits. *Education:* Brandeis University (B.A., 1985); Boston University (J.D., 1988). *PRACTICE AREAS:* Entertainment; Intellectual Property. *Email:* cburns@manatt.com

**CHRIS A. CARLSON,** born Milwaukee, Wisconsin, August 23, 1955; admitted to bar, 1982, Illinois; 1985, California and U.S. District Court, Central District of California. *Education:* Stanford University (B.A., 1977); University of California, Hastings College of the Law (J.D., 1982). *Member:* Century City and American Bar Associations. *PRACTICE AREAS:* Real Estate Law; Public Finance. *Email:* ccarlson@manatt.com

**CATHERINE A. CONWAY,** born San Francisco, California, January 26, 1953; admitted to bar, 1978, Indiana; 1979, U.S. District Court, District of Indiana; 1981, California; 1983, U.S. District Court, Northern District of California; 1985, U.S. District Court, Central District of California. *Education:* Purdue University (B.A., 1975); Indiana University (J.D., 1978). Phi Kappa Phi. Deputy Prosecuting Attorney for the 19th Judicial District, Indianapolis, Indiana, 1979-1983. Deputy General Counsel to the Independent Commission on the Los Angeles Police Department, 1991. *PRACTICE AREAS:* Labor and Employment Law; Litigation. *Email:* cconway@manatt.com

**JAY L. COOPER,** born Chicago, Illinois, January 15, 1929; admitted to bar, 1951, Illinois; 1953, California; 1965, U.S. Supreme Court; 1987, New York. *Education:* DePaul University (J.D., 1951). Author: Wihtol v. Crow: Fair Use Revisited," UCLA Law Review; "Acquiring Music Rights for Motion Pictures and Television," Annual Program on Legal Aspects of the Entertainment Industry, sponsored by Beverly Hills Bar Association and University of Southern California Law School; "Current Trends in Recording Contract Negotiation," Published by the NARAS' Institute Journal; "Recording Contract Negotiation: A Perspective," Entertainment Law Journal, Loyola Law School, 1981; "The Ownership and Protection of Performers' Names," published by the Beverly Hills Bar and UCLA, 1982. Co-Editor, "Record and Music Publishing Forms of Agreement in Current Use," published by Law-Arts Publishers, Inc., 1971. Guest Lecturer: California Copyright Conference, 1967, 1971, 1973, 1975 and 1977; Harvard Law School, 1985-1995; Practicing Law Institute Seminar on "Counseling Clients in the Entertainment Industry," 1977-1995; University of Southern California-Advanced Professional Program "Legal Aspects of the Music and Recording Industry"; MIDEM; Stanford Law School, 1987; Cannes Film Festival, 1994-1996; Florida Bar Association; Texas Bar Association, UCLA Seminar on New Multimedia Technologies. Instructor: Practical Aspects of the Music/Recording Industry," University of Southern California. Adjunct Professor, Entertainment Law, Loyola Law School. Entertainment Attorney of the Year, Billboard Magazine, listed in "The Best Lawyers in America," 1975. National President, National Academy of Recording Arts and Sciences, 1975-1977. President, California Copyright Conference, 1976. Chairman, ABA Forum Committee on the Entertainment and Sports Industries, 1983-1985. *Member:* Beverly Hills (Member, 1966— and Chairman, 1973-1977, Entertainment Law Committee), Los Angeles County, Illinois State, New York State and American Bar Associations; State Bar of California; International Bar Association. *PRACTICE AREAS:* Entertainment Law (Movie, Film, Television); Intellectual Property Law; Multimedia Law. *Email:* jcooper@manatt.com

**JUNE LANGSTON (WALTON) DEHART** (Resident, Washington, D.C. Office). *PRACTICE AREAS:* Legislative and Administrative; International Trading Policy. *Email:* dehart@manatt.com

**NEAL DITTERSDORF** (Resident, Washington, D.C. Office). *PRACTICE AREAS:* Trademark and Copyright; Litigation; Insurance. *Email:* ndittersdorf@manatt.com

**GENE R. ELERDING,** born Los Angeles, California, March 20, 1949; admitted to bar, 1975, California and U.S. District Court, Central District of California. *Education:* University of Southern California (B.A., 1971); Notre Dame University (J.D., 1974). Co-author, "California Law Reference Guide," 1996. Editor, Bank Advertising Law Guide. 1995 Recipient of Almon B. McCallum Award (California Bankers Association). Member, Consumer Financial Services Committee, State Bar of California. *PRACTICE AREAS:* Financial Services. *Email:* gelerding@manatt.com

*(This Listing Continued)*

**ROGER ELLISON,** born St. Paul, Minnesota, 1937; admitted to bar, 1965, New York; 1971, Massachusetts; 1978, California. *Education:* University of Minnesota (B.S.L., 1962; LL.B., cum laude, 1962). Phi Delta Phi. Editor, Minnesota Law Review, 1958-1960. *Member:* American Bar Association; State Bar of California; American College of Investment Counsel; National Association of Public Pension Attorneys. *PRACTICE AREAS:* Private Placements; Secured Financing; Securitization; Real Estate. *Email:* rellison@manatt.com

**DAVID ELSON,** born Chicago, Illinois, October 3, 1945; admitted to bar, 1971, California. *Education:* Occidental College (B.A., 1967); Stanford University (J.D., 1970). Member, Indigent Defense Panel, U.S. District Court for the Central District of California, 1974-1977. *Member:* Century City (Co-Chair, Environmental Law Section, 1990-1991), Los Angeles County (Member, 1975—, Secretary, 1976 and Chairperson, 1977-1978, Executive Committee, Human Rights Section) and American (Member, Sections on: Litigation; Criminal Justice; Member, Environmental Litigation Committee, 1990—, Co-Chair, Solid Waste Sub Committee, 1992—) Bar Associations; The State Bar of California (Member, Criminal Law and Procedure Committee, 1975-1977; Delegate to State Bar Conference of Delegates, 1977, 1978, 1979); Association of Business Trial Lawyers. *PRACTICE AREAS:* Litigation; White Collar Criminal Defense. *Email:* delson@manatt.com

**ANDREW ERSKINE,** admitted to bar, 1981, California. *Education:* University of Virginia and University of Southern California (A.B., 1978); University of Southern California (J.D., 1980). Author: Lecturer/Panelist: "Affiliate Transactions under FIRREA," National Law Journal Seminars/Press, 1989; "Fair Lending and the Business Lender," Los Angeles County Bar Association, Commercial Law and Bankruptcy Section Newsletter, Spring, 1995. Member, Attorneys Committee, Savings and Community Bankers of America. Member, Steering Committee, Debt Restructure and Enforcement Roundtable. *Member:* Los Angeles County (Member: Commercial Law Committee; Commercial Law and Bankruptcy and Real Property Sections) and American (Member, Business Law Section) Bar Associations; Financial Lawyers Conference. *PRACTICE AREAS:* Commercial Transactions; Secured Lending and Loan Workouts; Financial Institutions; Mortgage Banking. *Email:* aerskine@manatt.com

**DIANE L. FABER,** born Van Nuys, California, September 25, 1962; admitted to bar, 1987, California; 1988, U.S. District Court, Central District of California. *Education:* Yale University (B.A., summa cum laude, 1983); Harvard University (J.D., 1987). Phi Beta Kappa. Rotary International Foundation Scholar (University of Athens, Greece). *Member:* Century City Bar Association. *PRACTICE AREAS:* Entertainment Industry; Intellectual Property; Business Litigation. *Email:* dfaber@manatt.com

**PAUL H. FALON** (Resident, Washington, D.C. Office). *PRACTICE AREAS:* Insurance Regulation, Legislation, Transactions and Corporate Litigation; Reinsurance. *Email:* pfalon@manatt.com

**DONALD J. FITZGERALD,** born New York, N.Y., April 4, 1945; admitted to bar, 1973, District of Columbia; 1977, U.S. Tax Court; 1979, California. *Education:* University of North Carolina (A.B., 1967); Yale University; Duke University (J.D., 1973); Georgetown University (LL.M., 1977). Phi Beta Kappa. Author: "Does Service's Position on 'Stapled Stock' Open a Loophole for Foreign Operations?" Journal of Taxation, June, 1979. Adjunct Professor, University of San Diego School of Law, 1980-1988. *Member:* The District of Columbia Bar; State Bar of California. [LTJG, U.S. Navy, 1967-1970]. (Certified Specialist, Taxation Law, The State Bar of California Board of Legal Specialization) (Also at Washington, D.C. Office). *PRACTICE AREAS:* Taxation. *Email:* dfitzgerald@manatt.com

**JUDITH R. FORMAN, (P.C.),** born Philadelphia, Pennsylvania, April 7, 1942; admitted to bar, 1975, Pennsylvania; 1978, California; U.S. District Court, Eastern District of Pennsylvania and Central District of California; U.S. Court of Federal Claims. *Education:* University of Pennsylvania (B.A., with distinction, 1963; M.A., 1966); Université de Paris (Sorbonne, 1961); Villanova University (J.D., 1975). Author, Articles: "The Impact of Parental Alcoholism and Related Substance Abuse Issues in Custody Determinations,"; "The Effect of Parental Alcoholism in Custody Disputes," L.A. County Bar, Family Law Symposium Books, 1992-1993; Family Law: The Good Times and the Bad," Fourth Beverly Hills Bar Association Citizen's Law School, 1991. Member, Advisory Committee, Harriet Buhai Center for Family Law, 1990-1995. *Member:* Los Angeles County (Family Law Section; Family Law Mediation Panel; Family Law Symposium Panel, 1992) and American Bar Associations; Women Lawyers Association of Los Angeles; California Women Lawyers. (Certified Specialist, Family Law, The State Bar of California Board of Legal Specialization). *PRACTICE AREAS:* Family Law. *Email:* jforman@manatt.com

**HOWARD M. FRUMES,** born Long Beach, California, October 27, 1949; admitted to bar, 1974, California and U.S. District Court, Central District of California. *Education:* Claremont Men's College (B.A., magna cum laude with honors in Political Science, 1971); Harvard University (J.D., 1974). *PRACTICE AREAS:* Entertainment Law; International Law; Dispute Resolution. *Email:* hfrumes@manatt.com

**CYNTHIA FUTTER,** born Pomona, CA, 1959; admitted to bar, 1984, California. *Education:* University of Southern California (B.A., magna cum laude, 1980; J.D., 1983). Phi Beta Kappa. Order of the Coif. Law Clerk to the Honorable Robert J. Kelleher, U.S. District Court, Central District of California, 1983-1984. *PRACTICE AREAS:* Corporate Recovery/Insolvency; Financial Services. *Email:* cfutter@manatt.com

**PETER R. GILBERT** (Resident, Washington, D.C. Office). *PRACTICE AREAS:* Corporate; Securities; Political Risk Insurance. *Email:* pgilbert@manatt.com

**DONNA FIELDS GOLDSTEIN,** born New York, N.Y., November 2, 1947; admitted to bar, 1972, Pennsylvania; 1977, California; U.S. District Court, Central, Northern and Eastern Districts of California; U.S. Court of Appeals, Ninth Circuit. *Education:* Beaver College (B.A., 1968); Rutgers University (J.D., 1972). Trial Attorney, U.S. Department of Justice, Civil Rights Division, 1972-1977. Assistant U.S. Attorney, Central District of California, 1977-1980. *Member:* Century City (Co-Chair, Section on Employment Law), Los Angeles County and American (Member, Sections on: Labor and Employment Law; Litigation) Bar Associations. *PRACTICE AREAS:* Employment Law; Labor Law Litigation; Unfair Competition; Consumeration; General Business Litigation. *Email:* dgoldstein@manatt.com

**ANDREA JANE GREFE,** born Kew Gardens, New York, November 19, 1948; admitted to bar, 1978, California; 1979, Texas. *Education:* Northwestern University (B.A., 1970); Loyola University (M.Ed., 1974); Hastings College of the Law, University of California (J.D., 1978). Managing Editor, Hastings Constitutional Law Quarterly, 1977-1978. Author: "The Family Viewing Hour: An Assualt of the First Amendment?" 4 Hastings Constitutional Law Quarterly 935, 1977. *Member:* Los Angeles County Bar Association (Executive Committee, Intellectual Property and Unfair Competition Section, 1986-1990); State Bar of California; Los Angeles Copyright Society (President, 1993-1994). *PRACTICE AREAS:* Entertainment Law. *Email:* agrefe@manatt.com

**RICK L. GROSSMAN,** born Pasadena, California, December 22, 1955; admitted to bar, 1979, California; 1980, U.S. District Court, Central District of California and U.S. Tax Court. *Education:* University of California, Los Angeles (B.A., 1976); Southwestern University (J.D., 1979); Georgetown University (LL.M., 1981). Staff Member, Southwestern University Law Review, 1978-1979. Chair, State Bar of California, Taxation Section, Exempt Organizations Committee. Lecturer: "Ethical Issues for Health Care Lawyers," ABA Health Care Fraud National Institute, April, 1995; California Society for Healthcare Attorneys, November, 1995; "Unrelated Business Income," L.A. County Bar Association, Feb. 1996; California Association of Nonprofits Annual Institute, Oct. 1996. *Member:* State Bar of California (Member, Taxation Section; Business Law Section); American Bar Association (Member, Taxation Section; Business Law Section; Health Law Forum Committee); California Society of Healthcare Attorneys; National Health Lawyers Association; American Academy of Healthcare Attorneys. (Certified Specialist, Taxation Law, The State Bar of California Board of Legal Specialization). *PRACTICE AREAS:* Health; Taxation; Nonprofit/Tax Exempt Organizations. *Email:* rgrossman@manatt.com

**CARL GRUMER,** born Englewood, New Jersey, December 15, 1950; admitted to bar, 1975, California. *Education:* University of California at Los Angeles (B.A., magna cum laude, 1972; J.D., 1975). Phi Beta Kappa; Pi Gamma Mu; Psi Chi. Author: "Criminal Infringement of Copyright," Journal of the Beverly Hills Bar Association, July-August, 1976. University of California at Los Angeles Winner, Nathan Burkan Competition, 1974. *Member:* Beverly Hills and Los Angeles County (Member, Sections on: Commercial Law and Bankruptcy; Intellectual Property; Litigation) Bar Associations; State Bar of California; Los Angeles Bankruptcy Forum; Financial Lawyers Conference; Los Angeles Copyright Society. *PRACTICE AREAS:* Business Litigation. *Email:* cgrumer@manatt.com

**SCOTT D. HARRINGTON,** born Chicopee, Massachusetts, August 4, 1956; admitted to bar, 1984, California, U.S. District Court, Southern District of California and U.S. Supreme Court. *Education:* Northwestern Connecticut Community College (A.A., Fine Arts, with honors, 1976); University of Connecticut (B.A., summa cum laude, 1980); Duke University (J.D., 1983). Phi Kappa Phi; Phi Beta Kappa. Member, Duke Law Journal, 1981-1983. *Member:* Beverly Hills (Member, Entertainment Law Section), Los

*(This Listing Continued)*

## MANATT, PHELPS & PHILLIPS, LLP, Los Angeles—Continued

Angeles County and American (Member: Intellectual Property Law Committee; Forum Committee on Entertainment) Bar Associations. *PRACTICE AREAS:* Music. **Email:** sharrington@manatt.com

**ROBERT E. HINERFELD,** born New York, N.Y., May 29, 1934; admitted to bar, 1960, California; 1963, U.S. Supreme Court. *Education:* Harvard University (A.B., magna cum laude, 1956; LL.B., 1959). Clinical Lecturer, University of Southern California Law Center, 1980-1981. Guest Lecturer on Legal Ethics, 1993-1995. Lecturer on federal appellate and injuction practice and civil RICO for Los Angeles County and Federal Bar Associations and Continuing Education of the Bar, 1982-1984. Assistant U.S. Attorney, Los Angeles, 1960-1962. Member, Commercial Panel of Arbitrators, American Arbitration Association, 1966—. Critic, National Institute for Trial Advocacy, 1972. Director, 1974-1983 and Secretary, 1978-1980, Harvard Club of Southern California. Invited Witness, Advisory Committee for an Effective Publication Rule, Judicial Council of the State of California, 1978. Expert Witness on issues of Business Litigation, Legal Malpractice and Legal Ethics, 1987—. Fellow, American Bar Foundation, 1989—. Associate Independent Counsel of the United States (di Genova 1993-1995). *Member:* Los Angeles County Bar Association (Representative to Los Angeles City Attorney's Study Group on Conflicts of Interest By Public Law Offices, 1977-1978; Member, Special Committee on Judicial Evaluation, 1978-1982); The State Bar of California (Member, Criminal Law and Procedure Committee, 1973-1976; Reporter on Proposed Amendments to Federal Rules of Criminal Procedure, 1974-1975; Hearing Examiner/Referee in investigation, hearing and review depts. of state Bar court, 1974-1987; Chairman, Special Committee on Revision of Federal Criminal Code, 1975-1978; Member, Executive Committee, Litigation Section, 1983-1986; Member, Civil Litigation Consulting Group, 1985-1988); California Academy of Appellate Lawyers (Elected 1979); Association of Business Trial Lawyers (Member, Board of Governors, 1982-1984). *PRACTICE AREAS:* Litigation and Professional Responsibility. **Email:** rhinerfeld@manatt.com

**PAUL S. HOFFMAN,** born Chicago, Illinois, March 26, 1959; admitted to bar, 1985, California; 1986, U.S. District Court, Central District of California; 1988, U.S. District Court, Southern District of California; 1991, U.S. District Court, Northern District of California; 1992, U.S. Court of Appeals, Ninth Circuit. *Education:* Southern Illinois University (B.S., 1982); Southwestern University (J.D., 1985). Law Clerk to the Honorable Geraldine Mund, U.S. Bankruptcy Judge, Central District of California, 1985-1986. Judicial Extern to the Honorable Arthur L. Alarcon, U.S. Court of Appeals, Ninth Circuit, 1985. *Member:* Financial Lawyers Conference; Bankruptcy Forum. *PRACTICE AREAS:* Bankruptcy and Creditor-Debtor Rights; Commercial; Real Estate Workouts. **Email:** phoffman@manatt.com

**MARIA D. HUMMER, (P.C.),** admitted to bar, 1976, California; 1979, District of Columbia. *Education:* Scripps College (B.A., 1968); University of California at Los Angeles (J.D., 1976). Board of Editors, UCLA Law Review, 1975-1976. Los Angeles Regional Water Quality Control Board, 1976-1984; Board of Trustees, Pitzer College, 1983-1991; Board of Directors, Legal Aid Foundation of Los Angeles, 1984-1991; Board of Airport Commissioners, City of Los Angeles, Department of Airports, 1984-1989; Board of Trustees, California Museum Foundation, 1988-1992; Board of Directors, Music Center Operating Company, Music Center of Los Angeles County, 1992—; Board of Directors, Independent Colleges of Southern California, 1988—; Regents Council, Mount St. Mary's, 1988—; Board of Directors, Los Angeles Area Chamber of Commerce, 1994—; Board of Directors, Los Angeles County Bar Foundation. *Member:* Los Angeles County and American Bar Associations; The District of Columbia Bar. *PRACTICE AREAS:* Land Use; Administrative Law. **Email:** mhummer@manatt.com

**PHALEN G. HUREWITZ,** born Fall River, Massachusetts, November 25, 1936; admitted to bar, 1962, California; 1978, U.S. Supreme Court. *Education:* Dartmouth College (A.B., magna cum laude, 1958; Phi Beta Kappa); Stanford University (LL.B., 1961). Revising Chairman, Stanford Moot Court Board, 1960-1961. Recipient, American Jurisprudence Award in Mortgages. Law Clerk for the Honorable Justice Byrl Salsman, District Court of Appeal. Editor, Syllabus, 1968 Annual Program on Legal Aspects of the Entertainment Industry. Co-editor and Contributor, Annual Program on Legal Aspects of the Entertainment Industry. Commissioner, Los Angeles County Commission for Children's and Family Services, 1994—. President, Bureau of Jewish Education, 1994—. *PRACTICE AREAS:* Entertainment Law. **Email:** phurewitz@manatt.com

*(This Listing Continued)*

**LINDA M. IANNONE** (Resident, Washington, D.C. Office). *PRACTICE AREAS:* Corporate; Securities and Banking. **Email:** liannone@manatt.com

**PAUL H. IRVING,** born Los Angeles, California, May 23, 1952; admitted to bar, 1980, California and U.S. District Court, Central District of California. *Education:* New York University (B.F.A., with highest honors, 1975); Loyola Law School of Los Angeles (J.D., 1980). Member, 1978-1979 and Articles Editor, 1979-1980, Loyola of Los Angeles International and Comparative Law Annual First Place, 1979-1980, ABA Client Counseling Competition. Author, Publications: "Joint Accounts," Corporate Counsel, 1996; "Change in Congress Hits Financial Sector," California Law Business, 1995; "Financial Institution Directors-Mitigating Risks of Liability in Shareholder Actions," 109 The Banking Law Journal, 1992. Author, "Directors' Liability in Mergers and Acquisitions Causes New Concern," Corporate Finance News, 1990. Frequent speaker on Mergers and Acquisitions, Capital Markets, Financial Institutions, Corporate Directors' Obligations, Shareholders' Rights and Strategic Business Opportunities. Adjunct Professor, Loyola University School of Law, 1981-1985. Attorneys Committee, Western League of Savings Institutions (Chairman, 1993-1994). Attorneys Committee, America's Community Bankers. *PRACTICE AREAS:* Banking; Corporate Finance; Entertainment and Media. **Email:** pirving@manatt.com

**CLARENCE L. JAMES** (Resident, Washington, D.C. Office). *PRACTICE AREAS:* Taxation; Government Contracts; Real Estate Development.

**ROSALYN EVELYN JONES,** born Frankfurt, Germany, April 26, 1961; admitted to bar, 1987, California; 1988, District of Columbia. *Education:* Harvard-Radcliffe Colleges (A.B., magna cum laude, 1983) Phi Beta Kappa; Oxford University, England (Harvard Knox Fellow, 1983-1984); Harvard Law School (J.D., 1987). Author: "Personal Service Contracts," International Media Law, Vol. 6, Numbers 4 and 5, April and May, 1988. *Member:* Beverly Hills and American Bar Associations; Black Entertainment and Sports Lawyers Association (Officer, Board of Directors, Annual Conference Chairperson, 1994 and 1995). *PRACTICE AREAS:* Music. **Email:** rjones@manatt.com

**ROBERT J. KABEL** (Resident, Washington, D.C. Office). *PRACTICE AREAS:* Legislative; Administrative. **Email:** rkabel@manatt.com

**ANDREW M. KATZENSTEIN,** born Pennsylvania, October 13, 1957; admitted to bar, 1982, California; 1990, New York. *Education:* University of Michigan (B.A., magna cum laude, 1979; J.D., cum laude, 1982); University of San Diego (LL.M. in Taxation, 1985). Member, Mortar Board. Writing and Advocacy Instructor, University of Michigan Law School, 1980-1981, 1981-1982. Adjunct Professor, Estate Tax, UCLA School of Law. *Member:* Beverly Hills, Los Angeles County (Chair, Fiduciary Income Tax Committee, Death and Gift Tax Section, 1985—; Member, Section on Tax) and American (Member, Sections on Taxation; Probate and Trust Law) Bar Associations; State Bar of California (Member, Sections on Tax; Probate). (Certified Specialist, Estate Planning, Trust and Probate Law, The State Bar of California Board of Legal Specialization). *PRACTICE AREAS:* Health Law; Estates and Trusts. **Email:** akatzenstein@manatt.com

**GEORGE DAVID KIEFFER,** born New York, N.Y., November 17, 1947; admitted to bar, 1973, California. *Education:* University of California at Santa Barbara (B.A., 1969); University of California at Los Angeles (J.D., 1973). Outstanding Man, UC Santa Barbara, 1969. Extern Clerk, Chief Judge David L. Bazelon, U.S. Court of Appeals, District of Columbia Circuit, 1972. Regent, University of California, 1979-1980. Member, 1981-1987 and President, 1984-1985, Board of Governors, California Community Colleges. Member, and Chairman, Bd. of Directors, Center for the Study of Democratic Institutions, 1983-1993. Member, Commission for the Review of the Master Plan for Higher Education of California, 1985-1987. Bd. of Directors, Los Angeles Urban League, 1989-1995. Bd. of Directors, Constitutional Rights Foundation, 1994—. Bd. of Directors, California Chamber of Commerce, 1996—. Bd. of Directors, Los Angeles Export Terminal, Inc., 1996—. *Member:* Los Angeles County Bar Association. *PRACTICE AREAS:* Government; Administrative; Regulatory; Legislative. **Email:** gkieffer@manatt.com

**SANDRA R. KING,** born Buffalo, New York, November 19, 1955; admitted to bar, 1980, District of Columbia; 1982, California. *Education:* State University of New York at Albany (B.A., summa cum laude, 1977); George Washington University (J.D., with honors, 1980). Phi Beta Kappa. Member, 1978-1980 and Notes Editor, 1979-1980, George Washington Law Review. *Member:* Los Angeles County and American Bar Associa-

*(This Listing Continued)*

tions; The District of Columbia Bar. *PRACTICE AREAS:* Employment Law and Litigation. *Email:* sking@manatt.com

**DAVID M. KLAUS** (Resident, Washington, D.C. Office). *PRACTICE AREAS:* Government. *Email:* dklaus@manatt.com

**KENNETH L. KRAUS** (Resident, Nashville, Tennessee Office). *PRACTICE AREAS:* Music.

**BARRY S. LANDSBERG,** born Long Beach, New York, March 27, 1955; admitted to bar, 1980, Georgia and District of Columbia; 1985, California. *Education:* University of Maryland (B.A., summa cum laude, 1977); Emory University (J.D., 1980). Phi Beta Kappa. Emory Law Journal, 1979-1980. Co-Author: with Terri D. Keville, "Courts Hostile to Insurers Reneging on Hospital Payments". Lecturer: "Physician Integrity in Credentialing," NHLA seminar on physicians and hospitals, April, 1996; "Resident's Rights Under OBRA 1987," NHLA Seminar on Long Term Health Care and the Law, January 1996. Lecturer: "Transfer Trauma as a Legal Issue in Long Term Health Care," NHLA Seminar on Long Term Health Care and the Law, January 1994. *Member:* District of Columbia Bar; State Bar of California. *PRACTICE AREAS:* Health Care; Business Litigation. *Email:* blandsberg@manatt.com

**DAVID H. LARRY** (Resident, Washington, D.C. Office). *PRACTICE AREAS:* Litigation. *Email:* dlarry@manatt.com 43500

**JOHN P. LECRONE,** born San Francisco, California, December 30, 1957; admitted to bar, 1984, California. *Education:* University of Southern California (B.S., 1980); Institute of European Studies, Vienna, Austria (1978); Southwestern University (J.D., 1984). Member, Moot Court Honors Program. Member, Executive Committee of the Barristers of Los Angeles County Bar Association, 1990-1994. *Member:* Century City, Los Angeles County and American Bar Associations. *PRACTICE AREAS:* Labor/Employment Law; Litigation. *Email:* jlecrone@manatt.com

**MARK S. LEE,** born Christopher, Illinois, June 19, 1954; admitted to bar, 1980, California; 1981, U.S. District Court, Central District of California. *Education:* University of Illinois (B.A., 1977; J.D., 1980). Author: "Japan's Approach to Copyright Protection For Computer Software," Loyola of Los Angeles Int'l and Comp. Law Journal, Vol. 16 No. 3, June 1994; "Prejudgment Asset Freezes Against Software Pirates," The Computer Lawyer, Vol. 9 No. 10, October 1992. Adjunct Professor, Copyright Law, McGeorge School of Law. *Member:* The State Bar of California; American Bar Association. *LANGUAGES:* Japanese. *PRACTICE AREAS:* Intellectual Property; Litigation; International. *Email:* mlee@manatt.com

**TIN KIN LEE,** born Hong Kong, December 22, 1961; admitted to bar, 1987, California; 1988, District of Columbia, U.S. Court of Appeals for the District of Columbia Circuit and U.S. Court of Appeals for the Federal Circuit; 1989, U.S. District Court for the District of Columbia. *Education:* University of Southern California (B.S., cum laude, 1983); Columbia Law School (J.D., 1986). *Member:* State Bar of California; The District of Columbia Bar. *PRACTICE AREAS:* Healthcare; Finance; Corporate; Real Estate. *Email:* tlee@manatt.com

**MARGARET LEVY,** born Louisville, Kentucky, March 11, 1951; admitted to bar, 1975, California. *Education:* Michigan State University (B.A., with highest honors, 1972); University of California at Los Angeles (J.D., 1975). UCLA Law Review. Author: "Current Coverage Issues in Health Insurance Law: Is There Coverage When There Is No Coverage?" 26 Tort & Ins. L.J. 621 (1991). *Member:* Los Angeles County (Litigation Section) and American (Litigation and Tort and Insurance Practice Sections; Chair; Committee on Health Insurance Law, 1994-1995) Bar Associations; Defense Research Institute (Vice-chair, Life, Health and Disability Insurance Law Committee). *PRACTICE AREAS:* Disability Insurance Litigation; Life Insurance Litigation; Health Insurance Litigation; Employment Litigation. *Email:* mlevy@manatt.com

**JOHN F. LIBBY,** born Hempstead, New York, July 11, 1958; admitted to bar, 1984, District of Columbia; 1987, California. *Education:* Stanford University (A.B., 1980); Yale University (J.D., 1984). Assistant U.S. Attorney, Central District of California, 1989-1995. *PRACTICE AREAS:* Health Law; Business Litigation; White-Collar Criminal Defense. *Email:* jlibby@manatt.com

**EDWARD L. LUBLIN** (Resident, Washington, D.C. Office). *PRACTICE AREAS:* Financial Services. *Email:* elublin@manatt.com

**EILEEN LYON,** born Lynwood, California, September 18, 1957; admitted to bar, 1987, California, U.S. Court of Appeals, Ninth Circuit and U.S. District Court, Central District of California. *Education:* University of California at Los Angeles (B.A., 1983); University of Southern California (J.D., 1987). Member, Southern California Law Review, 1985-1986. Instructor,

*(This Listing Continued)*

Legal Writing Program, University of Southern California, 1985-1987. *Member:* Los Angeles County (Business and Corporate Law Section; Member, Delegation to the State Conference of Delegates, 1994-1995) and American (Section of Business Law; Banking Law Committee; Committee on Federal Regulation of Securities) Bar Associations; State Bar of California (Member, Business Law Section). *PRACTICE AREAS:* Corporate Law; Securities Law; Banking Law. *Email:* elyon@manatt.com

**BARRY E. MALLEN,** born Los Angeles, California, July 22, 1960; admitted to bar, 1985, California and U.S. District Court, Central District of California; 1986, U.S. Court of Appeals, Ninth Circuit; 1994, U.S. District Court, Eastern District of California. *Education:* University of California at Los Angeles (B.A., 1982); McGeorge School of Law, University of the Pacific (J.D., 1985). Phi Alpha Delta. Member, International Moot Court Honors Board. *Member:* Los Angeles County (Member, Sections on: Litigation; Intellectual Property) and American (Member, Sections on: Litigation; Business Law; Intellectual Property) Bar Associations; State Bar of California (Member, Sections on: Litigation; Intellectual Property). *PRACTICE AREAS:* Entertainment; Copyright; Business Litigation. *Email:* bmallen@manatt.com

**LAURENCE M. MARKS,** born London, England, August 22, 1947; admitted to bar, 1978, California, U.S. District Court, Central District of California and U.S. Court of Appeals, Ninth Circuit. *Education:* University of California at Los Angeles (B.A., summa cum laude, 1975; J.D., 1978). Phi Beta Kappa; Phi Alpha Delta. Member, Communications Bar Journal, 1977-1978. *Member:* Century City (Member, Entertainment Section) and Beverly Hills (Member, Entertainment Section) Bar Associations; L.A. Copyright Society. *PRACTICE AREAS:* Entertainment Law; Book Publishing; Motion Picture Finance. *Email:* lmarks@manatt.com

**GERALD A. MARGOLIS,** born Brooklyn, New York, August 18, 1943; admitted to bar, 1969, New York, U.S. District Court, Southern District of New York; 1974, California, U.S. District Court, Northern, Central, Eastern and Southern Districts of California; U.S. Court of Appeals, Ninth Circuit. *Education:* Harvard University (A.B., 1965); Fordham University (J.D., 1968). *Member:* Los Angeles County, New York State and American Bar Associations; State Bar of California. *PRACTICE AREAS:* Entertainment; Intellectual Property Transactions; Litigation Matters. *Email:* gmargolis@manatt.com

**THOMAS J. MCDERMOTT JR.,** born California, 1931; admitted to bar, 1959, California, U.S. District Court, Southern, Central, Northern and Eastern Districts of California and U.S. Court of Appeals, Ninth and Tenth Circuits and U.S. Supreme Court. *Education:* University of California at Los Angeles (B.A., 1953); University of California School of Law (J.D., 1958). Phi Delta Phi; Order of the Coif. Articles Editor, U.C.L.A. Law Review, 1957-1958. President, U.C.L.A. Law Alumni Association, 1961-1962. Chair, Ninth Circuit Judicial Conference, 1996-1997; Lawyer Representative Chair, 1995-1996. State Bar Litigation Section Executive Committee, Chair, 1993-1994. Adjunct Professor of Law, Corporate Directors' and Officers' Liability, Southwestern University School of Law, 1984—. President, Association of Business Trial Lawyers, 1980-1981. Fellow, American College of Trial Lawyers. [with U.S. Army, 1953-1956]. *PRACTICE AREAS:* High Technology Litigation; Securities Litigation; Antitrust. *Email:* tmcdermott@manatt.com

**THOMAS R. MCMORROW,** born Glendale, California, October 15, 1963; admitted to bar, 1989, California and U.S. Court of Appeals, Ninth Circuit; 1991, District of Columbia. *Education:* University of California at Los Angeles (B.A., with honors, 1985); George Washington University (J.D., 1989). Phi Delta Phi (Magister of Marshall Inn, 1988-1989). Coro Fellow, 1985-1986. Leadership Los Angeles Fellow, 1990-1991. Van Vleck Appellate Moot Court Board. Associate Editor, George Washington Journal of International Law and Economics, 1988-1989. Judge Samuel Green Memorial Scholar. *Member:* Century City, Los Angeles County and American (Student Representative) Bar Associations. *PRACTICE AREAS:* Government; Administrative Banking; General Corporate. *Email:* tmcmorrow@manatt.com

**SHERWIN L. MEMEL, (P.C.),** born Buffalo, New York, March 28, 1930; admitted to bar, 1955, California; 1963, U.S. Supreme Court; 1979, District of Columbia. *Education:* University of California at Los Angeles (B.A., 1951; J.D., 1954). Order of the Coif; Nu Beta Epsilon (President, 1953-1954). Associate Editor-in-Chief, U.C.L.A. Law Review, 1952-1954. Member: Health Insurance Benefits Advisory Council, 1970-1973. California Board of Medical Quality Assurance, 1973-1977, President, 1976-1977. *Member:* Century City, Los Angeles County and American Bar Associations; National Health Lawyers Association; American Society of Law and Medicine; California Society for Healthcare Attorneys (President, 1983);

*(This Listing Continued)*

**MANATT, PHELPS & PHILLIPS, LLP,** Los Angeles—
*Continued*

American Academy of Healthcare Attorneys. *PRACTICE AREAS:* Health Law. *Email:* smemel@manatt.com

**PETER M. MENARD,** born Denver, Colorado, September 14, 1953; admitted to bar, 1979, California. *Education:* University of Santa Clara (B.A., 1974; B.S., 1974); University of Michigan (M.S., 1976; J.D., 1979). Member, Michigan Journal of Law Reform, 1978-1979. *PRACTICE AREAS:* Corporate Law; Securities Law; Technology Transfer. *Email:* pmenard@manatt.com

**ALAN E. MORELLI,** born Morristown, New Jersey, August 4, 1961; admitted to bar, 1987, Delaware; 1989, California. *Education:* Rutgers University (B.S., magna cum laude, 1983); Georgetown Law Center (J.D., 1986). Recipient: G.L. Scholar Honors Award; Scholar Athlete Award. *Member:* Los Angeles County (Member, Business Law and Intellectual Property Law Sections), Delaware State (Member, Corporate Law Sections, 1987—) and American Bar Associations; State Bar of California (Member, Executive Committee, Business Law Section, 1995—; Chair, Online Project Task Force, 1994-1995; Member, Corporations Committee, Business Law Section, 1992-1995; Vice Chair, 1993-1994, Co-Chair, 1994-1995). *PRACTICE AREAS:* Corporate Securities; Technology/Electronic Commerce. *Email:* amorelli@manatt.com

**JAMES P. MULKEEN,** born Cambridge, Massachusetts, November 28, 1945; admitted to bar, 1970, Oklahoma; 1972, District of Columbia; 1975, U.S. Supreme Court; 1977, California. *Education:* Parsons College (B.A., 1967); University of Tulsa (J.D., 1970). Phi Delta Phi. Member, University of Tulsa Law Review, 1969-1970. Trial Attorney: Bureau of Competition, Federal Trade Commission, 1970. Civil Rights Division, U.S. Department of Justice, 1970-1972. President, City of Los Angeles Labor Board of Civil Service Commissioners. *Member:* Century City (Labor Section), Los Angeles County (Member, Labor Law and Litigation Sections) and American (Member, Sections on Labor and Employment Law; Litigation) Bar Associations; The District of Columbia Bar. *PRACTICE AREAS:* Labor; Employment Litigation; Business Litigation. *Email:* jmulkeen@manatt.com

**KEVIN O'CONNELL,** born Boston, Massachusetts, September 4, 1933; admitted to bar, 1961, California; 1976, U.S. Supreme Court. *Education:* Harvard University (A.B., magna cum laude, 1955; J.D., cum laude, 1960). Member, Board of Editors, Harvard Law Review, 1958-1960. Assistant U.S. Attorney (Criminal Division), Central District of California, 1963-1965. Staff Counsel, McCone Commission on the Los Angeles Riots, 1965. Member: Board of Directors, California Supreme Court Historical Society. *Member:* Los Angeles County and American (Litigation, Antitrust, and Corporate Law Sections) Bar Associations; American Law Institute; Association of Business Trial Lawyers. *PRACTICE AREAS:* Litigation; Antitrust and Unfair Business Practices. *Email:* koconnell@manatt.com

**THOMAS P. ONDECK** (Resident, Washington, D.C. Office). *PRACTICE AREAS:* Trade; Administrative Law; Civil Litigation; Computers and Technology. *Email:* tondeck@manatt.com

**ROBERT H. PLATT,** born New York, N.Y., October 19, 1957; admitted to bar, 1983, New York and California. *Education:* Cornell University, New York State School of Industrial and Labor Relations (B.S., 1979); Fordham University (J.D., 1982). General Counsel, Los Angeles Clippers Basketball Club. Member, Steering Committee, Bet Tzedek Legal Services; Steering Committee, UCLA Unicamp. *PRACTICE AREAS:* Labor/Employment Law; Sports; Litigation. *Email:* rplatt@manatt.com

**WILLIAM T. QUICKSILVER, (P.C.),** born St. Louis, Missouri, July 26, 1952; admitted to bar, 1978, California. *Education:* Princeton University (A.B., magna cum laude, 1974); University of Chicago (J.D., 1978). Phi Delta Phi. Associate Editor, University of Chicago Law Review, 1977-1978. *Member:* Century City and American Bar Associations. *PRACTICE AREAS:* Banking Law; Corporate Securities; Corporate Law. *Email:* wquicksilver@manatt.com

**B. MICHAEL RAUH** (Resident, Washington, D.C. Office). *PRACTICE AREAS:* Business; Civil Litigation. *Email:* mrauh@manatt.com

**JOHN L. RAY** (Resident, Washington, D.C. Office). *PRACTICE AREAS:* Healthcare; Business; Real Estate. *Email:* jray@manatt.com

**HAROLD P. REICHWALD,** born New York, New York, August 28, 1936; admitted to bar, 1962, New York; 1979, California. *Education:* Queens College of the City University of New York (B.A., 1957); New York University (J.D., 1962; LL.M., 1969). [With USAR, 1957-1962]. *PRACTICE AREAS:* Corporate Securities; Financial Services; Insurance Industry; Fashion Industry. *Email:* hreichwald@manatt.com

**JAMES H. ROBERTS III** (Resident, Washington, D.C. Office). *PRACTICE AREAS:* Governmental Contracts; Litigation; International Business; Business. *Email:* jroberts@manatt.com

**CHRISTOPHER L. RUDD,** born Cheverly, Maryland, July 31, 1962; admitted to bar, 1987, California. *Education:* University of Pennsylvania (B.A., 1984); Duke University (J.D., 1987). *PRACTICE AREAS:* Entertainment Law; General Business Litigation. *Email:* clrudd@manatt.com

**ALAN U. SCHWARTZ,** born Mt. Vernon, New York, 1933; admitted to bar, 1957, New York; 1985, California. *Education:* Cornell University (B.A., with honors, 1953); Oxford University; Yale Law School (LL.B., 1956). *Member:* Los Angeles County and New York State Bar Associations. *PRACTICE AREAS:* Entertainment; Financing. *Email:* aschwartz@manatt.com

**BRAD WILLIAM SEILING,** born Elgin, Illinois, August 5, 1964; admitted to bar, 1989, California; 1990, U.S. District Court, Central District of California, U.S. Court of Appeals, Ninth Circuit. *Education:* Georgetown University (B.S.F.S., cum laude, 1986); University of California at Los Angeles (J.D., 1989). Staff Counsel, Independent Commission on the Los Angeles Police Department, 1992. *Member:* Century City and American Bar Associations; California Association of Political Attorneys; Lawyers for Human Rights. *PRACTICE AREAS:* Commercial Litigation; Election Law. *Email:* bseiling@manatt.com

**MARTIN SHULMAN** (Resident, Washington, D.C. Office). *PRACTICE AREAS:* Trusts and Estates; Real Estate; Litigation. *Email:* mshulman@manatt.com

**LAURIE L. SORIANO,** born Bridgeport, Connecticut, October 13, 1961; admitted to bar, 1986, California. *Education:* University of Pennsylvania, Wharton School of Business (B.S., 1983); University of Pennsylvania, College of Arts and Sciences (B.A., 1983); University of California at Davis (J.D., 1986). Order of the Coif. Recipient, American Jurisprudence Awards in Property and Constitutional Law. Editor-in-Chief, University of California at Davis Law Review, 1985-1986. Judicial Clerk, Hon. Harry Pregerson, U.S. Court of Appeals, Ninth Circuit, 1986-1987. *PRACTICE AREAS:* Entertainment Law. *Email:* lsoriano@manatt.com

**LISA SPECHT,** born Los Angeles, California, December 5, 1945; admitted to bar, 1976, California. *Education:* University of La Verne, San Fernando Valley College of Law (J.D., 1976). Editor-in-Chief, Law Review. Los Angeles Recreation and Parks Commissioner. Los Angeles Coliseum Commissioner. IPAC Board, U.S. Department of Commerce. Trustee, Pitzer College. Vice President, Bet Tzedek Legal Services. Vice President, NOW Legal Defense and Education Fund. Founder and Director, Women's Political Committee. Former Board Member, The Urban League. Los Angeles Business Journal. *Who's Who in the Law,* 1995 and 1996. Chair, Administrative Law Section. *PRACTICE AREAS:* Government. *Email:* lspecht@manatt.com

**DONALD S. STEIN** (Resident, Washington, D.C. Office). *PRACTICE AREAS:* Customs; International Trade. *Email:* dstein@manatt.com

**ROBERT L. SULLIVAN** (Resident, Nashville, Tennessee Office). *PRACTICE AREAS:* Entertainment; Litigation.

**TIMOTHY M. THORNTON,** born Boston, Massachusetts, April 2, 1929; admitted to bar, 1955, Massachusetts; 1958, California. *Education:* Boston College (B.S., 1952; J.D., 1955). Assistant U.S. Attorney, 1959-1964 and Chief, Special Prosecution Section, 1961-1964, Southern District of California. Adjunct Professor, University of Southern California, Pre-Trial Advocacy, 1993-1996. [Captain, USNR, Ret.]. *PRACTICE AREAS:* Litigation. *Email:* tthornton@manatt.com

**RONALD B. TUROVSKY,** born Whittier, California, March 25, 1957; admitted to bar, 1983, California. *Education:* University of California at Berkeley (B.A., Great Distinction in General Scholarship, 1979); Columbia University Graduate School of Journalism (M.S., 1980); Boalt Hall School of Law, University of California (J.D., 1983). Phi Beta Kappa. Associate Editor, California Law Review, 1982-1983. Treasurer, California Political Attorneys Association. *PRACTICE AREAS:* Election and Governmental Litigation. *Email:* rturovsky@manatt.com

**LEONARD D. VENGER,** born Los Angeles, California, November 20, 1942; admitted to bar, 1967, California. *Education:* University of California at Los Angeles (B.A., 1964; J.D., 1967). Arbitrator for the Los Angeles Superior Court. Consultant to Author for the California Continuing Education of the Bar (CEB). *Member:* Los Angeles County Bar Association; The

*(This Listing Continued)*

## PROFESSIONAL BIOGRAPHIES — CALIFORNIA—LOS ANGELES

State Bar of California; Association of Business Trial Lawyers. (Chairman, Business Litigation Practice Group). *PRACTICE AREAS:* Business Litigation. *Email:* lvenger@manatt.com

**VINCENT M. WALDMAN,** born Tulsa, Oklahoma, July 27, 1959; admitted to bar, 1984, California. *Education:* Princeton University (A.B., magna cum laude, 1980); Stanford Law School (J.D., 1983). Phi Beta Kappa; Order of the Coif. Member, 1981-1983 and Topics and Developments Editor, 1982-1983, Stanford Law Review. Law Clerk, Hon. John Minor Wisdom, Senior Circuit Judge, U.S. Court of Appeals, Fifth Circuit, 1983-1984. *PRACTICE AREAS:* Entertainment and Intellectual Property Law; Closely-Held Business; Strategic Business Planning. *Email:* vwaldman@manatt.com

**CHARLES E. WASHBURN JR.,** born Kenmore, New York, December 5, 1952; admitted to bar, 1979, California. *Education:* University of California, Santa Barbara (B.A., 1974); University of California, Los Angeles (M.B.A., 1979; J.D., 1979). *PRACTICE AREAS:* Banking Law; Consumer Compliance Law. *Email:* cwashburn@manatt.com

**H. LEE WATSON,** born Tuscaloosa, Alabama, December 8, 1938; admitted to bar, 1975, California; 1976, U.S. District Court, Central and Northern Districts of California; 1985, U.S. District Court, Southern District of California; 1987, U.S. Court of Appeals, Ninth Circuit. *Education:* Northwestern University (B.S., with highest distinction, 1961); University of California at San Diego (Ph.D., 1965); Boalt Hall School of Law, University of California (J.D., 1975). Order of the Coif. Recipient, American Jurisprudence Award, Torts, 1973. Member of Staff, 1973-1975 and Managing Editor, 1974-1975, California Law Review, 1975. *PRACTICE AREAS:* Litigation. *Email:* lwatson@manatt.com

**NANCY H. WOJTAS,** born Dearborn, Michigan, November 28, 1951; admitted to bar, 1976, New York; 1981, Illinois; 1983, California. *Education:* University of Michigan (B.A., 1972); Wayne State University (J.D., 1976); New York University (LL.M., 1977). Attorney-Advisor, 1977-1979 and Counsel to Chairman, 1979-1981, Securities and Exchange Commission. *PRACTICE AREAS:* Corporate Law; Securities Law; Health Law. *Email:* nwojtas@manatt.com

**SHARI MULROONEY WOLLMAN,** born Los Angeles, California, September 14, 1963; admitted to bar, 1988, California, U.S. District Court, Central District of California and U.S. Court of Appeals, Ninth Circuit; 1991, U.S. District Court, Southern District of California; 1993, U.S. District Court, Northern District of California and U.S. District Court, District of North Dakota. *Education:* University of California at Los Angeles (B.A., 1985); University of Southern California (J.D., 1988). Member, Computer Law Journal. Member, Major Tax Planning Journal. Member: Los Angeles County, Federal and American Bar Associations; State Bar of California (Intellectual Property Section). *PRACTICE AREAS:* Intellectual Property; Computer Law; Entertainment; Commercial Litigation. *Email:* swollman@manatt.com

**STEVEN J. YOUNGER,** born Temple City, California, September 9, 1962; admitted to bar, 1987, California. *Education:* Loyola Marymount University (B.A., summa cum laude, 1984); University of California at Los Angeles (J.D., 1987). Chief Comment Editor, UCLA Law Review, Vol. 34, 1986-1987. Author: "Alcoholic Beverage Advertising on the Airwaves: Alternatives to a Ban or Counteradvertising," 34 UCLA Law Review 1139, 1987. *Member:* Beverly Hills (Member: Committee for the Arts; Entertainment Law Section) and Los Angeles County Bar Associations; State Bar of California. *PRACTICE AREAS:* Entertainment Law. *Email:* syounger@manatt.com

**STEVEN L. ZELINGER** (Resident, Washington, D.C. Office). *PRACTICE AREAS:* Civil Litigation; Criminal Defense; Employment; Federal Regulation. *Email:* szelinger@manatt.com

### OF COUNSEL

**DENNIS B. FRANKS,** born Klamath Falls, Oregon, November 22, 1957; admitted to bar, 1983, California. *Education:* Stanford University (A.B., honors, 1979); University of Southern California (J.D., 1983). Judicial Extern Clerk, Hon. Robert J. Kelleher, U.S. District Court, Central District of California, 1983. *PRACTICE AREAS:* Antitrust and Trade Regulation Law; Business Litigation; Financial Institution Litigation. *Email:* dfranks@manatt.com

**JOSEPH HORACEK III, (P.C.),** born Atlanta, Georgia, May 18, 1941; admitted to bar, 1967, California. *Education:* Occidental College and University of California, Los Angeles (B.A., 1963) Phi Delta Theta; University of California at Los Angeles (LL.B., 1966). Phi Alpha Delta. Member, Board of Editors, University of California at Los Angeles Law Review, 1964-1965. Member, Advisory Committee, California Motion Picture Council, 1981-1983. Member, Board of Trustees, California Museum Foundation, 1988-1991. Executive Director, Celebrities for the President, 1971-1972. Founding Trustee, The Mentor Foundation–Youth Substance Abuse Prevention Fund, 1993—. *Member:* Beverly Hills (Member, Entertainment Law Committee, 1970—) and Los Angeles County (Secretary-Treasurer, 1969-1971 and Member, Executive Committee, 1971-1972, Intellectual Property and Unfair Competition Section; Vice Chairman, 1973-1974) Bar Associations; Los Angeles Copyright Society (Treasurer, 1972-1973). *PRACTICE AREAS:* Entertainment; Motion Picture and Television. *Email:* jhoracek@manatt.com

**ARNOLD D. KASSOY,** born New York, N.Y., September 29, 1943; admitted to bar, 1969, California. *Education:* University of California at Los Angeles (B.S., 1964; M.B.A., 1965; J.D., 1968); London School of Economics and Political Science, University of London (LL.M., 1969). Author: "The Private Annuity & The Foreign Situs Trust," 16 UCLA Law Review 86, 1968; "Estate Planning for Americans Residing Abroad," VI International Tax Institute 108, 1971; "International Estate Planning," Trusts & Estates, 1973; "Tax Planning for Professional Athletes," Practicing Law Institute, 1976. Lecturer, Advanced Professional Programs, University of Southern California Law Center, 1971. *Member:* Beverly Hills (Member, Board of Governors, 1972-1973), Los Angeles and American Bar Associations. *PRACTICE AREAS:* Entertainment; Taxation; Estate Planning. *Email:* akassoy@manatt.com

**KEVIN KEENAN,** born San Diego, California, March 17, 1958; admitted to bar, 1985, California. *Education:* University of California at San Diego; University of California at Berkeley (B.S., 1980); Hastings School of Law, University of California (J.D., 1985). *PRACTICE AREAS:* Health Law; Corporate Law; Corporate Securities. *Email:* kkeenan@manatt.com

**SPENCER L. KIMBALL,** born Thatcher, Arizona, August 26, 1918; admitted to bar, 1950, Utah; 1965, Michigan; 1968, Wisconsin and U.S. District Court, Western District of Wisconsin; 1983, U.S. Supreme Court; 1986, U.S. Court of Appeals, 9th Circuit (Not admitted in California). *Education:* University of Arizona (B.S., with distinction, 1940); University of Utah; Oxford University (B.C.L., with first class honors, 1949); University of Wisconsin (S.J.D., 1958). Phi Beta Kappa; Phi Kappa Phi. Rhodes Scholar. Author: "Insurance & Public Policy," University of Wisconsin Press, 1960; "Historical Introduction to the Legal System," West Publishing Co., 1966; "The Regulation of Insurance Companies in the United States and The European Communities: A Comparative Study," (with W. Pfennigstort), U.S. Chamber of Commerce, 1981; "The Purpose of Insurance Regulation: A Preliminary Inquiry in the Theory of Insurance Law," 45 Minnesota Law Review 471, 1961. Associate Professor, Dean and Professor, University of Utah, 1949-1957. Professor, University of Michigan, 1957-1968. Dean and Professor, University of Wisconsin, 1968-1972. Professor, University of Chicago, 1972-1988; Professor Emeritus, 1988—. Executive Director, American Bar Foundation, 1972-1982. *Member:* Utah State Bar; State Bar of Michigan; State Bar of Wisconsin; American Bar Association; American Law Institute. Fellow, American Bar Foundation. (Also at Washington, D.C. Office). *PRACTICE AREAS:* Insurance. *Email:* skimball@manatt.com

**ELLIOT B. KRISTAL,** born Boston, Massachusetts, March 25, 1953; admitted to bar, 1977, California. *Education:* University of California at Los Angeles (B.A., magna cum laude, 1974; J.D., 1977). Phi Beta Kappa, Pi Gamma Mu. *Member:* Beverly Hills, Los Angeles County (Member, Sections on Probate, Trust and Taxation Law) and American Bar Associations. *PRACTICE AREAS:* Health Law; Estates and Trusts. *Email:* ekristal@manatt.com

**ROBERT A. PALLEMON,** born California, 1949; admitted to bar, 1976, California; 1978, U.S. District Court, Central District of California and U.S. Court of Appeals, Ninth Circuit. *Education:* University of Notre Dame (A.B., 1971); University of California (J.D., 1976). Assistant United States Attorney, Central District of California, 1977-1990. *Member:* American Bar Association. *PRACTICE AREAS:* Family Law; White Collar Criminal Defense; Litigation. *Email:* rpallemon@manatt.com

**MARTIN E. STEERE,** born Tucson, Arizona, July 11, 1956; admitted to bar, 1980, California; 1981, U.S. District Court, Eastern, Northern and Central Districts of California and U.S. Court of Appeals, Ninth Circuit; 1982, U.S. District Court, Southern District of California. *Education:* University of Virginia (B.A. with high distinction, 1977; J.D., 1980). *Member:* Los Angeles County Bar Association. *PRACTICE AREAS:* Real Estate Law. *Email:* msteere@manatt.com

**ABBY B. WAYNE,** born October 8, 1957; admitted to bar, 1986, Massachusetts; 1990, California. *Education:* University of California at Santa

*(This Listing Continued)*

**MANATT, PHELPS & PHILLIPS, LLP,** Los Angeles—
*Continued*

Cruz (B.A., 1980); Boston University School of Law (J.D., 1986). Editor-in-Chief, American Journal of Law and Medicine, 1985-1986. Author: "Kartell v. Blue Shield of Massachusetts, Inc.: An Antitrust Analysis of Blue Shield's Reimbursement Schemes," 11 Am. J. Law & Med., 465 (1986). *PRACTICE AREAS:* Health Law. *Email:* awayne@manatt.com

**GAIL ANDERSON WINDISCH,** born Pomona, California, April 24, 1952; admitted to bar, 1980, California. *Education:* University of California at Santa Cruz (B.A., with college honors, 1974); University of California at Los Angeles (J.D., 1980). (Firm General Counsel). *Email:* gwindisch@manatt.com

**ANGELA WONG,** born Hong Kong, July 24, 1951; admitted to bar, 1979, California and U.S. Court of Appeals, Ninth Circuit. *Education:* University of California at Berkeley (B.A., 1974); Georgetown University Law School (J.D., 1979); Harvard University Law School. Staff Member, Georgetown Law Journal, 1977-1978. *PRACTICE AREAS:* Health Law; Estates and Trusts. *Email:* awong@manatt.com

**THOMAS A. ZACCARO,** born Bridgeport, Connecticut, September 13, 1959; admitted to bar, 1984, Connecticut; 1985, District of Columbia and U.S. District Court for the District of Columbia; 1993, U.S. Supreme Court; 1996, California and U.S. District Court, Central District of California; U.S. Court of Appeals, Second, Ninth and Tenth Circuits. *Education:* Georgetown University (B.A., Phi Beta Kappa, magna cum laude, 1981; Boston College Law School (J.D., cum laude, 1984). Executive Editor, Boston College International and Comparative Law Review, 1984. Assistant United States Attorney, 1988-1994. Deputy Chief Appellate Attorney, Southern District of New York, 1991-1994. Trial Attorney, U.S. Department of Justice, Organized Crime and Racketeering Section, 1994-1995. *Member:* American Bar Association. *PRACTICE AREAS:* General Business Litigation. *Email:* tzaccaro@manatt.com

## ASSOCIATES

**ERIN K. ATKINS,** admitted to bar, 1992, California. *Education:* Loyola Marymount University (B.A., 1987); Southwestern University (J.D., magna cum laude, 1992). *PRACTICE AREAS:* Litigation. *Email:* eatkins@manatt.com

**ELIZABETH H. BELLAMY,** (admission pending). *Education:* University of California at Los Angeles (B.A., 1992); University of California at Los Angeles School of Law (J.D., 1995). *PRACTICE AREAS:* Corporate Securities; Financial Services. *Email:* ebellamy@manatt.com

**MATTHEW D. BERGER,** admitted to bar, 1992, California. *Education:* Cornell University (B.A., 1987); University of California, Hastings College of the Law (J.D., 1992). *PRACTICE AREAS:* Intellectual Property; High Technology/Electronic Commerce. *Email:* mberger@manatt.com

**KATRINA L. BREUNER,** admitted to bar, 1990, California. *Education:* University of California at Los Angeles (B.S., 1983); Hastings College of the Law, University of California (J.D., 1990). *PRACTICE AREAS:* Healthcare; Long-Term Care. *Email:* kbreuner@manatt.com

**DONALD BROWN,** admitted to bar, 1991, California. *Education:* Swarthmore College (B.A., 1978); New York School of Law (J.D., 1989). *PRACTICE AREAS:* Litigation. *Email:* dbrown@manatt.com

**CYNTHIA F. CATALINO,** admitted to bar, 1993, California. *Education:* Vassar College (B.A., 1988); Pepperdine University School of Law (J.D., 1993). *PRACTICE AREAS:* Trusts and Estates. *Email:* ccatalino@manatt.com

**ANDREW CUSHNIR,** admitted to bar, 1993, California. *Education:* University of California at Los Angeles (B.A., 1986); Hastings College of the Law, University of California (J.D., 1993). *PRACTICE AREAS:* Financial Services. *Email:* acushnir@manatt.com

**LEAH E. DELANCEY,** admitted to bar, 1990, California. *Education:* University of California at Los Angeles (B.A., 1986); University of Southern California (J.D., 1990). *PRACTICE AREAS:* Tax; Estate and Trust. *Email:* ldelancey@manatt.com

**KATHLEEN D. DE VANEY,** admitted to bar, 1991, California. *Education:* University of California at Berkeley (B.A., 1986); Loyola Law School (J.D., 1991). *PRACTICE AREAS:* Business Litigation; Bankruptcy Law. *Email:* kdevaney@manatt.com

*(This Listing Continued)*

**KATIA T. DIEHL,** admitted to bar, 1993, California. *Education:* University of California (B.A., 1989); Hastings College of the Law (J.D., 1992). *PRACTICE AREAS:* Family Law; Litigation. *Email:* kdiehl@manatt.com

**DAN FORMAN,** admitted to bar, 1991, California. *Education:* Indiana University (B.A., 1986); Georgetown University Law Center (J.D., 1991). *PRACTICE AREAS:* General Business Litigation. *Email:* dforman@manatt.com

**SETH GOLD,** admitted to bar, 1992, California. *Education:* Cornell University (B.A., 1989); Boston University (J.D., 1992). *PRACTICE AREAS:* General Business Litigation. *Email:* sgold@manatt.com

**MARC P. GOODMAN,** admitted to bar, 1990, California. *Education:* University of California at Los Angeles (B.A., 1986); University of Southern California (M.A., 1990; J.D., 1990). *PRACTICE AREAS:* Litigation. *Email:* mgoodman@manatt.com

**JAY R. GRANT,** admitted to bar, 1993, California. *Education:* Harvard University (A.B., cum laude, 1989); Boalt Hall School of Law, University of California at Berkeley (J.D., 1992). *PRACTICE AREAS:* Labor and Employment Law. *Email:* jgrant@manatt.com

**ALLISON B. GRUETTNER,** admitted to bar, 1993, California. *Education:* University of California at Berkeley (A.B., cum laude, 1989); Loyola University (J.D., 1993). *PRACTICE AREAS:* Litigation. *Email:* agruettner@manatt.com

**DANIEL B. HAYES,** admitted to bar, 1992, California. *Education:* University of Miami at Florida (B.B.A., 1989); University of Southern California (J.D., 1992). *PRACTICE AREAS:* Music. *Email:* dhayes@manatt.com

**TERRI DONNA KEVILLE,** admitted to bar, 1992, California. *Education:* University of Pennsylvania (B.A., 1972); University of Southern California (J.D., 1992). *PRACTICE AREAS:* Healthcare Law; Litigation. *Email:* tkeville@manatt.com

**BRIAN S. KEYS,** admitted to bar, 1994, California. *Education:* University of California at Berkeley, Haas School of Business (B.A., 1991); Leland Stanford Jr. University Law School (J.D., 1994). *PRACTICE AREAS:* Corporate Law; Securities Law. *Email:* bkeys@manatt.com

**COBY A. KING,** admitted to bar, 1992, California. *Education:* University of California at Los Angeles (B.A., 1985); Georgetown University (J.D., cum laude, 1991). *PRACTICE AREAS:* Election and Political Reform Law; Governmental and Administrative Law. *Email:* cking@manatt.com

**JOHN I. LAZAR,** admitted to bar, 1992, California. *Education:* Tufts University (B.A., 1984); University of Michigan (J.D., cum laude, 1990). *Email:* jlazar@manatt.com

**MONTE M. LEMANN II,** admitted to bar, 1994, California. *Education:* Harvard University (A.B., cum laude, 1983; J.D., 1987). *PRACTICE AREAS:* General Corporate; Corporate Finance. *Email:* mlemann@manatt.com

**SUZANNE K. LIST,** admitted to bar, 1992, California. *Education:* University of California at Davis (B.A., Economics, 1987); University of Santa Clara (J.D., 1992). *PRACTICE AREAS:* Corporate Securities. *Email:* slist@manatt.com

**LISA CATHLEEN MCARTHUR,** admitted to bar, 1993, California. *Education:* University of California at Los Angeles (B.A., cum laude, 1990); University of California at Los Angeles School of Law (J.D., 1993). *PRACTICE AREAS:* Estate Planning; Probate; Taxation Law. *Email:* lmcarthur@manatt.com

**CRAIG D. MILLER,** admitted to bar, 1993, California. *Education:* Occidental College (A.B., summa cum laude, 1990); Loyola University (J.D., magna cum laude, 1993). *PRACTICE AREAS:* Corporate Law; Financial Services. *Email:* cmiller@manatt.com

**JAY M. MILLER,** admitted to bar, 1993, California. *Education:* London School of Economics and Political Science, London, England; University of Michigan (B.A., with highest distinction, 1990); University of California at Los Angeles (J.D., 1993). *PRACTICE AREAS:* Litigation. *Email:* jmiller@manatt.com

**VIBIANA MOLINA,** admitted to bar, 1994, California. *Education:* University of California at Los Angeles (B.A., cum laude, 1989); Columbia University (J.D., 1994). *PRACTICE AREAS:* Entertainment Law; Music. *Email:* vmolina@manatt.com

**EUGENE E. MUELLER,** admitted to bar, 1992, California. *Education:* University of Southern California (B.Sc., cum laude, 1987; M.B.A., 1992;

*(This Listing Continued)*

# PROFESSIONAL BIOGRAPHIES

## CALIFORNIA—LOS ANGELES

J.D., 1992). *PRACTICE AREAS:* Insurance. *Email:* emueller@manatt.com

*BRENDA B. NELSON,* admitted to bar, 1992, California. *Education:* Lewis & Clark College (B.A., 1977); Yale University (M.A., 1981); University of Southern California (Ph.D., 1991; J.D., 1992). *PRACTICE AREAS:* Corporate Securities. *Email:* bnelson@manatt.com

*SEEMA L. NENE,* admitted to bar, 1994, California. *Education:* Case Western Reserve University (B.A., 1991); University of California at Los Angeles School of Law (J.D., 1994). *PRACTICE AREAS:* Corporate Securities. *Email:* snene@manatt.com

*ALBERT Y. PARK,* (admission pending). *Education:* University of California at Berkeley (A.B., 1993) Phi Beta Kappa; New York University (J.D., 1996). *PRACTICE AREAS:* Corporate Securities. *Email:* apark@manatt.com

*JOHN P. PHILLIPS,* admitted to bar, 1994, California. *Education:* Dartmouth College (B.A., 1990); Boalt Hall School of Law, University of California, Berkeley (J.D., 1994). *PRACTICE AREAS:* Litigation. *Email:* jphillips@manatt.com

*JILL M. PIETRINI,* admitted to bar, 1988, California; registered to practice before U.S. Patent and Trademark Office. *Education:* University of California at Berkeley (B.A., 1983); Santa Clara University (J.D., 1988). *PRACTICE AREAS:* Intellectual Property Litigation. *Email:* jpietrini@manatt.com

*ADAM PINES,* admitted to bar, 1994, California. *Education:* University of Pennsylvania (B.A., 1990); New York University (J.D., 1994). *PRACTICE AREAS:* Banking Law; Litigation. *Email:* apines@manatt.com

*STEVEN J. PLINIO,* admitted to bar, 1988, California. *Education:* Colgate University (B.A., 1985); Northwestern University School of Law (J.D., 1988). *PRACTICE AREAS:* Music. *Email:* splinio@manatt.com

*CAMERON A. PORT,* (admission pending). *Education:* Columbia University (B.A., 1993); University of California at Los Angeles (J.D., 1996). *PRACTICE AREAS:* General Business Litigation. *Email:* cport@manatt.com

*HARVEY ROCHMAN,* admitted to bar, 1992, California. *Education:* University of California at Los Angeles (B.A., magna cum laude, 1989; M.A., 1989); University of Southern California (J.D., 1992). *Email:* hrochman@manatt.com

*CIEMA LILI SALEM,* admitted to bar, 1992, California. *Education:* University of California at Los Angeles (B.A., 1986); Southwestern University School of Law (J.D., cum laude, 1991). *PRACTICE AREAS:* Intellectual Property. *Email:* csalem@manatt.com

*KELLEY L. SBARBARO,* admitted to bar, 1993, California. *Education:* University of California at Los Angeles (B.A., 1989); University of Southern California (J.D., 1993). *Email:* ksbarbaro@manatt.com

*MARLENE R. SCHWARTZ,* admitted to bar, 1993, California. *Education:* Pennsylvania State University (B.A., 1990); The American University, Washington College of Law (J.D., 1993). *PRACTICE AREAS:* Health Law. *Email:* mschwartz@manatt.com

*GREGORY S. SINGER,* (admission pending). *Education:* University of California at Santa Barbara (B.A., 1992); Southwestern University, School of Law (J.D., 1995). *PRACTICE AREAS:* Real Estate. *Email:* gsinger@manatt.com

*LAURIE JILL SLOSBERG,* admitted to bar, 1993, California. *Education:* Tufts University (B.A., 1990); Boston University (J.D., 1993). *PRACTICE AREAS:* Bankruptcy; Creditor's Rights; Commercial Litigation. *Email:* lslosberg@manatt.com

*ALLEN Z. SUSSMAN,* admitted to bar, 1988, California. *Education:* Cornell University (B.S., 1985); Boston University (J.D., 1988). *PRACTICE AREAS:* Corporate Securities; Financial Services and Banking. *Email:* asussman@manatt.com

*SANDRA A. TAYLOR,* (admission pending). *Education:* University of California at Los Angeles (B.A., 1990); Harvard Law School (J.D., 1993). *PRACTICE AREAS:* Litigation. *Email:* staylor@manatt.com

*ALISON S. ULLENDORFF,* (admission pending). *Education:* Harvard College (A.B., 1988); London School of Economics and Political Science, London, England (M.A., 1991); University of the Pacific, McGeorge School of Law (J.D., 1993). *PRACTICE AREAS:* Litigation; Intellectual Property; Entertainment Law. *Email:* aullendorff@manatt.com

*(This Listing Continued)*

*GAIL G. WOODBURY,* (admission pending). *Education:* University of California at Los Angeles (B.A., summa cum laude, 1992) Phi Beta Kappa; Stanford Law School (J.D., 1995). *PRACTICE AREAS:* Music. *Email:* gwoodbury@manatt.com

*MARY E. WRIGHT,* admitted to bar, 1989, California. *Education:* Webster College (B.A., 1977); Trinity University (M.F.A., 1982); University of San Francisco (J.D., 1989). *PRACTICE AREAS:* Labor and Employment. *Email:* mwright@manatt.com

*CANDACE ANNE YOUNGER,* admitted to bar, 1993, California. *Education:* Vassar College (B.A., honors, 1990); University of California at Los Angeles School of Law (J.D., 1993). *PRACTICE AREAS:* Business and Insurance Litigation. *Email:* cyounger@manatt.com

Unless otherwise indicated All Members and Associates of the Firm are Members of The State Bar of California.

(For Biographical Data on Washington D.C. and Nashville, TN Personnel, See Professional Biographies at this City.)

---

## MANDEL & NORWOOD

### LOS ANGELES, CALIFORNIA

(See Santa Monica)

*Business Litigation Practice including Unfair Competition, Antitrust, Real Property, Partnership, Corporate, Copyright, Entertainment and Equine Law.*

---

## MANNING, LEAVER, BRUDER & BERBERICH

Established in 1923

SUITE 655, 5750 WILSHIRE BOULEVARD
LOS ANGELES, CALIFORNIA 90036
Telephone: 213-937-4730
Fax: 213-937-6727
Email: ManningLeaver@msn.com

*General Civil and Trial Practice, in all State and Federal Courts. Corporation, Insurance, Automobile Dealer Law, Probate and Estate Planning, Automotive Finance, Business Purchases and Sales, Real Property and Bankruptcy, Association and Commercial Law.*

FIRM PROFILE: Manning, Leaver, Bruder & Berberich was founded in the mid 1920's. At Manning Leaver, Bruder & Berberich specialization in the automotive industry and commercial law has been our continuous specialty since the firm began.

Over the years, Manning, Leaver Bruder & Berberich has developed a special expertise in the business and personal needs of automobile dealers and the automotive finance industry. The quality of the firm's representation is highly regarded by many in the automotive industry.

Manning, Leaver, Bruder & Berberich is counsel to the California Motor Car Dealers Association, the largest state association of new motor vehicle dealers in the nation. The firm also represents dealers advertising associations and other dealer-related businesses and financial institutions. In addition, the firm has a general civil and business litigation practice.

*CAMERON B. AIKENS* (1916-1966).

*DEWITT M. MANNING* (1909-1992).

*GEORGE E. LEAVER* (Retired).

*WALTER F. BRUDER, JR.* (Retired).

### PARTNERS

*JOSEPH E. BERBERICH,* born San Jose, California, November 6, 1937; admitted to bar, 1969, California. *Education:* San Luis Rey College (B.A., 1960); Loyola Law School, Los Angeles (J.D., 1968). *Member:* Los Angeles County and American Bar Associations; State Bar of California. *PRACTICE AREAS:* Automotive Dealer Law; Business Purchases and Sales; Association and Commercial Law.

*ROBERT D. DANIELS,* born Binghamton, New York, December 3, 1952; admitted to bar, 1979, California and U.S. District Court, Central District of California. *Education:* State University of New York at Binghamton (B.A., 1976); University of California at Los Angeles (J.D., 1979). *Member:* Los Angeles County and American Bar Associations; State Bar of

*(This Listing Continued)*

CAA947B

## MANNING, LEAVER, BRUDER & BERBERICH, Los Angeles—Continued

California. **PRACTICE AREAS:** Automotive Dealer Law; Civil Trial; Bankruptcy; Commercial Law.

**BRENT W. SMITH,** born Tucson, Arizona, July 11, 1954; admitted to bar, 1979, California and U.S. District Court, Central District of California. *Education:* University of California at Los Angeles (B.A., summa cum laude, 1976; J.D., 1979). Phi Beta Kappa. *Member:* State Bar of California. **PRACTICE AREAS:** Automotive Dealer Law; Civil Trial; Business Purchase and Sales; Association and Commercial Law.

**PENNY L. REEVES,** born Glendale, California, January 31, 1953; admitted to bar, 1982, California. *Education:* University of California at Los Angeles (B.A., 1975); Loyola Law School, Los Angeles (J.D., cum laude, 1982). *Member:* Board of Editors, Loyola Law Review, 1981-1982; St. Thomas More Law Honor Society. *Member:* State Bar of California. **PRACTICE AREAS:** Automotive Dealer Law; Probate; Business Purchase and Sales; Real Property; Commercial Law.

**MICHAEL D. VAN LOCHEM,** born Amsterdam, The Netherlands, January 3, 1959; admitted to bar, 1983, California and U.S. District Court, Central District of California. *Education:* University of California at Berkeley (B.A., 1980); Loyola Law School, Los Angeles (J.D., 1983). Phi Alpha Delta. *Member:* State Bar of California. **PRACTICE AREAS:** Automotive Dealer Law; Civil Trial; Bankruptcy; Commercial Law.

**HALBERT B. RASMUSSEN,** born Santa Monica, California, March 25, 1959; admitted to bar, 1983, California. *Education:* University of California at Los Angeles (A.B., 1980); Loyola Law School, Los Angeles (J.D., cum laude, 1983). *Member,* St. Thomas More Law Honor Society. *Member:* Beverly Hills, Los Angeles County and American (Member, Antitrust and Business Law Sections and Forum on Franchising) Bar Associations; The State Bar of California. **PRACTICE AREAS:** Automotive Dealer Law; Civil Trial; Business Purchase and Sales; Corporation; Association and Commercial Law.

### ASSOCIATES

**TIMOTHY D. ROBINETT,** born Long Beach, California, March 27, 1967; admitted to bar, 1993, California and U.S. District Court, Central, Southern, Northern and Eastern Districts of California. *Education:* University of California at Berkeley (B.A., 1989); Loyola Law School, Los Angeles (J.D., 1993). *Member:* State Bar of California. **PRACTICE AREAS:** Civil Trial.

**REX L. MILLS,** born Arcadia, California, October 8, 1966; admitted to bar, 1995, California. *Education:* University of California at Santa Cruz (B.A., 1990); Loyola Law School, Los Angeles (J.D., 1995).

**DANA E. MALARNEY,** born Hartford, Connecticut, March 6, 1969; admitted to bar, 1996, California and U.S. District Court, Central, Southern, Northern and Eastern Districts of California. *Education:* Syracuse University (B.A., 1991); Southwestern University School of Law (J.D., 1995). *Member:* State Bar of California; Student Bar Association. **PRACTICE AREAS:** Business Litigation; Bankruptcy.

**ALAN W. FORSLEY,** born Pittsburgh, Pennsylvania, January 13, 1961; admitted to bar, 1995, California and U.S. District Court, Central District of California; 1996, U.S. District Court, Southern District of California. *Education:* University of California at Irvine (B.S., 1992); University of San Diego School of Law (J.D., 1995). **PRACTICE AREAS:** Civil Litigation; Bankruptcy.

**SEAN J. BALLARD,** born Lynwood, California, February 13, 1967; admitted to bar, 1992, California; 1993, U.S. District Court, Central District of California and U.S. Court of Appeals, Ninth Circuit. *Education:* University of California at Los Angeles (B.A., 1989); University of Southern California (J.D., 1992). Phi Alpha Delta. *Member:* Beverly Hills and Federal Bar Associations. **PRACTICE AREAS:** Business Litigation.

REPRESENTATIVE CLIENTS: Ford Dealers Advertising Assn.; General Motors Acceptance Corp.; General Motors Corp.; California Motor Car Dealers Association; California Motor Car Dealers Association Employee Benefits Trust; Mercedes Benz of North America, Inc.; Nissan Motor Acceptance Corp.; Southern California Chevrolet Dealers Association; Southern California Toyota Dealers Advertising Association; Mitsubishi Motors Credit of America; Inc.; Toyota Motor Credit Corp.; Volkswagen Credit Inc.; Greater Los Angeles Motor Car Dealers Association; Various New Motor Vehicle Dealers.
REFERENCE: Bank of America (Olympic & Flower Branch, Los Angeles, Calif.)

## MANNING, MARDER & WOLFE
### 45TH FLOOR AT FIRST INTERSTATE TOWER
### 707 WILSHIRE BOULEVARD
### LOS ANGELES, CALIFORNIA 90017
Telephone: 213-624-6900
Fax: 213-624-6999
Email: rfs@mmw.com
URL: http://www.mmw.com

*Irvine, California Office:* 19800 MacArthur Boulevard, Suite 1450. Telephone: 714-556-0552. Facsimile: 714-724-4575.
*San Diego, California Office:* 964 Fifth Avenue, Suite 214. Telephone: 619-699-5933.

*Insurance Defense, Police Civil Liability, General Civil Litigation, Private Security Litigation, Corporate Law, Business Formation and Securities Offerings, Employment Litigation, Entertainment Law, Workers' Compensation Defense, Professional Liability (Medical Malpractice, Legal Malpractice, Construction Malpractice), Appellate Law, Health Law, Bad Faith, Insurance Coverage, Loss Prevention and Risk Management.*

### MEMBERS OF FIRM

**STEVEN D. MANNING,** born October 21, 1953; admitted to bar, 1979, California. *Education:* California State University at Los Angeles (B.S., 1976); Whittier College (J.D., cum laude, 1979). Member, MM&W Karate Team. **PRACTICE AREAS:** Police Civil Liability Defense; Public Entity Defense Law; Complex Civil Litigation.

**JOHN A. MARDER,** born January 17, 1960; admitted to bar, 1985, California. *Education:* Bates College (B.A., 1982); California Western University School of Law (J.D., 1985). Member, MM&W Karate Team. **PRACTICE AREAS:** Civil Litigation Defense; Insurance Fraud Defense; Entertainment Law.

**DENNIS B. KASS,** born April 4, 1962; admitted to bar, 1988, California. *Education:* University of California at Los Angeles (B.A., 1984); Loyola Marymount University (J.D., 1988). **PRACTICE AREAS:** Insurance Fraud Litigation; Civil Litigation; Insurance Coverage Analysis; Bad Faith; Legal Malpractice; Construction Litigation.

**ANTHONY J. ELLROD,** born August 16, 1961; admitted to bar, 1988, California. *Education:* University of South Florida (B.A., 1984); Pepperdine University School of Law (J.D., 1987). Head Instructor, MM&W Karate Team. **PRACTICE AREAS:** Insurance Fraud; Complex Business; Securities Litigation; Insurance Coverage; Recreational and Sports Litigation.

**EUGENE P. RAMIREZ,** born February 3, 1960; admitted to bar, 1988, California. *Education:* California State University (B.A., 1983); Whittier College School of Law (J.D., 1987). **PRACTICE AREAS:** Police Civil Liability Defense; Civil Litigation; Public Entity Defense; Police Canine Litigation.

**MARTHA A. SHEN,** born Taipei, Taiwan, May 15, 1962; admitted to bar, 1987, California. *Education:* University of California at Davis (B.A., 1984); University of California at Santa Cruz (B.A., 1984); Whittier College (J.D., 1987). Member, MM&W Karate. **PRACTICE AREAS:** Police Civil Liability Defense; Medical Malpractice; Public Entity Defense.

**BARRY A. BRADLEY,** born June 14, 1960; admitted to bar, 1986, California. *Education:* San Diego State University (B.S., with distinction, 1983); Loyola Law School (J.D., 1986). Member, MM&W Karate Team. **PRACTICE AREAS:** Private Security Litigation; Premises Liability; Police Civil Liability; General Civil Liability.

**LAWRENCE D. ESTEN,** born May 16, 1961; admitted to bar, 1986, California. *Education:* University of California at Irvine (B.A., 1983); Loyola Law School (J.D., 1986). Managing Partner, Orange County Office.

### ASSOCIATES

**DAVID C. ADDISON,** born Fort Sill, Oklahoma, December 18, 1957; admitted to bar, 1989, California and U.S. District Court, Central District of California. *Education:* University of Hawaii at Manoa (B.A., 1981); University of Hawaii, William S. Richardson School of Law (J.D. 1988). Member and Assistant Editor, University of Hawaii Law Review, 1985-1987. *Member:* State Bar of California.

**TINA M. ALLEGUEZ,** born March 2, 1961; admitted to bar, 1988, California. *Education:* University of California at San Diego (B.A., Drama, 1983); Pepperdine University (J.D., 1987). Member, MM&W Karate. **LANGUAGES:** Spanish; French.

*(This Listing Continued)*

**ANNE E. ARVIN,** born Shreveport, Louisiana, November 6, 1959; admitted to bar, 1995, California and U.S. District Court, Central District of California. *Education:* Abilene Christian University (B.A., cum laude, 1980; M.A. in English, 1988); Pepperdine University School of Law (J.D., cum laude, 1995).

**STEVEN D. BLADES,** born January 28, 1954; admitted to bar, 1990, California. *Education:* California Polytechnic State University (B.S., cum laude, 1982); Southwestern University School of Law (J.D., cum laude, 1990).

**CATHERINE CONVY,** born October 3, 1957; admitted to bar, 1995, California. *Education:* Douglass College (B.A., 1979); Pepperdine University School of Law (J.D., cum laude, 1995).

**KEVIN E. COVENTON,** born October 14, 1963; admitted to bar, 1992, California. *Education:* Pepperdine University (B.S., cum laude, 1986); Rutgers Law School (J.D., 1992). Certified Public Accountant, California, 1986.

**ALFRED M. DE LA CRUZ,** born June 19, 1961; admitted to bar, 1990, California. *Education:* University of California at Irvine (B.S., 1984); University of California, Boalt Hall School of Law (J.D., 1990). Member, MM&W Karate.

**NICOLE M. FOOS,** born Los Angeles, California, October 25, 1959; admitted to bar, 1985, California and U.S. District Court, Central District of California. *Education:* University of California at Berkeley (B.A., Psychology, 1981); Boston University (J.D., 1984).

**RANDEL P. FRIEDMAN,** born Englewood, New Jersey, November 11, 1968; admitted to bar, 1994, California. *Education:* Dartmouth College (B.A., 1991); University of Miami (J.D., 1994). Member, MM&W Karate.

**THOMAS R. GILL,** born July 28, 1955; admitted to bar, 1988, California. *Education:* California State University at Northridge (B.A., 1983); Loyola Law School at Los Angeles (J.D., 1986).

**FINOLA G. HALLORAN,** born February 9, 1969; admitted to bar, 1995, California. *Education:* University of California at San Diego (B.A., 1990); Pepperdine University School of Law (J.D., magna cum laude, 1995).

**PAMELA S. HICKS,** born February 22, 1964; admitted to bar, 1994, California. *Education:* California State University, Northridge (B.S., 1991); Pepperdine University (J.D., 1994). Member, MM&W Karate.

**KATHLEEN A. KELLEHER,** born January 8, 1964; admitted to bar, 1990, California; 1992, New York. *Education:* College of William & Mary (B.A., 1986); George Washington University, National Law Center (J.D., 1989). Member, MM&W Karate.

**MARGUERITE T. LIEU,** born October 17, 1964; admitted to bar, 1989, California. *Education:* University of Washington (B.A., 1986); Pepperdine University (J.D., 1989). *Member:* Los Angeles County and American Bar Associations; State Bar of California.

**BRIAN T. MOSS,** born June 15, 1963; admitted to bar, 1991, Texas and California. *Education:* San Diego State University (B.A., in Economics, 1987); University of San Diego (J.D., 1990). Member, Orange County Office.

**G. ANDREW NAGLE,** born Long Beach, California, June 12, 1954; admitted to bar, 1983, California. *Education:* California State University at Long Beach (B.A., 1977); Southwestern University (J.D., 1983). Instructor, Insurance Education Association, 1988—. Member, Southwestern University Law Review, 1981-1982. *Member:* Long Beach, Los Angeles County and Orange County Bar Associations; State Bar of California; Association of Southern California Defense Counsel.

**ERWIN A. NEPOMUCENO,** born December 3, 1962; admitted to bar, 1989, California. *Education:* University of California at Irvine (B.A., 1985); Loyola Marymount University (J.D., 1989). Adjunct Professor, Workers' Compensation Law, Western State University School of Law, 1991—. Member, MM&W Karate.

**M. LAUREN OLANDER,** born November 22, 1966; admitted to bar, 1991, California. *Education:* Boston University (B.A., 1988); Pepperdine University School of Law (J.D., 1991).

**MILDRED K. O'LINN,** born May 4, 1960; admitted to bar, 1986, Ohio; 1991, Texas; 1992, California. *Education:* Kent State University (B.S., cum laude, 1982); University of Akron (J.D., 1985). Member, MM&W Karate.

**DAVID A. PECK,** born Inglewood, California, December 27, 1968; admitted to bar, 1994, California and U.S. District Court, Central District of California. *Education:* University of Southern California (B.A., 1991); Loyola Law School (J.D., 1994). *Member:* Los Angeles County and American Bar Associations; State Bar of California; Association of Southern California Defense Counsel. *PRACTICE AREAS:* Insurance Defense Litigation.

**UZZI O. RAANAN,** born New York, N.Y., June 11, 1966; admitted to bar, 1992, California; 1993, U.S. District Court, Central District of California; 1995, District of Columbia and U.S. Court of Appeals, 9th Circuit. *Education:* McGeorge School of Law (J.D., 1992). Member, MM&W Karate. *LANGUAGES:* Hebrew.

**STEVEN J. RENICK,** born January 19, 1956; admitted to bar, 1981, California. *Education:* Dartmouth College (A.B., 1978); Boston University (J.D., 1981). Law and Motion Department Team Leader. *LANGUAGES:* Spanish.

**JOHN REVELLI,** born October 5, 1967; admitted to bar, 1994, California. *Education:* California State University at Los Angeles (B.A., 1991); California Western School of Law (J.D., 1994). Member, Orange County Office.

**JONATHAN A. ROSS,** born February 25, 1960; admitted to bar, 1987, New York; 1990, California. *Education:* American University (B.S., 1982); George Washington University (J.D., 1986).

**PATRICIA M. SCOLES,** born August 3, 1958; admitted to bar, 1988, California. *Education:* California State University at Northridge (B.A., 1981); Loyola Marymount University (J.D., 1988). Member, MM&W Karate.

**PHILIP L. SOTO,** born May 4, 1959; admitted to bar, 1987, California. *Education:* Stanford University (B.A., 1981); Loyola University of Los Angeles Law School (J.D., 1986). Deputy District Attorney, Los Angeles County District Attorney's Office, 1987-1992.

**BARRY G. THORPE,** born August 27, 1960; admitted to bar, 1986, California. *Education:* California State University at Long Beach (B.A., 1983); Southwestern University (J.D., 1986). Member, MM&W Karate.

**JAMES URBANIC,** born July 4, 1964; admitted to bar, 1992, California. *Education:* University of California at Berkeley (B.A. with honors, 1988); Pepperdine University (J.D., 1992). Phi Alpha Delta. Member, MM&W Karate. *PRACTICE AREAS:* Insurance Defense.

**CHRISTOPHER A. WILSON,** born Albany, New York, February 15, 1967; admitted to bar, 1993, California and U.S. District Court, Central District of California. *Education:* Duke University (B.A., 1989); Loyola Law School (J.D., 1993). Member, MM&W Karate.

**DAVID J. WILSON,** born November 14, 1955; admitted to bar, 1988, California. *Education:* University of California, Santa Barbara (B.A., with honors, 1977); University of Southern California (J.D., 1988). *PRACTICE AREAS:* Writs and Appeals; Business Litigation; Insurance Bad Faith; Employment and Disability.

*OF COUNSEL*

**WILLIAM J. LOPSHIRE,** born June 7, 1963; admitted to bar, 1989, California; U.S. District Court, Central and Southern Districts of California; U.S. Tax Court. *Education:* Michigan State University (B.A., 1985); Pepperdine University (J.D., 1988). Member, MM&W Karate. *PRACTICE AREAS:* Corporate Finance; Securities; Venture Capital; Business Law.

**GERALD F. PHILLIPS,** born Brooklyn, New York, May 3, 1925; admitted to bar, 1950, New York; 1988, California. *Education:* Dartmouth College (A.B., 1947); Cornell University Law School (J.D., 1950). Counsel to, 1951-1979, and Vice-President, 1976-1979, United Artists Corporation. General Counsel of the J. Arthur Rank Organization, 1955-1968. Adjunct Professor of Law, Pepperdine School of Law. Senior Vice-President of American Multi Cinema, Inc., 1988-1990. Chair, Exhibition and Ancillary Market Division of the ABA Forum, 1989—. (Also of Counsel, Mannis and Bauman).

---

# MANNIS & PHILLIPS, L.L.P.
*2029 CENTURY PARK EAST, SUITE 1200*
**LOS ANGELES, CALIFORNIA 90067-2913**
*Telephone: 310-277-7117*
*Fax: 310-286-9182*

*Family Law, Entertainment Law and General Civil Litigation.*

**JOSEPH MANNIS,** born Boston, Massachusetts, September 18, 1944; admitted to bar, 1972, California and U.S. District Court, Southern District

*(This Listing Continued)*

## MANNIS & PHILLIPS, L.L.P., Los Angeles—Continued

of California. *Education:* University of Southern California (A.B., 1967); Loyola Marymount University (J.D., 1971). Member, St. Thomas More Law Honor Society. *Member:* Beverly Hills and Los Angeles County Bar Associations; State Bar of California. **PRACTICE AREAS:** Family Law; Sports Law; Art Law.

**STACY D. PHILLIPS,** born New York, N.Y., September 5, 1958; admitted to bar, 1984, California, U.S. District Court, Central District of California and U.S. Court of Appeals, Ninth Circuit. *Education:* Dartmouth College (A.B., cum laude, with high distinction, 1980); Columbia University (J.D., 1983). Representative, Pro Bono Panel for Abused and Neglected Children, 1984-1986. Mediator: Divorce Mediators Association, 1984-1986; Pacific Associates, Mediators of Children's Issues in Divorce, 1986—. *Member:* Beverly Hills (Member, Sections on: Family Law; Member, Alternative Dispute Resolutions Committee), Los Angeles County (Member, Family Law Section) and American (Member, Section of Family Law) Bar Associations; State Bar of California (Member, Child Custody and Visitation Committee). **PRACTICE AREAS:** Family Law; Custody; Arbitration; Mediation.

### OF COUNSEL

**GERALD F. PHILLIPS,** born Brooklyn, New York, May 3, 1925; admitted to bar, 1950, New York; 1988, California, U.S. Supreme Court, U.S. District Court, Southern and Eastern Districts of New York, U.S. District Court, Central District of California and U.S. Court of Appeals, Second Circuit. *Education:* Dartmouth College (A.B., 1947); Amos Tuck School, Hanover, N.H. (M.C.S., 1947); Cornell University Law School (J.D., 1950). Counsel to, 1951-1979, and Vice-President, 1976-1979, United Artists Corporation. General Counsel of the J. Arthur Rank Organization, 1955-1968. Author: "The Recent Acquisition of Theatre Circuits by Major Distributors," Entertainment and Sports Lawyer, American Bar Association Forum Committee on the Entertainment and Sports Industries, Fol. 5, No. 3, Winter, 1987; "Block Booking - Perhaps Forgotten, Perhaps Misunderstood, But Still Illegal," Entertainment and Sports Lawyer, American Bar Association Forum Committee on the Entertainment and Sports Industries, Vol. 6, No. 1, Summer, 1987. Adjunct Professor, Pepperdine University School of Law. Lecturer, The John E. Anderson Graduate School of Management at UCLA. Director, 1982-1988 and Chairman, 1984-1988, WNYC Foundation. Chairman, Law Committee of Motion Picture Association of America, 1975-1984. Senior Vice President of American Multi Cinema, Inc., 1988-1990. Member, Panel of Arbitrators, American Arbitration Association and American Film Marketing Association. *Member:* State Bar of California (Member, Sections on: Antitrust and Trade Regulation; Family Law; Intellectual Property); Beverly Hills (Member: Family Law Section; Dispute Resolution Committee), Los Angeles County (Member, Family Law Section) and American (Chairman: Forum Committee on The Entertainment and Sports Industries, 1986-1989; Chairman of the Exhibition and Ancillary Market Division of the Forum, 1989—; Motion Pictures, Television and Radio Division, 1982-1986) Bar Associations. (Also Member of Phillips & Salman and Of Counsel to Manning Marder & Wolfe, Los Angeles, CA). **PRACTICE AREAS:** Entertainment Law; Family Law; Arbitration; Mediation.

**ALLAN S. MORTON,** born New York, N.Y., February 2, 1944; admitted to bar, 1969, California and U.S. District Court, Central District of California. *Education:* Cornell University (A.B., 1965); University of California at Los Angeles (J.D., 1968). Senior Editor, University of California at Los Angeles Law Review, 1966-1968. *Member:* Beverly Hills (Member, Sections on: Real Property; Family Law; Alternative Dispute Resolution) and Los Angeles County (Member, Sections on: Litigation; Real Property; Family Law; Commercial Law, Alternative Dispute Resolution) Bar Associations; State Bar of California. (Also practicing individually). **Email:** morton4law@aol.com

---

**PETER A. LAUZON,** born Montreal, Canada, April 5, 1958; admitted to bar, 1991, California. *Education:* University of California, Los Angeles (B.A., 1986); Pepperdine University (J.D., 1990). *Member:* Beverly Hills (Member, Family Law Section) and Los Angeles County (Member, Family Law Section) Bar Associations; State Bar of California (Member, Family Law Section). **PRACTICE AREAS:** Family Law.

**JON S. SUMMERS,** born Syracuse, New York, September 22, 1964; admitted to bar, 1989, California and U.S. District Court, Central District of California. *Education:* University of Southern California (B.A., 1986); Southwestern University (J.D., 1989). *Member:* Beverly Hills (Member,

*(This Listing Continued)*

---

Family Law Section, 1990-1993, 1996—) and Los Angeles County Bar Associations; State Bar of California. **PRACTICE AREAS:** Family Law; Custody.

## MARCUS, WATANABE, SNYDER & DAVE, LLP

SUITE 300, 1901 AVENUE OF THE STARS
LOS ANGELES, CALIFORNIA 90067-6005
Telephone: 310-284-2020
Facsimile: 310-284-2025

*Real Property, Business and Commercial Litigation, General Business Transactions, Title Insurance Claims and Litigation.*

### MEMBERS OF FIRM

**DAVID M. MARCUS,** born Los Angeles, California, November 29, 1952; admitted to bar, 1979, California. *Education:* University of California at Berkeley (A.B., 1974); Loyola Law School (J.D., 1979). *Member:* State Bar of California. **PRACTICE AREAS:** Title Insurance Law; Real Property and General Business; Litigation; Real Property Law; Commercial Law.

**WENDY Y. WATANABE,** born Los Angeles, California, October 1, 1955; admitted to bar, 1980, California. *Education:* University of California at Santa Barbara (B.A., 1977); Loyola Law School (J.D., 1980). Member, Loyola International Comparative Law Annual, 1979-1980. Faculty, Title Insurance, Practising Law Institute, 1994-1996. *Member:* Los Angeles County Bar Association (Member: Real Property Section Executive Committee, 1993-1996; Title Insurance Subsection Steering Committee, 1991-1996); Japanese-American Bar Association. **PRACTICE AREAS:** Title Insurance Law; Real Property and General Business Litigation.

**PATRICIA M. SNYDER,** born Orange, California, June 18, 1957; admitted to bar, 1982, California and U.S. District Court, Central, Northern, Eastern and Western Districts of California; U.S. Court of Appeals, Ninth Circuit; 1993, Colorado. *Education:* Loyola Marymount University (B.A., magna cum laude, 1979; J.D., 1982). Alpha Sigma Nu. *Member:* Los Angeles County and American (Member, Title Insurance Subsection Steering Committee) Bar Associations. **PRACTICE AREAS:** Real Property Litigation; General Business Litigation.

**MICHAEL G. DAVE,** born Amherst, Ohio, May 24, 1939; admitted to bar, 1965, California. *Education:* University of California at Los Angeles (B.S., 1961); California School of Law, University of California (J.D., 1964). Licensed Certified Public Accountant, California, 1965. **PRACTICE AREAS:** Corporate Partnership; Real Property; Construction Law; Business Law.

**JUSTIN E. BUDARE,** born Ain Queny, Lebanon, February 7, 1959; admitted to bar, 1984, California; 1985, U.S. District Court, Central District of California and U.S. Court of Appeals, Ninth Circuit. *Education:* University of Michigan (A.B., 1980); University of California School of Law at Los Angeles (J.D., 1983). *Member:* Los Angeles County Bar Association (Co-Chair, Title Insurance Subsection Steering Committee).

**KATHLEEN M. COLLINS,** born Coronado, California, March 14, 1962; admitted to bar, 1989, California and U.S. District Court, Central District of California. *Education:* American University (B.A., 1984); Loyola Law School (J.D., 1988). **PRACTICE AREAS:** Real Estate Title; Business Law.

**RICHARD I. ARSHONSKY,** born Skokie, Illinois, March 12, 1967; admitted to bar, 1991, California and U.S. District Court, Central District of California; 1992, Nevada. *Education:* DePauw University (B.Mus., 1988); Loyola Law School (J.D., 1991). Member, Loyola Law Review. **PRACTICE AREAS:** Real Property; Business Law.

## MARKOWITZ, FERNANDEZ & URIARTE

811 WEST SEVENTH STREET
SUITE 1100
LOS ANGELES, CALIFORNIA 90017
Telephone: 213-362-0350
Facsimile: 213-362-0359

*Civil Trials, Appeals and Dispute Resolution including Commercial, Real Estate, Intellectual Property, Employment and Entertainment Law. Bankruptcy, Workouts, Debtor and Creditor. International Business Transactions and Litigation.*

*(This Listing Continued)*

## MEMBERS OF FIRM

**JOSEPH C. MARKOWITZ,** born New York, N.Y., March 2, 1954; admitted to bar, 1980, New York; 1990, California. *Education:* Columbia University (B.A., 1976); University of Chicago (J.D., cum laude, 1979). Order of the Coif. Associate Editor, University of Chicago Law Review. Law Clerk to Judge Bernard M. Decker, U.S. District Court, Northern District of Illinois, 1979-1980. *PRACTICE AREAS:* Litigation.

**JOSEFINA FERNANDEZ MCEVOY,** born Santiago, Dominican Republic, March 28, 1960; admitted to bar, 1990, California. *Education:* Temple University (B.A., 1982; M. Ed., 1983; J.D., 1989). Member, Moot Court Honor Society. Law Clerk to Chief Judge William J. Lasarow, U.S. Bankruptcy Court, Central District of California, 1989-1991. Member, Financial Lawyers Conference. U.S. Liaison, Monterey Bankers' Association (Mexico). Founder and Coordinator, Bankruptcy Oral History Program Ninth Judicial Circuit Historical Society. *Member:* Los Angeles County (Member, Sections on: Bankruptcy and Commercial Law) American (Member, Section On, Business Law) and Hispanic National Bar Associations; American Bankruptcy Institute (Member, International Trade and Finance). *LANGUAGES:* Spanish. *PRACTICE AREAS:* Bankruptcy.

**ROBERT G. URIARTE,** born Los Angeles, California, November 16, 1955; admitted to bar, 1983, California. *Education:* Loyola Marymount University (B.A., 1980); University of California at Los Angeles (J.D., 1983). Member, Moot Court Honors. Law Clerk to the Honorable William J. Lasarow, Chief Judge, U.S. Bankruptcy Court, Central District, 1983-1985. Judge Pro Tem, Los Angeles Superior Court. Member, Financial Lawyers Conference. Chapter 7 and 11 Bankruptcy Trustee Panel Member, Central District of California, 1991—. Receiver, Los Angeles Superior Court. *Member:* Los Angeles County (Member, Sections on Bankruptcy and Commercial Law) and Mexican-American Bar Associations; The State Bar of California; American Bankruptcy Institute. *LANGUAGES:* Spanish. *PRACTICE AREAS:* Creditor's Rights; Bankruptcy; Commercial Litigation.

---

## MARKS & MURASE L.L.P.

*Established in 1963*

THE WELLS FARGO CENTER
333 SOUTH GRAND AVENUE
SUITE 1570
**LOS ANGELES, CALIFORNIA 90071-1535**
Telephone: 213-620-9690
FAX: 213-617-9109

*New York, New York Office:* 399 Park Avenue. Telephone: 212-318-7700.
*Washington, D.C. Office:* Suite 750, 2001 L Street, N.W. Telephone: 202-955-4900.

*General Practice.*

*FIRM PROFILE: Marks & Murase engages in the general practice of law, representing diverse American and foreign clients in a broad spectrum of domestic and international legal matters. Practice groups include antitrust, banking & finance, corporate & corporate finance, creditors' rights & bankruptcy, employee benefits & executive compensation, government relations/international trade, immigration & nationality law, import/export issues, intellectual property, labor & employment, litigation, real estate and tax.*

### PARTNERS IN LOS ANGELES, CALIFORNIA

**SHU TOKUYAMA,** born Tokyo, Japan, April 18, 1948; admitted to bar, 1979, California; 1980, New York. *Education:* Columbia University (B.S., 1971; J.D., 1977); Stanford University Graduate School of Business (M.B.A., 1973). Tau Beta Pi. *Member:* State Bar of California; American Bar Association. *LANGUAGES:* Japanese.

**MATTHEW E. DIGBY,** born San Diego, California, November 10, 1951; admitted to bar, 1979, New York; 1984, California. *Education:* University of Notre Dame (B.A. magna cum laude, 1973); Sophia University, Tokyo, Japan (M.A., 1975); Columbia University (J.D., 1978). Rotary Foundation Graduate Fellow, Japan, 1973-1975. *Member:* The Association of the Bar of the City of New York; Los Angeles County Bar Association; State Bar of California (Member, International Law Section). *LANGUAGES:* Japanese.

*(This Listing Continued)*

---

### ASSOCIATES IN LOS ANGELES, CALIFORNIA

**TANYA K. DANFORTH,** born Des Moines, Iowa, March 14, 1945; admitted to bar, 1985, Hawaii (Not admitted in California). *Education:* California State University at Los Angeles (B.S., 1967; M.S., 1973); University of California at Los Angeles (M.P.H., 1978); Whittier College at Los Angeles (J.D., 1983). *Member:* Hawaii State, Federal and American Bar Associations; American Immigration Lawyers Association.

**JOHN J. DEL PROPOST,** born Wooster, Ohio, July 5, 1962; admitted to bar, 1989, California; 1990, U.S. District Court, Central and Northern Districts of California. *Education:* The College of Wooster (B.A., with honors, 1984); The Ohio State University College of Law; Pepperdine University School of Law (J.D., magna cum laude, 1989). Phi Beta Kappa. *Member:* State Bar of California.

**CRAIG L. SHELDON,** born Long Beach, New York, April 15, 1953; admitted to bar, 1978, California; 1985, New York. *Education:* Cornell University (B.S., 1975); Hastings College of the Law, University of California (J.D., 1978). Publications Editor, Hastings Constitutional Law Quarterly, 1977-1978. Arbitrator, National Association of Securities Dealers, Pacific Stock Exchange and Los Angeles County Superior Courts. *Member:* Los Angeles County and American Bar Associations; State Bar of California. *LANGUAGES:* Japanese.

---

## VICTOR I. MARMON

WATT PLAZA
*1875 CENTURY PARK EAST, SUITE 1600*
**LOS ANGELES, CALIFORNIA 90067**
Telephone: 310-551-8120
Telecopier: 310-551-8113

*Real Property, Business and Entertainment Law.*

**VICTOR I. MARMON,** born Los Angeles, California, March 1, 1951; admitted to bar, 1975, California. *Education:* Yale University (B.A., cum laude, 1972); University of Chicago (J.D., 1975). Adjunct Professor, Whittier College School of Law, 1979. *Member:* Los Angeles County (Member, Sections on: Business and Corporations Law; Intellectual Property and Unfair Competition; Real Property and Taxation; Vice-Chair, 1995-1996, Treasurer, 1994-1995, Secretary, 1993-1994 and Member, 1987—, Executive Committee, Real Property Section; Chair, Commercial Development Subsection of Real Property Section, 1983-1986) and American (Member, Sections on: Real Property, Probate and Trust Law; Business Law; International Law and Practice; and the Entertainment and Sports Industries Forum Committee) Bar Associations; State Bar of California (Member: Conference of Delegates, 1989, 1990 and 1991; Sections on: Business Law; Taxation; Real Property).

---

## MARQUEZ & TEPERSON, P.C.

**LOS ANGELES, CALIFORNIA**

(See Pasadena)

*General Civil Litigation and Appellate Practice in State and Federal Courts and Arbitration Tribunals, General Insurance, Casualty, Products Liability, Legal Malpractice and Labor and Employment.*

---

## MARRONE ROBINSON FREDERICK & FOSTER

**LOS ANGELES, CALIFORNIA**

(See Burbank)

*General Civil and Trial Practice in all State and Federal Courts. Corporation, Business, Insurance and Probate Law.*

## HAROLD MARSH, JR.

Established in 1988

P.O. BOX 251739
**LOS ANGELES, CALIFORNIA 90025**
Telephone: 310-458-0433
Fax: 310-458-0433

*Practice Limited to Consultation with other Law Firms and Acting as Co-Counsel, Expert Witness and Arbitrator in the Fields of Corporations, Securities and Commercial Law.*

**HAROLD MARSH, JR.,** born Tyler, Texas, November 30, 1918; admitted to bar, 1942, Texas; 1951, New York; 1955, California. *Education:* Rice University (B.A., 1939); University of Texas (LL.B., 1942); Columbia University (LL.M., 1947; J.S.D., 1951). Phi Beta Kappa; Phi Delta Phi; Order of the Coif. Author, with R. Roy Finkle, *Marsh's California Corporation Law*, 4 Vols., 3d Ed., Law and Business, Inc., 1996; with: R.H. Volk, *Practice Under California Securities Laws Revisers*, Matthew-Bender & Co., 3 vols., Revised 1996; R.W. Jennings and John C. Coffee. *Securities Regulation - Cases and Materials*, 7th Edition, 1992. Professor of Law, University of California, Los Angeles, 1958-1969. Member, National Bankruptcy Conference, 1961—. Chairman, Commission on the Bankruptcy Laws of the U.S., 1970-1973. Chairman, Business Law Section, 1978-1979 and Member, Committees on Corporations, 1974-1978, Uniform Commercial Code, 1960-1974 and Revision of the Nonprofit Corporation Law, 1977, State Bar of California. Member of Council, Section of Corporation, Banking and Business Law, American Bar Association, 1972-1976; Member, Article 9 Review Committee, 1967-1971 and Advisory Committee, Federal Securities Code Project, 1969-1978. *Member:* American Law Institute. Fellow, American Bar Foundation.

---

## MARTIN & HUDSON

**LOS ANGELES, CALIFORNIA**

(See Pasadena)

*Taxation, Civil Tax Litigation, Estate and Trust Planning, Corporation and Real Estate Law.*

---

## MARTINEAU & KNUDSON

**LOS ANGELES, CALIFORNIA**

(See San Marino)

*General Civil and Trial Practice. Corporation, Business, Probate and Trusts, Real Property, Estate Planning, Federal and State Tax Law.*

---

## STEFAN M. MASON

A LAW CORPORATION

Established in 1979

27TH FLOOR, 1999 AVENUE OF THE STARS
**LOS ANGELES, CALIFORNIA 90067**
Telephone: 310-553-3500
Fax: 310-553-3563

*Management and Individual Labor Relations, Employment Discrimination, Wrongful Termination, Sexual Harassment, Wage and Hour, and Contracts Law. Mediation, Arbitration, Administrative, State and Federal Litigation and Appellate Practice.*

*FIRM PROFILE: The firm's staff represent management and individuals in all aspects of the employment relationship. Acting both as advocates and neutrals, it emphasizes utilization of alternative dispute resolution techniques such as mediation and arbitration.*

**STEFAN M. MASON,** born Maywood, California, May 10, 1939; admitted to bar, 1967, California; 1983, U.S. Supreme Court. *Education:* Dartmouth College (A.B., 1962); Columbia University (Graduate Study, 1962); University of California at Los Angeles School of Law (J.D., 1967). Order of the Coif; Phi Alpha Delta. Editor in Chief, University of California at Los Angeles Law Review, 1966-1967. Certification of Training in Mediation, Collaborative Negotiation and Conflict Resolution Techniques, Center for Dispute Resolution, Santa Monica, California, 1991; Certification of Training in Mediation Skills and Settlement Conference Advocacy, Institute for Dispute Resolution, Pepperdine University School of Law, Malibu, California, 1993. Contributing Editor, California Practice Handbook, Employment Discrimination Litigation, Matthew Bender, 1992. Lecturer for MCLE Credit in Employment Discrimination Litigation, 1992-1993. Visiting Lecturer: University of California at Los Angeles School of Law, 1985. Author: "Labor's Antitrust Exemptions; Limitations Placed Upon Anticompetitive Conduct By Unions and Employers," *Antitrust Advisor*, 3rd Edition, McGraw-Hill, Inc., 1985. Co-Author, "Public Policy Wrongful Termination Actions," Los Angeles Lawyer, October, 1992. Board Member, UCLA Institute of Industrial Relations Association, Los Angeles, California, 1991-1996. Member, Southern California Mediation Association, 1992—. Member, Society for Professionals in Dispute Resolution, 1991. Associate, Munger, Tolles, Hills & Rickershauser, 1967-1970. Partner, Munger, Tolles & Olson, 1970-1979. *Member:* Century City (Member, Labor Law Section), Los Angeles County (Member: Alternative Dispute Resolution Section, 1993—; Ethics Committee, 1974-1977; Client Relations and Fee Disputes Arbitration Committee, 1974—; Labor Law Section, 1976—; Executive Committee, 1984—; Attorney-Client Relations Dispute Resolution Services, 1974—) and American (Member: Committee on Labor Arbitration and the Law of Collective Bargaining Agreements, Labor and Employment Law Section, 1976—; International Law and Practice Section, 1989—) Bar Associations; State Bar of California; American Arbitration Association (Mediator/Arbitrator Panel); National Employment Lawyers Association; California Employment Lawyers Association; American Employment Law Council. **PRACTICE AREAS:** Litigation; Negotiation and Mediation; Labor and Employment Law.

OF COUNSEL

**STEVEN P. KRAKOWSKY,** born Los Angeles, California, August 19, 1955; admitted to bar, 1980, California; U.S. Court of Appeals, Ninth Circuit; U.S. District Court, Central and Southern Districts of California. *Education:* University of California at Los Angeles (B.A., 1976); Southwestern University (J.D., cum laude, 1980). Phi Alpha Delta. Member, 1978-1979 and Executive Note and Comment Editor, 1979-1980, Southwestern University Law Review. *Member:* Los Angeles County (Member, Litigation Section) and American Bar Associations; State Bar of California. **PRACTICE AREAS:** Trials and Appeals.

---

## MASTERS & RIBAKOFF

**LOS ANGELES, CALIFORNIA**

(See Santa Monica)

*Employment Disputes Before Administrative, State and Federal Tribunals, Prosecution of Wrongful Termination, Discrimination, Sexual Harassment and Related Claims, Counseling and Training of Employers and Employees Regarding Prevention of Workplace Related Disputes and Effective Utilization of Older Workers, Alternative Employment Dispute Resolution, Services as a Neutral in Conducting Fact Finding Investigations and Mediating Employment Related Disputes.*

---

## RICHARD J. MATHIAS & ASSOCIATES

611 WEST SIXTH STREET, SUITE 2880
**LOS ANGELES, CALIFORNIA 90017**
Telephone: 213-955-9700
Fax: 213-955-9711

*Labor and Employment Law, Commercial Litigation, Commercial Contracts, General Civil Litigation in all State and Federal Courts, Alternative Dispute Resolution.*

*FIRM PROFILE: Founded in 1996, Richard J. Mathias & Associates is a full-service Labor & Employment Law specialty firm that also offers expertise in commercial litigation, appropriate dispute resolution ('ADR'), and all aspects of civil appellate practice. The Firm's attorneys are specialists in Labor & Employment Law counseling, human resource management, and effective litigation of all forms of employment-related lawsuits (wrongful termination, discrimination claims, class action defense, breach of contract matters, and all other labor and employment-related actions). The Firm's attorneys are committed to providing cost-effective counseling and other appropriate services to employers designed to prevent employment-related litigation. Significantly, the Firm takes pride in representing large and small employers with specially-tailored, personalized services of the highest quality available.*

*(This Listing Continued)*

*(This Listing Continued)*

**RICHARD J. MATHIAS,** born Las Vegas, Nevada, August 8, 1963; admitted to bar, 1988, California. *Education:* Georgetown University (B.S.F.S., 1985; J.D., 1988). Executive Editor, The Tax Lawyer, 1987-1988. Author: Incorporating Partnerships Under Revenue Ruling 84-111: A New Literal Code Application Approach," 40 Tax Lawyer 779 (1987); "The Actual Entitlement Doctrine: Attorneys Fees in Contract Cases," 1 Litigation Section Newsletter, No. 3, p.5 (Los Angeles County Bar Association 1990); "Section 128.5 Sanctions: The Conflict Rages On," 8 Litigation Section Newsletter, No. 4, p.1 (L.A. County Bar Association 1992); "Section 128.5 Sanctions: Should the 'Detailed' Order Requirement Be Reformed," 9 Litigation Section Newsletter, No. 3, p1 (L.A. County Bar Association 1992); "The Conversion to Individual Calendar Courts in Los Angeles: Practical Tips From the Bench," 9 Litigation Section Newsletter, No. 4, p.1 (L.A. County Bar Association 1993); "Practice Tips & Judicial Perspectives from Judge Paul Boland," 10 Litigation Section Newsletter, No. 3, p.1 (L.A. County Bar Association 1994); "Elimination of Bias In The Legal Profession," California State Bar Journal, December, 1994; "Trial Tips From The Master: A Conversation With Gerry Spence," 11 Litigation Section Newsletter, No. 2, p.1 (L.A. County Bar Association, 1995. Instructor, Legal Research and Writing, Georgetown University, 1986-1987. *Member:* State Bar of California (Member, Board of Governors, 1993-1994; Vice-Chairman, Committee on Minimum Continuing Legal Education, 1993; Committee Member, 1991-1993); California Young Lawyers Association (President, 1992-1993 and Member, Board of Director, 1989-1994); Los Angeles County (Member, Executive Committee, Litigation Section, 1995-1998; Member, Legislation and Programs Committees; Co-Editor, Section Newsletter) and American (Member, Labor and Employment Law Section) Bar Associations. *LANGUAGES:* Spanish. *PRACTICE AREAS:* Labor and Employment Law; Wrongful Termination Litigation; Civil Rights; Gay and Lesbian Rights; Employee Benefits; Disabilities Law; Civil Litigation; Appellate Practice.

---

## MYLES M. MATTENSON
*TWO CENTURY PLAZA*
*SUITE 1800*
*2049 CENTURY PARK EAST*
**LOS ANGELES, CALIFORNIA 90067**
*Telephone: 310-553-1160*
*Fax: 310-277-2755*

*Franchise Law. Corporate, Business, Uniform Commercial Code, Construction and Real Estate Law. Insurance Bad Faith, General Civil and Trial Practice.*

**MYLES M. MATTENSON,** born St. Paul, Minnesota, December 13, 1941; admitted to bar, 1968, California and U.S. District Court, Central District of California; 1971, U.S. Tax Court. *Education:* University of California at Los Angeles (B.S., 1964); Loyola University School of Law (J.D., 1967). Phi Alpha Delta (President, Ford Chapter, 1966-1967). President, District Four B'nai B'rith, 1981-1982. Chair, Board of Directors, San Fernando Valley Child Guidance Clinic, 1986-1987. Judge Pro Tem: Los Angeles Municipal Court, 1982—; Burbank Municipal Court, 1984—. Arbitrator, Los Angeles County Superior Court, 1980—. *Member:* Century City and Los Angeles County (Chair, Law Office Management Section, 1993-1995) Bar Associations; State Bar of California.

REPRESENTATIVE CLIENTS: Wienerschnitzel Cooperative Corporation of Los Angeles; Ardmor Vending Co.; Jeffries Truck Parts and Equipment Co. Inc.
REFERENCE: Bank of America (Century City Branch).

---

## MATTHIAS & BERG LLP
*Established in 1988*
*SEVENTH FLOOR*
*515 SOUTH FLOWER STREET*
**LOS ANGELES, CALIFORNIA 90071**
*Telephone: 213-895-4200*
*Telecopier: 213-895-4058*

*Corporate, Corporate Finance, Securities, Mergers and Acquisitions, Commercial Transactions, Asset Securitization, Municipal Finance, Securities Litigation, Tax Litigation, Business and Commercial Litigation, U.S. and International Taxation, including Expert Testimony.*

FIRM PROFILE: *Matthias & Berg LLP was founded in 1988 as a corporate law firm specializing in all securities matters, general commercial, securities and tax litigation, international commercial transactions and U.S. and international taxation. The firm's practice has grown to include a number of U.S. and foreign companies actively engaged in acquisitions and all aspects of corporate finance transactions. Areas of the firm's current practice include its traditional finance work, taxation and litigation, Sino-foreign joint ventures, derivatives financing and acquisition and financing of health care facilities.*

**MICHAEL R. MATTHIAS,** born Chicago, Illinois, June 19, 1947; admitted to bar, 1973, California; U.S. Supreme Court; U.S. Court of Appeals, Ninth and Tenth Circuits, U.S. Tax Court and U.S. District Court, Northern, Central and Southern Districts of California. *Education:* University of California at Los Angeles (B.A., magna cum laude, 1969); Loyola University (J.D., magna cum laude, 1973). Member, Loyola Law Review, 1972-1973. Lecturer, University of California Continuing Education of the Bar, 1981. Judge Pro Tem, Los Angeles Municipal Court, 1980-1996. Arbitrator, Business Law Arbitration Panel, Los Angeles County Superior Court, 1982-1996. *Member:* Los Angeles County and American Bar Associations; State Bar of California; Los Angeles Business Trial Lawyers Association; The Association of Trial Lawyers of America. *PRACTICE AREAS:* Securities Litigation; Tax Litigation; Business Litigation; Commercial.

**JEFFREY P. BERG,** born Los Angeles, California, September 11, 1948; admitted to bar, 1974, California; U.S. Supreme Court; U.S. Court of Appeals, Ninth and Tenth Circuits; U.S. Tax Court. *Education:* California State University at Northridge (B.A., 1970); University of New Mexico (M.A., 1971); Southwestern University School of Law (J.D., 1974). Phi Alpha Delta. Delta Theta Phi. *Member:* Los Angeles County and American Bar Associations; State Bar of California. *PRACTICE AREAS:* Corporate Finance; Mergers and Acquisitions; Asset Securitization; Municipal Finance; Securities; Tax Litigation.

**STUART R. SINGER,** born Boston, Massachusetts, May 25, 1941; admitted to bar, 1968, New York; 1975, California; 1979, U.S. Tax Court and U.S. Supreme Court; U.S. Court of Appeals, Tenth Circuit. *Education:* Dartmouth College (A.B., 1962); Columbia Law School (LL.B., 1965). Editor: "Foreign Investment in the United States," Practicing Law Institute, 1979, 1980, 1981 and 1982; "Regulation of Foreign Investments in the United States," Practicing Law Institute, 1976. Author: U.S. International Tax Forms Manual: Compliance and Reporting, Warren Gorham and Lamont; "When the Internal Revenue Service Abuses the System," 10 Virginia Tax Review 113, Summer, 1990; "Multinationals and New Customs Law will have Broad Impact on Intercompany Pricing," Journal of Taxation, April, 1983; "Tax Planning and Patent Assets," Les Nouvelles, December, 1982; "Captive Offshore Insurance Companies--An Endangered Species?" Tax Management International Journal, December, 1981; "Tax Treatment of an Individual Resident's Foreign Expropriation Losses: An Analysis," Journal of Taxation, November, 1980; "Current Issues in Federal Taxation of Nonresident Aliens," The Review of Taxation of Individuals, Summer, 1978; "Aspects of Foreign Investments in the United States," Tax Planning International, April, 1977; "Current Problems of Structuring Petrodollar Loans," Mercer Law Review, Winter, 1976; "Taxation of Foreign Entertainers," Los Angeles Bar Bulletin, 1976; "The IET Extension Act," Journal of Taxation, 1971; "Business and International Aspects of Proposed Canadian Tax Reform," Journal of Taxation, July, 1970; "Proposed Canadian Tax Reform has Far-Reaching Implications for U.S. Investors," Journal of Taxation, June, 1970; "U.S. Balance of Payments Policy: 1945-1969," Tax Executive, 1970; "Selecting an International Finance Subsidiary," Journal of Taxation, 1969; "The Eurodollar Route to Expansion Abroad," Management Review, 1969; "General Guide to Foreign Direct Investment Controls," Monograph, 1968, Third Edition Published, 1969. Member: Association of the Bar of the City of New York; The State Bar of California (Member, Committee of Bar Examiners, 1982-1986). *LANGUAGES:* French and Spanish. *PRACTICE AREAS:* U.S. and International Tax; Estate Planning.

**KENNETH M. H. HOFF,** born Chicago, Illinois, October 28, 1958; admitted to bar, 1983, California, U.S. Court of Appeals, Ninth Circuit and U.S. District Court, Central District of California. *Education:* University of California at Berkeley (A.B., 1980); University of California at Davis (J.D., 1983). Member, University of California at Davis Law Review, 1982-1983. Author: "Two-Way Cable Television and Informational Privacy," 6 COMMENT 797, 1984. *Member:* State Bar of California. *PRACTICE AREAS:* Corporate Law; Securities Law.

**MICHAEL D. BERGER,** born Oak Park, Illinois, July 27, 1946; admitted to bar, 1985, California; U.S. District Court, Northern and Central Districts of California. *Education:* University of Illinois (B.A., 1968); University of Wisconsin-Madison (M.A., 1978); Brigham Young University (J.D., cum laude, 1984); Columbia University (Certificate of Achievement with Honors, Parker School of International Law, December, 1984). Member,

*(This Listing Continued)*

### MATTHIAS & BERG LLP, Los Angeles—Continued

Board of Editors, Brigham Young University Journal of Legal Studies, 1983-1984. Author: "Soviet Divorce Law and the Role of the Russian Family," 3 Brigham Young University Law Review 821, 1986. *Member:* State Bar of California. [With U.S. Army Security Agency, 1969-1972 - SP/5]. *LANGUAGES:* Chinese (Mandarin), Russian and French. *PRACTICE AREAS:* Securities Offerings; Commercial Litigation.

REPRESENTATIVE CLIENTS: Synagro Technologies, Inc.; Mexalit, S.A.; Maxitile, Inc.; Allstar Inns; Chatsworth Products, Inc.; International Meta Systems, Inc.; Residential Resources, Inc.; AVIC Group Intl., Inc.; AutoBitter Group, Inc.; Greater China Corp.; HBO Ole; National Quality Care, Inc.
REFERENCE: First Professional Bank.

## LAW OFFICES OF JEFFREY A. MATZ
23822 VALENCIA BOULEVARD
SUITE 210
**LOS ANGELES, CALIFORNIA 91355**
*Telephone: 805-222-9131*

*Scottsdale, Arizona Office:* 6711 East Camelback Road, Suite 8. Telephone: 602-955-0900. Fax: 602-970-3172.

*Trial and Civil Practice in Personal Injury, Toxic Chemical Contamination, Products Liability, Insurance Bad Faith, Employment Discrimination and Wrongful Discharge, Construction Accidents, Maritime Accidents, Air Crash Litigation, F.E.L.A. Litigation, Medical Malpractice and Business Fraud.*

*FIRM PROFILE:* Trial experience includes 116 civil jury trials in several states to a verdict and lead counsel in the McColl Dump Site litigation. The firm is listed in Martindale-Hubbell Bar Register of Preeminent Lawyers in Civil Trial.

**JEFFREY A. MATZ,** born Cleveland, Ohio, March 15, 1942; admitted to bar, 1972, California. *Education:* California State University at Northridge (B.A., 1966; M.A., 1967); University of San Fernando (J.D., cum laude, 1971). Sigma Alpha Epsilon. Member, Blue Key. California Blue Key Man of the Year, 1966. *Member:* Beverly Hills, Los Angeles County and San Fernando County Bar Associations; The State Bar of California; California Trial Lawyers Association; The Association of Trial Lawyers of America; Board of Governors, Los Angeles Trial Lawyers Association; American Board of Professional Liability Attorneys. (Board Certified Civil Trial Advocate by the National Board of Trial Advocacy.)

## MICHAEL P. MAXWELL
10100 SANTA MONICA BOULEVARD, SUITE 300
**LOS ANGELES, CALIFORNIA 90067**
*Telephone: 310-556-1511*
*Fax: 310-556-1513*

*Customs and International Trade Law.*

**MICHAEL P. MAXWELL,** born Atlantic City, New Jersey, October 5, 1949; admitted to bar, 1979, Florida; 1981, New York and U.S. Court of Appeals, Sixth Circuit; 1982, U.S. District Court, Southern District of New York and U.S. Court of International Trade; 1983, U.S. Court of Appeals for the Federal Circuit; 1989, California. *Education:* Memphis State University (B.A., 1974; J.D., 1978); University of Pennsylvania (LL.M., 1980). Notes Editor, Memphis State University Law Review, 1977-1978. Member: Order of the Barristers; Moot Court Board; Moot Court Team. Recipient, American Jurisprudence Award in Contracts. Customs House Broker, License No. 11959, 1990. Law Clerk to: Hon. Gus J. Solomon, U.S. District Judge, District of Oregon, 1980; Hon. Nathaniel R. Jones, U.S. Circuit Judge, U.S. Court of Appeals, Sixth Circuit, 1980-1981. Author: "Better Read Than Shread: Customs Recordkeeping Requirements for Importers," 25 The International Lawyer 91, 1991; "Formulating Rules of Origin for Imported Merchandise: Transforming the Substantial Transformation Test," 23 The George Washington Journal of International Law and Economics 669, 1990. Trial Attorney, U.S. Department of Justice, Civil Division, Commercial Litigation Branch, International Trade Field Office, 1982-1985, 1986-1988. *Member:* The Florida Bar; Los Angeles County (Chair, Custom Law Committee, 1993-1994), New York State and American (Member, Litigation Section) Bar Associations; Customs and International Trade Bar Association. *REPORTED CASES:* Aviall of Texas v. United States, 861 F.Supp. 100, CIT, 1994; Sulzer Escher Wyss, Inc. v. United States, 17 CIT, Slip Op. 93-113, June 22, 1993.

## MAYER, BROWN & PLATT
350 SOUTH GRAND AVENUE, 25TH FLOOR
**LOS ANGELES, CALIFORNIA 90071-1503**
*Telephone: 213-229-9500*
*Facsimile: 213-625-0248*
*Telex: 188089*
*Cable: LEMAYLA*
*URL: http://www.mayerbrown.com*

*Chicago, Illinois Office:* 190 South La Salle Street, 60603-3441. Telephone: (312) 782-0600. Facsimile: (312) 701-7711. Telex: 190404. Cable: LEMAY.
*Berlin, Germany Office:* Spreeufer 5, 10178. Telephone: 011-49-30-247-3800. Facsimile: 011-49-30-247-38044.
*Brussels, Belgium Office:* Square de Meeûs 19/20, Bte. 4, 1050. Telephone: 011-32-2-512-9878. Facsimile : 011-3 2-2-511-3305.
*Houston, Texas Office:* 700 Louisiana Street, Suite 3600, 77002-2730. Telephone: (713) 221-1651. Facsimile: (723) 224-6410. Telex: 775809. Cable: LEMAYHOU.
*London, England Office:* 162 Queen Victoria Street, EC4V 4DB. Telephone: 011-44-171-248-1465. Facsimile: 011-44-171-329-4465. Telex: 8811095. Cable: LEMAYLDN.
*New York, New York Office:* 1675 Broadway, 10019-5820. Telephone: (212) 506-2500. Facsimile: (212) 262-1910. Telex: 701842. Cable: LEMAYEN.
*Washington, D.C. Office:* 2000 Pennsylvania Avenue, N.W., 20006-1882. Telephone: (202) 463-2000. Facsimile: (202) 861-0473. Telex: 892603. Cable: LEMAYDC.
*Representative Offices:*
*Almaty, Republic of Kazakhstan:* 162 Tulebaev Street #32. Telephone: 011-7-3272-636388. Facsimile: 011-7-3272-507828.
*Bishkek, Kyrgyz Republic:* Suite 405, Prospekt Manasa 55, 720001. Telephone: 011-7-3312-222970. Facsimile: 011-7-3312-620980.
*Köln, Germany:* An Lyskirchen 14, 50676. Telephone: 011-49-221-921-5210. Facsimile: 011-49-221-921-5514.
*Tashkent, Republic of Uzbekistan:* 5th Floor, 1 Turab Tula Street, 700003. Telephone: 011-7-3712-891179. Facsimile: 011-7-3712-891178.
*Mexico City, Mexico, D.F., Independent Mexico Correspondent:* Jáuregui, Navarrete, Nader y Rojas, S.C. Abogados, Paseo de la Reforma 199, Pisos 15, 16 y 17, 06500, Mexico. Telephone: 011-525-591-16-55. Facsimile: 011-525-535-80-62, 011-525-703-22-47. Cable: JANANE.

*General Practice.*

### PARTNERS

**TERESA A. BEAUDET,** born Los Angeles, California, February 7, 1953; admitted to bar, 1980, California and U.S. District Court, Central District of California; 1991, U.S. Court of Appeals, Ninth Circuit; 1992, U.S. District Court, Eastern, Northern and Southern Districts of California. *Education:* Loyola Marymount University of Los Angeles (B.A., magna cum laude, 1974; M.A., 1976); Loyola Law School (J.D., cum laude, 1980). *Email:* tbeaudet@mayerbrown.com

**LOUIS P. EATMAN,** born Montgomery, Alabama, November 16, 1948; admitted to bar, 1974, California. *Education:* Georgetown University (B.S.F.S., cum laude, 1970); Stanford University (J.D., 1974). *Email:* leatman@mayerbrown.com

**L. BRUCE FISCHER,** born Long Beach, California, November 16, 1957; admitted to bar, 1982, California. *Education:* University of California at San Diego (B.A., cum laude, 1979); University of Southern California (J.D., 1982). *Email:* lfischer@mayerbrown.com

**MICHAEL F. KERR,** born Cleveland, Ohio, February 28, 1953; admitted to bar, 1982, Illinois and U.S. District Court, Northern District of Illinois; 1995, California. *Education:* Boston College (A.B, summa cum laude, 1974); University of Chicago (A.M., 1975; J.D., 1982). *Email:* mkerr@mayerbrown.com

**KENNETH E. KOHLER,** born Auburn, California, May 28, 1953; admitted to bar, 1981, California. *Education:* University of California, Berkeley (B.S., with highest honors, 1977); Yale University (J.D., 1980). *Email:* kkohler@mayeerbrown.com

**ALEC G. NEDELMAN,** born Los Angeles, California, January 25, 1955; admitted to bar, 1980, Hawaii; 1981, California. *Education:* University of California at San Diego (B.A., summa cum laude, 1977); University of California at Los Angeles (J.D., 1980). *Email:* anedelman@mayerbrown.com

**BRIAN E. NEWHOUSE,** born Galion, Ohio, February 22, 1953; admitted to bar, 1978, Connecticut; 1984, Illinois; 1985, California. *Education:*

*(This Listing Continued)*

Denison University (B.A., with honors, 1975); University of Michigan (J.D., cum laude, 1978). *Email:* bnewhouse@mayerbrown.com

**M. ELLEN ROBB,** born Ames, Iowa, September 7, 1951; admitted to bar, 1982, New York; 1983, U.S. Tax Court; 1988, California. *Education:* University of Iowa (B.A., with high distinction, 1972); University of Kansas (M.S.W., 1977); Yale Law School (J.D., 1980); New York University (LL.M., 1987). *Email:* mrobb@mayerbrown.com

**KEVIN L. SHAW,** born Gibson City, Illinois, May 28, 1955; admitted to bar, 1980, Texas; 1982, Colorado; 1989, California. *Education:* University of Texas (B.A., with honors, 1976); University of Houston (J.D., cum laude, 1980). *Email:* kshaw@mayerbrown.com

**NEIL M. SOLTMAN,** born Philadelphia, Pennsylvania, July 20, 1949; admitted to bar, 1975, California. *Education:* Temple University (B.A., magna cum laude, 1971); Catholic University of America (J.D., 1975). *Email:* nsoltman@mayerbrown.com

**ROBERT A. SOUTHERN,** born Independence, Missouri, July 17, 1930; admitted to bar, 1955, Illinois (Not admitted in California). *Education:* Northwestern University (B.S., 1952; LL.B., 1954). *Email:* rsouthern@mayerbrown.com

**JAMES R. WALTHER,** born San Francisco, California, August 10, 1945; admitted to bar, 1972, California. *Education:* Stanford University (A.B., 1967); University of California, Los Angeles (J.D., 1972). *Email:* jwalther@mayerbrown.com

**DON L. WEAVER,** born Inglewood, California, December 1, 1951; admitted to bar, 1977, California. *Education:* University of California at Santa Barbara (B.A., with highest honors, 1973); University of Southern California (J.D., 1977). *Email:* dweaver@mayerbrown.com

### SPECIAL COUNSEL

**JOHN SHEPARD WILEY, JR.,** born February 26, 1953; admitted to bar, 1981, California. *Education:* University of California at Davis (A.B., 1975); Boalt Hall School of Law, University of California (M.A., J.D., 1980). *Email:* jwiley@mayerbrown.com

### COUNSEL

**CHRISTOPHER P. MURPHY,** born Sydney, Australia, May 28, 1949; admitted to bar, 1985, California and U.S. District Court, Central District of California; 1987, U.S. District Court, Eastern District of California; 1991, U.S. District Court, Northern and Southern Districts of California; 1992, U.S. Court of Appeals, Ninth Circuit. *Education:* University of Sydney, Sydney, Australia (B.A., 1969); Latrobe University (Ph.D., 1982); University of California at Los Angeles School of Law (J.D., 1985). *Email:* cmurphy@mayerbrown.com

### ASSOCIATES

Andrei A. Baev; David C. Bolstad; Jacqueline R. Brady; Christopher D. Chen; Boise A. Ding; Henry Einar Fink; Douglas B. Frank; Anthony G. Graham; Richard Greta; Lorie S. Griffen; Jerome M.F.J. Jauffret; Fredrick S. Levin (Not admitted in CA); Bruce H. Levine; John Nadolenco; A. Ken Okamoto; Maria M. Rabassa; Mary Beth Rhoden; Nina E. Scholtz; Carl J. Thomas; Kimberly S. Winick.

## MAYER, GLASSMAN & GAINES

A Partnership including Professional Corporations

Established in 1971

SUITE 400, 11726 SAN VICENTE BOULEVARD
**LOS ANGELES, CALIFORNIA 90049-5006**
*Telephone: 310-207-0007*
*Telecopier: 310-207-3578*

*Entertainment, Corporate, Business, Civil Litigation, Real Estate, Insolvency and Family Law.*

**FREDERICK J. GLASSMAN, (P.C.),** born Iowa City, Iowa, September 30, 1939; admitted to bar, 1966, California; 1971, U.S. Supreme Court. *Education:* State University of Iowa (B.A.B.S., 1961); University of California at Los Angeles (LL.B., 1965). Hearing Officer, Los Angeles Superior Court. *Member:* Los Angeles County, Beverly Hills (Member, Executive Committee, Family Law Section) and American (Member, Family Law Section) Bar Associations; State Bar of California (Member, Family Law Section; Alternative Dispute Resolution Standing Committee South); Academy of Family Mediators. *PRACTICE AREAS:* Family Law; Mediation; Divorce Litigation.

*(This Listing Continued)*

**ROBERT D. MAYER, (P.C.),** born Long Beach, California, July 27, 1939; admitted to bar, 1967, California; 1971, U.S. Supreme Court. *Education:* University of California at Berkeley (B.S., 1961); Boalt Hall School of Law, University of California at Berkeley (LL.B., 1966). Negotiating Strategies Extension Instructor, University of California at Los Angeles, 1985—. Author: "Power Plays-How to Negotiate, Persuade and Finesse Your Way to Success in Any Situation," Times Books/Random House, 1996. *PRACTICE AREAS:* Real Estate Law; Insolvency Law.

**FREDERIC N. GAINES,** born New York, N.Y., October 1, 1940; admitted to bar, 1966, California and U.S. District Court, Central District of California. *Education:* Hobart College (B.A., 1961); University of California at Los Angeles (LL.B., 1965). Phi Beta Kappa; Pi Gamma Mu; Phi Alpha Delta. Author: "From Pitch to Profit: An Overview of the Motion Picture Production Process," Los Angeles Lawyer, April, 1986. Judge Pro Tempore of the Beverly Hills Municipal Court, 1973 and 1974. Guest Entertainment Forum Lecturer, York University, Toronto, Practicing Law Institute and International Music Industry Conferences, 1976-1980. Guest Lecturer: Australian American Chamber of Commerce, 1986—; Entertainment Forum, Sydney, Australia, 1986—. *Member:* Beverly Hills (Member, Entertainment Law Committee, 1978—), Los Angeles County (2nd Vice President, Intellectual Property Committee, 1977-1978) and American Bar Associations; State Bar of California; Los Angeles Copyright Society. *PRACTICE AREAS:* Entertainment Law; Television Law; Motion Picture Law; Publishing Law; Intellectual Property Law.

**RICHARD P. SOLOMON,** born Miami, Florida, June 9, 1950; admitted to bar, 1983, California; U.S. District Court, Central District of California. *Education:* University of Georgia (B.A., 1975); California Western School of Law (J.D., 1982). *Member:* The State Bar of California. *PRACTICE AREAS:* Entertainment Law; Television Law; Motion Picture Law; Intellectual Property Law.

**MARC A. LIEBERMAN,** born Cincinnati, Ohio, April 22, 1964; admitted to bar, 1991, California and U.S. District Court, Central District of California; 1992, U.S. District Court, Southern, Eastern and Northern Districts of California. *Education:* University of Madrid, Madrid, Spain; Brown University (A.B., with honors, 1986); University of California at Los Angeles (J.D., 1991). *Member:* Beverly Hills (Member, Executive Committee, Bankruptcy Section, 1994-1995) and Los Angeles County (Member: Financial Lawyers Conference; California Bankruptcy Forum) Bar Associations. *LANGUAGES:* Spanish, French and Portuguese. *REPORTED CASES:* In re Barakat, 173 B.R. 672 (Bkrptcy. C.D. CAL. 1994). *PRACTICE AREAS:* Bankruptcy Litigation; Creditors Rights Law.

**STEVEN M. MAYER,** born Los Angeles, California, January 4, 1968; admitted to bar, 1994, California and U.S. District Court, Central, Northern, Southern and Eastern Districts of California; 1995, U.S. Court of Appeals, Ninth Circuit. *Education:* University of California at Santa Barbara (B.A., 1990); Tulane University of Louisiana (J.D., 1993). *Member:* Beverly Hills (Member, Executive Committee, Bankruptcy Law Section) and Los Angeles County Bar Associations; State Bar of California. *PRACTICE AREAS:* Bankruptcy Law; Litigation; Creditor's Rights Law.

REFERENCE: City National Bank, Brentwood Branch.

## W. MICHAEL MAYOCK
**LOS ANGELES, CALIFORNIA**

(See Pasadena)

*Criminal Trial Practice in all State and Federal Courts.*

## ARTHUR MAZIROW
*3415 SEPULVEDA BOULEVARD*
*SUITE 1200*
**LOS ANGELES, CALIFORNIA 90034**
*Telephone: 310-398-6227*
*Email: AM@FFSLAW.COM*

*Real Estate Development, Purchases, Sales, Leases, Financing and Joint Ventures.*

**FIRM PROFILE:** *Mr. Mazirow is the author of more than 100 articles on legal aspects of real estate transactions. He co-authored a textbook for real estate brokers and has written extensively for "The National Real Estate Investor*

*(This Listing Continued)*

**ARTHUR MAZIROW**, *Los Angeles—Continued*

*Magazine"* and *"Shopping Center World Magazine"*. He is a principal author of the lease and purchase forms published by the American Real Estate Association. Lecturer and participant in more than 300 seminars sponsored by the University of California, the State Bar of California and various real estate industry groups concerning the law and practice in real estate transactions. He has spoken before the University of Edmonton, Calgary, Canada and was a shareholder for 10 years and chairman of the real estate department for four years with the firm of Buchalter, Nemer, Fields & Younger. Mr. Mazirow is currently of counsel to Freeman, Freeman and Smiley, LLP.

**ARTHUR MAZIROW,** born New York, N.Y., July 20, 1933; admitted to bar, 1959, California. *Education:* University of California at Los Angeles (B.S., 1955; J.D., 1958). Member, California Housing Finance Agency 1981-1988. *Member:* Beverly Hills, Los Angeles County and American Bar Associations; State Bar of California. (Also Of Counsel, Freeman, Freeman & Smiley, LLP).

## MAZURSKY, SCHWARTZ & ANGELO
*Established in 1988*
SUITE 600, 10877 WILSHIRE BOULEVARD
**LOS ANGELES, CALIFORNIA 90024-4341**
*Telephone: 310-824-7725*
*Facsimile: 310-824-2735*

*Major Tort Litigation emphasizing Major Personal Injury, Insurance Bad Faith, Product Liability, Premise Liability, Professional Malpractice, Medical Malpractice and Business Torts. Civil Trial and Appellate Practice and Toxic Tort Litigation.*

**CHARLES J. MAZURSKY,** born Madison, Wisconsin, August 12, 1941; admitted to bar, 1970, California. *Education:* University of Wisconsin-Madison (B.A., 1963); Hastings College of Law, University of California (J.D., 1969). Author: "A Former Defense Attorney Looks at Product Liability Cases," Forum, 1980; "Securing Substantial Damages for False Arrest," The Advocate, 1983. Lecturer, CEB Annual Review of Torts, 1989-1990. Faculty Lecturer: "Insurance Litigation," California Judges Association, 1989; "Bad Faith Litigation," Defense Research Institute, 1990. Presentations: "Practical Considerations in the Use of Demonstrative Evidence at Trial," Los Angeles Trial Lawyers Association, Evidence Seminar, June 1991; "Punitive Damages in Bad Faith Cases: Successful Themes and Trial Tactics," South Dakota Trial Lawyers Association, May 1992; "Punitive Damages in Bad Faith Cases," Pasadena Bar Association, May 1992; "Orchestrating Your Case," Los Angeles Trial Lawyers Association and California Trial Lawyers Association, Anatomy of a Civil Trial, September 1992; "Developing a Bad Faith Case Through Critical Discovery and Choice of Experts," Los Angeles Trial Lawyers Association 10th Annual Las Vegas Convention, October 1992; "Getting Critical Claims File Materials - Hurdling Privilege Claims," California Trial Lawyers Association, November 1992; "Bad Faith Insurance Litigation in California - A Plaintiff's Perspective," National Business Institute, Inc., May 1993; "Insurance Bad Faith - The Excess Liability Case," Los Angeles Trial Lawyers Association - Mandatory Continuing Legal Education Fair, May 1993; "Bad Faith and Uninsured Motorist Claims: Can You Settle and Sue?" The Advocate, April 1996. Named Alumnus of the Year, Hastings College of the Law, Los Angeles Chapter, 1993. *Member:* Los Angeles County Bar Association (Member, Public Counsel, 1983—); State Bar of California; Consumer Attorneys Association of Los Angeles (formerly LATLA); President, 1995; Member, Board of Governors, 1983—; Vice President, Executive Board, 1992-1993; President-Elect, 1993); California Trial Lawyers Association; The Association of Trial Lawyers of America (Sustaining Member); National Board of Trial Advocacy (Diplomate); Los Angeles Trial Lawyers Association (Trial Lawyer of the Year, 1991). [With U.S. Army, 1963-1966]. *PRACTICE AREAS:* Insurance Bad Faith Law; Products Liability Law; Medical Malpractice.

**ARNOLD W. SCHWARTZ,** born New York, N.Y., August 9, 1945; admitted to bar, 1974, California; 1978, U.S. District Court, Central District of California; 1980, U.S. Supreme Court, U.S. Court of Appeals, Ninth Circuit and U.S. District Court, Southern and Northern Districts of California. *Education:* State University of New York at Albany (B.S., 1967); Southwestern University (J.D., 1974). Contributing Editor, CEB Litigation Reporter, Wrongful Discharge Litigation, 1985—. Author: "Expanding Concepts in Bad Faith: Construction Surety Bonds," The Advocate No. 2, March, 1984; "Wrongful Discharge: Statute of Limitation," CEB Civil Litigation Reporter, July, 1986; "The Statute of Frauds-A Potential Bar to

*(This Listing Continued)*

Wrongful Discharge Cases," 8 CEB Litigation Reporter 58, March, 1986; "Cole v. Fair Oaks Fire Protection District: Does the Workers' Compensation Exclusive Remedy Rule Bar Damages for Emotional Distress in Wrongful Termination Cases?" 9 CEB Litigation Reporter 132, June 1987; "Wrongful Termination Update-Workers Compensation Preemption," CEB Litigation Reporter, September, 1987; "Protecting the Industrial Worker Using Labor Code 4558," The Advocate, July/August, 1992; "Cross-Examining the Expert In Product Liability Cases," The Advocate, June 1993; "Proving The Intentional Discrimination Case," The Advocate, April 1995. *Member:* Los Angeles County (Former Member, Judicial Appointments Committee) and American (Member, Arbitration Panel, 1977—) Bar Associations; State Bar of California; The Association of Trial Lawyers of America; California Trial Lawyers Association; Consumer Attorneys Association of Los Angeles (formerly LATLA, Treasurer, 1994, Secretary, 1995, First Vice President, 1996); Board Member, Consumer Attorneys of California (formerly California Trial Lawyers Association). *PRACTICE AREAS:* Products Liability Law; Major Personal Injury; Insurance Bad Faith Law; Business Torts; Professional Liability Law.

**CHRISTOPHER E. ANGELO,** born Los Angeles, California, December 19, 1949; admitted to bar, 1976, California; 1995, U.S. Supreme Court. *Education:* University of California at Riverside (B.A., with honors, 1972); Loyola University of Los Angeles (J.D., 1975). Recipient, University of California Highlander Scholarship, 1968-1972. Member, Loyola University of Los Angeles Law Review, 1974-1975. Author: "Spoliation: Plaintiff's Perspective," Forum, V. 26, N.1, Jan/Feb 1996; "Why Reinsurance Made Moradi Shalal Unnecessary and Ineffectual," Forum, Vol. 20, No. 9, November 1990; "Nuisance and Other Tort Theories: New Tactics to Make Industry Environmentally Accountable," 31st Annual CTLA Convention Syllabus, San Francisco, November 1992; "In Defense of the Common Law Jury: Long May It Live," Forum, v. 24, No. 9, November 1994. Contributing Author, California Judges Association's Benchbook on Insurance Litigation. Faculty Lecturer, "Insurance Litigation," California Judges Association, 1989. Faculty Lecturer, Sierra Club International Symposium on Environmental Law, 1991. Lecturer: Guest Orator, "Arguments by the Masters, Bad Faith and Spoliation," Seminar, Consumer Attorneys Association of Los Angeles/Consumer Attorneys of California (formerly LATLA and CTLA), June 18, 1994; "Creative and Expanding Concepts of Landowner Liability," 9th Annual Consumer Attorneys Association of Los Angeles Convention, (formerly LATLA) October 18-20, 1991, Las Vegas, Nevada; Discovery Seminar, "Spoliation: Plaintiffs Perspective," June 3, 1995; "Recent Developments in Bad Faith Law," October 8, 1995, Las Vegas Convention. . Listed, Who's Who in American Law. Co-Founder, Officer and Director, "The Christopher Sampson Nonprofit Foundation for the Catastrophically Injured". General Counsel, Special Opportunities: Providing Recreation Activities for Disabled Children. *Member:* Los Angeles County and American Bar Associations; State Bar of California (Judge, State Bar Court, 1982-1983); Italian-American Lawyers Association; Consumer Attorneys Association of Los Angeles; Consumer Attorneys of California. *REPORTED CASES:* Trial and appellate counsel: Mora v. Baker Commodities (1989) 210 Cal.App. 3d 771, 258 Cal. Rptr. 699 (Also Basi; 8. 20. 1); Street v. Superior Court (1990) 224 Cal. App. 3d 1397, 274 Cal. Rptr. 595; Moore v. Regents of the University of California (1990) 51 Cal. 3d 120, 271 Cal. Rptr. 146; Lipton v. Lawyers Mutual, 56 Cal. Rptr. 2d 341; Lehito v. Allstate Ins. Co. (1994) 31 Cal. App. 4th 60, 36 Cal Rptr 2d 814. *PRACTICE AREAS:* Insurance Law; Commercial Bad Faith Law; Products Liability Law; Environmental Torts; Professional Liability Law.

---

**SCOTT A. MARKS,** born Skokie, Illinois, June 26, 1956; admitted to bar, 1990, California. *Education:* University of California, Irvine (B.A., 1978); University of Southern California (M.S.W., 1980); Loyola Marymount University (J.D., 1990). Speaker: Slip and Fall Seminar, Los Angeles Trial Lawyers Association, September, 1994; Seminar, Written Advocacy, Consumer Attorneys of Los Angeles, September, 1995. Speaker, "Consumer Legal Remedies Act," Consumer Attorneys Association of Los Angeles, 1995. Author, Civil Code Section 1750, "The Consumer Legal Remedies Act - A Powerful Weapon in the Fight for Consumers and Protection of the General Public," Advocates, June 1996. *Member:* Los Angeles County and American Bar Associations; Consumer Attorneys Association of Los Angeles (Member, Board of Governors); Consumer Attorneys Association of California; The Association of Trial Lawyers of America. *PRACTICE AREAS:* Insurance Law; Bad Faith Law; Product Liability Law; Medical Malpractice Law; Business Torts.

**DEBRA JANE WEGMAN,** born Los Angeles, California, May 20, 1954; admitted to bar, 1983, California; 1987, U.S. District Court, Central District of California; 1989, U.S. Court of Appeals, Ninth Circuit and U.S.

*(This Listing Continued)*

District Court, Southern and Eastern Districts of California. *Education:* California State University; University of California at Berkeley (B.A., 1976); Loyola Law School (J.D., 1982). *Member:* Beverly Hills, Century City, Los Angeles County and American Bar Associations; State Bar of California; California Women Lawyers; Association of Business Trial Lawyers; Consumer Attorneys Association of Los Angeles. *REPORTED CASES:* National & International Brotherhood, etc. et al vs. Superior Court, 215 Cal. App. 3d 934, 264 Cal. Rptr. 44. *PRACTICE AREAS:* Insurance Coverage and Bad Faith; Professional Liability Law; Major Tort Litigation.

## McBIRNEY & CHUCK, P.C.
611 WEST SIXTH STREET, SUITE 2500
LOS ANGELES, CALIFORNIA 90017
Telephone: 213-236-2750
Telecopier: 213-236-2700

*Commercial Leasing, Corporate, Real Estate, Nonprofit Organizations, Estate Planning and Probate Practice, Civil Litigation.*

*FIRM PROFILE:* McBirney & Chuck is a downtown Los Angeles law firm with a wide range of experience in business and real estate transactions, civil litigation, nonprofit organizations law, probate and estate planning. The firm's highly skilled and experienced team of attorneys emphasizes the prompt, personal delivery of the highest quality legal services in an efficient, cost-effective manner.

**BRUCE H. McBIRNEY,** born Los Angeles, California, June 16, 1954; admitted to bar, 1979, California. *Education:* Loyola Marymount University (B.A., summa cum laude, 1976); Boalt Hall School of Law, University of California (J.D., 1979). Alpha Sigma Nu. Associate Editor, California Law Review, 1977-1979. Author: "Quern v. Jordan: A Misdirected Bar to Section 1983 Civil Rights Suits Against States," 67 California Law Review 407, 1979. *Member:* Los Angeles County Bar Association (Member, Real Property Section); The State Bar of California; Building Owners and Managers Association of Greater Los Angeles. *PRACTICE AREAS:* Real Estate; Commercial Leasing; Landlord/Tenant.

**CATHERINE ENDO CHUCK,** born Oakland, California, November 8, 1956; admitted to bar, 1985, California; 1986, U.S. District Court, Central District of California. *Education:* University of California at Los Angeles (B.A., 1978); Loyola Law School (J.D., 1985). *Member:* Los Angeles County (Member: Executive Committee, Business and Corporate Law Section) and American (Member, Sections on: Corporation, Banking and Business Law; Real Property, Probate and Trust Law) Bar Associations; State Bar of California (Member: Business Law Section; Former Member, Committee on Non Profit Corporations and Unincorporated Associations, Business Law Section); Japanese-American Bar Association; National Asian Pacific American Bar Association. *PRACTICE AREAS:* Corporate; Non Profit Organizations; Probate and Estate Planning.

### OF COUNSEL

**MICHAEL E. REZNICK,** born Los Angeles, California, July 15, 1953; admitted to bar, 1984, California. *Education:* California State University, Northridge (B.A., summa cum laude, 1981); Loyola Law School, Law School (J.D., cum laude, 1984). Member, Loyola University of Los Angeles Law Review. *Member:* Los Angeles County and American Bar Associations; State Bar or California. *PRACTICE AREAS:* Civil Litigation.

## McBREEN, McBREEN & KOPKO
SUITE 922, 9841 AIRPORT BOULEVARD
LOS ANGELES, CALIFORNIA 90045
Telephone: 310-410-2887
Fax: 310-410-0735

*Chicago, Illinois:* Suite 2520, 20 North Wacker Drive. Telephone: 312-332-6405. Fax: 312-332-2657.
*Philadelphia, Pennsylvania Office:* 1760 Market Street, Suite 900. Telephone: 215-864-2600. Fax: 215-864-2610.
*Montvale, New Jersey Office:* 110 Summit Avenue. Telephone: 201-573-1508. Fax: 201-573-0574.

*General Practice, Corporate, Mergers and Acquisitions, Securities, Commodities, Real Estate, Aviation, General and Commercial Litigation, Toxic Torts, Products Liability, Medical Malpractice and Environmental Law.*

(For complete biographical data on all personnel, see Professional Biographies at Chicago, Illinois)

## McCAMBRIDGE, DEIXLER & MARMARO
Established in 1984
2029 CENTURY PARK EAST, SUITE 2700
LOS ANGELES, CALIFORNIA 90067
Telephone: 310-277-2650
Telecopier: 310-203-8304

*Commercial and Entertainment related Litigation, White Collar Criminal Defense, General Corporate matters and Corporate and Regulatory matters for Banks and other Financial Institutions.*

### MEMBERS OF FIRM

**GEORGE R. McCAMBRIDGE,** born Los Angeles, California, June 5, 1945; admitted to bar, 1973, California. *Education:* University of San Francisco (A.B., 1967); University of California at Los Angeles (J.D., 1973). Chief Articles Editor, UCLA Law Review, 1972-1973. Member, Peace Corps, 1967-1969. Member, Board of Directors, UCLA Law Alumni Association, 1979-1982. Member, Board of Directors, Lawyers' Mutual Insurance Company, 1992—. Member, Board of Directors, Public Counsel, 1994—. *Member:* Century City, Los Angeles County and American Bar Associations; State Bar of California (Member, Financial Institutions Committee, 1982-1985).

**BERT H. DEIXLER,** born Bronx, New York, November 8, 1952; admitted to bar, 1976, California; 1982, District of Columbia and U.S. Supreme Court. *Education:* George Washington University (B.A., with special honors and distinction, 1973); Columbia University (J.D., 1976). Phi Beta Kappa. Harlan Fiske Stone Scholar. Assistant U.S. Attorney, Criminal Division, 1978-1981 and Special Assistant to the U.S. Attorney, 1981, Central District of California. Author: "Discovery Approaches in Financial Institution Failure Cases: A Defense Perspective," Papers on Prosecuting Savings and Loan/Bank Fraud Cases, Georgetown University Law Center, 1992. Co-Author: "RICO: Taking the Stress Out of Fraudulent Claims," Papers collected in Manual for California Workers' Compensation Defense Attorney's Association, 1992. Member, Federal Criminal Indigent Defense Panel, 1983-1987. Judge Pro Tempore, Los Angeles Municipal Court, 1983—. Member, Panel of Settlement Arbitrators, Los Angeles Superior Court (West District). Consultant, Ethics Commission, City of Los Angeles, 1989-1990. Counsel, Independent Commission on the Los Angeles Police Department, 1991 ("Christopher Commission"). Counsel, Special Advisor to the Board of Police Commissions ("Judge Webster Study"). *Member:* Century City, Los Angeles County (Member, Task Force on Worker's Compensation Fraud, 1993) and American (Member, White Collar Crime Committee, 1990—; Co-Chair, Financial Institutions Fraud Subcommittee, 1990-1992) Bar Associations; State Bar of California; District of Columbia Bar.

**RICHARD MARMARO,** born Bronx, New York, February 20, 1951; admitted to bar, 1976, New York, U.S. District Court, Southern District of New York and U.S. Court of Appeals, Second Circuit; 1979, California and U.S. Supreme Court; 1980, U.S. District Court, Central District of California and U.S . Court of Appeals, Ninth Circuit; 1981, U.S. Court of Appeals, Fifth Circuit; 1986, U.S. District Court, Southern District of California; 1990, U.S. Court of Appeals, Eleventh Circuit. *Education:* George Washington University (B.A., with highest honors in History, 1972); New York University (J.D., 1975). Phi Beta Kappa. Executive Editor, Journal of International Law and Politics, New York University Law School, 1974-1975. Law Clerk to Hon, I.B. Cooper, Southern District of New York, 1975-1977. Author: "Domestic Criminal Proceedings Against Product Counterfeiting," Product Counterfeiting: Remedies, P.L.I., 1984; "The Criminal Law and Technology Protection: Prosecuting a Dishonest Employee," The Computer Lawyer, Vol. 2, No. 12, December, 1985; "Protecting the Results of Internal Corporate Investigations," White-Collar Crime Reporter, Vol. 1, No. 4, July, 1987. Co-Author: "The Procedural Rights of Third Parties in RICO's Post-Forfeiture Third-Party Ancillary Hearing," White-Collar Crime Reporter, Vol. 3, No. 10, November-December, 1989; "Government Procurement Fraud: The Ever-Expanding Scope of Liability and Methods of Damage Control," Corporate Criminal Liability-Representing Corporations, CEOs, Corporate Officers and the Impact of Sentencing Guidelines, P.L.I., 1991; "Contract Fraud: Minimizing Corporate Damage," Defense Contract Litigation Reporter, Vol. 5, No. 9, May, 1992. Adjunct Professor of Law, Southwestern Law School, 1981-1984. Faculty Member: Attorney General's Advocacy Institute, U.S. Department of Justice, Washington, D.C., 1981-1984; P.L.I. Product Counterfeiting Program, 1984. P.L.I. Corporate Criminal Liability Program, 1991. Assistant U.S. Attorney, Criminal Division, 1980-1984 and Assistant Chief, Criminal Division, 1984, Cen-

*(This Listing Continued)*

## McCAMBRIDGE, DEIXLER & MARMARO, Los Angeles—Continued

tral District of California. Member, Board of Editors, Business Crimes Bulletin: Compliance and Litigation. *Member:* Century City, Los Angeles County, Federal and American Bar Associations; State Bar of California; Association of Business Trial Lawyers.

**LARY A. RAPPAPORT,** born Los Angeles, California, August 20, 1954; admitted to bar, 1979, California; 1981, U.S. Court of Appeals, Ninth Circuit; 1996, U.S. Supreme Court. *Education:* University of California at Los Angeles (A.B., magna cum laude, 1976); University of California at Davis (J.D., 1979). Order of the Coif. Judge Pro Tempore, Los Angeles Municipal Court, 1985—. Member, Board of Directors, University of California at Davis Law Alumni Association, 1983-1986. *Member:* Century City, Los Angeles County, and American (Member, Litigation Section) Bar Associations; State Bar of California; Association of Business Trial Lawyers.

**MICHAEL A. FIRESTEIN,** born Los Angeles, California, August 8, 1958; admitted to bar, 1983, California. *Education:* Brown University (A.B., 1980); Northwestern University (J.D., 1983). Development Editor, Northwestern Journal of International Law and Business, 1982-1983. *Member:* Century City, Los Angeles County and American Bar Associations; State Bar of California; Association of Business Trial Lawyers.

**LARRY S. GREENFIELD,** born New Brunswick, New Jersey, July 11, 1950; admitted to bar, 1975, New Jersey; 1976, New York; 1977, U.S. District Court, Southern and Eastern Districts of New York; 1980, California, U.S. District Court, Central District of California and U.S. Court of Appeals, Ninth Circuit; 1986, U.S. District Court, Southern, Eastern and Northern Districts of California; 1987, U.S. Supreme Court; 1991, U.S. District Court, Western District of New York and U.S. Court of Appeals, Second Circuit. *Education:* Cornell University (A.B., 1972); New York University (J.D., 1975). Law Clerk to Hon. Lawrence Bilder, Judge, Superior Court of New Jersey, Hudson County, Civil Law Division, 1975-1976. Judge Pro Temore, Los Angeles Municipal Court, 1984—. Moot Court Judge, N.Y.U. School of Law and U.C.L.A. Law School. *Member:* Century City, Los Angeles County and American (Member: Section on Litigation; Forum Committee on the Entertainment and Sports Industries, 1983—; Section of Intellectual Property Law) Bar Associations; State Bar of California (Member, Section on Litigation).

### ASSOCIATES

**JOHN W. CRUMPACKER,** born Woodland, California, May 22, 1957; admitted to bar, 1983, Colorado; 1990, California; 1991, Oregon. *Education:* University of Colorado (B.A., 1979); Lewis and Clark (J.D., with honors in Environmental Law, 1983). Assistant District Attorney, State of Colorado, 1983-1987. *Member:* Century City, Los Angeles County and Colorado Bar Associations; Oregon State Bar; State Bar of California (Member, Criminal and Litigation Sections); Association of Business Trial Lawyers.

**MELISSA L. BURNS,** born Honolulu, Hawaii, June 8, 1966; admitted to bar, 1992, California. *Education:* Smith College (B.A., cum laude, 1988); University of California at Los Angeles (J.D., 1992). Senior Staff, Environmental Law Journal, 1987-1988. *Member:* State Bar of California.

**HAYES F. MICHEL,** born Lafayette, Louisiana, January 25, 1963; admitted to bar, 1988, California. *Education:* Northwestern University (B.S., 1985); University of California at Los Angeles (J.D., 1988). Law Clerk, Hon., Earl E. Vernon, Western District of Louisiana. *Member:* Century City, Los Angeles County and American Bar Associations; State Bar of California; Association of Business Trial Lawyers.

**NATASHA A. KOTTO,** born Bronx, New York, March 23, 1965; admitted to bar, 1992, California and U.S. District Court, Central, Eastern Nort hern and Southern Districts of California. *Education:* Dartmouth College; University of Washington (B.A., 1988); Georgetown University (J.D., 1992). Member, George Washington American Inn of Court. *Member:* Beverly Hills, Century City, Los Angeles County and American Bar Associations; State Bar of California.

**MICHAEL H. WEISS,** born San Jose, California, November 5, 1956; admitted to bar, 1983, California. *Education:* University of California at Berkeley (A.B., 1979); Boalt Hall School of Law, University of California (J.D., 1983). Recipient: American Jurisprudence Award in Civil Procedure. *Member:* Los Angeles County Bar Association; State Bar of California.

**BRYAN C. ALTMAN,** born Los Angeles, California, August 9, 1960; admitted to bar, 1986, California and U.S. District Court, Central District of California. *Education:* University of California at Berkeley (A.B., with highest honors, 1982); Columbia University (J.D., 1985). Phi Beta Kappa. Member, Columbia Human Rights Law Review, 1983-1985. *Member:* State Bar of California (Member, Criminal Section).

**CAMERON J. TALLEY,** born Los Angeles, California, August 12, 1959; admitted to bar, 1993, California. *Education:* University of California, San Diego (B.A., magna cum laude, 1990); University of California at Berkeley, Boalt Hall School of Law (J.D., 1993). Author: "In Favor of Capital Punishment: A Rebuttal of Abolitionist Arguments," Western State Law Review, Fullerton, California, 1996. Orange County Deputy District Attorney, 1994-1996.

**DAVID J. BECKER,** born Washington, D.C., October 2, 1966; admitted to bar, 1994, California, U.S. District Court, Central, Northern, Southern and Eastern Districts of California and U.S. Court of Appeals, Ninth Circuit. *Education:* University of California, Berkeley (B.A., 1991); University of California, Boalt Hall School of Law (J.D., 1994). Recipient, American Jurisprudence Awards in Contracts, Property, Writing and Supreme Court Seminar. *Member:* Los Angeles County Bar Association; State Bar of California. **LANGUAGES:** French.

### OF COUNSEL

**JONATHAN E. RICH,** born Brooklyn, New York, December 22, 1954; admitted to bar, 1980, New York and U.S. District Court, Southern and Eastern Districts of New York; 1985, Pennsylvania; 1989, U.S. District Court, Eastern District of Pennsylvania; 1991, U.S. Court of Appeals, Third Circuit; 1997, California. *Education:* Hobart College (B.A., cum laude, 1976), Phi Beta Kappa; Pi Gamma Mu; University of Chicago (J.D., 1979). Member, Criminal Defense Division, The Legal Aid Society of New York, 1981-1986. (Also Member Cordes, King & Rich, Newtown, PA).

REPRESENTATIVE CLIENTS: American Honda Motor Co., Bear, Stearns & Co., Inc.; City of Simi Valley; DIC Animation City, Inc.; Elektra Entertainment, Inc.; Fidelity Investments; Fleet National Bank; Hughes Aircraft Co.; Jane Fonda Health & Fitness, Inc.; Lockheed Corp.; Medaphis Corp.; Mercantile National Bank; Metro Commerce Bank, N.A.; Merrill Lynch; R & B Realty Group; Revlon, Inc.; State Compensation Insurance Fund; St. Louis Rams; Teledyne Electronics; TI United States Limited; WEA Latina; USA Network; Viacom Inc.; Zenith Insurance Co.

---

## McCASHIN & ASSOCIATES
### A PROFESSIONAL CORPORATION
Established in 1981

**12400 WILSHIRE BOULEVARD, SUITE 450**
**LOS ANGELES, CALIFORNIA 90025-1061**
Telephone: 310-207-0266
Fax: 310-207-8767

*Products Liability, Insurance Defense, Construction, Business, Real Estate, and Professional Malpractice Litigation, Motor Sports Law and Litigation.*

**JAMES P. MCCASHIN, II,** born Norwalk, Connecticut, July 7, 1943; admitted to bar, 1975, California and U.S. District Court, Central, Southern and Northern Districts of California; 1980, U.S. Supreme Court; 1989, U.S. Court of Appeals, Ninth Circuit. *Education:* Amherst College (B.A., 1965); California Western School of Law (J.D., 1975). Phi Delta Phi. Associate Editor, International Law Journal, 1974-1975. Judge Pro Tem, Municipal Court of the Los Angeles Judicial District, 1980—. Faculty Member, Practicing Law Institute and New York Law Journal, Seminars/Press, 1977-1981. *Member:* American Bar Association (Member, Litigation Section); State Bar of California; Product Liability Advisory Council; Association of Southern California Defense Counsel; National Order of Barristers.

---

## McCLAUGHERTY & ASSOCIATES
### LOS ANGELES, CALIFORNIA
(See Pasadena)

*Insurance Defense, General Civil Trial in all State and Federal Court.*

# McCLINTOCK, WESTON, BENSHOOF, ROCHEFORT, RUBALCAVA & MacCUISH LLP

**444 SOUTH FLOWER STREET, 43RD FLOOR**
**LOS ANGELES, CALIFORNIA 90071**
Telephone: 213-623-2322
FAX: 213-623-0824

*General Civil and Environmental Litigation and Environmental Law, including the Regulation of Air and Water Quality, Hazardous and Solid Waste, Land Use and California Environmental Quality Act/National Environmental Policy Act, Oil and Gas, Contracts, Construction, Labor, Products Liability, Toxic Torts, Real Estate, Banking and Insurance Disputes.*

*FIRM PROFILE: McClintock, Weston, Benshoof, Rochefort, Rubalcava & MacCuish law firm was formed in 1984 by five partners of a major Los Angeles law firm and is today a growing firm of more than 50 attorneys engaged in a broad-based litigation and environmental practice. Their client base includes many Fortune 500 companies as well as new growth industries and entrepreneurs engaged in a wide variety of businesses. The firm's clients are engaged in such diverse industries as energy, oil and gas, steel, solid waste management, aerospace and automotive manufacturing. They also represent clients involved in the manufacturing of consumer products and pharmaceuticals, the development of new technologies, the entertainment industry, real estate, construction and banking.*

**GREGORY R. McCLINTOCK,** born Glendale, California, August 8, 1943; admitted to bar, 1969, California; 1972, U.S. Supreme Court. *Education:* Loma Linda University (B.A., 1965); University of Southern California (J.D., 1968). Member, Southern California Law Review, 1967-1968. Member, Attorney General's Honor Law Graduate Program, 1968-1972. Assistant to Director of Operations, Antitrust Division, United States Department of Justice, 1970-1972. Chairman, Institute for Business Law's Annual Conference on Calif. Environmental Regulation, 1978-1994. General Counsel, Western States Petroleum Association, 1992—. *Member:* Los Angeles County and American (Vice Chairman, Air Quality Committee, Natural Resources Section, 1987—) Bar Associations; State Bar of California. *PRACTICE AREAS:* Environmental Law; Hazardous Waste Law; Superfund; Antitrust Law; Trade Regulation Law. *Email:* gmcclintock.mw@mcimail.com

**STEVEN W. WESTON,** born Oakland, California, May 31, 1946; admitted to bar, 1972, California; 1979, U.S. Supreme Court. *Education:* University of California, Berkeley (B.A., 1968); Boalt Hall School of Law, University of California (J.D., 1971). Member of Faculty: College of Advocacy, Center for Trial and Appellate Advocacy, Hastings College of the Law, University of California, 1984-1990. *Member:* Los Angeles County and American Bar Associations; State Bar of California. *PRACTICE AREAS:* Land Use; Environmental Litigation; Commercial Litigation; Trials and Appeals; California Environmental Quality Act (CEQA); National Environmental Policy Act (NEPA). *Email:* sweston.mw@mcimail.com

**WARD L. BENSHOOF,** born Detroit Lakes, Minnesota, May 13, 1946; admitted to bar, 1973, California. *Education:* Macalester College (B.A., 1968); New York University (J.D., 1972). Root Tilden Scholar. Note and Comment Editor, New York University Law Review, 1971-1972. *Member:* Los Angeles County Bar Association; State Bar of California. *REPORTED CASES:* Cose v. Getty Oil Co., 4 F.3d 700 (9th Cir. 1993); Ascon Properties, Inc. v. Mobil Oil Co., 866 F 2d 1149 (9th Cir. 1989); Abujdeh v. Mobil, 841 F. 2d 310 (9th Cir. 1988); Davis v. Gulf Oil, 572 F. Supp. 1393 (D.C. Calif. 1983); People v. Mobil Oil Corp., 143 Cal. App.3d 261, 192 Cal. Rptr. 155 (1983); California Federal v. Superior Court, 189 Cal. App. 3d 267, 239 Cal. Rptr. 413 (1987). *PRACTICE AREAS:* Environmental/Superfund Litigation; Business Litigation; Petroleum Marketing; Trade Regulation; Unlawful Termination. *Email:* wbenshoof.mw@mcimail.com

**JOHN M. ROCHEFORT,** born Olney, Maryland, September 4, 1947; admitted to bar, 1973, California. *Education:* University of Southern California (A.B., 1969); Hastings College of Law, University of California (J.D., 1972). Order of the Coif. *Member:* Los Angeles County and American Bar Associations; State Bar of California. *PRACTICE AREAS:* Business and Commercial Litigation; Antitrust and Franchise Law; Construction Law; Environmental Litigation; Toxic Tort; Products Liability. *Email:* mrochefort.mw@mcimail.com

**SHARON F. RUBALCAVA,** born Los Angeles, California, November 16, 1946; admitted to bar, 1975, California. *Education:* University of California, Los Angeles (B.A., 1968; J.D., 1975). Law Clerk to Francis C. Whelan, U.S. District Court, 1975-1976. *Member:* Los Angeles County and American (Vice Chairman, Air Quality Committee, Natural Resources Section) Bar Associations; State Bar of California. *PRACTICE AREAS:* Environmental Law; Air Pollution; Water Quality; Administrative Law; CEQA. *Email:* srubalcava.mw@mcimail.com

**DAVID S. MACCUISH,** born Abington, Pennsylvania, July 12, 1947; admitted to bar, 1972, California. *Education:* Stanford University (A.B., 1969); University of Pennsylvania (J.D., 1972). Associate Editor, 1970-1971 and Comment Editor, 1971-1972, University of Pennsylvania Law Review. Law Clerk to William P. Gray, U.S. District Court, 1972-1973. *Member:* Los Angeles County Bar Association; State Bar of California; Association of Business Trial Lawyers. *PRACTICE AREAS:* Commercial Litigation; Oil and Gas Law; Trade Regulation; Environmental Litigation. *Email:* dmacuish.mw@mcimail.com

**JONATHAN M. GORDON,** born Boston, Massachusetts, June 11, 1952; admitted to bar, 1978, California. *Education:* Claremont McKenna College (B.A., 1974); Northwestern University (J.D., 1978). Member: Los Angeles County Superior Court; Court-ordered Mediation panel; CPR Institute for Dispute Resolution; Center for Public Resources' Legal Program for ADR. ADR Specialty: Mediator. *Member:* Los Angeles County and American Bar Associations; State Bar of California. *REPORTED CASES:* Savers Federal Savings & Loan Assoc. v. Home Federal Savings & Loan Assoc., 721 F. Supp. 940 (W.D. Tenn. 1989); Resolution Trust Corporation v. State of California, 1944 WL 172267 (C.D.CAL.). *PRACTICE AREAS:* Business Litigation and Dispute Resolution; Mediation/Arbitration; Intellectual Property; Entertainment Disputes; Employment Law/Confidential Investigations; Insolvent Financial Institutions; Medical Practice Disputes. *Email:* jgordon.mw@mcimail.com

**VERNON T. MEADOR, III,** born Norwood, Massachusetts, November 24, 1953; admitted to bar, 1978, California. *Education:* University of California, Los Angeles (B.A., 1975; J.D., 1978). *Member:* Los Angeles County (Member, Environmental Law Section) and American (Member, Litigation and Torts and Insurance Sections) Bar Associations; State Bar of California; Maritime Law Association of the United States. *PRACTICE AREAS:* Environmental Litigation; Toxic Torts; Insurance; Product Liability. *Email:* tmeador.mw@mcimail.com

**SAMUEL C. TAYLOR,** born Fukuoka, Japan, September 15, 1952; admitted to bar, 1979, California. *Education:* Stanford University (B.A., 1975); Harvard University (J.D., 1978). *Member:* Los Angeles County (Litigation Section), Federal and American (Sections on: Litigation, Tort and Insurance Practice) Bar Associations; State Bar of California. *PRACTICE AREAS:* Environmental Litigation; Product Law; Toxic Torts; Business Litigation; Construction Law; Trials and Appeals. *Email:* staylor.mw@mcimail.com

**JOHN P. ZAIMES,** born Boston, Massachusetts, June 14, 1949; admitted to bar, 1980, California; 1985, U.S. Supreme Court. *Education:* University of California, Los Angeles (A.B., cum laude, 1971); Northwestern University (M.A.T., 1973); Georgetown University (J.D., 1979). *Member:* State Bar of California (Member, Labor and Employment Law Section). *LANGUAGES:* Spanish. *SPECIAL AGENCIES:* Cal/OSHA Appeals Board; Cal/OSHA Standards Board. *REPORTED CASES:* Meghrig v. KFC Western, Inc., 1996 U.S. Lexis 1955; 1996 Westlaw 117012; KFC Western, Inc. v. Meghrig, 49F3d5186 (9th Cir. 1995); Cory v. Western Oil & Gas Assn., 471 U.S. 81, 105 S.Ct. 1859 (1985); Western Oil & Gas Assn. v. Cory, 726 F. 2d 1340 (9th Cir. 1984); KFC Western, Inc. v. Meghrig, 23 Cal. App. 4th 1167, 28 Cal. Rptr. 676 (1994). *PRACTICE AREAS:* Environmental Litigation; Labor and Employment Counseling and Litigation; Oil and Gas Litigation; Business Litigation; Trials and Appeals. *Email:* jzaimes.mw@mcimail.com

**GEORGE C. ROUX,** born Teaneck, New Jersey, June 2, 1955; admitted to bar, 1981, California. *Education:* University of California, Berkeley (B.A., 1977); University of Virginia (J.D., 1981). *Member:* Los Angeles County Bar Association; State Bar of California. *PRACTICE AREAS:* Hazardous Waste and Environmental Litigation; Construction Litigation; Business Litigation; Trials and Appeals. *Email:* croux.mw@mcimail.com

**LOUIS A. KARASIK,** born Los Angeles, California, August 16, 1956; admitted to bar, 1981, California. *Education:* University of California, Los Angeles (B.A., magna cum laude, 1978); Stanford University (J.D., 1981). Phi Beta Kappa. Law Clerk to the Honorable Frank K. Richardson, California Supreme Court, 1980-1981. *Member:* Los Angeles County and American Bar Associations; State Bar of California. *LANGUAGES:* Spanish. *SPECIAL AGENCIES:* Cal-OSHA Appeals Board. *REPORTED CASES:* Ohandjanian v. Mobil Oil Corp., 1984 Bus. Franchise Rep. (CCH) §8249 (C.D. Cal. 1984). *PRACTICE AREAS:* Labor & Employment; Liti-

*(This Listing Continued)*

**McCLINTOCK, WESTON, BENSHOOF, ROCHEFORT, RUBALCAVA & MacCUISH LLP, Los Angeles—** *Continued*

gation and Trial; Alternative Dispute Resolution; Business Litigation; Environmental Litigation. *Email:* lkarasik.mw@mcimail.com

**KURT V. OSENBAUGH,** born Palo Alto, California, February 11, 1957; admitted to bar, 1982, California. *Education:* Stanford University (B.A., 1979); University of California, Los Angeles (J.D., 1982). Order of the Coif. *Member:* Los Angeles County Bar Association; State Bar of California. *PRACTICE AREAS:* Business Litigation; Environmental Litigation; Employment Litigation. *Email:* kosenbaugh.mw@mcimail.com

**JOCELYN NIEBUR THOMPSON,** born California, September 7, 1956; admitted to bar, 1982, California. *Education:* University of California at Santa Barbara (B.A., magna cum laude, 1978); University of California School of Law at Los Angeles (J.D., 1982). *Member:* Los Angeles County and American (Member, Natural Resources Law Section; Vice-Chair, Water and Wetlands Committee) Bar Associations; State Bar of California. *LANGUAGES:* Spanish. *PRACTICE AREAS:* Environmental Law; Air Quality; Water Quality; California Environmental Quality Act (CEQA); Proposition 65. *Email:* jocelynt.mw@mcimail.com

**MALCOLM C. WEISS,** born Richmond, Virginia, August 9, 1956; admitted to bar, 1983, California. *Education:* University of California at Santa Barbara (B.A., with honors, 1979); Northwestern University School of Law, Lewis and Clark College (J.D., honors certificate in Environmental and Natural Resources Law, 1982). Phi Alpha Delta. Member: Steering Committee, Environmental Auditing Forum. *Member:* Los Angeles County (Member, Executive Committee and Vice-Chair, Environmental Law Section) and American (Member, Natural Resources Law Section) Bar Associations; State Bar of California; Air and Waste Management Association. *SPECIAL AGENCIES:* South Coast Air Quality Management District; Department of Toxic Substances Control; California Regional Water Quality Control Board; U.S. EPA; Cal-EPA. *PRACTICE AREAS:* Environmental Law; Air Quality Issues; Environmental Due Diligence; Environmental Auditing; Lease Disputes; Facility Siting and Closure; Emissions Trading; Environmental Policy. *Email:* mweiss.mw@mcimail.com

**THOMAS J.P. MCHENRY,** born New York, N.Y., April 22, 1955; admitted to bar, 1985, New York; 1987, California. *Education:* Yale University (B.A., 1977; M.F.S., 1980); New York University (J.D., 1983). Journal of International Law and Politics; Research Fellow, National Park Dept., Taiwan, R.O.C., 1984. Law Clerk, Honorable Lawrence K. Karlton, Chief Judge, U.S. District Court, Eastern District of California, 1985-1986. Legislative Consultant, Food and Agriculture Organization, Rome, Italy, 1986-1987. Special Counsel, Northrop Corporation, 1990. President, Hazardous Waste Association of California, 1991-1994. Adjunct Professor of Environmental Law, Claremont McKenna College, 1992—. Vice Chairman, International, ABA Section on Energy and Environmental Law, 1993—. *Member:* Los Angeles County and American Bar Associations; State Bar of California. *LANGUAGES:* French. *SPECIAL AGENCIES:* California Environmental Protection Agency; Regional Water Quality Control Boards; State Department of Toxic Substances Control; South Coast Air Quality Management District. *PRACTICE AREAS:* Environmental Law; Air Quality; Hazardous Waste; Forestry; International Natural Resources. *Email:* tmchenry.mw@mcimail.com

**MICHAEL D. YOUNG,** born February 12, 1960; admitted to bar, 1985, California. *Education:* University of California, Santa Barbara (B.A., with high honors, 1981); University of Southern California (J.D., 1985). Member, Major Tax Planning Journal and Computer Law Journal, 1984-1985. President, Student Bar Association, 1984-1985. Member Board of Directors, 1985-1993, Vice President, 1990-1991 and President, 1991-1992, Legion Lex. Trained Professional Mediator. Superior Court Mediator. Municipal Court Judge Pro Tem. *Member:* Los Angeles County and American Bar Associations; State Bar of California. *REPORTED CASES:* United States v. Rogers, 769 F 2d 1418 (9th Cir. 1985); Cose v. Getty Oil Co., 4 F.3d 700 (9th Cir. 1993). *PRACTICE AREAS:* Environmental Litigation; Commercial and General Business Litigation; Employment Litigation; Mediation; ADR. *Email:* myoung.mw@mcimail.com

**STEVEN J. VINING,** born Springfield, Massachusetts, 1957; admitted to bar, 1985, California. *Education:* University of Massachusetts (B.A., 1980); University of Southern California (J.D., 1985). Los Angeles County Municipal Court Judge Pro Tem. *Member:* Los Angeles County Bar Association; State Bar of California. *PRACTICE AREAS:* Land Use Counseling and Litigation; CEQA and NEPA Counseling and Litigation; Hazardous Waste Litigation; General Business Litigation. *Email:* svining.mw@mcimail.com

**THOMAS L. VAN WYNGARDEN,** born Los Angeles, California, March 16, 1962; admitted to bar, 1987, California. *Education:* University of California at Los Angeles (B.A., 1984); Hastings College of the Law, University of California (J.D., 1987). David E. Snodgrass Moot Court Award. Technical Editor, Hastings Journal of Communications and Entertainment Law. *Member:* Los Angeles County and American Bar Associations; State Bar of California (Member, Litigation Section); Civil Trial Lawyers Association. *PRACTICE AREAS:* Environmental and Commercial Litigation; Toxic Torts; Environmental Insurance Coverage Litigation. *Email:* twyngarden.mw@mcimail

**ELAINE M. LEMKE,** born Lima, Ohio, October 4, 1958; admitted to bar, 1987, California. *Education:* Drake University (B.A., magna cum laude, 1980); Northwestern University (J.D., 1987). *Member:* State Bar of California; American Bar Association. *PRACTICE AREAS:* Business Litigation; Environmental Litigation. *Email:* elemke.mw@mcimail.com

**EDWARD J. CASEY,** born Rockville Center, New York, May 7, 1960; admitted to bar, 1985, California. *Education:* Hofstra University (B.A., magna cum laude, 1982) Phi Beta Kappa; University of Chicago (J.D., cum laude, 1985). Associate Editor, University of Chicago Law Review, 1984-1985. *Member:* Los Angeles County Bar Association (Member, Environmental Litigation Section); State Bar of California; Los Angeles Headquarters Association (Member, Board of Directors and Chair, Environmental Committee). *PRACTICE AREAS:* Hazardous Waste; Environmental Litigation; CEQA Litigation. *Email:* ecasey.mw@mcimail.com

**GERALD E. GOSCH,** born Omaha, Nebraska, June 30, 1953; admitted to bar, 1983, Nebraska and U.S. District Court, District of Nebraska; 1984, U.S. Court of Appeals, Eighth Circuit; 1986, U.S. Claims Court; 1987, U.S. Court of Appeals for the Federal Circuit; 1988, Minnesota and U.S. District Court, District of Minnesota; 1995, California and U.S. District Court, Central District of California. *Education:* University of Nebraska (B.A., 1975; M.A., 1978; J.D., 1982). *Member:* Nebraska State and American (Member: Litigation Section, Forum on the Construction Industry; Tort and Insurance Practice Section, Fidelity and Surety Law Committee) Bar Associations; State Bar of California. *PRACTICE AREAS:* Construction and Surety Law; Federal Government - Contract Law. *Email:* ggosch.mw@mcimail.com

**BARBARA BILES,** born Long Beach, California, September 24, 1954; admitted to bar, 1980, California and U.S. District Court, Central and Southern Districts of California. *Education:* University of California at Davis (B.A., with highest honors, 1977); University of California at Los Angeles (J.D., 1980). Order of the Coif; Phi Beta Kappa; Pi Kappa Phi. *Member:* Los Angeles County Bar Association (Member, Environmental Law Section); State Bar of California (Member, Sections on: Environmental Law; Real Property Law). *LANGUAGES:* Spanish. *PRACTICE AREAS:* Real Estate Law; Environmental Law. *Email:* bbiles.mw@mcimail.com

**EDWARD P. MANNING,** born Yonkers, New York, May 22, 1960; admitted to bar, 1985, California. *Education:* Rider College (B.A., magna cum laude, 1982); Loyola Law School (J.D., 1985). Author: "Primary Election," L.A. Daily Journal, June 23, 1995; "Water Fight," L.A. Daily Journal, Oct. 26, 1995; "Deterrence and Financial Incentives Vital to Cleanup of Toxic Wastes," L.A. Daily Journal, February 27, 1986. General Counsel, Lieutenant Governor Leo McCarthy, 1989-1992. Alternate Member, State Lands Commission, 1989-1992. Deputy City Attorney, Santa Monica City Attorney's Office, 1987-1989. Deputy District Attorney, Los Angeles County District Attorney's Office, 1986-1987. Co-Chair, Mono Lake Committee and Appointed Member, Los Angeles Environmental Affairs Commission, Lopez Canyon Landfill Task Force, Mayor's Blue Ribbon Commission on Water Rates. Co-Chair, L.A. Headquarters Association, Environmental Section. *Member:* Los Angeles County Bar Association; State Bar of California (Member, Environmental Section). *PRACTICE AREAS:* Environmental Compliance; Legislative and Regulatory Advocacy; Environmental Litigation; Environmental Criminal Defense. *Email:* emanning.mw@mcimail.com

**ROBERT I. MCMURRY,** born Sterling, Illinois, August 5, 1947; admitted to bar, 1982, California; 1983, Illinois; 1988, Nebraska. *Education:* University of Denver (B.S., 1970); Illinois State University (M.S., 1971); University of California School of Law (J.D., 1982). Order of the Coif. Managing Editor, University of California at Los Angeles Law Review, 1981-1982. Law Professor, Loyola Law School, 1984-1990. *Member:* State Bar of California; Nebraska State Bar Association. *Email:* rmcmurry.mw@mcimail.com

*(This Listing Continued)*

**ANDREW M. GILFORD,** born Los Angeles, California, May 13, 1963; admitted to bar, 1989, California. *Education:* University of California at Los Angeles (B.A., cum laude, 1986; J.D., 1989). *Member:* State Bar of California. *PRACTICE AREAS:* Civil Appellate Practice; Environmental Litigation; Commercial and General Business Litigation. *Email:* agilford.mw@mcimail.com

## ASSOCIATES

**ELIOT L. TEITELBAUM,** born Pasadena, California, December 10, 1961; admitted to bar, 1987, Connecticut and New York; 1989, U.S. District Court, Southern District of New York; 1991, U.S. District Court, Eastern District of New York; 1993, California and U.S. District Court, Central District of California; 1994, U.S. District Court, Eastern District of California. *Education:* Clark University (B.A., cum laude with high honors in History, 1983); George Washington University National Law Center (J.D., 1986). *Member:* The Association of the Bar of the City of New York; Los Angeles County and American (Member, ABA Forum Construction Industry) Bar Associations. *PRACTICE AREAS:* Construction and Environmental Litigation; General Business and Commercial Litigation. *Email:* eteitelbaum.mw@mcimail

**H. ELLIOTT HEIDE,** born Whittier, California, October 15, 1961; admitted to bar, 1989, California. *Education:* University of Texas (B.S., 1984); Loyola Marymount University (J.D., 1989). Instructor, Environmental Laws, Regulatory Framework, UCLA Extension, 1991-1994. *Member:* Los Angeles County (Member, Environmental Section; Past Chair, Legislative Review Committee; Air Quality Committee; Member, Executive Committee) and American (Member, Natural Resources, Energy and Environmental Law Section) Bar Associations; State Bar of California. *SPECIAL AGENCIES:* California and United States EPA, California Water Boards, California Air Board and local Air Districts. *PRACTICE AREAS:* Environmental and Corporate Compliance; Environmental Litigation. *Email:* eheide.mw@mcimail.com

**MARTHA SCHREIBER DOTY,** born Morristown, New Jersey, September 20, 1962; admitted to bar, 1989, California. *Education:* University of California at Berkeley (B.A., magna cum laude, 1984); University of California School of Law at Los Angeles (J.D., 1989). Member, UCLA Law Review, 1987-1988. *Member:* Los Angeles County and American Bar Associations; State Bar of California. *PRACTICE AREAS:* Civil Appellate Practice; Business Litigation; Employment Law; Petroleum Marketing/Franchise Litigation. *Email:* mdoty.mw@mcimail.com

**CLIFTON J. MCFARLAND,** born March 21, 1958; admitted to bar, 1989, California; 1993, Ohio. *Education:* Massachusetts Institute of Technology (B.S., 1981); Columbia University School of Law (J.D., 1981). *Member:* State Bar of California; Ohio State and American (Member, Editorial Board of Natural Resources & Environmental) Bar Associations. *PRACTICE AREAS:* Environmental Compliance; Environmental Litigation. *Email:* cmcfarland.mw@mcimail.com

**MARTIN "KELLY" J. MCTIGUE, JR.,** born Milwaukee, Wisconsin, July 23, 1959; admitted to bar, 1990, California and U.S. District Court. *Education:* University of Idaho (B.S., 1981); Southwestern University School of Law (J.D., cum laude, 1990). Note and Comment Editor, Southwestern University Law Review, 1989-1990. Co-Author: California Environmental Law Handbook, Government Institutes, Inc. 4th-6th editions. *Member:* Los Angeles County (Member, Environmental Law Section) and American (Section of Natural Resources, Energy, and Environmental Law) Bar Associations; State Bar of California (Member, Environmental Law Section). *SPECIAL AGENCIES:* U.S. EPA; California Air Resources Board; Cal-EPA Department of Toxic Substances Control; South Coast Air Quality Management District; California Coastal Commission. *PRACTICE AREAS:* Environmental compliance; Air Quality; Hazardous Waste. *Email:* kmctigue.mw@mcimail.com

**JAMES J. HEVENER,** born Greenwich, Connecticut, June 12, 1964; admitted to bar, 1990, California. *Education:* College of William & Mary (B.A., 1986); University of Washington (J.D., 1990). *Member:* State Bar of California. *PRACTICE AREAS:* Commercial and General Business Litigation; Employment Litigation; Environmental Litigation. *Email:* jhevener.mw@mcimail.com

**NICKI MARIE VARYU CARLSEN,** born Chicago, Illinois, June 9, 1961; admitted to bar, 1990, California. *Education:* University of Illinois (B.S., 1983; M.S., 1985); University of Southern California (J.D., 1990). Member, Computer Law and Major Tax Planning Journals, 1988-1989. *Member:* Los Angeles County Bar Association (Member, Real Property Section); State Bar of California (Member, Real Property Law Section).

*(This Listing Continued)*

*PRACTICE AREAS:* Business Litigation; Environmental Litigation; Land Use Litigation. *Email:* ncarlsen.mw@mcimail.com

**LAWRENCE P. BRENNAN, JR.,** born New York, N.Y., February 23, 1964; admitted to bar, 1991, California. *Education:* Brown University (A.B., 1988); University of California at Los Angeles, School of Law (J.D., 1991). Chief Justice, UCLA Moot Court Honors Program, Spring, 1991. Co-Author: Handbook of Appellate Advocacy, 3d Ed. *Member:* State Bar of California. [Captain, Judge Advocate General Corps, U.S. Army Reserve]. *PRACTICE AREAS:* Business Litigation; Real Estate; Environmental Litigation. *Email:* lbrennan.mw@mcimail.com

**EUGENE A. BURRUS,** born Lancaster, California, April 19, 1964; admitted to bar, 1991, California. *Education:* University of Oklahoma (B.S.A.E., with distinction, 1986); University of Virginia (J.D., 1991). Tau Beta Pi; Sigma Gamma Tau. *Member:* State Bar of California (Member, Sections on: Litigation; Antitrust; Air and Space Law Forum). *PRACTICE AREAS:* Commercial and Business Litigation; Franchise Litigation; Antitrust; Environmental Litigation. *Email:* eburrus.mw@mcimail.com

**JOHN D. ARYA,** born La Jolla, California, August 22, 1966; admitted to bar, 1991, California. *Education:* University of California (B.A., summa cum laude, 1988); University of California School of Law (J.D., 1991). Phi Beta Kappa. *Member:* State Bar of California (Member, Litigation Section). *REPORTED CASES:* Stell v. Jay Hayes Development Co., 11 Cal. App. 4th 1214, 15 Cal. Rptr. 2d 220, 1992. *PRACTICE AREAS:* Business Litigation; Franchise Litigation. *Email:* jarya.mw@mcimail.com

**KURT WEISSMULLER,** born Los Angeles, California, April 16, 1958; admitted to bar, 1984, California. *Education:* California State University at Northridge (B.A., 1980); Loyola Law School (J.D., 1984). St. Thomas More Law Honor Society. Contributing Author, Environmental Law Practice Guide, Mathew Bender, 1992. *Member:* State Bar of California (Member, Environmental Law Section). *PRACTICE AREAS:* Environmental Litigation; Environmental Compliance. *Email:* kweissmuller.mw@mcimail.com

**ROBERT M. MAHLOWITZ,** born Boston, Massachusetts, February 24, 1965; admitted to bar, 1992, California; 1993, Massachusetts. *Education:* University of Pennsylvania (B.A., cum laude, 1987); Boston College (J.D., magna cum laude, 1992). Order of the Coif. Member, Boston College Law Review, 1991-1992. Author: Comment, "The End of Political Patronage in Governmental Employment: Rutan v Republican Party of Illinois". *Member:* State Bar of California. *PRACTICE AREAS:* Civil Litigation; Federal Litigation; Franchise Termination; Contract Litigation; Environmental Law; CEQA; Toxic Torts; Underground Storage Tanks. *Email:* bmahlowitz.mw@mcimail.com

**WILLIAM E. BERNER, JR.,** born Dayton, Ohio, May 24, 1967; admitted to bar, 1993, California, U.S. District Court, Central, Northern, Southern and Eastern Districts of California and U.S. Court of Appeals, Ninth Circuit. *Education:* University of Cincinnati (B.S.M.E., 1990); University of Southern California (J.D., 1993). *Member:* State Bar of California. *PRACTICE AREAS:* Commercial Litigation; Environmental Litigation. *Email:* bberner.mw@mcimail.com

**JOON-SOO KIM,** born Los Angeles, California, November 16, 1967; admitted to bar, 1993, California. *Education:* University of California, Berkeley (B.A., 1989); Loyola Law School of Los Angeles (J.D., 1993). Managing Editor, Loyola of Los Angeles Law Review, 1992-1993. *Member:* Los Angeles County Bar Association; State Bar of California; Korean-American Bar Association. *PRACTICE AREAS:* Environmental Compliance and Litigation. *Email:* jskim.mw@mcimail.com

**GIDEON KRACOV,** born New York, N.Y., March 16, 1971; admitted to bar, 1995, California. *Education:* University of California, Berkeley (B.A., with high honors, 1992); University of California, Boalt Hall School of Law (J.D., 1995). Member, Environmental Law Certificate Program. *Member:* State Bar of California. *PRACTICE AREAS:* Environmental Litigation; Toxic Tort Litigation; Employment Litigation. *Email:* gkracov.mw@mcimail.com

**NICOLE RIVAS,** born Los Angeles, California, December 9, 1969; admitted to bar, 1995, California. *Education:* University of Southern California (B.A., 1992; J.D., 1995). *Member:* State Bar of California. *PRACTICE AREAS:* Environmental and General Business Litigation. *Email:* nrivas.mw@mcimail.com

## THOMAS E. McCURNIN
333 SOUTH GRAND AVENUE, 37TH FLOOR
LOS ANGELES, CALIFORNIA 90071
Telephone: 213-626-5800
Fax: 213-626-5868

General Civil Litigation in all State and Federal Courts, Banking and Finance, Bankruptcy, Commercial Law, Real Property.

FIRM PROFILE: Mr. McCurnin has specialized in the representation of financial institutions and leasing companies in the areas of bank operations, defense, collection, litigation, SBA loans, bankruptcy, and real property issues for over 20 years. Mr. McCurnin has served as an expert in the areas of collection and leasing in many contexts, including malpractice suits. Mr. McCurnin has been featured in the publications of Los Angeles Daily Journal, Los Angeles Lawyer, and Equipment Leasing Today. He is a frequent speaker to industry groups regarding issues which affect financial institutions.

**THOMAS E. McCURNIN,** born Cedar Rapids, Iowa, August 16, 1950; admitted to bar, 1976, Iowa; 1977, Wisconsin; 1982, California; U.S. District Court, Northern, Eastern, Southern and Central Districts of California, U.S. Court of Appeals, Ninth Circuit. *Education:* University of Iowa (B.A., 1972); Drake University (J.D., 1975). Member, Moot Court. Author: "A Guide to Marshal's Sales," Los Angeles Lawyer, January, 1990; "Pre-Judgement Writs of Possession-Effective Claim and Delivery of Personal Property," Los Angeles Lawyer, October, 1991; "Current Issues in Real Estate Lines and Title Insurance in California," PESI, 1991; "Don't Lien on Me - Water Liens and Financial Institutions," Los Angeles Lawyer, February, 1995; "Letters of Credit in Leasing Transactions," Equipment Leasing Today, February, 1996; "Letters of Credit and Leasing," The Monitor, March, 1996; "Yours Truly - New Revisions to Letter of Credit Law," Los Angeles Lawyer, May, 1996. Partner, Ross & Ivanjack, 1982-1995. *Member:* State Bar of California; Federal Bar Association; The Association of Trial Lawyers of America; California Bankruptcy Forum; Commercial Law Institute; Los Angeles Financial Lawyers Conference; Equipment Leasing Association; Western Association of Equipment Lessors; Independent Bankers Association; California Bankers Association. **PRACTICE AREAS:** Collections; Bank Operations; Real Estate; Lender Liability; Leasing Litigation; Small Business Loan Litigation; Bankruptcy.

## McCUTCHEN, DOYLE, BROWN & ENERSEN
355 SOUTH GRAND AVENUE
SUITE 4400
LOS ANGELES, CALIFORNIA 90071-1560
Telephone: 213-680-6400
Facsimile: 213-680-6499
Email: postmaster@mdbe.com
URL: http://www.mccutchen.com

*San Francisco, California Office:* Three Embarcadero Center, 94111-4066. Telephone: 415-393-2000. Facsimile: 415-393-2286 (G I, II, III). Telex: 340817 MACPAG SFO.

*San Jose, California Office:* Market Post Tower, Suite 1500, 55 South Market Street, 95113-2327. Telephone: 408-947-8400. Facsimile: 408-947-4750. Telex: 910 250 2931 MACPAG SJ.

*Walnut Creek, California Office:* 1331 North California Boulevard, Post Office Box V, 94596-4502. Telephone: 510-937-8000. Facsimile: 510-975-5390.

*Palo Alto, California Office:* One Embarcadero Place, 2100 Geng Road, 94303-0913. Telephone: 415-846-4000. Fax: 415-846-4086.

*Washington, D.C. Office:* The Evening Star Building, Suite 800, 1101 Pennsylvania Avenue, N.W., 20004-2514. Telephone: 202-628-4900. Facsimile: 202-628-4912.

*Taipei, Taiwan Republic of China Office:* International Trade Building, Tenth Floor, 333 Keelung Road, Section 1, 110. Telephone: 886-2-723-5000. Facsimile: 886-2-757-6070.

*Affiliated Offices In:* Bangkok, Thailand; Beijing, China; Shanghai, China.

General Practice.

FIRM PROFILE: *Commercial litigation and business practice, including complex, securities and environmental litigation; environmental and natural resources; healthcare; intellectual property; biotechnology; antitrust and trade regulation; torts; product liability; insurance; maritime; agribusiness; white-collar crime; appellate; corporate; banking; finance; insolvency; real estate and land use; construction; tax and employee benefits; labor and employment; international trade law; estate planning and trusts; alternative dispute resolution.*

### MEMBERS OF FIRM

**JOSEPH R. AUSTIN,** born Davenport, Iowa, March 25, 1939; admitted to bar, 1965, California. *Education:* Coe College (A.B., 1961); Harvard University (LL.B., 1964). Phi Beta Kappa. Lecturer in Law, University of Nigeria, Nsukka, Nigeria, 1965-1966. Law Clerk to Judge William C. Mathes, U.S. District Court, California, 1964-1965. Trustee, 1974-1975, President, Barristers, Los Angeles County Bar Association, 1974-1975. Trustee, Coe College, 1976-1986. Trustee, Los Angeles County Bar Foundation, 1986—. President, 1996-1997, Chair, Board of Trustees, Lax-The Los Angeles Exhibitions, Inc., 1993—. Trustee, Museum of Contemporary Art, 1988-1996. (Managing Partner). **PRACTICE AREAS:** Business Litigation. *Email:* jaustin@mdbe.com

**COLLEEN P. DOYLE,** born Philadelphia, Pennsylvania, October 8, 1953; admitted to bar, 1985, California. *Education:* University of California at Berkeley (A.B., 1976); University of California at Los Angeles (M.P.H., Environmental Health Sciences, 1979); Loyola University of Los Angeles (J.D., 1985). **PRACTICE AREAS:** Environmental Law. *Email:* cdoyle@mdbe.com

**JAMES J. DRAGNA,** born Los Angeles, California, 1953; admitted to bar, 1979, California. *Education:* University of California at Irvine (B.A., cum laude, 1976); Loyola University of Los Angeles (J.D., 1979). Senior Trial Attorney, U.S. Department of Justice, Land and Natural Resources Division, 1983-1986. Attorney Advisor, U.S. Environmental Protection Agency, 1980-1982. (Also at San Francisco Office). **PRACTICE AREAS:** Environmental Law. *Email:* jdragna@mdbe.com

**DEBRA L. FISCHER,** born Westwood, New Jersey, August 25, 1964; admitted to bar, 1989, California. *Education:* University of California at Davis (A.B., summa cum laude, 1986); Boalt Hall School of Law, University of California (J.D., 1989). Phi Beta Kappa. Managing and Executive Editor, Berkeley Womens' Law Journal. **PRACTICE AREAS:** Employment and General Commercial Litigation. *Email:* dfischer@mdbe.com

**KARLA A. FRANCKEN,** born San Diego, California, January 2, 1967; admitted to bar, 1994, Wisconsin and U.S. District Court, Eastern and Western Districts of Wisconsin; 1995, California and U.S. District Court, Eastern, Northern and Southern Districts of California. *Education:* University of Wisconsin-Madison (B.S., 1988; M.S., 1989); Marquette University (J.D., magna cum laude, 1994). Executive Editor, Marquette Law Review, 1993-1994. Case Reporter, Commercial Law League, Bankruptcy and Insolvency Section, 1994—. Author: Lead-Based Paint Poisoning: Wisconsin Realtors, Residential Property, Sellers and Landlords Beware, 77(3) Marquette Law Review 550 (1994). Law Clerk to Hon. Dale E. Ihlenfeldt, U.S. Bankruptcy Court for the Eastern District of Wisconsin, 1994-1995. *Member:* State Bar of Wisconsin; Marquette University Law School Health Law Society (President, 1992-19930. **PRACTICE AREAS:** Healthcare; Corporate/Business. *Email:* kfrancken@mdbe.com

**WILLIAM H. FREEDMAN,** born June 6, 1957; admitted to bar, 1982, California and U.S. District Court, Northern District of California; 1989, U.S. District Court, Central District of California; 1990, District of Columbia. *Education:* Washington University (B.S., 1979); Emory University (J.D., 1981). Author: "Corporate Strategy in Shaping Environmental Requirements: A Proposition 65 Study Case," Air and Waste Management Association Monograph; "California Does It Again: The Environmental Protection Initiative 1990," Chemical Times & Trends, April, 1990; "Regulating to Reduce Stormwater Pollutants," California Environmental News, April, 1991; "Eco-Nomic Implications for Business: The New United States Clean Air Act," Malente Symposium IX, Federal Republic of Germany, November, 1991; "Reclaim: Be Careful For What You Ask," Air & Waste Management Association Annual Meeting Proceedings, 1993; "Potential Changes In The CERCLA (SuperFund) Legislation That May Affect Multinational Corporation," The Legal Environment, ASD Publishing Limited, Hong Kong, Issue Number One, November, 1994. *Member:* Los Angeles County (Member, Environmental Section, Executive Committee; Newsletter Editor, 1989-1990; Co-Chair, Air Quality Subcommittee, 1990-1991), International Section and American (Member, Natural Resources Law Section; Co-Chair, Environmental Subcommittee, Business Law Section, 1988-1990) Bar Associations; Asian American Bar Association, 1993; Environmental Law Institute; Air and Waste Management Association; American Hospital Association; California-Southeast Asia Business Council, 1992; Southern California Chinese Lawyers' Association, 1993. *Email:* wfreedman@mdbe.com

*(This Listing Continued)*

**MELINDA L. HAYES,** born Minneapolis, Minnesota, February 14, 1960; admitted to bar, 1986, California. *Education:* University of Minnesota (B.S.B., with distinction, 1982); University of California at Los Angeles (M.B.A., 1986; J.D., 1986). Author: "Practical Applications of Stark II to Hospital Operations," Healthcare Financial Management, December 1993, with D. Higgins. *Member:* National Health Lawyers Association; American Academy of Hospital Attorneys; Healthcare Financial Management Association; Catholic Health Association; Health Care Executives of Southern California; Women in Health Administration. **PRACTICE AREAS:** Healthcare. *Email:* mhayes@mdbe.com

**SUSAN L. HOFFMAN,** born Montreal, Canada, October 28, 1948; admitted to bar, 1979, California. *Education:* McGill University, University of California at Los Angeles (B.A., cum laude, 1969); Stanford University (Ph.D., 1974); Yale University (J.D., 1979). Note Editor, Yale Law Journal, 1978-1979. Lecturer, Stanford University, 1973; Lecturer, University of Southern California Law Center, 1980. Director, Mental Health Advocacy Services, 1979-1984. **PRACTICE AREAS:** General Business Litigation; Securities Litigation; Health Care Related Litigation. *Email:* shoffman@mdbe.com

**MICHAEL B. LUBIC,** born November 9, 1960; admitted to bar, 1986, California and U.S. District Court, Central District of California. *Education:* Yale University (B.S., cum laude, 1981; M.A., 1981); University of Chicago (J.D., 1985; M.B.A., 1985). Co-Author: "Bankruptcy and Reorganization," Chapter 24 to *Energy Law And Transactions,* Matthew (1990). Adjunct Lecturer, Golden Gate University, 1993. Los Angeles County Bar Association (Member, Subcommittee on Bankruptcy Law, 1990-1993). **PRACTICE AREAS:** Insolvency; Corporate Finance. *Email:* mlubic@mdbe.com

**JOHN C. MORRISSEY,** born San Francisco, California, April 5, 1958; admitted to bar, 1985, California. *Education:* Yale University (B.A., cum laude, 1980); Pembroke College, Oxford University (M.A., 1982); University of Chicago (J.D., cum laude, 1985). Law Clerk, Honorable Charles L. Brieant, Jr., U.S. District Court, Southern District of New York, 1985-1986. **PRACTICE AREAS:** Commercial Litigation; Intellectual Property Law. *Email:* jmorrissey@mdbe.com

**JAMES FRANKLIN OWENS,** born March 20, 1961; admitted to bar, 1986, Georgia; 1989, California. *Education:* Emory University (B.A., 1983); Stetson University College of Law (J.D., 1986). Teaching Assistant, Legal Research and Writing, Stetson University College of Law, 1984-1985. Notes Editor, Stetson Law Review, 1985-1986. *Member:* Los Angeles County Bar Association (Health Care Section Vice Chair); National Health Lawyers Association; American Association of Hospital Attorneys. **PRACTICE AREAS:** Healthcare Law. *Email:* jfowens@mdbe.com

**RICK R. ROTHMAN,** born Syracuse, New York, April 8, 1963; admitted to bar, 1989, California; 1991, District of Columbia. *Education:* University of Michigan (B.A., 1985); Georgetown University Law Center (J.D., cum laude, 1989). **PRACTICE AREAS:** Environmental. *Email:* rrothman@mdbe.com

**PATRICIA L. SHANKS,** born Salt Lake City, Utah, April 3, 1940; admitted to bar, 1978, California. *Education:* Stanford University (B.A., microbiology, with honors, 1962); University of Colorado (J.D., 1978). Order of the Coif. Stork Scholar. Recipient, West Publishing Award. **PRACTICE AREAS:** Environmental Law. *Email:* pshanks@mdbe.com

## COUNSEL

**KAREN A. CAFFEE,** born Manhasset, New York, May 26, 1958; admitted to bar, 1990, New York; 1992, District of Columbia; 1994, California. *Education:* Colorado College (B.A., cum laude, 1980); London School of Economics (M.Sc., 1981); Georgetown University (J.D., 1989). Author: "Environmental Liabilities: Practical Approaches to Secured Lending," Practicing Law Institute, 591 PLI/Comm 475, December 1991. *Member:* Los Angeles County, New York State (Member, Environmental Section) and American Bar Associations; District of Columbia Bar (Member, Environmental Section); State Bar of California; Constitutional Rights Foundation. **LANGUAGES:** French. **PRACTICE AREAS:** Environmental and Transactional; Environmental and Compliance. *Email:* kcaffee@mdbe.com

**PETER HSIAO,** born Pocatello, Idaho, April 5, 1960; admitted to bar, 1985, California and U.S. District Court, Central District of California; 1987, U.S. Court of Appeals, Eighth Circuit; 1988, U.S. COurt of Appeals, Ninth Circuit; 1989, U.S. District Court, Eastern District of California. *Education:* University of Utah (B.S., Chemical Eng., magna cum laude, 1982); Boalt Hall School of Law, University of California, Berkeley (J.D., 1985). Assistant U.S. Attorney, U.S. Department of Justice, 1990-1994. Judge Pro Tem, Los Angeles County Municipal Court, 1994—. Co-Author: "California Environmental Law Handbook," Government Institute, First Through Third Editions, 1987-1989. Contributing Author: "Environmental Litigation Study Materials," American Law Institute, American Bar Association, 1994. Adjunct Professor of Law, Environmental Law, Southwestern University School of Law, 1995—. Instructor, Clean Air Act Litigation and Enforcement, Office of Legal Education, U.S. Department of Justice, 1991-1994. Lecturer, Environmental Law Enforcement Priorities, U.S. Attorney's Office Environmental Law Enforcement Conference, 1994. Instructor: Environmental Recordkeeping and Reporting, Government Institute, 1987—; Corporations, Honorable Robert M. Takasugi Bar Review, 1991—. *Member:* Los Angeles County and American (Member, Section on: Natural Resources and Environmental Law; Vice Chair, Solid and Hazardous Waste Committee, 1996—; Marine Resources Committee) Bar Associations; State Bar of California (Member, Executive Committee, Environmental Law Section, 1996—; Member, Legal Services Section, 1986-1995, Chair, 1992-1993; Vice Chair, 1991-1992, Standing Committee on Legal Services to The Poor); American Institute of Chemical Engineers. **REPORTED CASES:** Gerritsen v. Consulado General De Mexico, 989 F. 2d 340 (9th Cir. Cal.) Mar. 30, 1993) (NO. 82-55226); Animal Lovers Volunteer Ass'n. Inc. v. Cheney, 795 F. Supp. 994 (C.D. Cal., Apr. 07, 1992) (No. CV 86-4992-RJK); Animal Lovers Volunteer Ass'n. Inc. v. Cheney, 795. Supp. 991 (C.D. Cal., Feb. 10, 1992); (NO. CV 86-4992-RJK); U.S. v. Montrose Chemical Corp. of California, 788 F. Supp. 1485, 35 ERC 1089, 22 Envtl. L. Rep. 21,333 (C.D. Cal., Mar. 31, 1992) (NO. CV 90-3122 AAH); U.S. v. Shell Oil Co., 1992 WL 144296, 60 USLW 2528, 34 ERC 1342, 22 Envir. L. Rep. 20, 791 (C.D. CAl., Jan. 16, 1992); U.S. v. Montrose Chemical Corp. of California, 1991 WL 183147, 33 ERC 1207 (C.D.Cal., Mar. 29, 1991( (NO. CV 90-3122 AAH JRX). **PRACTICE AREAS:** Environmental Litigation; NEPA/CEQA/Land-Use Planning. *Email:* phsiao@mdbe.com

**DIANA PFEFFER MARTIN,** born Chicago, Illinois, October 14, 1959; admitted to bar, 1990, California. *Education:* University of Wisconsin, Madison (B.S., 1982); University of San Diego (J.D., cum laude, 1990). **PRACTICE AREAS:** Environmental Regulatory Work. *Email:* dmartin@mdbe.com

**DOUGLAS R. PAINTER,** born Topeka, Kansas, September 27, 1957; admitted to bar, 1988, California. *Education:* University of Maryland at College Park (B.S., cum laude, 1984); University of California at Davis (J.D., 1987). Best Oral Advocate, Spring, 1986. First Place Winner, Neumiller Moot Court Competition, 1986. Editor, University of California Davis Law Review, 1986-1987. Clerk, Chief Judge Lawrence Luoma, U.S. Department of Interior, 1985. Author: 1996 C.E.B. Action Guide, "Meeting Statutory Deadlines, Antitrust.". **LANGUAGES:** Spanish. **PRACTICE AREAS:** Litigation. *Email:* dpainter@mdbe.com

**CLAYTON J. VREELAND,** born Tucson, Arizona, March 22, 1955; admitted to bar, 1983, California. *Education:* University of Southern California (B.S., magna cum laude, 1977); University of California, Los Angeles (J.D., 1983). Comment Editor, UCCLA Law Review, 1982-1983. Certified Public Accountant, California, 1980. Member, Tax Section, Exempt Organizations Committee, State Bar of California, 1996—). *Member:* Los Angeles County (Health Care Law Section, Executive Committee, 1995—; Tax Section, Executive Committee, 1995—); Healthcare Financial Management Association. **PRACTICE AREAS:** Healthcare; Tax. *Email:* cvreeland@mdbe.com

## ASSOCIATES

**JEFFREY M. ANDERSON,** born Norfolk, Virginia, October 3, 1964; admitted to bar, 1991, Maryland; 1996, California. *Education:* Colgate University (B.A., 1986); George Mason University University (J.D., 1991). *Member:* National Health Lawyers Association. **PRACTICE AREAS:** Health Care; General Corporate.

**P. SCOTT BURTON,** born San Gabriel, California, April 6, 1966; admitted to bar, 1994, California. *Education:* University of California at Irvine (B.A., magna cum laude, 1989); University of California at Los Angeles School of Law (J.D., 1994). Phi Delta Phi. UCLA Journal of Environmental Law and Policy; Federal Communications Law Journal. **PRACTICE AREAS:** Environmental Law. *Email:* sburton@mdbe.com

**GREG A. CHRISTIANSON,** born Bismarck, North Dakota, September 25, 1966; admitted to bar, 1995, California; 1996, U.S. District Court, Central District of California and U.S. Court of Appeals, Ninth Circuit. *Education:* Princeton University (B.A., 1989); Yale School of Architecture; Stanford University (J.D., 1995). *Member:* Los Angeles County Bar Association (Member, Litigation Section); State Bar of California. **PRACTICE AREAS:** Environmental. *Email:* gchristianson@mdbe.com

*(This Listing Continued)*

## McCUTCHEN, DOYLE, BROWN & ENERSEN, Los Angeles—Continued

**JILL F. COOPER,** born Santa Monica, California, December 10, 1965; admitted to bar, 1991, California. *Education:* Princeton University (B.A., magna cum laude, 1987); University of California at Los Angeles (J.D., 1991). Member: Moot Court Honors Program; Moot Court Executive Board of Judges. Author: "Setting the Scene for Big Green," Agrichemical Age, vol. 34, No. 9 (Oct. 1990). *Email:* jcooper@mdbe.com

**I-FAN CHING GO,** born Iowa City, Iowa, November 6, 1970; admitted to bar, 1995, California and U.S. Court of Appeals, 9th Circuit. *Education:* Stanford University (B.A., with distinction, 1992); University of California School of Law, Los Angeles (J.D., 1995). *LANGUAGES:* Chinese. *PRACTICE AREAS:* Health Care Transactions. *Email:* igo@mdbe.com

**TIFFANY R. HEDGPETH,** born Greenbrae, California, July 8, 1969; admitted to bar, 1994, California. *Education:* University of California, Davis (B.S., with high honors, 1991); University of California School of Law, Los Angeles (J.D., 1994). Managing Editor, UCLA Journal of Environmental Law and Policy, 1992-1994. Member, Moot Court Board, 1993-1994. *Member:* Los Angeles County Bar Association; State Bar of California. *PRACTICE AREAS:* Environmental Counseling and Litigation. *Email:* thedgpeth@mdbe.com

**HEATHER HOECHERL,** born Minneapolis, Minnesota; admitted to bar, 1996, California. *Education:* Macalester College (B.A., 1990); Stanford Law School (J.D., 1996). Phi Beta Kappa. *PRACTICE AREAS:* Environmental. *Email:* hhoecherl@mdbe.com

**ASHER D. ISSACS,** born Binghamton, New York, May 27, 1968; admitted to bar, 1995, California. *Education:* Colgate University (B.A., 1990); University of California at Los Angeles (J.D., 1995). Articles Editor, University of California at Los Angeles Law Review. *PRACTICE AREAS:* Business Litigation. *Email:* aissacs@mdbe.com

**MICAH R. JACOBS,** born Dublin, Ireland, July 22, 1964; admitted to bar, 1994, California. *Education:* University of California, Los Angeles (B.A., 1991); Boalt Hall School of Law, University of California (J.D., 1994). *PRACTICE AREAS:* General and Commercial Litigation. *Email:* mjacobs@mdbe.com

**JERILYN LÓPEZ MENDOZA,** born Montebello, California, August 16, 1968; admitted to bar, 1996, California. *Education:* Stanford University (A.B., with departmental honors, 1990); University of California, Los Angeles (J.D., 1996). Editor-in-Chief, Chicano-Latino Law Review, 1995-1996. Editor, UCLA Journal of Environmental Law and Policy, 1994-1996. Recipient: American Jurisprudence Awards in Criminal Law and Lawyering Skills. *PRACTICE AREAS:* Commercial Litigation. *Email:* jmendoza@mdbe.com

**NEAL A. RUBIN,** born New York, N.Y., June 11, 1967; admitted to bar, 1994, California. *Education:* Amherst College (B.A., cum laude, 1989); University of Southern California (J.D., 1994). Moot Court Editor, Best Brief Winner. *LANGUAGES:* Spanish. *PRACTICE AREAS:* Commercial Litigation; Employment Litigation. *Email:* nrubin@mdbe.com

**JOHN D. SCHLOTTERBECK,** born Flint, Michigan, August 21, 1961; admitted to bar, 1993, California; 1994, U.S. District Court, Central District of California. *Education:* University of California, San Diego; University of Santa Clara (B.S., cum laude, 1984); Hastings College of the Law, University of California (J.D., 1993). Phi Beta Kappa. Recipient, American Jurisprudence Award in Legal Writing and Research. Staff Member, Hastings Law Journal, 1992-1993. Extern to U.S. District Judge Robert M. Takasugi, Central District of California, 1992. *Member:* Los Angeles County Bar Association (Member, Environmental Law Section); State Bar of California (Member, Environmental Law Section). *PRACTICE AREAS:* Environmental Law. *Email:* jschlotterbeck@mdbe.com

**ALLYSON W. SONENSHINE,** born Pittsburgh, Pennsylvania, March 15, 1971; admitted to bar, 1996, California. *Education:* University of Pennsylvania (B.A., cum laude, 1993); University of Southern California (J.D., 1996). Staff Member, Review of Law and Women's Studies. *LANGUAGES:* French. *PRACTICE AREAS:* Litigation and Employment Law.

**CHARLES E. SHELTON, II,** born Newport News, Virginia, June 5, 1963; admitted to bar, 1992, California and U.S. District Court, Central District of California. *Education:* University of Virginia (B.A., 1985); Yale University (J.D., 1990). *LANGUAGES:* Spanish. *PRACTICE AREAS:* Environmental Law; Litigation. *Email:* cshelton@mdbe.com

*(This Listing Continued)*

**SANDRA HUGHES WADDELL,** born New York, N.Y., February 18, 1958; admitted to bar, 1993, California. *Education:* Parsons School of Design; University of Florida; Baruch College; Columbia University (J.D., 1992). Articles Editor, Columbia Journal of Environmental Law, 1991-1992. Co-Author: "California Spill Reporting Manual" (Government Institutes, 1996). *PRACTICE AREAS:* Environmental Law. *Email:* swaddell@mdbe.com

**CORY WURTZEL,** born Brooklyn, New York, July 29, 1969; admitted to bar, 1996, California. *Education:* University of California, Los Angeles (B.A., 1991); Boalt Hall School of Law, University of California, Berkeley (J.D., 1996). *Member:* Los Angeles County Bar Association. *PRACTICE AREAS:* Environmental. *Email:* cwurtzel@mdbe.com

**KENNETH J. YOOD,** born Buffalo, New York, December 28, 1963; admitted to bar, 1989, New York and Massachusetts; 1990, California. *Education:* Haverford College (B.A., 1986); State University of New York, Buffalo (J.D., 1989); Harvard School of Public Health (M.P.H., 1990). *LANGUAGES:* Spanish. *PRACTICE AREAS:* Healthcare Law. *Email:* kyood@mdbe.com

All Members and Associates are Members of The State Bar of California.

---

## McDERMOTT, WILL & EMERY

A Partnership including Professional Corporations

*Established in 1934*

**2049 CENTURY PARK EAST**
**LOS ANGELES, CALIFORNIA 90067-3208**
Telephone: 310-277-4110
Facsimile: 310-277-4730
URL: http://www.mwe.com

*Chicago, Illinois Office:* 227 West Monroe Street. Telephone: 312-372-2000. Facsimile: 312-984-7700.

*Boston, Massachusetts Office:* 75 State Street, Suite 1700. Telephone: 617-345-5000. Facsimile: 617-345-5077.

*Miami, Florida Office:* 201 South Biscayne Boulevard. Telephone: 305-358-3500. Facsimile: 305-347-6500.

*Washington, D.C. Office:* 1850 K Street, N.W. Telephone: 202-887-8000. Facsimile: 202-778-8087.

*Newport Beach, California Office:* 1301 Dove Street, Suite 500. Telephone: 714-851-0633. Facsimile: 714-851-9348.

*New York, N.Y. Office:* 50 Rockefeller Plaza. Telephone: 212-547-5508. Facsimile: 212-547-5444.

*St. Petersburg, Russia Office:* AOZT McDermott, Will & Emery, Griboyedova Canal 36, 191023, St. Petersburg, Russia. Telephone: (7) (812) 310-52-44; 310-55-44; 310-59-44; 850-20-45. Facsimile: (7) (812) 310-54-46; 325-84-50.

*Vilnius, Lithuania Office:* Smetonos 6, 2600 Vilnius, Lithuania. Telephone: 370 2 61-43-08. Facsimile: 370 2 22-79-55.

*General Practice (including Corporate, Employee Benefits, Estate Planning, Health, Litigation and Tax Law).*

*FIRM PROFILE:* McDermott, Will & Emery is an international law firm founded in 1934. Originally a Chicago tax law practice, the firm has established a full-service presence in seven domestic and three international offices with more than 600 attorneys. Clients include large corporations and individuals as well as small and medium-sized businesses. The firm represents a wide range of industrial, financial and commercial enterprises, both publicly and privately held. Firm attorneys represent clients in every state as well as numerous foreign jurisdictions.

The firm is organized by legal specialization: corporate, employee benefits, estate planning, health law, legislative/government regulation, international, litigation and tax. Many firm attorneys also practice interdepartmentally distinguishing us from many other large law firms.

### MEMBERS OF FIRM

**CHRIS M. AMANTEA,** born December 22, 1955; admitted to bar, 1989, Illinois; 1990, California. *Education:* University of California, Davis (B.S., 1977); ITT Chicago-Kent College of Law (J.D., 1989). Order of the Coif. Instructor, ITT Chicago-Kent College of Law, 1989-1990.

**†PAUL A. BECK,** born 1950; admitted to bar, 1976, Missouri; 1978, California. *Education:* Harvard University (B.A., cum laude, 1972); George Washington University (J.D., with honors, 1975). Managing Editor, Journal of International Law and Economics, 1974-1975. Law Clerk, Hon. John W. Oliver, U.S. District Court, Western District of Missouri, 1975-1977. *Member:* Los Angeles County Bar Assn.; Bar Assns.; Missouri Bar; State

*(This Listing Continued)*

Bar of California; Financial Lawyers Conference; California Bankruptcy Forum. *PRACTICE AREAS:* Bankruptcy; Insolvency; Litigation.

**JOEL M. BERNSTEIN,** born July 31, 1945; admitted to bar, 1970, Illinois; 1971, California. *Education:* University of Michigan (B.A., with distinction, 1966); University of Chicago (J.D., 1969). Phi Beta Kappa. Author: "Is Security a Security? Daniel vs. Teamsters," Trust and Estates, Vol. 116, No. 12, December, 1977; "What to Watch for in Negotiating a Computer Contract for Your Hospital," Prentice-Hall Cost Management Service, 1982. *Member:* Illinois State Bar Assn.; State Bar of California. *PRACTICE AREAS:* Corporate Law; Finance; Securities.

**LEE L. BLACKMAN,** born August 28, 1950; admitted to bar, 1975, California. *Education:* University of Southern California (B.A., cum laude, 1973; J.D., 1975). Member, Southern California Law Review, 1974-1975. Author: Voting Rights for the Uninitiated—Evaluating Challenges to At-Large Elections Systems: A Practical Guide for the 1990's," 32 Muni. Atty. 118, Sept./Dec. 1991. Member, Editorial Advisory Board Airport Noise Report. Judge Pro Tem, Los Angeles Superior Court, 1987-1990. *Member:* State Bar of California (Member, Litigation Section); American Bar Assn. (Member, Litigation Section). *PRACTICE AREAS:* Constitutional Law; Environmental; Litigation.

**TIMOTHY P. BLANCHARD,** born April 12, 1960; admitted to bar, 1986, California. *Education:* Oklahoma State University (B.S., with honors, 1982); St. Louis University (M.H.A., 1986; J.D., cum laude, 1986). Order of the Woolsack. Health Law Editor, St. Louis University Law Journal, 1984-1985. *Member:* State Bar of California; American Bar Assn.; National Health Lawyers Assn.; Healthcare Financial Management Assn.; American Academy of Hospital Attorneys. *PRACTICE AREAS:* Health Care; Medicare and Medicaid.

**PETER M. BRANSTEN,** born April 16, 1957; admitted to bar, 1984, California. *Education:* University of California, Berkeley (B.A., 1979); University of Southern California (J.D., 1983).

**MARK A. CONLEY,** born November 22, 1951; admitted to bar, 1978, New York; 1989, California. *Education:* University of Pennsylvania (B.A., 1973); Columbia University (J.D., 1977). Member: Advisory Committee, University of Southern California Corporate Counsel Institute; Advisory Board, Entrepreneurship Institute, Southern California Chapter. *Member:* Los Angeles County and American Bar Assns.; State Bar of California.

**MARSHA S. CRONINGER,** born May 9, 1947; admitted to bar, 1977, California. *Education:* Connecticut College (B.A., 1972); McGeorge School of Law (J.D., 1977). Staff Counsel, State Department of Health Services, California, 1977-1988.

**JOHN E. CURTIS, JR.,** born June 12, 1945; admitted to bar, 1970, Maryland; 1972, District of Columbia; 1976, California. *Education:* Trinity College (B.A., 1967); University of Virginia (J.D., 1970); Georgetown University (LL.M., in Taxation, 1974). Counsel, United States Senate Committee on Finance, 1977-1980. Member, Editorial Board, Journal of Pension Planning & Compliance. Member, Advisory Board, Tax Management Compensation Planning Journal. *Member:* The District of Columbia Bar; State Bar of California; Maryland State Bar Assn. *PRACTICE AREAS:* ESOPS Law; ERISA.

**KATHLEEN L. HOUSTON DRUMMY,** born January 25, 1951; admitted to bar, 1977, California. *Education:* University of California at Berkeley (B.A., with honors, 1973); UCLA (M.A., 1974; J.D., 1977). Executive Editor, UCLA-Alaska Law Review, 1976-1977. Member, Moot Court. *Member:* State Bar of California. *PRACTICE AREAS:* Health Care; Hospitals; Medicare and Medicaid.

**GARY B. GERTLER,** born June 15, 1959; admitted to bar, 1986, California. *Education:* UCLA (B.S., 1982; M.P.H., 1983); University of Southern California (J.D., 1986). Articles Editor, Major Tax Planning, 1985-1986; Notes and Articles Editor Computer Law Journal, 1985-1986. Recipient, American Jurisprudence Award. Co-Author: "Navigating Your Way Through the Federal Physical Self-Referral Law," AIS, 1995; "State Laws and Regulations Governing Preferred Provider Organizations," Rand, 1986. Author: "Brain Birth: A Proposal for Defining When a Fetus is Entitled to Human Life Status," 59 Southern California Law Review, 1061, 1986; "Think Twice Before Revising Medical Staff Bylaws Under HCQIA," 3 Quality Resource Monitor, 5, 1987. *Member:* State Bar of California; National Health Lawyers Assn.; California Society of Healthcare Attorneys. *PRACTICE AREAS:* Health Care; Hospitals; Mergers, Acquisitions and Divestitures.

**DONALD A. GOLDMAN,** born September 11, 1947; admitted to bar, 1972, California. *Education:* UCLA (B.A., 1969; J.D., 1972). Deputy Attorney General, State of California, 1972-1979. *Member:* State Bar of California; American Bar Assn.; American Academy of Hospital Attorneys; National Health Lawyers Assn. *PRACTICE AREAS:* Administrative Law; Health Care; Regulatory.

**ERIC B. GORDON,** born October 19, 1961; admitted to bar, 1990, California. *Education:* Brown University (A.B., magna cum laude, 1982; M.D., 1986); UCLA (J.D., 1990). Order of the Coif; Phi Beta Kappa. Author: "Teaching and Research Hospitals," in Health Care Corporate Law Facilities and Transactions, Little, Brown 1996; "Faculty Practice Plans," BNA Health Law and Business Series, 1996. *Member:* State Bar of California; National Health Lawyers Assn. *PRACTICE AREAS:* Health Care.

**MICHAEL I. GOTTFRIED,** born November 19, 1955; admitted to bar, 1988, New York and U.S. District Court, Southern and Eastern Districts of New York; U.S. District Court, Central District of California; 1990, California. *Education:* State University of New York at Stony Brook (B.A., 1976); Columbia University (M.L.S., 1977); Brooklyn Law School (J.D., 1987). *Member:* Association of the Bar of the City of New York; State Bar of California; American Bar Assn.; Financial Lawyers Conference. *PRACTICE AREAS:* Bankruptcy; Debtor and Creditor.

**†DAVID GOULD,** born February 19, 1940; admitted to bar, 1966, California. *Education:* UCLA (A.B., 1962); University of California at Berkeley, Boalt Hall (LL.B., 1965). Author: with Bankruptcy Judge Lisa Hill Fenning, Local Bankruptcy Practice Manual, PESI, 1991. Deputy Attorney General, California, 1965-1968. Member, Board of Governors, 1977-1980; Secretary-Treasurer, 1980-1981; Vice President, 1981-1982; President, 1982-1983, Financial Lawyers Conference. Adjunct Associate Professor of Law, Southwestern University School of Law, Los Angeles, 1978-1980. Adjunct Professor of Law, Pepperdine University School of Law 1982-1983. Member, Personal and Small Business Bankruptcy Law Advisory Commission, Board of Legal Specialization, State Bar of California. Member, Board of Directors, 1989-1990; Secretary, 1990-1991; Second Vice President, 1991-1992; First Vice President, 1992-1993; President, 1993-1994, Los Angeles Bankruptcy Forum. Member, Board of Directors, California Bankruptcy Forum, 1993—. Lawyer-Delegate, Ninth Circuit Judicial Conference, 1990-1994. Mediator, U.S. Bankruptcy Court, Central District of California, 1995—. *Member:* Century City, Los Angeles County (Member, Federal Courts Committee, 1987—; Chair, 1990-1991), American (Member, Business Bankruptcy Committee, Section on Business Law, 1982—; Vice Chair, Rules Subcommittee, 1986-1992; Chair, 1992-1995; Chair, Task Force on International Money Laundering and Asset Training, International Bankruptcy Sub Committee) and Federal Bar Assns.; State Bar of California (Member, Debtor Creditor Relations and Bankruptcy, 1984-1987; Chair, 1987-1988; Advisor, 1988-1989; Member, Uniform Commercial Code Committee, 1988-1991. *PRACTICE AREAS:* Bankruptcy.

**DANIEL GRUNFELD,** born November 20, 1959; admitted to bar, 1987, California. *Education:* Drexel University (B.S., summa cum laude, 1982); Cornell University (J.D., 1986). Phi Kappa Phi; Beta Gamma Sigma; Phi Alpha Theta. Captain, Jessup Moot Court Team. National Securities Moot Court Competition. *Member:* State Bar of California; American Bar Assn. *PRACTICE AREAS:* Environmental Law; Franchises and Franchising; Litigation.

**MARY ELLEN HOGAN,** born September 13, 1955; admitted to bar, 1980, Pennsylvania; 1983, Illinois; 1988, California. *Education:* Northwestern University (B.A., 1977; M.S., 1977); Indiana University (J.D., 1980). Member, Board of Editors, Indiana Law Journal, 1978-1980. Contributing Editor: Airport Environmental Management Handbook, 1994. Co-Author: "A Land Use Analysis of Existing and Potential Coal Surface Mining Areas in the Ohio River Basin Energy Study Region," U.S. Environmental Protection Agency, 1980. *Member:* State Bar of California. *PRACTICE AREAS:* Environmental Law; Aviation and Aerospace; Toxic Torts.

**DOUGLAS A. JAQUES,** born September 20, 1958; admitted to bar, 1984, California. *Education:* Stanford University (B.A., with distinction, 1980); UCLA (J.D./M.B.A., 1984). *Member:* Los Angeles County and American Bar Assns.; The State Bar of California. *PRACTICE AREAS:* Nonprofit and Charitable Organizations; Health Care; Taxation.

**†IVAN L. KALLICK,** born November 28, 1955; admitted to bar, 1981, California, U.S. District Court, Central District of California and U.S. Court of Appeals, Ninth Circuit. *Education:* UCLA (B.S., 1977); University of San Francisco (J.D., 1980). *Member:* Los Angeles County and American Bar Assns.; State Bar of California; Financial Lawyers Conference; California Hotel & Motel Assn.; California Bankruptcy Forum. *PRACTICE AREAS:* Bankruptcy; Debtor and Creditor; Hotels.

*(This Listing Continued)*

## McDERMOTT, WILL & EMERY, Los Angeles—Continued

**DAVID L. KLATSKY,** born March 28, 1962; admitted to bar, 1990, California; 1991, U.S. District Court, Central District of California and U.S. Court of Appeals, Ninth Circuit. *Education:* Brown University (B.A., 1984); Institut D'Etudes Politiques, Universite de Paris, Paris, France; University of California at Los Angeles (J.D., 1990). *Member:* State Bar of California. *LANGUAGES:* Italian and French.

**STEPHEN A. KROFT,** born January 18, 1944; admitted to bar, 1969, California. *Education:* University of California at Berkeley (B.A., 1965); Stanford University (LL.B., 1968). Phi Beta Kappa. Fellow, American College of Trial Lawyers. Member, California Academy of Appellate Lawyers. Member, Ninth Circuit Advisory Rules Committee, 1992-1995. Guest Lecturer, Copyright Law, Stanford Law School, 1980, 1982, 1984, 1986, 1989, 1990, 1991, 1992 and 1993. Board of Trustees (1985-1991), Treasurer (1991-1992), Secretary (1992-1993), Vice President (1993-1994) (President (1995-1996), Los Angeles Copyright Society. Lawyer Delegate 1987-1990 and Co-Chair, Central District Delegation, 1989-1990, Ninth Circuit Judicial Conference. Panelist: PLI How to Handle Basic Copyright and Trademark Problems, 1991, 1992 and 1993; ABA National Institute on Appellate Advocacy, 1988; Continuing Education of the Bar's Federal Practice Institute, 1987-1996. Author: *Copyright Litigation Overview,* How to Handle Basic Copyright & Trademark Problems (Practicing Law Institute 1991, 1992 and 1993). *Member:* Los Angeles County and American Bar Assns.; The State Bar of California. *PRACTICE AREAS:* Complex Business Litigation; Intellectual Property Litigation and Counseling; Entertainment Litigation and Counseling; Legal Malpractice Defense.

**LEWIS R. LANDAU,** born April 6, 1963; admitted to bar, 1989, California, U.S. District Court, Central and Northern Districts of California and U.S. Court of Appeals, Ninth Circuit. *Education:* State University of New York at Albany (B.A., 1985); Loyola Marymount University (J.D., 1989). Phi Alpha Delta. *Member:* State Bar of California.

**RODGER M. LANDAU,** born December 21, 1963; admitted to bar, 1990, California. *Education:* Haverford College (B.A., 1985); University of Chicago (J.D., 1990).

**JEFFREY W. LEMKIN,** born June 15, 1945; admitted to bar, 1972, Massachusetts; 1978, California. *Education:* Bowdoin College (A.B., 1966); Northwestern University (M.A., 1968); Boston University (J.D., cum laude, 1972). Editor, Boston University Law Review, 1970-1972. *Member:* State Bar of California; American Academy of Hospital Attorneys; National Health Lawyers Assn.; California Society of Healthcare Attorneys. *PRACTICE AREAS:* Business Law; Corporate Law; Health Care.

**ROBERT P. MALLORY,** born November 1, 1943; admitted to bar, 1971, California; 1978, U.S. Court of Appeals, Ninth Circuit; 1980, U.S. Supreme Court; 1981, U.S. Court of Appeals, Tenth Circuit; 1982, U.S. Court of Appeals, Third Circuit; 1983, U.S. Court of Appeals for the Federal Circuit. *Education:* California State University, Sacramento (B.S., magna cum laude, 1966); University of California at Davis (J.D., 1970). Associate Editor, UCD Law Review, 1969-1970. Vice Chairman, Ninth Circuit Litigation Management Committee, 1971, 1974. *Member:* Los Angeles County and American (Member, Sections on: Litigation; Antitrust) Bar Assns.; The State Bar of California. *PRACTICE AREAS:* Antitrust and Trade Regulation; Professional Liability; Unfair Competition.

**DOUGLAS M. MANCINO,** born May 8, 1949; admitted to bar, 1974, Ohio; 1981, California; 1982, District of Columbia. *Education:* Kent State University (B.A., cum laude, 1971); Ohio State University (J.D., summa cum laude, 1974). Order of the Coif. Associate Editor, Ohio State Law Journal, 1973-1974. Author: "Taxation of Hospitals and Health Care Organizations," Warren, Gorham & Lamont, 1995. Co-Author: "Joint Ventures Between Hospitals and Physicians," Aspen Systems, 1987; "Navigating Your Way Through the Federal Physician Self-Referral Law," Atlantic Information Systems, 1995. *Member:* Cleveland, Ohio State and American (Chair, Exempt Organizations Committee, Tax Section, 1993— ) Bar Assns.; State Bar of California; District of Columbia Bar; American Academy of Hospital Attorneys (Member, Board of Directors, 1988-1995; President, 1993-1994); National Health Lawyers Assn. *PRACTICE AREAS:* Health Care; Federal Tax.

**MARK J. MIHANOVIC,** born August 24, 1960; admitted to bar, 1986, New York; 1988, California. *Education:* University of Michigan (A.B., with high honors, 1982; J.D., 1985). Member and Contributing Editor, University of Michigan Law Review, 1983-1985. *Member:* State Bar of California; Financial Lawyers Conference. *PRACTICE AREAS:* Corporate Law; Securities; Finance.

*(This Listing Continued)*

CAA966B

**TERESE A. MOSHER-BELURIS,** born January 2, 1958; admitted to bar, 1983, California and U.S. District Court, Northern, Eastern, Central and Southern Districts of California; 1987, District of Columbia. *Education:* Tufts University (B.A., magna cum laude, 1979); Loyola Law School, Los Angeles (J.D., 1982). Judge Pro Tem, Los Angeles Superior Court, 1989— . *Member:* Beverly Hills Bar Assn.; State Bar of California; District of Columbia Bar. *PRACTICE AREAS:* Commercial Litigation; Arbitration.

**DENISE G. PAULLY,** born June 9, 1950; admitted to bar, 1976, New York; 1982, California. *Education:* Vassar College (A.B., cum laude, 1971); Fordham Law School (J.D., 1975); New York University (LL.M., 1979). Associate Editor, Fordham Law Review, 1974-1975. *Member:* State Bar of California.

**IRA J. RAPPEPORT,** born January 13, 1954; admitted to bar, 1978, California. *Education:* Washington University (B.A., cum laude, 1975); Villanova University (J.D., cum laude, 1978). Order of the Coif. Recipient, Scribes Award. Member and Managing Editor, Villanova Law Review, 1977-1978. *Member:* State Bar of California; American Bar Assn.; National Health Lawyers Assn.; American Academy of Hospital Attorneys.

**J. PETER RICH,** born July 28, 1953; admitted to bar, 1977, California. *Education:* UCLA (A.B., summa cum laude, 1974); Harvard Law School (J.D., 1977). Phi Beta Kappa; Pi Gamma Mu. Author: "Direct Employer Contracting with Provider Networks in Managed Care and Alternative Delivery Systems," McGraw-Hill, 1995; "IPAs and Physician-Owned PPOs: Legal Implications of Alternative Forms of Organization," in Making Managed Care Work: A Practical Guide to Strategies and Solutions, McGraw Hill, 1991; "Managed Mental Health: Key Legal Issues," Managed Mental Health Services, Charles C. Thomas, 1991; "PPOs and Price Fixing," 6 Whittier Law Review, 1984. Co-Author: "State Laws and Regulations Governing Preferred Provider, Organizations," Rand Corporation, 1986. *Member:* State Bar of California; American Academy of Hospital Attorneys; National Health Lawyers Assn. *LANGUAGES:* French. *PRACTICE AREAS:* Health Care; Hospitals; Corporate Law.

**ROBERT H. ROSENFIELD,** born New York, N.Y., November 2, 1942; admitted to bar, 1976, California. *Education:* University of Wisconsin (B.S., 1964); Harvard University (LL.B., 1967); London School of Economics (LL.M., 1970). Phi Beta Kappa. Member, Board of Directors, 1977-1981, President, 1980 and Vice President, 1979, Beverly Hills Bar Association Scholarship Foundation. *Member:* American Bar Assn. (Member, Section of Corporation, Banking and Business Law); State Bar of California.

**ROBERT H. ROTSTEIN,** born June 28, 1951; admitted to bar, 1976, California. *Education:* UCLA (A.B., summa cum laude, 1973; J.D., 1976). Phi Beta Kappa; Order of the Coif. Lawyer Delegate, Ninth Circuit Judicial Conference, Central District, 1991-1993. Article Editor, UCLA Law Review, 1975-1976. Author: "Beyond Metaphor: Copyright Infringement and the Fiction of the Work," 68 Chicago Kent L. Rev. 701, 1993; "A Comment on Resolving Priority Disputes in Intellectual Property Collateral," 1 Journal of Intellectual Property 167, 1993. Law Clerk, Hon. Anthony M. Kennedy, Circuit Judge, U.S. Court of Appeals for the Ninth Circuit, 1976-1977. *Member:* Beverly Hills, Los Angeles County and American Bar Assns.; The State Bar of California (Member, Executive Committee, Intellectual Property Section, 1994—). *PRACTICE AREAS:* Complex Business Litigation; Intellectual Property Law; Copyright Law; Entertainment Litigation.

**THOMAS A. RYAN,** born February 14, 1964; admitted to bar, 1989, California. *Education:* Princeton University (A.B., 1986); University of California at Berkeley (J. D., 1989). *Member:* Los Angeles County Bar Assn. (Member, Litigation Section); Inns of Court; Association of Business Trial Lawyers. *PRACTICE AREAS:* Litigation.

**ALLAN L. SCHARE,** born November 9, 1961; admitted to bar, 1986, California. *Education:* University of California at Berkeley (A.B., with high distinction, 1983); Boalt Hall School of Law, University of California, Berkeley (J.D., 1986). Phi Beta Kappa; Order of the Coif. Executive Editor, High Technology Law Journal, 1985-1986. *Member:* State Bar of California. *PRACTICE AREAS:* Litigation.

**RICHARD K. SIMON,** born October 26, 1944; admitted to bar, 1970, California. *Education:* Claremont Men's College (B.A., 1966); University of Pennsylvania (LL.B., 1969). Member, Legal Committee, Airports Association Council International, 1975— . *Member:* State Bar of California; Los Angeles Copyright Society.

**†STEVEN M. SPECTOR,** born February 12, 1947; admitted to bar, 1972, California. *Education:* UCLA (A.B., 1968); Loyola University at Los Angeles (J.D., 1971). Phi Delta Phi (Vice-Magister, 1971). Member, St.

*(This Listing Continued)*

Thomas More Society. Member, 1970, and Associate Editor, 1971, Loyola University of Los Angeles Law Review. Author: Note, 3 Loyola University at Los Angeles Law Review 431, 1970. *Member:* Beverly Hills, Century City, Los Angeles County (Member, Commercial Law and Bankruptcy Section, 1972—) and American Bar Assns.; State Bar of California; Association of Business Trial Lawyers; California Bankruptcy Forum; Financial Lawyers Conference. *PRACTICE AREAS:* Bankruptcy; Banks and Banking; Debtor and Creditor.

**VIRGINIA VANCE SULLIVAN,** born August 27, 1961; admitted to bar, 1986, Florida; 1988, California. *Education:* Florida State University (B.S., magna cum laude, 1983); University of Florida (J.D., with honors, 1986). Junior Articles Editor, University of Florida Law Review, 1985. *Member:* Los Angeles County Bar Assn.; State Bar of California; The Florida Bar. *PRACTICE AREAS:* Health Care; Hospitals; Mergers, Acquisitions and Divestitures.

### COUNSEL

**MARTIN J. SCHNITZER,** born December 21, 1928; admitted to bar, 1953, California. *Education:* UCLA (B.A., 1950; LL.B., 1952). Member, UCLA Law Review, 1951-1952. Member, Panel of Arbitrators, American Arbitration Association. *Member:* State Bar of California; National Health Lawyers Assn.; California Society for Healthcare Attorneys (Director, 1990-1994). *PRACTICE AREAS:* Alternative Dispute Resolution; Health Care; Insurance.

---

**ALLISON SHER ARKIN,** born July 17, 1963; admitted to bar, 1992, New York; 1994, California. *Education:* Wesleyan Univ. (B.A., 1985); Fordham Univ. (J.D., 1991).

**JANE E. BOUBELIK,** born June 4, 1964; admitted to bar, 1991, California. *Education:* UCLA (B.A., 1987); McGeorge School of Law (J.D., 1991).

**ALEXANDER H. BROMLEY,** born May 27, 1966; admitted to bar, 1995, California. *Education:* New York Univ. (B.F.A., 1991); Univ. of California, Santa Cruz; Columbia Univ. (J.D., 1995).

**BRYAN T. CASTORINA,** born June 7, 1966; admitted to bar, 1992, California. *Education:* Univ. of California (B.A., 1988); Boalt Hall School of Law, Univ. of California (J.D., 1992).

**JUAN CARLOS DOMINGUEZ,** born June 17, 1963; admitted to bar, 1989, California. *Education:* Univ. of Southern California (B.A.B.S., cum laude, 1985); Univ. of California at Los Angeles (J.D., 1989). *LANGUAGES:* Spanish.

**DAVID R. GABOR,** born November 5, 1964; admitted to bar, 1989, California and U.S. District Court, Central District of California; 1992, U.S. District Court, Northern District of California. *Education:* Vassar College (B.A., 1986); UCLA (J.D., 1989). *LANGUAGES:* Hungarian.

**JAMES T. GRANT,** born March 25, 1965; admitted to bar, 1991, California. *Education:* Stanford Univ. (B.A., with distinction, 1987); Univ. of Michigan (J.D., 1991). *Member:* Los Angeles, Los Angeles County and American Bar Assns.

**GENEVIEVE M. KELLY,** born October 21, 1967; admitted to bar, 1993, California; 1996, District of Columbia. *Education:* Brown Univ. (A.B., magna cum laude and departmental honors, 1989); Katholieke Universiteit Leuven (M.A., magna cum laude, 1990; LL.M., magna cum laude, 1994); Georgetown Univ. (J.D., cum laude, 1993). *LANGUAGES:* French.

**HYONG S. KOH,** born June 14, 1959; admitted to bar, 1989, California. *Education:* Harvard Univ. (B.A., 1983); Univ. of California at Davis (J.D., 1989). *Member:* State Bar of California. (Also Foreign Legal Consultant to CJ International, Seoul, Korea). *LANGUAGES:* Korean.

**DANIEL B. LANTRY,** born December 8, 1965; admitted to bar, 1991, California. *Education:* Univ. of California, Riverside (B.S., summa cum laude, 1988); Univ. of California, Boalt Hall School of Law (J.D., 1991). *Member:* Los Angeles County Bar Assn.; State Bar of California.

**PAUL F. LAWRENCE,** born March 3, 1967; admitted to bar, 1991, California; 1992, U.S. District Court, Central District of California, U.S. Court of Appeals, Ninth Circuit and U.S. Tax Court. *Education:* UCLA (B.A., summa cum laude, 1988) Phi Beta Kappa; Harvard Univ. (J.D., 1991). *Member:* Los Angeles County Bar Assn. (Co-Chair, West Los Angeles Young Tax Lawyer's Committee, 1993-1995).

**MICHAEL L. MEEKS,** born July 24, 1968; admitted to bar, 1994, California. *Education:* Pepperdine Univ. (B.A., 1990); UCLA (J.D., 1994).

*(This Listing Continued)*

**AJAY A. PATEL,** born March 15, 1969; admitted to bar, 1994, California. *Education:* UCLA (B.A., 1991); Univ. of Southern California (J.D., 1994).

**JAMES B. RYAN,** born July 16, 1968; admitted to bar, 1993, California and U.S. District Court, Central District of California. *Education:* Univ. of California (B.A., 1990); UCLA (J.D., 1993).

**THEODORE R. SCHNECK,** born April 4, 1964; admitted to bar, 1991, California and U.S. District Court, Southern District of California. *Education:* Haverford College (B.A., 1986); Univ. of Michigan (J.D., 1990); John F. Kennedy School of Government, Harvard Univ. (M.P.A., 1991).

**CHRISTINA ANNE SLAWSON,** born January 19, 1969; admitted to bar, 1993, California; 1994, U.S. District Court, Central District of California; 1995, U.S. District Court, Northern, Eastern and Southern Districts of California. *Education:* Reed College (B.A., 1990); Harvard Univ. (J.D., 1993).

**JENNIFER L. SPAZIANO,** born May 18, 1971; admitted to bar, 1995, California. *Education:* Boston College (A.B., 1992); Pepperdine Univ. (J.D., 1995).

**SARAH TRIMBLE,** born December 27, 1969; admitted to bar, 1995, Louisiana; 1996, California. *Education:* Trinity Univ. (B.A., 1991); Louisiana State Univ. (J.D., 1994).

**ANNE H. WEST,** born December 13, 1968; admitted to bar, 1993, California. *Education:* Columbia College (B.A., 1990); UCLA (J.D., 1993); New York Univ. (LL.M., 1994).

**JANE CHOTARD WHEELER,** born January 14, 1952; admitted to bar, 1990, California. *Education:* University of Arizona (B.A., 1986); UCLA (J.D., 1990). *Member:* State Bar of California; National Health Lawyers Assn.

†Denotes a lawyer employed by a Professional Corporation which is a member of the Firm

(For Biographical data on all firm personnel, see Professional Biographies listings at other office locations)

---

## JANIS M. McDONALD
SUITE 2700, 1900 AVENUE OF THE STARS
**LOS ANGELES, CALIFORNIA 90067**
Telephone: 310-556-2028
Fax: 310-286-1728

*Family Law.*

**JANIS M. MCDONALD,** born Fargo, North Dakota; admitted to bar, 1975, California and U.S. District Court, Northern and Central Districts of California. *Education:* Stanford University (B.A., 1971); California State University at Hayward; University of San Francisco (J.D., 1975). Los Angeles County Bar Association: (Author: "Privilege and Confidentiality in Custody Disputes," Custody and Visitation Handbook, Child Custody Colloquium, 1982 and 1983. Lecturer/Author: Child Custody Colloquium, "Domestic Violence," 1991.) Continuing Education of the Bar; (Lecturer/Author; "Discovery in Family Law Cases," 1987; Lecturer: "Handling Spousal Child Support, 1988). American Woman's Society of Certified Public Accountants: (Lecturer/Author: "Marriage and Dissolution In a Community Property State," 1985). Beverly Hills Bar Association: (Lecturer/Author: Family Law Symposiums, Workshops and Seminars: "Planning and Drafting Marital Settlement Agreements," 1987; "Employees Benefits Practicum," 1990; "Real Estate/Fair Rental Values/Commercial Property Issues," 1992; "Bankruptcy/Family Law," 1992; "Hot Tips from the Experts," 1992, 1993, 1995; "The Impact of Bankruptcy on Family Law," 1993; "How to Comply with 4800.10 and 4800.11," 1993; "Valuation of Real Property," Beverly Hills Bar Association Journal, Vol. 27, No. 1 Winter, 1993; "Post Judgment Modification of Child and Spousal Support," 1994). *Member:* Century City, Beverly Hills (Member, Resolution Committee, 1983—; Board of Governors, 1988—; Delegate to State Bar Conference, 1983—; Legislative Committee, 1986—; Citizen's Law School, Lecturer, 1994; Member, Family Law Section, 1981—, Chair, 1987-1988, Vice-Chair, 1986-1987, Chair, Family Law Symposium, 1984, 1987; Officer, Executive Committee, 1983-1988; Member, Executive Committee, 1981—; Family Law Section Committees: Legislative, Resolution, Mediation, Mental Health, 1983—; Symposium Committee, 1984—; Workshop Committee, 1987—; Parents and Children Together Court Program Liaison, 1992—), San Fernando Valley (Member, Family Law Section, 1981—, Mediation Committee, 1983—, Judge Pro Tem Program, 1983—), Los Angeles County (Member, Family Law Section, 1981—; Executive Committee, 1990—; Member,

*(This Listing Continued)*

### JANIS M. McDONALD, Los Angeles—Continued

Symposium Committee, 1990-1991; Conciliation Court Services Liaison, 1991—; Chair, Finance and Grants Committee, 1992-1993; Child Custody Colloqium Committee, 1990—; Ethics Committee, 1992—; Mediator-/ADR Committee, 1992—; Family Law Institute University of Southern California/LACBA Committee, 1992—; Chair, 1994, 1995), Orange County (Member, Family Law Section, 1981—) and American (Member, Family Law Section, 1981—) Bar Associations; State Bar of California (Member: Family Law Section, Committee on Property South, 1985—); California Women Lawyers; Women Lawyers Association of Los Angeles. (Certified Specialist, Family Law, The State Bar of California Board of Legal Specialization).

REFERENCES: Wells Fargo Bank; First Interstate Bank; Great Western Bank.

---

### MARY J. McELROY
**LOS ANGELES, CALIFORNIA**
(See Templeton)

*Construction Transactions, Mediation, Arbitration and Litigation.*

---

### McGARRY & LAUFENBERG
**LOS ANGELES, CALIFORNIA**
(See El Segundo)

*Personal Injury Defense and Insurance Law, Probate and Estate Planning, Wills and Trusts, Taxation, Business and Commercial Litigation.*

---

### McGAUGHEY & SPIRITO
**LOS ANGELES, CALIFORNIA**
(See Torrance)

*General Civil Litigation. Family Law, Business Litigation, Real Estate, Probate and Estate Planning, Personal Injury and Contract Law.*

---

### PATRICK E. McGINNIS
924 WESTWOOD BOULEVARD, SUITE 725
**LOS ANGELES, CALIFORNIA 90024**
Telephone: 310-208-6625
Fax: 310-209-7444

*Tax Planning and Tax Litigation, Estate Planning and Bankruptcy.*

**PATRICK E. MCGINNIS,** born Chicago, Illinois, September 28, 1950; admitted to bar, 1976, Arizona; 1977, U.S. Tax Court; 1987, California; 19912, U.S. District Court, Central District of California and U.S. Court of Appeals, 9th Circuit; 1995, U.S. Bankruptcy Court. *Education:* University of California at Riverside (B.S. Economics, with honors, 1972); Arizona State University (J.D., cum laude, 1976). Member, Arizona State University Law Review, 1976. Guest Lecturer, Citizen's Law School, Beverly Hills, California, 1992 and 1993. Panelist, Los Angeles County Bar Continuing Legal Education Seminar on State Local Procedure in September 1993 and on Tax Fraud in June, 1992. Tax Trial Attorney, Office of the District Counsel for the Internal Revenue Service, Oklahoma City, Oklahoma, 1977-1983, Los Angeles, California, 1983-1984 and Laguna Niguel, California, 1984-1989. *Member:* Los Angeles County Bar Association (Chairman, Procedure and Litigation Subcommittee of the Taxation Section, 1993); State Bar of Arizona; State Bar of California; Irish-American Bar Association (Member and Board of Governors). (Certified Specialist, Taxation Law, California Board of Legal Specialization). **PRACTICE AREAS:** Federal and State Taxation Law; Civil Tax Litigation; Tax Controversies Law; Tax Collection; Civil and Criminal Tax Fraud.

---

### McHALE & CONNOR
*A PROFESSIONAL CORPORATION*
SUITE 300, 600 WILSHIRE BOULEVARD
**LOS ANGELES, CALIFORNIA 90017**
Telephone: 213-629-1131
Fax: 213-627-9736

*General Civil and Trial Practice in all State and Federal Courts. Insurance, Products Liability, Medical Legal and Malpractice Law.*

**MICHAEL J. MCHALE,** born Cleveland, Ohio, June 29, 1940; admitted to bar, 1965, Ohio; 1969, California. *Education:* John Carroll University (A.B., cum laude, 1962); University of Michigan (LL.B., 1965). Arbitrator, Los Angeles Superior Court Special Arbitration Panel, 1974—. *Member:* Los Angeles County Bar Association; State Bar of California; American Board of Trial Advocates; Association of Southern California Defense Counsel. [Capt., Judge Advocate, U.S. Marine Corps, 1965-1968]. **PRACTICE AREAS:** Insurance Defense; Products Liability; Construction.

**JAN ALLEN CONNOR,** born Lamar, Missouri, November 18, 1932; admitted to bar, 1966, California. *Education:* Los Angeles City College (A.A., 1957); Los Angeles State College (B.S., 1960); Loyola University and Southwestern University (LL.B., 1965). Deputy City Attorney, Los Angeles, 1966-1970. Arbitrator, Los Angeles Superior Court Special Arbitration Panel, 1977—. *Member:* Los Angeles County Bar Association; State Bar of California; American Board of Trial Advocates; Association of Southern California Defense Counsel. **PRACTICE AREAS:** Insurance Defense; Products Liability; Construction.

**PHILIP C. ALLEN,** born New York, N.Y., February 17, 1953; admitted to bar, 1977, California. *Education:* California State University at Los Angeles (B.A., 1974); University of San Diego (J.D., 1977). *Member:* Los Angeles County Bar Association; State Bar of California; Association of Southern California Defense Counsel. **PRACTICE AREAS:** Insurance Defense; Products Liability; Construction.

**BRUCE JANGER,** born Houston, Texas, November 8, 1950; admitted to bar, 1977, California. *Education:* Duke University and Stanford University (A.B., 1972); University of California at Los Angeles (J.D., 1976). Moot Court Honors Program. *Member:* Los Angeles County Bar Association; State Bar of California; Association of Southern California Defense Counsel. **PRACTICE AREAS:** Insurance Defense; Products Liability; Construction.

**KARA ANN PAPE,** born Pasadena, California, November 13, 1962; admitted to bar, 1987, California. *Education:* Loyola Marymount University (B.A., magna cum laude, 1984; J.D., 1987). *Member:* Los Angeles County Bar Association; State Bar of California; Association of Southern California Defense Counsel. **PRACTICE AREAS:** Insurance Defense; Products Liability; Commercial Carriers.

---

**MYRNA LINETT STRAPP,** born Pittsburgh, Pennsylvania, April 8, 1948; admitted to bar, 1975, Ohio; 1988, California. *Education:* Ohio State University (B.S., 1970); Capital University Law School (J.D., 1975). Order of the Curia. Business Editor, Capital University Law Review, 1974-1975. Author: "Mandatory Maternity Leave For Teachers-Now A Thing of the Past?" 3 Capital University Law Review 323, 1975. *Member:* Los Angeles County Bar Association; State Bar of California; Association of Southern California Defense Counsel.

**LAWRENCE A. WALTER,** born Chicago, Illinois, January 22, 1951; admitted to bar, 1986, California. *Education:* University of California at Santa Barbara (B.A., 1973); Western State University (J.D., 1977). *Member:* Los Angeles County Bar Association; State Bar of California; Association of Southern California Defense Counsel.

**SHERRY GRGURIC,** born Parma, Ohio, January 25, 1964; admitted to bar, 1992, California, U.S. District Court, Central District of California and U.S. Court of Appeals, Ninth Circuit. *Education:* Grove City College (B.A., magna cum laude, 1986); City of London Polytechnic; Whittier College School of Law (J.D., 1992). Delta Mu Delta. Recipient, American Jurisprudence Award. *Member:* Los Angeles County and American Bar Associations; State Bar of California; Association of Southern California Defense Counsel.

REPRESENTATIVE CLIENTS: Allstate Insurance Company; Alpha Beta Markets; Associated Claims Management, Inc.; Black Angus Restaurants; Boys Markets; Crawford & Company; Crum & Forster; ITT/Hartford Insurance; Ingersoll Rand; Lancer Insurance Company; Leaseway Transportation Corporation; Liberty Mutual Insurance Company; Los Angeles County Metropolitan

*(This Listing Continued)*

## PROFESSIONAL BIOGRAPHIES

CALIFORNIA—LOS ANGELES

Transportation Authority; Lucky Stores, Inc.; Ralph's Grocery Company; Reliance Electric Company; Ryder Truck; Schindler Elevator Corporation; The Velvet Turtle Restaurant.
REFERENCE: First Interstate Bank, Los Angeles Main Office.

## McKAY, BYRNE & GRAHAM
Established in 1976

**3250 WILSHIRE BOULEVARD, SUITE 603**
**LOS ANGELES, CALIFORNIA 90010**
Telephone: 213-386-6900
Fax: 213-381-1762

*Insurance Law (Reinsurance and Excess Insurance Included), Personal Injury, Product Liability, Premises Liability, Construction, Land Subsidence, Motor Vehicle, Medical and Legal Malpractice and Intentional Torts Law. General Civil and Trial Practice in all State and Federal Courts.*

*FIRM PROFILE: McKay, Byrne & Graham is located in the mid-Wilshire area of Los Angeles County. Our attorneys are experienced litigators in all State and Federal Courts in Central and Southern California.*

*We recognize that ninety percent of all Superior Court cases filed in the Central and Southern California Courts are resolved without trial. For that reason, it is our strategy to evaluate liability and damages in every case at the earliest possible opportunity in order to determine if the case can be resolved by negotiated settlement, motion for summary judgement or voluntary dismissal. If the matter is not amenable to an early resolution, we immediately undertake discovery of relevant facts and issues in order to prepare the case for trial. Our belief is that a well-prepared case will result in a successful resolution, whether by settlement or by jury verdict.*

*McKay, Byrne & Graham is a member of Eagle International Associates, which is an international network of law firms concentrating in the defense of all types of litigation, and adjusters who provide multiline adjusting services. Thus, we are able to offer to our clients referrals to qualified attorneys and adjusters throughout the United States, Canada and Europe.*

**JOHN P. McKAY,** born Oakland, California, July 27, 1940; admitted to bar, 1969, California and U.S. District Court, Central and Northern Districts of California; 1977, U.S. District Court, Eastern Districts of California; U.S. Supreme Court. *Education:* California State University at Fullerton (B.A., 1963); Pepperdine University (J.D., 1968). Judge Pro Tem: Los Angeles Municipal Court, 1981-1982; Orange County Superior Court, 1985—. Member: Panel of Arbitrators, American Arbitration Association; Panel of Arbitrators, Los Angeles Superior Court; Panel of Arbitrators, Orange County Superior Court; Joint Association Settlement Officer, Los Angeles County Superior Court. Lecturer: How to Handle a Motor Vehicle Case, 1978; How to Prepare a Case for Trial, 1979; Primary and Excess Carrier Duties, 1980; Punitive Damages, 1981; Negotiating Settlement in Personal Injury Litigation, 1981; Calculating and Proving Damages in Personal Injury and Wrongful Death Cases, 1985; Negotiating Settlements in Personal Injury Litigation, 1986, California Continuing Education of the Bar Programs; Management of Catastrophic Injuries, Craig Hospital, 1988; Determining, Proving & Limiting Damages, National Business Institute, 1989; Trial Practice, 1994-1995; Violence in the Workplace, Pacific Claims Executive Association, 1995; Ultimate Trial Notebook, American Board of Trial Advocates Masters of Trial, 1995. *Member:* Los Angeles County (Member: Special Committee of the Bench and Bar on Discovery, 1978-1979; Law and Discovery Subcommittee, 1979-1980; Superior Court Committee, 1979-1980; State Court Committee, 1989-1991; Judicial Committee, 1989-1991) and American (Member, Special Committee on Excess and Reinsurance, 1983-1989) Bar Associations; State Bar of California; Defense Research Institute (Lecturer, Industry Wide Litigation, 1980); Association of Southern California Defense Counsel; American Board of Trial Advocates; Robert A. Banyard Inn of Court. **PRACTICE AREAS:** Civil Trial; Insurance Defense; Personal Injury.

**MICHAEL A. BYRNE,** born Chicago, Illinois, December 13, 1941; admitted to bar, 1969, California; 1972, U.S. District Court, Central District of California; 1976, U.S. District Court, Northern District of California; 1977, U.S. Court of Appeals, Ninth Circuit and U.S. Supreme Court; 1983, U.S. Court of Appeals, Fifth Circuit; 1986, U.S. District Court, Southern District of California; 1987, U.S. District Court, Eastern District of California. *Education:* University of Wisconsin (B.A., 1964); Loyola University, Chicago (J.D., 1967). Member, Panel of Arbitrators, Los Angeles Superior Court. *Member:* Los Angeles County and American (Member, Torts and Insurance Practice Section) Bar Associations; State Bar of California; Association of Southern California Defense Counsel (Lecturer, 1982—); Defense

*(This Listing Continued)*

Research Institute; American Board of Trial Advocates. **PRACTICE AREAS:** Civil Trial; Insurance Defense; Personal Injury.

**ROBERT L. GRAHAM,** born Baltimore, Maryland, September 10, 1940; admitted to bar, 1972, California and U.S. District Court, Central District of California; 1980, U.S. District Court, Southern District of California; 1987, U.S. Supreme Court. *Education:* Colorado College (B.A., 1963); Loyola University of Los Angeles (J.D., 1971). Judge Pro Tem, Los Angeles Municipal Court, 1983—. Member, Panel of Arbitrators, Los Angeles Superior Court. *Member:* Los Angeles County and American (Member, Insurance, Negligence and Compensation Law Section) Bar Associations; State Bar of California; Association of Southern California Defense Counsel; Defense Research Institute. [With U.S. Army (Security Agency), 1963-1967]. **PRACTICE AREAS:** Civil Trial; Products Liability.

**BARRY HASSENBERG,** born Los Angeles, California, January 20, 1952; admitted to bar, 1976, California; U.S. District Court, Central and Eastern Districts of California. *Education:* California State University at Northridge (B.A., 1973); Southwestern University (J.D., 1976). *Member:* Los Angeles County Bar Association; State Bar of California; Association of Southern California Defense Counsel. **PRACTICE AREAS:** Civil Trial; Insurance Defense; Products Liability.

**MARK G. CUNNINGHAM,** born Fort Wayne, Indiana, June 17, 1959; admitted to bar, 1985, California; 1986, U.S. District Court, District of California. *Education:* Loyola Marymount University (B.B.A., cum laude, 1981); Syracuse University (J.D., 1984). Alpha Sigma Nu; Phi Alpha Delta. *Member:* Los Angeles County and American Bar Associations; Association of Southern California Defense Counsel. **PRACTICE AREAS:** Civil Trial; Insurance Defense; Personal Injury.

**PAUL A. DE LORIMIER,** born Salinas, California, July 12, 1954; admitted to bar, 1983, California, U.S. District Court, Central and Eastern Districts of California and U.S. Court of Appeals, Ninth Circuit. *Education:* California State University at Los Angeles (B.A., 1978); Southwestern University (J.D., 1982). *Member:* State Bar of California. **PRACTICE AREAS:** Civil Trial; Insurance Defense; Products Liability; Construction Law.

---

**JEFFREY CABOT MYERS,** born New York, N.Y., September 16, 1961; admitted to bar, 1990, California; 1991, U.S. District Court, Central District of California; 1993, U.S. Court of Appeals, Ninth Circuit; 1995, U.S. Supreme Court. *Education:* American University (B.A., with honors, 1983); Southwestern University School of Law (J.D., 1990). Dean's Honor List; Wildeman Scholar. Recipient, American Jurisprudence Award, Constitution Law, 1988. Member, Screen Actors Guild, 1983—; Actors Equity Association, 1983—; AFTRA, 1983—. *Member:* Beverly Hills Bar Association; State Bar of California. **PRACTICE AREAS:** Appellate Practice; Insurance Defense; Personal Injury.

**MICHAEL L. FOX,** born Encino, California, January 6, 1969; admitted to bar, 1994, California and U.S. District Court, Central District of California. *Education:* University of Pennsylvania (B.S., 1991); Pepperdine University (J.D., 1994). Judicial Extern for the Hon. David V. Kenyon, U.S. District Court, Central District of California, 1993. *Member:* Los Angeles County and American Bar Associations; State Bar of California.

### OF COUNSEL

**GAIL D. SOLO, (A PROFESSIONAL CORPORATION),** born Sacramento, California, August 29, 1950; admitted to bar, 1975, California; 1976, U.S. District Court, Central and Northern Districts of California. *Education:* University of California at Los Angeles (B.A., 1972; J.D., 1975). Clerk, Presiding U.S. Magistrate Venetta Tassupulos, 1974. Aide, California State Senate, 1975. Personnel Committee, Big Sisters of Los Angeles. Supervising Attorney, First African Methodist-Episcopal/Temple Isaiah Law Project. Judge Pro Tem, Los Angeles Municipal Court, 1984-1985. Civil Litigation Trainer, YWCA Rape Crisis Center. *Member:* Los Angeles County Bar Association (Member, Trial Lawyers Section); State Bar of California; Consumer Attorneys Association of Los Angeles; Los Angeles Women Lawyers Association. **LANGUAGES:** Spanish. **PRACTICE AREAS:** Labor and Employment; Civil Trial; Personal Injury; Medical Malpractice.

REPRESENTATIVE CLIENTS: American Reinsurance Co.; Avis Rent A Car System, Inc.; California Insurance Group; Canadian Reinsurance Co.; Central Life Assurance Co.; Cincinnati Insurance Company; Coats Co.; Condor Insurance Co.; General Casualty Co.; Golden Nugget/Las Vegas; Golden Nugget/Laughlin; Groupement Francais D'Assurances; Guaranty National Insurance Co.; Hafnia Forsikring; Hesssen Nassauische; Hyster Company; Mirage Casino-Hotel; Monfort of Colorado; Mutuelles Unies; North American Reinsurance Co.; Ohio Farmers Insurance Co.; Progressive Insurance Companies; Reli-

*(This Listing Continued)*

CAA969B

**McKAY, BYRNE & GRAHAM, Los Angeles—Continued**

ance Insurance Co.; Scottsdale Insurance Company; The Sherwin-Williams Co.; Swiss Reinsurance Co.; Treasure Island Casino-Hotel; United Pacific Insurance Co.; Uni-Europe; Vereinigte Aachen-Berlinische; Vesta Forsikring; Westfield Insurance Co.; Zenith Insurance Co.

## CAROL L. McKELVY

1925 CENTURY PARK EAST, SUITE 2000
**LOS ANGELES, CALIFORNIA 90067**
Telephone: 310-277-2236
Fax: 310-556-5653

*Contracts, Civil Trial, Real Estate, Entertainment Law.*

**CAROL L. MCKELVY,** born 1959; admitted to bar, 1990, California. *Education:* University of Southern California (B.S., 1981); Loyola University (J.D., 1989).

## McKENNA & CUNEO, L.L.P.

*Established in 1940*

444 SOUTH FLOWER STREET
**LOS ANGELES, CALIFORNIA 90071**
Telephone: 213-688-1000
Telecopier: 213-243-6330
URL: http://www.mckennacuneo.com

*Washington, D.C. Office:* 1900 K Street, N.W. Telephone: 202-496-7500.
*San Francisco, California Office:* One Market, Steuart Street Tower, Twenty-Seventh Floor. Telephone: 415-267-4000.
*Denver, Colorado Office:* 370 Seventeenth Street, Suite 4800. Telephone: 303-634-4000.
*San Diego, California Office:* Symphony Towers, Suite 3200, 750B Street. Telephone: 619-595-5400.
*Dallas, Texas Office:* 5700 Bank One Center, 1717 Main Street. Telephone: 214-746-5700.
*Brussels, Belgium Office:* 56, rue des Colonies, Box 14, B-1000. Telephone: 011-322-278-1211.

General Civil, Criminal and Trial Practice in all State and Federal Courts, Federal Departments and Agencies. Government Contracts, White Collar Crime, Environmental, Labor and Employment and Health Care Law.

### RESIDENT PARTNERS

**THOMAS M. ABBOTT,** born Hillsboro, Texas, June 11, 1954; admitted to bar, 1984, California. *Education:* United States Naval Academy (B.S., 1976); George Washington University (J.D., 1984). *Member:* The State Bar of California; American Bar Association (Public Contract Law Section). *PRACTICE AREAS:* Government Contracts; Litigation; White Collar Criminal Defense; International Arbitration. *Email:* thomas_abbott@mckennacuneo.com

**JOHN E. CAVANAGH,** born Winnipeg, Canada, November 15, 1918; admitted to bar, 1949, District of Columbia; 1957, California. *Education:* University of Oregon (B.A., 1941); George Washington University (J.D., 1949; LL.M., 1952). Order of the Coif; Delta Theta Phi. Member, George Washington Law Review, 1948-1949. Lecturer in Government Contract Law, University of Santa Clara Law School, 1964-1968. Counsel, 1958-1961, Company Counsel, 1961-1968, Chief Counsel, 1968-1973, Vice President-General Counsel, 1971-1978, Senior Vice President-General Counsel, 1978-1983 and Senior Vice President-Special Assistant, 1983, Lockheed Corporation. *Member:* Los Angeles County, Federal and American (Member, Special Committee to Study Product Liability, 1982; Member of Council, 1969-1972 and Chairman of General Counsels Committee, 1982-1984, Section on Public Contracts Law; Chairman, Committee on Aerospace Law, Section on International Law, 1970-1974; Member, Committee on Corporate Law Departments, 1980-1983, Chairman of Subcommittee on Product Liability, 1982-1983 and Member, Ad Hoc Committee on Tort Law Reform, 1983-1988, Section on Corporation, Banking and Business Law) Bar Associations; American Institute of Aeronautics and Astronautics; National Contract Management Association (Member, National Board of Advisors, 1991—); The State Bar of California. [Major, U.S. Army, 1941-1945] *Email:* john_cavanaugh@mckennacuneo.com

**THOMAS CURTISS, JR.,** born Buffalo, New York, November 4, 1941; admitted to bar, 1971, California. *Education:* Phillips Exeter Academy (1959); Yale University (B.A., 1963); Harvard University (J.D., 1970). Adjunct Professor, Estate Planning, Loyola of Los Angeles School of Law, 1983-1993. Member, Editorial Board, *Los Angeles Lawyer,* 1993. Author, Publications: "Administering an Insolvent Estate: There is More Than Meets the Eye, Parts I, II and III," Estate Planning, Trust & Probate News, Summer 1990 and Fall 1990. Co-authored with John A. Payne, Jr., Esq. "Estate Planning for the United States Citizen Residing Abroad: A Case Study," Estate Planning, Trust & Probate News, Winter 1991; "The Pros and Cons of Living Trust," Los Angeles Lawyer, September 1991; "Passing Wealth to Grandchildren-How to Minimize or Avoid the Generation-skipping Transfer Tax," Los Angeles Lawyer, November 1993, Co-authored with Maryann S. Meggelin, Esq.; "Estate Planning After Dad Dies: Should Mom Gift or Disclaim?" California Trusts and Estates Quarterly, Summer 1996, Co-authored with Charles A. Shultz, Esq. *Member:* Los Angeles County (Chairman, Executive Committee, Trust and Estates Sections, 1991-1992) and American (Member, Section of Real Property, Probate and Trust Law) Bar Associations; State Bar of California (Member: Probate Administration Subcommittee, Probate Section, 1981—). Fellow, The American College of Trust and Estate Counsel. (Certified Specialist, Estate Planning, Trust and Probate Law, The State Bar of California Board of Legal Specialization). *PRACTICE AREAS:* Trusts and Estates; Conservatorships and Guardianships; Estate Planning.

**JAMES J. GALLAGHER,** born Washington, D.C., June 17, 1939; admitted to bar, 1966, District of Columbia and U.S. Tax Court; 1970, U.S. Supreme Court; 1971, U.S. Claims Court; 1979, California. *Education:* University of Notre Dame (B.B.A., 1961); Georgetown University (LL.B., 1965). Author: "Renegotiation at the Court of Claims: The Government's Struggle with the Burden of Proof," 46 George Washington Law Review 376, 1978. Adjunct Professor of Law, Georgetown Law Center, 1973-1977. Lecturer of Law, Catholic University of America, Columbus School of Law, 1975-1977. *Member:* The District of Columbia Bar; Bar Association of the District of Columbia; Los Angeles County and American (Member, Public Contract Law Section) Bar Associations; The State Bar of California. *Email:* james_gallagher@mckennacuneo.com

**MICHAEL T. KAVANAUGH,** born Milwaukee, Wisconsin, January 28, 1947; admitted to bar, 1971, Wisconsin; 1980, District of Columbia; 1982, California. *Education:* United States Military Academy and Marquette University (B.B.A., 1969); Marquette University (J.D., 1971). Phi Alpha Delta. *Member:* State Bar of Wisconsin; The District of Columbia Bar; American Bar Association (Member, Public Contract Law Section); The State Bar of California. [Capt., U.S. Army, Judge Advocate General Corps, 1971-1976]. *PRACTICE AREAS:* Government Contracts Law. *Email:* michael_kavanaugh@mckennacuneo.com

**STANLEY W. LANDFAIR,** born Elwood, Indiana, July 9, 1954; admitted to bar, 1978, Virginia; 1984, District of Columbia; U.S. Supreme Court; 1992, California. *Education:* Butler University (B.A., magna cum laude, 1975); Georgetown University (J.D., 1978). Editor, Journal of Law and Policy in International Business, 1978. Co-Author: *Pesticide Regulation Handbook,* Executive Enterprises Publications, Inc., New York, N.Y., 1987 (Revised Edition); *TSCA Handbook,* Government Institutes, 1991 (Second Edition). Author: "TSCA Reporting and Recordkeeping Requirements: EPA's Focus for Enforcement," 6 Env. Mgmt. Report, VII, 1987; "The Toxic Substances Control Act: Recent Enforcement Trends: Chemical Regulation Reporter. Vol. 15, No. 28, Bureau of National Affairs, 1991; "The AB-2588 'Toxic Hot Spots' Health Risk Assessment Requirement: A Trap For the Unwary Under Proposition 65," Prop 65 News, Vol. VI, Nos. 11 and 12, November and December, 1992; "Legal and Practical Considerations in Defending Citizen Suits under Section 313 of the Emergency Planning and Community Right-To-Know Act," Vol. 2, No. 2, 1993. Member, Board of Editors, Proposition 65 News. Contributor: *Environmental Law Handbook,* Government Institutes, Twelfth Edition, 1993. Law Clerk, U.S. Court of Appeals, Fourth Circuit, 1981-1982. Commissioner, Fairfax County, Virginia Human Rights Commission, 1977-1978. *Member:* The District of Columbia Bar; Virginia State Bar; American Bar Association (Member, Sections on Litigation; Administrative Law; Natural Resources Law). [LCDR, JAGC, USNR, active duty, 1978-1981]. *PRACTICE AREAS:* Environmental Law. *Email:* stan_landfair@mckennacuneo.com

**ROBERT L. LAYTON,** born Napa, California, December 19, 1948; admitted to bar, 1974, California and U.S. Court of Appeals, Ninth Circuit. *Education:* University of California at Davis (B.A., 1971; J.D., 1974). Instructor, Legal Research and Writing, University of California at Davis, 1973-1974. *Member:* State Bar of California; American Bar Association (Member, Sections On: Tort and Insurance Practice; Forum Committee on Health Law); Association of Business Trial Lawyers. *PRACTICE AREAS:* Health Care; Civil Litigation; Business Law. *Email:* robert_layton@mckennacuneo.com

*(This Listing Continued)*

**STEPHANIE BERRINGTON MCNUTT,** born Vancouver, British Columbia, November 3, 1952; admitted to bar, 1981, California; 1982, U.S. District Court, Central District of California; 1987, U.S. District Court, Northern and Eastern Districts of California; 1992, U.S. Court of Appeals, Ninth Circuit; 1994, U.S. District Court, Southern District of California. *Education:* University of California at Los Angeles; University of California at Davis (B.A., 1975); Southwestern University (J.D., 1980). Lead Articles Editor and Chair, Antitrust Symposium, Southwestern University Law Review, 1978-1980. Pro Bono Counsel, Los Angeles Superior Court Child Advocate's Office, 1983—. Speaker, CEB Program, Laying Evidentiary Foundations, Los Angeles County Bar Association, Fundamentals of Discovery. *Member:* Los Angeles County and American (Member, Section on Litigation) Bar Associations; State Bar of California (Member, Litigation Section); Los Angeles Women Lawyers Association. *Email:* stephanie_mcnutt@mckennacuneo.com

**SUSAN A. MITCHELL,** born Kansas City, Kansas, November 20, 1954; admitted to bar, 1981, California. *Education:* University of Minnesota (B.A., 1977; J.D., 1980). Member, 1978-1979 and Managing Editor, 1979-1980, Minnesota Law Review. *Member:* The State Bar of California. *Email:* susan_mitchell@mckennacuneo.com

**ROBERT JON NEWMAN,** born 1950; admitted to bar, 1976, Missouri; 1994, California. *Education:* Wesleyan University (B.A., 1972); Washington University (J.D., 1975). *Member:* State Bar of California; American Bar Association (Member, Sections on: Public Contract and International Law); National Contract Management Association. *PRACTICE AREAS:* Government (Public) Contract Law; International Law; Environmental Law. *Email:* rob_newman@mckennacuneo.com

**MARLO S. OLIVER,** born Cocoa, Florida, June 14, 1950; admitted to bar, 1980, District of Columbia; 1982, U.S. Claims Court; 1986, California. *Education:* Wright State University (B.S., summa cum laude, 1970); Harvard University (J.D., 1980). *Member:* The District of Columbia Bar; Federal Bar Association; The State Bar of California. *Email:* marlo_oliver@mckennacuneo.com

**RICHARD B. OLIVER,** born Lansing, Michigan, November 11, 1951; admitted to bar, 1977, Georgia; 1980, District of Columbia; 1984, California. *Education:* University of Virginia (B.A., with high honors, 1974); Harvard University (J.D., 1977). Phi Beta Kappa. Note Editor, Harvard Journal on Legislation, 1976-1977. Co-Author: "Flow-Down Clauses in Subcontracts," Briefing Papers, Federal Publications, 85-5. *Member:* American and Federal Bar Associations; The District of Columbia Bar; The State Bar of Georgia; The State Bar of California. [Capt., USAF, 1977-1980] *Email:* richard_oliver@mckennacuneo.com

**CHARLES H. POMEROY, IV,** born Burbank, California, November 13, 1957; admitted to bar, 1988, California. *Education:* California State University at Northridge (B.A., 1980; B.S., 1983; M.S., 1984; B.A., 1984); Southwestern University (J.D., 1987). Phi Alpha Delta. Instructor, Environmental Health, California State University at Northridge, 1987-1995. California Registered Environmental, Health Specialist. California Registered Environmental Assesor. *Member:* Los Angeles County Bar Association; State Bar of California. *Email:* charles_pomeroy@mckennacuneo.com

**MARK R. TROY,** born Los Angeles, California, May 22, 1960; admitted to bar, 1985, California. *Education:* University of California, Los Angeles (B.A., 1982); Loyola University of Los Angeles (J.D., 1985). Member, Loyola of Los Angeles International and Comparative Law Journal, 1983-1984. Co-Author: "Qui Tam Provisions of the False Claims Act: Congress Should Limit the Power of Citizen Plaintiffs," Los Angeles Lawyer, March 1992. Judge Pro Tem, Los Angeles County Superior Court. *Member:* Los Angeles County and American (Member, Section on Public Contract Law) Bar Associations. *Email:* mark_troy@mckennacuneo.com

**GAIL FRULLA ZIRKELBACH,** born Phoenix, Arizona, July 9, 1962; admitted to bar, 1986, Maryland; 1988, District of Columbia; 1995, California. *Education:* Princeton University, Woodrow Wilson School of Public and International Affairs (B.A., cum laude, 1983); University of Virginia (J.D., 1986). *Member:* District of Columbia Bar; State Bar of California; American Bar Association (Member, Sections on: Public Contract; Litigation). *Email:* gail_zirkelbach@mckennacuneo.com

### RESIDENT OF COUNSEL

**JOHN A. BURKHOLDER,** born Mansfield, Ohio, February 15, 1949; admitted to bar, 1978, District of Columbia; 1992, California. *Education:* Yale University (B.A., 1971); Washington College of Law The American University (J.D., 1978). Law Clerk to Judge Smith, District of Columbia Superior Court, 1978-1979. Chief Counsel, 1986-1987, Administrative Judge, 1987-1988, General Services Administration Board of Contract Appeals. *PRACTICE AREAS:* Administrative Law; Civil Practice; Contract Law; Government Contract Law; Litigation. *Email:* john_burkholder@mckennacuneo.com

**ROBERT R. PLANK,** born Santa Monica, California, December 20, 1928; admitted to bar, 1979, California. *Education:* Whittier College (B.A., 1950); University of Connecticut (M.A., 1952); Valley University School of Law (J.D., cum laude, 1979). *Member:* The State Bar of California (Member, Public Law Section); American Bar Association (Member, Public Contract Law Section, Government Contracts); National Contract Management Association. [With U.S. Army, 1953-1955] *Email:* robert_plank@mckennacuneo.com

### RESIDENT ASSOCIATES

**BARBARA J. BACON,** born Los Angeles, California, February 8, 1966; admitted to bar, 1992, California. *Education:* San Diego State University (B.S., magna cum laude, 1989); Harvard University (J.D., 1992). *Member:* Los Angeles County and American Bar Associations; The State Bar of California. *Email:* barbara_bacon@mckennacuneo.com

**CYNTHIA BECKWITH,** born Toronto, Ontario, Canada, January 3, 1955; admitted to bar, 1992, California and U.S. District Court, Central District of California; 1994, U.S. Court of Appeals, Ninth Circuit; 1995, U.S. Court of Federal Claims. *Education:* Queen's University (B.A., 1977); Pepperdine University (J.D., cum laude, 1991). Member, Moot Court Board. Research Attorney, Los Angeles Superior Court, Law and Motion Department, 1991-1992. *Member:* Los Angeles County and American Bar Associations. *Email:* cynthia_bechwith@mckennacuneo.com

**CAROL R. BROPHY,** born San Diego, California; admitted to bar, 1991, California, U.S. Court of Appeals, Ninth Circuit and U.S. District Court, Central and Southern Districts of California. *Education:* Stanford University (A.B., 1968); Yale University (M.F.A., 1975); Southwestern University School of Law (J.D., 1991). Delta Theta Phi. Registered Environmental Assessor, California, 1989—. Author: "The Forgotten Factor: Environmental Implications of Military Activities," Adelphi Law Journal, Vol. 6, 1990. Member, California Aerospace Environmental Association, 1987-1991. *Member:* Los Angeles (Member, Litigation and Environmental Law Sections) and American (Member, Sections on: Business; Administrative; Natural Resources; Litigation) Bar Associations; State Bar of California (Member: International Law Section; Environmental Law Section). *PRACTICE AREAS:* Environmental; Litigation; Administrative Law. *Email:* carol_brophy@mckennacuneo.com

**ELIZABETH COPPAGE BROWN,** born Midland, Michigan, June 14, 1963; admitted to bar, 1992, California. *Education:* Trinity University (B.S., 1985); University of California School of Law, Davis (J.D., 1992). *Email:* elizabeth_brown@mckennacuneo.com

**TERRY L. BROWN,** born Ulm, Germany, August 29, 1955; admitted to bar, 1991, California; 1992, U.S. District Court, Central and Eastern Districts of California. *Education:* University of California at Los Angeles (B.A., 1977); Golden Gate University (M.B.A., 1983); Loyola Marymount University (J.D., 1991). Associate in Risk Management Certificate, 1987. Member: Risk and Insurance Management Society, 1985-1991; Public Risk Management Association, 1985-1991. *Member:* Los Angeles County, American and National Bar Associations; State Bar of California (Member: Labor and Litigation Sections); Black Women Lawyers Association. *PRACTICE AREAS:* Labor and Employment Law; Litigation. *Email:* terry_brown@mckennacuneo.com

**TRACEY A. CALVER,** born Garden Grove, California, September 11, 1962; admitted to bar, 1996, California. *Education:* California State University, Fullerton (B.A., 1985); California State University, Long Beach (M.S., 1991); University of San Diego (J.D., 1996). Editor: University of San Diego Law Review; Journal of Contemporary Legal Issues. *PRACTICE AREAS:* Government Contracts; Civil Litigation. *Email:* tracey_calver@mckennacuneo.com

**EDWIN A. CARLSON,** born Berkeley, California, December 6, 1963; admitted to bar, 1996, California. *Education:* McGill University (B.S., 1985); University of California, Los Angeles (J.D., 1996). Recipient, American Jurisprudence Award, Civil Procedure. Member, Moot Court. [Lt., U.S. Navy, 1987-1993]. *PRACTICE AREAS:* Environmental. *Email:* edwin_carlson@mckennacuneo.com

**NICOLE CARSON,** born Farmington, Michigan, May 9, 1969; admitted to bar, 1995, California; U.S. District Court, Central District of California; U.S. Court of Appeals, Ninth Circuit. *Education:* University of Michigan (B.A., 1991); University of California, Hastings (J.D., 1995). *Member:*

*(This Listing Continued)*

## McKENNA & CUNEO, L.L.P., Los Angeles—Continued

State Bar of California; Women Lawyer Association of Los Angeles. *PRACTICE AREAS:* Litigation; Government Contracts; Criminal Defense; Constitutional Law. *Email:* nicole_carson@mckennacuneo.com

**LAURA O. DOYLE,** born Harbor City, California, June 29, 1960; admitted to bar, 1993, California, U.S. District Court, Central District of California and U.S. Court of Appeals, Ninth Circuit. *Education:* California State University, Long Beach (B.S., Finance, with distinction, 1983; M.S., Finance, with great distinction, 1985); University of Southern California (J.D., 1993). Beta Gamma Sigma; Golden Key. Member, Hale Moot Court Honors Program. Recipient, American Jurisprudence Award in Real Property. *Member:* Los Angeles County and American (Member, Public Contract Law Section) Bar Associations; National Contract Management Association. *PRACTICE AREAS:* Government Contracts. *Email:* laura_doyle@mckennacuneo.com

**N. KEMBA EXTAVOUR,** born Port-of-Spain, Trinidad & Tobago, November 9, 1972; admitted to bar, 1996, California. *Education:* Stanford University (B.A., 1993); Boalt Hall School of Law, University of California (J.D., 1996). *PRACTICE AREAS:* Litigation; Government Contracts. *Email:* n_kemba_extavour@mckennacuneo.com

**DANA FITZGIBBONS,** born St. Louis, Missouri, November 1, 1962; admitted to bar, 1989, California and U.S. Court of Appeals, Ninth Circuit; 1990, U.S. District Court, Central District of California; 1991, District of Columbia. *Education:* West Virginia University (B.S., summa cum laude, 1984); Loyola Law School (J.D., 1988). Beta Gamma Sigma; Phi Kappa Phi. Member: Mortar Board Honor Society; St. Thomas More Law Honor Society. *Member:* State Bar of California (Member: Litigation Section, 1989-1990, 1995-1996; Public Contract Law Section, 1990-1995); District of Columbia Bar (Member, Government Contracts Section, 1991-1995); American Bar Association (Member, Section of Public Contract Law); Women's Law Association. *PRACTICE AREAS:* Government Contracts Law. *Email:* dana_fitzgibbons@mckennacuneo.com

**TARA A. FLANAGAN,** born Elizabeth, New Jersey, October 6, 1958; admitted to bar, 1987, California. *Education:* H. Sophie Newcomb Memorial College of Tulane University (B.A., with honors, 1980); Pepperdine University (J.D., cum laude, 1987). Recipient, American Jurisprudence Awards in Civil Procedure and Trial Practice. Lead Articles Editor, Pepperdine University Law Review, 1986-1987. Author: "The Grand Jury Subpoena, Is It the Prosecutor's 'Ultimate Weapon' Against Defense Attorneys and Their Clients?" Pepperdine Law Review, Vol. 13, 1986; "Sanctions Under California Code of Civil Procedure Section 128.5-How to Avoid 'Eating a Piece of Humble Pie'" Pepperdine Law Review, Vol. 13, 1986. Pro Bono Counsel, Public Counsel of Los Angeles, Children's Rights. *Member:* Los Angeles County and American (Member, Public Contracts Law Division) Bar Associations; The State Bar of California. *Email:* tara_flanagan@mckennacuneo.com

**EVELYN F. HEIDELBERG,** born Philadelphia, Pennsylvania, January 11, 1951; admitted to bar, 1991, California. *Education:* University of Delaware (B.A., magna cum laude, 1972); University of Pittsburgh (M.U.R.P., 1977); University of the Pacific (J.D., 1991). Valedictorian; Phi Beta Kappa; Order of the Coif. Member, Pacific Law Journal, 1989-1991. Author: "Parent Corporation Liability Under CERCLA: Toward a Uniform Federal Rule of Decision," 22 Pacific Law Journal 854, April, 1991. *Member:* Los Angeles County and American (Member, Section on Environmental Law); State Bar of California (Member, Legislative Committee, Environmental Section). *PRACTICE AREAS:* Environmental; Litigation. *Email:* evelyn_heidelberg@mckennacuneo.com

**R. CRAIG HOLMAN,** born Brigham City, Utah, August 15, 1954; admitted to bar, 1989, California and U.S. Court of Appeals, Ninth Circuit; 1990, U.S. District Court, Central District of California; U.S. Court of Federal Claims. *Education:* University of Utah (B.A., cum laude, 1978); Utah State University (M.B.A., 1980); Brigham Young University (J.D., 1989). *Member:* State Bar of California; American Bar Association (Member, Sections on: Public Contracts and Litigation). *LANGUAGES:* Portuguese. *PRACTICE AREAS:* Government Contracts Law; Litigation; Commercial Contracts; Construction. *Email:* craig_holman@mckennacuneo.com

**KARIN L. KEUTZER,** born Eugene, Oregon, October 4, 1962; admitted to bar, 1988, California; U.S. District Court, Central and Northern Districts of California and U.S. Court of Federal Claims. *Education:* University of Oregon (B.A., magna cum laude, 1985); Georgetown University Law Center (J.D., cum laude, 1988). Phi Beta Kappa. *Member:* Los Angeles

*(This Listing Continued)*

County and American Bar Associations; The State Bar of California (Litigation Section). *Email:* karin_keutzer@mckennacuneo.com

**PHILIP BRUNO KUMPIS,** born Halifax, England, December 20, 1953; admitted to bar, 1989, California. *Education:* United States Naval Academy (B.S.E.E., 1976); George Mason University (J.D., 1988). *Member:* American Bar Association; State Bar of California; The District of Columbia Bar. [Captain, USMC, 1976-1982] *Email:* phil_kumpis@mckennacuneo.com

**PAMELA D. LAUNDER,** born St. Louis, Missouri, February 12, 1967; admitted to bar, 1996, California and U.S. District Court, Central District of California. *Education:* Claremont McKenna College (B.A., 1989); Loyola Marymount University (J.D., cum laude, 1996). Alpha Sigma Nu; Phi Delta Phi; Order of the Coif; St. Thomas More Law Society. . Member, 1994-1995 and Executive Editor, 1995-1996, Loyola Of Los Angeles Entertainment Law Journal. *PRACTICE AREAS:* Government Contracts. *Email:* pamela_launder@mckennacuneo.com

**CHARLOTTE R. MAYA,** born Livermore, California, March 17, 1968; admitted to bar, 1993, California. *Education:* Rice University (B.A., 1990); University of California, Los Angeles (J.D., 1993). Editor, UCLA Women's Law Journal. Author: "Sexual Harassment Hits Home," UCLA Women's Journal. *Member:* Los Angeles County Bar Association; State Bar of California. *PRACTICE AREAS:* Estate and Trust Planning; Probate and Estate Settlement.

**KAREN POSTON MILLER,** born Burbank, California, October 24, 1962; admitted to bar, 1990, California; 1991, District of Columbia. *Education:* San Diego State University (B.S., 1986); Loyola Law School (J.D., 1990). Phi Delta Phi. Staff Writer, 1988-1989 and Executive Editor, 1989-1990, Loyola of Los Angeles Entertainment Law Journal. Author: "All Puff and No Stuff: Avoiding the Idea/Expression Dichotomy," Volume 9, Loyola of Los Angeles Entertainment Law Journal. *Member:* Federal and American Bar Associations. *PRACTICE AREAS:* Government Contracts; Litigation. *Email:* karen_miller@mckennacuneo.com

**ROBERT F. MILLER,** born Camden, New Jersey, September 26, 1959; admitted to bar, 1986, Virginia; 1988, California; 1989, District of Columbia. *Education:* Claremont Men's College (B.A., 1981); University of Southern California (M.S., 1985); McGeorge School of Law, University of Pacific (J.D., 1986). Recipient, National Contract Management Association Scholarship, 1986. Author: "Prospectively Pricing Subcontractor Impact and Dodging the Criminal Bullet," Guide to Government Contracting, Commerce Clearing House, 1992. *Member:* National Contract Management Association; American Bar Association (Member, Forum Committee on the Construction Industry and Section of Public Contract Law); Virginia State Bar; The District of Columbia Bar; The State Bar of California. *LANGUAGES:* French. *PRACTICE AREAS:* Construction; Government Contracts. *Email:* robert_miller@mckennacuneo.com

**KATHLEEN A. MORAN,** born Hobbs, New Mexico, March 12, 1967; admitted to bar, 1992, California; U.S. Court of Federal Claims. *Education:* University of Notre Dame (B.A., summa cum laude, 1989); University of Texas (J.D., with honors, 1992). Phi Beta Kappa. *PRACTICE AREAS:* Business Litigation; Government Contracts Litigation. *Email:* kathleen_moran@mckennacuneo.com

**THOMAS A. MYERS,** born Camden, New Jersey, October 20, 1964; admitted to bar, 1994, California. *Education:* Amherst College (B.A., 1987); Harvard University (J.D., cum laude, 1994). Articles Editor, Harvard Civil Rights Civil Liberties Law Review, 1993-1994. *PRACTICE AREAS:* Labor and Employment Law. *Email:* tom_myers@mckennacuneo.com

**JIN S. PARK,** born Seoul, Korea, September 10, 1968; admitted to bar, 1995, California. *Education:* Stanford University (B.A., 1991); University of California School of Law (J.D., 1995). Author: "Pink Asylum: Political Asylum Eligibility of Gay Men and Lesbians Under U.S. Immigration Policy," 42 UCLA Law Review, April, 1995. *LANGUAGES:* Korean. *PRACTICE AREAS:* Litigation; Government Contracts; International Law. *Email:* jin_park@mckennacuneo.com

**BRIAN M. REGAN,** born Inglewood, California, July 14, 1965; admitted to bar, 1990, California. *Education:* California State University at Long Beach (B.S., 1987); Loyola Marymount University (J.D., 1990). Member: St. Thomas Moore Law Honor Society; Catholic Law Society, 1987-1990. *Member:* The State Bar of California; American Bar Association. *PRACTICE AREAS:* Government Contracts; White Collar Criminal Defense; General Litigation. *Email:* brian_regan@mckennacuneo.com

**KAREN RINEHART,** born Colorado; admitted to bar, 1996, California and U.S. District Court, Central District of California. *Education:* Loyola

*(This Listing Continued)*

# PROFESSIONAL BIOGRAPHIES

## CALIFORNIA—LOS ANGELES

Marymount University (J.D., 1996). Phi Delta Phi (President, 1994-1995). Recipient, American Jurisprudence Awards. Member, Moot Court. Member, 1994-1995 and Editor-in-Chief, 1995-1996, Loyola of Los Angeles Entertainment Law Journal. Professional Certification in Government Contract Management, UCLA, 1985. Committee Member, Board of Governors, Loyola Law School, 1996—. *Member:* Los Angeles County and American (Member, Public Contract Law Section) Bar Associations; State Bar of California; Los Angeles Women Lawyers Association; National Contract Management Association; Association of Government Accountants. *PRACTICE AREAS:* Government Contracts. *Email:* karen_rinehart@mckennacuneo.com

**MARTIN A. RIPS,** born Omaha, Nebraska, November 22, 1962; admitted to bar, 1989, California and U.S. Court of Appeals, Ninth Circuit. *Education:* Northwestern University (B.A., 1985); George Washington University (J.D., with honors, 1989). Member, Journal of International Law and Economics, 1988-1989. *Member:* State Bar of California; American Bar Association (Member, Public Contract Law Section); National Contracts Management Association. *PRACTICE AREAS:* Government Contracts Law; Litigation; International Arbitration. *Email:* marty_rips@mckennacuneo.com

**MICHAEL R. RIZZO,** born Pasadena, California, May 21, 1967; admitted to bar, 1992, California and U.S. District Court, Central District of California. *Education:* Georgetown University (B.S., 1989; J.D., 1992). Associate Editor, Law of Policy in International Business Journal, 1992. Instructor, "Street Law, Corrections," 1991. *Member:* Los Angeles County and American Bar Associations; State Bar of California. *LANGUAGES:* Spanish. *PRACTICE AREAS:* Litigation; Government Contracts; White Collar Criminal Defense. *Email:* michael_rizzo@mckennacuneo.com

**DAWN SELLERS,** born Houston, Texas, September 27, 1966; admitted to bar, 1994, California. *Education:* Scripps College (B.A., 1988); University of California at Los Angeles (J.D.,1994). Phi Beta Kappa. *Email:* dawn_sellers@mckennacuneo.com

**DAVID A. SONNER,** born Lafayette, Indiana, December 22, 1957; admitted to bar, 1988, California. *Education:* Harvey Mudd College (B.S., 1980); Claremont Graduate School (M.A., 1981); Southwestern University School of Law (J.D., cum laude, 1988). Western Regional Winner, Giles Sutherland Rich Moot Court Competition, 1988. Member and Oralist, Moot Court Honors Program, 1987-1988. Staff Member, 1986-1987 and Note and Comment Editor, 1987-1988, Southwestern University Law Review. Author: "Apple Corp. v. Leber: Did Beatlemania Infringe the Beatles' Right of Publicity?" 17 Southwestern University Law Review 755, 1988. Extern Clerk to the Honorable Arthur Alarcon, U.S. Court of Appeals, Ninth Circuit, Fall, 1987. *Member:* State Bar of California; American Bar Association. *PRACTICE AREAS:* Government Contracts Law; Litigation. *Email:* david_sonner@mckennacuneo.com

**ELIZABETH A. STAMPER,** born Fayetteville, North Carolina, May 17, 1965; admitted to bar, 1992, California. *Education:* Miami University (B.A., cum laude, 1987); Boston University (J.D., 1991). Recipient, American Jurisprudence Award in Professional Responsibility. *Email:* elizabeth_stamper@mckennacuneo.com

**ROBERT R. VALENCIA,** born Los Angeles, California, June 3, 1965; admitted to bar, 1994, California. *Education:* California Polytechnic State University, San Luis Obispo (B.S.B.A., 1987); Pepperdine University School of Law (J.D., cum laude, 1994). Phi Alpha Delta. Recipient: American Jurisprudence Awards in Constitutional Law and Advanced Legal Research. Law Clerk to Judge Robert M. Takasugi, U.S. District Court, Central District of California, 1994-1995. *Member:* Los Angels County, American and Mexican American Bar Associations. *PRACTICE AREAS:* Litigation; Health Care. *Email:* robert_valencia@mckennacuneo.com

**DANIEL E. WAX,** born New York, N.Y., May 9, 1940; admitted to bar, 1989, California and U.S. District Court, Eastern and Central Districts of California. *Education:* Polytechnic Institute of New York (B.S., Chem. Eng., 1961); University of California, Berkeley; McGeorge School of Law, University of the Pacific (J.D., 1988). Member, American Association of Chemical Engineers, 1961-1964. *Member:* Los Angeles Bar Association (Executive Committee, Environmental Law Section); State Bar of California. *Email:* dan_wax@mckennacuneo.com

**MICHAEL E. WEINSTEN,** born New York, November 29, 1965; admitted to bar, 1991, California; U.S. District Court, Central District of California. *Education:* Tulane University of Louisiana (B.A., cum laude, 1987); London School of Economics, London, England; George Washington University (J.D., with honors, 1991). *Member:* State Bar of California; American Bar Association (Member, Section on Public Contract Law); National

*(This Listing Continued)*

Contract Management Association; Business Executive for National Security. *PRACTICE AREAS:* Government Contracts; Litigation; White Collar. *Email:* michael_weinsten@mckennacuneo.com

(For Biographical Data on other Firm Personnel, see Professional Biographies at Washington, D.C., San Francisco and San Diego, California, Denver, Colorado, Dallas, Texas and Brussels, Belgium.)

---

## McKINLEY & CAPELOTO
### LOS ANGELES, CALIFORNIA

(See Pasadena)

*Financial Institutions, Creditor Rights, Bankruptcy, Real Estate, Workouts, Commercial Law, Civil Litigation, Elder Law, Construction Law.*

---

## RICHARD W. McLAIN
### A PROFESSIONAL CORPORATION
### LOS ANGELES, CALIFORNIA

(See Glendale)

*General Practice.*

---

## McLAUGHLIN AND IRVIN
### 818 WEST SEVENTH STREET, SUITE 920
### LOS ANGELES, CALIFORNIA 90017

Telephone: 213-629-1414
Cable Address: "Loclinlaw"
Telefacsimile: 213-629-3008

*General Business Matters. Litigation in State and Federal Courts. Labor and Employment Law. Employment Benefits Law, ERISA, Antitrust, Estates and Trusts.*

### MEMBERS OF FIRM

**JOSEPH M. MCLAUGHLIN,** born Los Angeles, California, July 10, 1928; admitted to bar, 1955, California; 1959, U.S. Supreme Court. *Education:* University of Southern California; Loyola University of Los Angeles (J.D., 1955). Phi Delta Phi. Lecturer in Labor Relations, Loyola University, 1958-1960. Contributing Author: "Labor Law for General Practitioners," University of California, 1960. President, Food Employers Council, Inc., 1984-1989. Member, Board of Visitors, Loyola Law School, 1987—. *Member:* Bar Association of San Francisco; Long Beach, Los Angeles County, Federal, American (Member, Sections of: Business Law; Labor and Employment Law; Antitrust Law; Taxation; International Law and Practice; Litigation) and Inter-American Bar Associations; The State Bar of California; American Judicature Society; American Society of International Law; International Bar Association; Association of Business Trial Lawyers.

**WILLIAM B. IRVIN,** born Chicago, Illinois, October 23, 1918; admitted to bar, 1949, California; 1970, U.S. Supreme Court. *Education:* University of California at Los Angeles (B.A., 1941); Stanford University (J.D., 1949). Panel Arbitrator, American Arbitration Association. Judicial Arbitrator and Mediator, Los Angeles Superior Court. *Member:* Bar Association of San Francisco; Los Angeles County and American (Member, Sections of: Administrative Law; Antitrust Law; Labor and Employment Law; Real Property; Law Practice Management) Bar Associations; The State Bar of California.

**LAWRENCE J. MCLAUGHLIN,** born Long Beach, California, September 3, 1952; admitted to bar, 1978, California; 1982, U.S. Supreme Court. *Education:* University of Southern California (B.A., cum laude, 1974); Loyola University (J.D., 1978). President, Board of Governors, Loyola Law School. *Member:* Los Angeles County (Member, Federal Courts Committee), American (Member, Sections of: Litigation and Labor and Employment Law) and Federal Bar Associations; State Bar of California; Association of Business Trial Lawyers.

REFERENCE: Bank of America National Trust & Savings Assn. (Los Angeles Main Office).

## LAW OFFICES OF
## CARL A. McMAHAN
827 MORAGA DRIVE
LOS ANGELES, CALIFORNIA 90049
Telephone: 310-472-8078
Fax: 310-472-7014

*Medical Malpractice, Products Liability, Tort Law, Negligence, Complex Personal Injury Law. Civil Trials and Appeals in all State and Federal Courts.*

**CARL A. McMAHAN,** born Ridgecrest, California, August 31, 1953; admitted to bar, 1983, California and U.S. District Court, Central, Southern, Northern and Eastern Districts of California; 1985, Colorado; 1988, District of Columbia and The District of Columbia Court of Appeals. *Education:* San Diego State University (B.A., with honors, 1975); McGeorge School of Law, University of the Pacific (J.D., 1982). Moot Court Honors. Judge Pro Tem, Los Angeles County Superior Court. Arbitrator, Orange County Superior Court. *Member:* Los Angeles County, Colorado, District of Columbia Bar Associations; State Bar of California; American Board of Trial Advocates. Association of Trial Lawyers of America. (Also Of Counsel to Peter J. McNulty). **PRACTICE AREAS:** Civil Trial; Product Liability Law; Medical Malpractice Law.

### OF COUNSEL

**PETER J. McNULTY,** born Boston, Massachusetts, June 15, 1954; admitted to bar, 1979, California and U.S. District Court, Central District of California; 1983, U.S. District Court, Northern and Southern Districts of California; 1984, U.S. District Court, Eastern District of California; 1986, U.S. District Court, Northern District of Illinois; 1987, U.S. District Court, Central District of Illinois, U.S. District Court, Southern District of Texas, U.S. District Court, District of Massachusetts and U.S. Court of Appeals, Ninth Circuit; 1988, U.S. Court of Appeals, First Circuit and U.S. Supreme Court. *Education:* University of Vermont (B.A., 1976); Boston College Law School (J.D., 1979). Phi Beta Kappa. Assistant Editor, American Journal of Law and Medicine, 1978-1979. Instructor, Attorney Assistant Training Program, University of California at Los Angeles, 1980—. *Member:* Los Angeles County and American Bar Associations; State Bar of California; Lawyers-Pilots Bar Association; The Association of Trial Lawyers of America; Los Angeles Trial Lawyers Association; California Trial Lawyers Association; Bel-Air Trial Lawyers Association. (Also practicing individually at same address). **REPORTED CASES:** Herrera-Diaz vs. U.S. Department of Navy 845 F2d 1534 (9th Circuit 1988); Rodriguez vs. Superior Court of Kern County 221 Cal. App. 3d 1371.

REFERENCE: City National Bank, Beverly Hills, California.

## McMAHON & SPIEGEL
355 SOUTH GRAND AVENUE, SUITE 3290
LOS ANGELES, CALIFORNIA 90071-1591
Telephone: 213-628-9800
Fax: 213-628-9813

*Business Litigation in Federal and State Courts and before Federal, State and Local Regulatory Agencies; Oil, Energy and Pipeline Law; Antitrust and Trade Regulation; Business Contracts.*

### MEMBERS OF FIRM

**M. BRIAN McMAHON,** born East Orange, New Jersey, June 1, 1942; admitted to bar, 1978, California. *Education:* Queen of Apostles Seminary and College (B.A., 1963); University of Wisconsin-Madison (Ph.D., 1972); University of California at Los Angeles (J.D., 1978). Extern to Judge Ozell M. Trask, U.S. Court of Appeals, Ninth Circuit, 1977. Staff Attorney, U.S. Court of Appeals, Ninth Circuit, 1978-1979. *Member:* State Bar of California. **PRACTICE AREAS:** Anti Trust; Complex Litigation; Oil; Energy; Pipeline Law; Business Litigation.

**CRAIG R. SPIEGEL,** born Des Moines, Iowa, April 15, 1953; admitted to bar, 1980, Illinois; 1981, Texas; 1985, California. *Education:* St. Olaf College (B.A., summa cum laude, 1975); Harvard University (J.D., cum laude, 1979). Phi Beta Kappa. Editor: "Antitrust Laws and Trade Regulation," Matthew Bender, 1988-1993. Instructor, University of Miami, Coral Gables, Florida, 1979-1980. Professor, Pepperdine University School of Law, 1985-1990. *Member:* Illinois State Bar Association; State Bar of Texas; State Bar of California. **PRACTICE AREAS:** Business Litigation; Antitrust Law; Securities; Class Actions.

**MARILYN K. PACE,** born Akron, Ohio, October 21, 1949; admitted to bar, 1990, California. *Education:* University of Michigan (B.A., 1971); University of California at Los Angeles (J.D., 1989). Phi Beta Kappa; Alpha Lambda Delta. *Member:* Los Angeles County and American Bar Associations; State Bar of California.

REFERENCES: The Bank of California (Los Angeles Main Office).

## H. VINCENT McNALLY
10920 WILSHIRE BOULEVARD
SUITE 650
LOS ANGELES, CALIFORNIA 90024
Telephone: 310-208-7313
Fax: 310-824-1930

*Insurance Bad Faith, Commercial and Business and Real Estate Litigation. Fidelity and Surety Law.*

**H. VINCENT McNALLY,** born New York, N.Y., April 14, 1941; admitted to bar, 1967, California. *Education:* Loyola University (B.A., 1963; LL.B., 1966). Phi Delta Phi. Author: "The Free Speech Issue in the Subscription Television Controversy," Loyola Law Digest, Vol. 1 Number 1, 1965. *Member:* Los Angeles County and American Bar Associations; The State Bar of California.

## McNAMARA & SPIRA
LOS ANGELES, CALIFORNIA
(See Santa Monica)

*Business Litigation including Employment and Insurance Related Litigation, Antitrust, Unfair Competition, Tort, Intellectual Property, Libel, Slander, Defamation, Entertainment Law and Shareholder Litigation.*

## LAW OFFICES OF
## MALCOLM S. McNEIL
5777 WEST CENTURY BOULEVARD
SUITE 1475
LOS ANGELES, CALIFORNIA 90045-7400
Telephone: 310-216-0747
Facsimile: 310-216-5736

*General Business, International Transactional Work, Corporate, Bankruptcy, Insurance, Real Estate, Commercial Court Litigation, Wills and Trusts and Family Law.*

**FIRM PROFILE:** The Law Offices of Malcolm S. McNeil was founded in 1984 by Malcolm S. McNeil. The firm maintains a general practice of law, advising businesses and individuals in a variety of matters. The firm now serves clients in a wide range of legal services, including all aspects of Business and Business Litigation, International Transactional Law, Estate Planning and Commercial Law. The firm has also developed a sub-specialty of litigating and protecting Trademarks and Copyrights. The firm has developed a substantial Chinese Clientele and Advises U.S. Firms seeking to invest in China and also represents Chinese firms establishing branches in the U.S. for trade and investment.

**MALCOLM S. McNEIL,** born San Francisco, California, January 7, 1956; admitted to bar, 1983, California; 1984, U.S. District Court, Central District of California; 1989, U.S. Court of Appeals, Ninth Circuit; 1991, U.S. District Court, Northern District of California. *Education:* Los Angeles City College (A.A., 1976); Antioch School of Law (B.A., 1980); Loyola Marymount University (J.D., 1983). Sigma Tau Sigma; Phi Alpha Delta. Instructor, Northrop University, Los Angeles, California, 1987-1988. Executive Committee, 1991— and Presidential Delegate, 1993—, Association International Jeunes Avocats. Mediator, Attorney-Clients Relations Section, Los Angeles County Bar Association. *Member:* Los Angeles County and American Bar Associations; State Bar of California; Los Angeles Trial Lawyers Association. **LANGUAGES:** French. **PRACTICE AREAS:** Business Law; Dissolution of Marriage; Estate Planning; International Transactional Law; Emphasizing China.

**ALAN M. O'CONNOR,** born Chicago, Illinois, May 10, 1963; admitted to bar, 1993, California, U.S. District Court, District of California and U.S. Court of Appeals, Ninth Circuit. *Education:* University of Miami (B.S., honors program, 1986); Whittier College School of Law (J.D., 1992). Recipient, American Jurisprudence Award in Criminal Law. *Member:* Los

*(This Listing Continued)*

Angeles County Bar Association. **PRACTICE AREAS:** Bankruptcy Law; Commercial Law; Debt Recovery; Trademark and Copyright Law; Criminal Law.

**MING MA,** born Shenyang Liaoning, China, October 20, 1954; (admission pending).; (Not admitted in California). *Education:* China University of Politics and Laws (B.S., 1984; M.A., 1987); Columbia University M.A., 1993). Assistant Professor, China University of Politics and Laws, 1987-1991. *Member:* China Procedural Law Association. **LANGUAGES:** Chinese and Mandarin. **PRACTICE AREAS:** Civil Litigation; Contracts; Criminal; Immigration; Chinese Law Consultation.

## McNICHOLAS & McNICHOLAS

10866 WILSHIRE BOULEVARD
**LOS ANGELES, CALIFORNIA 90024**
Telephone: 310-474-1582
FAX: 310-475-7871

*Jury Trials of Personal and Business Tort Cases in State and Federal Courts.*

### MEMBERS OF FIRM

**JOHN P. MCNICHOLAS,** born Los Angeles, California, August 18, 1936; admitted to bar, 1962, California and U.S. District Court, Central and Southern Districts of California; 1976, U.S. Supreme Court; 1982, U.S. Court of Appeals for the Ninth Circuit; 1984, U.S. Court of Appeals for the Tenth Circuit; 1986, District of Columbia. *Education:* University of California at Los Angeles (B.A., History, 1958); Loyola Law School, Los Angeles, 1958-1962. Phi Delta Phi. Faculty: Adjunct Professor, Trial Advocacy, Loyola Law School, 1991—. Judge Pro Tem: Los Angeles Superior Court, 1991—; Beverly Hills Municipal Court, 1985; Los Angeles Municipal Court, 1982—. Arbitrator: National Panel of Arbitrators, American Arbitration Association. Master, Inns of Court, 1990. Lawyer Representative, Ninth Circuit Judicial Conference, 1990-1995. Panelist: "Liability for Employment Practice - Discrimination, Sexual Harassment and Wrongful Discharge," ABA National Institute of Tort Liability for Charitable, Religious, and Non-Profit Institutions, New York, NY, 1992; "The Masters in Trial, Medical Malpractice Trial Demonstration," American Board of Trial Advocates, Washington, D.C., 1992; "Cross Examination of Plaintiff in a Products Liability Case," California Trial Lawyers Association, Lake Tahoe, CA, 1991; "Responsibility of the Religious Institutional Entity for Its Officers for Sexual (Mis)Conduct of the Clergy-Recent Developments, 1989-1990," ABA National Institute of Tort and Religion, Boston, MA, 1990; "Defense of the Religious Institutional Entity for Sexual Conduct of the Clergy - An Overview," ABA National Institute of Tort and Religion, San Francisco, CA, 1989. Panelist: "Defense Strategies Under Proposition 51," Los Angeles Trial Lawyers, May 20, 21 and 22, 1993, Los Angeles; Los Angeles County Bar Association, Litigation Section, "What Every Litigator Should Know About Punitive Damages," 1992. *Member:* Los Angeles County and American Bar Associations; State Bar of California; St. Thomas More Law Society; American Board of Trial Advocates (Diplomate, 1968); American Board of Professional Liability Attorneys (Diplomate, 1992). Fellow, American College of Trial Lawyers. Certified Civil Trial Advocate, National Board of Trial Advocacy. **LANGUAGES:** Spanish. **REPORTED CASES:** Rita M. v. Roman Catholic Archbishop (1986) 187 Cal. App. 1453; Spectrum Fin. Cos. v. Marconsult, Inc. (9th Cir. 1979) 608 F.2d 377, cert. den., 446 U.S. 936, 100 S.Ct. 2153, 64 L.Ed.2d 788; Deaile v. General Telephone Company (1974) 40 Cal.App.3d 841. **PRACTICE AREAS:** Jury Trials of Personal Injury and Business Tort Cases in State and Federal Courts.

**PATRICK MCNICHOLAS,** born Los Angeles, California, February 6, 1961; admitted to bar, 1986, California. *Education:* University of San Francisco (B.A., 1983); McGeorge School of Law, University of the Pacific (J.D., 1986). "The Masters in Trial," Trial Demonstration, American Board of Trial Advocates, Beverly Hills, California, 1993. "The Masters in Trial", Trial Demonstration of Medical Malpractice Case, American Board of Trial Advocates, Morgantown, West Virginia, 1995. Adjunct Professor of Law, Whittier College School of Law, 1991-1993. *Member:* Los Angeles County Bar Association; State Bar of California; Los Angeles Trial Lawyers Association; California Trial Lawyers Association; The Association of Trial Lawyers of America. **PRACTICE AREAS:** Bad Faith Law; Defective Products; Employment Discrimination; Malpractice Law; Personal Injury Law.

**DAVID M. RING,** born Syracuse, New York, January 16, 1965; admitted to bar, 1990, California, U.S. District Court, Central District of California and U.S. Court of Appeals, Ninth Circuit. *Education:* University of

*(This Listing Continued)*

Southern California (B.S., cum laude, 1987); University of Southern California Law Center (J.D., 1990). Order of the Coif.

### ASSOCIATES

**MARK K. FLORES,** born Los Angeles, California, December 10, 1964; admitted to bar, 1993, California; 1994, U.S. District Court, Central District of California. *Education:* University of Southern California (B.S., 1986); Loyola University of Los Angeles (J.D., 1993). *Member:* Los Angeles County Bar Association; State Bar of California; Consumer Attorneys Association of Los Angeles; Consumer Attorneys of California.

**ERIC A. GOWEY,** born Los Angeles, California, May 8, 1967; admitted to bar, 1994, California and U.S. District Court, Central District of California. *Education:* University of California at Santa Barbara (B.A., 1989); Santa Clara University (J.D., 1994). *Member:* State Bar of California; Consumer Attorneys Association of Los Angeles; California Trial Lawyers Association.

## PETER J. McNULTY

Established in 1983
827 MORAGA DRIVE (BEL AIR)
**LOS ANGELES, CALIFORNIA 90049**
Telephone: 310-471-2707
Fax: 310-472-7014

*Gilroy, California Office:* Suite F-2, 8352 Church Street. Telephone: 408-848-5900. Fax: 408-848-1391.

*Aurora, Illinois Office:* 8 East Galena Street.

*Civil Litigation, Trial Practice, Medical Malpractice, Products Liability, Personal Injury and Commercial Torts.*

**PETER J. MCNULTY,** born Boston, Massachusetts, June 15, 1954; admitted to bar, 1979, California and U.S. District Court, Central District of California; 1983, U.S. District Court, Northern and Southern Districts of California; 1984, U.S. District Court, Eastern District of California; 1986, U.S. District Court, Northern District of Illinois; 1987, U.S. District Court, Central District of Illinois, U.S. District Court, Southern District of Texas, U.S. District Court, District of Massachusetts and U.S. Court of Appeals, Ninth Circuit; 1988, U.S. Court of Appeals, First Circuit and U.S. Supreme Court. *Education:* University of Vermont (B.A., 1976); Boston College Law School (J.D., 1979). Phi Beta Kappa. Assistant Editor, American Journal of Law and Medicine, 1978-1979. Instructor, Attorney Assistant Training Program, University of California at Los Angeles, 1980—. *Member:* Los Angeles County and American Bar Associations; State Bar of California; Lawyers-Pilots Bar Association; The Association of Trial Lawyers of America; Los Angeles Trial Lawyers Association; California Trial Lawyers Association; Bel-Air Trial Lawyers Association. (Also of Counsel to Carl A. McMahan). **REPORTED CASES:** Herrera-Diaz vs. U.S. Department of Navy 845 F2d 1534 (9th Circuit 1988); Rodriguez vs. Superior Court of Kern County 221 Cal. App. 3d 1371. **PRACTICE AREAS:** Civil Litigation; Trial Practice; Medical Malpractice; Products Liability Law; Personal Injury Law; Commercial Torts.

### ASSOCIATES

**MICHAEL L. ORAN, (A PROFESSIONAL CORPORATION),** born Encino, California, June 24, 1957; admitted to bar, 1983, California; 1984, U.S. District Court, Central District of California and U.S. Court of Appeals, Ninth Circuit. *Education:* University of California at Santa Barbara (B.A., 1979); Southwestern University School of Law (J.D., 1983). President, The Sherman Oaks Nursery School, 1989-1990. *Member:* San Fernando Valley and Los Angeles County Bar Associations; State Bar of California (Member, Litigation Section); Los Angeles Trial Lawyers Association; The Association of Trial Lawyers of America; California Trial Lawyers Association. **PRACTICE AREAS:** Civil Litigation; Trial Practice; Medical Malpractice; Products Liability; Personal Injury; Commercial Torts.

### OF COUNSEL

**JOHN A. ALVAREZ,** born Brawley, California, March 22, 1943; admitted to bar, 1984, California; 1985, U.S. District Court, Eastern and Northern Districts of California. *Education:* University of California at Riverside (B.S., 1973); University of Santa Clara (J.D., 1978). *Member:* Santa Clara County Bar Association; State Bar of California. (Resident, Gilroy Office). **LANGUAGES:** Spanish. **PRACTICE AREAS:** Personal Injury.

**ROBERT M. FOOTE,** born Cambridge, Massachusetts, July 17, 1954; admitted to bar, 1979, Illinois; 1986, Wisconsin (Not admitted in Califor-

*(This Listing Continued)*

**PETER J. McNULTY, Los Angeles—Continued**

nia). *Education:* Harvard University (B.A., 1976); University of Wisconsin-Madison (J.D., 1979). *Member:* Kane County, Illinois State and American Bar Associations; Illinois Trial Lawyers Association; The Association of Trial Lawyers of America. (Also Member, Murphy, Hupp, Foote, Mielke and Kinnally, Aurora, Illinois).

**ROBERT P. FRIEDMAN,** born Los Angeles, California, September 21, 1952; admitted to bar, 1978, California. *Education:* University of California at Berkeley (A.B., with honors, 1975); Georgetown University (J.D., cum laude, 1978). Member, Board of Directors, Public Counsel, 1983-1986 and Board of Editors, 1983-1988, Shopping Center Legal Update. Member, Board of Editors, Commercial Leasing Law and Strategy, 1988—. *Member:* Century City, Beverly Hills, Los Angeles County and American Bar Associations; State Bar of California. (Also practicing individually). **PRACTICE AREAS:** Real Estate Law; Corporate Law; Business Law; Civil Litigation.

**CARL A. McMAHAN,** born Ridgecrest, California, August 31, 1953; admitted to bar, 1983, California and U.S. District Court, Central, Southern, Northern and Eastern Districts of California; 1985, Colorado; 1988, District of Columbia and U.S. Court of Appeals for the District of Columbia. *Education:* San Diego State University (B.A., with honors, 1975); McGeorge School of Law, University of the Pacific (J.D., 1982). Moot Court Honors. Judge Pro Tem, Los Angeles County Superior Court. Arbitrator, Orange County Superior Court. *Member:* Los Angeles County and Colorado Bar Associations; District of Columbia Bar; State Bar of California; The Association of Trial Lawyers of America; American Board of Trial Advocates. (Also practicing individually at same address). **PRACTICE AREAS:** Civil Trial; Product Liability Law; Medical Malpractice Law.

REFERENCE: City National Bank (Beverly Hills, California).

---

## McNULTY & SAACKE
**LOS ANGELES, CALIFORNIA**
(See Torrance)

*Insurance Litigation, General Casualty Litigation, Insurance Fraud Defense Litigation, Governmental Agency Tort Liability Litigation.*

---

## McPHERSON & KALMANSOHN
**1801 CENTURY PARK EAST, 24TH FLOOR**
**LOS ANGELES, CALIFORNIA 90067**
Telephone: 310-553-8833
Fax: 310-553-9233

*Entertainment and Business Litigation in all State and Federal Courts. Libel and Slander, Rights of Privacy and Publicity, Music, Copyright, Licensing, Sports, Insurance, Legal Malpractice.*

### MEMBERS OF FIRM

**EDWIN F. McPHERSON,** born Boston, Massachusetts, January 16, 1957; admitted to bar, 1982, California and U.S. District Court, Central District of California; 1983, Hawaii, U.S. District Court, Northern, Southern and Eastern Districts of California and U.S. Court of Appeals, Ninth Circuit. *Education:* University of Southern California (B.A., cum laude, 1978; B.M., Music, 1978); University of San Diego (J.D., 1982). Phi Alpha Delta. Winner, University of San Diego, Nathan Burkan (ASCAP) Memorial Copyright Law Competition. Recipient: American Jurisprudence Awards for Federal Income Taxation and Communications Law. Certified NFL Player's Agent. Author: "Conflicts in the Entertainment Industry... Not," The Entertainment and Sports Lawyer, Vol. 10, No. 4, Winter 1993; "Conflict Malpractice and Causation - The Forgotten Element," U.C.L.A. Ent. Law Review, Vol. 3, Issue 1 (October, 1995); "How Talent Representatives Can Fight Client Flight," Entertainment Law and Finance, Vol. XI, No. 4 (July, 1995). Judge Pro Tem, Beverly Hills Municipal Court, 1987—. Arbitrator, Attorney-Client Fee Disputes, State Bar of California. *Member:* Beverly Hills (Member, Entertainment Law Committee), Los Angeles County and American (Member: Section on Tort and Insurance Practice; Sports Law Committee; Forum Committee on Entertainment and Sports Law) Bar Associations; State Bar of California; Hawaii State Bar Association; Sports Lawyers Association. **REPORTED CASES:** People v. Von Villas, 10 Cal. App. 4th 201 (1992); Selleck v. Globe, 166 Cal. App. 3d 1123

*(This Listing Continued)*

---

(1985); Republic Corp. v. Superior Court (Delfino), 160 Cal.App. 3d 1253, 207 Cal.Rptr 241 (1984).

**MARK E. KALMANSOHN,** born Alexandria, Virginia, June 17, 1953; admitted to bar, 1977, California, District of Columbia and U.S. District Court for the District of Columbia; 1979, U.S. Court of Appeals, Ninth Circuit and U.S. District Court, Central District of California; 1988, U.S. Supreme Court. *Education:* Cornell University; University of California at Los Angeles (B.A., summa cum laude, 1974; J.D., 1977); Cambridge University, Cambridge, England (Diploma in International Law, 1984). Phi Beta Kappa; Pi Gamma Mu. Recipient, University of California Regents Honors Scholarship. Author: "Application of ECC Articles 85 and 86 to Foreign Multinationals," Legal Issues of European Integration, 1984; "The Law, Lawyers and Literature," Lex Et Scientia, Vol. 12, No. 4, 1976. Trial Attorney, Antitrust Division, U.S. Department of Justice, Washington, D.C., 1977-1979. Assistant U.S. Attorney, Criminal Division, Central District, 1979-1983. Assistant Division Chief, Trial Supervisor, 1982-1983. Director, North American Antipiracy Operations (Motion Picture Association of America), 1987-1991. *Member:* American Bar Associations (Member, Section on Intellectual Property); State Bar of California; The District of Columbia.

REFERENCE: City National Bank (Century City Office)

---

## KEVIN MEENAN
**LOS ANGELES, CALIFORNIA**
(See Pasadena)

*Civil Trial Practice in all State and Federal Courts. General Tort Litigation, Injury and Death, Negligence, Product Liability, Professional Negligence, Premises, Carriers and Insurance.*

---

## MENDES & MOUNT, L.L.P.
**CITICORP PLAZA**
**725 SOUTH FIGUEROA STREET**
**NINETEENTH FLOOR**
**LOS ANGELES, CALIFORNIA 90017**
Telephone: 213-955-7700
Telecopy: 213-955-7725
Telex: 6831520
Cable Address: "MNDMT"

*New York, N.Y. Office:* 750 Seventh Avenue. Telephone: 212-261-8000. Fax: 212-261-8750.

*Newark, New Jersey Office:* 1 Newark Center. Telephone: 201-639-7300. Fax: 201-639-7350.

*General Practice. Insurance and Re-Insurance Law. Admiralty, Aviation and Space, Medical, Legal, Negligence, Products Liability and Public Utilities Law. Trials and Appeals.*

### MEMBERS OF FIRM

**WILLIAM BLANC MENDES** (1891-1957).

**RUSSELL THEODORE MOUNT** (1881-1962).

**CHARLES G. CARLUCCIO, III,** born Teaneck, New Jersey, January 8, 1962; admitted to bar, 1986, California and U.S. District Court, Southern District of California; 1987, U.S. District Court, Eastern, Northern and Central Districts of California; 1990, New Jersey and U.S. District Court, District of New Jersey. *Education:* Fordham University (B.S., 1983); California Western School of Law (J.D., 1986). *Member:* San Diego County, Los Angeles County and American (Member, Sections on: Litigation; Tort and Insurance Practice; Environmental Law) Bar Associations; State Bar of California; San Diego Trial Lawyers Association. **Email:** CHACAR@MENDES.COM

**JAMES W. HUNT,** born Brooklyn, New York, September 7, 1944; admitted to bar, 1976, New Jersey and U.S. District Court, District of New Jersey; 1977, New York; 1979, U.S. District Court, Southern and Eastern Districts of New York; 1986, California, U.S. Court of Appeals, Fourth and Ninth Circuits and U.S. District Court, Central, Eastern, Northern and Southern Districts of California; 1987, U.S. Supreme Court. *Education:* Siena College (B.A., 1966); Seton Hall University Law School (J.D., 1976). *Member:* New York State and American (Sections on Aviation and Space; Litigation; Tort and Insurance Practice, 1990—) Bar Association; State Bar of California; Lawyer-Pilots Bar Association; Defense Research Institute. [Capt., U.S. Army, 1966-1970] **Email:** JAMHUN@MENDES.COM

*(This Listing Continued)*

**JOAN E. COCHRAN,** born Columbus, Ohio, May 29, 1959; admitted to bar, 1987, California. *Education:* Capital University (B.A., 1981); Capital University School of Law (J.D., 1985). *Member:* Los Angeles County and American (Sections: Tort and Insurance Practice; Litigation; Intellectual Property) Bar Associations; State Bar of California. *Email:* JOACOC@MENDES.COM

**MARK S. FACER,** born Caldwell, Idaho, September 21, 1954; admitted to bar, 1983, California; 1984, U.S. District Court, Northern, Eastern Central and Southern Districts of California and U.S. Court of Appeals, 9th Circuit. *Education:* Brigham Young University (B.S., 1980; J.D., 1982). Member, Moot Court National Team, 1982. Individual Winner, Moot Court Competition, 1981. Law Clerk to the Honorable Judge Donald K. Fitzpatrick, California Superior Court, 1983-1984. *Member:* Los Angeles County and American (Member, Sections on: Litigation; Tort and Insurance Practice) Bar Associations; State Bar of California. *Email:* MARFAC@MENDES.COM

**SHALEM A. MASSEY,** born Hollywood, California, November 4, 1963; admitted to bar, 1989, California, U.S. District Court, Eastern District of California and U.S. Court of Appeals, 9th Circuit; 1990, U.S. District Court, Central, Northern and Southern Districts of California. *Education:* University of California at Los Angeles (B.A., cum laude, 1986); University of San Diego (J.D., cum laude, 1989). *Member:* Los Angeles County (Member, Litigation Section), Orange County (Member, Aviation Section) and American Bar Associations; The State Bar of California; Defense Research Institute. *LANGUAGES:* Urdu, Hindi and Punjabi. *Email:* SHAMAS@MENDES.COM

**RICHARD R. NELSON,** born Glendale, California, April 19, 1956; admitted to bar, 1987, California, U.S. District Court, Northern, Eastern, Central and Southern Districts of California and U.S. Court of Appeals, 9th Circuit; U.S. District Court, Northern District of Texas; 1992, Texas and U.S. Supreme Court. *Education:* Art Center College of Design (B.S., with honors, 1981); Whittier College School of Law (J.D., 1986). Phi Alpha Delta. *Member:* Los Angeles County and American (Member, Sections on: Litigation; Tort and Insurance Practice; Member, Forum Committee on Air and Space Law) Bar Associations; State Bar of California. *Email:* RICNEL@MENDES.COM

**ROBERT B. SCHULTZ,** born Buffalo, New York, January 19, 1947; admitted to bar, 1983, California, New York and U.S. District Court, Central, Southern, Northern and Eastern Districts of California; 1986, U.S. Court of Appeals, 9th Circuit. *Education:* Antioch College (B.S., 1969); State University of New York at Buffalo School of Law and Jurisprudence (J.D., 1982). Commercial Pilots License, 1972. Flight Instructor, Airplane, Instrument and Multiengine, 1973. *Member:* State Bar of California; New York State and American Bar Associations; Lawyer-Pilots Bar Association. [USNR, 1969-1971] *Email:* BOBSCH@MENDES.COM

**TY S. VANDERFORD,** born Carmichael, California, September 27, 1963; admitted to bar, 1987, California; 1988, U.S. District Court, Central, Eastern, Northern and Southern Districts of California. *Education:* University of Southern California (B.A., 1984); McGeorge School of Law, University of the Pacific (J.D., 1987). Staff Writer, 1985-1986; Member, Board of Editors, 1986-1987, Pacific Law Journal. *Member:* State Bar of California; American Bar Association. *LANGUAGES:* French and Russian. *Email:* TYXVAN@MENDES.COM

## ASSOCIATES

**GARTH W. AUBERT,** born Los Angeles, California, July 28, 1967; admitted to bar, 1992, California; 1993, U.S. District Court, Central, Eastern, Northern and Southern Districts of California. *Education:* University of Southern California (B.A., 1989); McGeorge School of Law, University of the Pacific (J.D., 1992). Phi Delta Phi. Moot Court Written Brief Finalist. Assistant Managing Editor, Pacific Law Journal, 1991-1992. Author, Review of Selected 1990 California Legislation, Pacific Law Journal, 1990. *Member:* Los Angeles County Bar Association. *Email:* GARAUB@MENDES.COM

**FELIX AVILA,** born Los Angeles, California, October 9, 1968; admitted to bar, 1994, California and U.S. District Court, Central, Southern, Northern and Eastern Districts of California. *Education:* California State Polytechnic University (B.A., 1991); University of California at Berkeley (J.D., 1994). Co-Editor in Chief, La Raza Law Journal. *Member:* Los Angeles County and American Bar Associations; Mexican-American Bar Association. *Email:* FELAVI@MENDES.COM

*(This Listing Continued)*

**JOHN FRANCIS BAZAN,** born Los Angeles, California, January 10, 1961; admitted to bar, 1994, California. *Education:* California State Polytechnic University (B.A., cum laude, 1987); University of California at Los Angeles (J.D., 1993). Phi Delta Phi. Extern to the Hon. Dickran Tevrizian, U.S. District Court, Central District of California, 1992. *Member:* Los Angeles County and American Bar Associations. [Capt., U.S. Army/U.S. Army Reserve, 1982-1994] *Email:* JOHBAZ@MENDES.COM

**JOHN G. CAHILL,** born Youngstown, Ohio, September 10, 1963; admitted to bar, 1989, Arizona; 1990, District of Columbia; 1994, California; 1995, U.S. District Court, Central, Northern, Eastern and Southern Districts of California. *Education:* American University (B.A., 1985); Arizona State University (J.D., 1989). Adjunct Professor, Paralegal Studies Program, University of California, Irvine, 1995—. *Member:* State Bar of Arizona; District of Columbia Bar; State Bar of California. [U.S. Navy, 1989-1994; Lt. (SW), JAGC, USNR]

**ALAN H. COLLIER,** born Bay Shore, New York, December 25, 1964; admitted to bar, 1990, California; 1991, U.S. District Court, Central, Eastern, Northern and Southern Districts of California. *Education:* Abilene Christian University (B.A., summa cum laude, 1987); Pepperdine University School of Law (J.D., cum laude, 1990). University Scholar. Recipient: Presidential Excelling Award; American Jurisprudence Award for Insurance Law. *Member:* State Bar of California (Member, Litigation Section, 1991—); American Bar Association; Defense Research Institute. *Email:* ALACOL@MENDES.COM

**CORY D. ESTERS,** born Bethesda, Maryland, May 22, 1968; admitted to bar, 1994, California. *Education:* University of California at Berkeley (B.A., 1990); Loyola Law School (J.D., 1994). *Email:* COREST@MENDES.COM

**JILL CHIANG FUNG,** born Taipei, Taiwan, August 15, 1971; admitted to bar, 1996, California. *Education:* Smith College (B.A., 1993); Loyola Law School (J.D., 1996). Psi Chi. Author, "Can Mickey Mouse Prevail in the Court of the Monkey King? Enforcing Foreign Intellectual Property Rights in The People's Republic of China," Loyola International & Comparative Law Journal, issue 18:3, 1996. Board of Directors, Asian Pacific American Legal Center, 1995-1996. Award of Honor by Board of Supervisors in Los Angeles County for "Excellent Work Done in Asian American Relations". *Member:* Southern California Chinese American Lawyers' Association. *LANGUAGES:* Mandarin, Shanghainese, Taiwanese.

**MARLYN M. GATES,** born Los Angeles, California, October 28, 1969; admitted to bar, 1994, California; 1995, U.S. District Court, Central, Eastern and Southern Districts of California. *Education:* Pepperdine University (B.A., 1990; J.D., 1994). *Member:* Los Angeles County and American Bar Associations; State Bar of California. *Email:* MARGAT@MENDES.COM

**RENEE A. HAUPT,** born Palmerton, Pennsylvania, June 30, 1970; admitted to bar, 1995, California, U.S. Court of Appeals, Ninth Circuit and U.S. District Court, Central, Northern, Eastern and Southern Districts of California. *Education:* University of Southern California (B.S., 1992; J.D., 1995). Beta Gamma Sigma.

**LYDIA A. HERVATIN,** born Hammond, Indiana, November 25, 1958; admitted to bar, 1992, California. *Education:* DePaul University (B.S., 1981); Loyola Law School (J.D., 1991). Note and Comment Editor, Loyola Law Review. Author: "Arbitration of Securities Disputes: Rodriquez de Quidas v. Shearson/American Express, Inc., Speedy Justice or Just Speed," 24 Loyola Law Review 757. *Email:* LYDHER@MENDES.COM

**MARK R. IRVINE,** born Denver, Colorado, March 9, 1963; admitted to bar, 1988, California; 1989, U.S. District Court, Eastern, Central, Northern and Southern Districts of California and U.S. Court of Appeals, Ninth Circuit. *Education:* University of California at Los Angeles (B.A., 1985); McGeorge School of Law, University of the Pacific (J.D., 1988). Comment Staff Member, 1986-1987, and Articles Editor, 1987-1988, Pacific Law Journal. Co-Author: "The Money Laundering Control Act of 1986: Tainted Money and the Criminal Defense Lawyer," Pacific Law Journal, 1987-1988. *Member:* State Bar of California; American Bar Association. *Email:* MARIRV@MENDES.COM

**CHARLES S. KROLIKOWSKI,** born Bellflower, California, May 5, 1970; admitted to bar, 1996, California. *Education:* University of California at Davis (B.S., 1992); University of Southern California (J.D., 1996).

**KIPP A. LANDIS,** born Oceanside, California, September 2, 1966; admitted to bar, 1995, California and U.S. District Court, Northern, Southern, Eastern and Central District of California. *Education:* Pepperdine University (B.A., 1989; J.D., 1995). Phi Alpha Theta.

*(This Listing Continued)*

## MENDES & MOUNT, L.L.P., Los Angeles—Continued

**ERIN K. MCGONAGLE,** born Elizabeth, New Jersey, March 7, 1965; admitted to bar, 1991, California; 1992, U.S. District Court, Central, Eastern, Northern and Southern Districts of California and U.S. Court of Appeals, Ninth Circuit. *Education:* University of North Carolina at Chapel Hill (B.A., 1987); Pepperdine University School of Law (J.D., 1991). Phi Delta Phi. Staff Member, 1989-1990 and Note and Comment Editor, 1990-1991, Pepperdine Law Review. Author: "California Supreme Court Survey," Pepperdine Law Review, Vol. 18, 1990-1991. Judicial Extern to the Honorable Stephen R. Reinhardt, U.S. Court of Appeals, Ninth Judicial Circuit, Sept., 1990 to December, 1990. *Member:* Los Angeles County and American Bar Associations; State Bar of California (Member, Litigation Section). *Email:* ERIMCG@MENDES.COM

**SUZANNE NAATZ MCNULTY,** born Syracuse, New York, August 14, 1960; admitted to bar, 1989, California. *Education:* University of Massachusetts (B.A., 1982); La Universidad de Santus, Spain; University of San Diego (J.D., 1988). *Member:* State Bar of California. **LANGUAGES:** Spanish. *Email:* SUZMCN@MENDES.COM

**PATRICK T. MICHAEL,** born Santa Clara, California, August 30, 1967; admitted to bar, 1993, California and U.S. District Court, Central District of California; 1994, Northern, Southern, Western and Eastern Districts of California. *Education:* University of California at Santa Barbara (B.A., 1989); Pepperdine University (J.D., cum laude, 1993). Note and Comment Editor, Pepperdine Law Review. Author, "Natural Resource Damages Under CERCLA: The Emerging Champion of Environmental Enforcement," 20 Pepperdine Law Review, 1992. *Email:* PATMIC@MENDES.COM

**DENNIS MORRIS,** born Los Angeles, California, December 15, 1963; admitted to bar, 1993, California; registered to practice before U.S. Patent and Trademark Office. *Education:* University of California at Los Angeles (B.S., 1986); Pepperdine University (J.D., 1993). Regents Full Scholarship. Women Lawyers Scholarship. Gunnar Nicholson Scholarship. Alumni Scholar. Chancellor's Honorarium. Chancellor's Marshall. Best Legal News TV Anchor, TV-3 News. Student Pilot. Author, Legal News Telecasts, TV-3 News Malibu, 1991-1993. Member: UCLA School of Engineering Alumni; Screen Actors Guild. Treasurer, Santa Monica Bar Association, 1995. Editor-in-Chief, "Amicus Curiae" a publication of the Santa Monica Bar Association, 1995. International Who's Who of Professionals (1995). Who's Who in American Law (1995). *Member:* Beverly Hills and Los Angeles County Bar Associations; Italian-American Bar Association; Irish-American Bar Association. **LANGUAGES:** Italian, Spanish and French. *Email:* DENMOR@MENDES.COM

**DAVID A. ROBINSON,** born Boulogne Sur Seine, France, December 17, 1967; admitted to bar, 1992, California. *Education:* University of Redlands (B.A., 1989); Loyola Law School (J.D., 1992). Author: "A Fair Use Analysis of Trademark Parody: Cliffs Notes, Inc. v. Bantam Doubleday Dell Publishing Group," 11 Loyola Entertainment Law Journal 223, 1991. **LANGUAGES:** French. *Email:* DAVROB@MENDES.COM

**HENRY L. SANCHEZ,** born Albuquerque, New Mexico, November 20, 1967; admitted to bar, 1995, California and U.S. District Court, Central, Eastern, Northern and Southern Districts of California. *Education:* University of New Mexico (B.A., 1991); University of Notre Dame (J.D., 1994). **LANGUAGES:** Spanish.

**YVONNE T. SIMON,** born Albuquerque, New Mexico, March 9, 1966; admitted to bar, 1995, California. *Education:* University of California at Los Angeles (B.A., departmental honors in Philosophy, 1989); Loyola Law School (J.D., 1994). Co-Founder/President, A.C.L.U. Student Chapter, Loyola Law School, 1992-1994. *Email:* YVOSIM@MENDES.COM

**MARLA A. SMITH,** born Kansas City, Missouri, May 12, 1962; admitted to bar, 1993, California, U.S. District Court, Central, Northern, Eastern and Southern Districts of California and U.S. Court of Appeals, Ninth Circuit. *Education:* University of Kansas (B.A., 1985); University of Southern California (J.D., 1993). Extern for the Honorable Justice Robert Boochever, Ninth Circuit Court of Appeals.

(For Complete Biographical Data on all Personnel, See Professional Biographies at New York, New York)

CAA978B

## LAW OFFICES OF JOYCE S. MENDLIN
1901 AVENUE OF THE STARS
SUITE 1600
**LOS ANGELES, CALIFORNIA 90067-6080**
Telephone: 310-553-5005
Telecopier: 310-553-5085

*Federal and State Court Litigation and Civil Appeals, involving Business, Real Property, Insurance Coverage and Unfair Competition.*

**JOYCE S. MENDLIN,** born Washington, D.C., February 11, 1954; admitted to bar, 1980, California. *Education:* St. John's College (B.A., 1975); Southwestern University (J.D., 1979). Member, Southwestern University Law Review, 1978-1979. Law Clerk Extern, California Court of Appeal Second Appellate District, 1979. Lecturer, Continuing Legal Education of the Bar, 1990, 1992. Judge Protem, Los Angeles Municipal and Superior Courts, 1987—. Member, Panel of Arbitrators, American Arbitration Association. *Member:* Los Angeles County (Member, Sections on Litigation and Real Property) and American Bar Associations; State Bar of California.

## MENES LAW CORPORATION
Established in 1982

1801 CENTURY PARK EAST, SUITE 1560
**LOS ANGELES, CALIFORNIA 90067**
Telephone: 310-286-1313
Cable Address: "Showlaw"
Telex: 317948 MLC LSA
Fax: 310-556-5695

*Entertainment, Contracts, Entertainment and Business Litigation, Intellectual Property, Business and Corporate Law.*

**FIRM PROFILE:** Menes Law Corporation is a full service entertainment law firm, providing international transactional and litigation services for music, music publishing, video, television, motion picture, licensing and intellectual property clients. It represents a broad range of institutional and individual clients, based in Japan, the United States, Europe and Canada. Members of the firm have extensive experience and substantial client base in Japanese and European music-related entertainment endeavors.

**BARRY A. MENES,** born Chicago, Illinois, May 19, 1947; admitted to bar, 1973, California. *Education:* California State University at Northridge (B.A., 1969); University of San Diego (J.D., 1973). Member of Editorial Board and Country Correspondent from USA, Entertainment Law Review. Judge Pro Tem Beverly Hills Bar Association. Speaker, International Association of Music. *Member:* Beverly Hills and Los Angeles County Bar Associations; State Bar of California; California Trial Lawyers Association. **LANGUAGES:** French. **PRACTICE AREAS:** Entertainment Law and Litigation; Business Law and Litigation; Intellectual Property Law.

**PAUL I. MENES,** born Chicago, Illinois, January 10, 1955; admitted to bar, 1981, California and U.S. District Court, Central District of California. *Education:* University of California at Los Angeles (B.A., 1976); Southwestern University (J.D., 1980). Special Award, Judge Pro Tem, 1987, Century City Bar Association. Listed in: Who's Who in American Law, 6th Edition, 7th Edition, 8th Edition; Who's Who Among Young American Professionals. *Member:* Beverly Hills, Century City, Los Angeles County and American Bar Associations; State Bar of California; The Association of Trial Lawyers of America; California Lawyers for the Arts. **PRACTICE AREAS:** Entertainment Law and Litigation; Business Law; Intellectual Property Law.

**MARC M. MESSINEO,** born Killeen, Texas, January 9, 1968; admitted to bar, 1993, California. *Education:* Boston College (B.A., 1989); Pepperdine University (M.B.A., 1992; J.D., 1993). Phi Alpha Delta. *Member:* Beverly Hills, Century City, Los Angeles County and American Bar Associations; State Bar of California. **PRACTICE AREAS:** Entertainment Law and Litigation; Intellectual Property Law; Business Law.

*(This Listing Continued)*

## OF COUNSEL

**JOHN R. CLIMACO** (Not admitted in California; Also Member, Climaco, Climaco, Seminatore, Lefkowitz & Garofoli Co., L.P.A., Cleveland, Ohio).

**EDWARD M. BERNSTEIN** (Not admitted in California; Also practices individually at Las Vegas, Nevada).

---

# MERCHANT & GOULD
### SUITE 400
### 11150 SANTA MONICA BOULEVARD
### LOS ANGELES, CALIFORNIA 90025
Telephone: 310-445-1140
Facsimile: 310-445-9031
Email: info@merchant-gould.com
URL: http://www.merchant-gould.com

*Minneapolis, Minnesota Office:* Merchant, Gould, Smith, Edell, Welter & Schmidt, Professional Association, 3100 Norwest Center, 90 South 7th Street. Telephone: 612-332-5300. Facsimile: 612-332-9081.

*St. Paul, Minnesota Office:* Merchant, Gould, Smith, Edell, Welter & Schmidt, Professional Association, One Thousand Norwest Center, 55 E. 5th Street. Telephone: 612-298-1055. Facsimile: 612-298-1160.

Patent, Trademark and Copyright Law, Licensing, Trade Secrets, Unfair Competition, Computer Law and Related Litigation.

**RAYMOND A. BOGUCKI,** born Minneapolis, Minnesota, August 13, 1922; admitted to bar, 1952, Minnesota; 1957, California; 1961, U.S. Court of Appeals, 9th Circuit; 1975-1982, U.S. Court of Customs and Patent Appeals; 1986, U.S. Court of Appeals for the Federal Circuit; registered to practice before U.S. Patent and Trademark Office. *Education:* University of Notre Dame (B.S. in M.E., magna cum laude, 1948); University of Minnesota (LL.B., 1952). Member, University of Minnesota Law Review, 1951-1952. *Member:* Los Angeles County and American Bar Associations; The State Bar of California.

**GREGORY B. WOOD,** born Indianapolis, Indiana, April 7, 1945; admitted to bar, 1975, California; registered to practice before U.S. Patent and Trademark Office. *Education:* University of California at Los Angeles (B.S., 1967; M.S., 1971) Tau Beta Pi; University of San Fernando Valley College of Law (J.D., 1975). Law Review, 1974-1975. Author: "California's New Anti-counterfeiting Statute," New Matter, Spring, 1984; "Criminalizing Counterfeiting in California," IACC Bulletin, August-September/October-November, 1984. Adjunct Professor of Law: Southwestern Law School, 1980-1981; Loyola Law School, 1981-1982. Patent and Resources Group, Claim Drafting Instructor, 1992—. Los Angeles City Commissioner (Commission on Disabilities). Judge Pro Tem, Los Angeles Municipal Court. *Member:* Los Angeles County Bar Association( Executive Committee, Delegate to State Bar Annual Meeting; Chair of Los Angeles Delegation, 1988); State Bar of California (Executive Committee, Intellectual Property Section and Resolutions Committee); Los Angeles Patent Law Association; Association of Business Trial Lawyers.

**GEORGE HENRY GATES, III,** born Akron, Ohio, March 17, 1957; admitted to bar, 1989, Minnesota; 1990, California; registered to practice before U.S. Patent and Trademark Office. *Education:* The Ohio State University (B.S.C.I.S., Engineering, 1980); William Mitchell College of Law (J.D., cum laude, 1989). Member: William Mitchell Law Review, 1988-1989; Moot Court. *Member:* State Bar of California; Minnesota State Bar Association.

**CHARLES BERMAN,** admitted to bar, 1969, Republic of South Africa; 1978, California; registered to practice before U.S. Patent and Trademark Office. *Education:* Witwatersrand University (B.S., 1964; LL.B., 1967). Member, Editorial Board, Patent World, Managing Intellectual Property. *Member:* Los Angeles County and American Bar Associations; State Bar of California (Member, Intellectual Property Section EPO/US Bar Liaison Council); American Intellectual Property Law Association (Board Member, 1994—, Japan/US Study Group; Chair, Foreign and International Law Committee, 1992-1994); Los Angeles Patent Law Association (Board Member, 1994—); International Trademark Association; Licensing Executive Society; International Federation of Industrial Property Attorneys; Associatio Internationale pour la Protection de la Propriete Industrielle. *Email:* cberman@merchant-gould.com

**JAI HO RHO,** born Seoul, South Korea, January 24, 1959; admitted to bar, 1986, California, U.S. Court of Appeals, Federal Circuit and U.S. District Court, Central and Northern Districts of California. *Education:* Harvard University (B.A., cum laude, 1981); University of California at Los Angeles (J.D., 1984). Member, Moot Court Honors Program. Co-Author: "Misappropriation Blues," Los Angeles Lawyer, Vol. 8, No. 2, 1985; "Don't Trade on Me," Los Angeles Lawyer, July, 1986; "Is the Counterfeiter's 'Waterloo' At Hand," Merchandising Reporter, November/December, 1984. *Member:* Korean American Bar Association. *PRACTICE AREAS:* Intellectual Property. *Email:* jrho@merchant-gould.com

---

**JANICE A. SHARP,** born Sydney, New South Wales, Australia, November 17, 1951; admitted to bar, 1990, California; registered to practice before U.S. Patent and Trademark Office. *Education:* University of New South Wales (B.Sc., with honors, 1975; Ph.D., 1978); Western State University (J.D., cum laude, 1989); Yale University (Postdoctoral Fellow, 1978-1983). Member, Western State University Law Review, 1988-1989. Author: "Of Transgenic Mice and Men," Western State University Law Review, Vol. 16, pp. 737-752, 1989. Research Specialist, University of California, Irvine, 1983-1984. *Member:* State Bar of California; Los Angeles Intellectual Property Law Association. *PRACTICE AREAS:* Patent Law; Trademark Law; Copyright Law; Biotechnology Law.

**MICHAEL B. FARBER,** born Cleveland, Ohio, September 22, 1947; admitted to bar, 1987, California and U.S. District Court, Central District of California; registered to practice before U.S. Patent and Trademark Office. *Education:* California Institute of Technology (B.S., with honors, 1969); Harvard University (Ph.D., 1975); Southwestern University School of Law (J.D., magna cum laude, 1987). Author, " 'Actual Malice' and the Standard of Proof in Defamation Cases in California," Southwestern University Law Review, 1987. *Member:* State Bar of California; American Bar Association; American Intellectual Property Law Association; American Association for the Advancement of Science. *PRACTICE AREAS:* Patents; Trademarks.

**SARAH B. ADRIANO,** born May 22, 1960; admitted to bar, 1990, New York; registered to practice before U.S. Patent and Trademark Office (Not admitted in California). *Education:* University of Maine (B.A., 1981); University of San Diego (J.D., 1988). *Member:* American Intellectual Property Law Association; New York Patent, Trademark and Copyright Law Association.

**VICTOR G. COOPER,** born Chicago, Illinois, November 28, 1956; admitted to bar, 1994, California; registered to practice before U.S. Patent and Trademark Office. *Education:* California State University (B.S.E., 1980); University of Southern California (M.S.E.E., 1984) Loyola Law School (J.D., 1994). Phi Delta Phi; Tau Beta Pi; Order of the Coif. *PRACTICE AREAS:* Patent Law; Copyright Law; Trademark Law.

**BEN M. DAVIDSON,** born Tehran, Iran, October 1, 1968; admitted to bar, 1995, California; registered to practice before U.S. Patent and Trademark Office. *Education:* Union College (B.S.E.E., 1990); George Washington University (J.D., with high honors, 1995). Order of the Coif. Member, George Washington University Law Review. *LANGUAGES:* French and Japanese. *PRACTICE AREAS:* Litigation; Patent Prosecution.

**ALBERT F. DAVIS,** born Chicago, Illinois; admitted to bar, 1995, Wisconsin, Minnesota and U.S. District Court, Western District of Wisconsin (Not admitted in California). *Education:* University of Illinois (B.S.C.E., Civil Engineer, 1990); University of Wisconsin (J.D., 1995). Managing Editor, University of Wisconsin Law Review, 1994-1995. *Member:* Hennepin County, National and American Bar Associations. *PRACTICE AREAS:* Patent; Trademark; Entertainment; Copyright. *Email:* adavis@mail.merchant-gould.com

**KAREN S. CANADY,** born Denver, Colorado; admitted to bar, 1996, California. *Education:* Pacific University (B.S., cum laude, 1983); University of Washington (J.D., 1995). Member, NIH Fellowship. Member, Washington Law Review Editorial Board.

REPRESENTATIVE CLIENTS: AT&T Global Information Solutions; Airtouch Communications; Bristol Myers Squibb Co.; University of California.

(For Complete Biographical data on all Personnel, see Professional Biographies at Minneapolis, Minnesota.)

*(This Listing Continued)*

## MESERVE, MUMPER & HUGHES

A Partnership
*Established in 1889*

**555 SOUTH FLOWER STREET, 18TH FLOOR**
**LOS ANGELES, CALIFORNIA 90071-2319**
Telephone: 213-620-0300
Telecopier: 213-625-1930
Email: mmhla@ix.netcom.com

*Irvine, California Office:* 2301 Dupont Drive, Suite 410. Telephone: 714-474-8995. Telecopier: 714-975-1065.
*San Diego, California Office:* 701 "B" Street, Suite 1080. Telephone: 619-237-0500. Telecopier: 619-237-0073.

General Civil and Trial Practice in all State and Federal Courts. Banking, Corporate, Real Estate, Labor, Life Insurance, Probate, Estate Planning, Family Law and Bankruptcy.

### MEMBERS OF FIRM

**EDWIN A. MESERVE** (1863-1955).

**SHIRLEY E. MESERVE** (1889-1959).

**HEWLINGS MUMPER** (1889-1968).

**CLIFFORD E. HUGHES** (1894-1981).

**DENNETT F. KOURI,** born 1938; admitted to bar, 1963, California. *Education:* University of Southern California (B.S., 1959; LL.B., 1962). Phi Delta Phi; Blue Key. *Member:* Los Angeles County and American Bar Associations.

**BERNARD A. LECKIE,** born Los Angeles, California, December 10, 1932; admitted to bar, 1960, California; 1979, U.S. Supreme Court and U.S. Court of Appeals, 9th Circuit. *Education:* University of Southern California (B.S., 1957; LL.B., 1959). Phi Delta Phi. Recipient, Law Week Award, University of Southern California Law School, for highest scholastic progress in senior year, 1959. Member, National Panel of Arbitrators, American Arbitration Association. Weekly Chairman for Indigent Defense Panel, 1964-1967. Examiner for State Bar, 1967-1968. Examiner in disciplinary proceedings, 1967-1968; Member, Disciplinary Committee #16, 1969-1971 and Chairman, 1972-1973; Local Administrative Committee #2, 1973—; Member and Chairman, Preliminary Investigation Panel #7, 1978—, State Bar of California. *Member:* Orange County, Los Angeles County and American Bar Associations; The Association of Trial Lawyers of America; American Judicature Society; California Trial Lawyers Association; Los Angeles Trial Lawyers Association; Association of Deputy District Attorneys of Los Angeles County; Orange County Trial Lawyers Association. (Irvine Office).

**LINDA M. LAWSON,** born San Mateo, California, January 26, 1952; admitted to bar, 1977, California. *Education:* Stanford University (B.A., 1974); University of Southern California (J.D., 1977). Chairman, Hale Moot Court Honors Program, 1976-1977. *Member:* Los Angeles County and American Bar Associations.

**DAVID R. EICHTEN,** born New Ulm, Minnesota, November 8, 1948; admitted to bar, 1973, California, U.S. District Court, Southern District of California and U.S. Supreme Court; 1984, Minnesota. *Education:* University of Minnesota (B.A., cum laude, 1970); University of San Diego (J.D., cum laude, 1973). (San Diego and Irvine Offices).

**WILLIAM E. VON BEHREN,** born Springfield, Illinois, October 4, 1955; admitted to bar, 1980, Missouri and U.S. District Court, Western District of Missouri; 1981, Illinois; 1982, California; 1983, U.S. District Court, Central District of California and Central District of Illinois. *Education:* Washington University (B.A., 1977); St. Louis University (J.D., 1980). Phi Delta Phi. Member, Moot Court Board. Staff Associate, St. Louis University Law Journal, 1978. *Member:* Los Angeles County, Illinois State and American Bar Associations; The Missouri Bar.

**JOAN E. AARESTAD,** born Fargo, North Dakota, June 1, 1953; admitted to bar, 1980, California and U.S. District Court, Central District of California. *Education:* Concordia College and California State Polytechnic University at Pomona (B.S., 1975); University of Southern California (J.D., 1980). Phi Kappa Phi. Member, University of Southern California Law Review, 1978-1980. *Member:* Los Angeles County and American Bar Associations.

**TIMOTHY A. GRAVITT,** born Los Angeles, California, January 28, 1957; admitted to bar, 1984, California; 1985, U.S. District Court, Central District of California and U.S. Court of Appeals, Ninth Circuit. *Education:* University of California at San Diego (B.A., 1981) Hastings College of Law,

*(This Listing Continued)*

University of California (J.D., 1984). *Member:* Orange County, San Diego County, Los Angeles County and American Bar Associations. (Los Angeles, Irvine and San Diego Offices).

**E. AVERY CRARY,** born 1939; admitted to bar, 1968, California. *Education:* Georgetown University (B.S., 1961); Southwestern University (LL.B., 1967). Phi Delta Phi. *Member:* Los Angeles County and American Bar Associations. (Irvine Office).

**PATRICIA A. ELLIS,** born American Falls, Idaho, April 19, 1959; admitted to bar, 1987, California and U.S. District Court, Central District of California. *Education:* Idaho State University (B.A., 1981); Southwestern University School of Law (J.D., 1987). *Member:* Los Angeles County and American Bar Associations.

**LISA A. ROQUEMORE,** born Ridgecrest, California, July 10, 1962; admitted to bar, 1989, California and U.S. District Court, Central District of California; 1992, U.S. District Court, Southern and Northern Districts of California; 1994, U.S. Court of Appeals, Ninth Circuit; 1996, U.S. District Court, Eastern District of California; U.S. Supreme Court. *Education:* San Diego State University (B.A., with distinction in Psychology, 1985); California Western School of Law (J.D., 1988). Sigma Nu Phi. William P. Gray Legion Lex Inns of Court. Intern to Hon. Louise DeCarl Malugen, U.S. Bankruptcy Judge, Southern District of California. Lecturer: Ethics in Bankruptcy, Orange County Bankruptcy Forum, June 12, 1993 (Participant and Contributor); The Most Important Thing You Need to Know About Bankruptcy, Orange County Women Lawyers Association, September 12, 1994 (Panel Member and General Bankruptcy Lectures to Practitioners). Member, Orange County Bankruptcy Forum. *Member:* Orange County (Publicity Chairperson, Commercial Law and Bankruptcy Section, 1995, 1996) and Federal (Orange County Section) Bar Associations; Orange County Bankruptcy Forum. (Irvine Office). *PRACTICE AREAS:* Bankruptcy; Commercial and Business Litigation.

### OF COUNSEL

**J. ROBERT MESERVE,** born 1916; admitted to bar, 1942, California. *Education:* University of California (A.B., 1938); Hastings College of Law (LL.B., 1941). Phi Delta Phi. *Member:* Orange County, Los Angeles County and American Bar Associations; American College of Trust and Estate Counsel; International Academy of Estate and Trust Law. (Irvine Office).

**THOMAS E. KELLETT,** born Minneapolis, Minnesota, 1926; admitted to bar, 1952, Minnesota; 1955, California; 1965, U.S. Supreme Court. *Education:* University of Minnesota (B.A., 1949; B.S., 1950; J.D., 1952); University of Southern California (LL.M., 1964). Delta Theta Phi. Member, Board of Editors, Minnesota Law Review, 1950-1952. Law Clerk to: Chief Justices, Minnesota Supreme Court, 1952-1954; U.S. District Judge, Southern District of California, 1954-1955. *Member:* American Bar Association (Member, Corporation, Banking and Business Law Section; Real Property, Probate and Trust Law Section).

**JULIAN SCHEINER,** born St. Louis, Missouri, July 9, 1937; admitted to bar, 1972, California and U.S. District Court, Central District of California. *Education:* Washington University (B.S.E.E., 1961; J.D., 1970). Member, Real Property and Business Law Sections, State Bar of California.

**GARY V. SPENCER,** born Vernon, Texas, September 2, 1944; admitted to bar, 1970, California and U.S. District Court, Central District of California; 1976, U.S. District Court, Southern District of California; 1989, U.S. District Court, Eastern District of California. *Education:* University of Southern California (B.A., cum laude, 1966); Boalt Hall School of Law, University of California (J.D., 1969). Instructor, La Verne College of Law, 1972-1974. *Member:* San Bernardino County, San Bernardino County West End (Member, Board of Directors, 1972-1974), Orange County and American Bar Associations; California Trial Lawyers Association; Orange County Trial Lawyers Association (Member, Board of Directors, 1980-1981); Society of Professionals in Dispute Resolution; Southern California Mediation Association. (Irvine Office). *PRACTICE AREAS:* Construction Law; Mediation; Trademark Licensing; General Business.

### ASSOCIATES

**JOSEPH B. MCGINLEY,** born Lynwood, California, December 18, 1955; admitted to bar, 1982, California, U.S. Court of Appeals, Ninth Circuit and U.S. District Court, Central District of California; 1983, U.S. District Court, Northern and Southern Districts of California. *Education:* University of Southern California (A.B., 1979; J.D., 1982). Quarter Finalist, Hale Moot Court Honors Program, 1980-1981. Publications Editor, Major Tax Planning Journal, Volume 33, 1981. Notes and Articles Editor, Major Tax Planning Journal, Volume 34, 1981-1982. Publications Editor, Com-

*(This Listing Continued)*

puter Law Journal, 1981-1982. Board of Directors, 1989-1990, Legion Lex. Legion Lex, Inns of Court. Law Clerk Extern for Justice Lynn Compton, California Court of Appeals, Second District, 1981. *Member:* Orange County Bar Association. (Irvine Office).

*BRIAN K. MAZEN,* born Glendale, California, February 5, 1962; admitted to bar, 1987, California and U.S. District Court, Central District of California. *Education:* California Polytechnic State University (B.S., 1984); Loyola Marymount University (J.D., 1987). *Member:* Los Angeles County and American Bar Associations.

*CAROL B. BURNEY,* born Stamford, Connecticut, February 19, 1962; admitted to bar, 1987, California. *Education:* University of Rochester (B.A., 1984); Loyola University of Los Angeles (J.D., 1987). Phi Alpha Delta. Extern to the Hon. Cruz Reynoso, Associate Justice California Supreme Court, 1986. *Member:* Los Angeles County Bar Association.

*GEOFFREY T. TONG,* born Santa Monica, California, July 9, 1962; admitted to bar, 1988, California; 1989, U.S. District Court, Central District of California. *Education:* University of California at Los Angeles (B.A., 1985); Loyola Marymount University (J.D., 1988). Author: "Matsushita Elec. Indus. Corp. v. Zenha Radio Corp.: Supreme Court Leaves Extraterritorial Antitrust Questions Unanswered," 10 Loyola of Los Angeles International & Comparative Law Journal 401, 1988. *Member:* American Bar Association.

*CHRISTOPHER M. STEVENS,* born Providence, Rhode Island, November 30, 1965; admitted to bar, 1991, California and U.S. District Court, Southern District of California. *Education:* Boston University (B.A., 1987); Syracuse University College of Law (J.D. , 1991). Member, Jessup International Law Appellate Team, 1988-1989. *Member:* Los Angeles County Bar Association.

*BRIAN M. HOLBROOK,* born Columbus, Ohio; admitted to bar, 1989, California. *Education:* University of Virginia (B.A., high distinction, 1985); Stanford University (J.D., 1989). Member, Labor and Employment Law Section, State Bar of California. *PRACTICE AREAS:* Wrongful Termination; Employment Discrimination; Personal Policy Counseling; Wage and Hour.

*MATTHEW T. CURRIE,* born San Jose, California, December 20, 1963; admitted to bar, 1991, California. *Education:* University of California, Los Angeles (B.A., 1987); Loyola Law School (J.D., 1991).

*KENDRA S. MEINERT HODSON,* born New York, N.Y., December 21, 1967; admitted to bar, 1993, California. *Education:* Wells College (B.A., 1989); Southwestern University (J.D., 1993). Law Review Research Editor.

*ANDREW L. SATENBERG,* born Bronxville, New York, April 13, 1969; admitted to bar, 1994, California. *Education:* University of North Carolina at Chapel (B.A., 1991); New York University (J.D., 1994). Phi Beta Kappa.

*WENDY C. SATULOFF,* born Van Nuys, California, August 5, 1966; admitted to bar, 1992, California, U.S. District Court, Central District of California and U.S. Court of Appeals, Ninth Circuit; 1994, U.S. District Court, Southern District of California; 1996, U.S. District Court, Eastern District of California. *Education:* University of California at Los Angeles (B.A., 1988); Loyola Law School of Los Angeles (J.D., 1992). *Member:* Orange County (Commercial Law and Bankruptcy Section; Publicity Committee, Commercial Law and Bankruptcy Section; Law and Technology Committee) and American Bar Associations; Orange County Bankruptcy Forum; Peter M. Elliot Inn of Court. (Irvine Office). *PRACTICE AREAS:* Bankruptcy.

*BECKY J. BELKE,* born Shawano, Wisconsin, April 21, 1967; admitted to bar, 1995, California and U.S. District Court, Northern, Southern, Eastern and Central Districts of California. *Education:* University of Wisconsin, Oshkosh (B.S., 1989); Southwestern University School of Law (J.D., 1995). Delta Theta Phi (Vice President, 1995). Law Review. Author: Case Note "Kerins v. Hartley: A Patient's Silent Cry for Mandatory Disclosure By HIV-Positive Physicians," 25 Southwestern University Law Review 205, 1995; Book Note, "Your Doctor Is Not In: Healthy Skepticism About National Health Care" by Jane M. Orlent, M.D., 24 Southwestern University Law Review 501, 1995. *Member:* American Bar Association (Litigation Section). *PRACTICE AREAS:* Insurance Bad Faith Defense; Labor (Management Defense).

*DENNETT F. KOURI, JR.,* born Pasadena, California, September 20, 1968; admitted to bar, 1995, California. *Education:* University of California, Santa Barbara (B.A., 1990); Southwestern University School of Law (J.D., 1995). Delta Theta Phi (Officer, 1995). *Member:* Los Angeles County Bar

*(This Listing Continued)*

Association. *LANGUAGES:* Spanish. *PRACTICE AREAS:* Civil Litigation.

All Resident Members and Associates of the Firm are Members of the State Bar of California.

## MESSINA, LALAFARIAN & MANNING

### LOS ANGELES, CALIFORNIA

(See Glendale)

*General Liability Defense, Products Liability, Insurance Defense, Insurance Coverage.*

## MEYER & ASSOCIATES

*1875 CENTURY PARK EAST, SUITE 600*
### LOS ANGELES, CALIFORNIA 90067
*Telephone: 310-551-2045*
*Facsimile: 310-551-1416*

*Bankruptcy, Litigation.*

FIRM PROFILE: *Meyer & Associates practices in the areas of bankruptcy, insolvency, debtor/creditor rights, real estate litigation and general commercial and business litigation. The firm provides enhanced representation of clients by virtue of its relationship-oriented approach, which is characterized by a global view of the transaction and/or litigation engagement in the context of the client's overall business operations and extensive, prompt and ongoing communication with the client as to the direction of each matter. Meyer & Associates represents a wide range of public companies, private companies, financial firms and individuals.*

*JEFFREY P. MEYER,* born New York, N.Y., October 11, 1951; admitted to bar, 1977, New York; 1979, U.S. District Court, Southern and Eastern Districts of New York; 1981, California; 1982, U.S. District Court, Northern, Eastern, Central and Southern Districts of California. *Education:* New York University (B.A., 1973); Rutgers University at Camden (J.D., 1976). Editor-in-Chief, Rutgers Camden Law Journal, 1975-1976. *Member:* Los Angeles County Bar Association; State Bar of California. *PRACTICE AREAS:* Bankruptcy; Reorganization; Commercial Litigation.

## MEYERS, BIANCHI & McCONNELL

*A PROFESSIONAL CORPORATION*

Established in 1980

*11859 WILSHIRE BOULEVARD, FOURTH FLOOR*
### LOS ANGELES, CALIFORNIA 90025-6601
*Telephone: 310-312-0772*
*Cable Address: "Trialaw"*
*Facsimile: 310-312-0656*

*New York, New York Office:* 400 Madison Avenue. Telephone: 212-509-1663. Facsimile: 212-269-5927.

*General Civil and Trial Practice in all State and Federal Courts. Products Liability, Professional Malpractice Defense. Construction, Insurance, Reinsurance and Business Law.*

*JEFFREY G. MEYERS,* born Brooklyn, New York, April 16, 1943; admitted to bar, 1968, New York and U.S. District Court, Southern and Eastern Districts of New York; 1975, California and U.S. District Court, Central and Southern Districts of California. *Education:* Hofstra University (B.A., 1964); Brooklyn Law School (LL.B., 1967). Co-Chairman, Reinsurance Sub-Committee, Tort and Insurance Section, American Bar Association. *Member:* The Association of the Bar of the City of New York; Los Angeles County Bar Association; State Bar of California; Association of Southern California Defense Counsel; Asian-Pacific Lawyers Association (Chairman, Product Liability, Committee, 1990—). *PRACTICE AREAS:* Product Liability; Coverage; Reinsurance Issues; Professional Liability.

*JOHN W. McCONNELL III,* born San Bernardino, California, August 19, 1949; admitted to bar, 1974, California and U.S. District Court, Southern, Central and Eastern Districts of California. *Education:* University of Southern California (B.A., 1971); California Western School of Law (LL.B., 1974); University of Southern California Law Center. Member, California Western Law Review, 1972-1973. *Member:* Los Angeles County and American Bar Associations; State Bar of California; Association of Southern Cal-

*(This Listing Continued)*

**MEYERS, BIANCHI & McCONNELL,** A PROFESSIONAL CORPORATION, Los Angeles—Continued

ifornia Defense Counsel; Product Liability Advisory Council; Defense Research Institute. *PRACTICE AREAS:* Litigation; Product Liability; Professional Liability; Environmental, Professional and CGL Coverage.

**MARTIN E. PULVERMAN,** born Santa Monica, California, December 9, 1953; admitted to bar, 1981, California; 1982, U.S. District Court, Central District of California; 1989, U.S. Supreme Court. *Education:* University of California, Los Angeles; University of California, Santa Barbara (B.A., 1975); Hastings College of the Law, University of California (J.D., 1979). Executive Editor, Research, Hastings COMM/ENT Communications and Entertainment Law Journal, 1978-1979. Licensed California State Real Estate Broker. Staff Attorney, Kern County Superior Court Law and Motion Department, 1983-1984. *Member:* Los Angeles County Bar Association; State Bar of California. *PRACTICE AREAS:* Litigation; Professional Liability; Product Liability; Appellate Practice.

**ELIZABETH A. KOOYMAN,** born Des Moines, Iowa, December 22, 1959; admitted to bar, 1984, Iowa; 1989, California, U.S. District Court, Central District of California and U.S. Court of Appeals, Ninth Circuit. *Education:* Grand View College (A.A., 1980); Drake University (B.A., 1981; J.D., 1984). Phi Alpha Delta. *Member:* Los Angeles County and American Bar Associations; State Bar of California; Iowa State Bar; Women's Law Association of Los Angeles; Professional Liability Underwriting Society. *PRACTICE AREAS:* Litigation; Professional Liability; Products Liability; Coverage; Construction.

---

**PATRICK D. BINGHAM,** born Salt Lake City, Utah, August 24, 1956; admitted to bar, 1981, California; 1982, U.S. District Court, Northern, Central, Southern and Eastern Districts of California; 1983, U.S. Court of Appeals, Ninth Circuit. *Education:* Stanford University (B.A., 1978); University of California at Los Angeles (M.A., 1981); University of California at Los Angeles School of Law (J.D., 1981). *Member:* State Bar of California. *PRACTICE AREAS:* Product Liability; Insurance Related Issues.

**FREDERICK S. REISZ,** born Los Angeles, California, January 1, 1964; admitted to bar, 1989, California. *Education:* Franklin & Marshall College (B.A., 1986); Pepperdine University School of Law (J.D., 1989). *Member:* Los Angeles County Bar Association; State Bar of California. *PRACTICE AREAS:* Insurance Bad Faith; Environmental Pollution; Coverage.

**ELIZABETH S. AGMON,** born Santa Monica, California, October 8, 1961; admitted to bar, 1988, California and U.S. Court of Appeals, Ninth Circuit. *Education:* University of California at Davis (A.B., 1983); Pepperdine University (J.D., 1987). Phi Delta Phi. *Member:* San Fernando Valley, Beverly Hills and Los Angeles County Bar Associations; State Bar of California. *PRACTICE AREAS:* Litigation; Professional Liability; Products Liability; General Liability; Insurance Coverage.

**JAMES M. FOWLER,** born Kalamazoo, Michigan, December 17, 1957; admitted to bar, 1992, California. *Education:* University of West Los Angeles (B.S., 1987; J.D., 1992). *Member:* State Bar of California. *PRACTICE AREAS:* Product Liability; Insurance Related Issues.

**CAROL J. KNOBLOW,** born Meadville, Pennsylvania, May 30, 1965; admitted to bar, 1990, California. *Education:* Allegheny College (B.A., with honors, 1987); Pepperdine University (J.D., 1990). *Member:* Beverly Hills and American Bar Associations; State Bar of California. *PRACTICE AREAS:* Litigation; Professional Liability; Products Liability; General Liability; Insurance Coverage; Construction.

**HEIDI M. YOSHIOKA,** born Gardena, California, March 13, 1964; admitted to bar, 1990, California and U.S. District Court, Central District of California; 1994, U.S. District Court, Northern District of California. *Education:* Loyola Marymount University (B.S.B.A., 1986); Southwestern University School of Law (J.D., 1989). *Member:* Japanese American Bar Association; Southern California Defense Counsel. *PRACTICE AREAS:* Insurance Defense.

*OF COUNSEL*

**JAMES S. BIANCHI,** born Los Angeles, California, March 3, 1945; admitted to bar, 1970, California and U.S. District Court, Central District of California; 1977, U.S. District Court, Eastern District of California; 1983, U.S. District Court, Northern District of California; 1990, U.S. District Court, Southern District of California. *Education:* University of California at Los Angeles (B.S., 1966; J.D., 1969). *Member:* Los Angeles County (Member, Litigation Section) and American (Member, Sections on:

*(This Listing Continued)*

Torts and Insurance Practice; Construction Law; Litigation) Bar Associations; State Bar of California; Association of Southern California Defense Counsel; National Transportation Safety Board Bar Association (Member, Product Liability Advisory Council). *PRACTICE AREAS:* Litigation; Product Liability; Professional Liability; Coverage.

**HARRIS ZEITZEW,** born Philadelphia, Pennsylvania, November 3, 1925; admitted to bar, 1976, California; registered to practice before U.S. Patent and Trademark Office. *Education:* University of Southern California (B.S., 1950; M.S., 1958); Loyola Law School, Loyola Marymount University (J.D., 1975). Registered Professional Engineer, California, 1956. Author: "Liability for Personal Injury Damages: A New Problem for Industrial Waste Generators," Purdue Industrial Waste Conference, 1984. *Member:* Los Angeles County and American (Member, Sections on: Torts and Insurance Practice; Litigation) Bar Associations; State Bar of California; Association of Southern California Defense Counsel. *PRACTICE AREAS:* Product Liability; Consumer Protection.

**ANDREW FELDMAN,** born London, England, March 26, 1943; admitted to bar, 1969, New York (Not admitted in California). *Education:* University of Buffalo (B.A., 1965; J.D., 1968). Author: "Medical and Legal Dimensions," Management for Physicians, 1983. Lecturer at Niagara University, State University of New York at Buffalo and New York State Bar Association and Author on Medical-Legal Topics, 1976—. Member, Panel of Arbitrators, American Arbitration Association. *Member:* Erie County, New York State, International and American Bar Associations; Western New York Trial Lawyers Association; International Association of Insurance Counsel. *PRACTICE AREAS:* Insurance; Professional Malpractice; Medical Malpractice; Environmental; Toxic Tort.

**CAROLE D. BOS,** born Grand Rapids, Michigan, May 31, 1949; admitted to bar, 1981, Michigan and U.S. District Court, Eastern and Western Districts of Michigan; U.S. Court of Appeals, Sixth Circuit (Not admitted in California). *Education:* Grand Valley State University (B.A., summa cum laude, 1977); Thomas M. Cooley Law School (J.D., cum laude, 1981). Student Award, 1981. Faculty: ICLE, University of Michigan Law; ICLE Advocacy Institute, Spring, Summer and Fall programs, 1990—. Faculty and Steering Committee Member, Hillman Advocacy Program, 1991—. Lecturer, National CLE Programs on environmental coverage and trial advocacy issues. Co-Author: "How to Use Video in Litigation," Prentice-Hall, Inc., 1986. Contributing Author, "Women Trial Lawyers: How They Succeed in Practice and in the Courtroom," Prentice-Hall, Inc., 1986. *Member:* Grand Rapids, Federal (Regional Director, 1985-1989) and American (Member, Task Force on Environmental Insurance Coverage Litigation; Co-Chair, Insurance Coverage Committee, Section of Litigation) Bar Associations; State Bar of Michigan (Member, Standing Committee on Professionalism); Defense Research Institute; American Judicature Society. Fellow, Michigan State Bar Foundation. (Also Member Bos & Glazier at Grand Rapids, MI). *PRACTICE AREAS:* Environmental Insurance Defense Litigation; Insurance Coverage Litigation; Personal Injury.

REPRESENTATIVE CLIENTS: Furnished on Request.
REFERENCE: Bank of America (Century City Branch).

---

## DALE R. MICHAEL

*6300 WILSHIRE BOULEVARD*
*SUITE 1630*
**LOS ANGELES, CALIFORNIA 90048**
*Telephone: 213-782-1027*
*Fax: 213-651-4868*

*General Civil Litigation, Appellate Practice in all State and Federal Courts. Insurance Bad Faith, Employment Discrimination, Sexual Harassment, Wrongful Termination.*

**DALE R. MICHAEL,** born St. Thomas, U.S. Virgin Islands, October 1, 1942; admitted to bar, 1968, New York; 1969, California. *Education:* Manhattan College (B.S., Chemical Engineering, 1962); Columbia University (J.D., 1967; M.B.A.; M.S.Ch.E., 1968). *LANGUAGES:* Spanish.

## MICHAELIS, MONTANARI & JOHNSON
*A PROFESSIONAL LAW CORPORATION*

**LOS ANGELES, CALIFORNIA**

(See Westlake Village)

*General Civil and Trial Practice in all State and Federal Courts. Business Litigation, Insurance, Aviation, Space, Environmental, General Casualty, Maritime, Product Liability and Toxic Torts.*

---

## MICHAELSON & LEVINE
**1901 AVENUE OF THE STARS, SUITE 1708**
**LOS ANGELES, CALIFORNIA 90067**
Telephone: 310-278-4984
Fax: 310-286-9969

*Trials and Appeals in State and Federal Courts, specializing in White Collar Criminal Defense, and the representation of professionals accused of crimes.*

### MEMBERS OF FIRM

**ALVIN S. MICHAELSON,** born Jersey City, New Jersey, May 13, 1939; admitted to bar, 1964, New Jersey and U.S. District Court, District of New Jersey; 1969, California, U.S. District Court, Central District of California and U.S. Court of Appeals, 9th Circuit; 1972, U.S. Supreme Court; 1974, U.S. District Court, Southern District of California; 1979, U.S. Court of Appeals, 3rd Circuit and U.S. Tax Court; 1981, U.S. District Court, Northern District of California; 1995, U.S. District Court, Eastern District of California. *Education:* Columbia University (B.A., cum laude, 1960); Harvard University (J.D., 1963). Assistant Prosecutor, Hudson County, New Jersey, 1964-1967. Trial Attorney, U.S. Department of Justice, Antitrust Division, 1967-1969. *Member:* Los Angeles County and Federal Bar Associations; State Bar of California; Criminal Courts Bar Association; National Association of Criminal Defense Lawyers; Los Angeles Trial Lawyers Association; California Attorneys for Criminal Justice. **LANGUAGES:** Spanish.

**JANET I. LEVINE,** born Los Angeles, California, March 22, 1955; admitted to bar, 1980, California; 1981, U.S. District Court, Central District of California and U.S. Court of Appeals, 9th Circuit; 1985, U.S. Supreme Court; 1987, U.S. District Court, Northern District of California; 1990, U.S. District Court, Southern District of California; 1992, U.S. District Court, Eastern District of California and District of Arizona. *Education:* University of California at Los Angeles (B.A. cum laude, 1977); Loyola University (J.D., summa cum laude, 1980). Member, 1978-1980 and Chief Articles Editor, 1979-1980, Loyola Law Review. Author: "The Contract Clause, A Constitutional Basis for Invalidating State Legislation," 12 Loyola Law Review, 927, 1979. Law Clerk to the Hon. Arthur L. Alarcon, U.S. Court of Appeals, 9th Circuit, 1980-1982. Deputy Federal Public Defender, Central District of California, 1982-1984. Judge Pro Tem, 1986—. Lawyer-Delegate, Ninth Circuit Judicial Conference, 1993-1995. *Member:* Los Angeles County, Federal and American Bar Associations; State Bar of California; California Attorneys for Criminal Justice; California Public Defenders Association; National Association of Criminal Defense Lawyers.

### ASSOCIATE

**BRENDA LIGORSKY,** born Stratford, New Jersey, August 20, 1968; admitted to bar, 1993, California and U.S. District Court, Southern District of California; 1996, U.S. District Court, Central and Eastern Districts of California. *Education:* Tufts University (B.A., 1990); University of Southern California (J.D., 1993). *Member:* Los Angeles County Bar Association; National Association of Criminal Defense Lawyers. **LANGUAGES:** French, Spanish and Italian.

### OF COUNSEL

**ROGER L. COSSACK,** born Boston, Massachusetts, April 16, 1941; admitted to bar, 1967, California, U.S. District Court, Central District of California and U.S. Court of Appeals, Ninth Circuit; 1976, U.S. Supreme Court; 1985, U.S. Court of Appeals, Tenth Circuit; 1992, U.S. Court of Appeals, Second Circuit. *Education:* University of California, Los Angeles (B.A., Pol. Sc., 1963); University of California School of Law at Los Angeles (J.D., 1966). Assistant Dean, University of California, School of Law at Los Angeles, 1969-1971. Deputy District Attorney, Los Angeles, California, 1967-1969. Legal analyst, Cable News Network, 1995—. *Member:*

*(This Listing Continued)*

---

Los Angeles County Bar Association; State Bar of California; National Association of Criminal Defense Lawyers; Criminal Courts Bar Association; Society of Professional Journalists.

REFERENCE: City National Bank (Century City Branch).

---

## MITCH MORIYASU MICHINO
**SUITE 313, 880 WEST FIRST STREET**
**LOS ANGELES, CALIFORNIA 90012**
Telephone: 213-680-2533
Telecopier: 213-680-3832

*International Corporate Law, Immigration and Naturalization.*

**MITCH MORIYASU MICHINO,** born Osaka, Japan, September 18, 1942; admitted to bar, 1973, Washington; 1974, California and Hawaii. *Education:* Keio University, Tokyo, Japan (B.A., 1966); University of California at Los Angeles (B.A., 1969); California Western School of Law (J.D., 1972); University of Washington (LL.M., 1973). Phi Alpha Delta. Managing Editor, California Western International Law Journal, 1971. *Member:* Los Angeles County, Washington State (inactive), Hawaii State and American Bar Associations; State Bar of California; Japan America Society of Southern California. **LANGUAGES:** Japanese. **PRACTICE AREAS:** International Corporate Law.

### OF COUNSEL

**JAMES W. O'NEIL,** born Erie, Pennsylvania, March 2, 1931; admitted to bar, 1962, California. *Education:* University of Notre Dame (A.B., 1952); Loyola University (LL.B., 1961). *Member:* State Bar of California. **PRACTICE AREAS:** Corporate Law; Banking Law.

---

## MIHALY, SCHUYLER & MITCHELL
An Association including Professional Corporations

*Established in 1972*

**SUITE 1201, 1801 CENTURY PARK EAST**
**LOS ANGELES, CALIFORNIA 90067**
Telephone: 213-879-5600; 310-556-3500
Telecopier: 310-556-0413; 310-284-7982

*General Civil and Trial Practice. Tax, Corporation, Real Property, Oil and Gas, Estate Planning, Trust, Probate, Immigration, Nationality and International Business Law.*

**ZOLTAN M. MIHALY,** born Bratislava, Czechoslovakia, March 25, 1926; admitted to bar, 1962, California; 1968, U.S. Tax Court. *Education:* Bratislava University, Czechoslovakia; Harvard University (LL.B., 1960); University of Budapest, Hungary (J.D., 1950). *Member:* Los Angeles County (Chairman, International Law Section, 1969) and American Bar Associations; State Bar of California; Foreign Law Association of Southern California (President, 1973—). (Member, Mihaly & Schuyler, A Professional Corporation).

**ROB R. SCHUYLER, A PROFESSIONAL CORPORATION,** born Mamaroneck, New York, August 13, 1932; admitted to bar, 1958, California; 1962, U.S. Supreme Court and U.S. Court of Military Appeals. *Education:* University of Paris, France and University of Southern California (B.A., 1955); University of Michigan (J.D., 1958). Delta Theta Phi. *Member:* Century City, Los Angeles County (Chairman, International Law Section, 1972-1973), Wilshire (Director, 1968—; President, 1970) and American (Member, Sections on: Corporation, Banking and Business Law; Family Law; International Law ) Bar Associations; State Bar of California; The Association of Trial Lawyers of America; American Immigration Lawyers Association. **LANGUAGES:** French. **PRACTICE AREAS:** International Business Clients doing Business in United States and Europe; Visa and Immigration Law; Trial Practice; Estate Planning; Airline Law.

**J. H. MITCHELL, JR., A PROFESSIONAL CORPORATION,** born Los Angeles, California, October 31, 1924; admitted to bar, 1951, California and U.S. District Court, Central District of California; 1959, U.S. Supreme Court; 1961, U.S. Tax Court; 1982, U.S. Court of Appeals, Ninth Circuit. *Education:* University of Southern California (B.S., 1947; LL.B., 1951). Phi Delta Phi. Member of National Panel, American Arbitration Association, 1961-1967. *Member:* Los Angeles County and American (Member, Section of Corporation, Banking and Business Law) Bar Associations; The State Bar of California; Chancery Club; American Judicature Society. (Also Vice President, Clary Broadcasting Group, Inc., Los Angeles).

*(This Listing Continued)*

CAA983B

## MIHALY, SCHUYLER & MITCHELL, Los Angeles—Continued

**STEPHEN A. MIHALY,** born Cambridge, Massachusetts, March 24, 1957; admitted to bar, 1984, California. *Education:* Stanford University (B.S., 1979); University of San Diego (J.D., 1982). Member: Beverly Hills Bar Association Journal, Winter, 1981; Tax Management International Journal, January, 1982; The International Lawyer, Winter, 1982. *Member:* Beverly Hills, Los Angeles County and American Bar Associations; State Bar of California.

**WILLIAM R. HESS,** born Los Angeles, California, February 25, 1954; admitted to bar, 1981, California; 1982, U.S. District Court, Central District of California. *Education:* Brandeis University (B.A., magna cum laude, 1976); Benjamin Cardozo School of Law, Yeshiva University (J.D., 1980). *Member:* Los Angeles County Bar Association; State Bar of California.

REPRESENTATIVE CLIENTS: Activision; Aerojet-General Corp.; Air France; Allergan Pharmaceuticals; American Hospital Supply Corp.; Applied Magnetics Corp.; Bell & Howell; Bobrick, Corp.; Bourns, Inc.; CFS Continental, Inc.; Consulate General of Switzerland, Los Angeles; Cutter Laboratories, Inc.; Data Products Corp.; Elf Petroleum Corp., U.S.A.; Exchange & Investment Bank, Geneva, Switzerland; Fairchild Camera & Instrument Corp.; U.T.A., French Airlines, Los Angeles; Gelco Corp.; General Telephone & Electronics; Global Marine, Inc.; ILC Technology; ICN Pharmaceuticals, Inc.; International Harvester; LH Research; Maxtor Corp.; Measured Marketing Services, Inc.; Microdata Corp.; Monogram Industries, Inc.; National Semiconductor Corp.; Pacific Architects and Engineers, Inc.; Park-Davis & Co.; Plessey Peripheral Systems, Inc.; Quantum Corp.; Qume Corp.; Rain Bird Sprinkler Mfg. Corp.; Raychem Corp.; Redken Laboratories, Inc.; Smithkline Beckman Corp.; Swiss Bank Corp; Syntex; TRW, Inc.

## MILBANK, TWEED, HADLEY & McCLOY

**601 SOUTH FIGUEROA STREET
LOS ANGELES, CALIFORNIA 90017**
Telephone: 213-892-4000
Fax: 213-629-5063 ABA/net: MilbankLA

*New York, New York Office:* 1 Chase Manhattan Plaza, 10005. Telephone: 212-530-5000. Fax: 212-530-5219. ABA/net: MilbankNY; MCI Mail: MilbankTweed.

*Midtown Office:* 50 Rockefeller Plaza, 10020. Telephone: 212-530-5800. Fax: 212-530-0158.

*Washington, D.C. Office:* International Square Building, Suite 1100, 1825 Eye Street, N.W., 20006. Telephone: 202-835-7500. Fax: 202-835-7586. ABA/net: MilbankDC.

*Tokyo, Japan Office:* Nippon Press Center Building, 2-1, Uchisaiwai-cho 2-chome, Chiyoda-ku, Tokyo 100. Telephone: 011-81-3-3504-1050. Fax: 011-81-3-3595-2790, 011-81-3-3502-5192.

*London, England Office:* Dashwood House, 69 Old Broad Street, London, EC2M 1Q5. Telephone: 011-44-171-448-3000. Fax: 011-44-171-448-3029.

*Hong Kong Office:* 3007 Alexandra House, 16 Charter Road. Telephone: 011-852-2571-4888. Fax: 011-852-2840-0792, 011-8522-845-9046. ABA/net: MilbankHK.

*Singapore Office:* 14-02 Caltex House, 30 Raffles Place, 048622. Telephone: 011-65-534-1700. Fax: 011-65-534-2733. ABA/net: EDNANG.

*Moscow, Russia Office:* 24/27 Sadovaya-Samotyochnya, Moscow, 103051. Telephone: 011-7-501-258-5015. Fax: 011-7-501-258-5014.

*Jakarta, Indonesia Correspondent Office:* Makarim & Taira S., 17th Floor, Summitmas Tower, Jl, Jend. Sudirman 61, Jakarta. Telephone: 011-62-21-252-1839 or 1272. Fax: 011-62-21-252-4740 or 2750.

*General Practice.*

### RESIDENT PARTNERS

**KENNETH J. BARONSKY,** born San Jose, California, 1962; admitted to bar, 1988, California. *Education:* University of Washington (B.A., with distinction, 1985; J.D., 1988).

**PAUL S. ARONZON,** born Los Angeles, California, 1954; admitted to bar, 1979, California; 1995, District of Columbia. *Education:* California State University at Northridge (B.A., cum laude, 1976); Southwestern University (J.D., 1979). *Member:* Los Angeles County (Member, Uniform Commercial Code Committee, 1985—) and American (Member, Commercial Law and Bankruptcy Sections) Bar Associations; State Bar of California (Member, Uniform Commercial Code Committee, Business Law Section, 1984-1988; Co-Chair, Article 2 A Subcommittee, 1987-1988); The District of Columbia Bar; Financial Lawyers Conference; Bankruptcy Study Group.

*(This Listing Continued)*

**EDWIN F. FEO,** born Los Angeles, California, 1952; admitted to bar, 1977, California. *Education:* Claremont McKenna College; University of California at Los Angeles (B.A., 1974); University of California School of Law (J.D., 1977). *Member:* Los Angeles County and American Bar Associations; State Bar of California. (Managing Partner, Los Angeles Office). *Email:* efeo@milbank.com

**DAVID C. L. FRAUMAN,** born Dallas, Texas, 1946; admitted to bar, 1976, New York; 1988, California. *Education:* Columbia University (B.A., magna cum laude, 1972), Phi Beta Kappa; Rutgers University (J.D., 1975). Editor, Rutgers Law Review. *Member:* The Association of the Bar of the City of New York; Los Angeles County, New York State and American Bar Associations; State Bar of California; Financial Lawyers Conference.

**C. STEPHEN HOWARD,** born Evansville, Indiana, 1940; admitted to bar, 1969, California; 1972, U.S. Supreme Court. *Education:* Yale University (B.A., summa cum laude, 1962; LL.B., cum laude, 1966). *Member:* Los Angeles County Bar Association (Trustee, 1975-1976, 1982-1984; President, Barristers, 1975-1976; Litigation Section, Executive Committee, 1989-1992); State Bar of California (Member, Joint Commission on Discovery, 1984-1986); Association of Business Trial Lawyers (Member, Board of Governors, 1981-1983).

**DAVID A. LAMB,** born Ventura, California, 1953; admitted to bar, 1979, California. *Education:* Santa Clara University (B.S.C., 1975; M.B.A., 1976); University of California at Los Angeles (J.D., 1979). *Member:* Los Angeles County Bar Association.

**TED OBRZUT,** born Hatfield, England, 1949; admitted to bar, 1974, California; 1990, New York. *Education:* Columbia University; University of California at Santa Barbara (B.A., summa cum laude, 1971); University of California School of Law (J.D., 1974). *Member:* Los Angeles County and American Bar Associations; State Bar of California.

**ERIC H. SCHUNK,** born Boston, Massachusetts, 1955; admitted to bar, 1981, California; 1990, New York. *Education:* Georgetown University (B.S., magna cum laude, 1977); UCLA School of Management (M.B.A., 1981); UCLA School of Law (J.D., 1981). (Managing Partner, Los Angeles Corporate Department).

**PETER P. WALLACE,** born Bronxville, New York, 1946; admitted to bar, 1983, New York; 1987, California. *Education:* United States Military Academy (B.S., 1968); Institut D'Etudes Politiques, Paris, France (Diplome, 1974); Harvard University (J.D., cum laude, 1982). *Member:* State Bar of California; New York State Bar Association.

**KAREN B. WONG,** born Los Angeles, California, 1961; admitted to bar, 1986, California. *Education:* University of Southern California (B.S., 1982; J.D., 1986).

### OF COUNSEL

**ALAN M. FENNING,** born San Bernardino, California, 1950; admitted to bar, 1975, Illinois; 1976, California, U.S. District Court, Northern District of Illinois and U.S. District Court, Central District of California. *Education:* Claremont McKenna College (B.A., magna cum laude, 1972); Boalt Hall School of Law, University of California, Berkeley (J.D., 1975). Order of the Coif. Member, 1973-1975, and Note and Comment Editor, 1974-1975, California Law Review. Author: Note, "Responsible Relative Laws and Equal Protection," Vol. 63, California Law Review, p. 85 (1975). *Member:* Los Angeles, Federal, American (Member: Coordinating Group on Energy Law, 1989-1994; Section on Natural Resources, Energy and Environmental Law, 1988—; Vice Chair, Special Committee on International Energy Law, 1994—) and International (Member, Committee on Electricity Law, 1995—) Bar Associations; State Bar of California.

### SENIOR COUNSEL

**NEIL J WERTLIEB,** born New York, New York, 1958; admitted to bar, 1984, California. *Education:* University of California at Berkeley (B.S., with honors, 1980); University of California Boalt Hall School of Law (J.D., 1984). *Member:* Los Angeles County and American Bar Associations; State Bar of California.

**HARRY L. USHER,** born Jersey City, New Jersey, 1939; admitted to bar, 1965, California. *Education:* Brown University (A.B., 1961); Stanford University (LL.B., 1964). Order of the Coif; Phi Beta Kappa. *Member:* The State Bar of California.

*(This Listing Continued)*

## RESIDENT ASSOCIATES

Taline A. Aharonian
Dino Barajas
Devan D. Beck
Amy Bersch
Scott M. Brown
Gregory L. Call
Veronica Davies
Michael Dayen
Jose M. Deetjan
Ada E. Ejikeme
R. Lee Garner III
Lawrence B. Gill
David J. Impastato
  (Not admitted in CA)
Patricia K Jones
Nicholas L. Kondoleon
Melainie K. Mansfield
Allan T. Marks
Jeffrey D. McFarland
Eddy Ching-Liang Meng
John A. Mitchell
Fred Neufeld
Gloria M. Noh
William J. Peters
Eric R. Reimer
Kendrick F. Royer
Eileen Driscoll Rubens
Deborah Ruosch
Roger K. Smith
Scot Tucker
Scott Vick
Paul T. Wrycha
Andrew H.T. Wu

(For Biographical Data on all Personnel, see Professional Biographies at New York, New York)

## MILLARD, PILCHOWSKI, HOLWEGER & CHILD, P.C.

A Partnership including Professional Corporations

Established in 1978

12TH FLOOR, 655 SOUTH HOPE STREET
**LOS ANGELES, CALIFORNIA 90017-3211**
Telephone: 213-627-3113
Fax: 213-623-9237
Email: mphc@loop.com

*General Civil Trial Practice in all Courts. Insurance, Personal Injury, Products Liability, Malpractice and Corporation Law.*

*FIRM PROFILE: Millard, Pilchowski, Holweger & Child is a Los Angeles based firm of civil trial attorneys serving all of Southern California. The firm's practice includes general civil, trial and appellate work in state and federal courts.*

*Founded in 1978, Millard, Pilchowski, Holweger & Child has earned a reputation as one of California's top defense firms. Originally, the firm was formed for the purpose of representing major U.S. manufacturers in litigation matters based in Southern California. As the litigation needs of our clients increased in breadth, the area of the firm's expertise has expanded to include virtually all types of civil actions, including insurance coverage and bad faith, as well as the handling of general civil litigation for insurance company clients.*

*Millard, Pilchowski, Holweger & Child adheres to a philosophy of personal service. At MPH&C, each client matter is handled by a partner in the firm who has a relationship with the client and is available to answer all questions promptly and knowledgeably.*

**L. RAYMOND MILLARD, (P.C.),** born Portland, Oregon, July 21, 1927; admitted to bar, 1958, California. *Education:* University of California at Los Angeles (A.B., 1953; J.D., 1957). Phi Delta Phi. Deputy District Attorney of Los Angeles, 1958-1960. *Member:* Los Angeles County and American Bar Associations; The State Bar of California; Defense Research Institute; American Board of Trial Advocates; Association of Southern California Defense Counsel. *PRACTICE AREAS:* Insurance Defense; Civil Litigation.

**THOMAS S. PILCHOWSKI, (P.C.),** born Detroit, Michigan, September 11, 1938; admitted to bar, 1974, California. *Education:* Detroit Institute of Technology (B.S.E.E., 1966); University of California at Los Angeles; Western State University (J.D., 1974). Recipient, American Jurisprudence Award. *Member:* Los Angeles County and American Bar Associations; The State Bar of California; Association of Southern California Defense Counsel. *PRACTICE AREAS:* Insurance Defense; Civil Litigation.

**MARIE POLIZZI HOLWEGER,** born Upland, California, December 31, 1954; admitted to bar, 1980, California. *Education:* Loyola Marymount University (B.S., magna cum laude, 1977); Loyola University of Los Angeles (J.D., 1980). Alpha Sigma Nu. *Member:* Los Angeles County and American Bar Associations; The State Bar of California. *PRACTICE AREAS:* Insurance Defense; Civil Litigation.

*(This Listing Continued)*

**BRADFORD T. CHILD,** born Minneapolis, Minnesota, September 13, 1954; admitted to bar, 1980, California; 1981, Minnesota. *Education:* University of the Pacific (B.A., 1977); McGeorge School of Law (J.D., 1980). Staff Writer, Pacific Law Journal, 1979-1980. *Member:* State Bar of California; Minnesota State Bar Association. *PRACTICE AREAS:* Insurance Defense; Civil Litigation.

---

**BRADLEY P. CHILDERS,** born Indianapolis, Indiana, May 20, 1964; admitted to bar, 1989, California. *Education:* University of California at Davis (B.A., 1986); Pepperdine University (J.D., 1989). *Member:* Los Angeles County Bar Association; State Bar of California. *PRACTICE AREAS:* Insurance Defense; Civil Litigation.

**ELIZABETH T. FITZGERALD,** born Maywood, Illinois, February 21, 1963; admitted to bar, 1992, California. *Education:* American College in Paris (1981-1982); University of Paris, The Sorbonne, Paris, France (Superior Certificate of the French Language, 1983); University of California at Irvine (B.A. in french, with honors, 1986); Loyola Marymount University (J.D., 1989). *Member:* Los Angeles County, American and Irish American Bar Associations; State Bar of California. *LANGUAGES:* French, German. *PRACTICE AREAS:* Insurance Defense; Civil Litigation. *Email:* mphc@loop.com

**JENIFFER A. WILDER,** born Detroit, Michigan, 1967; admitted to bar, 1993, Michigan; 1995, California. *Education:* Michigan State University (B.A., 1990); Thomas M. Cooley Law School (J.D., 1992). *Member:* Los Angeles County and Michigan State Bar Associations; State Bar of California. *PRACTICE AREAS:* Insurance Defense; Civil Litigation.

**RUSSELL W. SCHATZ, JR.,** born Santa Monica, California, July 15, 1960; admitted to bar, 1991, California. *Education:* Loyola Marymount University (B.S., 1983); California State University at Northridge (M.S., in environmental and occupational health, 1987); Western State University (J.D., 1991). *Member:* Los Angeles County Bar Association; State Bar of California. *PRACTICE AREAS:* Insurance Defense; Civil Litigation.

REPRESENTATIVE CLIENTS: Rockwell International Corp.; Royal Insurance Cos.; Travelers Insurance Cos.; Design Professional Insurance Co.; Blue Shield; Koehring Co.; Clark Equipment Co.; Delta International Machinery Corp.; Porter-Cable Corp.; AETNA Insurance Co.

---

## KIMBERLY A. MILLER

10960 WILSHIRE BOULEVARD
10TH FLOOR
**LOS ANGELES, CALIFORNIA 90024**
Telephone: 310-445-4600
Fax: 310-444-6420

*General Civil Trial, Personal Injury, Products Liability, Employment Law, Sexual Discrimination, FELA, Jones Act and Family Law.*

**KIMBERLY A. MILLER,** born Ridley, Pennsylvania, November 30, 1953; admitted to bar, 1981, California; 1982, U.S. District Court, Central District of California. *Education:* University of California at Los Angeles (B.A., 1976); Southwestern University (J.D., 1980). *Member:* Federal and American Bar Associations; The Association of Trial Lawyers of America; Consumers Attorneys Association of Los Angeles; Consumer Attorneys of California; Women Lawyers of California.

---

## HOWARD B. MILLER

**LOS ANGELES, CALIFORNIA**

(See El Segundo)

*Mediation and Arbitration, Civil Trials, Appellate, Intellectual Property, Patents, Copyright, Trademarks, Trade Secrets, Venture Capitol, Real Estate, Bankruptcy.*

## THE MILLER LAW OFFICES
### LOS ANGELES, CALIFORNIA
(See Studio City)

*Practice limited to Immigration and Nationality Law.*

---

## MITCHELL R. MILLER
### LOS ANGELES, CALIFORNIA
(See Beverly Hills)

*Taxation Law, Administrative Law and Estate Planning Law.*

---

## MILLER & NOLAN
### INCORPORATED
### LOS ANGELES, CALIFORNIA
(See Howrey & Simon)

---

## RICHARD F. MILLER
### A PROFESSIONAL CORPORATION
### LOS ANGELES, CALIFORNIA
(See Pasadena)

*Probate, Estate Planning, Trust and Conservatorship Law.*

---

## MILLIKAN AND THOMAS
### LOS ANGELES, CALIFORNIA
(See Pasadena)

*General Civil and Trial Practice in all State and Federal Courts. Corporate, Taxation, Construction, Government Contracts, Real Estate, Family, Estate Planning and Probate Law.*

---

## LAW OFFICES OF
## LYLE R. MINK
Established in 1976
SUITE 1700
2029 CENTURY PARK EAST
### LOS ANGELES, CALIFORNIA 90067
Telephone: 310-553-1010
Fax: 310-284-5743

*General Civil Trial and Appellate Practice in all State and Federal Courts.*

**LYLE R. MINK,** born Chicago, Illinois, October 7, 1944; admitted to bar, 1972, California; U.S. Court of Appeals, Ninth Circuit and U.S. District Court, Northern and Southern Districts of California; 1975, U.S. Court of Appeals for the District of Columbia Circuit and U.S. Supreme Court; 1981, U.S. Tax Court; 1982, U.S. Court of Appeals, Tenth Circuit. *Education:* University of Illinois and California State University, Northridge (B.S., 1967); Loyola University of Los Angeles (J.D., 1971). Phi Delta Phi. Member, St. Thomas More Society. Articles Editor, Loyola University Law Review, 1970-1971. Author: Note, "Reasonable Investigations and the Financial Responsibility Law—Protecting the Innocent Third Party," 3 Loyola University Law Review 169, 1970. Law Clerk to Presiding Justice John J. Ford, Court of Appeal of California, Second Appellate District, Division Three, 1970. Teaching Fellow in Legal Writing and Research, Loyola University Law School, 1970-1971. Law Clerk to Chief Justice Donald R. Wright, Supreme Court of California, 1971-1972. Assistant Professor of Business Law, California State University, Northridge, 1976-

*(This Listing Continued)*

1978. State Court Receiver, Referee, and Provisional Director, Los Angeles County Superior Court, 1983—. Arbitrator, Los Angeles County Judicial Arbitration Program, 1981-1985. *Member:* State Bar of California. [Capt., USMCR, 1967-1973]. **REPORTED CASES:** Kimmel v. Goland, 51 Cal. 3d 202 (1990); Hospital Building Co. v. Trustees of Rex Hospital, 425 U.S. 738 (1976); Fish v. Los Angeles Dodgers Baseball Club, 56 Cal. App. 3d 620 (1976); Paramount Convalescent Center, Inc. v. Department of Health Care Services, 15 Cal. 3d 489 (1975).

---

## MINTON, MINTON AND RAND LLP
Established in 1977
510 WEST SIXTH STREET
### LOS ANGELES, CALIFORNIA 90014
Telephone: 213-624-9394
Fax: 213-624-9323

*Corporation Law, Estate Planning, Trust and Probate Law, Real Estate Law. General Business Practice.*

### MEMBERS OF FIRM

**CARL W. MINTON** (1902-1974).

**CARL MINTON,** born Los Angeles, California, March 7, 1928; admitted to bar, 1955, California; 1960, U.S. Supreme Court. *Education:* Stanford University (B.A., 1949); University of Southern California (J.D., 1955). Phi Alpha Delta. Member, University of Southern California Law Review, 1954-1955. *Member:* Los Angeles County (Member, Sections on: Corporation; Probate) and American (Member, Sections on: Corporation Banking and Business Law; Real Property Probate and Trust Law) Bar Associations; State Bar of California. **PRACTICE AREAS:** Corporation Law; Estate Planning; Trust and Probate Law; Real Estate Law; Business Law.

**DAVID E. RAND,** born New York, N.Y., December 27, 1936; admitted to bar, 1962, California. *Education:* University of California at Los Angeles (B.A., with honors, 1958); Harvard University (J.D., 1961). *Member:* Beverly Hills and Los Angeles County Bar Associations; State Bar of California. [With U.S. Army, 1961-1963]. **PRACTICE AREAS:** Corporation Law; Estate Planning; Trust and Probate Law; Real Estate Law; Business Law.

REPRESENTATIVE CLIENTS INCLUDE: Meissner Mfg. Co., Inc.
REFERENCE: Bank of America National Trust & Savings Assn. (525 South Flower, Los Angeles, Calif.).

---

## ROBERT E. MITCHELL
### LOS ANGELES, CALIFORNIA
(See Norwalk)

*Corporate, Estate Planning, Real Estate and Business Litigation Law.*

---

## MITCHELL, SILBERBERG & KNUPP LLP
A Partnership including Professional Corporations
11377 WEST OLYMPIC BOULEVARD
### LOS ANGELES, CALIFORNIA 90064
Telephone: 310-312-2000
Fax: 310-312-3100

*General Civil, Appellate and Trial Practice. Corporation, Securities, Entertainment, Labor, Probate, Estate Planning, Trust, Federal and State Tax, Bankruptcy, Environmental, Antitrust, Financial Institutions, Administrative and International Law.*

### MEMBERS OF FIRM

**SHEPARD MITCHELL** (1908-1979).

**M. B. SILBERBERG** (1908-1965).

**GUY KNUPP** (1907-1970).

**ARTHUR GROMAN,** *(A PROFESSIONAL CORPORATION),* born Los Angeles, California, September 13, 1914; admitted to bar, 1939, California. *Education:* University of Southern California (A.B., magna cum laude, 1936) Phi Beta Kappa; Yale University (J.D., 1939). Order of the Coif. Member, Board of Editors, Yale Law Journal, 1938-1939. Instructor in the Graduate Law School, University of Southern California, 1957-1958.

*(This Listing Continued)*

Founding Member, Planning Committee, Tax Institute, University of Southern California. Member, Board of Councilors, University of Southern California Law School, 1968-1991. Attorney, General Counsel's Office, Treasury Department, 1939-1941. Senior Attorney, Chief Counsel's Office, Bureau of Internal Revenue, 1941-1944. President, Yale Law School Association of Southern California, 1972-1975. President, California Institute of Cancer Research, 1974-1976. Member, Board of Directors, Cedars Sinai Medical Center, 1983—. *Member:* Los Angeles County and American Bar Associations; The State Bar of California; Los Angeles Copyright Society. Fellow, American College of Trial Lawyers. **PRACTICE AREAS:** Litigation.

**CHESTER I. LAPPEN,** *(A PROFESSIONAL CORPORATION),* born Des Moines, Iowa, May 4, 1919; admitted to bar, 1943, Iowa and California. *Education:* University of California at Los Angeles (B.A., with highest honors, 1940); Harvard University (LL.B., magna cum laude, 1943). President, and Editor-in-Chief, Harvard Law Review, 1942-1943. President, Junior Bar of Los Angeles County, 1953. Chairman, Harvard Alumni Association of Southern California, 1972-1983. National Vice President, Harvard Alumni Association, 1972-1977. Chairman of the Board, Immaculate Heart College, 1975-1988. President, Los Angeles Junior Bar, 1953. Trustee, UCLA Foundation, 1970—. *Member:* Beverly Hills, Los Angeles County (Member, Board of Trustees, 1953) and American (Chairman, Procedural Reform Committee of Southern California, 1953-1955) Bar Associations; The State Bar of California. **PRACTICE AREAS:** Corporate Law; Real Estate Law. *Email:* cil@msk.com

**HAROLD FRIEDMAN,** *(A PROFESSIONAL CORPORATION),* born Newark, New Jersey, December 4, 1924; admitted to bar, 1952, California. *Education:* Harvard University (A.B., cum laude, 1948); Yale University (J.D., 1951). Law Clerk to Judge Albert Lee Stephens, Sr., U.S. Court of Appeals for the Ninth Circuit, 1952-1954. *Member:* The State Bar of California; American Bar Association; Los Angeles Copyright Society. **PRACTICE AREAS:** Corporate Law; Motion Picture Television Law; Real Estate Law; Banking Law; International Law. *Email:* hhf@msk.com

**ALLAN E. BIBLIN,** *(A PROFESSIONAL CORPORATION),* born Chicago, Illinois, August 21, 1938; admitted to bar, 1963, California. *Education:* University of Illinois (B.S., 1959); University of Chicago (J.D., 1962). Order of the Coif. Lecturer, University of Southern California Tax Institute, 1966, 1969 and 1978. Adjunct Professor of Law, University of San Diego Law School, 1980, 1981. *Member:* The State Bar of California. **PRACTICE AREAS:** Taxation Law; Estate Planning Law; Business Planning Law.

**EDWARD M. MEDVENE,** *(A PROFESSIONAL CORPORATION),* born Philadelphia, Pennsylvania, August 14, 1930; admitted to bar, 1957, District of Columbia and Pennsylvania; 1961, California. *Education:* Temple University (A.B., 1952); University of Pennsylvania (LL.B., 1957). Co-author: *Sentencing of White Collar Offenders in Federal Court,* White Collar Crimes, Practising Law Institute, 1978. Author: "The Use and Abuse of Repeated In Camera Filings," Federal Bar Association Seminar, Federal Enforcement Policies, Defense Considerations and Judicial Overviews on White Collar Prosecution for the Nineties, 1990; "Direct and Cross-Examination of Witnesses," Fifth Annual Fall Meeting, Section of Litigation, ABA, 1980; "Pre-Trial Motions in Federal Court," 10th Annual Defending Criminal Cases Forum, Practising Law Institute, 1979. Speaker, "Witness Examination and Cross Examination," 15th Annual Seminar on Advanced Trial Skills, Association of Business Trial Lawyers, 1988. Panelist, "Special Problems Affecting the Defense Perspective," Federal Bar Association Seminar, 1990. Contributor, *West's California Criminal Law,* West Publishing Co., 1995. Instructor, San Fernando College of Law, 1965-1969; 1972-1974. Adjunct Professor of Law, University of Southern California, 1991—. Trial Attorney, Antitrust Division, U.S. Department of Justice, 1957-1960. Assistant U.S. Attorney, Southern District of California, 1960-1962. Consultant, Office of Economic Opportunity, Neighborhood Legal Center Program, 1961—. Judge Pro-Tempore, Municipal Court, Beverly Hills, 1969-1970. *Member:* Los Angeles County and American (Member, Sections on, Antitrust Law, Family Law, Individual Rights and Responsibilities and Criminal Justice) Bar Associations; The State Bar of California. Fellow, American Bar Foundation. **PRACTICE AREAS:** White Collar Crime Law; Antitrust Litigation; Securities Litigation.

**RUSSELL J. FRACKMAN,** *(A PROFESSIONAL CORPORATION),* born New York, N.Y., July 3, 1946; admitted to bar, 1971, California, U.S. District Court, Central District of California and U.S. Court of Appeals, Ninth Circuit; 1980, U.S. District Court, Northern District of California, U.S. Court of Appeals, Second Circuit and U.S. Supreme Court; 1984, U.S. District Court, Eastern District of California. *Education:* Northwestern

*(This Listing Continued)*

University (B.A., 1967); Columbia University (J.D., cum laude, 1970). Member, Board of Editors, Columbia Law Review, 1969-1970. Contributor: *Counseling Clients in the Entertainment Industry,* Practising Law Institute, 1978; *Litigating Copyright, Trademark and Unfair Competition Cases,* Practising Law Institute, 1983— (Co-Chairman, 1992—); *False Advertising and Commercial Speech,* Practising Law Institute, 1993. Author: "The Failure to Pay Wages and Termination of Entertainment Contracts in California: Some Implications of the Labor Code," 52 Southern California Law Review 333, 1979; "The Chess Catalog Litigation," Los Angeles Lawyer, Vol. 16, No. 2 (April 1993) p. 28; Book Review, Intellectual Property Law Review, 1984; 7 COMM/ENT Law Journal 547, 1985. *Member:* The State Bar of California; American Bar Association (Member, Litigation Section, Committee on Intellectual Property, Chairman, Copyright Subcommittee, 1990-1992; Member, Forum Committee on the Entertainment and Sports Industries). **PRACTICE AREAS:** Intellectual Property Litigation; Entertainment Litigation. *Email:* rjf@msk2.msk.com

**THOMAS P. LAMBERT,** *(A PROFESSIONAL CORPORATION),* born Kankakee, Illinois, October 14, 1946; admitted to bar, 1971, California. *Education:* Loyola University of Los Angeles (B.A., 1968); University of California at Los Angeles (J.D., 1971). Member, 1969-1970, and Note and Comment Editor, 1970-1971, University of California at Los Angeles Law Review. Author: "Bid Shopping and Peddling in the Subcontract Construction Industry," 18 University of California at Los Angeles Law Review 389, 1971. *Member:* Beverly Hills, Los Angeles County and American (Member, Sections on: Antitrust Law; Litigation) Bar Associations; The State Bar of California. **PRACTICE AREAS:** Securities Litigation; Intellectual Property Litigation; Antitrust Litigation. *Email:* tpl@msk2.msk.com

**EUGENE H. VEENHUIS,** *(A PROFESSIONAL CORPORATION),* born Hutchinson, Minnesota, January 23, 1944; admitted to bar, 1971, California. *Education:* University of Minnesota (B.S., 1968); Stanford University (J.D., 1971). *Member:* Beverly Hills (Chairman, Income Tax Committee, 1976-1977), Los Angeles County (Member, Section on Taxation) and American (Member, Section on Taxation) Bar Associations; The State Bar of California (Member, Tax Section). **PRACTICE AREAS:** Taxation Law; ERISA; Business Planning Law. *Email:* ehv@msk.com

**PHILIP DAVIS,** *(A PROFESSIONAL CORPORATION),* born Pottstown, Pennsylvania, August 24, 1945; admitted to bar, 1971, California. *Education:* University of California at Los Angeles (A.B., cum laude, 1967); University of Southern California (J.D., 1970). Phi Beta Kappa. *Member:* Century City (Co-Chairman, Entertainment Law Section, 1991-1992) and Los Angeles County (Member, Executive Committee, Section on Patent, Trademark and Copyright Law, 1979-1984) Bar Associations; Los Angeles Copyright Society (Member, Board of Trustees, 1980-1984; 1994—); The State Bar of California. **PRACTICE AREAS:** Entertainment Law.

**ROY L. SHULTS,** *(A PROFESSIONAL CORPORATION),* born Cincinnati, Ohio, June 10, 1948; admitted to bar, 1973, California. *Education:* University of California at Los Angeles (B.A., summa cum laude, 1970); Harvard University (J.D., 1973). Phi Beta Kappa; Pi Gamma Mu; Pi Kappa Delta. Member, Board of Student Advisors, 1971-1973. Author: "Selected Recent Developments in Insider Trading: Private Litigation, S.E.C. Enforcement and Legislation," in *II Corporate Litigation: Substantive Trends and Management Techniques* (ABA Litigation Section, National Institute, 1991); "California's Draft Form Interrogatories--Two Steps Forward or One Step Back?" Recent Developments in Civil Procedure, California Continuing Education of the Bar, February/March, 1983. Co-author: *Sentencing of White Collar Offenders in Federal Court,* White Collar Crimes, Practising Law Institute, 1978. Judge Pro Tem, Small Claims Court, 1980-1990. Member, ABA Antitrust Section Task Force on Monograph No. 9, "Refusal to Deal and Exclusive Distributorships," 1983. *Member:* Century City, Los Angeles County (Member: Executive Committee, Antitrust Section, 1981-1988; First Vice-Chair, 1986-1987) and American (Member, Section on Antitrust Law) Bar Associations; The State Bar of California (Member, Executive Committee, Antitrust Section, 1978-1988; Vice-Chairperson, 1984-1985; Chairperson, 1985-1986). Member, Board of Regents of the University of California, 1992-1994. **PRACTICE AREAS:** Federal and State Antitrust and Trade Regulation Litigation and Counseling; Trademark and Unfair Competition Litigation and Counseling; Business Tort and Contract Litigation. *Email:* rls@msk2.msk.com

**STEVEN M. SCHNEIDER,** *(A PROFESSIONAL CORPORATION),* born Duluth, Minnesota, June 30, 1948; admitted to bar, 1973, California, Massachusetts and U.S. District Court, Central District of California; 1974, U.S. District Court, Northern District of California and U.S. Court of Ap-

*(This Listing Continued)*

**MITCHELL, SILBERBERG & KNUPP LLP, Los Angeles— Continued**

peals, Ninth Circuit; 1983, U.S. Supreme Court; 1986, U.S. District Court, Eastern and Southern Districts of California. *Education:* Cornell University (B.S., 1970); Harvard Law School (J.D., 1973). Phi Kappa Phi. Author: "The Unprotected Minority: Employers and Civil Rights Compliance," 49 Los Angeles Bar Bulletin No. 11, September, 1974. Contributor: *Employment Discrimination Law*, by Barbara Schlei and Paul Grossman, published by Bureau of National Affairs, 1976. Co-author: 1979 Supplement to *Employment Discrimination Law*, Chapter 27, "Title VII Jurisdiction;" *Advising California Employers*, Chapter 9, "Grievance Procedures and Arbitration," published by the California Continuing Education of the Bar, 1979; Chapter 12, "Wrongful Hiring?" The Employee Termination Handbook, published by John Wiley & Sons, 1986. *Member:* Los Angeles County and American (Member, Labor and Employment Law Section) Bar Associations; The State Bar of California. **PRACTICE AREAS:** Labor Law; Litigation; Employment Discrimination Law; Litigation; Wrongful Discharge Litigation. *Email:* sms@msk2.msk.com

**MARVIN LEON, (A PROFESSIONAL CORPORATION)**, born Chicago, Illinois, May 5, 1929; admitted to bar, 1953, Illinois; 1956, California. *Education:* University of Illinois (B.S. in Accountancy, 1950); Northwestern University (J.D., 1953); University of Southern California (LL.M., in Taxation, 1956). Order of the Coif; Tau Epsilon Rho. Lecturer, Continuing Education of the Bar, Practising Law Institute. Governor, American College of Real Estate Lawyers. Member, Anglo-American Real Property Institute. *Member:* Beverly Hills (Chairman, Committee on Real Estate, 1969), Los Angeles County (Member, Trustee and Treasurer, Chairman Audit Committee, 1982-1984; Member, Executive Committee and Chairman, Real Property Section, 1980-1981), Illinois State and American (Member, Sections on: Taxation and Real Property, Probate and Trust Law) Bar Associations; The State Bar of California (Member and Vice Chairperson, Executive Committee, Real Property Section, 1981-1985). Fellow, American College of Real Estate Lawyers. **PRACTICE AREAS:** Real Estate Property Law; Real Estate Development Law; Real Estate Syndications Law. *Email:* mxl@msk.com

**PATRICIA H. BENSON, (A PROFESSIONAL CORPORATION)**, born Santa Monica, California, May 23, 1949; admitted to bar, 1974, California and U.S. District Court, Central and Northern Districts of California; 1977, U.S. Court of Appeals, Ninth Circuit. *Education:* Smith College and Stanford University (B.A., with great distinction, 1971); University of Southern California (J.D., 1974). Phi Beta Kappa; Order of the Coif. *Member:* Los Angeles County (Member, Intellectual Property and Unfair Competition Section) and American (Member, Litigation Section) Bar Associations; The State Bar of California; Association of Business Trial Lawyers (Member, Board of Governors). Trustee, Los Angeles County Bar Foundation, 1991— (Director, Public Counsel). **PRACTICE AREAS:** Securities Litigation; Intellectual Property Litigation; Employment Litigation. *Email:* phb@msk2.msk.com

**ARTHUR FINE, (A PROFESSIONAL CORPORATION)**, born New York, N.Y., August 17, 1942; admitted to bar, 1968, California and U.S. District Court, Central, Northern and Southern Districts of California; U.S. Court of Appeals, Ninth Circuit. *Education:* University of California at Berkeley (A.B., 1964); Boalt Hall School of Law, University of California (J.D., 1967). Phi Alpha Delta. Author: "The Due-On-Sale Clause - Dawn: The California View," Los Angeles Lawyer, October, 1982; "Informed Consent - Liability Without Negligence," LACMA Physician, Sept., 1979; "Informed Consent - Latent Liability Without Negligence," The Western Journal of Medicine, August, 1977; "Reconsideration of Due-on-Sale - An Opportunity to Reemphasize the Difference Between an Outright Sale and an Installment Contract," Los Angeles Bar Journal, June, 1977. Visiting Lecturer in Law, Faculty of Law, University of Auckland, Auckland, New Zealand, February 1968-November 1968. Instructor: University of Southern California Continuing Education Short Course, "Subsurface Migration of Hazardous Wastes," May, 1984; University of California at Los Angeles Extension Short Course, "Hazardous Waste," October, 1982. *Member:* Los Angeles County and American Bar Associations; The State Bar of California. **PRACTICE AREAS:** Litigation; Environmental Law; Administrative Law. *Email:* abf@msk2.msk.com

**HAYWARD J. KAISER, (A PROFESSIONAL CORPORATION)**, born Los Angeles, California, February 10, 1950; admitted to bar, 1975, California. *Education:* University of California at Los Angeles (B.A., in Mathematics, with Departmental Honors, magna cum laude 1972; J.D., 1975). Order of the Coif; Phi Beta Kappa. Member, University of California at Los Angeles Law Review, 1973-1975. *Member:* The State Bar of Califor-

*(This Listing Continued)*

nia; American Bar Association (Member, Sections on: Litigation; Torts and Insurance Practice; Member, Insurance Coverage Committee). **PRACTICE AREAS:** Insurance Law; Contractual Litigation; Unfair Competition Law; Antitrust Litigation; Products Liability Law; Toxic Tort Litigation; Real Estate Litigation. *Email:* hjk@msk2.msk.com

**DEBORAH P. KOEFFLER, (A PROFESSIONAL CORPORATION)**, born Springfield, Massachusetts, August 18, 1948; admitted to bar, 1975, California. *Education:* University of Wisconsin (B.A., 1970); University of California at Los Angeles (J.D., 1975). Phi Beta Kappa; Phi Kappa Phi; Order of the Coif. Member, University of California at Los Angeles Law Review, 1973-1975. Author: "Employer Domination or Assistance to Labor Organization," The Developing Labor Law 1976 Supplement. Co-author: "Grievance Procedures and Arbitration," California Continuing Education of the Bar, 1981. Author: "Hospital Bargaining Units," Practising Law Institute, Appropriate Units for Collective Bargaining, published, 1979. Chairman, 1985 Southern California Labor Law Symposium. *Member:* Los Angeles County (Member, Executive Committee, Labor Law Section, 1983-1989) and American (Member, Discrimination Committee, 1978) Bar Associations; The State Bar of California; American Hospital Association (Member, Labor Relations Committee, 1983—). **PRACTICE AREAS:** Labor Law; Employment Litigation; Public Entity Labor Relations Law; Health Care Law. *Email:* dpk@msk2.msk.com

**JOHN M. KUECHLE, (A PROFESSIONAL CORPORATION)**, born Minneapolis, Minnesota, December 18, 1951; admitted to bar, 1977, California. *Education:* Occidental College (A.B., magna cum laude, 1974); Harvard University (J.D., cum laude, 1977). Phi Beta Kappa; Omicron Delta Epsilon. Executive Editor, Harvard Journal on Legislation, 1975-1976. *Member:* The State Bar of California. **PRACTICE AREAS:** Real Estate Law; Corporate Law; Commercial Law. *Email:* jmk@msk.com

**WILLIAM L. COLE, (A PROFESSIONAL CORPORATION)**, born Los Angeles, California, May 13, 1952; admitted to bar, 1977, California. *Education:* University of California at Irvine (A.B., magna cum laude, 1974); Stanford University (J.D., 1977). Phi Beta Kappa; Order of the Coif. *Member:* Los Angeles County (Member, Executive Committee, Labor Law Section, 1989-1990) and American Bar Associations; The State Bar of California. Managing Partner, 1991—. **PRACTICE AREAS:** Labor Law; Employment Litigation; Employee Benefits Law. *Email:* wlc@msk2.msk.com

**RICHARD S. HESSENIUS, (A PROFESSIONAL CORPORATION)**, born San Pedro, California, January 15, 1951; admitted to bar, 1977, California. *Education:* Pomona College (B.A., summa cum laude, 1974); University of Southern California (J.D., 1977). Phi Beta Kappa; Order of the Coif. Articles Editor, Southern California Law Review, 1976-1977. *Member:* The State Bar of California. **PRACTICE AREAS:** Real Estate Litigation; Insurance Litigation; Municipal Administrative Law. *Email:* rsh@msk2.msk.com

**JOSEPH CIASULLI, (A PROFESSIONAL CORPORATION)**, born Orange, New Jersey, April 22, 1952; admitted to bar, 1978, California. *Education:* University of Pennsylvania (B.S. in Econ., magna cum laude, 1974); Columbia University (J.D., 1978). Beta Gamma Sigma. Harlan Fiske Stone Scholar. *Member:* The State Bar of California. **PRACTICE AREAS:** Corporate Law; Securities Law; Motion Picture Financing Law. *Email:* jxc@msk.com

**FRIDA POPIK GLUCOFT, (A PROFESSIONAL CORPORATION)**, born Kfar Saba, Israel, June 10, 1953; admitted to bar, 1979, California. *Education:* University of Southern California (B.A., 1975); University of California at Los Angeles (J.D., 1978). Phi Beta Kappa; Phi Alpha Delta (McKenna Chapter). Author: "Temporary Employment for Foreign Artists," 5 Int'l Media Law 20 (March 1987) and 5 Entertainment and Sports Lawyer (ABA) 1 (Summer 1986). Adjunct Associate Professor of Law, Southwestern University School of Law, 1981-1982. *Member:* Los Angeles County Bar Association (Member, Immigration Section); The State Bar of California; Association of Immigration and Nationality Lawyers (Chapter Treasurer, 1986; Vice Chairperson, 1987; Chair, Entertainers and Athletes Committee, 1988; Member, Task Force on R.N.'s, 1989); Women in Film. **PRACTICE AREAS:** Immigration and Nationality Law; Employment Law. *Email:* fpg@msk.com

**JEAN PIERRE NOGUES, (A PROFESSIONAL CORPORATION)**, born Pomona, California, August 4, 1953; admitted to bar, 1978, California; 1979, U.S. Court of Appeals, Ninth Circuit and U.S. District Court, Central District of California; 1980, U.S. District Court, Northern District of California; 1985, U.S. Supreme Court; 1992, U.S. District Court, Eastern and Southern Districts of California. *Education:* California State Polytechnic University, Pomona (B.A., 1975); University of California at Los Angeles (J.D., 1978). Order of the Coif; Phi Alpha Delta. Managing Editor,

*(This Listing Continued)*

UCLA Law Review, 1977-1978. Author: Comment, "Defects in the Current Forcible Entry and Detainer Laws of the United States and England," 25 UCLA Law Review 1067, 1978. Law Clerk to Hon. Herbert Y.C. Choy, U.S. Circuit Judge, 9th Circuit, 1978-1979. *Member:* The State Bar of California; Association of Business Trial Lawyers. *PRACTICE AREAS:* General Business Litigation; Securities Litigation; Accountant's Liability Law; Engineering and Construction Litigation. *Email:* jpn@msk2.msk.com

**DAVID WHEELER NEWMAN, (A PROFESSIONAL CORPORATION),** born Salt Lake City, Utah, April 5, 1952; admitted to bar, 1978, California and U.S. District Court, Central District of California; 1979, U.S. Tax Court. *Education:* Claremont Men's College (B.A., magna cum laude, 1973); University of California at Los Angeles (J.D., 1977); New York University (LL.M., in Taxation, 1979). Omicron Delta Epsilon. Author: "Planning Opportunities for Expatriates under the Final Section 911 Regulations," 63 Taxes 805, 1985; "Financial Planning Techniques Using Charitable Gifts," 38 Major Tax Plan. 9-1, 1986; "FIRPTA Primer," 42 Major Tax Plan, 20-1, 1990; "Charitable Remainder Trusts Funded with S Corporation Assets," 4 The Exempt Organization Tax Review 1320 (1991). Co-Author: "Charitable Remainder Trusts Funded with Encumbered Property," 5 The Exempt Organization Tax Review 418 (1992); "Charitable Gifts of Retirement Plan Assets," 9 The Exempt Organization Tax Review 1301 (1994); "Coordinating Charitable Gifts of Retirement Plan Assets With Lifetime Distribution Requirements," 10 The Exempt Organization Tax Review 1335 (1994). Director, National Committee on Planned Giving, 1994— and Member, Executive Committee, 1995—. Member, American Council on Gift Annuities Task Force on State Regulation of Charitable Gift Annuities, 1994—. *Member:* Beverly Hills (Chairman, Taxation Committee, 1982-1983), Los Angeles County (Chairman, Foreign Tax Committee, 1991-1992; Chairman, Tax Exempt Organizations Committee, 1992—; Vice Chairman, Taxation Section, 1994—; Member, Taxation Section, Foreign Tax Committee and Tax Exempt Organizations Committee, 1980—) and American (Member, Taxation Section, 1982—) Bar Associations; The State Bar of California. *PRACTICE AREAS:* Taxation Law; Estate Planning Law; Business Planning Law. *Email:* dwn@msk.com

**ROGER SHERMAN, (A PROFESSIONAL CORPORATION),** born New York, N.Y., September 4, 1932; admitted to bar, 1960, California. *Education:* Yale University (B.A., magna cum laude, 1954; LL.B., 1959). Phi Beta Kappa; Phi Alpha Delta; Pi Sigma Alpha. Director, Los Angeles Copyright Society, 1981-1985, 1986-1988; Officer, 1988-1992; President, 1992-1993. *Member:* Beverly Hills, Los Angeles County and American Bar Associations; The State Bar of California; Los Angeles Copyright Society. *PRACTICE AREAS:* Entertainment Law; Copyright Law. *Email:* rxs@msk.com

**ALAN L. PEPPER, (A PROFESSIONAL CORPORATION),** born New York, N.Y., February 1, 1942; admitted to bar, 1973, California; U.S. District Court, Central District of California. *Education:* University of California at Los Angeles (B.S., 1963); University of La Verne College of Law (J.D., summa cum laude, 1973). *Member:* The State Bar of California. *PRACTICE AREAS:* Corporate Law; Business Acquisitions Law; Telecommunication Law; Consumer Protection; Warranty Law. *Email:* alp@msk.com

**JOHN E. HATHERLEY, (A PROFESSIONAL CORPORATION),** born San Jose, California, June 24, 1944; admitted to bar, 1974, California. *Education:* University of California at Berkeley (A.B., 1967); Princeton Theological Seminary (M.Div., 1971); University of California at Davis (J.D., 1974). Member, 1972-1973, Articles Editor, 1973-1974, University of California at Davis Law Review. *Member:* Beverly Hills and Los Angeles County Bar Associations; The State Bar of California. *PRACTICE AREAS:* Real Estate Law; Business Law.

**LAWRENCE A. GINSBERG, (A PROFESSIONAL CORPORATION),** born Boston, Massachusetts, September 11, 1952; admitted to bar, 1980, California, U.S. District Court, Central District of California and U.S. Court of Appeals, Ninth Circuit; 1983, Massachusetts. *Education:* Brandeis University (B.A., 1975); Boston University (J.D., cum laude, 1980). Moot Court Judge/Advisor, 1979-1980. Austin T. Stickells Scholar. Editor, Boston University Law Review, 1979-1980. *Member:* Los Angeles County and American (Member, Labor and Employment Law Section) Bar Associations; The State Bar of California. *PRACTICE AREAS:* Labor Law; Employment Law; Litigation; Discrimination Law; Litigation. *Email:* lag@msk2.msk.com

**DANIEL M. PETROCELLI, (A PROFESSIONAL CORPORATION),** born East Orange, New Jersey, August 15, 1953; admitted to bar, 1981, California, U.S. District Courts, Central and Northern Districts of California, U.S. Court of Appeals, Ninth Circuit and U.S. Supreme Court.
*(This Listing Continued)*

*Education:* University of California at Los Angeles (B.S., cum laude, 1976); Southwestern University (J.D., magna cum laude, 1980). Member, 1978-1979 and Editor-in-Chief, 1979-1980, Southwestern University Law Review. Author: "Opening Statements in California Civil Cases," Los Angeles Lawyer, March, 1989. *Member:* Los Angeles County (Member, Antitrust and Unfair Competition Section) and American (Member, Section of Litigation, Corporate Counsel Committee) Bar Associations; The State Bar of California (Member, Antitrust and Unfair Competition Section); Association of Business Trial Lawyers. *PRACTICE AREAS:* Litigation. *Email:* dmp@msk2.msk.com

**MARK A. WASSERMAN, (A PROFESSIONAL CORPORATION),** born Los Angeles, California, December 16, 1955; admitted to bar, 1981, California. *Education:* University of California at Berkeley (A.B., with great distinction, 1977); University of Chicago (J.D., with honors, 1980). Phi Beta Kappa; Order of the Coif. Associate Editor, University of Chicago Law Review, 1979-1980. Contributing Editor, *The Developing Labor Law,* 3rd Edition, 1992. Author: "Agency Consultants and Administrative Law," Administrative Law Review, Vol. 63, 1981. Law Clerk to Judge Robert S. Vance, Fifth Circuit Court of Appeals, 1981-1982. *Member:* Los Angeles County (Member, Labor and Employment Law Section) and American (Member, Committee on the Development of Law under the National Labor Relations Act) Bar Associations; The State Bar of California. *PRACTICE AREAS:* Employment Law Litigation; Equal Employment Law; Labor Law. *Email:* maw@msk2.msk.com

**ALLEN J. GROSS, (A PROFESSIONAL CORPORATION),** born Wheeling, West Virginia, 1948; admitted to bar, 1974, Pennsylvania; 1989, California. *Education:* The Ohio State University (B.S., 1970); Georgetown University (J.D., 1974). Executive Editor, The Tax Lawyer, 1973-74. *Member:* The State Bar of California. *PRACTICE AREAS:* Labor Law; Employment Law. *Email:* ajg@msk2.msk.com

**ANTHONY A. ADLER, (A PROFESSIONAL CORPORATION),** born Los Angeles, California, March 29, 1950; admitted to bar, 1979, California. *Education:* Claremont McKenna College (B.A., 1972); Harvard Business School (M.B.A., 1974); University of Southern California (J.D., 1979). *Member:* Order of the Coif. *Member:* The State Bar of California; American Bar Association. *PRACTICE AREAS:* Loan Workouts; Mergers and Acquisitions Law; Corporate Law. *Email:* aaa@msk.com

**ELIA WEINBACH, (A PROFESSIONAL CORPORATION),** born Tientsin, China, May 24, 1945; admitted to bar, 1973, New York; 1978, California. *Education:* New York University (B.A., 1967); Harvard University (J.D., 1972). Fulbright Scholar, Oxford University, 1967-1969. Phi Beta Kappa. Trial Attorney, Federal Trade Commission, 1973-1975. Assistant U.S. Attorney, Eastern District of New York, Criminal Division, 1975-1978. Judge Pro Tem, Los Angeles Municipal Court, 1986. Co-Author: "Contorts," *Business Torts Litigation,* (1992). Contributing Columnist, "Trial Strategy," Los Angeles Daily Journal, 1989—. *Member:* Los Angeles County (Member: Los Angeles County Bar Delegation to State Bar Conference, 1984-1986; Federal Courts and Practices Committee, 1983—; Member and Chair, Travel Committee, 1983) and American (Member, Sections on: Antitrust; Litigation; Vice-Chair, Committee on Corporate Counsel) Bar Associations; The State Bar of California. *PRACTICE AREAS:* Securities Litigation; Employment Litigation; Business Litigation. *Email:* exw@msk2.msk.com

**ALLAN B. CUTROW, (A PROFESSIONAL CORPORATION),** born Hollywood, California, July 19, 1946; admitted to bar, 1972, California, U.S. Tax Court and U.S. Court of Appeals, Ninth Circuit. *Education:* University of California at Los Angeles (B.A., 1968; J.D., 1971); University of Southern California (M.B.T., 1977). Certified Public Accountant, California, 1969. Lecturer in Law, Program for Legal Paraprofessionals, University of Southern California School of Law, 1975-1981. Director, Los Angeles Jewish Federation-Council of Greater Los Angeles, 1982—. Director, Jewish Community Foundation, 1985—; President, 1985-1989. *Member:* Beverly Hills (Member, Probate and Trust Section) and Los Angeles County (Member, Executive Committee, Probate Section, 1981) Bar Associations; The State Bar of California. Fellow, American College of Trust and Estate Counsel. *PRACTICE AREAS:* Estate Planning; Estate and Trust Administration and Litigation. *Email:* abc@msk.com

**LAURA A. LOFTIN, (A PROFESSIONAL CORPORATION),** born Jacksonville, Florida; admitted to bar, 1981, California. *Education:* Duke University (A.B., summa cum laude, 1976); Harvard University (J.D., 1981). Phi Beta Kappa. *Member:* The State Bar of California. *PRACTICE AREAS:* Corporate Law; Securities Regulation Law; Mergers and Acquisitions Law. *Email:* lal@msk.com
*(This Listing Continued)*

*MITCHELL, SILBERBERG & KNUPP LLP, Los Angeles—Continued*

**PETER B. GELBLUM,** *(A PROFESSIONAL CORPORATION),* born Philadelphia, Pennsylvania, February 24, 1952; admitted to bar, 1982, California and U.S. District Court, Central District of California; U.S. Court of Appeals, Ninth Circuit. *Education:* Wesleyan University (B.A., 1974); Southwestern University (J.D., summa cum laude, 1982). Member, 1979-1980 and Editor-in-Chief, 1980-1981, Southwestern University Law Review. Chairperson, Mental Health Advocacy Services, 1992—. Director, Inner City Law Center, 1994—. *Member:* The State Bar of California. *PRACTICE AREAS:* Litigation; Business Torts; Alternative Dispute Resolution; Estate and Trust Litigation. *Email:* pbg@msk2.msk.com

**DAVID P. SCHACK,** *(A PROFESSIONAL CORPORATION),* born Huntsville, Alabama, December 21, 1957; admitted to bar, 1982, California. *Education:* Stanford University (B.A., honors with distinction, 1979); University of California at Los Angeles (J.D., 1982). Phi Beta Kappa. Member, 1980-1982 and Article Editor, 1981-1982, UCLA Law Review. Member, 1979-1981 and Article Editor, 1980-1981, UCLA Journal of International Law. Author: "The Right to Privacy for Business Entities," 24 Santa Clara Law Review 53, 1984; "Reinsurance and Insurer Insolvency: The Problem of Direct Recovery by the Original Insured or Injured Claimant," 29 UCLA Law Review 872, 1982. Extern to the Hon. Stephen Reinhardt, U.S. Court of Appeals, Ninth Circuit, Fall, 1981. *Member:* Los Angeles County and American Bar Associations; The State Bar of California (Member, Legislative Committee, Litigation Section, 1993-1996). *PRACTICE AREAS:* Litigation; Insurance; Real Estate Law. *Email:* dps@msk2.msk.com

**LAWRENCE A. MICHAELS,** *(A PROFESSIONAL CORPORATION),* born Chicago, Illinois, July 30, 1955; admitted to bar, 1982, California. *Education:* University of California at Los Angeles (B.A., 1978); University of Southern California (J.D., 1982). Order of the Coif. Member, Southern California Law Review, 1980-1982. Judicial Extern to Hon. Malcolm Lucas, U.S. District Court, Central District of California. *Member:* Los Angeles County and American Bar Associations; The State Bar of California. *PRACTICE AREAS:* Labor Law; Employment Law. *Email:* lam@msk2.msk.com

**RONALD A. DiNICOLA,** *(A PROFESSIONAL CORPORATION),* born Erie, Pennsylvania, June 10, 1956; admitted to bar, 1982, Pennsylvania, U.S. District Court, Western District of Pennsylvania and U.S. Court of Appeals, Third Circuit; 1985, California and U.S. District Court, Central District of California; 1985, U.S. Court of Appeals, Ninth Circuit; 1989, U.S. Supreme Court. *Education:* Harvard College (A.B., 1979); Georgetown University (J.D., 1982). Associate Editor, The Tax Lawyer Law Journal, 1980-1982. Law Clerk to Chief United States District Judge Gerald J. Weber, United States District Court for the Western District of Pennsylvania, 1982-1984. Legal Counsel, Independent Commission on the Los Angeles Police Department, 1991. Author: "The Use and Abuse of Repeated In Camera Filings," Federal Bar Association Seminar, Federal Enforcement Policies, Defense Considerations and Judicial Overviews of White Collar Prosecution for the Nineties, 1990; Note, "Attorney's Fees in Tax Cases After the Tax Equity and Fiscal Responsibility Act of 1982," 36 Tax Lawyer 123, 1982; Article, "Controlling Violence in Prof. Sports: Rule Reform & Fed. Prof. Sports Violence Commission," 21 Duquesne Law Review 843, 1983. *Member:* Erie County, Los Angeles County, Pennsylvania and American Bar Associations; The State Bar of California; National Association of Criminal Defense Attorneys. [Corporal, U.S. Marine Corps, 1974-1976]. *PRACTICE AREAS:* Litigation; Entertainment Law. *Email:* rad@msk2.msk.com

**ANDREW E. KATZ,** *(A PROFESSIONAL CORPORATION),* born Brooklyn, New York, November 6, 1947; admitted to bar, 1972, California; 1981, U.S. Supreme Court. *Education:* University of California at Los Angeles (B.S., cum laude, 1969; J.D., 1972). Member of Staff, University of California at Los Angeles Law Review, 1970-1972. Author: "The General Revision of the Copyright Law— From Bare Bones to Corpulence— A Partial Overview," 4 Pepperdine Law Review 213, 1977; "The Due-on-Sale Clause-Fidelity Federal: The U.S. View," 5 Los Angeles Lawyer, October, 1982; "Asset Securitization Can Be A Significant Source of Working Capital," 7 The Investment Reporter 13, No. 1, 1996. Co-Author: "Is Asset Securitization a Good Source of Expansion Funds?" 26 Security Distributing & Marketing 60, No. 3, 1996. *Member:* Los Angeles County and American Bar Associations; The State Bar of California. *PRACTICE AREAS:* Financial Institutions Law; Securities Offerings; Business Law. *Email:* aek@msk.com

*(This Listing Continued)*

**JAMES O. THOMA,** *(A PROFESSIONAL CORPORATION),* born Weatherford, Texas, August 23, 1956; admitted to bar, 1981, Texas; 1987, California. *Education:* University of Texas at Arlington (B.A., with highest honors, 1977); University of Texas at Austin (J.D., 1980). *Member:* State Bar of Texas; The State Bar of California; American Bar Association (Member, Section on Litigation). *LANGUAGES:* Portuguese. *Email:* jot@msk2.msk.com

**KEVIN GAUT,** *(A PROFESSIONAL CORPORATION),* born Baltimore, Maryland, December 27, 1957; admitted to bar, 1985, California. *Education:* Harvard University (B.A., 1980; J.D., magna cum laude, 1984). Recipient, Sears Prize. Finalist Ames Moot Court Competition. *Member:* Los Angeles County Bar Association; The State Bar of California. *PRACTICE AREAS:* Litigation; Business Torts; Securities Regulation. *Email:* keg@msk2.msk.com

**DANNA L. COOK,** *(A PROFESSIONAL CORPORATION),* born Muncie, Indiana, June 9, 1959; admitted to bar, 1985, California, U.S. Court of Appeals, Ninth Circuit and U.S. District Court, Central District of California; 1989, U.S. Claims Court. *Education:* Occidental College (B.A., with distinction in English, magna cum laude, 1981); Yale University (J.D., 1984). Phi Beta Kappa. Law Clerk to Hon. Arthur L. Alarcon, U.S. Circuit Judge, 9th Circuit, 1984-1985. *Member:* Los Angeles County and American Bar Associations; The State Bar of California. *LANGUAGES:* Spanish. *PRACTICE AREAS:* Music Law; General Entertainment Law; Entertainment Litigation. *Email:* dlc@msk.com

**LARRY C. DRAPKIN,** *(A PROFESSIONAL CORPORATION),* born Lynwood, California, January 25, 1956; admitted to bar, 1981, California; U.S. Court of Appeals, Ninth Circuit; U.S. District Court, Central, Southern and Northern Districts of California. *Education:* University of California at Santa Barbara (B.A., with highest honors, 1977); University of California at Berkeley (M.P.H., 1981); Boalt Hall School of Law, University of California (J.D., 1981). Phi Beta Kappa. Research and Developments Editor, Industrial Relations Law Journal, 1980. Author: "Arbitration Pacts May Ease Employment Disputes," The National Law Journal, May 15, 1995; "Law Firms Embrace Arbitration Clauses to Avoid Employee Law Suits," Los Angeles Business Journal, October 31, 1994; "The Right to Refuse Hazardous Work After Whirlpool," 4 Industrial Relations Law Journal 29, 1980. Co-Author: "Health and Safety Provisions in Union Contracts: Power or Liability?" 65 Minnesota Law Review 635, 1981. Author: "OSHA's General Duty Clause: Its Use Is Not Abuse--A Response to Morgan and Duvall," 5 Industrial Relations Law Journal 322, 1983. *Member:* Los Angeles County (Member, Labor Law Section) and American Bar Associations; The State Bar of California. *PRACTICE AREAS:* Labor Law; Employment Litigation. *Email:* lcd@msk2.msk.com

**STEVEN E. SHAPIRO,** born Dover, Delaware, March 26, 1958; admitted to bar, 1983, New York; 1985, California; registered to practice before U.S. Patent and Trademark Office. *Education:* Columbia University (B.S.E.E., 1982; J.D., 1982). Tau Beta Pi; Eta Kappa Nu; Pi Upsilon Delta. Author: "Application of Proposition 51 to Intentional Misconduct," CTLA Forum, Vol. 19, Issue No. 10, Dec., 1989; "Preliminary Injunctions in Patent Litigation," New Matter, Vol. 18, No. 1, Spring 1993. Member, Board of Directors, Columbia Public Interest Law Foundation, 1980-1982. Member, Board of Governors, Women Lawyers' Association of Los Angeles, 1989-1991. *Member:* State Bar of California. *Email:* ses@msk2.msk.com

**LUCIA E. COYOCA,** *(A PROFESSIONAL CORPORATION),* born Grand Rapids, Michigan, January 7, 1961; admitted to bar, 1986, California; U.S. District Court, Central District of California. *Education:* University of California, Los Angeles (B.A., 1983); University of California School of Law, Davis (J.D., 1986). *Member:* Beverly Hills, Los Angeles County and American Bar Associations; The State Bar of California; California Women Lawyers; Women Lawyers of Los Angeles Bar Association. *PRACTICE AREAS:* Business Litigation; Insurance Coverage; Entertainment Litigation. *Email:* lec@msk2.msk.com

**REGINA T. SHANNEY-SABORSKY,** *(A PROFESSIONAL CORPORATION),* born Jersey City, New Jersey, October 4, 1949; admitted to bar, 1980, California. *Education:* University of Southern California (B.A., 1974; M.A., 1976); Whittier College School of Law (J.D., 1980). Member, Executive Committee, Moot Court Honors Board, 1978-1980. Member, 1978-1980 and Associate Editor, 1979-1980, Whittier Law Review. *Member:* Beverly Hills (Vice-Chairman, Employee Benefits Committee, 1991—) and American (Member: Employee Benefits Committee, 1995—; Individual Investment and Workouts Committee, 1995—; Exempt Organizations Committee, 1995—) Bar Associations; State Bar of California; The ESOP Association (Member, Legislative Regulatory Advisory Committee, 1994-

*(This Listing Continued)*

1995). *PRACTICE AREAS:* Employee Benefits/ERISA; Business Planning Law; Succession Planning Law. *Email:* rss@msk.com

**ROBERT C. WELSH, (A PROFESSIONAL CORPORATION),** born Lancaster, Pennsylvania, December 5, 1947; admitted to bar, 1987, California; 1988, U.S. District Court, Central District of California. *Education:* University of California, Santa Barbara (B.A., 1969; Ph.D., 1979); University of California at Los Angeles (J.D., 1987). Author: "Up From Calandra, The Exclusionary Rule As A Constitutional Right," Minn. L. Rev., 1974; "Reconsidering The Constitutional Common Law," Harv. L. Rev, 1978; "Interrogational Rights: Reflections on Miranda," So. Cal. L. Rev., 1978; "Whose Federalism? - The Burgers Court's Treatment of State Civil Liberties Judgments," Hast. Con. L.Q., 1978; "Reconsidering The Constitutional Relationship Between State and Federal Courts: A Critique of Michigan v. Long," Notre Dame. L. Rev., 1984; "Vicarious Triumphs," Los Angeles Daily Journal, (April 27, 1995). Assistant Professor, Constitutional Law and American Judicial Process, Department of Political Science, UCLA, 1977-1987. *Member:* Los Angeles County and American Bar Associations; The State Bar of California; Association of Business Trial Lawyers. *PRACTICE AREAS:* Business Litigation; Copyright Law; Trademark Law; Antitrust Law. *Email:* rcw@msk2.msk.com

**J. EUGENE SALOMON, JR. (A PROFESSIONAL CORPORATION),** born Brooklyn, New York, September 27, 1962; admitted to bar, 1987, California; U.S. District Court, Central District of California and U.S. Court of Appeals, Ninth Circuit. *Education:* Tufts University; University of Pennsylvania (B.S., 1984); University of Southern California (J.D., 1987). Phi Alpha Delta. Member, USC Entertainment Law Society, 1984-1987. Staff Member, Southern California Law Review, 1985-1986. Author: "The Right of Publicity Run Riot: The Case for a Federal Statute," 60 Southern California Law Review 1179, 1987. Member, Board of Directors, Bobby Brooks Foundation, 1992—. *Member:* The State Bar of California. *LANGUAGES:* Spanish. *PRACTICE AREAS:* Music Law; Entertainment Law. *Email:* jes@msk.com

**JOHN L. SEGAL, (A PROFESSIONAL CORPORATION),** born Los Angeles, California, August 16, 1960; admitted to bar, 1988, California, U.S. Court of Appeals, Eleventh Circuit and U.S. District Court, Central District of California. *Education:* Williams College (B.A., 1982); University of Southern California Law Center (J.D., 1987). Order of the Coif. Executive Articles Editor, Southern California Law Review, 1986-1987. Author: "Proposition 8 and the California Supreme Court: Interpretation Run Riot?" 60 S. Cal. L. Rev. 539, 1987; "Pollution Police Pursue Chemical Criminals," Bus. & Soc'y Rev., Fall, 1985. Law Clerk to the Honorable Robert S. Vance, U.S. Court of Appeals for the Eleventh Circuit, 1987-1988. Judge Pro Tem, Los Angeles County Municipal Court, 1993—. *Member,* Los Angeles County Bar Association Delegation to the State Bar Conference of Delegates (Member, Executive Committee; Chair, Legislation Committee), 1994-1995. *Member:* Los Angeles County (Member, Appellate Courts Committee) and American (Member, Special Publications Committee and Appellate Practice Committee, Section of Litigation) Bar Associations; The State Bar of California (Delegate, State Bar Convention, 1991—); Association of Business Trial Lawyers. *PRACTICE AREAS:* Litigation; Appeals. *Email:* jsl@msk2.msk.com

**GEORGE M. BORKOWSKI, (A PROFESSIONAL CORPORATION),** born Buffalo, New York, August 16, 1962; admitted to bar, 1988, California; 1989, U.S. District Court, Central, Southern and Northern Districts of California; U.S. Court of Appeals, Ninth Circuit. *Education:* State University of New York at Buffalo (B.A., summa cum laude, 1984); Harvard University (J.D., magna cum laude, 1987). Phi Beta Kappa. Author: "Use of Force: Interception of Aircraft," 27 Harv. Int'l L.J. 761, 1986. Law Clerk to the Hon. John F. Gerry, Chief Judge, U.S. District Court, District of New Jersey, 1987-1988. *Member:* The State Bar of California (Member, Intellectual Property Section); American Bar Association (Sections on: Litigation; Intellectual Property; Antitrust). *LANGUAGES:* Polish. *PRACTICE AREAS:* Intellectual Property; Antitrust and Securities Litigation. *Email:* gmb@msk2.msk.com

**DAVID A. STEINBERG, (A PROFESSIONAL CORPORATION),** born New York, New York, September 29, 1962; admitted to bar, 1987, California; U.S. District Court, Central and Southern Districts of California. *Education:* State University of New York at Binghamton (B.A., 1984); University of California at Los Angeles (J.D., 1987). *Member:* The State Bar of California. *PRACTICE AREAS:* Litigation. *Email:* das@msk2.msk.com

**CHRISTOPHER B. LEONARD, (A PROFESSIONAL CORPORATION),** born Pontiac, Michigan, October 17, 1962; admitted to bar, 1988, California; 1989, U.S. District Court, Central District of California; 1990, U.S. Court of Appeals, Ninth Circuit and U.S. District Court, Northern District of California; 1991, U.S. District Court, Southern District of California. *Education:* University of Michigan (B.A., 1984); University of California at Los Angeles (J.D., 1988). *Member:* The State Bar of California. *PRACTICE AREAS:* Litigation. *Email:* cbl@msk2.msk.com

*OF COUNSEL*

**EDWARD RUBIN, (A PROFESSIONAL CORPORATION),** born Brooklyn, New York, April 30, 1912; admitted to bar, 1937, New York; 1941, California. *Education:* University of California at Los Angeles (A.B., 1933); Duke University (LL.B., 1936). Phi Beta Kappa; Order of the Coif. Editor-in-Chief, Duke Bar Association Journal, 1936. Author: "Preventive Law" by Louis M. Brown and Edward Rubin, Prentice-Hall, Inc., 1950. Lecturer, Entertainment Law, University of Southern California School of Law, 1978-1979. Member, Advisory Council to Provost, U.C.L.A. College of Letters and Science, 1982-1985. U.C.L.A. Foundation Advisory Trustee, 1983—. Public Counsel, Board of Directors, 1987-1992. *Member:* Beverly Hills (Chairman, Entertainment Law Committee, 1958-1965; Member, Board of Governors, 1962-1964; 1966-1972; President, 1971-1972; General Counsel, 1990—; Entertainment Lawyer of the Year, 1987; Distinguished Service Award, 1981), Los Angeles County (Member, Board of Trustees, 1973-1974; 50 Year Club, 1991) and American (Member, House of Delegates, 1972-1974; Chairman, Forum Committee on Entertainment and Sports Industries, 1979-1980; Member, 1980— and Chairman, 1981, Standing Committee on Forum Committees; Member, Patent, Trademark and Copyright Section) Bar Associations; The State Bar of California (Vice Chairman, Executive Committee, Conference of Delegates, 1970; Board of Governors, 1974-1977; Vice President and Treasurer, 1976-1977; President, 1977; Committee of Bar Examiners, 1987-1991); Los Angeles Copyright Society (Member, Board of Trustees, 1966-1968); World Peace Through Law Center (Secretary, Section on Intellectual Property, 1972); Beverly Hills Bar Association Foundation (President, 1983); Beverly Hills Bar Foundation (Member, Board of Directors, 1982—); Los Angeles County Bar Foundation (Member, Board of Directors, 1979-1986); World Association of Lawyers; National Conference of Bar Presidents. Fellow, American Bar Foundation (Co-Chairman for California, 1986—). *PRACTICE AREAS:* Entertainment Law; Copyright Law; Intellectual Property Law.

**WILLIAM M. KAPLAN, (A PROFESSIONAL CORPORATION),** born Brooklyn, New York, July 20, 1924; admitted to bar, 1952, New York; 1968, California. *Education:* Syracuse University (B.A., 1948); Yale University (LL.B., 1951). *Member:* The State Bar of California; Los Angeles Copyright Society. *PRACTICE AREAS:* Music Publishing Law; Motion Picture Music Law; Copyright Law.

**LESSING E. GOLD, (A PROFESSIONAL CORPORATION),** born Chicago, Illinois, March 21, 1932; admitted to bar, 1957, California; 1973, U.S. Supreme Court. *Education:* Northwestern University (B.S., 1953); University of Southern California (J.D., 1956). Business Law Arbitrator, Los Angeles County Superior Court, 1979—. Member of Panel, American Arbitration Association. *Member:* Beverly Hills, Los Angeles County and American Bar Associations; The State Bar of California. *PRACTICE AREAS:* General Corporate Law; Corporate Acquisitions; Representation of International Companies. *Email:* leg@msk.com

**DOUGLAS R. RING, (A PROFESSIONAL CORPORATION),** born Rochester, New York, July 24, 1944; admitted to bar, 1977, California. *Education:* La Verne College (B.A., 1973); University of West Los Angeles (J.D., 1977). Author: "Law and Real Estate Column," Los Angeles Times, 1981-1985; "Coping with Bureaucracy," Los Angeles Lawyer Magazine, April, 1978. Deputy County Supervisor, Los Angeles County, 1975-1980. Member, Board of Editors: California State Bar Journal, 1979-1980; Los Angeles Lawyer Magazine, 1980-1982. Member, 1980-1984 and Vice President, 1983-1984, Board of Trustees, California Administrative Law. Vice Chair, 1983 and Chair, 1984-1988, Western Center on Law and Poverty. Vice President, 1983 and President, 1984-1986, Los Angeles Actors Theatre. Board Member: Center Theater Group (Mark Taper Forum and Ahmanson Theater), 1986-1992; American Arts Alliance, 1987-1991. Member: Board of Trustees, Hebrew Union College, 1991—; Full Member, Urban Land Institute, 1990; Los Angeles City Library Commission, 1990-1993; Los Angeles Children's Museum Board, 1994—; Los Angeles Theater Works Board, 1994—; Los Angeles County Bar Foundation Board of Directors, 1994—; Los Angeles Library Foundation Board of Directors, 1993—. *Member:* The State Bar of California. *PRACTICE AREAS:* Real Estate Law; Land Use Law; Administrative Law. *Email:* douglasr8@aol.com

**STEPHEN D. MARKS, (A PROFESSIONAL CORPORATION),** born Philadelphia, Pennsylvania, August 21, 1941; admitted to bar, 1968,

*(This Listing Continued)*

**MITCHELL, SILBERBERG & KNUPP LLP**, Los Angeles—*Continued*

California; 1973, U.S. Supreme Court. *Education:* University of Southern California and University of California at Los Angeles (A.B., 1964); Hastings College of Law, University of California (J.D., 1967). Author: "Legal Ethics: The Criminal Case," Los Angeles County Bar Journal, 1973. Co-Author: "The Contrasting Ethical Duties of the Prosecutor and Defense Attorney in Criminal Cases," University of West Los Angeles Law Review, Winter, 1975. Professor of Law: Torts, California College of Law, 1968-1971; Criminal Law, LaVerne College Law Center, 1971-1974. *Member:* The State Bar of California. *Email:* slm@msk2.msk.com

**H. WAYNE TAYLOR,** born Los Angeles, California, November 27, 1945; admitted to bar, 1971, California. *Education:* Stanford University (A.B. with great distinction, 1967); Harvard University (J.D., cum laude, 1970). Phi Beta Kappa. Member, Board of Editors, Harvard Law Review, 1969-1970. *Member:* The State Bar of California. *PRACTICE AREAS:* Securities Law; Mergers and Acquisitions; Corporate Law. *Email:* hwt@msk.com

**MARVIN A. DEMOFF, (A PROFESSIONAL CORPORATION),** born Los Angeles, California, October 28, 1942; admitted to bar, 1969, California; 1981, U.S. Tax Court. *Education:* University of California at Los Angeles (A.B., 1964); Loyola University of Los Angeles (J.D., 1967). Phi Delta Phi. Author: "Eligibility Requirements for Young Athletes," 4 Los Angeles Lawyer 34, 1981. Lecturer, "Representing Professional and Amateur Athletes," University of California at Los Angeles, 1984-1987. Member of Faculty and Speaker: "Representation of Women Athletes," Golden State Law School National Conference of Women and the Law, 1980. Speaker: "Representing Amateur and Professional Athletes," National Association of Collegiate Athletic Directors Annual Convention, 1980; "Contract Negotiations for Athletes and Sportscasters," Practicing Law Institute, Entertainment and Sports Industries, 1981; The Sports Industries "Representing the Professional Athlete," American Bar Association Seminar, 1981; "Negotiating Sports Contracts with Management," Pepperdine Law School Symposium, 1983-1986. "Introduction to Sports Law," California Trial Lawyers Association Annual Convention, 1983; "Current Issues in Collegiate Athletics," National Association of College and University Attorneys, 1985. Speaker: "Olympics and the Law," International Bar Association Seminar, 1988; "Future Relationship of Employer and Employee in Professional Sports," American Bar Association, 1989; Super Bowl Sports Law Symposium, Continuing Legal Education, 1990. Adjunct Professor, Sports Law, University of California School of Law, Davis, 1993. Member, Los Angeles Olympic Organizing Committee, 1982-1984. Member, 1985— and Chairman, 1988-1993, Board of Trustees, The Curtis School. *Member:* The State Bar of California; American Bar Association (Member, Forum Committee on Entertainment and Sports Industries, 1981—). *PRACTICE AREAS:* Sports Law.

**JEFFREY B. WHEELER,** born Fullerton, California, July 16, 1952; admitted to bar, 1978, California. *Education:* University of California at Irvine (B.A., 1975); Pepperdine University (J.D., 1978). Adjunct Professor of Law, Pepperdine University School of Law, 1983—. *Member:* Beverly Hills (Member, Probate, Trust and Estate Planning Section) and Los Angeles County (Member, Section on: Probate and Trust Law; Death and Gift Tax Law) Bar Associations; The State Bar of California. *PRACTICE AREAS:* Estate Planning Law; Probate Law; Trust Administration Law; Non-Profit Organizations Law. *Email:* jbw@msk.com

**BERNARD DONNENFELD, (A PROFESSIONAL CORPORATION),** born Brooklyn, New York, October 28, 1926; admitted to bar, 1950, New York; 1974, California and U.S. District Court, Central District of California. *Education:* New York University (B.A., 1948; J.D., 1950). Member, New York University Law Review, 1949-1950. Adjunct Professor of Law, Western State Law School, 1983-1984. Panelist, American Arbitration Association. *Member:* Los Angeles County Bar Association; The State Bar of California. [With U.S. Navy, 1944-1946]. *PRACTICE AREAS:* Entertainment Law; Intellectual Property and Copyright Law. *Email:* bxd@msk.com

**DOUGLAS W. BORDEWIECK,** born Weymouth, Massachusetts, September 11, 1954; admitted to bar, 1984, California, U.S. District Court, Central District of California; 1985, U.S. District Court, Eastern, Southern and Northern Districts of California and U.S. Court of Appeals, Ninth Circuit; 1990, U.S. District Court, Eastern District of Michigan, U.S. Court of Appeals, Sixth Circuit. *Education:* Swarthmore College (B.A., with distinction, 1977); Harvard University (J.D., cum laude, 1983). Author: "The Post-Petition, Pre-Rejection, Pre-Assumption Status of an Executory Contract,"

*(This Listing Continued)*

59 The American Bankruptcy Law Journal 197, 1985. Co-Author: "The Rejection of Collective Bargaining Agreements by Chapter 11 Debtors," 57 The American Bankruptcy Law Journal 293, 1983. Instructor, Cornell Law School, 1983-1984, 1990-1992, 1996. *Member:* The State Bar of California. *PRACTICE AREAS:* Civil Litigation; Trademark; Patent Law; Environmental Law; Bankruptcy Law. *Email:* dwbithaca@aol.com

**A. CATHERINE NORIAN,** born St. Louis, Missouri, September 10, 1948; admitted to bar, 1977, California. *Education:* Stanford University (B.A., 1970); University of California at Los Angeles (J.D., 1977). Member, Cap and Gown, Stanford University; Moot Court, UCLA. Member, 1975-1976 and Editor, 1976-1977, UCLA-Alaska Law Review. *Member:* Los Angeles County and American (Member, Litigation Section) Bar Association; The State Bar of California. *PRACTICE AREAS:* Litigation. *Email:* acn@msk.com

**KIM H. SWARTZ,** born Washington, D.C., April 25, 1954; admitted to bar, 1981, Georgia; 1987, California. *Education:* University of Georgia (B.A., cum laude, 1976); Emory University (J.D., 1981). Solo Entertainment Practitioner, 1981-1986; Associate, Nelson, Guggenheim, Felker & Levine, 1986-1989; Senior Production Counsel, MGM/UA Communications Co., 1989; Vice President, Business Affairs and Assistant General Counsel, Saban Entertainment, Inc., 1990-1993; Vice President, Business and Legal Affairs, Republic Entertainment, Inc., 1993-1995. *Member:* Beverly Hills and Los Angeles Bar Associations; The State Bar of California; State Bar of Georgia. *PRACTICE AREAS:* Entertainment Law. *Email:* khs@msk.com

**RICHARD E. ACKERKNECHT,** born Los Angeles, California, May 20, 1961; admitted to bar, 1987, California and U.S. Court of Appeals, Ninth Circuit. *Education:* University of Southern California (B.S., magna cum laude, 1983; J.D., 1987). Staff Member, Computer/Tax Law Journals, 1986-1987. *Member:* Beverly Hills Bar Association (Member, Sections on: Business Law; Real Estate); The State Bar of California (Member, Business Law Section). *PRACTICE AREAS:* Corporate Law; Commercial Law. *Email:* rna@msk.com

## ASSOCIATES

**SCOTT H. BAUMAN,** born Lake Success, New York, February 10, 1964; admitted to bar, 1989, California and U.S. Court of Appeals, Ninth Circuit; 1990, U.S. District Court, Central District of California; 1991, U.S. District Court, Eastern District of California. *Education:* Rice University (B.A., cum laude, 1986); Boalt Hall School of Law, University of California (J.D., 1989). Phi Beta Kappa. Moot Court Executive Board. Co-Author: "The Chess Catalog Litigation: How MCA Records Won a Key Battle Against Unauthorized Recordings," 16 Los Angeles Lawyer 28 (April 1993). *Member:* Los Angeles County Bar Association; The State Bar of California. *PRACTICE AREAS:* Litigation; Copyright Law. *Email:* shb@msk2.msk.com

**YVETTE MOLINARO,** born Teaneck, New Jersey, March 22, 1963; admitted to bar, 1990, California and U.S. District Court, Central District of California; 1991, U.S. District Court, Eastern and Southern Districts of California and U.S. Court of Appeals, Ninth Circuit. *Education:* John Jay College of Criminal Justice, The City University of New York (B.A., summa cum laude, 1987); Southwestern University School of Law (J.D., cum laude, 1990). Delta Theta Phi. Salutatorian. Women in Criminal Justice Scholarship; Paul Wildman Scholarship. Chairperson, Board of Governors Moot Court Honors Program. Member, Southwestern University Law Review, 1988-1989. *Member:* Century City, Los Angeles County, Federal and American Bar Associations; The State Bar of California. *PRACTICE AREAS:* Civil Litigation; Criminal Defense. *Email:* yxm@msk2.msk.com

**RICHARD B. SHELDON, JR.,** born Gainesville, Florida, September 1, 1964; admitted to bar, 1990, California and U.S. District Court, Central District of California; 1991, U.S. District Court, Northern District of California. *Education:* Louisiana State University and A. & M. College (B.A., 1986); Pepperdine University (J.D., cum laude, 1990). Member, Pepperdine University Law Review, 1989-1990. Member: Moot Court Honor Board; Roger Traynor Moot Court Competition. *Member:* Beverly Hills and American Bar Associations; The State Bar of California. *PRACTICE AREAS:* Litigation. *Email:* rbs@msk2.msk.com

**YAKUB HAZZARD,** born Los Angeles, California, November 3, 1964; admitted to bar, 1990, California; 1991, U.S. District Court, Central District of California and U.S. Claims Court. *Education:* Stanford University (B.A., 1986); University of California at Los Angeles (J.D., 1990). Certified Player-Agent, National Basketball Player's Association. *Member:* Century City and John Langston Bar Associations; The State Bar of California (Member, Litigation Section); Black Entertainment and Sports Law Associ-

*(This Listing Continued)*

ation. *PRACTICE AREAS:* Intellectual Property; Litigation; Sports Law. *Email:* yxh@msk2.msk.com

**MARY COURTNEY BURKE,** born Torrance, California, November 26, 1963; admitted to bar, 1992, California. *Education:* Stanford University (A.B., with honors, 1986); Georgetown University Law Center (J.D., cum laude, 1991). *Member:* The State Bar of California (Member, Labor Law Section). *PRACTICE AREAS:* Employment Law; Labor Law. *Email:* mmc@msk2.msk.com

**JEFFREY H. FRANKEL,** born Brooklyn, New York, March 19, 1965; admitted to bar, 1991, California. *Education:* Cornell University (B.S., 1986); University of California School of Law (J.D., 1991). *Member:* The State Bar of California. *PRACTICE AREAS:* Entertainment Law; Entertainment Industry Transactions; Copyright Law. *Email:* jhf@msk.com

**JEFFREY D. GOLDMAN,** born Los Angeles, California, September 23, 1966; admitted to bar, 1991, California; 1992, U.S. District Court, Central District of California; 1993, U.S. Court of Appeals, Ninth Circuit. *Education:* University of California at Los Angeles (B.A., 1988); University of California, Hastings College of Law (J.D., 1991). Note and Article Editor, Hastings Law Journal, 1990-1991. Co-Author: "Federal Antitrust Law in the Supreme Court and the Ninth Circuit: 1990-1995," Hot Topics for Corporate Counsel (American Bar Association Center for Continuing Legal Education 1995); "Vicarious Triumph: Manufacturers Are Finding That Indirect Theories of Liability Can Be a Potent Weapon in the War on Counterfeit Goods," Los Angeles Daily Journal (April 27, 1995); "9th Circuit Says Laches Applies to Copyright Claim," National Law Journal (October 31, 1994). *Member:* Los Angeles County Bar Association; The State Bar of California. *PRACTICE AREAS:* Antitrust; Intellectual Property Litigation. *Email:* jdg@msk2.msk.com

**ANN S. LEE,** born Seoul, South Korea, November 27, 1967; admitted to bar, 1992, California. *Education:* University of California at Berkeley (B.A., with distinction, 1989); Cornell University (J.D., 1992). Recipient, American Jurisprudence Award, Contracts. *Member:* The State Bar of California; Korean American Bar Association. *PRACTICE AREAS:* Litigation. *Email:* asl@msk2.msk.com

**BRENDA S. BARTON,** born Phoenix, Arizona, October 12, 1963; admitted to bar, 1992, California. *Education:* University of California at Los Angeles (B.A., cum laude, 1987); University of Chicago Law School (J.D., 1992). Recipient, Edwin F. Mandel Award. *Member:* The State Bar of California (Delegate, State Bar Conference of Delegates, 1994, 1995, 1996); Women Lawyers Association of Los Angeles. *PRACTICE AREAS:* General Civil; Bankruptcy Litigation. *Email:* bsb@msk2.msk.com

**BRIAN S. ARBETTER,** born Skokie, Illinois, August 4, 1966; admitted to bar, 1992, California and Illinois. *Education:* Washington University (B.S., 1988); University of Chicago (J.D., 1991). Tau Beta Pi; Omicron Delta Kappa. Development Editor, The University of Chicago Legal Forum, 1990-1991. Co-Author: "Arbitration Pacts May Ease Employment Disputes," National Law Journal, May 15, 1995. Law Clerk for the Hon. Charles L. Levin, Michigan Supreme Court, 1991-1992. *Member:* Century City, Illinois State and American (Member: Planning Board of the ABA Young Lawyers Division Labor and Employment Law Committee, 1993—; Federal Labor Standards Committee, 1995—) Bar Associations; The State Bar of California. *PRACTICE AREAS:* Labor Law; Employment Law; Employment Discrimination Law. *Email:* bsa@msk2.msk.com

**MICHELLE ABEND BAUMAN,** born New York, N.Y., January 14, 1967; admitted to bar, 1993, California. *Education:* Claremont McKenna College (B.A., with honors, 1989); University of Southern California (J.D., 1992). Member, University of Southern California Law Review. Law Clerk to the Honorable Edward C. Reed, Jr., District of Nevada. *Member:* The State Bar of California. *PRACTICE AREAS:* Labor Law; Employment Law. *Email:* mla@msk2.msk.com

**JEFFREY L. RICHARDSON,** born Portland, Oregon, April 3, 1968; admitted to bar, 1993, California. *Education:* Willamette University (B.S., 1990); University of Southern California (J.D., 1993). *Member:* The State Bar of California. *PRACTICE AREAS:* Litigation. *Email:* jlr@msk2.msk.com

**MATT J. RAILO,** born Kauniainen, Finland, July 18, 1969; admitted to bar, 1993, California. *Education:* University of Southern California (B.S., 1990); Stanford University; University of California at Los Angeles School of Law (J.D., 1993). Phi Alpha Delta. Order of the Coif. Extern to the Honorable Stephen V. Wilson, Central District of California, 1992. *Member:* The State Bar of California. *LANGUAGES:* Finnish, German. *PRACTICE AREAS:* Litigation. *Email:* mjr@msk2.msk.com

*(This Listing Continued)*

**ADAM LEVIN,** born Seattle, Washington, May 23, 1966; admitted to bar, 1991, California and U.S. District Court, Central District of California; 1993, U.S. District Court, Northern and Southern Districts of California. *Education:* Claremont McKenna College (B.A., 1988); University of San Diego (J.D., magna cum laude, 1991). Member, San Diego Law Review, 1989-1991. Co-Author: "Courts Are Divided on Drug Tests," National Law Journal, October 24, 1994. Law Clerk to the Honorable A. Andrew Hauk, U.S. District Court, Central District of California, 1991-1992. Extern to the Honorable J. Clifford Wallace, U.S. Court of Appeals, 9th Circuit, 1990. *Member:* The State Bar of California; American Bar Association. *PRACTICE AREAS:* Employment Law; Labor Law; Litigation. *Email:* a11@msk2.msk.com

**TAMMY CAIN BLOOMFIELD,** born Wilmington, Delaware, November 26, 1964; admitted to bar, 1991, Nevada; 1994, California. *Education:* State University of New York at Binghamton (B.A., with honors, 1987); Boston University School of Law (J.D., 1991); Boston University School of Communication (M.S. in Mass Communication, 1992). Clerk to the Honorable District Court Judge Edward C. Reed, Jr., Federal District Court, District of Nevada. *Member:* State Bar of California; State Bar of Nevada. *PRACTICE AREAS:* Litigation. *Email:* tcc@msk2.msk.com

**MICHAEL TSAO,** born October 3, 1969; admitted to bar, 1994, California and U.S. District Court, Central District of California. *Education:* Dartmouth College (A.B., 1991); University of California School of Law at Los Angeles (J.D., 1994). Member, University of California Law Review. Member, Moot Court Executive Board. Recipient, American Jurisprudence Award. *Member:* State Bar of California. *PRACTICE AREAS:* Litigation. *Email:* mht@msk2.msk.com

**DAVID J. KATZ,** born Los Angeles, California, July 9, 1963; admitted to bar, 1990, California. *Education:* California State University, Northridge (B.S., 1987); Loyola Law School (J.D., 1990). Saint Thomas Moore Law Honor Society, 1990. Reserve Los Angeles County Deputy Sheriff, Member, Malibu Search and Rescue Team. Co-Author: "Going Public, an Awakening Experience," American Law Institute-American Bar Association, *The Audio Lawyer,* 1991. *Member:* The State Bar of California. *PRACTICE AREAS:* Corporate; Securities; International Securities; Real Estate. *Email:* djk@msk.com

**JEFFREY D. DAVINE,** born Los Angeles, California, April 25, 1960; admitted to bar, 1985, California and U.S. District Court, Central District of California; 1991, U.S. Tax Court. *Education:* University of California at Berkeley (B.S., with honors, 1982); University of California School of Law at Los Angeles (J.D., 1985). Phi Beta Kappa. Moot Court Honors. Chairman, Los Angeles County Bar Association Young Tax Lawyers Committee, 1993-1994. *Member:* Los Angeles County Bar Association (Secretary, Entertainment-Tax Committee, 1995-1996); The State Bar of California. *PRACTICE AREAS:* Taxation; Tax Controversy and Litigation; Exempt Organizations-Nonprofit. *Email:* jdd@msk.com

**JEFFREY K. EISEN,** born Brooklyn, New York, June 21, 1967; admitted to bar, 1991, California. *Education:* Wharton School of the University of Pennsylvania (B.S., summa cum laude, 1988), Beta Gamma Sigma; New York University (J.D., magna cum laude, 1991). Order of the Coif. Recipient, American Jurisprudence Award in Criminal Law and Trusts and Estate. Co-Author: "Like-Kind Exchanges of Personal Property: A Practical Tour Through Uncharted Territory," Taxes Magazine, February 1994. *Member:* The State Bar of California. *PRACTICE AREAS:* Estate Planning and Probate. *Email:* jke@msk.com

**TRACY L. THORNBURG,** born Pasadena, California, November 24, 1964; admitted to bar, 1992, California, U.S. Court of Appeals, Ninth Circuit and U.S. District Court, Central District of California; 1993, U.S. District Court, Southern and Eastern Districts of California and U.S. District Court, District of Arizona. *Education:* Yale College (B.A., 1986); University of Southern California Law Center (J.D., 1992). Recipient, American Jurisprudence Award in Trial Advocacy. Author: "Special Rules for Schools: The Family and Medical Leave Act of 1993," *Public Risk* (Sept. 1993). Co-Author: "Court Announces New Drug Testing Standard," *The California Labor Letter,* Vol. V, No. 3 (Mar. 1994); "California Family Rights Update," The California Labor Letter, Vol. VI, No. 9 (Sept. 1995); "When Are Office No-Dating Policies Enforceable?" The National Law Journal, April 3, 1996. Member: Professionals in Human Resources Association, 1995; Society for Human Resource Management, 1995. *Member:* Los Angeles County Bar Associations; State Bar of California. *PRACTICE AREAS:* Employment Litigation; Management Labor Relations; Wage and Hour Law. *Email:* tlt@msk2.msk.com

**HOWARD D. SHAPIRO,** born Philadelphia, Pennsylvania, November 23, 1966; admitted to bar, 1992, California. *Education:* Rice University

*(This Listing Continued)*

**MITCHELL, SILBERBERG & KNUPP LLP,** *Los Angeles—Continued*

(B.A., 1989); Lewis & Clark Northwestern School (J.D., 1992). Cornelius Honor Society. *Member:* The State Bar of California; American Immigration Law Association. **LANGUAGES:** Mandarin. **PRACTICE AREAS:** Immigration; Employment Immigration; Immigration Discrimination. **Email:** hds@msk.com

**JEANNETTE HAHM,** born Korea, 1968; admitted to bar, 1992, California. *Education:* University of California at Berkeley (B.A., with highest honors, 1989); University of California School of Law at Los Angeles (J.D., 1992). *Member:* Beverly Hills Bar Association (Member, Executive Committee, 1995-1996, Chair, Legislative Committee, 1995-1996, Chair, Guardianship Section, 1994-1995 and Vice-Chair, Legislative Committee, Probate, Trusts and Estates Section); The State Bar of California. **LANGUAGES:** Korean. **PRACTICE AREAS:** Estate Planning; Wills; Trusts; Probate Law; Conservatorship. **Email:** jxh@msk.com

**JEFFREY M. LOWY,** born Los Angeles, California, May 13, 1963; admitted to bar, 1992, California and U.S. District Court, Central District of California. *Education:* University of Arizona (B.A., 1986); Southwestern University School of Law (J.D., 1992). Author: "When Does the Renewal Term Vest: Before and After The Copyright Renewal Act of 1992," Loyola of Los Angeles Entertainment Law Journal, Vol. 13, No. 3. *Member:* Beverly Hills (Member, Entertainment Law Section), Los Angeles County (Member, Entertainment Law Section) and American (Member, Entertainment Law Section) Bar Associations. **PRACTICE AREAS:** Music Law; Entertainment Law; Intellectual Property Law. **Email:** jml@msk.com

**TIMOTHY R. COLLINS, JR.,** born Washington, D.C., 1968; admitted to bar, 1995, California. *Education:* Stanford University (B.A., 1990); Yale Law School (J.D., 1995). Member, Yale Law and Policy Review. *Member:* The State Bar of California. **PRACTICE AREAS:** Motion Picture and Television Law. **Email:** trc@msk.com

**KIM Y. RICHARDSON,** born Tokyo, Japan, June 11, 1969; admitted to bar, 1995, California. *Education:* University of California at Los Angeles (B.A., magna cum laude, 1991); Harvard University (J.D., 1995). Phi Beta Kappa. *Member:* The State Bar of California. **PRACTICE AREAS:** Civil Litigation. **Email:** kyr@msk2.msk.com

**JENNIFER LIGHTMAN WESSELS,** born Carlisle, Pennsylvania, October 17, 1970; admitted to bar, 1995, California. *Education:* University of Pennsylvania (B.A., summa cum laude, 1992); Harvard Law School (J.D., cum laude, 1995). Phi Beta Kappa. *Member:* The State Bar of California. **PRACTICE AREAS:** Labor and Employment. **Email:** jlw@msk2.msk.com

**WAYNE KAZAN,** born Brooklyn, New York, October 10, 1968; admitted to bar, 1995, California. *Education:* University of Colorado (B.S.B.A., magna cum laude, 1990); University of Southern California (J.D., 1995). Recipient, American Jurisprudence Awards in Ethics, Constitutional Law, Torts. University of Southern California Law Review. *Member:* The State Bar of California. **PRACTICE AREAS:** Music and Entertainment Law. **Email:** w1k@msk.com

**HABIB A. BALIAN,** born Pasadena, California, March 15, 1970; admitted to bar, 1995, California. *Education:* University of Southern California (B.S., magna cum laude, 1992; J.D., 1995). Member, University of Southern California Law Review, Executive Editor, 1994-1995. *Member:* The State Bar of California. **PRACTICE AREAS:** Litigation. **Email:** hab@msk2.msk.com

**HARRY H.W. KIM,** born Seoul, Korea, February 28, 1964; admitted to bar, 1992, California. *Education:* Harvard University (A.B., 1986); New York University School of Law (J.D., 1991). *Member:* The State Bar of California; Korean-American Bar Association. **PRACTICE AREAS:** Corporate; Securities. **Email:** hhk@msk.com

**MICHAEL J. ZERMAN,** born New York, N.Y., January 3, 1960; admitted to bar, 1994, California; 1995, New York. *Education:* Wesleyan University (B.A., 1981); University of Arizona (J.D., 1993). Attorney, Resolution Trust Corporation, Federal Deposit Insurance Corporation, 1993-1994. *Member:* The State Bar of California. **PRACTICE AREAS:** Commercial Real Estate Law; Mortgage Finance Law; Corporate Law. **Email:** mjz@msk.com

**CAROLYN S. JAVIER,** born Miami Beach, Florida, March 13, 1968; admitted to bar, 1993, California. *Education:* Emory University (B.A., 1989); Loyola School of Law (J.D., 1992). Moot Court. *Member:* The State Bar of California. **LANGUAGES:** Spanish, French. **PRACTICE AREAS:** Music Law; Music Publishing; Entertainment Law. **Email:** csj@msk.com

**ROGER A. SANDAU,** born Los Angeles, California, September 29, 1966; admitted to bar, 1992, California. *Education:* University of California at Los Angeles (B.A., 1988); University of California Hastings College of the Law (J.D., 1992). *Member:* The State Bar of California. **PRACTICE AREAS:** Music Law; Entertainment Law; Music Publishing. **Email:** ras@msk.com

**SHERI E. COHEN,** born Los Angeles, California, March 17, 1962; admitted to bar, 1995, California; 1996, New York. *Education:* San Diego State University (A.B., 1986); Loyola Law School, Los Angeles (J.D., 1995); New York University School of Law (LL.M. in Taxation, 1996). Phi Alpha Delta (Justice, 1994; Vice-Justice, 1992-1993). Order of the Coif. Sayre Macneil Scolar. St. Thomas More Honor Society. *Member:* The State Bar of California; American Bar Association. **PRACTICE AREAS:** Federal Taxation; Employment Taxation; Tax Exempt Organizations. **Email:** sec@msk.com

**KARL J. DE COSTA,** born Honolulu, Hawaii, November 16, 1971; admitted to bar, 1996, California. *Education:* The Colorado College (B.A., magna cum laude, 1993); University of California School of Law, Los Angeles (J.D., 1996). Phi Delta Phi. Recipient: Award for Most Outstanding Senior Thesis; The J. Juan Reid Award for Excellence in the Liberal Arts; American Jurisprudence Awards: Constitutional Law; Commercial Law; Gift and Estate Taxation. Judicial Extern to the Honorable Chief Judge Calvin K. Ashland, U.S. Bankruptcy Court for the Central District of California, Bankruptcy Appellate Panel. *Member:* The State Bar of California. **PRACTICE AREAS:** Trusts and Estates; Probate; Civil Litigation. **Email:** kjd@msk2.msk.com

**LEE ANNE STEINBERG,** born Torrance, California, December 3, 1965; admitted to bar, 1996, California. *Education:* Williams College (B.A., 1988); University of California, Los Angeles (M.A., 1993); University of California, Boalt Hall School of Law (J.D., 1996). Phi Beta Kappa. Order of the Coif. Member, California Law Review, 1994-1996. *Member:* The State Bar of California. **PRACTICE AREAS:** Labor and Employment Law. **Email:** las@msk2.msk.com

**STEFANO G. MOSCATO,** born Paris, France, February 25, 1970; admitted to bar, 1996, California. *Education:* University of California, Berkeley (A.B., 1991); University of California School of Law, Los Angeles (J.D., 1996). Order of the Coif. *Member:* The State Bar of California. **LANGUAGES:** French, Italian. **PRACTICE AREAS:** Labor and Employment Law. **Email:** sgm@msk2.msk.com

**STACIE L. FELDMAN,** born Los Angeles, California, February 4, 1971; admitted to bar, 1996, California. *Education:* University of California, San Diego (B.A., summa cum laude, 1993); Boston University School of Law (J.D., cum laude, 1996). Member, 1994-1996 and Executive Editor, 1995-1996, Boston University Law Review. *Member:* The State Bar of California. **PRACTICE AREAS:** Civil Litigation. **Email:** sxf@msk2.msk.com

**JASON KRISCHER,** born Cambridge, Massachusetts, November 6, 1970; admitted to bar, 1996, California. *Education:* University of Illinois (B.S., 1992); Southwestern University (J.D., summa cum laude, 1996). Extern, The Honorable Thomas L. Steffen, Supreme Court of Nevada. Extern, The Honorable Harry Pregerson, Ninth Circuit Court of Appeals. *Member:* The State Bar of California. **PRACTICE AREAS:** Civil Litigation. **Email:** jbk@msk.com

**SUZANNE M. STEINKE,** born Vallejo, California, June 23, 1969; admitted to bar, 1996, California. *Education:* Stanford University (A.B., 1991); University of Wisconsin-Madison (J.D., 1996). Articles Editor, 1995-1996 and Member, 1994-1995, University of Wisconsin Law Review. Author: Comment, "The Exception to the Rule: Wisconsin's Fundamental Right to Education and Public School Financing," 1995 Wis. L. Rev. 1387. *Member:* The State Bar of California. **PRACTICE AREAS:** Labor and Employment Law. **Email:** s1s@msk2.msk.com

**JEREMY A. LAPPEN,** born Hollywood, California, April 25, 1970; admitted to bar, 1996, California. *Education:* University of California, Santa Barbara (B.A., with honors, 1993); University of Southern California (J.D., 1996). Order of the Coif. University of Southern California Law Review. *Member:* The State Bar of California. **PRACTICE AREAS:** Corporate. **Email:** jal@msk.com

**D. JAMES CHUNG,** born Seoul, Korea, January 4, 1963; admitted to bar, 1995, California. *Education:* University of Michigan (B.S.C.E., 1985); University of Southern California (J.D., 1995). Tau Beta Pi; Eta Kappa Nu.

*(This Listing Continued)*

# PROFESSIONAL BIOGRAPHIES

CALIFORNIA—LOS ANGELES

Senior Editor, Southern California Interdisciplinary Law Journal. *Member:* State Bar of California; American Bar Association. *LANGUAGES:* Korean. *Email:* djc@msk2.msk.com

REFERENCES: Wells Fargo Bank, N.A.; Merrill, Lynch.

## MOFFITT, WEAGANT & LOO LLP

1900 AVENUE OF THE STARS, SUITE 1900
**LOS ANGELES, CALIFORNIA 90067**
Telephone: 310-201-7575
Fax: 310-553-6437

General Civil and Trial Practice. Securities, Corporate Finance, Corporate, Commercial and Business Law, Real Property, Federal and State Taxation, Estate Planning, Trust and Probate Law.

### MEMBERS OF FIRM

**JOHN P. MOFFITT,** born Compton, California, October 12, 1942; admitted to bar, 1967, California; 1969, U.S. Tax Court; U.S. District Court, Central District of California; U.S. Court of Appeals, Ninth Circuit. *Education:* Occidental College (B.A., 1964); California Western University (J.D., 1967). Phi Alpha Delta. Managing Editor, California Western Law Review, 1967. Author: "Landlord Liability for Gratuitous Promises to Repair," II Calif.W.L.Rev. 126, Spring, 1966. Judge Pro Tem, Los Angeles Municipal Court, (1980-1984). *Member:* Century City (Member, Board of Governors, 1972-1975), Los Angeles County and American (Member, Section on Corporation, Banking and Business Law) Bar Associations; American Judicature Society. *PRACTICE AREAS:* Civil Trial; Appellate Practice; Commercial Law; Real Estate; Business.

**LANCE M. WEAGANT,** born Lynwood, California, March 13, 1950; admitted to bar, 1976, California; 1977, U.S. District Court, Central District of California; 1979, U.S. District Court, Southern District of California; 1980, U.S. Tax Court and U.S. Court of Appeals, Ninth Circuit. *Education:* University of Southern California (A.B., magna cum laude, 1972; J.D., 1976); University of San Diego School of Law (Diploma in Taxation, 1979). Phi Beta Kappa. Co-Chairperson and Lecturer, Hamline University Law School, Advanced Legal Education Program, "Life Insurance: Uses in Business and Tax Planning," 1982. Panelist and Co-Author: "Probate, Trust and Estate Planning Developments," Beverly Hills Bar Association, Third Annual Update of the Law Program, 1983. Contributing Author: "How to Live -- And Die -- With California Probate," Gulf Publishing Company, 1984. Lecturer, "Fundamentals of Estate Administration," California Continuing Education of the Bar, 1984. Co-Author: "Transfer of Assets and Discharge of Representative," Chapter 21, California Decedent Estate Practice, 1986. Panelist, "Tax Planning with Trusts," State Bar of California, 1990. Moderator, "Estate and Income Tax Planning for Entertainment Law Clients," Beverly Hills Bar Association, 1990. Instructor, Golden Gate University Masters in Taxation Program, Executive Compensation, 1988; Estate and Gift Taxation, 1988—. Coordinating Attorney, Beverly Hills Bar Association, Los Angeles County Superior Court Guardianship Assistance Program, 1991-1992. *Member:* Beverly Hills (Member: Probate, Trust and Estate Planning Section, Chair, 1989-1990 and Taxation Section), Los Angeles County and American (Member, Sections on: Taxation; Real Property, Probate and Trust Law) Bar Associations; The State Bar of California (Member, Probate, Estate Planning and Trust Law Sections); Beverly Hills Estate Planning Council. (Certified Specialist, Taxation Law and Probate, Estate Planning and Trust Law, The State Bar of California Board of Legal Specialization). *PRACTICE AREAS:* Estate Planning; Taxation Law; Probate, Trust and Tax Litigation.

**JOHN LOO,** born Toledo, Ohio, April 28, 1944; admitted to bar, 1976, California; 1977, U.S. District Court, Central District of California; 1991, U.S. Tax Court. *Education:* University of Toledo (B.S.E.E., 1966); University of Pittsburgh (M.B.A., 1967); Loyola University of Los Angeles (J.D., cum laude, 1976). Tau Beta Pi. Co-Author, "Transfer of Assets and Discharge of Representative," Chapter 21, California Decedent Estate Practice, 1986. *Member:* Beverly Hills (Member, Corporate and Commercial Law Section), Los Angeles County (Member, Sections on: Business and Corporations Law; Commercial Law and Real Property) and American (Member, Sections on: Corporation, Banking and Business Law; Taxation) Bar Associations; The State Bar of California (Member, Partnership Committee, Business Law Section, 1984-1987); Financial Lawyers Conference; Association of Real Estate Attorneys. *PRACTICE AREAS:* Corporate Law; Commercial Law; Business Planning Law.

## LAW OFFICES OF SHAHROKH MOKHTARZADEH

Established in 1990

2049 CENTURY PARK EAST, SUITE 720
**LOS ANGELES, CALIFORNIA 90067-3283**
Telephone: 310-788-0370
Fax: 310-788-0353

Business and Real Estate Litigation, Family Law, Insurance and Insurance Related Litigation.

FIRM PROFILE: Mr. Mokhtarzadeh specializes in handling cases within the range of $30,000 to $300,000.

**SHAHROKH MOKHTARZADEH,** born Tehran, Iran, August 2, 1961; admitted to bar, 1988, California. *Education:* University of California at Los Angeles (B.A., 1983); Golden Gate University (J.D., 1986). *Member:* Beverly Hills and Los Angeles County Bar Associations; State Bar of California. *LANGUAGES:* Persian/Farsi. *PRACTICE AREAS:* Real Estate Litigation; Business Litigation; Insurance Defense Litigation; Family Law.

## THE LAW FIRM OF RICHARD M. MONEYMAKER

Established in 1970

SUITE 2102 BROADWAY PLAZA
700 FLOWER STREET
**LOS ANGELES, CALIFORNIA 90017**
Telephone: 213-622-1088
Telecopier: 213-622-7002

Bankruptcy, Insolvency and Corporate Reorganization Law. General Commercial Litigation.

**RICHARD M. MONEYMAKER,** born Los Angeles, California, May 17, 1936; admitted to bar, 1961, California; 1967, U.S. Supreme Court. *Education:* Yale University (B.A., 1957); University of California at Berkeley (J.D., 1960). Member, Moot Court Board. *Member:* Los Angeles County (Member, Executive Committee, Commercial Law and Bankruptcy Section, 1972-1977) and Federal Bar Associations; State Bar of California. [With U.S. National Guard, 1960-1963; Air Force Reserve, 1963-1966]. *PRACTICE AREAS:* Bankruptcy.

### ASSOCIATES

**VINCENT B. MONEYMAKER,** born Los Angeles, California, June 11, 1964; admitted to bar, 1991, California. *Education:* University of California at Los Angeles (B.A., 1987); University of California at Davis (J.D., 1991). Extern to Honorable Calvin K. Ashland, U.S. Bankruptcy Court, Central District of California, Bankruptcy Appellate Panel, Ninth Circuit Court of Appeals, 1989; Extern to Honorable R. Clive Jones, U.S. Bankruptcy Court, District of Nevada, Bankruptcy Appellate Panel, Ninth Circuit Court of Appeals, 1990. *Member:* Los Angeles County and Federal Bar Associations; State Bar of California. *PRACTICE AREAS:* Bankruptcy.

**SHERI R. HANDEL,** born Los Angeles, California, August 2, 1968; admitted to bar, 1995, California. *Education:* University of California at Los Angeles (B.A., 1991); Loyola Law School (J.D., 1995). Extern to Honorable Kathleen T. Lax, U.S. Bankruptcy Court, Central District of California. *Member:* Los Angeles County and American Bar Associations. *PRACTICE AREAS:* Bankruptcy.

### OF COUNSEL

**FRANK W. MOLLOY,** born Cincinnati, Ohio, October 14, 1946; admitted to bar, 1972, California. *Education:* Dartmouth College (A.B., 1968); University of Pennsylvania (J.D., 1971). Order of the Coif. Member, University of Pennsylvania Law Review, 1970-1971. *Member:* Los Angeles County and Federal Bar Associations; State Bar of California. *PRACTICE AREAS:* Business Law and Litigation.

REFERENCE: Bank of America (Los Angeles Main Office).

## MONTELEONE & McCRORY

A Partnership including Professional Corporations

*Established in 1958*

**725 SOUTH FIGUEROA STREET
SUITE 3750
LOS ANGELES, CALIFORNIA 90017-5402**
Telephone: 213-612-9900
FAX: 213-612-9930

*Santa Ana, California Office:* Suite 750, 1551 North Tustin Avenue, 92705. Telephone: 714-565-3170. Fax: 714-565-3184.

Construction, Negligence and Product Defense, Environmental/OSHA, Federal, State and Municipal Government Contract Law. Transactional, International Business. General Civil and Trial Practice in all State and Federal Courts, Administrative Courts, Court of Claims, Arbitration and Alternative Dispute Resolution, Appellate Practice.

FIRM PROFILE: Monteleone & McCrory was founded in 1958 when Darrell McCrory joined Stephen Monteleone in his growing construction practice. Since that time the firm and its areas of practice have expanded and the firm now represents clients in a variety of commercial settings including construction.

### MEMBERS OF FIRM

**STEPHEN MONTELEONE** (1886-1962).

**G. ROBERT HALE, (P.C.),** born Carnegie, Pennsylvania, March 17, 1936; admitted to bar, 1964, California. *Education:* El Camino College (A.A., 1959); Hastings College of Law, University of California (LL.B., 1963). Order of the Coif. Member, Thurston Society. *Member:* The State Bar of California; American Bar Association. **PRACTICE AREAS:** Construction Litigation; Government Contracts; Appellate Practice.

**PATRICK J. DUFFY, III (P.C.),** born Los Angeles, California, July 20, 1944; admitted to bar, 1970, California. *Education:* Loyola University of Los Angeles (B.A., 1966; J.D., 1969). Article Author, Loyola University Law Review, 1969. Panelist and Speaker: Construction Law Forum; AGC Conferences; American Arbitration Association Conferences; International Arbitration Conferences. *Member:* Wilshire, Los Angeles County and American Bar Associations; State Bar of California. **PRACTICE AREAS:** Contract Litigation; Construction Litigation; Business Litigation; Contract Formation and Negotiation; Real Estate Transactions and Litigation; Administrative Law; Courts and Arbitration Proceedings; Court and Jury Trials.

**MICHAEL F. MINCHELLA, (P.C.),** born Los Angeles, California, January 8, 1945; admitted to bar, 1970, California. *Education:* Loyola University of Los Angeles (B.S., 1966; J.D., 1969). Deputy District Attorney, Los Angeles County, 1969-1974. Panelist/Speaker, "Construction Law," California Judges Conference, 1991. Member, Large Complex Case Panel, American Arbitration Association. *Member:* State Bar of California; American Bar Association. **PRACTICE AREAS:** Business Litigation; Commercial Litigation; Alternative Dispute Resolution; Construction Law; General Civil Trial Practice, State and Federal Courts.

**THOMAS P. MCGUIRE, (P.C.),** born Washington State; admitted to bar, 1975, California. *Education:* University of California at Los Angeles (B.A., 1972); Hastings College of Law, University of California (J.D., 1975). *Member:* State Bar of California. **PRACTICE AREAS:** Construction Law; OSHA; Environmental Law; Commercial Law.

**WILLIAM J. INGALSBE, (P.C.),** born Guam, June 5, 1947; admitted to bar, 1975, California. *Education:* California State University of San Diego (B.A., 1969); Southwestern University (J.D., 1975). Delta Theta Phi. Editor-in-Chief, Southwestern Law Review, 1974-1975. Author: "The Plaintiff's Burden of Proof?" 6 Southwestern Law Review 661, 1974. Panelist and Speaker: "Identifying a Claim," Associated General Contractors of California, Inc. Construction Contract Claims Seminar, 1988. Co-Author: "Common Bases for Claims on Construction Projects," Associated General Contractors of California, Inc. Construction Law Manual, 1989. Member, Legal Advisory Committee, Associated General Contractors of California, Inc., 1980—. *Member:* Los Angeles County (Volunteer, 1984-1989 and Vice-Chair, 1989-1995, Client Relations Committee; Volunteer Judge Pro Tem, Municipal Courts Committee, 1985—) and Orange County Bar Associations; The State Bar of California (Volunteer Investigative Attorney Program, 1986); The American Society of Writers on Legal Subjects; American Judicature Society. (Resident, Santa Ana Office). **REPORTED CASES:** Weeshoff Construction Co. v. L.A. County Flood Control Dist. (1979) 88 Cal. App. 3d 579, 152 Cal. Rptr. 19; Dallas-Fort Worth Regional Airport Board v. Superior Court (1976); 63 Cal. App. 3d 482, 133 Cal. Rptr. 720. **PRACTICE AREAS:** Construction Law; General Trial; Employee Wrongful Termination; Business Litigation; Commercial Law.

**PHILIP C. PUTNAM, (P.C.),** born Charlottesville, Virginia, December 7, 1954; admitted to bar, 1980, California, U.S. Claims Court, U.S. Tax Court, U.S. District Court, Northern, Southern, Eastern and Central Districts of California and U.S. Court of Appeals, Ninth Circuit. *Education:* University of Southern California (B.S., with honors, 1977; J.D., 1980). Beta Alpha Psi; Phi Alpha Delta. Recipient, Best Brief Award, 1978-1979, Hale Moot Court Competition. Certified Public Accountant, Illinois, 1978. Judge Pro Tem: Los Angeles County Municipal Court, 1987—; Los Angeles County Superior Court, 1991—. *Member:* Wilshire (Treasurer, 1988-1989; Vice President, 1989-1990; President, 1990-1991), Los Angeles County (Member: Taxation and Business Law Section; State Appellate Judicial Evaluations Committee; Tax Court Pro Se Settlement Program) and American (Member: Taxation Section; Business Law Section; Forum on the Construction Industry) Bar Associations; State Bar of California; Illinois Certified Public Accountant Society; American Institute of Certified Public Accountants. **REPORTED CASES:** Rain Bird Sprinkler Mfg. Corp. v. Franchise Tax Board (1991, 4th Dist.) 229 Cal. App. 3d 784, 280 Cal. Rptr. 362; Ronald v. 4'C's Electronic Packaging, Inc. (1985, 2d Dist.) 168 Cal. App. 3d 290, 214 Cal. Rptr. 225; County of Los Angeles v. Superior Court (T.G.I. Constr. Corp.) (1984, 2d Dist.) 155 Cal. App. 3d 798, 202 Cal. Rptr. 444. **PRACTICE AREAS:** Business/Corporate Law; Tax Law; Estate Planning; Employment Law; Construction.

**JOSEPH A. MILLER, (P.C.),** born Los Angeles, California, May 15, 1955; admitted to bar, 1980, New Mexico; 1981, California. *Education:* Yale University (B.A., 1977); Hastings College of Law, University of California (J.D., 1980). *Member:* State Bar of California. **PRACTICE AREAS:** Litigation.

**DIANA M. DRON,** born Whittier, California, December 1, 1953; admitted to bar, 1979, California. *Education:* The College of Idaho (B.S., 1975); Pepperdine University (J.D., 1979). In House Counsel, Stang Hydronics Inc., 1979-1984. Member, Legal Advisory Committee, Associated General Contractors of California, Inc., 1980—. *Member:* Orange County Bar Association; State Bar of California. (Resident, Santa Ana Office). **PRACTICE AREAS:** Construction Law; Business Law; Construction Defects; Minority Business Enterprises; Woman-Owned Business Enterprises; Mechanic's Liens/Stop Notices; Suretyships; Business Litigation; General Litigation.

**DONALD J. SHIELDS,** born Chuquicamata, Chile, September 6, 1933; admitted to bar, 1962, California; registered to practice before U.S. Patent and Trademark Office. *Education:* University of Santa Clara; University of California at Berkeley (B.S.E.E., 1956); Boalt Hall School of Law, University of California (LL.B., 1961). Associate Editor, California Law Review, 1960-1961. *Member:* State Bar of California. **PRACTICE AREAS:** Construction Law; Construction Litigation; Business Litigation; Alternative Dispute Resolution.

### ASSOCIATES

**DAVID C. ROMYN,** born San Francisco, California, May 5, 1961; admitted to bar, 1989, California. *Education:* University of California at Berkeley (B.A., 1984); Hastings College of the Law (J.D., cum laude, 1989). Recipient, American Jurisprudence Award, Criminal Law. *Member:* State Bar of California; American Bar Association. **PRACTICE AREAS:** Construction Litigation; Construction Defects.

**BARRY J. JENSEN,** born Livonia, Michigan, February 21, 1963; admitted to bar, 1989, California. *Education:* Wayne State University (B.A., 1985); University of Michigan (J.D., 1988). *Member:* Orange County (Member, Sections on Construction Law; Business Litigation) and American (Member, Public Contract Law Section) Bar Associations; State Bar of California. (Resident, Santa Ana Office). **PRACTICE AREAS:** Construction Litigation; Public Contract Law (State and Federal); General Business Litigation; Conflicts/Interstate Litigation; Appeals.

**W. JEFFREY BURCH,** born Clovis, New Mexico, May 4, 1964; admitted to bar, 1991, California; 1992, U.S. District Court, Central and Southern Districts of California. *Education:* Colorado State University (B.A., magna cum laude, 1987); Hastings College of Law (J.D., 1991). Phi Alpha Delta. *Member:* Los Angeles County and Wilshire (Member, Board of Governors) Bar Associations; State Bar of California. **PRACTICE AREAS:** General Business Litigation; Construction; Construction Defect.

**ANDREW W. HAWTHORNE,** born Van Nuys, California, September 6, 1963; admitted to bar, 1989, California and U.S. District Court, Central District of California. *Education:* Occidental College (A.B. in psychology, 1985); Loyola University of Los Angeles (J.D., 1989). St. Thomas More

*(This Listing Continued)*

## PROFESSIONAL BIOGRAPHIES

Law Honor Society. Recipient, American Jurisprudence Award for Criminal Procedure. *Member:* Los Angeles County and American Bar Associations; State Bar of California. **PRACTICE AREAS:** Construction Law; Business Litigation.

**STEPHEN L. DUBIN,** born Milwaukee, Wisconsin, May 30, 1963; admitted to bar, 1992, California and U.S. District Court, Central District of California. *Education:* University of Michigan (B.A., 1985); Loyola University (J.D., 1992). *Member:* Wilshire, Los Angeles County and American Bar Associations; State Bar of California. **PRACTICE AREAS:** Business Litigation; Construction Law; Business Law; Corporate Law.

**ERICA S. BEHRENS,** born Los Angeles, California, October 21, 1969; admitted to bar, 1995, California and U.S. District Court, Central District of California. *Education:* University of California at Berkeley (B.A., 1992); University of California, Hastings College of the Law (J.D., 1994). Judicial Extern to the Honorable Arthur W. Greenwald, U.S. Bankruptcy Court, Central District of California, 1994. *Member:* Wilshire, Los Angeles County and American Bar Associations; California State Bar. **LANGUAGES:** Spanish. **PRACTICE AREAS:** Construction Law; Business Litigation; Business Law; Corporate Law.

*OF COUNSEL*

**DARRELL P. MCCRORY,** born Milwaukee, Wisconsin, June 21, 1922; admitted to bar, 1949, California. *Education:* University of Wisconsin (Ph.B., 1946); Stanford University (LL.B., 1949). Phi Alpha Delta. Author: "The Legal Requirements for the Production of Documents in California," Los Angeles Bar Journal, 1953. Deputy City Attorney, Criminal Prosecutor, 1949-1953. Deputy City Attorney, Department, Water and Power, 1953-1955. *Member:* The State Bar of California; American Bar Association (Member, Section of Public Contract Law).

All Partners and Associates are Members of the Los Angeles County Bar Association.

REPRESENTATIVE CLIENTS: Granite Construction Co.; J.F. Shea Co., Inc.; Zurn Industries; Environmental Industries; Taft Electric Company; C.A. Rasmussen, Inc.; North Pacific Lumber Co.; Owl Rock Products; Kajima Development Corporation; DMJM; Vidal Sassoon Salons and Academies; Victor Valley Water District.

### MICHAEL B. MONTGOMERY
*A LAW CORPORATION*

**LOS ANGELES, CALIFORNIA**

(See El Monte)

Civil and Trial Practice in State and Federal Courts. Eminent Domain, Municipal Bond, Community Development, Municipal and Real Property Law, Gaming Law.

### F. BENTLEY MOONEY, JR.
*A LAW CORPORATION*

**LOS ANGELES, CALIFORNIA**

(See North Hollywood)

Practice Limited to Business Law, Estate Planning and Probate Law.

### CHRISTOPHER M. MOORE & ASSOCIATES
*A LAW CORPORATION*

**LOS ANGELES, CALIFORNIA**

(See Torrance)

Family Law, Estate Planning, Trust and Probate Law.

### MOORE, RUTTER & EVANS

**LOS ANGELES, CALIFORNIA**

(See Long Beach)

*General Civil, Maritime and Trial Practice in all State and Federal Courts, Appellate Practice, Automobile Negligence, Business Torts, Casualty Defense, Commercial Litigation, Construction Defect Litigation, Environmental Torts, Estate Planning, Insurance Coverage, Inverse Condemnation, Law Enforce-*
*(This Listing Continued)*

## CALIFORNIA—LOS ANGELES

*ment Defense, Municipality Defense, Premises Liability, Products Liability and Wrongful Termination.*

### MICHAEL R. MORALES

**LOS ANGELES, CALIFORNIA**

(See Torrance)

*Personal Injury.*

### MORGAN, LEWIS & BOCKIUS LLP
*801 SOUTH GRAND AVENUE*

**LOS ANGELES, CALIFORNIA 90017-4615**

Telephone: 213-612-2500
Telex: 67-3270
Fax: 213-612-2554
Email: postmaster@mlb.com
URL: http://www.mlb.com

*Philadelphia, Pennsylvania Office:* 2000 One Logan Square, 19103-6993. Telephone: 215-963-5000. Fax: 215-963-5299.

*Washington, D.C. Office:* 1800 M Street, N.W., 20036-5869. Telephone: 202-467-7000. Fax: 202-467-7176.

*New York, New York Office:* 101 Park Avenue, 10178-0060. Telephone: 212-309-6000. Fax: 212-309-6273.

*Miami, Florida Office:* 5300 First Union Financial Center, 200 South Biscayne Boulevard, 33131-2339. Telephone: 305-579-0300. Fax: 305-579-0321.

*Harrisburg, Pennsylvania Office:* One Commerce Square, 417 Walnut Street, 17101-1904. Telephone: 717-237-4000. Fax: 717-237-4004.

*Pittsburgh, Pennsylvania Office:* One Oxford Centre, 301 Grant Street, 32nd Floor, 15219-6401. Telephone: 412-560-3300. Fax: 412-560-3399.

*Princeton, New Jersey Office:* 100 Overlook Center, 08540-7814. Telephone: 609-520-6600. Fax: 609-520-6639.

*London, England Office:* Morgan, Lewis & Bockius, 4 Carlton Gardens, Pall Mall, London SW1Y 5AA. Telephone: 44-171-839-1677. Fax: 44-171-839-3650.

*Frankfurt, Germany Office:* Guiollettstraβe 54, Frankfurt/Main 60325. Telephone: (49-69) 71 40 07-0. Fax: (49-69) 71 40 07-10.

*Brussels, Belgium Office:* 7 Rue Guimard, B-1040. Telephone: 32-2/512.55.01. Fax: 32-2/512.58.88.

*Tokyo, Japan Office:* Yurakucho Denki Building S-556, 7-1 Yurakucho 1-chome, Chiyoda-ku, Tokyo 100. Telephone: 81-03-3216-2500. Fax: 81-03-3216-2501.

*Singapore Office:* 80 Raffles Place, #14-20 UOB Plaza 2, Singapore, 048624. Telephone: 65-438-2188. Fax: 65-230-7100.

*General Practice.*

*MEMBERS OF FIRM IN LOS ANGELES*

**JEFFREY N. BROWN,** born May 30, 1957; admitted to bar, 1982, California. *Education:* University of California, Los Angeles (B.A., 1979); Loyola Law School of Los Angeles (J.D., 1982). **Email:** brow1116@mlb.com

**ANTHONY CIASULLI,** born April 14, 1957; admitted to bar, 1982, California. *Education:* Haverford College (B.A., 1979); University of California School, at Los Angeles (J.D., 1982). Co-Author, "There's Gold in Those Greens", Developments, October, 1989; "Lowering the Golf Boom on No-Equity Member", Club Director, October, 1990. **Email:** cias1324@mlb.com

**CYNTHIA M. COHEN,** born September 5, 1945; admitted to bar, 1971, New York; 1975, U.S. Supreme Court; 1980, California. *Education:* Cornell University (A.B., 1967); New York University (J.D., 1970). Pomeroy Scholar. Member, Order of the Coif. Recipient, American Jurisprudence Awards and New York University Founder's Day Award. Member, New York University Law Review, 1968. Chairperson, Class Action Committee, 1979, New York State Bar Association. Member, Financial Lawyers Conference. *Member:* The Association of the Bar of the City of New York (Member, Committee on Trade Regulation, 1976-1979); Los Angeles County Bar Association (Member, Sections on: Commercial Law and Bankruptcy and Antitrust; Member, Bankruptcy Committee); American Bar Association (Member, Sections on: Litigation and Antitrust Law; Section 7, Clayton Act Committee and Private Antitrust Litigation Commit-
*(This Listing Continued)*

CAA997B

**MORGAN, LEWIS & BOCKIUS LLP,** Los Angeles—
*Continued*

tee); State Bar of California (Member, Sections on: Antitrust Law; Business Law); Association of Business Trial Lawyers. *Email:* cohe2505@mlb.com

**LINDA VAN WINKLE DEACON,** born December 14, 1948; admitted to bar, 1974, California. *Education:* Whitman College (A.B., 1970); University of Chicago (J.D., 1973). Associate Editor, University of Chicago Law Review, 1971-1973. Visiting Associate Professor of Law, University of Chicago, 1982. *Email:* deac1126@mlb.com

**LOYD P. DERBY,** born August 4, 1939; admitted to bar, 1967, California; 1988, Nevada. *Education:* University of California, Berkeley (A.B., 1963; J.D., 1966). Order of the Coif. Member, California Law Review. Member, Panel of Arbitrators: Pacific Stock Exchange; National Association of Securities Dealers, Inc.; Los Angeles County Superior Court; Clark County, Nevada District Court. *Email:* derb2556@mlb.com

**DOUGLAS A. DODDS,** born August 1, 1950; admitted to bar, 1976, California; 1983, New York. *Education:* University of California at Berkeley (A.B., 1972; Masters in City and Regional Planning, 1977); University of California at Davis (J.D., 1976). *Member:* New York State and American Bar Associations; State Bar of California. *Email:* dodd1320@mlb.com

**PETER BROWN DOLAN,** born March 25, 1939; admitted to bar, 1967, California; 1986, U.S. Supreme Court. *Education:* United States Naval Academy (B.S., 1960); University of Southern California (J.D., 1967). Deputy Los Angeles County Counsel, 1967-1969. *Email:* dola1177@mlb.com

**WILLIAM D. ELLIS,** born May 6, 1957; admitted to bar, 1982, California. *Education:* Occidental College (A.B., 1979); University of Michigan (J.D., 1982). *Email:* elli2612@mbl.com

**DAVID G. ELLSWORTH,** born January 20, 1941; admitted to bar, 1966, California; 1982, District of Columbia. *Education:* University of Southern California (B.S., 1962; LL.B., 1965). Co-Author: "The Law and Business of Resort Development," Clarke Boardman, 1987; "The Golf Development Life Cycle: Legal Issues and Strategies", Developments, April/May, 1992; "An American Developer's Guide To International Real Estate Investment", Vacation Industry Review, Spring, 1992; "Mexico Welcomes Foreign Tourist Development", Urban Land, August, 1991; "Master Planned Golf Communities," Golf Enterprise Europe, October, 1992; "Impact of the New Foreign Investment Law on Real Estate Investment and Development," Latin American Law and Business Report, June 1994; "Inside the Mexican Casino Debate," International Gaming & Wagering Business, February & March, 1996. Member, Board of Directors, American Resort Development Association, 1974-1976; 1978-1987. Chairman and Member, Board of Commissions of Los Angeles County Housing Authority, 1978-1985. Member, Executive Group, Urban Land Institute, 1976—. *Email:* ells1330@mlb.com

**WILLIAM J. EMANUEL,** born October 31, 1938; admitted to bar, 1963, Nebraska; 1965, California; 1976, U.S. Supreme Court. *Education:* Marquette University (A.B., 1960); Georgetown University (J.D., 1963). Co-Author: "California Employment Law," Merchants and Manufacturers Association, 1989. Chairman, Labor Law Section, Los Angeles County Bar Association, 1983-1984. Chairman, Southern California Labor Law Symposium, 1980-1981. Member, National Labor Relations Board Advisory Committee, 1994—. Member, Federal Mediation and Conciliation Service Labor-Management Advisory Committee for the Health Care Industry, 1980-1983. Member, Labor Relations Advisory Committee, American Hospital Association, 1974—. *Email:* eman2550@mlb.com

**STEPHEN R. ENGLISH,** born November 25, 1946; admitted to bar, 1975, California. *Education:* University of California, Los Angeles (A.B., 1971); Harvard University (J.D., 1975). Co-Author: "Reducing Delays in Civil Cases," Los Angeles Lawyer, December, 1987. President, Board of Directors, Public Counsel, the Public Interest Law Office of the Los Angeles and Beverly Hills Bar Associations, 1988-1989. Member: Board of Trustees, Los Angeles County Bar Association, 1990-1992; Executive Committee, Litigation Section, Los Angeles County Bar Association; Panel of Arbitrators, American Arbitration Association; NASD Board of Arbitrators. *Member:* Association of Business Trial Lawyers. *Email:* engl2536@mlb.com

**BARRY V. FREEMAN,** born April 18, 1938; admitted to bar, 1963, California. *Education:* University of California at Los Angeles (A.B., 1959; J.D., 1962). American Bar Association, Chair, Loan Documentation Sub Committee on Business Law Section, 1994—. Business Law Section, State Bar of California, Chairperson, Agribusiness Committee, 1994-1995; Vice Chair, Debtor/Credit Relations and Bankruptcy Committee, 1978-1979; Instructor, California Bar Continuing Education of the Bar: Bankruptcy Reorganizations, Debtor-Creditor Rights, Secured Transactions, 1967-1976. Banking Law Institute, Chairperson, Professional Education Programs; Member, Advisory Council, 1985—; Permanent Faculty Member, Banking Law Institute for presentations on Workouts, Loan Restructures, Bankruptcy and Loan Documentation. Faculty Member: Southern Methodist University School of Law and Southeastern Graduate School of Banking, Loan Workout, 1989—. Member, Board of Governors, Financial Lawyers Conference, 1979-1981; Member, Executive Committee, American Jewish Committee, Los Angeles. Member, American College of Commercial Finance Lawyers. *Email:* free1157@mlb.com

**JEFFREY L. GRAUSAM,** born September 21, 1943; admitted to bar, 1969, California; 1970, New York; 1972, U.S. Tax Court; 1981, U.S. Supreme Court. *Education:* Wesleyan University (B.A., 1965); University of Chicago (J.D., 1970); New York University (LL.M. Taxation, 1975). Law Clerk to Chief Justice Roger J. Traynor, California Supreme Court, 1968-1969. Author: "Current Developments in Partnership Taxation," 10 U.S.C. Major Tax Planning 16 (1988). Lecturer in Law, University of Southern California Law School, 1986-1987. Chairman, Pass-Through Entities Committee, Taxation Section, Los Angeles County Bar Association, 1994-1995. *Email:* grau1172@mlb.com

**JOHN F. HARTIGAN,** born June 16, 1950; admitted to bar, 1975, District of Columbia; 1984, California. *Education:* University of Illinois (B.S., in Finance, 1972); Georgetown University (J.D., 1975). Attorney, 1975-1978, Branch Chief, 1978-1981 and Assistant Director, 1981-1984, Division of Enforcement, Securities and Exchange Commission. Fmr. Vice Chair, Treasurer and Member, Executive Committee, Business Law Section, State Bar of California. Chairman, Education Committee, Business Law Section, State Bar of California, 1988-1990. Member, Executive Committee, Los Angeles County Bar Association. Editor, 1986 Legislation and Other Recent Developments of Interest to California Business Lawyers for Business Law Section of the State Bar of California. *Email:* hart2630@mlb.com

**J. DEAN HELLER,** born December 19, 1944; admitted to bar, 1969, District of Columbia; 1973, California; 1982, U.S. Supreme Court. *Education:* Duke University (B.A., 1966); Yale University (LL.B., 1969). *Email:* hell1068@mlb.com

**JOSEPH E. HERMAN,** born September 29, 1942; admitted to bar, 1966, Illinois; 1974, California. *Education:* Harvard University (A.B., 1963; LL.B., 1966). *Email:* herm1049@mlb.com

**KATHLEEN C. JOHNSON,** born October 19, 1949; admitted to bar, 1982, California. *Education:* University of California, Riverside (B.A., 1971); University of California, Los Angeles (J.D., 1982). *Email:* john2608@mlb.com

**MICHAEL J. A. KARLIN,** born August 27, 1952; admitted to bar, 1977, Solicitor of the Supreme Court of England and Wales; 1980, California. *Education:* Trinity College, University of Cambridge (B.A., 1973; M.A., 1977). Author: "The Portfolio Interest Exemption," Taxation of International Operations, ¶5014 and 5015 Warren, Gorham & Lamont, 1994; "Tax Planning for Doing Business in Mexico," How to Profit under NAFTA, Business & Law Reports, 1994. *Email:* karl2614@mlb.com

**RAYMOND R. KEPNER,** born August 3, 1952; admitted to bar, 1977, Ohio; 1979, California. *Education:* Indiana State University (B.A., 1974); University of Michigan (J.D., 1977). *Email:* kepn2652@mlb.com

**JACK CHI-HUSAN LIU,** born Taipei, Taiwan, Republic of China, June 2, 1958; admitted to bar, 1988, District of Columbia; 1990, California. *Education:* National Taiwan University Law School (LL.B., 1981); University of Pennsylvania Law School (LL.M., 1984); University of Chicago Law School (M.C.L., 1985). *LANGUAGES:* Chinese.

**STEPHEN M. LOWRY,** born December 19, 1944; admitted to bar, 1980, Pennsylvania; 1981, California and Nevada. *Education:* Willamette University (B.A., 1966); University of Pennsylvania (Ph.D., 1974; J.D., 1980). Law Clerk to Judge Elmer Gunderson, Chief Justice, Nevada Supreme Court, 1980. *Email:* lowr2538@mlb.com

**C. G. GORDON MARTIN,** born August 31, 1950; admitted to bar, 1975, California; 1980, U.S. Supreme Court. *Education:* Occidental College (A.B., 1972); Duke University (J.D., 1975). *Email:* mart1092@mlb.com

**ANDREA SHERIDAN ORDIN,** born January 4, 1940; admitted to bar, 1966, California. *Education:* University of California, Los Angeles (B.A., 1963); University of California Law School (LL.B., 1965). Adjunct Professor, Law, University of California at Los Angeles, 1981-1982. Chief Assis-

*(This Listing Continued)*

tant Attorney General, State of California, Division of Public Rights, 1983-1991. U.S. Attorney, Central District of California, 1977-1981. Assistant District Attorney, 1975-1977. President, Los Angeles County Bar Association, 1991-1992. Director, Los Angeles County Bar Association, 1973-1975. Deputy Attorney General, State of California, 1965-1972. **Email:** ordi1090@mlb.com

**ANDREW C. PETERSON,** born February 26, 1941; admitted to bar, 1972, California. *Education:* Wesleyan University (A.B., 1963); University of Chicago (J.D., 1971). Author: *California OSHA Compliance Handbook*, Government Institutes, Inc., 1992. **Email:** pete1032@mlb.com

**MARK S. RAPAPORT,** born July 31, 1947; admitted to bar, 1973, Wisconsin; 1974, New York; 1981, California. *Education:* University of Wisconsin (B.A., 1968; J.D., 1973). Certified Specialist, Probate, Estate Planning and Trust Law, California Board of Legal Specialization. **Email:** rapa1102@mlb.com

**ROBERT D. REDFORD,** born August 20, 1932; admitted to bar, 1957, California. *Education:* Stanford University (B.A., 1954; LL.B., 1956). **Email:** redf2588@mlb.com

**PAUL A. RICHLER,** born March 4, 1946; admitted to bar, 1974, California. *Education:* McGill University; Osgoode Hall Law School (LL.B., 1970); London School of Economics and Political Science, London, England (LL.M., 1971). **Email:** rich1104@mlb.com

**ANTHONY RUSSO,** born April 19, 1950; admitted to bar, 1980, California. *Education:* California State University, Northridge (B.A., 1972; M.A., 1973); University of California, Los Angeles (Ph.D., 1979); Loyola Law School of Los Angeles (J.D., 1980). **Email:** russ2626@mlb.com

**JOHN D. SHULTZ,** born October 9, 1939; admitted to bar, 1968, New York; 1978, California. *Education:* University of Arizona (A.B., 1964); University of California, Berkeley (J.D., 1967). **Email:** shul2602@mlb.com

**FRANK H. SMITH, JR.,** born August 3, 1943; admitted to bar, 1969, California. *Education:* University of Notre Dame (B.A., 1965; J.D., 1968). **Email:** smit1016@mlb.com

**ROSEANN C. STEVENSON,** born June 15, 1954; admitted to bar, 1979, California. *Education:* Rutgers College (B.A., 1976); University of Southern California (J.D., 1979). **Email:** stev2566@mlb.com

**ANNE E. STONE,** born October 3, 1961; admitted to bar, 1986, California. *Education:* Cornell University (A.B., 1983); University of Michigan (J.D., 1986). **Email:** ston1054@mlb.com

**THOMAS L. TAYLOR, III,** born San Antonio, Texas, April 15, 1946; admitted to bar, 1973, Texas; 1977, New York; 1982, California. *Education:* Cornell University (A.B., 1968); University of Texas (J.D., 1972). **PRACTICE AREAS:** Litigation of Securities, Commodities and Corporate Matters; Securities and Commodities Regulatory and Enforcement Matters. **Email:** tayl2522@mlb.com

**RANDOLPH C. VISSER,** born August 3, 1949; admitted to bar, 1975, California. *Education:* Northwestern University (B.A., 1971); University of California, Los Angeles (J.D., 1974). Lecturer in Law, Clinical Program, Trial Advocacy, University of California at Los Angeles Law School, 1978-1980. UCLA Journal of Environmental Law & Policy Advisory Board Member. Author: "Green Light for L.A. Mass Transit," 6 L.A. Lawyer 35, May, 1983. Co-author, "Sometimes All You Need is the Air That You Breathe," Orange County Lawyer, June, 1993. **Email:** viss2632@mlb.com

**JAMES WAWRO,** born August 27, 1944; admitted to bar, 1969, New York; 1973, California. *Education:* LeMoyne College (A.B., 1966); Cornell University (J.D., 1969). Order of the Coif. Author: "A Primer on Representing International Parties in United States Litigation," International Litigation Quarterly, December 1986. Columnist, Los Angeles Daily Journal, "Creditors' Claims", 1987; "Conflicts of Jurisdiction Model Act," adopted in Connecticut, 1991. Panelist: Los Angeles County Bar Association, "Litigating International Disputes in U.S. Courts," March, 1992; Practice Law Institute, "Lender Liability Litigation," 1990-1992. Panelist, Banking Law Institute, "Lender Liability -- 1992 Update"; White Paper, "Lender Liability - 1994 Update." Chairman, International Litigation Committee, International Law and Practice Section, American Bar Association, (1990—); Council Member, (1994—). **Email:** wawr2698@mlb.com

**MICHAEL L. WOLFRAM,** born November 24, 1945; admitted to bar, 1971, Texas; 1973, California; 1979, U.S. Supreme Court. *Education:* Harvard University (A.B., 1967); Columbia University and University of Texas (J.D., 1971). Law Clerk to Hon. John C. Godbold, U.S. Court of Appeals, Fifth Circuit, 1971-1972. Co-Author: "California Employment Law: A Guide To California's Laws Regulating Employment in the Private Sector,"

*(This Listing Continued)*

Merchants and Manufacturers Association, 1989. **Email:** wolf2570@mlb.com

**KENNETH B. WRIGHT,** born June 5, 1934; admitted to bar, 1961, California; 1979, U.S. Supreme Court. *Education:* Pomona College (B.A., 1956); Stanford University (J.D., 1960). Chairman, 1977-1981, Board of Editors, American Bar Journal; Division Director, 1977-1981 and Member of Council, 1981-1987, Section of Litigation. Chairman, ABA Standing Committee on Association Communications 1987-1988. **Email:** wrig2540@mlb.com

## *OF COUNSEL IN LOS ANGELES*

**JOHN S. BATTENFELD,** admitted to bar, 1985, California. *Education:* Haverford College (B.A., 1981); University of California, Los Angeles (J.D., 1985). **Email:** batt1018@mlb.com

**RICHARD W. ESTERKIN,** born September 6, 1951; admitted to bar, 1976, California. *Education:* Claremont Mens College (B.A., 1973); University of California at Los Angeles (J.D., 1976). Author, "Balance Due Courts Continue to Struggle with the Status Accorded Environmental Clean up Costs in Bankruptcy Proceedings," Los Angeles Lawyer Vol. 18, No. 5 (August 1995). Judge Pro Tempore, Los Angeles Municipal Court, 1982—. Settlement Officer, Los Angeles County Superior Court, 1988—. Arbitrator and Mediator, Los Angeles County Superior Court, 1989—. Mediator, United States Bankruptcy Court, Central District of California. **Email:** este1163@mlb.com

**Y. PETER KIM,** born October 13, 1947; admitted to bar, 1978, Pennsylvania; 1982, California. *Education:* Seoul National University (B.A., 1972); Temple University School of Law (J.D., 1978). **Email:** kim-2661@mlb.com

**RICHARD J. MAIRE, JR.,** admitted to bar, 1983, California. *Education:* University of California, Los Angeles (B.A., 1980); University of Southern California (J.D., 1983). Co-Author: Chapter 13, *Pre-Litigation Remedies* and Chapter 14, *Litigation Remedies*, in Sales and Leases in California Commercial Law Practice, (CEB, 1993). **Email:** mair1134@mlb.com

**MICHAEL A. VACCHIO,** admitted to bar, 1983, California. *Education:* Whittier College (B.A., 1980); University of California, Hastings College of the Law (J.D., 1983). **Email:** vacc1150@mlb.com

## *COUNSEL IN LOS ANGELES*

**EDWARD C. CAZIER, JR.,** born December 25, 1924; admitted to bar, 1952, California. *Education:* University of California, Berkeley (A.B., 1945); University of Paris; University of Aix-Marseille; University of Southern California (LL.B., 1952); New York University (LL.M., in Taxation, 1956). Trustee, Practicing Law Institute, 1987—. **Email:** cazi1084@mlb.com

## *ASSOCIATES IN LOS ANGELES*

**EDWARD T. ATTANASIO,** admitted to bar, 1985, California. *Education:* Cornell University (B.S., 1981); Stanford University (J.D., 1985). **Email:** atta1174@mlb.com

**ANDRE Y. BATES,** admitted to bar, 1995, California. *Education:* United States Naval Academy (B.S., 1982); University of California School of the Law (J.D., 1995). **Email:** bate1038@mlb.com

**MAGARA LEE CROSBY,** admitted to bar, 1982, California. *Education:* University of California, Riverside (B.A., 1974); University of California, Los Angeles (J.D., 1982). **Email:** cros2694@mlb.com

**LISA ANN DETRICK,** admitted to bar, 1983, Texas; 1990, California. *Education:* University of North Carolina at Chapel Hill (B.A., 1980); Vanderbilt University School of Law (J.D., 1983). **Email:** detr1072@mlb.com

**SUSAN R. ESSEX,** admitted to bar, 1990, California. *Education:* University of Redlands (B.A., 1985); Georgetown University (J.D., M.S.F.S., 1990). **Email:** esse2668@mlb.com

**ANN HALEY FROMHOLZ,** admitted to bar, 1994, California. *Education:* Dartmouth College (B.A., 1990); University of Southern California (J.D., 1994). **Email:** from2575@mlb.com

**STEVEN J. GLOUBERMAN,** admitted to bar, 1995, California. *Education:* University of California at Los Angeles (B.A., 1991); Loyola Law School (J.D., 1995). **Email:** glou1014@mlb.com

**KEITH D. GROSSMAN,** admitted to bar, 1987, California. *Education:* Tufts University (B.A., 1984); New York University (J.D., 1987). **Email:** gros1080@mlb.com

**ROBERT JON HENDRICKS,** admitted to bar, 1995, California. *Education:* University of California (A.B., 1990); Boalt Hall School of Law, University of California (J.D., 1995). **Email:** hend2692@mlb.com

*(This Listing Continued)*

**MORGAN, LEWIS & BOCKIUS LLP, Los Angeles—**
*Continued*

**J. MICHAEL JACK,** admitted to bar, 1986, California. *Education:* California State University, Northridge (B.S., 1983); Georgetown University (J.D., 1986). *Email:* jack1058@mlb.com

**WENDY K. KILBRIDE,** admitted to bar, 1994, California. *Education:* California State University, Northridge (B.A., 1989); Georgetown University Law Center (J.D., 1994). *Email:* kilb1106@mlb.com

**JEFFREY JAMES LEWIS,** admitted to bar, 1990, California. *Education:* Carleton College (B.A., 1985); Boalt Hall School of Law, University of California (J.D., 1989). *Email:* lewi1358@mlb.com

**MICHAEL C. LIEB,** admitted to bar, 1986, California. *Education:* Emory University (B.A., 1983); University of Michigan (J.D., 1986). *Email:* lieb1062@mlb.com

**DEREK B. LIPSCOMBE,** admitted to bar, 1994, New Jersey and Pennsylvania (Not admitted in California). *Education:* Northwestern University (B.S.M.S., 1988); University of Michigan School of Law (J.D., 1994). *Email:* lips7287@mlb.com

**DAVID D. MARSHALL,** admitted to bar, 1989, California. *Education:* Occidental College (A.B., 1985); Duke University (J.D., 1989). *Email:* mars1138@mlb.com

**ROBERT D. MING,** admitted to bar, 1996, California. *Education:* Azusa Pacific University (B.A., 1992); Pepperdine University (J.D., 1995). *Email:* ming2654@mlb.com

**STEVEN J. OPPENHEIMER,** admitted to bar, 1986, California. *Education:* Miami University (A.B., 1966); New Mexico Highlands University (M.S., 1978 ); University of New Mexico (J.D., 1986). *Email:* oppe2672@mlb.com

**RAUL PEREZ,** born June 18, 1968; admitted to bar, 1994, California. *Education:* Harvard College (B.A., 1990); Harvard Law School (J.D., 1994). *Email:* pere2519@mlb.com

**RANDI PAULA PERRY,** admitted to bar, 1993, California and Florida. *Education:* University of Florida (B.S.B.A., 1989; J.D., 1992). *Email:* perr1132@mlb.com

**MARK W. PUGSLEY,** admitted to bar, 1994, California. *Education:* University of Utah (B.S., 1991); Duke University (M.A., J.D., 1994). *Email:* pugs2679@mlb.com

**JEFFREY M. REISNER,** admitted to bar, 1989, California; 1990, District of Columbia. *Education:* Cornell University (B.S., 1985); New York University (M.B.A., 1989; J.D., 1989). *Email:* reis2507@mlb.com

**DAWN PATRICE ROSS,** admitted to bar, 1990, California. *Education:* Wayne State University (B.S., 1987); Harvard Law School (J.D., 1990). *Email:* ross2655@mlb.com

**NANCY M. SAUNDERS,** admitted to bar, 1983, California. *Education:* Pomona College (B.A., 1980); University of California, Hastings College of Law (J.D., 1983). *Email:* saun2670@mlb.com

**THEODORE G. SPANOS,** admitted to bar, 1986, California. *Education:* University of California, Los Angeles (B.A., 1983); University of California, Hastings College of the Law (J.D., 1986). *Email:* span1144@mlb.com

**STEVEN W. SPECTOR,** admitted to bar, 1991, California. *Education:* University of Pennsylvania (B.A., 1987; J.D., 1991). *Email:* spec1352@mlb.com

**ERIC M. STEINERT,** admitted to bar, 1993, California. *Education:* Rice University (B.A., 1990); Boalt Hall School of Law, University of California (J.D., 1993). *Email:* stei1048@mlb.com

**JAMES R. STEWART,** admitted to bar, 1982, California. *Education:* California State University, San Jose (B.A., 1968); University of California, Los Angeles (J.D., 1982). *Email:* stew1146@mlb.com

**MARK J. STUBINGTON,** admitted to bar, 1992, California. *Education:* University of California at Los Angeles (B.A., 1988); University of Michigan (J.D., 1992). *Email:* stub1026@mlb.com

**ADAM TREIGER,** admitted to bar, 1994, California. *Education:* University of California, Los Angeles (B.A., 1991); Georgetown University Law Center (J.D., 1994). *Email:* trei1182@mlb.com

*(This Listing Continued)*

**JASON HARUO WILSON,** admitted to bar, 1989, California. *Education:* Pomona College (B.A., 1984); Harvard Law School (J.D., 1987). Law Clerk to Hon. Diarmuid O'Scannlain, U.S. Court of Appeals for the Ninth Circuit, 1987-1988. Law Clerk to Hon. Thomas Tang, U.S. Court of Appeals for the Ninth Circuit, 1989-1990. *Email:* wils1076@mlb.com

**JOSEPH S. WU,** admitted to bar, 1990, California. *Education:* University of California at Irvine (B.A., 1986); University of California at Los Angeles (J.D., 1990). *Email:* wu--2648@mlb.com

Members of the Firm, Counsel, Of Counsel and Associates in Philadelphia, Harrisburg and Pittsburgh, Pennsylvania, Washington, D.C., New York, New York, Miami, Florida, Princeton, New Jersey, London, England, Brussels, Belgium, Frankfurt/Main, Germany, Tokyo, Japan and Singapore are listed in the Biographical Section respectively.

## DAVID J. MORRIS

1900 AVENUE OF THE STARS, SUITE 2430
**LOS ANGELES, CALIFORNIA 90067**
Telephone: 310-277-6244
Telecopier: 310-556-2366

*General Civil Trial Practice, Business, Corporate and Real Estate Law.*

**DAVID J. MORRIS,** born Helena, Montana, February 6, 1941; admitted to bar, 1966, California and U.S. District Court, Central and Northern Districts of California. *Education:* University of Montana (B.A. with honors, 1963); Boalt Hall, University of California at Berkeley (J.D., 1966). Phi Delta Phi. Judge Pro Tem, Los Angeles Municipal Court, 1983—. Arbitrator, Los Angeles Superior Court. *Member:* Los Angeles County (Member, Sections on: Litigation; Real Property; Corporations; International Law) and American (Member, Litigation Section) Bar Associations; The State Bar of California (Member, Sections on: Business Law and Real Estate Litigation); Association of Business Trial Lawyers.

REFERENCE: Bank of America (Century City Branch).

## MORRIS, POLICH & PURDY

Established in 1969

1055 WEST SEVENTH STREET
SUITE 2400
**LOS ANGELES, CALIFORNIA 90017**
Telephone: 213-891-9100
Facsimile: 213-488-1178

*Orange County Office:* 500 North State College Boulevard, 11th Floor, Orange, California. Telephone: 714-939-1100. Facsimile: 714-939-9261.
*San Diego County Office:* 501 W. Broadway, Suite 500, San Diego, California. Telephone: 619-557-0404. Facsimile: 619-557-0460.

*General Civil Trial and Appellate Practice in all State and Federal Courts. Construction Law, Insurance Law, Environmental Law, Products Liability, Architect and Engineer Liability, Government Tort Liability, Police Civil Liability, Pharmaceutical and Medical Device Liability, Toxic Tort Litigation and Commercial Litigation.*

### MEMBERS OF FIRM

**JEFFREY S. BARRON,** born Pasadena, California, October 4, 1949; admitted to bar, 1975, California. *Education:* U.C. Irvine (B.S., 1972); U.C.-L.A. (J.D., 1975).

**ANTHONY G. BRAZIL,** born Mallow, Ireland, October 2, 1953; admitted to bar, 1978, California. *Education:* University of Southern California (B.S., cum laude, 1975); Loyola University of Los Angeles (J.D., 1978). Arbitrator and Court Appointed Referee, Los Angeles Superior Court.

**JAMES M. CHANTLAND,** born Los Angeles, California, September 3, 1955; admitted to bar, 1980, California. *Education:* University of Southern California (B.A., cum laude, 1977); Loyola University of Los Angeles (J.D., cum laude, 1980).

**MICHAEL T. COLLIAU,** born Inglewood, California, December 8, 1955; admitted to bar, 1985, California. *Education:* U.C. Berkeley; Oregon State University (B.S., 1979); University of Utah (J.D., 1984); University of Melbourne Law School, Melbourne, Australia. Staff Member, 1982-1983 and Administrative Editor, 1983-1984, Journal of Energy Law and Policy/-Journal of Contemporary Law.

**DOUGLAS J. COLLODEL,** born Milan, Italy, June 9, 1959; admitted to bar, 1984, California. *Education:* University of Notre Dame (A.B., 1980); McGeorge School of the Law (J.D., 1983).

*(This Listing Continued)*

**STEVEN M. CRANE,** born Denver, Colorado, March 17, 1956; admitted to bar, 1980, Colorado; 1983, California. *Education:* University of Colorado (B.A., 1977; J.D., 1980).

**CAROL ANN HUMISTON,** born Covina, California, May 19, 1954; admitted to bar, 1984, California. *Education:* California Polytechnic University (B.S., 1977); Loyola Marymount University (J.D., 1984).

**MARC S. KATZ,** born Los Angeles, California, January 10, 1957; admitted to bar, 1981, California. *Education:* U.C. San Diego (B.A., summa cum laude, 1978); University of California at Los Angeles (J.D., 1981). Phi Beta Kappa.

**THEODORE D. LEVIN,** born Denver, Colorado, November 29, 1957; admitted to bar, 1986, California. *Education:* University of Colorado at Boulder (B.S., 1980); U.C.F. (J.D., 1986). Comments Editor, University of San Francisco Law Review, 1985-1986. Registered Civil Engineer, 1983.

**WALTER J. LIPSMAN,** born Davenport, Iowa, October 19, 1952; admitted to bar, 1977, California. *Education:* U.C.L.A. (B.A., cum laude, 1974); Loyola University of Los Angeles (J.D., cum laude, 1977). Member, 1975-1976, Articles Editor, 1976-1977, Loyola Law Review. Arbitrator, Construction Industry, American Arbitration Association.

**LANDON MORRIS** (1904-1991).

**DEAN A. OLSON,** born Rockford, Illinois, January 20, 1961; admitted to bar, 1986, California; 1987, Arizona. *Education:* Arizona State University (B.S., 1983); Southwestern University (J.D., 1986).

**THEODORE P. POLICH, JR.,** born Los Angeles, California, February 2, 1935; admitted to bar, 1961, California. *Education:* Stanford University (B.A., 1956); University of Southern California (J.D., 1960). Deputy City Attorney, Los Angeles, 1961-1962. Arbitrator, Los Angeles County Superior Court, 1984—. *Member:* American Board of Trial Advocates.

**DOUGLAS C. PURDY,** born Los Angeles, California, April 28, 1944; admitted to bar, 1970, California. *Education:* U.C.L.A. (B.A., 1966; J.D., 1969). Deputy District Attorney, 1970-1971. Arbitrator, Los Angeles Superior Court, 1981—. Recipient, Wiley W. Manuel Pro Bono Award, 1991-1992. Director and President, Catholic Charities Community Development Corporation.

**DONALD L. RIDGE,** born Murray, Utah, June 18, 1960; admitted to bar, 1987, California. *Education:* Occidental College (A.B., in Economics and Psychology, 1982); University of Southern California (J.D., 1987).

**NICHOLAS M. WIECZOREK,** born Los Angeles, California, September 8, 1958; admitted to bar, 1983, California. *Education:* University of Southern California (B.A., magna cum laude, 1980); U.C.L.A. (J.D., 1983). Phi Beta Kappa. Senior Staff Member, UCLA Law Review, 1982-1983.

*ASSOCIATES*

**MICHAEL F. AVILA,** born Tucumán, Argentina, January 12, 1966; admitted to bar, 1992, California. *Education:* U.C.L.A. (B.A., cum laude, 1987); University of Southern California (J.D., 1991).

**MARK C. CARLSON,** born Ojai, California, May 28, 1968; admitted to bar, 1993, California. *Education:* California Lutheran University (B.A., 1990); Southwestern University (J.D., 1993). **PRACTICE AREAS:** Real Estate Law; Insurance Law; Commercial Law.

**PENELOPE D. DOHERTY,** born Arlington Heights, Illinois, April 15, 1967; admitted to bar, 1993, California. *Education:* Arizona State University (B.A., 1989); University of Arizona (J.D., 1993).

**PHILIP M. DREWRY,** born Roanoke, Virginia, April 16, 1965; admitted to bar, 1994, California. *Education:* University of Virginia (B.A., 1987); Pepperdine University (J.D., 1994).

**MICHAEL A. FOX,** born Wilmington, Delaware, October 6, 1964; admitted to bar, 1991, California. *Education:* Oklahoma State University (B.S., 1986); Seton Hall University (J.D., 1990).

**HAL D. GOLDFLAM,** born Van Nuys, California, January 8, 1970; admitted to bar, 1995, California. *Education:* University of California at Irvine (B.A., 1992); Southwestern University School of Law (J.D., 1995).

**BRIAN G. HANNEMAN,** born Banning, California, February 19, 1965; admitted to bar, 1993, California. *Education:* Embry-Riddle Aeronautical University (B.S., summa cum laude, 1989); Southwestern University (J.D., magna cum laude, 1993). Articles Editor, Southwestern Law Review.

**CARLA M. HOFFMAN,** born Long Beach, California, April 23, 1965; admitted to bar, 1991, California. *Education:* U.C.L.A. (B.S., 1987); Loyola Law School (J.D., cum laude, 1991).

*(This Listing Continued)*

**CHRISTINE A. HULL,** born Inglewood, California, February 9, 1968; admitted to bar, 1995, California. *Education:* Trinity College (B.A., 1990); Southwestern University (J.D., 1944).

**BETH A. KAHN,** born Pasadena, California, October 7, 1961; admitted to bar, 1988, California. *Education:* Occidental College (A.B., with departmental honors, 1983); Arizona State University (J.D., 1987).

**CYNTHIA L. KEENER,** born Teaneck, New Jersey, October 23, 1958; admitted to bar, 1988, Florida, California and Georgia. *Education:* Eastern Michigan University (B.B.E., magna cum laude, 1980); Emory University (J.D., 1987).

**KATHERINE E. KLIMA LINER,** born Prague, Czechoslovakia, July 23, 1964; admitted to bar, 1989, California. *Education:* University of Illinois (B.A., 1986; J.D., 1989).

**JASON LEVIN,** born Seattle, Washington, June 12, 1968; admitted to bar, 1992, Washington and California. *Education:* Pomona College (B.A., 1989); University of San Diego (J.D., 1992).

**CORRINE L. MIX,** born Bellflower, California, December 23, 1966; admitted to bar, 1993, California. *Education:* University of Southern California (B.A., 1989); University of Nebraska (J.D., 1992).

**MARILYN MUIR,** born Salt Lake City, Utah, October 17, 1963; admitted to bar, 1989, California. *Education:* Utah State University (B.S., 1985); University of Utah (J.D., 1989). Staff Member and Associate Editor Journal of Contemporary Law, 1989.

**RICHARD H. NAKAMURA JR.,** born Kailua, Hawaii, April 10, 1957; admitted to bar, 1982, District of Columbia; 1988, Virginia; 1990, California. *Education:* Syracuse University; U.C. Berkeley (B.A., cum laude, 1979); Antioch School of Law (J.D., 1982). Phi Beta Kappa.

**DERRICK H. NGUYEN,** born Saigon, Vietnam, April 29, 1964; admitted to bar, 1992, California. *Education:* University of California at Los Angeles (B.A., 1987); University of Southern California (J.D., 1991).

**DAVID B. OLSON,** born San Diego, California, February 13, 1962; admitted to bar, 1992, California. *Education:* California State University at Pomona (B.S., 1985); University of Southern California (J.D., 1992).

**LEE I. PETERSIL,** born Santa Monica, California, November 5, 1962; admitted to bar, 1988, California. *Education:* U.C.L.A. (B.A., 1985); Loyola Law School, Los Angeles (J.D., 1988). Member, Loyola Law Review.

**JANET M. RICHARDSON,** born Torrance, California, November 28, 1967; admitted to bar, 1992, California. *Education:* Northwestern University (B.A., 1989); University of San Diego (J.D., 1992).

**JEFFREY T. WOODRUFF,** born Worcester, Massachusetts, August 5, 1964; admitted to bar, 1990, California. *Education:* University of Colorado (B.A., 1987); Hastings College of the Law, (J.D., 1990).

**MEGAN S. WYNNE,** born Framingham, Massachusetts, June 17, 1968; admitted to bar, 1993, Massachusetts; 1996, California. *Education:* Johns Hopkins University (B.A., 1990); Boston College (J.D., 1993).

ORANGE COUNTY OFFICE
MEMBERS OF FIRM

Gary L. Hoffman; Randall F. Koenig; John P. Miller; Steven C. Miller.

ORANGE COUNTY OFFICE
ASSOCIATES

William M. Betley; Kay Ann Connelly; Stephen J. McGreevy; Daniel J. McNamee; Thierry R. Montoya; Kristen Kay Nelson; Carlos A. Prietto, III; Paul S. Sienski.

SAN DIEGO OFFICE
MEMBERS OF FIRM

Gary L. Jacobsen; Gerald P. Schneeweis.

SAN DIEGO OFFICE
ASSOCIATES

Diana L. Cuomo; William C. Getty; Mark Hellenkamp; Joseph C. Lavelle; Matthew J. Liedle; Margot Sanguinetti; William C. Wilson.

REPRESENTATIVE CLIENTS: Beech Aircraft Co.; Boyle Engineering Corp.; Commerce Construction Co.; Converse Consultants; Crown, Cork & Seal Co.; Daniel, Mann, Johnson & Mendenhall (DMJM); Dow Chemical Co.; Eli Lilly and Co.; Ellerbe Becket, Inc.; Holmes and Narver, Inc.; Hybritech, Inc.; Jacobs Engineering Group; James M. Montgomery Consulting Engineers, Inc.; League of Cities; LeRoy, Crandall & Associates; Leighton and Associates; Pepperdine University; Southern Pacific Transportation Co.; Vons Grocery Co.; West Bend

*(This Listing Continued)*

## MORRIS, POLICH & PURDY, Los Angeles—Continued

Co.; The Roman Catholic Archdiocese; Los Angeles County; Cities of Costa Mesa, Huntington Beach, Lancaster, Los Angeles, Ontario, Pomona and Redondo Beach; Lloyd's of London; Allstate Insurance Co.; CNA; Continental Insurance Co.; Design Professionals Insurance Co.; Farmers Insurance Co.; Harbor Insurance Co.; Safeco Insurance Co.; St. Paul Insurance Co.; Transamerica Insurance Co.; 20th Century Insurance Co.; Zurich American Insurance Co.

(For Complete Biographical data on all Personnel, See Professional Biographies at Orange County and San Diego, California)

## MORRISON & FOERSTER LLP

Established in 1883

555 WEST FIFTH STREET, SUITE 3500
LOS ANGELES, CALIFORNIA 90013-1024

Telephone: 213-892-5200
Facsimile: 213-892-5454
URL: http://www.mofo.com

*Other offices located in:* San Francisco, New York, Washington, D.C., London, Brussels, Hong Kong, Tokyo, Sacramento, Palo Alto, Walnut Creek, Orange County and Denver.

*FIRM PROFILE:* Morrison & Foerster is one of the world's largest international law firms with over 500 lawyers in 13 offices worldwide. The firm's legal practice encompasses every major area of commercial law, including corporate finance, project finance, institutional lending, financial services, real estate, environmental and land use planning, mining and natural resources, multimedia, intellectual property, energy, communications, computer technology, insurance, alternative dispute resolution, product liability, bankruptcy and workouts, estate planning, probate, trust administration, financial transactions, labor and employment, immigration, civil, criminal and securities litigation, entertainment and sports, food and beverage, health care, hotel and resort, antitrust, international business, international litigation and arbitration, trade regulation, transportation and tax.

### MEMBERS OF FIRM

**DAVID B. BABBE,** born April 16, 1955; admitted to bar, 1981, California. *Education:* University of California, Irvine (B.A., 1978); University of California, Los Angeles School of Law (J.D., 1981). Order of the Coif. **PRACTICE AREAS:** Business Litigation. **Email:** dbabbe@mofo.com

**CHARLES S. BARQUIST,** born September 22, 1953; admitted to bar, 1979, New York; 1988, California; 1993, Japan as a Gaikokuho-Jimu-Bengoshi. *Education:* University of Michigan (A.B., with high distinction, 1975); Harvard Law School (J.D., cum laude, 1978). Phi Beta Kappa. Law Clerk to Judge Milton Pollack, U.S. District Court, Southern District of New York, 1978-1979. *Member:* Association of the Bar of the City of New York (Chairman, Committee on State Legislation, 1984-1986); Los Angeles County Bar Association (Secretary/Treasurer, Intellectual Property and Entertainment Law Section); American Intellectual Property Law Association (Member, U.S./Japan Practice Committee); Los Angeles Intellectual Property Law Association (Chair, Programs Committee, 1996-1997). **PRACTICE AREAS:** Intellectual Property Litigation; Product Liability; Business Litigation; Alternative Dispute Resolution. **Email:** cbarquist@mofo.com

**DONALD I. BERGER,** born February 8, 1957; admitted to bar, 1982, California. *Education:* University of California, Los Angeles (A.B., magna cum laude, 1979); University of California, Los Angeles School of Law (J.D., 1982). Phi Beta Kappa. **PRACTICE AREAS:** Land Use; Environmental; Real Estate. **Email:** dberger@mofo.com

**JERRY R. BLOOM,** born October 8, 1952; admitted to bar, 1981, Florida and District of Columbia; 1984, New York; 1988, California. *Education:* George Washington University (B.A., 1974; M.A., 1976); University of Miami School of Law (J.D., 1980). **PRACTICE AREAS:** Energy; Project Development. **Email:** jbloom@mofo.com

**MICHAEL J. CONNELL,** born July 27, 1938; admitted to bar, 1965, California. *Education:* Harvard University (A.B., cum laude, 1961); Harvard Law School (LL.B., cum laude, 1964). Associate Director, Division of Corporation and Finance, Securities and Exchange Commission, Washington, D.C., 1979-1980. Attorney Fellow, Office of the General Counsel, Securities and Exchange Commission, 1978-1979. Member, Executive Committee, Business and Corporations Law Section, Los Angeles County Bar Association, 1981-1988. **PRACTICE AREAS:** Corporate Finance; Securities. **Email:** mconnell@mofo.com

*(This Listing Continued)*

**MICHÈLE B. CORASH,** born May 6, 1945; admitted to bar, 1971, District of Columbia; 1982, California. *Education:* Mount Holyoke College (B.A., 1967); New York University School of Law (J.D., cum laude, 1970). Listed in Best Lawyers in America. General Counsel, U.S. Environmental Protection Agency, 1979-1981. Deputy General Counsel, U.S. Department of Energy, 1979. Member: Board of Editors, *Toxics Law Reporter*; Board of Advisors, Ecology Law Quarterly and Board of Advisors, Journal of Environmental Law and Corporate Practice. Member, Vice President Bush's Regulatory Reform Task Force, 1981. Legal Advisor to the Chairman, U.S. Federal Trade Commission, 1970-1972. Member: American Bar Association, Standing Committee on the Environment, 1988-1991, Chair, Committee on Environmental Crimes, 1990; Board of Directors of California Counsel on Environment and Economic Balance, 1991—; National Editorial Advisory Board, *Prop 65 News* (AEI); Member, Blue Ribbon Commission, California Environmental Protection Agency Unified Environmental Statute. Chair, Inter-Pacific Bar Association Environmental Law Committee. (Los Angeles and San Francisco Offices). **LANGUAGES:** French. **PRACTICE AREAS:** Land Use; Environmental; Health and Safety. **Email:** mcorash@mofo.com

**JEROME H. CRAIG,** born May 20, 1942; admitted to bar, 1967, California. *Education:* University of Southern California (B.S., magna cum laude, 1964; J.D., 1967). Phi Kappa Phi; Beta Gamma Sigma; Phi Delta Phi; Order of the Coif. Associate Editor, University of Southern California Law Review, 1966-1967. *Member:* Los Angeles County (Chairman, Continuing Education of the Bar, 1973-1974), Federal (Director, Los Angeles Chapter and Chair, Federal Appellate Practice Group, 1994—) and American Bar Associations; The State Bar of California (Member, Committee on Professional Ethics, 1974-1977; Referee, Review Department, State Bar Court, 1982-1985; Assistant Presiding Referee and Chair, 1987-1988; Special Deputy Trial Counsel, 1990—; Member, 1981-1986 and Chair, 1984-1985, Committee on Administration of Justice). **PRACTICE AREAS:** Business Litigation; Alternative Dispute Resolution. **Email:** jcraig@mofo.com

**R. STEPHEN DOAN,** born October 11, 1949; admitted to bar, 1974, California. *Education:* University of California at Los Angeles (B.A., summa cum laude, 1971); University of California at Los Angeles School of Law (J.D., 1974). Phi Beta Kappa. *Member:* Los Angeles County Bar Association (Member, Sections on: Taxation, Probate and Trust Law). **PRACTICE AREAS:** Business; Real Estate; Tax; Estate Planning; Probate. **Email:** rdoan@mofo.com

**HENRY M. FIELDS,** born February 11, 1946; admitted to bar, 1973, New York; 1974, New Jersey; 1981, California. *Education:* Harvard College (B.A., magna cum laude, 1968); Yale Law School (J.D., 1972). Phi Beta Kappa. Lecturer on Banking Law, Practising Law Institute, 1981—. Law Clerk to Judge Leonard I. Garth, United States Court of Appeals, Third Circuit, 1972-1973. Member, Board of Governors, Institute for Corporate Counsel, 1996. Chair, Subcommittee on Banking and Financial Transactions, International Law Section, State Bar of California, 1988-1989. **LANGUAGES:** French. **PRACTICE AREAS:** International Banking and Investment; Financial Services; Corporate Finance. **Email:** hfields@mofo.com

**THOMAS R. FILETI,** born November 2, 1956; admitted to bar, 1981, California. *Education:* Cornell University (A.B., with distinction, 1978); University of Pennsylvania Law School (J.D., cum laude, 1981). Order of the Coif. **PRACTICE AREAS:** Real Estate. **Email:** tfileti@mofo.com

**RICHARD D. FYBEL,** born April 7, 1946; admitted to bar, 1972, California. *Education:* University of California, Los Angeles (A.B., 1968); University of California, Los Angeles School of Law (J.D., 1971). Order of the Coif. Judge Pro Tempore: Los Angeles County Superior Court, 1988—; Los Angeles County Municipal Court, 1979—. **PRACTICE AREAS:** Business Litigation; Alternative Dispute Resolution. **Email:** rfybel@mofo.com

**JOSEPH GABAI,** born August 11, 1952; admitted to bar, 1976, California. *Education:* Pennsylvania State University (B.A., with highest distinction, 1973); University of Pennsylvania Law School (J.D., cum laude, 1976). Phi Beta Kappa. Member: Financial Institutions Committee, 1982-1985; Consumer Financial Services Committee, 1985-1988, State Bar of California. **PRACTICE AREAS:** Financial Services. **Email:** jgabai@mofo.com

**MARVIN D. HEILESON,** born January 29, 1941; admitted to bar, 1966, California; 1985, Utah and New York; 1995, Wyoming. *Education:* University of Idaho (B.A., summa cum laude, 1963); Harvard Law School (J.D., cum laude, 1966). Co-Author: "Private Subordination Agreements and the UCC: Is Section 1-209 An Un-Wyse Solution?" 38 Bus. Law 555, 1983; "Selected Problems Under the UCC: A Potpourri of Pitfalls Facing the (Paranoid?) Article 9 Practitioner—'Proceeds', Subordination and Participation Agreements and Pledges of Restricted Securities," 2 ALI-ABA

*(This Listing Continued)*

Banking and Commercial Lending Law, 1981. *Member:* Los Angeles County (Member, Commercial and Bankruptcy Law Executive Committee, 1992-1995) and American (Member, Banking Law Committee, 1992—, Chairman of Workout and Bankruptcy Subcommittee, 1993—; Uniform Commercial Code Committee, 1983—; Business Bankruptcy Committee, 1993—; Commercial Financial Services Committee; Vice Chairman of Creditors Rights Subcommittee, 1987-1990 and Vice Chairman of Acquisition Finance Subcommittee, 1990-1993) Bar Associations; State Bar of California (Chairman, 1981-1982, Uniform Commercial Code Committee). Fellow, American College of Commercial Finance Lawyers. *PRACTICE AREAS:* Banking and Financial Transactions; Loan Workouts; Bankruptcy and Insolvency; Creditors' Rights. *Email:* mheileson@mofo.com

**KATHRYN I. JOHNSTONE,** born February 26, 1957; admitted to bar, 1986, California. *Education:* Walla Walla College (B.S.B.A., cum laude, 1979); Golden Gate University (M.B.A., cum laude, 1983); Harvard Law School (J.D., cum laude, 1986). Certified Public Accountant, California, 1981. *Member:* State Bar of California (Member, Uniform Commercial Code Committee, Business Law Section); Financial Lawyers Conference. *PRACTICE AREAS:* Business-Financial Transactions. *Email:* kjohnstone@mofo.com

**GREGORY B. KOLTUN,** born October 8, 1962; admitted to bar, 1987, California. *Education:* Claremont McKenna College (B.A., magna cum laude, 1984); University of Chicago Law School (J.D., 1987). Phi Beta Kappa. Law Clerk to the Hon. Harry Hupp, U.S. District Judge, Central District of California, 1987-1988. *PRACTICE AREAS:* Litigation. *Email:* gkoltun@mofo.com

**MARC B. LEH,** born Pasadena, California, October 19, 1959; admitted to bar, 1986, California, U.S. District Court, Central District of California and U.S. Court of Appeals, Ninth Circuit. *Education:* University of Colorado (B.A., 1982); University of Southern California Law Center (J.D., 1986). Member: Computer Law Journal, 1984-1985; Major Tax Planning Institute, 1984-1985. *Member:* Los Angeles County (Member: Business, Corporations and International Law Sections) and American (Member, Business Law Section) Bar Associations; Financial Lawyers Conference; International Bankers Association of California. *PRACTICE AREAS:* Real Estate; Finance; Corporate Law; Mergers and Acquisitions. *Email:* mleh@mofo.com

**DAN MARMALEFSKY,** born October 4, 1955; admitted to bar, 1980, California. *Education:* University of California, Berkeley (A.B., 1976); Yale Law School (J.D., 1980). Phi Beta Kappa. *Member:* Los Angeles County Bar Association (Member, Criminal Justice Section, Executive Committee, 1985-1986; Co-Chair, Indigent Criminal Defense Appointments Committee, 1995-1996); The State Bar of California; Federal and American Bar Associations; California Attorneys for Criminal Justice; California Public Defenders Association; National Association of Criminal Defense Lawyers. *LANGUAGES:* Spanish and French. *PRACTICE AREAS:* Criminal Defense; Civil Litigation; Appellate Litigation. *Email:* dmarmalefs@mofo.com

**MARK R. MCDONALD,** born January 24, 1963; admitted to bar, 1988, California. *Education:* Princeton University (A.B., magna cum laude, 1985); Harvard Law School (J.D., cum laude, 1988). Counsel, Independent Commission on the Los Angeles Police Department, 1991-1992. *Member:* Los Angeles County Bar Association Barristers (Member: Young Lawyer Section; Executive Committee, 1993-1995); State Bar of California. *PRACTICE AREAS:* Business Litigation; Securities Litigation. *Email:* mmcdonald@mofo.com

**MARGOT A. METZNER,** born April 10, 1951; admitted to bar, 1976, New York; 1980, California. *Education:* Northwestern University (B.A., 1972); Duke University School of Law (J.D., with honors, 1975). Member, Editorial Staff, Duke Law Journal, 1974-1975. Author: "Choice of Law Choices in Environmental Coverage Suits: A Game of Blindman's Bluff?" 5 Mealey's Insurance Reports No. 30, June 11, 1991; "Traps for the Unwary: The Expanding Liability Under CERCLA for Past Owners, Current Owners and Arrangers," Toxics Law Reporter (BNA), Jan. 24, 1990; "The Due Diligence Requirement For Plaintiffs Under Rule 10b-5" Duke Law Journal 753, 1975; "The Controlling Persons' Liability of Broker-Dealers For Their Employees' Federal Securities Violations," Duke Law Journal 824, 1974. *Member:* Los Angeles County and American Bar Associations; State Bar of California. *PRACTICE AREAS:* Business Litigation; Insurance Coverage; Environmental Litigation. *Email:* mmetzner@mofo.com

**J. ROBERT NELSON,** born April 3, 1944; admitted to bar, 1972, California; 1973, U.S. Court of Military Appeals; 1985, Utah. *Education:* University of Utah; University of California, Los Angeles (B.S., 1968); University of California, Los Angeles School of Law (J.D., 1971). Order of the Coif. Note and Comment Editor, U.C.L.A. Law Review, 1970-1971. Member: Los Angeles County and American Bar Associations; State Bar of California; Utah State Bar. [Lieut., JAGC, USN, 1972-1975]. *LANGUAGES:* German. *PRACTICE AREAS:* Bankruptcy Law; Debtor/Creditors Rights Law. *Email:* jnelson@mofo.com

**MAREN E. NELSON,** born March 30, 1956; admitted to bar, 1981, California. *Education:* Occidental College (A.B., magna cum laude, 1978); University of Southern California Law Center (J.D., 1981). Phi Beta Kappa; Order of the Coif. Arbitrator: National Futures Association; National Association of Securities Dealers. *PRACTICE AREAS:* Securities Litigation. *Email:* mnelson@mofo.com

**RENA L. O'MALLEY,** born April 10, 1957; admitted to bar, 1983, California. *Education:* Stanford University (A.B., with distinction, 1979); University of California, Berkeley, Boalt Hall School of Law (J.D., 1983). Phi Beta Kappa. Delegate, Conference of Delegates, Los Angeles County Bar Association, 1984-1985. *PRACTICE AREAS:* Business-Corporate Finance. *Email:* romalley@mofo.com

**DENNIS M. PERLUSS,** born May 12, 1948; admitted to bar, 1973, California. *Education:* Stanford University (B.A., with great distinction, 1970); Harvard Law School (J.D., magna cum laude, 1973). Phi Beta Kappa. Articles Editor, Harvard Law Review, 1972-1973. Visiting Professor, University of California at Los Angeles School of Law, Fall, 1994. Lecturer, University of Southern California Law Center, Spring, 1983. Law Clerk to Hon. Shirley M. Hufstedler, U.S. Court of Appeals, 9th Circuit, 1973-1974. Law Clerk to Justice Potter Stewart, U.S. Supreme Court, 1974-1975. Deputy General Counsel, Independent Commission on the Los Angeles Police Department, 1991-1992. Member, U.S. District Court, Magistrate Judge Selection Panel, 1991. Member, Board of Directors, Public Counsel, 1979-1982, 1996—. Judge, Pro Tem Los Angeles Municipal Court/Los Angeles County Bar Association Pro Tem Program, 1981-1989. Member, Los Angeles Superior Court Business Litigation Arbitration Program, 1981-1985. Member, Board of Directors, Justicia, 1982-1985. Trustee, Los Angeles County Bar Foundation, 1982-1985. Member, Board of Directors, Western Center on Law and Poverty, 1989-1994. *Member:* Los Angeles County (Member, Executive Committee, State Bar Delegation, 1988-1990; President, Barristers, 1980-1981; Member, Board of Trustees, 1979-1981; Member, Barristers Executive Committee, 1977-1981) and American Bar Associations; State Bar of California; Association of Business Trial Lawyers (Member, Board of Governors, 1987-1989, 1996—). *PRACTICE AREAS:* Securities; Complex Business Litigation (Trial and Appellate). *Email:* dperluss@mofo.com

**JOHN G. PETROVICH,** born December 8, 1955; admitted to bar, 1980, California. *Education:* University of Southern California (B.S., summa cum laude, 1977); University of California, Los Angeles School of Law (J.D., 1980). Phi Beta Kappa. *PRACTICE AREAS:* Corporate Finance; Multimedia. *Email:* jpetro@mofo.com

**MARCIA B. PINE,** born July 3, 1941; admitted to bar, 1979, California. *Education:* Cornell University (B.A., 1963); Loyola Law School of Los Angeles (J.D., cum laude, 1979). St. Thomas More Law Honor Society. Chair, U.S. Trustee Subcommittee, American Bankruptcy Institute, 1994-1997. Member, Board of Directors, Los Angeles Bankruptcy Forum, 1994-1997. Author: "Pre-Bankruptcy Automatic Stay Agreement," Los Angeles Lawyer, September 1993. Faculty Member, Advanced Bankruptcy Workshop, Practising Law Institute, January 1995. *PRACTICE AREAS:* Bankruptcy. *Email:* mpine@mofo.com

**ANTHONY L. PRESS,** born October 20, 1958; admitted to bar, 1986, California. *Education:* Yale University (B.A., cum laude, 1981); University of California, Los Angeles School of Law (J.D., 1986). Chief Managing Editor, UCLA Law Review, 1985-1986. *PRACTICE AREAS:* Litigation. *Email:* apress@mofo.com

**STEPHEN P. ROTHMAN,** born Madison, Wisconsin, February 11, 1957; admitted to bar, 1985, California. *Education:* Yale University (B.A., cum laude, 1982); Harvard Law School (J.D., cum laude, 1985). *PRACTICE AREAS:* Corporate Finance; Mergers and Acquisitions; Business Law; Sports; Retail; Health Care; Insurance; Manufacturing. *Email:* srothman@mofo.com

**SUSAN E. RULE,** born October 15, 1964; admitted to bar, 1990, California. *Education:* Brown University (A.B., with honors, 1986); Columbia University School of Law (J.D., 1989). Staff Member, Columbia Business Law Review, 1987-1988. *PRACTICE AREAS:* Litigation. *Email:* srule@mofo.com

**TIMOTHY F. RYAN,** born October 13, 1946; admitted to bar, 1972, California; 1979, U.S. Supreme Court. *Education:* University of California at Santa Barbara (B.A., 1968); The Hague Academy of International Law,

*(This Listing Continued)*

**MORRISON & FOERSTER LLP, Los Angeles—Continued**

The Hague, The Netherlands (Special Certificate of Study, 1970); Loyola University (J.D., 1971). *Member:* State Bar of California (Member, Labor Section); American Bar Association (Member, Sections on: Litigation; Employment and Labor Law, Subcommittee on the Developing Labor Law); The American Academy of Hospital Attorneys. **PRACTICE AREAS:** Labor and Employment. *Email:* tryan@mofo.com

**DARRELL L. SACKL,** born September 26, 1948; admitted to bar, 1973, California; 1990-1993, Japan as a Gaikokuho-Jimu-Bengoshi and registered as a member of the Japan Federation of Bar Associations. *Education:* Cambridge University, Cambridge, England; St. Olaf College (B.A., 1970); Stanford Law School (J.D., 1973). Phi Beta Kappa. Law Clerk, U.S. Court of Appeals, Ninth Circuit, 1973-1974. Special Assistant to Chief Justice Rose Elizabeth Bird, California Supreme Court, 1977-1978. **PRACTICE AREAS:** Real Estate; Commercial Finance; Secured Transactions. *Email:* dsackl@mofo.com

**JANIE F. SCHULMAN,** born September 19, 1962; admitted to bar, 1987, California. *Education:* University of California, Berkeley (A.B., with distinction, 1983); University of California, Berkeley, Boalt Hall School of Law (J.D., 1987). Order of the Coif. Author: "Violence in the Workplace: Tips for Avoiding Catastrophe," Los Angeles Business Journal, April 11, 1994. Member, Labor and Employment Law Section, Co-Chair, Barrister's Children's Rights Committee, 1989-1990, Los Angeles County Bar Association. **PRACTICE AREAS:** Labor and Employment Law. *Email:* jschulman@mofo.com

**JOHN R. SHINER,** born September 8, 1943; admitted to bar, 1969, California. *Education:* University of Southern California (B.A., 1965); University of San Diego School of Law (J.D., 1968). **PRACTICE AREAS:** Litigation; Labor; Business. *Email:* jshiner@mofo.com

**B. SCOTT SILVERMAN,** born February 27, 1949; admitted to bar, 1975, California. *Education:* Stanford University (B.A., with distinction and honors, 1971); University of California, Hastings College of the Law (J.D., 1975). Order of the Coif. Thurston Honor Society. Law Clerk to Associate Justice Raymond L. Sullivan, California Supreme Court, 1975-1977. Editor and Co-Author: "Wrongful Employment Termination Practice," California Continuing Education of the Bar and Supplements. **PRACTICE AREAS:** Labor and Employment. *Email:* bsilverman@mofo.com

**ROBERT S. STERN,** born March 10, 1950; admitted to bar, 1975, California. *Education:* University of Illinois (B.S., magna cum laude, 1972); University of Chicago Law School (J.D., 1975). Comment Editor, University of Chicago Law Review, 1974-1975. Certified Public Accountant, Illinois, 1972. Law Clerk to Judge John Minor Wisdom, U.S. Court of Appeals, Fifth Circuit, 1975-1976. **PRACTICE AREAS:** Accountants' Liability; Securities Litigation; Financial Institutions Litigation. *Email:* rstern@mofo.com

**PAULINE M. STEVENS,** born February 28, 1947; admitted to bar, 1973, California. *Education:* Vassar College (A.B., 1969); University of Pennsylvania Law School (J.D., 1972). **PRACTICE AREAS:** Financial Transactions; Derivatives; Workouts; Entertainment Finance. *Email:* pstevens@mofo.com

**MARCUS A. TORRANO,** born June 6, 1961; admitted to bar, 1988, California. *Education:* Pacific Union College (B.S., 1983); University of California, Berkeley, Boalt Hall School of Law (J.D., 1988). **PRACTICE AREAS:** Labor. *Email:* mtorrano@mofo.com

**LAURIE D. ZELON,** born November 15, 1952; admitted to bar, 1977, California. *Education:* Cornell University (A.B., with distinction, 1974); Harvard Law School (J.D., 1977). *Member:* Los Angeles County (Trustee, 1990-1992; Vice President, 1992; Senior Vice President, 1993; President-Elect, 1994; President, 1995) and American (Chair: Standing Committee on Lawyers Public Service Responsibility, 1987-1990; Standing Committee on Legal Aid and Indigent Defendants, 1993—) Bar Associations. **PRACTICE AREAS:** Environmental Litigation; Geotechnical Litigation; Business Litigation. *Email:* lzelon@mofo.com

**DONNA J. ZENOR,** born January 23, 1945; admitted to bar, 1973, California. *Education:* Arizona State University (B.A., summa cum laude, 1968); Cornell University (J.D., 1973). Vice Chairman, Executive Committee, Business Law Section, State Bar of California, 1983. Fellow, American College of Investment Counsel. **PRACTICE AREAS:** Banking Transactions; Structured Finance; Asset Securitization. *Email:* dzenor@mofo.com

*(This Listing Continued)*

*SENIOR OF COUNSEL*

**SETH M. HUFSTEDLER,** born September 20, 1922; admitted to bar, 1950, California. *Education:* University of Southern California (B.A., 1944); Stanford University (LL.B., 1949). Delta Theta Phi; Phi Beta Kappa; Phi Kappa Phi; Order of the Coif. President, Chancery Club, 1974-1975. Legislation Editor, Stanford Law Review, 1947-1949. Chairman, Board of Visitors, Stanford Law School, 1972-1973. Co-Chairman, Public Commission on County Government, 1975-1976, 1989. Member, California Citizens' Commission on Tort Reform, 1976-1977. Member, Judicial Council of California, 1977-1979. *Member:* Los Angeles County (Member, Board of Trustees, 1963-1965; 1966-1970; President, 1970; Shattuck Price Award, 1976) and American (Chairman, Senior Lawyers Section, 1987-1988; Chairman, ABA Action Commission to Reduce Court Costs and Delay, 1979-1981) Bar Associations; The State Bar of California (Member, Board of Governors, 1971-1974; President, 1973-1974); American Law Institute. Fellow: American Bar Foundation (Member, Board of Trustees, 1975-1985 and President, 1982-1984); American College of Trial Lawyers. **PRACTICE AREAS:** Trial and Appellate Practice. *Email:* sethhufs@mofo.com

**SHIRLEY M. HUFSTEDLER,** born August 24, 1925; admitted to bar, 1950, California. *Education:* University of New Mexico (B.B.A., 1945); Stanford University (LL.B., 1949). Awarded Honorary Doctorates from: Claremont University Center, Columbia University; Georgetown University; Gonzaga University; Hood College; University of the Pacific; University of New Mexico; Occidental College; University of Pennsylvania; Rutgers University; University of Southern California; Syracuse University; Smith College; Tufts University; Tulane University; University of Wyoming; Yale University; Mt. Holyoke University; University of California at Los Angeles Medal; Earl Warren Medal, University of Judaism; Louis Brandeis Medal, University of Louisville; Dr. Humane Letters, Hebrew Union College; Fordham Stein Prize, Fordham University; American Bar Association Medal, 1995. Phi Alpha Delta; Order of the Coif. Article and Book Review Editor, Stanford Law Review, 1948-1949. Associate: Charles E. Beardsley, 1951-1954; Beardsley, Hufstedler & Kemble, 1955-1960. Special Legal Consultant to the Attorney General of California, 1960-1961. Judge, Los Angeles County Superior Court, 1961-1966. Associate Justice, California Court of Appeals, 1966-1968. United States Circuit Judge, U.S. Court of Appeals for the Ninth Circuit, 1968-1979. United States Secretary of Education, 1979-1981. Faculty Member, Appellate Judges Seminar, Institute of Judicial Administration, 1970-1971. Phleger Professor of Law, Stanford Law School, 1982. Member of the Board: Occidental College, 1972-1979, 1981-1990; Aspen Institute, 1973-1979, 1981-1995; American Law Institute, 1974-1985; California Institute of Technology, 1975-1979, 1981—; Colonial Williamsburg Foundation, 1976-1994; Institute for Civil Justice, 1981-1988; Center For National Policy, 1981-1986; Natural Resources Defense Council, 1983-1985; Carnegie Endowment for International Peace, 1985—; Institute for Advanced Study, 1985-1986; John D.C. Catherine T. MacArthur Foundation, 1983—. Chair, Law Faculty, Salzburg Seminar in American Studies, Austria, 1976. Member, Board of Trustees, Salzburg Seminar, 1986-1990. Director: Hewlett Packard Co., 1982-1996; US West, Inc., 1983-1996; Harman Industries International, Inc., 1986—. Chair, U.S. Commission on Immigration Reform, 1996—. Author: "Woman and The Law," Equal Justice Under Law, United States Department of Justice, Bicentennial Lecture Series; "Comity and The Constitution, The Changing Role of The Federal Judiciary," 47 N.Y.U.L. Rev. 841, 1972; "The Directions and Misdirections of a Constitutional Right of Privacy," Benjamin Cardozo Lecture (Association of the Bar of the City of New York): published by the Association of the Bar, 1971; "New Blocks For Old Pyramids: Reshaping The Judicial System," (Charles Evans Hughes Address for the New York County Bar Association), 44 S. Cal. L. Rev. 901, 1971; "Invisible Searches for Intangible Things," 127 U. Pa. L. Rev. 1483, 1979; "Constitutional Revision and Appellate Court Decongestants," 44 Washington Law Review 577, 1969. *Member:* Association of the Bar of the City of New York (Honorary Member); Los Angeles County and American Bar Associations; The State Bar of California; American Bar Foundation; International Federation of Women Lawyers; Women Lawyers Association; Institute of Judicial Administration; Council on Foreign Relations. Fellow: American Academy of Arts and Sciences; St. Catherine's College, Oxford, England. **PRACTICE AREAS:** Appellate Practice. *Email:* shirhufs@mofo.com

**PATRICIA DOMINIS PHILLIPS,** born July 21, 1934; admitted to bar, 1968, California. *Education:* University of California at Santa Barbara (B.A., 1956); Loyola Law School, Los Angeles (J.D., 1967). Phi Alpha Delta. Recipient, Stalhut Award. CEB and Rutter Group Lecturer, 1980-1985. Member, Board of Visitors, 1985— and Chair, 1988-1989, Loyola Law School. Member, Board of Councillors, University of Southern Cali-

*(This Listing Continued)*

fornia Law Center, 1983—. Member, Judicial Council, State of California, 1990-1993. *Member:* Los Angeles County (President, 1984-1985; Recipient, Shattuck-Price Award, 1991; Board of Trustees and Officer, 1979-1985; Family Law and Trial Lawyers Section; Delegate to State Bar Convention, 1972-1986) and American (Member: Family Law; Individual Rights and Responsibilities and General Practice Sections) Bar Associations; The State Bar of California (Member, Board of Governors, 1986-1989; Vice-President, 1988-1989; Chair, Commission on the Future of the Legal Profession and the State Bar, 1993-1995; Committee on Bar Examiners, Member, 1978-1982 and Chair, 1981-1982; Ninth Circuit Judicial Conference Delegate, 1991-1993); Women Lawyers Association of Los Angeles; California Women Lawyers Association; Black Women Lawyers of California; American Academy of Matrimonial Lawyers; National Conference of Bar Presidents; Chancery Club (Secretary). Fellow, American Bar Foundation (Member, Los Angeles County Commission on Judicial Procedures, 1991-1996). *PRACTICE AREAS:* Family Law; Civil Litigation; Mediation and Arbitration. *Email:* pphillips@mofo.com

**JOSEPH L. WYATT, JR.,** born February 21, 1924; admitted to bar, 1950, California. *Education:* Northwestern University (A.B., with honors, 1947); Harvard University (LL.B., 1949). Phi Beta Kappa. Author: Nossaman, Wyatt and McDaniel, *Trust Administration and Taxation* (2nd Revised Edition), Matthew Bender & Co., 1996. Author and Lecturer, University of California Program of Continuing Education of the Bar, 1957, 1962, 1964-1966, 1974, 1978-1981, 1996. Lecturer: Fiduciary Law, Preventive Law - Avoiding and Managing Litigation, Pacific Coast Banking School, 1963-1992; Southwest Graduate School of Banking, 1987-1989; Texas Professional Development Program, 1978; University of Miami, 14th Estate Planning Institute, 1980; "Divorce and Estate Planning in an Uncertain Marital Climate," presented at 1984 ABA Annual Meeting; "Drafting Arbitration and Other Clauses for Alternative Dispute Resolution in Wills and Trusts," presented at 1986 ABA Annual Meeting; "Escape From Bleak House: Alternative Dispute Resolution ("ADR") in Wills and Trusts—Can You? Should You? How Do You?" presented at 1989 ABA Annual Meeting; "The Fiduciary Responsibilities of a Public Retirement System Board Trustee—Old Ideas with New Twists," presented at 1989 Annual Meeting of National Association of Public Pension Attorneys; "Protecting the Fiduciary: Prepare Now or Pay Later," presented at the National Institute of The American Bankers' and American Bar Associations, 1989; "The Hague Convention on Succession: A United States Lawyer's Perspective," 1990 biennial meeting of the International Academy of Estate and Trust Law; "Compensation of Fiduciaries and Their Attorneys; Herein of Fee Fights and Tax Fee Fights," 1991 ABA Annual Meeting; "The Fiduciary Goes to War: What Kind of War; Managing the War; Financing the War," 1990 National Trust & Financial Services Conference, American Bankers Association; "Fiduciary Prudence and the Environment—What Do Fiduciaries of a Public Retirement System Need to Know—and Why Do They Need to Know It?" presented to the National Association of State Retirement Administrators, 1995 Conference; "Ethics and Conflicts: Duties and Dilemmas in Estate Planning—and Some Solutions," University of Missouri Annual Estate Planning Symposium, Kansas City, 1992. Member, 1961-1971 and President, 1965-1967, California State Personnel Board. Member, Board of Administration, California Public Employees Retirement System, 1963-1971. Adviser, American Law Institute Restatement of the Law of Trusts 3d, Prudent Investor Rule, 1988-1990 and Restatement of the Law of Trusts, 1990—. *Member:* Los Angeles County (Member, Board of Trustees, 1956) and American (Member, Sections on: Taxation; Real Property, Probate and Trust Law; Member, Special Committee on Professional Responsibility, Probate and Trust Law Division; Chair, Committee on Estate and Trust Litigation; Business Law, Vice-Chair, Credit Union Electronic Fund Transfers Committee) Bar Associations; The State Bar of California; American Judicature Society. International Academy of Estate and Trust Law (Academician; Member, Executive Council, 1982-1986, Treasurer, 1990-1996; American Law Institute. Fellow, American College of Trust and Estate Counsel. [1st Sgt., USAAF, 1942-1945]. *PRACTICE AREAS:* Tax; Trust; Probate; Ethics; Public Pension; Fiduciary Counsel; Litigation. *Email:* jwyatt@mofo.com

## OF COUNSEL

**BURTON J. GINDLER,** born January 31, 1927; admitted to bar, 1951, California; 1962, U.S. Supreme Court. *Education:* University of Minnesota (B.S.L., 1949; J.D., 1950). Deputy Attorney General, State of California, 1955-1968. Partner, Hufstedler & Kaus, 1968-1995. Of Counsel, Morrison & Foester, 1995—. Member, Panel, drafting California Water Code S3 13000 et seq., California Porter-Cologne Water Control Act, 1970. Member, California Regional Water Quality Control Board, Los Angeles Region, 1970-1973. Member, 1973-1975; President, 1974-1975, Board of Water and Power Commissioners, City of Los Angeles. Executive Assistant to Secretary of Education, 1979-1980. *Member:* Los Angeles County and American Bar Associations; The State Bar of California (Presiding Disciplinary Referee, Disciplinary Board, 1976-1977). *PRACTICE AREAS:* Environmental Law; Water Resources; Water Quality Law; Service Duplication Under California Public Utility Code; Privatization of Municipal Utilities; Attorney Fees; Malpractice and Ethics; Expert Witness. *Email:* bgindler@mofo.com

**JIM G. GRAYSON,** born February 18, 1948; admitted to bar, 1974, California. *Education:* Arizona State University (B.S., 1970); Arizona State University College of Law (J.D., magna cum laude, 1973); Harvard University (LL.M., 1974). Assistant Articles Editor, Arizona State University Law Journal, 1972-1973. Instructor, Boston University College of Law, 1973-1974. *PRACTICE AREAS:* Real Estate; Public Finance. *Email:* jgrayson@mofo.com

**JOHN P. OLSON,** born May 8, 1947; admitted to bar, 1972, California. *Education:* University of California, Los Angeles (B.A., with honors, 1969); University of Southern California Law School (J.D., 1972). Note and Comment Editor, University of Southern California Law Review, 1971-1972. *Member:* Los Angeles and American (Member, Tort and Insurance Practice Section) Bar Associations; The State Bar of California. *PRACTICE AREAS:* Business Litigation; Environmental; Toxic Tort; Bad Faith Insurance Litigation. *Email:* jolson@mofo.com

**J. TIMOTHY SCOTT,** born February 27, 1957; admitted to bar, 1985, California. *Education:* University of Scranton (B.S., cum laude, 1979); Fordham University School of Law (J.D., 1985). Member, Advisory Board, Institute for Corporate Counsel, 1995. *Member:* Los Angeles County (Member, Business and Corporations Law Section) and American (Member, Corporation, Banking and Business Law Section) Bar Associations. *PRACTICE AREAS:* Corporate Finance; Corporate; Real Estate. *Email:* jscott@mofo.com

**JOHN SOBIESKI,** born November 19, 1932; admitted to bar, 1958, California. *Education:* Stanford University (A.B., 1954; LL.B., 1958). Member, Board of Editors, Stanford Law Review, 1957-1958. Law Clerk to Honorable Albert Lee Stephens, Sr., Court of Appeals, 9th Circuit, 1959. *Member:* Los Angeles County (Member: Appellate Courts Committee and Amicus Briefs Committee, 1995-1997) and American Bar Associations; The State Bar of California. *PRACTICE AREAS:* Appellate Practice and Business Litigation. *Email:* jsobieski@mofo.com

**MICHAEL V. TOUMANOFF,** born November 4, 1952; admitted to bar, 1982, California. *Education:* Harvard University (A.B., magna cum laude, government, 1975); University of California, Boalt Hall School of Law (J.D., 1982). Member, Moot Court Board. *Member:* Los Angeles County Bar Association; The State Bar of California. *PRACTICE AREAS:* Public Pension Law; Business Litigation. *Email:* mtoumanoff@mofo.com

## ASSOCIATES

**JOHN W. (JACK) ALDEN JR.,** born October 27, 1965; admitted to bar, 1990, California. *Education:* Stanford University (A.B., 1987); Duke University (M.A., Public Policy Sciences, 1990; J.D., with honors, 1990). Member, Professional Responsibility and Ethics Committee, Los Angeles County Bar Association, 1994-1997. *Email:* jalden@mofo.com

**LORIE M. ALEXANDER,** born July 31, 1966; admitted to bar, 1992, California. *Education:* University of California, Irvine (B.A., 1989); University of California, Hastings College of the Law (J.D., 1992). *Email:* lalexander@mofo.com

**SARVENAZ BAHAR,** born August 5, 1966; admitted to bar, 1994, California. *Education:* University of Pennsylvania (B.A., summa cum laude, 1988); Yale Law School (J.D., 1991). Phi Beta Kappa. Law Clerk, Chief Judge Barefoot Sanders, U.S. District Court, Northern District of Texas, 1991-1992. *LANGUAGES:* French and Persian. *Email:* sbahar@mofo.com

**DAVID K. BARRETT,** born May 27, 1965; admitted to bar, 1990, California. *Education:* Stanford University (A.B., with distinction, 1987); University of California, Los Angeles School of Law (J.D., 1990). Extern to Hon. Harry Pregerson, U.S. Court of Appeals, Ninth Circuit, 1989. Deputy Public Defender, County of Los Angeles, 1990-1992. *Member:* Los Angeles County (Member, Appellate Courts Committee), Federal and American Bar Associations; State Bar of California. *Email:* dbarrett@mofo.com

**MARK R. BATEMAN,** born San Mateo, California, September 15, 1966; admitted to bar, 1991, California. *Education:* University of Southern California (B.S., magna cum laude, 1988); University of California, Hastings College of the Law (J.D., 1991). Order of the Coif. *Member:* State Bar of California.

*(This Listing Continued)*

**MORRISON & FOERSTER LLP,** Los Angeles—Continued

**LAURA R. BOUDREAU,** born August 15, 1965; admitted to bar, 1994, California. *Education:* Swarthmore College (B.A., with high honors, 1987); Harvard Law School (J.D., cum laude, 1994). Phi Beta Kappa. Editor, Human Rights Journal, 1993-1994. Law Clerk to Justice Steven Levinson, Hawaii State Supreme Court, 1994-1996. **LANGUAGES:** Japanese. **Email:** lboudreau@mofo.com

**LAURA D. CASTNER,** born July 30, 1966; admitted to bar, 1992, New Jersey; 1994, California; 1995, New York. *Education:* Rutgers University (B.A., with highest honors, 1988); Columbia University School of Law (J.D., 1992). Phi Beta Kappa. **LANGUAGES:** French. **Email:** lcastner@mofo.com

**MICHAEL S. CHAMBERLIN,** born January 25, 1966; admitted to bar, 1994, California. *Education:* University of California, Los Angeles (B.A., cum laude, 1989); University of California, Los Angeles School of Law (J.D., 1994). Legal Intern, Office of the Secretary of Defense, General Counsel's Office (International Affairs and Intelligence), Fall 1993. **Email:** mchamber@mofo.com

**RANDALL L. CLARK,** born May 19, 1969; admitted to bar, 1994, California. *Education:* Pepperdine University (B.S., summa cum laude, 1991); Duke University School of Law (J.D., with honors, 1994). *Member:* Los Angeles County and Federal Bar Associations. **LANGUAGES:** Spanish and German. **Email:** rclark@mofo.com

**THOMAS R. DAVIS,** born January 20, 1969; admitted to bar, 1995, California. *Education:* Brown University (B.A., magna cum laude, 1991); Princeton University (M.P.A., 1995); New York University School of Law (J.D., 1995). Phi Beta Kappa; Order of the Coif. **LANGUAGES:** Spanish. **Email:** tdavis@mofo.com

**ELIZABETH A. DEERE,** born February 23, 1957; admitted to bar, 1992, California. *Education:* Cornell University (B.S., 1983); University of California, Los Angeles School of Law (J.D., 1992). **Email:** edeere@mofo.com

**ANDREE D. DELGADO,** born May 21, 1966; admitted to bar, 1991, California. *Education:* University of North Carolina, Chapel Hill (B.A., with distinction, 1988); University of California, Los Angeles School of Law (J.D., 1991). Phi Beta Kappa. **Email:** adelgado@mofo.com

**YVONNE D. DENENNY,** born January 25, 1969; admitted to bar, 1994, California. *Education:* Wellesley College (B.A., magna cum laude, 1991); University of California, Los Angeles School of Law (J.D., 1994). **Email:** ydenenny@mofo.com

**STEVEN J. DETTMANN,** born March 18, 1967; admitted to bar, 1995, California. *Education:* University of California, Los Angeles (B.A., 1990); Loyola Law School, Los Angeles (J.D., 1995). **Email:** sdettmann@mofo.com

**GAVIN FRIEDMAN,** born December 19, 1967; admitted to bar, 1995, California. *Education:* University of Cape Town, South Africa (B.BS., second class honors, 1989); University of California, Berkeley, Boalt Hall School of Law (J.D., 1995). **Email:** gfriedman@mofo.com

**HECTOR G. GALLEGOS,** born May 20, 1962; admitted to bar, 1994, California. *Education:* Loyola Marymount University (B.S.E.E., 1984; M.S.E.E., 1988); University of California, Los Angeles School of Law (J.D., 1994). **LANGUAGES:** Spanish. **Email:** hgallegos@mofo.com

**MARK T. GILLETT,** born November 24, 1962; admitted to bar, 1990, California. *Education:* Pacific Christian College (B.A., 1984); Harvard Law School (J.D., 1990). **Email:** mgillett@mofo.com

**LAURIE B. GRANIEZ,** born April 26, 1959; admitted to bar, 1988, California. *Education:* University of Southern California (B.A., with honors, 1982); University of Southern California Law Center (J.D., 1988). Editor-in-Chief: Major Tax Planning, USC Tax Institute, 1987-1988; Computer/Law Journal, 1987-1988. **Email:** lgraniez@mofo.com

**RICHARD W. GRIME,** born September 24, 1964. admitted to practice, 1990, England; admitted to bar, 1991, California. *Education:* Oxford University, England (Law, first class honors, 1986); Guildford, England (Solicitor's Finals, 1987). **Email:** rgrime@mofo.com

**RONEN GROSS,** born October 31, 1969; admitted to bar, 1995, California. *Education:* University of California, Santa Barbara (B.A., with honors, 1991); Loyola Law School, Los Angeles (J.D., 1995). **LANGUAGES:** Hebrew. **Email:** rgross@mofo.com

**ANN HABERFELDE,** born August 19, 1955; admitted to bar, 1993, California. *Education:* University of California, Berkeley (B.A., 1977); University of California, Hastings College of Law (J.D., cum laude, 1993). Order of the Coif; Thurston Society. Note Editor, Hastings Law Journal, 1992-1993. *Member:* Federal Bar Association; Association Business Trial Lawyers. **Email:** haberfelde@mofo.com

**STEVEN M. HAINES,** born June 27, 1968; admitted to bar, 1993, California. *Education:* Boston College (B.A., magna cum laude, 1990); University of California, Los Angeles School of Law (J.D., 1993). **Email:** shaines@mofo.com

**SAHELI DATTA HARVILL,** born June 28, 1965; admitted to bar, 1990, California. *Education:* University of California, Berkeley (B.S., with honors, 1987); Columbia University School of Law (J.D., 1990). Harlan Fiske Stone Scholar. **Email:** sharvill@mofo.com

**AMY A. HOFF,** born April 10, 1964; admitted to bar, 1990, California. *Education:* University of California, Los Angeles (B.A., 1986); University of Southern California (J.D., with honors, 1990). Extern to Judge Miriam Vogel, Los Angeles Superior Court, 1990. *Member:* Los Angeles County Bar Association; Women Lawyers Association of Los Angeles. **Email:** ahoff@mofo.com

**SHANE Y. KAO,** born September 16, 1970; admitted to bar, 1995, California. *Education:* University of California, Berkeley (B.S., Electrical Engineering and Computer Science, 1991); Georgetown University Law Center (J.D., 1995). **Email:** skao@mofo.com

**MICHAEL KATZ,** born December 3, 1964; admitted to bar, 1993, New York; 1995, California. *Education:* Harvard University (A.B., cum laude, 1987); New York University School of Law (J.D., 1992). Law Clerk to Chief Judge Barbara B. Crabb, U.S. District Court, Western District of Wisconsin, 1992-1993. **Email:** mkatz@mofo.com

**CHARLES S. KAUFMAN,** born October 25, 1954; admitted to bar, 1994, California. *Education:* University of California (B.A., cum laude, 1975); San Francisco State University (M.A., 1978); University of California, Los Angeles School of Law (J.D., 1994). **Email:** ckaufman@mofo.com

**HOWARD S. LIBERSON,** born May 2, 1967; admitted to bar, 1995, California. *Education:* University of California, Los Angeles (B.A., cum laude, 1990); Loyola Law School, Los Angeles (J.D., 1995). Order of the Coif. Law Clerk to Judge James M. Ideman, U.S. District Court, 1995-1996. Certified Public Accountant, California. **Email:** hliberson@mofo.com

**JOHN P. LODISE,** born March 24, 1961; admitted to bar, 1988, California. *Education:* Williams College (B.A., cum laude, 1983); University of California, Los Angeles School of Law (J.D., 1988). Phi Beta Kappa. Editor, University of California at Los Angeles Law Review, 1987-1988. **Email:** jlodise@mofo.com

**LIZABETH RHODES,** born August 25, 1966; admitted to bar, 1991, California. *Education:* Smith College (A.B., cum laude, 1988); University of California, Los Angeles School of Law (J.D., 1991). **Email:** lrhodes@mofo.com

**P. RUPERT RUSSELL,** born June 29, 1958; admitted to bar, 1984, England; 1995, California. *Education:* Oxford University (B.A., 1980; M.A., 1985). **Email:** prussell@mofo.com

**KRIS G. VYAS,** born July 13, 1966; admitted to bar, 1992, California. *Education:* University of California, Berkeley (B.A., high honors, 1988); University of California, Los Angeles School of Law (J.D., 1992). **Email:** kvyas@mofo.com

**DEREK H. WILSON,** born April 30, 1959; admitted to bar, 1987, California; 1989, District of Columbia. *Education:* University of Wisconsin (B.A., 1982); Harvard Law School (J.D., 1986). **Email:** dwilson@mofo.com

**DAVID C. WRIGHT,** born December 29, 1968; admitted to bar, 1994, California. *Education:* Atlantic Union College (B.S., summa cum laude, 1991); Pepperdine University School of Law (J.D., magna cum laude, 1994). Law Clerk to Judge Stephen S. Trott, U.S. Court of Appeals, Ninth Circuit, 1994-1995. **Email:** dwright@mofo.com

**LESTER I. YANO,** born September 6, 1957; admitted to bar, 1994, California. *Education:* Washington University (B.S.C.E., cum laude, 1979); University of California, Irvine (M.S.E., 1981); University of California, Los Angeles School of Law (J.D., 1994). Tau Beta Pi. Member, UCLA Moot Court Honors Program. Recipient: American Jurisprudence Award in Property. Comment Editor, UCLA Law Review, 1993-1994. Author: "Protection of the Ethnobiological Knowledge of Indigenous Peoples," 41 UCLA L. Rev. 41, 1993. Co-Author: with Lawrence P. Ebiner, "Discovery

*(This Listing Continued)*

of Computer Records," California Deposition and Discovery Practice, 1996; with Cedrick Chao, et al., "Pretrial Motions," 1995 California Litigation Review, Litigation Section, State Bar of California, June 1996. *Member:* Los Angeles and American Bar Associations; State Bar of California; Japanese American Bar Association. *Email:* lyano@mofo.com

**ROWENA A. W. YEUNG,** born March 19, 1966; admitted to bar, 1991, California. *Education:* Swarthmore College (B.A., 1988); Columbia University School of Law (J.D., 1991). Editor, Columbia Law Review, 1990-1991. *LANGUAGES:* Cantonese. *Email:* ryeung@mofo.com

**MARC D. YOUNG,** born July 16, 1963; admitted to bar, 1993, California. *Education:* University of Utah (B.S., 1986); University of Utah College of Law (J.D., 1991). Order of the Coif. Editor-in-Chief, Utah Law Review, 1990-1991. Law Clerk to Hon. David K. Winder, U.S. District Court, District of Utah, 1992. *Email:* myoung@mofo.com

*LEGAL SUPPORT PERSONNEL*

**BROOKE C.F. ASHWORTH,** born August 4, 1955. *Education:* University of California, Davis (B.S., 1979). Registered Environmental Assessor, California, 1991—. Member, Air and Waste Management Association, 1989—. Member, Committee E-50, ASTM, 1991—. (Environmental Analyst). *PRACTICE AREAS:* Environmental Law. *Email:* bashworth@mofo.com

(For biographical data on San Francisco, Sacramento, Walnut Creek, Palo Alto and Irvine, CA, New York, NY, Washington, DC, Denver, CO, London, England, Brussels, Belgium, Hong Kong and Tokyo, Japan see professional biographies at each of those cities.)

---

## *ALLAN S. MORTON*

Established in 1983

**2029 CENTURY PARK EAST, SUITE 1200**
**LOS ANGELES, CALIFORNIA 90067**
Telephone: 310-277-8946
Fax: 310-277-8944
Email: morton4law@aol.com

*General Civil Practice. Business Litigation and Family Law. Arbitration and Mediation.*

**ALLAN S. MORTON,** born New York, N.Y., February 2, 1944; admitted to bar, 1969, California and U.S. District Court, Central District of California. *Education:* Cornell University (A.B., 1965); University of California at Los Angeles (J.D., 1968). Senior Editor, University of California at Los Angeles Law Review, 1966-1968. *Member:* Beverly Hills (Member, Sections on: Real Property; Family Law, Alternative Dispute Resolution) and Los Angeles County (Member, Sections on: Litigation; Real Property; Family Law; Commercial Law, Alternative Dispute Resolution) Bar Associations; State Bar of California. (Also of Counsel to Mannis & Phillips).

---

## *MOSKATEL LAW CORPORATION*

Established in 1980

**SUITE 950, 10100 SANTA MONICA BOULEVARD**
**LOS ANGELES, CALIFORNIA 90067**
Telephone: 310-282-8383; 310-556-3847
Email: mlc@moskatel.com
URL: http://www.moskatel.com/

*Taxation, Technology, Computer, Corporate Law.*

**IRA D. MOSKATEL,** born Los Angeles, California, November 18, 1950; admitted to bar, 1975, California. *Education:* California Institute of Technology (B.S., 1972); University of Southern California (J.D., 1975). Order of the Coif. Note and Article Editor, Southern California Law Review, 1974-1975. Author: "Panacea or Placebo? Actions for Negligent Non-Compliance under the Federal Fair Credit Reporting Act," 47 Southern California Law Review, 1974. Chairman, Cal Tech/M.I.T Enterprise Forum, 1992-1994. Adjunct Faculty, Golden Gate University, 1995—. *Member:* Beverly Hills, Los Angeles County (Chairman, Committee on Technology Transfer Law, 1980-1984; Chair, Law and Technology Section, 1984-1986) and American (Chair: Committee of Artificial Intelligence, 1983-1989; Task Force on Reengineering Law Practice, 1993—) Bar Associations; State Bar of California (Member, Conference of Delegates, 1985-1986); Association for Computing Machinery; Institute of Electrical and Electronic Engineers; Association for Computing Machinery. (Certified Specialist, Taxation Law, The State Bar of California Board of Legal Specialization).

*(This Listing Continued)*

---

## *MOSS, LEVITT & MANDELL, LLP*

**1901 AVENUE OF THE STARS**
**19TH FLOOR**
**LOS ANGELES, CALIFORNIA 90067**
Telephone: 310-284-8900
Telecopier: 310-284-6660

*Construction, Real Estate, Surety, Commercial Corporate and Business Law. Family Law. Title Insurance Defense. General Civil and Trial Practice.*

**RONALD J. MANDELL,** born Los Angeles, California, March 25, 1942; admitted to bar, 1968, California, U.S. District Court, Central District of California. *Education:* University of Southern California (B.S., 1964; J.D., 1967). Blue Key. Co-Author: "California Mechanics Liens and Other Remedies," 2nd Ed. Continuing Education of the Bar, 1988; "Who is the Contractor that Civil Code Section 3097 (b) Exempts from Giving a Preliminary 20 Day Notice," California Real Property Journal, Winter, 1992. "Member, Panel of Arbitrators, American Arbitration Association. *Member:* Century City and Los Angeles County (Member, Arbitration Committee, 1972—, Real Property Section [Construction and Title Insurance Subsection]; Dispute Resolution Section) and American Bar Associations; State Bar of California; Southern California Mediation Association. *REPORTED CASES:* J.A. Jones Construction Co. v. Superior Court, 27 Cal. App. 4th 1568 (1994). *PRACTICE AREAS:* Construction; Real Estate; General Business Law.

**MEYER S. LEVITT,** born New York, N.Y., May 16, 1938; admitted to bar, 1966, California and U.S. District Court, Southern District of California; 1973, U.S. Supreme Court. *Education:* University of California at Los Angeles (B.S., 1961); University of Southern California (J.D., 1965). *Member:* Beverly Hills and Los Angeles County (Member, Domestic Relations Section) Bar Associations; State Bar of California (Family Law Study Group). *PRACTICE AREAS:* Family Law; General Trial Law; Civil Litigation; Construction Litigation.

**RODNEY MOSS,** born Los Angeles, California, December 13, 1935; admitted to bar, 1961, California. *Education:* University of California at Los Angeles (B.S., 1957; LL.B., 1960). Certified Public Accountant, California, 1961. Author: "Joint Checks, Practices in the Construction Industry," 1968, "Mechanic's Liens and Related Remedies," 1968 and "Bond Practices in the Construction Industry," 1969, California State Bar Journal; "Protecting a Contractor's License in an Administrative Disciplinary Proceeding," 1971, "The Stop Notice Remedy in California —Updated," 1972 and "Application of the Doctrine of Estoppel in Construction Industry Litigation," 1974, Los Angeles Bar Bulletin; "Preliminary Notices in Construction Industry Litigation —A Trap for the Unwary," Los Angeles Bar Journal, 1976; "Construction Delays, Disputes & Damages," Los Angeles Lawyer, 1978; "Construction Industry Litigation in the 1990's," Los Angeles Lawyer, 1993; "A Proposal for Summary Determination of Mechanic's Liens & Stop Notice Claims," California Construction Law Reporter, 1993; "The Little Miller Act," California Construction Law Reporter, Premier Issue, 1991; "Lis Pendens and the Enforcement of Mechanic's Liens," California Construction Law Reporter, Vol. 5, #1, Feb. 1995. Co-author: "California Mechanics Lien Law," Continuing Education of the Bar, 1988. Member, Public Works Contract Arbitration Committee, State of California, 1986—. *Member:* Beverly Hills, Los Angeles County (Member, Arbitration Committee, 1970-1973; Executive Committee, Real Property Section, 1972-1979; Chairman, 1981-1982) and American Bar Associations; The State Bar of California. *PRACTICE AREAS:* Real Property Law; Commercial Law; Construction Litigation.

*OF COUNSEL*

**HOWARD B. BROWN,** born Bisbee, Arizona, February 8, 1922; admitted to bar, 1949, California; 1973, U.S. Supreme Court; 1984, U.S. Claims Court. *Education:* University of California at Los Angeles (B.A., 1943); University of Southern California (J.D., 1948). Member, University of Southern California Law Review, 1947-1948. Co-Author: "Mechanic's Liens and California and Federal Public Works," Los Angeles County Bar Association Publication, 1967; "California Mechanics Lien Law," Continuing Education of the Bar, 1972. Author: "Mechanic's Lien Priorities," California Real Property Journal, Winter, 1985. Member, Public Works Contract Arbitration Committee, State of California, 1986—. Former Board Member, Association of General Contractors, San Fernando Chapter.

*(This Listing Continued)*

**MOSS, LEVITT & MANDELL, LLP,** Los Angeles—Continued

Panel Member, Building Industry Credit Association Seminar, "General Contractors: Recognizing, Making & Defending Against Claims," 1994. Member, Panel of Arbitrators, American Arbitration Association. *Member:* Los Angeles County (Member, State Advisory Committee to Redraft California Mechanics Lien and Bond Laws, 1964-1968) and American (Member: Committee on Fidelity and Surety Law, 1973—; Forum Committee of the Construction Industry, 1982—; TIPS Title Insurance Committee, 1993—) Bar Associations; State Bar of California. **REPORTED CASES:** J.A. Jones Construction Co. v. Superior Court, 27 Cal.App.4th 1568 (1994); Sawyer Nurseries v. Galardi, 181 Cal.App.3d 663 (1986); Sukut Const. Co. v. Cabot, Cabot & Forbes Land Trust, 95 Cal.App.3d 527 (1979); Rodeffer Industries v. Chambers Estates, 263 Cal.App. 2d 116 (1968); Avalon Painting Co. v. Alert Lumber Co., 234 Cal.App.2d 178 (1965); Bumb v. Bennett, 51 Cal.2d 294 (1958). **PRACTICE AREAS:** Construction Law; Title Insurance Law; General Trial Law; Civil Litigation.

REPRESENTATIVE CLIENTS: Admarketing, Inc.; Associated Concrete Products, Inc.; Atelier Construction Services; Beverly Hills Medical Plaza; Cleveland Wrecking Co.; Commonwealth Land Title Insurance Co.; Conejo Ready Mix, Inc.; Construction Protective Services, Inc.; Credit Managers Association of Southern California; Dal-Tile Co.; Dynamic Builders; G&J Financial Services; Glendale Ready Mix; Grinnell Corp.; HAR-BRO, Inc.; Institute of Cancer and Blood Research; L.A. Roofing Materials; Learned Lumber Co.; McWane, Inc. dba Pacific States Cast Iron Pipe Co.; Mullin Lumber Co.; National Cement of California, Inc.; Rodney Spears, Architect; Smith Emery Co.; Southdown, Inc.; Sovereign Construction Co.; Star Inc.; The System Design; TrusJoist; Tumer Construction Co.; Underground Construction Co.; Wagnild Ready Mix, Inc.; White Consolidated Industries.

## MOSTEN & TUFFIAS

*Established in 1988*

**10990 WILSHIRE BOULEVARD, SUITE 940**
**LOS ANGELES, CALIFORNIA 90024**
Telephone: 310-473-7611
Facsimile: 310-473-7422
Email: FMostenn@counsel.com

*Practice Concentrating on Family Law, Litigation Mediation.*

**FIRM PROFILE:** *All three partners of the firm are Certified Family Law Specialists as determined by the California Board of Legal Specialization.*

*The Firm will continue its practice in child custody, support, property, family law appeals, adoptions, representation of children and other areas of family law, estate planning, probate and conservatorships.*

*The firm is nationally recognized for its expertise in mediation, private adjudication and ADR consultation and training in family law, civil litigation, employment, real estate, business, professional malpractice and public policy issues.*

### MEMBERS OF FIRM

**FORREST S. MOSTEN,** born 1947; admitted to bar, 1972, California. *Education:* University of California at Riverside (A.B., 1969); University of California, Los Angeles (J.D., 1972). Phi Beta Kappa. Adjunct Professor, Pepperdine School of Law. *Member:* Beverly Hills Bar Association (Chair, Alternate Dispute Resolution Committee); State Bar of California; National Center for Preventive Law (Trustee); Association of Certified Family Law Specialists (Chair-Elect-South). (Certified Specialist, Family Law, The State Bar of California Board of Legal Specialization). **PRACTICE AREAS:** Litigation and Mediation; Family Law; Real Estate; Business; Legal Malpractice. *Email:* FMostenn@counsel.com

**HEIDI S. TUFFIAS,** born Palo Alto, California, February 10, 1966; admitted to bar, 1990, California. *Education:* University of California (B.A., 1987); University of Southern California (J.D., 1990). Editor: Computer Law Journal; Major Tax Planning. Outstanding Woman Law Student, 1990. *Member:* State Bar of California; Women Lawyers Association (Board of Governors). (Certified Specialist, Family Law, The State Bar of California Board of Legal Specialization). **PRACTICE AREAS:** Family Law; Child Custody; Mediation; Representation of Children.

## F. PATRICIA MUDIE

*A PROFESSIONAL CORPORATION*

**12100 WILSHIRE BOULEVARD, SUITE 1900**
**LOS ANGELES, CALIFORNIA 90025-1506**
Telephone: 310-820-5505
Fax: 310-207-1030

*Family Law, Divorce, Domestic Relations and Matrimonial Law.*

**F. PATRICIA MUDIE,** born Greenville, South Carolina, July 31, 1940; admitted to bar, 1977, California and U.S. District Court, Central and Southern Districts of California. *Education:* University of Pennsylvania (B.A., 1962); University of Southern California (J.D., 1977). Phi Alpha Delta. Member, 1975-1977 and Notes Editor, 1976-1977, Southern California Law Review. Lecturer, Family Law, CEB, State Bar MCLE Institute and Beverly Hills Bar Association. Arbitrator, Los Angeles County Bar Association Dispute Resolution Services. Judge Pro Tem, Family Court. Panelist, Los Angeles Superior Court, West Court District. *Member:* Beverly Hills (Chair, Executive Committee; Family Law Section), Los Angeles County (Member, Sections on: Litigation; Family Law) and American (Member, Litigation Section) Bar Associations.

## MUNGER, TOLLES & OLSON

*A Law Partnership including Professional Corporations*

**355 SOUTH GRAND AVENUE**
**35TH FLOOR**
**LOS ANGELES, CALIFORNIA 90071**
Telephone: 213-683-9100
Cable Address: "Muntoll"
Telex: 677574
Telecopier: 213-687-3702

*San Francisco, California Office:* 33 New Montgomery Street, Suite 1900. Telephone: 415-512-4000. FAX: 415-512-4077.

*General Practice. Corporation, Securities and Business Law. Litigation, Labor Relations, Antitrust Law, Taxation, Real Property, Trust and Probate Law, Savings and Loan Law, Environmental Law.*

### MEMBERS OF FIRM

**RICHARD D. ESBENSHADE, (A PROFESSIONAL CORPORATION),** born Ashland, Ohio, March 19, 1929; admitted to bar, 1958, California. *Education:* Stanford University (A.B., 1950); Harvard University (LL.B., magna cum laude, 1956). Phi Beta Kappa. Member, Board of Editors, 1954-1956 and Article Editor, 1955-1956, Harvard Law Review. *Member:* Los Angeles County and American Bar Associations; The State Bar of California. *Email:* Esbenshaderd@MTO.COM

**FREDERICK B. WARDER, JR.** (1932-1972).

**PETER R. TAFT, (A PROFESSIONAL CORPORATION),** born Cincinnati, Ohio, March 3, 1936; admitted to bar, 1963, District of Columbia; 1969, California. *Education:* Yale University (B.A., magna cum laude, 1958; LL.B., 1961). Phi Delta Phi; Phi Beta Kappa. Managing Editor, Yale Law Journal, 1960-1961. Law Clerk to Judge Richard T. Rives, U.S. Court of Appeals, Fifth Circuit, 1961-1962. Law Clerk to Chief Justice Earl Warren, U.S. Supreme Court, 1962-1963. Assistant Attorney General, Land and Natural Resources Division, U.S. Department of Justice, 1975-1977. *Member:* The State Bar of California. *Email:* Taftpr@MTO.COM

**ROBERT K. JOHNSON, (A PROFESSIONAL CORPORATION),** born New York, N.Y., April 7, 1939; admitted to bar, 1965, California and New York; 1968, U.S. Supreme Court. *Education:* Harvard University (A.B., 1961); Stanford University (LL.B., 1964). Order of the Coif. Note Editor, Stanford Law Review, 1963-1964. Co-Author: Article, "Legislative Proposal on Classification of Workers as Employees or Independent Contractors," 55 Tax Notes 821 (1992); "Equity Incentives: Strategic, Tax and Other Issues Surrounding Plan Design," 44 Major Tax Planning," (U.S.C. Tax Institute, 1992); "Executive Compensation Deferred: Should The Rabbi Be Trusted," 41 Major Tax Planning §900 (U.S.C. Tax Institute, 1989). Author: "How The New Tax Law Will Affect Executive Compensation," 65 Journal of Taxation 318 (1986). Special Assistant to the Assistant Attorney General, Antitrust Division, U.S. Department of Justice, 1965-1968. *Member:* Los Angeles County (Trustee, 1992-1994; Member, Taxation Section; Executive Committee, 1987-1994; Chair, 1992-1993; Chair, Employee Benefits Committee, 1988-1989) and American Bar Associations; The State Bar of California (Member: Taxation Section; Executive Committee, 1990-1994;

*(This Listing Continued)*

Chair, 1993-1994). Fellow, American College of Tax Counsel. (Certified Specialist, Taxation Law, The State Bar of California Board of Legal Specialization).

**ALAN V. FRIEDMAN, (A PROFESSIONAL CORPORATION),** born Akron, Ohio, September 9, 1938; admitted to bar, 1963, Ohio; 1967, California. *Education:* University of Pennsylvania (A.B., 1960); Case Western Reserve University (LL.B., 1963); Georgetown University (LL.M., 1966). Phi Delta Phi. Member, Board of Editors, Case Western Reserve Law Review, 1962-1963. Associate Editor for Labor Law, Law Notes, American Bar Association, 1968-1973. Office of the Solicitor, U.S. Department of Labor, Washington, D.C., 1963-1966. Mayor's Labor-Management Advisory Committee, 1973-1983. Member, 1984-1988 and President, 1985-1986, Los Angeles Board of Civil Service Commissioners. Board Member: Bet Tzedek Legal Services and President, 1990-1991; Board Member, Constitutional Rights Foundation, 1984— and President, 1992-1994. *Member:* Los Angeles County (Chairman, 1987-1988; Labor Law Section) and American (Member, Committees of: International Labor Law, 1984—; Labor Arbitration, 1981—, Section of Labor and Employment Law) Bar Associations; The State Bar of California. *Email:* Friedmanav@MTO.COM

**RONALD L. OLSON, (A PROFESSIONAL CORPORATION),** born Carroll, Iowa, July 9, 1941; admitted to bar, 1966, Wisconsin; 1969, California. *Education:* Drake University (B.S., 1963); University of Michigan (J.D., 1966); Oxford University (Dipl. L. 1967). Beta Gamma Sigma; Phi Eta Sigma; Omicron Delta Kappa; Barristers. Assistant Editor, Michigan Law Review, 1965-1966. Ford Foundation Fellowship for International Legal Study, 1966-1967. Attorney, U.S. Department of Justice, 1967. Law Clerk to Chief Judge David L. Bazelon, U.S. Court of Appeals for the District of Columbia, 1967-1968. Member, Executive Committee, 1987-1990, Delegate, 1984-1990 and Chairman of Lawyer Delegates, 1985-1986, Ninth Circuit Judicial Conference. *Member:* Los Angeles County (President, Barristers, 1975-1976; Trustee, 1975-1977) and American (Chairman, Litigation Section, 1981-1982; Council, 1975-1981; Chairman, Special Committee on Dispute Resolution, 1978-1985; Member, House of Delegates, 1987—; Member, 1988-1992 and Chairman, Federal Judiciary Committee, 1991-1992) Bar Associations; The State Bar of California (Vice President and Treasurer, 1986-1987; Governor, 1984-1987); Chancery Club; American Law Institute; American Judicature Society. Fellow: American College of Trial Lawyers; American Bar Foundation.

**DENNIS E. KINNAIRD, (A PROFESSIONAL CORPORATION),** born El Centro, California, August 27, 1936; admitted to bar, 1965, California. *Education:* San Diego State College (B.A., 1961); Boalt Hall School of Law, University of California (LL.B., 1964). Order of the Coif; Beta Gamma Sigma. Assistant United States Attorney for the Central District of California, 1967-1971, Chief, Special Prosecution Section. Lawyer Delegate, Ninth Circuit Judicial Conference. *Member:* Los Angeles County Bar Association; The State Bar of California; Chancery Club. Fellow, American College of Trial Lawyers.

**RICHARD S. VOLPERT,** born Cambridge, Mass., February 16, 1935; admitted to bar, 1960, California. *Education:* Amherst College (B.A., 1956); Columbia Law School (LL.B., 1959). Phi Alpha Delta. Harlan Fiske Stone Scholar. Editor, Los Angeles County Bar Bulletin, 1965-1967. Editor and Chairman, California State Bar Journal, 1972-1973. Chairman, Board of Councilors, University of Southern California Law Center, 1979-1985. Author: "Creation and Maintenance of Open Spaces in Subdivisions: Another Approach," 12 U.C.L.A. Law Review 830. President, 1978-1984 and Chairman of Board, 1992—, Los Angeles County Natural History Museum Foundation. Vice-President, 1978-1992 and President, 1993-1995, Los Angeles Wholesale Produce Market Development Corporation. Chairman, 1977-1980 and Member, 1965—, Community Relations Committee of Jewish Federation - Council of Los Angeles. Vice President, 1978-1981; 1984-1986, Jewish Federation - Council of Los Angeles. Publisher, The Jewish Journal of Greater Los Angeles, 1986-1987. Board Member, Western Center on Law and Poverty, 1971-1975. *Member:* Los Angeles County (Member, Board of Trustees, 1968-1970; Chairman, Real Property Section, 1974-1975) and American Bar Associations; The State Bar of California; American College of Real Estate Lawyers; Anglo-American Real Property Institute (Treasurer, 1995—). Fellow: American Bar Foundation.

**DENNIS C. BROWN, (A PROFESSIONAL CORPORATION),** born Long Beach, California, September 29, 1939; admitted to bar, 1971, California. *Education:* University of California at Los Angeles (A.B., 1961; J.D., 1970). Order of the Coif. Note and Comment Editor, U.C.L.A. Law Review, 1969-1970. Law Clerk to Justice William O. Douglas, U.S. Supreme Court, 1970-1971. Visiting Professor of Law, The National Law Center,

The George Washington University, 1990-1991. *Member:* Los Angeles County and American Bar Associations; The State Bar of California.

**JEFFREY I. WEINBERGER,** born New York, N.Y., March 12, 1947; admitted to bar, 1971, New York; 1973, California. *Education:* City College of New York (B.A., 1967); Columbia University (J.D., magna cum laude, 1970). Harlan Fiske Stone Scholar, 1968-1969; James Kent Scholar, 1969-1970. Staff Member, 1968-1969 and Articles Editor, 1969-1970, Columbia Law Review. *Member:* Los Angeles County and American (Member, Sections on: Antitrust Law; Litigation) Bar Associations; State Bar of California; Association of Business Trial Lawyers (President, 1995-1996 and Member, Board of Governors, 1989—). *Email:* Weinbergerji@MTO.COM

**MELVYN H. WALD** (1947-1992).

**EDWIN V. WOODSOME, JR., (A PROFESSIONAL CORPORATION),** born Chicago, Illinois, October 20, 1946; admitted to bar, 1972, Massachusetts; 1973, District of Columbia and California. *Education:* College of the Holy Cross (A.B., summa cum laude, 1968); Harvard Law School (J.D., magna cum laude, 1971). Member, Board of Editors, Harvard Law Review, 1970-71. Law Clerk to Judge James R. Browning, U.S. Court of Appeals for the Ninth Circuit, 1971-1972. *Member:* Los Angeles County (Member, Labor Law Section) and American (Member, Sections of: Natural Resources, Energy and Environmental Law; Labor and Employment Law; Litigation) Bar Associations; The State Bar of California.

**ROBERT L. ADLER,** born New York, N.Y., October 14, 1947; admitted to bar, 1974, California. *Education:* Harvard University (A.B., magna cum laude, 1969; J.D., cum laude, 1973). Phi Beta Kappa. Member, 1971-1973 and Articles Editor, 1972-1973, Harvard Law Review. Executive Assistant, Orange County Board of Supervisors, 1970-1971. Legislative Assistant to Member of Congress, 1973-1974. President and Chief Executive Officer, Ray Wilson Co., 1985. *Member:* Los Angeles County and American Bar Associations; State Bar of California.

**CARY B. LERMAN,** born Chicago, Illinois, January 26, 1948; admitted to bar, 1972, California; 1973, District of Columbia. *Education:* University of Illinois (B.S., 1969); University of California at Los Angeles (J.D., 1972). Member, 1970-1972 and Note and Comment Editor, 1971-1972, University of California at Los Angeles Law Review. *Member:* Los Angeles County and American Bar Associations; The District of Columbia Bar; State Bar of California.

**WILLIAM L. CATHEY,** born Gastonia, North Carolina, October 2, 1947; admitted to bar, 1977, California. *Education:* University of North Carolina (B.S., 1969); Central Michigan University (M.A., 1974); University of Michigan (J.D., magna cum laude, 1977). Beta Gamma Sigma; Order of the Coif. Associate Editor, 1975-1976 and Managing Editor, 1976-1977, Michigan Law Review. *Member:* Los Angeles County and American (Member, Corporation, Banking and Business Law Section) Bar Associations; The State Bar of California.

**CHARLES D. SIEGAL,** born Pittsburgh, Pennsylvania, February 14, 1946; admitted to bar, 1976, California. *Education:* Carnegie-Mellon University (B.S., with honors, 1967; M.S., 1969; Ph.D., 1972); Stanford University (J.D., 1975). Sigma Xi. Member, 1973-1974 and Senior Note Editor, 1974-1975, Stanford Law Review. Law Clerk to Judge Shirley M. Hufstedler, U.S. Court of Appeals for the Ninth Circuit, 1975-1976. Attorney-Advisor, U.S. Department of State, 1976-1977. Visiting Professor, University of Pittsburgh Law School, 1988. Lecturer at Law, 1981-1984, 1992-1993, University of Southern California Law School. Lecturer at Law, 1991, UCLA Law School. Author: "Individual Rights Under Self-Executing Extradition Treaties: Dr. Alvarez Machain's Case," 13 Loyola (L.A.) Int. & Comp. L.J. 765 (1991); "Deference and Its Dangers: Congress' Power to Define Offenses Against the Law of Nations," 21 Vand. J. Transnat'l. L. 685 (1988). *Member:* Los Angeles County (Trustee, 1987-1989) and American Bar Associations; State Bar of California. *Email:* Siegalcd@MTO.COM

**RONALD K. MEYER,** born Decorah, Iowa, January 28, 1951; admitted to bar, 1976, California. *Education:* Stanford University (A.B., with university distinction, 1973; J.D., 1976). Phi Beta Kappa; Order of the Coif. Law Clerk to Judge Stanley A. Weigel, U.S. District Court for the Northern District of California, 1976-77. Clinical Lecturer in Law, University of Southern California Law Center, 1980-1981. *Member:* American Bar Association; State Bar of California.

**GREGORY P. STONE,** born Ventura, California, July 21, 1952; admitted to bar, 1977, California. *Education:* California Institute of Technology (B.S., 1974; M.S., 1974); Yale University (J.D., 1977). Tau Beta Pi. Law Clerk to Judge Wm. Matthew Byrne, Jr., U.S. District Court, Central Dis-

*(This Listing Continued)*

**MUNGER, TOLLES & OLSON, Los Angeles—Continued**

trict of California, 1977-1978. *Member:* Los Angeles County and American Bar Associations; The State Bar of California.

**VILMA S. MARTINEZ,** born San Antonio, Texas, October 17, 1943; admitted to bar, 1968, New York; 1975, California. *Education:* University of Texas (B.A., 1964); Columbia University (LL.B., 1967). John Hay Whitney Fellow, 1964. Honorary Doctor of Laws, Amherst College, 1983. Samuel Rubin Fellow, Columbia University School of Law, 1983. Recipient: Medal for Excellence, Columbia Law School, 1992; Distinguished Alumnus Award, University of Texas, 1988; University Medal of Excellence, Columbia University, 1978; Jefferson Award, American Institute for Public Service, 1976. Regent, 1976-1990 and Chairman of the Board, 1984-1986, University of California. President and General Counsel, Mexican American Legal Defense and Educational Fund, Inc., 1973-1982. Member: California Federal Judicial Selection Committee 1977-1980. Presidential Advisory Board on Ambassadorial Appointments, 1977-1981. Consultant: U.S. Commission on Civil Rights, 1969-1973; Immigration and Naturalization Service, 1975-1977; United States Bureau of Census, 1975-1981; United States Treasury Department, 1976. Lawyer Delegate, Ninth Judicial Conference, 1988-1992. *Member:* Los Angeles County Bar Association (Member, Board of Trustees, 1982-1984); State Bar of California.

**LUCY T. EISENBERG,** born New York, N.Y., March 6, 1941; admitted to bar, 1975, California. *Education:* Radcliffe College (A.B., 1961); Oxford University, Oxford, England (M.A., 1964); University of California at Los Angeles (J.D., 1975). Phi Beta Kappa. *Member:* Los Angeles County and American Bar Associations; The State Bar of California.

**BRAD D. BRIAN,** born Merced, California, April 19, 1952; admitted to bar, 1977, California; 1978, U.S. Court of Appeals, Third Circuit and U.S. District Court, Central District of California; 1980, U.S. Court of Appeals, Ninth Circuit. *Education:* University of California at Berkeley (B.A., 1974) Phi Beta Kappa; Harvard University (J.D., magna cum laude, 1977). Member, Board of Editors, 1975-1977 and Managing Editor and Treasurer, 1976-1977, Harvard Law Review. Lecturer in Law, University of Southern California Law Center, 1983. Guest Instructor, Harvard Law School Trial Advocacy Program, 1983. Instructor, National Institute of Trial Advocacy, 1986. Co-editor: *Internal Corporate Investigations: Conducting Them, Protecting Them* (ABA Section of Litigation, 1992). Co-author: "Vicarious Liability of Corporations and Corporate Enterprises under RICO," Civil RICO, Practising Law Institute, 1988. Law Clerk to Honorable John J. Gibbons, U.S. Court of Appeals, Third Circuit, 1977-1978. Assistant United States Attorney for the Central District of California, 1978-1981. Hearing Examiner, Los Angeles City Police Commission, 1982. *Member:* Beverly Hills (Board Member), Los Angeles County (Member, Federal Practice Standards Committee, 1980-1982), Federal (Vice President, Los Angeles Chapter, 1995-1996) and American (Chairman, Committee on Pre-Trial Practice and Discovery, Litigation Section, 1987-1989; Liaison with Federal Judicial Conferences, 1989-1991; Council Member, 1993—; Chair, Task Force on State of the Justice System, 1993; Chair, Task Force on Civil Justice Reform Act of 1990-1992) Bar Associations; State Bar of California.

**BRADLEY S. PHILLIPS,** born Los Angeles, California, March 1, 1954; admitted to bar, 1979, California. *Education:* Stanford University (B.A., 1975); Yale University (J.D., 1978). Phi Beta Kappa. Member, Board of Editors, Yale Law Journal, 1977-1978. Author: "Limiting the Peremptory Challenge: Representation of Groups on Petit Juries," 86 Yale Law Journal 1715, 1977. Adjunct Professor of Law, Loyola Law School, 1983-1988; Law Clerk to Judge Wm. Matthew Byrne, Jr., U.S. District Court, Central District of California, 1978-1979. Member, Board of Directors, Legal Aid Foundation of Los Angeles, 1985-1993; President, 1992-1993. *Member:* Los Angeles County (Member, Board of Trustees, 1992-1993; Chairperson, Amicus Briefs Committee, 1983-1986; Member, Legal Services for Poor Committee, 1983-1990, Chairperson, 1988-1990) and American Bar Associations; The State Bar of California.

**GEORGE M. GARVEY,** born Glen Cove, New York, June 30, 1954; admitted to bar, 1979, California. *Education:* Yale University (B.A., cum laude, 1976); Harvard University (J.D., cum laude, 1979). Industry-Affiliated Member of Arbitration Panels of the New York Stock Exchange, National Association of Securities Dealers and National Futures Association. *Member:* Los Angeles County and American Bar Associations; The State Bar of California; Association of Business Trial Lawyers of Los Angeles; Securities Industry Association (Legal and Compliance Division).
*Email:* Garveygm@MTO.COM

*(This Listing Continued)*

**RITA J. MILLER,** born New York, N.Y.; admitted to bar, 1979, California and U.S. District Court, Central District of California; 1982, U.S. Court of Appeals, Ninth Circuit; 1984, U.S. District Court, Northern District of California; 1987, U.S. District Court, Southern District of California; 1991, U.S. Court of Appeals, Tenth Circuit. *Education:* Connecticut College (A.B.); Loyola Law School of Los Angeles (J.D., summa cum laude, 1979). Member, St. Thomas More Law Honor Society. Member, 1977-1978 and Chief Articles Editor, 1978-1979, Loyola of Los Angeles Law Review. Author: "Shaffer v. Heitner: Reshaping the Contours of State Court Jurisdiction," 11 Loyola of Los Angeles Law Review, 1977. Member, Loyola Law School Board of Governors, 1980-1984. Member, Board of Directors, Family Assistance Involving the Homeless, 1990—. Hearing Examiner, Los Angeles City Police Commission, 1987—. *Member:* Los Angeles County Bar Association (Secretary, Human Rights Section, 1980-1982); The State Bar of California (Member, Standing Committee on Group Insurance, 1991-1994); Cowboy Lawyers Association(Member, 1994—).

**D. BARCLAY EDMUNDSON,** born Los Angeles, California, October 23, 1947; admitted to bar, 1979, California. *Education:* University of Southern California (A.B., magna cum laude, 1969); University of California at Los Angeles (J.D., 1979). Order of the Coif; Order of the Barristers; Phi Beta Kappa. Law Clerk to Hon. William Matthew Byrne, U.S. District Court, Central District of California, 1979-1980. *Member:* Los Angeles County Bar Association; State Bar of California. *Email:* Edmundsondb@MTO.COM

**WILLIAM D. TEMKO,** born Washington, D.C., April 21, 1954; admitted to bar, 1979, District of Columbia; 1981, California. *Education:* Williams College (B.A., magna cum laude, 1976); Columbia University (J.D., 1979). Phi Beta Kappa. Articles Editor, Columbia Journal of Law and Social Problems, 1978-1979. Author: "Weber v. Kaiser Aluminum & Chemical Corp.: The Challenge to Voluntary Compliance Under Title VII," 14 Colum. Journal of Law and Social Problems, 123, 1978. Law Clerk to Judge Frank A. Kaufman, U.S. District Court, District of Maryland, 1979-1980. *Member:* The District of Columbia Bar; State Bar of California.

**STEVEN L. GUISE, (A PROFESSIONAL CORPORATION),** born Harrisburg, Pennsylvania, December 10, 1946; admitted to bar, 1971, Michigan; 1974, Georgia; 1975, U.S. Tax Court; 1978, California. *Education:* University of Michigan (A.B., 1968); Vanderbilt University (J.D., 1971); Georgetown University (LL.M. in Taxation, 1976). Law Clerk, Michigan Court of Appeals, 1971-1972. *Member:* Los Angeles County (Member, Tax Section) and American (Member, Section of Taxation and Member, Section of Real Property, Probate and Trust Law) Bar Associations; State Bar of Michigan; State Bar of Georgia; State Bar of California. *Email:* Guisesl@MTO.COM

**ROBERT B. KNAUSS,** born New York, N.Y., August 6, 1953; admitted to bar, 1981, California. *Education:* Harvard University (A.B., magna cum laude, 1975); University of Michigan (J.D., magna cum laude, 1979). Order of the Coif. Note Editor, Michigan Law Review, 1978-1979. Law Clerk to: Judge Walter R. Mansfield, U.S. Court of Appeals, Second Circuit, 1979-1980; Justice William H. Rehnquist, U.S. Supreme Court, 1980-1981. *Member:* Los Angeles County Bar Association (Executive Committee, Business and Corporations Law Section); State Bar of California. *Email:* Knaussrb@MTO.COM

**R. GREGORY MORGAN,** born Long Beach, California, January 24, 1954; admitted to bar, 1981, California; 1982, U.S. District Court, Central District of California. *Education:* University of California at Los Angeles (B.A., summa cum laude, 1976); University of Michigan (J.D., 1979). Phi Beta Kappa. Member, 1977-1979 and Article and Book Review Editor, 1978-1979, Michigan Law Review. Author: "Using Finance Theory to Measure Damages in Fraud on the Market Cases," 37 UCLA Law Review 883, 1990 (with Bradford Cornell); "Securities Law Considerations Affecting Employee Benefit Plans," Corporate Practice Series, No. 44, BNA, 1985 (with Simon Lorne); "Roe v. Wade and the Lesson of the Pre-Roe Case Law," 77 Michigan Law Review 1724, 1979; Note," Racial Vote Dilution in Multimember Districts: The Constitutional Standard after Washington v. Davis," 76 Michigan Law Review 694, 1978. Law Clerk to: Honorable J. Edward Lumbard, U.S. Court of Appeals, Second Circuit, 1979-1980; Honorable Lewis F. Powell, Jr., U.S. Supreme Court, 1980-1981. Lecturer in Law, University of Southern California Law Center, 1986-1988. Visiting Professor, UCLA Law School, 1988-1989. Lecturer, UCLA Graduate School of Management, 1991, 1992. *Member:* State Bar of California; American Bar Association.

**STEPHEN M. KRISTOVICH,** born Los Angeles, California, February 23, 1953; admitted to bar, 1978, California; 1980, District of Columbia. *Education:* Stanford University (A.B., with distinction, 1975); Boalt Hall

*(This Listing Continued)*

School of Law, University of California at Berkeley (J.D., 1978). Phi Beta Kappa. Associate Editor, 1976-1977; Research Editor, 1977-1978, California Law Review. Author: Note, "United States v. Barker: Misapplication of the Reliance on an Official Interpretation of the Law Defense," 66 California Law Review 809, 1978. Visiting Fellow, Center for Law in the Public Interest, 1978-1979. *Member:* The District of Columbia Bar; State Bar of California; American Bar Association (Member, Sections on: Litigation; Natural Resources).

**JOHN W. SPIEGEL,** born San Francisco, California, October 23, 1948; admitted to bar, 1977, California; 1978, District of Columbia. *Education:* Stanford University (A.B., with great distinction, 1970; M.A., Economics, 1972; M.S., Statistics, 1972); Yale Law School (J.D., 1976). Phi Beta Kappa. Editor-in-Chief, Yale Law Journal, 1975-1976. Law Clerk to Justice Byron R. White, U.S. Supreme Court, 1976-1977. Special Assistant to Deputy Secretary of State Warren Christopher, 1977-1979. Assistant U.S. Attorney, Central District of California, Los Angeles, 1979-1982. General Counsel to the Independent Commission on the Los Angeles Police Department (Christopher Commission), 1991. Stanford Law School Board of Visitors, 1995-1997; ABA Litigation Section: Co-Chair, Committee on Class Actions and Derivative Suits, 1989-1992; Chair, Coordinating Group on Civil Justice Reform, 1992-1993. Chair, Committee on Professionalism, Los Angeles County Bar Association, 1990-1992. Trial Advocacy Instructor: National Institute for Trial Advocacy, 1984-1986; University of Southern California Law Center, 1980-1982; The Hastings Center for Trial and Appellate Advocacy, 1983-1985. Faculty Member: ABA National Institute on Taking Depositions, 1987-1988; CEB Federal Practice Institute, 1987-1997. *Member:* Los Angeles County and American Bar Associations; State Bar of California. Fellow, American Bar Foundation. *Email:* Spiegeljw@MTO.COM

**TERRY E. SANCHEZ,** born North Hollywood, California, February 14, 1956; admitted to bar, 1981, California; 1982, U.S. District Court, Central District of California and U.S. Court of Appeals, Ninth Circuit; 1987, U.S. District Court, Southern District of California; 1988, U.S. District Court, Northern District of California; 1995, U.S. Supreme Court. *Education:* Claremont Mens College (B.A., summa cum laude, 1978); Stanford University (J.D., 1981). Order of the Coif. *Member:* Los Angeles County and American Bar Associations; State Bar of California.

**STEVEN M. PERRY,** born Myrtle Beach, South Carolina, July 19, 1956; admitted to bar, 1982, California and U.S. District Court, Central District of California; 1983, U.S. Court of Appeals, Ninth Circuit; 1986, U.S. Court of Appeals for the Federal Circuit and U.S. District Court, Southern District of California; 1990, U.S. District Court, Northern District of California. *Education:* University of North Carolina (B.A.,1978); Yale University (J.D., 1981). Phi Beta Kappa. *Member:* Los Angeles County and American Bar Associations; The State Bar of California.

**RUTH E. FISHER,** born Frankfurt, Germany, December 12, 1955; admitted to bar, 1980, California and U.S. District Court, Central District of California; 1986, U.S. Court of Appeals, Ninth Circuit. *Education:* Scripps College (B.A., 1976); University of California at Los Angeles School of Law (J.D., 1980). Phi Beta Kappa. Member, 1978-1980 and Comment Editor, 1979-1980, UCLA Law Review. Law Clerk to Judge Malcolm M. Lucas, U.S. District Court, Central District of California, 1980-1982. *Member:* Los Angeles County and American Bar Associations; The State Bar of California. *Email:* Fisherre@MTO.COM

**MARK B. HELM,** born Burbank, California, October 4, 1956; admitted to bar, 1984, California and U.S. District Court, Central District of California; 1985, U.S. Court of Appeals, Ninth and District of Columbia Circuits; 1987, U.S. District Court, Southern District of California; 1989, U.S. Supreme Court; 1991, U.S. Court of Appeals, Fifth Circuit; 1992, U.S. District Court, Eastern District of Michigan. *Education:* Harvard University (A.B., magna cum laude, 1978; J.D., magna cum laude, 1982). President, Harvard Law Review, 1981-1982. Law Clerk to: Judge Carl McGowan, U.S. Court of Appeals, District of Columbia Circuit, 1982-1983; Chief Justice Warren E. Burger, U.S. Supreme Court, 1983-1984. Adjunct Professor of Law, Loyola Law School, 1991-1992. Member, Ninth Circuit Indigent Appellate Panel. *Member:* Los Angeles County (Secretary, 1989-1990, Vice Chair, 1990-1992 and Chair, 1992-1993, Committee on Professional Responsibility and Ethics) and American Bar Associations; State Bar of California.

**JOSEPH D. LEE,** born Los Angeles, California, September 6, 1957; admitted to bar, 1983, California. *Education:* University of California at Los Angeles (B.A., magna cum laude, 1979); Boalt Hall School of Law, University of California (J.D., 1982). Order of the Coif. Associate Editor, 1981 and Managing Editor, 1981-1982, Ecology Law Quarterly. Member,

Board of Editors, Leader's Legal Tech Newsletter. Law Clerk to the Hon. Roger Robb, U.S. Court of Appeals, D.C. Circuit, 1982-1983. *Member:* Los Angeles County Bar Association; State Bar of California (Chair, Law Technology Committee, Litigation Section).

**MICHAEL R. DOYEN,** born Pomona, California, March 24, 1955; admitted to bar, 1984, New York; 1985, California; 1995, U.S. Court of Appeals, Ninth Circuit, Fourth and Eleventh Circuits. *Education:* University of California at Berkeley (B.A., magna cum laude, 1979); Harvard University (J.D., 1982). Phi Beta Kappa. Articles Editor, Harvard Law Review, 1981-1982. Law Clerk for Hon. J. Edward Lumbard, U.S. Court of Appeals, 2nd Circuit, New York, N.Y., 1982-1983. *Member:* Los Angeles County, New York State and American Bar Associations; State Bar of California; American Association for the Advancement of Science; Los Angeles World Affairs Council.

**MICHAEL E. SOLOFF,** born Orange, New Jersey, December 31, 1958; admitted to bar, 1984, California. *Education:* Brown University (B.A., magna cum laude, 1980); Harvard University (J.D., magna cum laude, 1983). Member, Harvard Law Review, 1981-1982 and Developments Office Head, 1982-1983. Law Clerk to the Honorable Ruth Bader Ginsburg, U.S. Court of Appeals, District of Columbia Circuit, 1983-1984. *Member:* Los Angeles County and American Bar Associations; State Bar of California.

**GREGORY D. PHILLIPS,** born Los Angeles, California, September 12, 1949; admitted to bar, 1985, California and U.S. District Court, Central District of California. *Education:* Stanford University (B.A., with great distinction, 1971); Harvard University (M.A., 1973; Ph.D., 1976); Yale Law School (J.D., 1983). Phi Beta Kappa. Law Clerk to the Hon. William A. Norris, U.S. Court of Appeals for the Ninth Circuit, 1983-1984. *Member:* Los Angeles County Bar Association; State Bar of California.

**JOHN B. FRANK,** born Boston, Massachusetts, June 8, 1956; admitted to bar, 1985, California and U.S. District Court, Central District of California. *Education:* Wesleyan University (B.A., with honors in history, 1978); University of Michigan (J.D., magna cum laude, 1983). Order of the Coif. Associate Editor, 1981-1982 and Managing Editor, 1982-1983, Michigan Law Review. Author: Note, "Intent or Impact: Proving Discrimination Under Title VI of the Civil Rights Act of 1964," 80 Michigan Law Review 1095, 1982. Legislative Assistant to the Honorable Robert F. Drinan, Member of Congress, 1978-1980; Law Clerk to the Honorable Frank M. Coffin, U.S. Court of Appeals, First Circuit, 1983-1984. Member, Advisory Board, Institute for Corporate Counsel. *Member:* Los Angeles County (Member, Business and Corporations Law Section) and American (Member, Business Law Section) Bar Associations; State Bar of California. *Email:* Frankjb@MTO.COM

**LAWRENCE C. BARTH,** born New York, N.Y., April 22, 1954; admitted to bar, 1985, New York and U.S. Court of Appeals, Second Circuit; 1986, California, U.S. Court of Appeals, Ninth Circuit and U.S. District Court, Central, Southern and Eastern Districts of California. *Education:* Cooper Union; Cardozo Law School, Yeshiva University (J.D., summa cum laude, 1984). Member, 1982-1983 and Articles Editor, 1983-1984, Cardozo Law Review. Law Clerk to the Hon. Irving R. Kaufman, U.S. Court of Appeals, Second Circuit, 1984-1985. *Member:* State Bar of California; New York State and American Bar Associations.

**KATHLEEN M. MCDOWELL,** born LaCrosse, Wisconsin; admitted to bar, 1984, California; 1986, U.S. District Court, Southern and Central Districts of California; 1996, U.S. Court of Appeals, Ninth Circuit. *Education:* University of Wisconsin; University of Massachusetts (B.A., 1978); University of Southern California (J.D., 1984). Order of the Coif. Staff Member, 1982-1983 and Editor-in-Chief, 1983-1984, Southern California Law Review. Law Clerk to Chief Judge Gordon Thompson, Jr., U.S. District Court, Southern District of California, 1984-1986. *Member:* Los Angeles County and American Bar Associations; State Bar of California; Women Lawyers Association of Los Angeles. *Email:* Mcdowellkm@MTO.COM

**GLENN D. POMERANTZ,** born North Tarrytown, New York, February 2, 1958; admitted to bar, 1984, California and U.S. District Court, Central District of California; 1985, District of Columbia; 1986, U.S. Court of Appeals, Third Circuit; 1989, U.S. Court of Appeals, Ninth Circuit. *Education:* University of California at Berkeley (A.B., summa cum laude, 1980); Harvard University (J.D., cum laude, 1983). Phi Beta Kappa. Law Clerk to Hon. David V. Kenyon, U.S. District Court, Central District of California, 1983-1985. *Member:* State Bar of California; American Bar Association.

**THOMAS B. WALPER,** born Salem, Oregon, May 15, 1954; admitted to bar, 1980, California. *Education:* University of Southern California (B.S., 1976; M.B.A., 1977); Loyola University of Los Angeles (J.D., 1980). Contributor: "Bankruptcy Practice and Procedure," Practising Law Institute,

*(This Listing Continued)*

**MUNGER, TOLLES & OLSON,** Los Angeles—Continued

1986-1990; *The Substantive and Procedural Basics,* Practising Law Institute, 1987-1989; *Dealing with the Reorganizing Debtor,* Practising Law Institute, 1986; *Current Developments in Bankruptcy and Reorganization,* Practising Law Institute, 1987-1990. Contributor and Panelist: "Current Developments in Bankruptcy," Practising Law Institute, 1986; Chair, "Bankruptcy Law Update," Practising Law Institute, 1993-1994. Lecturer in Law: University of Southern California Law School, 1993—; Practising Law Institute Panelist, *Current Issues in Negotiating Commercial Leases, 1994—;* CLE International Panelist, Negotiating Leases, 1994—; American Conference Institute Panelist, *Understanding Commerical Leases, 1995—.* Author, *Creditors' Committee Manual,* Warren, Gorham & Lamont, 1994. Member, Board of Contributors, "The Bankruptcy Strategist," 1987—; Member: Advisory Committee, UCLA Bankruptcy Institute, 1994; Member: Attorneys' Committee, United States League of Savings Institutions, 1987-1989; Subcommittee, Supervisory Enforcement and Receiverships, 1987-1989. *Member:* Los Angeles County (Member, Executive Committee, Commercial Law and Bankruptcy Section, 1993—; Secretary, 1996—; Chairman, 1992-1994, Program Chairman,1991-1992 of Bankruptcy Committee) and American Bar Associations; The State Bar of California; Financial Lawyers Conference and American Bankruptcy Institute.

**RONALD C. HAUSMANN,** born Aurora, Illinois, May 29, 1947; admitted to bar, 1974, District of Columbia; 1980, U.S. Supreme Court; 1981, California. *Education:* Washington University (A.B., 1969); Georgetown University (J.D., 1973). Associate Editor, Class Action Reports, 1972-1973. Attorney, Office of Pesticide Programs, 1973-1974, and Office of the General Counsel, 1974-1979, U.S. Environmental Protection Agency. Trial Attorney, U.S. Department of Justice, Pollution Control and Environmental Enforcement Sections, Washington, D.C., 1979-1981. Member, Natural Resources Law and Litigation Sections, American Bar Association. *Member:* State Bar of California; The District of Columbia Bar. (Resident, San Francisco Office).

**PATRICK J. CAFFERTY, JR.,** born New York, N.Y., May 17, 1951; admitted to bar, 1976, New Jersey; 1980, U.S. Supreme Court; 1982, California. *Education:* Brown University (B.S., 1973); Fordham University (J.D., cum laude, 1976). Trial Attorney, U.S. Department of Justice, Pollution Control and Environmental Defense Sections, Washington, D.C., 1976-1982. Member, Natural Resources Law and Litigation Sections, American Bar Association. (Resident, San Francisco Office).

**JAY MASA FUJITANI,** born Wailuku, Hawaii, November 16, 1959; admitted to bar, 1987, California. *Education:* University of California at Los Angeles (B.A., 1981) Phi Beta Kappa; Boalt Hall School of Law, University of California (J.D., 1984). Order of the Coif. Law Clerk to: Hon. Stanley A. Weigel, U.S. District Court, Northern District of California 1984-1985; Hon. William J. Brennan, Jr., U.S. Supreme Court, 1985-1986. Co-author: "Securities Law Considerations Affecting Employee Benefit Plans," BNA Corporate Practice Series, No. 44-2nd, 1993. *Member:* State Bar of California (Member, Corporations Committee). *Email:* Fujitanijm@MTO.COM

**O'MALLEY M. MILLER,** born Santa Monica, California, September 25, 1951; admitted to bar, 1976, California. *Education:* Stanford University (B.A., with distinction, 1973); University of Southern California Law Center (J.D., 1976). Co-Author: *In re BFP: In the Ninth Circuit, the Price Obtained at a Nonconclusive Foreclosure Sale Is Now Irrebuttable Evidence of "Reasonably Equivalent Value,"* CEB Real Property Law Reporter, Vol. 15, No. 8, November, 1992; *"Legal Opinions in California Real Estate Transactions,"* The Business Lawyer, Vol. 42, No. 4, August, 1987; *Opinions of Counsel in Real Property Transactions,* a Joint Committee Report by The Real Property Law Section of the State Bar of California and the Real Property Section of the Los Angeles County Bar Association; Author: *Transferable Development Rights-The Los Angeles Experience,* California Real Property Law Journal, Fall, 1982. Co-Chair, Commercial and Industrial Subsection of the Real Property Section of The State Bar of California, 1986-1989. *Member:* Los Angeles County (Member, Executive Committee, 1979-1993, Chair, General Practice Subsection, 1979-1980; Vice Chair, 1988-1991 and Chair, 1991-1992, Real Property Section) and American (Member, Business Law Section and Real Property, Probate and Trust Section) Bar Associations; State Bar of California (Member, Executive Committee, Real Property Section, 1989-1990); American College of Real Estate Lawyers.

**SANDRA A. SEVILLE-JONES,** born Hazel Grove, England, July 17, 1960; admitted to bar, 1986, California. *Education:* Harvard University (B.A., 1982); University of California at Los Angeles (J.D., 1986). *Member:* State Bar of California.

**MARK H. EPSTEIN,** born Santa Monica, California, November 11, 1959; admitted to bar, 1985, California and U.S. District Court, Northern District of California; 1989, U.S District Court, Central District of California; 1990, U.S. District Court, Southern District of California; U.S. District Court, Eastern District of California; 1991, U.S. Court of Appeals, Ninth Circuit; 1994, U.S. Supreme Court. *Education:* University of California at Los Angeles (B.A., 1981); Boalt Hall School of Law, University of California (J.D., 1985). Order of the Coif. Note and Comment Editor, California Law Review, 1984-1985. Law Clerk to: Hon. Stanley A. Wiegel, U.S. District Court, Northern District of California, 1985-1986; Hon. Edward Panelli, Associate Justice, California Supreme Court, 1986-1987; Hon. William J. Brennan, Jr. Associate Justice, Supreme Court of the United States, 1987-1988. *Member:* State Bar of California; American Bar Association.

**HENRY WEISSMANN,** born Rio De Janeiro, Brazil, October 28, 1962; admitted to bar, 1987, California; 1988, U.S. District Court, Central District of California. *Education:* Claremont McKenna College (B.A., summa cum laude, 1984); Yale University (J.D., 1987). Phi Beta Kappa. Law Clerk: Hon. James L. Buckley, U.S. Court of Appeals for the District of Columbia Circuit; Hon. Antonin Scalia, Associate Justice, Supreme Court of the United States. *Member:* State Bar of California; American Bar Association (Member, Public Utility, Communications and Transportation Law and Litigation Sections); Los Angeles County Bar (Member, Professional Responsibility and Ethics Committee). Chairperson, Los Angeles Lawyers' Division, Federalist Society.

**KEVIN S. ALLRED,** born Evanston, Illinois, August 22, 1960; admitted to bar, 1986, California and U.S. District Court, Central District of California; 1991, U.S. District Court, Southern District of California. *Education:* University of Illinois (B.A., 1982); University of California at Berkeley (M.A., 1986); Boalt Hall School of Law, University of California (J.D., 1986). Order of the Coif. Member, California Law Review, 1983-1984. Law Clerk to Judge Irving Hill, U.S. District Court, Central District of California, 1986-1988. *Member:* State Bar of California.

**MARC A. BECKER,** born La Charite Sur Loire, France, September 9, 1964; admitted to bar, 1988, California and U.S. District Court, Central District of California. *Education:* University of Toronto, Canada (B. Mus. Perf., 1984); Boalt Hall School of Law, University of California (J.D., 1988). Order of the Coif. Member, California Law Review, 1986-1987. Law Clerk to Honorable Stephen V. Wilson, U.S. District Judge, Central District of California. *Member:* State Bar of California; American Bar Association (Member, Litigation and Public Contract Sections); Federal Bar Association, Los Angeles Chapter (Member, Board of Directors).

**CYNTHIA L. BURCH,** born Wichita, Kansas, September 21, 1952; admitted to bar, 1979, California. *Education:* University of Kansas (A.B., 1974); Washburn University School of Law (J.D., 1977); Institute of International Law, Paris, France. Issue Editor, Washburn Law Journal. *Member:* State Bar of California; American Bar Association (Member, Natural Resource Section). *PRACTICE AREAS:* Environmental.

**BART H. WILLIAMS,** born Orleans, France, October 24, 1962; admitted to bar, 1988, California and U.S. District Court, Central District of California. *Education:* Yale University (B.A., 1984; J.D., 1987). Potter Stewart Prize, Yale Moot Court Appeals. Assistant U.S. Attorney, Central District of California, U.S. Department of Justice, 1991-1994, Major Frauds Section, Securities Fraud, Mail and Wire Fraud, Money Laundering, Bank Fraud. Associate, Munger Tolles & Olson, 1987-1991 *Member:* State Bar of California; American Bar Association (Member, Sections on Litigation; Criminal Law). *PRACTICE AREAS:* Commercial Litigation; White Collar Criminal Defense.

**JEFFREY A. HEINTZ,** born Sidney, Ohio, June 15, 1960; admitted to bar, 1985, Ohio; 1986, California. *Education:* Ohio Northern University (B.S., highest honors, 1982); The Ohio State University (J.D., summa cum laude, 1985). Order of the Coif. Articles Editor, Ohio State Law Journal, 1984-1985. *Member:* Los Angeles County Bar Association (Member, Steering Committee of Real Estate/Commercial Section); State Bar of California. *PRACTICE AREAS:* Real Estate.

**JUDITH T. KITANO,** born Gardena, California, February 9, 1961; admitted to bar, 1988, California; 1989, U.S. District Court, Central District of California. *Education:* University of California at Los Angeles (B.A., magna cum laude, 1984); Stanford Law School (J.D., 1988); Stanford University Graduate School of Business (M.B.A., 1988). Phi Beta Kappa. *Member:* State Bar of California.

*(This Listing Continued)*

**KRISTIN A. LINSLEY,** born Boston, Massachusetts, July 27, 1960; admitted to bar, 1988, Massachusetts; 1989, New York; 1990, U.S. Court of Appeals, Ninth Circuit; 1991, California and U.S. District Court, Central District of California. *Education:* Harvard University (A.B., magna cum laude, 1982; J.D., magna cum laude, 1988). Law Clerk to Hon. Douglas H. Ginsburg, U.S. Court of Appeals, District of Columbia Circuit, 1988-1989; Law Clerk to Hon. Antonin Scalia, Supreme Court of the United States, 1989-1990. *Email:* Linsleyka@MTO.COM

**MARC T. G. DWORSKY,** born South Africa, May 22, 1961; admitted to bar, 1989, New York; 1990, British Columbia; 1991, California; 1995, U.S. Supreme Court. *Education:* Hebrew University of Jerusalem, Israel; University of Toronto; York University (B.A., with distinction, 1983); Osgoode Hall Law School (LL.B., Gold Medalist, 1986); Harvard University (LL.M., 1988). Law Clerk to Justice G.V. LaForest, Supreme Court of Canada, 1986-1987. Viscount Bennett Fellow. Member, Lawyers Committee for Human Rights, 1989-1990. *Member:* Association of the Bar of the City of New York (Secretary, International Law Committee, 1989-1990); Los Angeles County and American Bar Associations. *LANGUAGES:* Hebrew and Afrikaans. *Email:* Dworskymt@MTO.COM

**JEROME C. ROTH,** born Brooklyn, New York, January 7, 1958; admitted to bar, 1985, New York; 1992, California. *Education:* Harvard University (B.A., magna cum laude, 1979; J.D., magna cum laude, 1983). Editor, Harvard Law Review, 1982-1983. Law Clerk, Hon. William W Schwarzer, Northern District of California, 1983-1984. Author: Note, "Civil RICO: The Temptation and Impropriety of Judicial Restriction," 95 Harvard Law Review 1101 (1982). Assistant U.S. Attorney, Eastern District of New York, 1987-1991. Chair, Subcommittee on Privileges of Criminal Law and Procedures Committee of Litigation Section, American Bar Association, 1993. *Member:* Association of the Bar of the City of New York; Bar Association of San Francisco; American Bar Association (Chair, White Collar Crime Subcommittee for Northern California, 1995-1996). (Resident, San Francisco Office). *LANGUAGES:* French, Spanish, Italian. *PRACTICE AREAS:* White Collar Criminal Law; Commercial Civil Litigation. *Email:* Rothjc@MTO.COM

**STEVEN D. ROSE,** born New York, N.Y., November 21, 1961; admitted to bar, 1991, California; 1992, U.S. Tax Court. *Education:* University of California at San Diego (B.A., with distinction, 1986); University of California at Berkeley (M.B.A., 1990); Hastings College of the Law, University of California (J.D., 1990); New York University (LL.M., in Taxation, 1991). Graduate Editor, New York University Tax Law Review, 1990-1991. Recipient, American Jurisprudence Awards in Criminal Law, Federal Income Taxation and Corporations. Winner of Arthur Andersen & Co. Prize in Tax :aw. 1989. Recipient, New York University Tax Law Review Scholarship. Co-Author: State Bar of California Taxation Section Proposal, "'Check the Box' Elective Partnership Taxation and Reduced Cost Entity Conversions: A Proposal for Simplicity and Horizontal Equity" 95 TNT 147-46 (July 28, 1995); Article, "Legislative Proposal on Classification of Workers as Employees or Independent Contractors," 55 Tax Notes 821 (1992); Article, "Classification of Workers as Employees or Independent Contractors: A Proposed Legislative Solution," 10 Am. J. Tax Policy 1 (1992). *Member:* Los Angeles County Bar Association (Member, Business Law and Taxation Sections); The State Bar of California (Member, Business Law and Taxation Sections; Chair, 1995-1996, Corporate Tax Committee and Chair, 1996-1997, Partnership and Real Estate Tax Committee). *Email:* Rosesd@MTO.COM

**JEFFREY L. BLEICH,** born Neubruke, Germany, May 17, 1961; admitted to bar, 1989, California; 1990, U.S. Court of Appeals, District of Columbia Circuit; 1991, District of Columbia; 1993, U.S. Supreme Court. *Education:* Amherst College (B.A., magna cum laude, 1983); Harvard University (M.P.P., 1986); Boalt Hall School of Law, University of California, Berkeley (J.D., 1989). Order of the Coif. Member, 1987-1989 and Editor-in-Chief, 1988-1989, California Law Review. Author: *A New Direction for the Permanent Court of Arbitration,* 5 Leiden J. Int.L. (1993); Mikva & Bleich, *When Congress Overrules the Court,* 79 Calif. L. Rev. 729 (1991); Comment, *The Politics of Prison Crowding,* 77 Calif. L. Rev. 1125 (1989); Comment, *Chrome on the Range:* Off-Road Vehicles on Public Lands, 15 Ecol. L.Q. 159 (1988); M. Moore & J. Bleich, 1 From Children to Citizens, Springer-Verlag: New York (1987); *Towards an Effective Policy for Handling Dangerous Juvenile Offenders,* 3 From Children to Citizens, F. Hartmann (ed.) (1987); *Treatment of Dangerous Juvenile Offenders,* Governance: Harv. J. of Pub. Pol'y (1987). Law Clerk to: Hon. Abner J. Mikva, U.S. Court of Appeals, D.C. Circuit, 1989-1990; Chief Justice William H. Rehnquist, U.S. Supreme Court, 1990-1991; Hon. Howard M. Holtzmann, U.S.-Iran Claims Tribunal, The Hague, 1991-1992. Board Member, Bar Association of San Francisco (1994-1995); President, Barristers Club of San Francisco

*(This Listing Continued)*

(1995); Barrister of the Year (1995); Boalt Hall Recent Alumnus of the Year (1996); Vice-Chair, American Bar Association/Section on Individual Rights and Responsibilities Committee on Human Rights (1995-1996). (Resident, San Francisco Office).

**GARTH T. VINCENT,** born Evanston, Illinois, May 15, 1961; admitted to bar, 1990, California and U.S. District Court, Central, Northern and Eastern Districts of California and U.S. Court of Appeals, Ninth Circuit. *Education:* Harvard University (B.A., magna cum laude, 1985); Boalt Hall School of Law, University of California (J.D., 1988). Member, Ecology Law Quarterly, 1985-1986 and California Law Review, 1987. Law Clerk to Honorable Patrick E. Higginbotham, U.S. Court of Appeals, Fifth Circuit, 1988-1989. *Member:* State Bar of California; Los Angeles County, Federal and American Bar Associations; J. Reuben Clark Law Society; Association of Business Trial Lawyers; Los Angeles Business Council and Los Angeles County Bar Trial Inn of Court. *LANGUAGES:* Spanish.

**TED DANE,** born Yonkers, New York, July 9, 1964; admitted to bar, 1989, California and U.S. District Court, Central District of California. *Education:* Harvard University (A.B., magna cum laude, 1986); Stanford University (J.D., 1989). Phi Beta Kappa. Order of the Coif. Law Clerk, Hon. Harry T. Edwards, U.S. Court of Appeals, District of Columbia Circuit, 1990-1991.

## ASSOCIATES

**MARSHA HYMANSON,** born Los Angeles, California, April 22, 1946; admitted to bar, 1989, California and U.S. Court of Appeals, Ninth Circuit. *Education:* University of Southern California (B.A., cum laude, 1966; J.D., 1989). Order of the Coif. Member, Southern California Law Review, 1988-1989. Law Clerk, Hon. Edward Rafeedie, U.S. District Judge, Central District of California, 1989-1990. Author: "Borrower Beware: D'Oench, Duhme and Section 1823 Overprotect the Bank Insurer When Banks Fail," 62 So. Cal. Law Review, 1988. *Member:* Los Angeles County Bar Association; State Bar of California.

**STUART N. SENATOR,** born New York, N.Y., July 16, 1962; admitted to bar, 1990, California; 1991, U.S. District Court, Central, Eastern and Northern Districts of California; 1992, U.S. Court of Appeals, Ninth Circuit; 1993, U.S. District Court, Northern District of Texas. *Education:* Princeton University (A.B., cum laude, 1984); University of California at Berkeley (M.A., 1987); Boalt Hall School of Law, University of California at Berkeley (J.D., 1989). Order of the Coif. Member, 1987-1988 and Executive Editor, 1988-1989, California Law Review. Law Clerk to Hon. Charles E. Wiggins, U.S. Court of Appeals, 9th Circuit, 1989-1990.

**EVA ORLEBEKE CALDERA,** born Lansing, Michigan, October 8, 1963; admitted to bar, 1989, Illinois; 1990, District of Columbia and U.S. District Court for the District of Columbia; 1991, California. *Education:* Harvard University (A.B., cum laude in Philosophy, 1985; J.D., cum laude, 1989). Phi Beta Kappa. Co-Author: Article, "The Application of Per-Occurrence Limits From Successive Policies," with Thomas Baker, Environmental Claims Journal, Vol. 3, No. 4 (Summer 1991). *LANGUAGES:* French.

**MONICA WAHL SHAFFER,** born Shelby, Ohio, May 15, 1961; admitted to bar, 1991, California. *Education:* Miami University (B.S., 1983); University of Chicago (J.D., with honors, 1989). Order of the Coif. Member, University of Chicago Law Review. Law Clerk: Judge Patrick Higginbotham, U.S. Court of Appeals, Fifth Circuit, 1989-1990; Chief Justice William H. Rehnquist, U.S. Supreme Court, 1990-1991.

**LEONARD P. LEICHNITZ,** born San Jose, California, January 11, 1963; admitted to bar, 1991, California. *Education:* Occidental College (B.A., with honors, 1985); King's College, London, England (M.A., 1986); University of California at Los Angeles (J.D., 1991). Order of the Coif. Member, 1989-1990 and Editor, 1990-1991, UCLA Law Review. *PRACTICE AREAS:* Real Estate.

**ANDREW J. THOMAS,** born Hays, Kansas, September 20, 1965; admitted to bar, 1992, California. *Education:* Stanford University (B.A., 1988); Harvard Law School (J.D., 1991). Phi Beta Kappa. Member, Board of Editors, Harvard Law Review, 1989-1991. Author: Note, "Clarifying the Copyright Misuse Defense," 104 Harvard Law Review 1289 (1991). Law Clerk, Hon. Alfred T. Goodwin, U.S. Court of Appeals, Ninth Circuit, 1991-1992. *Email:* Thomasaj@MTO.COM

**ROBERT L. DELLANGELO,** born California, August 2, 1961; admitted to bar, 1992, California; 1993, U.S. District Court, Central District of California. *Education:* Columbia College (B.A., 1983); College of Physicians and Surgeons, Columbia University (M.D., 1987); University of California, Los Angeles (J.D., 1992). Order of the Coif. Member, vol. 38, 1990-

*(This Listing Continued)*

**MUNGER, TOLLES & OLSON, Los Angeles—Continued**

1991 and Editor, Vol. 39, 1991-1992, UCLA Law Review. California Medical License, 1991. Surgical Intern and Resident, St. Luke's Roosevelt Hospital, New York, 1987-1989.

**BRUCE A. ABBOTT**, born Berkeley, California, June 3, 1966; admitted to bar, 1992, California and U.S. District Court, Central District of California. *Education:* Pomona College (B.A., summa cum laude, 1988); Yale Law School (J.D., 1991). Phi Beta Kappa. Senior Editor, Yale Law Journal., V. 100, 1990-1991. Law Clerk, Honorable William D. Keller, U.S. District Court, Central District of California, 1991-1992. Special Prosecutor, Office of Independent Counsel: In Re United States Secretary of Agriculture Alphonso Michael (Mike) Espy, 1994-1996.

**MARTIN D. BERN**, born Boston, Massachusetts, April 2, 1962; admitted to bar, 1991, California; 1992, U.S. Court of Appeals, Ninth Circuit; U.S. District Court, Central District of California; 1995, U.S. District Court, Northern District of California. *Education:* Tufts University (B.A., summa cum laude, 1984); University of California at Berkeley (M.A., Political Science, 1986); Boalt Hall School of Law, University of California, Berkeley (J.D., 1990). Phi Beta Kappa; Order of the Coif. Author: Comment, "Government Regulation and the Development of Environmental Ethics Under the Clean Air Act," Ecology Law Quarterly 17:3. Law Clerk to: Hon. Charles A. Legge, U.S. District Court, Northern District of California, 1990-1991; Hon. J. Clifford Wallace, U.S. Court of Appeals, Ninth Circuit, 1991-1992. *Member:* State Bar of California. (Resident, San Francisco Office).

**MARGARET ELIZABETH DEANE**, born Lima, Ohio, August 28, 1963; admitted to bar, 1993, California. *Education:* University of Cincinnati (B.A., summa cum laude, 1987); Yale Law School (J.D., 1991). Phi Beta Kappa. Book Review Editor, Yale Law Journal, 1990-1991. Author: "City of Richmond v. J.A. Croson Co.: A Federal Legislative Answer," 100 Yale L. J. 451 (1990). (Resident, San Francisco Office). *LANGUAGES:* Spanish. *PRACTICE AREAS:* Environmental Law.

**DEANNE B. KYLE**, born Ft. Worth Texas, June 7, 1967; admitted to bar, 1993, California. *Education:* University of Georgia (B.B.A., magna cum laude, with honors certificate, 1990); University of Texas (J.D., 1992); New York University (LL.M., 1994). Notes Editor, American Journal of Criminal Law, Board of Advocates. *PRACTICE AREAS:* Tax; Trusts and Estates.

**SUSAN R. SZABO**, born Hollywood, California, April 17, 1957; admitted to bar, 1991, California; 1993, U.S. District Court, Central District of California and U.S. Court of Appeals, Ninth Circuit. *Education:* University of California at Santa Cruz (B.A., with highest honors, 1986); Boalt Hall School of Law, University of California (J.D., 1991). Order of the Coif. Law Clerk to: Honorable Harry Pregerson, United States Court of Appeals, Ninth Circuit, 1992-1993; Honorable A. Wallace Tashima, United States District Court, Central District of California, 1991-1992. Los Angeles County Bar Association, Trial Attorney Program. *Member:* Los Angeles County and American Bar Associations; National Lawyers Guild. *LANGUAGES:* Spanish.

**INEZ D. HOPE**, born New York, N.Y., June 11, 1952; admitted to bar, 1992, California. *Education:* Massachusetts Institute of Technology (S.B., 1973; S.M., 1975); University of Texas at Austin (Ph.D., 1983); University of California at Los Angeles (J.D., 1991). Sigma Xi; Phi Kappa Phi; Phi Alpha Delta. *Member:* State Bar of California; American Bar Association; National Association of Counsel for Children. [French]

**BERNARDO SILVA**, born Los Angeles, California, January 9, 1966; admitted to bar, 1993, California and U.S. District Court, Central District of California. *Education:* Stanford University (A.B., with distinction, 1988) Stanford Law School (J.D., 1993). Associate Editor, Stanford Law Review. Law Clerk to Hon. Stephen V. Wilson, U.S. District Court, Central District of California, 1994-1995. *Member:* Mexican-American Bar Association. *LANGUAGES:* Spanish.

**KRISTIN SHERRATT ESCALANTE**, born Los Angeles, California, July 29, 1963; admitted to bar, 1994, California. *Education:* University of Southern California (B.Arch., 1987; J.D., 1992). Order of the Coif. Editor-in-Chief, Southern California Law Review, 1991-1992. Legal Writing Instructor, University of Southern California, 1990-1991. Law Clerk to Judge Diarmuid F. O'Scannlain, U.S. Court of Appeals, Ninth Circuit, 1992-1993.

**MANUEL A. ABASCAL**, born Los Angeles, California, October 22, 1965; admitted to bar, 1994, California. *Education:* Claremont McKenna College (B.A., magna cum laude, Mathematics and Economics, 1987); Yale Law School (J.D., 1992). Articles Editor, Yale Law Journal. Author: "Guideline Developments, 5 Federal Sentencing Reporter 254," Co-Author: "Insurance Coverage for Intellectual Property Claims: The California vs the New York Approach," 19 AIPLA Quarterly, 189. Law Clerk, Judge Pamela A. Rymer, U.S. Court of Appeals, Ninth Circuit. *LANGUAGES:* Spanish.

**JONATHAN E. ALTMAN**, born New York, City, N.Y.; admitted to bar, 1994, California. *Education:* Columbia College (B.A., 1981); Georgetown University Law Center (J.D., magna cum laude, 1992). Order of the Coif. Senior Articles Editor, Georgetown Law Journal. Law Clerk to Hon. Arthur Alarcon, U.S. Court of Appeals, Ninth Circuit (1992-1993).

**GREGG W. KETTLES**, born Heraklion, Greece, April 7, 1966; admitted to bar, 1994, California. *Education:* Washington and Lee University (B.A., summa cum laude, Phi Beta Kappa, 1988); Yale University (J.D., 1991). Co-Editor-in-Chief, Yale Journal on Regulation, 1990-1991. Senior Editor, Yale Law Journal, 1990-1991. John M. Olin Law and Economics Fellow. Law Clerk to Hon. J. Clifford Wallace, Chief Judge, U.S. Court of Appeals, Ninth Circuit (1991-1992). Law Clerk to Hon. Irma E. Gonzalez, U.S. District Court, Southern District of California (1992-1993).

**STEVEN B. WEISBURD**, born Los Angeles, California, April 6, 1966; admitted to bar, 1994, California. *Education:* University of California, Berkeley; University of California, Los Angeles (B.A., magna cum laude, Phi Beta Kappa, 1988); Stanford Law School (J.D., with distinction, 1992); University of Cambridge, Cambridge, England (LL.M., first class honors, 1994). Member, 1990-1991 and Notes Editor, 1991-1992, Stanford Law Review. Evan Lewis-Thomas Scholar, Sidney Sussex College, University of Cambridge. Co-Author, Article: "On the Basis of Sex'; 'Recognizing Gender-Based Bias Crimes," 5 Stanford Law and Policy Review 21 (Spring 1994). Law Clerk to Hon. Alfred T. Goodwin, U.S. Court of Appeals, Ninth Circuit (1992-1993).

**ILANA B. RUBENSTEIN**, born New Haven, Connecticut, December 2, 1968; admitted to bar, 1994, California and U.S. District Court, Central District of California. *Education:* The College of William and Mary (B.A., with honors, Phi Beta Kappa, 1990); University of Michigan (J.D., magna cum laude, 1993). Order of the Coif. Member, Michigan Law Review, 1991-1993. Law Clerk to the Honorable John G. Davies, U.S. District Court, Central District of California, 1993-1994.

**MARY ANN LYMAN**, born California, May 12, 1968; admitted to bar, 1994, California. *Education:* University of California at Berkeley (A.B., with high honors, 1990); Yale Law School (J.D., 1993). Phi Beta Kappa. Articles Editor, Yale Law Journal, 1992-1993. Law Clerk to The Honorable Alex Kozinski, U.S. Court of Appeals, Ninth Circuit, 1993-1994.

**CARLA N. JONES**, born Norfolk, Virginia, September 1, 1968; admitted to bar, 1995, California. *Education:* Princeton University (A.B., cum laude, 1990); Yale Law School (J.D., 1993). John M. Olin Law and Economics Fellow. Law Clerk for the Honorable William A. Norris, U.S. Court of Appeals, Ninth Circuit, 1993-1994.

**JOHN C. ULIN**, born New York, New York, August 17, 1965; admitted to bar, 1993, California. *Education:* Brown University (A.B., 1987); University of California at Los Angeles (J.D., 1992); Harvard University (LL.M., 1995). Order of the Coif. Law Clerk, Hon. William Matthew Byrne, Jr., U.S. District Court, Central District of California, 1992-1993; Hon. Ferdinand F. Fernandez, U.S. Court of Appeals, Ninth Circuit, 1993-1994. Author: "First Amendment Crossroads Extending and Constitutional Defamation Protection to Commercial Speech," 39 University of California at Los Angeles Law Review, 633. *LANGUAGES:* French.

**JAMES H. ELLIS**, born Woburn, Massachusetts, May 10, 1963; admitted to bar, 1995, California. *Education:* Harvard College (A.B., cum laude, 1985); University of California at Los Angeles (J.D., 1995). Order of the Coif.

**BURTON A. GROSS**, born Watertown, Massachusetts, July 21, 1967; admitted to bar, 1993, California. *Education:* Duke University (B.A., summa cum laude, 1989); Stanford University (J.D., 1993). Phi Beta Kappa. Associate Editor, Stanford Law Review. Law Clerk to Hon. Douglas H. Ginsburg, U.S. Court of Appeals, District of Columbia Circuit, 1994-1995. (Resident, San Francisco Office).

**ANDREA J. WEISS**, born Brooklyn, New York, November 22, 1969; admitted to bar, 1996, California. *Education:* Duke University (A.B., 1991); Stanford Law School (J.D., 1994). Phi Beta Kappa. Associate Editor, Stanford Law Review. Clerk to the Honorable Harry L. Hupp, U.S. District Court, Central District of California, 1994-1995. *Member:* State Bar of California. *PRACTICE AREAS:* Litigation. *Email:* Weissaj@MTO.COM

*(This Listing Continued)*

**STEVEN W. HAWKINS,** born San Jose, California, February 20, 1966; admitted to bar, 1994, California. *Education:* Stanford University (A.B., with distinction, 1988; M.A., 1989); University of California at Los Angeles (J.D., 1994). Order of the Coif. Author: Note, The Constitution and the Item Veto, Journal of Law & Politics, 1994. Law Clerk to the Honorable Pamela A. Rymer, U.S. Court of Appeals, Ninth Circuit, 1994-1995. *Email:* Hawkinssw@MTO.COM

**DAVID M. ROSENZWEIG,** born Palo Alto, California, March 5, 1964; admitted to bar, 1995, California. *Education:* Harvard College (A.B., 1986); Georgetown University Law Center (J.D., magna cum laude, 1994). Order of the Coif. Primary Editor, Georgetown Law Journal. Author: Note, Confession of Error in the Supreme Court by the Solicitor General, 82 Georgetown Law Journal 2079 (1994). Law Clerk, Hon. Cynthia Holcomb Hall, U.S. Court of Appeals, Ninth Circuit, 1994-1995. *LANGUAGES:* French. *Email:* Rosenzweigdm@MTO.COM

**DAVID C. DINIELLI,** born Long Beach, California, August 27, 1968; admitted to bar, 1995, California. *Education:* Harvard College (A.B., magna cum laude, 1990); University of Michigan Law School (J.D., magna cum laude, 1994). Order of the Coif. Managing Editor, Michigan Law Review, 1993-1994. Law Clerk to the Honorable Cynthia Holcomb Hall, U.S. Court of Appeals, Ninth Circuit, 1994-1995.

**PETER A. DETRE,** born Montreal, Quebec, Canada, June 25, 1958; admitted to bar, 1996, California; 1996, U.S. District Court, Northern District of California. *Education:* McGill University (B.Sc., 1980); University of California, Berkeley (Ph.D., Mathematics, 1988); Yale University (J.D., 1994). Law Clerk to Hon. Kimba M. Wood, U.S. District Court, Southern District of New York. *LANGUAGES:* Hungarian, French. *PRACTICE AREAS:* Litigation.

**ELIZABETH EARLE BESKE,** born Honolulu, Hawaii, August 20, 1967; admitted to bar, 1993, Hawaii; 1996, California. *Education:* Princeton University (A.B., 1989); Columbia Law School (J.D., 1993). James Kent Scholar; Harlan Fiske Stone Scholar. Recipient, John Ordroneaux Prize. Editor-in-Chief, Columbia Law Review. Law Clerk to Hon. Sandra Day O'Connor, U.S. Supreme Court, 1994-1995; Hon. Patricia M. Wald, U.S. Court of Appeals, District of Columbia Circuit, 1993-1994. (Resident, San Francisco Office). *PRACTICE AREAS:* Litigation.

**EDWARD C. HAGEROTT, JR.,** born Inglewood, California, August 14, 1965; admitted to bar, 1990, California. *Education:* University of Southern California (B.A., 1987; J.D., 1990). Managing Editor, Southern California Law Review, 1989-1990. Recipient, American Jurisprudence Award in Real Estate Transactions. Co-author: "Junior Trust Deeds: A Primer for Senior and Junior Lenders," 11 California Real Property Journal #3 (Summer, 1993).

**KEVIN S. MASUDA,** born Los Angeles, California, March 15, 1967; admitted to bar, 1992, California. *Education:* University of California at Berkeley (A.B., with highest honors, Phi Beta Kappa, 1988); Harvard Law School (J.D., cum laude, 1992). Phi Beta Kappa; Omicron Delta Epsilon. *Member:* Los Angeles County Bar Association. *PRACTICE AREAS:* Corporate Finance; General Corporate.

**DANIEL P. COLLINS,** born Brooklyn, New York, July 4, 1963; admitted to bar, 1989, California, U.S. District Court, Central District of California and U.S. Court of Appeals, Ninth Circuit; 1991, District of Columbia. *Education:* Harvard University (A.B., summa cum laude, 1985); Stanford University (J.D., with honors, 1988). First Marshall, Phi Beta Kappa; Order of the Coif. Note Editor, Stanford Law Review, 1986-1988. Author: *Farwell Miranda?,* 1995 Pub. Interest L. Rev. 185; *Summary Judgement and Circumstantial Evidence,* 40 Stan. L. Rev. 491 (1988); *Islamization of Pakistani Law: A Historical Perspective,* 24 Stan. J. Int'l L. 511 (1988). Law Clerk to: Hon. Dorothy W. Nelson, U.S. Court of Appeals, Ninth Circuit, 1988-1989; Hon. Antonin Scalia, Supreme Court of the United States, 1991-1992. Assistant U.S. Attorney, Criminal Appeals Section, Central District of California, U.S. Department of Justice, 1992-1996. Attorney-Advisor, Office of Legal Counsel, U.S. Department of Justice, Washington, D.C., 1989-1991. Vice Chairman for Publications, Federalism and Separation of Powers Practice Group, Federalist Society. *Member:* Los Angeles, Federal and American Bar Associations; State Bar of California; District of Columbia Bar.

**ROBERT E. HOLO,** born Palo Alto, California, November 29, 1966; admitted to bar, 1993, New York (Not admitted in California). *Education:* University of California, Santa Cruz (B.A., with honors, 1987); University of California, Los Angeles (J.D., 1991). Phi Beta Kappa; Order of the Coif. Comment Editor, UCLA Law Review, 1990-1991. Law Clerk, Judge Pamela A. Rymer, U.S. Court of Appeals, Ninth Circuit, 1991-1992.

*(This Listing Continued)*

**MICHAEL J. O'SULLIVAN,** born Fullerton, California, September 10, 1965; admitted to bar, 1992, California. *Education:* University of Pennsylvania (B.A., with honors, 1987); University of Southern California (J.D., 1992). Order of the Coif. Staff Member, 1990-1991 and Executive Notes Editor, 1991-1992, Southern California Law Review. Legal Writing Instructor, University of Southern California law Center, 1991-1992. Author, "Artificial Unit Voting and the Electoral College," 65 Southern California Law Review 2421 (1992).

**STEVEN USDAN,** born Brooklyn, New York, June 5, 1972; admitted to bar, 1995, California. *Education:* Yeshiva University (B.A., magna cum laude, 1992); University of California at Los Angeles (J.D., 1995). Order of the Coif.

**PAUL J. WATFORD,** born Garden Grove, California, August 25, 1967; admitted to bar, 1996, California. *Education:* University of California, Berkeley (B.A., 1989); University of California, Los Angeles (J.D., 1994). *PRACTICE AREAS:* Litigation.

**TIMOTHY P. GRIEVE,** born Sacramento, California, June 8, 1964; admitted to bar, 1996, California. *Education:* Stanford University (B.A., 1986); Georgetown University Law Center (J.D., magna cum laude, 1995). Order of the Coif. Member, 1993-1994 and Notes and Comments Editor, 1994-1995, The Georgetown Law Journal. Law Clerk, Hon. A. Raymond Randolph, U.S. Court of Appeals, District of Columbia Circuit, 1995-1996. *PRACTICE AREAS:* Litigation. *Email:* grievetp@mto.com

**HOJOON HWANG,** born Seoul, Korea, September 7, 1969; admitted to bar, 1996, California. *Education:* Harvard College (B.A., 1993); Harvard Law School (J.D., magna cum laude, 1996). Phi Beta Kappa. (Resident, San Francisco Office). *PRACTICE AREAS:* Litigation.

**JENNIFER R. SCULLION,** admitted to bar, 1995, California. *Education:* Boston University (B.A., summa cum laude, 1991); University of California (J.D., 1995). Order of the Coif; Phi Beta Kappa. Coordinating Editor, 1993-1994 and Managing Editor, 1994-1995, Journal of Environmental Law and Policy. Recipient: American Jurisprudence Awards for Contracts, Federal Courts, Evidence and Community Property. Law Clerk to Hon Stephen V. Wilson, U.S. District Court, Central District of California, 1995-1996. *PRACTICE AREAS:* Litigation. *Email:* Scullionjr@MTO.COM

**DEVON A. GOLD,** born Annapolis, Maryland, April 3, 1970; admitted to bar, 1996, California. *Education:* University of California, Los Angeles (B.A., magna cum laude, 1992); University of Michigan (J.D., magna cum laude, 1995). Phi Beta Kappa; Order of the Coif. Law Clerk to the Hon. Mariana R. Pfaelzer, U.S. District Court, Central District of California, 1995-1996.

**JOSE F. SANCHEZ,** born Los Angeles, California, July 26, 1967; admitted to bar, 1992, California and U.S. District Court, Northern District of California; 1994, U.S. District Court, Central District of California. *Education:* Harvard College (B.A., 1989); Stanford Law School (J.D., 1992). Law Clerk to Hon. Richard A. Paez, U.S. District Court, Central District of California, 1994-1995; Law Clerk to Hon. Harry Pregerson, U.S. Court of Appeals, Ninth Circuit, 1995-1996. Recipient of two-year public interest law Skadden Arps Fellowship, 1992-1994. *Member:* American Bar Association. *LANGUAGES:* Spanish.

**SEAN A. MONROE,** born Indianapolis, Indiana, October 6, 1970; admitted to bar, 1996, California. *Education:* Georgetown University (B.A., 1992); Boalt Hall School of Law, University of California, Berkeley (J.D., 1996). Articles Editor, California Law Review, 1995-1996. *Member:* State Bar of California.

**JONATHAN R. LEVEY,** born St. Louis, Missouri, May 7, 1970; admitted to bar, 1995, Illinois; 1995, U.S. Court of Appeals, Seventh Circuit (Not admitted in California). *Education:* Princeton University (A.B., magna cum laude, 1991); Harvard Law School (J.D., cum laude, 1995). Phi Beta Kappa. Law Clerk to Hon. William J. Bauer, U.S. Court of Appeals, Seventh Circuit, 1995-1996. *PRACTICE AREAS:* Litigation. *Email:* Leveyjr@MTO.COM

**KELLY M. KLAUS,** born Encino, California, November 23, 1966; admitted to bar, 1992, California; 1996, U.S. Supreme Court. *Education:* University of California (B.A., magna cum laude, 1989); Stanford University (J.D., 1992). Phi Beta Kappa; Order of the Coif. Law Clerk to: Justice Anthony M. Kennedy, Supreme Court of the United States, 1995-1996; Judge Pamela Ann Rymer, U.S. Court of Appeals, Ninth Circuit, 1993-1994; Judge William H. Orrik, U.S. District Court, Northern District of California, 1992-1993. (Resident, San Francisco Office). *PRACTICE AREAS:* Litigation.

*(This Listing Continued)*

## MUNGER, TOLLES & OLSON, Los Angeles—Continued

**DENNIS M. WOODSIDE,** born Langhorne, Pennsylvania, February 28, 1969; admitted to bar, 1996, California. *Education:* Cornell University (B.S., 1991); Stanford Law School (J.D., 1996). Associate Editor, Stanford Law Review. Member, Kirkwood Moot Court Competition. Clerk to Hon. Dennis G. Jacobs, U.S. Court of Appeals, Second Circuit, 1995-1996.

**DOUGLAS A. AXEL,** admitted to bar, 1994, California; 1995, U.S. District Court, Central District of California; 1996, U.S. Court of Appeals, Ninth Circuit. *Education:* University of California, Los Angeles (B.S., 1991); Hastings College of the Law, University of California, San Francisco (J.D., summa cum laude, 1994). Order of the Coif.

**RACHEL M. CAPOCCIA,** born Greenville, Mississippi, February 9, 1961; admitted to bar, 1996, California. *Education:* Rochester Institute of Technology (B.S., 1984); University of Southern California (J.D., 1995). Order of the Coif. Executive Editor, Southern California Law Review, 1994-1995. Author: "Piercing the Veil of Tears: The Admission of Rape Crisis Counselor Records in Acquaintance Rape Trials," 68 S. Cal. L. Rev. 1335, 1995. Legal Writing Instructor, University of Southern California, 1993-1995. Law Clerk, Hon. Cynthia Holcomb Hall, U.S. Court of Appeals, Ninth Circuit, 1995-1996.

**BRUCE HAMILTON SEARBY,** born Caracas, Venezuela, September 28, 1968; admitted to bar, 1996, California. *Education:* Princeton University (B.A., magna cum laude, 1990); University of Michigan (J.D., cum laude, 1995). Law Clerk to Hon. A. Wallace Tashima, U.S. District Court, Central District of California and U.S. Court of Appeals, Ninth Circuit (1995-1996). Author: "Bay Islands" (feature article), Oceansports International, 1991. *LANGUAGES:* Spanish. *PRACTICE AREAS:* Litigation. *Email:* Searbybh@MTO.COM

REFERENCE: The Bank of California.

---

## ROBERTA L. MURAWSKI

SUITE 900
2049 CENTURY PARK EAST
**LOS ANGELES, CALIFORNIA 90067-3111**
Telephone: 310-551-6959
Fax: 310-556-5687

*General Civil Litigation, including Family Law.*

**ROBERTA L. MURAWSKI,** born Staunton, Virginia, June 6, 1958; admitted to bar, 1982, District of Columbia; 1984, Maryland; 1986, Virginia; 1989, California. *Education:* State University of New York at Buffalo (B.A., magna cum laude, 1979); George Washington University National Law Center (J.D., 1982). Phi Beta Kappa. Contributor: *Marriage and Family Law Agreements,* Shepard's/McGraw-Hill, 1984. Co-Author: *Dissolution of Marriage,* Shepard's/McGraw-Hill, 1986. *Member:* Los Angeles County and American Bar Associations.

---

## MURCHISON & CUMMING

*Established in 1952*
CHASE PLAZA
801 SOUTH GRAND AVENUE, 9TH FLOOR
**LOS ANGELES, CALIFORNIA 90017**
Telephone: 213-623-7400
Telex: 350 290
Fax: 213-623-6336

*Santa Ana, California Office:* 801 Park Tower, 200 West Santa Ana Boulevard. Telephone: 714-972-9977. Fax: 714-972-1404.
*San Diego, California Office:* Symphony Towers, 750 B Street, Suite 2550. Telephone: 619-544-6836. Fax: 619-544-1568.

*General, Civil, Trial and Appellate Practice in all State and Federal Courts. Negligence, Product Liability, Professional Liability, Intellectual Property, Employment Law, Insurance Coverage, Bad Faith and Business Litigation.*

### MEMBERS OF FIRM

**MICHAEL D. MCEVOY,** born Huntington Park, California, April 15, 1943; admitted to bar, 1969, California. *Education:* University of California at Berkeley; California State College at Los Angeles; Loyola University of Los Angeles (J.D., 1968). Arbitrator, Los Angeles Superior Court Special Arbitration Panel. *Member:* Los Angeles County, Orange County and American Bar Associations; State Bar of California; Association of South-

*(This Listing Continued)*

ern California Defense Counsel; American Board of Trial Advocates; Defense Research Institute. (Resident, Santa Ana Office). *PRACTICE AREAS:* Products Liability Litigation (Domestic and Foreign); Construction Defect; Homeowner Association Liability; Wrongful Termination.

**FRIEDRICH W. SEITZ,** born Regensburg, Germany, June 16, 1941; admitted to bar, 1972, California. *Education:* University of Southern California (B.A., 1965); Southwestern University (J.D., 1971). Senior Staff Member, Southwestern University Law Review, 1970-1971. Lecturer, Products Liability, Munich, Cologne, Braunschweig and Zurich. Arbitrator, Los Angeles Superior Court Special Arbitration Panel. *Member:* Los Angeles County and American Bar Associations; State Bar of California; Association of Southern California Defense Counsel; International Association of Defense Counsel; Defense Research Institute; American Board of Trial Advocates; Product Liability Advisory Counsel; Federation of Insurance and Corporate Counsel. *LANGUAGES:* German. *PRACTICE AREAS:* Domestic and International Products Liability Litigation; Catastrophic Injury Litigation; Toxic and Environmental Law.

**MICHAEL B. LAWLER,** born Los Angeles, California, October 23, 1942; admitted to bar, 1972, California. *Education:* Loyola University of Los Angeles (B.B.A., 1964); Southwestern University (J.D., 1971). Arbitrator, Los Angeles Superior Court Special Arbitration Panel. Settlement Officer, Los Angeles, Santa Monica and Van Nuys Superior Court Settlement Program. Speaker: California Trial Lawyers Association (CTLA); Association of Southern California Defense Counsel (ASCDC); Consumer Attorneys Association of Los Angeles, Santa Monica and Van Nuys. *Member:* Los Angeles County Bar Association; State Bar of California; Association of Southern California Defense Counsel (President, 1994); International Association of Defense Counsel (IADC); Federation of Insurance and Corporate Counsel (FICC); American Board of Trial Advocates (Member: Los Angeles Board of Directors, 1995; National Board of Directors, 1996—). *PRACTICE AREAS:* General Insurance Defense Litigation; Construction and Land Subsidence Law; Premises and Automobile Liability; Employment Law; Wrongful Termination; Discrimination; Sexual Harassment.

**GEORGE V. GENZMER, III,** born Los Angeles, California, April 21, 1943; admitted to bar, 1972, California. *Education:* University of Oregon (B.A., 1967); Southwestern University (J.D., 1971). Speaker: State Bar of California, Lawyers Professional Liability Insurance, 1977 and 1978; Los Angeles County Bar, Professional Liability Insurance, 1977. Testimony in front of California State Legislature regarding Lawyers Professional Liability Insurance, 1978-1987. Delegate from Los Angeles to California State Bar Conference of Delegates and Sergeant of Arms, 1972-1991. Arbitrator, Los Angeles Superior Court Special Arbitration Panel, 1976—. *Member:* Los Angeles County (Member, 1974-1976, Co-Chairman, 1977-1988, Insurance Programs Committee), Orange County, Federal and American (Vice Chair, 1989-1991, Chair-elect, 1992-1993 and Chair, 1993-1994, Professional, Officers' and Directors' Liability Law Committee, Tort and Insurance Practice Section; Standing Committee, Lawyers Professional Liability, Litigation Section) Bar Associations; State Bar of California; The Conference of Insurance Counsel; Association of Southern California Defense Counsel; International Association of Defense Counsel (Member: Excess and Reinsurance Committee; Professional Errors and Omissions Committee; Legal Malpractice Committee); Defense Research Institute; Ninth Judicial Circuit Historical Society. *PRACTICE AREAS:* Errors and Omissions Defense; Directors and Officers Defense; Excess and Reinsurance Liability; Lawyers Professional Liability Defense; Insurance Agents & Real Estate Professional Liability Defense; Drug Device and Medical Device Defense.

**BENJAMIN H. SEAL, II,** born San Diego, California, May 12, 1939; admitted to bar, 1975, California. *Education:* California State University at Northridge (B.A., 1965); University of San Fernando Valley (J.D., 1972). *Member:* Wilshire (Member, Board of Governors, 1976), Los Angeles County and American Bar Associations; State Bar of California; Association of Southern California Defense Counsel. *PRACTICE AREAS:* General Insurance Defense Litigation.

**TOM Y. K. MEI,** born Kuantan, Malaya, July 24, 1940; admitted to bar, 1976, California. *Education:* California State University at Los Angeles (B.A., 1963); Western State University (J.D., 1975). Recipient, American Jurisprudence Awards in Constitutional Law, Civil Procedure. *Member:* Orange County Bar Association; State Bar of California; Southern California Defense Counsel; American Board of Trial Advocates. (Resident, Santa Ana Office).

**STEVEN L. SMILAY,** born Chicago, Illinois, September 30, 1953; admitted to bar, 1979, California. *Education:* California State University, Northridge (B.A., magna cum laude, 1976); Loyola Law School of Los An-

*(This Listing Continued)*

geles (J.D., 1979). Phi Alpha Delta. Recipient, American Jurisprudence Award in Contracts. *Member:* Wilshire Bar Association (Member, Board of Governors, 1983-1985); State Bar of California; Association of Southern California Defense Counsel. **PRACTICE AREAS:** Intellectual Property; Litigation; Construction Litigation; General Business Tort Litigation.

**KENNETH H. MORENO,** born Indio, California, August 26, 1956; admitted to bar, 1983, California. *Education:* University of California at Los Angeles (B.A.,1979); University of Southern California (J.D., 1982). Member, Hale Moot Court Honors Program. *Member:* Los Angeles County, San Diego County and American Bar Associations; State Bar of California; Association of Southern California Defense Counsel; San Diego Defense Lawyers. (Resident, San Diego Office). **PRACTICE AREAS:** Environmental and Toxic Exposure Law; Product Liability Law; Wrongful Termination Law; Construction Law.

**RICHARD M. ARIAS,** born Los Angeles, California, January 2, 1946; admitted to bar, 1973, California. *Education:* Loyola University of Los Angeles (B.S., 1967; J.D., 1972). Phi Alpha Delta. Arbitrator, Los Angeles Superior Court Special Arbitration Panel. *Member:* Wilshire, Los Angeles County and American Bar Associations; State Bar of California; Association of Southern California Defense Counsel; Lawyers Club of Los Angeles County; Defense Research Institute; American Board of Trial Advocates. **PRACTICE AREAS:** General Insurance Defense Litigation.

**ROBERT A. GRANTHAM,** born Pasadena, California, December 21, 1952; admitted to bar, 1981, Colorado and California. *Education:* University of California at Santa Barbara (B.A., with honors, 1975); University of Bordeaux, Bordeaux, France; University of Denver (J.D., 1981). Author: "The Airline Merger Cases: CAB Application of Clayton§7 After Deregulation," 12 Transportation Law Journal 136, 1981. *Member:* The State Bar of California. **PRACTICE AREAS:** Business and Corporate Law; Products Liability; Environmental; International; Appeals.

**DAN L. LONGO,** born Los Angeles, California, September 25, 1956; admitted to bar, 1982, California and U.S. Supreme Court. *Education:* University of Southern California (B.A., 1978); Loyola Marymount University (J.D., 1982). *Member:* Los Angeles County and Orange County Associations; State Bar of California; American Board of Trial Advocates; Association of Southern California Defense Counsel. (Resident, Santa Ana Office). **PRACTICE AREAS:** Defense of Professionals; Directors and Officers Liability; Products Liability Law; Construction Defect Litigation.

**JEAN M. LAWLER,** born San Francisco, California, August 7, 1954; admitted to bar, 1979, California; 1981, Oregon; 1986, U.S. District Court, Central, Southern and Eastern Districts of California. *Education:* Riverside City College (A.A., 1974); Loyola Marymount University (B.B.A., 1976; J.D., 1979); University of San Francisco Law School. Member, Jessup International Honors Moot Court. Lecturer, Lane Community College, Legal Assistant Program, Eugene, Oregon, 1981-1982. Chairperson, Lane Community College, Legal Assistant Advisory Committee 1981-1982. *Member:* Los Angeles County Bar Association; State Bar of California; Oregon State Bar; Association of Southern California Defense Counsel (Director, 1994—); Federation of Insurance and Corporate Counsel; Defense Research Institute. **REPORTED CASES:** Michael Mitchell v. Scott Wetzel Services, 1991; Cristiano v. Hartford et al, 724 F Supp 732, 1989 (represented Arrow Coach). **PRACTICE AREAS:** Insurance Litigation; Insurance Coverage; Property Insurance; Casualty Insurance; Directors and Officers Liability; Excess Insurance; Environmental Insurance Coverage; Insurance Bad Faith Defense; Insurance Adjusters and Agents Errors and Omissions.

**EDMUND G. FARRELL III,** born Teaneck, New Jersey, September 10, 1955; admitted to bar, 1983, California and U.S. District Court, Central District of California; 1984, U.S. District Court, Southern and Northern Districts of California and U.S. Court of Appeals, Ninth Circuit. *Education:* University of California at San Diego (B.S., 1978); University of Santa Clara (J.D., 1982). Traynor Moot Court Participant. Associate Editor, Santa Clara Law Review, 1981-1982. *Member:* Los Angeles County Bar Association; State Bar of California; Association of Southern California Defense Counsel. **REPORTED CASES:** Danner v. Himmelfarb (1988) 858 F.2d 515; St. Mary Med. Center v. Cristiano (1989) 724 F.Supp 732; O'Dell v. Freightliner (1992) 10 CA 4th 645; Mitchell v. Scott Wetzel (1991) 227 CA 3d 1474; Semsch v. Henry Mayo Newhall Mem. Hospital (1985) 171 CA 3d 162; DeBlase v. Superior Court (1996) 41 CA 4 1279. **PRACTICE AREAS:** Appellate Practice; Professional Malpractice Defense.

*(This Listing Continued)*

## ASSOCIATES

**ROBERT M. SCHERK,** born Oceanside, New York, May 8, 1954; admitted to bar, 1980, California; 1981, U.S. Court of Appeals, Ninth Circuit and U.S. District Court, Central District of California; 1984, U.S. Supreme Court. *Education:* University of Colorado (B.A., 1976); Southwestern University (J.D., 1979). Judge, Pro Tem, Los Angeles Superior Court. Member, Attorney Settlement Panel Santa Monica Superior Court, 1988-1994. Member, Southwestern University Student-Alumni Mentor Program. Member, Los Angeles Olympic Citizen's Advisory Commission to the Los Angeles Olympic Organizing Committee, 1982-1984. *Member:* Los Angeles County and San Diego County Bar Associations; The State Bar of California; Association of Southern California Defense Counsel. (Resident, San Diego Office). **PRACTICE AREAS:** Professional Liability Law; Premises Liability; Personal Injury.

**RICHARD D. NEWMAN,** born Santa Monica, California, October 12, 1950; admitted to bar, 1978, Florida and California. *Education:* University of California at Berkeley (B.A., 1973); University of Miami (J.D., 1977). *Member:* Los Angeles County and Orange County Bar Associations; State Bar of California. (Resident, Santa Ana Office). **PRACTICE AREAS:** Law and Motion Law; Appellate Practice.

**BARBARA L. MCCULLY,** born McKeesport, Pennsylvania, October 14, 1950; admitted to bar, 1985, California and U.S. District Court, Southern and Eastern Districts of California; 1986, U.S. Court of Appeals, Ninth Circuit; 1987, U.S. District Court, Central District of California. *Education:* San Diego State University (B.A., with honors, 1973; M.P.A., 1978); University of San Diego (J.D., cum laude, 1984). Phi Alpha Delta. Member, Mortar Board. Recipient, American Jurisprudence Award. *Member:* San Diego County, Los Angeles County (Member: Los Angeles Lawyer Editorial Board; State Courts Committee; Errors and Omissions Prevention Committee; Legislative Review Committee and Litigation Legislative Review Subcommittee) and American (Member, Sections on: Labor and Employment Law; Administrative Law) Bar Associations; State Bar of California. **PRACTICE AREAS:** Law and Motion Law; Appellate Practice.

**RUSSELL S. WOLLMAN,** born Hollywood, California, July 2, 1958; admitted to bar, 1987, California; 1988, U.S. District Court, Central District of California. *Education:* University of California at Los Angeles (B.A., 1981); University of California at Santa Barbara; Southwestern University (J.D., 1987). Member, Order of Barristers; Moot Court Honor Society. Oralist: Marshall-Wyth Moot Court Competition, 1986; Benjamin Cardozo Moot Court Competition. *Member:* State Bar of California. **PRACTICE AREAS:** Products Liability Law.

**MARY JANE DELLAFIORA,** born Indiana, Pennsylvania, October 5, 1962; admitted to bar, 1987, California; 1988, U.S. District Court, Central and Northern Districts of California, U.S. Court of Appeals, Ninth Circuit and District of Columbia. *Education:* University of Virginia (B.A., 1984); Pepperdine University (J.D., 1987). Recipient, American Jurisprudence Award in Property. *Member:* Los Angeles County and American Bar Associations; State Bar of California; District of Columbia Bar. **PRACTICE AREAS:** Law and Motion Law; Appellate Practice; Insurance Coverage and Bad Faith Litigation.

**LAURA I. BAER,** born Los Angeles, California, November 3, 1958; admitted to bar, 1988, California; 1989, U.S. District Court, Central and Southern Districts of California. *Education:* University of Southern California (2 B.A.'s, 1980); Loyola Marymount University (M.A., 1982); Southwestern University; Northrop University (J.D., 1987). *Member:* Wilshire, Los Angeles County and American Bar Associations; State Bar of California; Association of Southern California Defense Counsel. **PRACTICE AREAS:** General Insurance Defense Litigation.

**KIM RODGERS WESTHOFF,** born Inglewood, California, March 27, 1957; admitted to bar, 1982, California; 1984, U.S. District Court, Central District of California. *Education:* University of Southern California (B.A., 1978); Southwestern University School of Law (J.D., 1981). Who's Who of American Women, 14th Edition. *Member:* State Bar of California. **REPORTED CASES:** In Re Bittelman, Debtor (Bankr. 9th Cir., 1988) 107 Bankr. 230; In Re Marvin A. Hartenaka Marvin Arthur Harten, Debtor (Bankr. 9th Cir., 1987) 7 8 Bankr. 252, 16 Bankr. Ct. Dec. (CRR) 686; Silbrico Corp. v. Raanan (1985) 170 Cal. App. 3d 202. **PRACTICE AREAS:** Law and Motion; Appellate.

**VICTOR A. LEE,** born Detroit, Michigan, January 22, 1963; admitted to bar, 1989, California and U.S. District Court, Central District of California. *Education:* University of California at Irvine (B.A., 1985); University of San Diego (J.D., 1988). *Member:* Orange County Bar Association; State Bar of California; Southern California Defense Counsel; Defense Research

*(This Listing Continued)*

*MURCHISON & CUMMING, Los Angeles—Continued*

Institute. (Resident, Santa Ana Office). *PRACTICE AREAS:* Personal Injury Defense; Construction Defect Law; Homeowner Association Litigation; Product Liability; Premises Liability.

**TERESA ANNA LIBERTINO,** born Brooklyn, New York, November 8, 1958; admitted to bar, 1987, California. *Education:* Mills College (B.A., 1981); McGeorge School of Law (J.D., 1986). *Member:* State Bar of California. *PRACTICE AREAS:* General Insurance Defense Litigation.

**ELIZABETH A. POLLOCK,** born Los Angeles, California, September 17, 1956; admitted to bar, 1982, Texas; 1983, California, U.S. Supreme Court, U.S. Court of Appeals, Ninth Circuit, U.S. District Court, Northern District of Texas and U.S. District Court, Districts of California, Georgia, Illinois, Kansas, Mississippi, New Jersey, North Carolina and Texas. *Education:* Stanford University (B.A., 1977); University of California at Los Angeles (M.B.A., 1982; J.D., 1982). Co-Founder and Research Editor, U.C.L.A. Pacific Basin Law Journal, 1981-1982. Student Editor-in-Chief, 1980-1981 and Student Executive Editor, 1979-1980, The International Lawyer. *Member:* State Bar of California (Member, International Section); State Bar of Texas (Member, International Section). *LANGUAGES:* German and Spanish. *PRACTICE AREAS:* Products Liability; Commercial Litigation.

**GEORGE G. ROMAIN,** born Port-au-Prince, Haiti, February 6, 1961; admitted to bar, 1989, California. *Education:* University of Virginia; State University of New York at Albany (B.A., 1983); Boston University School of Law (J.D., 1987). *Member:* Los Angeles County Bar Association; State Bar of California;. *LANGUAGES:* French. *PRACTICE AREAS:* Errors and Omissions; Liability of Directors and Officers; Attorney Malpractice.

**JAMES D. CARRAWAY,** born Toccoa, Georgia, March 1, 1959; admitted to bar, 1989, California; 1990, U.S. District Court, Central, Eastern and Southern Districts of California. *Education:* University of Hawaii (B.A., 1984); Pepperdine School of Law (J.D., 1989). Member, Moot Court Board. *Member:* State Bar of California. *PRACTICE AREAS:* Products Liability Law.

**THOMAS E. DIAS,** born Silver Spring, Maryland, September 18, 1963; admitted to bar, 1989, California; 1990, U.S. District Court, Central District of California; 1991, U.S. District Court, District of Arizona. *Education:* University of California at Los Angeles (B.A., 1986); Whittier College (J.D., 1989). *Member:* Orange County and American Bar Associations; State Bar of California. (Resident, Santa Ana Office). *PRACTICE AREAS:* Personal Injury Defense Law; Products Liability Law.

**SYDNEE R. SINGER,** born Chicago, Illinois, April 3, 1955; admitted to bar, 1988, California and U.S. District Court, Southern District of California; 1989, U.S. District Court, Central District of California. *Education:* University of Miami (B.M., cum laude, 1977; M.M., 1979; M.B.A., 1979); Indiana University (J.D., 1984). Member, Board of Editors, Indiana Law Journal, 1984. Mortarboard, Archontes. Author: "Satellite/Dish Antenna: Technology: A Copyright Owner's Dilemma," 59 Indiana Law Journal 417, 1983-1984. Co-Author with Don Howarth, "The Firing Line: Handling the Opposing Damage Expert," DRI Seminar, Las Vegas, Nevada, 1989. Co-Author with Suzelle M. Smith, "The Art of Negotiating: Assertiveness v. Aggressiveness, South Dakota Women "90", May 23, 1990 . Member: Board of Directors, Del Mar Highland; Board of Directors, East Bluff; Barristers Committee on Juvenile Justice, 1990-1994; Barristers Hospice Aids Project, 1991—. *Member:* Los Angeles County Bar Association; State Bar of California; Women Lawyers Association of Los Angeles (Member, Legislation Committee, 1990-1992). *PRACTICE AREAS:* Civil Litigation.

**BRYAN M. WEISS,** born Washington, D.C., August 29, 1960; admitted to bar, 1987, California and U.S. District Court, District of California. *Education:* Tulane University of Louisiana (B.S., 1982); Whittier College (J.D., cum laude, 1985). Editor-in-Chief, 1984 and Notes & Comments Editor, 1984-1985, Whittier Law Review. Recipient, American Jurisprudence Award, Contracts and Corporate Law. Author: "1983 California Court of Appeals Survey-Entertainment Law," 6 Whittier L. Rev. 391 (1984). Instructor, Advanced Legal Skills, Whittier College School of Law, 1991—. *PRACTICE AREAS:* Insurance Coverage and Litigation.

**SCOTT HENGESBACH,** born Berwyn, Pennsylvania, March 31, 1963; admitted to bar, 1990, California. *Education:* University of Redlands (B.A., 1985); McGeorge School of Law, University of the Pacific (J.D., with honors, 1989). Author: "The Degeneration of Failure to Warn Doctrine," *For the Defense,* Nov., 1991; Comment K: " A Prescription For the Over-the-Counter Drug Industry," 22 Pac. L.J. (1990). *Member:* Los Angeles County

and American Bar Associations. *PRACTICE AREAS:* Product Liability; Medical Device Litigation; Insurance Defense-General.

**GUY R. GRUPPIE,** born Los Angeles, California, January 6, 1962; admitted to bar, 1991, California and U.S. District Court, Central District of California. *Education:* University of Southern California (B.A., with honors in Journalism, 1986; B.A., Political Science, 1988); Loyola Law School (J.D., 1991). Recipient: American Jurisprudence Award in Trial Advocacy; Catholic Council Academic Achievement Award; National Italian American Federation Scholarship. Mediator, Los Angeles Superior Court. *Member:* American Bar Association; Italian American Lawyers Association of Los Angeles County; Association of Southern California Defense Counsel; American Board of Trial Advocates; Los Angeles Inns of Court (Associate Rank). *PRACTICE AREAS:* Products Liability; Construction; Accident; Construction Defect.

**LEE ANN KERN,** born Whittier, California, October 3, 1963; admitted to bar, 1991, California and U.S. District Court, Central District of California. *Education:* California State University, Fullerton (B.A., 1986); Southwestern University (J.D., 1991). *Member:* Los Angeles County and American Bar Associations; State Bar of California. *PRACTICE AREAS:* Insurance Defense-Litigation.

**MICHAEL J. RYAN,** born Los Angeles, California, December 22, 1963; admitted to bar, 1992, California. *Education:* University of California at Irvine (B.A., 1989); Southwestern University School of Law (J.D., cum laude, 1992). Moot Court Finalist. Member, Law Review. Recipient, American Jurisprudence Award in Contracts I and II. *PRACTICE AREAS:* General Liability.

**NANCY MORROW NORRIS,** born Pittsburgh, Pennsylvania, April 17, 1962; admitted to bar, 1992, California. *Education:* Washington & Jefferson College; California State University at Northridge (B.A., cum laude, 1989); Southwestern University School of Law (J.D., 1992). Staff Member, 1990-1991 and Note and Comment Editor, 1991-1992, Southwestern University Law Review. *PRACTICE AREAS:* General Liability.

**JEAN A. DALMORE,** born Chicago, Illinois, August 4, 1962; admitted to bar, 1994, California. *Education:* California State University, Los Angeles (B.S., 1991); University of Southern California (J.D., 1994). *Member:* State Bar of California. *PRACTICE AREAS:* Products Liability; Construction; General Civil Litigation; Toxic Tort; Insurance Coverage.

**SHARYN G. ALCARAZ,** born Van Nuys, California, June 16, 1967; admitted to bar, 1993, California. *Education:* University of California at San Diego (B.A., 1990); Santa Clara University (J.D., 1993). Moot Court Board, Administrative Chairperson. Comments Editor, Santa Clara Law Review. Recipient, American Jurisprudence Award in Criminal Procedure. *REPORTED CASES: Han v. City of Pomona*(1995) 37 Cal. App. 4th 552. *PRACTICE AREAS:* Law and Motion; Appellate.

**CORINE ZYGELMAN,** born Los Angeles, California, December 15, 1965; admitted to bar, 1995, California. *Education:* California State University Northridge (B.A., Speech Communication, 1988); University of La-Verne (J.D., 1994). Recipient, American Jurisprudence Awards in Federal Courts, Products Liability, Alternative Dispute Resolution, Family Law. Certified Paralegal, 1988. *PRACTICE AREAS:* Litigation.

**J. LYNN FELDNER,** born Los Angeles, California, March 5, 1961; admitted to bar, 1987, California; 1988, U.S. District Court, Central Districts of California; 1990, U.S. District Court, Southern District of California. *Education:* University of California at Santa Barbara (B.A., with honors, 1983); Pepperdine University (J.D., 1987). Phi Alpha Delta. Member, Mortar Board. *Member:* San Diego County and American Bar Associations; State Bar of California; Association of Southern California Defense Counsel. (Resident, San Diego Office). *PRACTICE AREAS:* Products Liability Law; Construction Defect Law; Premises Liability Law.

**JAMES S. WILLIAMS,** born Los Angeles, California, February 27, 1949; admitted to bar, 1977, California and U.S. District Court, Northern District of California; 1980, U.S. Court of Appeals, Ninth Circuit and U.S. District Court, Temporary Emergency Court of Appeals; 1981, U.S. District Court, Central District of California; 1986, U.S. District Court, Southern District of California. *Education:* University of California at Berkeley (B.A., 1971); Golden Gate University Law School (J.D., 1977). Author: A Complete Guide to the Petroleum Marketing Practices Act, Oil Express, 1980. *Member:* San Bernardino County Bar Association. *REPORTED CASES: United States v. Wickland* (1980) 619 F.2d 75; *Pacific Service Stations 6 v. Mobil Oil Corp.* (1982) F2d 1055; *Lerner v. Atlantic Richfield Co.* (1982) 690 F.2d 203; *Trans Tech Resources, Inc. v. Mobil Oil Corp.* (1985) 755 F.2d 1575; *National Metal & Steel Corp. v. Colby Crane & Mfg. Co.*

*(This Listing Continued)*

(1988) 200 Cal. App. 3d 1111. *PRACTICE AREAS:* Insurance Coverage; Insurance Bad Faith Litigation; Insurance Defense.

**JULIE F. SMITH,** born Lincoln, Nebraska, March 12, 1968; admitted to bar, 1995, California. *Education:* Brigham Young University (B.S., 1992; J.D., 1995). *LANGUAGES:* Spanish. *PRACTICE AREAS:* Personal Injury; Construction Defect.

**HUGH JEFFREY GRANT,** born Santa Monica, California, December 8, 1965; admitted to bar, 1991, California and U.S. District Court, Central District of California. *Education:* University of California at Berkeley; University of Southern California (B.S., Accounting, 1988); Loyola Marymount University (J.D., 1991). *Member:* Los Angeles County and American Bar Associations; State Bar of California; Association of Southern California Defense Counsel. *PRACTICE AREAS:* Product Liability; General Commercial Liability.

**LAWRENCE D. MARKS,** born Los Angeles, California, January 26, 1964; admitted to bar, 1991, California. *Education:* University of California at Riverside; University of California at San Diego (B.A., 1987); McGeorge School of Law, University of the Pacific (J.D., 1990). Phi Delta Phi. *Member:* Los Angeles County and Orange County Associations; State Bar of California; Southern California Defense Counsel. *PRACTICE AREAS:* Legal Malpractice Defense; Professional E & O Defense; General Liability Defense; Employment Litigation.

**CAROLINE M. ALBERT,** born Bethesda, Maryland, January 9, 1966; admitted to bar, 1993, California; 1994, U.S. District Court, Central District of California. *Education:* Duke University (B.S., cum laude, 1987); Loyola Marymount University (J.D., 1993). Member, Moot Court. Member, Entertainment Law Journal; St. Thomas More Law Honor Society. *Member:* Los Angeles County Bar Association; State Bar of California; Association of Southern California Defense Counsel. *PRACTICE AREAS:* Civil Litigation.

**JEFFERSON S. SMITH,** born San Diego, California, April 10, 1964; admitted to bar, 1991, California. *Education:* University of California, San Diego (B.A., 1987); University of San Diego (J.D., 1991). *Member:* Kern County and Orange County Bar Associations; State Bar of California. (Resident, San Diego Office). *PRACTICE AREAS:* Premises Liability; Auto Accidents; General Tort Defense; Medical Malpractice; Contractual Liability.

**ALLISON ROSE,** born Los Angeles, California, November 13, 1964; admitted to bar, 1989, California and U.S. District Court, Central District of California; 1993, U.S. Court of Appeals, 9th Circuit. *Education:* Pitzer College (B.A., 1986); Pepperdine University (J.D., cum laude, 1989). Phi Delta Phi. Note and Comment Editor, Pepperdine Law Review, 1988-1989. Author: "Mandatory Drug Testing of College Athletes: Are Athletes Being Denied Their Constitutional Rights?" Pepperdine Law Review 16:45. *Member:* Los Angeles County Bar Association; State Bar of California. *PRACTICE AREAS:* Professional Liability; Environmental Coverage; Appellate Practice.

**THOMAS R. MERRICK,** born Whittier, California, August 31, 1964; admitted to bar, 1995, California. *Education:* University of California, Santa Barbara (B.A., Political Science, with high honors and Distinction, 1986); California Western School of Law (J.D., magna cum laude, 1995). Recipient: American Jurisprudence Awards in, Insurance Law, Trial Practice, Advanced Legal Research, Advanced Criminal Procedure, Legal Skills I and II; Trustees' Award, 1995; Academic Excellence Award, 1995. Staff Writer, 1993-1994 and Editor-in-Chief, 1994-1995, California Western Law Review/California Western International Law Journal. *Member:* San Diego County and American Bar Associations. *PRACTICE AREAS:* Insurance Defense Litigation.

**KASEY A. COVERT,** born Escondido, California, July 3, 1964; admitted to bar, 1991, California and U.S. District Court, Central and Southern District of California. *Education:* California State University, Chico (B.A., Minor Latin American Studies, 1986); University of San Diego (J.D., 1990). Moot Court. Member, Advanced Trial Advocacy. *Member:* San Diego County and American Bar Associations; State Bar of California. *LANGUAGES:* Spanish. *PRACTICE AREAS:* Securities; Employment Litigation.

**MARY ANN ALSNAUER,** born Sharon, Pennsylvania, February 7, 1960; admitted to bar, 1985, Pennsylvania; 1987, California; 1995, Massachusetts. *Education:* Grove City College (B.A., 1982); Case Western Reserve University (J.D., 1985). *Member:* State Bar of California (Member, Litigation Section); Association of Trial Lawyers of America. *PRACTICE AREAS:* Trial Practice; Products Liability Law; Premises Liability; Inadequate Security; Business Litigation.

*(This Listing Continued)*

**GERHARD S. GACKLE,** born Kansas City, Kansas, May 25, 1955; admitted to bar, 1992, California. *Education:* University of Missouri, Kansas City (B.A., 1977); Loyola Law School, Los Angeles (J.D., 1991). Author: Does Deputy District Attorney Come Under This Category? (Ventura County, 1992). *Member:* State Bar of California. [Capt., USAF, 1978-1984]. *LANGUAGES:* German.

REPRESENTATIVE CLIENTS: *Domestic Insurance Clients:* Agricultural Farmers Surplus Ins. Co.; Allianz Insurance Co.; American Custom Insurance Services; American Empire Surplus Lines Insurance Co.; American States Insurance Co.; Argonaut Insurance Co.; Carl Warren & Co.; Chubb Group of Insurance Cos.; CIGNA; Colonia Insurance Co.; Commercial Union Insurance Cos.; Dearborn Insurance Co.; Fidelity & Deposit Company of Maryland; Fireman's Fund; First Financial Insurance Co.; First State Management Group; Golden Eagle Insurance Co.; Great American Insurance Co.; Guarantee National Cos.; ITT Hartford Insurance Co.; HCM Claim Management Co.; Insurance Corporation of Hannover; Interstate Insurance Group; Jefferson Insurance Co.; LMI Commercial Insurance Co.; LOBO Claims Management, Ins.; Northland Insurance Co.; Northwestern National Insurance Co.; Pacific National Insurance Co.; Philadelphia Insurance Co.; Progressive Insurance Co.; Reliance Insurance Co.; Risk Enterprise Management; Safeco Insurance Co.; Sentry Claims Service; Taisho Claims Service Corp.; TM Claims Service, Inc.; Tokyo Marine Management Inc.; Workmen's Auto Insurance Co.; The Yasuda Fire & Marine Insurance Company of America. *International Insurance Clients:* Albingia Versicherungs-AG; Allianz Versicherungs-AG; Bayerische Rueck Versicherung-AG; Bayerisohe Versicherungskammer; Colonia Versicherungs-AG; Deutscher Lloyd Versicherungs-AG; Donau Allgemeine Versicherungs-AG; Frankona Rueck Versicherung-Co.; Gothaer Allgemeine Versicherung-AG; Gothaer Versicherungsbank VVag; Haftpflichtverband der Deutschen Industrie V.a.G. (HDI); Malayan Overseas Insurance Corp.; Muenchener Reuckversicherungs-Gesellschaft; Seguros America, S.A.; Mitsui Marine & Fire Insurance Co., Limited; The Tokyo Marine & Fire Insurance Co., Limited; Swiss Reinsurance Co.; Wuertemberische Versicherung AG; Underwriters at Lloyds; Underwriters in London; Zurich RE (London); *Domestic Corporate Clients:* Arden Mayfair, Inc.; Besam, Inc.; Budget Rent-A-Car; Cargill, Inc.; Club Corp.; The Coleman Co.; Crompton & Knowles Corp.; Denny's Inc.; The First Gray Line Corporation and Grand Rent-A-Car Corp.; Freightliner Corp.; Gelson's Market; Gould, Inc.; Great Dane Trailers Inc.; Heidelberg West, Inc.; Heil-Quaker, Inc.; Hoechst Celanese Corp.; Kenworth Truck Company, an unincorporated division of PACCAR Inc.; KTI; LACMTA World Oil; Mannesmann AG; Mitsubishi Heavy Industries America, Inc.; Mitsubishi Heavy Industries, Ltd.; Mitsubishi International Corp.; Nissan Motor Corporation U.S.A.; Outboard Marine Corp.; PACCAR, Inc.; Peterbilt Motor Company, an unincorporated division of PACCAR Inc.; Public Storage; 3 M Co.; Vons Groceries, Inc.; Whirlpool Corp.

## MICHAEL M. MURPHY

*555 SOUTH FLOWER STREET, SUITE 2850*
**LOS ANGELES, CALIFORNIA 90071**
*Telephone: 213-488-3323*
*Fax: 213-689-0863*

*Practice Specializing in Real Estate Sales and Acquisitions, Commercial Leasing, Property Management, Real Estate Financing and Construction Law.*

**MICHAEL M. MURPHY,** born Los Angeles, California, July 21, 1939; admitted to bar, 1964, California. *Education:* University of Notre Dame (B.B.A. in Accounting, cum laude, 1960); University of California at Los Angeles (LL.B., 1963). Phi Delta Phi. Member, 1961-1963 and Editor, 1962-1963, University of California at Los Angeles Law Review. Associate, 1965-1970 and Partner, 1970-1982, Musick, Peeler & Garrett. Partner: Rogers & Wells, 1982-1990; Rudin, Appel & Rosenfeld, 1990-1992. *Member:* Los Angeles County and American Bar Associations; The State Bar of California. [Capt., U.S. Army, Artillery, 1963-1965]

## TAMELA J. MURPHY

*415 WASHINGTON BOULEVARD., SUITE 504*
**LOS ANGELES, CALIFORNIA 90292**
*Telephone: 310-822-4401*
*Fax: 310-822-4401*

*Entertainment, including Musicians and Film, Transactional and Litigation.*

**TAMELA J. MURPHY,** born Parkersburg, West Virginia, April 18, 1960; admitted to bar, 1992, Ohio (Not admitted in California). *Education:* Ohio University (B.B.A., 1982); Capital University (J.D., 1991). *Member:* Columbus Bar, Ohio State and American Bar Associations. *PRACTICE AREAS:* Entertainment Law (33%, 20); General Practice (66%, 50).

CAA1019B

## MURPHY, WEIR & BUTLER

*A PROFESSIONAL CORPORATION*

**2049 CENTURY PARK EAST, 21ST FLOOR**
**LOS ANGELES, CALIFORNIA 90067**

*Telephone: 310-788-3700*
*FAX: 310-788-3777*
*Email: lawyer@mwblaw.com*

*San Francisco, California Office:* 101 California Street, 39th Floor. Telephone: 415-398-4700. Telex: 705457 MWB UD. Telecopiers: 415-421-7879; 415-788-0783.

*Secured Financing and Commercial Lending, Real Estate Finance, Business Workouts and Bankruptcy Reorganizations, Creditors' Remedies. Trial Practice and Litigation.*

**LAWRENCE BASS,** born Los Angeles, California, March 24, 1950; admitted to bar, 1974, California. *Education:* University of California at Los Angeles (B.A., 1971); University of Southern California (J.D., 1974). Lecturer and Author: Banking Law Institute; CLE International; Frost & Sullivan; Los Angeles County Bar Association; Executive Enterprises. Member, Board of Directors and Vice President-Legal Counsel, California Special Olympics, Inc., 1982-1987. Board of Advisors, Commercial Property Law Digests, 1991-1992. *Member:* Los Angeles County (Chair, Bankruptcy Committee and Member, Executive Committee, Commercial Law and Bankruptcy Section, 1988—) and American (Member: Business Bankruptcy Committee, Chapter 11 Subcommittee, 1988—; Section on Corporation, Banking and Business Law) Bar Associations; State Bar of California (Member, Debtor/Creditor Relations and Bankruptcy Committee, 1990-1992). *PRACTICE AREAS:* Business Workouts; Bankruptcy Reorganizations; Creditors Remedies. *Email:* lbass@mwblaw.com

**N. DWIGHT CARY,** born Irvington, New Jersey, May 21, 1948; admitted to bar, 1975, California. *Education:* Pomona College (B.A., magna cum laude, 1970); Harvard University and Stanford University (J.D., 1975). Phi Beta Kappa. Consultant to 1981 Supplement and Author and Editor of 1982 and 1983 Supplements of *California Commercial Law: III,* published by California Continuing Education of the Bar. Author: *Legal Guide,* California Cattle Feeders Association, 1978. *Member:* State Bar of California (Member, Business Law Section); American Bar Association. *PRACTICE AREAS:* Secured Financing; Commercial Lending; Creditors Remedies; Real Estate Finance. *Email:* ncary@mwblaw.com

**SPENCER J. HELFEN,** born Los Angeles, California, August 4, 1961; admitted to bar, 1988, California. *Education:* University of California at Los Angeles (B.A., summa cum laude, 1984; M.A., 1984, Phi Beta Kappa, Departmental Scholar); Boalt Hall School of Law, University of California (J.D., 1987; Moot Court Honors). *Member:* Beverly Hills Bar Association (Executive Committee, Bankruptcy Section, 1993-1995; Chairman, Financial Lawyers Conference, 1995-1997). *PRACTICE AREAS:* Workouts; Bankruptcy Reorganization; Creditors Remedies. *Email:* shelfen@mwblaw.com

**JEAN B. LEBLANC, II,** born Detroit, Michigan, September 10, 1957; admitted to bar, 1987, California. *Education:* California State University at Northridge (B.A., summa cum laude, 1984); University of California at Los Angeles (J.D., 1987). Order of the Coif. Judicial Extern to Hon. Abner J. Mikva, U.S. Court of Appeals, District of Columbia Circuit. *PRACTICE AREAS:* Creditors Remedies; Commercial Lending; Secured Financing; Business Workouts. *Email:* jleblanc@mwblaw.com

**ROBERT JAY MOORE,** born Sentinel, Oklahoma, September 16, 1950; admitted to bar, 1977, California; 1980, District of Columbia. *Education:* University of North Carolina at Chapel Hill (A.B., with honors, 1974); University of California at Los Angeles (J.D., 1977). John Motley Morehead Foundation Scholar, University of North Carolina at Chapel Hill, 1968-1971 and 1973-1974. Member, Jessup Moot Court Team, 1975-1977. President, University of California at Los Angeles Society of International and Comparative Law, 1976-1977. Law Clerk to Judge Ozell M. Trask, U.S. Court of Appeals, Ninth Circuit, 1977. Author: "Preserving and Maximizing Value for the Equity Investor in Chapter 11 Bankruptcy Reorganizations," Venture Capital Institute, NVCA/NASBIC, 1996; "Representing a Committee of Unsecured Creditors in a Chapter 11 Case," *Bankruptcy Practice and Strategy,* Warren, Gorham & Lamont, 1987. Lecturer and Author: American Bar Association, American Bankruptcy Institute, Association of Insolvency Accountants, Turnaround Management Associations, NVCA/NASBIC Venture Capital Institute, Bond Buyer Symposium, National Federation of Municipal Analysts, Association of Real Estate Attorneys, Title Insurers Symposium, California Continuing Education of the Bar, Central California Bankruptcy Institute, Los Angeles County Bar Association, Orange County Bankruptcy Forum and Century City Bar Association. Member, Bankruptcy Judge Merit Screening Panel, U.S. District Court, Central District of California, 1987. Member, Lawyers' Advisory Council, Constitutional Rights Foundation, 1987-1992. Member, Board of Visitors, Southwestern University School of Law, 1988—. *Member:* Los Angeles County (Chair, Section on Commercial Law and Bankruptcy, 1986-1987; Vice Chair, 1985-1986; Secretary, 1983-1985; Member, Executive Committee, 1981—; Member, Bankruptcy Committee, 1981-1983; Chair, Publications Committee, 1981-1982; Member, Nominating Committee, 1980) and American (Member: Business Bankruptcy Committee, 1982—; Secured Creditors Subcommittee, 1984—; Chapter 11 Subcommittees, 1985—; Ad Hoc Subcommittee on the Suggested Interim Bankruptcy Rules, 1980) Bar Associations; State Bar of California (Member: Business Law Section; Debtor/Creditor Relations and Bankruptcy Committee, 1987-1989; Assignments for the Benefit of Creditors Subcommittee, 1987-1989). *PRACTICE AREAS:* Business Workouts; Bankruptcy Reorganizations; Creditors Remedies. *Email:* rmoore@mwblaw.com

**GARY B. ROSENBAUM,** born New York, New York, September 6, 1962; admitted to bar, 1988, California. *Education:* Northwestern University (B.A., 1984); University of California at Los Angeles (J.D., 1987). Member, UCLA Law Review, 1986-1987. *Member:* Beverly Hills, Century City, Los Angeles County (Member, Uniform Commercial Code Subcommittee and Commercial Financial Services Subcommittee) and American Bar Associations; State Bar of California (Member, Business Law Section); Financial Lawyers Conference. *PRACTICE AREAS:* Secured Financing; Commercial Lending; Business Workouts. *Email:* grosenbaum@mwblaw.com

**ADAM G. SPIEGEL,** born Los Angeles, California, January 16, 1964; admitted to bar, 1989, California. *Education:* University of California, Los Angeles (B.A., 1985); Georgetown University (J.D., cum laude, 1989). Member, Financial Lawyers Conference. *Member:* State Bar of California (Member, Business Law Section). *PRACTICE AREAS:* Secured Financing; Commercial Lending; Business Workouts. *Email:* aspiegel@mwbla.com

**ROLF S. WOOLNER,** born Alberta, Canada, 1957; admitted to bar, 1983, New York; 1989, California. *Education:* University of Calgary, Calgary, Alberta (B.A., first class honors and gold medalist, 1979); Yale University (J.D., 1982). *Member:* Los Angeles County (Member, Federal Courts Committee, 1992—) and American (Member, Litigation Section, Committee on Bankruptcy and Insolvency Litigation; Committee on Commercial and Banking Litigation) Bar Associations; State Bar of California; Association of Business Trial Lawyers (Member, Federal Court Committee). *Email:* rwoolner@mwblaw.com

**MARY L. TROKEL YOUNG,** born New York, New York, December 27, 1962; admitted to bar, 1989, New York; 1991, California. *Education:* Yale University (B.A., 1984); New York University (J.D., 1988). Moot Court Board, 1987-1988. Recipient, American Jurisprudence Award, Civil Procedure. Panel Mediator, Central District of California Bankruptcy Mediation Program. *Member:* Los Angeles County Bar Association (Member, Bankruptcy Committee, Commercial Law and Bankruptcy Section, 1996—); State Bar of California (Member, Partnerships and Unincorporated Business Associations, Committee of the Business Law Section, 1994-1997). *PRACTICE AREAS:* Business Workouts; Bankruptcy Reorganizations; Creditors Remedies. *Email:* myoung@mwblaw.com

---

**DEMETRA V. GEORGELOS,** born Oak Lawn, Illinois, December 6, 1967; admitted to bar, 1992, California. *Education:* Yale University (B.A., 1989); University of California, Los Angeles (J.D., 1992). *Email:* dgeorgelos@mwblaw.com

**ERIC S. KURTZMAN,** born London, England, November 3, 1970; admitted to bar, 1996, California. *Education:* University of California at Berkeley (B.A., 1992); University of California School of Law, Los Angeles (M.B.A./J.D., 1996). Member, California State Central Democratic Committee, 1992-1994. *Email:* ekurtzman@mwb.law

**WILLIAM W. NEUSCHAEFER,** born Oklahoma City, Oklahoma, March 18, 1969; admitted to bar, 1994, California. *Education:* University of Pennsylvania, The Wharton School (B.S., cum laude, 1991); University of California at Los Angeles (J.D., 1994). Benjamin Franklin Scholar. Judicial Extern, Honorable A. Wallace Tashima, U.S. District Court, Central District of California. *Member:* State Bar of California. *Email:* wneuschaefer@mwblaw.com

**PAUL P. SAGAN,** born Yonkers, New York, June 14, 1962; admitted to bar, 1991, California. *Education:* Brown University (B.A., 1984); John E.

*(This Listing Continued)*

Anderson Graduate School of Management, University of California, Los Angeles (M.B.A., 1991); University of California, Los Angeles (J.D., 1991). Member, Financial Lawyers Conference. *Member:* State Bar of California (Member, Sections on: Business Law and Real Property). *Email:* psagan@mwblaw.com

**ERIC E. SAGERMAN,** born Brooklyn, New York, October 20, 1966; admitted to bar, 1991, California. *Education:* London School of Economics, London (1986-1987); University of California at Santa Barbara (B.A., summa cum laude, 1988); University of California at Los Angeles (J.D., 1991). Member, Financial Lawyers Conference. *Member:* State Bar of California (Member, Business Law Section). *Email:* esagerman@mwblaw.com

**RICHARD VILLASEÑOR,** born Milwaukee, Wisconsin, January 6, 1967; admitted to bar, 1992, California. *Education:* University of Wisconsin (B.A., 1988); University of California, Los Angeles (J.D., 1992). Comment Editor, UCLA Law Review, 1991-1992. Recipient, American Jurisprudence Award, Legal Research & Writing. Member, Financial Lawyers Conference. *Member:* State Bar of California (Member, Business Law Section). **LANGUAGES:** Chinese, French, German and Spanish. *Email:* rvillasenor@mwblaw.com

*OF COUNSEL*

**BERNARD SHAPIRO,** born Brooklyn, New York, October 11, 1917; admitted to bar, 1946, California. *Education:* University of California at Berkeley (A.B., 1939); Boalt Hall School of Law, University of California, Berkeley (LL.B., 1942). Order of the Coif. Member, Board of Editors and Associate Editor, California Law Review, 1940-1942. Author: Chapter in "Assignments for the Benefit of Creditors," Continuing Education of the Bar, Remedies for Unsecured Creditors, 1957; "Tax Effects of Bankruptcy," U.S.C. Eleventh Tax Institute, Major Tax Planning, 1959. Co-Author with G. Bray: "Purchasing Financially Distressed Companies Before Bankruptcy--Pitfalls," in *Workouts and Turnarounds,* Irwin, 1991. Co-author: "Receivership, California Civil Procedure Before Trial," Continuing Education of the Bar, 1977. Lecturer, Hastings College of Law, San Francisco, California, 1946-1948. Visiting Professor, Creditors Remedies, Boalt Hall School of Law, University of California, Spring 1975 and 1978. Adjunct Professor, Reorganization under the New Bankruptcy Code, University of California at Los Angeles Law School, 1980. Member, 1962—, Vice Chair, 1984-1985 and Chair, 1992—, National Bankruptcy Conference. Member, Advisory Committee on Bankruptcy Rules, Judicial Conference of the United States. *Member:* Los Angeles County Bar Association (Chair, Commercial Law and Bankruptcy Section, 1971-1972); State Bar of California (Chair, UCC Committee, Business Law Section, 1979-1980). **PRACTICE AREAS:** Business Workouts; Bankruptcy Reorganizations; Creditors Remedies. *Email:* bshapiro@mwblaw.com

**ROBERT L. ORDIN,** born Los Angeles, California, December, 22, 1924; admitted to bar, 1949, California. *Education:* University of California at Los Angeles; University of Southern California (LL.B., 1949). Author: "Contesting Confirmation," Prentice Hall Law & Business, 1993. "The Good Faith Principle in the Bankruptcy Code," The Business Lawyer, Vol. 38, p. 1795, August, 1983. Associate Professor, Loyola Law School, 1977, 1978. Lecturer and Author, Prentice Hall Law & Business, Practising Law Institute, American Law Institute-American Bar Association. United States Bankruptcy Judge, Central District of California, 1973-1983. *Member:* State Bar of California (Chairman, State Bar Speaking Program, 1953-1954). **PRACTICE AREAS:** Business Workouts; Bankruptcy Reorganizations; Creditors Remedies. *Email:* rordin@mwblaw.com

(For Other Biographical Information, See Professional Biographies at San Francisco, California)

---

## MURRAY, BRADSHAW & BUDZYN

*A LAW CORPORATION*

**LOS ANGELES, CALIFORNIA**

(See Pasadena)

*Pension, Profit Sharing, Employment, Labor and Corporate Tax Law, ERISA and Business Litigation.*

---

## MUSICK, PEELER & GARRETT LLP

Established in 1954

SUITE 2000, ONE WILSHIRE BOULEVARD
**LOS ANGELES, CALIFORNIA 90017-3321**
*Telephone: 213-629-7600*
*Cable Address: "Peelgar"*
*Facsimile: 213-624-1376*

*San Diego, California Office:* 1900 Home Savings Tower, 225 Broadway. Telephone: 619-231-2500. Facsimile: 619-231-1234.
*San Francisco, California Office:* Suite 1300, Steuart Street Tower, One Market Plaza. Telephone: 415-281-2000. Facsimile: 415-281-2010.
*Sacramento, California Office:* Wells Fargo Center, Suite 1280, 400 Capitol Mall. Telephone: 916-557-8300. Facsimile: 916-442-8629.
*Fresno, California Office:* 6041 North First Street. Telephone: 209-228-1000. Facsimile: 209-447-4670.
*Irvine, California Office:* 2603 Main Street, Suite 1025. Telephone: 714-852-5122. Facsimile: 714-852-5128.

*General Practice. Trial and Appellate Practice. Corporation, Securities and Antitrust Law. Healthcare, Hospital, College and University Law. Insurance, Excess, Reinsurance and Coverage. Labor, Real Estate, Land Use, Environmental, Eminent Domain, Oil and Gas and Mining Law. Taxation, Trust, Probate, Estate Planning, Bankruptcy and Pension and Profit Sharing Law.*

*FIRM PROFILE: The Firm presently has attorneys practicing in eight major specialty groups: Litigation, Insurance, Tax and ERISA, Trusts and Estates, Corporate, Real Estate, Labor and Employment, and Healthcare. Musick, Peeler & Garrett represents a diverse clientele, ranging from individuals to private and publicly-traded, profit and non-profit, domestic and foreign businesses and institutions. The Firm also has offices in Fresno, Orange County, Sacramento, San Diego and San Francisco.*

*MEMBERS OF FIRM*

**ELVON MUSICK** (1890-1968).

**JOSEPH D. PEELER** (1895-1991).

**LEROY A. GARRETT** (1906-1963).

**WILLIAM L. ABALONA** (Resident at Sacramento Office; See Sacramento listing for full biographical information).

**DONALD P. ASPERGER** (Resident at Fresno Office; See Fresno listing for full biographical information).

**WILLIE R. BARNES,** born Dallas, Texas, December 9, 1931; admitted to bar, 1960, California. *Education:* University of California at Los Angeles (B.A., 1953; J.D., 1959). **PRACTICE AREAS:** Corporate Law; Securities; Franchises and Franchising.

**GRAHAM E. BERRY,** born Wellington, New Zealand, December 29, 1950; admitted to bar, 1973, New Zealand; 1979, New South Wales, Australia; 1981, New York; 1987, California. *Education:* University of Canterbury, Christchurch, New Zealand (LL.B., 1972).

**JAMES B. BERTERO** (Resident at San Diego Office; See San Diego listing for full biographical information).

**JAMES B. BETTS** (Resident at Fresno Office; See Fresno listing for full biographical information).

**HAL G. BLOCK** (Resident at Irvine Office; See Irvine listing for full biographical information).

**MARY CATHERINE M. BOHEN,** born Los Angeles, California, July 19, 1960; admitted to bar, 1985, California. *Education:* University of California at Irvine (B.A., cum laude, 1982); Hastings College of Law (J.D., cum laude, 1985). **PRACTICE AREAS:** Litigation; Insurance.

**EDUARDO A. GUERINI BOLT** (Resident at Irvine Office; See Irvine listing for full biographical information).

**WILLIAM A. BOSSEN,** born Clinton, Iowa, October 6, 1961; admitted to bar, 1987, California. *Education:* University of Iowa (B.G.S., 1984); Pepperdine University (J.D., 1987). **PRACTICE AREAS:** Litigation.

**GEOFFREY C. BROWN,** born Punxsutawney, Pennsylvania, October 2, 1949; admitted to bar, 1979, California. *Education:* University of California at Davis (A.B., with honors, 1976); University of California at Los Angeles (J.D., 1979). **PRACTICE AREAS:** Litigation.

**JOHN R. BROWNING,** born Norborne, Missouri, January 24, 1939; admitted to bar, 1965, California. *Education:* California State University, Long Beach (B.A., 1961); University of California, Los Angeles (LL.B.,

*(This Listing Continued)*

## MUSICK, PEELER & GARRETT LLP, Los Angeles—Continued

1964). *PRACTICE AREAS:* Healthcare; Hospitals; Corporate Law; Finance.

**LEONARD E. CASTRO,** born Los Angeles, California, March 18, 1934; admitted to bar, 1963, California. *Education:* University of California at Los Angeles (A.B., 1959; J.D., 1962). *PRACTICE AREAS:* Corporate Law; Securities.

**HARRY W. R. CHAMBERLAIN, II,** born Port Hueneme, California, February 12, 1957; admitted to bar, 1980, California; 1992, North Carolina; 1993, District of Columbia. *Education:* San Diego State University (B.A., summa cum laude, 1977); Hastings College of the Law, University of California (J.D., 1980). *PRACTICE AREAS:* Litigation; Insurance; Appellate Law.

**RICHARD S. CONN,** born Los Angeles, California, September 19, 1949; admitted to bar, 1975, California; 1976, U.S. Tax Court. *Education:* Brown University; Columbia University (B.A., magna cum laude, 1971); University of California at Los Angeles (J.D., 1975). *PRACTICE AREAS:* Litigation.

**R. JOSEPH DE BRIYN,** born Florida, December 9, 1948; admitted to bar, 1974, California. *Education:* Santa Clara University (B.S., 1970; J.D., 1973). (Chairman, Management Committee and Managing Partner). *PRACTICE AREAS:* Litigation; Insurance.

**DENNIS S. DIAZ,** born Los Angeles, California, July 20, 1952; admitted to bar, 1980, California. *Education:* University of California, Santa Barbara (B.A., with honors, 1975); University of California at Los Angeles School of Law (J.D., 1980). *PRACTICE AREAS:* Healthcare; Hospitals; Corporate Law.

**EDSELL M. EADY, JR.** (Resident at San Francisco Office; See San Francisco listing for full biographical information).

**STEVEN J. ELIE,** born Plainview, New York, January 30, 1962; admitted to bar, 1987, California. *Education:* State University of New York at Albany (B.A., cum laude, 1984); Hastings College of the Law, University of California (J.D., 1987). *PRACTICE AREAS:* Litigation; Insurance.

**PHILIP EWEN,** born New York, New York, May 4, 1961; admitted to bar, 1987, California. *Education:* Arizona State University (B.S., magna cum laude, 1982; M.S., 1983); University of Southern California (J.D., 1986). *PRACTICE AREAS:* Labor and Employment.

**SUSAN J. FIELD,** born Brooklyn, New York, September 20, 1954; admitted to bar, 1979, California; 1980, New York. *Education:* State University of New York at Albany (B.A., 1974); St. John's University (J.D., 1978). *PRACTICE AREAS:* Litigation; Insurance.

**MARTIN L. FINEMAN** (Resident at San Francisco Office; See San Francisco listing for full biographical information).

**CHARLES F. FORBES,** born Los Angeles, California, October 28, 1929; admitted to bar, 1956, California. *Education:* University of Southern California (B.S., 1951; J.D., 1956). *PRACTICE AREAS:* Healthcare; Hospitals; Corporate Law.

**ROBERT D. GIRARD,** born Pittsburgh, Pennsylvania, August 2, 1946; admitted to bar, 1971, California. *Education:* University of California, Los Angeles (A.B., 1967); Yale University (LL.B., 1970). *PRACTICE AREAS:* Healthcare; Hospitals; Corporate Law.

**MARK J. GRUSHKIN,** born Boston, Massachusetts, August 23, 1953; admitted to bar, 1978, California; 1985, U.S. Tax Court. *Education:* California State University at Los Angeles (B.S., 1975); Southwestern University School of Law (J.D., 1978). *PRACTICE AREAS:* Employee Benefits.

**STEPHEN A. HANSEN** (Resident at Fresno Office; See Fresno listing for full biographical information).

**LARRY C. HART,** born Lawton, Oklahoma, December 24, 1942; admitted to bar, 1974, California. *Education:* Colorado State University (B.S., 1967); Loyola University of Los Angeles (LL.B., 1974). *PRACTICE AREAS:* Litigation.

**JAMES M. HASSAN,** born Los Angeles, California, November 12, 1948; admitted to bar, 1973, California. *Education:* University of Southern California (B.S., cum laude, 1970); Hastings College of the Law, University of California (J.D., 1973). *PRACTICE AREAS:* Taxation; Estate Planning; Trusts and Estates; Non-Profit and Charitable Organizations.

**SUSAN J. HAZARD,** born San Bernardino, California, September 11, 1953; admitted to bar, 1978, California. *Education:* University of California at Riverside (B.A., 1975); University of California at Los Angeles (J.D., 1978). *PRACTICE AREAS:* Estate Planning; Trust and Estate Administration.

**PAUL D. HESSE,** born Las Vegas, Nevada, January 11, 1958; admitted to bar, 1983, California. *Education:* University of Nevada (B.S., 1980); University of Santa Clara (J.D., 1983). *PRACTICE AREAS:* Litigation; Insurance.

**MICHAEL J. HICKMAN** (Resident at San Diego Office; See San Diego listing for full biographical information).

**ANNE YEAGER HIGGINS,** born Riverside, California, May 21, 1959; admitted to bar, 1984, California. *Education:* University of California at Los Angeles (B.A., magna cum laude, 1981); Loyola Law School of Los Angeles (J.D., 1984). *PRACTICE AREAS:* Litigation; Insurance.

**THOMAS T. KAWAKAMI,** born Los Angeles, California, May 3, 1960; admitted to bar, 1986, California. *Education:* University of California at Los Angeles (B.A., 1983); University of San Diego (J.D., 1986). *PRACTICE AREAS:* Taxation; Business Law; Trusts and Estates.

**EDWARD A. LANDRY,** born New Orleans, Louisiana, March 29, 1939; admitted to bar, 1965, California. *Education:* Louisiana State University (B.A., 1961); University of California at Los Angeles (J.D., 1964). *PRACTICE AREAS:* Trusts and Estates; Non-Profit and Charitable Organizations.

**DAVID M. LESTER,** born Poughkeepsie, New York, 1960; admitted to bar, 1985, California; 1986, Arizona. *Education:* Cornell University (B.S., 1982); University of California at Los Angeles School of Law (J.D., 1985). *PRACTICE AREAS:* Labor and Employment.

**J. ROBERT LISET,** born Fall River, Massachusetts, February 2, 1945; admitted to bar, 1970, Virginia; 1973, District of Columbia; 1976, California. *Education:* Georgetown University (A.B., 1967; J.D., 1970). *PRACTICE AREAS:* Healthcare; Hospitals; Corporate Law; Litigation.

**WAYNE B. LITTLEFIELD,** born Waltham, Massachusetts, April 17, 1946; admitted to bar, 1976, California. *Education:* Lehigh University (B.A., cum laude, 1968); Washington State University (M.A., 1973); University of Idaho (J.D., 1975). *PRACTICE AREAS:* Litigation; Insurance.

**SETH B. MADNICK** (Resident at San Francisco Office; See San Francisco listing for full biographical information).

**DAVID G. MANN,** born Burlington, Ontario, Canada, April 28, 1961; admitted to bar, 1988, California. *Education:* University of California at Santa Barbara (B.A., with honors, 1983); University of Southern California (M.B.T., 1987; J.D., 1987). *PRACTICE AREAS:* Taxation; Corporate; Real Estate.

**C. DONALD MCBRIDE** (Resident at San Francisco Office; See San Francisco listing for full biographical information).

**JAMES W. MILLER,** born Santa Monica, California, 1948; admitted to bar, 1974, California. *Education:* University of California at Santa Barbara (B.A., with honors, 1970); Loyola University of Los Angeles (J.D., 1973). *PRACTICE AREAS:* Litigation.

**WILLIAM MCD. MILLER, III,** born Santa Monica, California, September 4, 1945; admitted to bar, 1971, California. *Education:* University of Oregon (B.A., 1967); Loyola University of Los Angeles (J.D., 1970). *PRACTICE AREAS:* Litigation.

**MICHAEL W. MONK,** born Grand Island, Nebraska, February 21, 1949; admitted to bar, 1974, Massachusetts; 1976, California. *Education:* Harvard University (B.A., in English, cum laude, 1971); University of Pennsylvania Law School (J.D., 1974). *PRACTICE AREAS:* Labor and Employment.

**ROBERT Y. NAGATA,** born Rohwer, Arkansas, April 27, 1945; admitted to bar, 1971, California. *Education:* University of Southern California (B.S., 1967); University of San Diego (J.D., 1970); Golden Gate University (M.S., 1977). (Certified Specialist, Taxation Law, The State Bar of California Board of Legal Specialization). *LANGUAGES:* Japanese. *PRACTICE AREAS:* Taxation; Business Law.

**LYNN A. O'LEARY,** born San Francisco, California, July 1, 1959; admitted to bar, 1983, California. *Education:* University of Santa Clara (B.S.C., 1980; J.D., 1983). *PRACTICE AREAS:* Litigation; Insurance.

**GARY F. OVERSTREET,** born Torrance, California, May 20, 1942; admitted to bar, 1972, California. *Education:* University of Oklahoma (B.S.,

*(This Listing Continued)*

Mathematics, 1964); Loyola University of Los Angeles (J.D., 1971). *PRACTICE AREAS:* Labor and Employment.

**ALAN R. PERRY** (Resident at San Diego Office; See San Diego listing for full biographical information).

**DAVID A. RADOVICH,** born Philadelphia, Pennsylvania, October 14, 1957; admitted to bar, 1988, California. *Education:* San Francisco State University (B.A., magna cum laude, 1980); Loyola University, Los Angeles (J.D., 1987). *PRACTICE AREAS:* Litigation.

**STUART W. RUDNICK,** born Sheboygan, Wisconsin, September 21, 1946; admitted to bar, 1972, Wisconsin; 1977, California. *Education:* University of Wisconsin-Madison (B.A., 1969); University of Michigan (J.D., 1972). *PRACTICE AREAS:* Labor and Employment.

**CHERYL L. SCHRECK,** born Pontiac, Michigan, September 20, 1959; admitted to bar, 1985, Tennessee; 1987, California. *Education:* Vanderbilt University (B.A., cum laude, 1981); University of Tennessee at Knoxville (J.D., 1984). *PRACTICE AREAS:* Labor and Employment.

**ROBERT L. SCHUCHARD,** born Los Angeles, California, February 14, 1952; admitted to bar, 1977, California. *Education:* Stanford University (B.A., 1974); University of Santa Clara (J.D., 1977). *PRACTICE AREAS:* Healthcare; Hospitals; Corporate Law; Mergers, Acquisitions and Divestitures.

**BRIAN J. SEERY,** born Flushing, New York, October 23, 1943; admitted to bar, 1969, New York; 1971, U.S. Tax Court; 1975, California. *Education:* St. John's University (B.A., 1965; J.D., 1968); New York University (LL.M., 1972). *PRACTICE AREAS:* Taxation; Tax Controversy.

**MARY BETH SIPOS,** born Geneva, New York, January 28, 1960; admitted to bar, 1986, California. *Education:* Universite de Paris IV-La Sorbonne, 1980-1981; Smith College (A.B., 1982); Boston University (J.D., 1986). *LANGUAGES:* French. *PRACTICE AREAS:* Litigation; Insurance.

**CHARLES E. SLYNGSTAD,** born Jersey City, New Jersey, February 20, 1954; admitted to bar, 1979, California; 1986, U.S. Tax Court. *Education:* University of California, Berkeley (A.B., 1976); Hastings College of Law, University of California (J.D., 1979). *PRACTICE AREAS:* Litigation.

**GERARD SMOLIN, JR.** (Resident at San Diego Office; See San Diego listing for full biographical information).

**W. CLARK STANTON** (Resident at San Francisco Office; See San Francisco listing for full biographical information).

**ROBERT M. STONE,** born Steubenville, Ohio, May 3, 1948; admitted to bar, 1974, New York; 1977, California. *Education:* Wesleyan University (B.A., 1970); Boston University (J.D., 1973). *PRACTICE AREAS:* Labor and Employment.

**DAVID A. TARTAGLIO,** born Orange, California, May 5, 1958; admitted to bar, 1984, California. *Education:* University of California at Irvine (B.A., magna cum laude, 1980); University of Southern California (J.D., 1984). *LANGUAGES:* Spanish. *PRACTICE AREAS:* Litigation; Insurance.

**JUAN A. TORRES,** born San Luis Rio Colorado, Sonora, Mexico, February 9, 1960; admitted to bar, 1987, California. *Education:* University of California at Berkeley (B.A., 1983); University of California, Boalt Hall School of Law, Berkeley (J.D., 1986). *LANGUAGES:* Spanish. *PRACTICE AREAS:* Litigation.

**ERIC L. TROFF,** born Kalamazoo, Michigan, September 14, 1952; admitted to bar, 1983, California. *Education:* The Colorado College; University of Michigan (B.A., Journalism, 1977); Loyola Marymount University (J.D., cum laude, 1983). *PRACTICE AREAS:* Litigation.

**MARK H. VAN BRUSSEL** (Resident at Sacramento Office; See Sacramento listing for full biographical information).

**DAVID L. VOLK,** born Avalon, California, March 14, 1945; admitted to bar, 1977, District of Columbia; 1980, California. *Education:* Antioch College (B.A., 1968); Antioch-Putney College (M.A.T., 1969); Georgetown University (J.D., 1977). *PRACTICE AREAS:* Healthcare Law; Hospitals; Corporate Law; Medicare and Medicaid.

**ROBERT G. WARSHAW,** born Los Angeles, California, July 26, 1961; admitted to bar, 1989, California. *Education:* California State University at Northridge (B.A., summa cum laude, 1984); Loyola University of Los Angeles (J.D., 1987). *PRACTICE AREAS:* Litigation.

*(This Listing Continued)*

**STEVEN D. WEINSTEIN,** born San Gabriel, California, October 24, 1948; admitted to bar, 1973, California. *Education:* University of California at Berkeley (B.A., 1970); University of Southern California (J.D., 1973). *PRACTICE AREAS:* Labor and Employment.

**J. PATRICK WHALEY,** born Los Angeles, California, December 6, 1934; admitted to bar, 1960, California. *Education:* Pomona College (A.B., 1956); Stanford University (LL.B., 1959); New York University (LL.M., 1961). (Certified Specialist, Taxation Law, The State Bar of California Board of Legal Specialization). *PRACTICE AREAS:* Taxation; Non-Profit and Charitable Organizations.

**GARY L. WOLLBERG** (Resident at San Diego Office, See San Diego listing for full biographical information).

**DAVID C. WRIGHT,** born Santa Ana, California, July 2, 1946; admitted to bar, 1972, California; 1981, U.S. Tax Court. *Education:* University of California at Santa Barbara (B.A., 1968); Loyola University of Los Angeles (J.D., 1972). *PRACTICE AREAS:* Employee Benefits; Business Law.

**JANET L. WRIGHT** (Resident at Fresno Office; See Fresno listing for full biographical information).

**ROBERT M. ZELLER,** admitted to bar, 1975, California. *Education:* University of California at Los Angeles (A.B., magna cum laude, 1972; J.D., 1975). *PRACTICE AREAS:* Real Property Law; Real Estate Law.

**ALAN J. ZUCKERMAN** (Resident at San Diego Office; See San Diego listing for full biographical information).

*OF COUNSEL*

**MARYANN LINK GOODKIND,** born Torrance, California, January 6, 1962; admitted to bar, 1987, California. *Education:* University of Southern California (B.S., cum laude, 1984; J.D., 1987). *PRACTICE AREAS:* Public Finance Law; Municipal Law.

**MARK KIGUCHI,** born Gillette, Wyoming, April 25, 1922; admitted to bar, 1958, California. *Education:* University of Southern California (B.S.L., 1956; J.D., 1958). *LANGUAGES:* Japanese.

**JAMES E. LUDLAM,** born Portland, Oregon, November 26, 1914; admitted to bar, 1940, California. *Education:* Stanford University (A.B., 1936); Harvard University (J.D., 1939).

**STEPHEN J. M. MORRIS,** born August 22, 1934; admitted to bar, 1962, California. *Education:* Pomona College (A.B., 1956); University of California Boalt Hall School of Law (LL.B., 1961).

**LAWRENCE E. STICKNEY,** born Los Angeles, California, September 18, 1943; admitted to bar, 1969, California. *Education:* University of Southern California (B.S.B.A., 1965; J.D., 1968).

*ASSOCIATES*

*Amy C. Bloom* (Resident at San Francisco Office); **Lisa M. Burkdall;** **Heather Bussing** (Resident at Fresno Office); **Bethany A. Cook; Dennis M. P. Ehling; Lauren Erickson; Edward T. Fenno; John T. Gilbertson; Michael R. Goldstein; Spencer Hamer; Peter T. Haven; Robin L. Hayward** (Resident at Irvine Office); **Kevin D. Jeter; Michael F. Klein; Daniel H. Lee; Kathleen A. McKnight** (Resident at Fresno Office); **Daniel Penserini** (Resident at Sacramento Office); **Gail A. Regenstreif; Michael D. Rountree; Dori K. Rybacki** (Resident at San Diego Office); **John J. Selbak; Sharon A. Siefert; Samuel H. Stein; Lawrence A. Tabb; Etta A. Talbot; Jeffrey R. Thomas; Stuart D. Tochner; Danny W. Wan** (Resident at San Francisco Office); **Monica Seine Wong.**

---

# SCOTT D. MYER
*1900 AVENUE OF THE STARS*
*SUITE 1070*
**LOS ANGELES, CALIFORNIA 90067**
*Telephone: 310-277-3000*
*Fax: 310-277-3510*

*Business, Real Estate, Bankruptcy, Personal Injury, Estate Planning. General Civil and Trial Practice in all Courts.*

**SCOTT D. MYER,** born Los Angeles, California, April 18, 1961; admitted to bar, 1986, California. *Education:* University of California at Los Angeles (B.A., magna cum laude, 1983; J.D., 1986). Phi Beta Kappa; Omicron Delta Epsilon; Phi Alpha Delta. Recipient, American Jurisprudence Award in Partnership Planning. *Member:* Los Angeles County and American Bar Associations; State Bar of California.

## MYERS & D'ANGELO

**LOS ANGELES, CALIFORNIA**

(See Pasadena)

*General Civil and Appellate Practice. Corporation, Taxation and Real Estate Law. Litigation. Estate Planning, Trust and Probate Law.*

---

## NACHSHIN & WESTON

A Partnership including Professional Corporations

*Established in 1990*

**SUITE 2240, 11755 WILSHIRE BOULEVARD**
**LOS ANGELES, CALIFORNIA 90025**
Telephone: 310-478-6868
Telefax: 310-473-8112

*Practice Limited to Family, Domestic Relations, Divorce and Matrimonial Law.*

**ROBERT J. NACHSHIN, (A PROFESSIONAL CORPORATION),** born New York, N.Y., June 3, 1950; admitted to bar, 1977, California. *Education:* Bucknell University (B.A., cum laude, 1972); Columbia University (M.I.A., 1976; J.D., 1976). Pi Sigma Alpha; Omicron Delta Kappa. Finalist, Jerome Michael Jury Trials. Lecturer, "How to Handle Family Law Litigation," CEB, January, 1984, January, 1986; "Enforcement of Family Law Judgments," CEB, January, 1984 and January, 1986; "Tracing and Apportionment," California Society of Certified Public Accountants, November, 1990; "What the Accountant Should Know About the Handling of Marriage Dissolutions," California Society of Certified Public Accountants, April and May, 1985; "Enforcement Options," Los Angeles County Bar-Los Angeles Superior Court, June, 1987; "The Management and Marketing of A Law Practice to Financial Success," USC Law Center, Spring, 1995. Author: "Effect of Divorce on Executive Compensation," Silicon Valley, June, 1985. *Member:* Los Angeles County Bar Association (Member, Executive Committee, Family Law Section, 1983-1989). (Certified Specialist, Family Law, The State Bar of California Board of Legal Specialization). **PRACTICE AREAS:** Family Law.

**SCOTT N. WESTON, (A PROFESSIONAL CORPORATION),** born New York, N.Y., May 8, 1962; admitted to bar, 1987, California. *Education:* University of California at Santa Barbara (B.A., cum laude, 1984); Loyola Law School of Los Angeles (J.D., cum laude, 1987). Phi Delta Phi (Member, 1984-1985). St. Thomas More Law Honor Society (Vice President, 1987). Author: "United States—Mexico: Coping with Environmental Problems at the Border," 9 Loy. L.A. Int'l. & Comp. L.J. 117, 1986. Lecturer, "Law and Ethics," The Association for Advanced Training Psychology, oral workshop, 1991; "Custody Litigation IV Advanced Psychological Litigation Issues," USC Law Center, April 1995. *Member:* Beverly Hills, Los Angeles County and American (Family Law Section) Bar Associations; State Bar of California. **PRACTICE AREAS:** Family Law.

### ASSOCIATES

**JOSEPH A. LANGLOIS,** born San Diego, California, August 9, 1958; admitted to bar, 1988, California. *Education:* University of California at San Diego; California State University at Northridge (B.A., magna cum laude, 1985); Brigham Young University (J.D., cum laude, 1988). Member, Board of Advocates Co-Curricular Program. Quarterfinalist, 1988 Fordham University Securities Law Moot Court Competition. *Member:* Los Angeles County Bar Association; State Bar of California. **LANGUAGES:** Spanish.

---

## TIMOTHY D. NAEGELE & ASSOCIATES

*Established in 1977*

**SUITE 2430**
**1900 AVENUE OF THE STARS**
**LOS ANGELES, CALIFORNIA 90067**
Telephone: 310-557-2300
Facsimile: 310-457-4014
Email: naegelewdc@aol.com
URL: http://www.naegele.com

*Washington, D.C. Office:* Suite 300, 1250 24th Street, N.W., 20037. Telephone: 202-466-7500. Facsimile: 202-466-3079 or 466-2888. Internet Web Site: http://www.naegele.com. Internet E-mail: naegelewdc@aol.com.

*General Practice. Financial Institutions Law. Banking, Savings and Loan, Savings Bank and Credit Union Law.*

*FIRM PROFILE:* Timothy D. Naegele & Associates is engaged in all phases of legal practice with respect to U.S. financial institutions, before federal and state courts, administrative agencies, executive branch departments and the United States Congress. The firm's founder, Timothy D. Naegele, offers 28 years of experience in this field, meeting the broad needs of corporate and individual clients. The firm specializes in matters pertaining to financial institution regulation and litigation, mergers and acquisitions, financial institution counseling and representation, and lobbying.

(For Complete Biographical data on all personnel, see Professional Biographies at Washington, D.C.)

---

## NAGLER & ASSOCIATES

**LOS ANGELES, CALIFORNIA**

(See Beverly Hills)

*Complex Multi-Party Litigation Practice in State and Federal Courts.*

---

## NAHAI LAW CORPORATION

A PROFESSIONAL CORPORATION

**SUITE 800**
**1875 CENTURY PARK EAST**
**LOS ANGELES, CALIFORNIA 90067**
Telephone: 310-201-6800
Fax: 310-201-6811

*Real Estate, Environmental. Corporate and Business Law and Civil Litigation.*

**HAMID NAHAI,** born Tehran, Iran, October 29, 1952; admitted to bar, 1976, England and Wales; 1979, California; 1980, U.S. District Court, Central District of California. *Education:* London School of Economics, England (LL.B., 1974; LL.M., 1975); Boalt Hall School of Law, University of California at Berkeley (LL.M., 1978, Visiting Scholarship, 1978-1979). Author: "Environmental Liability: Lenders Beware," The Secured Lender, December 1990 (Vol. 46 No. 6); "Riots and Natural Disasters: A Lease Law View," California Real Estate Journal, January 1993. *Member:* Los Angeles County Bar Association (Member, Real Property and Business Sections); The State Bar of California; The Bar of England and Wales; The Honorable Society of the Middle Temple, London. **LANGUAGES:** French and Persian. **PRACTICE AREAS:** Real Estate Law; Business Law; Corporate Law; Environmental Law.

**BEHZAD NAHAI,** born Tehran, Iran, April 3, 1958; admitted to bar, 1981, England and Wales; 1984, California. *Education:* London School of Economics, London, England (LL.B., 1979; LL.M., 1980); Boalt Hall School of Law, University of California (LL.M., 1982). *Member:* Los Angeles County and American Bar Associations; State Bar of California; Young Lawyers International Association; The Bar of England and Wales; The Honorable Society of the Middle Temple London, England. **LANGUAGES:** Persian and French. **PRACTICE AREAS:** Real Estate Law; Corporate Law; Civil Litigation.

PROFESSIONAL BIOGRAPHIES  CALIFORNIA—LOS ANGELES

## SILVIO NARDONI
*1925 CENTURY PARK EAST*
*SUITE 2000*
**LOS ANGELES, CALIFORNIA 90067**
*Telephone: 310-277-2236*
*Fax: 310-788-9290*

*Business Litigation, Bankruptcy, Elder Law, Personal Injury, Elder Abuse Litigation.*

**SILVIO NARDONI,** born Detroit, Michigan, September 14, 1946; admitted to bar, 1971, California and U.S. District Court, Central District of California; 1990, U.S. Court of Appeals, Ninth Circuit. *Education:* University of Redlands (B.A., 1967); University of Michigan (J.D.,1970); Harvard Divinity School (M.Div., 1981). Volunteer Arbitrator, Attorney-Client Fee Disputes, Los Angeles County Bar Association, 1990—. Volunteer Mediator, Los Angeles Municipal Court, 1990—. *Member:* Los Angeles County Bar Association (Member, Commercial Law and Bankruptcy Section); State Bar of California (Member Litigation Section); Commercial Law League of America; Consumer Attorneys of California.

---

## NASATIR, HIRSCH & PODBERESKY
**LOS ANGELES, CALIFORNIA**
(See Santa Monica)

*Trial and Appellate Practice Specializing in State and Federal Criminal Defense Litigation.*

---

## NASH & EDGERTON
**LOS ANGELES, CALIFORNIA**
(See Hermosa Beach)

*Commercial and Securities Litigation. Broker-Dealer Defense. General Business Practice. Corporate, Contract, Finance, Real Property Law, New Ventures and Partnership Law.*

---

## NEBENZAHL KOHN DAVIES & LEFF, LLP
*10940 WILSHIRE BOULEVARD*
*15TH FLOOR*
**LOS ANGELES, CALIFORNIA 90024**
*Telephone: 310-824-1700*
*Fax: 310-824-5676*

*General Civil Practice, Administrative, Real Estate, Financial Institutions, Legislative, Health Care, Employment, Secured Transactions, Shopping Centers, Commercial and Corporate Law. Trial and Appellate Practice.*

FIRM PROFILE: *Nebenzahl, Kohn, Davies & Leff is a six attorney firm founded in 1978. Lawyers of the firm have broad experience in business transactions, real estate, financial institutions, health care, employment, legislative matters, arbitration proceedings and civil litigation in both state and federal courts.*

*The firm's areas of practice include the purchase and sale of businesses and real property, regulatory and operational issues concerning financial institutions and other creditors, mergers and acquisition of financial institutions, health care, commercial leasing, corporate and partnership organization and dissolution, business, title and construction disputes, and employment law. Other areas of particular emphasis include secured and unsecured loan documentation, equipment leasing and collection and workout problems, foreclosures, and lender liability claims.*

**BERNARD B. NEBENZAHL, (A PROFESSIONAL CORPORATION),** born Mercedes, Texas, September 26, 1933; admitted to bar, 1963, California. *Education:* University of California at Los Angeles (B.A., 1955; J.D., 1962). Consultant, Judiciary Committee, California State Assembly, 1963-1964. General Counsel, California Association of Thrift and Loan Companies, 1972—. Vice President, 1968 and President, 1969, Barristers, Beverly Hills Bar Association. Member: Industrial Loan Advisory Committee, Department of Corporations, State of California, 1981-1989; National Consumer Finance Association Law Committee, 1981-1983; American Financial Services Association (AFSA), 1983-1988. Member and Draftsman, Industrial Loan Law Revision Committee, Department of Corporations,
*(This Listing Continued)*

State of California, 1984. Special Counsel, Thrift Guaranty Corporation of California, 1985-1994. California Department of Financial Institutions Organizational Task Force, 1996. *Member:* Beverly Hills (Vice Chairman, African Scholarship Committee, 1968; Member: Board of Governors, 1970-1972; Future of the Bar Association Committee, 1974; Federal Government Relations Committee, California Bankers Association, 1996; Sections on: Real Property; Commercial Law), Los Angeles County (Member, Sections on: Real Property; Commercial Law and Bankruptcy) and American (Member, Sections on: Corporation, Banking and Business Law; Real Property, Probate and Trust Law) Bar Associations; State Bar of California (Member, Sections on: Real Property Law; Business Law). **PRACTICE AREAS:** Banking; Financial Institutions Law; Real Property Law; Business Law.

**JAMES A. KOHN, (A PROFESSIONAL CORPORATION),** born Milwaukee, Wisconsin, June 17, 1936; admitted to bar, 1962, California. *Education:* Harvard University (A.B., 1958; LL.B., 1961). Adjunct Professor, La Verne University Law School, 1980—. Judge Pro Tem, Beverly Hills Municipal Court, 1968—. Member, National Panel, American Arbitration Association, 1963—. *Member:* Beverly Hills (Member: Board of Governors, Barristers, 1966-1972; Real Property, Probate and Trust Law Committee, 1978—), Los Angeles County and American (Member, Administrative Law Committee, 1973) Bar Associations; State Bar of California. **PRACTICE AREAS:** Real Estate Law; Business Litigation; Environmental Law; Corporation Law.

**M. RANDEL DAVIES,** born Los Angeles, California, November 27, 1951; admitted to bar, 1976, California; 1979, U.S. District Court, Central and Southern Districts of California. *Education:* University of California at Santa Barbara (B.A., cum laude, 1973); University of Southern California (J.D., 1976). Editor, Thrift Notes, California Association of Thrift and Loan Companies, 1988-1994. *Member:* Beverly Hills Bar Association; State Bar of California (Member, Sections on: Real Property Law; Business Law). **PRACTICE AREAS:** Real Property Law; Finance Law; Business Litigation.

**RANDALL S. LEFF,** born Long Beach, California, December 11, 1951; admitted to bar, 1977, California; 1980, District of Columbia. *Education:* Occidental College (B.A., 1974); Hastings College of Law, University of California (J.D., 1977). Review Editor, Hastings International and Comparative Law Review, 1976-1977. Author: "U.S. Policy Regarding Recognition of Foreign States," 1 Hastings International and Comparative Law Review 173. Staff Attorney: National Labor Relations Board, Washington, D.C., 1978-1979; Federal Trade Commission, Washington, D.C., 1979-1982. *Member:* Beverly Hills, Los Angeles County and American (Member, Sections on: Litigation and Employment; Member, Forum on Health Law) Bar Associations; District of Columbia Bar; State Bar of California; National Health Lawyers Association. **PRACTICE AREAS:** Health Care; Business Litigation; Employment Law.

---

**GERALD S. FRIM,** born Boston, Massachusetts, June 14, 1958; admitted to bar, 1984, Pennsylvania, New Jersey and U.S. District Court, District of New Jersey; 1987, California; 1988, U.S. District Court, Central, Northern, Eastern and Southern Districts of California; U.S. Claims Court. *Education:* University of Pennsylvania (B.A., magna cum laude, 1980; M.S., 1980; J.D., 1984); Hebrew College (B.H.L., magna cum laude, 1981). *Member:* Los Angeles County Bar Association; State Bar of California. **LANGUAGES:** Hebrew. **PRACTICE AREAS:** Business Law; Real Estate Litigation; Health Care.

**TRUDI J. LESSER,** born Roslyn, New York, March 24, 1959; admitted to bar, 1985, California and U.S. District Court, Central District of California. *Education:* State University of New York at Albany (B.A., magna cum laude, 1981); University of Southern California (J.D., 1984). Issue Editor, University of Southern California Entertainment Law Journal, 1983. Author: "Defining the Relevant Product Market: A Necessary First Step," Entertainment, Publishing and The Arts, Vol. 3, Clark Boardman, 1985. Chairperson, West Hollywood Rent Board, 1984-1986. Member, Board of Directors, West Hollywood Community Housing Corporation, 1986-1987. *Member:* Los Angeles County Bar Association; State Bar of California; Woman Lawyers Association of Los Angeles. **PRACTICE AREAS:** Business Law; Corporate Law; Real property Law; Business Litigation; Real Estate Litigation.

REPRESENTATIVE CLIENTS: California Association of Thrift and Loan Cos.; First Republic Bancorp, Inc.; First Republic Thrift and Loan; First Republic Savings Bank; Topa Thrift and Loan Assn.; Topa Savings Bank; Fremont General Corporation; Fremont Investment and Loan; Imperial Credit Industries, Inc.; Southern Pacific Thrift and Loan Assoc.; Westbrooke Inns Management, Inc.; Managed Care Innovations; Southern California Independent Practice

*(This Listing Continued)*

CALIFORNIA—LOS ANGELES

**NEBENZAHL KOHN DAVIES & LEFF, LLP,** Los Angeles—Continued

Association; Meredian Health Care Consultants; Physicians of Greater Long Beach; IPA; St. Bernardines Medical Center; Bay Area Medical Group, Inc.; Pacific Emergency Specialists; Coldwell Banker Residential Brokerage; Ray Charles Enterprises.
REFERENCES: Bank of America (Beverly Wilshire Branch); Metro Bank (Westwood Branch).

---

## JOSHUA C. NEEDLE
*Established in 1977*
SUITE 1800
1901 AVENUE OF THE STARS
**LOS ANGELES, CALIFORNIA 90067**
Telephone: 310-556-5676
FAX: 310-556-5654
Email: jcneedle@aol.com

*Criminal Defense, Trials and Appeals in all State and Federal Courts.*

**JOSHUA C. NEEDLE,** born Los Angeles, California, July 14, 1952; admitted to bar, 1977, California; 1978, Central, Southern and Eastern Districts of California; 1980, U.S. Court of Appeals, Ninth Circuit; 1982, U.S. Supreme Court. *Education:* Sonoma State University, (B.A., 1974); Loyola University of Los Angeles, (J.D., 1977). *Member:* Santa Monica Bar Association (Founder and Chair, Criminal Justice Section); National Association of Criminal Defense Lawyers; California Attorney's for Criminal Justice; California Public Defender's Association; Master. L.A. West Inn of Court.

---

## NEFF & ASSOCIATES
*A PROFESSIONAL LAW CORPORATION*
11693 SAN VICENTE BOULEVARD, SUITE 550
**LOS ANGELES, CALIFORNIA 90049**
Telephone: 310-540-6760
Fax: 310-540-0305
Email: Richard@Nefflaw.com
URL: http://www.Nefflaw.com

Torrance, California Office: Union Bank Tower, Suite 650, 21515 Hawthorne Boulevard. Telephone: 310-540-6760. Fax: 310-540-0305.

*Computers and Software, Licensing, International Law, Copyright, Intellectual Property, Corporate Transactions.*

FIRM PROFILE: Neff & Associates has a truly unique practice. We are a legal "boutique" specializing in International Transactional and Intellectual Property Law for a national (and international) client base. Virtually all of our clients are technology companies, or companies seeking assistance with technology-based issues. A majority of our clients are headquartered in California, many of them in Silicon Valley. Nonetheless, we also represent three important trade associations based in Washington, D.C., the Business Software Alliance (BSA), the Association of American Publishers (AAP), and the Interactive Digital Software Association (IDSA), handling copyright and trademark enforcement (anti-piracy) matters, particularly in Latin America. We have also done work for companies based in Brazil, Chile, Mexico, Singapore and the United Kingdom.

We have one of the finest technology-based practices in Southern California. We are leaders in anti-piracy enforcement activity for technology companies throughout the world. We believe that we engage in a higher percentage of international legal work than any other firm in Southern California, and perhaps in the State.

**RICHARD E. NEFF,** born Philadelphia, Pennsylvania, April 22, 1954; admitted to bar, 1980, District of Columbia; 1983, U.S. Court of International Trade; 1989, California. *Education:* Cornell University (B.A., with distinction, 1976); Yale University (J.D., 1980). Phi Beta Kappa. Editor, Yale Law Journal, 1979-1980. Co-Author: "NAFTA: Protecting and Enforcing Intellectual Property Rights in North America," Shepard's McGraw-Hill 1994; "Authors' Rights in Latin America," 34 The Quarterly Review of Economics & Finance, Journal of the Midwest Economics Ass'n 117, 1994. Author: "Mexican Copyright Protection: Proposals for Better Legislation and Enforcement," 2 U.S.-Mexico Law Journal 51, 1994; "Free Trade with Mexico," AMA Small Business Reports, 1993; "Prosecuting Software Piracy Internationally," 3 Cal. International Law Section Newsletter 17, 1990; "State Burdens on Resident Aliens: A New Preemption Analy-

*(This Listing Continued)*

CAA1026B

---

MARTINDALE-HUBBELL LAW DIRECTORY 1997

sis," 89 Yale Law Journal 940, 1980. Fulbright Scholar, Lima, Peru, 1976-1977. Chairman of the Board, Business Software Alliance, 1991. *Member:* State Bar of California; District of Columbia Bar; Computer Law Association. *LANGUAGES:* Spanish, Portuguese and French. *PRACTICE AREAS:* Computers and Software; Licensing; International law; Copyright; Intellectual Property; Corporate Transactions.

**SUSAN E. BUNNELL,** born San Gabriel, California, August 28, 1966; admitted to bar, 1994, California. *Education:* University of California, Berkeley (B.A., with distinction, 1988); University of California, Los Angeles, School of Law (J.D., 1993). *Member:* State Bar of California. *LANGUAGES:* Spanish. *PRACTICE AREAS:* Computers and Software; Licensing; International Law; Copyright; Intellectual Property; Corporate Transactions.

REPRESENTATIVE CLIENTS: Microsoft Corporation; Business Software Alliance; Association of American Publishers; Interactive Digital Software Assoc.; Unify Corporation; Intuit Inc.; Infinity Financial Technology, Inc.; ParcPlace-Digitalk, Inc.; Bristol Farms; Continuous Software Corporation; Davidson & Assoc., Inc.; Expersoft Corporation; Novell, Inc.; Symantec Corporation; El Camino Resources Ltd.; Rothenberg Systems International; MAI Systems Corporation; Quarterdeck Corp.; Media Vision.

---

## NEGELE & ASSOCIATES
*A LAW CORPORATION*
3800 BARHAM BOULEVARD, SUITE 403
**LOS ANGELES, CALIFORNIA 90068**
Telephone: 213-850-5100
Fax: 213-850-5505

*General Civil Litigation in all State and Federal Courts with Special Emphasis on Construction, Insurance, Corporate, Real Estate and Business Law.*

FIRM PROFILE: Negele & Associates, A Law Corporation is primarily a civil litigation firm that practices in all courts and specializes in the areas of construction and related liability and insurance matters. It has expertise in all phases of construction law, both private and public, including bidding, contracts, claims, liens, professional liability, mediation, arbitration and litigation. The firm also specializes in representing defendants and plaintiffs in complex and multi-party litigation of all types, toxic tort litigation, accident and personal injury litigation, business litigation, and all aspects of construction defect litigation. The firm also has substantial expertise in the areas of insurance law, insurance coverage, and related insurance defense matters. In addition to litigation the firm does transactional work in the areas of construction, real estate, partnerships and corporations.

**JAMES R. NEGELE,** born Chicago, Illinois, August 15, 1949; admitted to bar, 1981, California and U.S. District Court, Central, Northern, Eastern and Southern Districts of California; U.S. Court of Appeals, Ninth Circuit. *Education:* University of Illinois (B.S.C.E., 1971); Loyola University of Los Angeles (J.D., 1981). Co-Lecturer, with: James Acret, Legal Aspects of Construction, University of California at Los Angeles Extension, 1982. Lecturer: Construction Contract Administration of Public Works Projects and Resolving Construction Contract Disputes, University of California at Berkeley Extension, Institute of Transportation Studies, 1986-1994; Recovery For Impairment or Loss of Bonding Capacity, 1991 and Public Contracting: How Does It Work?, 1994, Associated General Contractors of California; Professional Standard of Care, 1991. American Institute of Architects, San Fernando Valley Chapter; Construction Lien Laws, Woodwork Institute of California, 1992. Author: "Articles, How to Respond to A Subpoena," Parts I and II, Resident and Staff Physician, Vol. 31, Nos. 6 & 7, June and July, 1985; "Contractors Project Guide to Public Agency Contracts," John Wiley & Sons, 1987. President, Board of Directors: Pediatric and Family Medical Center. Director, Building Division, Associated General Contractors of California. *Member:* American Society of Civil Engineers; American Society of Mechanical Engineers; National Society of Professional Engineers. *Member:* Beverly Hills, Los Angeles County and American Bar Associations; State Bar of California; Associated General Contractors of California (Member, Legal Advisory Committee); Engineering Contractors Association; Southern California Contractors Association. *REPORTED CASES:* Teitel v. First Los Angeles Bank (1991) 231 Cal. App.3d 1593. *PRACTICE AREAS:* Civil Litigation; Construction Law; Business Law; Wrongful Termination.

**THOMAS A. INGRAM, JR.,** born Oklahoma City, Oklahoma, January 16, 1954; admitted to bar, 1988, California, U.S. Court of Appeals, Ninth Circuit and U.S. District Court, Central, Northern, Southern, Eastern and Northern Districts of California and U.S. Court of Appeals, Ninth Circuit.

*(This Listing Continued)*

*Education:* California State University at Sonoma (B.A., 1978); Pepperdine University School of Law (J.D., 1988). Phi Alpha Delta. Member, Moot Court Honors Board. Recipient, American Jurisprudence Award in Trial Practice. *Member:* Los Angeles County and American Bar Associations; State Bar of California; California Trial Lawyers Association. **REPORTED CASES:** Charter Point Homeowners Association v. Superior Court (1992) 6 Cal. App. 4th 1167. **PRACTICE AREAS:** Commercial Construction Litigation; Complex Multi-party Litigation; Land Subsidence; Insurance Litigation; Construction Law.

**ADAM D. H. GRANT,** born Phoenix, Arizona, March 15, 1964; admitted to bar, 1991, California and U.S. District Court, Central District of California. *Education:* University of California at San Diego (B.A., 1986); Southwestern University School of Law (J.D., 1990). Moot Court Honors. Extern for the Honorable Barry Russell, Bankruptcy Appellate Panel, 1990. *Member:* Kern County and Los Angeles County Bar Associations; State Bar of California. **PRACTICE AREAS:** Commercial Construction Law; Residential Construction Law; Insurance Law; Products Liability; Interstate Commerce; Medical Malpractice.

**FELIX M. MARTIN,** born Quincy, Illinois, 1965; admitted to bar, 1995, California and U.S. District Court, Central District of California. *Education:* Illinois Wesleyan University (B.A., 1987); Pepperdine University (J.D., cum laude, 1995). Member, International Moot Court - London, England. Certified Public Accountant, California, 1987. *Member:* International Law Society; Latin American Law Students Association. **PRACTICE AREAS:** Litigation; Business Law; Construction Law.

*LEGAL SUPPORT PERSONNEL*

**LORRIE BUCHANAN ALVES,** born Los Angeles, California, January 8, 1951. *Education:* Pacific Oaks College (B.A., 1975); University of California at Los Angeles (Certificate in Litigation With Honors, 1976). (Litigation Paralegal).

**BEN DOWNING,** born Wabash, Indiana, January 5, 1951. *Education:* Point Loma College (B.A., 1974); Azusa Pacific University (Post Graduate Studies, 1975-1977; California State University at Los Angeles (Paralegal Certificate, 1994). Contractor's License, Class B-1, California, 1980.

REPRESENTATIVE CLIENTS: Admiral Insurance Company; American Beauty Homes, Inc.; Attorney Software, Inc.; Bain Hogg International; Beverly Hills Country Club; Bratton Corporation; Brian L. Cochran & Associates, Inc.; Chain Links; Cherokee Construction Company; City of Thousand Oaks; City of Simi Valley Landscape District No. 1; City of Simi Valley; Colich & Sons; Copley Real Estate Advisors; D.J. Scheffler, Inc.; D.W. Burhoe Construction, Inc.; Epsteen & Associates; Escudero-Fribourg Architects; First Oak Brook Corporation; First Financial Group, Inc.; GAF Materials, Inc.; GS Roofing Supplies Company, Inc.; J.A. Jones Construction Company; Joel L. Baumblatt, Inc.; Leahmia, Inc.; Morley Construction Company; Newhall Land and Farming Company; O'Leary Terasawa Partners; Pasadena Historical Society; Rebar Engineering, Inc.; Risk Administration & Management Co.; Rockwin Corporation; Scottsdale Insurance Co.; Shur Affordable Housing; Simi Valley Community Development Co.; Simi Valley County Sanitation District; Slater Waterproofing, Inc.; State Farm Fire & Casualty Co.; Studio Bauton; TCO Insurance Services; Thorn Automated Systems, Inc.; University Mechanical & Engineering, Inc.; Valverde Construction; Ventura County Waterworks District No. 8; Willo Products, Inc.; Witherow Construction; Woodwork Institute of California.

## JAMES C. NEIL

SUITE 670, 800 SOUTH FIGUEROA STREET
**LOS ANGELES, CALIFORNIA 90017**
Telephone: 213-689-1010
Facsimile: 213-622-9375
Email: jcnesq@sprynet.com

*International Business and Tax Planning, International Commercial Law, Corporation and Real Estate Law.*

**JAMES C. NEIL,** born Burbank, California, January 22, 1949; admitted to bar, 1974, California and U.S. Tax Court. *Education:* University of California at Los Angeles (B.A., 1970); Loyola University of Los Angeles (J.D., 1974). Member, Loyola Law Review, 1971-1972. Certified Public Accountant, California, 1974. *Member:* Los Angeles County (Chairman, Foreign Tax Committee, Section of Taxation, 1980-1981), American (Member: Committee on U.S. Activities of Foreigners and Tax Treaties, Section of Taxation, 1975-1980, 1985-1988; Section of International Law) and International Bar Associations; State Bar of California; American Institute of Certified Public Accountants.

## GERALD I. NEITER

A PROFESSIONAL CORPORATION
Established in 1981
SUITE 2000, 1925 CENTURY PARK EAST (CENTURY CITY)
**LOS ANGELES, CALIFORNIA 90067**
Telephone: 310-277-2236
Facsimile: 310-556-5653

*General Civil Trial Practice in all State and Federal Courts, and Family Law.*

**GERALD I. NEITER,** born Los Angeles, California, November 11, 1933; admitted to bar, 1958, California; 1970, U.S. Supreme Court. *Education:* University of California at Los Angeles and University of Southern California (B.S.L., 1957); University of Southern California (J.D., 1957). Lecturer, Attorneys' Fees and Ethics, California State Bar Continuing Legal Education Programs. Judge Pro Tem, Los Angeles Municipal Court, 1973-1993. Los Angles County Superior Court Family Law Mediator, 1984—. *Member:* Beverly Hills, Los Angeles County (Arbitrator, 1976—) and American Bar Associations; State Bar of California; Association of Business Trial Lawyers. **PRACTICE AREAS:** Civil Trial; Business Litigation; Matrimonial Law.

## NELSEN, THOMPSON, PEGUE & THORNTON

A PROFESSIONAL CORPORATION
**LOS ANGELES, CALIFORNIA**
(See Santa Monica)

*General Insurance Practice in California and Federal Trial and Appellate Courts. Bad Faith, Insurance, Aviation, Products and Professional Liability, Municipal and Business Defense.*

## NELSON & BROWN

550 SOUTH HOPE STREET
TWENTIETH FLOOR
**LOS ANGELES, CALIFORNIA 90071-2604**
Telephone: 213-891-9515
Fax: 213-689-7748

*General Civil Litigation in all State and Federal Courts, Insurance Defense, Construction, Real Estate, Labor and Employment including ERISA, Wrongful Termination, Discrimination and Employee Benefits.*

*FIRM PROFILE:* Our practice and style reflect the diverse interests, challenges and activities of our community and cover a distinct range of substantive legal areas including the representation of large, established Fortune 500 companies and smaller emerging business enterprises. Two aspects of our firm distinguish us from other firms. Specifically, Nelson & Brown are "trial lawyers" as opposed to "litigators". This gives us the ability and confidence to analyze the strengths and weaknesses of our clients' cases early in the litigation process, advise on various courses of action and, if appropriate, take the case to trial. Second, we deliver superior quality representation while maintaining a competitive fee structure.

**GLENN D. NELSON,** born Wichita, Kansas, March 23, 1951; admitted to bar, 1977, California and U.S. District Court, Central District of California; 1985, U.S. Supreme Court and U.S. Court of Appeals, 9th, 7th, 5th and D.C. Circuits. *Education:* University of the Pacific (B.A., 1973); University of California School of Law, Los Angeles (J.D., 1976). Member, Executive Board of Judges of UCLA Moot Court Honors Program, 1974-1976. Adjunct Professor, Western State University, College of Law, 1979-1983. *Member:* Los Angeles County and American Bar Associations; State Bar of California (Member, Litigation Section); Langston Bar Association. **LANGUAGES:** Japanese. **PRACTICE AREAS:** Business Litigation; Employment Law; Construction Litigation; Insurance Defense; Insurance Coverage.

**LOLITA BROWN FLETCHER,** born Los Angeles, California, December 16, 1962; admitted to bar, 1990, California and U.S. District Court, Central District of California. *Education:* University of California at Irvine (B.A., 1984); Loyola Marymount University (J.D., 1989). *Member:* Los Angeles County and American Bar Associations; State Bar of California (Member, Employment Law Section); Black Women Lawyers of Los An-

*(This Listing Continued)*

**NELSON & BROWN, Los Angeles**—Continued

geles. *PRACTICE AREAS:* Employment; Labor; Insurance Defense; Real Estate Construction; Banking.

*ASSOCIATE*

**LORITA M. CHAN,** born Los Angeles, California, July 25, 1967; admitted to bar, 1993, California. *Education:* University of California at Irvine (B.A., 1989); Loyola Marymount University (J.D., 1993). Phi Alpha Delta. *Member:* Los Angeles County and American Bar Associations. *LANGUAGES:* Cantonese, Spanish. *PRACTICE AREAS:* Construction Defect Litigation; Employment Litigation; Insurance Defense.

REPRESENTATIVE CLIENTS: Flagstar Corp.; Hughes Aircraft Corp.; McDonnell Douglas Corp.; Shell Oil Co.; Denny's, Inc.; State Farm Insurance; FDIC; RTC.

## NELSON • GRIFFIN

350 SOUTH FIGUEROA
SUITE 903
**LOS ANGELES, CALIFORNIA 90071**
Telephone: 213-626-4049
Fax: 213-626-4082
Email: nglaw@so.ca.com

*Insurance Coverage Analysis, Defense of Legal Malpractice, Insurance Fraud, Personal Injury and Construction Defect Cases.*

*MEMBERS OF FIRM*

**LARRY R. NELSON,** born Chicago, Illinois, April 5, 1947; admitted to bar, 1979, Nevada; 1980, California and U.S. District Court, Central District of California. *Education:* Carroll College (B.S., 1969); University of the Pacific, McGeorge School of Law (J.D., 1979). Law Clerk: Hon. Frank Gregory, First District Court of Nevada, 1977-1978; Hon. A. Andrew Hauk, Chief Judge, U.S. District Court, Central District of California, 1979-1980. Author: "Liability for Hazardous Substances in California," California Defense Journal, Summer 1988. *Member:* Los Angeles County Bar Association; State Bar of Nevada; The State Bar of California; Association of Southern California Defense Counsel. *PRACTICE AREAS:* Legal Malpractice; Insurance Fraud; Construction Defect.

**THOMAS J. GRIFFIN,** born Boston, Massachusetts, August 23, 1958; admitted to bar, 1989, California and U.S. District Court, Central District of California. *Education:* Providence College (B.A., 1980); Western State University (J.D., 1988). *Member:* Los Angeles County Bar Association; The State Bar of California. *PRACTICE AREAS:* Insurance Fraud Defense; Personal Injury.

## NELSON, GUGGENHEIM, FELKER & LEVINE

10880 WILSHIRE BOULEVARD, SUITE 2070
**LOS ANGELES, CALIFORNIA 90024**
Telephone: 310-441-8000
Fax: 310-441-8010

*Entertainment Law.*

*MEMBERS OF FIRM*

**PETER MARTIN NELSON,** born Lower Merion, Pennsylvania, April 6, 1954; admitted to bar, 1979, California; 1980, U.S. Court of Appeals, District of Columbia Circuit; 1981, New York; 1983, U.S. Court of Appeals, Second Circuit. *Education:* Williams College (B.A., cum laude, 1976); Hastings College of the Law, University of California (J.D., 1979). Order of the Coif. Note Editor, Hastings Law Journal, 1978-1979. Recipient, Lathers Class Prize. Author: "Discarding the Doctrine of Supervisory Domination," 30 Hastings Law Journal 767, 1979. Co-Author, "Representing Comedians: How to Protect Your Client's Material," Los Angeles Lawyer, April 1992, reprinted in Entertainment Law and Finance, April 1993 and Entertainment Publishing and the Arts Handbook, 1993. Law Clerk to the Hon. George E. MacKinnon, U.S. Court of Appeals, District of Columbia Circuit, 1979-1980. *Member:* Beverly Hills (Co-Chairman, Entertainment Law Section, 1990-1992) and Los Angeles County (Member, Intellectual Property and Entertainment Law Section) Bar Associations; American Film Institute, Third Decade Council. *PRACTICE AREAS:* Entertainment Law.

*(This Listing Continued)*

**ALFRED KIM GUGGENHEIM,** born Santa Monica, California, July 27, 1946; admitted to bar, 1972, California and U.S. District Court, Central District of California; 1979, U.S. District Court, Southern District of California; 1980, U.S. Supreme Court. *Education:* Pomona College (A.B., magna cum laude, 1968); Harvard Law School (J.D., cum laude, 1971). Phi Beta Kappa. Contributing Author: Songwriter's Magazine, "Song Protection - Your Options," 1978; "Attention A & R," Pomeranz & Muench, Alfred Publishing Co., 1988. *Member:* California Copyright Conference (President, 1981-1982; Member, Board of Directors, 1978—); Association of Independent Music Publishers; National Academy of Recording Arts and Sciences. Past Member, Executive Board of Directors, T. J. Martell Foundation. *Member:* Beverly Hills (Member, Entertainment Law Section), Los Angeles County (Member, Intellectual Property and Entertainment Law) and American (Member, Patent, Trademark and Copyright Law Section) Bar Associations. *LANGUAGES:* German. *PRACTICE AREAS:* Entertainment Law.

**PATTI C. FELKER,** born New York, N.Y., December 5, 1958; admitted to bar, 1983, California and U.S. District Court, Central District of California. *Education:* Union College (B.A., summa cum laude, 1980); Boalt Hall School of Law, University of California (J.D., 1983). Phi Beta Kappa; Omicron Delta Epsilon. *Member:* Los Angeles County and American Bar Associations. *PRACTICE AREAS:* Entertainment Law.

**JARED ELLIOTT LEVINE,** born Boston, Massachusetts, July 14, 1956; admitted to bar, 1981, California, U.S. District Court, Central District of California and U.S. Court of Appeals, Ninth Circuit. *Education:* Harvard University (A.B., cum laude, 1978; J.D., 1981). Phi Beta Kappa. *Member:* State Bar of California; American Bar Association. *PRACTICE AREAS:* Entertainment Law.

*ASSOCIATES*

**WARREN D. DERN,** born Los Angeles, California, June 20, 1964; admitted to bar, 1991, California and U.S. District Court, Central District of California. *Education:* Universidad Autonoma de Guadalajara, Mexico (1984); University of California at Los Angeles (B.A., 1987); University of Madrid, School of Law (1990); Southwestern University School of Law (J.D., 1991). *Member:* Beverly Hills and American Bar Associations; State Bar of California. *LANGUAGES:* Spanish. *PRACTICE AREAS:* Entertainment Law; Copyright Law; Communication Law.

**GEORGE M. DAVIS,** born New York, N.Y., December 30, 1957; admitted to bar, 1983, New York; 1991, California. *Education:* University of Miami (B.S., 1979; J.D., 1983). *PRACTICE AREAS:* Motion Pictures Law (100%).

## NELSON & NELSON

A PROFESSIONAL CORPORATION
2049 CENTURY PARK EAST, SUITE 4060
**LOS ANGELES, CALIFORNIA 90067**
Telephone: 310-556-1424
FAX: 310-556-1422

*Corporate, Real Estate, Securities and Business Law and Litigation.*

**WILLIAM L. NELSON,** born Ames, Iowa, August 19, 1945; admitted to bar, 1970, California. *Education:* University of Arizona (B.A., 1966); New York University (J.D., 1969). Phi Beta Kappa. Root-Tilden Scholar. Adjunct Professor, Southwestern University School of Law, 1976-1978. *Member:* Los Angeles County and American (Member, Section of Corporation, Banking, Business Law and Real Property) Bar Associations; The State Bar of California. *PRACTICE AREAS:* Corporate; Real Estate; Securities; Business Law; Litigation.

**KAY NEILL NELSON,** born Chickasha, Oklahoma, July 6, 1946; admitted to bar, 1978, California. *Education:* University of Arizona (B.A., 1967); Southwestern University (J.D., cum laude, 1978). Member, 1976-1977 and Associate Editor, 1977-1978, Southwestern University Law Review. Research Attorney for the Honorable Christian E. Markey, Jr., Los Angeles Superior Court Law and Discovery, 1978-1979. Member, Board of Women Lawyers Association of Los Angeles, 1985-1986. *Member:* Los Angeles County (Member, Sections on: Trial Lawyers and Economic Litigation) and American Bar Associations; The State Bar of California; Association of Business Trial Lawyers; California Women Lawyers Association (Member, Board of Governors, 1983-1985; Treasurer, 1984-1985). *PRACTICE AREAS:* Litigation; Corporate; Real Estate.

*(This Listing Continued)*

**E. SCOTT FRASER,** born Kansas City, Missouri, September 6, 1959; admitted to bar, 1984, California. *Education:* Stanford University (A.B., 1981); Loyola Law School of Los Angeles (J.D., 1984). Member, 1982-1983 and Chief Note and Comment Editor, 1983-1984, Loyola of Los Angeles International and Comparative Law Review. Author: "International Arbitration of Multi-Party Contract Disputes: The Need for Change," Vol. 6, No. 2, Loyola of Los Angeles International and Comparative Law Journal. Alumni, National Institute of Trial Advocacy. *Member:* Los Angeles County (Member, Fee Dispute Arbitration Panel) and American Bar Associations. **PRACTICE AREAS:** Litigation; Business; Personal Injury; Employment.

REFERENCE: Wells Fargo Bank, Camden and Santa Monica Branch, Beverly Hills, California.

## NEMECEK & COLE
### A PROFESSIONAL CORPORATION
### LOS ANGELES, CALIFORNIA
(See Sherman Oaks)

*Legal Malpractice Defense, Accountant Malpractice Defense, Errors and Omissions Defense, Wrongful Termination Defense, Insurance Coverage, Commercial Litigation, Real Estate Litigation, Banking and Creditors' Rights and General Business Litigation.*

## BEATRICE H. NEMLAHA, P.C.
### 11377 WEST OLYMPIC BOULEVARD
### LOS ANGELES, CALIFORNIA 90064-1683
Telephone: 310-914-7911
Fax: 310-312-3787

*Family Law. Prenuptial and Cohabitation Agreements, Dissolution Tax Planning. Inter-State, International Custody Disputes. Mediation.*

**BEATRICE H. NEMLAHA,** born Oak Park, Illinois, September 19, 1940; admitted to bar, 1979, California, U.S. Court of Appeals, 9th Circuit and U.S. District Court, Central District of California; 1982, U.S. District Court, Eastern and Northern Districts of California. *Education:* University of Michigan (B.A., cum laude, 1962); University of California at Berkeley; Boalt Hall School of Law, University of California (J.D., 1979). Phi Beta Kappa; Pi Sigma Alpha; Phi Kappa Phi; Alpha Lambda Delta. Member, Mortar Board. *Member:* Beverly Hills (Member, Family Law Section), Los Angeles County (Member, Family Law Section) and American (Member, Family Law Section) Bar Associations; The State Bar of California (Member, Family Law Section). (Certified Specialist, Family Law, The State Bar of California Board of Legal Specialization). **LANGUAGES:** Czech.

## LOUISE NEMSCHOFF
### LOS ANGELES, CALIFORNIA
(See Beverly Hills)

*Entertainment, Copyright and Trademark Law. International Law.*

## NEUMEYER & BOYD, LLP
### 2029 CENTURY PARK EAST, SUITE 1100
### LOS ANGELES, CALIFORNIA 90067
Telephone: 310-553-9393
Fax: 310-553-8437

*Appellate, Law and Motion and Related Trial Court Practice in all California and Federal Courts. Insurance, Insurance Coverage, Insurance "Bad Faith."*

FIRM PROFILE: Neumeyer & Boyd, LLP specializes in insurance coverage, insurance "bad faith," all areas of appellate practice and complicated law and motion matters, as well as the "problem" case. Representative cases in California state and federal courts which Neumeyer & Boyd, LLP lawyers briefed and argued on appeal: Crane v. Royal Insurance Co. (9th Cir. 1994) 17 F. 3d 1186; Globe Indemnity Co. v. Superior Court (1992) 6 Cal. App. 4th 725, 8 Cal. Rptr. 2d 251; Rose v. Royal Ins. (1991) 2 Cal. App 4th 709, 3 Cal. Rptr. 2d 483; St. Paul Mercury Ins. Co. v. Medical Lab. Network (C.D. Cal 1988) 690 F. Supp. 901; Mercury Casualty Co. v. Superior Court (1986) 179 Cal. App. 3d 1027, 225 Cal. Rptr. 100; Soto v. Royal Globe (1986) 184 Cal. App. 3d 420, 229 Cal. Rptr. 192; St. Paul Mercury Ins. Co. v. Ralee Engineering Co. (9th Cir. l986) 804 F. 2d 520; California Shoppers v. Royal Globe (1985) 175 Cal. App. 3d 1, 221 Cal. Rptr. 171; Guzman v. General Motors Corp. (1984) 154 Cal. App. 3d 438, 201 Cal. Rptr. 246; Zieman Mfg. Co. v. St. Paul Fire & Marine Ins. Co. (9th Cir. 1983) 724 F. 2d. 1343; City Products Corp. v. Globe Indemnity Co. (1979) 88 Cal. App. 3d 31, 151 Cal. Rptr. 494; Daly v. General Motors (1978) 20 Cal. 3d 725, 144 Cal. Rptr. 380; Endicott v. Nissan (1977) 73 Cal. App. 3d 917, 141 Cal. Rptr. 95; Self v. General Motors (1974) 42 Cal. App. 3d 1, 116 Cal. Rptr. 575.

### MEMBERS OF FIRM

**RICHARD A. NEUMEYER,** born Los Angeles, California, October 7, 1944; admitted to bar, 1970, California; U.S. District Court, Central, Northern, Southern and Eastern Districts of California; U.S. Court of Appeals, Ninth Circuit; U.S. Supreme Court. *Education:* Northwestern University (B.S., 1966); University of California at Los Angeles (J.D., 1969). Order of the Coif; Phi Delta Phi. Member, U.C.L.A. Moot Court Honors Program, 1967-1968. Associate Justice, U.C.L.A. Moot Court, 1968-1969. Attorney Settlement Officer, Court of Appeal Attorney Appellate Settlement Program, 1989—. Arbitrator, Los Angeles County Superior Court, 1983-1994. Judge Pro Tem, Los Angeles County Municipal Court, 1983-1990. Judge Pro Tem, Los Angeles Superior Court, 1992—. Expert Witness in Appellate, Insurance Coverage and Insurance "Bad Faith" Matters. *Member:* Los Angeles County and American Bar Associations; The State Bar of California; California Academy of Appellate Lawyers; Defense Research Institute. **PRACTICE AREAS:** Appellate Practice; Insurance Coverage; Insurance Bad Faith.

**CAROL BOYD,** born Nashville, Tennessee, November 9, 1945; admitted to bar, 1981, California; U.S. District Court, Central, Northern, Southern and Eastern Districts of California; U.S. Court of Appeals, Ninth Circuit; U.S. Supreme Court. *Education:* University of Florida; New College; San Fernando Valley College of Law (J.D., cum laude, 1981). Editor-in-Chief, University of San Fernando Law Review, 1980-1981. Author: Comment, "Malice in Wonderland, Taylor v. Superior Court," 8 S.F.V.L Rev. 219, 1980. Law Clerk to Presiding Justice Arleigh Maddox Woods, California Court of Appeal, Second District, 1982-1984. *Member:* Los Angeles County and American Bar Associations; State Bar of California; Los Angeles Women Lawyers Association. **PRACTICE AREAS:** Appellate Practice; Insurance Coverage; Insurance Bad Faith.

**LYDIA E. HACHMEISTER,** born Houston, Texas, July 12, 1949; admitted to bar, 1984, California; U.S. District Court, Central, Northern, Southern and Eastern Districts of California; U.S. Court of Appeals, Ninth Circuit. *Education:* Oklahoma State University (B.S., 1970); Oklahoma City University School of Law; Southwestern University School of Law (J.D., 1984). Phi Delta Phi. Member, Moot Court Honors Board. Recipient, American Jurisprudence Award in Torts. Nominated to Membership, Law Review. *Member:* State Bar of California; Los Angeles Women Lawyers Association. **PRACTICE AREAS:** Appellate Practice; Insurance Coverage; Insurance Bad Faith.

**STEVEN A. FREEMAN,** born Los Angeles, California, January 17, 1946; admitted to bar, 1970, California and U.S. District Court, Central District of California. *Education:* University of Southern California (B.S., 1965; J.D., 1969); University of California at Los Angeles (M.B.A., 1982). Beta Gamma Sigma. Chairperson, Department of Business Law, California State University, Northridge. *Member:* Los Angeles County Bar Association; State Bar of California. **PRACTICE AREAS:** Appellate Practice; Insurance Coverage; Insurance Bad Faith.

### ASSOCIATES

**KATHERINE TATIKIAN,** born Oklahoma City, Oklahoma, January 26, 1949; admitted to bar, 1990, California, U.S. District Court, Central, Northern and Southern Districts of California and U.S. Court of Appeals, Ninth Circuit. *Education:* Scripps College (B.A., 1970); Claremont Graduate School (M.A., 1975); Southwestern University School of Law (J.D., cum laude, 1989). Recipient, American Jurisprudence Awards; Who's Who Among American Law Students. *Member:* State Bar of California (Sections on: Litigation; Antitrust Law); Los Angeles County and American Bar Associations (Member, Sections on Tort and Insurance Law, Antitrust Law, Litigation). **PRACTICE AREAS:** Appellate Practice; Insurance Coverage; Insurance Bad Faith.

**SUSIE J. KATER,** born Valdosta, Georgia, June 28, 1946; admitted to bar, 1986, California and U.S. District Court, Central and Northern Dis-

*(This Listing Continued)*

## NEUMEYER & BOYD, LLP, Los Angeles—Continued

tricts of California. *Education:* University of Maryland (B.S., summa cum laude, 1983); University of the Pacific, McGeorge School of Law (J.D., with distinction, 1986). Traynor Honor Society. Assistant Comments Editor, Pacific Law Journal, 1985-1986. Author: "Sending Juveniles to the California Youth Authority: The Need for Effective Procedural Safeguards," 16 Pac. L.J., January, 1985. *Member:* Los Angeles County and American Bar Associations; State Bar of California. **PRACTICE AREAS:** Appellate Practice; Insurance Coverage; Insurance Bad Faith.

**DANIEL F. SANCHEZ,** born Tooele, Utah, November 8, 1952; admitted to bar, 1977, California, U.S. District Court, Central, Northern, Eastern and Southern Districts of California, U.S. Court of Appeals, Ninth Circuit and U.S. Supreme Court. *Education:* University of California at Riverside (B.A., 1974); Indiana University School of Law (J.D., 1977). *Member:* Los Angeles County Bar Association; State Bar of California. **PRACTICE AREAS:** Appellate Practice; Insurance Coverage; Insurance Bad Faith.

**STUART L. BRODY,** born Pomona, California, May 19, 1946; admitted to bar, 1972, California; 1978, U.S. Supreme Court. *Education:* University of California at Los Angeles (B.A., 1968); University of Southern California (J.D., 1971). Chairman, Moot Court Board. Research Attorney, Appellate Department, Los Angeles Superior Court, 1971-1973. Judge Pro Tem, Los Angeles Municipal Court, 1982-1985. Arbitrator, Los Angeles Superior Court, 1971-1973. *Member:* Los Angeles County Bar Association; State Bar of California. **REPORTED CASES:** Prudential-LMI Commercial Insurance v. Superior Court (1990) 51 Cal.3d 674, 274 Cal.Rptr. 387; Chu v. Canadian Indemnity Company (1990) 224 Cal.App.3d 86, 274 Cal.Rptr. 20; Home Insurance Company v. Landmark Insurance Company (1988) 205 Cal.App.3d 1388, 253 Cal. Rptr. 277; Preston v. Goldman (1986) 42 Cal.3d 108, 227 Cal.Rptr. 817; Poland v. Martin (9th Cir. 1985) 761 F.2d 546; Patillo v. Norris (1976) 65 Cal.App.3d 209, 135 Cal.Rptr. 210. **PRACTICE AREAS:** Appellate Practice; Insurance Coverage; Insurance Bad Faith.

**REID L. DENHAM,** born Provo, Utah, April 30, 1954; admitted to bar, 1987, California; 1989, U.S. District Court, Central District of California. *Education:* Brigham Young University (B.S., 1980); Pepperdine University (J.D., 1986). Member, Moot Court Honors Board, 1985-1986. Judicial Clerkship, U.S. District Court, District Court Judge Roger D. Foley, 1987-1988. Judicial Intern, Utah Supreme Court, Justice Richard C. Howe, 1985. *Member:* Los Angeles County and American Bar Associations; State Bar of California. **PRACTICE AREAS:** Appellate Practice; Insurance Coverage; Insurance Bad Faith.

REPRESENTATIVE CLIENTS: American Honda Motor Co., Inc.; Anglo American Underwriting Management, Ltd.; AXA Marine & Aviation; Calvert Insurance Co.; Commercial Union Assurance Company; Compass Insurance Co.; CNA International; Excess Insurance Company Limited; GAN Insurance Company Ltd.; General Accident; Honda Motor Co., Ltd.; IRISC London Ltd.; Northwestern National Insurance Co.; The Prudential; Royal Insurance Cos.; Royal Insurance Co. of Canada; The Salvage Association; Sirius (UK) Insurance PLC; St. Paul Insurance Cos.; Underwriters at Lloyds, London.
REFERENCE: City National Bank.

## NEWMAN & ASSOCIATES
10100 SANTA MONICA, SUITE 300
**LOS ANGELES, CALIFORNIA 90067**
*Telephone: 310-788-8937*
*Fax: 310-788-2709*

*Insurance Defense, Entertainment, Civil Litigation, Transactional Practice in Business.*

**PAUL ANDREW NEWMAN,** born New York, New York, December 15, 1960; admitted to bar, 1987, California; 1990, U.S. District Court, Central District of California. *Education:* Ithaca College (B.S., 1982); Loyola Marymount University (J.D., 1987). *Member:* Beverly Hills and Los Angeles County Bar Associations; State Bar of California; Southern California Defense Council. **PRACTICE AREAS:** Insurance Defense; Entertainment; Civil Litigation.

REPRESENTATIVE CLIENTS: Zurich American Ins.; Cosmair Inc.; Loreal Inc.; National Envelope Corp.; Ocean Bay Productions; Firmly in the Clouds Productions.

## FREDERICK M. NICHOLAS
**LOS ANGELES, CALIFORNIA**
(See Beverly Hills)
*Business and Real Estate Law.*

## GREGORY NICOLAYSEN
A PROFESSIONAL CORPORATION
**LOS ANGELES, CALIFORNIA**
(See Beverly Hills)
*Federal Criminal Defense, White Collar Defense.*

## W. PATRICK NOONAN
A PROFESSIONAL CORPORATION
**LOS ANGELES, CALIFORNIA**
(See Woodland Hills)

*Practice before all Courts, Government Agencies and International Regulatory Authorities involving Foods, Drugs, Cosmetics, Medical Devices and Consumer Products.*

## NORDMAN, CORMANY, HAIR & COMPTON
**LOS ANGELES, CALIFORNIA**
(See Oxnard)

*General Civil Litigation in all State and Federal Courts. Environmental and Hazardous Waste, Employment, Banking and Finance, Real Estate, Securities, Municipal and Special Districts, Creditors' Rights and Insolvency, Insurance Coverage, Commercial and Business, Corporation, Condemnation, Oil and Gas, Probate and Estate Planning, Taxation, Intellectual Property, Entertainment Litigation, Civil Service, Administrative Law, Education, State and Federal Appellate Practice.*

## NORDSTROM, STEELE, NICOLETTE AND JEFFERSON
A Partnership including a Professional Corporation
*Established in 1984*
FOURTEENTH FLOOR, 12400 WILSHIRE BOULEVARD
**LOS ANGELES, CALIFORNIA 90025**
*Telephone: 213-937-1000*
*Fax: 310-826-6968*

*Kenai, Alaska Office:* Suite 201, 215 Fidalgo Avenue. Telephone: 907-283-9187.
*Orange, California Office:* 770 The City Drive South, Suite 3000. Telephone: 704-750-1010.

*Personal Injury and Wrongful Death. Professional Negligence, Aviation, Construction, Industrial and Asbestos Law.*

FIRM PROFILE: Nordstrom, Steele and Jefferson was founded in 1984 by Russell E. Nordstrom (formerly a partner in Sherman & Nordstrom), Joseph W. Steele and Jeffrey D. Jefferson. The firm changed its name to Nordstrom, Steele, Nicolette and Jefferson in 1992.

The firm confines its practice to plaintiff's civil litigation with an emphasis on major injury and wrongful death cases arising from aviation, construction and product defect accidents. Asbestos-related cancers have been the subject of the office's attention since the mid-seventies.

Formal continuing legal education is a tradition in the firm. Mr. Nordstrom is a noted lecturer on various trial-related topics for the California Continuing Education of the Bar, Association of Trial Lawyers of America, Consumer Attorneys of California, Consumer Attorneys Association of Los Angeles and the Medical-Legal Institute.

*(This Listing Continued)*

## MEMBERS OF FIRM

**RUSSELL E. NORDSTROM, (A PROFESSIONAL CORPORATION),** born Salt Lake City, Utah, September 6, 1946; admitted to bar, 1974, California and U.S. District Court, Central, Eastern and Northern Districts of California; 1992, Nebraska; 1994, U.S. Court of Federal Claims. *Education:* University of Southern California (B.A., 1969); Loyola University of Los Angeles (J.D., 1974). Member, Panel of Arbitrators, American Arbitration Association; Continuing Education of the Bar, State of California. Author: "Damages--Their Many Faces," CTLA Forum, April 1979; "Apportionment of Damages in Wrongful Death Cases," LATLA Advocate, September 1992; "The Not So Peculiar Risk Doctrine," LATLA Advocate, May 1993. Speaker: Trial Related topics on more than 50 CLE Seminars. Consultant, California Government Tort Liability Practice, 3rd Ed., Regents of University of California, Continuing Education of the Bar, 1992. Member, Asbestos Litigation Group. Settlement Officer, LASC Settlement Project, 1985—. *Member:* Los Angeles County, Nebraska State and American Bar Associations; State Bar of California; Texas Trial Lawyers Association; Consumer Attorneys Association of Los Angeles, formerly LATLA (Member, Board of Governors, 1987—; Officer/Executive Board Member, 1992—); Consumer Attorneys of California, formerly CTLA (Sustaining Member, 1977—; Member, Board of Governors, 1996—; Member: Political Action Committee, 1977-1979; Legislative Action Committee, 1977—; Recognized experience in General Personal Injury, Products Liability and Professional Negligence Law); The Association of Trial Lawyers of America (Sustaining Member, 1981—); American Board of Trial Advocates (Advocate). *LANGUAGES:* Spanish. *PRACTICE AREAS:* Plaintiffs Trial Practice; Products Liability Law; General Negligence Trial Law; Appeals.

**JOSEPH W. STEELE, V,** born St. Louis, Missouri, October 16, 1949; admitted to bar, 1975, California. *Education:* Northern Arizona University (B.S., 1971); University of Utah (J.D., 1975). *Member:* State Bar of California; American Bar Association; Consumers Attorneys of California; Consumer Attorneys Association of Los Angeles; Consumer Attorneys of California. (Also Of Counsel to Guizot & Mouser). *PRACTICE AREAS:* Products Liability Law; Professional Malpractice Law; General Negligence Trials and Appeals.

**JEFFREY D. JEFFERSON,** born Grants Pass, Oregon, August 13, 1950; admitted to bar, 1976, Alaska, U.S. Trust Territory of the Pacific Islands, U.S. Claims Court, U.S. Supreme Court, U.S. District Court, District of Alaska and U.S. Court of Appeals, Ninth Circuit (Not admitted in California). *Education:* University of Oregon (B.S., 1973); Loyola Marymount University (J.D., 1976). Instructor of Law, University of Puget Sound, 1977-1978. Clerk to Justice Robert Erwin, Alaska Supreme Court, 1976-1977. *Member:* Alaska Bar Association; The Association of Trial Lawyers of America. (Resident, Kenai, Alaska Office).

**ALAN K. NICOLETTE,** born Grand Rapids, Michigan, May 6, 1956; admitted to bar, 1985, California and U.S. District Court, Central and Southern Districts of California. *Education:* Alma College (B.A., 1978); Southwestern University School of Law (J.D., 1984). *Member:* State Bar of California; Los Angeles County, Orange County and American Bar Associations; Consumer Attorneys of California, formerly CTLA; Consumer Attorneys Association of Los Angeles, formerly LATLA. *PRACTICE AREAS:* Plaintiffs Personal Injury.

**LUCIA NORDSTROM,** born Bogota, Colombia, January 19, 1959; admitted to bar, 1983, California and U.S. District Court, Central, Northern and Southern Districts of California; 1992, Nebraska. *Education:* California State University at Long Beach (B.S., 1979); University of Southern California (J.D., 1983). Phi Alpha Delta. *Member:* State Bar of California; American Bar Association; The Association of Trial Lawyers of America; Consumer Attorneys of California, formerly CTLA; Consumer Attorneys Association of Los Angeles, formerly LATLA (Member, Board of Governors, 1991—; Advocate Co-Editor, 1993—; Co-Chair, Education Committee, 1992—); Women Lawyers Association. *LANGUAGES:* Spanish and French. *PRACTICE AREAS:* Plaintiffs Personal Injury.

## ASSOCIATES

**ROBERT E. BLYTHE,** born Los Angeles, California, July 19, 1948; admitted to bar, 1981, California and U.S. District Court, Central District of California. *Education:* University of Southern California; California State University of Northridge (B.A., 1976); Southwestern University (J.D., 1980). *Member:* Los Angeles County and American Bar Associations; State Bar of California; Consumers Attorneys Association of Los Angeles; The Association of Trial Lawyers of America; Consumer Attorneys of California. [With U.S. Air Force, 1967-1968]

*(This Listing Continued)*

**MARIA IRIARTE-ABDO,** born Bogotá, Colombia, November 16, 1960; admitted to bar, 1990, California and U.S. District Court, Central District of California. *Education:* California State University at Long Beach (B.A., 1982); Loyola Marymount University (J.D., 1988). *Member:* Los Angeles County and American Bar Associations; State Bar of California; Consumer Attorneys Association of Los Angeles, formerly LATLA; Consumer Attorneys of California, formerly CTLA. *LANGUAGES:* Spanish. *PRACTICE AREAS:* Plaintiffs Personal Injury.

**FRANCIS P. PAPICA,** born Philippines, May 12, 1968; admitted to bar, 1992, California. *Education:* University of California, Los Angeles (B.A., cum laude, 1989); Syracuse University (J.D., cum laude, 1992). Mortar Board; Golden Key; Ford and Mellon Foundation Scholar. Moot Court Honors Program, 1990-1992. Law School Student Senate, 1990. Executive Editor, Syracuse Journal of International Law and Commerce, 1991-1992. Author, "Symbolic Sovereignty: The U.S. Bases in the Philippines." Delegate, State Bar Conference, 1993. *Member:* Orange County Bar Association; State Bar of California; Consumer Attorneys Association of Los Angeles, formerly LATLA; Consumer Attorneys of California, formerly CTLA. (Resident, Orange Office). *LANGUAGES:* Filipino (Tagalog). *PRACTICE AREAS:* Plaintiffs Personal Injury.

**TIMOTHY A. BLACK,** born Washington, D.C., March 15, 1964; admitted to bar, 1992, California and U.S. District Court, Central District of California; 1994, U.S. District Court, Eastern District of California. *Education:* University of California, Berkeley (B.A., 1986); Santa Clara University (J.D., 1991). Phi Delta Phi. *Member:* Orange County and Los Angeles County Bar Associations; Consumer Attorneys Association of Los Angeles, formerly LATLA. *PRACTICE AREAS:* Plaintiffs Litigation; Products Liability.

**PATRICK DEBLASE,** born Heidelberg, Germany, March 31, 1967; admitted to bar, 1993, California, U.S. District Court, Central District of California and U.S. Court of Appeals, Ninth Circuit. *Education:* University of California, Los Angeles (B.A., 1990); Whittier College School of Law, Los Angeles (J.D., 1993). Phi Delta Phi. *Member:* Los Angeles County and American Bar Associations; The Association of Trial Lawyers of America; Consumer Attorneys Association of Los Angeles. *PRACTICE AREAS:* Civil Litigation; Plaintiff Personal Injury.

**ANGELA G. KIM,** born Los Angeles, California, March 1, 1969; admitted to bar, 1995, California. *Education:* University of California at Los Angeles (B.A., 1991); California Western School of Law (J.D., 1994). Recipient: American Jurisprudence Award for Legal Skills. *Member:* Consumer Attorneys Association of Los Angeles. *PRACTICE AREAS:* Plaintiff's Personal Injury; Asbestos Litigation.

---

## FLOYD H. NORRIS

Established in 1946

SUITE 405 NORRIS BUILDING
714 SOUTH HILL STREET
**LOS ANGELES, CALIFORNIA 90014**
Telephone: 213-624-4088
FAX: 213-624-4080

*General Civil and Trial Practice in all State and Federal Courts. Corporation, Estate Planning, Trust and Probate Law.*

**FLOYD H. NORRIS,** born Tahlequah, Oklahoma, October 24, 1908; admitted to bar, 1935, Oklahoma and New Mexico; 1946, California. *Education:* Northeastern State College (B.S., 1932); University of Oklahoma (LL.D., 1935). Phi Delta Phi. Member, State Legislature, Oklahoma, 1937-1939. Member, Board of Trustees, University of Oklahoma Law Center, 1994—. *Member:* Los Angeles County and American Bar Associations; The State Bar of California. [Col., U.S., Army, 1940-1946; retired]

REPRESENTATIVE CLIENTS: Alice G. Harrison Memorial Trust; Norris Building, Inc.; Estate of Clara R. Hastings.
REFERENCES: Bank of America; Wells Fargo.

## LAW OFFICES OF LINDA L. NORTHRUP

A PROFESSIONAL CORPORATION
12424 WILSHIRE BOULEVARD, SUITE 900
**LOS ANGELES, CALIFORNIA 90025**
Telephone: 310-207-8300
Fax: 310-442-6400

*General Business Litigation and Appellate Practice concentrating in Business, Real Estate, Construction, Entertainment and Bankruptcy Litigation and General Legal advice in related areas.*

**LINDA L. NORTHRUP,** born Ashtabula, Ohio, September 14, 1956; admitted to bar, 1981, California; 1995, U.S. Supreme Court. *Education:* University of California at Los Angeles (B.A., cum laude, 1978); Hastings College of Law, University of California (J.D., 1981). Lecturer: Women Lawyers' Association of Los Angeles, Trial Advocacy Workshop, 1986; "Organizing Documents For Use at Trial", 1988; "Fundamentals of Law and Motion Practice," CEB/WLALA 1990. Judge Pro Tem: Los Angeles Municipal Court, 1987—; Los Angeles Superior Court, 1990—. *Member:* Los Angeles County (Member, Sections on: Business Law; Real Estate Law; Member, Committees on: Superior Court, 1986-1989; Appellate Courts, 1986-1989; Bridging the Gap, 1986-1993; Status of Women in the Legal Profession, 1988-1990; Continuing Legal Education, 1989-1991; Trial Practice Inn of Court, 1996—), Century City (Member, Business Litigation Section) and American (Member, Sections on: Corporation, Banking and Business Law; Real Property Law) Bar Associations; State Bar of California (Member, Sections on: Business Law; Real Estate Law); Women Lawyers' Association of Los Angeles (Member, Board of Governors, 1986-1991; Member, 1985— and Chair, 1986-1988, Committee on the Status of Women Lawyers; Chair, Special Projects and Legal Seminars, 1988-1989; Member, 1985—and Chair, 1989-1991, Trial Lawyers Section).

## NORTON & FAIRMAN

Established in 1974
515 SOUTH FIGUEROA, SUITE 1000
**LOS ANGELES, CALIFORNIA 90071**
Telephone: 213-683-1561
Telecopier: 213-683-0409
Email: Fairlaw@Linkonline.net

*Civil Trial and Appellate Practice in Federal and State Courts. Trial work involving Life, Health and Disability Insurance, ERISA matters, Casualty and Property Insurance, Real Property, Construction, Professional Liability, Wrongful Termination, Employment Law and Business Trial Law.*

FIRM PROFILE: *Founded in 1974, Norton & Fairman specializes in the defense of life, health, accident and disability insurance claims, the defense of bad faith, punitive damage actions, insurance coverage disputes and ERISA claims. We regularly handle trial matters relating to and including real estate matters, construction operations, broker-dealer matters, agent or employee disputes and the defense of wrongful termination claims.*

### MEMBERS OF FIRM

**THOMAS W. NORTON** (1910-1991).

**ROBERT L. FAIRMAN,** born Kansas City, Missouri, July 9, 1935; admitted to bar, 1963, California; U.S. District Court, Central, Northern, Eastern and Southern Districts of California; U.S. Court of Appeals, Ninth Circuit. *Education:* University of Southern California (A.B., 1957; LL.B., 1960). Phi Delta Phi. Deputy City Attorney, City of Los Angeles, 1963-1964. Arbitrator, Los Angeles Superior Court, 1978-1994, Mediator, Los Angeles Superior Court, 1994—. Judge Pro Tem, Los Angeles Municipal Court, 1974-1980. *Member:* Los Angeles County (Member: Trial Lawyer Section; Insurance Programs Committee, 1982-1989; Co-Chair, 1983-1989) and American (Member, Sections on: Litigation; Insurance, Negligence and Compensation Law) Bar Associations; The State Bar of California. (Also Of Counsel, James M. Donovan Law Office). **PRACTICE AREAS:** Insurance Bad Faith; Life Insurance; Health Insurance; Disability Insurance; ERISA; Professional and Insurance Errors and Omissions; Wrongful Termination; Construction Liability; Private Mediations.

### ASSOCIATES

**RICHARD J. KELLUM,** born Los Angeles, California, February 13, 1953; admitted to bar, 1979, California; U.S. District Court, Central District of California; U.S. Court of Appeals, Ninth Circuit. *Education:* University of Southern California (B.A., 1976); Loyola University of Los Angeles (J.D., 1979). Phi Beta Kappa. Member, Loyola Law Review,

*(This Listing Continued)*

1976-1977. *Member:* Los Angeles County Bar Association; State Bar of California. **PRACTICE AREAS:** Insurance Bad Faith; Insurance Coverage; Appellate Practice.

REPRESENTATIVE CLIENTS: The Equitable Life Assurance Society of the United States; Equitable Variable Life Insurance Company; General American Life Ins. Co.; Jackson National Life Insurance Co.; CIGNA Companies; Recovery Services International, Inc.; Insurance Company of North America; Equicor, Inc.; First Life Assurance Co.; First United Life Insurance Co.; Voluntary Plan Administrators, Inc.
REFERENCE: Bank of America.

## NOSSAMAN, GUTHNER, KNOX & ELLIOTT, LLP

THIRTY-FIRST FLOOR, UNION BANK SQUARE
445 SOUTH FIGUEROA STREET
**LOS ANGELES, CALIFORNIA 90071-1672**
Telephone: 213-612-7800
Telefacsimile: 213-612-7801
Telex: 67-4908
Cable Address: "Nossaman"

*San Francisco, California Office:* Thirty-Fourth Floor, 50 California Street. Telephone: 415-398-3600.
*Orange County, California Office:* Suite 1800, 18101 Von Karman Avenue, Irvine. Telephone: 714-833-7800.
*Sacramento, California Office:* Suite 1000, 915 L Street. Telephone: 916-442-8888.
*Washington, D.C. Office:* c/o French & Company, The Homer Building, Suite 370-S, 601 13th Street, N.W. Telephone: 202-783-7272.

*General Civil Practice, including Real Estate, Corporations and Litigation in all State and Federal Courts. Transportation, Bankruptcy, Municipal Finance, Land Use, Environmental, Hazardous Waste, Natural Resources, Health Care, Sports and Legislative Law.*

### MEMBERS OF FIRM

**WALTER L. NOSSAMAN** (1886-1964).

**WILLIAM E. GUTHNER, JR.,** born Denver, Colorado, February 3, 1932; admitted to bar, 1956, Michigan; 1959, California. *Education:* Northwestern University (B.S., 1953); University of Michigan (J.D., with distinction, 1956). Attorney Adviser, Tax Court of the United States, Washington, D.C., 1956-1958. *Member:* State Bar of California. **PRACTICE AREAS:** Corporations Law; Securities Law. **Email:** weg@ngke.com

**ALVIN S. KAUFER,** born Wilkes-Barre, Pennsylvania, August 12, 1932; admitted to bar, 1960, California. *Education:* Wesleyan University (B.A., 1954); University of Michigan (J.D., 1959). Law Associate, University of California at Berkeley, 1959-1960. *Member:* Los Angeles County Bar Association (Chairman, Superior Courts Committee, 1983-1984); State Bar of California; District of Columbia Bar; Chancery Club. Fellow, American Bar Foundation. **PRACTICE AREAS:** Litigation. **Email:** ask@ngke.com;

**JAMES C. POWERS,** born New York, N.Y., December 13, 1930; admitted to bar, 1960, California. *Education:* Yale University and Oxford University, England (B.A., in Jurisprudence, 1958; M.A., 1964). Judge Pro Tempore, Los Angeles Municipal Court, 1971—. *Member:* State Bar of California. **PRACTICE AREAS:** Litigation. **Email:** jcp@ngke.com

**HOWARD D. COLEMAN,** born Denver, Colorado, June 8, 1945; admitted to bar, 1970, California. *Education:* University of California at Berkeley (A.B., 1967); Boalt Hall School of Law, University of California (J.D., 1970). Member, California Law Review, 1968-1970. Lecturer, The Law of Coastal Zone Management, University of Southern California School of Law, 1974-1976. *Member:* State Bar of California. **PRACTICE AREAS:** Natural Resources Law; Real Property Law. **Email:** hdc@ngke.com

**ROBERT D. MOSHER,** born Inglewood, California, February 19, 1946; admitted to bar, 1972, California. *Education:* University of California at Los Angeles (A.B., cum laude, 1967; M.A., 1968; J.D., 1971). Order of the Coif. Member, 1969-1970 and Note and Comment Editor, 1970-1971, U.C.L.A. Law Review. *Member:* State Bar of California. **PRACTICE AREAS:** Corporations Law; Securities Law; Commercial Law. **Email:** rdm@ngke.com

**FREDERIC A. FUDACZ,** born Los Angeles, California, May 1, 1947; admitted to bar, 1972, California. *Education:* Stanford University (B.A., with distinction, 1968); Harvard Law School (J.D., cum laude, 1971). Phi

*(This Listing Continued)*

Beta Kappa. *Member:* State Bar of California; Association of Business Trial Lawyers. **PRACTICE AREAS:** Litigation. *Email:* faf@ngke.com

**RAYMOND J. STATON,** born Dallas, Texas, July 9, 1943; admitted to bar, 1974, California. *Education:* University of Dallas (B.A., 1965); Southern Methodist University (J.D., 1974). Order of the Coif. *Member:* State Bar of California. **PRACTICE AREAS:** Trusts Law; Estates Law. *Email:* rjs@ngke.com

**ISIDORO BERKMAN,** born Havana, Cuba, December 15, 1940; admitted to bar, 1964, Illinois; 1974, California and U.S. Tax Court. *Education:* Bradley University; De Paul University (B.S.C., 1961); Northwestern University (J.D., 1964). Member, Board of Editors, Northwestern University Law Review, 1963-1964. Certified Public Accountant, Illinois, 1963. Associate Professor, 1976-1978, Professor, 1978-1985 and Associate Dean, 1982-1984, Southwestern University School of Law. Chair, California Board of Legal Specialization, 1986-1987. *Member:* State Bar of California (Chair, Committee on Maintenance of Professional Competence, 1982-1984). **LANGUAGES:** Spanish. **PRACTICE AREAS:** Taxation Law. *Email:* ib@ngke.com

**JANET S. MURILLO,** born Los Angeles, California, April 6, 1953; admitted to bar, 1978, California. *Education:* University of Santa Clara (B.A., magna cum laude, 1975); University of California at Los Angeles (J.D., 1978). Order of the Coif. *Member:* State Bar of California. **PRACTICE AREAS:** Corporations Law; Securities Law; Commercial Law. *Email:* jsm@ngke.com

**FREDRIC W. KESSLER,** born Camden, New Jersey, January 28, 1952; admitted to bar, 1979, California. *Education:* Wesleyan University (B.A., magna cum laude, 1974); City of London Polytechnic, London, England; Hastings College of the Law (J.D., 1978). Order of the Coif. Member, Thurston Society. *Member:* State Bar of California. **PRACTICE AREAS:** Real Property Law. *Email:* fwk@ngke.com

**GEOFFREY S. YAREMA,** born Orlando, Florida, September 21, 1953; admitted to bar, 1978, California. *Education:* University of Florida (B.S., magna cum laude, 1975); University of Virginia School of Law (J.D., 1978). Phi Beta Kappa. Member, 1976-1977 and Articles Editor, 1977-1978, Virginia Journal of International Law. Lecturer, School of Urban and Regional Planning, University of Southern California, 1981-1982. National Chairman, U.S. Olympic Committee Job Opportunities Program, 1988—. *Member:* State Bar of California. **PRACTICE AREAS:** Natural Resources Law; Real Property Law; Transportation Law; Project Finance Law. *Email:* gsy@ngke.com

**HENRY S. WEINSTOCK,** born Brooklyn, New York, August 14, 1951; admitted to bar, 1979, California. *Education:* University of California at Los Angeles (B.A., magna cum laude, 1973); University of California at Los Angeles (J.D., 1979). Recipient, Charles F. Scott Fellowship. Associate Editor, U.C.L.A. Law Review, 1978-1979. Associate Editor, U.C.L.A.-Alaska Law Review, 1977-1979. Law Clerk to Judge Mariana R. Pfaelzer, U.S. District Court, Central District of California, 1979-1980. *Member:* State Bar of California. **PRACTICE AREAS:** Litigation. *Email:* hsw@ngke.com

**BARNEY A. ALLISON,** born Philadelphia, Pennsylvania, December 9, 1954; admitted to bar, 1979, California. *Education:* Amherst College (B.A., cum laude, 1976); University of Southern California (J.D., 1979). Deputy City Attorney, City of Cypress, 1979-1985. *Member:* State Bar of California; National Association of Bond Lawyers. **PRACTICE AREAS:** Municipal Finance Law. *Email:* baa@ngke.com

**ROBERT L. TOMS, SR.,** born Asheville, North Carolina, May 12, 1935; admitted to bar, 1965, North Carolina; 1966, California. *Education:* Bob Jones University (B.A., 1957); University of Southern California and Duke University (J.D., 1965). California State Commissioner of Corporations, 1974-1975. President, 1974-1975 and Member, Board of Directors, 1973-1988, Christian Legal Society. Member, Organized Crime Control Commission, 1977-1982. Member, Advisory Committee, U.S./China Joint Session on Trade, Investment and Economic Law, Beijing, 1987. *Member:* State Bar of California. **PRACTICE AREAS:** Corporation Law; Securities Law; Business Law; Regulatory Law; International Trade Law. *Email:* rlt@ngke.com

**NANCY C. SMITH,** born Gainesville, Florida, April 13, 1956; admitted to bar, 1981, California. *Education:* University of Florida (B.A., 1978); Yale University (J.D., 1981). Phi Beta Kappa. *Member:* State Bar of California. **PRACTICE AREAS:** Real Property Law; Transportation Law. *Email:* ncs@ngke.com

*(This Listing Continued)*

**DANIEL M. GRIGSBY,** born Bakersfield, California, February 20, 1954; admitted to bar, 1981, California. *Education:* San Diego State University and University of California at Los Angeles (B.A., 1977); Whittier College School of Law (J.D., cum laude, 1981). Member, Whittier Law Review, 1979-1981. *Member:* State Bar of California. **PRACTICE AREAS:** Sports Law; Entertainment Law; General Business Law. *Email:* dmg@ngke.com

**MICHAEL HEUMANN,** born Ellwood City, Pennsylvania, July 8, 1949; admitted to bar, 1975, California. *Education:* Princeton University (B.A., with honors, 1970; B.S.E., with honors, 1970); Stanford University (M.B.A., 1972); Boalt Hall School of Law, University of California (J.D., 1975). President, Southwest Museum Board of Trustees. *Member:* State Bar of California; Association of Business Trial Lawyers. **PRACTICE AREAS:** Litigation. *Email:* mh@ngke.com

**STEPHEN P. WIMAN,** born Los Angeles, California, May 29, 1947; admitted to bar, 1972, California. *Education:* University of California at Santa Barbara (B.A., 1969); International Christian University, Tokyo, Japan; Hastings College of the Law (J.D., 1972). Order of the Coif. Member, Thurston Society. Instructor, Legal Research and Writing, Hastings College of the Law, 1974-1975. Judge Pro Tem, Los Angeles Municipal Court, 1986-1988. *Member:* State Bar of California; Association of Business Trial Lawyers. **PRACTICE AREAS:** Commercial Litigation. *Email:* spw@ngke.com

**ALLAN H. ICKOWITZ,** born Brooklyn, New York, October 1, 1951; admitted to bar, 1975, New Jersey; 1978, California. *Education:* Columbia University (B.A., 1972; J.D., 1975). Managing Editor, Columbia Journal of Transnational Law, 1974-1975. *Member:* State Bar of California. **PRACTICE AREAS:** Debt Workout and Bankruptcy; Business Litigation; Real Estate Litigation. *Email:* ahi@ngke.com

**SAMUEL NORBER,** born Tel Aviv, Israel, December 5, 1948; admitted to bar, 1981, New York; 1988, California. *Education:* Brooklyn College of the City University of New York (B.S., 1970); Pratt Institute (M.S., 1973); Brooklyn Law School (J.D., cum laude, 1980). *Member:* New York State Bar Association; State Bar of California. **PRACTICE AREAS:** Municipal Finance Law; Taxation Law. *Email:* sn@ngke.com

**THOMAS D. LONG,** born Minneapolis, Minnesota, June 15, 1957; admitted to bar, 1982, California. *Education:* Stanford University (A.B., with distinction, 1979; J.D., 1982). Phi Beta Kappa. Member, Stanford Law Review, 1981-1982. *Member:* State Bar of California. **PRACTICE AREAS:** Litigation; Environmental Law; Insurance Coverage. *Email:* tdl@ngke.com

**JOHN OSSIFF,** born Los Angeles, California, July 1, 1953; admitted to bar, 1985, California. *Education:* United States Air Force Academy (B.S., 1975); University of California at Los Angeles (J.D., 1985). Order of the Coif. *Member:* State Bar of California. **PRACTICE AREAS:** Litigation. *Email:* jro@ngke.com

**JEFFREY A. STAVA,** born Torrance, California, July 9, 1958; admitted to bar, 1983, California. *Education:* Loyola University, Center for the Liberal Arts, Rome, Italy; Loyola Marymount University (B.A., 1980; J.D., 1983). *Member:* State Bar of California; National Association of Bond Lawyers. **PRACTICE AREAS:** Municipal Finance Law. *Email:* jas@ngke.com

**MARY LOU BYRNE,** born El Centro, California, September 26, 1958; admitted to bar, 1988, California. *Education:* Pepperdine University (B.S., 1983); University of Southern California (J.D., 1988). Staff Member, Southern California Law Review, 1986-1988. Legal Writing Instructor, USC Law Center, 1987-1988. *Member:* State Bar of California. **PRACTICE AREAS:** Litigation. *Email:* mlb@ngke.com

**WINFIELD D. WILSON,** born Pasadena, California, July 31, 1947; admitted to bar, 1972, California. *Education:* University of California at Davis (A.B., magna cum laude, 1968); University of California at Los Angeles (J.D., 1971). Phi Beta Kappa. Member, U.C.L.A. Law Review, 1969-1971. Lecturer, The Law of Coastal Zone Management, University of Southern California School of Law, 1974-1976. *Member:* State Bar of California. **PRACTICE AREAS:** Real Property Law; Litigation. *Email:* wdw@ngke.com

**SANDRA M. KANTER,** born Los Angeles, California, August 11, 1956; admitted to bar, 1981, California. *Education:* Brandeis University (B.A., magna cum laude, 1978); Harvard University (J.D., cum laude, 1981). Phi Beta Kappa. *Member:* State Bar of California. **PRACTICE AREAS:** Real Property Law. *Email:* smk@ngke.com

**RICHARD P. BOZOF,** born Washington, D.C., December 8, 1947; admitted to bar, 1977, California; 1980, District of Columbia. *Education:* Dartmouth College (B.A., magna cum laude, 1969); Yale University School of Medicine (M.D., 1973); Boalt Hall School of Law, University of Califor-

*(This Listing Continued)*

**NOSSAMAN, GUTHNER, KNOX & ELLIOTT, LLP, Los Angeles—Continued**

nia (J.D., 1977). Phi Beta Kappa. Attorney, Office of the General Counsel, U.S. Environmental Protection Agency, 1977-1985. *Member:* State Bar of California; District of Columbia Bar. *PRACTICE AREAS:* Environmental Law. *Email:* rpb@ngke.com

*ASSOCIATES*

**LINDA N. CUNNINGHAM,** born Spokane, Washington, March 7, 1953; admitted to bar, 1987, California. *Education:* University of Montana; University of Nevada (A.B., 1980); Hastings College of the Law (J.D., 1986). Member, Hastings Constitutional Law Quarterly, 1985-1986. *Member:* State Bar of California. *PRACTICE AREAS:* Real Property Law; Corporations Law. *Email:* lnc@ngke.com

**KARLA NEFKENS MACCARY,** born Urbana, Illinois, October 7, 1965; admitted to bar, 1990, California. *Education:* University of California at Berkeley (B.A., with high honors, 1987); University of California at Los Angeles School of Law (J.D., 1990). Phi Beta Kappa. *Member:* State Bar of California. *LANGUAGES:* French. *PRACTICE AREAS:* Real Property Law; Corporations Law. *Email:* knm@ngke.com

**DONNA M. GALLARELLO,** born Brooklyn, New York, December 9, 1965; admitted to bar, 1991, New York; 1992, California. *Education:* New York University (B.A., 1987); Brooklyn Law School (J.D., 1990). Law Clerk to Hon. Geraldine Mund, U.S. Bankruptcy Court, Central District of California, 1990-1992. *Member:* State Bar of California. *PRACTICE AREAS:* Bankruptcy. *Email:* dzg@ngke.com

**BRIAN G. PAPERNIK,** born Panama, March 7, 1964; admitted to bar, 1991, California. *Education:* Union College (B.S., 1985); Columbia University (J.D., 1991). Phi Beta Kappa; Harlan Fiske Stone Scholar. Administrative Editor, Columbia Business Law Review. *Member:* State Bar of California. *PRACTICE AREAS:* Real Property Law. *Email:* bgp@ngke.com

**SCOTT N. YAMAGUCHI,** born Oxnard, California, November 3, 1966; admitted to bar, 1991, California. *Education:* University of California, Berkeley (B.A., Phi Beta Kappa, 1988); University of California, Los Angeles (J.D., 1991). *Member:* State Bar of California. *PRACTICE AREAS:* Litigation. *Email:* sny@ngke.com

**CHRISTINE D. RYAN,** born Los Angeles, California, April 3, 1965; admitted to bar, 1992, California. *Education:* University of California, Los Angeles (B.A., 1988); University of Southern California Law Center (J.D., 1992). Editor, Interdisciplinary Law Journal, Tax Journal, 1990-1992. *Member:* State Bar of California. *LANGUAGES:* French and German. *PRACTICE AREAS:* Litigation. *Email:* cdr@ngke.com

**ALFRED E. SMITH,** born Torrance, California, March 30, 1972; admitted to bar, 1996, California. *Education:* University of California, Berkeley (B.A., high honors, 1993); Harvard Law School (J.D., 1996). Phi Beta Kappa. Executive Editor, Black Letter Law Journal, 1994-1996. *Member:* State Bar of California. *PRACTICE AREAS:* Litigation. *Email:* aes@ngke.com

*OF COUNSEL*

**WILLIAM D. MARKENSON,** born St. Louis, Missouri, September 9, 1941; admitted to bar, 1967, California. *Education:* University of California at Los Angeles (A.B., 1963); Boalt Hall School of Law, University of California (J.D., 1966). Order of the Coif. Member, California Law Review, 1965-1966. *Member:* State Bar of California. *PRACTICE AREAS:* Corporations Law; Securities Law; Commercial Law.

**KAREN J. HEDLUND,** born Chicago, Illinois, October 27, 1948; admitted to bar, 1974, Illinois; 1989, California; 1995, Colorado. *Education:* Radcliffe College (A.B., 1970); Georgetown University (J.D., 1974). *Member:* State Bar of California; National Association of Bond Lawyers. *PRACTICE AREAS:* Project Finance Law; Municipal Finance Law; Transportation Law. *Email:* kjh@ngke.com

REFERENCE: Union Bank (Los Angeles Headquarters Office).

(For Biographical Data of other Firm Personnel, see Professional Biographies at San Francisco, Irvine, Sacramento, California and Washington D.C.)

CAA1034B

---

## NOUSKAJIAN & CRANERT
*PROFESSIONAL CORPORATION*
**LOS ANGELES, CALIFORNIA**
(See South Pasadena)

*General Civil Trial and Appellate Practice in all State and Federal Courts. Insurance, Products Liability, Negligence and Professional Liability, Common Carrier. Probate, Family Law, Workers' Compensation.*

---

## BARRY NOVACK
**LOS ANGELES, CALIFORNIA**
(See Beverly Hills)

*Personal Injury. Wrongful Death Matters, Tort Actions.*

---

## EDWARD J. NOWAKOSKI
UNION BANK PLAZA
445 SOUTH FIGUEROA STREET, SUITE 2700
**LOS ANGELES, CALIFORNIA 90071-1603**
Telephone: 213-680-1425
Fax: 213-489-6897

Temecula, California Office: 27710 Jefferson Avenue, Suite 305. Telephone: 909-676-1424. Fax: 909-676-4796.

*International Finance and Business Law, Immigration and Naturalization, Asset Protection and Bankruptcy, Business and Real Estate Transactions and Litigation, Eminent Domain.*

**EDWARD J. NOWAKOSKI,** born Bayonne, New Jersey, June 1, 1952; admitted to bar, 1977, New Jersey; 1983, New York; 1987, California, U.S. Tax Court and U.S. Court of International Trade. *Education:* Fordham University (B.A., 1974); Rutgers University (J.D., 1977). Lecturer, Law and Banking, American Institute of Banking, Bloomfield, New Jersey, 1977-1987. *Member:* Riverside County, Southwest Riverside County (Past President), Los Angeles County (Member, Pacific Rim Committee) and American (Member, Delegation on Trade and Investment in China and Hong Kong, 1994) Bar Associations; American Immigration Lawyers Association. *LANGUAGES:* Mandarin Chinese, Spanish.

---

## OBERSTEIN, KIBRE & HORWITZ LLP
A Limited Liability Partnership
*Established in 1982*
1999 AVENUE OF THE STARS
SUITE 1850
**LOS ANGELES, CALIFORNIA 90067**
Telephone: 310-557-1213
Facsimile: 310-557-2460

*General Civil Trial and Appellate Litigation Practice; Entertainment, Family Law and General Business Litigation; Corporate, Mergers and Acquisitions.*

**NORMAN S. OBERSTEIN, (A PROFESSIONAL LAW CORPORATION),** born Oskaloosa, Iowa, November 5, 1940; admitted to bar, 1966, California; 1996, U.S. Supreme Court. *Education:* University of Iowa (B.A., magna cum laude, 1962); Boalt Hall School of Law, University of California at Berkeley (J.D., 1965). Phi Beta Kappa; Order of the Coif; Omicron Delta Kappa. Member, Board of Editors, California Law Review, 1964-1965. *Member:* Beverly Hills and Los Angeles County Bar Associations; State Bar of California.

**JOSEPH KIBRE,** born Los Angeles, California, February 17, 1946; admitted to bar, 1975, California. *Education:* University of California at Berkeley (B.A., with distinction, 1967); University of California at Los Angeles (M.A., 1969; C.Phil, 1972; J.D., 1975). Order of the Coif. *Member:* Beverly Hills (Member, Family Law Section) and Los Angeles County Bar Associations; State Bar of California.

**HOWARD L. HORWITZ,** born Los Angeles, California, June 27, 1957; admitted to bar, 1982, California; 1989, New York; 1996, U.S. Supreme Court. *Education:* University of California at Davis (B.A., 1979); Hastings
*(This Listing Continued)*

# PROFESSIONAL BIOGRAPHIES

College of the Law, University of California (J.D., 1982). Member, 1980-1981 and Editor-in-Chief, 1981-1982, Hastings Communications and Entertainment Law Journal (COMM/ENT). *Member:* Beverly Hills and Los Angeles County Bar Associations; State Bar of California.

## OF COUNSEL

**HENRY POLLARD,** born New York, N.Y., January 10, 1931; admitted to bar, 1954, New York; 1962, California. *Education:* Cooper Union College and College of the City of New York (A.B., 1953); Columbia University (J.D., 1954). Harlan Fiske Stone Scholar, 1952-1954. Member, Board of Editors, Columbia Law Review, 1953-1954. Lecturer, UCLA Paralegal Extension Program, 1968—. Judge Pro Tem, Los Angeles County Municipal Court, 1989—. Arbitrator/Mediator: American Arbitration Association (Large Complex Case Program); National Association of Securities Dealers; New York Stock Exchange; American Stock Exchange; Pacific Stock Exchange; Los Angeles County Bar Association Dispute Resolution Services. *Member:* Beverly Hills, Los Angeles County, New York State and American Bar Associations; State Bar of California.

**HAROLD J. STANTON,** born Columbus, Ohio, April 16, 1940; admitted to bar, 1966, California and U.S. District Court, Central District of California. *Education:* University of California, Los Angeles (B.S., 1962; J.D., 1965). Senior Editor, U.C.L.A. Law Review, 1964-1965. (Also Member Stanton Law Corporation; See Separate Listing for Biographical Information).

**MARIAN L. STANTON,** born New York, N.Y.; admitted to bar, 1981, California. *Education:* University of California, Los Angeles (B.A., 1962; M.A., 1967); Whittier College/Beverly School of Law (J.D., magna cum laude, 1980). (Also Member Stanton Law Corporation; See Separate Listing for Biographical Information).

## *OCHOA & SILLAS*

Established in 1978

**444 SOUTH, FLOWER STREET, 18TH FLOOR**
**LOS ANGELES, CALIFORNIA 90071**
Telephone: 213-362-1400
Fax: 213-622-0162

*Sacramento, California Office:* Wells Fargo Center, 400 Capitol Mall, Suite 1850. Telephone: 916-447-3383. FAX: 916-447-3495.

*Mexico City, Mexico Office:* Bosques de Duraznos, No. 65-507-B, Bosques de Las Lomas, 11700 Mexico, D.F. Telephone: 905-596-68-48.

*General Civil Trial, Appellate Practice, Corporate, Administrative and Municipal Law, Products Liability, Insurance Defense and Legislative Practice. Municipal Finance, Construction Law, Workers Compensation Defense. International Law, Labor, Real Estate and Education.*

FIRM PROFILE: *Ochoa & Sillas was founded in 1978 to meet the need for professional counsel in government law. From the inception, a substantial portion of the resources of the firm was devoted to legislative advocacy, administrative law and municipal law. Through the years, the firm has expanded to a full service law firm to include divisions in litigation, workers' compensation, educational law, and international law. Ochoa & Sillas has made a concentrated effort in its recruitment to have its work force reflect the diversity of the population of the state of California. The firm has offices in Los Angeles, Sacramento, Mexico City and Washington, D.C. The firm is a certified minority business enterprise.*

### MEMBERS OF FIRM

**RALPH M. OCHOA,** born Los Angeles, California, October 16, 1941; admitted to bar, 1970, California and U.S. District Court, Central District of California. *Education:* University of California at Los Angeles (B.A., 1963); University of California School of Law, Los Angeles (J.D., 1969); University of Pennsylvania. Phi Delta Phi. Member: Los Angeles County Revenue Sharing Commission, 1972-1976; State Commission of the California's, 1972-1983; California Building Standards Commission, 1982—. President, UCLA Alumni Association, 1990-1992. *Member:* Los Angeles County, Sacramento County and American Bar Associations; State Bar of California; Mexican-American Bar Associations. *LANGUAGES:* Spanish. *PRACTICE AREAS:* Legislative Advocacy; International Law.

**HERMAN SILLAS,** born Los Angeles, California, February 11, 1934; admitted to bar, 1960, California, U.S. District Court, Central, Eastern and Northern Districts of California and U.S. Court of Appeals, Ninth Circuit. *Education:* University of California at Los Angeles (B.A., 1956); University of California School of Law (J.D., 1959). Nu Beta Epsilon. Moot Court Finalist. Instructor, University of California School of Law at Davis, 1979.

*(This Listing Continued)*

# CALIFORNIA—LOS ANGELES

U.S. Attorney, California Eastern District, 1977-1980. Director, Department of Motor Vehicles, California, 1975-1977. Chairman, California Advisory Committee to U.S. Civil Rights Commission, 1966-1974. Member, Spanish Speaking Advisory Committee to U.S. Census Bureau, 1976-1980. *Member:* Sacramento County, Los Angeles County and American Bar Associations; State Bar of California (Member, Disciplinary Committee, 1968-1970). *LANGUAGES:* Spanish. *PRACTICE AREAS:* Civil Litigation; Government Law; Education Law; Legislative Advocacy.

**JESSE M. JAUREGUI,** born Los Angeles, California, November 11, 1956; admitted to bar, 1987, California and U.S. District Court, Central District of California; 1993, U.S. District Court, Northern, Southern and Eastern Districts of California. *Education:* Yale University (B.A., 1979); Loyola University of Los Angeles (J.D., 1986). Judicial Extern to the Honorable Mariana Pfaelzer, U.S. District Court, Central District of California, 1985. Member, State Central Committee, California Democratic Party. Board Director and Board of Trustees, 1995—, Latino Lawyers Association Inc. *Member:* Los Angeles County Bar Association; State Bar of California; Mexican-American Bar Association. *LANGUAGES:* Spanish. *REPORTED CASES:* Gonzalez v. Sup. Ct. 39 Cal Rptr 2d 896 (1995). *PRACTICE AREAS:* Civil Litigation; Construction Law.

**JACQUELINE RICH MOORE,** born Ontario, California, February 14, 1960; admitted to bar, 1993, California and U.S. District Court, Eastern and Northern Districts of California. *Education:* California State University, Sacramento (B.S., 1983); McGeorge School of Law, University of the Pacific (J.D., 1992). Moot Court; National Moot Court Competition. Vice President, Black American Law Students Association. Former Clerk, Department of Fair Employment and Housing. Formerly employed by the California Peace Officers' Association. *Member:* National Association of Female Executives; California Women Lawyers; Black American Political Association of California. *PRACTICE AREAS:* Litigation; Employment; Education.

### ASSOCIATES

**JACK T. MOLODANOF,** born San Jose, California, August 15, 1961; admitted to bar, 1987, California and U.S. District Court, Northern and Eastern Districts of California. *Education:* San Jose State University (B.S., 1983); McGeorge School of Law, University of the Pacific (J.D., with distinction, 1987). Member, Traynor Society. Recipient: American Jurisprudence Award in Business Associations and Corporations. Member: Sacramento Real Estate Board; Sacramento Legislative Committee; Sacramento County Assessment Appeals Board. Registered Lobbyist, State of California. *Member:* Sacramento and American (Member, Real Property Section) Bar Associations; State Bar of California. *LANGUAGES:* Greek. *PRACTICE AREAS:* Real Estate Litigation; Legislative Advocacy.

**FRANCISCO VALLES LOPEZ,** admitted to bar, 1951, Mexico (Not admitted in the United States). *Education:* Preparatoria de la Laguna; University of Durango (Law Degree). City Attorney and Director of Federal Projects, City of San Luis, Rio Colorado, Sonora. Member, Public Notary for the City of San Luis, Rio Colorado, Sonora, 1962—. Director, Administration for the Federal Lottery, 1970-1976. Director, Public Relations, Mexico City, 1979-1982. *PRACTICE AREAS:* Corporation Law; Real Estate; Public Notary; Administrative Legislation.

**TOMÁS R. LOPEZ,** born Dominican Republic, October 1, 1955; admitted to bar, 1981, District of Columbia; 1991, California; U.S. District Court, Central, Northern and Southern Districts of California, District of Columbia, Middle District of Maryland and Northern District of Alabama; U.S. Court of Appeals, Ninth, Eleventh and District of Columbia Circuits. *Education:* York College of the City University of New York (B.A., 1977); University of Strasbourg-Institute of International Human Rights; Georgetown University (J.D., 1980). Barrister, Los Angeles County Bar Inn of Court, 1991—. Charles E. Fahy Inn, 1983-1986. Lecturer and Moderator, 1992 CEB Panel, "How to Use and Present Demonstrative Evidence." Adjunct Professor, D.C. Law Students in Court, Georgetown University Law Center, 1988-1990. Commissioner, District of Columbia Commission on Latino Community Development. Delegate, District of Columbia Judicial Conference, 1982-1992. Member, Mandatory Arbitration Rules Advisory Committee, 1986. Member, Los Angeles County Bar Association Delegation to the State Bar Conference of Delegates, 1993-1994. *LANGUAGES:* Spanish. *PRACTICE AREAS:* Civil Litigation; Labor; Environmental.

**RITA A. REYES,** born Los Angeles, California, December 19, 1964; admitted to bar, 1991, California. *Education:* University of California, Los Angeles (B.A., 1987); Whittier College School of Law (J.D., 1990). President, Phi Alpha Delta, 1989-1990. *Member:* Los Angeles County and American Bar Associations; State Bar of California; Mexican-American Bar Association; California Trial Lawyers Association. *LANGUAGES:* Span-

*(This Listing Continued)*

CAA1035B

## OCHOA & SILLAS, Los Angeles—Continued

ish. *PRACTICE AREAS:* Workers' Compensation; Civil Litigation; Employment Law.

**CARLOS HILARIO,** born Manila, Philippines, March 2, 1963; admitted to bar, 1990, California. *Education:* California State University (B.A., 1985); University of West Los Angeles (J.D., 1989). Registered Radiological Technologist, 1981. *Member:* Los Angeles County Bar Association; State Bar of California; Philippine American Bar Association; American Society of Radiological Technologists. *LANGUAGES:* Pilipino and Spanish. *PRACTICE AREAS:* Workers Compensation; Civil Litigation.

**JOYCE E. EARL,** born Los Angeles, California, March 26, 1948; admitted to bar, 1988, California and U.S. District Court, Eastern and Central Districts of California. *Education:* University of California at Los Angeles (B.A., 1970); California State University of Northridge (M.A., 1974); McGeorge School of Law, University of the Pacific (J.D., with distinction, 1988). Order of the Coif. Traynor Society. Comment Staff Writer, Pacific Law Journal, 1987-1988. *Member:* Los Angeles County Bar Association (Member, Sections on: Labor and Employment Law; Public Agency); State Bar of California. *PRACTICE AREAS:* Education, Labor and Employment Law.

**CHRISTOPHER ERIC OCHOA,** born September 4, 1969; admitted to bar, 1994, California. *Education:* University of California, Los Angeles (B.A., History); U.S. Naval Academy; Harvard University; University of California, Davis, School of Law (J.D., 1994). Former Legislative Advocate, University of California, Los Angeles, Governmental Relations Department. Organizer and Legislative Advocate, Annual American Association of College Universities Legislative Conference, Sacramento, California. *PRACTICE AREAS:* Lobbying; Education; Hazardous Waste Land Acquisition.

**CHRISTOPHER GONZALEZ,** born Bronx, New York, July 4, 1968; admitted to bar, 1994, California; U.S. District Court, Southern District of California; U.S. Court of Appeals, Ninth Circuit. *Education:* University of California, Santa Barbara (B.A., 1991); Whittier College School of Law (J.D., 1994). Whittier Law Review, 1992-1994. President, Hispanic-American Law Students Association. Member, Puerto Rican Legal Defense and Education Fund. *Member:* Los Angeles County and American (Member, Young Lawyers Division) Bar Associations; California Young Lawyers Association; National Hispanic Bar Association; Mexican-American Bar Association. *LANGUAGES:* Spanish. *PRACTICE AREAS:* Civil Litigation; Education.

**EVAN F. HADNOT,** born Rockville Center, New York, May 1944; admitted to bar, 1989, California; 1990, U.S. District Court, Central District of California. *Education:* University of Missouri (B.S., 1970); Western State University (J.D., 1989). *Member:* State Bar of California. (Certified Specialist, Workers Compensation Law, The State Bar of California Board of Legal Specialization). *LANGUAGES:* Spanish. *PRACTICE AREAS:* Workers' Compensation; Personal Injury; Bankruptcy; Family Law.

**THOMAS J. JOY,** born Pasadena, California, October 22, 1951; admitted to bar, 1976, California; 1977 U.S. District Court, Central District of California; 1986, U.S. District Court, Eastern District of California. *Education:* Loyola University (B.B.A., 1973); Southwestern University School of Law (J.D., 1976). *Member:* Los Angeles County Bar Association; State Bar of California. American Immigration Lawyers Association. *PRACTICE AREAS:* Immigration Law; Litigation.

**MARIO CORDERO,** born Los Angeles, California, August 3, 1952; admitted to bar, 1980, California; U.S. District Court, Central District of California. *Education:* Long Beach State; Santa Clara (J.D., 1978). *Member:* State Bar of California; Mexican-American Bar Association. *LANGUAGES:* Spanish. *PRACTICE AREAS:* Workers Compensation.

### OF COUNSEL

**COCHRAN & LOTKIN**, Washington, D.C.

### LEGAL SUPPORT PERSONNEL

**MANUEL TEJEDA,** born Bishop, Texas, April 20, 1959. *Education:* Whittier College (B.A., 1982). (Paralegal). *LANGUAGES:* Spanish. *PRACTICE AREAS:* Workers Compensation.

**JEANETTE M. PALMA,** born Montebello, California, August 26, 1956. *Education:* Rio Hondo, Whittier (A.S., 1995). (Paralegal).

**LORI LEE MARINO,** born Wausau, Wisconsin, February 9, 1960. *Education:* Watterson College, Van Nuys (Paralegal Cert., 1987). (Paralegal). *PRACTICE AREAS:* Litigation Paralegal.

*(This Listing Continued)*

---

REPRESENTATIVE CLIENTS: American Golf; BKK Corp. (Toxic substance treatment); Chrysler; Department of Water and Power of Los Angeles; Sacramento Municipal Utility District; Department of Insurance; Metropolitan Water District, Los Angeles; General Motors; Hughes Aircraft; ICN Laboratories; K-Mart; Minnesota Mining & Manufacturing (3M); Metropolitan Transit Authority; Stewart Title; Lawyers Title; First American Title Company; Town of Los Gatos, California; County of San Bernardino, California; Cities of: Los Angeles, Pasadena, Sacramento, San Francisco, South Pasadena and Hawaiian Gardens; School Districts: Oxnard School District, Sacramento City Unified School District, Los Angeles Community College District, California State University, University of California, Richgrove Elementary School District, Rio Hondo Community College District; Von's Market.

## BERNARD E. O'CONNOR, JR.

### A LAW CORPORATION

### LOS ANGELES, CALIFORNIA

(See Torrance)

*Business and Commercial Law, International Trade and Transactions, Corporations and Partnerships, Real Estate and Construction Law, Estate Planning and Probate, Civil Litigation and Litigation in Probate and Trust Matters.*

## O'DONNELL, REEVES & SHAEFFER, LLP

633 WEST FIFTH STREET, SUITE 1700
### LOS ANGELES, CALIFORNIA 90071
Telephone: 213-532-2000
Facsimile: 213-532-2020

*Litigation, emphasis in areas of Antitrust, Complex Corporate, Complex Tort, Entertainment, Environmental, Intellectual Property, General Civil Litigation and Securities, Appellate in all Federal and State Courts.*

### PARTNERS

**PIERCE O'DONNELL,** born Troy, New York, March 5, 1947; admitted to bar, 1973, District of Columbia; 1976, U.S. Supreme Court; 1978, California. *Education:* Georgetown University (A.B., 1969; J.D., 1972); Yale University (LL.M., 1975). Topics Editor, Georgetown Law Journal, 1971-1972. Law Clerk to: Hon. Shirley M. Hufstedler, U.S. Court of Appeals, Ninth Circuit, 1972-1973; Justice Byron R. White, U.S. Supreme Court, 1973-1974. Co-Author: "The Hands of Justice: A Law Clerk Fondly Remembers Byron White," 33 Washburn L.J. 12, 1933; "Killing The Golden Goose, Hollywood's Death Wish," Beverly Hills Bar Journal, Summer, 1992; "Fatal Subtraction: The Inside Story of Buchwald v. Paramount," Doubleday, 1992; "Toward a Just and Effective Sentencing System: Agenda for Legislative Reform," Praeger Publishers, 1977; "A Poor Man in the Billion Dollar Wasteland: Proposals for a National Linkage Systems, Poor People's Bond, National Lottery Judibank," 59 Georgetown Law Journal 1015, 1971. Author: "Common Sense and the Constitution: Justice White and the Egalitarian Ideal," 58 Colorado Law Review 801, 1987; "Federal Chartering of Corporations: Constitutional Challenges," 61 Georgetown Law Journal 123, 1972; "Justice Byron R. White: Leading From The Center," American Bar Association Journal, Special Issue, June 15, 1986. Contributing Author: "Reflections on the ConArtist as a Young Man" in "The Private Diary of Lyle Menendez," Dove, 1995; "Prisoner of Justice" in "The Private Diary of an O.J. Juror," Dove, 1995. "Citibank: Ralph Nadar's Study Group Report On First National City Bank," Grossman Publishers, 1973. Member, Executive Committee, Washington Lawyers' Committee for Civil Rights Under Law, 1976-1978. Executive Assistant to U.S. Secretary of Education, 1979. *Member:* Los Angeles County (Vice Chair, Judicial Evaluation Committee, 1988-1989), Federal (Member, Federal Practice Committee, 1975-1977) and American (Member: Committee on Equal Protection of the Law, Section of Individual Rights and Responsibilities, 1974—) Bar Associations; State Bar of California (Public Counsel, Board of Directors, 1991—); District of Columbia Bar; American Law Institute; National Association of Criminal Defense Lawyers. *PRACTICE AREAS:* Business Torts; Complex Litigation; Constitutional Law; Contract Law; Entertainment Law; Environmental Law; Financial Institutions; Fraud; Intellectual Property; Products Liability; Racketeer Influenced and Corrupt Org Act; Real Estate; Securities Law; Tax Law.

**REX T. REEVES, JR.,** born Atlanta, Georgia, January 14, 1963; admitted to bar, 1988, California; 1989, U.S. District Court, Central District of California and U.S. Court of Appeals, 9th Circuit. *Education:* Brown University (A.B., magna cum laude, 1985); Harvard University (J.D., cum laude, 1988). Phi Beta Kappa. *Member:* Los Angeles County Bar Association; State Bar of California. *PRACTICE AREAS:* Litigation.

*(This Listing Continued)*

**JOHN J. SHAEFFER,** born San Francisco, California, July 30, 1963; admitted to bar, 1988, California. *Education:* Santa Clara University (B.S., 1985; J.D., magna cum laude, 1988). *Member:* State Bar of California; American Bar Association (Member, Sections on: Antitrust Law; Business Law). *PRACTICE AREAS:* Litigation.

### ASSOCIATES

**ANN MARIE MORTIMER,** born Los Angeles, California, July 31, 1966; admitted to bar, 1994, California. *Education:* Smith College (A.B., cum laude, 1988); London School of Econ. (M.Sc., 1989); University of California School of Law, Berkeley (J.D., 1992). Editor, California Law Review, 1992. Law Clerk to: Hon. Laughlin Waters, Central District of California, 1992-1993. *PRACTICE AREAS:* Litigation.

**BELYNDA RECK,** born Rockford, Illinois, February 28, 1964; admitted to bar, 1992, California. *Education:* Illinois State University (B.S., magna cum laude, 1986); University of Southern California (J.D., 1992). Order of the Coif. Member, University of Southern California Law Review. Law Clerk to: Judge Ronald S.W. Lew, Central District of California, 1992-1993. *PRACTICE AREAS:* Litigation.

**TIMOTHY J. TOOHEY,** born Bozeman, Montana, November 3, 1949; admitted to bar, 1987, New York; 1989, California. *Education:* Stanford University (B.A., 1972); Oxford University (B.A., 1975); Harvard University (Ph.D., 1980); Boalt Hall School of Law University of California at Berkeley (J.D., 1985). Law Clerk to: Hon. Francis D. Murnaghan, Jr., U.S. Court of Appeals, Fourth Circuit, 1985-1986. *PRACTICE AREAS:* Litigation.

**LISA R. BRANT,** born Monterey Park, California, July 7, 1969; admitted to bar, 1994, California. *Education:* University of California, Los Angeles (B.A., 1991); University of California School of Law, Los Angeles (J.D., 1994). *PRACTICE AREAS:* Litigation.

**BRIAN J. TUCKER,** born Kittery, Maine, October 11, 1960; admitted to bar, 1993, California and U.S. District Court, Central, Northern, Southern and Eastern Districts of California. *Education:* University of Notre Dame (B.A., 1982); Loyola Law School, Los Angeles (J.D., cum laude, 1993). Order of the Coif. Articles Editor, Loyola of Los Angeles Law Review, 1991-1993. Law Clerk to the Honorable Lisa Hill Fenning, U.S. Bankruptcy Court, Central District of California, 1993-1994. *Member:* Los Angeles County Bar Association (Member, Sections on: Litigation; Commercial Law). [Captain, U.S. Marine Corps, 1982-1988]. *PRACTICE AREAS:* Litigation.

### OF COUNSEL

**MICHAEL P. FLAHERTY,** born Fitchburg, Massachusetts, April 3, 1945; admitted to bar, 1972, District of Columbia (Not admitted in California). *Education:* Boston University (B.A., 1968); Catholic University School of Law (J.D., 1972). Counsel, 1972-1976 and General Counsel, 1976-1982, Committee on Banking Finance, Urban Affairs, U.S. House of Representatives, Washington, D.C. *Member:* District of Columbia Bar (Member, Corporations, Finance and Securities Committees); Federal (Executive Committee, Past Chairman, Banking Law Section) and American (Member, Corporations, Banking and Business Law Section) Bar Associations. *LANGUAGES:* German. *PRACTICE AREAS:* Litigation; Financial Institutions; Government Contracts; Regulatory Agency Law.

**HENRY S. ROSE,** born Los Angeles, California, July 20, 1924; admitted to bar, 1949, California, U.S. District Court, Northern District of California and U.S. Circuit Court, Ninth Circuit; 1960, U.S. Supreme Court. *Education:* University of Southern California (A.B. and B.S., 1947; J.D., 1949). Phi Beta Kappa; Nu Beta Epsilon. Chief Justice, Moot Court. Deputy Commissioner of Corps., California, 1950-1952. *Member:* Automotive Parts & Accessories Association. *PRACTICE AREAS:* International Law; Environmental Law.

**SUZANNE TRAGERT,** born Cambridge, Massachusetts, May 17, 1963; admitted to bar, 1988, California. *Education:* Boston University (B.A., with honors, 1985); Georgetown University (J.D., cum laude, 1988). Member, Georgetown International Environmental Law Review. *Member:* State Bar of California; American Bar Association. *PRACTICE AREAS:* Litigation.

## O'FLAHERTY & BELGUM
### LOS ANGELES, CALIFORNIA
(See Glendale)

*General Civil, Trial and Appellate Practice in State and Federal Courts. Medical and Dental Malpractice, Products Liability, General Insurance Law, Insurance Coverage, Wrongful Termination, Workers' Compensation, Business and Environmental Litigation.*

## OHASHI & PRIVER
### LOS ANGELES, CALIFORNIA
(See Pasadena)

*Business and Corporate Law. Real Estate, Federal and State Securities, Commercial and Tax Litigation.*

## OLDMAN & COOLEY, L.L.P.
Established in 1977

PENTHOUSE, SUITE A
16133 VENTURA BOULEVARD (ENCINO)
**LOS ANGELES, CALIFORNIA 91436**
Telephone: 818-986-8080
Fax: 818-789-0947
Email: ILAL@AOL.COM

*Probate, Conservatorships and Estate Planning, Tax, Trusts and Related Civil Trial and Appellate Practice in all State Courts.*

### MEMBERS OF FIRM

**MARSHAL A. OLDMAN,** born Santa Monica, California, September 30, 1951; admitted to bar, 1976, California. *Education:* University of Southern California (B.A., 1973); University of California at Los Angeles (J.D., 1976). Phi Beta Kappa; Phi Kappa Phi. President, San Fernando Valley Legal Foundation, 1981-1982. Author: "Estate Planning and Conservatorship Substituted Judgment Rule," Report, Daily Journal, July 17, 1981; "Published Articles: Probate and Estate Planning," Los Angeles Daily Journal, 1990—; Re Phelps-Dodge and Organized Labor in Bisbee & Douglas, Western Legal History, May 1992 edition. Lecturer: CEB, Fundamentals of Estate Planning, 1989; Probate Litigation, 1994; Estate Planning for Unmarried Couples. President, 1980-1989 and Board Member, 1990, San Fernando Valley Community Legal Foundation. Member, Board of Directors, San Fernando Valley Neighborhood Legal Services, Inc., 1986-1988. Member, Ninth Judicial Circuit Historical Society. *Member:* Los Angeles County (Secretary-Treasurer, 1985-1986, Vice Chairman, 1986-1987 and Chairman, 1987, Executive Committee and Chairman, Legislative Monitoring Committee, 1984—; Chair, Probate Section, 1988-1989; Member, Board of Trustees, 1988-1989; Reappointed to Executive Committee Probate Section, 1993-1996), San Fernando Valley (Chairman: Probate Section, 1981-1982; Probate Volunteer Panel, 1978—; Board of Trustees, 1979-1982; Delegate, State Bar Convention, 1979-1980; Chairman, Long Range Planning Committee, 1985—; Treasurer, 1986-1987; Secretary, 1987-1988; President-Elect, 1988-1989; President, 1989) and American Bar Associations; State Bar of California (Executive Committee, Estate Planning, Trust and Probate Section, 1996). *PRACTICE AREAS:* Probate and Trust Administration; Litigation; Conservatorships and Estate Planning.

**SUSAN J. COOLEY,** born Sacramento, California, November 7, 1952; admitted to bar, 1980, California. *Education:* University of California at Los Angeles (B.A. in Political Science, 1974); Southwestern University School of Law (J.D., 1979). Author: Contributing Editor, L.A. Daily Journal on Probate Law. Delegate, State Bar Convention, 1990. Member, Probate Volunteer Panel. *Member:* Los Angeles County Bar Association (Board Member, Probate and Trust Section Executive Committee, 1990-1993; Member, Probate Section); State Bar of California (Member, Estate Planning, Trust & Probate Law Section); Women Lawyers' Association of Los Angeles. *REPORTED CASES:* In re Estate of DiPinto, 188 Cal. App. 3d. 625 231 Cal Rptr. 612, 1986. *PRACTICE AREAS:* Probate; Conservatorship; Guardianship Administration; Trust Administration; Trust Litigation.

**SUSAN R. IZENSTARK,** born Bakersfield, September 8, 1952; admitted to bar, 1979, California and U.S. District Court, Central District of

*(This Listing Continued)*

## OLDMAN & COOLEY, L.L.P., Los Angeles—Continued

California. *Education:* University of California at Los Angeles (B.A., in Psychology, 1974); California Western School of Law (J.D., 1977). Member, California Western International Law Journal, 1976-1977. Co-Author: "Spouse's Death Raises Jurisdiction Problems," Los Angeles Daily Journal, 1990. Author: "Recent Trends in Spousal Support in Short Marriages," Family Law News Review, 1991; "Genetic Manipulation: Research, Regulation and Legal Liability Under International Law," 7 Cal. W. Int'l., L.J. 203, 1977. *Member:* Los Angeles County Bar Association (Member, Probate Section). **PRACTICE AREAS:** Probate and Trust; Litigation; Conservatorships; Guardianships.

### OF COUNSEL

**MICHAEL L. TROPE,** born Los Angeles, California, December 24, 1951; admitted to bar, 1987, California. *Education:* University of Southern California (B.A., 1973); Loyola Marymount University (J.D., 1981). (Also Member of Clinco, Fisher, Diamond & Trope, L.L.P., Los Angeles). **PRACTICE AREAS:** Probate Litigation; Child Custody.

REFERENCES: City National Bank (Encino Office); Industrial Bank (Van Nuys).

---

## OLINCY & KARPEL

10960 WILSHIRE BOULEVARD, SUITE 1111
**LOS ANGELES, CALIFORNIA 90024-3782**
Telephone: 310-478-1213
FAX: 310-478-1215

*Tax Law, Estate Planning, Probate and Trust.*

FIRM PROFILE: Olincy & Karpel (founded by George R. Olincy in 1930) specializes in the areas of Taxation Law and Probate, Estate Planning and Trust Law. It emphasizes planning (tax and estate), administration (estates, trusts and charitable organizations), and compliance/administrative (estate, gift and income tax returns; returns for charitable organizations; and IRS audits).

### MEMBERS OF FIRM

**GEORGE R. OLINCY** (1904-1982).

**J. DAN OLINCY,** born Los Angeles, California, November 12, 1929; admitted to bar, 1953, California. *Education:* University of California at Los Angeles; Stanford University (B.A., 1951; J.D., 1953). Certified Public Accountant, California, 1953. Chairman, Tax Advisory Commission, California Board of Legal Specialization, 1980-1983. Trustee, Sierra Club Legal Defense Fund, 1985—. Treasurer, UCLA Center on Aging, 1990—. *Member:* Westwood Village Bar Association (President, 1975); State Bar of California (Chair, Tax Committee, 1973-1974; V. Judson Klein Award, Tax Section, 1983). (Certified Specialist, Taxation Law and Estate Planning, Trust and Probate Law, The State Bar of California Board of Legal Specialization). **PRACTICE AREAS:** Tax; Estate Planning; Probate and Trust.

**PHILIP KARPEL,** born Detroit, Michigan, July 21, 1949; admitted to bar, 1977, California. *Education:* California State University at Northridge (B.A., cum laude, 1971; M.S., 1973); Loyola University of Los Angeles (J.D., 1977). Certified Public Accountant, California, 1972. Lecturer: California Continuing Education of the Bar, 1983, 1986; National Business Institute, 1993, 1995. Member, Board of Directors, 1987-1991, Treasurer, 1988-1991, Los Angeles Chapter of Juvenile Diabetes Foundation International. *Member:* Los Angeles County (Member, Tax Section) and American (Member, Tax Section) Bar Associations; The State Bar of California (Member, Tax Section). (Certified Specialist, Taxation Law and Estate Planning, Trust and Probate Law, The State Bar of California Board of Legal Specialization). **PRACTICE AREAS:** Tax Law; Estate Planning; Probate and Trust. *Email:* pkarpel0@counsel.com

### ASSOCIATE

**JOYCE RILEY,** born Long Beach, California, October 21, 1961; admitted to bar, 1989, California. *Education:* University of Southern California (B.S., 1983); University of California at Los Angeles (J.D., 1988). Certified Public Accountant, Colorado, 1990. *Member:* Los Angeles County (Member, Taxation Section, Trusts and Estates Section) and American (Member, Taxation Section and Real Property, Probate and Trusts Section) Bar Associations. **PRACTICE AREAS:** Tax Law; Estate Planning; Probate and Trust.

CAA1038B

---

## OLIVER, VOSE, SANDIFER, MURPHY & LEE

*A PROFESSIONAL CORPORATION*

THE PARK, SECOND FLOOR
281 SOUTH FIGUEROA STREET
**LOS ANGELES, CALIFORNIA 90012**
Telephone: 213-621-2000
Telecopier: 213-621-2211

*Litigation and Appellate Matters, Eminent Domain and Inverse Condemnation, Municipal Law, General Redevelopment Counsel Services, Land Use and Real Estate Development Services, Administrative Law Practice and Municipal/Personal Injury Defense Work.*

FIRM PROFILE: The firm, including its predecessor, was formed in 1966 and is presently comprised of 10 attorneys. Each attorney has brought to the firm unique experience in government which allows the firm to provide quality services to its clients. The firm is small enough to devote specialized attention to each of its clients, yet large enough to service the needs of large clients.

**CHARLES S. VOSE,** born Vallejo, California, June 7, 1947; admitted to bar, 1977, California. *Education:* Long Beach State College (B.A., 1972); Western State University College of Law (J.D., 1977). General/Special Counsel, Riverside Redevelopment Agency, 1984—. City Attorney: City of Covina, 1988—; City of South Pasadena, 1985-1991; City of Hermosa Beach, 1989-1994; City of Calabasas, 1991—. Deputy City Attorney, City of Colvina, 1978-1987. *Member:* Long Beach, Los Angeles County and American Bar Associations; State Bar of California. **PRACTICE AREAS:** Municipal; Land Use and Real Estate Development Services; General Redevelopment Counsel Services; Real Estate.

**CONNIE COOKE SANDIFER,** born Missoula, Montana, October 22, 1952; admitted to bar, 1978, California. *Education:* University of California at San Diego (B.A., 1973); University of San Diego (J.D., 1978). Assistant City Attorney, City of Covina, 1980—. Deputy City Attorney, City of Cudahy, 1980-1982. *Member:* Los Angeles County and American Bar Associations; State Bar of California. **PRACTICE AREAS:** Eminent Domain; Inverse Condemnation; Civil Litigation.

**JAMES DUFF MURPHY,** born Tucson, Arizona, February 21, 1954; admitted to bar, 1982, California, U.S. District Court, Central District of California and U.S. Court of Appeals, Ninth Circuit. *Education:* University of Southern California (A.B., magna cum laude, 1976); Loyola Law School (J.D., 1982). Phi Beta Kappa; Phi Kappa Phi. Adjunct Professor, Real Property Law, La Verne University College of Law, 1987-1988. *Member:* Los Angeles County (Member, Judicial Evaluation Committee, 1988—) and American Bar Associations; The State Bar of California (Committee on Condemnation, 1989—; Executive Committee, Los Angeles County Bar Barristers, 1988-1990). **PRACTICE AREAS:** Eminent Domain; Inverse Condemnation; Civil Litigation.

**EDWARD W. LEE,** born San Antonio, Texas, August 25, 1950; admitted to bar, 1987, California. *Education:* University of California at Davis (B.A.,1973); Southwestern University School of Law (J.D., 1985). Project Manager, Compton Redevelopment Agency, 1978-1981. Project Coordinator, Glendale Redevelopment Agency, 1981-1987. Assistant General Counsel, Riverside Redevelopment Agency, 1987-1995. Assistant City Attorney: City of Covina, 1987—City of Hermosa Beach, 1989-1994. City Attorney, City of South Pasadena, 1991-1996; City Attorney, City of Bell, 1994—. *Member:* Los Angeles County Bar Association; State Bar of California; Southern California Chinese Lawyers Association; National Association of Housing and Redevelopment Officials. **PRACTICE AREAS:** Municipal; Land Use and Real Estate Development Services; General Redevelopment Counsel Services; Real Estate.

**ROGER W. SPRINGER,** born Philadelphia, Pennsylvania, June 20, 1945; admitted to bar, 1973, California. *Education:* San Diego State University (B.A., 1969); University of San Diego (J.D., 1972). Assistant City Attorney, City of Covina, 1984-1990. *Member:* Los Angeles County Bar Association (Member, Litigation Section); State Bar of California; Association of Southern California Defense Counsel; California Trial Lawyers Association; Los Angeles Trial Lawyers Association. **PRACTICE AREAS:** Personal Injury; Appeals.

*(This Listing Continued)*

**MARY L. MCMASTER,** born Minneapolis, Minnesota, November 25, 1960; admitted to bar, 1990, California. *Education:* Occidental College (B.A., cum laude, 1983); University of California, Los Angeles Graduate School of Architecture and Urban Planning (M.A., Urban Planning, 1986); Boalt Hall School of Law, University of California, Berkeley (J.D., 1990). Phi Beta Kappa. Moot Court Board. Notes and Comments Editor, Ecology Law Quarterly, 1989-1990. *Member:* Los Angeles County Bar Association; State Bar of California; American Planning Association; International Right of Way Association. **PRACTICE AREAS:** Municipal Law; Land Use; Environmental; Eminent Domain.

**ARTHUR J. HAZARABEDIAN,** born Oakland, California, July 21, 1962; admitted to bar, 1988, California. *Education:* University of California at Davis (B.A, 1985); Loyola Marymount University (J.D., cum laude, 1988). Order of the Coif. Editor, Loyola Law Review, 1987-1988. Adjunct Professor of Remedies, University of La Verne Law School, 1992—. *Member:* Los Angeles County (Member, Eminent Domain and Land Valuation Committee) and American Bar Associations; Armenian-American Bar Association. **PRACTICE AREAS:** Eminent Domain; Inverse Condemnation; Land Use; Appeals.

**BRADLEY E. WOHLENBERG,** born Evanston, Illinois, July 18, 1966; admitted to bar, 1994, California. *Education:* University of California at Riverside (B.A., 1989); Loyola Law School (J.D., 1994). *Member:* Los Angeles County Bar Association; State Bar of California. **PRACTICE AREAS:** Municipal; General Redevelopment.

**TIMOTHY J. CHUNG,** born Los Angeles, California, June 24, 1963; admitted to bar, 1994, California. *Education:* Claremont McKenna College (B.A., 1985); Loyola Law School (J.D., 1994). Phi Beta Kappa. **PRACTICE AREAS:** Municipal Law.

**KRISTIN B. MENDENHALL,** born January 17, 1960; admitted to bar, 1992, California. *Education:* Stanford University (A.B., 1981); Loyola University of Los Angeles (J.D., 1992).

*OF COUNSEL*

**WILLIAM B. BARR,** born Glendale, California, March 24, 1939; admitted to bar, 1965, California. *Education:* University of Southern California (B.S.L., 1962; LL.B., 1964). Phi Delta Phi. Principal Deputy City Attorney, City of Los Angeles, 1965-1974. *Member:* Los Angeles County Bar Association; State Bar of California. **PRACTICE AREAS:** Eminent Domain; Inverse Condemnation; Civil Litigation.

REPRESENTATIVE CLIENT: Cities of Anaheim, Bell, Brea, Calabasas, Carson, Cathedral City, Compton, South Lake Tahoe.
AGENCY COUNSEL CLIENTS: Anaheim Housing Authority; Anaheim Redevelopment Agency; Brea Redevelopment Agency; Buena Park Redevelopment Agency; Compton Redevelopment Agency; Covina Redevelopment Agency; Glendale Redevelopment Agency; Los Angeles Community Redevelopment Agency; Riverside Redevelopment Agency; County of Santa Barbara; South Lake Tahoe Redevelopment Agency; Temple City Redevelopment Agency; West Covina Redevelopment Agency.

## GARY K. OLSEN

SUITE 1800
2049 CENTURY PARK EAST
LOS ANGELES, CALIFORNIA 90067
Telephone: 310-277-3603
Fax: 310-785-0506

*Family Law*

**GARY K. OLSEN,** born Reedley, California, May 25, 1943; admitted to bar, 1970, California and U.S District Court, Central District of California; 1975, U.S. Supreme Court. *Education:* University of Santa Clara (B.A., 1966); City of London College (International Law, with distinction and merit, 1968); University of California (J.D., 1969). Mediator, Family Law, Los Angeles Superior Court, Central District. *Member:* State Bar of California. (Certified Specialist, Family Law, The State Bar of California Board of Legal Specialization). **PRACTICE AREAS:** Divorce Law.

## ROGER M. OLSEN

A PROFESSIONAL CORPORATION
Established in 1989
UNION BANK PLAZA
445 SOUTH FIGUEROA, 24TH FLOOR
LOS ANGELES, CALIFORNIA 90071
Telephone: 213-488-1870
Telecopy: 213-488-1861

*Federal and State Taxation Law, Civil, Criminal and Tax Litigation.*

**ROGER MILTON OLSEN,** admitted to bar, 1969, California; 1977, District of Columbia. *Education:* University of California at Berkeley (A.B., 1964); Boalt Hall School of Law, University of California (J.D., 1968); George Washington University (LL.M., Taxation, 1977). Recipient, Edmund J. Randolph Award, 1987. Deputy District Attorney, Alameda County District Attorneys Office, 1969-1972. Deputy Assistant Attorney General, Criminal Division, U.S. Department of Justice, Washington D.C., 1981-1983. Trial Attorney, 1972-1976, Deputy Assistant Attorney General, 1983-1985 and Assistant Attorney General, 1985-1987, Tax Division, U.S. Department of Justice. Author: "Criminal Tax Procedure," Commerce Clearing House Tax Transactions Library, Vol. I 1989, Vol. II 1990; "Criminal Tax Procedure," Little, Brown & Co., 1995; "What Every Tax Lawyer Should Know About Representing Clients Accused of Tax Fraud, The Receipt of Illegal Income, or the Failure to Report Income," 40th U.S.C. Law Center Tax Institute, January, 1988. Advisor, The Department of Justice Manual, Prentice Hall Law and Business; Editorial Advisory Board, The DOJ Alert, Prentice Hall Law and Business. *Member:* Los Angeles County and American Bar Associations; State Bar of California (Member, Executive Committee, Taxation Section, 1992-1995); The District of Columbia Bar. Fellow, American College of Tax Counsel.

## O'MELVENY & MYERS LLP

Established in 1885
400 SOUTH HOPE STREET
LOS ANGELES, CALIFORNIA 90071-2899
Telephone: 213-669-6000
Cable Address: "Moms"
Facsimile: 213-669-6407
Email: omminfo@omm.com

*Century City, California Office:* 1999 Avenue of the Stars, 90067-6035. Telephone: 310-553-6700. Facsimile: 310-246-6779.
*Newport Beach, California Office:* 610 Newport Center Drive, 92660-6429. Telephone: 714-760-9600. Cable Address: "Moms". Facsimile: 714-669-6994.
*San Francisco, California Office:* Embarcadero Center West Tower, 275 Battery Street, 94111-3305. Telephone: 415-984-8700. Facsimile: 415-984-8701.
*New York, New York Office:* Citicorp Center, 153 East 53rd Street, 10022-4611. Telephone: 212-326-2000. Facsimile: 212-326-2061.
*Washington, D.C. Office:* 555 13th Street, N.W., 20004-1109. Telephone: 202-383-5300. Cable Address: "Moms". Facsimile: 202-383-5414.
*London, England Office:* 10 Finsbury Square, London, EC2A 1LA. Telephone: 0171-256-8451. Facsimile: 0171-638-8205.
*Tokyo, Japan Office:* Sanbancho KB-6 Building, 6 Sanbancho, Chiyoda-ku, Tokyo 102, Japan. Telephone: 03-3239-2900. Facsimile: 03-3239-2432.
*Hong Kong Office:* Suite 1905, Peregrine Tower, Lippo Centre, 89 Queensway, Central, Hong Kong. Telephone: 852-2523-8266. Facsimile: 852-2522-1760.
*Shanghai, Peoples Republic of China Office:* Shanghai International Trade Centre, Suite 2011, 2200 Yan An Road West, Shanghai, 200335, PRC. Telephone: 86-21-6219-5363. Facsimile: 86-21-6275-4949.

*General Civil Litigation, Appellate Practice, and Criminal Trials Practice in all State and Federal Courts. Administrative; Antitrust; Banking; Bankruptcy; Commercial; Communications; Construction; Corporation and Corporate Financing; Environmental; Immigration and Naturalization; Insurance Coverage Defense; Intellectual Property; International Business; Labor and Employment; Employment Benefits; Media and Entertainment; Municipal; Municipal Zoning and Municipal Finance; Natural Resources; Oil and Gas; Patent, Trademark, Copyright and Unfair Competition; Probate, Trusts and Estate Planning; Public Utilities; Real Estate; Securities; and Tax Law.*

(This Listing Continued)

CALIFORNIA—LOS ANGELES                          MARTINDALE-HUBBELL LAW DIRECTORY 1997

**O'MELVENY & MYERS LLP,** Los Angeles—Continued

FIRM PROFILE: *O'Melveny & Myers LLP, founded over 110 years ago on January 2, 1885, is the oldest law firm in Los Angeles. Since that time, we have grown from two attorneys in two rooms specializing in the local concerns of a frontier community to a firm of more than 500 lawyers involved in matters of regional, national and global concern.*

*Initially, the growth of our firm paralleled the growth of Los Angeles. Under founder Henry O'Melveny, the firm benefited from the first great California land and population booms that transformed a small outpost into one of the nation's most important cities. Our practice kept pace with the region's growth, and the early decades of the century saw O'Melveny attorneys working on behalf of clients in the aircraft, oil, motion picture and utility sectors. In the post-World War II period, leadership passed to John O'Melveny, who presided over the development of the modern firm until 1970. The ensuing years have seen a dramatic acceleration of our practice on both the national and international fronts: today O'Melveny ranks as one of the largest law firms in the world.*

*Each of our ten offices - Los Angeles, Century City, Newport Beach, San Francisco, Washington, D.C., New York, Tokyo, London, Hong Kong and Shanghai - is specifically located both to provide service affecting a particular region and to contribute important strengths and specializations to the firm as a whole.*

*Office-to-office collaborations are the norm, with attorneys on different coasts and different continents working together to structure complex transactions and to resolve important controversies.*

*Among our lawyers are many who have distinguished themselves through their leadership at the Bar or in public service. Our ranks include former Executive Branch and Capitol Hill policymakers; some of the nation's leading litigators and labor lawyers; recognized experts in public finance, financial institutions, corporate, securities, entertainment, real estate, bankruptcy, constitutional and tax law; and the nation's foremost practitioners in representations concerning the Europe, Latin America, and the Pacific Rim. This combination of highly skilled lawyers and a strategic presence in key economic centers enables O'Melveny to offer our clients the highest level of legal service and consultation.*

### SENIOR PARTNER

**WARREN CHRISTOPHER,** born Scranton, North Dakota, October 27, 1925; admitted to bar, 1949, California; 1953, U.S. Supreme Court; 1972, District of Columbia; 1984, New York. *Education:* University of Southern California (B.S., 1945); Stanford University (J.D., 1949). Order of the Coif. President, Stanford Law Review, 1947-1948. Law Clerk to Mr. Justice Douglas, Supreme Court of the United States, 1949-1950. Deputy Attorney General of the United States, 1967-1969. Deputy Secretary of State of the United States, 1977-1981. Secretary of State of the United States, 1993-1997. *Member:* Los Angeles County (President, 1974-1975) and American (Chairman, Judiciary Committee, 1975-1977) Bar Associations. Fellow, American College of Trial Lawyers. (Century City Office; also in Los Angeles and Washington, D.C. Offices).

### PARTNERS

**DOUGLAS W. ABENDROTH,** born Seattle, Washington, December 9, 1952; admitted to bar, 1982, California and U.S. District Court, Central District of California; 1983, U.S. District Court, Southern, Northern and Eastern Districts of California and U.S. Court of Appeals, Ninth Circuit; 1995, U.S. District Court, District of Arizona. *Education:* University of California at Los Angeles (B.A., magna cum laude, 1976); Loyola Law School of Los Angeles (J.D., magna cum laude, 1982). Member, St. Thomas More Law Honor Society. Staff Member, 1980-1981 and Chief Note and Comment Editor, 1981-1982, Loyola Los Angeles Law Review. Author: Comment, "Religious Meetings on Public School Property: The Constitutional Dimensions of Church-State Neutrality," 15 Loyola of Los Angeles Law Review 103, 1981. *Member:* Orange County (Member, Business Litigation Section), Federal Bar (Orange County) and American Bar Associations; Orange County Bar Foundation (Director, 1993-1994); Orange County Federal Bar Association (Director, 1994-1995). (Newport Beach Office). **PRACTICE AREAS:** Commercial Litigation; Intellectual Property, Real Estate and Bankruptcy Workouts; Lender Liability Litigation; Trademarks; Copyrights; Trade Secrets.

**WILLIAM G. ADAMS,** born Dallas, Oregon, July 26, 1939; admitted to bar, 1969, California; 1983, Conseil Juridique, France. *Education:* Stanford University (A.B., 1963); University of Utah (J.D., 1968). Order of the Coif; Phi Kappa Phi; Phi Delta Phi. Editor-in-Chief, Utah Law Review, 1967-1968. Member, Committee on Non Profit Corporations and Unincorporated Associations, State Bar of California, 1988-1992. *Member:* Orange County and American Bar Associations. (Newport Beach Office). **LAN-**

*(This Listing Continued)*

CAA1040B

**GUAGES:** French. **PRACTICE AREAS:** Corporate Law; Securities; International Law. **Email:** wadams@omm.com

**WALLACE M. ALLAN,** born Ridgecrest, California, April 17, 1954; admitted to bar, 1981, California. *Education:* University of California at Berkeley (A.B., 1976); George Washington University (J.D., 1981). *Member:* American Bar Association. **PRACTICE AREAS:** Automobile Manufacturers Dealers Disputes; General Commercial Litigation.

**RUSSELL G. ALLEN,** born Ottumwa, Iowa, November 7, 1946; admitted to bar, 1971, California. *Education:* Grinnell College (B.A., 1968); Stanford University (J.D., 1971). Order of the Coif. Member, Board of Editors, Stanford Law Review, 1969-1971. Member, Board of Visitors, Stanford Law School, 1993-1996. Fellow, American College of Trust and Estate Counsel. [Capt., U.S. Air Force, JAGC, 1971-1975]. (Certified Specialist, Probate, Estate Planning and Trust Law, The State Bar of California Board of Legal Specialization) (Newport Beach Office). **PRACTICE AREAS:** Trusts and Estates and related Transfer Tax; Fiduciary Law. **Email:** rallen@omm.com

**KERMIT W. ALMSTEDT,** born St. Louis County, Missouri, May 24, 1945; admitted to bar, 1970, Missouri; 1971, U.S. Court of Appeals, Eighth Circuit; 1974, U.S. District Court, Western District of Missouri; 1979, U.S. Supreme Court; 1981, District of Columbia. *Education:* Southeast Missouri University (B.S., 1967); University of Missouri-Kansas City (J.D., with honors, 1970). Member, Bench and Robe. Member, University of Missouri Law Review, 1969-1970. Trial Attorney, Anti-Trust Division, U.S. Department of Justice (honors program), 1970-1971. Assistant Attorney General, Chief Counsel, Antitrust Division, State of Missouri, 1971-1977. Legislative Assistant to U.S. Senator John C. Danforth, 1977-1981. *Member:* The District of Columbia Bar; The Missouri Bar; American Bar Association. (Washington, D.C. Office). **PRACTICE AREAS:** Antitrust; Customs Law; International Trade. **Email:** kalmstedt@omm.com

**JOHN L. ALTIERI, JR.,** born New Rochelle, New York, June 1, 1946; admitted to bar, 1972, New York, U.S. District Court, District of Columbia and U.S. Court of Appeals, Second Circuit; 1973, Connecticut, District of Columbia and U.S. District Court, Southern District of New York; 1977, U.S. District Court, Eastern District of New York; 1985, U.S. Supreme Court; 1989 , U.S. Court of Appeals, Sixth Circuit and Michigan; 1990, U.S. District Court, District of Connecticut; 1992, U.S. District Court, Northern District of New York and Vermont. *Education:* Georgetown University (A.B., 1968; J.D., 1971). Member, Executive Board and Lead Articles Editor, Georgetown Law Journal, 1970-1971. *Member:* Association of the Bar of the City of New York (Member: Committee on the Judiciary, 1983-1986; Committee on Transportation Law, 1979-1982; Secretary, Committee on Law Firm Management, 1987-1989); New York State Bar Association; The District of Columbia Bar. (New York, N.Y. Office). **PRACTICE AREAS:** Insurance Coverage Litigation; Business Fraud Litigation; Banking Litigation; Antitrust. **Email:** jaltieri@omm.com

**BRIAN C. ANDERSON,** born Berkeley, California, October 27,1959; admitted to bar, 1986, California; 1987, U.S. Court of Appeals, District of Columbia Circuit; 1988, District of Columbia; 1989, U.S. Court of International Trade; 1990, U.S. District Court, District of Columbia; 1994, U.S. Court of Appeals, Second Circuit; 1995, U.S. Court of Appeals, Eleventh Circuit; 1996, U.S. Court of Appeals, Fifth Circuit. *Education:* University of California at Berkeley (B.A., magna cum laude, 1982); Stanford University (J.D., with honors, 1986). Phi Beta Kappa. Note Editor, Stanford Law Review, 1984-1986. Law Clerk to Honorable Laurence H. Silberman, U.S. Court of Appeals, D.C. Circuit, 1986-1987. Special Assistant to the General Counsel, U.S. Department of Education, 1987-1989. (Washington, D.C. Office). **PRACTICE AREAS:** Litigation; Class Action Litigation. **Email:** banderson@omm.com

**D. STEPHEN ANTION,** born Oklahoma City, Oklahoma, September 8, 1961; admitted to bar, 1986, California and U.S. District Court, Central District of California. *Education:* University of California at Los Angeles (B.A., magna cum laude, 1983); Boalt Hall School of Law, University of California (J.D., 1986). Order of the Coif. *Member:* Los Angeles County Bar Association (Member, Federal Securities Subcommittee, 1986—; Member, Corporate and Securities Law and Regulation Committee, 1994—). **PRACTICE AREAS:** Corporate Law; Securities; Mergers, Acquisitions and Divestitures; Computers and Software. **Email:** santion@omm.com

**DALE M. ARAKI,** born Berkeley, California, March 23, 1960; admitted to bar, 1986, California and U.S. District Court, Central District of California; 1994, Japan, Gaikokuho-Jimu Bengoshi. *Education:* University of Hawaii (B.A., 1982); Harvard University (J.D., 1986). Phi Beta Kappa. Author: "Minority Investments in U.S. Companies," Journal of the Japanese Institute of International Business Law (Kokusai Shōji Hōmu) Vol. 18, No.

*(This Listing Continued)*

12 (1990). Administrative Partner of the Tokyo, Japan Office. *Member:* Tokyo Dai-Ni Bar Association. (Tokyo, Japan Office; may also be contacted at the Los Angeles Office). *LANGUAGES:* Japanese. *PRACTICE AREAS:* Corporate Law; Securities Law; International transactional Law. *Email:* daraki@omm.com

**SETH ARONSON,** born New York, N.Y., May 15, 1955; admitted to bar, 1981, California; 1983, U.S. District Court, Central District of California; 1985, U.S. District Court, Southern and Northern Districts of California and U.S. Court of Appeals, Ninth Circuit; 1987, U.S. Supreme Court; 1989, U.S. Court of Appeals, Eighth Circuit. *Education:* Ohio University (B.B.A., cum laude, 1978); Loyola of Los Angeles Law School (J.D., with honors, 1981). Member, National Panel of Arbitrators, American Arbitration Association. Author: "Emerging Theories of Liability: Corporate Fiduciaries Who Leave to Compete with Their Former Employers," The Journal of Proprietary Rights (April 1991, Prentice Hall). *Member:* Los Angeles County and American (Member, Litigation Section Committees on Federal Procedure, Class Actions and Derivative Suits, Trial Practice, Securities Litigation and Business Torts) Bar Associations; The Association of Business Trial Lawyers (Board of Governors, 1993—); Legal Aid Foundation of Los Angeles (Board of Directors, 1994—). *PRACTICE AREAS:* Securities Litigation; RICO; Professional Liability Defense; Advertising Liability; Unfair Competition; Directors and Officers Liability. *Email:* saronson@omm.com

**JAMES R. ASPERGER,** born Fresno, California, March 10, 1953; admitted to bar, 1978, California; 1980, District of Columbia. *Education:* University of California at Davis (B.A., with highest honors, 1975); University of California at Los Angeles (J.D., 1978). Phi Beta Kappa; Order of the Coif. Associate Editor, 1976-1977 and Editor-in-Chief, 1977-1978, UCLA Law Review. Law Clerk to: Justice Stanley Mosk, Supreme Court of the State of California, 1978-1979; Justice William H. Rehnquist, U.S. Supreme Court, 1979-1980. Assistant United States Attorney, Central District of California, 1983-1993 (Chief, Major Frauds Section, 1990-1993; Deputy Chief, Major Frauds Section, 1987-1990). Author: *"California's Energy Commission:* Illusions of a One-Step Power Plant Siting Agency," 25 UCLA Law Review 1313, 1977; Articles on Search Warrants, Arrest Warrants, Vagrancy Laws and Overruling, published in Encyclopedia of the American Constitution (L. Levy & K. Karst, 1985). Co-Author, *Forward and Afterward, Toward a Center For State and Local Legal Advocacy,* 31 Catholic University Law Review, 367 and 502 (1982). *Member:* The District of Columbia Bar; American Bar Association (Member: Criminal Justice Section; Litigation Section, Administrative Law and Regulatory Practice; and California Regional White Collar Crime Subcommittee, 1991—); Association of Business Trial Lawyers; Wong Sun Society. *PRACTICE AREAS:* Litigation; Securities Enforcement; White Collar Criminal Defense. *Email:* jasperger@omm.com

**GARY BARNETT,** born Chicago, Illinois, December 20, 1955; admitted to bar, 1981, Oklahoma; 1986, New York; 1989, California. *Education:* University of Tulsa (B.S., with honors, 1978; J.D., with honors, 1981); New York University (LL.M., 1986). Phi Delta Phi. Recipient, American Jurisprudence Awards. *Member:* American Bar Association. (New York, N.Y. Office).

**GEORGE M. BARTLETT,** born Tucson, Arizona, February 26, 1943; admitted to bar, 1973, California. *Education:* Stanford University (A.B., 1966); California Western School of Law (J.D., 1973). Editor-in-Chief, California Western Law Review, 1972-1973. Fellow, University of Pennsylvania Law School Center for Study of Financial Institutions, 1973-1974. *Member:* Los Angeles County and American (Member, Committee on Federal Regulation of Securities) Bar Associations. *PRACTICE AREAS:* Mutual Funds; Securities Regulation; Corporate Finance.

**THOMAS W. BAXTER,** born Los Angeles, California, October 9, 1954; admitted to bar, 1983, California; 1992, New York. *Education:* Colorado College (B.A., 1977); Hastings College of the Law, University of California (J.D., magna cum laude, 1983). Order of the Coif. Member, Thurston Society. Member, Hastings Communications and Entertainment Law Review, 1981-1982. *PRACTICE AREAS:* Corporate Banking; Corporate Finance; Securities; Structured Finance.

**JOHN H. BEISNER,** born Salina, Kansas, February 24, 1953; admitted to bar, 1978, California and U.S. District Court, Central District of California; 1980, District of Columbia and U.S. District Court, District of Columbia; 1985, U.S. Supreme Court. *Education:* University of Kansas (B.A., with distinction, 1975); University of Michigan (J.D., 1978). Phi Beta Kappa. Associate Editor, 1976-1977 and Administrative Editor, 1977-1978, Michigan Law Review. Author: "Conflicts of Interest and The Changing Concept of Marriage: The Congressional Compromise," 75 Michigan Law Review 1647, 1977. Member, State Colleges Coordinating Committee, Kansas Board of Regents, 1974-1975. *Member:* The District of Columbia Bar; Federal and American Bar Associations; American Law Institute; Federal Communications Bar Association. (Washington, D.C. Office). *PRACTICE AREAS:* Complex Litigation; Communications Law.

**CHARLES W. BENDER,** born Cape Girardeau, Missouri, October 2, 1935; admitted to bar, 1965, California; 1979, U.S. Supreme Court. *Education:* Harvard University (A.B., magna cum laude, 1960); Harvard Law School (LL.B., magna cum laude, 1963). Member, Board of Editors, 1961-1963 and Articles Editor, 1962-1963, Harvard Law Review. Sheldon Travelling Fellow from Harvard Law School, 1963-1964. Chairman of the Management Committee. *Member:* Los Angeles County and American Bar Associations.

**BEN E. BENJAMIN,** born Chicago, Illinois, August 26, 1941; admitted to bar, 1970, California; 1976, District of Columbia. *Education:* United States Military Academy (B.S., 1963); University of Texas (J.D., 1970). Chancellors. Associate Editor, Texas Law Review, 1968-1969. *Member:* The District of Columbia Bar; American Bar Association. (Washington, D.C. Office). *PRACTICE AREAS:* Taxation.

**KENDALL R. BISHOP,** born Los Angeles, California, March 3, 1939; admitted to bar, 1965, California. *Education:* Stanford University (A.B., with distinction, 1961); Boalt Hall School of Law, University of California (J.D., 1964). Order of the Coif. Member of Staff, 1962-1963 and Research Editor, 1963-1964, California Law Review. Partner-in-Charge, Century City Office. *Member:* Los Angeles County and American Bar Associations. (Century City and Los Angeles Offices). *PRACTICE AREAS:* Corporate Law; Securities; Mergers, Acquisitions and Divestitures. *Email:* kbishop@omm.com

**LEAH MARGARET BISHOP,** born New York, N.Y., November 2, 1954; admitted to bar, 1980, New York and U.S. District Court, Southern and Eastern Districts of New York; 1981, California and U.S. District Court, Central District of California. *Education:* Brandeis University (B.A., summa cum laude, 1975); Columbia University (J.D., 1979). Phi Beta Kappa. Staff Member, 1977-1978 and Editor, 1978-1979, Columbia Law Review. Law Clerk to the Honorable Edmund L. Palmieri, Senior, U.S. District Judge, Southern District of New York, 1979-1980. *Member:* Los Angeles County and American Bar Associations. Fellow, American College of Trust and Estate Counsel. (Century City Office). *PRACTICE AREAS:* Estate Administration; Taxation; Estate Planning; Tax Exempt Organizations, Nonprofit and Charitable Organizations. *Email:* lbishop@omm.com

**ROBERT D. BLASHEK, III,** born Columbus, Ohio, November 18, 1954; admitted to bar, 1980, New York, California and U.S. District Court, Central District of California. *Education:* Brown University (A.B., magna cum laude, 1976); Columbia University (J.D., 1979). Phi Beta Kappa. Staff Member, 1977-1978 and Editor, 1978-1979, Columbia Law Review. Harlan Fiske Stone Scholar. Clerk to Honorable Robert J. Kelleher, U.S. District Judge, Central District of California, 1979-1980. *Member:* Los Angeles County (Chairman, Corporate Tax Section, 1995-1996) and American Bar Associations. (Century City Office). *PRACTICE AREAS:* Federal Income Tax; California State Income Tax.

**DONALD T. BLISS, JR.,** born Norwalk, Connecticut, November 24, 1941; admitted to bar, 1967, Trust Territory of the Pacific Islands; 1969, New York; 1970, District of Columbia and U.S. Supreme Court (Not admitted in California). *Education:* Principia College (B.A. with highest honors, 1963); Harvard University (J.D. cum laude, 1966). Peace Corp Volunteer Lawyer, Micronesia, 1966-1968. Assistant to the Secretary of Health, Education and Welfare, 1969-1973. Special Assistant to the Administrator of the Environmental Protection Agency, 1973-1974. Assistant to the Administrator, Agency for International Development, U.S. Department of State, 1974-1975. Deputy General Counsel, U.S. Department of Transportation, 1975-1977. Acting General Counsel, U.S. Department of Transportation, 1976-1977. *Member:* The District of Columbia Bar (Co-Chair, Section on Administrative Law and Agency Practice, 1989-1990) ; Federal (Chair, Transportation Law Section, 1988-1990) and American Bar Associations; National Health Lawyers Association. (Washington, D.C. Office). *PRACTICE AREAS:* Aviation; Health Law; Appellate Litigation; Administrative Law. *Email:* dbliss@omm.com

**RICHARD A. BOEHMER,** born St. Louis, Missouri, June 26, 1951; admitted to bar, 1976, California. *Education:* Harvey Mudd College and University of Southern California (B.A., 1973); Loyola University School of Law, Los Angeles (J.D., 1976). Phi Beta Kappa, Phi Kappa Phi. Staff member, Loyola of Los Angeles Law Review, 1974. Recipient, Loyola University School of Law Academic Scholarship, 1974 and 1975. *Member:* Los Angeles County and American Bar Associations. *PRACTICE AREAS:*

*(This Listing Continued)*

**O'MELVENY & MYERS LLP, Los Angeles—Continued**

Corporate Finance; Mergers, Acquisitions and Divestitures; General Corporate Law.

**DANIEL H. BOOKIN,** born Ottumwa, Iowa, October 16, 1951; admitted to bar, 1978, California. *Education:* University of Iowa (B.A., 1973); Yale University (J.D., 1976). Phi Beta Kappa. Member, Board of Editors, Yale Law Journal, 1975-1976. Law Clerk to Honorable Charles B. Renfrew, United States District Court, Northern District of California, 1976-1977. Assistant United States Attorney, Southern District of New York, 1978-1982. *Member:* Bar Association of San Francisco (Member, Litigation Section); State Bar of California (Member, Criminal Law Section); American Bar Association (Member: Criminal Justice and Litigation Sections); California Trial Lawyers Association; Association of Business Trial Lawyers. Fellow, American College of Trial Lawyers. (San Francisco Office). *PRACTICE AREAS:* Criminal Defense; Civil Litigation.

**BRIAN DAVID BOYLE,** born Covina, California, July 27, 1960; admitted to bar, 1986, California; 1989, District of Columbia. *Education:* Georgetown University (A.B., summa cum laude, 1982); Harvard University (J.D., magna cum laude, 1986). Member, Harvard Law Review, 1984-1986. Law Clerk to: Justice Antonin Scalia, U.S. Supreme Court, 1991-1992; Judge Laurence H. Silberman, U.S. Court of Appeals for the District of Columbia Circuit, 1988-1989. [Assistant to the General Counsel, U.S. Army, 1986-1988 and 1989-1991]. (Washington, D.C. Office). *PRACTICE AREAS:* Regulatory Enforcement; Commercial Litigation; Class Action Litigation.

**GREYSON LEE BRYAN,** born Los Angeles, California, July 31, 1949; admitted to bar, 1976, California; 1978, New York; 1985, District of Columbia; 1987, Japan (Gaikokuho-Jimu-Bengoshi) withdrew, 1990. *Education:* Stanford University (B.A., with distinction, 1971); Harvard University (J.D., cum laude, 1976). Recipient, Harvard University Sheldon Travelling Fellowship, 1976-1977. Author: "Tax Implications of Japanese Multinational Corporations," 8 New York University Journal of International Law and Politics 153, 1975; "Developed Nation Tax Law and Investment in LDC's," 17 Columbia Journal of Transnational Law 211, 1978; "Taxing Unfair International Trade Practices," Lexington Books, 1980; Co-author: with D. Boursereau, "Antidumping Law in the European Communities and the United States," 18 George Washington Journal of International Law and Economics 631, 1985; "International Trade Disputes Are Won, Not Lost," 136 Italian-American Business 37, 1985; "1984 nen Tsushoo Kanzeihoo no Tsushoohoo Shokitei ni Kansuru Yobichishiki," Commentary on the Trade and Tariff Act of 1984 in Beikoku no 1984 nen Tsushoo Kanzeihoo, Matushita, ed., 1985. Director of Training, 1979-1981 and Research Associate, 1981-1982, Harvard Law School International Tax Program. Adjunct Professor of Law, UCLA School of Law, 1994-1996. Adjunct Professor of International Business Law, UCLA Anderson Graduate School of Management, 1995-1996. Member, Board of Advisors, Harvard International Law Journal, 1982-1987 and Loyola of Los Angeles International and Comparative Law Journal, 1993—. *Member:* The District of Columbia Bar; American Law Institute (Member, Tax Advisory Group, Federal Income Tax Project, 1982-1984). *LANGUAGES:* French and Japanese. *PRACTICE AREAS:* International Business Transactions; International Trade; General Corporate Law. *Email:* gbryan@omm.com

**FRANCIS J. BURGWEGER, JR.,** born Evanston, Illinois, July 5, 1942; admitted to bar, 1971, California; 1988, New York. *Education:* Yale University (B.A., 1964); University of Pennsylvania (J.D., 1970). Comment Editor, University of Pennsylvania Law Review, 1969-1970. Law Clerk to Judge Shirley M. Hufstedler, U.S. Court of Appeals, Ninth Circuit, 1970-1971. *Member:* Association of the Bar of the City of New York; American Bar Association. (New York, N.Y. Office). *PRACTICE AREAS:* Real Estate; Environmental Law.

**JOSEPH A. CALABRESE,** born Paterson, New Jersey, June 8, 1956; admitted to bar, 1981, California and U.S. District Court, Central District of California. *Education:* Boston College (A.B., summa cum laude, 1978); Cornell University (J.D., cum laude, with specialization in International Legal Affairs, 1981). Staff Member, 1979-1980 and Articles Editor, 1980-1981, Cornell International Law Journal; Arbitration Panel of the American Film Marketing Association. *Member:* American Bar Association. (Century City Office). *PRACTICE AREAS:* Entertainment Law; Media Law; Finance.

**JERRY W. CARLTON,** born Stamford, Texas, November 17, 1941; admitted to bar, 1968, California. *Education:* North Texas State University (B.B.A., 1964); University of Texas (LL.B., 1967). Partner-in-Charge, Newport Beach Office. *Member:* Orange County and American Bar Associations. (Newport Beach Office). *PRACTICE AREAS:* Taxation.

*(This Listing Continued)*

**CORMAC J. CARNEY,** born Detroit, Michigan, May 6, 1959; admitted to bar, 1987, California; 1991, Illinois. *Education:* University of California at Los Angeles (B.A., 1983); Harvard University (J.D., 1987). (Newport Beach Office).

**DAVID W. CARTWRIGHT,** born Park Ridge, Illinois, June 11, 1956; admitted to bar, 1981, California and U.S. District Court, Central District of California. *Education:* College of William and Mary (A.B., 1978); University of Illinois (J.D., magna cum laude, 1981). Omicron Delta Epsilon; Phi Alpha Theta; Order of the Coif; Phi Alpha Delta. Member, University of Illinois Law Review, 1979-1981. Author: Comment, "Toward Formation of a Legal Basis for Interstate Banking Transactions in Illinois," University of Illinois Law Review, No. 2, 1981. Co-Author: "Convertible and Shared Appreciation Loans: Unclogging the Equity of Redemption," 20 Real Property, Probate and Trust Journal 821, 1985; "Clogging the Equity of Redemption: Old Wine in New Bottles," Probate and Property, November, 1987. (Century City Office). *LANGUAGES:* French. *PRACTICE AREAS:* Real Estate; Government Contracts.

**DALE M. CENDALI,** born New York, N.Y., February 11, 1959; admitted to bar, 1985, New York and U.S. District Court, Southern and Eastern Districts of New York; U.S. District Court, Eastern District of Michigan; U.S. District Court, Northern District of California. *Education:* Yale University (B.A., summa cum laude, 1981); Harvard University (J.D., 1984). Phi Beta Kappa. Editor-in-Chief, The Harvard Journal of Legislation, 1983-1984. Author: "Of Things to Come: The Actual Impact of Herbert v. Lando and a Proposed National Correction Statute," 22 Harvard Journal of Legislation, 1985; "The Employee's Perspective: Entering and Leaving the Employer-Employee Relationship, Planning for Possible Litigation Strategic Aspects of Litigation," Trade Secret Law Reporter, Vol. II, Nos. 10-11 (1987); "In Search of Truth, A Review of Renata Adler's Reckless Disregard," 15 Northern Kentucky Law Review 227 (1987); "Representing The Employee In A Trade Secret Case," The Corporate Analyst, August 1989 (First Author); "Representing The Employee In A Trade Secret Case," The Corporate Counsel's Guide to Protecting Trade Secrets Ch. 7.1 (1989) (First Author); "Enjoining A Tender Offer for Misuse of Confidential Information: Is It A Show-Stopper or Can The Bidder Cure?" The Journal of Proprietary Rights, December 1989 (Part I); January 1990 (Part II) (First Author), Abstract Reprinted in April, 1990 Bowne Digest for Corporate & Securities Lawyers. Co-Author: "The Work for Hire Doctrine After CCNV vs. Reid," New York State Bar Journal, July 1990; *"Lotus* Case Highlights Copyright Issues and High-Tech Problems," The National Law Journal, November, 1993; "Federal Preemption of State Dilution Statutes," The New York Law Journal, April 12, 1993; *SEGA* Case Suggests Protection Strategies," The National Law Journal, January 18, 1993. Author: *Author:* "Book Publishing: The Writer's Side," University of Houston Law Foundation and University of California at Davis School of Law, July 1993; *"Ferrari* Case Shows Collision of Competing Protection Concepts," The National Law Journal, October 12, 1992; "Fact-Compilating Ruling May Hinder Protection," The National Law Journal, June 17, 1991; "In *Lotus,* the 1st Circuit Departed From Precedent, Narrowing Protection For Developed Software and Giving Crazy Litigators A Blank Disk on Which to Write," The National Law Journal, May 15, 1995; "The Book Publishing Industry: Intellectual Property, Privacy, Libel and Contract Issues," The Texas Bar Association, March 1995; Computer Interfaces Test Copyright Law's Scope," The National Law Journal, October 31, 1994. Co-Author: "You Name It: To What Extent Can a Surname Be Used As a Trademark?" The Los Angeles Daily Journal and The San Francisco Journal, April 25, 1996. Frequent Lecturer on Media, Intellectual Property and Litigation Topics. *Member:* The Association of the Bar of the City of New York (Member, Committees on: Communications and Media Law; Copyright and Literary Property; Trademarks and Unfair Competition); New York State (Member, Sections on: Commercial and Federal Litigation, Entertainment, Arts and Sports; Chair, Subcommittee on the Works For Hire Doctrine, 1989-1990) and American (Member, Litigation Section; Programming Co-Chair, 1993 Annual Meeting; Member, Trial Evidence Committee, 1985-1994) Bar Associations. (New York, N.Y. Office). *PRACTICE AREAS:* Litigation; Intellectual Property; Media Law.

**THERESA A. CEREZOLA,** born New York, N.Y., July 21, 1953; admitted to bar, 1979, New York. *Education:* Manhattanville College (A.B., with honors, 1975); Columbia University (J.D., 1978). Harlan Fiske Stone Scholar. Staff Member, 1976-1977 and Notes Editor, 1977-1978, Columbia Law Review. *Member:* The Association of the Bar of the City of New York (Secretary, Real Property Law Committee, 1988-1990); American Bar Association; Association of Real Estate Women. (New York, N.Y. Office). *Email:* tcerezola@omm.com

*(This Listing Continued)*

**HOWARD CHAO,** born Taipei, Taiwan, June 13, 1954; admitted to bar, 1980, California and U.S. District Court, Central District of California. *Education:* Purdue University (B.S., 1976); Boalt Hall School of Law, University of California (J.D., 1980). Phi Beta Kappa; Phi Kappa Phi; Order of the Coif. International Rotary Fellow, 1979-1980. Associate Editor, California Law Review, 1977-1980. Administrative Partner of the Hong Kong and Shanghai Offices. (Hong Kong and Shanghai Offices; may also be contacted at the Los Angeles Office). LANGUAGES: Mandarin Chinese, French. *Email:* hchao@omm.com

**MARTIN S. CHECOV,** born Chicago, Illinois, October 3, 1955; admitted to bar, 1981, California. *Education:* University of British Columbia (B.A., 1977); Northwestern University (J.D., 1980). Order of the Coif. Member, Northwestern University Law Review, 1978-1980. Co-author: Manual of Complex Insurance Coverage Litigation (1995) (with co-members of the Task Force of the Insurance Coverage Litigation Committee, American Bar Association, Litigation Section). *Member:* Bar Association of San Francisco; American Bar Association (Member, Insurance Committee, Torts and Insurance Practice Section). (San Francisco Office). *PRACTICE AREAS:* Commercial Litigation; Insurance Coverage; Insurance Coverage Litigation. *Email:* mchecov@omm.com

**DENISE M. CLOLERY,** admitted to bar, 1983, California. *Education:* University of California at Los Angeles (B.A., summa cum laude, 1979); Harvard Law School (J.D., cum laude, 1983). Phi Beta Kappa; Pi Gamma Mu. Governor's Scholar. Member, Women's Law Association, 1981-1983. *Member:* Los Angeles County Bar Association. (New York, N.Y. Office and Century City, California Offices). LANGUAGES: Spanish and German. *PRACTICE AREAS:* Entertainment Transactional; Entertainment and Media Finance; Telecommunications; Complex Media Acquisitions; Interactive Multimedia. *Email:* dclolery@omm.com

**ALAN M. COHEN,** born 1950; admitted to bar, 1980, New York and U.S. District Court, Southern District of New York; 1981, U.S. Court of Appeals, Second Circuit. *Education:* Temple University (B.A., magna cum laude, 1972); Rutgers University (Ph.D., Political Science, 1976; J.D., with highest honors, 1979). Recipient: John Marshall Award for Outstanding Performance and Directors Award by U.S. Department of Justice. Chairman, Preventing and Detecting Money Laundering for Securities Firms and Financial Institutions, Institute for International Research, 1993-1996. Lectures: RICO Seminars; Securities and Commodities Fraud and Racketeering Law Seminars, Practicing Law Institute, American Bar Association, Chicago-Kent Commodities Law Institute and Futures Industry Association. *Member:* Association of the Bar of the City of New York (Member, Ethics Committee); American Bar Association (Chair, Subcommittee of Securities and Commodities Fraud of the White Collar Crime Committee, Criminal Justice Section). (New York, N.Y. Office). *PRACTICE AREAS:* Litigation; White Collar Criminal; Securities Regulation and Enforcement. *Email:* acohen@omm.com

**JAMES W. COLBERT, III,** born New York, N.Y., September 1, 1945; admitted to bar, 1971, California; 1990, U.S. Supreme Court. *Education:* Yale University (A.B., magna cum laude, 1967); Harvard University (J.D., magna cum laude, 1970). Phi Beta Kappa. Member, Harvard Law Review, 1968-1970. Law Clerk to Judge Shirley M. Hufstedler, U.S. Court of Appeals, Ninth Circuit, 1970-1971. *Member:* Los Angeles County Bar Association.

**WILLIAM N. COONEY,** born Rochester, New York, September 18, 1942; admitted to bar, 1972, Wisconsin; 1974, Georgia; 1981, California; 1982, District of Columbia. *Education:* Purdue University (B.S.E.E., 1964); University of Wisconsin (J.D., cum laude, 1972). Member, Wisconsin Law Review, Editorial Board, 1971-1972. *PRACTICE AREAS:* Real Estate. *Email:* wcooney@omm.com

**BERTRAND M. COOPER,** born Detroit, Michigan, April 27, 1942; admitted to bar, 1970, California. *Education:* Yale University (B.A., 1964); Northwestern University (J.D., magna cum laude, 1969). Order of the Coif. Editor-in-Chief, Northwestern University Law Review, 1968-1969. Adjunct Professor of Law, Trade Regulations, 1982 and Antitrust, 1984-1985, Southwestern University School of Law. Contributing author: "Antitrust Considerations Relating to PPOs," The New Healthcare Market, Dow Jones-Irwin (1985). Panelist: "Lender Liability Litigation 1990: Recent Developments" (Practising Law Institute); "The Lender Liability Pendulum and Other Issues in Real Property Workouts and Foreclosures" (California Continuing Education of the Bar, 1995); "Pretrial Hearings, Before Trial Proceedings and Settlement," 11th Annual Federal Practice Institute (California Continuing Education of the Bar, 1988); "Motions in Limine," 7th Annual Federal Practice Institute (California Continuing Education of the Bar, 1984); and "Per se v. Rule of Reason: the Changing Standard; Standing: Antitrust Injury," Competitive Practices Institute (California Continuing Education of the Bar, 1986). *Member:* Los Angeles County Bar Association; Commercial Disputes. *Email:* bcooper@omm.com

**STEPHEN A. COWAN,** born Baltimore, Maryland, May 11, 1943; admitted to bar, 1970, California; 1970, District of Columbia. *Education:* University of Michigan; University of California at Berkeley (A.B., with distinction, 1965; M.B.A., cum laude, 1966); Harvard University (J.D., cum laude, 1969). Phi Beta Kappa; Beta Gamma Sigma. Angell Scholar, University of Michigan. Co-Author, "Attorney's Guide of California Professional Corporations," 2nd Edition, 1973; "Trends in Residential Mortgage Financing," Vol. 13, No. 4 Real Property, Probate and Trust Journal 1075, American Bar Association, Winter, 1978; "Bankruptcy Considerations in Drafting Real Estate Documents," California Real Property Journal, Vol. 1, No. 1, Winter, 1982; "Applicability of Securities Laws to Real Estate Investments Contract," ALI-ABA/American College of Real Estate Lawyers, October, 1983. Co-Author: "Debt/Equity Transactions: An Objective Approach to Recharacterization," 310 Real Estate Law and Practice, Practising Law Institute 153, April, 1988; "Cutting Through the Complexities of Partnership Bankruptcy Law: An Update," 349 Real Estate Workouts and Bankruptcies 7 (April, 1990); "Partner as Partnership Creditor: Practical Issues Raised by Dual Capacity in Default Situations," 368 Real Estate Workouts and Bankruptcies 79 (April, 1991); "Pledges of Partnership Interests: Panacea or Pandora's Box?" 368 Real Estate Workouts and Bankruptcies 121 (April, 1991). Partner-in-Charge, San Francisco Office. *Member:* Bar Association of San Francisco (Chairman, Corporations Committee, 1974 and Member, Board of Directors, 1975-1976, Barristers Club); State Bar of California (Chairman, Real Property Law Section, 1979-1981); American Bar Association (Chairman: Real Estate Specialization Committee, 1974-1980; Real Property Legal Practice Methods, 1974-1980; Real Property, Probate and Trust Section; Council Member, 1979-1986; Finance Officer, 1986-1992; Division Director, 1992-1994; Chair-Elect, 1994-1995; Chair, 1995-1996; Member, Standing Committee on Lawyers Title Guaranty Funds, 1979-1984); American College of Real Estate Lawyers (Member, Board of Governors, 1983-1985; 1990—); Anglo-American Real Property Institute. (San Francisco Office). *PRACTICE AREAS:* Real Estate; Bankruptcy; Insolvency. *Email:* scowan@omm.com

**ARTHUR B. CULVAHOUSE, JR.,** born Athens, Tennessee, July 4, 1948; admitted to bar, 1973, Tennessee; 1977, California and District of Columbia; 1988, U.S. Supreme Court. *Education:* University of Tennessee (B.S., with high honors, 1970); New York University (J.D., 1973). Root Tilden Scholar. Editor-in-Chief, NYU Annual Survey of American Law, 1972-1973. Chief Legislative Assistant to Senator Howard H. Baker, Jr., 1973-1976. Counsel to the President of the United States, 1987-1989. Partner-in-Charege, Washington, D.C. Office. (Washington, D.C. Office). *PRACTICE AREAS:* Litigation; Corporate Litigation. *Email:* aculvahouse@omm.com

**MICHAEL A. CURLEY,** born Philadelphia, Pennsylvania, June 14, 1958; admitted to bar, 1983, California and U.S. District Court, Central District of California; 1985, Pennsylvania and U.S. District Court, Eastern District of Pennsylvania; 1989, New York and U.S. District Court, Eastern and Southern Districts of New York. *Education:* Drexel University (B.S., with high honors, 1980); Villanova University (J.D., with honors, 1983). Order of the Coif. Member, Villanova Law Review, 1982-1983. Author: Comment: "Employee Solicitation in Health Care Institutions," Vill. Law Rev., 1983; "Employment At Will--Not Necessarily," American Banking Association Journal, 1985; "Health Care Unit Determination," Hofstra Labor Law Journal, 1985. *Member:* American Bar Association (Member, Labor and Employment Law Section). (New York, N.Y. Office). *PRACTICE AREAS:* Labor and Employment Law.

**BRIAN S. CURREY,** born San Pedro, California, October 26, 1956; admitted to bar, 1981, District of Columbia and U.S. Court of Appeals, District of Columbia Circuit; 1982, U.S. District Court, District of Columbia; 1983, California and U.S. District Court, Central District of California; 1993, U.S. Supreme Court. *Education:* University of California at Davis (B.A., with honors, 1978); University of Virginia (J.D., 1981). Phi Kappa Phi; Omicron Delta Epsilon. Member, Editorial Board, Virginia Law Review, 1979-1981. *Member:* Los Angeles County and American (Member, Litigation and Natural Resources, Energy and Environment Sections) Bar Associations; District of Columbia Bar. *PRACTICE AREAS:* Business Litigation; Environmental Litigation. *Email:* bcurrey@omm.com

**JOHN F. DAUM,** born Washington, D.C., May 9, 1943; admitted to bar, 1971, District of Columbia; 1972, California. *Education:* Harvard University (B.A., summa cum laude, 1965); Yale University (LL.B., 1969). Phi

*(This Listing Continued)*

## O'MELVENY & MYERS LLP, Los Angeles—Continued

Beta Kappa; Order of the Coif. Member, Yale Law Journal, 1967-1969. *Member:* Los Angeles County and American Bar Associations. (Washington, D.C. Office). *PRACTICE AREAS:* Litigation.

**F. AMANDA DEBUSK,** born Chilhowie, Virginia, December 20, 1955; admitted to bar, 1981, District of Columbia. *Education:* University of Richmond (B.A., summa cum laude, 1976); Harvard University (J.D., 1981). Phi Beta Kappa. *Member:* The District of Columbia Bar; American Bar Association. (Washington, D.C. Office). *PRACTICE AREAS:* International Trade. *Email:* adebusk@omm.com

**JAMES H. DE MEULES,** born Seattle, Washington, March 31, 1945; admitted to bar, 1971, California. *Education:* Whitman College (A.B., 1967); Columbia University (J.D., 1970). Phi Beta Kappa. Articles Editor, Columbia Journal of Law and Social Problems, 1969-1970. Chairman, Financial Institutions Committee, Business Law Section, State Bar of California, 1977-1978. Fellow, American College of Investment Counsel. *PRACTICE AREAS:* Banking; Financial Transactions; Project Finance; Corporate Law. *Email:* jdemeules@omm.com

**DANIEL A. DESHON, IV,** born Sandpoint, Idaho, January 5, 1961; admitted to bar, 1986, California and U.S. District Court, Central District of California. *Education:* Washington State University (B.A., cum laude, 1983); Cornell University (J.D., 1986). Lead Articles Editor, Cornell International Law Journal, 1985-1986. (San Francisco Office). *PRACTICE AREAS:* Public Finance.

**CHARLES P. DIAMOND,** born New York, N.Y., November 26, 1947; admitted to bar, 1973, California. *Education:* University of California at Los Angeles (B.A., 1969); New York University (J.D., cum laude, 1973). Editor-in-Chief, New York University Law Review, 1972-1973. Law Clerk to Judge William Matthew Byrne, Jr., U.S. District Court, 1973-1974. L.A. Business Journal, Top 100 Law "Who's Who" (1995-1996). Faculty Member, 1994 National Institute of Trial Advocacy, Western Regional; 1994 ABA Sports & Entertainment Section. *Member:* Beverly Hills, Los Angeles County and American Bar Associations. (Century City Office). *PRACTICE AREAS:* Litigation; Entertainment Litigation. *Email:* cdiamond@omm.com

**THOMAS E. DONILON,** born Providence, Rhode Island, May 14, 1955; admitted to bar, 1986, District of Columbia. *Education:* Catholic University of America (B.A., summa cum laude, 1977); University of Virginia School of Law (J.D., 1985). Recipient, Catholic University President's Award as Outstanding Graduate and Phi Beta Kappa; Editorial Board, Virginia Law Review, 1982-1983. Office of Congressional Liaison, The White House, 1977-1979. National Delegation Selection Coordinator, Carter-Mondale Presidential Campaign, 1979-1980. National Campaign Coordinator, Mondale for President, Campaign 1983-1984. General Counsel, Site Selection Committee, Democratic National Convention, 1985. Assistant Secretary of State for Public Affairs, 1993-1996. Chief of Staff to the Secretary of State, 1994-1996. Recipient, Secretary of State's Distinguished Service Award, 1996. *Member:* District of Columbia and American Bar Associations; Council on Foreign Relations. (Washington, D.C. Office).

**ROBERT S. DRAPER,** born Boulder, Colorado, February 18, 1942; admitted to bar, 1968, California. *Education:* University of California at Berkeley (A.B., 1964); Boalt Hall School of Law, University of California (J.D., 1967). Order of the Golden Bear, London School of Economics (Ford Foundation Fellowship), 1967-1968. Seminars: "Antitrust," Faculty Member, Columbia Law School (1981); "Antitrust," 35th Annual Antitrust Law Institute (1993); "Jury Trials in High Tech Intellectual Property Litigation," American Conference Institute (1993, 1994, 1995). Author: "English New Towns: A Lesson for America" (1968); "Handling Copyright and Patent Issues in Intellectual Property Litigation: How to Help Juries Understand What Lawyers and Judges May Not," Jury Trials in Patent and High Tech Litigation, American Conference Institute (1993). Member, Ninth Circuit Judicial Conference (1989-1990). Board of Trustees of the Exceptional Children's Foundation (1988-1991). *Member:* Los Angeles County and American Bar Associations. *PRACTICE AREAS:* Antitrust; Civil Trials; Accounting Law; Intellectual Property Litigation. *Email:* bdraper@omm.com

**KAREN K. DREYFUS,** born Palo Alto, California, April 3, 1961; admitted to bar, 1987, California. *Education:* Cornell University (B.A., 1982); Hastings College of the Law, University of California (J.D., cum laude, 1987). Order of the Coif. Member, Thurston Society. Member, 1985-1986 and Note Editor, 1986-1987, Hastings Law Journal. *Member:* Orange County and American Bar Associations. (Newport Beach Office). *PRACTICE AREAS:* Corporate Law. *Email:* kdreyfus@omm.com

*(This Listing Continued)*

CAA1044B

**SCOTT H. DUNHAM,** born Seattle, Washington, May 7, 1950; admitted to bar, 1975, California; 1976, U.S. District Court, Central District of California; 1977, U.S. Supreme Court. *Education:* Washington State University (B.A., with highest honors, 1972); University of Washington (J.D., 1975). Order of the Coif; Phi Beta Kappa; Phi Kappa Phi; Omicron Delta Kappa; Phi Delta Phi (Magister, Ballinger Inn Chapter, 1974). Editor-in-Chief, Washington Law Review, 1974-1975. Author: Note, "State Taxation--Privately Held Leaseholds in Publicly Owned Land," 49 Washington Law Review 913, 1974; "Avoiding and Defending Wrongful Discharge Claims," Clark, Boardman, Callaghan, 1987. Co-Author, "Designing An Effective Fair Hiring and Termination Compliance Program," Clark Boardman Callaghan, 1993. Contributing Author: American Bar Association, 1981-1995 Book on Occupational Safety and Health; West's California Criminal Law, West Publishing, 1995. *Member:* Los Angeles County and American (Member, Labor and Employment Law Section, Committee on Occupational Safety and Health) Bar Associations. *PRACTICE AREAS:* Labor and Employment Law. *Email:* sdunham@omm.com

**ROBERT N. ECCLES,** born Madison, Wisconsin, May 13, 1947; admitted to bar, 1972, Wisconsin; 1981, District of Columbia, U.S. Supreme Court and U.S. Court of Appeals, Second, Third, Fourth, Fifth, Sixth, Ninth, Tenth and Eleventh Circuits and District of Columbia. *Education:* Harvard University (A.B., magna cum laude, 1969; J.D., 1972). Trial Attorney, U.S. Department of Justice, 1972-1977. Trial Attorney, 1977-1980, Deputy Associate Solicitor, 1980-1982, and Associate Solicitor, 1982-1988, U.S. Department of Labor. Editor, ERISA Litigation Reporter (1991—). (Washington, D.C. Office). *PRACTICE AREAS:* ERISA; ERISA Litigation; Employee Benefits; Employee Benefits Litigation.

**STEVEN L. EDWARDS,** born New York, N.Y., September 9, 1947; admitted to bar, 1973, California and U.S. District Court, Central District of California. *Education:* Lehigh University (B.A., with high honors, 1969) Phi Beta Kappa; New York University (J.D., 1973). Root-Tilden Scholar. Editor, NYU Law Review, 1972-1973. Licensed Real Estate Broker, California, 1981. Member, Real Property Law Section, State Bar of California. *Member:* National Association of Review Appraisers and Mortgage Underwriters. (Newport Beach Office). *PRACTICE AREAS:* Real Estate. *Email:* sedwards@omm.com

**MICHAEL J. FAIRCLOUGH,** born Salt Lake City, Utah, September 23, 1944; admitted to bar, 1972, California. *Education:* University of Utah (J.D., 1972). Editor in Chief, Utah Law Review, 1971-1972. Conseil Juridique, France 1981-1984. Member, Board of Visitors, Brigham Young University Law School (1992-1994). *Member:* Los Angeles County (Member, Executive Committee, Business and Corporations Law Section, 1988-1993) and International Bar Associations. *LANGUAGES:* French. *PRACTICE AREAS:* Investment Companies; Investment Advisors; Mergers and Acquisitions; Partnerships; Securities; International Transactions; General Corporate.

**ROBERT E. FERDON,** born Nyack, New York, November 1, 1932; admitted to bar, 1958, New York; 1972, District of Columbia. *Education:* Harvard University (A.B., 1954); Columbia University (J.D., 1957). Member, Board of Governors, 1973-1976, President, 1975-1976, Municipal Forum of New York. *Member:* New York State and American Bar Associations; The District of Columbia Bar. (New York, N.Y. Office). *PRACTICE AREAS:* Public Finance. *Email:* rferdon@omm.com

**JOSÉ W. FERNANDEZ,** born Cienfuegos, Cuba, September 19, 1955; admitted to bar, 1981, New York, New Jersey and U.S. District Court, District of New Jersey; 1984, U.S. District Court, Southern District of New York. *Education:* Dartmouth College (A.B., 1977); Columbia University (J.D., 1980). Adjunct Professor of Law, New York Law School, 1984-1987. Secretary, U.S.-Spain Chamber of Commerce, 1988-1992. Member, Board of Directors, Columbia Law School Alumni Association, 1991-1994; Director, U.S.-Spain Chamber of Commerce, 1985—; Director, Brazilian-American Chamber of Commerce, 1995—; Council on Foreign Relations. *Member:* Association of the Bar of the City of New York (Member, Committee on Foreign and Comparative Law, 1984-1987); American Bar Association (Chairman, Section of InterAmerican Law, 1985-1988 and 1991-1994; Director, Central American Program, 1985-1989; Member, Presidential Commission on Latin America). (New York, N.Y. Office). *LANGUAGES:* Spanish, Portuguese and French. *PRACTICE AREAS:* Banking and Finance; Mergers and Acquisitions; Communications Law; Media Law; Corporate Law; Partnership Law; Latin American Trade; Communications and Media Law. *Email:* jfernandez@omm.com

**RICHARD N. FISHER,** born Los Angeles, California, October 28, 1943; admitted to bar, 1970, California. *Education:* University of Redlands (B.A., 1965); University of Wisconsin (M.A., 1966); University of Califor-

*(This Listing Continued)*

nia at Berkeley (J.D., 1969). Member, California Law Review, 1967-1969. *Member:* Los Angeles County and American (Member, Labor and Employment Law Sections) Bar Associations. **PRACTICE AREAS:** Labor and Employment.

**CLIFF H. FONSTEIN,** born Los Angeles, California, July 20, 1957; admitted to bar, 1984, California; 1994, District of Columbia and New York; U.S. District Court, Central, Northern and Eastern Districts of California, and Southern Districts of New York. *Education:* University of California at Berkeley (B.A., 1979); University of California at Los Angeles (J.D., 1983). *Member:* Los Angeles County, New York County and American Bar Associations. (New York, N.Y. Office). **PRACTICE AREAS:** Labor and Employment. *Email:* cfonstein@omm.com

**ANDREW J. FRACKMAN,** born New York, N.Y., May 31, 1956; admitted to bar, 1982, New York, U.S. Court of Appeals Second Circuit and U.S. District Court, Southern and Eastern Districts of New York; 1989, New Jersey, U.S. Court of Appeals, Third Circuit and U.S. District Court, District of New Jersey; 1990, U.S. Tax Court. *Education:* Harvard University (A.B., cum laude, 1977); Columbia University (J.D., 1981). Harlan Fiske Stone Scholar. Finalist, Harlan Fiske Stone Moot Court Competition, 1979-1980. Director, New York Lawyers for the Public Interest, Inc., 1991-1994. Author: "Restricting a Former Employee's Use of Trade Secrets In New York," 65 New York State Bar Journal 26 (Dec. 1993); "Shareholder Public Policy Proposals and The No-Action Letter Process," 27 Review of Securities and Commodities Regulation 43 (1994); "Shareholder Public Policy Proposals: An Update," 27 Review of Securities and Commodities Regulation 193 (1994); "ACTWU v. Wal-Mart: Is This the Cost of Corporate Democracy," Insights (August, 1995, at 2); "Despite the Supreme Court's 'Kodak 'Ruling, Manufacturers Continue to Fend Off ISO's Claims of Sherman Act Violations in Aftermarkets for Parts and Service," The National Law Journal (August 14, 1995, at B5). New York City Chair, New York State Bar Seminar "Federal Civil Court Practice" (April 26, 1995). *Member:* Association of the Bar of the City of New York (Member, Federal Legislation Committee, 1987-1990); New York State and American Bar Associations. (New York, N.Y. Office). **LANGUAGES:** Russian. **PRACTICE AREAS:** Civil Litigation. *Email:* afrackman@omm.com

**PATRICIA FROBES,** born Salt Lake City, Utah, March 12, 1947; admitted to bar, 1978, California. *Education:* Antioch College (B.A., 1970); University of Utah (J.D., 1978). Order of the Coif. Note and Comment Editor, Utah Law Review, 1977-1978. Graduate Research Fellow and Leary Scholar, University of Utah. Law Clerk to Hon. Chief Judge Aldon Anderson, U.S. District Court, District of Utah, 1978-1979. Chair, Real Property Law Section, Executive Committee, 1989 and Co-Chair, Joint Committee on Anti-Deficiency Laws, State Bar of California. Chair, Real Estate and Natural Resources Department. *Member:* American College of Real Estate Lawyers. (Newport Beach and Los Angeles Offices). **PRACTICE AREAS:** Real Estate. *Email:* pfrobes@omm.com

**TRAVIS C. GIBBS,** born Gainesville, Florida, August 9, 1956; admitted to bar, 1986, California. *Education:* University of Florida (B.S.B.A., 1977); University of Texas (J.D., 1985). Member and Lecturer, National Association of Bond Lawyers and Practising Law Institute. Member, Board of Directors, Barlow Respiratory Hospital, Los Angeles (1993-1996) and Foothill Family Services, Pasadena (1995-1996). *Member:* American Bar Association (Secretary, Committee on Tax-Exempt Financing, Section of Taxation, 1995-1996). **PRACTICE AREAS:** Federal Taxation; Municipal Finance. *Email:* tgibbs@omm.com

**MARTIN GLENN,** born New York, New York, October 3, 1946; admitted to bar, 1972, New York; 1973, California. *Education:* Cornell University (B.S., 1968); Rutgers University (J.D., 1971). Articles Editor, Rutgers Law Review, 1970-1971. Law Clerk to Judge Henry J. Friendly, U.S. Court of Appeals, Second Circuit, 1971-1972. *Member:* Association of the Bar of the City of New York (Member, Federal Courts Committee, 1989-1992); American Bar Association; Ninth Circuit Advisory Committee on Rules of Practice and Internal Operating Procedures, 1983-1989); National Institute for Trial Advocacy (Faculty Member, 1984—); Center for Public Resources (Member, Advisory Committee on Arbitration of Major Business Disputes, 1988—); American Law Institute. (New York, N.Y. Office). **PRACTICE AREAS:** Litigation. *Email:* mglenn@omm.com

**RICHARD B. GOETZ,** born Paw Paw, Michigan, August 1, 1960; admitted to bar, 1984, California, U.S. District Court, Central District of California and U.S. Court of Appeals, Ninth Circuit. *Education:* Dartmouth College (A.B., summa cum laude, 1981); University of Chicago (J.D., 1984). Phi Beta Kappa. Editor, University of Chicago Law Review, 1982-1984. Chairman, Hollywood Homeless Shelter, Advisory Board, 1990-1993; Member, Board of Directors, Program and Direction Setting Committees. Volunteers of America of Los Angeles, 1990-1995. *Member:* Association of Business Trial Lawyers. **PRACTICE AREAS:** Insurance Coverage; Environmental Law. *Email:* rgoetz@omm.com

**GREGORY W. GOFF,** born Glendale, California, January 30, 1952; admitted to bar, 1978, California. *Education:* University of California at Los Angeles (B.A., summa cum laude, 1975); Loyola University of Los Angeles (J.D., magna cum laude, 1978). Staff Member, 1976-1977 and Business Editor, 1977-1978, Loyola University of Los Angeles Law Review. Author: "REIT Revival - An Overview of Real Estate Investment Trusts as an Investment Vehicle," 39th U.S.C. Tax Institute ¶1900 (Matthew Bender 1987). Co-author: "REIT Revival II: Competitive Real Estate Investment Vehicle For the '90s or Short-Lived Arbitrage Strategy?" 46th U.S.C. Tax Institute (1994). *Member:* Los Angeles County and American Bar Associations. **PRACTICE AREAS:** Partnership and Real Estate Taxation, including Real Estate Investment Trusts.

**DAVID E. GORDON,** born Santa Monica, California, March 8, 1949; admitted to bar, 1972, California. *Education:* Harvard University (B.A., cum laude, 1969; J.D., magna cum laude, 1972). Member, Board of Editors, 1970-1972 and Articles Editor, 1971-1972, Harvard Law Review. Co-editor, ERISA Litigation Reporter, 1991—. *Member:* Los Angeles County (Chair, Tax Section, 1990-1991) and American (Co-Chair, Subcommittee on ERISA Litigation of Employee Benefits Committee of Section of Taxation, 1993-1994) Bar Associations; Western Pension Conference. Life Member: Los Angeles County Bar Foundation (President, 1985-1986). **PRACTICE AREAS:** Employee Benefits; Executive Compensation. *Email:* dgordon@omm.com

**KENT V. GRAHAM,** born Los Angeles, California, June 25, 1943; admitted to bar, 1970, California. *Education:* University of California at Los Angeles (B.A., 1964); Loyola University of Los Angeles (J.D., 1969). Member, Loyola University Law Review, 1968-1969. (Century City Office). **PRACTICE AREAS:** Family Business Law; Corporate Law; Venture Capital; Start-Ups; Mergers, Acquisitions and Divestitures. *Email:* kgraham@omm.com

**PAMELA C. GRAY,** born Salt Lake City, Utah, August 6, 1944; admitted to bar, 1976, California. *Education:* Wellesley College (B.A., 1966); Loyola University School of Law, Los Angeles (J.D., 1976). Alpha Sigma Nu. Member, St. Thomas More Law Honor Society, 1974-1976. Member, Jessup Moot Court Honors Board, 1975-1976. *Member:* Los Angeles County (Officer, Death and Gift Tax Subsection, 1983-1985; Chair, Foreign Tax Subsection of the Tax Section, 1987-1990) and American Bar Associations. (Certified Specialist, Estate Planning, Trusts and Probate Law, The State Bar of California Board of Legal Specialization) (Newport Beach and Los Angeles Offices). **PRACTICE AREAS:** Income Tax; International Income Tax; Estate and Gift Taxation. *Email:* pgray@omm.com

**LINDA BOYD GRIFFEY,** born Keokuk, Iowa, August 6, 1949; admitted to bar, 1980, California and U.S. District Court, Central District of California. *Education:* University of Iowa (B.S., with distinction, 1972); Duke University (J.D., with distinction, 1980). Administrative Law Editor, Duke Law Journal, 1979-1980. *Member:* Los Angeles County (Chair, Employee Benefits Committee, Taxation Section, 1995-1996) and American (Member, Tax Section and Employee Benefits Committee) Bar Associations; Western Pension and Benefits Conference (Officer and Member, Steering Committee and Program Chair); American Law Institute. **PRACTICE AREAS:** ERISA; Employee Benefits; Executive Compensation.

**STEVEN L. GROSSMAN,** born Chicago, Illinois, October 5, 1957; admitted to bar, 1982, California, U.S. District Court, Central District of California and U.S. Court of Appeals, Ninth Circuit; 1992, District of Columbia. *Education:* Stanford University (B.A., 1979); University of Southern California (J.D. 1982). Staff Member, 1980-1981 and Managing Editor, 1981-1982, Southern California Law Review. *Member:* American Bar Association. (New York, N.Y. Office). **PRACTICE AREAS:** Corporate Law; Securities; Mergers, Acquisitions and Divestitures; Aircraft Finance and Leasing.

**CATHERINE BURCHAM HAGEN,** born Long Beach, California, June 6, 1943; admitted to bar, 1978, California and U.S. District Court, Central District of California; U.S. Court of Appeals, Ninth Circuit; 1987, U.S. Supreme Court. *Education:* Occidental College (B.A., magna cum laude, 1964); Loyola University of Los Angeles (J.D., summa cum laude, 1978). Phi Beta Kappa (Mortar Board, 1964). Staff Member, 1976-1977 and Ninth Circuit Editor, 1977-1978, Loyola of Los Angeles Law Review. Chair, 1990 Southern California Labor Law Symposium. *Member:* Los Angeles County and American (Member, Labor and Employment Law Section) Bar Associations. (Newport Beach and Los Angeles Office). **PRAC-**

*(This Listing Continued)*

**O'MELVENY & MYERS LLP, Los Angeles—Continued**

TICE AREAS: Labor and Employment; Sexual Harassment and Disability Discrimination.

**CHRISTOPHER D. HALL,** born Watford, Hertfordshire, England, August 28, 1954; admitted to bar, 1977, District of Columbia; 1979, New York. *Education:* Oxford University, Oxford, England (B.A., first class honours, in Jurisprudence, 1976); George Washington University (M.C.L., 1977). Member, Editorial Board, International Banking Law, London, England, 1983-1990. *Member:* The Association of the Bar of the City of New York; The District of Columbia Bar; New York State Bar Association. (London, England and New York Offices). LANGUAGES: French and Spanish. PRACTICE AREAS: Banking; Securities; Corporate Law; Mergers and Acquisitions. *Email:* chall@omm.com

**THEODORE C. HAMILTON,** born San Rafael, California, February 14, 1956; admitted to bar, 1983, California. *Education:* Stanford University (A.B., with distinction, 1978; J.D., 1983). Book Review Editor, Stanford Journal of International Law, 1982-1983. (Newport Beach Office). PRACTICE AREAS: Taxation and Business Law. *Email:* thamilton@omm.com

**MARC P. HANRAHAN,** born Opelika, Alabama, June 27, 1954; admitted to bar, 1981, California; 1982, U.S. District Court, Central District of California; 1989, New York. *Education:* University of California at Santa Barbara (B.A., with highest honors, 1977); University of Texas (J.D., with honors, 1980). Member, Order of the Coif. (New York, N.Y. Office). PRACTICE AREAS: Corporate Law; Banking; Finance. *Email:* mhanrahan@omm.com

**STEPHEN J. HARBURG,** born Philadelphia, Pennsylvania, October 8, 1960; admitted to bar, 1985, Pennsylvania; 1987, District of Columbia. *Education:* Yale University (B.A., magna cum laude, 1982); University of Pennsylvania (J.D., magna cum laude, 1985). Order of the Coif. Associate Editor, University of Pennsylvania Law Review, 1983-1985. Law Clerk to Hon. Donald W. Van Artsdalen, U.S. District Judge, Eastern District of Pennsylvania, 1985-1986. *Member:* Pennsylvania and American Bar Associations; The District of Columbia Bar. (Washington, D.C. Office). PRACTICE AREAS: Insurance Coverage; Antitrust. *Email:* sharburg@omm.com

**JOHN D. HARDY, JR.,** born Hampton, Virginia, August 13, 1943; admitted to bar, 1972, California. *Education:* University of Virginia (B.M.E., 1965; J.D., 1972); Free University of Brussels, Belgium (Master of International and Comparative Law, 1973). Order of the Coif. Editorial Board, Virginia Law Review, 1970-1972. (San Francisco Office and Los Angeles Office). PRACTICE AREAS: Corporate Law; Securities; Securitization; Mergers and Acquisitions. *Email:* jhardy@omm.com

**ADAM C. HARRIS,** born East Orange, New Jersey, November 30, 1960; admitted to bar, 1987, New York and U.S. District Court, Southern and Eastern Districts of New York; U.S. Court of Appeals, Second Circuit. *Education:* Emory University (B.A., 1982); Georgetown University (J.D., magna cum laude, 1986). (New York, N.Y. Office). PRACTICE AREAS: Bankruptcy; Creditors' Rights; Out of Court Debt Restructuring.

**ROBERT D. HAYMER,** born Long Island, New York, January 27, 1956; admitted to bar, 1987, California; 1988, U.S. District Court, Central District of California. *Education:* University of California at Irvine (B.A., 1978); Loyola Marymount University (J.D., cum laude, 1987). Alpha Sigma Nu. Member, St. Thomas More Honor Society. Recipient, American Jurisprudence Awards in Trusts and Wills, Community Property and Business and Tax Planning. Staff Member, 1985-1986 and Note and Comment Editor, 1986-1987, Loyola of Los Angeles Law Review. Author: "Who Owns the Air: Unscrambling the Satellite Viewing Rights Dilemma," 20 Loyola of Los Angeles Law Review 1, 1986. (Century City Office). PRACTICE AREAS: Corporate Law; Securities; Partnerships; Joint Ventures; Mergers and Acquisitions. *Email:* rhaymer@omm.com

**PETER T. HEALY,** born New York, N.Y., 1951; admitted to bar, 1979, California. *Education:* University of Santa Clara (B.S., 1973); Cornell University (M.B.A., with distinction, 1975); Hastings College of Law, University of California (J.D., 1978). *Member:* Bar Association of San Francisco; American Bar Association. (San Francisco Office).

**HOWARD M. HEITNER,** born Jersey City, New Jersey, February 8, 1955; admitted to bar, 1982, California and U.S. District Court, Central District of California. *Education:* Bucknell University (B.A., summa cum laude, 1976); University of Chicago Graduate School of Business (M.B.A., 1982); University of Chicago (J.D., with honors, 1982). Phi Delta Phi. Articles Editor, California Real Property Law Journal, 1989-1991. Author:

*(This Listing Continued)*

"The Enforceable Guarantee: Illusion or Reality?" California Real Property Law Journal, Spring, 1990; "Junior Trust Deeds: A Primer For Senior and Junior Lenders," California Real Property Law Journal, Summer 1993. *Member:* Los Angeles County and American Bar Associations. PRACTICE AREAS: Real Estate; Purchases and Sales; Finance; Low Income Housing Tax Credits; Historic Preservation; Partnerships.

**JOSEPH J. HERRON,** born Lake City, Minnesota, October 29, 1954; admitted to bar, 1980, California and U.S. District Court, Central District of California. *Education:* University of California at Berkeley (B.S., 1977) Phi Beta Kappa; Beta Alpha Psi; Stanford University (J.D., 1980). Order of the Coif. (Newport Beach Office).

**JACK B. HICKS III,** born Lynwood, California, June 21, 1960; admitted to bar, 1986, California. *Education:* University of Southern California (B.A., 1983); Loyola of Los Angeles Law School (J.D., summa cum laude, 1986). Chief Note and Comment Editor, 1985-1986, Loyola of Los Angeles Law Review. Author: Note, "Easton v. Strassburger: Judicial Imposition of a Duty to Inspect on California Real Estate Brokers," 18 Loyola of Los Angeles Law Review 809, 1985; "Pension Fund Financing Activity in the Mid-1990s," CEB 12th Annual Real Property Institute, February 1995. Co-Author: "Partner As Partnership Creditor: Issues Raised ByDual Capacity in Default Situations," Vol. 368 Real Estate Workouts and Bankruptcies 23 (PLI 1991). *Member:* Los Angeles County Bar Association (Member, Real Property Section). PRACTICE AREAS: Real Estate.

**B. BOYD HIGHT,** born Lumberton, North Carolina, February 15, 1939; admitted to bar, 1967, California; 1981, District of Columbia; 1977, U.S. Supreme Court. *Education:* Duke University (B.A., 1960); Yale University (LL.B., 1966); University of Stockholm, Sweden (Dipl. in Comp. Law, 1967). Order of the Coif. Member, Board of Editors, Yale Law Journal, 1964-1966. Deputy Assistant Secretary of State, Transportation and Telecommunications, 1979-1981. Executive Vice President and General Counsel, Santa Fe International Corp., 1985-1989. PRACTICE AREAS: Tort Litigation; Commercial Litigation; Securities Litigation.

**BRUCE A. HILER,** born Watervliet, Michigan, June 4, 1952; admitted to bar, 1977, Illinois; 1995, District of Columbia. *Education:* University of Notre Dame (B.A., magna cum laude, 1974); University of Michigan (J.D., cum laude, 1977). Author: The SEC's Use of Its Cease-and-Desist Authority: a Survey Securities Regulations Law Journal (Fall, 1995); Retail Broker Compensation, Insights (Vol. 9, No. 10; October, 1995); "Management's Discussion and Analysis: Known Trends In SEC Enforcement," 8 (2) Insights (Dec. 1994); "The *Central Bank of Denver* Decision and the SEC: Effects of the Decision and the SEC's Possible Response," 8 Corp. Counsel Rev. 1 (May 1994); *The SEC and the Insider Trader/Tipper,* N.Y.L.J., August 29, 1991; *Basic Inc. v. Levinson:* The Supreme Court's Opinion on Disclosure of Merger Negotiations, in *Theory and Practice,* 7 Corp. Counsel Rev. 1 (May 1988); *The SEC and the Courts' Approach to Disclosure of Earnings Projections, Asset Appraisals and Other Soft Information: Old Problems, Changing Views,* 46 Md. L. Rev. 1401 (1987), cited in *Basic Inc. v. Levinson,* 485 U.S. 224 (1988); *Confidential Relationships and Insider Trading,* 18 Rev. Sec. Reg. 135 (June 19, 1985); *The Judiciary Considers the nature of Confidential Relationships in Insider Trading Cases - A Look at United States v. Reed,* 13 Sec. Reg. L. J. 128 (1985); *Dirks v. SEC: A Study in Cause and Effect,* 43 Md. L. Rev. 292 (1984). Adjunct Professor, Securities Law, Georgetown University Law Center, 1992—. Instructor, Civil Procedure, George Washington University Legal Assistant Program, Spring, 1987. Associate Director, March 1990-March 1994, Assistant Director, January 1985 to March 1990, Branch Chief, July 1981 to January 1985, Special Counsel, January 1981 to June 1981 and Staff Attorney, August 1978 to December 1980, United States Securities and Exchange Commission Division of Enforcement, Washington, D.C. Member, American Bar Association Task Force SEC Settlements. Member, Federal Regulations of Securities Committee, Business Law Section, American Bar Association. Member: Advisory Board of the Securities Regulation Law Journal. (Washington, D.C. Office). PRACTICE AREAS: Securities Law; Enforcement and Regulatory Counseling; Litigation.

**MICHAEL S. HOBEL,** born New York, N.Y., September 14, 1954; admitted to bar, 1981, California and U.S. District Court, Central District of California. *Education:* Harvard University (B.A., cum laude, 1977); New York University (J.D., 1981). Member, Editorial Staff, 1979-1980 and Note and Comment Editor, 1980-1981, New York University Law Review. *Member:* American Bar Association. (Century City Office).

**GARY N. HORLICK,** born Washington, D.C., March 12, 1947; admitted to bar, 1974, Connecticut; 1975, District of Columbia. *Education:* Dartmouth College (A.B., 1968); Cambridge University, Cambridge, England (M.A., Diploma of International Law, 1970); Yale University (J.D., 1973).

*(This Listing Continued)*

Phi Beta Kappa. Council on Foreign Relations, Visiting Lecturer: Yale Law School, 1983-1986; Georgetown Law Center, 1986—. Assistant Representative (Santiago, Chile and Bogota, Columbia), Ford Foundation, 1973-1976. International Trade Counsel, U.S. Senate Committee on Finance, 1981. Deputy Assistant Secretary of Commerce for Import Administration, 1981-1983. Advisory Committee, U.S. Council of International Trade (1994-1997). Member, Permanent Group of Experts (SCM Agreement), World Trade Organization; Chairman, 1996-1997. *Member:* The District of Columbia Bar (Member, Steering Committee, International Division, 1983-1985; Chairman, 1984-1985); American (Member, Committee on International Aspects of Antitrust Law, International Law Section, 1972—) and International (Vice Chairman, Antitrust and Trade Law Committee, 1987-1989) Bar Associations; American Branch, International Law Association (Member, Executive Council, 1984—); American Society of International Law (Member, Board of Review, 1987-1991); U.S. Court of International Trade (Advisory Committee, 1993-1995); Council on Foreign Relations. (Washington, D.C. Office). *REPORTED CASES:* Certain Table Wines from France and Italy, 49 Fed. Reg. 10,587 (Int'l Trade Comm'n 1984) (antidumping and countervailing duty allegations) (neg. prelim.), USITC Pub. No. 1502 (March 1984) (Represented Commission of the European Communities); Carbon and Certain Alloy Steel Products, 49 Fed. Reg. 30,-807 (Int'l Trade Comm'n 1984) (Section 201), USITC Pub. No. 1553 (July 1984) (Represented Japan Iron and Steel Exporters Association); Certain Table Wines from W. Germany, France and Italy, 50 Fed. Reg. 45,174 (Int'l Trade Comm'n 1985) (antidumping and countervailing duty allegations) (neg. prelim.), USITC Pub. No. 1771, appealed GATT Panel, SCM/71 (March 24, 1986) (Represented Commission of the European Communities); Steel Wheels From Brazil, 54 Fed. Reg. 21,456, (Dep't Comm. 1989) (Antidumping and Countervailing Duty Allegations) (Final, Affirm. In Part and Neg. In Part), USITC Pub. No. 2193 (May 1989) (Neg. Final) (Represented Rockwell International); Certain Fresh Atlantic Groundfish from Canada, 51 Fed. Reg. 10,041 (Dep't Comm. 1986) (countervailing duty allegation) (final affirm.), USITC Pub. No. 1844 (May 1986) (final affirm. in part and neg. in part) (Counsel to Government of Canada); Canada - United States Free Trade Agreement, Jan. 2, 1988, U.S.T., T.I.-.A.S. No., reprinted in 27 I.L.M. 281 (1988) (Counsel to the Government of. Canada); Fresh, Chilled, or Frozen Pork from Canada, 12 I.T.R.D. 1302 (1989) (appeal of Dep't. of Comm. decision), 12 I.T.R.D. 1380 (1989) (appeal of Int'l Trade Comm'n decision), 13 I.T.R.D. 1859 (1991) (Extraordinary Challenge Committee) (Represented Government of Alberta); Flat Panel Displays and Subassemblies from Japan, 56 Fed. Reg. 32,376 (Dep't. Comm. 1991) (antidumping allegation) (final, affirm. in part and neg. in part), USITC Pub. No. 2413 (August 1991) (Represented International Business Machines Co. (IBM)); Fresh and Chilled Atlantic Salmon from Norway, 56 Fed. Reg. 7,661 (Dep't Comm. 1991) (antidumping allegation) (final affirm.), appeal filed with GATT Panel, Requested by Norway for the Establishment of a Panel Under Article 15:5 of the Agreement (Sept. 25, 1991); 56 Fed. Reg. 7,678 (Dept Comm. 1991) (countervailing duty allegation) (final affirm.), appeal filed with GATT Panel, Requested by Norway for the Establishment of a Panel Under Article 17:3 of the Agreement (Aug. 28, 1991) (Counsel to the Government of Norway); Canada-Mexico-United States: North American Free Trade Agreement, December 1992, U.S.T., T.I.A.S. No., Reprinted in 32 I.L.M. 289 (1993) (Counsel to Government of Mexico); Agreement Establishing the World Trade Organization, in Final Act Embodying the Results of the Uruguay Round of Multilateral Trade Negotiations. 9 (General Agreement on Tariffs and Trade) (April 15, 1994) (Counsel to Emergency Committee for American Trade). *PRACTICE AREAS:* International Trade Law. *Email:* ghorlick@omm.com

**SANDRA SEGAL IKUTA,** born Los Angeles, California, June 24, 1954; admitted to bar, 1991, California. *Education:* University of California at Berkeley (B.A., 1976); Columbia University (M.S., 1978); University of California School of Law (J.D., 1988). Phi Beta Kappa. Order of the Coif. Chief Articles Editor, University of California at Los Angeles Law Review, 1987-1988. Author: " Non-Emergency" Environmental Reporting Under Leases, 4 LACBA R. Prop. Sec. News 7 (Nov/Dec 1993); "Liability of Passive Prior Owners of Contaminated Property Environmental Liability, Enforcement and Penalties Rep. (March 1993, at 79). Co-author: "Parent Corporation Liability Under CERCLA, Cal. L. (Nov 1995). Law Clerk: Circuit Judge Alex Kozinski, U.S. Court of Appeals, Ninth Circuit, 1988-1989; Justice Sandra Day O'Connor, U.S. Supreme Court, 1989-1990. *Member:* Los Angeles County Bar Association (Executive Committee, Environmental Section). *PRACTICE AREAS:* Real Estate Law; Natural Resources and Environmental Law. *Email:* sikuta@omm.com

**ROBERT S. INSOLIA,** born Huntington, New York, April 29, 1957; admitted to bar, 1985, New York. *Education:* State University of New York at New Paltz (B.A., 1979); Fordham University (J.D., 1984). (New York,

N.Y. Office). *PRACTICE AREAS:* Corporate Law; Corporate Finance; Corporate Real Estate; Corporate Securities; Finance; Structural Finance; Real Estate Finance; Commercial Real Estate; Real Estate Investment Trusts; Real Estate Securities. *Email:* rinsolia@omm.com

**PHILIP D. IRWIN,** born Madison, Wisconsin, September 6, 1933; admitted to bar, 1957, Wyoming; 1958, California. *Education:* University of Wyoming (B.A., 1954); Stanford University (LL.B., 1957). Phi Beta Kappa; Phi Delta Phi; Order of the Coif. Associate Comment Editor, Stanford Law Review, Vol. 9, 1956-1957. *Member:* Los Angeles County and American Bar Associations; Wyoming State Bar. (Certified Specialist, Taxation Law, The State Bar of California Board of Legal Specialization).

**WAYNE JACOBSEN,** born Landsthul, Germany, January 25, 1956; admitted to bar, 1982, California; 1983, U.S. District Court, Central District of California; 1989, U.S. Tax Court. *Education:* San Francisco State University; University of California at Los Angeles (A.B., magna cum laude, 1979); University of Southern California (J.D., 1982). Member, Order of the Coif. Member, 1980-1981 and Notes and Articles Editor, 1981-1982, Southern California Law Review. Author: "Withdrawal Liability for Double-Breasted Construction Employees Under the Multiemployer Pension Plan Amendments Act of 1982," 54 Southern California Law Review, 1981. (Newport Beach Office). *PRACTICE AREAS:* ERISA; Employee Benefits. *Email:* wjacobsen@omm.com

**TOM A. JERMAN,** born Salt Lake City, Utah, August 1, 1955; admitted to bar, 1981, California and U.S. District Court, Central District of California. *Education:* University of Utah (B.S., magna cum laude, 1978; J.D., 1981). Member, Order of the Coif. Staff Member, 1979-1980 and Executive Editor, 1980-1981, Utah Law Review. *Member:* Los Angeles County and American Bar Associations. (Washington, D.C. Office). *PRACTICE AREAS:* Labor and Employment.

**EVAN M. JONES,** born Washington, D.C., May 6, 1959; admitted to bar, 1984, California and U.S. District Court, Central District of California; 1989, District of Columbia; 1985, U.S. District Court, Northern District of California. *Education:* Duke University (B.A., magna cum laude, 1981); Boalt Hall School of Law, University of California (J.D., 1984). Member, Order of the Coif; Pi Sigma Alpha. Recipient, American Jurisprudence Awards in Civil Procedure and Corporations. Member, 1982-1983 and Research and Topics Editor, 1983-1984, California Law Review. *Member:* District of Columbia Bar; American Bar Association; Financial Lawyers Conference (Board of Governors). *PRACTICE AREAS:* Bankruptcy. *Email:* ejones@omm.com

**RICHARD M. JONES,** born Henderson, Texas, October 30, 1949; admitted to bar, 1976, California. *Education:* Rice University (B.A., 1972); University of Texas (J.D., 1976). Order of the Coif. Associate Editor, Texas Law Review, 1975-1976. *PRACTICE AREAS:* Government Finance; Government Infrastructure Projects. *Email:* rjones@omm.com

**PHILLIP R. KAPLAN,** born Downey, California, April 25, 1951; admitted to bar, 1977, California and U.S. District Court, Central District of California. *Education:* Yale College (B.A., 1973); University of Southern California (J.D., 1977). Order of the Coif. Staff Member, University of Southern California Law Review, 1975-1977. Author: "A Critique of the Penalty Limitation on Liquidated Damages," 50 Southern California Law Review 1055, 1977. Law Clerk to Hon. David W. Williams, U.S. District Court, Central District of California, 1977. *Member:* Orange County and American Bar Associations. (Newport Beach Office). *PRACTICE AREAS:* Securities Litigation; Insurance Coverage Defense; Bank Failures Litigation. *Email:* pkaplan@omm.com

**PETER C. KELLEY,** born Providence, Rhode Island, December 15, 1959; admitted to bar, 1986, California. *Education:* Yale University (B.A., with distinction, 1981); University of California at Los Angeles (J.D., 1986). Recipient: Shidler Grant (First Place, 1986). Member, UCLA Law Review, 1984-1986. *Member:* Los Angeles County Bar Association. (Century City Office). *LANGUAGES:* French. *PRACTICE AREAS:* Partnerships; Real Estate Transactions; Limited Liability Companies.

**HOLLY E. KENDIG,** born Oak Park, Illinois, July 30, 1947; admitted to bar, 1975, California; U.S. District Court, Central and Northern Districts of California. *Education:* DePauw University (B.A., 1969); Tufts University (M.A., 1970); Yale University (J.D., 1975). Phi Beta Kappa. Editor, 1973-1975 and Note Editor and Member, Board of Editors, 1974-1975, Yale Law Journal. *Member:* Women Lawyers Association of Los Angeles (Board Member, 1992-1994; Chair, Status of Women Committee, 1992-1994).

**DAVID E. KILLOUGH,** born Camp Gordon, Georgia, January 30, 1955; admitted to bar, 1983, California; 1984, U.S. District Court, Central

*(This Listing Continued)*

**O'MELVENY & MYERS LLP, Los Angeles—Continued**

District of California; 1985, U.S. Court of Appeals, Ninth Circuit; 1987, U.S. District Court, Northern District of California; 1991, U.S. Court of Appeals, Federal Circuit; 1994, U.S. Supreme Court. *Education:* North Texas State University (B.A., 1977); Southwestern University (J.D., magna cum laude, 1983). Member, Moot Court Board of Governors, 1981-1982. Special Projects Editor, Southwestern University Law Review, 1982-1983. (San Francisco and Los Angeles Offices). *PRACTICE AREAS:* Environmental Law; Patent Litigation.

**JOSEPH K. KIM,** born Seoul, Korea, November 26, 1959; admitted to bar, 1986, California. *Education:* University of California at Berkeley (B.A., with highest distinction, 1981); Harvard University (J.D., magna cum laude, 1986; M.B.A., 1986). Phi Beta Kappa. Editor, Harvard Law Review, 1984-1986. *Member:* Los Angeles County Bar Association; Korean American Bar Association. *LANGUAGES:* Korean. *PRACTICE AREAS:* Banking; Finance; Mergers, Acquisitions and Divestitures; Corporate Law. *Email:* jkkim@omm.com

**LOUIS B. KIMMELMAN,** born Cincinnati, Ohio, January 30, 1951; admitted to bar, 1975, New Jersey; 1977, New York. *Education:* Yale University (B.A., summa cum laude, 1972; J.D., 1975). Phi Beta Kappa. Law Clerk to Honorable Leonard I. Garth, U.S. Court of Appeals, Third Circuit, 1975-1976. *Member:* The Association of the Bar of the City of New York; New York State, American and International Bar Associations. (New York, N.Y. Office). *PRACTICE AREAS:* Litigation; Arbitration; Mediation. *Email:* bkimmelman@omm.com

**JAMES H. KINNEY,** born Oklahoma City, Oklahoma, March 2, 1937; admitted to bar, 1966, California. *Education:* California State University at Long Beach (B.S., cum laude, 1963); University of California at Los Angeles (LL.B., 1966). City Councilman, 1983-1990 and Mayor, 1985-1986; 1988-1989, Palos Verdes Estates, California. *Member:* Los Angeles County and American Bar Associations. (Century City Office). *PRACTICE AREAS:* Real Estate.

**MATTHEW T. KIRBY,** born Schenectady, New York, October 24, 1947; admitted to bar, 1974, California. *Education:* College of the Holy Cross, (A.B., 1969); University of San Francisco (J.D., 1974). Editor in Chief, University of San Francisco Law Review, 1973-1974. Recipient, Judge Haley Award, Outstanding Graduate, 1974. Co-Author: "Fraudulent Conveyance Concerns in Leveraged Buyout Lending," 43 Business Lawyer 27, 1987. *Member:* American Bar Association. (Los Angeles, California and New York, N.Y. Offices). *PRACTICE AREAS:* Banking and Creditor's Rights.

**F. CURT KIRSCHNER, JR.,** born San Diego, California, March 12, 1960; admitted to bar, 1986, California. *Education:* University of California, Berkeley (B.A., cum laude, 1982); University of Michigan (J.D., cum laude, 1985). Phi Beta Kappa. Author: Thesis, "Labor Unions and Governmental Policy: A Comparison of United States and Britain," 1982. Clara Belfield and Henry Bates Fellowship, University of Michigan Law School. (San Francisco Office).

**PAUL R. KOEPFF,** born Morristown, New Jersey, February 16, 1947; admitted to bar, 1974, New York, U.S. District Court, Southern and Eastern Districts of New York and U.S. Court of Appeals, First, Second, Third, Fourth, Fifth, Sixth and Ninth Circuits; 1978, U.S. Supreme Court; 1992, New Jersey; 1994, U.S. District Court, Western District of Michigan. *Education:* Lehigh University (B.A., Economics, cum laude, 1969; M.B.A., 1970); Duke University (J.D., cum laude, 1973). *Member:* American Bar Association (Litigation Section and Tort and Insurance Practice Section); Federation of Insurance and Corporate Counsel; Defense Research Institute. Past Member: New York State Bar Association; Association of the Bar of the City of New York. (New York, N.Y. Office). *PRACTICE AREAS:* Litigation; Insurance Coverage Litigation.

**JEFFREY I. KOHN,** born New York, New York, March 10, 1959; admitted to bar, 1985, New York and U.S. District Court, Southern and Eastern Districts of New York; 1988, New Jersey; 1991, U.S. Court of Appeals, Second Circuit; 1992, U.S. Court of Appeals, Third Circuit; 1993, U.S. Supreme Court. *Education:* Cornell University (B.S., with honors, 1981); George Washington University (J.D., with high honors, 1984). Order of the Coif. Managing Editor, George Washington Law Review, 1982-1984. Supplemental Author: Modern Law and Employment Relationships, Prentice Hall Law and Business (1990-1994), Adjunct Professor, New York Law School. *Member:* American Bar Association (Member, Employment and Labor Law Committee). (New York, N.Y. Office). *PRACTICE AREAS:* Labor and Employment. *Email:* jkohn@omm.com

*(This Listing Continued)*

**C. DOUGLAS KRANWINKLE,** born Elgin, Illinois, October 27, 1940; admitted to bar, 1966, California; 1995, New York. *Education:* Northwestern University (B.A., 1962); University of Michigan (J.D., 1965). Order of the Coif. Member, Barristers. Articles Editor, Michigan Law Review, 1964-1965. Law Clerk to Chief Justice Earl Warren, U.S. Supreme Court, 1966-1967. Professor of Law, University of Michigan, Winter Term, 1993. *Member:* Los Angeles County, New York State and American Bar Associations; American Law Institute. (New York, N.Y. and Los Angeles, California Offices). *PRACTICE AREAS:* Securities; Mergers and Acquisitions; Complex Business Transactions.

**DAVID A. KRINSKY,** born August 7, 1948; admitted to bar, 1973, California. *Education:* University of Southern California (B.A., 1969; J.D., 1973); Rutgers University (M.A., 1970). Member, Southern California Law Review; 1972-1973. (Newport Beach Office). *PRACTICE AREAS:* Corporate Law; Securities Law; Business Law. *Email:* dkrinsky@omm.com

**GORDON E. KRISCHER,** born Chicago, Illinois, December 9, 1946; admitted to bar, 1972, California; 1991, New York. *Education:* University of Illinois (B.S., 1968); Harvard University (J.D., magna cum laude, 1971). Phi Beta Kappa. Member, Board of Editors, Harvard Law Review, 1969-1971. Chairman, Labor and Employment Department. *Member:* Los Angeles County (Member, Executive Committee, Labor Law Section, 1987-1988) and American (Management Co-Chair, Labor Law Section Practice and Procedure Committee Under the National Labor Relations Act, 1992-1994) Bar Associations. *PRACTICE AREAS:* Trial Practice; Labor and Employment Law; Toxic Torts; Civil Litigation.

**THOMAS J. LEARY,** born Van Nuys, California, May 24, 1963; admitted to bar, 1988, California and U.S. District Court, Central District of California. *Education:* University of California at Los Angeles (B.A., Economics and Business, magna cum laude, 1985; J.D., 1988). Phi Eta Sigma. Staff Member, UCLA Law Review, 1986-1988. *PRACTICE AREAS:* Corporate Law; Securities Matters. *Email:* tleary@omm.com

**PERRY A. LERNER,** born Riverside, California, April 20, 1943; admitted to bar, 1969, California; 1992, New York. *Education:* Claremont McKenna College (B.A., cum laude, 1965); Harvard Law School (J.D., cum laude, 1968). Law Clerk to Judge Arnold Raum, U.S. Tax Court, 1968-1970. Attorney-Advisor, Office of the International Tax Counsel, U.S. Treasury Department, 1973-1976. *Member:* State Bar of California; Los Angeles County, New York State and American (Committee on International Law and Taxation) Bar Associations. (New York, N.Y. and Century City, California Offices).

**C. JAMES LEVIN,** born Belleville, Illinois, May 8, 1954; admitted to bar, 1981, California and U.S. District Court, Central District of California. *Education:* DePauw University (B.A., 1976); Northwestern University (M.M., 1981; J.D., cum laude, 1981). Staff Member, 1979-1980 and Member, Editorial Board, 1980-1981, Northwestern University Law Review. Member, Corporations Committee, State Bar of California, 1987-1990. *Member:* Los Angeles County and American Bar Associations. *PRACTICE AREAS:* Corporate Law; Executive Compensation; Corporate Governance; Securities; Mergers, Acquisitions and Divestitures.

**DOUGLAS P. LEY,** born Santa Cruz, California, July 20, 1951; admitted to bar, 1977, California. *Education:* Haverford College (B.A., magna cum laude, 1973); Harvard University (M.P.P., 1977; J.D., cum laude, 1977). Phi Beta Kappa. *Member:* State Bar of California (Partnerships Committee, 1991-1995; Vice Chair, 1993-1994; Chair, 1994-1995); Bar Association of San Francisco; American Bar Association. (San Francisco Office). *PRACTICE AREAS:* Corporate Law; Securities; Partnerships; Limited Liability Companies.

**CHARLES C. LIFLAND,** born New York, N.Y., May 14, 1957; admitted to bar, 1983, California and U.S. District Court, Central District of California; 1984, U.S. District Court, Northern District of California; 1985, U.S. District Court, Southern District of California; 1987, U.S. Court of Appeals, Ninth Circuit. *Education:* Yale University (B.A., magna cum laude, with distinction in Economics, 1979); Harvard University (J.D., magna cum laude, 1982). Editor, Harvard Environmental Law Review, 1981. Law Clerk to Hon. Mariana R. Pfaelzer, U.S. District Court, Central District of California, 1982-1983. *Member:* Los Angeles County and American Bar Associations. *PRACTICE AREAS:* Antitrust; Securities; Mass Torts; Business Litigation; Appellate Practice; Class Action Litigation. *Email:* clifland@omm.com

**BEN H. LOGAN, III,** born Medina, Ohio, July 21, 1951; admitted to bar, 1976, California; 1978, U.S. District Court, Central District of California; 1984, District of Columbia; 1986, U.S. District Court, Northern and Southern Districts of California; 1990, U.S. District Court, District of Ari-

*(This Listing Continued)*

zona; 1991, U.S. District Court, Eastern District of California and U.S. Court of Appeals, Second Circuit; 1994, U.S. Court of Appeals, Ninth Circuit. *Education:* Duke University (B.A., 1973); Stanford University (J.D., 1976). Phi Beta Kappa. Member, 1974-1976 and Note Editor, 1975-1976, Stanford Law Review. Member, Debtor/Creditor Relations and Bankruptcy Subcommittee, Commercial Law and Bankruptcy Section, State Bar of California, 1988-1991. *Member:* Los Angeles County Bar Association (Bankruptcy Committee, 1989-1992); Financial Lawyers Conference. *PRACTICE AREAS:* Creditors' Rights; Bankruptcy; Bankruptcy Workouts; Out of Court Debt Restructuring. *Email:* blogan@omm.com

**WARREN R. LOUI,** born Philadelphia, Pennsylvania, July 1, 1956; admitted to bar, 1982, New York; 1987, California. *Education:* Massachusetts Institute of Technology (B.S., 1977); Stanford University (M.B.A., J.D., 1981). Member, 1979-1980 and Associate Editor, 1980-1981, Stanford Law Review. Author: "Measuring Offsets and Eliminating Inequities in the Charitable Contribution Deduction," Stanford Law Review Vol. 33, pp. 893-904. *Member:* State Bar of California (Corporations Committee); Los Angeles County Bar Association (Committee on Minorities in the Legal Profession); Joint Minority Bar Task Force on Diversity (Co-Chair). (Century City Office). *PRACTICE AREAS:* Banking; Asset Securitization; Entertainment Finance. *Email:* wloui@omm.com

**PATRICK LYNCH,** born Pittsburgh, Pennsylvania, November 11, 1941; admitted to bar, 1967, California and U.S. District Court, Central District of California; 1972, U.S. Supreme Court; 1974, U.S. District Court, Northern District of California; 1986, U.S. District Court, Eastern District of California. *Education:* Loyola University of Los Angeles (B.A., 1964; LL.B., magna cum laude, 1966). Alpha Sigma Nu. Instructor (1981-1996), at the Antitrust Institute, which is sponsored by the Practising Law Institute. *Member:* Los Angeles County and American Bar Associations; American College of Trial Lawyers. *PRACTICE AREAS:* General Civil Litigation; Antitrust Law; Trademarks; Copyrights; Intellectual Property.

**JOSEPH M. MALKIN,** born New York, N.Y., January 26, 1947; admitted to bar, 1972, California and U.S. District Court, Central and Northern Districts of California; 1973, U.S. Court of Appeals, Ninth Circuit; 1976, U.S. Supreme Court. *Education:* Claremont Men's College (B.A., 1968); Yale Law School (J.D., 1972). Editor, Yale Law Journal, 1970-1972. Recipient, Carter, Ledyard and Milburn Prize, Yale Law School, 1970. Reporter, Ninth Circuit Judicial Conference Ad Hoc Civil Discovery Committee (1977-1978); Speaker, California Chamber of Commerce Conference on the Public Trust Doctrine (1983); Speaker, Los Angeles County Bar Association Land Use Planning Subsection (1984); Speaker, Conference on Utility Prudence Reviews (April 1987); Speaker, Edison Electric Institute Prudence Group (Oct. 1988); Featured Speaker, Energy Daily Annual Utility Conference (Nov. 1988). Invited Participant, California Public Utilities Commission Workshop on "The Evolving Regulatory Environment" (May 1995). *Member:* Bar Association of San Francisco; American Bar Association (Litigation Section Discovery Committee, 1983—). (San Francisco Office).

**JAMES P. MARLIN,** born Brooklyn, New York, August 29, 1945; admitted to bar, 1971, New York; 1979, District of Columbia. *Education:* Manhattan College (B.A., cum laude, 1967); Villanova University (J.D., 1970). *Member:* New York State Bar Association; The District of Columbia Bar. (New York, N.Y. Office). *PRACTICE AREAS:* Public Finance. *Email:* jmarlin@omm.com

**LOWELL C. MARTINDALE, JR.,** born Little Rock, Arkansas, August 25, 1940; admitted to bar, 1969, California. *Education:* California State College at Long Beach (B.A., 1962); University of Southern California (J.D., 1969). Phi Alpha Delta. Comment Editor, Southern California Law Review, 1968-1969. Author: "Testing the Limits of State Power to Alter Contracts by Eminent Domain," The National Law Journal (May 22, 1995). *Member:* Orange County (Member, Real Property Section) Los Angeles County (Member, Real Property Section) and American Bar Associations. (Newport Beach Office).

**MARIE L. MARTINEAU,** born Suffern, New York, July 25, 1959; admitted to bar, 1983, California and U.S. District Court, Central District of California. *Education:* Providence College (B.A., summa cum laude, 1980); Boston University School of Law (J.D., cum laude, 1983). *Member:* Los Angeles County and American Bar Associations; National Association of Bond Lawyers. (New York, N.Y. and Los Angeles California Offices). *PRACTICE AREAS:* Asset Securitization; Corporate Finance; Public Finance. *Email:* mmartineau@omm.com

**CHERYL WHITE MASON,** born Champaign, Illinois, January 16, 1952; admitted to bar, 1977, California and U.S. District Court, Central and Northern Districts of California; 1978, U.S. Court of Appeals, Ninth

*(This Listing Continued)*

Circuit. *Education:* Purdue University (B.A., summa cum laude, 1972); University of Chicago (J.D., 1976). Phi Beta Kappa; Phi Kappa Phi. Adjunct Professor, Loyola Law School, 1983. Chair, Legal Services Trust Fund Commission, State Bar of California, 1988-1989. *Member:* Langston, Los Angeles County (Trustee, 1985-1987) and American Bar Associations; Women Lawyers of Los Angeles. (San Francisco and Los Angeles Offices). *PRACTICE AREAS:* Public Utilities; Environmental and Civil Litigation; Litigation; Alternative Dispute Resolution. *Email:* cmason@omm.com

**JILL H. MATICHAK,** born Glen Cove, New York, April 25, 1954; admitted to bar, 1980, California; 1981, U.S. District Court, Central District of California. *Education:* University of California at Los Angeles (B.A., summa cum laude, 1977); Leeds University, Leeds, England; Stanford University (J.D., 1980). Phi Beta Kappa. Member, Stanford Law Review, 1979-1980. (San Francisco and Los Angeles Offices). *PRACTICE AREAS:* Banking; Securities; Corporate Law. *Email:* jmatichak@omm.com

**EDWARD J. MCANIFF,** born New York, N.Y., June 29, 1934; admitted to bar, 1961, New York; 1963, California; 1978, District of Columbia. *Education:* College of the Holy Cross (A.B., with honors, 1956) Alpha Sigma Nu; New York University (LL.B., 1961). Order of the Coif. Member, Board of Editors, New York University Law Review, 1960-1961. Clerk to Associate Justice Alfred T. Goodwin, Supreme Court of Oregon, 1961-1962. Adjunct Professor, Boalt Hall (1990—); Stanford University (1992—); and UCLA (1995—). Chair, Financial Institutions, Committee, Business Law Section, 1990-1991 and Member, Executive Committee, 1991-1994, State Bar of California. *Member:* Los Angeles County and American (Chair, Long-Range Planning Subcommittee, Banking Law Committee) Bar Associations. (Los Angeles and San Francisco Offices). *PRACTICE AREAS:* Banking Law; Securities Law.

**MICHAEL G. MCGUINNESS,** born Brooklyn, New York, June 23, 1962; admitted to bar, 1988, California and U.S. District Court, Central District of California. *Education:* University of Washington (B.A., Political Science, 1984); Loyola Law School, Los Angeles (J.D., 1987). Phi Beta Kappa; Alpha Sigma Nu. Member, St. Thomas More Law Honor Society. Recipient: American Jurisprudence Awards in Civil Procedure, Constitutional Law, Property and Practice and Procedure; Bancroft Whitney Award, Society of Writers on Legal Subjects Award. Staff Member, 1985-1986 and Editor-in-Chief, 1986-1987, Loyola of Los Angeles Law Review. Law Clerk to Honorable William Mathew Byrne, Jr. U.S. District Court, Central District of California, 1987-1988. Author: "Sliding Scale Settlements: The Need For a Minimum Contribution To Comply With the Reasonable Range Test For Good Faith," 19 Loyola of Los Angeles Law Review 995, 1986. *PRACTICE AREAS:* Labor and Employment.

**FREDERICK B. MCLANE,** born Long Beach, California, July 24, 1941; admitted to bar, 1967, California. *Education:* Stanford University (B.A., 1963); Yale University (LL.B., 1966). Order of the Coif. Editor, Yale Law Journal, 1964-1966. Chairman, Corporations Department. *Member:* Los Angeles County and American Bar Associations. *PRACTICE AREAS:* Corporate Law; Banking; Securities.

**JULIE A. MCMILLAN,** born Orange, California, September 30, 1959; admitted to bar, 1984, California and U.S. District Court, Central District of California; 1990, New York, U.S. Court of Appeals, 9th Circuit and U.S. District Court, Northern District of California. *Education:* University of California at Los Angeles (B.A., magna cum laude, 1981); Stanford University (J.D., 1984). Phi Beta Kappa. *Member:* Bar Association of San Francisco (Litigation Section); American Bar Association (Member, Litigation, Tort and Insurance Sections); Association of Business Trial Lawyers; Defense Research Institute. (San Francisco Office). *PRACTICE AREAS:* Litigation; Public Utilities; Insurance Coverage Defense.

**PAUL G. MCNAMARA,** born New York, N.Y., April 1, 1956; admitted to bar, 1982, California and U.S. District Court, Central District of California. *Education:* University of Redlands (B.A., magna cum laude, 1978); Stanford University (J.D., 1982); Trinity College, University of Dublin, Ireland (Higher Diploma of Letters, 1979). Phi Beta Kappa. Faculty, National Institute of Trial Advocacy (1992-1996). *Member:* Los Angeles County (Member, Litigation Section) and American (Member, Litigation Section) Bar Associations; Association of Business Trial Lawyers. *PRACTICE AREAS:* Civil Litigation; Defense Litigation; Federal Litigation. *Email:* pmcnamara@omm.com

**MITCHELL B. MENZER,** born Santa Monica, California, September 30, 1956; admitted to bar, 1984, California and U.S. District Court, Central District of California. *Education:* Amherst College (B.A., magna cum laude, 1978); University of California at Los Angeles (J.D., 1984). Order of the Coif. Law Clerk for the Hon. Pamela Ann Rymer, U.S. District Court, Central District of California, 1984. *Member:* Los Angeles County and

*(This Listing Continued)*

**O'MELVENY & MYERS LLP, Los Angeles—Continued**

American (Real Property and Environmental Law Sections) Bar Associations. *PRACTICE AREAS:* Real Estate Law; Environmental Law. *Email:* mmenzer@omm.com

**SCOTT A. MEYERHOFF,** born Chicago, Illinois, April 14, 1958; admitted to bar, 1984, California and U.S. District Court, Central District of California. *Education:* California State University at Northridge (B.S., magna cum laude, 1981); Loyola Marymount University (J.D., cum laude, 1984). Alpha Sigma Nu. Member, St. Thomas More Law Society. Recipient, American Society of Writers on Legal Subjects Award, 1984. Staff Member, 1982-1983 and Editor-in-Chief, 1983-1984, Loyola of Los Angeles Law Review. *Member:* Los Angeles County (Real Property Section), Orange County (Real Property Section) and American Bar Associations. (Newport Beach Office). *PRACTICE AREAS:* Real Estate.

**PAUL E. MOSLEY,** born Phoenix, Arizona, December 28, 1959; admitted to bar, 1986, California and U.S. District Court, Central District of California. *Education:* Brigham Young University (B.A., magna cum laude, 1982; B.S., 1982; J.D., magna cum laude, 1986). Order of the Coif. Member, 1984-1985 and Lead Articles Editor, 1985-1986, Brigham Young University Law Review. *Member:* American Bar Association (Section of Natural Resources, Energy and Environmental Law); Environmental Law Institute. (Newport Beach Office). *LANGUAGES:* Spanish. *PRACTICE AREAS:* Real Estate; Natural Resources; Environmental Law. *Email:* pmosley@omm.com

**F. THOMAS MULLER, JR.,** born St. Louis, Missouri, September 14, 1953; admitted to bar, 1982, New York; 1985, California. *Education:* Yale College (B.A., 1975); New York University (M.U.P., 1982; J.D., cum laude, 1981). Order of the Coif. Recipient, William Miller Award for Excellence in Municipal Law, 1981. Member, 1979-1980 and Articles Editor, 1980, New York University Law Review. Member, Real Property Section, State Bar of California. *Member:* Los Angeles County Bar Association (Member, Real Property Section). *PRACTICE AREAS:* Real Estate Finance; Land Use; Land Development. *Email:* tmuller@omm.com

**CHRISTOPHER C. MURRAY,** born Winchester, Virginia, October 11, 1949; admitted to bar, 1975, California. *Education:* University of Illinois (B.A., 1971); University of Southern California (J.D., 1974). Phi Beta Kappa; Order of the Coif. Executive Editor of Lead Articles, Southern California Law Review, 1973-1974. Law Clerk to Judge Walter Ely, U.S. Court of Appeals, Ninth Circuit, 1974-1975. Adjunct Professor, Entertainment Industry Transactions Seminar, Stanford Law School (1984-1990). Author: "An Overview of United States Intellectual Property Law," A Chapter In *Foreign Direct Investment In The United States* (Sweet & Maxwell, 1994). Chairman, Entertainment Department. Member, Intellectual Property and International Law Sections, State Bar of California. (Century City Office). *PRACTICE AREAS:* Intellectual Property; Entertainment Law. *Email:* cmurray@omm.com

**MICHAEL NEWMAN,** born Los Angeles, California, October 25, 1948; admitted to bar, 1975, California. *Education:* Pomona College (B.A., 1970); Hastings College of the Law, University of California (J.D., 1975). Order of the Coif. Member, Thurston Honor Society. Member of Staff, 1973-1974 and Associate Articles Editor, 1974-1975, Hastings Law Journal. *Member:* American Bar Association. *PRACTICE AREAS:* Banking; Public Finance.

**CHARLES F. NIEMETH,** born Lorain, Ohio, November 25, 1939; admitted to bar, 1966, California; 1984, New York. *Education:* Harvard University (B.A., 1962); University of Michigan (J.D., 1965). Order of the Coif. Note and Comment Editor, Michigan Law Review, 1964-1965. *Member:* Los Angeles County and New York County Bar Associations. (New York, N.Y. and Century City, California Offices). *PRACTICE AREAS:* Corporate Law; Mergers, Acquisitions and Divestitures; Securities.

**JOHN G. NILES,** born Dallas, Texas, October 5, 1943; admitted to bar, 1968, Texas; 1969, California; 1970, U.S. Court of Military Appeals; 1973, U.S. District Court, Central District of California; 1979, U.S. Supreme Court. *Education:* Stanford University (B.A., 1965); University of Texas (LL.B., 1968). Phi Kappa Phi; Order of the Coif; Phi Delta Phi. Member, Chancellors. Member, 1966-1968 and Casenote Editor, 1967-1968, Texas Law Review. *Member:* State Bar of Texas; Los Angeles County and American Bar Associations. *PRACTICE AREAS:* General Business Litigation; Insurance Law; Insurance Regulation; Professional Malpractice. *Email:* jniles@omm.com

**JEFFERY L. NORTON,** born Boston, Massachusetts, October 13, 1960; admitted to bar, 1985, California (Inactive); U.S. District Court, Central District of California; 1992, District of Columbia (Inactive); 1993, New York. *Education:* University of Washington (B.A., cum laude, with distinction, 1981; M.A., 1982); Cornell Law School (J.D., cum laude, 1985). Associate, 1983-1984 and Senior Editor, 1984-1985, Cornell Law Review. Author: "Removal Doctrine Reaffirmed: Franchise Tax Board v. Construction Laborers Vacation Trust," 70 Cornell Law Review 557, 1985. *Member:* New York State Bar Association; State Bar of California; District of Columbia Bar. (New York, N.Y. Office). *PRACTICE AREAS:* Corporate Law; Banking; Reorganization; Media Law.

**CHRISTINE M. OLSEN,** born Grand Rapids, Michigan, January 16, 1949; admitted to bar, 1976, New York and U.S. District Court, Southern District of New York (Inactive); 1978, California. *Education:* Mount Holyoke College (A.B., great distinction, 1971); Boston University (J.D., cum laude, 1975). Editor, Boston University Law Review, 1974-1975. *Member:* Los Angeles County and American Bar Associations. *PRACTICE AREAS:* Corporate Law; Banking.

**M. RANDALL OPPENHEIMER,** born Baltimore, Maryland, February 21, 1952; admitted to bar, 1977, California. *Education:* Harvard University (A.B., summa cum laude, 1974); University of Chicago (J.D., 1977). Comment Editor, University of Chicago Law Review, 1976-1977. *Member:* American Bar Association. (Century City Office).

**KENNETH R. O'ROURKE,** born Los Angeles, California, June 26, 1959; admitted to bar, 1985, California and U.S. District Court, Central District of California; 1986, U.S. Court of Appeals, Ninth Circuit and U.S. District Court, Northern and Southern Districts of California; 1988, U.S. District Court, Eastern District of California; 1991, U.S. Court of Appeals, Federal Circuit; 1994, U.S. Supreme Court. *Education:* University of California, Los Angeles (B.A., 1982); Loyola Marymount University (J.D., 1985). Member, St. Thomas More Law Honor Society. Staff Member, 1983-1984 and Editor-in-Chief, 1984-1985, Loyola of Los Angeles International and Comparative Law Journal. Author: Comment, "A Shipowner's Lien on Sub-sub-freight in England and the United States: New York Produce Exchange Time Charter Party Clause Eighteen," 7 Loyola of Los Angeles International and Comparative Law Journal 73, 1984. Extern: Los Angeles County Superior Court, 1983; U.S. Securities and Exchange Commission, 1985. *Member:* Los Angeles County Bar Association; American Intellectual Property Law Association. *PRACTICE AREAS:* Business Litigation; Intellectual Property Litigation. *Email:* ko'rourke@omm.com

**PETER V. PANTALEO,** born Brooklyn, New York, October 26, 1956; admitted to bar, 1983, New York. *Education:* Columbia University (B.A., 1978); New York University (J.D., 1982). Member, New York University Journal of International Law and Politics, 1981-1982. Contributing Co-author with Joel B. Zweibel, "Bankruptcy Practice and Strategy," A Resnick, Ed., 1987. *Member:* Association of the Bar of the City of New York (Secretary, Committee on Bankruptcy and Corporate Reorganization, 1987-1990); New York State Bar Association. (New York, N.Y. Office). *PRACTICE AREAS:* Bankruptcy and Commercial Law.

**RICHARD G. PARKER,** born St. Paul, Minnesota, June 27, 1948; admitted to bar, 1974, California; 1980, District of Columbia. *Education:* University of California at Davis (A.B., with highest honors, 1970); University of California at Los Angeles (LL.B., 1974). Phi Beta Kappa; Phi Kappa Phi; Order of the Coif. Comment Editor, U.C.L.A. Law Review, 1973-1974. Law Clerk to U.S. District Judge William Matthew Byrne, Jr., 1974-1975. *Member:* District of Columbia Bar; State Bar of California; American Bar Association (Antitrust Section). (Washington, D.C. Office). *PRACTICE AREAS:* Litigation; Antitrust Law.

**STEPHEN P. PEPE,** born Paterson, New Jersey, October 30, 1943; admitted to bar, 1969, California. *Education:* Montclair State College (B.A., 1965); Duke University (J.D., 1968). Editor, Duke Law Journal, 1967-1968. Co-Author: "Avoiding and Defending Wrongful Discharge Claims," Clark Boardman Callaghan, 1987; "Designing an Effective Fair-Hiring and Terminations Compliance Program," 9 Corporate Compliance Series, Clark Boardman Callaghan, 1993. Co-Editor "O'Melveny & Myers Guide to Acquiring and Managing a U.S. Business" Eurostudy Publ. Co. 1992 (and IPC Japanese Edition); California Employment Law Letter, 1990-1995. Co-Author: "Privacy in the Workplace," Employers Group, 1992; "Defamation in the Workplace," L. Smith & Co. 1993. Board of Visitors, Duke Law School, 1992-1996; Board of Trustees, Montclair State College Foundation. *Member:* Los Angeles County and American (Management Co-Chair, Labor and Employment Law Section, Committee on Individual Rights and Responsibilities, 1982-1985) Bar Associations; American Hospital Association (Member, Labor Advisory Committee, 1975-1990; Chair, Employers Group Legal Committee, 1988-1993); I.I.R.A. (President, 1991-1993); O'Melveny & Myers (Chair, Labor and

*(This Listing Continued)*

Employment Law Department, 1989-1992). (Newport Beach and Los Angeles Offices). *PRACTICE AREAS:* Labor and Employment. *Email:* spepe@omm.com

**DONALD V. PETRONI,** born Reno, Nevada, April 22, 1931; admitted to bar, 1959, California. *Education:* University of Nevada (B.A., 1952); Stanford University (LL.B., 1958). Order of the Coif. Note Editor, Stanford Law Review, 1957-1958. *Member:* Los Angeles County and American Bar Associations. (Century City Office). *PRACTICE AREAS:* Entertainment Law; Communications and Media Law.

**DAVID G. POMMERENING,** born Milwaukee, Wisconsin, March 22, 1960; admitted to bar, 1986, New York; 1992, District of Columbia. *Education:* Duke University (A.B., magna cum laude, 1982); University of Virginia (J.D., 1985). *Member:* New York State Bar Association; District of Columbia Bar. (Washington, D. C. Office). *PRACTICE AREAS:* General Corporate Law; Corporate Transactional Law.

**JOHN B. POWER,** born Glendale, California, November 11, 1936; admitted to bar, 1962, California. *Education:* Occidental College (A.B., magna cum laude, 1958); New York University (J.D., 1961). Root-Tilden Scholar, 1958-1961. Phi Beta Kappa. Associate Editor, New York University Law Review, 1960-1961. Member, 1980-1983 and Chair, 1982-1983, Partnership Committee; Chair, 1984-1985, Uniform Commercial Code Committee; Member, 1987-1991 and Chair, 1990-1991, Executive Committee, Business Law Section; Chair: Council of Section Chairs, State Bar of California, 1992-1993. President, Financial Lawyers Conference, 1985-1986. *Member:* Los Angeles County, American and International Bar Associations; American College of Commercial Financial Lawyers. *PRACTICE AREAS:* General Corporate Law; Banking; Securities Law; Insolvency Matters; Mergers, Acquisitions and Divestitures; International Finance.

**LAURENCE G. PREBLE,** born Denver, Colorado, April 24, 1939; admitted to bar, 1969, California and U.S. District Court, Central District of California; 1983, District of Columbia; 1987, New York. *Education:* Colorado School of Mines (Petroleum Refining Engineer, 1961); Loyola University of Los Angeles (J.D., cum laude, 1968). Alpha Sigma Nu; Phi Alpha Delta. Student Teaching Fellow, Loyola University, 1967-1968. Adjunct Professor: Southwestern University, 1970-1975; Loyola Law School, 1984-1992. Fordham University School of Law, 1992—. Co-Author: "Convertible and Shared Appreciation Loans: Unclogging the Equity of Redemption," Real Property, Probate and Trust Journal, 1985; "Legal Opinions in California Real Estate Transactions," The Business Lawyer, 1987; "Recent Changes in California and Federal Usury Laws: New Opportunities for Real Estate and Commercial Loans?" Loyola Law Review, 1979; *Member:* Los Angeles County and American Bar Associations; Association of the Bar of the City of New York; American College of Real Estate Lawyers; Anglo-American Real Property Institute. (New York, N.Y. and Los Angeles, California Offices). *PRACTICE AREAS:* Real Estate Law. *Email:* lpreble@omm.com

**ALAN RADER,** born New York, N.Y., November 28, 1944; admitted to bar, 1970, California; 1975, Massachusetts. *Education:* University of California at Los Angeles (B.A., 1966); Stanford University (J.D., 1969). Member, Editorial Board, Stanford Law Review, 1968-1969. *Member:* Los Angeles County Bar Association. (Century City Office). *PRACTICE AREAS:* Intellectual Property Litigation; Music and General Business Litigation. *Email:* arader@omm.com

**IRA H. RAPHAELSON,** born Chicago, Illinois, July 3, 1953; admitted to bar, 1977, Illinois; 1996, District of Columbia; U.S. District Court, Northern District of Illinois including Trial Bar and District of Maryland; U.S. Court of Appeals, Seventh Circuit; U.S. Supreme Court. *Education:* Northwestern University (B.A., 1974; J.D., 1977). First Presidentially-appointed Special Counsel for Financial Institutions Crime U.S. Department of Justice, 1991-1993. Counselor to the Attorney General of the United States, 1992-1993. Chairman (Banking), Senior Interagency Group, 1991-1993. United States Attorneys Office, Northern District of Illinois: United States Attorney, 1989-1990; First Assistant U.S. Attorney, 1989-1991; Chief, Special Prosecutions Division, 1987-1989; Chief, Criminal Litigation Division, 1987; Deputy Chief, Special Prosecutions Division, 1986-1987; Assistant U.S. Attorney, 1980-1991. Adjunct Faculty, John Marshall Law School, 1979-1990, Attorney General's Advocacy Institute, 1988-1993. Assistant States Attorney, Cook County, Illinois, 1978-1980. (Washington, D.C. Office). *PRACTICE AREAS:* Complex Litigation; Corporate Compliance and Special Investigations; Antitrust; White Collar Defense; Health Care; Financial Institutions.

**GILBERT T. RAY,** born Mansfield, Ohio, September 18, 1944; admitted to bar, 1972, California; 1984, New York. *Education:* Ashland University (B.A., 1966); University of Toledo (M.B.A., 1968); Howard University Law

*(This Listing Continued)*

School (J.D., magna cum laude, 1972). Editor in Chief, Howard Law Journal, 1971-1972. *Member:* Los Angeles County, American and National Bar Associations. *PRACTICE AREAS:* Corporate Law and Public Finance. *Email:* gray@omm.com

**CHARLES C. READ,** born Pasadena, California, September 9, 1949; admitted to bar, 1975, California; 1983, District of Columbia; 1984, New York. *Education:* Harvard University (A.B., magna cum laude, 1971); University of California at Los Angeles (J.D., 1975). Member, U.C.L.A. Law Review, 1973-1975; Chief Comment Editor, 1974-1975. *Member:* Los Angeles County and American Bar Associations; Association of Business Trial Lawyers.

**FREDERICK A. RICHMAN,** born Pasadena, California, October 18, 1945; admitted to bar, 1971, California. *Education:* Harvard University (A.B., cum laude, 1967); New York University (J.D., cum laude, 1970). Order of the Coif. Member, 1968-1970 and Note and Comment Editor, 1969-1970, New York University Law Review. (Century City Office). *PRACTICE AREAS:* State Taxation and Federal Taxation Litigation; Tax Planning for Technology Firms and Entertainment Clients. *Email:* rrichman@omm.com

**GEORGE A. RILEY,** born Memphis, Tennessee, March 9, 1957; admitted to bar, 1984, Tennessee; 1985, California. *Education:* Princeton University (A.B., summa cum laude, 1979); Harvard Law School (J.D., cum laude, 1983). Phi Beta Kappa. Author: "The Mining of Law of 1872" (*Amicus Journal,* Spring, 1981); "The Crises in Public Interest Law" (*Barrister, Spring, 1981);* Public Domain, Private Dominion, Sierra Club Books, 1985; "Section 1983 Update: Public Employers Beware," 27th Annual Pacific Coast Labor Law Conference University of Washington, 1994; "Civil Liability of Prosecutors," California District Attorneys Association Proceedings, 1996. Adjunct Professor, Memphis State University Law School, 1984. Law Clerk to Hon. Bailey Brown, U.S. Court of Appeals for the Sixth Circuit, 1983-1984. *Member:* State Bar of California. (San Francisco Office). *PRACTICE AREAS:* Litigation; Intellectual Property. *Email:* griley@omm.com

**ROBERT A. RIZZI,** born Madison, Wisconsin, December 25, 1949; admitted to bar, 1978, California. *Education:* Dartmouth College; Princeton University (A.B., 1972); Oxford University, Oxford, England (M.Litt., 1975); Harvard University (J.D., cum laude, 1978). Phi Beta Kappa. Member: Harvard Board of Student Advisers, 1975-1978; Board of Contributing Editors, Journal of Corporate Taxation, 1987—. Adjunct Faculty, Golden Gate University Law School, 1991-1994. *Member:* American Bar Association (Tax Section). (Washington, D.C. Office). *PRACTICE AREAS:* Tax Law. *Email:* rrizzi@omm.com

**JEFFREY J. ROSEN,** born New York, N.Y., May 13, 1949; admitted to bar, 1980, District of Columbia; 1987, New York. *Education:* Harvard University (B.A., magna cum laude, with highest honors, 1971; J.D., magna cum laude, 1978). Member, Board of Editors, 1976-1977 and Supreme Court Editor, 1977-1978, Harvard Law Review. Law Clerk to: Chief Judge J. Skelly Wright, U.S. Court of Appeals for the District of Columbia Circuit, 1978-1979; Associate Justice William J. Brennan, Jr., U.S. Supreme Court, 1979-1980. Special Assistant to the Secretary of Treasury, 1980-1981. *Member:* The District of Columbia Bar; American Bar Association (Member, Taxation Section). (Washington, D.C. and New York, N.Y. Offices). *PRACTICE AREAS:* Taxation; Corporate Law; Mergers and Acquisitions. *Email:* jrosen@omm.com

**RICHARD R. ROSS,** born New Brunswick, New Jersey, October 13, 1946; admitted to bar, 1974, California. *Education:* University of California at Los Angeles (B.A., 1968); Loyola University of Los Angeles (J.D., cum laude, 1973). Member, St. Thomas More Law Honor Society. Comment Editor, Loyola University of Los Angeles Law Review, 1972-1973. *Member:* Beverly Hills, Century City (Board of Governors, 1992-1997), Los Angeles County and American Bar Associations. (Century City Office). *PRACTICE AREAS:* Entertainment Law. *Email:* rrross@omm.com

**FRANK L. RUGANI,** born California, May 3, 1948; admitted to bar, 1978, California. *Education:* Occidental College (A.B., with honors, 1970); University of California at Davis (J.D., 1978). Participant, Roger Traynor Moot Court Competition, 1978. Thomas J. Watson Fellow, 1970. Member, University of California at Davis Law Review, 1977-1978. Clerk-Extern, Judge Philip C. Wilkins, U.S. District Court, Eastern District of California, 1977-1978. Co-Author: "Counselling on Vacation-Property Time Sharing," California Lawyer, February 1982; "Analysis of the Regulations of the Department of Real Estate, State of California, Regulating Real Property Time Share Sales," Time Sharing Industry Review, December 1981/January 1982; "Time Sharing of Real Property," Real Property News, Fall, 1980. *Member:* Los Angeles County, Orange County and American Bar Associa-

*(This Listing Continued)*

CAA1051B

**O'MELVENY & MYERS LLP,** *Los Angeles—Continued*

tions. (Newport Beach Office). *PRACTICE AREAS:* Real Estate. *Email:* frugani@omm.com

**MARK A. SAMUELS,** born Los Angeles, California, September 5, 1957; admitted to bar, 1982, California and U.S. District Court, Central District of California; 1983, U.S. Court of Appeals, Ninth Circuit; 1984, U.S. District Court, Southern and Northern Districts of California; 1987, U.S. District Court, Eastern District of California; 1991, U.S. Court of Appeals, Federal Circuit. *Education:* University of California at Berkeley (A.B., 1979); University of California at Los Angeles (J.D., 1982). Phi Beta Kappa; Order of the Coif. Member, 1980-1981 and Chief Managing Editor, 1981-1982, UCLA Law Review. Deputy Chair, Litigation Department. *Member:* Los Angeles County and American (Liaison, ABA Lawyers Conference Task Force on Reduction of Litigation Cost and Delay, 1993) Bar Associations. *PRACTICE AREAS:* Litigation; Intellectual Property. *Email:* msamuels@omm.com

**KATHRYN A. SANDERS,** born Fresno, California, November 29, 1958; admitted to bar, 1985, California, U.S. District Court, Central District of California and U.S. Court of Appeals, Ninth Circuit. *Education:* University of California at Los Angeles (B.A., 1980); University of Southern California (J.D., 1985). Order of the Coif. Member, Southern California Law Review, 1983-1985. Co-Author: "Registration of Taxable Obligations: An Examination of Rule 131," Municipal Finance Journal, Vol. 8, No. 1, 1987. *Member:* Los Angeles and American Bar Associations; National Association of Bond Lawyers. *PRACTICE AREAS:* General Corporate Law; Securities; Public Finance; Project Finance. *Email:* ksanders@omm.com

**WILLIAM H. SATCHELL,** born San Francisco, California, March 24, 1953; admitted to bar, 1979, California; 1992, District of Columbia. *Education:* University of Chicago; University of California at Berkeley (A.B., 1974); University of Southern California (J.D., 1979). Order of the Coif. (Washington, D.C. and New York, N.Y. Offices). *PRACTICE AREAS:* Banking. *Email:* wsatchell@omm.com

**STEPHEN SCHARF,** born Albany, New York, December 6, 1949; admitted to bar, 1975, California. *Education:* Colgate University (B.A., magna cum laude, 1971); Stanford University (J.D., 1975). Phi Beta Kappa. Editor, Stanford Law Review, 1973-1974. Author: "Inverse Condemnation: Its Availability in Challenging the Validity of a Zoning Ordinance," 26 Stanford Law Review 1439, 1974. Law Clerk to Hon. Fred J. Cassibry, U.S. District Court, Eastern District, Louisiana, 1975-1976. (Century City Office). *PRACTICE AREAS:* Entertainment Law; Intellectual Property Law. *Email:* sscharf@omm.com

**CARL R. SCHENKER, JR.,** born Portland, Oregon, February 28, 1949; admitted to bar, 1974, California: 1977, District of Columbia; 1978, U.S. Supreme Court. *Education:* Stanford University (B.A., with great distinction, 1971; J.D., 1974). Phi Beta Kappa. President, Stanford Law Review, 1973-1974. Law Clerk to: Hon. Shirley M. Hufstedler, U.S. Court of Appeals, Ninth Circuit, 1974-1975; Hon. Lewis F. Powell, Jr., U.S. Supreme Court, 1975-1976. *Member:* The District of Columbia Bar; American Bar Association. (Washington, D.C. Office). *PRACTICE AREAS:* Civil Litigation; Appellate Litigation. *Email:* cschenker@omm.com

**PATRICIA A. SCHMIEGE,** born Evanston, Illinois, December 2, 1953; admitted to bar, 1984, California; 1985, U.S. District Court, Central District of California; 1989, U.S. Court of Appeals, Ninth Circuit and U.S. District Court, Northern District of California. *Education:* University of Wisconsin-Madison (B.S., 1975); Loyola Law School of Los Angeles (J.D., magna cum laude, 1984). Alpha Sigma Nu. Recipient, American Jurisprudence Award in Civil Procedure. Member, St. Thomas More Law Honor Society. Staff Writer, 1982-1983 and Chief Ninth Circuit Editor, 1983-1984, Loyola of Los Angeles Law Review. Author: "Criminal Law in the Ninth Circuit: Recent Developments," Vol. 16:3, Loyola of Los Angeles Law Review, 1983. Law Clerk to the Honorable William Matthew Byrne, Jr., U.S. District Court, Central District of California, 1984-1985. *Member:* Bar Association of San Francisco. (San Francisco Office). *PRACTICE AREAS:* Complex Business Litigation; Intellectual Property Litigation; Public Utility Regulation. *Email:* pschmiege@omm.com

**ROBERT M. SCHWARTZ,** born Los Angeles, California, March 13, 1959; admitted to bar, 1984, California and U.S. District Court, Central District of California; U.S. Court of Appeals, Ninth Circuit; 1987, District of Columbia. *Education:* Williams College; University of California at Los Angeles (B.A., 1980); University of Southern California (J.D., 1984). Member, Hale Moot Court Honors Program. *Member:* Beverly Hills, Los Angeles County and American Bar Associations. (Century City Office).

*(This Listing Continued)*

*PRACTICE AREAS:* Litigation; Entertainment and Intellectual Property Litigation. *Email:* rschwartz@omm.com

**JAMES V. SELNA,** born Santa Clara, California, February 22, 1945; admitted to bar, 1971, California. *Education:* Stanford University (A.B. with distinction, 1967); Stanford University (J.D., 1970). Phi Beta Kappa; Order of the Coif. Article and Book Review Editor, Stanford Law Review, 1969-1970. *Member:* State Bar of California (Member, Standing Committee on Federal Courts, 1982-1985; Executive Committee, Litigation Section, 1986-1989; Executive Committee, Antitrust Section, 1992-1995, and Advisor, 1995—); Los Angeles County (Member, Executive Committee, Antitrust Law Section, 1981-1983) Orange County and American Bar Associations; Orange County Federal Bar Association (Director, 1991-1993). (Newport Beach Office). *PRACTICE AREAS:* Antitrust; Complex Business Litigation; Construction Defects. *Email:* jselna@omm.com

**RALPH J. SHAPIRA,** born Pittsburgh, Pennsylvania, September 24, 1946; admitted to bar, 1975, California. *Education:* Oberlin College (B.A., 1968); Boalt Hall School of Law, University of California (J.D., 1975). Associate Editor, California Law Review, 1974-1975. Recipient, American Jurisprudence Award, Commercial Law, 1975. Extern Law Clerk to Judge Charles B. Renfrew, United States District Court, Northern District, 1974. *Member:* Los Angeles County Bar Association.

**ROBERT A. SIEGEL,** born St. Louis, Missouri, September 7, 1949; admitted to bar, 1975, California and U.S. District Court, Central District of California; 1979, U.S. Court of Appeals, Ninth Circuit; 1984, U.S. Court of Appeals, Tenth Circuit; 1988, New York; 1992, U.S. Supreme Court and U.S. Court of Appeals, Second Circuit; 1994, U.S. Court of Appeals, Eleventh Circuit; 1995, U.S. Court of Appeals, District of Columbia Circuit. *Education:* University of California at Berkeley (A.B., with great distinction, 1971); University of Michigan (J.D., magna cum laude, 1974). Order of the Coif; Phi Beta Kappa. Chair, Railway and Airline Labor Law Committee, American Bar Association, 1989-1992. Senior Editor, "The Railway Labor Act" (Bureau of National Affairs), 1995. *Member:* Los Angeles County and American Bar Associations. *PRACTICE AREAS:* Litigation; Labor and Employment Law.

**GARY J. SINGER,** born Los Angeles, California, October 8, 1952; admitted to bar, 1977, California. *Education:* University of California at Irvine (B.A., magna cum laude, 1974); Loyola of Los Angeles (J.D., cum laude, 1977). Alpha Sigma Nu; Phi Beta Kappa. Member, St. Thomas More Law Honor Society. Editor-in-Chief, Loyola of Los Angeles Law Review, 1976-1977. Author: Case Note, "Gordon v. New York Stock Exchange," 9 Loyola of Los Angeles Law Review 226, 1975. *Member:* Orange County and American Bar Associations. (Newport Beach Office). *PRACTICE AREAS:* Corporate Law; Securities; Mergers, Acquisitions and Divestitures. *Email:* gsinger@omm.com

**LINDA JANE SMITH,** born Burlington, Vermont, August 1, 1952; admitted to bar, 1977, California; 1978, U.S. District Court, Central District of California; 1981, U.S. Court of Appeals, Ninth Circuit; 1984, District of Columbia; 1987, U.S. District Court, Northern District of California; 1988, U.S. District Court, Eastern District of California; U.S. Supreme Court. *Education:* Cornell University (B.A., magna cum laude, 1974); University of California at Los Angeles (J.D., 1977). Order of the Coif; Phi Beta Kappa. Staff Member, U.C.L.A. Law Review, 1976-1977. Law Externship to Hon. Carl McGowen. U.S. Court of Appeals, District of Columbia Circuit, 1976. *Member:* Los Angeles County and American Bar Associations. (Century City and Los Angeles Offices).

**STEVEN L. SMITH,** born Monterey, California, September 26, 1956; admitted to bar, 1984, California, U.S. District Court, Central, Northern and Southern Districts of California and U.S. Court of Appeals, Ninth Circuit. *Education:* University of Pennsylvania (B.A., cum laude, 1978); Cambridge University, England (M.Phil, 1979; LL.M., 1981); Boalt Hall School of Law, University of California at Berkeley (J.D., 1983). Founder and Editor-in-Chief, International Tax and Business Lawyer, 1982-1983. Author: "Badger Revisited: Implications for the Implementation of the Transfer of Technology Code," 1 International Tax and Business Lawyer 117, 1983; "The London Court of International Arbitration and English Arbitration Reform," In *ILEX Monograph #7: Report of the Delegation to International Arbitration Centers: An Update on Commercial Dispute Resolution Developments in London and Paris (May 1993);* "Advocacy and Tactics in International Commercial Arbitration," 5 *The California International Practitioner* 64 (Spring-Summer 1994). *Member:* American (Member, International Law Section) and International Bar Associations. (San Francisco Office). *PRACTICE AREAS:* Litigation; Intellectual Property; International Arbitration and Dispute Resolution. *Email:* ssmith@omm.com

*(This Listing Continued)*

**DARIN W. SNYDER,** born Kansas City, Missouri, July 17, 1963; admitted to bar, 1988, California. *Education:* Georgetown University (B.A., cum laude, 1985); University of Chicago (J.D., cum laude, 1988). Bradley Law and Government Fellow, 1987-1988. Champion Hinton Moot Court Competition, 1987. Co-Author, with Glad and Strout, of "Continuing Property Damage: The Manifestation Trigger," Underwriters Report 22 Dec 1988; with Glad, "AIDS and Insurance: The Regulatory Response," Insurance Litigation Reporter 27 Feb 1989; "Continuing Property Damage: The Pre-Manifestation Sequel," Underwriters Report 16 Aug 1989; "The One-Year Suit Limitation and Trigger of Coverage in Progressive Losses: Rules to Live By," Underwriters Report 20 Dec 1990. Author: "Polluters Should Pay to Clean Up Environment," Los Angeles Daily Journal, Aug 1990. (San Francisco Office). *PRACTICE AREAS:* Litigation; Insurance Coverage; Intellectual Property. *Email:* dsnyder@omm.com

**MASOOD SOHAILI,** born New Caledonia, January 9, 1958; admitted to bar, 1982, California, U.S. District Court, Central District of California and U.S. Court of Appeals, Ninth Circuit. *Education:* University of California at Santa Barbara (B.A., Econ., with highest honors, 1979); University of Southern California (M.A., Econ, 1982; J.D., 1982). Order of the Coif. Member: Southern California Law Review, 1980-1982. *PRACTICE AREAS:* Bond Counsel; Multi-Family Housing. *Email:* msohaili@omm.com

**STEPHANIE I. SPLANE,** born Bakersfield, California, April 13, 1956; admitted to bar, 1986, California; 1995, District of Columbia and New York. *Education:* University of Redlands (B.A., summa cum laude, 1977); University of California, Irvine (Ph.D., 1981); Yale University (J.D., 1984). Phi Beta Kappa. Note Editor, Yale Law Journal, 1983-1984. Law Clerk for Patricia M. Wald, U.S. Court of Appeals, District of Columbia Circuit, 1984. Author: Note, "Tort Liability of the Mentally Ill in Negligence Actions," 93 Yale Law Journal 153, 1983. (New York, N.Y. and Newport Beach, California Offices). *PRACTICE AREAS:* Banking; Securities; General Corporate Law; Mergers and Acquisitions.

**JOHN W. STAMPER,** born New Castle, Indiana, December 23, 1946; admitted to bar, 1974, California and U.S. District Court, Central District of California; 1979, U.S. Court of Appeals, Ninth Circuit; 1980, U.S. District Court, Eastern and Northern District of California; 1982, U.S. Supreme Court. *Education:* Indiana University (B.A., magna cum laude, 1969); Northwestern University (J.D., magna cum laude, 1972). Order of the Coif; Phi Beta Kappa. Editor-in-Chief, Northwestern University Law Review, 1971-1972. Law Clerk to Judge Carl McGowan, U.S. Court of Appeals, District of Columbia Circuit, 1972-1973. Adjunct Faculty Member, Southwestern University School of Law, 1980-1982. Member of Board of Directors of the Center for International Commercial Arbitration. *Member:* Los Angeles County (Board of Trustees, 1992-1993; Chair, Federal Courts Committee, 1989-1990; Chair, Pro Bono Council, 1992-1993), International and American Bar Associations; American Law Institute. *PRACTICE AREAS:* Litigation; Mediation; International Arbitration; Alternative Dispute Resolution.

**STEPHEN J. STERN,** born Los Angeles, California, December 31, 1940; admitted to bar, 1966, California, U.S. District Court, Central District of California and U.S. Court of Appeals, Ninth Circuit; 1985, New York. *Education:* University of Arizona; University of California at Berkeley (A.B. in Economics, 1962); University of San Francisco (LL.B., 1965). Member, Moot Court Board, 1965. *Member:* Los Angeles County, New York State and American Bar Associations; National Association of Bond Lawyers. *PRACTICE AREAS:* Public Finance; Project Finance.

**DRAKE S. TEMPEST,** born Denver, Colorado, September 15, 1953; admitted to bar, 1980, New York, U.S. District Court, Southern District of New York; Colorado. *Education:* Williams College (B.A., magna cum laude and highest honors, 1974); Oxford University, England; Yale University (J.D., 1979). (New York, N.Y. Office). *PRACTICE AREAS:* Securities; General Corporate Law.

**GREGORY B. THORPE,** born Los Angeles, California, December 5, 1953; admitted to bar, 1982, California. *Education:* University of California at Santa Barbara (B.A., cum laude, 1977); Loyola Law School, Los Angeles (J.D., cum laude, 1982). Member, St. Thomas More Law Society, 1980-1982. Staff Member and Chief Article Editor, Loyola of Los Angeles Law Review, 1980-1982. *Member:* Los Angeles County and American Bar Associations.

**HENRY C. THUMANN,** born Chicago, Illinois, January 6, 1935; admitted to bar, 1961, California. *Education:* University of Illinois (B.A., with honors, 1957); Harvard University (LL.B., magna cum laude, 1960). Member, Board of Editors, Harvard Law Review, 1958-1960. Chair, Litigation Department. *Member:* Los Angeles County and American Bar Associa-

*(This Listing Continued)*

tions. Fellow, American College of Trial Lawyers. *PRACTICE AREAS:* General Business Litigation; Antitrust; Securities.

**STUART P. TOBISMAN,** born Detroit, Michigan, June 5, 1942; admitted to bar, 1970, California. *Education:* University of California at Los Angeles (A.B., 1966); Boalt Hall School of Law, University of California (J.D., 1969). Phi Beta Kappa; Order of the Coif. Staff Member and Chief Note and Comment Editor, California Law Review, 1967-1969. Chairman, Tax Department. *Member:* Los Angeles County and American Bar Associations. Fellow, American College of Trust and Estate Counsel. (Century City and Los Angeles Offices). *PRACTICE AREAS:* Tax Law; Estate Planning; Trusts and Estates. *Email:* stobisman@omm.com

**LAWRENCE P. TU,** born New York, New York, August 23, 1954; admitted to bar, 1983, District of Columbia; 1986, U.S. Supreme Court (Not admitted in California). *Education:* Harvard University (A.B., summa cum laude, 1976; J.D., magna cum laude, 1981); Magdalen College, Oxford University, Oxford, U.K. (B.A., with honors, 1978). Rhodes Scholar. Editor, Harvard Law Review, 1979-1981. Author: "Complex Enforcement: Unconstitutional Prison Conditions," 94 Harvard Law Review 626, 1981. Law Clerk to: Judge Walter R. Mansfield, U.S. Court of Appeals for the Second Circuit, 1981-1982; Justice Thurgood Marshall, U.S. Supreme Court, 1982-1983. Attorney-Adviser, 1983-1985 and Special Assistant to the Legal Adviser, 1985-1986, Office of the Legal Adviser, U.S. Department of State. Associate, 1986-1989 and Partner, 1989-1994, O'Melveny & Myers, District of Columbia. *Member:* District of Columbia Bar. (Hong Kong Office). *LANGUAGES:* Chinese (Mandarin). *PRACTICE AREAS:* Securities; Finance; Corporate Law; Project Finance; International Finance and Joint Ventures. *Email:* ltu@omm.com

**KO-YUNG TUNG,** born Peking, China, February 20, 1947; admitted to bar, 1973, New York. *Education:* Harvard University (B.A., magna cum laude, 1969; J.D., 1973). Phi Beta Kappa. Recipient, Detur Prize, 1969. Editor, Harvard Journal of International Law, 1970-1973. Fellow, Faculty of Law, Tokyo University, 1971-1972. Adjunct Associate Professor of Law, New York University School of Law, 1974-1989. Member, Trilateral Commission. Chair, Board of Governors, East West Center, Honolulu, Hawaii. Board of Directors, Asian American Legal Defense and Education Fund. Member: The Brookings Institution; United States National Committee for Pacific Economic Cooperation; Council on Foreign Relations; National Committee on United States-China Relations; United States-China Business Council; Japan Society; Asian Society; Overseas Development Council; and Commercial Panel of Arbitrators, American Arbitration Association. Member, Presidential Commission on United States-Pacific Trade and Investment Policy (1996—). Chairman, Global Practice Group. *Member:* The Association of the Bar of the City of New York (Member: International Law Committee, 1973-1976; Special Committee on Asian Affairs, 1989); Japanese-American Society of Legal Studies. (New York, N.Y. Office). *LANGUAGES:* Japanese and Chinese (Mandarin). *PRACTICE AREAS:* Corporate Law; Mergers, Acquisitions and Divestitures; Corporate Finance; International Business. *Email:* kytung@omm.com

**SUZZANNE UHLAND,** born Oakland, California, October 2, 1962; admitted to bar, 1988, California and U.S. District Court, Central District of California; 1989, U.S. District Court, Eastern District of California. *Education:* Stanford University (A.B., with distinction, 1984; M.A., 1986); Yale University (J.D., 1988). Phi Beta Kappa; Cap and Gown. Recipient, Greenberg Prize. Managing Editor and Editor-in-Chief, Yale Journal on Regulation. Law Clerk to the Honorable Mariana R. Pfaelzer, U.S. District Court, Central District of California, 1989-1990. Adjunct Professor, Secured Transactions, Southwestern University School of Law, 1990. *Member:* State Bar of California (Business Law Section); Financial Lawyers Conference (1989—). *LANGUAGES:* Spanish, Italian and Latin. *PRACTICE AREAS:* Bankruptcy Law.

**JAMES R. UKROPINA,** born Fresno, California, September 10, 1937; admitted to bar, 1966, California; 1980, District of Columbia. *Education:* Stanford University (A.B., 1959; M.B.A., 1961); University of Southern California (LL.B., 1965). Editor-in-Chief, Vol. 38, Southern California Law Review. *Member:* Los Angeles County and American Bar Associations. *PRACTICE AREAS:* Corporate Law.

**ROBERT C. VANDERET,** born Brooklyn, New York, April 12, 1947; admitted to bar, 1973, California; 1986, New York. *Education:* University of California at Los Angeles (A.B., cum laude, 1969) Regents Scholar, 1967-1969; Stanford University (J.D., 1973). Class President. Order of the Coif. Managing Editor, 1972-1973 and Editor, 1971-1972, Stanford Journal of International Studies. Law Clerk to Mr. Justice Mathew O. Tobriner, California Supreme Court, 1972 (Externship). Special Transition Aide to Chief Justice Rose Elizabeth Bird, California Supreme Court, 1977. Chair,

*(This Listing Continued)*

**O'MELVENY & MYERS LLP,** *Los Angeles—Continued*

Committee on Administration of Justice, California State Bar Association, 1996-1997. *Member:* Los Angeles County and American (Chair, Committee on Media Law and Defamation Torts, TIPS Section, 1991-1992) Bar Associations. *REPORTED CASES:* Crane vs. Arizona Republic, 729 F.Supp. 698 (C.D.Cal.1989); Fresno Rifle and Pistol Club vs. Van de Kamp, 965 F.2d 723 (9th Cir. 1992); Galloway vs. CBS, 18 Med.L.Rep. 1161 (Cal. App. 1987); Kruse vs. Bank of America, 202 Cal.App.3d 38 (1988); Maheu vs. CBS, 201 Cal.App.3d 662 (1988); Lewis v. Columbia Pictures, 20 Med.L.Rep. 1807 (Cal. Super. 1992); Miyata v. Bungei Shunju, 19 Med.L.Rep 1400 (Cal. App. 1991); Phillips v. Syufy Enterprises, 20 Med.L.Rep. 1199 (Cal. Super. 1992); Raye v. Letterman, 18 Med.L.Rep. 2047 (Cal. Super. 1987); SEC vs. Carter Hawley Hale Stores, Inc., 587 F.Supp. 1248 (C.D.Cal. 1984); Walker vs. Superior Court, 47 Cal. 3d 112 (1988). *PRACTICE AREAS:* First Amendment Litigation; Securities Litigation; Media Law; Libel, Slander and Defamation. *Email:* bvanderet@omm.com

**FRAMROZE M. VIRJEE,** born London, England, December 30, 1960; admitted to bar, 1984, California and U.S. District Court, Central, Southern and Northern Districts of California. *Education:* University of California at Santa Barbara (B.A., summa cum laude, 1982); Hastings College of Law, University of California (J.D., cum laude, 1985). Alpha Kappa Delta; Phi Delta Phi; Order of the Coif. Member: Order of Omega; Thurston Society. Watts Scholar. Mortar Board Honors. Co-Author, "Privacy in the Workplace" (Merchants and Manufacturers Association, 1992). Adjunct Professor (Personal and Labor Law) Drucker Management Center of the Claremont Graduate School, 1991—. *Member:* Los Angeles County and American (Labor and Employment Sections) Bar Associations. *PRACTICE AREAS:* Labor and Employment.

**ULRICH WAGNER,** born Siegerdorf, West Germany, September 14, 1943; admitted to bar, 1974, California; 1984, New York. *Education:* University of Frankfurt (Referendarexamen, 1968; Dr. iur., summa cum laude, 1972); University of California at Berkeley (LL.M., 1972; J.D., 1974). Articles and Book Reviews Editor, California Law Review, 1973-1974. Author: *Hypothetische Schadensverursachung,* 1974. Member: Los Angeles County, New York State and American Bar Associations. (New York, N.Y. Office). *LANGUAGES:* German.

**DIANA L. WALKER,** born Grand Haven, Michigan, October 14, 1941; admitted to bar, 1970, California. *Education:* University of Michigan (A.B., 1963); University of California at Los Angeles (J.D., 1969). Phi Beta Kappa; Order of the Coif. Articles Editor, U.C.L.A. Law Review, 1968-1969. Trustee, Institute for Corporate Counsel, 1989—. Member, State Bar of California Business Law Section Chair of Corporation Committee, 1979-1980; Vice Chair Executive Committee, 1983-1984. *Member:* Los Angeles County and American Bar Associations; State Bar of California. *PRACTICE AREAS:* Corporate Finance; Securities Disclosure; Financial Institutions Law; Corporate Governance; Executive Compensation; Mergers, Acquisitions and Divestitures.

**RICHARD C. WARMER,** born Los Angeles, California, August 12, 1936; admitted to bar, 1963, California; 1976, District of Columbia. *Education:* Occidental College (A.B., magna cum laude, 1958); Fletcher School of Law & Diplomacy (M.A., 1959); New York University (LL.B., cum laude, 1962). Editor-in-Chief, New York University Law Review, 1961-1962. Phi Beta Kappa; Order of the Coif. Root-Tilden Scholar. *Member:* The District of Columbia Bar; Bar Association of San Francisco; State Bar of California; American Bar Association. (San Francisco Office). *PRACTICE AREAS:* Antitrust Law; Commercial Litigation. *Email:* rwarmer@omm.com

**STEPHEN H. WARREN,** born Pasadena, California, February 25, 1961; admitted to bar, 1988, California; 1989, U.S. District Court, Central District of California. *Education:* Pomona College; Stanford University (B.A., with distinction, 1983; J.D., with distinction, 1988). Phi Beta Kappa; Pi Sigma Alpha; Order of the Coif; Pomona College Scholar. Urban A. Sontheimer Scholar. Law Clerk to the Honorable Harry L. Hupp, U.S. District Judge, Central District of California, 1988-1989. Author: "A Creditor's Bargain Perspective of FDIC Policy for Handling Bank Failures (Or, the Bargain That Is No Bargain AT All)," Financial Services Yearbook, Volume 1, Berkeley Press, 1988*Member:* State Bar of California; Los Angeles County and American Bar Associations. *PRACTICE AREAS:* Bankruptcy Law.

**DAVID D. WATTS,** born Shreveport, Louisiana, November 13, 1941; admitted to bar, 1967, California. *Education:* Rhodes College (B.A., 1963); New York University (J.D., 1966). Order of the Coif. Note and Comment Editor, New York University Law Review, 1964-1966. Member: Los Angeles County Bar Association; American College of Trust and Estate Counsel. *PRACTICE AREAS:* Trusts and Estates. *Email:* dwatts@omm.com

**DAVID I. WEIL,** born Los Angeles, California, April 8, 1950; admitted to bar, 1980, District of Columbia and California; 1981, U.S. District Court, Central District of California. *Education:* Stanford University (B.A., 1972); Brandeis University (M.A., 1975); Georgetown University (J.D., 1979). Phi Beta Kappa. Syllabus Editor, 1986. Co-Chair, University of Southern California Entertainment Law Institute, 1987-1988. Adjunct Professor, Negotiations Seminar, Pepperdine Law School, 1984-1986. Staff Director, Subcommittee on International Trade of the Committee on Banking, U.S. House of Representatives, 1974-1979. (Century City Office). *PRACTICE AREAS:* Media Law; Entertainment Law; Intellectual Property Law. *Email:* dweil@omm.com

**DEAN M. WEINER,** born Worcester, Massachusetts, September 25, 1947; admitted to bar, 1976, California; 1977, U.S. District Court, Central District of California. *Education:* University of California at Los Angeles (B.S., 1970); McGeorge School of Law (J.D., magna cum laude, 1975); Harvard University (LL.M., 1977). Director, National Association of Bond Lawyers, 1983-1984. Chair, Los Angeles County Bar Tax section, 1991-1992. Chair, ABA Committee on Tax-Exempt Financing, 1990-1992. *PRACTICE AREAS:* Municipal Finance and Derivatives; Taxation; Corporate Law; Low Income Housing Tax Credits; Mortgage Securitization; Partnerships. *Email:* dweiner@omm.com

**JACQUELINE A. WEISS,** born Heidelberg, Germany, July 23, 1958; admitted to bar, 1984, New York. *Education:* Queens College of the City University of New York (B.A., magna cum laude, 1980); Fordham University (J.D., 1983). Regents Scholar, 1976-1980. Associate Editor, Fordham Law Review, 1982-1983. Author: "Beyond Upjohn: Achieving Certainty by Expanding the Scope of the Corporate Attorney-Client Privilege," 50 Fordham L. Rev. 1185, 1982. *Member:* Association of the Bar of the City of New York; New York State (Member, Real Property Section) and American Bar Associations. (New York, N.Y. Office). *PRACTICE AREAS:* Real Estate. *Email:* jweiss@omm.com

**JOHN E. WELCH,** born Gothenburg, Nebraska, December 23, 1954; admitted to bar, 1982, California and U.S. District Court, Central District of California; 1987, District of Columbia. *Education:* University of Nebraska-Lincoln (B.A. summa cum laude, 1977); Harvard Law School (J.D., magna cum laude, 1982). Phi Beta Kappa. Member of Board of Editors, Harvard Law Review, 1980-1982. Author: Note, "Police Liability for Negligent Failure to Prevent Crime," 94 Harvard Law Review 821, 1981. Co-Author with J. Rosen: "Leveraged Buyouts: A Legal Perspective," Directory of Intermediaries for Buyouts, Mergers and Acquisitions 5th Ed. 1989; S.P. Galante and J.A. Chiappinelli, Eds. *Member:* District of Columbia Bar; State Bar of California (currently inactive); Federal Communications Bar Association. (Washington, D.C. Office). *PRACTICE AREAS:* Communications Law; General Corporate Law. *Email:* jwelch@omm.com

**PAMELA LYNNE WESTHOFF,** born Redondo Beach, California, December 24, 1960; admitted to bar, 1986, California, U.S. District Court, Central District of California and U.S. Court of Appeals, Ninth Circuit. *Education:* Loyola Marymount University (B.B.A., summa cum laude, 1982); University of Southern California Graduate School of Business (M.B.A., 1986); University of Southern California Law Center (J.D., 1986). Alpha Sigma Nu; Beta Gamma Sigma; Order of the Coif. Finalist, Hale Moot Court Honors Competition, 1983-1984. Chairman, Moot Court Executive Board, 1984-1985. Member, National Moot Court Team, 1985. *Member:* Los Angeles County Bar Association (Real Property Section); State Bar of California (Landlord-Tenant Subsection). *Email:* pwesthoff@omm.com

**ROBERT J. WHITE,** born Chicago, Illinois, November 1, 1946; admitted to bar, 1972, California; 1985, New York. *Education:* University of Illinois (B.S., 1968); University of Michigan (J.D., magna cum laude, 1972). Order of the Coif; Beta Alpha Psi. Member, 1970-1972 and Comment Editor, 1971-1972, Michigan Law Review. Co-Author: "Advanced Chapter 11 Practice," PESI, 1987. Adjunct Lecturer, Michigan Law School, 1986. Author: Leveraged Buyouts and the Fraudulent Conveyance Laws Under the Bankruptcy Laws--Like Oil and Water, They Just Don't Mix," N.Y.U. Annual Survey of American Law 357, 1991. Co-Chair, Bankruptcy Department. *Member:* Los Angeles County (Chair, Federal Courts Committee, 1978; Member, Executive Committee, Commercial Law and Bankruptcy Section, 1982-1984; 1989-1991), and American Bar Associations; Financial Lawyers Conference (President, 1990-1991, Board of Governors, 1986—); Conferee, National Bankruptcy Conference. Fellow, American College of Bankruptcy. *PRACTICE AREAS:* Bankruptcy; Loan Restructuring; Out of Court Debt Restructuring.

*(This Listing Continued)*

**ROBERT E. WILLETT,** born Glendale, California, June 21, 1943; admitted to bar, 1974, California; 1987, U.S. Supreme Court; 1988, U.S. Tax Court. *Education:* San Fernando Valley State College (B.A., 1971); University of California at Berkeley (J.D., 1974). Order of the Coif. Associate Editor, California Law Review, 1972-1973. Notes and Comment Editor, California Law Review, 1973-1974. Member, State Bar Committee for the Administration of Justice, 1987-1990. *Member:* Los Angeles County (Vice-Chair, Court Improvements Committee, 1985-1987) and American Bar Associations. **PRACTICE AREAS:** Antitrust Law; Patent Litigation; Trade Secrets; Securities Litigation; General Commercial Litigation. *Email:* rwillett@omm.com

**JONATHAN P. WILLIAMS,** born Crawfordsville, Indiana, November 18, 1949; admitted to bar, 1981, California; 1991, New York. *Education:* Yale University (B.A., 1971); Hastings College of the Law, University of California (J.D., 1980). Member: Order of the Coif; Thurston Society. Recipient, Roger J. Traynor Award, 1980. Participant, 1978-1979 and Associate Editor, 1979-1980, Hastings Law Journal. (New York, N.Y. and Los Angeles, California Offices). **LANGUAGES:** Korean. *Email:* jwilliams@omm.com

**MICHAEL A. WISNEV,** born St. Louis, Missouri, July 3, 1956; admitted to bar, 1980, California. *Education:* University of Missouri (B.S., summa cum laude, 1977); Stanford University (J.D., 1980). Phi Kappa Phi; Beta Gamma Sigma; Order of the Coif. Nathan Abbott Scholar, 1980.

**CHARLES C. WOLF,** born Boston, Massachusetts, October 29, 1952; admitted to bar, 1980, Massachusetts; 1984, California. *Education:* Boston University (B.S., summa cum laude, 1977); Boston College Law School (J.D., cum laude, 1980). Member, Boston College Law Review. *Member:* American Bar Association; Financial Lawyers Conference. **REPORTED CASES:** In re Maxicare Health Plans; In re Drexel Burnham Lambert Group, Inc.; In re Prime Motor Inns; In re Phar-Mor, Inc.; In re Orange County. **PRACTICE AREAS:** Bankruptcy; Municipal Finance. *Email:* cwolf@omm.com

**THOMAS E. WOLFE,** born Jacksonville, Florida, July 1, 1952; admitted to bar, 1981, California and U.S. District Court, Central District of California. *Education:* University of California (A.B., 1976); Loyola Marymount University (J.D., magna cum laude, 1981). Alpha Sigma Nu. Staff Member, 1979-1980 and Managing Editor, 1980-1981, Loyola Law Review. Member, St. Thomas More Law Honor Society, 1979-1981. Extern for the Honorable Wm. Matthew Byrne, Jr., U.S. District Judge, Central District of California, 1981. (Newport Beach Office). **PRACTICE AREAS:** Corporate Law. *Email:* twolfe@omm.com

**W. MARK WOOD,** born Traverse City, Michigan, November 30, 1942; admitted to bar, 1968, California; 1985, District of Columbia. *Education:* University of Santa Clara (B.A., 1964); University of Southern California (J.D., 1967). Phi Delta Phi; Order of the Coif. Associate Editor, University of Southern California Law Review, 1966-1967. Judge Advocate, United States Marine Corps. *Member:* Los Angeles County and American Bar Associations; The District of Columbia Bar. **PRACTICE AREAS:** Civil Litigation; Aviation; Insurance Coverage Defense. *Email:* mwood@omm.com

**MICHAEL G. YODER,** born Lynwood, California, November 12, 1953; admitted to bar, 1978, California. *Education:* University of Southern California (A.B., 1975); Stanford University (J.D., 1978). Phi Beta Kappa; Order of the Coif; First Year Honor. *Member:* Orange County (Chair-Elect, Business Litigation Section, 1996) and American (Litigation Section, Business Torts Committee, 1992-1995; Co-Chair, Fraud Subcommittee, and Chair, California Region, 1996—) Bar Associations. (Newport Beach Office). **PRACTICE AREAS:** Complex Business Litigation; Land Use Litigation; Business Torts; Trade Secrets.

**JOEL B. ZWEIBEL,** born Bronx, New York, February 7, 1935; admitted to bar, 1959, New York. *Education:* College of the City of New York (B.B.A., 1955); Yale University (LL.B., 1958). Beta Gamma Sigma. Co-Author: Herzog's Bankruptcy Forms and Practice, 6th Ed., 1980: "Venue and Consolidation of Arrangement (Chapter XI) Proceedings Under the Bankruptcy Act Involving Related Corporations," The Business Lawyer, January, 1961; "The Supreme Court Puts the Trustee in Bankruptcy in His Place," The Business Lawyer, April, 1961; "The Equitable Subordination of Claims in Bankruptcy," Vanderbilt Law Review Vol. 15 No. 1, December, 1961. Author: *The Creditors' Rights Handbook;* "Equipment Financing," Uniform Commercial Code Law Journal, Vol. 2 No. 3, Winter, 1970; "Fixtures, Real Estate Mortgages Covering Personal Property, Corporate Mortgages and Utility Mortgages," The Banking Law Journal, Vol. 87 No. 4, April, 1970; "Work-Out Problems and Solutions," The Bankers Magazine Vol. 159, No. 2, Spring, 1976. Law Lecturer, 2nd Annual Uniform Commercial Code Law Institute, 1968. Co-Chair, Bankruptcy Department.

*Member:* The Association of the Bar of the City of New York (Chairman, Committee on Bankruptcy and Corporate Reorganization, 1981-1984); American Bar Association; Federal Bar Council (Chairman, Committee on Liaison with Supreme Court Committee on Bankruptcy Rules, 1969-1970); National Bankruptcy Conference (Chairman, Committee on Avoiding Powers, 1983—, Executive Committee and Treasurer, 1991—); Regent for the Second Circuit, American College of Bankruptcy (1994—). (New York, N.Y. Office). **PRACTICE AREAS:** Bankruptcy and Creditors' Rights.

### SENIOR COUNSELLOR

**WILLIAM T. COLEMAN, JR.,** born Philadelphia, Pennsylvania, July 7, 1920; admitted to bar, 1947, Pennsylvania; 1977, District of Columbia; 1955, U.S. Supreme Court. *Education:* University of Pennsylvania (A.B., summa cum laude, 1941); Harvard Law School (LL.B., magna cum laude, 1946). Phi Beta Kappa; Pi Gamma Mu. Editor, Harvard Law Review, 1942-1943 and 1946-1947. Law Secretary to: Judge Herbert F. Goodrich, 1947-1948; Justice Felix Frankfurter, 1948-1949. Trustee, Trilateral Commission. Secretary, U.S. Department of Transportation, 1975-1977. Officer, de la Légion d' Honneur, 1980. Recipient, Presidential Medal of Freedom, 1995. *Member:* Pennsylvania, Federal Power and American Bar Associations; District of Columbia Bar; American College of Trial Lawyers; Council, American Law Institute. (Washington, D.C. Office). **PRACTICE AREAS:** Constitutional Law; Trial and Appellate Practice; Corporate Business Law; International Transactional Law.

### SENIOR COUNSEL

**EDWARD W. HIERONYMUS,** born Davenport, Iowa, June 13, 1943; admitted to bar, 1968, Iowa; 1969, California. *Education:* Knox College (A.B., cum laude, 1965); Duke University (J.D., cum laude, 1968). Recent Developments Editor, Duke Law Journal, 1967-1968. Judge Advocate, U.S. Army, 1968-1974. Co-Chairman, Natural Resources Subsection, Real Property Section, State Bar of California, 1986-1987. *Member:* Los Angeles County, Iowa and American Bar Associations. **PRACTICE AREAS:** Real Property; Natural Resources; Water Law; Environmental Law.

### OF COUNSEL

**BARTON BEEK,** born Pasadena, California, January 23, 1924; admitted to bar, 1955, California. *Education:* California Institute of Technology (B.S., 1944); Stanford University (M.B.A., 1948); Loyola University (LL.B., 1955). *Member:* Los Angeles County and American Bar Associations. (Newport Beach Office). **PRACTICE AREAS:** Corporate Finance; Mergers and Acquisitions; Emerging Hi-Tech Companies.

**R. BRADBURY CLARK,** born Des Moines, Iowa, May 11, 1924; admitted to bar, 1952, California. *Education:* Harvard University (A.B., 1946); Harvard Law School (LL.B., 1951); Oxford University (Dip.L., 1952); Church Divinity School of the Pacific (D.H.L., 1983). Phi Beta Kappa. Member, Board of Editors, Harvard Law Review, 1950-1951. Editor, Ballantine and Sterling, California Corporation Laws, 6 Vols., 1976—. Member, Chancery Club. Chair: State Bar Committee on Corporations, 1976-1977; State Bar Drafting Committee on General Corporation Law, 1973-1981; Executive Committee, Business Law Section, 1984-1987, Secretary, 1986-1987; State Bar Committee on Revision of Nonprofit Corporation Law, 1980-1984, 1991—. *Member:* Los Angeles County (Real Property Section, Chair, 1969-1970, and Corporations Section) and American (Member: Business Law Section, Committee on Law and Accounting, Subcommittee on Audit Inquiry Responses and Committee on Legal Opinions) Bar Associations. **PRACTICE AREAS:** Corporations; Nonprofit Corporations; Limited Liability Companies; Limited Liability Partnerships; Project Finance; Public Utilities; Financial Institutions.

**OWEN OLPIN,** born Idaho Falls, Idaho, July 10, 1934; admitted to bar, 1959, California; 1979, District of Columbia; 1973, U.S. Supreme Court. *Education:* Brigham Young University (B.S., 1955); Columbia University (LL.B., 1958). Phi Beta Kappa; Phi Kappa Phi; Order of the Coif. Member, Board of Editors, Columbia Law Review, 1957-1958. Visiting Professor, University of Texas School of Law, 1969-1970. Farr Presidential Endowed Chair in Environmental Law, University of Utah College of Law, 1970-1976. *Member:* Los Angeles County and American (Council Member, Section of Administrative Law and Regulatory Practice) Bar Associations; American Law Institute; Senior Conference Fellow of the United States Administrative Conference. **PRACTICE AREAS:** Natural Resources; Environmental Law.

**LAWRENCE J. SHEEHAN,** born San Francisco, California, July 23, 1932; admitted to bar, 1960, California. *Education:* Stanford University (A.B., 1957; LL.B., 1959). Phi Alpha Delta; Order of the Coif. President, Stanford Law Review, 1958-1959. Law Clerk to Chief Judge Clark, U.S. Court of Appeals, 2nd Circuit, 1959-1960. *Member:* Los Angeles County

# O'MELVENY & MYERS LLP, Los Angeles—Continued

and American Bar Associations. (Century City Office). *PRACTICE AREAS:* Mutual Funds; Investment Management.

**CLYDE E. TRITT,** born Ordway, Colorado, January 23, 1920; admitted to bar, 1949, California. *Education:* Colorado College (A.B., 1941); Stanford University (LL.B., 1949). Order of the Coif; Delta Theta Phi. Member, Board of Editors, Stanford Law Review, 1947-1948. *Member:* Los Angeles County (Chairman, Tax Committee, 1963—) and American (Chairman, Employee Benefits Committee, Tax Section) Bar Associations. (Certified Specialist, Taxation Law, The State Bar of California Board of Legal Specialization).

**WILLIAM W. VAUGHN,** born Los Angeles, California, August 29, 1930; admitted to bar, 1956, California. *Education:* Stanford University (A.B., 1952); University of California at Los Angeles (LL.B., 1955). Order of the Coif. Member, Board of Editors, U.C.L.A. Law Review, 1953-1955. Recipient, Learned Hand Award, The American Jewish Committee, 1991. *Member:* Los Angeles County (Member, Board of Trustees, 1976-1978, 1980-1982; Chairman, Committee on Professionalism, 1988-1990) and American (Co-Chair: First Amendment and Media Litigation Committee, Litigation Section, 1985-1987; Securities Litigation Committee, Litigation Section, 1981-1984) Bar Associations; Los Angeles County Bar Foundation (Member, Board of Directors, 1992-1995); Association of Business Trial Lawyers (Member, Board of Governors, 1978-1982); Chancery Club. Fellow: American College of Trial Lawyers (Member, Board of Regents, 1991-1995). *PRACTICE AREAS:* Litigation.

## SPECIAL COUNSEL

**PETER B. ACKERMAN,** born Agana, Guam, June 23, 1954; admitted to bar, 1984, California and U.S. District Court, Central District of California; 1989, U.S. District Court, Northern District of California; 1990, U.S. Court of Appeals, Ninth Circuit. *Education:* University of California at Berkeley (B.A., 1981); Boston University School of Law (J.D., cum laude, 1984). Staff Member, 1982-1983 and Editor, 1983-1984, Boston University Law Review.

**SUSAN E. AKENS,** born Wilmington, Delaware, September 9, 1962; admitted to bar, 1988, California and U.S. District Court, Central District of California; 1991, District of Columbia. *Education:* Rutgers University (B.S., Pharmacy, with highest honors, 1985); University of Virginia (J.D., 1988). Rho Chi; Phi Delta Phi. Recipient, American Jurisprudence Awards in Civil Procedure and Federal Tax. Licensed Pharmacist, New Jersey, 1985. *Member:* Beverly Hills, Los Angeles County and American Bar Associations; District of Columbia Bar; American Pharmaceutical Association. (Century City Office). *PRACTICE AREAS:* Entertainment Law.

**KEVIN RAY BAKER,** born Kirksville, Missouri, July 1, 1961; admitted to bar, 1989, California, U.S. District Court, Central District of California and U.S. Court of Appeals, Ninth Circuit. *Education:* Claremont McKenna College (B.A., cum laude, with honors in Economics and Accounting, 1984); Harvard University Law School (J.D., cum laude, 1989). Omicron Delta Epsilon. Certified Public Accountant, Texas, 1986. *Member:* Orange County (Member, Business Law Section) and American (Member, Business Law and Taxation Sections) Bar Associations. (Newport Beach Office). *PRACTICE AREAS:* Mergers and Acquisitions; Securities Offerings; Franchise Law and General Corporate Matters.

**DAVID T. BEDDOW,** born Logan, West Virginia, April 13, 1955; admitted to bar, 1979, District of Columbia; 1982, U.S. Court of Appeals, Third Circuit; 1983, U.S. District Court, District of Columbia; 1985, U.S. Court of Appeals, District of Columbia Circuit and U.S. Claims Court. *Education:* Colgate University (A.B., magna cum laude, high honors in History, 1976); University of Virginia (J.D., 1979). Phi Beta Kappa; Phi Alpha Theta. Member, University of Virginia Law Review, Editorial Board, 1977-1979. Co-Author: "Should The Shipping Act of 1984 Be Amended To Eliminate Conference Antitrust Immunity?" Federal Bar News & Journal-volume 36, no. 8, Oct, 1989, pg. 357. *Member:* District of Columbia Bar; Federal (Officer, Transportation Law Section) and American (Member, Antitrust and Administrative Law and Regulatory Practice Sections) Bar Associations. (Washington, D.C. Office). *PRACTICE AREAS:* Antitrust; Aviation; Transportation.

**STAN BLUMENFELD,** born Patchogue, New York, March 7, 1962; admitted to bar, 1989, California and U.S. District Court, Central District of California. *Education:* State University of New York at Binghamton (B.A., 1984); New York University (M.A., 1985); University of California School of Law, Los Angeles (J.D., 1988). Phi Beta Kappa; Order of the Coif. Editor-in-Chief, UCLA Law Review. Law Clerk for the Honorable Cynthia Holcomb Hall, U.S. Court of Appeals, Ninth Circuit. Member, U.S. Attorney's Office, Civil Division, Los Angeles, 1989-1993. *Member:* American Bar Association; The State Bar of California. *PRACTICE AREAS:* Litigation. *Email:* sblumenfeld@omm.com

**ROSEMARY B. BOLLER,** born New York, N.Y., July 30, 1958; admitted to bar, 1984, New York and U.S. District Court, Eastern and Southern Districts of New York; 1992, U.S. District Court, Western District of Michigan. *Education:* St. Bonaventure University (B.A., 1980); St. John's University (J.D., 1983). Senior Notes and Comments Editor, St. John's Law Review, 1982-1983. Law Clerk to Honorable Frank X. Altimari, Eastern District of New York, 1983-1985. *Member:* Association of the Bar of the City of New York; American Bar Association; Federal Bar Council. (New York, N.Y. Office). *PRACTICE AREAS:* Insurance Coverage Litigation; General Commercial Litigation. *Email:* rboller@omm.com

**JENNIFER L. BOROW,** born New York, N.Y., January 6, 1964; admitted to bar, 1988, California and U.S. District Court, Central District of California. *Education:* Smith College (B.A., cum laude, 1985); Yale Law School (J.D., 1988). Current Topics Editor, Yale Law and Policy Review, 1987-1988. *Member:* Los Angeles County and American Bar Associations. (Century City Office). *PRACTICE AREAS:* Corporate Law; Corporate Acquisitions and Dispositions.

**MARK L. BRADSHAW,** born Waterloo, Iowa, January 18, 1962; admitted to bar, 1988, California and U.S. District Court, Central District of California; 1989, U.S. District Court, Eastern District of California; 1992, U.S. District Court, Northern and Southern Districts of California. *Education:* University of Iowa (B.B.A., with highest distinction, 1983); University of Texas at Austin (M.B.A., 1985; J.D., 1988). Beta Gamma Sigma; Phi Kappa Phi. Recipient, Certificate of Achievement, University of Iowa, 1983. Dean's Award for Academic Excellence, University of Texas Graduate School of Business, 1985. Staff Member, Legal Research Board, 1986-1988. *Member:* State Bar of California; American Bar Association. (San Francisco and Los Angeles Offices). *PRACTICE AREAS:* Bankruptcy Law.

**AVERY R. BROWN,** born New York, N.Y., September 19, 1964; admitted to bar, 1989, California, U.S. District Court, Central District of California and U.S. Court of Appeals, Ninth Circuit. *Education:* The Wharton School, University of Pennsylvania (B.S., Economics, 1986); University of California at Los Angeles School of Law (J.D., 1989). Order of the Coif. Recipient, American Jurisprudence Award, Civil Procedure. Staff Member, UCLA Law Review, 1987-1988. *Member:* American Bar Association. *LANGUAGES:* French. *PRACTICE AREAS:* Mergers and Acquisition Transactions.

**DEBORAH J. BROWN,** born Los Angeles, California, July 5, 1963; admitted to bar, 1988, California and U.S. District Court, Central District of California. *Education:* University of California at Berkeley (B.A., with distinction, 1984); University of California at Los Angeles (J.D., 1988). Member, Moot Court Board. Co-Author with Howard Heitner: "The Enforceable Guarantee: Illusion or Reality?" California Real Property Law Journal, Spring 1990. Law Externe to Honorable Laurence H. Silberman, U.S. Court of Appeals, District of Columbia Circuit, 1987. *Member:* State Bar of California (Real Estate Section); Los Angeles County Bar Association; Century City Bar Association; Los Angeles County Barristers. (Century City Office). *PRACTICE AREAS:* Real Estate Law.

**RICHARD W. BUCKNER,** born Alexandria, Virginia, September 13, 1954; admitted to bar, 1982, California; 1983, U.S. District Court, Central District of California; 1985, U.S. District Court, Northern District of California. *Education:* George Mason University (B.S., with distinction, 1976); University of Southern California (J.D., 1981). Order of the Coif. Staff Member, University of Southern California Law Review, 1979-1981. Law Clerk to the Hon. Walter Ely, U.S. Court of Appeals for the Ninth Circuit, 1981-1982. *Member:* Los Angeles County and American Bar Associations. *PRACTICE AREAS:* Insurance Litigation; Business Law.

**DONALD G. CARDEN,** born Knoxville, Tennessee, November 28, 1961; admitted to bar, 1987, New York; 1995, New Jersey. *Education:* Georgetown University (B.A., magna cum laude, 1983); Georgetown University Law Center (J.D., magna cum laude, 1986). Order of the Coif. Member, 1984-1985 and Associate Editor, 1985-1986, The Tax Lawyer. Author: Note, Availability of Tax-Free Reorganization Treatment For Mergers Involving Hybrid Securities, 39 Tax Lawyer 349 (1986). (New York, N.Y. Office). *PRACTICE AREAS:* Federal Income Tax. *Email:* dcarden@omm.com

**THOMAS G. CARRUTHERS,** born Bristol, Connecticut, September 1, 1953; admitted to bar, 1981, Connecticut, New York and U.S. District

*(This Listing Continued)*

Court, Southern and Eastern Districts of New York; 1989, California. *Education:* Dickinson College (B.A., magna cum laude, 1976); The American University, Washington College of Law (J.D., 1980). Member, American University Law Review, 1979-1980. Court Clerk, District of Columbia Court of Appeals, 1980-1981. *Member:* State Bar of California. (New York, N.Y. Office). **PRACTICE AREAS:** Litigation; Environmental Insurance Coverage Litigation. **Email:** tcarruthers@omm.com

**K. LEIGH CHAPMAN,** born Shelby, North Carolina, April 24, 1964; admitted to bar, 1989, California. *Education:* Duke University (A.B., Economics, magna cum laude, 1985); Columbia University (J.D., 1988). Phi Beta Kappa. Harlan Fiske Stone Scholar. Editor, Columbia University Business Law Review, 1987-1988. Author: Note, "Statutory Responses to Boardroom Fears," Columbia Business Law Review, Vol. 1987, No. 3. **PRACTICE AREAS:** Labor and Employment Law.

**CHRISTINE E. COLEMAN,** born Palo Alto, California; admitted to bar, 1989, California, U.S. Court of Appeals, Ninth Circuit and U.S. District Court, Central District of California. *Education:* Stanford University (A.B., 1976); California State University at Los Angeles (M.A., 1982)); Stanford Law School (J.D., 1989). Member: Stanford Law Review, 1987-1989; Stanford Journal of International Law, 1986-1987. (Century City Office). **PRACTICE AREAS:** Entertainment Law.

**FIONA M. CONNELL,** born Godalming, England, August 25, 1957; admitted to bar, 1987, California; 1988, U.S. District Court, Southern District of California and U.S. Court of Appeals, Ninth Circuit. *Education:* Duke University (B.A., magna cum laude, 1979); Zhongshan University, P.R.C.; University of California at Los Angeles (J.D., 1987). Order of the Coif. Editor-in-Chief, UCLA Pacific Basin Law Journal, 1984-1985. Member, Asia Society, 1987—. (Hong Kong Office). **LANGUAGES:** Chinese (Mandarin). **PRACTICE AREAS:** Corporate Law; Banking; Transactions in China and Southeast Asia. **Email:** fconnell@omm.com

**STEVEN M. COOPER,** born Los Angeles, California, August 18, 1964; admitted to bar, 1989, California, U.S. District Court, Central District of California and U.S. Court of Appeals, Ninth Circuit. *Education:* University of California at San Diego (B.A., cum laude, 1986); Hastings College of Law, University of California (J.D., magna cum laude, 1989). Order of the Coif. Articles Editor, Hastings Law Journal. Law Clerk to U.S. District Court Judge A. Andrew Hauk. **PRACTICE AREAS:** Toxic Tort Litigation; Employment Discrimination.

**REGINAM (GINGER) COVITT,** born Morristown, New Jersey, January 6, 1952; admitted to bar, 1981, California; 1982, U.S. District Court, Central District of California and U.S. Court of Appeals, Ninth Circuit; 1990, U.S. Tax Court. *Education:* University of Massachusetts (B.A., magna cum laude, 1973); University of California at Los Angeles (M.A., 1976; J.D., 1981). Author: "Funding Children's Education After the Trust Reform Act of 1984," California State Bar Estate Planning, Trust and Probate News, Spring, 1985. Co-Author: "Permanent Trusts," Drafting California Irrevocable Living Trusts, CEB, 1987. "Revocable Trusts and Other Property Arrangements," in Drafting California Revocable Living Trusts, CEB, 1984; "What Is Community Property?" in How To Live— And Die— With California Probate, Gulf Publishing Co., 1984. Guest Lecturer, UCLA Estate Planning Clinical Program, Fall, 1984, 1986, 1987, 1988. (Century City Office). **PRACTICE AREAS:** Trusts and Estate.

**JOHN A. CROSE, JR.,** born Seattle, Washington, October 27, 1959; admitted to bar, 1984, California and U.S. District Court, Central District of California; 1987, U.S. District Court, Southern District of California; 1988, U.S. District Court, Northern District of California; 1988, U.S. Court of Appeals, Ninth Circuit; 1993, U.S. Court of Appeals, Federal Circuit; 1994, U.S. Supreme Court. *Education:* University of California at Los Angeles (B.A., magna cum laude, 1981; J.D., 1984). Phi Beta Kappa; Order of the Coif. Recipient, American Jurisprudence Awards in Property, 1982 and Family Wealth Transactions, 1983. Executive Board of Judges Moot Court Honors Program, 1983-1984. Extern for Hon. Arthur L. Alarcon, U.S. Court of Appeals, Ninth Circuit, 1983-1984. *Member:* American Bar Association (Member, Litigation Section); Association of Business Trial Lawyers. **PRACTICE AREAS:** Litigation; Intellectual Property; Mass Torts; Insurance Coverage; Commercial Contracts.

**GEORGE C. DEMOS,** born La Mesa, California, October 5, 1962; admitted to bar, 1989, California, U.S. District Court, Central District of California and U.S. Court of Appeals, Ninth Circuit. *Education:* University of California at San Diego (B.A., cum laude, Departmental honors, with highest Distinction, 1984); University of Southern California (J.D., 1989). Order of the Coif; Alpha Beta Psi; Beta Gamma Sigma. *Member:* Los Angeles County (Tax Section) and American Bar Associations. (Newport Beach Office). **PRACTICE AREAS:** Health Care.

*(This Listing Continued)*

**DOUGLAS E. DEXTER,** born Honolulu, Hawaii, January 21, 1960; admitted to bar, 1984, California and U.S. District Court, Central District of California; 1988, U.S. Court of Appeals, Ninth Circuit. *Education:* San Jose State University (B.S., 1981); University of San Diego (J.D., magna cum laude, 1984). Comments Editor, San Diego Law Review, 1983-1984. Contributing Author: "Litigating the Employment Case: A Tort Guide for Plaintiff and Defense Attorneys," American Bar Association (1995). (San Francisco Office). **PRACTICE AREAS:** Wrongful Termination; Severance Agreements; Employment Litigation; Collective Bargaining. **Email:** ddexter@omm.comm

**MARIAN J. DILLON,** born New York, N.Y., November 2, 1961; admitted to bar, 1988, California and U.S. District Court, Central District of California. *Education:* University of Notre Dame (B.B.A., summa cum laude, 1983); Stanford Law School (J.D., with honors, 1988). Order of the Coif; Beta Gamma Sigma. Member, 1986-1987 and Associate Managing Editor, 1987-1988, Stanford Law Review. Certified Public Accountant, Texas, 1985. *Member:* Texas Society of Certified Public Accountants. (New York, N.Y. and Los Angeles, California Offices). **PRACTICE AREAS:** Corporate Law.

**SUZANNE F. DUFF,** born Port Chester, New York, January 12, 1937; admitted to bar, 1981, California and U.S. District Court, Central District of California; 1983, U.S. Temporary Emergency Court of Appeals; 1984, U.S. Court of Appeals, Ninth Circuit; 1986, U.S. District Court, Eastern District of California; 1988, U.S. District Court, Northern District of California; 1989, U.S. Court of Appeals, District of Columbia Circuit. *Education:* Green Mountain College (A.A., 1956); Southwestern University (J.D., magna cum laude, 1981). Staff Member, 1978-1979 and Note and Comment Editor, 1979-1980, Southwestern University Law Review. *Member:* Los Angeles County and American Bar Associations. **PRACTICE AREAS:** Business Litigation.

**DAVID P. ENZMINGER,** born Breckenridge, Minnesota, September 10, 1963; admitted to bar, 1988, California and U.S. District Court, Central District of California; 1989, Arizona. *Education:* University of the Redlands (B.A., cum laude, 1985); Arizona State University (J.D., cum laude, 1988). Phi Beta Kappa; Omicron Delta Epsilon. Staff Member, 1986-1987 and Associate Editor, 1987-1988, Arizona State Law Journal. Author: "Waive Goodbye to Law in the Public Interest - The Use of Coercive Fee Waivers in Civil Rights Actions, Evans v. Jeff D." 19 Arizona State Law Journal 749, 1987. *Member:* Los Angeles County and American (Section of Antitrust Law) Bar Associations. **LANGUAGES:** German. **PRACTICE AREAS:** Litigation.

**DAVID G. ESTES,** born Monterey, California, February 16, 1957; admitted to bar, 1984, California. *Education:* University of California at Los Angeles (B.A., 1980); University of San Francisco (J.D., valedictorian, 1984). Adjunct Professor, University of San Francisco, 1988. (San Francisco Office). **PRACTICE AREAS:** Real Estate; Real Estate Securities. **Email:** destes@omm.com

**THOMAS A. FERRIGNO,** born New Haven, Connecticut, April 3, 1949; admitted to bar, 1975, District of Columbia. *Education:* Georgetown University (A.B., 1971); Georgetown University Law Center (J.D., 1975). Co-Author: with Ralph C. Ferrara and David S. Darland, "Hardball! The SEC's New Arsenal of Enforcement Weapons," 47 The Business Lawyer 33 (1991). Chief Counsel, Division of Enforcement, U.S. Securities and Exchange Commission, 1988-1989. *Member:* American Bar Association. (Washington, D.C. Office). **PRACTICE AREAS:** Securities Enforcement Law; Securities Regulation Law. **Email:** tferrigno@omm.com

**CHARLES W. FOURNIER,** born St. Louis, Missouri, December 16, 1953; admitted to bar, 1983, New York; 1986, U.S. District Court, Southern and Eastern Districts of New York; 1988, U.S. Court of Appeals, Fifth Circuit and U.S. District Court, Southern District of Texas. *Education:* Trinity University (B.A., summa cum laude, 1976); Yale University (M.A., J.D., 1981). Phi Beta Kappa. Editor, Yale Law Journal, 1980-1981. Author: Note, "The Case for Special Juries in Complex Civil Litigation," 89 Yale Law Journal 1155 (1980). Law Clerk to Hon. Robert A. Sprecher, U.S. Court of Appeals, Seventh Circuit, 1981-1982. *Member:* The Association of the Bar of the City of New York; American Bar Association. (New York, N.Y. Office). **PRACTICE AREAS:** Litigation; Labor and Employment.

**DANIEL M. FREEDMAN,** born New Rochelle, New York, January 19, 1953; admitted to bar, 1979, New York (Not admitted in California). *Education:* Vassar College (A.B., 1975); Boston University (J.D., 1978); New York University School of Law. *Member:* The Association of the Bar of the City of New York (Member, Committee on the Profession, 1988-

*(This Listing Continued)*

CAA1057B

**O'MELVENY & MYERS LLP, Los Angeles—Continued**

1992). (Century City Office). *PRACTICE AREAS:* Securities; Corporate Finance; Mergers and Acquisitions. *Email:* dfreedman@omm.com

**DAVID R. GARCIA,** born Tampa, Florida, March 5, 1954; admitted to bar, 1980, District of Columbia; 1981, Florida and U.S. District Court for the District of Columbia ; 1984, New York and U.S. District Court, Southern District of New York; 1990, California, U.S. District Court, Central District of California and U.S. Court of Appeals, Ninth Circuit. *Education:* Harvard University (B.A., 1976); Georgetown University Law School (J.D., 1979). Law Clerk to The Honorable Constance Baker Motley, U.S. District Court, Southern District of New York, 1980-1981. *PRACTICE AREAS:* Securities Litigation; SEC Enforcement; Antitrust Counseling and Litigation.

**JAMES H. GIANNINOTO,** born Greenwich, Connecticut, July 9, 1952; admitted to bar, 1984, Connecticut; 1985, New York and U.S. District Court, Southern and Eastern Districts of New York. *Education:* Bard College (B.A., 1974); New York Law School (J.D., cum laude, 1984). Executive Editor, Journal of International and Comparative Law, 1983-1984. Author: Note, "Sovereignty Under Reservation, American Indian Tribal Sovereignty in Law and Practice," 4 New York Law School Journal of International and Comparative Law 589, 1983. *Member:* New York State and American Bar Associations. (New York, N.Y. Office). *PRACTICE AREAS:* Litigation.

**JOSEPH G. GIANNOLA,** born Brooklyn, New York, September 21, 1941; admitted to bar, 1968, New York; 1970, U.S. Tax Court; 1971, U.S. Claims Court. *Education:* St. John's University (B.B.A., 1964; J.D., 1967); Georgetown University (LL.M., in Taxation, 1971). Articles Editor, St. John's Law Review, 1966-1967. Attorney, Office of Chief Counsel, Internal Revenue Service, 1967-1971. *Member:* New York State Bar Association. (New York, N.Y. Office). *PRACTICE AREAS:* Tax Law.

**ROBERT A. GRAUMAN,** born New York, N.Y., October 19, 1949; admitted to bar, 1974, New York. *Education:* State University of New York at Stony Brook (B.A., magna cum laude, 1970); Columbia Law School (J.D., 1973). Harlan Fiske Stone Scholar, 1973. Volunteer Arbitrator, New York City Small Claims Court, 1983-1990. Author: "Net Capital Requirements for Broker-Dealers, "Financing Broker Dealers, PLI, 1972. *Member:* New York State and American (Member, Section on Corporation, Banking and Business Law) Bar Associations. (New York, N.Y. Office). *PRACTICE AREAS:* Corporate Law; Securities; International Mergers and Acquisitions; International Corporate Finance; Mergers, Acquisitions and Divestitures; Mortgage Securitization. *Email:* rgrauman@omm.com

**EDWARD G. GREGORY,** born Teaneck, New Jersey, March 25, 1949; admitted to bar, 1987, California; 1988, U.S. District Court, Central District of California. *Education:* Stevens Institute of Technology (B.E., 1970); Loyola Marymount Law School of Los Angeles (J.D., cum laude, 1986). Member, St. Thomas More Law Honor Society. Recipient, American Jurisprudence Awards in Labor Law 1985 and in Patent Law and Corporations Law, 1986. *Member:* American Bar Association; American Society for Metals. *PRACTICE AREAS:* Labor and Employment Law. *Email:* egregory@omm.com

**ALLAN I. GROSSMAN,** born Brooklyn, New York, October 13, 1945; admitted to bar, 1970, California; 1971, U.S. Tax Court; 1981, New York. *Education:* Brooklyn College (B.S., 1966); Harvard University (J.D., 1969). Editor, Harvard Law Review, 1967-1969. Clerk to Judge John W. Kern III, District of Columbia Court of Appeals, 1969-1970. *Member:* Los Angeles County Bar Association (Member, Employee Benefits Committee, 1981; Secretary, 1982; Vice-Chairman, 1983; Chairman, 1984); The State Bar of California (Member, Tax Section); Western Pension and Benefits Conference. *PRACTICE AREAS:* Employee Benefits; ERISA; Employee Stock Ownership Trusts; Pension and Profit Sharing Plans. *Email:* agrossman@omm.com

**KAREN R. GROWDON,** born Lebanon, Tennessee, June 27, 1948; admitted to bar, 1978, California and U.S. District Court, Central District of California. *Education:* Vanderbilt University (B.A., cum laude, 1969; M.A.T., 1971); Loyola University (J.D., cum laude, 1978). Staff Member, 1976-1977 and Articles Editor, 1977-1978, Loyola University of Los Angeles Law Review. Author: Note, "Extraterritorial Application of the Sherman Act," 10 Loyola University of Los Angeles Law Review 677, 1977. *Member:* American Bar Association; Women Lawyers Association of Los Angeles. *PRACTICE AREAS:* Civil Litigation; Environmental Insurance Coverage Litigation.

**HAROLD HENDERSON,** born Idaho Falls, Idaho, August 12, 1960; admitted to bar, 1990, New York and District of Columbia. *Education:* Gustavus Adolphus College (B.A., magna cum laude, 1982); University of Hawaii (M.A., 1985); Georgetown University (J.D., magna cum laude, 1989). Order of the Coif. Associate Editor, Georgetown Law Journal, 1988-1989. *Member:* The District of Columbia Bar; American Bar Association. (Washington, D. C. Office). *PRACTICE AREAS:* Corporation Law.

**MARGARET C. HENRY,** born Washington, D.C., November 24, 1951; admitted to bar, 1977, New Mexico; 1980, District of Columbia; 1986, New York. *Education:* Georgetown University (B.A., cum laude, 1974); George Washington University (J.D., 1977; LL.M., 1980). Visiting Assistant Professor (Corporate Tax and Antitrust Law), University of New Mexico, 1980. Visiting Assistant Professor (Federal Income Tax and Estate and Gift Tax Law), Catholic University Law School, 1980-1981. Author: "Reissuance Revisited," Tax Notes (January 2, 1989); "The Impact of Reeves v. Comm'r on the Creeping Control 'B' Reorganization: The Need for Legislative Re-examination of Section 368 (a) (1) (B)," Journal of Corporate Taxation, 195 (1983). *Member:* National Association of Bond Lawyers and American Bar Association. (New York, N.Y. Office). *PRACTICE AREAS:* Tax-Exempt Finance. *Email:* mhenry@omm.com

**DAVID A. HOLLANDER,** born New York, N.Y., July 17, 1961; admitted to bar, 1985, California and U.S. District Court, Central District of California. *Education:* Wharton School of Business (B.S., summa cum laude, 1982); Stanford Law School (J.D., 1985). Associate Editor, Stanford Law Review, 1984-1985. Author: "The Economics of Libel Litigation," The Cost of Libel 257 E. Dennis Ed. 1989. *PRACTICE AREAS:* Bankruptcy; Banking and Finance.

**CHRIS HOLLINGER,** born Glendale, California, June 13, 1964; admitted to bar, 1990, California and U.S. District Court, Central District of California. *Education:* Dartmouth College (B.A., summa cum laude, 1986); University of Chicago (J.D., 1989). Phi Beta Kappa. *Member:* American Bar Association (Member, Sections on: Labor and Employment, Litigation, Criminal Justice). *PRACTICE AREAS:* Railway Labor Act Litigation.

**MARK C. HOLSCHER,** born Inglewood, California, October 27, 1962; admitted to bar, 1988, California and U.S. District Court, Central District of California. *Education:* University of California at Berkeley (B.S., 1985); Boalt Hall School of Law, University of California (J.D., 1988). Law Clerk to Judge William Keller, U.S. District Court, Central District of California. Assistant U.S. Attorney, U.S. Attorney's Office, 1989-1994.

**DAVID I. HURWITZ,** born Freeport, New York, August 8, 1963; admitted to bar, 1988, Illinois; 1989, U.S. District Court, Northern District of Illinois; 1993, U.S. Court of Appeals, Seventh Circuit; 1994, U.S. District Court, Central District of California (Not admitted in California). *Education:* University of Pennsylvania (B.A., summa cum laude, 1984); University of Chicago (J.D., cum laude, 1988). Order of the Coif. Associate Editor, University of Chicago Law Review, 1987-1988. *Member:* Chicago Bar Association. *PRACTICE AREAS:* Commercial Trial and Appellate Practice; Class Action Litigation.

**KENNETH E. JOHNSON,** born Pittsburgh, Pennsylvania, October 19, 1955; admitted to bar, 1983, District of Columbia; 1984, California, U.S. District Court, Central and Northern Districts of California and U.S. Court of Appeals, Ninth Circuit and District of Columbia Circuits. *Education:* Harvard College (B.A., cum laude, 1977); Columbia University (J.D., 1982). Notes and Comments Editor, Columbia Law Review, 1981-1982. Law Clerk for Hon. Cynthia Holcomb Hall, U.S. District Court, Central District of California, 1982-1984. Author: Comment, "Limiting the Legislative Veto," 81 Columbia Law Review 1721, 1981. *Member:* Los Angeles County (Member, Labor Law Section) and American Bar Associations. *PRACTICE AREAS:* Labor and Employment; Employee Benefits Litigation.

**CAROL A. JOHNSTON,** born Indianapolis, Indiana, July 31, 1954; admitted to bar, 1979, California. *Education:* Middlebury College (B.A., magna cum laude, 1976); University of Chicago (J.D., 1979). *Member:* Los Angeles County Bar Association (Member, Sections on: Probate and Trust Law; Taxation). (Century City Office). *PRACTICE AREAS:* Trusts and Estates.

**JEFFREY M. JUDD,** born Butte, Montana, April 27, 1954; admitted to bar, 1988, California. *Education:* Harvard College (B.A., 1976); Hastings College of Law, University of California (J.D., cum laude, 1988). Order of the Coif. Member, Thurston Society. Recipient: Arnheim Award; David McCord Prize. Staff Member, 1986-1987 and Senior Research Editor, 1987-1988, Hastings Law Journal. Author: "The Implied Covenant of Good Faith & Fair Dealing: Employees' Good Faith Duties," 39 Hast. L.J. 453.

*(This Listing Continued)*

Law Clerk for Justice Marcus M. Kaufman, California Supreme Court, 1988-1989. (San Francisco Office). *PRACTICE AREAS:* Environmental Law and Disputes involving Property, including Real and Intellectual Property.

**CHRISTOPHER N. KANDEL,** born Baltimore, Maryland, May 11, 1960; admitted to bar, 1985, California; 1986, Maryland; 1987, District of Columbia. *Education:* Yale University (B.A., magna cum laude); Cornell Law School (J.D., cum laude, 1985). Member, Cornell International Law Journal, 1983-1985. Co-Author: "Fraudulent Conveyance Concerns in Leveraged Buyout Lending," The Business lawyer, Vol. 43, No. 1, November, 1987. (London, England Office). *PRACTICE AREAS:* Corporate Law; Financial Institutions. *Email:* ckandel@omm.com

**JEFFREY W. KILDUFF,** born Washington, D.C., September 26, 1958; admitted to bar, 1988, Virginia; 1991, District of Columbia. *Education:* University of Maryland (B.S., cum laude, 1981); Georgetown University Law Center (J.D., cum laude, 1988). Beta Gamma Sigma. Staff Member, The Tax Lawyer, 1986-1987. Author: Note, "The 'Internal Consistency' Test is Alive and Well: *Tyler Pipe Industries, Inc. v. Washington Department of Revenue,"* The Tax Lawyer, Vol. 41, No. 2, Winter, 1988. *Member:* The District of Columbia Bar; Virginia State Bar; American Bar Association. (Washington, D.C. Office). *PRACTICE AREAS:* Litigation.

**MALCOLM M. KRATZER,** born New Haven, Connecticut, March 21. 1964; admitted to bar, 1989, New Jersey; 1990, New York. *Education:* Princeton University (B.A., 1986); New York University (J.D., 1989). Order of Barristers. Editor-in-Chief, Moot Court Casebook, 1988-1989. Author: "Brady v. Friday," 12 N.Y.U. Moot Court Casebook 45, 1988. *Member:* New York State, New Jersey State and American Bar Associations. (New York, N. Y. Office). *PRACTICE AREAS:* Real Estate Financings and Restructurings.

**STANFORD G. LADNER,** born Bay St. Louis, Mississippi, February 19, 1951; admitted to bar, 1977, Mississippi; 1980, New York; U.S. Supreme Court. *Education:* The Catholic University of America (B.A., cum laude, 1973; M.A., J.D., 1976). Member, Board of Directors, National Water Resources Association, 1986-1992. (New York, N.Y. Office). *PRACTICE AREAS:* Public Finance. *Email:* sladner@omm.com

**ELIZABETH A. LECKIE,** born Bournemouth, England, October 28, 1961; admitted to bar, 1987, England and Wales as Solicitor; 1990, New York. *Education:* St. Anne's College, Oxford, England (B.A. Law, 1984; M.A., 1990); The Law Society's College of Law, London (1985); University of Illinois (1988). *Member:* American Bar Association (Member, Business Law Section); The Law Society (England and Wales). (New York, N. Y. Office). *PRACTICE AREAS:* Banking; Corporate Law. *Email:* eleckie@omm.com

**DAVID G. LITT,** born Boston, Massachusetts, October 10, 1962; admitted to bar, 1989, California, U.S. Court of Appeals, Ninth Circuit and U.S. District Court, Central District of California; 1991, District of Columbia. *Education:* Yale University (B.A., in Economics, summa cum laude, 1984); University of Chicago (J.D., with honors, 1988). Phi Beta Kappa; Order of the Coif. Recipient, Floyd R. Mechem Scholarship and William R. Massee Award. Member, Chicago Law Review, 1986-1987. Law Clerk for: Chief Judge Alfred T. Goodwin U.S. Court of Appeals, Ninth Circuit, 1988-1989; Hon. Anthony M. Kennedy, Associate Justice, U.S. Supreme Court, 1990-1991. Co-Author, with Litt, Macey, Miller and Rubin, "Politics, Bureaucracies and Financial Markets: Bank Entry Into Commercial Paper Underwriting in the United States and Japan," 139 U. Pa. L. Rev. 369 (1990). Author: "Work in Progress at the Ministry of Finance: Proposals for Restructuring the Japanese Financial Services Industry," 12 U. Pa. J. Int'l. Bus. L. 711 (1991). *Member:* American Bar Association (Business Law Section). (Washington, D.C. Office). *LANGUAGES:* Japanese. *PRACTICE AREAS:* Banking and Finance; Corporate Law; International Law. *Email:* dlitt@omm.com

**FRANCES ELIZABETH LOSSING,** born Dallas, Texas, June 10, 1944; admitted to bar, 1978, California and U.S. District Court, Central District of California. *Education:* University of Michigan (B.A. with distinction, 1966); University of California at Los Angeles (J.D., 1978). Order of the Coif. Staff Member, 1976-1977 and Comment Editor, 1977-1978, U.C.L.A. Law Review. *Member:* Los Angeles County and American (Business Law Section) Bar Associations; State Bar of California. *PRACTICE AREAS:* Banking and Finance; Public Utilities. *Email:* flossing@omm.com

**HELEN P. MAC DONALD,** born Dublin, Ireland, March 11, 1965; admitted to bar, 1989, New York; 1994, California. *Education:* Trinity College, Dublin (LL.B., with honors, 1986); University of Cambridge (LL.M., with honors, 1987). (London, England Office; may also be contacted at Los Angeles Office). *PRACTICE AREAS:* Banking and Finance. *Email:* hmacdonald@omm.com

**MARCY JO MANDEL,** born Morristown, New Jersey, October 14, 1955; admitted to bar, 1981, California; 1982, U.S. Court of Appeals, Fourth and Ninth Circuits and U.S. District Court, Central, Northern and Southern Districts of California; 1983, District of Columbia and U.S. District Court, Eastern District of California; 1984, U.S. Tax Court and U.S. Court of Federal Claims; 1991, New York. *Education:* Vassar College (A.B., 1976); University of Chicago (M.A., 1977; J.D., 1981). Co-Chair, Hinton Moot Court Committee, 1980-1981. Law Clerk to Hon. Francis D. Murnaghan, Jr., U.S. Court of Appeals, Fourth Circuit, 1981-1982. *Member:* Los Angeles County and New York Bar Associations. *PRACTICE AREAS:* Tax Controversies and Litigation; State Taxation; Local Taxation.

**JOSEPH G. MCHUGH,** born Oakland, California, October 20, 1962; admitted to bar, 1987, California; 1988, U.S. District Court, Central District of California. *Education:* University of Notre Dame (B.A., with honors, 1984); Duke University School of Law (J.D., 1987). Staff Member, Duke Law Journal, 1986-1987. *PRACTICE AREAS:* Real Estate Law. *Email:* jmchugh@omm.com

**GREGORY R. OXFORD,** born Pontiac, Michigan, November 21, 1949; admitted to bar, 1974, California and U.S. District Court, Northern District of California; 1976, U.S. District Court Central District of California; 1980, U.S. District Court, Eastern and Southern Districts of California; 1985, U.S. Court of Appeals, Ninth Circuit. *Education:* University of Michigan (B.A., with high distinction, 1971); Stanford University (J.D., 1974). Phi Beta Kappa. Member of Staff, 1972-1974 and Note Editor, 1973-1974. Stanford Law Review. Law Clerk to Judge Ben C. Duniway, U.S. Court of Appeals, Ninth Circuit, 1974-1975. *Member:* State Bar of California; American Bar Association. *PRACTICE AREAS:* Business Litigation.

**ACHILLES M. PERRY,** born New York City, New York, July 20, 1964; admitted to bar, 1989, New Jersey and U.S. District Court, District of New Jersey; 1990, New York. *Education:* Brandeis University (B.A., cum laude, 1986); Fordham University (J.D., 1989). Articles Editor, Fordham Law Review, 1988-1989. Law Clerk, Hon. Alfred J. Lechner, Jr., U.S. District Court, District of New Jersey, 1989-1990. *Member:* New Jersey State and New York State Bar Associations. (New York, N.Y. Office). *PRACTICE AREAS:* Litigation; Regulatory Enforcement and Criminal Practice.

**DIANE E. PRITCHARD,** born Sacramento, California, May 22, 1954; admitted to bar, 1981, California. *Education:* Northeastern University (B.A., with highest honors, 1975); Columbia University (M.A., 1976); New York University (J.D., cum laude, 1980). Order of the Coif. Editor-in-Chief, New York University Law Review, 1979-1980. Law Clerk to the Honorable James L. Oakes, U.S. Court of Appeals, Second Circuit, 1980-1981. Author, "Procedures for Probate Contests in the Central District," Metropolitan News, February 1992. *Member:* State Bar of California; Los Angeles County Bar Association; Association of Business Trial Lawyers; Women Lawyers Association of Los Angeles. *PRACTICE AREAS:* Business Litigation.

**ERIC A. S. RICHARDS,** born Detroit, Michigan, January 1, 1965; admitted to bar, 1989, California, U.S. Court of Appeals, Ninth Circuit and U.S. District Court, Central District of California. *Education:* Yale University (B.A., 1986); Harvard University (J.D., cum laude, 1989). *Member:* Los Angeles County, National and American Bar Associations. *LANGUAGES:* Spanish. *PRACTICE AREAS:* Airport Project Finance; International Joint Ventures; Corporate and Securities.

**JOHN A. ROGOVIN,** born Washington, D.C., July 10, 1961; admitted to bar, 1989, New York and U.S. District Court, Southern District of New York; 1990, District of Columbia and U.S. District Court, Eastern District of New York; 1991, U.S. District Court, District of Columbia Circuit. *Education:* Columbia University (A.B., 1983; University of Virginia (J.D., 1987). Articles Editor, Virginia Journal of International Law, 1987. Deputy Assistant Attorney General, Civil Division, U.S. Justice Department, 1993-1996. Assistant to the Attorney General, U.S. Justice Department, 1993-1996. Deputy Transition Counsel, Presidential Transition, 1992-1993. Law Clerk, The Hon. Laurence H. Silberman, U.S. Court of Appeals for the District of Columbia Circuit, 1987-1988. Vice Chair, Transportation Committee, ABA Section of Administrative Law, 1996—. *Member:* New York State and American Bar Associations; The District of Columbia Bar. (Washington, D.C. Office). *PRACTICE AREAS:* Litigation; Telecommunications.

**TANCRED V. SCHIAVONI, III,** born Huntington, New York, November 4, 1961; admitted to bar, 1989, New York; 1991, U.S. District Court, Southern District of New York. *Education:* Georgetown University

*(This Listing Continued)*

## O'MELVENY & MYERS LLP, Los Angeles—Continued

(B.S.B.A., 1984); Georgetown University Law Center (J.D., 1988). Member, Georgetown Journal of Legal Ethics, 1985-1988. (New York, N.Y. Office). **PRACTICE AREAS:** Insurance Coverage Defense; Accountants Malpractice; Civil Litigation. **Email:** tschiavoni@omm.com

**PETER O. SHINEVAR,** born Jackson, Michigan, October 3, 1955; admitted to bar, 1982, District of Columbia; U.S. Supreme Court and U.S. Court of Appeals, First, Fifth, Sixth, Eighth, Ninth, Eleventh and Federal and District of Columbia Circuits; 1994, New York. *Education:* University of Michigan (A.B., with high distinction, 1977; J.D., summa cum laude, 1980). Phi Eta Sigma; Phi Beta Kappa; Order of the Coif. Senior Editor, Michigan Law Review, 1979-1980. Winner, Henry M. Campbell Moot Court Competition, 1980. Recipient, Henry M. Bates Scholarship; Emmett E. Egan Award. Author: Note, 78 Michigan Law Review 1116, 1980. Law Clerk to Judge Harry T. Edwards, U.S. Court of Appeals for the District of Columbia Circuit, 1981-1982. Contributing Author of: "Employee Benefits Law," ABA Section of Labor and Employment. *Member:* The District of Columbia Bar; New York State and American Bar Associations. (New York, N.Y. Office). **PRACTICE AREAS:** ERISA; Pension and Profit Sharing Law; Employee Benefits; Labor Law. **Email:** pshinevar@omm.com

**EDWARD J. SZCZEPKOWSKI,** born Camden, New Jersey, August 24, 1962; admitted to bar, 1988, California and U.S. District Court, Central District of California; 1993, U.S. Court of Appeals, Ninth Circuit. *Education:* University of Pennsylvania, The Wharton School of Finance (B.S.E., 1984); Boston University Law School (J.D., cum laude, 1987); Boston University Graduate School of Management (M.B.A., 1988). Edward F. Hennessey Distinguished Scholar. Recipient, Book Awards for Contracts, Corporate Tax and Family Law. *Member:* Los Angeles County Bar Association (Committee on Eminent Domain); State Bar of California. **PRACTICE AREAS:** Litigation.

**TODD R. TRILLER,** born Oakland, California, February 23, 1964; admitted to bar, 1989, Virginia; 1990, Virginia Supreme Court and District of Columbia. *Education:* University of Virginia (B.S., 1986; J.D., 1989). Beta Gamma Sigma; Order of the Coif. Member, University of Virginia Law Review, 1988-1989. (New York, N.Y. Office). **PRACTICE AREAS:** Corporations Law.

**BRETT J. WILLIAMSON,** born Newport Beach, California, October 12, 1963; admitted to bar, 1989, California, U.S. Court of Appeals, Ninth Circuit and U.S. District Court, Central District of California; 1990, U.S. District Court, Northern, Southern and Eastern Districts of California. *Education:* University of California at Irvine (B.A., with honors, 1986); University of Southern California (J.D., 1989). Order of the Coif. Recipient, American Jurisprudence Awards in Constitutional Law II and Local Government Law. Staff Member, 1987-1988 and Articles Editor, 1988-1989, Southern California Law Review. Author: "Constitutional Privacy After Bowers v. Hardwick: Rethinking the Second Death of Substantive Due Process," 62 Southern California Law Review 1297, March/May, 1989. *Member:* Orange County and American (Member, Litigation Section) Bar Associations. (Newport Beach Office). **PRACTICE AREAS:** Litigation.

**ALFRED M. WURGLITZ,** born Chicago, Illinois, June 25, 1948; admitted to bar, 1976, Colorado; 1980, District of Columbia; 1981, Illinois; 1983, Maryland; 1985, Virginia. *Education:* United States Air Force Academy (B.S., 1970); Oxford University (B.Phil., 1973); New York University; Loyola University of Los Angeles (J.D., 1976). Author: "Developments in Computer Software Licensing Litigation," 8th Annual Advanced Computer Law Institute, Georgetown University Law Center; "Source Selection Issues in the Federal ADP Environment," Sixth Annual Program on ADP & Telecommunications Procurement," Section of Public Contract Law, ABA, April, 1993. Law Clerk to Hon. John Minor Wisdom, U.S. Court of Appeals, Fifth Circuit, 1976; Hon. William E. Doyle, U.S. Court of Appeals, Tenth Circuit, 1976-1977. Assistant General Counsel, President's Council on Wage & Price Stability, 1979-1980. *Member:* District of Columbia Bar (Member, Steering Committee, Computer and Telecommunications Law Section); American Bar Association (Member, Sections on: Litigation; Intellectual Property Law; Public Contract Law; Science and Technology); District of Columbia Computer Law Forum. [Capt., USAF, 1966-1976]. (Washington, D.C. Office). **PRACTICE AREAS:** Litigation; Computer Law; Government Contracts Law; Employment Law; Intellectual Property Law. **Email:** awurglitz@omm.com

*(This Listing Continued)*

## ASSOCIATES

*Christine M. Adams; Paul M. Alfieri* (New York, N.Y. Office); *Hubert L. Allen* (San Francisco Office); *Terrence R. Allen; Eric E. Amdursky; Iman Anabtawi* (Century City Office); *K. Allen Anderson* (Newport Beach Office); *Martine N. Apollon* (Washington, D.C. Office); *James D. Arbogast* (New York, N.Y. Office); *Barton S. Aronson* (Washington, D.C. Office); *Felipe J. Arroyo; Christine L. Bacon* (New York, N.Y. Office); *Linda A. Bagley* (San Francisco Office); *Patrick J. Bannon* (San Francisco Office); *Bernard C. Barmann, Jr.; Alfredo Barrios, Jr.; Steven Basileo; Evelyn Becker* (Washington, D.C. Office); *Angela M. Bellanca; Richard D. Beller; Carla J. Bennett; Laura B. Berger* (Century City Office); *Jay Blaivas* (New York, N.Y. Office); *Corey A. Boock; Michael G. Bosko* (Newport Beach and San Francisco Offices); *Lisa M. Bossetti; Debra L. Boyd; Laura C. Bremer* (San Francisco and Los Angles Offices); *Brian P. Brooks* (Washington, D.C. Office); *George H. Brown; J. Taylor Browning; Sharon Bunzel* (San Francisco Office); *Nadia St. George Burgard* (New York, N.Y. Office); *Walter R. Burkley, III; Andrea L. Campbell* (New York, N.Y. Office); *Bruce L. Campbell; Cannon Quigley Campbell; William A. Candelaria; Paul P. Canfield* (New York, N.Y. Office); *Jeffrey J. Carlisle* (Washington, D.C. Office); *Sean M. Carney; Christine L. Carr; Kevin B. Carter; Pinaki Chakravorty; John B. Chang* (San Francisco Office); *Gary A. Chodosh* (New York, N.Y. Office); *Apalla U. Chopra; Carla J. Christofferson* (Century City Office); *Peggy Ann Clarke* (Washington, D.C. Office); *Craig J. Coleman; Charles F. Connolly* (Washington, D.C. Office); *Craig A. Corman* (Century City Office); *Colleen Cox* (Newport Beach Office); *Frank M. Crance* (Newport Beach Office); *Andrea L. Crowe* (New York, N.Y. Office); *Brian Daly* (New York, N.Y. Office); *Scott J. Daruty* (Newport Beach Office); *Robert L. Davis* (Newport Beach Office); *Teresa E. Dawson* (Washington, D.C. Office); *Elizabeth A. Delaney* (Washington, D.C. Office); *Antonio A. Del Pino* (New York, N.Y. Office); *Ralph P. DeSanto* (New York, N.Y. Office); *Rafael Diaz-Granados* (New York, N.Y. Office); *Thomas J. Di Resta* (New York, N.Y. Office); *Mary P. Donlevy* (Newport Beach Office); *Erica K. Doran* (New York, N.Y. Office); *Kate W. Duchene; Bradford David Duea* (Century City Office); *Daniel M. Dunn* (New York, N.Y. Office); *Loryn D. Dunn; Martha Dye* (Washington, D.C. Office); *Mark C. Easton; Steven G. Eisner; John M. Farrell* (Century City Office); *Stephen P. Fattman* (Washington, D.C. Office); *Marcia A. Fay* (San Francisco Office); *John M. Fedorko* (New York, N.Y. Office); *Marc F. Feinstein; Aaron F. Fishbein* (New York, N.Y. Office); *Jeanne Morales Flynn* (Century City Office); *Suzanne Rich Folsom* (Washington, D.C. Office); *Michael Friedman* (New York, N.Y. Office); *Jess B. Frost; Lisa E. Funk* (New York, N.Y. Office); *Anne Elizabeth Garrett; Katherine E. Garrett; Neil K. Gilman* (Washington, D.C. Office); *John A. Gliedman* (New York, N.Y. Office); *Robin L. Gohlke; Gary R. Gold* (Washington, D.C. Office); *David B. Goldman; Jason P. Gonzalez* (San Francisco Office); *Victoria A. Graff; Todd A. Green* (Newport Beach Office); *Dionne C. Greene* (New York, N.Y. Office); *Jennifer G. Grenert* (New York, N.Y. Office); *Jonathan L. Griffith* (Washington, D.C. Office); *Alyssa A. Grikscheit* (New York, N.Y. Office); *Lawrence M. Hadley; Afshin Hakim; Andrea Hanneman* (New York, N.Y. Office); *Clint M. Hanni; Maria Snyder Hardy* (Century City Office); *Kevin M. Harr; David L. Hayes* (Newport Beach Office); *Judith A. Heinz; Krista Helfferich; David L. Herron; Lawrence J. Hilton* (Newport Beach Office); *Bruce R. Hirsh* (Washington, D.C. Office); *Mark Ho* (Shanghai Office; China Counsel); *Bonnie L. Hobbs* (Hong Kong Office); *Michael J. Holden* (New York, N.Y. Office); *Richard J. Holmstrom* (New York, N.Y. Office); *Carl D. Howard* (New York, N.Y. Office); *Lane Huang* (Shanghai Office; China Counsel); *Yongjin Im* (New York, N.Y. and Los Angeles, California Offices); *Mary A. Inman* (San Francisco Office); *Jill Irvin* (New York, N.Y. Office); *Bruce Gen Iwasaki; Neil Scot Jahss; Lynn A. Jansen; James Paul Jenal; Tonya Jenerette* (Washington, D.C. Office); *Nicholas G. Jenkins; Victor Jih* (Century City Office); *Teresa L. Johnson* (London, England Office); *Thomas J. Karr* (Washington, D. C. Office); *Allison M. Keller* (Century City Office); *Alice J. Kim* (Not admitted in CA; Century City Office); *Jonathan J. Kim; Patricia H. Kim* (New York, N.Y. Office); *Stuart Y. Kim; Susanna M. Kim* (Newport Beach Office); *Kathleen E. Kinney* (Newport Beach Office); *David S. Kitchen; Sandra R. Klein; Stephanie I. Klein* (New York, N.Y. Office); *Lonnie L. Kocontes; Hayley J. Kondon; Stephen V. Kovarik* (New York, N.Y. Office); *Peter Kozinets* (San Francisco Office); *Lisa E. Krim; Teresa Kwong* (District of Columbia Office); *John A. Laco; John M. Lambros; Jose Lau Dan* (New York, N.Y. Office); *Courtney A. Lederer* (New York, N.Y. Office); *James C. Lee; Mimi Lee* (New York, N.Y. Office); *Priscila Castillo Lemus* (admission pending).; *Michelle M. Leonard* (Century City Office); *Michael Cary Levine; Barry P. Levinson* (New York, N.Y. Office); *Alfred P. Levitt* (New York, N.Y. Office); *Warren H. Lilien* (San Francisco Office); *George C. Lin; Barry Littman* (Century City Office); *Lisa Litwiller* (Newport

*(This Listing Continued)*

# PROFESSIONAL BIOGRAPHIES

Beach Office); **Robert G. Loewy** (Newport Beach Office); **Joseph C. Lombard** (Washington, D.C. Office); **Monique Janelle London** (San Francisco Office); **Eva M. Luchini; Michael M. Maddigan; Andrew S. Mansfield; Lisa H. Marino** (Washington, D.C. Office); **Dennis J. Martin** (New York, N.Y. Office); **Carlos M. Matos** (Newport Beach Office); **Greg K. Matson; Lori A. Mazur** (New York, N.Y. Office); **Marion K. McDonald** (Washington, D.C. Office); **Patricia A. McKenna** (New York, N.Y. Office); **Susan M. McNeill** (New York, N.Y. Office); **Ann Catherine Menard; Michael A. Meyer** (Washington, D.C. Office); **John F. Milani; Eric S. Miller** (San Francisco Office); **Jessica Davidson Miller** (Washington, D.C. Office); **Angela C. Mok** (San Francisco Office); **Luc Moritz; Robert C. Murray; Vicki A. Nash** (Newport Beach Office); **David B. Newdorf** (San Francisco Office); **John F. Niblock; Anthony R. G. Nolan** (New York, N.Y. Office); **Brent J. North** (Newport Beach Office); **Peter Obstler** (San Francisco Office); **Arthur J. Ochoa; John C. Oehmke; Geoffrey D. Oliver** (Washington, D.C. Office); **Kevin Oliver; David L. Orlic; Dean Pappas** (Century City Office); **Troy A. Paredes; Jeehye Park** (New York, N.Y. Office); **Kenneth G. Parker** (Newport Beach Office); **Lisa J. Parnell** (Century City Office); **Lynn E. Parseghian** (Washington, D.C. Office); **Gregory P. Patti, Jr.** (New York, N.Y. Office); **Mark D. Peterson** (Newport Beach Office); **George R. Phillips, Jr.; Claire J. Philpott** (San Francisco Office); **Steven Lee Pickering** (San Francisco Office); **Annette L. Poblete** (New York, N.Y. Office); **Stuart S. Poloner** (New York, N.Y. Office); **Karen Craig Poltrock** (Newport Beach Office); **Sean H. Porter** (New York, N.Y. Office); **Henry K. Prempeh** (Washington, D.C. Office); **Mark R. Pronk** (New York, N.Y. Office); **Yash A. Rana** (New York, N.Y. Office); **Anthony D. Ratner** (San Francisco Office); **Claudia E. Ray** (New York, N.Y. Office); **Michael C. Ray** (Newport Beach Office); **David J. Reis** (San Francisco Office); **Jendi B. Reiter** (New York, N.Y. Office); **Donald M. Remy** (Washington, D.C. Office); **Laurel A. Remington; Ramon E. Reyes, Jr.** (New York, N.Y. Office); **Thomas M. Riordan; Patrick R. Rizzi** (Washington, D.C. Office); **James Gerard Rizzo** (New York, N.Y. Office); **Deborah Rogers** (Century City Office); **Lori E. Romley** (San Francisco Office); **Allison M. Rose; Eric N. Roth** (Century City Office); **Valerie Granfield Roush** (Washington, D.C. Office); **Lynda M. Ruiz** (San Francisco Office); **Rogelio M. Ruíz** (San Francisco Office); **Carlos P. Salas; Deborah J. Saltzman; Paul Salvaty; Pamela D. Samuels; Philip C. Scheurer** (Washington, D.C. Office); **Christine A. Schnabel** (Washington, D.C. Office); **Scott Schrader** (New York Office); **Daniel A. Schulze** (New York, N.Y. Office); **Nancy L. Shackleton** (Newport Beach Office); **Nina Shafran** (Washington, D.C. Office); **Sam S. Shaulson** (New York, N.Y. Office); **Gregory B. Shean; Katherine Sieck** (Newport Beach Office); **James P. Sileneck** (New York, N.Y. Office); **Gulwinder S. Singh** (Newport Beach Office); **Thomas Singher** (New York, N.Y. Office); **John F. Slusher** (Century City Office); **Craig W. Smith; Ellen M. Smith** (New York, N.Y. Office); **Gary M. Smith** (New York, N.Y. Office); **Valerie A. Smith; Albert J. Solecki, Jr.** (New York, N.Y. Office); **Steven E. Soule; Geoffrey J. Spolyar; Irene E. Stewart; William J. Stuckwisch** (Washington, D.C. Office); **Christine H. Suh; Dean Sussman; Nancy E. Sussman** (Century City Office); **Janet I. Swerdlow; Christine Tam; Jadene M.W. Tamura** (Newport Beach Office); **Mark Christopher Teuton** (Newport Beach Office); **Mark E. Thierfelder** (New York, N.Y. Office); **Diana M. Torres; Glenn A. Trager; Gloria Trattles** (New York, N.Y. Office); **Dana S. Treister; Kenneth J. Turnbull** (New York, N.Y. Office); **George A.H. Turner** (Newport Beach Office); **Harry E. Turner** (San Francisco Office); **Mark T. Uyeda; Debra J. Vella; Scott M. Voelz; Karen Mary Wahle** (Washington, D.C. Office); **Kent D. Wakeford** (Century City Office); **Jeffrey W. Walbridge** (Newport Beach Office); **Ellen R. Waldorf** (Washington, D.C. Office); **Larry A. Walraven** (Newport Beach Office); **Stephanie M. Walter; Todd R. Watkins; Stephen J. Watson** (New York, N.Y. Office); **Aimee S. Weisner** (Newport Beach Office); **Kevin M. Wernick; Heather G. White; Molly M. White; Ronan M. Wicks** (New York, N.Y. Office); **Michael A. Williamson; David A. Wimmer; Robert Winter** (New York, N.Y. Office); **Jeffrey A. Wortman; Todd R. Wulffson** (Newport Beach Office); **Richard Xu** (Hong Kong Office; China Counsel); **Kevin Yamaga-Karns; Masami Yamamoto; Keith K. Yang** (Century City Office); **Stephanie K. Yonekura; Spencer H.C. Yu**.

All Members and Associates of the firm are members of The State Bar of California, except where otherwise indicated.

## CALIFORNIA—LOS ANGELES

# O'NEILL, HUXTABLE & ABELSON

Established in 1930

800 WEST FIRST STREET, SUITE 400
LOS ANGELES, CALIFORNIA 90012
Telephone: 213-627-5017
Fax: 213-617-0196
Email: EmDOM@aol.com

Eminent Domain, Inverse Condemnation, Regulatory Takings, Property Taxation and Assessment Appeals, Real Property Litigation, Trusts and Estates, Probate and Probate Litigation, Civil Litigation and Trial Practice.

*FIRM PROFILE: Since 1930, the firm has a long history of legal tenacity, aggressive advocacy and consistent achievement. Great pride is taken in the individual attention and personal service provided to each client.*

### MEMBERS OF FIRM

**FRANCIS H. O'NEILL** (1912-1992).

**RICHARD L. HUXTABLE** (1927-1984).

**LEROY A. ABELSON**, born Mason City, Washington, February 25, 1942; admitted to bar, 1973, California, U.S. Court of Appeals, Ninth and Federal Circuits and U.S. Claims Court. *Education:* Washington State University (B.S., 1965); Loyola University (J.D., 1973). Registered Civil Engineer, California, 1969. Lecturer, 'Eminent Domain Law,' Loyola Law School, 1988; 'Foreign Takings,' UKNCCL, University of Oxford, England, 1990. Author: "Foreign Takings by the United States: How Far Does the Protection of the Just Compensation Clause Extend and to Whom," Published Proceedings of World Conference of the United Kingdom National Committee of Comparative Law (1990); republished in 'Nichols on Eminent Domain' (1993). *Member:* State Bar of California; Los Angeles County Bar Association. *PRACTICE AREAS:* Eminent Domain; Direct and Inverse Condemnation; Related Fields.

**GAVIN M. ERASMUS**, born Durban, South Africa, August 17, 1958; admitted to bar, 1983, Supreme Court of South Africa; 1986, California; 1987, U.S. District Court, Central District of California and U.S. Court of Appeals, Ninth Circuit; 1990, U.S. Supreme Court; 1991, U.S. Court of Appeals, Eleventh Circuit; 1996, U.S. District Court, Southern District of California. *Education:* University of Natal (B.Comm., 1978; LL.B., 1981; LL.M., Eminent Domain, 1983); Harvard Law School (Visiting Researchership in Eminent Domain, 1985-1986); Oxford University (Ph.D., Comparative Eminent Domain Law, 1995). Member: United Kingdom National Committee of Comparative Law; Eminent Domain Faculty of American Law Institute of the American Bar Association (ALI-ABA); Institute of Advanced Legal Studies, London. Lecturer: Chairman, World Conference on Eminent Domain, University of Oxford, 1990. Lecturer on eminent domain to National Conferences of ALI-ABA (New Orleans, 1993 and Phoenix 1994), Los Angeles County Bar Association (1995), American Society of Appraisers (1996), International Society of Land Economics (1996), and California Society of CPA's (1996). Author: Doctoral Thesis 'Comparative Compensation Systems for Eminent Domain,' Oxford 1994. General Editor, 'Compensation for Expropriation,' two volumes, Oxford, 1990. Masters Thesis, 'Eminent Domain and the Social Contract,' 1983. 'Eminent Domain Worldwide,' ALI-ABA, Florida, 1997. 'Eminent Domain Globally,' ASA, California, 1996. 'The Jurisprudence of Eminent Domain,' ALI-ABA, New Orleans 1993 and Phoenix 1994. Nichols, Chapter 1A, 'Comparative Eminent Domain,' 1996; Nichols, Chapter 1B, 'Eminent Domain Law-and-Economics,' 1995; Nichols, Chapter 13A, 'Eminent Domain and Environmentally Contaminated Properties,' 1994. Nichols, Chapter 26, "Eminent Domain, Powerlines, and Electromagnetic Field," (1993). *Member:* State Bar of California; American Bar Association. *PRACTICE AREAS:* Eminent Domain; Just Compensation; Direct Takings and Inverse Condemnation; Compensation for Expropriation (Nationally, Comparatively and Internationally); Related Fields.

**MARY L. O'NEILL**, born Los Angeles, California, January 26, 1957; admitted to bar, 1981, California; 1982, Idaho. *Education:* University of California at Irvine (B.A., 1978); Southwestern University (J.D., cum laude, 1981. Law Clerk, Supreme Court of Idaho, 1981-1983. Lecturer, National Business Institute, 'Property Tax Law in California,' Anaheim, California, 1996. *Member:* Los Angeles County Bar Association (Member, Condemnation and Land Valuation Litigation Committee, 1988—; Vice-Chair, 1992-1993, Chair, 1994-1996); State Bar of California; Idaho State Bar; Irish-American Bar Association (Member, Board of Directors, 1984—; President, 1989); Association of Real Estate Attorneys (Member, Board of Governors, 1989-1994, President, 1992). *PRACTICE AREAS:* Eminent Do-

*(This Listing Continued)*

CAA1061B

**O'NEILL, HUXTABLE & ABELSON,** Los Angeles—
*Continued*

main; Inverse Condemnation; Assessment Tax and Appeals; Probate; Civil Litigation; Trial Practice.

*ASSOCIATE*

**CHRISTINA E. JACKSON,** born District of Columbia, February 28, 1969; admitted to bar, 1994, New Jersey; 1996, California. *Education:* Siena College (B.A., cum laude, 1991); University of Miami (J.D., 1994). Author: Contributor to Nichols, Chapter 1A, 'Comparative Eminent Domain,' 1996; Contributor to Nichols, Chapter 1, "Eminent Domain Law-and-Economics," 1995; Contributor to Nichols, Chapter 26, 'Eminent Domain, Powerlines, and Electromagnetic Fields,' 1993. *Member:* State Bar of California; New Jersey State and American Bar Associations. **REPORTED CASES:** People v. Ricciardi, 23 Cal.2d 390 (1943); People v. Superior Court, 145 Cal.App.2d 683 (1956); People v. Faus, 48 Cal.2d 672 (1957); Redevelopment Agency v. Gilmore, 38 Cal.3d 790 (1985); Gasser v. United States, 14 Cl.Ct. 476 (1988); Southern Pacific Pipelines v. State Board of Equalization, 14 Cal.App.4th 42 (1993). *PRACTICE AREAS:* Eminent Domain; Direct and Inverse Condemnation; Land Use; Assessment Tax and Appeals; General Civil and Trial Practice.

REPRESENTATIVE CLIENTS: Goldrich & Kest; Los Angeles Athletic Club; Barrick Goldstrike Gold Mines; Chicago Title Company; Golden West Refining Company.
REFERENCE: Bank of America (Grand/Wilshire Branch Office, Los Angeles).

---

# O'NEILL, LYSAGHT & SUN
## LOS ANGELES, CALIFORNIA
(See Santa Monica)
*Business and Commercial Litigation and White-Collar Criminal Defense.*

---

# OPPENHEIMER POMS SMITH
*2029 CENTURY PARK EAST, 38TH FLOOR*
**LOS ANGELES, CALIFORNIA 90067**
*Telephone: 310-788-5000*
*FAX: 310-277-1297*
*Email: owdlaw.com*

*Orange County Office:* 1920 Main Street, Suite 1050, Irvine, California, 92714. Telephone: 714-263-8250. FAX: 714-263-8260.
*San Jose, California Office:* 333 West Santa Clara Street, Suite 1000, 95113. Telephone: 408-275-8790. FAX: 408-275-8793.
Oppenheimer Wolff & Donnelly:
*Brussels, Belgium Office:* Avenue Louise 250, Box 31, 1050. Telephone: 32-2-626-0500. FAX: 32-2-626-0510.
*Chicago, Illinois Office:* Two Prudential Plaza, 45th Floor, 180 North Stetson Avenue, 60601.
*Minneapolis, Minnesota Office:* 3400 Plaza VII, 45 South Seventh Street, 55401. Telephone: 612-344-9300. FAX: 612-344-9376.
*New York, N.Y. Office:* Citicorp Center, 153 East 53rd Street, 10022. Telephone: 212-826-5000. Telecopier: 212-486-0708.
*Paris, France Office:* 53 Avenue Montaigne, 75008. Telephone: (33/1) 44 95 03 50. FAX: (33/1) 44 95 03 40.
*St. Paul, Minnesota Office:* 3800 First Bank Building, 55101. Telephone: 612-223-2500. FAX: 612-223-2596.
*Washington, D.C. Office:* 1020 Nineteenth Street, N.W., Suite 400, 20036. Telephone: 202-293-6300. FAX: 202-293-6200.
*Detroit, Michigan Office:* Timberland Office Park, Suite 250, 5445 Corporate Drive, 48098. Telephone: 810-267-8500. FAX: 810-267-8559.
*Affiliated Offices:*
*Goudsmit & Branbergen, J.J. Viottastraat, 46 Amsterdam 1071.* Telephone: 31-20-662-30-31. FAX: 31-20-673-65-58.
*Pisano, DeVito, Maiano & Catucci, Piazza Del Duomo, 20, Milan 20122.* Telephone: 39-2-878281. FAX: 39-2-861275.
*Pisano, DeVito, Maiano & Catucci, Via G. Borsi, 3, Rome 00197.* Telephone: 39-6-8079087. FAX: 39-6-8078407.

*Medical Device, Health Care, Business/Technology, Labor and Employment, Antitrust, professional Liability and Securities, Banking and Finance, Real Estate, Corporate Finance, Employee Benefits, International Corporate, Tax-/Trust and Estate, Environmental Law and Toxic Torts, Insurance, Products Liability, Transportation, Dispute Resolution/Arbitration, European Community, International Tax.*

**RICHARD L. GAUSEWITZ,** born June 4, 1925; admitted to bar, 1950, Wisconsin; 1952, California; registered to practice before U.S. Patent and Trademark Office. *Education:* University of Wisconsin (B.S. in E.E., 1946); Stanford University (LL.B., 1949). Author: "Patent Pending," a book on the history of the Patent System. (Resident, Irvine Office). **Email:** RGausewitz@owdlaw.com

**MICHAEL A. KONDZELLA,** born June 9, 1927; admitted to bar, 1955, District of Columbia; 1979, California; registered to practice before U.S. Patent and Trademark Office. *Education:* University of Illinois (A.B., 1948; M.S., 1953); Rutgers University (J.D., 1955). (Resident, Irvine Office). *PRACTICE AREAS:* Intellectual Property. **Email:** MKondzella@owdlaw.com

**ALAN C. ROSE,** born June 2, 1922; admitted to bar, 1952, District of Columbia; 1957, U.S. Supreme Court; 1961, California; registered to practice before U.S. Patent and Trademark Office. *Education:* Dartmouth College; Massachusetts Institute of Technology (B.S., Physics, 1944; B.S., 1948); George Washington University (J.D., 1951). Chief Patent Attorney, for Litton Industries, Inc., 1968-1976. *PRACTICE AREAS:* Patents, Trademarks, Copyrights, Licensing, Unfair Competition. **Email:** ARose@owdlaw.com

**WILLIAM POMS,** born January 13, 1928; admitted to bar, 1959, California; 1965, U.S. Supreme Court; registered to practice before U.S. Patent and Trademark Office. *Education:* Catholic University of America (B.S.M.E., 1953); Georgetown University (J.D., 1957). Member, Panel of Arbitrators, American Arbitration Association. *PRACTICE AREAS:* Intellectual Property and International. **Email:** WPoms@owdlaw.com

**GUY PORTER SMITH,** born September 8, 1933; admitted to bar, 1959, Illinois; 1960, California; U.S. District Court, Central District of California; 1961, U.S. Court of Appeals, Ninth Circuit and U.S. Court of Appeals for the Federal Circuit; registered to practice before U.S. Patent and Trademark Office. *Education:* Northwestern University (B.S.I.E., 1955; J.D., 1959). *PRACTICE AREAS:* Intellectual Property Litigation and Prosecution. **Email:** GSmith@owdlaw.com

**GARY E. LANDE,** born June 12, 1934; admitted to bar, 1966, District of Columbia; 1967, California; registered to practice before U.S. Patent and Trademark Office. *Education:* University of South Dakota (B.S., Chemistry, 1957); American University (J.D., 1965). *PRACTICE AREAS:* Intellectual Property. **Email:** GLande@owdlaw.com

**LOUIS J. BOVASSO,** born August 16, 1935; admitted to bar, 1967, District of Columbia; 1971, California; registered to practice before U.S. Patent and Trademark Office. *Education:* Newark College of Engineering (B.S.M.E., 1961); Catholic University of America (J.D., 1966). Member, Law Review, 1965-1966. *PRACTICE AREAS:* Intellectual Property. **Email:** LBovasso@owdlaw.com

**EDWARD F. O'CONNOR,** born December, 2, 1944; admitted to bar, 1970, Indiana; 1971, Florida; 1973, U.S. Supreme Court; 1984, Connecticut; 1986, California; registered to practice before U.S. Patent and Trademark Office. *Education:* University of Michigan (B.S., Physics, 1966); Indiana University (J.D., 1969). (Resident, Irvine Office). *PRACTICE AREAS:* Intellectual Property Litigation. **Email:** EOConnor@owdlaw.com

**BERNARD R. GANS,** born November 18, 1948; admitted to bar, 1973, California; registered to practice before U.S. Patent and Trademark Office. *Education:* University of California at Santa Barbara (B.S.M.E., with honors, 1970); University of California at Los Angeles (J.D., 1973). Judge Pro Tem, Los Angeles Municipal Court, 1978-1980. Papers and Presentations: "State Antidilution Statutes: Are They Worth the Cost?" ABA Annual Meeting, August 10, 1991; "Intellectual Property and Medical Staff," American Bar Association Division for Professional Education, National Institute on Medical Staff Law Update, November 11-12, 1989; "Parallel Imports," Licensing Executives Society Mexico, January 28, 1991; "Use of U.S. Patent, Trademark and Copyright Rights to Prevent the Importation of Gray Market Imports," American Intellectual Property Law Association, May 2, 1991; "Intellectual Property and the Medical Staff," National Health Lawyers Association, September 28, 1991; "Inter Partes Trademark Proceedings in the Patent and Trademark Office," Los Angeles Intellectual Property Law Association, November 5, 1991; "Ten Important Things to Know When Conducting Trademark Oppositions and Cancellations," American Bar Association, Section of Patent, Trademark and Copyright Law, Annual Spring CLE Program, March 30, 1992; "Dilution," American Bar Association, Section of Patent, Trademark and Copyright Law, Annual

*(This Listing Continued)*

Spring CLE Program, April 5-6, 1993. Publications: Copyright Commentary, "Pac-Man Gobbles Up K.C. Munchkin in the Seventh Circuit," Vol. 7, No. 1, Journal of the Century City Bar Association, Summer, 1982; "Lawsuits of the Rich and Famous: Stars' Exert Right of Publicity," American Advertising, Spring, 1993; "Protection Against Infringing Imports," The Lightbulb, Vol. 15, No. 3, May/June 1987; "Hey, Isn't That So-and-So? Pushing the Limits of California's Right of Privacy," Los Angeles Lawyer, April 1993. *Member:* American Bar Association (Member, Intellectual Property Section; Council Member, 1995-1999; Chair, Trademark Division, 1991-1992; Chair, Parallel Imports Subcommittee, 1986-1987, 1987-1988, 1988-1989, 1989-1990, 1990-1991; Chair, State Trademarks Committee, 1988-1989, 1989-1990 1990-1991; Member; Industrial Design Committee, 1987-1988; International Copyright Treaties and Laws, 1988-1989; Unfair Competition-Trade Identity Committee, 1988-1989; Chair, Trademark Offices Affairs Committee, 1992-1993, 1993-1994; Chair, Unfair Competition Committee, 1994-1995; Member, Section Council, 1995—). *Email:* BGans@owdlaw.com

**MICHAEL D. HARRIS,** born March 16, 1946; admitted to bar, 1973, District of Columbia; 1974, California; registered to practice before U.S. Patent and Trademark Office. *Education:* Purdue University (B.S., 1969); American University (J.D., 1972). Examiner, U.S. Patent Office, 1969-1973. *PRACTICE AREAS:* Intellectual Property. *Email:* MHarris@owdlaw.com

**JERRY R. POTTS,** born January 13, 1940; admitted to bar, 1974, California; registered to practice before U.S. Patent and Trademark Office. *Education:* California State University at Long Beach (B.S.E., 1962; M.S.E.E., 1970); Southwestern University (J.D., 1974). *Member:* Institute of Electrical and Electronic Engineering. *PRACTICE AREAS:* Patent Prosecution with emphasis on Computer and Integrated Circuit Technologies.

**MARK P. WINE,** born January 6, 1949; admitted to bar, 1974, Iowa; 1976, Minnesota (Not admitted in California). *Education:* Princeton University (A.B., 1971); University of Iowa (J.D., 1974). Law Clerk to R.L. Stephenson, U.S. Circuit Judge for the 8th Circuit Court of Appeals, 1974-1976. *PRACTICE AREAS:* Intellectual Property; Business and Commercial Litigation. *Email:* MWine@owdlaw.com

**CHRISTOPHER DARROW,** born November 17, 1945; admitted to bar, 1976, California and U.S. District Court, Central, Eastern, Southern Districts of California and Western District of Texas; registered to practice before U.S. Patent and Trademark Office. *Education:* University of Toledo (B.S.M.E., 1968); Whittier College (J.D., 1976). Judge, Pro Tem, L.A. Municipal Court, 1982-1983. *PRACTICE AREAS:* Intellectual Property. *Email:* CDarrow@owdlaw.com

**JANE SHAY WALD,** admitted to bar, 1976, Illinois; 1978, U.S. Court of Appeals for the Federal Circuit; 1982, New York; 1996, California. *Education:* De Paul University (B.A., magna cum laude, 1973; J.D., cum laude, 1976). *PRACTICE AREAS:* Intellectual Property. *Email:* JWald@owdlaw.com

**DOUGLAS N. LARSON,** born March 11, 1952; admitted to bar, 1977, Maryland; 1984, District of Columbia; 1994, California; registered to practice before U.S. Patent and Trademark Office. *Education:* Rensselaer Polytechnic Institute (B.S.C.E., 1974); University of Missouri at Columbia (J.D., 1977); George Washington University (LL.M. in Patent, Trade and Regulation Law, 1983). *PRACTICE AREAS:* Patent Law. *Email:* DLarson@owdlaw.com

**DAVID J. OLDENKAMP,** born September 28, 1950; admitted to bar, 1978, California; registered to practice before U.S. Patent and Trademark Office. *Education:* University of Southern California (B.S., 1973); Whittier College (J.D., 1978). *PRACTICE AREAS:* Intellectual Property. *Email:* DOldenkamp@owdlaw.com

**MARC E. BROWN,** born September 7, 1952; admitted to bar, 1979, California; registered to practice before U.S. Patent and Trademark Office. *Education:* Case Western Reserve University (B.S.E.E., magna cum laude, 1975); George Washington University (J.D., cum laude, 1978). Law Clerk and Technical Advisor to U.S. Court of Claims, 1978-1979. *PRACTICE AREAS:* Intellectual Property; Computer Law; Litigation. *Email:* MBrown@owdlaw.com

**TERRY L. MILLER,** born January 23, 1948; admitted to bar, 1979, Indiana; 1987, Arizona; 1993, California; registered to practice before U.S. Patent and Trademark Office. *Education:* Indiana Institute of Technology (B.S.M.E., 1970); Valparaiso University (J.D., 1978). (Resident, Irvine Office). *PRACTICE AREAS:* Intellectual Property. *Email:* TMiller@owdlaw.com

*(This Listing Continued)*

**KURT A. MACLEAN,** born October 22, 1953; admitted to bar, 1982, California; 1983, U.S. District Court, Central District of California and U.S. Court of Appeals, Ninth Circuit; 1984, U.S. Court of Appeals for the Federal Circuit; registered to practice before U.S. Patent and Trademark Office. *Education:* California State University, Long Beach (B.A., Chem. with high honors, 1978); University of California, Los Angeles (J.D., 1982). (Resident, Irvine Office). *PRACTICE AREAS:* Intellectual Property. *Email:* KMaclean@owdlaw.com

**J. PATRICK WEIR,** born August 31, 1954; admitted to bar, 1982, California. *Education:* University of California, Irvine (B.S., 1979); Hastings College of Law, University of California (J.D., 1982). *Member:* American Society for Microbiology. *PRACTICE AREAS:* Intellectual Property. *Email:* JWeir@owdlaw.com

**CHARLES ROSENBERG,** born June 12, 1948; admitted to bar, 1983, Illinois; 1984, California; registered to practice before U.S. Patent and Trademark Office. *Education:* University of Illinois (B.S. in Engineering, 1971; M.S. in Engineering, 1972); The John Marshall Law School (J.D., 1983). Patent Examiner, 1983-1984. Technical Law Clerk to Judge Jean Galloway Bissell, U.S. Court of Appeals for the Federal Circuit, 1984-1985. *PRACTICE AREAS:* Intellectual Property. *Email:* CRosenberg@owdlaw.com

**JAMES A. HENRICKS,** born December 25, 1956; admitted to bar, 1984, California; registered to practice before U.S. Patent and Trademark Office. *Education:* University of Arizona (B.S., with distinction in Nuclear Engineering, 1979; J.D., 1983). Tau Beta Pi. *PRACTICE AREAS:* Intellectual Property. *Email:* JHenricks@owdlaw.com

**ALAN P. BLOCK,** born November 29, 1964; admitted to bar, 1989, California; 1992, District of Columbia; registered to practice before U.S. Patent and Trademark Office. *Education:* Cornell University (B.S., Chem. Eng., 1986); University of California at Los Angeles (J.D., 1989). *PRACTICE AREAS:* Intellectual Property. *Email:* ABlock@owdlaw.com

**JAMES W. INSKEEP,** born September 9, 1961; admitted to bar, 1990, Virginia: 1994, California; registered to practice before U.S. Patent and Trademark Office. *Education:* University of Illinois (B.S., Aero. Eng., 1983); Washington College of Law, The American University (J.D., 1989). *PRACTICE AREAS:* Intellectual Property; Medical Devices. *Email:* JInskeep@owdlaw.com

**STEVEN W. SMYRSKI,** born June 20, 1960; admitted to bar, 1992, California; practice before U.S. Patent and Trademark Office. *Education:* Purdue University (B.S.M.E., 1982); University of Southern California (M.S.E.E., 1986); Southwestern University School of Law (J.D., 1992). *PRACTICE AREAS:* Intellectual Property. *Email:* SSmyrski@owdlaw.com

**SCOTT R. HANSEN,** born January 2, 1963; admitted to bar, 1993, California; registered to practice before U.S. Patent and Trademark Office. *Education:* University of California, San Diego (B.S., 1985); University of California, Santa Barbara (M.S., 1987); Indiana University (J.D., cum laude, 1992). *Email:* SHansen@owdlaw.com

**PETER L. HOLMES,** born July 2, 1964; admitted to bar, 1994, California; registered to practice before U.S. Patent and Trademark Office. *Education:* Ohio State University (B.S.E.E., 1986); Southwestern University School of Law (J.D., 1993). *PRACTICE AREAS:* Intellectual Property. *Email:* PHolmes@owdlaw.com

**CRAIG A. SLAVIN,** born January 29, 1965; admitted to bar, 1994, California; registered before U.S. Patent and Trademark Office. *Education:* California Polytechnic State University (B.S.M.E., 1988); George Mason University School of Law (J.D., 1993). *PRACTICE AREAS:* Patent and Trademark Prosecution, Litigation and Licensing. *Email:* CSlavin@owdlaw.com

**JOEL D. VOELZKE,** born July 31, 1961; admitted to bar, 1995, California. *Education:* Harvey Mudd College (B.S., 1983); University of Southern California (J.D., 1995). *PRACTICE AREAS:* Intellectual Property; Litigation. *Email:* JVoelzke@owdlaw.com

REFERENCE: City National Bank (Century Plaza Office, Century City).

## ORD & NORMAN

*1901 AVENUE OF THE STARS, SUITE 1250*
**LOS ANGELES, CALIFORNIA 90067**
*Telephone: 310-282-9900*
*Telecopier: 310-282-9917*

*San Francisco, California Office:* 120 Montgomery Street, Suite 1055. Telephone: 415-274-3800. Telecopier: 415-274-3838.

Taxation (Federal, Foreign, State and Local), Tax Audits, International Business Transactions, Foreign Investment in the United States, Export Tax Incentives (FSC and DISC) Overseas Investment, NAFTA, Limited Liability Company, Corporation, Partnership and Statutory Trust Formations, Business Acquisitions, Technology Transfers, Business Startups, Family Owned Businesses, Real Estate, Cross Border Financing, Estate Planning, Foreign Trusts and Business and Investment Immigration and Expatriation.

### MEMBERS OF FIRM

**WILLIAM K. NORMAN,** born Beatrice, Nebraska, January 25, 1938; admitted to bar, 1967, California, U.S. District Court, Northern District of California and U.S. Court of Appeals, 9th Circuit; 1976, U.S. Tax Court; 1989, U.S. Claims Court; 1996, Wyoming. *Education:* University of California at Berkeley (B.A., 1962; J.D., 1965); University of California Graduate School of Business Administration, 1965-1967; New York University (LL.M. in Taxation, 1970). Senior Adjunct Professor, Graduate School of Taxation, Golden Gate University, 1979—. Instructor: U.C.L.A. Extension, Department of Business and Management, 1977-1987; Advanced Professional Program, University of Southern California, 1983-1984. Tax Management Advisory Board on Foreign Income, 1981-1994. *Member:* Beverly Hills (Vice-Chair, Business Law, 1991), Los Angeles County (Section Chairman, Tax Section, 1987-1988; Chair, International Law Section, 1990-1991; Member, Executive Committee, 1984—), American (Member, Committees on: Foreign Activities of U.S. Taxpayers, Section of Taxation; U.S. Activities of Foreigners and Tax Treaties, 1982—, Section on Taxation) and International (Member, Taxes Committee of Section on Business Law, 1984—; Chair, Committee on Closely Held and Growing Business Enterprises, General Practice Section, 1988-1994) Bar Associations; State Bar of California (Taxation Section: Vice Chair, 1989-1991; Chairman: Foreign Taxation Subcommittee, 1977-1979; Member, Taxation Section Advisory Committee to CEB, 1986—; Chair, Taxation Subcommittee, 1988-1990); International Fiscal Association (Regional Vice President, Southern California Branch, 1988-1990); Attorneys for Family-Held Enterprises, International Tax Planning Association. (Certified Specialist, Taxation Law, The State Bar of California Board of Legal Specialization).

**EDWARD O. C. ORD** (Resident at San Francisco).

### ASSOCIATES

**EDI S. STILES,** born Denver, Colorado, June 7, 1961; admitted to bar, 1993, California and U.S. District Court, Central District if California; 1996, U.S. Tax Court. *Education:* University of Southern California (B.S., 1983); Pepperdine University (J.D., cum laude, 1993); New York University School of Law (LL.M., Taxation, 1995). *Member:* State Bar of California (Member, Taxation Section). **PRACTICE AREAS:** Taxation; Estate Planning; General Business.

**CHRISTIAN M. WINTHER** (Resident at San Francisco).

---

## O'ROURKE, ALLAN & FONG

**LOS ANGELES, CALIFORNIA**
(See Glendale)

General Civil and Trial Practice in all State and Federal Courts. Real Estate, Construction, Business, Probate, Personal Injury, Family Law and Negligence Law, and Entertainment Law.

---

## ORRICK, HERRINGTON & SUTCLIFFE LLP

*Established in 1863*
**777 SOUTH FIGUEROA STREET, SUITE 3200**
**LOS ANGELES, CALIFORNIA 90017**
*Telephone: 213-629-2020*
*Telecopier: 213-612-2499*
*URL: http://www.orrick.com*

*San Francisco, California Office:* Old Federal Reserve Bank Building, 400 Sansome Street. Telephone: 415-392-1122. Telecopier: 415-773-5759.

*New York, New York Office:* 666 Fifth Avenue. Telephone: 212-506-5000. Telecopier: 212-506-5151.
*Sacramento, California Office:* 400 Capitol Mall. Telephone: 916-447-9200. Telecopier: 916-329-4900.
*Washington, D.C. Office:* Washington Harbour, 3050 K Street, N.W. Telephone: 202-339-8400. Telecopier: 202-339-8500.
*Menlo Park, California Office:* 1020 Marsh Road. Telephone: 415-833-7800. Telecopier: 415-614-7401.
*Singapore Office:* 10 Collyer Quay, #23-08 Ocean Building, Singapore. Telephone: 011-65-538-6116. Telecopier: 011-65-538-0606.

General Practice, including Corporate and Municipal Finance, Domestic and International Commercial Law, Banking and Commercial Finance, Project Finance, Structured Finance, Mergers and Acquisitions, Commercial Litigation, Insurance, Insurance Insolvency, White Collar Criminal Defense, Tax, Employee Benefits and Personal Estates, Antitrust, Distribution, and Trade Regulation, Intellectual Property, Real Estate, Environmental and Energy, Labor and Employment Law and Bankruptcy.

### RESIDENT PARTNERS

**ALAN G. BENJAMIN,** born New York, New York, 1953; admitted to bar, 1977, California; 1990, New York. *Education:* University of California, Los Angeles (A.B., 1974; M.B.A., 1977; J.D., 1977). Phi Beta Kappa; Order of the Coif. *Member:* State Bar of California. **PRACTICE AREAS:** Banking and Finance.

**WILLIAM W. BOTHWELL,** born Springfield, Missouri, 1950; admitted to bar, 1980, Colorado; 1984, California. *Education:* Washington University (A.B., 1972); University of Colorado (J.D., 1980). *Member:* State Bar of California. **PRACTICE AREAS:** Public Finance Law.

**LORI A. BOWMAN,** born Jersey Shore, Pennsylvania, 1955; admitted to bar, 1984, California. *Education:* Indiana University (A.B., 1976; J.D., 1984); University of Illinois (M.A., 1979). Managing Editor, Indiana Law Journal, 1983-1984. *Member:* State Bar of California. **PRACTICE AREAS:** Labor and Employment Law.

**WILLIAM B. CAMPBELL,** born Sioux City, Iowa, 1936; admitted to bar, 1963, California and District of Columbia; 1993, Wyoming. *Education:* Iowa State University (B.S., 1958); Stanford University (LL.B., 1962). Member, Board of Editors, Stanford Law Review, 1961-1962. Faculty: Tactics & Strategy in Major Litigation, Practicing Law Institute, 1980-1985; Federal Practice Institute, California Continuing Legal Education of the Bar, 1983—; Lawyer Delegate, Ninth Circuit Judicial Conference, 1982-1984. Member, Committee to Develop Settlement Procedures, 1995, and Subcommittee Chairman, Civil Justice Advisory Group, 1991—, United States District Court, Central District of California. *Member:* Los Angeles County (Member, Board of Trustees, 1972-1973; Chairman, Federal Practice Standards Committee, 1982-1984), Federal and American (Chairman, Committee on Liaison with the Judiciary, Litigation Section, 1984-1985; Co-Chairman, Committee on National Institutes, 1985-1987) Bar Associations; State Bar of California (Chairman, Committee on Administration of Justice, 1975-1977); Los Angeles County Barristers (Chairman, 1971-1972); Association of Business Trial Lawyers (Member, Board of Governors, 1977-1979). Fellow, American College of Trial Lawyers (Southern California State Committee, 1991—; Vice Chairman, 1985-1986 and Member, Emil Gumpert Award Committee, 1991—).

**EUGENE J. CARRON,** born New York, New York, 1946; admitted to bar, 1972, New York; 1980, South Carolina; 1985, California. *Education:* St. John's University (B.S., 1968; J.D., 1972). Member, St. John's Law Review, 1971-72. **PRACTICE AREAS:** Public Finance Law.

**ROBERT E. FREITAS,** born San Jose, California, 1952; admitted to bar, 1977, Oregon; 1978, California and U.S. Court of Appeals, Ninth Circuit; 1979, U.S. District Court, Northern District of California; 1980, U.S. Supreme Court; 1982, U.S. District Court, Central and Eastern Districts of California; 1985, U.S. Court of Appeals for the Federal Circuit; 1986, U.S. District Court, Southern District of California; 1992, U.S. Court of Appeals, Tenth Circuit. *Education:* University of Oregon (B.S., 1974); Hastings College of the Law, University of California (J.D., 1977). Phi Beta Kappa; Order of the Coif. Note and Comment Editor, Hastings Law Journal, 1976-1977. Law Clerk to Hon. Ralph M. Holman, Supreme Court of Oregon, 1977-1978. Public Counsel, Director, 1995—, and Member of Executive Committee, 1996—. Trustee, Hastings College of the Law 1066 Foundation 1993—. *Member:* State Bar of California. **PRACTICE AREAS:** Litigation; Antitrust Law; Insurance Coverage.

**EARL A. GLICK,** born Chicago, Illinois, 1930; admitted to bar, 1953, Illinois; 1962, California; 1973, U.S. Supreme Court. *Education:* University of Illinois (B.S., 1951); Northwestern University (J.D., 1953). Tau Epsilon

*(This Listing Continued)*

Rho. Member, Board of Governors, 1965 and President, 1971-1972, Financial Lawyers Conference. *Member:* Beverly Hills (Chairman, Commercial Law Committee, 1968-1969) and American (Chair, Programs Subcommittee, Business Law Section, 1992-1995); American College of Commercial Finance Lawyers. **PRACTICE AREAS:** Secured Transactions; Asset-based Lending; Workouts; Creditor Representation in Bankruptcy Proceedings.

**TODD E. GORDINIER,** born Pasadena, California, 1953; admitted to bar, 1978, California. *Education:* Harvard College (B.A., magna cum laude, 1975); University of California, Boalt Hall (J.D., 1978). Order of the Coif. *Member:* State Bar of California. **PRACTICE AREAS:** Complex Litigation.

**GREG HARRINGTON,** born Las Vegas, Nevada, 1953; admitted to bar, 1980, California. *Education:* University of California, Los Angeles (B.A., 1977); University of Southern California (J.D., 1980). Order of the Coif. *Member:* State Bar of California; National Association of Bond Lawyers. **PRACTICE AREAS:** Public Finance Law.

**W. DOUGLAS KARI,** born Berkeley, California, 1955; admitted to bar, 1985, California. *Education:* University of California at Berkeley (A.B., 1980); Hastings College of the Law, University of California (J.D., 1985). Order of the Coif. Thurston Honor Society. Editor staff, Hastings Law Journal, 1984-1985. Author: "Once Upon A Time In The West," Los Angeles Lawyer (July-August 1996); "Resolving Conflicts: Corporate Affiliations Pose Ethical Dilemmas for Counsel," Los Angeles Lawyer (March 1995); "Bassinger in a Box: Verbal Contracts in the Film Industry," Entertainment Law Reporter (1993); "Ready Willing and Able: The Court of Appeal Breathes New Life into a Forgotten Contract Doctrine," Los Angeles County Bar Association Litigation Newsletter (Fall 1993); "Problem Child: Contract Renegotiation in the Entertainment Industry," L.A. County Bar Association Litigation Newsletter (Fall 1992); "Buchwald v. Paramount: Minding Hollywood's Business," Entertainment Publishing and The Arts Handbook (1991). *Member:* State Bar of California. **PRACTICE AREAS:** Litigation and Entertainment Law.

**MICHAEL A. McANDREWS,** born Los Angeles, California, January 17, 1947; admitted to bar, 1972, California and U.S. District Court, Central District of California; 1981, District of Columbia. *Education:* St. Mary's College (B.A., magna cum laude, 1968); University of California School of Law, Los Angeles (J.D., 1971). Order of the Coif. Member, 1969-1970, Board of Editors and Articles Editor, 1970-1971, UCLA Law Review. Author: Comment, "Constitutional Validity of Attachment in Light of Sniadach v. Family Finance Corp.," 17 UCLA Law Review 835, 1970; "California Debt Collection Practice" (1972 Supplement), California Continuing Education of the Bar, 1972. *Member:* Los Angeles County (Member, Real Property Law Section, Executive Committee, 1986-1990) and American Bar Associations; State Bar of California. [Capt., U.S. Air Force, Department of Judge Advocate General, 1972-1975]. **PRACTICE AREAS:** Real Property Law; Real Property Finance Law.

**RICHARD C. MENDELSON,** born Patterson, New Jersey, 1954; admitted to bar, 1978, New Jersey; 1979, New York and U.S. District Court, Southern District of New York; 1981, California. *Education:* Rutgers University (A.B., 1975); University of Pennsylvania Law School (J.D., cum laude, 1978). Editor, University of Pennsylvania Law Review, 1977-1978. **PRACTICE AREAS:** Real Estate LAw.

**LAWRENCE PEITZMAN,** born 1947; admitted to bar, 1974, California. *Education:* University of California at Riverside (B.A., 1969); Harvard University (M.A., 1970); Boalt Hall School of Law, University of California (J.D., 1974). Phi Beta Kappa; Order of the Coif. Associate Editor, California Law Review, 1973-1974. Author: "Jurisdiction Venue and Structure of the Bankruptcy Court," Bankruptcy Practice after the 1984 Amendments, CED, 1985. Co-author: "The Impact of Sales Law on Business Transactions," CEB, 1985; "Obtaining Use of Cash Collateral," Bankruptcy Practice and Strategy, A. Resnick, ed., 1987; "Drafting Bankruptcy Provisions in Commercial Contracts and Leases," 2 Calif. Bus. Law. Prac. 32, 1987. Contributing Editor, Bankruptcy, California Business Law Reporter, 1983—. Adjunct Professor, San Francisco Law School, 1978-1981. *Member:* Los Angeles County Bar Association (Member, Bankruptcy Committee, Section of Bankruptcy and Commercial Law, 1987—; Chair of Subcommittee on Local Bankruptcy Rules, 1987-1990; Vice-Chair of Committee, 1990—); State Bar of California; Financial Lawyers Conference (Member, Board of Governors, 1987-1994; President, 1994). **PRACTICE AREAS:** Bankruptcy; Workouts.

**GARY D. SAMSON,** born Los Angeles, California, 1948; admitted to bar, 1974, California. *Education:* University of Southern California (A.B., 1970); Hastings College of Law, University of California (J.D., 1973). Order of the Coif. Member, Thurston Society. Associate Editor, Hastings Law Journal, 1972-1973. Co-Author: "Checklist for Secured Commercial Loans," 1983 edition, Financial Lawyers Conference. Lecturer, Uniform Commercial Code, Los Angeles County Bar Association, 1982. Member, Board of Governors of the Financial Lawyer's Conference. Panel Chair: California Bankers Association, 1985 Bank Counsel Seminar Panelist, National Commercial Finance Association, Western 1988 Seminar on Bankruptcy Developments. Panelist: California Bankers Association, 1986 Bank Counsel Seminar; Basic Skills, Articles 5 & 9, Practising Law Institute, 1986-1993; Commercial Law League Fund for Continuing Education, 1987 Satellite Program; Commercial Loan Documentation, Banking Law Institute, 1987; Banking Law Institute, Accounts Receivable and Inventory Financing, 1989. Lecturer, Los Angeles County Bar Association, 1990—; Legal Issues for the Health Care Industry, 1990. National Commercial Finance Association of California (Panel Chair, Chapter 11 Developments). Judge Pro Tem, Century City Bar Association, 1986. *Member:* Los Angeles County Bar Association (Arbitrator, 1986-1987; Chair, 1990-91, Vice-Chair, 1989-1990, Secretary, 1988-89 and Chair of Legislative Committee, Commercial and Bankruptcy Section); State Bar of California ( Vice-Chair, Subcommittee on Fraudulent Conveyances, Committee on Debtor Creditor Relations and Bankruptcy, 1984-1987, Member, Committee on the Uniform Commercial Code, 1981-1984). **PRACTICE AREAS:** Secured Transactions; Banking; Commercial Law; Bankruptcy.

**LARRY D. SOBEL,** born Philadelphia, Pennsylvania, 1951; admitted to bar, 1976, Pennsylvania; 1984, New York and California; 1985, District of Columbia. *Education:* Drexel University (B.S., magna cum laude, 1973); University of Pennsylvania (J.D., cum laude, 1976). *Member:* State Bar of California; American Bar Association (Member, Section on Taxation and Committee on Tax Exempt Financing); National Association of Bond Lawyers. **PRACTICE AREAS:** Taxation Law; Public Finance Law.

**PAYNE L. TEMPLETON,** born Richland, Washington, 1957; admitted to bar, 1987, California. *Education:* Harvard College (A.B., magna cum laude, 1979); University of California, Boalt Hall School of Law (J.D., 1985). Order of the Coif. Law Clerk to the Honorable Harry L. Hupp, U.S. District Court, Central District of California, 1985-1986. *Member:* State Bar of California. **PRACTICE AREAS:** Complex Litigation.

**PAUL A. WEBBER,** born Yakima, Washington, 1934; admitted to bar, 1962, California. *Education:* University of Washington (B.A., 1956; LL.B., 1961). Order of the Coif. Member, Washington Law Review, 1960-1961. *Member:* State Bar of California. **PRACTICE AREAS:** Public Finance Law; Corporate Law.

**HOWARD J. WEG,** born 1954; admitted to bar, 1979, California. *Education:* University of California at Los Angeles (B.A., 1976); Southwestern Law School (J.D., cum laude, 1979); Yale Law School (LL.M., 1980). Associate Editor, Southwestern University Law Review, 1978-1979. Editor, California Legislative Bulletin, 1988-1992. Author: "Strategies for Obtaining Injunctions in Bankruptcy," 3 Bankruptcy Litigation 26, Summer 1995; "The Secured Creditor's Rights to Rents From Real Property," 17 Real Estate Law Journal 29, Summer, 1988; "Introduction to Federal Regulation of Plant Closings and Mass Layoffs," 94 Commercial Law Journal 123, Summer 1989. Extern to the Attorney General for the State of California, 1978-1979; Hon. Justice Otto M. Kaus, 1979. *Member:* Los Angeles County (Member, Commercial Law and Bankruptcy Section, Executive Committee, Lawyer Referral Service, 1980-1981) and American (Member, Business Bankruptcy Committee, Section of Corporation, Banking and Business Law) Bar Associations; State Bar of California (Member: Business Law Section; Executive Committee, 1994—; Education Committee, Vice-Chair, 1992-1993; Co-Chair, 1993-1994; Chair, 15th Annual Spring Program, Business Law Section, 1993); Financial Lawyers Conference. **PRACTICE AREAS:** Bankruptcy; Commercial; Creditor Bankruptcy; Debtor Creditor Law; Lender Rights; Financial Restructuring.

## RESIDENT OF COUNSEL

**JEFFREY S. ALLEN,** born Orange, California, 1948; admitted to bar, 1975, California. *Education:* Stanford University (B.S., 1970); University of California, Boalt Hall School of Law (J.D., 1975). Order of the Coif. Note and Comment Editor, California Law Review, 1974-1975. Author: "Discovery of Complaints Alleging Police Brutality," 63 California Law Review 181, 1975. *Member:* Los Angeles County and American Bar Associations; State Bar of California. [U.S. Army, Active Duty, 1970-1971; USAR, 1971-1975]. **PRACTICE AREAS:** Real Estate Law.

**JOHN P. KREIS,** born Scranton, Pennsylvania, 1948; admitted to bar, 1973, Pennsylvania; 1975, District of Columbia; 1978, U.S. Supreme Court; 1982, California; 1984, New York; U.S. District Court, Southern, Northern, Eastern and Central Districts of California and U.S. Court of Appeals, Ninth Circuit. *Education:* University of Notre Dame (B.A., 1970; J.D.,

*(This Listing Continued)*

**ORRICK, HERRINGTON & SUTCLIFFE LLP,** Los Angeles—Continued

1973). Contributing Author: Steinberg, Bankruptcy Litigation (1990 Edition); Author: "The Reorganized City on A Hill: An Essay on the American Philosophy of Bankruptcy Reorganization," 6 ABI Newsletter No. 1 (1987). Member, American Bankruptcy Institute, 1984. *Member:* Century City, Beverly Hills and Los Angeles County Bar Associations; Financial Lawyers Conference. **PRACTICE AREAS:** Bankruptcy and Corporate Reorganization Litigation; Debt Restructure; Workouts.

**MARY H. NEALE,** born Wichita, Kansas, 1961; admitted to bar, 1989, New York and California. *Education:* University of California, Berkeley (B.A., with honors, 1983); Columbia University (J.D., 1988; M.B.A., 1988). *Member:* State Bar of California; New York State Bar Association; National Association of Bond Lawyers. **PRACTICE AREAS:** Public Finance; Banking; Project Finance.

**MICHAEL E. SILVER,** born New York, New York, 1958; admitted to bar, 1984, New York; 1988, California; U.S. District Court, Southern and Eastern Districts of New York. *Education:* Harvard University (A.B., cum laude, 1980); New York University (J.D., 1983). Member, Editorial Board, 1981-1982, Project Editor, 1982-1983, Journal of International Law and Politics. *Member:* Los Angeles County Bar Association (Member, Real Property Section); State Bar of California (Member, Real Property Section). **PRACTICE AREAS:** Secured Transactions; Real Estate Law.

### RESIDENT ASSOCIATES

**ELLA L. BROWN,** born Beverly, Massachusetts, 1962; admitted to bar, 1989, Virginia; 1992, California. *Education:* Bowdoin College (A.B., magna cum laude, 1984); University of Virginia (J.D., 1989). Phi Beta Kappa. *Member:* State Bar of California.

**DIANA K. CHUANG,** born Buffalo, New York, 1972; admitted to bar, 1996, California. *Education:* Stanford University (B.A., 1993); Duke University School of Law (J.D., 1996). *Member:* State Bar of California.

**CHRISTOPHER L. DAVIS,** born Orange, California, 1966; admitted to bar, 1992, California. *Education:* Stanford University (B.A., 1989); University of California at Los Angeles (J.D., 1992). *Member:* State Bar of California.

**ANDREW D. GARELICK,** born Indianapolis, Indiana, 1969; admitted to bar, 1994, California. *Education:* San Diego State University (B.S., Economics, magna cum laude, 1991); Hastings College of the Law, University of California (J.D., cum laude, 1994). *Member:* State Bar of California.

**MARGARET H. GILLESPIE,** born Boston, Massachusetts, 1965; admitted to bar, 1990, California and U.S. District Court, Central District of California. *Education:* Stanford University (B.A., with distinction, 1987); University of California at Los Angeles School of Law (J.D., 1990). *Member:* State Bar of California.

**OWEN P. GROSS,** born Redondo Beach, California, 1966; admitted to bar, 1995, California. *Education:* University of Southern California (A.B., cum laude, 1988; J.D., 1994).

**BRETT HEALY,** born New York, New York, 1970; admitted to bar, 1995, California. *Education:* Cornell University (B.A., 1992); University of Southern California (J.D., 1995). Order of the Coif. Member, Southern California Law Review, 1993-1994.

**VICTOR HSU,** born Baldwin Park, California, 1961; admitted to bar, 1987, California; 1988, U.S. District Court, Central District of California. *Education:* Princeton University (A.B., 1983); Yale University (M.P.P.M., 1987; J.D., 1987). Editor, Yale Law and Policy Review, 1985-1986. Author: "The Ease of Entry Doctrine in Merger Law: Managing the Waste of In re Echlin," 20 Pac. L.J. 75, 1988, reprinted in 31 Corporate Practice Commentator 273, 1989. *Member:* State Bar of California.

**ALISA JARDINE,** born Heidelberg, Germany, 1991; admitted to bar, 1996, California. *Education:* University of California at San Diego (B.A., summa cum laude, 1993), Phi Beta Kappa; University of Los Angeles School of Law (J.D., 1996).

**JULIE E. KNIPSTEIN,** born Chicago, Illinois, 1965; admitted to bar, 1990, Illinois; 1993, California. *Education:* Indiana University (B.A., 1987); University of Illinois College of Law (J.D., cum laude, 1990). *Member:* Illinois State Bar Association; State Bar of California. **PRACTICE AREAS:** Public Finance Law.

**LINDA S. KOFFMAN,** born Kadoma, Okinawa, August 22, 1963; admitted to bar, 1989, California. *Education:* University of California at Berkeley (A.B., 1985); University of California, Hastings College of the Law (J.D., 1988).

**SCOTT G. LAWSON,** born Whittier, California, 1962; admitted to bar, 1994, California. *Education:* University of California at Berkeley (B.A., 1984; M.A., 1987 ); University of Utah (J.D., 1994). Articles Editor, Utah Law Review. Member, National Moot Court Team. Extern to the Hon. Dee V. Benson, United States District Court, District of Utah. *Member:* State Bar of California.

**VICTORIA A. LEVIN,** born Chicago, Illinois, 1967; admitted to bar, 1993, California. *Education:* Stanford University (B.A., 1989); University of California at Los Angeles (J.D., 1993). Managing Editor, UCLA Law Review, 1992-1993. Author: "The Substantial Compliance Doctrine in Tax Law: Equity vs. Efficiency," 40 UCLA L. Rev. 6, 1993. *Member:* State Bar of California. **LANGUAGES:** Italian, French, Spanish. **PRACTICE AREAS:** Litigation.

**DOUGLAS E. LOVE,** born Sacramento, California, 1967; admitted to bar, 1996, California. *Education:* University of Southern California (B.S., 1991); McGeorge School of Law (J.D., with great distinction, 1995). Order of the Coiu. Robert Traynor Honor Society. Law Clerk, Honorable William B. Shubb, Chief Judge, U.S. District Court, Eastern District of California, 1995-1996.

**LISA GIRAND MANN,** born Palo Alto, California, 1967; admitted to bar, 1993, California. *Education:* Duke University (A.B., 1989); University of California at Los Angeles (J.D., 1993). *Member:* State Bar of California. **PRACTICE AREAS:** Litigation.

**PAUL T. MARTIN,** born Arlington, Massachusetts, 1964; admitted to bar, 1991, California and U.S. District Court, Central District of California; 1994, U.S. District Court, Northern District of California. *Education:* Amherst College (B.A., 1986); University of Southern California (J.D., 1991).

**ANTONIO D. MARTINI,** born New York, N.Y., 1964; admitted to bar, 1991, California; 1992, U.S. District Court, Northern District of California and U.S. Court of Appeals, Ninth Circuit; 1993, U.S. Tax Court. *Education:* Union College (B.A., summa cum laude, 1986); Columbia University (J.D., 1991). Phi Beta Kappa. Notes Editor, Columbia Law Review, 1991-92. Law Clerk, Hon. Jerome Farris, U.S. Court of Appeals, Ninth Circuit, 1991-92. *Member:* State Bar of California; American Bar Association.

**BRADLEY SCOTT MILLER,** born Dayton, Ohio, 1970; admitted to bar, 1996, California; U.S. District Court, Northern, Eastern, Southern and Central Districts of California. *Education:* University of Michigan (B.A., 1993; J.D., 1995). Author: "The Big Chill: Third Party Documents and the Reporter's Privilege," Michigan Journal of Law Reform, Vol. 29, Issue 1 & 2 at 613. *Member:* State Bar of California.

**MELANIE MURAKAMI,** born Santa Monica, California, 1970; admitted to bar, 1995, California. *Education:* University of California at Los Angeles (B.A., summa cum laude, 1992); Boalt Hall School of Law, University of California, Berkeley (J.D., 1995). Phi Beta Kappa. Articles Editor, 1993-1994 and Senior Articles Editor, 1994-1995, *Asian Law Journal.*.

**WILLIAM W. OXLEY,** born Fresno, California, 1963; admitted to bar, 1988, California. *Education:* California State University, Chico (B.A., 1985); University of the Pacific (J.D., with distinction, 1988). Order of the Coif. Order of Barristers. Note Writer and Associate Editor, Pacific Law Journal, 1987-1988. Associate Editor, The Transnational Lawyer, 1987-1988. *Member:* State Bar of California. **LANGUAGES:** Spanish.

**LUAN PHAN,** born Nha Trang, Vietnam, 1971; (admission pending). *Education:* Loyola Marymount University (B.S., magna cum laude, 1992), Presidential Scholarship; Loyola University of Los Angeles (J.D., 1996), Sayre Scholarship, Presidential Scholarship.

**GEORGIANA ROSENKRANZ,** born Inglewood, California, 1966; admitted to bar, 1993, California. *Education:* Occidental College (B.A., 1988); Loyola Law School (J.D., 1993). Moot Court Honors Board Traynor Competitor. *Member:* California Council of School Attorneys. **PRACTICE AREAS:** Public Finance; School District Debt Finance.

**CHRISTOPHER S. RUHLAND,** born Los Angeles, California, 1970; admitted to bar, 1994, California. *Education:* University of California at Irvine (B.A., 1991); University of California at Los Angeles School of Law (J.D., 1994). Phi Beta Kappa. Managing Editor, UCLA Law Review, 1993-1994. *Member:* State Bar of California.

**JOHN P. SHARKEY,** born Bayonne, New Jersey, 1954; admitted to bar, 1991, California. *Education:* University of South Carolina (B.A., 1976); Southwestern University (J.D., magna cum laude, 1991). Member, South-

*(This Listing Continued)*

# PROFESSIONAL BIOGRAPHIES — CALIFORNIA—LOS ANGELES

western University Law Review. *Member:* Los Angeles County and American Bar Associations; State Bar of California.

**DAVID B. SHEMANO,** born San Francisco, California, 1965; admitted to bar, 1992, New York and U.S. District Court, Southern and Eastern Districts of New York; 1995, California and U.S. District Court, Central and Northern Districts of California. *Education:* University of California at Santa Barbara (B.A., cum laude, 1987); Hastings College of the Law, University of California (J.D., cum laude, 1991). Order of the Coif; Thurston Society. Articles Editor, Hastings Constitutional Law Quarterly, 1990-1991. Member, Hastings International and Comparative Law Journal, 1989-1990.

**BRIDGETTE M. SMITH,** born East St. Louis, Illinois, 1968; admitted to bar, 1994, California. *Education:* University of California at Los Angeles (B.A., 1991); University of Southern California. Phi Delta Phi. Member, Hale Moot Court Program. *Member:* State Bar of California.

**WINNIE TSIEN,** born Oahu, Hawaii, 1968; admitted to bar, 1994, California. *Education:* Pitzer College (B.A., 1989); University of California at Davis (J.D., 1994). Order of the Coif. Editor, *UC Davis Law Review*. *LANGUAGES:* Chinese. *PRACTICE AREAS:* Litigation; Municipal Law; Public Finance.

**BRADLEY S. WHITE,** born Inglewood, California, 1957; admitted to bar, 1983, California. *Education:* University of Southern California (A.B., 1980); Loyola Law School (J.D., 1983). Phi Alpha Delta. Member, 1981-1982 and Note and Comment Editor, 1982-1983, Loyola of Los Angeles International and Comparative Law Journal. *Member:* State Bar of California.

## MENLO PARK, CALIFORNIA
### MEMBERS OF FIRM

W. Reece Bader
G. Hopkins Guy, III
Lynne C. Hermle
Terrence P. McMahon
Christopher R. Ottenweller
Jon B. Streeter
Gary E. Weiss

### ASSOCIATES

David J. Anderman
Carl W. Chamberlin
Erin Farrell
Kenneth J. Halpern
Leslie Y. Kimball
Wendy Kosanovich
Amy L. Landers
Joseph C. Liburt
Sean A. Lincoln
Alexandra McClure
Peter C. McMahon
Matthew H. Poppe
Eve T. Saltman
Shelley J. Sandusky
Graeme Ellis Sharpe
Eric L. Wesenberg
Thomas H. Zellerbach

## NEW YORK, NEW YORK
### MEMBERS OF FIRM

Paul B. Abramson
Charles W. Bradley
Bradford S. Breen
Peter R. Bucci
Charles N. Burger
Colman J. Burke
Fred C. Byers, Jr.
Richard Chirls
Katharine I. Crost
Bruce S. Cybul
Duncan N. Darrow
Michael Delikat
Edward M. De Sear
Rubi Finkelstein
Robert A. Fippinger
Lawrence B. Fisher
Adam W. Glass
Lawrence B. Goodwin
F. Susan Gottlieb
William A. Gray
Arnold Gulkowitz
Eileen B. Heitzler
Robyn A. Huffman
Laurence Bryan Isaacson
Robert M. Isackson
John J. Keohane
Alan M. Knoll
Peter J. Korda
Jeffrey A. Lenobel
Herbert J. Levine
Carl F. Lyon, Jr.
Daniel A. Mathews
Sam Scott Miller
Kathleen H. Moriarty
Barbara Moses
David Z. Nirenberg
Joshua E. Raff
Jill L. Rosenberg
Stephen K. Sawyier
Albert Simons, III
Louis H. Singer
Michael Voldstad
Richard Weidman
Neil T. Wolk

### SPECIAL COUNSEL

Donald J. Robinson

*(This Listing Continued)*

### OF COUNSEL

Stanley L. Amberg
Thomas Barr, IV
Susan L. Barry
Michael E. Emrich
William H. Horton, Jr.
John A. MacKerron
Robert B. Michel
Martin R. Miller
Amy Moskowitz
Richard H. Nicholls

### ASSOCIATES

Craig T. Beazer
Jonathan K. Bender
Thomas J. Benison
Leon J. Bijou
Colette Bonnard
Patti Lynn Boss
Eric R. Bothwell
Whitney R. Bradshaw
Karen M. Braun
Jarrett D. Bruhn
Juliet F. Buck
Benjamin C. Burkhart
Lawton M. Camp
Anthony Carabba, Jr.
Michael B. Carlinsky
Jennifer M. Clapp
Joseph M. Cohen
Caterina A. Conti
Robert A. Cote
Kyle W. Drefke
Joseph Evall
Marguerite J. Felsenfeld
Jeffrey J. Fessler
John D. Giansello, III
Michael A. Gilbert
Howard M. Goldwasser
Meryl A. Griff
Tzvi Hirshaut
Kiran J. Kamboj
René A. Kathawala
Joseph T. Kennedy
Jaemin Kim
Steven L. Kopp
Diane Krebs
Kenneth R. Linsk
Christopher Locke
Jonathan B. Lurvey
Michael D. Maline
Joseph E. Maloney
David A. Marple
Edward Mayfield
Lisa K. McClelland
Thomas N. McManus
James H. McQuade
Aimee B. Meltzer
Ronald Millet
Bradford E. Monks
Christopher J. Moore
C. Rochelle Moorehead
P. Quinn Moss
Bryan Jay Neilinger
William O'Brien
John F. Olsen
Edwin Gerard Oswald
Scott M. Pasternack
Marc J. Pensabene
Sheryl Lynn Pereira
Gail Pflederer
Nanci Prado
Ruth D. Raisfeld
Marlene Watts Reed
Marni J. Roder
Ira G. Rosenstein
Sidney M. Ruthenberg
Hooman Sabeti-Rahmati
David J. Sack
Al B. Sawyers
Martin L. Schmelkin
Patricia A. Seddon
William C. Seligman
Ronit Setton
Katherine A. Simmons
Corey A. Tessler
David M. Traitel
Sandra L. Tsang
Robert A. Villani
Steven I. Weinberger
Bradley E. Wolf
Michael J. Zeidel

## SACRAMENTO, CALIFORNIA
### MEMBERS OF FIRM

R. Michael Bacon
Norman C. Hile
Perry E. Israel
Cynthia J. Larsen
Marc A. Levinson
Timothy J. Long
John R. Myers
Cynthia L. Remmers

### SPECIAL COUNSEL

William E. Donovan

### OF COUNSEL

E. Randolph Hooks
Iain Mickle

### ASSOCIATES

Jennifer P. Brown
Jordon Lee Burch
James T. Cahalan
Virginia M. Christianson
John P. Cook
William T. Darden
Stephen L. Davis
Edward P. Dudensing
Lynn T. Ernce
Kelcie M. Gosling
Trish Higgins
Christopher E. Krueger
Constance L. LeLouis
Kim Mueller
Charles W. Nugent
Andrew W. Stroud
Susan R. Thompson
Margaret Carew Toledo

*(This Listing Continued)*

CAA1067B

# CALIFORNIA—LOS ANGELES

## ORRICK, HERRINGTON & SUTCLIFFE LLP, Los Angeles—Continued

Eric J. Glassman  
Thomas J. Welsh

### SAN FRANCISCO, CALIFORNIA
### MEMBERS OF FIRM

John E. Aguirre  
William F. Alderman  
Ralph H. Baxter, Jr.  
Elaine R. Bayus  
Daniel R. Bedford  
Michael J. Bettinger  
Steven A. Brick  
Frederick Brown  
Charles Cardall  
Thomas Y. Coleman  
Mary A. Collins  
Dean E. Criddle  
Roger L. Davis  
Stanley J. Dirks  
William M. Doyle  
Raymond G. Ellis  
Robert P. Feyer  
Carlo S. Fowler  
David S. Fries  
Richard A. Gilbert  
Robert J. Gloistein  
Richard E. V. Harris  
Richard D. Harroch  
Gary A. Herrmann  
Patricia K. Hershey  
Richard I. Hiscocks  
William L. Hoisington  
Leslie P. Jay  
John H. Kanberg  
Lawrence T. Kane  
Dana M. Ketcham  
John H. Knox  
Geoffrey P. Leonard  
Mark R. Levie  
Michael H. Liever  
Peter Lillevand  
Dora Mao  
John E. McInerney, III  
Michael R. Meyers  
Thomas C. Mitchell  
William G. Murray, Jr.  
Noel W. Nellis  
M. J. Pritchett  
Greg R. Riddle  
Marie B. Riehle  
William L. Riley  
Paul J. Sax  
John F. Seegal  
Thomas R. Shearer, Jr.  
Gary R. Siniscalco  
Richard V. Smith  
Stephen A. Spitz  
Alan Talkington  
Ralph C. Walker  
Jeffrey S. White  
Kenneth G. Whyburn  
Jeffrey D. Wohl  
George G. Wolf  
Cameron W. Wolfe, Jr.  
George A. Yuhas

### OF COUNSEL

Bruce S. Klafter  
Philip C. Morgan  
Catherine K. O'Connell  
Douglas C. Sands  
Samuel A. Sperry  
Timothy P. Walker

### ASSOCIATES

Melody A. Barker  
Pamela H. Bennett  
Gregory D. Bibbes  
Scott D. Blickenstaff  
Paul C. Borden  
Kerry Anne Bresnahan  
Susan J. Briscoe  
Jessica L. Cahen  
David Malcolm Carson  
David J. Castillo  
Kevin Shih-Chun Chou  
Brett E. Cooper  
Robert E. Curry, III  
Mark Davis  
Kirsten J. Day  
Ana Marie del Rio  
Mary Patricia Dooley  
Scott D. Elliott  
Gabriela Franco  
David K. Gillis  
Carlos E. Gonzalez  
Mary Elizabeth Grant  
Maria Gray  
Adam J. Gutride  
John M. Hartenstein  
Dolph M. Hellman  
Mats F. Hellsten  
Tanya Herrera  
Lynne T. Hirata  
Laura A. Izon  
Stephen J. Jackson, Jr.  
Andrew P. Johnson  
Daniel Judge  
Susan R. Kelley  
Hera Lie Kim  
Thomas P. Klein  
William J. Kramer  
Kathleen Hughes Leak  
Nancy M. Lee  
Gary Louie  
Ashley E. Lowe  
Steven C. Malvey  
Douglas D. Mandell  
Karen L. Marangi  
George P. Miller  
James W. Miller Jr.  
Genevieve M. Moore  
Lowell D. Ness  
Mark F. Parcella  
Anthony B. Pearsall  
David C. Ritchey  
Peter E. Root

(This Listing Continued)

CAA1068B

---

# MARTINDALE-HUBBELL LAW DIRECTORY 1997

### ASSOCIATES (Continued)

Christian J. Rowley  
Paul I. Rubin  
Dave A. Sanchez  
Michelle W. Sexton  
Usha Rengachary Smerdon  
David Sobul  
Lawrence N. Tonomura  
Adrienne Diamant Weil  
Stephen E. Whittaker

### SINGAPORE
### MEMBER OF FIRM

William R. Campbell

### ASSOCIATES

Kenneth S. Aboud  
M. Tamara Box  
Nicholas Chan Kei Cheong  
Bruce R. Schulberg  
David Z. Vance  
Eleanor Wong

### WASHINGTON, D.C.
### MEMBERS OF FIRM

Cameron L. Cowan  
Felicia B. Graham  
Keith W. Kriebel  
Lorraine S. McGowen  
Paul Weiffenbach

### OF COUNSEL

David S. Katz  
Dianne Loennig Stoddard

### ASSOCIATES

Michele E. Beasley  
Mark S. Dola  
Michael H. Freedman  
Rohit H. Kirpalani  
Douglas Madsen  
Thomas D. Salus  
Adam B. Tankel

---

## RONALD E. OSTRIN

**11377 WEST OLYMPIC BOULEVARD, SUITE 900**  
**LOS ANGELES, CALIFORNIA 90064-1625**  
Telephone: 310-914-7991  
Fax: 310-914-7907

*General Civil Practice in all State and Federal Courts with emphasis on Bankruptcy, Real Estate and Entertainment Law.*

**RONALD E. OSTRIN,** born Santa Monica, California, March 23, 1954; admitted to bar, 1979, California. *Education:* University of California at Los Angeles (B.A., cum laude, 1976); Hastings College of Law, University of California (J.D., 1979). *Member:* Los Angeles County Bar Association (Member, Bankruptcy and Solvency Section), State Bar of California; California Lawyers for the Arts. **PRACTICE AREAS:** Bankruptcy Litigation; Business Litigation; Real Estate Litigation; Entertainment Law; General Civil Litigation; Title Insurance Defense.

REPRESENTATIVE CLIENTS: First American Title Co. of Los Angeles; Coast Savings and Loan Association; Chicago Title Insurance Co.; Channel Islands Development Co.; Beechwood Services, Inc.

---

## OSTROVE, KRANTZ & OSTROVE

*A PROFESSIONAL CORPORATION*

Established in 1960

(Successor To: Ostrove and Lancer, A Professional Corporation; David Ostrove, A Professional Corporation)

**5757 WILSHIRE BOULEVARD, SUITE 535**  
**LOS ANGELES, CALIFORNIA 90036-3600**  
Telephone: 213-939-3400  
Fax: 213-939-3500  
Email: OSTROVE@AOL.COM

*Complex Business Litigation, General Civil Litigation, Real Estate Transactions and Real Estate Litigation, Buying and Selling Businesses, Mergers, Consolidations, Tax-Free Reorganizations, Commercial Transactions, Civil RICO, Tax Matters and Tax Litigation, Probate, Wills, Trusts, Estate Planning, Litigation Support and Expert Testimony, Legal and Accounting Education. Maritime Law, Insurance Defense.*

FIRM PROFILE: 37 year History. Ostrove, Krantz & Ostrove is a firm of legal professionals who specialize in solving all types of problems. We represent clients, large and small, for a variety of purposes. Typical Ostrove, Krantz & Ostrove engagements range from prosecuting and defending all types of lawsuits

(This Listing Continued)

to negotiating and preparing contracts for buying and selling businesses and property. We serve hundreds of clients from small start-up ventures to major corporations. We also advise many legal and accounting firms. We strive to achieve total autonomy and independence and approach many of our tasks as a team to best serve our clients needs.

**DAVID OSTROVE,** born Los Angeles, California, 1929; admitted to bar, 1960, California. *Education:* Los Angeles City College (A.A., 1950); University of California; Southwestern University School of Law (J.D., 1958). Certified Public Accountant, California, 1957. Lecturer and author for the California CPA Society and Continuing Education of the Bar: Advanced Corporate Tax Problems, 1990, 1991; Fiduciary Accounting for Estates and Trusts, 1988-1996; Forensic Accounting 1989-1996; Community Property 1989-1996. Senior Adjunct Professor of Law, Southwestern University School of Law, 1968—. Litigation Consultant and Expert Witness including Attorney and Accountant Malpractice, Business Valuations, Tax Accounting Issues and Damages. President, American Association of Attorneys-Certified Public Accountants, 1991-1992. *REPORTED CASES:* Edenfield v. Fane, 113 S. Ct. 1792, 1993; Sylvia S. Ibanez v. Florida Board of Accountancy, 114 Sup. Ct. 2084 (1994), Amicus Briefs, The American Association of Attorney CPAs in support of Commercial Free Speech. *TRANSACTIONS:* Tax Free Merger-Reorganization: System Parking and ABM, 1993-1994. *PRACTICE AREAS:* Taxation; Tax Litigation; Probate; Trusts; Business Litigation; Business Transactions; Professional Malpractice; Litigation Support; Expert Testimony.

**DAVID S. KRANTZ,** born Los Angeles, California, May 10, 1948; admitted to bar, 1978, California; 1980, U S. Court of Appeals, 9th Circuit and U.S. District Court, Central District of California. *Education:* University of California at Berkeley (B.A., 1970); Southwestern University School of Law (J.D., 1978). *PRACTICE AREAS:* Business Litigation; Business Transactions; Real Estate Litigation; Real Estate Transactions; Corporate Law; Wrongful Termination; Fraudulent Conveyances; Civil RICO; Tax; Maritime Law; Insurance Defense.

**KENNETH E. OSTROVE,** born Los Angeles, California, May 13, 1957; admitted to bar, 1983, California. *Education:* University of California at Los Angeles; Humboldt State (B.A., 1979); Southwestern University School of Law (J.D., 1982). Lecturer: "Durable Powers of Attorney for Health Care," 27th Annual Convention of American Association of Attorney-CPA's, 1991; "Expert Witness Testimony," 31st Annual Meeting of AAA-CPA, Palm Springs CA, November, 1995. *Member:* Los Angeles County Bar Association; State Bar of California (Member, Sections on: Taxation and Estate Planning, 1989-1992). *PRACTICE AREAS:* Probate; Estate Planning.

REPRESENTATIVE CLIENTS: Jefferson Insurance Group; Monticello Insurance Co.; Chicago Title; Century Oldsmobile, Inc.; Rally Automotive Group; Superior Rubbish Company, Inc.; TransAmerica Insurance Group; Parker Land and Timber; Special-T Fasteners; First State Insurance; General Accident Insurance; Universal Underwriters; The Hartford Insurance; California Accountants Mutual Insurance Co.; The California Society of CPA's; The State Bar of California; The Jack Hazard Trusts; System Property Management; Estate of Jasha Heifetz; Estate of Josephine Hixson; Cal Farm Insurance; Century Automotive Group, Inc.; Century Chevrolet, Inc.; Husac Intl Inc.; Century National Insurance; CNA Insurance; Intercargo Insurance Co.; U.S. Government - U.S. Attorney's Office - Los Angeles, California; State of California - California State Attorney General's Office; Tulare County District Attorney's Office; Sants Clara County; Los Angeles County.
REFERENCE: First Business Bank.

## THE O'TOOLE LAW FIRM

*601 SOUTH FIGUEROA STREET, SUITE 4100*

**LOS ANGELES, CALIFORNIA 90017**

Telephone: 213-630-4200

Facsimile: 213-683-1148

*Environmental and Worker Health and Safety Law.*

FIRM PROFILE: Patricia M. O'Toole practiced in the environmental, health and safety section at one of the largest and most prestigious law firms for five years and was the major oil and gas corporation for eight years prior to establishing The O'Toole Law Firm. Ms. O'Toole has over 15 years experience in counseling and management in the environmental, health and safety section at one of the largest and most prestigious law firms for five years, and was with a major oil and gas corporation for eight years before that. Patricia M. O'Toole has over 15 years experience in counseling and management in the environmental, health and safety fields. Ms. O'Toole has represented Fortune 500 companies, small and medium-sized businesses, real estate developers, and governmental entities in a variety of environmental, health and safety matters. Ms. O'Toole's experience also includes the development and drafting of legal and technical comments on legislative and regulatory proposals relating to

*(This Listing Continued)*

environmental, health and safety issues. She has represented clients in negotiations with the United States Congress and EPA on environmental legislation, including reauthorization of CERCLA/SARA, the Clean Air Act, The Resource Conservation and Recovery Act, and the Clean Water Act. Ms. O'Toole has represented clients in business and trade organizations, including the American Petroleum Institute, the Chemical Manufacturers Association, the U.S. Chamber of Commerce, the National Association of Manufacturers, The Business Roundtable (national and California), the National Environmental Development Association, the Air and Waste Management Association, the Western States Petroleum Association, the California Council on Environmental and Economic Balance, the California Manufacturers Association, the California Mining Association, the Los Angeles Area Chamber of Commerce, the International Forum of the World Environment Center, the International Petroleum Industry Environmental Conservation Association, and the World Industry Conference on Environmental Management (UNEP, Paris, November 1984).

**PATRICIA M. O'TOOLE,** born Chicago, Illinois, January 30, 1953; admitted to bar, 1982, California, U.S. District Court, Central District of California and U.S. Court of Appeals, 9th Circuit. *Education:* Occidental College (B.A., with honors, 1975); University of California School of Law at Los Angeles (J.D., 1980). *Member:* Los Angeles County Bar Association (Member, Environmental Law Section); State Bar of California (Member, Environmental Law Section). *LANGUAGES:* French. *SPECIAL AGENCIES:* U.S. EPA (Environmental Protection Agency); Federal Occupational Safety and Health Administration (OSHA); California Occupational Safety and Health Administration (Cal OSHA); California OSH Appeals Board; South Coast Air Quality Management District (SCAQMD); San Joaquin Valley Unified Air Pollution Control District (SJVUAPCD); California Department of Toxic Substances Control; California Regional Water Quality Control Boards.

## OTT & HOROWITZ

**LOS ANGELES, CALIFORNIA**

(See Glendale)

*General Civil, Trial and Appellate Practice in State and Federal Courts and Arbitration Tribunals, Commercial Litigation, Labor, Real Estate and Corporate.*

## OVERLANDER, LEWIS & RUSSELL

**LOS ANGELES, CALIFORNIA**

(See Pasadena)

*Business and Commercial Litigation. Personal Injury, Insurance Defense, Commercial and Tort Law, Civil Rights, Police Misconduct Defense, Public Entity Defense. General Civil Trial Practice.*

## OVERTON, LYMAN & PRINCE, LLP

A Registered Limited Liability Partnership including Professional

Corporations

*Established in 1877*

*777 SOUTH FIGUEROA STREET, 37TH FLOOR*

**LOS ANGELES, CALIFORNIA 90017**

Telephone: 213-683-1100

Cable Address: "Olap"

Telecopier: 213-627-7795

*General Civil Trial and Appellate Practice in all State and Federal Courts. Corporation, Labor, Real Property and Construction Law, Employment, Literary Property, Trademark, Estate Planning, Trust and Probate Law. State and Federal Taxation, Water Rights, Business, Banking and International Business Law emphasizing Mexico and Japan. Bankruptcy and Creditors' Rights, Securities and Commodities Law.*

MEMBERS OF FIRM

**EUGENE OVERTON** (1880-1970).

**EDWARD DEAN LYMAN** (1881-1962).

**GEORGE W. PRINCE, JR.** (1887-1971).

*(This Listing Continued)*

OVERTON, LYMAN & PRINCE, LLP, Los Angeles—
Continued

DONALD H. FORD, born Chicago, Illinois, December 5, 1906; admitted to bar, 1932, California. *Education:* Oregon State University (B.S., 1929); University of Michigan (J.D., with distinction, 1932). Order of the Coif. *Member:* Los Angeles County and American Bar Associations. *PRACTICE AREAS:* Oil and Gas; Corporate Law; Farm and Ranch Law.

DENNIS B. HANSEN, (P.C.), born Preston, Idaho, November 4, 1944; admitted to bar, 1972, California. *Education:* Brigham Young University (B.S., 1969); University of California at Los Angeles (J.D., 1972). Beta Gamma Sigma; Order of the Coif. *Member:* Los Angeles County and American Bar Associations. *PRACTICE AREAS:* Business Law; Probate; Trusts and Estates; Estate Planning.

ROY E. POTTS, born Vincennes, Indiana, December 24, 1918; admitted to bar, 1952, California; 1967, U.S. Supreme Court. *Education:* Purdue University (B.S.M.E., 1940); Loyola University at Chicago; Yale Law School (LL.B., 1951). *PRACTICE AREAS:* Labor Law; Literary Property Law; Business Litigation.

FREDERICK W. HILL, born Kalamazoo, Michigan, September 24, 1937; admitted to bar, 1965, California, U.S. District Court, Northern District of California and U.S. Court of Appeals, 9th Circuit. *Education:* Western Michigan University (B.A., 1960); Hastings College of Law, University of California (J.D., 1964). Phi Alpha Delta. Co-Author: "U.S. Business for Japanese Businessmen," The Simul Press, 1972. Editor, "Mexican Law Syllabus," Los Angeles County Bar Association, 1972, 1980, 1989, 1991. Member, Hill, Gould & Pearson, 1977-1983. *Member:* Los Angeles County (Chairman, International Law Section, 1974-1975), American (Member, International Law and Practice Section) and International Bar Associations. *PRACTICE AREAS:* Banking Law; General Corporate Law; International Business Law; Mexico Trade; Japan Trade.

GREGORY C. GLYNN, born Albany, New York, December 9, 1940; admitted to bar, 1967, California and Connecticut; 1975, District of Columbia; 1980, U.S. Supreme Court; 1984, Maryland. *Education:* College of the Holy Cross (B.S., summa cum laude, 1962); Yale University (M.S., 1963; LL.B., 1966). Member, Board of Editors, Yale Law Journal, 1964-1966. Adjunct Professor, Washington College of Law, American University, 1977-1978. Law Clerk to Hon. M. Joseph Blumenfeld, U.S. District Court, District of Connecticut, 1966-1967. Assistant U.S. Attorney, Central District of California, 1971-1975. Assistant Chief Trial Attorney, Securities and Exchange Commission, 1975-1979. Associate General Counsel, Litigation, Commodity Futures Trading Commission, 1979-1983. *Member:* The District of Columbia Bar; Los Angeles County, Connecticut, Maryland State and American Bar Associations. *PRACTICE AREAS:* Securities Litigation; Commodities; Business Litigation. *Email:* 71342.3174@compuserve.com

GERALD R. WHITT, born Tachikawa, Japan, July 11, 1950; admitted to bar, 1976, California. *Education:* Duke University (B.S.E.E., summa cum laude, 1972); Stanford University (J.D., 1976). Phi Beta Kappa; Tau Beta Pi. *Member:* Los Angeles County and American Bar Associations. *PRACTICE AREAS:* Business Law; Commercial Law; Creditors Rights; Bankruptcy Law.

(All Members of the Firm are Members of the State Bar of California)

REFERENCES: Union Bank of California (550 S. Hope St., Los Angeles); Daiichi Kangyo Bank, Ltd.; Asahi Bank, Ltd.

## OWENS & GACH RAY

Established in 1987

**10351 SANTA MONICA BOULEVARD, SUITE 400**
**LOS ANGELES, CALIFORNIA 90025**
Telephone: 310-553-6611
Telecopier: 310-553-2179
Email: ogrlaw@aol.com

General Civil Practice with emphasis on Commercial Litigation, Real Estate Litigation and Creditors' Rights in Bankruptcy Matters, Conservatorship Matters and Entertainment Litigation.

FIRM PROFILE: Owens & Gach Ray, founded in 1987, specializes in all aspects of commercial litigation, including real estate, employment, business torts, and bankruptcy litigation. The founding partners of the firm maintain direct control over each client matter and consistently keep clients apprised of all case developments. The firm is committed to delivering top quality legal services, and to being responsive, accountable and accessible to the firm's clients.

### MEMBERS OF FIRM

ROBERT B. OWENS, born Chicago, Illinois, November 15, 1951; admitted to bar, 1977, California. *Education:* University of Southern California (B.S., magna cum laude, 1972); M.B.A., 1974; J.D., 1977). Phi Kappa Phi. Note and Article Editor, Southern California Law Review, 1977. *Member:* Beverly Hills and Los Angeles County Bar Associations; State Bar of California.

LINDA GACH RAY, born Los Angeles, California, December 15, 1954; admitted to bar, 1979, California. *Education:* University of California at Los Angeles (B.A., 1976); Loyola University and University of California at Los Angeles (J.D., 1979). Associate Editor, UCLA Law Review, 1978-1979. *Member:* Beverly Hills and Los Angeles County Bar Associations; State Bar of California.

REPRESENTATIVE CLIENTS: Equifax, Inc.; Fox, Inc.; Gruen Marketing Corp.; Barbara Lazaroff and Wolfgang Puck; Mosler Inc.; Resolution Trust Corporation; Sysco Corp.

## LLOYD C. OWNBEY, JR.

**LOS ANGELES, CALIFORNIA**

(See Pasadena)

Labor and Employment Law, Public and Private Sectors.

## PACHULSKI, STANG, ZIEHL & YOUNG

PROFESSIONAL CORPORATION

**SUITE 1100, 10100 SANTA MONICA BOULEVARD**
**LOS ANGELES, CALIFORNIA 90067**
Telephone: 310-277-6910
Telecopier: 310-201-0760

San Francisco, California Office: 350 California Street, Suite 2020.
Telephone: 415-263-7000. Facsimile: 415-263-7010.

Bankruptcy, Corporate Reorganization, Debtor-Creditor Matters, Insurance Insolvency, Civil Litigation, Business, Commercial Law, General Real Estate, and Corporate and Entertainment Transactions.

FIRM PROFILE: Pachulski, Stang, Ziehl & Young P.C. is a firm of thirty-five attorneys which specializes in corporate reorganization, bankruptcy and insolvency law, and insurance insolvency, business and commercial litigation, and general real estate matters.

The Firm's bankruptcy attorneys are experienced in representing all major constituencies in out-of-court workouts and bankruptcy cases, including debtors, trustees, receivers, creditors' committees, secured creditors, bondholders, asset purchasers and third party plan proponents.

The Firm's litigation attorneys have a wide range of experience in complex business litigation in state and federal courts, including litigating claims relating to securities laws, insurance insolvencies, insurance coverage, director and officer liability, banking, real estate and breach of contract.

The Firm's demonstrated ability to effectively combine its bankruptcy and litigation disciplines distinguishes it from other practitioners in the insolvency area. While our primary objective is to seek business solutions to our clients' problems, when results cannot be achieved by other means, the Firm's attorneys are highly experienced in prosecuting and defending complex litigation.

While the Firm has acted as insolvency counsel for debtors and creditors in numerous industries, it has developed a particular expertise in the financial services, insurance, computers and high technology, real estate, entertainment and retailing industries.

Creditors' Committees: Members of the Firm have represented numerous out-of-court and official bankruptcy creditors' committees comprising various creditor groups, including trade creditors, bondholders and other holders of unsecured debt. In the financial services area, the Firm has represented the official bankruptcy creditors' committees for First Executive Corporation (parent company to Executive Life Insurance Company and Executive Life Insurance Company of New York); First Capital Holdings Corp. (parent company to First Capital Life Insurance Company and Fidelity Bankers Life Insurance Company); Westwood Equities Corporation (parent company to the Ticor Title Group of Companies); and HomeFed Corp. (parent company to HomeFed

(This Listing Continued)

Bank). The Firm has also represented numerous official creditors' committees and subcommittees in entertainment bankruptcy cases, including those formed in the matters of National Peregrine, Inc.; MCEG, Inc.; Qintex Entertainment, Inc.; Weintraub Entertainment, Inc.; and Fries Entertainment, Inc. Other current or recent significant committee representations include committees for the employees of Orange County, California Leisure Technology, Inc. and subsidiaries; C&R Clothiers, Inc.; DAK Industries, Inc.; Specialty Restaurants Corporation; The Clothestime, Inc.; House of Fabrics, Inc.; and Tallon Termite and Pest Control.

*Special Interest Committees:* The Firm has developed a particular expertise in representing specialized creditors' committees and subcommittees, such as equity security, franchisee and membership committees. Typical representations in this area include: co-counsel to the Official Franchisee Committee of Pioneer Take-Out Corporation; counsel to the Official Committee of Equity Holders of Sun Corporation; counsel to the Official Committee of Equity Holders of House of Fabrics, Inc.; counsel to the Official Committee of Marketing Representatives of FundAmerica, a multi-level international marketing organization; counsel to the Official Committee of Membership Creditors of American Adventure, a national recreational campground operator; and counsel to a committee of petitioning creditors for Eastern Airlines Secured Equipment Trust.

*Debtors:* Members of the Firm have represented a broad spectrum of debtors in successful out-of-court workouts and chapter 11 reorganizations. Representations by members of the firm in this area include: Sizzler International, Inc. and Related Entities (A National Franchisor and Restaurant Chain); Gateway Educational Products, Ltd., Manufacturer of Hooked on Phonics; Penguin's Frozen Yogurt, Inc./Penguin's Place, Inc. (a regional food franchisor and licensor); Imperial Hotels Corporation (a regional hotel owner/operator); TreeSweet Juice Co. (a national beverage manufacturer and retailer); Buffums, Inc. (a regional department store chain); Commonwealth Equity Trust (publicly held real estate investment trust); Film Ventures (a motion picture distributor); TSL Holdings, Inc. (publicly held computer hardware company); and F&C International, Inc. (publicly held company in the fragrance and flavor manufacturing industry).

*Trustees:* The Firm or its members have acted as general and special counsel for numerous chapter 7 and chapter 11 trustees. In particular, the Firm or its members have represented trustees for Triad America Corporation and related entities; Oppenheimer Industries, Inc.; National Lumber and Supply Co.; Rogersound Labs; Triad Healthcare; Hiuka America Corporation and Papaho Corporation. The Firm is especially experienced in representing trustees in cases involving complicated fraud and asset misappropriation.

*Secured and Major Unsecured Creditors/Bondholders:* Members of the Firm routinely render advice to secured creditors and major unsecured creditors in transactions in which insolvency issues are of concern and have frequently represented such constituencies in bankruptcy proceedings. Typical secured and unsecured creditor clients of the Firm include: National Broadcasting Company, Inc.; The Hahn Company; First Nationwide Bank; Sony Pictures Entertainment, Inc.; Holiday Inns, Inc.; Barclays Bank; and Paine Webber, Inc.

*Purchasers and Investors:* Members of the Firm have represented asset purchasers and outside investors in successful acquisitions of the stock or assets of troubled or insolvent companies. Successful representations in this area include the acquisition of the stock or assets of: Hiller Aviation Inc., an aircraft manufacturing company; Irvine Ranch Farmer's Market, a high-end food market chain; and Eaton Leonard Corporation. Members of the Firm have also provided insolvency advice to major bondholders and asset purchasers in the following matters: Eastern Airlines; Hillsborough Holdings; BiCoastal Corporation; and General Development Corporation.

*Receivers and Receiverships:* James Stang, a name shareholder of the Firm, has served on the Los Angeles County Superior Court's Receivership Panel for several years. His major receiverships have included commercial, office and retail properties; hotels; automobile dealerships; and manufacturing operations. Mr. Stang has served as receiver for numerous banks and other financial institutions, including: Bank of America; First National Bank of Chicago; Sears Savings Bank; Fidelity Federal Bank; and Tokai Credit Corporation.

*Bankruptcy Litigation:* The Firm prides itself on its ability to effectively litigate in the specialized forum of the bankruptcy court. The Firm is particularly experienced in prosecuting fraudulent transfer claims, especially in the context of failed leveraged buyouts and complicated preference litigation. The Firm has also successfully defended E.F. Hutton and Alexander Hamilton Life Insurance Companies against lender liability claims exceeding $200 million asserted by debtors in chapter 11 cases.

*Insurance Litigation:* The Firm represents holders of over $750 million in group pension annuity contracts issued by Executive Life Insurance Company of California in one of the nation's largest life insurance conservatorships.

*(This Listing Continued)*

These contract-holders have actively participated throughout the proceeding, including a trial concerning the priority classification of various groups of policyholders and proceedings testing the Insurance Commissioner's proposed plan of rehabilitation. The Firm participated on the steering committee for the pension group contract holders in the Mutual Benefit Life Insurance Company conservation proceeding. A member of The Firm participated in the demutualization of Equitable Life Assurance Society of America representing the American Bar Retirement Association in the distribution of Equitable's assets. Members of Firm represented pension policyholders in a trial with Mutual Life of New York, resulting from its attempted unilateral restructuring of insurance contracts. The Firm is handling liability insurance coverage issues for professional negligence claims of $250 million in conjunction with its representation of the Creditors' Committee of the Pannell Kerr Forster successor partnership. A member of the Firm handled numerous insurance coverage matters for Travelers Insurance Company pertaining to professional errors and omissions policies.

*General Litigation:* General business and insurance related litigation is also a significant part of the Firm's practice. The Firm has developed a number of litigation specialties, including the prosecution and defense of lender liability claims and major fraud actions. In addition, the Firm offers expertise in the resolution of insurance coverage disputes, director and officer liability claims, and bank operation matters. Successful representations include: protecting the rights of over $700 million in Executive Life pension contract holders in the Executive Life conservation proceedings; recovering a $9 million judgment against the largest private diagnostic laboratory in the United States and its owner based upon breach of an oral agreement; recovering of $7 million Judgement arising out of a failed corporate acquisition transaction; recovering for numerous financial institutions on fidelity bond claims; successfully Defending directors and officers of a number of failed financial institutions; obtaining a substantial settlement for a real estate development company in a fraud and breach of contract action brought against Bank of America; and successfully defending the developers of a major residential subdivision in litigation arising from land subsidence affecting hundreds of single-family homes.

*Real Estate:* Our Firm's Transactional practice includes the representation of clients in general real estate matters, including the acquisition, disposition, development and subdivision of real property; the leasing of commercial, industrial and retail space and the negotiation of acquisition, construction and permanent financing and workouts.

*Business and Entertainment Transactions:* The Firm's practice also includes general business and entertainment transactions, the representation of motion picture producers, filmakers and distributors and clients involved in corporate acquisition and financing transactions.

### SHAREHOLDERS

**MARC A. BEILINSON,** born Los Angeles, California, May 20, 1958; admitted to bar, 1983, California and U.S. District Court, Central, Northern, Eastern and Southern Districts of California. *Education:* University of California at Los Angeles (B.A., 1980); University of California at Davis (J.D., 1983). *Member:* Los Angeles County and American Bar Associations; State Bar of California; Financial Lawyers Conference.

**ANDREW W. CAINE,** born Tulsa, Oklahoma, October 21, 1958; admitted to bar, 1983, California; U.S. District Court, Central, Northern, Southern and Eastern Districts of California; U.S. Court of Appeals, Ninth Circuit. *Education:* Northwestern University (B.A., 1980); University of California at Los Angeles (J.D., 1983). Phi Beta Kappa. Member, Mortar Board. Recipient, American Jurisprudence Award in Administrative Law. Co-Author: "The Influence of Outcomes and Procedures on Formal Leaders," 41 Journal of Personality and Social Psychology, No. 4, 1981. Extern to Judge Arthur L. Alarcon, U.S. Court of Appeals, Ninth Circuit, 1982. Member, Los Angeles Superior Court Arbitration Panel (1991-1993). *Member:* Los Angeles County and American Bar Associations; Association of Business Trial Lawyers; American Bankruptcy Institute (Member, Board of Directors, 1995—). *REPORTED CASES:* In re Madison Associates, 183 B.R. 206 (Bankr. C.D. California 1995); Gregorian v. National Convenience Stores, Inc., 174 Cal. App. 3d 944 (1985). *TRANSACTIONS:* Represented Official Creditors Committee of Madison Associates, FKA Pannell Kerr Foster; Merisel, Inc. and Advanced Research Laboratories in defense of various preference actions; Paine Webber Partnerships in guarantee litigation; Holiday Inns, Inc. in contract litigation.

**LINDA F. CANTOR,** born Detroit, Michigan, April 23, 1956; admitted to bar, 1988, Illinois and U.S. District Court, Northern District of Illinois; 1991, California and U.S. District Court Central, Northern, Southern and Eastern District of California; 1994, U.S. Court of Appeals, Ninth Circuit. *Education:* University of Michigan (A.B., with high distinction, 1979; M.S.W., 1982; J.D., cum laude, 1987). Author: "The Impact of Bankruptcy

*(This Listing Continued)*

CAA1071B

**PACHULSKI, STANG, ZIEHL & YOUNG,** PROFESSIONAL CORPORATION, Los Angeles—Continued

on Entertainment License Agreements: Protecting the Rights of Debtor Licensees," 19 California Bankruptcy Journal 225, 1991. *Member:* Los Angeles County and American Bar Associations; Financial Lawyers Conference.

**LARRY W. GABRIEL,** born Chicago, Illinois, September 12, 1948; admitted to bar, 1974, Illinois; 1976, California. *Education:* Southern Illinois University (B.A., 1970); De Paul University (J.D., 1974). Member, De Paul Law Review, 1972-1973. Author: "1994 Receivers and Guaranty Funds in Life Insurance Insolvency Proceedings: The Need For Reform," ABA National Institute; "Solvency Concerns With Foreign Insurers and Reinsurers/Recent Developments/US Reform Efforts," 1994; "Pension Phantasmagoria," Business Insurance, September 6, 1993. Co-Author: "Check Kiting - The Implications of a Discovering Bank's Actions on Its Right of Recovery," Banking News, November 15, 1982, reprinted Independent Banker, January, 1983; "Ramifications of a Check Kite-Liability Between Banks," Pacific Banker and Business, March, 1983. Planning Commissioner, City of Hidden Hills, 1991-1993. Adjunct Professor of Law, Banking, Pepperdine University, 1987-1989. Judge Pro Tem, Beverly Hills Municipal Court, 1982-1990. *Member:* Los Angeles County and American (Member: Business Law Section, Commercial Financial Services Committee, Insurance Insolvency Task Force; Tort and Insurance Practice Section) Bar Associations; State Bar of California; Los Angeles Business Trial Lawyers Association. **REPORTED CASES:** In re County of Orange, Orange County Employers Assn., et al. v. County of Orange, 1995 WL 95157 (Bankr. C.D. Cal); Quackenbush as Insurance Commissioner, Etc., Plaintiff and Respondent, v. Aurora, et al., Defendants and Respondents, Commercial National Bank in Shreveport, et al., Defendants and Appellants (32 Cal. App. 4th 344, 38 Cal Rptr. 2d 453); Commercial National Bank in Shreveport, et al., v. Garamendi, 14 Cal. App. 4th 393, 17 Cal. Rptr. 2d 884 (1993); Texas Commerce Bank v. Garamendi, 11 Cal. App. 4th 460, 491, 14 Cal. Rptr. 854, 874 (1992); Federal Deposit Insurance Corporation v. Imperial Bank, 859 F.2d p.101 (9th Cir. 1988); Seven Elves, Inc. v. Eskinazi, et al, 635 F.2d 396 (5th Cir. 1981); Seven Elves, Inc. v. Eskinazi, et al., 704 F.2d 241 (5th Cir. 1983).

**BRAD R. GODSHALL,** born Sellersville, Pennsylvania, July 31, 1957; admitted to bar, 1982, California; U.S. District Court, Central, Northern, Southern and Eastern Districts of California; 1996, Nevada. *Education:* Juniata College (B.A., summa cum laude, 1979); University of Pennsylvania (J.D., cum laude, 1982). Captain, National Moot Court Team, 1981. Associate Editor, University of Pennsylvania Law Review, 1980-1981. Co-Author: "Plan Wars-The Use of Chapter 11 to Coax Continued Financing From A Reluctant Lender," Commercial Law and Practice, Number A-738; "Chapter 11: The Bank of Last Resort," The Business Lawyer, November 1989; "Wading 'Upstream' in Leveraged Transactions: Traditional Guarantees v. 'Net Worth' Guarantees." 46 The Business Lawyer 391, 1991; "Two Years Later: Eight Questions Left Unanswered (or Extremely Confused) by Deprizio," California Bankruptcy Law Journal, Spring 1991. *Member:* Los Angeles County Bar Association; Financial Lawyers Conference. **REPORTED CASES:** In re Outlook Century Ltd., 127 B.R. 65.

**STANLEY E. GOLDICH,** born Philadelphia, Pennsylvania, May 19, 1955; admitted to bar, 1980, California; U.S. District Court, Central, Northern, Southern and Eastern Districts of California; U.S. Court of Appeals, Ninth Circuit. *Education:* Trinity College (B.A., 1976); Stanford University (J.D., 1979). Extern, Center for Law in the Public Interest. Associate Editor, Stanford Environmental Law Annual, 1979. Judge Pro Tem, Small Claims Court, Temporary Judge Program, Los Angeles Municipal Court, 1988-1993. *Member:* Los Angeles County Bar Association (Member, Professional Responsibility and Ethics Committee); Financial Lawyers Conference. **REPORTED CASES:** In re Reed, 89 B.R. 100; In re Westworld Community Healthcare, Inc. 95 B.R. 730; In re Reed 940 F.2d 1317. **TRANSACTIONS:** Represented New West Federal Savings and Loan in Hollywood Roosevelt Hotel chapter 11 and sale; Truck Insurance Exchange in Maxicare chapter 11; Official Committee of Creditors Holding Unsecured Membership Claims in American Adventure, Inc. chapter 11; Commonwealth Equity Trust.

**RICHARD J. GRUBER,** born Paterson, New Jersey, September 24, 1955; admitted to bar, 1982, California. *Education:* Brandeis University (B.A., magna cum laude, 1977); University of California at Los Angeles (J.D., 1982). Recipient, American Jurisprudence Awards in Constitutional Law and Criminal Law. *Member:* Los Angeles County Bar Association; State Bar of California.

*(This Listing Continued)*

**IRA D. KHARASCH,** born Chicago, Illinois, May 14, 1955; admitted to bar, 1983, California and Alaska; U.S. District Court, Northern, Eastern, Southern and Central Districts of California. *Education:* University of Illinois (B.A., cum laude, 1977); University of California at Los Angeles (J.D., 1982). Phi Beta Kappa. Law Clerk to Alaska Supreme Court Chief Justice Edmond Burke, 1982-1983. *Member:* Los Angeles County Bar Association; Financial Lawyers Conference.

**ALAN J. KORNFELD,** born Los Angeles, California, 1955; admitted to bar, 1987, California and U.S. District Court, Northern, Southern, Eastern and Central Districts of California; 1990, U.S. Court of Appeals, Ninth Circuit and Arizona; 1995, U.S. District Court, Eastern, Southern, Northern and Central Districts of California. *Education:* University of California at Los Angeles (A.B., 1976); University of California at Los Angeles (J.D., 1987). Phi Beta Kappa, Pi Gamma Mu. **LANGUAGES:** Hebrew.

**ROBERT B. ORGEL,** born Elizabeth, New Jersey, September 5, 1955; admitted to bar, 1981, California; U.S. District Court, Northern, Eastern and Central Districts of California. *Education:* Rutgers University (B.A., 1977); University of California at Los Angeles (J.D., 1981). Phi Beta Kappa. Associate Editor, UCLA Journal of Environmental Law and Policy, 1980-1981. Law Clerk to Senior Judge Martin Pence, U.S. District Court, District of Hawaii, 1981-1982. *Member:* Los Angeles County and American (Chairman, Task Force on Health Care-Related Bankruptcy Issues, 1995—) Bar Associations; State Bar of California (Member, Franchise Law Committee, 1992-1994); Financial Lawyers Conference.

**RICHARD M. PACHULSKI,** born Los Angeles, California, October 29, 1956; admitted to bar, 1979, California; U.S. Court of Appeals, Ninth Circuit and U.S. District Court, Northern, Central, Eastern and Southern Districts of California. *Education:* University of California at Los Angeles (B.A., summa cum laude, 1976); Stanford University (J.D., 1979). Phi Beta Kappa. Pi Gamma Mu. Extern to Judge Robert M. Takasugi, U.S. District Court, Central District of California, 1978-1979. Co-Author: "Chapter 11- The Bank of Last Resort," 45 Bus. Law. 261, 1989; "Plan Wars-The Use of Chapter 11 To Coax Continued Financing From A Reluctant Lender," Commercial Law and Practice, Number A-738. *Member:* Los Angeles County and American (Member, Section of Business Law) Bar Associations; Association of Business Trial Lawyers; Financial Lawyers Conference (Member, Board of Governors, 1989-1992). **REPORTED CASES:** In re F.A.B. Industries, 147 B.R. 763 (C.D. Cal. 1992). **TRANSACTIONS:** Represented the Creditors' Committees of Weintraub Entertainment, Inc. and First Executive Corporation; Represented or Representing the Debtors in TSL Holdings, Inc.; Penguin's Frozen Yogurt, Inc./Penguin's Place, Inc.; Commonwealth Equity Trust; and Sizzler International, Inc. and Affiliated Debtors.

**JEFFREY N. POMERANTZ,** born Brooklyn, New York, March 10, 1965; admitted to bar, 1989, California and U.S. District Court, Central, Northern, Eastern and Southern Districts of California. *Education:* New York University (B.A., 1986; J.D., 1989). Phi Beta Kappa; Order of the Coif. **REPORTED CASES:** In re AEG Acquisition Corp.; In re F.A.B. Industries.

**JEREMY V. RICHARDS,** born London, England, June 27, 1958; admitted to bar, 1982, California; U.S. District Court, Central, Northern, Eastern and Southern Districts of California. *Education:* Oxford University (B.A., first class honors, Jurisprudence, 1979; B.C.L., first class honors, Law, 1980); Harvard University (LL.M., 1981). David Blank Open Scholarship in Jurisprudence, 1976-1979. Frank Knox Fellowship, 1980-1981. *Member:* Los Angeles County Bar Association; Financial Lawyers Conference. **REPORTED CASES:** Carolco Television Inc. vs. National Broadcasting Co. (In re DeLaurentiis Entertainment Group, Inc.), 963 F.2d 1269 (9th Cir. 1992); In re Davey Roofing, Inc. 167 B.R. 604 (Bankr. C.D. 1994). **TRANSACTIONS:** Represented the Creditors Committees in Qintex Entertainment Inc.; Weintraub Entertainment, Inc.; Leisure Technology, Inc.; First Capital Holdings, Inc.; Represented or represents the Trustee in Triad America Corporation and Oppenheimer Industries, Inc.

**JAMES I. STANG,** born Neptune, New Jersey, September 28, 1955; admitted to bar, 1980, California; U.S. District Court, Northern, Southern, Central and Eastern Districts of California. *Education:* Franklin & Marshall College; University of California at Berkeley (B.A., with honors, 1977); Hastings College of Law, University of California (J.D., 1980). Order of the Coif. Editor-in-Chief, Hastings International and Comparative Law Review, 1979-1980. *Member:* Los Angeles County Bar Association; Financial Lawyers Conference. **TRANSACTIONS:** Represented Official Subcommittee of Employee Organizations in Orange County chapter 9 Case; Debtor Representation of Gateway Educational Products, Ltd., Manufacturer of Hooked on Phonics.

*(This Listing Continued)*

**THOMSEN YOUNG,** born Los Angeles, California, August 5, 1946; admitted to bar, 1974, California; U.S. District Court, Central District of California. *Education:* University of California at Los Angeles (B.A., cum laude, 1967); Columbia University (M.A., 1968); Rutgers University; University of California at Los Angeles (J.D., 1974). Phi Beta Kappa. Woodrow Wilson Fellow. Member, UCLA Law Review, 1973-1974. Lécole De Cordon Bleu (Certificate De Cuisine De Base, 1996). Co-Author: "Need Post-Confirmation Injunctive Relief? Get Some Class," American Bankruptcy Institute Journal, Vol. XIV, No. 9, November 1995; "Trademarks and Tradenames in Bankruptcy," American Bar Section of Business Law, Fall Meeting of Business Bankruptcy Committee, November 1995. *Member:* Los Angeles County (Past Chairman, Section on Commercial Law and Bankruptcy) and American (Member, Bankruptcy Subcommittee, Section on Business Law; Chairman, Entertainment Bankruptcy Task Force; Subcommittee on Partnerships in Bankruptcy and the Task Force on Limited Liability Entities in Bankruptcy, 1995—) Bar Associations; Financial Lawyers Conference (Member, 1986-1988, 1993— and Secretary, 1996, Board of Governors). *REPORTED CASES:* In re Madison Associates, 183 B.R. 206 (Bankr. C.D. California 1995). *TRANSACTIONS:* Represented Creditors Committee in Qintex Entertainment, Inc., Madison Associates (Formerly Pannell Kerr Forster), represented the chapter 11 Trustee in 21st Century Film Corporation and NSB Film Corporation (formerly Hemdale Entertainment).

**DEAN A. ZIEHL,** born Washington, D.C., July 18, 1952; admitted to bar, 1978, California; U.S. Court of Appeals, Ninth Circuit and U.S. District Court, Northern, Southern, Central and Eastern Districts of California. *Education:* University of California at Berkeley (B.A., magna cum laude, 1975); Loyola University of Los Angeles (J.D., 1978). Member, Editorial Staff, Loyola Law Review, 1976-1977. Law Clerk to Chief Judge Albert Lee Stephens, Jr., U.S. District Court, Central District of California, 1978-1980. Author: "Grand Juries— Administrative Agency Access to Secret Materials— Requirements and Safeguards," 12 Beverly Hills Bar Association Journal 257, 1978; "Developments in Criminal Law and Procedure in the Ninth Circuit," 10 Loyola Law Review 885, 1977. Lawyer Representative, Ninth Circuit Judicial Conference, Chair, 1995-1996). *Member:* Beverly Hills, Los Angeles County (Member, Executive Committee, Litigation Section) and American (Member: Commercial Financial Services Committee; Steering Committee, Task Force on Insurance Insolvency, 1992—) Bar Associations; Association of Business Trial Lawyers.

---

**DEBRA GRASSGREEN,** born Livingston, New Jersey, June 16, 1966; admitted to bar, 1992, Florida, U.S. District Court, Southern District of Florida and U.S. Court of Appeals Fifth Circuit; 1994, California and U.S. District Court, Central District of California; 1995, U.S. District Court, Northern, Southern and Eastern Districts of California. *Education:* University of Florida (B.S.B.A., 1988; J.D., with honors, 1991). President, Florida Blue Key, 1991. Outstanding Female Graduate, University of Florida, 1988. *Member:* Dade County, Los Angeles County, Federal and American (Member, Mass Torts Subcommittee; Legislation Subcommittee) Bar Associations; The Florida Bar (Member: Business Law Section; Bankruptcy/UCC Committee); State Bar of California; Dade County Bankruptcy Bar Association; American Bankruptcy Institute (Member: Legislation Subcommittee; Mass Tort Subcommittee); Financial Lawyers Conference. *PRACTICE AREAS:* Bankruptcy.

**RACHELLE S. VISCONTE,** born Rochester, New York, May 5, 1971; admitted to bar, 1995, California; 1996, U.S. Bankruptcy Court; U.S. District Court, Central, Southern, Northern and Eastern Districts of California. *Education:* University of California, Irvine (B.A., summa cum laude, 1992); Boalt Hall School of Law, University of California, Berkeley (J.D., 1995). Phi Beta Kappa. Member: Golden Key National Honor Society. Recipient: American Jurisprudence Award, Bankruptcy; Order of Merit for Excellence in Economics. Solicitations Editor, 1993-1995 and Administrative Editor, 1994-1995, Berkeley Journal of Employment and Labor Law. Law Clerk to the Hon. Thomas B. Donovan, U.S. Bankruptcy Court, Central District of California, 1995-1996. Extern to the Hon. Arthur S. Weissbrodt, U.S. Bankruptcy Court, Northern District of California, 1993. *Member:* State Bar of California (Member, Business Section). *PRACTICE AREAS:* Bankruptcy.

### SENIOR COUNSEL

**HARRY D. HOCHMAN,** born Detroit, Michigan, September 26, 1958; admitted to bar, 1987, California and U.S. District Court, Central, Northern, Southern and Eastern Districts of California; 1993, U.S. Court of Appeals, Ninth Circuit. *Education:* University of Michigan (A.B., with high distinction, 1982); University of California at Los Angeles (J.D., 1987).

*(This Listing Continued)*

Editor-in-Chief, UCLA Pacific Basin Law Journal, 1986-1987. Extern for the Hon. W. Mathew Byrne, Jr., U.S. District Court, Central District Of California, 1986. Clerk for the Hon. William J. Rea, U.S. District Court, Central District of California, 1987-1989. *Member:* Los Angeles County Bar Association; Association of Business Trial Lawyers. *REPORTED CASES:* Kelly v. Gordon (In re Gordon) 988 F.2d 1000 (9th Cir. 1993); Greyhound Real Estate Finance Co. v. Official Unsecured Creditors' Committee (In re Northview Corp.) 130 B.R. 543 (9th Cir. BAP 1991).

**CATHERINE A. STEINER,** born Los Angeles, California, March 6, 1962; admitted to bar, 1987, California and U.S. Court of Appeals, Ninth Circuit; 1988, U.S. District Court, Central, Northern, Eastern and Southern Districts of California. *Education:* University of California at Davis (A.B., with honors, 1984); University of California at Los Angeles (J.D., 1987). Phi Beta Kappa; Order of the Coif. Member, Moot Court Honors Program. Law Clerk to Judge Arthur L. Alarcon, Ninth Circuit, U.S. Court of Appeals, 1987-1988. *Member:* Los Angeles County (Member: Commercial Law and Bankruptcy Section; Bankruptcy Sub-Committee), Ventura County and American (Member, Section on: Law Practice Management; Business Law) Bar Associations; California Women Lawyer's Association.

### OF COUNSEL

**ELLEN M. BENDER,** born Denver, Colorado, 1957; admitted to bar, 1984, California and U.S. District Court, Northern, Eastern and Central Districts of California. *Education:* University of Notre Dame (B.A., summa cum laude, 1979); University of California at Los Angeles School of Law (J.D., 1983). *Member:* Los Angeles County and American Bar Associations.

**BRADLEY E. BROOK,** born Shaker Heights, Ohio, April 5, 1960; admitted to bar, 1986, California and U.S. District Court, Central District of California. *Education:* Northwestern University (B.S., 1982); Ohio State University; Hastings College of the Law, University of California (J.D., 1986). Co-Author, "Two Years Later: Eight Questions Left Unanswered (Or Extremely Confused) by Deprizio," California Bankruptcy Law Journal, Spring 1991. *Member:* Los Angeles County Bar Association.

**JAMES K. T. HUNTER,** born Montreal, Canada, April 4, 1951; admitted to bar, 1976, California. *Education:* New College (B.A., 1973); Harvard University (J.D., cum laude, 1976). *Member:* Los Angeles County Bar Association. (Also Of Counsel, Robert Arnold, Tustin, California).

**GEORGE A. JUAREZ,** born Los Angeles, California, July 4, 1949; admitted to bar, 1977, California; U.S. District Court, Northern, Central, Eastern and Southern Districts of California; U.S. Court of Appeals, Ninth Circuit. *Education:* University of California at Berkeley (B.A., 1973); Boalt Hall School of Law, University of California at Berkeley (J.D., 1976); Oxford University, Oxford, England (Dip. Law, 1977). Member, Oxford University Law Society. Associate Editor, 1974-1975 and Note and Comment Editor, 1975-1976, California Law Review. Author: "Modifying the Indeterminate Sentence: The Changing Emphasis in Criminal Punishment," 64 California Law Review, 1976. *Member:* Beverly Hills (Member, Resolutions Committee, Trial Lawyers Section), Los Angeles County (Member, Court Improvements Committee, Trial Lawyers Section) and American (Member, Sections on: Antitrust Law; International Law and Practice; Litigation) Bar Associations; The State Bar of California (Member, Committee on Administration of Justice, 1982-1985; Examiner, 1982-1985); The Association of Trial Lawyers of America; California Trial Lawyers Association; Association of Business Trial Lawyers; International Law Society.

**LINDA A. KIRIOS,** born Lynn, Massachusetts; admitted to bar, 1981, California and U.S. District Court, Central District of California; 1982, U.S. Court of Appeals, Ninth Circuit. *Education:* Salem State College (B.A.Chem., cum laude, 1972); University of California School of Law at Los Angeles (J.D., 1981). Recipient, American Jurisprudence Award in Contracts. Clinical Program Participant, Federal Public Defender's Office-Appellate Division, 1980. Author: "Precise Planning Averts Title Insurance Legal Woes," Los Angeles Business Journal, December 11, 1989. Member: Commercial Real Estate Women; Board of Trustees, Camp Ronald McDonald For Good Times. *Member:* Los Angeles County and American Bar Associations; Women Lawyers' Association of Los Angeles; Hellenic-American Chamber of Commerce. *PRACTICE AREAS:* Real Property Law.

**SAMUEL R. MAIZEL,** born Paterson, New Jersey, April 9, 1955; admitted to bar, 1985, Pennsylvania, Army Court of Military Review and Court of Military Appeals (Not admitted in California). *Education:* United States Military Academy (B.S. 1977); Georgetown University (M.A., 1983); George Washington University National Law Center (J.D., 1985). Recipi-

*(This Listing Continued)*

**PACHULSKI, STANG, ZIEHL & YOUNG, PROFESSIONAL CORPORATION, Los Angeles—Continued**

ent, Jacob Burns Prize for excellence in Appellate Advocacy. President, Moot Court Board, 1984-1985. Co-Author: *The Government's Contractual Rights and Bankruptcy's Automatic Stay,* Public Contract Law Journal, Vol. 25, No. 4 (Summer 1996); *The Medicare Contract In Bankruptcy: In Which Direction Does University Medical Center Lead?,* Bankruptcy Developments Journal, Vol 11, No. 2 (1994-1995); *"1994 Contract Law Developments - The Year In Review,* The Army Lawyers, February 1996 (contributed section discussing bankruptcy cases with potential impact on government contract law); *1994 Contract Law Developments - The Year in Review,"* The Army Lawyer, February 1995 (contributed section discussing bankruptcy cases with potential impact on government contract law); *"Does An Open House Turn a Military Installation Into A Public Forum?"* The Army Lawyer, August 1986; *Intervention in Grenada,"* Naval Law Review, Vol. 35, No. 1 (Spring 1986). Adjunct Professor in Trial Advocacy and Bankruptcy for The Judge Advocate General's School, US Army, Charlottesville, Virginia, 1991-1996. *Member:* Pennsylvania and American (Member: ABA Subcommittee on Claims, Exemptions and Priorities; ABA Task Force on Health Care Related Bankruptcy Issues) Bar Associations; American Bankruptcy Institute. [U.S. Army, 1973-1996; Lieutenant Colonel, Judge Advocate General's Corps]. **LANGUAGES:** French. **REPORTED CASES:** In re Buckner, 66 F.3d 263 (10th Cir. 1995); United States Postal Service v. Dewey Freight Systems, Inc., 31 F.3d 620 (8th Cir. 1994); In re Trans World Airlines, Inc., 18 F.3d 208 (3d Cir. 1994); United States Agricultural Stabilization and Conservation Service v. Gerth, 991 F.2d 1428 (8th Cir. 1993); In re St. Johns Home Health Agency, Inc., 173 B.R. 238 (Bankr. S.D. Fla. 1994); Hall v. Thwing, 30 M.J. 583 (A.C.M.R. 1990). **PRACTICE AREAS:** Bankruptcy; Government Contracts.

**IAIN A.W. NASATIR,** born New York, N.Y., May 7, 1957; admitted to bar, 1983, New York and U.S. District Court, Eastern and Southern Districts of New York; 1985, U.S. Court of Appeals, Second Circuit; 1987, U.S. Court of Appeals, Ninth Circuit; 1991, California and U.S. District Court, Central and Northern Districts of California; 1993, U.S. District Court, Eastern and Southern Districts of California; 1995, U.S. Supreme Court. *Education:* Williams College; Columbia University (B.A., 1979); Benjamin Cardozo School of Law (J.D., cum laude, 1982). Member, The Order of Barristers; National Moot Court Team. Author: "Insurer's Collapse Highlights Hazards to Investors," National Law Journal, April, 1995; "Whose Contract is it Anyway?" Mealey's Litigation Reports Reinsurance, August, 1994; "For All The Wrong Reasons D & O Claims Should Diminish," Risk Management, October, 1994. Co-Author, with J. Bank: "Communications Under Wraps," Best's Review, September 1992; "Late Notice: In Harm's Way," Best's Review, September 1991. *Member:* New York State and American (Member, Torts and Insurance Practice Section) Bar Associations; State Bar of California; Conference of Insurance Counsel. **Email:** l.nasatir@counsel.com

**ARNOLD M. QUITTNER,** born Los Angeles, California, February 12, 1927; admitted to bar, 1952, California; 1956, U.S. Supreme Court; 1960, U.S. Court of Military Appeals. *Education:* University of California at Los Angeles (A.A., 1948); California Maritime Academy (B.S., 1947); Loyola University of Los Angeles (J.D., 1951). Author: "Indebtedness of Naval Personnel," The J.A.G. Journal, November, 1960; "Unsecured Creditor Representation in Bankruptcy and Reorganization," 2 Legal Notes and Viewpoints Quarterly 15, August, 1982; "Franchises in Bankruptcy: Termination, Rejection and Assumption," Commercial Law Journal, February, 1984; "Corporate Reorganization Proceedings in the United States," (Japanese translations) 628 The Hanrei Times, (Special Edition) 43, April, 1987; "Corporate Reorganizations in the United States, A Summary," 15 Journal of the Japanese Institute of International Business Law (Kokusai Shoji Homu) 293, April, 1987. Editor and Co-Author: "Litigation with the Bankruptcy and Reorganization Receiver and Trustee," Practising Law Institute, New York, 1975; "Current Developments in Bankruptcy, Reorganization and Arrangement Proceedings," Practising Law Institute, New York, 1976; "Current Developments in Bankruptcy 1977," Practising Law Institute, New York; "Current Developments in Bankruptcy, Reorganization and Arrangement Proceedings, 1978," Practising Law Institute, New York; "Current Developments in Bankruptcy and Reorganization 1980," Practising Law Institute, New York; "Current Developments in Bankruptcy and Reorganization 1982," Practising Law Institute, New York; "Current Developments in Bankruptcy and Reorganization 1983," Practising Law Institute, New York; "Current Developments in Bankruptcy and Reorganization 1984," Volumes I and II, Practising Law Institute, New York; "Current Developments in Bankruptcy and Reorganization," Volumes I and II, Practising Law Institute, New York, 1985; "Current Developments in Bankruptcy and Reorganization 1986," Volumes, I and II, Practising Law Institute, New York, 1986; "Dealing With the Reorganizing Debtor-Transactions, Negotiations and Litigation," Practising Law Institute, New York, 1986. "Current Developments in Bankruptcy and Reorganization, 1987," Volumes I and II, Practising Law Institute, New York, 1987; "Current Developments in Bankruptcy and Reorganization," 1988; "Current Development in Bankruptcy and Reorganization, 1989," Volume I & II, Practising Law Institute, New York; Current Developments in Bankruptcy and Reorganization, 1990," Volumes I and II; "Current Developments in Bankruptcy and Reorganization, 1991," Volumes I and II; "Dealing With The Reorganizing Debtor: Transactions, Negotiations and Litigation 1990," Volumes II and II; "Current Developments in Bankruptcy and Reorganization 1991," Volumes I and II; "Doing Business With Troubled Companies, 1991," A Satellite Program; "Current Developments in Bankruptcy and Reorganization 1992," Volumes I and II; "Current Developments in Bankruptcy and Reorganization 1993" - Volumes I and II; "Understanding the 1994 Amendments to the Bankruptcy Code," 1995; "Current Developments in Bankruptcy and Reorganization 1995" - Volumes I and II; "Current Developments in Bankruptcy and Reorganization 1996" - Volumes I, II and III; "Current Developments in Bankruptcy and Reorganization 1994" - Volumes I and II. Co-author: "Bankruptcy Practice and Procedure 1977," Practising Law Institute, New York; "Bankruptcy Practice and Procedure 1978," Practising Law Institute, New York; "Bankruptcy Reform Act of 1978," Practising Law Institute, New York; Bankruptcy Practice and Procedure under the New Bankruptcy Act," Practising Law Institute, New York, 1979; "Business Reorganization and Rehabilitation: The New Chapter 11" Practising Law Institute, New York, 1979; "The New Bankruptcy Code" Practising Law Institute, New York, 1980; "Bankruptcy Practice and Procedure," Practising Law Institute, New York, 1982; "Bankruptcy Practice and Procedure," Practising Law Institute, New York, 1983; "Bankruptcy Practice and Procedure," Volumes I and II, Practising Law Institute, New York, 1984; "Creative Uses of Chapter 11, Pitfalls and Tactics," Practising Law Institute, New York, 1984; "Bankruptcy Practice and Procedure, 1985" Practising Law Institute, New York, 1985; "Bankruptcy and Reorganization, 1986," Volumes I and II, Practicing Law Institute, New York, 1986; "Bankruptcy and Reorganization 1987 The Substantive and Procedural Basics," Vols. I & II; "The Basics of Bankruptcy and Reorganization, 1988," Volumes I & II, Practising Law Institute, New York; "The Basics of Bankruptcy and Reorganization, 1989, Volumes I & II; Basics of Bankruptcy and Reorganization, 1990," Volumes I and II; "Basics of Bankruptcy and Reorganization, 1991" Volumes I and II, 1992. Lecturer: Practicing Law Institute Programs on Bankruptcy and Reorganization; International Bar Association, Section on Business Law; American Bar Association, Forum Committee on Franchising; Commercial Law League of America, Fund for Public Education; University of London, Queen Mary College (Centre for Commercial Law Studies); Southeastern Bankruptcy Law Institute; Tokyo Bar Association; Japanese Institute of International Business Law, Inc.; The Japanese Institute for Financial Affairs, Inc.; Colorado CLE; National Conference of Bankruptcy Judges; Federal Judicial Center: Seminar for Bankruptcy Judges; Advanced Bankruptcy Seminars (Iowa); Prentice Hall Law and Business; Practicing Law Institute International Bankruptcy Program; American Bar Association Section on International Law and Practice; The Insolvency Institute of Canada; California Bankruptcy Forum; Southwestern University, School of Law; Turnaround Management Association; Central California Bankruptcy Association; Inter-Pacific Bar Association; International Association of Insolvency Practitioners (INSOL); Hong Kong University; Adilet, School of Law, Almaty, Kazakhstan; United States Agency for International Development - Kazakhstan and Kyrgyzstan seminars; Hong Kong Society of Chartered Accountants; Insolvency Interest Group (IIG), Hong Kong. Chairman, Bankruptcy Study Group Los Angeles, 1961. *Member:* Beverly Hills, Los Angeles County, American and International Bar Associations; State Bar of California.

**WILLIAM L. RAMSEYER,** born Stillwater, Oklahoma, April 6, 1950; admitted to bar, 1980, California. *Education:* University of California at Los Angeles (B.S., 1976); University of Southern California (J.D., 1980). Order of the Coif. *Member:* The State Bar of California.

**ADRIAN F. ROSCHER,** born Freeport, New York, August 19, 1960; admitted to bar, 1985, New York; 1986, California. *Education:* Columbia University (B.A., cum laude, 1981); Stanford University (J.D., 1984). Founding Member, Stanford Law School Entertainment Law Society. *Member:* Beverly Hills and Century City Bar Associations; State Bar of California (Member, Intellectual Property Section). **LANGUAGES:** German. **PRACTICE AREAS:** Entertainment and Business Transactions; Motion Picture Production and Distribution.

*(This Listing Continued)*

**DON WILLENBURG,** born Belleville, Illinois, October 15, 1956; admitted to bar, 1984, California and U.S. District Court, Central District of California; 1989, U.S. Court of Appeals, First Circuit; 1992, U.S. District Court, Southern, Northern and Eastern Districts of California and U.S. Court of Appeals, Ninth Circuit. *Education:* Loyola University (B.A., magna cum laude, 1978); Stanford University (J.D., 1984). Pi Sigma Alpha; Alpha Sigma Nu. Editor and Senior Note Editor, Stanford Law Review and Article Editor, Stanford Journal of International Law, 1983-1984. Co-Author: "Single Asset Real Estate Cases After the Bankruptcy Reform Act of 1994," Journal of Bankruptcy Law and Practice, Jan./Feb. 1996. *Member:* Los Angeles County (Conference of Delegates, 1989—) and American (Member, Sections on Litigation and Business Law) Bar Associations; State Bar of California. **REPORTED CASES:** In re Pub. Serv. Co. of N.H., 884 F. 2d 11 (1st Cir. 1989); Greyhound Real Estate Finance Co. v. Official Unsecured Creditors' Committee (In re Northview Corp.) 130 B.R. 543 (9th Cir. BAP 1991). **TRANSACTIONS:** Sale of Ticor Title Co. to Chicago Title Co.; 21st Century Film Library.

---

## PADILLA & O'LEARY
*ONE WILSHIRE BOULEVARD, SUITE 2100*
**LOS ANGELES, CALIFORNIA 90017-3383**
*Telephone: 213-489-2003*
*Fax: 213-489-2323*

Civil Litigation in all State and Federal Courts, Business and Commercial Law, Labor and Employment, Real Estate, Environmental and Casualty, Bankruptcy, Admiralty and Maritime, Insurance, Products Liability, Personal Injury and Toxic Torts.

### MEMBERS OF FIRM

**STEPHEN M. PADILLA,** born Boulder City, Nevada, February 8, 1958; admitted to bar, 1986, California and U.S. District Court, Central, Eastern, Northern and Southern Districts of California. *Education:* University of Southern California (B.S., cum laude, 1981); University of Michigan (J.D., 1985). Hispanic Business Association. *Member:* Los Angeles County and Mexican-American Bar Associations; State Bar of California. **LANGUAGES:** Spanish. **PRACTICE AREAS:** Employment and Labor Law; Commercial Litigation; Business Litigation; Civil Litigation; Real Property Litigation; Bankruptcy.

**KEVIN D. O'LEARY,** born San Francisco, California, December 25, 1956; admitted to bar, 1983, District of Columbia; 1984, Connecticut; 1987, California. *Education:* Middlebury College (B.A., 1979); International Institute, Madrid, Spain; Georgetown University (J.D., 1982). Extern Law Clerk to Hon. Rita C. Davidson, Associate Judge, Maryland Court of Appeals, 1980-1981. Special Appointments: Senate Committee Counsel, 1984 Legislative Session, Maryland General Assembly; Special Assistant State's Attorney, State of Connecticut, 1985-1986. Litigation Attorney, Shell Oil Company, 1988-1990. Director, Western States Petroleum Association Associates, Southern California Chapter, 1994—. *Member:* Los Angeles County Bar Association; State Bar of California (Member, Committee on Federal Courts); Maritime Law Association of the United States. **LANGUAGES:** Spanish. **REPORTED CASES:** State of Connecticut vs. Willie Milledge, 8 Conn. App. 119; 511 A.2d 366 (1986). **PRACTICE AREAS:** Business Litigation; Real Estate; Environmental; Admiralty; Maritime; Labor and Employment Law; Products Liability; Personal Injury.

REPRESENTATIVE CLIENTS: Exxon Co., U.S.A.; Exxon Corp.; Mesa Environmental Services, Inc.; Mesa Environmental Consulting & Technologies, Inc.; Mesa Mechanical Services, Inc.; SeaRiver Maritime, Inc.; SeaRiver Maritime Financial Holdings, Inc.; K2-M Environmental, Inc.; Mad Science Media, Inc.; Commercial Filter Cleaning Systems; Central Plastics, Inc.; L.T. Lewis, Inc.; DataCom West, Inc.
APPROVED COUNSEL FOR: Federal Deposit Insurance Corp. (FDIC); Shell Oil.

---

## ROBERT P. PALAZZO
*3002 MIDVALE AVENUE, SUITE 209*
**LOS ANGELES, CALIFORNIA 90034**
*Telephone: 310-474-5483*
*Fax: 310-474-6736*

*Inyo County Law Office:* 230 South Main Street, Darwin, California 93522.
Telephone: 619-876-5941.

State, Local, Federal and International Taxation, Corporation, Entertainment, Church, Mining and Oil and Gas Law.

*(This Listing Continued)*

---

**ROBERT P. PALAZZO,** born Los Angeles, California, April 14, 1952; admitted to bar, 1976, California; 1977, U.S. Tax Court; 1978, U.S. Court of Appeals, Ninth Circuit; 1980, U.S. Supreme Court. *Education:* University of California at Los Angeles (B.A., cum laude, 1973); University of Southern California (M.B.A., 1976; J.D., 1976). Contributing Author: Vol. 17C and Vol. 17E, *Business Organizations, Eaton-Professional Corporations and Associations,* Matthew Bender, 1979, 1981. Certified Public Accountant: California, 1975; Nevada, 1979; Colorado, 1980. Member, Board of Directors, California Cancer Foundation, 1978-1987. Judge Pro Tem, Los Angeles Municipal Court, 1982—. Member, William S. Hart Museum Advisory Council, 1990-1993. *Member:* State Bar of California. **REPORTED CASES:** Soto v. Wisconsin Department of Revenue, WTAC, No. 88-I-16, August 29, 1989 CCH §203-092 (Wisconsin Tax Appeals Commission).

---

## PANSKY & MARKLE
*SUITE 4050, 333 SOUTH GRAND AVENUE*
**LOS ANGELES, CALIFORNIA 90071**
*Telephone: 213-626-7300*
*Fax: 213-626-7330*

Lawyer Disciplinary and Admissions Matters, Legal Malpractice, Professional Liability, General Civil Trial and Appellate Practice, Defense of Professional Licensing proceedings.

FIRM PROFILE: Pansky & Markle specializes in the representation of attorneys and bar applicants in State Bar Proceedings, in the defense and prosecution of legal and other professional malpractice, and in ethics consultations and advice. The firm also represents other professionals in disciplinary and licensure proceedings. The firm is a California State Bar approved Minimum Continuing Legal Education provider.

### MEMBERS OF FIRM

**R. GERALD MARKLE,** born Syracuse, New York, May 2, 1950; admitted to bar, 1976, California; 1977, U.S. District Court, Southern District of California; 1986, U.S. District Court, Central District of California; 1987, U.S. Court of Appeals, Ninth Circuit. *Education:* University of California at Santa Barbara (B.A., 1972); University of Puget Sound (J.D., cum laude, 1976). Assistant Chief Trial Counsel, Office of Trial Counsel, State Bar of California, 1983-1986. Senior Trial Counsel, Office of Trial Counsel, State Bar of California, 1979-1983. Former Ex-Officio Member, California State Bar Board of Governors' Select Committee re Expediting the Disciplinary Process. *Member:* Los Angeles County Bar Association (Member, Committee on the State Bar); Association of Professional Responsibility Lawyers. **REPORTED CASES:** Grossman v. State Bar (1983) 34 Cal.3d 73; In Re Morales (1983) 35 Cal.3d 1; In re Possino (1984) 37 Cal.3d 163; Leoni v. State Bar (1985) 39 Cal.3d 609; In the Matter of Hagen (Rev. Dept. 192) 2 Cal. State Bar Ct.Rptr. 153; In the Matter of Respondent J (Rev. Dept. 1993) 2 Cal. State Bar Ct.Rptr. 273; In the Matter of Chen (Rev. Dept. 1993) 2 Cal. State Bar Ct.Rptr. 571; In the Matter of Langfus (Rev. Dept. 1994) 3 Cal. State Bar Ct.Rptr. 161; In the Matter of Twitty (Rev. Dept. 1994) 2 Cal. State Bar Ct.Rptr. 664. **PRACTICE AREAS:** Lawyer Disciplinary Defense and Admissions; Legal Malpractice; Ethics Consultations and Testimony.

**ELLEN A. PANSKY,** born Los Angeles, California, May 7, 1953; admitted to bar, 1977, California and U.S. District Court, Central and Southern Districts of California; U.S. Court of Appeals, Ninth Circuit. *Education:* University of California at Los Angeles (B.A., summa cum laude, 1974); Loyola University of Los Angeles (J.D., 1977). Contributing Editor, Attorney Ethics, California Practice Handbook, Matthew Bender, 1993. Author: "Client Trust Account Procedures: How to Ensure Proper Compliance," *Los Angeles Lawyer Magazine,* December, 1992; "An Attorney's Expanding Fiduciary Duties to Opposing Parties and Non-Clients," Fall, 1992; "Barred for Life? Permanent Sanction for Ethics Abuses Won't Cure Profession's Ills," *Los Angeles Daily Journal,* May 1995; "Mitigation of Disciplinary Sanctions: Justice and Fairness Require Analysis of Each Individual Attorney," *American Bar Association 21st Ethics Symposium,* June 1995. Assistant General Counsel, Office of General Counsel, State Bar of California, 1983-1985; Senior Trial Counsel, Office of Trial Counsel, State Bar of California, 1978-1983. Member, Advisory Rules Revision Committee of the Executive Committee of State Bar Court, 1992-1994. *Member:* Los Angeles County Bar Association (Member, Committee on the State Bar and Chair, Committee on Professional Responsibility and Ethics); California Women Lawyers (Director); Women Lawyers Association of Los Angeles; Association of Professional Responsibility Lawyers (Immediate Past President); National Association of Women Lawyers (Chair, Gender Bias Committee); ABA Center for Professional Responsibility (Charter Member). **RE-**

*(This Listing Continued)*

PANSKY & MARKLE, Los Angeles—Continued

**PORTED CASES:** Rimel v. State Bar (1983) 34 Cal.3d 128; Greene v. Zank (1984) 158 Cal.App.3d 497; Palomo v. State Bar (1984) 36 Cal.3d 758; Tarver v. State Bar (1984) 37 Cal.3d 122; Leoni v. State Bar (1985) 39 Cal.3d 609; Ritter v. State Bar (1985) 40 Cal.3d 595; Trousil v. State Bar (1985) 38 Cal.3d 337; Lister v. State Bar (1990) 51 Cal.3d 1117; Sternlieb v. State Bar (1990) 52 Cal.3d 317. **PRACTICE AREAS:** Lawyers Disciplinary Defense and Admissions; Legal Malpractice; Ethics Consultations and Testimony; Professional Licensure Defense.

**DENNIS W. RIHN,** born Pasadena, California, February 10, 1957; admitted to bar, 1986, California, U.S. District Court, Central District of California and U.S. Court of Appeals, Ninth Circuit. *Education:* California Institute of the Arts (B.F.A., 1979); Loyola Law School (J.D., cum laude, 1986). Member, St. Thomas More Law Honor Society. Attorney-client fee arbitrator, Los Angeles County Bar Association. *Member:* Los Angeles County and American Bar Associations; State Bar of California. **REPORTED CASES:** ITT v. Niles (1994) 9 Cal.4th 245. **PRACTICE AREAS:** Legal Malpractice; Professional Liability; General Civil Trial and Appellate Practice.

---

## LAW OFFICES OF RONALD M. PAPELL

*A PROFESSIONAL CORPORATION*

FIFTEENTH FLOOR, 1875 CENTURY PARK EAST
**LOS ANGELES, CALIFORNIA 90067**
Telephone: 310-553-4767
Fax: 310-553-8002

*Civil Litigation, Professional Liability, Personal Injury, Products Liability, Sexual Harassment, Wrongful Termination, and Insurance Coverage Litigation.*

**RONALD M. PAPELL,** born New York, N.Y., May 28, 1947; admitted to bar, 1974, California; 1978, U.S. Supreme Court. *Education:* California State University at Northridge; Southwestern University School of Law (J.D., 1974). Member, Southwestern University Law Review, 1973-1974. Author: "An Overview of California Condominium Law," Southwestern University Law Review, Vol. 6 No. 3, Fall, 1974. Member, Los Angeles Superior Court Arbitration Plan, 1981—. Member, Los Angeles Superior Court Settlement Officer Program, 1979—. Member, Joint Liaison Committee, Los Angeles County Medical Association/Los Angeles County Bar Association, 1981-1984; Member, Los Angeles Superior Court Ad Hoc Uniform Arbitration and Pretrial Procedures Committee, 1981-1983. Member, Panel of Arbitrators, American Arbitration Association. *Member:* Beverly Hills (Member, Litigation Section), Century City, Los Angeles County and American (Member, Negligence Section) Bar Associations; State Bar of California; Los Angeles Trial Lawyers Association (Member, Superior Court Settlement Officer Program, 1979—); California Trial Lawyers Association; The Association of Trial Lawyers of America. **LANGUAGES:** French. **PRACTICE AREAS:** Civil Litigation; Professional Liability; Personal Injury; Products Liability; Sexual Harassment; Wrongful Termination.

REFERENCE: City National Bank.

---

## DAYTON B. PARCELLS III

2049 CENTURY PARK EAST
SUITE 2790
**LOS ANGELES, CALIFORNIA 90067**
Telephone: 310-201-9882
Fax: 310-201-9855

*Civil Trial and Appellate Practice in all State and Federal Courts. Emphasis in the Areas of Business Litigation, Products Liability, Personal Injury, Medical Malpractice Law and Employment.*

**DAYTON B. PARCELLS, III,** born Summit, New Jersey, November 11, 1960; admitted to bar, 1987, California, U.S. District Court, Central, Eastern and Southern Districts of California and U.S. Court of Appeals, Ninth Circuit. *Education:* University of Richmond (B.A., 1983); Pepperdine University School of Law (J.D., 1986). Associate Editor, Pepperdine Law Review, 1985-1986. Author: "California Supreme Court Survey," Pepperdine Law Review, Vol. 13, No. 2, 1985. Instructor: Torts and Products Liability, Santa Monica College Paralegal Program, 1987-1989; Contract/-

*(This Listing Continued)*

---

Commercial Law, and Trial and Appellate Practice, Attorney Assistant Training Program, U.C.L.A. Extension, 1991—. Judge Pro Tem, Los Angeles Municipal Court, 1993—. *Member:* Los Angeles County and American Bar Associations; State Bar of California; Los Angeles Trial Lawyers Association; The Association of Trial Lawyers of America; California Trial Lawyers Association.

**KENTON E. MOORE,** born Long Beach, California, May 8, 1958; admitted to bar, 1989, California and U.S. Court of Appeals, Ninth Circuit. *Education:* California State University at Northridge (B.S., 1985); University of La Verne at San Fernando Valley (J.D., 1989). *Member:* Los Angeles County Bar Association; State Bar of California; Association of the Southern California Defense Counsel. **PRACTICE AREAS:** Medical Malpractice; General Liability.

---

## WILLIAM R. PARDEE

6255 SUNSET BOULEVARD
SUITE 2000
**LOS ANGELES, CALIFORNIA 90028**
Telephone: 213-464-6026

*General Practice.*

**WILLIAM R. PARDEE,** born 1935; admitted to bar, 1961, California. *Education:* Santa Clara University (B.S.C.; LL.B.).

---

## JOHN K. PARK & ASSOCIATES

445 SOUTH FIGUEROA, TWENTY-SEVENTH FLOOR
**LOS ANGELES, CALIFORNIA 90071-1603**
Telephone: 213-612-7730
Fax: 213-426-2171

*Intellectual Property, Patent, Trademarks, Copyright, Contracts and Licensing.*

**JOHN K. PARK,** born 1960; admitted to bar, 1994, California; registered to practice before U.S. Patent and Trademark Office. *Education:* Harvey Mudd College (B.S.E., 1982); California State University at Long Beach (M.S.M.E., 1988); Drexel University (M.B.A., 1991); Southwestern University (J.D., 1994). **LANGUAGES:** Korean. **PRACTICE AREAS:** Patent; Trademark; Copyright; Trade Secrets; Contracts.

---

## PARKER, MILLIKEN, CLARK, O'HARA & SAMUELIAN

*A PROFESSIONAL CORPORATION*

Established in 1913

TWENTY SEVENTH FLOOR, SECURITY PACIFIC PLAZA
333 SOUTH HOPE STREET
**LOS ANGELES, CALIFORNIA 90071**
Telephone: 213-683-6500
Telecopier: 213-683-6669

*General Civil, Business, and Construction Litigation in State and Federal Courts. Environmental Civil, Criminal and Administrative Litigation, including government initiated and private party Superfund Litigation. Hazardous Materials Management and Compliance. Labor Relations and Employment Discrimination Law. Corporation, Partnership, Securities, Commercial and Business Law. Mergers and Acquisitions, Employee Benefits and Real Estate Law. Taxation (Federal, State and Local), Estate Planning, Probate, Banking, Government Contracts, Insurance and Eminent Domain Law. Bankruptcy/Reorganization, Creditors' Rights.*

**FIRM PROFILE:** Founded in 1913, Parker, Milliken, Clark, O'Hara & Samuelian is a prominent downtown Los Angeles law firm. The firm's principal offices are located in the heart of the business district in Los Angeles, adjacent to both state and federal courts and many governmental agencies. In addition to representing a number of publicly-held corporations whose operations are national and international in scope, the firm represents governmental entities and a diverse clientele of smaller, privately-held businesses, entrepreneurs and individuals. The firm encourages involvement in professional, civic or public service activities. Many of our attorneys have made significant commitments on behalf of political candidates of both major parties, bar organizations, civic groups, colleges and universities.

**CLAUDE I. PARKER** (1871-1952).

*(This Listing Continued)*

**JOHN B. MILLIKEN** (1893-1981).

**RALPH KOHLMEIER** (1900-1976).

**MARK TOWNSEND** (1921-1989).

**LESLIE W. MULLINS** (1951-1990).

**FRANK W. CLARK, JR.,** born Los Angeles, California, November 17, 1917; admitted to bar, 1946, California. *Education:* University of California, Los Angeles (B.S., 1939); University of California (J.D., 1946). Regent, University of California, 1980—. Chairman, Regents of University of California, 1987-1988. *Member:* Los Angeles County and American Bar Associations; The State Bar of California.

**N. MATTHEW GROSSMAN,** born Boston, Massachusetts, May 22, 1934; admitted to bar, 1959, Massachusetts; 1960, California. *Education:* Harvard University (A.B., cum laude, 1956); Columbia University (LL.B., 1959). Member, 1984-1993 and President, 1990, 1991 and 1993, Los Angeles Memorial Coliseum Commission. Member, Board of Directors, 1983-1993 and President, 1985 and 1986, California Museum of Science and Industry. Member, Board of Directors, Cedars Sinai Medical Center, 1985-1990 and 1993. *Member:* Los Angeles County, Massachusetts and American Bar Associations; The State Bar of California. *TRANSACTIONS:* Attorney for: Western Gear Corporation sale to Bucyrus-Erie Company; Bayly, Martin & Fay sale to Bass Brothers; BWIP International, Inc. purchase of United Centrifugal Pumps. *PRACTICE AREAS:* Estates and Trust; Business Law; Mergers and Acquisitions; Tax.

**KARL M. SAMUELIAN,** born Philadelphia, Pennsylvania, March 8, 1932; admitted to bar, 1957, California. *Education:* University of California at Los Angeles (B.A., 1953; LL.B., 1956). Trial Attorney, Office of Chief Counsel, Internal Revenue Service, 1957-1962. *Member:* Los Angeles County and American (Member, Sections on: Business Law; Taxation; Senior Lawyers Division) Bar Associations; The State Bar of California. *TRANSACTIONS:* Counsel For Belridge Oil Company in $3.65 Billion dollar merger with Shell Oil Company. *PRACTICE AREAS:* Corporate and General Business; General Taxation; Real Estate; Political Campaign Contribution Law.

**ANTHONY T. OLIVER, JR.,** born San Jose, California, July 19, 1929; admitted to bar, 1954, California; 1979, U.S. Supreme Court. *Education:* Santa Clara University (B.S., 1951; J.D., 1953). Alpha Sigma Nu. Vice President, 1959-1963 and Director, 1974-1976 The Law Society. Member, Santa Clara Law School Board of Visitors, 1983—. Recipient, Edwin J. Owens Lawyer of the Year Award, 1976, Santa Clara University, College of Law. *Member:* Los Angeles County (Chairman, 1985, Labor Law Section) and American (Co-Chairman, Committee on Labor Arbitration and the Law of Collective Bargaining Agreements, 1985-1988, Labor and Employment Law Section) Bar Associations; The State Bar of California (Member, Labor and Employment Law Section); Chancery Club. *SPECIAL AGENCIES:* National Labor Relations Board; Department of Labor; Wage and Hour Administrator; Equal Employment Opportunity Commission; Office of Federal Contract Compliance; California Department of Fair Employment and Housing; Federal Mediation and Conciliation Service; California Conciliation Service. *PRACTICE AREAS:* Labor and Employment Law; Employment Discrimination; Wrongful Termination; Labor Arbitrations; Collective Bargaining Negotiations.

**EVERETT F. MEINERS,** born Elgin, Illinois, December 27, 1939; admitted to bar, 1965, California and U.S. District Court, Central District of California; 1974, U.S. Court of Appeals, Ninth Circuit and U.S. District Court, Southern District of California; 1980, U.S. Supreme Court; 1981, U.S. District Court, Northern District of California. *Education:* University of California at Riverside (B.A., 1961); University of California at Los Angeles (LL.B., 1964). Law Clerk to Justice Gordon L. Files, California Court of Appeals, 1964-1965. *Member:* Los Angeles County and American (Member, Sections on: Corporation, Banking and Business Law; International Law; Labor Law) Bar Associations; State Bar of California. *SPECIAL AGENCIES:* National Labor Relations Board; Equal Employment Opportunity Commission; Agricultural Labor Relations Board; California Department of Fair Employment and Housing; American Arbitration Association; Occupational Safety and Health Administration, CAL-OSHA. *REPORTED CASES:* (all Employment and Labor Law related cases) Clayton v. UAW and ITT Gilfillan, United States Supreme Court, 451 U.S. 679 (1981); Bratton v. Bethlehem Steel Corp., 649 F.2d 658 (9th Cir. 1980); Sahara-Tahoe Corp. v. NLRB, 533 F. 2d 1125, (9th Cir. 1976); Belridge Farms v. ALRB and UFW, 21 Cal.3d 551 (1978); Iron Workers, Local 433 v. Superior Court, 80 C.A.3d 346 (1978). *PRACTICE AREAS:* Employment, Labor Law and Litigation on behalf of Management; Commercial UCC Law; International Law.

*(This Listing Continued)*

**RICHARD A. CLARK,** born Los Angeles, California, February 22, 1941; admitted to bar, 1966, California. *Education:* University of California at Santa Barbara (A.B., 1962); University of California, Hastings College of Law (LL.B., 1966). *Member:* Los Angeles County and American (Member, Litigation Section) Bar Associations; The State Bar of California. *PRACTICE AREAS:* Civil Litigation; Securities Litigation; Directors and Officers Liability Defense.

**CLAIRE D. JOHNSON,** born Tilden, Nebraska, November 28, 1931; admitted to bar, 1958, Nebraska; 1962, California. *Education:* University of Nebraska (B.S., 1954; J.D., 1958). Order of the Coif; Delta Theta Phi. Associate Editor, University of Nebraska Law Review, 1957-1958. Teaching Associate, Evidence, Pleading, Practice and Procedure, University of Nebraska College of Law, 1958-1959. *Member:* Los Angeles County, Nebraska State and American Bar Associations; The State Bar of California. Fellow, American College of Trial Lawyers. [1st Lieut., U.S. Army, 1954-1956]. *SPECIAL AGENCIES:* California Department of Insurance. *REPORTED CASES:* Canadian Commercial Bank v. Findley, 229 Cal. App. 3d 1139; Shapiro v. United California Bank, 133 CA 3d 256. *PRACTICE AREAS:* Commercial Litigation; Class Action Defense; Securities Litigation; Directors and Officers Liability Defense.

**FRANK ALBINO,** born New York, N.Y., August 6, 1945; admitted to bar, 1970, California. *Education:* St. John's University (B.A., magna cum laude, 1966); Harvard University (J.D., cum laude, 1969). Former Member, Medical Board of California, State of California and Former President of Board's Division of Medical Quality. *Member:* Los Angeles County and American (Member, Section on Health Law) Bar Associations; The State Bar of California. *TRANSACTIONS:* $100 million sale of liquor manufacturing company; Structuring and documentation of partnership and financing for development and operation of major Atlantic City Hotel Casino; Structuring and documentation of partnership for mixed-use commercial development of Farmer's Market property in Los Angeles. *PRACTICE AREAS:* Health Law (Defense of Physicians in licensing-disciplinary proceedings; Mergers, Contracts and Structuring of Modern Health-care practices & delivery systems); Professional Corporations Practice; Real Estate; ERISA/Employee Benefits.

**NOWLAND C. HONG,** born Los Angeles, California, December 7, 1934; admitted to bar, 1961, California; 1974, U.S. Supreme Court. *Education:* Pomona College (B.A., 1956); University of Southern California (J.D., 1959). Phi Alpha Delta. Assistant City Attorney and Chief Counsel, Port of Los Angeles, 1970-1973. *Member:* Los Angeles County and American Bar Associations; State Bar of California; American Board of Trial Advocates; Southern California Chinese Lawyers Association (President, 1978, 1983); Chancery Club. *PRACTICE AREAS:* Business Litigation; Insurance Coverage Litigation; Representation of and Litigation against Public Entities.

**CARLO SIMA,** born San Pedro, California, February 20, 1948; admitted to bar, 1973, California. *Education:* University of Southern California (A.B., 1970; J.D., 1973). Member, Southern California Law Review, 1971-1973. *Member:* Los Angeles County and American Bar Associations; State Bar of California. *PRACTICE AREAS:* Real Property Law; Estate Planning and Probate Law.

**STEPHEN T. HOLZER,** born Palo Alto, California, March 31, 1948; admitted to bar, 1974, Illinois; 1977, California. *Education:* Yale College (B.A., magna cum laude, 1970); Yale Law School (J.D., 1974). Phi Beta Kappa; Pi Sigma Alpha. Member, Board of Editors, Yale Law Journal, 1972-1974. *Member:* Illinois State Bar Association; The State Bar of California. *PRACTICE AREAS:* Environmental Law; Hazardous Materials Management.

**BRENTON F. GOODRICH,** born Plainfield, New Jersey, January 27, 1942; admitted to bar, 1968, California; U.S. Supreme Court; U.S. Court of Appeals, Ninth Circuit and U.S. District Court, Central, Northern and Southern Districts of California. *Education:* Wesleyan University (A.B., 1964); Stanford University (J.D., 1967). Phi Beta Kappa. Member, Governing Board, Palos Verdes Peninsula Unified School District. Trustee, Palos Verdes Peninsula Education Foundation. *Member:* Los Angeles County and American Bar Associations; Computer Law Association; Association of Business Trial Lawyers. *PRACTICE AREAS:* Construction; Civil Litigation.

**LINDA S. KLIBANOW,** born New Rochelle, New York, August 20, 1950; admitted to bar, 1977, California. *Education:* Radcliffe College (B.A., cum laude, 1972); Yale Law School (J.D., 1975). Phi Beta Kappa. Author: "The Developing Labor Law," Contributing Editor (BNA); "Employment Discrimination" (Matthew Bender California Practice Handbook Series). *Member:* Los Angeles County (Member, Executive Committee, Labor and

*(This Listing Continued)*

**PARKER, MILLIKEN, CLARK, O'HARA & SAMUELIAN,**
*A PROFESSIONAL CORPORATION, Los Angeles—Continued*

Employment Law Section) and American (Member: Subcommittee on Development of the Law under the National Labor Relations Act, Labor Law Section, 1982—; Individual Rights and Responsibilities Section) Bar Associations; The State Bar of California. **SPECIAL AGENCIES:** National Labor Relations Board; U.S. Equal Opportunity Commission; California Department of Fair Employment and Housing; U.S. Department of Labor; U.S. Department of Justice. **REPORTED CASES:** Sahara-Tahoe Corporation v. NLRB, 648 F.2d 553, 9th Cir. (1980); Universal Paper Goods Company v. NLRB, 638 F.2d 1159, 9th Cir. (1979); NLRB v. Solar Turbines, Inc., 302 NLRB No. 3, (1991); Arbitration of Heinz Pet Products, 90-2 ARB ¶8468. **PRACTICE AREAS:** Labor and Employment Law.

**RICHARD D. ROBINS,** born Los Angeles, California, February 6, 1951; admitted to bar, 1977, California. *Education:* University of California at Los Angeles (A.B., cum laude, 1972); Texas Tech University; Boalt Hall School of Law, University of California (J.D., 1977). Phi Delta Phi; Order of the Coif. Associate Editor, Boalt Hall School of Law, University of California Industrial Relations Law Journal, 1976-1977. *Member:* Los Angeles County and American (Chairman, Individual Investments and Workouts Committee, Tax Section, 1991-1993; Chairman, Subcommittee on Asset Protection Devices and Member of the Task Force on Limited Liability Companies) Bar Associations; The State Bar of California. **TRANSACTIONS:** Represent major parking companies, real estate development, medical related companies and computer reseller in Tax Law, General Corporate, Real Estate and Litigation. **PRACTICE AREAS:** Tax; General Corporate; Real Estate; Litigation.

**WILLIAM V. MCTAGGART, JR.,** born Philadelphia, Pennsylvania, May 16, 1943; admitted to bar, 1978, California; 1982, U.S. Supreme Court; 1989, New York; 1985, U.S. Court of International Trade. *Education:* Northeastern University (A.B., with honors, 1966); Loyola University (J.D., cum laude, 1978). Alpha Sigma Nu; Pi Sigma Alpha. Member, Loyola University Moot Court Team. Author: "The Medical Director and Company Liability Beyond the Insurance Policy," 25 Journal of Insurance Medicine 420, Winter 1993; "Movement of Money Across National Borders," International Business Transactions by D.T. Wilson. *Member:* Los Angeles County, New York State and American (Member, Torts, Insurance and International Law Sections) Bar Associations; State Bar of California. [1st. Lt., U.S. Army Medical Service Corps, 1967-1968]. **REPORTED CASES:** Evans v. Safeco Life Ins. Co., 916 F.2d 1437 (9th Cir. 1990). **PRACTICE AREAS:** Business Litigation; Insurance Coverage/Bad Faith; ERISA; Banking and Finance Litigation.

**GARY A. MEYER,** born Los Angeles, California, August 16, 1953; admitted to bar, 1980, California and District of Columbia. *Education:* University of California at Los Angeles (B.A., departmental honors in Philosophy, summa cum laude, 1975; J.D., 1979). Phi Beta Kappa. Member, Moot Court Honors Program, 1978. Member, University of California at Los Angeles Law Review, 1979. Instructor and Lecturer, University of California at Los Angeles Hazardous Materials Certificate Program, 1990—. *Member:* Beverly Hills (Chairperson, Environmental Law Section, 1987-1990), Los Angeles County (Member, Environmental Law Section) and American (Member, Natural Resources Section) Bar Associations; State Bar of California. **REPORTED CASES:** Los Angeles Chemical Company v. Superior Court, 226 Cal. App. 3d 703 (1990). Torrance Redevelopment Agency v. Solvent Coating Company, 763 F. Supp. 1060 (C.D. Cal. 1991). **PRACTICE AREAS:** Environmental Civil, Criminal and Administrative Litigation; Environmental/Hazardous Materials Management and Compliance.

**WILLIAM W. REID,** born Oakland, California, June 3, 1954; admitted to bar, 1980, California. *Education:* University of California at Irvine (B.A., cum laude, 1975; M.S., 1977); University of California at Davis (J.D., 1980). *Member:* Los Angeles County and American Bar Associations; State Bar of California. **SPECIAL AGENCIES:** Internal Revenue Service; California Franchise Tax Board; California Attorney General. **REPORTED CASES:** Clayton v. Automobile Workers, 451 U.S. 679 (1981); Wright v. Commissioner, 67 T.C.M. 3125 (1994). **TRANSACTIONS:** San Joaquin Hills Transportation Corridor; Harvard School/Westlake School for Girls Merger; I Have a Dream Foundation-Los Angeles; Galef Institute; California Tourism Corporation; California Economic Development Corp.; Governor's Residence Foundation. **PRACTICE AREAS:** General Corporate Law; Taxation Law; Non-Profit Organizations; Employee Benefits Law; Executive Compensation Law.

*(This Listing Continued)*

CAA1078B

**CAMERON H. FABER,** born Walnut Creek, California, December 9, 1955; admitted to bar, 1981, California; 1982, U.S. District Court, Central District of California; 1989, U.S. Court of Appeals, Ninth Circuit. *Education:* University of California at Los Angeles (B.A., 1978); Loyola Marymount University (J.D., cum laude, 1981). Pi Sigma Alpha. Member, St. Thomas More Law Honor Society. Recipient, American Jurisprudence Award in Criminal Law. Member, Loyola Law Review, 1979-1980. *Member:* Los Angeles County and American Bar Associations; The State Bar of California. **PRACTICE AREAS:** Commercial Litigation.

**REBECCA M. ARAGON,** born Los Angeles, California, May 30, 1957; admitted to bar, 1987, California; 1990, U.S. District Court, Central District of California; 1991, U.S. District Court, Eastern District of Wisconsin. *Education:* Yale University (B.A., 1979); Georgetown University (J.D., 1984). Editor, Georgetown Immigration Law Reporter, 1983-1984. Law Clerk to Hon. T. J. Hatter, Jr., U.S. District Court, Central District of California, 1984-1986. *Member:* Los Angeles County and American Bar Associations; State Bar of California; Mexican-American Bar Association; California Trial Lawyers Association. **LANGUAGES:** Spanish. **SPECIAL AGENCIES:** California Department of Fair Employment and Housing; Equal Employment Opportunity Commission. **PRACTICE AREAS:** Employment; Labor Law and Litigation; Management; Civil Litigation.

**JOSEPH G. MARTINEZ,** born Arcadia, California, January 6, 1958; admitted to bar, 1984, California and U.S. District Court, Northern District of California; 1985, U.S. District Court, Central District of California. *Education:* University of California at Berkeley (B.A., 1980; M.B.A., 1984); University of California at Davis (J.D., 1984). Member, City of Torrance Planning Commission, 1992—(Chairman, 1993-1994). Member, Board of Managers of Torrance-South Bay YMCA. *Member:* Los Angeles County (Member, Business and Corporate Law Section) and American Bar Associations; The State Bar of California. **TRANSACTIONS:** Initial and subsequent public offerings and public reports of several public companies; Acquisitions of several high technology companies; Organization of numerous corporations, limited liability companies and partnerships. **PRACTICE AREAS:** General Corporate Law; Securities Law; Commercial Law.

**CARL E. KOHLWECK,** born Los Angeles, California, November 21, 1946; admitted to bar, 1979, California and U.S. District Court, Central District of California; 1982, U.S. Court of Appeals, Ninth Circuit; 1993, U.S. Tax Court. *Education:* University of California at Los Angeles (B.A., 1968); University of West Los Angeles (J.D., 1979). Recipient: Corpus Juris Secundum Award; American Jurisprudence Awards. Member, University of West Los Angeles Law Review, 1978-1979. Member, Board of Directors, UWLA Alumni Association, 1980-1981. Licensed Real Estate Broker, California, 1987—. Author: "Manhart v. City of Los Angeles - A Statutory Decision Without a Constitutional Basis," UWLA Law Review, 1979. *Member:* Los Angeles County and American Bar Associations; State Bar of California. **PRACTICE AREAS:** Complex Commercial Litigation including Construction; Real Property; Trade Secrets, Unfair Business Practices and RICO; Computer Technology Licensing and Real Estate Transactions; Class Action Litigation.

**MICHAEL M. MULLINS,** born Norton, Virginia, January 15, 1951; admitted to bar, 1976, Virginia, U.S. District Court, Western District of Virginia; 1977, U.S. Court of Appeals, 4th Circuit; 1980, Minnesota, U.S. District Court, District of Minnesota and U.S. Court of Appeals, 8th Circuit; 1988, California; 1989, U.S. District Court, Central, Eastern, Northern and Southern Districts of California and U.S. Court of Appeals, 9th Circuit. *Education:* Brown University (A.B., 1973); University of Virginia (J.D., 1976). *Member:* Los Angeles County (Member, Appellate Courts Committee) Minnesota State and American Bar Associations; State Bar of California; Virginia State Bar. **REPORTED CASES:** Westinghouse v. Newman & Holtzinger, 46 Cal. Rptr. 2d 151 (Cal. App. 1995); Westinghouse v. Newman & Holtzinger, 992 F. 2d 932 (9th Cir. 1993); Canadian Commercial Bank v. Ascher Findley Co., 280 Cal. Rptr. 521 (Cal. App. 1991); In re City of Northfield, 386 N.W.2d 748 (Mn. App. 1986); Soo Line RR Co. v. Commissioner of Revenue, 377 N.W. 2d 453 (Mn. 1985); District 28, UMWA v. Wellmore Coal Co., 609 F. 2d 1083 (4th Cir. 1979); Compton v. Nationwide Insurance Co., 480 F. Supp. 1254 (W.D. Va. 1979). **PRACTICE AREAS:** Commercial and Business Litigation; Public Entities Litigation; Appellate Practice.

**ARSINE B. PHILLIPS,** born Sophia, Bulgaria, July 16, 1961; admitted to bar, 1986, California; 1987, U.S. District Court, Central District of California. *Education:* University of California at Los Angeles (B.A., summa cum laude, 1983); University of Southern California (J.D., 1986). Phi Beta Kappa; Alpha Lambda Delta; Phi Delta Phi. Member, Moot Court Honors Program. *Member:* Los Angeles County and American Bar Associations;

*(This Listing Continued)*

State Bar of California. *LANGUAGES:* Armenian. *PRACTICE AREAS:* Business Litigation.

**MICHAEL S. SIMON,** born Los Angeles, California, April 18, 1963; admitted to bar, 1989, California. *Education:* University of California at Davis (B.A., 1985; J.D., 1989). *Member:* Los Angeles County and American (Member, Sections on: Litigation; Business Law) Bar Associations. *PRACTICE AREAS:* Litigation; Government Benefits; Construction Litigation; Insurance.

**GREGORY M. SALVATO,** born Newark, New Jersey, March 24, 1954; admitted to bar, 1986, California and U.S. District Court, Central District of California. *Education:* Claremont McKenna College (B.A., magna cum laude, 1976); Loyola Law School, Los Angeles (J.D., 1986). Member, St. Thomas More Law Honor Society. Member, 1984-1985 and Chief Articles Editor, 1985-1986, Loyola of Los Angeles Law Review. *Member:* Los Angeles County (Member: Executive Committee, Provisional and Post-Judgment Remedies Section, 1991—; Commercial Law and Bankruptcy Committee) and American (Member, Sections on: Real Estate; Litigation) Bar Associations; American Bankruptcy Institute; Financial Lawyers Conference; Los Angeles Bankruptcy Forum. *PRACTICE AREAS:* Bankruptcy/Reorganization; Creditors' Rights; Real Estate Litigation.

---

**LARON J. LIND,** born Boise, Idaho, January 19, 1962; admitted to bar, 1990, California; 1991, U.S. District Court, Central District of California. *Education:* Boise State University (B.B.A., cum laude, 1985); University of Utah (J.D., 1990). *Member:* Los Angeles County and American Bar Associations; State Bar of California. *PRACTICE AREAS:* Commercial Litigation; Business Litigation.

**MARINA GATTI,** born Camerino, Italy, January 29, 1961; admitted to bar, 1992, California; 1993, U.S. District Court, Central and Eastern Districts of California and U.S. Court of Appeals, Ninth Circuit. *Education:* University of California at Berkeley (A.B., 1982; M.P.P., 1985); University of Virginia (J.D., 1992). Author: "Proposition 65: 'Shoot First, Ask Question's Later' - Do the Bullets Really Work? Have We Shot the Wrong Party? Will They Call Out the Bazookas?" Food and Drug Law Journal, Vol. 47, No. 6, 1992. *Member:* Los Angeles County Bar Association (Member, Labor and Litigation Sections); State Bar of California (Member Sections on: Labor and Employment; Litigation). *LANGUAGES:* Italian. *PRACTICE AREAS:* Labor and Employment Law; Litigation.

**FAYE CHEN BARNOUW,** born Boston, Massachusetts, November 11, 1968; admitted to bar, 1993, California, U.S. Court of Appeals, Ninth Circuit and U.S. District Court, Central District of California. *Education:* Harvard University (A.B., 1990); Boalt Hall School of Law, University of California (J.D., 1993). Book Review Editor, Berkeley Women's Law Journal, 1992-1993. Law Clerk to the Honorable Warren J. Ferguson, Ninth Circuit Court of Appeals, 1993-1994. *Member:* Los Angeles County (Member, Commercial Law and Bankruptcy Section) and American (Member, Litigation Section) Bar Associations; State Bar of California (Member, Litigation Section); Southern California Chinese Lawyers Association. *LANGUAGES:* Mandarin Chinese, French, Portuguese. *PRACTICE AREAS:* Litigation; Bankruptcy Law; Commercial Law.

**ASTEGHIK KHAJETOORIANS,** born Tehran, Iran, September 21, 1965; admitted to bar, 1993, California. *Education:* George Washington University (B.S., 1987); Whittier Law School (J.D., summa cum laude, 1993). Recipient, American Jurisprudence Awards in Federal Courts, Remedies, Civil Procedure, Torts and Legal Skills. Research Editor, Whittier Law Review, 1992-1993. *Member:* Beverly Hills, Los Angeles County (Member, Environmental Section) and American (Member, Section of Natural Resources, Energy and Environmental Law) Bar Associations. *PRACTICE AREAS:* Environmental.

**MARK E. ELLIOTT,** born Vallejo, California, September 3, 1966; admitted to bar, 1992, California. *Education:* University of California at Los Angeles (B.A., 1988); University of California, Hastings College of the Law (J.D., 1991). *Member:* Los Angeles County Bar Association; State Bar of California.

**STEVEN P. HELLER,** born Los Angeles, California, August 1, 1967; admitted to bar, 1995, California. *Education:* University of California at Berkeley (B.A., 1990); Boalt Hall School of Law, University of California (J.D., 1995). Phi Beta Kappa. Associate Editor, Ecology Law Quarterly.

**MICHAEL D. STEVENS,** born Verdun, France, January 25, 1963; admitted to bar, 1991, California; 1992, U.S. District Court, Central District of California and U.S. Court of Appeals, Ninth Circuit. *Education:* University of California at Irvine (B.S., Biology, with honors, 1985); University of

*(This Listing Continued)*

Michigan (M.S., Natural Resources, 1986); Hastings College of the Law, University of California (J.D., 1991). *Member:* Los Angeles County Bar Association (Member, Environmental Law Section); State Bar of California (Member, Environmental Law and Litigation Sections). *PRACTICE AREAS:* Environmental Law; Environmental Insurance Coverage; Litigation.

**JOHN PETER SCHAEDEL,** born Long Island, New York, June 19, 1970; admitted to bar, 1995, California, U.S. District Court, Central District of California and U.S. Court of Appeals, Ninth Circuit. *Education:* Cornell University (B.S., 1992); University of California at Los Angeles (J.D., 1995). Phi Alpha Delta. Articles Editor, UCLA Entertainment Law Review. Author: "Harassment Law: A Hostile Environment for Speech?" The Defender, May 1995. *LANGUAGES:* Spanish, French, German. *PRACTICE AREAS:* Labor and Employment; Labor Relations.

**PAIGE E. BUDD,** born Rumson, New Jersey, September 8, 1967; admitted to bar, 1992, Texas; 1993, U.S. District Court, Southern and Northern District of Texas; 1994, U.S. Court of Appeals, Fifth Circuit and U.S. District Court, Western District of Texas; 1996, California. *Education:* College of William & Mary (B.A., 1989; J.D., 1992). Member, National Moot Court Board. *REPORTED CASES:* Bill-Rea v. National Fin. Serv., 860 F. Supp. 1181 (WD. TX. 1994). *PRACTICE AREAS:* Litigation; General Transactional/Contract (in area of Telecommunications).

*OF COUNSEL*

**JOHN F. O'HARA,** born Oakland, California, November 29, 1917; admitted to bar, 1946, California. *Education:* University of Santa Clara (Ph.B., cum laude, 1939); Hastings College of Law, University of California (J.D., 1946). Member: Board of Regents, 1959-1971; Board of Trustees, 1971-1977, 1988-1993. Santa Clara University. Member, 1976 and Chairman, 1982-1983, Board of Managers, National Conference of Bar Examiners. *Member:* Los Angeles County (Chairman, Labor Law Committee, 1973-1974) and American Bar Associations; The State Bar of California (Member, Committee of Bar Examiners, 1974-1978, Chairman, 1977-1978); Chancery Club (President, 1983-1984). Fellow: American Bar Foundation; Los Angeles County Bar Foundation (Member, Board of Directors, 1980-1985; President, 1983-1984). *PRACTICE AREAS:* Labor Relations; Employment Law.

**FLOYD M. LEWIS,** born U.S.A., July 23, 1927; admitted to bar, 1955, California. *Education:* Occidental College and University of California at Los Angeles (B.S., 1951); University of California at Los Angeles (LL.B., 1954). *Member:* Los Angeles County Bar Association (Member, Probate and Trust Law Section); The State Bar of California. *SPECIAL AGENCIES:* Internal Revenue Service. *TRANSACTIONS:* Decedent Trust and probate court administration. I.R.S. Estate and Gift Tax Return examination procedures. Fiduciary income tax planning. *PRACTICE AREAS:* Trusts and Estates; Federal Estate and Gift Tax proceedings; Financial and Estate Planning; Trust and Estate Litigation; Charitable Trusts and Deferred Giving.

**A. ALBERT SPAR,** born New York, N.Y., February 21, 1916; admitted to bar, 1939, Florida; 1944, California; 1945, U.S. District Court, Central District of California; 1956, U.S. Supreme Court; 1979, U.S. Court of Appeals, Ninth Circuit. *Education:* Syracuse University; University of Miami (B.A., 1937; J.D., 1939). Contributor: Matthew Bender, California Forms of Pleading and Practice. Arbitrator, American Arbitration Association. Mediator, Los Angeles Superior Court. *Member:* Hollywood (Governor) and Los Angeles County Bar Associations. *REPORTED CASES:* In re Arstein (Probate); Buck v. Buck - Domestic Relations; Participation in recent automobile appellate cases: BMW of North America, Inc. v. New Motor Vehicle Board (Hal Watkins Chevrolet Inc. 209 Cal.Rept.50, 162 CA3d 980); Piano v. New Motor Vehicle Board, 163 Cal.Rept.41, 103 CA3d 412; Champian Motorcycles v. New Motor Vehicle Board (Yamaha); American Isuzu Motors, Inc. v. New Motor Vehicle Board (Ray Fladeboe Lincoln Mercury Inc.) 1986 230 Cal.Rptr. 769 186 CA3d 464; Ri-Joyce, Inc. v. New Motor Vehicle Board (Mazda), 2 Cal.App. 4th 445, 3 Cal.Rptr. 2d 546 (1992); Zint v. Topp Industries, Inc., 184 CA2d 240, 7 Cal.Rptr. 302 (1960). *PRACTICE AREAS:* General Civil Litigation; Automobile Dealer Transactions and Litigation.

**SIDNEY I. PILOT,** born Dallas, Texas, March 3, 1933; admitted to bar, 1958, California. *Education:* Southern Methodist University (B.A., 1951); University of California at Los Angeles; Southwestern University (LL.B., 1957). Certified Public Accountant, Texas, 1954. [1st. Lt., USAF, 1955-1957]. *REPORTED CASES:* Gardner v. Gardner - Domestic Relations; BMW of North American, Inc. v. New Motor Vehicle Board 209 Cal.-Rept.50, 162 CA3d 980); Piano V. New Motor Vehicle Board, 163 Cal.Rptr. 41, 103 CA3d 412; American Isuzu Motors, Inc. v. New Motor

*(This Listing Continued)*

**PARKER, MILLIKEN, CLARK, O'HARA & SAMUELIAN,**
*A PROFESSIONAL CORPORATION, Los Angeles—Continued*

Vehicle Board, 1986 230 Cal.Rept. 769 186 CA3d 464. *PRACTICE AREAS:* Automobile Dealerships.

**RICHARD L. FRANCK,** born Los Angeles, California, October 10, 1926; admitted to bar, 1953, California. *Education:* East Los Angeles Junior College; Whittier College; Loyola University of Los Angeles (J.D., 1952). Phi Delta Phi. Attorney, 1953-1971 and Assistant Chief Counsel, 1964-1971, State Department of Transportation Law Department. *Member:* Orange County (Member, Administration of Justice Committee, 1966-1986) Los Angeles County (Member, Condemnation Committee, 1975—) and American (Member, Urban, State and Local Government Law Section, Chairman, Condemnation Committee, 1984-1987) Bar Associations; The State Bar of California (Member, Condemnation Committee, 1969-1972; 1983-1986; Chairman, 1985-1986); Orange County Trial Lawyers Association; California Condemnation Attorneys Group; Association of Business Trial Lawyers. Advocate, American Board of Trial Advocates. *PRACTICE AREAS:* Condemnation; Inverse Condemnation; Real Estate Valuation Litigation.

REPRESENTATIVE CLIENTS: ALCOA House of Fabrics; American Bankers Insurance Group; Anheuser-Busch, Inc.; ARCO; Bankers Life Nebraska; Bay Enterprises, Inc.; The Bryna Company (Kirk Douglas); California Hardware Co.; Calprop Corp.; Carrier Clearing Services; The Central National Life Insurance Company of Omaha; First Interstate Bank; Forest Lawn Co,; Fred S. James & Co., Inc.; Gilmore Commercial and Savings Bank; A. F. Gilmore Co.; International Telephone and Telegraph Corp.; Jardine Insurance Brokers, Inc.; Laurantian Capital Corp.; Maxwell Laboratories, Inc.; Nissho-Iwai American Corp.; Old Republic Life Insurance Co.; Oxford Properties, Inc.; Santa Fe Southern Pacific Corp.; The Sheraton Hotel Corp.; Sierracin Corp.; Solar Turbines Inc.; Star-Kist Foods, Inc.; Taco Bell; Union Bank; Western Motor Tariff Bureau; Western Pacific Life Insurance Co.; M.H. Whittier Corp.; Wrather Corp. (Hotels); Wells Fargo Bank; Diceon Electronics Corp.; Earle M. Jorgensen, Co.; Five Star Parking; House of Packaging; Holiday Inns, Inc.
REFERENCE: Bank of California (Los Angeles, California, Main Office).

## PARKER STANBURY

A Partnership including a Professional Corporation

*Established in 1927*

**THIRTY-THIRD FLOOR, 611 WEST SIXTH STREET
LOS ANGELES, CALIFORNIA 90017-3101**
Telephone: 213-622-5124
Fax: 213-622-4858

*Orange County Office:* 888 North Main Street, Seventh Floor Santa Ana, California. Telephone: 714-547-7103. Fax: 714-547-3428.
*San Bernardino, California Office:* 290 North D Street, Suite 400. Telephone: 909-884-1256. Fax: 909-888-7876.
*San Diego, California Office:* 3131 Camino Del Rio North, Suite 1200. Telephone: 619-528-1259. Fax: 619-528-1419.

General Civil, Trial and Appellate Practice in all State and Federal Courts. Insurance Law, Products Liability, Governmental Liability, Construction Accidents, Construction Defects; Land Subsidence, Toxic Torts, Wrongful Termination; Professional Malpractice, Coverage, Bad Faith, Transportation Law, Uninsured Motorist, First Party Claims, Vehicular Liability, Corporation, Family and Criminal Law.

FIRM PROFILE: Parker Stanbury is proud to have recently celebrated its 69th anniversary of legal service to the insurance industry and business community of Southern California. The firm was founded in 1927 when Harry Parker began practicing law in the casualty defense field. In the years that followed, he was joined by such outstanding scholars and advocates as Ray Stanbury and White McGee, Jr. Today with offices in Los Angeles, Santa Ana, San Bernardino and San Diego, we proudly continue that tradition of service.

All human and material resources of the firm are directed toward the goals of providing the highest quality of legal service at the most reasonable cost. In pursuit of these goals, we utilize the latest technology, including a 24-hour paging system, to respond immediately to our clients' needs.

**HARRY D. PARKER** (1891-1976).
**RAYMOND G. STANBURY** (1904-1966).

### MEMBERS OF FIRM

**THOMAS LEE WADDELL, (A PROFESSIONAL CORPORATION),** born Pittsburgh, Pennsylvania, July 11, 1933; admitted to bar, 1962, California; U.S. District Court, Southern and Central Districts of California. *Education:* Dartmouth College (A.B., 1955); Harvard University *(This Listing Continued)*

sity (LL.B., 1961). *Member:* Los Angeles County Bar Association; The State Bar of California; Association of Southern California Defense Counsel.

**DOUGLASS H. MORI,** born Los Angeles, California, October 13, 1951; admitted to bar, 1978, California; U.S. District Court, Southern and Central Districts of California. *Education:* Pomona College (B.A., 1973); Occidental College; Vanderbilt University (J.D., 1976). *Member:* Los Angeles County and American Bar Associations; State Bar of California; Association of Southern California Defense Counsel; Japanese-American Bar Association.

**JOHN D. BARRETT, JR.,** born Ossining, New York, February 7, 1951; admitted to bar, 1976, California; U.S. District Court, Southern and Central Districts of California. *Education:* Loyola University of Los Angeles (B.A., 1973); Southwestern University (J.D., 1976). Phi Alpha Theta. Judge Pro Tem: Los Angeles Municipal Court, 1984—; Los Angeles Superior Court, 1988—. Member, Panel of Arbitrators; Los Angeles County Bar Association Fee Dispute Resolution Services, Contractors State Licensing Board, American Arbitration Association, Los Angeles Superior Court. *Member:* South Bay, Los Angeles County (Member, Litigation and Criminal Justice Sections) and American (Member, Litigation and Criminal Justice Sections) Bar Associations; State Bar of California; Association of Southern California Defense Counsel; Defense Research Institute; American Board of Trial Advocates. Certified, Civil Trial Advocate, National Board of Trial Advocacy.

**RAYMOND F. KILLION,** born New York, N.Y., February 18, 1941; admitted to bar, 1969, California. *Education:* Williams College (B.A., 1963); Vanderbilt University (J.D., 1966). *Member:* Orange County and American Bar Associations; State Bar of California; Association of Southern California Defense Counsel; American Board of Trial Advocates. (Santa Ana Office).

**ROBERT L. LOPRESTI,** born Los Angeles, California, October 4, 1951; admitted to bar, 1976, California; U.S. District Court, Southern and Central Districts of California. *Education:* California State University at Northridge (B.S., 1973); Southwestern University (J.D., 1976). Delta Theta Phi; Blue Key. *Member:* Los Angeles County and American (Member, Litigation Section) Bar Associations; The State Bar of California; Association of Southern California Defense Counsel; American Board of Trial Advocates; Federation of Insurance and Corporate Counsel; Defense Research Institute.

**JACK A. LUCAS,** born Lakeport, California, October 31, 1945; admitted to bar, 1975, California; 1980, U.S. Supreme Court. *Education:* California State University at Long Beach (B.S., 1970); Pepperdine University (J.D., 1975). *Member:* Orange County Bar Association; The State Bar of California; Association of Southern California Defense Counsel. (Santa Ana Office).

**JOHN W. DANNHAUSEN,** born Lima, Ohio, October 6, 1949; admitted to bar, 1980, California; U.S. District Court, Central District of California. *Education:* The Ohio State University (B.A., 1976); Ohio Northern University (J.D., 1979). Delta Theta Phi. *Member:* Los Angeles County Bar Association; The State Bar of California; Association of Southern California Defense Counsel.

**RONALD L. SMITH,** born Los Angeles, California, March 2, 1954; admitted to bar, 1980, California; U.S. District Court, Southern and Central Districts of California. *Education:* University of California at Los Angeles (B.A., 1976); Southwestern University (J.D., 1980). *Member:* The State Bar of California; American Bar Association; Association of Southern California Defense Counsel; American Prepaid Legal Services Institute.

**GRAHAM J. BALDWIN,** born London, England, January 29, 1945; admitted to bar, 1976, California. *Education:* California State University at Long Beach (B.A., 1971); Western State University (J.D., 1976). Instructor, Paralegal Studies, Cerritos College, Norwalk California, 1977-1982. *Member:* Riverside County Bar Association; State Bar of California; Association of Southern California Defense Counsel. (San Bernardino Office).

**TIMOTHY D. LUCAS,** born Modesto, California, September 18, 1953; admitted to bar, 1978, California; 1980, U.S. Court of Appeals, Ninth Circuit; 1982, U.S. District Court, Central District of California; 1984, U.S. Supreme Court. *Education:* University of Southern California (B.A., cum laude, 1975); Pepperdine University (J.D., 1978). *Member:* Orange County and American Bar Associations; State Bar of California; Association of Southern California Defense Counsel. (San Diego Office).

**DOUGLAS M. DE GRAVE,** born Rochester, New York, May 23, 1954; admitted to bar, 1981, California; 1982, U.S. District Court, Central Dis- *(This Listing Continued)* trict of California; 1985, U.S. District Court, Southern District of California; 1986, U.S. Court of Appeals, Ninth Circuit; 1987, U.S. Supreme Court. *Education:* University of Hawaii (A.S., 1976); California State University, Long Beach (B.A., honors, 1978); Loyola Law School of Los Angeles (J.D., 1981). Phi Alpha Delta. Scott Moot Court Honors Program. Co-winner, Loyola Trial Advocacy Competition, 1981. *Member:* Orange County Bar Association; The State Bar of California; Association of Southern California Defense Counsel; International Association of Defense Counsel; Defense Research Institute; American Board of Trial Advocates. (Santa Ana Office).

**RICHARD A. JONES,** born Los Angeles, California, June 28, 1958; admitted to bar, 1985, California. *Education:* University of California at Irvine (B.A., 1980); Southwestern University School of Law (J.D., 1984). Recipient, American Jurisprudence Award in Torts. *Member:* Orange County Bar Association; State Bar of California; Association of Southern California Defense Counsel; American Board of Trial Advocates. (Santa Ana Office).

**J. LUIS GARCIA,** born Los Angeles, California, July 29, 1959; admitted to bar, 1986, California; U.S. District Court, Central District of California. *Education:* University of Southern California (B.A., cum laude, 1981); Loyola Marymount University (J.D., 1984). *Member:* Los Angeles County and Mexican-American Bar Associations; State Bar of California. *LANGUAGES:* Spanish.

## ASSOCIATES

**CRAIG J. FRILOT,** born Baton Rouge, Louisiana, April 17, 1946; admitted to bar, 1983, California. *Education:* California State University at Long Beach (B.S., 1978); Western State University (J.D., 1983). *Member:* San Bernardino County Bar Association; State Bar of California; Association of Southern California Defense Counsel. (San Bernardino Office).

**DANA C. CLARK,** born Fullerton, California, March 24, 1958; admitted to bar, 1988, California, U.S. Supreme Court, U.S. District Court, Central District of California and U.S. Court of Appeals, Ninth Circuit. *Education:* Point Loma College (B.A., 1979); Western State University (J.D., 1986). Delta Theta Phi. Recipient, Four American Jurisprudence Awards. Member, Western State University Law Review, 1984. Author: "Cordet, Preston & Becker: Recent California Decisions Impacting Landowner Tort Liability," Western State University Law Review, Vol. 13, No. 1, 1985. *Member:* Orange County and American Bar Associations; State Bar of California; Association of Southern California Defense Counsel. (Santa Ana Office).

**MICHAEL E. MCCABE,** born Lake Charles, Louisiana, March 1, 1963; admitted to bar, 1988, California; 1989, U.S. District Court, Central District of California; U.S. Court of Appeals, Ninth Circuit. *Education:* George Washington University (B.A., 1985); Loyola Marymount University (J.D., 1988). *Member:* State Bar of California; Association of Southern California Defense Counsel.

**RICHARD R. THERRIEN,** born Biddeford, Maine, July 11, 1949; admitted to bar, 1988, California, U.S. District Court, Central and Southern Districts of California and U.S. Court of Appeals, Ninth Circuit. *Education:* Barry University (B.S., 1977); Western State University (J.D., 1987). Delta Theta Phi. *Member:* Orange County Bar Association (Member, Sections on: Business Litigation; Real Estate); State Bar of California; Association of Southern California Defense Counsel. (Santa Ana Office).

**WALTER DEMYANEK, JR.,** born Torrance, California, August 19, 1960; admitted to bar, 1990, California. *Education:* Northern Arizona University (B.S., 1982); University of Southern California (M.A., 1983); Southwestern University (J.D., 1990). *Member:* State Bar of California; Association of Southern California Defense Council.

**JAMES M. LEDAKIS,** born Great Falls, Montana, August 2, 1958; admitted to bar, 1987, California, Montana, U.S. District Court, District of Montana, Colorado, U.S. District Court, District of Colorado and U.S. District Courts, Central and Southern Districts of California. *Education:* University of Montana (B.A., 1981); California Western School of Law (J.D., 1985). Phi Alpha Theta. *Member:* San Diego County and Colorado Bar Associations; State Bar of Montana; Association of Southern California Defense Counsel. (San Diego Office).

**MICHAEL GOULD,** born San Francisco, California, June 21, 1964; admitted to bar, 1990, California; 1991, U.S. District Court, Central District of California. *Education:* University of Manitoba (B.S.C., 1986); Western State University College of Law (J.D., 1991). *Member:* State Bar of California; Association of Southern California Defense Counsel. (Santa Ana Office).

*(This Listing Continued)*

**PATRICIA L. BLANTON,** born Roanoke, Virginia, February 18, 1958; admitted to bar, 1984, California; 1990, Virginia and District of Columbia; U.S. District 1990, Virginia and District of Columbia; U.S. District Court, Central District of California. *Education:* Roanoke College (B.A., 1980); Pepperdine University (J.D., 1983). *Member:* Los Angeles, Orange County and American Bar Associations; State Bar of California; Southern California Defense Counsel. *PRACTICE AREAS:* Insurance Defense Law; General Liability Law.

**SUSAN E. PRICE,** born Beverly, Massachusetts, September 25, 1963; admitted to bar, 1989, California and U.S. Court of Appeals, Ninth Circuit. *Education:* Drew University (B.A., in History, 1985); University of the Pacific, McGeorge School of Law (J.D., 1988). *Member:* Beverly Hills, Los Angeles County and American Bar Associations; Irish-American Bar Association; Southern California Defense Counsel.

**STANLEY A. CALVERT,** born Paterson, New Jersey, April 8, 1954; admitted to bar, 1991, California, U.S. District Court, Southern District of California and U.S. Court of Appeals, Ninth Circuit; 1992, U.S. District Court, Southern District of California. *Education:* Brown University (B.A., 1976); California Western School of Law (J.D., 1988). *Member:* San Diego County and American Bar Associations; State Bar of California; Defense Research Institute; California Defense Counsel. (San Diego Office).

**GERARD L. GARCIA-BARRON,** born Los Angeles, California, November 29, 1965; admitted to bar, 1992, California and U.S. District Court, Central District of California. *Education:* University of California, Los Angeles (B.A., 1987); Whittier College School of Law (J.D., 1990). Delta Theta Phi. *Member:* Los Angeles and Orange County Bar Associations; State Bar of California; Mexican-American Bar Association. *LANGUAGES:* Spanish. *PRACTICE AREAS:* Civil Litigation.

**GALA E. DUNN,** born Santa Barbara, California, March 12, 1953; admitted to bar, 1989, California, 1990, U.S. District Court, Southern and Central Districts of California and U.S. Court of Appeals, Ninth Circuit. *Education:* California State University/Los Angeles (B.S., 1981); Loyola University of Los Angeles (J.D., 1988). *Member:* Los Angeles County and American Bar Associations; State Bar of California; The Black Women Lawyers Association. *PRACTICE AREAS:* Litigation.

**KARIE E. SCHRODER,** born Hollywood, California, January 16, 1963; admitted to bar, 1988, California and U.S. District Court, Central District of California; 1990, U.S. Court of Appeals, Ninth Circuit. *Education:* University of California at Los Angeles (B.A., 1985); Loyola Marymount University (J.D., 1988). *Member:* State Bar of California. *PRACTICE AREAS:* Insurance Defense.

**NICOLE T. SAADEH,** born Canoga Park, California, December 25, 1963; admitted to bar, 1989, California, Supreme Court of California and U.S. Court of Appeals, Ninth Circuit; 1990, U.S. District Court, Central District of California. *Education:* University of Southern California (B.A., with honors, 1986); Loyola Law School, Los Angeles (J.D., 1989). Extern to the Honorable Lisa Hill Fenning, United States Bankruptcy Judge, Central District of California, Summer 1987. *Member:* Los Angeles County, Federal and American Bar Associations; State Bar of California; Financial Lawyers Conference; Los Angeles Bankruptcy Forum; California Women Lawyers. *LANGUAGES:* Spanish.

**EVANGELINA P. FIERRO HERNANDEZ,** born Los Angeles, California, March 17, 1966; admitted to bar, 1993, California and U.S. District Court, Central District of Florida. *Education:* Stanford University (B.A., 1988); Arizona State University College of Law (J.D., 1993). *LANGUAGES:* Spanish.

**JENNA LEA GRANT,** born Pueblo, Colorado, July 7, 1965; admitted to bar, 1992, California and U.S. District Court, Southern District of California. *Education:* San Diego State University (B.A., cum laude, 1988); University of San Diego School of Law (J.D., 1992). Phi Beta Kappa. *Member:* San Diego County Bar Association. (San Diego Office).

**MARY CRENSHAW TYLER,** born San Diego, California, January 24, 1953; admitted to bar, 1991, California. *Education:* Brigham Young University (B.A., 1974); Western State University College of Law (J.D., 1990). *Member:* San Diego County Bar Association; State Bar of California. (San Diego Office).

**GORMAN J. DEGRAVE,** born Rochester, New York, January 4, 1953; admitted to bar, 1993, California. *Education:* Western State University (J.D., 1993). *Member:* Orange County Bar Association; Association of Southern California Defense Counsel. (Santa Ana Office).

**LUCY G. MENDOZA,** born Los Angeles, California, October 11, 1966; admitted to bar, 1994, California. *Education:* California State University,

*(This Listing Continued)*

CAA1081B

CALIFORNIA—LOS ANGELES  MARTINDALE-HUBBELL LAW DIRECTORY 1997

**PARKER STANBURY,** Los Angeles—Continued

Los Angeles (B.S., 1989); Southwestern University School of Law (J.D., 1994). Recipient, Exceptional Achievement Award, Wills and Trusts. Governor, Southwestern's Hispanic Law Students, 1993-1994. *Member:* Los Angeles County and American Bar Associations; Mexican-American Bar Association. *LANGUAGES:* Spanish and French. *PRACTICE AREAS:* General Practice.

**RICHARD LEUNG,** born Sheffield, England, United Kingdom, December 3, 1966; admitted to bar, 1992, California. *Education:* University of California, Los Angeles (B.A., 1989); University of Southern California (J.D., 1992).

**MAXINE H. PARK,** born Seoul, Korea, October 16, 1964; admitted to bar, 1991, California; 1994, New York. *Education:* Loma Linda University (B.S., 1987); University of Southern California (J.D., 1991). *Member:* State Bar of California; New York State Bar Association. *PRACTICE AREAS:* Personal Injury; Government Benefits; Family Law.

**LEONOR C. GONZALES,** born Guanajuato, Mexico, April 27, 1957; admitted to bar, 1988, California. *Education:* California State University, Dominguez Hills (B.A., 1980); University of San Diego (J.D., 1987). *PRACTICE AREAS:* General Civil; Family Law; Government Benefits.

**KATE A. WILLMORE,** born Shell Lake, Wisconsin, February 23, 1947; admitted to bar, 1991, California and U.S. District Court, Southern District of California; 1994, U.S. District Court, Central District of California. *Education:* University of California at San Diego (B.A., Sociology, cum laude, 1988); University of San Diego School of Law (J.D., 1991). *Member:* Los Angeles County, San Diego County and American Bar Associations; State Bar of California. *PRACTICE AREAS:* Civil Litigation; Bankruptcy; General Civil.

*OF COUNSEL*

**ROBERT H. BERGSTEN,** born Glendale, California, April 3, 1932; admitted to bar, 1964, California; U.S. District Court, Southern and Central Districts of California. *Education:* Los Angeles City College and University of Southern California (B.S., 1959); University of Southern California (J.D., 1962). Phi Delta Phi. *Member:* Orange County Bar Association; The State Bar of California; Association of Southern California Defense Counsel; International Association of Defense Counsel; American Board of Trial Advocates; Defense Research Institute. (Santa Ana Office).

COUNSEL FOR: County of Orange; Loss Management Professionals, Inc.; Pre-Paid Legal Service; Self Insured Management Services, Inc.
REPRESENTATIVE CLIENTS: Allied Group Insurance; Allstate Ins. Co.; American Bankers Ins. Group; American Family; American Liberty; Armed Forces Ins. Exch.; Auto Owners Ins. Co.; California Ins. Group; Celina Mutual; Country Mutual Ins. Co.; Crawford & Co.; Crum & Forster Inc.; Employers Mutual Insurance Co.; General Adjustment Bureau; Golden Eagle Insurance Company; Great American Ins. Co.; Guarantee Natl. Co.; Home Mutual Ins. Co.; Hawkeye-Security; Meridian Mutual Ins. Co.; Minnehoma Ins. Co.; Nationwide/Wausau; Northbrook Ins. Co.; Northland Ins. Co.; Northwestern National Ins. Co.; Ohio Cas. Ins. Group; Oregon Auto Ins. Co.; Protective Ins. Co.; T.I.G.; Transport Ins. Co.; United States Fidelity & Guaranty Co.; Western Heritage Insurance Co.; Zurich-American Ins. Co.
TRANSPORTATION CLIENTS: Allied Van Lines; Arkansas Best Freight; National Car Rental; Rocket Rent-A-Car; Watkins Motor Lines.

## PARSONS AND DESTIAN

Established in 1981

**1055 WILSHIRE BOULEVARD, SUITE 1750
LOS ANGELES, CALIFORNIA 90017**

Telephone: 213-975-0064
Telecopier: 213-975-1172
Email: dparsla@gnn.com

*London, England Office:* Guild House, 36-38 Fenchurch Street. EC3M 3DQ. Telephone: 071-929-5252. Telecopier: 071-283-4466. Telex: 914561.

*Litigation and General Insurance Practice. Coverage Excess and Reinsurance; Bad Faith Law; Fire Insurance Law; Products and Professional Liability; Asbestos, Hazardous Waste, Environmental Pollution and Other Toxic Tort Defense; Employment Wrongful Termination Liability; Equine Law, Mass Disaster Litigation; Municipal and Public Officials Liability; Landslide and Subsidence Law; Non-Marine, Marine and Inland Marine Insurance Law.*

*FIRM PROFILE: The firm was established on 1 October 1981 by David W. Parsons. With offices in both Los Angeles and London, Parsons & Destian serves both the domestic and international insurance communities emphasizing insurance law, both substantive and defense. The firm members have considerable expertise and experience in the representation of primary, excess, surplus*

*(This Listing Continued)*

CAA1082B

*and reinsurance carriers. In addition to the firm's expertise in the areas of coverage and mass litigation, Parsons & Destian has vast experience in the defense of personal lines, products, commercial, environmental, toxic torts, and professional negligence cases.*

*MEMBERS OF FIRM*

**DAVID W. PARSONS,** born London, England, February 8, 1936; admitted to bar, 1969, California and U.S. District Court, Central, Northern, Southern and Eastern Districts of California. *Education:* London University, London England; Golden Gate University (J.D., 1968). *Member:* State Bar of California (Member, Committee on Insurance, 1978-1980). *PRACTICE AREAS:* Complex Coverage; Professional Liability; Reinsurance; General Insurance Litigation.

**TONY DESTIAN,** born New York, N.Y., August 21,1959; admitted to bar, 1989, California and U.S. District Court, Central District of California. *Education:* University of Massachusetts at Amherst (B.A., 1981); Southwestern University School of Law (J.D., 1988). *Member:* Los Angeles County and American Bar Associations; State Bar of California. *PRACTICE AREAS:* General Insurance Litigation; Complex Coverage; Writs and Appeals.

*OF COUNSEL*

**G. DAVID RUBIN,** born Los Angeles, California, May 24, 1970; admitted to bar, 1995, California and U.S. District Court, Central District of California. *Education:* University of California at Los Angeles (B.A., 1992); Loyola Law School (J.D., 1995). Member, Federalist Society, 1995—. *Member:* Los Angeles County Bar Association. *LANGUAGES:* Spanish. *PRACTICE AREAS:* Complex Coverage; Excess and Reinsurance Litigation; General Insurance Litigation.

## PASCOTTO & GALLAVOTTI

Established in 1987

**1800 AVENUE OF THE STARS, 6TH FLOOR
LOS ANGELES, CALIFORNIA 90067-4276**

Telephone: 310-203-7515
Facsimile: 310-284-3021

*Rome, Italy Associated Office:* Studio Legale Gallavotti Honorati & Pascotto, Via Po n. 9, 00198. Telephone: (06) 8530.1100. Facsimile: (06) 854.1323. E-Mail: MGAL@STAR.FLASHNET.IT

*International, Corporate, Business, Investment Taxation, Entertainment, Real Estate and Aviation Law. General Practice United States and Europe.*

**ALVARO PASCOTTO,** born Rome, Italy, March 8, 1949; admitted to bar, 1976, Italy; 1987, California. *Education:* Le Roche College, Crans, Switzerland (Ginnasio, 1964); Liceo Mameli, Rome, Italy (B.A., 1967); University of Rome (J.D., 1973). Member, Italy-America Chamber of Commerce, Inc., 1987. *Member:* Los Angeles County and American Bar Associations; State Bar of California; National Italian American Bar Association; Italian American Lawyers Association. (Also Of Counsel to Irell & Manella). *LANGUAGES:* English, French, Spanish and Italian. *PRACTICE AREAS:* International; Entertainment; Real Estate; Aviation; Corporate; Business; Investment Taxation.

*OF COUNSEL*

**AVV. MARIO GALLAVOTTI** (Not admitted in the United States).

## PATTERSON, RITNER, LOCKWOOD, GARTNER & JURICH

A Partnership including Professional Corporations

**SUITE 900, 3580 WILSHIRE BOULEVARD
LOS ANGELES, CALIFORNIA 90010**

Telephone: 213-487-6240
FAX: 213-380-8681

*Ventura, California Office:* Suite 231, 260 Maple Court. Telephone: 805-644-1061.
*Bakersfield, California Office:* Suite 522, 1415 Eighteenth Street. Telephone: 805-327-4387.
*San Bernardino, California Office:* 325 Hospitality Lane, Suite 204. Telephone: 909-885-6063.

*Insurance, Personal Injury, Products Liability, Casualty and Medical Malpractice Law. Trials. Legal Malpractice.*

*(This Listing Continued)*

## MEMBERS OF FIRM

**HOBART G. PATTERSON** (1922-1973).

**WILLIAM F. RITNER, (A PROFESSIONAL CORPORATION),** born Nebraska, July 22, 1937; admitted to bar, 1966, California. *Education:* University of Nebraska; Nebraska State University; Southwestern University (J.D., cum laude, 1965). *Member:* State Bar of California; American Bar Association; American Board of Trial Advocates.

**CLYDE E. LOCKWOOD, (A PROFESSIONAL CORPORATION),** born San Francisco, California, May 30, 1932; admitted to bar, 1964, California. *Education:* Pasadena City College and Fresno State College; Southwestern University (LL.B., cum laude, 1963). Member, Board of Governors, Los Angeles Legal Aid Society, 1968. *Member:* Los Angeles County Bar Association (Member, Board of Governors, 1966); State Bar of California; Association of Trial Lawyers of America.

**HAROLD H. GARTNER, III, (A PROFESSIONAL CORPORATION),** born Los Angeles, California, June 23, 1948; admitted to bar, 1972, California. *Education:* Pasadena City College; George Williams College; California State University of Los Angeles; Loyola University (J.D., cum laude, 1972). Member, St. Thomas More Legal Aid Society. City Attorney, Los Angeles, California, 1972-1973. *Member:* State Bar of California; American Bar Association; St. Thomas More Society (Member, Board of Governors, 1972-1973).

**JOHN A. JURICH,** born Minneapolis, Minnesota, January 13, 1945; admitted to bar, 1978, California. *Education:* California State University at Northridge (B.A., cum laude, 1973); Loyola University of Los Angeles (J.D., 1978). *Member:* State Bar of California. (Resident, Bakersfield Office).

**ROBERT R. SCHOLL,** born Chicago, Illinois, August 9, 1946; admitted to bar, 1981, California; 1982, U.S. District Court, Central District of California and U.S. Court of Appeals, Ninth Circuit. *Education:* University of Texas (B.A., 1968); Southwestern University (J.D., 1981). *Member:* Los Angeles County and American Bar Associations; State Bar of California.

## OF COUNSEL

**JAMES F. MCGAHAN, (A PROFESSIONAL CORPORATION),** born Philadelphia, Pennsylvania, January 3, 1931; admitted to bar, 1965, California and U.S. District Court, Southern District of California. *Education:* Loyola University of Los Angeles; University of California at Los Angeles; University of Southern California (LL.B., 1964). Phi Alpha Delta. Recipient, American Jurisprudence Award. Member, Staff, University of Southern California Law Review, 1963-1964. Deputy District Attorney, Ventura, California, 1965-1966. Member, Ventura Superior Court Arbitration Panel, 1980—. Member, Panel of Arbitrators, American Arbitration Association. *Member:* Ventura County and American Bar Associations; The State Bar of California; Association of Southern California Defense Counsel; American Society of Law and Medicine. [Capt., U.S. Marine Corp, 1951-1962]. (Resident, Ventura Office).

---

**CAROL J. ADAMS,** born California, August 25, 1952; admitted to bar, 1985, California. *Education:* California State University at Long Beach (B.A., 1975); Southwestern University School of Law (J.D., 1985). *Member:* State Bar of California.

**CAROLYN WADE DORAN,** born Riverside, California, November 12, 1956; admitted to bar, 1982, California and U.S. District Court, Central District of California. *Education:* Occidental College (B.A., 1979); Whittier College School of Law (J.D., 1982). *Member:* State Bar of California; American Bar Association.

**CHRISTOPHER W. GARDNER,** born Jacksonville, Florida, February 5, 1947; admitted to bar, 1972, Florida; 1983, California and U.S. District Court, Central District of California. *Education:* University of the South (B.A., 1969); Florida State University (J.D., 1972).

**ANN BIRGITTA GUSTAFSSON,** born Stockholm, Sweden, May 11, 1951; admitted to bar, 1990, California; 1991, U.S. District Court, Central District of California. *Education:* University of California at Berkeley (B.A., 1974); University of San Francisco (J.D., 1990). *Member:* State Bar of California. **LANGUAGES:** Swedish.

**TOBIE B. WAXMAN,** born Washington, D.C., June 26, 1963; admitted to bar, 1993, California. *Education:* George Washington University (B.A., 1985); Loyola Marymount University (J.D., 1993). Staff Editor, Loyola International and Comparative Law Journal.

*(This Listing Continued)*

**REPRESENTATIVE CLIENTS:** California Insurance Guarantee Assn.; Chubb-/Pacific Indemnity Group; Cooperative of American Physicians, Inc.; Doctors Co.; Employers Casualty Co.; Fremont Indemnity Co.; Great American Insurance Co.; Guarantee National Insurance Co.; Hartford Insurance Cos.; Kemper Insurance Cos.; Liberty Mutual Insurance Co.; Physicians Interindemnity; Professional Risk Management; Royal Insurance; St. Paul Insurance Co.; Southern California Physicians Insurance Exchange; Travelers Insurance Co.; Western Employers.

---

# JACK PAUL
### 1801 AVENUE OF THE STARS
### SUITE 932
## LOS ANGELES, CALIFORNIA 90067
### Telephone: 310-277-1322
### Facsimile: 310-277-1333

*Government Contract Law, Construction Litigation, Commercial and International Contract Disputes.*

**JACK PAUL,** born Los Angeles, California, July 31, 1928; admitted to bar, 1953, California and District of Columbia; 1961, U.S. Claims Court; 1963, U.S. Supreme Court. *Education:* University of California at Los Angeles (A.B., 1950); Stanford University (LL.B., 1952); Harvard University (LL.M., 1953). Phi Beta Kappa; Phi Alpha Delta. Member, Board of Editors, Stanford Law Review, 1952. Author: *United States Government Contracts and Subcontracts,* book published by American Law Institute and American Bar Association, 1964; Chapter on "Claims and Remedies," published in *Basic Techniques of Public Contracts Practice,* Continuing Education of the State Bar of California, 1977. Started the Government Contracts Extension Program, University of California, Los Angeles. Member, Department of Defense-Industry Procurement Training Advisory Committee, 1964-1966. Member, 1967-1975 and President, 1970 and 1973-1974, Beverly Hills Board of Education. *Member:* Los Angeles County, Federal and American Bar Associations; State Bar of California. [With the Air Materiel Command, U.S. Air Force, 1954-1956]. **TRANSACTIONS:** Lead counsel for complex public construction claims litigation in Federal and State courts and arbitration; counsel for substantial recovery on behalf of contractor for changes and cost impact claims, Parsons of California, 82-1 BCA ¶15,659; estoppel against the Government, Inet Power, a Division of Teledyne, 68-1 BCA ¶7020; resolution of cost determination and damages claims and disputes. **PRACTICE AREAS:** Government Contract Law; Construction Litigation.

---

# PAUL, HASTINGS, JANOFSKY & WALKER LLP

A Limited Liability Partnership including Professional Corporations

*Established in 1951*

### TWENTY-THIRD FLOOR, 555 SOUTH FLOWER STREET
## LOS ANGELES, CALIFORNIA 90071-2371
### Telephone: 213-683-6000
### FAX: 213-627-0705
### Email: info@PHJW.com
### URL: http://www.phjw.com

*Orange County, California Office:* Seventeenth Floor, 695 Town Center Drive, Costa Mesa. Telephone: 714-668-6200.

*Washington, D.C. Office:* Tenth Floor, 1299 Pennsylvania Avenue, N.W. Telephone: 202-508-9500.

*Atlanta, Georgia Office:* 24th Floor, 600 Peachtree Street, N.E. Telephone: 404-815-2400.

*Santa Monica, California Office:* Fifth Floor, 1299 Ocean Avenue. Telephone: 310-319-3300.

*Stamford, Connecticut Office:* Ninth Floor, 1055 Washington Boulevard. Telephone: 203-961-7400.

*New York, New York Office:* 31st Floor, 399 Park Avenue. Telephone: 212-318-6000.

*Tokyo, Japan Office:* Ark Mori Building, 30th Floor, 12-32 Akasaka, P.O. Box 577, 1-Chome, Minato-Ku. Telephone: (03) 3586-4711.

*General Practice.*

**ROBERT PUSEY HASTINGS** (1910-1996).

### COUNSEL

**OLIVER F. GREEN** (Costa Mesa, California; See Costa Mesa listing for biographical information).

*(This Listing Continued)*

**PAUL, HASTINGS, JANOFSKY & WALKER LLP,** Los Angeles—Continued

**LEONARD S. JANOFSKY** (Santa Monica, California; See Santa Monica listing for biographical information).

**LEE G. PAUL** (Costa Mesa, California; See Costa Mesa for biographical information).

**CHARLES M. WALKER** (Santa Monica, California; See Santa Monica listing for biographical information).

### MEMBERS OF FIRM

**NANCY L. ABELL** (Santa Monica, California; See Santa Monica listing for biographical information).

**CARL T. ANDERSON** (Stamford Connecticut; See Stamford listing for biographical information).

**TOSHIYUKI ARAI,** born Hokkaido, Japan, November 25, 1956; admitted to bar, 1985, Japan; 1989, New York, Michigan and California. *Education:* Tokyo University (B.A., 1980; B.A., 1982); The Legal Research and Training Institute of the Supreme Court of Japan (Diploma, 1985); Cornell Law School (LL.M., 1988). *Email:* TArai@PHJW.com

**RICHARD M. ASBILL** (Atlanta, Georgia; See Atlanta listing for biographical information).

**R. LAWRENCE ASHE, JR., (P.C.)** (Atlanta, Georgia; See Atlanta listing for biographical information).

**MARK W. ATKINSON,** born Beaver Falls, Pennsylvania, February 9, 1949; admitted to bar, 1974, California. *Education:* Stanford University (B.A., with distinction, 1971); University of California at Los Angeles (J.D., 1974). Phi Beta Kappa. Member, UCLA Law Review, 1972-1974. *Email:* MWAtkinson@PHJW.com

**JESSE H. AUSTIN, III** (Atlanta, Georgia; See Atlanta listing for biographical information).

**E. LAWRENCE BARCELLA, JR.** (Washington, D.C.; See District of Columbia listing for biographical information).

**CHRISTOPHER A. BARRECA** (Stamford, Connecticut; See Stamford listing for biographical information).

**ALAN J. BARTON,** born New York, New York, September 2, 1938; admitted to bar, 1964, California. *Education:* University of California at Berkeley (A.B., 1960); University of California, Boalt Hall (LL.B., 1963). Order of the Coif. Member, 1961-1962 and Associate Editor, 1962-1963, California Law Review. *Email:* AJBarton@PHJW.com

**KEITH W. BERGLUND** (Atlanta, Georgia; See Atlanta listing for biographical information).

**DANIEL G. BERGSTEIN** (New York, New York; See New York listing for biographical information).

**STEPHEN L. BERRY,** born Fort Worth, Texas, June 22, 1954; admitted to bar, 1981, California. *Education:* Brigham Young University (B.S., cum laude, 1978; J.D., 1981). Order of the Barristers. Associate Editor, Utah Bar Journal, 1980-1981. [Captain, JAGC, U.S. Army, 1982-1985] *Email:* SLBerry@PHJW.com

**WOODSON TOLIVER BESSON, (P.C.)** (Santa Monica, California; see Santa Monica listing for biographical information).

**JONATHAN BIRENBAUM** (Stamford, Connecticut; See Stamford listing for biographical information).

**THOMAS P. BRENNAN, (P.C.),** born New York, New York, June 26, 1941; admitted to bar, 1966, District of Columbia; 1969, California; 1983, Connecticut. *Education:* Fordham University (B.S., magna cum laude, 1962); Harvard University (LL.B., 1965). Phi Beta Kappa. Member, Panel of Arbitrators, American Arbitration Association. [Capt., USMC, 1965-1969] *Email:* TPBrennan@PHJW.com

**JOHN H. BRINSLEY,** born New York, New York, December 29, 1933; admitted to bar, 1961, California. *Education:* Cornell University (B.A., 1958; LL.B., 1960). Recipient, 1994 Maynard Toll Award, Los Angeles County Bar Association. Member, Board of Trustees, 1974-1980 and President, 1979-1980, Los Angeles County Bar Association. Member, Board of Governors, 1975-1978 and President, 1976-1977, Association of Business Trial Lawyers. Member, Board of Directors, Constitutional Rights Foundation, 1983-1989. Member, 1983-1990 and Chair, 1988-1990, Board of Directors, Western Center on Law and Poverty. Member, Chancery Club. Member: Board of Directors, California Supreme Court Historical Society, 1993—; Executive Committee, Antitrust and Trade Regulation Law Section, State Bar of California, 1993—, Treasurer, 1995-1996. Fellow: American College of Trial Lawyers; American Bar Foundation. *Member:* American Law Institute. *Email:* JHBrinsley@PHJW.com

**JAMIE BRODER,** born Oakland, California, December 17, 1949; admitted to bar, 1976, New York; 1977, California. *Education:* Brandeis University (A.B., magna cum laude, 1972); Boston College and New York University (J.D., cum laude, 1975). Phi Beta Kappa. Member, Moot Court Board, 1973-1975. Member, Special Committee on Cooperation with the American Newspaper Publishers Association, American Bar Association, 1982-1988. Member, Committee on Alternative Dispute Resolution, Litigation Section, American Bar Association, 1990—. Panelist: Center for Public Resources Panel of Distinguished Neutrals, 1992—; Editorial Board of Alternatives, 1994—. *Email:* JBroder@PHJW.com

**BARRY A. BROOKS** (New York, New York; See New York listing for biographical information).

**BARBARA BERISH BROWN** (Washington, D.C.; See District of Columbia listing for biographical information).

**DARYL R. BUFFENSTEIN** (Atlanta, Georgia; See Atlanta listing for biographical information).

**THOMAS G. BURCH, JR.** (Atlanta, Georgia; See Atlanta listing for biographical information).

**SIOBHAN MCBREEN BURKE,** born Northbrook, Illinois, March 7, 1958; admitted to bar, 1983 Illinois; 1984, Florida; 1986, California. *Education:* Smith College (A.B., with high honors, 1980); University of Illinois (J.D., 1983). Member, Moot Court Board. *Email:* SMBurke@PHJW.com

**PAUL W. CANE, JR.,** born San Francisco, California, March 3, 1954; admitted to bar, 1981, California. *Education:* Dartmouth College (A.B., summa cum laude, 1976); University of California, Boalt Hall (J.D., 1979). Editor-in-Chief, California Law Review, 1978-1979. Editor-in-Chief, *Employment Discrimination Law* (3d ed.), Bureau of National Affairs, 1995. Co-Author: N.L. Abell and P.W. Cane, "An Employer's Guide to the Americans with Disabilities Act," 1991. Law Clerk: Hon. Carl McGowan, U.S. Court of Appeals, District of Columbia Circuit, 1979-1980; Hon. Lewis F. Powell, Jr., Supreme Court of the United States, 1980-1981. Member, Executive Committee, Labor Law Section, Los Angeles County Bar Association, 1988-1993. Faculty: Practising Law Institute; Defense Research Institute; American Employment Law Council. Member, EEO Law Committee, Labor and Employment Law Section, American Bar Association, 1988—. Member, Board of Directors, Constitutional Rights Foundation, 1989—. *Email:* PWCane@PHJW.com

**ROBERT E. CARLSON,** born Brooklyn, New York, October 11, 1930; admitted to bar, 1959, California. *Education:* University of Oregon (B.S., 1953); University of California, Hastings (LL.B., 1958); Harvard University (LL.M., 1963). Order of the Coif. Member, Hastings Law Journal, 1957-1958. Recipient, Griffin Bell Award, Dispute Resolution Services, Inc., 1992. Chair of the Board, Skid Row Housing Trust of Los Angeles, 1988—. Recipient, Katherine Krause Award, Inner City Law Center, 1996. *Member:* Los Angeles County (Member, Executive Committee, Business and Corporation Law Section, 1982-1989; Chair, Committee on Continuing Legal Education, 1983-1985) and American (Chair, Youth Education for Citizenship Committee, 1982-1985; Member, Steering Committee, Public Education Division, 1985-1989; Vice Chair, Committee on Developments in Investment Services, Business Law Section; Member, ABA Task Force on Guidelines for Mutual Fund Directories) Bar Associations; Los Angeles County Bar Foundation (Member, 1985— and President, 1988-1989, Board of Trustees). Fellow, American Bar Foundation. *Email:* RECarlson@PHJW.com

**GRACE A. CARTER,** born Wichita, Kansas, October 5, 1955; admitted to bar, 1981, California. *Education:* University of California at Berkeley (B.A., 1977); University of California, Boalt Hall (J.D., 1981). Phi Beta Kappa. Member: Moot Court Board. Co-author: *Environmental Insurance Handbook,* Government Institutes, 1992. Faculty: Practising Law Institute, 1995; Rutter Group, 1996. Delegate, California State Bar Conference of Delegates, 1986, 1988; Executive Committee, Los Angeles County Bar Association Barristers, 1987-1989; Committee on Administration of Justice, State Bar of California, 1988-1991. Chair, Society of 1912, Boalt Hall School of Law. Member: Board of Directors, Legal Aid Foundation of Los Angeles, 1995—. Board of Directors, Western Center on Law and Poverty, 1994—. *Email:* GACarter@PHJW.com

*(This Listing Continued)*

**EVE MARY CODDON,** born San Diego, California, April 17, 1961; admitted to bar, 1986, California. *Education:* University of California at San Diego (B.A., 1983); University of San Diego (J.D., magna cum laude, 1986). Member, San Diego Law Review, 1984-1986. **Email:** EMCoddon@PHJW.com

**RONALD T. COLEMAN, JR.** (Atlanta, Georgia; See Atlanta listing for biographical information).

**KEVIN CONBOY** (Atlanta, Georgia; See Atlanta listing for biographical information).

**PAUL J. CONNELL** (Atlanta, Georgia; See Atlanta listing for biographical information).

**DOUGLAS C. CONROY** (Stamford, Connecticut; See Stamford listing for biographical information).

**STEPHEN D. COOKE** (Costa Mesa, California; See Costa Mesa listing for biographical information).

**JAMES H. COX** (Atlanta, Georgia; See Atlanta listing for biographical information).

**VICTORIA A. CUNDIFF** (New York, New York; See New York listing for biographical information).

**GLENN D. DASSOFF** (Costa Mesa, California; See Costa Mesa listing for biographical information).

**DONALD A. DAUCHER,** born Buffalo, New York, April 2, 1945; admitted to bar, 1972, California. *Education:* University of Rochester (B.S., 1967); Duke University (J.D., 1971). Beta Gamma Sigma. Order of the Coif. Recent Developments Editor, Duke Law Journal, 1970-1971. **Email:** DADaucher@PHJW.com

**JANET TOLL DAVIDSON** (Costa Mesa California; See Costa Mesa listing for biographical information).

**BARBRA L. DAVIS,** born Chicago, Illinois, January 16, 1945; admitted to bar, 1984, California. *Education:* University of California at Los Angeles (B.A., cum laude, 1966; M.A., with highest honors, 1970; J.D., 1984). Order of the Coif. Management Co-Chair, Trial Advocacy Subcommittee, Employee Rights and Responsibilities Committee, Labor and Employment Section, American Bar Association, 1994—. **Email:** BLDavis@PHJW.com

**JOHN F. DELLA GROTTA** (Costa Mesa, California; See Costa Mesa listing for biographical information).

**NICHOLAS DEWITT,** born Boston, Massachusetts, July 4, 1950; admitted to bar, 1979, California. *Education:* Indiana University (B.S., 1972); Loyola Law School, Los Angeles (J.D., cum laude, 1979). Note and Comment Editor, Loyola of Los Angeles Law Review, 1978-1979. Assistant U.S. Attorney, Criminal Division, 1980-1984. Adjunct Professor of Law: Trial Advocacy, Criminal Procedure, Loyola Law School, Los Angeles, 1985-1987. Member, Board of Directors, Western Law Center for Disability Rights, 1983—. **Email:** NDewitt@PHJW.com

**ROBERT A. DEWITT, (P.C.),** born Santa Monica, California, December 19, 1931; admitted to bar, 1963, California. *Education:* Columbia University and University of California at Los Angeles (A.B., 1954); Stanford University (LL.B., 1962). Order of the Coif. Revising Editor, Stanford Law Review, 1961-1962. Chair, Taxation Section, Los Angeles County Bar Association, 1975-1976. Member, Planning Committee, University of Southern California Institute on Federal Taxation, 1973-1988. **Email:** RADewitt@PHJW.com

**R. BRUCE DICKSON** (Washington, D.C. and New York, New York; See District of Columbia and New York listings for biographical information).

**ROBERT M. DUDNIK** (Santa Monica, California; see Santa Monica listing for biographical information).

**WILLIAM E. EASON, JR.** (Atlanta, Georgia; See Atlanta listing for biographical information).

**E. DONALD ELLIOTT** (Washington, D.C.; See District of Columbia listing for biographical information).

**RALPH B. EVERETT** (Washington, D.C.; See District of Columbia listing for biographical information).

**ZACHARY D. FASMAN** (Washington, D.C.; See District of Columbia listing for biographical information).

**PHILIP N. FEDER,** born Santa Monica, California, June 17, 1954; admitted to bar, 1979, California; 1991, New York. *Education:* Stanford University (A.B., 1976); Columbia University (J.D., 1979). Harlan Fiske Stone Scholar. Member, Moot Court Board. **Email:** PNFeder@PHJW.com

**HYDEE R. FELDSTEIN,** born Hato Rey, Puerto Rico, July 17, 1958; admitted to bar, 1982, California. *Education:* Swarthmore College (B.A., 1979); Columbia University (J.D., 1982). Harlan Fiske Stone Scholar, 1979-1982. Member, Board of Editors, Columbia Law Review, 1980-1982. Extern, Hon. Pierre N. Leval, U.S. District Court, Southern District of New York. **Email:** HRFeldstein@PHJW.com

**ALFRED G. FELIU** (New York, New York; See New York listing for biographical information).

**ESTEBAN A. FERRER, III** (Stamford, Connecticut; See Stamford listing for biographical information).

**BRUCE W. FRASER,** born Glen Cove, New York, September 4, 1957; admitted to bar, 1981, California. *Education:* Columbia University (A.B., summa cum laude, 1978); Harvard University (J.D., cum laude, 1981). Phi Beta Kappa. **Email:** BWFraser@PHJW.com

**JOHN C. FUNK,** born Washington, D.C., July 18, 1944; admitted to bar, 1972, California. *Education:* United States Air Force Academy and University of Southern California (A.B., cum laude, 1966); Harvard University (J.D., 1971). Phi Kappa Phi. Lecturer: Administrative Law, University of Southern California, 1979, 1980, 1982; Environmental Law, University of California at Los Angeles, 1991 and 1992; California Continuing Education of the Bar, Real Estate Law, 1988. Member, Board of Directors, Central City Association of Los Angeles and the Western Center on Law and Poverty. Member, Executive Committee, Urban Land Institute, Los Angeles District Council. **Email:** JCFunk@PHJW.com

**NORMAN A. FUTAMI,** born Hermosa Beach, California, January 5, 1960; admitted to bar, 1984, California. *Education:* Yale University (B.A., summa cum laude, 1981); Harvard University (J.D., 1984). Phi Beta Kappa. **Email:** NAFutami@PHJW.com

**JOHN J. GALLAGHER** (Washington, D.C.; See District of Columbia listing for biographical information).

**JON A. GEIER** (Washington, D.C.; See District of Columbia listing for biographical information).

**DAVID L. GERSH,** born Atlanta, Georgia, January 7, 1942; admitted to bar, 1967, California; 1979, District of Columbia. *Education:* University of California at Los Angeles (B.S., with honors, 1962; M.B.A., 1963); Harvard Law School (J.D., cum laude, 1966). Certified Public Accountant, California, 1963. **PRACTICE AREAS:** Corporate Law; Securities Law; Acquisitions, Divestitures and Mergers Law. **Email:** DLGersh@PHJW.com

**JOHN S. GIBSON,** born Ann Arbor, Michigan, November 10, 1960; admitted to bar, 1987, Pennsylvania; 1989, California. *Education:* Harvard University (A.B., 1982); University of Michigan (J.D., 1986). Associate Editor, Michigan Law Review. Law Clerk to Hon. John Feikens, U.S. District Court, Eastern District of Michigan. **Email:** JSGibson@PHJW.com

**MICHAEL GLAZER,** born Los Angeles, California, October 10, 1940; admitted to bar, 1967, California; 1980, District of Columbia. *Education:* Stanford University (B.S., 1962); Harvard University (M.B.A., 1964); University of California at Los Angeles (J.D., 1967). Phi Beta Kappa; Order of the Coif. Articles Editor, UCLA Law Review, 1966-1967. Law Clerk to Chief Justice Roger J. Traynor, California Supreme Court, 1967-1968. Assistant Administrator, National Oceanic and Atmospheric Administration, U.S. Department of Commerce, 1978-1980; Chairman, California Water Commission, 1976-1978; Commissioner, Los Angeles Department of Water and Power, 1973-1976. Director, Metropolitan Water District of Southern California, 1984-1991. Member, Committee on Corporations, 1986-1987, State Bar of California. Chair, Federal Securities Regulation Committee, 1988-1990, Member, Executive Committee, Business and Corporation Law Section, 1989—, Los Angeles County Bar Association. **Email:** MGlazer@PHJW.com

**GEORGE L. GRAFF** (New York, New York; See New York listing for biographical information).

**PAUL GROSSMAN,** born Palo Alto, California, August 26, 1939; admitted to bar, 1965, California. *Education:* Amherst College (A.B., 1961); Yale University (LL.B., 1964). Member, Board of Editors, Yale Law Journal, 1962-1964. Co-Author: Schlei and Grossman, *Employment Discrimination Law,* Bureau of National Affairs, 1976, 1979, 1983, 1984, 1985, 1987, 1989, 1991 and 1996. President, Legal Aid Foundation of Los Angeles, 1982-1983. General Counsel, California Employment Law Council

*(This Listing Continued)*

**PAUL, HASTINGS, JANOFSKY & WALKER LLP,** Los Angeles—Continued

(CELC), 1984—. Member, Board of Trustees, Greater Los Angeles Zoo Association, 1977—. *Email:* PGrossman@PHJW.com

**WILLIAM M. HART** (New York, New York; See New York listing for biographical information).

**LAWRENCE J. HASS** (Washington, D.C.; See District of Columbia listing for biographical information).

**JOHN D. HAWKINS, JR.** (Stamford, Connecticut; See Stamford listing for biographical information).

**HOWARD C. HAY** (Costa Mesa, California; See Costa Mesa listing for biographical information).

**WILLIAM B. HILL, JR.** (Atlanta, Georgia; See Atlanta listing for biographical information).

**MATTHEW A. HODEL** (Costa Mesa, California; See Costa Mesa listing for biographical information).

**MICHAEL A. HOOD** (Costa Mesa, California; See Costa Mesa listing for biographical information).

**JUDITH RICHARDS HOPE** (Washington, D.C.; See District of Columbia listing for biographical information).

**JOHN P. HOWITT** (New York, New York; See New York listing for biographical informaTion).

**MARIO J. IPPOLITO** (Stamford, Connecticut; See Stamford listing for biographical information).

**NANCY L. IREDALE, (P.C.),** born Pasadena, California, November 27, 1947; admitted to bar, 1973, District of Columbia; 1977, California. *Education:* Georgetown University (B.S.F.S., summa cum laude, 1969); Yale University (J.D., 1972). Phi Beta Kappa. Vice President, Executive Committee, Yale Law School Association, 1982-1985. Councilor, Alpha Associates of Phi Beta Kappa Alumni in Southern California, 1986. Member: Commissioner's Advisory Group, 1990-1991; Planning Committee, USC Tax Institute, 1988—. Director, California Taxpayers' Association (Cal-Tax), 1992—. *Email:* NLIredale@PHJW.com

**EUCLID A. IRVING** (New York, New York; See New York listing for biographical information).

**JOHN GRIFFITH JOHNSON, JR.** (Washington, D.C.; see District of Columbia listing for biographical information).

**WEYMAN T. JOHNSON, JR.** (Atlanta, Georgia; See Atlanta listing for biographical information).

**ERIC H. JOSS** (Santa Monica, California; See Santa Monica listing for biographical information).

**MARGUERITE R. KAHN** (New York, New York; See New York listing for biographical information).

**JAMES W. KENNEDY** (New York, New York; See New York listing for biographical information).

**RONALD KREISMANN** (New York, New York; See New York listing for biographical information).

**THOMAS R. LAMIA** (New York, New York and Washington, D.C.; See New York and District of Columbia listings for biographical information).

**J. AL LATHAM, JR.,** born Kinston, North Carolina, September 16, 1951; admitted to bar, 1976, California; 1980, Georgia; 1984, District of Columbia. *Education:* Yale University (B.A., cum laude, 1973); Vanderbilt University (J.D., 1976). Order of the Coif. Articles Editor, Vanderbilt Law Review, 1975-1976. Lecturer in Law, University of Southern California Law Center, 1990—. Staff Director, U.S. Commission on Civil Rights, 1985-1986. Chief Counsel to National Labor Relations Board Member Dennis, 1983-1985. *Email:* JALatham@PHJW.com

**CHARLES T. LEE** (Stamford, Connecticut; See Stamford listing for biographical information).

**MICHAEL K. LINDSEY,** born Houston, Texas, June 27, 1951; admitted to bar, 1976, California. *Education:* Texas A & M University (B.S., summa cum laude, 1973); Stanford University (J.D., 1976). Phi Kappa Phi. Co-author: "Franchise Protection: Laws Against Termination and the Establishment of Additional Franchises," American Bar Association (1990). Law Extern to Hon. Raymond L. Sullivan, Associate Justice, California Supreme Court, 1975-1976. Chair, 1993—, Vice Chair, 1989-1993, Franchise and Dealership Committee, Section of Antitrust Law, American Bar Association. Member, 1987-1991, Chair, 1989-1990, Franchise Legislation Committee, State Bar of California. *Email:* MKLindsey@PHJW.com

**ETHAN LIPSIG,** born New York, New York, December 11, 1948; admitted to bar, 1974, California. *Education:* Pomona College (B.A., 1969); Oxford University, Oxford, England; University of California at Los Angeles (J.D., 1974). Order of the Coif. Comment Editor, UCLA Law Review, 1973-1974. Author: "Downsizing," BNA Books (1996). Member, Employee Benefits Committee, 1976—; Chair, Subcommittee on Federal Preemption, 1978-1979; Chair, Subcommittee on Investments and Funding, 1981, Section on Labor and Employment Law; Member, Committee on Employee Benefits, 1982—; Subcommittee on Governmental Submissions, 1992—, Section on Taxation, American Bar Association. Chair, Employee Benefits Committee, Tax Section, State Bar of California, 1981-1984. Member, Health Policy Committee, California Chamber of Commerce, 1992—. *Email:* ELipsig@PHJW.com

**G. HAMILTON LOEB** (Washington, D.C.; See District of Columbia listing for biographical information).

**KEVIN C. LOGUE** (New York, New York; See New York listing for biographical information).

**M. GUY MAISNIK,** born Burbank, California, September 28, 1957; admitted to bar, 1984, California. *Education:* University of California at Santa Barbara (B.A., 1980); Loyola Law School, Los Angeles (J.D., 1984). *Email:* MGMaisnik@PHJW.com

**PHILIP J. MARZETTI** (Atlanta, Georgia; See Atlanta listing for biographical information).

**JOHN S. McGEENEY** (Stamford, Connecticut; See Stamford listing for biographical information).

**ROGER M. MILGRIM** (New York, New York; See New York listing for biographical information).

**NANCY KENNERLY MILLER,** born San Diego, California, October 13, 1954; admitted to bar, 1980, California. *Education:* Stanford University (B.A., 1976); University of San Diego (J.D., 1979). Member, San Diego Law Review, 1978-1979. Chair, Committee on Commercial Development, Real Estate Section, Los Angeles County Bar Association, 1996—. *Email:* NNKennerly@PHJW.com

**ROBERT A. MILLER, JR.,** born Los Angeles, California, July, 30, 1954; admitted to bar, 1984, California. *Education:* University of North Dakota (B.S.B.A., 1976); Loyola Law School, Los Angeles (J.D., 1983). Member, St. Thomas More Law Honor Society. *Email:* RAMiller@PHJW.com

**CHRIS D. MOLEN** (Atlanta, Georgia; See Atlanta listing for biographical information).

**DONALD L. MORROW** (Costa Mesa, California; See Costa Mesa listing for biographical information).

**JULIAN D. NEALY** (Atlanta, Georgia; See Atlanta listing for biographical information).

**GREG M. NITZKOWSKI,** born Long Beach, California, February 22, 1957; admitted to bar, 1984, California. *Education:* Harvard College (B.A., cum laude, 1979); University of California at Los Angeles (J.D., 1984). *Email:* GMNitzkowski@PHJW.com

**CARL W. NORTHROP** (Washington, D.C.; see District of Columbia listing for biographical information).

**BELINDA K. OREM,** born Raton, New Mexico, April 15, 1951; admitted to bar, 1981, California. *Education:* University of Montana (B.A., magna cum laude, 1978); University of San Diego (J.D., magna cum laude, 1980). Associate Editor, San Diego Law Review, 1979-1980. Extern, Hon. Clifford J. Wallace, U.S. Court of Appeals, Ninth Circuit, 1980. *Email:* BKOrem@PHJW.com

**BRENDAN J. O'ROURKE** (New York, New York; See New York listing for biographical information).

**CHARLES B. ORTNER** (New York, New York; See New York listing for biographical information).

**KEVIN J. O'SHEA** (New York, New York; See New York listing for biographical information).

**RONALD M. OSTER, (P.C.),** born Bismarck, North Dakota, April 6, 1948; admitted to bar, 1973, California. *Education:* Stanford University

*(This Listing Continued)*

(A.B., with distinction, 1970; J.D., 1973). Phi Beta Kappa. Co-Chair, Stanford Moot Court Board, 1973. **Email:** RMOster@PHJW.com

**MICHAEL L. OWEN,** born Los Angeles, California, August 17, 1942; admitted to bar, 1968, California and New York. *Education:* Stanford University (A.B., with distinction, 1964); Harvard University (LL.B., 1967). Member, Executive Committee, Asia/Pacific Center for the Resolution of International Business Disputes, 1990—. Member, American Arbitration Association's International Task Force on NAFTA, 1994. **Email:** MLOwen@PHJW.com

**JOHN G. PARKER** (Atlanta, Georgia; See Atlanta listing for biographical information).

**CHARLES A. PATRIZIA** (Washington, D.C.; See District of Columbia listing for biographical information).

**PAUL L. PERITO** (Washington, D.C.; See District of Columbia listing for biographical information).

**THOMAS R. POLLOCK** (New York, New York; See New York listing for biographical information).

**JOHN E. PORTER,** born Cincinnati, Ohio, October 23, 1958; admitted to bar, 1983, California. *Education:* Stanford University (B.S., with distinction, 1980; J.D., 1983). Law Clerk, Hon. Procter Hug, U.S. Court of Appeals, Ninth Circuit, 1983-1984. **Email:** JEPorter@PHJW.c0m

**PATRICK A. RAMSEY,** born Los Angeles, California, December 11, 1950; admitted to bar, 1976, California. *Education:* University of Southern California (B.A., magna cum laude, 1973; J.D., 1976). Phi Beta Kappa; Phi Kappa Phi; Order of the Coif. Member, Southern California Law Review, 1974-1976. **Email:** PARamsey@PHJW.com

**CLAYTON S. REYNOLDS** (Stamford, Connecticut; See Stamford listing for biographical information).

**DAVID M. ROBERTS,** born Cambridge, Massachusetts, September 18, 1951; admitted to bar, 1976, California. *Education:* University of California at Davis (A.B., 1973); University of the Pacific (J.D., 1976). Managing Editor, 1975-1976, Pacific Law Journal. Law Clerk to Hon. A. Andrew Hauk, U.S. District Court, Central District of California, 1976-1977. **Email:** DMRoberts@PHJW.com

**SAMUEL D. ROSEN** (New York, New York; See New York listing for biographical information).

**BRUCE D. RYAN** (Washington, D.C.; See District of Columbia listing for biographical information).

**LEIGH P. RYAN** (New York, New York; See New York listing for biographical information).

**CHERYL R. SABAN** (New York, New York; See New York listing for biographical information).

**DOUGLAS A. SCHAAF** (Costa Mesa, California; See Costa Mesa listing for biographical information).

**WILLIAM A. SCHMIDT** (Washington, D.C.; See District of Columbia listing for biographical information).

**WILLIAM F. SCHWITTER, JR.** (New York, New York; See New York listing for biographical information).

**W. ANDREW SCOTT** (Atlanta, Georgia; See Atlanta listing for biographical information).

**CHARLES T. SHARBAUGH** (Atlanta, Georgia; See Atlanta listing for biographical information).

**PATRICK W. SHEA** (Stamford, Connecticut; See Stamford listing for biographical information).

**ROBERT L. SHERMAN** (New York, New York; see New York listing for biographical information).

**ANDREW M. SHORT** (New York, New York; See New York listing for biographical information).

**WAYNE H. SHORTRIDGE** (Atlanta, Georgia See Atlanta, listing for biographical information).

**MARC L. SILVERMAN** (New York, New York; See New York listing for biographical information).

**JOEL M. SIMON** (New York, New York; See New York listing for biographical information).

**WILLIAM J. SIMPSON** (Costa Mesa, California; See Costa Mesa listing for biographical information).

*(This Listing Continued)*

**DAVID E. SNEDIKER** (Stamford, Connecticut; See Stamford listing for biographical information).

**ROBERT S. SPAN** (Santa Monica, California; See Santa Monica listing for biographical information).

**JOHN H. STEED** (Tokyo, Japan; See Tokyo listing for biographical information).

**ALAN K. STEINBRECHER,** born Detroit, Michigan, April 13, 1946; admitted to bar, 1977, California; 1991, New York. *Education:* University of North Carolina (A.B., 1968); Duke University (J.D., 1977). Research and Managing Editor, Duke Law Journal, 1976-1977. Member, Moot Court Board. Planning Advisor and Moderator, "Product Liability," 1986. Faculty, Trial Practice Institute, California Continuing Education of the Bar, 1987. Judge Pro Tem, Los Angeles County Small Claims Court, 1986, 1987, 1988. Member, Product Liability Advisory Council. Arbitrator, Los Angeles County Superior Court, 1994—. Deputy District Attorney, Los Angeles County, 1995—. **Email:** AKSteinbrecher@PHJW.com

**GEORGE E. STEPHENS, JR., (P.C.),** born Lawrence, Kansas, March 26, 1936; admitted to bar, 1963, California. *Education:* University of Colorado; Stanford University (LL.B., 1962). Fellow: International Academy of Estate and Trust Law; American College of Trust and Estate Counsel; American Bar Foundation. **Email:** GEStephens@PHJW.com

**HARVEY A. STRICKON** (New York, New York; See New York listing for biographical information).

**KAORUHIKO SUZUKI,** born Tokyo, Japan, June 5, 1947; admitted to bar, 1975, California. *Education:* Harvard College (A.B., magna cum laude, 1971); Harvard University (J.D., 1975). Lecturer, Law and Information, Seikei University, Tokyo, Japan, 1988. (Also at Tokyo, Japan). **Email:** KSuzuki@PHJW.com

**PETER J. TENNYSON** (Costa Mesa, California; See Costa Mesa listing for biographical information).

**GEOFFREY L. THOMAS, (P.C.),** born Lindsay, California, May 12, 1944; admitted to bar, 1972, California. *Education:* Harvard College (A.B., cum laude, 1967); Stanford University (J.D., 1971). Member, Board of Editors, Stanford Law Review, 1970-1971. **Email:** GLThomas@PHJW.com

**CHARLES V. THORNTON,** born Takoma Park, Maryland, July 18, 1942; admitted to bar, 1969, California. *Education:* Cornell University (A.B., 1964); University of Michigan (J.D., 1967). Assistant Editor, Michigan Law Review, 1966-1967. Instructor, University of Pennsylvania Law School, 1967-1968. Lecturer, California Continuing Education of the Bar, 1980—. President, Board of Directors, Information and Referral Federation of Los Angeles County, 1989-1995. **Email:** CVThornton@PHJW.com

**NEIL A. TORPEY** (New York, New York; See New York listing for biographical information).

**GARY F. TORRELL,** born Buffalo, New York, May 8, 1955; admitted to bar, 1983, California. *Education:* State University of New York at Buffalo (B.S.B.A., 1977); University of Toledo; University of Virginia (J.D., 1983). **Email:** GFTorrell@PHJW.com

**JOHN E. TRINNAMAN** (Costa Mesa, California; See Costa Mesa listing for biographical information).

**DENNIS H. VAUGHN** (Santa Monica, California; See Santa Monica listing for biographical information).

**WILLIAM STEWART WALDO,** born Battle Creek, Michigan, October 10, 1951; admitted to bar, 1977, California. *Education:* Georgetown University (A.B., summa cum laude, 1973); University of Michigan (J.D., magna cum laude, 1976). Phi Beta Kappa. Associate Editor, 1974-1975; Administrative Editor, 1975-1976, Michigan Law Review. Law Clerk to Hon. Ellsworth A. Van Graafeiland, U.S. Court of Appeals, Second Circuit, 1976-1977. **Email:** WSWaldo@PHJW.comm

**ELIZABETH W. WALKER,** born Medford, Oregon, January 19, 1955; admitted to bar, 1984, California. *Education:* University of Oregon (B.S., 1977); University of San Diego (J.D., cum laude, 1983). **Email:** EW Walker@PHJW.com

**PAUL R. WALKER,** born Bronx, New York, February 6, 1945; admitted to bar, 1970, New York; 1972, California. *Education:* University of Notre Dame (A.B., 1966); University of Pennsylvania (LL.B., 1969). **Email:** PRWalker@PHJW.com

**ROBERT F. WALKER** (Santa Monica, California; see Santa Monica listing for biographical information).

*(This Listing Continued)*

**PAUL, HASTINGS, JANOFSKY & WALKER LLP, Los Angeles—Continued**

**ALAN WADE WEAKLAND,** born Palo Alto, California, February 7, 1958; admitted to bar, 1983, California. *Education:* Duke University (B.A., magna cum laude, 1980); University of Southern California (J.D., 1983). Articles Editor, Southern California Law Review, 1982-1983. *Email:* AWeakland@PHJW.com

**LAWRENCE I. WEINSTEIN** (New York, New York; See New York listing for biographical information).

**C. GEOFFREY WEIRICH** (Atlanta, Georgia; See Atlanta listing for biographical information).

**MICHAEL A. WIEGARD** (Washington, D.C.; See District of Columbia listing for biographical information).

**THOMAS S. WISIALOWSKI,** born Milwaukee, Wisconsin, March 4, 1960; admitted to bar, 1985, California. *Education:* University of Wisconsin-Whitewater (B.B.A., summa cum laude, 1982); Stanford University (J.D., 1985). Phi Kappa Phi. Adjunct Professor, Partnership Taxation, University of San Diego Law School, LL.M. in Taxation Program, 1987-1989 and University of Southern California School of Law, 1996—. Co-Chair, Subcommittee on Portfolio Investments and Withholding Tax Committee of U.S. Activities of Foreigners and Tax Treaties, Section of Taxation, American Bar Association, 1988-1996. Chair, Foreign Tax Committee, Section of Taxation, Los Angeles County Bar Association, 1993-1994. *Email:* TSWisialowski@PHJW.com

**SETH M. ZACHARY** (New York, New York; See New York listing for biographical information).

**JAMES A. ZAPP,** born Chicago, Illinois, December 27, 1946; admitted to bar, 1980, California. *Education:* Stanford University (B.S. with distinction, 1968); Loyola Law School, Los Angeles (J.D., cum laude, 1980). Phi Beta Kappa. St. Thomas More Law Honor Society. *Email:* JAZapp@PHJW.com

**HARRY A. ZINN** (Santa Monica, California; See Santa Monica listing for biographical information).

*SENIOR COUNSEL*

**ROBERT R. BURGE** (Costa Mesa, California; See Costa Mesa listing for biographical information).

**JAMES W. HAMILTON** (Costa Mesa, California; See Costa Mesa listing for biographical information).

*OF COUNSEL*

**JOHN M. BERGIN** (New York, New York; See New York listing for biographical information).

**THEODORE W. BROWNE, II** (New York, New York; See New York listing for biographical information).

**ROXANNE E. CHRIST,** born Tucson, Arizona, August 31, 1960; admitted to bar, 1985, California. *Education:* University of California at Los Angeles (B.A., 1982); Loyola Law School, Los Angeles (J.D., 1985). Staff Member, 1983-1984 and Articles Editor, 1984-1985, Loyola of Los Angeles International and Comparative Law Journal. *Email:* REChrist@PHJW.com

**EDWIN I. COLODNY** (Washington, D.C.; See District of Columbia listing for biographical information).

**MARY L. CORNWELL** (Costa Mesa, California; See Costa Mesa listing for biographical information).

**JONATHAN C. CURTIS,** born Glendale, California, April 14, 1959; admitted to bar, 1986, California; 1990, Washington. *Education:* University of California at Los Angeles (B.A., 1982); Loyola Law School, Los Angeles (J.D., cum laude, 1986). St. Thomas More Law Honor Society. *Email:* JCCurtis@PHJW.com

**JULIAN B. DECYK,** born Ellwangen, Germany, May 29, 1950; admitted to bar, 1984, California. *Education:* Amherst College (B.A., 1974); Harvard University (J.D., 1984). Adjunct Professor of Law, Income Taxation of Estates and Trusts, University of San Diego School of Law, 1987 and 1989. Member, 1975-1981 and Chairman, 1975-1979, Rhode Island Employment and Training Council. Chair, Income Tax Committee, Tax Section, Los Angeles County Bar Association, 1993-1994. *Email:* JBDecyk@PHJW.com

*(This Listing Continued)*

**WILLIAM D. DEGRANDIS** (Washington, D.C.; See District of Columbia listing for biographical information).

**LESLIE A. DENT** (Atlanta, Georgia; See Atlanta listing for biographical information).

**BRIAN J. DONNELLY,** born Youngstown, Ohio, October 27, 1937; admitted to bar, 1966, Virginia; 1972, District of Columbia; 1975, California; 1987, Texas. *Education:* Youngstown University (A.B., 1961); American University (J.D., 1965). Speaker, Capital Formation in Health Funds, Official Proceedings, International Federation of Health Funds, 15th International Conference, Auckland, New Zealand, February 1994. Member, Executive Committee, Association of California Life Insurance Companies, 1983-1993. Trustee, California Kids Trust. Delegate, California State Bar Conference of Delegates, 1977-1982. Member, Executive Committee, Los Angeles Delegation, 1981-1982. Past President, Conference of Insurance Counsel of Los Angeles. Member, Dean's Advisory Council, American University Law School, 1981-1985. *Member:* Los Angeles County Bar Association (Member, Executive Committee, Corporate Counsel Section; Co-Chair, Insurance Programs Committee, 1978-1983); Association of Life Insurance Counsel (Member, Board of Governors, 1995-1998; Chair, General Corporate Section, 1990-1993). *Email:* BJDonnelly@PHJW.com

**JANE ELIZABETH EAKINS** (Santa Monica, California; See Santa Monica listing for biographical information).

**JASON O. ENGEL** (Costa Mesa, California; See Costa Mesa listing for biographical information).

**ELLIOT K. GORDON** (Santa Monica, California; See Santa Monica listing for biographical information).

**ANNA M. GRAVES,** born Arlington, Virginia, September 26, 1959; admitted to bar, 1985, California. *Education:* Cornell University (A.B., cum laude, 1981); University of Virginia (J.D., 1985). *Email:* AMGraves@PHJW.com

**KURT W. HANSSON** (Stamford, Connecticut; See Stamford listing for biographical information).

**ANDREW S. HOLMES** (Stamford, Connecticut; See Stamford listing for biographical information).

**GAGE RANDOLPH JOHNSON** (Washington, D.C.; See District of Columbia listing for biographical information).

**STEVEN D. JOHNSON** (New York, New York; See New York listing for biographical information).

**RICK S. KIRKBRIDE,** born Torrance, California, September 25, 1954; admitted to bar, 1983, California. *Education:* University of Southern California (B.A., 1979); Loyola Law School, Los Angeles (J.D., 1983). Certified Public Accountant, California, 1983. *Email:* RSKirkbride@PHJW.com

**THOMAS J. KNAPP** (Washington, D.C.; See District of Columbia for biographical information).

**PETER W. LAVIGNE** (New York, New York; See New York listing for biographical information).

**SCOTT N. LESLIE** (Costa Mesa, California; See Costa Mesa listing for biographical information).

**A. ALAN MANNING,** born Los Angeles, California, September 12, 1961; admitted to bar, 1986, California. *Education:* University of Southern California (B.S., summa cum laude, 1982); University of California at Los Angeles (J.D., 1986). President, Blackstonian Honor Society, 1982-1983. Junior Staff Member, 1984-1985 and Editor, 1985-1986, UCLA Law Review. Extern, Hon. Malcolm M. Lucas, Associate Justice, California Supreme Court, Spring, 1985. Chairman, Business and Corporate Law Section, Orange County Bar Association, 1993. *Email:* AAManning@PHJW.com

**DEBORAH A. MARLOWE** (Atlanta Georgia; See Atlanta listing for biographical information).

**NEAL D. MOLLEN** (Washington, D.C.; See District of Columbia for biographical information).

**ROBERT C. MOOT, JR.** (Atlanta, Georgia; See Atlanta listing for biographical information).

**SEAN A. O'BRIEN** (Costa Mesa, California; See Costa Mesa listing for biographical information).

**TETSUYA OGAWA** (Tokyo, Japan; See Tokyo listing for biographical information).

*(This Listing Continued)*

***CRAIG K. PENDERGRAST*** (Atlanta, Georgia; See Atlanta listing for biographical information).

***GLORIA C. PHARES*** (New York, New York; See New York listing for biographical information).

***DAVID S. PHELPS,*** born Los Angeles, California, March 7, 1960; admitted to bar, 1987, California. *Education:* Stanford University (B.A., with honors, 1982); University of Southern California (J.D., 1986). *Email:* DSPhelps@PHJW.com

***ROBERT S. PLOTKIN*** (Washington, D.C.; See District of Columbia listing for biographical information).

***ROBERT E. POKUSA*** (Washington, D.C.; See District of Columbia listing for biographical information).

***LUCY PRASHKER*** (New York, New York; See New York listing for biographical information).

***DAVID E. RABIN*** (Stamford, Connecticut; see Stamford listing for biographical information).

***WILLIAM THOMAS REEDER, JR.*** (Washington, D.C.; See District of Columbia listing for full biographical information).

***ANTHONY J. ROSSI,*** born Los Angeles, California, October 11, 1932; admitted to bar, 1961, California. *Education:* University of Southern California (B.A., 1957; J.D., 1960); New York University (LL.M., 1961). Order of the Coif. Member, Board of Editors, University of Southern California Law Review, 1958-1959. Member, and Chairman-Elect, 1996-1997, Executive Committee of Real Property Section, Los Angeles County Bar Association. Member, Board of Visitors, Southwestern University School of Law. Member, Advisory Committee, University of Southern California School of Urban and Regional Planning. *Email:* AJRossi@PHJW.com

***CHRISTINE A. SCHEUNEMAN,*** born Kansas City, Missouri, December 30, 1950; admitted to bar, 1981, Illinois; 1984, California. *Education:* Cottey College (A.A., 1970); University of Kansas (B.A., 1972); De Paul University (J.D., 1981). Order of the Barristers. Member, Moot Court Society Executive Board. Law Clerk to Hon. Albert Green, Chancery Circuit Court, Chicago, Illinois, 1981-1983. Member, National Panel of Arbitrators, American Arbitration Association. President, Board of Directors, Orange County Chamber Orchestra, 1989-1992. *Email:* CAScheuneman@PHJW.com

***CHARLES A. SHANOR*** (Atlanta, Georgia and Washington, D.C.; see District of Columbia and Atlanta listings for biographical information).

***MARGARET H. SPURLIN*** (Washington, D.C.; See District of Columbia listing for biographical information).

***TAKASHI SUZUKI*** (Tokyo Japan; See Tokyo listing for biographical information).

***JEFFREY G. VARGA,*** born Budapest, Hungary, December 22, 1950; admitted to bar, 1978, California. *Education:* University of California at Los Angeles (B.A., 1972); University of San Diego (J.D., cum laude, 1978). Executive Editor, San Diego Law Review, 1977-1978. Trial Attorney, U.S. Department of Justice, Tax Division, Criminal Section, 1978-1981. Assistant United States Attorney, Tax Division, Central District of California, 1981-1988. Chair, State and Local Tax Committee, Taxation Section, Los Angeles County Bar Association, 1993-1994. [LTJG, U.S. Navy, 1972-1975] *Email:* JGVarga@PHJW.com

***WILLIAM P. WADE,*** born Los Angeles, California, March 31, 1947; admitted to bar, 1972, California. *Education:* University of Southern California (B.S., cum laude, 1969); University of California at Los Angeles (J.D., 1972). Member, UCLA Law Review, 1971-1972. *Email:* WPWade@PHJW.com

***PHILIP R. WEINGOLD*** (New York, New York; See New York listing for biographical information).

***PATRICK J. WHITTLE*** (Washington, D.C.; see District of Columbia listing for biographical information).

***KENNETH M. WILLNER*** (Washington, D.C.; See District of Columbia listing for biographical information).

***MICHAEL S. WOODWARD,*** born Huntington Park, California, May 22, 1950; admitted to bar, 1976, California. *Education:* California State University at Northridge; University of California at Los Angeles (B.A., 1971); Georgetown University (J.D., 1976). Deputy City Attorney, Los Angeles City Attorneys' Office, 1979-1988. *Email:* MSWoodward@PHJW.com

*(This Listing Continued)*

***GERALD H. YAMADA*** (Washington, D.C.; See District of Columbia listing for biographical information).

***DARLA L. YANCEY*** (Costa Mesa, California; See Costa Mesa listing for biographical information).

***CLARISSE W. J. YOUNG,*** born Tokyo, Japan, October 18, 1957; admitted to bar, 1982, California. *Education:* University of Hawaii (B.A., with high honors, 1979); University of Michigan (J.D., 1982). Phi Beta Kappa; Phi Kappa Phi. *Email:* CWYoung@PHJW.com

*ASSOCIATES*

***LESLIE ABBOTT*** (Santa Monica, California; See Santa Monica listing for biographical information).

***GEORGE W. ABELE,*** born Rockville Centre, New York, October 16, 1963; admitted to bar, 1990, California. *Education:* University of Virginia (B.A., with distinction, 1985); University of California at Los Angeles (J.D., 1990). Member and Associate Editor, UCLA Law Review, 1988-1990. Intern, National Labor Relations Board, Office of Appeals, 1989. *Email:* GWAbele@PHJW.com

***ELIOT J. ABT*** (Atlanta, Georgia; See Atlanta listing for biographical information).

***ELIZABETH A. ADOLFF*** (Stamford, Connecticut; See Stamford listing for biographical information).

***TERRY JON ALLEN*** (Costa Mesa, California; See Costa Mesa listing for biographical information).

***STEVEN D. ALLISON*** (Costa Mesa, California; See Costa Mesa listing for biographical information).

***KENNETH T. ARAKI,*** born Santa Monica, California, April 24, 1963; admitted to bar, 1990, California. *Education:* University of Hawaii (B.A., 1985); University of California at Berkeley (M.B.A., 1990); University of California, Boalt Hall (J.D., 1990). *Email:* KTAraki@PHJW.com

***PETER ARONSON,*** born Port Elizabeth, South Africa, December 29, 1967; admitted to bar, 1992, California. *Education:* American University (B.A., magna cum laude, 1988); Georgetown University (J.D., cum laude, 1991). Phi Beta Kappa. *Email:* PAronson@PHJW.com

***ELENA R. BACA,*** born Santa Monica, California, February 4, 1967; admitted to bar, 1992, California. *Education:* Arizona State University (B.S., 1988); University of Notre Dame (J.D., 1992). *Email:* ERBaca@PHJW.com

***JENNIFER STIVERS BALDOCCHI,*** born Bayonne, New Jersey, April 5, 1968; admitted to bar, 1993, California. *Education:* University of California at Berkeley (B.A., cum laude, 1990); Loyola Law School, Los Angeles (J.D., 1993). Order of the Coif; St. Thomas More Law Honor Society. Member, 1991-1992 and Note and Comment Editor, 1992-1993, Loyola of Los Angeles Law Review. *Email:* JSBaldocchi@PHJW.com

***TRACEY T. BARBAREE*** (Atlanta, Georgia; See Atlanta listing for biographical information).

***MICHELE L. BARBER,*** born Carlisle, Pennsylvania, November 19, 1969; admitted to bar, 1995, California. *Education:* University of California at Los Angeles (B.A.,1992); University of Southern California (J.D., 1995). *Email:* MLBarberPHJW.com

***KIRBY D. BEHRE*** (Washington, D.C.; See District of Columbia listing for biographical information).

***BRENT J. BELNAP*** (New York, New York; See New York listing for biographical information).

***DAVID S. BENYACAR*** (New York, New York; See New York listing for biographical information).

***PATRICIA M. BERRY,*** born Havana, Cuba, September 30, 1953; admitted to bar, 1991, California. *Education:* University of Redlands (B.A., 1975); University of Washington (M.F.A., 1981); University of Southern California (J.D., 1990). Order of the Coif. Member, University of Southern California Law Review, 1988-1990. *Email:* PMBerry@PHJW.com

***JAMES R. BLISS*** (Stamford, Connecticut; See Stamford listing for biographical information).

***STEPHANIE A. BOHM*** (Atlanta, Georgia; See Atlanta listing for biographical information).

***BRENT R. BOHN*** (Costa Mesa, California; See Costa Mesa listing for biographical information).

*(This Listing Continued)*

CAA1089B

**PAUL, HASTINGS, JANOFSKY & WALKER LLP**, Los Angeles—Continued

**DAVID B. BOOKER** (New York, New York; See New York listing for biographical information).

**ROBERT L. BOYD** (New York, New York; See New York listing for biographical information).

**DEBORAH M. BRADLEY** (Atlanta, Georgia; see Atlanta listing for biographical information).

**MARIAN L. BRANCACCIO** (New York, New York; See New York listing for biographical information).

**GLENN L. BRIGGS** (Costa Mesa, California; See Costa Mesa listing for biographical information).

**MARK BRONSON**, born Denver, Colorado, February 10, 1963; admitted to bar, 1989, California. *Education:* University of California at Santa Barbara (B.A., with highest honors, 1985); Stanford University (J.D., 1989). Editor, Stanford Environmental Law Journal, 1987-1989. *Email:* MLBronson@PHJW.com

**SHERYL J. BROWN** (Washington, D.C.; See District of Columbia listing for biographical information).

**ROBERT P. BRYANT** (Costa Mesa, California; See Costa Mesa listing for biographical information).

**DAVID D. BURNS** (Washington, D.C.; see District of Columbia listing for biographical information).

**CHRISTINE E. CAHILL** (Atlanta, Georgia; See Atlanta listing for biographical information).

**JOSEPH A. CALLARI** (Stamford, Connecticut; See Stamford listing for biographical information).

**GWYNETH A. CAMPBELL**, born Long Beach, California, February 5, 1964; admitted to bar, 1989, California. *Education:* Baylor University (B.A., with honors, 1986); University of Texas, Austin (J.D., 1989). *Email:* GACampbell@PHJW.com

**ROBERT R. CARLSON**, born August 24, 1970; admitted to bar, 1995, California. *Education:* University of California at Berkeley (A.B., 1992), Phi Beta Kappa; Harvard University (J.D., cum laude, 1995). *Email:* RRCarlson@PHJW.com

**DIANNE C. CARRAWAY** (Washington, D.C.; See District of Columbia listing for biographical information).

**PATRICIA M. CARROLL** (New York, New York; See New York listing for biographical information).

**MARIE CENSOPLANO** (New York, New York; See New York listing for biographical information).

**SARKA CERNA-FAGAN** (New York, New York; See New York, New York listing for biographical information).

**VERONICA J. CHERNIAK** (Atlanta, Georgia; See Atlanta listing for biographical information).

**ALPA PATEL CHERNOF**, born Toledo, Ohio, December 10, 1966; admitted to bar, 1991, California; 1992, District of Columbia. *Education:* University of Miami (B.A., cum laude, 1988); Georgetown University (J.D., cum laude, 1991). Phi Beta Kappa; Phi Kappa Phi. Member, American Criminal Law Review, 1989-1991. Member, Board of Directors, Los Angeles Commission on Assaults Against Women, 1995—. *Email:* APChernof@PHJW.com

**TANYEE CHEUNG** (New York, New York; See New York listing for biographical information).

**JUSTIN C. CHOI** (New York, New York; See New York listing for biographical information).

**JOHN H. CLAYTON** (New York, New York; see New York listing for biographical information).

**A. CRAIG CLELAND** (Atlanta, Georgia; See Atlanta listing for biographical information).

**MICHELLE WEISBERG COHEN** (Washington, D.C.; See District of Columbia listing for biographical information).

**CHRISTOPHER H. CRAIG** (Stamford, Connecticut; See Stamford listing for Biographical information).

*(This Listing Continued)*

**SANDRA A. CRAWSHAW** (New York, New York; See New York listing for biographical information).

**CHRISTINE M. CROWE** (Washington, D.C.; see District of Columbia listing for biographical information).

**KATHLEEN O. CURREY** (Atlanta, Georgia; see Atlanta listing for biographical information).

**MARC A. DANIEL** (New York, New York; see New York listing for biographical information).

**BARBARA R. DANZ** (Costa Mesa, California; See Costa Mesa listing for biographical information).

**CINDY J.K. DAVIS** (Atlanta, Georgia; See Atlanta listing for biographical information).

**ERIC B. DAVIS** (New York, New York; See New York listing for biographical information).

**JEANNE R. DAWSON**, born Artesia, California, January 8, 1947; admitted to bar, 1984, California. *Education:* California State University at Long Beach (B.A., 1970); Loyola Law School, Los Angeles (J.D., cum laude, 1984). St. Thomas More Law Honor Society. *Email:* JRDawson@PHJW.com

**BEHNAM DAYANIM** (Washington, D.C.; See District of Columbia listing for biographical information).

**DANIEL P. DELANEY**, born Anchorage, Alaska, December 31, 1965; admitted to bar, 1992, California. *Education:* Stanford University (A.B., with distinction, 1988); University of California at Los Angeles (J.D., 1992). *Email:* DPDelaney@PHJW.com

**S. MARK DENHAM**, born Sao Paulo, Brazil, November 7, 1967; admitted to bar, 1995, California. *Education:* Liberty University (B.S., 1990); University of Virginia (J.D., 1994). *Email:* SMDenham@PHJW.com

**ALEJANDRO J. DIAZ** (Stamford, Connecticut; See Stamford listing for biographical information).

**KRISTINA H. DINERMAN**, born New York, New York, March 14, 1969; admitted to bar, 1994, California. *Education:* Loyola Marymount University (B.A., cum laude, 1991); Loyola Law School, Los Angeles (J.D., 1994),. *Email:* KHDinerman@PHJW.com

**MARY C. DOLLARHIDE** (Stamford, Connecticut; See Stamford listing for biographical information).

**JESSICA S. DORMAN-DAVIS** (Costa Mesa, California; See Costa Mesa listing for biographical information).

**PATRICIA A. DRISCOLL** (Stamford, Connecticut; See Stamford listing for biographical information).

**MICHAEL W. DUBUS** (Atlanta, Georgia; See Atlanta listing for biographical information).

**JOHN C. DWORKIN** (New York, New York; see New York listing for biographical information).

**HAROLD N. EDDY, JR.** (Stamford, Connecticut; See Stamford listing for biographical information).

**LINDA M. EDWARDS** (Santa Monica, California; See Santa Monica listing for biographical information).

**SUSAN LANGLEY ELLIOT** (Atlanta, Georgia; See Atlanta listing for biographical information).

**DENNIS S. ELLIS**, born San Diego, California, October 30, 1967; admitted to bar, 1995, California. *Education:* California State University (B.B.A., cum laude, 1990); Howard University (J.D., 1995). *Email:* DSEllis@PHJW.com

**JEWELL L. ESPOSITO** (Washington, D.C.; See District of Columbia listing for biographical information).

**WILLIAM P. EWING** (Atlanta, Georgia; See Atlanta listing for biographical information).

**MALINDA A. FABER** (Costa Mesa, California; See Costa Mesa listing for biographical information).

**WENDELL M. FARIA** (Washington, D.C.; See District of Columbia listing for biographical information).

**ELIZABETH A. FEALY** (New York, New York; See New York listing for biographical information).

*(This Listing Continued)*

## PROFESSIONAL BIOGRAPHIES — CALIFORNIA—LOS ANGELES

*ALAN M. FELD* (New York, New York; see New York listing for biographical information).

*BENJAMIN J. FERRON* (New York, New York; See New York listing for biographical information).

*VIOLET F. FIACCO* (Costa Mesa, California; See Costa Mesa listing for biographical information).

*REGINA M. FLAHERTY* (Stamford, Connecticut; See Stamford listing for biographical information).

*SCOTT M. FLICKER* (Washington, D.C.; See District of Columbia listing for biographical information).

*LAURA A. FORBES* (Costa Mesa, California; See Costa Mesa listing for biographical information).

*MICHELE FREEDENTHAL,* born Waterbury, Connecticut, September 16, 1963; admitted to bar, 1990, California. *Education:* University of Pennsylvania (B.S., cum laude, 1984); University of Texas at Austin (M.S., 1990; J.D., with honors, 1990). Member, The Review of Litigation, 1989-1990. *Email:* MFreedenthal@PHJW.com

*MARGO E. FREEDMAN,* born Detroit, Michigan, May 19, 1966; admitted to bar, 1992, California. *Education:* University of Michigan (B.B.A., 1988; J.D., 1991). *Email:* MEFreedman@PHJW.com

*PHILIP E. FRIED* (New York, New York; See New York listing for biographical information).

*INTRA L. GERMANIS* (Washington, D.C.; See District of Columbia listing for biographical information).

*DAVID E. GEVERTZ* (Atlanta, Georgia; See Atlanta listing for biographical information).

*LISA M. GIGLIOTTI* (New York, New York; See New York listing for biographical information).

*RONALD K. GILLER,* born New York, New York, October 27, 1963; admitted to bar, 1989, California. *Education:* University of California at Los Angeles (B.A., magna cum laude, 1986; J.D., 1989). Phi Beta Kappa. *Email:* RKGiller@PHJW.com

*MARGARET A. GILLERAN* (New York, New York; See New York listing for biographical information).

*MARK A. GLOADE* (New York, New York; See New York listing for biographical information).

*KAREN K. GREENWALT,* born San Diego, California, March 6, 1945; admitted to bar, 1993, California. *Education:* Occidental College (B.A.); Loyola Law School, Los Angeles (J.D., 1993). *Email:* KKGreenwalt@PHJW.com

*E. JEFFREY GRUBE,* born Putnam, Connecticut, December 5, 1964; admitted to bar, 1993, California. *Education:* University of California, Irvine (B.A., 1988); University of Southern California (J.D., 1993). Executive Editor, Southern California Law Review, 1992-1993. *Email:* EJGrube@PHJW.com

*DELIA GUEVARA,* born Hollywood, California, May 23, 1964; admitted to bar, 1990, California. *Education:* University of California at San Diego (B.A., cum laude, 1986); University of California at Los Angeles (J.D., 1989). *Email:* DYGuevara@PHJW.com

*JOHN W. HAMLIN* (Stamford, Connecticut; See Stamford listing for biographical information).

*ANDREW P. HANSON* (Costa Mesa, California; See Costa Mesa listing for biographical information).

*SUSAN E. HIMMER* (Atlanta, Georgia; See Atlanta listing for biographical information).

*ERIC J. HOFFMAN,* born Washington, D.C., August 13, 1969; admitted to bar, 1996, California. *Education:* University of California at Irvine (B.A., 1991); University of Southern California (J.D., 1994). Order of the Coif. *Email:* EJHoffman@PHJW.com

*STACY M. HOPKINS,* born Cape Girardeau, Missouri, May 10, 1958; admitted to bar, 1994, California. *Education:* California State University (B.A., 1991); Pepperdine University (J.D., magna cum laude, 1994). Associate Editor, 1993-1994, Staff Member, 1992-1993, Pepperdine Law Review. Judicial Clerk to Hon. Alan M. Ahart, U.S. Bankruptcy Judge, Central District of California, 1994-1996. *Email:* SMHopkins@PHJW.com

*ALAN B. HOROWITZ* (Washington, D.C.; See District of Columbia listing for biographical information).

*JAMES CHE-MING HSU* (New York, New York; See New York listing for biographical information).

*SCOTT N. HUDSON* (New York, New York; See New York listing for biographical information).

*LISA G. HUFFINESS* (New York, New York; See New York listing for biographical information).

*JAMES JUDSON JACKSON* (Stamford, Connecticut; see Stamford listing for biographical information).

*MARCIA N. JACKSON* (Santa Monica, California; See Santa Monica listing for biographical information).

*MICHAEL B. JAFFE* (Stamford, Connecticut; See Stamford listing for biographical information).

*EDWARD S. JOHNSON, JR.* (Atlanta, Georgia; See Atlanta listing for biographical information).

*JARRET L. JOHNSON* (Costa Mesa, California; See Costa Mesa listing for biographical information).

*E. ASHTON JOHNSTON* (Washington, D.C.; see District of Columbia listing for biographical information).

*GEORGE R.A. JONES* (Washington, D.C.; See District of Columbia listing for biographical information).

*KAREN E. JORIK* (Atlanta, Georgia; see Atlanta listing for biographical information).

*MICHAEL B. KAUFMAN* (New York, New York; see New York listing for biographical information).

*DEIDRE M. KELLY,* born Los Angeles, California, January 10, 1966; admitted to bar, 1989, California. *Education:* University of Southern California (B.A., cum laude, 1986); Loyola Law School of Los Angeles (J.D., 1989). *Email:* DMKelly@PHJW.com

*TARA K. KELLY,* born Lakewood, Ohio, October 9, 1968; admitted to bar, 1995, California. *Education:* Tufts University (B.A., 1990); University of Southern California (J.D., 1995). Member, Southern California Law Review, 1993-1994. Member, Editorial Board, Southern California Review of Law and Women's Studies. *Email:* TKKelly@PHJW.com

*ANN T. KENNY* (New York, New York; see New York listing for biographical information).

*MARC E. KENNY,* born Bloomington, Indiana, March 29, 1969; admitted to bar, 1995, California. *Education:* Bucknell University; Boston University (J.D., cum laude, 1995). *Email:* MEKenny@PHJW.com

*JONG HAN KIM,* born Seoul, Korea, August 1, 1963; admitted to bar, 1989, California. *Education:* Georgetown University (B.S.F.S., magna cum laude, 1986; J.D., cum laude, 1989). *Email:* JHKim@PHJW.com

*KEN KIMURA* (New York, New York; See New York listing for full biographical information).

*EILEEN M. KING* (New York, New York; See New York listing for biographical information).

*ROSEMARY MAHAR KIRBACH,* admitted to bar, 1990, California. *Education:* Pennsylvania State University (B.S., with high distinction, 1986); Columbia University (J.D., 1990). Harlan Fiske Stone Scholar. Certified Public Accountant, Illinois, 1988. *Email:* RMKirbach@PHJW.com

*JANET L. KISHBAUGH* (Atlanta, Georgia; See Atlanta listing for biographical information).

*KAREN L. KLEIDERMAN,* born New York, New York, June 16, 1962; admitted to bar, 1987, California. *Education:* University of California at Los Angeles (B.A., 1984); George Washington University (J.D., with high honors, 1987). Order of the Coif. Member, 1985-1986 and Managing Editor, 1986-1987, George Washington Law Review. *Email:* KLKleiderman@PHJW.com

*JUDITH M. KLINE,* born St. Louis, Missouri, February 24, 1966; admitted to bar, 1991, California. *Education:* University of Notre Dame (B.A., summa cum laude, 1988); Harvard University (J.D., 1991). Phi Beta Kappa. *Email:* JMKline@PHJW.com

*CHERYL L. KOPITZKE* (Santa Monica, California; see Santa Monica listing for biographical information).

*(This Listing Continued)*

**PAUL, HASTINGS, JANOFSKY & WALKER LLP**, Los Angeles—Continued

*LISA M. LAFOURCADE* (Costa Mesa, California; See Costa Mesa listing for biographical information).

*DOUGLAS E. LAHAMMER,* born Moorhead, Minnesota, November 16, 1963; admitted to bar, 1990, California. *Education:* University of Minnesota (B.A., summa cum laude, 1986; J.D., cum laude, 1989). Phi Beta Kappa. Associate Editor, Minnesota Law Review, 1988-1989. Law Clerk, Hon. Peter S. Popovich, Chief Justice, Minnesota Supreme Court, 1989-1990. *Email:* DELahammer@PHJW.com

*GREGORY F. LANG* (Stamford, Connecticut; See Stamford listing for biographical information).

*LISA J. LAPLACE* (New York, New York; See New York listing for biographical information).

*ARIC H. LASKY,* born Los Angeles, California, September 20, 1967; admitted to bar, 1994, California. *Education:* University of California at Irvine (B.A., 1989); University of Southern California (J.D., M.R.E.D., 1994). *Email:* AHLasky@PHJW.com

*DAVID S. LEVIN* (New York, New York; See New York listing for biographical information).

*ERIC T. LEVINE* (Stamford, Connecticut; See Stamford listing for biographical information).

*BRIGITTE P. LIPPMANN* (New York, New York; see New York listing for biographical information).

*KATHERINE B. LIPTON* (New York, New York; See New York listing for biographical information).

*VINCENT D. LOWDER* (Costa Mesa, California; See Costa Mesa listing for biographical information).

*ROBERT L. MADOK,* born Los Angeles, California, November 11, 1963; admitted to bar, 1991, California. *Education:* Georgetown University (B.A., 1985); University of Southern California (J.D., 1991). *Email:* RLMadok@PHJW.com

*JENIFER A. MAGYAR* (Stamford, Connecticut; See Stamford listing for biographical information).

*CHRISTOPHER J. MANFREDI,* born Santa Monica, California, November 28, 1969; admitted to bar, 1995, California. *Education:* Pomona College (B.A., cum laude, 1991), Phi Beta Kappa; New York University (J.D., 1995). *Email:* CJManfredi@PHJW.com

*PAUL C. MARAZITA* (Stamford, Connecticut; See Stamford listing for biographical information).

*MICHAEL S. MARX,* born Sacramento, California, December 21, 1962; admitted to bar, 1988, California. *Education:* University of Southern California (B.S., 1985); University of California, Boalt Hall (J.D., 1988). *Email:* MSMarx@PHJW.com

*ANDREW M. MAYER* (New York, New York; See New York listing for biographical information).

*KATHLEEN L. MCACHRAN,* born St. Louis, Missouri, May 5, 1966; admitted to bar, 1990, California; 1993, District of Columbia. *Education:* Texas Christian University (B.A., magna cum laude, 1987); Harvard University (J.D., 1990). Phi Beta Kappa. *Email:* KLMcAchran@PHJW.com

*P. CASEY MCGANNON,* born Palo Alto, California, March 22, 1966; admitted to bar, 1993, California. *Education:* Stanford University (B.A., 1988); University of Southern California, Los Angeles (J.D., 1993). *Email:* PCMcGann@PHJW.com

*DENISE MARIE MCGORRIN,* born Lansing, Michigan, November 3, 1959; admitted to bar, 1985, Michigan; 1988, California. *Education:* Western Michigan University (B.A., magna cum laude, 1981); College of William & Mary (J.D., 1985). Staff Member, William & Mary Law Review, 1984-1985. *Email:* DMMcGorrin@PHJW.com

*SARAH M. MCWILLIAMS* (Washington, D.C.; See District of Columbia listing for biographical information).

*MARTIN C. MEAD,* born Arab, Alabama, July 15, 1965; admitted to bar, 1990, California. *Education:* Birmingham-Southern College (B.S., summa cum laude, 1987); Harvard University (J.D., 1990). Phi Beta Kappa. *Email:* MCMead@PHJW.com

*(This Listing Continued)*

*JON DOUGLAS MEER,* born Amherst, New York, December 8, 1963; admitted to bar, 1989, California. *Education:* Cornell University (B.S., with honors, 1986); Boston University (J.D., 1989). Phi Kappa Phi. *Email:* JDMeer@PHJW.com

*MICHAEL T. MERVIS* (New York, New York; See New York listing for biographical information).

*INGRID M. MESA* (New York, New York; See New York listing for biographical information).

*CARA D. MILLER* (Santa Monica, California; See Santa Monica listing for biographical information).

*J. CLARK MILLER,* born Sacramento, California, June 2, 1965; admitted to bar, 1995, California. *Education:* University of Southern California (B.S., 1987); University of Virginia (J.D., 1995). *Email:* JCMiller@PHJW.com

*SCOTT R. MILLER* (Costa Mesa, California; See Costa Mesa listing for biographical information).

*HARUKI MINAKI,* born Honolulu, Hawaii, June 5, 1962; admitted to bar, 1990, California. *Education:* Princeton University (B.A., 1985); University of Southern California (J.D., 1990). Member, Computer Law and Major Tax Planning Journals, 1988-1989. *Email:* HMinaki@PHJW.com

*HEATHER MORGAN* (Santa Monica, California; See Santa Monica listing for biographical information).

*JAY A. MORRISON* (Washington, D.C.; See District of Columbia listing for biographical information).

*MELINDA L. MOSELEY* (Atlanta, Georgia; See Atlanta listing for biographical information).

*JOHN J. NEELY, III* (Atlanta, Georgia; See Atlanta listing for biographical information).

*ELIZABETH A. NEWELL* (New York, New York; See New York listing for biographical information).

*ELIZABETH HARDY NOE* (Atlanta, Georgia; See Atlanta listing for biographical information).

*J. YOHEVED NOVOGRODER* (New York, New York; see New York listing for biographical information).

*ROBERT J. ODSON,* born Los Angeles, California, December 15, 1963; admitted to bar, 1992, California. *Education:* Occidental College (B.A., cum laude, 1986); University of Southern California (J.D., 1992). Managing Editor, Southern California Law Review. *Email:* RJOdson@PHJW.com

*JOHN C. O'MALLEY,* born Pittsburgh, Pennsylvania, May 21, 1964; admitted to bar, 1989, California. *Education:* Amherst College (B.A., 1986); Boston College (J.D., cum laude, 1989). *Email:* JCOmalley@PHJW.com

*MAUREEN E. O'NEILL* (Atlanta, Georgia; See Atlanta listing for biographical information).

*JOSEPH P. OPICH* (New York, New York; See New York listing for biographical information).

*DEANNE H. OZAKI,* born Yokosuka, Japan, August 6, 1966; admitted to bar, 1991, California. *Education:* University of California at Los Angeles (B.A., magna cum laude, 1988); University of California, Boalt Hall (J.D., 1991). Phi Beta Kappa. Associate Editor, High Technology Law Journal, 1990-1991. Member, U.S. Regulatory Subcommittee, Regulatory Analysis Committee, International Trademark Association, 1996-1997.

*VINCENT J. PASQUARIELLO* (New York, New York; See New York listing for biographical information).

*SUSAN M. PAVLIN* (Atlanta, Georgia; See Atlanta listing for biographical information).

*JOSEPH D. PENACHIO* (New York, New York; See New York listing for biographical information).

*SUZANNE MARIE PEPE-ROBBINS* (Stamford, Connecticut; See Stamford listing for biographical information).

*BONNIE PIERSON-MURPHY* (Stamford, Connecticut; See Stamford listing for biographical information).

*ALEXIS PINTO* (New York, New York; See New York listing for biographical information).

*SARA RABINOWITZ PINTO* (New York, New York; See New York listing for biographical information).

*(This Listing Continued)*

**LESLIE A. PLASKON** (Stamford, Connecticut; See Stamford listing for biographical information).

**TRACY S. PLOTT** (Atlanta, Georgia; See Atlanta listing for biographical information).

**LISA A. POPOVICH,** born Whittier, California, May 19, 1960; admitted to bar, 1985, California. *Education:* University of Southern California (B.S., cum laude, 1982); Loyola Law School, Los Angeles (J.D., 1985). Editor, Loyola of Los Angeles International and Comparative Law Journal, 1984-1985. *Email:* LAPopovich@PHJW.com

**NANCY E. RAFUSE** (Atlanta, Georgia; See Atlanta listing for biographical information).

**PHILIP J. RAGONA** (New York, New York; See New York listing for biographical information).

**LYNNE H. RAMBO** (Atlanta, Georgia; See Atlanta listing for biographical information).

**T. ROBERT REID** (Atlanta, Georgia; see Atlanta listing for biographical information).

**ELLEN C. RICE** (Washington, D.C.; See District of Columbia listing for biographical information).

**PETER J. ROTH,** born Cook County, Illinois, February 3, 1968; admitted to bar, 1993, California. *Education:* Duke University (A.B., cum laude, 1990; J.D., 1993). Member, Alaska Law Review, 1992-1993. *Email:* PJRoth@PHJW.com

**JOEL H. ROTHSTEIN,** born New York, New York, October 10, 1963; admitted to bar, 1990, California; 1993, District of Columbia and Colorado. *Education:* University of California at Los Angeles (B.A., magna cum laude, 1985); Columbia University (M.S., 1987); New York University (J.D., 1990). Phi Beta Kappa. Associate Editor, 1989-1990 and Member, 1988-1989, New York University Review of Law and Social Change. *Email:* JHRothstein@PHJW.com

**DENA T. SACCO** (Washington, D.C.; See District of Columbia listing for biographical information).

**ALFRED SANCHEZ, JR.,** born El Paso, Texas, October 17, 1966; admitted to bar, 1995, California. *Education:* California State University at Fullerton (B.A., 1992); University of Southern California (J.D., 1995). Articles Editor, Southern California Law Review. *Email:* ASanchez@PHJW.com

**ALLYSON G. SAUNDERS,** born New York, New York, March 7, 1954; admitted to bar, 1987, California. *Education:* State University of New York at Buffalo (B.A., cum laude, 1977); Loyola Law School, Los Angeles (J.D., 1987). Extern, Hon. Wm. Matthew Byrne, Jr., U.S. District Court, Central District of California, 1986. *Email:* AGSaunders@PHJW.com

**MATHEW ANTHONY SCHUH** (Atlanta, Georgia; See Atlanta listing for biographical information).

**GLORI J. SCHULTZ,** born Bay City, Michigan, March 11, 1970; admitted to bar, 1995, California. *Education:* University of Michigan (B.S., 1992); University of Southern California (J.D., 1995). Member: Southern California Law Review, 1994-1995; Review of Law and Women's Studies, 1993-1995. *Email:* GJSchultz@PHJW.com

**SUSAN E. SCHWARTZ,** born Long Island, New York, January 20, 1962; admitted to bar, 1994, California. *Education:* Pennsylvania State University (B.A., magna cum laude, 1984); Loyola Law School, Los Angeles (J.D., 1993). Phi Beta Kappa. *Email:* SESchwartz@PHJW.com

**CRAIG S. SELIGMAN,** born Boston, Massachusetts, July 5, 1960; admitted to bar, 1990, California. *Education:* Dartmouth College (B.A., 1981; B.E., 1982); Southwestern University School of Law (J.D., magna cum laude, 1990). *PRACTICE AREAS:* Corporate Law; Securities Law; Acquisitions, Divestitures and Mergers Law. *Email:* CSSeligman@PHJW.com

**LEE R. SELTMAN,** born Lincoln, Nebraska, November 12, 1968; admitted to bar, 1994, California. *Education:* Andrews University (B.A., summa cum laude, 1990); University of Southern California (J.D., 1993). Order of the Coif. Member, 1991-1992, Articles Editor, 1992-1993, Southern California Law Review. *Email:* LRSeltman@PHJW.com

**NANCY E. SHALLOW** (Washington, D.C.; See District of Columbia listing for biographical information).

**JOSEPH C. SHARP** (Atlanta, Georgia; See Atlanta listing for biographical information).

**ERIC M. SHERBET** (New York, New York; See New York listing for biographical information).

**GLENN C. SHRADER,** born San Francisco, California, January 15, 1960; admitted to bar, 1989, California. *Education:* University of California at Santa Cruz (B.A., with honors, 1983); Georgetown University (J.D., cum laude, 1989). Executive Editor, The Tax Lawyer, 1988-1989. *Email:* GCShrader@PHJW.com

**BETTY M. SHUMENER,** born Haifa, Israel, October 14, 1952; admitted to bar, 1988, California. *Education:* University of California at Los Angeles (B.A., cum laude, 1974; M.A., with honors, 1976; Ph.D., 1983); Loyola Law School, Los Angeles (J.D., cum laude, 1988). Order of the Coif. St. Thomas More Law Honor Society. *Email:* BMShumener@PHJW.com

**DEREK E. SMITH,** born Salt Lake City, Utah, February 25, 1964; admitted to bar, 1991, California. *Education:* Brigham Young University (B.S., 1988); Cornell University (J.D., 1991). *Email:* DESmith@PHJW.com

**NAOMI WEYAND SMITH** (Atlanta, Georgia; see Atlanta listing for biographical information).

**NANCY L. SOMMER** (New York, New York; See New York listing for biographical information).

**STEPHEN P. SONNENBERG,** born New York, New York, October 20, 1952; admitted to bar, 1993, California. *Education:* State University of New York at Binghamton (B.A., cum laude, 1974); University of Michigan (M.S.W., 1977); University of Southern California (J.D. 1992). Senior Editor, Southern California Interdisciplinary Law Journal. Licensed Clinical Social Worker, California, 1985. *Email:* SPSonnenberg@PHJW.com

**E. GARY SPITKO** (Atlanta, Georgia; See Atlanta listing for biographical information).

**DAVID H. STEINBERG** (New York, New York; See New York listing for biographical information).

**JOHN B. STEPHENS** (Costa Mesa, California; See Costa Mesa listing for biographical information).

**JOSHUA H. STERNOFF** (Washington, D.C.; See District of Columbia listing for biographical information).

**RANDALL M. STONE** (Washington, D.C.; See District of Columbia listing for biographical information).

**BRIAN D. SULLIVAN** (Atlanta, Georgia; See Atlanta listing for biographical information).

**KRISTEN K. SWARTZ** (Atlanta, Georgia; See Atlanta listing for biographical information).

**GREGORY J. SWEDELSON,** born Los Angeles, California, November 24, 1966; admitted to bar, 1994, California. *Education:* University of California at Santa Barbara (B.A., with high honors, 1988); University of Southern California (J.D., with honors, 1994). Staff Writer, Southern California Inter-disciplinary Law Journal. *Email:* GJSwedelson@PHJW.com

**ERIN M. SWEENEY** (Washington, D.C.; See District of Columbia listing for biographical information).

**ERIC JON TAYLOR** (Atlanta, Georgia; See Atlanta listing for biographical information).

**KATHERINE A. TRAXLER,** born Slidell, Louisiana, January 9, 1965; admitted to bar, 1990, California. *Education:* University of Notre Dame (B.A., magna cum laude, 1987); University of California at Los Angeles (J.D., 1990). Phi Beta Kappa. Intern, International Trade Commission, 1989. *Email:* KATraxler@PHJW.com

**MICHAEL W. TRAYNHAM,** born Fredericksburg, Virginia, July 10, 1958; admitted to bar, 1991, California; 1993, Texas. *Education:* Mary Washington College (B.A., 1982); University of Texas, Tyler (M.B.A., 1985); University of Southern California (J.D., 1991). Executive Notes Editor, Major Tax Planning and Computer Law Journal. *Email:* MWTraynham@PHJW.com

**RICHARD M. VICENZI** (Stamford, Connecticut; See Stamford listing for biographical information).

**MICHAEL T. VOYTEK** (Atlanta, Georgia; See Atlanta listing for biographical information).

**STANLEY F. WASOWSKI** (Atlanta, Georgia; See Atlanta listing for biographical information).

*(This Listing Continued)*

**PAUL, HASTINGS, JANOFSKY & WALKER LLP**, Los Angeles—Continued

**L. KENT WEBB** (Atlanta, Georgia; See Atlanta listing for biographical information).

**DEBORAH S. WEISER** (Santa Monica, California; See Santa Monica listing for biographical information).

**TIMOTHY J. WELLMAN** (Washington, D.C.; See District of Columbia listing for biographical information).

**ELISE M. WHITAKER** (Atlanta, Georgia; See Atlanta listing for biographical information).

**CRYSTAL L. WILLIAMS** (Atlanta, Georgia; See Atlanta listing for biographical information).

**S. REGINALD WILLIAMS** (New York, New York; See New York listing for biographical information).

**JONATHAN B. WILSON** (Atlanta, Georgia; See Atlanta listing for biographical information).

**IVAN J. WOLPERT** (New York, New York; See New York listing for biographical information).

**SCOTT M. WORNOW** (New York, New York; See New York listing for biographical information).

**SHANNON P. WRIGHT,** born Huntington Park, March 15, 1971; admitted to bar, 1995, California. *Education:* University of California at Los Angeles (B.A., 1991); Loyola Law School, Los Angeles (J.D., 1994). Order of the Coif. Staff Member, 1992-1993 and Note and Comment Editor, 1993-1994, Loyola of Los Angeles Law Review. Law Clerk, Hon. William J. Rea, U.S. District Court, Central District of California, 1994-1995. *Email:* SPWright@PHJW.com

**JOSHUA G. WROBEL,** born Missoula, Montana, September 29, 1970; admitted to bar, 1996, California. *Education:* Claremont McKenna College (B.A., 1992); University of Michigan (J.D., 1995). *Email:* JGWrobel@PHJW.com

**JENNY C. WU** (Washington, D.C.; See District of Columbia listing for biographical information).

**STEPHEN A. YAMAGUCHI,** born Long Beach, California, February 29, 1964; admitted to bar, 1989, California. *Education:* Stanford University (B.A., 1986); International Christian University; Columbia University (J.D., 1989). *Email:* SAYamaguchi@PHJW.com

**JULIE ARIAS YOUNG,** born New York, New York, March 16, 1968; admitted to bar, 1993, California. *Education:* University of California at Los Angeles (B.A., cum laude, 1990); Georgetown University (J.D., 1993). Member, American Criminal Law Review, 1991-1993. Extern, Hon. Stephen Reinhardt, U.S. Court of Appeals, Ninth Circuit, 1991-1992. *Email:* JAYoung@PHJW.com

**ARTHUR L. ZWICKEL,** born Los Angeles, California, April 8, 1964; admitted to bar, 1993, California. *Education:* Loyola Marymount University (B.S., 1986); Loyola Law School, Los Angeles (J.D.,1993). Order of the Coif. St. Thomas More Law Honor Society. Member, 1991-1992 and Note and Comment Editor, 1992-1993, Loyola of Los Angeles Law Review. Certified Public Accountant, California, 1989. *Email:* ALZwickel@PHJW.com

---

## PAUL & JANOFSKY
### LOS ANGELES, CALIFORNIA
(See Santa Monica)

*Civil Trial. Product Liability, Negligence, Professional Malpractice, Wrongful Death, Civil Misconduct, Business Torts, Sexual Harassment, Insurance Bad Faith, Wrongful Termination and Employment Discrimination, Construction Accidents, Business Disputes, Entertainment Law.*

---

## PEARLMAN, BORSKA & WAX
### LOS ANGELES, CALIFORNIA
(See Encino)

Employment Litigation, Workers Compensation Defense, Liability Defense, Subrogation, Insurance Coverage, Special Investigation Claims.

CAA1094B

---

## ALBERT PEREZ, JR.
### LOS ANGELES, CALIFORNIA
(See Covina)

*Civil and Criminal Litigation.*

---

## PERKINS COIE

A Law Partnership including Professional Corporations
Strategic Alliance with Russell & DuMoulin
Strategic Alliance with So Keung Yip & Sin

**1999 AVENUE OF THE STARS, NINTH FLOOR**
**LOS ANGELES, CALIFORNIA 90067-6109**
Telephone: 310-788-9900
Telex: 32-0319 PERKINS SEA
Facsimile: 310-788-3399
URL: http://www.perkinscoie.com

**REVISERS OF THE WASHINGTON LAW DIGEST FOR THIS DIRECTORY.**

*Seattle, Washington Office:* 1201 Third Avenue, 40th Floor. Telephone: 206-583-8888. Facsimile: 206-583-8500. Cable Address: "Perkins Seattle". Telex: 32-0319 PERKINS SEA.

*Anchorage, Alaska Office:* 1029 West Third Avenue, Suite 300. Telephone: 907-279-8561. Facsimile: 907-276-3108. Telex: 32-0319 PERKINS SEA.

*Denver, Colorado Office:* Mellon Financial Center, 1775 Sherman Street, Suite 2950. Telephone: 303-863-8686. Facsimile: 303-863-0423.

*Washington, D.C. Office:* 607 Fourteenth Street, N.W. Telephone: 202-628-6600. Facsimile: 202-434-1690. Telex: 44-0277 PCSO.

*Portland, Oregon Office:* 1211 Southwest Fifth Avenue, Suite 1500. Telephone: 503-727-2000. Facsimile: 503-727-2222. Telex: 32-0319 PERKINS SEA.

*Bellevue, Washington Office:* Suite 1800, One Bellevue Center, 411 - 108th Avenue N.E. Telephone: 206-453-6980. Facsimile: 206-453-7350, After April 29, 1997, Area Code will Change to 425. Telex: 32-0319 PERKINS SEA.

*Spokane, Washington Office:* North 221 Wall Street, Suite 600. Telephone: 509-624-2212. Facsimile: 509-458-3399. Telex: 32-0319 PERKINS SEA.

*Olympia, Washington Office:* 1110 Capitol Way South, Suite 405. Telephone: 360-956-3300. Facsimile: 360-956-1208.

*Hong Kong Office:* 23rd Floor Asia Pacific Finance Tower, Citibank Plaza, 3 Garden Road. Telephone: 852-2878-1177. Facsimile: 852-2524-9988.

*London, England Office:* 3/4 Royal Exchange Buildings, EC3V 3NL. Telephone: 171-369-9966. Facsimile: 171-369-9968.

*Taipei, Taiwan Office:* 8/F, TFIT Tower, 85 Jen Ai Road, Sec. 4, Taipei 106, Taiwan, R.O.C. Telephone: 011-886-2-778-1177. Facsimile: 011-886-2-777-9898.

*Canada:* Strategic Alliance with Russell & DuMoulin, 1700-1075 West Georgia Street, Vancouver, B.C. V6E 3G2. Telephone: 604-631-3131.

*Strategic Alliance with, So Keung Yip & Sin, 1501 Edinburgh Tower, The Landmark, 15 Queen's Raod Central, Hong Kong. Telephone:* 852-2810-8908. Facsimile: 852-2801-4148.

*General Trial and Appellate Practice in State and Federal Courts and before various Federal and State Administrative Tribunals. Corporate, Real Estate, Securities, General Business and Commercial, Corporate Finance, Taxation, Philanthropic Law, Aviation, Environmental, Natural Resources, Labor, Insolvency, Bankruptcy, Reorganization, Creditors' Rights, Administrative, Insurance and Antitrust Law.*

FIRM PROFILE: *Although Perkins Coie is the largest law firm headquartered in the Pacific Northwest, we are a national and international firm. We have 330 lawyers in 11 offices located in Asia, Europe and North America. We can tap a reservoir of experienced practitioners to handle demanding projects and react swiftly to emergencies around the world.*

*Our business clients include 96 Fortune 500 corporations and 48 of their subsidiaries, privately held businesses, partnerships and enterprises in emerging industries, such as life sciences, internet law, telecommunications and high technology.*

*As well as a strong U.S. presence, Perkins Coie has and extensive international practice. In the past five years alone, our lawyers have completed transactions in over 50 countries.*

(This Listing Continued)

Perkins Coie is committed to providing high-quality, cost-effective legal services that exceed our clients' expectations. In order to serve our clients better, the firm has undertaken a total quality management process called Total Client Satisfaction. In Fact, we are one of only a few law firms to implement this process. Moreover we are constantly exploring alternative billing options that are mutually beneficial for both clients and the firm.

## RESIDENT MEMBERS/SHAREHOLDERS

**DAVID T. BIDERMAN, A PROF. CORP.,** born Montgomery, Alabama, October 12, 1954; admitted to bar, 1981, California. *Education:* Emory University (B.A., 1977); University of Virginia (J.D., 1981). Articles Editor, Virginia Journal of Natural Resources Law, 1980-1981. *Member:* Los Angeles County, Century City (Member, Board of Governors) and American (Member, Section on Litigation) Bar Associations; State Bar of California. *PRACTICE AREAS:* Commercial Litigation; Bankruptcy Law. *Email:* bided@perkinscoie.com

**RONALD A. MCINTIRE,** born Glendale, California, July 26, 1960; admitted to bar, 1986, California. *Education:* Dartmouth College (B.A., cum laude, 1982); University of California at Los Angeles (J.D., 1986). Member, Environmental Law Journal, 1984-1986. Law Clerk to Hon. Harry L. Hupp, U.S. District Court, Central District of California, 1986-1987. *Member:* State Bar of California; American Bar Association. *PRACTICE AREAS:* Airplane Crash Litigation; Asbestos Litigation; Business Torts; Product Liability Law; Tort Law. *Email:* mcinr@perkinscoie.com

**THOMAS E. MCLAIN,** born Kansas City, Missouri, August 19, 1946; admitted to bar, 1974, California; U.S. Court of Appeals, Ninth Circuit. *Education:* Duke University (B.A., with highest honors, 1968; J.D., with highest honors, 1974). Nihon Kenkyu Center, Tokyo. Japan Foundation Fellow, 1974-1975. Articles Editor, Duke Law Journal, 1973-1974. Co-Author: *The Japanese Legal System,* 1977; Lecturer, Japanese Legal System, University of Southern California Law School, 1977-1978. Foreign Law Consultant, Nagashima & Ohno, Tokyo, 1974-1975 and 1978-1979. Commissioner and Financial Advisor, Japan-United States Friendship Commission; Commissioner, United States-Japan Conference on Cultural and Educational Interchange. Member: Board of Visitors, Stanford Institute of Public Policy, Duke University, 1987—; Financial Advisory Board, Inter-University Center, Yokohoma, Japan; Advisory Board, *The International Computer Lawyer.* Delegate and Fellow, British-American Project, Oxford, England. *Member:* State Bar of California. [With U.S. Army, 1969-1972]. *LANGUAGES:* Japanese. *PRACTICE AREAS:* International Business Transactions; Location Based Entertainment; Investments, Financings; Mergers and Acquisitions; Franchising; Licensing; Real Estate; Transportation Law. *Email:* mclah@perkinscoie.com

**CHARLES F. PALMER,** born Los Angeles, California, October 4, 1946; admitted to bar, 1973, California. *Education:* University of California at Berkeley (A.B., with honors, 1969); Yale Law School (J.D., 1973). Author: "Placing Pro Bono Publico in the National Legal Services Strategy," American Bar Association Journal, 1980. Member, Board of Directors: California Alumni Association, 1985-1988; Legal Aid Foundation of Los Angeles, 1986-1995. President, 1993-1994. Member, Board of Trustees, Los Angeles County Bar Association, 1988-1990. *Member:* Beverly Hills, Los Angeles County (Delegate, State Bar Conference of Delegates, 1974, 1976 and 1979-1985; Chairman, Housing and Urban Development Committee, 1980-1982; Chair, Special Committee on the Homeless, 1988-1989; Committee on Judicial Appointments, 1992-1993; Labor and Employment Section) and American (Member, Labor and Employment Law and Litigation Sections) Bar Associations; State Bar of California (Member, Labor and Employment Law Section; Chair, Legal Services Section, 1982-1983); Association of Business Trial Lawyers. *Email:* palmc@perkinsoie.com

**BRUCE ERIC SHERMAN,** born Santa Monica, California, August 10, 1956; admitted to bar, 1982, California. *Education:* University of California at Los Angeles (B.A., cum laude, 1979); University of California, Hastings College of Law (J.D., 1982). Member, 1980-1981 and Note and Comment Editor, 1981-1982, Hastings Law Journal. *Member:* Los Angeles County (Member, Real Property Section); State Bar of California. *Email:* sherb@perkinscoie.com

**DOUGLAS L. THORPE,** born Wahoo, Nebraska, January 25, 1937; admitted to bar, 1969, California. *Education:* University of Nebraska (B.S.C.E., 1959); Southern Methodist University (J.D., cum laude, 1968). Order of the Coif; Barristers; Phi Delta Phi; Sigma Tau; Tau Beta Pi; Chi Epsilon. Member, Board of Directors, Public Counsel, 1980-1983. *Member:* Century City (Member, Board of Governors, 1982-1985), Los Angeles County (Delegate to State Bar Conference of Delegates, 1981, 1983-1984; Member, Executive Committee, Section on Antitrust Law, 1981-1983) and American (Member, Sections on: Antitrust Law; Corporation, Banking and Business Law; Litigation; Economics of Law Practice) Bar Associations; State Bar of California. *Email:* thord@perkinscoie.com

## OF COUNSEL

**SANDRA J. CHAN,** born Los Angeles, California, August 18, 1956; admitted to bar, 1979, California. *Education:* University of California at Los Angeles (A.B., 1976); University of California at Davis (J.D., 1979). Phi Delta Phi. Member, U.C. Davis Law Review, 1979. *Member:* Beverly Hills, Century City, Los Angeles County and American Bar Associations; State Bar of California (Advisor, Estate Planning, Trust and Probate Law Section Executive Committee). Fellow, American College of Trust and Estate Counsel. (Also Member, Ambrecht, Chan & Cummins, L.L.P., Santa Barbara, California). *LANGUAGES:* Mandarin. *PRACTICE AREAS:* Estate Planning; Probate Law; Decedents Trust Administration. *Email:* chan@perkinscoie.com

## RESIDENT ASSOCIATES

**WENDY S. ALBERS,** born Los Angeles, California, August 7, 1966; admitted to bar, 1993, California. *Education:* University of California at Santa Barbara (B.A., 1988); Loyola Marymount University (J.D., cum laude, 1993). Order of the Coif; St. Thomas More Society. Author: Comment, "Lujan v. Defenders of Wildlife: Closing the Courtroom Door to Environmental Plaintiffs - The Endangered Species Act Remains Confined to United States Borders," 15 Loy. L.A. Int'l. & Comp. L.J. 203 (1992). *Member:* State Bar of California; California Women Lawyers. *PRACTICE AREAS:* Litigation. *Email:* albew@perkinscoie.com

**JASON K. AXE,** born Los Angeles, California, August 25, 1971; (admission pending). *Education:* University of California at Los Angeles (B.A., 1993); University of California at Los Angeles School of Law (J.D., 1996). Managing Editor, UCLA Law Review, 1994-1996. Author: "Computer Bulletin Boards and Software Piracy: Are System Operators to Blame for Acts of Copyright Infringement by Their Users?" Entertainment, Publishing and Arts Handbook, 1996-1997 Edition. *LANGUAGES:* Spanish. *PRACTICE AREAS:* Civil Litigation.

**MARK BIRNBAUM,** born Queens, New York, November 21, 1966; admitted to bar, 1991, California. *Education:* State University of New York at Binghamton (B.A., 1988); University of California at Los Angeles (J.D., 1991). Judicial Extern to Judge Irving Hill, U.S. District Court, Central District of California, 1990. *Member:* Los Angeles County Bar Association; State Bar of California. *PRACTICE AREAS:* Real Estate Law. *Email:* birnm@perkinscoie.com

**KAREN M. BRAY,** born Glendale, California, January 10, 1967; admitted to bar, 1993, California. *Education:* University of California at Los Angeles (B.A./B.A., magna cum laude, 1990; J.D.,1993). Editor in Chief, UCLA Law Review, 1992-1993. Law Clerk to Hon. Arthur L. Alarcon, U.S. Court of Appeals, Ninth Circuit, 1993-1994. *PRACTICE AREAS:* Litigation. *Email:* brayk@perkinscoie.com

**DAMON R. FISHER,** born Berkeley, California, March 29, 1969; admitted to bar, 1995, California. *Education:* University of California, San Diego (B.A., 1992); Loyola Law School, Los Angeles (J.D., 1995). Judicial Extern to the Honorable Dickran Tevrizian, U.S. District Court, Central District of California, 1994. Staff Member, Loyola of Los Angeles International and Comparative Law Journal, 1993-1994. Participant, Trial Advocacy Project. *Member:* Los Angeles County Bar Association. *PRACTICE AREAS:* General Litigation. *Email:* fishd@perkinscoie.com

**MARK JAY GOLDZWEIG,** born Los Angeles, California; admitted to bar, 1994, California. *Education:* University of California at Santa Cruz (B.A., 1987); Loyola Law School of Los Angeles (J.D., 1994). Chief Note and Comment Editor, Loyola of Los Angeles International and Comparative Law Journal, 1993-1994. *Member:* State Bar of California. *Email:* goldzweig@perkinscoie.com

**ELIZABETH E. KRUIS,** born Whittier, California, September 14, 1966; admitted to bar, 1993, California. *Education:* University of California at Irvine (B.A., with honors, 1988); Loyola Law School (J.D., 1993). Order of the Coif. Chief Note and Comment Editor, Loyola of Los Angeles International and Comparative Law Journal, 1992-1993. Author: "The United States Embargo on Mexican Tuna: A Necessary Conversationalist Measure or Unfair Trade Barrier?" 14 Loy. L.A. Int'L & Comp. L.J. 903 (1992). *Member:* State Bar of California. *PRACTICE AREAS:* Litigation; Employment Law. *Email:* kruie@perkinscoie.com

**RANDI MAURER,** born New York, N.Y., February 28, 1953; admitted to bar, 1988, California. *Education:* University of California at Los Angeles (B.A., cum laude, with honors, 1975); Loyola Law School (J.D., cum laude,

*(This Listing Continued)*

## PERKINS COIE, Los Angeles—Continued

1988). Order of the Coif; Phi Delta Phi. Member, St. Thomas More Law Honor Society. Recipient, American Jurisprudence Award in Analysis, Research and Writing and Procedure and Practice. Staff and Note and Comment Editor, Loyola of Los Angeles Law Review, 1986-1988. Author: "Bowers v. Hardwick: A Giant Step Back for Privacy Rights," 20 Loyola of Los Angeles Law Review 1013 (1987). *Member:* Los Angeles County (Labor and Employment Law Section) and American Bar Associations; State Bar of California. *PRACTICE AREAS:* Litigation; Labor and Employment Law. *Email:* maurr@perkinscoie.com

LESLIE N. MURDOCK, born Richmond Hill, New York, September 16, 1943; admitted to bar, 1985, California. *Education:* University of California at Los Angeles (B.A., 1965); Loyola Law School (J.D., 1985). Member, Board of Trustees, 1981-1985 and President, 1983-1984, Hermosa Beach City School District Board. Legal Extern for Judge Terry Hatter, U.S. District Court, Central District of California, 1984. *Member:* State Bar of California; American Bar Association. *PRACTICE AREAS:* Loan Modifications/Workout; Real Estate; General Corporate. *Email:* murdl@perkinscoie.com

COLLEEN M. REGAN, born Tacoma, Washington, September 20, 1956; admitted to bar, 1985, California. *Education:* St. John's College (B.A., 1978); Loyola Law School (J.D., 1985). Recipient, American Jurisprudence Award in Debtor-Credit Relations Law. Staff Member and Note and Comment Editor, Loyola of Los Angeles Law Review, 1983-1985. Author, "Criminal Law in the Ninth Circuit: Recent Developments, Sentencing," 18 Loyola of Los Angeles Law Review 517, 1985. *Member:* Los Angeles County and American Bar Associations; State Bar of California. *PRACTICE AREAS:* Civil Litigation. *Email:* regac@perkinscoie.com

BENJAMIN E. SOFFER, born Tel Aviv, Israel; admitted to bar, 1995, California. *Education:* Pennsylvania State University (B.S., Civil Engineering, 1978); Loyola Law School (J.D., cum laude, 1995). Phi Delta Phi; Order of the Coif. St. Thomas More Law Society. Recipient, American Jurisprudence Awards in Remedies and Ethics. *PRACTICE AREAS:* Bankruptcy; Litigation. *Email:* soffb@perkinscoie.com

MICHAEL I. SOROCHINSKY, born Odessa, Ukraine, April 30, 1968; admitted to bar, 1993, California. *Education:* University of California at Irvine (B.A., magna cum laude, 1990); University of California at Los Angeles School of Law (J.D., 1993). Phi Beta Kappa. *Member:* State Bar of California. *LANGUAGES:* Russian. *PRACTICE AREAS:* Bankruptcy; Litigation. *Email:* sorom@perkinscoie.com

PETER STOUGHTON, born Newport Beach, California, June 11, 1966; admitted to bar, 1993, California. *Education:* University of California at Berkeley (B.A., 1988); University of California at Los Angeles School of Law (J.D., 1993). *Member:* State Bar of California. *PRACTICE AREAS:* Real Estate. *Email:* stoup@perkinscoie.com

REPRESENTATIVE CLIENTS: ACL Holdings Limited (The Dragon Funds); Adams Rite Sabre International; Alaska Airlines, Inc.; Bank of Montreal; Bank One Management and Consulting Corp.; (The) Boeing Co.; Bugle Boy Industries; The Capital Group (The New Asia East Investment Fund); Carbon Mesa Advisors, Inc.; Computer Business Applications; Delta Benefit Plans; Elsinore Aerospace Systems; Garrett Corporation (Allied Signal); Gucci America, Inc.; Horsemen's Quarter Horse Assn.; Hughes Electronics; Isuzu Motors; Landmark Theatre Corp.; MCA Enterprises International; Northwest Airlines, Inc.; Omega Environmental, Inc.; O'Melveny & Myers; Paramount Pictures Corp.; Smart & Final Stores Corp.; Sportcap, Inc.; Square LA, Inc.; Tiger Shark Golf, Inc.; Tombo Aviation; U.S. Aviation Underwriters; U S WEST, Inc.; Wall Data Inc.; W.R. Grace; Zausner Foods, Inc.

REVISERS OF THE WASHINGTON LAW DIGEST FOR THIS DIRECTORY.

(For biographical data on Seattle personnel, see Professional Biographies, Seattle, Washington)
(For biographical data on Washington, D.C. personnel, see Professional Biographies, Washington, D.C.)
(For biographical data on Bellevue personnel, see Professional Biographies, Bellevue, Washington)
(For biographical data on Portland personnel, see Professional Biographies, Portland, Oregon)
(For biographical data on Spokane personnel, see Professional Biographies, Spokane, Washington)
(For biographical data on Anchorage, Alaska personnel, see Professional Biographies, Anchorage, Alaska)
(For biographical data on Denver personnel, see Professional Biographies, Denver, Colorado)
(For biographical data on Hong Kong personnel, see Professional Biographies, Hong Kong)

*(This Listing Continued)*

(For biographical data on Taipei personnel, see Professional Biographies, Taipei)
(For biographical data on London personnel, see Professional Biographies at London, England)

## PERKINS, ZARIAN & DUNCAN, P.C.

1801 CENTURY PARK EAST, SUITE 1100
**LOS ANGELES, CALIFORNIA 90067**
Telephone: 310-203-4646
Fax: 310-203-4647

Irvine, California Office: 2030 Main Street, Suite 660. Telephone: 714-475-1700. Fax: 714-475-1800.

*Business Litigation including Securities, Real Estate, Construction, Insurance, Antitrust, Environmental and Commercial Disputes.*

ADAM D. DUNCAN, JR., born Salt Lake City, Utah, January 4, 1964; admitted to bar, 1990, California. *Education:* University of Utah (B.A., cum laude, 1986); University of Southern California (J.D., 1990). Phi Beta Kappa; Phi Kappa Phi. Member, University of Southern California Law Review, 1988-1990. Commissioner, City of Los Angeles, Department of Public Works, 1993-1995. *Member:* Los Angeles County Bar Association; State Bar of California. *PRACTICE AREAS:* Real Estate, Environmental, Securities and Commercial Litigation.

## PERONA, LANGER & BECK

A PROFESSIONAL CORPORATION
9255 SUNSET BOULEVARD, SUITE 920
**LOS ANGELES, CALIFORNIA 90069**
Telephone: 800-435-7542

Long Beach, California Office: 300 East San Antonio. Telephone: 310-426-6155. Facsimile: 310-490-9823.

*Personal Injury, Products Liability, Malpractice, Insurance (Bad Faith), Commercial Litigation and Trial Practice in all Courts and Administrative Agencies. Landslide and Subsidence Law.*

(For complete Biographical Data on all Personnel, see Professional Biographies at Long Beach, California)

## CAROL A. PETERS

**LOS ANGELES, CALIFORNIA**
(See Pasadena)

*Probate, Estate Planning, Bio-Ethics, Conservatorship and Related Litigation.*

## PETERSON & ROSS

333 SOUTH GRAND AVENUE, SUITE 1600
**LOS ANGELES, CALIFORNIA 90071-1520**
Telephone: 213-625-3500
Telecopy: 213-625-0210
Telex: 19-4545 EPALAW LSA

Chicago, Illinois Office: 200 East Randolph Drive, Suite 7300, 60601-6969. Telephone: 312-861-1400.
New York, N.Y. Office: 33 Whitehall Street, 27th Floor, 10004. Telephone: 212-820-7700.
Springfield, Illinois Office: 600 South Second Street, Suite 400, 62704. Telephone: 217-525-0700.
Morristown, New Jersey Office: 55 Madison Avenue, Suite 200, 07960. Telephone: 201-993-9668.
Austin, Texas Office: 101 East Ninth Street, Suite 1000, 78701. Telephone: 512-472-5587.

*General Civil Trial and Appellate Practice, Insurance (Corporate, Regulatory and Coverage Defense), Government Affairs, Antitrust, Aviation, Banking, Corporation, Employment Discrimination, Estate Planning, Insurance Law, International, Probate, Real Estate, Securities and Taxation Law.*

*(This Listing Continued)*

## MEMBER OF FIRM

**VIVIAN RIGDON BLOOMBERG,** born Long Island, New York, April 22, 1954; admitted to bar, 1986, California and U.S. District Court, Central District of California; 1987, U.S. District Court, Southern District of California; 1992, U.S. District Court, Northern District of California and U.S. Court of Appeals, Ninth Circuit. *Education:* American University (B.A., cum laude, 1976); George Washington University (J.D., cum laude, 1985). Kappa Tau Alpha. Member, George Washington Law Review, 1984-1985. Editor, ABTL Report, published by The Association of Business Trial Lawyers, 1980—. Author: "GlenFed Versus Wells Fargo—Stirring the Controversy," ABTL Report, September, 1994; "Tactical Disqualification of Attorneys," ABTL Report, May 1993; "Federal Discovery Rules: Kinder, Simpler Procedures," ABTL Report, January 1992. *Member:* Los Angeles County Bar Association; State Bar of California; Association of Business Trial Lawyers (Member, Board of Governors); The Association of Trial Lawyers of America. *Email:* VBloomberg@PetersonRoss.com

## ASSOCIATES

**GINA M. BROWN,** born East St. Louis, Illinois, October 6, 1962; admitted to bar, 1988, Massachusetts and U.S. District Court, District of Massachusetts; 1989, District of Columbia and California; 1990, U.S. District Court, Central, Southern and Northern Districts of California and U.S. Court of Appeals, Ninth Circuit. *Education:* Yale University (B.A., 1984); Harvard University (J.D., 1987). *Member:* Beverly Hills, Los Angeles County, Massachusetts and American Bar Associations; State Bar of California; The District of Columbia Bar; California Association of Black Lawyers. *Email:* GBrown@PetersonRoss.com

**DAVID T. GLUCK,** born Van Nuys, California, September 19, 1965; admitted to bar, 1994, California and U.S. District Court, Central District of California; U.S. Court of Appeals, Ninth Circuit. *Education:* California State University, Sacramento (B.S., magna cum laude, 1991); University of California at Los Angeles (J.D., 1994). Member, 1991-1992 and Assistant Editor, 1992-1993, UCLA Pacific Basin Law Journal. *Member:* Los Angeles County Bar Association; State Bar of California. *Email:* DGluck@PetersonRoss.com

**LAINE T. WAGENSELLER,** born Santa Monica, California, February 23, 1968; admitted to bar, 1993, California, U.S. District Court, Central District of California and U.S. Court of Appeals, Ninth Circuit. *Education:* Duke University (A.B., 1990); University of Southern California (J.D., 1993). Law Clerk to the Hon. Richard C. Neal and the Hon. Melvin B. Grover, Los Angeles, Superior Court, 1993-1994. *Member:* Los Angeles County Bar Association (Member: Litigation; Business Law, 1993—). *LANGUAGES:* French. *Email:* LWagenseller@PetersonRoss.com

**BRETT P. WAKINO,** born West Covina, California, March 27, 1967; admitted to bar, 1992, California; U.S. District Court, Central District of California; 1993, U.S. Tax Court. *Education:* University of California (B.A., 1989); Hastings College of the Law, University of California (J.D., 1992). *Member:* Orange County, American and Orange County Asian-American Bar Associations; State Bar of California. *Email:* BWakino@PetersonRoss.com

(For complete biographical data on all personnel, see Professional Biographies at Chicago, Illinois)

---

# PETILLON & HANSEN

### LOS ANGELES, CALIFORNIA

(See Torrance)

*General Practice, Corporate, Securities, Bankruptcy Reorganization.*

---

# R. EDWARD PFIESTER, JR.

*A LAW CORPORATION*

**2000 RIVERSIDE DRIVE**
**LOS ANGELES, CALIFORNIA 90039-3707**
Telephone: 213-384-0880
FAX: 213-669-8549

*Personal Injury, Federal Employers Liability, Railroad, Products Liability, Bad Faith and Wrongful Death Litigation.*

(This Listing Continued)

---

**R. EDWARD PFIESTER, JR.,** born Fort Stockton, Texas, November 18, 1943; admitted to bar, 1970, Texas; 1972, California; 1974, U.S. Supreme Court, U.S. Court of Appeals, Ninth and Fifth Circuits and U.S. District Court, Central, Northern, Eastern and Southern Districts of California and U.S. District Court, Western and Northern Districts of Texas; U.S. District Court, District of Arizona; U.S. District Court, District of New Mexico. *Education:* New York University; University of Texas (B.B.A., with honors, 1966; J.D., 1970). Phi Eta Sigma; Phi Delta Phi. Best Brief, Moot Court. Crier Clerk to Hon. D.W. Suttle, Judge, U.S. District Court, Western District of Texas, 1970. Senior Law Clerk, Hon. Albert L. Stephens, Jr., Chief Judge, U.S. District Court, Central District of California, 1970-1972. Author: "Railroad Cases- Liability, Damages, Verdicts and Settlements under the FELA," 20 Texas Trial Lawyers Forum 3, 1985; "Liability, Damages and Settlements Under the FELA," 13 Los Angeles Trial Lawyers Advocate, 1986; "Railroad Cases Under the FELA," 9 Indiana Trial Lawyers Verdict 59, 1987. Lecturer, How to Settle Personal Injury Cases, Texas Trial Lawyers Association, 1985. Handling FELA Cases, Texas Trial Lawyers Association, 1987. Member, Panel of Arbitrators, American Arbitration Association. *Member:* Pecos County, Los Angeles County, Federal and American Bar Associations; Los Angeles Trial Lawyers Association; Texas Trial Lawyers Association; The Association of Trial Lawyers of America (Member, Railroad Section, 1976—); Lawyers Club of Los Angeles County; National Board of Trial Advocacy (Diplomate); Academy of Rail Labor Attorneys (National Secretary, 1988-1989, 1993-1994; National Treasurer, 1992-1993; Board of Managers, 1988—). Certified as a Civil Trial Advocate by the National Board of Trial Advocacy. (Board Certified, Personal Injury Trial Law, Texas Board of Legal Specialization). *LANGUAGES:* Spanish. *PRACTICE AREAS:* Personal Injury; FELA; Railroad Law.

---

**VICTOR A. RUSSO,** born Cleveland, Ohio, January 20, 1959; admitted to bar, 1984, California and U.S. District Court, Central and Southern Districts of California and District of Arizona. *Education:* University of California at Los Angeles (B.A., 1980); Arizona State University (J.D., 1984). *Member:* State Bar of California; California Trial Lawyers Association; The Association of Trial Lawyers of America; Academy of Rail Labor Attorneys. *PRACTICE AREAS:* Civil Litigation; FELA.

**ANTHONY M. ONTIVEROS,** born Mountain Home, Idaho, May 25, 1964; admitted to bar, 1991, California. *Education:* University of New Mexico (B.A., Economics and English, 1987); Boalt Hall School of Law, University of California (J.D., 1990). *Member:* Los Angeles County and American Bar Associations; State Bar of California. *PRACTICE AREAS:* Civil Litigation; FELA.

COUNSEL FOR: *FELA:* Brotherhood Railway Carmen of the United States and Canada; Brotherhood Maintenance of Way Employee's; Brotherhood of Locomotive Engineers; Transportation Communications Union; United Transportation Union; International Brotherhood of Electrical Workers.
REFERENCES: Sanwa Bank California (Headquarters Office); Espee Federal Credit Union.

---

# PHILLIPS & BRANCH

*EIGHTEENTH FLOOR*
*1901 AVENUE OF THE STARS (CENTURY CITY)*
**LOS ANGELES, CALIFORNIA 90067**
Telephone: 213-930-0986
Fax: 213-937-2964
Email: attyphil@aol.com

*Will Contests, Class Action Anti-trust and Securities Actions, Major Construction Cases, matters involving Charitable Foundations, Purchase and Sale of Businesses, Employment related matters, Commercial Disputes.*

## MEMBERS OF FIRM

**THOMAS P. PHILLIPS,** born Los Angeles, California, December 25, 1940; admitted to bar, 1966, California. *Education:* Pomona College (B.A., 1962); Hastings College of Law, University of California (J.D., 1965). Author: "Negligence vs. Fraud in Commodity Hearings," 2 Los Angeles Lawyers 39; "How to Survive the Insurance/Product Liability Crisis," 1986. Lecturer, University of California, Continuing Education of the Bar, "How to Handle a Short Non-Jury Trial," 1976. Delegate to Conference of State Bar Delegates, 1967, 1976, 1977, 1979. Faculty Member, Los Angeles College of Trial Advocacy, Pepperdine University School of Law, 1979-1980. Member, Special Committee to prepare Civil Trial Manual for the Los Angeles Superior Court, 1975. Member, Bench and Bar Council, Los Angeles Superior Court, 1976-1977. Judge Pro Tem, Los Angeles Municipal Courts,

(This Listing Continued)

## PHILLIPS & BRANCH, Los Angeles—Continued

1977-1980. Arbitrator, Los Angeles County Superior Court, 1981-1985. Member, Panel of Arbitrators, American Arbitration Association. *Member:* Los Angeles County (Member, 1973-1981, Secretary, 1973-1975, Vice-Chairman, 1975-1976 and Chairman, 1976-1977, Executive Committee, Trial Lawyers Section; Founding Member and Co-Chairperson, Appellate Courts Committee, 1977-1979; Member: Lawyers Referral Committee, 1978-1980; By-laws Committee, 1981-1982) and American (Southern California Membership Chairman, 1966-1968) Bar Associations; The State Bar of California; Association of Business Trial Lawyers; The Association of Trial Lawyers of America.

**K. CHRISTOPHER BRANCH,** born Los Angeles, California, November 8, 1962; admitted to bar, 1988, California and U.S. District Court, Central District of California; 1990, U.S. District Court, Southern District of California; 1991, U.S. District Court, Eastern District of California; 1994, U.S. District Court, Northern District of California; 1995, U.S. Court of Appeals, 9th Circuit; 1996, U.S. Supreme Court. *Education:* University of Southern California (A.B., 1983); Loyola Law School, Los Angeles (J.D., 1987). Phi Alpha Delta (Clerk 1985-1986). Business Law and Litigation Society (President, 1986-1987). Served on: U.S. Trade Representative's Committee on Trade In Services, 1983; Office of Management and Budget's International Economic Affairs Division, 1983. *Member:* Los Angeles County Bar Association; State Bar of California (Member, Litigation Section). *PRACTICE AREAS:* Insurance Coverage; Bad Faith; Commercial Litigation.

## PHILLIPS & SALMAN

2029 CENTURY PARK EAST, SUITE 1200
**LOS ANGELES, CALIFORNIA 90067-2957**
Telephone: 310-277-7117
Fax: 310-286-9182

*New York, N.Y. Office:* 111 Broadway, Thirteenth Floor. Telephone: 212-571-6500. Fax: 212-571-6533.

*Corporate and Commercial and Entertainment Law. Litigation in all Courts. Arbitration and Mediation.*

### PARTNERS

**GERALD F. PHILLIPS,** born New York, May 3, 1925; admitted to bar, 1950, New York; 1988, California, U.S. Supreme Court, U.S. District Court, Southern and Eastern Districts of New York, U.S. District Court, Central District of California and U.S. Court of Appeals, Second Circuit. *Education:* Dartmouth College (A.B., 1947); Amos Tuck School, Hanover, N.H. (M.C.S., 1947); Cornell University Law School (J.D., 1950). Counsel to, 1951-1979, and Vice-President, 1976-1979, United Artists Corporation. General Counsel of the J. Arthur Rank Organization, 1955-1968. Adjunct Professor of Law, Pepperdine School of Law. Member, Arbitration Panels of The American Film Marketing Association and the American Arbitration Association. Chairman, Law Committee of the MPAA, 1975-1984. Senior Vice President of American Multi Cinema, Inc., 1988-1990. *Member:* Beverly Hills, Los Angeles County and American (Chairman: Forum on The Entertainment and Sports Industries, 1986-1989; Chairman of the Exhibition and Ancillary Market Division of the Forum, 1989—; Member Sections on: Antitrust, Family Law, Alternative Dispute Resolution) Bar Associations. (Resident). (Also Of Counsel to Mannis & Phillips, and Manning Marder & Wolfe, Los Angeles, CA). *PRACTICE AREAS:* Entertainment Law; Family Law; General Commercial Litigation; Arbitration; Mediation.

**ROBERT R. SALMAN,** born New York, December 26, 1939; admitted to bar, 1965, New York; 1967, U.S. Court of Appeals, Second Circuit; 1974, U.S. Supreme Court. *Education:* Columbia College (B.A., magna cum laude, 1961; LL.B., cum laude, 1964). Phi Beta Kappa. Harlan Fiske Stone Scholar, 1962-1963. Adjunct Professor, Seton Hall University School of Law, 1995—. Member: Panel of Arbitrators, American Arbitration Association, The American Film Marketing Association and NASDAQ. *Member:* New York State (Member: Courts and Community Committee) and American (Member, Sections on: Litigation, Antitrust; Alternative Dispute Resolution) Bar Associations. (Resident, New York City Office). *PRACTICE AREAS:* Corporate and Commercial Litigation; Antitrust; Accountants' Liability; Securities; Environmental Litigation; Entertainment Litigation; Arbitration. *Email:* rrsalman@aol.com

*(This Listing Continued)*

### ASSOCIATE

**SUZANNE A. SALMAN,** born August 7, 1970; admitted to bar, 1995, New Jersey; 1996, New York and U.S. District Court, Southern and Eastern Districts of New York. *Education:* Boston University (B.A., magna cum laude, 1992); Brooklyn Law School (J.D., 1995). *Member:* New York State and New York Women's Bar Associations; New York County Lawyer's Association. (Resident, New York City Office).

REPRESENTATIVE CLIENTS: Amrep Corp.; Deloitte & Touche, LLP.; Sandvik, Inc.; Soap Opera Festivals, Inc.; Transamerica Insurance Finance Corporation.

## PICK & BOYDSTON

A Partnership including a Professional Corporation
800 WEST SIXTH STREET, SUITE 400
**LOS ANGELES, CALIFORNIA 90017**
Telephone: 213-624-1996
Telecopier: 213-624-9073

*General Civil Trial and Appellate Practice. Antitrust, Business Regulation, Copyright and Trademark, Corporate, Real Estate, Securities, Taxation and Trust Law.*

**ALAN B. PICK,** born Seattle, Washington, January 8, 1945; admitted to bar, 1971, California and District of Columbia. *Education:* University of Washington (B.A., 1966); Stanford University (J.D., 1970). Trial Attorney, Antitrust Division, U.S. Department of Justice, 1970-1973. Special Consultant, Federal Trade Commission, 1978-1979. President, Stanford Law Society of Southern California, 1983-1985. Member: Stanford Law School Board of Visitors, 1991-1994; Stanford Law School Advocacy Skills Workshop Faculty, 1994—. Member, Board of Trustees, University of Washington President's Club, 1993—. Panelist and Moderator, California Continuing Education of the Bar Program, "Punitive Damages," 1993—. *Member:* State Bar of California.

**BRIAN BOYDSTON,** born Leavenworth, Kansas, June 12, 1964; admitted to bar, 1991, California; 1992, U.S. District Court, Central District of California; 1994, U.S. District Court, Northern District of California; U.S. Court of Appeals, Ninth Circuit. *Education:* University of California at Los Angeles (B.A., 1986); Loyola Law School (J.D., 1991). Member, Loyola Law School International and Comparative Law Journal, 1990-1991. *Member:* State Bar of California; American Bar Association.

**JOAN I. SAMUELSON,** born San Diego, California, April 5, 1950; admitted to bar, 1977, California and U.S. District Court, Northern District of California. *Education:* University of California at Los Angeles (B.A., cum laude, 1972); University of California at Berkeley (J.D., 1977). Recipient: "California Lawyer 1996," A Lawyer of the Year; Distinguished Service Award, 1996 University of California Law School at Berkeley, Boalt Hall Alumni Association. Member, California Law Review, 1976-1977. Author: "Employment Rights of Women in the Toxic Workplace," 65 California Law Review 1113, 1977. Member, Board of Directors, Berkeley Law Foundation, 1977-1978. Member, Citizens Advisory Committee on Community Development, City and County of San Francisco, 1979-1982. Panelist, "Occupational Safety and Health Law," Practising Law Institute, 1978, 1981. Founder and President, Parkinson's Action Network, 1991—. *Member:* The State Bar of California.

**IRVING C. PARCHMAN,** born Los Angeles, California, August 20, 1958; admitted to bar, 1984, California and U.S. District Court, Northern and Central Districts of California. *Education:* Stanford University (A.B., 1980; J.D., 1983). Past Co-President and Member, Stanford Alumni in Entertainment. *Member:* State Bar of California. *PRACTICE AREAS:* Entertainment Law; Intellectual Property; Civil Litigation.

**PATRICK E. MICHELA,** born Long Beach, California, June 20, 1966; admitted to bar, 1994, California and U.S. District Court, Central District of California. *Education:* University of California, Los Angeles (B.A., 1989); Pepperdine University School of Law (J.D., 1994). Member, 1992-1993 and Note and Comment Editor, 1993-1994, Pepperdine Law Review. Author: "'You May Already Have Won...': Telemarketing Fraud and the Need for a Federal Legislative Solution," 21 Pepp L. Rev. 553, 1994. *Member:* State Bar of California. *Email:* pmichela@ix.netcom.com

**TREVOR L. ALT,** born Indianapolis, Indiana, October 9, 1968; admitted to bar, 1994, California and U.S. District Court, Central District of California. *Education:* California State University at Sacramento (B.S., 1990); Pepperdine University (J.D., 1994). Member, Pepperdine Roundtable. Extern to the Honorable Edward Rafeedie, United States District

*(This Listing Continued)*

Court Judge, Central District of California, 1993. Extern to the Honorable Vincent P. Zurzolo, United States Bankruptcy Court Judge, Central District of California, 1993. *Member:* American Bar Association; State Bar of California. *PRACTICE AREAS:* Bankruptcy; Civil Litigation; Telemarketing Law.

MARK K. DREW, born Manhattan, Kansas, November 9, 1962; admitted to bar, 1995, California and U.S. District Court, Central District of California. *Education:* University of California at Los Angeles (B.A., 1990); Loyola Law School (J.D., 1993). Recipient: American Jurisprudence Awards, Civil Procedure and Trial Advocacy. Member, Byrne Trial Advocacy Team, 1992-1993. Assistant Coach, Loyola Law School Byrne Intermural Trial Advocacy Team, 1994—. *Member:* Los Angeles County Bar Association; State Bar of California. *PRACTICE AREAS:* Insurance Coverage; Complex Securities Litigation; Criminal Law; ERISA and Tort Litigation.

### LEGAL SUPPORT PERSONNEL

BEVERLY HOPKINS, born Bakersfield, California, March 29, 1946. *Education:* California State University, Los Angeles, Paralegal Program. Member: National and Local Paralegal Associations. *PRACTICE AREAS:* Pre-judgment remedies; Post-judgment collections; Attachments; Telemarketing registration and compliance.

---

## PIERRY & MOORHEAD, LLP
A Partnership including a Professional Corporation
**301 NORTH AVALON BOULEVARD**
**LOS ANGELES, CALIFORNIA 90744-5888**
Telephone: 310-834-2691, 213-775-8348, 714-636-2970
FAX: 310-518-5814

*General Personal Injury Litigation, Maritime, Medical Malpractice, Products Liability.*

### MEMBERS OF FIRM

THOMAS J. PIERRY, SR., born 1937; admitted to bar, 1965, California, U.S. District Court, Central District of California, U.S. District Court of appeals, 9th Circuit, U.S. Supreme Court. *Education:* Purdue University (B.S.); University of Southern California (LL.B.). *Member:* Los Angeles County and Long Beach Bar Associations; State Bar of California. *PRACTICE AREAS:* Maritime; Personal Injury; Products Liability (Plaintiff); Workmans Compensation.

MICHAEL D. MOORHEAD, (P.C.), born Sault Ste. Marie, Michigan, January 24, 1948; admitted to bar, 1975, California, U.S. District Court, Northern, Central and Southern Districts of California and U.S. Court of Appeals, 3rd, 7th, 9th and 10th Circuits. *Education:* Whittier College (B.A., 1970); Loyola University of Los Angeles (J.D., 1975). Adjunct Professor of Law, Loyola University School of Law, 1978—. *Member:* Los Angelea County, Century City and Los Angeles Bar Associations; State Bar of California. *PRACTICE AREAS:* Personal Injury; Medical Malpractice; Labor; Employment; Products Liability.

---

JAMES M. MCADAMS, born Hobbs, New Mexico, 1945; admitted to bar, 1975, California, U.S. District Court, Central District of California, U.S. Court of Appeals, 9th Circuit, U.S. Supreme Court. *Education:* University of New Mexico (B.A., 1967; M.A., 1968); University of Southern California (J.D., 1975). *Member:* Los Angeles County and Long Beach Bar Associations; State Bar of California. [Lt. U.S. Navy, 1969-1972]. *PRACTICE AREAS:* Admiralty/Maritime; Personal Injury; Products Liability (Plaintiff); Workmans Compensation.

F. JOSEPH FORD, JR., born Omaha, Nebraska, 1950; admitted to bar, 1977, California, U.S. District Court, Central District of California. *Education:* University of Nebraska at Omaha (B.S.); Pepperdine University (J.D.). *Member:* Los Angeles County Bar Association; State Bar of California. *PRACTICE AREAS:* Admiralty/Maritime; Personal Injury; Products Liability (Plaintiff).

ROBERT W. FORD, born Omaha, Nebraska, April 25, 1956; admitted to bar, 1980, California. *Education:* University of Southern California (B.A., magna cum laude, 1977); Pepperdine School of Law (J.D., 1980). *Member:* Orange County, Los Angeles County and American Bar Associations; State Bar of California; Orange County Trial Lawyers Association; Association of Southern California Defense Counsel. *LANGUAGES:* Spanish. *PRACTICE AREAS:* Admiralty/Maritime; Personal Injury; Products Liability (Plaintiff); Workmans Compensation.

*(This Listing Continued)*

F. JAVIER TRUJILLO, born Guayaquil Ecuador, South America, March 12, 1952; admitted to bar, 1983, New Jersey and U.S. District Court, District of New Jersey; 1986, California, U.S. District Court, Central District of California. *Education:* Fairleigh Dickinson University (B.A., 1980); New York Law School (J.D., 1983). *Member:* Los Angeles County Bar Association; State Bar of California. [Sargent, USAF, 1974-1978]. *LANGUAGES:* Spanish. *PRACTICE AREAS:* Admiralty/Maritime; Personal Injury; Products Liability (Plaintiff); Workmans Compensation.

THOMAS J. PIERRY, III, born Torrance, California, 1962; admitted to bar, 1987, California, U.S. District Court, District of California, U.S. Court of Appeals, 9th Circuit, U.S. Supreme Court. *Education:* University of Washington (B.A.); University of Southern California (J.D.). *Member:* Los Angeles County Bar Association; State Bar of California. *PRACTICE AREAS:* Admiralty/Maritime; Personal Injury; Products Liability (Plaintiff); Workmans Compensation.

JOSEPH P. PIERRY, born Passaic, New Jersey, March 17, 1961; admitted to bar, 1986, New Jersey; 1988, California, U.S. District Court, Central District of California. *Education:* Boston College (B.A., 1983); Seton Hall University (J.D., 1986). *Member:* Los Angeles County Bar Association; State Bar of California. *PRACTICE AREAS:* Admiralty/Maritime; Personal Injury; Products Liability (Plaintiff); Workmans Compensation.

---

## JOHN K. PIERSON
**THE GATEWAY**
**12424 WILSHIRE BOULEVARD, SUITE 900**
**LOS ANGELES, CALIFORNIA 90025-1043**
Telephone: 310-826-8009
Fax: 310-442-6400
Email: Pierson.law@aol.com

Minneapolis, Minnesota Office: 5100 Gamble Drive, Suite 398. Telephone: 612-545-6326.

*Civil and Trial Practice in all Courts. Business Litigation, Entertainment Law, Bankruptcy, Criminal Defense and Negligence.*

JOHN K. PIERSON, born Redondo Beach, California, December 7, 1963; admitted to bar, 1990, California; 1992, Minnesota, U.S. District Court, Northern, Eastern, Southern and Central Districts of California, U.S Court of Appeals, 9th Circuit and U.S. Bankruptcy Court, Central and Southern Districts of California. *Education:* Cambridge University; St. Olaf College (B.A., 1986); Pepperdine University (J.D., 1989). *Member:* Los Angeles County, Hennepin County and Minnesota State Bar Association; State Bar of California; California Trial Lawyers Association; Consumer Attorneys Association of Los Angeles. (Also Of Counsel to Raymond Kirk Kolter, Los Angeles, California). *PRACTICE AREAS:* Business Litigation; Bankruptcy; Entertainment; Criminal Defense; Negligence.

### OF COUNSEL

ROBERT M. DE FEO, born Las Vegas, Nevada, August 28, 1965; admitted to bar, 1990, California; 1991, U.S. District Court, Central District of California; 1993, U.S. District Court, Southern District of California. *Education:* Northwestern University (B.A., 1987); Pepperdine University (J.D., 1990). *Member:* Beverly Hills, Orange County and American Bar Associations; State Bar of California. *LANGUAGES:* Finnish and Russian. *PRACTICE AREAS:* Civil Litigation.

RAYMOND KIRK KOLTER, born Wichita Falls, Texas, November 6, 1962; admitted to bar, 1991, California and U.S. District Court, District of California and U.S. Court of Appeals, 9th Circuit. *Education:* Midwestern State University (B.A., 1986); St. Mary's University; Pepperdine University (J.D., 1989). *Member:* Los Angeles County and American Bar Associations; State Bar of California; Consumer Attorneys Association of Los Angeles; California Trial Lawyers Association. (Also practicing individually, Los Angeles, California). *PRACTICE AREAS:* Family Law; Personal Injury.

J. ERIC KIRKLAND, born Nashville, Tennessee, June 25, 1964; admitted to bar, 1990, California; 1991, U.S. District Court, Central District of California. *Education:* University of Tennessee; David Lipscomb College (B.S., 1986); Pepperdine University (J.D., 1990). Litigation Associate, Paul & Stuart, 1991-1994. *PRACTICE AREAS:* Products Liability Law.

REPRESENTATIVE CLIENTS: Math Teachers Press, Inc.; Wincom Wirless; Chinin, U.S.A.; Ruthless Records; Reco, Inc.; Los Angeles Police Protective League; Nissan Financial Ltd.; Gersten Companies, Closets By Design; Struther's Industries.
RECORDING ARTISTS: Flesh N' Bone; Bone Thugs N' Harmony; Above The Law; Century Club; The Gate.

CALIFORNIA—LOS ANGELES — MARTINDALE-HUBBELL LAW DIRECTORY 1997

# PILLSBURY MADISON & SUTRO LLP

*CITICORP PLAZA*
*725 SOUTH FIGUEROA STREET, SUITE 1200*
**LOS ANGELES, CALIFORNIA 90017-2513**
*Telephone: 213-488-7100*
*Fax: 213-629-1033*

*Costa Mesa, California Office:* Plaza Tower, Suite 1100, 600 Anton Boulevard, 92626. Telephone: 714-436-6800. Fax: 714-662-6999.

*Silicon Valley Office:* 2700 San Hill Road, Menlo Park, 94025. Telephone: 415-233-4500. Fax: 415-233-4545.

*Sacramento, California Office:* 400 Capitol Mall, Suite 1700, 95814. Telephone: 916-329-4700. Fax: 916-441-3583.

*San Diego, California Office:* 101 West Broadway, Suite 1800, 92101. Telephone: 619-234-5000. Fax: 619-236-1995.

*San Francisco, California Office:* 235 Montgomery Street, 94104. Telephone: 415-983-1000. Fax: 415-983-1200.

*Washington, D.C. Office:* 1100 New York Avenue, N.W., Ninth Floor, 20005. Telephone: 202-861-3000. Fax: 202-822-0944.

*New York, New York Office:* 520 Madison Avenue, 40th Floor, 10022. Telephone: 212-328-4810. Fax: 212-328-4824. One Liberty Plaza, 165 Broadway, 51st Floor. Telephone: 212-374-1890. Fax: 212-374-1852.

*Hong Kong Office:* 6/F Asia Pacific Finance Tower, Citibank Plaza, 3 Garden Road, Central. Telephone: 011-852-2509-7100. Fax: 011-852-2509-7188.

*Tokyo, Japan Office:* Pillsbury Madison & Sutro, Gaikokuho Jimu Bengoshi Jimusho, 5th Floor, Samon Eleven Building, 3-1, Samon-cho, Shinjuku-ku, Tokyo 160 Japan. Telephone: 800-729-9830; 011-813-3354-3531. Fax: 011-813-3354-3534.

*General Civil Practice and Litigation in all State and Federal Courts. Business: Banking and Corporate Finance; Commercial Transactions/Energy; Corporate, Securities and Technologies; Creditors' Rights and Bankruptcy; Employee Benefits; Employment and Labor Relations; Environment, Health & Safety; Estate Planning; Finance and Commercial Transactions; Food and Beverage Regulation; Health Care; Political Law; Real Estate; Tax (domestic and international); and Telecommunications. Litigation: Alternative Dispute Resolution; Antitrust/Trade Regulation; Appellate; Banking/Financial Institutions; Commercial Disputes; Construction/Real Estate; Creditors' Rights, Bankruptcy and Insurance Insolvency; Energy Matters; Employment/Equal Opportunity; Environmental/Land Use; ERISA; Insurance; Intellectual Property; Maritime/Admiralty; Media/Entertainment/Sports; Securities; Tort/-Product Liability; and White Collar Defense. Intellectual Property: Aesthetic Design & Trade Dress Protection; Biotechnology; Computer Law; Copyright Law; Intellectual Property Audits and Strategic Planning; International Trade Commission; Licensing and Technology Transfer; Procurement of Property Rights; Patent Prosecution; Trade Secrets and Unfair Competition; Trademark Law; Interference Practice; Mechanical/Biomed/Aeronautical; and Physics/Optics.*

FIRM PROFILE: Founded in 1874, Pillsbury Madison & Sutro LLP has grown to become one of the largest law firms in the United States, with more than 560 attorneys and expertise in virtually every area of the law. With offices in seven California cities, New York, Washington, D.C., and two offices in Asia, Hong Kong and Tokyo, the firm combines a strong domestic practice with a dynamic presence in the rapidly changing international markets. The firm's corporate expertise encompasses all aspects of business law and covers the full range of legal needs. Our litigation practice is conducted by trial lawyers who have handled landmark cases in the federal and state courts. Our intellectual property practices focuses on litigation, patent and trademark prosecution, licensing and copyright protection. Pillsbury attorneys also work in other legal areas where technology interacts with law, including international trade, environmental protection and food and drug regulation. The firm's clients range from large national and international corporations to start-up companies, the U.S. and foreign governments to universities to individuals. The Cushman Darby & Cushman Intellectual Property Group of Pillsbury Madison & Sutro LLP has practiced intellectual property law since 1892, concentrating on United States and international patent, trademark, copyright and unfair competition law, other technology-associated matters, and related litigation in all courts and administrative agencies. Our patent attorneys have degrees in technical disciplines, and a number hold advanced degrees. Many have practical experience as engineers, microbiologists, physicists, computer experts and chemists.

*(This Listing Continued)*

CAA1100B

*MEMBERS OF FIRM*

**LAWRENCE D. BRADLEY, JR.,** born Santa Monica, California, February 19, 1920; admitted to bar, 1951, California. *Education:* U.S. Coast Guard Academy (B.S., 1941); Stanford Law School (J.D., 1950). **Email:** bradley_ld@pillsburylaw.com

**JOHN R. CADARETTE, JR.,** born Birmingham, Michigan, November 29, 1958; admitted to bar, 1983, California. *Education:* University of Michigan (B.B.A., 1980); University of Notre Dame (J.D., 1983). **Email:** cadarette_jr@pillsburylaw.com

**ANTHON S. CANNON, JR.,** born Salt Lake City, Utah, August 26, 1938; admitted to bar, 1966, New York; 1974, U.S. Supreme Court; 1976, California and U.S. Tax Court. *Education:* University of Utah (B.S., 1962); Harvard University (J.D., 1965); New York University (LL.M., in Taxation, 1971). **Email:** cannon_as@pillsburylaw.com

**KENNETH R. CHIATE,** born Phoenix, Arizona, June 24, 1941; admitted to bar, 1967, California; 1970, Arizona. *Education:* Claremont Men's College (B.A., 1963); Columbia University (LL.B., 1966). **Email:** chiate_kr@pillsburylaw.com

**ANTHONY R. DELLING,** born London, England, January 13, 1953; admitted to bar, 1978, California. *Education:* Stanford University (B.A., 1975); Stanford Law School (J.D., 1978). **Email:** delling_ar@pillsburylaw.com

**WILLIAM K. DIAL,** born Cincinnati, Ohio, February 17, 1940; admitted to bar, 1968, California. *Education:* Yale University (B.A., 1961); Boalt Hall School of Law, University of California (J.D., 1967). **Email:** dial_wk@pillsburylaw.com

**BLASE P. DILLINGHAM,** born Los Angeles, California, December 16, 1946; admitted to bar, 1976, California. *Education:* Stanford University (B.A., 1968); Vanderbilt University (M.A., 1976); University of Southern California (J.D., 1976). **Email:** dillingha_bp@pillsburylaw.com

**JOHN J. DUFFY,** born New York, N.Y., May 19, 1939; admitted to bar, 1973, California. *Education:* St. Josephs College (B.A., 1960); Gregorian University, Rome Italy (S.T.L., 1964); Manhattan College (M.A., 1969); New York University (J.D., 1973). **Email:** duffy_jj@pillsburylaw.com

**JERONE J. ENGLISH,** born Cambridge, England, September 12, 1952; admitted to bar, 1981, California. *Education:* California State University at Sacramento (B.S., 1978); McGeorge School of Law, University of the Pacific (J.D., 1981). **Email:** english_jj@pillsburylaw.com

**MICHAEL J. FINNEGAN,** born Los Angeles, California, December 14, 1962; admitted to bar, 1988, California. *Education:* Loyola Marymount University (B.B.A., 1985; J.D., 1988). **Email:** finnegan_mj@pillsburylaw.com

**L. GAIL GORDON,** born Vancouver, British Columbia, Canada, February 23, 1941; admitted to bar, 1975, California. *Education:* University of British Columbia (B.Ed., 1968); University of Southern California (J.D., 1974). **Email:** gordon_lg@pillsburylaw.com

**KENT B. GOSS,** born Pasadena, California, June 30, 1961; admitted to bar, 1987, California. *Education:* Occidental College (B.A., 1983); Hastings College of the Law, University of California (J.D., 1987). **Email:** goss_kb@pillsburylaw.com

**T.J. (MICK) GRASMICK,** born Lincoln, Nebraska, June 15, 1948; admitted to bar, 1976, California. *Education:* University of Nebraska (B.A., 1970); University of Michigan (J.D., 1976). **Email:** grasmick_tj@pillsburylaw.com

**DAVID L. HAYUTIN,** born Phoenix, Arizona, April 19, 1930; admitted to bar, 1958, California. *Education:* University of Southern California (A.B., 1952; J.D., 1958). **Email:** hayutin_dl@pillsburylaw.com

**JEFFREY W. HILL,** born Madison, Wisconsin, February 3, 1955; admitted to bar, 1980, California. *Education:* Princeton University (A.B., 1977); University of Southern California (J.D., 1980). **Email:** hill_jw@pillsburylaw.com

**AMY D. HOGUE,** born Ellwood City, Pennsylvania, May 3, 1952; admitted to bar, 1979, California. *Education:* Duke University (A.B., 1974); Cambridge University, Cambridge, England (M.Phil., 1975); Graduate Fellow, Harvard University (1976); Duke University (J.D., 1979). **Email:** hogue_ad@pillsburylaw.com

**CAROLYN M. HUESTIS,** born Dallas, Texas, May 27, 1949; admitted to bar, 1975, California. *Education:* University of California at Berkeley

*(This Listing Continued)*

## PROFESSIONAL BIOGRAPHIES — CALIFORNIA—LOS ANGELES

(B.A., 1971); Loyola Law School (J.D., 1975). *Email:* huestis_cm@pillsburylaw.com

**YUJI IWANAGA,** born Osaka, Japan, April 3, 1941; admitted to bar, 1981, Japan; 1984, California. *Education:* University of Tokyo (LL.B., 1964); Legal Training and Research Institute of the Supreme Court of Japan; Columbia Business School (Special Student, 1965); Boalt Hall School of Law, University of California (LL.M., 1984). *Email:* iwanaga_y@pillsburylaw.com

**SIDNEY K. KANAZAWA,** born Honolulu, Hawaii, October 4, 1952; admitted to bar, 1978, California; 1981, Hawaii. *Education:* University of Hawaii (B.Ed., 1974); University of Southern California (J.D., 1978). *Email:* kanazawa_sk@pillsburylaw.com

**RALPH D. KIRWAN,** born Albany, California, August 30, 1942; admitted to bar, 1969, California. *Education:* University of California at Berkeley (A.B., 1966); University of San Francisco (J.D., 1969). *Email:* kirwan_rd@pillsburylaw.com

**STEVEN O. KRAMER,** born St. Louis, Missouri, December 18, 1947; admitted to bar, 1973, Illinois; 1978, California. *Education:* University of Colorado (B.A., 1969); Illinois Institute of Technology, Chicago-Kent College of Law (J.D., 1973). *Email:* kramer_so@pillsburylaw.com

**JENNIE L. LA PRADE,** born Gallup, New Mexico, January 6, 1953; admitted to bar, 1978, California. *Education:* University of California at Berkeley (A.B., 1975); University of Southern California (J.D., 1978). *Email:* laprade_jl@pillsburylaw.com

**THOMAS R. LARMORE,** born Miami Beach, Florida, January 6, 1944; admitted to bar, 1969, California. *Education:* University of California at Los Angeles (B.S., 1965; J.D., 1968). *Email:* larmore_tr@pillsburylaw.com

**PETER V. LEPARULO,** born Plainfield, New Jersey, December 4, 1958; admitted to bar, 1985, California. *Education:* Colgate University (B.A., 1980); Case Western Reserve University (J.D., 1984). *Email:* leparulo_pv@pillsburylaw.com

**JOHN Y. LIU,** born New York, New York, March 26, 1963; admitted to bar, 1983, California. *Education:* University of California at Berkeley (B.A., 1980); University of California at Los Angeles School of Law (J.D., 1983). *Email:* liu_jy@pillsburylaw.com

**CHRISTOPHER J. McNEVIN,** born Davenport, Iowa, September, 6, 1958; admitted to bar, 1983, California. *Education:* University of Miami (B.S., 1979); Stanford Law School (J.D., 1983). *Email:* mcnevin_cj@pillsburylaw.com

**DONALD W. MEADERS,** born Dahlonega, Georgia, May 3, 1947; admitted to bar, 1973, California. *Education:* Harvard University (A.B., cum laude, 1969); Harvard University (J.D., 1973). *Email:* meaders_dw@pillsburylaw.com

**CATHERINE D. MEYER,** born Seattle, Washington, March 27, 1951; admitted to bar, 1979, California. *Education:* Bryn Mawr College (A.B., 1973); Northwestern University (J.D., 1979). *Email:* meyer_cd@pillsburylaw.com

**MICHAEL E. MEYER,** born Chicago, Illinois, October 23, 1942; admitted to bar, 1968, California. *Education:* University of Wisconsin (B.S., 1964); University of Chicago (J.D., 1967). *Email:* meyer_me@pillsburylaw.com

**RUTH MODISETTE,** born St. Charles, Illinois, June 21, 1946; admitted to bar, 1972, California. *Education:* Vassar College (B.A., 1968); Stanford Law School (J.D., 1971). *Email:* modisette_r@pillsburylaw.com

**NANCY G. MORRISON,** born Omaha, Nebraska, March 16, 1951; admitted to bar, 1977, California. *Education:* University of California at Santa Barbara (B.A., 1972; M.A., 1973); University of San Francisco (J.D., 1977). *Email:* morrison_ng@pillsburylaw.com

**ROBERT L. MORRISON,** born Waukegan, Illinois, February 26, 1947; admitted to bar, 1972, California. *Education:* DePauw University (B.A., 1969); University of Michigan (J.D., 1972). *Email:* morrison_rl@pillsburylaw.com

**J. RICHARD MORRISSEY,** born Los Angeles, California, January 8, 1941; admitted to bar, 1966, California; 1967, U.S. Court of Military Appeals; 1980, U.S. Supreme Court. *Education:* University of Santa Clara (A.B., 1963); Boalt Hall School of Law, University of California (LL.B., 1966). *Email:* morrissey_jl@pillsburylaw.com

**DANA P. NEWMAN,** born Los Angeles, California, June 13, 1952; admitted to bar, 1981, California. *Education:* Yale University (B.A., 1974); University of New Haven (M.S., Taxation, 1978 ); Boalt Hall School of Law, University of California (J.D., 1981). *Email:* newman_dp@pillsburylaw.com

**F. JOHN NYHAN,** born Philadelphia, Pennsylvania, January 10, 1944; admitted to bar, 1972, California; 1975, U.S. Supreme Court. *Education:* Tufts University (B.A., 1965); Villanova University (J.D., 1971). *Email:* nyhan_fj@pillsburylaw.com

**HENRY Y. OTA,** born Gila River, Arizona, December 31, 1942; admitted to bar, 1970, California. *Education:* Dartmouth College (B.A., 1964); University of Southern California (J.D., 1969). *Email:* ota_hy@pillsburylaw.com

**JACKIE K. PARK,** born Pusan, Korea, November 11, 1959; admitted to bar, 1986, Illinois; 1990, California. *Education:* Brown University (B.A., 1982); Northwestern University (J.D., 1985). *Email:* park_jk@pillsburylaw.com

**CHARLES E. PATTERSON,** born Rockford, Illinois, January 4, 1941; admitted to bar, 1966, Missouri; 1985, California. *Education:* University of Kansas (A.B., 1963); University of Michigan (J.D., 1966). *Email:* patterson_ce@pillsburylaw.com

**EDWARD A. PERRON,** born Washington, D.C., January 19, 1954; admitted to bar, 1979, California. *Education:* Harvard College (A.B., 1975); Harvard Law School (J.D., 197 9). *Email:* perron_ea@pillsburylaw.com

**TERESA M. QUINN,** born Logan, Utah, April 27, 1952; admitted to bar, 1979, California. *Education:* Pomona College (B.A., 1974); Boston University (J.D., 1978). *Email:* quinn_tm@pillsburylaw.com

**JAMES M. RISHWAIN, JR.,** born Stockton, California, April 28, 1959; admitted to bar, 1984, California. *Education:* University of California at Los Angeles (B.A., 1981); Pepperdine University (J.D., 1984). *Email:* rishwain_jm@pillsburylaw.com

**PATRICK G. ROGAN,** born New Haven, Connecticut, May 4, 1944; admitted to bar, 1972, California. *Education:* Claremont Men's College (B.A., 1966); Loyola University of Los Angeles (J.D., 1972). *Email:* rogan_pg@pillsburylaw.com

**MATTHEW R. ROGERS,** born New York, New York, September 30, 1961; admitted to bar, 1987, California. *Education:* Hamilton College (B.A., 1983); Boston University School of Law (J.D., 1986). *Email:* rogers_mr@pillsburylaw.com

**KENNETH N. RUSSAK,** born Downey, California, March 28, 1957; admitted to bar, 1982, California. *Education:* Amherst College (B.A., magna cum laude, 1979); University of Southern California (J.D., 1982). *Email:* russak_kn@pillsburylaw.com

**KARL A. SCHMIDT,** born Stockton, California, September 18, 1947; admitted to bar, 1974, California. *Education:* University of California at Berkeley (B.S., 1969); Boalt Hall School of Law, University of California (J.D., 1974). *Email:* schmidt_ka@pillsburylaw.com

**FAISAL SHAH,** born Port-of-Spain, Trinidad, October 31, 1960; admitted to bar, 1987, California. *Education:* University of Colorado (B.S., 1982); University of San Francisco (J.D., 1986). *Email:* shah_f@pillsburylaw.com

**ROBERT V. SLATTERY JR.,** born Chicago, Illinois, July 28, 1950; admitted to bar, 1977, California. *Education:* Stanford University (A.B., 1972); Columbia University (M.B.A., 1976; J.D., 1976). *Email:* slattery_rv@pillsburylaw.com

**SHERYL E. STEIN,** born Brooklyn, New York, April 20, 1952; admitted to bar, 1979, California. *Education:* University of Miami (B.A., 1974); Southwestern University (J.D., 1978). *Email:* stein_se@pillsburylaw.com

**WILLIAM E. STONER,** born Elgin, Illinois, May 16, 1956; admitted to bar, 1981, California; 1982, Illinois. *Education:* Wittenberg University (B.S., 1978); Duke University (J.D., 1981). *Email:* stoner_we@pillsburylaw.com

**MARSHALL M. TAYLOR,** born Pasadena, California, December 27, 1947; admitted to bar, 1974, California. *Education:* Yale University (B.A., 1969); University of California at Los Angeles School of Law (J.D., 1974). *Email:* taylor_mm@pillsburylaw.com

**REED S. WADDELL,** born Sacramento, California, June 24, 1957; admitted to bar, 1982, California. *Education:* University of California at Santa

*(This Listing Continued)*

## PILLSBURY MADISON & SUTRO LLP, Los Angeles—Continued

Barbara (B.A., 1979); University of California at Los Angeles School of Law (J.D. 1982). *Email:* waddell_rs@pillsburylaw.com

**ROBERT L. WALLAN,** born Los Angeles, California, September 16, 1960; admitted to bar, 1986, California. *Education:* University of California at Los Angeles (B.A., 1982); University of San Diego (J.D., 1986). *Email:* wallan_rl@pillsburylaw.com

**WILLIAM S. WALLER,** born Pasadena, California, November 19, 1957; admitted to bar, 1984, California. *Education:* University of California at Los Angeles (B.A., 1979); University of Southern California (J.D., 1983). *Email:* waller_ws@pillsburylaw.com

**DON R. WEIGANDT,** born Memphis, Tennessee, February 25, 1947; admitted to bar, 1975, New York; 1979, California. *Education:* Yale University (B.A., 1969); Columbia University (J.D., 1974). *Email:* weigandt_dr@pillsburylaw.com

**JOHN W. WHITAKER,** born Los Angeles, California, April 7, 1942; admitted to bar, 1968, California. *Education:* Stanford University (A.B., 1964); University of Southern California (J.D., 1967). *Email:* whitaker_jw@pillsburylaw.com

**JOHN G. WIGMORE,** born Los Angeles, California, March 14, 1928; admitted to bar, 1958, California. *Education:* Stanford University (B.S., 1949); University of California at Los Angeles School of Law (LL.B., 1958). *Email:* wigmore_jg@pillsburylaw.com

**THOMAS E. WORKMAN, JR.,** born Los Angeles, California, August 20, 1927; admitted to bar, 1958, California. *Education:* Loyola University of Los Angeles (B.B.A., 1951; J.D., 1957). *Email:* workman_te@pillsburylaw.com

**GORDON K. WRIGHT,** born St. Louis, Missouri, February 19, 1920; admitted to bar, 1948, California. *Education:* University of Southern California (A.B., 1941; LL.B., 1948). *Email:* wright_gk@pillsburylaw.com

### OF COUNSEL

**CHARLES E. ANDERSON,** born May 24, 1930; admitted to bar, 1955, California. *Education:* University of Southern California (B.S., 1958; LL.B., 1964); Northwestern University.

**ROLAND G. SIMPSON,** born Phoenix, Arizona, August 6, 1950; admitted to bar, 1975, California; 1976, U.S. Tax Court; 1980, U.S. Supreme Court. *Education:* University of Notre Dame (B.A., 1972); University of California at Los Angeles (J.D., 1975). *Email:* simpson_rg@pillsburylaw.com

**DEBORAH S. THOREN-PEDEN,** born Rockford, Illinois, March 28, 1958; admitted to bar, 1982, California, U.S. District Court, Central District of California and U.S. Court of Appeals, Ninth Circuit. *Education:* University of Michigan (B.A., 1978); University of Southern California (J.D., 1982). *Email:* thoren_ds@pillsburylaw.com

### SENIOR COUNSEL

**A. TODD LITTLEWORTH,** born Riverside, California, July 11, 1955; admitted to bar, 1980, California. *Education:* University of California at Riverside (B.A., 1977); Loyola Law School (J.D., 1980). *Email:* littleworat@pillsburylaw.com

**STEVEN M. NAKASONE,** born Chicago, Illinois, January 26, 1946; admitted to bar, 1975, California. *Education:* University of California at Berkeley (B.S., 1970); Loyola University of Los Angeles (J.D., 1975). *Member:* State Bar of California. *Email:* nakasone_sm@pillsburylaw.com

### ASSOCIATES

Keith A. Allen-Niesen
Farhad Bahar
Brett H. Bailey
Ian R. Barrett
J. Keith Biancamano
Dimitrios P. Biller
J. Douglas Bishop
Dawn S. Brookey
Jan H. Cate
J. Mark Childs
Barbara L. Croutch
Michael J. Crowley
Douglas H. Deems
Sybille Dreuth
Julie G. Duffy
Sheri F. Eisner
Douglas C. Emhoff
Jason R. Erb
Michael J. Erlinger
Alyssa First
Eric B. Foker
William B. Freeman
Jeffrey D. Frost
William T. Gillespie
Tracy Birnkrant Gray
Stewart S. Harrison
L. Keven Hayworth
Sabina A. Helton
Karen L. Hermann
Julia R. Johnson
Kelly A. Kightlinger
Lynne E. Mallya
Tohru Masago
Jennifer E. Mayo
Mary T. Michelena-Monroe
Margaret L. Milam
David S. Rauch
Jeffrey A. Rich
Julia Ellen Richards
Lori A. Ridley
Susan M. St. Denis
Kalman Steinberg
John T. Vangel
David J. Westgor
Marcus G. Whittle
Christopher T. Williams
Andrew M. Winograd

(For biographical data on San Francisco, San Diego, Sacramento, San Jose, Costa Mesa and Menlo Park, CA, Washington, DC, Tokyo, Japan, New York, NY and Hong Kong personnel, see Professional Biographies at each of those cities).

---

## PINE & PINE

SUITE 1520, 15760 VENTURA BOULEVARD (ENCINO)
**LOS ANGELES, CALIFORNIA 91436**
Telephone: 818-379-9710
Fax: 818-379-9749

Appellate and Related Trial Court Practice. Litigation Consulting and Briefwriting, Business Litigation in State and Federal Courts. False Claims Act (Whistleblowing), Antitrust Law, Unfair Trade Practices. Entertainment.

### MEMBERS OF FIRM

**NORMAN PINE,** born New York, N.Y., September 21, 1949; admitted to bar, 1975, California; 1980 U.S. Court of Appeals, 9th Circuit; 1996, U.S. Supreme Court. *Education:* University of California at Los Angeles (B.A., summa cum laude, 1971); University of Sussex, Sussex, England, Phi Beta Kappa; Boalt Hall School of Law, University of California (J.D., 1975). Note and Comment Editor, California Law Review, 1974-1975. Author: "The Impoundment Dilemma: Crisis in Constitutional Government," Yale Review of Law and Social Action, Vol. 3, No. 2, Winter, 1973; "Implied Warranty of Habitability as a Defense to Unlawful Detainer Actions," California Law Review, Vol. 63, No. 1, January, 1975. *Member:* Los Angeles County Bar Association (Member, Appellate Courts Committee); State Bar of California; Los Angeles Complex Litigation Inn of Court; Consumer Attorneys Association of Los Angeles; Association of Business Trial Lawyers.

**BEVERLY TILLETT PINE,** born Brooklyn, New York, October 28, 1948; admitted to bar, 1980, California. *Education:* Indiana University (B.S., 1970); Loyola Law School, Los Angeles (J.D., cum laude, 1980). Member, St. Thomas More Law Honor Society. Member, Moot Court Honors Board. Co-recipient, Best Appellant Brief Award, Traynor Moot Court Competition. Member, Loyola Law Review, 1979-1980. Author: "Recent Ninth Circuit Developments in Securities Law Pursuant to Section 10 (B) and Rule 10 B-5," 13 Loyola Law Review, 1981; "Pending Cases Testing the Copyright Holder's Exclusive Right of Public Performance," 18 Beverly Hills Bar Journal 127, 1984. *Member:* Los Angeles County Bar Association; State Bar of California; Women Lawyers Association of Los Angeles.

---

## LAW OFFICES OF DAVID A. PINES

**LOS ANGELES, CALIFORNIA**

(See Woodland Hills)

Construction, Surety, Collections, Business Litigation and Business Transactions.

---

## PIRCHER, NICHOLS & MEEKS

1999 AVENUE OF THE STARS
**LOS ANGELES, CALIFORNIA 90067**
Telephone: 310-201-8900
FAX: 310-201-8922

*Chicago, Illinois Office:* 900 North Michigan Avenue. Telephone: 312-915-3112. FAX: 312-915-3348; 312-915-3354.

(This Listing Continued)

Real Estate Law including Representation of Partnerships, Limited Liability Companies and Tax-Exempt Organizations in Acquisition, Development and Financing. Corporation, Federal and State Securities, Federal and State Taxation, Partnership, Municipal Finance, Environmental Law, Litigation, Bankruptcy and Limited Liability Company, Multimedia and Entertainment Law, Sports Law.

## MEMBERS OF FIRM

**STEVENS A. CAREY,** born Los Angeles, California, March 30, 1951; admitted to bar, 1978, California; 1988, New York. *Education:* University of California at Berkeley (B.A., Honors Program, summa cum laude, 1973; M.A., with distinction, 1975); Boalt Hall School of Law, University of California (J.D., 1978). Phi Beta Kappa. Author: "Profit Participations: Coping With the Limitations Faced by Pension Funds and REITs," Volume 14, Journal of Real Estate Taxation, 35-53, Fall, 1986; "Shared Appreciation Loans by Tax-Exempt Pension Funds," Volume 6, Real Estate Finance Journal, 19-23, Spring, 1991; "Workouts: A Borrower's Guide to Deferrals and Cash Flow Payments," Volume 7, Real Estate Finance Journal, 5-14, Summer, 1991; "Prorations: Watch Out For Real Estate Taxes Paid in Arrears," Volume 8, Real Estate Finance Journal, 11-22, Spring 1993. Contributing Editor, Real Estate Finance Journal. Regular Contributor and Member of Board of Advisers, Real Estate Workouts and Asset Management. *Member:* Los Angeles County (Member, Real Estate Section) and American Bar Associations; The State Bar of California. ***PRACTICE AREAS:*** Real Estate Law.

**DAVID E. CRANSTON,** born Los Angeles, California, July 16, 1959; admitted to bar, 1986, California, U.S. District Court, Central District of California and U.S. Court of Appeals, Ninth Circuit. *Education:* San Diego State University (B.A., cum laude, 1981); University of California at Davis (J.D., 1985). Contributing Editor, California Environmental Law Reporter, 1993—. Author: Chapter 59, "Insurance Coverage for Environmental Claims, Losses, and Liabilities," California Environmental Law and Land Use Practice," Matthew Bender, 1996; "Environmental Insurance Coverage Disputes—Issues and Strategies for Resolution from the Policyholder's Perspective," California Environmental Law Reporter (April 1992). Instructor, National Institute on Hydrocarbon Fingerprinting, sponsored by University of Wisconsin (March 1995). Instructor: Proving the Technical Case: Soil and Groundwater Contamination Litigation, Sponsored by Hawaii Department of Health, Solid and Hazardous Waste Branch and University of Wisconsin (May 1993); Instructor, Environmental Litigation, Hydrocarbons, Chlorinated Solvents and Visual Display of Evidence, Sponsored by University of Wisconsin (December 1995). Co-Chair and Instructor, Resolving Environmental Disputes through Mediation, Sponsored by University of Wisconsin (May 1996). *Member:* Los Angeles County (Member, Environmental Section) and American (Member, Section on Natural Resources, Energy and Environmental Law) Bar Associations; State Bar of California (Member, Environmental Section). ***PRACTICE AREAS:*** Environmental Law and Litigation; Insurance Coverage.

**ALFRED F. DELEO,** born New York, N.Y., November 25, 1952; admitted to bar, 1978, New York; 1983, California. *Education:* Georgetown University (B.S.L., cum laude, 1974); George Washington University (J.D., with honors, 1977). Order of the Coif; Phi Alpha Delta; Delta Phi Epsilon (The National Professional Foreign Service Fraternity). Lecturer in Law: Boalt Hall School of Law, University of California at Berkeley; University of California at Los Angeles School of Law. Author: "New Tax Law Changes Rule for Debt Discharge Income," Real Estate Workouts & Asset Management, October 1993; UPwhats: Umbrella Partnership Real Estate Investment Trusts," REITs & Securitization, January 1994. Member, Board of Advisors, Faculty of Languages & Linguistics, Georgetown University, Washington, D.C. Member, Board of Governors, National Association of Real Estate Investment Trusts, 1989-1992. Member, 1988—and Chairman, 1992-1995, Board of Trustees, The Peninsula Heritage School, Rolling Hills Estates, California. *Member:* Los Angeles County (Chair, Committee on Pass-through Entities, Taxation Section, 1993-1994), New York State (Member, Taxation Section) and American (Member, Taxation Section) Bar Associations; The State Bar of California (Chair, Committee on Pass-Through Entities/Real Estate, Taxation Section, 1995-1996). *LANGUAGES:* French and German. ***PRACTICE AREAS:*** Tax Law.

**JAMES L. GOLDMAN,** born Santa Monica, California, September 25, 1948; admitted to bar, 1973, California and U.S. District Court, Central District of California; 1975, U.S. Court of Appeals, Ninth Circuit; 1976, U.S. District Court, Northern District of California; 1982, U.S. District Court, Southern District of California. *Education:* University of California at Santa Barbara (B.A., with highest honors, 1970); University of California at Los Angeles (J.D., 1973). Order of the Coif. Author: "Legal Tender: Valuing A Law Practice in Divorce," Los Angeles Lawyer 26, March 1995;

*(This Listing Continued)*

"'Soliciting' Your Former Partners' Clients: Legitimate Competition or Bad Faith?" Vol. XIV, No. 1, Association of Business Trial Lawyers ABTL Report 3, September; 1991; "Standards Governing Client Solicitation," Vol. XIV, No. 1, Association of Business Trial Lawyers ABTL Report 5, September 1991; "Settlement: An Unsettled and Unsettling Question for the Ninth Circuit," Vol. XII, No. 1, Association of Business Trial Lawyers ABTL Report 4, November 1989; "Distribution of the Unclaimed Portion of an Award of Monetary Damages in a Securities Fraud Class Action," Class Action Reports, Fourth Quarter, 1985. Member, Board of Editors, Class Action Reports, 1986—. Member, Editorial Board, Los Angeles Lawyer, 1992—. *Member:* Los Angeles County (Member, Litigation Law Section), Federal (Los Angeles Chapter, Member, Executive Board, 1990—; Treasurer, 1993-1994; Vice President, 1994—) and American (Member, Litigation Section) Bar Associations; State Bar of California; Association of Business Trial Lawyers (Member, Board of Governors, 1987-1989). ***PRACTICE AREAS:*** Commercial Litigation.

**SHELDON A. HALPERN,** born Philadelphia, Pennsylvania, November 24, 1945; admitted to bar, 1970, Pennsylvania (inactive status); 1976, Ohio; 1983, California. *Education:* University of Pennsylvania (B.A., cum laude, 1967; J.D., 1970). Co-Chairman, Moot Court Board. Member, Advisory Board, Institute of Corporate Counsel. *Member:* Century City and Los Angeles County Bar Associations; The State Bar of California. ***PRACTICE AREAS:*** Real Estate Law.

**KATHLEEN M. HOGABOOM,** born Berkeley, California, March 2, 1951; admitted to bar, 1980, California. *Education:* University of California at Santa Barbara (B.A., with high honors, 1973); University of California at Los Angeles (J.D., 1980). Member, Order of the Coif. Member, Moot Court. *Member:* Los Angeles County Bar Association; The State Bar of California. ***PRACTICE AREAS:*** Real Estate Law; Real Estate Finance; Corporate.

**JERRY A. KATZ,** born Los Angeles, California, March 18, 1958; admitted to bar, 1983, California. *Education:* University of California at Berkeley (B.S., 1980); Hastings College of the Law, University of California (J.D., cum laude, 1983). *Member:* Los Angeles County and American Bar Associations; The State Bar of California. ***PRACTICE AREAS:*** Real Estate Law; Sports and Entertainment.

**GARY M. LAUGHLIN,** born Kansas City, Missouri, August 5, 1952; admitted to bar, 1978, New York; 1982, California. *Education:* Syracuse University (B.A., with honors, 1974); University of Connecticut (J.D., with honors, 1977). *Member:* The State Bar of California. ***PRACTICE AREAS:*** Real Estate Law.

**EUGENE J. M. LEONE,** born Glen Cove, New York, August 5, 1957; admitted to bar, 1983, New York; 1995, Illinois. *Education:* Cornell University (B.A., 1979); George Washington University (J.D., 1982). Co-Author: "Friendly Foreclosures: A Borrower's Checklist," Real Estate Workouts and Asset Management, Vol. 5, No. 7, January, 1995. Author: "Financing a Regional Mall: Tradition as Sources Versus Securitization," The Real Estate Finance Journal, Vol. II, No. 3, Winter 1996. *Member:* New York State and Illinois State Bar Associations. (Resident Partner, Chicago Office). ***PRACTICE AREAS:*** Real Estate Law.

**LARRY M. MEEKS,** born Thomaston, Georgia, June 10, 1943; admitted to bar, 1968, New York; 1980, California. *Education:* Washington & Lee University (B.A., cum laude, 1965); Columbia University (LL.B., cum laude, 1968). Co-Author: Regulation D, BNA Corporate Practice Series, 1994. *Member:* The State Bar of California. ***PRACTICE AREAS:*** Corporate Law; Securities Law.

**PHILLIP G. NICHOLS,** born Los Angeles, California, March 3, 1946; admitted to bar, 1974, California. *Education:* Occidental College (A.B., cum laude, 1968); University of California at Los Angeles School of Law (J.D., 1974). Order of the Coif. Author: "Texas Draws and Self-Inflicted Wounds," Volume 5, Number 3, Commercial Investment Real Estate Journal 6-9, Summer, 1986; "Making Corporate Assets Work: Practical Tips on Making a Lease Financeable," Volume 10, Number 6, Corporate Real Estate Executive, July/August 1995. Member, Board of Directors, Shelter Partnership. *Member:* Los Angeles County and American Bar Associations; The State Bar of California. ***PRACTICE AREAS:*** Real Estate Law.

**LEO J. PIRCHER,** born Berkeley, California, January 4, 1933; admitted to bar, 1958, California; 1985, New York. *Education:* University of California at Berkeley (B.S., 1954); Boalt Hall School of Law, University of California (J.D., 1957). Phi Beta Kappa; Phi Alpha Delta. Instructor in Law, Loyola University School of Law, 1959-1962. *Member:* Los Angeles County, New York State and American Bar Associations; The State Bar of California. (Certified Specialist, Taxation Law, The State Bar of California

*(This Listing Continued)*

*PIRCHER, NICHOLS & MEEKS, Los Angeles—Continued*

Board of Legal Specialization). *PRACTICE AREAS:* Real Estate Law; Tax Law.

**MICHAEL E. SCHEINBERG,** born Chicago, Illinois, July 15, 1957; admitted to bar, 1983, California. *Education:* Northwestern University (B.A., 1979; M.M., 1983; J.D., 1983). Author: "Mortgageable Ground Leases," 22 Shopping Center World 40, October 1993; "Anticipating Tenant Bankruptcy," 23 Shopping Center World 16, April 1994; "Using Discounted Payoffs," 2 Real Estate Workouts and Asset Management, August 1993; "Are Partial Payments Worth the Trouble," The Secured Lender, Jan./Feb. 1996. *Member:* California State Bar. *PRACTICE AREAS:* Real Estate Finance.

**URBAN J. SCHREINER,** born Madison, Wisconsin, January 6, 1931; admitted to bar, 1959, California. *Education:* Dartmouth College (A.B., 1953); University of California at Los Angeles (J.D., 1959). Phi Alpha Delta. Author: "Proposition 9, Big Trouble in a Small Package," Journal of the American Industrial Real Estate Association, 1968. Assistant City Attorney, Belmont, California, 1959-1960. *Member:* State Bar of California; National Association of Bond Lawyers. *PRACTICE AREAS:* Municipal Bond Law; Finance Law.

**RANDALL C. SINGLE,** born Albuquerque, New Mexico, July 31, 1963; admitted to bar, 1988, California. *Education:* Illinois Wesleyan University (B.A., magna cum laude, 1985); Stanford University (J.D., 1988). Phi Kappa Phi; Blue Key. Member, Moot Court Board. *Member:* The State Bar of California. *PRACTICE AREAS:* Real Estate Law.

## ASSOCIATES

**MARC A. BENJAMIN,** born New York, N.Y., October 19, 1964; admitted to bar, 1989, Illinois. *Education:* University of Wisconsin (B.A., with honors, 1986); Harvard University (J.D., 1989). Phi Beta Kappa. (Resident Associate, Chicago Office). *PRACTICE AREAS:* Real Estate Law.

**BRUCE J. GRAHAM,** born Los Angeles, California, August 27, 1954; admitted to bar, 1983, California. *Education:* Claremont McKenna College (B.A., magna cum laude, 1976); University of California at Los Angeles (J.D., 1983). *Member:* State Bar of California; National Association of Bond Lawyers. *PRACTICE AREAS:* Public Finance Law.

**JOHN H. IRONS, JR.,** born Yokosuka, Japan, November 28, 1961; admitted to bar, 1987, California and U.S. District Court, Central District of California. *Education:* University of California at Los Angeles (B.A., Philosophy, magna cum laude, 1984); University of California at Los Angeles (J.D., magna cum laude, 1987). Phi Beta Kappa; Phi Kappa Psi; Blue Key. Recipient, American Jurisprudence Awards in Torts and Criminal Law. Author: "Using Discounted Payoffs," Vol. 2, Real Estate Workouts and Asset Management, August 1993; "Analyzing Promissory Notes for Negotiability," Vol. 11, No. 1, Real Estate Finance Journal, Summer 1995. *PRACTICE AREAS:* Real Estate Law and Finance.

**WILLIAM HOWARD JACKSON,** born Cincinnati, Ohio, April 18, 1964; admitted to bar, 1990, California. *Education:* Stanford University (B.A., 1986); Stanford University Law School (J.D., 1989). *Member:* State Bar of California. *PRACTICE AREAS:* Real Estate Law; Sports; Entertainment; Multimedia.

**ROBERT D. JAFFE,** born May 11, 1964; admitted to bar, 1992, California. *Education:* University of California (B.A., 1986); Loyola Law School (J.D., 1992). Recipient, American Jurisprudence Award, Civil Procedure. Staff Member, Loyola Law Review, 1990-1991. *Member:* State Bar of California; Constitutional Rights Foundation (Member, Sports and Law Committee). *PRACTICE AREAS:* Real Estate Law; Entertainment; Sports; Multimedia.

**JAY S. LAIFMAN,** born Los Angeles, California, July 1, 1963; admitted to bar, 1988, California; U.S. District Court, Central, Northern, Eastern and Southern Districts of California and U.S. Court of Appeals, Ninth Circuit. *Education:* University of California at Santa Cruz (B.A., 1985); Hastings College of the Law, University of California (J.D., 1988). Recipient, American Jurisprudence Award, Real Property, 1985-1986. Participant, 1986-1987 and Chief Managing Editor, 1987-1988, Hastings International and Comparative Law Review. Author: "Treaties and Nationalization: The People's Republic of China Experience," 11 Hastings International and Comparative Law Review 325, 1988; "Bankruptcy: The 1111 (b) Election," Real Estate Finance Journal, Fall 1993. *Member:* Beverly Hills and Los Angeles County Bar Associations; State Bar of California. *PRACTICE AREAS:* Real Estate Law.

*(This Listing Continued)*

**EMILY B. MILLER,** born Cody, Wyoming, September 20, 1946; admitted to bar, 1988, California, U.S. District Court, Central District of California and U.S. Court of Appeals, Ninth Circuit. *Education:* Swarthmore College (A.B., 1968); New York University (Ph.D., 1983); University of California at Los Angeles (J.D., 1988). Member, Archaeological Institute of America, 1970-1983. Law Clerk, Hon. Ferdinand F. Fernandez, U.S. District Judge, Central District of California and U.S. Court of Appeals, Ninth Circuit. *Member:* Los Angeles County and American Bar Associations; State Bar of California. *LANGUAGES:* French, German and Greek.

**RALPH L. OLIVI, JR.,** born Oakland, California, June 9, 1927; admitted to bar, 1955, California; 1980, U.S. Supreme Court. *Education:* University of California at Berkeley (A.B., 1951); Hastings College of Law, University of California (J.D., 1954). *Member:* The State Bar of California; American Bar Association. (Resident Associate, Chicago Office). *PRACTICE AREAS:* Real Estate Law.

**DAVID L. PACKER,** born Springfield, Illinois, August 19, 1959; admitted to bar, 1985, California. *Education:* Georgetown University (B.A., magna cum laude, 1982); University of Virginia (J.D., 1985). Order of the Coif. Member, Editorial Board, 1983-1984, and Executive Editor, 1984-1985, Virginia Law Review. *PRACTICE AREAS:* Real Estate Law; Real Estate Finance.

**TODD OLEN PICCUS,** born Encino, California, June 22, 1965; admitted to bar, 1993, California. *Education:* University of California, Santa Barbara (B.A., summa cum laude, 1987); The University of Texas, Austin (M.B.A., 1990; J.D., 1992). Associate Editor, 1992-1993, and Member, 1991-1992, Texas Law Review. Extern to the Honorable Nathan Hecht, Texas Supreme Court, Fall 1992, and to General Counsel, Directors Guild of America, Summer 1992. Author: "Demystifying the Least Understood Branch: Opening the Supreme Court to Broadcast Media," 71 Texas Law Review 1053 (1993), reprinted in Supreme Court Politics: The Institution And Its Procedures, West Publishing (1994); "The Small Business Exemption and the Realities of the Home-Electronic Marketplace," The Entertainment and Sports Lawyer, Winter 1993, at 8; "An Inside Look at the Directors Guild of America," Art Law and Accounting Reporter, Summer 1992, at 1; "Preserving Rights to Redevelop," Shopping Center World, May 1996 at 84; "Landlord and Tenant Law," California Department of Real Estate Reference Guide, 1995-1996; "Insurance Intrinsics," Shopping Center World, August 1996. *Member:* State Bar of California. *PRACTICE AREAS:* Real Estate Law; Entertainment; Multimedia.

**MICHELE A. POWERS,** born Oconomowoc, Wisconsin, September 2, 1964; admitted to bar, 1994, Wisconsin and California. *Education:* Oberlin College (B.A., cum laude, 1988); University of Wisconsin (J.D., 1994). Articles Editor and Staff Writer, Wisconsin International Law Journal, 1992-1994. Author: "The United Nations Framework Convention on Biological Diversity: Will Biodiversity Preservation Be Enhanced Through Its Provisions Concerning Biotechnology Intellectual Property Rights?" Wisconsin International Law Journal, Vol. 12, No. 1, Fall 1993. *Member:* State Bar of California; American Bar Association. *LANGUAGES:* Spanish. *PRACTICE AREAS:* Civil Litigation; Water Law; Environmental Law.

**MIRYAM ROSIE REES,** born Bremen, Germany, August 23, 1951; admitted to bar, 1981, Illinois. *Education:* Northeastern Illinois University (B.A., with high honors, 1973); Loyola University (J.D., with honors, 1981). Recipient, Edward B. White Scholarship Award. Lead Article Editor, Loyola University Law Journal, 1980-1981. Teaching Assistant, Loyola University, September, 1980-1981. *Member:* Illinois State Bar Association. (Resident Associate, Chicago Office). *PRACTICE AREAS:* Real Estate Law.

**STEVEN A. RIVERS,** born Los Angeles, California, March 3, 1970; admitted to bar, 1995, California. *Education:* University of California at Los Angeles (B.A., cum laude, 1991); University of California at Los Angeles School of Law (J.D., 1995). National Merit Scholar; Regent's Scholar; Dean's Honors List. Member, The Thurston Society. Recipient: Milton D. Green "Top Ten" Award, Hastings College of the Law, University of California, (Spring, 1993). *Member:* The State Bar of California (Member, Real Property Section). *PRACTICE AREAS:* Real Estate Law. *Email:* river swild@aol.com

**MICHAEL F. SMETANA,** born Oak Park, Illinois, July 8, 1962; admitted to bar, 1987, Illinois and U.S. District Court, Northern District of Illinois. *Education:* University of Illinois (B.A., 1984; J.D., 1987). Phi Beta Kappa; Phi Kappa Phi. *Member:* Chicago and Illinois State Bar Associations. (Resident Associate, Chicago Office). *PRACTICE AREAS:* Real Estate Law; Zoning Law; Land Use Regulation Law.

*(This Listing Continued)*

**ANNE K. SMITH,** born Lafayette, Indiana, November 8, 1958; admitted to bar, 1987, Indiana and U.S. District Court, Northern and Southern Districts of Indiana; 1994, Illinois. *Education:* DePauw University (B.Mus., 1981); Indiana University (J.D., 1987). Phi Delta Phi. (Resident Associate, Chicago Office). *PRACTICE AREAS:* Shopping Center Law; Commercial Law; Leases and Leasing.

**VALERIE H. WULF,** born Cambridge, Massachusetts, March 23, 1969; admitted to bar, 1994, California, Wisconsin and U.S. District Court, Southern District of California. *Education:* University of Wisconsin, Madison (B.B.A., with honors, 1991); University of Wisconsin Law School (J.D., 1994). Member, Moot Court Board. *Member:* San Diego County and American Bar Associations; The State Bar of California; State Bar of Wisconsin. (Resident Associate, Chicago Office).

*OF COUNSEL*

**STEVEN B. ARBUSS,** born New York, N.Y., July 26, 1959; admitted to bar, 1984, California. *Education:* Cornell University (B.S., 1981); University of California at Los Angeles School of Law (J.D., 1984). Associate Editor, University of California at Los Angeles Law Review, 1983-1984. Judicial Extern to the Honorable Winslow Christian, California Court of Appeals, Spring, 1983. Author: Comment, "The Unruh Civil Rights Act: An Uncertain Guarantee," 31 UCLA Law Review 443, 1983. Co-Author: "Foreclosure Bidding Strategies," Real Estate Workouts & Asset Management, September, 1993. Author: "Giving Tenant Self-Help Rights," Shopping Center World, June 1993. Co-Author: "Structuring Public Agency Participation in Redevelopment Projects," Real Estate Review, Winter 1991. Panel Speaker and Round-Table Leader, International Council of Shopping Centers Law Conference, 1991, 1990, and 1989. Instructor, program in Multimedia and Digital Arts, UCLA Extension Department of Entertainment Studies and Performing Arts. *Member:* The State Bar of California. *PRACTICE AREAS:* Real Estate Law; Entertainment; Multimedia.

**DEBRA SPANGLER BARBANEL,** born Gary, Indiana, June 20, 1957; admitted to bar, 1982, California. *Education:* St. Mary's College of Notre Dame (B.A., magna cum laude, 1979); University of San Diego (J.D., cum laude, 1982). Notes and Comment Editor, San Diego Law Review, 1981-1982. Recipient, American Jurisprudence Award in Torts, Civil Procedure and Criminal Procedure. Judicial Law Clerk for Judge James Moody, U.S. District Court, Northern District of Indiana, 1980. *Member:* Los Angeles County and American Bar Associations; The State Bar of California. *PRACTICE AREAS:* Real Estate Law; Finance.

**ERIK C. GOULD,** born Youngstown, Ohio, October 19, 1961; admitted to bar, 1986, Illinois. *Education:* Georgetown University (B.A., magna cum laude, 1983); University of Chicago Law School (J.D., 1986). *Member:* Chicago and American Bar Associations. (Resident Of Counsel, Chicago Office).

**BARBARA A. KAYE,** born New York, New York, December 25, 1950; admitted to bar, 1982, California; 1983, U.S. District Court, Central District of California and U.S. Court of Appeals, Ninth Circuit. *Education:* State University of New York at Buffalo (B.A., summa cum laude, 1971); University of Iowa (M.A., 1972); Pepperdine University (J.D., 1982). Phi Delta Phi. Managing Editor, Pepperdine Law Review, 1981-1982. *Member:* Los Angeles County Bar Association; State Bar of California (Member, Real Property Section). *PRACTICE AREAS:* Real Estate; Business Law; Secured Creditors Rights; Mediation.

**MICHAEL J. KRETZMER,** born San Francisco, California, December 16, 1952; admitted to bar, 1983, California. *Education:* University of California at Berkeley (A.B., 1976); Loyola Law School (J.D., 1982). Recipient, William B. Hogoboom Award for Excellence in Clinical Juvenile Justice. *Member:* Los Angeles County Bar Association (Member, Committee on Juvenile Justice, 1988-1990); Association of Business Trial Lawyers. *PRACTICE AREAS:* Real Estate; Litigation; Family Law.

**E. THOMAS MORONEY, JR.,** born Highland Park, Illinois, March 10, 1959; admitted to bar, 1984, Ohio; 1986, California. *Education:* Miami University, Ohio (B.A., 1981); University of Southern California (J.D., magna cum laude, 1984; M.A., 1994; A.B.D., 1996). Order of the Coif. Executive Articles Editor, Southern California Law Review, 1985. Author: "Military Dissent and the Law of War," 58 Southern California Law Review 871, 1985. *PRACTICE AREAS:* Litigation.

**STEPHANIE C. SILVERS,** born New York, N.Y., April 1, 1952; admitted to bar, 1977, California. *Education:* Queens College of the City University of New York (B.A., magna cum laude, 1973); University of California at Los Angeles (J.D., 1977). Phi Beta Kappa. *Member:* The State Bar of California. *PRACTICE AREAS:* Real Estate Law.

*(This Listing Continued)*

**CRAIG A. SMITH,** born Arlington, Virginia, July 27, 1952; admitted to bar, 1979, California. *Education:* California State University at Humboldt (A.B., summa cum laude, 1974); University of California at Los Angeles School of Law (J.D., 1979). Order of the Coif. Distinguished Advocate, Moot Court Honors Program. Finalist, Roscoe Pound Moot Court Tournament. Recipient, American Jurisprudence Awards in Contracts, Wills and Trusts and Business Associations. Author: "Rights of First Refusal: Practical Negotiating and Drafting Techniques," Volume 3, Number 2, Real Estate Finance 55-62, Summer, 1986. *Member:* The State Bar of California. *PRACTICE AREAS:* Real Estate Law.

**DANIEL H. WILLICK,** born St. Louis, Missouri, September 4, 1942; admitted to bar, 1973, California; 1982, District of Columbia. *Education:* University of California, Los Angeles (A.B., with highest honors, 1964; J.D., 1973); University of Chicago (A.M., 1966; Ph.D., 1968). Phi Beta Kappa; Order of the Coif. Russell Sage Foundation Resident in Law and Social Science, University of California, Los Angeles School of Law, 1970-1972. National First Prize, Association of Trial Lawyers of America Environmental Law Essay Contest, 1973. Co-Author: "Attacks on Medical Staff Self-Governance Intensify," Southern California Psychiatrist, April, 1989. Adjunct Professor of Law, Loyola Law School, Los Angeles, 1977-1978. Lecturer, 1993-1996, Assistant Clinical Professor, 1996—, U.C.L.A. School of Medicine, Los Angeles. Member, Board of Directors, 1981-1994 and Vice President, 1983-1989, Constitutional Rights Foundation. *Member:* Los Angeles County and American Bar Associations; State Bar of California; The District of Columbia Bar (inactive). (Also practicing individually). *PRACTICE AREAS:* Litigation; Healthcare Law.

REPRESENTATIVE CLIENTS: Ahmanson Developments, Inc.; Ahmanson Commercial Development Company; The Alexander Haagen Company; Alper Development, Inc.; American Fidelity Assurance Company; American General Investment Corporation; American Savings Bank; American Stores Properties, Inc.; AMLI Residential Properties Trust; Baril Hotels, Ltd.; Beverly Pavilion Hotel; Catellus Development Corporation; City National Bank; Colony Advisors, Inc.; Community Redevelopment Agency of Los Angeles; Donaldson, Lufkin & Jenrette; Financo, Inc.; First Boston Corp.; First Dearborn Properties; GAP Portfolio Partners; Goldman, Sachs & Co.; Guiness Peat Properties Inc.; Grubb & Ellis; The Hampstead Group; Heitman Financial, Ltd.; Heron Financial Corporation; Home Savings of America; Housing Authority of the City of Los Angeles; ING Capital Corp.; Interstate Brands Corporation; J.E. Robert Companies; J.H. Snyder Company; JMB Realty Corporation; JMB/Urban Development Company; Kraft General Foods; LaSalle Partners; Long Term Credit Bank of Japan; Maguire Thomas Partners; Marcus & Millichap Pension Ventures; Merrill Lynch & Co.; Merrill Lynch Capital Markets Group; Mountain AMD L.P.; Nomura Securities International, Inc.; Rosamond Community Services District; Oppenheimer & Co., Inc.; Pacific Mutual Life Insurance Company; R & B Realty Group; Residential Asset Trust I; The RREEF Funds; RTC Mortgage Trust 1993-N-2; Sacramento Kings Professional Basketball Club; Secured Capital; Shutters on the Beach Hotel; Smith, Barney, Harris Upham & Co., Inc.; Southern Pacific Transportation Co.; Stanford Ranch, Inc.; Starwood Capital Partners; Urban Shopping Centers, Inc.; Varco International Inc.; The Vons Companies, Inc.; Walton Street Capital; Wells Fargo Bank; West Coast Acquisition Partners; Wilshire Pacific Realty & Management Company.

## PIZER & MICHAELSON INC.

2029 CENTURY PARK EAST, SUITE 600
**LOS ANGELES, CALIFORNIA 90067**
*Telephone: 310-843-9729*
*Fax: 310-843-9619*

Santa Ana, California Office: 2122 North Broadway, Suite 100, 92706. Telephone: 714-558-0535. Telecopier: 714-550-0841.

*General Civil Practice in all State and Federal Courts. Business Transactions and Litigation, Representing and Advising Financial Institutions, Credit Unions, Corporations and Partnerships, Creditor Rights in Bankruptcy, Collections, Real Estate, Family Law, Conservatorships, Estate Planning, Wills, Trusts, and Probate.*

(For complete biographical data on all personnel, see Professional Biographies at Santa Ana, California)

## MICHAEL E. PLOTKIN

**LOS ANGELES, CALIFORNIA**

(See Pasadena)

*Business Litigation, Bankruptcy, Personal Injury and Criminal Law.*

## POINDEXTER & DOUTRÉ, INC.

*Established in 1972*

ONE WILSHIRE BUILDING, SUITE 2420
624 SOUTH GRAND AVENUE
**LOS ANGELES, CALIFORNIA 90017-3325**
*Telephone: 213-628-8297*
*Telecopier: 213-488-9890*

*San Francisco, California Office:* 44 Montgomery Street, Suite 1300. Phone: 415-398-5811. Fax: 415-398-5808.

*General Civil and Trial Practice. Corporation, Real Property, Insurance, Construction, Securities, Estate Planning, Trust, Probate, Federal, State and Local Tax Law.*

**WILLIAM M. POINDEXTER,** born Los Angeles, California, June 16, 1925; admitted to bar, 1952, California. *Education:* Yale University (B.A., 1946); University of Chicago and University of California at Berkeley (J.D., 1949). President, San Marino School Board, 1967-1968. President, Conference of Insurance Counsel, 1974. *Member:* Los Angeles County (Chairman, Law Office Management Section, 1978-1980; Chairman, State and Local Tax Committee, 1984-1985) and American Bar Associations; The State Bar of California. Fellow, American College of Trust and Estate Counsel. **PRACTICE AREAS:** Probate; Trust Litigation; State and Local Tax.

**ALFRED B. DOUTRÉ** (1927-1980).

**EVAN G. WILLIAMS,** born New York, N.Y., April 24, 1943; admitted to bar, 1969, California. *Education:* University of California at Los Angeles (A.B., 1965; J.D., 1968). Blue Key. *Member:* Los Angeles County Bar Association; State Bar of California. **PRACTICE AREAS:** Corporate; Securities; Alternative Energy; Real Estate.

**JAMES P. DRUMMY,** born San Diego, California, August 22, 1948; admitted to bar, 1973, California. *Education:* University of California at Los Angeles (A.B., cum laude, 1970); University of California at Berkeley (J.D., 1973). Assistant Managing Editor, California Law Review, 1972-1973. *Member:* Los Angeles County Bar Association; State Bar of California. **PRACTICE AREAS:** Real Estate; Commercial Transactions; Corporate.

**JEFFREY A. KENT,** born Inglewood, California, February 27, 1952; admitted to bar, 1976, California. *Education:* University of California at Los Angeles (B.S., 1973); Loyola University of Los Angeles School of Law (J.D., cum laude, 1976). Member, Loyola Law Review, 1974-1975. Arbitrator: Los Angeles Superior Court Business Law Panel, 1982—. *Member:* Los Angeles County Bar Association (Chairperson, Construction Law Subsection, Real Property Section, 1988-1990); State Bar of California. **PRACTICE AREAS:** Construction Litigation; Commercial Litigation.

**BENNETT M. SIGMOND,** born Chicago, Illinois, February 21, 1957; admitted to bar, 1983, California. *Education:* University of Illinois (A.B., with honors, 1979); University of California at Los Angeles (J.D., 1983). Phi Beta Kappa. *Member:* Los Angeles County Bar Association; State Bar of California. **PRACTICE AREAS:** Commercial Litigation; Bankruptcy; Real Estate; Secured Transactions.

**JAMES W. POINDEXTER,** born San Rafael, California, December 4, 1952; admitted to bar, 1980, California. *Education:* Yale University (B.A., cum laude, 1975); University of California at Davis (J.D., 1980). (Resident, San Francisco Office). **PRACTICE AREAS:** Landlord and Tenant Law; Construction Law; Business Litigation; Real Estate.

**ANTHONY J. TAKETA,** born Los Angeles, California, March 9, 1958; admitted to bar, 1983, California. *Education:* Loyola Marymount University (B.A., summa cum laude, 1980); University of California at Los Angeles (J.D., 1983). Pi Gamma Mu. Contributing Editor, Agricultural Law Update, 1985. *Member:* Los Angeles County and American Bar Associations; State Bar of California. **PRACTICE AREAS:** Insurance Defense; Construction Law; Civil Litigation; Probate Litigation.

---

**CHRISTINE KIM,** born Indianapolis, Indiana August 17, 1966; admitted to bar, 1994, California; 1995, U.S. District Court, Central District of California. *Education:* Mount Holyoke College (B.A., 1988); Boston University (J.D., 1993). Author, "The Collateral Source Rule," Product Liability Advisory Council, Deskbook Series Compensatory Damages, Vol. I, Section I pp. 1-44. *Member:* Los Angeles County Bar Association; State Bar of California. **PRACTICE AREAS:** Commercial Litigation; Insurance Defense; Probate Litigation.

*(This Listing Continued)*

**MARK A. FELDMAN,** born Los Angeles, California, September 4, 1965; admitted to bar, 1991, California, U.S. District Court, Central, Northern, Southern and Eastern Districts of California and U.S. Court of Appeals, Ninth Circuit. *Education:* University of California, Los Angeles (B.A., cum laude, 1987); University of Southern California (J.D., 1990). Phi Alpha Delta. Legion Lex Scholar. Author: "Selecting an Entity for Acquiring and Holding Title to Property," Real Estate Transactions, The Michie Company, 1993. Panel Member, Building Industry Credit Association Seminar, "General Contractors: Recognizing, Making & Defending Against Claims," 1994. *Member:* Los Angeles County and American Bar Associations; State Bar of California. **PRACTICE AREAS:** Construction Law; Surety Law; Real Estate; Probate Litigation.

*OF COUNSEL*

**RICHARD H. PATTERSON, JR.,** born Arcadia, California, September 7, 1958; admitted to bar, 1984, California; 1986 Texas. *Education:* Duke University (A.B., cum laude, 1980); Southern Methodist University (J.D., 1983). *Member:* Pasadena and Los Angeles County Bar Associations; The State Bar of California; State Bar of Texas. **PRACTICE AREAS:** Insurance Defense; Civil Litigation; Probate Litigation.

REPRESENTATIVE CLIENTS: Braille Institute of America, Inc.; Cambrian Energy Development; Childrens Hospital of Los Angeles; Citicorp North America, Inc.; Glass Incorporated International; Hospital Management Services, Inc.; Key Air Conditioning Contractors; Motors Insurance Corp.; Textron Financial Corporation; Westinghouse Electric Corporation; Western Air & Refrigeration.
REFERENCE: Bank of California (Sixth/Flower).

---

## MICHAEL R. POLIN

THE WILSHIRE LANDMARK BUILDING
11755 WILSHIRE BOULEVARD
SUITE 1400
**LOS ANGELES, CALIFORNIA 90025-1520**
*Telephone: 310-477-5455*
*Fax: 310-417-5058*
*Email: rmgn00a@prodigy.com*

*Santa Ana, California Office:* 5 Hutton Centre, 11th Floor. Telephone: 714-445-9261. Fax: 714-825-8517.

*International Business Law, Offshore Banking including the establishment of Foreign Corporation and Banking Relations, Estate Planning emphasizing Living Trusts and Wills, General Business Law, Entertainment Law, Sports Representation.*

**MICHAEL R. POLIN,** born Los Angeles, California, September 17, 1959; admitted to bar, 1987, California. *Education:* University of California at Berkeley (B.S., Philosophy and Business, 1983); University of West Los Angeles (J.D., 1987). *Member:* American Bar Association; State Bar of California (Member, Sections on: Estate Planning, International Law, Litigation, Business Law and Entertainment). **PRACTICE AREAS:** International Business Law; Entertainment Law; Estate Planning; Business Law; Litigation.

---

## DAVID POLINSKY

1901 AVENUE OF THE STARS, SUITE 200
**LOS ANGELES, CALIFORNIA 90067**
*Telephone: 310-553-0555*
*Fax: 310-203-8753*

*Construction and General Business Litigation.*

**DAVID POLINSKY,** born Norwich, Connecticut, July 16, 1961; admitted to bar, 1986, California. *Education:* Yale University (B.A., 1983); University of California at Los Angeles (J.D., 1986). *Member:* Beverly Hills, Los Angeles County and American Bar Associations; State Bar of California. **PRACTICE AREAS:** Construction; General Business Litigation; Civil Litigation; Arbitration; Mediation.

---

## POLITIS & POLITIS

865 S. FIGUEROA STREET, SUITE 1388
**LOS ANGELES, CALIFORNIA 90017**
*Telephone: 213-630-8800*
*Telecopier: 213-630-8818*

*Customs Law, International Trade Law, Insurance Defense, Business Litigation. General Civil Litigation, Commercial Litigation and Contracts.*

*(This Listing Continued)*

## MEMBERS OF FIRM

**JOHN N. POLITIS,** born Zanesville, Ohio, April 3, 1935; admitted to bar, 1969, California and U.S. District Court, Southern District of California; 1970, U.S. Circuit Court of Appeals, Ninth Circuit; 1971, U.S. District Court, Central District of California; 1972, U.S. Customs Court; 1973, U.S. Court of Customs and Patent Appeals; 1980, U.S. Court of International Trade. *Education:* U.S. Military Academy (B.S., 1957); University of San Diego (J.D., 1968). Trial Attorney, Department of Justice, 1972-1976. *Member:* Los Angeles County Bar Association (Member, 1978-1987, Vice Chairman, 1980 and Chairman, 1981-1983, Customs Law Committee); State Bar of California; Wilshire Bar Association (Director, 1981-1986). [1st Lt., U.S. Army, 1957-1960]. *PRACTICE AREAS:* Customs Law; International Trade.

**NICHOLAS J. POLITIS,** born Frankfurt, West Germany, November 25, 1958; admitted to bar, 1985, California; 1986, U.S. District Court, Central District of California; 1987, U.S. Court of Appeals, Ninth Circuit and U.S. Court of International Trade. *Education:* Pepperdine University (B.A. 1980); Whittier College School of Law (J.D., 1983). Phi Alpha Delta. Recipient, American Jurisprudence Award in Real Property. Member: Moot Court Honors Board; Whittier Law Review, 1982-1983. *Member:* The State Bar of California; American Bar Association; Association of Southern California Defense Counsel; The ABOTA Inns of Court. *PRACTICE AREAS:* Customs Law; Commercial Insurance.

## LAW OFFICES OF ELON A. POLLACK

*A PROFESSIONAL CORPORATION*

865 SOUTH FIGUEROA STREET, SUITE 1388
**LOS ANGELES, CALIFORNIA 90017**
Telephone: 213-630-8888
Fax: 213-630-8890
URL: http://www.dutylaw.com

*Customs, International Trade Law and Related Matters.*

**FIRM PROFILE:** *Law Offices of Elon A. Pollack provides over 20 years of combined expertise in International Trade and Customs Law to those companies needing counsel in this increasingly specialized international economy. Each member has extensive experience with both governmental and administrative requirements as well as private corporate concerns. The firm's Los Angeles location makes for easy international access and members of their staff speak Italian, French and Hebrew for easy communication with their clients.*

**ELON A. POLLACK,** born Brooklyn, New York, September 22, 1950; admitted to bar, 1973, Virginia and U.S. District Court, Eastern District of Virginia; 1974, Louisiana and U.S. Court of International Trade; 1977, U.S. District Court, Eastern District of Louisiana; 1978, U.S. Court of Appeals, Fifth Circuit; 1980, California; 1981, U.S. District Court, Central District of California and U.S. Court of Appeals, Ninth Circuit; 1982, U.S. Court of Appeals for the Federal Circuit. *Education:* Tulane University (B.A., 1971; J.D., 1973). Phi Delta Phi. Lecturer, "Importing & Exporting Wearing Apparel," University of California at Los Angeles, 1986. *Member:* Los Angeles County (Vice Chairman, 1986-1987, 1988-1990, 1993-1994 and Chairman, 1987-1988, Customs Law Committee), Louisiana State (Member, Committee on Legal Aid, 1975-1978) and American (Member, Sections on: Administrative Law; Patent, Trademark and Copyright Law) Bar Associations; Virginia State Bar; State Bar of California; U.S. Court of International Trade (Member, Advisory Committee, 1993—); Customs and International Trade Bar Association. *PRACTICE AREAS:* Customs Law; International Trade.

---

**HEATHER C. LITMAN,** born Los Angeles, California, October 12, 1966; admitted to bar, 1991, California; 1996, U.S. District Court, Central District of California and U.S. Court of International Trade. *Education:* University of California, Berkeley (B.A., 1988); Tulane University (J.D., cum laude, 1991). Law Clerk to the Honorable Harvey Schneider and Stephen O'Neil, Los Angeles Superior Court. *LANGUAGES:* French, Italian. *PRACTICE AREAS:* Customs Law; International Trade.

## POLLAK, VIDA & FISHER

1801 CENTURY PARK EAST, 26TH FLOOR
**LOS ANGELES, CALIFORNIA 90067**
Telephone: 310-551-3400
Fax: 310-551-1036

*Civil Litigation in State and Federal Trial and Appellate Courts, Insurance Coverage, Insurance Bad Faith, Casualty, Property, Governmental Tort Liability, Federal Civil Rights and Professional Negligence.*

### MEMBERS OF FIRM

**MICHAEL M. POLLAK,** born Milwaukee, Wisconsin, October 25, 1953; admitted to bar, 1979, California, U.S. Court of Appeals, Ninth Circuit and U.S. District Court, Central, Southern and Eastern Districts of California. *Education:* University of California at Santa Barbara (B.A., with honors, 1976); University of California at Davis (J.D., 1979). Neumiller Honors Moot Court; Moot Court Board. Author: "Practical Considerations in Section 998 Compromise Offers," California Association of Independent Insurance Adjusters, Summer, 1985. *Member:* State Bar of California.

**SCOTT J. VIDA,** born Los Angeles, California, October 30, 1956; admitted to bar, 1982, California; 1985, U.S. District Court, Central District of California; 1986, U.S. Court of Appeals, Ninth Circuit; 1989, U.S. District Court, Southern District of California. *Education:* University of California at Irvine (B.A., 1979); Benjamin N. Cardozo School of Law, Yeshiva University (J.D., 1982). *Member:* Los Angeles County and American Bar Associations; State Bar of California; Association of Southern California Defense Counsel.

**GIRARD FISHER,** born San Diego, California, November 6, 1945; admitted to bar, 1973, California, U.S. District Court, Central, Eastern, Northern and Southern Districts of California, U.S. Court of Appeals, Ninth Circuit and U.S. Supreme Court. *Education:* University of California at Berkeley (A.B., 1967); California State University (M.A., 1977); University of San Diego (J.D., 1973). Author, Article, "Design Immunity for Public Entities," 28 University of San Diego L. Rev. 241, 1991. Speaker: "Liability of Adjoining Landowners," Consumer Attorneys Association of Los Angeles, 1996; "Recent Developments in Municipal Liability," League at California Cities, 1995; "Police Liability," International Association of Claims Administrators, 1994; "Roadway Design Cases," California Conference of County Counsel, 1992; "Governmental Claims Procedures," California League of Cities, 1991; "Design Immunity," City Attorneys of Los Angeles County Association, 1991; CEB Panel on "Attorney's Fees," 1984. Law Clerk, U.S. District Court, Southern District of California, 1974-1975. Arbitrator: National Association of Securities Dealers, 1979—; Los Angeles Superior Court, 1984—. *Member:* Los Angeles County and American (Member, Sections on: Litigation; Tort and Insurance Practice Law; Urban State and Local Government Law) Bar Associations; State Bar of California.

**WAYNE D. PARISER,** born Los Angeles, California, July 27, 1962; admitted to bar, 1987, California; 1988, U.S. District Court, Central, Eastern and Southern Districts of California. *Education:* University of California at Los Angeles; Occidental College (A.B., cum laude, 1984); University of San Diego (J.D., 1987). *Member:* American Bar Association; State Bar of California.

**J. SUSAN GRAHAM,** born Los Angeles, California, August 13, 1962; admitted to bar, 1987, California and U.S. District Court, Central, Northern, Southern and Eastern Districts of California. *Education:* University of California at Los Angeles (B.A., 1983; J.D., 1986). *Member:* Los Angeles County and American Bar Associations; State Bar of California.

### ASSOCIATES

**GERARD A. LAFOND, JR.,** born Dunkirk, New York, April 27, 1954; admitted to bar, 1986, California; 1987, U.S. District Court, Central District of California; 1988, U.S. District Court, Northern, Southern and Eastern Districts of California and U.S. Court of Appeals, Ninth Circuit. *Education:* University of California at San Diego (B.A., 1982); University of California at Los Angeles; Southwestern University School of Law (J.D., 1986). *Member:* Los Angeles County and American Bar Associations; State Bar of California.

**MICHAEL R. NEBENZAHL,** born Santa Monica, California, December 7, 1955; admitted to bar, 1983, California; U.S. District Court, Central District of California. *Education:* California State College, Sonoma; University of California at Santa Barbara (B.A., 1978); Loyola Law School of Los Angeles (J.D., 1983). *Member:* Los Angeles County Bar Association; State Bar of California.

*(This Listing Continued)*

## POLLAK, VIDA & FISHER, Los Angeles—Continued

**DAVID A. HADLEN,** born Ventura, California, August 27, 1947; admitted to bar, 1972, California; 1978, U.S. District Court, Central District of California; 1986, U.S. Court of Appeal, Ninth Circuit. *Education:* St. Mary's College; Loyola University (B.A., 1969; J.D., 1972). Judge, U.C.-L.A. Moot Court Program, 1986-1994. Judge Pro Tem, Los Angeles Municipal Court, 1984—. Member, Legal and Regulatory Subcommittee, Association of California Insurance Companies, 1984. *Member:* Los Angeles County (Arbitrator, Attorney-Client Relations Committee, 1982-1993) and American Bar Associations; State Bar of California.

**DANIEL P. BARER,** born Walla Walla, Washington, April 24, 1965; admitted to bar, 1990, California; 1991, U.S. District Court, Central District of California. *Education:* University of California at Los Angeles (B.A. in Political Science, 1987); University of California, Hastings College of the Law (J.D., cum laude, 1990). Phi Eta Sigma; Pi Gamma Mu; Gold Key Honor Society. *Member:* State Bar of California; American Bar Association.

**JUDY L. MCKELVEY,** born London, England, April 19, 1957; admitted to bar, 1991, California and U.S. District Court, Central District of California. *Education:* University of California at Santa Cruz (B.A., with honors, 1980); University of California at Berkeley (M.A., with honors, 1982); New York University School of Law (J.D., 1991). *Member:* Los Angeles County and American Bar Associations; State Bar of California (Member, Litigation Section).

**LAWRENCE J. SHER,** born Brooklyn, New York, August 4, 1955; admitted to bar, 1992, California; U.S. District Court, Eastern and Central Districts of California. *Education:* Queens College of the City University of New York (B.A., magna cum laude, 1977); University of California, Davis School of Law (J.D., 1992). Recipient, Nathan Burkan Memorial Competition in Copyright Law, First Place, University of California, Davis School of Law, 1992. Senior Research Editor, University of California, Davis Law Review. Author: "The Search for a Suitable Standard of Substantial Similarity: The Ninth Circuit's Application of the Krofft Test," 25 U.C. Davis Law Review 229 (1991). Judicial Extern to Honorable Edward J. Garcia, U.S. District Court, Eastern District, 1991. *Member:* Los Angeles County Bar Association; State Bar of California; Association of Defense Counsel of Southern California.

**KATHLEEN K. ANDREWS,** born Burbank, California, June 23, 1960; admitted to bar, 1987, California, U.S. District Court, Central and Southern Districts of California and U.S. Court of Appeals, Ninth Circuit. *Education:* University of Southern California; University of California at Los Angeles (B.A., 1982); Southwestern University School of Law (J.D., 1987). Phi Delta Phi. Recipient, American Jurisprudence Awards in Community Property and Legal Profession. Note and Comment Editor, Southwestern University Law Review, 1986-1987. Author: Comment, "The Next Best Thing to Being There? Foreseeability of Media-Assisted Bystanders," 17 S.W.U. L. Rev. 65, 1987. Judicial Extern to Hon. Cynthia Holcomb Hall, U.S. Court of Appeals, Ninth Circuit, 1986. *Member:* Los Angeles County and American Bar Associations; State Bar of California (Member, Litigation Section).

**NEIL R. ANAPOL,** born Camden, New Jersey, February 21, 1962; admitted to bar, 1989, California; 1991, U.S. District Court, Central District of California. *Education:* Northwestern University (B.S., 1984; M.A., 1984); University of California at Los Angeles (J.D., 1988). *Member:* State Bar of California; American Bar Association.

**ERICA M. BROIDO,** born Los Angeles, California, March 2, 1966; admitted to bar, 1992, California. *Education:* University of California, Davis (B.A., magna cum laude, 1988); Santa Clara University (J.D., magna cum laude, 1992). Phi Beta Kappa. Recipient, American Jurisprudence Award in Family Law. Associate Editor, Santa Clara Law Review.

**NICOLE A. GREENWALD,** born Toronto, Canada, May 9, 1968; admitted to bar, 1994, California. *Education:* Yeshiva University/Stern College (B.A., cum laude, 1990); Loyola Law School of Los Angeles (J.D., 1994). Recipient, American Jurisprudence Awards in Property and Trial Advocacy.

REPRESENTATIVE CLIENTS: Allstate Insurance Co.; Authority For California Cities' Excess Liability ("ACCEL"); Balboa Insurance Co.; Big Independent Cities' Excess Pool ("BICEP"); Carl Warren & Co.; City of Beverly Hills; City of Coachella; City of Pasadena; City of Santa Monica; City of Ventura; Commercial Union Insurance Companies; County of Los Angeles; GAB Business Services, Inc.; Los Angeles Community Development Commission; Philadelphia Insurance Companies; Southern California Joint Powers Insurance Authority; Travelers Insurance Company; Tristar Risk Management.

CAA1108B

## JULIAN A. POLLOK

A PROFESSIONAL CORPORATION

1000 WILSHIRE BOULEVARD, SUITE 620
LOS ANGELES, CALIFORNIA 90017
Telephone: 213-688-7795
Telecopier: 213-688-1080

*General Civil Trial, Commercial Litigation, Business Litigation including Contracts, Real Estate, and Unfair Competition in all State and Federal Courts.*

**JULIAN A. POLLOK,** born Los Angeles, California, March 22, 1942; admitted to bar, 1971, California and U.S. District Court, Central District of California; 1973, U.S. District Court, Southern District of California; 1975, U.S. Court of Appeals, Ninth Circuit; 1982, U.S. District Court, Northern and Eastern Districts of California. *Education:* Glendale College (A.A., 1962); California State University, Northridge (B.A., 1967); University of California, Los Angeles (J.D., 1970). Pi Sigma Alpha. Managing Editor, University of California, Los Angeles, Alaska Law Review, 1969-1970. *Member:* Los Angeles County Bar Association (Member, Executive Committee, Trial Lawyers Section, 1981-1984); The State Bar of California.

## POMS, SMITH, LANDE & ROSE

LOS ANGELES, CALIFORNIA

(See Oppenheimer Poms Smith)

## CHAD T-W PRATT

Established in 1991

4929 WILSHIRE BOULEVARD, SUITE 300
LOS ANGELES, CALIFORNIA 90010
Telephone: 213-936-9002
Fax: 213-938-6069

Pasadena, California Office: 221 East Walnut Street, Suite 245. Telephone: 818-441-CHAD. Fax: 818-577-4561.

*Civil Trial and Appellate Practice in State and Federal Courts. Landlord and Tenant Law, Uninhabitability, Labor Law, Family Law, Personal Injury, Premises Liability and Torts Law.*

(For Complete Biographical Data on all Personnel, see Professional Biographies at Pasadena, California)

## PRAY, PRICE, WILLIAMS & RUSSELL

LOS ANGELES, CALIFORNIA

(See Long Beach)

*General Civil and Criminal Trial Practice. Corporation, Real Estate, Estate Planning, Trust, Taxation, Probate, Negligence and Family Law.*

## PRESTHOLT, KLEEGER, FIDONE & VILLASENOR

SUITE 1600, 1055 WEST 7TH STREET
LOS ANGELES, CALIFORNIA 90017
Telephone: 213-895-4811
FAX: 213-895-4817

San Francisco, California Office: 989 Market Street, 6th Floor. Telephone: 415-267-6362. Fax: 415-267-6275.

*General Civil Trial Practice with emphasis on Insurance Litigation and Coverage Issues. Personal Injury, Casualty, Professional Negligence, Governmental Tort Liability and Insurance Company Practices and Procedures Law.*

(This Listing Continued)

*FIRM PROFILE:* The law firm of Prestholt, Kleeger, Fidone & Villasenor, located in downtown Los Angeles, specializes in general civil trial work with major emphasis in the field of insurance litigation and coverage issues. The practice includes cases in several areas including, but not limited to, casualty, professional negligence, governmental tort liability and insurance company practices and procedures.

### MEMBERS OF FIRM

**DAVID A. PRESTHOLT,** born August 11, 1956; admitted to bar, 1983, California. *Education:* University of California at Irvine (B.A., cum laude, 1979); University of California at Los Angeles School of Law (J.D., 1982). Member, Moot Court Honors Program, 1980-1981. Extern to Honorable James Fitzgerald, U.S. District Court, Anchorage, Alaska, 1981. *Member:* Los Angeles County and American Bar Associations; State Bar of California; Association of Southern California Defense Counsel. *PRACTICE AREAS:* Insurance Defense; Bad Faith; Trials.

**KENNETH S. KLEEGER,** born December 1, 1954; admitted to bar, 1982, California. *Education:* California State University/Los Angeles (B.S., 1978); Southwestern University (J.D., 1981). Delta Theta Phi. *Member:* Los Angeles County and American Bar Associations; State Bar of California; Association of Southern California Defense Counsel. *PRACTICE AREAS:* Products Liability; Premises Liability; Governmental Torts; Business Torts; Trials.

**GARY P. FIDONE,** born March 6, 1946; admitted to bar, 1974, California; 1978, U.S. Supreme Court; U.S. District Court, Central District of California. *Education:* California Polytechnic State University (B.S., 1970); Loyola Law School (J.D., 1974). Member, Los Angeles Superior Court Panel of Arbitrators, 1986-1987. Referee: Santa Monica Superior Court, 1986—; Van Nuys Superior Court, 1989—. *Member:* Los Angeles County and American Bar Associations; State Bar of California; Italian-American Lawyers Association; Southern California Defense Counsel. *PRACTICE AREAS:* Insurance Defense Litigation; Complex Commercial Trial Practice.

**LISA A. VILLASENOR,** born July 27, 1958; admitted to bar, 1988, California. *Education:* California State University at Long Beach (B.S., 1981); Loyola University of Los Angeles (J.D., 1987). Member, Loyola Law School Alumni. *Member:* Los Angeles County Bar Association; State Bar of California; Association of Southern California Defense Counsel. *PRACTICE AREAS:* Insurance Defense Litigation; Special Investigations Unit Trials.

**BRIAN D. HOLMBERG,** born April 7, 1942; admitted to bar, 1974, California. *Education:* University of Southern California (B.S., cum laude, 1970); California Western School of Law (J.D., 1973). *Member:* Los Angeles County and American Bar Associations; State Bar of California; American Board of Trial Advocates; Association of Southern California Defense Counsel. [E-4, USAF, 1961-1966]. *PRACTICE AREAS:* Civil Trial Litigation; Insurance Casualty Defense.

**WILLI H. SIEPMANN,** born November 15, 1946; admitted to bar, 1982, California and Nevada. *Education:* Brigham Young University (B.A., 1970); University of Utah (J.D., 1981). *Member:* Los Angeles County Bar; The State Bar of California; State Bar of Nevada; Association of Southern California Defense Counsel. *PRACTICE AREAS:* Personal Injury; General Practice.

**DAVID CRAWFORD, III,** born January 31, 1955; admitted to bar, 1985, California. *Education:* University of Nevada, Las Vegas (B.A., 1977); Pepperdine University School of Law (J.D., 1980). *Member:* San Fernando Valley and Los Angeles County Bar Associations; State Bar of California. *PRACTICE AREAS:* Insurance Defense Law; Plaintiff Personal Injury Law; General Practice Law.

**LISA L. LOVERIDGE,** born December 14, 1964; admitted to bar, 1992, California. *Education:* University of California, Santa Barbara (B.A., cum laude, 1987); Southwestern University School of Law (J.D., 1992). *Member:* Los Angeles County and American Bar Associations; State Bar of California; Association of Southern California Defense Counsel. *PRACTICE AREAS:* Premises Liability; Bad Faith; Insurance Defense Law.

**ARCHIE CHIN,** born September 15, 1958; admitted to bar, 1989, California. *Education:* University of California at Los Angeles (B.A., 1980); Whittier College School of Law (J.D., 1987). *Member:* Los Angeles County and American Bar Associations; State Bar of California; Southern California Defense Counsel and Southern California Chinese Lawyers Association. *PRACTICE AREAS:* Insurance Defense; Products Liability.

**ROBERT J. SCOTT, JR.,** born February 16, 1961; admitted to bar, 1990, California. *Education:* University of California, Berkeley (A.B., 1987); Santa Clara University (J.D., 1990). *Member:* San Mateo County Bar Association; State Bar of California (Member, Tort and Insurance Practice Section). *PRACTICE AREAS:* General Civil Litigation; Insurance Coverage; Insurance Bad Faith.

**AVIGAL HORROW,** born Norway, April 17, 1965; admitted to bar, 1992, California; 1993, U.S. District Court, Central District of California. *Education:* University of Maryland (B.S., 1987); California Western School of Law (J.D., 1992). Member, Board of Directors, Sojourn Battered Women's Shelter, 1993. *Member:* State Bar of California; American Bar Association. *PRACTICE AREAS:* Insurance Defense; Civil Litigation.

**JAMIE ANN LOUIE,** born February 9, 1964; admitted to bar, 1992, California. *Education:* California State University, Los Angeles (B.S., 1987); Western State University College of Law, Fullerton (J.D., 1991). *Member:* Southern California Chinese Lawyers Association. *PRACTICE AREAS:* Personal Injury; Workers Compensation.

**ROBERT S. PUTNAM,** born Plainfield, New Jersey, July 1, 1953; admitted to bar, 1992, California; 1993, U.S. District Court, Northern, Central, Eastern and Southern Districts of California. *Education:* Lincoln University (J.D., 1992). *Member:* Santa Monica and Los Angeles County Bar Associations. *PRACTICE AREAS:* Insurance Bad Faith; Construction Litigation; Civil Defense Litigation.

**ARNIE E. GOLDSTEIN,** born August 30, 1965; admitted to bar, 1996, California. *Education:* Arizona State University (B.A., magna cum laude, 1992, Phi Beta Kappa); Southwestern University School of Law (J.D., 1995). *Member:* State Bar of California; American Bar Association; Association for Southern California Defense Counsel.

**BRIAN J. FINN,** born New York, N.Y., December 7, 1958; admitted to bar, 1989, California and U.S. Court of Appeals, Ninth Circuit. *Education:* University of Nevada-Reno (B.A., with distinction, 1985); Hastings College of the Law, University of California (J.D., 1989). Phi Kappa Phi; Pi Sigma Alpha. *Member:* San Francisco and American Bar Associations. *PRACTICE AREAS:* Civil Defense Litigation; Products Liability; Bad Faith.

REPRESENTATIVE CLIENTS: Argonaut Insurance, Clarendon; California Casualty Insurance Company; Civil Service Employees Insurance Company; The Regents of the University of California; Del Amo Fashion Center; Ward-THG.

---

## *PRESTON GATES & ELLIS*
### SUITE 2100
### 725 SOUTH FIGUEROA STREET
### LOS ANGELES, CALIFORNIA 90017
*Telephone: 213-624-2395*
*Facsimile: 213-624-5924*

*Anchorage, Alaska Office:* Suite 400, 420 L Street, 99501-1937. Telephone: 907-276-1969. Facsimile: 907-276-1365.

*Coeur d'Alene, Idaho Office:* 1200 Ironwood Drive, Suite 315. 83814. Telephone: 208-667-1839. Facsimile: 208-765-2494.

*Washington, D.C. Office:* Preston Gates Ellis & Rouvelas Meeds, Suite 500, 1735 New York Avenue, N.W., 20006-4759. Telephone: 202-628-1700. Facsimile: 202-331-1024.

*Portland, Oregon Office:* 3200 US Bancorp Tower 111 S.W. Fifth Avenue, 97204-3688. Telephone: 503-228-3200. Facsimile: 503-248-9085.

*Seattle, Washington Office:* 5000 Columbia Seafirst Center, 701 Fifth Avenue. Telephone: 206-623-7580. Facsimile: 206-623-7022.

*Spokane, Washington Office:* 1400 Seafirst Financial Center, 601 West Riverside Avenue, 99201-0636. Telephone: 509-624-2100. Facsimile: 509-456-0146.

*Hong Kong Office:* 2901 Central Plaza, 18 Harbour Road, Hong Kong. Telephone: 852-2511-5100. Facsimile: 852-2511-9515.

*General Practice.*

### MEMBERS OF FIRM

**JANE H. BARRETT,** born Dayton, Ohio, December 13, 1947; admitted to bar, 1972, California. *Education:* California State University (B.A., 1969); University of Southern California (J.D., 1972). Outstanding Alumni, California University, Long Beach, 1988. Member: USC Legion Lex Board of Directors, 1990—. Advisory Council, Harriet Buhai Law Center, 1990—. *Member:* Los Angeles County (Chairperson, Special Committee on Detoxification Reform, 1975-1978; Conference of Delegates Executive Committee, 1976-1978) and American (Member, Board of Governors, 1981-1984; Finance Secretary, Torts and Insurance Practice, 1980-1981; Chairperson, Young Lawyers Division, 1980-1981; Advisor, Standing Committee on the Federal Judiciary; Member, Special Committee on Insur-

*(This Listing Continued)*

## PRESTON GATES & ELLIS, Los Angeles—Continued

ance Legislation, 1977-1979; Chairperson, Section Officers Conference, 1981-1982; Member, Committee on London Meeting, 1983-1985; Chairperson, Torts and Insurance Practice Special Committee, 1981-1983; Chairperson, Special Committee on Delivery of Legal Services, 1985-1989; Member, Executive Council Legal Education and Admissions, 1985-1989) Bar Associations; The State Bar of California (Member: Committee on Equal Rights, 1975-1976; Committee on Administration of Justice, 1976-1979; Coordinating Committee, Conference of Delegates, 1977); American Judicature Society (Member, Board of Directors, 1977-1984). Fellow, American Bar Foundation; American Bar Endowment (Secretary, 1985-1990; Treasurer, 1995—; Member Board, 1990—).

**ROGER LANE CARRICK**, born High Point, North Carolina, July 28, 1951; admitted to bar, 1980, California. *Education:* Harvard College (A.B., magna cum laude, 1973); Boalt Hall School of Law, University of California (J.D., 1980). Instructor in Computer Law, Boalt Hall School of Law, 1984-1989, and UCLA Law School, 1988—. Deputy Assistant to the Governor of California, 1980-1983. Special Assistant Attorney General for Policy, California, 1984-1986. Special Review Task Force on Proposition 65, appointed by California Secretary of EPA, 1992. *Member:* Los Angeles County (Member, Environmental Law Section) and American (Member, Natural Resources Section) Bar Associations; State Bar of California.

**GREGORY LAWRENCE EVANS**, born Chico, California, December 20, 1960; admitted to bar, 1990, California, U.S. District Court, Central, Eastern and Northern Districts of California and U.S. Court of Appeals, Seventh and Ninth Circuits. *Education:* University of Southern California (B.S., 1984); University of California at Berkeley (M.S., 1986); University of Notre Dame (J.D., 1989). Recipient, 1993 State Bar of California Wiley W. Manuel Award. Author: "Meeting the Diverse Needs of the Poor," 16 Journal of Legislation 127, 1990; "Federal Emergency Shelter Assistance to the Homeless: Mandating a Standard of Decency," 4 Notre Dame Journal of Law, Ethics & Public Policy 325, 1989; "School Crime and Violence: Achieving Deterrence Through Tort Law," 3 Notre Dame Journal of Law, Ethics & Public Policy 501, 1988. Contributing Author: "Child Welfare League of America, Standards of Excellence for Residential Group Care Services," Child Welfare League of America, Washington, D.C. (1991). Fellowship/Extern, U.S. Department of Justice, Office of Juvenile Justice and Delinquency Prevention, 1987. Member, Board of Catholic Charities of Los Angeles. Member, Los Angeles County Bar Association, Committees on Childrens' Rights; Juvenile Justice. *LANGUAGES:* Spanish. *PRACTICE AREAS:* Civil Litigation. *Email:* gregory@prestongates.com

**HOWARD A. KROLL**, born Los Angeles, California, November 7, 1956; admitted to bar, 1981, California. *Education:* Claremont McKenna College (B.A., 1978); University of Southern California (J.D., 1981).

**PHILIP NELSON LEE**, born Stockton, California, June 18, 1945; admitted to bar, 1973, Virginia; 1976, California, U.S. Supreme Court and U.S. Court of Appeals, Fourth Circuit. *Education:* Foothill College; University of Southern California (A.B., 1967); Harvard Law School (J.D., 1970). Attorney: Division of Corporation Finance, 1973-1976, Securities and Exchange Commission; Office of The General Counsel, 1976-1977, Securities and Exchange Commission. *Member:* State Bar of California; The Virginia State Bar; American Bar Association; National Association of Bond Lawyers. *PRACTICE AREAS:* Municipal Finance; Corporate Law.

**JOHN P. PETRULLO**, born Brooklyn, New York, May 6, 1955; admitted to bar, 1988, California, District of Columbia, U.S. Court of Appeals, Second and Ninth Circuits. *Education:* State University of New York at Stony Brook (B.A., 1977, M.A., 1978); New York University (M.A., 1982); Whittier College School of Law (J.D., 1987). Phi Alpha Delta. Moot Court Honors. *Member:* Los Angeles County and American (Member, Sections on: Business Law; Environmental Law; Litigation) Bar Associations; The State Bar of California; Southern California Defense Counsel; The Association of Trial Lawyers of America; California Trial Lawyers Association; International Association of Defense Counsel; Los Angeles County Superior Court Judges Inn of Court for Complex Litigation. *PRACTICE AREAS:* Products Liability Law.

**DAVID B. SADWICK**, born St. Paul, Minnesota, April 15, 1961; admitted to bar, 1986, California; 1989, District of Columbia. *Education:* University of California at San Diego (B.A., magna cum laude, 1983); Stanford Law School (J.D., with distinction, 1986). Author: "Inactive Sites-The Superfund Process," Environmental Law Practice Guide. Law Clerk to Hon. David R. Thompson, U.S. Court of Appeals, Ninth Circuit, 1986-1987. *Member:* Los Angeles County Bar Association; State Bar of California.

*(This Listing Continued)*

nia. *PRACTICE AREAS:* Environmental Law; Pharmaceutical; Technology.

### OF COUNSEL

**ELIZABETH C. GREEN**, born Alamogordo, New Mexico, April 9, 1953; admitted to bar, 1978, Texas; 1981, California. *Education:* Yale University (A.B., with honors, 1975); University of Chicago (J.D., 1978). *Member:* American Bar Association (Member, Section on Corporation, Banking and Business Law).

### ASSOCIATES

**KATHERINE M. MARELICH**, born Sacramento, California, March 31, 1967; admitted to bar, 1993, California, U.S. District Court, Central District of California and U.S. Court of Appeals, Ninth Circuit. *Education:* University of California at Los Angeles (B.A., 1989); University of Southern California (J.D., 1993). Phi Delta Phi. *Member:* Los Angeles County Bar Association; State Bar of California; Defense Research Institute. *PRACTICE AREAS:* Litigation.

**GARY STEVEN SEDLIK**, born Colorado Springs, Colorado, September 3, 1968; admitted to bar, 1995, California, U.S. District Court, Central District of California and U.S. Court of Appeals, Ninth Circuit. *Education:* Middlebury College (B.A., 1990); Washington College of Law of American University (J.D., magna cum laude, 1995). Recipient: Belva A. Lockwood Scholarship for Academic Excellence and Service to the Law School, 1995; Willian Brinks Hofer Gilson & Lione Award for Excellence in Intellectual Property, 1995. Member, Journal of International Law and Policy. *Member:* Los Angeles County Bar Association (Member, Sections on: Litigation; Intellectual Property; Environment); State Bar of California (Member, Litigation Section). *LANGUAGES:* Japanese and Spanish. *REPORTED CASES:* Makell v. State, 104 Md.App. 334, 656 A.2d 348 (Md. Ct. Spec. App. 1995). *PRACTICE AREAS:* Litigation.

**MARK B. TUVIM**, born Atlanta, Georgia, May 1, 1955; admitted to bar, 1992, California and U.S. District Court, Central District of California; 1993, U.S. Court of Appeals, Ninth Circuit; 1996, U.S. District Court, Southern District of California. *Education:* University of North Carolina (B.A., with honors, 1977); University of California at Los Angeles (J.D., 1992). Phi Beta Kappa; Phi Eta Sigma; Order of the Old Well. *Member:* Los Angeles County and American Bar Associations. *PRACTICE AREAS:* Labor and Employment Law; General Litigation.

Languages: Chinese, French, German, Italian, Japanese, Portuguese, Russian, Spanish and Taiwanese.

REPRESENTATIVE CLIENTS: City of Anaheim; City of Oakland; Cooper Industries Inc.; GEC/Alsthom; Kerr-MGee Corp.; Los Angeles County Transportation Authority; Microsoft; National Railroad Passenger Corp. (Amtrak); SmithKline Beecham Consumer Healthcare; Southwest Airlines Co.; Univar Insurance Reserve; Van Waters & Rogers Scientific Corp.

(For complete Biographical data on all Personnel, see Professional Biographies at Seattle, Spokane and Tacoma, Washington, Anchorage, Alaska, Portland, Oregon and Washington, D.C., Coeur d'Alene, Idaho)

---

## PRETTY, SCHROEDER & POPLAWSKI

*A PROFESSIONAL CORPORATION*
SUITE 2000, 444 SOUTH FLOWER STREET
**LOS ANGELES, CALIFORNIA 90071**
*Telephone: 213-622-7700*
*Telecopier: 213-489-4210*

*Patents, Trademarks, Copyrights and Unfair Competition Law. Litigation.*

*FIRM PROFILE: Pretty, Schroeder, Brueggemann & Clark was founded in 1984 by the four named members, who had worked together for nearly a decade before starting their own firm. Since 1984, the firm has continued to grow in size and experience.*

*The philosophy behind the creation of the firm has been to provide services at the highest quality level in the intellectual property area. Recognizing that the field of litigation is adversarial, the firm has focused on representing its clients aggressively without compromising high ethical standards and professional courtesy. The firm places particular emphasis on prompt service, knowing that business decisions dependent on legal input should not be delayed.*

*The major portion of the firm's work has been, and continues to be, intellectual property litigation, primarily patent and trademark lawsuits. It is one of California's most active patent and trademark litigation firms, with ongoing litigation in California and throughout the United States.*

*(This Listing Continued)*

**LAURENCE H. PRETTY,** admitted to bar, 1969, District of Columbia; 1970, New York; 1973, California; registered to practice before U.S. Patent and Trademark Office. *Education:* London University (B.S., with honors, 1958); George Washington University (J.D., with honors, 1968). Order of the Coif. Law Clerk, U.S. Court of Customs and Patent Appeals, 1969. Adjunct Lecturer, Patent and Trademark Law, UCLA School of Law, 1974-1984 and 1996. Chairperson, Practising Law Institute program in "Patent Litigation," 1989-1996. Author: "Where the Veil Against Discovery In Patent Litigation Falls" Vol. 76, No. 2 Journal of the Patent and Trademark Office Society (Feb. 1994); "Patent Litigation: It's No Mystery," Vol. 26 TRIAL No. 3, 1990; "Patent Litigation," Vol. II, No. 4, Litigation 32, 1985; "Inequitable Conduct Before the PTO," 13 AIPLA Quarterly Journal, Nos. 3 & 4, 1985; "Patent Law for the Business Lawyer," California Continuing Education of the Bar, 1980; "A Forecast of C.A.F.C. Holdings," 10 APLA Quarterly Journal, No. 4, 1982; "Harnessing a Personal Computer to Win Cases," 69 ABA Journal 1438, 1983. Lawyer Delegate, Ninth Circuit Judicial Conference, 1993-1994. *Member:* State Bar of California (Chairperson, Intellectual Property Section, 1987); American Bar Association (Member of Council, Patent, Trademark and Copyright Section, 1987-1991); American Intellectual Property Law Association (Member, Board of Directors, 1984-1986); Association of Business Trial Lawyers (President, 1983-1984); Los Angeles Intellectual Property Law Association (President, 1981-1982). **PRACTICE AREAS:** Patents; Trademarks; Copyrights; Unfair Competition; Litigation.

**ROBERT A. SCHROEDER,** born Woodridge, New Jersey, September 2, 1942; admitted to bar, 1969, New York; 1977, California; registered to practice before U.S. Patent and Trademark Office. *Education:* Clarkson University (B.S., with distinction, 1964); Cornell University (J.D., 1967). Author: "Licensing of Rights to Intellectual Property," Vol. 50, No. 3, Albany Law Review, Symposium on Intellectual Property, 1986. Member, Panel of Patent Arbitrators, American Arbitration Association. *Member:* Licensing Executive Society; Association of Business Trial Lawyers; American Intellectual Property Law Association. **PRACTICE AREAS:** Patents; Trademarks; Copyrights; Unfair Competition; Litigation.

**EDWARD G. POPLAWSKI,** born Scranton, Pennsylvania, June 18, 1957; admitted to bar, 1984, California and District of Columbia; registered to practice before U.S. Patent and Trademark Office. *Education:* Drexel University (M.S.M.E. and B.S.M.E., summa cum laude, 1980); Villanova University School of Law (J.D., 1983). Author: "The Impact of Federal Circuit Precedent on the 'On-Sale' and 'Public Use' Bars to Patentability," 44 American University Law Review 2351 (1995); "Obtaining and Defending Against TROs and Preliminary Injunctions in Trademark Cases," American Intellectual Property Law Association, Selected Legal Papers Vol. X, 1992. *Member:* District of Columbia Bar; American Institute of Astronautics and Aeronautics; American Intellectual Property Law Association (Member, Board of Directors, 1996); Association of Business Trial Lawyers; Los Angeles Intellectual Property Law Association (Member, Board of Directors, 1992—; Vice President and President Elect, 1996—; Treasurer, 1994—). Los Angeles Complex Litigation Inn of Court. **PRACTICE AREAS:** Patents; Trademarks; Copyrights; Trade Secrets; Unfair Competition; Litigation.

**MARK GARSCIA,** born St. Paul, Minnesota, April 4, 1955; admitted to bar, 1985, New York; 1988, California; registered to practice before U.S. Patent and Trademark Office. *Education:* University of Minnesota (B.S., with distinction, 1978); New York Law School (J.D., cum laude, 1984). Member, New York Law School Law Review, 1982-1984. *Member:* Los Angeles County and American Bar Associations (Member, Intellectual Property Section); State Bar of California; American Intellectual Property Law Association. **PRACTICE AREAS:** Patents; Trademarks; Copyrights; Unfair Competition; Litigation.

**JEFFREY F. CRAFT,** born Chicago, Illinois, May 26, 1954; admitted to bar, 1981, Michigan; 1982, Delaware; 1990, California; registered to practice before U.S. Patent and Trademark Office. *Education:* University of Michigan (B.S., 1976); Wayne State University (J.D., 1981). Author: "Prejudgment Interest Under 35 U.S.C. Section 284," Journal of the Patent Office Society, Vol. 64, No. 5, 1982. *Member:* American Bar Association; American Intellectual Property Law Association. **PRACTICE AREAS:** Patents; Trademarks; Copyrights; Unfair Competition; Litigation.

**MICHAEL J. MACDERMOTT,** born Dearborn, Michigan, November 2, 1950; admitted to bar, 1975, California; registered to practice before U.S. Patent and Trademark Office. *Education:* University of Michigan (B.S., Physics and Mathematics, 1972); University of California at Los Angeles (J.D., 1975). Co-Author: "The Fifth Amendment and Its Impact on Civil Actions Under the Trademark Counterfeiting Act of 1984," AIPLA Quar-

*(This Listing Continued)*

terly Journal, Vol. 14, No. 4, 1986; "Searching and Clearing Trademarks and Company Names," Los Angeles Lawyer, Vol. 8, No. II, 1986; "Federal Registration and Incontestability," 79 Trademark Reporter 373, 1989. Contributor to State Trademark and Unfair Competition Law. *Member:* Wilshire (Vice President, Board of Directors), Los Angeles County and American Bar Associations; The State Bar of California; International Trademark Association. **PRACTICE AREAS:** Patents; Trademarks; Copyrights; Unfair Competition.

**SUZANNE R. JONES,** born Houston, Texas, April 23, 1962; admitted to bar, 1988, California. *Education:* University of California at Irvine (B.S., 1985); Loyola Marymount University (J.D., 1988). Senior Note and Comment Editor, Loyola of Los Angeles Law Review, 1987-1988. Author: "Whelan Associates v. Jaslow Dental Laboratory: Copyright Protection for the Structure and Sequence of Computer Programs," 21 Loy. L.A. L. Rev. 255, 1987. *Member:* Los Angeles County and American Bar Associations; State Bar of California. **PRACTICE AREAS:** Patents; Trademarks; Copyrights; Unfair Competition; Litigation.

## COUNSEL

**RICHARD A. WALLEN,** born Glendale, California, July 16, 1937; admitted to bar, 1963, California; registered to practice before U.S. Patent and Trademark Office. *Education:* University of California at Los Angeles (B.A., Physics, 1959); University of Southern California (J.D., 1962). Phi Delta Phi. Member, Chancery Club, 1970. Co-Author: "The Fifth Amendment and Its Impact on Civil Actions Under the Trademark Counterfeiting Act of 1984," AIPLA Quarterly Journal, Vol. 14, No. 4, 1986; "Federal Registration and Incontestability," 79 Trademark Reporter 373, 1989. Contributor to State Trademark and Unfair Competition Law. *Member:* Los Angeles County (Chairman, Intellectual Property and Unfair Competition Section, 1971-1972) and American (Chairman: State Trademark Committee, Patent, Trademark and Copyright Section, 1970-1971; Patent Office Affairs Committee, 1971-1972; Trademark Division Chairman, 1972-1973) Bar Associations; The State Bar of California (Member, Executive Committee, Patent, Trademark and Copyright Section 1981-1983); American Judicature Society; International Trademark Association (Member, Board of Directors, 1981-1983; Trademark Review Commission, 1985-1988). **PRACTICE AREAS:** Patents; Trademarks; Copyrights; Unfair Competition.

## OF COUNSEL

**WALTON EUGENE TINSLEY,** born Vanceburg, Kentucky, January 22, 1921; admitted to bar, 1954, California; 1971, U.S. Supreme Court; registered to practice before U.S. Patent and Trademark Office. *Education:* University of Cincinnati (E.E., 1943); New York University (M.A.E., 1947); University of Southern California (J.D., 1953). Tau Beta Pi. Phi Alpha Delta. Member, American Institute of Aeronautics and Astronautics. Associate Member, Institute of Electrical and Electronic Engineers. *Member:* Los Angeles County and American Bar Associations; The State Bar of California. **PRACTICE AREAS:** Patents; Trademarks; Unfair Competition.

---

**PAUL D. TRIPODI, II,** born Latrobe, Pennsylvania, November 23, 1966; admitted to bar, 1992, California. *Education:* Pennsylvania State University (B.S., with honors and distinction, 1987); California Institute of Technology (M.S., 1990); University of California, Los Angeles (J.D., 1992). Phi Beta Kappa. *Member:* State Bar of California. **PRACTICE AREAS:** Patents; Trademarks; Copyrights; Unfair Competition; Litigation.

**MARC H. COHEN,** born Fond du Lac, Wisconsin, September 22, 1963; admitted to bar, 1993, California. *Education:* Western Michigan University (B.S.E.E., 1987); Case Western Reserve University (J.D., 1993). Phi Delta Phi (President). Mock Trial Team. **PRACTICE AREAS:** Patents; Trademarks; Copyrights; Unfair Competition; Litigation.

**KEITH A. NEWBURRY,** born Kalamazoo, Michigan, October 8, 1965; admitted to bar, 1993, California. *Education:* University of Michigan (B.S.M.E., cum laude, 1987); University of Southern California (J.D., 1993). Pi Tau Sigma; Tau Beta Pi. **PRACTICE AREAS:** Patents; Trademarks; Copyrights; Unfair Competition; Litigation.

**SHARON M. FUJITA,** born Los Angeles, California, October 10, 1961; admitted to bar, 1994, California. *Education:* University of Southern California (B.S., Chemical Engineering, Magna Cum Laude, 1983); University of California at Berkeley (M.S., Chemical Engineering, 1986); Hastings College of the Law (J.D., 1994). Tau Beta Pi. Phi Kappa Phi. Phi Beta Kappa. Note Editor, Hastings Law Journal. *Member:* State Bar of California. **PRACTICE AREAS:** Patents; Trademarks; Copyrights; Unfair Competition; Litigation.

*(This Listing Continued)*

## PRETTY, SCHROEDER & POPLAWSKI, A PROFESSIONAL CORPORATION, Los Angeles—Continued

**J. CHRIS JAMES,** born Tokyo, Japan, November 21, 1965; admitted to bar, 1994, California. *Education:* Purdue University (B.S.M.E., 1989); University of Texas (J.D., 1994). Member, Texas Intellectual Property Law Journal. *Member:* State Bar of California. *PRACTICE AREAS:* Patents; Trademarks; Copyrights; Unfair Competition; Litigation.

**JOHN A. GRIECCI,** born Evanston, Illinois, October 11, 1960; admitted to bar, 1994, California. *Education:* University of Illinois (B.S., 1982; M.S., 1987); Cornell Law School (J.D., 1994). Member, Cornell International Law Journal. *PRACTICE AREAS:* Patents; Trademarks; Copyrights; Unfair Competition; Litigation.

**ANNE WANG,** born Taipei, Taiwan, July 11, 1962; admitted to bar, 1990, California, U.S. District Court, Central District of California and U.S. Court of Appeals, Ninth Circuit; registered to practice before U.S. Patent and Trademark Office. *Education:* University of California (B.S., Sigma Pi Sigma 1985); University of Southern California Law Center (J.D., 1990). Moot Court Honors Program. *Member:* Los Angeles County and American Bar Associations; State Bar of California; Southern California Chinese Lawyers' Association; Los Angeles Intellectual Property Law Association; Lawyers' Club of Los Angeles County. *LANGUAGES:* Chinese (Mandarin). *PRACTICE AREAS:* Patent Law; Trademark Law.

**JEANINE L. HAYES,** born Williamsport, Pennsylvania, September 11, 1968; admitted to bar, 1996, California. *Education:* University of Rochester (B.S., 1992); Loyola Law School (J.D., 1995). Articles Editor, Loyola Law Review.

**MARC E. HANKIN,** born Queens, New York, 1961; admitted to bar, 1994, New Jersey, California, U.S. District Court, District of New Jersey and U.S. District Court, Central District of California; registered to practice before U.S. Patent and Trademark Office. *Education:* Boston University (B.A., 1984); Iona College (M.S., 1987); University of Pennsylvania (J.D., 1992). *Member:* Los Angeles County, Federal and American Bar Associations; Los Angeles Intellectual Property Law Association; American Intellectual Property Law Association. *PRACTICE AREAS:* Patent Litigation and Prosecution; Trademark Litigation and Registration; Copyright Litigation and Registration; Trade Secrets Litigation.

**JEFFREY A. FINN,** born Chicago, Illinois, December 28, 1963; admitted to bar, 1996, California. *Education:* University of Illinois (B.S.E.E., 1988); University of Southern California (J.D., 1996). Tay Beta Pi; ETA Kappa Nu. *PRACTICE AREAS:* Intellectual Property; Patent Litigation and Prosecution; Trademark Litigation and Prosecution.

---

## PRINDLE, DECKER & AMARO

### LOS ANGELES, CALIFORNIA

(See Long Beach)

*General Litigation Practice including Asbestos Personal Injury and Property Damage, Personal Injury, Products Liability, Recreation and Amusement Park Litigation, Environmental, Admiralty, Business Transaction, Real Estate Transaction, Superfund, Workers Compensation, Construction Litigation and Coverage.*

---

## ROBERT C. PROCTOR, JR.

### A PROFESSIONAL CORPORATION

### LOS ANGELES, CALIFORNIA

(See Pasadena)

*Personal Injury and Products Liability. Trial Practice in all State Courts. Third Party Cases, Medical Malpractice and Americans Disability Act.*

CAA1112B

---

## PROSKAUER ROSE GOETZ & MENDELSOHN LLP

### 2121 AVENUE OF THE STARS, SUITE 2700
### LOS ANGELES, CALIFORNIA 90067-3003

Telephone: 310-557-2900
FAX: 310-557-2193
Email: info@proskauer.com
URL: http://www.proskauer.com

*New York, N.Y. Office:* 1585 Broadway. Telephone: 212-969-3000.
*Washington, D.C. Office:* 1233 Twentieth Street, N.W., Suite 800. Telephone: 202-416-6800.
*Boca Raton, Florida Office:* One Boca Place, Suite 340 West, 2255 Glades Road. Telephone: 407-241-7400.
*Clifton, New Jersey Office:* 1373 Broad Street, P.O. Box 4444. Telephone: 201-779-6300.
*Paris, France Office:* Proskauer Rose Goetz & Mendelsohn, 9 rue Le Tasse. Telephone: (33-1) 44 30 25 30.

*General Practice.*

### RESIDENT PARTNERS

**HOWARD D. BEHAR,** born New York, New York, October 23, 1950; admitted to bar, 1982, California. *Education:* Columbia University (B.S., 1972); Stanford Law School (J.D., 1982). *PRACTICE AREAS:* Entertainment Law.

**HENRY BEN-ZVI,** born Haifa, Israel, May 16, 1953; admitted to bar, 1982, California. *Education:* Immaculate Heart College (B.A., 1976); University of Oregon (M.A., 1979); University of California at Los Angeles School of Law (J.D., 1982). Member, 1980-1981 and Comment Editor, 1981-1982, UCLA Law Review. Law Clerk to Hon. Howard B. Wiener, California Court of Appeal, Fourth District, 1982-1983. *PRACTICE AREAS:* Litigation.

**JEFFREY A. BERMAN,** born Los Angeles, California, September 3, 1946; admitted to bar, 1972, California. *Education:* University of California at Santa Barbara (B.A., with honors, 1968); University of California at Los Angeles (J.D., 1971). Associate Editor, U.C.L.A. Law Review, Vol. 18, 1971. *PRACTICE AREAS:* Labor and Employment Law.

**HAROLD M. BRODY,** born Chicago, Illinois, June 19, 1950; admitted to bar, 1975, Illinois; 1979, California. *Education:* University of Pennsylvania (A.B., cum laude, 1972); Northwestern University (J.D., cum laude, 1975). Phi Beta Kappa. President, Board of Directors, Westside Legal Services, 1985-1986. *PRACTICE AREAS:* Alternative Dispute Resolution; Employment Discrimination Law; Equal Employment Law.

**SCOTT P. COOPER,** born Evanston, Illinois, October 6, 1955; admitted to bar, 1981, California. *Education:* University of Notre Dame (B.A., 1977); Georgetown University (J.D., 1980). *PRACTICE AREAS:* Litigation.

**THOMAS W. DOLLINGER,** born Rochester, New York, April 18, 1950; admitted to bar, 1979, New York; 1984, California. *Education:* Gannon University (B.A., 1972); Brooklyn Law School (J.D., 1978). Articles Editor, Brooklyn Law Review. *PRACTICE AREAS:* Corporate.

**HOWARD D. FABRICK,** born Milwaukee, Wisconsin, June 30, 1938; admitted to bar, 1963, California. *Education:* Stanford University (B.A., 1960; J.D., 1962). Phi Sigma Alpha; Phi Delta Phi. Instructor, Peter Stark Producer Program, University of Southern California, Collective Bargaining in the Entertainment Industries, 1981-1991. Attorney, National Labor Relations Board, 1962-1964. *PRACTICE AREAS:* Labor; Entertainment Law.

**MITCHELL M. GASWIRTH,** born Queens, New York, February 10, 1957; admitted to bar, 1982, California and U.S. District Court, Central District of California; 1983, U.S. Court of Appeals, Ninth Circuit and U.S. Tax Court. *Education:* University of California at Santa Barbara (B.A., 1979); Boalt Hall School of Law, University of California (J.D., 1982). Member: Order of the Coif; University of California Law Review, 1981-1982. Extern to Hon. Allen E. Broussard, Associate Justice of the California Supreme Court, 1982. *PRACTICE AREAS:* Taxation.

**BERNARD D. GOLD,** born New York, New York, December 12, 1930; admitted to bar, 1955, New York; 1975, California. *Education:* Cornell University (B.S., 1952); Harvard University (J.D., magna cum laude, 1955). Editor, Harvard Law Review, 1954-1955. *PRACTICE AREAS:* Labor and Employment Law.

*(This Listing Continued)*

**BARRY C. GROVEMAN,** born Ellenville, New York, July 23, 1953; admitted to bar, 1978, California and U.S. Court of Appeals, Ninth Circuit. *Education:* Clark University; University of Wisconsin (B.A., 1975); Southwestern University (J.D., 1978). Author: "Environmental Crime and Corporate Liability," Business and Society Magazine, Oct., 1985; "Air Pollution Litigation," National Institute of Municipal Law Offices, 1980 Quarterly. Professor, Environmental Law and Hazardous Waste Litigation, Southwestern University, 1982-1989. Assistant Los Angeles City Attorney, 1979-1984. Special Assistant to the District Attorney, Los Angeles County, 1984-1986. Chief Environmental Prosecutor, Los Angeles County, 1982-1986. Founder and Head, Los Angeles Toxic Waste Strike Force, 1982-1986. Advisory Member, Environmental Health Committee, Los Angeles County Medical Association, 1986-1989. *Member:* Los Angeles County Bar Association (Founder and Chair, Environmental Law Section, 1986-1988); State Bar of California. *PRACTICE AREAS:* Environmental Law.

**PAUL D. RUBENSTEIN,** born Los Angeles, California, April 7, 1946; admitted to bar, 1971, California. *Education:* Georg-August-Universitat, Gottingen, West Germany; University of California at Los Angeles (B.A., 1967); Harvard University (J.D., 1970). *PRACTICE AREAS:* Real Estate; Partnership Law.

**DAVID R. SCHEIDEMANTLE,** born White Plains, New York, June 3, 1960; admitted to bar, 1987, New York; 1990, California. *Education:* Juilliard School of Music (B.A., 1982); Fordham University Law School (J.D., cum laude, 1985). *PRACTICE AREAS:* Securities; Banking; Antitrust Litigation.

**MARVIN SEARS,** born Philadelphia, Pennsylvania, June 11, 1927; admitted to bar, 1953, New York; 1955, California. *Education:* New York University (A.B., cum laude, 1948); Harvard University (LL.B., magna cum laude, 1951). Law Clerk to Hon. Harrie B. Chase, U.S. Court of Appeals, Second Circuit, 1951-1952. Member, Board of Editors, Harvard Law Review, 1949-1951. Special Master, U.S. District Court, Central District of California, 1970-1971. *PRACTICE AREAS:* Corporate; Real Estate; Entertainment Law.

**LOIS D. THOMPSON,** born New York, New York, March 6, 1946; admitted to bar, 1970, New York; 1980, California; U.S. Court of Appeals, Ninth and Second Circuits. *Education:* Smith College (B.A., cum laude, 1966); Columbia University (J.D., cum laude, 1969). *PRACTICE AREAS:* Litigation; Alternative Dispute Resolution.

**MARTIN S. ZOHN,** born Denver, Colorado, October 22, 1947; admitted to bar, 1972, California; 1973, Indiana and U.S. Tax Court; 1977, U.S. Supreme Court and U.S. Claims Court; 1980, U.S. Court of Appeals, Ninth Circuit. *Education:* Indiana University (A.B., 1969), Phi Beta Kappa; Harvard Law School (J.D., 1972). *PRACTICE AREAS:* Bankruptcy; Corporate; Litigation.

*SPECIAL COUNSEL*

**WALTER COCHRAN-BOND,** born Palo Alto, California, February 18, 1948; admitted to bar, 1974, California. *Education:* Swarthmore College (B.A., 1970); University of California at Los Angeles (J.D., 1974). *PRACTICE AREAS:* Labor; Employment Discrimination.

**KENNETH KRUG,** born Brooklyn, New York, October 25, 1958; admitted to bar, 1982, California; 1983, Florida. *Education:* Duke University (A.B., summa cum laude, 1979); University of Chicago (J.D., 1982). *PRACTICE AREAS:* Real Estate; Corporate.

**W. HERBERT YOUNG,** born Los Angeles, California, August 28, 1937; admitted to bar, 1963, California; 1968, U.S. Supreme Court. *Education:* University of California at Los Angeles (B.S., magna cum laude, 1959; J.D., 1962). Beta Gamma Sigma. Guest Lecturer, Environmental Law, Pepperdine Law School, April, 1987. Vice President and General Counsel, Powerine Oil Co., 1981-1986. Founding Partner, Groveman & Young, 1986-1992. *Member:* Los Angeles County Bar Association; The State Bar of California. *PRACTICE AREAS:* Environmental Law.

*RESIDENT ASSOCIATES*

Aaron P. Allan
Christopher M. Brock
Yun Y. Choi
Nicholas P. Connon
James F. Dunn
Daniel E. Eaton
Steven J. Elkins
Alan H. Finkel
Maria E. Grecky

Gloria Ching-hua Jan
Elizabeth J. Kruger
Carol E. Kurtz
Erick Kwak
Dana Hirsch Lipman
David S. Lippman
Matthew J. Lopez (admission pending).
Seth A. Miller

(This Listing Continued)

*RESIDENT ASSOCIATES (Continued)*

Gregory J. Patterson
Mary H. Rose
Jane E. Rudofsky
Lori E. Sambol
Christopher J. Tricarico

Tal O. Vigderson
Hao-Nhien Q. Vu
James M. Wakefield
Leslie A. Wederich
Scott J. Witlin

(For biographical data on all personnel, see Professional Biographies at New York, New York)

## QUAN, COHEN, KURAHASHI, YANG, SCHOLTZ & HIRANO

*A PROFESSIONAL CORPORATION*

Established in 1975

**777 SOUTH FIGUEROA STREET, 38TH FLOOR**
**LOS ANGELES, CALIFORNIA 90017**
Telephone: 213-892-7550
Telecopier: 213-892-7567

General Civil and Trial Practice. Real Property, Banking, Commercial and Business Law and Related Litigation.

**RICHARD K. QUAN,** born Los Angeles, California, May 10, 1936; admitted to bar, 1964, California and U.S. District Court, Central District of California; 1968, U.S., Court of Appeals, Ninth Circuit. *Education:* University of California at Los Angeles (B.A., 1960; LL.B., 1963). Deputy City Attorney, City of Los Angeles, 1964-1965. Law Clerk to Hon. Shirley Hufstedler, 1965. Deputy Attorney General, State of California, 1965-1968. *Member:* Los Angeles County Bar Association; State Bar of California; Southern California Chinese Lawyers Association. *PRACTICE AREAS:* Business Law; Real Estate; Banking.

**KENNETH P. SCHOLTZ,** born Los Angeles, California, March 24, 1938; admitted to bar, 1964, California; 1965, U.S. District Court, Central District of California; 1972, U.S. Supreme Court and U.S. Court of Appeals, Ninth Circuit. *Education:* California Institute of Technology (B.S., 1960); University of California at Berkeley (LL.B., 1963). Deputy Attorney General, State of California, 1964-1968. Member, Board of Directors, Alzheimer's Association of Los Angeles County. *Member:* Los Angeles County Bar Association; State Bar of California. *PRACTICE AREAS:* Administrative Law; Business; Commercial; Insurance; Real Estate Litigation; Appellate Practice.

**ARTHUR D. COHEN,** born Los Angeles, California, April 14, 1927; admitted to bar, 1954, California and U.S. District Court, Central District of California; 1959, Southern District of California; 1960, U.S. Court of Appeals, Ninth Circuit. *Education:* University of California at Los Angeles (B.S., 1950); University of Southern California (LL.B., 1953). Attorney, Inheritance Tax Department, State of California, 1954-1958. *Member:* Los Angeles County Bar Association; State Bar of California; Southern California Chinese Lawyers Association. *PRACTICE AREAS:* Commercial Litigation; Business Law.

**EILEEN KURAHASHI,** born Poston, Arizona, October 16, 1943; admitted to bar, 1975, California; 1976, U.S. District Court, Central District of California and U.S. Court of Appeals, Ninth Circuit. *Education:* Mills College (B.A., 1965); University of Southern California (J.D., 1975). *Member:* State Bar of California (Board of Governors, 1993-1996; Member, Judicial Nominee Evaluation Commission, 1985-1988); Los Angeles County (Member, Board of Trustees, 1988-1990) and American Bar Associations; Southern California Chinese Lawyers Association. *PRACTICE AREAS:* Commercial Litigation; Employment Law; Family Law.

**RICHARD P. YANG,** born Seattle, Washington, April 10, 1949; admitted to bar, 1974, California and U.S. District Court, Central District of California; 1982, U.S. District Court, Northern District of California; 1983, U.S. Court of Appeals, Ninth Circuit. *Education:* University of California at Los Angeles (A.B., 1971; J.D., 1974). Phi Beta Kappa. Deputy Attorney General, State of California, 1974-1981. *Member:* Los Angeles County Bar Association; State Bar of California; Southern California Chinese Lawyers Association (Member, Board of Governors, 1976-1977; Secretary, 1977); Japanese American Bar Association. *PRACTICE AREAS:* Real Estate; Banking; Debtor and Creditor Remedies; Business Law.

**RONALD M. HIRANO,** born Amache, Colorado, April 7, 1943; admitted to bar, 1983, California and U.S. District Court, Central District of California; 1989, U.S. District Court, Eastern District of California. *Education:* University of California at Berkeley (A.B., 1967); University of South-

(This Listing Continued)

## QUAN, COHEN, KURAHASHI, YANG, SCHOLTZ & HIRANO A PROFESSIONAL CORPORATION, Los Angeles—Continued

ern California (M.P.A., 1970); Loyola Marymount University (J.D., 1982). *Member:* Los Angeles County and American Bar Associations; State Bar of California; Japanese American Bar Association. **PRACTICE AREAS:** Business Law; Commercial Litigation; Employment Law.

REPRESENTATIVE CLIENTS: American Telephone & Telegraph Co.; Aurora National Life Assurance Co.; California State Insurance Commissioner; Cathay Bank; China & Asia (U.S.) Travel Service, Inc.; China Tourist Administration; Desert Community Bank; Edwards Properties, Inc,; Federal Deposit Insurance Corp.; Iwata Electric Co., Ltd. (Japan); Los Angeles National Bank; Los Angeles Unified School District; Pacific BMW & Infiniti; Resolution Trust Corp.; Sears Roebuck and Co.; The Tom James Co.; Trust Bank; Valley-Hi Toyota-Honda; Wing Tai (Group).

## QUATEMAN & ZIDELL LLP
### 1901 AVENUE OF THE STARS, SUITE 1505
### LOS ANGELES, CALIFORNIA 90067
Telephone: 310-556-7755
Fax: 310-556-7750

*Corporate, Finance, Real Estate and Environmental. General Business.*

FIRM PROFILE: *Quateman & Zidell LLP is committed to serving our clients with the utmost quality service. The firm represents individuals and domestic and multi-national firms doing business in a wide range of industries, as well as financial institutions and governmental entities.*

**LISA GREER QUATEMAN,** born Los Angeles, California, November 27, 1953; admitted to bar, 1978, California; 1979, New York. *Education:* University of California at Los Angeles (B.A., summa cum laude, 1974; J.D., 1978). Phi Beta Kappa; Phi Delta Phi. Director, Arthritis Foundation, Southern California Chapter, 1987—. National Delegate for CREW-LA, the Los Angeles member organization of Commercial Real Estate Women. Past President of Women in Commercial Real Estate. Director, California Association of Bond Lawyers. *Member:* Beverly Hills, Los Angeles County and New York State Bar Associations; State Bar of California (Member, Sections on: Business Law; Real Property; Environmental Law; Public Law; Member, Education Committee); National Association of Bond Lawyers; National Association of Women Business Owners; Women Lawyers Association of Los Angeles (Vice-Chair, Corporate Law Section).

**STEVEN H. ZIDELL,** born Los Angeles, California, July 21, 1960; admitted to bar, 1985, California. *Education:* University of California at Los Angeles (B.A., summa cum laude 1982; J.D., 1985). Phi Beta Kappa. Editor-in-Chief, UCLA Environmental Law Journal. Licensed Real Estate Broker, California. Member, Century City Chamber of Commerce. *Member:* Los Angeles County Bar Association, State Bar of California (Real Property Law Section).

---

**MATTHEW P. SEEBERGER,** born St. Charles, Missouri, January 14, 1960; admitted to bar, 1988, California. *Education:* Swarthmore College (B.A., 1981); Brooklyn Law School; The Ohio State University (J.D., with honors, 1987). Phi Alpha Delta. Director, Asian Business League of Southern California. *Member:* Los Angeles County Bar Association (Member, Real Property Section); State Bar of California.

REPRESENTATIVE CLIENTS: BANC ONE Management and Consulting Corp.; Countrywide Home Loans, Inc.; Federal Deposit Insurance Corp.; State Teachers' Retirement System; City National Bank; First Regional Bank; Honda North America, Inc.; American Honda Motor Co., Inc.; Ports of Los Angeles and Long Beach; Swiss Bank Corp.

## QUINN EMANUEL URQUHART & OLIVER, LLP
### 865 SOUTH FIGUEROA STREET, 10TH FLOOR
### LOS ANGELES, CALIFORNIA 90017
Telephone: 213-624-7707
Telecopier: 213-624-0643

*Palm Desert, California Office:* 74-090 El Paseo, Suite 101. Telephone: 619-340-2276. Telecopier: 619-346-1368.

*Business Litigation and Trial Practice, including Antitrust; Banking; Construction; Copyright, Trademark and Patent Litigation; Employment; ERISA; Government Contracts; Health Care; Intellectual Property; Product Liability; Real Estate; Securities; Unfair Competition; White Collar Crime.*

### MEMBERS OF FIRM

**JOHN B. QUINN,** born Ft. Belvoir, Virginia, June 20, 1951; admitted to bar, 1978, New York; 1979, California. *Education:* Claremont Men's College (B.A., magna cum laude, 1973); Harvard University (J.D., cum laude, 1976). Editor, Harvard Law Review, 1974-1976. Knox Fellow, Harvard University, 1976-1977. Instructor in Law, J. Reuben Clark School of Law, 1977. Lecturer on Federal Practice, California Continuing Education of the Bar. Associate, Cravath, Swaine & Moore, New York, NY, 1976-1979. General Counsel, Academy of Motion Picture Arts and Sciences, 1987—. Named "One of the Top 3 Trial Lawyers of Choice by General Counsel in California" by California Law Business, 1994. Named "One of the Top 15 Litigators in California" by The Los Angeles Daily Journal, 1995. Selected as "One of the Top 45 Lawyers Under the Age of 45 in the United States" by The American Lawyer, 1995. *Member:* Los Angeles County (Member, Federal Courts and Practices Committee) and American (Member, Sections on: Corporation, Banking and Business Law; Litigation; Patent, Trademark and Copyright Law; Member, Forum Committees on: Health Law; Construction Industry) Bar Associations; State Bar of California (Member, Committee on Federal Courts). (Also at Palm Desert Office). **REPORTED CASES:** Ficalora v. Lockheed Corp., 193 Cal. App. 3d 489 (1987); America's Cup Properties, Inc. v. America's Cup Club, Inc., 8 U.S.P.Q. 2d (BNA) 2025 (1988); Academy of Motion Picture Arts and Sciences v. Creative House Promotions, Inc., 944 F.2d 1446 (9th Cir. 1991) and 728 F. Supp. 1442 (C.D. Cal. 1989); Cinemateca Uruguaya v. Academy of Motion Picture Arts and Sciences, 826 F.Supp. 323 (C.D.Cal. 1993). **PRACTICE AREAS:** Employment; Intellectual Property; Unfair Competition; Real Estate; General Commercial Litigation; General Trial Practice. *Email:* jquinn05@counsel.com

**DALE H. OLIVER,** born Lansing, Michigan, June 26, 1947; admitted to bar, 1973, District of Columbia; 1991, California. *Education:* Michigan State University (B.A., with highest honors, 1969); Harvard University (J.D., cum laude, 1972). Member, Ames Moot Court Championship Team, 1971. Editor, Harvard Journal on Legislation, 1971-1972. Attorney Advisor, Office of General Counsel, U.S. Air Force, 1973-1975. Member: Jones, Day, Reavis & Pogue, 1979, 1987-1992; Crowell & Moring, 1979-1984; Gibson, Dunn & Crutcher, 1984-1987. *Member:* Los Angeles County (Member, Sections on: Litigation; Public Law) and American (Member and Vice Chairman, Procurement Fraud Committee; Chairman, Profit Policy Committee, Public Contract Law Section, 1987-1989) Bar Associations; District of Columbia Bar (Member, Sections on: Public Contracts; Litigation); State Bar of California. **SPECIAL AGENCIES:** Armed Services Board of Contract Appeal; U.S. Court of Federal Claims; General Services Board of Contract Appeals; London Court of International Arbitration; U.S. General Accounting Office. **PRACTICE AREAS:** Government Contracts and Regulations; General Commercial Litigation; White Collar Crime.

**A. WILLIAM URQUHART,** born Forest Hills, New York, February 20, 1947; admitted to bar, 1978, New York; 1989, California and U.S. Tax Court. *Education:* Fordham College (B.A., 1969); Fordham Law School (J.D., cum laude, 1977). Member, Fordham Law Review, 1976-1977. Vice President, General Counsel and Secretary, New York Insurance Exchange, Inc., 1985-1988. Associate, Cravath, Swaine & Moore, New York, NY, 1977-1980. Associate, Willkie Farr and Gallagher, New York, NY, 1980-1985. *Member:* The Association of the Bar of the City of New York; State Bar of California; New York State and American (Member, Sections on: Antitrust; Litigation) Bar Associations. **PRACTICE AREAS:** Intellectual Property; Unfair Competition; General Commercial Litigation; Government Contracts and Regulations; Antitrust Law; Securities; General Trial Practice.

**GARY A. FEESS,** born Alliance, Ohio, March 13, 1948; admitted to bar, 1974, California. *Education:* The Ohio State University (B.A., cum laude, 1970); University of California at Los Angeles (J.D., 1974). Phi Beta Kappa; Order of the Coif. Comment Editor, UCLA Law Review, 1973-1974. Adjunct Professor in Trial Advocacy, Southwestern University Law School, 1983-1984. Instructor, United States Attorney General's Advocacy Institute, 1983-1985. Assistant U.S. Attorney, 1979-1987, Chief Assistant U.S. Attorney, 1988-1989, U.S. Attorney, Central District of California, 1989. Deputy General Counsel, Christopher Commission, 1991. Member, Jones, Day, Reavis and Pogue, 1987-1988, 1989-1992, Head of Litigation, Los Angeles Office, 1991-1992. *Member:* American (Member, Sections on: Litigation; Criminal Justice; Member, Committee on White Collar Crime,

*(This Listing Continued)*

1991) and Federal Bar Associations; State Bar of California. *REPORTED CASES:* U.S. v. Schaflander, 743 F.2d 714 (9th Cir. 1984); U.S. v. Michaels, 796 F.2d 1112 (9th Cir. 1986); U.S. v. Stafford, 831 F.2d 1479 (9th Cir. 1987); U.S. v. Flewitt, 874 F.2d 669 (9th Cir. 1989); U.S. ex rel. Madden, et al. v. General Dynamics Corp., 4 F.3d 827 (9th Cir. 1993); U.S. v. Hughes Aircraft Co., 20 F.3d 974 (9th Cir. 1994). *PRACTICE AREAS:* White Collar Crime; Appellate Litigation; Government Contracts and Regulations; Employment; General Trial Practice.

**ERIC EMANUEL,** born West Point, Nebraska, February 11, 1952; admitted to bar, 1981, California; 1989, U.S. Supreme Court. *Education:* St. John's University (B.A., 1974); University of California at Los Angeles (J.D., 1981). *Member:* American Bar Association (Member, Sections on: Economics of Law Practice; Litigation; Member, Forum Committee on Construction Industry); State Bar of California. *REPORTED CASES:* Zimmerman v. Stotter, 160 Cal. App. 3d 1067 (1984); Youngblood v. Wilcox, 207 Cal. App. 3d 1368 (1989); Chamberlain v. Cocola Associates, 958 F.2d 282 (9th Cir. 1992); Downey Community Hosp. v. Wilson, 977 F.2d 470 (9th Cir. 1992). *PRACTICE AREAS:* Employment; Construction; ERISA.

**STEVEN G. MADISON,** born Brooklyn, New York, September 4, 1955; admitted to bar, 1981, California. *Education:* University of Santa Clara (B.A., 1978); Boston College (J.D., cum laude, 1981); University of Southern California (Visiting Student, Law Center, 1980-1981; M.P.A., 1996). Member, Boston College Law Review, 1979-1981. Adjunct Professor in Evidence and Trial Advocacy, University of Southern California Law Center, 1990—. Lecturer and Group Leader, United States Attorney General's Trial Advocacy Institute. Judge Pro Tem, Beverly Hills Municipal Court. Assistant U.S. Attorney, Central District of California, Criminal Division, 1987-1996. Assistant Division Chief, Criminal Division, 1990-1996. Associate, Memel, Jacobs & Ellsworth, Los Angeles, California, 1981-1987. Alternate Member, Los Angeles County Criminal Justice Coordination Committee, 1991-1996. *Member:* Los Angeles County and American (Member, Sections on: Litigation; Criminal Law) Bar Associations; State Bar of California; California Peace Officers Association. *PRACTICE AREAS:* General Trial Practice; White Collar Crime; Appellate Litigation.

**PHYLLIS KUPFERSTEIN,** born New York, New York, September 9, 1958; admitted to bar, 1982, California. *Education:* University of California at Los Angeles (B.A., 1978); Loyola Marymount University (J.D., cum laude, 1982). Articles Editor, Loyola of Los Angeles Law Review, 1981-1982. Judicial Extern to the Hon. Stephen R. Reinhardt, U.S. Court of Appeals, Ninth Circuit, 1981. *Member:* Los Angeles County and American (Member, Sections on: Litigation; Labor and Employment Law; Member, Forum Committee on Health Law) Bar Associations; State Bar of California; National Health Lawyers Association; Women Lawyers Association of Los Angeles. *REPORTED CASES:* Simon Oil Co., Ltd. v. Norman, 789 F.2d 780 (9th Cir. 1986); Mitsui Manufacturers Bank v. Texas Commerce Bank, 159 Cal. App. 3d 1051 (1984). *PRACTICE AREAS:* Employment; Health Care; ERISA; General Commercial Litigation; General Trial Practice.

**DAVID W. QUINTO,** born New York, New York, June 11, 1955; admitted to bar, 1982, California; 1983, Arizona. *Education:* Amherst College (B.A., magna cum laude, 1977); Harvard University (J.D., 1982). *Member:* Los Angeles County and American Bar Associations; State Bar of California; State Bar of Arizona; Los Angeles Intellectual Property Lawyers. (Also at Palm Desert Office). *LANGUAGES:* Spanish. *REPORTED CASES:* Quinto v. Legal Times of Washington, Inc., 506 F. Supp. 554 and 511 F. Supp. 579 (1981); Ficalora v. Lockheed Corp., 193 Cal. App. 3d 489 (1987); America's Cup Properties, Inc. v. America's Cup Club, Inc., 8 U.S.P.Q. 2d (BNA) 2025 (1988); Academy of Motion Picture Arts and Sciences v. Creative House Promotions, Inc., 944 F.2d 1446 (9th Cir. 1991) and 728 F. Supp. 1442 (C.D. Cal. 1989); Cinemateca Uruguay v. Academy of Motion Pictures Arts and Sciences, 826 F.Supp. 323 (C.D. Cal. 1993); Florentine Art Studio v. Vedet K Corp., 891 F. Supp. 532 (C.D. Cal. 1995). *PRACTICE AREAS:* Copyright and Trademark; Real Property Litigation.

**KAREN A. ROONEY,** born Los Angeles, California, November 10, 1955; admitted to bar, 1980, California. *Education:* University of California at Santa Barbara (B.A., 1977); University of San Diego (J.D., magna cum laude, 1980). Judicial Extern to the Hon. J. Clifford Wallace, U.S. Court of Appeals, Ninth Circuit, 1979. Judicial Law Clerk to the Hon. William B. Enright, U.S. District Court, Southern District of California, 1980-1981. Staff Attorney, United States Commodity Futures Trading Commission, Division of Enforcement, 1984-1986. *Member:* South Bay, Los Angeles County (Member, Sections on: Business; Labor; Litigation) and American (Member, Sections on: Litigation; Tort and Insurance Practice) Bar Associ-

*(This Listing Continued)*

ations; State Bar of California. *PRACTICE AREAS:* General Commercial Litigation; Employment; Securities.

**WILLIAM C. PRICE,** born Bristol, Virginia, October 28, 1956; admitted to bar, 1983, California. *Education:* Duke University (B.A., valedictorian, 1978); Yale University (J.D., 1981). Judicial Law Clerk to the Hon. Stanley A. Weigel, U.S. District Court, Northern District of California, 1981-1982. Assistant U.S. Attorney, Major Crimes Unit and Public Fraud and Corruption Unit, 1985-1988. *Member:* State Bar of California. *REPORTED CASES:* U.S. v. Pulido-Baquerizo, 800 F.2d 899 (9th Cir. 1986). *PRACTICE AREAS:* General Trial Practice; Employment; White Collar Crime; Appellate Litigation.

**ADRIAN M. PRUETZ,** born Chicago, Illinois, November 13, 1948; admitted to bar, 1982, Wisconsin; 1985, California. *Education:* University of Wisconsin; Loyola University (B.A., 1972); Marquette University (J.D., magna cum laude, 1982). Co-Author: "Intellectual Property Protection and Compliance: A Practical Guide for Management," Los Angeles Lawyer, August, 1994; "Recent Developments in Intellectual Property Law in the European Community," Los Angeles Lawyer, December, 1993; Amendments to Sections 2030 (l), 2031 (l) and 2033 (l) of the California Code of Civil Procedure and Section 3334 of the California Civil Code. Lecturer and Advisor, Price Waterhouse Intellectual Property Leadership Forum; Licensing Executives Society. Member, Panel of Arbitrators, American Arbitration Association. *Member:* American Bar Association (Chair, Committee on Patent Litigation Affecting International Treaties and Laws); State Bar of California. *REPORTED CASES:* Constant v. Advanced Micro-Devices, Inc., 848 F.2d 1560 (Fed. Cir. 1988). *PRACTICE AREAS:* Intellectual Property, Complex Commercial and Construction Litigation.

**RICHARD A. SCHIRTZER,** born New York, New York, February 16, 1957; admitted to bar, 1985, New York; 1990, California. *Education:* State University of New York at Binghamton (B.A., 1978); University of Michigan (M.A., Philosophy, 1983; J.D., cum laude, 1983). Phi Beta Kappa. Counsel to Governor Mario Cuomo's New York State Housing Task Force, 1988. Associate, Willkie Farr and Gallagher, New York, NY, 1984-1990. *Member:* State Bar of California; New York State Bar Association. *PRACTICE AREAS:* Securities; Banking.

**DOMINIC SURPRENANT,** born Kankakee, Illinois, November 3, 1955; admitted to bar, 1986, New York; 1993, California. *Education:* Illinois State University (B.A., with highest honors, 1977); University of Wisconsin at Madison (M.A., 1980); Harvard University (J.D., cum laude, 1985). Editor, 1983-1984, Articles Editor, 1984-1985, Harvard Law Review. Author: "Freedom of Speech," in "Developments in the Law--Public Employment," 97 Harv. L. Rev. 1611 (1984). Associate, Cravath, Swaine & Moore, New York, NY, 1985-1992. *Member:* New York State and American Bar Associations; State Bar of California. *PRACTICE AREAS:* Complex Commercial Litigation; Antitrust; Intellectual Property.

**DOUGLAS A. KUBER,** born New York, New York, May 27, 1960; admitted to bar, 1987, California; 1988, District of Columbia. *Education:* California State University at Northridge (B.A., 1984); University of California, Hastings College of the Law (J.D., 1987). Staff Member, 1985-1986, Articles Editor, 1986-1987, Hastings International and Comparative Law Review. Judicial Extern to the Hon. Laughlin E. Waters, U.S. District Court, Central District of California, 1987. Author: "A Sewing Lesson in Political Offense Determinations: Stitching-Up The International Terrorist's Loophole," 10 Hast. Int'l & Comp. L. Rev. 499 (1987). Associate, Jones, Day, Reavis & Pogue, Los Angeles, CA, 1987-1992. *Member:* State Bar of California; District of Columbia Bar; American Bar Association. *REPORTED CASES:* Macaulay v. Norlander, 12 Cal. App. 4th 1 (1992). *PRACTICE AREAS:* General Commercial Litigation; Securities; Real Property Litigation.

**SCOTT B. KIDMAN,** born Los Angeles, California, July 27, 1959; admitted to bar, 1985, California. *Education:* University of California at Los Angeles (B.A., cum laude, 1982); Loyola Marymount University (J.D., magna cum laude, 1985). Staff Member, Loyola of Los Angeles Law Review, 1983-1984. Editor, Loyola International and Comparative Law Journal, 1984-1985. *Member:* State Bar of California. *PRACTICE AREAS:* Employment; General Commercial Litigation.

**ANN KOTLARSKI,** born Palos Verdes, California, March 9, 1960; admitted to bar, 1985, California. *Education:* Northwestern University (B.A., 1982); University of San Francisco (J.D., cum laude, 1985). *Member:* State Bar of California; American Bar Association; Women Lawyers Association of Los Angeles. *PRACTICE AREAS:* Employment.

**CHARLES K. VERHOEVEN,** born Ames, Iowa, June 19, 1963; admitted to bar, 1989, New York; 1994, California. *Education:* University of

*(This Listing Continued)*

CAA1115B

## QUINN EMANUEL URQUHART & OLIVER, LLP, Los Angeles—Continued

Iowa (B.B.A., with distinction, 1985; J.D., with high distinction, 1988). Member, 1986-1987, Articles Editor, 1987-1988, Iowa Law Review. Author, "South Carolina v. Catawba Indian Tribe: Terminating Federal Protection with 'Plain' Statements," 72 Iowa L. Rev. 1117 (1987). *Member:* The Association of the Bar of the City of New York; New York State and American Bar Associations; State Bar of California. **PRACTICE AREAS:** General Commercial Litigation; Intellectual Property; Unfair Competition; Real Property Litigation; Antitrust Law.

**JOHN P. D'AMATO,** born Worcester, Massachusetts, December 21, 1963; admitted to bar, 1989, California. *Education:* Georgetown University (B.A., cum laude, 1985); Boston College Law School (J.D., cum laude, 1989). Managing Editor, Boston College Law Review, 1988-1989. Author: "Statistical Evidence of a Manifest Imbalance in a Traditionally Segregated Job Category Can Protect a Voluntary Affirmative Action Plan From a Title VII Challenge: Johnson v. Transportation Agency, Santa Clara, California," 30 B.C.L. Rev. 271 (1988); "Selected Developments in Massachusetts Corporate Law," 30 B.C.L. Rev. 748 (1989). *Member:* State Bar of California; American Bar Association. **PRACTICE AREAS:** General Commercial Litigation; Securities; Antitrust Law; Unfair Competition; Employment.

### OF COUNSEL

**DAVID C. HENRI,** born Bronx, New York, August 16, 1943; admitted to bar, 1972, Oklahoma; 1978, Texas; 1983, California. *Education:* Fairleigh Dickinson University (B.S., 1965; M.B.A., 1966); University of Tulsa (J.D., 1972). Author: "Employer Searches of Employees," Vol. 2, No. 3, Journal of the Corporate Counsel Section, State Bar of Texas, June 1979; "As Companies Fret, ADR Can Save Costs," California Law Business, June 1993; "If You Must Litigate, Litigate Efficiently," California Law Business, June 1993; "Engagement Letters Can Make Marriage," California Law Business, July 1993; "Outside Counsel Must Shift Marketing Focus in These Tough Times," California Law Business, September 1993; "Ethics Rules Must Be Periodically Reviewed," California Law Business, October 1993; "A Manager's Priority Must be Management," California Law Business, November 1993; "Procedures Can Help Attorneys Make Critical Conflict Decisions," California Law Business, January 1994; "Organization Key to Managing Litigation," California Law Business, February 1994; "Basic Understanding of Insurance a 'Must'," California Law Business, March 1994. Counsel, Transamerica Investment Group, 1972-1974. Division Attorney, Getty Oil Co., 1974-1984. Executive Vice President and General Counsel, California Federal Bank, 1984-1994. President and Director, American Corporate Counsel Association, Southern California Chapter, 1993 and 1994. Director, Public Counsel, 1993-1996. Chairman, California League of Savings Institutions Attorneys Committee, 1993. *Member:* Los Angeles County and Oklahoma Bar Associations; State Bar of California; State Bar of Texas. **PRACTICE AREAS:** Employment; General Commercial Litigation.

### ASSOCIATES

**HAROLD W. HOPP,** born Takoma Park, Maryland, March 25, 1960; admitted to bar, 1986, California. *Education:* Pacific Union College (B.S., 1983); University of Southern California (J.D., 1986). Staff Editor, 1984-1985, Articles Editor, 1985-1986, Southern California Law Review. *Member:* Desert and American Bar Associations; State Bar of California. (Resident, Palm Desert, California).

**KURT MICHAEL CHEN,** born Hong Kong, November 5, 1954; admitted to bar, 1979, California. *Education:* University of Southern California (B.A., magna cum laude, 1976); Southwestern University (J.D., 1979). *Member:* State Bar of California.

**ARPIE BALEKJIAN,** born Pasadena, California, October 30, 1961; admitted to bar, 1989, California. *Education:* Occidental College (B.A., 1983); Loyola Marymount University (J.D., 1989). Staff Member, 1987-1988, Executive Editor, 1988-1989, Loyola Entertainment Law Journal. Author: "Navigating Public Access and Owner Control on the Rough Waters of Popular Music Copyright Law," 8 Loy. L.A. Ent. L.J. 369 (1988). *Member:* State Bar of California; Armenian Bar Association.

**STEVEN M. ANDERSON,** born Ogden, Utah, April 24, 1964; admitted to bar, 1989, California; registered to practice before U.S. Patent and Trademark Office. *Education:* University of California at Irvine (B.S., magna cum laude, 1986); Harvard Law School (J.D., cum laude, 1989). Phi Beta Kappa. Editor, Harvard Journal of Law and Technology, 1987-1989. Law Clerk to the Hon. William D. Keller, U.S. District Court, Central District of California, 1989-1990. Co-author: "Intellectual Property Law in the European Community," Los Angeles Lawyer, December, 1993. *Member:* Beverly Hills, Los Angeles County and American Bar Associations; State Bar of California; Computer Law Association. **PRACTICE AREAS:** Intellectual Property.

**WARRINGTON S. PARKER,** born Detroit, Michigan, May 23, 1964; admitted to bar, 1990, California. *Education:* Princeton University (A.B., 1986); Harvard Law School (J.D., 1989). Editor, Harvard Law Review, 1988-1989. Law Clerk to the Hon. Cecil F. Poole, U.S. Court of Appeals, Ninth Circuit, 1989-1990. Assistant U.S. Attorney, Central District of California, Criminal Division, 1992-1996. Staff Member, Kolts Commission, 1991-1992. Author: "Military Contractor Defense," 102 Harv. L. Rev. 288 (1988); "The Limits of Racial Equality: The Fourteenth Amendment and the Criminal Justice System" in "Developments in the Law--Race and the Criminal Process," 101 Harv. L.Rev. 1479 (1988). *Member:* State Bar of California.

**CHRISTOPHER TAYBACK,** born Burbank, California, November 11, 1963; admitted to bar, 1989, California. *Education:* Oxford University (1984); University of Notre Dame (B.A., magna cum laude, 1985); Harvard Law School (J.D., cum laude, 1989). Assistant U.S. Attorney, Central District of California, 1991-1996. Author: "Initial Appearance and Arraignment Bail, and Detention" in *Federal Criminal Litigation: A Practical and Strategic Guide to Key Issues,* American Bar Association, 1994. *Member:* State Bar of California. **PRACTICE AREAS:** Criminal Law (100%).

**RANDA A. F. OSMAN,** born Alexandria, Egypt, December 5, 1964; admitted to bar, 1990, California. *Education:* University of Hawaii at Manoa (B.A., 1987); University of California, Hastings College of the Law (J.D., cum laude, 1990). Order of the Coif. Member, Thurston Society. Note Editor, 1989-1990, Staff Member, 1988-1989, The Hastings Law Journal. *Member:* Los Angeles County and American Bar Associations; State Bar of California.

**WILLIAM O. STEIN,** born Los Angeles, California, June 21, 1964; admitted to bar, 1990, California. *Education:* University of California at Los Angeles (B.A., 1987); Loyola Marymount University (J.D., 1990). Member, St. Thomas More Law Honor Society. Staff Member, 1988-1989, Editor, 1989-1990, Loyola International and Comparative Law Journal. Law Clerk to the Hon. Robert J. Kelleher, U.S. District Court, Central District of California, 1990-1991. Extern to the Hon. Stephen V. Wilson, U.S. District Court, Central District of California, 1988. Counsel, Webster Commission, 1992. *Member:* State Bar of California.

**KIMBERLY S. STENTON,** born Los Angeles, California, May 1, 1965; admitted to bar, 1992, California. *Education:* University of California at Santa Barbara (B.A., 1987); Loyola Marymount University (J.D., cum laude, 1991). Order of the Coif. Staff Member, Loyola International and Comparative Law Journal, 1989-1990. Law Clerk to the Hon. William J. Rea, U.S. District Court, Central District of California, 1991-1993. *Member:* State Bar of California.

**JOHN S. PURCELL,** born Vinton, Iowa, December 9, 1963; admitted to bar, 1992, California. *Education:* University of Illinois (B.S., cum laude, 1986); New York University School of Law (J.D., 1991). Member, New York University Review of Law and Social Change, Student Bar Association Board of Governors. *Member:* State Bar of California.

**JESSICA M. NEILSON,** born Lynnwood, Washington, November 9, 1967; admitted to bar, 1992, Oregon; 1994, California. *Education:* Whitworth College (B.A., cum laude, 1988); University of Oregon (J.D., 1991). Order of the Coif. Executive Editor, Journal of Environmental Law & Litigation, 1990-1991. Law Clerk to the Hon. George C. Pratt, U.S. Court of Appeals, Second Circuit, 1992-1993. Co-author: "Shot In The Dark: The Ninth Circuit Pulls the Wrong 'Trigger'in California Insurance Law," 1 Stan. J.L. Bus. & Fin. 333 (1995). *Member:* Oregon State Bar; State Bar of California.

**SAMUEL BROOKS SHEPHERD,** born New Haven, Connecticut, January 25, 1966; admitted to bar, 1992, California. *Education:* Bowdoin College (B.A., summa cum laude, 1988); University of Chicago (J.D., M.B.A., 1992). Phi Beta Kappa. Recipient: University of Chicago Business Fellow; Jefferson Davis Award; James Bowdoin Cup; Pray English Prize; Nixon Class of 1868 Prize; James Bowdoin Collection Scholar; Shakespeare Prize. *Member:* State Bar of California. (Also at Palm Desert Office).

**TRICIA J. HARTMAN,** born Brookville, Pennsylvania, August 27, 1964; admitted to bar, 1993, California; 1994, Illinois. *Education:* University of California at Santa Barbara (B.A., summa cum laude, 1989); Harvard University (J.D., cum laude, 1992). *Member:* Illinois State Bar Association; State Bar of California.

*(This Listing Continued)*

# PROFESSIONAL BIOGRAPHIES

**REBECCA DELFINO,** born Bakersfield, California, August 9, 1968; admitted to bar, 1993, California. *Education:* University of California at Los Angeles (B.A., magna cum laude, 1988); University of California at Davis (J.D., 1992). Phi Beta Kappa. Member, Moot Court Board; National Trial Advocacy Team; Order of the Barristers. Extern to the Hon. William B. Shubb, U.S. District Court, Eastern District of California, 1992. Law Clerk to the Hon. Clifford C. Young, Nevada Supreme Court, 1992-1993. *Member:* Los Angeles County and American Bar Associations; State Bar of California.

**JOHN R. CALL,** born Dallas, Texas, July 18, 1946; admitted to bar, 1993, California. *Education:* University of Arizona (B.A., with high honors, 1974); Stanford University (J.D., 1992). Phi Beta Kappa; Phi Kappa Phi. Executive Editor, Stanford Law Review, 1991-1992. *Member:* State Bar of California. [LT. Col., U.S. Army (retired)]. *LANGUAGES:* Castilian Spanish.

**DAVID J.P. KALOYANIDES,** born Brooklyn, New York, July 31, 1964; admitted to bar, 1992, California. *Education:* University of California at Los Angeles (B.A., 1986); Loyola Marymount University (J.D., 1992). Member, Scott Moot Court Honors Board; Jessup International Moot Court Team. Staff Member, Loyola of Los Angeles Law Review, 1991-1992. Extern to the Hon. William J. Rea, U.S. District Court, Central District of California, 1991. Author: "The Depraved Sexual Instinct Theory: An Aberrant Application of Federal Rule of Evidence 404(b)," 25 Loy. L.A.L. Rev 1297 (1992). *Member:* Beverly Hills, Federal and American Bar Associations; State Bar of California.

**MARSHALL M. SEARCY,** born Austin, Texas, January 30, 1968; admitted to bar, 1993, California. *Education:* University of Texas (B.A., with highest honors, 1990); Harvard Law School (J.D., 1993). Phi Beta Kappa. Oralist, Ames Moot Court Championship Team, 1993. Editor, Harvard Journal of Law and Technology, 1992-1993. *Member:* State Bar of California.

**JAMES J. WEBSTER,** born Melbourne, Australia, November 11, 1967; admitted to bar, 1992, Victoria, Australia; 1993, California. *Education:* University of Melbourne (B.Com., 1989; LL.B., with honors, 1990); Harvard University (LL.M., 1993). Member Editorial Board, 1987-1990 Law Reform Editor, 1990, Melbourne University Law Review. *Member:* State Bar of California.

**SUSAN L. BARNA,** born Pasadena, California, September 10, 1965; admitted to bar, 1993, California. *Education:* University of California at Berkeley (B.A., high honors, 1988); New York University School of Law (J.D., magna cum laude, 1993). Order of the Coif. Staff Member, 1991-1992, Note and Comment Editor, 1992-1993, New York University Law Review. Recipient, Ann Petluck Poses Memorial Prize. *Member:* State Bar of California.

**GRADY LEE WHITE,** born Memphis, Tennessee, November 20, 1963; admitted to bar, 1993, California. *Education:* Northwestern University (B.S., 1985); University of California at Los Angeles (J.D., 1993). Production Manager, 1992-1993, Editor, 1991-1992, UCLA Law Review. *Member:* State Bar of California. *PRACTICE AREAS:* High-tech Intellectual Property; Computer Law.

**LEE J. PAPAGEORGE,** born New York, New York, January 10, 1965; admitted to bar, 1995, California. *Education:* Princeton University (A.B., summa cum laude, 1987); Stanford Law School (J.D., 1994). Associate Editor, 1993-1994, Member, 1992-1993, Stanford Law Review. Recipient, Johnson & Gibbs Law Review Award. *Member:* State Bar of California.

**ANNA Y. JOO,** born Pusan, South Korea, February 14, 1969; admitted to bar, 1996, California. *Education:* Carleton College (B.A., magna cum laude, 1991); Harvard Law School (J.D., cum laude, 1994). Phi Beta Kappa. Editor, Harvard Journal on Legislation, 1992-1993. Adjunct Professor, William S. Richardson School of Law at the University of Hawaii, 1995. Law Clerk to the Hon. Herbert Y.C. Choy, U.S. Court of Appeals, Ninth Circuit, 1994-1995. Author: "Broadening the Scope of Counselor-Patient Privilege to Protect the Privacy of the Sexual Assault Survivor," 32 Har. J. on Legis. 225 (1995). *Member:* State Bar of California.

**GARY H. LOEB,** born Las Vegas, Nevada, April 21, 1969; admitted to bar, 1996, California. *Education:* Stanford University (B.A., B.S., 1991); Columbia University (J.D., 1994). Harlan Fiske Stone Scholar, 1991-1994. Administrative Editor, 1993-1994, Staff Member, 1992-1993, Columbia Journal of Law and Social Problems. Law Clerk to the Hon. A. Joe Fish, U.S. District Court, Northern District of Texas, 1994-1995. Author: "Protecting the Right to Informational Privacy for HIV-Positive Prisoners," 27 Colum. J.L. & Soc. Probs. 269 (1994). *Member:* State Bar of California.

*(This Listing Continued)*

**PAUL E. VAN HORN,** born Princeton, New Jersey, October 17, 1966; admitted to bar, 1995, New York (Not admitted in California). *Education:* Yale University (B.A., cum laude, 1989); Columbia University (J.D., 1994). Harlan Fiske Stone Scholar. Editor, Columbia Journal of Law and Social Problems, 1992-1993. Law Clerk to the Hon. David R. Thompson, U.S. Court of Appeals, Ninth Circuit, 1995-1996. Law Clerk to the Hon. Rudi M. Brewster, U.S. District Court, Southern District of California, 1994-1995. Author: "Revocation of Conditional Release in New York State: What Process is Due?," 27 Colum. J.L. & Soc. Probs. 523 (1994). *Member:* New York State Bar Association.

**LINDA J. KIM,** born Seoul, South Korea, August 28, 1970; admitted to bar, 1995, California. *Education:* Yale University (B.A., magna cum laude, 1992); Harvard Law School (J.D., 1995). Phi Beta Kappa. Editor, Harvard International Law Journal, 1994-1995. *Member:* State Bar of California.

**NADIA M. BISHOP,** born London, England, March 18, 1969; admitted to bar, 1996, California. *Education:* University of Toronto (B.A., magna cum laude, 1991); Stanford Law School (J.D., 1995). Associate Managing Editor, Stanford Journal of International Law, 1992-1993. *Member:* State Bar of California.

**KRISTIN L. WETENKAMP,** born Manitowoc, Wisconsin, July 26, 1964; admitted to bar, 1996, California. *Education:* University of Utah (B.A., 1992); Brigham Young University (J.D., 1995). *Member:* State Bar of California. [Capt., U.S. Army]. *LANGUAGES:* Arabic.

**PAUL S. CHAN,** born San Francisco, California, April 13, 1970; admitted to bar, 1995, California. *Education:* Harvard College (A.B., magna cum laude, 1991); Harvard Law School (J.D., cum laude, 1995). Technical Editor, Harvard Journal of Legislation, 1993-1995. Law Clerk to the Hon. Rudi M. Brewster, U.S. District Court, Southern District of California, 1995-1996. *Member:* State Bar of California.

**SCOTT R. EMERY,** born Burbank, California, March 23, 1970; admitted to bar, 1995, California. *Education:* University of California at Los Angeles (B.A., summa cum laude, 1992); Harvard Law School (J.D., 1995). Phi Beta Kappa. Law Clerk to the Hon. Linda H. McLaughlin, U.S. District Court, Central District of California, 1995-1996. *Member:* State Bar of California.

**MICHAEL ERNEST WILLIAMS,** born Los Angeles, California, November 28, 1970; admitted to bar, 1995, California. *Education:* University of Southern California (B.A., 1992); Harvard Law School (J.D., 1995). Phi Beta Kappa. Staff Member, Harvard Journal of Law and Technology, 1994. Extern to the Hon. Ronald S. W. Lew, U.S. District Court, Central District of California, 1993. *Member:* State Bar of California.

**SHON MORGAN,** born Redondo Beach, California, December 31, 1967; (admission pending). *Education:* University of California at Los Angeles (B.A., summa cum laude, 1992); Harvard Law School (J.D., magna cum laude, 1995). Supervising Editor, 1994-1995, Editor, 1993-1994, Harvard Law Review. Law Clerk to the Hon. Michael Boudin, U.S. Court of Appeals, First Circuit, 1995-1996. Author: "Unenforced Boundaries: Illegal Immigration and the Limits of Judicial Federalism," 108 I Harv. L. Rev. 1643 (1995); Comment, Eckstein v. Balcor Film Investors, 107 Harv. L. Rev. 1170 (1994).

**ADAM D. SAMUELS,** born Salford, England, January 14, 1971; admitted to bar, 1995, California. *Education:* University of California at San Diego (B.A., magna cum laude, 1992); The George Washington University National Law Center (J.D., honors, 1995). Staff Member, The George Washington Law Review, 1993-1995. Recipient, Corpus Juris Secundum Award for Scholastic Excellence in Property. Author: "Reliability of Natural Gas Service for Captive End-Users Under the Federal Energy Regulatory Commission's Order No. 636," 62 Geo. Wash. L. Rev. 718 (1994). *Member:* State Bar of California.

**JAMES P. BERKLAS, JR.,** born Pomona, California, February 5, 1971; (admission pending). *Education:* University of California at Los Angeles (B.A., summa cum laude, 1993); Harvard Law School (J.D., 1996). Phi Beta Kappa. Recipient, Chancellor's Service Award. Senior Editor and Case Comment Author, Harvard Journal of Law and Public Policy, 1993-1995.

**SHALIN N. MEHTA,** born Ahmadabad, India, September 27, 1971; (admission pending). *Education:* H.L. Commerce College, India (B.Com., First Class Honors, 1992); Siddhartha Law College, India (LL.B., Class Valedictorian, First Class Honors, 1994); Columbia Law School (LL.M., 1996). Editor, Siddhartha Law Review, 1993-1994. Gujarat University Gold Medal Recipient, Indian Government National Merit Scholar. Author: "Reservation Policy: A Poor Tool for the Uplift of the Poor," Siddhartha

*(This Listing Continued)*

## QUINN EMANUEL URQUHART & OLIVER, LLP, Los Angeles—Continued

Law Review, 1993; "Doctrine of Reasonableness under the Indian Constitution," *Siddhartha Law Review,* 1994. LANGUAGES: Hindi and Gujarati.

**JON D. COREY,** born Delta, Utah, July 8, 1970; (admission pending). *Education:* Utah State University (B.A., cum laude, 1993); J. Reuben Clark Law School, Brigham Young University (J.D., magna cum laude, 1996). Member, 1994-1995. Executive Editor, 1995-1996, *Brigham Young University Law Review.* . LANGUAGES: Spanish.

**KIM Y. GOHATA,** born Encino, California, March 20, 1972; (admission pending). *Education:* University of California at Los Angeles (B.A., summa cum laude, 1993); Yale Law School (J.D., 1996). Phi Beta Kappa. Member, *Yale Journal of International Law,* 1993-1994.

**JENNIFER L. KELL,** born San Antonio, Texas, January 9, 1969; (admission pending). *Education:* Universidad de Sevilla, Spain (1989-1990); Amherst College (B.A., magna cum laude, 1991); Harvard Law School (J.D., cum laude, 1996). Phi Beta Kappa. LANGUAGES: Spanish.

REPRESENTATIVE CLIENTS: Academy of Motion Picture Arts and Sciences; Avery Dennison; Bank of America; California Institute of Technology; Computer Sciences Corp.; Countrywide Credit; Federal Home Mortgage Corp.; General Motors Corporation; GranCare, Inc.; H.F. Ahmanson & Co.; Hughes Aircraft Company; Johnson Controls, Inc.; Litton Industries, Inc.; Lockheed Martin Corp.; Lewis Homes; Maguire Thomas Partners; Marriott Corp.; Mattel, Inc.; Northrop Grumman Corp.; The Parsons Corporation; Sizzler International, Inc.; Teledyne, Inc.; Texaco, Inc.; Ticket Master, Inc.; Toyota Motor Sales, U.S.A., Inc.; TRW, Inc.; WMX Technologies, Inc.

REFERENCE: Bank of California.

---

## QUISENBERRY & BARBANEL
### 2049 CENTURY PARK EAST
### SUITE 2200
### LOS ANGELES, CALIFORNIA 90067
Telephone: 310-785-7966
FAX: 310-785-0254

**San Diego, California Office:** Emerald Shapery Center, 402 West Broadway, Suite 400. Telephone: 619-595-4866. Fax: 619-595-3166.

*Civil Litigation practice in State and Federal Courts, Trials and Appeals. Insurance Coverage and Litigation, including Casualty, Property and Environmental Claims. Business and Commercial Litigation. Unfair Competition and Business Torts Litigation.*

**JOHN N. QUISENBERRY,** born Jackson, Mississippi, December 9, 1942; admitted to bar, 1980, California, U.S. Court of Appeals, Ninth Circuit and U.S. District Courts, Northern, Southern, Central and Eastern Districts of California. *Education:* United States Naval Academy (B.S., 1965); Occidental College (M.A., 1972); Heidelberg University, Heidelberg, West Germany; University of California at Los Angeles (J.D., 1980). *Member:* Los Angeles County and American (Member, Section of Tort and Insurance Practice) Bar Associations; State Bar of California; Association of Business Trial Lawyers; Lawyer-Pilots Bar Association. [Cmdr., USNR; active duty, Navy Pilot, 1965-1972]

**ALAN H. BARBANEL,** born Boston, Massachusetts, April 29, 1955; admitted to bar, 1983, California, U.S. District Court, Central, Northern, Eastern and Southern Districts of California and U.S. Court of Appeals, Ninth Circuit. *Education:* Northeastern University (B.S., magna cum laude, 1978); University of California, San Diego; University of San Diego (J.D., 1982). Phi Alpha Delta. Member, 1980-1982 and Lead Articles Editor, 1981-1982, San Diego Law Review. Co-Author: "Settlement of Professional Liability Claims," Professional Liability Insurance for Attorneys, Accountants and Insurance Brokers, Practicing Law Institute, 1984-1986. Co-Author: "The Right to Settle Claims," Introduction to Business Insurance-Law and Litigation, Practising Law Institute, 1985. Member, Editorial Board, The Los Angeles Lawyer Magazine, published by Los Angeles County Bar Association, 1985-1986. *Member:* Los Angeles County, San Diego County and American (Member, Torts and Insurance Practice Section; Insurance Coverage Litigation Committee) Bar Associations; State Bar of California; The Association of Trial Lawyers of America; California Trial Lawyers Association; Defense Research Institute; Practicing Law Institute. (Also at San Diego Office). *REPORTED CASES:* North Star Reinsurance Corporation v. Superior Court, 10 Cal. App. 4th 1815 (1992); General Star Indemnity Company v. Superior Court, 96 Daily Journal D.A.R. 9263 (1996).

**STEPHEN D. TREUER,** born Fort Bragg, North Carolina, August 3, 1954; admitted to bar, 1984, Arizona; 1988, California; U.S. District Court, Central District of California and U.S. Court of Appeals, Ninth Circuit; U.S. District Court, District of Arizona. *Education:* Hampshire College (B.A., 1976); University of California at Berkeley (M.A., 1980); Boalt Hall School of Law, University of California (J.D., 1984). *Member:* State Bar of California; State Bar of Arizona; American Bar Association (Member, Tort and Insurance Practice Section). *REPORTED CASES:* North Star Reinsurance Corporation v. Superior Court, 10 Cal. App. 4th 1815 (1992).

### ASSOCIATES

**BRIAN S. KABATECK,** born Los Angeles, California, August 15, 1961; admitted to bar, 1990, California; 1991, U.S. District Court, Southern, Central, Northern Districts of California and U.S. Court of Appeals, 9th Circuit. *Education:* University of Southern California (B.A., Political Science, 1985); Loyola of Los Angeles Law School (J.D, cum laude, 1989). Order of the Coif. Phi Alpha Delta. Recipient: American Jurisprudence Award; Bronze Key Award. Member, Loyola of Los Angeles Law Review. Author: "Attorney Direct Mail Solicitation: Regulating After Shapiro v. Kentucky Bar Association," 23 Loyola Law Review 851 (1989). *Member:* Los Angeles County and American Bar Associations; State Bar of California.

**AMY DANTZLER,** born Durham, North Carolina, July 6, 1964; admitted to bar, 1990, California. *Education:* Pomona College (B.A., 1986); Loyola University of Los Angeles (J.D., 1990). *Member:* Los Angeles County and American Bar Association; State Bar of California; California Women Lawyers.

**TERRY R. BAILEY,** born Van Nuys, California, September 20, 1960; admitted to bar, 1990, California and United States District Court, Central District of California. *Education:* California State University, Northridge (B.A., History, magna cum laude, 1987); University of California, Davis (J.D., 1990). Member, Board of Directors, Child Abuse and Neglect, Inc., Ventura County (CAAN). *Member:* Ventura County Bar Association; State Bar of California. *REPORTED CASES:* Fleming v. Gallegos 23 Cal.App.4th 68 (1994).

**ORA D. KRAMER,** born San Francisco, California, March 6, 1962; admitted to bar, 1988, California; 1989, U.S. District Court, Central and Southern Districts of California. *Education:* University of California at Davis (B.S., 1984); Loyola University of Los Angeles (J.D., 1988).

**JENNY Y. LI,** born Atlanta, Georgia, March 26, 1966; admitted to bar, 1992, California. *Education:* University of Illinois (B.A., 1987); Georgetown University (J.D., 1991). *Member:* State Bar of California.

**DAVID C. PARISI,** born Pasadena, California, November 23, 1966; admitted to bar, 1992, California. *Education:* California State University, Fullerton (B.A., Business Administration, minor Philosophy, 1989); Boston University (J.D., 1992). *Member:* Los Angeles County and American (Member, Insurance Coverage Litigation Committee; Torts and Insurance Practice Section) Bar Association; State Bar of California. PRACTICE AREAS: Insurance Coverage.

**KATHRYN PAIGE FLETCHER,** born Bellevue, Washington, June 24, 1966; admitted to bar, 1992, Washington and U.S. District Court, Western District of Washington; 1996, California. *Education:* University of Washington (B.A., Political Science, 1988; J.D., with honors, 1992). *Member:* State Bar of California; Washington State Bar Association.

**BARBARA CIOLINO,** born Teaneck, New Jersey, February 13, 1959; admitted to bar, 1989, California. *Education:* University of Massachusetts (B.A., 1981); Boston College (J.D., 1989). *Member:* State Bar of California. PRACTICE AREAS: General Business Litigation.

**SUSAN E. ABITANTA,** born Newark, New Jersey, September 9, 1949; admitted to bar, 1983, California. *Education:* University of Louisville (B.A., 1971); Southern Methodist University (J.D., cum laude, 1983). Phi Delta Phi. Order of the Coif. Assistant Editor-in-Chief, Southwestern Law Journal, 1982-1983. Author, "Bifurcation of Liability and Damages in Rule 23 (b) (3) Class Actions, History, Policy, Problems and a Solution", 36 Sw. L.J. 759 (1983) *Member:* Westwood and Los Angeles County Bar Associations; Women Lawyers Association of Los Angeles. PRACTICE AREAS: Civil Litigation; Insurance Coverage.

**PHYLLIS J. BERSCH,** born Ann Arbor, Michigan, December 12, 1954; admitted to bar, 1979, California; 1980, U.S. District Court, Central District of California; 1981, U.S. Court of Appeals, Ninth Circuit; 1985, U.S. District Court, Eastern District of California. *Education:* University of California at Berkeley (B.A., with distinction, 1976); University of California at Los Angeles (J.D., 1979). Member, U.C.L.A. Law Review, 1978-1979. *Member:* Los Angeles County and American (Member, Litigation

*(This Listing Continued)*

Section) Bar Associations; The State Bar of California (Member, 1982-1987 and Vice-Chair, 1985-1987, Conference of Delegates Resolutions Committee; Member, 1987-1990 and Vice-Chair, 1989-1990, Conference of Delegates Executive Committee); Women Lawyers' Association of Los Angeles (Member, Board of Governors, 1980-1984; Co-Chair, Judicial Evaluations Committee, 1983-1984; Chair, Legislative Drafting Committee, 1982-1983; Chair, WLALA Delegation to State Bar Conference, 1981-1982; Vice-Chair, WLALA Delegation to State Bar Conference, 1980-1981; Member, WLALA Delegation to State Bar Conference, 980-1985); California Women Lawyers Association (Member: Board of Governors, 1982-1984). **PRACTICE AREAS:** Family Law; Business Litigation.

**JOHN R. LISENBERY,** born San Pedro, California, November 2, 1962; admitted to bar, 1988, California and U.S. District Court, Central District of California; 1995, U.S. District Court, Northern District of California. *Education:* University of Southern California (B.A., Political Science and International Relations, 1985); Loyola Marymount University (J.D., 1988). Phi Alpha Delta. *Member:* Los Angeles County (Member, Section on Litigation) and American Bar Associations; State Bar of California. **REPORTED CASES:** Simmons v. West Covina Medical Clinic, 212 Cal.App. 3d 696 (1989); Denny's, Inc. v. Chicago Ins. Co., 234 Cal.App. 3d 1786 (1991); American Arbitration Association v. Superior Court, 8 Cal.App. 4th 1131 (1992); Fireman's Fund Ins. Co. v. McDonald, Hecht & Solberg, 30 Cal. App. 4th 1371 (1994); General Star Indem. Co. v. Schools Excess Liability Fund, 888 F. Supp. 1022 (N.D. Cal. 1995). **PRACTICE AREAS:** Insurance Coverage; Insurance Defense; Commercial Litigation.

**CAROLYN PIERCE BELL,** born Los Angeles, California, April 6, 1947; admitted to bar, 1991, California and U.S. District Court, Central District of California; 1992, U.S. District Court, Southern District of California; 1993, U.S. Court of Appeals, Ninth Circuit. *Education:* Mount Holyoke College; University of California at Los Angeles (B.S.N., 1970; M.S.N., 1985); Southwestern University (J.D., cum laude, 1991). Registered Nurse, California, 1970. *Member:* Los Angeles County and American (Tort and Insurance Law Section) Bar Associations; West Los Angeles Bar Association. **PRACTICE AREAS:** Business Litigation; Insurance Coverage; Bankruptcy.

**JOSHUA A. GRATCH,** born Los Angeles, California, May 1, 1967; admitted to bar, 1993, California. *Education:* University of California at Berkeley (B.A., 1989); University of California School of Law, Los Angeles (J.D., 1993). Moot Court Honors Program. Extern to Judge Pregerson, U.S. Court of Appeals, Ninth Circuit, Spring, 1992). *Member:* State Bar of California.

**DEREK W. STARK,** born Burbank, California, August 15, 1967; admitted to bar, 1994, California; U.S. District Court, Central District of California. *Education:* University of California at Berkeley (B.A., 1989); Loyola Law School (J.D., 1994). *Member:* Los Angeles County and American Bar Associations; State Bar of California. **PRACTICE AREAS:** Business Litigation; Real Estate Litigation; Insurance Coverage.

## OF COUNSEL

**JOHN A. GRANIEZ,** born Tarrytown, New York, June 22, 1948; admitted to bar, 1979, California; 1980, U.S. District Court, Central District of California; 1985, New York. *Education:* Fordham University (B.A., 1970); University of Chicago Graduate School of Business; Loyola University (J.D., 1979). *Member:* Los Angeles County and American Bar Associations; State Bar of California; Association of Business Trial Lawyers; Conference of Insurance Counsel; Defense Research Institute. **PRACTICE AREAS:** Insurance Coverage Litigation.

REPRESENTATIVE CLIENTS: Alper Development; American Insurance Adjustment Agency; American Multi-Cinema, Inc.; Browning-Ferris Industries; California Insurance Guarantee Association; Ceredyne, Inc.; Computer Systems of America; First City Properties, Inc.; General Reinsurance Corporation; General Star Indemnity Company; General Star Management Corporation; Grand American, Inc.; Great American Bank; Halliburton Company; Highlands Insurance Company; Insurance Company of the West; Maryland Casualty Insurance Company; MSR Exploration, Ltd.; Nonprofits Insurance Alliance of California; North Star Reinsurance Corporation; Sanncor Industries, Inc.; Schlumberger, Ltd.; Southern World Airlines; Torrance Unified School District; Turner Industries; Unigard Mutual Insurance Company; United Capital Insurance Company; United National Insurance Company; Wells Fargo Bank.
REFERENCE: Bank of California.

# RADCLIFF, FRANDSEN & DONGELL
*Established in 1988*

40TH FLOOR, 777 SOUTH FIGUEROA STREET
**LOS ANGELES, CALIFORNIA 90017**
*Telephone: 213-614-1990*
*Facsimile: 213-489-9263*

*San Francisco, California Office:* 88 Kearny Street, Suite 1475. Telephone: 415-399-8393. Facsimile: 415-989-5465.
*Rome, Italy Office:* Via Tacito, 7. Telephone: (39) 06-323-5588. Facsimile: (39) 06-324-3392.

General Civil, Trial and Appellate Practice in all State and Federal Courts, Corporate, Environmental, Administrative, Regulatory, Telecommunications, Real Estate, Insurance, Professional Liability, Trademark and Trade Name, Competitive Business Practices, Fiduciary, Financial Institutions, Securities and Finance, Commercial, International, Tax, Construction, Labor and Employment, Employment Benefits, Product Liability.

FIRM PROFILE: *The firm's practice is devoted largely to business and commercial law, government regulation, and related litigation.*

*Among the firm's clients are national and international corporations and companies involved in broadcasting, transportation, insurance, real estate, manufacturing, electronics, computer software development, health care, food processing and distribution, and financial services.*

*Radcliff, Frandsen & Dongell's seasoned trial lawyers have vigorously represented clients in federal and state courts, having extensive experience at the appellate level. The firm has represented clients in connection with proceedings before committees of the United States Congress, federal agencies, and various offices, agencies, and departments of California state government, with expertise in matters involving the Securities and Exchange Commission, the U.S. Environmental Protection Agency, the Federal Communications Commission, the Internal Revenue Service, and state environmental agencies.*

*The firm is nationally known for its expertise in compliance with storm water regulations and represents more than 15 associations of industrial and manufacturing concerns.*

*Real estate clients include landlords, tenants, owner-operators, and creditors. The firm actively represents clients in merger and acquisition transactions.*

## MEMBERS OF FIRM

**JULES G. RADCLIFF, JR.,** born Morgantown, West Virginia, September 16, 1947; admitted to bar, 1976, California. *Education:* California State University at Northridge (B.S., summa cum laude, 1973); University of California at Los Angeles (J.D., 1976). Contributing Editor, "International Court of Justice Opinion Briefs," American Bar Association, 1978. Chief of Staff and Executive Assistant to California Lt. Governor, 1983-1984. Member, Los Angeles County Courthouse Corporation, 1989—. *Member:* State Bar of California; District of Columbia Bar.

**RUSSELL MACKAY FRANDSEN,** born Gunnison, Utah, February 25, 1949; admitted to bar, 1976, California; 1982, U.S. Court of Appeals, Ninth Circuit and U.S. Tax Court. *Education:* Brigham Young University (B.A., high honors, magna cum laude, 1973); Duke University (J.D., 1976). Author: "Mexico Relaxes Restrictions on Foreign Technology Transfers," California International Law Section Newsletter, Vol. 3, No. 2, June 1990. Member, Board of Directors, 1987-1994 and Vice-Chairman, 1989-1990, Los Angeles County Private Industry Council. Member, Board of Directors, 1987-1993 and President, 1990-1991, La Cañada-Flintridge Educational Foundation. Section Chair, Science and Technology, Town Hall of California, 1989-1993. Member, Executive Committee, Caltech MIT Enterprise Forum, 1990—. Member, Board of Directors, Pasadena Young Musicians Orchestra, 1991—. *Member:* State Bar of California; American Bar Association (Member, Sections on: Business Law; Tax; Science and Technology; Real Estate). **LANGUAGES:** German.

**RICHARD A. DONGELL,** born Hagerstown, Maryland, November 26, 1961; admitted to bar, 1987, California. *Education:* Pennsylvania State University (B.A., 1983); Temple University (J.D., 1986); Institute of Comparative Law, University of Rome, Italy. Consecutive Member, Temple Law Review, 1984-1986. Author: "Insurance Law-Gender-Based Automobile Insurance Rates Violate Casualty and Surety Rate Regulatory Act interpreted In Light of Pennsylvania Equal Rights Amendment--Hartford Accident & Indemnity Co. v. Insurance Commissioner," 58 Temp. L.Q. 457, 1985, republished, National Insurance Law Review, Vol. l, 1985; "Criminal Procedure-Defense Attorney Is Under Reciprocal Duty to Disclose Witnesses' Pretrial Statements, If Requested, To Commonwealth At Trial-Commonwealth v. Brinkley," 58 Temp. L.Q. 377, 1985. Chief Legal Coun-
*(This Listing Continued)*

## RADCLIFF, FRANDSEN & DONGELL, Los Angeles—Continued

sel, Business Finance Council of the California Democratic Party. Member: California Insurance Commissioner Garamendi's Environmental Insurance Task Force; Environment Crimes Sentencing Guidelines Task Force, Los Angeles County District Attorney's Office and the Los Angeles City Attorney's Office. *Member:* Los Angeles County Bar Association (Former Member: Steering Committee; Real Estate Litigation Section); State Bar of California.

### OF COUNSEL

**TAL CLIFTON FINNEY,** born Lancaster, Pennsylvania, March 21, 1964; admitted to bar, 1991, California. *Education:* University of California at Los Angeles (B.A., 1986); Loyola Marymount University (J.D., 1991). Deputy Director, South Africa Constitution Watch Commissions. Legal Counsel, Global Rights. Elected Controller and Chair of Finance Committee, California Democratic Party. Member, California State Child Support Task Force. Board Member, Children's Rights 2000, Oceansafe Coalition. *Member:* Los Angeles County and American Bar Associations; State Bar of California.

### ASSOCIATES

**FRANCIS P. ASPESSI,** born Milton, Massachusetts, September 9, 1956; admitted to bar, 1985, California and U.S. District Court, Central District of California; 1989, U.S. District Court, Northern District of California; 1995, U.S. District Court, Southern District of California. *Education:* Columbia University (B.A., 1980); University of Southern California (J.D., 1984). Recipient, American Jurisprudence Award, Remedies. *Member:* State Bar of California.

**RUBEN A. CASTELLON,** born Okinawa, Japan, June 7, 1963; admitted to bar, 1991, California, U.S. District Court, Northern, Eastern and Central Districts of California and U.S. Court of Appeals, Ninth Circuit; 1994, Hawaii. *Education:* Saint Mary's College of California (B.S., B.A, 1985); University of California at Los Angeles (J.D., 1991). Author: "Refugee Redefined: An Inquiry into Mexican Legal Standards Relating to Asylum and Non-Reoulment," Chicano Latino Review, Spring, 1992. Member, Federal Communications Law Journal, 1991. Member, Moot Court Honors Program, University of California at Los Angeles. *Member:* Los Angeles County Bar Association; State Bar of California. *LANGUAGES:* Spanish.

**WILLIAM W. FUNDERBURK, JR.,** born Washington, D.C., August 21, 1961; admitted to bar, 1991, Pennsylvania and District of Columbia; 1995, California. *Education:* Yale University (B.A., 1985); Georgetown University Law Center (J.D., 1990). Co-Author: "California's Storm Water Regulations: A Practical Review of the Regulations and their Enforcement," Cal.Env.L.Rep. 384, Nov., 1993. Contributing Commentator, California Environmental Law Reporter. Mondale for President, 1984. John Ray for Mayor (Finance Director), 1990. Bob Kerrey for President, 1991-1992 (Finance Committee). Appointed by: U.S. Environmental Protection Agency to National Phase II Storm Water Advisory Board, 1992-1993; Environmental Liability Insurance Justice Force, California Insurance Commissioner, 1992-1994; Environmental Crimes Sentencing Task Force, Los Angeles County District Attorney and Los Angeles City Attorney, 1993-1995; Thompson Publishing National Stormwater Advisory Board, 1994—. *Member:* District of Columbia Bar; State Bar of California; American Bar Association (Member, Sections on: Natural Resources Energy and Environmental Law; Labor and Employment Law; Administrative Law and Regulatory Practice).

**JEFFREY A. GAGLIARDI,** born Jersey City, New Jersey, June 26, 1965; admitted to bar, 1991, California and U.S. District Court, Central, Southern and Northern Districts of California; U.S. Court of Appeals, Ninth Circuit. *Education:* University of Maryland, College Park (B.S., 1988, Beta Gamma Sigma); University of California, Hastings College of the Law (J.D., cum laude, 1991). Order of the Coif; Thurston Society; Golden Key; Phi Eta Sigma. Recipient, American Jurisprudence Awards in Insurance Law, Constitutional Criminal Procedure, and Evidence Advocacy Workshop. *Member:* State Bar of California; District of Columbia Bar.

**DAVID K. LEE,** born Seoul, Korea, August 20, 1963; admitted to bar, 1992, California. *Education:* University of California at Los Angeles (B.A., 1988); McGeorge School of Law (J.D., 1991). Latin Honors, U.C.L.A. *Member:* State Bar of California. *LANGUAGES:* Korean.

**MARIA ANNA MANCINI,** born Los Angeles, California, April 14, 1966; admitted to bar, 1994, California and U.S. District Court, Central District of California. *Education:* Loyola Marymount University (B.A.,

*(This Listing Continued)*

1988; J.D., 1992). Alpha Sigma Nu; Pi Gamma Mu. *Member:* State Bar of California; American Bar Association (Member, International Law Section). *LANGUAGES:* Italian, Spanish and French.

**JEFFREY C. MAYES,** born Los Angeles, California, November 28, 1968; admitted to bar, 1993, California; 1996, Arizona, U.S. District Court, Central District of California and U.S. District Court, District of Arizona. *Education:* University of Southern California (B.S., 1989); Syracuse University (J.D., 1993). *Member:* State Bar of California; State Bar of Arizona.

**MARISA A. MORET,** born Los Angeles, California, December 31, 1969; admitted to bar, 1994, California; 1995, U.S. District Court, Northern and Central Districts of California. *Education:* Georgetown University (B.A., 1991); University of California at Los Angeles (J.D., 1994). *Member:* Los Angeles County and American Bar Associations; State Bar of California; Mexican American Bar Association.

**DANIEL E. PARK,** born Seoul, Korea, June 15, 1969; admitted to bar, 1994, California, U.S. District Court, Central District of California and U.S. Court of Appeals, Ninth Circuit. *Education:* University of California at Los Angeles (B.A., with honors, 1991; J.D., 1994). Phi Delta Phi. Gail McKinney Wheat Scholarship. Member, Moot Court Honors Program. Articles Editor, Asian Pacific American Law Journal. Author: "The Fallout From the Baker Cases: Sexual Harassment and the Korean-American Community," KoreAm Journal, Feb., 1995. *Member:* Los Angeles County Bar Association; State Bar of California (Member, Litigation Section); Korean-American Bar Association. *LANGUAGES:* Korean.

**SCOTT D. PINSKY,** born Los Angeles, California, October 29, 1957; admitted to bar, 1985, California and U.S District Court, Central District of California; 1986, U.S. District Court, Northern, Southern and Eastern Districts of California and U.S. Court of Appeals, Ninth Circuit. *Education:* Pomona College (B.A., 1979); Rutgers University (M.A., 1980); University of California at Los Angeles (J.D., 1985). Member, UCLA Moot Court Honors Program, 1983-1984. Comment Editor, Federal Communications Law Journal, 1983-1984. Extern: Hon. A. Wallace Tashima, U.S. District Court, Central District of California, 1983; Hon. Stephen Reinhardt, U.S. Court of Appeals, Ninth Circuit, 1984. *Member:* State Bar of California. *LANGUAGES:* French.

**ERIC H. SAIKI,** born Los Angeles, California, November 5, 1965; admitted to bar, 1991, California; 1992, U.S. District Court, Central District of California and U.S. Court of Appeals, Ninth Circuit; 1993, U.S. District Court, Northern and Southern Districts of California. *Education:* University of California at Los Angeles (B.A., 1987); University of California, Hastings College of the Law (J.D., 1991). *Member:* Los Angeles County Bar Association; State Bar of California.

**STEVE R. SEGURA,** born Lompoc, California, November 16, 1965; admitted to bar, 1991, California; 1993, U.S. District Court, Central and Eastern Districts of California; 1994, U.S. Court of Appeals, Ninth Circuit. *Education:* University of California at Los Angeles (B.A., 1988); University of California at Los Angeles School of Law (J.D., 1991). Phi Alpha Delta. Member: Moot Court Honors Program; National Criminal Justice Student Trial Advocacy Competition. *Member:* Los Angeles County Bar Association; State Bar of California.

**GLENN M. WHITE,** born El Paso, Texas, August 26, 1958; admitted to bar, 1989, California. *Education:* University of Texas at Austin (B.A., 1984; J.D., 1987). *Member:* State Bar of California.

---

## RAMSEY, BRONSTEIN & DAYTON
### 5959 WEST CENTURY BOULEVARD, SUITE 1410
### LOS ANGELES, CALIFORNIA 90045
Telephone: 310-641-8900
FAX: 310-641-7377

*General Civil Litigation Practice, Products Liability, Tractor/Trailer Litigation, Construction Litigation, Drug Product Liability, Automotive Dealer Litigation, Workers' Compensation.*

### MEMBERS OF FIRM

**CHRISTOPHER P. RAMSEY,** born Los Angeles, California, May 13, 1952; admitted to bar, 1977, California; 1979, U.S. District Court, Central District of California. *Education:* University of California at Los Angeles (B.A. in Political Science, cum laude, 1974); Hastings College of Law, University of California (J.D., 1977). *Member:* State Bar of California; Association of Southern California Defense Counsel. *PRACTICE AREAS:* Municipality; Products Liability; General Negligence; Workers' Compensation Defense.

*(This Listing Continued)*

**JOHN D. BRONSTEIN,** born Los Angeles, California, May 28, 1956; admitted to bar, 1981, California. *Education:* University of California at Los Angeles (B.A., 1978); Loyola Marymount University (J.D., 1981). Member, Scott Moot Court Honor Society. *Member:* Los Angeles County Bar Association; State Bar of California; Association of Southern California Defense Counsel. *PRACTICE AREAS:* Tractor-Trailer; Automotive Dealers Litigation; Products Liability Litigation; Negligence.

**LEE W. DAYTON,** born Greenwich, Connecticut, February 6, 1951; admitted to bar, 1982, California and U.S. District Court, Central District of California. *Education:* Brigham Young University (B.A., 1976); Western State University (J.D.1980). Recipient, American Jurisprudence Awards in: Criminal Law and Procedure; Contracts; Uniform Commercial Code. *Member:* Los Angeles County and American Bar Associations; State Bar of California; Association of Southern California Defense Counsel. *LANGUAGES:* Spanish. *PRACTICE AREAS:* Municipality; Products Liability; General Negligence.

### ASSOCIATES

**ALAN L. SOBEL,** born Bridgeport, Connecticut, November 5, 1963; admitted to bar, 1988, Connecticut; 1989, U.S. District Court, District of Connecticut; 1991, California; 1992, U.S. District Court, Central District of California. *Education:* Clark University (B.A., 1985); Washington College of Law-American University (J.D., 1988). Judicial Clerkship, State of Connecticut Superior Court, 1990-1991. *PRACTICE AREAS:* Tractor-Trailer Litigation; General Products Negligence.

### OF COUNSEL

**GREGG H. ROBIN,** born Los Angeles, California, December 12, 1951; admitted to bar, 1980, California. *Education:* University of California at Los Angeles (B.A., magna cum laude, 1974); Southwestern University School of Law (J.D., 1980). *Member:* State Bar of California. *PRACTICE AREAS:* Workers Compensation Defense Law (100%).

REPRESENTATIVE CLIENTS: Alexsis Risk Management Services; Interstate National Corp.; World Oil Co.; Chicago Insurance Co.; ESIS, Inc.; Protective Insurance Co.; Mercury Casualty Co.; Sandoz Pharmaceuticals Corp.; Crawford & Co.; Carl Warren and Co.; Motor Cargo Co.; Carolina Casualty; D. Longo, Inc.; Longo Toyota; Penske Corporation; Penske Truck Leasing Co.; Leaseway Transportation; CSK Trucking; CSX International; City of Lancaster; United Southern Assurance Co.; Baldwin & Lyons, Inc.; Homebase, Inc.

---

## RAPORE AND LOWE

### LOS ANGELES, CALIFORNIA

(See Santa Monica)

*General Civil Litigation, Franchise Relations, Real Property, Probate, Trust, Entertainment, Business and Intellectual Property Law.*

---

## THOMAS J. READY

*333 SOUTH GRAND AVENUE, 33RD FLOOR*
### LOS ANGELES, CALIFORNIA 90071-1504
Telephone: 213-229-9009
Facsimile: 213-229-9010
Email: TJRLA@AOL.com

*Business Litigation.*

**THOMAS J. READY,** born Oakland, California, October 7, 1937; admitted to bar, 1966, California; 1974, U.S. Supreme Court. *Education:* University of California at Berkeley (A.B., 1959); Stanford University (LL.B., 1965). *Member:* Los Angeles County (Member, Trial Lawyers and Antitrust Sections), Federal and American (Member, Sections on: Antitrust; Litigation; Committee on Insurance Coverage Litigation) Bar Associations; State Bar of California (Member, Sections on: Litigation; Real Property Law); Association of Business Trial Lawyers. Fellow, American Bar Foundation.

---

## REBACK, HULBERT, McANDREWS & KJAR, LLP

### LOS ANGELES, CALIFORNIA

(See Manhattan Beach)

*Civil Litigation Defense, Insurance Defense, Professional Liability, Personal Injury, Product Liability, Business Litigation, Real Estate, Commercial Litigation, Risk Management, Loss Prevention, Mediation, Legal and Medical Malpractice.*

---

## REBOUL, MacMURRAY, HEWITT, MAYNARD & KRISTOL

*SUITE 1500*
*1801 CENTURY PARK EAST*
### LOS ANGELES, CALIFORNIA 90067
Telephone: 310-551-3070
Telecopier: 310-551-3071

New York, N.Y. Office: 45 Rockefeller Plaza. Telephone: 212-841-5700.
Washington, D.C. Office: Suite 406, 1111 Nineteenth St., N.W., 20036. Telephone: 202-429-0004.

*General Practice.*

### RESIDENT PARTNER

**ANDREW P. TASHMAN,** born New York, N.Y., August 30, 1944; admitted to bar, 1968, New York; 1981, District of Columbia; 1987, California. *Education:* Columbia College (B.A., 1965); Columbia Law School (LL.B., 1968). Editor, Columbia Law Review, 1967-1968. Law Clerk to Hon. Charles D. Breitel, New York Court of Appeals, 1968-1970. Special Litigation Counsel, Civil Division, U.S. Department of Justice, Washington, D.C., 1979-1982. Assistant General Counsel and Deputy General Counsel, U.S. Synthetic Fuel Corp., 1982-1986. *Member:* American Bar Association.

### RESIDENT ASSOCIATES

**JOEL J. BERNSTEIN,** born Washington, D.C., September 27, 1963; admitted to bar, 1989, California; 1990, District of Columbia. *Education:* Columbia College (A.B., 1985); University of Pennsylvania (J.D., 1989). *Member:* Century City, Beverly Hills and Los Angeles County Bar Associations; State Bar of California. *LANGUAGES:* Spanish.

**NAOMI A. HENTSCHEL,** born Washington, D.C., September 28, 1954; admitted to bar, 1984, California. *Education:* University of California at Los Angeles (B.A., 1981); Boalt Hall School of Law, University of California (J.D., 1984). *Member:* Los Angeles County Bar Association; State Bar of California.

### STAFF ATTORNEY

**KEVIN S. WATTLES,** born Seattle, Washington, December 28, 1962; admitted to bar, 1990, Massachusetts; 1994, California. *Education:* Harvard University (B.A., 1986); Pepperdine University School of Law (J.D., 1990). *Member:* Massachusetts and American Bar Associations; State Bar of California.

(For Biographical data on all Personnel, see Professional Biographies at New York, New York)

---

## REHWALD RAMESON LEWIS & GLASNER

### LOS ANGELES, CALIFORNIA

(See Woodland Hills)

*General Civil and Trial Practice. Corporation, Real Property, Estate Planning, Trusts, Probate, Negligence, Workplace Litigation, Family Law, Appeals.*

## HARVEY REICHARD

*501 SHATTO PLACE, SUITE 100*
*LOS ANGELES, CALIFORNIA 90020*
*Telephone: 213-386-3860*
*Fax: 213-386-5583*

*Workers Compensation Law.*

**HARVEY REICHARD,** born Plainfield, New Jersey, June 8, 1937; admitted to bar, 1963, California. *Education:* University of California at Los Angeles (B.S., 1959); University of California School of Law, Los Angeles (J.D., 1962); University of Southern California (LL.M., 1965). President, Phi Alpha Delta, 1962. *Member:* Los Angeles County Bar Association (Member, Workers Compensation Section, 1964—; Chairman, Workers Compensation Section, 1981); State Bar of California (Chairman, Workers Compensation Law Advisory Commission, 1989); California Applicant Attorney Association; Southern California Applicant Attorneys Association (President, 1976). ***PRACTICE AREAS:*** Worker's Compensation Law.

---

## REINIS & REINIS

*550 SOUTH HOPE STREET, 20TH FLOOR*
*LOS ANGELES, CALIFORNIA 90071*
*Telephone: 213-624-4246*
*Facsimile: 213-624-4709*

*General Corporate, Commercial, Litigation, Intellectual Property and Real Estate Law.*

### MEMBERS OF FIRM

**MITCHELL N. REINIS,** born New York, N.Y., October 1, 1939; admitted to bar, 1965, California and U.S. District Court, Central, Northern and Southern Districts of California; U.S. Court of Appeals, Ninth Circuit and U.S. Supreme Court. *Education:* University of California at Berkeley (B.S., 1961); Boalt Hall School of Law, University of California (LL.B., 1964). Phi Delta Phi. Judge Pro Tempore, Beverly Hills Municipal Court, 1970-1973. *Member:* Beverly Hills and Los Angeles County Bar Associations; State Bar of California (Member, Intellectual Property Section). ***REPORTED CASES:*** Russell vs. Price, 612 F.2d 1123,205 USPQ 206; Lew vs. Moss, 797 F.2d 747; McCaffrey vs. Diversified Land, 564 F.2d 1241; Southwestern Publishing vs. Simons, 651 F.2d 653; Golden West Melodies vs. Capitol Records, 274 CA2d 713; Estate of Johnson, 162 CA3d 917; People vs. Elinson, 70 CA3d Supp. 19. ***PRACTICE AREAS:*** Business Transactions; Litigation; Intellectual Property.

**RICHARD G. REINIS,** born Great Neck, New York, October 9, 1944; admitted to bar, 1970, California and U.S. District Court, Central District of California. *Education:* Princeton University (B.A., 1966); University of Southern California (J.D., 1969). Member, University of Southern California Law Review, 1968-1969. Chief Justice, Moot Court. Author: "Small Claims Court," University of Southern California Law Review, 1969. Judge Pro Tem, Los Angeles Superior Court, 1985. Public Counsel, Board of Directors, Legal Aid Foundation, 1986-1994. President, 1989-1990 and Chairman, 1990-1991, Board of Trustees, Los Angeles Children's Museum. Board of Directors, Maxwell Gluck Foundation. Founder and Acting Executive Director, Compliance Alliance. *Member:* Beverly Hills, Los Angeles County and American (Member, Real Property, Probate and Trust Law Section) Bar Associations; State Bar of California. ***TRANSACTIONS:*** License agreements respecting trademarks "Bum Equipment", "Let's Get Ready to Rumble," Professional Sports and other national brands; quoted expert on apparel industry matters. ***PRACTICE AREAS:*** Licensing Law; Labor; Business Organization; Business Acquisitions; Real Estate; Apparel Industry Matters; Business Litigation.

### ASSOCIATES

**LAURA P. WORSINGER,** born Long Beach, California, March 26, 1947; admitted to bar, 1972, California, U.S. District Court, Central District of California and U.S. District Court, Southern District of New York. *Education:* California State University at Fullerton (B.A., with honors, 1968); University of California at Los Angeles (J.D., 1971). Author: "Vertical Restraint After Repeal of Fair Trade," Fordham Law Journal, March 1977; "New Technologies and Antitrust," New York State Bar Journal, December, 1985, reprinted Case and Comment, September 1986. Co-Director with Professor Barry Hawk, Clinical Program in Antitrust Law, Fordham University Law School, 1976. Assistant Director, New York Office of the Federal Trade Commission, 1974-1976. Member, Board of Governors, Braemar Country Club, 1995—. *Member:* Association of the Bar of the City of New York (Member, Trade Regulation Committee, 1975-1977); State

*(This Listing Continued)*

Bar of California. ***PRACTICE AREAS:*** Business Litigation; Commercial Litigation; Insurance Law; Antitrust; Trade Regulation.

**STEVEN M. HARRISON,** born Los Angeles, California, December 11, 1944; admitted to bar, 1970, California, U.S. District Court, Central and Southern Districts of California and U.S. Court of Claims. *Education:* University of California at Berkeley (B.S., 1966); University of Southern California (J.D., 1969). Judge Pro Tempore, Los Angeles Municipal Court, 1982. Justice of Moot Court, University of California, Los Angeles, 1983. *Member:* San Fernando Valley (Member, Real Estate Section) and Los Angeles County Bar Associations; State Bar of California (Member, Real Estate and Litigation Sections, Lis Pendens Sub-committee); Association of Business Trial Lawyers. ***TRANSACTIONS:*** Real Estate, Partnership, Corporate, Limited Liability, Business Purchase and Sales, and License Agreements. ***PRACTICE AREAS:*** Real Estate; Business Litigation; Trade Secret; Unfair Competition Litigation; Securities Litigation; Construction Litigation.

**GREGORY N. WEISMAN,** born San Diego, California, November 20, 1968; admitted to bar, 1994, California and U.S. District Court, Central and Southern Districts of California. *Education:* University of California at Berkeley (B.A., 1991); University of San Diego (J.D., 1994). *Member:* State Bar of California. ***TRANSACTIONS:*** Trademark, Copyright and License Agreements. ***PRACTICE AREAS:*** Medical Malpractice; Insurance Litigation; Construction Defect Litigation; Product Liability; Business Litigation; Apparel Industry Matters; Intellectual Property.

### OF COUNSEL

**L. DOUGLAS BROWN,** born Fairmont, West Virginia, July 17, 1943; admitted to bar, 1970, California and U.S. District Court, Central District of California; 1971, U.S. Court of Appeals, Ninth Circuit; 1981, U.S. Supreme Court and U.S. Claims Court. *Education:* University of Southern California (B.A., with honors, 1966; J.D., 1969). Editor in Chief, Los Angeles Bar Journal, 1977. Real Estate Broker, California, 1990. Assistant U.S. Attorney, Central District of California, 1971-1974; Special Counsel, U.S. Department of Housing and Urban Development, 1974-1977; City Councilman, Torrance, 1976-1982. Executive Vice President and Director, Taiyo Development U.S.A., 1990. *Member:* Los Angeles County (Ethics Committee, 1974-1976, Judicial Appointments Committee, 1974-1977) Bar Association; State Bar of California (Member, Litigation, Real Estate and Taxation Sections). ***TRANSACTIONS:*** Sale of Northrop Corporation Headquarters Building, 1989; Purchase of Ford Motor Company Pico Rivera Facility, 1982. ***PRACTICE AREAS:*** Business and Commercial Litigation; Insolvency Practice and Reorganizations; Real Estate; General Business and Corporate Law.

---

## REINSTEIN, PANTELL & CALKINS

A Partnership of Professional Corporations
*Established in 1989*

*10940 WILSHIRE, SUITE 1600*
*LOS ANGELES, CALIFORNIA 90024*
*Telephone: 310-443-4299*

*Business and Commercial Transactions, Corporate and Partnership Law, Taxation, Real Estate, Health Care, Estate Planning, Trust, Probate, Civil and Criminal Tax Litigation, Employee Benefits and Relationships.*

### PARTNERS

**TODD RUSSELL REINSTEIN, (P.C.),** born Chicago, Illinois, July 30, 1937; admitted to bar, 1963, California and U.S. Tax Court; 1969, U.S. Claims Court; 1973, U.S. Court of Appeals Ninth Circuit; 1975, U.S. Supreme Court. *Education:* University of California at Los Angeles (B.S., cum laude, 1959; J.D., 1962). Phi Alpha Delta; Beta Gamma Sigma; Beta Alpha Psi. Member, Board of Editors, University of California at Los Angeles Law Review, 1960-1962. Co-Author: "Planning the Disposition of Real Estate After the Tax Reform Act of 1986," Fortieth Annual Tax Institute, University of Southern California; "Deconglomeration—Tax and Business Problems Associated with The Divestiture of a Recently Acquired Business," Twenty-Fourth Tax Institute, University of Southern California. Certified Public Accountant, California, 1964. Professor, Tax Law, California State University at Northridge, 1967—. *Member:* Beverly Hills, Los Angeles County and American (Member, Section of Taxation) Bar Associations; State Bar of California. (Certified Specialist, Taxation Law, The State Bar of California Board of Legal Specialization). ***PRACTICE AREAS:*** Taxation Law; Real Estate Law; Health Care Law; Estate Planning and Probate Law; Commercial and Business Law.

*(This Listing Continued)*

# PROFESSIONAL BIOGRAPHIES

## CALIFORNIA—LOS ANGELES

**COLLEEN DAPHNE CALKINS, (P.C.),** born Los Angeles, California, March 28, 1955; admitted to bar, 1978, California; 1981, U.S. Court of Appeals, Ninth Circuit; 1982, U.S. Tax Court and U.S. District Court, Central District of California. *Education:* University of California at Los Angeles (B.A., magna cum laude, 1975); University of Southern California (J.D., 1978). Phi Beta Kappa. Mortar Board. Contributing Author: "Planning the Disposition of Real Estate After the Tax Reform Act of 1986," Fortieth Annual Tax Institute, University of Southern California. *Member:* Beverly Hills, Century City, Los Angeles County and American (Member, Taxation Section) Bar Associations; State Bar of California. *PRACTICE AREAS:* Employee Benefits Law; Business Law; Corporate Law; Estate Planning and Probate Law; Health Care Law; Tax Law.

**LLOYD S. PANTELL, (P.C.),** born Los Angeles, California, December 8, 1951; admitted to bar, 1977, California and U.S. District Court, Central District of California. *Education:* University of California at Los Angeles (B.A., 1973); Pepperdine University (J.D., 1977); Georgetown University (LL.M., 1978). National Association of Securities Dealers, Inc., Series 27 Financial Operations Principal License, 1987. Adjunct Professor, Pepperdine University School of Law, 1989—. *Member:* Beverly Hills (Member, Sections on: Business Law and Natural Resources, Energy and Environmental Law) and American (Member, Sections on Natural Resources and Energy) Bar Associations; State Bar of California (Member, Business Law Section); California Society for Health Care Attorneys; National Health Lawyers Association. *PRACTICE AREAS:* Business Law; Commercial Law; Health Care Law; Partnership Law; Corporate Law.

### OF COUNSEL

**WILLIAM L. FEINSTEIN,** born Los Angeles, California, February 18, 1957; admitted to bar, 1981, California; 1982, U.S. Tax Court, U.S. District Court, Central District of California; U.S. Court of Appeals, Ninth Circuit. *Education:* Claremont McKenna College (B.A., magna cum laude, 1977); University of California at Los Angeles (J.D., 1981; M.B.A., 1981). Member: National Paralegal Instructional Courses; Editorial Review Board. Licensed Real Estate Broker, California, 1987. Author, Estate Planning Syllabus. Author: "Allen vs. Commissioner of Internal Revenue," 92 TC 1, 1989; "MacPherson vs. United States," 614 F. Supp 589, DC C.Cal., 1985; "Olsen vs. Commissioner of Internal Revenue," 1984 TC Memo No. 411. Co-Author: "Planning the Disposition of Real Estate After the Tax Reform Act of 1986," Fortieth Annual Tax Institute, University of Southern California. *Member:* Beverly Hills, Los Angeles County and American Bar Associations; State Bar of California. *PRACTICE AREAS:* Taxation Law; Probate; Estate Planning.

**JONATHAN B. KLINCK,** born Los Angeles, California, June 12, 1957; admitted to bar, 1985, California; U.S. Court of Appeals for the Ninth Circuit; U.S. District Court, Central, Southern and Eastern Districts of California. *Education:* University of Virginia (B.A., 1979; J.D., 1985). Elected Member, Jefferson Society. Volunteer Arbitrator, Los Angeles Superior Court. Judge Pro Tem, Los Angeles Municipal Court. *Member:* Los Angeles County and American Bar Associations; The Association of Trial Lawyers of America; Association of Business Trial Lawyers; Los Angeles Complex Litigation Inn of Court. *PRACTICE AREAS:* Business Litigation; Trademark and Copyright Law; Arbitration.

REFERENCE: Wells Fargo Bank, San Diego, California.

## REISH & LUFTMAN

*A PROFESSIONAL CORPORATION*

Established in 1985

11755 WILSHIRE BOULEVARD
10TH FLOOR
**LOS ANGELES, CALIFORNIA 90025**
Telephone: 310-478-5656
Facsimile: 310-478-5831
URL: http://www.benefitslink.com/reish/

Washington, D.C. Office: One Massachusetts Avenue, N.W., Suite 800, 20001. Telephone: 202-745-0024. Facsimile: 202-745-0005.

Corporate, Real Estate, Business and Real Estate Litigation, ERISA Litigation, Pension and Welfare Benefits, Taxation, Employment Law, Estate Planning and Probate. Civil Tax Controversies.

FIRM PROFILE: Reish & Luftman was founded in 1985 as a firm concentrating on a tax and business practice for businesses and professional firms. Our law firm has since added real estate and litigation (business, real estate, employment and ERISA) to its practice. We cover substantially all of the legal needs of businesses, by a team of specialized and experienced attorneys. Our clients range from public corporations to private foundations, from financial institutions to incorporated individuals, and from successful families to first generation entrepreneurs.

**BRUCE L. ASHTON,** admitted to bar, 1971, California. *Education:* Rice University (B.A., 1967); Southern Methodist University (J.D., 1970). Order of the Coif. Co-Author: "Actuarial Audits: A Legal and Tactical Analysis," American Society of Pension Actuaries, 1990; "Actuarial Audit Program," Journal of Taxation, August, 1991; "IRS Closing Agreement Program," Journal of Taxation, September, 1992. *Member:* Los Angeles County and American Bar Associations; American Society of Pension Actuaries (Member, Government Affairs Committee; Chair, Enforcement Subcommittee); ESOP Association (Member, Legislative and Regulatory Committee); Western Pension and Benefits Conference. *PRACTICE AREAS:* Employee Benefits; ESOPs; Employee Relations. *Email:* bruceashton@reish.com

**ROLAND M. ATTENBOROUGH,** admitted to bar, 1965, California. *Education:* University of California at Berkeley (B.S., 1961); Hastings College of Law, University of California (LL.B., 1965); New York University (LL.M., in Taxation, 1966). Certified Public Accountant, California, 1969. *Member:* Los Angeles County and American Bar Associations; ESOP Association; National Center for Employee Ownership; Western Pension and Benefits Conference; California Society of CPAs. *PRACTICE AREAS:* ESOPs; Financing Law; Business and Corporate Law. *Email:* rolandattenborough@reish.com

**JOSEPH C. FAUCHER,** admitted to bar, 1988, California. *Education:* University of Iowa (B.A., 1985); University of California at Davis (J.D., 1988). Member, Pension Rights Center, Washington D.C. *Member:* Los Angeles County and American Bar Associations. *PRACTICE AREAS:* Business Litigation; Employee Benefits Litigation; Employment Law. *Email:* joefaucher@reish.com

**MARTIN M. HEMING,** admitted to bar, 1972, California. *Education:* Rutgers University (A.B., 1964); National University (M.B.A., 1981); Boston University (J.D., 1967; LL.M. in Taxation, 1982). Member, Boston University Journal of Tax Law, 1981-1982. Author: "Footnote 37 of Crane Revived," Boston University Journal of Tax Law, 65, 1983. *Member:* Los Angeles and American (Member, Committee on Employee Benefits, Section on Taxation, 1984—) Bar Associations. *PRACTICE AREAS:* Employee Benefits Law; ESOPs. *Email:* martyheming@reish.com

**JONATHAN A. KARP,** admitted to bar, 1976, California; 1979, U.S. District Court, Central District of California; 1984, U.S. Tax Court. *Education:* University of California at Berkeley (B.S., 1973); University of Michigan (J.D., 1976). Phi Beta Kappa. Certified Public Accountant, California, 1980. Author: "How Will My Debts Be Paid?" How to Live and Die with California Probate, Third Edition, Beverly Hills Bar Association, 1992. Adjunct Professor, Masters of Business in Taxation Program, University of Southern California, 1985. *Member:* Beverly Hills, Los Angeles County and American Bar Associations. *PRACTICE AREAS:* Business Law; Estate Planning; Tax. *Email:* jonkarp@reish.com

**MICHAEL B. LUFTMAN,** admitted to bar, 1973, California; 1977, U.S. Tax Court. *Education:* Wharton School, University of Pennsylvania (B.S., 1966; M.S., 1967); Loyola University of Los Angeles (J.D., 1973). Certified Public Accountant, California. Lecturer: Master of Business Taxation, University of Southern California, 1975-1982; Estate Planning For The Owners of Closely Held Businesses, Continuing Education of the Bar, 1984; Tax and Financial Planning for Individuals, Continuing Education of the Bar, 1985. *Member:* Los Angeles County (Taxation Section Executive Committee, 1979-1981; Secretary, 1978-1979, Vice Chairman, 1979-1980, Chairman, 1980-1981, Death and Gift Tax Subsection; Chairman, 1977-1978, Fiduciary Income Tax Committee) and American Bar Associations; State Bar of California. (Certified Specialist, Taxation Law, State Bar of California, Board of Legal Specialization). *PRACTICE AREAS:* Tax, Estate Planning and Probate. *Email:* michaelluftman@reish.com

**JAMES R. MCDANIEL,** admitted to bar, 1981, California. *Education:* California State University at Sacramento (B.A., with honors, 1975); State University of New York at Binghamton (M.A., 1978); University of California at Los Angeles (J.D., 1981). Member, UCLA Law Review. Co-Author, Nossaman, Wyatt and McDaniel, Trust Administration and Taxation, 2nd Ed. Matthew Bender, 1987-1994. Contributing Author: California Closely Held Corporations, Tax Planning and Practice Guide, Matthew Bender, 1987. Author: "Protecting Your Property From Taxes and Lawsuit Judgments," WMA Reporter, June 1994; "Revaluing Prior Taxable Gifts on the Estate Tax Returns - The Controversy Continues," Estate Planning,

*(This Listing Continued)*

## CALIFORNIA—LOS ANGELES

**REISH & LUFTMAN**, A PROFESSIONAL CORPORATION, Los Angeles—Continued

WGL, 1990; "Funds on Front Lines: Plans Weigh Risks of Controlling Boards," Pensions & Investment Age, Nov., 1988. Lecturer: UCLA Estate Planning Institute; CEB Estate Planning Programs. *Member:* Los Angeles County Bar Association (Member, Executive Committee, Trusts and Estates Section, 1993-1994). **PRACTICE AREAS:** Estate and Tax Planning; Probate; Tax Controversy; Employee Benefits. **Email:** jimmcdaniel@reish.com

**LELAND J. REICHER,** admitted to bar, 1975, California. *Education:* University of Southern California (B.S., 1972); University of California at Los Angeles (J.D., 1975). Certified Public Accountant, California, 1976. Instructor: Real Estate Finance and Real Estate Syndications, UCLA, Irvine and Riverside Extensions, 1979-1982. *Member:* Los Angeles County and American Bar Associations; California Society of CPAs; American Institute of CPAs. **PRACTICE AREAS:** Real Estate; Business Law. **Email:** leereicher@reish.com

**C. FREDERICK REISH,** admitted to bar, 1969, Arizona; 1971, California; 1994, District of Columbia. *Education:* Arizona State University (B.S., 1966); University of Arizona (J.D., 1969). Author: "Fiduciary Standards Under ERISA," Los Angeles Bar Bulletin, April, 1975; "Qualified Retirement Plans; What Are the Options?," Chapter 14, Withdrawal, Retirement and Disputes, American Bar Association, 1986; "Actuarial Audit Program," Journal of Taxation, 1991. Lecturer: National Institute of Pension Administrators: "Protection of Plan Assets from Creditors (and Related Subjects)," 1990; "Fiduciary Responsibility and Professional Liability for Plan Service Providers," 1991. American Society of Pension Actuaries, Annual Conference: "Prohibited Cut-Backs Under Section 411(d) (6)," 1989; "IRS Audits of Defined Benefit Plans," 1990. Enrolled Actuaries Annual Conference, "Fiduciary Responsibility and Professional Liability Under ERISA." University of Southern California Annual Institute on Federal Taxation, "Estate Planning for IRA and Qualified Plan Benefits," 1991. Co-Chair, Los Angeles District IRS Benefits Conference 1992-1995. Speaker: "ERISA Issues In Bankruptcy," 1992; "IRS Benefits Litigation, 1993. *Member:* Los Angeles County Bar Association (Member, Executive Committee, Taxation Section, 1982-1986; Chair, Employee Benefits Committee, 1982-1986); State Bar of California. **REPORTED CASES:** Amicus Briefs on behalf of the American Society of Pension Actuaries, Patterson v. Shumate, U.S. 112 S.Ct 2242 (1992); Citrus Valley Estates, Inc., et al. v. Commissioner of Internal Revenue, 99 T.C. 379 (1992). **PRACTICE AREAS:** Employee Benefits; ERISA Litigation. **Email:** fredreish@reish.com

**MARK E. TERMAN,** admitted to bar, 1983, California; 1984, U.S. District Court, Central, Northern, Eastern and Southern Districts of California and U.S. Court of Appeals, Ninth Circuit; 1985, District of Columbia. *Education:* University of California at Los Angeles (B.S., 1979); Loyola Law School (J.D., 1983); Hastings College of Law, University of California. Extern, Hon. Clarke Stephens, California Court of Appeals, 1982. Author: "Hidden Danger-Unwary Attorneys May Face Liability Under ERISA," ABA Journal, August 1993; "Employer Duties and Liabilities Under ERISA," Employee Benefit News, September 1992; "Survey of Labor Law," Loyola of Los Angeles Law Review, 1982-1983. *Member:* Board of Directors and Volunteer Relations Chair, Scholarship Programs, UCLA Alumni Association. *Member:* Los Angeles and American Bar Associations; Association of Business Trial Lawyers. **PRACTICE AREAS:** ERISA Litigation; Employment; Business; Unfair Competition Litigation. **Email:** markterman@reish.com

**MICHAEL A. VANIC,** admitted to bar, 1976, California. *Education:* University of Southern California (A.B., magna cum laude, 1973); Loyola University of Los Angeles (J.D., cum laude, 1976). Alpha Sigma Nu. Member, St. Thomas More Honor Society. *Member:* Los Angeles County and American Bar Associations; Los Angeles Trial Lawyers Association; The Association of Trial Lawyers of America; Western Pension and Benefits Conference. **REPORTED CASES:** Swoboda vs. Pala Min., Inc. 844 F.2d 654 (9th Cir. 1988); Seedman vs. U.S. District Court for the Cent. Dist. of California, 837 F.2d 413 (9th Cir. 1988); Columbus Line, Inc. vs. Gray Line Sight-Seeing Companies Associated, Inc., 120 Cal. App. 3d 622, 174 Cal. Rptr. 527 (1981); and Merry vs. Coast Community College Dist., 97 Cal. App. 3d 214, 158 Cal. Rptr. 603 (1979). **PRACTICE AREAS:** Appellate; Business; ERISA Litigation. **Email:** mikevanic@reish.com

**LYNN B. WITTE,** admitted to bar, 1979, Oregon; 1988, California. *Education:* The Principia College (B.A., cum laude, 1973); Northwestern School of Law at Lewis and Clark College (J.D., 1979). Issue Editor, Environmental Law, 1978-1979. Co-Author: "Qualified Plan Benefits and the

*(This Listing Continued)*

CAA1124B

## MARTINDALE-HUBBELL LAW DIRECTORY 1997

Debtor Participant in the Ninth Circuit in Light of the U.S. Supreme Court's Ruling in Patterson v. Shumate," California Bankruptcy Journal, Vol. 20, No. 4, 1992; "After Patterson: Which Pension Benefits Are Protected?" Journal of Taxation for Employee Benefits, Vol. 1, No. 8, July/August, 1994. Lecturer, Employee Benefits: McGladdrey & Pullen, 1993; ASPA, 1989, 1990; WEB, 1990; Corbel, 1989. *Member:* Oregon State Bar; Los Angeles County and American Bar Associations; Los Angeles Bankruptcy Forum; Financial Lawyers Conference. **PRACTICE AREAS:** Employee Benefits Consulting and Litigation; Taxation. **Email:** lynnwitte@reish.com

---

**FERNANDO L. DELMENDO,** admitted to bar, 1993, California. *Education:* University of California at Berkeley (B.A., 1989); University of San Francisco (J.D., 1993). *Member:* State Bar of California. **PRACTICE AREAS:** Employee Benefits Law. **Email:** fernandodelmendo@reish.com

**ILENE HIRSCH FERENCZY,** admitted to bar, 1992, California. *Education:* University of California at San Diego; University of California at Los Angeles (A.B., magna cum laude, 1977); Western State University College of Law (J.D., summa cum laude, 1992). Author: "Protection of Pension Assets After Patterson," Plan Horizons, 1994. Lecturer: Coping With Problems in Pension and Profit Sharing Plans, California Society of CPAs; ERISA Section 404 (C) and Fiduciary Responsibilities, ASPA. *Member:* Los Angeles County and American Bar Associations; American Society of Pension Actuaries. **PRACTICE AREAS:** Pension/Employee Benefits. **Email:** ileneferenczy@reish.com

**NELSON J. HANDY,** admitted to bar, 1990, California. *Education:* California State University at Northridge (B.S., 1987); Loyola Marymount University (J.D., 1990). Member: St. Thomas More Law Honor Society; Loyola of Los Angeles Entertainment Law Journal. Author: "All Events Test Proves Taxing to Magazine Publisher," Vol. 9-1 Loyola Entertainment Law Journal. Certified Public Accountant, California. *Member:* State Bar of California. **PRACTICE AREAS:** Estate Planning; Taxation; Business Law. **Email:** nelsonhandy@reish.com

---

## GERALD G. REPPETTO

EQUITABLE BUILDING
3435 WILSHIRE BOULEVARD, SUITE 640
**LOS ANGELES, CALIFORNIA 90010**
Telephone: 213-388-4320
FAX: 213-383-1231

*Personal Injury Defense, Products Liability Defense, Insurance Coverage.*

**GERALD G. REPPETTO,** born Chicago, Illinois, August 24, 1932; admitted to bar, 1963, California. *Education:* University of Southern California (B.S., 1955; LL.B., 1961). Member, Board of Directors, Chevy Chase Country Club, 1988—. *Member:* Los Angeles County Bar Association; State Bar of California. [LTJG, USN, Deck Officer, 1956-1959]

REPRESENTATIVE CLIENTS: PARATRANSIT Insurance Co.; Farmers Home Mutual Ins. Co.; Clarendom National Ins. Co.; National Auto & Casualty Co.; Risk Management Co.; Self Insured Trucking Companies; Assurance Alliance Co.; Paratransit Insurance Co.

---

## RESCH POLSTER ALPERT & BERGER LLP

A Limited Liability Partnership including Professional Corporations
*Established in 1980*

10390 SANTA MONICA BOULEVARD, FOURTH FLOOR
**LOS ANGELES, CALIFORNIA 90025-5058**
Telephone: 310-277-8300
FAX: 310-552-3209

*Business Law, Real Estate, Corporate, Financing, Securities Regulation, Federal, State and International Taxation and Commercial Litigation.*

### ATTORNEYS

**PETER H. ALPERT, (PROFESSIONAL CORPORATION),** born New York, N.Y., January 25, 1948; admitted to bar, 1974, California. *Education:* University of California at Los Angeles (B.A., 1970); Hastings College of Law, University of California (J.D., 1974). Lecturer: Probate, Tax and Estate Planning Considerations in Marital Dissolution, Beverly Hills Bar, 1978; Secured Real Property Transactions, California Continuing Education of the Bar, 1980; Withholding Responsibilities of U.S. Companies, Income Tax Section of the State Bar of California, 1980; and Low-Income

*(This Listing Continued)*

Housing Tax Credits, USC Real Estate and Tax Accounting Conference, 1990, 3rd and 4th Annual Conferences of Affordable Housing Forum, 1994 and 1995. *Member:* Beverly Hills, Los Angeles County (Member, Sections on: Real Property Law; Tax; Probate and Trust) and American (Member, Section on Real Property, Probate and Trust Law; Affordable Housing Forum) Bar Associations; The State Bar of California. *PRACTICE AREAS:* Real Estate; Business Law.

*SHELDON P. BERGER, (PROFESSIONAL CORPORATION),* born Scranton, Pennsylvania, April 14, 1949; admitted to bar, 1974, California. *Education:* University of Pittsburgh (B.A., 1971; J.D., cum laude, 1974). Order of the Coif. Vice-Chairman, University of Pittsburgh Moot Court Program, 1973-1974. Lecturer, Developments in Real Property Law, California Continuing Education of the Bar. Author: "California Construction Liens," Construction Liens, Construction Publications, Inc., 1992. *Member:* Beverly Hills, Los Angeles County (Member, Real Property Finance Subcommittee) and American (Member, Mortgage and Secured Financing Committee, Section on Real Property, Probate and Trust Law) Bar Associations; The State Bar of California (Member, Taxation Section). *PRACTICE AREAS:* Real Estate; Business Law.

*DAVID GITMAN, (PROFESSIONAL CORPORATION),* born Chicago, Illinois, July 4, 1952; admitted to bar, 1977, Illinois; 1979, California; 1980, District of Columbia; 1980, U.S. Tax Court. *Education:* University of Illinois (B.A., 1974); Loyola University (J.D., 1977); New York University (LL.M., Taxation, 1978). Phi Alpha Delta. *Member:* Beverly Hills, Century City, Los Angeles County (Member, Taxation Section) and American (Member, Taxation Section) Bar Associations; The State Bar of California (Member, Taxation Section); The District of Columbia Bar (Member, Taxation Section). *PRACTICE AREAS:* Taxation; Business Law.

*KELI N. OSAKI,* admitted to bar, 1995, California. *Education:* University of California at Los Angeles (B.A., 1987); Pepperdine University (J.D., magna cum laude, 1995). Pepperdine University Law Review, 1993-1995. Recipient, American Jurisprudence Awards for Legal Research and Writing and Constitutional Law, 1994. Extern to the Honorable Arthur L. Alarcon, Senior Circuit Judge, 9th Circuit Court of Appeals, 1994. Author: "Madsen vs. Women's Health Center - An Unequal Balance Between the Right of Women to obtain and the Rught to Pro-Life Groups to Freedom of Expression," Pepperdine Law Review, Volume 24, 1995-1996. *Member:* Beverly Hills, Los Angeles County and American Bar Associations. *PRACTICE AREAS:* Business Litigation.

*LEE M. POLSTER, (PROFESSIONAL CORPORATION),* born Los Angeles, California, November 14, 1948; admitted to bar, 1973, California. *Education:* University of Pennsylvania (B.S., 1970); Southwestern University (J.D., 1973). Editor-in-Chief, Southwestern University Law Review, 1972-1973. Co-Author: "Zoning: Monopoly Effects and Judicial Abdication," 4 Southwestern University Law Review 1, 1972. Adjunct Associate Professor, Corporations and Partnership Law and Taxation, Southwestern University, 1975-1979. *Member:* Los Angeles County and American (Member, Section on Corporation, Banking and Business Law) Bar Associations; The State Bar of California. *PRACTICE AREAS:* Corporate and Partnership Law; Securities Regulation; Business Law.

*NICOLAS RAMNICEANU,* born New York, N.Y., November 16, 1957; admitted to bar, 1984, California. *Education:* Amherst College (B.A., 1980); Stanford University (J.D., 1983). Phi Beta Kappa. Co-Author: "Dealing with the Unexpected: Marital Dissolution or the Business Break-Up," Third Annual Institute on Advanced Tax Planning for Real Property Transactions, Pages 51-105, Continuing Education of the Bar, 1985. Author: "From Pro-Growth to No-Growth: Mountain View, California from 1968 to 1980," Stanford Environmental Law Annual, Volume IV, Pages 50-67, 1982. *Member:* Century City Bar Association; State Bar of California (Member, Affordable Housing Section); Urban Land Institute. *LANGUAGES:* French. *PRACTICE AREAS:* Real Estate; Business Law.

*RONALD M. RESCH, (PROFESSIONAL CORPORATION),* born Bronx, New York, May 20, 1945; admitted to bar, 1970, California; 1979, District of Columbia. *Education:* University of California at Los Angeles (B.A., 1966); California Western University (J.D., 1969). Phi Sigma Delta; Phi Delta Phi. Member, California Western Law Review, 1968-1969. Author: "Arguing the Guidelines for Conglomerate Mergers," California Western Law Review, Fall, 1968. *Member:* Century City, Los Angeles County (Member, Supervisory Committee of the Credit Union, 1978-1980; Member, Sections on: Business and Corporation Law; Real Property Law) and American (Member, Sections on: Corporation, Banking and Business Law; Real Property, Probate and Trust Law; Taxation) Bar Associations; The State Bar of California; The District of Columbia Bar. *PRACTICE AREAS:* Real Estate; Business Law.

*(This Listing Continued)*

## OF COUNSEL

*MARVIN G. BURNS, (PROFESSIONAL CORPORATION),* born Los Angeles, California, July 3, 1930; admitted to bar, 1955, California. *Education:* Arizona University (B.A., 1951); Harvard University (J.D., 1954). *Member:* Los Angeles County and American (Member, Litigation Section) Bar Associations; State Bar of California. *PRACTICE AREAS:* Land Use Law; Entertainment Litigation; Business Litigation; Real Estate Litigation.

*AARON A. GRUNFELD,* born Winsheim, Germany, December; admitted to bar, 1972, California. *Education:* University of California at Los Angeles (A.B., with honors, 1968); Columbia University (J.D., 1971). Phi Delta Phi. Harlan Fiske Stone Scholar and Charles Evans Hughes Fellow. *Member:* Beverly Hills, Los Angeles County and American (Member, Sections on: Taxation; Real Property, Probate and Trust Law; Corporation, Banking and Business Law) Bar Associations; State Bar of California. *PRACTICE AREAS:* Corporate and Partnership Law; Securities Regulation.

*NICHOLAS T. HARITON,* born Ann Arbor, Michigan, August 22, 1956; admitted to bar, 1984, California, U.S. District Court, Central District of California and U.S. Court of Appeals, Ninth Circuit. *Education:* University of California at Berkeley (B.A., 1979); University of Lund, Sweden; University of Southern California Law Center (J.D., 1983). *Member:* Society of English and American Lawyers (London, England). *LANGUAGES:* Swedish; Danish. *PRACTICE AREAS:* Business Law; Banking; Admiralty Law.

*LAWRENCE R. RESNICK, (PROFESSIONAL CORPORATION),* born Toledo, Ohio, September 27, 1934; admitted to bar, 1962, Ohio; 1964, California and U.S. District Court, Central District of California; 1973, U.S. Court of Appeals, Ninth Circuit; 1976, U.S. District Court, Eastern District of California and U.S. Supreme Court. *Education:* Ohio State University (B.A., 1958); University of Toledo (LL.B., 1962). Phi Alpha Delta. *Member:* Los Angeles County (Member, Litigation Section) and American (Member, Litigation Section) Bar Associations; State Bar of California (Member, Litigation Section). *PRACTICE AREAS:* Business Litigation; Real Estate Litigation; Construction Industry Litigation.

*CHARLES S. TIGERMAN, (PROFESSIONAL CORPORATION),* born Kansas City, Missouri, February 21, 1942; admitted to bar, 1969, Missouri; 1970, California; 1983, U.S. Tax Court. *Education:* University of Missouri (B.A., cum laude, 1964); St. Louis University (J.D., 1969). Phi Eta Sigma; Sigma Rho Sigma. Author: "Computer Litigation: Recent Cases," Los Angeles Lawyer, Vol. 1 No. 6, 1978. Member, Governing Body of Jewish Homes for the Aging of Greater Los Angeles. Member, National Panel of Arbitrators, Computer Law Disputes, American Arbitration Association. *Member:* Beverly Hills (Member, Committees on: Taxation, 1974—; Probate, 1974—) and Los Angeles County (Member, Committee on Computer Technology, 1978—) Bar Associations; State Bar of California; The Missouri Bar; Computer Law Association; Data Processing Management Association. (Certified Specialist, Estate Planning, Trust and Probate Law, California Board of Legal Specialization). *PRACTICE AREAS:* Computer Law; Estate Planning; Business Law.

REFERENCE: Imperial Bank, Beverly Hills, Calif.

## *REUBEN & NOVICOFF*

### LOS ANGELES, CALIFORNIA

(See Beverly Hills)

*Business Litigation, including Real Estate, Entertainment, International Commercial Disputes, Intellectual Property, Securities, Complex Civil Matters, Bankruptcy, Insurance, Environmental.*

## REXON, FREEDMAN, KLEPETAR & HAMBLETON

*A PROFESSIONAL CORPORATION*

Established in 1984

**12100 WILSHIRE BOULEVARD, SUITE 730**
**LOS ANGELES, CALIFORNIA 90025**
Telephone: 310-826-8300
FAX: 310-826-0333

Labor and Employment Relations Law, Wrongful Termination Litigation, Equal Opportunity Law and OSHA.

FIRM PROFILE: Rexon, Freedman, Klepetar & Hambleton exclusively represents management in all areas of labor and employment relations law. The firm's lawyers provide preventative labor relations counsel and litigation services, with an emphasis on practical and cost-effective approaches to problems. The firm represents employers in litigation and before administrative agencies at the federal, state and local levels. Clients of the firm represent an array of industries, including, among others, manufacturing, city and county government, food and grocery wholesale and retail operators, hospitality, power and utility, health care and electronics. These businesses range in size from closely-held organizations to large multi-national corporations.

**BRIAN L. REXON,** born Los Angeles, California, November 22, 1943; admitted to bar, 1970, California. *Education:* University of California at Berkeley (B.S., 1966); University of California at Los Angeles (M.S., 1969; J.D., 1969). Phi Delta Phi. *Member:* Los Angeles County (Member, Labor Law Section) and American (Member, Labor Relations Law Section) Bar Associations; State Bar of California. **PRACTICE AREAS:** Labor Negotiation; Arbitration; National Labor Relations Board Proceedings.

**JEFFREY C. FREEDMAN,** born Los Angeles, California, August 18, 1944; admitted to bar, 1969, California, U.S. District Court, Central, Northern, Southern and Eastern Districts of California, U.S. Court of Appeals, Ninth Circuit and U.S. Supreme Court. *Education:* Occidental College (B.A., 1966); University of California at Los Angeles (J.D., 1969). Author: "Sex Discrimination in Law Partnership Decisions," Los Angeles Lawyer Magazine, June, 1991; "Maternity Leave and Parental Leave; Concepts Leading for Collision," Los Angeles Lawyer Magazine, February, 1991; "Drug Testing By Private Employers," Los Angeles Lawyer Magazine, October, 1990; "Discharging Law Firm Partners: Courts May Apply Employment Discrimination Laws," Legal Economics Magazine, October, 1989, and Los Angeles Lawyer, March, 1988; "Commuting and Polluting: New Rules Require Employers to Promote Ridesharing," February, 1990; "The Public Safety Officers Procedural Bill of Rights: An Analysis," CPER, No. 54, September, 1982; "Cumulative Stress Claims Put Strain on City Coffers," Western City Magazine, January 1984; A Symposium on "The Memphis Decision: The Big Impact Will Be on Settlement Negotiations," CPER No. 62, September, 1984; "Recent Development in Public Employee Labor Relations: Due Process Rights of Public Employees," The Urban Lawyer, Fall, 1984; "Analysis: Supreme Court Decision on Lybarger v. L.A. City," CPER, No. 69, June, 1986. Deputy Attorney General, California, 1969-1974. *Member:* Los Angeles County (Member, Board of Trustees, 1982-1984 and 1985-1987), Century City (Member, Board of Governors, 1976-1983; President, 1981) and American (Member: Labor and Employment Law Section; Urban, State and Local Governmental Law Section) Bar Associations; State Bar of California. **PRACTICE AREAS:** Labor and Employment Litigation; Public and Private Sectors.

**RONALD J. KLEPETAR,** born Chicago, Illinois, April 8, 1946; admitted to bar, 1971, Illinois; 1972, California, U.S. District Court, Central District of California, U.S. Court of Appeals, Ninth Circuit and U.S. Supreme Court. *Education:* Knox College and University of Illinois (B.A., 1968); De Paul University (J.D., 1971); New York University (LL.M. in Labor Law, 1973). *Member,* De Paul University Law Review, 1969-1970. Attorney, National Labor Relations Board, 1973-1975. *Member:* Los Angeles County, Century City and American (Member, Labor and Employment Law Section) Bar Associations; State Bar of California. **PRACTICE AREAS:** Labor Negotiation; Arbitration; Labor Litigation; National Labor Relations Board Proceedings.

**DEBBY R. HAMBLETON,** born Reno, Nevada, January 17, 1959; admitted to bar, 1984, California; 1985, Nevada, U.S. District Court, Central District of California and U.S. Court of Appeals, Ninth Circuit; 1986, U.S. District Court, District of Nevada; 1989, U.S. District Court, Northern District of California, 1991, U.S. District Court, Arizona and U.S. Court of Appeals, Fifth Circuit; 1993, U.S. Supreme Court. *Education:* University of

*(This Listing Continued)*

Nevada (B.A., 1981); Pepperdine University (J.D., cum laude, 1984). Phi Alpha Delta (Treasurer, 1983-1984). Recipient, American Jurisprudence Award in Labor Law. *Member:* Los Angeles County (Member, Labor Law Section) and American Bar Associations; State Bar of California; State Bar of Nevada. **PRACTICE AREAS:** Labor and Employment Litigation.

**WENDY K. GENZ,** born Milwaukee, Wisconsin September 30. 1957; admitted to bar, 1989, California, U.S. District Court, Southern, Eastern, Northern, Western and Central Districts of California and U.S. Court of Appeals, Ninth Circuit. *Education:* Brigham Young University (B.A./A.S., 1980); Marquette University; University of Louisville (J.D., 1988). Sigma Delta Phi. Member, Journal of Family Law, University of Louisville Law Review, 1987-1988. *Member:* Los Angeles County (Member, Labor and Employment Law Section) and American Bar Associations; State Bar of California; California Young Lawyers Association. **LANGUAGES:** Spanish. **PRACTICE AREAS:** Labor and Employment Litigation; Administrative Proceedings.

---

**STEVEN J. PROUGH,** born Pacific Palisades, California, November 6, 1966; admitted to bar, 1992, Illinois and U.S. District Court, Northern District of Illinois; 1994, California. *Education:* Colgate University (B.A., 1988); De Paul University (J.D., 1992). Member, De Paul University Law Review and Arts and Entertainment Law Journal, 1991-1992. *Member:* Chicago, Illinois State and American Bar Associations; State Bar of California. **PRACTICE AREAS:** Litigation.

**STEPHANIE J. HART,** born Butler, Pennsylvania, July 19, 1959; admitted to bar, 1987, California, U.S. District Court, Central, Southern, Eastern and Northern Districts of California and U.S. Court of Appeals, Ninth Circuit. *Education:* University of California at Los Angeles (B.A., 1981); Pepperdine University (J.D., 1985). *Member:* Los Angeles County Bar Association; State Bar of California; Women's Lawyers' Association of Los Angeles. **PRACTICE AREAS:** Litigation; Labor and Employment Law; Employee Benefits; Family Law.

The firm is a member of LABNET, Labor Attorneys for Business Network. LABNET is a nationwide organization of labor and employment law firms representing business and management interests exclusively. Member firms coordinate case handling, and share information and resources on labor law and practice-related issues. LABNET has member firms in Chicago; Cleveland and Columbus, Ohio; Flint, Michigan; Las Vegas; Memphis; New York; Portland, Oregon; San Antonio; San Francisco; Spartanburg, South Carolina; Springfield, Massachusetts; Washington, D.C.

REFERENCE: Santa Monica Bank.

---

## REZNIK & REZNIK

*A LAW CORPORATION*

Established in 1982

**15456 VENTURA BOULEVARD, FIFTH FLOOR (SHERMAN OAKS)**
**LOS ANGELES, CALIFORNIA 91403-3023**
Telephone: 213-872-2900; 818-907-9898
Telecopier: 818-907-8465

Environmental, Hazardous Waste, Zoning and Land Use, Real Estate Transactions and Litigation, Insurance Coverage, Utilities and Energy.

FIRM PROFILE: Reznik & Reznik specializes in matters pertaining to hazardous waste compliance, regulatory and litigation matters (CERCLA/SUPERFUND), environmental insurance coverage, land use and zoning. The firm also represents property owners in the pursuit of building entitlements before planning commissions, city councils and other governmental bodies. Firm members actively participate in professional and civic affairs and serve as lecturers/panelists in legal seminars.

**BENJAMIN M. REZNIK,** born Haifa, Israel, June 18, 1951; admitted to bar, 1976, California; 1977, U.S. Court of Appeals, Ninth Circuit and U.S. District Court, Central District of California. *Education:* University of California at Los Angeles (B.A., Pol. Sc., 1973); University of Southern California (J.D., 1976). Judge Pro-Tem, Los Angeles Municipal Court, Landlord/Tenant, 1982-1983. Director, 1985-1990 and President, 1989, Encino Chamber of Commerce. Member, Sign Advisory Committee for the City of Los Angeles, 1986—. Chair, Mayor's Business Advisory Committee for Economic Redevelopment, 1994—. Board Member, 1994—, Co-Chair, 1994-1996, Economic Development Alliance. Member, Development Reform Committee, 1995-1996 (Appointed by Mayor). President, Valley Job Recovery Corporation, Non-Profit, 1994—. Member, Ventura Boulevard Citizens Advisory, Ventura Boulevard Specific Plan, 1986-1990. Director,

*(This Listing Continued)*

Greater Los Angeles Building Industry Association, 1989-1990. Chair, Valley Industry and Commerce Association, 1992-1993, Vice-Chair, 1991; Director; Chairperson, Land Use Committee, 1990-1992. Member, Board of Directors, 1992 and Chair, Political and Regulatory Committee, 1991-1992, The 2000 Partnership. Member, Board of Trustees, Encino Hospital, 1989-1991; Director, The Cultural Foundation, 1990—. Member, Los Angeles Host Committee, World Cup Soccer '94. Recipient, Resolution Commendations from U.S. House of Representatives, California State Assembly, California Lieutenant Governor; California Attorney General, Los Angeles County Board of Supervisors, Los Angeles County District Attorney's Office, Mayor, City of Los Angeles, Los Angeles City Council, Los Angeles City Attorney's Office. Profiled in Los Angeles Times, 1993. *Member:* Los Angeles County and San Fernando Valley Bar Associations; State Bar of California. *LANGUAGES:* Hebrew. *SPECIAL AGENCIES:* Los Angeles County Metropolitan Transit Authority (MTA); Federal Deposit Insurance Corporation (FDR). *REPORTED CASES:* Jama Construction Co. v. City of Los Angeles, 938 F2d 1045 (9th Cir. 1991); Save Our Residential Environment v. City of West Hollywood, 9 Cal.App. 4th 1745 (1992). *PRACTICE AREAS:* Zoning, Land Use; Environmental Law; Utilities and Energy.

**JANICE M. KAMENIR-REZNIK,** born Rantoul, Illinois, March 17, 1952; admitted to bar, 1982, California; 1984, U.S. District Court, Central District of California; 1989, U.S. Court of Appeals, Ninth Circuit. *Education:* University of California at Los Angeles (B.A., 1973; J.D., 1982); University of Southern California (M.S.W., 1975); Hebrew Union College (M.A., 1975). President, California Womens Law Center, 1995—; Commissioner, Los Angeles County Commission on Judicial Procedures, 1996—; Commissioner, Legal Services Trust Fund, State of California, 1993-1996;Chair, University of California, Los Angeles, Hillel Advisory Board, 1993—; Chair, Lawyer Referral and Information Services, Los Angeles County Bar Association, 1993-1994; Found Chair, Committee on the Future of The Small Law Office and Sole Practitioner, 1989-1993; Chair, Environment Committee, Valley Industry and Commerce Association (VICA), 1992; Board Member, Valley Community Legal Foundation, 1991-1995; California Women Lawyers, President, 1988-1989;Judge Pro Tem, Los Angeles Municipal Court, 1985-1988. March of Dimes Premier Parents Award, 1994. Recipient, Maccabee Award for Leadership, 1993. Honoree, Los Angeles Commission for Women. Recipient, San Fernando Valley Bar Association President's Award. Women of the Year, 43rd Assembly District, State of California Legislature. Recipient, Encino Chamber of Commerce "Athena" Award. Recipient, Resolutions of Commendation: House of Representatives of the United States Congress, California State Senate, California State Assembly, Los Angeles County Board of Supervisors, Los Angeles City Council, Los Angeles City Attorney's Office. *Member:* San Fernando Valley and Los Angeles County Bar Associations; State Bar of California. *LANGUAGES:* Hebrew. *SPECIAL AGENCIES:* Federal Deposit Insurance Corporation (FDIC); Los Angeles County Metropolitan Transit Authority (MTA). *REPORTED CASES:* Haskel vs. Superior Court, 33 Cal. App. 4th, 963, Mod. 34 Cal. App. 4th 199e, rev. den. (June 29, 1995). *PRACTICE AREAS:* Environmental Law; Regulatory Compliance; Administrative Law; Hazardous Waste, State and Federal Superfund.

**PENNY GROSZ-SALOMON,** born Los Angeles, California, June 19, 1955; admitted to bar, 1980, California; 1981, U.S. District Court, Central District of California; 1982, U.S. District Court, Northern District of California; 1988, U.S Court of Appeals, Ninth Circuit; 1992, U.S. Supreme Court. *Education:* University of California at Santa Barbara (B.A., 1977); Loyola University of Los Angeles (J.D., 1980). Judge Pro Tem, Los Angeles Municipal Court, 1987-1992. Arbitrator, Los Angeles Superior Court, 1993—. *Member:* Los Angeles County (Member, Litigation Section, Environmental Insurance Subsection) and Beverly Hills (Chair, Litigation Section, 1985-1986) Bar Associations; State Bar of California. *PRACTICE AREAS:* Environmental Insurance Coverage; Real Estate Litigation.

**ALAN J. KHEEL,** born Los Angeles, California, September 5, 1957; admitted to bar, 1982, California and U.S. District Court, Central District of California. *Education:* Claremont McKenna College; University of Southern California (B.A., 1979); Loyola Marymount University (J.D., cum laude, 1982). Phi Beta Kappa. St. Thomas More Law Honor Society. Recipient, American Jurisprudence Awards in Property and Criminal Law. *Member:* Los Angeles County Bar Association (Member, Sections on: Real Property and Environmental Law); State Bar of California (Member, Sections on Real Property and Business Law). *SPECIAL AGENCIES:* Federal Deposit Insurance Corporation (FDIC). *PRACTICE AREAS:* Real Estate Transactions; Subdivision Compliance and Environmental Matters.

**FRED N. GAINES,** born Los Angeles, California, August 31, 1959; admitted to bar, 1986, California; 1987, U.S. District Court, Central and Northern Districts of California and U.S. Court of Appeals, Ninth Circuit; 1991, U.S. Supreme Court. *Education:* University of California, Los Angeles (B.A., cum laude, 1981); Harvard University, John F. Kennedy School of Government (M.P.P., 1983); Boalt Hall School of Law, University of California (J.D., 1986). President, University of California, Los Angeles Undergraduate Student Body, 1980-1981. Kennedy Fellowship in Government and Public Service, 1981-1983. Extern Clerk, Hon. Marilyn Hall Patel, U.S. Judge, Northern District of California, 1985. Member, University of California Board of Regents, 1984-1985; California Lexington Group (President, 1990-1992); Citizen's Advisory Panel on Transportation Solutions for the San Fernando Valley, 1988; Valley Industry and Commerce Association, Land Use Committee, 1989—; Board of Directors, 1993—; UCLA Alumni Association Governmental Relations Steering Committee, 1989—; Pacific Southwest Regional Board of Directors, Anti-Defamation League of B'Nai-B'rith, 1989—; California Building Industry Association Select Committee on Industry Litigation, 1991—; Valley Development Forum, President, 1995; Board of Trustees, San Fernando Valley Bar Association, 1993—; Treasurer, 1995-1996; Secretary, 1996-1997; Member, Regional Advisory Council, Southern California Association of Governments (SCAG), 1993-1996 (Chair, 1995-1996); Sherman Oaks Town Council (President, 1995); Adjunct Professor of Law, University of West Los Angeles School of Law, 1993—. Member, Los Angeles County Public Library Commission, 1995—. *Member:* Los Angeles County, San Fernando Valley and American (Member, Section of Urban, State and Local Government Law) Bar Associations; State Bar of California (Member, Public Law Section). *SPECIAL AGENCIES:* Los Angeles County Metropolitan Transit Authority (MTA). *REPORTED CASES:* Jama Construction Co. v. City of Los Angeles, 938 F.2d 1045 (9th Cir. 1991); Save Our Residential Environment v. City of West Hollywood, 9 Cal App. 4th 1745, 12 Cal. Rptr. 2d 308 (1992). *PRACTICE AREAS:* Zoning and Land Use; Environmental Law; Administrative Law and Related Litigation.

**RICHARD A. MCDONALD,** born San Jose, California, June 24, 1958; admitted to bar, 1986, California; 1987, U.S. District Court, Central, Southern, Northern and Eastern Districts of California and U.S. Court of Appeals, Ninth Circuit; 1992, U.S. Supreme Court. *Education:* University of California at Berkeley (B.A., 1979); University of Southern California (M.P.A., 1981); Loyola University of Los Angeles (J.D., 1986). Pi Alpha Alpha. Member, St. Thomas More Law Honor Society. *Member:* Los Angeles County and American (Member, Litigation Section) Bar Associations; State Bar of California; Association of Business Trial Lawyers; Los Angeles Superior Court Volunteer Arbitration Program. *SPECIAL AGENCIES:* Los Angeles County Metropolitan Transit Authority (MTA).

---

**JOHN M. BOWMAN,** born Kearney, Nebraska, January 12, 1959; admitted to bar, 1988, California and U.S. District Court, Central District of California; 1991, Illinois; 1992, U.S. Court of Appeals, Ninth Circuit. *Education:* Iowa State University (B.S., Community and Regional Planning, 1981); Southwestern University School of Law (J.D., 1988). Paul W. Wildman Scholar; Dean's Scholar. Recipient: Bankruptcy Judge Barry Russell Federal Bar Association Award for Excellence in the Field of Federal Practice; American Jurisprudence Awards in Federal Courts and Criminal Law. Board of Directors, Valley Leadership Institute, 1993—. Select Committee on Industry Litigation, California Building Industry, 1992—. *Member:* Pierce College Community Advisory Committee, 1995—. Member Program Advisory Board for Land Use Planning Certificate Program, State University at Northridge, 1996—. *Member:* Los Angeles County Bar Association; State Bar of California; American Planning Association; Valley Industry and Commerce Association (Member, Land Use Committee, 1989—). *PRACTICE AREAS:* Zoning and Land Use; Environmental Administrative Law and Litigation.

**KENNETH A. EHRLICH,** born Los Angeles, California, October 16, 1965; admitted to bar, 1990, California; 1991, U.S. Court of Appeals, Ninth Circuit, U.S. District Court, Central, Eastern and Northern Districts of California. *Education:* University of California at Davis (B.A., with high honors, 1987); Santa Clara University (J.D., 1990). Regents Scholar, University of California at Davis, 1985-1987. Recipient, California Air and Waste Management Association Award. Comments Editor, Santa Clara Law Review, 1989-1990. Author: "The Supreme Court Speaks In Meghrig! For RCRA Recovery, Sue First And Clean Up Later," 1996 Cal. Envtl. L.Rptr., 143 (May 1996); "Maximizing Damages in Environmental Contamination Cases: Cleanup Costs, Dimunition in Value and the Emergence of Stigma Dames," Vol. 7 No. 3, Real Estate/Environmental Liability News, p.16 (November 3, 1995); "National Contingency Plan's Public Comment Requirement and New RCRA Case Law Make CERCLA Yesterday's News," 1995 California Environmental Law Reporter 81 (April 1995);

*(This Listing Continued)*

**REZNIK & REZNIK,** A LAW CORPORATION, Los Angeles—
Continued

"Reaping the Fruits of a Ripe Property Takings Challenge: Eliminating the Ripeness Problem in Facial Regulatory Takings Cases," 30 Santa Clara Law Review 865 (1990). *Member:* Beverly Hills and Los Angeles County (Assistant Secretary, Environmental Section, 1996-1997; Chair, Environmental Programs, 1995-1996; Vice-Chair, 1994-1995, Chair: Environmental Litigation Committee, 1993-1994; Legislation Review Committee, 1992-1993; Member, Real Property and Environmental Sections) Bar Associations; State Bar of California (Member, Environmental Litigation and Real Property Sections, 1990—; Board Member, 1994—, Heal the Bay; Secretary, 1995—; Chair, Legal Committee, 1992-1996 ); Los Angeles Trial Lawyers Association; California Trial Lawyers Association. *LANGUAGES:* French. *SPECIAL AGENCIES:* Federal Deposit Insurance Corporation (FDIC). *PRACTICE AREAS:* Environmental and Land Use Litigation. *Email:* 75022.3611@compuserve.com

**JEFFREY S. RASKIN,** born Los Angeles, California, April 20, 1964; admitted to bar, 1993, California, U.S. District Court, Central and Southern Districts of California and U.S Court of Appeals, Ninth Circuit. *Education:* University of California, Los Angeles (B.A., 1987); Santa Clara University (J.D., 1993). Recipient, Certificate of Excellence, Legal Analysis, Research & Writing, 1990-1991. Comments Editor, Santa Clara Law Review, 1992-1993. Author, "Dancing on the Outer Perimeters: The Supreme Court's Precarious Protection of Expressive Conduct," Santa Clara Law Review, Vol. 33. *PRACTICE AREAS:* Environmental Litigation; Real Estate Litigation; Business Litigation.

**L. ELIZABETH STRAHLSTROM,** born Ventura, California, November 8, 1968; admitted to bar, 1994, California. *Education:* University of California at Santa Barbara (B.A., with honors, 1990); McGeorge School of Law (J.D., 1994). Recipient, John A. McCarthy Academic Scholarship, 1992. Dean's List, University of the Pacific, McGeorge School of Law, 1994. Comment Staff Writer and Legislative Review Staff Writer, San Fernando Valley and McGeorge - Pacific Law Journal. Member: Environmental Law Forum, McGeorge School of Law; Valley Development Forum, 1995-1996, Women Lawyers of Los Angeles, San Fernando Valley, Litigation Section (Membership Co-Chair Valley Leadership Institute, 1995-1996, California Building Industry Association, 1995-1996. *Member:* Beverly Hills and Los Angeles County Bar Associations. *LANGUAGES:* Spanish. *PRACTICE AREAS:* Land Use; Environmental Law; Administrative Law; Water Law.

**REBECCA ANN THOMPSON,** born Inglewood, California, January 15, 1961; admitted to bar, 1992, California; 1993, U.S. District Court, Central District of California; 1995, U.S. District Court, Northern and Southern Districts of California. *Education:* University of Southern California (B.A., 1982); University of Notre Dame (J.D., 1992). *Member:* State Bar of California. *SPECIAL AGENCIES:* Los Angeles County Metropolitan Transit Authority (MTA). *PRACTICE AREAS:* Environmental Litigation; Environmental Compliance; Energy.

**ROBERT B. KEELER,** born Provo, Utah, September 11, 1942; admitted to bar, 1973, California; 1976, U.S. District Court, Central District of California: 1978, U.S. Court of Appeals, Ninth Circuit. *Education:* Brigham Young University (B.A., 1967); University of Washington, Seattle (M.A., 1969); University of Washington (M.A., 1969); Boalt Hall School of Law (J.D., 1973). Delta Phi Alpha; German Honor Society, Brigham Young University, 1966-1968. Blue Key National Honor Fraternity, Brigham Young University, 1966-1968. California, Attorney Generals Office, 1973-1978; Pacific Enterprises Law Department, 1978-1995.Auth or, "Recent California Planning Statutes and Mountain Area Subdivisions," 3 Ecology Law Qu 107 (1972-1973). President, Conference of California Public Utility Counsel, 1990-1991. Member, Board of Directors, J. Reuben Clark Law Society, Los Angeles Chapter, 1994—. *Member:* Los Angeles County and American (Member, Sections on: Natural Resources, Energy and Environmental Law) Bar Associations; State Bar of California. *LANGUAGES:* German. *SPECIAL AGENCIES:* California Public Utility Commission. *PRACTICE AREAS:* Public Utility Law; Energy Law; Administrative.

**KEVIN M. KEMPER,** born Camarillo, California, December 25, 1966; admitted to bar, 1994, California and U.S. District Court, Southern District of California; 1996, U.S. District Court, Central District of California. *Education:* University of California at Los Angeles (B.A., 1991); University of San Diego (J.D., 1994). Member, San Diego Law Review. Outstanding Intern, USD Environmental Law Society, 1994. Author, "Judicial Review Under the California Environmental Quality Act," California State Bar, Environmental Law Institute, October 1993. *Member:* San Diego County
*(This Listing Continued)*

Bar Association; State Bar of California (Member, Environmental Law Section). *SPECIAL AGENCIES:* Los Angeles County Metropolitans Transit Authority (MTA). *PRACTICE AREAS:* Land Use; Zoning; Environmental; Administrative.

**MONICA WITT,** born Redlands, California, May 11, 1964; admitted to bar, 1992, California. *Education:* University of California at Los Angeles (B.A., 1986); University of Southern California (M.A., 1989); Loyola University of Los Angeles (J.D., with honors, 1992). Recipient, Annenberg Research Grant, University of Southern California, 1989). Past employment, Stein, Hanger, Levine & Young (1992-1994); Laskin & Graham (1994-1996). *Member:* Los Angeles County, San Fernando Valley (Member, Sections on: Business and Real Property Law) and Los Angeles County Bar Associations. *PRACTICE AREAS:* Real Estate Litigation; Eminent Domain; Inverse Condemnation; Land Use.

**ANDREW VOGEL,** born New Haven, Connecticut, March 3, 1971; admitted to bar, 1996, California. *Education:* Dartmouth College (B.A., 1993); University of California (J.D., 1996). Editor-in-Chief, University of California, Los Angeles, Journal of Environmental Law and Policy. *Member:* State Bar of California. *PRACTICE AREAS:* Environmental.

**DIANA NG,** born Chicago, Illinois, July 29, 1971; admitted to bar, 1996, California. *Education:* University of California at Berkeley (B.A., 1993); University of Southern California (J.D., 1996). Executive Editor, Southern California Law Review. Author: "Debating The Wisdomof Placing Superfund Costs on Municipalities," 69 Southern California Law Review.

*OF COUNSEL*

**ROBERT M. HERTZBERG,** born Los Angeles, California, November 19, 1954; admitted to bar, 1979, California. *Education:* University of Redlands (B.A., magna cum laude, 1976); Hastings College of Law, University of California at San Francisco (J.D., 1979). Co-Author: "California Lis Pendens Practice," University of California, Continuing Education of the Bar, 1983.; Publications: "A Commonsense Approach to Good English," 400 Pages, 1976, University of Redlands;"The Catalyst and the King: Frank E. Brown and East San Bernardino Water Development," 1871-1893, Redlands Historical Society, 1976. Member, California State Assembly 40th AD, November, 1996. *Member:* Los Angeles and American Bar Association; State Bar of California.

*LEGAL SUPPORT PERSONNEL*

*PARALEGALS*

**SERENA A. BURNETT,** born Los Angeles, California, February 5, 1959. *Education:* California State University, Northridge; California State University, Long Beach (B.S., 1981); University of California at Los Angeles (Paralegal Certificate, 1989). Instructor, UCLA Attorney Assistant Training Program, 1994. *Member:* Los Angeles Paralegal Association; California Alliance of Paralegal Association; National Association of Female Executives (NAFE). (Paralegal). *PRACTICE AREAS:* Environmental Litigation; Business Litigation.

**KATHY HOFFMAN,** born Dayton, Ohio, August 25, 1962. *Education:* Pierce College (A.A., 1982); Watterson College (Paralegal Cert, 1983). Member: Los Angeles Paralegal, 1983; Associate Member of American Bar Association, 1992. (Paralegal). *PRACTICE AREAS:* Complex Litigation Management; Insurance Coverage; Research; Trial Preparation.

REPRESENTATIVE CLIENTS: MCA Development Company (subsidiary of MCA); Citicorp Real Estate, Inc. (subsidiary of Citicorp); Service Corporation International, New York Stock Exchange; BET Plant Services; Tokai Credit Corporation (subsidiary of Tokai Bank); Weyerhaeuser; RTC (Resolution Trust Corporation); Mitsubishi Electronics America, Budget Rent-A-Car, AT&T Wireless Services; Federal Deposit Insurance Corporation (FDIC);Los Angeles County Metropolitan Transit Authority (MTA).

# RUFUS VON THÜLEN RHOADES

*Established in 1975*

*633 WEST FIFTH STREET, 20TH FLOOR*
**LOS ANGELES, CALIFORNIA 90071**
*Telephone: 213-896-2491*
*Fax: 213-362-2957*
*Email: rufustax@ix.netcom.com*

*Federal and California Taxation Law.*

**RUFUS VON THÜLEN RHOADES,** born Oakland, California, October 30, 1932; admitted to bar, 1960, New York; 1962, California. *Education:* Stanford University Law School (A.B., 1954); Stanford University (LL.B., 1959). Member, Board of Editors, Stanford Law Review, 1958-
*(This Listing Continued)*

## PROFESSIONAL BIOGRAPHIES

## CALIFORNIA—LOS ANGELES

1959. Co-Author: "Income Taxation of Foreign Related Transactions," 5 Vols., Matthew Bender & Co., Revised 1996 (four times a year). Recipient, Dana Latham Memorial Award for Lifetime Achievement in Tax, Tax Section, Los Angeles County Bar Association. Appointed to Internal Revenue Service List of Mediators, 1996—. *Member:* Los Angeles County (Member, Real Estate Section; Chair, Taxation Section, 1975-1976 ), New York State and American Bar Associations; State Bar of California; Society of Professionals in Dispute Resolution (SPIDR).

REFERENCE: City National Bank (3rd and Fairfax Branch).

---

### CLAUDIA RIBET

11661 SAN VICENTE BOULEVARD, SUITE 1015
**LOS ANGELES, CALIFORNIA 90049**
Telephone: 310-826-2313
FAX: 310-826-8242
Email: Ribet@appellatelaw.com
*Appellate Practice and Complex Civil Litigation.*

**CLAUDIA RIBET,** born New York, N.Y., August 17, 1953; admitted to bar, 1978, District of Columbia; 1982, Virginia; 1986, Massachusetts; 1991, California. *Education:* Oberlin College (B.A., high honors, 1974); Antioch Law School (J.D., 1977). Faculty Member: Southern California Regional National Institute of Trial Advocacy, 1988-1996; Harvard Law School Trial Advocacy Program, 1988-1990. Former Partner: McDermott & Rizzo, Boston, Massachusetts. Former Associate: Wilmer, Cutler & Pickering, Washington, D.C.; Former of Counsel: Keck, Mahin & Cate, Los Angeles, California. Judge Pro Tempore: Small Claims Court, Santa Monica. *Member:* State Bar of California; District of Columbia Bar (Chair, Division of Courts, Lawyers and the Administration of Justice, 1980; Member, Ethics Committee, 1984-1985); Los Angeles West Inns of Court. (Also Of Counsel, Kulik, Gottesman & Mouton, L.L.P.)

---

### RICH & EZER

**LOS ANGELES, CALIFORNIA**
(See Ezer & Williamson)

---

### RICHARDS, WATSON AND GERSHON

PROFESSIONAL CORPORATION
THIRTY-EIGHTH FLOOR
333 SOUTH HOPE STREET
**LOS ANGELES, CALIFORNIA 90071**
Telephone: 213-626-8484
Telecopiers: 213-626-0078; 617-1144
Cable Address: "Richwat"

*The Firm Specializes in the Areas of Civil Litigation, Public Law, Municipal Finance, Insurance, Environmental Law, Oil and Gas, Corporation, Banking, Securities, State and Federal Tax, Estate Planning, Trust and Probate, Unfair Competition, Entertainment, Real Estate, Public Utilities, Administrative and Employment Law.*

**RICHARD RICHARDS** (1916-1988).

**GLENN R. WATSON,** born Ada, Oklahoma, May 2, 1917; admitted to bar, 1939, Oklahoma; 1946, California. *Education:* Oklahoma East Central University; University of Oklahoma (LL.B., 1939). Order of the Coif; Phi Delta Phi. City Attorney: Cerritos, California, 1956-1964; City of Industry, California, 1957-1967; 1978-1983; Rosemead, California, 1960-1976; Carson, California, 1968—; Seal Beach, California, 1971-1978. Member, City Attorneys' Department, League of California Cities, 1956—. *Member:* Los Angeles County (Member, Section of Oil and Gas Law) and American (Member, Section of Natural Resources Law) Bar Associations; The State Bar of California; Lawyers' Club of Los Angeles County (President, 1957); American Judicature Society. *PRACTICE AREAS:* Oil and Gas Law; Public Law; Litigation; Environmental.

**ROBERT G. BEVERLY,** born Belmont, Massachusetts, July 1, 1925; admitted to bar, 1952, California. *Education:* University of California at Los Angeles; Loyola University (LL.B., 1951). Phi Delta Phi. City Attor-

*(This Listing Continued)*

ney: City of Industry, California, 1964-1967; Cerritos, California, 1964-1965; Artesia, California, 1959-1962; Bell Gardens, 1961-1965; Lawndale, 1965-1967. Councilman, 1958-1967, Mayor, 1959-1960, 1964-1967, City of Manhattan Beach, California. President, Los Angeles Division, League of California Cities, 1966-1967. Member of Assembly, 1967-1976, Minority Floor Leader, 1973-1976, Member of Senate, 1976—, Vice Chairman, Senate Finance Committee, 1982-1985 and Vice Chairman, Senate Appropriations Committee, 1985—, California State Legislature. *Member:* Los Angeles County Bar Association; The State Bar of California.

**HARRY L. GERSHON,** born San Francisco, California, May 29, 1922; admitted to bar, 1949, California. *Education:* University of California (A.B., 1942); University of Southern California (LL.B., 1949). Nu Beta Epsilon; Order of the Coif. Member, Editorial Board, 1947-1949 and Editor in Chief, 1948, Southern California Law Review. Lecturer, University of Southern California School of Law, 1951-1955. Law Clerk, Hon. Roger J. Traynor, Associate Justice, Supreme Court of California, 1949-1950. *Member:* Beverly Hills, Los Angeles County and American (Member, Section of Antitrust Law) Bar Associations; The State Bar of California; Los Angeles Copyright Society. *PRACTICE AREAS:* Antitrust Law; Intellectual Property Law; Business Litigation; Land Use; Environmental Litigation.

**DOUGLAS W. ARGUE,** born Los Angeles, California, August 20, 1931; admitted to bar, 1956, Texas; 1963, California. *Education:* University of Texas (B.A., 1956; LL.B., 1956). Phi Delta Phi. Co-Author: "Tax Practice in California (Chapter 6)," Continuing Education of the Bar, University of California, 1984; "Tax Court Practice," ALI/ABA Publication, 1981; "Tax Aspects of Property Divisions in Divorce," 45 Los Angeles Bar Bulletin No. 7, May, 1970, p. 288; "Organization of the Tax Court under the Tax Reform Act of 1969," 16 The Practical Lawyer No. 5, May, 1970, p. 61; Chapter 9, "Life Insurance: Employee Benefits," *California Marital Termination Settlements,* Continuing Education of Bar, University of California, 1971. Author: "Recent Legislative Changes in Estate, Trust and Gift Taxation," 24th Title Insurance Tax and Probate Forum, 1972. Lecturer: Tax Procedure Institute, California Continuing Education of the Bar, May, 1987; Federal Tax Procedure, University of Southern California Law School, 1966-1968: PLI Federal Tax Practice and Procedure, 1974; "Tax and Estate Planning Highlights," Continuing Education of the Bar, University of California, 1976; "Compliance with Section 89," Merchants & Manufacturers Association, 1989; California C.P.A. Education Program, 1993. Attorney, Internal Revenue Service, Office of Chief Counsel, Washington, D.C., 1957-1959; Regional Counsel's Office, Los Angeles, 1959-1964. *Member:* Los Angeles County Bar Association (Chairman, Section of Taxation, 1973-1974); The State Bar of California. (Certified Specialist, Taxation Law, The State Bar of California Board of Legal Specialization). *PRACTICE AREAS:* Federal Income and Estate Taxation; State Income; Sales, Employment and Property Taxation; Tax Planning; Administrative Practice; Tax Litigation; Arbitrations.

**MARK L. LAMKEN,** born Los Angeles, California, January 26, 1933; admitted to bar, 1961, California. *Education:* University of California at Berkeley (A.B., 1954); University of California at Los Angeles (LL.B., 1960). Order of the Coif; Phi Alpha Delta. Editor, University of California at Los Angeles Law Review, 1959-1960. Author: "A Lender's Rights in and to Fire Insurance Proceeds," The Los Angeles Bar Bulletin No. 8, 1968, reprinted 41 California Savings and Loan Journal No. 7; "Condominium Conversions in the 1980's: An Historical Perspective," 55 California State Bar Journal 162, No. 4, April, 1980. Panelist: California Continuing Education of the Bar, 1974, 1975, 1978, 1983, 1984, 1985, 1986, 1987, 1989, 1990; Practising Law Institute, 1977, 1978, 1979, 1980, 1981, 1982, 1984, 1986, 1987, 1988, 1989, 1990; California Association of Judges Conference, 1991; American College of Real Estate Attorneys, 1992, 1993. Member, Board of Directors, Mountain Restoration Trust, 1982—. *Member:* Los Angeles County Bar Association (Chair, Real Property Section, 1988-1989); The State Bar of California; Association of Real Estate Attorneys (President, 1969-1970); American College of Real Estate Lawyers; Community Associations Institute. *PRACTICE AREAS:* Real Estate Development and Finance; Common Interest Developments.

**ERWIN E. ADLER,** born Flint, Michigan, July 22, 1941; admitted to bar, 1966, Michigan; 1967, California. *Education:* University of Michigan (B.A., 1963; LL.M., 1967); Harvard University (J.D., 1966). Phi Beta Kappa; Phi Kappa Phi. *Member:* State Bar of California; American Bar Association (Vice-Chairman, Appellate Advocacy Committee, 1982-1987). *PRACTICE AREAS:* Trial Law; Appellate Litigation; Insurance Coverage.

**DAROLD D. PIEPER,** born Vallejo, California, December 30, 1944; admitted to bar, 1971, California. *Education:* University of California at Los Angeles (A.B., 1967); University of Southern California (J.D., 1970).

*(This Listing Continued)*

## RICHARDS, WATSON AND GERSHON, PROFESSIONAL CORPORATION, Los Angeles—Continued

Phi Alpha Delta. Comment Editor, Southern California Law Review, 1969-1970. Author: "Condominiums and the 1968 Housing and Urban Development Act," 43 Southern California Law Review 309, 1970; "Estate Planning for Owners of the Family or Closely Held Business," California Continuing Education of the Bar, 1978, 1982, Lecturer, California Continuing Education of the Bar, 1978, 1982. Contributing Author: "The California Municipal Law Handbook," League of California Cities, 1993. Commissioner, 1983— and President, 1987—, Los Angeles County Delinquency and Crime Commission. Chairman, Los Angeles County Delinquency Prevention Planning Council, 1987-1990. Trustee, California City Management Foundation, 1992—; Chairman of the Board, 1990—, Youth Opportunities United, Inc. *Member:* Los Angeles County and American Bar Associations; The State Bar of California. **PRACTICE AREAS:** Public Law; Public Contracts Law; Public Transportation Law.

**ALLEN E. RENNETT,** born Philadelphia, Pennsylvania, January 25, 1948; admitted to bar, 1973, California. *Education:* University of Pennsylvania (B.A., 1969; J.D., 1973). Research & Writing Editor, University of Pennsylvania Law Review, 1972-1973. *Member:* Los Angeles County and American (Member, Sections on: Corporation, Banking and Business Law; Real Estate Law) Bar Associations; The State Bar of California. **PRACTICE AREAS:** Real Estate Law; Corporate Law; Partnership Law. **Email:** ARennett@mail.rwglaw.com

**STEVEN LEE DORSEY,** born Beckley, West Virginia, May 28, 1948; admitted to bar, 1973, California. *Education:* Stanford University (A.B., 1970; J.D., 1973). Note and Research Editor, Stanford Law Review, 1972-1973. Author: "Regulation of Interstate Land Sales," 25 Stanford Law Review 605, 1973. Agency Counsel, Palm Desert Redevelopment Agency, 1977—. City Attorney: Cudahy, 1982-1987; Rancho Palos Verdes, 1982-1989; South El Monte, 1973-1992; San Marino, 1986—; Norwalk, 1989—. President, City Attorneys Department, League of California Cities, 1989-1990. *Member:* Los Angeles County Bar Association (Member, 1982— and Chairman, 1986, Law of Local Government Section); The State Bar of California. **PRACTICE AREAS:** Public Law; Government Contracts Law.

**WILLIAM L. STRAUSZ,** born Spokane, Washington, December 12, 1946; admitted to bar, 1973, California; 1975, Washington. *Education:* University of Washington (B.A., 1969); Loyola University of Los Angeles (J.D., cum laude, 1973). Member, St. Thomas More Law Honor Society. Associate Editor, Loyola University Law Review, 1972-1973. *Member:* State Bar of California; Washington State Bar Association. **PRACTICE AREAS:** Public Finance Law; Public Law.

**ANTHONY B. DREWRY,** born Santa Monica, California, January 6, 1947; admitted to bar, 1972, California. *Education:* Stanford University (B.A., 1968); University of California at Los Angeles (J.D., 1971). Phi Delta Phi. Staff Member, U.C.L.A.-Alaska Law Review, 1969-1970. Member, Panel of Arbitrators, Los Angeles Superior Court. *Member:* Los Angeles County and American (Member, Litigation Section; Tort and Insurance Section) Bar Associations; State Bar of California; Association of Southern California Defense Counsel (Chairman, Legislative Committee, 1986); Association of Business Trial Lawyers; Defense Research Institute. **PRACTICE AREAS:** General Litigation.

**MITCHELL E. ABBOTT,** born Tulare, California, July 24, 1950; admitted to bar, 1975, Virginia and California; 1978, District of Columbia. *Education:* University of California at Davis (A.B., magna cum laude, 1972); University of Virginia (J.D., 1975). Phi Beta Kappa; Phi Kappa Phi. Member, Editorial Board, 1973-1974 and Notes Editor, 1974-1975, Virginia Journal of International Law. Author: Note, "Epidemiology in the Americas: International Treaties for the Prevention of Diseases," 15 Va. J. Int'l. L. 151, 1974. Contributing Author: *California Civil Appellate Practice*, 3d Ed. CEB, 1996. Editorial Consultant, California Civil Practice, Bancroft-Whitney, 1992. Special Assistant to U.S. Senator John V. Tunney, 1971-1973. *Member:* The State Bar of California; American Bar Association (Member, Sections on: Litigation and Forum Committee on Franchising). **PRACTICE AREAS:** Environmental Litigation; Unfair Competition Law; Appeals.

**TIMOTHY L. NEUFELD,** born Glendale, California, April 23, 1947; admitted to bar, 1975, California. *Education:* Brown University (A.B., 1969); Boston University (J.D., 1975). Member, Moot Court Administrative Board. *Member:* Los Angeles County Bar Association; The State Bar of California. [Lieut. (jg), U.S. Naval Reserve, 1969-1972]. **PRACTICE AREAS:** Business Litigation.

*(This Listing Continued)*

**GREGORY W. STEPANICICH,** born San Francisco, California, July 30, 1951; admitted to bar, 1977, California. *Education:* University of California at Riverside (A.B., with highest honors, 1973); Hastings College of Law, University of California (J.D., 1977). Order of the Coif. Associate Articles Editor, Hastings Law Journal, 1976-1977. Author: "Rondeau v Mosinee Paper Corp and Implied Private Rights of Action," 28 Hastings Law Journal 93, 1976. City Attorney, Agoura Hills, 1982—; Beverly Hills, 1987—; Seal Beach, 1982-1992. *Member:* The State Bar of California. **PRACTICE AREAS:** Public Law; Land Use Law.

**ROCHELLE BROWNE,** born Chicago, Illinois, December 23, 1938; admitted to bar, 1977, California. *Education:* University of California at Los Angeles (A.B., 1960; J.D., 1977). Phi Beta Kappa; Order of the Coif. Member, UCLA Law Review, 1975-1977. Extern Law Clerk to the Honorable Harry Pregerson, U.S. District Court, Los Angeles, 1977. *Member:* Los Angeles County Bar Association (Member, Sections on: Governmental Law; Land Use; Chair, Land Use Section, 1987-1988, 1988-1989; Member, Executive Committee, Real Property Section, 1989-1991; Delegate to State Bar Conference, 1989-1991); American Bar Association (Member, Sections on: Urban, State and Local Government; Natural Resources; Litigation); The State Bar of California (Member, Committee on Zoning and Land Use Regulation, 1985-1987, Sections on Real Property, Public Law and Litigation); Women Lawyers Association of Los Angeles; California Women Lawyers. **PRACTICE AREAS:** Litigation; Public Law; Land Use Law.

**MICHAEL JENKINS,** born New York, N.Y., March 16, 1953; admitted to bar, 1978, California. *Education:* Haverford College (B.A., 1975); Duke University (J.D., 1978). Executive Editor, Duke Law Journal, 1977-1978. Co-Author: "Contracting For Services: Where Do We Stand" Western City, Vol. LXX, No 7, August, 1994. Author: "The Quiet Explosion in Inverse Condemnation Liability," Western City, Vol. LX, No. 9, Sept, 1984. Lecturer in Law, University of Southern California Law Center, 1982-1995. Faculty Member, California Institute of Trial Advocacy, 1983-1987. City Attorney: Cities of Diamond Bar, Rolling Hills, Hermosa Beach and West Hollywood. President, City Attorneys Department of League of California Cities, 1994. President, City Attorneys Association of Los Angeles County, 1992. *Member:* State Bar of California (Member, Executive Committee, Public Law Section and Co-Editor, Public Law News, 1984-1988). **PRACTICE AREAS:** Public Law; Land Use Law; Litigation.

**WILLIAM B. RUDELL,** born Los Angeles, California, November 10, 1939; admitted to bar, 1968, New York; 1969, California. *Education:* Princeton University (A.B., cum laude, 1961); Graduate Institute of International Studies, Geneva, Switzerland; Yale Law School (LL.B., 1965). Crown Counsel and Director of Public Prosecutions, Republic of Botswana, Africa, 1965-1967. Member, 1970-1972 and Chairman, 1972, Planning Board, Burbank, California. Consul of the Republic of Botswana for the State of California, 1971—. Member, 1973-1977 and Mayor, 1975-1976, City Council, Burbank, California. Member, 1973-1977 and Chairman, 1975-1976, Redevelopment Agency, Burbank, California. Commissioner, 1977-1985 and President, 1978-1984, Burbank-Glendale-Pasadena Airport Authority. City Attorney: City of Burbank, California, 1982-1985; City of Palmdale, 1988—; City of South Gate, 1990-1993; City of Lynwood, 1993—. Member, City Attorneys Department, League of California Cities, 1982—. *Member:* Los Angeles County (Member, Government Law Section) and American (Member, Section on Urban, State and Local Government Law) Bar Associations; The State Bar of California. **PRACTICE AREAS:** Municipal Law; Municipal Finance; Aviation Law; Land Use Law.

**QUINN M. BARROW,** born Chicago, Illinois, October 31, 1955; admitted to bar, 1980, California; 1982, U.S. District Court, Central District of California; 1983, U.S. Court of Appeals, Ninth Circuit; 1995, U.S. Supreme Court. *Education:* State University of New York at Brockport (A.B., summa cum laude, 1976); Boston University (J.D., 1980). Member, 1977-1978 and Editor, 1978-1980, Boston University Law Review. City Attorney: City of Adelanto, 1990-1992; City of Seal Beach, 1992—; City of South El Monte, 1993—. *Member:* Los Angeles County and American Bar Associations; The State Bar of California; Orange County City Attorneys Association; City Attorney's Association of Los Angeles County; City Attorneys Department, League of California Cities. **PRACTICE AREAS:** Public Law; Litigation; Land Use Law.

**CAROL W. LYNCH,** born Pasadena, California, May 31, 1951; admitted to bar, 1981, California. *Education:* University of California at Los Angeles (B.A., cum laude, 1973); Loyola University of Los Angeles (J.D., 1981). City Attorney, La Puente and Rancho Palos Verdes. *Member:* State Bar of California. **PRACTICE AREAS:** Public Law; Land Use Law.

*(This Listing Continued)*

**JEFFREY A. RABIN,** born Los Angeles, California, December 15, 1956; admitted to bar, 1981, California. *Education:* University of California at Los Angeles (B.A., 1978); Boalt Hall School of Law, University of California (J.D., 1981). *Member:* Los Angeles County Bar Association (Member, Real Property Section); State Bar of California. **PRACTICE AREAS:** Real Property Law; Business Law.

**GREGORY M. KUNERT,** born Kansas City, Missouri, November 7, 1954; admitted to bar, 1980, California, U.S. District Court, Central District of California and U.S. Court of Appeals, Ninth Circuit; 1983, U.S. District Court, Southern District of California. *Education:* Occidental College (A.B., 1977); University of Southern California (J.D., 1980). *Member:* Los Angeles County and American Bar Associations; State Bar of California. **PRACTICE AREAS:** Civil Litigation and Trials; Civil Rights Litigation; Land Use Litigation.

**THOMAS M. JIMBO,** born Tokyo, Japan, September 27, 1957; admitted to bar, 1982, California; 1983, U.S. District Court, Central District of California; 1984, U.S. District Court, Northern, Southern and Eastern Districts of California; 1987, U.S. Court of Appeals, Ninth Circuit. *Education:* University of California at Los Angeles (B.A., summa cum laude, 1979); Loyola University of Los Angeles (J.D., cum laude, 1982). Phi Beta Kappa. *Member:* Los Angeles County and American Bar Associations; State Bar of California. **PRACTICE AREAS:** Litigation; Insurance Coverage Law.

**MICHELE BEAL BAGNERIS,** born Los Angeles, California, March 7, 1959; admitted to bar, 1984, California; 1985, U.S. District Court, Central District of California. *Education:* Stanford University (A.B., 1980); Boalt Hall School of Law, University of California (J.D., 1983). City Attorney, City of Monrovia. *Member:* Los Angeles County and American Bar Associations; State Bar of California; San Fernando Valley Legal Services Association (Member, Board of Directors); Black Women Lawyers Association. **PRACTICE AREAS:** Public Law.

**AMANDA F. SUSSKIND,** born Palo Alto, California, January 1, 1957; admitted to bar, 1982, California and U.S. District Court, Central District of California; 1983, U.S. District Court, Southern District of California. *Education:* Stanford University (B.S., 1978); Hastings College of Law, University of California (J.D., 1981). Note Editor, Hastings Constitutional Law Quarterly, 1979-1981. Judicial Extern to Justice Allison Rouse, California Court of Appeals, 1980. Senior Deputy County Counsel, Office of County Counsel of Los Angeles, 1984-1990. City Attorney, City of Hidden Hills, 1991—. Commissioner, Los Angeles County Parks and Recreation Commission, 1992-1996. Author: "Providing Affordable Housing Through Redevelopment," Public Law News, Annual Issue, 1991, Vol. 15, No. 2. *Member:* State Bar of California; Los Angeles County Bar Association (Chair, Executive Committee of Government Law Section, 1992-1996); California Women Lawyers Association; Women Lawyers Association of Los Angeles; National Association of Bond Lawyers; League of California Cities (Chair, Legislative Committee, 1992-1996; Jewish Federation Legislative Committee, 1996—). **LANGUAGES:** French and German. **PRACTICE AREAS:** Public Law; Public Finance; Redevelopment Law; Litigation.

**ROBERT C. CECCON,** born Boston, Massachusetts, January 11, 1960; admitted to bar, 1984, California; U.S. District Court, Central District of California; U.S. Court of Claims. *Education:* Columbia University (B.A., 1981); University of California at Los Angeles (J.D., 1984). *Member:* UCLA Moot Court Honors Program. Member, Federal Communications Law Journal, 1981-1982. *Member:* Los Angeles County Bar Association (Member, Litigation Section); State Bar of California. **PRACTICE AREAS:** Insurance Coverage; Litigation.

**SAYRE WEAVER,** born Bangkok, Thailand, May 13, 1952; admitted to bar, 1984, California; 1985, U.S. District Court, Central District of California. *Education:* Wellesley College; University of North Dakota; Yale University (B.A., 1975; J.D., 1984). Member, Board of Editors, Yale Journal of International Law, 1983-1984. *Member:* Los Angeles County and Federal Bar Associations; State Bar of California; Women Lawyers Association of Los Angeles; National Association of Women Lawyers. **PRACTICE AREAS:** Civil Rights and Land Use Litigation; Eminent Domain.

**WILLIAM K. KRAMER,** born Los Angeles, California, February 7, 1934; admitted to bar, 1964, California. *Education:* St. John's College (B.A., 1955); Loyola University of Los Angeles (J.D., 1963). *Member:* State Bar of California. **PRACTICE AREAS:** Municipal Finance.

**STEVEN H. KAUFMANN,** born Los Angeles, California, January 18, 1949; admitted to bar, 1974, California and U.S. District Court, Central District of California; 1984, U.S. Court of Appeals, Ninth Circuit; 1985, U.S. Supreme Court. *Education:* University of California at Los Angeles

*(This Listing Continued)*

(B.A., 1971); Loyola University School of Law, Los Angeles (J.D., 1974). Member, 1972-1973, and Associate Editor, 1973-1974, Loyola of Los Angeles Law Review. Deputy Attorney General, Office of California Attorney General, 1974-1991. Recipient, California Attorney General's Award for Excellence in Legal Services, 1990. Member, Los Angeles Superior Court Ad Hoc Committee on CEQA Writs of Mandate, 1994-1995. *Member:* Los Angeles County Bar Association; State Bar of California. **PRACTICE AREAS:** State and Municipal Land Use and CEQA Litigation; Writs and Appellate Practice; Administrative Law; Coastal Law.

**GARY E. GANS,** born Los Angeles, California, November 13, 1953; admitted to bar, 1979, California and U.S. District Court, Central District of California; 1980, U.S. District Court, Eastern District of California; 1984, U.S. District Court, Northern District of California; 1992, U.S. District Court, Southern District of California and U.S. Court of Appeals, Ninth Circuit; 1995, U.S. Court of Appeals, Tenth Circuit. *Education:* Wesleyan University (B.A., 1975); Boalt Hall School of Law, University of California, Berkeley (J.D., 1979). *Member:* Los Angeles County and American Bar Associations; State Bar of California. **PRACTICE AREAS:** Business Litigation; Entertainment Litigation; Intellectual Property Litigation.

**JOHN JOSEPH HARRIS,** born Cheverly, Maryland, May 28, 1952; admitted to bar, 1980, California; 1981, U.S. District Court, Central, Eastern, Northern and Southern Districts of California; 1987, U.S. Court of Appeals, Ninth Circuit. *Education:* University of California at Santa Barbara (B.A., with high honors, 1974); Hastings College of the Law, University of California (J.D., 1980). *Member:* Los Angeles County (Member, Section on Environmental Law) and American (Member, Sections on: Litigation; Natural Resources, Energy and Environmental Law) Bar Associations; State Bar of California (Member, Sections on: Real Property; Business, Natural Resources and Environmental); Rocky Mountain Mineral Law Foundation; California Independent Producers Association. **PRACTICE AREAS:** Environmental Law; Oil and Gas Law; Business Litigation.

**KEVIN G. ENNIS,** born Los Angeles, California, March 28, 1960; admitted to bar, 1986, California. *Education:* Claremont McKenna College (B.A., cum laude, 1982); Loyola Marymount University (J.D., 1985). Phi Alpha Delta. General Counsel, Green Valley County Water District, 1987—. Deputy City Attorney, City of Artesia, 1989—. Assistant City Attorney, City of Rolling Hills, 1989—. Assistant City Attorney, City of Palmdale, 1990-1994, 1994—. *Member:* Los Angeles County (Member, Sections on Local Government and Real Property) and American (Member, Public Law Section) Bar Associations; State Bar of California. **PRACTICE AREAS:** Public Law; Water Law.

**ROBIN D. HARRIS,** born Chicago, Illinois, February 26, 1959; admitted to bar, 1987, California and U.S. District Court, Central District of California. *Education:* Illinois State University (B.S., summa cum laude, 1981); University of Illinois College of Law (J.D., magna cum laude, 1986). Phi Alpha Delta. Member, University of Illinois Law Review, 1984-1986. Author: "Federal Jurisdiction Over Declaratory Judgment Suits - Federal Preemption of State Law," 1986 University of Illinois Law Review 127. *Member:* State Bar of California. **PRACTICE AREAS:** Public Law; Public Finance.

**MICHAEL ESTRADA,** born Los Angeles, California, May 6, 1956; admitted to bar, 1987, California; 1988, U.S. District Court, Central District of California. *Education:* University of California at San Diego (B.A., 1979); University of California at Los Angeles (M.A. Urban Planning, 1981); Boalt Hall School of Law, University of California at Berkeley (J.D., 1986). Extern Law Clerk to Hon. Judith N. Keep, U.S. District Court, Southern District of California, 1985. City Planner, San Francisco, Department of City Planning, 1981-1984. City Attorney: Bell Gardens, 1993-1994; San Fernando, 1995—. *Member:* Los Angeles County Bar Association; Mexican-American Bar Association. **LANGUAGES:** Spanish. **PRACTICE AREAS:** Municipal; Redevelopment; Solid Waste; Affordable Housing.

**LAURENCE S. WIENER,** born Los Angeles, California, December 15, 1961; admitted to bar, 1987, California. *Education:* Princeton University (A.B., 1983); University of California at Los Angeles (J.D., 1987). Order of the Coif. Editor-in-Chief, UCLA Journal of Environmental Law and Policy, 1986-1987. Extern Law Clerk to Justice Allen E. Broussard, California Supreme Court. Author: Case Note, "A Growing Loophole in the Clean Water Act," 4 UCLA Journal of Environmental Law and Policy 251; Note, "'People Not Trees': A Proposal for an Environmentalist/Housing Advocacy Coalition," 5 UCLA Journal of Environmental Law and Policy 49. Contributing Author: "Municipal Law Handbook," League of California Cities, 1993. Editor: "Municipal Law Handbook," League of California Cities, 1995-1997 Updates. Consultant, "Practice Under the California Environmental Quality Act," Continuing Education of the Bar. City Attorney,

*(This Listing Continued)*

## RICHARDS, WATSON AND GERSHON, PROFESSIONAL CORPORATION, Los Angeles—Continued

City of Westlake Village, 1993—. Member, Board of Advisors, UCLA Journal of Environmental Law and Policy. *Member:* Beverly Hills Bar Association; State Bar of California; City Attorney's Association of Los Angeles County. *PRACTICE AREAS:* Public Law; Municipal Law; Land Use Law; California Environmental Quality Act.

**STEVEN R. ORR,** born New Haven, Connecticut, November 3, 1962; admitted to bar, 1988, California and U.S. District Court, Central District of California; 1989, U.S. District Court, Northern, Eastern and Southern Districts of California and U.S. Court of Appeals, Ninth Circuit. *Education:* University of Southern California (A.B., magna cum laude, 1985); Harvard University (J.D., 1988). Phi Beta Kappa; Phi Kappa Phi. Book Review Editor, Harvard Civil Rights-Civil Liberties Law Review, 1987-1988. Adjunct Professor, University of Southern California Law Center, 1996. *Member:* Los Angeles County and American Bar Associations; State Bar of California. *PRACTICE AREAS:* Civil Litigation; Insurance Coverage; Dispute Resolution.

**MICHAEL G. COLANTUONO,** born Mt. Lebanon, Pennsylvania, October 13, 1961; admitted to bar, 1989, California and U.S. Court of Appeals, Ninth Circuit; 1990, U.S. District Court, Central District of California. *Education:* Harvard University (B.A., magna cum laude, 1983); Boalt Hall, University of California at Berkeley (J.D., 1988). Order of the Coif. Recipient, Thelen-Marin Award for Highest Rank Graduate. Articles Editor, *California Law Review,* 1987-1988. Contributor, *The California Municipal Law Handbook,* League of California Cities (1993). Author: "The Revision of American State Constitutions—Popular Sovereignty, Legislative Power, and Constitutional Change," 75 *California Law Review* 1473 (1987); "Methods of State Constitutional Revision," 7 *Legal Reference Services Quarterly* 45 (1987). Adjunct Professor of Law, Boalt Hall School of Law, 1995. Law Clerk to Ninth Circuit Judge James R. Browning, 1988-1989. City Attorney, Cudahy, California, 1992—. General Counsel, Big Bear City Community Services District, 1994—. City Attorney, La Habra Heights, 1995—. *Member:* Los Angeles County Bar Association (Member, Real Property and Government Law Sections); State Bar of California. *PRACTICE AREAS:* Public and Municipal Law; Land Use Law.

**C. EDWARD DILKES,** born Philadelphia, Pennsylvania, June 14, 1942; admitted to bar, 1971, California; 1972, U.S. District Court, Central District of California; 1973, U.S. Court of Appeals, Ninth Circuit; 1975, U.S. Supreme Court. *Education:* Occidental College (A.B., 1966) University of Southern California (J.D., 1969). Phi Alpha Delta. Alpha Chi Sigma. Author: "The 'Duchy' of LA," LA Planning Report 1993. City Attorney: City of Rosemead, 1976-1980; City of Maywood, 1980-1984; City of Bradbury, 1990—. *Member:* American Bar Association. *REPORTED CASES:* HFH v. Superior Court (Vons) 15 Cal 3rd 508 (1975); Regus v. Baldwin Park 70 Cal App. 3d 968 (1977). *PRACTICE AREAS:* Eminent Domain; Municipal Law; Environmental Law; Litigation.

**PETER M. THORSON,** born Santa Monica, California, December 22, 1951; admitted to bar, 1978, California; 1979, U.S. District Court, Central District of California. *Education:* University of California at Los Angeles (B.A., 1974); Loyola University of Los Angeles (J.D., 1978). Deputy General Counsel, The Metropolitan Water District of Southern California, 1978-1979. City Attorney: Azusa, 1983-1992; Downey, 1988-1994; Mission Viejo, 1991—; Temecula, 1994—. *Member:* Los Angeles County (Chair, Government Law Section, 1991-1992) and American Bar Associations; The State Bar of California; City Attorneys Association of Los Angeles County. *PRACTICE AREAS:* Municipal Law; Redevelopment Law; Land Use Law.

**BRENDA L. DIEDERICHS,** born Long Beach, California, April 30, 1957; admitted to bar, 1991, California; 1993, Minnesota. *Education:* California Polytechnic State University (B.A., 1979); Loyola Marymount University (J.D., 1989). *PRACTICE AREAS:* Labor Law; Employment.

**DEBORAH R. HAKMAN,** born Los Angeles, California, September 3, 1961; admitted to bar, 1988, California and U.S. District Court, Central District of California; 1989, U.S. District Court, Eastern, Southern and Northern Districts of California and U.S. Court of Appeals, Ninth Circuit. *Education:* University of California at Los Angeles (B.A., magna cum laude, 1984); Loyola Law School of Los Angeles (J.D., 1988). Phi Beta Kappa. Member, St. Thomas More Law Honor Society. Recipient, American Jurisprudence Awards. Member and Editor, Loyola of Los Angeles International and Comparative Law Journal, 1986-1988. *Member:* Santa Monica, Los Angeles County and American Bar Associations; State Bar of California; Women Lawyers Association of Los Angeles. *LANGUAGES:* Hebrew. *PRACTICE AREAS:* Public Law.

**B. TILDEN KIM,** born Seoul, Korea, May 27, 1963; admitted to bar, 1989, California. *Education:* University of California at Davis (B.S., Biochemistry Major-English Minor, 1985; J.D., 1989). Senior Notes and Comments Editor, University of California at Davis Law Review, 1988-1989. Author: "Peculiar Risk Doctrine: A Criticism of its Application in California," 22, University of California Davis Law Review 215, 1988. Member, California State Judicial Nominee Evaluation Committee, 1990. *Member:* Los Angeles County Bar Association; State Bar of California (Member: Sections on: Real Estate, International Law, Litigation). *LANGUAGES:* Korean. *PRACTICE AREAS:* Litigation; Insurance Coverage.

**RUBIN D. WEINER,** born Philadelphia, Pennsylvania, December 5, 1964; admitted to bar, 1991, California. *Education:* Harvard University (A.B., cum laude, 1986); University of Pennsylvania Law School/Wharton School of Management (J.D., cum laude, 1990; M.A., 1990). Senior Editor, Journal of International Business Law, 1989-1990. Recipient, Milton C. Sharp Prize in Urban Renewal and Land Use Planning, 1990. *Member:* Los Angeles County Bar Association; State Bar of California. *PRACTICE AREAS:* Municipal Law; Municipal Finance.

**SASKIA TSUSHIMA ASAMURA,** born London, England, April 15, 1957; admitted to bar, 1991, California. *Education:* London School of Economics, London, England (B.Sc., Hons., 1979); University of California at Los Angeles (J.D., 1991). UCLA Moot Court Distinguished Advocate Award, 1989. First Place and Best Brief Awards, National Moot Court Competition, Regional Championships, 1990. Member, 1989-1990 and Member, Executive Board of Judges, 1990-1991, UCLA Moot Court Honors Program. *Member:* State Bar of California; Los Angeles County and American Bar Associations; Japanese American Bar Association. *LANGUAGES:* French. *REPORTED CASES:* Sinaloa Lake Owners Assoc. v. Stephenson, 805 F.Supp. 824 (C.D. Cal. 1992). *PRACTICE AREAS:* Litigation.

**KAYSER O. SUME,** born Ankara, Turkey, March 3, 1966; admitted to bar, 1991, California and U.S. District Court, Central District of California. *Education:* Stanford University (A.B., 1988); Boston College (J.D., cum laude, 1991). *Member:* State Bar of California. *PRACTICE AREAS:* Insurance Coverage; Civil Litigation.

**SAUL JAFFE,** born Johannesburg, South Africa, May 3, 1964; admitted to bar, 1991, California; 1992, U.S. District Court, Southern and Central Districts of California. *Education:* University of Texas (B.A., 1986); University of Houston (M.B.A., 1991); McGeorge School of Law (J.D., 1991). Phi Alpha Delta (Justice, 1991). Assistant Comment Editor, 22 Pacific Law Journal, 1991. Staff Writer, Legislative Review, 21 Pacific Law Journal, 1990. *Member:* State Bar of California.

**CRAIG A. STEELE,** born Los Angeles, California, May 18, 1962; admitted to bar, 1992, California. *Education:* University of Southern California (B.A., 1984; J.D., 1992). President, Student Bar Association, 1991-1992. Member, Southern California Law Review, 1990-1992. Extern Law Clerk, City of Los Angeles Ethics Commission, 1992. *PRACTICE AREAS:* Litigation; Public Law; Political Law.

**T. PETER PIERCE,** born Gainesville, Florida, July 30, 1964; admitted to bar, 1992, California; 1993, U.S. Court of Appeals, Fifth Circuit and U.S. District Court, Central District of California. *Education:* Cornell University (B.A., 1986); Syracuse University (M.S., 1987); Tulane University (J.D., cum laude, 1992). Member: Order of the Barristers; Moot Court Board; National Moot Court Competition, semifinalist, National Championships, Finalist and Best Brief Awards, Regional Championships. Law Clerk to the Honorable Marcel Livaudais, Jr., U.S. District Court, Eastern District of Louisiana, 1992-1993. *PRACTICE AREAS:* Municipal Law; Municipal Litigation.

**BENJAMIN BARNOUW,** born New Haven, Connecticut, July 7, 1967; admitted to bar, 1993, California; 1994, U.S. District Court, Central District of California; 1995, U.S. Court of Appeals, Tenth Circuit; U.S. District Court, Southern District of California. *Education:* University of Texas at Austin (B.A., B.S., 1989); Boalt Hall School of Law, University of California at Berkeley (J.D., 1993). Phi Beta Kappa. Law Clerk to Honorable Lawrence T. Lydick, U.S. District Court, Central District of California, 1993-1994. *PRACTICE AREAS:* Insurance Coverage; Business Litigation.

**TERENCE R. BOGA,** born Hollywood, California, April 1, 1969; admitted to bar, 1994, California. *Education:* Princeton University (A.B., 1991); Harvard University (J.D., 1994). Author: "Turf Wars: Street Gangs, Local Governments, and the Battle for Public Space," 29 Harv. C.R.- C.L. L.Rev. 477 (1994). *PRACTICE AREAS:* Public Law.

*(This Listing Continued)*

**DANIEL L. PINES,** born Los Angeles, California, April 16, 1969; admitted to bar, 1994, California and U.S. District Court, Central District of California; 1995, U.S. Court of Appeals, Ninth Circuit. *Education:* Georgetown University (B.S.F.S., magna cum laude, 1991); Boalt Hall School of Law, University of California (J.D., 1994). Phi Beta Kappa. Member, California Law Review. *PRACTICE AREAS:* Litigation.

**LISA BOND,** born Fort Worth, Texas, February 26, 1969; admitted to bar, 1994, California. *Education:* University of Texas, Austin (B.B.A., 1990; J.D./M.B.A., 1994). *PRACTICE AREAS:* Environmental Litigation; Oil and Gas Law.

**DIANE ARKOW GROSS,** born New York, N.Y., April 2, 1968; admitted to bar, 1994, California. *Education:* Duke University (B.A., 1990); University of Southern California (J.D., 1993). Phi Beta Kappa. Recipient: Robert S. Rankin Award in American State and Local Government; Shattuck Award. Board Member, USC Public Interest Law Foundation, 1991-1993. Editor, Review of Law and Women's Studies, 1992-1993. Law Clerk to the Honorable Ewing Werlein Jr., U.S. District Judge, Southern District of Texas, 1993-1995. *Member:* Los Angeles County and American Bar Associations; State Bar of California. *PRACTICE AREAS:* Litigation; Labor and Employment.

**ROXANNE DIAZ MONTGOMERY,** born Burbank, California, July 30, 1967; admitted to bar, 1995, California. *Education:* California State University at Fullerton (B.A., 1992); Hastings College of Law, University of California (J.D., 1995). *PRACTICE AREAS:* Litigation; Municipal Law.

REFERENCE: Bank of California, N.A. (Los Angeles Regional Main Office).

---

## RICHMAN, LAWRENCE, MANN, GREENE, CHIZEVER, FRIEDMAN & PHILLIPS

### A PROFESSIONAL CORPORATION

### LOS ANGELES, CALIFORNIA

(See Beverly Hills)

*Transactional Business, Securities, Labor, Entertainment, Real Estate and Environmental Law. Litigation in all Courts.*

---

## RICHMAN, LUNA, KICHAVEN & GLUSHON

12424 WILSHIRE BOULEVARD, SUITE 900
**LOS ANGELES, CALIFORNIA 90025**
Telephone: 310-207-4880
Telecopier: 310-207-4889, 310-442-6400

*General Business Transaction and Civil Litigation Practice, with special expertise in Corporate and Real Estate Transactions, Land Use, Natural Resource Matters and Federal and State Trial Practice.*

### MEMBERS OF FIRM

**JAMES D. RICHMAN,** born Los Angeles, California, September 11, 1948; admitted to bar, 1974, California. *Education:* Occidental College (B.A., magna cum laude, 1970); Boalt Hall School of Law, University of California at Berkeley (J.D., 1974). Phi Beta Kappa. Associate Editor, California Law Review. Law Clerk: Hon. Stanley Mosk, California Supreme Court, 1974; Hon. Harry Pregerson, U.S. Court of Appeals, Ninth Circuit, 1975. Author: "Negotiating Operating Expense Provisions in Office Building Leases," Lead Article, CEB Real Property Law Reporter, Volume 11, No. 4, June, 1988 and in Real Estate Review, Vol. 18 No. 3, Fall, 1988; "Negotiating Leases of Non-Residential Property under the Bankruptcy Code: Drafting Strategies," Lead Article, CEB Real Property Law Reporter, Volume X, No. 2, March, 1987; "Anticipatory Lease Drafting Strategies," Chapter 26B, The Law of Distressed Real Estate, Clark Boardman. Real Estate Editor, Warrens Forms of Agreement, Matthew Bender. Contributing Editor, The Law of Distressed Real Estate. Editor, LACBA Real Property Review, 1994—. *Member:* Los Angeles County Bar Association (Member, Executive Committee, Real Property Section, 1990—). *PRACTICE AREAS:* Real Estate; Taxation; Business Law; Finance. *Email:* Beckrich@aol.com

**DENNIS R. LUNA,** born Los Angeles, California, August 21, 1946; admitted to bar, 1974, California and U.S. District Court, Central District of California; 1985, U.S. Tax Court. *Education:* University of Southern California (B.S., in Petroleum Engineering, 1968; M.S., 1969; M.B.A., 1971); Harvard University (J.D., 1974). Chairman of the Board, Angels Flight

*(This Listing Continued)*

Railway Foundation, 1995—. Trustee, Hollywood Sign Trust, 1992—. Director and Member of Executive Committee, Economic Development Corporation of Los Angeles County, 1990—. Commissioner and Treasurer, Los Angeles Community Redevelopment Agency, 1989-1993. Los Angeles City Board of Recreation and Parks Commission, 1984-1989. Alternate Commissioner, Los Angeles Memorial Coliseum Commission, 1987-1989. Member, Los Angeles County Supervisory District Boundary Review Committee, 1990-1991. *Member:* Los Angeles County and American Bar Associations. *PRACTICE AREAS:* Corporate; Business Law; Real Estate; Taxation; Natural Resources; Arbitration. *Email:* Dennis_Luna@msn.com

**JEFFREY G. KICHAVEN,** born Los Angeles, California, June 14, 1956; admitted to bar, 1980, California, U.S. Supreme Court, U.S. Court of Appeals, Ninth Circuit and U.S. District Court, Central, Northern and Southern Districts of California. *Education:* University of California at Berkeley (A.B., with great distinction in general scholarship, 1977); Harvard University (J.D., cum laude, 1980). Phi Beta Kappa. Author: "Using Alternative Dispute Resolution," Chapter 30, California Forms of Pleading and Practice: Alternative Dispute Resolution, Matthew Bender, 1996; "Rule 16 to the Rescue: An Opportunity to Redefine the Dispute Resolution Mission of the Federal Courts," 29 Tort & Ins. L.J. 507, ABA, 1994. Co-Author (with V. Stone)," Preparing for Mediation," 18:1 Litigation 40, ABA, 1991. Adjunct Professor, Straus Institute for Dispute Resolution, Pepperdine University School of Law, 1995—. Speaker and Writer: ADR and Civil Litigation Topics, American Bar Association, Los Angeles County Bar Association, Beverly Hills Bar Association, California Continuing Education of the Bar and the Practising Law Institute. Vice-President, Los Angeles Chapter, 1994—, Member: National Legal Affairs Committee, 1995—, National Church-State Subcommittee, 1990—, American Jewish Committee. *Member:* Beverly Hills, Century City, Los Angeles County (Chair, ADR Section, 1995—; Member, Committee on Professionalism, 1992—; Member, Nominating Committee, 1994) and American (Member, Council of the Section of Dispute Resolution, 1995—; Chair, Committee on Dispute Resolution, Section of Business Law, 1995—) Bar Associations; State Bar of California; Association of Business Trial Lawyers (Member, Board of Governors, 1986-1988); American Arbitration Association (Member, Panel of Mediators and Arbitrators, 1993—). Los Angeles Superior Court Panel of Mediators. *PRACTICE AREAS:* Mediation; Arbitration; Alternative Dispute Resolution. *Email:* JGKichaven@aol.com

**ROBERT L. GLUSHON,** born Los Angeles, California, September 15, 1953; admitted to bar, 1980, California. *Education:* University of Southern California and University of California at Los Angeles (B.A., Political Science with emphasis in Local Government, 1976); Loyola University (J.D., 1980). City Commissioner and Vice-Chair of the Board, Zoning Appeals, City of Los Angeles, 1996—. Commissioner, Citizens Economy and Efficiency Commission, County of Los Angeles, 1996—. Member, Advisory Council of Progress L.A., 1994—. Commissioner and President, Environmental Quality Board, Telecommunications Commission, City of Los Angeles, 1985-1988. Deputy to Marvin Braude, Los Angeles City Councilman, 1977-1981. *Member:* Los Angeles County Bar Association (Member, Real Estate Section); State Bar of California (Member, Real Property Section). *PRACTICE AREAS:* Real Estate; Real Property; Land Use; Governmental; Business Law. *Email:* RGlushon@ix.netcom.com

### ASSOCIATE

**LUZ AURORA ORTIZ,** born Guadalajara, Mexico, July 19, 1967; admitted to bar, 1996, California and New York. *Education:* Princeton University (B.A., Political Science, with Certificate in Latin American Studies, 1992); University of Michigan (J.D., 1995).

REFERENCES: Coast Federal Savings & Loan Assn. (Westwood Branch); City National Bank (Beverly Hills, Calif.).

---

## RICKLESS & WOLF

Established in 1976

SUITE 1900
1900 AVENUE OF THE STARS
**LOS ANGELES, CALIFORNIA 90067**
Telephone: 310-201-7577
Telecopier: 310-277-5143

*London, England Office:* Trafalgar House, ll Waterloo Place. Telephone: 071-839 3226. Telex: 917881 WITSOM G. Telecopier: 071-839-6741.

*General and International Law Practice. Entertainment, Corporate, Copyright and Tax Law.*

*(This Listing Continued)*

**RICKLESS & WOLF, Los Angeles—Continued**

**MICHAEL B. WOLF,** born Los Angeles, California, January 26, 1942; admitted to bar, 1969, California. *Education:* University of California at Berkeley (A.B., 1963; J.D., 1968); Oxford University, England (B.A., 1965; M.A., 1971). *Member:* Beverly Hills, Los Angeles County and American Bar Associations; The State Bar of California.

---

## LAW OFFICES OF
## ROBERT GORE RIFKIND

Established in 1955

10100 SANTA MONICA BOULEVARD, SUITE 215
**LOS ANGELES, CALIFORNIA 90067**
Telephone: 310-552-0478
FAX: 310-552-0478

*Corporate Securities and Real Estate and Related Litigation. Estate Planning and Probate.*

**ROBERT GORE RIFKIND,** born Beverly Hills, California, July 12, 1928; admitted to bar, 1955, California; 1977, U.S. Supreme Court. *Education:* University of California at Los Angeles (B.A., 1950); Harvard University (LL.B., 1954). Author, "Securities Problems of The Locked-in Estate," The Business Lawyer, November 1969; "Wild Passion at Midnight: German Expressionist Art," Art Journal, Summer, 1980. Co-author: "SEC Registration of Real Estate Interests: An Overview," The Business Lawyer, April 1972; "Private Placement and Proposed Rule 146," The Hastings Law Journal, January 1974; "Pre-Mortem Planning For Unique and Unusual Assets," New York Law Journal Seminars-Press, June 1979; "Setting Business Development and Other Long-Range Planning Policies for the Smaller-Medium Size Firm: Fact or Fantasy," for the Eighth Annual Conference of American Legal Executives, 1979. Recipient, Order of Merit, First Class, Federal Republic of Germany, 1979. Member: Board of Trustees, California Institute of the Arts, 1983-1985; Art Book Committee, University of California Press, 1983—. Distinguished Adjunct Professor of Art History, University of California at Los Angeles, 1986-1988. Created Robert Gore Rifkind Center for German Expressionist Studies, 1985. *Member:* American (Section of Corporation, Banking and Business Law) and International (Section on Business Law) Bar Associations; The State Bar of California (Examiner, 1961-1962 and Chairman, 1964-1970, Local Administrative Committee); American Judicature Society; Association of Lawyers of the World Peace Through Law Center. Life Fellow, Los Angeles County Bar Foundation.

---

## RING & GREEN

SUITE 2300, 1900 AVENUE OF THE STARS
**LOS ANGELES, CALIFORNIA 90067**
Telephone: 310-201-0777
Fax: 310-556-1346

*Business, Commercial and Real Estate Litigation. General Business Transactions and Corporate Law. Trial Practice in all Courts.*

### MEMBERS OF FIRM

**ROBERT A. RING,** born Los Angeles, California, January 10, 1955; admitted to bar, 1981, California, U.S. District Court, Central District of California and U.S. Court of Appeals, Ninth Circuit; 1985, U.S. District Court, Eastern, Northern and Southern Districts of California. *Education:* University of California at Los Angeles; University of California at Berkeley (B.A., with distinction and honors, 1977); University of San Diego (J.D., 1980). Phi Alpha Delta. Judge Pro Tem, Beverly Hills Municipal Court, 1988—. *Member:* Beverly Hills (Member, Litigation Section), Century City (Member, Litigation Section), Los Angeles County (Member, Litigation and Real Property Sections) and American (Member, Sections of: Litigation; Real Property) Bar Associations; The State Bar of California; Association of Business Trial Lawyers. **PRACTICE AREAS:** General Business; Commercial and Real Estate Litigation; General Business Transactions; Corporate Law.

**SUSAN H. GREEN,** born Tulsa, Oklahoma, October 24, 1956; admitted to bar, 1981, California and U.S. District Court, Central and Southern Districts of California. *Education:* Northwestern University (B.A., 1978); University of California at Los Angeles (J.D., 1981). Member: Order of the

*(This Listing Continued)*

---

Barristers; UCLA Journal of International Law, 1980-1981. *Member:* Los Angeles County Bar Association; State Bar of California. **PRACTICE AREAS:** Business; Commercial; Corporate Litigation.

REFERENCE: Union Bank (Century City Office).

---

## RINTALA, SMOOT, JAENICKE & REES

Established in 1981

10351 SANTA MONICA BOULEVARD, SUITE 400
**LOS ANGELES, CALIFORNIA 90025-6937**
Telephone: 310-203-0935
Facsimile: 310-556-8921

*Civil Trial and Appellate Practice.*

**FIRM PROFILE:** *Rintala, Smoot, Jaenicke & Rees is a firm engaged in a sophisticated litigation and employment law practice which includes business and entertainment litigation involving breach of contracts, franchising, copyright and trademark, unfair competition and trade secrets, cable franchising, First Amendment and privacy rights issues, insurance coverage disputes, wrongful termination and employment discrimination, construction, product liability, creditor's rights, shareholder and partnership disputes and motion picture profit participation.*

*The firm's employment practice encompasses litigation and administrative proceedings, grievance and arbitration hearings, union contract negotiations, as well as counseling and advice in all employment-related matters.*

### MEMBERS OF FIRM

**WILLIAM T. RINTALA,** born San Francisco, California, May 29, 1938; admitted to bar, 1967, California; 1976, U.S. Supreme Court. *Education:* Stanford University (A.B., 1961); University of California at Berkeley; Harvard University; Boalt Hall School of Law, University of California (J.D., 1967). Order of the Coif. Executive Editor, California Law Review, 1966-1967. Author: Comment, "The Mere Evidence Rule: Limitations on Seizure Under the Fourth Amendment," 54 California Law Review 2099, 1966; Chapter on Copyright in CEB, Attorney's Guide to Competitive Practices, Second, Edition 1991. Co-Author: Chapter on Copyright in CEB, Attorney's Guide to the Law of Competitive Business Practices, 1981; "Review by California Supreme Court," CEB, California Civil Appellate Practice, 2nd Edition, 1985. Member, Board of Directors, Public Counsel, 1977-1980. *Member:* Beverly Hills (Chair, Amicus Briefs Committee, 1980-1990), Los Angeles County and American (Member, Sections on: Litigation; Intellectual Property Law) Bar Associations; State Bar of California (Member, Committee on Appellate Courts, 1981-1984). *Email:* WTR@RSJR.COM

**PETER C. SMOOT,** born Los Angeles, California, July 10, 1945; admitted to bar, 1971, California; 1976, U.S. Supreme Court. *Education:* University of California at Berkeley (B.A., 1967); University of Southern California (J.D., 1970). Pi Sigma Alpha; Order of the Coif. Topics and Projects Editor, Southern California Law Review, 1969-1970. Author: Comment, "Never Trust a Bureaucrat: Estoppel Against the Government," 42 Southern California Law Review 391, 1969. Consultant, CEB, California Civil Procedure During Trial, 1982. Co-Author: "Review by California Supreme Court," CEB, California Civil Appellate Practice, 2nd Edition, 1985. *Member:* Los Angeles County Bar Association; State Bar of California. *Email:* PCS@RSJR.COM

**J. LARSON JAENICKE,** born Greenville, Alabama, August 5, 1947; admitted to bar, 1972, New York; 1976, Virginia; 1977, California. *Education:* University of the South (B.A., 1969); New York University (J.D., 1972). Phi Beta Kappa. *Member:* Los Angeles County and American Bar Associations; State Bar of California. *Email:* JLJ@RSJR.COM

**ROBERT A. REES,** born Tucson, Arizona, September 15, 1955; admitted to bar, 1980, California. *Education:* Stanford University (A.B., 1976); University of Arizona and Loyola University of Los Angeles (J.D., cum laude, 1980). Member, St. Thomas More Law Honor Society. Member, Consumer Attorneys Association of Los Angeles. *Member:* Los Angeles County and American Bar Associations; State Bar of California; American Trial Lawyers Association. *Email:* RAR@RSJR.COM

**MELODIE K. LARSEN,** born Moscow, Idaho, November 16, 1951; admitted to bar, 1983, California. *Education:* California State University at Los Angeles (B.A., 1978); Loyola Law School; University of California at Berkeley (J.D., 1983). Member and Associate Editor, Industrial Relations Law Journal, 1982-1983. Judicial Extern to The Honorable Stephen Reinhardt, U.S. Court of Appeals, Ninth Circuit, 1981. *Member:* State Bar of California.

*(This Listing Continued)*

**FRANK E. MELTON,** born Oceanside, NY, December 16, 1954; admitted to bar, 1980, CA. *Education:* Yale University (B.A., 1976); Stanford University (J.D., 1980). Phi Beta Kappa. Author: "The State Action Antitrust Defense for Local Governments: A State Authorization Approach," 12 Urban Lawyer 315 (1980). Legislative Assistant, U.S. Senator John C. Danforth, 1977-1978. Law Clerk to Judge David V. Kenyon, U.S. District Court, Central District of California, 1980-1981. Member, Board of Directors, Bet Tzedek Legal Services, 1993—. Vice President and Member, Board of Directors, Sinai Temple, 1987—. President, Stanford Law Society of Southern California, 1989-1992. *Member:* Los Angeles County (Member, Labor and Employment Law Section) and American (Member, Labor and Employment Law Section) Bar Associations; State Bar of California (Member, Labor and Employment Law Section).

### ASSOCIATES

**ROBERT W. HODGES,** born Los Angeles, California, January 14, 1963; admitted to bar, 1988, California. *Education:* University of Southern California (B.A., 1985; J.D., 1988). Order of the Coif; Member, Southern California Law Review, 1986-1987. Judicial Clerkship with Richard A. Gadbois, U.S. District Court, Central District of California, 1988-1989. *Member:* Los Angeles County Bar Association; State Bar of California.

**MARC D. MOOTCHNIK,** born Los Angeles, California, November 29, 1963; admitted to bar, 1989, California. *Education:* California State University at Long Beach (B.A., 1986); Loyola Law School, Los Angeles (J.D., 1989). St. Thomas More Society. Associate Editor, International and Comparative Law Journal, 1987-1989. Landlord Tenant Dispute Settlement Officer, 1990-1991. *Member:* Los Angeles County and American Bar Associations; State Bar of California.

**MICHAEL B. GARFINKEL,** born Detroit, Michigan, May 3, 1966; admitted to bar, 1991, California. *Education:* University of Michigan (B.A., 1988); University of California at Los Angeles (J.D., 1991). Judicial Extern to the Honorable Robert C. Bonner, United States District Court, Central District of California, Spring 1990. *Member:* Los Angeles County and American Bar Associations; State Bar of California. *Email:* MBG@RSJR.COM

**EMILY PETERS,** born June 23, 1968; admitted to bar, 1994, California. *Education:* Stanford University (B.A., 1990); University of Michigan (J.D., 1994). *Member:* Los Angeles County Bar Association; State Bar of California.

REPRESENTATIVE CLIENTS: ARCO; Broadcast Music, Inc.; Century Communications; Continental Airlines, Inc.; Dollar Rent A Car Systems, Inc.; Eaton Corp.; Host Marriott Services Corporation; International Creative Management, Inc.; Kellwood Company; NestléUSA, Inc.; Northwest Airlines, Inc.; Public Storage, Inc.; Warner Bros. Inc.; William Morris Agency, Inc.
REFERENCE: Western Bank.

---

## RIORDAN & McKINZIE

*A PROFESSIONAL LAW CORPORATION*

CALIFORNIA PLAZA
29TH FLOOR, 300 SOUTH GRAND AVENUE
**LOS ANGELES, CALIFORNIA 90071**
*Telephone: 213-629-4824*
*FAX: 213-229-8550*

*Westlake Village, California Office:* 5743 Corsa Avenue, Suite 116.
Telephones: 818-706-1800; 805-496-4688. FAX: 818-706-2956.
*Costa Mesa, California Office:* 695 Town Center Drive, Suite 1500.
Telephone: 714-433-2900. FAX: 714-549-3244.

*General Civil and Trial Practice in all State and Federal Courts. Corporation, Corporate Securities, Real Estate, Antitrust, Patent, Trademark, Copyright and Unfair Competition Law. Taxation, Estate Planning, Trust and Probate Law.*

**RICHARD J. RIORDAN** (Retired).

**CARL W. MCKINZIE,** born Lubbock, Texas, December 3, 1939; admitted to bar, 1967, California. *Education:* Texas Technological University (B.B.A., 1962; M.B.A., 1963); Southern Methodist University (J.D., 1966). Member, 1964-1965; Associate Editor, 1965-1966, Southwestern Law Journal. Member: Executive Board, Southern Methodist University School of Law, 1979-1982, 1990—; Board of Advisors, The University of Wyoming College of Law, 1987-1991; Law Society's Board of Directors, Arizona State University College of Law, 1990—; Board of Governors, California Community Foundation, 1994—; Board of Governors, The National Association of Real Estate Investment Trusts, 1986-1989. *Member:* Los Angeles County and American (Chairman, Current Developments Subcommittee of the Real Estate Tax Problems Committee, Taxation Section, 1978-1980) Bar Associations; State Bar of California. *Email:* cwm@riordan.com

**JAMES A. HAMILTON,** born Rochester, New York, December 22, 1944; admitted to bar, 1970, California; U.S. Court of Appeals, Ninth Circuit and Federal Circuit; U.S. Supreme Court. *Education:* University of Rochester (B.A., 1967); University of Texas School of Law (J.D., with honors, 1969). Order of the Coif. Member, Chancellors. Member, University of Texas Law Review, 1968-1969. *Member:* Los Angeles County and American Bar Associations; State Bar of California. *Email:* jah@riordan.com

**JEFFREY L. DUROCHER,** born Oak Park, Illinois, March 9, 1945; admitted to bar, 1971, California. *Education:* Northwestern University (B.S., 1967); Columbia Law School (J.D., 1970); New York University (LL.M. in Taxation, 1971). Member, Board of Editors, Columbia Law School, Journal of Law and Social Problems, 1969-1970. Lecturer, Golden Gate University Graduate School of Taxation, 1974-1979. *Member:* Los Angeles County and American Bar Associations; State Bar of California. *Email:* jld@riordan.com

**JEFFREY L. GLASSMAN,** born New York, N.Y., April 11, 1947; admitted to bar, 1972, California. *Education:* University of California at Los Angeles (B.A., 1969); Loyola University of Los Angeles (J.D., magna cum laude, 1972). Alpha Sigma Nu. Member, 1970-1972 and Associate Editor, 1971-1972, Loyola University Law Review. Co-Author: "Overcoming the Uncertainty Caused By the Family Partnership Rules for Freezes," The Journal of Taxation, April, 1985; "The Riddle of Taxation on Income Tax Defective Trusts," Los Angeles Lawyer (November, 1995). *Member:* Los Angeles County and American Bar Associations; State Bar of California. *Email:* jlg@riordan.com

**L. ANDREW GIFFORD,** born Dayton, Ohio, April 19, 1946; admitted to bar, 1972, California; 1974, U.S. Court of Military Appeals. *Education:* Miami University (B.S., cum laude, 1968); University of Michigan (J.D., cum laude, 1971). Phi Beta Kappa; Beta Gamma Sigma; Omicron Delta Kappa; Order of the Coif. Member, 1969-1970 and Associate Editor, 1970-1971, University of Michigan Law Review. Author: "Jurisdiction—Atomic Energy—Federal Preemption and State Regulation of Radioactive Air Pollution: Who is the Master of the Atomic Genie?" 68 University of Michigan Law Review 1294, 1970. Lecturer, Continuing Legal Education of the Bar, 1981, 1983, 1985, 1988-1995; Seminar Leader, Thirty-First Tax Institute, University of Southern California; Lecturer, University of Southern California Probate and Trust Conference, 1981, 1985, 1992, 1995. Commissioner: City of Los Angeles Board of Telecommunications, 1994-1995; City of Los Angeles Board of Information Technology, 1995—. *Member:* Los Angeles County Bar Association (Member, Section on Probate and Trust Law, Executive Committee, 1984-1991, 1993-1995; Chair, 1989-1990); State Bar of California. Fellow, American College of Trust and Estate Counsel. [Lt., U.S. Naval Reserve, Judge Advocate General Corps, 1972-1975] *Email:* lag@riordan.com

**ROGER H. LUSTBERG,** born Brookline, Massachusetts, March 25, 1948; admitted to bar, 1973, California. *Education:* Yale University (A.B., magna cum laude, 1970); Harvard University (J.D., cum laude, 1973). Phi Beta Kappa. *Member:* State Bar of California. *Email:* rhl@riordan.com

**MARTIN J. THOMPSON,** born Seattle, Washington, November 11, 1948; admitted to bar, 1973, California; 1981, District of Columbia. *Education:* University of the Pacific; University of California at Davis (A.B., 1970); University of California at Berkeley (J.D., 1973). Phi Beta Kappa; Order of the Coif. Associate Editor, California Law Review, 1972-1973. Author: "Antitrust and the Health Care Provider," Aspen Systems, 1979; "Health Planning and Antitrust Exemptions," 2 Whittier Law Review 649, 1980; "Antitrust Considerations and Defenses in Reorganizing for Multi-Institutional Activities," 26 St. Louis Law Journal 465. Co-Author: CH. 13, ABA Antitrust Law Section, State Antitrust Practice and Statutes (1990). *Member:* Los Angeles County and American (Member, Antitrust Law Section) Bar Associations; State Bar of California; District of Columbia Bar; National Health Lawyers Association (Member, Board of Directors, 1981-1987). (Resident, Orange County Office). *Email:* mjt@riordan.com

**LAWRENCE C. WEEKS,** born Los Angeles, California, December 20, 1951; admitted to bar, 1976, California. *Education:* University of California at Irvine (B.A., 1973); University of California at Los Angeles (J.D., 1976). Order of the Coif. Member, U.C.L.A. Law Review, 1974-1976. *Member:* Los Angeles County Bar Association (Member, Executive Committee, Business and Corporations Law Section, 1992-1995); State Bar of California. (Resident, Westlake Village Office). *Email:* lcw@riordan.com

*(This Listing Continued)*

**RIORDAN & McKINZIE, A PROFESSIONAL LAW CORPORATION, Los Angeles—Continued**

**KENNETH D. KLEIN,** born Philadelphia, Pennsylvania, October 4, 1947; admitted to bar, 1973, New York; 1979, California. *Education:* University of Michigan (B.A., with honors, 1968); Columbia University (J.D., 1973). Assistant District Attorney, New York County, 1973-1977. Assistant Deputy Chief Counsel, U.S. House of Representatives Select Committee on Assassinations, 1977-1979. Trustee, Los Angeles County Law Library. *Member:* Los Angeles County Bar Association; State Bar of California. *Email:* kdk@riordan.com

**THOMAS L. HARNSBERGER,** born Berkeley, California, July 1, 1949; admitted to bar, 1974, California. *Education:* University of California at San Diego (B.A., 1971); University of Michigan (J.D., magna cum laude, 1974). *Member:* State Bar of California; American Bar Association. *Email:* tlh@riordan.com

**RICHARD J. WELCH,** born Kewanee, Illinois, February 2, 1952; admitted to bar, 1977, California. *Education:* Duke University (A.B., magna cum laude, 1974); Stanford University (J.D., 1977). Chairman, Los Angeles Sports and Entertainment Commission. Member: Los Angeles Convention and Visitors Bureau - Executive Committee; Special Advisory Committee to the Mayor of the City of Los Angeles - Fiscal Administration (1993-1994); Board of Advisors of the Entrepreneurial Studies Center - The John E. Anderson Graduate School of Management at UCLA; The Coalition of 100 Los Angeles; Los Angeles Duke University Development Council. *Member:* Los Angeles County Bar Association; State Bar of California. *Email:* rjw@riordan.com

**JANIS B. SALIN,** born Glendale, California, June 12, 1953; admitted to bar, 1979, California. *Education:* University of California at Los Angeles (B.A., summa cum laude, 1976; J.D., 1979). Phi Beta Kappa; Order of the Coif. Member, 1977-1978 and Articles Editor, 1978-1979, U.C.L.A.-Alaska Law Review. *Member:* State Bar of California. *Email:* jbs@riordan.com

**JOHN J. QUINN,** born Rockville Centre, New York, August 26, 1950; admitted to bar, 1976, New York; 1987, California. *Education:* Adelphi University (B.A., 1972); Albany Law School of Union University (J.D., 1975); New York University (LL.M. in Corporation Law, 1982). *Member:* State Bar of California. *PRACTICE AREAS:* Trial Practice; White Collar Criminal Fraud. *Email:* jjq@riordan.com

**ANGELO C. FALCONE,** born Buffalo, New York, February 21, 1951; admitted to bar, 1978, California. *Education:* University of California at Los Angeles (B.A., 1974); Southwestern University (J.D., 1978); New York University (LL.M. in Taxation, 1984). Author: Chapter 12 of *A Practical Guide to the Tax Act of 1984,* entitled "Impact of Tax Laws on Overseas Operations of High Technology Companies," Law & Business, Inc., Harcourt Brace Jovanovich; "United States Federal Income Tax Considerations Applicable to a Mexican Maquiladora Investment After the 1986 Tax Act," Taxes, March, 1987; "California Tax Planning After Adoption of Water's Edge Legislation," The International Business Lawyer, June/July, 1987; "A U.S. Tax Planning Checklist for Foreign Nationals on Assignment in the United States," The Tax Executive, January, 1987; "Structuring U.S. Operations of Foreign Corporations After the Tax Reform Act of 1986," Taxes International, November, 1986. Instructor, Income Taxation of Foreign Related Transactions, UCLA Graduate School of Management, 1983-1991. *Member:* Los Angeles County (Chairman, Foreign Tax Committee, 1984-1985) and American (Member, Committee on Foreign Activities of United States Taxpayers, 1985—) Bar Associations; State Bar of California; International Fiscal Association. *PRACTICE AREAS:* International Business; Tax Law. *Email:* acf@riordan.com

**WILLIAM H. EMER,** born Los Angeles, California, October 30, 1946; admitted to bar, 1972, California. *Education:* University of California at Los Angeles (B.A., 1969); University of California School of Law at Los Angeles (J.D., 1972). Recipient, Charles F. Scott Fellowship. *Member:* Los Angeles County and American (Member, Labor Law Section) Bar Associations; State Bar of California. *SPECIAL AGENCIES:* National Labor Relations Board, Office of Federal Contract Compliance Program, Equal Employment Opportunity Commission, Department of Labor. *PRACTICE AREAS:* Traditional Labor Law; Employment Discrimination; Employment Law; Wrongful Termination. *Email:* whe@riordan.com

**KIRK F. MALDONADO,** born Omaha, Nebraska, March 7, 1950; admitted to bar, 1978, Nebraska; 1982, California. *Education:* Cornell College; University of Nebraska at Omaha (B.A., 1975); Creighton University (J.D., 1978) Georgetown University (M.L.T., 1981). Staff Editor, Creighton Law Review, 1977-1978. Member, Editorial Advisory Board, Benefits Law Journal, 1993—. Member, Committee on Continuing Professional Education, ALI-ABA, 1995—. Author of more than forty articles dealing with executive compensation and employee benefits matters, including Tax Management Portfolio 362, *Securities Laws Aspects of Employee Benefit Plans.* Attorney, Employee Plans and Exempt Organizations Division, Office of Chief Counsel, Internal Revenue Service, 1978-1981. Member: Employee Benefits Committee, Section of Taxation, State Bar of California, Chair-Elect, 1996; Employee Benefits Committee, Section of Taxation, American Bar Association; Western Pension and Benefits Conference, Program Chair, 1994-1996. (Resident, Orange County Office). *Email:* kfm@riordan.com

**JAMES W. LOSS,** born Kenosha, Wisconsin, April 2, 1953; admitted to bar, 1983, California. *Education:* Princeton University (A.B., cum laude, 1976); Yale Law School (J.D., 1980). Law Clerk to the Honorable Malcolm M. Lucas, U.S. District Judge for the Central District of California, 1981-1983. *Member:* State Bar of California. (Resident, Orange County Office). *Email:* jwl@riordan.com

**DANA M. WARREN,** born San Bernardino, California, January 18, 1955; admitted to bar, 1983, California. *Education:* Montana State University (B.S., with highest honors, 1978); Stanford University (J.D., 1981). Phi Kappa Phi. Senior Editor, Stanford Journal of International Law, 1980-1981. Law Clerk to Hon. Procter R. Hug, Jr., U.S. Court of Appeals, Ninth Circuit, 1981-1982. *Member:* State Bar of California. (Resident, Westlake Village Office). *Email:* dmw@riordan.com

**EUGENE G. COWAN,** born Los Angeles, California, October 3, 1955; admitted to bar, 1981, California; 1984, U.S. Tax Court. *Education:* University of California at San Diego (B.A., 1977); Northwestern University (M.A.T., 1978); Boalt Hall School of Law, University of California (J.D., 1981); New York University (LL.M., in Taxation, 1983). Adjunct Professor of Law, Graduate Tax Program, University of San Diego School of Law, 1985-1988. Lecturer, University of California at Los Angeles School of Law, 1989-1990. *Member:* Los Angeles County (Member, Taxation Section) and American (Member, Taxation Section) Bar Associations; State Bar of California. *LANGUAGES:* Spanish. *Email:* egc@riordan.com

**SCOTT R. MILLER,** born Lincoln, Nebraska, October 9, 1958; admitted to bar, 1983, California; registered to practice before U.S. Patent and Trademark Office. *Education:* University of Nebraska (B.S.M.E., with distinction, 1980); University of Southern California (J.D., 1983). Tau Beta Pi; Pi Tau Sigma. Quarterfinalist, 1981-1982 and Editor, 1982-1983, Hale Moot Court Honors Competition, 1981-1982. Co-Author: Note, "An Appraisal of the Court of Appeals for the Federal Circuit," 57 So. Cal. L. Rev. 301, 1984. *Member:* Los Angeles County and American Bar Associations; State Bar of California; American Intellectual Property Law Association. *Email:* srm@riordan.com

**MICHAEL P. WHALEN,** born Detroit, Michigan, December 3, 1954; admitted to bar, 1981, California. *Education:* Princeton University (A.B., cum laude, 1977); University of California at Berkeley (M.A. in Mathematics, 1978); Harvard University (J.D., cum laude, 1981). Author: "Causation and Reliance in Private Actions Under SEC Rule 10b-5," 14 Pacific Law Journal 101, 1982. *Member:* State Bar of California; State Bar of Wisconsin. (Resident, Orange County Office). *LANGUAGES:* German. *Email:* mpw@riordan.com

**CYNTHIA M. DUNNETT,** born Illinois, November 9, 1957; admitted to bar, 1985, California. *Education:* University of California at Santa Cruz (B.A., 1979); Hastings College of the Law, University of California (J.D., 1985). Staff Member, 1983-1984 and Editor, 1984-1985, Hastings Law Journal. *Member:* Los Angeles County Bar Association (Member, Business Law Section); State Bar of California. *Email:* cmd@riordan.com

**AAFTAB P. ESMAIL,** born Nairobi, Kenya, November 16, 1962; admitted to bar, 1986, California. *Education:* University of California at Los Angeles (B.A., 1983); Harvard University (J.D., 1986). Phi Beta Kappa. *Member:* Los Angeles County Bar Association (Member, Real Property Section); State Bar of California. *Email:* ace@riordan.com

**SANDRA J. LEVIN,** born Salem, Massachusetts, March 24, 1963; admitted to bar, 1987, California and U.S. District Court, Central District of California. *Education:* University of California at Berkeley (B.A., high honors, 1984) Phi Beta Kappa; Boalt Hall School of Law, University of California (J.D., 1987). Member, California Law Review, 1985-1987. Senior Editor, High Technology Law Journal, 1986-1987. Chairperson, Boalt Hall Womens' Association, 1985-1986. Founder, Boalt Hall Fund for Diversity. Author: "Examining Restraints on Freedom to Contract as an Approach to Purchaser Dissatisfaction in the Computer Industry," Volume 74, Issue 6, California Law Review, December, 1986. Extern, Hon. William Norris, Ninth Circuit Court of Appeals, Fall, 1986. Member, Culver City Council.

*(This Listing Continued)*

*Member:* Los Angeles County Bar Association; State Bar of California; Women Lawyers Association of Los Angeles; Association Business Trial Lawyers. *Email:* sjl@riordan.com

**LANCE S. BOCARSLY,** born Los Angeles, California, August 12, 1962; admitted to bar, 1988, California. *Education:* University of California at Los Angeles (B.A., cum laude, 1984); University of California, Los Angeles School of Law (J.D., 1987). Governing Committee Member, ABA Forum on Affordable Housing and Community Development Law. Co-Author: "Real Property Tax Exemptions in Affordable Housing Transactions," ABA Journal of Affordable Housing and Community Development Law, Winter 1993. Author: "Scenic Rivers Designation Maintained," UCLA Journal of Environmental Law and Policy, Vol. 4, No. 2, 1985. *Member:* Los Angeles County (Real Property Section) and American (Affordable Housing and Community Development Forum) Bar Associations; State Bar of California. *Email:* lsb@riordan.com

**ELAINE R. LEVIN,** born Chicago, Illinois, June 9, 1957; admitted to bar, 1986, New York; 1992, California. *Education:* Stanford University (A.B., 1979); IIT Chicago-Kent College of Law (J.D., with high honors, 1985). Note and Comment Editor, 1984-1985 and Member, 1983-1985, Chicago-Kent Law Review. Co-Author: "Legislative Intervention: The Assembly's 'Anti-Referral' Bill," Northern California Medicine, 1992; "Self Referral Laws: Understanding the Limits on Health Care Professionals," California Business Law Reporter, 1994. *Member:* Los Angeles County (Member, Healthcare Law Section) and American (Member: Business Law Section; Forum on Health Law) Bar Associations; State Bar of California (Member, Business Law Section). (Resident, Orange County Office). *Email:* erl@riordan.com

**DONALD J. KULA,** born Chicago, Illinois, December 25, 1963; admitted to bar, 1989, California, U.S. Court of Appeals for the Ninth Circuit and U.S. District Court, Central District of California; 1990, U.S. District Court, Northern District of California; 1991, District of Columbia. *Education:* University of Illinois at Chicago (B.A., 1986); University of Michigan (J.D., 1989). Phi Beta Kappa. *Member:* Los Angeles County and American Bar Associations; State Bar of California; District of Columbia Bar. *Email:* djk@riordan.com

**THOMAS M. CLEARY,** born Whittier, California, May 28, 1963; admitted to bar, 1989, California and U.S. District Court, Central District of California. *Education:* University of Notre Dame (B.S., Chemical Engineering, with honors, 1985); University of California, Boalt Hall School of Law (J.D., 1989). Tau Beta Pi. *Member:* State Bar of California. *Email:* tmc@riordan.com

---

**JANINE Y. ARIEY,** born Los Angeles, California, November 28, 1949; admitted to bar, 1980, California. *Education:* University of Southern California; University of California at Los Angeles (B.A., 1972; M.A., 1976); University of California School of Law (J.D., 1980). *Member:* State Bar of California. *PRACTICE AREAS:* Real Estate. *Email:* jya@riordan.com

**JAMES H. SHNELL,** born Los Angeles, California, August 19, 1950; admitted to bar, 1981, California. *Education:* Stanford University (A.B., 1972); Harvard Business School (M.B.A., 1978); University of California at Berkeley (J.D., 1981). Associate Editor, California Law Review, 1980-1981. (Resident, Orange County Office). *PRACTICE AREAS:* Corporate; Mergers and Acquisitions; Financings. *Email:* jhs@riordan.com

**TIMOTHY F. SYLVESTER,** born March 21, 1959; admitted to bar, 1984, California. *Education:* Tufts University (B.A., magna cum laude, 1981); University of California at Los Angeles (J.D., 1984). Editor, UCLA Law Review, 1983-1984. Law Clerk, Honorable Robert J. Kelleher, Senior District Judge, U.S. District Court, Central District of California, 1984-1985. *Member:* State Bar of California. *Email:* tfs@riordan.com

**ROBERT W. STOCKSTILL, JR.,** born Baton Rouge, Louisiana, June 20, 1962; admitted to bar, 1987, Texas and Louisiana; 1989, California. *Education:* Louisiana State University (B.A., 1984; J.D., 1987). Beta Alpha Psi; Beta Gamma Sigma; Phi Eta Sigma. Recipient, Chancellor's Award. Order of the Coif. Member, Louisiana State Law Review, 1985-1987. *Member:* Louisiana State Bar Association; State Bar of Texas; State Bar of California. *Email:* rws@riordan.com

**BART GREENBERG,** born Garden Grove, California, January 14, 1963; admitted to bar, 1989, California. *Education:* University of California at Los Angeles (B.A., magna cum laude, 1986); University of California, Boalt Hall School of Law (J.D., 1989). Phi Beta Kappa. President and Director, Arroyo Maintenance Corporation, 1990—. *Member:* Orange County (Member, Business Law Section) and American (Member, Business Law

*(This Listing Continued)*

Section) Bar Associations; State Bar of California (Member, Business Law Section). (Resident, Orange County Office). *PRACTICE AREAS:* Business and Finance. *Email:* bg@riordan.com

**MISARA C. SHAO,** born Hong Kong; admitted to bar, 1990, California. *Education:* Stanford University (B.A., 1981); University of Southern California (J.D., 1989). Member, Hale Moot Court Honors Program, 1987-1988. Member, University of Southern California Journal of Law and the Environment, 1988-1989. Judicial Extern to the Honorable Robert M. Takasugi, U.S. District Court, Central District of California, 1989. *Member:* Los Angeles County Bar Association; State Bar of California (Member, Litigation and Real Property Sections). *PRACTICE AREAS:* Litigation. *Email:* mcs@riordan.com

**GINA M. CALVELLI,** born Mineola, New York, October 4, 1956; admitted to bar, 1991, California. *Education:* Earlham College (B.A., 1978); Stanford Law School (J.D., 1991). Member, International Alliance of Theatrical Stage Employees, 1983—. Member: Bay Area Lawyers for Individual Freedom, 1989-1992; Lawyers for Human Rights, 1993—. *Member:* Los Angeles County (Member, Appellate Courts Committee) and American (Member, Litigation Section, Committee on Appellate Practice) Bar Associations; State Bar of California (Member, Litigation Section). *Email:* gmc@riordan.com

**BRUCE C. GEYER,** born Wilkinsburg, Pennsylvania, June 24, 1962; admitted to bar, 1991, California. *Education:* University of Pittsburgh (B.S., magna cum laude, 1984); University of Southern California (J.D., 1991). *Member:* State Bar of California. *PRACTICE AREAS:* Real Estate. *Email:* bcg@riordan.com

**BRENDA L. WHITE,** born Kansas City, Missouri, April 24, 1965; admitted to bar, 1990, Missouri; 1991, Kansas, U.S. District Court, District of Kansas and U.S. Court of Appeals, Tenth Circuit; 1993, California. *Education:* University of Kansas (B.A., with distinction, 1987); Harvard Law School (J.D., cum laude, 1990). Phi Beta Kappa; Phi Kappa Phi. Law Clerk to The Honorable G. T. Van Bebber, U.S. District Court, District of Kansas, 1990-1992. *Member:* The Missouri Bar; Kansas Bar Association; State Bar of California.

**ROBERT N. DURAN,** born Los Angeles, California, January 18, 1956; admitted to bar, 1987, California, U.S. District Court, Central and Northern Districts of California and U.S. Tax Court. *Education:* University of Utah; California State University at Fullerton (B.A., 1983); Santa Clara University (J.D., 1987); New York University (LL.M., 1990). Associate Editor, Santa Clara Computer & High Technology Law Journal. *Member:* Los Angeles County Bar Association; State Bar of California (Member, Tax Law Section); Mexican-American Bar Association. *PRACTICE AREAS:* International Business and Tax Planning; Corporation; Limited Liability Company; Partnership Taxation. *Email:* rnd@riordan.com

**KAREN C. GOODIN,** born Los Angeles, California, February 27, 1963; admitted to bar, 1991, California. *Education:* University of Southern California (A.B., summa cum laude, 1985); University of Pennsylvania (M.A., 1987); University of California, Boalt Hall School of Law (J.D., 1991). Phi Beta Kappa. Member, International Tax & Business Lawyer, 1989-1990. *Member:* State Bar of California. (Resident, Orange County Office). *PRACTICE AREAS:* General Corporate; Securities. *Email:* kcg@riordan.com

**REYNOLDS T. CAFFERATA,** born San Francisco, California, May 25, 1966; admitted to bar, 1992, California; 1994, Nevada. *Education:* George Washington University (B.A., summa cum laude, 1989); University of Southern California (J.D., 1992). Phi Beta Kappa. Order of the Coif. Recipient, American Jurisprudence Award, Constitutional Law II. Member, Southern California Law Review, 1991. Editor, Southern California Interdisciplinary Journal, 1992. Member, Southern California Planned Giving Roundtable, 1995—. Director, Nevada Planned Giving Roundtable, 1995—. Author: "A Proposal for an Empirical Interpretation of Canon 5," 65 S. Cal. L. Rev. 1939 (1992); "Transfers of Family Real Estate," 45 Major Tax Planning ¶2000 (1993). Co-Author: "Equal Treatment of Jurors is Everyone's Responsibility," Los Angeles Daily Journal and San Francisco Daily Journal, April 29, 1993, page 7; "Challenges and Objections Need Intelligent Preparation," Los Angeles Daily Journal and San Francisco Daily Journal, April 30, 1993, page 9. Author: "Home Office Deductions after *Soliman*," 1 The Tax Reporter 7 (May 1993); "Cobra Notice Requirements," 7 Employee Benefit News 39 (October 39); "Charitable Gifts of Retirement Plan Assets," *Exempt Organization Tax Review* (June, 1994), co-author David Wheeler Newman; "New Charitable Deduction Reporting Requirements," *Los Angeles Lawyer* (October, 1994); "Coordinating Charitable Gifts of Retirement Plan Assets with Lifetime Distribution Requirements," *Exempt Organization Tax Review* (December, 1994), co-author David Wheeler Newman; "Putting More Flexibility Into Net Income Limitation

*(This Listing Continued)*

**RIORDAN & McKINZIE,** A PROFESSIONAL LAW CORPORATION, Los Angeles—Continued

on Charitable Remainder Unitrusts," *Journal of Taxation of Exempt Organizations* (July/Aug. 1995); "The Riddle of Taxation of Income Tax Defective Trusts," Los Angeles Lawyer (November 1995), co-author Jeffrey L. Glassman. *Member:* Los Angeles County Bar Association (Exempt Organizations Committee of Tax Section, Secretary, 1995-1996, Vice Chair, 1996—); State Bar of California (Chair, Westside Young Tax Lawyers Committee, 1992-1994, Member, Editorial Board, Los Angeles Lawyer, 1994-1996). *PRACTICE AREAS:* Estate Planning; Planned Charitable Giving; Probate Litigation. *Email:* rtc@riordan.com

**ERIC J. SMITH,** born Seattle, Washington, January 26, 1962; admitted to bar, 1991, California; 1992, Utah. *Education:* Evergreen State College (B.A., 1985); University of California, Davis (J.D., 1991); University of Florida College of Law (LL.M. Taxation, 1993). Editor, University of Florida Tax Review, 1993. Recipient: American Jurisprudence Award in International Business Transactions. *Member:* Los Angeles County and American Bar Associations; State Bar of California; Utah State Bar. *LANGUAGES:* Spanish. *PRACTICE AREAS:* International and Domestic Corporate Law and Taxation. *Email:* ejs@riordan.com

**PAMELA SMITH KELLEY,** born Westminster, California, July 28, 1967; admitted to bar, 1992, California and U.S. District Court, Central District of California. *Education:* University of California at Irvine (B.A., summa cum laude, 1989) Phi Beta Kappa; Yale University (J.D., 1992). Author: "Regulating Confidentiality of Surrogacy Records: Lesson From The Adoption Experience," 31 University of Louisville Journal of Family Law 65, 1992. *Member:* State Bar of California. *PRACTICE AREAS:* Litigation. *Email:* psk@riordan.com

**THOMAS A. WALDMAN,** born Los Angeles, California, November 15, 1965; admitted to bar, 1993, California. *Education:* Harvard University (B.A., magna cum laude, 1987); University of California School of Law at Los Angeles (J.D., 1992). Order of the Coif. Editor, UCLA Law Review. Law Clerk to The Hon. David R. Thompson, U.S. Court of Appeals, Ninth Circuit, 1992-1993. *Member:* State Bar of California. *PRACTICE AREAS:* Corporate. *Email:* taw@riordan.com

**DAVID M. JANET,** born Baltimore, Maryland, August 16, 1966; admitted to bar, 1993, Pennsylvania; 1994, District of Columbia; 1996, California. *Education:* College of William & Mary (B.A., summa cum laude, 1989); Duke University School of Law (J.D., with high honors, 1992). Phi Beta Kappa. *Member:* Los Angeles County Bar Association; District of Columbia Bar; State Bar of California. *PRACTICE AREAS:* Corporate Transactional; Securities. *Email:* dmj@riordan.com

**SUNG HUI KIM,** born Seoul, South Korea, June 8, 1968; admitted to bar, 1993, California; 1994, District of Columbia. *Education:* Emory University (B.A., summa cum laude, 1988; M.A., summa cum laude, 1988); Harvard Law School (J.D., cum laude, 1992). Phi Beta Kappa. *Member:* State Bar of California; District of Columbia Bar. *LANGUAGES:* German and Korean. *PRACTICE AREAS:* General Corporate; Securities. *Email:* shk@riordan.com

**DIANE M. LAMBILLOTTE,** born Toledo, Ohio, March 29, 1955; admitted to bar, 1993, California; 1994, U.S. District Court, Central District of California and U.S. Court of Appeals, Ninth Circuit. *Education:* California State Polytechnic University, Pomona (B.A., magna cum laude, 1980); Loyola Law School (J.D., 1993). Member, 1991-1992 and Production Editor, 1992-1993, Entertainment Law Journal. *Member:* State Bar of California. *Email:* dml@riordan.com

**ERIC REED HATTLER,** born Philadelphia, Pennsylvania, May 14, 1965; admitted to bar, 1993, California. *Education:* Amherst College (B.A., magna cum laude, 1987); University of Chicago (M.B.A., 1993; J.D., 1993). Phi Beta Kappa. *Member:* State Bar of California. *Email:* erh@riordan.com

**JONATHAN GLUCK,** born Los Angeles, California, September 25, 1965; admitted to bar, 1993, California, U.S. District Court, Central District of California and U.S. Court of Appeals, Ninth Circuit. *Education:* Rabbinical College of America (B.A., 1987); University of Southern California (J.D., 1993). Recipient, American Jurisprudence Awards: Contracts; Federal Procedure/Jurisprudence. Staff Member, 1991-1992 and Articles Editor, 1992-1993, Southern California Law Review. *Member:* State Bar of California. *LANGUAGES:* Spanish, Hebrew, German. *PRACTICE AREAS:* Litigation. *Email:* jg@riordan.com

**JACQUELINE A. COOKERLY,** born Los Angeles, California, March 25, 1966; admitted to bar, 1993, California. *Education:* University of California at Santa Barbara (B.A., 1988); University of California School of Law (J.D., summa cum laude, 1993). Phi Alpha Delta. Moot Court Honors; American Jurisprudence Awards Recipient. Member, Woman's Law Journal, 1992-1993. *Member:* State Bar of California. *Email:* jac@riordan.com

**KYLE B. ARNDT,** born January 12, 1967; admitted to bar, 1994, California. *Education:* University of California at Santa Cruz (B.A., 1989); UCLA Graduate School of Architecture and Urban Planning (M.A., 1991); UCLA School of Law (J.D., 1994). Editor-in-Chief, UCLA Law Review. *Member:* State Bar of California. *Email:* kba@riordan.com

**DOUGLAS C. CARLETON,** born Oak Park, Illinois, October 29, 1963; admitted to bar, 1994, California. *Education:* University of Virginia (B.A., 1985); University of Southern California (J.D., 1994). Associate Editor and Editor, University of Southern California Law Review, 1992-1994. *Member:* State Bar of California. *Email:* dcc@riordan.com

**GRACE C. LIANG,** born Los Angeles, California, March 14, 1968; admitted to bar, 1994, California. *Education:* University of California at Los Angeles (B.A., 1990); Columbia University School of Law (J.D., 1994). *Member:* State Bar of California. *Email:* gcl@riordan.com

**MICHAEL G. McKINNON,** born Newport Beach, California, May 27, 1968; admitted to bar, 1994, California. *Education:* Cornell University (B.S., 1990); Pepperdine University (J.D., cum laude, 1994). *Member:* State Bar of California; National Health Lawyers Association. (Resident, Orange County Office). *LANGUAGES:* Spanish. *PRACTICE AREAS:* Corporate; Securities. *Email:* mgmck@riordan.com

**RYAN S. HONG,** born Seoul, South Korea, October 19, 1968; admitted to bar, 1994, California. *Education:* University of California at Irvine (B.S., B.A., 1991); Columbia Law School (J.D., 1994). Harlan Fiske Stone Scholar. *Member:* State Bar of California. *PRACTICE AREAS:* Corporate. *Email:* rsh@riordan.com

**AMY E. GREENBERG,** born Norwalk, Connecticut, February 16, 1968; admitted to bar, 1994, California. *Education:* University of Michigan (B.A., 1990); Loyola Law School (J.D., 1994). *Member:* Los Angeles County (Member, Labor and Employment Section) and American Bar Associations; State Bar of California; Women Lawyers of Los Angeles. *PRACTICE AREAS:* Labor and Employment. *Email:* aeg@riordan.com

**BARBARA A. KRIEG,** born Jersey City, New Jersey, June 23, 1958; admitted to bar, 1995, California. *Education:* University of Notre Dame (B.A., 1979); University of California School of Law at Los Angeles (J.D., 1995). Recipient, American Jurisprudence Award in Real Property. *Member:* State Bar of California. *PRACTICE AREAS:* Litigation. *Email:* bak@riordan.com

**RONN S. DAVIDS,** born Cincinnati, Ohio, February 10, 1965; admitted to bar, 1995, California. *Education:* Tufts University (B.A., 1987); Hebrew Union College (M.A.H.L. and Rabbinic Ordination, 1992); Columbia University (J.D., 1995). *Member:* State Bar of California. *LANGUAGES:* Hebrew. *Email:* rsd@riordan.com

**JEANNE MILLER-ROMERO,** born San Luis Obispo, California, June 7, 1965; admitted to bar, 1995, California. *Education:* University of California at Los Angeles (B.A., magna cum laude, 1987); University of California School of Law, Davis (J.D., 1995). Phi Beta Kappa; Phi Delta Phi; Order of the Coif. Recipient, American Jurisprudence Award, Legal Writing, Labor Law. *Member:* Orange County Bar Association; State Bar of California. (Resident, Orange County Office). *PRACTICE AREAS:* Corporate Securities. *Email:* jm-r@riordan.com

**ASHLEY S. NEWSOM,** born Dallas, Texas, June 16, 1970; admitted to bar, 1995, California. *Education:* University of California, Santa Barbara (B.A., with high honors, 1992); University of California School of Law, Los Angeles (J.D., 1995). Phi Beta Kappa. Order of the Coif. Member, UCLA Law Review. Law Clerk to Hon. Emilio M. Garza, Court of Appeals for the Fifth Circuit, 1995-1996. *Member:* State Bar of California. *PRACTICE AREAS:* Corporate. *Email:* asn@riordan.com

**KRISTI L. COBB,** born Tyler, Texas, July 21, 1968; admitted to bar, 1996, California. *Education:* Duke University (A.B., 1990); University of California School of Law, Los Angeles (J.D., 1995). Recipient, American Jurisprudence Award in Community Property. Member and Editor, UCLA Women's Law Journal. Law Clerk to the Honorable William J. Rea, U.S. District Court, Los Angeles, California, 1995-1996. *Member:* State Bar of California. *LANGUAGES:* Japanese. *PRACTICE AREAS:* Labor and Employment Litigation. *Email:* klc@riordan.com

*(This Listing Continued)*

**KAREN A. BERK,** born San Francisco, California, November 15, 1969; (admission pending). *Education:* Stanford University (A.B., with honors, 1991); University of California School of Law, Los Angeles (J.D., 1995). Member, UCLA Law Review. *Email:* kab@riordan.com

**KARL H. CHRISTIANSON,** born Royal Oak, Michigan, April 5, 1964; (admission pending). *Education:* University of Michigan (B.A., with honors, 1986); University of California, Hastings College of the Law (J.D., 1996). Member, Hastings Law Journal. Primary Associate Antilles Editor, Hastings Law Review. Extern to Honorable Judge William W. Schwarzer, Northern District of California. Member, Bay Area Lawyers for Individual Freedom (BALIFF). *Email:* khc@riordan.com

*OF COUNSEL*

**THOMAS L. CAPS,** born Evanston, Illinois, September 15, 1926; admitted to bar, 1955, California. *Education:* University of California at Los Angeles (B.S., 1951; LL.B., 1954). Phi Delta Phi. *Member:* Los Angeles County and American Bar Associations; State Bar of California. *Email:* tlc@riordan.com

**JOSEPH A. CARBONE,** born Providence, Rhode Island, October 5, 1924; admitted to bar, 1962, California. *Education:* Providence College (B.S., 1949); University of Southern California (LL.B., 1961). Order of the Coif; Phi Alpha Delta. Member, Board of Editors, Southern California Law Review, 1959-1960. *Member:* Los Angeles County and American Bar Associations; State Bar of California. *Email:* jac@riordan.com

**PATRICK C. HADEN,** born Westbury, New York, January 23, 1953; admitted to bar, 1983, California. *Education:* University of Southern California (B.A., 1975); Oxford University, Oxford England (B.A., 1978); Loyola Law School (J.D., 1982). Phi Beta Kappa. Recipient, Rhodes Scholarship. *Member:* State Bar of California. *Email:* pah@riordan.com

REFERENCE: Citibank, 333 S. Grand Avenue, Los Angeles, Calif.

---

## *CLAY ROBBINS, III*

700 SOUTH FLOWER STREET, SUITE 500
**LOS ANGELES, CALIFORNIA 90017**
Telephone: 310-553-6630
Fax: 310-785-9143

*General Civil Litigation.*

**CLAY ROBBINS, III,** born Los Angeles, California, February 4, 1955; admitted to bar, 1981, California. *Education:* University of California at Los Angeles (B.A., 1978); Loyola University (J.D., 1981). Psi Chi. *Member:* Los Angeles County and American Bar Associations; State Bar of California; Defense Research Institute; Association of Southern California Defense Counsel; Ninth Circuit Historical Society; United States Historical Society. (Also of Counsel to Fish, Falkenhainer & Downer, Pasadena). *PRACTICE AREAS:* Civil Litigation; Wrongful Discharge; Governmental Tort Liability; Premises Liability; Trademark Infringement; Corporate and Business Litigation; Unfair Competition; Public Utility Liability; Products Liability; Insurance Coverage Disputes; Civil Rights.

---

## *ROBBINS, BERLINER & CARSON*

FIFTH FLOOR, FIGUEROA PLAZA
201 NORTH FIGUEROA STREET
**LOS ANGELES, CALIFORNIA 90012-2628**
Telephone: 213-977-1001
Telecopier: 213-977-1003

*Patent, Trademark, Copyright and Unfair Competition Law. Trial and Appellate Practice in all Federal and State Courts.*

FIRM PROFILE: *Located in central Los Angeles, the Firm is active in all aspects of intellectual property law with special emphasis on litigation, transactional, and international matters. Dating back to 1956, the Firm has a history of serving clients effectively with many outstanding accomplishments. Members have actively participated in professional activities, both of the general bar and the specialty of the Firm.*

*MEMBERS OF FIRM*

**BILLY A. ROBBINS,** born Hot Springs, Arkansas, October 18, 1926; admitted to bar, 1958, California and U.S. Supreme Court; registered to practice before U.S. Patent and Trademark Office. *Education:* University of Arkansas (B.S.E.E., 1951); University of Southern California (J.D., 1957). Phi Delta Phi; Blue Key. Member, Southern California Law Review, 1956-1957. Author: "Patents-Patentability-Anticipation-Meaning" of "Known" as used in 35, U.S.C. Section, 102, Volume 30, #2, Southern California Law Review, 1957; "What Every Engineer Should Know About Patents," Los Angeles Section, IRE Bulletin, December, 1959 and January, 1960; "Educational Institutions and the New Copyright Act," Ventura Community College, 1978. Co-Author: "The New Copyright Act," Los Angeles Lawyer, July, 1978; "Protecting Trade Secrets 1985," Practising Law Institute; "Is It Time For Trade Sanctions Against China," Pacific Economic Review, Fall 1994. Adjunct Professor, Southwestern University School of Law, 1972-1990. Elected to College of Fellows, Institute for Advancement of Engineering, 1972—. *Member:* Los Angeles County and American Bar Associations; The State Bar of California; Lawyers Club of Los Angeles; Los Angeles Patent Law Association (Member, Board of Directors, 1979-1981); Asia Pacific Lawyers Association; Institute of Electrical and Electronic Engineers. *PRACTICE AREAS:* Patent Law; Trademark Law; Copyright Law; Trade Secret Law; Unfair Competition Law; Technology Licensing and Transfer Law; International and Domestic Patent and Trademark Licensing.

**ROBERT BERLINER,** born New York, N.Y., August 16, 1935; admitted to bar, 1962, Michigan; 1967, California. *Education:* College of the City of New York (B.S., 1956); DePaul University and Detroit College of Law (J.D., 1961). Co-Author: "The New Copyright Act," Los Angeles Lawyer, July, 1978. Lecturer, Patent and Franchise Law, University of California, 1968—. Author: "GATT's Effect on Patents," Orange County Business Journal, June 1995; "Provisional Patent Application Protects Technology Abroad," Metropolitan News, August 1995. Panelist on "The Futurist Conference of Biotechnology and Biomedical Developments," Irvine, California, June 1995. Elected to College of Fellows, Institute for Advancement of Engineering, 1972—. Adjunct Professor, Southwestern University School of Law, 1979-1982. Judge Pro Tem, Municipal Court, 1980—. *Member:* Los Angeles County (Delegate, Conference of Delegates, 1982—) and American (Member, Patent, Trademark and Copyright Law Section; Chair, Patent Expert Subcommittee, 1994—) Bar Associations; The State Bar of California; American Intellectual Property Law Association; American Chemical Society. *PRACTICE AREAS:* Patents Law; Copyright Law; Trademark Law; Federal Litigation; Licensing Law.

**JOHN CARSON,** born Wilmington, North Carolina, May 9, 1942; admitted to bar, 1968, California. *Education:* University of Santa Clara (B.S., 1964); Hastings College of Law, University of California (J.D., 1967). Governor, Hastings College of Law Alumni Association, 1972-1973. Co-author: "The New Copyright Act," Los Angeles Lawyer, July, 1978; "Misappropriation Blues," Los Angeles Lawyer, April, 1985; "Don't Tread on Me," Los Angeles Lawyer, July, 1986; "The Counterfeiter's 'Waterloo' ," The Merchandising Reporter, November, 1984; "California's Anti-Counterfeiting Statute," Los Angeles Lawyer, February, 1984; "Anti-Counterfeiting Law," Civil-Business and Professions Code Sections 14340-14342, Criminal-Penal Code Section 350; "Trade Secret Act," Civil Code Section 3426 et seq.; Code of Civil Procedure Section 2036.5 et seq.; "Trademark Use on Collateral Products," Business and Professions Code Section 14330; "Employee Rights in Inventions," Labor Code Section 2870; "Prior Trademark Use," Business and Professions Code Section 14342. Professor, Loyola University of Los Angeles Law School, 1978-1982. Governor, Patent Law Association of Los Angeles, 1975-1977. Judge Pro Tem, Municipal and Superior Courts, 1980—. Director, 1983-1996, , President, 1990, Los Angeles County Bar Foundation. *Member:* Los Angeles County (President, 1994-1995; Trustee, 1976-1978, 1981-1983; Chair: Trial Attorney's Project, 1977-1980; Jails Committee, 1974-1977; Ethics Committee, 1978—; Committee on Evaluation of Professional Standards, 1981-1986, 1989—; Coordinating Committee 1976-1980; Delegation to State Bar Conference, 1979; Planning Chair, Advisory Committee, 1983-1985; Committee on the State Bar, 1985-1987; Legislation Committee, 1989-1994; Delegate, Conference of Delegates, 1971—) and American (Member, Sections on: Patent, Trademark and Copyright Law; International Law; Litigation) Bar Associations; State Bar of California (Member, Executive Committee, 1981-1984; Chair, Committee on Specialization, 1982-1983; Member, State Bar Board of Legal Specialization, 1979-1982); American Intellectual Property Law Association; Los Angeles Intellectual Property Law Association (Chair, Ethics Committee, 1973-1975; Governor, 1975-1977). *PRACTICE AREAS:* Patent Law; Trademark Law; Copyright Law; Trade Secret Law; Unfair Competition Law.

**MICHAEL S. ELKIND,** born Milwaukee, Wisconsin, July 30, 1948; admitted to bar, 1974, California; registered to practice before U.S. Patent and Trademark Office. *Education:* University of California at Berkeley (B.S., in Electrical Engineering and Computer Science, with honors, 1970); Massachusetts Institute of Technology (M.S.E.E., 1971); Harvard Law School (J.D., 1974). Tau Beta Pi; Eta Kappa Nu; Phi Beta Kappa. *Member:*

*(This Listing Continued)*

## ROBBINS, BERLINER & CARSON, Los Angeles—Continued

Los Angeles County (Member, Barristers Executive Committee, 1982-1983; Delegate Conference of Delegates, 1991—) and American (Member, Patent, Trademark and Copyright Law Section) Bar Associations; State Bar of California; Los Angeles Intellectual Property Law Association. *PRACTICE AREAS:* Patent Law; Trademark Law; Copyright Law; Trade Secret Law; Unfair Competition Law.

**LEONARD D. MESSINGER,** born Philadelphia, Pennsylvania, February 21, 1953; admitted to bar, 1979, California and U.S. Court of Appeals, Ninth Circuit; U.S. District Court, Central, Northern, Southern and Eastern Districts of California. *Education:* Temple University (B.A., cum laude, 1974); Southwestern University (J.D., 1978). Member, Southwestern University Law Review, 1977-1978. *Member:* Los Angeles County and American (Member, Patent, Trademark and Copyright Law and Litigation Sections) Bar Associations; State Bar of California (Member, Intellectual Property Section); Los Angeles Intellectual Property Law Association; Lawyers Club of Los Angeles County. *REPORTED CASES:* Dolco Packaging Corp. v. Creative Industries, Inc. 1 USPQ 2d 1538 (C.D.CA. 1986) Gassaway v. Business Machine Security, 9 USPQ 2d 1572 (C.D.CA. 1988). *PRACTICE AREAS:* Trademark Law; Copyright Law; Transactions Law; Litigation; Unfair Competition Law; Trade Secret Law.

**JOHN M. MAY,** born Farnborough, England, November 26, 1941; admitted to bar, 1966, California; 1973, U.S. Supreme Court; registered to practice before U.S. Patent and Trademark Office. *Education:* California Institute of Technology (B.S., 1963); University of California at Los Angeles (LL.B., 1966). *Member:* The State Bar of California; Computer Law Association; Los Angeles Intellectual Property Law Association. *LANGUAGES:* French, German, Russian (reading only). *PRACTICE AREAS:* Patents; Trademarks; Copyrights; Licensing.

**CLARK D. GROSS,** born Glendale, California, November 25, 1952; admitted to bar, 1987, California; 1988, U.S. District Court, Southern, Central, Eastern and Northern Districts of California and U.S. Court of Appeals, Ninth and Federal Circuits. *Education:* University of California at Irvine; University of California at Berkeley; Whittier College (J.D., summa cum laude, 1987) Valedictorian. Phi Alpha Delta. Member, Whittier Law Review, 1985-1986. Director, Bridging the Gap Program for New Attorneys, 1992—. Member, Board of Directors, Whittier Alumni Association, 1994; Whittier College "Alumni of the Year", 1993. *Member:* Los Angeles County and American Bar Associations; State Bar of California (Member, Intellectual Property Section); Lawyers Club of Los Angeles County (Member, Board of Governors and President-Elect, 1995). *PRACTICE AREAS:* Patent, Trademark and Copyright Litigation.

### ASSOCIATES

**YING-KIT LAU,** born Hong Kong, March 20, 1953; admitted to bar, 1986, New Jersey; 1987, New York; 1990, California, U.S. District Court for the Central District of California and U.S. Court of Appeals, Ninth Circuit; registered to practice before U.S. Patent and Trademark Office. *Education:* University of Wisconsin (B.S., cum laude, 1974; Ph.D., 1979); Columbia University (J.D., 1986). Member, Columbia Law School Alumni Association, 1986—. *Member:* Los Angeles County, New York County, New York State, New Jersey State, California State and American Bar Associations; Southern California Chinese Lawyers Association; American Chemical Society. *LANGUAGES:* Chinese (Mandarin and Cantonese). *PRACTICE AREAS:* International Technology Transfers Law; Pharmaceutical and Chemical Technology Law; Business Planning Law; Litigation in the Peoples' Republic of China.

**HORACIO A. FARACH,** born Buenos Aires, Argentina, June 18, 1955; admitted to bar, 1989, Texas; 1990, U.S. Court of Appeals, Fifth and Federal Circuits and U.S. District Court, Southern District of Texas; 1991, District of Columbia; 1993, California. *Education:* University of South Carolina (B.S., Biology, 1978); Medical College of Virginia (Ph.D., Biochemistry, including Interference Practice, 1983); South Texas College of Law (J.D., 1989). Phi Alpha Delta. Adjunct Associate Professor of Law, Southwestern University School of Law, 1993—. *Member:* Houston, Los Angeles County and American Bar Associations; State Bar of California; American Intellectual Property Law Association. *LANGUAGES:* Spanish. *PRACTICE AREAS:* Patent Law (Biotechnology); Trademark Law; Copyright Law; Federal Litigation.

**SHARON WONG,** born Los Angeles, California, January 19, 1964; admitted to bar, 1992, California; registered to practice before U.S. Patent and Trademark Office. *Education:* University of California at Los Angeles (B.S., Electrical Engineering, 1986); Loyola Law School (J.D., 1992). Phi Delta Phi. *Member:* State Bar of California; Los Angeles County and American Bar Associations; Southern California Chinese Lawyers Association; Women Lawyers Association of Los Angeles. *LANGUAGES:* Chinese (Cantonese). *PRACTICE AREAS:* Patent Law; Trademark Law; Copyright Law; Unfair Competition Law.

**DEBORAH M. NESSET,** born Chicago, Illinois, October 3, 1951; admitted to bar, 1979, California. *Education:* California State University at Northridge (B.A., 1974); Southwestern University School of Law (J.D., 1978). Recipient, American Jurisprudence Awards in Contracts, 1975, Insurance Law, 1976 and Federal Estate Gift Tax, 1977. Author: "The Delaware Controversy - The Legal Debate," Delaware Journal of Corporate Law, 1979. *Member:* State Bar of California. *PRACTICE AREAS:* Entertainment; Commercial; Business Litigation.

**PETE A. SMITS,** born Detroit, Michigan, August 20, 1961; admitted to bar, 1990, California; 1991, U.S. District Court, Central District of California; 1992, U.S. District Court, Eastern District of California; 1993, U.S. District Court, Northern and Southern Districts of California; registered to practice before U.S. Patent and Trademark Office. *Education:* Michigan State University (B.S.E.E., 1983); University of Dallas (M.B.A., 1986); University of Texas (J.D., 1990). Sigma Iota Epsilon. *Member:* State Bar of California; American Bar Association. *LANGUAGES:* Latvian and Spanish. *PRACTICE AREAS:* Litigation; Trademark Law; Copyright Law; Patent Law; Intellectual Property.

**WEAN KHING WONG,** born Pasir Mas, Kelantan, Malaysia, March 29, 1960; admitted to bar, 1987, California and U.S. District Court, Central District of California; registered to practice before U.S. Patent and Trademark Office. *Education:* Massachusetts Institute of Technology (B.S., 1984); Southwestern University School of Law (J.D., 1987). Author: "Protecting American Software in Japan," Computer Law Journal, Vol. VIII, No. 2, Spring 1988. *Member:* Los Angeles County Bar Association; State Bar of California; American Intellectual Property Law Association. *LANGUAGES:* Mandarin, Cantonese and Malay. *PRACTICE AREAS:* Patent Law; Trademark Law; Copyright Law.

**LISA N. PARTAIN,** born Denver, Colorado, August 10, 1967; admitted to bar, 1995, California. *Education:* Westmont College (B.A., magna cum laude, 1989); Southwestern University School of Law (J.D., summa cum laude, 1995). Writer and Oralist, Moot Court Honors Program; Semifinalist, Pace Environmental Moot Court Competition. Recipient, American Jurisprudence Awards for Excellence in Legal Research & Writing, Property, Remedies, Bankruptcy, and Real Estate Sales Transaction; Excellent Achievement Awards in Computer Law and Employment Law; Corpus Juris Secundum Award in Property. Managing Editor, Southwestern Law Review. Judicial Extern for U.S. District Judge Stephen V. Wilson. Author: "Better Late Than Never: The Role of After-Acquired Evidence in Employment Discrimination Claims," California Labor and Employment Law Quarterly, Summer, 1995. *Member:* Los Angeles County and American Bar Associations; State Bar of California (Member, Intellectual Property Section). *PRACTICE AREAS:* Litigation; Patent, Trademark and Copyright.

### OF COUNSEL

**JOHN P. SPITALS,** born Newark, New Jersey, June 21, 1953; admitted to bar, 1980, New York; 1988, California; registered to practice before U.S. Patent and Trademark Office. *Education:* Brown University (Sc.B., 1975); Yale University (M.S., 1977); New York Law School (J.D., magna cum laude, 1980). Author: "Intellectual Property Decisions of the European Court of Justice," 1 N.Y.J. Int'l & Comp. L. 58, 1979; "The UNCTAD Report on the Role of Trademarks in Developing Countries; An Analysis," 3 N.Y.J. Int'l & Comp. L. 369, 1981. *Member:* American Bar Association; State Bar of California. *LANGUAGES:* French, German, Italian, Spanish. *PRACTICE AREAS:* Patent Prosecution Law (Biological and Chemical).

---

## *ROBIE & MATTHAI*

*A PROFESSIONAL CORPORATION*

Established in 1987

BILTMORE TOWER
500 SOUTH GRAND, SUITE 1500
**LOS ANGELES, CALIFORNIA 90071**
Telephone: 213-624-3062
Fax: 213-624-2563

*Products Liability, Insurance and Bad Faith Litigation, Legal Malpractice Defense, General Civil Litigation. Appellate Litigation.*

(This Listing Continued)

## PROFESSIONAL BIOGRAPHIES

### CALIFORNIA—LOS ANGELES

*FIRM PROFILE: Robie & Matthai emphasizes the handling of complex or "problem" cases. The firm offers aggressive handling of these matters, both at the trial court and appellate levels.*

*Although the firm expects to continue to expand on a limited basis, we are determined to remain a small firm, able to provide personalized, efficient and economical handling of litigated matters.*

**JAMES R. ROBIE,** born Los Angeles, California, December 10, 1949; admitted to bar, 1975, California; U.S. District Court, Southern, Central, Eastern and Northern Districts of California and U.S. Court of Appeals, Ninth and Eighth Circuits; U.S. Supreme Court. *Education:* Claremont Men's College (B.A., cum laude, 1972); Loyola University of Los Angeles (J.D., 1975). Phi Alpha Delta (Marshal, 1973-1974; Chief Justice, 1974-1975). Member: International Law Society; St. Thomas More Law Honor Society. Member, Board of Governors, Loyola University School of Law, 1987-1989. Co-Author: "Business Interruption and Indirect Loss," Insuring Real Property, Matthew Bender, 1989. Panelist, "Hot Issues In Insurance Law," Orange County Bar Association, April, 1995. Speaker: "Bad Faith and Punitive Damages In Insurance Claims," American Conference Institute Seminar, April, 1995; "Bad Faith Claims and Punitive Damages," American Conference Institute Seminar, March 1996. Panelist, "Insurance Litigation Update," Orange County Bar Association, April 1996. Member, Panel of Arbitrators, Los Angeles Superior Court, 1994—. *Member:* Los Angeles County (Member, Executive Committee, Law Office Management Section, 1984-1986) and American Bar Associations; State Bar of California; Association of Southern California Defense Counsel (Annual Program Chairman, 1984; Member, Board of Directors, 1985-1986). *REPORTED CASES:* Allegro v. Superior Court; Austero v. National Casualty Co.; Omaha Paper Stock v. Harbor Ins. Co.; Prudential LMI v. Superior Court; von der Leith v. State Farm; Federal Ins. Co. v. Public Service Co. of Colorado; Pamela W. v. Milsom; Winans v. State Farm; Almon v. State Farm; Hung v. Wang; Orr v. Byers; Smith v. Superior Court. *PRACTICE AREAS:* Insurance Bad Faith; Legal Malpractice.

**EDITH R. MATTHAI,** born Taft, California, September 20, 1950; admitted to bar, 1975, California, U.S. District Court, Northern, Southern, Eastern and Central Districts of California, U.S. Court of Appeals, 9th Circuit and U.S. Tax Court; U.S. Supreme Court. *Education:* University of California at Santa Barbara (B.A., cum laude, 1971); Hastings College of Law, University of California (J.D., 1975). Articles Editor, Hastings Constitutional Law Quarterly, 1973-1975. Faculty Member, Hastings College of Advocacy, 1983—; Member, Advisory Board, 1991—. Co-Chairman Business Litigation College, 1992. Panelist: Rutter Group-Trial Practice Program; Los Angeles Trial Lawyers Association, Association of Trial Lawyers of America and Southern California Defense Counsel Trial Practice Seminars; Deposition Skills, CEB; Association of Trial Lawyers of America Trial College; CEB, Ethics, Products Liability; Los Angeles Trial Lawyers Association, "Argument of the Masters." Member, Panel of Arbitrators, Los Angeles Superior Court, 1983—. *Member:* Los Angeles County and American Bar Associations; State Bar of California; Women Lawyers Association of Los Angeles; Association of Southern California Defense Counsel (Board of Directors, 1993—); Defense Research Institute; American Board of Trial Advocates. *PRACTICE AREAS:* Legal Malpractice; Products Liability; Business Litigation.

**MICHAEL J. O'NEILL,** born Santa Cruz, California, August 9, 1954; admitted to bar, 1982, California; U.S. District Court, Eastern, Central and Southern Districts of California; U.S. Supreme Court. *Education:* University of California at Berkeley (B.A., 1977); McGeorge School of Law, University of the Pacific (J.D., 1982). Phi Alpha Delta. Judicial Intern to Associate Justice Edward J. Regan, Court of Appeal, Third District, 1981. Co-Author: "Business Interruption and Indirect Loss," Insuring Real Property, Matthew Bender, 1989. *Member:* Los Angeles County and American Bar Associations; State Bar of California; Defense Research Institute; Association of Southern California Defense Counsel. *REPORTED CASES:* Smith v. Superior Court (1990) 217 Cal. App. 950; Orr v. Byers (1988) 198 Cal. App. 3d 666. *PRACTICE AREAS:* Insurance Bad Faith; Insurance Agency Malpractice; Insurance Coverage.

**KYLE KVETON,** born Huntington, New York, January 7, 1959; admitted to bar, 1983, California and U.S. District Court, Central, Southern and Eastern Districts of California. *Education:* State University of New York at Binghamton (B.A., 1980); University of Southern California (J.D., 1983). Hale Moot Court Honors Program, 1982. *Member:* Los Angeles County and American (Member, Section of Business Law) Bar Associations; State Bar of California. *PRACTICE AREAS:* Business Litigation; Directors and Officers Errors and Omissions.

*(This Listing Continued)*

**MARIA LOUISE COUSINEAU,** born Pasadena, California, August 4, 1959; admitted to bar, 1985, California; 1986, U.S. District Court, Central and Southern Districts of California and U.S. Court of Appeals, Ninth Circuit; 1987, Nevada and U.S. District Court, Eastern District of California and District of Nevada. *Education:* University of California at Irvine (B.A., 1981); Southwestern University (J.D., cum laude, 1984). Member, Board of Governors, Moot Court Honors Program, 1983-1984. Recipient, American Jurisprudence Awards in Civil Procedure and Criminal Procedure. Judicial Extern to Judge Arthur Alarcon, U.S. Court of Appeals, Ninth Circuit, 1983. Judicial Clerk to Chief Justice Charles E. Springer, Nevada Supreme Court, 1984-1986. *Member:* Los Angeles County (Volunteer, AIDS Hospice Panel) Bar Association; State Bar of California; State Bar of Nevada; Women Lawyers Association of Los Angeles; Lawyers for Human Rights. *REPORTED CASES:* In Re Couch (Taxel v. Equity General) 80 B.R. 512 (1987); Orr v. Byers (1988) 198 Cal. App 3d 666. *PRACTICE AREAS:* Insurance Bad Faith; Insurance Agency Malpractice; Professional Malpractice.

**PAMELA E. DUNN,** born Washington, D.C., April 27, 1949; admitted to bar, 1985, California; 1986, U.S. District Court, Central and Southern Districts of California; 1987, Nevada, U.S. District Court, District of Nevada and U.S. Court of Appeals, Ninth Circuit; 1989, U.S. Supreme Court. *Education:* University of South Florida (B.A., 1972); Southwestern University School of Law (J.D., 1984). Chair, Board of Governors, Moot Court Honors Program, 1983-1984. Member, Board of Governors, 1982-1983. Senior Law Clerk to Associate Justice E. M. Gunderson, Nevada Supreme Court, 1984-1985. Extern to Judge Edward Rafeedie, U.S. District Court, Central Division, 1983. Associate Adjunct Professor of Law, Southwestern University School of Law, 1986—; Adjunct Professor of Law, Loyola Law School, 1991-1992. Member, Executive Committee, 1988—, Secretary, 1992-1993; Vice Chair, 1993-1994; Chair, 1994-1995; Los Angeles County Bar Association Conference of Delegates. Member: Lawyers for Human Rights; Los Angeles County Bar Association, Ad Hoc Committee Studying Sexual Orientation Bias. Volunteer, AIDS Hospice Panel, Los Angeles County Bar, 1989—. Delegate to the State Bar Conference, 1986—; Chair, Committee on Appellate Courts, 1995—. Consultant, California Civil Writ Practice, C.E.B., 2d ed., 1987. *Member:* Los Angeles County (Member, Appellate Courts Committee, 1986—; Vice Chair, 1992; Chair, 1993-1995; Member, Board of Trustees, 1995—; Chair, State Appellate Judicial Evaluation Committee, 1991-1992) and American Bar Associations; State Bar of California; State Bar of Nevada; National Order of the Barristers; Women Lawyers of Los Angeles; California Women Lawyers. (Certified Specialist, Appellate Law, The State Bar of California Board of Legal Specialization). *REPORTED CASES:* Waller v. Truck Insurance Exchange 1995 11 Cal. 4th; Kasparian v. County of Los Angeles 1995 386 App. 4th 242; State Farm v. Superior Court 1994 45 Cal. App. 4th 1093; Winans v. State Farm Fire and Casualty Co., 968 F 2d 884 (9th Cir. 1992); Almon v. State Farm Fire and Casualty Co., 724 F. Supp. 765 (S.D. Cal. 1989); Christensen v. Superior Court, 54 Cal. 3d 868, 2 Cal. Rptr. 2d 79 (1991); Prudential-LMI Commercial Insurance v. Superior Court, 51 Cal 3d 674, 274 Cal. Rptr. 387 (1990); Pamela W. v. Millsom, 25 Cal. App. 4th 940, 30 Cal. Rptr. 2d 690 (1994); Kaiser Foundation Hospitals, Inc. v. Superior Court, 19 Cal. App. 4th 513, 23 Cal. Rptr. 2d 431 (1994); Hung v. Wang, 8 Cal. App. 4th 908, 11 Cal. Rptr. 2d 113 (1992); Fisher v. San Pedro Peninsula Hospital, 214 Cal. App. 3d 590, 262 Cal. Rptr. 842 (1989); Rojes v. Riverside General Hospital, 203 Cal. App. 3d 1151, 250 Cal. Rptr. 435 (1988). *PRACTICE AREAS:* Appellate Law.

---

**CRAIG W. BRUNET,** born Los Angeles, California, July 25, 1956; admitted to bar, 1983, California; 1984, Nevada and U.S. District Court, Southern, Central, Eastern and Northern Districts of California. *Education:* Loyola Marymount University (B.S., 1978); McGeorge School of Law, University of the Pacific (J.D., with distinction, 1983). Member, Roger J. Traynor Honor Society. Judicial Clerk for Justice Charles E. Springer, Nevada Supreme Court, 1983-1984. *Member:* Los Angeles County and American Bar Associations; The State Bar of California; State Bar of Nevada; Association of Southern California Defense Counsel; The Association of Trial Lawyers of America. *PRACTICE AREAS:* Insurance Coverage; Construction Defect.

**KIM W. SELLARS,** born Lewiston, Idaho, June 17, 1949; admitted to bar, 1988, California and U.S. District Court, Central and Southern Districts of California. *Education:* University of California at Irvine (B.A., cum laude, 1985); Loyola Marymount University (J.D., 1988). *Member:* State Bar of California; American Bar Association. *PRACTICE AREAS:* Litigation.

*(This Listing Continued)*

CALIFORNIA—LOS ANGELES     MARTINDALE-HUBBELL LAW DIRECTORY 1997

*ROBIE & MATTHAI, A PROFESSIONAL CORPORATION, Los Angeles—Continued*

**TERESA J. FRIEDERICHS,** born San Diego, California, September 6, 1959; admitted to bar, 1992, California and U.S. District Court, Central, Eastern, Northern and Southern Districts of California. *Education:* University of West Los Angeles (J.D., 1992). *Member:* Los Angeles County Bar Association (Volunteer, Domestic Violence Project, 1996); State Bar of California. *PRACTICE AREAS:* Civil Litigation.

**BERNADINE J. STOLAR,** born Los Angeles, California, January 20, 1952; admitted to bar, 1987, California; 1990, U.S. District Court, Central District of California; 1994, U.S. District Court, Southern District of California. *Education:* Loyola Marymount University (B.A., 1974; J.D., 1987); Texas Tech University (M.A., 1977). *Member:* Los Angeles County and American Bar Associations; State Bar of California; Southern California Defense Counsel; California Womens Bar Association; California Trial Lawyers Association. *PRACTICE AREAS:* Insurance Defense.

**CLAUDIA SOKOL,** born Buenos Aires, Argentina, April 26, 1963; admitted to bar, 1993, California and U.S. District Court, Central, Southern and Eastern Districts of California; 1994, U.S. Court of Appeals, Ninth Circuit. *Education:* Southwestern University School of Law (J.D., magna cum laude, 1993). Chair, Board of Governors, 1992-1993. Member, Moot Court Honors Program, 1991-1992. Extern to Judge Robert M. Takasugi, U.S. District Court, 1992. Volunteer, AIDS Legal Services Project and Homeless Shelter Project, Los Angeles County Bar Association. *Member:* Los Angeles County (Member, Appellate Courts Committee), Federal and American Bar Associations; State Bar of California. *LANGUAGES:* Spanish. *PRACTICE AREAS:* Appellate Practice; Civil Litigation.

**KAREN R. PALMERSHEIM,** born Los Angeles, California, February 21, 1966; admitted to bar, 1994, California. *Education:* University of California at Berkeley (B.A., 1988); Southwestern University School of Law (J.D., magna cum laude, 1994). Articles Editor, 1993-1994 and Member, Southwestern University Law Review Executive Board. Dean's List, 1992-1994. Recipient: American Jurisprudence Book Awards-Constitutional Law and Legal Professions; Wall Street Journal Student Achievement Award, 1994. Author, "Lucas v. South Carolina Coastal Council: How Lucas' Effect on Regulatory Takings Will Change California Coastal and Endangered Species Regulation," 23 S.W.U.L. Rev. 177. *Member:* Los Angeles County Bar Association. *PRACTICE AREAS:* Civil Litigation.

**BRIAN D. HUBEN,** born Inglewood, California, May 14, 1962; admitted to bar, 1988, California, U.S. District Court, Central, Eastern, Northern and Southern Districts of California and U.S. Court of Appeals, Ninth Circuit; 1989, District of Columbia; 1994, U.S. District Court, District of Arizona; 1996, U.S. Supreme Court. *Education:* Loyola Marymount University (B.A., cum laude, 1984); Loyola Law School, Los Angeles (J.D., 1987). Member, Institutional Review Board, Torrance Memorial Medical Center, 1990-1995. Special Master for the State Bar of California (Los Angeles County) 1995—. *Member:* Los Angeles County (Member, Delegation to State Bar Convention, 1990—) and Federal Bar Associations; State Bar of California; District of Columbia Bar. *PRACTICE AREAS:* Commercial Litigation; Creditor Rights in Bankruptcy; Business Litigation; Banking.

**WENDY L. SCHNEIDER,** born Atlanta, Georgia, November 27, 1967; admitted to bar, 1995, California. *Education:* The College of William & Mary (B.A., 1989); University of California School of Law, Los Angeles (J.D., 1995). Editor, Environmental Law Journal, Pacific Basin Law Journal, 1993-1995. Externship, U.S. Agency for International Development, Office of the General Counsel. *Member:* Los Angeles County Bar Association; Barristers Domestic Violence Project. *LANGUAGES:* Italian and French. *PRACTICE AREAS:* Civil Litigation.

**NATALIE A. KOUYOUMDJIAN,** born New York City, New York, September 12, 1969; admitted to bar, 1994, California. *Education:* University of Southern California (B.A., 1991); Southwestern University School of Law (J.D., 1994). Staff Member, 1992-1993 and Research Editor, 1993-1994, Southwestern University Law Review. Recipient, Mable Wilson Richards Scholarship. Judicial Externship, Judge Edward Rafeedie, U.S. District Court, Central District of California, 1992. *Member:* State Bar of California; American Bar Association. *LANGUAGES:* Armenian. *PRACTICE AREAS:* Civil Litigation.

**GABRIELLE M. JACKSON,** born Los Angeles, California, February 18, 1961; admitted to bar, 1993, California; U.S. District Court, Central and Eastern Districts of California; U.S. Court of Appeals, Ninth Circuit. *Education:* University of San Francisco (B.S., 1983); University of California at Los Angeles (J.D., 1993). *PRACTICE AREAS:* Civil Litigation.

*(This Listing Continued)*

CAA1142B

REPRESENTATIVE CLIENTS: State Farm Fire & Casualty Co.; The Travelers; American Integrity Ins. Co.; Lawyers Mutual Ins. Co.; Continental Casualty Co.; National Fire Insurance Company of Hartford; American Casualty Company of Reading, PA; CNA Casualty of California; Transcontinental Insurance Co.; Transportation Insurance Co.; Valley Forge Insurance Co.; CNA Casualty of Puerto Rico; Columbia Casualty Co.; Washington National Insurance Co.; New England Ins. Co.; Cameron & Colby Co.; First State Insurance Co.; Bituminous Casualty Co.; Constitutional State Insurance Co.; United Technologies Maytag; Liberty Mutual Insurance Co.; U.S.A.A. Insurance Co.; Southland Life Insurance Co.; Central Life Assurance Co.; Interamerican Ins. Co.; Carrier Corp.; State Farm Mutual Automobile Insurance Co.; 20th Century Insurance Co.; McCarthy Construction.
REFERENCE: First Professional Bank.

---

## *ROBINS, KAPLAN, MILLER & CIRESI*

Established in 1938

*2049 CENTURY PARK EAST, SUITE 3700*
**LOS ANGELES, CALIFORNIA 90067**
*Telephone: 310-552-0130*
*Fax: 310-229-5800*

*Atlanta, Georgia Office:* 2600 One Atlanta Plaza, 950 East Paces Ferry Road NE. Telephone: 404-233-1114. Fax: 404-233-1267.
*Boston, Massachusetts Office:* Suite 2200, 222 Berkeley Street. Telephone: 617-267-2300. Fax: 617-267-8288.
*Chicago, Illinois Office:* Suite 1400, 55 West Wacker Drive. Telephone: 312-782-9200. Fax: 312-782-7756.
*Costa Mesa Office:* 600 Anton Boulevard, Suite 1600. Telephone: 714-540-6200. Fax: 714-545-6915.
*Minneapolis, Minnesota Office:* 2800 LaSalle Plaza, 800 LaSalle Avenue. Telephone: 612-349-8500. Fax: 612-339-4181.
*San Francisco, California Office:* Suite 2700, 444 Market Street. Telephone: 415-399-1800. Fax: 415-391-1968.
*Washington, D.C. Office:* Suite 1200, 1801 K Street, N.W. Telephone: 202-775-0725. Fax: 202-223-8604.

*Trials and Appeals in all Federal and State Courts. Administrative, Antitrust, Appellate, Banking, Bankruptcy and Reorganization, Construction, Communications, Corporate, Employment and Employee Benefits, Environmental, Estate Planning and Probate, Franchising, Finance, Health, Insurance Law, Intellectual Property, International Litigation and Trade, Medical Malpractice, Personal Injury, Products Liability, Real Estate, Securities, Tax, Transportation.*

FIRM PROFILE: *The California offices (Costa Mesa, Los Angeles and San Francisco) focus on insurance, business, and personal injury/mass tort litigation. The insurance practice includes property and liability coverage disputes, subrogation, bad faith claims, environmental claims, crime and fidelity disputes, excess and reinsurance issues. The business litigation practice involves complex disputes in areas of antitrust and trade regulation, intellectual property, employment law, communications litigation, finance and other commercial matters. The personal injury/mass tort practice involves representation of plaintiffs in mass torts and large-scale personal injury cases.*

### MEMBERS OF FIRM

**STEVEN D. ARCHER,** born Boston, Massachusetts, November 11, 1948; admitted to bar, 1975, California, U.S. District Court, Central District of California and U.S. Supreme Court. *Education:* University of California at Los Angeles (B.A., 1970); Loyola University of Los Angeles (J.D., 1974). *Member:* Los Angeles County Bar Association; State Bar of California; Los Angeles Trial Lawyers Association; California Trial Lawyers Association; The Association of Trial Lawyers of America; Consumer Attorneys Association of Los Angeles; Trial Lawyers for Public Justice. *PRACTICE AREAS:* Medical Malpractice; Product Liability Law; Professional Liability; Tort and Personal Injury; Workers Compensation.

**ROMAN M. SILBERFELD,** born Munich, Germany, August 3, 1949; admitted to bar, 1974, California, U.S. District Court, Central District of California and U.S. Court of Appeals, Ninth Circuit; 1993, Arizona. *Education:* University of California at Los Angeles (B.A., cum laude, 1971); Loyola University of Los Angeles (J.D., 1974). Associate Editor, Loyola University Law Review, 1973-1974. *Member:* Los Angeles County Bar Association; State Bar of California; Los Angeles Trial Lawyers Association; California Trial Lawyers Association; The Association of Trial Lawyers of America. *LANGUAGES:* German. *PRACTICE AREAS:* Commercial and Business Litigation; Medical Malpractice; Product Liability Law; Professional Liability; Tort and Personal Injury.

**J. KEVIN SNYDER,** born Cleveland, Ohio, 1956; admitted to bar, 1982, California, U.S. District Court, Central and Southern Districts of California and U.S. Court of Appeals, Ninth Circuit. *Education:* University

*(This Listing Continued)*

of Southern California (B.A., cum laude, 1979; J.D., 1982). *PRACTICE AREAS:* Construction Law; Insurance Defense; Intellectual Property; Business Litigation.

**DAVID C. VEIS,** born Long Beach, California, January 24, 1953; admitted to bar, 1978, California, U.S. District Court, Southern, Central and Northern Districts of California and U.S. Court of Appeals, 9th Circuit. *Education:* University of California at Los Angeles (B.A., 1974); University of Southern California (M.A., 1975); Southwestern University (J.D., 1978). *PRACTICE AREAS:* General Corporate; Insurance; Intellectual Property Law; Litigation.

### ASSOCIATES

**JOSEPH C. CANE, JR.,** born Buffalo, New York, September, 19, 1968; admitted to bar, 1994, California. *Education:* Cornell University; Loyola Law School (J.D., 1994). *Member:* State Bar of California; American Bar Association; Los Angeles Trial Lawyers Association. *PRACTICE AREAS:* General Civil Practice; Litigation; Medical Malpractice; Product Liability Law.

**BERNICE CONN,** born New York, New York, December 12, 1953; admitted to bar, 1992, California and U.S. District Court, Central District of California; 1993, U.S. Court of Appeals, Ninth Circuit. *Education:* University of California at Los Angeles (B.A., 1974); Loyola Marymount University (J.D., 1992). Associate Justice, Scott Moot Court Honors Board, 1991-1992. Member, International and Comparative Law Journal, Loyola Marymount University, 1991-1992. *Member:* Los Angeles County Bar Association; State Bar of California; Los Angeles Trial Lawyers Association; Women Lawyers Association of Los Angeles. *PRACTICE AREAS:* General Civil Practice; Litigation; Medical Malpractice; Product Liability Law; Tort and Personal Injury.

**MICHAEL GEIBELSON,** born Van Nuys, California, December 25, 1970; admitted to bar, 1995, California. *Education:* University of California, Berkeley (B.A., 1991); Loyola Law School, Los Angeles (J.D., 1995). *PRACTICE AREAS:* Medical Malpractice; Product Liability Law; Mass Tort.

**DOUGLAS A. GREER,** born Los Angeles, California, May 2, 1949; admitted to bar, 1987, California; 1988, U.S. District Court, Central and Southern Districts of California; U.S. Court of Appeals, Ninth Circuit. *Education:* University of California at Riverside (B.A., cum laude, 1972); Loyola Law School, Los Angeles (J.D., 1987). Author: "Workers Compensation Premium, Dividend and Claims Disputes," Recent Developments in Insurance Law (Lorman Education Services, 1993). *Member:* State Bar of California; American Bar Association (Member, Sections on: Litigation; Tort and Insurance Practice; Business Law). *PRACTICE AREAS:* Insurance Coverage Law; Bad Faith Litigation; Business Litigation.

**DOUGLAS A. MASTROIANNI,** born McKeesport, Pennsylvania, 1965; admitted to bar, 1991, California; 1992, U.S. District Court, Central and Northern Districts of California. *Education:* Arizona State University (B.S., 1983); University of Pennsylvania (J.D., 1990).

**RANDY H. MCMURRAY,** born Los Angeles, California, October 17, 1953; admitted to bar, 1986, California; 1987, U.S. District Court, Central District of California. *Education:* California Polytechnic University (B.A., 1982); Southwestern University School of Law (J.D., 1986). Member: Moot Court Honors Program. *Member:* Los Angeles County, John B. Langston and National Bar Associations; State Bar of California; Los Angeles Trial Lawyers Association; California Trial Lawyers Association; The Association of Trial Lawyers of America; Consumer Lawyers of Los Angeles. *PRACTICE AREAS:* Medical Malpractice; Product Liability Law; Professional Liability; Tort and Personal Injury.

**EDWARD T. MURAMOTO,** born Los Angeles, California, 1962; admitted to bar, 1989, California; 1993, U.S. District Court, Central District of California; 1996, U.S. District Court, Southern District of California and U.S. Court of Appeals, Ninth Circuit. *Education:* University of California at Los Angeles (B.A., 1985); University of California School of Law (J.D., 1988). *PRACTICE AREAS:* Insurance; Construction Litigation; Fidelity and Surety Practice and Litigation.

**LAURA P. NASH,** born Mexico City, Mexico, November 10, 1962; admitted to bar, 1988, California; 1989, U.S. District Court, Central and Northern Districts of California; 1990, U.S. Court of Appeals, 9th Circuit; 1992, U.S. District Court, Southern District of California. *Education:* Loyola Marymount University (B.A., cum laude, 1985); University of California School of Law at Los Angeles (J.D., 1988). *PRACTICE AREAS:* Litigation.

*(This Listing Continued)*

**SHANN D. WINESETT,** born Anaheim, California, October 2, 1966; admitted to bar, 1993, California and U.S. District Court, Central District of California; 1994, Nevada. *Education:* University of Nevada, Las Vegas (B.A., summa cum laude, 1988); University of Munich, Munich, Germany; Loyola Marymount University (J.D., 1993). *Member:* Los Angeles County Bar Association; Los Angeles Trial Lawyers Association; Nevada Trial Lawyers Association. *LANGUAGES:* German. *PRACTICE AREAS:* Medical Malpractice; Product Liability Law; Professional Liability; Tort and Personal Injury.

(For other biographical data, see Professional Biographies at all other offices)

## LAW OFFICES OF
## MARK P. ROBINSON

ONE WILSHIRE BOULEVARD, 22ND FLOOR
**LOS ANGELES, CALIFORNIA 90017-3383**
*Telephone: 213-485-1798*
*FAX: 213-236-0791*

*General Civil and Criminal Litigation, Business, Personal Injury, Legal and Medical Malpractice and Products Liability Litigation, Trial and Appellate Practice, Family Law.*

**MARK P. ROBINSON,** born Santa Monica, California, November 25, 1924; admitted to bar, 1950, California. *Education:* Loyola University of Los Angeles (LL.B., 1950). Author: "Square Pegs in Round Holes," Products Liability, California State Bar Journal, 1977; and "Products Liability," New York Law Review, 1974. President, American Board of Trial Advocates, 1958-1959. President, International Society of Barristers, 1988. Member of Judicial Council of the State of California, 1975-1976. Superior Court Judge, Orange County, 1982-1984. *Member:* Los Angeles County and American Bar Associations; State Bar of California (Member, Board of Governors, 1971-1974; Vice President, 1974). [With U.S. Air Force, 1942-1945]. *PRACTICE AREAS:* Civil Litigation; Torts; Business Litigation.

## PETER E. ROBINSON

2049 CENTURY PARK EAST, 26TH FLOOR
**LOS ANGELES, CALIFORNIA 90067**
*Telephone: 310-556-9200*
*Fax: 310-556-9229*
*Email: per@protonet.com*

*Real Estate Law, Corporate Law, Business Law.*

**PETER E. ROBINSON,** born Santa Monica, California, June 19, 1943; admitted to bar, 1977, California. *Education:* University of California at Los Angeles (B.A., 1966); California State University at Northridge (M.A., 1970); University of Southern California (J.D., 1977). *Member:* Los Angeles County (Member: Continuing Legal Education Committee, 1981-1983; Real Property Section; Executive Committee, 1987—; Chairman: General Real Estate Subsection, Real Property Section, 1986-1987; Secretary, 1992, Treasurer, 1993-1994, Vice-Chairman, 1994-1996 and Chairman, 1996-1997, Real Property Section) and American (Member, Real Property, Probate and Trust Law Section) Bar Associations; State Bar of California. *PRACTICE AREAS:* Real Estate Law; Corporate Law; Business Law.

## ROBINSON, DIAMANT, BRILL & KLAUSNER

A PROFESSIONAL CORPORATION
*Established in 1962*

SUITE 1500, 1888 CENTURY PARK EAST (CENTURY CITY)
**LOS ANGELES, CALIFORNIA 90067**
*Telephone: 310-277-7400*
*Telecopier: 310-277-7584*

*Bankruptcy, Insolvency, Reorganization and Commercial Litigation Law. General Civil and Trial Practice in all State and Federal Courts.*

*FIRM PROFILE:* Robinson, Diamant, Brill & Klausner, A Professional Corporation, has specialized in the areas of Insolvency, Bankruptcy and Corporate Reorganization since its inception, in 1962. The firm represents Debtors, secured and unsecured Creditors, Creditors' Committees, Trustees in Bankruptcy and other interested parties in all facets of Bankruptcy and Reorganization cases. Two members of the firm, Lawrence A. Diamant and Edward M.

*(This Listing Continued)*

**ROBINSON, DIAMANT, BRILL & KLAUSNER,** A PROFESSIONAL CORPORATION, Los Angeles—Continued

Wolkowitz, regularly serve as Trustees and Receivers. The firm is listed in The Bar Register of Preeminent Lawyers.

**GILBERT ROBINSON** (1927-1991).

**ELLIOTT LISNEK** (1939-1992).

**LAWRENCE A. DIAMANT,** born Newark, New Jersey, January 3, 1942; admitted to bar, 1967, California. *Education:* University of California at Los Angeles (B.A., 1963; LL.B., 1966). Phi Delta Phi. Member, Moot Court. Contributing Editor, California Practice Handbook on Basic Bankruptcy. Adjunct Professor of Law, San Fernando Valley College of Law, 1979—. Judge Pro Tempore, Los Angeles Municipal Court, 1975. *Member:* Beverly Hills, Century City and Los Angeles County (Past Chairman, Executive Committee, Commercial Law and Bankruptcy Section, 1991-1992) and American (Member: Sections on Corporation, Banking and Business Law; Subsections on Business Bankruptcies and Creditors Rights; Vice-Chair, Subsection on Administration and U.S. Trustee; Reporter, Bankruptcy Ethics Task Force) Bar Associations; State Bar of California; Financial Lawyers Conference. *PRACTICE AREAS:* Bankruptcy Law; Insolvency; Reorganization.

**MARTIN J. BRILL,** born Newark, New Jersey, May 9, 1946; admitted to bar, 1972, California. *Education:* University of California at Los Angeles (B.A., cum laude, 1969; J.D., 1972). Associate Editor, U.C.L.A. Law Review, 1971-1972. Co-Author: "Collective Bargaining and Politics in Public Employment," 19 U.C.L.A. Law Review 887, 1972. *Member:* Beverly Hills (Member, Executive Committee on Bankruptcy, 1991-1994), Century City (Member, Committee on Bankruptcy and Creditors Rights), Los Angeles County (Member, Sections on: Commercial Law; Bankruptcy) and American (Member, Business Law Section) Bar Associations; The State Bar of California; Financial Lawyers Conference; Los Angeles Bankruptcy Forum. *PRACTICE AREAS:* Bankruptcy Law; Insolvency; Reorganization.

**EDWARD M. WOLKOWITZ,** born Kassel, Germany, March 11, 1949; admitted to bar, 1976, California. *Education:* California State University at Northridge (B.A., 1971); Southwestern University (J.D., cum laude, 1975); University of Michigan (LL.M., 1976). Note Editor, Southwestern University Law Review, 1974-1975. Author: "Land Use Controls: Is There A Place For Everything?" 6 Southwestern University Law Review 607, 1974; Book Review, "Legislative Analysis—Land Use Proposals," 8 Southwestern University Law Review 216, 1976; "Bankruptcy and Family Law: A Marriage of Irreconcilable Differences," 24 B.H. Bar Assn. J. 83, 1990. Contributing Author: "Land Use Controls: The Power To Exclude," 5 Environmental Law 529, 1975; Book Review, "Planning Without Prices," 10 Southwestern University Law Review 297, 1978. Adjunct Professor of Law, Southwestern University School of Law, 1979—. Member, Board of Directors, 1978— and President, 1990, Los Angeles Bankruptcy Forum. Member, Board of Directors, California Bankruptcy Forum, 1990—. Executive Editor, California Bankruptcy Journal, 1989—. Planning Commissioner, City of Culver City, 1989-1994, Chairman, 1991. Council Member, City of Culver City, 1994—. *Member:* Century City, Los Angeles County (Member, Sections on: Commercial Law; Bankruptcy; Real Property) and American Bar Associations; State Bar of California; Financial Lawyers Conference (Member, Board of Governors, 1990-1993; Executive Committee, 1991). *PRACTICE AREAS:* Bankruptcy Law; Reorganization; Commercial Transactions.

**GARY E. KLAUSNER,** born Baltimore, Maryland, October 29, 1949; admitted to bar, 1974, Maryland; 1976, California; 1980, U.S. Supreme Court. *Education:* University of Maryland (B.A., 1971; J.D., with honors, 1974). Omicron Delta Kappa; Pi Sigma Alpha. Staff Member, University of Maryland Law Review, 1972-1973. Author: "Section 1111 (b) Look Before You Leap," Bankruptcy Study Group Journal 15, 1986. Co-Author: "Chapter 11-The Bank of Last Resort," The Business Lawyer, November 1989, Vol. 45, No. 1; "The New Bankruptcy Rules," 4 Bankruptcy Study Group Journal 64, 1987. Adjunct Professor of Law, Southwestern University School of Law, 1982-1986. *Member:* Century City (Member, Committee on Bankruptcy and Creditors Rights, 1984—), Los Angeles County (Member, Executive Committee, Section on Commercial Law and Bankruptcy, 1985—; Vice-Chair, Bankruptcy Committee, 1988—) and American (Member, Section on Business Law; Chairman Task Force on the Economics of Chapter 11 practice) Bar Associations; The State Bar of California; Financial Lawyers Conference (Member, Board of Governors, 1983-1986, 1987—; Secretary, 1990; Vice President, 1991; President, 1992). *REPORTED CASES:* In re Southeast Company, 868 F.2d 335 (9th Cir. 1989); In re Rubin, 769 F.2d 611 (9th Cir. 1986); In re Softalk Pub. Co., Inc., 856 F.2d 1328 (9th Cir. 1988); In re Victory Construction Co., 37 B.R. 222 (9th Dir. BAP 1984). *PRACTICE AREAS:* Bankruptcy Law; Insolvency; Reorganization.

**IRVING M. GROSS,** born Germany, June 10, 1947; admitted to bar, 1972, California. *Education:* University of California at Los Angeles (B.A., cum laude, 1968); Boalt Hall School of Law, University of California (J.D., 1972). Pi Sigma Alpha. Law Clerk to Judge Robert Firth, U.S. District Court, Central District of California, 1973-1975. *Member:* Los Angeles County (Member, Sections on: Labor Law and Employment; Litigation) and American (Member, Sections on: Labor and Employment; Litigation) Bar Associations; State Bar of California. *REPORTED CASES:* First Pacific Bancorp., Inc. v. Bro, 847 F.2d 542 (9th Cir. 1988); In re Rossi, 86 B.R. 220 (9th Cir. BAP, 1988); In re Qintex Entertainment, Inc., 950 F.2d 1492 (9th Cir. 1991); Bergman v. Rifkind & Sterling, Inc., 227 Cal. App. 3d 1380 (1991); In re Qintex Entertainment, Inc., 8 F. 3d 1353 (9th Cir. 1993; In re Advent Management Corp., 178 B.R. 480 (9th Cir. BAP, 1995).. *PRACTICE AREAS:* Bankruptcy Law; Insolvency; Commercial Litigation; Employment Litigation.

**DOUGLAS D. KAPPLER,** born Santa Barbara, California, February 26, 1942; admitted to bar, 1971, California. *Education:* Westmont College (B.A., 1964); Boalt Hall School of Law, University of California (J.D., 1970). Author: "Post-Petition Appreciation Belongs to Debtor," The Los Angeles Daily Journal, August 16, 1990; *Bankruptcy Basics,* 1981. *Member:* Century City and Los Angeles County Bar Associations; Financial Lawyers Conference; Los Angeles Bankruptcy Forum; State Bar of California; California Trial Lawyers Association. *REPORTED CASES:* In re Tepper Industries, 74 B.R. 713 (9th Cir. BAP 1987) affirmed 840 F.2d 22; In re Matthews, 724 F.2d 798 (9th Dir. 1984). *PRACTICE AREAS:* Insolvency; Bankruptcy Law.

**PHILIP A. GASTEIER,** born Sandusky, Ohio, May 29, 1952; admitted to bar, 1977, Pennsylvania; 1987, California, U.S. District Court, Central, Eastern and Northern Districts of California and U.S. Court of Appeals, Third and Ninth Circuits. *Education:* The Ohio State University (B.A., 1974); University of Pennsylvania (J.D., 1977). Pi Sigma Alpha. *Member:* Beverly Hills, Century City, Los Angeles County (Member, Bankruptcy Committee of Commercial Law and Bankruptcy Section, 1991-1994) and American (Member, Section of Corporation, Banking and Business) Bar Associations; State Bar of California; American Bankruptcy Institute. *REPORTED CASES:* In re Qintex Entertainment, Inc., 950 F.2nd 1492 (9th Cir. 1991); in re Mercon Industries, Inc., 37 B.R. 549 (Bankr. E.D. Pa., 1984). *PRACTICE AREAS:* Bankruptcy Law; Insolvency; Reorganization.

**KARL E. BLOCK,** born Boston, Massachusetts, December 3, 1958; admitted to bar, 1983, California and U.S. District Court, Central, Northern, Eastern and Southern Districts of California. *Education:* Johns Hopkins University (B.A., 1980); University of Southern California (J.D., 1983). Phi Delta Phi; Omicron Delta Epsilon. Recipient, American Jurisprudence Award in Bankruptcy. Extern to the: Honorable Barry Russell, United States Bankruptcy Judge, United States Bankruptcy Court, Central District of California, 1982; Honorable Robert L. Ordin, United States Bankruptcy Judge, Central District of California, 1983. Author: "The Assignment of Avoiding Power Claims in Bankruptcy Cases (Who Gets The Windfall)" published in ABA Insolvency and Bankruptcy Committee Newsletter; "The Effect of Bankruptcy Cases on the Division of Property in Dissolution Proceedings, Selected Problems," 1990. *Member:* Los Angeles County (Chair, Legislative Subcommittee, 1988-1991; Member, Commercial Law and Bankruptcy Subcommittees; Member, Executive Committee and Secretary, Vice-Chair and Chair, 1996-1997, Commercial Law and Bankruptcy Section) and American (Co-Chair, Subcommittee on Creditor's Rights for Bankruptcy and Insolvency Committee, Litigation Section) Bar Associations; State Bar of California (Member, U.C.C. Committee, 1995—); Financial Lawyers Conference; Los Angeles Bankruptcy Forum. *LANGUAGES:* French. *REPORTED CASES:* In re Commercial Consortium of California, 135 B.R. 120 (Bankr C.D. Cal. 1991);In re Hathaway Ranch Partnership, 127 B.R. 859 (Bankr C.D. Cal. 1990); In re Altabon Foods, Inc., 998 F. 2d 718 (9th Cir., 1993). *PRACTICE AREAS:* Bankruptcy Law; Insolvency Law; Creditors' Rights Law; Commercial Law.

**LESLIE A. COHEN,** born St. Louis, Missouri, January 27, 1956; admitted to bar, 1980, California, U.S. District Court, Central, Eastern, Northern and Southern Districts of California and U.S. Court of Appeals, Ninth Circuit. *Education:* University of California at San Diego (B.A., 1977); University of California at Los Angeles (J.D., 1980). Staff Member, 1978-1980, Associate Editor, 1980, U.C.L.A. Law Review. Author: Comment, 27 UCLA Law Review, 1438, 1980; "Bankruptcy and Contractual Relations in the Entertainment Industry--An Overview," 1990 Entertainment Publishing

*(This Listing Continued)*

and the Arts Handbook; "A Survey of Recent Bankruptcy Decisions Impacting Upon the Entertainment Industry," 1992 Entertainment Publishing and the Arts Handbook; "Asset Protection Strategies, 1992," University of Southern California Real Estate Tax and Accounting Conference, November, 1992. Speaker: "Promoting Fairness in the Bankruptcy Courts," Century City Bar Association, December, 1991; "A Survey of Bankruptcy Decisions Impacting Upon the Entertainment Industry," Century City Bar Association, May, 1992; "Recent Developments in Dischargeability Litigation," June, 1986 and "The Impact of Bankruptcy Proceedings on Contractual Relations in the Entertainment Industry," Century City Bar Association, July 1987; "Managing Your Caseload," Women Lawyers Association of Los Angeles Mentor Network, March, 1987; "Intellectual Property and Bankruptcy," Financial Lawyers Conference, January, 1989; "Issues in Partnership Bankruptcy Cases," American Bar Association Midyear Meeting, April, 1990; "Asset Sales in Bankruptcy," Financial Lawyers Conference, April, 1996. Member, Board of Governors, Financial Lawyers Conference, 1992—. *Member:* Century City (Co-Section Chair, Bankruptcy and Creditors' Rights, 1992—), Los Angeles County and American Bar Associations; State Bar of California; Financial Lawyers Conference (Member, Board of Governors, 1991-1994); Women Lawyers Association of Los Angeles (Chair, Mentor Network, 1986-1987; Member, Board of Directors, 1988-1989); Los Angeles Bankruptcy Forum (Member, Board of Directors, 1988-1989). *REPORTED CASES:* In re Oak Creek Energy Farms, Ltd., Debtor. Energy Enterprises, Inc., Plaintiff, v. Oak Creek Energy Systems, Inc., Dean Beckett, Steve Cummings, Oak Creek Energy Farms, Ltd., Defendant, No. 187-00644-A-11 Chapter 11, Adv. No.; In re Skyler Ridge, Debtor, No. LA 87-13216-SB Chapter 11, United States Bankruptcy Court for the Central District of California, 80 Bankr. 500; 1987 Bankr. Lexis 1935; Bankr. L. Rep. (CCH) P72,167; 16 Bankr. Ct. Dec. (CRR) 1122, November 2, 1987, December 15, 1987; In re George A. Safren, Debtor; In re Helen Safren, Debtor; In re Ronald I. Safren, Debtor; In re Rosa Jean Safren, Debtor, Nos. LA-82-18569-SB, LA-86-00846-SB, LA-82-18570-SB, LA-86-00847-SB Chapter 11, United States Bankruptcy Court for the Central District of California, 65 Bankr. 566; Bankr. L. Rep. (CCH) P71,478; 16 Collier Bankr. Cas. 2d (MB) 315; 14 Bankr. Ct. Dec. (CRR) 1261, September 26, 1986; In re Moses N. Aslan, Debtor, No. LA 86-03637-GM, Chapter 11, United States Bankruptcy Court for the Central District of California, 65 Bankr. 826; Bankr. L. Rep. (CCH) P71,536; 15 Bankr. Ct. Dec. (CRR) 136, September 15, 1986. *PRACTICE AREAS:* Bankruptcy.

**GREGG D. LUNDBERG,** born Miami, Oklahoma, September 23, 1957; admitted to bar, 1990, California, U.S. District Court, Central, Southern and Eastern Districts of California and U.S. Court of Appeals, Ninth Circuit. *Education:* University of Southern California (B.S., 1980); Loyola Marymount University (M.B.A., 1987); Southwestern University School of Law (J.D., 1987). Law Clerk to the Hon. Calvin K. Ashland, U.S. Bankruptcy Court, Central District of California, 1988-1990; Extern to the Hon. Robert Boochever, Circuit Judge, Ninth Circuit Court of Appeals. Automation and Technology Committee of the National Conference of Bankruptcy Judges, Financial Lawyers Conference. *Member:* South Bay and Los Angeles County Bar Associations; State Bar of California. *REPORTED CASES:* In re Advent Management Corp., 178 B.R. 480 (Bankr. 9th Cir.). *PRACTICE AREAS:* Bankruptcy Law.

**SANDFORD L. FREY,** born New York, N.Y. August 7, 1955; admitted to bar, 1982, California and U.S. District Court, Central, Northern and Southern Districts of California. *Education:* California State University at Northridge (B.A., 1979); University of West Los Angeles School of Law (J.D., 1982). Recipient, Award for Outstanding Legal Journalism, 1982; Business Reorganization, University of Southern California, 1983. Associate Editor, Law Review, 1982-1983. Judicial Clerkship, Hon. James R. Dooley, 1982-1985 and Hon. Richard Mednick, 1982, U.S. Bankruptcy Court, Central District of California. Member, Bankruptcy Local Rules Committee, Central District of California, 1988—. Co-Author: "'Trust Me' or Trustee? The Requirements for Appointment of a Trustee or Examiner Under 11 U.S.C. §1104," 17 Cal. Bankr. J. 34, 1989. Speaker: "Chapter 11-Changes in Attitudes and Latitudes," New York Institute of Credit and Business, 1994; "Acquisitions Through Chapter 11 - The Good, the Bad and the Ugly," Los Angeles County Bar Association, 1991; "You Say Potato, I Say Potato - Calculating Claims under Section 507(a)(4) for contributions to employee benefit plans," Client Briefing Conference, Los Angeles, 1995; "Dances with Wolves - Warn, Golden Parachutes and other Labor Issues in Bankruptcy," Client Briefing Conference, Los Angeles, 1993. *Member:* Los Angeles County Bar Association; State Bar of California; Financial Lawyers Conference; Bankruptcy Forum; Los Angeles Venture Association.

**JEFFREY A. RESLER,** born Brooklyn, New York, March 23, 1962; admitted to bar, 1988, New York; 1990, U.S. District Court, Eastern and *(This Listing Continued)* Southern Districts of New York; 1991, California and U.S. District Court, Central District of California. *Education:* Wesleyan University (B.A., 1984); New York University (J.D., cum laude, 1987). Order of the Coif. *PRACTICE AREAS:* Bankruptcy Law; Corporate Reorganizations; Corporate Law.

---

**JUDITH E. MILLER,** born Glendale, California, April 24, 1959; admitted to bar, 1989, California and U.S. Court of Appeals, Ninth Circuit. *Education:* Brandeis University (A.B., cum laude, 1982); University of Southern California (J.D., 1989). Phi Alpha Delta. Publications Editor, University of Southern California Computer Law Journal, 1988-1989. Member, Editorial Board, National Paralegal Instructional Course Compendium and Syllabus Series, 1990—. *Member:* Beverly Hills, Los Angeles County and American Bar Associations; Financial Lawyers Conference; California Bankruptcy Conference. *PRACTICE AREAS:* Bankruptcy Law.

**SANDRO F. PIEDRAHITA,** born Los Angeles, California, May 17, 1964; admitted to bar, 1990, California; 1992, U.S. District Court, Central District of California. *Education:* Yale University (B.A., cum laude, 1986); Harvard University (J.D., 1990). *Member:* Century City Bar Association. *LANGUAGES:* French and Spanish. *REPORTED CASES:* In re Altabon Foods, Inc., 998 F. 2d 718 (9th Cir., 1993). *PRACTICE AREAS:* Commercial Litigation; Bankruptcy Law; Creditors' Rights Law; Real Estate.

**CHRISTOPHER E. JONES,** born Los Angeles, California, March 24, 1969; admitted to bar, 1994, California, U.S. District Court, Central District of California and U.S. Court of Appeals, Ninth Circuit. *Education:* Georgetown University (B.S.B.A., cum laude, 1991); University of California School of Law, Los Angeles (J.D., 1994). Phi Delta Phi. Extern to the Honorable Barry Russell, U.S. Bankruptcy Court, Central District of California. *Member:* Los Angeles County Bar Association; State Bar of California. *PRACTICE AREAS:* Bankruptcy.

**NICOLE D. LANCE,** born Wiesbaden, Germany, March 4, 1966; admitted to bar, 1993, California. *Education:* University of California at Los Angeles (B.A., cum laude, 1988); University of California School of Law, Davis (J.D., 1991). Law Clerk to the Honorable Vincent P. Zurzolo, U.S. Bankruptcy Judge, Central District of California, 1991-1993. *Member:* Los Angeles County Bar Association; State Bar of California. *PRACTICE AREAS:* Bankruptcy.

**ROBYN B. SOKOL,** born Philadelphia, Pennsylvania, February 12, 1964; admitted to bar, 1992, California. *Education:* University of Colorado (B.S., cum laude, 1986); Boston University (J.D., 1991). Extern to the Honorable William H. Yohn, Court of Common Pleas, Montgomery County, Pennsylvania. Judicial Law Clerk to the Honorable Robin L. Riblet, U.S. Bankruptcy Judge, Central District of California, 1991-1992. Staff Law Clerk to the Honorable Kathleen Lax, Honorable Kathleen March, Honorable Vincent P. Zurzolo, Honorable Alan M. Ahart and Honorable William Lasarow, U.S. Bankruptcy Judges for the Central District of California, 1992. *Member:* Beverly Hills Bar Association; State Bar of California; Financial Lawyers Conference.

**JEFFREY W. DULBERG,** born Queens, New York, January 8, 1970; admitted to bar, 1995, California. *Education:* Swarthmore College (B.A., with honors, 1991); University of California, Los Angeles (J.D., 1995). *Member:* Los Angeles County Bar Association; State Bar of California. *PRACTICE AREAS:* Bankruptcy.

**SETH D. GARLAND,** born Poughkeepsie, New York, October 13, 1970; admitted to bar, 1995, California, U.S. District Court, Central District of California and U.S. Court of Appeals, Ninth Circuit. *Education:* University of Pennsylvania (B.A., cum laude, 1992); University of California, Los Angeles (J.D., 1995). *Member:* Los Angeles County Bar Association; State Bar of California. *PRACTICE AREAS:* Bankruptcy.

---

REFERENCES: Fidelity & Deposit Co.; Home Savings of America (Century City Office); Bergen Brunswig Corp.; Metrobank (Los Angeles Regional Office); Wells Fargo Bank (Century City Office).

## ROBINSON, DI LANDO & WHITAKER

*A PROFESSIONAL LAW CORPORATION*

Established in 1991

800 WILSHIRE BOULEVARD
SUITE 1300
**LOS ANGELES, CALIFORNIA 90017-2687**
Telephone: 213-229-0100
Facsimile: 213-229-0114

*San Francisco, California Office:* 465 California Street. Suite 510. 94104. Telephone: 415-391-9475. Fax: 415-391-3799.

*General Insurance Defense Practice Including Civil, Business and Insurance Litigation in both State and Federal Courts, Self Insured, Professional Liability and Products Liability, Entertainment and Sports, Employment and Labor, Corporations and Coverage.*

*FIRM PROFILE: Robinson, Di Lando & Whitaker was founded in 1991 by Michael Robinson, Jr., Michael Di Lando and Ronald S. Whitaker. The firm has experienced steady growth by providing superior legal services to its clients in all phases of litigation and appeals. Because of their central office location and extensive litigation experience, each attorney is able to efficiently handle cases throughout California. The firm also uses a team approach to litigation. Robinson, Di Lando & Whitaker is comprised of exceptional attorneys dedicated to providing quality legal services. The firm takes pride in its ability to successfully represent each and every client's individual needs. Responsiveness to these needs is the essence of the practice of law at Robinson, Di Lando & Whitaker.*

**MICHAEL C. ROBINSON, JR.,** born Santa Monica, California, June 17, 1956; admitted to bar, 1985, California; 1986, U.S. Court of Appeals, Ninth Circuit and U.S. District Court, Central District of California. *Education:* California State University at Los Angeles (B.A., 1981); Loyola University of Los Angeles (J.D., 1985). *Member:* Los Angeles County Bar Association; Association of Southern California Defense Counsel. **PRACTICE AREAS:** Professional Errors and Omissions; Products Liability; Insurance Coverage.

**MICHAEL A. DI LANDO,** born Van Nuys, California, July 8, 1959; admitted to bar, 1985, California; 1986, U.S. District Court, Central District of California, U.S. Tax Court and U.S. Court of Appeals for the Federal Circuit. *Education:* California State University at Northridge (B.A., cum laude, 1981); Loyola Marymount University (J.D., 1984). Phi Sigma Alpha. *Member:* Association of Southern California Defense Counsel. **PRACTICE AREAS:** Professional Errors and Omissions; Product Liability.

**RONALD S. WHITAKER,** born Cleveland, Ohio, October 26, 1957; admitted to bar, 1983, California; 1984, U.S. District Court, Central, Northern and Southern Districts of California and U.S. Court of Appeals, Ninth Circuit. *Education:* University of California at Los Angeles (B.A., 1980; J.D., 1983). Distinguished Advocate, Moot Court Honors Program. *Member:* American Bar Association; Association of Southern California Defense Counsel; Defense Research Institute; American Board of Trial Advocates. **PRACTICE AREAS:** Professional Errors and Omissions; Products Liability; Insurance Coverage; General Litigation.

**JACK M. LIEBHABER,** born Great Neck, New York, April 6, 1958; admitted to bar, 1984, California and U.S. District Court, Central District of California. *Education:* Tulane University; State University of New York at Binghamton (B.A., in Political Science and History, 1980); Pepperdine University (J.D., 1983). *Member:* Los Angeles County Bar Association; State Bar of California; Association of Southern California Defense Counsel. **PRACTICE AREAS:** General Litigation.

---

**GEORGE E. ORDONEZ,** born La Paz, Bolivia, October 30, 1964; admitted to bar, 1992, California; 1993, U.S. District Court, Central District of California. *Education:* Loyola Marymount University (B.B.A., 1986); Hastings College of the Law, University of California, San Francisco (J.D., 1991). *Member:* Los Angeles County Bar Association; Mexican American Bar Association; Association of Southern California Defense Counsel. **LANGUAGES:** Spanish. **PRACTICE AREAS:** General Litigation; Insurance Coverage; Professional Errors and Omissions.

**STEVE H. YU,** born Seoul, South Korea, August 7, 1967; admitted to bar, 1992, California; 1996, U.S. District Court, Central District of California. *Education:* University of California at Berkeley (B.A., 1989); Arizona State University (J.D., 1992).

*(This Listing Continued)*

**KEVIN K. BROERMAN,** born Phoenix, Arizona, November 22, 1961; admitted to bar, 1993, California. *Education:* Arizona State University (B.S., 1983); Western State University College of Law (J.D., 1992). *Member:* State Bar of California. [1st Lt., U.S. Army, 1984-1989]. **PRACTICE AREAS:** Litigation; Insurance Law; Products Liability; Personal Injury; Tort Defense.

**KENNETH W. JOHNSON,** born Tacoma, Washington, April 19, 1965; admitted to bar, 1991, California. *Education:* Harvard University (A.B., 1987); University of California, Boalt Hall School of Law (J.D., 1991). **PRACTICE AREAS:** Civil Litigation; Legal Malpractice.

**MARK KANE,** born New York, N.Y., July 12, 1956; admitted to bar, 1994, California. *Education:* Queens College of the City University of New York (B.A., 1978); Boston University (M.S., 1981); Southwestern University School of Law (J.D., cum laude, 1993). Editor, Southwestern Law Review, 1992-1993. **PRACTICE AREAS:** Litigation.

**LESLIE ANNE DENNY,** born Ada, Oklahoma, June 15, 1963; admitted to bar, 1988, California and U.S. District Court, Central District of California. *Education:* University of Oklahoma (B.B.A., 1984; J.D., 1987). Member, Oklahoma Law Review, 1986-1987. Author: Note "Constitutional Law, Privacy, Personal Autonomy and the Freedom of Intimate Association: Hardwick v. Bowers," 39 Oklahoma Law Review 233, 1986; Recent Development, "Constitutional Law: Memphis Community School District v. Stachura," 40 Oklahoma Law Review 177, 1987. *Member:* Beverly Hills and Los Angeles County Bar Associations; State Bar of California. **PRACTICE AREAS:** General Civil Trial and Appellate Practice in all State and Federal Courts; Insurance; Products Liability; Negligence and Professional Liability; Common Carrier.

**ROBERT G. MENDOZA,** born Orange, California, July 23, 1953; admitted to bar, 1993, California. *Education:* University of California, Irvine (B.A., 1975); California Western School of Law (J.D., 1978). *Member:* State Bar of California. **LANGUAGES:** Spanish. **PRACTICE AREAS:** Personal Injury; Insurance Defense; Product Liability.

*OF COUNSEL*

**TIMOTHY L. SALAZAR,** born Burbank, California, December 28, 1957; admitted to bar, 1984, New Mexico; 1990, Texas; U.S. District Court, District of New Mexico, U.S. District Court, Eastern District of Michigan, U.S. District Court, Northern District of Texas and U.S. Court of Appeals, Fifth, Sixth and Tenth Circuits (Not admitted in California). *Education:* California State University (B.A., 1981); University of California at Los Angeles (J.D., 1984). *Member:* Albuquerque and American (Member, Sections on: Litigation; Labor and Employment Law; Member, State Labor Law Developments Committee; Chairman, State Right to Know Laws, Subcommittee, 1990—) Bar Associations; State Bar of New Mexico; State Bar of Texas. (Also practicing individually, Albuquerque, New Mexico). **PRACTICE AREAS:** Labor Law; Employment Law.

---

## ROBINSON, PHILLIPS & CALCAGNIE

**LOS ANGELES, CALIFORNIA**

(See Laguna Niguel)

*Automobile Product Liability Litigation, Toxic Tort, Corporate Fraud, Serious Injury and Death Cases.*

---

## RODARTE & GERINGER

10880 WILSHIRE BOULEVARD
SUITE 1050
**LOS ANGELES, CALIFORNIA 90024**
Telephone: 310-441-8020
Fax: 310-441-8021
Email: 104457.513@compuserve.com

*Product Liability, Medical Device and Toxic Tort Litigation.*

**DANIEL D. RODARTE,** born Pasadena, California, May 29, 1954; admitted to bar, 1979, California and U.S. District Court, Central District of California; 1980, U.S. District Court, Southern and Northern Districts of California. *Education:* University of California at Santa Cruz (A.B., with honors in Politics, 1976); Harvard University (J.D., 1979). Member, Arbitration Panel, Los Angeles County Superior Court. *Member:* Los Angeles County and American Bar Associations; State Bar of California; Southern

*(This Listing Continued)*

California Defense Counsel. *PRACTICE AREAS:* Products Liability; Medical Device Litigation.

**AYLENE M. GERINGER,** born Los Angeles, California, December 23, 1950; admitted to bar, 1984, California, U.S. District Court, Central District of California and U.S. Court of Appeals, Ninth Circuit. *Education:* University of California at Los Angeles (B.A., 1973); Southwestern University School of Law (J.D., 1984). Law Clerk to the Honorable Arthur Alarcon, U.S. Court of Appeals, Ninth Circuit, 1984-1985. Extern to Hon. Edward Rafeedie, U.S. District Court, Central District of California. *Member:* Los Angeles County Bar Association; State Bar of California; Southern California Defense Counsel. *PRACTICE AREAS:* Toxic Tort/Environmental Litigation; Products Liability; Medical Device Litigation.

## LAW OFFICES OF
## MICHELLE M. RODENBORN
### LOS ANGELES, CALIFORNIA
(See Long Beach)

*Customs, International Trade and Transportation Law. Trial and Appellate Practice in all State and Federal Courts. Practice before Federal Administrative Agencies. Export Licensing.*

## RODGERS & GREENFELD
### 660 SOUTH FIGUEROA STREET
### 23RD FLOOR
### LOS ANGELES, CALIFORNIA 90017
Telephone: 213-955-4850
Fax: 213-955-4851

*General Business Law, Real Estate, Land Use and Development, Corporate, International, Antitrust, General Civil, Trial and Appellate Practice in all State and Federal Courts.*

### MEMBERS OF FIRM

**RONALD L. RODGERS, JR.,** born Brawley, California, February 2, 1956; admitted to bar, 1982, California; U.S. District Court, Central District of California. *Education:* University of Southern California (B.A., magna cum laude, 1979); Hebrew University of Jerusalem, Jerusalem, Israel; George Washington University (J.D., 1982). *Member:* Los Angeles County and American (Member, Real Property, Probate and Trust Law, Corporation, Banking and Business Law and Urban State and Local Government Law Sections) Bar Associations; State Bar of California (Member, Real Property Law Section); National Association of Bond Lawyers. *PRACTICE AREAS:* General Business Law; Real Estate; International; Land Use and Development; Corporate.

**J. STEVEN GREENFELD,** born Miami, Florida, July 14, 1952; admitted to bar, 1977, California, U.S. District Court, Southern, Central and Eastern Districts of California, U.S. Court of Appeals, Ninth Circuit and U.S. Supreme Court. *Education:* Kenyon College (A.B., cum laude, 1974); Hastings College of Law, University of California (J.D., 1977). *Member:* Los Angeles County Bar Association; State Bar of California. *PRACTICE AREAS:* General Civil Trial Practice; Appellate Practice.

## RODI, POLLOCK, PETTKER, GALBRAITH
## & CAHILL
### A LAW CORPORATION
Established in 1969
### SUITE 400
### 801 SOUTH GRAND AVENUE
### LOS ANGELES, CALIFORNIA 90017
Telephone: 213-895-4900; 680-0823
Telecopiers: 213-895-4921; 895-4922; 895-4750

*General Civil and Trial Practice, State and Federal Courts. Corporate, Securities, Business, Taxation, Real Estate and Banking Law. Estate Planning, Probate, Products Liability and Environmental and Employment Law.*

FIRM PROFILE: Rodi Pollock is a full-service law firm located in the downtown Los Angeles financial district. Approximately half of Rodi Pollock's lawyers are experienced trial attorneys, with the remaining lawyers practicing corporate, tax, real estate and environmental law, estate planning and
*(This Listing Continued)*

administration and employment law. Most of Rodi Pollock's practice is centered in California and the surrounding states.

**KARL B. RODI** (1908-1982).

**JOHN D. CAHILL,** born Niagara Falls, New York, May 12, 1929; admitted to bar, 1954, New York; 1957, California; 1958, U.S. Supreme Court. *Education:* Canisius College; State University of New York at Buffalo (LL.B., 1953); University of California at Los Angeles School of Law; University of Southern California Law School. Phi Delta Phi. National Vice President, 1965-1968, National President, 1968-1971, 1983-1987 and Member of the Executive Committee, 1971-1989, Alpha Kappa Psi. Trial Attorney, 1957-1970 and Chief of Tax Section, 1967-1970, Office of Los Angeles County Counsel. Chairman, Arcadia General Plan Citizens Committee, 1966-1967. Legislative Representative for Los Angeles County, 1967-1970. Counsel, California Association of County Assessors, 1967-1970. Member, 1967-1971 and Chairman, 1968-1970, Arcadia Planning Commission. Member, 1971-1974 and President, 1971-1973, Holy Angels School Board, Arcadia. Member, Legal Committee, Institute of Property Taxation, 1983—. *Member:* Los Angeles County (Chairman, State and Local Taxation Section, 1972-1974, 1980-1981), New York State and American Bar Associations; The State Bar of California (Chairman, State and Local Taxation Section, 1983-1984; Chairman, Property, Estate Trust, Sales and Use Tax Committee, 1984); International Association of Assessing Officers (IAAO). [Captain, USNR]. *PRACTICE AREAS:* Real and Personal Property Tax Litigation; Sales and Use Tax Litigation; Probate Litigation.

**JOHN D. PETTKER,** born Los Angeles, California, November 1, 1942; admitted to bar, 1968, California. *Education:* Stanford University (A.B., with distinction, 1964; J.D., 1967). Co-Author: "Legal Problems of Family Businesses," Family Business Research Conference, University of Southern California Graduate School of Business Administration, 1985; "The New Anti-Freeze Law: A Meltdown for the Family Firm," Family Business Review, Vol. II, No. 2, Summer 1989. listed in The Best Lawyers in America, by Woodward/White. *Member:* Los Angeles County (Member, Sections on: Probate and Trust Law; Real Property; Taxation) and American (Member, Section on Real Property, Probate and Trust Law) Bar Associations; The State Bar of California (Member, Section on Taxation). (Certified Specialist, Probate, Estate Planning and Trust Law, The State Bar of California Board of Legal Specialization). *PRACTICE AREAS:* Estate Planning and Probate Administration; Succession Planning for Family-Owned Businesses; Counseling Private Foundations.

**DANIEL C. BOND** (1942-1977).

**WILLIAM R. CHRISTIAN,** born Columbia, South Carolina, March 18, 1950; admitted to bar, 1974, California. *Education:* University of South Carolina and California State College at Fullerton (B.A., 1970); Hastings College of Law, University of California (J.D., 1973). Member, 1971-1972 and Associate Editor, 1972-1973, Hastings Law Journal. Lecturer: Tax Law, University of Southern California, 1976—; University of California at Los Angeles, 1979; Golden Gate University Masters in Tax Program, 1985—. Co-Author: Grant and Christian, *Subchapter S Taxation,* 3nd Ed. Shepard's McGraw-Hill, 1992; "Recent Developments in S Corporations," 48th U.S.C. Am. Institute on Fed. Tax, Chapter 5 . *Member:* Los Angeles County (Member, Sections on: Taxation, Executive Committee; Business and Corporations Law; Real Property and Probate) and American (Member, Sections on: Corporations, Banking and Business Law; Real Property, Probate and Trust Law; Taxation; Member, Subchapter S Corporations Subcommittee) Bar Associations; State Bar of California (Member Sections on: Taxation; Business; Real Property; Taxation; Estate Planning). *PRACTICE AREAS:* Closely Held Business and Individual Tax and Business Planning; Estate Planning; Real Estate; Tax Law.

**HENRY P. PRAMOV, JR.,** born Bridgeton, New Jersey, September 26, 1947; admitted to bar, 1974, Virginia and California; 1976, U.S. Tax Court. *Education:* Georgetown University (A.B., 1969; LL.M., in Taxation, 1976); Catholic University of America (J.D., 1974). Lecturer, Tax Law, University of Southern California Masters in Business Taxation Program, 1978-1982. Adjunct Professor, Corporate Tax Law, University of San Diego School of Law, Graduate Tax Program, 1985-1987. *Member:* Los Angeles County (Member, Sections on: Business and Corporations Law; Real Property; Taxation; Member, Executive Committee, 1979) and American (Member, Sections on: Corporation, Banking and Business Law; Real Property, Probate and Trust Law; Taxation) Bar Associations; Virginia State Bar; State Bar of California (Member, Sections on: Business Law; Real Property; Taxation). *PRACTICE AREAS:* General Business, Tax and Real Estate.

**ROBERT A. YAHIRO,** born Los Angeles, California, July 17, 1950; admitted to bar, 1976, California and U.S. Tax Court; 1982, U.S. Supreme
*(This Listing Continued)*

## RODI, POLLOCK, PETTKER, GALBRAITH & CAHILL, A LAW CORPORATION, Los Angeles—Continued

Court. *Education:* University of California at Los Angeles (A.B., cum laude, 1973); University of Southern California (J.D., 1976). Certified Public Accountant, California, 1973. Lecturer on Tax Law, University of Southern California, 1978-1979. *Member:* Los Angeles County and American Bar Associations; The State Bar of California; American Institute of Certified Public Accountants; California Society of Certified Public Accountants. *PRACTICE AREAS:* Corporate; Taxation; Employee Benefits; Environmental Law.

**ELIZABETH B. BLAKELY,** born Dhahran, Saudi Arabia, August 9, 1953; admitted to bar, 1978, California. *Education:* Occidental College (A.B., cum laude, 1975); University of Southern California (J.D., 1978). Phi Alpha Delta. *Member:* Los Angeles County (Member, Sections on: Taxation; Business and Corporations Law) and American (Member: Sections on Corporation, Banking and Business Law and Taxation) Bar Associations; State Bar of California. *PRACTICE AREAS:* Corporate; Partnership and Real Estate Transactions; Tax Planning.

**ROBERT C. NORTON,** born San Francisco, California, September 25, 1948; admitted to bar, 1979, California; 1981, U.S. Tax Court. *Education:* San Francisco State College (B.A., 1972); Golden Gate University (J.D., 1978); Georgetown University (LL.M., in Taxation, 1981). *Member:* Los Angeles County and American (Member: Sections on Taxation and Corporation, Banking and Business Law; Forum Committee on Franchising) Bar Associations; State Bar of California (Member, Sections on: Taxation; Real Property); American Society of Corporate Secretaries. *PRACTICE AREAS:* General Business, Corporate and Securities Law.

**JOHN F. CERMAK, JR.,** born New Bedford, Massachusetts, November 27, 1956; admitted to bar, 1982, District of Columbia; 1989, Pennsylvania; 1990, California. *Education:* Boston University (B.A., summa cum laude, 1979); American University (J.D., magna cum laude, 1982). Phi Beta Kappa. Associate Editor, American University Law Review, 1980-1982. Author, "Tackling 'Big Green': An Analysis and Critique of the Environmental Protection Act of 1990," published by California Environmental Insider, 1991. Law Clerk to Judge Zampano, U.S. District Court for the District of Connecticut, 1982 term. Law Clerk to Judge Trask and Judge Beezer, U.S. Court of Appeals, Ninth Circuit, 1983 term. Trial Attorney, Land and Natural Resources Division, Environmental Defense Section, U.S. Department of Justice, 1984-1987. *LANGUAGES:* German. *REPORTED CASES:* Long Beach Unified School District v. Dorothy B. Goodwin, 32 F. 3d 1364 (9th Cir. 1994); AISI v. EPA, 886 F.2d 390 (D.C. Cir. 1989); Center for Auto Safety v. Thomas, 847 F. 2d 843 (D.C. CIr. 1988); Phillips Petroleum Co. v. EPA, 803 F.2d 545 (10th Cir. 1986); B.R. MacKay & Sons v. EPA, 633 F. Supp. 1290 (D. Utah 1986); In Re Commonwealth Oil Refining Co., 58 Bkrptcy. 608, 22 Envir. Rep. Cas. (BNA) 1069 (Bkrptcy. W.D. Tex. 1985); Aff'd Official Committee of Uninsured Creditors v. EPA, 23 Envir. Rep. Cas (BNA) 1606 (W.D. Tex. Nov. 5, 1985); Aff'd, 805 F.2d 1175 (5th Cir. 1986), Cert. Denied, 483 U.S. 1005 (1987); Ciba-Geigy Corp. v. EPA, 607 F. Supp. 1467 (D.D.C. 1985); Vacated, 801 F. 2d 430 (D.C. Cir. 1986); In Re Professional Sales Corp., 56 Bkrptcy. 753 (N.D. Ill. 1985). *PRACTICE AREAS:* Environmental; Health and Safety; Civil Litigation.

**TIM G. CEPERLEY,** born Philadelphia, Pennsylvania, December 19, 1950; admitted to bar, 1984, California. *Education:* Dickinson College (B.A., 1973); Georgetown University (M.S., 1975); Loyola Law School (J.D., 1983). *Member:* Los Angeles County and American Bar Associations; State Bar of California; Association of Business Trial Lawyers. *PRACTICE AREAS:* Civil Litigation; Products Liability Construction and Insurance Law.

**CORALIE KUPFER,** born San Gabriel, California, July 8, 1948; admitted to bar, 1974, California. *Education:* University of Southern California (B.A., cum laude, 1970); University of Santa Clara (J.D., 1973). Author, "The Impact of Indirect Source Control on Local Authority Over Land Use," California Environmental Law Reporter, September, 1992; "Reclaim Elements of the New Scaqud Program-Will It be a Hit or a Miss," California Environmental Law Reporter, February, 1994. Instructor: Air Quality Regulatory Framework, UCLA Extension, 1991, 1993, 1995; UCLA, UCI and ICR Regulatory Update, 1991, 1992, 1993, 1994, 1995. Chairman, South Coast Air Quality Management District Hearing Board, 1984-1988. *Member:* Los Angeles County Bar Association (Member, Environmental Section); State Bar of California (Member, Environmental Section). *PRACTICE AREAS:* Environmental Law; Air Quality Regulation; Transportation; Health and Safety.

**CRIS K. O'NEALL,** born Denver, Colorado, December 9, 1959; admitted to bar, 1986, California; 1987, U.S. District Court, Central District of California and U.S. Court of Appeals, Ninth Circuit; 1991, U.S. District Court, Eastern District of California. *Education:* Claremont McKenna College (B.A., summa cum laude, 1982); University of California, Los Angeles (J.D., 1986). *Member:* Los Angeles County (Member, State and Local Tax Committee) and South Bay Bar Associations; State Bar of California; Institute of Property Taxation. *SPECIAL AGENCIES:* County Assessment Appeals Boards; City Tax Boards. *PRACTICE AREAS:* State and Local Tax Counselling and Litigation; Environmental Litigation; Probate and Trust Litigation; Business and Commercial Litigation.

**JOHN S. CHA,** born Seoul, Korea, February 7, 1961; admitted to bar, 1987, California; 1988, U.S. District Court, Central District of California; 1992, U.S. District Court, Eastern District of California; 1993, U.S. Court of Appeals, Ninth Circuit; 1994, U.S. District Court, Southern District of California. *Education:* Northwestern University (B.A. 1983); Washington University (J.D., 1986). *Member:* The State Bar of California; American Bar Association (Member, Section on Urban, State and Local Government Law). *LANGUAGES:* Korean. *PRACTICE AREAS:* Commercial Litigation; Insurance Law; Environmental Law; Professional Malpractice; Construction Law; Products Liability Law.

**SCOTT E. ADAMSON,** born Los Angeles, California, January 23, 1963; admitted to bar, 1988, California. *Education:* University of California, Los Angeles (B.A., 1985); University of Southern California (J.D., 1988). Phi Delta Phi. Publication Editor, Major Tax Planning, 1987-1988. Publication Editor, Computer/Law Journal, 1987-1988. Recipient, American Jurisprudence Award. Co-Author: "Recent Developments in S Corporations," 48th USC Am. Institute on Fed. Tax, Chapter 5.; Tax Benefits of NOLS Can Be Lost Due to the Impact of the AMT, 44 Taxation for Accountants 22, 1990. *Member:* State Bar of California.

---

**SONJA A. INGLIN,** born Salinas, California, August 2, 1954; admitted to bar, 1979, California. *Education:* California Polytechnic State University, Pomona; University of California at San Diego (B.A., with highest honors, 1976); Boalt Hall School of Law, University of California (J.D., 1979). Associate Editor, Industrial Relations Law Journal, 1978-1979. *Member:* Los Angeles County and American Bar Associations; State Bar of California.

**THOMAS J. YOO,** born Seoul, Korea, October 7, 1968; admitted to bar, 1994, California, U.S. District Court, Central District of California and U.S. Court of Appeals, Ninth Circuit. *Education:* University of California, Los Angeles (B.A., 1991); University of California School of Law (J.D., 1994). UCLA Alumni School Scholarship. Moot Court Honor Program. *Member:* State Bar of California; Consumer Attorneys Association of Los Angeles. *LANGUAGES:* Korean. *PRACTICE AREAS:* Business Litigation; Products Liability; Professional Errors and Omissions.

**RICHARD NESSARY,** born Lynwood, California, August 7, 1969; admitted to bar, 1995, California and U.S. District Court, Central District of California. *Education:* University of California at Los Angeles (B.A., with honors, 1992); Chicago-Kent College of Law (J.D., 1995). Member, 1993-1995 and Vice-President, 1994-1995, Chicago-Kent Moot Court Honor Society. Recipient, American Jurisprudence Award. *Member:* State Bar of California (Member, Litigation Section). *PRACTICE AREAS:* Business Litigation; Environmental Litigation; Corporate Transactions.

**MARK MCCLEARY,** born Athens, Georgia, October 3, 1969; admitted to bar, 1995, California. *Education:* University of California at Berkeley (B.S., 1991); Loyola Law School (J.D., 1995); New York University (LL.M., 1996). Treasurer, 1994-1995, Phi Delta Phi. *PRACTICE AREAS:* Corporate Law; Taxation.

*OF COUNSEL*

**JOHN P. POLLOCK,** born Sacramento, California, April 28, 1920; admitted to bar, 1949, California; 1954, U.S. Supreme Court. *Education:* Stanford University (A.B., 1942); Harvard University (J.D., 1948). Co-author, "Federal Civil Practice," Continuing Education of the Bar, California, 1961. Author: *When is an Engineering Geologist Liable,* 1966. President, Chancery Club, 1967-1968. Fellow, American College of Trial Lawyers. Trustee, Pacific Legal Foundation, 1984-1991. *Member:* The State Bar of California (Member, Committee on Federal Courts, 1959-1963; Chairman, 1960-1961 and 1962-1963; Vice Chairman, 1962-1963; Member, Committee on Administration of Justice, 1963-1969); Los Angeles County (Member, Board of Trustees, 1964-1966; Chairman: Trial Lawyers Section, 1969-1970; Chairman, Superior Courts Committee, 1970-1971) and American Bar Associations.

*(This Listing Continued)*

**MARGARET ROSENTHAL,** born Romania, May 6, 1956; admitted to bar, 1979, Illinois; 1985, District of Columbia; 1989, California. *Education:* Queen's College of the City University of New York (B.A., cum laude, 1977); Chicago Kent College of Law, Illinois Institute of Technology (J.D., with high honors, Valedictorian, 1979). Recipient: Meritorious Service Award; West Hornbook Award; Law Week Award; Kent Memorial Scholarship; Decalogue Society Scholarship; U.S. Department of Health and Human Services Office of the Secretary, Certificate of Meritorious Service, 1981; Office of the Mayor Certificate of Appreciation in Recognition of Significant and Valuable Service, District of Columbia, 1989 and DHS Certificate of Award, 1989. Legis Fellow, 1982-1983. *Member:* Illinois State Bar Association; District of Columbia Bar; State Bar of California. *LANGUAGES:* French, Hungarian and Romanian. *PRACTICE AREAS:* Employment Law; Health Care Law.

REPRESENTATIVE CLIENTS: AeroVironment; American National Can Co.; Ameron, Inc.; Arco; Bank of Montreal; Beazer East, Inc.; Bechtel Investments Realty (Bechtel Corporation); Boy Scouts of America (Los Angeles Area Council); Browning-Ferris Industries; California Congress of Parents, Teachers and Students, Inc.; Carter, Hawley, Hale; DFS Group, Ltd. (Duty Free Shoppers); Diacon; Duty Free Shoppers Group Limited; Eaton Leonard Technologies, Inc.; Ernest W. Hahn Companies; Flintridge Foundation; Golden West Refining Company; Host International; Host Marriott Corporation; International Paper; Isuzu Motors America; Jos. Schlitz Brewing Co.; Kilroy Industries; KKW Trucking, Inc.; Little Joe's Restaurant; Marten Management Company (Tishman West Properties); Market City Cafe Restaurants; May Department Stores Company; Mercedes-Benz of North America; Mobil Oil Corporation; Northrop Grumman Corporation; Northwestern Mutual Life Insurance Co.; Occidental Petroleum Services; Oil Process Company; Pan Pacific Hotels; Paramount Petroleum; The Pasha Group/Pasha Maritime Services; Powerine Oil Co.; Prime Time Shuttle International; Rollins Environ. Srv.; Sabre Industries, Inc.; Santa Fe Energy Resources; Seal Furniture & Systems; Shell Oil Co.; Shell Western E & P, Inc. (Shell Oil Company); Six Flags Magic Mountain; Sterer Eng. & Mfg., Inc.; The Stroh Brewery Company; The Coastal Corporation; The Fletcher Jones Foundation; The May Department Stores Co.; The Stroh Brewery Co.; Texaco; Tina C. Foundation; Trinova (Aeroquip); TRW; Union Oil Company of California; Unisys Corporation; Unocal Corporation; Vickers Incorporated; WesTech Gear Corporation; ZHI International, Inc.

---

## RODRÍGUEZ, HORII & CHOI
### 777 SOUTH FIGUEROA STREET, SUITE 4207
### LOS ANGELES, CALIFORNIA 90017
Telephone: 213-892-7700
Fax: 213-892-7777

*Tax Law including California State and Local Taxation, Tax Exempt Organizations, Tax Litigation and International Taxation.*

*FIRM PROFILE: The firm engages in the general practice of law with emphasis on California State and local taxation and nonprofit corporations. The firm's expertise in California State and local taxation includes all matters before the Franchise Tax Board, State Board of Equalization, Employment Development Department, and includes local real and personal property tax matters and local business and payroll tax matters. The firm's work with nonprofit corporations includes all legal issues relating to associations, charities, churches, museums, private foundations, cemeteries, social clubs, hospitals, scientific research organizations, educational organizations and amateur sports organizations. The firm also has expertise in the representation of clients before the U.S. Internal Revenue Service and U.S. Tax Court, including the representation of foreign entities in disputes involving transfer pricing, effectively connected income, withholding and other international tax issues.*

### MEMBERS OF FIRM

**ALBERT R. RODRÍGUEZ,** born Los Angeles, California, December 27, 1951; admitted to bar, 1978, California. *Education:* University of California at Irvine (B.A., 1974); Yale University (J.D., 1978). Author: "1986 Legislative Changes Affecting California Nonprofit Corporations," 21 U.S.F.L. Rev. 831, 1987. With Latham & Watkins, 1978-1996, (Partner, 1986-1995). *Member:* Los Angeles County and American (Member, Exempt Organization Committee, Taxation Section, 1981—) Bar Associations; State Bar of California (Member: Nonprofit and Unincorporated Organizations Committee, 1984-1989, 1994—; Chair, 1986-1987; Section on Taxation); Fellow, American Bar Foundation.

**DWAYNE M. HORII,** born Inglewood, California, November 16, 1960; admitted to bar, 1986, California. *Education:* University of California at Berkeley (B.S., 1982); University of Michigan (J.D., 1985). Adjunct Lecturer, (Multistate Corporate Tax, Golden Gate University Schools of Accounting and Taxation, 1996—. With: Latham & Watkins, 1985-1992; Wilson, Sonsini, Goodrich & Rosati, 1992-1996. *Member:* Los Angeles County (Chair/Vice-Chair, State and Local Tax Committee, 1992), Santa Clara County (Member, Tax Section) and American (Member, Tax Section) Bar

*(This Listing Continued)*

---

Associations; State Bar of California (Member: Executive Committee, Taxation Section, 1995—; State and Local Tax Committee).

**WILLIAM C. CHOI,** born Seoul, Korea, June 15, 1959; admitted to bar, 1985, California. *Education:* San Jose State University (B.S., Highest Honors, 1981); University of Southern California (J.D., 1985). Member, University of Southern California Law Review, 1983-1984. With: Latham & Watkins, Law Firm, Los Angeles, California, 1985-1992; Kim & Chang Law Firm, 1992-1995; Coudert Brothers Law Firm, Hong Kong, 1995. Deloitte, Haskins & Sells, (Deloitte & Touche) Accounting Firm, San Jose, California, 1981-1982. Passed C.P.A. Examination, 1982. *Member:* Los Angeles County (Member, Tax Section) and American (Member, Tax Section, Committee on U.S. Activities of Foreigners and Tax Treaties, 1989-1992) Bar Associations; State Bar of California (Member, Tax Section). *LANGUAGES:* Korean.

---

## ROGERS & WELLS
### 444 SOUTH FLOWER STREET
### LOS ANGELES, CALIFORNIA 90071-2901
Telephone: 213-689-2900
Facsimile: 213-689-2999

### REVISERS OF THE NEW YORK LAW DIGEST FOR THIS DIRECTORY.

*New York, N.Y. Office:* Two Hundred Park Avenue, New York, N.Y. 10166-0153. Telephone: 212-878-8000. Facsimile: 212-878-8375. Telex: 234493 RKWUR. E-Mail: email@rw.com.

*Washington, D.C. Office:* 607 Fourteenth Street, N.W., Washington, D.C. 20005-2018. Telephone: 202-434-0700. Facsimile: 202-434-0800.

*Paris, France Office:* 47, Avenue Hoche, 75008-Paris, France. Telephone: 33-1-44-09-46-00. Facsimile: 33-1-42-67-50-81. Telex: 651617 EURLAW.

*London, England Office:* 40 Basinghall Street, London EC2V 5DE, England. Telephone: 44-171-628-0101. Facsimile: 44-171-628-6111.

*Frankfurt, Germany Office:* Westendstrasse 16-22, 60325 Frankfurt/Main, Federal Republic of Germany. Telephone: 49-69-97-14-78-0. Facsimile: 49-69-97-14-78-33.

*Hong Kong:* One Exchange Square, 8 Connaught Place, Central, Hong Kong. Telephone: 852-2844-3500. Facsimile: 852-2844-3555.

*General Practice.*

### PARTNERS

**MICHAEL D. BERK,** born Chicago, Illinois, August 4, 1943; admitted to bar, 1967, California; 1981, District of Columbia. *Education:* University of California, Berkeley (B.A., 1964); University of California School of Law (J.D., 1967). Order of the Coif; Phi Delta Phi. Note and Comment Editor, UCLA Law Review, 1966-1967. Author: "The Bargaining Lockout: The Great Equalizer," 13 UCLA Law Review 381, 1966; "Darr v. Yellow Cab Co.: The Advent of the Consumer Class Action in California," 10 University of San Francisco Law Review 651, 1976. Co-Author: *California Lis Pendens Practice, Second Edition,* California Continuing Education of the Bar. Law Clerk to the Hon. Raymond L. Sullivan, California Supreme Court, 1967-1968. Panelist, Continuing Education of the Bar, Real Property Remedies, 1976 and 1980. Judge Pro Tem, Los Angeles Municipal Court, 1981—. Arbitrator, Superior Court of the State of California, 1981—. *Member:* Los Angeles County (Member: Sections on Trial Lawyers, Executive Committee, 1985-1988; Real Property, Real Property Litigation Steering Committee, 1995—), American (Member, Sections on Litigation; Business Law; Tort and Insurance Practice) Bar Associations; State Bar of California; District of Columbia Bar (inactive); The Association of Business Trial Lawyers. *PRACTICE AREAS:* Banking Litigation; Business Litigation; Business Insurance; Business Torts; Real Estate Litigation. *Email:* berkm@rw.com

**ALLAN E. CERAN,** born Jersey City, New Jersey, March 6, 1954; admitted to bar, 1980, California. *Education:* Boston University (B.A., with distinction, 1976); University of California School of Law (J.D., 1979). Phi Beta Kappa. Associate Editor, 1977-1978, Chief Article Editor, 1978-1979, UCLA Law Review. Author: "The Insurer's Duty of Good Faith and Fair Dealing," 25 UCLA Law Review 1413, 1978. Co-Author: "Lis Pendens: A Provisional Remedy," 6 Los Angeles Lawyer 10, March, 1983; "Depositions," California Continuing Education of the Bar, September, 1983. Law Clerk to the Hon. John F. Gerry, U.S. District Judge, District of New Jersey, 1979-1980. *Member:* Los Angeles County Bar Association; State Bar of California; Association of Business Trial Lawyers. *Email:* cerana@rw.com

**JOHN I. FORRY,** born February 9, 1945; admitted to bar, 1970, California; 1977, U.S. Tax Court; 1979, U.S. Supreme Court. *Education:* Am-

*(This Listing Continued)*

CAA1149B

## ROGERS & WELLS, Los Angeles—Continued

herst College (A.B., 1966); Harvard University (J.D., 1969). Author/Editor: *A Practical Guide to Foreign Investment in the United States*, BNA International, Inc., 1st Edition 1979, edition in French 1980, 2nd edition 1982, edition in Japanese 1983, edition in German 1983, loose leaf 3rd edition 1989. Member, Advisory Group to the U.S. Commissioner of Internal Revenue, 1985-1986. **PRACTICE AREAS:** International Taxation; Foreign Investment in the United States; Project Finance. **Email:** forryj@rw.com

**JOHN A. KARACZYNSKI,** born Brooklyn, New York, January 23, 1953; admitted to bar, 1978, New York; 1980, California. *Education:* Cornell University (B.A., magna cum laude, 1974; J.D., cum laude, 1977). Member, Board of Editors, Cornell Law Review, 1976-1977. Author: "Standards For the Suppression of Evidence Under the Supreme Court's Supervisory Power," 62 Cornell Law Review 364, 1977. *Member:* New York State, Federal and American Bar Association; The State Bar of California; Association of Business Trial Lawyers (Member, Board of Governors, 1988-1989). **PRACTICE AREAS:** Antitrust; Complex Commercial Litigation; Media and First Amendment. **Email:** karaczyj@rw.com

**JOHN K. KEITT, JR.,** born Boston, Massachusetts, April 17, 1954; admitted to bar, 1979, South Carolina; 1985, New York (Not admitted in California). *Education:* Dartmouth College (A.B., History, 1976); University of South Carolina (J.D., 1979); Cambridge University, Sidney Sussex College (LL.B., 1981). *Member:* The Association of the Bar of the City of New York; New York State, American and International (Member, Committee on International Computer and Technology Law) Bar Associations. **Email:** keittj@rw.com

**TERRY O. KELLY,** born Baltimore, Maryland, July 21, 1945; admitted to bar, 1970, District of Columbia; 1973, California. *Education:* Georgetown University (B.A., 1967); New York University (J.D., 1970). Member, Board of Editors, New York University Law Review, 1969-1970. *Member:* Los Angeles County, Federal and American Bar Associations; District of Columbia Bar; State Bar of California. [Capt. U.S. Marine Corps, Judge Advocate Division, 1970-1973]. **PRACTICE AREAS:** Business Litigation; Environmental; Intellectual Property. **Email:** kellyt@rw.com

**EUGENE Y. C. LU,** born Shanghai, China, May 29, 1942; admitted to bar, 1978, California. *Education:* Dalhousie University (B.S., 1963; M.S., 1964); Cambridge University (Ph.D., 1967); University of Southern California (J.D., 1977). Order of the Coif. Staff, Southern California Law Review, 1976-1977. Extern Law Clerk to Hon. Shirley M. Hufstedler, U.S. Court of Appeals, Ninth Circuit, 1977. Special Consultant to U.S. Secretary of Education, Shirley M. Hufstedler, 1980. *Member:* Los Angeles County and American Bar Associations; State Bar of California. **PRACTICE AREAS:** Banking and Project Finance. **Email:** lueyc@rw.com

**RICHARD A. SHORTZ,** born Chicago, Illinois, March 11, 1945; admitted to bar, 1971, California. *Education:* Indiana University (B.S., 1967); Harvard University (J.D., 1970). *Member:* State Bar of California. **Email:** shortzr@rw.com

**CARL W. SONNE,** born Palo Alto, California, April 30, 1958; admitted to bar, 1984, California. *Education:* Brigham Young University (B.A., with high honors, 1981; J.D., 1984). Member and Note and Comment Editor, B.Y.U. Law Review, 1982-1984. Author: "Civil Antitrust Liability Based on Apparent Authority: American Society of Mechanical Engineers v. Hydrolevel Corp." 1983 B.Y.U. Law Review 483. Lecturer: "Recent Developments In Civil Procedure," C.E.B., 1993—. *Member:* State Bar of California. **Email:** sonnec@rw.com

**I. BRUCE SPEISER,** born Jersey City, New Jersey, September 8, 1948; admitted to bar, 1974, California. *Education:* Rutgers University (B.A., 1969); George Washington University (J.D., with honors, 1973). Managing Editor, George Washington Law Review, 1972-1973. *Member:* Los Angeles County Bar Association; State Bar of California. **PRACTICE AREAS:** Bankruptcy Litigation; Foreclosures; Receiverships; Loan Workouts; Business Litigation; Secured Creditor Rights. **Email:** speiseib@rw.com

### ASSOCIATES

**CHRISTOPHER R. BAKER,** born Saigon, Vietnam, September 19, 1969; admitted to bar, 1996, California. *Education:* University of South Carolina (B.S., magna cum laude, 1992); University of Virginia (J.D., 1995). Phi Beta Kappa; Phi Delta Phi. Member, Editorial Board: Virginia Environmental Law Journal; Virginia Tax Review; Virginia Journal of Social Policy and The Law. *Member:* State Bar of California. **Email:** bakerc@rw.com

*(This Listing Continued)*

**DAVID B. COHEN,** born Washington, D.C., February 24, 1960; admitted to bar, 1986, California. *Education:* University of Pennsylvania (B.A., 1981; B.A.S., 1981; M.A., 1981; M.B.A., 1986; J.D., 1986). Associate Editor, 1984-1985 and Editor, 1985-1986, University of Pennsylvania Law Review. Co-Author: *Modern Business Law and the Regulatory Environment*, McGraw-Hill, Inc., 1996; *Business and its Legal Environment*, Prentice-Hall, Inc., 1992; Article, "Advising Project Lenders on Proposition 65," *Los Angeles Lawyer*, May, 1989. Lecturer, Department of Finance, Real Estate and Law, California State University, Long Beach, 1991-1995. *Member:* State Bar of California. **Email:** cohend@rw.com

**ALAN H. FAIRLEY,** admitted to bar, 1995, California. *Education:* University of California at Los Angeles (B.A., summa cum laude, 1990); University of California School of Law, Los Angeles (J.D., 1995). Phi Beta Kappa. Member and Editor, UCLA Law Review, 1993-1995. *Member:* State Bar of California. **Email:** fairleya@rw.com

**RICHARD C. JUN,** born December 3, 1970; admitted to bar, 1996, New York (Not admitted in California). *Education:* Harvard College (A.B., cum laude, 1992); Columbia Law School (J.D., 1995). **Email:** junr@rw.com

**STEVEN M. RUSKIN,** born White Plains, New York, October 7, 1965; admitted to bar, 1990, California. *Education:* University of Michigan (A.B., 1986); University of Michigan Law School (J.D., 1990). *Member:* State Bar of California. **Email:** ruskins@rw.com

**JULIE A. SHEPARD,** born San Francisco, California, May 4, 1965; admitted to bar, 1994, California. *Education:* University of California, Berkeley (B.A., 1988); McGeorge School of Law (J.D., 1994). Valedictorian. Order of the Coif. Recipient, American Jurisprudence Awards in: Constitutional Law; Sales and Leases; Bankruptcy; Decedents's Estates and Trusts; Legal Writing and Research. Outstanding Graduating Senior. Traynor Honor Society. Symposium Editor, The Transnational Lawyer, 1993-1994. Author: "Using United States Antitrust Laws Against the Keiretsu as a Wedge into the Japanese Market," 6 Transnat'l Law. 345 (1993). *Member:* Los Angeles County Bar Association; State Bar of California. **Email:** shepardj@rw.com

**STEVEN S. SPITZ,** born Southampton, New York, February 8, 1968; admitted to bar, 1994, California. *Education:* Brown University (A.B., magna cum laude, with highest honors, 1990); Columbia University (J.D., 1994). Phi Beta Kappa. Head Articles Editor, Columbia Human Rights Law Review, 1993-1994. Author: "The Norplant Debate: Birth Control or Woman Control?" 25 Columbia Human Rights Law Review 131 (1993). *Member:* Los Angeles County Bar Association; State Bar of California. **Email:** spitzs@rw.com

### REVISERS OF THE NEW YORK LAW DIGEST FOR THIS DIRECTORY.

(For biographical data of all partners, see Professional Biographies at New York, New York)

---

## ALAIN G. ROGIER

**12100 WILSHIRE BOULEVARD, SUITE 1900**
**LOS ANGELES, CALIFORNIA 90025-1722**
*Telephone: 310-207-0421*
*Fax: 310-826-3210*

*Family Law Dissolutions, Domestic and International Custody, Paternity, Support.*

**ALAIN G. ROGIER,** born Paris, France, May 15, 1947; admitted to bar, 1976, California. *Education:* University of California at Berkeley (B.A., 1969); Loyola University of Los Angeles (J.D., 1974). Lecturer: "How to Increase the Spousal and Child Support," Beverly Hills Bar, Family Symposium, 1995; "Family Law and Estate Planning Aspects of Prenuptial Agreements," California Bar, 1995; "Out of State Jurisdiction: A Review of Uniform Child Custody Jurisdiction Act, the Hague Convention and the Federal Parental Kidnapping Act," California State Bar Convention, San Diego, California, 1993; "Child Support, Spousal Support, Attorney's Fees," State Bar MCLE Institute San Diego, California, Fall 1993; "Family Law Practice," Beverly Hills Bar Association Young Barristers Division, Fall 1993; "Hot Tips," Beverly Hills Bar Association Family Law Section, Spring 1993; "Custody and the Use of Psychological Testimony in Custody Cases," State Bar of California MCLE Institute, San Diego, California, Fall 1992; "The Relation Between Family Law and Estate Planning/Probate," Los Angeles County Bar, Family Law Section/Probate Section, 1992; "Financial Considerations in Family Law," State Bar of California MCLE Institute, Monterey, California, Spring 1992. Author: "Critical Distinctions Between Family Law vs. Civil Litigation," American Bar Family Law

*(This Listing Continued)*

Subcommittee Journal. Consultant, Continuing Education of the Bar, California State Bar, Family Law Publications. Contributor, Family Law Mentors Program, "Handling a Marital Dissolution." Deputy City Attorney, City of Los Angeles, California, 1976-1979. President's Ad Hoc Committee on the Status of the Bar, Los Angeles County Bar, 1993. *Member:* Beverly Hills (Member: Family Law Section; Executive Committee, 1995—), Los Angeles County (Member, Family Law Section) and American (Chair, Family Law Subcommittee, General Practice Division, 1993) Bar Associations; State Bar of California (Chair, Executive Committee, General and Solo Practice Section, 1993; Member: Family Law Section; Continuing Education Dept., Family Law Advisory Committee, 1993—); Cardozo Society (Member, Executive Steering Committee). *LANGUAGES:* French.

REFERENCE: French Consulate, Beverly Hills, California.

---

## LAW OFFICES OF
## DANIEL ROMANO

### LOS ANGELES, CALIFORNIA

(See Santa Monica)

*Business Litigation, Real Estate Litigation, Environmental Law, Land Use, Entertainment Litigation, Insurance Coverage Litigation and Toxic Torts.*

---

## S. ROGER ROMBRO

*A LAW CORPORATION*

10866 WILSHIRE BOULEVARD, SUITE 500
### LOS ANGELES, CALIFORNIA 90024
Telephone: 310-475-4088
Fax: 310-475-5543

*Business and Family Law and Civil Litigation*

**S. ROGER ROMBRO,** born Buffalo, New York, April 23, 1944; admitted to bar, 1973, California; 1974, U.S. District Court, Central District of California and U.S. Court of Appeals, Ninth Circuit; 1984, U.S. District Court, Southern District of California. *Education:* University of Pennsylvania (B.A., 1966); Tulane University (J.D., 1972). Phi Alpha Delta. Law Clerk to the Honorable Stanley Nelson Barnes, Circuit Judge, U.S. Court of Appeals, Ninth Circuit, 1972-1973. *Member:* Beverly Hills and Los Angeles County Bar Associations; State Bar of California (Member, Committee on Custody and Visitation, 1984—). (Certified Specialist, Family Law, The State Bar of California Board of Legal Specialization).

---

## JOHN R. RONGE

10866 WILSHIRE BOULEVARD, 15TH FLOOR
### LOS ANGELES, CALIFORNIA 90024
Telephone: 310-441-4100
Fax: 310-470-1360
Email: RONGEJOHN@aol.com

*Tax, Probate and Estate Planning, Real Estate, Business.*

**JOHN R. RONGE,** born Chicago, Illinois, March 28, 1948; admitted to bar, 1984, California and U.S. District Court, Central District of California; 1993, U.S. Tax Court. *Education:* Illinois Institute of Technology (B.S., 1970); University of California (M.B.A., 1973); Loyola Law School (J.D., 1983). Tau Beta Pi. Certified Public Accountant, California, 1979. *Member:* American Bar Association (Member, Sections on: Taxation, Real Property, Probate and Trust Law); State Bar of California (Member, Sections on: Taxation, Estate Planning, Trust and Probate); California Society of Certified Public Accountants (Member, The Westside Technology Users Group of the Los Angeles Chapter).

---

## ROPER & FOLINO
*Established in 1974*

SUITE 1700, 3255 WILSHIRE BOULEVARD
### LOS ANGELES, CALIFORNIA 90010-1420
Telephone: 213-388-3181
Telecopier: 213-388-2600
Email: legalkix@ix.netcom.com

*Insurance, Trial and Appellate Practice in all State and Federal Courts. Negligence, Products Liability, Malpractice, Casualty and Fire Insurance Law, Professional Negligence, Landslide and Subsidence Law, Construction Litigation, Municipality and Public Entities, Excess and Surplus Lines, Bad Faith and Wrongful Termination, Insurance, Coverage and Litigation and Reinsurance Law, Toxic Torts, Construction Defect Defense, Subrogation Law.*

### MEMBERS OF FIRM

**JAMES L. ROPER,** born Los Angeles, California, May 24, 1935; admitted to bar, 1961, California, U.S. District Court, Central and Southern Districts of California and U.S. Court of Appeals, 9th Circuit; 1968, U.S. Supreme Court. *Education:* University of California at Los Angeles (A.B., cum laude, 1957; J.D., 1961). Phi Delta Phi; Phi Beta Kappa. Member, National Panel of Arbitrators, American Arbitration Association. Appointee of Presiding Judge, Los Angeles Attorneys' Special Arbitration Group, 1972. *Member:* Los Angeles County and American Bar Associations; The State Bar of California; Association of Southern California Defense Counsel (Member, Board of Directors, 1971-1973; Membership Chairman, 1970-1971); American Board of Trial Advocates (Diplomate). *PRACTICE AREAS:* Agent E & O; Construction Defect Litigation; Legal Malpractice Law; Excess Insurance Law; Real Estate Errors and Omissions.

**DOMENIC FOLINO,** born Watertown, New York, January 17, 1938; admitted to bar, 1964, New York; 1966, California. *Education:* Syracuse University (B.A., 1960; LL.B., 1963). Phi Alpha Delta. *Member:* The State Bar of California; Association of Southern California Defense Counsel. [With U.S. Army Reserve, 1963-1969]. *PRACTICE AREAS:* Construction Insurance; Insurance Subrogation; Trial Practice; Environmental Law; Environmental Insurance Litigation.

**MICHAEL J. IRWIN,** born Chicago, Illinois, June 26, 1946; admitted to bar, 1978, California; 1979, U.S. District Court, Central District of California. *Education:* University of Texas at Austin (B.A., 1968); Southwestern University (J.D., 1978). Staff Member, Southwestern University Law Review, 1977-1978. *Member:* The State Bar of California; Association of Southern California Defense Counsel. *PRACTICE AREAS:* Products Liability Law; Tort Law; Legal Malpractice Law; Subrogation Law; Real Estate Errors and Omissions.

**JOHN B. LARSON,** born Denver, Colorado, February 14, 1954; admitted to bar, 1983, California. *Education:* Mankato State University (B.S., 1976); Southwestern University (J.D., 1982). Dean's List, Southwestern University, 1982. Member, Moot Court. Superior Court Arbitrator. *Member:* Los Angeles County, Central District, Federal and American Bar Associations; The State Bar of California. *PRACTICE AREAS:* Environmental Insurance Litigation; Government Law; Construction Defect Litigation; Public Entity Law; Subrogation Law.

**JOSEPH L. STARK,** born Los Angeles, California, May 23, 1958; admitted to bar, 1984, California; U.S. District Court, Central and Southern Districts of California. *Education:* University of California at Santa Barbara (B.A., 1981); Southwestern University (J.D., cum laude, 1984). Recipient, American Jurisprudence Awards in Civil Procedure, Legal Responsibility, Insurance Law and Health Care Practices. *Member:* The State Bar of California. *PRACTICE AREAS:* Appellate Practice; Insurance Coverage; Public Entity Law; Nursing Home; Administrative Hearings and Appeals.

**RAYMOND J. FARGO,** born Glendale, California, March 27, 1938; admitted to bar, 1975, California and U.S. District Court, Central District of California. *Education:* California State University at Los Angeles (B.A., 1970); Southwestern University School of Law (J.D., 1974). Arbitrator, Personal Injury Panel of Los Angeles Superior Court. *Member:* The State Bar of California; Association of Southern California Defense Counsel. *PRACTICE AREAS:* Accidents; Personal Injury; Malpractice Defense; Uninsured Motorist; Products Liability Law; Litigation Defense.

**MICHAEL A. KRUPPE,** born Hinsdale, Illinois, May 14, 1959; admitted to bar, 1986, California. *Education:* Vanderbilt University (B.A., 1982); John Marshall Law School (J.D., 1985). Staff Editor, John Marshall Law Review, 1984-1985. Quarterfinalist, Irving Kaufman National Securities Law Moot Court Competition. *Member:* Los Angeles County and American Bar Associations; The State Bar of California; Association of

*(This Listing Continued)*

## ROPER & FOLINO, Los Angeles—Continued

Southern California Defense Counsel. *PRACTICE AREAS:* Appellate Practice; Automobile Negligence; Construction Defect Litigation; Construction Accidents; Civil Rights Actions.

**JOHN M. BERGERSON,** born Eugene, Oregon, October 27, 1960; admitted to bar, 1986, California. *Education:* University of Southern California (B.A., 1982); Southwestern University (J.D., 1986). *Member:* Los Angeles County and American Bar Associations; The State Bar of California; Association of Southern California Defense Counsel. *PRACTICE AREAS:* Accidents; Personal Injury; Construction Defect Litigation; Defamation; Intentional Torts; Premises Liability.

**TAMAR D. TUJIAN,** born September 30, 1967; admitted to bar, 1993, California; U.S. District Court, Central District of California. *Education:* University of California at Los Angeles (B.A., magna cum laude, 1989) Phi Beta Kappa; Loyola Law School (J.D., 1993). Recipient, American Jurisprudence Awards in Comparative Law and Conflicts of Law. *Member:* State Bar of California; American Bar Association. *PRACTICE AREAS:* Construction and Design; Insurance Defense Law; Public Entity Law; Litigation Defense; Wrongful Death Law.

REPRESENTATIVE CLIENTS: Central Mutual Insurance Co.; CIGNA; ESIS; Housing Authority Risk Retention Group; National Car Rental Systems Inc.; First State Insurance Co.; ITT-Hartford Insurance Co.; Zenith Insurance Co. (Special Situations); Cal-Farm Insurance Co.; Maine Bonding and Casualty Co.; Maxson-Young Associates, Inc.; Michigan Millers Mutual Insurance Co.; Old Republic Insurance Co.; Northland Insurance Co.; IT Corporation; Ryder Truck Rental & Ryder Systems; Commercial Underwriters Insurance Co.; Shapell Industries Inc.; S&S Construction Co.; CNA Insurance Co.; Superior National Insurance Co.; IT-New England Management Co.; Pepsi Cola Bottling Co. of Los Angeles & Pepsico Inc.; Hawkeye Insurance Co.; Quincy Mutual Insurance Co.
REFERENCES: First Interstate Bank (Wilshire Blvd. Bevends Office); American Savings and Loan Assn. (Wilshire Center).

---

## ROPERS, MAJESKI, KOHN & BENTLEY

*A PROFESSIONAL CORPORATION*
550 SOUTH HOPE STREET, SUITE 1900
**LOS ANGELES, CALIFORNIA 90071**
Telephone: 213-312-2000
Fax: 213-312-2001

*Redwood City, California Office:* 1001 Marshall Street. Telephone: 415-364-8200. Fax: 415-367-0997.
*San Jose, California Office:* 80 North 1st Street. Telephone: 408-287-6262. Fax: 408-297-6819.
*San Francisco, California Office:* 670 Howard Street. Telephone: 415-543-4800. Fax: 415-512-1574.
*Santa Rosa, California Office:* Fountaingrove Center, Suite 300, 3558 Round Barn Boulevard. Telephone: 707-524-4200. Fax: 707-523-4610.
*Sacramento, California Office:* 1000 G. Street, Suite 400. Telephone: 916-556-3100. Fax: 916-442-7121.

Arbitration and Mediation, Appellate Services, Banking and Financial Institutions Services, Bankruptcy, Commercial Litigation, Construction Litigation, Employment Law, Environmental Compliance and Litigation, Estate Planning, Trusts Probate and Elder Law, Fidelity and Surety Law, Health Care Law, Insurance Coverage and Litigation, Insurance Regulatory and Reinsurance, Intellectual Property Protection and Litigation, Products Litigation, Professional Malpractice Litigation, Real Estate Law, Trials and Antitrust.

**STEPHEN J. ERIGERO,** born San Francisco, California, December 7, 1959; admitted to bar, 1985, California. *Education:* Loyola Marymount University (B.A., 1982); Hastings College of the Law, University of California (J.D., 1985). Phi Delta Phi. *Member:* State Bar of California. *PRACTICE AREAS:* Insurance Coverage; Construction and General Civil Litigation; Bad Faith Litigation.

**FRANK T. SABAITIS,** born Scranton, Pennsylvania, June 2, 1954; admitted to bar, 1980, Illinois; 1983, California. *Education:* Boston College (A.B., cum laude, 1976); De Paul University College of Law (J.D., 1980). *Member:* Bar Association of San Francisco; Chicago, Illinois State and American Bar Associations; The State Bar of California. (Resident). *PRACTICE AREAS:* Construction Litigation; Products and General Civil Litigation; Bad Faith Litigation.

**MARTA B. ARRIANDIAGA,** born Havana, Cuba, February 25, 1953; admitted to bar, 1985, California. *Education:* University of Delaware (B.A., 1975); West Chester College (M.A., 1980); University of San Francisco (J.D., 1985). *Member:* Alameda County and American Bar Associations;

*(This Listing Continued)*

State Bar of California. *LANGUAGES:* Spanish. *PRACTICE AREAS:* Insurance Coverage and Bad Faith Litigation.

**SUE CAROL ROKAW,** born New York, N.Y., October 28, 1949; admitted to bar, 1985, California; U.S. District Court, Northern, Eastern and Central Districts of California. *Education:* University of Rochester (B.A., 1971); Southern Connecticut State College (M.L.S., 1975); University of San Francisco (J.D., 1984). Phi Beta Kappa; Beta Phi Mu. Recipient, Russell Mumford Tuttle Award for Excellence in Greek. Member, University of San Francisco Law Review. Author: "Shedding the Cloak of Ancillary Administration: Application of Summary Probate Procedures to Estates of Decedents Formerly Domiciled in Foreign Countries," Univ. of S.F. Law Review (Summer 1983). Instructor, Hastings College of the Law, Legal Writing and Research Program, 1989-1990. *Member:* Los Angeles County Bar Association; Women Lawyers Association of Los Angeles. *PRACTICE AREAS:* Insurance Coverage and Bad Faith Litigation; Business Litigation.

**CAROL KURKE LUCAS,** born Washington, D.C., September 4, 1957; admitted to bar, 1983, New York and U.S. District Court, Southern and Eastern Districts of New York; 1990, California. *Education:* University of Rochester (B.A., magna cum laude, 1979); New York University (J.D., cum laude, 1982). Phi Beta Kappa; Order of the Coif. Chapter Author: Widger & Moffat, Standards of Care in Emergency Medicine (Little, Brown, 1994). Author: "Liability for Utilization Review Decisions," Managing Employee Health Benefits," Autumn, 1994; "Do Managed Care Incentives Increase Liability?" LACMA Physician, May 16, 1994. *Member:* Los Angeles County Bar Association; State Bar of California; National Health Lawyers Association. *PRACTICE AREAS:* Health Care; Securities; Corporate.

**ALLAN E. ANDERSON,** born Berkeley, California, August 14, 1961; admitted to bar, 1988, California. *Education:* University of California at Berkeley (A.B., 1983); University of San Francisco (J.D., 1987). Phi Delta Phi. *Member:* Bar Association of San Francisco; Los Angeles County, San Mateo County and American Bar Associations. (Resident). *PRACTICE AREAS:* Civil Litigation.

---

**MICHAEL W. PARKS,** born Lewiston, New York, December 3, 1965; admitted to bar, 1991, California. *Education:* Cornell University; Arizona State University (B.A., 1987); University of the Pacific, McGeorge School of Law (J.D., 1991). Phi Alpha Delta. Legislative Review Staff, 1989, Comment Staff, 1989-1990 and Board of Editors, 1990-1991, Pacific Law Journal. Settlement Officer, Second District Court of Appeals, Settlement Conference Program. *Member:* Los Angeles County (Member, Appellate Courts Committee) and American (Member, Tort and Insurance Practice Section) Bar Associations; State Bar of California.

**SEAN S. VARNER,** born San Bernardino, California, August 14, 1966; admitted to bar, 1993, California. *Education:* University of California, Los Angeles (B.A., 1989); Cambridge University; Pepperdine University (J.D., cum laude, 1993). Editor, Pepperdine Law Review. Recipient, Sorensen Outstanding Author Award, 1992. Author, "The California Environmental Quality Act (CEQA) After Two decades: Relevant Problems and Ideas for Necessary Reform," 19 Pepperdine Law Review 1447 (reprinted, National Law Anthology, Environmental Law Anthology October, 1992). *PRACTICE AREAS:* Corporate Transactions.

**ERNEST E. PRICE,** born Baltimore, Maryland, May 30, 1962; admitted to bar, 1993, California and U.S. Court of Appeals, 9th Circuit. *Education:* University of California at Berkeley (B.A., 1984); University of San Francisco (J.D., 1992). Recipient, NROTC Scholarship. Moot Court Championship, Second Place. National Moot Court Competition. [U.S. Marine Corps., 1984-1989, Capt.; Activated Desert Storm, 1990-1991, Capt. (Marine Corps Reserves)]. *PRACTICE AREAS:* General Civil Litigation; Environmental Coverage; Construction Defect; Real Property; Civil Rights; Insurance Coverage; Personal Injury.

**ANDREW D. CASTRICONE,** born Albany, New York, September 30, 1963; admitted to bar, 1991, California; 1993, Massachusetts and New York. *Education:* State University of New York at Cortland (B.S., 1985); University of the Pacific, McGeorge School of Law (J.D., 1991). Phi Delta Phi. Member, Moot Court Honors Board. Recipient, Emil Gumpert Trial Advocacy Award for Outstanding Achievement as Student Advocate. *Member:* State Bar of California. *PRACTICE AREAS:* Litigation.

**CHARLENE RUDIO CULVER,** born Helena, Montana, January 24, 1943; admitted to bar, 1988, California and U.S. District Court, Northern, Central, Eastern and Southern Districts of California. *Education:* College of Notre Dame (B.A., cum laude, 1981); Golden Gate University (J.D., 1987). Associate Editor, Golden Gate University Law Review, 1987. Member,

*(This Listing Continued)*

National Association of Securities Dealers Arbitration Panel; U.S. Diving Law and Legislation. *Member:* Los Angeles County Bar Association (Member, Sections on: Probate and Litigation); State Bar of California (Member, Sections on: Litigation and Environmental). **PRACTICE AREAS:** Environmental Coverage Litigation; Business Litigation; Probate and Trust Litigation.

**I. PAUL BAE,** born Seoul, Korea, July 11, 1964; admitted to bar, 1991, California and U.S. District Court, Northern District of California; 1996, U.S. District Court, Central and Southern Districts of California. *Education:* University of California, Los Angeles (B.A., 1988); McGeorge School of Law (J.D., 1991). Finalist, International Moot Court, Best Memorial. County of Santa Clara, Deputy District Attorney, 1991-1992. (Resident). **LANGUAGES:** Korean. **PRACTICE AREAS:** Products and General Civil Litigation.

**BRADLEY P. BOYER,** born Lansing, Michigan, August 12, 1970; admitted to bar, 1995, California and U.S. District Court, Southern District of California. *Education:* Michigan State University (B.A., 1992); University of San Diego (J.D., 1995). Judicial Extern: Hon. John S. Rhoades, U.S. District Court, Southern District of California; Hon. Ruben Brooks, Supervising Judge, U.S. District Court, Southern District of California; Hon. Suzanne Knoff, San Diego North County municipal Court (Drug Court). Law Clerk: U.S. Attorney's Office, Southern District of California (Drug Task Force); U.S. Attorney's Office, Western District of Michigan, Northern Division.

**MICHAEL T. O'CALLAGHAN,** born Los Angeles, California, December 6, 1963; admitted to bar, 1993, California and U.S. District Court, Central District of California; 1995, District of Columbia. *Education:* University of Southern California (B.S., Business, 1986); Loyola Law School (J.D., 1993); Georgetown University Law Center. Recipient, American Jurisprudence Award for Evidence. Author, "Resolving The Conflicts In Our Lives and In Our Communities," Loyola Lawyer, Fall 1994. *Member:* Los Angeles County (Member, Section on Litigation and Taxation) and American Bar Associations; State Bar of California; District of Columbia Bar. **PRACTICE AREAS:** Construction Defect; Litigation.

**ROBIN L JACOBS,** born Winston-Salem, North Carolina, July 25, 1969; admitted to bar, 1995, California and U.S. District Court, Central District of California. *Education:* Wake Forest University (B.A., 1991); Pepperdine University (J.D., cum laude, 1995). Recipient: Dean's Academic Merit Scholarship; N.C. Academic Merit Scholarship. *Member:* Los Angeles County (Member, Sections on: Litigation and Environmental) and Santa Monica Bar Associations. **PRACTICE AREAS:** Litigation.

**GERALD B. MALANGA,** born Santa Monica, California, January 16, 1964; admitted to bar, 1993, California. *Education:* University of Southern California (B.A., 1986); Pepperdine University (J.D., 1993). Phi Delta Phi. **LANGUAGES:** Spanish. **PRACTICE AREAS:** General Civil Liability Defense.

**ROBIN J. DEVEREUX,** born Phoenix, Arizona, December 10, 1964; admitted to bar, 1994, California. *Education:* Princeton University (B.A. in History, 1987); Pepperdine University School of Law (J.D., 1994). Phi Delta Phi. Participant: Fall Individual Advocacy Tournament, 1992 and 1993; Dalsimer Moot Court Competition, 1993. *Member:* State Bar of California. **PRACTICE AREAS:** Insurance Defense; Malpractice.

REPRESENTATIVE CLIENTS: Aetna Life & Casualty Co.; Aetna Casualty & Surety Co.; Alamo Rent A Car, Inc.; ALCOA; Alta Bates Corp.; American International Group; Avemco; Bank of America; Bank of California; Bedford Properties, Inc.; Black Mountain Spring Water Co.; Cadence Design Systems Inc.; California Casualty; California Micro Devices; California State Automobile Assn.; Chubb Group; CIGNA; Continental Insurance Cos.; Continental National Assurance; County of San Mateo; Employers Reinsurance; Farmers Insurance Group; Fireman's Fund American Insurance Co.; First American Title Insurance, Co.; First Interstate Bank; Granite Construction Co.; Grinnell Corp.; Hallmark Cards, Inc.; Hartford Insurance Co.; Holiday Inn Corp.; Home Insurance; Industrial Indemnity; Intel Corp.; Kelly Moore Paint Co.; Kinetic Systems, Inc.; Certain Lloyd's Underwriters; Lucky Stores; Mansville Trust; Metropolitan Life & Casualty; Montgomery Ward; Nationwide Insurance Co.; North American Van Lines, Inc.; Orion Group; PMI Mortgage Insurance Co.; Prudential Property & Casualty; Reliance Insurance Cos.; Royal Globe Insurance Cos.; San Mateo Co.; Santa Clara County; Santa Cruz County; Service Corporation International (SCI); Shand Morahan & Co.; Signetic Corp.; Southern Pacific Transportation Co.; Stanford University Hospital; State Farm Insurance Cos.; TeleVideo Systems, Inc.; Transport Insurance Co.; Truck Insurance Exchange; The Travelers; USAA; Volvo Corporation of America; Watkins Johnson; Westinghouse; White Consolidated Industries; Zimpro.

(For Data on all Firm Personnel, see Professional Biographies at Redwood City, San Jose, Sacramento, San Francisco and Santa Rosa, California.)

## LAW OFFICES OF STEVEN A. ROSEMAN

12011 SAN VINCENTE BOULEVARD, SUITE 600
**LOS ANGELES, CALIFORNIA 90049-4948**
Telephone: 310-440-3144
Fax: 310-440-3140
Email: sarinla@aol.com

*Construction, Real Estate, Community Associations, Landlord-Tenant, Business, Civil Litigation.*

**STEVEN A. ROSEMAN,** born South Africa, January 20, 1963; admitted to bar, 1989, Supreme Court of South Africa; 1993, California. *Education:* University of the Witwatersrand, South Africa (B.S., 1986; J.D., 1989). Certified by Los Angeles County Bar, Trial Advocacy Project, 1996. *Member:* Century City and Los Angeles County Bar Associations; State Bar of California; Community Associations Institute. **PRACTICE AREAS:** Construction Litigation; Real Estate Litigation; Community Association Law.

## ROSEN & ASSOCIATES

SUITE 5850
633 WEST FIFTH STREET
**LOS ANGELES, CALIFORNIA 90071**
Telephone: 213-362-1025
Fax: 213-362-1026

*General Civil Practice, Commercial Litigation, Mergers and Acquisitions, Real Estate, Legal Malpractice.*

**ROBERT C. ROSEN,** born Valley Forge, Pennsylvania, October 4, 1945; admitted to bar, 1970, Pennsylvania (Not admitted in California). *Education:* University of Minnesota (B.S., 1967); Duquesne University (J.D., 1970); Harvard University (LL.M., 1979). Phi Alpha Delta. General Editor, International Securities Regulation, 5 Volumes Oceana Publications, Inc., 1986. Author: "Commercial Business and Trade Laws: India," Oceana Publications, Inc., 1982; "The Myth of Self Regulation or the Dangers of Securities Regulation Without Administration—The Indian Experience," Journal of Comparative Corporate Law and Securities Regulation, Volume 2, No. 4, December, 1979; "Law and Population Growth in Jamaica," The Fletcher School of Law and Diplomacy, Tufts University, Monograph Series No. 10, 1973. *Member:* Los Angeles County (Chair, Business and Corporations Law Section and Securities Law Enforcement Subcommittee), American (Member, Sections on: International Law and Banking and Business Law; Former Member, ABA Special Task Force on Securities Arbitration), International (Member, Committee on Issues and Trading in Securities, Section of Business Law) and Inter-American Bar Associations; State Bar of California (Member, Sections on: Business Law; International Law; Litigation and Real Property Law). **PRACTICE AREAS:** Business Law; Securities.

*OF COUNSEL*

**DAVID E. KRONEMYER,** born Chicago, Illinois, March 12, 1953; admitted to bar, 1976, California, U.S. District Court, Southern District of California and U.S. Court of Appeals, Ninth Circuit; 1977, U.S. District Court, Central District of California; 1980, U.S. District Court, Northern and Eastern Districts of California and U.S. Supreme Court; 1987, New York; 1995, Tennessee. *Education:* University of California at Berkeley (A.B., in Philosophy and Mathematics with great distinction, 1973); University of Southern California (J.D., 1976). Adjunct Associate Professor, Commercial Law and Corporate Law, Southwestern University, 1985-1990. Vice President, Business Affairs, Capitol Records, Inc. *Member:* State Bar of California; American Bar Association (Member, Sections on: Litigation; Corporation, Banking and Business Law); Association of Interstate Commerce Commission Practitioners; Motor Carrier Lawyers Association. **PRACTICE AREAS:** Entertainment Law; Corporate Law; Business Law.

## CHARLES B. ROSENBERG

1901 AVNEUE OF THE STARS
SUITE 1600
**LOS ANGELES, CALIFORNIA 90067**
Telephone: 310-286-3002
Fax: 310-286-3032

*Complex civil and business litigation in state and federal courts. Litigation Management, including selection of counsel. Commercial arbitration. Expert witness on reasonableness of legal fees in large cases.*

(This Listing Continued)

CAA1153B

## CHARLES B. ROSENBERG, Los Angeles—Continued

**CHARLES B. ROSENBERG,** born Pittsburgh, Pennsylvania, March 12, 1945; admitted to bar, 1972, California; 1980, District of Columbia. *Education:* Antioch College (B.A., 1968); Harvard University (J.D., 1971). Case Editor, Harvard Law Review. Author: "The Law After O.J.," American Bar Association Journal, June, 1995; "The Trial of O.J.: How to Watch the Trial and Understand What's Really Going On," Publishing Partners, Los Angeles, 1994; "Uncharted Areas in Commercial Arbitration: The Impact of Rapid Case Growth, Involuntary Arbitration and the Professionalization of Arbitrators," Proceedings of the ABA Conference on Critical Issues in Arbitration, November, 1993; "An L.A. Lawyer Replies (concerning L.A. Law) 98 Yale Law Journal, 1625 June 1989; "The Legal Environment of Business," Management Magazine, May 1985; "An Interview with Bernie Witkin," Los Angeles Lawyer, September 1984; "Learning the Litigation Game," Management Magazine, April 1982; "The Lawyer as Hired Gun," Los Angeles Lawyer, July 1979. Member, Board of Directors, American Judicature Society, 1992—. Member, National Panel of Arbitrators, American Arbitration Association, 1986—. Alternate Delegate, Ninth Circuit Judicial Conference, 1989-1990. Visiting Professor (full time), University of California at Los Angeles, 1982-1983. Adjunct Professor (part time), Southwestern School of Law, 1980. Visiting Instructor (part time), University of California at Los Angeles, Graduate School of Management, 1983-1986. *Member:* State Bar of California; American Bar Association. (Litigation Section Taks Force on Public Dialogue, 1995—; Co-chair, Training the Advocate Committee, 1992-1995; Editor, Pre-Trial Practice and Discovery Committee Newsletter, 1989-1992). **LANGUAGES:** French.

---

## ANDREW M. ROSENFELD

### LOS ANGELES, CALIFORNIA

(See Torrance)

*General Civil Litigation in all State and Federal Courts including Business Litigation, Consumer Bankruptcy, Insurance Bad Faith, Wrongful Termination and Employment Discrimination, and Family Law.*

---

## ROSENFELD, MEYER & SUSMAN, LLP

### LOS ANGELES, CALIFORNIA

(See Beverly Hills)

*General Civil, Trial and Appellate Practice in all State and Federal Courts. Banking and Savings and Loan Law, Copyright, Corporate, Employee Benefits, Entertainment (Motion Picture, Television and Music) Transactions, Errors and Omissions Clearance, Estate Planning, Family Law, Insurance Coverage and Defense Litigation, International Business Law, Labor and Employment Law, Motion Picture Financing, New Media Technologies, Real Estate, Real Property, Securities, Succession Planning, Taxation (Federal, State and International), Trademark, Trusts and Probate, Unfair Competition, Intellectual Property and Media Finance.*

---

## ROSENFELD & WOLFF

*A PROFESSIONAL CORPORATION*

2049 CENTURY PARK EAST, SUITE 600

### LOS ANGELES, CALIFORNIA 90067

Telephone: 310-556-1221

Fax: 310-556-0401

*Corporate, Corporate Securities, Real Estate, General Business.*

**FIRM PROFILE:** Clients of Rosenfeld & Wolff include publicly and privately held corporations and partnerships, including American Stock Exchange-listed companies, as well as high net worth individuals engaged in sophisticated business ventures that encompass financial services, real estate, product distribution, health and fitness, food services, entertainment, high technology and the environment. The law firm is listed in the Bar Register of Preeminent Lawyers and Canadian Directory.

**MORTON M. ROSENFELD,** born St. Louis, Missouri, February 23, 1948; admitted to bar, 1972, California. *Education:* Princeton University (A.B., 1969); University of Michigan (J.D., 1972). Order of the Coif. Note and Comment Editor, University of Michigan Journal of Law Reform, 1971-1972. Author: "SEC Rule 146: A Preliminary View," Los Angeles Bar Bulletin, Vol. 49, No. 9, July, 1974; "Rule 146 Leaves Private Offering Waters Still Muddied," 2 Securities Regulation Law Journal 195, Fall, 1974. *Member:* Los Angeles County Bar Association; The State Bar of California. **PRACTICE AREAS:** Corporate Law; Corporate Securities.

**STEVEN G. WOLFF,** born Rockville Centre, New York, June 8, 1956; admitted to bar, 1981, California; 1983, U.S. Tax Court. *Education:* University of California at Los Angeles (B.A., magna cum laude, 1978); Boalt Hall School of Law, University of California (J.D., 1981). Phi Beta Kappa; Pi Gamma Mu. *Member:* Beverly Hills, Los Angeles County and American Bar Associations; State Bar of California. **PRACTICE AREAS:** Real Estate Law.

**ALAN D. ARONSON,** born Seattle, Washington, July 3, 1962; admitted to bar, 1987, California. *Education:* Stanford University (A.B., 1984); University of California at Los Angeles (J.D., 1987). Member, Order of the Coif. Member, Order of the Barristers. Chief Justice, UCLA Moot Court Honors Program, 1986-1987. *Member:* Los Angeles County Bar Association; State Bar of California. **PRACTICE AREAS:** Corporate Law; Real Estate Law.

---

## ROSS, IVANJACK, LAMBIRTH & ARANOFF

### LOS ANGELES, CALIFORNIA

(See Ivanjack & Lambirth)

---

## S. K. ROSS & ASSOC., P.C.

5777 WEST CENTURY BOULEVARD, SUITE 520

### LOS ANGELES, CALIFORNIA 90045-5659

Telephone: 310-410-4414

FAX: 310-410-1017

Email: skohnxro@counsel.com

URL: http://www.skralaw.com

*Customs, International Trade, Transportation, Admiralty and Maritime, Business and Commercial Law.*

**SUSAN KOHN ROSS,** born Plymouth, England, November 10, 1945; admitted to bar, 1978, California; 1979, U.S. Court of International Trade; 199 0, U.S. Supreme Court. *Education:* University of California at Los Angeles (B.A., 1967); Southwestern University School of Law (J.D., 1977). *Member:* Los Angeles County (Member and Past Vice Chair, Customs Law Committee) and American Bar Associations; State Bar of California; Customs and International Trade Bar Association; Inter-Pacific Bar Association; International Bar Association. **SPECIAL AGENCIES:** U.S. Customs Service; Food and Drug Administration; Department of State; Department of Commerce and U.S. Trade Representative. **PRACTICE AREAS:** International Trade Law; Customs Law; Transportation Law; Business Law.

**JOHN W. SHI,** born Xi'an, P. R. China, January 4, 1963; admitted to bar, 1995, Minnesota, Connecticut and California. *Education:* Xi'an Foreign Languages Institute (B.A., 1985); Brigham Young University (J.D., 1993). **LANGUAGES:** Mandarin. **PRACTICE AREAS:** International Trade; Customs Law; Transportation Law; Business Law.

Languages: German, Mandarin Chinese.

Representative Clients and References available upon request.

---

## ROSS, SACKS & GLAZIER

Established in 1991

SUITE 3900

300 SOUTH GRAND AVENUE

### LOS ANGELES, CALIFORNIA 90071

Telephone: 213-617-2950

Fax: 213-617-9350

*Estate, Trust and Conservatorship Litigation. Business Litigation. Professional Responsibility Litigation. Appellate Practice. Probate and Estate Planning.*

*(This Listing Continued)*

## MEMBERS OF FIRM

**BRUCE S. ROSS,** born Los Angeles, California, February 1, 1947; admitted to bar, 1972, California. *Education:* Oberlin College (A.B., cum laude, 1968); University of California at Berkeley (J.D., 1971). Order of the Coif. Member, 1969-1971, and Note and Comment Editor, 1970-1971, California Law Review. Author: *California Practice Guide: Probate,* The Rutter Group, 2 vols. with annual supplements. Participant, Temporary Judge Program, Los Angeles Municipal Court, 1989-1995. JASOP Settlement Officer, Los Angeles Superior Court, 1992—. *Member:* Los Angeles County (Member: Executive Committee, Taxation Section, 1984-1985; Executive Committee, Estates and Trusts Section, 1994—; Executive Committee, Alternative Dispute Resolution Section, 1996—) and American (Chair, Task Force on State and Local Tax Regulation, Committee on Exempt Organizations, Section of Taxation, 1984-1988; Chair, Estate and Trust Litigation Committee, 1991-1993; Group Chair, Litigation and Controversy Committees, 1996—; Real Property, Probate and Trust Law Section) Bar Associations; State Bar of California (Member, 1987-1989, Vice Chair, 1989-1990 Chair, 1990-1991 and Advisor, 1991-1994, Executive Committee, Estate Planning, Trust and Probate Law Section). Fellow, American College of Trust and Estate Counsel (Member, Board of Regents, 1995—, Member, 1987— and Chair, 1990-1994, Professional Standards Committee; Member, Fiduciary Litigation Committee, 1993—). (Certified Specialist, Estate Planning, Trust and Probate Law, The State Bar of California Board of Legal Specialization). *PRACTICE AREAS:* Estate, Trust and Conservatorship Litigation; Professional Responsibility Litigation; Probate; Appellate Practice; Mediation.

**KENNETH M. GLAZIER,** born Toronto, Ontario, May 17, 1948; admitted to bar, 1973, California. *Education:* Harvard College (B.A., magna cum laude, 1969); Yale Law School (J.D., 1973). Editor, Yale Law Journal, 1972. *Member:* Los Angeles County and American Bar Associations. *PRACTICE AREAS:* Business Litigation; Estate, Trust and Conservatorship Litigation.

**ROBERT N. SACKS,** born Oberlin, Ohio, October 29, 1960; admitted to bar, 1986, California. *Education:* University of Wisconsin (B.A., with distinction, 1981); University of California at Los Angeles (J.D., 1986). Member, Moot Court Honors Program. Teaching Assistant, University of California at Los Angeles School of Law, 1984-1985. Arbitrator, Los Angeles County Superior Court, 1993—. Participant, Temporary Judge Program, Los Angeles County Municipal Court, 1994—. *Member:* Beverly Hills, Los Angeles County and American Bar Associations. *LANGUAGES:* Spanish. *PRACTICE AREAS:* Estate, Trust and Conservatorship Litigation; Business Litigation; Appellate Practice.

**JOHN T. ROGERS, JR.,** born St. Louis, Missouri, April 2, 1955; admitted to bar, 1981, California. *Education:* Stanford University (B.S. with distinction, 1978); University of California at Los Angeles (J.D., 1981). Tau Beta Pi. Managing Editor, Federal Communications Law Journal, 1980-1981. *Member:* Los Angeles County (Chair, Trusts and Estates Section, 1995-1996; Member, Executive Committee, Taxation Section, 1988-1990) and American Bar Associations; State Bar of California (Member, Environmental Subcommittee, Estate Planning, Trust and Probate Law Section, 1993—); Los Angeles Estate Planning Council (President, 1993-1994). Fellow, American College of Trust and Estate Counsel. (Certified Specialist, Estate Planning, Trust and Probate Law, The State Bar of California Board of Legal Specialization). *PRACTICE AREAS:* Trusts and Estates; Taxation Law.

**TERRENCE M. FRANKLIN,** born Chicago, Illinois, September 29, 1963; admitted to bar, 1989, California. *Education:* Northwestern University (B.S., 1984); University of Paris, Paris, France; Harvard Law School (J.D., 1989). Member, Board of Student Advisors, Harvard Law School Moot Court Board, 1987-1989. Member, International Law Journal, Harvard Law School, 1987. *Member:* Los Angeles County and American Bar Associations (Litigation Section); State Bar of California (Member, Estate Planning, Trust & Probate Law Advisory Commission of the Board of Legal Specialization; Member, Litigation Subcommittee of Executive Committee, Estate Planning, Trust and Probate Law Section). *PRACTICE AREAS:* Estate, Trust and Conservatorship Litigation; Appellate Practice; Business Litigation.

## COUNSEL

**CHRISTINA M. JACOBS,** born Los Angeles, California, November 4, 1950; admitted to bar, 1978, Louisiana; 1979, California. *Education:* University of California at Los Angeles (B.A., cum laude, 1972); Loyola University of New Orleans (J.D., 1978). Note Editor, Loyola Law Review, 1977-1978. *Member:* Los Angeles County Bar Association; State Bar of California; Women Lawyers Association of Los Angeles. *PRACTICE AREAS:* Estate, Trust and Conservatorship Litigation; Business Litigation.

**JERYLL S. COHEN,** born San Diego, California, September 2, 1959; admitted to bar, 1986, California. *Education:* University of California at Los Angeles (B.A., magna cum laude, 1981); Loyola University of Los Angeles (J.D., cum laude, 1986). *Member:* Los Angeles County and American Bar Associations. *PRACTICE AREAS:* Estate Planning; Probate and Trust Administration.

## ASSOCIATES

**MARGARET G. LODISE,** born Stockton, California, 1963; admitted to bar, 1988, California. *Education:* Pomona College (B.A., cum laude, 1985); University of California at Los Angeles (J.D., 1988). Member, Moot Court Honors Program. *Member:* Los Angeles County and American Bar Associations; Women Lawyers Association of Los Angeles (Secretary, 1996-1997; Board of Governors, 1993-1996; Chair, Adopt-A-School Committee, 1993-1995; Chair, Special Events Committee, 1995—). *PRACTICE AREAS:* Estate, Trust and Conservatorship Litigation; Appellate Practice; Business Litigation.

**JANA W. BRAY,** born Springfield, Ohio, December 23, 1965; admitted to bar, 1991, California. *Education:* Mount Holyoke College (B.A., 1988); University of Virginia (J.D., 1991). Member, Raven Society. Editorial Board, Virginia Tax Review. *Member:* Los Angeles County and American Bar Associations. *PRACTICE AREAS:* Estate, Trust and Conservatorship Litigation; Business Litigation.

**JOHN F. EYRICH,** born Anaheim, California, July 11, 1967; admitted to bar, 1994, California. *Education:* San Francisco State University (B.S., summa cum laude, 1991); Santa Clara University School of Law (J.D., 1994). *Member:* Los Angeles County and American Bar Associations.

# LAW OFFICES OF
# WILLIAM D. ROSS

*A PROFESSIONAL CORPORATION*

520 SOUTH GRAND AVENUE, SUITE 300
**LOS ANGELES, CALIFORNIA 90071**
Telephone: 213-892-1592
Telecopier: 213-892-1519

*Palo Alto, California Office:* 425 Sherman Avenue, Suite 310. Telephone: 415-617-5678. Fax: 415-617-5680.

*Civil Trial and Appellate Practice in State and Federal Courts. Business Litigation, Employment Rights, Land Use, Real Property, Environmental, Water Rights, Public Finance, State and Local Administrative Law.*

**FIRM PROFILE:** *Governmental, corporate and individual clients are assisted in the areas of local government, real estate development and real property title litigation. Governmental clients are advised and represented in administrative and litigation proceedings issues including employment rights, environmental compliance, real estate development, proceedings before Local Agency Formation Commission (LAFCO), formation, administration and dissolution of joint power authorities, public finance and administration of claims under the California Tort Claims Act.*

*The firm advises and represents developers and owners of residential, commercial and industrial properties and public entities in administrative and litigation proceedings in land use, California Environmental Quality Act (Public Resources Code §21000 et seq., "CEQA") compliance and LAFCO matters. The firm has been involved as lead counsel on several published appellate cases and trial court cases concerning land use and CEQA compliance issues. The firm also has extensive experience in obtaining land use entitlements from local, environmental, state and federal agencies. In connection with these matters, the firm has performed analyses of environmental documentation required under CEQA, including but not limited to, procedural notices, draft and final environmental impact reports.*

**WILLIAM D. ROSS,** born Cedar Rapids, Iowa, April 27, 1948; admitted to bar, 1975, California and U.S. District Court, Central District of California; 1978, U.S. Claims Court and U.S. District Court, Southern District of California; 1981, U.S. District Court, Eastern District of California; 1982, U.S. Court of Appeals, Tenth Circuit; 1983, U.S. Court of Appeals, Ninth Circuit, U.S. District Court, Northern District of California. *Education:* Stanford University (B.A., with honors in History, 1970); University of Santa Clara (J.D., 1974). Deputy County Counsel, County of Los Angeles, 1976-1981. Member, 1981-1989, and Chairman, 1986-1988, City of Pasadena Planning Commission. *Member:* Los Angeles County (Member,

*(This Listing Continued)*

## LAW OFFICES OF WILLIAM D. ROSS A PROFESSIONAL CORPORATION, Los Angeles—Continued

Sections on: Real Property; Environmental Law; Member, Committee on Municipal Courts, 1979-1980) and American (Member, Sections on: Natural Resources Law; Administrative Law and Regulatory Practice) Bar Associations. (Also at Palo Alto Office). *REPORTED CASES:* William S. Hart Union High School Dist. v. Regional Planning Commission, 226 Cal. .App.3d 1612 (1991); Long Beach Unified School District v. State of California, 225 Cal.App.3d 155 (1990), Petition for Review denied February 28, 1991; City of Sacramento v. State of California, 50 Cal.3d 51, 266 Cal.Rptr. 139 (1990); American River Fire Protection Dist. v. Board of Supervisors, 211 Cal.App.3d 1076, 259 Cal.Rptr. 858 (1989); Carmel Valley Fire Protection Dist. v. State of California, 190 Cal.App.3d 521, 234 Cal.Rptr. 795 (1987); City of Anaheim v. State of California, et al., 189 Cal.App.3d 1478, 235 Cal.Rptr. 101 (1987); Division of Occupational Safety and Health v. State Board of Control, 189 Cal.App.3d 794, 234 Cal.Rptr. 661 (1987); County of Los Angeles, et al. v. State of California, et al.; City of Sonoma, et al. v. State of California, et al., 43 Cal.3d 46, 233 Cal.Rptr. 38 (1987); Las Virgenes Homeowners Federation, Inc., et al. v. County of Los Angeles, (Currey-Riach Company, Real Party-In-Interest), 177 Cal.App.3d 300, 223 Cal.Rptr. 18 (1986) (CEQA action); Rapid Transit Advocates v. Southern California Rapid Transit District, 752 F.2d 373 (9th Cir. 1985) (NEPA action); San Bernardino Valley Audubon Society v. County of San Bernardino, et al., (Gold. Mountain Memorial Park, Real Property-In-Interest), 155 Cal.App.3d 738, 202 Cal.Rptr. 424 (1984) (CEQA action). *PRACTICE AREAS:* Land Use; Municipal and Zoning; Real Estate.

**DIANE C. DEFELICE,** born Redwood City, California, October 12, 1962; admitted to bar, 1990, California. *Education:* University of California at Los Angeles; University of California at Berkeley (B.A., 1984); Pepperdine University (J.D., 1990). Real Estate Sales License, California, 1985. *Member:* Los Angeles County (Member, Sections on: Litigation; Real Property) and American Bar Associations; State Bar of California. *PRACTICE AREAS:* Business; Civil Trial; Real Estate.

**MYRA J. PRESTIDGE,** born San Francisco, California, April 25, 1956; admitted to bar, 1984, California and U.S. District Court, Northern District of California. *Education:* University of California at Santa Cruz (B.A., 1981); University of Santa Clara (J.D., 1984). Assistant and Senior Assistant City Attorney City of Mountain View, 1990-1996. *Member:* San Matco County and Santa Clara County Bar Associations; State Bar of California (Member, Sections on: Labor Law and Public Law). (Also at Palo Alto Office). *REPORTED CASES:* City of Redwood City v. Dalton Construction Company, 221 Cal. App.3d 1570 (1990). *PRACTICE AREAS:* Municipal Law.

### OF COUNSEL

**CAROL B. SHERMAN,** born Bronx, New York, April 4, 1951; admitted to bar, 1981, California; 1982, U.S. District Court, Central, Northern, Eastern and Southern Districts of California; 1986, U.S. Court of Appeals, Ninth Circuit. *Education:* Douglass College, (B.A., cum laude, 1973); Loyola Law School of Los Angeles (J.D., 1980). Member, Loyola Law Review, 1978-1980. Author: "Labor Law in the Ninth Circuit: Recent Developments Section IV Collective Bargaining," 13 Loyola of Los Angeles Law Review No. 2, 1980. Law Clerk to Hon. Thelton E. Henderson, U.S. District Court for the Northern District of California, 1981. *Member:* Los Angeles County Bar Association; State Bar of California; Association of Business Trial Lawyers.

**LISABETH D. ROTHMAN,** born Los Angeles, California, December 4, 1957; admitted to bar, 1982, California; 1984, U.S. District Court, Central District of California; 1985, U.S. Court of Appeals, Ninth Circuit; 1987, U.S. District Court, Northern and Southern Districts of California; 1988, U.S. District Court, Eastern District of California. *Education:* Pomona College (B.A., cum laude, 1979); Columbia University (J.D., 1982). Notes and Comments Editor, Columbia Journal of Environmental Law. Law Clerk to the Honorable Gus J. Solomon, U.S. District Court, District of Oregon, 1982-1983. *Member:* Los Angeles County Bar Association; The State Bar of California. *PRACTICE AREAS:* Appellate Practice; Business; Civil Trial; Commercial Litigation; Securities; Antitrust; Insurance; Sports and Entertainment.

CAA1156B

## ROSSBACHER & ASSOCIATES
UNION BANK PLAZA, TWENTY-FOURTH FLOOR
445 SOUTH FIGUEROA STREET
**LOS ANGELES, CALIFORNIA 90071**
Telephone: 213-895-6500
Fax: 213-895-6161

*Civil, Criminal and Appellate Litigation in all State and Federal Courts and Administrative Tribunals.*

*FIRM PROFILE: Reported Cases: Ayeni v. CBS, Inc., 848 F.Supp. 362 (E.D.N.Y. 1994), aff'd, Ayeni v. Mottola, 35 F.3d 680 (2nd Cir. 1994), cert. denied, 115 S.Ct. 1689 (1995); U.S. v. Sanusi, 813 F.Supp. 149 (E.D.N.Y. 1992); Walbrook Ins. Co. Ltd. v. Spiegel, (1994 Transfer Binder) Fed. Sec. L. Rep. (CCH) ¶98, 020 (C.D.Cal. Aug. 6, 1993); In re Price/Costco Shareholder Litigation, (1995 Transfer Binder) Fed. Sec. L. Rep. (CCH ¶98, 955 (W.D.Wash. Oct. 30, 1995); Sosinsky v. Grant, 6 Cal.App.4th 1548 (Cal.App. 5 Dist. 1992); U.S. v. Blaylock, 20 F.3d 1458 (9th Cir. 1994); U.S. v. Gordon, 987 F.2d 902 (2nd Cir. 1993); Lentz v. Woolley, (1989 Transfer Binder) Fed. Sec. L. Rep. (CCH) ¶84, 498 (C.D.Cal. June 12, 1989).*

### MEMBERS OF FIRM

**HENRY H. ROSSBACHER,** born Plainfield, New Jersey, August 1, 1943; admitted to bar, 1969, New York; 1970, U.S. Court of Appeals, Second Circuit and U.S. District Court, Southern District of New York; 1972, U.S. Supreme Court and U.S. Court of Appeals, Ninth Circuit; 1974, California and U.S. District Court, Central and Southern Districts of California; 1975, U.S. Claims Court; 1987, Federal Circuit and U.S. District Court, Eastern District of California; 1989, U.S. District Court, Northern District of California; 1992, U.S. District Court, Eastern District of New York; 1994, U.S. Court of Appeals, Third Circuit. *Education:* Wharton School of Finance and Commerce, University of Pennsylvania (B.S.Ec., 1965); University of Virginia (LL.B., 1968). Phi Delta Phi. Member, Editorial Board, University of Virginia Law Review, 1967-1968. Author: "Civil Commitment for Narcotics Addiction to the California Rehabilitation Center," N.I.D.A., 1974. Adjunct Professor of Law and Director, UCLA Program In Corrections Law, UCLA Law School, 1972-1974. Deputy General Counsel, New York State Special Commission on Attica, 1971-1972. Assistant U.S. Attorney and Senior Litigation Counsel, U.S. Attorney's Office, Central District of California, 1978-1985. Advisory Counsel, Office of Independent Counsel in re Secretary of Agriculture Espy, 1996—. *Member:* Los Angeles County (Member, Federal Courts and Practices Committee, 1982-1983) and American (Antitrust Section - Member, Civil RICO Subcommittee of the Private Antitrust Litigation Committee, 1989—; Criminal Justice Section - Member, White Collar Crime Committee, 1990—) Bar Associations; The State Bar of California (Member, Committee on Correctional Facilities and Services, 1972-1974). *PRACTICE AREAS:* Civil Litigation; Criminal Litigation; Appellate Litigation; Securities Litigation; Constitutional Law.

### OF COUNSEL

**GEORGE M. SNYDER,** born Seattle, Washington, February 1, 1939; admitted to bar, 1980, California and U.S. District Court, Central District of California; 1984, U.S. District Court, Northern and Eastern Districts of California and U.S. Court of Appeals, Ninth Circuit; 1985, U.S. District Court, Southern District of California; 1996, U.S. Supreme Court. *Education:* University of Washington (B.S., Aeronautical Engineering, 1960; M.S., Aeronautics and Astronautics, 1964); Loyola University of Los Angeles (J.D., cum laude, 1980). Member, St. Thomas More Law Society. Associate Professor, General Engineering, University of Washington, 1963-1964. *Member:* Los Angeles County and American Bar Associations; The State Bar of California. *PRACTICE AREAS:* Civil Litigation; D&O; Insurance; Warranty; ERISA; Class Actions; Constitutional Law; Religion; Commercial Law.

### ASSOCIATES

**JAMES S. CAHILL,** born Columbus, Nebraska, October 22, 1951; admitted to bar, 1976, California, U.S. Court of Appeals, Ninth Circuit, U.S. District Court, Central, Eastern and Southern Districts of California. *Education:* University of California, Santa Barbara (B.A., with highest honors, 1973); Loyola University of Los Angeles (J.D., 1976); University of Birmingham-United Kingdom (1971-1972). Phi Alpha Delta. Member: Board of Governors for Loyola University of Los Angeles Law School (1990-1993). *Member:* Los Angeles County and American Bar Associations; State Bar of California. *PRACTICE AREAS:* Complex Commercial, Class Action and Labor Litigation; Business Transactions.

*(This Listing Continued)*

**LINDA L. GRIFFIS,** born Lake Forest, Illinois, March 29, 1949; admitted to bar, 1981, California, U.S. District Court, Central and Eastern Districts of California and U.S. Court of Appeals, Ninth Circuit; 1991, U.S. Court of International Trade; 1993, U.S. Supreme Court. *Education:* University of Arizona (B.A., 1972); Loyola University of Los Angeles (J.D., with honors, 1981). *Member:* Los Angeles County Bar Association; State Bar of California; California Attorneys for Criminal Justice. *LANGUAGES:* French. *PRACTICE AREAS:* Federal Habeas Corpus; Complex Business Litigation.

**KAREN D. KERNER,** born Huntsville, Alabama, October 5, 1962; admitted to bar, 1989, California; 1990, U.S. District Court, Central District of California; 1992, U.S. Court of Appeals, Ninth Circuit. *Education:* California State University, Northridge (B.A., summa cum laude, 1985); Boalt Hall School of Law, University of California, Berkeley (J.D., 1989). Phi Kappa Phi. *Member:* State Bar of California.

**NANCI E. NISHIMURA,** born Los Angeles, California, June 28, 1953; admitted to bar, 1991, California, U.S. District Court, Central District of California, U.S. Court of Appeals, Ninth Circuit and Second Circuit. *Education:* University of Southern California (B.A., 1975, M.A. International Relations, 1978); Waseda University, Tokyo, Japan (1974-1975); U.S.C. London Program (Summer, 1977); The Columbus School of Law at The Catholic University, Washington, D.C. (J.D., 1989). Legislative Analyst for Senate Select Committee for Indian Affairs, Washington, D.C., 1988. Law Clerk, Overseas Private Investment Corporation, Office of the General Counsel, Washington, D.C., 1988; Member, U.S. International Trade Commission, Office of Unfair Import Practices, Washington, D.C., 1987. *Member:* Los Angeles County Bar Association (Member, Business, Litigation, International Law Sections); The State Bar of California. *LANGUAGES:* Japanese.

**TRACY W. YOUNG,** born New York, New York, February 26, 1955; admitted to bar, 1984, New York and U.S. District Court, Southern and Eastern Districts of New York; 1987, California; 1988, U.S. District Court, Central District of California; 1989, U.S. Court of Appeals, Ninth Circuit. *Education:* New York University (B.A., cum laude, 1977); Benjamin N. Cardozo School of Law, New York (J.D., 1983). Assistant District Attorney, Office of the District Attorney of Kings County, Brooklyn, New York, 1983-1987. *Member:* Los Angeles County Bar Association; The Association of the Bar of the City of New York; State Bar of California. *REPORTED CASES:* People v. Kramer, 132 A.D.2d 708, 518 N.Y.S.2d 189 (N.Y.A.D. 2 Dept. 1987); Sosinsky v. Grant, 6 Cal.App.4th 1548 (Cal.App. 5 Dist. 1992); U.S. v. Blaylock, 20 F.3d 1458 (9th Cir. 1994). *PRACTICE AREAS:* Appellate Law; Litigation.

**JULIE A. LANGSLET,** born Long Beach, California, April 18, 1954; admitted to bar, 1986, California, U.S. District Court, Central District of California, U.S. Court of Appeals, Ninth Circuit; 1993, U.S. Supreme Court. *Education:* University of Southern California (Pharm.D., 1978; M.P.A., Health Services Adm., 1986; J.D. 1986). Participant, Moot Court Honors Program. Co-Author: "The Aminoglycoside Antibiotics," 81 Am.-Jour.Nursing, (1981). *Member:* Los Angeles County and American Bar Associations; State Bar of California; California Attorneys for Criminal Justice; American Society for Pharmacy Law. *PRACTICE AREAS:* Appellate; Business Litigation; Federal Habeas Corpus.

**DAVID F. DESMOND,** born Brooklyn, New York, May 23, 1964; admitted to bar, 1993, California, U.S. District Court, Central District of California and U.S. Court of Appeals, Ninth Circuit. *Education:* William College (B.A., cum laude, 1986); University of California at Los Angeles (J.D., 1993). Comment Editor, UCLA Pacific Basin Law Journal. Author: Book Note, 11 UCLA Pacific Basin Law Journal, 188 (1992), (reviewing Kenneth B. Pyle, "The Japanese Question: Power and Purpose in a new Era" (1992). *Member:* State Bar of California. *LANGUAGES:* French.

*LEGAL SUPPORT PERSONNEL*

**LINDA CONNELL** (Legal Administrator).

**JOAN A. DEGENKOLB** (Paralegal).

**MARTHA E. GUILMETTE** (Paralegal).

## LAW OFFICES OF MICHAEL DUNDON ROTH

*THE WILSHIRE LANDMARK BUILDING*
*11755 WILSHIRE BOULEVARD, SUITE 1400*
**LOS ANGELES, CALIFORNIA 90025-1520**
Telephone: 310-477-5455
Facsimile: 310-477-1979

*Practice Limited to Health Care and Related General Practice Areas.*

**MICHAEL DUNDON ROTH,** born New York, N.Y., February 16, 1952; admitted to bar, 1977, Massachusetts; 1978, District of Columbia; 1984, California; 1986, Texas. *Education:* University of Massachusetts (B.A., magna cum laude, 1974); Boston College Law School (J.D., 1977). Phi Kappa Phi. Author: "What Every Perinatologist Should Know About Medicolegal Problems," Contemporary OB/GYN, Medical Economics, October, 1981; "Tarasoff: Patient Privacy vs. Public Protection," Maryland State Medical Journal, April, 1981; "Medical, Legal and Ethical Issues in Critical Care," Critical Care Magazine, Vol. 10, No. 1; "Dilemma of Tarasoff: Must Physicians Protect the Public or Their Patients?" Law, Medicine and Health Care, American Society of Law and Medicine, Fall, 1982; "Informed Consent: The Need to Keep Lawyers and Physicians Informed of One Another," The Health Lawyer, Fall, 1982; "Are Nurses Practicing Medicine in the ICU?" Dimensions of Critical Care Nursing, J.P. Lippincott Company, July/August, 1984; "Dealing with Unsafe Requests," Dimension of Critical Care Nursing, J.B. Lippincott Co., January/February, 1985; "Legal Aspects of Utilization Review: How to Reduce Potential Liability," Professional Liability Newsletter, Insurance Corporation of America, December, 1985; "Utilization Review: Lowering Costs and Liability," California Health Law News, California Society for Healthcare Attorneys, December, 1986; "Corporate Restructuring: What Adoption of a Multicorporate Structure Offers a Home Health Agency," Caring Magazine, National Association for Home Care, January, 1987; Article, "Problems of Physician Referral Services," American Medical News, American Medical Association, October 23, 1987 and November 6, 1987; "Utilization Review Employed by Managed Care Programs: A Legal Perspective," Medical Interface, Medicom International, Inc., January, 1988; "Exclusive Provider Organizations: A Legal Perspective," Contract Healthcare, Johnson & Johnson, Inc., November, 1988; "Computer Contracting for Ambulatory Care Providers," The Journal of Ambulatory Care Management, Aspen Publishers, May, 1989; "Peer Review Pitfalls: The Data Bank and Beyond," 13 Whittier L. Rev. 381 1992. Co-editor, The Health Lawyer, American Bar Association Forum Committee on Health Law, 1981-1983. Member, Board of Directors, Jewish Social Service Agency of Metropolitan Washington, 1982-1983. Member, Editorial Board, Journal of Ambulatory Care, Aspen Systems Corp., 1987-1995. Co-Chair, New Medical Staff: Legal Issues Update sponsored by National Health Lawyers Association, 1991-1993. Member, Board of Trustees, Stephen S. Wise Temple, 1995—. *Member:* The State Bar of California; American Bar Association (Chairman, 1981-1983 and Vice-Chairman, 1983-1987, Health Care Law Committee, Young Lawyers Division; Vice-Chairman, 1984-1988, 1991-1995, Chair-Elect, 1988-1989, Chair, 1989-1990 and Past Chair, 1990-1991, Medicine and Law Committee, Tort and Insurance Practice Section; Appointed to Special Committee on Medical Professional Liability, 1994—; Member, Medicine and Law Subcommittee on Medical Malpractice and Health Law Issues, 1987-1991); National Health Lawyers Association (Member, Board of Directors, 1987-1993); American Academy of Hospital Attorneys; California Society for Healthcare Attorneys (Member: Publications Committee and Editor, California Health Law News, 1986-1992; Chairperson Membership Committee, 1994-1995. *PRACTICE AREAS:* Health Care Law.

---

**SHARON F. ROTH,** born Canton, Ohio, May 19, 1958; admitted to bar, 1989, California. *Education:* University of Cincinnati (B.A., magna cum laude, 1980; M.A., 1981); Loyola Law School (J.D., 1989). Phi Beta Kappa. *Member:* Los Angeles County Bar Association; State Bar of California; National Health Lawyers Association. *PRACTICE AREAS:* Health Care Law.

REFERENCE: Marathon National Bank.

CAA1157B

## LAW OFFICES OF
## WILLIAM I. ROTHBARD

12424 WILSHIRE BOULEVARD, SUITE 900
**LOS ANGELES, CALIFORNIA 90025-1043**
Telephone: 310-207-4603
Facsimile: 310-442-6400

*Business and Civil Litigation in all State and Federal Trial and Appellate Courts, Antitrust, Unfair Competition, Advertising, Trade Regulation, Copyright, Trademark, Election Law, Legislative and Regulatory Representation.*

**WILLIAM I. ROTHBARD,** born Indianapolis, Indiana, December 17, 1950; admitted to bar, 1976, California; 1977, District of Columbia. *Education:* University of Michigan (B.A., 1972); Hastings College of Law, University of California (J.D., 1976). Editor, "Competition," State Bar of California, Antitrust and Trade Regulation Section (Vol. 5, No. 2, 1996). Author: "The FTC's Revised Telemarketing Rule: A 'Graceful Retreat'," American Bar Association, Antitrust Law Section: Consumer Protection Update (Vol. 4 No. 2, Summer 1995); "Qualified Jurists or Savvy Politicos," Los Angeles Times, December 8, 1994; "Reorganizing the FTC Back Into the Future," Legal Times, July 5, 1993; "Despite Victories, the Fight Against the Deadliest Drug is Far From Over," Los Angeles Times, November 19, 1989; "Antitrust Developments in the Insurance Industry," Antitrust Litigator (ABA Litigation Section), June 1989. Co-author: "The Impact of Proposition 103's Partial Repeal of the Insurance Industry's Immunity from California Antitrust and Trade Regulation Laws," Practicing Law Institute, Corporate Law and Practice Course Handbook, September, 1989; "Consumer Protection: The Federal Trade Commission," America's Transition: Blueprint for the 1990's, published by Democracy Project, 1989; "GM, FTC: David Is No Match for Goliath After All," Legal Times, May 16, 1983; "Antitrust Law Developments," (1978 Supplement), Consumer Law Chapter, published by the ABA. Of Counsel: Davis Wright Tremaine, 1992-1993; Irell & Manella, 1989-1990, 1984-1987. Senior Counsel to United States Senate Judiciary Committee, Subcommittee on Antitrust, Monopolies and Business Rights, 1987-1988. Attorney-Advisor to Chairman and Commissioner, Federal Trade Commission, 1980-1984. Chair, Santa Monica Mountains Conservancy, 1995. President, Americans for Nonsmokers' Rights, 1989-1993. Member, Board of Directors, Bet Tzedek Legal Services, 1996—. Chair, Bet Tzedek Legal Services Managing Committee, 1993-1995. Legal Counsel, Pacific Palisades Education Complex, 1990—. *Member:* Los Angeles County (Member, Executive Committee, Antitrust Section, 1989—) and American (Chairman, Litigation Section Subcommittee on Antitrust Legislation and Regulation, 1988-1991; Member, Consumer Protection Committee of Antitrust Section) Bar Associations; State Bar of California (Member, Executive Committee, Antitrust and Trade Regulation Law Section, 1995—); The District of Columbia Bar.

---

## LARRY A. ROTHSTEIN
**LOS ANGELES, CALIFORNIA**
(See Woodland Hills)

*Business and Construction Litigation in all State and Federal Courts. Commercial, Surety and Fidelity, Bad Faith.*

---

## ROUP, LOOMIS & JOHNSON LLP
**LOS ANGELES, CALIFORNIA**
(See Lake Forest)

*Real Estate, Civil Litigation and Bankruptcy.*

---

## RUBEN & McGONIGLE LLP
Established in 1993

1999 AVENUE OF THE STARS, 15TH FLOOR
**LOS ANGELES, CALIFORNIA 90067-6045**
Telephone: 310-772-2950
Fax: 310-772-2955

*General Civil Litigation, Professional Liability, Securities, Trial Appellate, Corporations, Insurance, Probate, Family and Entertainment Law, Administrative and Legislative Practice in all State and Federal Courts.*

**STEVEN J. RUBEN,** born Pittsburgh, Pennsylvania, April 28, 1944; admitted to bar, 1970, California. *Education:* University of California at Los Angeles (A.B., 1966); Loyola University of Los Angeles (J.D., 1969). Phi Alpha Delta. Editor, Loyola University of Los Angeles Law Review, 1968-1969. Author: "Insurance Aspects of Physical Abuse Cases," 1991; "Ethical Issues In Psychotherapist/Patient Contracts," 1991; "Overview of Recent Cases Involving Insurance Issues in Sexual Abuse Cases," 1991; "Spoliation of Evidence in Legal Malpractice Cases," 1992; "Attorney as a Witness in the Legal Malpractice Case," 1992; "Presenting Damages in Legal Malpractice Cases," 1992; "Potential Liability of Insurance Agents and Brokers for Insolvency of Non-Admitted Carrier," 1993; "You've Paid High Premiums, So Why Aren't You Covered? Understanding Coverage Gaps," 1993; "Ethical Issues in Professional Liability Cases," 1995. Judge Pro Tem, Los Angeles Municipal Court (Beverly Hills). **PRACTICE AREAS:** Business Litigation; Professional Liability; Insurance Law.

**TIMOTHY D. McGONIGLE,** born Santa Monica, California, September 26, 1958; admitted to bar, 1984, California. *Education:* University of Notre Dame (B.B.A., 1980); Pepperdine University School of Law (J.D., 1983); Georgetown University Law Center (LL.M., Securities Regulation, 1984). Recipient, American Jurisprudence Award in Wills and Trusts. Author: "The Class Action: A Solution to the Dilemma of Certification After Judgement," 1984. **PRACTICE AREAS:** Business Litigation; Securities Litigation; Insurance Bad Faith; Professional Liability.

**JUDITH R. SELIGMAN,** born Brooklyn, New York, March 1, 1944; admitted to bar, 1984, California. *Education:* Ohio University (B.S., summa cum laude, 1966); California State University at Northridge (M.A., 1976); University of California at Los Angeles (J.D., 1984). Moot Court Honors Program (Distinguished Advocate Award). Co-Author, "In Re Marriage of Fabian," Los Angeles Lawyer Magazine, December 1986; "A Guide to Community Property," Family Law and Practice, Matthew Bender, 1987. **PRACTICE AREAS:** Family Law; Civil Litigation; Professional Liability.

**MARK JONES,** born San Diego, California, March 6, 1960; admitted to bar, 1988, California. *Education:* University of California at Santa Barbara (B.A., 1983); Loyola Law School of Los Angeles (J.D., with honors, 1988). **PRACTICE AREAS:** Business Litigation; Professional Liability; Appellate Advocacy.

**RUSSELL W. CLAMPITT,** born Washington, D.C., June 19, 1956; admitted to bar, 1986, California; 1987, U.S. District Court, Central District of California and U.S. Court of Appeals, Ninth Circuit; 1988, District of Columbia. *Education:* Northwestern University (B.S., 1978); Loyola University of Los Angeles (J.D., 1986). Editor-in-Chief, Loyola Entertainment Law Journal, 1985-1986. **PRACTICE AREAS:** Business Litigation; Professional Liability; Appellate Advocacy.

**PETER M. KUNSTLER,** born New York, New York, January 15, 1948; admitted to bar, 1984, California and U.S. District Court, Central and Northern Districts of California; U.S. Court of Appeals, Ninth Circuit. *Education:* Université Libre de Bruxelles; University of Southern California (M.A., 1980 ); University of California at Los Angeles School of Law (J.D., 1984). Board Member, Moot Court Honors Program. Associate Editor, UCLA Journal of Environmental Law and Policy. President, UCLA Environmental Law Society. *Member:* State Bar of California; The Association of Trial Lawyers of America; California Trial Lawyers Association; Lawyers Alliance for World Security. **PRACTICE AREAS:** Civil Litigation.

**ANGELI CUESTA ARAGON,** born Manila, Philippines, March 17, 1960; admitted to bar, 1995, California and U.S. District Court, Central District of California. *Education:* University of California at Los Angeles (B.A., 1982; J.D., 1990). Member, Moot Court Honors Program. Externship, Ninth Circuit Court of Appeals, Treasurer, Student Body Association. **PRACTICE AREAS:** Business Litigation; Professional Liability; Appellate Advocacy.

*(This Listing Continued)*

## OF COUNSEL

**BRYAN J. AXELROOD,** born Los Angeles, California, July 26, 1954; admitted to bar, 1980, California; 1984, District of Columbia. *Education:* University of California at Los Angeles (B.A., magna cum laude, 1977); Loyola Law School at Los Angeles (J.D., 1980); Georgetown University Law Center (LL.M. in Taxation, 1981; LL.M. in Securities Regulation, 1985). Phi Beta Kappa; Pi Gamma Mu. Member: St. Thomas More Society; Georgetown Tax Lawyer Law Review, 1980-1981. Author: "Federal Income Taxation and The Marriage Penalty," Jan., 1981; "Federal Taxation and the Starker Trilogy-An Analysis of Deferred Tax Free Exchanges," June, 1981. *Member:* Beverly Hills, Los Angeles County and American (Member: Taxation Section; Securities Regulation Committee, 1985) Bar Associations. (Certified Specialist, Taxation Law, State Bar of California Board of Legal Specialization). *PRACTICE AREAS:* Federal and California Taxation; Estate Planning; Corporate Formation; Dissolution; Mergers and Acquisitions.

**ROBERT M. SILVERMAN,** born Brooklyn, New York, August 29, 1946; admitted to bar, 1973, District of Columbia; 1980, California. *Education:* University of Wisconsin-Madison (B.A., with honors, 1968); George Washington University (J.D., 1972). Pi Sigma Alpha; Order of the Coif. Senior Trial Attorney, United States Department of Justice, Antitrust Division, 1974-1980. Adjunct Professor of Banking Law, Pepperdine University School of Law, 1987—. *Member:* The District of Columbia Bar; The Bar Association of the District of Columbia; State Bar of California; American Bar Association. *PRACTICE AREAS:* Antitrust Law; Securities Litigation; White Collar Criminal Defense.

**GEORGE J. WANG,** born Washington, D.C., February 20, 1958; admitted to bar, 1986, New York; 1987, California. *Education:* New York University (B.A., 1979); Pepperdine University (J.D., 1984); Georgetown University (LL.M., Securities Regulation, 1986). Law Clerk to the Honorable Ronald S.W. Lew, U.S. District Court, Central District of California, 1987-1988. Author: "Outsider's Guide To Insider Trading Liability Under Rule 10b-5," 1985. *LANGUAGES:* Chinese. *PRACTICE AREAS:* Civil Litigation; Securities; International Transactions.

**CAROL L. NEWMAN,** born Yonkers, New York, August 7, 1949; admitted to bar, 1977, District of Columbia; 1979, California. *Education:* Brown University (A.B., summa cum laude, 1971; M.A., 1971); Harvard Law School; George Washington University (J.D., cum laude, 1977). Phi Beta Kappa, Order of the Coif. Topics Editor, George Washington Law Review, 1976-1977. Member, Antitrust Division, U.S. Department of Justice, 1977-1980. Member, Los Angeles City Board of Transportation Commissioners, 1993—. *Member:* Los Angeles County and American Bar Associations; State Bar of California; The District of Columbia Bar; Lawyers for Human Rights (Co-President, 1991); California Women Lawyers (Board of Governors, 1991-1994). *PRACTICE AREAS:* Business Law; Commercial Litigation; Antitrust Law.

## RUBENSTEIN & FINCH

2049 CENTURY PARK EAST, SUITE 1200
**LOS ANGELES, CALIFORNIA 90067-3114**
Telephone: 310-277-1646
FAX: 310-277-4259

*Litigation Practice in the areas of Real Estate, Entertainment, Business and Personal Injury Law. Insurance Defense.*

**STEVEN M. RUBENSTEIN,** born Flint, Michigan, June 16, 1953; admitted to bar, 1978, California. *Education:* University of Michigan (B.A., with high distinction, 1974); University of California, Los Angeles (J.D., 1978). Recipient: Distinguished Advocate Award, Moot Court Honors Program, University of California, Los Angeles. *Member:* State Bar of California. *PRACTICE AREAS:* Civil Litigation; Entertainment Litigation; Real Estate Litigation; Business Litigation; Insurance Defense.

**ROXANNE P. FINCH,** born Los Angeles, November 8, 1962; admitted to bar, 1987, California, U.S. District Court, Central District of California and U.S. Court of Appeals, Ninth Circuit. *Education:* University of California, Los Angeles (B.A., Economics, cum laude, 1984); University of Southern California (J.D., 1987). Hale Moot Court. *Member:* Los Angeles County Bar Association; State Bar of California. *PRACTICE AREAS:* Civil Litigation; Real Estate Litigation; Personal Injury Litigation; Business Litigation; Insurance Defense.

REPRESENTATIVE CLIENTS: A List of Clients Furnished Upon Request.

## RUBIN & EAGAN, P.C.

**LOS ANGELES, CALIFORNIA**

(See Beverly Hills)

*Civil Practice. State and Federal Litigation. Controversies and Disputes involving Insurance, Real Property, and Commercial Matters. Insurance Controversies including Insurance Bad Faith, Title Insurance, Property Insurance, Professional Liability Insurance, Directors and Officers Insurance, Suretyship, Subrogation, Mortgage Guaranty Insurance and Reinsurance. Real Property Controversies including Financing, Title, Foreclosure, Construction, Lien, Easement, Legal Description, Specific Performance and Escrow.*

## RUBINSTEIN & PERRY

A PROFESSIONAL CORPORATION

355 SOUTH GRAND AVENUE, 31ST FLOOR
**LOS ANGELES, CALIFORNIA 90071**
Telephone: 213-346-1000
Fax: 213-680-3275
Email: info@rplaw.com
URL: http://www.rplaw.com

San Francisco, California Office: 101 California Street, Suite 4090.
Telephone: 415-658-0800. Fax: 415-399-1407.

*General Civil Practice, Insolvencies, General Corporate, Insurance, Reinsurance Litigation, Real Estate, Real Estate Litigation, Workouts and Reorganization, Intellectual Properties, Bankruptcy and Taxation.*

FIRM PROFILE: Rubinstein & Perry is a business law firm specializing in all forms of commercial and real estate law, litigation and problem solving. Our expertise includes Banking, Bankruptcy, General Corporate, Insurance, Insurance Insolvencies, Insurance Rate-Making, Lending, Litigation, Mergers & Acquisitions, Real Estate, Reinsurance and Workouts & Reorganizations, Taxation, and Tax Controversies.

**DANA CARLI BROOKS,** born Los Angeles, California, August 28, 1958; admitted to bar, 1986, California, U.S. Court of Appeals, Ninth Circuit and U.S. District Court, Northern and Central Districts of California. *Education:* University of Southern California (A.B., cum laude, 1980); Loyola Marymount University (J.D., cum laude, 1983). Phi Alpha Delta. St. Thomas More Law Honor Society. *Member:* Los Angeles County and American Bar Associations; State Bar of California. *REPORTED CASES:* Quackenbush California Insurance Commissioner v. Allstate Ins. Co. 116 S.Ct.1712 (1996); In re Mission Insurance Company (Imperial Casualty), 41 Cal. App. 4th 828 (1995); In re Executive Life (Ins. Co.), 32 Cal. App. 4th 344 (1995); Sunburst Bank N.A. v. Executive Life, 24 Cal. App. 4th 1156 (1994); Garamendi v. Mission Ins. Co., 15 Cal. App. 4th 1277 (1993); Commercial Nat'l Bank v. Superior Court (Garamendi) 14 Cal. App. 4th 393 (1993); Garamendi v. Executive Life Ins. Co., 17 Cal. App. 4th 504 (1993); Prudential Ins. Co. v. Garamendi, 3 Cal. 4th 1118 (1992); California Automobile Assigned Risk Plan v. Garamendi, 232 Cal. App. 3d 904 (1991); Heckmann v. Ahmanson, 168 Cal. App. 3d 119 (1985); Quackenbush v. Mission Ins. Co. (Boozell), 46 Cal.App.4th 458 (1996). *PRACTICE AREAS:* Business and Commercial Litigation; Insurance; Reinsurance; Insurance Insolvency; Insurance Rate Regulation. *Email:* dcbrooks@rplaw.com

**MELISSA S. KOOISTRA,** born New Jersey, July 26, 1960; admitted to bar, 1986, California, U.S. Supreme Court, U.S. Court of Appeals, Ninth Circuit and U.S. District Court, Northern, Central and Southern Districts of California. *Education:* University of California at Los Angeles (B.A., 1982); Pepperdine University (J.D., 1985). *Member:* Los Angeles County and American Bar Associations; State Bar of California; International Association of Insurance Receivers. *REPORTED CASES:* Quackenbush California Insurance Commissioner v. Allstate Ins. Co. 116 S.Ct. 1712 (1996); In re Mission Insurance Company v. (Imperial Casualty) 41 Cal. App. 4th 828 (1995); Sunburst Bank, N.A. v. Executive Life, 24 Cal. App. 4th 1156 (1994); Prudential Ins. Co. v. Garamendi, 3 Cal. 4th 1118 (1992); California Automobile Assigned Risk Plan v. Garamendi, 232 Cal. App. 3d 904 (1991); Quackenbush v. Mission Ins. Co. (Boozell), 46 Cal.App.4th 458 (1996). *PRACTICE AREAS:* Litigation; Insurance Insolvency; Reinsurance.

**KATHLEEN MARY MCCAIN,** born La Porte, Indiana, December 17, 1957; admitted to bar, 1984, Illinois and Indiana; 1985, California, U.S. District Court, Central, Northern and Southern Districts of California, U.S. Court of Appeals, Ninth Circuit and U.S. Supreme Court. *Education:* The

*(This Listing Continued)*

**RUBINSTEIN & PERRY**, A PROFESSIONAL CORPORATION, Los Angeles—Continued

Sorbonne, Paris, France; Ohio Northern University (B.A., with high distinction, 1980); Valparaiso University (J.D., 1984). Phi Alpha Theta; Pi Delta Phi; Phi Alpha Delta. *Member:* Los Angeles County, Indiana State, Illinois State and American Bar Associations; State Bar of California. **REPORTED CASES:** Morgan Stanley Mortgage Capital, Inc. v. Insurance Commissioner of the State of California, 18 F.3d 790 (9th Cir. 1994), Bankr. L. Rep. (CCH) P.75, 755; Checker Motor Corp. v. Superior Court (Garamedi), 13 Cal. App. 4th 1007, (1993); Garamendi v. Executive Life, 17 Cal. App. 4th 504, Brookview Condominium Owners' Association v. Heltzer Enterprises - Brookview, 218 Cal. App. 3d 502, 267 Cal. Rptr. 76 (1990); Walton Insurance Company v. Chase Manhattan Bank, No. 90 Civ. 4714, 4715, 4797 & 4798 (JFK), 1990 U.S. Dist. LEXIS 10490, 1990 WL 121555 (S.D.N.Y. August 14, 1990); Prudential Reinsurance Company v. Superior Court (Gillespie), 265 Cal. Rptr. 386 (1989). **PRACTICE AREAS:** Litigation; Insurance Insolvency; Reinsurance; Real Estate. *Email:* kmmccain@rplaw.com

**ROBERT H. NUNNALLY, JR.,** born San Antonio, Texas, August 12, 1959; admitted to bar, 1984, Texas; 1988, California, U.S. District Court, Northern District of Texas and U.S. District Court, Central District of California; U.S. Supreme Court. *Education:* University of Arkansas (B.A., 1980); University of Arkansas at Little Rock (J.D., with high honors, 1984). Phi Delta Phi. Survey Editor, University of Arkansas at Little Rock Law Journal, 1983-1984. Author: Note, "Standing of Unsuccessful Bidders to Sue, Walt Bennett Ford, Inc. v. Pulaski County Special School District 274 Arkansas 208, 624 S.W.2d 426, 1981," 5 University of Arkansas at Little Rock Law Journal 431, 1982; Reprinted in Yearbook of Procurement Articles, 1983; Government Contracts Service, 1983. *Member:* State Bar of Texas; State Bar of California; American Bar Association. **REPORTED CASES:** In re Mission Insurance Company v. Imperial Casualty 41 Cal. App. 4th 828, (1995); Sunburst Bank v. Executive Life, 24 Cal. App. 4th 1156, (1994); Garamendi v. Mission Insurance Company (Appeal of Missouri Insurance Guaranty Association), 15 Cal. App. 4th 1277, (1993); Allegheny International Credit Corporation v. Segal, 735 S.W. 2d 552 (Texs. App.--Dallas 1987); Liquidation of Security Casualty Insurance Company, 127 Ill. 2d 434, 537 N.E.2d 775 (1989). **PRACTICE AREAS:** Insurance Insolvency; Intellectual Property.

**KARL L. RUBINSTEIN,** born Springfield, Illinois, July 15, 1943; admitted to bar, 1968, Texas; 1983, California; U.S. Supreme Court; U.S. Court of Appeals, Fifth Circuit; U.S. Court of Appeals, Ninth Circuit; U.S. District Court, Northern, Southern and Western Districts of Texas; U.S. District Court, Northern and Central Districts of California; U.S. District Court, Western District of Louisiana. *Education:* Texas A & M University (B.A., 1966); St. Mary's University of San Antonio (J.D., magna cum laude, 1968). Phi Delta Phi (Tarlton Inn). Recipient: James R. Norvell Moot Court Award and James P. Lytton Memorial Award, 1968. Outstanding Graduate Tarlton Inn, Phi Delta Phi, Delta Theta Phi Award for Contributions to School of Law, 1968. Finalist, Texas State Moot Court Competition, 1968. Co-Author: "Best Brief," Texas State Moot Court Competition, 1968. Author: "Personal Injuries and the Texas Survival Statute: The Case for Recovery of Damages for a Decedent's Lost Future Earnings," 12 St. Mary's Law Journal 49, 1980; "Calling Out Before the Flood," Best's Review, Vol. 93, No. 6, page 24, Oct. 1992. *Member:* Dallas, Travis County and American Bar Associations; State Bar of Texas (Member, Jury Service Committee, 1984—); State Bar of California; The Association of Trial Lawyers of America. [Capt., JAG, U.S. Air Force, 1969-1973]. (Board Certified, Civil Trial Law, Texas Board of Legal Specialization). **REPORTED CASES:** Quackenbush California Insurance Commissioner v. Allstate Ins. Co. 116 S. Ct. 1712 (1996); Sunburst Bank, N.A. v. Executive Life, 24 Cal. App. 4th 1156 (1994); Garamendi v. Executive Life, 17 Cal. App. 4th 504 (1993); Checkers Motor Corporation v. Superior Court (Garamendi), 13 Cal. App. 4th 1007 (1993); Commercial National Bank v. Superior Court (Garamendi), 14 Cal. App. 4th 393 (1993); Garamendi v. Mission Insurance Company, 15 Cal. App. 4th 1277 (1993); Prudential Reinsurance Co. v. Superior Court (Garamendi), 3 Cal. 4th 1118 (1992); Texas Commerce Bank v. Garamendi, 11 Cal. App. 4th 460 (1992); California Automobile Assigned Risk Plan v. Garamendi, 232 Cal. App. 3d 904 (1991); Stoffer Hotel Company v. Teachers Insurance and Annuity Association, 737 F. Supp. 1553 (M.D. Fla. 1990); Walton Insurance Company v. Chase Manhattan Bank, No. 90 Civ. 4714 (JFK), 1990 U.S. Dist. LEXIS 10490 (S.D.N.Y. August 14, 1990); Ohio Reinsurance Corporation v. Pacific Reinsurance Management Corporation, No. 85 Civ. 1412 (JFK), 1990 U.S. Dist. LEXIS 15169 (S.D.N.Y. November 13, 1990); In re Liquidation of Security Casualty Company, 127 Ill.2d 434 (1989); In re Liquidations of Reserve Insurance Company, 122 Ill.2d 555 (1988); Baldwin-United Corporation v. Garner, 283 Ark. 385, 678 S.W.2d 754 (1984); Mendel v. Garner, 283 Ark. 473, 678 S.W.2d 759 (1984); Whitson v. Harris, 682 S.W.2d 423 (Tex. Ct. App. 1984); Stroller v. Baldwin-United Corporation, 41 B.R. 884, Bankr. L. Rep. (CCH) ¶69, 850, 11 Collier Bankr. Cas. 2d (MB) 168 (S.D. Ohio 1984); Griffen v. Rowden, 26 Tex. Sup. Ct. J. 569, 654 S.W.2d 435 (1983); Central Bank v. Harris, 623 S.W.2d 807 (Tex. Civ. App. 1981); Southwest Offset, Inc. v. Hudco Publishing Company, 622 F.2d 149 (5th Cir. 1980); Hicks v. Wright, 564 S.W.2d 785 (Tex. Ct. App. 1978); Crook v. Malone, 571 S.W.2d 544 (Tex. Civ. App. 1978); Quackenbush v. Mission Ins. Co. (Boozell), 46 Cal. App.4th 458 (1996); In Re: Mission Ins. Co. (Imperial Casualty), 41 Cal.App.4th 828 (1995); In Re: Executive Life (Commercial Nat'l Bank) 32 Cal.App.4th 344 (1995). **TRANSACTIONS:** Final Liquidation Dividend Plan For Mission Insurance Companies (1996); Rehabilitation Plan for Executive Life Insurance Company (1994); Rehabilitation Plan for Mission American Insurance Company (1986); Rehabilitation Plan for Baldwin-United Insurance Companies (1984). **PRACTICE AREAS:** Business and Commercial Litigation; Intellectual Property; Workouts; Insurance; Reinsurance; Insurance Insolvencies. *Email:* klr@rplaw.com

**SANFORD I. MILLAR,** born Los Angeles, California, July 18, 1949; admitted to bar, 1975, California. *Education:* University of Southern California (A.B., 1971); Southwestern University School of Law (J.D., 1974); University of Southern California Graduate School of Business (M.B.T., 1981). Author: "I.R.C. Section 121 and the Grantor Trust," Beverly Hills Bar Association Volume 14, No. 3 (1980). Lecturer: California Continuing Education of the Bar, 1981, 1985, 1986: "Tax and Financial Planning for Professionals"; "Income Tax Consequences of Real Property Transaction," 1985; "Tax Planning for Family Businesses," 1985; "Tax Reform Act of 1986"; Practicing Law Institute: "The Closely Held Business Financial Planning for the Owners 1986 and 1987". Instructor: "Advanced Corporate Taxation," University of Southern California Graduate School of Business, 1983; "Tax Controversies under TRA '86," UCLA Extension, 1987. Chair, Economics Section, Town Hall West, 1987-1988. *Member:* Beverly Hills (Member, Sections on: Income Taxation; Real Property), Los Angeles County and American Bar Associations; The State Bar of California; Pacific Council on International Policy. (Certified Specialist, Taxation Law, The State Bar of California Board of Legal Specialization). **PRACTICE AREAS:** Taxation Law; Real Property Law; Corporation Law; International Transactions. *Email:* simillar@rplaw.com

---

**DAVID WAYNE JOHNSON, JR.,** born Petersburg, Virginia, June 1, 1965; admitted to bar, 1993, California; 1996, U.S. District Court, Central District of California. *Education:* Duke University (A.B., 1987); Wake Forest University (J.D., 1990). *Member:* Los Angeles County Bar Association; State Bar of California (Member, Litigation Section). **PRACTICE AREAS:** Litigation. *Email:* dwjohnson@rplaw.com

**SHANNON M. KEANE,** born Orange, California, October 3, 1968; admitted to bar, 1994, Wisconsin, Illinois and U.S. District Court, Northern District of Illinois; 1996, California. *Education:* Saint Mary's College, Notre Dame, Indiana (B.A., 1990); Marquette University Law School (J.D., 1994). *Member:* Chicago (Member, Young Lawyers Section) and American Bar Associations; Illinois State Bar Association; State Bar of California; State Bar of Wisconsin. **PRACTICE AREAS:** Commercial Litigation. *Email:* smkeane@rplaw.com

**DONALD B. SERAFANO,** born Detroit, Michigan, October 4, 1967; admitted to bar, 1993, California; 1994, Arizona; 1995, U.S. District Court, Central District of California, U.S. District Court, Eastern District of Arizona and U.S. Court of Appeals, Ninth Circuit. *Education:* Claremont McKenna College (B.A., 1990); University of California at Davis (J.D., 1993). Phi Delta Phi. *Member:* Long Beach and Los Angeles County Bar Associations; State Bar of California; State Bar of Arizona. **PRACTICE AREAS:** Civil Litigation. *Email:* dbserafano@rplaw.com

(For additional biographical data, see Professional Biographies at San Francisco)

*(This Listing Continued)*

## PROFESSIONAL BIOGRAPHIES

## CALIFORNIA—LOS ANGELES

### LAW OFFICES OF FRED RUCKER
10100 SANTA MONICA BOULEVARD, SUITE 300
**LOS ANGELES, CALIFORNIA 90067**
Telephone: 310-203-9330
Fax: 310-203-9332

*Complex Commercial, Securities, Real Estate and Insurance Coverage Litigation, White Collar Criminal Defense.*

**FRED RUCKER,** born Los Angeles, California, November 16, 1953; admitted to bar, 1978, California, U.S. District Court, Central, Southern and Northern Districts of California and District of Arizona. *Education:* Claremont Men's College (B.A., summa cum laude, 1975); Boston College (J.D., 1978). Editor, Boston College International and Comparative Law Journal, 1977. Member, Moot Court Board, 1976-1977. Author: "The Politics of Ocean Pollution, The Third Law of the Sea Conference, Comparative and International Structures for Environmental Protection," 1 Boston College International and Comparative Law Journal, 1977. Judge Pro Tem, Los Angeles and Beverly Hills Municipal Courts. *Member:* Los Angeles County (Member, Litigation Section) and American (Member, Sections on: Litigation; Business, Committee on Securities Litigation) Bar Associations; State Bar of California.

---

### RUNQUIST & ASSOCIATES
Established in 1985
10821 HUSTON STREET (NORTH HOLLYWOOD)
**LOS ANGELES, CALIFORNIA 91601-4613**
Telephone: 818-760-8986
Fax: 818-760-8314
Email: RUNQUIST@silicon.net

*Nonprofit Organizations, also as it relates to Health Care Law, Corporate Law and Securities.*

FIRM PROFILE: *Good communication and client relations are the heart of this "family like" firm. We represent a diverse clientele, ranging from individuals, small nonprofits and start-up business ventures, to major public benefit and religious corporations. Our goal is to provide the highest-quality legal representation possible to our clients. Our success is to provide it promptly and economically, while treating our clients as part of the family.*

**LISA A. RUNQUIST,** born Minneapolis, Minnesota, September 22, 1952; admitted to bar, 1977, Minnesota; 1978, California; 1985, U.S. District Court, Central District of California. *Education:* Hamline University (B.A., 1973); University of Minnesota (J.D., 1976). Author: "The Night The Sky Fell: Directors of Nonprofits Continue at Risk," Business Law News, Vol. 16, No. 2, Spring, 1994; "A Job Description For Directors," ABA-Business Law Today, Vol. 4, No. 2, November-December, 1994; "Responsibilities and Duties of a Nonprofit Organization, Charitable Giving and Solicitation," Updated 1991, MacMillan, Inc. Section 3, 1985; "The Government's Role in the Purification of Religious Organizations," 7 Pepperdine Law Review 355, 1980. Member, Advisory Board, Exempt Organizations Tax Review. Member, Advisory Board, California State University, Los Angeles, Continuing Education Accounting and Taxation Programs. Member, Editorial Board, Business Law Today. *Member:* Minnesota State and American (Member, Council of the Business Law Section, 1995—; Chair, Nonprofit Corporations Committee, of the Business Law Section, 1991-1995) Bar Associations; State Bar of California (Chair, Nonprofit Organizations Committee of the Business Law Section, 1989-1991); Christian Legal Society. *PRACTICE AREAS:* Nonprofit Organization Law; Corporate Law; Business Law; Securities.

---

**INGRID P. MITTERMAIER,** born Geneva, Switzerland, September 13, 1967; admitted to bar, 1994, California and U.S. District Court, Northern District of California. *Education:* Stanford University (B.A., with distinction, 1991); Boalt Hall School of Law, University of California, Berkeley (J.D., 1994). Phi Beta Kappa. Executive Editor, Berkeley Women's Law Journal. *Member:* Santa Clara County (Member, Women Lawyers Committee, 1995-1996) and American Bar Associations; State Bar of California. *LANGUAGES:* German. *PRACTICE AREAS:* Non-Profit Organization Law; Corporate Law; Business Law.

*(This Listing Continued)*

---

OF COUNSEL

**J. DIANE PARRISH,** born Los Angeles, California; admitted to bar, 1991, California; 1992, U.S. District Court, Central District of California. *Education:* University of Southern California (B.A., 1968); University of La Verne College of Law (J.D., cum laude, 1991). Recipient: American Jurisprudence awards in Criminal Law, Products Liability, Civil Procedure, Professional Responsibility, Criminal Procedure, Evidence, Constitutional Law, Wills and Trusts, Lawyering Skills Practicum; West Publishing Outstanding Scholastic Achievement Award. Adjunct Faculty, Legal Analysis and Writing, University of Laverne, 1994-1996. *Member:* State Bar of California.

REPRESENTATIVE CLIENTS: Northeast Valley Health Corporation; Church Development Fund; Pacific Christian College; Hargrave Family Ministries; Wildlands Conservancy; Gregg Manufacturing; Building & Construction Inspection Academy; Childcare Resource Center; Friends Investment Fund.

---

### RUSHFELDT, SHELLEY & DRAKE
**LOS ANGELES, CALIFORNIA**
(See Sherman Oaks)

*Civil Trial Practice. Medical Malpractice Defense and Wrongful Termination Defense.*

---

### RUSS, AUGUST & KABAT
A PROFESSIONAL CORPORATION
Established in 1982
SUITE 1200, 12424 WILSHIRE BOULEVARD
**LOS ANGELES, CALIFORNIA 90025**
Telephone: 310-826-7474
Fax: 310-826-6991

*Intellectual Property Litigation, Trademark, Copyright, Patent, Trade Secret, Product Licensing, Antitrust, Unfair Competition, Business Litigation, Real Estate Litigation and Transactions, Environmental, Entertainment Law.*

FIRM PROFILE: *Founded in 1982 with a practice focusing on unfair competition and antitrust, Russ, August & Kabat today is also a leader in the areas of real estate and general business transactions, intellectual property and complex business, securities and real estate litigation. The firm has attracted highly accomplished and experienced attorneys from large and mid-sized firms and represents clients ranging in size from individuals to multinational, public companies.*

**LARRY C. RUSS,** born Lakewood, New Jersey, April 21, 1953; admitted to bar, 1978, California; 1979, U.S. District Court, Central District of California and U.S. Court of Appeals, Ninth Circuit; 1988, U.S. Supreme Court. *Education:* University of California at Los Angeles; University of California at Berkeley (B.A., with high distinction, 1975); Hastings College of Law, University of California (J.D., 1978). Phi Delta Phi. Associate Editor, Association of Business Trial Lawyers Journal. *Member:* Los Angeles County (Member, Sections on: Antitrust and Unfair Competition and Environmental) and American (Member, Sections on: Antitrust Law; Environmental and Land Use Law; Patent and Trademark Law) Bar Associations; State Bar of California. *PRACTICE AREAS:* Unfair Competition Litigation; Trademark; Trade Secret; Antitrust Law; Real Property; Environmental Law; Complex Business Litigation; Intellectual Property.

**RICHARD LEE AUGUST,** born Chicago, Illinois, February 1, 1949; admitted to bar, 1974, California. *Education:* University of Illinois (B.S., 1969; B.A., 1969); University of Southern California (J.D., 1974). Phi Beta Kappa; Phi Kappa Phi; Psi Chi. Member, 1972-1973 and Note and Articles Editor, 1973-1974, Southern California Law Review. Member, Executive Committee, Executive Vice President and Secretary, Business Property Council, 1987-1991. *Member:* Beverly Hills and Los Angeles County Bar Associations; State Bar of California. *PRACTICE AREAS:* Real Estate Transactions; Business Transactions.

**JULES L. KABAT,** born Los Angeles, California, November 19, 1949; admitted to bar, 1974, California. *Education:* University of California at Los Angeles (A.B., 1971; J.D., 1974). *Member:* Beverly Hills (Member, Board of Governors) and Los Angeles County Bar Associations; State Bar of California. *PRACTICE AREAS:* Land Use Law; Real Property Law; Environmental Law; Complex Real Property and Business Litigation.

*(This Listing Continued)*

CAA1161B

## RUSS, AUGUST & KABAT, A PROFESSIONAL CORPORATION,
Los Angeles—Continued

**LAURA K. STANTON,** born Hollywood, California, October 14, 1955; admitted to bar, 1980, California and U.S. District Court, Central District of California; 1983, U.S. Court of Appeals, Ninth, Eighth and Federal Circuits. *Education:* California State University at Northridge (B.A., cum laude, 1975); Loyola University of Los Angeles (J.D., 1978). *Member:* Los Angeles County and American Bar Associations; State Bar of California; The Association of Trial Lawyers of America; Women Lawyers Association of Los Angeles. *PRACTICE AREAS:* Intellectual Property Litigation; Trade Secrets; Securities Litigation; Unfair Competition; Real Estate Litigation; Complex Business Litigation; Antitrust Law.

**EVAN M. KENT,** born Chicago, Illinois, March 19, 1955; admitted to bar, 1980, Illinois; 1983, U.S. Court of Appeals, Federal Circuit; 1988, U.S. Supreme Court; 1992, California; registered to practice before U.S. Patent and Trademark Office. *Education:* Stanford University (B.S., with distinction, 1977); University of Chicago (J.D., 1980). Tau Beta Pi. *Member:* Los Angeles County and American Bar Associations; State Bar of California; American Intellectual Property Law Association; Licensing Executives Society. *PRACTICE AREAS:* Trademark Law; Copyright Law; Patent Law; Trade Secrets; Unfair Competition; Intellectual Property Litigation.

**D. JOHN HENDRICKSON,** born Berkeley, California, July 16, 1955; admitted to bar, 1981, California; 1982, U.S. District Court, Central District of California and U.S. Court of Appeals, Ninth Circuit. *Education:* Stanford University (B.A., with distinction, 1977); University of California at Los Angeles; Pepperdine University (J.D., cum laude, 1981). Recipient, American Jurisprudence Prize in Constitutional Law, 1980 and Labor Law, 1981. *Member:* Los Angeles County Bar Association; State Bar of California (Member, Section on: Business Law). *PRACTICE AREAS:* Commercial Law; Communications; Entertainment; Product Licensing; General Business.

---

**JUDITH L. MEADOW,** born New York, N.Y., April 11, 1946; admitted to bar, 1979, California; U.S. District Court, Eastern, Northern, Southern and Central Districts of California; U.S. Court of Appeals, Ninth Circuit. *Education:* State University of New York at Binghamton (B.A., 1966); Loyola Law School, Los Angeles (J.D., 1979). St. Thomas More Law Honor Society. *Member:* Los Angeles County and American Bar Associations. *PRACTICE AREAS:* Business Litigation; Trade Secrets; Unfair Competition; Trademark Infringement; Real Property; Employment Law.

**EFRAT M. COGAN,** born Israel, November 30, 1962; admitted to bar, 1987, California, U.S. District Court, Central District of California and U.S. Court of Appeals, Ninth Circuit. *Education:* University of California at Los Angeles (B.A., with honors, 1983); University of Southern California (J.D., 1987). Order of the Coif. Articles Editor, Southern California Law Review, 1986-1987. Author: "Executive Nonacquiescence: Problems of Statutory Interpretation and Separation of Powers," 60 Southern California Law Review 1143, 1987. *Member:* Westwood and American Bar Associations; State Bar of California. *LANGUAGES:* Hebrew and French. *REPORTED CASES:* Cawdrey v. Redondo Beach. *PRACTICE AREAS:* Land-Use; Civil Rights; Commercial Litigation.

**FRANCE D. LEMOINE,** born Montreal, Quebec, Canada, August 22, 1964; admitted to bar, 1989, Quebec; 1993, California. *Education:* University of Montreal (D.E.C., 1984; LL.B., 1987); University of Southern California (M.A., 1989). *Member:* Los Angeles County Bar Association; State Bar of California (Member, Intellectual Property Law Section); Women Lawyers Association of Los Angeles; Los Angeles Intellectual Property Association; International Trademark Association. *LANGUAGES:* French. *PRACTICE AREAS:* Trademark; Copyright.

**ROBYN K. JOHNSON,** born Sterling, Illinois, February 13, 1966; admitted to bar, 1991, California; 1993, U.S. District Court, Central and Northern Districts of California; 1995, U.S. Supreme Court. *Education:* University of Illinois (B.A., Finance, with departmental distinction, 1988); Georgetown University (J.D., 1991). Member, Georgetown Journal of Law & Policy in International Law, 1989-1991. *Member:* Los Angeles County Bar Association; State Bar of California. *PRACTICE AREAS:* Commercial Litigation; Real Estate Litigation; Intellectual Property Litigation; Unfair Competition Litigation.

**BARRY D. KAYE,** born Plainview, New York, May 20, 1968; admitted to bar, 1995, New York, California and U.S. District Court, Central District of California. *Education:* Yeshiva University (B.A., 1990); Benjamin N. Cardozo School of Law (J.D., 1994). Member and Editor, Cardozo

*(This Listing Continued)*

Journal of International and Comparative Law, 1992-1994. Law Clerk to the Honorable A. Andrew Hauk, U.S. District Court, Central District of California. *PRACTICE AREAS:* Intellectual Property Litigation; Securities Litigation; Commercial Litigation; Bankruptcy.

### OF COUNSEL

**STEVEN M. SIEMENS,** born Euclid, Ohio, April 13, 1954; admitted to bar, 1982, California. *Education:* Stanford University (B.A., 1976); Hastings College of Law, University of California (J.D., 1982). Member, Hastings Constitutional Law Quarterly, 1980-1981. *Member:* Beverly Hills, Los Angeles (Member, Real Estate and Business Law Sections) and American Bar Associations; State Bar of California. *PRACTICE AREAS:* Real Estate Law; Administrative; Land Use.

> REPRESENTATIVE CLIENTS: Ocean Spray; Apple; Rampage; National Media; Western International Media; First Charter Bank; Windsor Financial; Magic Johnson; Positive Response Television; Westfield Inc.; Broadway Stores Inc.; California Mart; World Gym; Hewlett-Packard Company; Tribune Company.

---

## RUSSELL, HANCOCK & JEFFRIES
### LOS ANGELES, CALIFORNIA
(See Pasadena)

*General Civil and Trial Practice in all State and Federal Courts. Employment, Public Utility, Transportation, Interstate Commerce and Corporation Law.*

---

## RUSSELL & MIRKOVICH
### LOS ANGELES, CALIFORNIA
(See Long Beach)

*General Civil, Trial and Appellate Practice in State and Federal Courts, Admiralty, Maritime, International, Environmental and Commercial Law, Personal Injury and Business Litigation.*

---

## RUTAN & TUCKER, LLP
### LOS ANGELES, CALIFORNIA
(See Costa Mesa)

*General Civil and Trial Practice in all State and Federal Courts. Municipal Law, Real Estate, Corporate, Securities, Employment and Labor Relations (Management and Public Sector), Taxation, Estate Planning, Trust and Probate, Environmental and Land Use Law, Municipal Finance, Water Rights, Education Law, Bankruptcy and Creditors Rights.*

---

## RUTTER, GREENE & HOBBS
INCORPORATED
*Established in 1973*

1900 AVENUE OF THE STARS, SUITE 2700
### LOS ANGELES, CALIFORNIA 90067
Telephone: 310-286-1700
Telecopier: 310-286-1728

*General Civil and Trial Practice. Corporation, Securities, Partnership, Financial Institutions, Bankruptcy, Family, Taxation (International, Domestic, Litigation), Environmental, Probate, Estate Planning and Real Property Law.*

**CHRISTINE H. BELGRAD,** born Ottawa, Canada, October 28, 1964; admitted to bar, 1991, California. *Education:* University of Pennsylvania (B.S., 1987); University of Texas (J.D., 1991). *PRACTICE AREAS:* Litigation.

**BRIAN L. DAVIDOFF,** born Johannesburg, South Africa, November 7, 1956; admitted to bar, 1979, South Africa; 1982, California. *Education:* University of Witwatersrand, South Africa (B.Proc., 1979); University of Miami at Florida (LL.M., International, 1982). Author: Thesis "The European Economic Community on Foreign Exchange Controls - A Practical Approach," August, 1981; "Banking Report," University of Miami Journal of International Law, Fall, 1982; "Tax Residency of Foreign Nationals," BNA Investment U.S.A., April, 1984; "Let the Lenders Lighten Up—The Real Problem Lies With The Laws," California Real Estate Journal, 1993; "Lenders Beware: Borrowers Get Better 'Cramdown' Powers," Los Angeles

*(This Listing Continued)*

## PROFESSIONAL BIOGRAPHIES

Daily Journal, April 12, 1994. Co-Author: "Neue Definition Der Annasigkiet Nach U.S. - Steurrecht," Der Schweizer Treuhander, November, 1984; "Avoiding Late Fees in Bankruptcy," Los Angeles Lawyer, Oct., 1990. *Member:* Beverly Hills (Member, Bankruptcy Law Committee), Westwood (President, 1990-1992), Los Angeles County (Member, Sections on: Bankruptcy and Commercial) and American (Member, Business Law Section) Bar Associations; State Bar of California; Organization of Small Bar Associations (President, 1991-1992); American Bankruptcy Institute; Los Angeles Bankruptcy Forum; Turnaround Managers Association.

**GEOFFREY M. GOLD,** born Washington, D.C., April 26, 1964; admitted to bar, 1989, California. *Education:* University of Rochester (B.A., summa cum laude, 1986); Boalt Hall School of Law, University of California at Berkeley (J.D., 1989). Phi Beta Kappa. *Member:* Century City, Los Angeles County and American Bar Associations. *PRACTICE AREAS:* Business Litigation; Real Estate Law.

**OLIVIA GOODKIN,** born Los Angeles, California, September 21, 1956; admitted to bar, 1981, California. *Education:* University of California, Los Angeles (B.A., cum laude, 1977); University of Southern California (J.D., 1981). Member, Southern California Law Review, 1979-1981. Law Clerk to the Honorable William P. Gray, United States District Court, Central District of California, 1981-1982. *Member:* Los Angeles County and American (Member, Section on Litigation) Bar Associations; Association of Business Trial Lawyers. *PRACTICE AREAS:* Business Litigation; Employment Law.

**CURTIS A. GRAHAM,** born Los Angeles, California, June 12, 1953; admitted to bar, 1979, California; 1981, U.S. District Court, Central, Southern and Northern Districts of California. *Education:* University of Edinburgh; Monterey Institute of Foreign Studies; University of California at Irvine (B.A., magna cum laude, 1976); University of Pennsylvania (J.D., 1979). Phi Beta Kappa. Member, Board of Directors, Public Counsel, 1984-1987. Judge Pro Tem, Los Angeles Municipal Court, 1988—. *Member:* Beverly Hills, Los Angeles County and American Bar Associations. *PRACTICE AREAS:* Business Litigation; Real Estate Law; Business Planning.

**WARREN G. GREENE,** born Mexico, Missouri, June 13, 1949; admitted to bar, 1974, California. *Education:* Stanford University (A.B., with distinction, 1971); University of Southern California (J.D., 1974). Member, Business Law Panel of Arbitrators for the Superior Court, 1982—. Member, National Panel of Arbitrators (Commercial), American Arbitration Association, 1983—. *Member:* Los Angeles County and American (Member, Section on Litigation) Bar Associations; Association of Business Trial Lawyers. *PRACTICE AREAS:* Business Litigation.

**FRANKLIN D. HOBBS, III,** born Huntington Park, California, May 30, 1952; admitted to bar, 1977, California. *Education:* Claremont McKenna College (B.A., cum laude, 1974); University of California, Los Angeles (J.D., 1977). *Member:* Los Angeles County (Vice-Chair, Attorney-Client Relations Committee, 1982-1985; Member, Arbitration Committee, 1985—) and American (Member, Section on Litigation) Bar Associations; Association of Business Trial Lawyers. *PRACTICE AREAS:* Business Litigation; Real Estate Law.

**SHARON I. JUHN,** born Seoul, Korea, July 2, 1964; admitted to bar, 1991, California. *Education:* University of California, Berkeley (B.A., 1987); University of California, Los Angeles (J.D., 1991). Golden Key. Berkeley Alumni Scholarship. University Distinction Graduate. Judicial Extern, Honorable Irving Hill, U.S. District Court, Central District of California, 1989. *Member:* State Bar of California (Labor Section); American Bar Association. *LANGUAGES:* Korean and Spanish. *PRACTICE AREAS:* Labor; Employment; General Litigation.

**BRANDON L. KIRK,** born Urbana, Illinois, August 3, 1968; admitted to bar, 1994, California. *Education:* University of California, Santa Barbara (B.A., with honors, 1990); University of California, Davis (J.D., 1993). Staff Editor, University of California Davis Law Review, 1992-1993. *Member:* State Bar of California. *PRACTICE AREAS:* Litigation.

**TERENCE S. NUNAN,** born Palm Springs, California, March 21, 1949; admitted to bar, 1974, California. *Education:* Pomona College (B.A., cum laude, 1971); University of California at Los Angeles (J.D., 1974). Member, Taxation Section, Chairman, Death and Gift Tax Subsection, 1983-1984 and Editor, Tax Section Newsletter, 1980, Los Angeles County Bar Association. (Certified Specialist, Probate, Estate Planning and Trust Law, The State Bar of California Board of Legal Specialization). *PRACTICE AREAS:* Tax; Estate Planning; Probate.

**MARSHALL A. RUTTER,** born Pottstown, Pennsylvania, October 18, 1931; admitted to bar, 1960, California. *Education:* Amherst College (B.A., cum laude, 1954); University of Pennsylvania (J.D., 1959). *Member:* Los

*(This Listing Continued)*

Angeles County and American (Member, Sections on: Litigation; Corporation, Banking and Business Law) Bar Associations; Association of Business Trial Lawyers (Member, Board of Governors, 1977-1980). *PRACTICE AREAS:* Business Litigation; Family Law; Environmental Law.

**JOEL WEINSTEIN,** born Cleveland, Ohio, July 8, 1956; admitted to bar, 1981, Ohio; 1985, California. *Education:* University of Akron (B.A., 1978); Cornell University (J.D., 1981). Omicron Delta Kappa. *Member:* Los Angeles County, Ohio State and American (Member, Business Law Section) Bar Associations; State Bar of California. *PRACTICE AREAS:* Corporate Law; Securities; Banking and Commercial/Finance Law.

---

## STEPHEN R. RYKOFF

PROFESSIONAL LAW CORPORATION

SUITE 1400
11755 WILSHIRE BOULEVARD
**LOS ANGELES, CALIFORNIA 90025**
Telephone: 310-477-5455
Fax: 310-477-1966

*General Civil Trial and Appellate Practice, Attorney Malpractice Defense and Probate Litigation.*

**STEPHEN R. RYKOFF,** born Los Angeles, California, June 17, 1936; admitted to bar, 1961, California. *Education:* University of Michigan; Stanford University (B.A., 1958; J.D., 1960). Panel Member, Beverly Hills Bar Association Family Law Workshop Re: Attorneys Fees and Malpractice, 1994. Panel Member, USC 2nd Annual Family Law Institute. *Member:* Los Angeles County Bar Association; State Bar of California. *REPORTED CASES:* Pierce v. Lyman (1991) 3 Cal. Rptr. 2d 236. *PRACTICE AREAS:* Attorney Malpractice; Probate Litigation.

---

## NICHOLAS L. SAAKVITNE

A LAW CORPORATION

**LOS ANGELES, CALIFORNIA**
(See Santa Monica)

*Employee Benefits and General Business Law.*

---

## SABO & GREEN

A PROFESSIONAL CORPORATION

**LOS ANGELES, CALIFORNIA**
(See Calabasas)

*Municipal Law, Public Finance, Real Estate, Redevelopment, Condemnation, Litigation and Military Base Closures.*

---

## SACKS ZWEIG & BURRIS, LLP

**LOS ANGELES, CALIFORNIA**
(See Santa Monica)

*General Civil Practice in all State and Federal Courts. Business Law and Litigation, Entertainment, Real Estate, Corporation, Partnership Law and Personal Injury.*

---

## SALTZBURG, RAY & BERGMAN, LLP

A Partnership including Professional Corporations

TENTH FLOOR, 10960 WILSHIRE BOULEVARD
**LOS ANGELES, CALIFORNIA 90024**
Telephone: 213-879-8733; 310-473-8405
Fax: 310-473-3689; 310-444-9205

*Commercial Litigation, Bankruptcy, Federal and State Court Receiverships, Real Estate, Financial Institutions, Commercial Transactions and Financing, Mortgage Banking, Entertainment Industry, Insurance Defense, Probate and Estate Planning.*

*(This Listing Continued)*

## SALTZBURG, RAY & BERGMAN, LLP, Los Angeles— Continued

*FIRM PROFILE: The firm was founded in 1970 and specializes in representing clients in commercial, business and real estate transactions. Primary clients of the firm are institutional lenders, real estate owners and developers and entertainment related enterprises. David L. Ray is a nationally recognized Receiver who handles complex cases, including law firm dissolutions, manufacturing facilities, hotels, apartment complexes and government regulatory receiverships. Alan M. Bergman heads the transactional department which documents Entertainment Law Matters, real estate acquisition and sales, commercial leases, loan origination, workouts, HUD financing, environmental issues, alternative energy power source financing and various real estate, corporation and partnership transactions. The litigation department, headed by Henley L. Saltzburg, represents clients in complex commercial, business and real estate litigation. The firm is also active in insolvency matters representing trustees, creditors, debtors and creditor committees.*

### MEMBERS OF FIRM

**DAVID L. RAY,** born Los Angeles, California, June 17, 1929; admitted to bar, 1971, California and U.S. District Court, Central District of California; 1982, U.S. District Court, Southern District of California and U.S. Supreme Court. *Education:* University of California at Los Angeles (B.S., with honors, 1955); University of La Verne, San Fernando Campus (J.D., magna cum laude, 1970). Certified Public Accountant, California, 1957. Guest Lecturer: "Taxation", UCLA., 1980; "The Receivership Remedy," Beverly Hills Bar Association, 1985; "The In's and Outs of Receivership Practice," Los Angeles County Bar Association, 1986. Panelist, "Law Firms: How They Work and Don't Work," Beverly Hills Bar Association, April 1989; "Attachment Execution and Other Creditor Remedies," The Rutter Group, 1991; Benjamin S. Crocker Symposium, 1991; "Receiverships-Beyond the Basics," Los Angeles County Bar Association. 1994 Author: Articles, "Partnership Dissolutions and the Role of the Receiver,: part of *Partnerships in Trouble*, Prentiss Hall, 1991; "Breaking Up Is Hard To Do," California Lawyer, April, 1989; "Law Firm on the Rocks," The Complete Lawyer, Spring, 1989; "What To Do Following a Law Firm Dissolution," The Legal Management, May/June, 1989; "Law Office Economics & Management," Association of Legal Administrators, September/October, 1988; "Law Firms: How They Work," Beverly Hills Bar Association Journal, April, 1989. Member, Panel of Arbitrators, American Arbitration Association. Member, Board of Directors, National Association of Bankruptcy, Trustees, 1994—. Member, Los Angeles Superior Court Ad Hoc Committee on Receivership, 1993. *Member:* Los Angeles County (Past Chair, Executive Committee, Provisional & Post Judgment Remedies Section, 1991-1993) and American Bar Associations; State Bar of California; California Association of Certified Public Accountants; Financial Lawyers Conference. **PRACTICE AREAS:** State and Federal Court Receivership Practice; Bankruptcy Law; Partnership Law.

**HENLEY L. SALTZBURG,** born Cleveland, Ohio, September 30, 1937; admitted to bar, 1963, California and U.S. District Court, Central, Northern and Southern Districts of California. *Education:* University of California at Los Angeles (B.A., 1959); University of California School of Law (J.D., 1962). Instructor, Continuing Education of the Bar in conjunction with State Bar of California and University of California, 1973-1980. Lecturer, Lender Participation Agreements, Lender Liability, Construction Lending and Income Property Workouts, Foreclosures and REO, California League of Savings Institution and Mortgage Bankers Association on Secondary Market Transactions, 1980-1988. *Member:* State Bar of California; American Bar Association; Financial Lawyers Conference; Mortgage Bankers Association; California League of Savings Associations. **PRACTICE AREAS:** Litigation; Commercial Transactions; Bankruptcy Law; Real Estate Law.

**ALAN M. BERGMAN,** born Bayonne, New Jersey, January 5, 1941; admitted to bar, 1965, New Jersey and U.S. District Court, District of New Jersey; 1975, California and U.S. District Court, Central District of California. *Education:* Rutgers University at New Brunswick (A.B., 1962); Seton Hall University (LL.B., 1965; J.D., 1966). Member: California League of Savings and Loan Associations, 1975—; Board of Governors, Cedars Sinai Hospital, 1986—; Board of Governors, United Cerebral Palsy, 1986—. Board of Directors, Big Brothers of Greater Los Angeles, 1988. *Member:* Beverly Hills (Member, Fee Arbitration Committee, 1975—), Los Angeles County and American Bar Associations; State Bar of California; Financial Lawyers Conference; Mortgage Bankers Association of America. **PRACTICE AREAS:** Real Estate Law; Business Law; Partnership Law; Entertainment Law.

**GENISE R. REITER, (A PROFESSIONAL CORPORATION),** born Los Angeles, California, June 25, 1952; admitted to bar, 1978, California and U.S. District Court, Central, Southern, Eastern and Northern Districts of California. *Education:* University of California at Los Angeles (B.A., summa cum laude, 1974); Southwestern University (J.D., cum laude, 1977). Moot Court Honors Program. Instructor: University of West Los Angeles College of Law, 1985. Judge Pro Tem, Los Angeles Superior Court, 1985. *Member:* Beverly Hills, Century City, Los Angeles County (Arbitrator, Arbitration Committee, 1981) and American Bar Associations; State Bar of California. **PRACTICE AREAS:** Litigation; Business Law; Real Estate Law; Entertainment Law.

**PETER A. DAVIDSON,** born New York, N.Y., May 19, 1952; admitted to bar, 1977, California; U.S. District Court, Central, Northern, Southern and Eastern Districts of California and U.S. District Court, Northern District of Texas; U.S. Court of Appeals, Ninth Circuit and U.S. Supreme Court. *Education:* University of California at Los Angeles (B.A., cum laude, 1974; J.D., 1977). Managing Editor, UCLA-Alaska Review, 1976-1977. Member, Board of Directors, Los Angeles Bankruptcy Forum, 1989—. President, 1994-1995, Vice President, 1993-1994, Program Chair, 1992-1993, Secretary, 1991-1992, Editor and Member, Editorial Board, 1986—California Bankruptcy Journal. Member, Board of Directors, California Bankruptcy Forum, 1994—. Mediator, Bankruptcy Court, Central District of California. Member of Board of Directors, California Receivers Forum, 1995—. Editor-in-Chief, Receivership News, 1996—. Author: "Using Receivers in Arbitration Proceedings: the wrong way & the right way," L.A. County Bar Association Provisional & Post Judgement Remedies Newsletter, Summer 1994; "Updated Thoughts on Bayside and on Avoiding One Form of Action Problems in Receiverships," Los Angeles County Bar Association Real Property Section Newsletter (Nov./Dec. 1993); "Avoiding One Form of Action Problems when using a Receiver," Los Angeles County Bar Association Provisional and Post-Judgment Remedies Newsletter (Spring 1992); "ZZZZ Best-Ordinary Course Protection For Long Term Debt," 20 Cal.Bkrptcy.J. 45, 1992; "Grogan v. Garner: Nondischargeability By A Preponderance," 19 Cal.Bkrptcy.J.71, 1991; "Grandfinanciera, S.A., et al v. Norberg, et al: Jury Trials Come to the Bankruptcy Court—Maybe," 17 Cal.Bkrptcy.J.207 (Fall, 1989); Co-Author: "Answers to Common Receivership Questions," L.A. County Bar Association Provisional & Post-Judgement Remedies Newsletter, Summer, 1995. Co-Author: *"Jury Trials: The Bankruptcy Court Dilemma,"* Los Angeles Lawyer, July 1990, cited as reference in Collier Pamphlet Edition Bankruptcy Code, 1992-1996. Speaker: "Receiverships: Beyond the Basics," Los Angeles County Bar Association, April, 1994; "Fundamentals of Bankruptcy Law and Procedure in California," National Business Institute, November 1993; "Remedies During a Recession," Los Angeles County Bar CLE Convention, March 1993; "Basic Bankruptcy in California," National Business Institute, November 1992; "How to Obtain and Use a Receiver," Los Angeles County Bar CLE Convention, March 1992; Prejudgment Remedies I: A Primer Course," Los Angeles County Bar Association, May 1988. Member, Los Angeles Superior Court Ad Hoc Committee on Receiverships, 1993, 1995. *Member:* Los Angeles County Bar Association (Chair: Pre-Judgement Remedies Section, 1988-1989; Member, Executive Committee, Provisional and Post Judgment Remedies Section, 1985—); State Bar of California (Member, Debtor/-Creditor Relations and Bankruptcy Committee, Business Law Section, 1988-1991; Counsel of Delegates, 1989); National Association of Bankruptcy Trustees. **PRACTICE AREAS:** Receivership Law; Bankruptcy Law; Debtor Creditor Law.

**ERIC F. EDMUNDS, JR.,** born Pasadena, California, June 19, 1953; admitted to bar, 1978, California. *Education:* Princeton University (A.B., 1975); University of California at Los Angeles (J.D., 1978). Associate Editor, UCLA Law Review, 1977-1978. Author: "Disparity and Discretion in Sentencing: A Proposal for Uniformity," 25 University of California at Los Angeles Law Review 323, 1977. Judge Pro Tem; Los Angeles and Santa Monica Superior and Municipal Courts, 1986—. *Member:* Los Angeles County Bar Association; The State Bar of California; Million Dollar Advocates Forum. **PRACTICE AREAS:** Litigation; Real Estate Law; Business Law.

**SANDRA L. STEVENS,** born Los Angeles, California, July 12, 1950; admitted to bar, 1978, California; 1979, U.S. Court of Appeals, 9th Circuit and U.S. District Court, Central and Eastern Districts of California. *Education:* California State University at Northridge (B.A., 1975); Loyola University (J.D., 1978). *Member:* Los Angeles County Bar Association (Member, Sections on: Real Property, Commercial Law and Bankruptcy; Trial Lawyers); State Bar of California; Commercial Law League of America; Financial Lawyers Conference; Women's Lawyers Association of Los Angeles. **PRACTICE AREAS:** Litigation; Debtor Creditor Law; Commercial Law.

*(This Listing Continued)*

**PAUL T. DYE,** born Massapequa, New York, May 17, 1951; admitted to bar, 1978, California; 1979, U.S. District Court, Southern, Central and Northern Districts of California. *Education:* Cornell University (A.B., cum laude, 1973); University of Michigan (J.D., magna cum laude, 1978). Instructor in Environmental Law, University of Michigan, 1978. *Member:* Los Angeles County (Litigation Section) and American (Litigation and Intellectual Property Sections) Bar Associations; State Bar of California. **REPORTED CASES:** Steinberg v. Amplica, 42 Cal 3d 1198 (1986); California Digital v. Union Bank, 705 F.Supp 489 (CD Cal 1989). *PRACTICE AREAS:* Litigation; Business Law; Financial Institutions Law; Entertainment Law.

**BYRON Z. MOLDO,** born Los Angeles, California, September 26, 1956; admitted to bar, 1983, California; 1984, U.S. Tax Court, U.S. District Court, Central, Southern, Eastern and Northern Districts of California and U.S. Court of Appeals, Ninth Circuit. *Education:* University of California at Los Angeles (B.A., magna cum laude, 1979); Southwestern University School of Law (J.D., 1982). Bankruptcy Trustee, Central District of California, 1995—. *Member:* Westbrook (President, 1993-1995), Los Angeles County and American Bar Associations; State Bar of California; Commercial Law League of America; Financial Lawyers Conference; Los Angeles Bankruptcy Forum. *PRACTICE AREAS:* Receivership Law; Bankruptcy Law; Real Estate Law.

## ASSOCIATES

**NORMAN A. FAGIN,** born Los Angeles, California, July 12, 1951; admitted to bar, 1979, California; U.S. District Court, Central, Northern and Southern Districts of California. *Education:* California State University at Northridge (B.S., 1973); University of San Fernando Valley (J.D., with honors, 1979). Editor, USFV Law Review, 1977-1979. Recipient, American Jurisprudence Award. Co-Author: "Result-Oriented Adjudication, A Lasting Injury," 6 USFV Law Review 49. *Member:* Beverly Hills (Member, Probate and Trusts Section) and Los Angeles County (Member, Probate and Trust Law Section) Bar Associations; State Bar of California (Member, Estate Planning, Trust and Probate Section). *PRACTICE AREAS:* Estate Planning; Wills; Trusts; Probate.

**JENNY VAN LE,** born Los Angeles, California, October 13, 1961; admitted to bar, 1985, California. *Education:* Stanford University (B.A., with honors, 1982; J.D., 1985). Phi Beta Kappa; Pi Sigma Alpha; Omicron Delta Epsilon. Staff Attorney, Ways and Means Committee, Congress of the Federated States of Micronesia, 1987-1989. *Member:* State Bar of California. **LANGUAGES:** French and Vietnamese. *PRACTICE AREAS:* Business Transactions; Real Estate Law.

**SARA T. HARRIS,** born Los Angeles, California, October 20, 1952; admitted to bar, 1986, California and U.S. District Court, Northern, Central and Eastern Districts of California. *Education:* Glendale College of Law (J.D., 1985). Member, Glendale College Law Review, 1983-1984. *Member:* Los Angeles County Bar Association (Member, Children Rights Committee); State Bar of California (Member, Real Property Section); Women Lawyers Association of Los Angeles. *PRACTICE AREAS:* Litigation; Real Estate Law; Bankruptcy Law; Receivership Law.

**DEIRDRE HUGHES HILL,** born New York, N.Y., July 25, 1960; admitted to bar, 1987, California and U.S. District Court, Central District of California; 1988, District of Columbia; 1989, U.S. Court of Appeals, Ninth Circuit; 1990, U.S. District Court, Southern, Eastern and Northern Districts of California. *Education:* University of California at Santa Barbara (B.A., 1983); Loyola University of Los Angeles (J.D., 1985). Vice President, 1993-1995 and President, 1995—, Board of Police Commissioners, City of Los Angeles. *Member:* Los Angeles County and American Bar Associations; State Bar of California; The District of Columbia Bar; National Bar Association. *PRACTICE AREAS:* Litigation; Business Law; Commercial Law.

**STEVEN N. RUBY,** born Los Angeles, California, February 18, 1960; admitted to bar, 1987, California; U.S. District Court, Central District of California. *Education:* University of San Diego (B.A., 1981); Pepperdine University (J.D., 1986). *Member:* Los Angeles County Bar Association; State Bar of California; Financial Lawyers Conference; Los Angeles Bankruptcy Forum. *PRACTICE AREAS:* Bankruptcy Law; Litigation; Business Law.

**DAVID A. GREENE,** born Encino, California, May 16, 1963; admitted to bar, 1989, California, U.S. Court of Appeals, Ninth Circuit and U.S. District Court, Central, Eastern, Southern and Northern Districts of California. *Education:* Pepperdine University (B.A., 1985); Southwestern University (J.D., 1989). Phi Alpha Delta. Judicial Externship with the Honorable Barry Russell, Bankruptcy Judge, Central District of California. *Member:* Beverly Hills and Los Angeles County Bar Associations; State Bar of California; Los Angeles Bankruptcy Forum; Financial Lawyers Conference; Commercial Law League of America. *PRACTICE AREAS:* Bankruptcy Law; Debtor Creditor Law; Litigation.

**KARRIN FEEMSTER,** born Encino, California, April 19, 1962; admitted to bar, 1989, California, U.S. District Court, Central District of California and U.S. Court of Appeals, Ninth Circuit. *Education:* California State University at Northridge (B.A., 1986); Whittier College School of Law (J.D., summa cum laude, 1989) Valedictorian. Phi Alpha Delta. Member, Whittier College Law Review, 1988-1989. *Member:* Beverly Hills, Los Angeles County and American Bar Associations; State Bar of California. *PRACTICE AREAS:* Business Litigation; Bankruptcy Law; Receiverships; Debtor Creditor Law; Business Litigation.

**NANCY R. BINDER,** born Los Angeles, California, May 22, 1962; admitted to bar, 1990, California and U.S. District Court, Central District of California. *Education:* University of California at Los Angeles (B.A., 1986); Southwestern University (J.D., 1989). Member, Moot Court Board. Judicial externship, 1988 and Clerkship, 1989-1990, the Honorable Barry Russell, U.S. Bankruptcy Court, Central District of California. *Member:* Beverly Hills and Los Angeles County (Member, Sections on Litigation and Commercial Law and Bankruptcy) Bar Associations; State Bar of California; Los Angeles Bankruptcy Forum; Financial Lawyers Conference; Women Lawyers Association of Los Angeles. *PRACTICE AREAS:* Bankruptcy; Receiverships; Business Law.

**DAMON G. SALTZBURG,** born Los Angeles, California, May 7, 1967; admitted to bar, 1992, California and U.S. District Court, Central District of California. *Education:* University of California at Berkeley (B.A., 1989); Boston University School of Law (J.D., 1992). *Member:* Los Angeles County Bar Association; State Bar of California; Financial Lawyers Conference. *PRACTICE AREAS:* Bankruptcy; Debtor and Creditor Law; Litigation.

**GORDON P. STONE, III,** born Alabaster, Alabama, August 18, 1965; admitted to bar, 1993, California, U.S. District Court, Central District of California. *Education:* University of Virginia (B.S., 1987); Pepperdine University (J.D., 1993). *Member:* Los Angeles County and American Bar Associations; State Bar of California; Financial Lawyers Conference. *PRACTICE AREAS:* Bankruptcy; Debtor and Creditor Law; Litigation.

## OF COUNSEL

**ARTHUR M. KATZ,** born Brooklyn, New York, March 31, 1934; admitted to bar, 1960, California and U.S. District Court, Central District of California. *Education:* University College of New York University (B.A., Economics and History, 1954); Yale University (LL.B., with honors in International Law, 1957). Tau Kappa Alpha; Perstare et Praestare. Member, National Panel of Arbitrators, American Arbitration Association. *Member:* Los Angeles County and American Bar Associations; State Bar of California. *PRACTICE AREAS:* Business and Commercial Transactions; International.

**MARC E. PETAS,** born Buffalo, New York, June 3, 1945; admitted to bar, 1971, California and U.S. District Court, Central District of California. *Education:* University of California at Berkeley (B.S., 1967); University of Southern California (J.D., 1970). Phi Delta Phi. *Member:* State Bar of California; American Bar Association.

REPRESENTATIVE CLIENTS: Chase Manhattan Bank; Citibank; American Savings Bank, F.A.; Tishman International; R & B Realty Group; Pac Prop. Inc.; The Irvine Co.; Resolution Trust Corp.; Edward J. DeBartolo Construction Corp.; World Title Insurance Co.; Cal Fruit; City National Bank; Cathay Bank; Dai-Ichi Kangyo Bank; Tokai Bank; Glendale Federal Bank; Downey Savings; General Electric Capital Corp.; Crum & Forster; Hyatt Corp.; Delta Music; RHS Carpet Mills; Paoletti Vineyards; Nedwind; Hollandia B.V.; Pacific Guaranty Title; Coast Federal Bank; California Commerce Bank; Bank of Seoul; California Department of Real Estate; California Department of Corporations; Securities Exchange Commission; Hartford Life Insurance Co.; Morgan Stanley; Federal Trade Commission; Israel Discount Bank; National Canada Finance.

---

# ALICE A. SALVO

*18801 VENTURA BOULEVARD, SUITE 312 (TARZANA)*
**LOS ANGELES, CALIFORNIA 91356-3372**
Telephone: 818-705-1100
Fax: 818-705-0943

Probate, Estate Planning and Trust Law. Elder Law, Conservatorship, Probate, Trust Litigation.

*(This Listing Continued)*

### ALICE A. SALVO, Los Angeles—Continued

**ALICE A. SALVO,** born Port Jefferson, New York, November 10, 1955; admitted to bar, 1982, California; 1986, U.S. Tax Court. *Education:* State University of New York at Stony Brook (B.A., cum laude, 1976); Southwestern University (J.D., 1980); University of Miami (LL.M. in Estate Planning, 1981). *Member:* San Fernando Valley Bar Association; State Bar of California; National Academy of Elder Law Attorneys; San Fernando Valley Estate Planning Council (Past President); Southern California Council of Elder Law Attorneys (President, 1996—); Warner Center Estate Planning Council. (Certified Specialist, Estate Planning, Trust and Probate Law, The State Bar of California Board of Legal Specialization). *PRACTICE AREAS:* Elder Law; Conservatorship; Probate; Estate Planning; Conservatorship Probate; Trust Litigation.

---

## IRA M. SALZMAN
### LOS ANGELES, CALIFORNIA
(See Pasadena)

*General Civil Litigation in all State and Federal Courts with emphasis on the Defense of Professional Negligence, Personal Injury and Public Safety Employees, General Wrongful Termination, Criminal Defense in State and Federal Courts.*

---

## WILLIAM A. SAMPSON II & ASSOCIATES
### LOS ANGELES, CALIFORNIA
(See Pacific Palisades)

*Civil Trial Practice in all State and Federal Courts. Personal Injury, Products Liability, Medical Malpractice, Aviation and Admiralty Law. Criminal Law.*

---

## SAMUELS & SAMUELS
### 2029 CENTURY PARK EAST, SUITE 2718
### LOS ANGELES, CALIFORNIA 90067
Telephone: 310-201-0101
Facsimile: 310-201-0166

*General Business, Labor and Employment, Corporate and Entertainment Law, Business, Employment and Entertainment Litigation.*

### MEMBERS OF FIRM

**JACK D. SAMUELS,** born New York, N.Y., December 24, 1935; admitted to bar, 1960, New York; 1964, U.S. Supreme Court; 1976, California. *Education:* Brown University (A.B., cum laude, 1956); Columbia University (LL.B., 1960). Phi Alpha Delta. Harlan Fiske Stone Scholar. Adjunct Professor, Corporation Law, University of West Los Angeles, 1983-1986. Attorney, U.S. Department of Justice, 1960-1961. Special Assistant to Deputy Attorney General of the U.S., 1961-1962. Assistant U.S. Attorney, Southern District of New York, 1962-1965. Founding Director of Compliance and Practices, National Broadcasting Company, 1968-1975. Legal Counsel, Filmways, Inc., 1975-1978. Member, Panel of Arbitrators, American Arbitration Association. *Member:* Beverly Hills, Los Angeles County, New York State and American Bar Associations; The State Bar of California. *PRACTICE AREAS:* Business Law; Corporation Law; Business Litigation; Entertainment Law.

**DONALD L. SAMUELS,** born Washington, D.C., May 8, 1961; admitted to bar, 1986, California. *Education:* Brown University (B.A., Phi Beta Kappa, magna cum laude, 1983); Columbia University (J.D., 1986). James Kent Scholar; Harlan Fiske Stone Scholar. Editor, Columbia Journal of Law and Social Problems, 1985-1986. Co-author: "Injunctions: Why, When, How," California Continuing Education of the Bar, 1989. Law Clerk to Hon. William Keller, U.S. District Court, Central District of California, 1986-1987. Sidley & Austin, 1987-1995, Partner, 1994-1995. *Member:* American Bar Association (Chairman, State Legislation Committee, 1991-1994). *PRACTICE AREAS:* Employment Law; Civil Litigation; Intellectual Property Law.

CAA1166B

---

## SANCHEZ & AMADOR, LLP
### 601 SOUTH FIGUEROA STREET, SUITE 2300
### LOS ANGELES, CALIFORNIA 90017
Telephone: 213-891-1822
Facsimile: 213-891-1808

*Corporate, Securities and General Business Transactions, Employment, Trademark and General Business Litigation.*

**FIRM PROFILE:** Sanchez & Amador represents clients ranging from large, publicly-held corporations to entrepreneurs and non-profit organizations, with an emphasis in the following areas: BUSINESS TRANSACTIONS: Mergers and acquisitions, venture capital, public offerings, private placements, commercial loans, partnership and shareholder agreements, employment and consulting agreements; BUSINESS LITIGATION: employment lawsuits, including defense of sexual harassment and wrongful termination claims, trademark and trade secret protection, unfair business practices.

**RICHARD S. AMADOR,** born Sacramento, California, May 1, 1963; admitted to bar, 1988, California. *Education:* University of California at Los Angeles (B.A., 1985); University of California at Berkeley (J.D., 1988). Board Member, 1989-1993 and President, 1992-1993, Los Angeles Employee Retirement System. General Counsel, Latin Business Association. *Member:* Los Angeles County Bar Association (Member, Litigation and Employment Law Sections); State Bar of California (Member, Litigation Section); Association of Business Trial Lawyers. *PRACTICE AREAS:* Business Litigation; Employment; Trademark Protection; Unfair Business Practices.

**DAVID SANCHEZ,** born Santa Maria, California, January 16, 1962; admitted to bar, 1987, California. *Education:* Stanford University (B.A., 1984; J.D., 1987). President, Latino Lawyers Association. *Member:* Los Angeles County Bar Association (Member, Business and Corporations Law Section); State Bar of California (Member, Partnerships and Unincorporated Business Organizations Committee of the Business Law Section); California Lawyers for the Arts; Mexican-American Bar Association; Latino Lawyers Association. *PRACTICE AREAS:* Corporate Finance; Securities Law; Partnerships; Limited Liability Companies. *Email:* dsanchez@aol.com

### OF COUNSEL

**DELYNN Y. ARNESON,** born Hann, Germany, April 1, 1963; admitted to bar, 1994, California. *Education:* Northern Arizona University (B.S., cum laude, 1985); Pepperdine University (J.D., 1994). Phi Delta Phi. Magister, 1993-1994. *Member:* Beverly Hills and Los Angeles County Bar Associations. *LANGUAGES:* German. *PRACTICE AREAS:* Trademark Protection; Entertainment.

**ELIZABETH BRANDON-BROWN,** born Hamilton, Ontario, Canada, June 12, 1948; admitted to bar, 1991, Florida; 1992, District of Columbia, 1995, California. *Education:* University of Florida (B.S., 1969); Columbus School of Law, Catholic University (J.D., 1991). Recipient, National Association of Area Business Publications Award for Series on Venture Capital, 1981. Author: ABA Newsletter, Network 2nd, "Facsimiles Can Breach Confidentiality," 1993; "E-Mail Snoops May Breach Confidentiality," 1993; "Knock, Knock - It's the Government Calling," 1994. *Member:* The Florida Bar; District of Columbia Bar; State Bar of California (Sections on: Business Law and Intellectual Property). (Also Practicing Individually in Los Angeles). *PRACTICE AREAS:* Securities; Corporate; Business Law.

---

## SANDERS, BARNET, GOLDMAN, SIMONS & MOSK
### A PROFESSIONAL CORPORATION
Established in 1980

### SUITE 850, 1901 AVENUE OF THE STARS (CENTURY CITY)
### LOS ANGELES, CALIFORNIA 90067
Telephone: 310-553-8011
Telecopier: 310-553-2435

*Corporation, Securities, Business and Real Estate Law, Business and Commercial Litigation, Alternate Dispute Resolution, Federal and State Taxation Law, Administrative Law, International Arbitration, Estate Planning, Trust and Probate Law.*

**IRWIN G. BARNET,** born Rochester, New York, February 13, 1938; admitted to bar, 1962, New York; 1964, California. *Education:* Wesleyan University (B.A., 1959); Harvard University (LL.B., cum laude, 1962).
(This Listing Continued)

*Member:* Beverly Hills, Los Angeles County and American (Member, Sections on: Corporation, Banking and Business Law; Taxation) Bar Associations; The State Bar of California.

**JAMES R. ESKILSON,** born Los Angeles, California, November 28, 1959; admitted to bar, 1985, California. *Education:* California State University at Northridge (B.A., summa cum laude, 1982); Hastings College of the Law, University of California; University of California at Los Angeles (J.D., 1985). Order of the Coif. Milton D. Green Scholar. Recipient, Karen Dorey Award. *Member:* Beverly Hills and Los Angeles County Bar Associations; The State Bar of California.

**JERRY FINE,** born Los Angeles, California, February 8, 1923; admitted to bar, 1951, California. *Education:* Stanford University and University of California at Los Angeles (B.A., 1947); Loyola University (J.D., 1950). Phi Delta Phi. Co-Author, "New Forms and Old Problems," Savings and Loan League Journal, 1968. Author: "Representing The Athlete: Business and Contractual Considerations," Representing Professional Athletes and Teams — 1981, Practicing Law Institute. Professor, Loyola Law School, 1980-1983. Member, California Commission on Economic Development, 1972-1977. *Member:* Beverly Hills, Inglewood (President, 1955), Los Angeles County and American Bar Associations; The State Bar of California (Member, 1980-1982 and Chairman, 1981-1982, Governing Committee, Continuing Education of the Bar).

**KENNETH A. GOLDMAN,** born Los Angeles, California, May 29, 1942; admitted to bar, 1968, California. *Education:* Princeton University, Woodrow Wilson School of Public and International Affairs (A.B., cum laude, 1964); University of California at Berkeley (J.D., 1967). Order of the Coif. Note and Comment Editor, California Law Review, 1966-1967. *Member:* Los Angeles County Bar Association; The State Bar of California.

**DEBORAH L. GUNNY,** born Oakland, California, March 8, 1956; admitted to bar, 1981, California. *Education:* University of California at Davis (A.B., with honors, 1978; J.D., 1981). Member, 1979-1980 and Editor, 1980-1981, University of California at Davis Law Review. Co-Author: "The Substantial Compliance Doctrine: Preserving Limited Liability under the Uniform Limited Partnership Act," 13 University of California at Davis Law Review, 1980. *Member:* Century City and Los Angeles County Bar Associations; State Bar of California.

**RUTH N. HOLZMAN,** born Santa Monica, California, December 11, 1952; admitted to bar, 1977, California. *Education:* University of California at Riverside and University of California at Berkeley (A.B., 1974); Boalt Hall School of Law, University of California at Berkeley (J.D., 1977). Phi Beta Kappa; Order of the Coif. Member, California Law Review, 1975-1977. *Member:* Beverly Hills and Los Angeles County (Member, Sections on: Taxation; Corporation, Banking and Business Law) Bar Associations; The State Bar of California.

**EDWARD LEVINE,** born San Francisco, California, October 13, 1951; admitted to bar, 1978, California and U.S. District Court, Central District of California. *Education:* Hebrew University of Jerusalem; University of California at Berkeley (B.A., 1973); Northwestern University School of Law (J.D., magna cum laude, 1978). Order of the Coif. Author: "Agreements in Contemplation of Marriage," CCH Financial and Estate Planning Reporter, Forms and Planning Aid Volume, Paragraph 6100. *Member:* Beverly Hills and Los Angeles County Bar Associations; State Bar of California. (Certified Specialist, Estate Planning, Trust and Probate Law, The State Bar of California Board of Legal Specialization).

**LOUIS E. MICHELSON,** born Los Angeles, California, November 24, 1956; admitted to bar, 1988, California. *Education:* University of Chicago (B.A., with honors, 1977); DePaul University (M.S.A., 1982); University of California, Los Angeles (J.D., 1988). Certified Public Accountant, California, 1984. *Member:* Beverly Hills, Los Angeles County and American Bar Associations; State Bar of California; American Institute of Certified Public Accountants.

**RICHARD M. MOSK,** born Los Angeles, California, May 18, 1939; admitted to bar, 1964, California; 1970, U.S. Supreme Court, U.S. Court of Military Appeals, U.S. District Court, Central, Southern, Eastern and Northern Districts of California and U.S. Court of Appeals, Ninth Circuit. *Education:* Stanford University (A.B., with great distinction, 1960); Honorary Woodrow Wilson Fellow; Harvard University (J.D., cum laude, 1963) Roscoe Pound Prize. Phi Beta Kappa; Pi Sigma Alpha. Lecturer on Law, University of Southern California School of Law, 1978. Member of Staff, President's Commission on the Assassination of President Kennedy, 1964. Law Clerk to Justice Mathew Tobriner, Supreme Court of California, 1964-1965. Member, 1974-1982, Chairman, 1978, Los Angeles County Commission on Judicial Procedures. Special Deputy Federal Public Defender, 1975-1976. Member, Iran-U.S. Claims Tribunal, 1981-1984. Substitute Member, Iran-U.S. Claims Tribunal, 1984—. Member, Advisory Council of the Asia/Pacific Center for Resolution of International Trade Disputes. Commissioner of Independent Commission of the Los Angeles Police Department (Christopher Commission), 1991. Member, American Film Marketing Association, Hong Kong International Arbitration Centre and British Columbia Arbitration Centre, Asia-Pacific Center, Los Angeles Center for International Commercial Arbitration Panels. Arbitrator, International Chamber of Commerce cases. Member, Commercial and Large Complex Case Panels, American Arbitration Association. *Member:* Beverly Hills, Los Angeles County (Member: Federal Indigent Defense Panel, 1976-1977; Federal (President, Los Angeles Chapter, 1972) and American (Member, Litigation Section; Member of Council, Section of International Law and Practice, 1985-1990) Bar Associations; State Bar of California (Member, Executive Committee, Criminal Law Section, 1977); American Judicature Society; Association of Business Trial Lawyers; American Society of International Law; International Arbitration Commission.

**EDWARD SANDERS,** born New York, N.Y., April 4, 1922; admitted to bar, 1950, California. *Education:* University of California, Los Angeles (A.B., 1943); University of Southern California (LL.B., 1950). Order of the Coif. Member, University of Southern California Law Review, 1949-1950. Senior Advisor to President of the United States and Secretary of State, 1978-1980. *Member:* Beverly Hills, Los Angeles County and American Bar Associations; State Bar of California.

**MICHAEL SANDERS,** born Los Angeles, California, August 8, 1952; admitted to bar, 1977, California. *Education:* Northwestern University (B.S., 1974); Boalt Hall School of Law, University of California at Berkeley (J.D., 1977). Associate Editor, Industrial Relations Law Journal, 1976-1977. *Member:* Beverly Hills and Los Angeles County Bar Associations; State Bar of California.

**BERNARD P. SIMONS,** born New York, N.Y., November 14, 1942; admitted to bar, 1967, California, U.S. District Court, Central and Northern Districts of California and U.S. Court of Appeals, 9th Circuit; 1974, U.S. Supreme Court; 1994, U.S. District Court, District of Arizona; 1995, U.S. Court of Appeals for the Federal Circuit. *Education:* Rutgers University (B.A., 1964); Hastings College of Law, University of California (J.D., 1967). Order of the Coif. Member, Thurston Society. Member, Hastings Moot Court Board. Member, Hastings Law Review. Author: "Taxability of Testamentary Transfer Made For Adequate Consideration," Hastings Law Journal 440, 1967. C.E.B. Lecturer, 1979—. Faculty Member: Hastings College of the Law, Center for Trial and Appellate Advocacy, 1986-1993; Hastings College of The Law Advanced Advocacy Program, 1991—. Judge Pro Tempore, Beverly Hills Municipal Court, 1977-1980. Arbitrator, Los Angeles County Superior Court, 1979-1993. *Member:* Los Angeles County and American Bar Associations; State Bar of California; The Association of Trial Lawyers of America (Sustaining Member).

**RUSSELL L. VAN PATTEN, JR.,** born Willows, California, August 1, 1960; admitted to bar, 1987, California. *Education:* Stanford University (B.S., with distinction, 1983); Yale University (J.D., 1986). Member, 1983-1985 and Senior Editor, 1985-1986, Yale Law and Policy Review. *Member:* Beverly Hills, Century City and Los Angeles County Bar Associations; State Bar of California.

*OF COUNSEL*

**LOUIS M. BROWN,** born Los Angeles, California, September 5, 1909; admitted to bar, 1933, California; 1944, U.S. Supreme Court. *Education:* University of Southern California (A.B., 1930); Harvard University (J.D., 1933); Manhattan College (LL.D., 1977). Order of the Coif (Honorary Member). Recipient, Beverly Hills Bar Association Life Achievement Award, 1989. Author: "Manual of Preventive Law" (Prentice-Hall, Inc., 1950); "How to Negotiate a Successful Contract" (Prentice-Hall, Inc., 1955); "Manual for Periodic Legal Check-Up," (Butterworth Legal Publishers, 1983); "Lawyering Through Life: The Origin of Preventive Law," (Fred B. Rothman & Co., 1986). Co-author, "Planning by Lawyers: Materials on a Nonadversarial Legal Process," (Foundation Press, 1978). Co-author: "The Legal Audit: Corporate Internal Investigations" (Clark Boardman Callaghan, 1990). Editor, University of Southern California Tax Institute, 1949-1950-1951. Member, Planning Committee, University of Southern California Tax Institute, 1948-1969. Professor Emeritus, University of Southern California School of Law. Counsel, Reconstruction Finance Corporation, Washington, D.C., 1942-1944. Administrator, Hermione and Louis Brown Foundation, Preventive Law Prize Awards, 1963-1987. Chairman, Board of Trustees, National Center for Preventive Law, University of Denver College of Law, 1987-1995; Chairman, Emeritus, 1995—. *Member:* Beverly Hills (President, 1961), Los Angeles County (Member, Board of Trustees, 1963-

*(This Listing Continued)*

## SANDERS, BARNET, GOLDMAN, SIMONS & MOSK, A PROFESSIONAL CORPORATION, Los Angeles—Continued

1964) and American (Member, Accreditation Committee of Section of Legal Education, 1978-1981; Chairman, Client Counseling Competition Committee, 1973-1982; Chairman, Standing Committee, Legal Assistance to Military Personnel, 1969-1972) Bar Associations; State Bar of California.

**LAZARE F. BERNHARD,** born Ft. Worth, Texas, August 12, 1908; admitted to bar, 1932, California; 1943, U.S. Supreme Court. *Education:* Stanford University (A.B., cum laude, 1929; J.D., 1932). *Member:* Beverly Hills, Los Angeles County and American Bar Associations; State Bar of California; American College of Trust and Estate Counsel.

**GORDON R. KANOFSKY,** born Waterloo, Iowa, May 13, 1955; admitted to bar, 1980, District of Columbia; 1984, California. *Education:* Washington University at St. Louis (A.B., magna cum laude, 1977); Duke University (J.D., with distinction, 1980). Omicron Delta Kappa; Phi Beta Kappa. Member, Mortar Board. Recipient, The Ethan Shepley Award. Member of Staff and Member, Editorial Board, Duke Law Journal, 1978-1979. *Member:* Los Angeles County and American (Member, Business Law Section) Bar Associations. *PRACTICE AREAS:* Corporate Law; Commercial Law; Securities Law; Intellectual Property Law.

# SANDLER AND ROSEN

*Established in 1957*

SUITE 510 GATEWAY WEST
1801 AVENUE OF THE STARS (CENTURY CITY)
**LOS ANGELES, CALIFORNIA 90067**
Telephone: 310-277-4411; 213-879-9161
Cable Address: "Raynels"
Fax: 310-277-5954

*San Diego, California Office:* 701 B Street, 92101. Telephone: 619-231-0340. Facsimile: 619-231-8752.

*Business Law, Real Estate, Land Use, Construction, and Environmental Law. Corporate Law, Employment Law, Estate Planning, Trust and Probate Law. General Civil and Trial Practice in all State and Federal Courts.*

### MEMBERS OF FIRM

**NELSON ROSEN** (1910-1985).

**RAYMOND C. SANDLER,** born Reshitza, Latvia, August 24, 1913; admitted to bar, 1937, Oklahoma; 1938, California; 1962, U.S. Claims Court. *Education:* University of Oklahoma (B.A., 1935; LL.B., 1937). *Member:* Hollywood, Beverly Hills, Los Angeles County and American (Member Sections on: Taxation; Real Property, Probate and Trust Law; Corporation, Banking and Business Law) Bar Associations; State Bar of California.

**CHARLES L. BIRKE,** born New York, N.Y., July 20, 1937; admitted to bar, 1962, California. *Education:* University of Michigan and Washington University (B.A., 1958); Harvard Law School (LL.B., cum laude, 1961). Phi Eta Sigma; Phi Beta Kappa. Instructor of Law, Conflicts of Law and Domestic Relations, University of San Fernando Valley College of Law, 1967-1970. Member, Executive Committee, Regional Advisory Board, Anti-Defamation League, Pacific Southwest Region, 1968-1971. Judge, Pro Tem: Municipal Court, Los Angeles County, 1979-1984; Superior Court, Los Angeles County, 1989-1990. Member, Superior Court of Los Angeles County, arbitration panel and settlement conference panel. Member of panel of arbitrators, American Arbitration Association. Member, Legal Action Committee, California Building Industry Association. *Member:* Los Angeles County Bar Association; State Bar of California.

**STEVEN E. LEVY,** born Santa Monica, California, September 13, 1948; admitted to bar, 1973, California. *Education:* University of California at Los Angeles (A.B., cum laude, 1970; J.D., 1973). Order of the Coif. Chief Comment Editor, UCLA Law Review, 1972-1973. Adjunct Professor of Contract Law, Claremont School of Executive Management, 1985—. Member of Executive Board and Legal Advisor of Western Los Angeles County Council, Inc., Boy Scouts of America, 1994—. *Member:* Los Angeles County and American Bar Associations; State Bar of California.

**WILLIAM F. TISCH,** born Glendale, California, April 15, 1944; admitted to bar, 1970, California. *Education:* Pomona College (B.A., 1966); Loyola Law School (J.D., 1969). Recipient, American Jurisprudence Award in Corporations. *Member:* Los Angeles County and American Bar Associations; State Bar of California.

*(This Listing Continued)*

CAA1168B

**CRAIG C. BIRKER,** born Los Angeles, California, January 8, 1954; admitted to bar, 1979, California. *Education:* California State University at Northridge (B.A., cum laude, 1976); Loyola University of Los Angeles (J.D., cum laude, 1979). Phi Alpha Delta. Recipient: American Jurisprudence Award in Criminal Procedure, 1978; American Jurisprudence Award in Evidence, 1978. Member, Panel of Arbitrators, American Arbitration Association. *Member:* Los Angeles County Bar Association; State Bar of California.

### ASSOCIATES

**MING-CHU C. ROUSE,** born Taipei, Taiwan, November 7, 1951; admitted to bar, 1984, California. *Education:* Tunghai University (B.A., summa cum laude, 1973); Northwestern School of Law of Lewis & Clark College (J.D., 1983). Phi Tau Phi. *Member:* Los Angeles County Bar Association; State Bar of California. *LANGUAGES:* Mandarin Chinese.

**VIRGINIA A. JOHNSON,** born Muskogee, Oklahoma, September 12, 1944; admitted to bar, 1984, California. *Education:* Boise State University (B.A., 1974); University of California, Davis (J.D., 1984). Editor, University of California, Davis Law Review, 1983-1984. Author, Copyright Protection for Computer Program Algorithms Computer Law Journal, Fall, 1985. *Member:* Los Angeles County and American Bar Associations; The State Bar of California.

**IVAR E. LEETMA,** born Zurich, Switzerland, June 14, 1958; admitted to bar, 1985, New York and U.S. District Court, Southern and Eastern Districts of New York; 1986, California and U.S. District Court, Southern and Central Districts of California. *Education:* Colgate University; Boston University (B.A., 1981); Albany Law School of Union University (J.D., 1984). *Member:* San Diego County (Member, Sections on: Construction Law; Environmental Law), New York State (Member, Environmental Law Section) and American (Member, Environmental and Construction Law Section) Bar Associations; State Bar of California. (Resident, San Diego Office). *LANGUAGES:* Estonian and French. *PRACTICE AREAS:* Hazardous Waste; Environmental; Construction; Litigation; Transactions; Compliance.

**DONALD C. MILLER,** born Marshalltown, Iowa, January 23, 1962; admitted to bar, 1987, California, U.S. District Court, Central, Southern, Eastern and Northern Districts of California and U.S. Court of Appeals, Ninth Circuit. *Education:* Buena Vista College (B.A., summa cum laude, 1984) Alpha Chi; University of Southern California (J.D., 1987). Arbitrator, National Futures Association, 1991—. *Member:* Los Angeles County and American Bar Associations; State Bar of California.

### OF COUNSEL

**RICHARD V. SANDLER,** born Los Angeles, California, July 11, 1948; admitted to bar, 1973, California. *Education:* University of California at Berkeley (B.S., 1970); University of California at Los Angeles (J.D., 1973). Beta Gamma Sigma. *Member:* Beverly Hills, Los Angeles County and American Bar Associations; State Bar of California. (Also Member, Maron & Sandler).

REPRESENTATIVE CLIENTS: Pardee Construction Co.; Deane Homes; College Park Realty Co.; Weyerhaeuser Realty Investors; Weyerhaeuser Venture Co.; The Brown Organization; Hillcrest Motor Co.; Radio Stations KGB, KXOA, KKSF, KRWM, KDFC & KQPT; Carlsberg Management Co.; Carlsberg Realty, Inc.; Denso Sales California, Inc.; Aisin World Corp. of America; Carlsberg Financial Corp.; Los Angeles Chemical Co.; Luscombe Aircraft Corp.

# SANDS NARWITZ FORGIE LEONARD & LERNER

PROFESSIONAL CORPORATION
11100 SANTA MONICA BOULEVARD
SUITE 1770
**LOS ANGELES, CALIFORNIA 90025**
Telephone: 310-479-8826
Facsimile: 310-479-8834

*General Civil Litigation Practice in State and Federal Courts. Trials and Appeals. Admiralty and Maritime, Business Litigation, Personal Injury, Transportation, Inland Marine, Insurance Coverage and Defense.*

**NORMAN S. NARWITZ,** born Los Angeles, California, May 16, 1938; admitted to bar, 1964, California, U.S. District Court, Central and Southern Districts of California, U.S. Court of Appeals, Ninth Circuit and U.S. Supreme Court. *Education:* University of California at Los Angeles (B.S., 1960); Loyola University of Los Angeles (J.D., 1963); University of South-

*(This Listing Continued)*

ern California. Phi Alpha Delta. Member, St. Thomas More Law Society. Member, Los Angeles County Superior Court Arbitrator, 1981. Member, Panel of Arbitrators, American Arbitration Association. *Member:* Beverly Hills and San Diego County Bar Associations; State Bar of California; Maritime Law Association of the United States; Association of Southern California Defense Counsel; UCLA Chancellor's Associates.

**DONALD J. SANDS,** born Chicago, Illinois, June 20, 1939; admitted to bar, 1974, California, U.S. District Court, Central, Eastern, Northern and Southern Districts of California and U.S. Court of Appeals, Ninth Circuit. *Education:* Palomar College (A.A., 1959); California State University at San Diego; University of West Los Angeles (B.S.L., 1972; J.D., 1974). *Member:* Beverly Hills, Los Angeles County, San Diego County Bar Associations; State Bar of California; Maritime Law Association of the United States; Association of Transport Practitioner; Transportation Lawyers Association; American Trucking Association.

**PETER S. FORGIE,** born Los Angeles, California, October 24, 1949; admitted to bar, 1975, California; 1979, Guam; 1980, U.S. Court of Appeals, Ninth Circuit; 1983, U.S. District Court, Central and Southern Districts of California. *Education:* University of Southern California (B.A., 1971); Pepperdine University (J.D., 1975); University of London, London, England (LL.M., 1982). *Member:* State Bar of California; Guam Bar Association; Maritime Law Association of the United States.

**ARTHUR A. LEONARD,** born New Orleans, Louisiana, October 3, 1952; admitted to bar, 1981, Louisiana and U.S. District Court, Eastern District of Louisiana; 1983, California; 1984, U.S. District Court, Central, Northern and Southern Districts of California; 1991, U.S. Court of Appeals, Ninth Circuit. *Education:* University of California at Santa Barbara (B.A., 1976); Tulane University of Louisiana (J.D., cum laude, 1981). *Member:* Long Beach, Los Angeles County, Louisiana State and American Bar Associations; State Bar of California; Maritime Law Association of the United States.

**NEIL S. LERNER,** born Hewlett, New York, December 15, 1959; admitted to bar, 1986, New York; 1988, California; U.S. District Court, Central, Southern and Northern Districts of California. *Education:* Tulane University (B.A. in Political Science, 1982); Bristol University, Bristol, England; George Washington University (J.D., 1985). *Member:* Beverly Hills, San Diego, Los Angeles County and American Bar Associations; State Bar of New York; State Bar of California; Maritime Law Association of the United States.

---

**KELLY BENNETT HONIG,** born Barberton, Ohio, September 10, 1962; admitted to bar, 1990, California; 1991, Nebraska; 1992, U.S. District Court, Central, Southern and Northern Districts of California, U.S. Court of Appeals, Ninth Circuit. *Education:* University of California, Davis (B.A., 1984); University of the Pacific, McGeorge School of Law (J.D., 1990). Recipient, American Jurisprudence Award in Administrative Law. Staff Writer, 1988-1989 and Associate Comment Editor, 1989-1990, Pacific Law Journal. Author: "Mandatory Aids Testing: The Slow Death of 4th Amendment Protection," 20 Pacific Law Journal 1413, (1989). Judicial Clerk to the Honorable C. Thomas White, Supreme Court, Nebraska, 1990-1991. *Member:* Los Angeles, Ventura County and Nebraska Bar Associations; State Bar of California; Marine Underwriters of Southern California.

**HOWARD L. JACOBS,** born Pittsburgh, Pennsylvania, March 6, 1966; admitted to bar, 1990, California, U.S. District Court, Central and Southern Districts of California and U.S. Court of Appeals, Ninth Circuit. *Education:* Florida State University (B.S., 1987); College of William and Mary (J.D., 1990). Author, "Cruise Ship Litigation," Los Angeles Lawyer (March 1993). *Member:* Los Angeles County and American Bar Associations; State Bar of California.

**DANIELLE F. FURMAN,** born Los Angeles, California, December 5, 1968; admitted to bar, 1995, California; U.S. District Court, Central District of California. *Education:* University of California at Berkeley (B.A., 1990); Pepperdine University Law School (J.D., 1994). Best Brief, West Coast Regional Moot Court Competition. Judicial Extern to the Honorable Morio L. Fukuto, California Court of Appeal. *Member:* State Bar of California.

REPRESENTATIVE CLIENTS: American International Group; Assurance Foreningen Skuld; BBDO-New York; Bradshaw & Associates, Ltd.; California Cartage Co.; California MultiModal; Chubb Group of Insurance Cos.; CIGNA Property and Casualty Insurance Company; Continental Air Cargo; Continental Insurance Co.; Crowley Maritime Corp.; Cunard Line Ltd.; Farmer's Insurance Truck Exchange; Fireman's Fund Insurance Cos.; Gearbulk Container Services; GRE America; H.J. Heinz Co.; Highlands Insurance Group; Insurance Company of North America; International Marine Underwriters; Liberty

*(This Listing Continued)*

Mutual Insurance Co.; Liverpool & London Steamship Protection and Indemnity Association, Ltd; Marine Office of America Corp.; Marine Terminals Corp.; Newport Petroleum, Inc.; Pacific Mutual Marine Office; Pacific Refining Co.; Boat Owners Association of the United States; St. Paul Insurance Cos.; Stevedoring Services of America; Scandinavian Marine Claims; Somerset Insurance Services; T.W. Rice & Co., Inc.; The Coastal Corp.; Through Transport Mutual Insurance Association Ltd.; United Airlines Air Cargo; P.B.S. Inc.

---

## LAURA L. SANTOS

900 WILSHIRE BOULEVARD
SUITE 1012
LOS ANGELES, CALIFORNIA 90017-4711
Telephone: 213-689-9941
Fax: 213-589-9945
Email: LLS98775@AOL.com

*Family Law, Bankruptcy, Probate including Trusts and Wills, Real Estate.*

**LAURA L. SANTOS,** born Pueblo, Colorado, March 4, 1954; admitted to bar, 1990, California; 1991, U.S. District Court, Central District of California; 1992, U.S. District Court, Eastern District of California. *Education:* University of California at Los Angeles (B.A., 1979); University of California School of Law at Davis (J.D., 1987). *Member:* Los Angeles County Bar Association; Eastern Bar Association; Mexican American Bar Association; State Bar of California. **LANGUAGES:** Spanish.

---

## RICKARD SANTWIER

LOS ANGELES, CALIFORNIA

(See Pasadena)

*Criminal and Juvenile Defense in all State and Federal Courts.*

---

## SAPHIER AND HELLER

LAW CORPORATION

Established in 1986

SUITE 1900, 1900 AVENUE OF THE STARS
LOS ANGELES, CALIFORNIA 90067-4410
Telephone: 310-201-7555
Telecopier: 310-286-7821

*Hospital, Health Care and General Business Law.*

**MICHAEL D. SAPHIER,** born Los Angeles, California, March 3, 1942; admitted to bar, 1968, District of Columbia; 1971, California. *Education:* University of California at Berkeley (A.B., with honors, 1965); University of Michigan (J.D., cum laude, 1968); University of California at Los Angeles (LL.M., 1970). Member, Board of Editors, Journal of Law Reform, University of Michigan, 1967-1968. Recipient, UCLA Law School/Ford Foundation Fellowship, Law and Development Program, Santiago, Chile, 1968-1970. Member, Los Angeles City Attorney's Task Force on Nursing Homes, 1975. Member, Board of Governors, Beverly Hills Bar Association Law Foundation, 1974-1975. *Member:* American Bar Association (Member, Forum Committee on Health Law); State Bar of California; American Academy of Hospital Attorneys; California Society for Healthcare Attorneys; National Health Lawyers Association. **LANGUAGES:** Spanish. **PRACTICE AREAS:** Health Care Law.

**DONA L. HELLER,** born Hanover, New Hampshire, September 16, 1947; admitted to bar, 1974, Colorado and Vermont; 1977, New Hampshire; 1979, California. *Education:* Bryn Mawr College (A.B., cum laude, 1970); University of Pennsylvania (J.D., 1973). Assistant to the President, Dartmouth-Hitchcock Medical Center, 1977-1979. Instructor of Law and Medicine, Dartmouth Medical School, 1976-1979. *Member:* State Bar of California. **LANGUAGES:** Spanish and French. **PRACTICE AREAS:** Health Care Law.

---

**BETH A. KASE,** born Brooklyn, New York, July 11, 1951; admitted to bar, 1983, California. *Education:* Tufts University (B.A., magnum cum laude, 1973); California State University at San Francisco (M.A., 1978); University of Southern California (J.D., 1983). Shattuck Award, Hale Moot Court Honors Program Quarter-Finalist. Author: "How Law Firms Handle

*(This Listing Continued)*

CALIFORNIA—LOS ANGELES                MARTINDALE-HUBBELL LAW DIRECTORY 1997

SAPHIER AND HELLER, LAW CORPORATION, Los Angeles—Continued

Maternity Leaves," California Lawyer, December, 1982. *Member:* State Bar of California. **LANGUAGES:** Spanish. **PRACTICE AREAS:** Health Care Law.

## SCHAFFER & LAX
### A PROFESSIONAL CORPORATION
**SUITE 600, 5757 WILSHIRE BOULEVARD**
**LOS ANGELES, CALIFORNIA 90036-3664**
Telephone: 213-934-4300
Fax: 213-931-5680

*General Insurance Practice. Insurance Coverage, Products Liability, Medical Products, Bad Faith Litigation, Construction Litigation, Professional Liability, Environmental Law, State and Federal Courts.*

**CLIFFORD L. SCHAFFER,** born Los Angeles, California, August 15, 1939; admitted to bar, 1967, California, U.S. District Court, Central District of California and U.S. Court of Appeals, Ninth Circuit. *Education:* University of Southern California (B.S., in Mechanical Engineering, 1962); Boalt Hall School of Law, University of California (LL.B., 1966). Phi Alpha Delta; Pi Tau Sigma. Deputy Attorney General, California, 1967-1969. Arbitrator, Los Angeles Superior Court, 1980—. *Member:* Los Angeles County Bar Association (Member, Delegation to Conference of State Bar Delegates, 1981); State Bar of California; Southern California Defense Counsel; Defense Research Institute.

**STEPHEN A. LAX,** born Queens, New York, February 19, 1951; admitted to bar, 1979, California; 1980, U.S. District Court, Central District of California; 1982, U.S. Court of Appeals, Ninth Circuit. *Education:* State University of New York at Stony Brook (B.A., 1972; M.S.W., 1976); Loyola University of Los Angeles (J.D., cum laude, 1979). Member, Loyola Law Review, 1977-1978. Member, St. Thomas More Law Honor Society. *Member:* Los Angeles County Bar Association; State Bar of California; Association of Southern California Defense Counsel; Defense Research Institute.

**KEVIN J. MCNAUGHTON,** born Brooklyn, New York, August 2, 1952; admitted to bar, 1979, New York; 1980, California, U.S. Court of Appeals, Second Circuit and U.S. District Court, Eastern and Southern Districts of New York; 1983, U.S. District Court, Central and Northern Districts of California and U.S. Court of Appeals, Ninth Circuit. *Education:* Bernard M. Baruch College of the City University of New York (B.A., cum laude, 1975); Brooklyn Law School (J.D., 1978). Member, Moot Court Honor Society. Recipient, American Jurisprudence Award in Contracts. Assistant District Attorney, Kings County District Attorney's Office, 1978-1981. *Member:* Los Angeles County (Member, Trial Lawyers Section), New York State (Member, Sections on: Trial Lawyers; Insurance, Negligence and Compensation Law; Member, Committee on Toxic and Hazardous Substances, 1984-1989) and American (Member, Tort and Insurance Sections) Bar Associations; The State Bar of California (Member, Section on Litigation); Association of Southern California Defense Counsel.

**BARBARA C. FASISKA,** born Cleveland, Ohio, June 15, 1944; admitted to bar, 1981, Pennsylvania, California and U.S. District Court, Central District of California; 1984, U.S. Court of Appeals, Ninth Circuit. *Education:* University of Pittsburgh (B.S., Physics, 1968; M.S. Radiation Health Physics, 1969; J.D., 1980). President Elect, 1974-1975 and President, 1975-1976, Western Pennsylvania Chapter, Health Physics Society. *Member:* Wilshire, Los Angeles County, Pennsylvania and American (Member, Sections on: Litigation; Tort and Insurance Practice Law) Bar Associations; State Bar of California; Association of Southern California Defense Counsel; Defense Research Institute.

**ALEXANDER J. CHEN,** born Los Angeles, California, December 13, 1957; admitted to bar, 1982, California, U.S. District Court, Central District of California and U.S. Court of Appeals, Ninth Circuit. *Education:* University of California at San Diego (B.A., cum laude, 1978); Hastings College of Law, University of California (J.D., 1981). Staff Editor, COMM/ENT, Journal of Communications and Entertainment Law, 1980-1981. *Member:* Los Angeles County and American (Member, Litigation Section) Bar Associations; State Bar of California (Member, Sections on: Real Property; Litigation); Association of Southern California Defense Counsel; Defense Research Institute.

*(This Listing Continued)*

CAA1170B

**MARK D. SAYRE,** born Pittsburgh, Pennsylvania, April 23, 1957; admitted to bar, 1983, California; 1986, U.S. District Court, Central District of California. *Education:* University of California at Santa Barbara (B.A., 1979); Pepperdine University (J.D., 1983). Phi Delta Phi. *Member:* Los Angeles County and American Bar Associations; State Bar of California; Southern California Defense Counsel.

**JILL A. FRANKLIN,** born Boston, Massachusetts, March 10, 1959; admitted to bar, 1987, California and U.S. District Court, Central District of California. *Education:* Occidental College (A.B., 1980); Loyola Marymount University (J.D., 1986). *Member:* Los Angeles County Bar Association; State Bar of California; Association of Southern California Defense Counsel.

**JOHN H. HORWITZ,** born Kokomo, Indiana, May 6, 1947; admitted to bar, 1988, California. *Education:* University of California at Irvine (B.A., 1972); University of California at Los Angeles (M.A., 1978); Loyola Law School (J.D., 1988). *Member:* Wilshire (Board of Governors) and American Bar Associations; State Bar of California; Southern California Defense Council. [With U.S. Army, 1968-1970]. **PRACTICE AREAS:** Insurance Coverage; Bad Faith.

---

**MARJORIE E. MOTOOKA,** born Honolulu, Hawaii; admitted to bar, 1988, California. *Education:* University of Hawaii (B.A., 1983); University of Oregon (J.D., 1988). *Member:* Los Angeles County Bar Association; State Bar of California; Association of Southern California Defense Counsel; Japanese American Bar Association.

**G. CALVIN HUTCHINSON,** born Peekskill, New York, December 25, 1938; admitted to bar, 1988, California; 1989, U.S. District Court, Central District of California. *Education:* Carnegie Mellon University (B.S., 1962); Western State University (J.D., 1978). Aircraft Single, Multi-Engine and Helicopter Ratings, 1964; Instrument Rating, 1964. *Member:* Los Angeles County and American Bar Associations; State Bar of California; Association of Southern California Defense Counsel. [Capt., USMC, Naval Aviator, 1962-1967]

**MICHAEL M. WALSH,** born Minneapolis, Minnesota, December 19, 1963; admitted to bar, 1990, California; 1991, U.S. District Court, Central District of California. *Education:* University of California at Los Angeles (B.S., 1987); Loyola Law School (J.D., 1990). *Member:* Los Angeles Bar Association; State Bar of California; Association of Southern California Defense Counsel. **REPORTED CASES:** Goldrich v. Natural Y. Surgical Specialties, Inc. (1994) 25 Cal.App 4th 772. **PRACTICE AREAS:** Products Liability; Construction Defect; General Negligence.

**DAVID M. FRISHMAN,** born Chicago, Illinois, March 16, 1962; admitted to bar, 1987, California and U.S. District Court, Central District of California. *Education:* Illinois State University (B.S., 1984); Southwestern University School of Law (J.D., 1987). Recipient, American Jurisprudence Award in Administrative Law, Fall, 1987. *Member:* Los Angeles County and American Bar Associations; State Bar of California; Association of Southern California Defense Counsel.

**COURTNEY COLLEEN MCNICHOLAS,** born Los Angeles, California, April 23, 1962; admitted to bar, 1987, California and U.S. District Court, Central District of California. *Education:* University of California at Los Angeles (B.A., 1984); McGeorge School of Law, University of the Pacific (J.D., 1987). Phi Alpha Delta. *Member:* Los Angeles County Bar Association; State Bar of California; Association of Southern California Defense Counsel.

**SUZANNE R. FEFFER,** born Van Nuys, California, December 7, 1960; admitted to bar, 1985, California; 1986, U.S. District Court, Central District of California; 1987, U.S. Court of Appeals, Ninth Circuit. *Education:* California State University at Northridge (B.A., cum laude, 1982); Whittier College School of Law (J.D., cum laude, 1985); Pepperdine University (M.A., 1990). Pi Sigma Alpha; Pi Alpha Delta; Psi Chi. Member, Executive Committee, 1983-1985 and Chairperson's Award, 1985, Moot Court Honors Board. Recipient: WCSL Merit Scholarship, 1983-1985; First Place Winner, 1985 ACLU Writing Competition. Most Outstanding Graduate, 1985. Lead Articles Editor, Whittier Law Review, 1983-1985. Author: "The Denial of Rehabilitation Benefits Subsequent to a Permanent Disability Hearing Constitutes 'good cause' to Reopen the Hearing," 6 Whittier Law Review 889, 1984, reprinted in National Insurance Law Review 83, Winter 1985; "Gray Turns To Black: Further Expansion of Duties to Defend the Insured," 35 FIC Quarterly 351, Summer 1985. *Member:* Los Angeles County and American Bar Associations; State Bar of California; Association of Southern California Defense Counsel.

*(This Listing Continued)*

# PROFESSIONAL BIOGRAPHIES

CALIFORNIA—LOS ANGELES

**AMY W. LEWIS,** born Salt Lake City, Utah, August 28, 1963; admitted to bar, 1992, California and U.S. District Court, Central District of California. *Education:* Brigham Young University (B.A., 1985); Loyola Law School (J.D., 1991). *Member:* Los Angeles County and American Bar Associations; State Bar of California; Association of Southern California Defense Counsel.

**MARSHALL ZELAZNIK,** born Babylon, New York, April 6, 1965; admitted to bar, 1992, California and U.S. District Court, Central District of California. *Education:* California State University at Long Beach (B.A., Sociology, 1988); University of San Francisco (J.D., 1992). Staff Member, University of San Francisco Maritime Law Journal. *Member:* Los Angeles County Bar Association; State Bar of California; Association of Southern California Defense Counsel.

**STEVEN M. DAILEY,** born Lawrence, Kansas, June 14, 1965; admitted to bar, 1993, California. *Education:* University of Colorado at Boulder (B.S., Business-Finance, 1988); Loyola Marymount University (J.D., 1992). Finalist, Loyola Trial Advocacy Competition. Recipient: American Jurisprudence Award in Remedies and Torts; Loyola Marymount University Merit Scholarship. *Member:* Los Angeles County Bar Association; State Bar of California; Association of Southern California Defense Counsel. **PRACTICE AREAS:** Products Liability; Environmental Litigation; Business Litigation.

**JULIE A. AUGUST,** born Ann Arbor, Michigan, June 10, 1968; admitted to bar, 1993, California; 1994, U.S. District Court, Central District of California. *Education:* University of California, San Diego (B.A., 1990); University of San Francisco (J.D., 1993). Recipient, American Jurisprudence Award, Constitutional Law, 1991. *Member:* Los Angeles County, South Bay and American Bar Associations; State Bar of California; Association of Southern California Defense Counsel. **LANGUAGES:** Spanish.

**DAVID SWEI-CHUAN LIN,** born Keelung, Taiwan, October 21, 1966; admitted to bar, 1991, California; 1992, U.S. District Court, Northern, Central and Eastern Districts. *Education:* Cornell University (B.A., 1988); Boston University School of Law (J.D., 1991). *Member:* State Bar of California; American Bar Association; Asian Professional Exchange (Director, Corporate Relations, 1993—); Asian Business League (ABL); Southern California Chinese Lawyers Association (SCCLA); Southern California Defense Counsel Association. **LANGUAGES:** Chinese (Mandarin), Taiwanese and Spanish. **PRACTICE AREAS:** Insurance Coverage/Bad Faith.

**R. BRET BEATTIE,** born Torrance, California, January 23, 1960; admitted to bar, 1990, California and U.S. District Court, Northern, Eastern and Central Districts of California. *Education:* California Lutheran University (B.S., 1983); Golden Gate University (M.S., 1987); Pepperdine University (J.D., 1990). Dean's List: California Lutheran University, Golden Gate University and Pepperdine University. Member, State Board of Accountancy, 1985—. Certified Public Accountant, California, 1985. *Member:* Los Angeles County and American (Member: Sections on Litigation and Business Litigation) Bar Associations; State Bar of California (Member, Business Litigation Section); Defense Research Institute; Association of Southern California Defense Counsel. **PRACTICE AREAS:** Products Liability; Complex Personal Injury; Chemical Exposure; Business Interruption; Property Damage.

**SHARYL B. ZIMMERMAN,** born Sacramento, California, June 27, 1966; admitted to bar, 1994, California. *Education:* University of California at Berkeley (B.A., 1988); University of the Pacific, McGeorge School of Law (J.D., 1993). *Member:* Los Angeles County and American Bar Associations; Association of Southern California Defense Counsel. **PRACTICE AREAS:** Products Liability; Medical Products.

REPRESENTATIVE CLIENTS: American Home Assurance Co.; American International Group; American International Underwriters; American Medical Systems; Audubon Insurance Group; Carl Warren & Co.; California Insurance Guarantee Association; CIGNA Companies; Constitution State Service Co.; Crawford & Company; Employers Insurance of Wausau; GAB Business Services; General Accident Insurance Co.; General Star Insurance Co.; Granite State Insurance Co.; GRE American Ins. Group; Hamilton Resources Corp.; Home Insurance; Industrial Underwriters, Inc.; John Deere Insurance Co.; Lexington Insurance Co.; LWP Insurance Services; MacCready & Gutmann Insurance Services, Inc.; McLarens Toplis North America; National Union Fire Insurance Co.; New Hampshire Insurance Co.; Northbrook Property & Casualty Insurance Co.; Seibels, Bruce and Co.; Scott Wetzel Services; St. Paul Fire & Marine; Tokio Marine and Fire Insurance Co., Ltd.; Transamerica Insurance; United Capitol Insurance Co.; United National Insurance; Western Heritage Insurance Co.
REFERENCE: Union Bank, Downtown Los Angeles, California.

## LAW OFFICE OF
## LEONARD L. SCHAPIRA
### LOS ANGELES, CALIFORNIA
(See Hermosa Beach)

*Real Estate, Lender Liability, Debt Restructuring, Business, Consumer and Commercial Law.*

---

## NANCY R. SCHAUER
### 5601 WEST SLAUSON, SUITE 282
### LOS ANGELES, CALIFORNIA 90230
Telephone: 310-338-6670
Fax: 310-338-6673

*Business Law and Receivership Law.*

**NANCY R. SCHAUER,** born Detroit, Michigan, September 9, 1950; admitted to bar, 1976, California. *Education:* University of Michigan (A.B., 1972; J.D., 1976). Member: Mortar Board; University of Michigan Journal of Law Reform, 1976. Author: "Leveraged Buyouts and Fraudulent Conveyances", 1984; "A Close Call for a Small Corporation's Attorneys," 1991. President: Organization of Women Executives, 1981-1982; Association for Corporate Growth, 1989-1990. Panelist: Buy Sell Agreements for California Businesses; Representing California Corporations and Their Shareholders, Officers and Directors; Organizing and Advising Partnerships and Joint Ventures; Buying and Selling a Business, CEB.

---

## SCHELL & DELAMER, LLP
A Partnership including Professional Corporations
*Established in 1935*

### 865 SOUTH FIGUEROA STREET
### SUITE 2750
### LOS ANGELES, CALIFORNIA 90017
Telephone: 213-622-8181
Fax: 213-627-5252

*Thousand Oaks, California Office:* 100 East Thousand Oaks Boulevard, Suite 142. Telephone: 805-496-9533. Fax: 805-496-3424.

*Products Liability, Premise Liability and Security Issues, Insurance Coverage and Bad Faith, Public Entity and Government Liability, Automobile and Transportation, Truck and Heavy Equipment, Restaurant and Club Liability, Medical and Dental Malpractice, Wrongful Termination and Employers Liability, Defamation and Invasion of Privacy, Environmental (including EMF and RFI Exposure and Toxic Torts), Construction Defect and Land Subsidence, Business and Commercial Law, Professional Liability, Pharmaceutical Liability.*

FIRM PROFILE: *Schell & Delamer has been engaged in defense litigation in Southern California for more than 50 years. We are fully experienced in the defense and prosecution of all types of actions for our insured or self-insured clients.*

**GERALD F. H. DELAMER** (1892-1955).

**WALTER O. SCHELL** (1895-1981).

**ROLAND R. KASPAR, (PROFESSIONAL CORPORATION),** born Prague, Nebraska, October 10, 1928; admitted to bar, 1961, California. *Education:* University of Nebraska (B.S., 1952); University of California at Los Angeles (LL.D., 1960). Phi Delta Phi; Beta Gamma Sigma. Deputy District Attorney, Los Angeles County, 1961-1965. *Member:* State Bar of California; Association of Southern California Defense Counsel; American Board of Trial Advocates.

**GARRIN JAMES SHAW, (PROFESSIONAL CORPORATION),** born Riverside, California, July 2, 1943; admitted to bar, 1969, California. *Education:* University of Redlands (B.A., 1965); Hastings College of Law, University of California (J.D., 1968). Phi Delta Phi; Pi Gamma Mu. *Member:* Los Angeles County and American Bar Associations; State Bar of California; Lawyers Club of Los Angeles County; International Association of Insurance Counsel; American Board of Trial Advocats.

**ROBERT S. HAMRICK, (PROFESSIONAL CORPORATION),** born Detroit, Michigan, May 8, 1946; admitted to bar, 1973, California; U.S. District Court and Circuit Court of Appeals. *Education:* Michigan State University (B.A. in Economics, 1968); University of San Francisco (J.D.,

*(This Listing Continued)*

CAA1171B

## SCHELL & DELAMER, LLP, Los Angeles—Continued

1973). Arbitrator, American Arbitration Association and the Los Angeles Attorneys Arbitration Program. Settlement Officer, Los Angeles County Arbitration Program, 1979—. Member, Panel of Arbitrators, American Arbitration Association. *Member:* Los Angeles County Bar Association; The State Bar of California; Association of Southern California Defense Counsel.

**JEFFREY F. BRISKIN,** born Los Angeles, California, September 30, 1948; admitted to bar, 1978, California, U.S. Tax Court and U.S. Claims Court; 1981, U.S. Supreme Court. *Education:* University of Southern California (B.A., 1971); Western State University at Fullerton (J.D., 1977). *Member:* Los Angeles County and American Bar Associations; State Bar of California; The Association of Trial Lawyers of America; Association of Southern California Defense Counsel. **LANGUAGES:** Spanish.

**KATHERINE B. PENE,** born Alhambra, California, August 1, 1946; admitted to bar, 1979, California; 1980, U.S. District Court, Central District of California and U.S. Court of Appeals, Ninth Circuit; U.S. Court of Military Appeals, U.S. Claims Court and U.S. Tax Court; 1983, U.S. Supreme Court. *Education:* Immaculate Heart College; Pasadena City College; Los Angeles Valley College (A.A., 1976); University of LaVerne/San Fernando Valley College of Law (J.D., 1979). Arbitrator, Los Angeles Superior Court for Los Angeles, Van Nuys and Pomona. Judge Pro Tem, Los Angeles Municipal Court and Los Angeles Superior Court. Los Angeles County Panel of Arbitrators, Executive Committee of Los Angeles County Bar Association Delegation of California Bar Association. *Member:* Los Angeles County (Member, Superior Courts Committee) and American (Member, Tort and Insurance Practice Section) Bar Associations; State Bar of California; Southern California Adjusters Association.

### ASSOCIATES

**CANDACE E. AHRENS KALLBERG,** born Glendale, California, May 25, 1953; admitted to bar, 1983, California and U.S. District Court, Central District of California. *Education:* De Anza College (A.A., 1973); San Diego State University (B.S., cum laude, 1975); Loyola Law School (J.D., 1983). Beta Gamma Sigma. Staff Writer, Entertainment Law Journal, 1982-1983. *Member:* The State Bar of California; American Bar Association.

**DENISE A. NARDI,** born Inglewood, California, January 29, 1958; admitted to bar, 1987, California. *Education:* Brigham Young University; University of California at Los Angeles (B.A., 1980); Loyola Law School (J.D., 1987). *Member:* Los Angeles County and South Bay Bar Associations; Association of Southern California Defense Counsel; California Women Lawyers; California Trial Lawyers Association.

**RANDY A. BERG,** born Philadelphia, Pennsylvania, March 14, 1959; admitted to bar, 1987, California. *Education:* University of California at Los Angeles (B.A., cum laude, 1981); Loyola Marymount University (J.D., 1984). Author: 2 Articles, Loyola Entertainment Law Journal, 1984. *Member:* Los Angeles County Bar Association; State Bar of California; California Trial Lawyers Association.

**KENNETH S. MARKSON,** born Boston, Massachusetts, May 29, 1954; admitted to bar, 1989, California, U.S. District Court, Southern and Central Districts of California and U.S. Court of Appeals, Ninth Circuit. *Education:* University of Vermont (B.A., cum laude, 1976); Tulane Law School (J.D., cum laude, 1989). Phi Alpha Delta. Recipient, American Jurisprudence Award in Products Liability. *Member:* Los Angeles County and American (Member, Sections on: Tort and Insurance Practice; Business Law; Real Property, Probate and Trust Law; Young Lawyers Division) Bar Associations; State Bar of California; California Young Lawyers Association. **LANGUAGES:** French.

**JOSEPH P. SEPIKAS,** born Chicago, Illinois, October 20, 1952; admitted to bar, 1987, California and U.S. District Court, Southern, Eastern, Northern and Central Districts of California. *Education:* California State University at Northridge (B.A., cum laude, 1975); University of San Fernando College of Law (J.D., 1979). *Member:* Los Angeles County and American Bar Associations; Association of Southern California Defense Counsel; Lithuanian-American Bar Association; International Association of Defense Counsel Trial Academy.

**GREGORY J. AMANTIA,** born Encino, California, September 30, 1961; admitted to bar, 1989, California. *Education:* California State University at Northridge (B.A., 1984); Whittier College School of Law (J.D., 1989). *Member:* Los Angeles County Bar Association; State Bar of California. (Resident at Thousand Oaks Office).

*(This Listing Continued)*

CAA1172B

**JOHN J. LATZANICH, II.,** born Scranton, Pennsylvania, January 28, 1956; admitted to bar, 1986, California, Indiana, U.S. District Court, Northern and Southern Districts of Indiana, U.S. Tax Court and U.S. Court of Appeals, Seventh and Ninth Circuits; U.S. Supreme Court. *Education:* Widener University (B.S., 1978); University of LaVerne (J.D., 1984); Temple University (LL.M., 1985). T.A.P.S. graduate, nationally recognized trial advocacy program. Judge Pro Tem, Los Angeles County. Settlement Officer, Los Angeles County Arbitration Program. Arbitrator, Ventura County. Member, Los Angeles Attorneys Arbitration Program. *Member:* Los Angeles County and American Bar Associations; State Bar of California; Association of Southern California Defense Counsel; Irish American Bar Association; American Arbitration Association. (Resident at Thousand Oaks Office).

**LORI M. LEVINE,** born Los Angeles, California, October 5, 1951; admitted to bar, 1987, California. *Education:* University of California at Los Angeles (B.A., cum laude, 1973); Loyola Law School, Los Angeles (J.D., cum laude, 1987). Member, St. Thomas More Society. Recipient, American Jurisprudence Awards of Excellence in Evidence, Tax, Debtor-Creditor Relations, Trusts and Wills. *Member:* American Bar Association; State Bar of California.

**SYLVIA HAVENS,** born Heidelberg, Germany; admitted to bar, 1988, California. *Education:* Rutgers University (B.A., 1984); Southwestern University (J.D., 1988). *Member:* State Bar of California.

**ROMAN Y. NYKOLYSHYN,** born July 24, 1950; admitted to bar, 1988, California; 1989, U.S. District Court, Central District of California. *Education:* Kent State University (B.A., 1972); California State University at Dominguez Hills (M.B.A., 1981); Magdalen College, Oxford University, England (Certificate of Jurisprudence, 1987); Southwestern University (J.D., cum laude, 1988). Member, Moot Court Honors Program. Member, Southwestern University Law Review, 1987-1988. Recipient, American Jurisprudence Awards in Constitutional Law and Evidence. *Member:* State Bar of California.

REPRESENTATIVE CLIENTS: Alexsis Risk Management Services, Inc.; All Risk Claims Service Inc.; American International Group; Anthem Health Cos., Inc.; Balboa Insurance; California Fair Plan; Carl Warren & Co.; Century Surety; Chubb/Pacific Indemnity Group; Cigna-Aetna Insurance Group; CNA Insurance Cos.; Crawford and Company; Denny's, Inc.; Erie Insurance Co.; Fireman's Fund Insurance; Fruit of the Loom, Inc./Union Underwear, Inc.; GAB Business Services; Geico Annuity and Insurance; Hacienda-La Puente Unified School District; Hartford Insurance Group; Hertz Claims Management; Home Depot; House of Blues; Hughes Electronic Corp.; Hunt Wesson Inc.; Industrial Indemnity Co.; Insurance Company of North America; Keeling and Co.; Kemper Insurance Group; Liberty Mutual Group; Los Angeles Unified School District; Long Beach Unified School District; Marriott Casualty Claims; Motors Insurance Co.; National General Insurance Co.; Ontario-Montclair Unified School District; Pemco Insurance; Perrier Group; Safeco Insurance Co.; Transamerica Insurance Group; Travelers Insurance Co.; U.S. Borax & Chemical Corp.; United Pacific/Reliance Insurance Co.; University of Southern California; Vons Grocery Co.; Waltco Truck Equipment Co.; Wausau Insurance Cos.; W-D 40; Willis Corroon Administrative Services Corp.

## ROBERT L. SCHIBEL

A PROFESSIONAL CORPORATION

Established in 1987

SUITE 1000, 11111 SANTA MONICA BOULEVARD
**LOS ANGELES, CALIFORNIA 90025**
Telephone: 310-473-6888
Fax: 310-473-0906

*General Civil and Trial Practice in all State and Federal Courts. Family, Domestic Relations, Corporate, Real Property, Business and Entertainment Law.*

**ROBERT L. SCHIBEL,** born Duluth, Minnesota, July 27, 1938; admitted to bar, 1970, California and U.S. District Court, Central District of California; 1978, U.S. Supreme Court. *Education:* University of Minnesota (B.B.A., 1960); University of Southern California (J.D., 1969). Author: "The Doctrine of Constructive Change," NCMA Journal, Vol. 3, Fall, 1969. Co-Author: "The Great Record Rip-Off: Penal Sanctions and State Civil Remedies," University of West Los Angeles Law Review, Vol. VII, Winter, 1975. Instructor, Contracts, Entertainment and Family Law, University of West Los Angeles, 1971-1975. *Member:* Beverly Hills, Los Angeles County and American Bar Associations. (Certified Specialist, Family Law, The State Bar of California Board of Legal Specialization).

REPRESENTATIVE CLIENTS: Inco Homes; XIV Karats, Gallery Judaica; Dryer Productions, Inc.
REFERENCE: City National Bank (Beverly Hills Branch).

## LAW OFFICES OF JOEL P. SCHIFF

1801 CENTURY PARK EAST
TWENTY THIRD FLOOR
LOS ANGELES, CALIFORNIA 90067
Telephone: 310-201-2550
Fax: 310-201-2551

*Appellate Practice and Business Litigation, State and Federal, Mediation and Arbitration, Business Law.*

**JOEL P. SCHIFF,** born Brooklyn, N.Y., December 7, 1942; admitted to bar, 1966, New York and U.S. Court of Military Appeals; 1969, California; 1979, U.S. Court of Appeals, Ninth Circuit. *Education:* Cornell University (A.B., 1963; J.D., with distinction, 1965). Order of the Coif; Phi Beta Kappa; Phi Alpha Delta. Associate Editor, Cornell Law Quarterly, 1964-1965. Superior Court Arbitrator, 1981—. Private Mediator and Arbitrator, 1992—. *Member:* Beverly Hills (Chairman: Amicus Briefs Committee, 1992—; Attorney-Client Mediator Committee, 1994—; Resolutions Committee, 1985-1986; Member, Board of Governors, 1979-1981, 1985-1989) and Los Angeles County Bar Associations; The State Bar of California (Member, Committee on Administration of Justice, 1986-1989; Association of Business Trial Lawyers (Member, Board of Governors, 1982-1984).

## SCHIFFMACHER, WEINSTEIN, BOLDT & RACINE

PROFESSIONAL CORPORATION
LOS ANGELES, CALIFORNIA
(See Weinstein, Boldt, Racine, Halfhide & Camel)

*Federal and State Taxation, Employee Benefits, Estate Planning and Business Transactions.*

## SCHIFINO & LINDON

1901 AVENUE OF THE STARS, SUITE 251
LOS ANGELES, CALIFORNIA 90067
Telephone: 310-553-2600
Fax: 310-553-2625

*Corporate, Securities and General Business.*

### MEMBERS OF FIRM

**PAUL G. SCHIFINO,** born Washington, D.C., December 30, 1961; admitted to bar, 1989, California. *Education:* Loyola University (B.B.A., summa cum laude, 1984); University of Michigan (M.B.A., 1986); Georgetown University (J.D., 1989). Adjunct Professor, Corporate Finance, Georgetown University, 1987-1989. *Member:* State Bar of California. **PRACTICE AREAS:** Corporate Law; Securities Law; Acquisitions, Divestitures and Mergers Law.

**MARK L. LINDON,** born Los Angeles, California, June 23, 1960; admitted to bar, 1985, California. *Education:* Georgetown University (A.B., magna cum laude, 1982); University of California School of Law at Los Angeles (J.D., 1985). Executive Editor, Federal Communications Law Journal, 1984-1985. *Member:* Los Angeles County Bar Association; State Bar of California. **PRACTICE AREAS:** Corporate Law; Securities Law; Acquisitions, Divestitures and Mergers Law.

### OF COUNSEL

**JOLIE L. BUSCH,** born New York, N.Y., September 25, 1962; admitted to bar, 1988, New York (Not admitted in California). *Education:* Boston University (B.A., 1984); Benjamin Cardozo School of Law (J.D., 1987). Belkin Fellow. *Member:* New York State and American Bar Associations. **PRACTICE AREAS:** Securities Litigation; General Civil Litigation.

## SCHIMMEL, HILLSHAFER & LOEWENTHAL

LOS ANGELES, CALIFORNIA
(See Sherman Oaks)

*General Civil Litigation, Construction Law, Community Association Law, Personal Injury, Products Liability and Insurance Law, Real Estate Law.*

## ROBERT S. SCHLIFKIN

1925 CENTURY PARK EAST, SUITE 1250
LOS ANGELES, CALIFORNIA 90067-2713
Telephone: 310-553-5151
FAX: 310-553-7204

*Practice limited to Civil Litigation. Professional Liability, Personal Injury, Products Liability and Business Fraud.*

**ROBERT S. SCHLIFKIN,** born Chicago, Illinois, May 16, 1939; admitted to bar, 1969, California; 1973, U.S. Supreme Court. *Education:* Roosevelt University (B.S., 1962); University of San Fernando Valley (J.D., 1969). Member, Los Angeles Superior Court Arbitration Plan, 1973—. Chairman, Task Force #1, Civil Trials Manual, Los Angeles Superior Court, 1975-1976. Member, Rules Committee, Trial Delay Reduction Program, Member, Joint Association Settlement Office Program Committee. Member, Los Angeles City Attorney's Advisory Committee, 1981-1984. *Member:* Beverly Hills, Century City, Los Angeles County (Member: Executive Committee, Trial Lawyers Section, 1973-1974, 1983—; Court Congestion Committee, 1981-1987; Judicial Evaluations Committee, Sub Chair, 1988—; Trustee, 1984-1986) and American Bar Associations; State Bar of California; Los Angeles Trial Lawyers Association (Member, Board of Governors, 1976-1977, 1980-1984; President-Elect, 1986; President, 1987; Chairman, Superior Court Settlement Officer Program, 1979-1986); California Trial Lawyers Association (Member: Medical Malpractice Section; Board of Governors, 1981-1982; 1987-1988); National Board of Professional Liability Attorneys; The Association of Trial Lawyers of America (Member, Legislation Committee, 1976-1980). (Member of California Trial Lawyers Association, with recognized experience in the fields of General Personal Injury, Product Liability and Professional Negligence).

REFERENCE: First Los Angeles Bank.

## SCHLOTHAUER, COLLINS & MACALUSO

11661 SAN VICENTE BOULEVARD, SUITE 303
LOS ANGELES, CALIFORNIA 90049
Telephone: 310-820-8606
Fax: 310-820-7057

*Affiliated San Jose California Office:* Collins & Schlothauer, 60 South Market Street, Suite 1100. Telephone: 408-298-5161. Fax: 408-297-5766.

*Civil Litigation in all State and Federal Courts, Personal Injury, Medical Malpractice, Aviation Law including Plane Crashes, Products Liability.*

### PARTNERS

**THOMAS L. SCHLOTHAUER,** born Windsor, Colorado, August 11, 1942; admitted to bar, 1973, California. *Education:* University of Colorado; Colorado State University (B.S.C.E., 1966); University of Santa Clara (J.D., 1972). Phi Alpha Delta (Vice President, 1971-1972); Chi Epsilon. Member, 1974-1979 and President, 1976, Board of Examiners in Veterinary Medicine for State of California. Member, Judicial Settlement Panel, Superior Court, County of Los Angeles, 1985—. *Member:* Los Angeles County and American Bar Associations; State Bar of California; American Society of Civil Engineers; California Trial Lawyers Association; The Association of Trial Lawyers of America. (Also Of Counsel to Collins & Schlothauer, San Jose). **PRACTICE AREAS:** Torts (100%, 200); Products Liability Law; Professional Liability Law.

**MARK SCOTT COLLINS,** born Vallejo, California, January 11, 1949; admitted to bar, 1974, California. *Education:* California State University at Northridge (B.A., 1971); Hastings College of the Law, University of California (J.D., 1974). *Member:* Santa Clara County and American Bar Associations; State Bar of California; Association of Defense Counsel; California Trial Lawyers Association (Recognized Experience as a Trial Lawyer and in the fields of Professional Negligence, Products Liability, General Personal Injury Law and Insurance Bad Faith Litigation). (Member of C.T.L.A., with recognized experience in the fields of Trial Lawyer, Profes-

*(This Listing Continued)*

### SCHLOTHAUER, COLLINS & MACALUSO, Los Angeles—Continued

sional Negligence, Product Liability, General Personal Injury and Insurance Bad Faith) (Also Member Collins & Schlothauer, San Jose, California). **PRACTICE AREAS:** Civil Litigation; Insurance Defense Law; Personal Injury.

**TODD E. MACALUSO,** born Valley Stream, New York, October 11, 1962; admitted to bar, 1987, California; 1988, U.S. District Court, Central District of California. *Education:* Boston College (B.A., 1984); University of Detroit (J.D., 1987); Regents College, London, England (1987). National Institute of Trial Advocacy, Oxford University, England (1987). *Member:* Los Angeles County and American Bar Associations. **LANGUAGES:** Spanish.

#### ASSOCIATE

**JAMES PFLASTER,** born 1947; admitted to bar, 1973, California. *Education:* University of California at Los Angeles (B.A.); University of California School of Law at Los Angeles (J.D.). *Member:* State Bar of California. **LANGUAGES:** Spanish. **PRACTICE AREAS:** Personal Injury Law (60%); Workers Compensation Law (40%).

#### OF COUNSEL

**MALCOLM G. HEIB,** born Chicago, Illinois, February 16, 1934; admitted to bar, 1968, California; 1975, U.S. Supreme Court. *Education:* Fairleigh Dickinson University (B.A., 1962); Southwestern University (J.D., 1969). *Member:* Los Angeles County and American Bar Associations; State Bar of California; Southern California Defense Counsel; American Board of Trial Advocates (Advocate). **PRACTICE AREAS:** Trial Practice (100); Civil Practice (300); Insurance Defense; Personal Injury; Construction Defect Cases; Malpractice.

---

### SCHMELTZER, APTAKER & SHEPARD, P.C.

*1999 AVENUE OF THE STARS*
*TWENTY-SEVENTH FLOOR*
**LOS ANGELES, CALIFORNIA 90067-4095**
*Telephone: 310-557-2966*
*FAX: 310-286-6610*
*Email: sas@saslaw.com*
*URL: http://www.saspc.com*

Washington, D.C. Office: The Watergate, Suite 1000, 2600 Virginia Avenue, N.W., 20037-1905. Telephone: 202-333-8800. Facsimile: 202-342-3434.

Labor and Employment Law, Maritime, Equal Employment Opportunity, Civil Litigation, Employee Benefits, Franchise, Criminal, Health Care Law, Antitrust, Interstate Commerce and Corporate Law.

(For complete biographical data on all personnel, see Professional Biographies at Washington, D.C.)

---

### JAMES R. SCHOENFIELD

*A PROFESSIONAL CORPORATION*
*1801 CENTURY PARK EAST, SUITE 2400*
**LOS ANGELES, CALIFORNIA 90067**
*Telephone: 310-556-9605*
*FAX: 310-551-2814*

Business Transactions, Licensing, Real Estate and Entertainment Law.

**JAMES R. SCHOENFIELD,** born Evanston, Illinois, January 21, 1951; admitted to bar, 1976, California. *Education:* University of California at Los Angeles (B.A., summa cum laude, 1973; J.D., 1976). Phi Beta Kappa. *Member:* State Bar of California.

---

### KARL W. SCHOTH & ASSOCIATES

**LOS ANGELES, CALIFORNIA**

(See Pasadena)

Personal Injury, Specializing in medical malpractice and elder abuse law.

---

### MARK SCHREIBER

**LOS ANGELES, CALIFORNIA**

(See Encino)

Personal Injury, Elder Abuse, and Wrongful Death Defense, Copyright & Trademark.

---

### LAW OFFICES OF ALAN SCHUCHMAN

*1901 AVENUE OF THE STARS*
*20TH FLOOR*
**LOS ANGELES, CALIFORNIA 90067**
*Telephone: 310-556-2889*
*Fax: 310-556-0065*

Personal Injury, Medical Malpractice, Products Liability, Civil Litigation, Family Law.

**ALAN SCHUCHMAN,** born Brooklyn, New York, October 6, 1947; admitted to bar, 1976, New York; 1978, California. *Education:* Southampton College of Long Island University (B.A., 1969); Brooklyn Law School (J.D., 1975). Recipient, American Jurisprudence Award, 1969. *Member:* Consumer Attorneys of Los Angeles; Consumer Attorneys of California.

---

### J. BRIN SCHULMAN

*10866 WILSHIRE BOULEVARD*
*SUITE 970*
*WESTWOOD PLACE*
**LOS ANGELES, CALIFORNIA 90024**
*Telephone: 310-234-1933*
*Fax: 310-234-1943*

General Civil, Criminal, Trial and Appellate Practice in all State and Federal Courts. Business, Commercial, Entertainment, Real Estate, Conservatorship, Trust and Probate Litigation. White Collar Criminal Defense, Organ Transplantation and Family Law.

**J. BRIN SCHULMAN,** born Chicago, Illinois, January 20, 1934; admitted to bar, 1959, California, U.S. District Court, Northern District of California, U.S. Court of Military Appeals and U.S. Court of Appeals, 9th Circuit; 1960, U.S. District Court, Central District of California; 1965, U.S. Supreme Court. *Education:* University of California at Los Angeles (B.A., 1955); University of Southern California (J.D., 1958). Phi Alpha Delta. Justice (President) Ross Chapter. Winner, Hale Moot Court Competition, University of Southern California, 1958. Lecturer: "Liability Issues in Organ Transplantation," North American Transplant Coordinators Organization (NATCO), National Convention, Chicago, Illinois, 1981; "Legal Issues in Transplantation," American Operating Room Nurses Organization (AORN), National Convention, Anaheim, California, 1983; "Estates and Trusts, Dispute Resolution and Litigation," CEB, March and April, 1986, August and September, 1989; "Litigation in Probate, Pursuing Assets, Attorneys Fees and Resolution of Disputes as Viewed by Special Litigator of The Groucho Marx Estate, San Fernando Bar Association, 1990; "Legal and Ethical Issues in Transplantation, Point-Counter Point," Fourth Annual Symposium on Organ Transplantation, Hoag Hospital, Newport Beach, California, 1991; "Mock Trial - The Transplant Coordinator and the Law," North American Transplant Coordinators Organization (NATCO), Annual Meeting, Halifax, Nova Scotia, Canada, 1991; "Legal Issues Affecting Patients' Rights," Transplant Recipients International Organization (TRIO), 5th Annual Conference, Washington, D.C., 1993. Assistant U.S. Attorney, Central District of California, 1960-1966. Assistant Chief of Criminal Division, 1964-1966. Judge Pro Tempore, Beverly Hills Municipal Court, 1970-1977; Member, President, Anatomical Transplant Association of California (ATAC), 1980-1986; Member: UCLA Alumni Association; U.S.C. Law Alumni Association, Legion Lex. *Member:* Beverly Hills, Los Angeles County (Member, Sections on: Estate, Probate and Trust; Family Law; Law Office Management; Member, Executive Committee, Litigation Section, 1983-1986) Federal and American (Member, Sections on: Criminal Justice; Entertainment and Sports Industries; Family Law; Litigation; Real Property, Probate and Trust Law) Bar Associations; The State Bar of Cali-

*(This Listing Continued)*

fornia (Member, Sections on: Litigation; Estate Planning, Trust and Probate; Family Law). [U.S. Army, Office of Staff Judge Advocate, Ft. Ord., California, 1959-1960]

## DOUGLAS B. SCHWAB
**11845 WEST OLYMPIC BOULEVARD, SUITE 1000**
**LOS ANGELES, CALIFORNIA 90064**
Telephone: 310-444-5929
FAX: 310-312-8189

*Civil Litigation, Health Care, Business, Securities and Real Estate.*

**DOUGLAS B. SCHWAB,** born Los Angeles, California, July 15, 1944; admitted to bar, 1970, Massachusetts; 1971, California. *Education:* Williams College (B.A., 1966); Harvard University (J.D., 1969). Phi Beta Kappa. *Member:* Los Angeles County Bar Association; State Bar of California.

## SCHWARTZ, STEINSAPIR, DOHRMANN & SOMMERS
**6300 WILSHIRE BOULEVARD, SUITE 2000**
**LOS ANGELES, CALIFORNIA 90048**
Telephone: 213-655-4700
Fax: 213-655-4488

*Pittsburgh, Pennsylvania Office:* 3600 One Oxford Centre. Telephone: 412-456-2008. Fax: 412-456-2020.

*Labor Law, Trust and Employee Benefit Law (ERISA). Libel and Slander, General Civil and Trial Practice in all State and Federal Courts and Arbitrations, Real Estate Law, Credit Unions, Nonprofit Corporations, Political Campaign Finance Law.*

*FIRM PROFILE:* Schwartz, Steinsapir, Dohrmann & Sommers has represented local and international labor unions, teacher and other voluntary associations, Taft-Hartley and governmental employee benefit plans, and individual workers since 1954. In addition to representing unions and benefit plans in all aspects of state and federal labor and employee benefits law, we also provide the full range of legal services required by those organizations, including representation in real estate and business matters. The firm also represents individual plaintiffs in actions arising under state and federal civil rights law, ERISA, the Fair Labor Standards Act, and other state and federal laws governing employment and we also practice in the area of political campaign finance law. The firm represents clients throughout California, Nevada and neighboring states.

### MEMBERS OF FIRM

**LAURENCE D. STEINSAPIR,** born Cleveland, Ohio, September 27, 1935; admitted to bar, 1959, Ohio; 1960, California; 1970, U.S. Supreme Court. *Education:* Ohio University (B.S.C., 1957); Case Western Reserve University (J.D., 1959). Phi Eta Sigma. Association Counsel for the California Teachers Association (NEA), 1982—. *Member:* Cleveland (Ohio), Los Angeles County and American (Member, Section of Labor and Employment Law) Bar Associations; State Bar of California. *PRACTICE AREAS:* Labor Law; Education Law; Arbitration Law; Real Estate.

**ROBERT M. DOHRMANN,** born San Francisco, California, April 20, 1935; admitted to bar, 1963, California; 1970, U.S. Supreme Court. *Education:* University of Santa Clara (B.S., 1956); University of Southern California (LL.B., 1962). Phi Delta Phi. *Member:* Los Angeles County (Chairman, Labor Law Section, 1982-1983) and American (Member, Section of Labor and Employment Law; Council Member, 1986-1994; Co-Chairman, Committee on State and Local Government Bargaining, 1981-1984; Member, Board of Editors, The Labor Lawyer, 1984—; Co-Chair, Publications Committee, 1994—) Bar Associations; State Bar of California. *PRACTICE AREAS:* Labor and Employment Law; Employee Benefits Litigation; Public Sector Employment Relations; Collective Bargaining Law.

**RICHARD D. SOMMERS,** born St. Louis, Missouri, April 21, 1945; admitted to bar, 1971, California. *Education:* University of California at Berkeley and University of California at Los Angeles (A.B., 1967); Loyola University of Los Angeles (J.D., 1970). Member, Loyola University at Los Angeles Law Review, 1969-1970. Research Attorney to Presiding Justice John J. Ford, California Court of Appeal, 1970-1972. *Member:* Los Angeles County and American Bar Associations; State Bar of California. *PRACTICE AREAS:* ERISA; Employee Benefit Law; Labor and Employment Law.

*(This Listing Continued)*

**STUART LIBICKI,** born Celle, Germany, April 15, 1949; admitted to bar, 1973, California. *Education:* University of California at Berkeley (B.S., summa cum laude, 1970); Boalt Hall School of Law, University of California at Berkeley (J.D., 1973). Phi Beta Kappa. *Member:* Los Angeles County and American Bar Associations; State Bar of California. *PRACTICE AREAS:* Labor and Employment Law; Employee Benefits Litigation; Real Estate; Insurance.

**MICHAEL R. FEINBERG,** born Brooklyn, New York, November 1, 1952; admitted to bar, 1979, California. *Education:* University of Rochester, University of Southern California (B.A., 1974); University of California at Los Angeles (M.A., in American Labor History, 1977); Loyola University of Los Angeles (J.D., 1979). Member, AFL-CIO Lawyers Coordinating Committee, 1984—. *Member:* Los Angeles County (Member, Labor and Employment Section, Executive Committee) and American (Member: Labor and Employment Law Section) Bar Associations; State Bar of California; National Lawyers Guild (Member, Labor and Employment Committee). *REPORTED CASES:* Paramount Unified School Dist. v. Teachers Ass'n. of Paramount, Cal.App.4th, 32 Cal.Rptr.2d 311 (1994); Combs v. Rockwell International Corp., 927F.2d 486 (9th Cir. 1991); Wiman v. Vallejo City Unified School Dist., 221 Cal.App.3d 1486, 271 Cal.Rptr. 142 (1990); Dixon v. Bd. of Trustees of Saugus Union School Dist., 216 Cal.App.3d 1269, 265 Cal.Rptr. 511 (1989); California Teachers Ass'n. v. Cory, 155 Cal.App.3d 484, 202 Cal.Rptr. 611 (1984); Stanford v. Calif. Unemployment Ins. App. Bd., 147 Cal.App.3d 98, 195 Cal.Rptr. 1 (1983). *PRACTICE AREAS:* Labor and Employment Law; Employment Discrimination; Sexual Harassment; Wage and Hour Law; Education Law; Defamation; Public Employment Relations Law.

**MICHAEL D. FOUR,** born Chicago, Illinois, February 29, 1956; admitted to bar, 1981, California. *Education:* University of California at Berkeley (A.B., 1978); Loyola Marymount University, Los Angeles (J.D., 1981). *Member:* Los Angeles County Bar Association; State Bar of California. *PRACTICE AREAS:* Labor and Employment Law; Campaign Finance Law.

**MARGO A. FEINBERG,** born New York, N.Y., November 16, 1956; admitted to bar, 1981, California. *Education:* University of California at Berkeley (B.A.,1978); University of Sussex, England; Hastings College of Law, University of California (J.D., 1981). *Member:* Los Angeles County Bar Association; State Bar of California; National Lawyers Guild; Women Lawyers Association of Los Angeles. *PRACTICE AREAS:* Labor and Employment Law; Public Employment Relations Law; Sexual Harassment; Education Law; Employment Discrimination Law; Campaign Finance Law.

**HENRY M. WILLIS,** born Washington, D.C., October 8, 1952; admitted to bar, 1978, California; 1981, Arkansas. *Education:* Wesleyan University (B.A., 1974); Boalt Hall School of Law, University of California (J.D., 1978). Order of the Coif. *Member:* Los Angeles County Bar Association; State Bar of California; National Lawyers Guild. *PRACTICE AREAS:* Labor and Employment Law; Public Employment Relations Law; Employment Discrimination Law.

**DENNIS J. MURPHY,** born Alamogordo, New Mexico, February 1, 1955; admitted to bar, 1980, California. *Education:* San Jose State University (B.A., 1977); Hastings College of Law, University of California (J.D., 1980). *Member:* Los Angeles County Bar Association; State Bar of California; Japanese American Bar Association. *PRACTICE AREAS:* ERISA; Employee Benefit Law; Labor and Employment Law.

**D. WILLIAM HEINE, JR.,** born Buffalo, New York, February 28, 1953; admitted to bar, 1983, California; 1985, District of Columbia. *Education:* State University of New York at Buffalo (B.A., summa cum laude, 1975); University of California, Irvine (M.A., 1980); Boalt Hall School of Law, University of California (J.D., 1983). Articles Editor, Industrial Relations Law Journal, 1982-1983. *Member:* Los Angeles County Bar Association; State Bar of California; National Lawyers Guild. *PRACTICE AREAS:* Labor and Employment Law; Employment Discrimination Law; Campaign Finance Law; Employee Drug Testing.

**CLAUDE CAZZULINO,** born New York, N.Y., June 17, 1954; admitted to bar, 1985, California and U.S. District Court, Central District of California; 1988, U.S. Court of Appeals, Ninth Circuit; 1989, U.S. District Court, Southern District of California. *Education:* Brown University (B.A., 1976); Northeastern University (J.D., 1984). Author: "Effective QDRO'S," 15 Los Angeles Lawyer, p.26 (#3 May, 1992). *Member:* Los Angeles County Bar Association; State Bar of California; National Lawyers Guild. *PRACTICE AREAS:* ERISA; Employee Benefit Law; Labor and Employment Law.

*(This Listing Continued)*

## SCHWARTZ, STEINSAPIR, DOHRMANN & SOMMERS,
Los Angeles—Continued

**DOLLY M. GEE,** born Hawthorne, California, July 1, 1959; admitted to bar, 1984, California. *Education:* University of California at Los Angeles (B.A., summa cum laude, 1981); University of California at Los Angeles School of Law (J.D., 1984). Phi Beta Kappa. Law Clerk to Hon. Milton L. Schwartz, U.S. District Court, Eastern District of California, 1984-1986. Central District Lawyer Representative to the Ninth Circuit Judicial Conference, 1993-1996. Member, Federal Service Impasses Panel, 1994—. *Member:* Los Angeles County Bar Association (Member, Board of Trustees, 1993-1995); State Bar of California (Member, Judicial Nominees Evaluation Commission, 1996—); Southern California Chinese Lawyers Association (President, 1992-1993). **PRACTICE AREAS:** Labor and Employment Law; Public Employment Relations Law; Education Law.

**WILLIAM T. PAYNE,** born Pueblo, Colorado, April 25, 1953; admitted to bar, 1979, California; 1983, Pennsylvania. *Education:* University of Pittsburgh (B.A., summa cum laude, 1975); University of California - Berkeley, Boalt Hall School of Law (J.D., 1979). Associate Editor, Industrial Relations Law Journal, 1978-1979. Author: "Enjoining Employers Pending Arbitration," 3 Industrial Relations Law Journal 169, (1979); "Lawsuits Challenging Termination or Modification of Retiree Insurance Benefits: A Plaintiff's Perspective," 10 The Labor Lawyer 91, (1994). Assistant General Counsel, United Steelworkers of America, 1982-1991. *Member:* Los Angeles County (Member, Executive Committee, 1994-1995) and American (Co-Chair, Subcommittee for Benefit Claims and Individual Rights, Labor and Employment Law Section, 1988—; Member, AFL-CIO Lawyers Coordinating Committee, 1982—) Bar Associations; State Bar of California. (Resident at Pittsburgh, Pennsylvania Office). **PRACTICE AREAS:** Labor and Employment Law; ERISA; Employee Benefits Litigation; Age Discrimination; Pension and Profit Sharing Law.

### ASSOCIATES

**BRENDA E. SUTTON,** born Riverside, California, September 23, 1961; admitted to bar, 1993, California. *Education:* Drake University (B.A., 1984); University of California at Los Angeles (J.D., 1992). *Member:* Los Angeles County Bar Association (Member, Sections on: Labor and Employment); Langston Bar Association; State Bar of California; Black Women Lawyers Association; National Lawyers Guild. **PRACTICE AREAS:** Labor Law; Employment Discrimination; Civil Rights Law.

**ERIKA A. ZUCKER,** born Syracuse, New York, May 6, 1965; admitted to bar, 1993, California. *Education:* Oberlin College (B.A., 1987); Northeastern University (J.D., 1993). *Member:* Bar Association of San Francisco; State Bar of California; National Lawyers Guild. **PRACTICE AREAS:** Labor and Employment.

REFERENCE: Wells Fargo, Los Angeles, California.

---

## SCHWARTZ, WISOT & WILSON, LLP
### LOS ANGELES, CALIFORNIA
(See Beverly Hills)

*General Civil and Trial Practice in all State and Federal Courts. Business Corporate, Civil Litigation, Real Property and Commercial Transactions, Litigation, Title Insurance, Probate Litigation and Construction Litigation.*

---

## ARTHUR E. SCHWIMMER
2049 CENTURY PARK EAST, SUITE 1800
### LOS ANGELES, CALIFORNIA 90067
Telephone: 310-277-8448

*Appellate Practice in State and Federal Courts.*

**ARTHUR E. SCHWIMMER,** born Brooklyn, New York, March 12, 1941; admitted to bar, 1964, New York; 1965, U.S. Tax Court; 1966, U.S. Court of Appeals, Federal Circuit; 1969, California; 1972, U.S. Court of Appeals, 9th Circuit; 1974, U.S. Supreme Court. *Education:* Columbia University (A.B., 1961); Brooklyn Law School (LL.B., 1964). Represented Brooklyn Law School in National Moot Court Competitions of 1962 and 1963. Author: "Oral Argument" Chapter, California Civil Appellate Practice, 3d ed. Continuing Education of the Bar, 1996. Trial Attorney, U.S. Department of Justice: Civil Division, General Litigation Section, Washington, D.C., 1964-1966; Civil Division, Customs Section, New York, N.Y., 1966-1968. Panelist: "Preserving the Record for Appeal," Los Angeles

*(This Listing Continued)*

County Bar Association, 1979; "Appellate Practice," Federal Practice Institute, Continuing Education of the Bar, 1981, 1983, 1984 and 1986; "Step by Step, The Appellate Process," Continuing Education of the Bar, 1983; "Handling Civil Appeals," Continuing Education of the Bar, 1992. Lecturer, Appellate Courts Institute, Center for Judicial Education and Research, 1985. Member, Judicial Council Advisory Committee to Implement Proposition 32, 1984-1985. *Member:* Century City, Beverly Hills, Los Angeles County (Chair, Appellate Courts Committee, 1979-1980) and American (Member: Appellate Practice Committee, Litigation Section, 1978—; Appellate Advocacy Committee, Tort and Insurance Practice Section, 1979—) Bar Associations; State Bar of California (Member, Committee on Appellate Courts, 1981-1984); California Academy of Appellate Lawyers (President, 1984-1985); American Academy of Appellate Lawyers.

---

## ROBIN R. SCROGGIE
333 SOUTH GRAND AVENUE, 37TH FLOOR
### LOS ANGELES, CALIFORNIA 90071
Telephone: 213-620-9576
Facsimile: 213-625-1832

*Criminal Trial and Appellate Practice in all State and Federal Courts.*

**ROBIN R. SCROGGIE,** born Fort Benning, Georgia, April 7, 1957; admitted to bar, 1983, Iowa; 1984, Arizona, U.S. District Court, District of Arizona, California and U.S. District Court, Central, Southern, Northern and Eastern Districts of California; 1985, U.S. Court of Appeals, Ninth Circuit; 1995, U.S. Supreme Court. *Education:* University of Iowa (B.A., 1980; J.D., with distinction, 1983). Member, Board of Editors, Iowa Law Review, 1982-1983. Law Clerk to the Honorable Walter E. Craig, U.S. District Court, District of Arizona, 1983-1985. Assistant United States Attorney, Central District of California, Criminal Division, 1987-1990. *Member:* Los Angeles County (Member, White Collar Defense Committee) and American (Member, White Collar Crime Committee) Bar Associations; National Association of Criminal Defense Lawyers; California Attorneys for Criminal Justice. **PRACTICE AREAS:** Criminal Law.

---

## SEAVER & GILL, LLP
444 SOUTH FLOWER STREET, SUITE 2300
### LOS ANGELES, CALIFORNIA 90071
Telephone: 213-689-4700
Facsimile: 213-689-0330

*General Business Practice, Probate and Trust Administration, Conservatorship Law, Probate, Trust, Conservatorship and Elder Abuse Litigation, Civil Litigation, Estate Planning and Charitable Organizations.*

### MEMBERS OF FIRM

**MICHAEL J. GILL,** born Los Angeles, California, November 9, 1944; admitted to bar, 1970, California and U.S. District Court, Central District of California. *Education:* University of Redlands (A.B., 1966); Loyola University of Los Angeles (J.D., 1969). Phi Delta Phi. Deputy Inheritance Tax Referee, 1967-1969. Deputy County Counsel, County of Los Angeles, 1970-1972. *Member:* Los Angeles County (Member: Probate and Trust Law Section; Executive Committee, 1984-1987), Orange County (Member, Sections on: Probate and Estate Planning; Probate and Trust Law; Secretary and Vice Chairman, 1973-1975) and American (Member, Real Property, Probate and Trust Law Section) Bar Associations; State Bar of California. **PRACTICE AREAS:** Probate and Trust Administration; Conservatorships; Probate, Trust and Elder Abuse Litigation; Estate Planning.

**LAURA STERN SEAVER,** born Chicago, Illinois, July 21, 1950; admitted to bar, 1975, California. *Education:* University of California at Los Angeles (B.A., summa cum laude, 1972); Stanford University (J.D., 1975). Phi Beta Kappa. *Member:* Los Angeles County and American Bar Associations; State Bar of California. **PRACTICE AREAS:** Estate Planning; Charitable Organizations.

**R. CARLTON SEAVER,** born Oakland, California, February 24, 1947; admitted to bar, 1975, California; 1979, U.S. Supreme Court and U.S. Tax Court. *Education:* Princeton University (A.B., cum laude, 1968); Stanford University (J.D., 1975). *Member:* Pasadena, Los Angeles County and American Bar Associations; State Bar of California. **PRACTICE AREAS:** Business Law; Civil Litigation; Probate and Trust Litigation.

## LAW OFFICES OF SAVIZ SEBGHATI

*Established in 1990*

WILSHIRE BUNDY PLAZA
12121 WILSHIRE BOULEVARD
SUITE 401
LOS ANGELES, CALIFORNIA 90025
Telephone: 310-207-9706
Facsimile: 310-826-6696

*Business, Corporate and Real Estate Law.*

**SAVIZ SEBGHATI,** born Tehran, Iran, April 14, 1961; admitted to bar, 1986, California; 1987, U.S. District Court, Central District of California, and U.S. Court of Appeals, Ninth Circuit. *Education:* University of California at Berkeley (A.B., 1983); Boston University (J.D., 1986). *Member:* Los Angeles County Bar Association (Member, Sections on: International, Business and Corporations, Commercial Law and Bankruptcy, Real Estate and Taxation Law); State Bar of California (Member, Sections on: Corporate, Business and Banking, Real Estate, International and Labor Law).
**LANGUAGES:** Persian.

---

## SEDGWICK, DETERT, MORAN & ARNOLD

A Partnership including Professional Corporations

*801 SOUTH FIGUEROA STREET, 18TH FLOOR*
**LOS ANGELES, CALIFORNIA 90017-5556**
Telephone: 213-426-6900
Fax: 213-426-6921
Email: E-Mail@SDMA.com

*San Francisco, California Office:* 16th Floor, One Embarcadero Center. Telephone: 415-781-7900. Cable Address: "Sedma". Fax: 415-781-2635.
*Irvine, California Office:* 3 Park Plaza, 17th Floor. Telephone: 714-852-8200. Fax: 714-852-8282.
*New York, New York Office:* 41st Floor, 59 Maiden Lane. Telephone: 212-422-0202. Fax: 212-422-0925.
*Chicago, Illinois Office:* The Rookery Building, Seventh Floor, 209 South La Salle Street. Telephone: 312-641-9050. Fax: 312-641-9530.
*London, England Office:* Lloyds Avenue House, 6 Lloyds Avenue, EC3N 3AX. Telephone: 0171-929-1829. Fax: 0171-929-1808. Telex: 927037.
*Zurich, Switzerland Office:* Spluegenstrasse 3, CH-8002. Telephone: 011-411-201-1730. Fax: 011-411-201-4404.

*General Civil Litigation and Trial Practice. Aviation, Business, Construction, Directors and Officers Liability, Employment and Labor, Entertainment, Environmental, Fidelity and Surety, General Liability, Health Care, Pharmaceuticals, Insurance and Reinsurance, Intellectual Property, Products Liability and Professional Malpractice.*

### MEMBERS OF FIRM

**LANE J. ASHLEY,** born Spokane, Washington, April 12, 1952; admitted to bar, 1976, California and U.S. Supreme Court. *Education:* University of Illinois (B.A., 1973); University of California at Los Angeles (J.D., 1976). Author: "General Considerations in Settlement" and "Special Considerations in Settlement," CEB publication, California Liability Insurance Practice: Claims and Litigation, 1991; "Representation of the Insurer's Interests in an Environmental Damage Claim," Defense Counsel Journal, p. 11, January, 1987; "Guidelines for the Insurer in Avoiding Bad Faith Exposure," Federation of Insurance and Corporate Counsel Quarterly, p. 1, Winter, 1986; "Avoiding 'Bad Faith' Exposure," National Underwriters, p. 19, June, 1985.

**DAVID M. HUMISTON,** born Denver, Colorado, September 16, 1954; admitted to bar, 1979, California. *Education:* University of California at Los Angeles (B.A., magna cum laude, 1976); Hastings College of the Law, University of California (J.D., 1979). *Member:* Japanese Bar Association.

**N. DAVID LYONS,** born Worcester, Massachusetts, August 5, 1950; admitted to bar, 1975, California. *Education:* Harvard College (B.A., 1972); Georgetown University (J.D., 1975).

**MICHAEL R. VELLADAO,** born Gilroy, California, August 11, 1958; admitted to bar, 1983, California. *Education:* University of San Francisco (B.A., 1980); Pepperdine University (J.D., 1983).

**MICHAEL R. DAVISSON,** born Paso Robles, California, April 27, 1953; admitted to bar, 1978, California. *Education:* University of California

*(This Listing Continued)*

at Los Angeles; University of California at Berkeley (A.B., 1975); Hastings College of Law, University of California (J.D., 1978).

**EDWARD T. STORK,** born Rochester, Minnesota, April 11, 1951; admitted to bar, 1978, New York; 1983, California. *Education:* Vanderbilt University; Northeastern University (B.A., with highest honors, 1974); Albany Law School of Union University (J.D., 1977).

**T. EMMET THORNTON,** born New York, N.Y., September 4, 1948; admitted to bar, 1978, California. *Education:* New York University; Washington State University (B.S., 1973); McGeorge School of the Law, University of the Pacific (J.D., 1978).

**CRAIG S. BARNES,** born New York, N.Y., November 19, 1956; admitted to bar, 1986, California. *Education:* Hunter College of the City University of New York (B.A., 1980); Massachusetts Institute of Technology (M.C.P., 1982); University of California at Los Angeles (J.D., 1985). Author: "The African Development Bank Group Role in Regional Economic Integration in the ECOWAS," Boston College Third World Law Journal, Spring, 1985.

**ROBERT F. HELFING,** born Lorain, Ohio, January 2, 1954; admitted to bar, 1979, California. *Education:* University of California at Los Angeles (B.A., 1976); Southwestern University School of Law (J.D., 1979).

**THOMAS B. MCNUTT,** born Bakersfield, California, January 23, 1949; admitted to bar, 1975, California. *Education:* University of California at Los Angeles (B.A., Political Science, 1971); Loyola University (J.D., cum laude, 1975).

**KRISTIN E. MEREDITH,** born Richmond, Virginia, January 25, 1957; admitted to bar, 1983, California. *Education:* University of California at San Diego (B.A., 1979); University of Santa Clara (J.D., 1983); Georgetown University Law Center (LL.M., 1984). Author: "What Kind of Jury Is Most Likely to Find Insurance Fraud?" DRI Fraud Seminar, November 1993.

**ELLIOTT D. OLSON,** born Detroit, Michigan, April 25, 1941; admitted to bar, 1968, California. *Education:* University of California at Los Angeles (B.S., 1964; J.D., 1967). *Member:* American Board of Trial Advocates; American College of Trial Lawyers; Product Liability Advisory Counsel; Federation of Insurance and Corporate Counsel.

**WILLIAM A. BOECK,** born Santa Monica, California, October 29, 1960; admitted to bar, 1987, California. *Education:* Loyola Marymount University (B.A., cum laude, 1982); Loyola Law School, Los Angeles (J.D., 1986).

**DONNA D. MELBY,** born Los Angeles, California, October 9, 1950; admitted to bar, 1979, California. *Education:* Oxford University, Oxford, England; University of California at Santa Barbara (B.A., 1972); California Western University School of Law; Loyola University School of Law (J.D., 1978). *Member:* Glendale and Los Angeles County (Delegate, State Bar Conference, 1985-1992; Member, Executive Committee, 1992—) Bar Associations; State Bar of California (Counsel, 1985-1986, Legal Services Trust Fund Commission); Association of Southern California Defense Counsel (Chair, Program, Seminar, Legislative and Benefits Committees, 1984-1990).

**TOD I. ZUCKERMAN,** born San Francisco, California, September 18, 1954; admitted to bar, 1980, California. *Education:* University of Southern California (B.A., magna cum laude, 1975); Hastings College of Law, University of California (J.D., 1980). Lead-Author: "Environmental Insurance Litigation Law and Practice and Environmental Insurance Litigation: Practice Forms," Shepard's/McGraw-Hill, 1992; "Informal Discovery Strategies For Environmental Coverage Litigators," Mealey's Litigation Reports-Insurance, October 22, 1991; "The Pollution Exclusion in Liability Insurance Policies -- The Insurers' Perspective," Los Angeles Lawyer, March 1990; "Legal Damages Versus Equitable Relief in California Pollution Coverage Cases: What Does the Future Hold?" California Insurance Law & Regulation Reporter, January 1990. Author: "Insurers Are Not Liable for Pollution Damage," Los Angeles Daily Journal, September 24, 1990; "E & O Policies Will Vary: What Does Yours Cover?" Notary Viewpoint, February 1989; "Producers: Communicate Clearly!" Insurance Journal, March 14, 1988; "Claims-Made and Reported Policies and the Notice Prejudice Rule," San Mateo County Bar Association Journal, December-January 1987/88; "The Rise of Claims Made Policies," California Broker, December 1987; "Producers Beware - Protect Your Expirations," Underwriters' Report, December 17, 1987. Member, Shepard's/McGraw-Hill Environmental Law Advisory Board.

**REBECCA R. WEINREICH,** born Ann Arbor, Michigan, December 7, 1962; admitted to bar, 1986, Massachusetts; 1989, District of Columbia;

*(This Listing Continued)*

**SEDGWICK, DETERT, MORAN & ARNOLD,** Los Angeles—*Continued*

1991, California. *Education:* University of Michigan (B.A., 1982); Boston University School of Law (J.D., 1986).

### SPECIAL COUNSEL

**MARK A. GRAF,** born Evanston, Illinois, September 21, 1954; admitted to bar, 1979, Illinois; 1983, California. *Education:* Knox College; University of Dayton (B.A., 1975); University of Illinois (J.D., 1979).

**JOHN M. RADERS,** born Cedar Rapids, Iowa, February 24, 1953; admitted to bar, 1979, California. *Education:* Loyola University of Los Angeles (B.A., magna cum laude, 1975; J.D., cum laude, 1979).

**JEFFREY M. SMITH,** born Boston, Massachusetts, July 2, 1947; admitted to bar, 1979, Illinois; 1994, California. *Education:* Northeastern University (B.S.Chem.E., 1970); University of Michigan (M.B.A., 1974); Chicago-Kent University (J.D., 1978). Township Trustee, 1979-1984.

**BRUCE G. SHANAHAN,** born Scott Air Force Base, Belleville, Illinois, July 8, 1950; admitted to bar, 1981, California. *Education:* U.S. Air Force Academy; University of Texas, Austin (B.S., 1972; M.S., 1974); University of Southern California (J.D., 1980).

**LAWRENCE E. PICONE,** born Jersey City, New Jersey, March 26, 1958; admitted to bar, 1983, California. *Education:* Upsala College (B.A., cum laude, 1980); University of San Francisco School of Law (J.D., with honors, 1983).

**JORDON E. HARRIMAN,** born Massillon, Ohio, January 26, 1957; admitted to bar, 1984, California. *Education:* The Ohio State University (B.A., 1979); University of Southern California (J.D., 1984).

**KATHRYN M. TREPINSKI,** born Toledo, Ohio, August 2, 1959; admitted to bar, 1985, California; 1990, Florida. *Education:* Miami University (B.A., 1981); Southwestern University (J.D., 1984).

**JAMES J. S. HOLMES,** born Santa Monica, California, March 21, 1961; admitted to bar, 1986, California, U.S. Supreme Court. *Education:* Arizona State University (B.S., 1983; J.D., 1986). Recipient, California State Bar Commendation for Pro Bono Legal Services. **LANGUAGES:** French.

**GARY K. KWASNIEWSKI,** born Boonville, New York, October 6, 1951; admitted to bar, 1986, California and Ohio. *Education:* Clarkson University (B.S.Ch.E., 1973); Xavier University (M.B.A., 1979); Salmon P. Chase College of Law, Northern Kentucky University (J.D., 1985).

**CHARLES F. PETERSON,** born Brooklyn, New York, March 12, 1956; admitted to bar, 1986, California. *Education:* Boston College (B.A., 1978); University of Southern California (J.D., 1985).

**KATHLEEN CASWELL VANCE,** born Los Angeles, California, September 15, 1961; admitted to bar, 1987, California. *Education:* Loyola Marymount University (B.A., 1983); Loyola Law School (J.D., 1987).

### ASSOCIATES

**SUSAN F. HANNAN,** born Newark, New Jersey, May 30, 1949; admitted to bar, 1981, California. *Education:* Rutgers University (B.A., 1971; M.Ed., 1972); Loyola Law School (J.D., 1980).

**BRUCE S. BOLGER,** born San Diego, California, July 7, 1954; admitted to bar, 1982, California. *Education:* University of Southern California (B.M., 1976); Southwestern University School of Law (J.D., 1981).

**JANICE ROURKE HUGENER,** born Culver City, California, November 20, 1959; admitted to bar, 1986, California. *Education:* Loyola Marymount University (B.A., 1981; J.D., 1986).

**MARGRET G. PARKE,** born Atlanta, Georgia, November 26, 1959; admitted to bar, 1986, California; 1989, Colorado. *Education:* Colorado State University (B.A., with honors, 1982); Loyola Marymount University (J.D., 1986). **LANGUAGES:** German. **PRACTICE AREAS:** Insurance Fraud Law.

**KAREN L. SCHWARTZ,** born Los Angeles, California, June 25, 1951; admitted to bar, 1986, California. *Education:* California State University at Stanislaus (B.A., cum laude, 1981); Pepperdine University (J.D., 1985).

**JEANETTE L. VIAU,** born Los Angeles, California, February 24, 1960; admitted to bar, 1986, California. *Education:* University of California at Los Angeles (B.A., 1982); Loyola University (J.D., 1985).

*(This Listing Continued)*

**LISA A. CLARK,** born Cincinnati, Ohio, March 27, 1962; admitted to bar, 1988, California. *Education:* Claremont McKenna College (B.A., 1984); University of San Diego (J.D.,1987).

**H. ALIX EVANS,** born Charleston, West Virginia, November 28, 1958; admitted to bar, 1987, California; 1989, District of Columbia. *Education:* University of Virginia (B.A., 1981); Vanderbilt University (J.D., 1987); Vanderbilt Divinity School (M.Div., 1987).

**DOUGLAS L. STUART,** born Los Angeles, California, February 9, 1962; admitted to bar, 1987, California. *Education:* University of California at Los Angeles (B.A., 1983); McGeorge School of Law, University of the Pacific (J.D., 1987).

**RICHARD A. JANISCH,** born Los Angeles, California, February 23, 1960; admitted to bar, 1988, California. *Education:* Loyola Marymount University (B.A., cum laude, 1982); Southwestern University School of Law (J.D., 1986). Co-Author: "The Pollution Exclusion in Liability Insurance Policies," Los Angeles Lawyer, March, 1990.

**ANTHONY J. PARASCANDOLA,** born Perth Amboy, New Jersey, December 21, 1961; admitted to bar, 1989, California. *Education:* Eastern Illinois University (B.A., 1983); Saint Louis University School of Law (J.D., 1987).

**MARCO P. FERREIRA,** born Lisbon, Portugal, November 22, 1963; admitted to bar, 1990, California. *Education:* California State University, Northridge (B.A., cum laude, 1987); Loyola University of Los Angeles (J.D., 1990). **LANGUAGES:** Portuguese, Spanish and French.

**BIRGIT A. HUBER,** born Santa Monica, California, April 10, 1962; admitted to bar, 1990, California. *Education:* Pepperdine University (B.A., 1982); University of Southern California (M.S.Ed., 1985); University of California, Los Angeles School of Law (J.D., 1990). **LANGUAGES:** German.

**AMAND K. MINES,** born Clarksburg, West Virginia, September 22, 1965; admitted to bar, 1991, California. *Education:* College of William & Mary (B.A., 1987); Pepperdine University (J.D., 1991).

**JOHN W. MUSTAFA, II,** born Portland, Oregon, October 26, 1963; admitted to bar, 1991, District of Columbia; 1994, California. *Education:* University of California at Los Angeles (B.A., 1986); University of California School of Law (J.D., 1991). [with USMC, 1986-1987]

**THOMAS A. DELANEY,** born Pasadena, California, May 20, 1967; admitted to bar, 1992, California. *Education:* Loyola Marymount University (B.A., 1989); Loyola Law School, Los Angeles (J.D., 1992).

**STEVEN D. DI SAIA,** born New Haven, Connecticut, December 28, 1966; admitted to bar, 1992, California. *Education:* University of California at Berkeley (B.A., with honors, 1988); Hastings College of the Law, University of California (J.D., 1991).

**JAY E. FRAMSON,** born Bridgeport, Connecticut, April 9, 1958; admitted to bar, 1992, California. *Education:* Brown University (B.A., 1980); Stanford University (M.A., 1983); Loyola Law School of Los Angeles (J.D., 1992).

**WYNN CROSS KANESHIRO,** born Quezon City, Philippines, April 3, 1967; admitted to bar, 1992, Hawaii; 1993, California. *Education:* University of the Philippines (B.A., cum laude, 1987); University of California at Los Angeles (J.D., 1992). Managing Editor, UCLA Pacific Basin Law Journal, 1991-1992. **LANGUAGES:** Tagalog.

**CELIA D. MOUTES,** admitted to bar, 1992, California. *Education:* California State University, Northridge (B.A., summa cum laude, 1981); Loyola Law School (J.D., 1992).

**GREGORY J. NEWMAN,** born Hollywood, California, November 3, 1967; admitted to bar, 1993, California. *Education:* University of California, Santa Barbara (B.A., 1989); Southwestern University (J.D., 1993).

**TRACEY N. BROADHEAD,** born Oakland, California, November 26, 1967; admitted to bar, 1994, California. *Education:* University of California at Los Angeles (B.A., 1990); University of California, Hastings College of the Law (J.D., 1994).

**VICTOR A. BULLOCK,** born Arcadia, California, July 29, 1968; admitted to bar, 1994, California. *Education:* University of California at Los Angeles (B.A., 1991); Hastings College of the Law, University of California (J.D., 1994).

**SPENCER A. KRIEGER,** born Harbor City, California, April 21, 1965; admitted to bar, 1994, California. *Education:* University of California,

*(This Listing Continued)*

Berkeley (B.A., 1987); McGeorge School of Law, University of the Pacific (J.D., 1994). *LANGUAGES:* Spanish, French and Portuguese.

**BRANDON D. SMITH,** born Bremerhaven, Germany, November 25, 1967; admitted to bar, 1994, California. *Education:* University of California, Davis (B.A., 1990); University of San Francisco (J.D., 1994). Author: "Note, Lujan v. Defenders of Wildlife: A Slash & Burn Expedition Through the Law of Environmental Standing," USF Law Review (1994).

**JAMES NELSON,** born San Pedro, California, September 3, 1969; admitted to bar, 1995, California. *Education:* University of California at Los Angeles (B.A., 1991); Southwestern University School of Law (J.D., cum laude, 1995).

**TIMOTHY A. PICO,** admitted to bar, 1995, California. *Education:* University of California, Los Angeles (B.A., 1990); Pepperdine University School of Law (J.D., 1995).

**ERIC L. TANEZAKI,** admitted to bar, 1996, California. *Education:* University of Southern California (B.S., 1989); University of the Pacific, McGeorge School of Law (J.D., 1996).

All Partners and Associates are members of the State Bar of California

(For complete biographical data on all personnel at San Francisco and Irvine, California, Chicago, Illinois, New York, New York, London, England and Zurich, Switzerland, see Professional Biographies at those locations).

## WILLIAM A. SELIGMANN
ONE WILSHIRE BUILDING
624 SOUTH GRAND AVENUE
SUITE 2420
LOS ANGELES, CALIFORNIA 90017
Telephone: 213-892-1122
Fax: 213-488-9890

*Estate Planning, Wills, Trusts, Corporate, Tax, Corporate Organization, Mergers and Acquisitions, Qualified and Non Qualified Retirement Plans.*

**WILLIAM A. SELIGMANN,** born Milwaukee, Wisconsin, November 16, 1925; admitted to bar, 1974, California; 1976, U.S. Tax Court; 1980, U.S. Supreme Court. *Education:* University of Wisconsin (B.Com., 1950); University of San Diego (J.D., 1974). Author: "Distributions to Children in the Sprinkling Trust," Trusts and Estates, February, 1975; "Gifts Made on Installment Basis Can Reduce Gift Tax Liability," Taxation for Lawyers, May/June, 1976; "Defective Crummey Trusts - A Reflection on Irrevocable Gift and Insurance Trusts," T.S.A. Forum, 1984. President, Estate Counselors Forum, 1993-1994. *Member:* Los Angeles County and American Bar Associations; State Bar of California. [Capt., USAF, 1943-1961, retired]

## SELMAN • BREITMAN
11766 WILSHIRE BOULEVARD, SIXTH FLOOR
LOS ANGELES, CALIFORNIA 90025-6538
Telephone: 310-445-0800
Fax: 310-473-2525

*San Diego, California Office:* Emerald Plaza, 402 W. Broadway, Suite 400. Telephone: 619-595-4880. Facsimile: 619-595-4890.

*San Francisco, California Office:* Citicorp Center, One Sansome Street, Suite 1900. Telephone: 415-951-4646. Fax: 415-951-4676.

*General Civil and Trial Practice in all State and Federal Courts. Insurance, Products Liability and Toxic Substance Law.*

### MEMBERS OF FIRM

**NEIL H. SELMAN,** born New York, N.Y., June 12, 1949; admitted to bar, 1974, California and U.S. District Court, Northern, Central and Southern Districts of California and U.S. Supreme Court. *Education:* University of Southern California (B.A., magna cum laude, 1971; J.D., 1974). Phi Beta Kappa. Judge Pro Tem, Los Angeles Municipal Court, 1981, 1982 and 1983. Los Angeles Superior Court Arbitrator, 1980-1983. *Member:* Century City, Los Angeles County and American (Member, Sections on: Tort and Insurance Practice; Natural Resources; Chairman, Newsletter Subcommittee, 1987—; Committee Vice Chairman, 1988-1989) Bar Associations; State Bar of California; Defense Research Institute (Member, Committee on Industry Wide Litigation, 1974-1984); American Judicature Society; Association of Southern California Defense Counsel; Association of Business Trial Lawyers.

*(This Listing Continued)*

**CRAIG R. BREITMAN,** born Los Angeles, California, October 18, 1955; admitted to bar, 1982, California; 1983, U.S. District Court, Central, Northern, Eastern and Southern Districts of California and U.S. Court of Appeals, Ninth Circuit. *Education:* University of California at Los Angeles (B.A., Psychology, 1978); Southwestern University School of Law (J.D., 1982). *Member:* Southwestern University Law Review, 1981-1982; Board of Governors, Moot Court Honors Program. Recipient, American Jurisprudence Award in Remedies. *Member:* State Bar of California; American Bar Association; National Order of Barristers; Association of Southern California Defense Counsel; Defense Research Institute.

**ROBERT A. STELLER,** born Kansas City, Missouri, January 7, 1954; admitted to bar, 1977, California; 1978, U.S. District Court, Central District of California; 1983, Wisconsin and U.S. District Court, Western District of Wisconsin; 1985, U.S. District Court, Southern District of California and U.S Court of Appeals, Ninth Circuit; 1986, U.S. District Court, Northern District of California; 1987, U.S. District Court, Eastern District of California. *Education:* University of Missouri (B.B.A., with distinction, 1974); Boalt Hall School of Law, University of California at Berkeley (J.D., 1977). Phi Kappa Phi; Omicron Delta Kappa; Beta Gamma Sigma. Member, Panel of Arbitrators, American Arbitration Association. *Member:* Los Angeles County and American Bar Associations; State Bar of California; State Bar of Wisconsin; Association of Southern California Defense Counsel; Defense Research Institute, Inc.; Maritime Law Association of the United States of America. (Partner, San Diego Office).

**ALAN B. YUTER,** born Briarcliff Manor, New York, November 8, 1956; admitted to bar, 1981, California; 1982, U.S. District Court, Central and Southern Districts of California. *Education:* Cornell University (B.A., 1978); Georgetown University (J.D., 1981). Editor, Law and Policy in International Business, Georgetown University, 1980-1981. *Member:* Los Angeles County Bar Association; State Bar of California.

**NANCY W. SHOKOHI,** born Palo Alto, California, January 14, 1959; admitted to bar, 1986, California and U.S. District Court, Central and Southern Districts of California. *Education:* University of California at Los Angeles (B.A., with honors, 1981); Loyola Law School (J.D., 1985). *Member:* Beverly Hills, Los Angeles County (Member, Environmental Law Section) and American Bar Associations; State Bar of California.

**JEFFREY C. SEGAL,** born Toledo, Ohio, January 9, 1959; admitted to bar, 1986, California and U.S. District Court, Central and Southern Districts of California. *Education:* Occidental College (A.B., cum laude, Departmental Distinction in Political Science, 1981); American University, Washington College of Law (J.D., 1985). Member, Mortar Board. *Member:* Los Angeles County and American Bar Associations; State Bar of California.

**A. SCOTT GOLDBERG,** born Paterson, New Jersey, January 4, 1959; admitted to bar, 1985, California; 1986, U.S. District Court, Central District of California and U.S. Court of Appeals, Ninth Circuit. *Education:* California State University at Northridge (B.A., 1982); Pepperdine University (J.D., 1985). Phi Delta Phi. *Member:* Los Angeles County and American Bar Associations; State Bar of California; Defense Research Institute; Association of Southern California Defense Counsel.

**ELAINE K. FRESCH,** born Columbus, Ohio, August 8, 1960; admitted to bar, 1985, California and U.S. District Court, Central District of California. *Education:* University of California at Los Angeles (A.B., cum laude, 1982) Pi Gamma Mu; University of San Diego (J.D., 1985). *Member:* Los Angeles County and American Bar Associations; State Bar of California.

**NICHOLAS BANKO,** born Port Hueneme, California, December 1, 1952; admitted to bar, 1984, California; 1985, U.S. District Court, Central District of California and U.S. Court of Appeals, Ninth Circuit. *Education:* University of California at Berkeley (A.B., 1975); Loyola Law School of Los Angeles (J.D., 1984). *Member:* Orange County, Los Angeles County and American Bar Associations; State Bar of California. [Lieut., U.S. Navy, 1976-1980]

**BRAD D. BLEICHNER,** born St. Paul, Minnesota, April 3, 1953; admitted to bar, 1985, California, U.S. District Court, Central, Southern, Northern and Eastern Districts of California; 1995, Arizona. *Education:* Duquesne University; University of Maryland (B.A., 1975); Southern California Institute of Law (J.D., 1984). Delta Theta Phi. Recipient: American Jurisprudence Awards in Contracts and Torts; West Publishing Award. Judge Pro Tem, 1986—. Superior Court Arbitrator, 1991. *Member:* Simi Valley (Vice-President; Treasurer) and East Valley Bar Associations; State Bar of California.

**DAVID L. JONES,** born Santa Monica, California, January 18, 1957; admitted to bar, 1983, California; 1984, U.S. District Court, Central,

*(This Listing Continued)*

**SELMAN ● BREITMAN, Los Angeles—Continued**

Northern and Eastern Districts of California; 1992, U.S. District Court, Southern District of California. *Education:* Loyola Marymount University (B.A., 1979); Pepperdine University (J.D., 1983). Phi Delta Phi. Author: "California Supreme Court Survey," 9 Pepperdine Law Review 677, 1982. *Member:* State Bar of California; Southern California Defense Counsel. **PRACTICE AREAS:** Insurance Coverage; Insurance Bad Faith; Personal Injury; Product Liability.

**MARK L. JUBELT,** born Los Angeles, California, May 15, 1962; admitted to bar, 1987, California; 1988, U.S. District Court, Central, Southern and Eastern Districts of California. *Education:* California State University at Sacramento; California Polytechnic State University (B.A., 1984); University of California at Davis (J.D., 1987). *Member:* State Bar of California.

**MONICA CRUZ THORNTON,** born Los Angeles, California, December 29, 1959; admitted to bar, 1987, California; 1988, U.S. District Court, Central District of California. *Education:* University of California at Irvine (B.A., 1982); University of California at Davis (J.D., 1987). Phi Beta Kappa. *Member:* Los Angeles County and American Bar Associations; State Bar of California. **LANGUAGES:** Spanish.

**DAVID T. BAMBERGER,** born Berkeley, California, July 6, 1954; admitted to bar, 1979, California. *Education:* University of California at Davis (B.A., with honors, 1976; J.D., 1979). First Place Team, U.C. Davis Environmental Law Moot Court Competition. U.C. Davis Representative and Second Place Appellate Brief, Roger J. Traynor California State Moot Court Competition. *Member:* Los Angeles County and American (Member: Tort and Insurance Practice Section; Committee on Insurance Coverage Litigation, Tort and Insurance Practice Section, 1990-1993) Bar Associations; State Bar of California (Member, Litigation Section); Association of Southern California Defense Counsel; Defense Research Institute.

**STERLING TAO,** born Palo Alto, California, May 25, 1961; admitted to bar, 1988, California. *Education:* University of San Francisco (B.S., 1983); University of Santa Clara (J.D., 1988). *Member:* San Mateo County Bar Association; State Bar of California. (Partner, San Francisco Office). **LANGUAGES:** Mandarin Chinese.

---

**LYNETTE KLAWON,** born Willoughby, Ohio, September 15, 1962; admitted to bar, 1988, California; 1989, U.S. District Court, Central District of California. *Education:* Pitzer College (B.A., with honors, 1984); Cornell Law School (J.D., cum laude, 1988). Recipient, American Jurisprudence Award in Criminal Law. Member, Cornell Legal Aid Society, 1986-1988. *Member:* Los Angeles County and American Bar Associations; State Bar of California.

**RAMON Z. BACERDO,** born Manila, Philippines, August 22, 1959; admitted to bar, 1988, California. *Education:* University of California at Los Angeles (B.A., 1984); Hastings College of Law, University of California (J.D., 1988). Recipient, American Jurisprudence Award in Evidence Advocacy. *Member:* State Bar of California; Association of Southern California Defense Counsel. (Resident, San Francisco Office). **LANGUAGES:** Tagalog, French and Spanish.

**JOHN S. KNOWLTON,** born Seattle, Washington, October 25, 1957; admitted to bar, 1990, California. *Education:* University of California at San Diego (B.A., 1980); Southwestern University (J.D., 1989). Recipient: Moot Court Exceptional Achievement Award-Best Court Brief; American Jurisprudence Award in Medical Malpractice. *Member:* Los Angeles County Bar Association; State Bar of California.

**MURRAY M. SINCLAIR,** born Santa Monica, California, January 28, 1950; admitted to bar, 1990, California. *Education:* University of California at Santa Barbara (B.A. in English Lit with honors, 1972); University of Southern California at Los Angeles (M.F.A., 1980); Southwestern University School (J.D., 1990). Second Place, Best Brief, 1988, Intramural Moot Court Competition; Recipient: Exceptional Achievement Award: Unfair Competition & Consumer Protection; Exceptional Achievement Award: Entertainment Law; Exceptional Achievement Award: Mass Communications Law: Third Prize, Best Essay, 1990 Federation of Insurance & Corporate Counsel Foundation Essay Contest "Insurer Fiduciary Responsibility vs. Comparative Bad Faith: Recent Trends in the Developing Law of Reciprocal Duties Under the Implied Convent of Good Faith and Fair Dealing".

**JEFFREY A. SIMMONS,** born Los Angeles, California, June 17, 1956; admitted to bar, 1992, California. *Education:* California State University at Hayward (B.A., 1982; B.S., 1985); Southwestern University (J.D., 1990). Member, Moot Court Honors Program, 1988. Second Place, Best Brief, Intramural Moot Court Competition. *Member:* State Bar of California.

**MARK S. GRUSKIN,** born Los Angeles, California, January 28, 1958; admitted to bar, 1985, California; 1986, U.S. District Court, Central and Southern Districts of California; U.S. Court of Appeals, Ninth Circuit. *Education:* University of California at Santa Barbara (B.A., Environmental Studies, 1979); Pepperdine University (J.D., 1984). *Member:* Los Angeles County and American Bar Associations; State Bar of California. **PRACTICE AREAS:** Personal Injury; Construction Defect/Property Damage; Real Property.

**ANTHONY L. CIONE,** born Buffalo, New York, July 11, 1963; admitted to bar, 1992, California, U.S. District Court, Central District of California and U.S. Court of Appeals, Ninth Circuit. *Education:* College of William & Mary (B.B.A., 1986); University of Southern California (J.D., 1992). *Member:* Los Angeles County and American Bar Associations; State Bar of California.

**CHRISTOPHER J. HARRINGTON,** born Lowndes, Mississippi, June 30, 1966; admitted to bar, 1993, California; 1994, U.S. District Court, Central and Southern Districts of California. *Education:* Claremont McKenna College (B.A., 1988); University of San Diego (J.D., 1993). Founding Director, Barrister's Society, University of San Diego, 1992-1993. Honor Court Preliminary Examiner, University of San Diego, 1992-1993. *Member:* State Bar of California. [Corporal, U.S. Army, 1988-1990]. **PRACTICE AREAS:** Insurance Coverage; Insurance Coverage Litigation.

**SHERYL W. LEICHENGER,** born Chicago, Illinois, January 16, 1964; admitted to bar, 1992, California. *Education:* California State University at Northridge (B.S., Accounting, 1987); Loyola Law School (J.D., 1992). Beta Alpha Psi. Recipient, Judge Barry Russel Federal Practice Award, 1992. Certified Public Accountant, California, 1992. *Member:* Los Angeles County Bar Association; State Bar of California. **PRACTICE AREAS:** Insurance Coverage.

**THERESA ANN LOSS,** born Copiague, New York, December 17, 1956; admitted to bar, 1990, California; 1991, U.S. District Court, Central District of California and U.S. Court of Appeals, Ninth Circuit. *Education:* Arizona State University (B.A., 1986; J.D., 1989).

**JERRY C. POPOVICH,** born Bellflower, California, July 14, 1965; admitted to bar, 1988, California and U.S. District Court, Central District of California; 1991, U.S. Court of Appeals, Ninth Circuit. *Education:* Cypress Junior College (A.A., 1985); Western State University College of Law at Fullerton (B.S.L., 1987; J.D., 1988). Recipient, American Jurisprudence Award in Appellate Brief Writings. *Member:* American Bar Association (Member, Litigation Section, 1989—).

**LISA HANNAH KAHN,** born Long Beach, California, September 19, 1968; admitted to bar, 1993, California and U.S. District Court, Central and Southern Districts of California. *Education:* San Diego State University (B.A., 1990); University of San Diego (J.D., 1993).

**DAVID H. OKEN,** born Los Angeles, California, June 6, 1963; admitted to bar, 1994, California. *Education:* California State University, Northridge (B.S., 1987); Southwestern University School of Law (J.D., 1994). *Member:* State Bar of California.

**KATY A. NELSON,** born Amityville, New York, June 25, 1954; admitted to bar, 1994, California. *Education:* California State University, Northridge (B.A., 1986); Loyola Marymount University (J.D., 1994). Opinion Editor, Daily Sundial, California State University. Managing Editor, CSUN Magazine. Staff Member, Entertainment Law Journal. *Member:* State Bar of California.

**JAN LONG POCATERRA,** born Kansas City, Missouri, May 28, 1950; admitted to bar, 1986, Illinois and U.S. District Court, Northern District of Illinois; 1988, California; 1988, U.S. District Court, Central, Northern, Southern and Eastern Districts of California; 1991, U.S. Court of Appeals, Ninth Circuit and U.S. Supreme Court. *Education:* University of Kansas; National College of Education (B.A., with honors, 1983); DePaul University College of Law (J.D., 1986). *Member:* Los Angeles County, Illinois State and American (Chairperson, Environmental Coverage Subcommittee) Bar Associations; State Bar of California; California Women Lawyers; Defense Research Institute. **PRACTICE AREAS:** Insurance Coverage Law (including Environmental); Bad Faith; Appellate Law.

**KIM KARELIS,** born Waseca, Minnesota, October 30, 1953; admitted to bar, 1994, California; 1995, U.S. District Court, Central District of California and U.S. Court of Appeals, Ninth Circuit. *Education:* Winona State University (B.S., 1976); Southwestern University School of Law (J.D., cum

*(This Listing Continued)*

laude, 1993). Member, Southwestern University Law Review. Author: "Private Justice: How Civil Litigation is Becoming a Private Institution - The Rise of Private Dispute Centers," 23 SW U.L. Rev. 621. *Member:* State Bar of California. **PRACTICE AREAS:** Insurance Coverage.

**ASIM K. DESAI,** born Akron, Ohio, June 15, 1968; admitted to bar, 1994, California, U.S. District Court, Central District of California and U.S. Court of Appeals, Ninth Circuit. *Education:* University of California at Los Angeles (B.A., 1991); Southwestern University School of Law (J.D., 1994). Delta Theta Phi. Recipient: American Jurisprudence Awards in Torts; Exceptional Achievement Awards; Corpus Juris Secundum Awards; Best Brief Award. Author: "From The Standpoint of the Insured: Insured's Loophole or Insurer's Noose?" 23 S.W. U. Law Rev. 495. **PRACTICE AREAS:** Insurance Coverage.

**PAULINE A. NEW,** born Urbana, Ohio, September 9, 1962; admitted to bar, 1986, California and U.S. District Court, Northern and Central Districts of California. *Education:* Oberlin College (B.A., 1983); University of Michigan (J.D., 1986).

**DIANNE M. COSTALES,** born Encino, California, March 25, 1967; admitted to bar, 1992, California. *Education:* University of California at Los Angeles (B.A., 1989); University of Southern California (J.D., 1992). *Member:* Los Angeles County Bar Association; State Bar of California.

**ELDON S. EDSON,** born Los Angeles, California, September 16, 1966; admitted to bar, 1993, California and U.S. District Court, Central District of California. *Education:* University of California at Los Angeles (B.A., 1988); Pepperdine University (J.D., cum laude, 1993). Real Estate Sales License, California, 1989. *Member:* State Bar of California. **PRACTICE AREAS:** Personal Injury.

**JAMES B. KAMANSKI,** born Orange, California, October 23, 1967; admitted to bar, 1994, California; 1995, U.S. District Court, Northern District of California. *Education:* San Diego State University (B.A., 1991); McGeorge School of Law (J.D., 1994). Recipient, International Moot Court Competition, Best Brief Competition Finalist Award. **PRACTICE AREAS:** Litigation.

**MICHAEL L. MENGOLI,** born Honolulu, Hawaii, June 9, 1969; admitted to bar, 1994, California and U.S. District Court, Southern District of California. *Education:* University of California at Los Angeles (B.A., 1990); University of San Diego (J.D., 1993). **PRACTICE AREAS:** Construction Defect; Casualty.

**RITA H. ISSAGHOLIAN,** born Tehran, Iran, January 3, 1963; admitted to bar, 1992, California and U.S. District Court, Central District of California; 1993, U.S. Court of Appeals, Ninth Circuit; 1995, U.S. District Court, Northern District of California. *Education:* California State University at Northridge (B.A., Economics, 1987); Southwestern University (J.D., cum laude, 1992). Moot Court Honors Program (Member, 1990-1992; Board of Governors, 1991-1992). Recipient, American Jurisprudence Award, Legal Research and Writing. Member, 1990-1992 and Note and Comment Editor, 1991-1992, Law Review. Legal Extern to the Honorable Robert Boochever, Ninth Circuit Court of Appeals, 1991. *Member:* Los Angeles County Bar Association; State Bar of California; Women Lawyers' Association of Los Angeles; Defense Research Institute; Southern California Defense Counsel. **LANGUAGES:** French, Armenian, Farsi, Spanish, Italian. **PRACTICE AREAS:** Insurance Coverage; Insurance Litigation; Insurance Bad Faith; Intellectual Property Litigation.

**SARAH F. BURKE,** born Los Angeles, California, December 10, 1966; admitted to bar, 1992, California. *Education:* Bowdoin College (A.B., magna cum laude, 1989); University of San Diego (J.D., 1992). *Member:* San Diego County Bar Association; State Bar of California; San Diego Defense Lawyers Association. (Resident, San Diego Office). **LANGUAGES:** Russian and French. **PRACTICE AREAS:** Insurance Law.

**DARCY D. JORGENSEN,** born Lancaster, California, January 20, 1962; admitted to bar, 1994, California and U.S. District Court, Central District of California. *Education:* Cornell University (B.S., 1984); Southwestern University School of Law (J.D., 1994). *Member:* State Bar of California. **PRACTICE AREAS:** Insurance Defense.

**LINDA S. WENDELL,** born Lima, Peru, June 7, 1967; admitted to bar, 1992, California and U.S. District Court, Southern and Central Districts of California. *Education:* San Diego State University (B.A., 1989); University of San Diego (J.D., 1992). Golden Key; Order of Omega. Member, University of San Diego Law Review. Member, Womens Law Caucus, 1989-1992; Lawyers Club of San Diego, 1990-1993. (Resident, San Francisco Office). **PRACTICE AREAS:** Insurance Bad Faith; General Civil Litigation; Professional Negligence; Constitutional Claims; Sexual Harassment.

*(This Listing Continued)*

**JEFFREY S. BOLENDER,** born Covington, Kentucky, February 20, 1961; admitted to bar, 1995, California. *Education:* California State University, Northridge (B.A., 1991); Southwestern University School of Law (J.D., 1995). Recipient: American Jurisprudence Book Award, Insurance Law. *Member:* Los Angeles Bar Association. **PRACTICE AREAS:** Insurance Law; Personal Injury Litigation.

**JEFFREY T. BRIGGS,** admitted to bar, 1993, California. *Education:* University of California at Los Angeles (B.A., 1989); Southwestern University School of Law (J.D., 1993).

**MARCIE A. KEENAN,** born Daly City, California, December 22, 1969; admitted to bar, 1995, California. *Education:* University of California at San Diego (B.A., 1992); Loyola University of Los Angeles. *Member:* State Bar of California.

**LISA M. DYSON,** born Denver, Colorado, August 12, 1966; admitted to bar, 1992, California and U.S. District Court, Southern, Eastern, Northern and Central Districts of California. *Education:* University of California at Los Angeles (B.A. in Political Science, 1989); Santa Clara University (J.D., 1992). Member, Moot Court Board, 1988-1989. *Member:* State Bar of California; American Bar Association. (Resident, San Francisco Office).

**AIMEE Y. WONG,** born Los Angeles, California, November 20, 1970; admitted to bar, 1995, California. *Education:* University of California at Los Angeles (B.A., 1992); University of Southern California (J.D., 1995). Phi Alpha Delta. *Member:* Los Angeles County Bar Association; State Bar of California; Southern California Chinese Lawyers Association. **LANGUAGES:** Cantonese.

**GRACE HOROUPIAN,** born Beirut, Lebanon, April 8, 1969; admitted to bar, 1995, California. *Education:* California State University, Northridge (B.A., magna cum laude, 1992); Loyola University of Los Angeles (J.D., 1995). Phi Kappa Phi. Member, Golden Key Honor Society. Recipient, Judge Julian Beck Award. *Member:* State Bar of California. **PRACTICE AREAS:** Insurance Coverage; Litigation.

**KATHLEEN T. DEELEY,** born Torrance, California, October 16, 1954; admitted to bar, 1987, California and U.S. District Court, Central, Eastern, Northern and Southern Districts of California; 1991, U.S. Court of Appeals, Ninth Circuit. *Education:* University of Southern California (B.A., 1984); University of California at Los Angeles (J.D., 1987). *Member:* Los Angeles County and American Bar Associations; State Bar of California. **REPORTED CASES:** Austin v. Allstate Insurance Co. (1993) 16 Cal.App.4th 1812. **PRACTICE AREAS:** Environmental Law; Insurance Coverage.

**CHRISTOPHER A. PETROVIC,** born Los Angeles, California, August 10, 1969; admitted to bar, 1995, California, U.S. District Court, Central District of California and U.S. Court of Appeals, 9th Circuit. *Education:* Columbia University (B.A., 1991); Southwestern University School of Law (J.D., 1995). *Member:* Los Angeles County and American Bar Associations; State Bar of California. **LANGUAGES:** Serbo-Croatian. **PRACTICE AREAS:** Insurance.

**KIMBERLY D. ALLARIO,** born San Jose, California, April 7, 1968; admitted to bar, 1995, California and U.S. District Court, Southern District of California. *Education:* University of San Diego (B.A., 1991); Western State University (J.D., cum laude, 1994). *Member:* San Diego County Bar Association. (Resident, San Diego Office). **PRACTICE AREAS:** Insurance Law.

**WENDY WEN YUN CHANG,** born Taipei, Taiwan, Republic of China, October 4, 1970; admitted to bar, 1995, California. *Education:* University of California at Los Angeles (B.A., 1995); Loyola University of Los Angeles (J.D., 1995). Executive Editor and Chief Articles Editor, Loyola of Los Angeles Entertainment Law Journal, 1994-1995. *Member:* State Bar of California; Southern California Chinese Lawyers Association (Member, Board of Governors, 1996—). **LANGUAGES:** Mandarin (conversational; verbal). **PRACTICE AREAS:** Insurance Coverage; Construction Defect; Coverage Litigation.

**JACK M. ZAKARIAIE,** born Tehran, Iran, June 22, 1968; admitted to bar, 1993, California; 1994, U.S. District Court, Central District of California. *Education:* University of California at Los Angeles (B.A., 1990); Loyola University of Los Angeles (J.D., 1993). *Member:* State Bar of California. **LANGUAGES:** Persian. **REPORTED CASES:** Amex Life Assurance Company v. Slome Capital Corp., 43 CalApp 4th 1588. **PRACTICE AREAS:** Civil Litigation; Insurance Defense; Insurance Coverage.

*(This Listing Continued)*

## SELMAN • BREITMAN, Los Angeles—Continued

### OF COUNSEL

**THOMAS A. LEARY,** born Las Mesa, California, April 5, 1959; admitted to bar, 1985, Minnesota; 1986, California. *Education:* University of California (B.A., 1982); University of Minnesota (J.D., 1985). *Member:* Hennepin County Bar Association; State Bar of California; Minnesota Trial Lawyers Association; Minnesota Minority Lawyers Association. (Of Counsel, San Diego Office). *REPORTED CASES:* Parker vs. Ophelan, 414 N.W. 2d 534 (Minn 1987).

REPRESENTATIVE CLIENTS: Allianz Insurance Co.; American States Insurance Co.; Argonaut Insurance Co.; Associated International Insurance Co.; Avis Rent A Car System; Budget Rent a Car; CIGNA Cos.; Citation Insurance Group; CNA Insurance Co.; Commercial Union Insurance Co.; Explorer Insurance Co.; Fireman's Fund Insurance Co.; Furon Corp.; GAB Business Services, Inc.; Golden Eagle Insurance Co.; Gulf Insurance Co.; H. B. Fuller Co., Inc.; Insurance Company of the West; LMI Insurance Co.; National American Insurance Company of California; Precision Risk Management, Inc.; Scottsdale Insurance Co.; Sentry Insurance Co.; St. Paul Fire & Marine Insurance Company and Affiliates; TIG Insurance Co.; Vik Brothers Insurance Group; Western Mutual Insurance Co.; Zurich-American Insurance Group.
REFERENCE: City National Bank (Beverly Hills Branch).

---

## SELVIN & WEINER & WEINBERGER

*A Partnership of Professional Corporations*

*Established in 1975*

**12401 WILSHIRE BOULEVARD, SECOND FLOOR
LOS ANGELES, CALIFORNIA 90025**
Telephone: 310-207-1555
Fax: 310-207-3666

*General Civil, Trial, Appellate, Administrative and Legislative Practice in all State and Federal Courts. Corporation, Commercial, Real Property, Taxation, Health Care, Libel and Slander, Estate Planning, Probate, Family and Entertainment Law.*

FIRM PROFILE: Selvin & Weiner & Weinberger is a Los Angeles based Law firm, with a litigation and transactional practice. The firm represents clients before local, state and federal courts and before administrative and regulatory agencies. The firm counsels individuals, corporations, partnerships, labor unions and other organizations with respect to transactional matters. Its practice ranges in scope from local to international. The attorneys at Selvin & Weiner & Weinberger serve the bar as members, officers or chairpersons of county, state, specialty and national bar association committees. The firm is able to provide the services typically offered by larger firms, while still maintaining the intimacy of a smaller firm. The members of the firm reinforce each other to guarantee the highest quality client service.

**PAUL P. SELVIN** (1917-1987).

**BERYL WEINER, (PROFESSIONAL CORPORATION),** born Los Angeles, California, November 7, 1943; admitted to bar, 1970, California; 1971, U.S. Tax Court. *Education:* University of California (A.B., 1965); Loyola University (J.D., 1969). Phi Alpha Delta. Judge Pro-Tem, Beverly Hills Municipal Court, 1976—. Co-Author: "Limited Partner Liability and The General Partner: Corporations Code Section 15507 Rev.," Beverly Hills Bar Association Journal, 1990. *Member:* Beverly Hills, Los Angeles County and American (Member, Litigation Section) Bar Associations. *LANGUAGES:* Hebrew and Spanish. *REPORTED CASES:* Orient Handel v. United States Fidelity & Guaranty Company, 192 Cal.App.3d 684, (1987); Artesia Medical Development Company v. Regency Associates, Inc., 214 Cal.App.3d 957 (1989); Paramount General Hospital Company v. Jay, 213 Cal.App.3d 360 (1989); Marriage of Diller, Court of Appeal Case No. B035205 (1991), U.S. cert. den. at 112 S.Ct. 657, 116 L.Ed.2d 748, rehearing denied at 112 S.Ct. 1248, (1992); Gertz v. Unger, Court of Appeal Case No. B056074 (1992); Linda J. v. Butler, Court of Appeal Case No. B054215 (1992); Tobin v. Oris, 3 Cal.App.4d 814 (1992); Cho v. Rogow, Court of Appeal Case No. B072990 (1994). *PRACTICE AREAS:* Civil Litigation; Appeals; Family Law; Entertainment Law; Health Care; Real Estate; Corporations and Partnerships.

**WILLIAM E. WEINBERGER, (PROFESSIONAL CORPORATION),** born Cleveland, Ohio, March 16, 1955; admitted to bar, 1982, California. *Education:* Cornell University (B.A., cum laude, 1977); Stanford University (J.D., 1981). Author: Note, "Congressional Access to Grand Jury Transcripts," Stanford Law Review, November, 1980. Senior Editor, Stanford Journal of International Law, 1978-1981. Associate Editor, Stanford Law Review, 1979-1981. Law Clerk to Hon. Frank J. Battisti, Chief Judge, U.S. District Court, Northern District of Ohio, 1981-1982. Judge Pro-Tem, Beverly Hills Municipal Court, 1991—. Member, 1982— and President 1987, Los Angeles Lawyers for Human Rights. Member, 1988— and Co-Chair, 1993-1994, National Lesbian & Gay Law Association. *Member:* Los Angeles County and American Bar Associations. *REPORTED CASES:* Paramount General Hospital Company vs. Jay, 1989, 213 Cal.App.3d 360; Long Beach Lesbian and Gay Pride, Inc. v. City of Long Beach, 1992, 14 Cal.App. 4th 312. *PRACTICE AREAS:* Business Litigation; Appeals; Professional Liability; First Amendment Law.

### ASSOCIATES

**KATHRYN M. STANTON,** born Los Angeles, California, December 7, 1962; admitted to bar, 1989, California. *Education:* University of California at Berkeley (B.A., 1984); University of Southern California (J.D., 1989). *PRACTICE AREAS:* Estate Planning; Appeals; Business Litigation; Real Estate; Family Law.

**DARREN R. MARTINEZ,** born Santa Fe, New Mexico, December 9, 1966; admitted to bar, 1991, California. *Education:* University of Notre Dame, (B.A., 1984); University of California School of Law (J.D., 1991). *Member:* Los Angeles County and American Bar Associations. *LANGUAGES:* Spanish. *PRACTICE AREAS:* Bankruptcy; Business Litigation; Real Estate; Appeals.

**DAVID M. DE CASTRO,** born Los Angeles, California, September 7, 1964; admitted to bar, 1991, California. *Education:* University of California at San Diego; University of California at Los Angeles (B.S., 1987); Loyola Law School (J.D., 1991). *PRACTICE AREAS:* Civil Litigation.

REFERENCE: City National Bank, Brentwood Branch, Los Angeles, California.

---

## RICHARD F. SEONE

**1801 AVENUE OF THE STARS, SUITE 640
LOS ANGELES, CALIFORNIA 90067**
Telephone: 310-788-0477
Fax: 310-788-0923

*Family Law, Immigration, Criminal and Personal Injury.*

**RICHARD F. SEONE,** born Riverside, California, August 4, 1958; admitted to bar, 1994, California. *Education:* California State University at Long Beach (B.A., 1987); Whittier College School of Law (J.D., 1994). *PRACTICE AREAS:* Immigration and Naturalization; Family Law; Criminal Law.

### ASSOCIATE

**DAVID SCOTT RUGENDORF,** born Skokie, Illinois, January 29, 1965; admitted to bar, 1990, California; 1991, Illinois. *Education:* University of Wisconsin-Madison (B.A., 19087); University of Michigan (J.D., 1990). Guest Lecturer, University of Michigan Department of Womens Studies, 1990. Deputy Public Defender, Madera County, California, 1992-1993. Deputy Conflict Defender, Fresno County, California, 1993—. *Member:* State Bar of California; American Bar Association; California Public Defenders Association. *PRACTICE AREAS:* Criminal Law (100%, 350); Felonies (12); Appellate Practice (5).

---

## SERRITELLA & PAQUETTE

*A PROFESSIONAL CORPORATION*

**201 NORTH FIGUEROA STREET, SUITE 1050
LOS ANGELES, CALIFORNIA 90012**
Telephone: 213-250-1600
Facsimile: 213-250-0949

*Municipal Liability, Products Liability, Employment, Construction Defect and Appellate Practice.*

**ANTHONY P. SERRITELLA,** born Chicago, Illinois, January 3, 1951; admitted to bar, 1976, California; 1977, U.S. District Court, Central, Eastern, Northern and Southern Districts of California; 1980, U.S. Court of Appeals, Ninth Circuit; 1980, U.S. Supreme Court; 1985, U.S. Tax Court. *Education:* University of Southern California (A.B., magna cum laude, 1973; J.D., 1976); University of San Diego (LL.M., 1984). Member, Hale Moot Court Honors Program. Instructor, Police Civil Liability, Los Angeles Sheriffs Department, 1984-1985. Counsel, National Association of Government Employees, 1976-1977. Trial Attorney, Bureau of Investigations and Enforcement, I.C.C., 1977-1981. Deputy County Counsel, Courts and Law Enforcement Division, Los Angeles, 1981-1983. Senior Assistant City Attorney, Burbank, California, 1983-1986. Board of Editors, Matthew

*(This Listing Continued)*

## PROFESSIONAL BIOGRAPHIES

Bender Federal Evidence Practice Guide Register, 1996—. *Member:* State Bar of California; American Bar Association; American Board of Trial Advocates; California Peace Officers Association. *PRACTICE AREAS:* Trials; Appellate Litigation.

**PAUL N. PAQUETTE,** born Inglewood, California, June 8, 1950; admitted to bar, 1983, California; 1984, U.S. District Court, Central, Southern and Northern Districts of California; U.S. Court of Appeals, Ninth Circuit; U.S. Supreme Court. *Education:* California State University at Fullerton (B.A., 1979); Loyola Marymount University (J.D., 1983). Author: "Admissibility of Felony Convictions for Impeachment in Civil Trials," *Federal Evidence Guide Reporter,* Matthew Bender 1989; "Crashworthiness: The Second Collision Claim," *CC&F Legal Update,* Spring, Fall 1988; "Manufacturer Liability for Collision Claim, *CC&F Legal Update,* Spring 1989; "The PRA: Watchdog of the Government of Intruder on Personal Privacy Rights?" *C&C Legal Update,* Summer 1992; "Privacy Rights at Risk," *Los Angeles Daily Journal,* August 1992. *Member:* State Bar of California; American Bar Association; Association of Southern California Defense Counsel. *PRACTICE AREAS:* Products Liability Defense; Public Entity Defense; General Civil Litigation.

---

**DENNIS P. RILEY,** born Los Angeles, California, May 16, 1962; admitted to bar, 1988, California. *Education:* Santa Clara University (B.S., 1984; J.D., 1987). *Member:* Los Angeles County Bar Association; State Bar of California. *PRACTICE AREAS:* Trial; Appellate Litigation.

**GLORIA CARDENAS CONN,** born Santa Monica, California, February 9, 1964; admitted to bar, 1991, California, U.S. District Court, Central District of California and U.S. Court of Appeals, 9th Circuit. *Education:* University of California at Los Angeles (B.A., 1986); Hastings College of the Law (J.D., 1990). *Member:* Los Angeles Bar Association (Member, Litigation Section). *PRACTICE AREAS:* Civil and Business Litigation; Public Entity Defense.

**ALARICE M. GARCIA,** born Visalia, California, February 21, 1967; admitted to bar, 1993, California. *Education:* University of California at Los Angeles (B.A., 1989; J.D., 1993). *PRACTICE AREAS:* Government Defense Litigation; Appellate Law.

**AVA M. SANDLIN,** born Tokyo, Japan, October 14, 1955; admitted to bar, 1993, California; 1994, U.S. District Court, Central District of California; 1995, U.S. District Court, Southern District of California. *Education:* Southwestern University School of Law (J.D., 1992). *Member:* State Bar of California.

**KENNETH A. LEVINE,** born Toronto, Ontario, November 12, 1951; admitted to bar, 1988, California; 1989, U.S. District Court, Central District of California. *Education:* York University (B.A., 1975); University of Toronto (M.A., 1979); Loyola University, Los Angeles (J.D., 1987). Member, Loyola Law School Entertainment Law Journal, 1987. Author: "Utah's Cable Decency Act: An Indecent Act?" Loyola Entertainment Law Journal, 1987. Adjunct Professor, Jurisprudence, University of LaVerne, 1993. *Member:* State Bar of California.

---

## SEYFARTH, SHAW, FAIRWEATHER & GERALDSON

*Established in 1973*

**2029 CENTURY PARK EAST**
**LOS ANGELES, CALIFORNIA 90067-3063**
Telephone: 310-277-7200
Facsimile: 310-201-5219
URL: http://www.seyfarth.com

*Chicago, Illinois Office:* 55 E. Monroe Street, Suite 4200. Telephone: 312-346-8000. Facsimile: 312-269-8869.

*Washington, D.C. Office:* 815 Connecticut Avenue, N.W. Telephone: 202-463-2400. Facsimile: 202-828-5393.

*New York, N.Y. Office:* 900 Third Avenue, 16th Floor. Telephone: 212-715-9000. Facsimile: 212-752-3116.

*San Francisco, California Office:* Suite 2900, 101 California Street. Telephone: 415-397-2823. Facsimile: 415-397-8549.

*Sacramento, California Office:* 400 Capitol Mall, Suite 2350. Telephone: 916-558-4828. Facsimile: 916-558-4839.

*Houston, Texas Office:* 700 Louisiana Street, Suite 3900. Telephone: 713-225-2300. Facsimile: 713-225-2340.

*Atlanta, Georgia Office:* One Atlantic Center, 1201 West Peachtree Street, Suite 3260. Telephone: 404-892-6412. Facsimile: 404-892-7056.

*(This Listing Continued)*

*Brussels, Belgium Office:* Avenue Louise 500, Box 8. Telephone: (32) (2) 647.60.25. Fax: (32) (2) 640.70.71.

*Affiliated Law Firm:*
*Matray, Matray et Hallet:* 34/24, Boulevard Frère-Orban, 4000, Liege, Belgium. Telephone: (32) (41) 52 70 68. Telex: macoha 42330. Telecopier: (32) (41) 52 08 57.

*Labor and Employment Law, Employee Benefits, Employment Discrimination, Employment-at-Will, Health Care, Occupational, Safety and Health, Worker's Compensation. Government Contracts. White-Collar Criminal. Litigation, Administrative Law, Business Contract Disputes, Construction, Corporations and Partnerships, General Tort, Insurance, Intellectual Property, Product Liability, Professional Liability, Securities and Commodities. Corporate, Acquisitions, Antitrust, Bankruptcy and Creditors' Rights, Commercial and Financial Transactions, Contracts, Divestitures, Joint Ventures, Mergers, Real Estate, Tax Law, Trust and Probate. Environmental, Safety and Health.*

### PARTNERS

**STEPHEN A. BAUMAN,** born Los Angeles, California, January 25, 1935; admitted to bar, 1960, California. *Education:* UCLA (B.S., 1956); Stanford University (J.D., 1959); Harvard University (LL.M., 1960). Author: USC Tax Institute. Contributing Author: California CEB. Lecturer, Tax Law and Estate Planning: USC Tax Institute; Calif. CEB; PLI; USC Law Center Advanced Professional Program. *Member:* State Bar of California. (Certified Specialist, Taxation Law, The State Bar of California Board of Legal Specialization) (Resident). *PRACTICE AREAS:* Taxation Law; Estate Planning Law; Probate Law.

**ROBERT E. BUCH,** born 1946; admitted to bar, 1974, California. *Education:* University of Southern California (B.A., 1969; M.S., 1970); Loyola University School of Law (J.D., 1973). Recipient: Blue Key Achievement Award. Member, Loyola University Law Review. Member, St. Thomas More Law Honor Society. Associate Professor of Business Law, California State University, Northridge, 1976-1978. *Member:* State Bar of California (Vice-Chairman, Workers' Compensation Law Advisory Commission). (Certified Specialist, Workers' Compensation Law, The State Bar of California Board of Legal Specialization). *PRACTICE AREAS:* Workers' Compensation.

**GEORGEANNE HENSHAW,** born Detroit, Michigan, July 30, 1955; admitted to bar, 1980, Illinois; 1987, California. *Education:* Duke University (B.A., magna cum laude, 1977); University of Michigan (J.D., cum laude, 1980). *Member:* State Bar of California; American Bar Association. (Resident). *PRACTICE AREAS:* Labor Law; Employment Law. *Email:* henshge@la.seyfarth.com

**JERRY M. HILL,** born Abilene, Kansas, November 5, 1942; admitted to bar, 1967, California. *Education:* Kansas State University (B.A., 1964); University of Missouri (J.D., 1966). Phi Delta Phi. Deputy District Attorney, Los Angeles County, 1967-1969. Judge Pro Tem, Beverly Hills Municipal Court, 1983-1985. Member, Panel of Arbitrators, American Arbitration Association. *Member:* Century City, Beverly Hills, Los Angeles County and American (Member, Section on Litigation) Bar Associations; State Bar of California; Association of Business Trial Attorneys. *PRACTICE AREAS:* Litigation; Gaming.

**DAVID D. KADUE,** born Minneapolis, Minnesota, August 14, 1952; admitted to bar, 1978, Minnesota; 1984, California. *Education:* Yale University (B.A., cum laude, 1975); University of Minnesota (J.D., cum laude, 1978). Notes and Comments Editor, Minnesota Law Review, 1977-1978. Instructor, University of Miami Law School, 1978-1979. Law Clerk, United States Court of Appeals, 1979-1981. Co-Author: Public Employee Privacy, ABA Section of State and Local Government Law, 1995; Sexual Harassment in Employment Law, BNA Books, 1992. (Resident). *PRACTICE AREAS:* Labor and Employment Law; Civil Litigation. *Email:* kadueda@la.seyfarth.com

**STEVEN J. KMIECIAK,** born Baltimore, Maryland, October 13, 1953; admitted to bar, 1979, Maryland; 1981, Texas; 1991, District of Columbia; 1995, California. *Education:* University of Notre Dame (B.A., 1975); University of Maryland (J.D., 1979). Assistant Attorney General, Maryland Attorney General's Office, 1982-1986. *Member:* State Bar of Texas; District of Columbia Bar; State Bar of California; Maryland State and American Bar Associations. *PRACTICE AREAS:* Construction Law; Government Contracts Law.

**DAVID J. KUCKELMAN,** born Frankfort, Kansas, September 23, 1950; admitted to bar, 1976, Kansas; 1989, California. *Education:* Kansas State University (B.S., 1973; B.A., 1973); University of Kansas (J.D., 1976); The George Washington University, National Law Center (LL.M., 1981). Lecturer: "Contracting With NATO Agencies," Advanced Technology, Ltd.

*(This Listing Continued)*

**SEYFARTH, SHAW, FAIRWEATHER & GERALDSON,**
*Los Angeles—Continued*

(1984-1989); "Government Contracts Compliance Programs," Federal Publications, Inc. (1987—); "Contractual And Legal Strategies For Industrial Collaboration," Advanced Technology, Ltd. (1988-1989); "Contracting With United States Government," Tunnock & Parish, Ltd. (1989-1992). Author: "Contracting With The North Atlantic Treaty Organization," G. W. Journal Int'l. Law & Econ. (1987); "Guide To Contracting With United States Government," SSF&G (1989, 1990). *PRACTICE AREAS:* Government Contract Law; International Contract Law; Corporate Law.

**DANIEL G. MCINTOSH,** born Portland, Oregon, October 24, 1944; admitted to bar, 1972, California. *Education:* University of California at Berkeley (A.B., cum laude, 1967); Boalt Hall School of Law, University of California at Berkeley (J.D., 1972). Adjunct Professor of Law, Southwestern University, 1982-1984. *Member:* Beverly Hills (President, 1995-1996; Board of Governors, 1990-1991; Chairman, Legislative Committee, 1991-1993), Los Angeles County (Member, Board of Trustees, 1992-1993) and American Bar Associations; State Bar of California. (Resident). *PRACTICE AREAS:* Corporation Law; Real Estate Law; Business Law.

**JOSEPH M. MILLER,** born Los Angeles, California, November 21, 1940; admitted to bar, 1965, California. *Education:* Harvard University (A.B., cum laude, 1962); Boalt Hall School of Law, University of California (J.D., 1965); New York University (LL.M., 1967). Past Chair, Workers' Compensation Law Advisory Commission. Past Member, California Board of Legal Specialization. *Member:* State Bar of California; Workers' Compensation Defense Attorneys Association. (Certified Specialist, Workers' Compensation Law, The State Bar of California Board of Legal Specialization) (Resident).

**F. SCOTT PAGE,** born New York, N.Y., March 20, 1957; admitted to bar, 1983, California. *Education:* Rutgers College (B.A., with high distinction in Political Science, 1979); Boston University (J.D., 1982). Phi Beta Kappa; Pi Sigma Alpha; Henry Rutgers Scholar. Case and Note Editor, Boston University International Law Journal, 1981-1982. *Member:* Los Angeles County and American Bar Associations; State Bar of California. (Resident). *Email:* pagesc@la.seyfarth.com

**EDWARD J. PIERCE,** born Peekskill, New York, September 21, 1951; admitted to bar, 1979, California. *Education:* Yale University (A.B., magna cum laude, 1973); Brown University (M.A.T., 1975); Harvard University (J.D., cum laude, 1979). Phi Beta Kappa. *Member:* Century City, Los Angeles County and American Bar Associations; State Bar of California. (Resident). *PRACTICE AREAS:* Corporations Law; Securities Law; Real Estate Law.

**GEORGE E. PREONAS,** born Dayton, Ohio, October 5, 1943; admitted to bar, 1968, Illinois; 1969, Nevada; 1974, California. *Education:* Stanford University (B.A., 1965); University of Michigan (J.D., 1968). Member, Editorial Board: University of Michigan Law Review, 1968-1969; Prospectus, Journal of Law Reform, 1968-1969. *Member:* Los Angeles County (Member, Executive Committee, Labor Law Section, 1984-1987) and American Bar Associations; State Bar of California. (Resident).

**STACY D. SHARTIN,** born Minneapolis, Minnesota, March 10, 1949; admitted to bar, 1973, California. *Education:* University of California at Los Angeles (A.B., cum laude, 1970; J.D., 1973). *Member:* Los Angeles County and American Bar Associations; State Bar of California (Member, Executive Committee, Labor and Employment Law Section). (Resident).

**KENNETH D. SULZER,** born Urbana, Illinois, November 3, 1960; admitted to bar, 1985, California. *Education:* Occidental College (A.B., magna cum laude, 1982); Harvard University (J.D., cum laude, 1985). Co-Author: *Public Employee Privacy, A Legal and Practical Guide to Issues Affecting the Workplace* (ABA Section of State and Local Government Law, 1985). *Member:* State Bar of California. (Resident).

**DIANA TABACOPOULOS,** born New York, N.Y., May 21, 1960; admitted to bar, 1987, California. *Education:* University of Southern California (B.A., magna cum laude, 1982); Northwestern University (J.D., 1985). Author: "ERISA Plaintiffs Strike Out: The Supreme Court and Congress Explicitly Reject Punitive Damages," Los Angeles Lawyer Magazine, Vol. 18, No. 4, page 17. *Member:* State Bar of California. *PRACTICE AREAS:* Business Litigation; ERISA Litigation; Employment Litigation. *Email:* tabacdi@la.seyfarth.com

**THOMAS LARRY WATTS,** born Los Angeles, California, April 15, 1939; admitted to bar, 1972, California. *Education:* Claremont McKenna College (B.A., cum laude, 1960); London School of Economics; University of California at Los Angeles (J.D., 1972). Member, UCLA Law Review, 1971-1972. *Member:* Los Angeles County and American Bar Associations; State Bar of California. *PRACTICE AREAS:* Litigation; Financial Institution Litigation; Securities Litigation; Insurance Coverage; Environmental Litigation; Land Use; Construction Litigation.

**THOMAS J. WEISS,** born Fargo, North Dakota, February 19, 1941; admitted to bar, 1974, California; 1984, U.S. Court of Appeals, Ninth Circuit; 1988, U.S. Supreme Court. *Education:* University of Notre Dame (A.B., 1962); University of Chicago (Ph.D., 1969); Harvard Law School (J.D., cum laude, 1974). Assistant and Associate Professor, California State University at Northridge, 1969-1976. Judge, Protem, Los Angeles Municipal Court. Arbitrator, Los Angeles Superior Court. *Member:* Los Angeles County (Vice-Chair, Committee on Attorney-Client Relations) and American Bar Associations; State Bar of California. (Resident). *PRACTICE AREAS:* Litigation; Healthcare Law.

**MITCHEL D. WHITEHEAD,** born Los Angeles, California, August 31, 1953; admitted to bar, 1978, California. *Education:* University of California at Riverside (B.A., cum laude, 1975); University of Kent, Canterbury, England; Loyola University (J.D., cum laude, 1978). Phi Beta Kappa. *Member:* Los Angeles County and American Bar Associations; State Bar of California. (Resident).

**KENWOOD C. YOUMANS,** born Seattle, Washington, June 25, 1946; admitted to bar, 1974, Illinois; 1976, California. *Education:* University of California at Santa Barbara (B.A., magna cum laude, 1968); University of Michigan (M.A., Economics, 1971; J.D., 1974). *Member:* Illinois State and American Bar Associations; State Bar of California. (Resident). *PRACTICE AREAS:* Labor and Employment.

## OF COUNSEL

**BARBARA T. LINDEMANN,** born New York, N.Y.; admitted to bar, 1957, New York; 1961, District of Columbia; 1982, California. *Education:* Sarah Lawrence College (B.A., 1954); Yale Law School (J.D., 1956). Order of the Coif. Member, Board of Editors, Yale Law Journal, 1955-1956. Author: Lindemann and Kadue, *Sexual Harassment,* Bureau of National Affairs, 1992; Schlei and Grossman, *Employment Discrimination Law,* BNA, 1976, 1979 and 1983. Police Commissioner, City of Los Angeles, 1984-1988. Adjunct Professor, Loyola University School of Law, 1972-1977. Instructor, University of Southern California Law Center, 1967-1977. Administrator, Agricultural Marketing Service, U.S. Department of Agriculture, 1977-1981. Member: The U.S. Trade Representative's Service Advisory Committee, 1985-1993; The California Commission for Economic Development's Advisory Council on Asia. *PRACTICE AREAS:* Employment Law.

**ALEXANDER H. POPE,** born New York, N.Y., June 4, 1929; admitted to bar, 1952, Illinois; 1954, Korea; 1955, California; 1970, U.S. Supreme Court; 1975, U.S. Court of Appeals, Ninth Circuit. *Education:* University of Chicago (A.B., 1948; J.D., 1952). Phi Beta Kappa; Order of the Coif. Legislative Secretary to Governor of California, 1959-1961. Los Angeles County Assessor, 1978-1986. *PRACTICE AREAS:* Property Tax Law; Litigation; Administrative Law.

**CONWARD E. WILLIAMS,** born Premier, West Virginia, January 22, 1937; admitted to bar, 1961, West Virginia; 1984, District of Columbia; 1987, California. *Education:* West Virginia University (A.B., 1959; J.D., 1961); George Washington University (LL.M., 1972). Lecturer: "Government Approval of Subcontracts and Contractor Purchasing Systems," Annual Western Briefing Conference, Federal Bar Association and Bureau of National Affairs (1983); "Contracting with the Government, Selection of Contract Type," University of Central Florida, College of Business Administration (1988). Author: "Use of Dispositive Motions Before Government Boards of Contract Appeals, 5 Public Contract Law Journal 151 (1972)" and "The Return to Parallel Development," 5 National Contract Management Journal 35 (1971). *Member:* American Bar Association (Member: Public Contract Law Section; Vice Chair, Accounting, Cost and Pricing Committee, 1984-1990; Chair, Small Business Committee, 1993—). *PRACTICE AREAS:* Government Contract Law; International Law; Litigation; Boards of Contract Appeals.

## RESIDENT ASSOCIATES

**BRIAN T. ASHE,** born April 24, 1961; admitted to bar, 1989, California. *Education:* Boston College (B.A., cum laude, 1984); Oxford University, England, 1985; National Law Center, George Washington University (J.D., with honors, 1988). *PRACTICE AREAS:* Labor and Employment Law. *Email:* ashebr@la.seyfarth.com

*(This Listing Continued)*

**W. MICHAEL BATTLE,** born Cleveland, Ohio, August 27, 1964; admitted to bar, 1992, California. *Education:* University of Southern California (A.B., 1987; J.D., 1991). *Member:* State Bar of California. *PRACTICE AREAS:* Labor and Employment.

**JEFFREY L. BRAKER,** born Palo Alto, California, May 24, 1961; admitted to bar, 1988, California. *Education:* Columbia College, Columbia University (A.B., 1983); University of Michigan (J.D., cum laude, 1988; M.P.P., 1988). *Member:* State Bar of California. *PRACTICE AREAS:* Corporate/Business Law; Real Estate Law. *Email:* brakeje@la.seyfarth.com

**JAMES A. BRESLO,** born Clearwater, Florida, February 24, 1967; admitted to bar, 1992, California. *Education:* University of California, Irvine (B.S., cum laude, 1989); Northwestern University (J.D., 1992). Student Body Vice President, University of California, Irvine, 1987-1988. Note and Comment Editor, Northwestern Law Review. Author: "Taking the Punitive Damage Windfall Away From the Plaintiff: An Analysis," 86 Northwestern Law Review 1130 (Summ. 1992); "Singled Out: When Is An Individual Manager Exposed to Liability in an Employment Claim?" L.A. Daily Journal (July 27, 1995). *Member:* State Bar of California. *PRACTICE AREAS:* Employment; Labor; Litigation. *Email:* breslja@la.seyfarth.com

**JOHN G. CORRENTI,** born Boulder, Colorado, April 19, 1963; admitted to bar, 1996, California. *Education:* University of California, Irvine (B.A., 1986); Whittier College School of Law (J.D., cum laude, 1996). Member and Executive Editor, Whittier Law Review, 1994-1996. Member, Moot Court Honors Board, 1995-1996. *Member:* Los Angeles County Bar Association; State Bar of California. *PRACTICE AREAS:* Government Contract Law. *Email:* correjg@la.seyfarth.com

**BARBARA A. FITZGERALD,** born June 4, 1960; admitted to bar, 1990, California, U.S. District Court, Central, Southern and Northern Districts of California and U.S. Court of Appeals, Ninth Circuit. *Education:* University of California, Davis (B.S., 1983); University of California, Los Angeles (M.P.H., 1986); University of Southern California (J.D., 1990). *Member:* Los Angeles County and American Bar Associations; State Bar of California. *PRACTICE AREAS:* Employment Litigation.

**SEAN J. GALLAGHER,** born Queens, New York, November 29, 1963; admitted to bar, 1989, Florida; 1990, District of Columbia; 1996, California. *Education:* Boston University (B.S., 1985); University of Miami (J.D., 1989). Recipient, Moot Court Board Director Competitor Best Brief Award. *Member:* The Florida Bar; District of Columbia Bar; State Bar of California; American Bar Association. *PRACTICE AREAS:* Workers Compensation; Labor and Employment. *Email:* gallagsj@la.seyfarth.com

**JUDITH A. GORDON,** born Washington, D.C., August 16, 1954; admitted to bar, 1979, Pennsylvania and U.S. District Court, Eastern District of Pennsylvania; 1987, California. *Education:* Brown University (A.B., with honors, 1976); University of Virginia (J.D., 1979). *Member:* Los Angeles County Bar Association; State Bar of California. *PRACTICE AREAS:* Pension and Employee Benefits Law. *Email:* gordonju@la.seyfarth.com

**DAVID M. GRUENBERG,** born Los Angeles, California, December 14, 1964; admitted to bar, 1991, California. *Education:* University of California, Berkeley (B.A., 1987); University of San Francisco (J.D., cum laude, 1991). *Member:* State Bar of California. *PRACTICE AREAS:* Workers' Compensation Defense; Labor. *Email:* gruenda@la.seyfarth.com

**PHILECIA L. HARRIS,** born Springfield, Missouri, December 7, 1962; admitted to bar, 1994, California. *Education:* United States Air Force Academy (B.S., 1985); The Ohio State University (J.D.). *Member:* State Bar of California. [U.S. Air Force, 1985-1994, Capt.]

**GAYE E. HERTAN,** born Denver, Colorado, March 7, 1961; admitted to bar, 1987, California and U.S. District Court, Central District of California; 1991, U.S. District Court, Northern District of California; 1992, U.S. District Court, Eastern District of California. *Education:* University of California at Los Angeles (B.A., 1984); University of Southern California (J.D., 1987). *PRACTICE AREAS:* Labor and Employment Law.

**DAVID D. JACOBSON,** born Rochester, Minnesota, July 21, 1955; admitted to bar, 1987, Oklahoma; 1989, California. *Education:* Winona State University (B.A., 1983); University of Arkansas (J.D., with honors, 1986). *Member:* State Bar of California. *PRACTICE AREAS:* Litigation.

**STEVEN B. KATZ,** born Boonton, New Jersey, March 20, 1962; admitted to bar, 1988, California and U.S. District Court, Central, Northern and Southern and Eastern Districts of California. *Education:* University of Southern California (A.B., summa cum laude, 1984; M.A., 1987; J.D., 1987); Stanford University (J.S.M., 1988). Phi Beta Kappa; Order of the Coif. *PRACTICE AREAS:* Commercial; Real Estate; Employee Benefits; Employment Litigation. *Email:* katzst@la.seyfarth.com

*(This Listing Continued)*

**THOMAS R. KAUFMAN,** born East Chicago, Indiana, November 17, 1970; admitted to bar, 1995, California. *Education:* University of Illinois at Chicago (B.A., 1992); University of California School of Law, Los Angeles (J.D., 1995). *LANGUAGES:* Spanish and Japanese. *PRACTICE AREAS:* Litigation; Employment and Labor.

**PATRICIA KINAGA,** born Santa Monica, California, November 28, 1953; admitted to bar, 1986, California; U.S. District Court, Central District of California; U.S. Court of Appeals, Ninth Circuit; U.S. Supreme Court. *Education:* University of California at Los Angeles (B.A., cum laude, 1975); University of California at Berkley (M.A., 1977); Georgetown University Law Center (J.D., 1984). *Member:* Los Angeles County and Japanese American Bar Associations; State Bar of California (Member, State Bar Committee on Women); Women Lawyers Association. *PRACTICE AREAS:* Public Sector; Employment Discrimination; Wrongful Termination; Discipline.

**LORRAINE H. O'HARA,** born Elmhurst, Illinois, August 17, 1962; admitted to bar, 1988, Ohio; 1994, California. *Education:* Wheaton College (B.A., 1983); University of Cincinnati (J.D., 1988). Student Articles Editor, University of Cincinnati Law Review. *PRACTICE AREAS:* Employment Law; Labor Law.

**ALLAN S. ONO,** born Honolulu, Hawaii, February 12, 1961; admitted to bar, 1987, California, U.S. Court of Appeals, Ninth Circuit and U.S. District Court, Central District of California; 1991, U.S. District Court, Northern, Eastern and Southern Districts of California. *Education:* University of Hawaii (B.A., 1984); George Washington University (J.D., 1987). *PRACTICE AREAS:* Commercial Litigation; Bankruptcy/Creditors' Rights.

**LAURA WILSON SHELBY,** born Santa Monica, California, March 8, 1964; admitted to bar, 1991, California and U.S. District Court, Central District of California. *Education:* University of California at Los Angeles (B.A., 1986); University of California School of Law, Davis (J.D., 1990). Board Editor, University of California at Davis Law Review, 1989-1990. *Member:* State Bar of California.

**DAVID T. VAN PELT,** born Wichita, Kansas, October 13, 1964; admitted to bar, 1993, California. *Education:* Davidson College (B.A., cum laude, 1987); Duke University (J.D., 1992). Senior Editor, The Alaska Law Review. Member, Moot Court Board.

**JAN A. YOSS,** born Scottsbluff, Nebraska, November 20, 1963; admitted to bar, 1989, California and U.S. District Court, Central District of California. *Education:* University of Illinois, Urbana (B.A., 1986, Phi Beta Kappa); University of California at Los Angeles (J.D., 1989). President, Los Angeles County Bar Association Barristers, 1994-1995. *PRACTICE AREAS:* Commercial, Tort and Employment Litigation. *Email:* yossja@la.seyfarth.com

(For complete biographical data on personnel at Chicago, Illinois, Washington, D.C., New York, New York, San Francisco, California, Sacramento, California, Houston, Texas and Brussels, Belgium, see Professional Biographies at those locations)

---

## SHAPIRO, HINDS & MITCHELL LLP

*11100 SANTA MONICA BOULEVARD*
*SUITE 900*
**LOS ANGELES, CALIFORNIA 90025**
*Telephone: 310-445-9888*
*Fax: 310-445-9899*

*Alternative Dispute Resolution, Appellate, Commercial Litigation, Commercial Policyholders Mass Tort Exposure Dispute Resolution, Environmental, First Amendment, Insolvency, Insurance Coverage, Intellectual Property and Partnership and Shareholder Disputes.*

**CARL W. SHAPIRO,** born Boston, Massachusetts, September 6, 1949; admitted to bar, 1976, California. *Education:* Yale University (B.A., magna cum laude, 1971); Harvard University (J.D., 1976). *Email:* CShapiro@SH_M.Com

**JAMES ANDREW HINDS, JR.,** born Berkeley, California, April 6, 1951; admitted to bar, 1976, California; 1977, U.S. Court of Appeals, Ninth Circuit; 1988, U.S. Court of Appeals, Fourth Circuit. *Education:* University of California at Berkeley; Dartmouth College (A.B., 1973); Harvard University (J.D., 1976). Book Review Editor, Harvard Journal on Legislation, 1975-1976. Staff Member, Harvard Civil Rights Civil Liberties Law Review, 1975-1976. Co-author: "Buying Hotel Properties in Bankruptcy: Goldmine or Trap for the Unwary," 3 Journal of Bankruptcy Law and Prac-

*(This Listing Continued)*

## SHAPIRO, HINDS & MITCHELL LLP, Los Angeles— Continued

tice, 627, 1944. Author: "To Right Mass Wrongs: A Federal Consumer Class Action Act," 13 Harvard Journal on Legislation 776, 1976. Lecturer: 14th Annual Real Property Retreat, Real Property Law Section of The California State Bar, 1995; The Orange County Bankruptcy Forum, 1990; The Group Health Association of America, Group Health Institute, 1989; California Society for Healthcare Attorneys, Annual Meeting, 1987; Century City Bar Association, 1983. Member of Board, Association of Business Trial Lawyers, 1986-1988. President, 1989-1995 and Treasurer, 1986-1988, Harvard Law School Association of Southern California. *Email:* JHinds@SH__M.Com

**BRIANE NELSON MITCHELL,** born Seattle, Washington, July 4, 1953; admitted to bar, 1978, Idaho; 1982, New York; 1984, California. *Education:* Columbia University (A.B., 1975); University of Idaho (J.D., 1978). Law Clerk, Hon. J. Blaine Anderson, U.S. Court of Appeals, Ninth Circuit, 1978-1980. Author: "Summary Judgment: A Solution to Court Congestion?" Los Angeles Lawyer, Vol. 13, No. 9, December 1990; "Another Important Tort Basic," California Lawyer, Vol. 12, No. 11, November 1992; "Litigation Terrorism," California Lawyer, Vol. 11, No. 2, February 1991; "Foreign Judgements," Litigation, Vol. 22, No. 4, Summer 1996. *Email:* NMitchell@SH__M.Com

**NORMAN A. DUPONT,** born Sherman, Texas, October 4, 1953; admitted to bar, 1979, California. *Education:* Stanford University (B.A., with distinction, 1975); Georgetown University (J.D., magna cum laude, 1978). Phi Beta Kappa. Member, 1976-1977 and Staff Editor, 1977-1978, Georgetown Law Journal. Law Clerk to Hon. Oscar H. Davis, U.S. Court of Claims, 1978-1979. Author: "Chapter 31: Waste Site Liability," Environmental Law Practice Guide, M. Gerrand, ed., Matthew Bender; "Municipal Solid Waste: The Endless Disposal of American Municipalities Meets the CERCLA Strict Liability Dragon," 24 Loyola of Los Angeles Law Review 1183 (1991). *Email:* NDupont@SH__M.Com

**KEITH A. MEYER,** born Los Angeles, California, August 22, 1957; admitted to bar, 1982, California. *Education:* Claremont McKenna College (B.A., cum laude, 1979); Loyola Law School, Los Angeles (J.D., 1982). Member, St. Thomas More Law Honor Society. Chairman, Jessup International Moot Court, 1981-1982. Extern, Hon. William Matthew Byrne, Jr., U.S. District Court, Central District of California, 1981. Co-Author: "Environmental Insurance Handbook," Government Institutes, Inc., 1992. Author: "Securing Insurance Coverage for EMF Claims," Public Utilities Fortnightly, February 1992; "California's Shield Law - The California Supreme Court Clarifies the Scope of Protection for Journalists," Los Angeles Lawyer, April 1991. Lecturer, *Transmission & Distribution,* Magazine, Annual Conference, 1994; Ameican Bar Association Section of Natural Resources, Energy and Environmental Law, Annual Conference on Electricity Law and Regulation, 1993; Risk and Insurance Management Society, Los Angeles Chapter, 1993; National Rural Electric Cooperative Association, Generation and Transmission Section, 1992; Edison Electric Institute, Annual Meeting, 1992. *Email:* KMeyer@SH__M.Com

### OF COUNSEL

**CINDY F. FORMAN,** born New York, N.Y., November 30, 1957; admitted to bar, 1985, New York; 1988, California. *Education:* Wesleyan University; Barnard College (B.A., magna cum laude, 1979); Georgetown University (J.D., magna cum laude, 1984). Member, Law and Policy in International Business, 1983-1984. *Email:* CForman@SH__M.Com

**LEORA D. FREEDMAN,** born New Haven, Connecticut, July 19, 1959; admitted to bar, 1987, California and U.S. District Court, Central District of California; 1991, U.S. Court of Appeals, Ninth Circuit. *Education:* Wesleyan University (B.A., 1981); University of California at Los Angeles (J.D., 1987). Law Clerk to the Honorable Harry L. Hupp, U.S. District Court, Central District of California, 1987-1988. *LANGUAGES:* French. *Email:* LFreedman@SH__M.Com

### ASSOCIATE

**SUZANNE HARMATZ MITCHELL,** born Los Angeles, California, June 24, 1952; admitted to bar, 1980, California; 1981, New York. *Education:* Stanford University (B.A., 1975); University of California School of Law, Davis (J.D., 1980).

**COLLEEN E. CURTIN,** born Poughkeepsie, New York, July 13, 1970; admitted to bar, 1995, California and U.S. District Court, Southern District of California. *Education:* Colgate University (B.A., 1992); University of San Diego (J.D., cum laude, 1995). Order of the Coif. Phi Alpha Delta. Vice Justice, 1994-1995. *Member:* San Diego County Bar Association; State Bar of California; San Diego Defense Lawyer's Association. *LANGUAGES:* Spanish. *PRACTICE AREAS:* Medical Malpractice; Legal Malpractice; Products Liability; Personal Injury.

## SHAPIRO, ROSENFELD & CLOSE
### A PROFESSIONAL CORPORATION
Established in 1971

SUITE 2600, ONE CENTURY PLAZA
2029 CENTURY PARK EAST
LOS ANGELES, CALIFORNIA 90067
Telephone: 310-277-1818
Telecopier: 310-201-4776
Email: src__law@ix.netcom.com

*General Business Practice. Franchising, Entertainment, Copyright, Corporation, Bankruptcy and Reorganization, Taxation, Estate Planning and Real Estate Law. Antitrust, Trade Regulation, Land Use, Unfair Competition and Administrative Law. Civil Litigation.*

FIRM PROFILE: Shapiro, Rosenfeld & Close, a Professional Corporation, is located in Century City, Los Angeles, California, Since the inception of the firm in 1971. The law firm is an aggressive well rounded firm that believes that a lawyer, client relationship is very important and is never jeopardized. The firm works as a team and takes great pride in its victories. The law firm is listed in the Bar Register of Preeminent Lawyers. Present size of eighteen attorneys (six partners, six associates and six of counsels). The varied backgrounds and areas of specialty of the firm and its attorneys enable the firm to conduct an active and broad-based business practice, which includes franchise, bankruptcy, antitrust, commercial and securities litigation and counseling, copyright, environmental tort litigation, trademark and unfair competition litigation, insurance coverage work (particularly in environmental tort law), other civil litigation, entertainment, real estate, estate planning, regulatory work, taxation, corporations, and general business.

**MITCHELL S. SHAPIRO,** born Warsaw, New York, April 7, 1940; admitted to bar, 1965, California; 1971, U.S. Supreme Court and U.S. Tax Court. *Education:* Syracuse University (B.A., 1961); University of Chicago (J.D., 1964). Instructor: Franchising, California State University at Northridge, 1983—; California Continuing Education of the Bar, 1981. Deputy Attorney General, State of California, 1964-1966. Past President, University of Chicago Law School Alumni Association for Southern California. *Member:* Beverly Hills, Century City, Los Angeles County and American (Member, Forum Committee on Franchising, 1979—) Bar Associations; State Bar of California (Member, Committee on Franchise Law, Business Law Section; State Bar Referee, 1983—); International Franchise Association (Member, Advisory Committee to California Legislature on Franchising, 1987—). *Email:* src__law@ix.netcom.com

**EDWARD M. ROSENFELD,** born Terre Haute, Indiana, April 3, 1940; admitted to bar, 1964, New York; 1971, California. *Education:* Wharton School of Finance and Commerce, University of Pennsylvania (B.S., in Economics, 1961); Columbia University (J.D., 1964). General Counsel, Technicolor, Inc., 1970-1972. Member, U.S. Holocaust Memorial Council, 1987-1992; Lecturer, Securities Law, Practicing Law Institute, 1991—. *Member:* New York County, Los Angeles County and American Bar Associations (Member, Corporation, Banking and Business Law Section); State Bar of California. *PRACTICE AREAS:* Litigation. *Email:* src__law@ix.netcom.com

**RICHARD H. CLOSE,** born Boston, Massachusetts, January 24, 1945; admitted to bar, 1969, Massachusetts; 1971, U.S. Tax Court; 1972, California. *Education:* Wharton School of Finance and Commerce at the University of Pennsylvania (B.S., 1966); Boston University (J.D., magna cum laude, 1969). Editor, Boston University Law Review, 1968-1969. Director, California United Bank, Encino, California, 1982—. *Member:* Beverly Hills and Los Angeles County Bar Associations; State Bar of California. *Email:* src__law@ix.netcom.com

**HELMUT F. FURTH,** born Vienna, Austria, September 12, 1930; admitted to bar, 1956, New York; 1987, California. *Education:* Harvard College (B.A., magna cum laude, 1952); Harvard University (J.D., magna cum laude, 1955). Articles Editor, Harvard Law Review, 1954-1955. Author: "Price-Restrictive Patent Licenses Under the Sherman Act," 71 Harvard Law Review 815, 1958; "Applying the Merger Guidelines," 53 Antitrust Law J. 335, 1984. Deputy Assistant Attorney General, Antitrust Division, Department of Justice, 1982-1984. Official Reporter, Judicial Conference of the State of New York, prepared official Forms for New York Civil Practice Law & Rules, 1970-1971. *Member:* The Association of the Bar of The City

*(This Listing Continued)*

of New York; Los Angeles County and American Bar Associations; State Bar of California; New York County Lawyers Association (Former Chairman, Federal Courts Committee). *LANGUAGES:* German. *PRACTICE AREAS:* Litigation. *Email:* src_law@ix.netcom.com

**ROCHELLE BUCHSBAUM SPANDORF,** born New York, N.Y., July 17, 1951; admitted to bar, 1976, New York and U.S. District Court, Southern District of New York; 1977, California and U.S. District Court, Central District of California. *Education:* Cornell University (B.S., with distinction, 1973); New York University; Washington University (J.D., 1976). Phi Kappa Phi. Associate Editor, 1988-1992 and Topics and Articles Editor, 1985-1988, ABA Franchise Law Journal. Author: "What Every Lender Should Know About The Legal Aspect of Franchising," 76 Journal of Commercial Lending, No. 4, Dec. 1993; "The Case Against Courtney v. Waring: An Analytical Response to Due Diligence Proponents," 11 ABA Franchise Law Journal, No. 2, Fall, 1991; "Implications of the Covenant of Good Faith: Its Extension to Franchising," 5 ABA Franchise Law Journal, No. 2, Fall, 1985. Instructor: Franchising Course, University of California at Santa Barbara, Extension, 1988, 1990; California State University, Dominguez Hills Extension, 1986-1988. *Member:* State Bar of California (Member, Executive Committee, Business Law Section, 1990-1993; Franchise Law Committee, 1985-1988; Chair, Franchise Law Committee, 1987-1988); American Bar Association (Member, Forum on Franchising, 1981—, Governing Committee, 1992-1995, Chair, 1995—, Program Chair 1994 Annual Forum on Franchising; Co Vice-Chair, Franchising Subcommittee of Business Law Section, 1987-1988; Member, Sections on Antitrust, Business Law; Intellectual Property). *PRACTICE AREAS:* Domestic and international franchising and licensing matters in all industries. *Email:* src_law@ix.netcom.com

**DOUGLAS L. CARDEN,** born Bismarck, North Dakota, October 4, 1951; admitted to bar, 1977, California; 1978, U.S. District Court, Central District of California; 1984, U.S. Court of Appeals, Ninth Circuit. *Education:* University of Chicago (B.A., 1974); University of Santa Clara (J.D., summa cum laude, 1977). Articles Editor, Santa Clara Law Review, 1976-1977. Law Clerk to Hon. Francis C. Whelan, U.S. District Court, Central District of California, 1977-1978. Law Clerk Extern to Hon. William P. Clark, California Supreme Court, 1976. *Member:* Los Angeles County (Member, Conference of Delegates, 1982—) and American (Member, Forum Committee on Franchising, 1987—, Litigation Section, 1980—) Bar Associations; State Bar of California (Member, Litigation Section, 1980—). *PRACTICE AREAS:* Business Litigation and Franchising Law. *Email:* src_law@ix.netcom.com

**JONATHAN J. PANZER,** born Bronx, New York, December 20, 1949; admitted to bar, 1981, California; 1984, New York. *Education:* State University of New York at Stony Brook (B.A., 1972); Claremont Graduate School (M.A., 1977); University of California at Los Angeles (J.D., 1981). *Member:* Los Angeles County and New York State Bar Associations; State Bar of California. *Email:* src_law@ix.netcom.com

**CATHRYN S. GAWNE,** born Lake Forest, Illinois, July 4, 1957; admitted to bar, 1982, California. *Education:* Stanford University (A.B., 1979); University of California at Los Angeles (J.D., 1982). Assistant Comment Editor, UCLA Law Review, 1981-1982. Co-Author: "Creative Funding for High Technology Ventures," Los Angeles Lawyer, June, 1988. Lecturer, Business Law, California American Womens Economic Development Corporation, 1991—, USC Entrepreneur Program, 1994. *Member:* Beverly Hills, Los Angeles County (Member, Business and Corporations Section) and American (Member Business Law Section) Bar Associations; Women Lawyers of Los Angeles; State Bar of California. *PRACTICE AREAS:* Corporate Law; Securities Law. *Email:* src_law@ix.netcom.com

**JULIE J. BISCEGLIA,** born Fresno, California, November 23, 1946; admitted to bar, 1985, California; 1986, U.S. District Court, Central, Eastern, Northern and Southern Districts of California, District of Hawaii and U.S. Court of Appeals, Ninth Circuit. *Education:* Stanford University (B.A., 1968); University of California at Los Angeles (M.A., 1974; Ph.D., 1980; J.D., 1985). Author: "Practical Aspects of Directors and Officers Liability Insurance-Allocating and Advancing Legal Fees and the Duty to Defend," 32 UCLA Law Review 690 (1985); "Parody and Copyright Protection: Turning The Balancing Act Into a Juggling Act," 34 ASCAP Copyright Law Symposium (1987); "Summary Judgment on Substantial Similarity in Copyright Actions," 16 Comm/Ent 51 (1993); "Parody and Fair Use: 2 Live Crew Meets the Supremes," 15 Entertainment Law Rptr. 13, (May 1994). *Member:* Los Angeles County Bar Association; State Bar of California. *LANGUAGES:* French and Italian. *PRACTICE AREAS:* Commercial and Entertainment Litigation. *Email:* src_law@ix.netcom.com

*(This Listing Continued)*

**LISA K. SKAIST,** born Los Angeles, California, November 3, 1961; admitted to bar, 1987, California; 1988, U.S. District Court, Central District of California. *Education:* University of California at Los Angeles; Tufts University (B.A., 1983); Loyola Law School (J.D., 1987). *Member:* Century City, Los Angeles County and American Bar Associations; State Bar of California. *PRACTICE AREAS:* Business Litigation; Franchising Law. *Email:* src_law@ix.netcom.com

**RHONDA H. MEHLMAN,** born Anaheim, California, November 3, 1963; admitted to bar, 1989, California. *Education:* University of California at Berkeley (B.A., 1985); Universite De Paris III (Sorbonne-Nouvelle); University of California at Los Angeles (J.D., 1989). Member, Associate Editor, University of California Law Review, 1987-1989. *Member:* Los Angeles County and American Bar Associations; Women Lawyers Association of Los Angeles; State Bar of California. *LANGUAGES:* French. *REPORTED CASES:* Anaconda Minerals Co. v. Stoller Chemical Co., 990 F.2d 1175 (10th Cir. 1993). *PRACTICE AREAS:* Litigation; Franchise Law. *Email:* src_law@ix.netcom.com

**MARNA F. MILLER,** born Los Angeles, California, August 29, 1964; admitted to bar, 1994, California. *Education:* University of California at Santa Barbara (B.A., 1987); Whittier College School of Law (J.D., 1994). *Email:* src_law@ix.netcom.com

**JENNIFER A. DEMARRAIS,** born Teaneck, New Jersey, June 26, 1969; admitted to bar, 1995, California. *Education:* Williams College (B.A., 1991); Georgetown University (J.D., 1995). *Email:* src_law@ix.netcom.com

*OF COUNSEL*

**ALAN D. JACOBSON,** born Perth Amboy, New Jersey, August 10, 1940; admitted to bar, 1965, California and U.S. Court of Appeals, Third Circuit; 1970, U.S. Supreme Court. *Education:* Cornell University (A.B., 1961); Yale University (LL.B., cum laude, 1964); Stanford University (M.S.M., 1984). Phi Beta Kappa; Order of the Coif. Editor, Yale Law Journal, 1962-1964. Associate, Gibson, Dunn & Crutcher, 1965-1969. Assistant General Counsel, 1969-1971, General Counsel, 1971-1985, Whittaker Corporation. Adjunct Professor, Cardozo Law School, New York, 1990-1991. *Member:* Los Angeles County (Member, 1977-1986 and Officer, 1985-1986, Executive Committee, Corporate Law Section) and American Bar Associations; State Bar of California. *PRACTICE AREAS:* Corporate Law; Mergers and Acquisitions. *Email:* src_law@ix.netcom.com

**ALAN G. DOWLING,** born Houston, Texas, May 28, 1951; admitted to bar, 1976, California; 1977, U.S. District Court, Central District of California; 1980, U.S. Court of Appeals, 9th Circuit. *Education:* University of Michigan (B.A., cum laude, 1973); University of Southern California (J.D., 1976). Member, 1974-1975 and Executive Editor, Topics and Assignments, 1975-1976, Southern California Law Review. Author: "A Right to Adequate Assurance of Performance in All Transactions: U.C.C. Section 2-609 Beyond Sales of Goods," 48 So. Cal. Law Review 1358, 1975. Awarded Certificates in, Entertainment Litigation, 1987, Federal Civil Trial Practice, 1981 and Litigation and Settlement of Marital Disputes, 1977, University of Southern California Law Center Advanced Professional Program. *Member:* Beverly Hills, Los Angeles County and American Bar Associations; State Bar of California; Copyright Society of Los Angeles. *LANGUAGES:* French. *PRACTICE AREAS:* Litigation; Entertainment Law.

**BARRY KURTZ,** born Buffalo, New York, July 5, 1948; admitted to bar, 1973, California and U.S. District, Central District of California; 1974, U.S. District Court, Southern District of California; 1978, U.S. Supreme Court. *Education:* University of California at Los Angeles (B.A., 1970); Southwestern University (J.D., 1973). Note and Comment Editor, Southwestern University Law Review, 1972-1973. Lecturer: American Bar Association, Forum Committee on Franchise, Fundamental of Franchising Program, 1987-1988; University of California at Los Angeles Business and Management Extension Education, Fast Food and Restaurant Management, 1988-1989. *Member:* Los Angeles County, American (Member: Section on Antitrust Law; Forum Committee on Franchising, 1982—) and International (Member, Section on Business Law-International Franchising) Bar Associations; State Bar of California (Member, Corporation, Banking and Business Law Section); International Franchise Association (Member, Legal/Legislative Committee). *PRACTICE AREAS:* Franchise Law; Business Law. *Email:* src_law@ix.netcom.com

REPRESENTATIVE CLIENTS: Nittetsu Shohi America, Inc.; Numero Uno Franchise Corp.; Midas Mufflers; Dunkin' Donuts; Subway; Obayashi America, Inc.; Velcro USA, Inc.; Pay-Fone Systems, Inc.; Uniglobe International; Highlands Insurance Co.; United Capitol Insurance Co.; American Reinsurance Co.; Future Kids, Inc.; Jetro Cash & Carry; Conroys; 1-800-Flowers.

## LEONARD SHARENOW
*1901 AVENUE OF THE STARS, 20TH FLOOR*
**LOS ANGELES, CALIFORNIA 90067**
Telephone: 310-203-8100
Fax: 310-277-9430

*White Collar Crime, Criminal Tax, Environmental Defense, Securities Litigation, Complex Civil Trials.*

**LEONARD SHARENOW,** born New York, N.Y., September 7, 1944; admitted to bar, 1970, New York; 1971, U.S. District Court, Southern and Eastern Districts of New York; 1973, U.S. Supreme Court and U.S. Court of Appeals, Second Circuit; 1974, California, U.S. Court of Appeals, Ninth Circuit and U.S. District Court, Central District of California; 1990, U.S. District Court, Southern District of California. *Education:* University of Rochester (A.B., 1966); New York University Law School (J.D., 1969). Assistant U.S. Attorney, Assistant Chief, Criminal Division and Member, Fraud and Special Prosecutions Section, Central District of California, 1974-1978. U.S. Department of Justice Award for Superior Performance as an Assistant U.S. Attorney. Counsel, Report of The Special Advisor to The Board of Police Commissioner on the Civil Disorder in Los Angeles-October 21 , 1992. *Member:* Los Angeles County, New York State, Federal and American (Member: White Collar Crime Committee, California Regional Subcommittee; Executive Committee) Bar Associations; State Bar of California. *PRACTICE AREAS:* Business Crimes; Criminal Trial Practice; Civil Trial; Environmental; Tax Fraud; Health Care; Fraud.

## SHAUB & WILLIAMS
*12121 WILSHIRE BOULEVARD, SUITE 205*
**LOS ANGELES, CALIFORNIA 90025**
Telephone: 310-826-6678
Telefax: 310-826-8042
Email: 74577.1544@compuserve.com
Email: dshaub@earthlink.net

*Associated With:* Hurt, Sinisi & Papadakis in San Diego, Atlanta, Rome and Milan, Italy, Athens, Greece.

*General and International Practice. Business and Investment Transactions. Business and Transnational Litigation in all Courts. E.U. Law, Intellectual Property Protection and Licensing, Computer Software and Telebroadcast Law, Entertainment. Foreign Companies and Trusts. Real Estate. International Insurance Transactions, Foreign Joint Ventures. Immigration.*

**DAVID R. SHAUB,** born Detroit, Michigan, 1935; admitted to bar, 1962, California; 1965, U.S. Tax Court; U.S. Court of Appeals, Ninth Circuit; U.S. Claims Court; U.S. Supreme Court. *Education:* University of Michigan (B.S., Math, 1958; J.D., 1960). Author: "A Review of Some of the Major Statutory Regimes, Other Than the Federal Antitrust Laws, That Regulate Unfair Trade Practices by Foreign Companies Doing Business in the United States and California," CEB International Business Law Institute, 1991; "International Litigation, Obtaining Evidence Abroad," 1991; "International Litigation Jurisdiction and Immunities," 1992. Arbitrator, American Arbitration Association. *Member:* Los Angeles County Bar Association (Executive Committee Chair, International Law Section, Pacific Rim Committee); State Bar of California (Member, International and Business Law Sections, Partnership Committee, 1990-1991); Inter-Pacific Bar Association. *PRACTICE AREAS:* Transnational and Domestic Business; Intellectual Property; International Litigation and Tax Related Matters; Pacific Basin Trade and Investment; Offshore Trusts and Corporations.

**LESLIE GAIL WILLIAMS,** born Boise, Idaho; admitted to bar, 1980, California. *Education:* Occidental College (B.A., cum laude, 1974); College of Europe, Bruges, Belgium (M.A., 1975); University of California at Davis (J.D., 1980). Research Fellow, Max Planck Institute for Foreign and International Industrial Property and Copyright Law, 1980-1982. Legal Translator for C.G. Beck Verlag, Munich, West Germany (1983—), "Pharmon v. Hoechst: Limits on the Community Exhaustion Principle in Respect of Compulsory Patent Licenses," Fordham Corporation Law Institute, 1987; "Exporting the California Franchise to the EC", The California International Practitioner, Vol. 2, No. 1, 1990-1991, p. 18; "Aspects of Intellectual Property law in the European Community," Hastings Int'l & Comparative Law Review, 1993; "The European Community in View of Maastricht," Los Angeles County Bar Association Seminar, June 1993; "Current Legal Developments in the EU," Thirteenth Whittier International Law Symposium, 1996. Appointee, Team Europe. *Member:* Los Angeles County Bar Association; State Bar of California (Member, Intellectual Property Section); International Association of Young Lawyers (AIJA); American Intellectual Property Law Association. *LANGUAGES:* French, German and Spanish. *PRACTICE AREAS:* European Union; International Business and Intellectual Property Transactions; and Related Litigation.

**EDWARD EVERETT VAILL,** born June 23, 1940; admitted to bar, 1970, California and 1966, District of Columbia; U.S. Supreme Court. *Education:* University of Oslo; Colgate University (A.B., 1962); University of Chicago Law School (J.D., 1965). Author, Publications: "How to Use the Smoking Gun: A Case Study of MDL-417" and "The An Tai Bao Coal Mine Joint Venture Arbitration: Litigation Avoidance in Foreign Lands," International Litigation: Case Studies Home and Abroad, L.A. County Bar Symposium, April, 1995; "Lessons from the Front Line: Experiences of An In-House Counsel," International Joint Ventures, Federal Publications, Inc., November, 1993; "Wind up By Mutual Agreement: Effect of Local Law, Continuing Liability of Ventures (and Venturers)," Dealing With Failing International Joint Ventures, International Law Section, State Bar of California, July 1993; "International Insurance Coverage Issues," Minimizing the Risks in International Business Transactions, CEB, April 1991; Symposium: "Changing Perspectives in Antitrust Litigation - The Role of the Federal Trade Commission," 12 Southwestern U.L. Rev., 1989-1981; "The Federal Trade Commission: Should it Continue as Both Prosecutor and Judge in Antitrust Proceedings?, 10 Southwestern U.L. Rev. 763, 1978. *Member:* Malibu, Los Angeles County (Executive Committee, International Law Section; Pacific Rim Committee) and American Bar Associations; State Bar of California. *REPORTED CASES:* Scranton v. Litton Industries Leasing Corporation, 494 F.2d 778 (5th Cir., 1974), cert. den., 95 Sup. Ct. 774 (1975). *TRANSACTIONS:* Successfully concluded 23 negotiations with the Federal Trade Commission or the Antitrust Division, including all Hart-Scott-Rodino Premerger Notification filings. *PRACTICE AREAS:* Litigation; Insurance Coverage; Tax; International Insurance Transactions; Foreign Joint Venture Laws.

**ALAN M. KINDRED,** born Sydney, Australia, 1952; admitted to bar, 1977, (Barrister, 1987) New South Wales, High Court of Australia; 1986, New York; 1988, California. *Education:* University of Sydney (B.A., 1973; LL.B., 1976; M.A., 1979). Author: "Enforcing Money Judgements," New South Wales College of Law, 1986; The Hamburg Rules: Variations and Metamorphoses on Existing Themes," published on the Worldwide Web; articles on the Warsaw Convention and the Death On The High Seas Act. Arbitrator, Local Court of New South Wales, 1986-1988. *Member:* Los Angeles County Bar Association (Member, Executive Committee, International Law Section); American Bar Association; New South Wales Bar Association; International Trade Club of Southern California; Transportation Lawyers Association (Member, Committee on Bankruptcy and Creditors' Rights, Committee on Freight Claims); International Bar Association; American Bankruptcy Institute. *LANGUAGES:* German. *PRACTICE AREAS:* Transportation Litigation; Commercial and International Litigation; Bankruptcy Litigation.

*OF COUNSEL*

**INGO LEETSCH,** born Bremen, Germany, 1948; admitted to bar, 1979, Germany (Not admitted in the United States). *Education:* University of Gottingen, Gottingen, Germany (Law Degree); University of Michigan, Ann Arbor (LL.M., 1975). *LANGUAGES:* English and Japanese. *PRACTICE AREAS:* International Investment with Japan; German Real Property; Restitution.

**HONG SUN,** born Beijing, China; admitted to bar, 1994, California. *Education:* Yunan University, Yunan China, (B.A., History, 1978); Chinese Academy of Social Sciences (Juris Doctorate Equivalent, 1986); University of California School of Law, Los Angeles; University of California at Santa Barbara (M.A., 1991); Whittier College School of Law (J.D., 1994). Assistant Professor of Law, Law Institute of China, Chinese Academy of Social Sciences, 1986-1987. *Member:* State Bar of California; Chinese Law Society; Chinese Association of Legal History. *LANGUAGES:* Chinese-Mandarin, Shanghai, Sichuan, Tianjing, Hubei, Yunnan, Hunan. *PRACTICE AREAS:* Immigration; Trademarks; Copyright; International Business; Litigation.

## SHAWN, MANN & NIEDERMAYER, L.L.P.
*2029 CENTURY PARK EAST*
*SUITE 1690*
**LOS ANGELES, CALIFORNIA**
Telephone: 310-553-8065
Fax: 310-557-0729

*Washington, D.C., Government Affairs Office:* 499 S. Capitol Street, S.W., Suite 420. Telephone: 202-842-3000. Fax: 202-547-7161.

*(This Listing Continued)*

*Washington, D.C. Office:* 1850 M Street, N.W., Suite 280. Telephone: 202-331-7900. Fax: 202-331-0726.

*San Diego, California Office:* 401 West "A" Street, Suite 1850. Telephone: 619-236-0303. Fax: 619-238-8181.

*San Francisco, California Office:* The Fox Plaza, 1390 Market Street, Suite 1204. Telephone: 415-982-0150. Fax: 415-522-0513.

*Bloomington, Minnesota Office:* 2090 West 98th Street. Telephone: 612-881-6577. Fax: 612-881-6894.

*Business Law and Litigation before Courts and Government Agencies. Legislative Advocacy, Corporate, Intellectual Property, International, Procurement, Real Estate, Trade Association, Transactional and Transportation Law.*

(For Complete Biographical data on all personnel, see Professional Biographies at Washington, D.C.)

## SHEARMAN & STERLING
*777 SOUTH FIGUEROA STREET, 34TH FLOOR*
**LOS ANGELES, CALIFORNIA 90017-5418**
Telephone: (213) 239-0300
Fax: (213) 239-0381, 614-0936

*New York, N.Y. Office:* 599 Lexington Avenue, New York, New York 10022-6069 and Citicorp Center, 153 East 53rd Street, New York, New York 10022-4676. Telephone: (212) 848-4000. Telex: 667290 Num Lau. Fax: 599 Lexington Avenue: (212) 848-7179. Citicorp Center: (212) 848-5252.

*Abu Dhabi, United Arab Emirates Office:* P.O. Box 2948. Telephone: (971-2) 324477. Fax: (971-2) 774533.

*Beijing, People's Republic of China Office:* Suite #2205, Capital Mansion, No. 6, Xin Yuan Nan Lu. Chao Yang District, Beijing, 100004. Telephone: (86-10)6465-4574. Fax: (86-10) 6465-4578.

*Budapest, Hungary Office:* Szerb utca 17-19, 1056 Budapest. Telephone: (36-1) 266-3522. Fax: (36-1) 266-3523.

*Düsseldorf, Federal Republic of Germany Office:* Couvenstrasse 8 40211 Düsseldorf. Telephone: (49 211) 178 88-0. Fax: (49 211) 178 88-88. Telex: 8588294 NYLO.

*Frankfurt, Federal Republic of Germany Office:* Bockenheimer Landstrasse 55, 60325 Frankfurt am Main. Telephone: (49-69) 97107-0. Fax: (49-69) 97107-100.

*Hong Kong Office:* Standard Chartered Bank Building, 4 Des Voeux Road, Central. Telephone: (852) 2978-8000. Fax: (852) 2978-8099.

*London, England Office:* 199 Bishopsgate, London EC2M 3TY. Telephone: (44-171) 920-9000. Fax: (44-171) 920-9020.

*Paris, France Office:* 114 avenue des Champs-Elysées, 75008. Telephone: (33-1) 53-89-7000. Fax: (33-1) 53-89-7070. Telex: 282964 ROYALE.

*San Francisco, California Office:* 555 California Street, 94104-1522. Telephone: (415) 616-1100. Fax: (415) 616-1199.

*Singapore Office:* 80 Raffles Place #16-21, UOB Plaza 2. Singapore 048624. Telephone: (65) 230-3800. Fax: (65) 230-3899.

*Tokyo, Japan Office:* Shearman & Sterling (Grant Finlayson Gaikokuho-Jimu-Bengoshi Jimusho), Fukoku Seimei Building, 5th Fl. 2-2-2, Uchisaiwaicho, Chiyoda-ku, Tokyo 100, Japan. Telephone: (81 3) 5251-1601. Fax: (81 3) 5251-1602.

*Toronto, Ontario, Canada Office:* Commerce Court West, Suite 4405, P.O. Box 247, M5L 1E8. Telephone: (416) 360-8484. Fax: (416) 360-2958.

*Washington, D.C. Office:* 801 Pennsylvania Avenue, N.W., 20004-2604. Telephone: (202) 508-8000. Fax: (202) 508-8100.

General Practice.

FIRM PROFILE: *Shearman & Sterling, founded in 1873, has more than 600 lawyers in 15 offices throughout the world. The firm's practice encompasses most major areas of business law, including: Antitrust and Trade Regulation; Banking; Bankruptcy and Corporate Reorganization; Compensation and Benefits; Environmental; Finance (including Corporate Finance, Domestic Private Finance, Financial Institutions, International Private Finance and Project Finance); Individual Clients, Trusts and Estates; Insurance; International Trade and Government Relations; Litigation and Arbitration; Mergers and Acquisitions; Oil and Gas; Privatizations; Real Estate; and Tax. The Firm is also engaged in the practice of French, German and Hungarian law through its offices in France, Germany and Hungary.*

RESIDENT PARTNERS

**RONALD M. BAYER,** born Los Angeles, California, 1948; admitted to bar, 1972, California. *Education:* University of California at Los Angeles (A.B., 1969; J.D., 1972). (Managing Partner). *Email:* rbayer@shearman.com

*(This Listing Continued)*

**JACULIN AARON,** born Wichita, Kansas, 1958; admitted to bar, 1985, New York; 1988, California. *Education:* Wichita State University (B.A., 1981); University of Kansas (J.D., 1984). *Email:* jaaron@shearman.com

**RICHARD B. KENDALL,** born Princeton, New Jersey, 1952; admitted to bar, 1979, California. *Education:* Wesleyan University (B.A., 1974); University of Southern California (J.D., 1979). Law Clerk to the Hon. J. Clifford Wallace, U.S. Court of Appeals, Ninth Circuit, 1979-1980. Assistant U.S. Attorney, 1980-1985. Assistant Chief, Criminal Division, Los Angeles, 1983-1985. *Email:* rkendall@shearman.com

**DARRYL SNIDER,** born Grand Rapids, Michigan, 1949; admitted to bar, 1974, California; 1984, U.S. Supreme Court. *Education:* University of Michigan (B.A., 1971; Ph.D. in Econ., 1975; J.D., 1974). *Email:* dsnider@shearman.com

(For Biographical data of all partners, see Professional Biographies at New York, N.Y.)

## KEVIN D. SHEEHY
**LOS ANGELES, CALIFORNIA**
(See Santa Monica)

*Civil Trial and Appellate Practice in all State and Federal Courts, including Business Tort, Commercial, Partnership and Joint Venture, Entertainment, Professional Liability, Hazardous Waste, Toxic Tort, Environmental and Insurance Litigation, Arbitration, Mediation and Alternative Dispute Resolution.*

## BRYAN KING SHELDON
*11400 WEST OLYMPIC BOULEVARD, 9TH FLOOR*
**LOS ANGELES, CALIFORNIA 90064**
Telephone: 310-575-4111
FAX: 310-575-1520

*Civil Litigation in State and Federal Courts. Trials, Appeals and Administrative Agency Practice. Emphasizing Litigation of Complex Business Disputes, Unfair Trade Practices, Intellectual Property, Entertainment and Real Estate Disputes.*

**BRYAN KING SHELDON,** born Rhinelander, Wisconsin, July 10, 1958; admitted to bar, 1984, California and U.S. District Court, Central District of California; 1985, U.S. Court of Appeals, Ninth Circuit; 1987, U.S. Tax Court; 1989, U.S. District Court, Northern and Southern Districts of California. *Education:* University of Wisconsin (B.S., 1980); Southwestern University School of Law (J.D., 1984). Judge Pro Tem, Los Angeles Municipal Court, 1995—. *Member:* Beverly Hills and Los Angeles County Bar Associations; The Association of Trial Lawyers of America.

## SHEPPARD, MULLIN, RICHTER & HAMPTON LLP
A Limited Liability Partnership including Professional Corporations
*Established in 1927*
*FORTY-EIGHTH FLOOR, 333 SOUTH HOPE STREET*
**LOS ANGELES, CALIFORNIA 90071-1448**
Telephone: 213-620-1780
Telecopier: 213-620-1398
Cable Address: "Sheplaw"
Email: info@smrh.com
URL: http://www.smrh.com

*Orange County, California Office:* 650 Town Center Drive, 4th Floor, Costa Mesa. Telephone: 714-513-5100. Telecopier: 714-513-5130. Home Page Address: http://www.smrh.com.

*San Francisco, California Office:* Seventeenth Floor, Four Embarcadero Center. Telephone: 415-434-9100. Telecopier: 415-434-3947. Home Page Address: http://www.smrh.com.

*San Diego, California Office:* Nineteenth Floor, 501 West Broadway. Telephone: 619-338-6500. Telecopier: 619-234-3815. Home Page Address: http://www.smrh.com.

*General Civil Trial and Appellate Practice in all State and Federal Courts; Financial Institutions Law; Commercial Law; Banking; Bankruptcy and Reorganization; Corporate; Securities; Antitrust; Intellectual Property; Unfair Competition; Labor and Employment; Pension and Employee Benefits; Federal, State and Local Taxation; Real Estate; Land Use; Environmental; White*

*(This Listing Continued)*

**SHEPPARD, MULLIN, RICHTER & HAMPTON LLP,** Los Angeles—*Continued*

Collar Criminal Defense; International Business; Administrative; Probate; Trust; and Estate Planning.

### COUNSEL

**GORDON F. HAMPTON** (1912-1996).

**J. STANLEY MULLIN,** born Los Angeles, California, July 14, 1907; admitted to bar, 1933, California; 1950, U.S. Supreme Court. *Education:* Stanford University (A.B., 1930); Harvard Law School (LL.B., 1933). Member, Chancery Club; President, 1958-1959. *Member:* Los Angeles County (Member, Board of Trustees, 1955-1957) and American (Chairman, Section of Real Property, Probate and Trust Law, 1958-1959, Honorary Member of Council; Member, House of Delegates, 1959-1960; 1968-1976; Co-Chairman, National Conference of Lawyers, Title Companies and Abstracters, 1972-1977; Chairman, Standing Committee on Clients Security Fund, 1970-1973) Bar Associations; State Bar of California (Chairman, Client Security Fund Committee, 1975-1976). Fellow: American Bar Foundation; American College of Trust and Estate Counsel. (Retired). *Email:* jmullin@smrh.com

**GEORGE R. RICHTER, JR.,** born Blue Island, Illinois, July 8, 1910; admitted to bar, 1933, California; 1950, U.S. Supreme Court. *Education:* University of Southern California (A.B., 1930; LL.B., 1933). Order of the Coif. Member, Chancery Club. President, National Conference of Commissioners on Uniform State Law, 1959-1961. Member, 1951-1973 and 1986— and Chairman, 1956-1973, California Commission on Uniform State Laws. Member, Permanent Editorial Board, Uniform Commercial Code, 1953-1985. Chairman, Commercial Law and Bankruptcy Section, Los Angeles County Bar Association, 1967-1969. *Member:* Orange County and American (Chairman: Section of Corporation, Banking and Business Law, 1962-1963; Ad Hoc Committee on Class Actions, 1973-1975; Member, House of Delegates, 1959-1961, 1980-1982) Bar Associations; American Law Institute. Fellow, American Bar Foundation. (Retired). *Email:* grichter@smrh.com

**JAMES C. SHEPPARD** (1898-1963).

†**MYRL R. SCOTT,** born Elburn, Illinois, February 5, 1928; admitted to bar, 1956, California; 1963, U.S. Supreme Court. *Education:* University of California (A.B., with highest honors, 1952); Stanford University (J.D., 1955). Phi Beta Kappa. Co-Author: "The Lawyer's Basic Corporate Practice Manual," ALI-ABA, 1978, as supplemented; "Organizing Corporations In California," CEB, 1983, as supplemented; "Legal Opinions in California Real Estate Transactions," The Business Lawyer, August, 1987. *PRACTICE AREAS:* Corporate Law; Real Estate Law. *Email:* mscott@smrh.com

**FRANK SIMPSON, III** (1926-1993).

### MEMBERS OF FIRM

**CHARLES F. BARKER,** born Los Angeles, California, September 19, 1951; admitted to bar, 1976, California. *Education:* University of Southern California (A.B., 1973); University of California at Los Angeles (J.D., 1976). Order of the Coif. Author, "Employees Rights and Duties during an Internal Investigation," *Internal Corporate Investigations* (ABA 1992). *PRACTICE AREAS:* Labor and Employment Law. *Email:* cbarker@smrh.com

**ROBERT S. BEALL,** admitted to bar, 1987, California. *Education:* University of Southern California (J.D., 1987). Executive Editor of Articles, Major Tax Planning, 1986-1987. Executive Editor of Articles, Computer Law Journal, 1986-1987. (Orange County Office). *Email:* rbeall@smrh.com

**JOHN D. BERCHILD, JR.,** born Superior, Wisconsin, April 4, 1942; admitted to bar, 1972, California. *Education:* Wisconsin State University (B.S., 1965); University of Minnesota (J.D., cum laude, 1971). Member and Board of Editors, Minnesota Law Review, 1970-1971. Co-Author: Chapters on, Equipment Financing, Chattel Paper Financing and Equipment Leasing for "Asset Based Financing-A Transactional Guide," (H. Ruda, ed., 1985). Member, PEB Study Committee, UCC Article 9. *Member:* Los Angeles County (Executive Committee, Commercial Law Committee) and American (Member, Committee on Commercial Financial Services) Bar Associations; State Bar of California (Member, Uniform Commercial Code Committee); Financial Lawyers Conference; American College of Commercial Finance Lawyers. *PRACTICE AREAS:* Commercial Secured Transactions; UCC Law; Bankruptcy Law; Debtor/Creditor Law; Finance Law. *Email:* jberchild@smrh.com

**ANTHONY J. BISHOP,** born Long Beach, California, February 26, 1956; admitted to bar, 1981, California. *Education:* University of Southern California (A.B., magna cum laude, 1978; J.D., 1981). Phi Beta Kappa. Co-Author: "Organizing California Corporations," California Continuing Education of the Bar, 1983. Resident Partner in Hong Kong, 1989-1990. *Email:* abishop@smrh.com

**JOHN R. BONN,** born Newton, New Jersey, November 5, 1949; admitted to bar, 1976, California. *Education:* Princeton University (A.B., 1972); Boalt Hall School of Law, University of California (J.D., 1976). Author: *Partnership Taxation,* 2 Vols. published, Clark Boardman Callaghan, 1987. (San Diego Office). *PRACTICE AREAS:* Taxation Law; Partnership Law; Corporate Acquisitions Law. *Email:* jbonn@smrh.com

**BARBARA L. BORDEN,** born Kansas City, Missouri, June 19, 1959; admitted to bar, 1984, Arizona; 1987, California. *Education:* University of Virginia (B.A., with high distinction, 1981); Arizona State University (J.D., magna cum laude, 1984). Clerk: Honorable William C. Canby, Jr., Ninth Circuit Court of Appeals. (San Diego Office). *PRACTICE AREAS:* Corporate; Securities; Technology Licensing. *Email:* bborden@smrh.com

**DAVID M. BOSKO,** born Denver, Colorado, September 17, 1940; admitted to bar, 1965, California. *Education:* Stanford University (B.S., 1962; J.D., 1965). Member, Moot Court Board, 1965. (Orange County Office). *PRACTICE AREAS:* Corporate Law; Mergers and Acquisitions; Securities Law. *Email:* dbosko@smrh.com

**LAWRENCE M. BRAUN,** born New Jersey, December 24, 1954; admitted to bar, 1981, California. *Education:* Rutgers College (B.A., Economics/Accounting, 1977); Northwestern University (M.B.A. in Finance, 1981; J.D., 1981). *Member:* Los Angeles County (Member, Executive Committee, Business and Corporations Law Section) and American Bar Associations; State Bar of California. *PRACTICE AREAS:* Corporate Law; Mergers and Acquisitions; Venture Capital. *Email:* lbraun@smrh.com

**ARTHUR WM. BROWN, JR.,** born Denver, Colorado, March 8, 1946; admitted to bar, 1975, California. *Education:* Northwestern University (B.S., 1968); University of Southern California (M.B.A., 1972; J.D., 1975). Order of the Coif. Note and Article Editor, Southern California Law Review, 1974-1975. Member, Executive Committee, Business and Corporations Law Section, Los Angeles County Bar. *PRACTICE AREAS:* Corporate and Securities Law; Acquisitions, Divestitures and Mergers; International Business Law. *Email:* abrown@smrh.com

**JAMES R. BRUEGGEMANN,** born Long Beach, California, November 9, 1946; admitted to bar, 1975, California; registered to practice before U.S. Patent and Trademark Office. *Education:* University of California at Los Angeles (B.S., magna cum laude, 1968; M.S., 1971; J.D., 1975). *Member:* American Intellectual Property Law Association; Los Angeles Intellectual Property Law Association (Member, Board of Directors, 1986-1993; President, 1991-1992). *PRACTICE AREAS:* Patents; Trademarks; Copyrights; Unfair Competition. *Email:* jbrueggemann@smrh.com

**RICHARD W. BRUNETTE, JR.,** born Green Bay, Wisconsin, February 14, 1953; admitted to bar, 1978, California. *Education:* University of Wisconsin (B.A., 1974); Duke University (J.D., 1978). Order of the Coif. Articles Editor, Duke Law Journal, 1977-1978. *PRACTICE AREAS:* Bankruptcy Law; Commercial Law; Creditors Rights Law. *Email:* rbrunette@smrh.com

**STEVEN W. CARDOZA,** born Walnut Creek, California, October 6, 1961; admitted to bar, 1987, California. *Education:* University of California, Berkeley (J.D., 1987; M.B.A., 1987). *Member:* Orange County and American Bar Associations; Financial Lawyers Conference. (Orange County Office). *PRACTICE AREAS:* Finance and Banking Law; Commercial Law; Problem Loan Workouts. *Email:* scardoza@smrh.com

†**JAMES J. CARROLL, III,** born Los Angeles, California, September 29, 1946; admitted to bar, 1974, California. *Education:* Stanford University (A.B., 1968); Hastings College of the Law, University of California (J.D., 1974). *Member:* Los Angeles County and American Bar Associations; State Bar of California. *PRACTICE AREAS:* Business Litigation; Estate Planning Law. *Email:* jcarroll@smrh.com

**MICHAEL J. CHANGARIS,** born Yuba City, California, June 17, 1954; admitted to bar, 1979, California. *Education:* University of California, Berkeley (B.A., 1976); Hastings College of the Law, University of California (J.D., 1979); New York University (LL.M., Taxation, 1981). Attorney Advisor to U.S. Tax Court, 1981-1982. (San Diego Office). *Email:* mchangaris@smrh.com

*(This Listing Continued)*

**DENNIS CHILDS,** born Corning, New York, June 10, 1958; admitted to bar, 1982, Texas; 1987, California. *Education:* Trinity University; University of Texas (B.A., with high honors, 1979; J.D., with honors, 1982). Phi Beta Kappa. *Member:* San Diego County and American (Section of Labor and Employment Law) Bar Associations; State Bar of Texas; State Bar of California; Idaho State Bar. (San Diego Office). *PRACTICE AREAS:* Labor and Employment Law; Employment Discrimination; Wrongful Discharge; Civil Rights. *Email:* dchilds@smrh.com

**GARY A. CLARK,** born Huntington Park, California, November 26, 1948; admitted to bar, 1975, California; registered to practice before U.S. Patent and Trademark Office. *Education:* California State University at Long Beach (B.S.E., summa cum laude, 1970); Stanford University (M.S., 1971); University of California at Los Angeles (J.D., 1975). Contributing Author: "Protecting Trade Dress," John Wiley & Sons, Inc., 1992. *Member:* Association of Business Trial Lawyers (Member, Board of Governors, 1981-1983); American Intellectual Property Law Association; Los Angeles Intellectual Property Law Association (Member, Board of Directors, 1982-1984); American Arbitration Association (Member, Intellectual Property Panel). *PRACTICE AREAS:* Patents; Trademarks; Copyrights; Unfair Competition; Litigation. *Email:* gclark@smrh.com

**†JOHN D. COLLINS,** born Topeka, Kansas, May 20, 1944; admitted to bar, 1970, California. *Education:* Stanford University (A.B., 1966; J.D., 1969). Recipient, San Diego Trial Lawyers Association Outstanding Trial Lawyer Award, 1982. Author: "Multi-Employer Bargaining Units," Appropriate Units for Collective Bargaining, PLI, 1979. Instructor, Collective Bargaining, Masters Program, University of Redlands, 1980—. (San Diego Office). *PRACTICE AREAS:* Labor Employment Law; Unfair Competition Law; Civil Litigation. *Email:* jcollins@smrh.com

**JOSEPH F. COYNE, JR.,** born Springfield, Massachusetts, February 26, 1955; admitted to bar, 1980, California. *Education:* University of Notre Dame (B.B.A., magna cum laude, 1977); Stanford University (J.D., 1980). Beta Alpha Psi; Beta Gamma Sigma. Recipient, Notre Dame Scholar Award. Member, Board of Visitors, Stanford Law School. *Member:* Los Angeles County and American Bar Associations; State Bar of California. *PRACTICE AREAS:* Government Contracts Law; Antitrust Law; Commercial Litigation. *Email:* jcoyne@smrh.com

**ANDRÉ J. CRONTHALL,** admitted to bar, 1984, California. *Education:* University of Southern California (J.D., 1984). Editor, Hale Moot Court Honors Program, 1983-1984. *Member:* Los Angeles County and American Bar Associations; State Bar of California; Association of Business Trial Lawyers. *PRACTICE AREAS:* Insurance Law; Product Liability Law; Business Litigation. *Email:* acronthall@smrh.com

**JOSEPH A. DARRELL,** born Los Angeles, California, February 4, 1945; admitted to bar, 1972, California; 1981, U.S. Supreme Court. *Education:* University of Florida (B.A., with high honors, 1969); University of Michigan (J.D., cum laude, 1972). Phi Delta Phi. Contributor: "A Practitioner's Guide to the Litigation and Defense of Hazardous Substance Cases," 1983. Member, Panel of Arbitrators, American Arbitration Association. (San Francisco Office). *PRACTICE AREAS:* Environmental Law. *Email:* jdarrell@smrh.com

**PHILLIP A. DAVIS,** born Pasadena, California, September 30, 1958; admitted to bar, 1983, California; 1984, U.S. District Court, Central District of California; 1987, U.S. Court of Appeals, Ninth Circuit; 1993, U.S. District Court, Southern District of California. *Education:* Stanford University (B.A., 1980); Trinity College, Oxford, England; Hastings College of the Law, University of California (J.D., 1983). Note Writer and Editor, Hastings Constitutional Law Quarterly, 1981-1983. *PRACTICE AREAS:* Securities, Business, Commercial and Real Estate Litigation. *Email:* pdavis@smrh.com

**DEAN A. DEMETRE,** born Pasadena, California, March 6, 1955; admitted to bar, 1980, California. *Education:* University of California at Irvine (B.A., 1977); University of California at Los Angeles (J.D., 1980). Phi Beta Kappa. Member, University of California at Los Angeles Law Review, 1979-1980. *Member:* Orange County and American Bar Associations; State Bar of California. (Orange County Office). *PRACTICE AREAS:* Finance and Banking Law; Commercial Law; Problem Loan Workouts. *Email:* ddemetre@smrh.com

**POLLY TOWILL DENNIS,** born Plymouth, Connecticut; admitted to bar, 1985, California. *Education:* The University of Connecticut (B.A., magna cum laude, Phi Beta Kappa, 1981); Georgetown University Law Center (J.D., 1985). Law Clerk of Chief Judge Manuel L. Real, Central District. *PRACTICE AREAS:* Litigation; Government Contracts Law. *Email:* pdennis@smrh.com

*(This Listing Continued)*

**DOMENIC C. DRAGO,** born Redwood City, California, October 13, 1958; admitted to bar, 1984, California and U.S. District Court, Northern District of California. *Education:* University of California at Los Angeles (B.A., 1981); Hastings College of the Law, University of California (J.D., 1984). (San Diego Office). *Email:* ddrago@smrh.com

**JULIETTE M. EBERT,** admitted to bar, 1986, California. *Education:* Hastings College of the Law, University of California (J.D., 1986). Bronze Tablet; Phi Kappa Phi; Beta Gamma Sigma. Member, Constitutional Law Quarterly, 1985-1986. Extern to Honorable Justice Racanelli, California Court of Appeals, Division 1, Fall, 1985. (San Francisco Office). *PRACTICE AREAS:* Real Estate; Finance; Secured Transactions. *Email:* jebert@smrh.com

**FRANK FALZETTA,** born Detroit, Michigan, May 2, 1961; admitted to bar, 1986, California. *Education:* Dartmouth College (B.A., 1983); University of Michigan (J.D., 1986). *Member:* Los Angeles County and American Bar Associations; State Bar of California. *PRACTICE AREAS:* Litigation. *Email:* ffalzetta@smrh.com

**ROBERT B. FLAIG,** born Pasadena, California, December 15, 1941; admitted to bar, 1967, California; 1987, U.S. Supreme Court. *Education:* University of Southern California (A.B., cum laude, 1963; J.D., 1966). Chair, Los Angeles County Bar Association Litigation Section, 1985-1986. Author: "Advanced Course on Construction Claims," 1979-1980; chapter, "Owner," California Mechanics Liens, Continuing Education of the Bar, 1988. *PRACTICE AREAS:* Construction Law; Construction and Commercial Litigation. *Email:* rflaig@smrh.com

**†MERRILL R. FRANCIS,** born Iowa City, Iowa, January 28, 1932; admitted to bar, 1960, California; 1976, U.S. Supreme Court. *Education:* Pomona College (B.A., magna cum laude, 1954); Stanford University (J.D., 1959). Phi Beta Kappa; Order of the Coif. Member, Board of Governors, 1970—. President, Financial Lawyers Conference, 1972-1973. *PRACTICE AREAS:* Insolvency Law; Bankruptcy Law; Creditors Rights Law; Secured Transactions. *Email:* mfrancis@smrh.com

**GERALDINE A. FREEMAN,** born San Francisco, California, February 10, 1958; admitted to bar, 1983, California. *Education:* University of California at Berkeley (A.B., 1979); Boalt Hall School of Law, University of California (J.D., 1983). *Member:* Bar Association of San Francisco; State Bar of California; American Bar Association. (San Francisco Office). *PRACTICE AREAS:* Bankruptcy; Commercial; Real Estate Law. *Email:* gfreeman@smrh.com

**†RICHARD M. FREEMAN,** born El Paso, Texas, January 28, 1948; admitted to bar, 1974, California. *Education:* Claremont Mens College (B.A., cum laude, 1970); Duke University (J.D., with distinction, 1974). Author: "Federal and State Court Injunctions," Practicing Law Institute, 1981. Co-Author: "Creative Approaches in Employment Termination Cases," The Rutter Group, 1985; "Jury Trial Techniques In Employment Cases: Wrongful Discharge and Discrimination," Labor and Employment Law Section of the State Bar of California, 1985. (San Diego Office). *PRACTICE AREAS:* Labor Relations Law; Construction Law. *Email:* rfreeman@smrh.com

**MARSHA D. GALINSKY,** born Philadelphia, Pennsylvania, February 22, 1958; admitted to bar, 1984, California, U.S. Supreme Court, U.S. Court of Appeals, Ninth Circuit and U.S. District Court, Central, Northern, Southern and Eastern Districts of California. *Education:* Harvard University (B.A., cum laude, 1979); University of Southern California (J.D., 1984). Recipient, Federal Bar Association Judge Barry Russell Award. *PRACTICE AREAS:* Bankruptcy, Workouts and Commercial Litigation. *Email:* mgalinsky@smrh.com

**JOHN J. GIOVANNONE,** born Culver City, California, April 8, 1950; admitted to bar, 1975, California. *Education:* Princeton University (A.B., 1972); Hastings College of the Law, University of California (J.D., 1975). Attorney, Office of Chief Counsel, Division of Trading and Markets, Commodity Futures Trading Commission, 1975-1977. Arbitrator: National Association of Securities Dealers; National Futures Association. (Orange County Office). *PRACTICE AREAS:* Commodities Law; Securities Law; Life Sciences. *Email:* jgiovannone@smrh.com

**RANDOLPH B. GODSHALL,** born Phoenixville, Pennsylvania, March 10, 1952; admitted to bar, 1979, California. *Education:* Yale University (B.A., magna cum laude, 1974); University of California at Berkeley (J.D., 1979). Order of the Coif. Fellow, ACTEC; Adjunct Professor, USD Law School. (Orange County Office). *PRACTICE AREAS:* Litigation; Estate Planning; Probate Law; Trust Law. *Email:* rgodshall@smrh.com

*(This Listing Continued)*

CAA1191B

**SHEPPARD, MULLIN, RICHTER & HAMPTON LLP,** Los Angeles—Continued

**GERALD N. GORDON,** born Pittsburgh, Pennsylvania, April 4, 1934; admitted to bar, 1958, Ohio; 1961, California; 1967, U.S. Supreme Court; 1981, U.S. Claims Court. *Education:* Case Western Reserve University (B.A., 1955; LL.B., 1958). Member, Board of Editors, Western Reserve Law Review, 1957-1958. Instructor: Construction Law, Business Administration Extension, University of California at Los Angeles, 1967-1970; Legal Aspects of Management, Summer Management Program, Graduate School of Management, University of California at Los Angeles Extension, 1976-1986. *PRACTICE AREAS:* Government Contract Law; Business Litigation; Construction Litigation. *Email:* ggordon@smrh.com

†**JOSEPH G. GORMAN, JR.,** born Chicago, Illinois, September 27, 1939; admitted to bar, 1967, California. *Education:* Georgetown University and University of California at Berkeley (B.A., 1961); University of California at Los Angeles (M.B.A., 1963; J.D., 1966). Member, Board of Editors, UCLA Law Review, 1964-1966. Co-author: "Special Problems of Trust Administration for Closely Held Businesses, Real Property, and Tax Shelters," 3 UCLA—CEB Estate Planning Institute 191, 1981; "The Marital Deduction: Beyond The Basics," 35th U.S.C. Major Tax Planning, Chapter 16, 1983; "Estate Planning During Divorce and Remarriage," University of Miami 17th Institute on Estate Planning, Chapter 4, 1984. Member: Advisory Committee, University of Miami Institute on Estate Planning, 1976—; Planning Committee, U.S.C. Probate and Trust Conference, 1975—; Advisory Board, UCLA—CEB Estate Planning Institute, 1987—. Lecturer in Law, U.S.C. Law Center's Advance Professional Program, 1976-1977. *Member:* Los Angeles County (Chairman, Committee on Federal and California Death and Gift Taxation, 1974-1975; Chairman, Probate and Trust Law Section, 1980-1981) and American Bar Associations; State Bar of California (Chairman, Death and Gift Tax Committee Tax Section, 1976-1977); American College of Trust and Estate Counsel (Fellow, 1977—, and Regent, 1992—); International Academy of Estate and Trust Law (Academician). *PRACTICE AREAS:* Estate Planning Law; Taxation Law. *Email:* jgorman@smrh.com

**GORDON A. GREENBERG,** born Chicago, Illinois, July 2, 1954; admitted to bar, 1980, Illinois, U.S. District Court, Northern District of Illinois and U.S. Court of Appeals, Seventh Circuit; 1984, California and U.S. Court of Appeals, Ninth Circuit. *Education:* University of Illinois, Champaign-Urbana (B.A., 1976); Illinois Institute of Technology/Chicago Kent College of Law (J.D., with honors, 1980). Assistant United States Attorney, Chief of Financial Investigations Unit, 1983-1989. Assistant State's Attorney, 1980-1983. Special Assistant U.S. Attorney, Northern District of Illinois, 1982-1983. Recipient: Directors Award for Outstanding Performance by U.S. Department of Justice. Ninth Circuit Lawyer Representative, 1993-1996. Editor, Leader Publications Newsletter, "Money Laundering Law Report,". *Member:* Los Angeles County (Chairman, White Collar Defense Committee) and American (Member, RICO and White Collar Crime Sections; Co-Chair, Subcommittee of Money Laundering of White Collar Crime Section) Bar Associations. *PRACTICE AREAS:* Antitrust Law; Criminal Law; Business Crimes; Trial Practice. *Email:* ggreenberg@smrh.com

**ANDREW J. GUILFORD,** born Santa Monica, California, November 28, 1950; admitted to bar, 1975, California; 1979, U.S. Supreme Court. *Education:* University of California at Los Angeles (A.B., summa cum laude, 1972; J.D., 1975). Phi Beta Kappa. Member, 1973-1974 and Associate Editor, 1974-1975, UCLA Law Review. Fellow, American College of Trial Lawyers. President, Orange County Bar Association, 1991. (Orange County Office). *PRACTICE AREAS:* Business Litigation; Appellate Practice; Arbitration Law. *Email:* aguilford@smrh.com

**GUY N. HALGREN,** born San Diego, California, April 18, 1956; admitted to bar, 1984, California. *Education:* University of California at Davis (B.A., with honors, 1977); University of California at Los Angeles (J.D., 1984). Order of the Coif. Extern Law Clerk to Judge Gordon Thompson, Jr., U.S. District Court, Southern District of California, 1983. (San Diego Office). *PRACTICE AREAS:* Employment Discrimination Law; Management Labor Law; Wrongful Discharge Law. *Email:* ghalgren@smrh.com

**GARY L. HALLING,** born Los Angeles, California, September 10, 1950; admitted to bar, 1975, California; 1977, District of Columbia. *Education:* University of California at Los Angeles (B.A., cum laude, 1972); University of San Francisco (J.D., 1975). Extern, Justice Louis H. Burke, California Supreme Court, 1974. Articles Editor, University of San Francisco Law Review, 1974-1975. Law Clerk for U.S. District Judge William B. Enright, Southern District of California, 1975-1976. Trial Attorney, U.S. Department of Justice, Antitrust Division, Washington, D.C., 1976-1981. *Member:* Bar Association of San Francisco; American Bar Association (Member: Antitrust Law Section). (San Francisco Office). *PRACTICE AREAS:* Antitrust; Unfair Competition; Business Litigation. *Email:* ghalling@smrh.com

**HAROLD E. HAMERSMITH,** born Dixon, Illinois June 9, 1955; admitted to bar, 1979, California. *Education:* University of Illinois, Urbana-Champaign (A.B., cum laude, 1976); University of Michigan Law School (J.D., cum laude, 1979). Phi Beta Kappa. Lecturer: Effective Discovery in Construction Disputes (LACBA), 1993; Recent Developments in WBE, MBE, and DBE Issues (LACBA), 1993; Construction Litigation Superconference, 1987; Cambridge Institute Seminar on Architect-Engineer Liability Under California Law, 1988-1991. Author: What's Happening in the Area of Architect/Engineer Liability? (LACBA), 1996; Public Works: Contracts & Litigation (Cal. CEB), 1995; Update on Mechanics' Lien Issues (LACBA), 1995. *PRACTICE AREAS:* Business Litigation; Construction Law; Public Contract Law. *Email:* hhamersmith@smrh.com

**DOUGLAS R. HART,** born Billings, Montana, April 6, 1958; admitted to bar, 1984, California. *Education:* Montana State University (B.S., with highest honors, 1980; M.S., with highest honors, 1981); University of Nebraska (J.D., with highest honors, 1984). Order of the Coif. Managing Editor, Nebraska Law Review, 1983-1984. *PRACTICE AREAS:* Employment Law. *Email:* dhart@smrh.com

**DON T. HIBNER, JR.,** born Boone, Iowa, April 5, 1934; admitted to bar, 1963, California; 1980, District of Columbia. *Education:* Stanford University (B.A., 1955; J.D., 1962). Member, Council, ABA Antitrust Section, 1982-1985. Chair, Franchise and Private Litigation Committees. Executive Committee, Los Angeles Bar Section of Antitrust Law. *PRACTICE AREAS:* Antitrust and Trade Regulation Law; Product Distribution Law; Domestic and International Competition Law. *Email:* dhibner@smrh.com

†**JAMES BLYTHE HODGE,** born Pasadena, California, June 4, 1946; admitted to bar, 1972, California. *Education:* University of Washington (B.A., with honors, 1968); Columbia University (J.D., 1971). Harlan Fiske Stone Scholar. Articles Editor, 1969 and Member, 1969-1971, Columbia Journal of Transnational Law. *Member:* Bar Association of San Francisco; State Bar of California; American Bar Association. (San Francisco Office). *PRACTICE AREAS:* Business Law; Real Estate Law; Securities Law. *Email:* jhodge@smrh.com

†**ROBERT JOE HULL,** born Ft. Monmouth, New Jersey, December 16, 1944; admitted to bar, 1969, Texas; 1970, California; 1971, U.S. Tax Court. *Education:* University of Texas (B.A., 1966; J.D., with honors, 1969). Order of the Coif. Member, Chancellors. Reviews Editor, Texas Law Review, 1968-1969. Co-Author: "Personal Tax Planning," California Continuing Education of the Bar, 1983; "R & D Partnerships," Clark Boardman Company, Ltd., 1985; "Representing Start-Up Companies," Clark, Boardman Callaghan, 1992. Editorial Board, Journal of Multistate Taxation, 1991—. Member, Executive Committee, National Association of State Bar Tax Sections, 1981-1983. *PRACTICE AREAS:* Taxation Law; Partnership Law; Corporate Law. *Email:* rhull@smrh.com

†**JOHN D. HUSSEY,** born Los Angeles, California, October 13, 1935; admitted to bar, 1961, California. *Education:* Pomona College (B.A., 1957); University of California at Berkeley (LL.B., 1960). Member, Board of Editors, California Law Review, 1959-1960. Member, Chancery Club. *PRACTICE AREAS:* Corporate Law; Securities Regulation Law; Venture Capital Law. *Email:* jhussey@smrh.com

**BRENT R. LILJESTROM,** born Pasadena, California, March 24, 1956; admitted to bar, 1981, California. *Education:* University of California at Los Angeles (B.A., 1977; J.D., 1981). *Member:* Orange County and American Bar Associations; State Bar of California. (Orange County Office). *PRACTICE AREAS:* Real Estate Law; Real Estate Finance Law; Tax Exempt Bond Financing. *Email:* bliljestrom@smrh.com

**JAMES A. LONERGAN,** born Loma Linda, California, May 18, 1953; admitted to bar, 1980, California. *Education:* Vassar College and University of California at Irvine (B.A., summa cum laude, 1977); University of Southern California (J.D., 1980). Member, Southern California Law Review, 1978-1980. *Member:* Los Angeles County Bar Association; State Bar of California. *PRACTICE AREAS:* Real Estate Development Law; Finance Law; Landlord and Tenant Law. *Email:* jlonergan@smrh.com

†**GREGORY A. LONG,** born San Francisco, California, August 28, 1948; admitted to bar, 1973, California; 1976, U.S. Court of Appeals, Ninth Circuit; 1977, U.S. Supreme Court; 1984, U.S. Court of Appeals for the Federal Circuit. *Education:* Claremont Men's College (B.A., magna cum laude, 1970); Harvard University (J.D., cum laude, 1973). Member, House

*(This Listing Continued)*

of Delegates, 1983-1989 and Executive Counsel, Litigation Section, 1981-1983, American Bar Association. Trustee, 1979-1982, Executive Counsel, Trial Lawyers Section, 1984-1988 and Chair, Amicus Briefs Committee, 1989-1992, Los Angeles County Bar Association. *PRACTICE AREAS:* Civil Trial and Appellate Practice. *Email:* glong@smrh.com

**†RICHARD L. LOTTS,** born Van Nuys, California, March 30, 1941; admitted to bar, 1967, California. *Education:* University of California at Santa Barbara (B.A., 1963); University of Michigan (J.D., 1966). Order of the Coif. Assistant Editor, Michigan Law Review, 1965-1966. *Member:* Los Angeles County and American (Member, Labor Law Section) Bar Associations; State Bar of California. *PRACTICE AREAS:* Labor Law; Employment Law. *Email:* rlotts@smrh.com

**JAMES M. LOWY,** born New York, N.Y., February 23, 1951; admitted to bar, 1977, California. *Education:* Wharton School, University of Pennsylvania (B.S., 1973); University of California at Los Angeles (M.B.A., 1977; J.D., 1977). Beta Gamma Sigma. Adjunct Lecturer, Partnership Taxation, Golden Gate University Graduate School of Taxation, 1992—. Co-Author: "Real Property Tax Shelter Syndications," Real Property Tax Planning 1984, California Continuing Education of the Bar, 1984. (San Francisco Office). *Email:* jlowy@smrh.com

**CHARLES H. MACNAB, JR.,** born Pasadena, California, November 6, 1946; admitted to bar, 1972, California. *Education:* University of California at Los Angeles (B.A., 1968); University of Southern California (J.D., 1971). Order of the Coif. Comment Editor, Southern California Law Review, 1970-1971. *Member:* Bar Association of San Francisco; Los Angeles County and American Bar Associations; State Bar of California. (San Francisco Office). *PRACTICE AREAS:* Commercial Law; Real Estate Law; Corporate Trust Law; Municipal and Public Debt Litigation. *Email:* cmacnab@smrh.com

**†DAVID A. MADDUX,** born Artesia, California, January 27, 1933; admitted to bar, 1960, California. *Education:* University of Southern California (B.S., 1954; LL.B., 1959). Order of the Coif. Managing Editor, Southern California Law Review, 1958-1959. *PRACTICE AREAS:* Labor and Employment Law. *Email:* dmaddux@smrh.com

**PAUL S. MALINGAGIO,** born Los Angeles, California, February 19, 1952; admitted to bar, 1979, California. *Education:* University of California at Los Angeles (B.A., 1975); Loyola Law School (J.D., cum laude, 1979). Member, Loyola University of Los Angeles Law Review, 1978-1979. Member, 1977-1979 and Treasurer, 1978-1979, St. Thomas More Law Honor Society. *PRACTICE AREAS:* Litigation; Civil Trials and Arbitrations; Creditors' Rights and Commercial Law. *Email:* pmalingagio@smrh.com

**ALAN H. MARTIN,** admitted to bar, 1987, California. *Education:* University of Virginia (B.A., 1984; J.D., 1987). *Member:* Orange County (Member, Commercial Law and Bankruptcy Section) and American Bar Associations; Orange County Bankruptcy Forum (Member, Board of Directors, 1995—); American Bankruptcy Institute. (Orange County Office). *PRACTICE AREAS:* Bankruptcy Law; Commercial Litigation; Creditors Rights and Workouts. *Email:* amartin@smrh.com

**DAVID J. MCCARTY,** admitted to bar, 1977, California. *Education:* Claremont Men's College (B.A., summa cum laude, 1974); Harvard University (J.D., cum laude, 1977). Member, Executive Committee, Former Chair, Commercial Law and Bankruptcy Section, Los Angeles County Bar Association. *PRACTICE AREAS:* Bankruptcy Law; Loan Workouts. *Email:* dmccarty@smrh.com

**CHARLES E. MCCORMICK,** born Dearborn, Michigan, October 6, 1939; admitted to bar, 1969, California. *Education:* University of Michigan (B.A., 1961; J.D., magna cum laude, 1968); University of Oxford (Dipl.L., 1969). Order of the Coif. Article Editor, Michigan Law Review, 1967-1968. Fulbright Scholar, 1968-1969. *PRACTICE AREAS:* Banking Law; Corporate Financing Law; Business Acquisitions Law. *Email:* cmccormick@smrh.com

**RYAN D. MCCORTNEY,** admitted to bar, 1987, California. *Education:* Occidental College (B.A., magna cum laude, 1984); University of Southern California (J.D., 1987). Phi Beta Kappa. Labor and Employment Section, Los Angeles County Bar Association. *Member:* American Bar Association (Labor and Employment and Litigation Sections). *PRACTICE AREAS:* Labor and Employment Law. *Email:* rmccortney@smrh.com

**M. ELIZABETH MCDANIEL,** admitted to bar, 1984, California. *Education:* Vanderbilt University (B.A., 1966); Hastings College of the Law, University of California (J.D., 1984). Phi Alpha Delta. Member, 1982-1984 and Executive Research Editor, 1983-1984, Hastings International and Comparative Law Review. Law Clerk, Associate Justice Malcolm M.

*(This Listing Continued)*

Lucas, California Supreme Court, 1985-1986. *Email:* mmcdaniel@smrh.com

**JAMES F. MCSHANE,** born Pittsburgh, Pennsylvania, December 10, 1954; admitted to bar, 1986, California. *Education:* Cornell University (J.D., 1985). *Email:* jmcshane@smrh.com

**JAMES J. MITTERMILLER,** born Washington, D.C., April 13, 1953; admitted to bar, 1978, California. *Education:* Claremont Men's College (B.A., magna cum laude, 1975); Boalt Hall School of Law, University of California (J.D., 1978); University of Heidelberg, Germany. Associate Editor, Industrial Relations Law Journal, 1977-1978. Author: "Preferential Treatment Remedies in Employment Discrimination Cases: An Analysis of Institutional Limitations," 3 Indus. Rel. L.J. 387 (1979). (San Diego Office). *PRACTICE AREAS:* Business and Finance Litigation; Class Actions; Construction Litigation; Intellectual Property. *Email:* jmittermiller@smrh.com

**CHRISTOPHER B. NEILS,** born Evansville, Indiana, September 5, 1944; admitted to bar, 1969, Washington and U.S. District Court, Western District of Washington; 1972, California; 1974, U.S. District Court, Southern District of California. *Education:* University of Washington (B.A., with honors, 1966); Harvard University (J.D., 1969). (San Diego Office). *PRACTICE AREAS:* Real Estate Development Law; Finance Law; Land Use Law; Corporate Law; Partnership Law; Business Transactions. *Email:* cneils@smrh.com

**MARK L. NELSON,** born Columbus, Ohio, September 10, 1954; admitted to bar, 1979, California. *Education:* California State College, Stanislaus (B.A., 1976); University of California at Davis (J.D., 1979). *Member:* Los Angeles County and American Bar Associations; State Bar of California. *PRACTICE AREAS:* Real Estate Development Law; Finance Law. *Email:* mnelson@smrh.com

**JON W. NEWBY,** born Los Angeles, California, March 20, 1961; admitted to bar, 1986, California. *Education:* University of California at Los Angeles (B.A., summa cum laude, 1983); Harvard University (J.D., cum laude, 1986). Phi Beta Kappa. *Member:* Los Angeles County and American Bar Associations; State Bar of California. *PRACTICE AREAS:* Corporate Law; Securities Law; Mergers and Acquisitions. *Email:* jnewby@smrh.com

**†WESLEY L NUTTEN, III** (1929-1993).

**KATHYLEEN A. O'BRIEN,** born Portsmouth, New Hampshire, December 31, 1952; admitted to bar, 1978, Massachusetts, 1979, New York; 1980, California. *Education:* Emmanuel College (B.A., magna cum laude, 1972); Georgetown University (J.D., with honors, 1978). Kappa Gamma Pi National Honor Society. *PRACTICE AREAS:* Complex Business Counseling and Litigation; Intellectual Property; False Advertising; Unfair Trade Practices; Antitrust Law. *Email:* kobrien@smrh.com

**JOEL R. OHLGREN,** born Minneapolis, Minnesota, July 21, 1942; admitted to bar, 1969, California. *Education:* University of California at Los Angeles (B.A., 1965; J.D., 1968). Order of the Coif. Member, University of California at Los Angeles Law Review, 1967-1968. Fellow, American College of Bankruptcy. *Member:* Los Angeles County (Past Chair, Commercial Law and Bankruptcy Section) and American Bar Associations; State Bar of California. *PRACTICE AREAS:* Bankruptcy Law; Commercial Law; Creditors Rights Law. *Email:* johlgren@smrh.com

**MARK T. OKUMA,** born Chicago, Illinois, January 18, 1956; admitted to bar, 1984, California. *Education:* University of Illinois (B.S., 1977); Northwestern University School of Law (J.D., 1984). *Member:* Los Angeles County Bar Association; State Bar of California; Japan America Society; Asian Business League; The Asia Society; Pension Real Estate Association. *PRACTICE AREAS:* Real Estate; Finance. *Email:* mokuma@smrh.com

**†PRENTICE L. O'LEARY,** born Los Angeles, California, May 6, 1942; admitted to bar, 1969, California. *Education:* University of California, Los Angeles (B.A., 1965; J.D., 1968). Order of the Coif. *Member:* Los Angeles County (Chairman, Bankruptcy Committee, Commercial Law and Bankruptcy Section, 1983-1984; Vice Chair, Commercial Law and Bankruptcy Section, 1984-1985; Chair, Commercial Law and Bankruptcy Section, 1985-1986) and American (Member, Business Bankruptcy Committee) Bar Associations; State Bar of California; Financial Lawyers Conference; Legal Aid Foundation of Los Angeles (Member, Board of Directors, 1987-1994); Los Angeles Bankruptcy Forum (Member, Board of Directors, 1988-1990). *PRACTICE AREAS:* Commercial Law; Creditors' Rights Law; Insolvency Law; Bankruptcy Law. *Email:* poleary@smrh.com

**STEPHEN J. O'NEIL,** born Chicago, Illinois, December 9, 1960; admitted to bar, 1986, California. *Education:* University of Notre Dame (B.A., 1983); University of California, Los Angeles (J.D., 1986). *Member:*

*(This Listing Continued)*

## SHEPPARD, MULLIN, RICHTER & HAMPTON LLP, Los Angeles—Continued

Los Angeles County and American Bar Associations; State Bar of California. *PRACTICE AREAS:* Litigation. *Email:* soneil@smrh.com

**T. WILLIAM OPDYKE,** born Greeley, Colorado, August 26, 1948; admitted to bar, 1974, California. *Education:* University of Colorado (B.S., magna cum laude, 1970); University of Michigan (J.D., magna cum laude, 1974). Panelist, "The Problems of Indenture Trustees and Bondholders - Defaulted Bonds, High Yield Issues and Bankruptcy," Practising Law Institute, San Francisco, California, 1990-1994. Co-Author: Chapter 4: "Offering, Selling and Issuing Securities," *Organizing Corporations in California,* Second Edition, California Continuing Education of the Bar. Certified Public Accountant. *PRACTICE AREAS:* Corporate Trust Law; Public Finance Law; Corporate Securities Law; Mergers and Acquisitions. *Email:* topdyke@smrh.com

**JOHN R. PENNINGTON,** born Eugene, Oregon, January 26, 1952; admitted to bar, 1977, California. *Education:* University of Oregon (B.S., 1974); University of California at Los Angeles (J.D., 1977). Beta Gamma Sigma. *Member:* Los Angeles County and American (Member, Trial Practice Committee) Bar Associations; State Bar of California (Lecturer, Continuing Education of the Bar, 1981—); Association of Business Trial Lawyers (Board of Governors). *PRACTICE AREAS:* Business Litigation. *Email:* jpennington@smrh.com

**JOSEPH E. PETRILLO,** born Tuckahoe, New York, October 15, 1939; admitted to bar, 1965, New York; 1975, California. *Education:* Fordham University (B.S., 1962; J.D., 1965). Adjunct Professor of Law, University of San Francisco, 1989. Chief Counsel, California Coastal Commission, 1973-1975. Consultant, Land Use Management Committee, California State Senate, 1976-1977. Executive Officer, State Coastal Conservancy, 1977-1985. *Member:* State Bar of California; American Bar Association. (San Francisco Office). *Email:* jpetrillo@smrh.com

**SARA PFROMMER,** born Santa Monica, California, August 5, 1953; admitted to bar, 1978, California; 1979, Illinois; 1980, U.S. District Court, Northern District of Illinois; 1983, U.S. District Court, Southern District of California; 1985, U.S. District Court, Central District of California; 1988, U.S. District Court, Northern District of California. *Education:* University of California at Los Angeles (B.A., magna cum laude, 1974; J.D., 1978). Phi Beta Kappa. Member, UCLA Law Review, 1977-1978. *PRACTICE AREAS:* Bankruptcy Law; Creditors' Rights Law; Financial Institutions Litigation. *Email:* spfrommer@smrh.com

**ROBERT H. PHILIBOSIAN,** born San Diego, California, September 29, 1940; admitted to bar, 1968, California; 1980, U.S. Supreme Court. *Education:* Stanford University (A.B., 1962); Southwestern University (J.D., 1967). Former District Attorney, Los Angeles County. Former Chief Deputy Attorney General, California. Commissioner, California State World Trade Commission. *PRACTICE AREAS:* Government; Administrative Law. *Email:* rphilibosian@smrh.com

**FRED R. PUGLISI,** born Duluth, Minnesota, January 16, 1960; admitted to bar, 1985, California. *Education:* University of Minnesota, Minneapolis (J.D., magna cum laude, Order of the Coif, 1985). *PRACTICE AREAS:* Litigation. *Email:* fpuglisi@smrh.com

**KENT R. RAYGOR,** born Minneapolis, Minnesota, November 6, 1952; admitted to bar, 1984, California; 1985, U.S. District Court, Central District of California; 1989, U.S. Court of Appeals, Ninth Circuit; 1993, U.S. Court of Appeals, Federal Circuit. *Education:* University of Minnesota (B.A., summa cum laude, 1976; J.D., cum laude, 1984). *PRACTICE AREAS:* Intellectual Properties Law; Unfair Competition Law; Computer Law. *Email:* kraygor@smrh.com

**NANCY BALDWIN REIMANN,** born Springfield, Massachusetts, February 4, 1958; admitted to bar, 1983, California, U.S. District Court, Central District of California and U.S. Court of Appeals, Ninth Circuit. *Education:* University of Santa Clara (B.S.C., magna cum laude, 1980); University of California at Los Angeles (J.D., 1983). Beta Gamma Sigma. *PRACTICE AREAS:* Banking and Finance Law; Secured Transactions Law; Estate Planning Law. *Email:* nreiman@smrh.com

**†PAUL M. REITLER,** born Vienna, Austria, October 3, 1936; admitted to bar, 1964, California, U.S. District Court, Central District of California and U.S. Court of Appeals, Ninth Circuit. *Education:* Stanford University (A.B., 1958); Harvard University (LL.B., 1963). Phi Beta Kappa. *PRACTICE AREAS:* Business Litigation. *Email:* preitler@smrh.com

*(This Listing Continued)*

**MARK RIERA,** born Covina, California, August 20, 1957; admitted to bar, 1985, California and U.S. District Court, Central District of California; 1986, U.S. Court of Appeals, Ninth Circuit; 1989, U.S. Supreme Court. *Education:* Pomona College (B.A., with honors, 1979); Cornell University (1979-1981); Stanford Law School (J.D., 1984). *PRACTICE AREAS:* Antitrust and Trade Regulation; Condemnation Law. *Email:* mriera@smrh.com

**SCOTT F. ROYBAL,** born Laguna Beach, California, August 10, 1959; admitted to bar, 1987, California; 1991, U.S. Court of Federal Claims. *Education:* University of Utah (B.A., 1983); Columbia University (J.D., 1986). Phi Beta Kappa. *Member:* Los Angeles County and American Bar Associations; The State Bar of California. *PRACTICE AREAS:* Litigation; Government Contracts Law. *Email:* sroybal@smrh.com

**JACK H. RUBENS,** born New Orleans, Louisiana, November 18, 1957; admitted to bar, 1982, California. *Education:* University of California at Los Angeles (B.A., magna cum laude, 1979; J.D., 1982). Distinguished Advocate, Moot Court Honors Program. Co-Author: "A Preservationist's Guide to the California Environmental Quality Act". *PRACTICE AREAS:* Land Use Law; Real Estate Law; Secured Transactions. *Email:* jrubens@smrh.com

**JOHN F. RUNKEL, JR.,** born Redlands, California, April 27, 1955; admitted to bar, 1981, California and U.S. District Court, Central District of California; 1987, U.S. District Court, Northern District of California; 1992, U.S. District Court, Eastern District of California and U.S. Court of Appeals, Ninth Circuit; 1993, U.S. Court of Appeals, Seventh and Eight Circuits; 1994, U.S. District Court, District of Arizona. *Education:* University of California, Los Angeles (B.A., 1978; J.D., 1981). (San Francisco Office). *PRACTICE AREAS:* Business; Franchise; Intellectual Property Litigation. *Email:* jrunkel@smrh.com

**THEODORE A. RUSSELL,** born Los Angeles, California, August 31, 1943; admitted to bar, 1970, California, U.S. District Court, Northern, Eastern, Central and Southern Districts of California and U.S. Court of Appeals, Ninth Circuit. *Education:* University of California at Berkeley (A.B., 1965); Boalt Hall School of Law, University of California (J.D., 1969). *PRACTICE AREAS:* Business Litigation. *Email:* trussell@smrh.com

**D. RONALD RYLAND,** born Ashland, Ohio, March 22, 1945; admitted to bar, 1971, California. *Education:* College of Wooster (B.A., 1967); Columbia University (J.D., 1970). Editor and Business Manager, Columbia Law Review, 1969-1970. Associate-in-Law, University of California at Berkeley, 1970-1971. Judicial Arbitrator, San Francisco Superior Court, 1981—. (San Francisco Office). *PRACTICE AREAS:* Commercial Law; Business Litigation; Bankruptcy Law; Consumer Credit Law. *Email:* dryland@smrh.com

**JAMES L. SANDERS,** born Seattle, Washington, March 5, 1948; admitted to bar, 1974, Illinois and U.S. District Court, Northern District of Illinois; 1986, California and U.S. District Court, Central District of California. *Education:* Drake University (B.S., Finance, 1970); University of Tulsa (J.D., 1973). Attorney, Chicago Regional Office, U.S. Securities and Exchange Commission, 1974-1980. Assistant U.S. Attorney, Chicago, Illinois, 1980-1985. Assistant U.S. Attorney, Los Angeles, California, 1985-1989. Regional Administrator, Los Angeles Regional Office, U.S. Securities and Exchange Commission, 1989-1991. *PRACTICE AREAS:* Criminal Law; Securities Regulation Law and Litigation; Criminal Trial Practice. *Email:* jsanders@smrh.com

**WILLIAM M. SCOTT IV,** born Greensburg, Pennsylvania, April 20, 1960; admitted to bar, 1985, Massachusetts; 1986, California. *Education:* Dartmouth College (A.B., 1982); Albany Law School of Union University (J.D., 1985); Boston University (LL.M., Banking Law, 1986). *PRACTICE AREAS:* Commercial Law and Banking Law. *Email:* wscott@smrh.com

**†PIERCE T. SELWOOD,** born Evanston, Illinois, July 31, 1939; admitted to bar, 1965, California. *Education:* Princeton University (A.B., 1961); Harvard University (LL.B., 1964). *Member:* Los Angeles County and American Bar Associations; State Bar of California (Member, Board of Governors, Association of Business Trial Lawyers, 1977-1979). *PRACTICE AREAS:* Litigation; Class Actions; RICO. *Email:* pselwood@smrh.com

**†THOMAS R. SHEPPARD,** born Pasadena, California, August 8, 1934; admitted to bar, 1962, California. *Education:* Stanford University (A.B., 1956); Harvard University (LL.B., 1961). *Member:* Los Angeles County and American Bar Associations; State Bar of California; American Law Institute; American College of Real Estate Lawyers. *PRACTICE AREAS:* Real Estate Law; Taxation Law. *Email:* tsheppard@smrh.com

*(This Listing Continued)*

**RANDAL B. SHORT,** born Kansas City, Missouri, November 24, 1945; admitted to bar, 1972, California. *Education:* University of Missouri (A.B., 1967); Stanford University (J.D., 1971). Phi Beta Kappa. President, Stanford Moot Court Board, 1970-1971. *Member:* Bar Association of San Francisco; American Bar Association (Business Law Section). (San Francisco Office). *Email:* rshort@smrh.com

**RICHARD J. SIMMONS,** born Brockton, Massachusetts, November 26, 1951; admitted to bar, 1976, California. *Education:* University of Massachusetts (B.A., summa cum laude, 1973) Phi Kappa Phi; Commonwealth Scholar; University of California, Boalt Hall School of Law (J.D., 1976). Reviews Editor, 1974-1975 and Editor-in-Chief, 1975-1976, Industrial Relations Law Journal. Author: *Wrongful Discharge and Employment Practices Manual,* 1989 and 1994 editions. *Employee Handbook and Personnel Policies Manual,* 1994, 1992, 1987 and 1983 editions; *Wage and Hour Manual for California Employers,* 1994, 1991, 1989, 1988, 1986 and 1982 editions; *Employment Discrimination and EEO Practice Manual for California Employers,* 1996, 1991, 1985 and 1982 editions; *Employer's Guide to the Americans with Disabilities Act,* 1992, 1991 and 1990 editions. *Member:* Los Angeles County (Member, Sections on: Tax; Labor) and American (Member, Sections on: Labor and Employment Law; Taxation) Bar Associations; The State Bar of California; Western Pension and Benefits Conference; California Society for Health Care Attorneys; The American Society for Health Care Attorneys. *Email:* rsimmons@smrh.com

†**JOHN R. SIMON,** born Los Angeles, California, September 16, 1939; admitted to bar, 1965, California. *Education:* University of Michigan and University of California at Berkeley (B.S., 1961); Boalt Hall School of Law, University of California (LL.B., 1964). Phi Beta Kappa; Beta Gamma Sigma; Order of the Coif. (Orange County Office). *PRACTICE AREAS:* Real Property Law; Partnership Law; Real Estate Development Law. *Email:* jsimon@smrh.com

**JAMES J. SLABY, JR.,** born Aberdeen, South Dakota, July 3, 1940; admitted to bar, 1968, California. *Education:* University of South Dakota (B.S., 1962); University of Minnesota (J.D., 1967). Member, Board of Directors, Legal Aid Foundation of Los Angeles, 1981-1985. *Member:* Los Angeles County Bar Association (Member, Executive Committee, Business and Corporations Law Section, 1987-1990; 1992-1995); State Bar of California. *PRACTICE AREAS:* Corporate Law; Securities Law; Mergers and Acquisitions. *Email:* jslaby@smrh.com

**MARK K. SLATER,** admitted to bar, 1987, California. *Education:* University of California at Los Angeles (J.D., 1987). Phi Beta Kappa. (San Francisco Office). *Email:* mslater@smrh.com

**ANN KANE SMITH,** born New York, N.Y., April 1, 1945; admitted to bar, 1976, California; 1977, U.S. District Court, Central District of California; 1980, U.S. Supreme Court; 1986, U.S. Court of Appeals, Tenth Circuit; 1988, U.S. Court of Appeals, Ninth Circuit. *Education:* Manhattanville College (B.A., 1967); Southwestern University (J.D., cum laude, 1976). Moot Court. Phillip C. Jessup International Law Competition, Pacific Region, Best Oralist 1975. Member, Southwestern University Law Review, 1974, 1975. *PRACTICE AREAS:* Labor/Employment; Litigation. *Email:* asmith@smrh.com

**DIANNE BAQUET SMITH,** born New Orleans, Louisiana, May 15, 1955; admitted to bar, 1980, California. *Education:* University of California Boalt Hall School of Law (J.D., 1980). Judge Pro Term, Los Angeles Municipal Court, 1988—. *Member:* Women Lawyers of California, 1982-1987; Black Women Lawyers, Northern California, 1980-1982. *Member:* Los Angeles Bar Association. *Email:* dsmith@smrh.com

**MARTIN J. SMITH,** born Beverly Hills, California, October 29, 1956; admitted to bar, 1981, California. *Education:* University of Southern California (A.B., summa cum laude, 1978); University of California at Los Angeles (J.D., 1981); New York University (LL.M., Tax, 1983). Phi Beta Kappa; Phi Kappa Phi. Moot Court Honors Program. Staff Member, UCLA Law Review, 1980-1981. Member, Executive Committee, Taxation Section, Los Angeles County Bar Association. *Member:* American Bar Association (Member, Taxation Section). (Certified Specialist, Taxation Law, The State Bar of California Board of Legal Specialization). *PRACTICE AREAS:* Employee Benefits; ERISA. *Email:* msmith@smrh.com

**RICHARD L. SOMMERS,** born Waukegan, Illinois, October 30, 1952; admitted to bar, 1977, California. *Education:* University of Illinois (B.S., 1974); University of Michigan (J.D., 1977). Order of the Coif. Note Editor, Michigan Law Review, 1976-1977. *Member:* Los Angeles County and American Bar Associations; State Bar of California. *PRACTICE AREAS:* Commercial Law; Banking Law; Real Estate Finance Law. *Email:* rsommers@smrh.com

*(This Listing Continued)*

**MARK A. SPITZER,** admitted to bar, 1986, California. *Education:* Duke University (J.D., with honors, 1986). *Email:* mspitzer@smrh.com

**RICHARD L. STONE,** born Hammond, Indiana, June 1, 1959; admitted to bar, 1983, California. *Education:* University of California at Los Angeles (B.A., cum laude, 1980); Loyola Law School (J.D., cum laude, 1983). Phi Alpha Delta. Member, St. Thomas More Honor Society. *PRACTICE AREAS:* Commercial Law; Investment Fraud Law; Litigation. *Email:* rstone@smrh.com

**JOAN H. STORY,** born Parsons, Kansas, February 7, 1944; admitted to bar, 1977, California. *Education:* Occidental College (A.B., 1965); University of California at Los Angeles (M.A., 1967); University of California at Davis (J.D., 1977). Phi Kappa Phi. Volume Editor, University of California at Davis Law Review, 1976-1977. *Member:* Practicing Law Institute (Real Estate Advisory Board). (San Francisco Office). *Email:* jstory@smrh.com

**R. MARSHALL TANNER,** born Santa Monica, California, December 4, 1946; admitted to bar, 1977, California. *Education:* Brigham Young University (B.A., magna cum laude, 1970); University of California at Los Angeles (J.D., 1977). Phi Kappa Phi. Comment Editor, UCLA Law Review, 1976-1977. *Member:* Orange County Bar Association; State Bar of California (Real Estate and Business Law Section). [Lt., USNR, 1970-1974]. (Orange County Office). *Email:* rmtanner@smrh.com

†**FINLEY L. TAYLOR,** born Florence, Alabama, August 31, 1945; admitted to bar, 1971, California. *Education:* University of California at Santa Barbara (B.A., 1967); Vanderbilt University (J.D., 1970). Order of the Coif. Articles Editor, Vanderbilt Law Review, 1969-1970. *Member:* Orange County and American Bar Associations; State Bar of California. (Orange County Office). *PRACTICE AREAS:* Business Litigation. *Email:* ftaylor@smrh.com

**LAURA S. TAYLOR,** born Winston Salem, North Carolina, July 9, 1958; admitted to bar, 1983, California. *Education:* University of North Carolina at Chapel Hill (B.A., with highest honors, 1979); Duke University (J.D., with honors, 1983). Phi Beta Kappa. Author: Action Guide: Litigating in the Shadow of Bankruptcy: CEB 1993. (San Diego Office). *PRACTICE AREAS:* Bankruptcy; Special Education Law. *Email:* ltaylor@smrh.com

†**STEPHEN C. TAYLOR,** born Chicago, Illinois, May 20, 1932; admitted to bar, 1961, California. *Education:* Princeton University (A.B., 1954); University of California at Los Angeles (LL.B., 1960). Member, Board of Editors, UCLA Law Review, 1959-1960. *Member:* Los Angeles County and American Bar Associations; State Bar of California; Association of Business Trial Lawyers. *PRACTICE AREAS:* Business Law; Environmental Law. *Email:* staylor@smrh.com

**TIMOTHY B. TAYLOR,** born Burbank, California, February 6, 1959; admitted to bar, 1984, California, U.S. District Court, Central District of California and U.S. Court of Appeals, Ninth Circuit; 1985, U.S. District Court, Southern District of California; 1989, U.S. Supreme Court; 1990, District of Columbia. *Education:* University of Southern California (A.B., cum laude, 1981); Georgetown University (J.D., magna cum laude, 1984). (San Diego Office). *PRACTICE AREAS:* Litigation; Environmental Law; Securities. *Email:* ttaylor@smrh.com

**ROBERT A. THOMPSON,** born Chicago, Illinois, February 11, 1943; admitted to bar, 1970, California. *Education:* Stanford University (B.A., 1965); University of Vienna, Austria; Harvard Law School (J.D., 1969). Phi Beta Kappa; Lambda Alpha. Fulbright Scholar. Author: "Real Estate Opinion Letter Practice," Wiley Law Publications, 1993; "Opinions in Real Estate Transactions," Drafting Legal Opinion Letters, Wiley Law Publications, 1988. Co-Author: "Negotiating Loan Transactions," Negotiating Real Estate Transactions, Wiley Law Publications, 1988. ABA, Real Property, Probate and Trust Section, Co-Chair, Legal Opinion Committee. State Bar of California, Chair, Committee on the Environment, 1977-1978; Executive Committee, Real Property Section, 1980-1982. Member, Board of Directors: San Francisco Legal Aid Society, 1973—; Youth Law Center, 1973—. Member, 1973— and Member, Executive Committee, 1986-1990, San Francisco Lawyers Committee for Urban Affairs. (San Francisco Office). *Email:* rthompson@smrh.com

†**CARLTON A. VARNER,** born Creston, Iowa, July 14, 1947; admitted to bar, 1972, California. *Education:* University of Iowa (B.A., 1969); University of Minnesota (J.D., magna cum laude, 1972). Order of the Coif. Member, 1970-1971 and Editor, 1971-1972, Minnesota Law Review. Chair, Antitrust Section, Los Angeles County Bar Association, 1993-1994. Contributor: "Antitrust Law Developments," (Second) 1984; "Antitrust Ad-

*(This Listing Continued)*

CAA1195B

**SHEPPARD, MULLIN, RICHTER & HAMPTON LLP,** Los Angeles—*Continued*

viser," Third Edition, 1985. *PRACTICE AREAS:* Business Litigation; Antitrust Law. *Email:* cvarner@smrh.com

**VICTOR A. VILAPLANA,** born San Diego, California, December 21, 1946; admitted to bar, 1973, California; 1974, U.S. District Court, Southern District of California. *Education:* San Diego State University (B.A., with honors, 1968); George Washington University (M.A., with highest honors, 1970); Stanford University (J.D., 1973). Managing Editor, Stanford Journal of International Studies, 1972. (San Diego Office). *PRACTICE AREAS:* Bankruptcy Law; International Business Transactions; Creditors Rights Law. *Email:* vvilaplana@smrh.com

**PERRY JOSEPH VISCOUNTY,** born Orange, California, September 29, 1962; admitted to bar, 1987, California; U.S. District Court, Central, Southern, Northern and Eastern Districts of California, U.S. Court of Appeals, Ninth Circuit and U.S. Supreme Court. *Education:* University of Southern California (B.S., Business Administration and Finance, 1984; J.D., 1987). (Orange County Office). *PRACTICE AREAS:* Litigation; Intellectual Property Law. *Email:* pviscounty@smrh.com

**EDWARD D. VOGEL,** born Sandusky, Ohio, April 21, 1959; admitted to bar, 1983, California, U.S. District Court, Central, Southern and Eastern Districts of California, U.S. Court of Appeals, Ninth Circuit and U.S. Supreme Court. *Education:* Pomona College; Claremont Men's College (B.A., cum laude, 1980); Boalt Hall School of Law, University of California (J.D., 1983). (San Diego Office). *PRACTICE AREAS:* Creditors' Rights Law; Litigation and Appellate Practice. *Email:* evogel@smrh.com

**L. KIRK WALLACE,** born Whittier, California, May 8, 1948; admitted to bar, 1973, California. *Education:* Stanford University (B.A., 1970); University of California at Los Angeles (J.D., 1973). Member, U.C.L.A. Law Review, 1971-1972. *Member:* Los Angeles County and American Bar Associations; State Bar of California. *PRACTICE AREAS:* Real Estate Law; Secured Transactions. *Email:* kwallace@smrh.com

†**MICHAEL J. WEAVER,** born Bakersfield, California, February 11, 1946; admitted to bar, 1973, California; 1975, U.S. Court of Appeals, Ninth Circuit; 1977, U.S. Supreme Court. *Education:* California State University (A.B., 1968); University of San Diego (J.D., magna cum laude, 1973). Law Clerk to Judge Gordon Thompson, Jr., U.S. District Court, 1973-1975. Fellow, American College of Trial Lawyers. *Email:* mweaver@smrh.com

**WILLIAM V. WHELAN,** born Palo Alto, California, June 28, 1959; admitted to bar, 1984, California and U.S. District Court, Southern and Central Districts of California. *Education:* Pomona College (B.A., 1981); University of California at Los Angeles (J.D., 1984). Member, State Bar Committee on Professional Responsibility and Conduct, 1990-1993. *Member:* San Diego County and American Bar Associations; The State Bar of California. (San Diego Office). *Email:* wwhelan@smrh.com

**ROBERT E. WILLIAMS,** born La Jolla, California, July 18, 1951; admitted to bar, 1976, California. *Education:* University of California, Santa Barbara (B.A., with highest honors, 1973); Harvard Law School (J.D., 1976). Phi Beta Kappa. *Member:* Los Angeles County Bar Association; State Bar of California; American College of Real Estate Lawyers. *PRACTICE AREAS:* Real Estate Law; Secured Transactions. *Email:* rwilliams@smrh.com

**DARRYL M. WOO,** born San Francisco, California, February 7, 1955; admitted to bar, 1981, California. *Education:* University of California at Berkeley (B.A., Biology, with honors, 1977); Georgetown University (J.D., 1981). Extern to Hon. Stanley B. Frosh, Circuit Judge, Maryland, 1979. *Member:* Bar Association of San Francisco; American Bar Association. (San Francisco Office). *PRACTICE AREAS:* Business; Securities; Antitrust; Intellectual Property Litigation. *Email:* dwoo@smrh.com

**ROY G. WUCHITECH,** born Chicago, Illinois, March 21, 1946; admitted to bar, 1972, California; 1980, District of Columbia; 1986, U.S. Supreme Court; 1988, U.S. Court of Military Appeals. *Education:* University of Chicago (B.A., 1967); University of Texas (J.D., cum laude, 1972). Staff Member, Texas Law Review, 1968. Assistant General Counsel, U.S. Department of Energy, 1986-1987. Deputy General Counsel and Acting General Counsel, U.S. Air Force, 1987-1989. *PRACTICE AREAS:* Environmental Law. *Email:* rwuchitech@smrh.com

**WILLIAM R. WYATT,** born Evanston, Illinois, November 2, 1956; admitted to bar, 1982, California. *Education:* Purdue University (B.S.M.E., with distinction, 1977; M.S.M.E., 1979); Stanford University (J.D., 1982). *Member:* Bar Association of San Francisco; American Bar Association.

*(This Listing Continued)*

(San Francisco Office). *PRACTICE AREAS:* Secured Transactions; Real Estate Law. *Email:* wwyatt@smrh.com

**JOHN A. YACOVELLE,** admitted to bar, 1987, California. *Education:* Southwestern University School of Law (J.D., magna cum laude, 1987). Moot Court Honors. Member, Board of Governors, Moot Court Honors Program, 1986-1987. Member, Southwestern Law Review, 1985-1986. *Member:* Associated Builders and Contractors of San Diego. (San Diego Office). *PRACTICE AREAS:* Business Litigation; Construction Litigation. *Email:* jyacovelle@smrh.com

*SPECIAL COUNSEL*

**FREDRIC I. ALBERT,** born Philadelphia, Pennsylvania, August 1, 1961; admitted to bar, 1987, Pennsylvania; 1988, California, U.S. District Court, Central, Southern, Northern and Eastern Districts of California; U.S. Court of Appeals, Ninth Circuit; U.S. Supreme Court. *Education:* Pennsylvania State University (B.A., 1983); University of Toledo (J.D., 1987); University of Notre Dame London Law Centre, 1985. Member, The National Order of the Barristers. The U.S. Department of Justice Attorney General's Honor Law Program. *Member:* Orange County, Los Angeles County and American Bar Associations; State Bar of California (Litigation and Criminal Justice Sections). (Orange County Office). *PRACTICE AREAS:* Civil and Business Litigation; White Collar Criminal Defense. *Email:* falbert@smrh.com

**PHILIP F. ATKINS-PATTENSON** (San Francisco Office).

**THOMAS M. BROWN,** born Los Angeles, California, May 20, 1957; admitted to bar, 1985, California. *Education:* Loyola Marymount University (B.A., with honors, 1979; M.A., 1981); Loyola Law School (J.D., 1984). Editor-in-Chief, Loyola of Los Angeles International Law Journal, 1983-1984. Law Clerk to Judge Donald Gates, California Court of Appeal, 1984-1985. Law Clerk to Judge Arthur L. Alarcon, U.S. Court of Appeals, Ninth Circuit, 1986-1987. Assistant United States Attorney, Central District of California, Major Frauds Section, 1991-1995. *Member:* Los Angeles County (White Collar Defense Committee) and American (Member, White Collar Crime Section) Bar Associations; State Bar of California (Member, Criminal Justice Section). *PRACTICE AREAS:* Criminal Law and Parallel Civil Proceedings; Internal Corporate Investigations; Criminal Trial Practice. *Email:* tbrown@smrh.com

**FREDERICK V. GEISLER,** born Geneva, New York, April 15, 1952; admitted to bar, 1976, California; 1986, Washington. *Education:* Stanford University (B.A., with honors, 1973); Hastings College of Law, University of California (J.D., 1976). *Member:* Beverly Hills, Los Angeles County and American Bar Associations; State Bar of California. *Email:* fgeisler@smrh.com

**LAURENCE K. GOULD, JR.,** born Covina, California, February 16, 1946; admitted to bar, 1972, California. *Education:* Yale University (B.A., cum laude, 1967); Stanford University (J.D., 1971). Member, Stanford Moot Court Board, 1969-1971. *PRACTICE AREAS:* Administrative, Probate and Estate Planning. *Email:* lgould@smrh.com

**REBECCA V. HLEBASKO** (San Francisco Office).

**SCOTT J. LOCHNER,** born Philadelphia, Pennsylvania, 1956; admitted to bar, 1984, New York and Massachusetts; 1987, District of Columbia; 1988, California. *Education:* Lehigh University (B.A., with high honors, 1978); London School of Economics and Political Science (1976-1977); New York University (J.D., 1982). *PRACTICE AREAS:* Corporate Law, International Business Law and High Technology Law. *Email:* slochner@smrh.com

**STEVEN C. NOCK** (Orange County Office).

**ETHNA M. S. PIAZZA** (San Diego Office).

**MARIA C. PRACHER** (San Francisco Office).

**BRIAN G. PRENTICE,** born Downey, California, September 23, 1940; admitted to bar, 1966, California. *Education:* University of Southern California (A.B., 1962; LL.B., 1965). Phi Delta Phi. *Member:* Los Angeles County and American Bar Associations. *PRACTICE AREAS:* Real Estate Law; Land Use; Finance Law; Environmental Law. *Email:* bprentice@smrh.com

**DAVID A. PURSLEY** (San Francisco Office).

**PAUL F. RAFFERTY** (Orange County Office).

*SENIOR ATTORNEYS*

**DAVID M. BECKWITH** (San Diego Office).

*(This Listing Continued)*

# PROFESSIONAL BIOGRAPHIES
## CALIFORNIA—LOS ANGELES

**DONNA L. HUECKEL,** admitted to bar, 1981, California. *Education:* University of Southern California (J.D., 1981). *Email:* dhueckel@smrh.com

**HAROLD S. MARENUS,** admitted to bar, 1989, California. *Education:* University of California at Los Angeles (J.D., 1988). *PRACTICE AREAS:* Commercial Law, Creditors' Rights Law and Bankruptcy Law. *Email:* hmarenus@smrh.com

**RENÉE LOUISE ROBIN** (San Francisco Office).

**STEVEN A. ROSS,** admitted to bar, 1982, California. *Education:* Yale University (J.D., 1982). *Email:* sross@smrh.com

**BETTY J. SANTOHIGASHI** (San Diego Office).

**SHELDON M. SIEGEL** (San Francisco Office).

**ALAN VAN DERHOFF** (San Diego Office).

**KARIN A. VOGEL** (San Diego Office).

**LORETTA A. WIDER** (San Francisco Office).

### ASSOCIATES

Nancy McAniff Annick
Cindy Thomas Archer (Orange County Office)
Karin L. Backstrom (San Diego Office)
John O. Beanum
Scott A. Brutocao
James M. Burgess
Dennis A. Calderon (San Diego Office)
Justine Mary Casey (Orange County Office)
David B. Chidlaw (San Diego Office)
Gene R. Clark (Orange County Office)
Ronald S. Cohen
Araceli K. Cole
Sharli Colladay
Thomas A. Counts (San Francisco Office)
S. Ellen D'Arcangelo
Brian M. Daucher (Orange County Office)
Wendi J. Delmendo
Julie A. Dunne (San Diego Office)
Teresa F. Elconin
Phillip J. Eskenazi
Grant P. Fondo (San Francisco Office)
Linda D. Fox (San Diego Office)
Travis M. Gemoets
Robert S. Gerber (San Diego Office)
Anna E. Goodwin (San Francisco Office)
Kurt L. Gottschall
Kelly L. Hensley
Paula A. Hobson
Frank W. Iaffaldano
Kristen A. Jensen (San Francisco Office)
Beverly A. Johnson (Orange County Office)
Frank J. Johnson, Jr. (San Diego Office)
Mark D. Johnson
Sarah D. Keller
Tracey A. Kennedy
Jay T. Kinn
Greg S. Labate (Orange County Office)
James F. Lam
Bub-Joo S. Lee
Steven J. Lehrhoff
Ted C. Lindquist, III (San Francisco Office)
Michael L. Ludwig
Philip A. Magen (San Diego Office)
I. Kenneth Magid (San Diego Office)
Aaron J. Malo (Orange County Office)
Candace L. Matson
Susan S. Matsui (Orange County Office)
Susan Freeman McCortney
Leslie J. McShane
Michael Paul Mihalek (San Francisco Office)
Justine Witt Milani
Paul M. Miloknay
Michael G. Morgan
Elena Muravina
Christie M. Musser (San Francisco Office)
Thomas D. Nevins (San Francisco Office)
Patricia V. Ostiller
Richard H. Otera
Tyler M. Paetkau (San Francisco Office)
Kimberly N. Papillon
Jeffrey J. Parker
Kathleen M. Ratz
Felicia R. Reid (San Francisco Office)
James M. René
Michael J. St. Denis
Lara A. Saunders (Orange County Office)
Michael J. Shea (San Diego Office)
Michelle Sherman
Robert M. Shore
Angela Dahl Sisney (San Diego Office)
Michael D. Stewart (Orange County Office)
Robert T. Sturgeon

*(This Listing Continued)*

### ASSOCIATES (Continued)

Barry Sullivan
Turner Swan
Stanley Sze
Amy L. Tranckino (San Diego Office)
Lei K. Udell (San Diego Office)
David A. Urban
Holly O. Whatley
Tara L. Wilcox (San Diego Office)
Tawnya R. Wojciechowski (Orange County Office)
Timothy J. Yoo

†Professional Corporation

All Los Angeles Attorneys are Members of the State Bar of California and Los Angeles County Bar Associations.

---

## SHERIN AND LODGEN LLP
### 11300 WEST OLYMPIC BOULEVARD
### SUITE 700
### LOS ANGELES, CALIFORNIA 90064
Telephone: 310-914-7891
Fax: 310-552-5327
Email: lawyers@sherin.com

*Boston, Massachusetts Office:* 100 Summer Street. Telephone: 617-426-5720. Telecopier: 617-542-5186.

*General Civil Practice. Banking, Business, Computer, Construction, Creditors' Rights and Bankruptcy, Environment, Estate Planning and Probate, Labor, Litigation and Appeals in all Courts, Products Liability, Real Estate, Commercial Leasing and Lending, Securities, Taxation, Maritime Law, Trade Regulation and Antitrust Law.*

(For complete data on all personnel, see Professional Biographies at Boston, Massachusetts)

---

## SHERMAN, DAN & PORTUGAL
### A PROFESSIONAL CORPORATION
### LOS ANGELES, CALIFORNIA
(See Beverly Hills)

*Practice Limited to Personal Injury, Products Liability, Malpractice, Environment, and Aviation Law, Mass Tort Litigation.*

---

## SHERNOFF, BIDART & DARRAS
### LOS ANGELES, CALIFORNIA
(See Claremont)

*Practice Limited to Plaintiff's Insurance Bad Faith, Automobile Insurance, Fire Insurance, Commercial Liability Insurance, Homeowners Insurance, Accident and Health Insurance, Catastrophic Personal Injury, Wrongful Death, Wrongful Termination, Lender's Liability and Consumer Law Litigation.*

---

## SHERWOOD AND HARDGROVE
A Partnership including a Professional Corporation
Established in 1987
### SUITE 240, 11990 SAN VICENTE BOULEVARD
### LOS ANGELES, CALIFORNIA 90049-5004
Telephone: 310-826-2625
FAX: 310-826-6055

*Real Estate and Business Litigation. General Civil, Trial and Appellate Practice in all State and Federal Courts.*

*FIRM PROFILE:* Sherwood and Hardgrove is a 6 attorney firm with an emphasis on real estate related litigation and the negotiation and drafting of real property leases.

**DON C. SHERWOOD, (P.C.),** born Dallas, Texas, September 3, 1947; admitted to bar, 1971, Texas; 1972, California and U.S. District Court, Central District of California. *Education:* Randolph-Macon College (B.A., 1969); University of Texas (J.D., cum laude, 1971). Pi Gamma Mu; Delta Sigma Rho; Tau Kappa Alpha; Phi Kappa Phi; Phi Delta Phi; Order of the Coif. Associate Editor, Texas Law Review, 1970-1971. *Member:* Santa Monica, Los Angeles County and American Bar Associations; State Bar of Texas; State Bar of California. *PRACTICE AREAS:* Real Estate Litiga-

*(This Listing Continued)*

### SHERWOOD AND HARDGROVE, Los Angeles—Continued

tion; Business Litigation; Negotiation and Drafting of Real Property Leases.

**KENNETH M. HARDGROVE,** born Somerville, New Jersey, December 31, 1951; admitted to bar, 1979, California; 1980, U.S. District Court, Central District of California; 1984, U.S. District Court, Northern District of California and U.S. Court of Appeals, Ninth Circuit; 1985, U.S. District Court, Southern and Eastern Districts of California. *Education:* Fairleigh-Dickinson University (B.A., cum laude, 1976); Pepperdine University (J.D., 1979). Lead Articles Editor, Pepperdine Clinical Law Reporter, 1978-1979. *Member:* Santa Monica, Los Angeles County and American Bar Associations; State Bar of California; The Association of Trial Lawyers of America. *PRACTICE AREAS:* Real Estate Litigation; Business Litigation; Negotiation and Drafting of Real Property Leases.

#### ASSOCIATES

**CHARLES G. BRACKINS,** born Florala, Alabama, October 2, 1948; admitted to bar, 1973, Florida; 1987, California and U.S. District Court, Northern, Southern and Central Districts of California. *Education:* University of Florida (B.A., 1970; J.D., with honors, 1973). Order of the Coif. *Member:* Los Angeles County Bar Association; State Bar of California. *PRACTICE AREAS:* Real Estate Litigation; Business Litigation.

**TIMOTHY S. PLUM,** born Alliance, Ohio, November 11, 1959; admitted to bar, 1985, California; 1986, U.S. District Court, Central District of California and U.S. Court of Appeals, Ninth Circuit; 1991, U.S. District Court, Southern District of California. *Education:* Ventura College (A.A., 1979); University of Southern California (B.A., 1981); University of Santa Clara (J.D., 1985). Recipient: Bancroft-Witney American Jurisprudence Award; Emery Law Scholarship; Owens Law Scholarship. *Member:* Los Angeles County Bar Association; State Bar of California. *PRACTICE AREAS:* Real Estate Litigation; Business Litigation.

**CHET A. CRAMIN,** born Los Angeles, California, May 29, 1962; admitted to bar, 1986, California and U.S. District Court, Central District of California; 1987, U.S. District Court, Northern and Southern Districts of California and U.S. Court of Appeals, Ninth Circuit. *Education:* University of California at Los Angeles (B.A., 1983); University of the Pacific, McGeorge School of Law (J.D., 1986). *Member:* Los Angeles County and American Bar Associations; State Bar of California. *PRACTICE AREAS:* Real Estate Litigation; Business Litigation.

**DARLENE R. DAVID,** born Glendale, California, May 1, 1961; admitted to bar, 1986, California and U.S. District Court, Central District of California; 1987, U.S. Court of Appeals, Ninth Circuit. *Education:* University of Southern California (B.A., cum laude, 1983); Pepperdine University (J.D., cum laude, 1986). Phi Delta Phi. *Member:* Los Angeles County Bar Association; State Bar of California. *PRACTICE AREAS:* Real Estate Litigation; Business Litigation.

---

## WILLIAM H. SHIBLEY
### LOS ANGELES, CALIFORNIA
(See Long Beach)

*General Civil, Business Intellectual Property and Criminal Trial Practice with emphasis on Plaintiff Personal Injury, Criminal Defense, Maritime Injury, Longshore Compensation.*

---

## SHIOTANI & INOUYE
*11100 SANTA MONICA BOULEVARD, SUITE 1820*
### LOS ANGELES, CALIFORNIA 90025
Telephone: 310-575-3688
Telecopier: 310-575-4095

*General Business Practice. Real Estate, Corporate, Tax, Estate Planning, Probate and Oil and Gas Law.*

#### MEMBERS OF FIRM

**BARNEY B. SHIOTANI,** born Hilo, Hawaii, May 11, 1934; admitted to bar, 1969, California. *Education:* University of Hawaii (B.B.A., 1956); University of Southern California (J.D., 1968). *Member:* Beverly Hills and Los Angeles County Bar Associations; State Bar of California; California Society of Certified Public Accountants. [1st. Lt., U.S. Army Signal Corps.,

*(This Listing Continued)*

CAA1198B

1956-1958]. *PRACTICE AREAS:* Tax; Corporate; Real Estate; Oil and Gas Law.

**LAWRENCE G. INOUYE,** born Los Angeles, California, September 17, 1955; admitted to bar, 1981, California. *Education:* University of Southern California (B.S., 1978); University of Santa Clara (J.D., 1981). *Member:* Los Angeles County and American Bar Associations; State Bar of California. *PRACTICE AREAS:* Corporate Law; Real Estate; Taxation; Estate Planning.

#### ASSOCIATE

**NICOLE GRATTAN PEARSON,** born Detroit, Michigan, November 15, 1969; admitted to bar, 1995, California. *Education:* George Washington University (B.A., magna cum laude, 1992); University of Southern California (J.D., 1995). Omicron Delta Kappa. *PRACTICE AREAS:* Business Law; Probate; Estate Planning; Real Estate Law; Tax Law.

#### LEGAL SUPPORT PERSONNEL

**GABRIELA VELASQUEZ,** born Mexico City, Mexico, March 24, 1966. *Education:* San Diego State University (B.A., 1993); University of California at Los Angeles (Paralegal Certificate, 1995). Member, Los Angeles Paralegal Association. (Paralegal). *LANGUAGES:* Spanish.

REFERENCES: First Los Angeles Bank (Airport Office); Bank of California.

---

## GEORGE G. SHORT
*A PROFESSIONAL CORPORATION*
Established in 1980
*815 MORAGA DRIVE*
### LOS ANGELES, CALIFORNIA 90049
Telephone: 310-440-4299
Telecopier: 805-564-6646

Santa Barbara, California Office: 1421 State Street, Suite A. Telephone: 805-564-6644. Fax: 805-564-6646.

*Tax, Estate and Retirement Planning. Corporate, Partnership and Limited Liability Company Law. Tax Dispute Resolution. Closely-Held Business Planning. Financial Planning.*

*FIRM PROFILE: George G. Short, A Professional Corporation provides legal services to privately-held and family businesses and their owners, professional and amateur athletes, entertainment industry executives, talent and production personnel, people in transition, whether due to divorce, marriage, family death or other life-changing events, professional service providers and business executives and entrepreneurs. The firm serves as outside general counsel for many private businesses and wealthy families, responding to all of their legal needs either by providing services directly or by coordinating the services of other law firms and professional advisers with special skills. While the firm takes pride in its ability to promptly and efficiently handle legal problems from the mundane to the complex, the firm adds value in its attention to the counseling and emotional aspects of lawyering and its mission of providing clients with peace of mind and access to the increasingly complex legal system in a timely, compassionate and "user friendly" manner.*

(For Complete Biographical Data on all Personnel, see Professional Biographies at Santa Barbara)

---

## SHUMAKER & SRAGOW, LLP
*865 SOUTH FIGUEROA, SUITE 850*
### LOS ANGELES, CALIFORNIA 90017
Telephone: 213-622-4441
Fax: 213-622-1444
Email: shumaker@pmplaw.com

*General Practice, Business and Commercial Transactions, Employee Relations, Real Estate Development and Finance, Hospitality Law, Non-Profit Law, Election Law and the Law of Politics, Complex Commercial Litigation in all Courts.*

#### MEMBERS OF FIRM

**CHARLES M. SHUMAKER III,** born New York, N.Y., August 4, 1955; admitted to bar, 1982, California. *Education:* Bryn Mawr College; Tufts University (B.A., 1976); Columbia University (M.A., 1979); University of Michigan (J.D., 1982). Fellow of the Graduate School of Arts and Sciences, Columbia University. Recipient, George Rice Carpenter Fellowship Award in Art History, Columbia University. Adjunct Professor of Law, Pepperdine University School of Law, Law and the Visual Arts,

*(This Listing Continued)*

1986—. Chief Operating Officer and General Counsel, Walter Hotel and Casino Corp., 1993-1995. Parks Commissioner, Rolling Hills Estates, 1995—. Director, Tracy Austin Tennis Tournament, 1996—. Founder, Palos Verdes Peninsula Library Foundation. *Member:* Beverly Hills, Los Angeles County and American Bar Associations; State Bar of California.

**DARRY A. SRAGOW,** born New York, N.Y., May 17, 1946; admitted to bar, 1983, California, U.S. District Court, Central District of California and U.S. Court of Appeals, Ninth Circuit. *Education:* Cornell University (B.S., 1966); University of Pennsylvania (M.A., 1968); Georgetown University (J.D., cum laude, 1982). Editor, Law and Policy in International Business, 1981-1982. Co-Author with Lynn Soukup: "The Customs Courts Act of 1980," Law and Policy in International Business, Vol. 13, No. 1. Professional Staff Member, U.S. Senate Committee on Veterans' Affairs, 1973. Special Assistant to Senator Birch Bayh, 1973-1978. Assistant to the President, U.S. Railway Association, 1978-1982. Associate: Mannatt, Phelps, Rothenberg & Tunney, 1982-1984; O'Melveny & Myers, 1984-1985. Consultant to California statewide political campaigns, 1985-1990 and 1994-1996. Chief of Staff to Chairman, State Board of Equalization, 1991-1992. Deputy Insurance Commissioner, 1993. *Member:* State Bar of California. [Lt., U.S. Naval Reserve, 1969-1970]

### ASSOCIATE

**MATTHEW S. MEZA,** born Santa Monica, California, October 2, 1962; admitted to bar, 1987, California and U.S. District Court, Central District of California. *Education:* University of California at Berkeley (A.B., 1984); University of Michigan (J.D., 1987). *Member:* Los Angeles County (Member, Real Property Section) and American Bar Associations; State Bar of California (Member: Real Property and Corporate Law Sections). *PRACTICE AREAS:* Real Property Law; Corporate Law; Insurance Regulation.

### OF COUNSEL

**DAVID B. PARKER**

**WILLIAM K. MILLS**

**JAYESH PATEL**

**RINA J. PAKULA**

REPRESENTATIVE CLIENTS: The Cimarron Group; CBO Communications, LLC; Pacific Restaurant Innovations; Mr. Tony Danza; Philadelphia Bulldogs; Premiere Home Video, Inc.; Flagship Communications, Inc.; Hollywood Palladium; La Natura; Futuretronics; Vivorx, Inc.; Ring of Fire Advanced Media; Rose Works, LLC; George Elkins Property Management Co.; Palm Springs Hilton Resorts.

# LAW OFFICES OF
# CARL SHUSTERMAN

*ONE WILSHIRE BUILDING*
**624 SOUTH GRAND AVENUE, SUITE 1608**
**LOS ANGELES, CALIFORNIA 90017**
*Telephone: 213-623-4592*
*Fax: 213-623-3720*
*Email: visalaw@ix.netcom.com*
*URL: http://websites.earthlink.net/~visalaw*

Immigration and Naturalization.

FIRM PROFILE: *Specializing in immigration law, the Law Offices of Carl Shusterman offer decades of experience in the field to individual and corporate clients. The firm's attorneys have achieved positions of leadership in the American Immigration Lawyers Association and are frequently quoted as authorities on immigration law by the national media.*

**CARL SHUSTERMAN,** born Los Angeles, California, March 26, 1949; admitted to bar, 1973, California; 1977, U.S. District Court, Central District of California; 1978, U.S. Court of Appeals, Ninth Circuit; 1979, U.S. Supreme Court. *Education:* University of Edinburgh, Scotland; University of California at Los Angeles (B.A., cum laude, 1969); University of California at Los Angeles School of Law (J.D., 1973). Phi Beta Kappa. General Attorney and Trial Attorney, U.S. Immigration and Naturalization Service, 1976-1982. Editor, Immigration Law Review, Healthcare Association, 1989—. Author: "Bills Toughen Standards for Hiring Alien Workers," The National Law Journal, November 1995; "Closing the Asylum Door," California Lawyer, November 1995; "Survey and Analysis of H-1B LCA Decisions," Interpreter Releases, January 1995; "International Medical Graduates and the Foreign Residency Requirement," Journal of the American Medical Association, March 1994; "Recruiting International Talent," Los Angeles Lawyer, November 1993. Speaker: National and local conferences

*(This Listing Continued)*

of the American Immigration Lawyers Association; American Management Association; Los Angeles County Bar Association. *Member:* Los Angeles County (Member, Immigration Section; Executive Committee) and American Bar Associations; American Immigration Lawyers Association (Member, National Board of Governors). (Certified Specialist, Immigration and Nationality Law, The State Bar of California Board of Legal Specialization). *PRACTICE AREAS:* Immigration and Naturalization Law.

### ASSOCIATES

**ELAHE NAJFABADI,** born Tehran, Iran, August 16, 1958; admitted to bar, 1991, California; 1992, U.S. District Court, Central District of California. *Education:* Bombay University; University of West Los Angeles (J.D., 1991). Speaker, American Immigration Lawyers Association, Local Conference, Los Angeles County Bar Association. Volunteer Attorney: Harriet Buhai Family Law Center, 1994—; Los Angeles County Bar, Pro Bono Domestic Violence Project, 1995—. *Member:* Los Angeles County (Member, Executive Committee, Immigration Section, Immigration Legal Assistant Project), American and Mexican Bar Associations; American Immigration Lawyers Association. *LANGUAGES:* Spanish, Farsi and Hindi. *PRACTICE AREAS:* Immigration and Naturalization Law.

**CLAIRE H. KIM,** born Seattle, Washington, November 23, 1965; admitted to bar, 1993, California and U.S. District Court, Central District of California; 1996, U.S. Court of Appeals, Ninth Circuit. *Education:* University of California at Los Angeles (B.A., 1989); Northwestern School of Law at Lewis and Clark College (J.D., 1992). *Member:* Los Angeles County Bar Association; American Immigration Lawyers Association. *LANGUAGES:* Korean. *PRACTICE AREAS:* Immigration and Naturalization Law.

**ELLEN MA LEE,** born Manila, Philippines, August 16, 1948; admitted to bar, 1975, California, U.S. District Court, Central District of California; 1977, U.S. Court of Appeals, Ninth Circuit. *Education:* Occidental College (B.A., 1971); Loyola University of Los Angeles (J.D., 1974). Staff Attorney, Long Beach Legal Aid, 1974-1977. Staff Attorney and Directing Attorney, One Stop Immigration Center, 1977-1981. Seminar: "Immigrant and Nonimmigrant Waivers: Exceptions to the Rule," American Immigration Lawyers Association (AILA). *Member:* Los Angeles County Bar Association (Member, Immigration Section, Executive Committee); American Immigration Lawyers Association (Member, National Board of Governors). *LANGUAGES:* Chinese. *PRACTICE AREAS:* Immigration and Naturalization Law.

# SIDLEY & AUSTIN

*A Partnership including Professional Corporations*
*Established in 1866*
**555 WEST FIFTH STREET, 40TH FLOOR**
**LOS ANGELES, CALIFORNIA 90013-1010**
*Telephone: 213-896-6000*
*Telecopier: 213-896-6600*

*Chicago, Illinois Office:* One First National Plaza 60603. Telephone: 312-853-7000. Telecopier: 312-853-7036.
*New York, New York Office:* 875 Third Avenue 10022. Telephone: 212-906-2022. Telecopier: 212-906-2021.
*Washington, D.C. Office:* 1722 Eye Street, N.W. 20006. Telephone: 202-736-8000. Telecopier: 202-736-8711.
*Dallas, Texas Office:* 4500 Renaissance Tower, 1201 Elm Street 75270. Telephone: 214-939-4500. Telecopier: 214-939-4600.
*London, England Office:* Royal Exchange, EC3V 3LE. Telephone: 011-44-171-360-3600. Telecopier: 011-44-171-626-7937.
*Tokyo, Japan Office:* Taisho Seimei Hibiya Building, 7th Floor, 9-1, Yurakucho, 1 Chome, Chiyoda-ku, 100. Telephone: 011-81-3-3218-5900. Facsimile: 011-81-3-3218-5922.
*Singapore Office:* 36 Robinson Road, #18-01 City House, Singapore 0106. Telephone: 011-65-224-5000. Telecopier: 011-65-224-0530.

*General Practice.*

### RESIDENT PARTNERS

**AMY L. APPLEBAUM,** born New York, N.Y., March 18, 1944; admitted to bar, 1980, California. *Education:* William Smith College (B.A., magna cum laude, 1965), Phi Beta Kappa; University of California at Los Angeles (J.D., with honors, 1980). Order of the Coif. *Member:* State Bar of California (Member, Committee on Administration of Justice, 1990-1993); Women Lawyers Association of Los Angeles; Association of Business Trial Lawyers. *PRACTICE AREAS:* Litigation; Insurance Coverage Disputes. *Email:* aappleba@sidley.com

*(This Listing Continued)*

## SIDLEY & AUSTIN, Los Angeles—Continued

**PHILIP M. BATTAGLIA,** born Pasadena, California, 1935; admitted to bar, 1959, California. *Education:* University of Southern California (B.S.L., 1955; J.D., 1958). Executive Assistant to California Governor Ronald Reagan, 1967. Mayor, City of Rolling Hills, 1974-1975. *Member:* Los Angeles County Bar Association; The State Bar of California; Chancery Club of Los Angeles. Fellow, American College of Trust and Estate Counsel. *Email:* pbattalg@sidley.com

**DAVID W. BURHENN,** born Grand Rapids, Michigan, April 27, 1953; admitted to bar, 1982, California. *Education:* University of Michigan (A.B., 1975; J.D., cum laude, 1982). Executive Editor, Michigan Law Review, 1981-1982. Co-Editor, *California Environmental Law Handbook,* 2nd Edition, 1988. Co-Author: "Lender Liability," California Real Property Journal, Spring, 1988. *Member:* Los Angeles County Bar Association (First Vice-Chair, Environmental Law Section, 1994-1995). **PRACTICE AREAS:** Environmental Law. *Email:* dburhenn@sidley.com

**GARY J. COHEN,** born New York, N.Y., April 20, 1946; admitted to bar, 1975, California. *Education:* Polytechnic University-Brooklyn (B.S., 1967); University of California-Berkeley (M.S., 1969; J.D., 1974). Eta Kappa Nu; Order of the Coif. Recipient, Bartley Cavanaugh Crum Boalt Hall Scholarship (First in Class). Associate Editor, California Law Review, 1972-1974. Law Clerk to Hon. Wilfred Feinberg, U.S. Court of Appeals, Second Circuit, 1974-1975. **PRACTICE AREAS:** Business Transactions and Corporation Law. *Email:* gcohen@sidley.com

**RONALD C. COHEN,** born Santa Monica, California, November 8, 1962; admitted to bar, 1987, California. *Education:* Pomona College (B.A., magna cum laude, 1984); University of Chicago (J.D., with honors, 1987). Phi Beta Kappa; Order of the Coif. **PRACTICE AREAS:** Litigation. *Email:* rcohen@sidley.com

**STEPHEN G. CONTOPULOS,** born Los Angeles, California, February 9, 1946; admitted to bar, 1972, California, U.S. District Court, Central District of California, U.S. Court of Appeals, Ninth Circuit and U.S. Supreme Court; 1981, New York. *Education:* California State University at Los Angeles (B.A., 1967); Loyola University (J.D., 1971). *Member:* State Bar of California; The Copyright Society of the USA. *Email:* scontopu@sidley.com

**M. SCOTT COOPER,** born Burbank, California, January 24, 1950; admitted to bar, 1979, California and U.S. District Court, Northern, Central and Southern Districts of California. *Education:* University of California at Los Angeles (A.B., 1976); University of California at Los Angeles School of Law (J.D., 1979). Order of the Coif. Member, Board of Editors, UCLA Law Review, 1978-1979. Author: "Financial Penalties Imposed Directly Against Counsel in Litigation Without Resort to the Contempt Power," 26 UCLA Law Review 855, 1979; "Unsecured Environmental Indemnity Agreements," Real Property Law Reporter, April 1989; "New California Statutes Enhance Rights of Lenders in Mortgage Transactions Involving Letters of Credit and Guaranties," Journal of International Banking Law, Vol. 10, No. 1, Jan. 1995. Adjunct Professor of Law, Real Estate Finance, Whittier College School of Law, 1980-1984. *Member:* Los Angeles County (Member, Real Property Section) and American (Member: Committee on Legal Opinions in Real Property Transactions, Section on Real Property, Probate and Trust Law; Section on Business Law) Bar Associations; State Bar of California (Member, Real Property Section). **PRACTICE AREAS:** Real Estate; Finance. *Email:* scooper@sidley.com

**GEORGE DEUKMEJIAN,** born Albany, New York, June 6 1928; admitted to bar, 1952, New York; 1956, California. *Education:* Siena College (B.A., 1949); St. John's University (J.D., 1952). Deputy County Counsel, Los Angeles County, 1956-1958. Attorney General, 1979-1983 and Governor, 1983-1991, State of California. Partner: Lucas, Lucas & Deukmejian, 1963-1970; Riedman, Dalessi, Deukmejian & Woods, 1970-1979. Member, State Assembly, 1963-1966. State Senator, 1967-1979. **PRACTICE AREAS:** Business Transactions; Governmental Consultation. *Email:* gdeukeme@sidley.com

**LORI HUFF DILLMAN,** born San Francisco, California, November 27, 1958; admitted to bar, 1983, California; 1984, U.S. District Court, Central District of California and U.S. Court of Appeals, Ninth Circuit; 1985, U.S. District Court, Northern District of California; 1987, U.S. District Court, Southern District of California. *Education:* University of California-Davis (B.A., 1980); University of California-Los Angeles (J.D., 1983). Phi Alpha Delta. Editor-in-Chief, UCLA Law Review, 1982-1983. Author: "Conflicts of Interest," Civil Procedure Before Trial, California Continuing Education of the Bar, 1990. Law Clerk to Hon. William P. Gray, U.S. District Court, Central District of California, 1983-1984. *Member:* Los Angeles County Bar Association; Women Lawyers Association of Los Angeles; Association of Business Trial Lawyers. **PRACTICE AREAS:** Business Litigation; Products Liability; Reinsurance. *Email:* ldillman@sidley.com

**EDWARD D. EDDY III,** born Ithaca, New York, March 1, 1951; admitted to bar, 1983, New York; 1984, New Jersey; 1990, California. *Education:* Yale University (B.A., 1974); Cornell University (M.S., 1979); University of Michigan (J.D., 1981). *Member:* American Bar Association (Member, Commercial Financial Services Committee, Section on Business Law, 1987—). **LANGUAGES:** French. **PRACTICE AREAS:** Banking Law; Corporate Law. *Email:* eeddy@sidley.com

**BRADLEY H. ELLIS,** born Moline, Illinois, December 31, 1957; admitted to bar, 1983, California, U.S. Court of Appeals, Ninth Circuit and U.S. District Court, Central, Eastern, Northern and Southern Districts of California; 1985, Illinois. *Education:* University of Illinois (B.A., summa cum laude, with highest distinction in Political Science, 1980); Paedagogische Akademie des Bundes in Niederosterreich; University of Illinois College of Law (J.D., cum laude, 1983). Phi Beta Kappa; Phi Kappa Phi; Bronze Tablet. *Email:* bellis@sidley.com

**ROBERT FABRIKANT,** born Elizabeth, New Jersey, September 22, 1943; admitted to bar, 1968, New Jersey; 1974, District of Columbia; 1993, California. *Education:* University of Pennsylvania (B.A., 1965); Georgetown University (J.D., 1968). Research Editor, Georgetown Law Journal 1967-1968. Law Clerk, Judge Warren E. Burger, U.S. Court of Appeals for the D.C. Circuit, 1968-1969. Senior Law Clerk to Chief Justice Warren E. Burger, 1969-1970. Legal Advisor, Monetary Authority of Singapore, 1970-1972. Law Lecturer, University of Singapore Law Faculty, 1970-1974. Assistant United States Attorney, District of Columbia, 1974-1977. Acting and Assistant Chief, Energy Section, Antitrust Division, U.S. Department of Justice, 1978-1981. Special Bar Counsel, District of Columbia Board on Professional Responsibility, 1988-1991. Chairman, Health Care Fraud and Abuse Subcommittee, White Collar Crime Committee, ABA Criminal Justice Section, 1990—. *Member:* District of Columbia Bar; New Jersey State Bar Association. **PRACTICE AREAS:** Health Care; Antitrust; White Collar Criminal; Complex Commercial Litigation. *Email:* rfabrica@sidley.com

**HOWARD D. GEST,** born Bergenfield, New Jersey, January 24, 1952; admitted to bar, 1977, California, U.S. District Court, Northern District of California and U.S. Court of Appeals, Ninth Circuit; 1978, U.S. District Court, Central District of California. *Education:* University of California-Berkeley (A.B., 1974); University of California-Hastings College of Law (J.D., 1977). Order of the Coif. Thurston Society. Adjunct Professor of Law, Southwestern University, 1990-1992. Staff Attorney, U.S. Court of Appeals, Ninth Circuit, 1977-1978. Assistant U.S. Attorney, Central District of California, 1978-1983. **PRACTICE AREAS:** Environmental Law. *Email:* hgest@sidley.com

**RICHARD J. GRAD,** born Brooklyn, New York, February 19, 1957; admitted to bar, 1983, Massachusetts; 1984, District of Columbia; 1985, California, U.S. District Court, District of Massachusetts and U.S. District Court, Central, Southern, Northern and Eastern Districts of California; 1986, U.S. Court of Appeals, Ninth Circuit; 1990, U.S. Supreme Court. *Education:* University of California-Los Angeles (B.A., summa cum laude, 1980); Northeastern University (J.D., 1983). Phi Beta Kappa. Author: "The Enforceability of Contracts: A Practitioner's Playbook," 7 Loyola Marymount Law Journal, 1987. Law Clerk to Hon. Howard G. Munson, U.S. District Court, Northern District of New York, 1983-1985. **PRACTICE AREAS:** Business Litigation. *Email:* rgrad@sidley.com

**JOHNNY D. GRIGGS,** born Chicago, Illinois, December 17, 1957; admitted to bar, 1983, California. *Education:* Lewis & Clark College (B.S., 1980); Yale University (J.D., 1983). Director, Yale Moot Court Board of Appeals, 1982-1983. Recipient, 1991 Langston Bar Association Loren Miller Lawyer-of-the Year Award. *Member:* State Bar of California; Los Angeles County (Member, Fair Judicial Election Practices Committee on Minority Representation in the Legal Profession; Joint Minority Bar Diversity Task Force of Los Angeles County) and National Bar Associations. **PRACTICE AREAS:** Business Litigation. *Email:* jgriggs@sidley.com

**LARRY G. GUTTERRIDGE,** born Danville, Illinois, August 5, 1945; admitted to bar, 1971, Illinois; 1974, U.S. Supreme Court, U.S. Court of Appeals, First, Second, Fourth, Fifth, Sixth, Seventh, Eighth, Ninth, Tenth and District of Columbia Circuits; 1979, Pennsylvania (inactive); 1982, California; 1989, U.S. District Court, Southern District of California; 1990, U.S. District Court, Northern District of California. *Education:* University of Illinois (B.S., with high honors, University honors and Bronze Tablet, 1967; J.D., 1971). Advisor to the Executive Committee of the California State Bar Environmental Law Section. *Member:* American Bar Association

*(This Listing Continued)*

(Member, Natural Resources, Energy and Environmental Law and Litigation Sections). *PRACTICE AREAS:* Environmental Law; Health and Safety Law. *Email:* lgutterr@sidley.com

**JENNIFER C. HAGLE,** born Cincinnati, Ohio, May 6, 1961; admitted to bar, 1987, California. *Education:* University of California-Los Angeles (B.A., 1983); University of California, Hastings College of the Law (J.D., 1987). *LANGUAGES:* French. *PRACTICE AREAS:* Bankruptcy Law. *Email:* jhagle@sidley.com

**KENT A. HALKETT,** born San Diego, California, May 28, 1956; admitted to bar, 1982, California; U.S. District Court, Central, Southern and Northern Districts of California; U.S. Court of Appeals, Ninth Circuit; U.S. District Court, Northern District of Ohio; U.S. Court of Appeals, Sixth Circuit. *Education:* University of California-Berkeley (B.S., 1978); Vanderbilt University (J.D., 1981). *Member:* Los Angeles, American and International Bar Associations; Association of Business Trial Lawyers. *PRACTICE AREAS:* Commercial and International Litigation. *Email:* khalkett@sidley.com

**ADAM M. HANDLER,** born Newark, New Jersey, May 14, 1959; admitted to bar, 1984, California; 1991, U.S. Tax Court; 1992, U.S. District Court, Central District of California. *Education:* Yale University (B.S., summa cum laude, with distinction in Chemistry, 1981); Stanford University (J.D., 1984). Phi Beta Kappa. Author: "Empowerment Zones and Other Business Incentives May Provide Only Limited Benefits," 79 Journal of Taxation 274, 1993; "Proposal Regulations Coordinate Deferred Exchange and Installment Sale Rules," 79 Journal of Taxation 44, 1993; "Final Regulations on Deferred Like-Kind Exchanges Provides Additional Clarifications," 75 Journal of Taxation 10, 1991. Attorney-Advisor, Office of Tax Legislative Counsel, U.S. Department of the Treasury, 1988-1990. Member, Commissioner of Internal Revenue's Executive Task Force on Civil Tax Penalties, 1988-1989. *Member:* American Bar Association (Chairman Subcommittee on Section 1031 Exchanges of the Committee on Sales, Exchanges and Basis Tax Section). *PRACTICE AREAS:* Taxation Law. *Email:* ahandler@sidley.com

**THOMAS P. HANRAHAN,** born Brooklyn, New York, April 23, 1950; admitted to bar, 1975, Illinois and U.S. District Court, Northern District of Illinois; 1977, U.S. Court of Appeals, Seventh Circuit; 1979, U.S. Court of Appeals, Fifth Circuit; 1983, California. *Education:* Fordham University (B.A., summa cum laude, 1972); Columbia University (J.D., 1975). Articles Editor, Columbia Journal of Law and Social Problems, 1974-1975. *Member:* Los Angeles County (Member, Sections on: Litigation and Antitrust) and American (Member, Executive Committee, Sections on: Antitrust Law; Litigation; Intellectual Property) Bar Associations; Association of Business Trial Lawyers. *PRACTICE AREAS:* Business Litigation. *Email:* thanraha@sidley.com

**JAMES M. HARRIS,** born Evanston, Illinois, August 13, 1951; admitted to bar, 1976, District of Columbia and U.S. District Court, District of Columbia; 1977, U.S. Court of Appeals, District of Columbia Circuit; 1980, U.S. Court of Appeals, Fourth and Ninth Circuits; 1981, U.S. Court of Appeals, Second Circuit; 1982, California. *Education:* Brown University (A.B., with honors, 1973); University of Chicago (J.D., cum laude, 1976). Order of the Coif. Editor-in-Chief, University of Chicago Law Review, 1975-1976. Author: "Titles I & IV of the LMRDA: A Resolution of the Conflict of Remedies," 43 University of Chicago Law Review. Law Clerk to Hon. David L. Bazelon, Chief Judge, U.S. Court of Appeals, District of Columbia Circuit, 1976-1977. Instructor: Journalism Law, University of Virginia, 1977-1979. *PRACTICE AREAS:* Appellate and Civil Litigation. *Email:* jharris@sidley.com

**RICHARD W. HAVEL,** born Fairmont, Minnesota, September 20, 1946; admitted to bar, 1972, California. *Education:* University of Notre Dame (B.A., 1968); University of California-Los Angeles (J.D., 1971). Order of the Coif. Note and Comment Editor, U.C.L.A. Law Review, 1970-1971. Author: "Foreclosure Litigation," Chapter 11 Reporter Vol. 5, No. 10, Business Laws, Inc., 1988. Instructor in Creditors Rights, Loyola Marymount University, Fall, 1975-1980. Member, Board of Governors, Financial Lawyers Conference, 1991-1994. Member, Board of Industrial Development Authority for the City of Los Angeles, 1994—. *Member:* Los Angeles County (Member, Executive Committee, Commercial Law and Bankruptcy Section, 1989-1992; Lawyer Assistance Committee; Executive Committee, 1986-1989; Bankruptcy Committee, 1986-1989) and American Bar Associations. *PRACTICE AREAS:* Corporate Reorganization Law; Bankruptcy Law. *Email:* rhavel@sidley.com

**MARC I. HAYUTIN,** born Denver, Colorado, April 6, 1944; admitted to bar, 1969, California. *Education:* Stanford University (B.A., with distinction, 1965); Harvard University (J.D., cum laude, 1968). Phi Beta Kappa.

*(This Listing Continued)*

*LANGUAGES:* French. *PRACTICE AREAS:* Commercial Real Estate Financial and Acquisitions; Partnerships; Corporate Mergers and Acquisitions; Computer; Telecommunications Technology. *Email:* mhayutin@sidley.com

**MICHAEL C. KELLEY,** born Providence, Rhode Island, May 8, 1954; admitted to bar, 1979, California and U.S. District Court, Central District of California; 1982, U.S. District Court, Northern and Southern Districts of California; 1984, U.S. Court of Appeals, Ninth Circuit; 1985, U.S. Supreme Court. *Education:* University of Southern California (A.B., summa cum laude, 1976); Yale University (J.D., 1979). Phi Beta Kappa. Author: "Preliminary Injunctions in F.T.C. Merger Cases: A Proposal for Expanded Use of Preliminary Structural Decrees," 14 University of San Francisco Law Review 1, 1980; "Toward A National Statute of Limitations in 10b-5 Cases," Association of Business Trial Lawyers Report, August, 1988. Chairperson, Barristers Trial Attorneys Project, 1981-1982. *Member:* State Bar of California; Association of Business Trial Lawyers (Member, Board of Governors, 1989-1993). *PRACTICE AREAS:* General Litigation; Antitrust; Securities Litigation. *Email:* mkelley@sidley.com

**MOSHE J. KUPIETZKY,** born Brooklyn, New York, May 17, 1944; admitted to bar, 1969, New York; 1970, California. *Education:* City College of the City University of New York (B.B.A., cum laude, 1965); Harvard University (LL.B., magna cum laude, 1968). Beta Gamma Sigma. Member, Board of Editors, Harvard Law Review, 1967-1968. Author: Note, "UMW vs. Gibbs and Pendent Jurisdiction," 81 Harvard Law Review 657, 1968. Law Clerk to Hon. William B. Herlands, U.S. District Court, Southern District of New York, 1968-1969. *LANGUAGES:* Hebrew. *PRACTICE AREAS:* Corporate Law; Mergers and Acquisitions; Banking Law. *Email:* mkupiet@sidley.com

**PERRY L. LANDSBERG,** born Chicago, Illinois, May 7, 1956; admitted to bar, 1982, California. *Education:* University of California-Santa Barbara (B.A., 1978); University of California-Hastings College of Law (J.D., magna cum laude, 1982). Order of the Coif. Member, Board of Advisors Bankruptcy Law Review, 1989-1992. Member, Committee on Business Bankruptcy, American Bar Association Section of Business Law, 1991—. *PRACTICE AREAS:* Bankruptcy Law. *Email:* plandsbe@sidley.com

**KENNETH H. LEVIN,** born Chicago, Illinois, April 17, 1953; admitted to bar, 1978, California. *Education:* University of Illinois (A.B., summa cum laude, 1975); Harvard University (J.D., cum laude, 1978). Phi Beta Kappa. *Member:* Beverly Hills and Los Angeles County Bar Associations; The State Bar of California. *PRACTICE AREAS:* Corporate Law; Securities Law; Commercial Law. *Email:* klevin@sidley.com

**GEORGE M. MEANS,** born Inglewood, California, January 23, 1963; admitted to bar, 1988, California. *Education:* Gordon College (B.A., summa cum laude, 1985); University of San Diego (J.D., magna cum laude, 1988). Executive Editor, San Diego Law Review, 1987-1988. Author: Comment, "Sherman v. Lloyd and Mutual Selection in California Limited Partnership Law," 24 San Diego L. Rev. 1185, 1987. *PRACTICE AREAS:* Real Estate and Business Transactions. *Email:* gmeans@sidley.com

**THEODORE N. MILLER,** born Chicago, Illinois, October 9, 1942; admitted to bar, 1967, Illinois; 1972, U.S. Supreme Court; 1991, California. *Education:* University of Michigan (B.A., 1964); Yale University (LL.B., 1967). Order of the Coif. Staff member, Yale Law Journal, 1966-1967. Law Clerk to Hon. Luther M. Swygert, U.S. Court of Appeals, Seventh Circuit, 1967-1968. *Member:* Chicago Council of Lawyers. *PRACTICE AREAS:* Antitrust Law; Securities Law; Complex and Commercial Litigation. *Email:* tmiller@sidley.com

**SALLY SCHULTZ NEELY,** born Los Angeles, California, March 2, 1948; admitted to bar, 1972, Arizona; 1977, California. *Education:* Stanford University (B.A., 1970; J.D., 1971). Order of the Coif. Law Clerk to Hon. Ozell M. Trask, U.S. Court of Appeals, Ninth Circuit, 1971-1972. Assistant Professor of Law, Harvard Law School, 1975-1977. Faculty: NYU School of Law Workshop on Bankruptcy & Business Reorganization, 1992—; ALI-ABA Chapter 11 Business Reorganizations, 1989—; Federal Judicial Center Workshops for Bankruptcy Judges, 1989-1990, 1994-1995; Southeastern Bankruptcy Law Institute, 1990, 1994. Lawyer Representative, Ninth Circuit Judicial Conference, 1989-1991. Member, National Bankruptcy Conference (Executive Committee). Fellow, American College of Bankruptcy. Member, Board of Visitors, 1990-1992 and Chair, Reunion Giving, Stanford Law School, 1986. Member, Board of Directors, Organization of Women Executives, 1985-1987. *Member:* State Bar of California (Member, Debtor-Creditor Relations and Bankruptcy Subcommittee, Business Law Section, 1985-1987). *PRACTICE AREAS:* Chapter 11 Reorganization Law. *Email:* sneely@sidley.com

*(This Listing Continued)*

CAA1201B

**SIDLEY & AUSTIN, Los Angeles—Continued**

**EDWIN L. NORRIS,** born Columbus, Ohio, October 6, 1946; admitted to bar, 1973, New York; 1979, U.S. Tax Court; 1987, California. *Education:* Duke University (B.A., 1968); Yale University (J.D., 1972); New York University (LL.M. in Taxation, 1978). Phi Beta Kappa. Co-author: "1994 Federal Regulations on Transfer Pricing," Warren, Gorham & Lamont's *U.S. Taxation of International Operations* (August 24, 1994); "IRS Addresses Transfer-Pricing Abuses," The National Law Journal, April 5, 1993, p. 21; "California Taxation of Multinational Businesses: Important Developments in the Worldwide Combined Reporting and Water's Edge Methods," 10 California Business Law Reporter 215, April, 1989. *Member:* Los Angeles County and American (Member, Committee on Foreign Activities of U.S. Taxpayers, Section on Taxation 1984—) Bar Associations; State Bar of California (Member, Tax Section). *PRACTICE AREAS:* Taxation Law. *Email:* enorris@sidley.com

**PETER I. OSTROFF,** born Washington, D.C., December 15, 1942; admitted to bar, 1967, Illinois; 1970, California. *Education:* Washington University (B.A., 1964); University of Chicago (J.D., 1967). Law Clerk to Hon. Shirley M. Hufstedler, U.S. Court of Appeals, Ninth Circuit, 1969-1970. Teaching Fellow in Law, Monash University, Melbourne, Australia. *Member:* Los Angeles County (Member, Board of Trustees, 1974-1976; Chairperson, Human Rights Section, 1975-1976; Member, Ethics Committee, 1982-1984 and American (Director, Division of Substantive Law, 1982-1983; Chairman, Commercial Transactions Litigation Committee, 1976-1980; Council Member, 1980-1983; Chairman, Computer Litigation Committee, Litigation Section, 1985-1989; Director, Programs Division, 1990-1993) Bar Associations; State Bar of California (Member, Executive Committee: Intellectual Property Section, 1988-1989 and Litigation Section, 1990-1993); Association of Business Trial Lawyers (President, 1988-1989). *PRACTICE AREAS:* Complex Commercial Litigation; Intellectual Property; Employment and Computer Technology. *Email:* posteroff@sidley.com

**THOMAS E. PATTERSON,** born Winnipeg, Canada, January 25, 1960; admitted to bar, 1987, California. *Education:* University of Manitoba (B.A. Honors, 1982); Oxford University, England (B.A., with first class honors, 1984; B.C.L., with first class honors, 1985); Loyola Law School. Recipient, Rhodes Scholar. Bigelow Fellow and Lecturer in Law, University of Chicago Law School, 1985-1986. Author: "Current Issues Involving Adequate Protection in Real Estate Bankruptcies," 22 California Bankruptcy Journal 75, 1994. *Member:* Los Angeles County Bar Association (Bankruptcy Subcommittee, Commercial Law and Bankruptcy Committee, 1991-1994); State Bar of California (Debtor-Creditor Relations Committee, Business Law Section); Financial Lawyers Conference. *PRACTICE AREAS:* Bankruptcy Law; Reorganizations Law; Creditor's Rights Law. *Email:* tpatters@sidley.com

**RICHARD T. PETERS,** born La Mesa, California, September 24, 1946; admitted to bar, 1972, California. *Education:* Santa Clara University (B.A., 1968); University of California-Los Angeles (J.D., 1971). Order of the Coif. Managing Editor, U.C.L.A. Law Review, 1970-1971. Member, Board of Governors, Financial Lawyer's Conference, 1976-1980. Consultant, Continuing Legal Education of the Bar, 1984—. *Member:* State Bar of California (Member, 1979-1982 and Chair, 1981-1982, Debtor Creditor Relations and Bankruptcy Subcommittee of the Business Law Section; Member, 1982-1985 and Vice-Chair, 1984-1985, Executive Committee, Business Law Section). Fellow, American College of Bankruptcy. *PRACTICE AREAS:* Bankruptcy Law; Chapter 11 Reorganization; Debtor-Creditors' Rights Law; Commercial Litigation. *Email:* rpeters@sidley.com

**LINDA S. PETERSON,** born Grand Forks, North Dakota, March 15, 1952; admitted to bar, 1977, North Dakota; 1978, District of Columbia; 1986, California. *Education:* University of North Dakota (B.A., summa cum laude, 1973); Yale University (J.D., 1977). Phi Beta Kappa. Law Clerk to Hon. Frank Q. Nebeker, District of Columbia Court of Appeals, 1977-1978. Member, Board of Trustees, Southwestern University School of Law, 1995—. Deputy General Counsel to the Special Advisor to the Los Angeles Board of Police Commissioners, 1992. *Member:* Los Angeles County Bar Association (Member, Conference of Delegates, 1987-1990); State Bar of California (Member, Rules of Court Committee, 1988-1992); Women Lawyers Association of Los Angeles (Member of Board, 1989-1994). *PRACTICE AREAS:* Civil Litigation. *Email:* lpeters@sidley.com

**JUDITH M. PRAITIS,** born Omaha, Nebraska, December 14, 1962; admitted to bar, 1989, California. *Education:* University of Chicago (A.B., 1985); Harvard University (J.D., cum laude, 1988). Phi Beta Kappa. *Member:* Los Angeles County and American (Member, Section on Natural Resources, Energy and Environmental Law) Bar Associations; State Bar of California. *LANGUAGES:* Spanish. *PRACTICE AREAS:* Environmental Law. *Email:* jpraitis@sidley.com

**HOWARD J. RUBINROIT,** born Newark, New Jersey, April 23, 1944; admitted to bar, 1969, New Jersey; 1971, California. *Education:* Rutgers University (B.A., 1966); University of Pennsylvania (LL.B., 1969). Editor, University of Pennsylvania Law Review, 1967-1969. Law Clerk to Hon. Nathan Jacobs, New Jersey Supreme Court, 1969-1970. *Member:* Beverly Hills Bar Association (Member: Board of Governors, 1977-1978; Board of Governors of the Barristers, 1975-1979); Association of Business Trial Lawyers. *PRACTICE AREAS:* Business Litigation; Real Estate and Construction Litigation; Insurance Coverage Disputes; Product Liability. *Email:* hrubinro@sidley.com

**JOEL G. SAMUELS,** born Los Angeles, California, November 6, 1959; admitted to bar, 1984, California. *Education:* Princeton University (A.B., magna cum laude, 1981); Stanford University (J.D., 1984). Phi Beta Kappa. Order of the Coif. Co-author: "Federal Appellate Practice Guide-Ninth Circuit," Lawyers Cooperative Publishing (1994); "Survey of the New Value Exception to the Absolute Priority Rule," unpublished paper presented to the NYU Bankruptcy Seminar (1992-1994). Law Clerk to Hon. James R. Browning, U.S. Court of Appeals, Ninth Circuit, 1984-1985. *PRACTICE AREAS:* Bankruptcy Law; Corporate Reorganizations Law; Insolvency Law; Debtor-Creditor Relations Law. *Email:* jsamuels@sidley.com

**SHERWIN L. SAMUELS,** born Chicago, Illinois, June 22, 1935; admitted to bar, 1960, California. *Education:* Harvard University (A.B., magna cum laude, 1956); Boalt Hall, University of California, Berkeley (LL.B., 1959). Phi Beta Kappa. Member Board of Editors, California Law Review, 1958-1959. Associate, 1959-1967, Partner, 1967-1992, Mitchell, Silberberg & Knupp. *Member:* Los Angeles County and American Bar Associations; The State Bar of California. *PRACTICE AREAS:* Corporate Law; Mergers and Acquisitions; Corporate Securities Law; Real Estate Law. *Email:* ssamuels@sidley.com

**RONIE M. SCHMELZ,** born Los Angeles, California, July 11, 1961; admitted to bar, 1987, California. *Education:* University of California-Los Angeles (B.A., 1984); University of California, Hastings College of the Law (J.D., 1987). Temporary Judge, Municipal Court of California, Los Angeles. Arbitrator, Municipal/Superior Court of California, County of Los Angeles. *Member:* Los Angeles County and American (Member, White Collar Crime Committee and Health Care Fraud and Abuse Subcommittee) Bar Associations; State Bar of California. *LANGUAGES:* Hebrew. *PRACTICE AREAS:* Civil Litigation; Health Care Litigation. *Email:* rschmelz@sidley.com

**D. WILLIAM WAGNER,** born Dixon, Illinois, January 14, 1943; admitted to bar, 1968, Illinois and U.S. District Court, Northern District of Illinois; 1969, U.S. Court of Appeals, Seventh Circuit; 1982, California. *Education:* Northwestern University (B.A., 1965; J.D., cum laude, 1968). Member, Editorial Board, Northwestern University Law Review, 1967-1968. Co-author: "Subdivisions and Subdivision Controls," Illinois Municipal Law Handbook, Illinois Institute for Continuing Legal Education, 1978 and supp., 1981. *Member:* Chicago (Chairman, Land Use and Real Property Committee, 1979-1981) and Beverly Hills (Chairman, Real Property Section, 1986-1987) Bar Associations. *PRACTICE AREAS:* Real Estate Law. *Email:* dwagner@sidley.com

**MICHAEL D. WRIGHT,** born Danville, Illinois, December 13, 1962; admitted to bar, 1988, Illinois; 1993, California. *Education:* Purdue University (B.S., 1985); Indiana University (J.D., cum laude, 1988). Articles Editor, Indiana Law Review, 1987-1988. Law Clerk to Hon. John L. Coffey, U.S. Court of Appeals, Seventh Circuit, 1988-1990. *PRACTICE AREAS:* Banking and Commercial Law. *Email:* mwright@sidley.com

### COUNSEL

**JAMES F. DONLAN,** born Brooklyn, New York, December 29, 1952; admitted to bar, 1978, California. *Education:* Princeton University (A.B., magna cum laude, 1974); University of California-Berkeley (M.A., 1976); Harvard University (J.D., 1978). Phi Beta Kappa. *Member:* State Bar of California (Member, Partnerships Committee of Business Law Section, 1993—). *LANGUAGES:* French and Italian. *PRACTICE AREAS:* Business Transactions; Real Estate Law. *Email:* jdonlan@sidley.com

**STUART L. KADISON,** born Richmond, Virginia, November 17, 1923; admitted to bar, 1948, California. *Education:* New York University; University of Maryland (A.B., 1942); Stanford University (LL.B., 1948). Member, Board of Editors, University of Maryland Law Review, 1942. Lecturer on Law: Southwestern University, 1949-1952; Stanford University School of Law, 1977-1982. Phleger Visiting Professor of Law, Stanford University

*(This Listing Continued)*

School of Law, 1994. Professor of Law, J.R. Clark School of Law, Brigham Young University, 1995—. *Member:* Los Angeles County Bar Association (President, 1971-1972); State Bar of California (Member, Board of Governors, 1973-1976); American Law Institute (Life Member); Chancery Club. Fellow; American College of Trial Lawyers; American Bar Foundation. *PRACTICE AREAS:* General Litigation. *Email:* skadison@sidley.com

**RICHARD SCHAUER,** born Los Angeles, California, September 18, 1929; admitted to bar, 1955, California. *Education:* Occidental College (B.A., 1951); University of California-Los Angeles (J.D., 1955). Order of the Coif; Phi Delta Phi. Editor-in-Chief, UCLA, Law Review, 1954-1955. Lecturer, Judicial Continuing Education and Orientation, 1968-1977. Author: *Writs and Receivers Manual,* 1970. Editor, *Civil Trial Manual,* Superior Court of California Los Angeles County, 1976; "The Ubiquitous California Civil Pretrial Conference," 9 U.C.L.A. Law Review 1, 1977. Professor, Real Property and Agency Law, Loyola of Los Angeles School of Law, 1955-1964. Urban Project Model Neighborhood Commission on Justice, U.S. Department of Housing and Urban Development, 1958-1959. Member, Unauthorized Practice of Law Committee, California State Bar, 1960-1962. Judge: Los Angeles County Court, 1963-1965; Superior Court of California, 1965-1982 and Presiding Judge, 1979-1980. Supervising Judge, Central Criminal Division, 1968. Presiding Justice, California Court of Appeals, 1982-1984. Vice Chairman, Superior Court Committee on Standard Jury Instruction, Criminal 1968-1974. Member, No-Fault Insurance Commission, California Senate Judicial Committee, 1971-1973. Presiding Justice, California Court of Appeal, 1982-1984; California Judicial Council, 1979-1980. Commissioner, California Fair Judicial Elections Practice Committee, 1975-1977. Justice pro tem, California Supreme Court, 1981. *Member:* American Bar Association (Chairman: National Conference of State Trial Judges, Judicial Administration Division, 1972-1973; California Judicial Council Advisory Commission on Economical Litigation Project, 1977-1982); California Judges Association. Fellow, American Bar Foundation. *PRACTICE AREAS:* Judicial Administration Litigation. *Email:* rschauer@sidley.com

**YEE-YOONG YONG,** born Singapore, May 19, 1956; admitted to bar, 1987, California. *Education:* Raffles Institution; National University of Singapore (LL.B. Hons., 1979). *Member:* State Bar of California; Law Society of Singapore. *LANGUAGES:* Chinese. *Email:* yyong@sidley.com

## RESIDENT ASSOCIATES

**MARK ANCHOR ALBERT,** born Los Angeles, California, March 13, 1961; admitted to bar, 1988, California; U.S. Court of Appeals, Ninth Circuit; U.S. District Court, Northern, Southern, Eastern and Central Districts of California. *Education:* University of California at Berkeley (A.B., with high distinction in General Scholarship, 1984); Boalt Hall School of Law, University of California (J.D., 1988). Phi Beta Kappa. Dean's Honor Roll, 1979-1984; Commendation, Excellent Brief and Excellent Oral Argument, 1986 Boalt Hall Moot Court. Member, 1987 and Associate Editor, 1988, California Law Review. Author: "Deregulation and the Thrifts: The Case for Dismantling The Current Regulatory Structure," National Center of Financial Services, Boalt Hall School of Law, 1988; "Forma e Conteudo Em O Sonho da Terra," A UNIÃO, Bimonthly review of literary criticism, S220 Paulo, Brazil, 1984. *Member:* State Bar of California (President's Pro Bono Service Award and Wiley W. Manual Pro Bono Award, 1992); American Bar Association. *LANGUAGES:* French, Spanish, Portuguese, Italian. *PRACTICE AREAS:* Commercial and International Litigation. *Email:* malbert@sidley.com

**ALAN AU,** born Youngstown, Ohio, September 29, 1967; admitted to bar, 1992, California. *Education:* Cornell University (B.A., cum laude, with distinction, 1989); University of California-Berkeley (J.D., 1992). Golden Key National Honor Society. *PRACTICE AREAS:* Environmental Law. *Email:* aau@sidley.com

**LEE L. AUERBACH,** born Orlando, Florida, November 18, 1955; admitted to bar, 1990, California; 1991, U.S. District Court, Central District of California; 1992, New Mexico. *Education:* Ithaca College (B.S., 1977); Loyola Law School (J.D., 1990). Order of the Coif; Alpha Sigma Nu. Law Clerk to Hon. Manuel L. Real, U.S. District Court, Central District of California, 1990-1991. *PRACTICE AREAS:* Civil Litigation; Environmental Litigation; Tort and Insurance Coverage Litigation. *Email:* lauerbac@sidley.com

**RANDEE J. BARAK,** born Los Angeles, California, September 10, 1967; admitted to bar, 1993, California. *Education:* University of California-Los Angeles (B.A., History, summa cum laude, 1989; J.D., 1992); University of California-Hastings College of the Law (1989-1990). Phi Beta Kappa; Order of the Coif. UCLA Moot Court Program, 1990. Recipient: Dean's Book Award, 1989; Section Scholarship Award, 1990; Milton T.

*(This Listing Continued)*

Green Top Ten Citation Award, 1990; American Jurisprudence Award, Torts. Co-Author: (R. Fabrikant and R. Barak), "The Use of the Health Care Anti-Kickback Statute in Civil Litigation," ABA Health Care Fraud and Abuse Conference Materials, February, 1994; (R. Fabrikant, J. Diesenhaus and R. Barak), "The Criminal Medicare & Medicaid Anti-Kickback Statute: The Intent Defense," ABA White Collar Crime Conference Materials, March 1994. Law Clerk to Judge Arthur L. Alarcon, U.S. Court of Appeals, Ninth Circuit, 1992-1993. *Member:* Los Angeles County and American Bar Associations; Women Lawyers' Association of Los Angeles. *PRACTICE AREAS:* General Civil, Health Care and Employment Litigation. *Email:* rbarak@sidley.com

**LESLIE KENT BECKHART,** born Pasadena, California, March 23, 1961; admitted to bar, 1993, California; U.S. Court of Appeals, Ninth Circuit; U.S. District Court, Central District of California. *Education:* Harvard University (A.B., cum laude, 1982); University of Southern California (J.D., 1993). Order of the Coif. Member, Southern California Law Review. Author: "No Intrinsic Value: The Failure of Traditional Real Estate Appraisal Methods to Value Income-Producing Real Estate," Southern California Law Review, Vol. 66, July 1993, No. 5. *Member:* Beverly Hills and American Bar Associations. *PRACTICE AREAS:* Taxation. *Email:* lbeckhar@sidley.com

**ELLIE MASK BERTWELL,** born Baltimore, Maryland, August 11, 1957; admitted to bar, 1989, California. *Education:* University of Maryland (B.A., 1979); Loyola Law School (J.D., cum laude, 1989). Order of the Coif; St. Thomas More Society. Note and Comment Editor, Loyola of Los Angeles International and Comparative Law Journal, 1987-1989. *PRACTICE AREAS:* Environmental Law. *Email:* ebertwel@sidley.com

**JONATHAN M. BRENNER,** born Los Angeles, California, June 28, 1966; admitted to bar, 1992, California and U.S. District Court, Central District of California. *Education:* University of California-San Diego (B.A., with distinction, 1988); University of California, Hastings College of the Law (J.D., magna cum laude, 1992). Order of the Coif. *PRACTICE AREAS:* Litigation. *Email:* jbrenner@sidley.com

**STEVEN A. ELLIS,** born Buffalo, New York, April 7, 1964; admitted to bar, 1994, California. *Education:* Harvard University (A.B., 1986); University of California at Berkeley (J.D., 1991). Order of the Coif. Articles Editor, California Law Review. Law Clerk to Hon. Douglas H. Ginsburg, U.S. Court of Appeals for the District of Columbia Circuit, 1991-1992. *PRACTICE AREAS:* Litigation. *Email:* sellis@sidley.com

**ADAM G. ENGELSKIRCHEN,** born Los Angeles, California, August 12, 1968; admitted to bar, 1994, California, U.S. Court of Appeals, Ninth Circuit and U.S. District Court, Central District of California. *Education:* Claremont McKenna College (B.A., 1990); University of Southern California (J.D., 1994). Senior Editor, Interdisciplinary Law Journal, 1993. *LANGUAGES:* French, Spanish. *PRACTICE AREAS:* Real Estate. *Email:* aengelsk@sidley.com

**JEFFREY M. FISHER,** born Chicago, Illinois, August 11, 1966; admitted to bar, 1991, California. *Education:* Northwestern University (B.A., 1988); University of Illinois (J.D., summa cum laude, 1991). Order of the Coif. Harno Scholar. Staff Member, 1989-1991 and Notes and Comments Editor, 1990-1991, University of Illinois Law Review. Author: "In the Wake of Lorance v. AT&T Technologies, Inc: Interpreting Title VII's, Statute of Limitations for Facially Neutral Seniority Systems," University of Illinois Law Review, 1991. *PRACTICE AREAS:* Litigation. *Email:* jfisher@sidley.com

**LISA A. FONTENOT,** born New Orleans, Louisiana, September 7, 1968; admitted to bar, 1994, California. *Education:* Georgetown University (B.S.F.S., 1990); University of Virginia (M.A., 1994; J.D., 1994). Order of the Coif. Edward Cohen Tax Award. Member, Articles Review Board, Virginia Journal of International Law. *LANGUAGES:* French. *PRACTICE AREAS:* Corporate. *Email:* lfonteno@sidley.com

**JOHN E. FRIEDRICHS,** born Baton Rouge, Louisiana, August 2, 1968; admitted to bar, 1994, California and U.S. District Court, Central District of California. *Education:* Tulane University of Louisiana (B.A., summa cum laude, 1990); University of California, Berkeley, Boalt Hall School of Law (J.D., 1994). Phi Beta Kappa; Phi Eta Sigma, Moot Court Board, 1993-1994. Managing Editor, International Tax and Business Lawyer, 1993-1994. *Member:* Los Angeles County Bar Association. *LANGUAGES:* French and Spanish. *PRACTICE AREAS:* Litigation. *Email:* jfriedri@sidley.com

**STEPHEN W. GEARY,** born Palo Alto, California, Jun2 4, 1966; admitted to bar, 1995, California. *Education:* Stanford University (A.B., 1990); Boalt Hall School of Law, University of California (J.D., 1994). Member, Moot Court Board, 1993-1994. Member, 1992-1994, Executive

*(This Listing Continued)*

## SIDLEY & AUSTIN, Los Angeles—Continued

Editor, 1993-1994, California Law Review. Law Clerk to Judge Oliver Wagner, U.S. District Court, Eastern District of California, 1994-1995. **LANGUAGES:** German. **PRACTICE AREAS:** Litigation. **Email:** sgeary@sidley.com

**MARLO ANN GOLDSTEIN,** born Bethesda, Maryland, September 27, 1967; admitted to bar, 1994, California. *Education:* Wharton School, University of Pennsylvania (B.S., Econ., summa cum laude, 1989); University of Virginia (J.D., 1994). Beta Gamma Sigma. *Member:* State Bar of California. **PRACTICE AREAS:** Real Estate. **Email:** mgoldste@sidley.com

**ROBERT A. HOLLAND,** born Portsmouth, Virginia, July 17, 1968; admitted to bar, 1994, California and U.S. District Court, Central District of California. *Education:* University of California, Irvine (B.A., summa cum laude, 1990); Boalt Hall School of Law, University of California, Berkeley (J.D., 1993). Order of the Coif; Phi Beta Kappa; Pi Sigma Alpha. Recipient: American Jurisprudence Award; Moot Court Writing Award, 1991. Notes and Comments Editor, California Law Review, 1992-1993. Student Instructor, Legal Writing and Research, 1992. Author: "A Theory of Establishment Clause Adjudication: Individualism, Social Contract and the Significance of Coercion in Identifying Threats to Religious Liberty," 80 Cal. L. Rev. 1595, 1992. Law Clerk to Hon. James R. Browning, U.S. Court of Appeals, Ninth Circuit, 1993-1994. **PRACTICE AREAS:** Civil and Appellate Litigation. **Email:** rholland@sidley.com

**ROBERT W. KADLEC,** born Winston-Salem, North Carolina, July 17, 1963; admitted to bar, 1988, Illinois and U.S. District Court, Northern District of Illinois; 1994, California and U.S. District Court, Central District of California. *Education:* University of North Carolina (B.S., 1985); New York University (J.D., 1988). Alpha Beta Psi. Certified Public Accountant, 1988. *Member:* American Bar Association. **PRACTICE AREAS:** Corporate Law. **Email:** rkadlec@sidley.com

**JENNIFER LANDAU,** born San Francisco, California, March 15, 1965; admitted to bar, 1991, California and U.S. District Court, Central District of California. *Education:* Amherst College (B.A., magna cum laude, 1987); University of Chicago (J.D., cum laude, 1990). Member, 1988-1990, Associate Editor, 1989-1990, Chicago Law Review. Law Clerk to Judge Wm. Matthew Byrne, Jr., U.S. District Court, Central District of California, 1990-1991. *Member:* Los Angeles County and American Bar Associations. **PRACTICE AREAS:** Litigation. **Email:** jlandau@sidley.com

**KEVIN T. LANTRY,** born Nevada, Iowa, May 16, 1958; admitted to bar, 1991, California. *Education:* Pacific Union College (B.A., 1980); Loma Linda University M.A., 1982); University of California at Berkeley (J.D., 1991). **PRACTICE AREAS:** Bankruptcy Law. **Email:** klantry@sidley.com

**JOEL K. LIBERSON,** born Park Ridge, Illinois, September 2, 1963; admitted to bar, 1993, California and U.S. District Court, Central District of California. *Education:* University of Illinois (B.S., 1984); Loyola University (J.D., 1992). Order of the Coif. Deans Scholar. Deans List. Member, Loyola Law Review. Certified Public Accountant, California, 1984. Law Clerk to Judge Arthur L. Alarcon, U.S. Court of Appeals, Ninth Circuit, 1993-1994. *Member:* State Bar of Texas. **PRACTICE AREAS:** Litigation. **Email:** jliberso@sidley.com

**JEFFERSON K. LOGAN,** born Denver City, Texas, April 11, 1960; admitted to bar, 1988, California. *Education:* University of Texas (B.S., Pharm., with highest honors, 1983; J.D., with honors, 1988). *Member:* Los Angeles County and American Bar Associations; Texas State Board of Pharmacy; American Pharmaceutical Association. **PRACTICE AREAS:** Business Litigation; Professional Liability; Products Liability Law. **Email:** jlogan@sidley.com

**AIMEE D. LONG,** born Pasadena, California, January 13, 1969; admitted to bar, 1995, California. *Education:* University of California at Davis (B.A., 1991); Northwestern University (J.D., 1995).

**SUSANNE M. MACINTOSH,** born Philadelphia, Pennsylvania, June 18, 1970; admitted to bar, 1995, California. *Education:* Scripps College (B.A., 1992); Northwestern University (J.D., 1995). Author: Note, "Fourth Amendment - The Plain Touch Exception to the Warrant Requirement," Journal of Criminal Law and Criminology, Vol. 84, No. 4, 1994.

**THOMAS A. MCWATTERS III,** born Bethpage, New York, January 26, 1959; admitted to bar, 1986, Ohio; 1990, California. *Education:* Taylor University (B.S., cum laude, 1982); University of Toledo (J.D., magna cum laude, 1986). Order of the Coif. Order of the Barristers. Editor, University of Toledo Law Review, 1984. Law Clerk to Hon. James Harvey, U.S. District Court, Eastern District of Michigan, 1986-1988; Hon. Charles E. Wiggins, U.S. Court of Appeals, Ninth Circuit, 1988-1989. Author: Comment, "An Attempt to Regulate Pornography Through Civil Rights Legislation: Is It Constitutional?," 16 University of Toledo Law Review, 231, 1984. *Member:* Los Angeles County and American Bar Associations. **PRACTICE AREAS:** Commercial and Real Estate Litigation; Appellate Practice. **Email:** tmcwater@sidley.com

**CATHY OSTILLER,** born Los Angeles, California, October 24, 1970; admitted to bar, 1994, California. *Education:* University of California at Berkeley (B.S., 1991; J.D., 1994). Member, 1992-1993, Executive Editor, 1993-1994, California Law Review. Instructor, Legal Research and Writing, 1993. Law Clerk to Hon. James M. Ideman, U.S. District Court, Los Angeles. *Member:* Los Angeles County Bar Association; Sta te Bar of California. **LANGUAGES:** French, Spanish.

**OCTAVIO A. PEDROZ,** born Los Angeles, California, February 12, 1969; admitted to bar, 1995, California. *Education:* Stanford University (B.A., 1991); Harvard University (J.D., 1995). Member, Harvard Legal Aid Society. **LANGUAGES:** Spanish.

**JOHN E. POLICH,** born Covina, July 3, 1963; admitted to bar, 1995, California. *Education:* University of Redlands (B.A., 1984); University of Southern California (J.D., 1995). Staff Member, 1993-1994, Executive Editor, 1994-1995, Southern California Law Review. Author: Note, "The Ambiguity of Plain Meaning: Smith v. United States and the New Textualism," 58 Southern California Law Review 259, 1995.

**SCOTT PRESTON,** born Grand Rapids, Michigan, February 4, 1970; admitted to bar, 1995, California. *Education:* University of Michigan (A.B., 1992); Harvard University (J.D., 1995). Article Editor, 1994-1995, Associate Editor, 1993-1994, Harvard International Law Journal. Articles Editor, 1994-1995, Supervising Editor, 1993-1994, Harvard Latino Law Review. **LANGUAGES:** Spanish.

**JOHN V. PRIDJIAN,** born Chicago, Illinois, July 24, 1964; admitted to bar, 1991, California; 1992, U.S. Tax Court, U.S. Court of Appeals, Ninth Circuit and U.S. Supreme Court. *Education:* University of Illinois (B.S., 1986; J.D., 1991); University of Chicago (M.B.A., 1988). J. Nelson Young Scholar in Tax Law. Certified Public Accountant, Illinois, 1991. Author: "1994 Final Regulations on Transfer Pricing," U.S. Taxation of International Operations, August 1994; "IRS Addresses Transfer-Pricing Abuses," The National Law Journal, April 5, 1993; "No Incentives in the Film Industry," International Tax Review, November 1992; "Treaty Shopping and U.S. Tax Policy: New Approaches," Tax Planning International Review, October 1992; "Recent Developments in Foreign Direct Investment in the United States: Financing, Transfer Pricing and Information Reporting," Major Tax Planning, 1992; "Using a Shotgun When a Pistol Would Do - An Examination of the Reporting and Record Keeping Requirements for Foreign-Owned Corporations (Section 6038A Regulations)," University of Virginia Tax Review, Fall 1991. *Member:* Los Angeles County and American Bar Associations; State Bar of California. **LANGUAGES:** French. **PRACTICE AREAS:** Tax. **Email:** jpridjia@sidley.com

**JAMES ROBERTSON,** born San Diego, California, 1955; admitted to bar, 1995, California. *Education:* Lewis and Clark College (B.A., cum laude, 1978); San Francisco Theological Seminary (M.Div., 1982); Stanford University (J.D., 1995). Managing Editor, Stanford Journal of International Law, 1994-1995. Symposium Editor, Stanford Law and Policy Review, 1993-1994. **LANGUAGES:** Japanese, Dutch. **PRACTICE AREAS:** Corporate Banking. **Email:** jroberts@sidley.com

**JAY D. ROCKEY,** born Centralia, Washington, August 9, 1958; admitted to bar, 1986, California; 1987, U.S. District Court, Central District of California; 1994, Arizona. *Education:* University of Utah (B.A., 1980); California Western School of Law (J.D., 1986). Member: Roger Traynor Moot Court Competition; George Gafford Moot Court Competition. **PRACTICE AREAS:** Real Estate; Land Use; Leasing. **Email:** jrockey@sidley.com

**MATTHEW E. SLOAN,** born Detroit, Michigan, December 11, 1964; admitted to bar, 1993, California and U.S. District Court, Central District of California; 1994, U.S. District Court, Eastern District of California. *Education:* Hebrew University, Jerusalem, Israel; Yale University (B.A., magna cum laude, 1987); Harvard University (J.D., cum laude, 1991). Recent Developments Editor, Harvard Civil Rights-Civil Liberties Law Review, 1990-1991. Co-author, "Reconstruction, Deconstruction and Legislative Response: The 1988 Supreme Court Team and The Civil Rights Act of 1990," 25 Harvard Civil Rights-Civil Liberties Law Review 475, 1990. Law Clerk to the Hon. David V. Kenyon, U.S. District Court, Central District of California, 1991-1993. **Email:** msloan@sidley.com

*(This Listing Continued)*

**GLENN E. SOLOMON,** born Encino, California, January 21, 1967; admitted to bar, 1991, California and U.S. District Court, Central District of California. *Education:* University of California-Berkeley (B.A., 1988); Harvard University (J.D., cum laude, 1991). Phi Beta Kappa; Phi Alpha Delta (Treasurer, 1989-1990). *Member:* American Bar Association. *PRACTICE AREAS:* Complex Business Litigation; Employment Law; Real Estate Law. *Email:* gsolomo@sidley.com

**SARAH V. J. SPYKSMA,** born Princeton, New Jersey, March 5, 1962; admitted to bar, 1987, California. *Education:* University of California-Santa Barbara (B.A., with highest honors, 1984); Harvard University (J.D., cum laude, 1987). Phi Beta Kappa. *Member:* Los Angeles County Bar Association; State Bar of California. *PRACTICE AREAS:* Real Estate Transactions. *Email:* sspyksma@sidley.com

**SONYA SUD,** born Knoxville, Tennessee, September 4, 1970; admitted to bar, 1995, California. *Education:* University of Illinois (B.S., 1991); Northwestern University (J.D., 1995). Phi Beta Kappa. Julius H. Minor Moot Court Finalist, 1994. Member, Northwestern Moot Court National Team, 1994-1995. *Email:* ssud@sidley.com

**HOLLY L. SUTTON,** born Oakland, California, December 12, 1966; (admission pending). *Education:* University of California at Los Angeles (B.A., summa cum laude, 1989); Stanford University (J.D., 1993). Phi Beta Kappa. Member, Stanford Law Review. Co-Chair, Women of Stanford; Stanford Environmental Law Society. Law Clerk to Judge John S. Rhoades, Sr., U.S. District Court, Southern District of California, 1993-1994. *LANGUAGES:* Spanish. *PRACTICE AREAS:* Environmental Law. *Email:* hsutton@sidley.com

**LAURINE E. TULEJA,** born Philadelphia, Pennsylvania, May 13, 1957; admitted to bar, 1991, California, U.S. District Court, Central District of California and U.S. Court of Appeals, Ninth Circuit; 1993, U.S. Court of Appeals, Tenth Circuit. *Education:* Harvard University (A.B., magna cum laude, 1979); University of California-Berkeley (J.D., 1990). Executive Editor and Staff Member, California Law Review, 1988-1990. Law Clerk to Hon. Alfred T. Goodwin U.S. Court of Appeals, Ninth Circuit, 1990-1991. *Member:* Los Angeles County Bar Association; State Bar of California (Member, Legislation Committee, Environmental Law Section, 1993—); Women Lawyers Association of Los Angeles. *PRACTICE AREAS:* Environmental Law. *Email:* ltuleja@sidley.com

**CATHERINE M. VALERIO BARRAD,** born San Diego, California, November 8, 1960; admitted to bar, 1993, California; 1994, U.S. District Court, Central, Eastern, Northern and Southern Districts of California and U.S. Court of Appeals, Ninth Circuit. *Education:* University of California, San Diego (B.A., 1982); University of California at Los Angeles (M.B.A., 1984); Northwestern University (J.D., magna cum laude, 1993). Order of the Coif. U.C. Regents Scholar, Bank of America Scholar, 1978-1982; COGME Fellow, 1982-1984; AAUW Education Foundation Fellow, 1991-1993. Member, Northwestern University Law Review, 1991-1993. Author: "Genetic Information and Property Theory," 87 Northwestern Law Review 1037, 1993. Contributing Author: "50 State Survey on Media Privacy and Related Claim," LDRC, 1995. Contributor: Federal Appellate Practice Guide, Ninth Circuit, 1994. Clerk to Hon. D.H. Ginsburg, U.S. Court of Appeals for the District of Columbia Circuit, 1993-1994. *Member:* American Bar Association. *LANGUAGES:* Spanish. *PRACTICE AREAS:* Litigation; Appellate. *Email:* cvalerio@sidley.com

**STANLEY J. WALLACH,** born Columbia, Missouri, August 24, 1965; admitted to bar, 1992, California; 1994, Missouri. *Education:* Duke University (A.B., cum laude, 1987); University of Chicago (J.D., 1992). *LANGUAGES:* Russian. *Email:* swallach@sidley.com

**DARON WATTS,** born Chicago, Illinois, June 5, 1968; admitted to bar, 1994, California. *Education:* University of San Diego (B.A., 1991); University of Southern California (J.D., 1994). Phi Beta Phi. Legion Lex Scholar, 1991-1994. Hale Moot Court Honors Program, 1992-1993. *LANGUAGES:* Spanish. *PRACTICE AREAS:* Litigation. *Email:* dwatts@sidley.com

(For Biographical Data of all Personnel, see Professional Biographies, Chicago, Illinois).

## LAW OFFICES OF ALLAN A. SIGEL

GAYLEY CENTER - WESTWOOD
1125 GAYLEY AVENUE
LOS ANGELES, CALIFORNIA 90024
Telephone: 310-824-4070
Telecopier: 310-208-7271

*Civil Trial and Criminal Litigation. Corporate, Business, Personal Injury, Medical Malpractice, Legal Malpractice, Product Liability, Real Estate, Family Law and Appellate Practice.*

**ALLAN A. SIGEL,** born Atlantic City, New Jersey, June 11, 1927; admitted to bar, 1953, California. *Education:* Los Angeles City College (A.A., 1950); Loyola Law School (J.D., highest honors, 1953). Phi Delta Phi. Arbitrator, Los Angeles Superior Court, 1980-1987. Member, Panel of Arbitrators, American Arbitration Association. *Member:* Los Angeles County Bar Association; The State Bar of California; Los Angeles County Trial Lawyers Association. *PRACTICE AREAS:* Corporate Transactions; Civil Trial; White Collar Criminal Litigation; Officer and Director Liability; Real Estate; Entertainment Law; Defamation; Legal Malpractice; Medical Malpractice; Personal Injury; Products Liability; Toxic Tort; Family.

**PHILLIP R. POLINER,** born Los Angeles, California, May 12, 1966; admitted to bar, 1991, California. *Education:* University of California at Santa Barbara (B.A., cum laude, 1988); Southwestern University (J.D., 1991). *Member:* Los Angeles County Bar Association; State Bar of California; Los Angeles Trial Lawyers Association. *PRACTICE AREAS:* Civil Trial; Personal Injury; Medical Malpractice; Products Liability; Real Estate; Corporate; Family.

OF COUNSEL

**JEFFREY D. MARKEL,** born Los Angeles, California, September 21, 1962; admitted to bar, 1992, California, U.S. District Court, Central District of California and U.S. Court of Appeals, Ninth Circuit. *Education:* University of California, Berkeley (B.A., 1984; M.A., 1987); University of Southern California (J.D., 1992). *Member:* Los Angeles County Bar Association; State Bar of California. *PRACTICE AREAS:* Business Transactions; Civil; Appellate; Contracts; Interstate Law; Products Liability.

REPRESENTATIVE CLIENTS: Westwood Village Development Co.; Ogner Porsche Audi; Porsche Audi Dealers (State of California); Western Bank; Advantage Life Products; American Packaging Products; A. Morgan Maree, Inc.
REFERENCE: Western Bank, Los Angeles, California.

## KENNETH M. SIGELMAN AND ASSOCIATES

LOS ANGELES, CALIFORNIA
(See San Diego)

*Civil Trial Practice, Negligence, Malpractice, Product Liability and Health Care Law.*

## SILVER & FREEDMAN

A PROFESSIONAL LAW CORPORATION

Established in 1975

1925 CENTURY PARK EAST, SUITE 2100
LOS ANGELES, CALIFORNIA 90067
Telephone: 310-556-2356
Telecopier: 310-556-0832

*General Civil, Trial and Appellate Practice in State and Federal Courts and Administration Agencies, Business, Corporate, Partnership, LLC, Commercial and Tax Law, Real Property Acquisitions, Sales, Exchanges, Leases and Development, Business Acquisitions, Sales and Mergers, Estate Planning and Probate, Management Employment Relations, Labor Law and Family Law.*

**NEIL H. FREEDMAN,** born Los Angeles, California, June 26, 1945; admitted to bar, 1971, California, U.S. District Court, Central District of California and U.S. Court of Appeals, Ninth Circuit. *Education:* University of California at Los Angeles (B.A., 1967); Loyola Law School (J.D., 1970). Phi Alpha Delta. Member, Loyola Law Review, 1969. Lecturer: University of Southern California, University Seminar, "Business Litigation," University of California at Los Angeles, University Extension, Business Management Seminar "Business Litigation," 1986. Referee, Los Angeles Superior

*(This Listing Continued)*

**SILVER & FREEDMAN,** A PROFESSIONAL LAW CORPORATION, Los Angeles—Continued

Court Fast Track Program, 1987. Judge Pro Tem, Los Angeles Municipal Court. Los Angeles County Bar Fee Arbitrator. *PRACTICE AREAS:* Business Litigation; General Civil Litigation; Family Law.

**PERRY S. SILVER,** born Bad Weresohfen, Germany, October 12, 1946; admitted to bar, 1971, California, U.S. District Court, Central District of California and U.S. Court of Appeals, Ninth Circuit; 1978, U.S. Tax Court. *Education:* University of California at Los Angeles (B.A., 1967); Loyola Law School (J.D., with honors, 1970). Phi Alpha Delta. Member, St. Thomas More Law Honor Society. Member, Loyola Law Review, 1970-1971. Author: "Alcoholism and the 8th Amendment," Loyola Law Review, 1969. Lecturer: University of Southern California, University Seminar, "Business Litigation," 1982; "Protecting Trade Secrets," 1996. *PRACTICE AREAS:* Business Law; Real Property Law; Commercial Law.

**JOEL SACHS,** born Jersey City, New Jersey, October 10, 1941; admitted to bar, 1966, Florida, U.S. District Court, Southern District of Florida and U.S. Court of Appeals, Fifth Circuit; 1974, California; 1978, U.S. District Court, Central District of California, U.S Court of Appeals, Ninth Circuit and U.S. Tax Court. *Education:* University of Florida (B.A., 1963; J.D., 1966). Phi Eta Sigma; Phi Alpha Delta; Florida Blue Key. Board Member, University of Florida, Law Review, 1965-1966. Instructor, Continuing Education, "Estate and Gift Taxation," University of West Los Angeles, 1976-1979. Lecturer, Practicing Law Institute, California Continuing Education of the Bar, 1986—. President, Beverly Hills Estate Counselors Forum, 1986—. [Capt., U.S. Army, 1967-1969]. *PRACTICE AREAS:* Estate Planning Law; Trust Law; Probate Law; Tax Law.

**MARGARET MCDONALD KANE,** born Long Beach, California, June 2, 1944; admitted to bar, 1980, California; 1981, U.S. District Court, Central District of California and U.S. Court of Appeals, Ninth Circuit. *Education:* University of Southern California (A.B., 1967); University of Southern California School of Business Administration (1976-1978); Southwestern University (J.D., 1980). Member, Southwestern University Curriculum Committee, 1980. Attorney-Client Fee Dispute Arbitrator, 1988—. *PRACTICE AREAS:* Business Law; Corporate Law; Real Property Law.

**MITCHELL B. STEIN,** born New York, New York, July 28, 1952; admitted to bar, 1978, California, U.S. District Court, Central District of California and U.S. Court of Appeals, Ninth Circuit. *Education:* University of Southern California; University of California at Irvine (B.A., 1974); Loyola Law School (J.D., 1978). Judge Pro-Tem, 1984— and Landlord-Tenant Mediator, 1986—, Los Angeles County Municipal Court. Los Angeles County Attorney-Client Fee Arbitrator, 1986—. *PRACTICE AREAS:* Commercial Insurance; General Civil Litigation; General Business Law; Real Property Law.

---

**EDWARD J. MCNAMARA,** born Columbus, Ohio, January 9, 1964; admitted to bar, 1991, California. *Education:* University of Southern California (B.A., 1986; J.D., 1991). Hale Moot Court Honors Program, Runner Up, Best Written Brief. *Member:* Los Angeles County Barristers AIDS Project. *PRACTICE AREAS:* General Civil Litigation; Employment; Probate.

**BRUCE H. LEISEROWITZ,** born Des Moines, Iowa, June 29, 1957; admitted to bar, 1984, California. *Education:* Stanford University (A.B., 1979); Boalt Hall School of Law, University of California (J.D., 1984). Phi Beta Kappa. Managing Editor, International Tax and Business Lawyer, 1983-1984. Author: "Coordination of Taxation Between the United States and Guam," 1 International Tax and Business Law 218, 1983. *Member:* Los Angeles County Bar Association; State Bar of California; Los Angeles County Bar Association Inns of Court. *LANGUAGES:* French. *PRACTICE AREAS:* Commercial Litigation; Insurance Litigation; Surety Litigation.

**BETH ACKERMAN SCHROEDER,** born Philadelphia, Pennsylvania, December 27, 1959; admitted to bar, 1985, California; 1987, U.S. District Court, Central District of California; 1988, U.S. Court of Appeals, Ninth Circuit. *Education:* University of Wisconsin (B.A., with distinction, 1981); University of California at Los Angeles (J.D., 1985). Phi Eta Sigma; Psi Chi. Member, U.C.L.A. Moot Court Honors Program, 1983-1985. Author: "Personnel Policies and Practices: What's Legal and What's Not," Dental Management, Sept. 1987; "Protecting Yourself From Wrongful Discharge Litigation," National Second Mortgage Association Journal, Sept. 1989; "Handling Sexual Harassment Claims," Limousine and Chauffer Magazine, Sept 1994; Employment Practices Liability Insurance Handbook, 1996.

*(This Listing Continued)*

CAA1206B

Member, Executive Committee, Los Angeles County Barristers AIDS Project, 1989—, Los Angeles County Attorney-Client Fee Arbitrator, 1993—. Instructor: Certificate in Management Effectiveness Program, University of Southern California, 1991; UCLA Workers' Compensation Institute, 1994. Lecturer, California State Dominguez Hills, MBA Program, 1966, 1997. *PRACTICE AREAS:* Management Employment Relations Law; Labor Law; General Business Litigation.

**LINDA T. PIERCE,** born Los Angeles, California, January 14, 1961; admitted to bar, 1992, California. *Education:* California State University at Sonoma; California State University at Northridge (B.A., 1984); Southwestern University (J.D., 1991). Member, Professional Liability Underwriting Society. *Member:* State Bar of California. *PRACTICE AREAS:* Employment Law; General Business Litigation; Civil Litigation.

REPRESENTATIVE CLIENTS: Four Seasons Hotel, L.A.; Goldberg and Solovy Foods, Inc.; Lithonia Lighting a division of National Service Industries; The Marmon Corporation; Music Express; Parks, Palmer, Turner & Yemenidjian, Certified Public Accountants; Paul Davril, Inc.; Printing Industries Association; Service Packing Co.; Southern California Broadcasting, Inc.; Browne of Los Angeles, Inc.; Bertelsmann Industry Services; Longwood Management; Advance Business Graphics; Mount Saint Mary's College; Kemper National Insurance Co.; Country Star, Inc.

---

## IRENE L. SILVERMAN

1840 CENTURY PARK EAST, EIGHTH FLOOR
**LOS ANGELES, CALIFORNIA 90067-2101**
Telephone: 310-553-4999
Fax: 310-553-2033
Email: ILS101@AOL.COM

*Estate Planning, Trusts and Probate Law. Conservatorships and Guardianships, Elder Law, Health Care and Elder Abuse Litigation. Probate Litigation.*

*FIRM PROFILE: Irene Silverman is the author of numerous articles relating to legal aspects of health care, probate and conservatorships and dementia. She is also a frequent guest speaker and lecturer for senior health care providers and health care professionals and legal professionals including, UCLA, USC, Veteran's Administration Medical Center, Century City Hospital, community mental health organizations, senior care facilities, alzheimer's organizations.*

**IRENE L. SILVERMAN,** born Santa Monica, California, February 11, 1942; admitted to bar, 1971, California. *Education:* University of California at Los Angeles; University of San Fernando Valley College of Law (J.D., magna cum laude, 1970). Member, University of San Fernando Valley Law Review, 1969-1970. Instructor: Probate, Conservatorships, Guardianships and Probate Administration, University of West Los Angeles, 1977-1980. Lecturer, "Legal Aspects of Aging and Incapacity," California Continuing Education of the Bar. *Member:* Beverly Hills (Member, Probate and Trust Section), Los Angeles County (Member: Executive Committee, Trusts and Estates Section, 1994—; Officer, Executive Committee, Trusts and Estates Section; Chairperson: Committee on Legal Aspects of Bioethics, 1982-1983; Chair, Sub-Committee of Chapter 10, Superior Court Probate Rules Revisions) and American (Member: Probate, Real Property and Trust, Human Rights, Taxation, General Practice and Corporate Sections) Bar Associations; State Bar of California (Member, Probate and Trust Section); Women Lawyers Association. (Certified Specialist, Estate Planning, Trust and Probate Law, The State Bar of California Board of Legal Specialization).

---

## SIMKE CHODOS

A Partnership of Professional Corporation
*Established in 1955*

SUITE 1511, 1880 CENTURY PARK EAST
**LOS ANGELES, CALIFORNIA 90067**
Telephone: 310-203-3888
Fax: 310-203-3866

*Civil and Business Litigation, Entertainment, Commercial, Real Estate, Personal Injury, Malpractice and Insurance Defense Law, Criminal Trial.*

*FIRM PROFILE: Simke Chodos and its predecessor firms, have been in existence since 1955. The firm limits its practice to litigation in the areas of civil, criminal and administrative trial and appellate practice. The law firm has successfully litigated thousands of cases on behalf of both plaintiffs and defendants at all levels of the state and federal courts.*

*The firm specializes in corporate, partnership, contract, commercial and real property disputes. The prosecution and defense of business torts, professional licensing and disciplinary proceedings, probate and will contest litigation.*

*(This Listing Continued)*

**STUART A. SIMKE,** born New York, N.Y., November 12, 1935; admitted to bar, 1961, California. *Education:* City College of the City University of New York and University of California at Los Angeles (B.A., cum laude, 1957); University of California at Los Angeles (LL.B., 1960). Phi Beta Kappa; Order of the Coif. Editor, U.C.L.A. Law Review, 1959-1960. *Member:* Beverly Hills Bar Association; State Bar of California. **PRACTICE AREAS:** Business Litigation; Entertainment Litigation; Administrative Law; Contract Litigation.

**DAVID M. CHODOS,** born Minneapolis, Minnesota, June 26, 1936; admitted to bar, 1967, California. *Education:* University of California at Los Angeles (B.A., 1960); Loyola University of Los Angeles (LL.B., 1966). Master Attorney and Member of Executive Committee of the Complex Litigation Inns of Court. *Member:* Beverly Hills and Los Angeles County Bar Associations; State Bar of California; Los Angeles Trial Lawyers Association; California Trial Lawyers Association; Association of Business Trial Lawyers. **PRACTICE AREAS:** Business Litigation; White Collar Crime; Fiduciary Malpractice; Administrative Law; Contract Litigation.

---

**RICHARD A. FOND,** born Los Angeles, California, April 8, 1948; admitted to bar, 1972, California. *Education:* University of Southern California (A.B., with honors, 1969; J.D., 1972). Phi Delta Phi. Member, Southern California Law Review, 1971-1972. Co-Author: "Claim and Delivery," California Civil Procedure Before Trial, 1977; "Judgments," California Civil Procedure During Trial, 1995. *Member:* Beverly Hills, Los Angeles County and American (Member, Section on Corporation, Banking and Business Law) Bar Associations; State Bar of California; Association of Business Trial Lawyers. **PRACTICE AREAS:** Business Litigation; Creditors' Rights and Remedies; Provisional Remedies.

**ELLEN RESINSKI ROSEN,** born Philadelphia, Pennsylvania, August 18, 1960; admitted to bar, 1985, Pennsylvania; 1986, U.S. District Court, Eastern District of Pennsylvania; 1987, U.S. Court of Appeals, Third Circuit; 1989, California and U.S. Court of Appeals, Ninth Circuit. *Education:* La Salle University (B.A., cum laude, 1982); Villanova University (J.D., 1985). Co-Author, "Judgements," California Civil Procedure During Trial, 1995. *Member:* Los Angeles County, Beverly Hills and American Bar Associations; State Bar of California; Women Lawyers Association of Los Angeles; Association of Business Trial Lawyers; California Women Lawyers. **PRACTICE AREAS:** Business Litigation; Entertainment Litigation; Fiduciary Malpractice.

**JAMES ROBERTSON MARTIN,** born Burbank, California, November 2, 1963; admitted to bar, 1994, California and U.S. District Court, Central District of California. *Education:* University of Massachusetts, Amherst (B.A., 1987); Loyola University of Los Angeles (J.D., 1994). Order of the Coif. Recipient: American Jurisprudence Awards: Legal Process, Civil Procedure, Constitutional Law I, Commercial Law, Sales and Payments. Member, 1992-1993; Articles Editor, 1993-1994, International and Comparative Law Journal. *Member:* State Bar of California; Association of Business Trial Lawyers; Consumer Attorneys Association of Los Angeles (Member, Real Property Litigation Section); Inns of Court. **PRACTICE AREAS:** Business Litigation; Civil Litigation; Criminal.

### OF COUNSEL

**JAMES L. KEANE,** born Los Angeles, California, February 24, 1947; admitted to bar, 1972, California. *Education:* University of California at Los Angeles (B.A., cum laude, 1968; J.D., 1971). Member, 1970-1971 and Senior Editor, 1971, University of California at Los Angeles Law Review. *Member:* State Bar of California. **PRACTICE AREAS:** Business and Commercial; Appellate Practice.

REFERENCE: City National Bank (Wilshire-La Cienega Branch).

---

## SIMMONS, RITCHIE & SEGAL

**555 SOUTH FLOWER STREET**
**SUITE 4640**
**LOS ANGELES, CALIFORNIA 90071**
Telephone: 213-624-7391
FAX: 213-489-7559

*General Civil and Trial Practice in all State and Federal Courts and Administrative Agencies. Corporations, Municipal, Corporate Securities, Eminent Domain, Real Estate, State and Federal Tax, Estate Planning, Trust and Probate Law.*

(This Listing Continued)

---

### MEMBERS OF FIRM

**FREDERICK L. SIMMONS,** born Los Angeles, California, November 11, 1928; admitted to bar, 1958, California. *Education:* University of California at Los Angeles (B.A., 1952; J.D., 1958). Phi Alpha Delta. Member, University of California at Los Angeles Law Review, 1956-1958. Author: "The Realities of Planning for Capital Gains," 44 Los Angeles Bar Bulletin 15, 1968; "The Requirements for Recognition of Multiple Trusts Through Separate Taxable Entities," 44 Los Angeles Bar Bulletin 304, 1969; "Community Property and the Migrant Executive," 7 Houston Law Journal 20, 1970; "The Effect of Community Property and Related Doctrines," Chapter IV, Estates Planning for the Migrant Executive Practicing Law Institute, 1970; "Planning for the Moderate Estate in which the Family Business is the Principal Asset," Chapter IV, Second Annual Estate Planning Institute, Practising Law Institute, 1971; "The Use of Trusts in Tax Planning for the Professional," 50 Taxes 420, 1972; "Estate Planning Considerations when the Family Business is the Principal Asset," 8 California Western Law Review 235, 1972; "Inter Vivos Trusts in Estate Planning for the Professional," Chapter 8, Third Annual Estate Planning Institute, Practising Law Institute, 1972; "Gift and Leaseback Arrangements Involving Property Used in a Professional Practice," 48 Los Angeles Bar Bulletin 62, 1972; "New Developments in the Gift and Leaseback," 51 Taxes 654, 1974; "Should the Revocable Trust Be Used to Avoid Probate In Community Property Jurisdictions," 1 Community Property Journal 4, 1974; "The Use Of Trusts In Estate Planning For the Corporate Executive," 52 Taxes 471, 1974; "The Use of Inter Vivos Trusts in Tax and Estate Planning for the Corporate Executives and the Professional," 11 California Western Law Review 255, 1975; "Resisting Continuing IRS Attacks on the Use of 'Gift and Leaseback' in Tax Planning for the Professional," 56 Taxes 195, 1978; "Tax Oriented Family Estate Planning: The Use of A Minority Trust to Effect Tax Free Transfers and Income Tax Savings Despite the Tax Reform Acts," The National Public Accountant, March 1979; "How to Save Taxes by Using an Income Redirecting Trust to Fund College Expenses," TAXES, The Tax Magazine, pp 567-573, August, 1980; "The Real Estate Partnership Freeze in Light of the Economic Recovery Tax Act of 1981: A Guide for the Perplexed," TAXES, The Tax Magazine, pp 476-485, June, 1982; "How the Proper Use of Gift and Borrowback Techniques May Make Children's Educational Expenses Deductible," TAXES-The Tax Magazine, pp 110-117, February, 1984. Member, Probate Mediation Panel. *Member:* Los Angeles County and American Bar Associations; State Bar of California. (Certified Specialist, Taxation Law and Probate, Trusts and Estate Planning, The State Bar of California Board of Legal Specialization). **PRACTICE AREAS:** Federal Taxation; State Taxation; Estate Planning; Trust Probate; Taxation; Corporate Law.

**JONATHAN L. SIMMONS,** born Los Angeles, California, May 24, 1967; admitted to bar, 1993, California. *Education:* University of California at Los Angeles (B.A., 1990); Pepperdine University (J.D., 1993). Phi Alpha Delta. Author: "Drafting Enforceable Non-Marital Partnership Agreements," Los Angeles Daily Journal, Vol 108, No. 143, July 31, 1995. *Member:* State Bar of California. **PRACTICE AREAS:** Estate Planning; Estate Probate; Corporate Law; Litigation; General Practice.

**WILLIAM D. SEGAL,** born Chicago, Illinois, November 23, 1934; admitted to bar, 1964, California. *Education:* University of California at Berkeley (B.S., 1956; J.D., 1963). Order of the Coif; Phi Delta Phi. Associate Editor, California Law Review, 1962-1963. *Member:* Los Angeles County and American Bar Associations; The State Bar of California. **PRACTICE AREAS:** Corporate Law; Business Law.

### OF COUNSEL

Graham A. Ritchie        Lee E. Stark
Michael W. Roberts

REFERENCE: South Bay Bank, Los Angeles.

---

## SIMON, McKINSEY, MILLER, ZOMMICK, SANDOR & DUNDAS

*A LAW CORPORATION*

**LOS ANGELES, CALIFORNIA**

(See Long Beach)

*General Civil and Civil Trial Practice. Corporation, Real Estate, Estate Planning, Trust, Taxation, Probate, Negligence, Family Law, Local Government Administrative Hearings and Appeals.*

CALIFORNIA—LOS ANGELES

## SIMON & SIMON, LTD.
### LOS ANGELES, CALIFORNIA
(See Manhattan Beach)

*General Civil Litigation, Family Law, Real Property, Probate, Estate Planning, Personal Injury, Business.*

---

## SINCLAIR TENENBAUM OLESIUK & EMANUEL
### LOS ANGELES, CALIFORNIA
(See Beverly Hills)

*Entertainment, Domestic and International Business, Corporate and Finance.*

---

## SINNOTT, DITO, MOURA & PUEBLA
550 SOUTH HOPE STREET
TWENTIETH FLOOR
### LOS ANGELES, CALIFORNIA 90071
Telephone: 213-312-1470
Fax: 213-892-8322

San Francisco, California Office: 1 Post Street, Suite 2680, 94104. Telephone: 415-352-6200. Fax: 415-352-6224.

Insurance Coverage Litigation, Bank and Finance Litigation, General Business Litigation and Trial and Appellate Practice.

FIRM PROFILE: Sinnott, Dito, Moura & Puebla was founded with the goal of providing the highest quality legal representation. The firm achieves this goal by aggressively upholding clients' interests while simultaneously streamlining litigation and controlling costs. Two offices located in Los Angeles and San Francisco provide a solid base from which to serve clients.

With expertise in complex practice areas, the firm has an extensive trial practice in all aspects of business law, insurance law and appellate litigation. Sinnott, Dito, Moura & Puebla has a recognized national reputation in insurance coverage litigation, as well as in the representation of businesses and municipalities.

### MEMBERS OF FIRM

**RANDOLPH P. SINNOTT,** born Mineola, New York, April 21, 1954; admitted to bar, 1982, California, U.S. Court of Appeals, Ninth Circuit and U.S. District Court, Central, Northern, Southern and Eastern Districts of California. *Education:* University of Michigan (A.B., cum laude, with distinction, 1976); University of Southern California (J.D., 1982). Recipient, Phillips Prize for Excellence in Greek, University of Michigan. Member, Southern California Law Review, 1980-1982. Executive Editor, Major Tax Planning Journal, 1981. Co-Author: "The Limits of Coverage Under Personal Injury Endorsements for Environmental Claims: An Insurer's Perspective," Mealey's Litigation Reports (July 31, 1990); "The Pollution Exclusion Clause: It Says What It Means and Means What It Says," Mealey's Litigation Reports (October 2, 1990). [USMCR, 1975—, Lieutenant Col. (Active Duty, 1976-1979)]. *PRACTICE AREAS:* Insurance Coverage Litigation; General Litigation; Trial Practice.

**JOHN A. DITO,** born Oakland, California, June 8, 1935; admitted to bar, 1962, California. *Education:* Stanford University (B.A., 1957); Harvard University (LL.B., 1961). Author, "Defense of Insurance Bad Faith Cases," Practising Law Institute, 1989. Lecturer: California CEB, 1978, 1980, 1981, 1985-1988; Practising Law Institute, 1987, 1988; Association of Business Trial Lawyers, 1985. Consultant, California CEB Civil Procedure Before Trial. *Member:* Los Angeles County and American Bar Associations; State Bar of California; Association of Business Trial Lawyers (Member, Board of Governors, 1991-1993; Member, Editorial Board, ABTL Report, 1991—; Irish American Bar Association (Member, Board of Directors, 1981—; President, 1992). *PRACTICE AREAS:* Insurance Coverage; General Litigation; Trial Practice.

**JOHN J. MOURA,** born Oakland, California, October 8, 1952; admitted to bar, 1978, California and U.S. District Court, Central District of California; 1981, U.S. Claims Court; 1982, U.S. Tax Court; 1984, U.S. District Court, Northern District of California; 1985, U.S. Court of Appeals, Ninth Circuit. *Education:* University of California at Berkeley (A.B., with distinction, 1974; J.D., 1978). *Member:* State Bar of California (Member,
*(This Listing Continued)*

CAA1208B

---

MARTINDALE-HUBBELL LAW DIRECTORY 1997

Litigation Section). *PRACTICE AREAS:* General Trial Practice; Insurance Coverage; Products Liability.

**DEBRA R. PUEBLA,** born Palo Alto, California, May 16, 1960; admitted to bar, 1986, California. *Education:* Cornell University (B.A., 1982; J.D., 1986). Member, Cornell University Moot Court Board. Co-Author, "The Pollution Exclusion Clause: It Says What it Means and Means What it Says," Mealey's Litigation Reports (October, 1990). *Member:* Los Angeles County and American Bar Associations; State Bar of California; Women's Law Association. *PRACTICE AREAS:* Insurance Coverage Litigation; General Litigation.

### ASSOCIATES

**SUZANNE M. RUFFLO,** born Akron, Ohio, May 10, 1961; admitted to bar, 1988, California; U.S. District Court, Northern and Central Districts of California. *Education:* University of Santa Clara (B.S., 1983); Loyola Marymount University (J.D., 1988). Editor-in-Chief, Entertainment Law Journal, 1987-1988. Author: Casenote, "Unfair Competition: Copy Cats Can No Longer 'Take the Money and Run' " Loyola Entertainment Law Journal, Vol. 7, No. 1. *Member:* Los Angeles County and American Bar Associations; State Bar of California. *PRACTICE AREAS:* General Business Litigation; Insurance Coverage Litigation.

**DAVID M. HARRIS,** born Santa Monica, California, March 19, 1964; admitted to bar, 1989, California; U.S. Court of Appeals, Ninth Circuit; U.S. District Court, Central District of California. *Education:* University of California, Los Angeles (B.A., 1986); University of Southern California (J.D., 1989). *Member:* Los Angeles County and American Bar Associations; State Bar of California. *PRACTICE AREAS:* Business Litigation; Trial Practice; Insurance Coverage Litigation; Real Property Law; Corporate Law.

**GAIL L. ORR,** born St. Paul, Minnesota, February 2, 1955; admitted to bar, 1991, California and U.S. District Court, Central and Eastern Districts of California. *Education:* University of Minnesota (B.A., magna cum laude, 1980; M.B.A., 1982) Phi Beta Kappa; University of Southern California (J.D., 1990). Participant, Hale Moot Court. *Member:* State Bar of California. *PRACTICE AREAS:* Insurance Coverage Litigation; Appellate Litigation.

**SHANE C. YOUTZ,** born Riverton, Wyoming, July 18, 1966; admitted to bar, 1991, California; U.S. Court of Appeals, Ninth Circuit and U.S. District Court, Central and Eastern Districts of California. *Education:* University of Wyoming (B.A., with honors, 1988); University of Minnesota (J.D., 1991). *PRACTICE AREAS:* Insurance Coverage Litigation; Business Litigation.

**WINNIE C. LOUIE,** born Hong Kong, December 1, 1964; admitted to bar, 1994, California, U.S. District Court, Central and Eastern Districts of California and U.S. Court of Appeals, Ninth Circuit. *Education:* Harvard-Radcliffe Colleges (B.A., with honors, 1987); University of California School of Law, Los Angeles (J.D., 1994). *PRACTICE AREAS:* Insurance Coverage Litigation.

---

## SKADDEN, ARPS, SLATE, MEAGHER & FLOM LLP
300 SOUTH GRAND AVENUE
### LOS ANGELES, CALIFORNIA 90071
Telephone: 213-687-5000
Fax: 213-687-5600

*Firm/Affiliate Offices:*
*New York, New York:* 919 Third Avenue, 10022. Telephone: 212-735-3000. Fax: 212-735-2000; 212-735-2001. Telex 645899 Skarslaw.
*Boston, Massachusetts:* One Beacon Street, 02108. Telephone: 617-573-4800. Fax: 617-573-4822.
*Washington, D.C.:* 1440 New York Avenue, N.W., 20005 Telephone: 202-371-7000. Fax: 202-393-5760.
*Wilmington, Delaware:* Skadden, Arps, Slate, Meagher & Flom (Delaware), One Rodney Square, P.O. Box 636, 19899. Telephone: 302-651-3000. Fax: 302-651-3001.
*Chicago, Illinois:* Skadden, Arps, Slate, Meagher & Flom (Illinois), 333 West Wacker Drive, 60606. Telephone: 312-407-0700. Fax: 312-407-0411.
*San Francisco, California:* Four Embarcadero Center, 94111. Telephone: 415-984-6400. Fax: 415-984-2698.
*Houston, Texas:* 1600 Smith Street, Suite 4460, 77002. Telephone: 713-655-5100. Fax: 713-655-5181.
*(This Listing Continued)*

*Newark, New Jersey:* One Newark Center, 07102. Telephone: 201-639-6800. Fax: 201-639-6858.

*Tokyo, Japan:* Skadden, Arps, Slate, Meagher & Flom (International), 403, ABS Building, 2-4-16 Kudan Minami, Chiyoda-ku, Tokyo 102. Telephone: 81-3-3221-9738. Fax: 81-3-3221-9753.

*London, England:* 25 Bucklersbury EC4N 8DA. Telephone: 011-44-171-248-9929. Fax: 011-44-171-489-8533.

*Hong Kong:* Skadden, Arps, Slate, Meagher & Flom (International), 30/F Peregrine Tower, Lippo Centre, 89 Queensway, Central. Telephone: 011-852-2820-0700. Fax: 011-852-2820-0727.

*Sydney, New South Wales, 2000, Australia:* Skadden, Arps, Slate, Meagher & Flom (International), Level 26-State Bank Centre, 52 Martin Place. Telephone: 011-61-2-9224-6000. Fax: 011-61-2-9224-6044.

*Toronto, Ontario:* Skadden, Arps, Slate, Meagher & Flom (International), Suite 1820, North Tower, P.O. Box 189, Royal Bank Plaza, M5J 2J4. Telephone: 416-777-4700. Fax: 416-777-4747.

*Paris, France:* 105 rue du Faubourg Saint-Honoré, 75008. Telephone: 011-33-1-40-75-44-44. Fax: 011-33-1-49-53-09-99.

*Brussels, Belgium:* 523 avenue Louise, Box 30, 1050. Telephone: 011-32-2-639-0300. Fax: 011-32-2-639-0339.

*Frankfurt, am Main, Germany:* MesseTurm, 27th Floor, 60308. Telephone: 011-49-69-9757-3000. Fax: 011-49-69-9757-3050.

*Beijing, China:* Skadden, Arps, Slate, Meagher & Flom (International), East Wing Office, Level 4, China World Trade Center, No. 1 Jian Guo Men Wai Avenue, 100004. Telephone: 011-86-10-6505-5511. Fax: 011-86-10-6505-5522.

*Moscow, Russia:* Pletshkovsky Pereulok 3/2, 107005. Telephone: 011-7-501-940-2304. Fax: 011-7-501-940-2511.

*Singapore, Singapore:* Skadden, Arps, Slate, Meagher & Flom (International), 9 Temasek Boulevard, Suite 29-01, Suntec City Tower Two, Singapore, 038989. Telephone: 011-65-434-2900. Fax: 011-65-434-2988.

General Practice.

PARTNERS

**JEROME L. COBEN,** born Cleveland, Ohio, 1944; admitted to bar, 1969, New York; 1977, District of Columbia; 1979, California. *Education:* Brown University (A.B., cum laude, 1966); New York University (J.D., 1969). Root-Tilden Scholar.

**RAND S. APRIL,** born Brooklyn, N.Y., 1951; admitted to bar, 1976, New York; 1989, California. *Education:* Northwestern University (B.A., 1972); Columbia University (J.D., 1975). Phi Beta Kappa. Harlan Fiske Stone Scholar.

**JOSEPH J. GIUNTA,** born Cleveland, Ohio, 1948; admitted to bar, 1977, New York; 1985, California. *Education:* Stanford University (B.S., 1972); Washington College of Law of American University (J.D., magna cum laude, 1976). Associate Editor, American University Law Review, 1975-1976.

**JOHN A. DONOVAN,** born New York, N.Y., 1942; admitted to bar, 1967, New York; 1982, California. *Education:* Harvard University (A.B., 1965); Fordham University (LL.B., 1967). Articles Editor, Fordham Law Review, 1966-1967.

**FRANK ROTHMAN,** born Los Angeles, Cal., 1926; admitted to bar, 1952, California; 1969, District of Columbia. *Education:* University of California at Los Angeles and University of Southern California (A.B., 1949); University of Southern California (LL.B., 1951). Member, Board of Editors, Southern California Law Review, 1950-1951.

**DOUGLAS B. ADLER,** born New York, N.Y., 1952; admitted to bar, 1978, New York; 1987, California. *Education:* Cornell University (A.B., with distinction, 1974); Boston College Law School (J.D., cum laude, 1977). Editor, Boston College Industrial and Commercial Law Review.

**BRIAN J. MCCARTHY,** born New York, N.Y., 1953; admitted to bar, 1979, New York; 1984, California. *Education:* Tufts University (B.A., magna cum laude, 1975); Fordham University (J.D., 1978).

**EDWARD E. GONZALEZ,** born Havana, Cuba, 1954; admitted to bar, 1980, New York; 1987, California. *Education:* Princeton University (A.B., summa cum laude, 1976); Columbia University (J.D., 1979).

**NICHOLAS P. SAGGESE,** born Passaic, N.J., 1947; admitted to bar, 1980, California. *Education:* University of California at Los Angeles (B.A., 1969; M.B.A., 1973); Loyola University of Los Angeles (J.D., cum laude, 1980). Beta Gamma Sigma. St. Thomas More Honor Society. Member, Loyola University of Los Angeles Law Review.

*(This Listing Continued)*

**RODRIGO A. GUERRA, JR.,** born Indianapolis, Ind., 1956; admitted to bar, 1983, California. *Education:* Stanford University (B.A., 1978); University of California School of Law, Anderson Graduate School of Management (M.B.A., J.D., 1982).

**DARREL J. HIEBER,** born Chicago, Ill., 1953; admitted to bar, 1981, District of Columbia and California. *Education:* University of California at Santa Barbara (B.A., 1977); University of California at Los Angeles (J.D., 1980). Order of the Coif. Editor, UCLA International Law Journal, Affiliated with ABA International Lawyer, 1980. Judicial Extern, to Judge J. Clifford Wallace, U.S. Court of Appeals, Ninth Circuit, 1979. Law Clerk to U.S. District Judge William Matthew Byrne, Jr., Central District California, 1980-1981.

**THOMAS C. JANSON, JR.,** born Yonkers, N.Y., 1956; admitted to bar, 1982, New York; 1985, California. *Education:* Massachusetts Institute of Technology (B.S., 1978); University of Miami (J.D., 1981).

**JOHN D. RAYIS,** born Baghdad, Iraq, 1954; admitted to bar, 1981, Michigan; 1985, Illinois; 1989, California. *Education:* Michigan State University (B.A., with honors, 1977; B.S., with honors, 1977) ; Wayne State University (J.D., cum laude, 1979); University of Michigan (LL.M., 1980).

**RAYMOND W. VICKERS,** born Wilmington, N.C., 1943; admitted to bar, 1969, New York (Not admitted in California). *Education:* Harvard University (A.B., 1965; LL.B., 1968).

**GREGG A. NOEL,** born Los Angeles, Cal., 1957; admitted to bar, 1982, California. *Education:* Loyola Marymount University (B.B.A., magna cum laude, 1979; B.A., magna cum laude, 1979; J.D., cum laude, 1982). Alpha Sigma Nu, St. Thomas More Law Honor Society.

**ERIC S. WAXMAN,** born Los Angeles, Cal., 1957; admitted to bar, 1982, California. *Education:* University of California at Los Angeles (B.A., magna cum laude, 1979); University of California at Davis (J.D., 1982). Pi Gamma Mu. Editor, University of California at Davis Law Review, 1981-1982.

**JEFFREY B. VALLE,** born Rochester, N.Y., 1955; admitted to bar, 1983, California. *Education:* University of California at Los Angeles (B.A., 1980); Boalt Hall School of Law, University of California (J.D., 1983).

**JEFFREY H. DASTEEL,** born Santa Monica, Cal., 1953; admitted to bar, 1983, California. *Education:* University of California at Davis (B.A., with honors, 1974); University of California at Los Angeles (M.A., 1978); Loyola Law School of Los Angeles (J.D., cum laude, 1983). St. Thomas More Law Honor Society. Ninth Circuit Editor, Loyola of Los Angeles Law Review, 1982-1983.

**HARRIET S. POSNER,** born Chicago, Ill., 1960; admitted to bar, 1984, California. *Education:* Harvard University (B.A., cum laude, 1980); University of California School of Law, Los Angeles (J.D., 1984).

**PETER SIMSHAUSER,** born Springfield, Ill., 1957; admitted to bar, 1984, Illinois; 1986, California. *Education:* Augustana College (A.B., summa cum laude, 1979); University of Illinois (B.S., 1980); Harvard University (J.D., cum laude, 1983). Law Clerk, Northern District of Illinois, 1983-1985.

**MICHAEL A. WORONOFF,** born New York, N.Y., 1960; admitted to bar, 1985, California. *Education:* Purdue University (B.S.I.M., with highest honors, 1982; M.S.I.A., 1982); University of Michigan (J.D., cum laude, 1985). Phi Beta Kappa.

**MICHAEL A. LAWSON,** born Little Rock, Ark., 1953; admitted to bar, 1978, District of Columbia; 1982, New York; 1990, California. *Education:* Loyola University of Los Angeles (B.A., 1975); Harvard University (J.D., 1978).

**JEFFREY H. COHEN,** born New York, N.Y., 1963; admitted to bar, 1988, California. *Education:* The Wharton School, University of Pennsylvania (B.S., cum laude, 1985); University of California at Los Angeles (J.D., 1988). First Place, Roscoe Pound Moot Court Competition.

**KAREN LEILI CORMAN,** born Los Angeles, Cal., 1962; admitted to bar, 1988, California. *Education:* University of California at Los Angeles (B.A., magna cum laude, 1984); Harvard University (J.D., 1987). Phi Beta Kappa.

**ALLAN G. MUTCHNIK,** born Winnipeg, Canada, 1963; admitted to bar, 1988, California. *Education:* University of California, Los Angeles (B.A., 1985); Cornell University (J.D., cum laude, 1988).

**JOHN E. MENDEZ,** born Brooklyn, New York, April 27, 1957; admitted to bar, 1983, New York; 1988, California. *Education:* Rutgers Univer-

*(This Listing Continued)*

CALIFORNIA—LOS ANGELES                              MARTINDALE-HUBBELL LAW DIRECTORY 1997

**SKADDEN, ARPS, SLATE, MEAGHER & FLOM LLP,** Los Angeles—Continued

sity (B.A., 1979); Harvard University (J.D., 1982). *Member:* New York State and American Bar Associations; State Bar of California.

### COUNSEL

**PETER W. CLAPP,** born Washington, D.C., 1946; admitted to bar, 1982, California; 1984, New York. *Education:* Columbia University (B.A., 1969); Hastings College of Law, University of California (J.D., 1982). Order of the Coif. Member, Hastings Law Journal, 1981-1982.

**LORI ANNE CZEPIEL,** born 1963; admitted to bar, 1987, California. *Education:* Northwestern University (B.A.); Boston University (J.D., 1987).

**MOSHE J. KUSHMAN,** born Oakland, Cal., 1956; admitted to bar, 1987, California. *Education:* University of California, Los Angeles (B.A., cum laude, 1976; M.A., Pol.Sc., 1978); University of Southern California (M.B.A., 1980; M.B.T., 1981); University of Judaism (B.L., 1980); The Jewish Theological Seminary of America (M.A., Hebrew Literature, 1983; Rabbinical Ordination, 1983); Loyola Law School (J.D., cum laude, 1987). Alpha Sigma Nu. St. Thomas More Law Honor Society. Executive Editor, Loyola of Los Angeles Law Review.

**WALTER S. LOWRY,** born Pascagoula, Miss., 1957; admitted to bar, 1984, New York; 1988, California. *Education:* Brown University (A.B., 1980); New York University (J.D., 1983). Member, New York University Law Review.

**GARRETT J. WALTZER,** born Nashville, Tenn.; admitted to bar, 1987, California. *Education:* Colorado College (B.A., 1983); University of California at Los Angeles (J.D., 1987).

### OF COUNSEL

**WARREN ETTINGER,** born Cleveland, Ohio, 1929; admitted to bar, 1956, California. *Education:* University of Southern California (B.S., 1952; LL.B., 1955).

(For Complete Biographical data on all Personnel, see New York, New York Professional Biographies).

## DANIEL M. SKLAR
*A PROFESSIONAL LAW CORPORATION*
1900 AVENUE OF THE STARS, SUITE 1450
**LOS ANGELES, CALIFORNIA**
Telephone: 310-277-2582
FAX: 310-277-5953

*General Practice. Entertainment and Copyright Law. Litigation.*

**DANIEL M. SKLAR,** born New York, N.Y., September 15, 1926; admitted to bar, 1953, New York; 1961, California. *Education:* University of Colorado (A.B., cum laude, 1949); Harvard University (LL.B., 1952). Phi Alpha Theta. Author: "Pour-Over Trusts," New York Law Journal, 1958; "How to Make $12,000 A Year By Doing Something," Beverly Hills Bar Association Journal, 1971; "Judicial Incompetence: A Plea for Reform," (A.B.A.S., Nov., 1983); "The Act of Persuasive Writing," California Litigation (Pub. Litig. Sect., Cal. St. Bar Assn, 1989-1993). Director, Legal and Business Affairs, United Artists TV, 1960-1963. Director, Business Affairs, CBS-TV, Hollywood, 1963-1964. Adjunct Instructor, Legal Research and Writing, Whittier College School of Law, 1988-1989. Visiting Associate Professor of Law, University of Tennessee College of Law, 1993. Trustee, Pension Plan, Writers Guild of America, 1961-1962. Member: Los Angeles Copyright Society; Academy of Television Arts and Sciences; Writer's Guild of America, West. *Member:* New York State and American Bar Associations; State Bar of California (Executive Committee, Litigation Section, 1986-1989; Chairman, 1985-1986). **PRACTICE AREAS:** Entertainment; Civil Litigation.

## SLAFF, MOSK & RUDMAN
*Established in 1965*
SUITE 825, 9200 SUNSET BOULEVARD
**LOS ANGELES, CALIFORNIA 90069**
Telephone: 310-275-5351
Telecopier: 310-273-8706

*Motion Picture, Entertainment, Television, Copyright and Trademark Law. Trials and Appeals in Federal and State Courts.*

*(This Listing Continued)*

CAA1210B

**GEORGE SLAFF** (1906-1989).

**EDWARD MOSK** (1916-1989).

### MEMBERS OF FIRM

**NORMAN G. RUDMAN,** born Chicago, Illinois, September 8, 1930; admitted to bar, 1956, California; 1963, U.S. Supreme Court. *Education:* University of California at Los Angeles (A.B., 1952); Boalt Hall School of Law, University of California (J.D., 1955). Order of the Coif. Revising Editor, California Law Review, 1954-1955. Author: Comment, "Estoppel under the Uniform Divorce Recognition Act," 40 California Law Review, 503, 1954; "Sitting in on the Omnibus— The 1961 Segregation Cases," 22 Law in Transition, 206, 1963; "Incorporation under the Fourteenth Amendment— The Other Side of the Coin," 3 Law in Transition, Q 141, 1966. Co-Author: Supplement, with W.T. Laube, "Collier on Bankruptcy," 1955; with R.C. Solomon, "Who loves a Parade? Walker v. City of Birmingham," 4 Law in Transition, Q 185, 1967; "Brambles, Nettles and Bees: Things That Sting the Film Investor" in Tax Shelters: How to Avoid Murphy's Law, Illinois Institute of Continuing Legal Education, 1974, reprinted in Practicing Law Institute Legal and Business Problems of Financing Motion Pictures, 1979: "The Completion Guaranty: Bait, Hook and Landing Net," Fourth Annual UCLA Entertainment Symposium, 1979; Chapter, "Over-Budget Protection and the Completion Guarantee," in Squire, The Movie Business Book, Prentice-Hall, 1983; "The Finishing Touch: The Completion Guarantee," in Squire, The Movie Business Book, Second Edition, Simon & Schuster, 1992. Member, Panel of Arbitrators, Producers-Writers Guild of America Basic Agreement of 1977. Member, Panel of Arbitrators, American Film Marketing Association. *Member:* Beverly Hills, Los Angeles County and American (Member, Litigation and Patent, Trademark and Copyright Section) Bar Associations; State Bar of California. **PRACTICE AREAS:** Motion Picture; Entertainment; Television; Copyright and Trademark; Transactions and Litigation.

**MARC R. STEIN,** born Passaic, New Jersey, March 18, 1947; admitted to bar, 1976, California; 1985, U.S. Supreme Court. *Education:* University of California at Berkeley (A.B., 1968); University of California at Los Angeles (J.D., 1976). Member, Board of Editors, University of California at Los Angeles Law Review, 1975-1976. Recipient, National First Prize, Nathan Burkan Memorial Competition, 1976. Author: Comment, "California's Common Law Defense Against Landlord Retaliatory Conduct," 22 UCLA Law Review 1161, 1975; "Termination of Transfers and Licenses under the New Copyright Act: Thorny Problems for the Copyright Bar," 24 UCLA Law Review 1141, 1977, also published in 26 ASCAP Copyright Law Symposium 1, Columbia University Press, 1981; "Motion Picture Exhibition Without A License: Alchemy in the Second Circuit?," 1 Hastings College of Law Journal of Communications and Entertainment Law 277, 1978; "Nimmer on Copyright," Book Review, 47 George Washington Law Review 339, 1978. Member, Panel of Arbitrators, American Film Marketing Association. Instructor, Peter Stark Program, USC School of Cinema-TV, 1989-1995. *Member:* Beverly Hills, Los Angeles County and American (Member, Sections on: Patent, Trademark and Copyright Law; Corporation, Banking and Business Law) Bar Associations; State Bar of California. **PRACTICE AREAS:** Entertainment Transactions; General Business Litigation; Copyright and Trademark.

**VALERIE V. FLUGGE,** born Sioux Falls, South Dakota, April 11, 1959; admitted to bar, 1983, California. *Education:* University of South Dakota (B.S., 1980); University of Southern California (J.D., 1983). Order of the Coif. Member, Editorial Board, University of Southern California Law Review, 1982-1983. Law Clerk to the Honorable Warren J. Ferguson, Ninth Circuit Court of Appeals, 1983-1984. Author: Note, "Works of Applied Art: An Expansion of Copyright Protection," 56 Southern California Law Review 241, 1982. *Member:* Beverly Hills, Los Angeles County and American Bar Associations; State Bar of California. **PRACTICE AREAS:** General Business Litigation; Entertainment; Copyright and Trademark.

REFERENCE: City National Bank.

## RONALD P. SLATES
### A PROFESSIONAL CORPORATION
Established in 1975

**548 SOUTH SPRING STREET, SUITE 1012**
**LOS ANGELES, CALIFORNIA 90013-2309**
Telephone: 213-624-1515; 213-654-1461
Fax: 213-624-7536; 213-654-1463

*Bankruptcy (Creditor), Commercial Debt Collection with Pre-Judgment Writs of Attachment and Possession, General Business and Commercial Litigation and Real Estate Transactional Litigation, Business Contractual Negotiations.*

FIRM PROFILE: Ronald P. Slates, P.C. was registered in 1980 as the professional law corporation successor to the sole practice of Ronald P. Slates which commenced practice in 1975 after Mr. Slates' return from one year in Thailand and three and one-half years of living and working in Europe. There he was a principal legal counsel in the United States Army Judge Advocate General's Corps. In 1974 he obtained a Masters of Law Degree at Kings College of the University of London.

Upon commencing practice in 1975, the firm emphasized commercial debt collection and business litigation. The firm's clientele have requested, and the firm has responded, with expert creditor bankruptcy, Real Estate, and financial institution litigation as well as developing an expertise in financial and real estate negotiations and transactional matters.

Ronald P. Slates, P.C. aggressively and ethically pursues its clients' objectives with close and careful personal service and attention being given to each individual and business client.

The firm offers foreign language capabilities - German, French and Spanish.

**RONALD P. SLATES,** born Los Angeles, California, November 24, 1943; admitted to bar, 1969, California; 1975, U.S. District Court, Central District of California; 1990, U.S. Court of Appeals, Ninth Circuit and U.S. Supreme Court. *Education:* University of California at Los Angeles (B.A., 1965; J.D., 1968); King's College, University of London, England (LL.M., 1974). Phi Alpha Delta. *Member:* Los Angeles County Bar Association (Member, Sections on: Business and Corporations; Pre-Judgment Writs; Real Estate); State Bar of California. LANGUAGES: German and French. **PRACTICE AREAS:** Creditors' Rights; Bankruptcy; Commercial Debt Collection; Business Litigation; Real Estate.

---

**G. MICHAEL JACKSON,** born Colorado Springs, Colorado, February 27, 1956; admitted to bar, 1985, Nevada and U.S. District Court, District of Nevada; 1988, California and U.S. District Court, Central District of California; 1990, U.S. Court of Appeals, Ninth Circuit; 1993, Georgia. *Education:* University of Nevada (B.S.B.A., 1980; M.P.A., 1982); California Western School of Law (J.D., 1985). Recipient, American Jurisprudence Award in Conflicts of Law. *Member:* Los Angeles County, Beverly Hills and American Bar Associations; State Bar of Nevada; State Bar of California; The Association of Trial Lawyers of America. LANGUAGES: Spanish. **PRACTICE AREAS:** Bankruptcy; Business Litigation; Creditors Rights; Commercial Transfers; Commercial Litigation.

REPRESENTATIVE CLIENTS: ABC Textile; Amertex International Ltd.; B.N.Y. Financial; Bruder Releasing, Inc.; C-Air Int'l, Inc.; California Textile Industry; Coleman Powermate, Inc.; Compensation Resources Group; Congress/Talcott Corp.; Continental Business Credit; CoreStates Bank, N.A.; Fabric Junction Inc.; Finova Financial Innovators; Fifth Third Bank of Toledo, N.A.; First Commercial Bank, California; Hamilton Adams Linen; Hong Kong Linen; Jalate, Ltd.; J.M. Leibowitz and Associates, Certified Public Accountants; Lafayette Textile; Law Offices of Knerr & Oyler; Law Offices of Poms, Smith, Lande and Rose, P.C.; Law Offices of Pretty, Schroeder, Brueggemann and Clark; Metropolitan Credit Services; Money Store, Inc.; National Spinning Co., Inc.; Neman Bros. and Associates; Rock Candy, Inc.; Salt Lake City Credit Union; Slater Roof Co., Inc.; Solomon Fabrics Co.; Streamline Shippers Assn.; Superior Assembly and Distribution; Swenvest Corp.; Tustin Thrift & Loan; UNIFI Textiles, Inc.; Von's Co., Inc.; Woodleaf Investment Co., Inc.

---

## SHELDON H. SLOAN
**1801 AVENUE OF THE STARS, SUITE 417**
**LOS ANGELES, CALIFORNIA 90067**
Telephone: 310-201-0622
Fax: 310-556-1620
Email: SSloanlaw@aol.com

*Governmental Affairs, Administrative and Legislative Advocacy, Business and Real Estate.*

*(This Listing Continued)*

---

**SHELDON H. SLOAN,** born Minneapolis, Minnesota, December 25, 1935; admitted to bar, 1962, California, U.S. Supreme Court, U.S. Court of Military Appeals and U.S. Claims Court. *Education:* University of California at Los Angeles (B.S., in Bus. Adm., 1958); University of Southern California (J.D., 1961). Phi Delta Phi. Author: "Maximum and Minimum Sentences for Common Misdemeanors and Infractions," Journal of Center for Judicial Education and Research, 1974-1976; "Handling Extradition Cases," Journal of Center for Judicial Education and Research, 1976. Attorney, U.S. Department of Justice, Washington, D.C., 1962-1963. Member, Regional Council, U.S. Small Business Administration, Los Angeles, 1972-1973. Public Member, State of California Board of Registration for Professional Engineers, 1972-1973. Judge of the Municipal Court, Los Angeles Judicial District, 1973-1976. Member: California College of Trial Judges, 1973; National College of the State Judiciary, 1975. Member of Faculty, California Trial Judges College, 1975. Member, Panel of Arbitrators, American Arbitration Association. Member, Los Angeles County Music and Performing Arts Commission, 1981—. Vice-President, State of California Museum of Science and Industry, 1992—. Chairman, 1983-1984 and Member, 1983—, Senator Pete Wilson Committee on Judicial Qualification, Central District of California. Member, Los Angeles Memorial Coliseum Commission, 1994. *Member:* Los Angeles County Bar Association (Trustee, 1991-1997; President, 1996-1997); Member: Arbitration Committee, 1969-1970; Committee on Municipal Courts, 1975; Special Committee on Court Reorganization, 1976-1982; Judicial Appointments Committee, 1982-1988, Chair, 1985-1987; Chair, Committee on Judicial Evaluation, 1989-1993; Chair, Committee on Judicial Resources, 1992-1993); State Bar of California (Member, Committee on Maintenance of Professional Competence, 1972-1973).

REFERENCE: 1st Business Bank.

---

## LAW OFFICES OF TODD M. SLOAN
**LOS ANGELES, CALIFORNIA**
(See Malibu)

*General Litigation, Unfair Competition Law, Banking Litigation.*

---

## SMALL LARKIN & KIDDÉ
**10940 WILSHIRE BOULEVARD, EIGHTEENTH FLOOR**
**LOS ANGELES, CALIFORNIA 90024**
Telephone: 310-209-4400
Fax: 310-209-4450
Cable Address: SLK MARK
Telex: 49616151
Email: SLK@SLKlaw.com
URL: http://www.lainet.com/legal/

*Domestic and International Intellectual Property Law, including Counseling, Due Diligence Investigations, Litigation and Licensing in Trademark, Patent, Copyright, Unfair Competition, Trade Secrets and related matters and Business and Commercial Litigation.*

FIRM PROFILE: Small Larkin & Kiddé was founded in 1992. The firm's major area of concentration is in intellectual property matters and its practice includes counseling, due diligence investigations, licensing and litigation in all areas of trademark, copyright, patent, trade secret and unfair competition law. The Firm has substantial experience in trademark, copyright, patent and trade secret litigation, and in the prosecution and counseling of trademark matters with an extensive domestic and International trademark practice.

### MEMBERS OF FIRM

**THOMAS M. SMALL,** born Sullivan, Indiana, March 4, 1933; admitted to bar, 1957, Indiana; 1960, Illinois; 1970, California; U.S. Court of Appeals, Sixth, Seventh, Ninth and Federal Circuits; registered to practice before U.S. Patent and Trademark Office. *Education:* Purdue University (B.S., 1957); Indiana University (J.D., 1957). Editor, Indiana Law Journal, 1956-1957. Teaching Associate, Indiana University School of Law, 1959-1960. Chairman, Patent, Trademark and Copyright Section of the State Bar of California, 1978-1979. President, Los Angeles Patent Law Association, 1975-1976. *Member:* Los Angeles County and American Bar Associations; State Bar of California; American Intellectual Property Law Association; Licensing Executive Society (U.S.A. and Canada; Trustee, 1980-1982; Vice President, 1987-1989 and 1993-1996; President Elect, 1996; International

*(This Listing Continued)*

## SMALL LARKIN & KIDDÉ, Los Angeles—Continued

Delegate). *PRACTICE AREAS:* Trademark, Patent and Copyright; Arbitration; Mediation. *Email:* TMS@SLKlaw.com

**JOAN KUPERSMITH LARKIN,** born New York, N.Y., January 30, 1953; admitted to bar, 1977, New York; 1978, District of Columbia and Florida; 1980, California; U.S. Court of Appeals, Sixth, Ninth, District of Columbia and Federal Circuits. *Education:* New York University (B.A., 1973); New England School of Law (J.D., 1976). Phi Alpha Delta. *Member:* Los Angeles County and American Bar Associations; State Bar of California (Member: Executive Committee, Patent, Trademark and Copyright Section, 1986-1989); International Trademark Association (Member: Board of Directors, 1987-1989; Member: U.S. Department of Commerce's Public Advisory Committee for Trademark Affairs, 1979—); Los Angeles Intellectual Property Law Association (Member: Board of Directors, 1992-1994); Women Lawyers Association of Los Angeles. *PRACTICE AREAS:* Trademark, Copyright and Unfair Competition. *Email:* JKL@SLKlaw.com

**THOMAS S. KIDDÉ,** born Pasadena, California, April 26, 1950; admitted to bar, 1974, California; 1985, Idaho; U.S. Supreme Court; U.S. Court of Appeals, Ninth, Tenth and Federal Circuits. *Education:* Stanford University (B.A., 1971); Hastings College of Law, University of California (J.D., 1974). Phi Delta Phi. *Member:* Panel of Arbitrators, American Arbitration Association. *Member:* Los Angeles County, Federal and American (Member: Litigation Section; Tort and Insurance Practice Section; Patent, Trademark and Copyright Section) Bar Associations; State Bar of California; Idaho State Bar; International Trademark Association; Defense Research Institute; Association of Business Trial Lawyers. *PRACTICE AREAS:* Intellectual Property Litigation; Unfair Competition and Commercial Litigation; Trademark; Arbitration. *Email:* TSK@SLKlaw.com

**CHRISTOPHER C. LARKIN,** born Stuttgart, Germany, 1955; admitted to bar, 1981, New York; 1985, California; U.S. Court of Appeals, Ninth and Federal Circuits; U.S. Supreme Court. *Education:* Stanford University (B.A., with distinction, 1977); Columbia University (J.D., 1980). Phi Beta Kappa. Harlan Fiske Stone Scholar. Recipient, Young B. Smith Award. *Member:* Los Angeles County and American (Member: Litigation Section; Patent, Trademark and Copyright Section) Bar Associations; International Trademark Association; American Intellectual Property Law Association; Los Angeles Intellectual Property Association (Member: Board of Directors, 1995—); United States Copyright Society. *LANGUAGES:* German. *PRACTICE AREAS:* Trademark; Copyright; Litigation. *Email:* CCL@SLKlaw.com

**JON E. HOKANSON,** born Manistee, Michigan, January 15, 1948; admitted to bar, 1980, District of Columbia; 1982, Texas; 1985, California; registered to practice before U.S. Patent and Trademark Office. *Education:* Albion College (B.A., with honors, 1970); University of Michigan (M.S.E., 1976); George Washington University (J.D., with honors, 1979). Clerk, Judge Jack R. Miller, U.S. Court of Customs and Patent Appeals, 1979-1981. Patent Examiner, U.S. Patent and Trademark Office, 1977-1979. *Member:* Los Angeles County and American Bar Associations; State Bar of California; American Intellectual Property Law Association; Los Angeles Intellectual Property Law Association (Member: Board of Directors, 1992—). *PRACTICE AREAS:* Patent, Trademark and Copyright. *Email:* JH@SLKlaw.com

**JANET A. KOBRIN,** born Chicago, Illinois, July 10, 1942; admitted to bar, 1985, California and U.S. Court of Appeals, Ninth and Federal Circuits. *Education:* Brandeis University (B.A., 1964); University of Chicago (M.S.T., 1965); University of California School of Law at Los Angeles (J.D., 1984). Staff Member, UCLA Law Review, 1982-1983. Chief Article Editor, UCLA Law Review, 1983-1984. Author, "Confidentiality of Genetic Information," 30 UCLA Law Review, 1283 (1983). Participant, Los Angeles Trial Attorneys Project, 1988-1989. Co-Chair, Los Angeles Trial Attorneys Project, 1989-1990. *Member:* Los Angeles County and American (Member: Patent, Trademark and Copyright, and Litigation Sections) Bar Associations; State Bar of California (Member: Patent, Trademark and Copyright and Litigation Sections); United States Copyright Society. *PRACTICE AREAS:* Intellectual Property; Unfair Competition; Trade Secrets; Commercial Litigation. *Email:* JAK@SLKlaw.com

---

**KENNETH L. WILTON,** born Encino, California, November 13, 1961; admitted to bar, 1986, California, U.S. Court of Appeals, Ninth, Eleventh and Federal Circuits and U.S. Tax Court. *Education:* University of California at Los Angeles (B.A., 1983); Hastings College of Law, University of California (J.D., 1986). Phi Alpha Delta. Editor-in-Chief, COMM/ENT,
*(This Listing Continued)*

Hastings Journal of Communications and Entertainment Law, 1985-1986. *Member:* Beverly Hills (Member: Intellectual Property Law and Litigation Sections), Los Angeles County (Participant, Los Angeles Trial Attorneys Project, 1989) and American Bar Associations; State Bar of California (Member: Patent, Trademark and Copyright and Litigation Sections); Computer Law Association. *PRACTICE AREAS:* Intellectual Property; Unfair Competition; Trade Secrets; Computer Law; Commercial Litigation. *Email:* KLW@SLKlaw.com

**BARRY C. SEATON,** born Toronto, Canada, May 3, 1962; admitted to bar, 1987, California and U.S. Court of Appeals, Ninth Circuit. *Education:* University of California at San Diego, Revelle College, Provost's List (B.A., with honors, 1984); University of Southern California (J.D., 1987). Phi Alpha Delta. *Member:* Beverly Hills Bar Association (Member: Intellectual Property Section); State Bar of California. *PRACTICE AREAS:* Trademark and Copyright.

**KAREN E. SAMUELS,** born Norfolk, Virginia, September 7, 1964; admitted to bar, 1992, California and U.S. Court of Appeals, Federal Circuit. *Education:* University of Virginia (B.A., with distinction, 1986); Harvard Law School (J.D., cum laude, 1991). Phi Beta Kappa. Law Clerk to Hon. Rebecca Beach Smith, U.S. District Court, Eastern District of Virginia, 1991-1992. Editor, Harvard Human Rights Journal, 1989-1990. *Member:* Beverly Hills and Los Angeles County Bar Associations; State Bar of California. *LANGUAGES:* French. *PRACTICE AREAS:* Trademark; Copyright; Litigation. *Email:* KES@SLKlaw.com

**DONALD J. COX, JR.,** born Trenton, New Jersey, April 27, 1963; admitted to bar, 1992, California and U.S. Court of Appeals, Federal Circuit; registered to practice before U.S. Patent and Trademark Office. *Education:* Rutgers University (B.S.E.E., 1985); University of the Pacific (J.D., 1992). *Member:* Los Angeles County Bar Association; State Bar of California; Institute of Electrical and Electronic Engineers; American Intellectual Property Law Association; Los Angeles Intellectual Property Law Association. [Capt., U.S. Air Force, 1985-1989]. *PRACTICE AREAS:* Patent, Copyright and Trademark; Computer Law. *Email:* COXD@SLKlaw.com

**MICHELLE A. COOKE,** born Queens, New York, August 18, 1967; admitted to bar, 1993, California and U.S. Court of Appeals, Ninth Circuit. *Education:* University of Virginia (B.A., 1989; J.D., 1992). *Member:* State Bar of California. *PRACTICE AREAS:* Trademark; Litigation. *Email:* MAC@SLKlaw.com

**SASHA E. FARRAH,** born Newport News, Virginia, September 26, 1962; admitted to bar, 1989, Pennsylvania; 1990, District of Columbia (Not admitted in California). *Education:* University of Madrid, Complutense (Certificate of Proficiency Advanced Level of Spanish Language and Culture, 1984-1985); American University (B.A., 1984); George Washington University (J.D., 1988). Omicron Delta Kappa Honor Society. *Member:* American Intellectual Property Law Association; International Trademark Association. *LANGUAGES:* Spanish. *PRACTICE AREAS:* Trademark; Copyright; Unfair Trade; Litigation.

### LEGAL SUPPORT PERSONNEL

**SUSAN BRADY BLASCO,** born Upland, California, March 12, 1954. *Education:* Chaffey College (A.A., 1974); University of California at Los Angeles (B.A., 1976); Attorney Assistant Training Program (Certificate with honors, 1977). Alpha Gamma Sigma. Speaker: Intellectual Property Law Section of the State Bar of California, "The Trademark Office Visits Los Angeles," 1994; Intellectual Property Law Section of the State Bar of California, "Going Abroad: Practical Solutions to Protecting Intellectual Property on the Changing International Scene," 1991. *Member:* International Trademark Association (Member: Meetings Committee). (Intellectual Property Administrator). *Email:* SBB@SLKlaw.com

---

## SMALTZ, ANDERSON & FAHEY

*A PROFESSIONAL LAW CORPORATION*
*333 SOUTH GRAND AVENUE, SUITE 3580*
**LOS ANGELES, CALIFORNIA 90071**
*Telephone: 213-625-1666*
*Telex: 213-625-8010*

*Complex Business Litigation including Antitrust, Environmental, Intellectual Property, Securities and White Collar Criminal Defense. Trial and Appellate Practice in State and Federal Courts.*

*(This Listing Continued)*

## PROFESSIONAL BIOGRAPHIES

## CALIFORNIA—LOS ANGELES

*FIRM PROFILE: Smaltz, Anderson & Fahey is a small but nationally prominent firm of trial lawyers who specialize in complex business litigation and white collar criminal defense. Its lawyers offer the trial capabilities of a major law firm.*

*Smaltz, Anderson & Fahey serves a diverse clientele, including major oil companies, manufacturing concerns, securities brokers, municipalities, computer software developers and individuals.*

*The firm practices primarily in southern California but has handled matters throughout the country.*

**DONALD C. SMALTZ,** born February 5, 1937; admitted to bar, 1961, Pennsylvania; 1965, California; 1971, U.S. Supreme Court. *Education:* Penn State University (B.A., 1958); Dickinson School of Law (LL.B., 1961). Author: "California and Federal Pretrial Criminal Procedure," 1978; "Due Process Limitations on Prosecutorial Discretion in Recharging Defendants: Pearce to Blackledge to Bordenkircher," 1979; "Tactical Considerations for Effective Representation During A Government Investigation," 1979; "Application of Government's Traditional Criminal Weapons to Corporations and Their Officers" and "The Racketeer Influenced and Corrupt Organizations Act," 1980; "Some Ethical Problems in the Defense of Criminal Cases," 1977. Asst. U.S. Attorney, So. Dist. of CA., 1964-1966. Special Asst. U.S. Attorney for Central Dist. of CA., 1967-1968. Independent Counsel, In Re Espy, 1994—. Adjunct Associate Professor of Law, Advanced Criminal Procedure, Southwestern University, Los Angeles, 1972-1980. Fellow, American College of Trial Lawyers. Chairman, Civil Justice Reform Act Advisory Group, Central District, CA, 1991-1994. Lawyer Representative, 1978-1981, Chairman, 1980-1981, 1991-1994, 9th Cir. Judicial Conference. **PRACTICE AREAS:** Complex Business Litigation; Antitrust; Environmental; White Collar Criminal Defense.

**LEIGHTON M. ANDERSON,** born December 28, 1953; admitted to bar, 1978, California. *Education:* Claremont Mens College (B.A., 1976); Columbia University (J.D., 1978). Chair, 1992-1996, Vice Chair, 1990-1991, 1996—, Oil Refining and Marketing Committee, ABA Section of Natural Resources, Energy and Environmental Law. **REPORTED CASES:** Rebel Oil Co., Inc. v. ARCO, 51 F.3d 1421 (9th Cir. 1995); Little Oil Co., Inc. v. ARCO, 852 F.2d 441 (9th Cir. 1988); Orloff v. Allman, 819 F.2d 904 (9th Cir. 1987); Dyke v. Gulf Oil Corp., 601 F.2d 557 (Em. Appl. 1979); Southern Nevada Shell Dealers Assoc. v. Shell Oil Co., 725 F. Supp. 1104 (D. Nov. 1989); Abadjian v. Gulf Oil Co., 602 F. Supp. 874 (C.D. Cal. 1984); California ARCO Distributors, Inc. v. ARCO, 158 Cal. App. 3d 349 (1984). **PRACTICE AREAS:** Complex Business Litigation; Antitrust; Environmental. *Email:* L8NANDERS@AOL.COM

**WILLIAM F. FAHEY,** born November 8, 1951; admitted to bar, 1976, California. *Education:* University of Southern California (B.S., magna cum laude, 1973); University of California, Los Angeles (J.D., 1976). Phi Alpha Delta. Law Clerk, Hon. Laughlin E. Waters, Central District of California, 1976-1978. Assistant U.S. Attorney, Central District of California, 1980-1992. Chief, Public Corruption and Government Fraud Section, 1986-1990 and First Assistant Chief, Criminal Division, 1990-1992. Recipient, John Marshall Award, 1991. *Member:* Federal and American Bar Associations. **PRACTICE AREAS:** White Collar Crime; Securities; Environmental; Complex Business Litigation.

**JAMES D. KOWAL,** born Los Angles, California, October 21, 1935; admitted to bar, 1960, California. *Education:* San Diego State University (A.B., 1956); Stanford University (J.D., 1959). Phi Alpha Delta (President, 1959). *Member:* State Bar of California. [Lt., U.S. Navy, 1959-1963]

**LELAND A. WAHL,** born Bay Shore, New York, January 17, 1959; admitted to bar, 1987, California and U.S. District Court, Central District of California. *Education:* Williams College (B.A., cum laude, 1981, Tyng Scholar); Vanderbilt University (J.D., 1986). **PRACTICE AREAS:** Complex Business Litigation; Environmental; Intellectual Property; Construction.

---

**LISA M. KERR,** born Orange, California, August 19, 1961; admitted to bar, 1995, California. *Education:* University of Oklahoma (B.A., summa cum laude, 1985); University of California, Boalt Hall School of Law (J.D., 1995). Articles Editor, California Law Review, 1994-1995. *Member:* Los Angeles County and American Bar Associations; State Bar of California. **PRACTICE AREAS:** Complex Business Litigation.

## LAW OFFICES OF
## MICHAEL R. SMENT
1800 AVENUE OF THE STARS, SUITE 1000
**LOS ANGELES, CALIFORNIA 90067-4212**
Telephone: 310-277-6361; 310-277-6362
Fax: 310-277-6517
Email: rockjr@aol.com

Ventura, California Office: 674 County Square Drive, Suite 108. Telephone: 805-654-0311. Telecopier: 805-984-2399.

Bankruptcy Litigation in Bankruptcy and Federal Courts, Creditors Rights and Insolvency, Business and Real Estate Litigation in State and Federal Courts. Bankruptcy, State and Federal Appellate Matters. Arbitrations, Mediations.

*FIRM PROFILE:* Listed in Bar Register of Preeminent Lawyers.

(For Complete Biographical Data on Personnel, see Professional Biography at Ventura, California)

## SMILAND & KHACHIGIAN
*Established in 1884*

SEVENTH FLOOR
ONE BUNKER HILL
601 WEST FIFTH STREET
**LOS ANGELES, CALIFORNIA 90071**
Telephone: 213-891-1010
Facsimile: 213-891-1414

San Clemente, California Office: 209 Avenida Del Mar, Suite 203, 92672. Telephone: 714-498-3879. Facsimile: 714-498-6197.

General Civil Trial and Appellate Practice in all State and Federal Courts, Corporation, Commercial and General Business Practice. Water Resources, Air Pollution, Environmental and Government Regulation Practice.

*FIRM PROFILE: Smiland & Khachigian practices public and private law on behalf of businesses, property owners and entrepreneurs. Continuing its predecessors' century-old tradition, the firm handles commercial and corporate disputes and transactions in the private market sector. Its lawyers also represent leading corporations in administrative proceedings before federal, state and local governments and in litigation with regulatory and environmental agencies relating to air, water and land use.*

### MEMBERS OF FIRM

**JOSEPH W. SWANWICK** (1858-1932).

**CHARLES E. DONNELLY** (1890-1973).

**ERNEST M. CLARK, JR.** (Emeritus).

**WILLIAM M. SMILAND,** born Los Angeles, California, June 15, 1942; admitted to bar, 1968, California. *Education:* Stanford University (A.B., 1964); Boalt Hall School of Law, University of California (J.D., 1967). Arbitrator, National Association of Securities Dealers, 1977-1990. Board Member, South Coast Air Quality Management District, Chairman, Small Business Committee, 1983-1987. *Member:* Los Angeles County Bar Association; The State Bar of California. **REPORTED CASES:** O'Neill v. U.S., 50 F 3d 677 (9th Cir. 1995) affirming Barcellos & Wolfsen v. Westlands Water District, 849 F. Supp. 717 (E.D. Cal. 1993); Westlands Water District v. U.S., 850 F. Supp. 1388 (E.D. Cal. 1994); Sumner Peck Ranch v. Bureau of Reclamation, 823 F. Supp. 715 (E.D. Cal. 1993); Dunn-Edwards Corp. v. South Coast Air Quality Management Dist., 19 Cal. App. 4th 519 (1993); Dunn-Edwards Corp. v. South Coast Air Quality Management Dist., 19 Cal. App. 4th 536 (1993); Dunn-Edwards Corp. v. Bay Area Air Quality Management District, 9 Cal. App. 4th 644 (1992); Colusa Air Pollution Control District v. Superior Court, 226 Cal. App. 3d 880 (1991); Barcellos & Wolfsen v. Westlands Water District, 899 F. 2d 814 (9th Cir. 1990); In re Westhaven Trust, Interior Sol. Op. M-36965 (1989); Shultz Steel Co. v. Hartford Accident & Indemnity Co., 187 Cal. App. 3d 513 (1986); Barcellos & Wolfsen v. Westlands Water District, 491 F. Supp. 263 (E.D. Cal. 1980); American Center For Education v. Cavnar, 80 Cal. App. 3d 476 (1978); In re Okamoto, 491 F. 2d 496 (9th Cir. 1974). **PRACTICE AREAS:** Public Law; Air Pollution; Water Resources; Commercial Litigation; Corporate Law.

**KENNETH L. KHACHIGIAN,** born Visalia, California, September 14, 1944; admitted to bar, 1970, California. *Education:* University of California at Santa Barbara (B.A., 1966); Columbia University (J.D., 1969). Staff As-

*(This Listing Continued)*

**SMILAND & KHACHIGIAN, Los Angeles—Continued**

sistant and Deputy Special Assistant to President Richard Nixon, 1970-1974. Special Consultant to President Ronald Reagan, 1981. Member, Advisory Board, National Institute of Justice, 1982-1984. Director, Armenian Assembly, 1983-1989. Member, Board of Overseers, Hoover Institution, Stanford University, 1985-1992. Director, California Council for Environmental and Economic Balance, 1986—. Director, Richard Nixon Library and Birthplace Foundation. Vice Chairman, Citizens for Common Sense, 1987-1990. *Member:* State Bar of California. **PRACTICE AREAS:** Public Law.

**THEODORE A. CHESTER, JR.,** born Pasadena, California, November 21, 1956; admitted to bar, 1982, California. *Education:* Stanford University (B.A., 1978); Loyola Law School (J.D., 1982). Member, Loyola of Los Angeles Law Review, 1981-1982. *Member:* The State Bar of California; American Bar Association. **REPORTED CASES:** Sumner Peck Ranch v. Bureau of Reclamation, 823 F. Supp. 715 (E.D. Cal. 1993); In re Westhaven Trust, Interior Sol. Op. M-36965 (1989). **PRACTICE AREAS:** Water Resources; Corporate Law; Tax Law; Estates; Trusts; Commercial Litigation.

**CHRISTOPHER G. FOSTER,** born Bethesda, Maryland, September 12, 1956; admitted to bar, 1985, California; 1987, U.S. District Court, Central District of California and U.S. Court of Appeals, Ninth Circuit. *Education:* Stanford University (B.S., 1978; M.S., 1979); University of California, Hastings College of the Law (J.D., 1984). Phi Delta Phi. *Member:* Los Angeles County Bar Association; State Bar of California. **REPORTED CASES:** Setliff v. E.I. DuPont de Nemours, 32 Cal. App. 4th 1525 (1995); Teitel v. First Los Angeles Bank, 231 Cal. App. 3d 1593 (1991). **PRACTICE AREAS:** Air Pollution; Water Resources; Commercial Litigation.

*OF COUNSEL*

**CHARLES H. CHASE,** born Omaha, Nebraska, December 20, 1921; admitted to bar, 1949, Nebraska; 1954, California. *Education:* University of Nebraska (B.S., 1948; LL.B., 1950). Phi Delta Phi; Order of the Coif. Assistant Professor of Law, Washington University School of Law, St. Louis, Missouri, 1950. Trial Attorney Office of Chief Counsel, Internal Revenue Service, Los Angeles, 1951-1954. *Member:* Los Angeles County and American Bar Associations; The State Bar of California. **PRACTICE AREAS:** Corporate Law; Tax Law; Estates; Trusts.

REPRESENTATIVE CLIENTS: AirTouch Communications; Alliance of Small Emitters/Metals Industry; Banning Residence Museum; Boston Ranch Company; Del-Tho, Inc.; Dunn-Edwards Corp.; Ellis Paint Co.; Great Western Steel; Henry Company; J.G. Boswell Co.; Laagco Sales; Mag-Tek, Inc.; Murrieta Farms; O'Neill Ranches; Pilibos Bros.; Shultz Steel Co.; Sumner Peck Ranch, Inc.; Smiland Paint Company; Triangle Coatings.
REFERENCE: First Business Bank, Los Angeles, California.

---

## SMITH & HILBIG LLP

LOS ANGELES, CALIFORNIA

(See Torrance)

*Banking, Bankruptcy, Commercial, Corporate, Employment, Environmental, Estate Planning, Probate, Real Property, Securities and Taxation Law, State and Federal Administrative, Trial and Appellate Practice.*

---

## SMITH & KAUFMAN LLP

601 SOUTH FIGUEROA STREET, 41ST FLOOR
LOS ANGELES, CALIFORNIA 90017
Telephone: 213-623-9704
Fax: 213-623-4619

*Business Litigation (Unfair Competition, Contract Disputes and Business Torts), Insurance Litigation, Environmental Coverage, Directors' and Officers' Coverage, Surety and Fidelity, Reinsurance, Political Campaign Finance and Election Law. Wills, Trusts and Estate Planning and Small Business Entity Formation.*

**PAUL K. SMITH,** born Kankakee, Illinois, September 18, 1958; admitted to bar, 1985, California and U.S. District Court, Central District of California; 1988, U.S. District Court, Eastern District of California; 1991, U.S. Court of Appeals, 9th Circuit; 1993, Minnesota. *Education:* Regis College; Loyola Marymount University (B.B.A., 1981); University of Southern California (M.B.A., 1985; J.D., 1985). Managing Editor, Major Tax Planning and Computer Law Journal, 1984-1985. Author: "Reinsurer Beware - Notice of Rescission Must Precede the Cedent's Complaint," Legal Ledger, Vol. 7, No. 1, Winter 1996; "Abra Cadabra - How A Reinsurer's Equitable Defenses May Disappear in the Cedent's Liquidation," Legal Ledger, Vol. 7, No. 1, Winter 1996. *Member:* Minnesota State and American (Member, Tort and Insurance Practice Section) Bar Associations; State Bar of California. **PRACTICE AREAS:** Business Litigation; Insurance Coverage; Estate Planning; Small Business Formation.

**STEPHEN J. KAUFMAN,** born New York, N.Y., October 4, 1962; admitted to bar, 1987, California and U.S. District Court, Central District of California; 1989, U.S. Court of Appeals, 9th Circuit. *Education:* University of California at Los Angeles (B.A., 1984); University of California, Hastings College of the Law (J.D., 1987). Recipient, State Bar of California Wiley W. Manuel Pro Bono Services Award. *Member:* Los Angeles County and American (Member, Sections on: Litigation; Torts and Insurance Practice; State and Local Government Law) Bar Associations; State Bar of California (Member, Public Law Section); California Political Attorneys Association. **PRACTICE AREAS:** Business Litigation; Campaign Finance; Election Law; Insurance Coverage; Insurance Defense; Surety and Fidelity Law.

---

## SOLISH, ARBITER & GEHRING, LLP

Established in 1977
12100 WILSHIRE BOULEVARD
15TH FLOOR
LOS ANGELES, CALIFORNIA 90025
Telephone: 310-826-2255
FAX: 310-207-3230

*Franchise, Intellectual Property, Labor, Insurance, Business, Real Estate, Corporate, Tort, Administrative Law and Litigation and Appellate Practice in all State and Federal Courts before Municipal Administration and Regulatory Boards, Agencies and Elected Councils, Banking and Finance.*

**JONATHAN CRAIG SOLISH,** born Monticello, New York, May 27, 1949; admitted to bar, 1975, California; 1977, U.S. District Court, Central District of California; 1979, U.S. Court of Appeals, Ninth Circuit; 1988, U.S. District Court, Southern District of California and U.S. Court of Appeals for the Federal Circuit; 1992, U.S. District Court, Eastern District of California; 1993, U.S. District Court, Northern District of California. *Education:* University of California at Santa Cruz (B.A., 1971); University of California at Los Angeles (J.D., 1975). Associate Editor, Franchise Law Journal, 1992—. Editor-in-Chief, Franchise Law Journal, August, 1997—. Author: "Litigation Strategies" American Bar Association (1989); "Hot Topics in Franchise Litigation," International Franchise Association Symposium (1991); "Collateral Estoppel in Franchise Law," Franchise Law Journal, Spring, 1991; "How to Turn Your Arbitration Instrument into a Stradivarius," Franchise Law Journal, Spring, 1992; "A Survey of Franchise Law in the Pacific Rim," Los Angeles County Bar Association, 1992; "Franchising in Twelve Countries of the Asian Pacific Rim," in Practical Guide to Trade & Investment in the Pacific Rim, State Bar of California, 1992; "Working Creatively With Franchise Relationship Laws," American Bar Association, 1993; "Deposing the Perpetrator, an Unlikely Source of Maximizing the Defense," Defense Research Institute, Inc., 1994; "Market Power in Per Se Franchise Tying Claims"; Virtual Maintenance Decision Addresses "Locked-In Buyers," Franchise Law Journal, Winter 1994; American Bar Association Forum on Franchising "The Perils of Controlling Franchisee Real Estate," 1994; "Antitrust Ramifications of Sourcing Requirements," International Franchise Association, 1995; "The Rise and Fall of Third Party Violence Liability," Defense Research Institute, 1996; "Franchisor Assumption of Liability," International Franchise Association, 1996, with Bailey & Schnell; "Antitrust Implications of Tying Arrangements, Rebates, Kickbacks and Exclusive Supplier Programs," American Bar Association, 1996, with McDavid; *"Expansion of Liability in Novel Tort Claims," Idaho Trial Lawyers Association, 1996. Member:* Los Angeles County (Member: Attorney-Client Relations Committee, 1985—, Antitrust Section, 1990—; Pacific Rim Committee, 1990—; Liaison to the American Bar Association, Appellate Practice, 1989—) and American (Member: Forum Committee on Franchising, 1984—; Tort and Insurance Practice Section; Antitrust Section, 1990—; Antitrust Subsection on Franchising, 1990—; Appellate Advocacy Committee, 1989—; Antitrust Task Force on Legislation and Regulation) Bar Associations; State Bar of California (Member: International Law Section, 1990—; Franchise Law Committee, 1991-1995). **REPORTED CASES:** Strang v. Cabrol, 37 Cal.3d 720, 209 Cal.Rptr. 347 (1984); Nelson v. Tiffany Industries, Inc. 778 F.2d 533 (9th Cir. 1985); 6th & K Ltd., v. Ramada Franchise Systems, Inc., Bus. Franchise Guide (CCH) 10,721 (S.D. Cal. 1995); O'Leary v. Mid Wilshire As-

*(This Listing Continued)*

sociates, 7 Cal. App. 4th 1450 (1992); 6th & K v. RFS, Inc., Bus. Franchise Guide (CCH) ¶10,721 (S.D.Cal. 1995); Garcia v. Midas International, Bus. Franchise Guide (CCH) ¶10,792 (Cal. Superior Court 1995); VICORP Restaurants, Inc. v. Village Inn Pancake House of Albuquerque, Bus. Franchise Guide ¶10,994 (D.N.M. 1996). *PRACTICE AREAS:* Franchise Law; Antitrust; Intellectual Property; Civil Trials; Appellate.

**ROSS ARBITER,** born Los Angeles, California, October 16, 1951; admitted to bar, 1977, California. *Education:* University of California at Los Angeles (A.B., 1973); University of Southern California (J.D., 1977). Phi Alpha Delta. Professor, Business Law, Los Angeles Community Colleges, 1983. *Member:* Los Angeles County and American Bar Associations; State Bar of California. *PRACTICE AREAS:* Business Transactions; Medical Compliance; Real Estate; Tax.

**STEVEN D. WIENER,** born Los Angeles, California, December 28, 1940; admitted to bar, 1975, California and U.S. District Court, Central District of California; 1985, U.S. Court of Appeals, Ninth Circuit. *Education:* Dartmouth College (B.A., with distinction, 1962); University of California, Los Angeles (M.A., 1964; J.D., 1974). Lecturer, English Language and Literature, Chinese University of Hong Kong, 1964-1967. Instructor, Legal Education Opportunities Program, University of California at Los Angeles Law School, 1970. Researcher, California Penal Code Revision Committee, 1968. *Member:* Los Angeles County (Member, Judiciary Committee, 1989-1990) and American (Member: Forum Committee on Franchising, 1985—; Sections on Administrative Law and Regulatory Practice, Litigation and Antitrust) Bar Associations; The State Bar of California (Member, Franchise Legislation Committee, 1988-1991); International Franchise Association, Council of Suppliers (1985—). *PRACTICE AREAS:* Franchise Law; Business Litigation.

**JUDITH B. GITTERMAN,** born Plainfield, New Jersey, September 7, 1957; admitted to bar, 1984, California and U.S. District Court, Southern District of California; 1985, U.S. District Court, Central District of California; 1986, U.S. Court of Appeals, Ninth Circuit; 1987, U.S. District Court, Eastern District of California. *Education:* University of Pennsylvania (B.A., magna cum laude, 1978); Cornell University (J.D., 1984). *Member:* Los Angeles County and American (Member, Forum Committee on Franchising, 1988—) Bar Associations; State Bar of California. *REPORTED CASES:* Cislaw v. 7-Eleven, 4 Cal. App. 4th 1284; Martin v. The Southland Corporation, Bus. Franchise Guide (CCH) ¶11,019 (Cal.App. 1996). *PRACTICE AREAS:* Franchise Law; Business Litigation; Appellate Law.

**THOMAS G. GEHRING,** born Baltimore, Maryland, June 18, 1954; admitted to bar, 1979, California; 1981, U.S. District Court, Central District of California; 1982, U.S. Court of Appeals, Ninth Circuit. *Education:* University of California at Santa Barbara (B.A., 1976); Pepperdine University (J.D., 1979). Member, Pepperdine University Law Review, 1978-1979. Author: "Another Citadel Has Fallen-This Time the Plaintiffs. California Applies Comparative Negligence to Strict Products Liability," 6 Pepperdine Law Review, 985, 1979; "Pretrial Basis: Ten Essential Principles of Preparation for Every Litigator," Los Angeles Daily Journal, June 14, 1996. Adjunct Professor of Law, Trial Preparation and Settlement and Health Law, Pepperdine University School of Law, 1988—. *Member:* Los Angeles County (Delegate to the 1988 State Bar Conference of Delegates; Member, Court Improvements Committee, 1985-1988) and American Bar Associations; State Bar of California.

---

**ROBERT M. PHILIPS,** born Los Angeles, California, March 9, 1955; admitted to bar, 1984, California; 1989, U.S. District Court, Central, Southern, Eastern and Northern Districts of California. *Education:* University of California at Irvine (B.A., 1978); University of California at Berkeley (M.C.P., 1984); Boalt Hall School of Law, University of California (J.D., 1984). *Member:* State Bar of California. *PRACTICE AREAS:* Commercial Litigation; Franchise Law; Intellectual Law; Property Law.

**GLENN J. PLATTNER,** born Los Angeles, California, August 1, 1963; admitted to bar, 1988, California; 1989, U.S. District Court, Central and Southern Districts of California and U.S. Court of Appeals, Ninth Circuit. *Education:* University of California at Berkeley (B.A., Economics, cum laude, 1985); University of California at Davis; Boalt Hall School of Law, University of California (J.D., 1988). Recipient, Prosser Prize, Corporations. *Member:* Los Angeles County and American Bar Associations; State Bar of California. *PRACTICE AREAS:* Insurance Defense; Insurance Coverage; Business Litigation; Franchise Law; Real Estate Law.

**JOEL D. SIEGEL,** born San Francisco, California, 1966; admitted to bar, 1991, California; 1992, U.S. District Court, Central, Southern and Eastern Districts of California. *Education:* University of California at Los Angeles (B.A., 1988); Hastings College of the Law, University of California (J.D., 1991). Note & Article Editor, The Hastings Law Journal, 1990-1991. Author, "Premises Liability for the Torts of a Stranger: Who Should Foot the Bill for Crime," 1st Quarter, Verdict, 1993. *Member:* Beverly Hills and Los Angeles County Bar Associations; State Bar of California. *PRACTICE AREAS:* Business Litigation; Real Estate Litigation; Trademark Law; Franchise Law.

REPRESENTATIVE CLIENTS: The Southland Corp.; Taco Bell Corp.; Midas International Corporation; Pearl Vision, Inc.; Motel 6; Alphagraphics; Paul Revere Life Insurance Co.; The Prudential Real Estate Affiliates, Inc.; Days Inn; Tony Roma's Romacorp, Inc.; Ramada Franchise Systems, Inc.; HFS Corporation; Howard Johnson Franchise Systems, Inc.; Pizza Hut; Days Inn; Forte Hotels; Holiday Inns; KMI Real Estate Group, Inc.; Speare & Company Insurance Agency; Saturn Fastners, Inc.; AAMCO; Little Caesar Enterprises; VICORP, Inc.; The Image Bank, Inc.; RE/MAX, International, Inc.
REFERENCES: Santa Monica Bank.

---

## MICHAEL C. SOLNER
### LOS ANGELES, CALIFORNIA
(See Encino)

*Estate Planning, Trust and Probate Law, Civil Litigation, Professional Negligence, Business, White Collar Criminal Litigation, Elder Law.*

---

## STEPHEN E. SOLOMON
1801 CENTURY PARK EAST
SUITE 2400
LOS ANGELES, CALIFORNIA 90067
Telephone: 310-556-0360
Fax: 310-556-0462

*Federal and state income tax planning and controversy matters.*

FIRM PROFILE: Mr. Solomon's practice is limited exclusively to federal and state income tax planning and income tax controversy matters. Prior to forming his own firm in 1997, Mr. Solomon's practice had been as a partner in (and of counsel to) major Los Angeles law firms.

Mr. Solomon has extensive experience in all areas of federal income taxation, including entertainment tax matters, real property income tax matters, insolvency and bankruptcy tax matters, corporate formations, reorganizations, liquidations and restructurings, partnership (limited liability company) taxation, and S corporation taxation.

Mr. Solomon obtains referrals from a number of smaller boutique law firms and CPA firms.

**STEPHEN E. SOLOMON,** born Detroit, Michigan, June 16, 1939; admitted to bar, 1966, California; 1971, U.S. Tax Court. *Education:* University of Michigan (B.B.A., 1962); Stanford Law School (LL.B., 1965). Order of the Coif. Member, Board of Editors, Stanford Law Review, 1964-1965. Lecturer in Law: University of Southern California Law Center, 1967-1972; Stanford Law School, 1972-1979. Member, Planning Committee, UCLA Entertainment Tax Institute, 1995-1996. Author: "The Current Status of the Income Tax Consequences of Advances and Recent Legislative Changes to the Income Forecast Method of Depreciation," 49 University of Southern California Tax Institute, 1997; "Recent Developments in Section 1031," 37 University of Southern California Tax Institute, 1985; "Tax Strategies for the Dealer," Third Annual Institute on Advanced Tax Planning for Real Property Transactions 261-309, 1984; "Multi-Party Exchanges and Other Recent Developments in Section 1031," 33 University of Southern California Tax Institute, 1981; "The Judicially Expanded 'F' Reorganization And Its Uncertain Operating Rules," 7 J. Corp. Tax 24, 1980; "Net Operating Losses in Consolidated Returns," Operating Losses, Practicing Law Institute 132, 1979; "Current Planning For Partnership Start Up, Including Special Allocations, Retroaction Allocations and Guaranteed Payments," 16th Annual Heart of America Ta Institute, Chapter 9, 1979; "Carryovers and Carrybacks of Net Operating Losses under Section 381," Operating Losses, Practicing Law Institute 132, 1979; "Current Planning For Partnership Start Up Including Special Allocations, Retroaction Allocations and Guaranteed Payments," 37 New York Tax Institute, Chapter 13, 1979; "Tax Benefits of Nonqualified Compensation Plans Increased Under Tax Reform Act of 1976," 19 Taxation for Accountants 226, 1977, 6 Taxation for Lawyers 24, 1977; "Tax-Free Reorganization, Practicing Law Institute Handbook," Acquisition 1975, 1975; "The Installment Sale-Qualification," University of Southern California Tax Institute, 1974; "How To Deal With Section 306," 20 University of Southern California Tax Institute 167, 1968;

*(This Listing Continued)*

**STEPHEN E. SOLOMON**, *Los Angeles—Continued*

"Tax Consequences on the Sale of Real Property - A New Approach," 19 University of Southern California Tax Institute 281, 1967. Co-Author: "The Confusing, Complex and Uncertain Tax World of Real Estate Workouts," University of Southern California Tax Institute, 1993; "The Passive Loss Rules; Guidance From the First Set of Regulations," 41 University of Southern California Tax Institute, 1989; "The Passive Loss Rules - The Initial Temporary Regulations," 8th Annual Institute on Advanced Planning for Real Property Transactions, Chapter 10, 1989; "Impact of the Passive Activity Rules on Real Estate," 40 University of Southern California Tax Institute, 1987. *Member:* Beverly Hills, Century City, Los Angeles County and American Bar Associations; State Bar of California.

---

## SONNENSCHEIN NATH & ROSENTHAL
**601 SOUTH FIGUEROA STREET, SUITE 1500**
**LOS ANGELES, CALIFORNIA 90017**
*Telephone:* 213-623-9300
*Telecopier:* 213-623-9924

*Chicago, Illinois Office:* Suite 8000 Sears Tower, 233 South Wacker Drive. Telephone: 312-876-8000. Cable Address: "Sonberk". Telex: 25-3526. Facsimile: 312-876-7934.

*New York, N.Y. Office:* 1221 Avenue of the Americas, 24th Floor. Telephone: 212-768-6700. Facsimile: 212-391-1247.

*Washington, D.C. Office:* 1301 K Street, N.W., Suite 600 East Tower. Telephone: 202-408-6400. Fax: 202-408-6399.

*San Francisco, California Office:* 685 Market Street, 10th Floor. Telephone: 415-882-5000. Facsimile: 415-543-5472.

*St. Louis, Missouri Office:* One Metropolitan Square, Suite 3000. Telephone: 314-241-1800. Facsimile: 314-259-5959.

*Kansas City, Missouri Office:* Suite 1100, 4520 Main Street, 64111. Telephone: 816-932-4400. Facsimile: 816-531-7545.

*London, England Office:* Sonnenscheins, Royex House, Aldermanbury Square, EC2V 7HR. Telephone: 0171-600-2222. Facsimile: 0171-600-2221.

Antitrust, Aviation Litigation, Banking, Bankruptcy, Commercial Financing, Construction, Corporate, Employee Benefits, Environmental, Estate Planning, Executive Compensation, First Amendment, Franchising, Government Contracts, Health Care, Insurance, Intellectual Property, International Trade, Labor and Employment, Land Use, Litigation, Media, Municipal Bonds, Probate, Product Liability, Professional Liability, Real Estate, Securities, Taxation, Trade Regulation, Venture Capital, White Collar Criminal Defense, Workouts, Zoning.

**PERCY ANDERSON**, born California, 1949; admitted to bar, 1975, California. *Education:* University of California at Los Angeles (B.A., 1970); University of California at Los Angeles School of Law (J.D., 1975). *Member:* State Bar of California; American Bar Association. **PRACTICE AREAS:** Litigation.

**MICHAEL J. BAYARD**, born San Bernardino, California, May 6, 1953; admitted to bar, 1979, California. *Education:* University of California at Berkeley (A.B., 1976); University of California Hastings College of Law (J.D., 1979). Phi Beta Kappa. Member and Associate Executive Editor, Hastings Law Journal, 1977-1979. Author: "Ten of the Most Common Legal Errors Made by California Contractors," 1983. Co-Author: "How to Pick an Expert in a Construction Dispute," 1984; Author: Supplement to the *Construction Industry Formbook*, 1987; "Answers to the Ten Most Common Construction Law Questions Asked by California Public Entities," 1988. *Member:* Los Angeles County (Member and Past Chairman, Subsection on Construction Law, Real Property Section, 1981—; Member, Executive Committee, Real Property Section, 1985—) and American (Member, Forum Committee on the Construction Industry, 1981—) Bar Associations; State Bar of California (Member, Subsection on Construction Law, Real Property Section, 1981—). **PRACTICE AREAS:** Construction Law; Alternative Dispute Resolution.

**ERNEST P. BURGER**, born Germany, 1947; admitted to bar, 1973, California; 1982, U.S. Tax Court. *Education:* Loyola University of Los Angeles (B.S., Economics, 1969); University of California at Los Angeles (J.D., 1972). *Member:* State Bar of California. **LANGUAGES:** German. **PRACTICE AREAS:** Corporate Law; Real Estate Transactions; Acquisition Law; Leasing Law; Construction Law. **Email:** epb@sonnenschein.com

**CHARLES R. CAMPBELL, JR.**, born Pasadena, California, January 19, 1957; admitted to bar, 1982, California; 1983, U.S. Court of Appeals,
*(This Listing Continued)*

CAA1216B

---

Ninth Circuit and U.S. District Court, Northern District of California; 1984, U.S. District Court, Central and Southern Districts of California. *Education:* University of California at Los Angeles (B.A., cum laude, 1979); University of Southern California (J.D., 1982). Phi Alpha Delta. *Member:* Los Angeles County (Member, Sections on: Real Property; Environmental) and American (Member, Sections on: Real Property, Probate and Trust Law; Natural Resources, Energy and Environmental) Bar Associations; State Bar of California. **PRACTICE AREAS:** Real Property; Corporate; Workouts; Environmental. **Email:** crc@sonnenschein.com

**MARTIN J. FOLEY**, born Omaha, Nebraska, November 7, 1946; admitted to bar, 1975, California and U.S. District Court, Central District of California; U.S. Court of Federal Claims; U.S. District Court, Northern, Southern and Eastern Districts of California and U.S. Court of Appeals, Ninth Circuit; U.S. Supreme Court. *Education:* University of Southern California (B.A., 1968; M.B.A., 1975; J.D., 1974); Cambridge University, Cambridge, England. Order of the Coif; Phi Beta Kappa; Phi Kappa Phi; Beta Gamma Sigma. Member, Southern California Law Review, 1972-1974. Delegate, State Bar Conference of Delegates, 1980-1993. Member, Los Angeles County Bar Association Delegation Executive Committee, 1985-1988. Vice-Chair, Law and Technology Section, 1978-1980; Chair, Products Liability Section, 1978-1980, Los Angeles County Bar Association. Senior Vice-Chair, Aviation and Aerospace Committee, Tort and Insurance Practice Section, 1979-1994; Member, Committee on Corporate Counsel, Litigation Section, American Bar Association. Member, Board of Governors, University of Southern California General Alumni Association, 1982-1984. *Member:* State Bar of California; Association of Business Trial Lawyers. [LTJG, USNR, 1968-1970]. **PRACTICE AREAS:** Aviation and Aerospace Litigation; Technology Law; Intellectual Property.

**MATTHEW C. FRAGNER**, born New York, N.Y., January 12, 1954; admitted to bar, 1978, California; 1979, U.S. District Court, Central District of California; 1980, U.S. Tax Court and U.S. Court of Appeals, Ninth Circuit. *Education:* Yale University (B.A., cum laude, 1975); Boalt Hall School of Law, University of California (J.D., 1978). Associate Editor: Industrial Relations Law Journal, 1976-1978; Ecology Law Quarterly, 1977-1978. Member, Berkeley Law Foundation, 1978. *Member:* Los Angeles County Bar Association (Member: Steering Committee, Commercial Law Subsection of Real Property Section; Legal Services for the Poor Committee; Commercial Property Subsection, Real Estate Section; Delegate to State Bar Convention, 1987); The State Bar of California. **LANGUAGES:** German. **PRACTICE AREAS:** Real Estate; Corporate. **Email:** MXF@sonnenschein.com

**BRENT MATTHEW GIDDENS**, born Burbank, California, January 15, 1962; admitted to bar, 1988, California, U.S. District Court, Northern, Southern, Eastern and Central Districts of California and U.S. Court of Appeals, Eighth and Ninth Circuits. *Education:* Columbia College (B.A., 1984); University of Southern California (J.D., 1987). *Member:* American Bar Association (Member, Section on Labor and Employment Law, Development of the Law Under the National Labor Relations Act Committee). **PRACTICE AREAS:** Labor/Employment for Management Law. **Email:** bg@sonnenschein.com

**PETER J. GURFEIN**, born September 13, 1948; admitted to bar, 1976, New York and U.S. Supreme Court; 1982, U.S. Court of International Trade; 1987, California; 1993, District of Columbia. *Education:* New York University (B.A., 1969); George Washington University (J.D., 1973). Author: "Liabilities in Correctional Volunteer Programs," American Bar Association Corrections Commission, Washington, D.C., 1975. Instructor, Benjamin Cardozo School of Law, 1980-1982. Assistant District Attorney, New York County, 1976-1981. Special Narcotics Prosecutor, New York, N.Y., 1976-1981. National Project Director, American Bar Association Corrections Commission, Washington, D.C., 1973-1975. Editor-in-Chief, California Bankruptcy Journal, 1995—. *Member:* Bar Association of San Francisco (Chair, Commercial Law and Bankruptcy Section, 1993); Los Angeles County (Member, Commercial Law and Bankruptcy Section); American (Member, Task Force on Special Financing in the Transportation Industry, Business Bankruptcy Committee, 1975—) Bar Associations. **PRACTICE AREAS:** Bankruptcy. **Email:** pjg@sonnenschein.com

**ELLIOTT J. HAHN**, born San Francisco, California, 1949; admitted to bar, 1974, New Jersey; 1976, California; 1979, District of Columbia. *Education:* University of Pennsylvania (B.A., cum laude, 1971; J.D., 1974); Columbia University (LL.M., 1980). Law Clerk to Judge Harry Hupp, Los Angeles County Superior Court, 1975-1976. Author: "Japanese Business Law and the Legal System," Greenwood Press, 1984; "Negotiating Contracts with the Japanese," 2 California Lawyer 21, 1982; "An Overview of the Japanese Legal System," 5 Northwestern Journal of International Law
*(This Listing Continued)*

and Business 517, 1983; "California Implications of the 1980 United Nations Convention on Contracts for the International Sale of Goods," 7 Business Law News 33, 1984. Professor of Law: California Western School of Law, 1980-1985; Santa Clara Law School Summer in Tokyo Program, 1981-1983. Adjunct Professor of Law: Pepperdine Law School, 1987—; Southwestern Law School, 1986—; Orientation in USA Law Program, University of California, Davis Law School, 1994—. *Member:* Los Angeles County Bar Association (Member, Executive Committee, International Law Section, 1987—; Secretary, 1995-1996; Second Vice-President, 1996—; Appointee, Pacific Rim Committee, 1990—, Chairman, 1991-1992; 1995—); State Bar of California (Legislative Chair, International Law Section, 1989-1992; Advisor, Executive Committee, International Law Section, 1990-1991; Appointee, Executive Committee, International Law Section, 1991—, Vice-Chair, 1992-1993; Chair, 1993-1994); Contrib. Ed. for Int'l L. The California Business Law Reporter (1994—). *LANGUAGES:* Japanese and Spanish. *PRACTICE AREAS:* International Corporate; Real Estate; Banking. *Email:* ejh@sonnenschein.com

**MARK T. HANSEN,** born Chicago Heights, Illinois, February 24, 1959; admitted to bar, 1984, California, U.S. District Court, Northern District of California; 1987, U.S. District Court, Central and Southern Districts of California and U.S. Court of Appeals, 9th Circuit; 1995, U.S. District Court, Eastern District of California. *Education:* Santa Clara University (B.S., cum laude, 1981); Hastings College of the Law, University of California (J.D., 1984). Hastings International and Comparative Law Review, 1982-1984. Extern, Judge Stanley A. Weigel, U.S. District Court, Northern District of California, 1983. *Member:* Los Angeles County and American Bar Associations; State Bar of California; Association of Business Trial Lawyers. *PRACTICE AREAS:* Litigation. *Email:* mth@sonnenschein.com

**SUE L. HIMMELRICH,** born Baltimore, Maryland, April 27, 1953; admitted to bar, 1983, California. *Education:* Harvard University (B.A., 1975); Columbia University (J.D., 1983). Civil Procedure Teaching Fellow, Journal of Law and Social Problems. Author: "Cyberlitigator," Los Angeles Daily Journal. Judicial Arbitrator, Los Angeles Superior Court. Member, Organization of Women Executives. *PRACTICE AREAS:* Litigation. *Email:* swh@sonnenschein.com

**RONALD D. KENT,** born Long Beach, California, March 29, 1956; admitted to bar, 1981, California, U.S. District Court, Central, Eastern, Northern and Southern Districts of California and U.S. Court of Appeals, Ninth Circuit. *Education:* University of California, Los Angeles (B.A., summa cum laude, 1978) Phi Beta Kappa; Boalt Hall School of Law, University of California, Berkeley (J.D., 1981). Order of the Coif. Member, California Law Review 1979-1981. Extern, Judge Stanley A. Weigel, United States District Court, Northern District of California, 1980. *Member:* State Bar of California. *PRACTICE AREAS:* Insurance Law; General and Environmental Litigation.

**LEE T. PATERSON,** born Washington, D.C., September 26, 1941; admitted to bar, 1967, California, U.S. Court of Appeals, Ninth Circuit and U.S. District Court, Northern District of California; 1979, U.S. Supreme Court; 1988, U.S. Court of Appeals for the District of Columbia Circuit; 1989, U.S. District Court, Central District of California; 1992, U.S. Court of Appeals, Eighth Circuit. *Education:* St. Mary's College of California and Oregon State University (B.A., 1964; B.S., 1964); University of California at Los Angeles (J.D., 1967). Author: "California Unemployment Insurance Guide," Parker Publications, 1990; "Cobra Compliance Manual," J.W. Wiley, 1990; "Documenting Employee Discipline," Parker Publications, 1988; "Employer's Compliance Review," Parker Publications, 1992; "Employer's Wage Manual," Parker Publications, 1992; "Employment Compliance Audit—California," Parker Publications, 1989; "Federal Workplace Posters," Parker Publications, 1989; "Mandatory Workplace Posters in California," Parker Publications, 1988; "Negotiating Employee Resignations," Parker Publications, 1990; "Public Employer's Compliance Review," Parker Publications, 1990; "Public Employer's Wage Guide," Parker Publications, 1990; "Sexual Harassment - What You Need to Know," Crisp Publications, 1992; "Supervisors Guide to Documenting Employee Discipline," Parker Publications, 1988; "Supervisors Guide to Employee Performance Reviews," Parker Publications, 1990. General Counsel: PIHRA, Professionals in Human Resources Association, 1990; State Council Society of Human Resource Managers, 1990. *Member:* Los Angeles County and American (Member, Labor and Employment Law Section) Bar Associations; State Bar of California. *PRACTICE AREAS:* Management Employment Law; Labor (Private and Public Sector) Law. *Email:* ltp@sonnenschein.com

**LAURA R. PETROFF,** born Cleveland, Ohio, July 7, 1955; admitted to bar, 1980, Illinois; 1986, California, U.S. District Court, Central, Southern and Northern Districts of California and U.S. Court of Appeals, Ninth Cir-

*(This Listing Continued)*

cuit. *Education:* Denison University (B.A., 1977); Vanderbilt (J.D., 1980). *Member:* Los Angeles County (Co-Chair, Education Committee of the Barristers, 1989-1991; Member, Executive Committee of the Barristers, 1990-1992) and American Bar Associations; State Bar of California. *PRACTICE AREAS:* Labor and Employment Litigation; Commercial Litigation. *Email:* lrp@sonnenschein.com

**ANDRIA K. RICHEY,** born Redding, California, July 14, 1955; admitted to bar, 1979, California; 1980, U.S. District Court, Central District of California and U.S. Court of Appeals, Ninth Circuit; 1982, U.S. Tax Court; 1983, U.S. Supreme Court; 1992, U.S. Claims Court; 1993, U.S. Court of Appeals for the Federal Circuit. *Education:* University of California at Berkeley (B.A., 1976); Boalt Hall School of Law, University of California (J.D., 1979). Phi Alpha Delta. Editor, Ecology Law Quarterly, 1978-1979. *Member:* Los Angeles County (President, Barristers Section; Trustee, 1986-1988, 1989-1992; Delegate, State Bar Conference of Delegates 1985-1990; Member, Delegation Executive Committee, 1987-1990; California Director, ABA/YLD Disaster Legal Services, 1986-1988), American (Member, Section on: Public Contract Law) and Federal Bar Associations; State Bar of California; Association of Business Trial Lawyers. *PRACTICE AREAS:* Commercial Litigation; Government Contracts Law; Intellectual Property Law. *Email:* akr@sonnenschein.com

**MICHAEL W. RING,** born Phoenix, Arizona, February 14, 1943; admitted to bar, 1969, California. *Education:* University of Washington (B.A., with high honors, 1964); Boalt Hall School of Law, University of California, Berkeley (J.D., 1968). *Member:* Los Angeles County (Member, Real Property Section) and American (Member, Section of Real Property, Probate and Trust Law) Bar Associations; The State Bar of California (Member, Real Property Law Section); American College of Real Estate Lawyers. *PRACTICE AREAS:* Real Estate and Real Estate Finance.

**ROBERT F. SCOULAR,** born Colorado, 1942; admitted to bar, 1968, Missouri, Colorado and North Dakota; 1972, U.S. Supreme Court; 1979, California. *Education:* St. Louis University (B.S.A.E., 1964; J.D., 1968). Law Clerk, Chief Judge Charles J. Vogel, U.S. Court of Appeals, Eighth Circuit, 1968-1969. *Member:* The Bar Association of Metropolitan St. Louis (Chairman, Young Lawyers Section, 1975-1976 and Vice President, 1978-1979); The Missouri Bar (Chairman, Young Lawyers Section, 1976-1977; Distinguished Service Award); American (Director, Young Lawyers Division, 1977-1978) Bar Association; State Bar of California; Association of Business Trial Lawyers; Computer Law Association. *PRACTICE AREAS:* Litigation; Government Contracts Litigation; Intellectual Property Law.

**NORBERT M. SEIFERT,** born Taunton, Massachusetts, March 29, 1956; admitted to bar, 1981, New York; 1989, California. *Education:* The Wharton School; University of Pennsylvania (B.S., 1977); New York University School of Law (J.D., 1980). Beta Alpha Psi. *Member:* Los Angeles County (Member, Real Estate Section) and New York State Bar Associations; The State Bar of California. *PRACTICE AREAS:* Real Estate and Real Estate Finance.

**J. A. SHAFRAN,** born Los Angeles, California, March 7, 1938; admitted to bar, 1964, California. *Education:* University of California at Berkeley (B.S., with honors, 1959); Boalt Hall School of Law, University of California (J.D., 1963). Order of the Coif; Phi Delta Phi; Tau Beta Pi. Note and Comment Editor, California Law Review, 1962-1963. Contributing Author: "Business Buy-Out Agreements," California Continuing Education of the Bar, 1976. Law Clerk to Justices Roger J. Traynor and Mathew O. Tobriner, California Supreme Court, 1963-1964. Chairman, Judge Pro Tem Panel, Small Claims Court, Beverly Hills Barristers, 1970-1971. *Member:* Los Angeles County and American Bar Associations; The State Bar of California (Member, Partnership Committee, Business Law Section, 1981-1984). *PRACTICE AREAS:* Real Estate; Corporate; General Business. *Email:* jas@sonnenschein.com

**ARTHUR F. SILBERGELD,** born St. Louis, Missouri, June 1, 1942; admitted to bar, 1976, New York; 1978, California; 1983, District of Columbia. *Education:* University of Michigan (B.A., 1968); University of Pennsylvania (M.C.P., 1971); Temple University (J.D., 1975). Author: "Title VII and the Collective Bargaining Agreement: Seniority Provisions Under Fire," 49 Temple Law Quarterly 288, 1976; *Doing Business in California: An Employment Law Handbook,* Executive Enterprises, Inc., 1989, 2d Ed. 1996; *Advising California Employers,* 1990, 1991, 1993, 1994 and 1995 Supplements, California Continuing Education of the Bar; *Americans With Disabilities Act Handbook: A Compliance Guide for Corporations,* 1992; "Wrongful Discharge and the At-Will Employee," The National Law Journal, May 21, 1984; "Federal Contractors Must Keep Work Place Free of Illegal Drugs," The National Law Journal, January 16, 1989; "Withdrawing Union Recognition," Employee Relations Law Journal, Vol. 16, No. 2,

*(This Listing Continued)*

**SONNENSCHEIN NATH & ROSENTHAL**, Los Angeles—
*Continued*

1990. "Private Sector Drug Testing: Legal Limitations in California" Employee Relations Law Journal, Vol. 16, No. 3, 1991; "WARN Act Litigation" Employment Relations Today, Winter, 1990/91; "NLRB Rules On The Legality of Employee Action Teams," 20 Employment Relations Today, No. 1, 1993; "Compelling Arbitration of Employee Disputes," 20 Employment Relations Today, No. 2, 1993; "Avoiding Wrongful Termination Claims: A Checklist for Employers," 20 Employment Relations Today, No. 3, 1993; "Harris v. Forklift Systems: The Court Relaxes the Burden of Providing Sexual Harassment Claims," 20 Employment Relations Today, No. 3, 1993; "The Use of Sexual Conduct Evidence in Harassment Cases," 21 Employment Relations Today, No. 4, 1994; "Accommodating Mental Disabilities Under the ADA," 22 Employment Relations Today, No. 3, 1995; "After-Acquired Evidence," The National Law Journal, March 18, 1996; "Hostile-Environment Litigation Since Maritor Savings," The National Law Journal, September 30, 1996. Contributing Editor: The Developing Labor Law, Bureau of National Affairs, 1976—. Lecturer, Labor Relations Law, University of California at Los Angeles, 1981-1989. Attorney, National Labor Relations Board, Los Angeles, California, 1977-1978. *Member:* Los Angeles County (Member, Alternative Dispute Resolution Section; Labor and Employment Law Section, Executive Committee, 1984—; Secretary, 1996—) and American (Member, Committee on Development of the Law Under the National Labor Relations Act, Section on Labor and Employment Law, 1976—; Committee on Employer-Employee Relations, Section of Tort and Insurance Practice) Bar Associations; The State Bar of California; The District of Columbia Bar. *PRACTICE AREAS:* Employment Law; Labor Law. *Email:* afs@sonnenschein.com

**SUSAN M. WALKER,** born Los Angeles, California, August 22, 1951; admitted to bar, 1987, California. *Education:* University of California at Los Angeles (B.A., 1972); University of Southern California (M.A., 1974); University of California at Davis (J.D., 1987). Order of the Coif. Executive Editor, University of California at Davis Law Review, 1986-1987. Recipient: American Jurisprudence Awards: Business Organization, Fall, 1985, Trust, Wills and Estates and Constitutional Law, Spring 1986 and Debtor-Creditor Law, Fall, 1986. *PRACTICE AREAS:* Litigation.

### OF COUNSEL

**NEAL R. MARDER,** born Encino, California, July 8, 1960; admitted to bar, 1986, California; U.S. Court of Appeals, Ninth and Tenth Circuits ; U.S. District Court, Central, Southern and Northern Districts of California. *Education:* University of California at Los Angeles (B.S., cum laude, 1982); Loyola University School of Law, Los Angeles (J.D., cum laude, 1986). Order of the Coif; St. Thomas More Law Honor Society. Formerly: Partner, Brookwell, Karic & Marder, Los Angeles, California; Associate, Buchalter, Nemer, Fields & Younger, Los Angeles, California. *Member:* Los Angeles County and American (Member, Inn of the Courts) Bar Associations; State Bar of California (Member, Litigation Section); Association of Business Trial Lawyers. *PRACTICE AREAS:* General Business and Commercial Litigation; Government Contracts; Labor.

**GRACE ELLEN MUELLER,** born Bethesda, Maryland, March 20, 1963; admitted to bar, 1988, California, U.S. District Court, Central, Eastern and Southern Districts of California and U.S. Court of Appeals, Ninth Circuit. *Education:* Oberlin College (B.A., 1985, Phi Beta Kappa); University of Southern California (J.D., 1988). Order of the Coif. Member, 1986-1987; Publications Editor, 1987-1988, Southern California Law Review. *Member:* State Bar of California. *PRACTICE AREAS:* Insurance Coverage; General Business Litigation.

**HENRY S. ZANGWILL,** born Paterson, New Jersey, October 25, 1944; admitted to bar, 1970, California, U.S. District Court, Central District of California and U.S. Court of Appeals, Ninth Circuit. *Education:* University of Alabama (B.S., 1966); University of Texas (J.D., with honors, 1969). Order of the Coif; Phi Delta Phi. Associate Editor, Texas Law Review, 1968-1969. Author: "Sex and Your Insurance Policy: Insurance Coverage for Sexual Harassment Claims," Los Angeles Lawyer (July/August, 1994); "Is the Insurance Companies 'Absolute' Pollution Exclusion Clause Absolute," Insurance Litigation Reporter (January 1992), California Insurance Law and Regulation Reporter (August 1991). *Member:* Los Angeles County and American Bar Associations; State Bar of California; Association of Business Trial Lawyers (Member, Board of Governors, 1978-1980). *PRACTICE AREAS:* Insurance Coverage; Business Litigation. *Email:* hsz@sonnenschein.com

*(This Listing Continued)*

CAA1218B

### ASSOCIATES

**JEFFRY BUTLER,** born Los Angeles, California, February 11, 1961; admitted to bar, 1995, California. *Education:* University of California (B.A., summa cum laude, 1992); University of California-Berkeley (J.D., 1995). *PRACTICE AREAS:* Litigation; Insurance. *Email:* jzb@sonnenschein.com

**ANTHONY CAPOBIANCO,** born Cleveland, Ohio, September 2, 1965; admitted to bar, 1992, California and U.S. District Court, Southern and Central Districts of California. *Education:* Arizona State University (B.S., summa cum laude, 1987); Hastings College of the Law, University of California (J.D., cum laude, 1992). Order of the Coif. Thurston Society. Executive Note Editor, Hastings International and Comparative Law Review, 1991-1992. *Member:* Los Angeles County Bar Association; State Bar of California. *PRACTICE AREAS:* Litigation. *Email:* axc@sonnenschein.com

**NARGIS CHOUDHRY,** admitted to bar, 1990, California. *Education:* Occidental College (B.A., 1975); University of Southern California (M.A., 1979); University of California at Los Angeles (J.D., 1990). Phi Kappa Phi. Editor-in-Chief, Pacific Basin Law Journal. Editor, U.C.L.A. Law Review. *Member:* State Bar of California (Member, Standing Committee on Minimum Continuing Legal Education); American Bar Association. *PRACTICE AREAS:* Real Estate. *Email:* nxc@sonnenschein.com

**STEPHEN J. CURRAN,** born San Francisco, California, June 6, 1963; admitted to bar, 1990, California and U.S. District Court, Central District of California; 1991, U.S. Court of Appeals, Ninth Circuit. *Education:* San Diego State University (B.A., magna cum laude, 1987); Georgetown University (J.D., magna cum laude, 1990). Order of the Coif. Recipient, American Jurisprudence Award in Criminal Justice. Lead Articles Editor, Georgetown Journal of Legal Ethics, 1989-1990. Author: "Regulating The Revolving Door: A Study of Proposed Restrictions on Post-Government Employment," Georgetown Journal of Legal Ethics, Vol. II, 1989. *Member:* The State Bar of California; American Bar Association (Member, Criminal Justice Section). *PRACTICE AREAS:* Litigation.

**WESTON A. EDWARDS,** born Summit, New Jersey, January 30, 1965; admitted to bar, 1992, California and U.S. District Court, Central District of California. *Education:* Brigham Young University (B.A., 1989); University of Texas (J.D., 1992). Lecturer, "Legal Aspects of the Construction Industry," Pacific Coast Regional's Entrepreneurial Institute, 1995-1996. *Member:* Los Angeles County Bar Association; State Bar of California. *PRACTICE AREAS:* Litigation; Construction Law. *Email:* wae@sonnenschein.com

**JONATHAN F. GOLDING,** born Oakland, California, July 24, 1962; admitted to bar, 1990, California; 1991, U.S. District Court, Central and Southern Districts of California; 1993, U.S. Court of Appeals, Ninth Circuit. *Education:* University of California at Los Angeles (B.A., 1984); Loyola Law School of Los Angeles (J.D., 1990). Alpha Sigma Nu; Phi Alpha Phi. Order of the Coif. Member, Saint Thomas More Law Honor Society. Senior Note and Comment Editor, Loyola of Los Angeles Law Review, 1989-1990. Author: "Fair-Value Limitations Applied to the Deficiency Judgments of Sold-Out Junior Lienholders: A Critical Analysis of the Courts' Application of California Code of Civil Procedure Section 580a," 23 Loyola of Los Angeles Law Review 313, 1989. *Member:* Los Angeles County Bar Association; State Bar of California. *PRACTICE AREAS:* Litigation; Creditor's Rights.

**MICHAEL S. GOULD,** born Los Angeles, California, September 11, 1971; (admission pending). *Education:* University of Colorado at Boulder (B.A. in History, 1993; Phi Beta Kappa); University of Southern California (J.D., 1996). Order of the Coif.

**CHARLES W. HOKANSON,** born San Diego, California, December 19, 1964; admitted to bar, 1992, California. *Education:* Stanford University (A.B., with honors, 1987); Hastings College of the Law, University of California (J.D., magna cum laude, 1992). Order of the Coif. Thurston Honor Society. Associate Executive Editor, Hastings Law Journal, 1991-1992. Extern, Judge A. Wallace Tashima, U.S. District Court, Central District of California, 1991.

**BRYAN C. JACKSON,** born Salt Lake City, Utah, August 5, 1955; admitted to bar, 1987, California and U.S. District Court, Central District of California. *Education:* Brigham Young University (B.A., 1983; J.D., 1986). Member, Moot Court and First Year Moot Court Finalist. President and Member, Natural Resources Law Forum, 1983-1986. Recipient, The Wiley W. Manuel Award for Pro Bono Legal Services presented by the Board of Governors of the State Bar of California, 1996. Author: "Public Construction Contracts: Are California's New Minority Goals on a Collision Course

*(This Listing Continued)*

with Croson?" 13 Public Law News 2 (Spring, 1989); "California's Minority Goals After Croson," 102 Los Angeles Daily Journal, No. 7 (April 10, 1989); "Can Stop-Notice Claimants Get at Interest Reserves?" 102 Los Angeles Daily Journal, No. 242, p. 7 (December 5, 1989); "Construction Contracts: Are California's New Minority Goals Unconstitutional?" 1 Los Angeles County Bar Association Newsletter, No., 1 (January, 1990); "New Real Property Bills," Los Angeles County Bar Association Real Property Section Review, Vol. 5, No. 4 and No. 5, Vol. 6, No. 1 and No. 2 (1994-1995). Adjunct Professor: Construction Management and Technology, Master of Real Estate Development, School of Urban Planning and Development, University of Southern California, 1990—. *Member:* Los Angeles County (Member, Executive Committee, Real Property Section; Past Chair, Subsection on Construction Law, Real Property Section, 1987—; Past Co-Editor, Real Property Section Review; Co-Chair, 26th Annual Benjamin S. Crocker Symposium) and American (Member: Forum Committee on the Construction Industry; Public Contract and Litigation Sections, 1987—) Bar Associations; State Bar of California (Member, Subsection on Construction Law, Real Property Section). *LANGUAGES:* Portuguese. *PRACTICE AREAS:* Construction Litigation; Construction Contracts; Real Estate Litigation. *Email:* bcj@sonnenschein.com

**SCOTT L. JONES,** born Racine, Wisconsin, March 19, 1957; admitted to bar, 1988, Virginia; 1989, District of Columbia; 1992, California. *Education:* American College of Switzerland; University of Idaho (B.Arch., 1981); Columbia University (M.S., 1982); Catholic University of America (J.D., 1988). Member, Moot Court. Recipient: John Harlin Scholarship; American Jurisprudence Awards: Corporations; Remedies; Navy Commendation Medal. Registered Architect, Wisconsin, 1986. Author: "A-E Government Contracts," Federal Publications, October, 1988; "Government Damages For Default," Federal Publications, June, 1989. *Member:* Federal (Secretary, Beverly Hills Chapter) and American (Public Contracts Section, 1990—) Bar Associations; Virginia State Bar; State Bar of California; The District of Columbia Bar. [LCDR, Civil Engineers Corps, U.S. Navy, 1981—]. *PRACTICE AREAS:* Government Contracts; Construction; Litigation. *Email:* slj@sonnenschein.com

**SUZANNE CATE JONES,** born Glendale, California, June 24, 1960; admitted to bar, 1991, California; 1992, U.S. District Court, Central District of California. *Education:* University of Southern California (A.B., 1982); Loyola Law School (J.D., 1991). Note and Comment Editor, Loyola of Los Angeles International and Comparative Law Journal, 1990-1991. *Member:* State Bar of California. *PRACTICE AREAS:* Litigation.

**MATTHEW I. KAPLAN,** born Chicago, Illinois, June 21, 1967; admitted to bar, 1993, Illinois; 1994, Missouri; 1995, California. *Education:* University of Michigan (B.A., 1989) University of Minnesota (J.D., cum laude, 1993). Author: "Exterior Access Routes in Residential Housing," Los Angeles County Bar Association Real Property Section Review, Vol. 7, No. 4, September/October, 1995. *Member:* Los Angeles County, Illinois State and American Bar Associations; The Missouri Bar; State Bar of California. *PRACTICE AREAS:* Insurance Law; Construction Law; Commercial Litigation. *Email:* mik@sonnenschein.com

**NAMYON KIM,** born South Korea, January 7, 1967; admitted to bar, 1992, Missouri; 1994, California. *Education:* University of Kansas (B.A., 1989); Columbia University (J.D., 1992). Phi Beta Kappa. *LANGUAGES:* Korean. *PRACTICE AREAS:* General Litigation.

**JESSIE A. KOHLER,** born Mt. Kisco, New York, September 11, 1970; admitted to bar, 1995, California. *Education:* University of California, Santa Barbara (B.A., magna cum laude, 1992); University of Southern California (J.D., 1995). Member, Southern California Interdisciplinary Law Journal.

**PAULINE NG LEE,** born Los Angeles, California, September 8, 1964; admitted to bar, 1989, California and U.S. Court of Appeals, Ninth Circuit; 1990, U.S. District Court, Central District of California; 1991, Texas and U.S. District Court, Southern District of Texas. *Education:* University of Southern California (B.S., in Accounting, 1986); Duke University (J.D., 1989). Alpha Lambda Delta. Member: Blue Key; Golden Key; Order of the Laurel; Skull and Dagger; Mortar Board; Moot Court Board. President, Duke Bar Association, 1988-1989. Author: "The Maze of Ad Valorem Taxes in Bankruptcy," Houston Bankruptcy Conference, 1992. *Member:* State Bar of California; State Bar of Texas (Member, Sections on: Business; Litigation); American Bar Association; Los Angeles Bankruptcy Forum; Southern California Chinese Lawyers Association. *PRACTICE AREAS:* Bankruptcy; Commercial and Lending Litigation. *Email:* pnl@sonnenschein.com

**JOHN R. MILLER,** born Burbank, California, June 22, 1964; admitted to bar, 1989, California and U.S. District Court, Central District of California; 1990, U.S. Court of Appeals, Ninth Circuit; 1991, District of Columbia. *Education:* University of California at Los Angeles (B.A., 1986); Loyola Marymount Law School (J.D., 1989). Judicial Extern to Chief Judge Loren A. Smith, U.S. Claims Court, Washington, D.C., 1986. *Member:* State Bar of California; The District of Columbia Bar. *PRACTICE AREAS:* Litigation; Insurance Coverage. *Email:* jm6@sonnenschein.com

**KAZUO MIWA,** born Hiroshima, Japan, December 25, 1962; (admission pending). *Education:* Waseda University, Japan (LL.B., 1986); New York University (M.C.J., 1996). *LANGUAGES:* Japanese. *Email:* k3m@sonnenschein.com

**DUNCAN E. MONTGOMERY,** born Berkeley, California; admitted to bar, 1985, California, U.S. District Court, Central District of California and U.S. Court of Appeals, Ninth Circuit. *Education:* University of California, Santa Barbara (B.A., 1979); Universite d'Aix-Marseille III (1987-1988); University of Denver (J.D., 1992). Editor-in-Chief, University of Denver Law Review (1991-1992). Law Clerk to Judge Myron H. Bright, U.S. Court of Appeals, Eighth Circuit (1992-1993). *LANGUAGES:* French. *PRACTICE AREAS:* Litigation; Appellate Law.

**TERRENCE R. PACE,** born Pensacola, Florida, July 30, 1966; admitted to bar, 1995, California. *Education:* University of Southern California (B.S., Mechanical Engineering, 1988; J.D., 1995). *PRACTICE AREAS:* Real Estate; Corporate Law. *Email:* trp@sonnenschein.com

**MICHAEL E. PAPPAS,** born Los Angeles, California, November 14, 1961; admitted to bar, 1987, California; 1988, U.S. District Court, Central, Northern, Eastern and Southern Districts of California. *Education:* University of California at Los Angeles (B.A. in Communications Studies, 1983); Hastings College of Law, University of California (J.D., 1987). Phi Delta Phi. Research Editor, Hastings International and Comparative Law Review, 1986-1987; Los Angeles County Bar Association Trial Attorney Project, 1990-1991. *Member:* Los Angeles County and American Bar Associations; State Bar of California. *PRACTICE AREAS:* Insurance and Commercial Litigation; Creditor's Rights. *Email:* mep@sonnenschein.com

**STACIE S. POLASHUK,** born Washington, D.C., April 30, 1970; admitted to bar, 1996, California. *Education:* University of California at Los Angeles (B.A., 1992); University of Southern California (J.D., 1996). *Member:* State Bar of California. *Email:* ssp@sonnenschein.com

**HENRY S. ROBLES,** born Big Lake, Texas, April 12, 1969; (admission pending). *Education:* University of Texas (B.A., 1991); Stanford University (J.D., 1996). *LANGUAGES:* Spanish and Portuguese. *Email:* hsr@sonnenschein.com

**LEONORA M. SCHLOSS,** born St. Louis, Missouri, December 18, 1961; admitted to bar, 1987, Texas; 1988, U.S. District Court, Northern District of Texas; 1989, California and U.S. District Court, Central District of California. *Education:* St. Louis University (A.B., 1984); Columbia University (J.D., 1987). Phi Beta Kappa; Alpha Sigma Nu. Who's Who Among Students in American Universities and Colleges. Finalist Harlan Fiske Stone Moot Court Competition. Winner: Best Brief One Round; Best Oral Argument, Two Rounds. Author: "The Evolution of the Rule Determining an Insurer's Duty to Defend - An Acknowledgment for Help in Editing," Environmental Claims Journal, Vol. VI, No. 3, Spring, 1994. *Member:* Dallas, Los Angeles County and American Bar Associations; State Bar of Texas; State Bar of California. *LANGUAGES:* Russian and German. *REPORTED CASES:* Local 21, International Federation of Professional & Technical Engineers, AFL-CIO, v. Thornton C. Bunch, Jr., Waldemar Rojas, et al. *PRACTICE AREAS:* Labor and Employment.

**DAVID SIMANTOB,** born Tehran, Iran, October 7, 1966; admitted to bar, 1991, California. *Education:* Brown University (B.A., 1988); University of California at Los Angeles (J.D., 1991). Phi Beta Kappa. Member, Moot Court Honors. Co-Author, with Lee Paterson: "Jury Verdicts in Employment Cases," Pira Scope: The Association of Human Resource Professionals, Vol. XLV, No. 5, May 1992; "Jury Verdicts in 1992 Employment Cases," Pira Scope: The Association of Human Resource Professionals, Vol. XLVI, No. 2, February 1993. *LANGUAGES:* Persian, French. *PRACTICE AREAS:* Litigation; Insurance Law.

**STEVEN R. SMITH,** born Salt Lake City, Utah, December 31, 1961; admitted to bar, 1989, California and U.S. Court of Appeals, Ninth Circuit; 1990, U.S. District Court, Central and Eastern Districts of California. *Education:* University of Utah (B.A., magna cum laude, 1985) Phi Beta Kappa; Boston University (J.D., 1989). Editor, Boston University International Law Journal. *Member:* Los Angeles County Bar Association (Board Member, AIDS Legal Services Project, 1994—); State Bar of California. *PRACTICE AREAS:* Litigation.

*(This Listing Continued)*

## SONNENSCHEIN NATH & ROSENTHAL, Los Angeles—Continued

**T. MARK SMITH,** born Bakersfield, California, June 27, 1966; admitted to bar, 1992, California. *Education:* Claremont McKenna College (B.A., magna cum laude, 1988); University of California at Los Angeles (J.D., 1992). Phi Alpha Delta. Member, Moot Court Honors. Extern, Honorable Edward Rafeedie (U.S. District Court, Central District of California) Fall 1991.

**STEVEN E. STONE,** born Los Angeles, California, March 5, 1971; (admission pending). *Education:* University of Redlands (B.A., summa cum laude, 1993); University of Southern California (J.D., 1996). Phi Beta Kappa. **PRACTICE AREAS:** General Litigation.

**DAVID W. TUFTS,** born Provo, Utah, October 10, 1967; admitted to bar, 1995, California. *Education:* Brigham Young University (B.S., Civil Engineering, 1992; J.D., 1995). Best Brief, Western Region, Giles Sutherland Rich Moot Court Competition, 1995. Executive Editor, Brigham Young University Law Review. Author: "Taking a Look at the Modern Takings Clause Jurisprudence: Finding Private Protection Under the Federal and Utah Constitutions," B.Y.U. L. Rev. 893, 1994. Member, American Society of Civil Engineers, 1990—. *Email:* dxt@sonnenschein.com

**JOHN E. WALKER,** born Holyoke, Massachusetts, August 26, 1968; admitted to bar, 1993, California; 1994, U.S. District Court, Central District of California. *Education:* University of California at Los Angeles (B.A., magna cum laude, Political Science, 1990); New York University (J.D., 1993). Phi Beta Kappa. Golden Key National Honor Society. Associate Editor, New York University Review of Law and Social Change, 1991-1993. *Member:* State Bar of California. **LANGUAGES:** German. **PRACTICE AREAS:** Litigation.

**VIVIAN L. WILLIAMS,** born Buffalo, New York, April 1, 1965; admitted to bar, 1994, California and U.S. District Court, Central District of California; 1996, U.S. District Court, Northern District of California. *Education:* Harvard University (B.A., 1987); New York University (J.D., 1993). **PRACTICE AREAS:** Labor and Employment. *Email:* vlw@sonnenschein.com

**LAUREN M. YU,** born Taipei, Taiwan, May 17, 1955; admitted to bar, 1982, Ontario; 1984, British Columbia; 1988, California; 1989, U.S. Court of Appeals, Ninth Circuit; 1990, U.S. District Court, Central District of California; 1991, U.S. Court of Appeals, Federal Circuit. *Education:* McGill University (B.Sc., 1977); Osgoode Hall (J.D., 1980). **LANGUAGES:** Chinese (Mandarin). **PRACTICE AREAS:** Litigation.

**CONSUELO A. ZERMENO,** born San Francisco, California, June 8, 1968; admitted to bar, 1994, California. *Education:* University of California at Davis (B.S., 1990); Stanford University (J.D., 1994). *Member:* Los Angeles County and American Bar Associations. **PRACTICE AREAS:** Labor and Employment. *Email:* caz@sonnenschein.com

(For Complete Biographical Data on all Personnel, see Chicago, Illinois; New York, N.Y.; St. Louis, Kansas City, Missouri; San Francisco, California; Washington, D.C. and London, England Professional Biographies)

---

## ANGELA M. SOUSA
### 1840 CENTURY PARK EAST
### EIGHTH FLOOR
### LOS ANGELES, CALIFORNIA 90067
Telephone: 310-553-1390
Telecopier: 310-553-1392

Business Litigation, Construction and Public Utilities Litigation.

**ANGELA M. SOUSA,** born Hong Kong, July 22, 1954; admitted to bar, 1980, California. *Education:* University of California, Berkeley (A.B., 1976); Massachusetts Institute of Technology (M.C.P., 1980); Harvard University (J.D., 1980). Phi Beta Kappa. Trial Attorney, U.S. Department of Justice, Civil Division, 1980-1983.

---

## LAW OFFICES OF RICHARD C. SPENCER
### ONE WILSHIRE BOULEVARD, SUITE 2100
### LOS ANGELES, CALIFORNIA 90017
Telephone: 213-629-7900
Fax: 213-629-7990

Civil Litigation, Business Law.

**RICHARD C. SPENCER,** born Queens, New York, May 2, 1943; admitted to bar, 1969, California and U.S. District Court, Northern and Central Districts of California; 1983, New York. *Education:* Syracuse University (A.B., 1964); University of New Hampshire (M.A., 1965); State University of New York at Buffalo (J.D., cum laude, 1968). Psi Chi. Special Projects Editor, Buffalo Law Review, 1967-1968. Author: "The Deductibility of Educational Expenses: Administrative Construction of Statute," 17 Buffalo Law Review 182, 1967. Co-Author: ABA Monograph: "Attorney-Client Privilege and Work Product Doctrine," 1980; "Conflicts of Interest: A Trial Lawyers Guide," Published by National Law Publishing Corp., 1984. Contributor, "Evidence in America; The Federal Rules in the State," Michie Company, 1987. Speaker, "The Hard Deposition," Beverly Hills Bar Association, Litigation Section Panel Seminar, 1985. Clerk, U.S. District Court, Central District of California, 1968-1969. Deputy District Attorney, Los Angeles County, 1969-1971. Arbitrator, Los Angeles County Bar Association Arbitration Committee, 1984—. *Member:* Los Angeles County and American (Member: Committee on Discovery, 1979-1984); Trial Practice Committee, 1980—; Special Publications Committee, 1994—; Co-Chairman, Subcommittee on Developments in Rules of Evidence, 1982-1984, Section on Litigation; Chairman, Softword MS Word User Group, Economics of Law Practice Section, 1986-1990; Member, Section on Insurance, Negligence and Compensation Law; Vice-Chair, Beginning Computer User's Interest Group Law Practice Management Section, 1990-1991) Bar Associations; State Bar of California; Los Angeles Trial Lawyers Association; California Trial Lawyers Association; The Association of Trial Lawyers of America. **PRACTICE AREAS:** Civil Litigation; Business Law.

---

## PETER SPERO
### PROFESSIONAL CORPORATION
### LOS ANGELES, CALIFORNIA
(See Santa Monica)

*Asset Protection, Pre-Bankruptcy Planning, Tax and Estate Planning Law, and Litigation Support.*

---

## SPILE & SIEGAL, LLP
### LOS ANGELES, CALIFORNIA
(See Encino)

*Insurance Defense, Real Estate, Professional Liability, Employment Law, Criminal Defense and Alternative Dispute Resolution.*

---

## SPOLIN & SILVERMAN
### LOS ANGELES, CALIFORNIA
(See Santa Monica)

*Business and Real Estate Litigation and Transactions, Environmental Litigation, Regulatory Matters, Employment Law, Corporate, Securities, Insurance Transactions and Professional Liability Litigation.*

---

## SPRAY, GOULD & BOWERS
### A PROFESSIONAL CORPORATION
### SUITE 1655, 3530 WILSHIRE BOULEVARD
### LOS ANGELES, CALIFORNIA 90010
Telephone: 213-385-3402

*Ventura, California Office:* Suite 300, 1000 Hill Road. Telephone: 805-642-8400.
*Tustin, California Office:* 17592 Seventeenth Street, Third Floor. Telephone: 714-544-7200.

*(This Listing Continued)*

General Civil Trial and Appellate Practice, State and Federal Courts. Insurance Law including Coverage and Bad Faith, Casualty and Products Liability, Construction Defect, Premises Liability and Motor Carrier. Commercial Litigation including Contract Disputes, Employment, Professional Liability, Franchise, Environmental, Taxation and Estate Planning.

**JOSEPH A. SPRAY** (1899-1971).

**CHARLES W. BOWERS** (1904-1974).

**ROBERT M. DEAN,** born Muskegon, Michigan, October 22, 1931; admitted to bar, 1966, California. *Education:* Michigan State University (B.S., 1957); Southwestern University (LL.B., 1963). (Tustin Office).

**BRUCE ALAN FINCK,** born Santa Barbara, California, July 31, 1949; admitted to bar, 1974, California. *Education:* University of California at Santa Barbara (B.A., summa cum laude, 1971) Phi Beta Kappa; University of California at Davis (J.D., 1974). (Ventura Office).

**KEITH E. WALDEN,** born Los Angeles, California, September 22, 1951; admitted to bar, 1976, California. *Education:* California State University at Fullerton (B.A., 1973); Loyola University of Los Angeles (J.D., 1976). (Tustin Office).

**RICHARD C. TURNER,** born Los Angeles, California, February 24, 1951; admitted to bar, 1977, California. *Education:* University of California, Los Angeles (B.A., 1973); Loyola University of Los Angeles (J.D., magna cum laude, 1977).

**JOSEPH G. YOUNG,** born Cameron, Missouri, July 9, 1951; admitted to bar, 1978, California. *Education:* San Diego State University (B.S., 1975); University of San Diego (J.D., 1978). (Ventura Office).

**STEVEN TOBIN,** born Detroit, Michigan, August 30, 1950; admitted to bar, 1976, California. *Education:* Eastern Michigan University (B.A., 1972); University of San Fernando Valley (J.D., 1976); Boston University (LL.M., Taxation, 1977).

**MICHAEL W. CHAMP,** born Fredonia, Kansas, November 28, 1953; admitted to bar, 1980, California. *Education:* California State University at Hayward (B.A., 1976); Pepperdine University (J.D., 1980).

**ROBERT D. BRUGGE,** born Salt Lake City, Utah, July 4, 1954; admitted to bar, 1980, California. *Education:* Loyola University (B.A., 1976); Southwestern University (J.D., 1979).

**JOEY P. MOORE,** born Malone, New York, November 26, 1954; admitted to bar, 1981, California. *Education:* St. Lawrence University (B.A., 1976); Pepperdine University (J.D., 1980). (Tustin Office).

**W. GLENN JOHNSON,** born Ridley Park, Pennsylvania, December 28, 1953; admitted to bar, 1980, California. *Education:* University of Utah (B.S., magna cum laude, 1976; J.D., 1980). (Tustin Office).

**MICHAEL D. CORTSON,** born Benton Harbor, Michigan, August 6, 1951; admitted to bar, 1985, California. *Education:* Western Michigan University (B.S., 1974); Northrop University (J.D., 1984).

*OF COUNSEL*

**CHARLES P. GOULD,** born Los Angeles, California, March 11, 1909; admitted to bar, 1932, California. *Education:* University of Chicago (Ph.B., 1930); University of Southern California (LL.B., 1932). Delta Theta Phi.

**ROBERT A. VON ESCH, III,** born Los Angeles, California, September 6, 1952; admitted to bar, 1977, California. *Education:* UCLA (A.B., 1974); Western St. University (J.D., 1977). (Tustin Office).

**JOHN CARPENTER OTTO,** born Chicago, Illinois, January 11, 1930; admitted to bar, 1959, California. *Education:* Ohio Wesleyan University (B.A., 1952); Southwestern University (J.D., 1958).

---

**LINDA L. ADAMS,** born Los Angeles, California, December 5, 1941; admitted to bar, 1985, California. *Education:* Los Angeles City College (A.A., 1961); Pacific Coast University (J.D., 1984). (Tustin Office).

**DONALD R. WOOD,** born Los Angeles, California, May 31, 1953; admitted to bar, 1988, California. *Education:* Fort Lewis College (B.A., 1980); Ventura College of Law (J.D., 1985). (Ventura Office).

**J. JANE FOX,** born Detroit, Michigan, August 19, 1936; admitted to bar, 1970, Iowa; 1979, California. *Education:* University of Michigan (B.A., 1958); University of Iowa (J.D., 1970). (Ventura Office).

**FRANCIS M. DRELLING,** born Cambridge, England, June 5, 1959; admitted to bar, 1985, Texas; 1986, California. *Education:* California State

*(This Listing Continued)*

University at Long Beach (B.A., with distinction, 1981); St. Mary's University (J.D., 1985). (Tustin Office).

**DAVID H. PIERCE,** born Charles City, Iowa, April 19, 1949; admitted to bar, 1984, California. *Education:* University of California at Los Angeles (B.A., 1971); California State University at Northridge (M.S., 1974); Southern California Institute of Law (J.D., 1983). (Ventura Office).

**MICHAEL P. FARRELL,** born Chicago, Illinois, December 29, 1955; admitted to bar, 1991, California. *Education:* University of California (B.S., 1979); Oxford University, Oxford, England; University of West Los Angeles (J.D., 1984). (Tustin Office).

**STEPHEN E. SESSA,** born Philadelphia, Pennsylvania, December 26, 1967; admitted to bar, 1993, California. *Education:* St. Joseph's University (B.A., 1990); Whittier College School of Law (J.D., 1993).

**CARLOS C. CABRAL,** born Oxnard, California, November 17, 1964; admitted to bar, 1992, California. *Education:* University of California (B.A., 1987); University of California at Los Angeles (J.D., 1990). **LANGUAGES:** Spanish.

**NICOLE M. KILGORE,** born San Francisco, California, May 31, 1970; admitted to bar, 1995, California. *Education:* Pepperdine University (J.D., 1995). (Ventura Office).

All Members and Associates of the Firm are Members of The State Bar of California.

REPRESENTATIVE CLIENTS: State Farm Mutual Automobile Insurance Co.; State Farm Fire and Casualty Co.; The Chubb Group of Insurance Cos.; AT&T Capital Corp.; Fireman's Fund Insurance Co.; Bayliner Marine Corp.; FHP, Inc.; Johnson Controls; Taco Bell, Inc.; U.S. Elevator Corp.; KFC, Inc.; Wal-mart Stores; United States Pollution Control, Inc.; Sears, Roebuck & Co.; Uniroyal/Goodrich Tire Co.; Overnight Transportation Co.; Viking Insurance Co.; J.I. Case; County of Ventura; City of Oxnard; Cincinnati Milacron; Industrial Indemnity; Mercury Insurance Group; Colonial Penn Insurance Co.

---

## PATRICK C. STACKER
### LOS ANGELES, CALIFORNIA

(See Long Beach)

*Real Estate, Corporate, Estate Planning and Dispute Resolution.*

---

## LAW OFFICES OF
## MARC R. STAENBERG
### A PROFESSIONAL CORPORATION

1801 CENTURY PARK EAST, TWENTY-THIRD FLOOR
**LOS ANGELES, CALIFORNIA 90067**
Telephone: 310-201-2550
Fax: 310-201-2551

*Business and Transactions, Entertainment and Sports Law. Civil Litigation.*

**MARC R. STAENBERG,** born Newark, New Jersey, November 21, 1947; admitted to bar, 1973, New Jersey and U.S. District Court, District of New Jersey; 1975, District of Columbia; 1976, U.S. District Court for the District of Columbia and U.S. Court of Appeals, District of Columbia; 1978, U.S. Supreme Court; 1981, California, U.S. District Court, Central District of California and U.S. Court of Appeals, Ninth Circuit. *Education:* University of Wisconsin (B.A., 1969); Rutgers University (J.D., 1973); Georgetown University (LL.M., 1977).

---

## MICHAEL N. STAFFORD
### LOS ANGELES, CALIFORNIA

(See Glendale)

*General Civil Trial Practice in all State and Federal Courts, Real Estate, Corporate and Business Law, Probate and Estate Planning, Arbitration and Mediation.*

## STAITMAN, SNYDER & TANNENBAUM

**LOS ANGELES, CALIFORNIA**

(See Encino)

*General Civil, Trial, Appellate Practice. Insurance Law; Litigation; Personal Injury, Products Liability, Premises Liability, Medical Malpractice, Legal Malpractice, Corporate Real Estate, Commercial and General Business.*

---

## STALL, ASTOR & GOLDSTEIN

PICO LAW BUILDING
10507 WEST PICO BOULEVARD
SUITE 200
**LOS ANGELES, CALIFORNIA 90064**
Telephone: 310-470-6852
Facsimile: 310-470-3673
Email: StAsGo@msn.com

*General Civil Trial and Appellate Practice in all State and Federal Courts. Transactional Services in Business, Real Estate, Labor, Entertainment Matters, Family Law, Insurance Defense, Intellectual Property, Patents, Trademarks and Copyrights.*

**RICHARD J. STALL, JR.,** born Covington, Kentucky, July 5, 1941; admitted to bar, 1967, California; 1971, U.S. Supreme Court; 1973, U.S. Tax Court. *Education:* Purdue University (B.S., with distinction, 1963); Stanford University (J.D., 1966). Tau Beta Pi. Recipient, President's Honor Award for 1963. Member, Panel of Arbitrators, American Arbitration Association, 1971—. Arbitrator, 1980— and Receiver, 1983—, Los Angeles Superior Court. Arbitrator, NASD Arbitration, 1996—. *Member:* Los Angeles (Member: Insurance Committee, 1972-1973; Arbitration Committee, 1972), Culver-Marina Del Rey (President, 1973), Santa Monica (Trustee, 1973-1974), Century City and American (Member, Section on Real Property, Probate & Trust Law and Chairman, 1972—) Bar Associations; State Bar of California (Member, Committee on Jury Instructions, 1978—). **PRACTICE AREAS:** General Business; Real Estate; Civil Litigation. **Email:** StAsGo@msn.com

**SANFORD ASTOR,** born St. Louis, Missouri, January 1, 1937; admitted to bar, 1963, California and U.S. District Court, Southern District of California; 1978, U.S. Supreme Court. *Education:* Purdue University (B.S.Ch.E., 1958); George Washington University (J.D., 1962). Family Law Mediator, Los Angeles County Superior Court, 1990—. Member, Panel of Arbitrators, American Arbitration Association, 1984—. *Member:* Beverly Hills, Los Angeles County and American (Chairman, Intellectual Property Law Committee of the Tort and Insurance Practice (TIPS) Section, 1996-1997) Bar Associations; State Bar of California (Member, Sections on: Family Law; Intellectual Property). **SPECIAL AGENCIES:** U.S. Patent and Trademark Office. **PRACTICE AREAS:** Civil Litigation; Corporate; Probate; Real Estate; Intellectual Property. **Email:** StAsGo@msn.com

**DON W. GOLDSTEIN,** born San Luis Obispo, California, September 26, 1941; admitted to bar, 1966, California; 1974, U.S. District Court, Central District of California and U.S. Court of Appeals, Ninth Circuit. *Education:* University of California at Berkeley (A.B., 1963); Boalt Hall School of Law, University of California (LL.B., 1966). Phi Delta Phi. Member, Panel of Arbitrators, American Arbitration Association. Judge, Pro-Tem, Los Angeles, Municipal Court, 1977—. Arbitrator, Los Angeles Superior Court, 1980—. Judge Pro Tem, Los Angeles Municipal Court, 1977—. *Member:* Santa Monica, Marina Del Rey (President, 1976-1977), Los Angeles County (Member, Family Law Section) and American Bar Associations; The State Bar of California. **PRACTICE AREAS:** Civil Litigation; Family Law; Insurance Defense. **Email:** StAsGo@msn.com

### ASSOCIATES

**CYNTHIA C. LAM,** born Los Angeles, California, December 2, 1961; admitted to bar, 1988, California and U.S. District Court, Central and Eastern Districts of California. *Education:* University of California at Santa Barbara (B.A., 1983); Pepperdine University (J.D., 1987). Borba Scholarship. *Member:* Century City and Los Angeles County Bar Associations; State Bar of California.

**CONSTANCE E. BOUKIDIS,** born Santa Monica, California, January 19, 1958; admitted to bar, 1992, California. *Education:* University of California at Santa Cruz (B.A., 1979); Boston University (J.D., 1990); The Fletcher School of Law and Diplomacy (M.A., 1992). *Member:* State Bar of California.

*(This Listing Continued)*

CAA1222B

---

REPRESENTATIVE CLIENTS: Associate International Insurance Co.; Atlantic Richfield Co.; Barco Aviation, Inc.; Consolidated International Automotive Co.; Creative Agricultural Packaging, Inc.; Gulf Insurance Group; King Meat, Inc.; Northern Telecom, Inc.; PacTel Meridian Systems; Photon Physics Services, Inc.; Radiator Specialty Co.; Red Carpet Real Estate Services, Inc.; SunBank; Suntan Hawaii, Ltd.; Teachers Magazine; Trans-Atlantic Entertainment, Inc.; United Labor Bank; Vanadium-Pacific Steel Co.; West LA Realty, Inc.
REFERENCE: Union Bank.

---

## STANARD, BLENDER & SCHWARTZ

**LOS ANGELES, CALIFORNIA**

(See Woodland Hills)

*General Civil Trial Practice in all State and Federal Courts. Corporation, Real Property, Radio (Entertainment), Estate Planning, Family Law, Probate and Taxation Law.*

---

## PAUL L. STANTON

11111 SANTA MONICA BOULEVARD
SUITE 1840
**LOS ANGELES, CALIFORNIA 90025-3352**
Telephone: 310-444-1840
Fax: 310-268-8444

*Fiduciary Litigation including Probate and Trust Litigation, Elder Abuse, Legal Malpractice. Estate Planning, Probate and Trust Administration, Alternative Dispute Resolution.*

**PAUL L. STANTON,** born Guadalajara, Jalisco, Mexico, August 16, 1947; admitted to bar, 1973, California; 1974, U.S. District Court, Central District of California. *Education:* Clark University (A.B., magna cum laude, 1969); University of California at Los Angeles (J.D., 1973). Member, Panel of Arbitrators, Los Angeles Superior Court. *Member:* Beverly Hills (Member, Sections on: Real Estate Law; Computer Law; Alternate Dispute Resolution Committee; Officer, Executive Committee, Probate and Trust Section; Co-Chair, Probate and Trust Litigation Sub-Committee) and Los Angeles County (Member, Section on: Litigation; Law Office Management) Bar Associations; State Bar of California (Member, Sections on: Litigation; Probate and Trust; Real Estate Law; Law Office Management; Member: Executive Committee, Management Section; Litigation Sub-Committee, Probate and Trust Section); Los Angeles Trial Lawyers Association; California Trial Lawyers Association; American Arbitration Association. **LANGUAGES:** Spanish. **PRACTICE AREAS:** Fiduciary Litigation.

### ASSOCIATES

**SHANNON H. BURNS,** born Fort Ord, California, July 25, 1952; admitted to bar, 1986, California; 1987, U.S. District Court, Central District of California. *Education:* University of California at Los Angeles (B.A., 1977); Whittier College School of Law (J.D., 1986). *Member:* Beverly Hills and Los Angeles County Bar Associations; State Bar of California (Member: Estate Planning, Trust and Probate Section; Subcommittee on Litigation, 1994—). **PRACTICE AREAS:** Estate Planning; Fiduciary Litigation.

---

## STANTON LAW CORPORATION

1999 AVENUE OF THE STARS
SUITE 1850
**LOS ANGELES, CALIFORNIA 90067**
Telephone: 310-789-1994
Fax: 310-282-0328

*Family Law, Personal Injury, Business Litigation, Business Law, Mediation and Arbitration.*

**HAROLD J. STANTON,** born Columbus, Ohio, April 16, 1940; admitted to bar, 1966, California and U.S. District Court, Central District of California. *Education:* University of California, Los Angeles (B.S., 1962; J.D., 1965). Senior Editor, U.C.L.A. Law Review, 1964-1965. Author: "The Celebrity's Right to Publicity," Family Advocate ABA journal Vol. 9 #2, 1986; "Community Property and the Right of Publicity," L.A. Lawyer, Vol. 9, 1986; "Comment on Land Use Planning," Vol. 12 U.C.L.A. Law Review, 1965. Deputy Attorney General, California Department of Justice, 1965-1967. Judge Pro Tem, Los Angeles and Beverly Hills Municipal Courts, 1980—. Family Law Mediator, Los Angeles Superior Court. Chair, Mediation Committee and Certified Family Law Arbitrator, American Academy of Matrimonial Lawyers. *Member:* Beverly Hills, Los Angeles County and American (Lecturer, N.Y., 1986) Bar Associations; State Bar of California

*(This Listing Continued)*

(Lecturer, San Diego, California, 1993); California Trial Lawyers Association; Los Angeles Trial Lawyers Association. *PRACTICE AREAS:* Family Law; Personal Injury; Business Litigation; Business Law; Mediation and Arbitration (Family Law).

**MARIAN L. STANTON,** born New York, N.Y.; admitted to bar, 1981, California. *Education:* University of California, Los Angeles (B.A., 1962; M.A., 1967); Whittier College/Beverly School of Law (J.D., magna cum laude, 1980). Recipient, American Jurisprudence Award, Family Law and Constitutional Law. Editor, Whittier Law Review, 1979-1980. Author: "California Diminishes Federally Protected Constitutional Rights," Whittier Law Review Vol. 2, No. 2., 1980. Instructor, Legal Research and Writing, Whittier College School of Law, 1982-1983. Judge Pro Tem: Family Law; Los Angeles Superior Court, North Valley. *Member:* Los Angeles County Bar Association (Member, Family Law Section); State Bar of California (Member, Family Law Section); San Fernando Valley Bar Association. *PRACTICE AREAS:* Family Law; Business Litigation.

OF COUNSEL

**OBERSTEIN, KIBRE & HORWITZ** Los Angeles, California.

LEGAL SUPPORT PERSONNEL

**STACEY STANTON BLACK** (Paralegal).

---

## STEVEN J. STANWYCK
*1900 AVENUE OF THE STARS, SUITE 1700*
**LOS ANGELES, CALIFORNIA 90067-4403**
*Telephone: 310-557-8390*
*Telecopier: 310-557-8391*

*Arbitration, Mediation and Litigation in Financial Matters, Computers, Business Information Systems and Telecommunications.*

**STEVEN J. STANWYCK,** born New York, N.Y., September 21, 1944; admitted to bar, 1971, California; 1972, New York; 1980, U.S. Supreme Court; 1982, U.S. Tax Court. *Education:* University of Denver (B.A., 1967); University of California at Berkeley (M.B.A., 1971); Boalt Hall School of Law, University of California (J.D., 1970). Phi Alpha Delta. Counsel for United Computer Systems in UCS v. AT&T. *Member:* Association of the Bar of the City of New York; Los Angeles County, New York State, Federal and American Bar Associations; State Bar of California; Association of Business Trial Lawyers. [U.S. Army Security Agency, 1962-1964]

---

## STARK, RASAK & CLARKE
**LOS ANGELES, CALIFORNIA**
(See Torrance)

*Personal Injury, Plaintiffs and Defense, Products Liability, Medical Malpractice, Real Estate & Family Law.*

---

## RONALD J. STAUBER
*1840 CENTURY PARK EAST, 8TH FLOOR*
**LOS ANGELES, CALIFORNIA 90067**
*Telephone: 310-556-0080*
*Telecopier: 310-556-3687*

*General Civil Practice. Real Estate, Corporation, Securities and Business Law. Litigation.*

**RONALD J. STAUBER,** born Toledo, Ohio, November 8, 1940; admitted to bar, 1967, California and U.S. District Court, Central District of California; 1972, U.S. District Court, Eastern District of California and U.S. Supreme Court. *Education:* University of Toledo (B.B.A., 1962); Ohio State University (J.D., 1965). Tau Epsilon Rho. Co-Author: "Smart Credit Repair," Paris Publishers, 1991. Corporations Counsel, Department of Investment, Division of Corporations, State of California, 1965-1967. Judge Pro Tem, Los Angeles County Bar Association, 1990—. *Member:* Beverly Hills (Member, Real Estate and Corporations Committee, 1968—), Los Angeles County (Member, Real Estate, Business and Corporate Law Section) and American (Member, Corporation and Business Law Section) Bar Associations; State Bar of California.

---

## RICHARD A. STAVIN AND ASSOCIATES
*1840 CENTURY PARK EAST, SUITE 800*
**LOS ANGELES, CALIFORNIA 90067**
*Telephone: 310-553-1144*

Encino, California Office: 15760 Ventura Boulevard, Suite 1600. Telephone: 818-385-1144. Fax: 818-385-1149.

*Business and Fraud Litigation, Insurance Defense, Unfair Competition, Wrongful Termination, Discrimination Litigation.*

(For Complete Biographical Data, See Professional Biography at Encino, California).

---

## STEGMAN & CARAGOZIAN
*1900 AVENUE OF THE STARS, SUITE 1750*
**LOS ANGELES, CALIFORNIA 90067**
*Telephone: 310-843-9338*
*Fax: 310-843-0438*

*General Civil Trial and Appellate Practice in all State and Federal Courts and Administrative Agencies.*

**DAPHNE M. STEGMAN,** born Jamaica, New York, September 27, 1948; admitted to bar, 1975, California. *Education:* Trinity College (A.B., cum laude, 1970); University of California at Los Angeles (J.D., 1974). Co-author, "Hanson v. Shell Oil Co.: A Straw in the Wind?" 38 Ohio State Law Journal 269, 1977; "Moderate-Cost Housing after Lafayette: A Proposal," 11 Urban Lawyer 209, 1979. Law Clerk to Honorable Roger G. Connor, Alaska Supreme Court, 1974-1975. *Member:* Los Angeles County (Chair, Antitrust Section, 1983-1984) and American (Member, Sections on: Antitrust Law; Litigation) Bar Associations; State Bar of California (Member, Executive Committee, Antitrust and Trade Regulation Law Section, 1987-1990) Women Lawyers Association of Los Angeles. *PRACTICE AREAS:* Antitrust; Intellectual Property; Business Litigation; Construction Disputes; Employment Law.

**JOHN S. CARAGOZIAN,** born March 23, 1953; admitted to bar, 1979, California. *Education:* University of California at Los Angeles (A.B., summa cum laude, 1975); Harvard University (J.D., cum laude, 1979). Phi Beta Kappa. *Member:* Los Angeles County Bar Association; State Bar of California. *PRACTICE AREAS:* Business Litigation; Real Estate Litigation; Business Torts; Arbitration.

**KAREN A. SHARE,** born Los Angeles, California, December 22, 1949; admitted to bar, 1975, California. *Education:* University of California at Los Angeles (B.S., 1971; Executive Program Cert., 1984) Hastings College (J.D., 1975). *Member:* State Bar of California. *PRACTICE AREAS:* Business Litigation; Arbitration.

OF COUNSEL

**DONALD E. WARNER, JR.,** born Glendale, California, December 26, 1941; admitted to bar, 1974, California. *Education:* University of California at Los Angeles (A.B., 1963; J.D., 1974). Order of the Coif. Associate Editor, UCLA Law Review, 1973-1974. Member, Executive Committee, Labor and Employment Law Section, State Bar of California, 1982—. *PRACTICE AREAS:* Labor Law; Employment Law.

---

## STEIN & KAHAN
*A LAW CORPORATION*
**LOS ANGELES, CALIFORNIA**
(See Santa Monica)

*General Civil and Trial Practice in all State and Federal Courts. Business, Corporate, Securities, Licensing and Franchise Law, Entertainment Litigation.*

---

## STEIN PERLMAN & HAWK
*9000 SUNSET BOULEVARD, SUITE 500*
**LOS ANGELES, CALIFORNIA 90069**
*Telephone: 310-247-9500*
*Telecopier: 310-247-0109*

*Business Litigation and Bankruptcy Law.*
(This Listing Continued)

## STEIN PERLMAN & HAWK, Los Angeles—Continued

**MITCHELL J. STEIN,** born Pittsburgh, Pennsylvania, August 17, 1958; admitted to bar, 1985, California; 1986, U.S. District Court, Central and Southern Districts of California. *Education:* Indiana University; Duquesne University; University of Pittsburgh (B.A., summa cum laude, 1982; J.D., 1985). Sole Recipient: United States Law Week Award, issued by the Bureau of National Affairs, the B.N.A. Civil Trial Manual, and the University of Pittsburgh for outstanding scholastic achievement. First Place Speaker, Moot Court Oral Argument. Speaker: "Leveraged Buyouts of Closely Held Corporations--The Levinson Steel Company, A Case Study," University of Pittsburgh, 1985. *Member:* Beverly Hills, Los Angeles County and American Bar Associations; State Bar of California; The Association of Trial Lawyers of America. *PRACTICE AREAS:* Business Litigation; Corporate Organization.

**DANA M. PERLMAN,** born West Covina, California, October 30, 1961; admitted to bar, 1986, California, U.S. District Court, Central District of California and U.S. Court of Appeals, Ninth Circuit; 1987, U.S. District Court, Northern, Southern and Eastern Districts of California. *Education:* University of California at Los Angeles (B.A., 1983); University of Southern California (J.D., 1986). Director, Los Angeles Regional Food Bank. *Member:* Los Angeles County and American Bar Associations; American Bankruptcy Institute. *PRACTICE AREAS:* Business Litigation (75%); Bankruptcy (25%).

**DENNIS J. HAWK,** born Elko, Nevada, December 31, 1959; admitted to bar, 1987, California. *Education:* California Polytechnic State University (B.S., 1984); Georgetown University (J.D., 1987). *Member:* Los Angeles County and American Bar Associations. *PRACTICE AREAS:* Entertainment (50%); Corporate (30%); Medical (10%); Real Estate (10%).

### ASSOCIATES

**DANIEL L. KRISHEL,** born 1963; admitted to bar, 1990, California. *Education:* California State University, Northridge; Loyola University of Los Angeles (J.D., 1990). *Member:* American Bar Association. *PRACTICE AREAS:* Business Litigation (100%).

## STEIN SHOSTAK SHOSTAK & O'HARA

*A PROFESSIONAL CORPORATION*
Established in 1933

*515 SOUTH FIGUEROA STREET, SUITE 1200*
**LOS ANGELES, CALIFORNIA 90071-3329**
*Telephone: 213-486-0010*
*Fax: 213-486-0011*

*Washington, D.C. Office:* Suite 807, 1620 L Street, N.W. Telephone: 202-223-6270. Fax: 202-659-4237.

*San Diego, California Office:* 2675 Customhouse Court, Suite B. Telephone: 619-661-6317. Fax: 619-661-1448.

*Customs and International Trade Law. Practice before Federal Administrative Agencies. Trials and Appeals.*

*FIRM PROFILE: The firm was established in 1933 as a law firm specializing in the practice of Customs and International Trade Law, representing clients located throughout the United States with importations from around the world including Pacific Rim countries, Mexico and Latin American countries. The firm represents importers and exporters in a variety of industries, including textiles, footwear, toys, chemicals, automotive and electronic products.*

*Active involvement in all phases of the international trade community has been a policy of the firm since its inception. Members of the firm serve in active leadership positions in many international trade organizations, including: the Foreign Trade Association of Southern California, the Los Angeles Area Chamber of Commerce, the American Association of Exporters and Importers, the Border Trade Alliance, the American Bar Association and the Los Angeles County Bar Association Customs Law Committees. Members of the firm also conduct and participate in seminars on customs and trade matters frequently.*

**PHILIP STEIN** (1899-1955).

**MARJORIE M. SHOSTAK,** born Lincoln, Nebraska; admitted to bar, 1945, California; 1946, U.S. Customs Court; 1949, U.S. District Court, Central District of California; 1951, U.S. Court of Customs and Patent Appeals and U.S. Supreme Court; 1980, U.S. Court of International Trade; 1982, U.S. Court of Appeals for the Federal Circuit. *Education:* University of Nebraska (A.B., 1935). Phi Beta Kappa; Alpha Lambda Delta. Author, "Customs Law Practice: Scope and Challenge," American Import & Export Bulletin, 1960. Collaborated with Philip Stein in preparation of textbook "U.S. Customs Administration and Procedure," 1949, 1950, and brochure "U.S. Customs Court," 1950. Assistant Instructor, U.S. Customs Procedure, University of Southern California, 1946-1953. Member, Industry Functional Advisory Committee on Customs Matters, U.S. Department of Commerce/ U.S. Trade Representative, 1980—. *Member:* Los Angeles County (Chairman, 1970-1972 and Member, 1973—, Customs Law Committee) and American (Member, Administrative Law Section, Customs Committee, 1970—) Bar Associations; State Bar of California (Member, International Law Section); Customs and International Trade Bar Association; California Women Lawyers; American Judicature Society. *REPORTED CASES:* United States v. Winkler-Koch Engineering, 209 F.2d 758, 41 CCPA 121, C.A.D. 540 (1953); United States v. Baltimore & Ohio RR a/c United China & Glass Co., 47 CCPA 1, C.A.D. 719 (1959); United States v. Quon Quon Co., 46 CCPA 70, C.A.D. 699 (1959); Mattel, Inc. v. United States, 926 F.2d 1116, 9 Fed. Cir. (T) 63 (1991). *PRACTICE AREAS:* Customs Law; International Trade Law.

**S. RICHARD SHOSTAK,** born Omaha, Nebraska, July 16, 1931; admitted to bar, 1956, California, U.S. Circuit Court of Appeals, Ninth Circuit and U.S. District Court, Northern District of California; 1957, U.S. Customs Court; 1960, U.S. District Court, Central District of California, U.S. Court of Customs and Patent Appeals and U.S. Supreme Court; 1980, District of Columbia; 1980, U.S. Court of International Trade; 1982, U.S. Court of Appeals for the Federal Circuit. *Education:* Northwestern University and University of California at Berkeley (A.B., 1953); Boalt Hall School of Law, University of California (J.D., 1956). Phi Eta Sigma. Author: *Simplification of U.S. Customs Laws and Regulations,* Organizational Dynamics, Inc., 1979; "The Evolution of Item 807.00 of the Tariff Schedules of the United States and The Resulting Revolution of the Customs Laws," University of West Los Angeles Law Review, Vol. 12, 1980. Deputy District Attorney, Sonoma County, California, 1957-1959. Hearing Examiner, Civil Service Commission, City of Los Angeles, 1975-1982. Secretary, Committee for Production Sharing, 1976-1990. *Member:* Los Angeles County (Member, International Law Section, 1968—), Federal Circuit (Chair, Court of International Trade Appeals Committee, 1986-1987; Director, 1987-1990) and American (Member, International Law Section) Bar Associations; State Bar of California (Member, International Law Section); District of Columbia Bar; Wilshire Bar Association; Customs and International Trade Bar Association (Co-Chair, Special Committee on Trade Agreements, 1991—). *REPORTED CASES:* Superscope v. United States, 727 F.Supp. 629, 13 CIT 997 (1989); Bushnell International v. United States, 49 Cust. Ct. 123, CD 2370 (1962); Rudolph Miles v. United States, 567 F.2d 979, 65 CCPA 32, CAD 1202 (1978); Authentic Furniturea Products, Inc. v. United States, 486 F.2d 1062, 61 CCPA 5, CAD 1109 (1974); O.L. Electronics, Inc. Arrow Sales, Inc. v. United States, 49 CCPA 111, CAD 804 (1962). *PRACTICE AREAS:* Customs Law; International Trade Law.

**JOSEPH P. COX,** born Ellensburg, Washington, April 10, 1948; admitted to bar, 1977, California and U.S. District Court, Southern District of California; 1978, District of Columbia and U.S. Court of Customs and Patent Appeals; 1980, U.S. Customs Court and U.S. Court of International Trade; 1982, U.S. Court of Appeals for the Federal Circuit. *Education:* University of California at San Diego and University of California at Los Angeles (B.A., 1970); University of San Diego (J.D., 1977). Recipient: Marquardt Corporation Scholarship; Outstanding Achievement Award, U.S. Customs Service, Los Angeles, 1973. Air Security Officer, U.S. Customs Service, Los Angeles, 1970-1973. Inspector, U.S. Customs Service, San Ysidro, California, 1974-1977. Attorney: Penalties Branch, 1977, Commercial Fraud Penalties Branch, 1977-1979; Penalties Task Force, 1978 and Classification Branch, 1979, Office of Regulations and Rulings, U.S. Customs Service, Washington, D.C.; Office of Regional Counsel, U.S. Customs Service, Los Angeles, 1979-1980. *Member:* The District of Columbia Bar; Los Angeles County (Member, 1981—, Chair, 1984-1985 and 1992-1993, Customs Law Committee) and American (Member, Administrative Law Section; Vice-Chair, Customs and Tariffs Committee, 1985-1988) Bar Associations; State Bar of California (Member, International Law Section); Customs and International Trade Bar Association. *PRACTICE AREAS:* Customs Law; International Trade Law; Export Law.

**STEVEN B. ZISSER,** born Los Angeles, California, May 21, 1959; admitted to bar, 1988, California; 1989, U.S. Court of International Trade; 1990, U.S. Court of Appeals for the Federal Circuit. *Education:* University of California at Berkeley (B.A., 1981); Loyola Marymount University (J.D., 1988). Author: "NAFTA Eligibility Begins with Classification," North American Trade Guide, 1994-1995, 1995-1996, 1996-1997; "Successful Importing Begins with Product Classification," Custom House Guide, 1995,

*(This Listing Continued)*

1996, 1997. *Member:* Los Angeles County Bar Association (Member: Sections on Law Office Management and International Law; Customs Law Committee; Chairman, 1996-1997); State Bar of California (Member, International Law Section); Customs and International Trade Bar Associations. **PRACTICE AREAS:** Customs Law; International Trade Law; Administrative Law.

### OF COUNSEL

**JAMES F. O'HARA,** born New York, N.Y., March 13, 1932; admitted to bar, 1959, New York; 1961, U.S. Customs Court and U.S. Court of Customs and Patent Appeals; 1972, U.S. District Court, Southern and Eastern Districts of New York; 1974, California and U.S. District Court, Central District of California; 1980, U.S. Court of International Trade; 1982, U.S. Court of Appeals for the Federal Circuit. *Education:* St. John's University (B.A., 1954; LL.B., 1959). Delta Theta Phi. Attorney, U.S. Customs Service, 1959-1961. Trial Attorney, U.S. Department of Justice, Customs Section, 1961-1962. General Counsel, Man-Made Fibre Producers Association, Inc., 1963-1971. *Member:* Los Angeles County (Member, 1975— and Chairman, 1978-1979, Customs Law Committee), New York State and American Bar Associations; State Bar of California; Association of the Customs Bar (Member: Discipline Committee, 1972; Committee on Practice, Procedure and Legislation, 1976-1980; Advisory Committee on Rules, U.S. Customs Court, 1980-1982); Customs and International Trade Bar Association (Member, Judicial Selection Committee, 1981-1986). [With U.S. Army, 1954-1956]. **PRACTICE AREAS:** Customs Law; International Trade Law.

(For additional biographical data, see Professional Biographies at San Diego and Washington, D.C.)

## STEINBERG BARNESS GLASGOW & FOSTER LLP

**LOS ANGELES, CALIFORNIA**

(See Manhattan Beach)

*General Business Practice, Corporation, Real Estate, Estate Planning, Trust and Probate Law, Civil Litigation, Bankruptcy, Creditor's Rights.*

## STEINBERG, NUTTER & BRENT

**LOS ANGELES, CALIFORNIA**

(See Santa Monica)

*Bankruptcy, Insolvency, Corporate Reorganization, Creditor's Rights, Real Estate, Commercial and Business Litigation. General Civil, Trial and Appellate Practice in all State and Federal Courts.*

## STEINER & SAFFER

A PROFESSIONAL LAW CORPORATION

2121 AVENUE OF THE STARS
TWENTY-SECOND FLOOR
**LOS ANGELES, CALIFORNIA 90067-5010**
Telephone: 310-557-8422
FAX: 310-556-0336

*New York, New York Affiliated Office:* Lynch Rowin Novack Burnbaum & Crystal, 300 East 42nd Street, 10th Floor. Telephone: 212-682-4001. Fax: 212-986-2907.

*Art, Entertainment, Intellectual Property and Commercial Litigation in all State and Federal Courts. Artist, Publisher, Gallery and Art Collector Transactions, Domestic and International Business, Insurance Coverage, Real Estate Litigation.*

**DAVID PAUL STEINER,** born San Mateo, California, March 17, 1949; admitted to bar, 1975, California; U.S. District Court, Northern and Central Districts of California; 1991, Colorado. *Education:* Stanford University (B.A., 1971); Hastings College of Law, University of California, San Francisco (J.D., 1974). Co-founder and Editor-in-Chief, Hastings Constitutional Law Quarterly, 1973-1974. Contributing Editor, Art Business News, 1984-1985. Co-editor, The Visual Artist's Manual - A Practical Guide to Your Career, Beverly Hills Bar Association Committee for the Arts (1981). Author: "Copyright - A Valuable Tool For the Art Business Community," September, October, November, December, 1984 and January, 1985 editions of

*(This Listing Continued)*

Art Business News. Speaker: Montreux Conference, Summer, 1987; L.A. Art Expo, Art Law in the Print Market, October, 1988; State Bar of California Section Institute, Monterey, California, May, 1993; Art Law issues, Pepperdine University Art Museum, Fall, 1993; Laguna Art Museum, June, 1994; University of Judaism Art Museum, Sept., 1994; Palm Springs Desert Museum, April, 1995. Adjunct Professor, "Art Law and Litigation," University of Southern California Law Center, 1995. Judge Pro Tem, Los Angeles Municipal Court, 1983-1984. *Member:* Beverly Hills (Member: Board of Governors, 1984-1986; Bi-Centennial Committee, 1986-1987; Barristers Board of Governors, 1981-1987; President, 1986-1987, Treasurer, 1985-1986 and Secretary, 1984-1985, Barristers; Chairman, Lawyers Referral and Information Service Committee, 1984-1987; Chairperson and Founder, Wine Auction Committee, 1984-1987; Member, Committee for the Arts, 1977-1986), Los Angeles County and American (Chairperson, Computer Law Committee, 1985-1986; Member, Organizational Committee, Affiliate's Outreach Project, Los Angeles, May, 1987; Young Lawyers Division) Bar Associations; State Bar of California (Member, Volunteer Investigative Attorney Program, Office of Legal Counsel, 1986-1987); International Bar Association (Member, Cultural Property Section). (Also Counsel to Lynch Rowin Novack Burnbaum & Crystal, P.C.).

**SHERRY M. SAFFER,** born Brooklyn, New York, August 9, 1958; admitted to bar, 1983, California; 1984, U.S. District Court, Northern and Central Districts of California; 1987, U.S. District Court, Eastern District of California. *Education:* University of California at Los Angeles (B.A., 1979); Syracuse University College of Law (International Program Abroad, 1981); Southwestern University School of Law (J.D., 1983). Phi Alpha Delta. Law Review Member, Southwestern University School of Law, 1982-1983. Judicial Extern to the Hon. Cynthia H. Hall, U.S. District Court, Central District of California (elevated to the 9th Circuit Court of Appeals), 1982. Commission on Judicial Nominees Evaluation, 1993-1996. Advisor, C.E.B.-C.Y.L.A., Action Guides Series Meeting Statutory Deadlines, 1987-1990. Moderator, The State Bar of California Section Institute, San Diego, California, November, 1992. *Member:* Beverly Hills Bar Association (Barristers Board of Governors, 1985-1993; President, 1991-1992; Vice President, 1990-1991; Secretary, 1989-1990; Treasurer, 1988-1989; Secretary, 1987-1988; Chairperson, Law Day, 1988-1991; Board of Governors, 1989—; Executive Committee Litigation Section, 1993-1994; Judge Pro Tem, Beverly Hills Municipal Court, 1991-1995), Los Angeles County and American Bar Associations; State Bar of California (Liaison, The Consortium on Competence, 1988-1990; Executive Committee General Practice Section, 1989-1993; Chair Elect, 1992-1993; Treasurer, 1991-1992); California Young Lawyers Association (Board of Directors, 1987-1990; Second Vice President, 1989-1990). **REPORTED CASES:** Gribin v. Hammer Galleries, a Division of Hammer Holdings, 793 F.Supp. 233 (C.D. Cal. 1992).

REPRESENTATIVE CLIENTS: Lloyds of London; Martin Lawrence Limited Editions, Inc.; Great Events Editions, Inc.; Galerie Michael, Inc.; Stygian Publishing, Inc.; Mercantile National Bank; Hang Ups Art Enterprises, Inc.; Tom Binder Fine Arts; Telemedia Network, Inc.; Texican Natural Gas Company, Inc.; Gregory Editions, Inc.; The Estate of Erté; G.H. Palmer Associates; George Hormel Enterprises; Fidelity Investments/Wentworth Gallery; Visage Fine Art; Pasquale Iannetti Art Gallery, Excel Programing Innovations; Miranda Art Gallery; David Lynch Collectors Edition; Art Imposium; The Garfield Foundation.
REFERENCE: Mercantile National Bank (Century City Branch).

## TERRAN T. STEINHART

4311 WILSHIRE BOULEVARD, SUITE 405
**LOS ANGELES, CALIFORNIA 90010-3708**
Telephone: 213-933-8263
FAX: 213-933-2391

*General Practice with emphasis on Business, Entertainment and Personal Injury Litigation. Appeals in State and Federal Courts and Dispute Resolution for Christian Ministries.*

**TERRAN T. STEINHART,** born Los Angeles, California, October 5, 1939; admitted to bar, 1965, California; U.S. District Court, Central and Northern Districts of California; U.S. District Court, Southern District of Texas and U.S. Court of Appeals, Ninth Circuit. *Education:* University of California at Los Angeles (B.A., with honors, 1961); Harvard University (J.D., cum laude, 1964). Phi Beta Kappa. *Member:* State Bar of California. **REPORTED CASES:** Frances T. vs. Village Green Owners' Association, 42 C.3d 490 (California Supreme Court 1986); Columbia Record Productions vs. Hot Wax Records, Inc., 966 F.2d 515 (9th Cir. 1992).

## STEPHENS, BERG & LASATER
A PROFESSIONAL CORPORATION
Established in 1977
1055 WEST SEVENTH STREET, TWENTY-NINTH FLOOR
**LOS ANGELES, CALIFORNIA 90017**
Telephone: 213-629-3111
Telecopy: 213-629-2302; 213-624-4734

General Civil Litigation Practice in State and Federal Courts, Alternate Dispute Resolution. Antitrust, Business and Commercial, Insurance, Environmental, Real Estate and Construction Litigation. Corporate, Securities and Real Estate Transactions. Federal, State and Local and International Taxation. Estate Planning, Trust and Probate.

FIRM PROFILE: Stephens, Berg & Lasater was founded in 1977. As a business law firm we pride ourselves on our ability to provide prompt, economical, personalized and quality legal services to our clients. Our emphasis on regular and frequent communication and cost-effective results has enabled us to develop and maintain long-term relationships with our clients. Our clients include individuals, small and medium-sized businesses and national and international Fortune 100 companies.

**LAWRENCE M. BERG** (1947-1995).

**R. WICKS STEPHENS II,** born Los Angeles, California, November 30, 1934; admitted to bar, 1963, California; 1967, U.S. Supreme Court. *Education:* University of California at Los Angeles (B.S., 1957); Stanford University (LL.B., 1962). *Member:* American Bar Association; State Bar of California. **PRACTICE AREAS:** Business Litigation; Professional Liability Litigation; Antitrust and Trade Regulation; Alternate Dispute Resolution.

**RICHARD W. LASATER II,** born Champaign, Illinois, October 2, 1948; admitted to bar, 1974, California. *Education:* Stanford University (B.A., 1971); Hastings College of Law, University of California (J.D., 1974). Order of the Coif. Research Editor, Hastings Law Journal, 1973-1974. Member, Thurston Society. *Member:* American Bar Association; State Bar of California; Inter-Pacific Bar Association. **PRACTICE AREAS:** Real Estate; Corporate and Corporate Securities; Probate; Estate Planning.

**MARK G. ANCEL,** born Pittsburgh, Pennsylvania, August 13, 1924; admitted to bar, 1951, California and U.S. Tax Court; U.S. Supreme Court. *Education:* Stanford University (B.A., 1948; LL.B., 1950). Phi Alpha Delta. *Member:* Los Angeles County (Chairman, Committee on State and Local Taxation, Section on Taxation, 1978-1979) and American (Chairman, Committee on State and Local Taxation, Section on Taxation, 1971-1973; Subcommittee on Standards of Tax Practice, 1978-1981, Chairman, 1980-1981) Bar Associations; State Bar of California. Fellow, American College of Tax Counsel. **PRACTICE AREAS:** State and Local Tax; Probate; Estate Tax Valuation.

**DUDLEY M. LANG,** born Chandler, Arizona, 1936; admitted to bar, 1963, California. *Education:* Loyola University of Los Angeles; University of California, Los Angeles (A.B., 1959; J.D., 1962). Lecturer on Tax Law, University of Southern California Law School, 1967-1988. Member, 1969-1992 and Chairman, 1974-1980, Planning Committee, University of Southern California Institute on Federal Taxation. *Member:* Los Angeles County (Chairman, Taxation Section, 1975-1976) and American (Chairman, Subchapter S Committee, 1978-1980 and Coordinator, Subchapter S Project, 1980-1982, Council Director, 1983-1986, Section of Taxation) Bar Associations; State Bar of California (Member, Taxation Advisory Commission, Pilot Program for Legal Specialization, 1971-1976). Fellow, American College of Tax Counsel. (Certified Specialist, Taxation Law, The State Bar of California Board of Legal Specialization). **PRACTICE AREAS:** Taxation Law.

**JOSEPH F. BUTLER,** born San Francisco, California, September 23, 1950; admitted to bar, 1975, California; 1976, U.S. District Court, Central District of California; 1977, U.S. Court of Appeals, Ninth Circuit. *Education:* University of California at Los Angeles (B.A., 1972); University of San Diego (J.D., 1975). Assistant U.S. Attorney, Central District of California, 1979-1987. Recipient, Attorney General's Special Commendation Award. Instructor, Attorney General's Trial Advocacy Institute, Washington, D.C. Panelist, 1994 California CEB Environmental Law Institute; 1995 Building Owners and Managers Association Environmental Forum. *Member:* State Bar of California. **PRACTICE AREAS:** Business Litigation; Employment Litigation; Environmental Litigation; Insurance Litigation.

**FREDERICK A. CLARK,** born San Francisco, California, September 17, 1942; admitted to bar, 1968, California. *Education:* Whitman College;

*(This Listing Continued)*

Stanford University (B.A., 1964); University of Southern California (J.D., 1967). Phi Delta Phi. Associate Editor, University of Southern California Law Review, 1966-1967. *Member:* Los Angeles County (Member, Antitrust Section) and American (Member, Sections on: Antitrust; Litigation; Patent, Trademark and Copyright Law) Bar Associations; State Bar of California (Member, Sections on: Antitrust, Trade Regulation and Intellectual Property Law); Association of Business Trial Lawyers; Chancery Club. **PRACTICE AREAS:** Antitrust and Trade Litigation; Business Litigation; Copyright and Trademark Litigation.

**JOEL A. GOLDMAN,** born New York, New York, May 27, 1942; admitted to bar, 1967, California. *Education:* Grinnell College (B.A., 1964); University of Southern California (J.D., 1967). Phi Delta Phi. *Member:* Los Angeles County (Member, Commercial Law and Bankruptcy Section; First Chairman, Provisional and Post Judgement Remedies Section, 1984-1985) and American (Member, Litigation Section) Bar Associations; The State Bar of California; Commercial Law League of America; Financial Lawyers Conference; Association of Business Trial Lawyers; Los Angeles Complex Litigation Inn of Court. **PRACTICE AREAS:** Complex Civil Litigation.

**C. STEPHEN DAVIS,** born Lubbock, Texas, April 29, 1955; admitted to bar, 1980, California; 1981, U.S. District Court, Central, Southern, Northern and Eastern Districts of California; 1986, U.S. Court of Appeals, Ninth Circuit. *Education:* University of California at Los Angeles (B.A., 1977); Loyola Marymount University, Los Angeles (J.D., 1980). Author: "Determining Market Value for Assessment Purposes Under Amended Revenue & Taxation Code § 110 (b): Does The Amended Statute Mean What It Says?", C.E.B. Real Property Law Reporter (November 1990); "Interest on California Property Tax Refunds: Dealing With The Problems," Journal of Multistate Taxation (September/October 1994). *Member:* Los Angeles County (Chairman, Committee on State and Local Taxation, Section on Taxation, 1994-1995) and American Bar Associations; State Bar of California; Institute of Property Taxation (Co-Chair, Legal Committee, 1995-1996). **SPECIAL AGENCIES:** California State Board of Equalization, Local Assessment Appeals Boards. **PRACTICE AREAS:** State and Local Tax; Commercial Litigation.

**KENNETH A. FEINFIELD,** born San Francisco, California, February 4, 1944; admitted to bar, 1975, California and U.S. District Court, Central District of California; 1976, U.S. Tax Court. *Education:* University of California at Los Angeles (B.A., 1966); University of LaVerne (J.D., with honors, 1972). Contributing Author: "How to Live -- And Die -- With California Probate," Gulf Publishing Company, 1983; Los Angeles Superior Court Guidelines on Attorney Fees in Probate; California Decedent Estate Practice, California Continuing Education of the Bar, 1986. Panelist, "Fundamentals of Estate Administration," 1984 and Probating an Estate in an Environment of a Changing Probate Code, 1986, California Continuing Education of the Bar. Instructor: Federal Estate and Gift Tax, UCLA Extension, 1993—; Probate Paralegal Program, University of Southern California, 1984-1985. *Member:* Los Angeles County (Chairman, 1992-1993, Executive Committee, 1984—, Trusts and Estates Section) and Beverly Hills (Chairman, 1984-1985, Probate, Trust and Estate Planning Section) Bar Associations; State Bar of California. Fellow, American College of Trust and Estate Counsel. (Certified Specialist, Estate Planning, Trust and Probate Law, The State Bar of California Board of Legal Specialization). **PRACTICE AREAS:** Estate Planning; Trust and Probate.

**JEAN-PAUL MENARD,** born Burbank, California, May 20, 1959; admitted to bar, 1984, California. *Education:* California State University at Northridge (B.A., magna cum laude, 1981); Loyola Marymount University (J.D., 1984). Phi Alpha Delta. Senior Associate and Cumulative Index Editor, International and Comparative Law Journal, 1983-1984. *Member:* Los Angeles County Bar Association; State Bar of California. **LANGUAGES:** French. **PRACTICE AREAS:** Business Litigation.

**MICHAEL J. KAMINSKY,** born New York, N.Y., April 25, 1958; admitted to bar, 1986, California and U.S. District Court, Central District of California. *Education:* Duke University (B.A., 1980); Boston University (J.D., 1986). Recipient, American Jurisprudence Award in Corporations, 1985. Co-author: CEB, "California Real Property Financing," Supplements, 1990 and 1991. Lecturer: "Legal Aspects of Condominiums and Planned Unit Developments," UCLA Extension Program, 1992. *Member:* Beverly Hills and Los Angeles County Bar Associations; State Bar of California. **PRACTICE AREAS:** Real Estate; Community Association Law.

**JOHN A. DRAGONETTE,** born Oakland, California, May 10, 1967; admitted to bar, 1993, California. *Education:* University of California, Los Angeles (B.A., Economics and Political Science, 1989); Loyola Marymount University (J.D., 1993). Phi Delta Phi. Recipient, American Jurisprudence Award, Remedies. *Member:* State Bar of California (Member, Business Law

*(This Listing Continued)*

Section); American Bar Association; California Young Lawyers Association. **PRACTICE AREAS:** Medical Malpractice.

### OF COUNSEL

**LOUIS R. BAKER,** born St. Paul, Minnesota, January 19, 1915; admitted to bar, 1938, California; U.S. Supreme Court. *Education:* University of California at Los Angeles (A.B., 1935); Boalt Hall School of Law, University of California (J.D., 1938). Special Hearing Officer, Department of Justice, 1957-1961. Member, L.A. Regional Export Expansion Council, 1962-1974. Lecturer, Legal Drafting, University of Southern California Law School, 1964-1965. *Member:* Los Angeles County (Member, Committee on International Transactions, 1961—), American (Member, Committee on Judicial Review, 1967-1975); State Bar of California. **PRACTICE AREAS:** Corporate; Health Care; Probate.

**J. LANE TILSON,** born Long Beach, California, November 5, 1934; admitted to bar, 1960, California. *Education:* University of California at Los Angeles (A.B., 1956; LL.B., 1959). Phi Delta Phi. Member, Board of Editors, University of California at Los Angeles Law Review, 1957-1959. *Member:* The State Bar of California. **PRACTICE AREAS:** Business Litigation; Professional Liability Litigation.

---

## STEPHENSON & STEPHENSON
### LOS ANGELES, CALIFORNIA
(See San Pedro)

*General Civil Practice. Trials and Appeals in all Courts. Probate, Family, Corporation, Criminal and Personal Injury Law.*

---

## STERN & GOLDBERG
### LOS ANGELES, CALIFORNIA
(See Beverly Hills)

*General Business Law with Emphasis in Business Litigation, Real Estate, Corporate, Taxation, Probate and Estate Planning.*

---

## STETTNER, EISENBERG & MORRIS
### LOS ANGELES, CALIFORNIA
(See Glendora)

*Family Law, including, Dissolutions, Prenuptials, Cohabitation Agreements, Spousal Support, Custody and Adoptions, International Custody Disputes.*

---

## STEVENS, KRAMER, AVERBUCK & HARRIS
### A PROFESSIONAL CORPORATION
*Established in 1994*

**1990 SOUTH BUNDY DRIVE, SUITE 340**
**LOS ANGELES, CALIFORNIA 90025**
Telephone: 310-442-8435
Fax: 310-442-8441

*Irvine, California Office:* 18400 Von Karman Avenue, Suite 615, 92612. Telephone: 714-253-9553. Fax: 714-253-9643.

*General Civil Litigation Defense in all State and Federal Courts. Commercial and Personal Lines, Construction Defect, Bad Faith, Insurance Coverage and Declaratory Relief, Medical Malpractice, Environmental Law, Legal Malpractice, Wrongful Termination, Governmental Entity Defense.*

**FIRM PROFILE:** *Stevens, Kramer, Averbuck & Harris, A Professional Corporation, was formed in 1994 by Carl R. Stevens, Jeffrey S. Kramer, Clayton C. Averbuck and Charles L. Harris. Our objective in establishing this firm is to provide the highest quality legal services to the insurance industry at a reasonable price, and provide an efficient and trial ready alternative to house counsel. We strive daily to achieve this objective for our growing client base. Our founders bring more than 50 years of combined legal experience to the firm. We are leaders in the legal community, noted for our trial skills, expertise in alternative dispute resolution, effective case management and cost control techniques. Our associates are trained in the same manner to ensure continuity of file handling with adherence to the firm's goals for client service and litigation guidelines.*

*In addition to our commitment to providing quality legal services at a reasonable price, we also work to develop long term relationships with our clients. We aggressively represent their interest, while always considering the cost factor.*

*Our offices in Los Angeles and Orange Counties serve clients in all of Southern California, including Los Angeles, Orange, San Diego, Santa Barbara, Ventura, Riverside, San Bernardino and Kern Counties.*

**CARL R. STEVENS,** born Newport Beach, California, July 29, 1953; admitted to bar, 1978, California and U.S. District Court, Northern District of California. *Education:* University of Southern California (B.A., 1975); California Western University (J.D., 1978). Phi Alpha Delta. *Member:* Association of Southern California Defense Counsel; Los Angeles and Orange County Bar Associations. **PRACTICE AREAS:** Defense of Legal and Medical Malpractice; General Insurance Defense Law; Insurance Coverage; Bad Faith; Wrongful Termination; Environmental Law; Premises Liability; Construction Defect.

**JEFFREY S. KRAMER,** born Santa Monica, California, December 16, 1954; admitted to bar, 1980, California; 1981, U.S. District Court, Central District of California. *Education:* San Jose State University (B.S., summa cum laude, 1977); Southwestern University (J.D., 1980). Judge Pro Tem, Los Angeles Municipal Court, 1986—. Mediator and Arbitrator, Los Angeles Superior Court. *Member:* Los Angeles County Bar Association (Member, Section on Litigation); State Bar of California; Southern California Defense Counsel. **REPORTED CASES:** Debbie Reynolds v. Superior Court (1994) 25 CA 4th 222, 30 C.R. 2nd 514. **PRACTICE AREAS:** Defense of General Liability; Construction Defect; Intellectual Property; Public Carrier; Entertainment; Wrongful Termination.

**CLAYTON C. AVERBUCK,** born Washington, D.C., October 3, 1950; admitted to bar, 1979, California; U.S. District Court, Central District of California. *Education:* Loyola University of Los Angeles and La Verne College (B.A., 1976); La Verne College (J.D., 1979). Mediator and Arbitrator, Los Angeles Superior Court. *Member:* The State Bar of California; Southern California Defense Counsel; American Board of Trial Advocates. **PRACTICE AREAS:** Defense of Legal and Medical Malpractice; Personal Casualty Liability; Commercial Casualty Liability; Public Entities.

**CHARLES L. HARRIS,** born Palm Springs, California, November 9, 1963; admitted to bar, 1990, California, U.S. District Court, Central and Southern Districts of California. *Education:* University of Southern California (B.S. Political Science, 1985); Pepperdine University (J.D., 1990). Member, United States Olympic Water Polo Team, 1984-1992. *Member:* Los Angeles County and Orange County (Construction and Environmental Law Sections) Bar Associations; State Bar of California. (Resident Partner, Irvine Office). **PRACTICE AREAS:** Construction Defect; Environmental; Coverage and Liability; Personal and Commercial Casualty.

---

**ANGELA M. ROSSI,** born Brooklyn, New York, June 2, 1960; admitted to bar, 1987, California; 1988, U.S. District Court, Central District of California. *Education:* State University of New York at Albany (B.A., 1982); Pepperdine University (J.D., 1987). *Member:* Los Angeles County and American Bar Associations; State Bar of California; The Association of Trial Lawyers of America; California Trial Lawyers Association; Italian American Lawyers Association; Inn of Court.

**CRAIG H. MARCUS,** born Los Angeles, California, July 6, 1966; admitted to bar, 1991, California, U.S. District Court, Central District of California and U.S. Court of Appeals, Ninth Circuit. *Education:* Loyola Marymount University (B.B.A., magna cum laude, 1988); St. Gallen Graduate School of Economics; Loyola Law School (J.D., 1991). *Member:* Los Angeles, Beverly Hills and American Bar Associations; State Bar of California; Barristers.

**VALERIE MCSWAIN,** admitted to bar, 1995, California. *Education:* University of Washington (B.A., in Economics, 1991); University of California at Davis (J.D., 1994). *Member:* State Bar of California. (Resident Irvine Office).

**CHRISTOPHER J. NEVIS,** born Carmel, California, August 25, 1967; admitted to bar, 1992, California. *Education:* University of California at Santa Barbara (B.A., 1989); McGeorge School of Law, University of the Pacific (J.D., 1992).

*(This Listing Continued)*

**STEVENS, KRAMER, AVERBUCK & HARRIS,** A PROFESSIONAL CORPORATION, Los Angeles—Continued

**LEE E. BURROWS,** born Glendale, California, July 7, 1966; admitted to bar, 1994, California and U.S. District Court, Central District of California. *Education:* University of California at Los Angeles (B.A., 1988); Southwestern University; Western State University (J.D., 1993). Phi Eta Sigma. Recipient, American Jurisprudence Award in Constitutional Law II. Member Southwestern University Moot Court. *Member:* Los Angeles and Orange County Bar Associations. (Resident, Irvine Office).

**MONICA A. BLUT,** born Los Angeles, California, October 26, 1967; admitted to bar, 1992, California and U.S. District Court, Central District of California. *Education:* University of California at Los Angeles (B.A., 1989); Hastings College of the Law, University of California (J.D., 1992). *Member:* Los Angeles County Bar Association; State Bar of California. *LANGUAGES:* Spanish.

**ANGIE Y. YOON,** born Seoul, Korea, July 9, 1970; admitted to bar, 1995, California. *Education:* University of California at San Diego (B.A., 1992); Loyola Marymount University (J.D., 1995). *Member:* Los Angeles County Bar Association; State Bar of California; Korean American Bar Association. *PRACTICE AREAS:* General Civil Litigation; Personal Injury; Construction Defect.

**CARRIE ANN MOFFETT,** born Toledo, Ohio, October 26, 1966; admitted to bar, 1994, California. *Education:* Marquette University (B.A., 1989); DePaul University (J.D., 1993). *Member:* State Bar of California; Women Lawyers Association of Los Angeles. *PRACTICE AREAS:* Insurance Defense.

**LYDIA R. BOUZAGLOU,** born Burbank, California, March 8, 1962; admitted to bar, 1988, California. *Education:* University of California at Los Angeles (B.A., 1983); McGeorge School of Law, University of the Pacific (J.D., 1987). Member, Moot Court Honors Board. Moot Court Top Oral Advocate Finalist and Best Written Brief. *Member:* Orange County and American Bar Associations; State Bar of California; Association of Southern California Defense Counsel. (Resident, Irvine Office). *PRACTICE AREAS:* Construction Defect.

**JOHN R. MARKING,** born National City, California, June 24, 1967; admitted to bar, 1994, California. *Education:* University of California, San Diego (B.A., 1989); Pepperdine University (J.D., 1994). *Member:* State Bar of California. (Resident, Irvine Office). *PRACTICE AREAS:* Construction Defect; Personal Injury.

**ROBERT A. FISHER, II,** born Covina, California, January 17, 1965; admitted to bar, 1991, California. *Education:* California State University, Chico (B.A., Political Science, 1988); Pepperdine University (J.D., 1991). *Member:* Orange Country Bar Association; State Bar of California. (Resident, Irvine Office). *PRACTICE AREAS:* Construction Defect Law; General Liability-Torts; Professional Liability; Products Liability; Litigation Defense.

**JEANNE E. PEPPER,** born San Diego, California, May 17, 1970; admitted to bar, 1995, California. *Education:* University of California, Santa Barbara (B.A., 1992); Pepperdine University (J.D., 1995). Recipient: Edward D. Diloreto-Odell S. McConnell Endowed Scholar, 1994-1995. *Member:* State Bar of California. (Resident, Irvine Office). *PRACTICE AREAS:* Construction Defect Litigation; Insurance Defense; General Liability Defense; Professional Malpractice.

**ADA BERMAN,** born Odessa, Ukraine, October 16, 1971; admitted to bar, 1996, California. *Education:* University of California, Los Angeles (B.A., magna cum laude, 1993); Loyola Law School (J.D., 1996). Golden Key Honor Society. Senior Production Editor, International and Comparative Law Journal, Loyola Law School, 1995-1996. *Member:* State Bar of California. *LANGUAGES:* Russian. *PRACTICE AREAS:* Personal Injury; Premises Liability; Construction Defects.

**MARISSA R. ARRACHE,** born Lancaster, California, November 17, 1970; admitted to bar, 1996, California. *Education:* University of California, Los Angeles (B.A., 1992); Santa Clara University (J.D., 1996; M.B.A., 1996). Associate Editor, Santa Clara Law Review, 1995-1996. Author: "Factor Representation in the Apportionment of Income from Intangibles," Santa Clara Law Journal, Volume 2, 1996. *Member:* State Bar of California. *PRACTICE AREAS:* Insurance Defense.

REPRESENTATIVE CLIENTS: American States Insurance Co.; County of Los Angeles; Gulf Insurance Group; Hartford Insurance Co.; Infinity Insurance Group; Motors Insurance Co.; State Farm Fire and Casualty; Reliance Insurance Co.; AIG; Vesta Insurance.

CAA1228B

## HUNSDON CARY STEWART

7377 WEST 85TH STREET
**LOS ANGELES, CALIFORNIA 90045-2456**
Telephone: 310-641-7320
Fax: 310-641-7320

*Civil Trial, Business, Real Estate, Professional Negligence and Family Law.*

**HUNSDON CARY STEWART,** born Richmond, Virginia, June 30, 1943; admitted to bar, 1970, California, U.S. District Court, Central District of California and U.S. Court of Appeals, Ninth Circuit; 1974, U.S. Supreme Court. *Education:* University of Oregon (B.A., 1965); The George Washington University (J.D., 1968). Delta Theta Phi. *Member:* The State Bar of California; American Bar Association (Member, Sections on: Litigation; Antitrust Law; Taxation). *LANGUAGES:* Spanish. *PRACTICE AREAS:* Civil Trial; Business Real Estate; Professional Negligence; Family Law.

## STILZ & BOYD

A PROFESSIONAL CORPORATION
SUITE 1000, WESTSIDE TOWERS
11845 WEST OLYMPIC BOULEVARD
**LOS ANGELES, CALIFORNIA 90064**
Telephone: 310-312-8100
Telecopy: 310-312-8189

*General Civil, Criminal and Appellate Practice in all State and Federal Courts. Corporate, Commercial and Family Law Practice.*

**RICHARD A. STILZ,** born Santa Monica, California, June 16, 1945; admitted to bar, 1971, California and U.S. District Court, Central District of California; 1972, U.S. Court of Appeals, Ninth Circuit; 1975, U.S. Supreme Court; 1978, U.S. District Court, Northern District of California. *Education:* University of California at Los Angeles (B.A., cum laude, 1967); Loyola University School of Law (J.D., 1970). Phi Alpha Delta. Member, St. Thomas More Law Honor Society. Member, Loyola Law School Law Review, 1969-1970. Assistant U.S. Attorney, Criminal Division, U.S. Department of Justice, 1971-1977. Assistant Division Chief, 1975-1977 and Chief, Criminal Complaints, 1976-1977. *Member:* Los Angeles County and American Bar Associations; State Bar of California.

**EARL E. BOYD,** born Pleasantville, Iowa, July 30, 1941; admitted to bar, 1966, Missouri; 1969, California, U.S. District Court, Central, Southern and Northern Districts of California and U.S. Court of Appeals, Ninth Circuit. *Education:* Northwest Missouri State College (B.A., 1963); University of Missouri (J.D., 1966). Phi Delta Phi; Blue Key. Member, University of Missouri Law Review, 1965-1966. Author: "Workmen's Compensation Injury by Act of God The Obsolescence of the Increased-Risk Doctrine," 31 Missouri Law Review 508, 1965; "The Inadequacy of Pretrial Discovery in Missouri Criminal Cases," 31 Missouri Law Review 424, 1966. Instructor, Contracts, Northrop University Law School, Inglewood, California, 1978-1982. Special Agent, Federal Bureau of Investigation, 1966-1970. Assistant U.S. Attorney, Criminal Division, U.S. Department of Justice, 1971-1977. *Member:* Los Angeles County Bar Association; The Missouri Bar; State Bar of California.

## STOCKWELL, HARRIS, WIDOM & WOOLVERTON

A PROFESSIONAL CORPORATION
*Established in 1957*
6222 WILSHIRE BOULEVARD, SIXTH FLOOR
P.O. BOX 48917
**LOS ANGELES, CALIFORNIA 90048-0917**
Telephone: 213-935-6669; 818-784-6222; 310-277-6669
Fax: 213-935-0198

*Santa Ana, California Office:* Suite 500, 1551 N. Tustin Avenue, P.O. Box 11979. Telephone: 714-479-1180. Fax: 714-479-1190.

*Ventura, California Office:* 2021 Sperry Avenue, Suite 46. Telephone: 805-654-8994; 213-617-7290. Fax: 805-654-1546.

*San Bernardino, California Office:* Suite 303, 215 North "D" Street. Telephone: 909-381-5553. Fax: 909-384-9981.

*San Diego, California Office:* Suite 400, 402 West Broadway. Telephone: 619-235-6054. Fax: 619-231-0129.

*(This Listing Continued)*

Grover Beach, California Office: Suite 307, 200 South 13th Street. Telephone: 805-473-0720. Fax: 805-473-0635.

*Workers Compensation Insurance and Employment Matters.*

**STEVEN I. HARRIS,** admitted to bar, 1967, California. *Education:* University of California at Los Angeles (B.A., 1962; LL.B., 1965). *Member:* Los Angeles County Bar Association. (Managing Attorney).

**PATRICIA A. OLIVE,** admitted to bar, 1972, California; U.S. District Court, Central District of California. *Education:* University of Oklahoma (B.A., 1958); Pepperdine University (J.D., 1971). *Member:* Los Angeles County Bar Association.

**DAVID L. SLUCTER,** admitted to bar, 1974, California. *Education:* University of Michigan (B.A., 1970); University of Minnesota (J.D., 1973). (Resident, San Bernardino Office).

**RICHARD M. WIDOM,** admitted to bar, 1977, California. *Education:* California State University at Northridge; University of San Fernando Valley (J.D., 1976). *Member:* American Bar Association. (Managing Attorney).

**JEFFREY T. LANDRES,** admitted to bar, 1977, California. *Education:* University of California at Berkeley (B.A., 1974); California Western School of Law (J.D., 1977). Author: "The Legal Efficacy of Probable Cause Complaints In Light Of People vs. Ramsey," California Western Law Review, Vol. XIII, No. 3, 1977. *Member:* American Bar Association. (Resident, Ventura Office).

**LINDA S. FREEMAN,** admitted to bar, 1983, California. *Education:* University of California at Riverside (B.A., 1974); Loyola Marymount University (J.D., 1981). *Member:* Orange County Bar Association. (Santa Ana and San Diego Offices).

**MICHAEL L. TERRY,** admitted to bar, 1981, California. *Education:* California State University at Los Angeles (B.A., 1975); Loyola Marymount University (J.D., 1980). *Member:* San Luis Obispo County Bar Association. (Resident, Grover Beach Office).

**WILLIAM M. CARERO,** admitted to bar, 1982, California. *Education:* Loyola Marymount University (B.A., 1977; J.D., 1980).

**BRIAN R. HORAN,** admitted to bar, 1979, California. *Education:* University of California at Los Angeles (B.A., 1975); Southwestern University (J.D., 1978). Member, Southwestern University Law Review, 1976-1978. *Member:* American Bar Association.

**DAVID F. GRANT,** admitted to bar, 1982, California. *Education:* California State University at San Bernardino (B.A., 1975); University of La Verne (J.D., 1981). (Resident, Santa Office Office).

**EDWARD S. MUEHL,** admitted to bar, 1975, California; U.S. District Court, Central District of California. *Education:* University of Missouri at Rolla (B.S.E.E., 1967); University of Southern California (M.S.E.E., 1969); Pepperdine University (J.D., 1974). *Member:* Orange County Bar Association. (Santa Ana and San Diego Offices).

**LAWRENCE S. MENDELSOHN,** admitted to bar, 1974, California. *Education:* California State University at Los Angeles (B.A., 1970); Southwestern University (J.D., 1973).

**EDWIN H. McKNIGHT, JR.,** admitted to bar, 1981, California and U.S. District Court, Southern District of California. *Education:* Creighton University (B.A., 1978); Western State University College of Law (J.D., 1981). (Resident, Santa Ana Office).

**STEVEN A. MELINE,** admitted to bar, 1986, California. *Education:* California Polytechnic State University at Pomona (B.S., 1969); California State University at Fullerton (M.S., 1977); Simon Greenleaf School of Law (J.D., 1985). *Member:* American Bar Association. (Resident, Santa Ana Office).

**TED L. HIRSCHBERGER,** admitted to bar, 1987, California and U.S. District Court, Central District of California. *Education:* C.W. Post College, Long Island University (B.S., 1972); University of Miami (M.B.A., 1977); Southwestern University (J.D., 1986).

**THEODORE G. SCHNEIDER, JR.,** admitted to bar, 1985, California. *Education:* University of La Verne (B.A., 1979; J.D., 1984). (Resident, San Bernardino Office).

**LAWRENCE B. MADANS,** admitted to bar, 1980, California; U.S. District Court, Central District of California. *Education:* Colorado State University (B.A., 1968); University of Massachusetts (M.A., 1970); Southwestern University (J.D., 1979).

*(This Listing Continued)*

**LESTER D. MARSHALL,** admitted to bar, 1990, California. *Education:* San Jose State University; University of Southern California (B.S., 1987); Loyola University (J.D., 1990).

**JOHN R. PAYNE,** admitted to bar, 1975, California. *Education:* University of Denver; California State University at Long Beach (B.S., 1972); University of California at Los Angeles (J.D., 1975). [With USN, STG2, 1966-1970]

**GEORGE WOOLVERTON,** admitted to bar, 1975, California. *Education:* California State University, Dominguez Hills (B.A., 1972); Southwestern University (J.D., 1975). Delta Theta Phi. *Member:* Beverly Hills, Long Beach and Los Angeles County Bar Associations.

**JAMES C. SHIPLEY,** admitted to bar, 1979, California; U.S. District Court, Central District of California. *Education:* University of California at Irvine (B.A.,1976); University of Oklahoma (J.D., 1979). *Member:* Los Angeles County Bar Association. (Resident, Ventura Office).

**JEFFREY EUGENE LOWE,** admitted to bar, 1990, California and U.S. District Court, Central District of California. *Education:* University of California at Irvine (B.S., 1980); Western State University (J.D., 1987). *Member:* Los Angeles County Bar Association. (Resident, Santa Ana Office).

All Attorneys are Members of the State Bar of California.

REPRESENTATIVE CLIENTS: Alexis Risk Management; Keenan & Assoc.; Owens-Illinois, Inc.; Highlands Insurance Co.; Greyhound Lines, Inc.; International Telephone & Telegraph; Browning Ferris Industries; The VIAD Corp; General Accident Ins. Co.; Pacific Rim Ins. Co.; Transamerican Ins. Co.; Cigna; E.S.I.S.; C.I.G.A.; Coca-Cola; Budget Rent-A-Car; Cedars Sinai Medical Center; B.C.I.S. Insurance Services; Ogden Allied; Pepsi-Cola; Thrifty Oil Co.; ARCO; Home Insurance Co.; Tokio Fire and Marine Insurance Co.; CNA Insurance Companies; City of Los Angeles.

---

## STOLPMAN • KRISSMAN • ELBER • MANDEL & KATZMAN LLP

A Partnership including Professional Corporations

*Established in 1952*

SUITE 1800, 10880 WILSHIRE BOULEVARD (WESTWOOD)
**LOS ANGELES, CALIFORNIA 90024**
Telephone: 310-470-8011

Long Beach, California Office: Nineteenth Floor, 111 West Ocean Boulevard. Telephone: 310-435-8300. Telecopier: 310-435-8304.

*Tort Litigation, Trials, Appeals and Workers Compensation.*

(For complete biographical data on all personnel, see Professional Biographies at Long Beach, California)

---

## STONE & DOYLE
**LOS ANGELES, CALIFORNIA**

(See Pasadena)

*Practice Limited to Estate Planning, Probate and Trust Administration, Corporation, Business and Tax Law, Business Litigation.*

---

## STONE & FEELEY, P.C.
**LOS ANGELES, CALIFORNIA**

(See Law Offices of Thomas J. Feeley, P.C.)

---

## STONE & HILES
**LOS ANGELES, CALIFORNIA**

(See Beverly Hills)

*General Civil Practice in State and Federal Courts. Civil, Business, Probate, and Corporate Litigation, Tort, Real Estate, Insurance, Personal Injury and Toxic Tort Law.*

## STONE & ROSENBLATT

*A PROFESSIONAL CORPORATION*

**LOS ANGELES, CALIFORNIA**

(See Encino)

*Insurance Defense Litigation, Premises Liability Defense, Construction Defect, Municipality Defense, Products, Employment, Corporate and Commercial Transactions.*

---

## STRAIN & ROSENBERGER

*A LAW CORPORATION*

**LOS ANGELES, CALIFORNIA**

(See Long Beach)

*International, Federal and State Taxation Law. Pension and Profit Sharing Law. Employee Benefit Law. Estate Planning.*

---

## HARVEY STRASSMAN

*1875 CENTURY PARK EAST, 15TH FLOOR*
**LOS ANGELES, CALIFORNIA 90067**
*Telephone: 310-277-6775*
*Fax: 310-552-3228*

*Practice Limited to Family Law and Civil Litigation.*

**HARVEY STRASSMAN,** born Los Angeles, California, November 6, 1933; admitted to bar, 1959, California. *Education:* University of California at Los Angeles (A.B., 1955); University of Southern California (LL.B., 1958). Nu Beta Epsilon (Vice President, 1957). Lecturer, Real Estate Law, U.C.L.A., 1962-1964. Hearing Officer, Los Angeles Police Commission, 1962-1964. Delegate to California State Bar Convention, 1969. Los Angeles Superior Court Family Law Mediator, 1979—. *Member:* Century City (Treasurer, 1969-1970; Member, Board of Trustees, 1969-1972), Beverly Hills (Member, Family Law Section) and Los Angeles County (Member: Family Law Section; Business Law Section) Bar Associations; State Bar of California (Member, Family Law Section); Los Angeles Trial Lawyers Association; The Association of Trial Lawyers of America.

---

## HERBERT J. STRICKSTEIN

*Established in 1960*

*2049 CENTURY PARK EAST, SUITE 1200*
**LOS ANGELES, CALIFORNIA 90067**
*Telephone: 310-553-4888*
*FAX: 213-879-5459*

*Real Estate, Condominium, Planned Development and Cooperative Housing Law.*

**HERBERT J. STRICKSTEIN,** born Detroit, Michigan, September 4, 1932; admitted to bar, 1957, California. *Education:* University of California at Los Angeles (A.A., 1952); Cornell University and University of Southern California (B.S.L., 1955); University of Southern California (J.D., 1956). Nu Beta Epsilon. President, Condominium Counsel Association of Southern California, 1964-1965. Member, Subdivision Advisory Committee, State of California Department of Real Estate, 1977-1995. Member, County of Los Angeles Small Craft Harbor Commission, 1983—. Listed, The Best Lawyers in America, 1987-1996. *Member:* Beverly Hills Bar Association; State Bar of California (Member, Common Interest Developments Subsection, Real Property Section, 1980—).

---

## STRINGFELLOW & ASSOCIATES

*A LAW CORPORATION*

*444 SOUTH FLOWER STREET, 31ST FLOOR*
**LOS ANGELES, CALIFORNIA 90071**
*Telephone: 213-538-3880*
*Fax: 213-538-3890*

*Litigation, Business, Construction, Environmental and Real Estate, and Representation of Doctors and Hospitals in Workers' Compensation.*

(This Listing Continued)

---

**WALTER A. STRINGFELLOW,** born Chicago, Illinois, June 20, 1945; admitted to bar, 1971, California. *Education:* Duke University (B.A., 1967; J.D., 1971). Editorial Board, Duke Law Journal, 1970-1971. *Member:* Los Angeles County and American (Section on Litigation; Forum Committee on the Construction Industry) Bar Associations.

---

**MANUEL J. DIAZ,** born Durango, Mexico, November 12, 1963; admitted to bar, 1992, California. *Education:* University of California, Berkeley (B.A., 1985); University of Exeter, Exeter, England; University of California School of Law, Los Angeles (J.D., 1992). *Member:* Los Angeles County Bar Association. **LANGUAGES:** Spanish.

**DAVID A. KEISNER,** born London, England, June 9, 1956; admitted to bar, 1980, England and Wales; 1985, California. *Education:* University of Southampton, England (LL.B., 1977); College of Law, London.

*OF COUNSEL*

**LISA SCHWARTZ TUDZIN,** born Forest Hills, New York, March 1, 1962; admitted to bar, 1987, California. *Education:* University of California at Los Angeles (B.A., cum laude, 1984); University of Southern California (J.D., 1987). Quarter-Finalist, Hale Moot Court Honors Program.

---

## STROOCK & STROOCK & LAVAN LLP

*SUITE 1800, 2029 CENTURY PARK EAST*
**LOS ANGELES, CALIFORNIA 90067-3086**
*Telephone: 310-556-5800*
*Telecopier: (310) 556-5959*
*Cable Address: "Plastroock, L.A."*
*Telex: Plastroock LSA 677190 (Domestic and International)*

*New York, N.Y. Office:* 180 Maiden Lane, New York, N.Y., 10038. Telephone: 212-806-5400. Telecopiers: (212) 806-5919; (212) 806-6006; (212) 806-6086; (212) 425-9509; (212) 806-6176.

*New York Conference Center:* 767 Third Avenue, New York, N.Y., 10017-2023. Telephones: 212-806-5767; 5768; 5769; 5770. Telecopier: (212) 421-6234.

*Boston, Massachusetts Office:* 100 Federal Street, 02110. Telephone: 617-482-6800. Fax: 617-330-5111.

*Budapest, Hungary Office:* East-West Business Center, Rákóczi ut 1-3, H-1088. Telephone: 011-361-266-9520 or 011-361-266-7770. Telecopier: 011-361-266-9279.

*Miami, Florida Office:* 200 South Biscayne Boulevard, Suite 3300, First Union Financial Center, 33131-2385. Telephone: 305-358-9900. Telecopier: (305) 789-9302.

*Washington, D.C. Office:* 1150 Seventeenth Street, N.W., Suite 600, 20036-4652. Telephone: 202-452-9250. Telecopier: (202) 293-2293.

*RESIDENT PARTNERS*

**RICHARD S. FORMAN,** born New York, N.Y., August 18, 1960; admitted to bar, 1986, New Jersey; 1987, New York; 1995, California. *Education:* University of Pennsylvania (B.A., 1986); New York University (J.D., 1986). *Member:* New York State Bar Association. **PRACTICE AREAS:** Securities; Corporate; Mergers and Acquisitions.

**SCHUYLER M. MOORE,** born New York, N.Y., June 12, 1955; admitted to bar, 1981, California; U.S. Tax Court. *Education:* University of California at Los Angeles (B.A., summa cum laude, 1978); University of California School of Law (J.D., 1981). Phi Beta Kappa; Order of the Coif (first in class). Member, Honors Department, UCLA College of Letters and Science and Psychology, 1977-1978. Author: *Taxation of the Entertainment Industry,* published by Warren Gorham Lamont. Licensed Real Estate Broker, California, 1982. *Member:* Los Angeles County Bar Association (Member, Executive Committee, Tax Section, 1987-1991; Chairman, Entertainment Tax Section, 1988-1991); State Bar of California (Member, Taxation Section). **PRACTICE AREAS:** Entertainment Contracts; Entertainment Finance; Entertainment Law; Taxation; Corporate Law.

**MARGARET A. NAGLE,** born Lynn, Massachusetts, August 4, 1950; admitted to bar, 1975, Massachusetts; 1978, California. *Education:* Boston College (A.B., summa cum laude, 1972); Columbia University (J.D., 1975). Phi Beta Kappa. *Member:* Los Angeles County and American Bar Associations. **PRACTICE AREAS:** Litigation; Environmental Law; Products Liability.

**MICHAEL F. PERLIS,** born New York, N.Y., June 3, 1947; admitted to bar, 1971, District of Columbia; 1980, California. *Education:* Georgetown University (B.S.F.S., 1968; J.D., 1971). Research Editor, Law & Pol-

(This Listing Continued)

icy in International Business, 1970-1971. Court Law Clerk, District of Columbia Court of Appeals, 1971-1972. Assistant Corporation Counsel, Washington, D.C., 1972-1974. Staff Attorney, 1974-1975, Branch Chief, 1975-1977 and Assistant Director, 1977-1980, Division of Enforcement Securities and Exchange Commission. Adjunct Faculty, Columbus School of Law, The Catholic University of America, 1979-1980. *Member:* State Bar of California; The District of Columbia Bar. *PRACTICE AREAS:* Litigation; Insurance.

**JULIA B. STRICKLAND,** born San Francisco, California, August 21, 1954; admitted to bar, 1978, California and U.S. District Court, Central, Northern and Southern Districts of California; 1979, U.S. Court of Appeals, Ninth Circuit. *Education:* Dartmouth College; University of California at San Diego (B.A., with honors, 1975); University of California, Los Angeles, School of Law (J.D., 1978). Member, Moot Court. *Member:* The State Bar of California. *PRACTICE AREAS:* Securities Litigation.

**MICHAEL M. UMANSKY,** born New York, N.Y., 1941; admitted to bar, 1967, New York; 1975, California. *Education:* University of Pennsylvania (B.S., Econ., 1963); Harvard University (J.D., 1966). Beta Gamma Sigma; Beta Alpha Psi. *Member:* Beverly Hills, Los Angeles County, New York State and American Bar Associations; The State Bar of California. *PRACTICE AREAS:* Corporate Law; Securities Law; Acquisitions, Divestitures and Mergers Law.

*OF COUNSEL*

**GERALD J. MEHLMAN,** born New York, N.Y., January 29, 1930; admitted to bar, 1954, District of Columbia and U.S. Court of Appeals, District of Columbia Circuit; 1958, U.S. Supreme Court; 1960, California. *Education:* University of Michigan (B.A., 1951); Yale University (LL.B., 1954). Member, Judge Advocate General's Office of U.S. Navy, Pentagon, Washington, D.C., 1955-1957. Attorney-Advisor, U.S. Tax Court, Washington, D.C., 1957-1959. Member, Task Force, Capitol Formation Committee, White House Conference on Small Business, 1979. Chairman of Board, Motion Picture and Television Tax Institute, 1977—. *Member:* Beverly Hills, Los Angeles County (Member at Large, Executive Committee, Section of Taxation, 1979, 1981) and American Bar Associations; State Bar of California. Fellow, American College of Tax Counsel. (Certified Specialist, Taxation Law, The State Bar of California Board of Legal Specialization). *PRACTICE AREAS:* Estate Planning Law; Taxation; Probate Law; General Practice; Corporate Law.

*RETIRED PARTNERS*

**MERRILL E. JENKINS,** born San Jose, California, July 15, 1925; admitted to bar, 1969, California. *Education:* Stanford University (B.A., 1949; M.A., 1950; J.D., 1969). Order of the Coif. Member, Board of Editors, Stanford Law Review, 1967-1968. *Member:* Los Angeles County Bar Association; The State Bar of California.

**WILLIAM H. LEVIT, (P.C.),** born San Francisco, California, January 11, 1908; admitted to bar, 1930, California; 1942, U.S. Supreme Court. *Education:* Stanford University (A.B., 1928; J.D., 1930). Judge, Superior Court of California for Los Angeles County, 1962-1976. Member: Judicial Council of California, 1969-1971; Governing Board, California Center for Judicial Education and Research, 1973-1976. Fellow, American College of Trial Lawyers. *Member:* The State Bar of California; Institute of Judicial Administration. [Lieut. Col., U.S. Army, JAGD, 1942-1945]

**ROBERT M. SHAFTON,** born Chicago, Illinois, February 18, 1931; admitted to bar, 1955, Arizona; 1956, California and U.S. District Court, Central District of California; 1962, U.S. Supreme Court. *Education:* University of Arizona (A.B., cum laude, 1952); Stanford University; University of Arizona (J.D., 1955). Phi Beta Kappa; Phi Delta Phi; Mensa. Member, Board of Visitors, University of Arizona College of Law, 1986—. Member, Board of Advisors, National Center for Preventive Law, University of Denver College of Law, 1986—. President, LAX International Business Council, 1989-1991; Chairman, Los Angeles Commission on World Jewry, 1990. Chair, Commission on the Middle East and International Affairs, 1992—. Assistant U.S. Attorney, Southern District of California, 1955-1957. Hearing Officer, Conscientious Objector Cases, Department of Justice, 1957-1968. Member, California Savings and Loan Commissioners Advisory Panel, 1981-1985. Member: Arbitration Panels of New York Stock Exchange; Panel of Arbitrators, for American Arbitration Association Large Complex Case Program. Member of the American Arbitration Association Center for Mediation Distinguished Panel of Mediators. *Member:* Los Angeles (Executive Committee, ADR Section), Beverly Hills (Vice-Chair, Dispute Resolution Committee) and American Bar Associations; State Bar of Arizona; State Bar of California. *PRACTICE AREAS:* Arbitrator-Mediator; Expert Witness.

*(This Listing Continued)*

Judith L. Anderson; Maryanne Carson; Wrenn E. Chais; James W. Denison; Karen R. Dinino; Joseph W. Dung; D. Wayne Jeffries; Nicholas F. Klein; David S. Lippes (Not admitted in CA); Mary D. Manesis; Andrew J. Matosich; Scott M. Pearson; Lisa M. Simonetti; Glenn D. Smith; Chauncey M. Swalwell; Matthew C. Thompson; Karynne G. Weiss.

(For Information on New York, Boston, Budapest, Miami and Washington, D.C., Personnel, see appropriate Professional Biographies state listings)

---

## LAW OFFICES OF
## JOHN J. STUMREITER
### LOS ANGELES, CALIFORNIA

(See Pasadena)

*General Practice with emphasis on Litigation and Bankruptcy.*

---

## STUTMAN, TREISTER & GLATT
*PROFESSIONAL CORPORATION*
**3699 WILSHIRE BOULEVARD, SUITE 900**
**LOS ANGELES, CALIFORNIA 90010**
Telephone: 213-251-5100
FAX: 213-251-5288

*Bankruptcy, Insolvency, Corporate Reorganization and Commercial Litigation.*

*FIRM PROFILE: Stutman, Treister & Glatt Professional Corporation is a firm of 29 attorneys, all of whom specialize in corporate reorganization, bankruptcy and insolvency law, as well as commercial litigation. Eighteen members of the firm are principals, six are associates, and four are of counsel.*

The firm is a national leader in its field, and is active in all aspects of the insolvency practice:

*Debtor Representation.* Whenever possible, the firm attempts to restructure a client's indebtedness out of court, thereby avoiding the need for a reorganization case. Only when an out-of-court solution is not feasible does the firm recommend commencing a case under the Bankruptcy Code. The firm's present and former chapter 9 and 11 debtor clients range from municipal governments and large publicly held corporations to considerably smaller privately held companies and individuals. The firm has acted as lead insolvency counsel in chapter 9 cases and numerous public and non-public cases in such business segments as agriculture, entertainment, franchising, gas and energy, health care, high technology, hotels, insurance holding companies, manufacturing, non-bank financial institutions, oil, real estate development, recreation, restaurants, retailing, transportation and wholesaling.

*Creditor Representation.* The Firm regularly represents secured and unsecured creditors, public debt holders, and indenture trustees, as well as landlords and other parties to executory contracts, in out-of-court restructurings and in chapter 11 cases. Many of the firm's former debtor clients have repeatedly retained the firm to represent them as creditors in insolvency matters. The firm also represents creditor committees in both chapter 11 cases and out-of-court restructurings. Accordingly, the firm is familiar with all perspectives on the reorganization process.

*Acquirer/Proponent Representation.* The firm is well known for its representation of acquirers of troubled business and as counsel to plan proponents in insolvency cases. In addition, the firm frequently advises arbitrageurs and other investors interested in the securities of entities experiencing financial difficulty or of chapter 11 debtors.

*Commercial Litigation/Lender Liability.* The firm maintains an outstanding commercial litigation capability with emphasis on bankruptcy and lender liability litigation. Its achievements include the successful prosecution of a lender liability action against a major financial institution resulting in a collected judgment in excess of $22 Million.

*Expert Witnesses.* Several members of the firm have qualified as expert witnesses on the subject of insolvency law in state and federal courts and before administrative agencies. A representative client is The Farmers Insurance Group.

The Firm prides itself on the academic and professional achievements of its lawyers. Ten members of the firm have taught on the faculties of Stanford, U.C.L.A., U.S.C., Loyola or Southwestern Law Schools. Many members teach

*(This Listing Continued)*

CAA1231B

**STUTMAN, TREISTER & GLATT,** PROFESSIONAL CORPORATION, Los Angeles—*Continued*

*specialized courses sponsored by the American Law Institute/American Bar Association, California Continuing Education of the Bar, and several other organizations. One member of the firm has taught at Harvard Law School (Robert Braucher Visiting Professor From Practice). Members of the firm include former law clerks to Mr. Justice Black and Mr. Justice Kennedy; several former law clerks to federal appeals and district court judges; several former editors and members to the Harvard, Yale, Stanford, California, U.C.L.A., Duke and Southern California Law Reviews; a former member of the Board of Governors of the State Bar of California; three members of the National Bankruptcy Conference; two former Chairpersons of the Business Bankruptcy Committee of the American Bar Association Section on Business Law; several past Presidents of the Los Angeles Financial Lawyers Conference; numerous chairpersons of State and Los Angeles County Bar Committees (on Debtor/Creditor Relations and Bankruptcy, UCC, and Bankruptcy Specialization); contributing editors to Collier on Bankruptcy (15th ed.) and one of the primary draftsmen of the Bankruptcy Code who served as minority counsel to the House Judiciary Committee.*

**JACK STUTMAN,** born Manchester, New Hampshire, May 27, 1914; admitted to bar, 1942, Massachusetts; 1947, California. *Education:* Harvard University (A.B. with honors, 1935); Boston College and Harvard University (LL.B., 1941). Co-author: "Insolvency Planning," University of California Extension, 1957; "The Voice of the Gavel," Business Lawyer, 1958 and republished in "The Practical Lawyer," 1959. Author, "Anatomy of a Bankruptcy," 1965; "Chapter X1/2 or Bust," 1973. Adjunct Professor of Law, Loyola University School of Law, 1975-1976. Chairman, Bankruptcy Study Group, 1952; Member, Committee on Continuing Education of the Bar, 1958-1961. *Member:* Beverly Hills, Los Angeles County (Member, Board of Trustees, 1971-1973, 1974-1975; Treasurer, 1971-1975) and American (Chairman, Business Bankruptcy Committee, 1971-1977; Member, Business Law Section) Bar Association; The State Bar of California (Member: Committee on Bankruptcy, 1957-1961; Debtor/Creditor Relations and Bankruptcy Committee, 1958-1960, 1963-1966; Member, Board of Governors, 1976-1979; Treasurer, 1978-1979); Los Angeles County Bar Foundation (President, 1975-1977; Recipient, Shattuck-Price Award, 1987). Life Fellow, American Bar Foundation. (Retired Founder).

**GEORGE M. TREISTER,** born Oxnard, California, September 5, 1923; admitted to bar, 1950, California. *Education:* University of California at Los Angeles (B.S., 1943); Yale University (LL.B., 1949). Order of the Coif; Phi Beta Kappa. Law Clerk for Honorable Phil S. Gibson, Chief Justice, California Supreme Court, 1949-1950. Law Clerk for Justice Hugo L. Black, U.S. Supreme Court, 1950-1951. Instructor in Law: University of Southern California Law School, 1955—; Stanford Law School, 1977-1981. Assistant U.S. Attorney, Southern District of California, 1951-1953. Deputy Attorney General, State of California, 1953. Member, 1958—; Vice Chairman, 1971-1984, National Bankruptcy Conference. Member, Advisory Committee on Bankruptcy Rules, Judicial Conference of the United States, 1963-1976. *Member:* Los Angeles County (Chairperson, Judicial Appointments Committee, 1976-1977) and American Bar Association (Member, Business Law Section); The State Bar of California; American Law Institute; American Judicature Society. **PRACTICE AREAS:** Bankruptcy; Insolvency; Corporate Reorganization.

**HERMAN L. GLATT,** born New York, N.Y., May 3, 1929; admitted to bar, 1953, District of Columbia; 1954, California. *Education:* Franklin & Marshall College and University of California at Los Angeles (B.A., 1950); Harvard University (LL.B., 1953). Lecturer, Southern California School of Law "Creditors Rights," 1957-1958. Adjunct Professor of Law, Loyola University School of Law "Corporate Reorganization," 1975-1983. Member, National Panel, American Arbitration Association, 1964—. Editor, Bankruptcy Study Group Bulletin, 1964. Chairman, Bankruptcy Study Group, 1966-1967. *Member:* Los Angeles County and American (Member, Business Bankruptcy Committee, 1973—; Chairperson, Business Bankruptcy Committee, 1981-1985; Member, Business Law Section) Bar Associations; The State Bar of California (Member, Debtor/Creditor Relations and Bankruptcy Committee, 1970-1972). Fellow, American College of Bankruptcy. **PRACTICE AREAS:** Bankruptcy; Insolvency; Corporate Reorganization; Commercial Litigation.

**RICHARD M. NEITER,** born Los Angeles, California, September 17, 1937; admitted to bar, 1963, California. *Education:* University of California at Los Angeles (B.S., with honors, 1959); University of Southern California (LL.B., 1962). Member, Board of Editors, Southern California Law Review, 1960-1962. Member, Board of Trustees, Law Center Alumni, 1986- 1987. *Member:* Los Angeles County (Executive Committee, Commercial Law and Bankruptcy Section, 1974-1976) and American Bar Associations (Business Law Section); The State Bar of California (Chairman, Debtor/Creditor Relations and Bankruptcy Committee, 1974-1975, 1977-1978; Executive Committee, Business Law Section, 1979-1981, Liaison to Committee on Debtor/Creditor Relations and Bankruptcy Committee, 1979-1980). **TRANSACTIONS:** Lead Bankruptcy Counsel to Debtors in Chapter 11 cases of Hamburger Hamlet Restaurants, Inc.; First City/Hunter's Ridge, the Doskocil Companies Incorporated; Wilson Foods Corporation; Sambo's Restaurants, Inc.; Federal Wholesale Toy Co.; Northern Specialty Sales; David Orgell, Inc.; to the trustees of Pacific Far East Line, Inc.; Pacific Homes; To the Creditors Committee of Triad America Corporation and Del Taco, Inc. **PRACTICE AREAS:** Bankruptcy; Insolvency; Corporate Reorganization; Commercial Litigation.

**ROBERT A. GREENFIELD,** born Los Angeles, California, May 28, 1941; admitted to bar, 1967, California. *Education:* University of California at Los Angeles (B.S., 1963); Harvard University (J.D., cum laude, 1966). Phi Beta Kappa. Author: "Lines v. Frederick: The Effect of Bankruptcy on a Bankrupt's Accrued Vacation Pay and Other Forms of Deferred Compensation," 47 Los Angeles Bar Bulletin 67, 1971; "Alternatives to Bankruptcy for the Business Debtor," 51 Los Angeles Bar Bulletin 135, 1975; "The Bankruptcy Code and the Article 9 Secured Creditor," The Business Lawyer, April, 1979; "The National Bankruptcy Conference's Position on the Court System Under the Bankruptcy Amendments and Federal Judgeship Act of 1984 and Suggestions for Rules Promulgation," 23 Harv. J. on Legis. 357, 1986. Adjunct Professor of Law, Loyola University School of Law, 1978-1983. Member, 1974—; Chairman, Committee on Procedure and Court System, 1983—, National Bankruptcy Conference. *Member:* Los Angeles County (Editor, Bankruptcy Law Matters, Commercial Law and Bankruptcy Digest, 1973-1975; Member: Section on Commercial Law and Bankruptcy, 1967—) and American (Member: Subcommittee on Secured Transaction, Section on Business Law, 1974—; Member: Joint Task Force on Bankruptcy Court Structure and Insolvency Process, Section of Business Law and Section of Litigation, 1989—; Member: Joint Task Force on Bankruptcy Court Structure and Insolvency Process, Section of Business Law and Section of Litigation, 1989—) Bar Associations; The State Bar of California (Member, Committee on Uniform Commercial Code, 1977-1979; Business Law Section; Member: Leadership Subcommittee of the Long Range Plan Implementation Committee of the United States Bankruptcy Court, Central District of California; Member: Financial Lawyers Conference (1967—; Past President); Member: Board of Trustees of The Center For Law In The Public Interest, 1982-1992, Past Chairman; Member: Board of Directors, 1996—, and Lawyers Advisory Board, 1995—, Constitutional Rights Foundation; Member: Advisory Board, Friends of the Graphic Arts at UCLA, Grunwald Center for the Graphic Arts, 1995—). **PRACTICE AREAS:** Bankruptcy; Insolvency; Corporate Reorganization; Commercial Litigation.

**CHARLES D. AXELROD,** born New York, N.Y., June 19, 1941; admitted to bar, 1967, California. *Education:* Colgate University (B.A., magna cum laude, 1963); Duke University (J.D., 1966). Order of the Coif; Phi Beta Kappa; Phi Alpha Delta. Editor, Duke Law Journal, 1965-1966. Member, Practicing Law Institute's Bankruptcy and Creditors Rights Advisory Committee, 1992—. Faculty Member, Ninth Annual Norton Bankruptcy Litigation Institute, 1995. Guest Lecturer, Financial Executives Institute, 1992. Facility Member, "Bankruptcy: Is It The Best Way Out?", Faculty Member, Prentice Hall Twelfth Annual Institute and Acquisitions and Takeovers, 1990. Practicing Law Institute (Faculty Member, Secured Creditors in Bankruptcy, 1977). Recording Secretary of the UCC Committee, Business Law Section, State Bar of California, 1977-1980. Member, Board of Governors, 1974-1979, 1981—, Secretary and Treasurer, 1975-1980 and Vice-President, 1980, President, 1981, Financial Lawyers Conference. *Member:* Los Angeles County (Member, Sections on: Corporate Law; Commercial Law; Bankruptcy) and American (Member, Section on Business Law, Committee on Business Bankruptcy, Subcommittee on International Bankruptcy, Subcommittee on Bankruptcy Committees and Subcommittee on Trust Indentures and Claims Trading) Bar Associations; The State Bar of California (Chairman, Committee on Bankruptcy Specialization, Business Law Section, 1978-1979). **PRACTICE AREAS:** Bankruptcy; Insolvency; Corporate Reorganization; Commercial Litigation.

**THEODORE B. STOLMAN,** born Philadelphia, Pennsylvania, August 21, 1941; admitted to bar, 1967, Pennsylvania; 1972, California. *Education:* Villanova University (B.S.Ex., 1963; LL.B., 1966). George Washington University. Trial Attorney, U.S. Department of Justice, Tax Division, Washington, D.C., 1967-1971. *Member:* Beverly Hills, Los Angeles County (Member, Commercial Law and Bankruptcy Section) and American Bar

*(This Listing Continued)*

Associations (Member, Business Law Section); The State Bar of California. *PRACTICE AREAS:* Bankruptcy; Insolvency; Corporate Reorganization; Commercial Litigation.

**ISAAC M. PACHULSKI,** born Los Angeles, California, August 18, 1950; admitted to bar, 1974, California. *Education:* University of California at Los Angeles (B.A., summa cum laude, 1971); Harvard University (J.D., summa cum laude, 1974). Phi Beta Kappa. Recipient: Sears Prize, 1972 and 1973; Fay Diploma, 1974, Harvard University. Member, Harvard Law Review, 1972-1973. Author: "Levy v. Cohen: Another Pitfall for Creditors in Bankruptcy Proceedings," 53 Los Angeles Bar Journal 278, 1977; "The Cram Down and Valuation Under Chapter 11 of The Bankruptcy Code," 58 N.C.L. Review, 925, 1981. *Member:* Los Angeles County (Member, Commercial Law and Bankruptcy Section) and American (Member, Business Law Section) Bar Associations; The State Bar of California (Member, Board of Editors, California State Bar Journal, 1978). *PRACTICE AREAS:* Bankruptcy; Insolvency; Corporate Reorganization.

**KENNETH N. KLEE,** born Los Angeles, California, April 12, 1949; admitted to bar, 1975, California and District of Columbia; 1995, U.S. Court of Appeals, Second Circuit; 1996, New York. *Education:* Stanford University (B.A., with great distinction, 1971); Harvard University (J.D., cum laude, 1974). Phi Beta Kappa. Captain, Ames Moot Court Competition Team, 1972-1973. Member, Board of Editors, Harvard Journal on Legislation, 1973-1974. Co-Author: *Business Reorganization in Bankruptcy,* West (1995). Co-Author: *Fundamentals of Bankruptcy Law,* ALI/ABA (4th ed. 1995). Author: Bankruptcy Chapter of *Glickman Franchising,* 1985. Consulting Editor, 1979 and Contributing Editor, 1980, *Collier on Bankruptcy* . Author: "Adjusting Chapter 11: Fine Tuning the Plan Process," 69 Am. Bankr. L.J. 551 (1995). Co-Author: Creditors Committees Under Chapter 11 of the Bankruptcy Code," 44 S.C. L. Rev. 995 (1993). Author: "Cram Down II," 64 Am. Bankr. L.J. (1990). Author: "Timber, Ahlers, and Beyond," 1989 Ann. Surv. Bankr. L.1. (1989). Co-Author: "Ignoring Congressional Intent: Eight Years of Judicial Legislation," 62 Am. Bankr. L.J.1 (1988). Co-Author: "Caveat Creditor: The Consumer Debtor Under the Bankruptcy Code," 58 N.C.L. Review, 681, 1980; 54 American Bankruptcy Law Journal 275, 1980; "A Lending Officer's Primer on the New Bankruptcy Code," 97 Bank. L.J. 388, 1980. Co-Author: "Secured Creditors Under the New Bankruptcy Code," 11 U.C.C.L.J. 312, 1979; "The Impact of the New Bankruptcy Code on the 'Bankruptcy Out' in Legal Opinions," 48 Fordham Law Review 277, 1979. Author: "All You Ever Wanted to Know About Cram Down Under the New Bankruptcy Code," 53 Am. Bankr. L.J. 133, 1979; "Legislative History of the New Bankruptcy Law," 28 De Paul Law Review 941, 1979; 1 Annual Survey of Bankruptcy Law 21, 1979. Articles: Defining Success in Business Bankruptcies (submitted for publication and to the Bankruptcy Review Commission); Adjusting Chapter 11: Fine Tuning the Plan Process, 69 American Bankruptcy Law Journal 551 (1995). Robert Braucher, Visiting Professor from Practice, Harvard Law School, 1995-1996: Bankruptcy and Chapter 11 Business Reorganizations. Adjunct Professor of Law: Bankruptcy and Business Reorganizations, University of California at Los Angeles, 1979-1994; University of Southern California School of Law, 1983. Associate Counsel, Committee on the Judiciary, 1974-1977 and Consultant, House Committee on the Judiciary, U.S. House of Representatives, 1977-1979, 1981-1982, U.S. Department of Justice, 1983-1985. Member, Judicial Conference Advisory Committee on Bankruptcy Rules, 1992—. Member, 1979—, Executive Committee, 1985-1988 and 1992—, and Chairman of Committee on Legislation, 1992—, National Bankruptcy Conference. Member, Board of Governors, Financial Lawyers Conference, 1981—. President, Financial Lawyers Conference, 1986-1987. Lawyer Representative from Central District of California to Ninth Circuit Judicial Conference, 1987-1991. *Member:* Los Angeles (Member, Executive Committee, 1982-1984, Commercial Law and Bankruptcy Sections) and American (Member, 1980 and Chairman 1985-1987, New & Pending Legislation, Subcommittee, Section on Business Law) Bar Associations; The State Bar of California (Chairman, Bankruptcy Law Consulting Group to Board of Legal Specialization, 1989-1993); American Law Institute (Advisor, Transnational Insolvency Project, 1994—); American College of Bankruptcy. *REPORTED CASES:* In re Standard Brands Paint Co., 154 B.R. 563 Bankr. C.D. Cal. 1993; In re Texaco Inc., 92 B.R. 38; In re Western Real Estate Fund, Inc., 75 B.R. 580, 17 Collier Bankr. Cas. 2d 577. *TRANSACTIONS:* Represented Pennzoil Co. in Texaco Chapter 11; Griffin Resorts, Inc. Noteholders' Committee in Resorts International, Inc. Chapter 11; Charter Medical Secured Bondholders' Group out-of-Court Restructuring; Bally's Inc. Junior Bondholders' Group out-of-Court Restructuring; Orion Pictures Bondholders' Group out-of-Court Restructuring; Creditors Committee Papercraft Corp. Chapter 11; Debtor in Possession Standard Brands Paint Co. Chapter 11; Creditors' Committee Del Taco, Inc. Chapter 11; Equity Security Holders' Committee Liberte'

*(This Listing Continued)*

Chapter 11; L.A. Kings, Ltd. out-of-court restructuring: Apollo Advisors in Hillsborough Chapter 11; Barney's Inc. Special Counsel to Debtor. *PRACTICE AREAS:* Bankruptcy; Insolvency; Corporate Reorganization; Commercial Litigation; Expert Witness.

**ALAN PEDLAR,** born Burbank, California, March 13, 1949; admitted to bar, 1976, California. *Education:* University of California at Los Angeles (B.S., summa cum laude, 1971); Stanford University (M.S., 1973); Boalt Hall School of Law, University of California (J.D., 1976). Phi Beta Kappa; Order of the Coif. Articles Editor, California Law Review, 1975-1976. Contributing Editor, Collier on Bankruptcy (15th ed. 1996). Author: "The Implications of the New Community Property Laws for Creditors' Remedies and Bankruptcy," 63 California Law Review 1610, 1975; "Community Property and the Bankruptcy Reform Act of 1978," 11 St. Mary's Law Journal 349, 1979; "When Transfers Between Husband and Wife are Fraudulent," 5 Family Advocate, No. 3, p. 32, 1983. Adjunct Professor of Law, Loyola University School of Law, 1978-1986. *Member:* Los Angeles County (Member, Commercial Law and Bankruptcy Section) and American Bar Associations (Member, Business Law Section); The State Bar of California (Chairman, Debtor/Creditor Relations and Bankruptcy Committee, 1980-1981; Member, Executive Committee of Business Law Section, 1981-1984); UCC Committee (Member, Business Law Section, 1990-1991). *TRANSACTIONS:* Attorney for Storage Technology Corporation, Chapter 11 Reorganization; Attorney for Carter Hawley Hale Stores, Inc., Chapter 11 Reorganization. *PRACTICE AREAS:* Bankruptcy; Insolvency; Corporate Reorganization; Commercial Litigation; Secured Transactions.

**GEORGE C. WEBSTER, II,** born Evanston, Illinois, January 16, 1953; admitted to bar, 1978, California. *Education:* University of California at Santa Cruz and University of California at Berkeley (B.A., with highest honors, 1974); Harvard University (J.D., cum laude, 1978). Phi Beta Kappa. Author: "Collateral Control Decisions in Chapter Cases-Clear Rules v. Judicial Discretion," 51 American Bankruptcy Law Journal 197, 1977; "The Utility of Section 366 of the Bankruptcy Code," 19 Beverly Hills Law Journal 15, 1985. Adjunct Professor of Law, Bankruptcy, Loyola University Law School, 1984. *Member:* The State Bar of California (Member, Debtor/Creditor Relations Committee, 1984-1987); American Bar Association (Member, Section on Business Law). *PRACTICE AREAS:* Bankruptcy; Insolvency; Corporate Reorganization; Commercial Litigation.

**STEPHAN M. RAY,** born Los Angeles, California, July 12, 1954; admitted to bar, 1979, California. *Education:* University of California at Berkeley and Los Angeles (B.A., summa cum laude, 1976); Stanford University (J.D., 1979). Phi Beta Kappa. Member, 1977-1978 and Associate Editor, 1978-1979, Stanford Law Review. Lecturer in Law, Corporate Reorganization, University of Southern California Law Center, 1989—. Adjunct Professor of Law, Bankruptcy, Loyola University Law School, 1984. Managing Editor, Annual Review of Recent Developments and Legislation of Interest to California Business Lawyers, Business Law Section of the State Bar of California, 1991-1992. Board of Visitors, Stanford Law School, 1995-1996. *Member:* Los Angeles County (Member, Committee on Law School Education, 1981-1982) and American (Member, Sections on Litigation and Business Law) Bar Associations; The State Bar of California (Member, Debtor/Creditor Relations and Bankruptcy Committee, 1981-1984; Member, Education Committee, Business Law Section, 1990-1994, and Chair, 1994-1995; Member, Executive Committee, Business Law Section, 1995—). *REPORTED CASES:* Committee of Creditors Holding Unsecured Claims v. Citicorp Venture Capital, Ltd. (In re Papercraft Corp.); 187 B.R. 486 (Bankr. W.D. Pa. 1995); National Peregrine, Inc. v. Capital Fed. Sav. & Loan Ass'n (In re Peregrine Entertainment, Inc.), 116 B.R. 194 (C.D. Cal. 1990). *PRACTICE AREAS:* Bankruptcy; Insolvency; Corporate Reorganization; Commercial Litigation.

**MICHAEL A. MORRIS,** born Memphis, Tennessee, May 6, 1954; admitted to bar, 1979, California. *Education:* Immaculate Heart College (B.A., 1976); University of California, Boalt Hall School of Law (J.D., 1979). Member: Order of the Coif; Moot Court Board. Associate Editor, Industrial Relations Law Journal, 1979. Member: Board of Governors and Officer, Financial Lawyers Conference, 1991-1996. President, Financial Lawyers Conference, 1996-1997. *Member:* Los Angeles County (Member, Executive Committee, 1988-1989; Section of Commercial Law and Bankruptcy) and American (Member, Business Law Section) Bar Associations; The State Bar of California (Member, Debtor/Creditor Relations Committee, 1989); Financial Lawyers Conference (Member, Board of Governors). *PRACTICE AREAS:* Bankruptcy; Insolvency; Corporate Reorganization; Commercial Litigation.

*(This Listing Continued)*

**STUTMAN, TREISTER & GLATT,** PROFESSIONAL CORPORATION, Los Angeles—Continued

**JEFFREY C. KRAUSE,** born Gardena, California, May 16, 1956; admitted to bar, 1980, California. *Education:* California State University at Northridge and University of California at Los Angeles (B.S., 1977); University of California at Los Angeles (J.D., 1980). Member: Order of the Coif; UCLA Law Review, 1979-1980. Contributing Author: "California Real Property Financing: Bankruptcy and Secured Real Property Transactions," CEB, 1989; Steinberg, Bankruptcy Litigation, 1989; Author: "The Bias of the Courts Against Single Asset Real Estate Cases is Creating Bad Law in the Area of Classification," 22 Cal. Bankr. J. 45, 1994; "United States Trustee Guidelines Regarding Prepetition Retainers, "18 Cal. Bankr. J. 135, 1990; "Treatment of Prepetition Retainers," 17 Cal. Bankr. J. 153, 1989; "Foreclosure Sales Should Not Be Treated As Fraudulent Transfers," 1 ABA Bankr. Litigation Newsletter 7 (1993); "Non-Collusive Foreclosure Sales of Real Property Are Not Avoidable As Fraudulent Transfers," 3 ABA Bankr. Litigation Newsletter 18 (1995); Consultant, Bernhardt, California Mortgage and Deed of Trust Practice (2d ed. 1989 CEB). Adjunct Professor, University of Southern California School of Law, 1994-1996, Loyola School of Law, 1987 and 1988. *Member:* Los Angeles County (Former Member of Executive Committee of Section on Commercial Law and Bankruptcy) and American (Member, Sections on Litigation and Business Law; Co-Chairman of Education Subcommittee of Debtor-Creditor Committee) Bar Associations; The State Bar of California (Former Member, UCC Committee, Business Law Section, 1987-1990; Former Member, Debtor-Creditor Committee, Business Law Section, 1992-1995); Los Angeles Bankruptcy Forum (President). *REPORTED CASES:* In re Felburg, 39 Bankr. 591 (Bankr. C.D. Cal. 1984); Pistole V. Mellor (In re Mellor), 734 F. 2d 1396 (19th Cir. 1984); In re Safren, 65 Bankr. 566 (Bankr. C.D. Cal. 1986); Black & White Cattle Co. V. Shamrock Farms Co. (In re Black & White Cattle Co.), 30 Bankr. 508 (Bankr. 9th Cir. 1983), Rev'd. 746 F. 2d 1484 (9th Cir. 1984); Black & White Cattle Co. V. Granada Services, Inc. (In re Black & White Cattle Co.), 783 F. 2d 1454 (9th Cir. 1986); In re Lindsay, 59 F. 3d 942 (9th Cir. 1995). *PRACTICE AREAS:* Bankruptcy; Insolvency; Corporate Reorganization; Commercial Litigation.

**MICHAEL H. GOLDSTEIN,** born Philadelphia, Pennsylvania, October 16, 1959; admitted to bar, 1984, California. *Education:* Franklin and Marshall College (B.A., magna cum laude, 1981); Harvard University (J.D., cum laude, 1984). Phi Beta Kappa. Contributing Author, 1994—*Collier on Bankruptcy,* Chapter 9. *Member:* Los Angeles County (Member, Commercial Law and Bankruptcy Section) and American (Member, Business Law Section) Bar Associations; The State Bar of California. *PRACTICE AREAS:* Bankruptcy; Insolvency; Corporate Reorganization; Commercial Litigation.

**LEE R. BOGDANOFF,** born Van Nuys, California, November 28, 1960; admitted to bar, 1985, California, U.S. Court of Appeals, Ninth Circuit and U.S. District Court, Southern, Northern and Central Districts of California. *Education:* University of California at Davis (A.B., 1982); Boalt Hall School of Law, University of California (J.D., 1985). Phi Beta Kappa; Order of the Coif. Regents Scholar. Associate Editor, California Law Review, 1984-1985. Author: Article, "The Purchase and Sale of Assets in Reorganization Cases - of Interest and Principal, of Principal and Interests," The Business Lawyer, 1992; "Exemptions Under the Bankruptcy Code: Using California's New Homestead Exemption as a Medium for Analysis," 72 California Law Review 922. Law Clerk, Hon. David R. Thompson, Ninth Circuit Court of Appeals, 1985-1986. Member, Board of Governors, Financial Lawyers Conference, 1996. *Member:* American Bar Association (Member, Business Law Section); The State Bar of California. *PRACTICE AREAS:* Bankruptcy; Insolvency; Corporate Reorganization; Commercial Litigation.

**FRANK A. MEROLA,** born Syracuse, New York, June 17, 1963; admitted to bar, 1988, California. *Education:* Georgetown University (B.S., cum laude, 1985); University of California at Los Angeles (J.D., 1988). Order of the Coif; Order of the Barristers. Co-Author: "Ignoring Congressional Intent: Eight Years of Judicial Legislation," 62 Am. Bankr. L.J. 1, 1988. *Member:* Los Angeles County (Member, Commercial Law and Bankruptcy Section) and American (Member, Business Law Section) Bar Associations; The State Bar of California; Turner and Managers Association. *PRACTICE AREAS:* Bankruptcy; Insolvency; Corporate Reorganization; Commercial Litigation.

**K. JOHN SHAFFER,** born Fontana, California, August 17, 1964; admitted to bar, 1991, California. *Education:* Stanford University (A.B., with honors and distinction, 1986); Boalt Hall School of Law, University of California (J.D., 1989). Order of the Coif. Max Thelen, Paul Marrin Award, 1989. Book Review Editor, California Law Review, 1988-1989. Law Clerk to the Honorable Alex Kozinski, U.S. Court of Appeals, Ninth Circuit, 1989-1990. Law Clerk to the Honorable Anthony M. Kennedy, Associate Justice, U.S. Supreme Court, 1990-1991. Author: "Creditors' Committee Under Chapter 11 of the Bankruptcy Code," 44 S.C. L. Rev. 995 (1993). *Member:* Los Angeles County Bar Association (Commercial Law and Bankruptcy Section); The State Bar of California (Business Law Section). *PRACTICE AREAS:* Bankruptcy; Insolvency; Corporate Reorganization; Commercial Litigation.

**MARETA C. HAMRE,** born Fort Collins, Colorado, November 30, 1963; admitted to bar, 1990, California. *Education:* Harvard University (B.A., cum laude, 1985); University of California Boalt Hall School of Law (J.D., 1990). Recipient, John Harvard Scholarship. Recipient, Elizabeth Carey Aggasiz Award. Editor, University of California Law Review, 1989-1990. Officer, Moot Court Board. *Member:* The State Bar of California (Member, Business Law Section); American Bar Association (Member, Business Law Section). *PRACTICE AREAS:* Bankruptcy; Insolvency; Corporate Reorganization; Commercial Litigation.

**MICHAEL L. TUCHIN,** born Los Angeles, California, January 14, 1965; admitted to bar, 1990, California. *Education:* Stanford University (A.B., with honors and distinction, 1987); University of California, Berkley, Boalt Hall School of Law (J.D., 1990). Extern to the Honorable Joseph T. Sneed, U.S. Court of Appeals, Ninth Circuit. *Member:* Los Angeles County (Member, Commercial Law and Bankruptcy Section) and American (Member, Business Law Section) Bar Associations; The State Bar of California (Member, Business Law Section). *PRACTICE AREAS:* Bankruptcy; Insolvency; Corporate Reorganization; Commercial Litigation.

**JEFFREY H. DAVIDSON,** born Brookline, Massachusetts, April 7, 1952; admitted to bar, 1977, California. *Education:* Harvard University (B.A., cum laude, 1973; J.D., cum laude, 1976). Phi Beta Kappa. *Member:* Los Angeles County (Chairman, Commercial Law and Bankruptcy Section, 1987-1988, Secretary, 1986-1987, Executive Committee, 1985—; Chairman, Bankruptcy Committee, 1984-1986, Member, 1983—; Member, Nominating Committee for County Bar Trustees and Officers, 1988) Federal Bar Association (Member, Bankruptcy Section, 1990—) and American (Member, Section on Business Law; Member, UCC Committee; Member, Business Bankruptcy Committee) Bar Associations; The State Bar of California (Chairman, UCC Committee, 1986-1987; Vice Chairman, UCC Committee, 1985-1986; Member, UCC Committee, Business Law Section, 1984-1987 and 1992-1995; Member, 1987-1990 and Treasurer, 1989-1990, Executive Committee, Business Law Section); Member, Bench/Bar Committee on Local Bankruptcy Rules for the Central District of California; Financial Lawyers Conference (Member, Board of Governors, 1988-1991; Executive Committee, 1990-1991). *SPECIAL AGENCIES:* Bankruptcy Court and Office of U.S. Trustee. *TRANSACTIONS:* Attorney for Debtor in Possession in Chapter 11 Reorganization of Barry's Jewelers, Inc.; Attorney for Debtor in Possession in Chapter 11 Reorganization of Lamont's Apparel, Inc.; Attorney for Debtor in Possession in Chapter 11 Reorganization of Castle Entertainment, Inc.; Attorney for Executive Life Insurance Co. in Chapter 11 Reorganization of Continental Airlines, Inc.; Attorney for Executive Life Insurance Co. in Restructuring of LVI Group, Inc.; Attorney for Debtor in Restructuring of Stars To Go, Inc.; Attorney for Southmark California, Inc. in Chapter 11 Reorganization of Southmark Corporation. *PRACTICE AREAS:* Business Bankruptcy; Insolvency; Corporate Reorganization.

**RONALD L. FEIN,** born Detroit, Michigan, August 26, 1943; admitted to bar, 1970, California. *Education:* University of California at Los Angeles (A.B., cum laude, 1966); University of San Diego (J.D., cum laude, 1969). Articles Editor, University of San Diego Law Review, 1968-1969; member, University of San Diego Law Review, 1967-1969. Author: "Chapter XIII of the Bankruptcy Act: As Maine Goes So Should the Nation" 5 U.S.D.L. Rev. 329 , (1968). Co-author: "The New California General Corporation Law: A Transactional Analysis,"; "ULOE: Comprehending the Confusion," 43 Business Lawyer 737, (February, 1988); "Leveraged Buy-Outs, Freeze Outs and Entire Fairness," Officers' and Directors' Liability: A Review of the Business Judgment Rule, Practicing Law Institute, (1986); "Officers and Directors as ERISA Fiduciaries," Officers' and Directors' Liability: A review of the Business Judgment Rule, Practicing Law Institute (1986); "State Securities Law Limited Offering Exemptions," an annual publication from 1982 through 1988; "Comparative Assessment of the Regulatory Constraints on Issuer Self Tender Offers and Issuer Open market Repurchase Programs," California Business Institute; "Private (Limited) Offerings: Existing State Exemptions," Blue Sky Laws: State Regulation of Securities, Practicing Law Institute, 1985; "State Regulation of Tenders and Takeovers." State Regulation of Capital Formation and Securities Transactions,

*(This Listing Continued)*

Practicing Law Institute, (1983); "Private Offerings: The General Spectrum of Regulation," State Regulation of Capital Formation and Securities transactions, Practicing Law Institute, (1983); "Integration of Securities Transactions" Review of Securities Regulation, (December, 1982). Adjunct Professor of Law, Loyola University School of Law, 1976—. *Member:* Los Angeles County (Member, Commercial Law and Bankruptcy Section; Executive Committee, Business and Corporate Law Section) and American (Corporation, Banking and Business Law Section: Vice Chairman, State Regulation of Securities Committee; Subcommittee Chairman, Private Offering Exemption and Simplification of Capital Formation; Ad Hoc Committee on Merit Regulation; Federal Regulation of Securities Committee; Ad Hoc Committee on the Uniform Limited Offering Exemption; Ad Hoc Committee on Regulation D; Subcommittee on Registration Statements-1933 Act; ABA Task Force on Lawyer Business Ethics and ABA Corporate Counsel Committee) Bar Associations; The State Bar of California (Member, Business Law Section); National Association of Securities Dealers, Inc. (Member: Arbitration Panel; Subcommittee on Indemnification, Commissioner's Circle Advisory Committee to the California Commissioner of Corporations); Financial Lawyers Conference. *PRACTICE AREAS:* General Corporate; Corporate Securities; Corporate Reorganization.

**MARK S. WALLACE,** born Paterson, New Jersey, January 2, 1954; admitted to bar, 1977, Arizona; 1991, California. *Education:* Princeton University (A.B., summa cum laude, 1976); Columbia University (J.D., 1977). Phi Beta Kappa. Notes and Comments Editor, Columbia Law Review, 1976-1977. Law Clerk to Judge William B. Enright, U.S. District Court, Southern District of California, 1977-1979. Author: "Is A Midstream Abandonment Taxable To The Estate?," 77 Journal of Taxation 26 (1992); "Practical Aspects of Representing the Failing Business," 44 Major Tax Planning R 400 (1992); "Reorganizing the Financially-Troubled Taxpayer," 46 Major Tax Planning¶800 (1994). Co-author: "Tax Procedure Considerations in Chapter 11 Reorgs.," 20 Taxation for Lawyers 289 (1992). Adjunct Professor of Law: Arizona State University, 1984-1986 and 1988; Golden Gate University, 1984. Chair-Elect, Bankruptcy/Insolvency Committee, California State Bar Tax Section. *Member:* Los Angeles County (Member, Commercial Law and Bankruptcy Section; Taxation) and American (Member, Sections of Taxation, Corporate Tax Committee, Section 108 Real Estate and Partnerships Task Force and Business Law) Bar Associations; The State Bar of California. *SPECIAL AGENCIES:* California Franchise Tax Board and State Board of Equalization; Internal Revenue Service. *PRACTICE AREAS:* Bankruptcy; Insolvency; Corporate Reorganization; Bankruptcy Tax.

**ERIC D. GOLDBERG,** born New York, New York, March 16, 1965; admitted to bar, 1992, California. *Education:* Cornell University (B.S., with honors, 1987); Harvard Law School (J.D., cum laude, 1991). *Member:* The State Bar of California (Business Law Section). *PRACTICE AREAS:* Bankruptcy; Insolvency; Corporate Reorganization.

**EVE H. KARASIK,** born Cambridge, Massachusetts, September 2, 1962; admitted to bar, 1991, California. *Education:* University of California, Berkeley (B.A., with High Honors, 1984); University of Southern California (J.D., 1991). Member, Order of the Coif. Managing Editor, University of Southern California Computer Law and Major Tax Planning Journals. Author, "A Normative Analysis Of Disclosure, Privacy, And Computers: The State Cases," 10 Computer/L.J. 603 , 1990. *Member:* Los Angeles County (Commercial Law and Bankruptcy Section) and American (Business Law Section) Bar Association; The State Bar of California (Business Law Section). *PRACTICE AREAS:* Bankruptcy; Insolvency; Corporate Reorganization; Commercial Litigation.

**THOMAS R. KRELLER,** born Chicago Heights, Illinois, October 21, 1964; admitted to bar, 1992, California and U.S. District Court, Central, Northern, Eastern and Southern Districts of California. *Education:* Millikin University (B.S., with high honors, 1986); University of California, Los Angeles, School of Law/Anderson Graduate School of Management (J.D./M.B.A., 1992). *Member:* Los Angeles County (Commercial Law and Bankruptcy Section) and American (Business Law Section) Bar Association; The State Bar of California (Business Law Section); Association of Insolvency Accountants; Turnaround Management Association. *PRACTICE AREAS:* Bankruptcy; Insolvency; Corporate Reorganization; Commercial Litigation.

**MARTIN R. BARASH,** born Los Angeles, California, February 10, 1968; admitted to bar, 1992, California; 1993, U.S. Court of Appeals, Ninth Circuit; 1994, U.S. District Court, Central, Southern, Northern and Eastern Districts of California. *Education:* Princeton University (A.B., magna cum laude, in Politics, 1989); University of California at Los Angeles (J.D.,

*(This Listing Continued)*

1992). Member, University of California Law Review, 1990-1991; Editor and Business Manager, 1991-1992. Law Clerk to the Honorable Proctor R. Hug, Jr., U.S. Ninth Circuit Court of Appeals, 1992-1993. *Member:* Los Angeles County and American Bar Associations (Member, Business Law Sections); The State Bar of California (Member, Business Law Section). *PRACTICE AREAS:* Bankruptcy; Corporate Reorganization; Corporate Insolvency; Commercial Litigation.

**JAMES O. JOHNSTON JR.,** born Glendale, California, August 14, 1968; admitted to bar, 1993, California. *Education:* Stanford University (B.A., 1990); University of Southern California (J.D./M. A., 1993). Order of the Coif. Author: 66 S. Cal. L. Rev. 659; 66 S. Cal. L. Rev. 977. *Member:* State Bar of California. *PRACTICE AREAS:* Bankruptcy; Insolvency; Corporate Reorganization.

**MICHAEL C. STANDLEE,** born Santa Barbara, California, December 3, 1968; admitted to bar, 1994, California. *Education:* Claremont McKenna College (B.A., cum laude, 1991); University of Southern California (J.D., 1994). Member, Southern California Law Review, 1992-1993. Senior Editor, Southern California Interdisciplinary Law Journal, 1993-1994. *Member:* State Bar of California. *PRACTICE AREAS:* Bankruptcy; Insolvency; Corporate Reorganization.

REPRESENTATIVE CLIENTS: County of Orange; Apollo Advisors; L.P. First American Title Insurance Company; MCA. Inc.; Fidelity Investments; First Executive Corporation; Wickes Companies, Inc.; Storage Technology Corp.; Pennzoil; Public Service Company of New Hampshire; Doskocil Companies, Inc.; Federated Stores, Inc.; Carter Hawley Hale Stores, Inc.; Standard Brands Paint Company; Griffin Resorts, Inc. Noteholders' Committee; Litton Industries, Inc.; Executive Life Insurance Co.; Papercraft Bondholders' Committee.

---

## STYSKAL, WIESE & MELCHIONE
### LOS ANGELES, CALIFORNIA
(See Glendale)

*General Corporate, Commercial and Consumer Insurance and Computer Law as it affects Credit Unions.*

---

## SULLIVAN & CROMWELL
### 444 SOUTH FLOWER STREET
### LOS ANGELES, CALIFORNIA 90071-2901
Telephone: 213-955-8000
Telecopier: 213-683-0457

*New York City Office:* 125 Broad Street, 10004-2498. Telephone: 212-558-4000. Telex: 62694. Telecopier: 212-558-3588.
*Washington, D.C. Office:* 1701 Pennsylvania Avenue, N.W., 20006-5805. Telephone: 202-956-7500. Telecopier: 202-293-6330.
*Paris Office:* 8, Place Vendôme, Paris 75001, France. Telephone: (011)(331)4450-6000. Telex: 240654. Telecopier: (011)(331)4450-6060.
*London Office:* St. Olave's House, 9a Ironmonger Lane, London EC2V 8EY, England. Telephone: (011)(44171)710-6500. Telecopier: (011)(44171)710-6565.
*Melbourne Office:* 101 Collins Street, Melbourne, Victoria 3000, Australia. Telephone: (011)(613)9654-1500. Telecopier: (011)(613)9654-2422.
*Tokyo Office:* Sullivan & Cromwell, Gaikokuho Jimu Bengoshi Jimusho, Akai Law Offices (Registered Associated Offices), Tokio Kaijo Building Shinkan, 2-1, Marunouchi 1-chome, Chiyoda-ku, Tokyo 100, Japan. Telephone: (011)(813)3213-6140. Telecopier: (011)(813)3213-6470.
*Hong Kong Office:* 28th Floor, Nine Queen's Road, Central, Hong Kong. Telephone: (011)(852)2826-8688. Telecopier: (011)(852)2522-2280.
*Frankfurt Office:* Oberlindau 54-56, 60323 Frankfurt am Main, Germany. Telephone: (011)(4969)7191-260. Telecopier: (011)(4969)7191-2610.

*General Practice.*

*PARTNERS IN LOS ANGELES*

**STANLEY F. FARRAR,** born Santa Ana, CA., 1943; admitted to bar, 1968, California; 1969, New York. *Education:* Univ. of California, Berkeley (B.S., 1964; J.D., 1967).

**FRANK H. GOLAY, JR.,** born Chicago, IL., 1948; admitted to bar, 1978, New York; 1988, California. *Education:* Cornell (B.A., 1970; M.A.T., 1972; J.D., 1977).

**ROBERT A. SACKS,** born Long Beach, NY., 1957; admitted to bar, 1983, New York; 1990, California. *Education:* Harvard (A.B., 1979); Univ. of Texas (J.D., 1982).

*(This Listing Continued)*

## SULLIVAN & CROMWELL, Los Angeles—Continued

**ALISON S. RESSLER,** born New York, NY., 1958; admitted to bar, 1984, New York; 1985, California. *Education:* Brown (A.B., 1980); Columbia (J.D., 1983).

**MICHAEL H. STEINBERG,** born Ft. Riley, KS., 1962; admitted to bar, 1988, California. *Education:* Univ. of California, Berkeley (A.B., 1983); Stanford (J.D., 1986).

**JOHN L. SAVVA,** born Swindon, England, 1960; admitted to bar, 1988, California. *Education:* Pitzer College (B.A., 1985); Loyola (J.D., 1988).

### ASSOCIATES IN LOS ANGELES

**ELIZABETH S. BLUESTEIN,** born Washington, D.C., 1968; admitted to bar, 1993, California. *Education:* Harvard (B.A., 1990); Boalt Hall School of Law (J.D., 1993).

**PATRICK S. BROWN,** born Hawthorne, CA., 1969; admitted to bar, 1995, California. *Education:* Univ. of California at Los Angeles (B.A., 1991; J.D., 1995).

**JULIUS G. CHRISTENSEN,** born Ely, NV., 1965; admitted to bar, 1995, California. *Education:* Univ. of California at Los Angeles (B.A., 1992); Harvard (J.D., 1995).

**VALERIE C. EDWARDS,** born Houston, TX., 1967; admitted to bar, 1995, California. *Education:* Stanford (B.A., 1989); Univ. of California at Los Angeles (J.D., 1994).

**KEN IKARI,** born Tokyo, Japan, 1964; admitted to bar, 1990, New York; 1995, California. *Education:* Univ. of California at Los Angeles (B.A., 1986); Harvard (J.D., 1989).

**BRIAN P.Y. LIU,** born Taipei, Taiwan, October 13, 1967; admitted to bar, 1996, California. *Education:* Univ. of California at Berkeley (A.B., 1990); Univ. of California at Los Angeles (J.D., 1996).

**MICHAEL L. PRESTON,** born Glendale, CA., 1964; admitted to bar, 1990, California. *Education:* Univ. of California at Los Angeles (B.A., 1987); Loyola Marymount (J.D., 1990).

**STEVIE PYON,** born Seoul, Korea, 1968; admitted to bar, 1995, California. *Education:* Claremont McKenna College (B.A., 1990); Univ. of Southern California (J.D., 1994).

**DANIEL E. SOBELSOHN,** born Los Angeles, CA., 1971; admitted to bar, 1995, California. *Education:* Columbia (B.A., 1992; J.D., 1995).

**THADDEUS G. STEPHENS,** born Pasadena, CA., 1969; admitted to bar, 1996, California. *Education:* Oberlin (B.A., 1991); Stanford (J.D., 1996).

**STEVEN B. STOKDYK,** born Mountain View, CA., 1967; admitted to bar, 1991, California. *Education:* Stanford (A.B., 1988); Univ. of California at Los Angeles (J.D., 1991).

**STEVEN W. THOMAS,** born East Point, GA., 1967; admitted to bar, 1993, California. *Education:* Univ. of Missouri-Kansas City (B.A., 1989); Duke (J.D., 1992).

(For Biographical Data on all Partners and Associates see Professional Biographies at New York, N.Y.)

---

## SULLIVAN LAW CORPORATION

545 SOUTH FIGUEROA STREET, SUITE 1216
**LOS ANGELES, CALIFORNIA 90071-1599**
Telephone: 213-488-9200
Telecopier: 213-488-9664

*Corporation, Taxation, Environmental, Commercial, Aviation, Insurance, Government Contracting and Litigation in all State and Federal Courts, Internal Revenue Service, National Transportation Safety Board, and Federal Government Boards of Contract Appeals.*

**MICHAEL R. SULLIVAN,** born Chicago, Illinois, August 17, 1947; admitted to bar, 1973, California and U.S. Court of Appeals, Ninth Circuit; U.S. District Court, Northern, Central, Eastern and Southern Districts of California; 1979, U.S. Supreme Court and U.S. Claims Court; 1985, U.S. District Court, Northern District of Texas and U.S. Court of Appeals for the Federal Circuit. *Education:* University of California, Berkeley (A.B., 1970); University of California, Los Angeles, School of Law (J.D., 1973). Phi Delta Phi. Member, UCLA Law Review, 1972-1973. Judge Pro Tem, Los Angeles Municipal Court, 1980-1988. Member, National Transportation Safety Board Bar; Panel of Arbitrators, Los Angeles Superior Court American Arbitration Association,. 1979-- American Arbitration Association, New York Stock Exchange. *Member:* Los Angeles County (Member, Business and Corporation Section) and American (Member Sections on: Aviation, Litigation and Corporation Law) Bar Associations; State Bar of California (Member, Section on Business Law; Acting Supervising Referee and Referee, Hearing Department, State Bar Court, 1980-1989); Aircraft Finance Association; Association of Business Trial Lawyers; Lawyer-Pilot Bar Association. **SPECIAL AGENCIES:** National Transportation Safety Board, State Bar of California. **PRACTICE AREAS:** Aviation; Business; Corporation.

---

**DOUGLAS G. CARROLL,** born Miami, Florida, October 1, 1944; admitted to bar, 1981, California; 1983, U.S. District Court, Central District of California. *Education:* California State University at Northridge (B.A., 1973); Loyola University of Los Angeles Law School (J.D., 1981). Alpha Mu Gamma. *Member:* St. Thomas More Law Honor Society; Loyola University of Los Angeles Law Review, 1979-1980. Co-Author: "Airport Noise Pollution Damages: The Case for Local Liability," 15 Urban Lawyer 621, 1983. *Member:* Los Angeles County and American Bar Associations; State Bar of California. **LANGUAGES:** German and Russian. **PRACTICE AREAS:** Business Litigation.

---

## SULLIVAN, WORKMAN & DEE

A Partnership including a Professional Corporation
TWELFTH FLOOR, 800 FIGUEROA STREET
**LOS ANGELES, CALIFORNIA 90017**
Telephone: 213-624-5544
Fax: 213-627-7128

*General Civil Practice including Trial and Appellate Litigation. Eminent Domain, Land Use and Real Property, Business, Securities and Corporate Matters, Entertainment Law, Probate, Trust and Estate Planning Law.*

### PARTNERS

**ROGER M. SULLIVAN, (A PROFESSIONAL CORPORATION),** born Los Angeles, California, October 27, 1926; admitted to bar, 1952, California. *Education:* Occidental College California; Loyola University of Los Angeles (J.D., 1952). Phi Delta Phi. Member, Chancery Club. Author: "Eminent Domain and Inverse Condemnation," Los Angeles Lawyer, January 1994; "Oakland v. The Raiders-Eminent Domain Law will Never be the Same," Probate and Property, 1984; "Oaklands Search for a Legal Touchdown," 6 Los Angeles Lawyer 8, July-August, 1983. Co-author: "Practical Aspects of Condemnation Proceedings," State Bar Conference of Barristers, 1953; "California Condemnation Practice," Continuing Education of the Bar, 1960. Advisor, Uniform Code Commission, Committee on Model Eminent Domain Code, 1973-1974. Lecturer, "Selected Problems in Condemnation Practice," California Continuing Education of the Bar, 1981. *Member:* Los Angeles County (Chairman, Committee on Condemnation Law and Procedure, 1970-1972) and American (Member, 1967— and Chairman, 1975-1977, Committee on Condemnation Law; Member, Council, Real Property, Probate and Trust Law Section, 1978-1980) Bar Associations; The State Bar of California (Vice President, Conference of Barristers, 1960; Member: Committee on Condemnation Law and Procedure, 1960-1968; Committee on Governmental Liability and Condemnation, 1970-1973; Chairman, Committee on Condemnation, 1975-1976); American College of Real Estate Lawyers. Fellow, American College of Trial Lawyers. **PRACTICE AREAS:** Eminent Domain Law; Land Use Regulation Law.

**HENRY K. WORKMAN,** born Los Angeles, California, February 5, 1926; admitted to bar, 1957, California. *Education:* University of Southern California (B.S., 1948); Loyola University of Los Angeles (LL.B., 1956). Phi Delta Phi. *Member:* Los Angeles County and American Bar Associations; The State Bar of California. **PRACTICE AREAS:** Estate Planning Law; Administration Law; Civil Appeals; Condemnation Law.

**JOHN J. DEE,** born Los Angeles, California, January 13, 1941; admitted to bar, 1970, California. *Education:* University of Santa Clara (B.A., 1963); Lincoln University (J.D., 1969). Member, Lincoln University Law Review, 1968-1969. Consultant/Co-Author: "California Condemnation Practice," Continuing Education of the Bar, 1981 Supplement. *Member:* Los Angeles County (Member: Committee on Condemnation Procedures, 1972—; Chairman, Committee on Condemnation and Land Valuation Litigation, 1980-1981; Land Use Subcommittee, 1974—, Real Property Section) and American (Member: Section of Litigation, Committee on Zoning and Condemnation, 1978—; Real Property Section, Committee on Con-

*(This Listing Continued)*

demnation, Vice Chair, 1989—) Bar Associations; The State Bar of California (Member: Committee on Condemnation, 1977-1980, 1982-1985, 1987-1990, Chair, 1989-1990; Condemnation Subcommittee of Public Law Section, 1980—; Delegate, State Bar Conference of Delegates, 1990-1993). *PRACTICE AREAS:* Eminent Domain Law; Zoning Law; Land Use Regulation Law; Real Estate Litigation.

**CHARLES D. CUMMINGS,** born Boise, Idaho, February 18, 1949; admitted to bar, 1974, California. *Education:* Loyola University of Los Angeles (B.A., cum laude, 1971; J.D., cum laude, 1974). Member, Board of Governors, St. Thomas More Law Honor Society, 1973-1974. *Member:* Los Angeles County (Member, Real Property Section) and American Bar Associations; The State Bar of California. *PRACTICE AREAS:* Real Estate Law; Business Litigation; Real Estate Transactions.

**CHARLES F. CALLANAN,** born Washington, D.C., January 12, 1942; admitted to bar, 1968, District of Columbia; 1979, California and U.S. District Court, Central District of California. *Education:* Fordham College (B.A., 1964); Catholic University Law School (J.D., 1967). *Member:* Los Angeles County and American Bar Associations; State Bar of California; The District of Columbia Bar. *PRACTICE AREAS:* Corporations Law; Real Estate Law; Commercial Law.

**GARY A. KOVACIC,** born Pasadena, California, November 16, 1951; admitted to bar, 1976, California; 1977, U.S. District Court, Central District of California; 1978, U.S. District Court, Eastern District of California; 1980, U.S. District Court, Southern District of California; 1985, U.S. Court of Appeals, Ninth Circuit. *Education:* University of California at Los Angeles (B.A., cum laude, 1973); Southwestern University School of Law (J.D., cum laude, 1976). Note and Comment Editor, Southwestern University Law Review, 1975-1976. Adjunct Professor, University of LaVerne, College of Law, 1987-1988. Planning Commissioner, City of Arcadia, California, 1984-1987, 1994. Speaker, American Planning Association: Zoning Institute, 1985; California Chapter Conference, 1986, 1994. *Member:* Los Angeles County (Member, 1986— and Chair, 1990-1992, Condemnation and Land Valuation Litigation Committee) and American (Member, Committee on Condemnation Law, 1978—) Bar Associations; The State Bar of California (Delegate, State Bar Convention, 1985-1988). *PRACTICE AREAS:* Eminent Domain Law; Zoning Law; Land Use Regulation Law; Environmental Law.

**JOSEPH S. DZIDA, JR.,** born Los Angeles, California, August 9, 1955; admitted to bar, 1979, California. *Education:* Loyola Marymount University (B.A., 1976); Loyola University of Los Angeles (J.D., 1979). Member, Board of Governors, Loyola Law School Alumni Association, 1987-1989. *Member:* Los Angeles County and American Bar Associations; The State Bar of California. *PRACTICE AREAS:* Business Law; Real Estate Litigation.

**JOHN E. MACKEL, III,** born Los Angeles, California, October 18, 1959; admitted to bar, 1985, California. *Education:* University of California at Los Angeles (B.A., in Economics, 1981); Loyola Marymount University (J.D., 1985). Law Clerk to the Hon. Manuel L. Real, Chief Judge of U.S. District Court, Central District of California, 1985-1986. *Member:* Los Angeles County and American Bar Associations; State Bar of California.

**PAUL C. EPSTEIN,** born Los Angeles, California, January 12, 1956; admitted to bar, 1986, California; 1987, U.S. District Court, Central District of California and U.S. Court of Appeals, Ninth Circuit. *Education:* University of California at Los Angeles (Biology, 1978); Southwestern University School of Law (J.D., 1986). Recipient, George Yanase Scholarship, 1986. Author: "How to Protect Your Client Before Condemnation Occurs," Los Angeles Lawyer, January 1994. *Member:* Los Angeles County and American Bar Associations; The Association of Trial Lawyers of America. *PRACTICE AREAS:* Civil Litigation; Real Estate Litigation; Eminent Domain Law.

**CHRISTOPHER K. COOPER,** born Los Angeles, California, March 7, 1960; admitted to bar, 1986, California and U.S. District Court, Central District of California. *Education:* University of California at Berkeley (A.B., 1982); Loyola Marymount University (J.D., 1985). Phi Alpha Delta. Scott Moot Court Honors. *Member:* Los Angeles County (Member, Real Estate Section) and American Bar Associations; State Bar of California. *PRACTICE AREAS:* Real Estate Transactions; Real Estate Acquisitions; Sales; Financing; Workouts; Commercial Leasing.

*(This Listing Continued)*

**SUSAN MAPEL KAHN,** born Los Angeles, California, July 12, 1948; admitted to bar, 1983, California. *Education:* University of Colorado (B.A., 1971); Loyola Marymount University (J.D., 1983). Member, St. Thomas More Law Honor Society. *Member:* Los Angeles County and American Bar Associations; The State Bar of California.

**EMIL J. WOHL,** born Pasadena, California, July 18, 1968; admitted to bar, 1994, California and U.S. District Court, Central District of California. *Education:* University of Southern California (B.A. with honors, 1990); University of San Diego (J.D., 1994). Alpha Lambda Delta. *Member:* Los Angeles County Bar Association (Member, Real Property Section); State Bar of California (Member, Real Property Section). *PRACTICE AREAS:* Real Estate Litigation; Eminent Domain Law; Land Use Regulation Law.

*OF COUNSEL*

**HENRY G. BODKIN, JR.,** born Los Angeles, California, December 8, 1921; admitted to bar, 1948, California; 1958, U.S. Supreme Court. *Education:* Loyola University of Los Angeles (B.S., cum laude, 1943; J.D., 1948). Phi Delta Phi. Member, Chancery Club, 1965; President, 1990-1991. Member, 1972-1974; President, 1973-1974, Board of Water and Power Commissioners, City of Los Angeles. Regent, Marymount College 1962-1967. Trustee, Loyola-Marymount University, 1967-1991. *Member:* Los Angeles County (Member, Board of Trustees, 1968-1971) and American (Member, Sections on: Business Law; Tort and Insurance Practice; Litigation) Bar Associations; The State Bar of California (Member, Executive Committee, Conference of Delegates, 1968-1970). Fellow, American College of Trial Lawyers. [Lt., U.S.N.R., 1943-1945; 1951-1953]. *PRACTICE AREAS:* Business Litigation.

**THOMAS E. O'SULLIVAN,** born Louisville, Kentucky, April 13, 1924; admitted to bar, 1955, California. *Education:* University of Southern California (B.S., 1949); Loyola University of Los Angeles (J.D., 1954). Revenue Agent, Internal Revenue Service, 1950-1955. *Member:* Los Angeles County, Beverly Hills and American Bar Associations. *PRACTICE AREAS:* Taxation Law; General Business Planning Law; Estate Planning Law; Probate Law.

REFERENCE: First Business Bank.

---

# SULMEYER, KUPETZ, BAUMANN & ROTHMAN

*A PROFESSIONAL CORPORATION*

Established in 1952

300 SOUTH GRAND AVENUE, 14TH FLOOR
**LOS ANGELES, CALIFORNIA 90071**
Telephone: 213-626-2311
Fax: 213-629-4520

Bankruptcy, Insolvency, Corporate Reorganization, Commercial Law and Creditor's Rights. General Civil and Trial Practice.

FIRM PROFILE: Sulmeyer, Kupetz, Baumann & Rothman foresaw the need for specialists in bankruptcy nearly forty years ago. Our experience and creative approach in representing creditors and debtors in reorganization cases has earned the firm a national reputation. Our insolvency attorneys represent secured creditors, creditor's committees, bankruptcy trustees, receivers and business debtors, purchasers of assets, trade and other unsecured creditors, governmental agencies and title insurance companies, among others.

**IRVING SULMEYER,** born New York, N.Y., July 22, 1927; admitted to bar, 1952, California; U.S. District Court, Central District of California; U.S. Court of Appeals, Ninth Circuit; U.S. Supreme Court. *Education:* California Institute of Technology (B.S., 1948); Stanford University (J.D., 1951). Phi Alpha Delta; Order of the Coif. Member, Board of Editors, Stanford Law Review, 1950-1951. Contributing Editor, Collier Bankruptcy Practice Guide, 1981-1983. Author: "Collier Handbook for Trustees," 1993; "Collier Handbook for Creditors' Committees," 1988. Adjunct Professor, Pepperdine Law School. *Member:* Los Angeles County and American Bar Associations; State Bar of California. Fellow, American College of Bankruptcy. [U.S.N.R., 1945-1946]. *PRACTICE AREAS:* Bankruptcy. **Email:** isulmeyer@skbr.com

**ARNOLD L. KUPETZ,** born Denver, Colorado, June 30, 1933; admitted to bar, 1956, Colorado; 1960, California; U.S. District Court, Central and Southern Districts of California and District of Colorado; U.S. Court of Appeals, Ninth Circuit. *Education:* University of Colorado and Univer-

*(This Listing Continued)*

## SULMEYER, KUPETZ, BAUMANN & ROTHMAN, A PROFESSIONAL CORPORATION, Los Angeles—Continued

sity of Denver (B.S., 1955); University of Denver (J.D., 1956). Clerk for Justice O. Otto Moore, Supreme Court of Colorado, 1955. Member: Panel of Trustees, United States Trustee's Office, Central District of California; "Approved/Qualified Receivers List," Los Angeles Superior Court. *Member:* Los Angeles County Bar Association; The State Bar of California. [Judge Advocate General Corps, U.S.A.F., 1956-1959]. *PRACTICE AREAS:* Bankruptcy; Federal and State Court Receiverships. *Email:* akupetz@skbr.com

**RICHARD G. BAUMANN,** born Chicago, Illinois, April 7, 1938; admitted to bar, 1964, Wisconsin; 1970, California; 1973, U.S. Supreme Court. *Education:* University of Wisconsin (B.S., cum laude, 1960; J.D., 1964). Phi Delta Phi. Author: "Legal Aspects of Collecting an Account Receivable," American Lawyers Quarterly, July, 1987. Judge Pro Tem, Los Angeles Municipal Court, 1980—. Contributing Editor, Commercial Law Journal. Board of Directors, National Institute on Credit Management. Board of Directors, Academy of Commercial and Bankruptcy Law Specialists. *Member:* Los Angeles County Bar Association; State Bar of Wisconsin; State Bar of California; Commercial Law League of America (Member, Board of Governors, 1986-1992; President, 1990-1991). Fellow, Commercial Law Foundation; National Conference of Bar Presidents. *PRACTICE AREAS:* Commercial Law. *Email:* rbaumann@skbr.com

**DON ROTHMAN,** born Chicago, Illinois, July 2, 1936; admitted to bar, 1966, California. *Education:* University of California at Berkeley and Coe College (B.A., 1957); University of Southern California (J.D., 1966). Phi Alpha Delta. Winner, Moot Court Competition. Chairman, Los Angeles County Housing Commission, 1982. *Member:* Los Angeles County Bar Association (Member, Commercial Law and Bankruptcy Section); State Bar of California. *PRACTICE AREAS:* Bankruptcy. *Email:* drothman@skbr.com

**ALAN G. TIPPIE,** born Massillon, Ohio, October 11, 1953; admitted to bar, 1979, California. *Education:* Kent State University and Ohio State University (B.A., 1976); Loyola Law School of Los Angeles (J.D., 1979). Member, St. Thomas More Law Honor Society. Member, Loyola Law Review, 1978-1979. Adjunct Professor, Loyola Law School, Los Angeles, 1987. Law Clerk to the Honorable Barry Russell, United States Bankruptcy Court, 1979-1980. *Member:* Los Angeles County Bar Association (Member, Commercial Law and Bankruptcy Section); State Bar of California; Financial Lawyers' Conference. *PRACTICE AREAS:* Financial Restructuring; Bankruptcy; Business Litigation. *Email:* atippie@skbr.com

**ISRAEL SAPERSTEIN,** born Los Angeles, California, May 8, 1945; admitted to bar, 1978, California. *Education:* California State University at Los Angeles (B.S., 1973); Whittier College School of Law (J.D., 1978). Judge Pro Tempore, Los Angeles Superior Court. Prior Speaker, CLLA/CLE Satellite Network Program. *Member:* Los Angeles County Bar Association (Member, Litigation Section; Commercial Law and Bankruptcy Section); State Bar of California; Financial Lawyers' Conference. (Certified Specialist, Small Business and Personal Bankruptcy, The State Bar of California Board of Legal Specialization). *PRACTICE AREAS:* Bankruptcy; Commercial Litigation. *Email:* isaperstein@skbr.com

**VICTOR A. SAHN,** born New York, N.Y., June 27, 1954; admitted to bar, 1980, California. *Education:* Syracuse University (B.A., cum laude, 1976); University of San Diego School of Law (J.D., 1979). Legal Intern to the Honorable Herbert Katz, United States Bankruptcy Court, San Diego, California, 1978-1979. Law Clerk to the Honorable Peter M. Elliott, United States Bankruptcy Court, Santa Ana, California, 1979-1981. *Member:* Los Angeles County Bar Association (Member, Bankruptcy Subcommittee); State Bar of California; Financial Lawyers' Conference. *PRACTICE AREAS:* Bankruptcy; Business Litigation. *Email:* vsahn@skbr.com

**STEVEN R. WAINESS,** born Culver City, California, February 2, 1950; admitted to bar, 1982, California. *Education:* Los Angeles Valley College (A.A., 1975); California State University, Northridge; San Fernando Valley College of Law (J.D., 1981). *Member:* State Bar of California; Association of Business Trial Lawyers; Commercial Law League of America; Los Angeles Bankruptcy Forum; Financial Lawyers Conference. *PRACTICE AREAS:* Bankruptcy; Commercial Litigation. *Email:* swainess@skbr.com

**DAVID S. KUPETZ,** born Los Angeles, California, January 17, 1961; admitted to bar, 1986, California. *Education:* University of California at Santa Barbara (B.S., 1983); University of California, Hastings College of the Law (J.D., 1986). Participant, COMM/ENT, Hastings Journal of Communications and Entertainment Law, 1984-1985. Note Editor, COMM/ENT, Hastings Journal of Communications and Entertainment Law, 1985-1986. Author: Note, "Cable's 'Non-Cable Communications Services': Cable Television as a Common Carrier," 8 COMM/ENT 75 (1985); Author: "Break Up Fees in Bankruptcy," Commercial Law Bulletin, Volume 9, No. 4 (July/August, 1994); "Sales of Substantially All Assets of Chapter 11 Bankruptcy Estates Outside of a Plan," Commercial Law Bulletin, Volume 9, No. 5 (September/October, 1994); "Basic Issues and Alternatives Facing Litigators When Bankruptcy Interrupts the Litigation Process," Commercial Law Journal, Volume 99, No. 4. pp. 401-45 (Winter 1994). "Chapter and Verse - An Analysis of Municipal Debt Adjustment Under the Bankruptcy Code," Los Angeles Daily Journal, pp. 7-8 (April 13, 1995). "Municipal Debt Adjustment - A Look at How Chapter 9 Allowed Orange County to Provide Essential Services While Undergoing Debt Restructuring," The Federal Lawyer, Volume 42, No. 4, pp. 18-24 (May 1995). "Intellectual Property Issues in Chapter 11 Bankruptcy Reorganization Cases," IDEA: The Journal of Law and Technology," Volume 35, No. 4, pp. 383-406 (1995). "Municipal Debt Adjustment Under the Bankruptcy Code," Government Finance Review, Volume 11, No. 3, pp. 27-29 (June 1995). "The Deficits of Orange County," Los Angeles Lawyer (July-August 1995). "Municipal Debt Adjustment Under the Bankruptcy Code," Municipal Attorney, Volume 36, No. 4 (July/August 1995), "City Limits - Legislature Considers Conditions on Chapter 9 Relief," Los Angeles Daily Journal (September 12, 1995). "Municipal Debt Adjustment Under the Bankruptcy Code," The Urban Lawyer, Volumbe 27, No. 3, pp. 531-604 (Summer 1995). Contributing Author: Collier Forms Manual, (Matthew Bender). *Member:* Los Angeles County Bar Association; State Bar of California; Financial Lawyers Conference; Los Angeles Bankruptcy Forum. *PRACTICE AREAS:* Bankruptcy. *Email:* dkupetz@skbr.com

**HOWARD M. EHRENBERG,** born New York, N.Y., February 19, 1961; admitted to bar, 1986, California. *Education:* University of California at Berkeley (B.A., 1983); University of Southern California School of Law (J.D., 1986). Phi Alpha Delta. *Member:* State Bar of California (Member, Panel of Chapter 7 Trustees for the Central District of California); Financial Lawyers' Conference; Los Angeles Bankruptcy Forum. (Certified in Business Bankruptcy Law by the American Board of Bankruptcy Certification). *PRACTICE AREAS:* Bankruptcy. *Email:* hehrenberg@skbr.com

**KATHRYN KERFES,** born Kansas City, Kansas, November 12, 1946; admitted to bar, 1981, California; 1984, U.S. District Court, Central District of California; 1985, U.S. Court of Appeals, Ninth Circuit. *Education:* University of California at Los Angeles (B.A., 1976); Whittier College (J.D., 1980). Recipient, American Jurisprudence Award in Criminal Procedure. *Member:* Los Angeles County Bar Association; State Bar of California; Financial Lawyers Conference; Los Angeles Bankruptcy Forum. (Certified in Business Bankruptcy Law by the American Board of Bankruptcy Certification). *PRACTICE AREAS:* Bankruptcy. *Email:* kkerfes@skbr.com

---

**NATHAN H. HARRIS,** born Boston, Massachusetts, October 20, 1944; admitted to bar, 1972, California. *Education:* San Diego State College (B.A., 1967); Hastings College of Law, University of California (J.D., 1972). Contributing Editor, California Continuing Legal Education, Enforcement of Civil Judgments. *Member:* Los Angeles County Bar Association; State Bar of California; Commercial Law League of America. *PRACTICE AREAS:* Commercial Law. *Email:* nharris@skbr.com

**SUSAN FRANCES MOLEY,** born England, May 7, 1963; admitted to bar, 1992, California. *Education:* Loyola Marymount University (B.S., Accounting, Honors Program, 1985); Georgetown University Law Center (J.D., 1991). Recipient, Adam Smith Economics Award, 1982. Licensed Certified Public Accountant, California. *Member:* State Bar of California; Financial Lawyers Conference. *PRACTICE AREAS:* Bankruptcy. *Email:* smoley@skbr.com

**MATTHEW ROTHMAN,** born Los Angeles, California, October 8, 1965; admitted to bar, 1991, California. *Education:* Pomona College (B.A., 1987); Loyola Law School (J.D., 1991). Phi Delta Phi. Member, Editor, Loyola Law Review, 1990-1991. Author: "Responsible Persons and Irresponsible Doctrine: The Allocation of the Bankrupt's Postpetition Payments on Unpaid Prepetition Federal Taxes," 95 Com. L.J. 24, 1990. *Member:* State Bar of California; Commercial Law League of America; Financial Lawyers Conference. *PRACTICE AREAS:* Bankruptcy; Insolvency. *Email:* mrothman@skbr.com

**WESLEY AVERY,** born Inglewood, California, September 18, 1958; admitted to bar, 1991, California. *Education:* University of California (B.A., 1980; J.D., 1984); Harvard University (M.B.A., 1984). Phi Beta Kappa. Phi

*(This Listing Continued)*

Kappa Phi. California Real Estate Broker's License, 1992. *Member:* State Bar of California. PRACTICE AREAS: Bankruptcy. *Email:* wavery@skbr.com

MARK S. HOROUPIAN, born Winnipeg, Manitoba, Canada, December 11, 1969; admitted to bar, 1994, California. *Education:* University of California, Santa Barbara (B.A., 1991); Loyola Law School, Los Angeles (J.D., 1994); University of San Diego Institute of International and Comparative Law (Paris, France). Member, Loyola Law Review, 1992-1993. *Member:* Los Angeles County Bar Association; State Bar of California; Financial Lawyers Conference. *Email:* mhoroupian@skbr.com

STEPHEN C. SETO, born Montreal, Quebec, Canada, January 13, 1967; admitted to bar, 1994, California. *Education:* Colgate University (B.A., 1988) Omicron Delta Epsilon (National Economics Honor Society); University of Southern California School of Law (J.D., 1994). Law Clerk to the Honorable John E. Ryan, United States Bankruptcy Court, Central District (1995). Judicial Extern to the Honorable James N. Barr, United States Bankruptcy Court, Central District (1992). *Member:* State Bar of California; Financial Lawyers Conference. PRACTICE AREAS: Bankruptcy Law; Business Litigation. *Email:* sseto@skbr.com

HOWARD N. MADRIS, born New York, N.Y., June 30, 1966; admitted to bar, 1991, California. *Education:* Cornell University (B.S., 1988); Boston University (J.D., 1991). First Place, Boston University Law Negotiation Competition, 1989; second place in Northeast Regional. Member: Financial Lawyers' Conference; Board of Directors of the Cornell University Southern California Alumni Association. *Member:* State Bar of California. PRACTICE AREAS: Bankruptcy Law; Business LItigation. *Email:* hmadris@skbr.com

TANYA M. VINCE, born Anaheim, California, December 3, 1969; admitted to bar, 1994, California. *Education:* University of California, Riverside (B.S., 1991); McGeorge School of Law (J.D., 1994). Law Clerk to the Honorable David N. Naugle, United State Bankruptcy Court (1994-1996). Judicial Extern to the Honorable Christopher M. Klein, United States Bankruptcy Court (1993). Judicial Extern to the Honorable Barry Russell, United States Bankruptcy Court, Ninth Circuit Bankruptcy Appellate Panel (1993). *Member:* State Bar of California; Financial Lawyers Conference. PRACTICE AREAS: Bankruptcy Law; Business Litigation. *Email:* tvince@skbr.com

*OF COUNSEL*

MARILYN S. SCHEER, born Mapleton, Iowa, June 10, 1954; admitted to bar, 1979, Iowa and U.S. District Court, Northern and Southern Districts of Iowa; 1983, U.S. Court of Appeals, Eighth Circuit; 1987, California, U.S. District Court, Southern and Northern Districts of California and U.S. Court of Appeals, Ninth Circuit. *Education:* University of South Dakota (B.A., with honors, 1976); Drake University (J.D., 1979). Phi Beta Kappa; Order of the Coif. Member, Drake University Law Review, 1978-1979. *Member:* Los Angeles, San Fernando Valley (Member, Executive Committee, Business Section, 1990-1993), Iowa State and American Bar Associations; State Bar of California; Financial Lawyers Association; Bankruptcy Forum. PRACTICE AREAS: Bankruptcy; Creditor's Rights; General Litigation. *Email:* mscheer@skbr.com

FRANK VRAM ZERUNYAN, born Istanbul, Turkey, September 17, 1959; admitted to bar, 1989, California, U.S. District Court, Central District of California; 1994, U. S. Court of International Trade; 1995, District of Columbia Court of Appeals. *Education:* College Samuel Moorat (French Baccalaureate, 1978); California State University at Long Beach (B.A., 1982); Western State University (J.D., 1985); University of Southern California Law Center (Certificate of Corporate Taxation, 1988). *Member:* Los Angeles (Member, Financial Lawyers Conference) Bar Association; State Bar of California. LANGUAGES: Armenian, French and Turkish. PRACTICE AREAS: Real Estate; Litigation; Loan Workouts; Reorganizations; Bankruptcy Litigation; Commercial Lease Practice; Tort Law; Business Law. *Email:* fzerunyan@skbr.com

SUZANNE L. WEAKLEY, born San Francisco, California, July 22, 1945; admitted to bar, 1979, Colorado; 1987, California, U.S. Court of Appeals, Ninth and Tenth Circuits and U.S. District Court, Central District of California and District of Colorado. *Education:* Stanford University (A.B., 1966); University of Denver (J.D., 1979). Member, Order of St. Ives. Member and General Editor, 1977-1979, Denver Law Journal. Author: "Title III of the Americans with Disabilities Act of 1990," 9 California Real Property Journal 46 (Fall, 1991); "Antitrust Overview: 5th Annual Tenth Circuit Survey, 1977-1978," 56 Denver Law Journal 395, 1979. Law Clerk to Hon. William E. Doyle, U.S. Court of Appeals, Tenth Judicial Circuit, Denver, Colorado, 1979-1980. *Member:* Los Angeles County (Member, Commercial Law Committee, Commercial Law and Bankruptcy Section, 1992—) and American (Member, Section of Business Law, Ad Hoc Committee on Payment Systems, 1988-1990) Bar Associations; State Bar of California. PRACTICE AREAS: Bankruptcy; Financial Transactions. *Email:* sweakley@skbr.com

ELISSA D. MILLER, born Los Angeles, California, October 11, 1955; admitted to bar, 1985, California. *Education:* University of California at Los Angeles (B.A., 1977); Southwestern University School of Law (J.D., with honors, 1985). Member, Moot Court Honors Program. Legal Extern to the Honorable Arthur Alarcon, United States Court of Appeals for the Ninth Circuit. Law Clerk to the Honorable Robert Devich, Justice of California Courts of Appeal, Second District, Division One, 1986. Judge Pro Tempore of the Los Angeles County Municipal Court. Board Member and Officer of Women's Clinic, a Los Angeles community based health and counseling center. Board Member, Project New Hope. *Member:* Los Angeles County and American Bar Associations; State Bar of California; Women Lawyers of Los Angeles; Financial Lawyers Conference; Bankruptcy Forum and Women Bankruptcy Professionals. PRACTICE AREAS: Bankruptcy Law; Business Litigation; Entertainment Litigation. *Email:* emiller@skbr.com

REPRESENTATIVE CLIENTS: General Electric Capitol Corp.; Bank; Continental Insurance Co.; MCC Powers, Inc.; California Southwest Management Co.; North American Phillips Corp.; Phillips Credit Corp.; The Selmer Company; Heller Financial Inc.; Transamerica Occidental Life Insurance Co.; Transamerica Realty Services, Inc.; Afco Acceptance Corp.; Pacific Business Bank; Integon Life Insurance Corp.; Body Glove International; Norwest Financial; Litton Industries; Litton Aerospace; Ventura Port District; Ocean Pacific Sunwear, Ltd.

---

# PAUL D. SUPNIK

### LOS ANGELES, CALIFORNIA

(See Beverly Hills)

*Domestic and International Copyright and Trademark Law, Motion Picture, Television, Publishing, Media and General Entertainment Law, Multimedia and Computer Law, Licensing, Related Litigation.*

---

# SWAIN & DIPOLITO

### LOS ANGELES, CALIFORNIA

(See Long Beach)

*General Civil, Trial and Appellate Practice in all State and Federal Courts. Admiralty and Maritime, Transportation, Labor and Employment, General Liability and Insurance Law.*

---

# SWERDLOW, FLORENCE & SANCHEZ

*A LAW CORPORATION*

### LOS ANGELES, CALIFORNIA

(See Beverly Hills)

*Management, Labor and Employment Law.*

---

# SYLVESTER & OPPENHEIM

Established in 1983

15260 VENTURA BOULEVARD, SUITE 1500 (SHERMAN OAKS)
### LOS ANGELES, CALIFORNIA 91403
Telephone: 818-905-5200
FAX: 818-789-6078

*General Trial and Appellate Litigation, Insurance Defense, Public Entity Defense, Entertainment and Intellectual Property Law.*

*MEMBERS OF FIRM*

LEE SYLVESTER, born Rochester, New York, October 26, 1930; admitted to bar, 1955, New York; 1967, California and U.S. District Court, Central District of California. *Education:* University of Rochester (A.B., 1952); Harvard Law School (J.D., 1955). *Member:* Los Angeles County Bar Association; State Bar of California (Member, Litigation Section and Intellectual Property Section); Association of Southern California Defense

*(This Listing Continued)*

## SYLVESTER & OPPENHEIM, Los Angeles—Continued

Counsel. *PRACTICE AREAS:* Trial Practice; Appellate Litigation; Insurance Defense Law; Public Entity Law.

**RICHARD D. OPPENHEIM, JR.,** born New York, N.Y., September 20, 1952; admitted to bar, 1977, California; 1978, U.S. District Court, Central District of California. *Education:* University of California at Santa Cruz and University of California at Los Angeles (B.A., cum laude, 1975); Loyola University of Los Angeles (J.D., 1977). Recipient: American Jurisprudence Awards in Trusts and Criminal Procedure. *Member:* Los Angeles County Bar Association; State Bar of California; Defense Research Institute; Southern California Defense Counsel. *PRACTICE AREAS:* Trial Practice; Appellate Litigation; Insurance Defense Law; Public Entity Law.

### ASSOCIATES

**RICHARD J. SCHLEGEL,** born Akron, Ohio, February 12, 1945; admitted to bar, 1974, California; 1975, U.S. District Court, Central District of California. *Education:* Miami University (B.S., 1967); Southwestern University (J.D., cum laude, 1974). Phi Alpha Delta. Note and Comment Editor, Southwestern University Law Review, 1973-1974. Author: "Silverhart v. Mount Zion Hospital. A Re-examination of the Hospital: Patient Relationship," 5 Southwestern University Law Review 279, 1973. *Member:* Los Angeles County Bar Association; State Bar of California; Association of Southern California Defense Counsel. *PRACTICE AREAS:* Insurance Defense.

**GARY R. KAPLAN,** born August 13, 1958; admitted to bar, 1983, California. *Education:* Seton Hall University (B.A., 1980); Southwestern University School of Law (J.D., 1982). *Member:* Los Angeles County and American Bar Associations; State Bar of California; California Trial Lawyers Association; American Trial Lawyers Association. *PRACTICE AREAS:* Governmental Tort Liability; Contracts; Bad Faith; Medical Malpractice; Legal Malpractice; Product Liability; Construction.

REPRESENTATIVE CLIENTS: Allstate Insurance Co.; American Hardware; American National Insurance Company; American National Property & Casualty Company; Argonaut Insurance; Carl Warren & Company; Farmers Insurance Group; Fireman's Fund Insurance Company; Industrial Indemnity; Maryland Casualty; Mini Storage Insurance Corporation; Philadelphia Insurance Companies; Royal Insurance Company; State Farm Fire & Casualty Insurance Company; State Farm Mutual Automobile Insurance Company; Transportation Casualty Insurance Company; Sisk II; HCM Claim Mgmt Corp.; ESIS, Inc.; Sedgwick James of CA., Inc.

---

## ERICA TABACHNICK

1200 WILSHIRE BOULEVARD, SUITE 400
**LOS ANGELES, CALIFORNIA 90017**
Telephone: 213-482-1600
Facsimile: 213-482-0515

Lawyer Disciplinary and Admissions Matters, Reinstatements, Ethics Consultations, Legal Malpractice, Professional Liability, Defense of Professional Licensing Proceedings.

FIRM PROFILE: *Erica Tabachnick specializes in the representation of attorneys and other professionals in licensing proceedings at both the trial and appellate levels. The firm also defends and prosecutes legal and other professional malpractice cases and provides ethics consultation and advice and expert testimony.*

**ERICA TABACHNICK,** born Biloxi, Mississippi, February 4, 1953; admitted to bar, 1980, California and U.S. District Court, Central District of California; 1988, U.S. Supreme Court. *Education:* University of California at Los Angeles (B.A., cum laude, 1975); Loyola University of Los Angeles (J.D., 1980). Senior Trial Counsel, State Bar of California, 1984-1991. Author, "Attorney-Client Pitfalls," LA Lawyer, November 1994. *Member:* Los Angeles County Bar Association (Errors and Omissions Prevention and Judicial Evaluations Committees); Los Angeles Consumer Attorney's Association; Los Angeles Women Lawyers Association; California Women Lawyers; California Academy of Attorneys for Health Care Professionals. *REPORTED CASES:* Read vs. State Bar, 53 Cal.3rd 394; Stanley vs. State Bar, 50 Cal.3rd 555; Billings vs. State Bar, 50 Cal.3rd 358; Farnham vs. State Bar, 47 Cal.3rd 429; Greenbaum vs. State Bar, 43 Cal.3rd 543; In the matter of Nelson 1 Cal. State Bar Ct.Rptr. 178. *PRACTICE AREAS:* Lawyer Disciplinary and Admissions Defense; Legal Malpractice; Mental Health Therapists Licensure Defense; Ethics Consultations and Testimony.

---

## TAKAKJIAN & SOWERS

Established in 1989

WESTSIDE TOWERS, SUITE 1000
11845 WEST OLYMPIC BOULEVARD
**LOS ANGELES, CALIFORNIA 90064**
Telephone: 310-312-8055
Telecopier: 310-312-8189

*San Fernando Valley, California Office:* 16501 Ventura Blvd, Encino, California. Telephone: 818-379-8588. Fax: 818-789-3391.
*Ventura County, California Office:* 300 Esplanade Drive, Oxnard, California. Telephone: 805-522-0720. Fax: 805-988-0570.
*Orange County, California Office:* 333 City Boulevard West, Suite 1700, Orange, California. Telephone: 714-456-9955. Fax: 714-938-3255.
*San Gabriel Valley, California Office:* 225 South Lake Avenue, 9th Floor, Pasadena, California. Telephone: 818-242-0042. Fax: 818-795-6321.
*South Bay, California Office:* World Trade Center, Suite 800, Long Beach, California. Telephone: 310-424-7337. Fax: 310-983-8199.

Criminal Law.

FIRM PROFILE: *The firm limits its practice to matters of criminal defense. Mr. Takakjian is one of only 318 Criminal Law Specialists out of over 117,000 attorneys practicing Law in the State of California. The firm has over 35 years of combined Criminal Investigation, Prosecution and Defense Trial Experience and concentrates in Criminal Law Litigation throughout Southern California. Both Mr. Takakjian and Mr. Sowers are former deputy district attorneys and Mr. Sowers is a former police detective and a current instructor at the Los Angeles County Sheriff's Academy.*

### MEMBERS OF FIRM

**PAUL TAKAKJIAN,** born Los Angeles, California, November 16, 1953; admitted to bar, 1979, California; 1980, U.S. District Court, Central District of California. *Education:* University of California at Los Angeles (B.A., cum laude, 1975); Loyola Marymount (J.D., 1979). Member, Loyola of Los Angeles Law Review, 1978-1979. Instructor: California New Prosecutor's College, 1985. Former Deputy District Attorney, Los Angeles County, 1981-1987. *Member:* Los Angeles County Bar Association (Member, Criminal Justice Section, 1988—); State Bar of California; Criminal Courts Bar Association; National Association of Criminal Defense Lawyers; California Attorneys for Criminal Justice. (Certified Specialist, Criminal Law, The State Bar of California Board of Legal Specialization). *LANGUAGES:* French. *REPORTED CASES:* P. v. Tamborrino (1989) 215 Cal. App. 3d 575 263 Ca. RPTR. 731. *PRACTICE AREAS:* Criminal Defense.

**DONALD G. SOWERS,** born Los Angeles, California, February 7, 1953; admitted to bar, 1986, California and U.S. District Court, Central District of California. *Education:* Moorpark College (A.S., 1983); Southwestern University School of Law (J.D., 1985). Phi Alpha Delta. Judge Pro Tem, Santa Monica and Malibu Municipal Courts. Recipient: Detective of the Year Award, Santa Monica, Police Department, 1985. Instructor, Laws of Arrest, Search and Seizure, Evidence, Los Angeles County Sheriff's Academy, 1988—. Police Detective, Santa Monica Police Department, 1977-1986. Chairman of the Board, Make-A-Wish Foundation of Los Angeles, 1984—. President, Student Bar Association, 1982-1983; President, Alumni Association; Member, Board of Trustees, Southwestern University School of Law. Deputy District Attorney, Los Angeles County, 1986-1989. *Member:* Malibu, Santa Monica, Los Angeles County (Vice-Chairman, Executive Committee, Criminal Justice Section) and American Bar Associations. *PRACTICE AREAS:* Criminal Defense.

---

## LAW OFFICES OF
## RONALD M. TAKEHARA

2049 CENTURY PARK EAST, SUITE 1100
**LOS ANGELES, CALIFORNIA 90067**
Telephone: 310-785-3880
Fax: 310-785-3882
Email: rmtlaw@aol.com

General Civil Litigation, Business, Entertainment, Insurance, Subrogation, Bad Faith and Personal Injury Law.

**RONALD M. TAKEHARA,** born Los Angeles, California, April 12, 1962; admitted to bar, 1987, California. *Education:* California State University at Northridge (B.A., 1984); McGeorge School of Law, University of the Pacific (J.D., 1987). Recipient, American Jurisprudence Award in Commu-

*(This Listing Continued)*

nity Property. *Member:* Los Angeles County and American Bar Associations. (Associate, Sedgwick, Detert, Moran & Arnold, 1992-1994).

REPRESENTATIVE CLIENTS: Toyota Motor Sales, USA Inc.; Toyota Motors Distributors, USA Inc. and Toyota Motor Credit Corporation ; Tokio Marine & Fire Insurance Company; Certain Underwriters at LLoyds, London; The Elliot Group; CBS, Inc.; Performance Textiles, Inc.; KingWorld Productions; Inside Edition; National Wildlife Federation.

## TALCOTT, LIGHTFOOT, VANDEVELDE & SADOWSKY

*Established in 1977*
THIRTEENTH FLOOR
655 SOUTH HOPE STREET
LOS ANGELES, CALIFORNIA 90017
Telephone: 213-622-4750
Fax: 213-622-2690

*General Civil and Criminal Trial and Appellate Practice in all State and Federal Courts.*

FIRM PROFILE: *The firm was formed in 1977 to specialize in criminal defense and related civil litigation, including civil rights litigation. It has grown to become one of the largest firms in Los Angeles to practice primarily in those areas. The attorneys have extensive experience in both the federal and state courts. There are three former Assistant United States Attorneys, two former Deputy Federal Public Defenders, two former law clerks to federal judges and one to a state court chief justice. They have a broad range of experience in the defense of corporations and individuals charged with white collar crime, including environmental cases, defense and other government contract cases, health care cases, investment and tax fraud cases, financial institution cases, and criminal antitrust cases. They have defended and prosecuted a variety of civil cases, including business fraud cases, and civil rights cases.*

### MEMBERS OF FIRM

**ROBERT M. TALCOTT,** born New Haven, Connecticut, September 18, 1932; admitted to bar, 1959, District of Columbia; 1962, U.S. Supreme Court; 1966, California. *Education:* University of Connecticut (B.A., 1954); Georgetown University (J.D., 1958; LL.M., 1961). Phi Alpha Delta. Adjunct Professor of Law, Loyola Law School, 1974-1984. Special Atty., Criminal Div., U.S. Dept. of Justice, Washington, D.C., 1961-1964. Asst. U.S. Atty. Criminal Div., Central District of California, U.S. Dept. of Justice, 1964-1967. Special Hearing Officer, U.S. Department of Justice, 1967-1968. President, Board of Police Commissioners, City of Los Angeles, 1984-1990. *Member:* Los Angeles County (Member, Board of Trustees, 1980-1982), Federal (President, Los Angeles Chapter, 1976-1977) and American Bar Associations; The State Bar of California (Member, Board of Governors and Vice President, 1988-1991); Los Angeles County Bar Foundation (Member Board of Directors, 1987-1993). Fellow, American College of Trial Lawyers. **PRACTICE AREAS:** Criminal Defense Law; Civil Litigation; Appellate Law.

**MICHAEL J. LIGHTFOOT,** born Brooklyn, New York, April 7, 1939; admitted to bar, 1964, Virginia; 1971, California. *Education:* Fordham University (A.B., 1960); University of Virginia (LL.B., 1964). Editor: Federal Criminal Practice Manual, California Public Defenders Association, 1974. Professor of Law, Loyola Law School, 1973-1985. Trial Attorney, U.S. Department of Justice, Civil Rights Division, 1964-1968. Assistant U.S. Attorney, Criminal Division, Central District of California, 1968-1971. Chief Deputy, Federal Public Defenders' Office, 1972-1973. *Member:* Los Angeles County Bar Association; The State Bar of California (Member, Judicial Nominees Evaluation Commission, 1989-1991); California Attorneys for Criminal Justice (Member, Board of Governors, 1984-1990). **PRACTICE AREAS:** Criminal Defense Law; Civil Litigation; Civil Rights Litigation; Appellate Law.

**JOHN D. VANDEVELDE,** born The Hague, Netherlands, March 30, 1946; admitted to bar, 1975, California; 1984, U.S. Supreme Court. *Education:* California Polytechnic State University (B.S., 1968); Loyola Law School (J.D., magna cum laude, 1975). Member, Loyola Law Review, 1974-1975. Teaching Fellow, Legal Research and Writing, Loyola Law School, 1974-1975. Author: "United States v. Robinson," 7 Loyola Law Review 516, 1974. Assistant United States Attorney, Central District of California, 1976-1980 (Assistant Chief of Criminal Division, 1979-1980). Member, Board of Directors, Legal Aid Foundation of Los Angeles, 1995—. *Member:* Los Angeles County (Chair: Law Enforcement and Justice Committee, 1991-1993; Chair, Ad Hoc Committee on 1991 Federal Crime Bill; Member, Federal Courts Committee), Federal (President, Los Angeles Chapter,

*(This Listing Continued)*

1979-1980; Chairperson, Federal Appointments Committee, 1980-1983; Program Coordinator, Federal Bridging-The-Gap Seminar, 1980-1982; Member, Federal Indigent Defense Panel, 1980-1983, 1985-1987) and American (Member, Vice Chair, White Collar Crime Committee, 1996—; Chair, Western Regional Subcommittee, 1994-1996) Bar Associations; California Attorneys for Criminal Justice; National Association of Criminal Defense Lawyers; Criminal Courts Bar Association. Fellow, American College of Trial Lawyers. [Lt. Cmdr., U.S. Coast Guard Reserve, 1968-1972]. **PRACTICE AREAS:** Criminal Defense Law; Civil Litigation; Appellate Law.

**STEPHEN B. SADOWSKY,** born Brooklyn, New York, December 29, 1948; admitted to bar, 1979, California. *Education:* Yeshiva University (B.A., magna cum laude, 1969); University of California at Berkeley (M.A., 1971); Boalt Hall School of Law, University of California (J.D., 1979). Teaching Associate, Legal Research and Writing, Boalt Hall School of Law, 1978-1979. Law Clerk to Hon. John C. Mowbray, Chief Justice, Nevada Supreme Court, 1979-1980. *Member:* Los Angeles County, Federal (Member, Federal Indigent Defense Panel, 1986-1989) and American Bar Associations; The State Bar of California; National Association of Criminal Defense Lawyers; California Attorneys for Criminal Justice. **REPORTED CASES:** United States v. City of Rancho Palos Verdes, 841 F.2d 329 (9th Cir. 1988); U.S. v. Helmandollar, 852 F.2d 498 (9th Cir. 1988); Chizen v. Hunter, 809 F.2d 560 (9th Cir. 1986); United States v. Duz-Mor Diagnostic Laboratory, Inc., 650 F.2d 223 (9th Cir. 1981). **PRACTICE AREAS:** Criminal Defense Law; Civil Litigation; Appellate Law.

**JOHN S. CROUCHLEY,** born Kittery, Maine, February 4, 1958; admitted to bar, 1984, California. *Education:* Creighton University (B.A., cum laude, 1980); Loyola Law School (J.D., cum laude, 1984). Member, St. Thomas More Honor Society. Law Clerk to Hon. William D. Keller, U.S. District Judge, Central District of California, 1984-1985. Member, Federal Indigent Defense Panel, 1988-1989. *Member:* Los Angeles County, Federal and American Bar Associations; State Bar of California; California Attorneys for Criminal Justice. **PRACTICE AREAS:** Criminal Defense Law; Civil Litigation; Appellate Law.

**JOHN P. MARTIN,** born Chicago, Illinois, August 20, 1958; admitted to bar, 1984, California; 1988, U.S. Supreme Court. *Education:* Stanford University (A.B., 1980); Loyola Law School (J.D., 1984); Freie Universitaet, West Berlin (Rotary Foundation Scholar, 1984-1985). Deputy Federal Public Defender, Central District of California, 1985-1988. Member, Federal Indigent Defense Panel, 1989-1992. *Member:* Los Angeles County, Federal and American (Member, Vice Chair, White Collar Crime West Coast Regional Subcommittee; Regional Liaison, White Collar Crime National Committee) Bar Associations; State Bar of California (Member, Client Security Fund Commission); National Association of Criminal Defense Lawyers; California Attorneys for Criminal Justice. **LANGUAGES:** German. **REPORTED CASES:** United States v. Delgadillo-Velasquez, 856 F.2d 1292 (9th Cir. 1988). **PRACTICE AREAS:** Criminal Defense Law; Appellate Law; Civil Litigation.

**MELISSA N. WIDDIFIELD,** born New York, N.Y., December 24, 1958; admitted to bar, 1987, California. *Education:* University of California at Los Angeles (B.A., 1983); Loyola Law School (J.D., 1987). Articles Editor, Loyola Entertainment Law Journal, 1985-1986. Author: Note, "Access of the Hearing Impaired to Television Programming," 5 Loy. Ent. L.J. 188, 1985. Law Clerk to Hon. Consuelo B. Marshall, U.S. District Judge, Central District of California, 1988-1989. *Member:* State Bar of California; California Attorneys for Criminal Justice (Member, Board of Governors); National Association of Criminal Defense Lawyers; Women Lawyers Association of Los Angeles (Member, Board of Governors; Chair, Criminal Law Section). **PRACTICE AREAS:** Criminal Defense Law; Civil Rights Law; Civil Litigation.

### ASSOCIATE

**JAMES H. LOCKLIN,** born Rochester, New York, July 12, 1968; admitted to bar, 1992, California. *Education:* Clarkson University (B.S., with great distinction, 1989); University of Southern California Law School (J.D., 1992). *Member:* Los Angeles County and American Bar Associations. **REPORTED CASES:** California Men's Colony, Unit II Men's Advisory Council v. Rowland, 939 F2d 854 (9th Cir. 1991). **PRACTICE AREAS:** Appellate Law; Criminal Defense Law; Civil Litigation.

REFERENCE: Sterling Bank, Los Angeles, California.

## FREDERIC B. TANKEL

*Established in 1973*

10507 WEST PICO BOULEVARD, SUITE 200
**LOS ANGELES, CALIFORNIA 90064**
Telephone: 310-470-6852
Fax: 310-470-3673

*General Civil and Trial Practice in all State and Federal Courts, Corporation, Real Estate, Trust and Probate Law.*

**FREDERIC B. TANKEL,** born Minneapolis, Minnesota, May 7, 1929; admitted to bar, 1954, Minnesota; 1956, California. *Education:* University of Minnesota (B.A., 1951); Harvard University (J.D., 1954). Examiner, State Bar of California, 1967-1968. *Member:* Beverly Hills, Los Angeles County and American (California Reporter for Committee on Significant Legislation, Real Property, 1973— ) Bar Associations; The State Bar of California.

REFERENCE: Far East National Bank.

---

## LAW OFFICES OF
## WILLIAM V. TARKANIAN

**LOS ANGELES, CALIFORNIA**

(See Pasadena)

*General Civil Trial in all State and Federal Courts. Family Law, Bankruptcy including Creditors, Debtors, Chapter 7, Chapter 11, Personal Injury.*

---

## LAW OFFICES OF
## BARRY TARLOW

A PROFESSIONAL CORPORATION

9119 SUNSET BOULEVARD
**LOS ANGELES, CALIFORNIA 90069**
Telephone: 310-278-2111
Cable Address: "Habeas"
Fax: 310-550-7055
Email: lobt@earthlink.net

*Criminal Trial and Appellate Practice, all State and Federal Courts.*

**BARRY TARLOW,** born Boston, Massachusetts, August 2, 1939; admitted to bar, 1965, California, U.S. Court of Appeals, 9th Circuit and U.S. District Court, Central, Southern and Northern Districts of California; 1971, U.S. Supreme Court. *Education:* Boston University (B.A., 1961; LL.B., cum laude, 1964). Editor, Boston University Law Review, 1962-1964. Recipient: Los Angeles Criminal Courts Bar Association, Special Award as a Zealous Defender of Constitutional Rights, 1993; National Association of Criminal Defense Lawyers Robert Heeney Memorial Award for Lifetime Achievement, 1992; Century City Bar Association Criminal Defense Lawyer of the Year, 1992; California State Bar Pro Bono Commendation, 1989. Assistant U.S. Attorney, Central District of California, Criminal Division, 1965. Author: "The Act of State Doctrine in American Courts," 44 Boston University Law Review 86, 1964; "Tarlow on Search Warrants," Courtroom Compendiums, 1972; "Admissibility of Polygraph Evidence in 1975: An Aid in Determining Credibility in a Perjury-Plagued System," 26 Hastings Law Journal, 917, 1975; "Witness for the Prosecution: A New Role For The Defense Attorney," 1 National Journal of Criminal Defense, 235, 1975; "Criminal Defendants and Abuse of Jeopardy Tax Procedures," 22 University of California at Los Angeles Law Review 1191, 1975; "Defense of A Federal Conspiracy Prosecution," 4 National Journal of Criminal Defense 183, 1978; "RICO: The New Darling of the Prosecutor's Nursery," 49 Fordham Law Review, 165, 1980; "RICO Revisited," 17 Georgia Law Review 291, 1983; "California Criminal Defense Practice," Vols. 1-6, Matthew Bender, 1980. Editor, National Directory of Criminal Lawyers, Gold Publishers, 1976— . Criminal Law Editor, Rico Litigation Reporter, 1985-1993. Member, Editorial Board, Sentencing Guidelines Law Reporter, 1989-1993. *Member:* Beverly Hills (Member, Criminal Law Committee, 1967-1991) and American (Member, Criminal Justice Section, Counsel, 1982-1983; Vice Chairman, 1983 and Chairman, RICO Criminal Law Subcommittee, 1981-1983, Committee on Prosecution and Defense of RICO Cases, 1982-1984) Bar Associations; The State Bar of California; California Attorneys for Criminal Justice (Member, Board of Governors, 1973-1975; Chairman, Seminar and Education Committee, 1974-1976;

*(This Listing Continued)*

President, 1977-1978; Chairman, RICO Committee, 1980-1990); National Association of Criminal Defense Lawyers (Member, Board of Directors, 1979-1990; Chairman, RICO Prosecutions Committee, 1978-1990; Chair, Committee to Free the Innocent Imprisoned, 1990-1995; Contributing Editor "The Champion" and Author "RICO Report", 1981— ). (Certified Specialist, Criminal Law, The State Bar of California Board of Legal Specialization). **PRACTICE AREAS:** Criminal Law.

---

**MARK O. HEANEY,** born Philadelphia, Pennsylvania, December 21, 1946; admitted to bar, 1972, California, U.S. District Court, Central District of California and U.S. Court of Appeals, Ninth Circuit. *Education:* Duke University (B.A., magna cum laude, 1968); University of Pennsylvania (J.D., magna cum laude, 1971). Phi Beta Kappa; Omicron Delta Kappa; Order of the Coif. Member, 1970-1971 and Articles Editor, 1971, University of Pennsylvania Law Review. Author: "Board of Public Instruction v. Finch: Unwarranted Compromise of Title VI'S Termination Sanction," 118 University of Pennsylvania Law Review 1113, 1970. Assistant U.S. Attorney, 1973-1979 and Assistant Division Chief, 1977-1979, Central District of California, Criminal Division. Lawyer Delegate, Ninth Circuit Judicial Conference, 1983-1985. *Member:* Federal and American Bar Associations; State Bar of California; National Association of Criminal Defense Lawyers (Member and Co-Chairman, Special Committee on the Currency Transaction Reporting Law, 1984— ). **PRACTICE AREAS:** Criminal Law.

**A. BLAIR BERNHOLZ,** born Fayetteville, North Carolina, May 16, 1964; admitted to bar, 1992, California, U.S. District Court, Central and Southern Districts of California and California Supreme Court. *Education:* Boston University (B.A., summa cum laude, 1987; M.A., summa cum laude, 1987); Harvard Law School (J.D., 1990). Phi Beta Kappa. *Member:* Beverly Hills (Member, Criminal Law Section, 1992— ), Los Angeles County and American (Litigation Section, Criminal Justice Section, 1992— ) Bar Associations; National Association of Criminal Defense Lawyers (Member, Public Affairs Committee, 1992— ); California Trial Lawyers Association; California Attorneys for Criminal Justice. **PRACTICE AREAS:** Criminal Law.

**EVAN A. JENNESS,** born Boston, Massachusetts, July 11, 1962; admitted to bar, 1988, California, U.S. District Court, Southern, Northern and Central Districts of California and U.S. Court of Appeals, Ninth and Eleventh Circuits. *Education:* Brandeis University (B.A., summa cum laude, 1984); London School of Economics and Political Science; Columbia University Law School (J.D., 1988). Phi Beta Kappa; Harlan Fiske Stone Scholar. Law Clerk to the Honorable Harry L. Hupp, U.S. District Judge, Central District of California, 1988-1989. *Member:* Los Angeles County Bar Association (Member, Litigation and Criminal Justice Sections; Professional Responsibility and Ethics Committee); National Association of Criminal Defense Lawyers. **PRACTICE AREAS:** Criminal Law.

**PAUL J. LOH,** born Taipei, Taiwan, April 29, 1967; admitted to bar, 1992, California, U.S. District Court, Southern, Central and Northern Districts of California and U.S. Court of Appeals, Ninth Circuit; 1995, District of Columbia. *Education:* University of California, Berkeley (A.B., summa cum laude, 1989); Harvard Law School (J.D., 1992). Phi Beta Kappa. Los Angeles District Attorney's Office, 1992. *Member:* State Bar of California (Member, Criminal Law Section, 1993— ); California Attorneys for Criminal Justice (Member, Federal Practice Committee, 1993— ); Southern California Chinese Lawyers Association; National Association of Criminal Defense Lawyers. **LANGUAGES:** Mandarin and Taiwanese. **PRACTICE AREAS:** Criminal Law.

---

## TAUBMAN, SIMPSON, YOUNG & SULENTOR

**LOS ANGELES, CALIFORNIA**

(See Long Beach)

*General Civil and Criminal Trial Practice, Business, Taxation, Real Estate, Environmental, Oil and Gas, Eminent Domain, Estate Planning and Probate, Commercial.*

## TAX CONSULTING GROUP
2029 CENTURY PARK EAST
SEVENTEENTH FLOOR
**LOS ANGELES, CALIFORNIA 90067**
*Telephone: 310-789-3250*
*Facsimile: 310-789-3210*

Tax Law, Bankruptcy, Intellectual Property, Employee Benefits, Patent, Trademark, Copyright and Trade Secrets. Corporate Structuring, Estate and Business Planning.

FIRM PROFILE: Tax Consulting Group, A.P.C. is a growing, boutique California firm headquartered in Los Angeles with offices in Century City, Irvine and Woodland Hills. Due to our unique firm structure, we are able to provide our clients with the most sophisticated legal advice and representation in extremely technical areas, while maintaining our uncharacteristically youthful, aggressive and personal approach to our client's causes.

Our organization renders professional services of the highest quality at the most reasonable cost. Our firm is regularly engaged by outside law firms to provide legal counselling and representation in certain of our specialities and areas of expertise. Our organization has a professional staff which includes attorneys from some of the most notable firms in their fields, former Internal Revenue Service District Counsel Attorneys, former Internal Revenue Service Collection personnel, and Certified Public Accountants. Our clients vary from individuals with a single matter to some of the world's largest corporations whose interests we advance around the globe. Nevertheless, we pride ourselves on offering each client the same respect and representation regardless of size.

Our organization strives to achieve a successful outcome on behalf of each client and we ensure that each client always receives the personal attention they deserve. Given the nature of our firm's practice and the necessary overlap of several very comprehensive areas of law, we typically must employ a team approach. We combine the talents of our various professionals while maintaining each client's personal relationship with the professional they feel most comfortable with. In this manner, each client has the personal contact with a single individual previously experienced with only small firms while having the most advanced legal resources available today. Furthermore, in support of our professionals, we have a team of highly trained and experienced paralegals and legal secretaries who provide quality support at a reduced cost to our clients. In summary, our firm offers thorough and efficient representation in all matters, regardless of the degree of complexity.

**JEFFREY ADAM SHERMAN,** born Flushing, New York, September 8, 1961; admitted to bar, 1987, California and U.S. District Court, Central District of California. *Education:* University of Florida (B.S., 1983); Southwestern University School of Law (J.D., 1986). *Member:* State Bar of California.

---

**KENNETH L. SHERMAN**

**JOHN A. HARBIN**

**VICTOR J. YOO**

**NORMAN J. KREISMAN**

---

## TAYLOR KUPFER SUMMERS & RHODES
**LOS ANGELES, CALIFORNIA**
(See Pasadena)

General Civil and Trial Practice in all State and Federal Courts. Estate Planning, Probate, Trust, Taxation, Business, Corporation, Securities and Real Estate Law.

---

## LAWRENCE TAYLOR
**LOS ANGELES, CALIFORNIA**
(See Long Beach)

Criminal Defense practice limited to Drunk Driving Defense.

---

## THARP & BERG
*Established in 1980*
555 SOUTH FLOWER STREET, SUITE 2850
**LOS ANGELES, CALIFORNIA 90071-2404**
*Telephone: 213-627-6227*
*Telecopier: 213-689-4651*

FIRM PROFILE: Ronny R. Tharp and Richard G. Berg founded the firm in 1980 after having met when both were associates at O'Melveny & Myers. The firm concentrates on probate, trust, guardianship and conservatorship administration; wills, trusts and other methods of estate planning; general commercial litigation including real estate, construction, collections and litigation of will contests and other contested fiduciary proceedings. The firm has been intentionally kept small so that each client receives the personal attention of a partner.

**RONNY R. THARP,** born Chariton, Iowa, December 25, 1944; admitted to bar, 1970, Iowa; 1971, California. *Education:* University of Iowa (B.M., 1967; J.D., 1970). Order of the Coif. Editor-in-Chief, Iowa Law Review, 1969-1970. *Member:* Los Angeles County Bar Association; The State Bar of California. **PRACTICE AREAS:** Probate, Trust, Guardianship and Conservatorship Administration; Wills, Trusts and other Methods of Estate Planning; Litigation of Will Contests and other Contested Fiduciary Proceedings.

**RICHARD G. BERG,** born Gary, Indiana, November 22, 1937; admitted to bar, 1971, California. *Education:* Purdue University (B.A., 1960); Southwestern University (J.D., magna cum laude, 1970). Associate Adjunct Professor of Law, Southwestern University School of Law, 1971-1976. *Member:* Los Angeles County Bar Association; The State Bar of California. **PRACTICE AREAS:** General Commercial Litigation; Litigation of Will Contests and other Contested Fiduciary Proceedings; Real Estate Law; Construction Law; Environmental Law.

---

## THARPE & HOWELL
15TH FLOOR, 12400 WILSHIRE BOULEVARD
**LOS ANGELES, CALIFORNIA 90025**
*Telephone: 310-826-4240*
*Fax: 310-207-1301*

*Santa Barbara, California Office:* 25 East Anapamu Street, Third Floor. Telephone: 805-962-4000. Fax: 805-965-5121.
*Newport Beach, California Office:* 4400 MacArthur Boulevard, Suite 500. Telephone: 714-261-8000. Fax: 714-955-4990.
*Santa Maria, California Office:* 910 East Stowell Road, Suite F. Telephone: 805-928-8600. Fax: 805-928-3550.
*Oxnard, California Office:* 300 Esplanade Drive, Suite 1820. Telephone: 805-485-2275. Fax: 805-988-7897.

Civil Trial and Arbitration Practice. Insurance, Casualty, Malpractice and Products Liability Law. Business Litigation. Wrongful Termination/Employment Litigation, Construction Litigation.

### MEMBERS OF FIRM

**TODD R. HOWELL,** born Burbank, California, July 3, 1948; admitted to bar, 1973, California and U.S. District Court, Southern District of California; 1974, U.S. District Court, Central District of California and U.S. Court of Appeals, 9th Circuit. *Education:* University of California at Santa Barbara (B.A., 1970); California Western School of Law (J.D., 1973). *Member:* Los Angeles County and American Bar Associations; State Bar of California; Association of Southern California Defense Counsel. (Also at Santa Maria Office). **PRACTICE AREAS:** General Casualty Defense; Coverage; Wrongful Termination; Contract Litigation; Sexual Harassment.

**EDGAR A. THARPE, III,** born Baton Rouge, Louisiana, June 9, 1945; admitted to bar, 1973, California; 1974, U.S. Court of Appeals, District of Columbia Circuit and U.S. Court of Appeals, 5th and 9th Circuits. *Education:* University of Southern California (B.S., 1969; J.D., 1972). *Member:* Los Angeles County Bar Association; State Bar of California; Association of Southern California Defense Counsel. **PRACTICE AREAS:** Construction Defect Litigation; Professional Malpractice; Product Liability.

**JONATHAN G. MAILE,** born Livermore, California, August 11, 1954; admitted to bar, 1979, California; 1980, U.S. District Court, Central District of California. *Education:* University of California at Santa Barbara (B.A., 1977); Southwestern University (J.D., 1979). Member, Southwestern University Law Review, 1978-1979. *Member:* Los Angeles County Bar Association (Member, Trial Lawyers Section); State Bar of California. **PRAC-**

*(This Listing Continued)*

## THARPE & HOWELL, Los Angeles—Continued

TICE AREAS: General Casualty Defense; Defense of Claims Against Truckers; Wrongful Termination; Sexual Harassment.

**TIMOTHY D. LAKE,** born Los Angeles, California, November 12, 1949; admitted to bar, 1974, California and U.S. District Court, Central District of California. *Education:* University of Southern California (B.A., 1971); Southwestern University (J.D., 1974). *Member:* Los Angeles County Bar Association; State Bar of California; Association of Southern California Defense Counsel; West Valley Claims Association; Southern California Adjusters Association. PRACTICE AREAS: Construction Accident Litigation; Complex Fire Litigation.

**PAUL V. WAYNE,** born Eglin Air Force Base, Florida, September 25, 1955; admitted to bar, 1981, California; 1988, U.S. District Court, Central District of California. *Education:* University of California at San Diego (B.A., 1977); University of San Diego (J.D., 1981). Member, University of San Diego Law Review, 1980-1981. Author: "Recent Developments in The Law of The Sea," University of San Diego Law Review, Vol. 18, 1979-1980, 1981. *Member:* State Bar of California. PRACTICE AREAS: Toxic Tort Litigation; Products Liability; Construction Defect Litigation; Personal Injury Litigation; Insurance Coverage.

**STEPHEN G. SCHERZER,** born Portland, Oregon, August 3, 1948; admitted to bar, 1973, California and U.S. District Court, Northern District of California; 1988, U.S. District Court, Central District. *Education:* University of Oregon (B.S., 1970); University of Santa Clara (J.D., 1973). (Also at Newport Beach Office). PRACTICE AREAS: Personal Injury Defense; Commercial Business Litigation; Construction Litigation (Defense); Intellectual Property Litigation (Defense).

**CHRISTOPHER S. MAILE,** born Burbank, California, August 31, 1958; admitted to bar, 1981, U.S. District Court, Central District of California; 1985, California; 1986, U.S. Court of Appeals, 9th Circuit. *Education:* University of California at Los Angeles (B.A., cum laude, 1980); Loyola Marymount University (J.D., 1984). Phi Alpha Delta. *Member:* State Bar of California. REPORTED CASES: Far West Financial Corp. vs. D & S Co., Inc., 46 Cal 3d 796, 1988. PRACTICE AREAS: Employment Litigation; Insurance Carrier/Agent Litigation; Employment Discrimination/Harassment; Construction Defect Litigation; Intellectual Property/Unfair Business Practices Litigation.

**CHRISTOPHER P. RUIZ,** born Hawthorne, California, December 14, 1954; admitted to bar, 1982, California; 1984, U.S. District Court, Central District of California and U.S. Court of Appeals, 9th Circuit. *Education:* California State University at Los Angeles (B.A., 1978); University of California at Los Angeles (J.D., 1982). *Member:* Los Angeles County Bar Association; State Bar of California; The Association of Trial Lawyers of America. PRACTICE AREAS: Construction Defect Litigation; Community/Homeowners Association.

**ROBERT B. SALLEY,** born Chicago, Illinois, July 17, 1959; admitted to bar, 1988, California and U.S. District, Central District of California. *Education:* University of California at Santa Barbara (B.A., 1982); Whittier College School of Law (J.D., magna cum laude, 1987). Recipient, American Jurisprudence Awards for Criminal Law, Advanced Criminal Procedure and Securities Regulations. *Member:* State Bar of California; California Young Lawyers Association.

**CHARLES D. MAY,** born Burbank, California, August 21, 1954; admitted to bar, 1985, Idaho and U.S. District Court, District of Idaho; 1987, California and U.S. District Court, Central District of California. *Education:* Loyola Marymount University (B.A., 1977); Southwestern University (J.D., 1984). Phi Alpha Delta. *Member:* Conejo Valley, Ventura County (Member, Board of Directors, Barristers Committee, 1988-1989) and American Bar Associations; State Bar of California; Idaho State Bar; Los Angeles Trial Lawyers Association; National Association of College and University Attorneys; Cryogenic Society of America; National Contract Management Association. (Also at Oxnard Office).

**ROBERT J. NEEDHAM,** born New York, New York, February 10, 1953; admitted to bar, 1982, Oregon; 1988, California; 1989, U.S. District Court, Central District of California. *Education:* University of Colorado (B.A., 1976); University of Oregon (J.D., 1982). Assistant Attorney General, State of Oregon, 1984-1985. Author: "Real and Demonstrative Evidence," Evidence, Oregon CLE, Artline, 1986. *Member:* Ventura County, Santa Barbara County and American Bar Associations; State Bar of California. (Also at Santa Barbara Office).

*(This Listing Continued)*

## ASSOCIATES

**WILLIAM P. O'KELLY,** born Eugene, Oregon, November 15, 1958; admitted to bar, 1984, Oregon; 1985, California and U.S. District Court, Eastern District of California. *Education:* Portland State University (B.S., 1981); Willamette University (J.D., 1984). *Member:* Oregon State Bar; State Bar of California; The Association of Trial Lawyers of America.

**PAUL W. BURKE,** born Syracuse, New York, June 28, 1959; admitted to bar, 1988, California; 1991, U.S. District Court, Central District of California. *Education:* Loyola Marymount University (B.A., 1981); Southwestern University School of Law (J.D., 1987). *Member:* State Bar of California.

**STUART K. SELLERS,** born Los Angeles, California, July 14, 1954; admitted to bar, 1984, California. *Education:* University of Wisconsin (B.A., 1976); University of West Los Angeles (J.D., 1984). *Member:* State Bar of California.

**ROBERT M. FREEDMAN,** born Los Angeles, California, March 21, 1949; admitted to bar, 1989, California, U.S. District Court Central District of California and U.S. Court of Appeals, 9th Circuit. *Education:* University of California at Los Angeles; Golden West University (B.S., 1978; J.D., 1980). Recipient, Bancroft Whitney Award in Corporations and Civil Procedure, 1979. *Member:* State Bar of California. LANGUAGES: French.

**DAVID BREITBURG,** born Cincinnati, Ohio, May 16, 1956; admitted to bar, 1981, Ohio; 1982, California; 1984, U.S. District Court, Central District of California. *Education:* University of Cincinnati (B.A., 1978); Southwestern University School of Law (J.D., 1981). *Member:* Cincinnati Bar Association; State Bar of California.

**MITCHELL I. COHEN,** born Inglewood, California, November 23, 1960; admitted to bar, 1988, California, U.S. District Court, Central and Northern Districts of California and U.S. Court of Appeals, Ninth Circuit. *Education:* University of California at Santa Barbara (B.A., 1982); Art Center College of Design; McGeorge School of Law (J.D., 1987).

**BRIAN J. FERBER,** born Los Angeles, California, May 19, 1965; admitted to bar, 1991, California. *Education:* San Diego State University (B.A., Journalism, 1988); Golden Gate University School of Law (J.D., 1991). Phi Alpha Delta. *Member:* State Bar of California; American Bar Association. PRACTICE AREAS: Insurance Defense; Wrongful Termination; Premises Liability.

**ROBERT L. CARDWELL,** born Richmond, Virginia, March 16, 1959; admitted to bar, 1985, California; 1986, U.S. District Court, Central District of California and U.S. Court of Appeals, 9th Circuit. *Education:* Wofford College (B.A., cum laude, 1982); Pepperdine University School of Law (J.D., 1985). Dalsimer Moot Court; Jessup International Moot Court. Member, Entertainment Law Society. *Member:* Los Angeles County Bar Association; State Bar of California.

**HELEN E. STRAND,** born Hartford, Michigan, March 30, 1941; admitted to bar, 1989, California. *Education:* University of Arizona (B.A., 1963; M.A., 1966); University of South California (M.A., 1969); University of California (Ph.D., 1980) Loyola Marymount University (J.D., 1988). Jessup International Law Trial and Competition Teams. Instructor, Pacific States University, 1989-1995. *Member:* Ventura County and Los Angeles County Bar Associations; Ventura Trial Lawyers Association. LANGUAGES: Chinese, Japanese, French. PRACTICE AREAS: Civil Litigation.

**DAVID B. WASSON,** born Burbank, California, October 7, 1959; admitted to bar, 1988, California; 1989, U.S. District Court, Central District of California. *Education:* California State University at Fullerton (B.A., 1983; M.P.A., 1985); Pepperdine University (J.D., 1988). Phi Delta Phi. Member, 1986-1988, and Lead Articles Editor, 1987-1988, Pepperdine University Law Review. PRACTICE AREAS: Personal Injury Defense; Construction Defect Defense; ERISA; Labor.

**LOUIS K. TSIROS,** born Boston, Massachusetts, May 9, 1962; admitted to bar, 1990, California. *Education:* Columbia University (A.B., 1984); Boston University (J.D., 1989). Staff Member, 1987-1988, Articles Editor, 1988-1989, Boston University International Law Journal. Author: "Exemption of Transportation Income from U.S. Taxation: How Will Changes in the Tax Reform Act of 1986 Affect Foreign Corporations?" 7 Boston University International Law Journal 379, Fall 1989. *Member:* State Bar of California. LANGUAGES: French and Spanish. PRACTICE AREAS: General Commercial Litigation; Insurance Coverage; Construction Law.

**WARREN J. HIGGINS,** born Niskayuna, New York, May 3, 1969; admitted to bar, 1995, California. *Education:* University of California, Los Angeles (B.A., magna cum laude, 1991); Hastings College of Law, Univer-

*(This Listing Continued)*

sity of California (J.D., 1994). Phi Beta Kappa. *PRACTICE AREAS:* Employment Litigation; Products Liability; Bad Faith Litigation; Construction Defect Litigation.

*J. JUNE CHANG,* born Harrisburg, Pennsylvania, June 27, 1967; admitted to bar, 1992, Illinois; 1993, U.S. District Court, Northern District of Illinois; 1995, California. *Education:* Bryn Mawr College (B.A., 1989); Temple University (J.D., 1992). *PRACTICE AREAS:* Insurance Defense.

*JEFFREY C. LYNN,* born Boston, Massachusetts, October 11, 1955; admitted to bar, 1981, California; 1982, U.S. District Court, Central District of California; 1987, U.S. District Court, Southern District of California; 1988, U.S. District Court, Northern District of California; 1990, U.S. District Court, Eastern District of California. *Education:* Whittier College (B.A., 1977); Southwestern University (J.D., 1980). Pi Sigma Alpha. *PRACTICE AREAS:* Insurance Coverage; Insurance Bad Faith.

*PAUL H. LASKY,* born San Francisco, California, November 6, 1940; admitted to bar, 1987, California. *Education:* Massachusetts Institute of Technology (Sc.B., 1960); University of Washington (M.S., 1965); University of West Los Angeles (J.D., 1987). Sigma Xi. Pre Doctoral Fellow. Recipient, American Jurisprudence Awards in Constitutional Law, Evidence and Civil Procedure. Editor, University of West Los Angeles Law Review, 1986-1987. *Member:* Los Angeles County Bar Association; State Bar of California; Association of Southern California Defense Counsel. *PRACTICE AREAS:* Construction Law; Toxic Tort; Product Liability; Professional Liability.

*CAROLE A. BUSCH,* born Granite City, Illinois, July 4, 1964; admitted to bar, 1991, California and U.S. District Court, Central District of California; 1992, Illinois. *Education:* University of Illinois (B.S., 1986); Washington University (J.D., 1991). Alpha Lambda Delta. Scholars in Law Scholarship Recipient. *PRACTICE AREAS:* Civil Litigation; Insurance Defense; Construction Defects.

*DIANE F. TAYLOR,* born Kishinev, Russia, September 3, 1970; admitted to bar, 1995, California; 1996, U.S. District Court, Central District of California. *Education:* University of California at LaJolla (B.A., 1992); University of San Diego (J.D., 1995). *PRACTICE AREAS:* Construction Defect; Insurance Defense.

*BRANDON K. TADY,* born Santa Monica, California, February 27, 1953; admitted to bar, 1978, California; 1984, U.S. District Court, Central District of California and U.S. Court of Appeals, Ninth Circuit. *Education:* University of Southern California (B.A., 1975; J.D., summa cum laude, 1978); Stanford University (M.A., 1984). *Member:* San Fernando Valley and Los Angeles County Bar Associations; State Bar of California; Southern California Defense Counsel; Defense Research Institute. *PRACTICE AREAS:* Insurance Coverage; Insurance Bad Faith; First Party Property; Liability Defense.

*RICHARD A. FERCH,* born Milwaukee, Wisconsin, September 19, 1950; admitted to bar, 1982, California; 1983, U.S. District Court, Central District of California. *Education:* California State University at Fullerton (B.A., cum laude, 1978); Loyola University of Los Angeles (J.D., 1982). *Member:* State Bar of California.

*DAVID K. STEWART,* born Gary, Indiana, January 21, 1965; admitted to bar, 1990, California and U.S. District Court, Central District of California. *Education:* University of California at Santa Barbara (B.A., 1987); Pepperdine University (J.D., 1990). *PRACTICE AREAS:* Automobile Accident; Construction Defect.

*STACEY A. MILLER,* born Midland, Texas, August 3, 1966; admitted to bar, 1992, California and U.S. District Court, Central District of California; 1993, U.S. Court of Appeals, Ninth Circuit. *Education:* Occidental College (A.B., 1988); Pepperdine University (M.B.A., 1991; J.D., 1992). *Member:* State Bar of California; Federal Bar Association.

## SANTA BARBARA OFFICE
## RESIDENT ASSOCIATES

*PAUL M. BIELACZYC,* born Petoskey, Michigan, November 9, 1952; admitted to bar, 1989, California. *Education:* Western Michigan University (B.S., 1984); University of California at Santa Barbara (J.D., 1988). *Member:* State Bar of California.

*HEATHER A. SCIACCA,* born Cheverly, Maryland, October 17, 1963; admitted to bar, 1989, California and U.S. Court of Appeals, 9th Circuit. *Education:* University of California at Santa Barbara (B.A., 1986); Universidad de Madrid; Arizona State University (J.D., 1989). *Member:* State Bar of California.

*(This Listing Continued)*

*STEVEN PATRICK LEE,* born Detroit, Michigan, May 23, 1966; admitted to bar, 1993, California and U.S. District Court, District of California. *Education:* University of California, Santa Barbara (B.A., 1988); Santa Clara University (J.D., 1992). *Member:* Bar Association of San Francisco; Barristers Club of San Francisco.

*ERIC B. KUNKEL,* born Delaware, Ohio, June 14, 1965; admitted to bar, 1990, California. *Education:* Indiana University (B.S., 1987); Ohio Northern University (J.D., 1990). Student Articles Editor, Editorial Board, Ohio Northern Law Review, 1989-1990. Author: Casenote, "The Inherent Dangers of the Ubiquitous Limiting Instruction," 15 Ohio Northern L.Rev. 131 (1988). *Member:* Santa Barbara Bar Association. *LANGUAGES:* Spanish. *PRACTICE AREAS:* Civil Litigation.

*P. MARK KIRWIN,* born Hamilton, Bermuda, May 21, 1963; admitted to bar, 1992, California and U.S. District Court, Southern District of California; 1994, Colorado. *Education:* University of Colorado at Boulder (B.A, History, 1987); California Western University (J.D., 1991). *Member:* Los Angeles County Bar Association; State Bar of California. *PRACTICE AREAS:* Civil Litigation.

*JILL RENEE MARKOTA,* born Glendale, California, April 7, 1967; admitted to bar, 1993, California. *Education:* California Polytechnic State University (B.A., Pol. Sc.), 1990); California Western School of Law (J.D., 1993). Member, Advisory Board. Sports and Entertainment Law Society, 1992-1993. Listed in: The World's Who Who of Women, 1993; International Who's Who of Professional and Business Women, 1993. *Member:* Santa Barbara and American Bar Associations; State Bar of California; Santa Barbara Barristers Club.

*ERIK B. FEINGOLD,* born Paterson, New Jersey, August 23, 1967; admitted to bar, 1993, California. *Education:* California State University, Chico (B.A., 1989); Western State University College of Law (J.D., 1993). Member, Western State University Law Review. Judicial Externship, California Court of Appeal. *PRACTICE AREAS:* Insurance Defense; Plaintiff's Personal Injury.

*DENISE M. KALE,* born Burbank, California, November 15, 1955; admitted to bar, 1991, California. *Education:* Santa Barbara City College (A.A., with honors, 1987); University of California at Santa Barbara (J.D., 1991). *Member:* Board of Directors, Santa Barbara County Bar Association, 1993-1994; Santa Barbara Women Lawyers, 1993-1994. *PRACTICE AREAS:* Insurance Defense; Civil Litigation; Government Law.

## OXNARD, CALIFORNIA OFFICE
## RESIDENT ASSOCIATES

*GENE B. SHARAGA,* born Bronx, New York, November 3, 1951; admitted to bar, 1987, California; 1988, U.S. District Court, Central, Southern and Eastern Districts of California. *Education:* Queens College of the City University of New York (B.A., 1973); Wayne State University (J.D., magna cum laude, 1987). Recipient: American Jurisprudence Awards in International Law and Equal Opportunity in Employment Law; New York Regents Scholarship. *PRACTICE AREAS:* Personal Injury; Subrogation; Construction Defect.

*DEBORAH MEYER-MORRIS,* born Los Angeles, California, March 1, 1964; admitted to bar, 1992, California; 1994, U.S. District Court, Central District of California. *Education:* California State University at Northridge (B.S., cum laude, 1986); Loyola Law School (J.D., 1991). Phi Delta Phi. *Member:* Ventura County and American Bar Associations; State Bar of California; Woman Lawyers of Ventura County. *PRACTICE AREAS:* Civil Litigation; Construction Defect Litigation.

REPRESENTATIVE CLIENTS: Allstate Insurance Company; Amex Assurance Company; Argonaut Insurance Company; E & O Professionals; Farmers Insurance Group of Companies; Financial Indemnity Insurance Company; Golden Eagle Insurance Company; McDonnel Douglas Corporation; Mercury Insurance Group of Companies; Nationwide Insurance Group; Ohio Casualty Insurance Company; Schneider National Trucking Company; State Farm Insurance Company; Stonewall Insurance Group; Utica Mutual Insurance Company; Walt Disney Company; Wausau Insurance Company; Workman's Auto Insurance Company; Worldwide Underwriters Insurance Group; Yellow Freight Systems, Inc.

(For complete biographical data on other personnel, see Professional Biographies at other office locations)

CALIFORNIA—LOS ANGELES                          MARTINDALE-HUBBELL LAW DIRECTORY 1997

# THELEN, MARRIN, JOHNSON & BRIDGES LLP

*Established in 1924*

**SUITE 3400, 333 SOUTH GRAND AVENUE
LOS ANGELES, CALIFORNIA 90071**
Telephone: 213-621-9800
Fax: 213-623-4742
Email: postmaster@tmjb.com

**San Francisco Office:** Two Embarcadero Center. Telephone: 415-392-6320. Fax: 415-421-1068.

**San Jose Office:** 17th Floor, 333 West San Carlos Street. Telephone: 408-292-5800. Fax: 408-287-8040.

**New York, New York Office:** Suite 1100, 330 Madison Avenue. Telephone: 212-297-3200. Fax: 212-972-6569.

*FIRM PROFILE: Thelen, Marrin, Johnson & Bridges is a national law firm with nearly 200 attorneys in its San Francisco, Los Angeles, San Jose, CA, and New York offices. Practices include: Antitrust and Trade Regulations; Bankruptcy; Business Litigation; Commercial Finance; Construction, Corporate; Environmental; Equipment Leasing; Franchising; Government Contracts; Insurance; Intellectual Property; Labor and Employment Relations; Mining; Project Finance; Real Estate and Land Use; Securities; Tax, Trusts and Estates and Tort Law.*

**DAVID L. BACON,** born Pittsburgh, Pennsylvania, January 26, 1944; admitted to bar, 1969, California. *Education:* Harvard University (A.B., magna cum laude, 1965; J.D., 1968). *Member:* Los Angeles County and American (Member, Sections of Labor and Employment Law; Tort and Insurance Practice) Bar Associations; State Bar of California; Defense Research Institute; Conference of Insurance Counsel. **PRACTICE AREAS:** Management Labor Law; Civil Rights Litigation; Employee Benefit Plan Law; Insurance Law; Appeals. *Email:* dlbacon@tmjb.com

**CHARLES S. BIRENBAUM,** admitted to bar, 1983, California. *Education:* Oberlin College (B.A., with honors, 1979); Georgetown University (J.D., 1982). Author: "Construction Labor Law Issues of the 1990's," *Construction Contractor's Handbook of Business and Law* (Wiley Law Pub., 1992); "Employee Screening Techniques: Advantages and Pitfalls," Proceedings of New York University 44th Annual Nat. Conf. on Labor (NYU, 1991). **PRACTICE AREAS:** Labor Litigation. *Email:* cbirenbaum@tmjb.com

**ROBERT G. CAMPBELL,** born Port Hueneme, California, December 2, 1956; admitted to bar, 1982, California. *Education:* University of California, Los Angeles (B.A., 1979); University of Southern California (J.D., 1982). Member, Hale Moot Court. *Member:* Los Angeles County and American Bar Associations. **PRACTICE AREAS:** Business and Construction Litigation; Representation of Professional Athletes. *Email:* rgcampbell@tmjb.com

**JOHN B. CLARK,** born Great Bend, Kansas, August 2, 1936; admitted to bar, 1962, New York; 1966, California; 1991, Colorado. *Education:* Stanford University (B.S., 1958; LL.B., 1961). Member, Board of Editors, Stanford Law Review, 1960-1961. Fellow of the American College of Construction Lawyers. **PRACTICE AREAS:** Construction Litigation. *Email:* jbclark@tmjb.com

**CURTIS A. COLE,** born Niles, MI., 1946; admitted to bar, 1972, California. *Education:* University of California, Los Angeles (A.B., 1968; J.D., 1972). *Member:* State Bar of California (Chair, Insurance Law Committee, 1991-1992); American Bar Association (Administrative Law and Regulatory Practice, Litigation, Torts and Insurance Sections, Appellate Advocacy Committee); National Health Lawyers Association. **PRACTICE AREAS:** Torts; Insurance; Health Care Law.

**W. GLENN CORNELL,** born Philadelphia, Pennsylvania, September 20, 1946; admitted to bar, 1973, California. *Education:* Franklin & Marshall College (A.B., 1968); University of North Carolina, Chapel Hill (M.A., 1970); Stanford University (J.D., 1973). Pi Gamma Mu; Phi Alpha Theta. **PRACTICE AREAS:** Torts; Insurance Law. *Email:* wgcornell@tmjb.com

**CHRISTINE C. FRANKLIN,** born Glens Falls, New York, July 4, 1949; admitted to bar, 1980, California. *Education:* Newton College (B.A., cum laude, 1971); University of Virginia (M.A., in foreign affairs, 1974); University of California at Los Angeles (J.D., 1979). Deputy Attorney General, State of California, 1979-1986. **PRACTICE AREAS:** Commercial Litigation; Insurance. *Email:* ccfranklin@tmjb.com

*(This Listing Continued)*

CAA1246B

**THOMAS E. HILL,** born Oakland, California, December 15, 1953; admitted to bar, 1981, California. *Education:* University of California at Los Angeles (B.A., 1976); Loyola Law School of Los Angeles (J.D., 1981). **PRACTICE AREAS:** Labor and Employment. *Email:* tehill@tmjb.com

**LINDA S. HUSAR,** born Chicago, Illinois, September 12, 1955; admitted to bar, 1980, California; 1981, U.S. District Court, Eastern, Northern, Southern and Central Districts of California and U.S. Court of Appeals, Ninth Circuit. *Education:* Boston University (B.S., summa cum laude, 1977); Loyola University of Los Angeles (J.D., magna cum laude, 1980). **PRACTICE AREAS:** Labor and Employment Law. *Email:* lshusar@tmjb.com

**REMY KESSLER,** born Alhambra, California, November 10, 1960; admitted to bar, 1986, California and U.S. District Court, Central District of California; 1988, U.S. District Court, Northern District of California; 1991, U.S. Court of Appeals, Ninth Circuit. *Education:* University of California at Berkeley (B.A., 1982); Loyola Marymount University (J.D., 1985). Associate Editor, Loyola of Los Angeles Entertainment Law Journal, 1984-1985. *Member:* Los Angeles County (Member, Labor Law Section) and American (Member, Labor and Employment Law and Litigation Sections) Bar Associations; State Bar of California (Member, Labor and Employment Law and Public Law Sections). **PRACTICE AREAS:** Labor and Employment; Litigation; Municipal Law; Commercial.

**HELEN J. LAUDERDALE,** born Maryland, 1960; admitted to bar, 1985, California. *Education:* Carleton College (B.A., cum laude, 1981); Northwestern University (J.D., 1985). Note and Comment Editor, Journal of Criminal Law and Criminology, 1983-1985. Author: "The Admissibility of Expert Testimony on Rape Trauma Syndrome," Journal of Criminal Law and Criminology, Winter, 1984. **PRACTICE AREAS:** Litigation; Construction Law. *Email:* hjlauderdale@tmjb.com

**JAMES J. MOAK,** born Los Angeles, California, August 3, 1953; admitted to bar, 1978, California. *Education:* Loyola University (B.A., 1975); University of California at Los Angeles (J.D., 1978). *Member:* Los Angeles County and American (Member, Tort and Insurance Practice Section) Bar Associations; State Bar of California; Conference of Insurance Counsel. **PRACTICE AREAS:** Life and Health Insurance; Disability Insurance; Extracontractual Insurance Claims; Unfair Insurance Practice; First Party Insurance Defense. *Email:* jjmoak@tmjb.com

**WALTER K. OETZELL,** born Evanston, Illinois, February 12, 1949; admitted to bar, 1983, California. *Education:* University of California at Los Angeles (B.A., 1978; J.D., 1983). Phi Beta Kappa. *Member:* American Bar Association; Financial Lawyers Conference. **PRACTICE AREAS:** Bankruptcy Law; Commercial Law.

**TIMOTHY M. TRUAX,** born Corpus Christi, Texas, September 17, 1960; admitted to bar, 1985, California. *Education:* San Jose State University (B.A., with distinction, 1982); University of Southern California (J.D., 1985). *Member:* Los Angeles County Bar Association. **PRACTICE AREAS:** Construction Law; Government Contracts Law. *Email:* tmtruax@tmjb.com

**JOHN L. VIOLA,** born Rockville Centre, New York, September 28, 1954; admitted to bar, 1980, New York; 1987, California; 1991, U.S. Supreme Court. *Education:* Columbia University (B.A., 1976); New York University (J.D., 1979). *Member:* American Bar Association; State Bar of California; Conference of Insurance Counsel. **PRACTICE AREAS:** Appellate Practice; ERISA Law; Life and Health Insurance; Insurance Bad Faith; Employment Claims. *Email:* jlviola@tmjb.com

**LONNIE E. WOOLVERTON, (P.C.),** born El Paso, Texas, November 28, 1932; admitted to bar, 1963, California. *Education:* University of California at Los Angeles (B.A., 1957); University of Southern California (J.D., 1962). Deputy City Attorney, Los Angeles, 1963-1964. *Member:* Los Angeles County and American Bar Associations; State Bar of California; Conference of Insurance Counsel. *Email:* lewoolverton@tmjb.com

*OF COUNSEL*

**WILLIAM F. HOLBROOK,** born Augusta, Maine, May 30, 1939; admitted to bar, 1985, California; 1993, Florida. *Education:* Bowdoin College (B.A., 1961); Harvard University (M.B.A., 1972); Loyola Law School (J.D., 1985). Member, Insurance Law Committee, Business Law Section, California State Bar, 1992-1995 (Vice-Chair, 1994-1995). *Member:* Los Angeles County and American Bar Associations. **PRACTICE AREAS:** Business and Insurance Litigation. *Email:* wfholbrook@tmjb.com

*(This Listing Continued)*

## ASSOCIATES

**JOHN N. CHILDERS,** born Los Angeles, California, June 8, 1969; admitted to bar, 1995, California. *Education:* University of California, San Diego (B.A., 1991); University of California, Los Angeles (J.D., 1995). *LANGUAGES:* French. *PRACTICE AREAS:* Business, Construction, Litigation and Insurance. *Email:* jchilders@tmjb.com

**GARY H. GREEN, II,** born Los Angeles, California, January 23, 1969; admitted to bar, 1994, California; 1995, U.S. District Court, Central District of California; 1995, U.S. District Court, Southern, Northern and Eastern Districts of California. *Education:* Washington & Lee University (B.A., magna cum laude, 1991); Harvard Law School (J.D., cum laude, 1994). *Member:* Century City, Beverly Hills and Los Angeles County Bar Associations; American Political Science Association. *PRACTICE AREAS:* Labor and Employment Law; Litigation; Federal Litigation. *Email:* ghgreen@tmjb.com

**LISA S. HALEBLIAN,** born Hollywood, California, June 17, 1970; admitted to bar, 1995, California, U.S. District Court, Central, Northern, Southern and Eastern Districts of California and U.S. Court of Appeals, Ninth Circuit. *Education:* California State University, Northridge (B.S., 1991); University of Southern California (J.D., 1995). Editor, Interdisciplinary Law Journal. *LANGUAGES:* Armenian. *PRACTICE AREAS:* Business Litigation; Insurance; Employment. *Email:* lshaleblian@tmjb.com

**MICHAEL D. HOLTZ,** born New York, N.Y., April 1, 1964; admitted to bar, 1990, California. *Education:* Suffolk Community College (A.A., 1985); University of Michigan (A.B., 1987); New York University (J.D., 1990). *PRACTICE AREAS:* Litigation. *Email:* mdholtz@tmjb.com

**GAYLE I. JENKINS,** born Anchorage, Alaska, March 21, 1968; admitted to bar, 1993, California and U.S. District Court, Central District of California; 1994, U.S. Court of Appeals, Ninth Circuit. *Education:* Chapman College (B.A., cum laude, 1990); Hastings College of the Law, University of California (J.D., 1993). Member, Editorial Board, Hastings Women's Law Journal. *Member:* State Bar of California Litigation and Labor and Employment Sections). *PRACTICE AREAS:* Insurance Litigation (Life, Health & Disability); Business Litigation. *Email:* gjenkins@tmjb.com

**MATTHEW LEVINSON,** born Los Angeles, California, January 2, 1969; admitted to bar, 1994, California. *Education:* Cornell University (B.A., 1991); University of California at Los Angeles (J.D., 1994). Managing Editor, University of California at Los Angeles Law Review. *PRACTICE AREAS:* Litigation.

**CHRISTINE L. LOFGREN,** born Fullerton, California, December 11, 1967; admitted to bar, 1993, California. *Education:* University of California, Los Angeles (B.A., magna cum laude, 1990); University of California, Davis (J.D., 1993). Phi Beta Kappa. Recipient, American Jurisprudence Award in Legal Writing. *PRACTICE AREAS:* Litigation. *Email:* cllofgren@tmjb.com

**MICHELLE LOGAN-STERN,** born San Diego, California, December 8, 1968; admitted to bar, 1995, California. *Education:* University of California, Berkeley (B.A., 1991); University of California, Los Angeles (J.D., 1995). Editor in Chief, UCLA Women's Law Journal. *PRACTICE AREAS:* Business Litigation. *Email:* loganstern@tmjb.com

**SHEA H. LUKACSKO,** born Laguna Beach, California, February 16, 1964; admitted to bar, 1991, California. *Education:* Pepperdine University (B.S., 1986); University of California, San Francisco, Hastings College of the Law (J.D., cum laude, 1991). Member and Editor, Hastings Law Journal, 1989-1991. *PRACTICE AREAS:* Business Litigation and Construction. *Email:* shlukacsko@tmjb.com

**VALARIE H. MACHT,** born Tucson, Arizona, April 25, 1961; admitted to bar, 1988, California; 1991, District of Columbia. *Education:* University of Virginia (B.A., cum laude, 1983); Georgetown University (J.D., 1988). Member, Committee on Federal Courts, State Bar of California. *Member:* Los Angeles County Bar Association; Financial Lawyers Conference; Women Lawyers Association of Los Angeles. *PRACTICE AREAS:* Bankruptcy Law and Commercial Litigation.

**BROOKS P. MARSHALL,** born Royal Oak, Michigan, September 16, 1963; admitted to bar, 1988, California. *Education:* Miami University (B.S., 1985); University of Michigan (J.D., 1988). Member, Order of the Barristers. *Member:* Beverly Hills and Los Angeles County Bar Associations. *PRACTICE AREAS:* Business Litigation. *Email:* bmarshall@tmjb.com

**DENNIS M. NAISH,** born Framingham, Massachusetts, November 14, 1964; admitted to bar, 1989, California. *Education:* University of Washing-

(*This Listing Continued*)

ton (B.A., with honors, 1986; J.D., with honors, 1989). *Member:* Los Angeles County (Commercial Law and Bankruptcy Section) and American (Construction Litigation Section) Bar Associations. *PRACTICE AREAS:* Construction and Government Contracts; Bankruptcy Law; General Commercial Litigation. *Email:* dmnaish@tmjb.com

**RICHARD C. RYBICKI,** born Sacramento, California, May 13, 1967; admitted to bar, 1992, California; 1993, U.S. District Court, Northern, Central, Eastern and Southern Districts of California. *Education:* University of California, Los Angeles (B.A., 1989); Cornell University (J.D., 1992). *PRACTICE AREAS:* Labor and Employment Law; Appellate Law. *Email:* rcrybicki@tmjb.com

**TERI L. VASQUEZ,** born Colorado Springs, Colorado, September 4, 1967; admitted to bar, 1994, California, U.S. District Court, Central, Southern, Northern and Eastern Districts of California and U.S. Court of Appeals, Ninth Circuit. *Education:* University of California at Los Angeles (B.A., 1989; J.D., 1994). *PRACTICE AREAS:* Insurance Litigation; Civil Litigation. *Email:* tvasquez@tmjb.com

**JASON G. WILSON,** born White Plains, New York, February 3, 1969; admitted to bar, 1994, California. *Education:* Princeton University (A.B., 1990); University of California at Los Angeles (J.D., 1994). *Member:* National Bar Association. *LANGUAGES:* French. *PRACTICE AREAS:* Business Litigation. *Email:* jgwilson@tmjb.com

**SUSAN Y. YOON,** born Seoul, Korea, July 9, 1970; (admission pending). *Education:* University of California, Berkeley (B.A., Psychology, 1992); University of Southern California (J.D., 1996). *PRACTICE AREAS:* Business Litigation. *Email:* syyoon@tmjb.com

All Partners and Associates are Members of The State Bar of California.

REPRESENTATIVE CLIENTS: Bank of America; Bank of California; The Bechtel Group of Companies; California State Automobile Assn.; Dillingham Construction N.A., Inc.; Homestake Mining; Hydril Company; Hyundai Electronics Industries; IBM; International Insurance Company; Kaiser Aluminum & Chemical Corporation; Louisiana-Pacific Corporation; Metlife Capital Corporation; Metropolitan Transit Authority; Monsanto Company; MPT/CAP; NEC Electronics; Pacific Theatres Corporation; Postal Instant Press; Seagate Technology, Inc.; Sequa Corporation; Sumitomo Construction America; Texas Commerce Bank NA Trustee; 20th Century Insurance Co.; Underwriters at Lloyd's, London; The Vendo Company; Wells Fargo Bank, N.A.; Westinghouse Electric Corporation.

(A complete list of the lawyers of this Firm will be found under the San Francisco, California Professional Biographies entry).

---

## THOMAS & PRICE
### LOS ANGELES, CALIFORNIA
(See Glendale)

Insurance Defense, Medical and Accounting Malpractice, Automobile Law, Product Liability, Construction and Premise Liability Law.

---

## THOMAS & WALTON LLP
### 550 SOUTH HOPE STREET, SUITE 1000
### LOS ANGELES, CALIFORNIA 90071
Telephone: 213-488-1600
Fax: 213-228-0256

General Practice.

### MEMBERS OF FIRM

**JOHN R. WALTON,** born Corvallis, Oregon, April 12, 1962; admitted to bar, 1987, California; 1996, Oregon. *Education:* Keo Gijyuku University, Tokyo, Japan; Stanford University (A.B., 1984); University of Michigan (J.D., cum laude, 1987); Kyoto University (LL.M., 1990). *LANGUAGES:* Japanese. *PRACTICE AREAS:* Business; International Litigation.

**ANDREW J. THOMAS,** born Glendale, California, October 19, 1958; admitted to bar, 1987, California. *Education:* University of California at Los Angeles (B.A., cum laude, 1983); University of San Diego (J.D., cum laude, 1986). Member, California Regulatory Law Reporter, 1984-1986. Judicial Clerk, Extern, California Court of Appeals, Fourth District, Division 1, Fall, 1985. *Member:* Glendale, Los Angeles County and American (Member, Sections of Litigation, Real Property and Intellectual Property) Bar Associations. *PRACTICE AREAS:* Business; Real Estate Litigation.

# CALIFORNIA—LOS ANGELES

## THOMPSON & WALDRON
### 1901 AVENUE OF THE STARS, SUITE 1901
### LOS ANGELES, CALIFORNIA 90067
Telephone: 310-553-7310
Facsimile: 310-553-6843

*Alexandria, Virginia Office:* 4th Floor. 1055 North Fairfax Street. 22314-1541. Telephone: 703-684-3340. Facsimile: 703-684-6225.

*General Civil Practice, Government Contract, Construction and Contract Law, Suretyship, Federal Administrative and Legislative Practice.*

(For complete Biographical Data on all Personnel, See Professional Biographies at Alexandria, Virginia)

---

## THOMSON & NELSON
### A PROFESSIONAL LAW CORPORATION
### LOS ANGELES, CALIFORNIA
(See Whittier)

*General Civil and Trial Practice. Taxation, Corporation, Partnership, Real Estate, Estate Planning, Nonprofit Corporation and Association Law, Trusts, Probate and Commercial Law.*

---

## THON, BECK, VANNI, PHILLIPI & NUTT
### A PROFESSIONAL CORPORATION
### LOS ANGELES, CALIFORNIA
(See Pasadena)

*Civil Trial and Appellate Practice. Personal Injury, Products Liability, Medical Malpractice and Maritime Law.*

---

## THORNE AND COMPANY
### A PROFESSIONAL LAW CORPORATION
### 1801 CENTURY PARK EAST, TWELFTH FLOOR
### LOS ANGELES, CALIFORNIA 90067
Telephone: 310-553-9000
Facsimile: 310-201-9190

*Entertainment Law.*

**FIRM PROFILE:** *Thorne and Company represents leading clients in the areas of domestic and international motion picture, television, multimedia, music, radio, touring, book publishing and licensing. The firm also represents and counsels A-list children talent and properties in all aspects of the entertainment industry.*

**ROBERT THORNE,** born Los Angeles, California, December 6, 1954; admitted to bar, 1980, California. *Education:* University of California at Berkeley (B.A., with highest honors and distinction, 1977); Hastings College of the Law, University of California (J.D., 1980). Phi Beta Kappa; Alpha Kappa Delta. Member, Editorial Board, 1978-1980 and Note and Comment Editor, 1979-1980, Hastings Constitutional Law Quarterly. Author: "Copyright Royalty Tribunal Increases Royalty Payable Under Compulsory Music Recording License," 6 Century City Bar Bulletin 1, May 1981; "Entertainment Law Update," 6 Century City Bar Bulletin 5, December 1981; "Compulsory Licensing: The Music Makers as Money Makers," 5 Los Angeles Lawyer 11, March 1982; "The Section 110 (5) Exemption For Radio Play in Commercial Establishments: A Narrowly Construed Music Copyright Haven," 3 Loyola Entertainment Law Journal 101, 1983. Co-Author: "International Aspects of United States Copyright Law: The Music Business," 1984 Symposium on Copyrights, Intellectual Property and Unfair Competition Section, Los Angeles County Bar Association. Syllabus Editor, Symposium on Production and Distribution of Videocassettes, Intellectual Property and Unfair Competition Section of the Los Angeles County Bar Association, 1986. Contributing Editor, 1981-1985 and Member, Advisory Editorial Board, 1985—, Entertainment Law Reporter. Editor-in-Chief, Century City Bar Association Journal, 1982-1985. Co-Editor, Entertainment, Publishing and The Arts Handbook, 1985—. Instructor, "The Law and Business of Music in the '80s: Developments and Trends," University of California at Los Angeles, 1985-1986. Symposium Chair and Moderator, "Lights, Camera, Trial: Do Cameras in the Courtroom Serve the Public Interest or Inhibit Justice?" Century City Bar Association, 1995. Former Partner, Loeb & Loeb, LLP. *Member:* Century City Bar Association (Member, Board of Governors, 1985-1988, Treasurer, 1989, Secretary, 1990, Vice President, 1991, President Elect, 1992, President, 1993, Chair, Entertainment Law Section, 1988-1990 and Chairman, Bar Journal Committee, 1982-1985); Los Angeles County Bar Association (Member, Executive Committee, 1986-1988 and 1986 Symposium Planning Committee, Intellectual and Unfair Competition Section); State Bar of California; Los Angeles Copyright Society. **PRACTICE AREAS:** Entertainment Law.

**GREGORY V. REDLITZ,** born Cambridge, Massachusetts, October 25, 1951; admitted to bar, 1977, California; 1980, New York. *Education:* Yale University (B.A., magna cum laude, 1973); Columbia University (J.D., 1977). Harlan Fiske Stone Scholar. Former Partner, Loeb & Loeb, LLP. *Member:* State Bar of California; Los Angeles Copyright Society. **PRACTICE AREAS:** Entertainment Law.

**MICHAEL R. FULLER,** born Lafayette, Indiana, July 1, 1968; admitted to bar, 1994, California. *Education:* University of Missouri (B.S., B.A., cum laude, 1991); Southwestern University School of Law (J.D., magna cum laude, 1994). Recipient, American Jurisprudence Award: Legal Writing, Wills and Trusts. Listed, Who's Who: American Law Students, 1992-1993 and 1993-1994. Staff Member, 1992-1993 and Editorial Board Member, 1993-1994, Southwestern University Law Review. Author: "Hollywood Goes Interactive: Licensing Problems Associated With Repurposing Motion Pictures Into Interactive Multimedia Video Games," 15 Loy. L.A. Ent. L. J. 599 (1995); "Just Whose Life Is It? Establishing a Constitutional Right For Physician Assisted Euthanasia," 23 Southwestern L. R. 103 (1993). *Member:* State Bar of California. **PRACTICE AREAS:** Entertainment Law.

---

## THORPE AND THORPE
### PROFESSIONAL CORPORATION
### ONE BUNKER HILL, SUITE 800
### 601 WEST 5TH STREET
### LOS ANGELES, CALIFORNIA 90071
Telephone: 213-680-9940
Telecopier: 213-680-4060

*Civil, Trial and Appellate Practice. Business, Corporate, Securities, Real Property, Estate Planning, Trusts and Probate, Taxation, Construction Insurance, Trade Regulation and Unfair Competition Law.*

**FIRM PROFILE:** *Thorpe and Thorpe is a Downtown Los Angeles Law firm with over a quarter century of experience in representing business and real estate clients in complex litigation and transactional matters.*

**TIMOTHY D. KEVANE,** born Rome, Italy, February 4, 1965; admitted to bar, 1991, California. *Education:* Georgetown University (B.S., 1987); Loyola Law School (J.D., 1991). St. Thomas More Law Honor Society. Member, Barristers Continuing Legal Education and Bench and Bar Relations Committees. *Member:* Los Angeles County Bar Association; State Bar of California; Association of Business Trial Lawyers. **LANGUAGES:** Spanish, French. **PRACTICE AREAS:** Business Litigation.

**REBECCA HAIRSTON LESSLEY,** born Fort Worth, Texas, April 10, 1958; admitted to bar, 1991, California; 1992, U.S. District Court, Central District of California; 1994, U.S. Court of Claims; 1996, U.S. District Court, Eastern and Southern Districts of California. *Education:* Baylor University (B.B.A., 1980); Loyola Law School (J.D., 1991). Phi Delta Phi. Member, Western Council of Construction Consumers (Member, Products and Services Committee) *Member:* Los Angeles County (Co-Vice Chair, Construction Law Subsection of the Real Property Section) and American (Member, Forum Committee on the Construction Industry) Bar Associations; State Bar of California. **PRACTICE AREAS:** Construction; Business Litigation.

**LEE NEW,** born Yorkton, Canada, June 17, 1957; admitted to bar, 1989, California. *Education:* California State University at Los Angeles (B.A., 1980); Loyola Law School (J.D., cum laude, 1989). Phi Delta Phi; Order of the Coif. Member: St. Thomas More Law Honor Society. Recipient, American Jurisprudence Award in Torts and Legal Writing. Member, City of Pasadena City Vote Task Force. Articles Consultant for Business Law Practitioner. *Member:* State Bar of California. **PRACTICE AREAS:** Business Litigation; Corporate Law.

**MARK R. STAPKE,** born 1955; admitted to bar, 1983, California. *Education:* University of California at Berkeley (A.B.,1977); University of Oregon (J.D., 1982). Phi Alpha Delta. Member, Moot Court Board. Certificate of Completion, Environmental and Natural Resources Law Program. Author: "Evaluating Oregon Legislative History: Tailoring An Approach to

*(This Listing Continued)*

the Legislative Process," Oregon Law Review, Vol. 61, No. 3, 1983. Judge Pro Tempore and Landlord-Tenant Settlement Officer, Superior Court, State of California for the County of Los Angeles, 1989—. Instructor, Oregon Police Academy, Monmouth, Oregon, 1982. Staff, Oregon Senate Committee on Environment, 1981. Staff: California Air Resources Board, 1981; Lane County District Attorney's Office, 1981-1982. Member: Associated General Contractors of California (Member, Legal Advisory Committee); Southern California Contractors Association; Western Council of Construction Consumers; Construction Lawyers Study Group. *Member:* Los Angeles County (Member, Construction Law Subsection of the Real Property Section) and American (Member: Construction Law Subsection, Litigation Section) Bar Association (Member, Litigation Section); State Bar of California. **PRACTICE AREAS:** Construction Litigation; Business Litigation.

**BRENDAN J. THORPE,** born Los Angeles, California, November 6, 1960; admitted to bar, 1988, California and U.S. District Court, Central, Eastern, Southern and Northern Districts of California. *Education:* Loyola Marymount University (B.A., 1984); Loyola Law School (J.D., 1988). Arbitrator, Los Angeles Superior Court. Volunteer, Bet Tzedik Legal Services. Member, Board of Governors, Loyola Law School Alumni Association. *Member:* Los Angeles County Bar Association (Member, Sections on: Real Estate); State Bar of California; Irish American Bar Association (Member, Board of Directors). **PRACTICE AREAS:** Business Litigation; Real Estate Litigation. *Email:* 75140.3054@Compuserve.com

**JOHN G. THORPE,** born San Francisco, California, September 5, 1924; admitted to bar, 1952, California. *Education:* Loyola University of Los Angeles (B.B.A., 1953; LL.B., 1951). Phi Delta Phi. Deputy District Attorney, Los Angeles County, 1952-1954. National Association of Real Estate Investment Trusts, 1982—. Member, St. Joseph's Medical Center Bio-Ethics Committee, 1983—. Member, Board of Directors, Metabolic Foundation, 1974—. Member, Board of Visitors, Loyola Law School, 1984—. *Member:* Los Angeles County and American Bar Associations; The State Bar of California. **PRACTICE AREAS:** Real Estate Law.

**VINCENT W. THORPE,** born Los Angeles, California, October 11, 1933; admitted to bar, 1960, California. *Education:* Loyola Marymount University (B.S., 1955; J.D., 1959); University of Bombay, India. Phi Delta Phi. Adjunct Professor of Law, Business Acquisitions, Loyola Law School, 1983-1989. Author, "Negotiating the Sale of Business," Continuing Education of the Bar, California, 1991. Contributing Author: "Drafting Business Contracts-Principles, Techniques & Forms," Continuing Education of the Bar, 1995. Assistant Attorney General, Antitrust and Consumer Fraud, State of California, 1960-1966. *Member:* Los Angeles County (Chairman, Committee on Law Office Management, 1972-1974; Member, Business and Corporate Law Section) and American (Member, Sections on: Litigation; Corporation, Banking and Business Law) Bar Associations; State Bar of California (Member, Business Law Section); Association of Business Trial Lawyers. **PRACTICE AREAS:** Business Litigation; Corporate Law.

## OF COUNSEL

**JOHN C. CARPENTER,** born Oakland, California, April 27, 1948; admitted to bar, 1976, California and U.S. District Court, Northern District of California; 1977, U.S. District Court, Central District of California; 1983, Alaska; 1996, U.S. District Court, Eastern District of California. *Education:* University of San Francisco (B.A., 1970; J.D., 1975). Phi Sigma Alpha; Phi Alpha Delta; Sigma Alpha Epsilon. Recipient: American Jurisprudence Award in Corporate Law; American Indian Scholarship. Licensed Real Estate Broker, California, 1987. *Member:* Los Angeles County Bar Association; State Bar of California. **PRACTICE AREAS:** Business; Corporate; Entertainment; Real Estate Law.

**SANFORD HOLO,** born Cincinnati, Ohio, January 18, 1939; admitted to bar, 1964, Illinois; 1967, California, U.S. Court of Appeals, Ninth Circuit and U.S. District Court, Northern District of California; 1969, New York, U.S. Supreme Court, U.S. Tax Court and U.S. Court of Appeals, Second Circuit. *Education:* University of Michigan (B.A., with honors in Economics, 1960); Harvard University (J.D., 1963); New York University (LL. M., in Taxation, 1968). Author: "Installment Sales in 1982—Seller Financing Possibilities & Difficulties-Real Property Tax Planning, 1982," California Continuing Education of the Bar, 1983; "The A-B Partnership: Planning for Differing Investor Objectives," 36 Annual Institute on Federal Taxation, University of Southern California Law Center, 1984; "The Home Office Deduction," 10 CEB Cal.-Bus. L. Prac. 121, Fall, 1995. Lecturer and Panelist: Income Tax Consequences and Tax Planning in Real Property Transactions, California Continuing Education of the Bar, 1979-1982, 1984-1985; "Tax Shelters Under Attack," California Continuing Education of the Bar, 1985; "Advanced Partnership Taxation," California CPA Foundation, 1985;

*(This Listing Continued)*

"Tax Deferred Real Property Exchanges," California Continuing Education of the Bar, 1987; "Passive Activity Loss and Internal Tracing Issues," Taxation Section, State Bar of California Annual Program, 1987. Adjunct Professor, Graduate School of Taxation, Golden Gate University, Los Angeles, California, 1977-1986. Assistant Professor, California State University, Los Angeles, Summer, 1996. Adjunct Faculty, Golden Gate University School of Law, LL.M (Tax) Fall, 1996. *Member:* The Association of the Bar of the City of New York; Los Angeles County and American (Member, Taxation Section) Bar Associations; State Bar of California (Member, Taxation Section). **PRACTICE AREAS:** Individual & Business Tax Planning & Business Transactions.

**JENNIFER HARRIS,** born Los Angeles, California, May 31, 1964; admitted to bar, 1989, California. *Education:* University of California at Los Angeles (B.A., 1986); Loyola Law School (J.D., 1989). Note and Comment Editor, Loyola Law Review, 1988-1989. Lecturer, California Bail Agents Associations, 1996-1997. *Member:* State Bar of California; American Bar Association (Member, Taxation Section). **LANGUAGES:** French, Spanish and Japanese. **PRACTICE AREAS:** Probate Law; Trusts and Estates; Corporate Law; Real Estate.

REFERENCE: Sanwa Bank.

## THROCKMORTON, BECKSTROM, OAKES & TOMASSIAN LLP
### LOS ANGELES, CALIFORNIA
(See Pasadena)

*Construction (claims and defects), Real Estate, Insurance, Business, Commercial and Medical Legal Law. General Civil Litigation, Defense of Religious Institutions. All aspects of Trial and Appellate Work.*

## THE LAW OFFICES OF JAMES P. TIERNEY, P.C.
*Established in 1975*

**800 TARCUTO WAY**
**LOS ANGELES, CALIFORNIA 90077**
*Telephone: 310-576-1260*
*Fax: 310-576-1270*

*Business and Entertainment Litigation.*

**JAMES P. TIERNEY,** born Montclair, New Jersey, August 23, 1942; admitted to bar, 1968, New York; 1973, California, U.S. District Court, Southern District of New York and Central District of California, U.S. Court of Appeals, Ninth Circuit and U.S. Supreme Court. *Education:* Rutgers University (B.A., 1965); New York Law School (J.D., cum laude, 1968). Member, New York Law School Law Review, 1967-1968. Law Clerk to the Hon. Edward C. McLean, U.S. District Judge, Southern District of New York. Assistant U.S. Attorney, Southern District of New York, 1970-1972. Special Attorney, U.S. Department of Justice, Los Angeles, 1972-1973. *Member:* Beverly Hills, Los Angeles County and New York State Bar Associations; State Bar of California. **REPORTED CASES:** Sid & Marty Krofft Television Productions, Inc. v. McDonald's Corp., 562 F.2d 1152 (9th Cir, 1977); Lutz v. De Laurentis, 211 Cal. App. 3d, 1317, 260 Cal. Rptr. 106 (1989). **PRACTICE AREAS:** Entertainment Litigation; Commercial Litigation.

**SUSAN CLARY,** born Houston, Texas, June 27, 1949; admitted to bar, 1978, California. *Education:* Rice University (B.A., 1971); University of Texas (J.D., with high honors, 1977). Member, Order of the Coif. Articles Editor, Texas Law Review, 1976-1977. Law Clerk to Hon. John C. Godbold, U.S. Court of Appeals, Fifth Circuit, 1977-1978. *Member:* State Bar of California (Member, Committee on Partnerships). **PRACTICE AREAS:** Entertainment Litigation; Commercial Litigation.

REPRESENTATIVE CLIENTS: Republic Pictures, Virgin Vision, LTD. (U.K.); Timothy Hutton; Brian Wilson; Geffen Records; Martin Poll, Herbert B. Leonard; Gloria Estefan; Randy Travis; Hercules Incorporated; Jane Seymour; Ray R. Irani, Chairman, Occidental Petroleum Corporation; All American Communications; Scotti Bros.; Bruce Karatz Chairman, Kaufman & Broad; Larry King; PolyGram (U.K.).

CALIFORNIA—LOS ANGELES — MARTINDALE-HUBBELL LAW DIRECTORY 1997

## TILEM WHITE & WEINTRAUB LLP
### LOS ANGELES, CALIFORNIA
(See Glendale)

*Bankruptcy, Workouts, Related Litigation, Creditor Rights in Marital Dissolution Proceedings, Bankruptcy Appellate Practice.*

---

## THE TIPLER LAW FIRM
8224 BLACKBURN AVENUE, SUITE 100
### LOS ANGELES, CALIFORNIA 90048-4216
Telephone: 213-651-3590
Fax: 213-651-4273
Email: TiplerFL@aol.com

*Andalusia, Alabama Office:* The Tipler Building. P.O. Drawer 1397. Telephone: 334-222-4148. Fax: 334-222-4086.
*Fort Walton Beach, Florida Office:* 348 Miracle Strip Parkway, Suite 18. Telephone: 904-664-0600. Fax: 904-664-6990.
*Atlanta, Georgia Office:* Garland Law Building. 3151 Maple Drive, N.E. Telephone: 404-814-9755. Fax: 404-365-5041.
*London, England Office:* 31 Bedford Square. WC1B 3SG. Telephone: 44-071-323-2722. Fax: 44-071-631-4659.

*Trial Practice, Negligence Law.*

(For Complete Biographical Data on all Personnel, see Professional Biographies at Andalusia, Alabama)

---

## TISDALE & NICHOLSON
Established in 1993
SUITE 755
2049 CENTURY PARK EAST
### LOS ANGELES, CALIFORNIA 90067
Telephone: 310-286-1260
Facsimile: 310-286-2351

*General Civil Trial and Administrative Practice before all State and Federal Courts and Regulatory Agencies. Civil Appeals, Banking, Corporate, Regulatory, Real Estate, Entertainment, International Business, Finance and Litigation Matters, Including Real Estate Workouts and Receiverships, Mergers and Acquisitions. Complex Business, Bankruptcy and Insolvency, Directors and Officers and Other Professional Liability, Trials and Appeals.*

FIRM PROFILE: *The law firm of Tisdale & Nicholson was established with a singular goal in mind: to provide to the financial services industry and general business community high quality legal services in the most efficient and cost-effective manner possible. At Tisdale & Nicholson we are dedicated to our clients and the advancement of their business opportunities.*

*Prior to this firm's formation, our attorneys have, over the course of many years at large nationally-known law firms, actively represented banks, savings institutions, thrift and loans, holding companies, investment banks and other business and financial entities. We therefore recognize the value of superior professional work - we know that by refusing to assign client matters to inexperienced attorneys or to over-staff matters, we are able to provide top-quality service. We are proud of the results we have obtained for our clients.*

### MEMBERS OF FIRM

**JEFFREY A. TISDALE,** born Akron, Ohio, February 10, 1949; admitted to bar, 1978, California and U.S. District Court, Southern District of California; 1979, Florida; 1992, U.S. Office of Financial Adjudications. *Education:* University of California at Santa Barbara (B.A., 1974); California Western Law School (J.D., 1977). Member, Moot Court Honors Board. Editor, California Western International Law Journal, 1976-1977. Attorney: Federal Deposit Insurance Corporation, Honors Program in Banking, Washington D.C., 1977-1979; Federal Home Loan Bank Board, Washington, D.C., 1979-1980. *Member:* State Bar of California; The Florida Bar; American Bar Association; Western League of Savings Institutions; Community Bankers of Southern California; California Association of Thrift and Loans. **PRACTICE AREAS:** Financial Institutions Regulatory Counseling; Corporate and Securities Law; Entertainment Law; International Business.

**GUY C. NICHOLSON,** born Van Nuys, California, April 9, 1955; admitted to bar, 1982, California and U.S. District Court, Central District of California; 1983, U.S. District Court, Southern District of California; 1986,

*(This Listing Continued)*

CAA1250B

U.S. District Court, Northern District of California; U.S. Court of Appeals, Ninth Circuit; 1992, U.S. Office of Financial Adjudications; 1995, U.S. Court of Federal Claims. *Education:* California State University at Northridge (B.A., summa cum laude, 1978); Loyola University of Los Angeles (J.D., 1982). Pi Sigma Alpha. Judge Pro Tem, Los Angeles Municipal Court, 1987—. *Member:* Los Angeles County, American and Federal Bar Associations; State Bar of California. **PRACTICE AREAS:** Financial Institutions Regulatory Litigation; Complex Business; Corporate and Real Estate Litigation; Appeals.

**SANDOR X. MAYUGA,** born Lynwood, California, November 23, 1948; admitted to bar, 1974, California and U.S. District Court, Central District of California. *Education:* University of California at Santa Barbara (A.B., magna cum laude, 1970); University of Pennsylvania (J.D., 1974); Academie du Droit Internationale de la Haye; Universite Libres de Bruxelles. Recipient, Raymond A. Speiser Award in Field Research, University of Pennsylvania, 1974. Author: "Law and Liberty," Long Beach Bar Association Bulletin, September, 1966. Member, California Association of Thrift and Loan Companies. *Member:* State Bar of California (Member, Business Law Section and Financial Institutions Committee, 1991-1994). [Maj., USAFR, Air Force Intelligence Service, 1970-1990]. **PRACTICE AREAS:** Banking and Financial Institutions; Regulatory Law; Corporations; Securities; General Business.

### ASSOCIATES

**PAUL S. COOLEY,** born Phoenix, Arizona, December 2, 1964; admitted to bar, 1990, California and U.S. District Court, Central District of California. *Education:* Loyola Marymount University (B.A., 1987); Loyola Law School (J.D., 1990). St. Thomas More Law Honor Society. Recipient: Frank Brick Memorial Academic Merit Scholarship. Case Note Editor, The Loyola of Los Angeles Entertainment Law Journal, 1988-1990. Constitutional Law Fellow, 1989-1990. **PRACTICE AREAS:** Business; Securities; Intellectual Property; Construction; Unfair Competition.

**ELIZABETH A. MCFARLAND,** born Santa Monica, California, March 28, 1965; admitted to bar, 1993, Maryland; 1994, California and District of Columbia; 1995, Arizona and U.S. District Court, Central District of California. *Education:* University of California at Los Angeles (B.A., 1987); Georgetown University (J.D., 1993). Author: "Czechoslovakia Links Economic and Immigration Policies," Immigration Law Journal, Vol. 5, No. 3. "The Schengen Agreement and Its Portent for the Freedom of Personal Movement in Europe," Georgetown Immigration Law Journal, Vol. 6, No. 1. Consultant to Government of Estonia regarding antitrust legislation, 1992. Visiting Professor, Santa Barbara College of Law, 1995. *Member:* Santa Barbara Women Lawyer's Association. **LANGUAGES:** Italian. **REPORTED CASES:** Marriage of Heikes, California Supreme Court, 1995; Alleco Inc. v. Alfred, Maryland Court of Appeals, 1993; The Maxima Corporation v. 6933 Arlington Development Limited Partnership, Maryland Court of Special Appeals, 1993. **PRACTICE AREAS:** Commercial Litigation; Appellate Practice; Financial Institutions; General Business.

### OF COUNSEL

**RICHARD A. KOLBER,** born Wantagh, Long Island, New York, August 2, 1961; admitted to bar, 1986, California and U.S. District Court, Central District of California; U.S. District Court, Southern District of California. *Education:* State University of New York at Binghamton (B.A., with honors, 1983); McGeorge School of Law, University of the Pacific (J.D., with distinction, 1986). Pi Sigma Alpha; Phi Delta Phi; National Order of Barristers. Recipient: New York State Merit Scholarship; American Jurisprudence Award in Evidence; Best Brief, Moot Court Competition. Member, National Moot Court Team and Moot Court Honors Board. *Member:* Los Angeles County Bar Association; State Bar of California. **PRACTICE AREAS:** Business, Corporate and Entertainment Litigation.

**DAVID KERN PETELER,** born Minneapolis, Minnesota, July 13, 1953; admitted to bar, 1981, California. *Education:* Leningrad University of Leningrad, USSR; Carleton College (B.A., cum laude, 1975); University of Michigan at Ann Arbor (M.A., 1978); Universite Paul Valerie at Montpellier, France; Columbia University Graduate School of Business Management at New York (M.B.A., 1981); Columbia University (J.D., 1981). Writing and Research Editor, Columbia Journal of Transnational Law. Author: "Recent Developments in Privatization in Russia," Privatization International Yearbook, 1992; "Perestroika in Transition," Los Angeles Lawyer, November, 1991. Member: Columbia Society of International Law; Russian and Commonwealth Business Forum; Russian Trade Association, California; California Central Coast World Trade Center. *Member:* State Bar of California. **LANGUAGES:** Russian. **PRACTICE AREAS:** Business Law; Securities; Corporate Finance; Mergers and Acquisitions; High Technology; International Business; International Joint Ventures.

*(This Listing Continued)*

**MARK J. PEARL,** born Burbank, California, October 23, 1958; admitted to bar, 1984, California. *Education:* University of California at Los Angeles (B.A., magna cum laude, 1980); University of California at Berkeley (M.B.A., 1984); Boalt Hall School of Law, University of California at Berkeley (J.D., 1984). Associate Editor and Founding Member, International Tax and Business Lawyer. *Member:* State Bar of California (Member, Real Property Section; Steering Committee, Affordable Housing Subsection). *PRACTICE AREAS:* Real Property; Community Development; Real Estate Exchanges; Real Estate Finance; Corporations; General Business.

**KENNETH S. FIELDS,** born Los Angeles, California, June 12, 1962; admitted to bar, 1989, California. *Education:* University of California at Los Angeles (B.A., 1986); Loyola University of Los Angeles (J.D., 1989). Member, St. Thomas More Law Honor Society. Staff Member, Loyola of Los Angeles Law Review. *Member:* Los Angeles County Bar Association (Member, Sections on: Real Property; Environmental and Business Law; Chairman, Heal The Bay Legal Committee); State Bar of California. *PRACTICE AREAS:* Real Property; Environmental Law; Insurance Law; Real Estate Finance; Corporate; General Business.

**PAUL H. MOELLER,** born Auburn, California, March 31, 1947; admitted to bar, 1972, California. *Education:* University of California at Los Angeles (B.A., 1969); Loyola University of Los Angeles (J.D., 1972). Former Counsel, Security Pacific National Bank. Former Assistant Regional Counsel, Federal National Mortgage Association. Former General Counsel, Countrywide Funding. *Member:* State Bar of California; Community Bankers of Southern California; Southern California Mortgage Bankers Association (Chairman, Income Property Roundtable); REOMAC. *PRACTICE AREAS:* Mortgage; Banking; Real Estate Law.

---

## LAWRENCE C. TISTAERT

11766 WILSHIRE BOULEVARD, SUITE 1580
**LOS ANGELES, CALIFORNIA 90025-6537**
Telephone: 310-312-0874
Fax: 310-312-1034
Email: lctist@ix.netcom.com

*Business, Real Estate, Probate/Trust and Trial Practice.*

FIRM PROFILE: *With emphasis on long-term representation as outside general counsel to moderate-size businesses and real estate owners. Transactional and litigation practice. Practice includes routine utilization of other specialized counsel on an as-needed basis.*

**LAWRENCE C. TISTAERT,** born Los Angeles, California, January 14, 1942; admitted to bar, 1967, California and U.S. District Court, Central District of California. *Education:* University of California at Los Angeles (B.A., 1964); University of California at Los Angeles School of Law (J.D., 1967). Phi Delta Phi. Moot Court Honors Program. *Member:* Los Angeles County Bar Association; State Bar of California (Member, Sections on: Business Law; Real Property; Estate Planning, Trust and Probate).

REPRESENTATIVE CLIENTS: Bell Foundry Co.; Brendan Tours; Franklin Telecommunications Corp.; Munro Properties; United States Tour Operators Association.
REFERENCE: Bank of America.

---

## TOURTELOT & BUTLER

A PROFESSIONAL LAW CORPORATION
SUITE 1090, 11835 WEST OLYMPIC BOULEVARD
**LOS ANGELES, CALIFORNIA 90064-5001**
Telephone: 310-575-5600
Fax: 310-575-5626

*General Civil and Trial Practice with special emphasis on Real Estate, Business, Partnership, Intellectual Property, Unfair Competition, Construction Litigation, Product Liability and Personal Injury Litigation, Geothermal Energy and Oil and Gas Related Matters, Labor and Employment Law.*

**ROBERT H. TOURTELOT,** born Evanston, Illinois, December 27, 1934; admitted to bar, 1965, California; 1972, U.S. Supreme Court; 1979, Hawaii. *Education:* University of Santa Clara (B.Sc., 1956); Hastings College of Law, University of California (J.D., 1964). Phi Delta Phi; Order of the Coif. Member, Thurston Society. Member, Board of Editors and Issue Editor, Hastings Law Journal, 1963-1964. Author: "Separate Tax Assessment of Condominiums," 14 Hastings Law Journal, May, 1963. Member, Attorney General's Volunteer Advisory Counsel, 1972. Judge Pro-Tem, *(This Listing Continued)*

Los Angeles County Municipal Court, 1984-1990. *Member:* Los Angeles County (Member, Judicial Evaluation Committee; Executive Committee of the Litigation Section; Attorneys Errors and Omissions Prevention Committee and Attorney Client Relations Program), Beverly Hills, Century City, Hawaii State and American (Member, Section of Labor and Employment Law) Bar Associations; State Bar of California; The Association of Trial Lawyers of America (Member, Employment Rights Section; Vice Chair, Small Office Practice Section); National College of Advocacy (Advocate). [With U.S. Navy, 1957-1959]. *PRACTICE AREAS:* Civil Litigation; Personal Injury Litigation; Product Liability Litigation; Corporate; Real Estate; Labor and Employment Law and related matters; Geothermal Energy and Oil and Gas related matters; Wrongful Death Litigation.

**LAURIE J. BUTLER, (P.C.),** born Burlington, Vermont, September 7, 1949; admitted to bar, 1978, California and U.S. District Court, Central and Eastern Districts of California; 1987, U.S. District Court, Northern District of California; 1987, U.S. Supreme Court. *Education:* Indiana University (B.A., 1971); University of Strasbourg, France; Loyola University of Los Angeles (J.D., cum laude, 1978); University of Grenoble, France. Member: Loyola Law Review Staff, 1976-1978; St. Thomas More Law Honor Society. Public Arbitrator, National Association of Securities Dealers, 1988—. *Member:* Los Angeles County Bar Association; State Bar of California. *LANGUAGES:* French and Spanish. *PRACTICE AREAS:* State and Federal Court Business Litigation; Defamation; Unfair Competition; Real Estate; Corporate; Employment and Labor related matters.

---

**MARLENA M. BLANKENSHIP,** born Los Angeles, California, October 2, 1954; admitted to bar, 1989, California; 1990, U.S. District Court, Central District of California. *Education:* University of California at Los Angeles (B.A., 1985); Loyola University of Los Angeles (J.D., 1989). *Member:* Los Angeles County Bar Association; State Bar of California.

OF COUNSEL

**PETER J. WILKE,** born St. Paul, Minnesota, November 10, 1948; admitted to bar, 1975, Spokane Indian Tribal Court; 1976, Swinomish Indian Tribal Community Court; 1977, Washington; 1978, U.S. District Court, Western District of Washington; 1992, California; 1994, U.S. District Court, Central District of California. *Education:* University of California at Los Angeles (B.A., 1971); Gonzaga University (J.D., 1976). *Member:* State Bar of California; Washington State Bar Association. *PRACTICE AREAS:* Business Litigation; Entertainment Law; Corporate Law; Securities (public filings and private offerings); Real Estate; Employment; Land Use.

REFERENCE: Bank of Los Angeles.

---

## RICHARD P. TOWNE

**LOS ANGELES, CALIFORNIA**
(See Woodland Hills)

*Business, Bankruptcy, Corporate and related Insolvency Litigation, Entertainment and First Amendment Litigation, Trials and Appeals in all State and Federal Courts.*

---

## D. MICHAEL TRAINOTTI,

A PROFESSIONAL LAW CORPORATION
**LOS ANGELES, CALIFORNIA**
(See Long Beach)

*General Tax Practice. Real Estate, Trust and Probate Law, Estate Planning, Corporation and Partnership Law. Real Estate Pass Through Entities.*

---

## TREDWAY, LUMSDAINE & DOYLE, LLP

**LOS ANGELES, CALIFORNIA**
(See Downey)

## TRESSLER, SODERSTROM, MALONEY & PRIESS

2049 CENTURY PARK EAST, SUITE 2140
**LOS ANGELES, CALIFORNIA 90067-3283**
Telephone: 310-226-7460
Fax: 310-226-7461

*Chicago, Illinois Office:* 233 Wacker Drive, 22nd Floor. Telephone: 312-627-4000. FAX: 312-627-1717.

*Wheaton, Illinois Office:* 2100 Manchester Road, Suite 950. Telephone: 630-668-2800. FAX: 630-668-3003.

*Waukegan, Illinois Office:* 415 Washington Street, Suite 203. Telephone: 847-623-2100. FAX: 847-623-9695.

*New York, New York Office:* 655 Madison Avenue, Suite, 1900. Telephone: 212-593-5050. FAX: 212-593-5404.

*General Civil Trial and Appellate Practice. Trusts and Estate Planning, Property and Casualty Insurance, Corporation, Real Estate, Health Care, Employment, Professional Liability, Environmental, Securities Law and Drug and Medical Device Litigation.*

### RESIDENT PARTNER

**MARY E. MCPHERSON,** born Fontana, California, March 1, 1961; admitted to bar, 1986, Colorado; 1989, Illinois; 1995, California. *Education:* Wellesley College; University of Notre Dame. *Member:* State Bar of California; Illinois Bar Association; Southern California Association and Defense Counsel; Defense Research Institute; Illinois Association of Defense Trial Counsel.

### ASSOCIATE

**JEFFREY J. CHRISTOVICH,** born New Orleans, Louisiana, February 5, 1959; admitted to bar, 1985, Louisiana; 1991, California. *Education:* Washington & Lee University; Tulane University of Louisiana.

**SHARON R. TERRIS,** born Los Angeles, California, April 3, 1964; admitted to bar, 1989, California and U.S. District Court, Central District of California. *Education:* University of California, San Diego; Loyola Law School.

Representatives Clients to be furnished upon request.

## TROOP MEISINGER STEUBER & PASICH, LLP

A Partnership including a Professional Corporation
*Established in 1975*
10940 WILSHIRE BOULEVARD
**LOS ANGELES, CALIFORNIA 90024-3902**
Telephone: 310-824-7000
Orange County: 714-953-6221
Telecopier: 310-443-7599

*Corporate Law, including Corporate Securities and Finance, Entertainment, Financial Services, Institutional Finance, International Transactions, Insurance Coverage Advice, Labor and Employment Law, Real Estate, Tax, and Litigation including, General Business and Securities Litigation, Environmental and Insurance Coverage Litigation.*

### MEMBERS OF FIRM

**SCOTT W. ALDERTON,** born Casper, Wyoming, February 14, 1959; admitted to bar, 1985, California; 1986, U.S. District Court, Central District of California. *Education:* University of California, Los Angeles (B.A., 1982); Loyola University of Los Angeles (J.D., cum laude, 1985). St. Thomas More Law Honor Society; Scott Moot Court. *Member:* State Bar of California (Member, Business Law Section). **PRACTICE AREAS:** General Corporate Law; Corporate Securities Law; Mergers and Acquisitions Law. *Email:* swa@tmsp.com

**MARTIN S. APPEL,** born Chicago, Illinois, March 15, 1933; admitted to bar, 1956, Illinois; 1958, California. *Education:* Northwestern University (B.S., 1953; J.D., 1956). Phi Alpha Delta; Beta Alpha Psi. Author: "Motion Picture Service Company: A Service to the Motion Picture Industry," 27th USC Tax Institute, 1975; 33rd USC Tax Institute, 1981; "The Personal Service Corporation - A Tax Planning Tool," 33rd USC Tax Institute, 1981. Executive Vice President, Motion Picture Television and Tax Institute, 1979—. Commissioner, Internal Revenue Advisory Committee, 1983 and 1984. President, Motion Picture Television Tax Institute, 1994—. Gubernatorial Appointment to the California State Council on Developmental Disabilities, 1995—. *Member:* Los Angeles County and American Bar Associations; The State Bar of California (Chairman, Subcommittee of Income Tax Section, 1975-1976). (Certified Specialist, Taxation Law, The State Bar of California Board of Legal Specialization). *Email:* msa@tmsp.com

**MARY K. BARNES,** born Los Angeles, California, July 31, 1958; admitted to bar, 1983, California; 1984, U.S. District Court, Central District of California; 1985, U.S. District Court, Southern District of California; 1986, U.S. District Court, Eastern District of California. *Education:* University of Southern California (A.B., magna cum laude, 1980); University of California at Los Angeles (J.D., 1983). Phi Beta Kappa. Member, Moot Court Honor Program, 1982-1983. *Member:* Westwood (Member, Board of Governors), Los Angeles County (Member, Committee on Professional Liability Insurance) and American Bar Associations; State Bar of California. **PRACTICE AREAS:** General Business Litigation; Insurance Coverage Litigation; Entertainment Litigation. *Email:* mkb@tmsp.com

**ANTHONY M. BASICH,** born Los Angeles, California, September 4, 1956; admitted to bar, 1981, California. *Education:* Stanford University (B.S., 1978); George Washington University (J.D., 1981). Member, George Washington University Law Review, 1979-1981. *Member:* Los Angeles County Bar Association; State Bar of California (Chairman, Litigation Section, Education Committee). **PRACTICE AREAS:** General Business Litigation; Environmental Litigation; Wrongful Termination Litigation; Entertainment Litigation. *Email:* amb@tmsp.com

**MARY CRAIG CALKINS,** born San Diego, California, February 16, 1950; admitted to bar, 1981, California and U.S. District Court, Central District of California; 1982, U.S. Court of Appeals, Ninth Circuit; 1983, U.S. District Court, Northern, Eastern and Southern Districts of California. *Education:* Occidental College; University of California at Los Angeles (B.A., 1972); Loyola Law School, Los Angeles (J.D., cum laude, 1981). Member: St. Thomas More Law Honor Society; Scott Moot Court Honors Board; Production Editor, Loyola of Los Angeles Law Review, 1981. Co-Author: "Avoiding Wrongful Termination in the 90's," American Somerset, Inc., 1989. *Member:* Los Angeles County (Former Member, Bench and Bar Committee) and American Bar Associations; State Bar of California (Member, Administration of Justice Committee, Litigation Section, 1990-1993). **PRACTICE AREAS:** Insurance Coverage Litigation; General Business Litigation; Entertainment Litigation; Employment Litigation. *Email:* mcc@tmsp.com

**ELIZABETH A. CASEY,** born Suffern, New York, December 31, 1962; admitted to bar, 1988, California; 1989, U.S. District Court, Central District of California; 1992, U.S. District Court, Northern District of California; 1994, U.S. District Court, District of Arizona. *Education:* Claremont McKenna College (B.A., cum laude, 1985); George Washington University (J.D., with high honors, 1988). Order of the Coif. Member, 1986-1987 and Notes Editor, 1987-1988, George Washington University Law Review. *Member:* State Bar of California. **PRACTICE AREAS:** General Commercial Litigation; Entertainment Litigation. *Email:* eac@tmsp.com

**TYRONE R. CHILDRESS,** born Cincinnati, Ohio, December 15, 1963; admitted to bar, 1988, California and U.S. District Court, Central District of California. *Education:* Georgetown University (B.S., cum laude, 1985); University of Virginia (J.D., 1988). Member, National Moot Court Team, 1987-1988. Member, Task Force on Environmental Insurance Coverage Litigation, 1991—, Torts and Insurance Practice Section, American Bar Association. Member, National Litigation Panel, Civil Litigation Principles and Practice Course, University of Virginia School of Law, 1994—. *Member:* Beverly Hills, Los Angeles County, American and International Bar Associations; State Bar of California; German-American Chamber of Commerce. **LANGUAGES:** German. **PRACTICE AREAS:** Insurance Coverage Litigation; General Business Litigation; International Law. *Email:* trc@tmsp.com

**JAMES J. CICCONE,** born Miami, Florida, September 10, 1963; admitted to bar, 1989, New York and U.S. District Court, Southern and Eastern Districts of New York; 1990, California and U.S. District Court, Central District of California. *Education:* Tufts University (B.S., cum laude, 1985); George Washington University (J.D., with honors, 1988). *Member:* Los Angeles Bar Association; State Bar of California. **PRACTICE AREAS:** Insurance Coverage Litigation; Business Litigation. *Email:* jjc@tmsp.com

**HARRISON J. DOSSICK,** born New York, N.Y., February 11, 1960; admitted to bar, 1987, California. *Education:* University of Michigan (B.G.S., with Distinction, 1982); Boston University School of Law (J.D., 1986). Extern Investigator, Public Defender Service for the District of Co-

*(This Listing Continued)*

lumbia, 1982. *Member:* State Bar of California. **PRACTICE AREAS:** Entertainment Litigation; Business Litigation. *Email:* hjd@tmsp.com

**ROBERT E. DUFFY,** born Buffalo, New York, August 22, 1946; admitted to bar, 1971, California. *Education:* University of St. Thomas (B.A., magna cum laude, 1967); University of Houston (J.D., magna cum laude, 1970). Articles Editor, Houston Law Review, 1969-1970. Member, Editorial Board, The Journal of Real Estate Development, 1985-1989. Author: "The Real Estate Settlement Procedures Act of 1974, An Overview of the Act and Selected Problems," 51 Los Angeles Bar Journal 164, 1975; "RESPA Refined and Revisited," Real Estate Review, Vol. 6, No. 4, at 82, 1977; "Art Law: Representing Artists, Dealers and Collectors," Practising Law Institute, 1977; "Residential Land Leases Provide New Opportunities," 1 The Journal of Real Estate Development 5, 1985. Lecturer in Law, University of Houston, 1969-1970. *Member:* Los Angeles County (Member, Real Property Section) and American (Member, Sections of: Real Property, Probate and Trust Law; Corporation, Banking and Business Law) Bar Associations; The State Bar of California. **PRACTICE AREAS:** Real Estate Law; Real Estate Finance Law. *Email:* red@tmsp.com

**JOHN M. GENGA,** born Detroit, Michigan, April 28, 1962; admitted to bar, 1986, California; 1987, U.S. District Court, Central and Eastern Districts of California; 1988, U.S. District Court, Northern and Southern Districts of California; 1988, U.S. Court of Appeals, Ninth Circuit; 1993, U.S. Supreme Court. *Education:* Stanford University (B.A., 1983); University of Michigan (J.D., 1986). Phi Beta Kappa. Member: Intellectual Property and Litigation Sections of Los Angeles County and American Bar Associations; State Bar of California. **PRACTICE AREAS:** Copyright Litigation; General Entertainment Litigation; General Business Litigation. *Email:* jmg@tmsp.com

**MARC J. GRABOFF,** born Brooklyn, New York, March 30, 1956; admitted to bar, 1983, California. *Education:* University of California at Los Angeles (B.A., 1977); Loyola Law School of Los Angeles (J.D., magna cum laude, 1983). Alpha Sigma Nu. St. Thomas More Law Honor Society. Staff, 1981-1982 and Note and Comment Editor, 1982-1983, Loyola Law Review. *Member:* Los Angeles County, Beverly Hills and American Bar Associations; State Bar of California. **PRACTICE AREAS:** Entertainment Law. *Email:* mjg@tmsp.com

**BLAINE ERIC GREENBERG,** born New York, N.Y., June 18, 1958; admitted to bar, 1982, California and U.S. District Court, Central District of California; 1985, U.S. Court of Appeals, Ninth Circuit; 1993, U.S. Supreme Court. *Education:* Vassar College (A.B., cum laude, 1979); Stanford University (J.D., 1982). Order of the Coif. Extern at the U.S. Attorney's Office, Northern District of California. Author: "The ABC's of Protecting Vanna White's Right of Publicity At Trial," and Speaker on "The Outer Limits of the Right of Publicity," at 1994 ABA Annual Meeting, New Orleans, La. *Member:* Los Angeles County Bar Association; State Bar of California. **PRACTICE AREAS:** Environmental/Toxic Tort Litigation; Commercial Litigation; Family Law Litigation. *Email:* beg@tmsp.com

**DAVID HALBERSTADTER,** born Elizabeth, New Jersey, September 1, 1957; admitted to bar, 1982, California and U.S. District Court, Central District of California; 1985, U.S. District Court, Eastern and Southern Districts of California. *Education:* Cornell University (B.A., 1979); Georgetown University (J.D., magna cum laude, 1982). Staff Member, 1980-1981 and Editor, 1981-1982, Law and Policy in International Business, The Georgetown International Law Journal. *Member:* Los Angeles County Bar Association (Arbitrator, Attorney Client Relations Program, Litigation, Intellectual Property and Entertainment Law Section); State Bar of California (Member, Section on Litigation); Los Angeles Copyright Society. **PRACTICE AREAS:** Entertainment Litigation; Intellectual Property/Unfair Competition Law; General Commercial Litigation. *Email:* dnh@tmsp.com

**FRED D. HEATHER,** born Philadelphia, Pennsylvania, October 8, 1943; admitted to bar, 1978, New York; 1983, California and U.S. Supreme Court. *Education:* Bucknell University (A.B., 1966); Columbia University (M.A., 1971); Hofstra Law School (J.D., 1977). Member, 1975-1977 and Editor-in-Chief, 1976-1977, Hofstra Law Review. Assistant U.S. Attorney, Central District of California, Criminal Division, 1983-1987. . Member, Federal Indigent Defense Panel, Central District of California, 1988—. Member, Advisory Board, Institute for Corporate Counsel, The Law Center, University of Southern California, 1994—. *Member:* Los Angeles County, New York State and American (Chair, Qui Tam/Procurement Fraud Subcommittee, White Collar Crime Committee) Bar Associations. [Capt., U.S. Army Intelligence, 1967-1969]. **PRACTICE AREAS:** White Collar Criminal Defense; Complex Civil Litigation; Civil False Claims Act Defense. *Email:* fdh@tmsp.com

*(This Listing Continued)*

**CLYDE M. HETTRICK, III,** born Salt Lake City, Utah, August 3, 1961; admitted to bar, 1987, Illinois and U.S. District Court, Northern District of Illinois; 1988, California and U.S. District Court, Central District of California; 1994, U.S. District Court, Northern District of California. *Education:* University of Chicago (A.B., with honors, 1984); Boalt Hall School of Law, University of California, Berkeley (J.D., 1987). *Member:* Illinois State Bar Association; State Bar of California. **PRACTICE AREAS:** Insurance Coverage; Business Litigation. *Email:* cmh@tmsp.com

**ROBERT M. JASON,** born New York, N.Y., March 4, 1956; admitted to bar, 1981, California and U.S. District Court, Central District of California. *Education:* Harvard University (A.B., cum laude, 1978; J.D., cum laude, 1981). Member, Board of Editors, Harvard Law Review, 1979-1981. Author: "IRS Issues Examination Guide Attacking Industry Deductions," 11 Entertainment Law & Finance No. 6 of 1 (September 1995); "IRS Finally Gives Blessing To The So-Called Rabbi Trust," Los Angeles Daily Journal, August 7, 1992; "Two Major Decisions Expand Definition of Change of Ownership," 3 Journal of California Taxation 41, Spring 1992; "California Sales Tax Aspects of Acquisitions, Reorganizations and Liquidations," 1 Journal of California Taxation 1990; "The Use of Surety Bonds to Secure Unfunded Deferred Compensation," 12 Tax Section News 12, Fall, 1985; "Proposition 13: Legal Entities and Changes in Ownership," 9 Tax Section News 1, Summer, 1983; "Determining Breach of Fiduciary Duty Under the Labor Management Reporting and Disclosure Act: Gabauer v. Woodcock," 93 Harvard Law Review 608, 1980. Member, Board of Contributing Editors, Entertainment Law & Finance, 1995—; Motion Picture and Television Tax Institute, 1994; Board of Advisors, The Journal of California Taxation, 1989-1992. *Member:* Los Angeles County (Member, Section on Taxation) and American (Member, Section on Taxation) Bar Associations; The State Bar of California (Member: Taxation Section; Executive Committee, 1984-1985). **LANGUAGES:** French. **PRACTICE AREAS:** Tax Law; Business Planning; Compensation Planning. *Email:* rmj@tmsp.com

**MARTIN D. KATZ,** born Chicago, Illinois, November 20, 1959; admitted to bar, 1983, California. *Education:* Northwestern University (B.A., 1980); University of Michigan (J.D., cum laude, 1983). Phi Beta Kappa. **PRACTICE AREAS:** Insurance Coverage Litigation; General Business Litigation; Products Liability Defense. *Email:* mdk@tmsp.com

**THOMAS GLEN LEO,** born Los Angeles, California, May 16, 1953; admitted to bar, 1978, California. *Education:* Massachusetts Institute of Technology (S.B. in Computer Science, 1975; S.B. in Management, 1975; S.B. in Mathematics, 1975); University of Southern California (J.D., 1978). Member, 1976-1978 and Executive Editor of Publication, 1977-1978, Southern California Law Review. *Member:* American Bar Association (Member, Section of Corporation, Banking and Business Law; Section of Intellectual Property, Member, Securitization Committee); State Bar of California. **PRACTICE AREAS:** Secured Transactions; Entertainment Finance. *Email:* tgl@tmsp.com

**C. DENNIS LOOMIS,** born Cleveland, Ohio, February 2, 1950; admitted to bar, 1978, California. *Education:* University of California at Los Angeles (B.A., cum laude, 1973); Hastings College of Law, University of California (J.D., 1978). Order of the Coif. Member, Thurston Society. Member, 1976-1977 and Note and Comment Editor, 1977-1978, Hastings Law Journal. Author: "Criminal Remedies May Take Wind Out of Sales," Los Angeles Daily Journal, Summer 1992; "Multimedia Productions: Beware The Pitfalls," The Strategist, January 1995. *Member:* Los Angeles County and American (Member, Section of Intellectual Property) Bar Associations; State Bar of California. **LANGUAGES:** Italian. **PRACTICE AREAS:** Domestic and International; Copyright and Trademark Protection, Registration Enforcement Law; Intellectual Property Litigation; General Commercial Litigation. *Email:* cdl@tmsp.com

**MURRAY MARKILES,** born Johannesburg, South Africa, October 30, 1961; admitted to bar, 1987, California. *Education:* University of California at Los Angeles (B.A., magna cum laude, 1983; J.D., 1986). Phi Beta Kappa. *Member:* State Bar of California. **PRACTICE AREAS:** Corporate Securities; Mergers and Acquisitions; High Technology; Intellectual Property Law; Antitrust. *Email:* mmm@tmsp.com

**ROBERT A. MARTIS,** born Cleveland, Ohio, June 29, 1963; admitted to bar, 1988, California and U.S. District Court, Central District of California. *Education:* Arizona State University (B.A., summa cum laude, 1985); University of Paris, Sorbonne; Georgetown University (J.D., magna cum laude, 1988). Order of the Coif. Editor, Georgetown University Law Review, 1987-1988. Author: "Children in the Entertainment Industry: Are They Being Protected? An Analysis of the California and New York Approaches," 8 Loyola University Law Journal 25, 1988. *Member:* Beverly

*(This Listing Continued)*

## TROOP MEISINGER STEUBER & PASICH, LLP, Los Angeles—Continued

Hills Bar Association (Chair, Entertainment Law Section; Past President Emeritus, Premiere Patrons and Board of Trustees, American Cinematheque); State Bar of California. *LANGUAGES:* French. *PRACTICE AREAS:* Transactional Entertainment Law. *Email:* ram@tmsp.com

**LOUIS M. MEISINGER,** born New York, N.Y., December 12, 1942; admitted to bar, 1968, California. *Education:* University of California at Los Angeles (B.A., 1964; J.D., 1967). Phi Beta Kappa; Order of the Coif; Sigma Delta Pi; Phi Delta Phi. Member and Editor, U.C.L.A. Law Review, 1965-1967. Co-author: "Trial Without Jury," California Continuing Education of the Bar, California Civil Procedure During Trial 2, 1984. Member, Panel of Arbitrators, American Arbitration Association. *Member:* Los Angeles County and Century City Bar Associations; The State Bar of California. *PRACTICE AREAS:* Entertainment Litigation; Intellectual Property Litigation; Commercial Litigation. *Email:* lmm@tmsp.com

**ROBERT S. METZGER,** born St. Louis, Missouri, September 27, 1950; admitted to bar, 1977, California; 1978, District of Columbia. *Education:* Middlebury College (B.A., 1972); Georgetown University (J.D., 1977). Research Fellow, Center for Science and International Affairs, Harvard University, 1977-1978. Author: "Segment Closing Rules Under The New CAS 413: Implications for Contractors," CP&A Report 95-6 (June 1995); "Reforming Post-Cold War Arms Sales Policy: The Crucial Link Between Exports and the Defense Industrial Base," 18 Journal of Strategic Studies No. 4 (Dec. 1995) (with Dr. Christopher Layne); "Retroactivity of the 1986 Amendments To The False Claims Act," Public Contracts Law Journal, Summer 1993. *Member:* The District of Columbia Bar; State Bar of California; American Bar Association. *PRACTICE AREAS:* Litigation; Government Contracts Law. *Email:* rsm@tmsp.com

**LEIGH B. MORRIS,** born Long Beach, California, July 13, 1946; admitted to bar, 1972, California. *Education:* University of California at Los Angeles (A.B., 1968; J.D., 1972). Order of the Coif. Associate of Law, Boalt Hall School of Law, University of California, 1972-1973. *Member:* The State Bar of California; American Bar Association (Member, Sections on: Corporation, Banking and Business Law; Real Property, Probate and Trust Law). *PRACTICE AREAS:* Real Estate Law; Real Estate and Commercial Finance Law; General Business; Franchising. *Email:* lbm@tmsp.com

**NEIL R. O'HANLON,** born New York, N.Y., August 11, 1950; admitted to bar, 1975, California; U.S. District Court, Central, Northern, Southern and Eastern Districts of California and U.S. Court of Appeals, Ninth and Federal Circuits. *Education:* Columbia University (A.B., 1972; J.D., 1975). Harlan Fiske Stone Scholar. Co-Author: *Officers and Directors: Liabilities and Resolutions* (Matthew Bender 1995). *Member:* Los Angeles County Bar Association (Member: Barristers Executive Committee, 1981-1983; Sections on: Litigation; Real Property); The State Bar of California. *PRACTICE AREAS:* Real Estate and Real Estate Finance Litigation; Financial Institutions Litigation; Bankruptcy Litigation; General Business Litigation. *Email:* nro@tmsp.com

**ANTHONY J. ONCIDI,** born Santa Monica, California, October 30, 1959; admitted to bar, 1985, California, U.S. District Court, Central and Southern Districts of California and U.S. Court of Appeals, Ninth Circuit. *Education:* Pomona College (B.A., cum laude, 1981); University of Chicago (J.D., 1984). Phi Beta Kappa. Semifinalist, Hinton Moot Court Competition. Faculty Member, National Employment Law Institute. Regular columnist on employment law issues for The Los Angeles Daily Journal and The California Labor and Employment Law Quarterly, the official publication of the State Bar of California Labor and Employment Law Section. Co-Author: "Campaign Finance Law: The PACs Strike Back," 12 L.A. Lawyer 50, June, 1989; Supplement to "Advising California Employers," California Continuing Education of the Bar, 1986 and 1987. *Member:* Los Angeles County and American Bar Associations; State Bar of California. *PRACTICE AREAS:* Labor and Employment Law; Litigation. *Email:* ajo@tmsp.com

**KIRK A. PASICH,** born La Jolla, California, May 26, 1955; admitted to bar, 1980, California; 1981, U.S. District Court, Central, Eastern, Northern and Southern Districts of California; 1982, U.S. Court of Appeals, Ninth Circuit; 1992, U.S. Court of Appeals, First Circuit. *Education:* University of California at Los Angeles (B.A., cum laude, 1977); Loyola Law School, Los Angeles (J.D., cum laude, 1980). Member, St. Thomas More Law Honor Society. Chief Ninth Circuit Editor, Loyola of Los Angeles Law Review, 1979-1980. Entertainment Law Columnist, 1988-1990 and Insurance Law Columnist, 1990—, Los Angeles Daily Journal and San Francisco Daily Journal. Member, Forum on Entertainment and Sports Industries, 1983—, Insurance Coverage Litigation Committee, Torts and Insurance Practice Section, 1989— and Task Force on Complex Insurance Coverage Litigation, 1990-1993, American Bar Association. Co-Author: *Manual for Complex Insurance Coverage Litigation* (Prentice Hall 1993); *Officers and Directors: Liabilities and Protections (Matthew Bender 1995).* Author: *including Casualty and Liability Insurance* (Matthew Bender 1990, 1992, 1996); Comment, "The Right of the Press to Gather Information Under the First Amendment," 12 Loyola of Los Angeles Law Review 357 (1979); "Insurance Coverage for Environmental Claims," Los Angeles Lawyer, Jan. 1989; "The Application of the Attorney-Client Privilege & the Work Product Doctrine to Insured-Insurer Communications," in *The Attorney-Client Privilege Under Siege* (ABA Press 1989); "Coverage Litigation Wages On," National Law Journal, May 15, 1989; "Insurance Coverage for the Asbestos Building Cases: There's More Than Property Damage," XXIV Tort & Insurance Law Journal 630 (1989); "Defining Pollution Exclusions," National Law Journal, March 19, 1990; "The Breadth of Insurance Coverage for Environmental Claims," 52 Ohio State Law Journal 1131 (1991); "Infringement vs. Parody: When Is It Fair Use?" Los Angeles Daily Journal, Dec. 19, 1991; "The Work Product Doctrine in the Context of Insurance Coverage Disputes," III Coverage No. 2 (1992); "Beware the Creeping Contract," National Law Journal, Mar. 2, 1992; "General Liability and Personal Injury Coverage for Business Losses: Maximizing Insurance Coverage," 4 The Corporate Analyst, No. 3 (May 1992); "Insurance Coverage After Corporate Mergers and Acquisitions," 6 Mealey's Litigation Reports—Insurance, No. 39, at 18 (Aug. 18, 1992); "Insurance Coverage For Environmental Claims Under Personal Injury Provisions," 7 Mealey's Litigation Reports - Insurance, No. 18, at 18 Mar. 9, 1993 & No. 19 at 22, Mar. 16, 1993; "Series: Insurance in The Aftermath of the Northridge Earthquake," Los Angeles Daily Journal, January 31 - February 3, 1994; "Disappearing Coverage: How To Avoid Being Left High And Dry By Insurers," ABA Journal (June 1994); "Measuring the True Value of Insurance Companies for Punitive Damage Purposes, 8 Mealey's Litigation Reports - Insurance, No. 46, at 17 (Oct. 11, 1994); "Blanket Coverage: An Insurer's Broad Duty to Defend," *Daily Journal* (May 3, 1995); "The 'Expected or Intended' Exclusion and California Insurance Code Section 533," 10 Mealey's Litigation Reports - Insurance, No. 21, at 20 (Apr. 2, 1996). Faculty Member: The Rutter Group, California State Bar Skills Training Workshop, 1987 and 1988; Attorney-Client Privilege Program, Torts and Insurance Practice Section, American Bar Association, 1989; Deposition Skills Workshop, The Practising Law Institute, 1989, Insurance Coverage for Environmental and Pollution Problems, Hawaii State Bar Association Corporate Counsel Section Retreat, 1990; J.A.M.S Environmental Judicial College, June 1994. Speaker: "Recent Developments In Insurance Law: "Resolving First Party Property Policy Environmental Claims," Executive Enterprises, Inc., San Francisco, February 1991; "General Liability and Personal Injury Coverage for Business Losses," The Business Insurance Law Institute, Executive Enterprises, Inc., San Francisco, November 1991; "The Personal Injury and Advertising Liability Endorsement," Insurance, Excess and Reinsurance Coverage Disputes Seminar, Practising Law Institute, San Francisco, February 1992; "The Work Product Doctrine in the Context of Insurance Coverage Disputes," American Bar Association Committee on Insurance Coverage Litigation Annual Meeting, Tucson, March 1992; "Insurance in the Aftermath," Los Angeles Public Counsel, Los Angeles, May 1992; "Will Your Client's Insurer Pay Your Bill," Los Angeles County Bar Association Litigation Section Meeting, Los Angeles, November 1992; "Applying the Principal Exclusions to Hazardous Waste Sites," First Party Property Policies Seminar, Executive Enterprises, Inc., Chicago, May 1993; "Insolvency Issues Arising From Natural Disasters," The Los Angeles Bankruptcy Forum, March 1994; "American Bar Association Section of Litigation, Insurance Coverage, Litigation Committee and Mid-Year Meeting, Tuscon, March 1995. Judge Pro Tem, Los Angeles County Superior Court, 1991—. Chairman, Board of Directors, The Woody Herman Foundation, 1988-1991. Honors: Listed By *California Law Business* as one of the Top 25 Litigators in California and by *The American Lawyer* as one of the Nation's Top 45 Lawyers Under the Age of 45. *PRACTICE AREAS:* Insurance Coverage; Entertainment Litigation; Real Estate Litigation; Commercial Litigation. *Email:* kap@tmsp.com

**DAVID T. PETERSON,** born San Francisco, California, January 27, 1944; admitted to bar, 1971, California and U.S. District Court, Central District of California; 1972, U.S. District Court, Northern, Eastern and Southern Districts of California and U.S. Court of Appeals, Ninth Circuit; 1981, U.S. Supreme Court. *Education:* University of California, Berkeley (B.S., 1965); Georgetown University (J.D., 1970). Editor, The Georgetown Law Journal, 1969-1970. Author: "Innovations & Considerations in Settling Toxic Tort Litigation," 3 Natural Resources and Environment, pg. 9, Spring, 1988. Faculty Member, Executive Enterprises, Inc., 1990—. *Mem-*

*(This Listing Continued)*

ber: Los Angeles County and American (Member, Natural Resources and Environment and Litigation Sections) Bar Associations; The State Bar of California. [1st Lt., U.S. Army, 1965-1967]. *PRACTICE AREAS:* Environmental Litigation; Business and Entertainment Litigation. *Email:* dtp@tmsp.com

**ROBERT J. PLOTKOWSKI,** born San Francisco, California, June 17, 1962; admitted to bar, 1987, California. *Education:* University of California at Los Angeles (B.A., magna cum laude, 1984); Boalt Hall School of Law, University of California (J.D., 1987). Author: Law Letter, "New Construction: Changes in the AIA Standard Form Construction Agreement," The Journal of Real Estate Development, Spring, 1988. Panelist, "Hazardous Waste and Real Estate Transactions," Region IX Hazardous and Solid Waste Regulation Briefing, San Francisco, California, June 1990. Guest Speaker, Warner Center CFO Forum, 1990. Guest Lecturer: University of California, Los Angeles Extension, 1990—; West Los Angeles College, 1991-1992. Panelist, "Real Asset Management," Region IX Federal/State Environmental Conference, San Francisco, California, December, 1990. Member, Board of Directors, Crestwood Hills Association, Brentwood, California, 1993—. *Member:* Beverly Hills (Member, Real Property Section) and Los Angeles County (Member, Real Estate Section) Bar Associations; State Bar of California (Member, Real Property Section). *PRACTICE AREAS:* Real Estate Law; Environmental Law; General Business Law. *Email:* rjp@tmsp.com

**CURTIS D. PORTERFIELD,** born Coral Gables, Florida, April 10, 1957; admitted to bar, 1981, California. *Education:* University of Georgia (A.B., magna cum laude, 1978); Vanderbilt University (J.D., 1981). Phi Beta Kappa; Phi Kappa Phi. President, Vanderbilt Bar Association, 1980-1981. Member, Los Angeles City Attorney's Task Force for Economic Recovery, Insurance Subcommittee. *Member:* Los Angeles County and American Bar Associations; State Bar of California. *PRACTICE AREAS:* Insurance Coverage Litigation; Business & Entertainment Litigation. *Email:* cdp@tmsp.com

**C. N. FRANKLIN REDDICK III,** born Quantico, Virginia, January 26, 1953; admitted to bar, 1980, California. *Education:* California State University at San Jose (B.A., with honors and great distinction, 1977); Hastings College of the Law, University of California (J.D., 1980). Member: Order of the Coif; Thurston Society. Member, 1978-1979 and Note and Comment Editor, 1979-1980, Hastings Law Journal. *PRACTICE AREAS:* Corporate Securities Law; Corporations Law. *Email:* cfr@Tmsp.com

**RONALD D. REYNOLDS,** born Greeley, Colorado, March 28, 1953; admitted to bar, 1981, New York and U.S. District Court, Southern and Eastern Districts of New York; 1982, U.S. Court of Appeals, Third Circuit; 1985, California and U.S. District Court, Central District of California; 1986, U.S. District Court, Northern and Eastern Districts of California and U.S. Court of Appeals, Ninth Circuit. *Education:* University of Colorado (B.A., cum laude, 1976); New York Law School (J.D., cum laude, 1980). Articles Editor, New York Law School Law Review, 1979-1980. *Member:* American Bar Association (Member, Litigation and Antitrust Sections). *PRACTICE AREAS:* Securities and Antitrust Litigation; General Commercial Litigation. *Email:* rdr@tmsp.com

**D. MATTHEW RICHARDSON,** born Seattle, Washington, August 17, 1952; admitted to bar, 1984, California; 1985, U.S. Tax Court and U.S. District Court, Central District of California; 1986, U.S. Claims Court. *Education:* University of Washington (B.A., 1981); Hastings College of Law, University of California (J.D., cum laude, 1984); New York University (LL.M., in Taxation, 1985). Co-Author: "California Professional Corporations," 1989 Supplement, California Continuing Education of the Bar. *Member:* Beverly Hills (Member, Taxation Section, Trust and Probate Section; Chair, Taxation Section, 1989-1990) and American (Member, Section on Taxation) Bar Associations; State Bar of California. *PRACTICE AREAS:* Taxation Law; Estate Planning; General Business Law. *Email:* dmr@tmsp.com

**JEFFREY A. ROSENFELD,** born Los Angeles, California, April 12, 1962; admitted to bar, 1988, California; 1989, U.S. District Court, Central District of California. *Education:* California State University at Northridge (B.A., magna cum laude, 1985); Pepperdine University School of Law (J.D., magna cum laude, 1988). *Member:* Los Angeles County and American Bar Associations; State Bar of California. *PRACTICE AREAS:* Business and Entertainment Litigation; Insurance Coverage Litigation. *Email:* jar@tmsp.com

**DAVID H. SANDS,** born Chappaqua, New York, March 2, 1962; admitted to bar, 1987, California. *Education:* Oberlin College (B.A., 1984); Boston University (J.D., 1987), G. Joseph Tauro Scholar. *Member:* State Bar of California (Chairman, Consumer Financial Services Committee,

*(This Listing Continued)*

1995-1996). *PRACTICE AREAS:* Financial Institutions Law; Corporate and Securities Law; Secured Transactions. *Email:* dhs@tmsp.com

**ALAN B. SPATZ,** born Charleston, West Virginia, May 19, 1954; admitted to bar, 1979, California. *Education:* University of Michigan (B.A., cum laude, 1976); Boalt Hall School of Law, University of California (J.D., 1979). Member, 1976-1979 and Executive Editor, 1978-1979, Ecology Law Quarterly. *Member:* American Bar Association; The State Bar of California (Member, Financial Institutions Committee of the Business Law Section of The State Bar of California, 1990-1993). *PRACTICE AREAS:* Financial Institutions Law; Corporate and Securities Law. *Email:* abs@tmsp.com

**DAVID W. STEUBER,** born Evanston, Illinois, January 22, 1949; admitted to bar, 1973, California. *Education:* Trinity College (B.A., 1970); (Student Body President, 1969); University of Virginia (J.D., 1973). Order of the Coif. Editor, Virginia Law Review, 1972-1973. Law Clerk to the Hon. Albert Lee Stephens, Jr., Chief Judge of the U.S. District Court for the Central District of California, 1973-1974. Faculty Member: Practising Law Institute; Executive Enterprises, Inc.; The Rutter Group and California Judges Association. Judge Pro Tem, Los Angeles County Small Claims Court, 1982-1985. *Member:* Los Angeles County and American (Member, Task Force Re Insurance Complex Litigation and Disputes, 1991-1995) Bar Associations; State Bar of California. *PRACTICE AREAS:* Insurance Coverage Litigation; Business and Corporate Litigation; Environmental and Toxic Tort Litigation. *Email:* dws@tmsp.com

**BRUCE D. TOBEY,** born Santa Monica, California, May 23, 1959; admitted to bar, 1984, California and U.S. District Court, Central District of California. *Education:* University of California at Los Angeles (B.A., cum laude, 1981; J.D., 1984). Order of the Coif. *Member:* State Bar of California. *PRACTICE AREAS:* Transactional; Entertainment Law. *Email:* bdt@tmsp.com

**JEFFREY A. TODER,** born New York, N.Y., June 3, 1957; admitted to bar, 1982, California; 1990, District of Columbia. *Education:* Princeton University (A.B., 1979); University of Pennsylvania (J. D., 1982). *Member:* Los Angeles County and American (Member, Sections on: Public Contracts; Litigation); State Bar of California; The District of Columbia Bar. *PRACTICE AREAS:* Government Contracts Law. *Email:* jat@tmsp.com

**RICHARD E. TROOP,** born Weehawken, New Jersey, July 5, 1941; admitted to bar, 1970, California. *Education:* University of Florida (B.E.E., 1963); Loyola University of Los Angeles (J.D., magna cum laude, 1969). Phi Alpha Delta. Comment Editor, Loyola Law Review, 1968-1969. Editor, Practice Under California Corporate Securities Law of 1968, 1970-1973. Member, Editorial Board, Los Angeles County Bar Bulletin, 1970-1973. *Member:* Los Angeles County (Member, Executive Committee, Corporate and Banking Section, 1975-1987) and American Bar Associations; The State Bar of California. *PRACTICE AREAS:* Corporate Securities Law; Corporate Law; Entertainment Law. *Email:* ret@tmsp.com

**RITA L. TUZON,** born Watsonville, California, April 25, 1959; admitted to bar, 1984, California and U.S. District Court, Central District of California. *Education:* Stanford University (A.B., 1981); Boalt Hall School of Law, University of California (J.D., 1984). *Member:* Los Angeles County (Member, Litigation Section) and American (Member, Litigation Section) Bar Associations; The State Bar of California. *PRACTICE AREAS:* Entertainment Litigation; Commercial Litigation; Securities/Banking Litigation. *Email:* rlt@tmsp.com

## PRINCIPAL ATTORNEYS

**MICHAEL T. ANDERSON,** born Nashville, Tennessee, January 10, 1963; admitted to bar, 1989, California, U.S. District Court, Central District of California and U.S. Court of Appeals, Ninth Circuit; 1994, U.S. Tax Court. *Education:* Harvard University (B.A., summa cum laude, 1984; J.D., cum laude, 1989). Phi Beta Kappa. Associate, Boston Consulting Group, 1984-1986. *Member:* State Bar of California. *PRACTICE AREAS:* Business Litigation; Entertainment Litigation. *Email:* mta@tmsp.com

**BRYAN B. ARNOLD,** born Syracuse, New York, January 23, 1965; admitted to bar, 1990, California. *Education:* Cornell College (B.A., magna cum laude, 1987); Georgetown University (J.D., cum laude, 1990). Phi Beta Kappa. *Member:* State Bar of California; American Bar Association (Member, Public Contracts Law Section). *PRACTICE AREAS:* Litigation and Government Contracts. *Email:* bba@tmsp.com

**ERIC A. BARRON,** born Detroit, Michigan, September 7, 1964; admitted to bar, 1990, California; 1991, Florida and U.S. District Court, Central District of California. *Education:* Harvard University (B.A., cum laude, 1985); University of Michigan (J.D., cum laude, 1990). Clerk to the Hon. Joseph W. Hatchett, Judge, United States Court of Appeals for the Elev-

*(This Listing Continued)*

## TROOP MEISINGER STEUBER & PASICH, LLP, Los Angeles—Continued

enth Circuit, 1990-1991. *Member:* State Bar of California (Member, Litigation Section); The Florida Bar (Member, Entertainment Artist Sports Law Section); American Bar Association. *PRACTICE AREAS:* General Business Litigation. *Email:* eab@tmsp.com

**AMY L. KINCAID BERRY,** born Gainesville, Florida, February 20, 1963; admitted to bar, 1988, California; 1989, U.S. District Court, Central District of California; 1991, District of Columbia. *Education:* Vanderbilt University (B.A., magna cum laude, with high honors, 1985); Duke University (J.D., with honors, 1988). Phi Beta Kappa. Member, Moot Court Board. Winner, Moot Court Best Brief Award. *PRACTICE AREAS:* Insurance Coverage and General Business Litigation. *Email:* a@tmsp.comkb

**SAMUEL E. BRAMHALL,** born Washington, D.C., April 7. 1960; admitted to bar, 1989, California and U.S. District Court, Central District of California; 1990, U.S. Court of Appeals, Ninth Circuit. *Education:* University of Maryland (B.A., summa cum laude, 1986); University of Virginia (J.D., 1989). Law Clerk to the Hon. Manuel L. Real, Chief Judge, U.S. District Court, Central District of California, 1989-1990. *Member:* Los Angeles County and American Bar Associations; State Bar of California. *PRACTICE AREAS:* Litigation. *Email:* seb@tmsp.com

**KAREN PALLADINO CICCONE,** born Riverside, California, January 21, 1964; admitted to bar, 1989, California and U.S. Court of Appeals, Ninth Circuit; 1991, U.S. District Court, Central District of California. *Education:* University of California at Los Angeles (B.A., cum laude, 1986); Loyola University of Los Angeles (J.D., 1989). Phi Delta Phi. Member, St. Thomas More Law Honor Society. Author: "Cercla Unclear About Lawyer Fee Recovery," Los Angeles Daily Journal, April 16, 1991; "It Never Rains in Southern California, But. . .," Los Angeles Daily Journal, September 30, 1991. Co-Author: "Innovations and Considerations in Settling Toxic Test Litigation," The Environmental Law Manual, 1992 and Chemical Waste Litigation Reporter, Vol. 25, No. 6, May 1993. *Member:* Los Angeles County and American Bar Associations; State Bar of California. *PRACTICE AREAS:* Insurance Coverage; Environmental Compliance and Litigation. *Email:* kpc@tmsp.com

**JON E. DRUCKER,** born New York, N.Y., January 1, 1955; admitted to bar, 1988, California; 1989, U.S. District Court, Central District of California. *Education:* University of California at Los Angeles (B.A., cum laude, 1976); Columbia University School of International Affairs (M.I.A., 1978); University of California at Los Angeles (J.D., 1988). Participant, Moot Court Honors Program, Fall 1986. Pacific Basin Law Journal Special Assignments Editor, 1986-1987. Extern to the Honorable David V. Kenyon, Federal District Court Judge for the Central District of California, 1987. Legislative Aide to U.S. Senator Carl Levin, Washington, D.C., 1979-1981. *Member:* Los Angeles County Bar Association; State Bar of California; Financial Lawyers Conference. *PRACTICE AREAS:* General Business Litigation; Insolvency and Creditors' Rights Law. *Email:* jed@tmsp.com

**CINDY ZIMMERMAN DUBIN,** born Los Angeles, California, April 10, 1962; admitted to bar, 1988, New York; 1990, California. *Education:* University of California at Berkeley (B.A., magna cum laude, 1983), Phi Beta Kappa; University of Chicago (J.D., 1987). *Member:* State Bar of California (Member, Franchise Committee of Business Law Section). *PRACTICE AREAS:* Corporate Law; Franchise Law. *Email:* czd@tmsp.com

**JOSEPH B. HERSHENSON,** born Boston, Massachusetts, August 2, 1961; admitted to bar, 1989, California. *Education:* Harvard University (A.B., magna cum laude, 1983); Stanford University (J.D., 1989). Phi Beta Kappa. *Member:* State Bar of California. *LANGUAGES:* French, Italian and German. *PRACTICE AREAS:* Corporate Law; Securities Law. *Email:* jbh@tmsp.com

**LOUIS M. KAPLAN,** born Los Angeles, California, April 29, 1960; admitted to bar, 1987, California. *Education:* University of California (B.S., Physics, 1982); Loyola Marymount at Los Angeles (J.D., 1987). Phi Delta Phi (Magister, 1985). Member: St. Thomas More Law Honor Society; Loyola International Law Journal, 1986-1987. *Member:* State Bar of California. *PRACTICE AREAS:* Real Estate Law. *Email:* lmk@tmsp.com

**STEPHEN V. MASTERSON,** born Suffern, New York, 1964; admitted to bar, 1989, Pennsylvania; 1992, California. *Education:* Amherst College (B.A., magna cum laude, 1986); George Washington University (J.D., with honors, 1989). Member, George Washington University Law Review, 1987-1989. *PRACTICE AREAS:* Insurance Coverage Litigation. *Email:* svm@tmsp.com

*(This Listing Continued)*

**CATHERINE L. RIVARD,** born Pensacola, Florida, October 11, 1958; admitted to bar, 1986, California; 1987, U.S. District Court, Central District of California; 1993, Florida. *Education:* Lake Forest College; Occidental College (A.B., cum laude, 1982); Northwestern University (J.D., 1986). Member, Julius H. Miner Moot Court Board, 1985-1986. *Member:* State Bar of California; The Florida Bar; American Bar Association. *PRACTICE AREAS:* Insurance Coverage Litigation. *Email:* clr@tmsp.com

**DANIEL J. SCHULTZ,** born Wabasha, Minnesota, March 28, 1956; admitted to bar, 1989, Wisconsin, California and U.S. District Court, Central District of California; 1990, District of Columbia. *Education:* United States Military Academy (B.S. 1978); University of Wisconsin Law School (J.D., 1988). Note and Comment Editor, Wisconsin International Law Journal. Author: "The Well Regulated Militia of the Second Amendment: An Examination of the Intentions of the Framers," *The LEAA Advocate,* Spring 1996. *Member:* State Bar of California; The District of Columbia Bar; State Bar of Wisconsin; The Lawyer's Second Amendment Society (President and Co-Founder). *PRACTICE AREAS:* Insurance Coverage Litigation. *Email:* djs@tmsp.com

**SUSAN PAGE WHITE,** born Riverside, California, November 24, 1961; admitted to bar, 1988, California; 1989, U.S. District Court, Central District of California. *Education:* Wheaton College (B.A., 1983); Loyola Law School, Los Angeles (J.D., cum laude, 1988). Order of the Coif; Member, St. Thomas More Honor Society. Member, International Law Journal. *Member:* Los Angeles County and American Bar Associations; State Bar of California. *PRACTICE AREAS:* Insurance Coverage Litigation; Entertainment Law. *Email:* spw@tmsp.com

### ASSOCIATES

**MEHRAN ARJOMAND,** born Tehran, Iran, September 9, 1969; admitted to bar, 1995, California. *Education:* University of California, Berkeley (B.S., high honors, Mechanical Engineering, 1991; J.D., 1995). *PRACTICE AREAS:* General Business Litigation. *Email:* ma@tmsp.com

**WHITNEY E. BAKLEY,** born New York, N.Y., November 4, 1964; admitted to bar, 1987, Florida; 1990, District of Columbia; 1991, Indiana (Not admitted in California). *Education:* Barry University (B.A., magna cum laude, 1984); Georgetown University (J.D., cum laude, 1987). *Email:* web@tmsp.com

**JESSICA R. BASS,** born Washington, D.C., November 7, 1969; admitted to bar, 1994, California. *Education:* University of California, Berkeley (B.A., 1991); Loyola Law School (J.D., 1994). Phi Kappa Phi. Associate Editor, Loyola Law Review. *Member:* Beverly Hills, Los Angeles and American Bar Associations. *PRACTICE AREAS:* Corporate. *Email:* jrb@tmsp.com

**WILLIAM F. BLY,** born Wilmington, Delaware, October 8, 1964; admitted to bar, 1993, Maryland; 1994, Pennsylvania; 1995, California. *Education:* University of Delaware (B.S./B.A., 1986); George Washington University (J.D., 1993). Judicial Clerk to the Honorable Moody R. Tidwell, U.S. Court of Federal Claims, 1993-1995. *PRACTICE AREAS:* Insurance Coverage; Litigation; Environmental. *Email:* wfb@tmsp.com

**MYLENE J. BROOKS,** born Pomona, California, December 3, 1963; admitted to bar, 1994, California. *Education:* California State Polytechnic University (B.S., 1989); California State University (M.A., 1991); Loyola Law School (J.D., 1994). Author: Lawyer Advertising: Is There Really a Problem? Loyola Entertainment Law Journal, Vol. 15, Issue 1. *PRACTICE AREAS:* Labor and Employment. *Email:* mb@tmsp.com

**ANTONY E. BUCHIGNANI,** born San Francisco, California, February 23, 1971; admitted to bar, 1996, California. *Education:* Saint Mary's College of California (B.A., Psychology, magna cum laude, 1993); University of California, Hastings College of the Law (J.D., 1996). Phi Alpha Delta. Recipient, American Jurisprudence Award in Legal Writing and Research, 1993. Member and Editor, Hastings Communications and Entertainment Law Journal, 1994-1996. Extern to Honorable Saundra Brown Armstrong, Federal District Court Judge for the Northern District of California, 1995. *PRACTICE AREAS:* Litigation; Insurance Coverage.

**MATTHEW F. BURKE,** born Dayton, Ohio, November 13, 1966; admitted to bar, 1993, California. *Education:* University of Colorado (B.A., 1989); University of California, Hastings College of the Law (J.D., cum laude, 1993). Phi Beta Kappa. *PRACTICE AREAS:* General Corporate; Securities; Mergers and Acquisitions.

**KENNETH L. BURRY,** born St. Paul, Minnesota, October 2, 1966; admitted to bar, 1993, Virginia; 1994, California. *Education:* University of Michigan (B.A., 1988), honors program; The American University (J.D., cum laude, 1993). Judicial Clerk to the Honorable Reginald W. Gibson,

*(This Listing Continued)*

U.S. Court of Federal Claims. *Member:* Los Angeles and American Bar Associations; State Bar of California; Virginia State Bar. **PRACTICE AREAS:** Entertainment and Business Litigation. *Email:* klb@tmsp.com

**RICHARD A. CHAPKIS,** born Encino, California, March 5, 1965; admitted to bar, 1991, California. *Education:* Brown University (B.A., 1988); Boalt Hall School of Law, University of California (J.D., 1991). Co-Author: "Acquisitions of Chapter 11 Debtors," PLI Commercial Law Series. **PRACTICE AREAS:** Insurance Coverage Litigation; General Business Litigation.

**ALISA M. CHEVALIER,** born Burbank, California, April 25, 1967; admitted to bar, 1993, California; 1994, U.S. District Court, Central District of California. *Education:* Mills College (B.A., 1989); Loyola Law School (J.D., 1993). **PRACTICE AREAS:** Labor and Employment; Litigation.

**MICHAEL R. CHIAPPETTA,** born Mineola, New York, September 8, 1970; admitted to bar, 1996, California. *Education:* Colgate University (B.A., 1992); University of Southern California (J.D., 1996). Order of the Coif. **PRACTICE AREAS:** General Litigation.

**BERT C. COZART,** born Concord, North Carolina, March 17, 1965; admitted to bar, 1992, California. *Education:* University of North Carolina (B.S., Business Administration with distinction, 1987); University of California at Los Angeles (J.D., 1992). Beta Gamma Sigma; Beta Alpha Psi. Certified Public Accountant, California, 1989. *Member:* Los Angeles County Bar Association (Member, Litigation Section). **PRACTICE AREAS:** Insurance Coverage Litigation; Business Litigation. *Email:* bcc@tmsp.com

**KRISTINA M. DIAZ,** born Covina, California, December 17, 1964; admitted to bar, 1990, California. *Education:* Claremont McKenna College (B.A., cum laude, 1987); Boalt Hall College of Law, University of California at Berkeley (J.D., 1990). *Member:* American Bar Association (Member, Antitrust Section). **PRACTICE AREAS:** General Business Litigation; Securities Litigation. *Email:* kmd@tmsp.com

**HILARI HANAMAIKAI ELSON,** born Los Angeles, California, September 2, 1969; admitted to bar, 1993, California and U.S. District Court, Central District of California. *Education:* University of California, Berkeley (A.B., summa cum laude, 1990); Harvard University (J.D., cum laude, 1993). Phi Beta Kappa. Articles Editor, *Harvard Environmental Law Review.* Member, Mortar Board Honor Society. **PRACTICE AREAS:** Litigation; Environmental; Insurance Coverage. *Email:* hhe@tmsp.com

**AMY J. FINK,** born Phoenix, Arizona, December 4, 1968; admitted to bar, 1993, California. *Education:* University of California (B.A., 1990); University of California, Hastings College of Law (J.D., 1993). Phi Delta Phi; Moot Court Board. *Member:* Los Angeles County Bar Association; State Bar of California. **LANGUAGES:** French and German. **PRACTICE AREAS:** Insurance Coverage. *Email:* ajf@tmsp.com

**HOWARD A. FISHMAN,** born Milwaukee, Wisconsin, August 31, 1966; admitted to bar, 1992, California. *Education:* University of Arizona (B.F.A., 1987); University of Southern California (J.D., 1992). *Member:* Beverly Hills Bar Association; State Bar of California. **PRACTICE AREAS:** Entertainment Finance. *Email:* haf@tmsp.com

**SCOTT D. GALER,** born Aberdeen, Washington, September 6, 1966; admitted to bar, 1992, California. *Education:* University of California at Los Angeles (B.A., Econ/Bus., summa cum laude, 1989); Harvard University (J.D., 1992). Phi Beta Kappa. *Member:* State Bar of California. **PRACTICE AREAS:** Corporate Law; Securities Law. *Email:* sdg@tmsp.com

**DANIELLE L. GILMORE,** born Waterbury, Connecticut, December 6, 1967; admitted to bar, 1994, California. *Education:* Northwestern University (B.S., 1989); George Washington University (J.D., with honors, 1993). Order of the Coif; Trial Court Board; Phi Delta Phi. Member, George Washington Journal of International Law and Economics. Judicial Clerk to Chief Justice Joseph F. Baca, Supreme Court of New Mexico. Author: Precision Guided Munitions Demonstrated Their Pinpoint Accuracy in Desert Storm; But Is a Country Obligated to Use Precision Technology to Minimize Collateral Civilian Injury and Damage?, 26 Geo. Wash. J. Int'l L.& Econ. 109 (1992) republished by *The Royal Australian Air Force Air Power Studies Centre,* May 1995. **PRACTICE AREAS:** Litigation; Insurance Coverage. *Email:* dlg@tmsp.com

**LINDA M. GIUNTA,** born Bridgeton, New Jersey, July 11, 1965; admitted to bar, 1990, California. *Education:* Ursinus College (B.A., Economics and Political Science, 1987); Emory University (J.D., 1990). **PRACTICE AREAS:** Corporate; Securities; Mergers and Acquisitions. *Email:* lg@tmsp.com

*(This Listing Continued)*

**LAURENCE L. GOTTLIEB,** born Montreal, Quebec, September 10, 1968; admitted to bar, 1993, California; 1994, U.S. District Court, Central District of California. *Education:* Boston University (B.S., cum laude, 1990); Benjamin N. Cardozo School of Law (J.D., 1993). Judicial Extern to the Honorable Garrett E. Brown, U.S. District Judge, District of New Jersey. Judicial Extern to the Honorable Cornelius Blackshear, U.S. Bankruptcy Judge, Southern District of New York. Student Law Clerk to the Honorable Gerard L. Goettel, U.S. District Judge, Southern District of New York. Judicial Law Clerk to the Honorable Kathleen T. Lax, U.S. Bankruptcy Judge, Central District of California. *Member:* Beverly Hills, Los Angeles County (Member, Litigation Section) and American Bar Assns.; Financial Lawyers Conference; Los Angeles Bankruptcy Forum. **PRACTICE AREAS:** Litigation. *Email:* llg@tmsp.come.com

**G. KARL GREISSINGER,** born Tacoma, Washington, May 2, 1966; admitted to bar, 1994, California. *Education:* University of California at Los Angeles (B.A., 1989); Loyola Law School (J.D., 1994). Phi Delta Phi. Member, Loyola Law Review. *Member:* Los Angeles County and American (Member, Business Law Section) Bar Associations; State Bar of California. **PRACTICE AREAS:** Corporate; Securities.

**JOY K. GUMPERT,** born Takoma Park, Maryland, September 30, 1968; admitted to bar, 1995, California. *Education:* Syracuse University (B.S., cum laude, 1990); American University, Washington College of Law (J.D., cum laude, 1993). *Member:* State Bar of California. **PRACTICE AREAS:** Litigation. *Email:* jkg@tmsp.com

**KATHLEEN M. HALLINAN,** born Portland, Oregon, January 20, 1967; admitted to bar, 1993, California, U.S. District Court, Northern District of California and U.S. Court of Appeals, Ninth Circuit; 1995, U.S. Court of Appeals for the Federal Circuit. *Education:* Stanford University (A.B., 1989); Columbia University (J.D., 1993). Harlan Fiske Stone Scholar. Author: "Restrictions on Co-employee Dating and Employer Liability," Journal of Law and Social Problems, Spring 1993. *Member:* State Bar of California; American Bar Association. **PRACTICE AREAS:** Intellectual Property Litigation; General Business Litigation.

**JACQUELINE JOURDAIN HAYES,** born New York, New York, September 1, 1967; admitted to bar, 1994, New York; 1995, Massachusetts (Not admitted in California). *Education:* Harvard/Radcliffe College (B.A., magna cum laude, 1989); Harvard Law School (J.D., 1992). *Member:* Massachusetts and New York State Bar Associations. **PRACTICE AREAS:** Corporate; Financial Services; Intellectual Property. *Email:* jjh@tmsp.com

**JEFFREY M. JACOBBERGER,** born San Francisco, July 3, 1964; admitted to bar, 1989, California. *Education:* Georgetown University (A.B., magna cum laude, 1986); University of Boalt Hall School of Law (J.D., 1989). *Member:* State Bar of California; American Bar Association. [Capt., U.S. Army JAG Corps, 1990-1993]. **PRACTICE AREAS:** Government Contracts; Insurance Coverage. *Email:* jmj@tmsp.com

**JOHN D. JENKINS,** born Las Vegas, Nevada, August 12, 1967; admitted to bar, 1992, California. *Education:* University of Southern California (J.D., 1992). Deputy District Attorney, Orange County, 1993-1995. **PRACTICE AREAS:** Corporate. *Email:* jdj@tmsp.com

**JULIE M. KAUFER,** born Los Angeles, California, August 10, 1964; admitted to bar, 1991, California. *Education:* Tufts University (B.S., computer science, 1986); Loyola Law School (J.D., 1991). Order of the Coif; St Thomas More Law Honor Society. Member, Loyola Law Review, 1991. **PRACTICE AREAS:** General Corporate Law. *Email:* jmk@tmsp.com

**ALYSSA TARA KENNEDY,** born Los Angeles, California, December 14, 1971; admitted to bar, 1996, California. *Education:* Cornell University (B.A., summa cum laude, 1993); Harvard Law School (J.D., 1996). Phi Beta Kappa. **LANGUAGES:** French, Spanish. **PRACTICE AREAS:** Corporate; Taxation.

**JOHN C. KIRKE,** born Pomona, California, October 30, 1968; admitted to bar, 1994, California. *Education:* University of California, Berkeley (B.A., 1990); University of California, Los Angeles (J.D., 1994). Managing Editor, UCLA Journal of Environmental Law and Policy, 1993-1994. Extern to the Honorable William J. Rea, U.S. Central District, 1993. **PRACTICE AREAS:** Insurance Coverage; Litigation. *Email:* jck@tmsp.com

**ABIGAIL KLEM,** born New York, N.Y., September 9, 1968; admitted to bar, 1996, California and U.S. District Court, Central District of California. *Education:* Indiana University (B.A., cum laude, 1990); Hastings College of the Law (J.D., cum laude, 1994). Member: Thurston Society; Hastings Law Journal. Clerk to Hon. Robert J. Kelleher, U.S. District Court, Central District of California, 1994-1995. *Member:* Los Angeles County

*(This Listing Continued)*

**TROOP MEISINGER STEUBER & PASICH, LLP,** Los Angeles—Continued

Bar Association; State Bar of California. **LANGUAGES:** French. **PRACTICE AREAS:** Entertainment.

**LAURI S. KONISHI,** born Chicago, Illinois, April 25, 1964; admitted to bar, 1992, California; U.S. Court of Appeals, Ninth Circuit; U.S. District Court, Central and Northern Districts of California. *Education:* University of Southern California (B.A., 1986); Boston University School of Law (J.D., cum laude, 1992). G. Joseph Tauro Scholar. Member, Boston University Law Review. *Member:* American Bar Association; Japanese American Bar Association. **PRACTICE AREAS:** Insurance Coverage Litigation; General Litigation. *Email:* lsk@tmsp.com

**LINDA D. KORNFELD,** born Encino, California, June 26, 1965; admitted to bar, 1991, California. *Education:* University of California at Los Angeles (B.A., 1988); George Washington University (J.D., with honors, 1991). Recipient, American Jurisprudence Award for Criminal Law and Basic Procedure. *Member:* Beverly Hills and Los Angeles County Bar Association; State Bar of California. **PRACTICE AREAS:** Insurance Coverage Litigation; General Litigation. *Email:* ldk@tmsp.com

**ANEETA KUMAR,** born Patna Bihar, India, January 23, 1966; admitted to bar, 1992, California; 1993, U.S. District Court, Central District of California. *Education:* Occidental College (A.B., 1988); University of California at Davis (J.D., 1992). Recipient, Phi Beta Kappa Award.; Mortar Board National Honor Society. Research Editor, University of California at Davis Law Review. Member, National Mock Trial Team. *Member:* Los Angeles County Bar Association; State Bar of California. **PRACTICE AREAS:** Insurance Coverage and General Litigation. *Email:* ak@tmsp.com

**GREG R. LANGER,** born Mineola, New York, May 8, 1956; admitted to bar, 1981, California. *Education:* Georgetown University (B.S.B.A., magna cum laude, 1978; J.D., cum laude, 1981). Executive Editor, American Criminal Law Review. **PRACTICE AREAS:** Real Estate. *Email:* grl@tmsp.com

**MICHAEL S. LUKE,** born Culver City, California, May 11, 1970; admitted to bar, 1995, California. *Education:* University of California, Los Angeles (B.A., 1992; J.D., 1995). *Member:* American Bar Association. **PRACTICE AREAS:** Corporate. *Email:* msl@tmsp.com

**JOHN J. MCILVERY,** born Vicenza, Italy, September 21, 1971; admitted to bar, 1995, California. *Education:* University of Southern California (B.S., summa cum laude, 1992); Boalt Hall School of Law, University of California (J.D., 1995). Phi Kappa Phi. **PRACTICE AREAS:** Corporate Law; Securities. *Email:* jjm@tmsp.com

**MARK A. MCLEAN,** born Arcola, Saskatchewan, Canada, November 22, 1959; admitted to bar, 1987, California. *Education:* Boston University (B.A., with honors, 1983); University of Notre Dame (J.D., 1987). *Member:* Los Angeles County and American Bar Associations. **PRACTICE AREAS:** Labor and Employment Law. *Email:* mam@tmsp.com

**BETH E. MACHLOVITCH,** born Montreal, Canada, May 31, 1968; admitted to bar, 1992, California. *Education:* McGill University (B.A., magna cum laude, 1989); New York University School of Law (J.D., 1992). **PRACTICE AREAS:** Litigation. *Email:* bem@tmsp.com

**CARY M. MEADOW,** born Dallas, Texas, June 9, 1969; admitted to bar, 1994, California. *Education:* University of Texas, Austin (B.B.A., Finance, cum laude, 1991); University of Southern California (J.D., 1994). Phi Kappa Phi. Recipient, Judge Dorothy Wright Nelson Award; American Jurisprudence Award for Federal Court. *Member:* Beverly Hills and Los Angeles County Bar Associations. **PRACTICE AREAS:** Transactional Entertainment Law. *Email:* cmm@tmsp.com

**PAUL B. NEINSTEIN,** born Van Nuys, California, January 22, 1969; admitted to bar, 1994, California and U.S. District Court, Central District of California. *Education:* University of California, Los Angeles (B.A., 1991); Loyola Law School of Los Angeles (J.D., 1994). Phi Delta Phi. Member, St. Thomas Moore Honors Society. Staff Writer, 1992-1993 and Business and Directory Editor, 1993-1994, Loyola of Los Angeles Entertainment Law Journal. *Member:* Beverly Hills and Los Angeles County Bar Associations. **PRACTICE AREAS:** Transactional Entertainment Law. *Email:* pbn@tmsp.com

**KATE E. OHLSON,** born Berkeley, California, January 31, 1968; admitted to bar, 1995, California. *Education:* Georgetown University (B.A., magna cum laude, 1990); University of California at Davis (J.D., 1995).

Senior Notes and Comments Editor, University of California, Davis Law Review, 1995. Law Clerk for Sonoma County Superior Court, 1995-1996. **PRACTICE AREAS:** Insurance Coverage.

**JASON S. REICHENTHAL,** born New York, N.Y., November 22, 1970; admitted to bar, 1996, New York and California. *Education:* University of California at Los Angeles (B.A., 1992); Loyola Law School, Los Angeles (J.D., 1995). **PRACTICE AREAS:** Corporate; Financial Institutions; Securities Law.

**MELISSA A. ROGAL,** born Downey, California, August 11, 1971; admitted to bar, 1996, California. *Education:* University of Pennsylvania (B.S. and B.A., 1993); New York University (J.D., 1996). **PRACTICE AREAS:** Entertainment.

**MICHAEL A. ROSSI,** born Orange, California, December 31, 1965; admitted to bar, 1991, California. *Education:* University of California at Los Angeles (B.A., cum laude, 1988); University of California at Berkeley (J.D., 1991). Phi Beta Kappa. Member, Moot Court Board. Author: "Bad Faith in the Absence of Coverage," TIPS Litigation Committee Mid-Year Meeting, February 1995. Co-Author: "The Products Hazard Exclusion: Negligent Failure to Warn Claims," The Environmental Claims Journal, Winter 1992/93: "Issues Involving Excess Liability Insurance Coverage," ABA Insurance Coverage Litigation Committee Midyear Meeting, March, 1993; "Risk Management And Insurance Coverage Issues That Should Be Considered Before And After A Corporate Merger Or Acquisition," Council of Chief Legal Officers Conference, May, 1994. Speaker, "Stop Taking Pennies on the Dollar -- Learn How Insurers Deprive You of Coverage," 33rd RIMS Annual Conference, San Francisco, 12995; "Hot Topics in Business Interruption, Property, Liability and D&D Insurance,' Price Waterhouse General Counsel Forum, Los Angeles, 1994; Environmental Damage as "Personal Injury," Institute for International Research Symposium on Environmental Insurance Claims, San Francisco, 1993. *Member:* State Bar of California; American and International Bar Associations; Lexis Counsel Connect (Moderator, Risk Management Discussion Forum); Risk Management and Insurance Coverage Council, RMICC (Founder). **PRACTICE AREAS:** Risk Management Consulting; Insurance Coverage: Advice, Claims Presentation, Alt. Dispute Resolution & Litigation. *Email:* mar@tmsp.com

**CHRISTINE A. SAMSEL,** born Hartford, Connecticut, November 16, 1964; admitted to bar, 1990, California. *Education:* Smith College (B.A., 1986); University of Virginia (J.D., 1990). Author: "Turning Over Client Files," LA Lawyer 2/93; Personnel & Employment Law in Calif; FED Publications Manual, Fall & Spring 1994 and 1995. *Member:* Los Angeles County and American Bar Associations. **PRACTICE AREAS:** Employment; General Litigation; Appellate. *Email:* cas@tmsp.com

**BARBRA E. SHERAK,** born Brooklyn, New York, October 9, 1970; admitted to bar, 1995, California. *Education:* Brandeis University (B.A., high honors in Psychology, 1992); Loyola Law School (J.D., 1995). **PRACTICE AREAS:** Financial Services; Corporate; Securities. *Email:* bes@tmsp.com

**CASSANDRA C. SHIVERS,** born Pasadena, California, January 27, 1965; admitted to bar, 1994, California. *Education:* University of California, Los Angeles (B.A., 1987); Loyola of Los Angeles (J.D., 1994). Note and Comment Editor, Loyola of Los Angeles Law Review. *Member:* Los Angeles County Bar Association; State Bar of California; Women Lawyers Association of Los Angeles. **PRACTICE AREAS:** Insurance Coverage; Litigation. *Email:* ccs@tmsp.com

**JESSICA CULLEN SMITH,** born Boston, Massachusetts, July 9, 1963; admitted to bar, 1992, Massachusetts (Not admitted in California). *Education:* Vassar College (B.A., with highest honors, 1985); Boston University (J.D., magna cum laude, 1991). **PRACTICE AREAS:** Corporate; Corporate Securities; Intellectual Property; Entertainment.

**LAURIE E. SMITH,** born Manassas, Virginia, May 11, 1971; admitted to bar, 1996, California. *Education:* University of California, Los Angeles (B.A., cum laude, 1993); University of Virginia (J.D., 1996). **PRACTICE AREAS:** Litigation.

**TINA M. TRAN,** born Saigon, Vietnam, November 1, 1971; admitted to bar, 1996, California. *Education:* University of Southern California (B.A., 1993); Boalt Hall School of Law, University of California (J.D., 1996). **PRACTICE AREAS:** Litigation.

**WILLIAM T. UM,** born Seoul, Korea, July 20, 1967; admitted to bar, 1993, California; 1993, U.S. District Court, Central District of California. *Education:* University of California at Irvine (B.A., 1990); Boston University (J.D., cum laude, 1993). Senior Editor, International Law Journal.

*(This Listing Continued)*

## PROFESSIONAL BIOGRAPHIES — CALIFORNIA—LOS ANGELES

Member: Los Angeles County and American Bar Associations; State Bar of California. LANGUAGES: Korean. PRACTICE AREAS: Commercial Litigation; Insurance Coverage Litigation; General Business Litigation. Email: wtu@tmsp.com

**ALISSA L. VRADENBURG,** born Orange, New Jersey, January 22, 1971; admitted to bar, 1996, California. Education: Cornell University (B.A., 1993); Harvard Law School (J.D., cum laude, 1996). Phi Beta Kappa; Phi Kappa Psi; Sigma Delta Tau; Golden Key National Honor Society. PRACTICE AREAS: Corporate; Entertainment.

**ERIC A. WANNON,** born Wheaton, Maryland, August 25, 1966; admitted to bar, 1991, Maryland; 1992, California; 1995, District of Columbia. Education: University of Maryland (B.S., Computer Science, 1988); Loyola University (J.D., 1991). Order of the Coif; St. Thomas More Honor Society. Note and Comment Editor, Loyola's International and Comparative Law Journal. Listed in Who's Who Among American Law Students. Member: State Bar of California. LANGUAGES: French. PRACTICE AREAS: Insurance Coverage; General Litigation. Email: eaw@tmsp.com

**JAMES D. WEISS,** born Los Angeles, California, June 14, 1968; admitted to bar, 1993, California; U.S. District Court, Central District of California. Education: University of Southern California (B.S., Business Administration, cum laude, 1990), Indiana University; University of California at Los Angeles (J.D., 1993). Phi Delta Phi. Member: Los Angeles County Bar Associations; State Bar of California. PRACTICE AREAS: General Litigation; Insurance Coverage Litigation. Email: jdw@tmsp.com

**MARK A. WIESENTHAL,** born Los Angeles, California, July 3, 1955; admitted to bar, 1996, California. Education: University of California at Los Angeles (B.A., 1977); Loyola Law School, Los Angeles (J.D., 1996). Order of the Coif; Sigma Alpha Nu. Sayre MacNeil Scholar. Member, St. Thomas More Law Honor Society. Recipient, American Jurisprudence Awards in Criminal Law and Remedies. Staff Member, 1994-1995 and Editor, 1995-1996, Loyola Law Review. PRACTICE AREAS: Real Estate.

**LORI M. YANKELEVITS,** born Los Angeles, California, September 5, 1966; admitted to bar, 1991, California. Education: University of California, Berkeley (A.B., 1988); Northwestern University (J.D., 1991). Member: Los Angeles County Bar Association; State Bar of California. PRACTICE AREAS: Insurance Coverage Litigation. Email: lmy@tmsp.com

**JULIE S. ZIMMERMAN,** born Los Angeles, California, October 6, 1968; admitted to bar, 1995, California. Education: University of California, Los Angeles (B.A., cum laude, 1990); George Washington University (J.D., with honors, 1995). PRACTICE AREAS: Insurance Coverage. Email: jsz@tmsp.com

### OF COUNSEL

**PETER M. EICHLER,** born Jersey City, New Jersey, October 9, 1936; admitted to bar, 1961, New York; 1970, California; registered to practice before U.S. Patent and Trademark Office. Education: Wesleyan University (A.B., 1957); Columbia University (J.D., 1960). Phi Alpha Delta. Chairman, Trademark Committee, Los Angeles Patent Law Association, 1974-1975. Legal Editor, "The Licensing Book." 1987—. Member: Beverly Hills and Los Angeles County (Member, International and Intellectual Property Sections) Bar Associations; State Bar of California (Member: Patent, Trademark and Copyright Law Section; International Law Section); Foreign Law Association of Southern California; Los Angeles Copyright Society; United States Trademark Association (Member, International Trademark Committee, 1980-1989); Los Angeles Patent Law Association. LANGUAGES: Spanish. PRACTICE AREAS: International Business Transactions; International Trademarks; World-wide Licensing and Merchandising. Email: pme@tmsp.com

**DENNIS D. HILL,** born Chicago, Illinois, March 5, 1941; admitted to bar, 1967, California. Education: University of California at Los Angeles (A.B., 1963; J.D., 1966). Order of the Coif; Phi Alpha Delta. Member, Board of Editors, 1964-1966 and Note and Comment Editor, 1965-1966, UCLA Law Review. Member: The State Bar of California (Chair, Financial Institutions, 1983-1984); American Bar Association; California League of Savings Associations; Federal National Mortgage Association (Member, National Advisory Council, 1988-1989); California Mortgage Bankers Association (Member Legislation Committee, 1990—); Mortgage Bankers of America. PRACTICE AREAS: Financial Institutions Law; Mortgage Banking Law; Real Estate Law. Email: ddh@tmsp.com

**PAUL R. KATZ,** born New York, N.Y., November 15, 1950; admitted to bar, 1975, California. Education: University of California (A.B., 1972); University of California School of Law (J.D., 1975). Member: State Bar of California (Member, Intellectual Property Section); American Bar Association (Member, Section of Patent, Trademark and Copyright Law, 1990-1993); Computer Law Association; American Corporate Counsel Association (Member, Board of Directors, Southern California Chapter, 1989-1993). PRACTICE AREAS: Computer Law; Multimedia; Electronic Commerce; Telecommunications. Email: prk@tmsp.com

**CHRIS ANN MAXWELL,** born New York, N.Y., February 9, 1950; admitted to bar, 1975, California. Education: University of California at Los Angeles (B.A., 1971); California Western University (J.D., 1975). PRACTICE AREAS: Entertainment. Email: cam@tmsp.com

**GLENN WARNER,** born Concordia, Kansas, April 15, 1924; admitted to bar, 1951, California. Education: Stanford University (B.A., 1948; J.D., 1950). Phi Beta Kappa; Order of the Coif. Managing Editor, Stanford Law Review, 1949-1950. Special Assistant Attorney General, State of Washington, 1975-1976. PRACTICE AREAS: Insurance Coverage Litigation; Business Litigation. Email: gzw@tmsp.com

---

# TROPE AND TROPE
### 12121 WILSHIRE BOULEVARD, SUITE 801
### LOS ANGELES, CALIFORNIA 90025
Telephone: 310-207-8228
Fax: 310-826-1122

*Family Law and General Civil Trial Work. Appellate, Custody.*

FIRM PROFILE: Trope and Trope was founded in 1949 by Sorrell Trope and Eugene Trope. From the inception, a substantial portion of the practice of the firm was devoted to divorce law (now referred to as Family Law). All of the firm's endeavors were involved in areas of litigation and trial work. At present, the firm's practice is almost exclusively devoted to the field of Family Law litigation, trials and appeals. Certain members of the firm continue to be involved in general civil trial work. Members of the firm participate in the Los Angeles County Superior Court's Mediation Program in Family Law and serve as Mediators, assisting the Court in resolving calendared cases by mediation, eliminating the necessity of such cases being tried within the Court system itself. Members of the firm are active in writing and teaching in the field of Family Law. The firm is listed in the Bar Register of Preeminent Lawyers.

### MEMBERS OF FIRM

**SORRELL TROPE,** born Albany, New York, June 9, 1927; admitted to bar, 1949, California; U.S. Court of Appeals, Ninth Circuit; 1952, U.S. Board of Immigration Appeals; 1954, U.S. Supreme Court; 1958, U.S. Court of Appeals, Seventh Circuit. Education: University of Southern California (A.B., 1947; J.D., 1949). Phi Kappa Phi. Bencher Emeritus of American Inns of Court, University of Southern California Legion Lex Chapter, 1985—. Author: "Preparing for Trial and Trials," California Marital Disso. Practice, 1983; "California Family Law Trial Technique," LA County Family Law Bar Symposium, 1984-1989; "Preparing for Trial and Trials," California Marital Dissolve Practice, 1983. Co-Author: "Initial Order to Show Cause," 1991, 1992, 1993, 1994, 1995 Family Law Reference Book, LA County Family Law Bar; Selected Topics in Divorce and Real Estate (Chapter 18, from proceedings of the University of Southern California Law Center 47th Annual Institute on Federal Taxation). Instructor: Family Law Litigation, University of Southern California, 1989; Advanced Family Law Program, Pepperdine University School of Law, 1983-1984; Advanced Domestic Relations Practice, University of Southern California Law School, March, 1882; The Masters Series, Advanced Family Law, Pepperdine School of Law, 1983, Banff, Canada; The Masters Series, Advanced Family Law, Pepperdine University School of Law, 1984, London, England; Dividing Property on Dissolution of Marriage, University of California Continuing Education of the Bar, August, 1980; Family Law Litigation, University of California Continuing Education of the Bar, November, 1981; Family Law Litigation, University of California Continuing Education of the Bar, January, 1986; University of Southern California School of Law, Settlement Litigation and Family Law, Spring Semester, 1989. Lecturer: Continuing Education of the Bar, Legal Seminars, University of California, 1970—; Family Law, The Rutter Group; Family Law Litigation, University of California Continuing Education of the Bar, January, 1986; University of Southern California School of Law, Advanced Professional Program, The Management and Marketing of a Family Practice, Fall Semester, 1991; University of Southern California School of Law, The High Asset Celebrity Divorce, Spring Semester, 1989; University of Southern California Family Law Institute-The Ethical Limits of Advocacy, June, 1993; Beverly Hills Bar Association Family Law Symposium-Cash Available and Unreported or Hidden Assets, November, 1992; University of Southern California Family Law Institute-The Ethics of Running a Law Practice, September, 1994; University of Southern California School of Law-The Management and

*(This Listing Continued)*

*TROPE AND TROPE, Los Angeles—Continued*

Marketing of a Family Law Practice, April, 1994; the Ethics of Custody Litigation, University of Southern California Family Law Institute, 1995; Divorce Trial By the Masters, University of Southern California Law Center Continuing Legal Education Program, 1995; The Management and Marketing of a Law Practice to Financial Success, University of Southern California Law School, 1996. Panelist: Family Law Litigation and Enforcement of Orders, University of California Continuing Education of the Bar, January, 1984; Los Angeles County Bar Family Law Symposium, May, 1981, May 1982, April, 1983; Los Angeles County Bar Family Law Symposium, Fiduciary Obligations, Disclosure and Set Asides, 1995; Evidentiary Problems in Family Law Trial Tactics and Techniques, Beverly Hills Bar Association and University of Southern California Family Law Symposium, October, 1983; Dividing Property on Dissolution of Marriage, University of California Continuing Education of the Bar, February, 1983; Family Law Practice-Major 1984 Legislation, The Rutter Group, Los Angeles County Bar, April, 1984; The Rutter Group- Los Angeles County Bar Family Law Workshop, November, 1983; The Rutter Group- Los Angeles County Bar Family Law Workshop, December, 1984; Los Angeles County Bar Family Law Symposium-Goodwill, Retirement Plans, Family Residence, May, 1981; Los Angeles County Bar Family Law Symposium-Tax Considerations, May. 1982; The Rutter Group, Los Angeles County Bar Family Law Workshop, November, 1985; Los Angeles County Bar Family Law Symposium Special Issues, May, 1984; Los Angeles County Bar Family Law Symposium, Presentation of Post-Judgment Order to Show Cause for Modification of Spousal and Child Support, April, 1989; University of California Continuing Education of the Bar, Dividing Property on Dissolution of Marriage, October, 1994; University of Southern California 47th Annual Institute on Federal Taxation, 1995. Judge Pro Tem, Los Angeles Superior Court, 1970-1972. Chairperson, Southern California Committee Family Law Commission of State Senate Judicial Committee, 1983. Member, State Assembly Family Law Advisory Committee, 1984. *Member:* Los Angeles County (Member, Executive Committee, Family Law Section, 1980-1996) and American Bar Associations. Fellow, American Academy of Matrimonial Lawyers. Fellow, International Academy of Matrimonial Lawyers. (Certified Specialist, Family Law, The State Bar of California Board of Legal Specialization). **REPORTED CASES:** Sokolow v. City of Hope, 41 Cal.2d 556, 1953; Arsenian v. Meketarian, 138 Cal. App.2d 627, 1956; Wunch v. Wunch, 184 Cal. App.2d 527, 1960; Rheuban v. Rheuban, 238 Cal. App.2d 552, 1965; Buck v. Superior Court of Orange, 232 Cal. App.2d 153, 1965; Buck v. Superior Court of Ventura, 245 Cal. App.2d 431, 1966; Escrow Owners v. Taft Allen, Inc., 252 Cal. App.2d 506, 1967; People v. Superior Court, 3 Cal. App.3d 648, 1970; Alonso Investment Corporation v. Doff, 17 Cal.3d 539, 1976; Care Construction v. Century Convalescent Centers, 54 Cal. App.3d 701, 1976; Marriage of Keeva, 66 Cal. App.3d 512, 1977; Marriage, of Clark, 80 Cal. App.3d 417, 1978; Marriage of Marx, 97 Cal. App.3d 552, 1979; Marriage of Marx, 92 Cal. App.3d 984, 1979; Marriage of Koppleman, 159 Cal. App.3d 627, 1984; Marriage of Garrity/Bishton, 181 Cal. App.3d 675, 1986; Marriage of Segal, 179 Cal. App.3d 602, 1986; Marriage of Segal, 177 Cal. App.3d 1030, 1986; Marriage of Okum, 195 Cal. App.3d 176, 1987; Marriage of Dick, 15 Cal. App.4th 144, 1993; Estevez v. Superior Court, 22 Cal. App.4th 423, 1994. **PRACTICE AREAS:** Family Law.

**EUGENE L. TROPE,** born Albany, New York, December 4, 1916; admitted to bar, 1946, California; U.S. District Court, Southern District of California; 1954, U.S. Supreme Court; 1958, U.S. Court of Appeals, Seventh Circuit; 1961, U.S. District Court, District of Hawaii; 1978, U.S. Court of Appeals, Ninth Circuit; 1980, U.S. Court of Customs and Patent Appeals; 1982, U.S. Court of International Trade; 1988, U.S. Claims Court. *Education:* University of Southern California (A.B., 1940); Pacific Coast Law (LL.B., 1941). Judge Pro Tem, Los Angeles Municipal and Superior Courts, 1993-1994. Alternative Dispute Resolution, American Bar Association and Beverly Hills Bar Associations, 1994-1995. *Member:* Beverly Hills and Los Angeles County Bar Associations; National Health Lawyers Association. [1st Lt., U.S. Infantry, 1942, 1943]. **PRACTICE AREAS:** Family Law; Civil Litigation; White Collar Defense.

**MARYANNE LA GUARDIA,** born New York, N.Y., November 4, 1943; admitted to bar, 1975, California; 1976, U.S. District Court, Central District of California. *Education:* San Jose State College (B.A., cum laude, 1965); University of Southern California (J.D., with honors, 1975). Phi Alpha Delta. Member, 1973-1974 and Note and Article Editor, 1974-1975, Southern California Law Review. *Member:* Beverly Hills, Los Angeles County (Member: Family Law Section; Family Law Executive Committee, 1984-1987) and American Bar Associations; State Bar of California (Member, Family Law Section); Association of Business Trial Lawyers (Member, Board of Governors, 1978—). **PRACTICE AREAS:** Family Law.

**STEVEN KNOWLES,** born Los Angeles, January 19, 1952; admitted to bar, 1977, California; 1978, U.S. District Court, Central District of California; 1979, U.S. Court of Appeals, Ninth Circuit. *Education:* University of Southern California (B.A., summa cum laude, 1973); Harvard Law School (J.D., cum laude, 1976). Phi Beta Kappa; Phi Kappa Phi. Member, Harvard Journal of Legislative Review, 1975-1976. Co-Author: "Enforcement of Foreign Judgments," LA County Family Law Bar Symposium Handbook, 1985-1986; "Initial Order to Show Cause," 1991-1995, Family Law Reference Book, LA County Family Law Bar. Adjunct Professor: San Fernando Valley College of Law, 1978-1979; Western States College of Law, 1980-1981. *Member:* State Bar of California (Member, Family Law Section); American Bar Association (Family Law Section). (Certified Specialist, Family Law, The State Bar of California Board of Legal Specialization). **PRACTICE AREAS:** Family Law; Civil Litigation.

**MARK S. PATT,** born Chicago, Illinois, December 13, 1948; admitted to bar, 1974, California and U.S. District Court, Northern District of California; 1978, U.S. District Court, Central District of California and U.S. District Court, Ninth Circuit. *Education:* University of California, Los Angeles (B.A., with honors, 1970); University of Michigan (J.D., 1974). Co-Author: "Initial Order to Show Cause," 1991-1995, Family Law Reference Book, LA County Family Law Bar. Author: "Practical Considerations Concerning California Child Support Guidelines-Rule 1274 and S.B. 101," California Law Monthly, Matthew Bender, 1992. Panelist, Law Office Management Seminar, State Bar of California, 1993. *Member:* Los Angeles County Bar Association (Member, Family Law Section). **PRACTICE AREAS:** Family Law; Civil Litigation.

**BRUCE E. COOPERMAN,** born Los Angeles, California, May 8, 1952; admitted to bar, 1977, California. *Education:* University of California at Irvine (B.A., summa cum laude, 1974); University of California at Los Angeles (J.D., 1977). Phi Beta Kappa; Order of the Coif. Contributing Editor, Hogoboom & King, California Practice Guide: Family Law 1, (TRG) 1988—. Co-Author: "Deposition - A Practical Approach," L.A. County Family Law Bar - Family Law Reference Book, 1996. *Member:* Los Angeles County and American Bar Associations; State Bar of California. (Certified Specialist, Family Law, The State Bar of California Board of Legal Specialization). **PRACTICE AREAS:** Family Law.

**MARK VINCENT KAPLAN,** born Chicago, Illinois, October 30, 1947; admitted to bar, 1973, California; 1974, U.S. District Court, Central District of California. *Education:* University of Illinois (B.A., 1969); Southwestern University (J.D., 1973). Moot Court. Recipient: George Huff Achievement Award; West Publishing Award. Member, Planning Committee, University of Southern California Family Law Institute, 1993-1994. *Member:* Beverly Hills and Los Angeles County Bar Associations; State Bar of California. (Certified Specialist, Family Law, The State Bar of California Board of Legal Specialization). **LANGUAGES:** Italian. **PRACTICE AREAS:** Family Law.

*ASSOCIATES*

**THOMAS PAINE DUNLAP,** born Oroville, California, June 4, 1949; admitted to bar, 1974, California and U.S. District Court, Central District of California; 1975, U.S. District Court, Eastern District of California; 1980, U.S. Supreme Court and U.S. Customs Court; U.S. Court of International Trade; 1989, U.S. District Court, Southern District of California. *Education:* University of California (B.A., 1971); University of California at Los Angeles (J.D., 1974). Phi Beta Kappa. Order of the Coif. Author: "Property Law of the Marshall Islands," Hawaii Bar Journal, Spring 1977; "Marshallese Property Law...," California State Bar Journal Nov-Dec 1977, Vol. 52, #6. *Member:* Los Angeles County Bar Association (Member, Appellate Courts Committee, 1996). **LANGUAGES:** Spanish and Arabic. **REPORTED CASES:** In Re Marriage of Templeton, 14 Cal 4th, 607 1993; In Re Marriage of Dick, 15 CA 4th 144, 1993; In Re Marriage of Quay, 18 CA 4th 961, 1993; Estevez v. Superior Court, 22 CA 4th 423. 1994; In Re Marriage of Gigliotti (1995) 33 CA App. 4th 518; In Re Marriage of Lurie-Marino (1995) 33 CA App. 4th 658; Trope & Trope v. Katz (1995) 11 CA 4th 274; Glade v. Glade (1995) 38 CA App. 4th 1441. **PRACTICE AREAS:** Family Law; Family and Civil Appeals; Business Litigation.

**DONNA BECK WEAVER,** born Long Beach, California, June 20, 1952; admitted to bar, 1977, California; 1980, U.S. District Court, Central District of California. *Education:* University of California, Berkeley (A.B., 1974); University of Bordeaux, Bordeaux, France; Golden Gate University (J.D., 1977). Lecturer: "Negotiating and Drafting Marital Settlement Agreements," Continuing Education of the Bar, 1993; "Ethics of Family Law," Continuing Education of the Bar, 1995; "Recent Developments,"

*(This Listing Continued)*

Continuing Education of the Bar, 1990 and 1991; "Family Law," University of California, 1983 and 1985; "Beyond Hubner and Catalano: Child and Spousal Support," California State Bar Family Law Section, 1989. *Member:* San Luis Obispo County (President, 1986); Los Angeles County (Member, Family Law Section, 1992—) and American Bar Associations; State Bar of California (Education Chair, Executive Committee, Family Law Section, 1989-1991; Chair, Law Practice Management Section, 1994); Women Lawyers of San Luis Obispo County (Founding President, 1981; Chair, Judicial Campaign); American Academy of Matrimonial Lawyers (Board of Directors, 1995—). (Certified Specialist, Family Law, The State Bar of California Board of Legal Specialization). **REPORTED CASES:** Glade v. Glade (1995) 38 CA 4th 1441. **PRACTICE AREAS:** Family Law.

**CAROLYN J. KOZUCH,** born Hartford, Connecticut, May 27, 1959; admitted to bar, 1985, California and U.S. District Court, Central District of California. *Education:* Brown University (A.B., 1981); University of Southern California (J.D., 1984). Member, Environmental Law Symposium, USC Law Center, 1981-1984. Board of Directors, Harriett Buhai Center for Family Law. *Member:* Los Angeles County Bar Association (Member, Family Law Section) Bar Associations; State Bar of California; Women Lawyers Association of Los Angeles (Board of Governors). **PRACTICE AREAS:** Family Law.

**ANNE CAMPBELL KILEY,** born Kalamazoo, Michigan, July 2, 1964; admitted to bar, 1990, California. *Education:* University of Michigan (B.A., with high honors, 1986; J.D., cum laude, 1989). Order of the Coif; Editor, Michigan Law Review. *Member:* American Bar Association. **PRACTICE AREAS:** Family Law.

**ROGER B. PEIKIN,** born Philadelphia, Pennsylvania, December 29, 1961; admitted to bar, 1991, California, U.S. District Court, Central District of California and U.S. Court of Appeals, Ninth Circuit. *Education:* Villanova University (B.S., 1982); Southwestern University School of Law (J.D., 1991). Delta Theta Phi. Recipient, Award of Exceptional Achievement in the Study of Juvenile Law. *Member:* Beverly Hills (Member, Family Law Section) and Los Angeles County (Member, Family Law Section) Bar Associations; State Bar of California (Member, Family Law Section). **PRACTICE AREAS:** Family Law.

**SALVADOR P. LAVIÑA,** born Los Angeles, California, February 9, 1962; admitted to bar, 1988, California. *Education:* University of California at Los Angeles (B.A., cum laude, 1983); Columbia University (J.D., 1987). Staff Member, 1985-1986 and Administrative Editor, 1986-1987, Columbia VLA Journal of Law and The Arts. Chief of Staff, Operation Hope, Los Angeles, 1992. Recipient, Wiley W. Manuel Award for Pro Bono Legal Services, 1993. *Member:* Los Angeles County Bar Associations; Mexican American Bar Association. **PRACTICE AREAS:** Real Estate; Commercial Litigation; Business Law.

**LORI A. HOWE,** born Belleville, New Jersey, November 5, 1965; admitted to bar, 1990, California. *Education:* State University of New York at Binghamton (B.S., 1987); Pepperdine University (J.D., 1990). *Member:* Beverly Hills and Los Angeles County Bar Associations.

**WARREN D. CAMP,** born Santa Barbara, California, May 29, 1964; admitted to bar, 1991, California and U.S. District Court, Central District of California. *Education:* University of Toronto (B.A., 1986); University of Windsor (LL.B., 1989); University of Detroit. Instructor, Juvenile Dependence Proceedings, Juvenile Courts Bar Association, 1994-1995. Member, American Professional Society on the Abuse of Children, 1995—. Los Angeles Superior Court Family Law Mediation Program, 1996—. *Member:* Los Angeles County Bar Association (Member, Family Law Section); Juvenile Courts Bar Association. (Certified Specialist, Family Law, The State Bar of California Board of Legal Specialization). **PRACTICE AREAS:** Family Law.

**ROBERT B. CLAYTON,** born Philadelphia, Pennsylvania, June 12, 1962; admitted to bar, 1988, California, U.S. District Court, Central District of California and U.S. Court of Appeals, Ninth Circuit; 1992, U.S. District Court, Southern District of California. *Education:* The Johns Hopkins University (B.A., 1984); University of Michigan (J.D., 1987). *Member:* State Bar of California. **PRACTICE AREAS:** Family Law; Civil Litigation.

**LESLIE M. JORDON,** born New York, N.Y., January 29, 1965; admitted to bar, 1990, Illinois; 1991, California. *Education:* Brown University (B.A., 1986); Northwestern University (J.D., 1990). *Member:* Los Angeles County and American Bar Associations; State Bar of California. **LANGUAGES:** French.

**NANCY CRONENWALT,** born Los Angeles, California, June 25, 1958; admitted to bar, 1988, California. *Education:* California State University at Northridge (B.A., cum laude, 1981); Loyola Law School of Los Angeles

*(This Listing Continued)*

(J.D., 1987). Member, St. Thomas More Law Honor Society. *Member:* Beverly Hills Bar Association; State Bar of California.

**ANDREA A. FUGATE,** born Frankfort, Indiana, August 20, 1970; admitted to bar, 1995, California. *Education:* University of Michigan (B.A., 1992); University of Southern California (J.D., 1995). Phi Alpha Delta. *Member:* State Bar of California; American Bar Association; California Family Law Bar Association. **LANGUAGES:** German. **PRACTICE AREAS:** Family Law; Civil Litigation.

**JEFF M. STURMAN,** born Seattle, Washington, September 24, 1961; admitted to bar, 1990, Washington; 1993, U.S. District Court, Western District of Washington and U.S. Tax Court; 1995, California; 1996, U.S. District Court, Central District of California. *Education:* University of Washington (B.A., 1987); University of Oregon (J.D., 1990); Georgetown University Law Center (LL.M., Taxation, 1991). Judicial Law Clerk to Judge Perry Shields, U.S. Tax Court, 1991-1993. *Member:* Washington State and American (Member, Tax Section) Bar Associations. **PRACTICE AREAS:** Family Law; Civil Litigation; Tax Law.

**SUSAN E. WIESNER,** born Kansas City, Missouri, October 17, 1961; admitted to bar, 1987, Nebraska and U.S. District Court, District of Nebraska; 1991, California and U.S. District Court, Central, Northern, Southern and Eastern Districts of California. *Education:* Creighton University (B.A., 1984; J.D., 1987); London School of Economics and Political Science (LL.M., 1989). Phi Alpha Theta (Treasurer, 1986-1987). Member, Moot Court Board. *Member:* State Bar of California; Nebraska State Bar Association; Los Angeles World Affairs Council. **LANGUAGES:** French. **PRACTICE AREAS:** Family Law.

**FAHI TAKESH,** born Tehran, Iran, September 12, 1969; admitted to bar, 1996, California. *Education:* University of California at Los Angeles (B.A., 1992); Loyola Law School (J.D., 1996). **LANGUAGES:** French, Farsi.

**DEREK JON REEVE,** born Thousand Oaks, California, September 16, 1970; admitted to bar, 1996, California. *Education:* University of Southern California (B.A., 1993; J.D., 1996). **PRACTICE AREAS:** Family Law.

**GENIVEVE JOAN RUSKUS,** born San Antonio, Texas, May 30, 1971; admitted to bar, 1996, California. *Education:* Stanford University (B.A., 1993); University of California School of Law at Los Angeles (J.D., 1996). **PRACTICE AREAS:** Family Law; Civil Trial.

**DANIEL B. RUBANOWITZ,** born Burbank, California, May 10, 1962; admitted to bar, 1990, California; 1991, U.S. District Court, Central District of California. *Education:* University of California, Los Angeles (B.A., 1986); Loyola Marymount University (J.D., 1989). Author: *NBA v. Basketball Club, Inc.:* Who Said "There's No Place Like Home" Franchise Relocation in Professional Sports, 10 Loyola Entertainment Law Journal 1, 163, 1990. *Member:* Los Angeles County and American Bar Associations; State Bar of California. **PRACTICE AREAS:** Family Law.

*OF COUNSEL*

**ROLAND L. TROPE,** born Los Angeles, California, September 25, 1947; admitted to bar, 1982, New York; 1984, Minnesota (Not admitted in California). *Education:* University of Southern California (B.A., 1969) Marshall Scholar; Brasenose College, Oxford University (B.A., 1972; M.A., 1976); Yale University (J.D., 1980). Recipient, U.S. Department of the Army Commander's Award for Public Service, 1994. Guest Lecturer: Defense Contracts and Intellectual Property, U.S. Military Academy at West Point, 1992—; U.S. Department of Defense, 1995—. *Member:* The Association of the Bar of the City of New York (Member, Committees on: Copyright and Literacy Property; Military Affairs and Justice). (Also Member, Trope and Trope, New York, N.Y.).

---

# TROY & GOULD

*PROFESSIONAL CORPORATION*

*16TH FLOOR, 1801 CENTURY PARK EAST*
**LOS ANGELES, CALIFORNIA 90067**
Telephone: 310-553-4441
Facsimile: 310-201-4746
Cable Address: "Tromalaw"

*Corporate, Securities, Real Property, Taxation, International, Bankruptcy and Entertainment Law. General Civil Trial and Appellate Litigation, including Financial Institutions, Intellectual Property, Employment and Environmental Litigation.*

*(This Listing Continued)*

**TROY & GOULD,** PROFESSIONAL CORPORATION, Los Angeles—Continued

FIRM PROFILE: Troy & Gould was founded in 1970 to specialize in corporate and securities law. The firm's expertise has since expanded to include mergers and acquisitions, business and personal taxation, real estate lending, leasing and development, business financing and equipment leasing, business, financial institutions, intellectual property, environmental and employment litigation, entertainment and bankruptcy law and international transactions.

**ISTVAN BENKO,** born Budapest, Hungary, August 13, 1954; admitted to bar, 1980, California. *Education:* University of California at Los Angeles (B.A., magna cum laude, 1977; J.D., 1980). Phi Beta Kappa. Member, Moot Court. Member, U.C.L.A. International and Comparative Law Society, 1979-1980. *Member:* Century City (Chairman, International Law Section, 1994), Los Angeles County and American (Member, Section on Corporation, Banking and Business Law) Bar Associations; State Bar of California. **PRACTICE AREAS:** Corporate Law; Securities Law; International Law.

**KENNETH R. BLUMER,** born Los Angeles, California, June 19, 1942; admitted to bar, 1967, California; 1972, U.S. Tax Court. *Education:* University of California at Berkeley (A.B., 1964); University of California at Los Angeles (J.D., 1967). Senior Editor, University of California at Los Angeles Law Review, 1966-1967. *Member:* Los Angeles County and American Bar Associations; State Bar of California. **PRACTICE AREAS:** Real Estate Development; Finance; Lease Law.

**YVONNE E. CHESTER,** born Hong Kong, June 23, 1958; admitted to bar, 1982, California. *Education:* University of California at Berkeley (B.S., 1979); Boalt Hall School of Law, University of California (J.D., 1982). Recipient, American Jurisprudence Award. Associate Editor, California Law Review, 1980-1982. *Member:* State Bar of California. **PRACTICE AREAS:** Corporate Law; Securities Law.

**THOMAS HENRY COLEMAN,** born Santa Monica, California, December 12, 1940; admitted to bar, 1966, California. *Education:* Stanford University (B.A., 1962); University of California, Los Angeles (J.D., 1965). Author, "Money and Bankruptcy: Permissible Cash Investments," *California Bankruptcy Journal,* Winter 1993; "Looking Out for Shareholders: The Role of the Equity Committee in Chapter 11 Reorganization Cases of Large, Publicly Held Companies," *American Bankruptcy Law Journal,* Summer 1994. Lecturer: "Investment Risks: Deceptive Practices and Available Remedies," Treasury '92, Los Angeles City Treasurer's Office; National League of Cities, Washington, DC, March 1992; California Municipal Treasurers' Association, April 1992; "The Legal Environment in Which Municipalities Currently Operate," Treasury '93. Chairperson, Judicial Appointments Committee, Los Angeles County Bar Association, 1987-1989. **PRACTICE AREAS:** Bankruptcy; Securities Litigation.

**GARY O. CONCOFF,** born Los Angeles, California, June 28, 1936; admitted to bar, 1962, California. *Education:* University of California at Los Angeles (B.S., 1958); Harvard Law School (LL.B., 1962). Author: "Motion Picture Secured Transactions Under the Uniform Commercial Code; Problems in Perfection," 13 University of California at Los Angeles Law Review 1214. Reprinted as Chapter 25 of *Secured Transactions* by Coogan, Hogan and Vagts. Lecturer on Law, Course entitled, "Motion Picture Transactions," UCLA Law School, 1979-1982; "Coproduction and Interim Financing: The United States Situation," presented in 1987 at the International Bar Association/International Chamber of Commerce motion picture program at the Cannes Film Festival and also published in French translation in magazine *Film Exchange* (No. 39); "International Co-Financing Arrangements," Los Angeles Lawyer, April, 1992. Author, Moderator and Presenter: "New Technologies: Their Influence on International Audiovisual Law," International Chamber of Commerce and the International Bar Association, Cannes, France, May 1994. Co-Founder and Co-Chairman, UCLA Entertainment Law Symposium, 1977-1979. *Member:* The State Bar of California; American Bar Association (Chairman, Motion Picture and Television Division, Forum Committee on the Sports and Entertainment Industries, 1987-1992; Member, Board of Governors, 1993—); Los Angeles Copyright Society (Member, Board of Trustees, 1976-1977, 1985-1986). **PRACTICE AREAS:** Entertainment Law; Motion Picture and Television Law; Finance Law; Intellectual Property Law.

**ALAN M. DETTELBACH,** born Philadelphia, Pennsylvania, July 18, 1961; admitted to bar, 1988, California. *Education:* University of Pittsburgh (B.S., 1983); Benjamin N. Cardozo School of Law; Loyola Law School (J.D., 1988). Judicial Extern to the Honorable Barry Russell, Central District of California, 1988. *Member:* Los Angeles County, Century City and American Bar Associations; State Bar of California. **PRACTICE AREAS:** Environmental Law; Securities and Real Estate Litigation.

**WILLIAM J. FEIS,** born New York, N.Y., February 4, 1931; admitted to bar, 1967, California. *Education:* Harvard University (A.B., magna cum laude, 1952; LL.B., magna cum laude, 1966). Member, Board of Editors, Harvard Law Review, 1965-1966. *Member:* Los Angeles County (Chairman, Executive Committee, Business and Corporations Law Section, 1976-1977) and American (Member: Section of Business Law; Committee on Federal Regulation of Securities, 1974—) Bar Associations; State Bar of California. **PRACTICE AREAS:** Corporate Law; Securities Law.

**RUSS M. FUKANO,** born Inglewood, California, September 12, 1957; admitted to bar, 1984, California. *Education:* California State University at Long Beach (B.S., 1980); University of Southern California (J.D., 1983). *Member:* Los Angeles County and Japanese American Bar Associations; State Bar of California; Association of Business Trial Lawyers. **PRACTICE AREAS:** Securities Litigation; Business Litigation; Real Estate Litigation.

**MARTIN T. GOLDBLUM,** born New York, N.Y., January 5, 1940; admitted to bar, 1963, New York; 1974, California. *Education:* City College of the City University of New York (B.A., 1960); New York University School of Law (LL.B., 1963). Order of the Coif. Executive Note and Comment Editor, New York University Law Review, 1962-1963. Law Clerk to U.S. Court of Claims Judge Oscar H. Davis, 1963-1964. Attorney, Appellate Section of the Tax Division, Department of Justice, 1964-1969. *Member:* Los Angeles County (Executive Committee, Taxation Section, 1992-1993; Real Estate Taxation Committee Chairman, 1992-1993) and New York State Bar Associations; State Bar of California. (Certified Specialist, Taxation Law, The State Bar of California Board of Legal Specializations). **PRACTICE AREAS:** Taxation Law.

**WILLIAM D. GOULD,** born Los Angeles, California, November 21, 1938; admitted to bar, 1964, California. *Education:* Loyola University of Los Angeles (B.A., 1960); University of California at Los Angeles (J.D., 1963). Order of the Coif; Phi Delta Phi. Editor-in-Chief, U.C.L.A. Law Review, 1962-1963. Co-author, "Mergers," a chapter of Operating Problems of California Corporations, CEB, 1978. *Member:* Los Angeles County (Chairman, Business and Corporations Law Section, 1983-1984; Member, Executive Committee, 1973—; Member, Board of Governors, Institute for Corporate Counsel, 1980-1987) and American Bar Associations; State Bar of California. **PRACTICE AREAS:** Corporate Law; Securities Law.

**SANFORD J. HILLSBERG,** born New York, N.Y., June 20, 1948; admitted to bar, 1973, California. *Education:* University of Pennsylvania (B.A., summa cum laude, 1970); Harvard University (J.D., cum laude, 1973). Phi Beta Kappa. Co-author: "Corporate Aspects of Dissolution," Chapter 13, *Closely Held Corporations,* Illinois Institute for Continuing Legal Education, 1977. *Member:* Los Angeles County and American (Member, Section of Corporation, Banking and Business Law) Bar Associations; State Bar of California. **PRACTICE AREAS:** Corporate Law; Securities Law.

**DEREK W. HUNT,** born Washington, D.C., June 15, 1943; admitted to bar, 1972, California. *Education:* Cornell University (A.B., 1965; J.D., 1972). Associate, 1970-1971, and Managing Editor, 1971-1972, Cornell Law Review. *Member:* Century City and Los Angeles County Bar Associations; State Bar of California; Los Angeles Association of Business Trial Lawyers; Complex Litigation Inns of Court. [1st Lt., U.S. Army, 1967-1969]. **PRACTICE AREAS:** Securities Litigation; Business Litigation; Real Estate Litigation.

**JEFFREY W. KRAMER,** born Evanston, Illinois, June 29, 1951; admitted to bar, 1976, California. *Education:* Indiana University (A.B., with honors, 1973); Stanford University (J.D., 1976). Phi Beta Kappa. Member, Stanford Law Review, 1975-1976. *Member:* Beverly Hills, Century City (Member, Board of Governors), Los Angeles County (Member, Section of Trial Lawyers) and American (Member, Securities Litigation Committee, Litigation Section and Labor and Employment Law Section) Bar Associations; State Bar of California; Los Angeles Association of Business Trial Lawyers; Los Angeles Complex Litigation Inn of Court. **PRACTICE AREAS:** Securities Litigation; Business and Financial Institutions Litigation; Real Estate Litigation; Employment Litigation.

**ALLYN O. KREPS,** born Cambridge, Massachusetts, May 4, 1930; admitted to bar, 1959, California; 1980, District of Columbia. *Education:* Harvard University (B.A., magna cum laude, 1952); Stanford University (LL.B., 1958). Order of the Coif. Comment Editor, Stanford Law Review. Special Counsel to Senate Majority Whip, U.S. Senate, 1977-1979. *Member:* The District of Columbia Bar. Fellow, American College of Trial Lawyers.

*(This Listing Continued)*

[Lt. JG U.S. Navy, 1952-1955]. *PRACTICE AREAS:* Complex Commercial; Corporate; Antitrust Litigation.

**JAMES C. LOCKWOOD,** born Saginaw, Michigan, December 30, 1937; admitted to bar, 1963, Georgia; 1967, California. *Education:* Georgia Institute of Technology (B.S., 1960); University of the South; Tulane University of Louisiana; University of Michigan (J.D., with distinction, 1963). Assistant Editor, Michigan Law Review, 1962-1963. Author: Note, "Insurance-State Regulation-Surplus Line Insurance," 61 Michigan Law Review 1171, 1963; "Protecting Corporate Officers and Directors from Liability," CEB Handbook, 1994. *Member:* Los Angeles County and American Bar Associations; State Bar of California. *PRACTICE AREAS:* Corporate Law; Securities Law.

**PATRICK R. OBEL,** born Wausau, Wisconsin, May 11, 1957; admitted to bar, 1984, California. *Education:* University of Southern California (B.S., magna cum laude, 1979); Harvard University (J.D., 1984). Phi Kappa Phi. Certified Public Accountant, California, 1982. *PRACTICE AREAS:* Real Estate; Finance Law; Environmental Law.

**RONALD S. ROSEN,** born Los Angeles, California, July 22, 1932; admitted to bar, 1958, California. *Education:* Stanford University (A.B., cum laude, 1954); London School of Economics, London, England; Stanford University (LL.B., 1957). Phi Delta Phi; Phi Beta Kappa; Pi Sigma Alpha. Author: "Litigating Copyright, Trademark and Unfair Competition Cases," Practising Law Institute, 1983-1995. Lecturer: Practising Law Institute, 1983-1995; California Continuing Education of the Bar, 1973, 1976, 1982 and 1994; University of Southern California Law Center, 1983; Georgetown University Law Center, 1984-1988; Stanford Law School, 1986-1993. Contributing Editor, California Continuing Education of the Bar, California Business Law Reporter, 1984—. Assistant U.S. Attorney, Southern District of California, 1958-1959. Member, National Panel of Arbitrators, American Arbitration Association, 1964—. *Member:* Beverly Hills, Hollywood, Los Angeles County and American Bar Associations; State Bar of California; ALAI-USA; American Judicature Society. *PRACTICE AREAS:* Entertainment Litigation; Business Litigation; Real Estate Litigation.

**DALE E. SHORT,** born Sioux City, Iowa, May 7, 1955; admitted to bar, 1980, California. *Education:* Iowa State University (B.S., with distinction, 1977); University of Southern California (J.D., 1980). Phi Beta Kappa; The Order of the Coif. Member, University of Southern California Law Review, 1979-1980. *Member:* Century City, Los Angeles County (Member, Executive Committee, Business and Corporate Law Section, 1993—) and American (Member, Section on Corporation, Banking and Business Law) Bar Associations; State Bar of California (Member, Partnerships Committee, Business Law Section, 1993—). *PRACTICE AREAS:* Corporate Law; Securities Law; Partnership Law.

**JOSEPH F. TROY,** born Wilkes-Barre, Pennsylvania, August 16, 1938; admitted to bar, 1964, California; 1978, District of Columbia. *Education:* Yale University (B.A., 1960); Harvard University (LL.B., 1963). Co-author: "Protecting Corporate Officers and Directors from Liability," California Continuing Education of the Bar Program Handbook, 1994; "A Specialized Business Court for the State of California," Report of the Business Court Committee of the Business Law Section of the State Bar of California, 1991; "How Section 2115 Affects Your Delaware Clients: A Comparison of Delaware and California Law Applicable to Quasi-California Corporations," 15 Business Law News 5, State Bar of California, Summer 1993. Author: "A Pilot Project for the Creation of Business and Commercial Law Divisions in the California Courts," 15 Business Law News 3, State Bar of California, Summer 1993; "Business Courts for California: A Status Report and the Argument for Change," 16 California Business Law Reporter (CEB), p. 24 (July 1994); "Homebuilder and Developer Public Offerings," the Stanger Report, January, 1992; "Accountability of Corporate Management," California Continuing Education of the Bar, 1979; Chapter 12, "Corporate Aspects of Dissolution," *Closely Held Corporations,* Illinois Institute for Continuing Legal Education, 1971 (Co-author of 1990 revision); "Dismissing D&O Suits," Business Insurance, July 7, 1980; "Issues in the Structuring of Master Limited Partnerships," 20th Annual Securities Regulation Seminar, October 1987; "Securitization of Mortgages and Receivables," California Bankers Association Lenders Conference, March 8, 1988. Chair, Business Court Committee of the Business Law Section of the State Bar of California. Chairman, American Electronics Association Annual Corporate Finance and Capital Sources Conference, 1983-1995. Chair, Los Angeles Council Lawyers Committee, American Electronics Association, 1986-1992. *Member:* Century City (Member, Board of Governors, 1982-1985), Los Angeles County (Chair, Business and Corporations Law Section, 1977-1978) and American (Member: Committee on Federal Regulation of Securities, Subcommittee on Securitization of Assets; Corporation, Banking and

*(This Listing Continued)*

Business Law Section) Bar Associations; State Bar of California (Member, Corporations Committee, 1990-1993); District of Columbia Bar. *LANGUAGES:* French. *PRACTICE AREAS:* Corporate Finance; Securities; Mergers and Acquisitions; Structured Finance.

*OF COUNSEL*

**FRANK V. CALABA,** born Glendale, California, December 27, 1945; admitted to bar, 1972, California; 1974, New York. *Education:* University of California at Los Angeles (B.S., 1968); Loyola University of Los Angeles (J.D., 1971); Harvard University (LL.M., 1973). *Member:* Beverly Hills, Century City, Los Angeles County (Member, Taxation Section), New York State and American (Member, Taxation Section) Bar Associations; State Bar of California. *PRACTICE AREAS:* Corporate Law; Taxation Law; Trusts and Estates Law.

**DAVID Y. HANDELMAN,** born New York, N.Y., July 2, 1938; admitted to bar, 1963, New York; 1977, California. *Education:* University of Pennsylvania (A.B., 1959); Harvard Law School (J.D., 1962). General Counsel, Twentieth Century Fox and Fox Inc., 1974-1993. *PRACTICE AREAS:* Corporate Law; Entertainment Law.

**JULIUS M. TITLE,** born New York, N.Y., August 26, 1915; admitted to bar, 1941, California. *Education:* University of Southern California (B.A., 1939; LL.B., 1941). Adjunct Professor, Trial Practice and Advocacy, Whittier College School of Law, Los Angeles, 1980—. Judge, Los Angeles Municipal Court, 1967-1970; Los Angeles Superior Court, 1970-1984. *Member:* State Bar of California. *PRACTICE AREAS:* Alternative Dispute Resolution.

**DAVID J. WOHLBERG,** born Los Angeles, California, September 13, 1953; admitted to bar, 1979, California. *Education:* University of California at Santa Cruz (B.A., with honors, 1975); Yale University (J.D., 1979). Editor, Yale Law Journal, 1978-1979. Co-author: "Suing the Police in Federal Court," 88 Yale Law Journal 781, 1979. Judge Pro Tem, Beverly Hills and Los Angeles Small Claims Courts, 1986—. Member, Telluride Association. *Member:* Beverly Hills and Century City Bar Associations; State Bar of California. *PRACTICE AREAS:* Corporate Law; Securities Law; Entertainment Law; Business Litigation.

---

**JENNIFER L. GENTIN,** born Boston, Massachusetts, September 19, 1962; admitted to bar, 1990, California. *Education:* Brown University (B.A., 1984); Benjamin Cardozo School of Law (J.D., 1989). Articles Editor, Benjamin Cardozo Arts and Entertainment Law Journal, 1988-1989. Judicial Extern to the Honorable Pierre N. Leval, Southern District of New York, 1988. *Member:* Beverly Hills, Los Angeles County and American Bar Associations; State Bar of California. *PRACTICE AREAS:* Business, Entertainment and Real Estate Litigation.

**SHARON R. GOLD,** born Denville, New Jersey, October 13, 1966; admitted to bar, 1990, Illinois and U.S. District Court, Northern District of Illinois; 1992, California; 1993, U.S. District Court, Central District of California; 1994, District of Columbia. *Education:* University of Illinois (B.S., with high honors, 1987); Columbia University (J.D., 1990). Harlan Fiske Stone Scholar. Recipient, American Jurisprudence Awards in Torts, Constitutional Law and Legal Writing. Member, Columbia Journal of Law and Social Problems, 1989-1990. Instructor, DePaul University School of Law, Fall 1991. *Member:* Illinois State and American Bar Associations; State Bar of California. *LANGUAGES:* German.

**ERIC G. GROEN,** (admission pending). *Education:* University of California at Santa Barbara (B.A., 1993); Harvard University (J.D., 1996).

**YOUNG J. KIM,** born Seoul, Korea, August 18, 1968; admitted to bar, 1994, Washington; 1995, California. *Education:* University of Washington (B.S./B.A., 1991); Columbia University (J.D., 1994). Tau Beta Pi; Phi Beta Kappa. *Member:* Los Angeles County and American Bar Associations. *LANGUAGES:* Korean. *PRACTICE AREAS:* Corporate; Mergers and Acquisitions; Securities.

**WILLIAM O. KNOX,** born New Rochelle, New York, January 3, 1958; admitted to bar, 1985, California. *Education:* University of Connecticut (B.A., summa cum laude, 1980); University of California, Los Angeles (J.D., 1985). Co-author: "Remedies in Computer Trade Secret Litigation," 3 Computer Law Reporter 213 (Sept., 1984). Author: Comment, "Cable Franchising and the First Amendment: Does the Franchising Process Controversy First Amendment Rights?" 36 Federal Communications Law Journal 317, 1984. *Member:* Century City and Los Angeles County Bar Associations; State Bar of California. *PRACTICE AREAS:* Securities Litigation; Business Litigation; Intellectual Property Litigation.

*(This Listing Continued)*

*TROY & GOULD, PROFESSIONAL CORPORATION, Los Angeles—Continued*

**KENNETH J. MACARTHUR,** born Los Angeles, California, November 1, 1962; admitted to bar, 1995, California. *Education:* University of California at Los Angeles (B.S., 1984); University of Southern California (J.D., 1994). Order of the Coif. Member, University of Southern California Law Review, 1992-1993. *Member:* Century City Bar Association; State Bar of California; Association of Business Trial Lawyers; Los Angeles Complex Litigation Inn of Court. [Lt., U.S. Navy, 1984-1990]. **PRACTICE AREAS:** Business Litigation; Real Estate Litigation.

**JAMES P. MENTON, JR.,** born New York, New York, August 9, 1962; admitted to bar, 1992, California; 1994, District of Columbia. *Education:* Northwestern University (B.A., 1984); University of California, Los Angeles School of Law (J.D., 1991). *Member:* Century City, Los Angeles County and American Bar Associations; State Bar of California. **PRACTICE AREAS:** Bankruptcy; Litigation.

**BENJAMIN ROZWOOD,** born Canal Zone, Panama, November 15, 1968; admitted to bar, 1996, California. *Education:* University of California at Los Angeles (B.A., magna cum laude, 1991); Harvard University (J.D., 1994). Phi Beta Kappa. Recipient: Regents Scholar; College Honors (Letters & Science); Departmental Scholar; Masonic Foundation Scholar; Reginold Lewis International Fellow. Co-Author: "Side Agreements, Sidesteps and Sideshows: Protecting Labor from Free Trade in North America, 34 Harvard International Law Journal 333 (1993). *LANGUAGES:* Spanish. **PRACTICE AREAS:** Securities Law; Corporate Law.

**LAWRENCE P. SCHNAPP,** born New York, New York, November 15, 1962; admitted to bar, 1988, California. *Education:* The Wharton School of the University of Pennsylvania (B.S., 1983); University of California at Los Angeles (J.D., 1988). Order of the Coif, University of California at Los Angeles School of Law. Certified Public Accountant, New York, 1985. *Member:* State Bar of California; American Bar Association. **PRACTICE AREAS:** Corporate Securities; General Corporate.

**ALLISON M. SUNDERLAND,** born Santa Monica, California, October 19, 1969; admitted to bar, 1994, California. *Education:* University of California at Los Angeles (B.A., 1991); Hastings College of the Law, University of California (J.D., 1994). *Member:* State Bar of California (Member, Real Property Law Section, 1994—). **PRACTICE AREAS:** Financial Institutions; Real Estate Litigation.

**MARK S. TORPOCO,** (admission pending). *Education:* Harvard University (A.B., 1993; J.D., 1996). **PRACTICE AREAS:** Litigation.

**NATASHA WAZZAN,** born Los Angeles, California, March 4, 1969; admitted to bar, 1995, California. *Education:* University of California at Berkeley (B.A., 1991); University of Southern California (J.D., 1995). Hale Moot Court Honors Program. *Member:* American Bar Association; State Bar of California. *LANGUAGES:* French, Japanese. **PRACTICE AREAS:** Corporate; Securities.

---

## PHYLLIS ALDEN TRUBY

12100 WILSHIRE BOULEVARD, SUITE 1600
LOS ANGELES, CALIFORNIA 90025
Telephone: 310-826-8136
Fax: 310-826-6715

*Business Law, Real Estate Law and Franchise Law.*

**PHYLLIS ALDEN TRUBY,** born Los Angeles, California, August 8, 1947; admitted to bar, 1976, California; 1977, U.S. District Court, Central District of California. *Education:* University of California at Los Angeles (B.A., 1969; M.J., 1970); Loyola University of Los Angeles (J.D., 1976). Member, Loyola University Law Review. Co-Author: "The Regulation of Non-Franchise Dealer Programs, Business Opportunities, Sales Agencies and Other Distribution Networks," American Bar Association Forum on Franchising Program Materials, 1994; "The Evolution of the California Negotiated Changes Rule," American Bar Association, Franchise Law Journal, Spring 1994; "Selected Issues in Franchising," California Continuing Education of the Bar Program Materials, March 1989; "Business Opportunity Laws: Traps for the Unwary," California State Bar Conference Program Materials, September, 1989. Consultant to California Continuing Education of the Bar for "California Commercial Sales and Leases," 1992. Real Estate Broker's License, California, 1989. *Member:* Los Angeles County (Member: Business Law Section and Real Property Section) and American (Member: Antitrust; Business; Real Property, Probate and Trust

*(This Listing Continued)*

Law Section; Forum Committee on Franchising; Business Law Section, Small Business Committee and Franchising Subcommittee, 1983—; Antitrust Law Section; Franchising Committee, 1990—; Real Property, Probate and Trust Law Section) Bar Associations; State Bar of California (Member: Business Law Section, 1976—; Executive Committee, 1992-1995; Vice-Chair, 1994-1995, Franchise Law Committee; Member, 1987-1992, Vice-Chair, 1990-1991, Chair, 1991-1992); Women Lawyers' Association of Los Angeles (Member, 1976—; Board Member, 1982-1988; Chair, Ad Hoc Committee on Long Range Planning, 1990-1991; Co-Chair, Legislation, 1987-1988; Chair, Pro-Choice, 1985-1987; Co-Chair, Appointive Office, 1994-1985; Co-Chair, Legislative Drafting, 1983-1984; Co-Chair, Amicus Briefs, 1982-1983; Public Action Grant Foundation Board Member, 1989-1992). **PRACTICE AREAS:** Business and Commercial Law; Franchise and Distribution Law; Real Property Law.

---

## LAWRENCE B. TRYGSTAD

A LAW CORPORATION
FOURTH FLOOR, 1880 CENTURY PARK EAST
LOS ANGELES, CALIFORNIA 90067-1600
Telephone: 310-552-0500
Fax: 310-552-1306

*General Civil and Criminal Trial Practice. Labor, Negligence and Family Law. Estate Planning and Probate, School Law and Administrative Practice.*

**LAWRENCE B. TRYGSTAD,** born Holton, Michigan, March 22, 1937; admitted to bar, 1968, California; 1969, U.S. Tax Court; 1974, U.S. Court of Appeals, 9th Circuit and U.S. Supreme Court. *Education:* University of Michigan (B.A., 1959); University of Southern California (J.D., 1967). Phi Alpha Delta. Recipient, American Jurisprudence Award in Remedies Legal and Equitable, 1967. *Member:* Century City, Beverly Hills, Los Angeles County and American Bar Associations; State Bar of California; Los Angeles Trial Lawyers Association; California Trial Lawyers Association; The Association of Trial Lawyers of America; National Organization of Lawyers for Education Associations.

---

**RICHARD J. SCHWAB,** born Charleston, West Virginia, November 23, 1951; admitted to bar, 1976, California. *Education:* University of California at Los Angeles (B.A., 1973); Loyola University (J.D., 1976). Phi Beta Kappa; Pi Gamma Mu. Recipient, American Jurisprudence Award, Trust and Wills, 1976. *Member:* State Bar of California.

**DAVID J. PENNER,** born Fresno, California, July 3, 1958; admitted to bar, 1984, California. *Education:* University of Southern California (B.S., 1981); University of Southern California (J.D., 1984). *Member:* Los Angeles County and American Bar Associations; The State Bar of California.

**ROSEMARY O. WARD,** born New York, N.Y., May 27, 1949; admitted to bar, 1991, California. *Education:* Franconia College (B.A.); State University of New York (M.A.); Pepperdine University (J.D., 1991). Recipient, American Jurisprudence Award, Administrative Law. *Member:* State B ar of California.

**SHANON TRYGSTAD,** born Los Angeles, California, August 12, 1967; admitted to bar, 1994, California; 1995, U.S. District Court, Central District of California and U.S. Court of Appeals, Ninth Circuit. *Education:* University of California, San Diego (B.A., 1990); University of Southern California (J.D., 1994). *LANGUAGES:* Spanish.

REPRESENTATIVE CLIENTS: United Teachers-Los Angeles; South Bay United Teachers; California Teachers Assn.; National Education Assn.
REFERENCE: City National Bank (Century City Branch).

---

## JOHN A. TUCKER, JR.

12TH FLOOR, 800 WILSHIRE BOULEVARD
LOS ANGELES, CALIFORNIA 90017
Telephone: 213-629-0060
FAX: 213-624-9441

*Real Property, Estate Planning and Probate Law.*

**JOHN A. TUCKER, JR.,** born Los Angeles, California, May 2, 1932; admitted to bar, 1961, California; 1971, District of Columbia. *Education:* Stanford University (A.B., 1954); University of Denver (J.D., 1959). Phi Delta Phi; Omicron Delta Kappa. Member, Board of Editors, University of

*(This Listing Continued)*

Denver Law Review, 1958-1959. *Member:* Los Angeles County and American Bar Associations; District of Columbia Bar; State Bar of California. (Also Of Counsel to Clark & Trevithick, A Professional Corporation).

## JOHN W. TULAC
### LOS ANGELES, CALIFORNIA
(See Claremont)

*International Business Law, International Trade Law, General Business and Corporate Law, Foreign Investment in the United States, International Arbitration, Mediation and Litigation, Business Litigation. Professional Mediator and Arbitrator.*

## STEVEN M. TURKOWITZ
### A PROFESSIONAL CORPORATION
### 1900 AVENUE OF THE STARS, SUITE 1800
### LOS ANGELES, CALIFORNIA 90067
Telephone: 310-788-0074
Telecopier: 310-788-0141

*Retail Development and Leasing, Land Use, Entitlements, Governmental Assistance, Environmental, Equity and Debt Financing, Joint Ventures, Partnerships and Limited Partnerships, Real Property Acquisition and Disposition, Commercial, Tenant Leases, Shopping Center Development and Corporate and Securities Law.*

FIRM PROFILE: *The firm's client base ranges from small restaurant pads to large department stores and disposition of improved and unimproved real estate.*

**STEVEN M. TURKOWITZ,** born New York, N.Y., October 19, 1946; admitted to bar, 1972, New York; 1980, California. *Education:* Yale University (B.A., 1968); Columbia Law School (J.D., 1971).

REPRESENTATIVE CLIENTS: Majestic Realty Co.; Virgin Entertainment Group; Westrust Financial.

## TURNER, GERSTENFELD, WILK, AUBERT & YOUNG, LLP
### LOS ANGELES, CALIFORNIA
(See Beverly Hills)

*General Civil Practice. Civil Litigation. Real Estate, Construction, Probate, Tax, Estate Planning and Family, Franchise, Entertainment, Cellular Communication, International, Corporation and Business Law.*

## TUTTLE & TAYLOR
### A LAW CORPORATION
### Established in 1941
### 355 SOUTH GRAND AVENUE
### FORTIETH FLOOR
### LOS ANGELES, CALIFORNIA 90071-3102
Telephone: 213-683-0600
Facsimile: 213-683-0225

Washington, D.C. Office: Tuttle, Taylor & Heron, 1025 Thomas Jefferson Street, N.W. 20007-5201. Telephone: 202-342-1300. Facsimile: 202-342-5880.

Sacramento, California Office: 1521 I Street, 95814-2016. Telephone: 916-441-2249. Facsimile: 916-441-2910.

*General Practice. Corporation, Securities, Real Property, Bankruptcy and Insolvency, Taxation and Antitrust Law. General Civil Litigation in all State and Federal Courts. Agricultural and Cooperative Law. Administrative and Labor Relations Practice. Estate Planning, Probate and Trust Law. Environmental and Natural Resources and Insurance Law. International Law.*

**EDWARD W. TUTTLE** (1877-1960).

**EDWARD E. TUTTLE** (1907-1996).

**ROBERT G. TAYLOR,** born Sacramento, CA, October 26, 1923; admitted to bar, 1949, CA; 1974, DC; 1994, U.S. Tax Court. *Education:* Wheaton College (A.B., 1947); Stanford University (J.D., 1949). Phi Beta

*(This Listing Continued)*

Kappa; Order of the Coif. Note Editor, Stanford Law Review, 1947-1949. *PRACTICE AREAS:* Agricultural Cooperatives; Cooperative Taxation; Business.

**MERLIN W. CALL,** born Long Beach, CA, November 25, 1931; admitted to bar, 1953, CA; 1957, U.S. Tax Court. *Education:* Pasadena City College; Stanford University (A.B., 1951; J.D., 1953). Phi Beta Kappa; Order of the Coif. Comment Editor, Stanford Law Review, 1952-1953. Trustee, Fuller Theological Seminary, 1963-1978, 1983—. Trustee, 1984— and Chairman, 1988-1994, Westmont College. Director, 1987— and Chairman, 1987-1994, The Fuller Foundation. *PRACTICE AREAS:* Trust and Probate Administration; Engineering; Business.

**FRANK C. CHRISTL,** born Tujunga, CA., June 4, 1922; admitted to bar, 1952, CA. *Education:* University of Southern California (A.B., 1943); Southwestern University (LL.B., 1951). Judge Pro Tempore, Los Angeles Municipal Court, 1968-1975. Arbitrator, Los Angeles County, 1979— and Orange County, 1984—, Superior Courts, Business Matters. Member, American Bar Association, Judicial Administration Division Lawyers Conference, State and Federal Committee, 1988-1989. Mediator, U.S. Bankruptcy Court Mediation Panel (Central District of CA), 1995-1996. *Member:* American Board of Trial Advocates; The Association of Trial Lawyers of America; Association of Attorney-Mediators (Southern California Chapter). *PRACTICE AREAS:* Civil Litigation; Bankruptcy and Creditors' Rights.

**PATRICK L. SHREVE,** born Minneapolis, MN., July 2, 1940; admitted to bar, 1966, CA. *Education:* Loyola (LA) University (B.S., 1962); University of California at Berkeley (LL.B., 1965). Order of the Coif. Editor-in-Chief, California Law Review, 1964-1965. *PRACTICE AREAS:* Real Estate; Business; Natural Resources.

**C. DAVID ANDERSON,** born Baltimore, MD, August 4, 1943; admitted to bar, 1967, WI; 1970, DC; 1972, CA; 1985, U.S. Tax Court. *Education:* Yale University (B.A., 1964); University of Chicago (J.D., 1967). Order of the Coif. Member, University of Chicago Law Review, 1965-1967. Author: "Tax Planning: The Missing Quantitative Dimension," 39 University of Southern California Tax Institute (1981); "Conventional Tax Theory and 'Tax Expenditures': A Critical Analysis of the Life Insurance Example," 57 Tax Notes 1417 (1992). Co-Author with Nancy E. Howard: "Real and Apparent Differences Between Employee and Partner/Sole Proprietor Compensation," 45 University of Southern California Tax Institute 500 (1993). Lecturer on Law: University of Southern California Law School, 1976-1978; Harvard Law School, 1983. Adjunct Professor of Law, University of California at Los Angeles Law School, 1979-1984. Member, Planning Committee, University of Southern California Tax Institute, 1980—. *PRACTICE AREAS:* Tax; Executive Employment Benefits.

**RICHARD S. BERGER,** born New York, NY, October 17, 1941; admitted to bar, 1967, CA; 1972, U.S. Supreme Court. *Education:* Stanford University (B.S., 1963); Hastings College of the Law, University of California (J.D., 1967). Phi Alpha Delta. Issue Editor, Hastings Law Journal, 1966-1967. Member: American Bar Association, Litigation Section, Bankruptcy and Insolvency Committee (Co-Chair, 1995—; Newsletter Co-Editor, 1993-1995; Business Law Section, Business BankrupTCy Committee; Section on International Law and Practice; International Creditors' Rights and Bankruptcy Committee); Los Angeles County Bar Association (Judicial Evaluation, Amicus Briefs and Federal Practice Committees; Commercial Law and Bankruptcy Section, Bankruptcy Committee); American Bankruptcy Institute; Association of Business Trial Lawyers; Financial Lawyers Conference; Los Angeles Bankruptcy Forum. *PRACTICE AREAS:* Civil Litigation; Bankruptcy and Creditors' Rights; Appellate Practice.

**JOHN R. LIEBMAN,** born Evanston, IL, March 9, 1935; admitted to bar, 1962, CA; 1966, U.S. Supreme Court; 1971, NY. *Education:* Dartmouth College (A.B., 1956); University of California at Los Angeles (J.D., 1961). Phi Alpha Delta. Recipient: National Order of the Southern Cross, Brazil, 1978; Stanley P. Olafson Bronze Plaque, Los Angeles Area Chamber of Commerce, 1989. Co-Author: "United States Export Controls," Aspen Law and Business. Attorney-Advisor and Chief, Program Development, Agency for International Development, U.S. Department of State, 1966-1968. Member, 1975-1995 and Chairman, 1982-1984, Southern California District Export Council. Member, California State World Trade Commission, 1983-1991. Lecturer in Law, UCLA School of Law, 1993-1995. Director: California Council of International Trade, 1991-1995; Los Angeles Child Guidance Clinic, 1980—. *Member:* Los Angeles County Bar Association (Chair, International Law Section, 1983); State Bar of California (Member, 1986—, Advisor, 1990— and Chair, 1989-1990, International Law Section). *LANGUAGES:* German. *PRACTICE AREAS:* Interna-

*(This Listing Continued)*

CAA1265B

**TUTTLE & TAYLOR, A LAW CORPORATION, Los Angeles—**
*Continued*

tional Trade Regulation; International Trade Finance; Technology Transfer; International Joint Ventures; International Commercial Transactions.

**ALAN E. FRIEDMAN,** born New York, NY, May 5, 1946; admitted to bar, 1971, CA. *Education:* Amherst College (B.A., 1967); Stanford University (J.D., 1970). Note Editor, Stanford Law Review, 1969-1970. Member, Board of Governors, 1996— and Chair, 1994-1996, Federal Courts Committee, Association of Business Trial Lawyers. Member, 1977-1985 and Chair, 1982-1983, Federal Courts and Practices Committee, Los Angeles County Bar Association. *PRACTICE AREAS:* Civil Business Litigation.

**TIMI ANYON HALLEM,** born New York, NY, October 24, 1946; admitted to bar, 1972, CA. *Education:* Smith College (A.B., 1968); New York University; University of California at Los Angeles (J.D., 1972). Order of the Coif. Managing Editor, UCLA Law Review, 1971-1972. Member, California Secretary of State's Los Angeles Corporate Citizen Advisory Council, 1975-1982. Trustee, 1979-1981, Vice-Chair, Arbitration Committee, 1979-1983 and Judicial Evaluation Committee, 1984-1985, Los Angeles County Bar Association. Member, Executive Committee, Conference of Delegates, State Bar of California, 1981-1984. President, Women Lawyers' Association of Los Angeles, 1979-1980. Director, Alumnae Association of Smith College, 1985-1988. President, Santa Monica-Malibu Education Foundation, 1987-1993. Member, Los Angeles County Child Care Advisory Board, 1989-1996. Director, YWCA of Santa Monica, 1996—. Member: Urban Land Institute, 1993—; International Council of Shopping Centers, 1991—. *PRACTICE AREAS:* Real Estate; Land Use; Secured Financing; Corporate Law.

**CHARLES L. WOLTMANN,** born Weehawken, NJ, July 23, 1947; admitted to bar, 1974, HI; 1975, DC; 1976, CA. *Education:* Yale University (B.A., 1969; J.D., 1973). Phi Beta Kappa. Articles Editor, Yale Law Journal, 1972-1973. Law Clerk to Judge Samuel P. King, U.S. District Court, District of Hawaii, 1973-1974. *PRACTICE AREAS:* Commercial Law; Agricultural Cooperatives.

**MARJORIE S. STEINBERG,** born Bethesda, MD, January 7, 1946; admitted to bar, 1975, CA. *Education:* Stanford University (A.B., 1968); Johns Hopkins University (M.A.T., 1970); University of California at Los Angeles (J.D., 1975). Order of the Coif. Editor-in-Chief, UCLA Law Review, 1974-1975. President, Women Lawyers Association of Los Angeles, 1985-1986. Trustee, Los Angeles County Bar Association, 1984-1986. Director, Constitutional Rights Foundation, 1990-1996. Vice Chair, Committee on Women in Law, The State Bar of California, 1992-1993. Legislative Assistant for Education and Legislative Director to U.S. Senator Jeff Bingaman, 1993-1995. *PRACTICE AREAS:* Bankruptcy; Corporate Law; Real Estate.

**DOUGLAS W. BECK,** born Kansas City, MO, September 3, 1949; admitted to bar, 1975, CA; 1977, U.S. Claims Court. *Education:* Princeton University (A.B., 1971); University of California at Berkeley (J.D., 1975). Order of the Coif. Research Editor, California Law Review, 1974-1975. Law Clerk to the Honorable J. Clifford Wallace, U.S. Court of Appeals, 9th Circuit, 1975-1976. *PRACTICE AREAS:* Civil Litigation; Real Estate and Environmental Litigation.

**JOHN ARTHUR MOE, II,** born Philadelphia, PA., July 7, 1950; admitted to bar, 1975, CA; 1985, U.S. Supreme Court. *Education:* University of Notre Dame (B.A., magna cum laude, 1972; J.D., 1975). Associate Editor, Notre Dame Journal of Legislation, 1974-1975. *Member:* Los Angeles County Bar Association (Member, Sections on Trial Lawyers, Commercial Law and Bankruptcy, Business and Corporations Law); The Association of Trial Lawyers of America; California and Los Angeles Trial Lawyers Associations; Financial Lawyers Conference. [Capt. USAF, JAG, 1976-1980]. *PRACTICE AREAS:* Civil Litigation; Bankruptcy and Creditors' Rights.

**ROBERT L. SHULER,** born Tempe, AZ, May 5, 1950; admitted to bar, 1975, AZ; 1983, CA; 1988, DC. *Education:* Arizona State University (B.S., 1972); University of Arizona (J.D., 1975). Member, Class XIII, California Agricultural Leadership Program. Chief Deputy Director, California Department of Food and Agriculture, 1991-1994. (Resident, Sacramento, California Office). *PRACTICE AREAS:* Government Relations; Agricultural Law.

**MARK A. BORENSTEIN,** born Brooklyn, NY, June 26, 1951; admitted to bar, 1976, VA; 1977, DC; 1978, CA; 1989, U.S. Tax Court; 1992, U.S. Supreme Court. *Education:* N.Y. State University at Buffalo (B.A., 1973); George Washington University (J.D., 1976); Georgetown University (LL.M., 1978). Phi Beta Kappa; Order of the Coif. Executive Editor,

*(This Listing Continued)*

George Washington Law Review, 1975-1976. Law Fellow, Institute for Public Interest Representation, Georgetown University Law Center, 1977-1978. Law Clerk to Judge Irving Hill, U.S. District Court, Central District of California, 1976-1977. Lecturer in Law, University of Southern California, 1980-1982. *PRACTICE AREAS:* Civil and Probate Litigation; Professional Liability Litigation.

**NANCY E. HOWARD,** born Fort Wayne, IN, August 13, 1951; admitted to bar, 1977, CA. *Education:* Stanford University (B.A., 1973; J.D., 1977). Phi Beta Kappa; Order of the Coif. Author: "Planning the Irrevocable Trust," Drafting California Irrevocable Living Trusts, CEB, 1988; "Using Revocable Trusts During Client's Lifetime" (Chapter 1), "Postmortem Advantages and Disadvantages" (Chapter 2), Drafting California Revocable Living Trusts, CEB, 1994. Co-Author with C. David Anderson: "Real and Apparent Differences Between Employee and Partner/Sole Proprietor Compensation," 45 University of Southern California Tax Institute 500 (1993); "The Mathematics of Estate Planning and Estate Freezing," Freeman, Estate Tax Freeze: Tools and Techniques, 1984. *PRACTICE AREAS:* Partnership Taxation; Probate and Estate Planning.

**MARC L. BROWN,** born Dallas, TX, September 24, 1951; admitted to bar, 1978, CA. *Education:* University of Wisconsin (B.A., 1973); Yale University (J.D., 1976). Phi Beta Kappa. Article and Book Review Editor, Yale Law Journal, 1975-1976. Law Clerk to: the Honorable Ozell M. Trask, U.S. Court of Appeals, 9th Circuit, 1976-1977; Judge William W. Schwarzer, U.S. District Court, Northern District of California, 1978-1979. Author: "The Legality of Bank-Sponsored Investment Services," 84 Yale Law Journal 1477 (1975). *PRACTICE AREAS:* Business Law; Securities.

**MICHAEL H. BIERMAN,** born Portland, OR, March 11, 1950; admitted to bar, 1976, OR; 1979, CA. *Education:* Harvard University (B.A., magna cum laude, 1972; J.D., cum laude, 1976). Co-Author: "Towards a Reformulation of the Test for Determining Trademark Infringement," 80 Trademark Reporter 1, 1990. Law Clerk to the Honorable Alfred T. Goodwin, U.S. Court of Appeals, 9th Circuit, 1976-1977. Trustee, Los Angeles County Bar Association, 1983-1984. Member, Patent, Trademark and Copyright Law and Litigation Sections, American Bar Association. Member, Board of Directors, 1988—and President, 1991-1996, San Fernando Valley Neighborhood Legal Services, Inc. *Member:* International Trademark Association. *PRACTICE AREAS:* Professional Liability Litigation; False Claims Act Litigation; Trademark; Copyright.

**LOUIS E. KEMPINSKY,** born Superior, WI, May 5, 1955; admitted to bar, 1979, CA. *Education:* Rice University (B.A., magna cum laude, 1979); Columbia University (J.D., 1979). Member, 1977-1978 and Associate Editor, 1978-1979, Columbia Journal of Transnational Law. *Member:* Los Angeles County Bar Association (Member, Amicus Briefs and Provisional and Postjudgment Remedies Committees); Public Counsel of California. *PRACTICE AREAS:* Civil Litigation; Bankruptcy and Creditors' Rights; Environmental Litigation.

**GORDON A. GOLDSMITH,** born Carbondale, IL, October 13, 1955; admitted to bar, 1980, IL; 1982, CA. *Education:* University of Illinois (B.A., with distinction, 1977); University of California at Los Angeles School of Law (J.D., 1980). Member, UCLA Law Review, 1979-1980. Chief Comment Editor, UCLA-Alaska Law Review, 1980. Law Clerk to Judge Cynthia H. Hall, U.S. District Court, Central District of California, 1981-1982. *PRACTICE AREAS:* Commercial Litigation; Environmental Litigation; Professional Liability Litigation.

**GREGORY D. SCHETINA,** born Denver, CO, November 8, 1955; admitted to bar, 1981, CO; 1984, CA;. *Education:* University of California at Berkeley (A.B., with great distinction, 1977); Loyola (LA) Law School (J.D., 1981). Phi Beta Kappa. Special Assistant U.S. Attorney, Central District of California, Major Frauds Section, Criminal Division and Special Counsel to the Office of Thrift Supervision, 1988-1992. Deputy General Counsel, Kolts Investigation of the Los Angeles County Sheriff's Department, 1992. *PRACTICE AREAS:* Civil and Professional Liability Litigation; White-Collar Criminal Defense.

**DIANN H. KIM,** born Minneapolis, MN, February 20, 1958; admitted to bar, 1985, CA; 1995, U.S. Supreme Court. *Education:* Harvard College (B.A., cum laude, East Asian Studies, 1980); University of Michigan (J.D., cum laude, 1983). Associate Editor, 1981-1982 and Senior Editor, 1982-1983, Michigan Yearbook of International Legal Studies. Law Clerk to Judge A. David Mazzone, U.S. District Court, District of Massachusetts, 1983-1984. Deputy General Counsel, Office of the Special Advisor to the Board of Police Commissioners (Webster Commission), 1992-1993. Contributor, *Jury Persuasion*, (Prentice-Hall, 1993). *PRACTICE AREAS:* Civil Litigation; Antitrust and Unfair Business Practices Litigation; Civil Trial.

*(This Listing Continued)*

**MARLA J. ASPINWALL,** born Los Angeles, CA, March 13, 1959; admitted to bar, 1984, CA. *Education:* University of Utah (B.A., 1980); University of Southern California (J.D., 1984). Order of the Coif. Member, Southern California Law Review, 1982-1983. . *Member:* Christian Legal Society; National Council of Farmer Cooperatives (Member, Legal Tax and Accountancy Committee); National Society of Accountants for Cooperatives (Member, Tax Committee). *PRACTICE AREAS:* Agricultural Cooperatives; Tax.

**ROBIN D. WIENER,** born New York, NY, January 11, 1954; admitted to bar, 1985, CA. *Education:* Brandeis University (A.B., magna cum laude, 1975); Cornell University (B.S., with distinction, 1977); Harvard University (J.D., magna cum laude, 1984). Phi Beta Kappa; Sigma Theta Tau. Editor: Harvard Law Review, 1982-1984; Harvard Women's Law Journal, 1983-1984. Registered Professional Nurse, NY, 1977-1981. Author: "Occupationally Induced Cancer Susceptibility: Regulating the Risk," 96 Harvard Law Review 697 (1983); "Limiting Your Exposure to Sexual Harassment Claims," Los Angeles Business Journal, Vol. 16, No. 14 (April 11, 1994). Law Clerk to the Honorable Stephen Reinhardt, U.S. Court of Appeals, 9th Circuit, 1984-1985. Fellow, Center for Law in the Public Interest, 1985-1986. (Resident, Sacramento, California Office). *PRACTICE AREAS:* Labor and Employment; Commercial Litigation; Appellate Practice.

**LAURA J. CARROLL,** born Racine, WI, January 18, 1951; admitted to bar, 1985, HI; 1986, CA, DC. *Education:* Miami University of Ohio (B.A., magna cum laude, 1973); Stanford University (M.A., 1976); Cornell University; University of California at Los Angeles (J.D., 1984). Phi Kappa Phi. Co-Author: "California Environmental Law Handbook," Government Institutes, Inc., 1990, 1991, 1992, 1993, 1994 and 1995 editions; "Understanding the Regulatory Status of Contaminated Environmental Media," Journal of Environmental Regulation (April, 1994). Extern to Judge Mariana R. Pfaelzer, U.S. District Court, Central District of California, 1983. *PRACTICE AREAS:* Environmental Law; Business; Real Estate; Toxic Tort Litigation.

**EDWARD A. MENDOZA,** born Chicago, IL, November 2, 1956; admitted to bar, 1981, CA. *Education:* University of Illinois, Champaign-Urbana (B.S., with high honors, 1978); University of Michigan (J.D., cum laude, 1981). Member: Barristers Society; The Association of Trial Lawyers of America. *PRACTICE AREAS:* Civil Litigation; Bankruptcy and Creditors' Rights; Accountants' Liability Litigation.

**JEFFREY D. WEXLER,** born Santa Monica, CA, March 10, 1962; admitted to bar, 1987, CA. *Education:* University of California at Los Angeles (B.A., summa cum laude, 1984); Harvard University (J.D., magna cum laude, 1987). Phi Beta Kappa. Editor, Harvard Law Review, 1985-1987. Author: Note, "Imposing Tort Liability on Real Estate Brokers Selling Defective Housing," 99 Harvard Law Review 1861 (1986); Comment, "Summary Judgment Standards," 100 Harvard Law Review 250 (1986). Co-Author: "Towards a Reformulation of the Test for Determining Trademark Infringement," 80 Trademark Reporter 1 (1990). Law Clerk to the Honorable Alfred T. Goodwin, Chief Judge, U.S. Court of Appeals, 9th Circuit, 1987-1988. *PRACTICE AREAS:* Civil Litigation; Patent, Trademark, Copyright; Agricultural Litigation; Franchisor-Franchisee Litigation; False Claims Litigation.

**JULIO A. THOMPSON,** born Detroit, MI, October 20, 1964; admitted to bar, 1990, CA. *Education:* Wayne State University (B.A., summa cum laude, 1986); University of Michigan (J.D., cum laude, 1989). Phi Beta Kappa; Delta Sigma Rho; Tau Kappa Alpha. Golden Key. Member, 1987-1988, and Executive Note Editor, 1988-1989, Michigan Law Review. Law Clerk to the Honorable Cynthia H. Hall, U.S. Court of Appeals, 9th Circuit, 1989-1990. Author: Casenote, "A Board Does Not a Bench Make," 87 Michigan Law Review 241 (1988). *Member:* Los Angeles County Bar Association (Employment Law Section); Los Angeles County Barristers; Pro Bono Council. *PRACTICE AREAS:* Labor and Employment Law; Trade Secrets; Unfair Business Practices; Commercial Litigation; Appellate Law; Law Enforcement Auditing.

---

**JOHN R. DENT,** born Los Angeles, CA, July 21, 1963; admitted to bar, 1990, CA. *Education:* University of California at Los Angeles (B.A., 1984); University of Chicago (J.D., 1990). Staff Member, 1988-1989 and Comment Editor, 1989-1990, University of Chicago Legal Forum.

**SUNG H. SHIN,** born Seoul, Korea, April 9, 1966; admitted to bar, 1991, CA. *Education:* University of California at Berkeley (B.A., 1988); Columbia University (J.D., 1991). *LANGUAGES:* Korean.

**MARNIE S. CARLIN,** born Redwood City, CA, November 18, 1964; admitted to bar, 1991, CA. *Education:* University of California at Los An-

*(This Listing Continued)*

geles (B.A., 1986); Loyola (LA) Law School (J.D., magna cum laude, 1991). Order of the Coif; Alpha Sigma Nu; St. Thomas More Law Honor Society. Articles Editor, Loyola (LA) Law Review, 1990-1991.

**KATE SCHNEIDER GOLD,** born Los Angeles, CA, April 15, 1966; admitted to bar, 1991, CA. *Education:* University of California at Berkeley (B.A., 1988); Boalt Hall, University of California, Berkeley (J.D., 1991). Phi Beta Kappa. Associate Editor, California Law Review, 1989-1990, 1990-1991.

**DAHNI K. TSUBOI,** born Los Angeles, CA, August 21, 1967; admitted to bar, 1992, CA; 1994, DC. *Education:* Wellesley College (B.A., magna cum laude, 1989); Yale University (J.D., 1992). *LANGUAGES:* Spanish.

**ANDREA V. RAMOS,** born Santiago, Chile, May 21, 1966; admitted to bar, 1992, CA; 1995, DC. *Education:* Arizona State University (B.A., 1988); University of Southern California (J.D., 1992). *LANGUAGES:* Spanish.

**SAM S. OH,** born Seoul, Korea, June 21, 1963; admitted to bar, 1993, CA. *Education:* University of California at Berkeley (B.A., 1986); Loyola (LA) Law School; University of California at Los Angeles (J.D., 1993). Order of the Coif. UCLA Law Review, 1991-1992. *LANGUAGES:* Korean.

**SHERRY L. APPEL,** born Los Angeles, CA, October 22, 1965; admitted to bar, 1993, CA. *Education:* University of California at Los Angeles (B.S., 1988); Boalt Hall School of Law, University of California at Berkeley (J.D., 1993).

**MALISSIA R. LENNOX,** born Tucson, AZ, November 14, 1968; admitted to bar, 1994, CA. *Education:* Arizona State University (B.A., summa cum laude, 1990); Stanford University (J.D., 1993). Phi Beta Kappa. Editor, Stanford Law Review, 1991-1993. Author: Note, "Refugees, Racism and Reparations: A Critique of the United States' Haitian Immigration Policy," 3 Stanford Law Review 687 (1993).

**KATHRYN E. OLSON,** born Stanford, CA, June 5, 1966; admitted to bar, 1994, CA. *Education:* University of Pennsylvania (B.A., cum laude, 1988); University of California at Berkeley (M.P.P., 1993); Boalt Hall School of Law, University of California at Berkeley (J.D., 1994).

**THOMAS I. DUPUIS,** born Elgin, IL, February 23, 1969; admitted to bar, 1994, CA. *Education:* Northwestern University (B.S.Ed., 1991); University of Southern California (J.D., 1994). Order of the Coif. Member, Southern California Law Review, 1992-1993. Associate Editor, Southern California Interdisciplinary Law Journal, 1993-1994.

**SHANNON SULLIVAN MARTINEZ,** born Los Angeles, CA, November 26, 1967; admitted to bar, 1994, CA. *Education:* University of California at Los Angeles (B.A., magna cum laude, 1991); Loyola (LA) Law School (J.D., 1994). Order of the Coif; St. Thomas More Law Honor Society. Editor-in-Chief, Loyola (LA) International and Comparative Law Journal, 1993-1994.

**DEAN A. BOCHNER,** born Los Angeles, CA, February 2, 1969; admitted to bar, 1994, CA. *Education:* Stanford University (A.B., with distinction, 1990); University of Michigan (J.D., cum laude, 1994). Phi Beta Kappa. Law Clerk to Judge Elaine E. Bucklo, U.S. District Court, Northern District of Illinois, 1994-1995.

**STEVEN M. ROGERS,** born Los Angeles, CA, July 19, 1970; admitted to bar, 1995, CA. *Education:* University of California at Berkeley (B.A., 1992); Loyola (LA) Law School (J.D., 1995). Order of the Coif.

**JEFFREY S. KARR,** born Fort Smith, AR, April 5, 1971; admitted to bar, 1996, CA. *Education:* Northwestern University (B.A., 1993); Hastings College of the Law, University of California at Berkeley (J.D., 1996).

*OF COUNSEL*

**JULIAN B. HERON, JR.,** born Washington, D.C, December 17, 1939; admitted to bar, 1965, KY; 1966, DC; 1968, MD. *Education:* University of Kentucky (B.S., 1962; LL.B., 1965). Phi Alpha Delta. Author: "Reparations Proceedings Under the Perishable Agricultural Commodities Act— Valuable Tool in Need of Change," 22 South Dakota Law Review No. 3 (Summer, 1977); "Pacific Rim as a Future Market for U.S. Agricultural Trade," 23 University of California at Davis Law Review No. 3 (Spring, 1990); "New Challenges for California Agriculture in World Export Markets," 1 San Joaquin Agricultural Law Review No. 1 (1991). Chairman, Agricultural Committee, Administrative Law Section, American Bar Association, 1974-1977. Fellow, American Bar Foundation. [Capt., J.A., USAF, 1965-1968]. (Resident, Washington, D.C. Office). *PRACTICE AREAS:* Administrative Law; International Law; Business Law.

*(This Listing Continued)*

**TUTTLE & TAYLOR, A LAW CORPORATION, Los Angeles—** Continued

**PHILLIP L. FRAAS,** born Independence, MO, September 30, 1943; admitted to bar, 1969, MO; 1974, DC; 1975, U.S. Supreme Court; 1993, U.S. Court of Claims. *Education:* Rockhurst College (A.B., 1965); University of Missouri at Kansas City (J.D., 1969). Chief Counsel, Committee on Agriculture, U.S. House of Representatives, 1985-1989. Member, American Agricultural Law Association, 1990—. (Resident, Washington, D.C. Office). *PRACTICE AREAS:* Agricultural Law; Federal Administrative Law; International Trade.

**PAMELA G. BOTHWELL,** born Los Angeles, CA, October 25, 1952; admitted to bar, 1985, CA. *Education:* Barnard College (B.A.; 1975); Columbia University (M.A., 1979); University of Colorado (J.D., 1984). Contributor: *California Trial Handbook* 2d (Bancroft Whitney 1986). Los Angeles Municipal Court Judge Pro Tempore, 1992—. LANGUAGES: French and Sanskrit. *REPORTED CASES:* Korea Exchange Bank vs. Yang, 200 Cal. App. 3d 1471 (1988). *PRACTICE AREAS:* Special Tax and Assessment Lien Foreclosures; Civil Trial; Real Estate.

REFERENCE: Union Bank, 455 South Figueroa Street, Main Office (Los Angeles, California).

## TUVERSON & HILLYARD

A Limited Liability Partnership, including Professional Corporations

*Established in 1979*

**12400 WILSHIRE BOULEVARD, SUITE 900**
**LOS ANGELES, CALIFORNIA 90025**
Telephone: 310-826-7855; 625-1234
Fax: 310-826-8738

*Newport Beach, California Office:* 4675 MacArthur Court, Suite 650, Newport Beach, California 92660. Telephone: 714-752-7855. Fax: 714-752-5437.

*Palm Springs, California Office:* 1800 Tahquitz Canyon Way, Palm Springs, California 92263. Telephone: 619-322-7855. Fax: 619-322-5121.

*San Diego, California Office:* 4365 Executive Drive, Suite 700, San Diego, California 92121. Telephone: 619-452-7855. Fax: 619-452-2153.

General Civil and Trial Practice in all State and Federal Courts. *Medical and Legal Malpractice Defense, Public Entity Defense, Construction Defect and Construction Site Injury Defense, Personal Lines, Transactional Services, Asset Management, Lender Liability and Director's and Officer's Liability.*

FIRM PROFILE: Founded in 1979 by Arthur W. Tuverson and Steven D. Hillyard, Tuverson & Hillyard has grown into a law firm comprising four offices strategically placed throughout Southern California. The firm offers a wide range of legal services and has established a reputation of trial attorneys who focus on early evaluation of cases, aggressive but cost efficient case management and successful trial results.

### MANAGING PARTNERS OF THE FIRM

**ARTHUR W. TUVERSON, (P.C.),** born Pasadena, California, January 2, 1946; admitted to bar, 1970, California and U.S. District Court, Central District of California; 1971, U.S. Court of Appeals, Ninth Circuit; 1993, Nevada. *Education:* University of Southern California (B.A., 1967); University of Southern California (J.D., 1970). *Member:* State Bar of California; American Board of Trial Advocates; Association of Southern California Defense Counsel. Certified as a Civil Trial Advocate by the National Board of Trial Advocates. (Managing Partner, Los Angeles Office). *PRACTICE AREAS:* Managed Care Litigation; Medical and Legal Malpractice Defense; Insurance Defense Law; Casualty Insurance Law; General Negligence Trials and Appeals.

**STEVEN D. HILLYARD, (P.C.),** born Orange, California, October 4, 1949; admitted to bar, 1975, California and U.S. District Court, Central District of California. *Education:* Santa Ana College (A.B., 1971); California State University, Long Beach; Western State University (B.S., 1973; J.D., 1975). *Member:* Orange County Bar Association; State Bar of California; American Board of Trial Advocates. (Managing Partner, Newport Beach Office). *PRACTICE AREAS:* Insurance Defense Law; Defense of Legal and Medical Malpractice; Fire Loss Litigation; Casualty Insurance Law; General Negligence Trials and Appeals.

**JEFFREY G. KEANE,** born Long Beach, California, December 15, 1949; admitted to bar, 1977, California. *Education:* University of San Diego (B.A., 1972); Western State University (J.D., 1976). Member, Moot Court. Recipient: Book Award in Evidence and Trial Practice; Corpus Juris Secundum Award in Significant Legal Scholarship. Member, Panel of Arbitrators, American Arbitration Association. *Member:* State Bar of California; American Bar Association; California Trial Lawyers Association; The Association of Trial Lawyers of America; Association of Southern California Defense Counsel. (Managing Partner, Palm Springs Office). *PRACTICE AREAS:* Defense of Legal and Medical Malpractice; Insurance Defense Law; Professional Malpractice Law; Homeowners Association Law; Business Torts.

**JOHN T. FARMER,** born Highland Park, Illinois, December 17, 1952; admitted to bar, 1977, Montana and U.S. District Court, District of Montana; 1979, California and U.S. District Court, Central District of California; 1982, U.S. Supreme Court; 1988, U.S. District Court, Southern District of California. *Education:* Marquette University (B.A., 1974); University of Montana (J.D., 1977). Phi Delta Phi; Pi Sigma Alpha; Phi Sigma Tau. Recipient, American Jurisprudence Award in Family Law. Deputy County Attorney, Gallatin County, Montana, 1978-1979. Arbitrator and Judge Pro-Tem, San Diego and Orange County Superior Courts. *Member:* San Diego County and Orange County Bar Associations; State Bar of California; State Bar of Montana; Association of Southern California Defense Counsel. (Managing Partner, San Diego Office). *PRACTICE AREAS:* Insurance Defense Law; Insurance Coverage; Tort Law; Construction Accidents; Products Liability Law.

### PARTNERS OF THE FIRM

**DEBORAH DEBOER,** born Cincinnati, Ohio, July 26, 1957; admitted to bar, 1983, California; 1984, U.S. District Court, Central, Northern and Eastern Districts of California. *Education:* California State University at Hayward (B.S., 1980); Pepperdine University (J.D., 1983). Phi Delta Phi. Note and Comment Editor, Pepperdine Law Review, 1982-1983. Author: "Aviation Litigation, Federal Preemption and the Creation of a Federal Remedy as a Means to Extinguish the Current Confusion in the Court," Vol. 9, No. 4, 1982. Arbitrator, Riverside County Superior Court. *Member:* Desert, Riverside County and American Bar Associations; State Bar of California; Association of Southern California Defense Counsel. (Resident Partner, Palm Springs Office). *PRACTICE AREAS:* Defense of Legal and Medical Malpractice; General Negligence Trials and Appeals; Insurance Defense Law; Litigation; Medical Malpractice Law.

**JERRY WAYNE HOWARD,** born Fresno, California, October 19, 1948; admitted to bar, 1983, California and U.S. District Court, Central District of California. *Education:* California State University at Fresno (B.S., 1970); Southwestern University (J.D., 1983). Arbitrator, Riverside County Superior Court. *Member:* Association of Southern California Defense Counsel; Desert Bar Association. (Resident Partner, Palm Springs Office). *PRACTICE AREAS:* Premise Liability; Professional Malpractice; Product Liability; Construction Defect.

**RICHARD G. HARRIS,** born Los Angeles, California, July 11, 1955; admitted to bar, 1981, California and U.S. District Court, Central District of California; 1989, U.S. District Court, District of Arizona. *Education:* University of California at Santa Cruz (B.A., 1977); University of Santa Clara (J.D., 1981). *Member:* Los Angeles County Bar Associations; State Bar of California; Southern California Defense Counsel. *PRACTICE AREAS:* Insurance Defense Law; Defense of Medical Malpractice; business Torts Litigation.

**MARK S. SIEGEL,** born Fresh Meadows, New York, April 19, 1960; admitted to bar, 1987, California and U.S. District Court, Southern District of California. *Education:* Arizona State University (B.A., 1983); University of San Diego (J.D., 1986). *Member:* San Diego County Bar Association; State Bar of California. (Resident Partner, San Diego Office).

### LOS ANGELES ASSOCIATES

**MICHAEL A. COLETTI,** born Worcester, Massachusetts, April 5, 1962; admitted to bar, 1988, California. *Education:* University of Massachusetts (B.A., 1984); Pepperdine University (J.D., 1987). *Member:* State Bar of California; American Bar Association; Italian American Lawyers Association; Association of Southern California Defense Counsel.

**CHRISTOPHER A. DATOMI,** born Los Angeles, California, December 30, 1955; admitted to bar, 1987, California and U.S. District Court, Central District of California. *Education:* University of Southern California (B.A., with honors, 1983); Loyola Law School (J.D., 1987). Phi Beta Kappa. Member, Loyola of Los Angeles Law Review, 1985-1986. *Member:* State Bar of California.

**MITCHELL L. FENTON,** born Cleveland, Ohio, December 17, 1956; admitted to bar, 1984, California and U.S. District Court, Southern and Central Districts of California. *Education:* San Diego State University

*(This Listing Continued)*

(B.A., with distinction, 1980); University of San Diego (J.D., 1983). *Member:* Los Angeles County and Orange County Bar Association; Association of Southern California Defense Counsel; Orange County Barristers.

**BRADLEY N. GIBSON,** born Anaheim, California, July 7, 1970; admitted to bar, 1996, California and U.S. District Court, Central District of California. *Education:* University of California, Irvine (B.S., 1993); Loyola Law School (J.D., 1996). *Member:* American Bar Association.

**KEVIN PAULEY HILLYER,** born Los Angeles, California, September 24, 1965; admitted to bar, 1992, California and U.S. District Court, Central District of California. *Education:* University of Colorado (B.S., 1989); Pepperdine University (J.D., cum laude, 1992). *Member:* National Association of Surfing Attorneys; Surfer's Medical Association. *LANGUAGES:* Spanish.

**MARIO A. IORILLO,** born Southington, Connecticut, July 6, 1939; admitted to bar, 1965, California. *Education:* Cornell University (B.A., 1961); Harvard University (LL.B., 1964). Arbitrator, Los Angeles Superior Court, 1976—. *Member:* Los Angeles County and American Bar Associations; The State Bar of California; Association of Southern California Defense Counsel; Defense Research Institute. *PRACTICE AREAS:* Insurance Defense; Bad Faith Defense; Personal Injury Defense; Automobile Liability; Automobile Law.

**HARMON B. LEVINE,** born Los Angeles, California, October 6, 1954; admitted to bar, 1980, California, U.S. District Court, Central District of California and U.S. Court of Appeals, Ninth Circuit. *Education:* University of California at Los Angeles (B.A., cum laude, 1977); University of San Diego (J.D., cum laude, 1980). *Member:* State Bar of California; American Bar Association.

**MICHAEL J. NUÑEZ,** born Encino, California, August 27, 1965; admitted to bar, 1992, California. *Education:* University of California, Los Angeles (B.A., 1988); Hastings College of the Law, University of California, San Francisco (J.D., 1992). Managing Editor, Hastings Law Journal, 1991-1992. Author: "Violence at our Borders: Rights & Status of Immigrant Victims of Hate Crimes & Violence," Hastings Law Journal, Vol. 43 Issue 6, 1992. *Member:* Los Angeles County Bar Association. *PRACTICE AREAS:* Civil Litigation.

## NEWPORT BEACH ASSOCIATES

**PATRICIA ANN CARMICHAEL,** born Cullman, Alabama, April 5, 1947; admitted to bar, 1990, California. *Education:* Western State University (B.S.L., 1989; J.D., cum laude, 1990). *Member:* Orange County Bar Association; State Bar of California; Orange County Women Lawyers Association.

**PETER A. HERZOG,** born Philadelphia, Pennsylvania, June 15, 1955; admitted to bar, 1981, California and U.S. District Court, Central District of California. *Education:* University of the Redlands (B.A., 1977); McGeorge School of Law, University of the Pacific (J.D., 1981). Omicron Delta Kappa; Pi Gamma Mu.

**MARGARET KRINSKY,** born Long Beach, California, October 23, 1969; admitted to bar, 1995, California. *Education:* University of California at San Diego (B.A., 1992); Santa Clara University (J.D., 1995). *PRACTICE AREAS:* Medical Malpractice; Insurance Defense.

**BRIAN M. MEADOWS,** born Long Beach, California, December 24, 1966; admitted to bar, 1994, California and U.S. District Court, Central District of California. *Education:* California State University, Fullerton (B.A., 1990); Western State University College of Law, Fullerton (J.D., 1994). Delta Theta Phi. Clerk of the Exchequer, 1992-1993. *Member:* State Bar of California. *PRACTICE AREAS:* Medical Malpractice; General Liability Defense.

**GEOFFREY T. MOORE,** born San Francisco, California, August 26, 1955; admitted to bar, 1987, California and U.S. District Court, Southern District of California. *Education:* University of California at Irvine (B.A., 1981); University of Southern California (M.A., 1986); McGeorge School of Law, University of the Pacific (J.D., 1987). *Member:* Bar Association of Northern San Diego County; San Diego County Bar Association; State Bar of California; San Diego Trial Lawyers Association; San Diego Defense Lawyers Association; Association of Southern California Defense Counsel.

**CHARLES J. NOREK,** born Chicago, Illinois, September 10, 1949; admitted to bar, 1978, Illinois; 1985, California. *Education:* Western Illinois University (B.S., 1972); John Marshall Law School (J.D., 1978). Member, Order of John Marshall. Instructor, National College of Education, 1984-1986. Adjunct Professor, Western State University, 1994—. *Member:* Orange County, Illinois State and American Bar Associations; State Bar of California.

## PALM SPRINGS ASSOCIATES

**RAYMOND E. BROWN,** born Newport News, Virginia, November 1, 1965; admitted to bar, 1993, California; 1996, Arizona. *Education:* Arizona State University (B.A., cum laude, Journalism, 1988; B.A. Psychology, 1990; J.D., 1992). *LANGUAGES:* German.

**GREGORY E. DEETMAN,** born San Gabriel, California, February 24, 1967; admitted to bar, 1994, California and U.S. District Court, Southern District of California. *Education:* San Diego State University (B.A. Political Science, with distinction, 1990); McGeorge School of Law (J.D., 1994). *PRACTICE AREAS:* Insurance Defense.

**JOANNA D. GORSAGE,** born West Covina, California, August 4, 1969; admitted to bar, 1995, California. *Education:* California State University, San Bernardino (B.A., 1991); McGeorge School of Law (J.D., 1995).

**JENNIFER R. JOHNSON,** born Springfield, Missouri, December 24, 1959; admitted to bar, 1992, California. *Education:* Evangel College (B.S., 1983); Mesa College (R.N., 1987); University of Arizona (J.D., 1992).

**JACK M. LAPEDIS,** born San Francisco, California, December 12, 1967; admitted to bar, 1995, California. *Education:* University of California at Irvine (B.A., 1991); Pepperdine University School of Law (J.D., 1995). Phi Alpha Delta. Member, Moot Court Board. *Member:* Los Angeles County and American Bar Associations; State Bar of California. (Palm Springs Office).

**ALEXANDER R. MARTINEZ,** born Hollywood, California, July 30, 1970; admitted to bar, 1995, California; 1996, U.S. Court of Appeals, Ninth Circuit and U.S. District Court, Central District of California. *Education:* University of California (B.A., 1992); Hastings College of the Law (J.D., 1995). Phi Alpha Delta. *Member:* Desert and American Bar Associations; State Bar of California. (Palm Springs Office). *LANGUAGES:* Spanish.

**DANIEL P. MARTZ,** born Jacksonville, North Carolina, April 21, 1964; admitted to bar, 1990, California and U.S. District Court, Southern District of California. *Education:* A.N.C. College (A.A., 1984); University of Arizona (B.A., 1986); University of San Diego (J.D., 1990). *Member:* Desert and San Diego County Bar Associations; State Bar of California.

**JENNIFER F. SWILLER,** born New York, N.Y., May 11, 1971; admitted to bar, 1995, California. *Education:* University of California, San Diego (B.A., 1992); McGeorge School of Law (J.D., 1995). Phi Delta Phi. Staff Writer and Associate Article Editor, McGeorge Law Review. Member, Traynor Society. Author: "The Secrets of Success: Confidential Business Information in the Czech and Slovak Republics," 7 Transnational Lawyer, 1995. *Member:* Los Angeles County Bar Association; State Bar of California.

## SAN DIEGO ASSOCIATES

**ANTHONY T. CASE,** born Bogota, Columbia; admitted to bar, 1990, California. *Education:* University of California at San Diego (B.A., 1987); University of San Diego (J.D., 1990). *Member:* State Bar of California.

**MARCI S. DANIELS,** born Marion County, Kentucky, July 9, 1948; admitted to bar, 1982, California. *Education:* St. Joseph Infirmary School of Nursing (Diploma, 1969); Point Loma College (B.S.N., 1977); Western State University (J.D., 1982). Editor, 1979-1980, and Business Editor, 1980-1981, Western State University Law Review. Registered Nurse: Arizona, 1969; Kentucky, 1970; California, 1973. Faculty, San Diego Inn of Court, 1988—.

**MARY AGNES MATYSZEWSKI,** born Syracuse, New York, March 15, 1963; admitted to bar, 1988, California and U.S. District Court, Southern District of California. *Education:* Villanova University (B.S., cum laude, 1985); Boston University (J.D., 1988). *Member:* San Diego County and American Bar Associations; State Bar of California; Lawyers Club of San Diego (Member, Community Relations Committee); San Diego Defense Lawyers; The Association of Trial Lawyers of America; Volunteer Lawyers.

**RENEE J. PALERMO,** born Lakes Charles, Louisiana, June 25, 1967; admitted to bar, 1996, California. *Education:* Southern Methodist University (B.A., 1990); California Western School of Law (J.D., 1996). Phi Alpha Delta (Beaumont Chapter). *PRACTICE AREAS:* Construction Defect; Premises Liability; General Liability.

**JEFFREY D. SCHREIBER,** born Provo, Utah, June 2, 1953; admitted to bar, 1983, Washington and U.S. District Court, Western District of Washington; 1990, California, U.S. District Court, Southern District of California and U.S. Court of Appeals, Ninth Circuit; 1991, U.S. District

*(This Listing Continued)*

**TUVERSON & HILLYARD, Los Angeles—**Continued

Court, Central, Eastern and Northern Districts of California; 1994, U.S. Supreme Court. *Education:* University of Utah (B.S., 1980); Seattle University School of Law (J.D., cum laude, 1983). Author, Published Opinions: *Fingers v. United States,* 170 B.R. 419 (Dist. Ct. S.D. Cal. 1994); *Fingers v. United States,* 148 B.R. 586 (Bkrptcy. S.D. Cal. 1993). *Member:* San Diego, Washington State and American (Member, Business Bankruptcy Committee) Bar Associations; State Bar of California.

**JONATHAN M. SHIFF,** born New York, N.Y., January 1, 1967; admitted to bar, 1991, California and U.S. District Court, Southern District of California; U.S. Court of Appeals, Ninth Circuit. *Education:* University of California, Berkeley (B.A., 1988); University of San Diego (J.D., cum laude, 1991). *Member:* San Diego County and American Bar Associations; San Diego Defense Lawyers.

**DAVID C. WEBER,** born Geneva, Illinois, September 14, 1952; admitted to bar, 1982, California and U.S. District Court, Southern District of California. *Education:* Whitworth College (B.A., 1975); Gonzaga University (J.D., 1980); California Western University. Member, San Diego Superior Court Arbitration Panel. *Member:* San Diego County Bar Association; State Bar of California.

REPRESENTATIVE CLIENTS: The Doctors Company; Southern California Physicians Insurance Exchange, ARISCO; County of Los Angeles; State Farm Insurance Co.; American States; Physicians and Surgeons; Reliance Insurance Company; Farmer Insurance Company; California Insurance Guarantee Association; Professional Liability Claims Management; Gulf Insurance Group; St. Paul Fire & Marine Insurance Company; Professional Risk Management; Champion Claims; Ralphs Grocery Company; Lucky Stores, Inc.; Kemper Group; Infinity Insurance; Mercury Insurance.

---

## LAW OFFICES OF
## JEANNETTE E. VALDIVIA

### LOS ANGELES, CALIFORNIA

(See Pasadena)

*Product Liability, Warranty, Insurance, Employer and Business Litigation. Health Management.*

---

## VALENSI, ROSE & MAGARAM

*PROFESSIONAL LAW CORPORATION*

**SUITE 1000, 1800 AVENUE OF THE STARS**
**LOS ANGELES, CALIFORNIA 90067-4212**

Telephone: 310-277-8011
Cable Address: "Valerose"
Telecopier: 310-277-1706

*General Business, Corporate, Real Estate, Tax, Labor and Entertainment Law, Related Civil Trial, Appellate, Arbitration and Administration Hearing Practice concerning: Mergers and Acquisitions, Business Agreements and Licenses, Corporate Securities and Corporate Finance, Real Estate Purchases, Sales, Development and Finance, Federal, State and Local Taxation, Estate, Gift and Asset Protection Planning, Trusts and Probate, Secured Transactions, Creditors Rights, Employer and Employee Representation, Wrongful Termination and Discrimination Matters, Music and Copyright Law and Related Entertainment Matters.*

**KENNETH L. HEISZ,** born Kansas City, Missouri, June 8, 1957; admitted to bar, 1989, California. *Education:* Kansas Wesleyan University (B.A., 1979); Claremont School of Theology (M.Div., cum laude, 1985); Loyola University of Los Angeles (J.D., 1989). Member, St. Thomas More Honor Society. Staff, 1987-1988 and Note and Comment Editor, 1988-1989, International and Comparative Law Journal. *Member:* Beverly Hills, Los Angeles County (Member: Litigation Section, 1989-1995; State Courts Committee, 1991-1995) and American Bar Associations; State Bar of California (Member, Conference of Delegates, 1992-1995). *PRACTICE AREAS:* Litigation; Business Litigation; Real Estate Litigation; Unfair Competition; Landlord/Tenant.

**MARGARET E. LENNON,** born Brooklyn, New York, February 26, 1959; admitted to bar, 1986, California and U.S. District Court, Southern District of California; 1989, U.S. Tax Court. *Education:* Barnard College, Columbia University (A.B., magna cum laude, 1981); University of Michigan (J.D., 1985). *Member:* Los Angeles County, Beverly Hills and Ameri-
*(This Listing Continued)*

can Bar Associations; State Bar of California. *PRACTICE AREAS:* Tax Law; Estate Planning Law.

**PHILIP S. MAGARAM,** born New York, N.Y., July 29, 1937; admitted to bar, 1962, California. *Education:* University of California at Los Angeles (B.S., with honors in Accounting, 1958; LL.B., 1961). Phi Alpha Delta (President, McKenna Chapter, 1961); Beta Gamma Sigma; Phi Eta Sigma. Author: "Trusts for Minors," Drafting California Irrevocable Living Trusts (C.E.B.), 1987; "Do You Trust Your Spouse? A Look at the Spousal Remainder Trust," T.S.A. 37th Annual Trust and Tax Forum, 1985. Co-Author: "Property Transfers— Gift and Death Tax Aspects," Tax Aspects of Marital Dissolutions (C.E.B.), 1979; "Transfers to Noncitizen Spouses Significantly Affected by RRA '89," The Journal of Taxation, May, 1990. Author: "The Use of Private Annuities Under the 1976 Tax Reform Act," University of Southern California Tax Institute, 1978; "Understanding Collapsible Corporations," *Tax Ideas,* Prentice Hall, 1975; "Determining Interests in Estate Distribution," II California Decedent Estate Administration (C.E.B.), 1975. Co-Author: "Income Deferral Lost on Disposition of Installment Obligations," Los Angeles Bar Bulletin, 1970. Author: "Loss, Expense and Interest Deductions with Respect to Related Taxpayers," Beverly Hills Bar Journal, March, 1969; "The Deductibility of Prepaid Interest," Los Angeles Bar Bulletin, November, 1968. Adjunct Professor of Law, University of San Diego, 1985-1988. Member, Board of Trustees, Greater Los Angeles County Chapter, Leukemia Society of America, Inc., 1970-1986. Member, Board of Governors and Former Chairman, Southern California Arthritis Foundation. Member, U.C.L.A. Foundation Board of Trustees, 1986—. National Foundation for Ileitis and Colitis (Vice President, Board of Directors, 1987-1990). *Member:* Beverly Hills (Member, Taxation Committee, 1963—), Century City (Member, Board of Governors, 1972-1975), Los Angeles County and American (Member, Section of Taxation) Bar Associations; The State Bar of California (Member, Taxation Section). (Certified Specialist, Taxation Law, The State Bar of California Board of Legal Specialization). *PRACTICE AREAS:* Tax Planning Law; Estate Planning Law; General Business Law.

**WARREN K. MILLER,** born Oklahoma City, Oklahoma, December 23, 1944; admitted to bar, 1973, Oklahoma and U.S. District Court, Western District of Oklahoma; 1983, U.S. Court of Appeals, Tenth Circuit; 1989, California, U.S. District Court, Central District of California and U.S. Court of Appeals, Ninth Circuit. *Education:* Westminster College (B.A., 1966); Oklahoma State University (M.B.A., 1968); University of Oklahoma (J.D., 1972). Phi Delta Phi. Outstanding Young Lawyer, Oklahoma Bar Association, 1976. *Member:* Beverly Hills, Century City, Cleveland County (Secretary-Treasurer, 1974; Vice President, 1975; President, 1976), Los Angeles County (Member, Litigation Section), Oklahoma (Chairman-Elect, 1978-1979 and Chairman, 1979-1980, Young Lawyers Division) and American (Member, Sections on: Litigation; Real Estate) Bar Associations; California Trial Lawyers Association; The Association of Trial Lawyers of America. *PRACTICE AREAS:* Business; Business Tort Litigation; Real Estate Litigation; Construction Litigation.

**MICHAEL R. MORRIS,** born New York, N.Y., July 12, 1953; admitted to bar, 1978, Arizona and U.S. Tax Court; 1980, U.S. District Court, Central District of California; 1981, California. *Education:* University of Pennsylvania, (B.A. magna cum laude, 1975; M.A. magna cum laude, 1975); University of Arizona (J.D., with highest distinction, 1978). Order of the Coif. Case Note Writer, Arizona Law Review, 1976. Trial Attorney, Internal Revenue Service Chief Counsel's Office, Los Angeles District, Los Angeles, California, 1978-1983. *Member:* State Bar of Arizona; State Bar of California. (Certified Specialist, Taxation Law, The State Bar of California Board of Legal Specialization). *PRACTICE AREAS:* Tax Law (Transactional and Litigation); Entertainment Law (Emphasizing Music, Copyright and related matters).

**M. LAURIE MURPHY,** born Buffalo, New York, April 14, 1952; admitted to bar, 1985, California; 1986, U.S. District Court, Northern, Southern, Eastern and Central Districts of California. *Education:* State University of New York at Buffalo (B.S., 1974); University of Wisconsin-Madison (M.S., 1976); Loyola Law School (J.D., 1985). Registered Professional Civil Engineer, California, 1979. *Member:* Beverly Hills and Los Angeles County Bar Associations; State Bar of California. *PRACTICE AREAS:* Litigation; Real Estate Litigation; Construction Litigation; Business Litigation; Insurance Coverage and Litigation; Landlord/Tenant; Unfair Competition; Intellectual Property.

**SIDNEY R. ROSE,** born Los Angeles, California, August 25, 1927; admitted to bar, 1952, California; 1973, U.S. Supreme Court. *Education:* University of New Mexico; University of California at Los Angeles; University of Southern California (J.D., 1951). President (1973), Member of Board of
*(This Listing Continued)*

Directors (1984-1986) and Steering Committee of Community and Charitable Organizations Counseling Project (1986-1988) of Public Counsel. Member of Board of Directors, Beverly Hills Bar Association Law Foundation (1984—). *Member:* Beverly Hills (President, 1980-1981; Officer, 1975-1979; Member, Sections on Real Estate, Corporations and Business Law; Recipient, 1985/86 Executive Directors' Award; Recipient, 1989 Beverly Hills Bar Foundation Distinguished Service Award) Los Angeles County (Member, Board of Trustees, 1979-1980, Section on Real Property; Neighborhood Justice Center Mediation Project Committee, 1983-1986) and American (Member, National Conference of Bar Presidents, 1980-1986; Sections on Real Estate and Law Practice Management) Bar Associations; The State Bar of California (Member, Conference of Delegates, 1968-1984, Sections on Business Law, Real Estate and Law Practice Management). Fellow: American Bar Foundation; American Judicature Society. *PRACTICE AREAS:* General Business Law; Real Estate Law.

**MARK HALLIWELL SMITH,** born Ft. Belvoir, Virginia, August 12, 1956; admitted to bar, 1981, California. *Education:* University of California at Los Angeles (B.S., summa cum laude, 1977); Harvard University (J.D., cum laude, 1980). Phi Beta Kappa; Tau Beta Pi. *Member:* Los Angeles County Bar Association; State Bar of California (Member, Sections on: Real Property Law; Business Law and Law Office Management). *LANGUAGES:* Spanish. *PRACTICE AREAS:* Corporate Law; Securities Law; Real Estate Law; General Business Law. *Email:* mhs@vrm.com

**STEPHEN G. VALENSI,** born New York, N.Y., August 11, 1918; admitted to bar, 1949, California. *Education:* Dartmouth College and University of California at Los Angeles (A.B., 1940); Loyola University of Los Angeles (J.D., 1949). Member, Commercial Arbitration Panel, American Arbitration Association. *Member:* Beverly Hills (Member, Board of Governors, 1979-1980), Los Angeles County and American Bar Associations; The State Bar of California (Member, California Continuing Education of the Bar Joint Advisory Committee, 1974-1988). *PRACTICE AREAS:* Real Estate Law; General Business Law.

**ELIZABETH ALLEN WHITE,** born Santa Monica, California, December 16, 1955; admitted to bar, 1982, California and Texas. *Education:* Faculte' de Pau, Pau, France; Sorbonne, University of Paris, France; University of California at Los Angeles (B.A., 1977); Loyola University of Los Angeles (J.D., 1981). Alpha Mu Gamma; Phi Alpha Delta. Judge Pro Tem, Los Angeles Municipal Court, 1987-1990. *Member:* Los Angeles County (Member, Section on Litigation) and American Bar Associations; State Bar of California; State Bar of Texas. *LANGUAGES:* French and Spanish. *PRACTICE AREAS:* Employment Litigation; General Business Litigation.

---

**DAVID HALM,** born Culver City, California, October 7, 1969; admitted to bar, 1995, California and U.S. District Court, Central District of California. *Education:* University of California at Los Angeles (B.A., 1991); Loyola Marymount University (J.D., 1995). *Member:* Los Angeles County Bar Association; State Bar of California; Korean American Bar Association. *PRACTICE AREAS:* Litigation.

**GERALDINE A. WYLE,** born New York, N.Y., May 4, 1953; admitted to bar, 1979, California; 1980, U.S. District Court, Central District of California. *Education:* Radcliffe College; University of California at Los Angeles (B.A., magna cum laude, 1976); University of California School of Law at Los Angeles (J.D., 1979). *Member:* Beverly Hills, Century City and American Bar Associations; Womens Lawyers Association. *PRACTICE AREAS:* Commercial Litigation; Probate.

REFERENCES: Northern Trust Bank (Los Angeles Office); Ticor Title Insurance Company of California (Los Angeles, California).

---

## VEATCH, CARLSON, GROGAN & NELSON

A Partnership including a Professional Corporation

*Established in 1952*

**3926 WILSHIRE BOULEVARD**
**LOS ANGELES, CALIFORNIA 90010**
Telephone: 213-381-2861
Telefax: 213-383-6370

General Civil and Trial Practice, State and Federal Courts. Insurance and Healthcare Law.

FIRM PROFILE: *General, Civil and Trial practice in State and Federal Courts. We specialize in personal injury defense, including medical, dental, legal and accounting malpractice, product liability, homeowners, auto, wrongful termination actions, commercial liability, insurance fraud and general insurance law.*

*Our technologically advanced legal and support staff are professionally managed to emphasize quality, efficiency and cost containment. The firm's clients include numerous professional liability carriers, general casualty insurance companies, commercial liability carriers and governmental self-insured entities.*

### MEMBERS OF FIRM

**JAMES C. GALLOWAY, JR. (A PROFESSIONAL CORPORATION),** born Pasadena, California, June 14, 1942; admitted to bar, 1970, California; 1976, U.S. Supreme Court. *Education:* University of Southern California (B.S., 1964); Southwestern University (J.D., 1969). Phi Alpha Delta. Judge Pro Tem, Los Angeles Municipal Court, 1980—. Arbitrator, Los Angeles Superior Court Arbitration Plan. Member, National Panel of Arbitrators, American Arbitration Association. *Member:* Los Angeles County and American Bar Associations; State Bar of California; American Judicature Society; Association of Southern California Defense Counsel. Certified Advocate by the National Board of Trial Advocacy (Associate Member). *REPORTED CASES:* Hector v. Cedars-Sinai Medical Center, 180 Cal.App.3d 493, 225 Cal.Rptr. 595, Prod. Liab. Rep. (CCH)P. 11,014 (Cal.App.2 Dist., Apr 29, 1986) (NO.CIV. B012677); Jones v. McCollister, 159 Cal.App.2d 708, 324 P.2d 639 (Cal.App., Apr 28, 1958) (NO. CIV. 17718). *PRACTICE AREAS:* Dental and Medical Malpractice; Construction Defects; Products Liability; Vehicle and Government Tort Liability Defense Law.

**ANTHONY D. SEINE,** born Los Angeles, California, May 30, 1938; admitted to bar, 1968, California. *Education:* University of Southern California (B.S., 1960); Southwestern University (LL.B., 1967). *Member:* Pasadena, Los Angeles County and American Bar Associations; The State Bar of California; Association of Southern California Defense Counsel. *PRACTICE AREAS:* Vehicle and Homeowner's Liability; Commercial Claims; Coverage Issues; Medical Malpractice; Products Liability Defense Law.

**MARK A. WEINSTEIN,** born Los Angeles, California, October 18, 1950; admitted to bar, 1975, California and U.S. District Court, Central District of California. *Education:* University of California at Los Angeles (B.A., cum laude, 1972); Loyola Marymount University (J.D., cum laude, 1975). Arbitrator, Los Angeles County Superior Court. *Member:* Los Angeles County Bar Association; State Bar of California. *REPORTED CASES:* Hacker (Eleanor) v. City of Glendale, Cal.Rptr.2d, 1993 WL 231478 (Cal.App. 2 Dist., Jun 29, 1993) (NO. B047989); Hacker v. City of Glendale, 7 Cal.App. 4th 120, 279 Cal.Rptr.371 (Cal.App. 2 Dist., Mar 22, 1991) (NO. B047989); Chevlin v. Los Angeles Community College Dist., 212 Cal.App.3d 382, 260 Cal.Rptr. 628, 54 Ed. Law Rep. 920 (Cal.App. 2 Dist., July 06, 1989) (NO. B031967); Leader v. State, 182 Cal.App.3d 1079, 226 Cal.Rptr. 207 (Cal.App. 2 Dist., May 19, 1986) (NO. CIV B009187); Kuykendall v. State, 178 Cal.App.3d 563, 223 Cal.Rptr. 763 (Cal.App. 2 Dist., Mar 06, 1986) (NO. B014924); State v. Meyer, 174 Cal.App.3d 1061, 220 Cal.Rptr. 884 (Cal.App. 2 Dist., Nov 25, 1985) (NO. CIV. B005540); Clemente v. State, 40 Cal.3d 202, 707 P.2d 818, 219 Cal.Rptr. 445 (Cal., Oct 28, 1985) NO. L.A. 31832); Van Truong v. James, 168 Cal.App.3d 833, 215 Cal.Rptr. 33 (Cal.App. 2 Dist., May 29, 1985) (NO. B008900); Clemente by Clemente v. State, 147 Cal.App.3d 49, 194 Cal.Rptr. 821 (Cal.App. 2 Dist., Aug 24, 1983) (NO. CIV. 65833); Clemente v. State, 101 Cal.App.3d 374, 161 Cal.Rptr. 799 (Cal.App. 2 Dist., Jan 24, 1980) (NO. CIV. 55769); Guess v. State, 96 Cal.App.3d 111, 157 Cal.Rptr. 618. (Cal.App. 4 Dist., Aug 20, 1979) (NO. CIV 20392). *PRACTICE AREAS:* Government Tort Liability; Police Misconduct; Vehicle Liability; Medical Malpractice Defense Law.

**JOHN A. PETERSON,** born Los Angeles, California, August 5, 1949; admitted to bar, 1974, California and U.S. District Court, Northern District of California; 1980, U.S. Supreme Court and U.S. District Court, Central District of California. *Education:* University of California at Irvine and University of California at Los Angeles (B.A., 1971); Hastings College of Law, University of California (J.D., 1974). Articles Editor, Hastings Constitutional Law Quarterly, 1973-1974. *Member:* Los Angeles County Bar Association; Association of Southern California Defense Counsel. *PRACTICE AREAS:* Vehicle Liability; General Casualty; Government Tort Liability; Coverage Issues and Uninsured Motorist Defense Law.

**GORDON F. SAUSSER,** born Los Angeles, California, July 2, 1933; admitted to bar, 1966, California. *Education:* Occidental College and University of California at Los Angeles (B.S., 1955); Southwestern University (LL.B., 1965). *Member:* Los Angeles County and American Bar Associations; The State Bar of California; Association of Southern California Defense Counsel (Committee Chairman and Board Member, 1982-1986); De-

*(This Listing Continued)*

## VEATCH, CARLSON, GROGAN & NELSON, Los Angeles—Continued

fense Research Institute. **PRACTICE AREAS:** Civil Litigation; Insurance Defense.

**THOMAS M. PHILLIPS,** born Amityville, New York, November 5, 1955; admitted to bar, 1983, California. *Education:* University of California at Los Angeles (B.A., 1978); Loyola Marymount University (J.D., 1982). Arbitrator in the Los Angeles County Superior Courts. *Member:* State Bar of California; American Bar Association; American Board of Trial Advocates; Association of Southern California Defense Counsel. **PRACTICE AREAS:** Insurance Defense; Business Litigation.

**AMY W. LYONS,** born Los Angeles, California, April 20, 1953; admitted to bar, 1982, California and U.S. District Court, Central and Southern Districts of California; 1983, Nevada; 1984, U.S. District Court, District of Nevada and U.S. Court of Appeals, Ninth Circuit; 1988, District of Columbia. *Education:* Dartmouth College; Smith College (A.B., cum laude, 1974); University of San Diego (J.D., 1981). Recipient, American Jurisprudence Awards for: Professional Responsibility; Evidence Agency and Partnership. *Member:* Clark County Bar Association; State Bar of Nevada; District of Columbia Bar; State Bar of California. **LANGUAGES:** Spanish. **REPORTED CASES:** Wilson v. Circus Circus Hotels, Inc., 101 Nev. 751-710 P.2d 77; Planet Insurance v. Transport Indemnity, 523 F.2d 285 (9th Cir. 1987). **PRACTICE AREAS:** Medical Malpractice Defense Law; General Casualty Defense Law.

**MICHAEL ERIC WASSERMAN,** born Los Angeles, California, January 8, 1953; admitted to bar, 1981, Oregon and U.S. District Court, District of Oregon; 1982, California; 1983, Washington; 1984, U.S. District Court, Central District of California. *Education:* University of California at Los Angeles (B.A., magna cum laude, 1975); University of Oregon (M.S., 1978; J.D., 1981). Phi Beta Kappa; Pi Gamma Mu. *Member:* Los Angeles County and American Bar Associations; Oregon State Bar; Oregon Trial Lawyers Association; Association of Southern California Defense Counsel. **REPORTED CASES:** Hector v. Cedars-Sinai Medical Center 180 Cal. App. 3d 493. **PRACTICE AREAS:** Dental Malpractice; General Casualty Defense Law.

**MICHAEL A. KRAMER,** born Winthrop, Massachusetts, September 1, 1953; admitted to bar, 1978, California; 1979, U.S. Court of Appeals, 9th Circuit. *Education:* University of Southern California (B.A., 1975); Southwestern University School of Law (J.D., 1978). Phi Beta Kappa. Recipient, American Jurisprudence Award in Remedies. *Member:* State Bar of California. **REPORTED CASES:** Mitchell v. Superior Court 37 Cal. 3rd, Page 591. **PRACTICE AREAS:** Product Liability; Vehicle Liability; Government Tort Liability; General Casualty Defense Law.

### ASSOCIATES

| | |
|---|---|
| Hollis O. Dyer | Dawn M. Costello |
| Mark M. Rudy | Daniel R. Brown |
| D. Michael Bush | Stephen D. Enerle |
| André S. Goodchild | John J. Nolan, III |
| Kevin L. Henderson | Steven W. Sedach |
| Gilbert A. Garcia | Joan E. Hewitt |
| William G. Lieb | Joanne M. Andrew |

### OF COUNSEL

David J. Aisenson  Lyn A. Woodward
(Judge Retired)

REPRESENTATIVE CLIENTS: Farmers Insurance Companies; Truck Insurance Exchange; Allstate Insurance Company; Northbrook Insurance Company; The Dentist Insurance Company (TDIC); County of Los Angeles; State of California; Los Angeles County Metropolitan Transit Authority (LACMTA); Professional Risk Management (PRM); Cedars-Sinai Medical Center; UniHealth America; AMEX Assurance Company; Cincinnati Insurance Companies; American Continental Insurance Company (MSA, Ltd.); Southern California Physicians Insurance Exchange (SCPIE); Shand, Morahan & Co., Inc.; Associated Claims Management, Inc.; Foundation Integrated Risk Mgt. Solutions, Inc.; (FIRM Solutions, Inc.); ARB, Inc.; Northland Insurance Companies; Fremont Indemnity.

CAA1272B

---

## VERBOON, WHITAKER, HARTMANN & PETER, LLP

*Established in 1984*

11100 SANTA MONICA BOULEVARD, SUITE 1950
**LOS ANGELES, CALIFORNIA 90025-3384**
Telephone: 310-445-5447
Facsimile: 310-445-9176

*Construction Defect Litigation*

**GARY W. VERBOON,** born Calgary, Alberta, Canada, February 14, 1957; admitted to bar, 1981, California and U.S. District Court, Central District of California. *Education:* Azusa Pacific University (B.A., Business and Theology, magna cum laude, 1978); Pepperdine University, Dean's List (J.D., 1981); University of Salzburg, Salzburg, Austria (LL.M. Candidate). Alpha Chi Honor Society. Finalist, Vincent Dalsimer Moot Court Competition. Advisory Board, Azusa Pacific University School of Business and Management. Author: "International Arbitration—Effective Dispute Resolution for the International Commercial Lawyer," Kluwer Law Publishers, 1988. Community Association Institute, 1991—. Founding Member, Los Angeles Superior Court Construction Defect Committee. *Member:* Los Angeles County and American Bar Associations; State Bar of California; Los Angeles Trial Lawyers. **PRACTICE AREAS:** Construction Defect Litigation.

**MICHAEL T. WHITAKER,** born San Diego, California, March 6, 1958; admitted to bar, 1984, California and U.S. District Court, Central District of California; U.S. Court of Appeals, Ninth Circuit. *Education:* California Polytechnic State University, San Luis Obispo (B.A, 1981); Southwestern University (J.D., 1984). Arbitrator, Los Angeles County Superior Court. *Member:* State Bar of California; Consumer Attorneys Association of Los Angeles. **PRACTICE AREAS:** Bad Faith Litigation; Professional Liability; Construction Litigation; Commercial Litigation.

**RONALD A. HARTMANN,** born Pittsburgh, Pennsylvania, July 18, 1958; admitted to bar, 1984, California, U.S. District Court, Central District of California and U.S. Court of Appeals, Ninth Circuit; 1993, U.S. District Court, Northern, Southern and Eastern Districts of California. *Education:* Arizona State University; University of Alabama (B.S., magna cum laude, 1981); University of Texas (J.D., 1984). Beta Gamma Sigma. *Member:* State Bar of California. **PRACTICE AREAS:** Construction Defects Litigation; Real Estate Litigation; Insurance Litigation.

**ALOIS PETER, JR.,** born Emmenbrücke, Switzerland, November 17, 1954; admitted to bar, 1987, California. *Education:* California State University at Sacramento (B.S., 1976; M.S., 1977); Lincoln College of Law (J.D., 1985). Professional Civil Engineer, California, 1978. Professional Structural Engineer, California, 1981. *Member:* Los Angeles County Bar Association; State Bar of California; Structural Engineers Association of California. **PRACTICE AREAS:** Construction Defect.

**M. THEREZA BRAGA,** born Campo Grande, MS, Brazil, September 4, 1962; admitted to bar, 1985, M.S., Brazil (Not admitted in California). *Education:* N.S. De Sion, Sao Paulo, Brazil (1979); Faculdade Unidas Catolicas, Campo Grande, Brazil (J.D., 1985). **LANGUAGES:** Portuguese, French, Italian and Spanish. **PRACTICE AREAS:** Construction Litigation.

**FRED ADELMAN,** born Long Island, New York, December 3, 1962; admitted to bar, 1987, California; 1988, U.S. District Court, Central District of California. *Education:* California Lutheran University (B.A., 1984); University of San Diego (J.D., 1987). *Member:* State Bar of California. **PRACTICE AREAS:** Complex Civil Litigation.

**MARK MILSTEIN,** born Los Angeles, California, May 11, 1964; admitted to bar, 1991, California and U.S. District Court, Southern District of California; 1994, Nevada. *Education:* University of California at Los Angeles (B.A., 1987); University of San Diego (J.D., 1991). Vice-Justice, Phi Alpha Delta, 1990-1991. *Member:* San Diego County and American Bar Associations; State Bar of California; San Diego Defense Lawyers Association. **PRACTICE AREAS:** Civil Litigation; Construction Defect Law.

### LEGAL SUPPORT PERSONNEL

**BRIAN ARTHUR NOTENARE,** born Stockton, California, June 10, 1954. *Education:* University of California (A.B., 1976); California Polytechnic State University (M.Arch., 1980). Registered Architect, 621514, 1990. Designed Numerous Buildings, Built 15 Homes. *Member:* American Society of Testing Materials; American Institute of Architects; Regional Master

*(This Listing Continued)*

Builders Association; California Council of Interior Designers; International Conference of Building Officials. (Architect). **PRACTICE AREAS:** In House Architect and General Building Contractor.

## ROBERT M. VICTOR
### LOS ANGELES, CALIFORNIA
(See Encino)

*Business Litigation, Personal Injury, Medical Malpractice, Product Liability, Family Law, Adoption, Corporation and Contract, Collections.*

## VITTAL AND STERNBERG
Established in 1989

2121 AVENUE OF THE STARS, 22ND FLOOR
### LOS ANGELES, CALIFORNIA 90067-5010
Telephone: 310-551-0900
Facsimile: 310-551-2710
Email: javittal@ix.netcom.com

Woodland Hills, California Office: 21700 Oxnard Street. Suite 1640. 91367-7326. Telephone: 818-710-7801. Facsimile: 818-593-6192.

*Resolution of Complex Business and Real Estate Disputes Through Litigation in the State and Federal Trial and Appellate Courts and ADR Techniques.*

*FIRM PROFILE:* Founded in 1989 by colleagues at the Los Angeles office of Shea & Gould to concentrate in complex business litigation and preventive business law. The firm has a demonstrated commitment to alternative dispute resolution and to pro bono publico services, both directly and through Public Counsel, the pro bono legal services arm of the Beverly Hills and Los Angeles County Bar Associations. Members of the firm serve as volunteer judicial arbitrators, mediators and judges pro tem of the Los Angeles Superior Court and are active in bar association sections and committees at the national, state, and local level. In order to maximize efficiency, the firm utilizes the services of contract and of counsel attorneys as required.

**J. ANTHONY VITTAL,** born Long Beach, California, November 8, 1943; admitted to bar, 1974, California and U.S. District Court, Central District of California; 1975, U.S. Court of Appeals, Ninth Circuit; 1976, U.S. District Court, Southern District of California; 1981, U.S. Supreme Court; 1982, U.S. District Court, Eastern District of California and U.S. Tax Court; 1984, U.S. District Court, Northern District of California. *Education:* Stanford University (A.B., 1971); University of California at Irvine; University of California at Los Angeles (J.D., 1974). Phi Alpha Delta. Member, Moot Court Honor Program. Vive President, California Association of Local Bars, 1996—. Director, Public Counsel, 1995—. Co-Chair, Statewide Bench-Bar Coalition, 1996—. Member, Beverly Hills Economic Development Council, 1992-1996. Master, McBurney Business Litigation Inn of Court, 1992—. *Member:* Beverly Hills (President, 1994-1995), Los Angeles County (Trustee, 1991-1992), Federal and American (Delegate, House of Delegates, 1995—) Bar Associations; State Bar of California (Delegate, Conference of Delegates, 1977—; Member, Committee on Administration of Justice, 1990—); Association of Business Trial Lawyers; National Conference of Bar Presidents (Member, Executive Council, 1996—). (Resident). **LANGUAGES:** German. **SPECIAL AGENCIES:** Beverly Hills City Council; California Senate and Assembly. **REPORTED CASES:** Garstang v. Superior Court, 39 Cal. App. 4th 526 (1995). **PRACTICE AREAS:** Business Litigation; Unfair Business Practices Litigation; Real Estate Litigation; Construction Litigation; Civil RICO Litigation.

**TERENCE M. STERNBERG,** born Los Angeles, California, April 24, 1950; admitted to bar, 1979, California and U.S. District Court, Central District of California; 1980, U.S. Court of Appeals, Ninth Circuit. *Education:* Whittier College School of Law (J.D., 1979). *Member:* Beverly Hills and Los Angeles County Bar Associations; State Bar of California; Association of Business Trial Lawyers. (Resident, Woodland Hills Office). **SPECIAL AGENCIES:** Malibu City Council; Malibu Planning Commission. **PRACTICE AREAS:** Unfair Business Practices Litigation; Business Litigation; Real Estate Litigation; Land Use Litigation.

## VOORHIES & KRAMER
A PROFESSIONAL CORPORATION
1122 WILSHIRE BOULEVARD
### LOS ANGELES, CALIFORNIA 90017
Telephone: 213-250-1122

*General Civil and Trial Practice in all State and Federal Courts. Insurance, Products Liability, Medical Malpractice and Negligence Law.*

**RICHARD C. VOORHIES,** born San Diego, California, August 10, 1928; admitted to bar, 1967, California. *Education:* Los Angeles County College (A.A., 1954); University of Southern California (B.A., 1959). Phi Alpha Delta (Secretary-Treasurer, 1961). *Member:* Wilshire and Los Angeles County Bar Associations; State Bar of California; Los Angeles Trial Lawyers Association; California Trial Lawyers Association (Member, Board of Governors, 1983-1984); The Association of Trial Lawyers of America. [With USMC]. **PRACTICE AREAS:** Civil Trial; Insurance; Product Liability; Medical Malpractice; Negligence Law.

**R. BRIAN KRAMER,** born Santa Monica, California, January 11, 1955; admitted to bar, 1980, California. *Education:* University of Southern California (B.A., 1977); Loyola University of Los Angeles (J.D., 1980). Phi Beta Kappa; Phi Kappa Phi. *Member:* Los Angeles County Bar Association; State Bar of California; California Trial Lawyers Association; The Association of Trial Lawyers of America. **PRACTICE AREAS:** Civil Trial; Insurance; Product Liability; Medical Malpractice; Negligence Law.

REFERENCE: Western Bank (Beverly Hills Branch).

## VORZIMER, GARBER, MASSERMAN & ECOFF
### LOS ANGELES, CALIFORNIA
(See Beverly Hills)

*General Civil, Trial and Appellate Practice in all State and Federal Courts and Administrative Agencies. Business Litigation, Corporate, Real Estate, Criminal Defense, Insurance Coverage, Entertainment, Wrongful Termination, Unfair Competition, Constitutional and Civil Rights Litigation.*

## DONALD R. WAGER
10960 WILSHIRE BOULEVARD, SUITE 1000
### LOS ANGELES, CALIFORNIA 90024
Telephone: 310-235-3939
Fax: 310-325-3949

*State and Federal Criminal Defense. Administrative Law.*

**DONALD R. WAGER,** born Rockford, Illinois, March 15, 1936; admitted to bar, 1963, California and U.S. District Court, Central District of California. *Education:* University of Southern California (B.A., 1968); Willamette University (LL.B., 1962). Contributor, Willamette Law Review, 1961-1962. *Member:* Los Angeles County Bar Association; State Bar of California (Member, Criminal Law Section); California Attorneys for Criminal Justice; Criminal Courts Bar Association of Los Angeles County (Vice-President, 1996).

REFERENCE: Bank of America, Santa Monica, California.

## CARL R. WALDMAN
A LAW CORPORATION
18TH FLOOR
1901 AVENUE OF THE STARS
### LOS ANGELES, CALIFORNIA 90067
Telephone: 310-785-9090
FAX: 310-201-0226

*Estate Planning, Tax Planning, General Business and Estate Administration Law.*

**CARL R. WALDMAN,** born La Chapelle, France, March 24, 1957; admitted to bar, 1983, California. *Education:* University of California at San Diego; Pomona College (B.A., 1979); University of California at Los Angeles (J.D., 1983). Co-Author: "Despite Complexity, Private Foundations Offer Advantages To Donors With Charitable Intentions," Estate Planning, July, 1985. Lecturer, Western Pension Conference, "Nonqualified Deferred

*(This Listing Continued)*

CALIFORNIA—LOS ANGELES

**CARL R. WALDMAN** A LAW CORPORATION, Los Angeles—Continued

Compensation Arrangements," 1988; California Society of Certified Public Accountants, Estate Planning Conference, "Charitable Planning," 1990. *Member:* Century City, Beverly Hills and American Bar Associations; State Bar of California. (Also Of Counsel, Ronald A. Litz & Associates). **PRACTICE AREAS:** Estate Planning Law; Tax Planning Law; General Business Law.

## ROBERT D. WALKER

A PROFESSIONAL CORPORATION

*Established in 1985*

SUITE 1208, ONE PARK PLAZA
3250 WILSHIRE BOULEVARD
**LOS ANGELES, CALIFORNIA 90010-1606**
Telephone: 213-382-8010
Fax: 213-388-1033

Civil Trial Practice in all State and Federal Courts. Professional Negligence, Products Liability and Medical-Legal Law, Unfair Competition and Defamation Law, Hospital Staff Privilege Law.

FIRM PROFILE: The firm was started on June 17, 1985. Consultant with other small firms regarding trials. Handles many trial cases for large downtown Los Angeles firms. The firm handles broad based commercial tort, Personal Injury specialization, mostly serious damages. The firm has tried around 300 civil trials. Represents physicians in hospital staff privilege law. The firm handles all trial cases except tax court and patent.

**ROBERT D. WALKER,** born Sacramento, California, December 4, 1937; admitted to bar, 1963, California; 1989, Nevada. *Education:* Dartmouth College; University of Southern California (B.A., 1959); University of California at Los Angeles (J.D., 1962). Phi Alpha Delta. Justice, Roscoe Pound Moot Court Competition, 1961-1962. *Member:* Pasadena, Los Angeles County (Member: Insurance Committee, 1968-1972; Legal Medical Relations Committee, 1969—; Trial Lawyers Section, 1972—; Delegate to State Bar Convention, 1972—) and American (Member, Sections on: Insurance, Negligence and Compensation Law; Litigation; Litigation Management and Economics Committee, 1978—) Bar Associations; State Bar of California; State Bar of Nevada; Nevada Trial Lawyers Association; American Board of Trial Advocates (Diplomate); American Judicature Society; Association of Business Trial Lawyers; American Board of Professional Liability Attorneys; American Society of Law and Medicine. **PRACTICE AREAS:** Professional Negligence; Products Liability; Medical-Legal Law; Unfair Competition; Defamation Law; Hospital Staff Privilege Law.

**DELIA FLORES,** born San Pedro, California, April 27, 1955; admitted to bar, 1981, California; 1989, Nevada. *Education:* Harvard University (A.B., cum laude, 1977); University of California School of Law at Los Angeles (J.D., 1981). Editor, Chicano Law Review, 1980-1981. *Member:* Los Angeles County and American Bar Associations; State Bar of California; Nevada Trial Lawyers Association; Mexican American Bar Association; American Judicature Society. **PRACTICE AREAS:** Employment Discrimination; Negligence; Product Liability; Medical-Legal Law; Unfair Competition; Defamation Law; Hospital Staff Privilege Law.

REFERENCE: Bank of America (Los Angeles Main Office)

## WALKER, WRIGHT, TYLER & WARD

A Partnership

*Established in 1923*

SUITE 900, 626 WILSHIRE BOULEVARD
**LOS ANGELES, CALIFORNIA 90017**
Telephone: 213-629-3571
Telecopier: 213-623-5160

General Civil and Trial Practice. Banking, Corporation, Real Estate, Estate Planning, Taxation and Probate Law.

FIRM PROFILE: Walker, Wright, Tyler & Ward was founded in 1923. The firm's practice is concentrated in business and real estate litigation, real estate and corporate transactional work, banking and finance work and estate planning. The firm deliberately has remained small by Los Angeles standards and

*(This Listing Continued)*

MARTINDALE-HUBBELL LAW DIRECTORY 1997

offers its clients responsive, quality services at rates below those charged by national firms. The firm's clientele ranges from small businesses to Fortune 1000 companies with emphasis on the middle market.

*MEMBERS OF FIRM*

**IRVING M. WALKER** (1885-1969).

**HOWARD W. WRIGHT** (1892-1977).

**J. RANDOLPH HUSTON,** born Santa Monica, California, December 24, 1941; admitted to bar, 1967, California. *Education:* Georgetown University (A.B., 1963); University of Southern California (J.D., 1966). Phi Delta Phi. Member, Southern California Law Review, 1964-1966. *Member:* State Bar of California. **PRACTICE AREAS:** Litigation; General Business Practice.

**ROBERT J. WITT,** born Chicago, Illinois, March 4, 1941; admitted to bar, 1966, California. *Education:* De Paul University (B.S.C., 1962); University of California at Los Angeles (J.D., 1965). Beta Alpha Psi; Beta Gamma Sigma. *Member:* Los Angeles County and American Bar Associations; The State Bar of California. [with U.S. Army, 1965-1967]. **PRACTICE AREAS:** Probate and Estate Planning; Taxation; Banking.

**JOHN M. ANGLIN,** born Boston, Massachusetts, June 19, 1947; admitted to bar, 1972, California. *Education:* University of Southern California (A.B., magna cum laude, 1969; J.D., 1972). Phi Beta Kappa. *Member:* Los Angeles County and American Bar Associations; The State Bar of California. **PRACTICE AREAS:** Real Estate; Corporate; Banking.

**ROBIN C. CAMPBELL,** born San Diego, California, August 19, 1951; admitted to bar, 1976, California. *Education:* Gottingen University, West Germany and University of California at Riverside (B.A., with highest honors, 1973); Columbia University (J.D., 1976). Phi Beta Kappa. Articles Editor, Columbia Human Rights Law Review, 1975-1976. *Member:* Los Angeles County and American Bar Associations; State Bar of California. **PRACTICE AREAS:** Litigation; General Business Practice.

**MARK T. FLEWELLING,** born Glendale, California, August 26, 1955; admitted to bar, 1980, California. *Education:* Occidental College (A.B., 1977); University of Southern California (J.D., 1980); Salzburg University, Austria. Phi Sigma Kappa. Recipient, American Jurisprudence Award for Criminal Procedure. *Member:* Los Angeles County and American Bar Associations; State Bar of California. **PRACTICE AREAS:** Banking; Litigation.

*RETIRED*

Don F. Tyler     Shirley C. Ward, Jr.
Stevens Weller, Jr.

*ASSOCIATES*

**JOHN S. WARD,** born Paterson, New Jersey, June 4, 1958; admitted to bar, 1986, California. *Education:* Connecticut College (B.A., 1981); University of Southern California (J.D., 1986). Phi Alpha Delta. Member, Southern California Law Review, 1984-1985. *Member:* Los Angeles County and American Bar Associations; State Bar of California. **PRACTICE AREAS:** Civil Practice.

**ROBERT A. ACKERMANN,** born Torrance, California, November 28, 1964; admitted to bar, 1991, California and U.S. District Court, Central, Northern and Southern Districts of California. *Education:* University of California at Berkeley (A.B., with high honors, 1987) Loyola Law School (J.D., 1991). Extern to the Honorable A. Andrew Hauk, Senior Judge and Chief Judge Emeritus, U.S. District Court, Central District of California. *Member:* Los Angeles County and American Bar Associations; State Bar of California.

**KATHERINE E. ADKINS,** born Franklin, Nebraska, September 9, 1962; admitted to bar, 1991, California. *Education:* University of Nebraska at Lincoln (B.A., 1984); Loyola Law School (J.D., 1991). Member, Innocent's Society. Staff Writer and Production Editor, Loyola Entertainment Law Journal, 1989. Extern to the Honorable Samuel Bufford, U.S. Bankruptcy Court, Central District of California. *Member:* Los Angeles County and American Bar Associations; State Bar of California.

**CHARLES J. KAO,** born Taipei, Taiwan, October 30, 1968; admitted to bar, 1994, California. *Education:* University of California at Los Angeles (B.A., 1990); Cornell University (J.D., 1994). *Member:* State Bar of California. **LANGUAGES:** Mandarin Chinese.

*(This Listing Continued)*

# PROFESSIONAL BIOGRAPHIES — CALIFORNIA—LOS ANGELES

*OF COUNSEL*

**JOHN J. MOLLOY, III,** born San Antonio, Texas, August 8, 1946; admitted to bar, 1972, California and U.S. Tax Court; 1973, U.S. District Court, Central District of California; 1975, U.S. Court of Appeals, Ninth Circuit; 1976, U.S. Supreme Court. *Education:* University of Southern California (B.S., 1968; J.D., 1972). *Member:* Los Angeles County and American Bar Associations; State Bar of California. **PRACTICE AREAS:** Corporate; Tax; Real Estate.

> REPRESENTATIVE CLIENTS: McDonald's Corp.; The Hong Kong & Shanghai Banking Corp.; Farmer Bros. Co.; Santa Catalina Island Co.; Higgins Brick Co.; Thor Industries West, Inc.; Dahsing Bank; First Union Mortgage Corp.; LTV Energy Products Co.; Penhall Co.
> REFERENCE: The Bank of California (Los Angeles Office).

---

## THOMAS EDWARD WALL
### LOS ANGELES, CALIFORNIA
(See Culver City)

*Personal Injury, Civil Trials and Appeals, Insurance Defense Disputes, Child Abuse Law.*

---

## WALLACE, BRENNAN & FOLAN
### LOS ANGELES, CALIFORNIA
(See Torrance)

*Labor and Employment Law, Business Litigation, General Corporate and Securities Law.*

---

## DAVID G. WALLER
### 600 WILSHIRE BOULEVARD, SUITE 300
### LOS ANGELES, CALIFORNIA 90017-3215
Telephone: 213-627-3141
FAX: 213-627-5938

Torrance, California Office: 24520 Hawthorne Boulevard, Suite 110. Telephone: 310-375-0077.

*General Civil and Trial Practice in all State and Federal Courts. Family Law, Mediation, Corporation, Probate and Real Property Law.*

**DAVID G. WALLER,** born Philadelphia, Pennsylvania, June 14, 1935; admitted to bar, 1962, California. *Education:* University of California at Los Angeles (B.S., 1958; LL.B., 1961). Order of the Coif. Member, Board of Editors, University of California at Los Angeles Law Review, 1960-1961. *Member:* Los Angeles County Bar Association (Member, Family Law Section); State Bar of California; Southern California Mediation Association.

> REFERENCE: Bank of America.

---

## WALSH, DONOVAN, LINDH & KEECH
### SUITE 2600, 445 SOUTH FIGUEROA STREET
### LOS ANGELES, CALIFORNIA 90071-1630
Telephone: 213-612-7757
Telefax: 213-612-7797
Telex: WU 401760 WADINH LSA ESL 62949341

San Francisco, California Office: Suite 2000, 595 Market Street. Telephone: 415-957-8700. Telefax: 415-543-9388. Telex: WU 384831 WADINH SFO; RCA 286833 WDL UR; ESL 62756007.
Long Beach, California Office: 301 East Ocean Boulevard, Suite 1200. Telephone: 310-901-4848. Telefax: 310-901-4850. Telex: 384-831.

*General Civil and Trial Practice. Admiralty, Commercial, Construction, Bankruptcy, Franchising, International Practice and Insurance Law.*

(For Complete Biographical Data on all Personnel, see San Francisco, California Professional Biographies)

---

## WALTER, FINESTONE & RICHTER
### A PROFESSIONAL CORPORATION
### SUITE 1900, 11601 WILSHIRE BOULEVARD
### LOS ANGELES, CALIFORNIA 90025
Telephone: 310-575-0800
Fax: 310-575-0170
Email: WFRLAW@Primenet.com

*General Civil and Trial Practice in all State and Federal Courts. Corporation, Estate Planning, Probate, Real Property, Franchise, Securities, Taxation, Exempt Organizations. Commercial, Antitrust and Unfair Competition Law.*

**JOHN F. WALTER,** born Buffalo, New York, November 3, 1944; admitted to bar, 1970, California, U.S. District Court, Central District of California and U.S. Court of Appeals, Ninth Circuit; 1972, U.S. District Court, Southern District of California; 1973, U.S. Supreme Court; 1984, U.S. District Court, Eastern District of California; 1986, U.S. District Court, Northern District of California; 1988, Hawaii; 1989, U.S. District Court, District of Hawaii; 1990, U.S. Claims Court. *Education:* Loyola University of Los Angeles (B.A., 1966; J.D., 1969). Assistant U.S. Attorney, Central District of California, 1970-1972. Judge Pro Tem, Los Angeles Municipal Courts, 1983—. *Member:* Los Angeles County, Federal and American Bar Associations; The State Bar of California; Association of Business Trial Lawyers. **PRACTICE AREAS:** Civil Litigation.

**WILLIAM FINESTONE,** born Los Angeles, California, November 7, 1943; admitted to bar, 1969, Oregon; 1970, California; 1976, U.S. Tax Court; 1990, U.S. District Court, Central District of California; U.S. Claims Court; U.S. Court of Appeals, Ninth Circuit; U.S. Supreme Court. *Education:* University of California at Los Angeles (B.S., 1965; M.B.A., 1966; J.D., 1969). Beta Gamma Sigma; Order of the Coif. Author: "Corporate-Owned Life Insurance and the Estate Tax— The New Majority Stockholder Rule," 1 J. Corp. Taxation 261, Autumn 1974; "The Tax Ramifications of Property Ownership," Real Estate Intelligence Report, October 1979; "Are Crummey Trusts Better After ERTA?" Title Ins. & Trust Co. Forum, 1982; "Charity Begins at Home," XVI Currents (February 1990); "Gift Giving Tips and Traps," 17th Ann. U.S.C. Prob. & Tr. Conf., (1991); "Irrevocable Life Insurance Trusts," L.A. County Bar Assoc. 1992 Probate Symposium. Co-Author: "Eligibility of Revocable Trust As 'S Corporation' Shareholder After Death of Co-Grantor Spouse," 4 J. S. Corp. Tax 106 (1992). Clerk to Chief Justice William C. Perry, Supreme Court of Oregon, 1969-1970. Instructor, Tax Aspects of Real Estate Investments, UCLA Extension, 1977—. *Member:* Los Angeles County and American Bar Associations; Oregon State Bar; The State Bar of California; American College of Trust and Estate Counsel. (Certified Specialist, Estate Planning, Trust and Probate Law, The State Bar of California Board of Legal Specialization). **PRACTICE AREAS:** Taxation Law; Estate Planning Law.

**JEFFREY R. RICHTER,** born Los Angeles, California, July 21, 1945; admitted to bar, 1971, California and U.S. District Court, Central District of California. *Education:* University of California at Los Angeles (A.B., 1967); University of Texas (J.D., 1970). Associate Editor, Texas Law Review, 1968-1970. Judge Pro Tem, Los Angeles Municipal Court, 1984—. *Member:* Beverly Hills, Los Angeles County (Member, Client Relations Committee) and American (Member, Corporation, Banking and Business Law Section) Bar Associations; The State Bar of California. **PRACTICE AREAS:** Corporate Law; Commercial Transactions; Business Planning; Mergers and Acquisitions; Federal and State Securities Law.

**CHRISTOPHER TESAR,** born New York, N.Y., June 9, 1950; admitted to bar, 1978, California and U.S. District Court, Central District of California. *Education:* University of California (B.A., summa cum laude, 1972); University of California at Los Angeles (J.D., 1978). Order of the Coif. Member, Moot Court. Author: "This Land is Our Land?" Los Angeles County Bar Journal, July, 1979; "Some Pitfalls of Strip Center Redevelopment," Southern California Commercial Property Owners Association Newsletter, February, 1986; "Avoiding Needless Eviction Losses and Delays," Southern California Commercial Property Owners Association Newsletter, May, 1986; "Supreme Court Requires Landlords to Act 'Reasonably'," Southern California Commercial Property Owners Association Newsletter, September, 1986. *Member:* Los Angeles County Bar Association (Member, Real Property Section); State Bar of California (Member, Real Property Law Section). **PRACTICE AREAS:** General Real Estate Law; Business Law.

**JEFF M. NOVATT,** born Brooklyn, New York, August 13, 1958; admitted to bar, 1983, California; 1984, U.S. Tax Court; 1990, U.S. District Court, Central District of California; U.S. Claims Court; U.S. Court of Ap-

*(This Listing Continued)*

**WALTER, FINESTONE & RICHTER**, *A PROFESSIONAL CORPORATION, Los Angeles—Continued*

peals, Ninth Circuit; U.S. Supreme Court. *Education:* Duke University (B.S., cum laude, 1980); University of Florida (J.D., with honors, 1983); New York University (LL.M., in Taxation, 1984). Phi Eta Sigma; Phi Delta Phi. Member, University of Florida Law Review, 1982-1983. Recipient, Book Awards in Income Taxation, 1982 and Income Taxation of Estates and Trusts, 1983, University of Florida. Co-Author: "Eligibility of Revocable Trust As 'S Corporation' Shareholder After Death of Co-Grantor Spouse," 4 J. S. Corp. Tax 106 (1992). Instructor, Tax Aspects of Real Estate Investments, UCLA Extension, 1988—. Panel Member, Tax Court Pro Se Program, 1985—. *Member:* Los Angeles County and American Bar Associations; State Bar of California (Member, Taxation Section). *PRACTICE AREAS:* Taxation Law; Business Law.

**JOHN J. WALLER, JR.,** born Pasadena, California, September 13, 1955; admitted to bar, 1980, California; 1981, U.S. District Court, Central District of California; 1986, Eastern, Northern and Southern Districts of California and U.S. Court of Appeals, Ninth Circuit; 1988, U.S. Supreme Court. *Education:* University of California at Berkeley (A.B., 1977); Hastings College of the Law, University of California (J.D., 1980); National Institute for Trial Advocacy, 1989. Supplement Editor, von Kalinowski's Antitrust Laws and Trade Regulation, 1993—. *Member:* Los Angeles County (Member, Antitrust and Litigation Sections) and American (Member, Antitrust and Litigation Sections) Bar Associations; State Bar of California (Member, Antitrust and Litigation Sections). *PRACTICE AREAS:* General Business Litigation; Antitrust Litigation and Counseling.

---

**NANCY R. BENVENISTE,** born Los Angeles, California, August 25, 1954; admitted to bar, 1984, California. *Education:* University of California at Santa Cruz (B.A., 1976); Hastings College of the Law, University of California (J.D., 1984). Chairman, Moot Court Board, Committee on Standards and Grading, 1983-1984. *Member:* Los Angeles County Bar Association; State Bar of California. *PRACTICE AREAS:* Corporate Law; Commercial Transactions; Employment Law; Non-Profit Corporations Law.

**JOSEPH L. GREENSLADE,** born Bronx, New York, May 30, 1963; admitted to bar, 1989, California and U.S. Court of Appeals, Ninth Circuit; 1990, U.S. District Court, Central District of California; 1992, U.S. District Court, Southern District of California. *Education:* University of California at Los Angeles (B.A., 1986); Loyola Law School (J.D., cum laude, 1989). Order of the Coif. Editor, Loyola of Los Angeles Law Review, 1988-1989. Author: Comment, "Labor Unions and The Sherman Act: Rethinking Labor's Nonstatutory Exemption," Loyola of Los Angeles Law Review, Vol. 22, No. 1, 1988. *Member:* Los Angeles County Bar Association; State Bar of California. *PRACTICE AREAS:* Litigation.

---

## LAW OFFICES OF
## PETER M. WALZER

SUITE 2610, 2029 CENTURY PARK EAST
**LOS ANGELES, CALIFORNIA 90067**
Telephone: 310-557-0915
Email: peterlaw@aol.com

*Practice Limited to Family Law.*

**PETER M. WALZER,** born Santa Monica, California, May 18, 1953; admitted to bar, 1981, California. *Education:* University of Santa Monica (M.A. Psych., 1990); University of California at Los Angeles (B.A., 1975); Southwestern University (J.D., 1980). Co-Author: "Innovative Prenuptial Agreements, Family Law and Estate Planning Perspectives," CEB Program Handbook, March 1996; "French Knots: Contrat de Marriage in California," Los Angeles Daily Journal, March 1996; "Pensions Simplified and Not So Simplified," "Obtaining More Than Half of the Community Property for Your Client" and "The Ins and Outs of Interstate Jurisdiction and Conflicts of Law," CEB Program Handbook, Selected Issues in Community Property, October 1993; "Jurisdiction - Maneuvering Through Complex Rules," Family Advocate, Winter 1990; "To Have and To Hold - Most Premarital Agreements are Binding and Enforceable," California Lawyer, September 1990; "When Fault Affects Fitness - How to Fight the Custody Battle," Family Advocate, Fall 1987; " Using Receiverships in California Marital Dissolutions," California Lawyer, February 1981. Lecturer, California Continuing Education of the Bar, 1993. Past President, Association of Certified

*(This Listing Continued)*

Family Law Specialists. Los Angeles Superior Court Family Law Department Hearing Officer, 1988, 1991, 1995 and 1996. Los Angeles County Municipal Court Judge Pro Tem, 1987-1991. Volunteer Attorney, Alliance for Children's Rights, 1995-1996. *Member:* Century City Bar Association (Chair, Law Office Management Section). State Bar of California (Chair, Family Law Section Property Committee, 1996-1997). Fellow, American Academy of Matrimonial Lawyers. (Certified Specialist, Family Law, State Bar of California Board of Legal Specialization). *PRACTICE AREAS:* Family Law.

---

## WARREN & HERMAN

*Established in 1992*

1901 AVENUE OF THE STARS, SUITE 300
**LOS ANGELES, CALIFORNIA 90067-6005**
Telephone: 310-843-9030
Telecopier: 310-843-9034

*Real Estate, Estate Planning, Probate and Corporations. General Civil Practice.*

### MEMBERS OF FIRM

**MICHAEL G. HERMAN,** born Los Angeles, California, March 16, 1953; admitted to bar, 1980, California; 1981, U.S. District Court, Central District of California and U.S. Court of Appeals, Ninth Circuit. *Education:* Stanford University (A.B., with distinction, 1976); University of California, Hastings College of Law (J.D., 1980). Note and Comment Editor, Hastings Journal of Communications and Entertainment Law, 1979-1980. Co-Author: "The SEC's New Regulation D," 5 Los Angeles Lawyer, September 1982; "Section 25102(f): California's New Counterpart to Regulation D," 5 Los Angeles Lawyer, October 1982. *Member:* Los Angeles County Bar Association; State Bar of California (Member, Business and Real Property Law Sections). *PRACTICE AREAS:* Real Property Law; General Corporate Practice; Commercial.

**JUDITH WARREN,** born Manhattan Beach, California, September 4, 1949; admitted to bar, 1979, California and U.S. District Court, Central District of California; 1980, U.S. Court of Appeals, Ninth Circuit; 1982, U.S. District Court, Southern District of California; 1985, U.S. District Court, Northern and Eastern Districts of California. *Education:* Stanford University (A.B., with distinction, 1971); University of Michigan (M.A., 1974); University of California at Los Angeles (J.D., 1979). Phi Beta Kappa; Alpha Lambda Delta. *Member:* Los Angeles County Bar Association (Member, Trusts and Estate Section); State Bar of California (Member, Sections on: Estate Planning, Trusts and Probate; Business Law). *PRACTICE AREAS:* Estate Planning Law; Probate Law; Professional Corporations; General Corporate Practice.

---

## KATHERINE BUTTS WARWICK

300 SOUTH GRAND AVENUE
14TH FLOOR
**LOS ANGELES, CALIFORNIA 90071**
Telephone: 213-346-9067
Fax: 213-346-9069

*Bankruptcy Litigation specializing in Creditors Rights.*

**KATHERINE BUTTS WARWICK,** born Spokane, Washington, April 1, 1941; admitted to bar, 1980, Indiana and U.S. District Court, Southern District of Indiana, Ohio and U.S. District Court, Southern District of Ohio; 1984, U.S. Court of Appeals, Sixth Circuit; 1985, California, U.S. District Court, Central District of California; 1989, U.S. District Court, Eastern and Northern Districts of California; 1990, U.S. Court of Appeals, Ninth Circuit; 1993, U.S. District Court, Southern District of California. *Education:* Wellesley College (A.B., 1963); Indiana University (J.D., magna cum laude, 1980). Articles Editor, Indiana University Law Review, 1979. Adjunct Faculty Member, University of Dayton Law School, 1980. *Member:* American Bar Association; State Bar of California.

## H. ANDREW WASMUND
### LOS ANGELES, CALIFORNIA
(See Manhattan Beach)

*General Civil and Criminal Litigation with emphasis in Federal Court. Arbitration and Mediation.*

---

## BONNIE STERN WASSER
*Established in 1988*
**12121 WILSHIRE BOULEVARD, SUITE 205**
**LOS ANGELES, CALIFORNIA 90025**
Telephone: 310-447-1684
Fax: 310-207-9374
Email: bwasser@earthlink.net
URL: http://www.ilw.com/wasser

*Immigration and Nationality Law and Employment Law.*

**BONNIE STERN WASSER,** born Los Angeles, California, June 8, 1957; admitted to bar, 1984, California and U.S. District Court, Central District of California; 1985, U.S. Court of Appeals, Ninth Circuit. *Education:* University of California at Irvine (B.A., 1979); Universite de Bordeaux, France (1977-1978); University of California at Los Angeles (M.A., 1981); Southwestern University School of Law (J.D., 1984). Extern: Hon. Robert M. Takasugi, U.S. District Judge, Los Angeles, 1983; Hon. Carol J. Fieldhouse and Hon. Florence T. Pickard, Judges Pro Tem, California Court of Appeals, Second Appellate District, 1984. Instructor, USC Law Center, 1987. Trial Attorney, U.S. Department of Justice, Immigration and Nationalization Service, 1984-1986. Associate, Barst & Mukamal, Los Angeles, 1986-1988. *Member:* Los Angeles County Bar Association (Member, Executive Committee, International Section, 1993—); L.A. Women's Appointment Collaboration (President, 1994-1995 ); American Immigration Lawyers Association; Women Lawyers Association of Los Angeles. (Certified Specialist, Immigration Law, The State Bar of California Board of Legal Specialization). **LANGUAGES:** French.

---

## WASSER, ROSENSON & CARTER
*Established in 1983*
**SUITE 1200, ONE CENTURY PLAZA**
**2029 CENTURY PARK EAST (CENTURY CITY)**
**LOS ANGELES, CALIFORNIA 90067**
Telephone: 310-277-7117
Fax: 310-553-1793

*Family Law, Divorce, Domestic Relations, Matrimonial Law.*

**FIRM PROFILE:** *Wasser, Rosenson & Carter practices exclusively in family law including palimony. The firm has represented many high profile clients. They are sensitive to the clients needs and the client is promised to be kept out of the public eye. Wasser, Rosenson & Carter has participated in numerous high profile cases.*

### MEMBERS OF FIRM

**DENNIS M. WASSER,** born Brooklyn, New York, August 27, 1942; admitted to bar, 1968, California. *Education:* University of California at Los Angeles (B.A., with honors, 1964); University of Southern California (J.D., 1967). Phi Delta Phi; Order of the Coif. Note and Comment Editor, Law Review. Listed in "Best Lawyers In America," 1987-1996. Author: "Spousal Support and The Wife's Desire and Ability to Work," *Beverly Hills Bar Journal,* Vol. 8, March 1974; "Increases in the Value of Property After Separation - Community or Separate Property," *Beverly Hills Bar Journal,* Vol. 9, July 1975; "Child Custody & Visitation Disputes: An Overview," *Los Angeles Lawyer,* Vol 1, No. 5, July, 1978; "The Impact of Potential Future Taxes on Community Property Divisions," *Beverly Hills Bar Journal,* July - August, 1978; "Child Custody & Visitation: Update," 1982. Lecturer: Continuing Education of the Bar, Beverly Hills Bar Family Law Symposium, Los Angeles County Bar Family Law Symposium, Community Property Journal - Fifth Annual Seminar, 1979, University of Southern California Law Center - 1978 Family Law Seminar, The Rutter Group Family Law Specialist Program, 1981, The Rutter Group Family Law Workshop - 1983-1985, University of California at Los Angeles Law School - Community Property. Program Participant: Pepperdine University School of Law - Masters Series Conference on Advanced Family Law Practice, 1984, Canada; American Bar Association Family Law Section, "Divorce and Estate Planning in an Uncertain Marital Climate," Beverly Hills, New York, 1983. Co-Instructor, University of Southern California Advanced Professional Program Family Law, 1989. *Member:* Beverly Hills (Chairperson, Family Law Section, 1978-1979), Los Angeles County (Chairperson, 1984; Member, Executive Committee, Family Law Section, 1978-1988) and American Bar Associations; State Bar of California; American Academy of Matrimonial Lawyers. (Certified Specialist, Family Law, The State Bar of California Board of Legal Specialization).

*(This Listing Continued)*

**S. DAVID ROSENSON,** born Los Angeles, California, September 24, 1936; admitted to bar, 1961, California and U.S. District Court, Central District of California; 1964, U.S. Supreme Court. *Education:* University of California at Los Angeles (B.A., 1958); Stanford University (LL.B., 1961); University of Southern California (Masters Program). Named in "Best Lawyers In America," 1989-1996, 1991-1992. Author: "Divorce California Style," Los Angeles Lawyer, 1981; "An Analysis of Property Presumptions in Family Law," State Bar Family News, 1982; "Use of Tax Returns in Domestic Relations Matters," 1980; Reimbursement of Pre-Existing Community Expenses," 1979; Divorce Courts in the Tax Planning Business," 1979; "Marriage of Sullivan - The Visible Becomes Invisible," 1982, Beverly Hills Bar Journal; Real and Personal Property Title Presumptions—1984 Style," 1984 Los Angeles Lawyer; "*Grinius* and Bear It - An Analysis of the Characterization of Loan Proceedings Made During Marriage," Beverly Hills Bar Journal, 1987; "Fonstein Failing" - An Analysis of Tax Considerations in Domestic Relations Matters," Los Angeles Lawyer, March, 1988; "Date of Valuation and Marriage of Green - It's Simple," Beverly Hills Bar Association Journal, Vol. 23, Number 3, Summer 1989; "Silver Spoon Child Support," Beverly Hills Bar Journal, Fall 1991; "Disposition of Community Property Partnership Interests," Los Angeles Lawyer, December 1992 and Bancroft-Whitney News Alert, April 1993. Lecturer, (Continuing Education of Bar, 1978-1996). *Member:* Beverly Hills (Member, Executive Committee, Family Law Section, 1987-1996; Chairman, 1989) and Los Angeles County (Member, Executive Committee, Family Law Section, 1980-1988; Judge Pro Tem Panel, 1980-1984) Bar Associations; State Bar of California. (Certified Specialist, Family Law, The State Bar of California Board of Legal Specialization). **PRACTICE AREAS:** Family Law.

**SUSAN K. CARTER,** born Baltimore, Maryland, November 10, 1941; admitted to bar, 1978, California. *Education:* University of California at Los Angeles (B.A., 1963); California State University at Northridge (M.A., with honors, 1969); University of San Fernando Valley College of Law (J.D., with honors, 1978). Judge Pro Tem, Panel, Small Claims Court, 1983-1991. Member, Mediation Panel, Los Angeles Superior Court, 1982, 1983, 1984, 1985, 1986, 1987, 1988. *Member:* Beverly Hills and Los Angeles County Bar Associations; The State Bar of California.

### ASSOCIATES

**JOHN A. FOLEY,** born Los Angeles, California, June 21, 1953; admitted to bar, 1982, California and U.S. District Court, Central District of California; 1983, U.S. Court of Appeals, Ninth Circuit. *Education:* Pasadena City College; California State University at Northridge (B.A., 1975); Southwestern University (J.D., 1979). Member, Mediation Panel, Los Angeles Superior Court, 1990—. Participant, Los Angeles Superior Court Family Law Walk Thru Program, 1991, 1993-1996. Panel Member, Beverly Hills Bar Association Family Law Section Workshop Seminars, 1991. Member, 1982-1987, Vice President, 1984-1985, 1986-1987 and Treasurer, 1985-1986, Pasadena Young Lawyers. *Member:* Beverly Hills (Member, Family Law Section), Los Angeles County (Member, Family Law Section) and American (Member, Family Law Section) Bar Associations; State Bar of California. (Certified Specialist, Family Law, The State Bar of California Board of Legal Specialization).

**LAURA LANDESMAN,** born Los Angeles, California, April 20, 1959; admitted to bar, 1982, California. *Education:* University of California at Irvine (B.A., 1979); University of California at Los Angeles (J.D., 1982). *Member:* Beverly Hills (Member, Family Law Section) and Los Angeles County (Member, Family Law Section) Bar Associations; State Bar of California. (Certified Specialist, Family Law, The State Bar of California Board of Legal Specialization).

**LAURA ALLISON WASSER,** born Los Angeles, California, May 23, 1968; admitted to bar, 1994, California. *Education:* University of California, Berkeley (B.A., 1991); Loyola Law School (J.D., 1994). *Member:* Beverly Hills (Member, Family Law Section) and Los Angeles County Bar Associations.

CAA1277B

## WASSERMAN, COMDEN & CASSELMAN L.L.P.

**LOS ANGELES, CALIFORNIA**

(See Tarzana)

*Insurance Defense, Product Liability and Landslide Litigation, Subrogation, Fire Insurance, Business Litigation and Real Estate Law.*

---

## WATERS, McCLUSKEY & BOEHLE

**LOS ANGELES, CALIFORNIA**

(See Santa Monica)

*Civil Litigation, Trial and Appellate Practice. Insurance and Negligence Law.*

---

## WATKINS & STEVENS

A Law Partnership

Established in 1991

SUITE 600
10877 WILSHIRE BOULEVARD
**LOS ANGELES, CALIFORNIA 90024**
Telephone: 310-824-5624
FAX: 310-824-2735

*Major Tort Litigation emphasizing Substantial Personal Injury, Employment Discrimination, Insurance Bad Faith, Product Liability, Professional Malpractice, Medical Malpractice and Business Torts. Civil Trial and Appellate Practice.*

### MEMBERS OF FIRM

**SHIRLEY K. WATKINS,** born Yokosuka, Japan, July 19, 1957; admitted to bar, 1982, California; 1991, U.S. Supreme Court. *Education:* University of California at San Diego (B.A., 1979); California Western School of Law (J.D., 1982). Author: "A Short Course in Malicious Prosecution", LATLA Advocate, September 1994; "Crucial Discovery in Third Party Cases", LATLA Las Vegas Seminar Syllabus, October 1992 and October 1994; "Discovery of Sexual Conduct of Plaintiff in Civil Sexual Harassment or Sexual Assault Case", LATLA Advocate, June 1992 (with Steven B. Stevens); "Discovery Privileges and Protections", LATLA MCLE Fair, April 1993; "Opposing Defendant's Motion for Discretionary Relief from Default", LATLA Advocate, January 1993 (with Steven B. Stevens). Recipient: American Jurisprudence Award in Remedies; Faculty Awards in Employment Law, Discrimination Law and Anti-trust. Contributing Editor, *The Advocate,* 1993—. Judge Pro Tem, Los Angeles Superior and Municipal Court, 1991—. President, Women's Law Association, 1979-1980. Member, Bench and Bar Committee, Los Angeles Superior Court. *Member:* State Bar of California; Japanese-American Bar Association; Consumer Attorneys Association of Los Angeles (Board of Governors, 1991—); The Association of Trial Lawyers of America; Consumer Attorneys of California; Women Lawyers Association of Los Angeles (Board of Governors, 1993-1996); California Women Lawyers; Trial Lawyers for Public Justice. **PRACTICE AREAS:** Employment Discrimination; Medical Malpractice; Product Liability.

**STEVEN B. STEVENS,** born Chicago, Illinois, April 19, 1956; admitted to bar, 1981, Illinois; 1982, California; 1985, U.S. Supreme Court. *Education:* Carleton College (B.A., magna cum laude, 1978); University of Illinois (J.D., 1981). Phi Beta Kappa. Judicial Law Clerk for Justice Jay J. Alloy, Illinois Appellate Court, 1981-1983. Editor-in-Chief, *The Advocate* . Author: "Professional Liability for Psychotherapist-Patient Sexual Relations," CTLA Forum, Vol. 19, Nos. 8 and 9, 1989; Statutory Settlement Offers," LATLA Annual Seminar, October, 1991; "Health Care Provider Liens," LATLA Ethics Seminar, July, 1991; "When the Doctor Says 'Yes' but the Client Says 'No': Health Care Provider Liens," LATLA Advocate (July/August 1992); "Code of Civil Procedure section 351: Its Use in Discovery and Defense in Court," CTLA Forum (November 1992); "Respondent Superior Liability: Unchanged Even After Proposition 51," Los Angeles Lawyers (December 1992). Co-Author: "Limited Partner Liability and The General Partner: Corporations Code Section 15507 Rev." Beverly Hills Bar Association Journal, 1990; "Discovery of Sexual Conduct of Plaintiff In Sexual Harassment or Sexual Assault Case," LATLA Advocate, Vol. 19,

*(This Listing Continued)*

---

no. 6 (1992). Co-Author: "Opposing Defendant's Motion for Discretionary Relief From Default," LATLA Advocate (January 1993), with Watkins, Shirley K; "Two Year Statute of Limitations for Public Policy Termination Claims", LATLA Advocate, June 1994, with Posner, Joseph; "Individual Liability Under the Fair Employment and Housing Act," Consumer Attorneys Association of Los Angeles *Advocate,* November 1994, with Posner, Joseph. *Member:* Los Angeles County (Member: Bioethics Committee, 1988-1992; Courts Committee, 1992—; Vice-Chair, Courts Committee, 1993-1994; Chair, 1994-1995), Illinois State and American (Member, Tort and Insurance Practice Section; Section of Litigation, 1982—) Bar Associations; State Bar of California; The Association of Trial Lawyers of America; Consumer Attorneys Association of Los Angeles (Board of Governors, 1993—); Consumer Attorneys of California. **PRACTICE AREAS:** Appellate Practice; Insurance Bad Faith; Professional Malpractice; Employment Discrimination.

---

## STEPHEN E. WEBBER

3435 WILSHIRE BOULEVARD
SUITE 1800
**LOS ANGELES, CALIFORNIA 90010**
Telephone: 213-386-2505
Fax: 213-386-4440

*Criminal Defense specializing in Sanity Issues, Mental Health Law.*

**STEPHEN E. WEBBER,** born Los Angeles, California, September 10, 1942; admitted to bar, 1974, California and U.S. Court of Appeals, Ninth Circuit; 1984, U.S. District Court, Central District of California; 1993, U.S. District Court, Eastern District of California. *Education:* California State University at Los Angeles (B.A., 1966); Hastings College of the Law, University of California (J.D., 1972). Phi Alpha Delta. Award Winner, Moot Court Legal Writing. Judge Pro Tem, Los Angeles and Alhambra Municipal Courts, 1985-1990. *Member:* Los Angeles County (Member, Juvenile Justice Committee, 1989-1995; Committee on State Bar 1988—), American and Federal (Member, 1994—and Vice Chair, 1996, Drug Law Enforcement Committee) Bar Associations; State Bar of California; California Attorneys for Criminal Justice; Association of Federal Defense Attorneys; Criminal Courts Bar Association of Los Angeles County. [U.S. Army, 1967-1969, Sp - 5]. **PRACTICE AREAS:** Mental Health Law; Criminal Defense.

---

## WEHNER AND PERLMAN

A Partnership of Professional Corporations

Established in 1983

11100 SANTA MONICA BOULEVARD, SUITE 800
**LOS ANGELES, CALIFORNIA 90025-3384**
Telephone: 310-478-3131
Facsimile: 310-312-0078

*General Civil Litigation. Trial and Appellate Practice in Federal and State Courts including Business, Securities, Insurance, Construction, Professional Liability, Business Crimes and Federal Criminal Fraud Defense.*

### MEMBERS OF FIRM

**CHARLES C. WEHNER, (P.C.),** born Morgantown, West Virginia, July 27, 1948; admitted to bar, 1973, West Virginia and U.S. District Court, Southern District of West Virginia; 1977, U.S. Court of Appeals, Seventh Circuit; 1979, U.S. Court of Appeals, Ninth Circuit; 1981, California and U.S. District Court Central District of California; 1982, District of Columbia and U.S. District Court, Southern District of California; 1995, U.S. Supreme Court. *Education:* West Virginia University (B.A., 1970; J.D., 1973). Member, West Virginia Law Review, 1971-1973. Trial Attorney, U.S. Department of Justice Organized Crime and Racketeering Section, Chicago, Illinois Regional Office, 1974-1978. Trial Attorney and Deputy Attorney-in-Charge, U.S. Department of Justice Organized Crime and Racketeering Section, Los Angeles, California Regional Office, 1979-1981. *Member:* The State Bar of California; The District of Columbia Bar; The West Virginia State Bar; American Bar Association.

**RODNEY M. PERLMAN, (P.C.),** born Valdosta, Georgia, September 13, 1951; admitted to bar, 1976, Georgia and U.S. Court of Appeals, Ninth Circuit; 1978, District of Columbia; 1981, California and U.S. District Court, Central District of California. *Education:* George Washington University (B.A., 1973); Emory University (J.D., 1976). Trial Attorney, U.S. Department of Justice Organized Crime and Racketeering Section, Los

*(This Listing Continued)*

Angeles, California Regional Office, 1977-1982. *Member:* The State Bar of California; The District of Columbia Bar; State Bar of Georgia; Defense Research Institute; The Association of Defense Trial Attorneys.

### ASSOCIATES

**STEVEN M. COHEN,** born Los Angeles, California, July 29, 1959; admitted to bar, 1985, California; 1986, U.S. District Court, Central District of California; 1987, U.S. District Court, Eastern District of California; 1988, U.S. District Court, Northern and Southern Districts of California; 1994, Oregon. *Education:* University of California at San Diego (B.A., 1982); Washington College of Law, The American University (J.D., cum laude, 1985). *Member:* State Bar of California (Member, Litigation Section); Oregon State Bar (Member, Litigation Section). *PRACTICE AREAS:* Business Litigation.

**STEVEN A. BERLINER,** born Detroit, Michigan, March 17, 1964; admitted to bar, 1991, California; 1992, U.S. Court of Appeals for the District of Columbia Circuit; 1993, U.S. District Court, Central District of California. *Education:* Wesleyan University (B.A., 1986); University of California at Los Angeles (J.D., 1990). Recipient, American Jurisprudence Award in Criminal Law. Extern for the Honorable Harry Pergerson, U.S. Court of Appeals, Ninth Circuit, 1988. Articles Editor and Member, Federal Communication Law Journal, 1989-1990. *Member:* American Bar Association; State Bar of California.

**DAVID EUM,** born Seoul, South Korea, August 3, 1961; admitted to bar, 1993, California and U.S. District Court, Central District of California; 1994, Utah. *Education:* University of California at Los Angeles (B.S., 1984); Georgetown University (M.S., 1987); J. Reuben Clark School of Law, Brigham Young University (J.D., 1993); Marriott School of Management, Brigham Young University (M.B.A., 1993). *Member:* State Bar of California; Utah State Bar. *LANGUAGES:* Korean.

**STEPHEN T. HODGE,** born Sacramento, California, September 13, 1963; admitted to bar, 1992, California and U.S. Claims Court; 1993, U.S. Court of Appeals, Ninth Circuit and U.S. District Court, Central and Southern Districts of California; 1995, U.S. Supreme Court. *Education:* Brigham Young University (B.S., 1988); J. Reuben Clark Law School, Brigham Young University (J.D., 1991). Phi Delta Phi (Magister, 1990-1991). Member, Brigham Young University National Moot Court Team, 1990-1991. Conference Editor, BYU Journal of Law & Education, 1990-1991. Law Clerk to Hon. Moody R. Tidwell, U.S. Claims Court, 1991-1992.

**JOHN C. STEELE,** born Provo, Utah, October 3, 1967; admitted to bar, 1995, California and U.S. District Court, Central District of California. *Education:* Brigham Young University (B.A., magna cum laude, 1992); J. Reuben Clark Law School, Brigham Young University (J.D., cum laude, 1995). Member, Jessup International Moot Court Team. Executive Editor, BYU Journal of Public Law. *Member:* State Bar of California. *LANGUAGES:* Korean.

---

## WEINHART & RILEY

*Established in 1992*

*12424 WILSHIRE BOULEVARD*
*SUITE 1200*
**LOS ANGELES, CALIFORNIA 90025**
*Telephone: 310-207-1234*
*Fax: 310-207-3775*

*Real Estate Litigation, Real Estate and Business Transactions, Commercial Litigation, Secured Creditors Rights, Bankruptcy, Administrative Law and Title Insurance Defense.*

FIRM PROFILE: *Weinhart & Riley specializes in representing financial institutions, master and special servicers of mortgage-backed securities, real estate developers, entrepreneurs and other businesses in connection with their real estate finance and commercial, employment and bankruptcy litigation needs. The firm has full-service capabilities in the area of real estate transactions, loan workouts and other corporate and business matters. The firm's lawyers also represent numerous community care facilities and mental health professionals in administrative and civil proceedings.*

**GRANT K. RILEY,** born Los Angeles, California, February 16, 1956; admitted to bar, 1984, California and U.S. District Court, Central, Eastern, Northern and Southern Districts of California. *Education:* University of California at Davis (B.A. Rhetoric, 1979); Southwestern University School of Law (J.D., cum laude, 1984). Associate Editor, Southwestern University Law Review. Recipient, American Jurisprudence Awards: Contracts, Real

*(This Listing Continued)*

Property and Antitrust. Associate, 1988, Litigation Partner, 1992, Christensen, White, Miller, Fink & Jacobs. Author: "It Ain't Over Till Its Over: Attacking The Private Retirement Plan Exemption, "Los Angeles County Bar Association PPRS Newsletter, Spring, 1995. *Member:* Los Angeles County (Executive Committee, Provisional and Post-Judgement Remedies Section) Bar Association; State Bar of California. *PRACTICE AREAS:* Real Estate Litigation; Bankruptcy; Secured Creditors Rights.

**BRIAN S. WEINHART,** born Los Angeles, California, September 26, 1960; admitted to bar, 1985, California and U.S. District Court, Central District of California. *Education:* University of Southern California (B.A. Philosophy, 1982; J.D., 1985). Member, Hale Moot Court. *Member:* State Bar of California; State Bar of California. *PRACTICE AREAS:* Real Estate Transactions; Business Transactions.

**LINDA RANDLETT KOLLAR,** born Malden, Massachusetts, November 24, 1944; admitted to bar, 1986, California; 1988, U.S. District Court, Central District of California and U.S. Court of Appeals, Ninth Circuit. *Education:* Scripps College (B.A. American Studies, 1966); Pepperdine University (J.D., cum laude, 1985). Phi Delta Phi; Order of Barristers. Member, 1983-1985 and Editor in Chief, 1984-1985, Pepperdine Law Review. Outstanding Young Woman of America. Who's Who in American Law Schools. Extern, California Court of Appeals, Second District, Sixth Division. Author: Note "Up or Out and Into the Supreme Court: A Forecast for Hishon v. King & Spalding," 11 Pepperdine L. Rev. 391, 1984; Note "California Supreme Court Survey," 11 Pepperdine L. Rev. 221, 1984; Comment, "Easton v. Strassburger: A Red Flag for California Real Estate Brokers," 20 B.H.B.J. 12, 1986. *Member:* Los Angeles County and American Bar Associations; State Bar of California. *PRACTICE AREAS:* Administrative Law; Commercial Litigation.

**WILLIAM W. STECKBAUER,** born Los Angeles, California, December 10, 1958; admitted to bar, 1984, California and U.S. District Court, Central District of California; 1986, U.S. Court of Appeals, Ninth Circuit. *Education:* University of California at Los Angeles (B.A., 1980); Southwestern University School of Law (J.D., 1984). Research Editor, 1983-1984 and Staff Member, 1982-1983, Southwestern University Law Review. *Member:* Los Angeles County Bar Association; State Bar of California. *PRACTICE AREAS:* Civil Litigation.

### ASSOCIATES

**DARIA A. DUB,** born Sewickley, Pennsylvania, June 26, 1965; admitted to bar, 1990, California and U.S. District Court, Central and Eastern Districts of California; 1991, Pennsylvania. *Education:* University of Pittsburgh (B.A. Philosophy, Rhetoric and Communications, magna cum laude, 1987); Pepperdine University (J.D., 1990). Recipient: American Jurisprudence Award in Uniform Commercial Code, Article II; West Publishing Company, Scholastic Achievement Award. *Member:* State Bar of California; Pennsylvania Bar Association; Los Angeles Bankruptcy Forum; Financial Lawyers Conference,. *PRACTICE AREAS:* Bankruptcy; Secured Creditor's Rights.

**ANTHONY E. GOLDSMITH,** born Los Angeles, California, August 20, 1960; admitted to bar, 1986, California. *Education:* University of California at Los Angeles (B.A., 1982); University of Southern California (J.D., 1986). Phi Beta Kappa. *Member:* Los Angeles County and American Bar Associations; State Bar of California. *PRACTICE AREAS:* Business Law; Real Property Law.

**MARGARET W. WOLFE,** born New Castle, Pennsylvania, September 6, 1945; admitted to bar, 1990, California. *Education:* University of Texas, Austin (B.A., 1967; M.L.S., Information Science, 1971); University of Southern California (J.D., 1990). Member, Hale Moot Court Honors Program. *Member:* State Bar of California.

**SUSAN M. FREEDMAN,** born Wilmington, Delaware, October 26, 1959; admitted to bar, 1991, California and U.S. District Court, Central District of California; 1992, U.S. Court of Appeals, Ninth Circuit. *Education:* Mount St. Mary's College (B.A., cum laude, 1987); Loyola Marymount University (J.D., 1990). Delta Sigma Chi. Extern for the Honorable Samuel L. Bufford, U.S. Bankruptcy Court, Central District of California, 1988. Law Clerk to the Honorable Samuel L. Bufford, U.S. Bankruptcy Court Judge, Central District of California, 1990-1991. *Member:* Los Angeles County and American (Member, Sections on: Business Law; General Practice; Litigation; Tort and Insurance Practice) Bar Associations; State Bar of California. *PRACTICE AREAS:* Business Litigation.

REPRESENTATIVE CLIENTS: Bank of America; Marine Midland Bank; Wells Fargo Bank; GE Capital; America Honda Finance; Crown Northcorp; Watson & Associates; Joigg Enterprises; FEDCO, Inc.; State Street Bank and Trust;

*(This Listing Continued)*

CAA1279B

WEINHART & RILEY, Los Angeles—Continued

Downey Savings; The Alexander Haagen Co.; Travelers Express; Fidelity National Title Insurance Co.; Benefit Land Title Company; R.W. Selby & Co.; Group Dynamics, Inc.; Walden Environment, Inc.; Children's Baptist Homes of Southern California and Florence Crittenden Center.

## WEINSTEIN, BOLDT, RACINE, HALFHIDE & CAMEL

PROFESSIONAL CORPORATION

Established in 1982

1801 CENTURY PARK EAST, SUITE 2200
LOS ANGELES, CALIFORNIA 90067-2336
Telephone: 310-203-8466
Cable Address: "Swbrtax"
Telex: 701-793
Telecopy: 310-552-7938

*Federal and State Taxation, Employee Benefits, Estate Planning and Business Transactions.*

**DAVID A. WEINSTEIN,** born Buffalo, New York, May 17, 1947; admitted to bar, 1973, New York; 1975, California. *Education:* State University of New York at Buffalo (B.A., 1969); Syracuse University (J.D., 1972); New York University (LL.M. in Taxation, 1973). Professor of Law, Taxation of Individuals, Golden Gate University, 1981-1986. Instructor, Corporate Taxation, University of California at Los Angeles, 1986—. *Member:* Beverly Hills, Los Angeles County and American Bar Associations; State Bar of California. **PRACTICE AREAS:** Tax; Estate Planning.

**RONALD M. BOLDT,** born Rupert, Idaho, December 6, 1947; admitted to bar, 1977, California. *Education:* University of California at Los Angeles (A.B., 1970; M.S., 1973); University of California at Davis (J.D., 1977); New York University (LL.M., in Taxation, 1980). Order of the Coif. Adjunct Professor of Law, University of San Diego School of Law, 1982-1984. *Member:* Los Angeles County and American Bar Associations; State Bar of California. **PRACTICE AREAS:** Tax; Business Law; Business Transactions.

**SCOTT H. RACINE,** born Chicago, Illinois, March 26, 1951; admitted to bar, 1978, California. *Education:* Bradley University (B.A., 1972); Pepperdine University (J.D., cum laude, 1978); New York University (LL.M., in Taxation, 1979). Student Writings Editor, Pepperdine Law Review, 1976-1978. Law Clerk to Judge William M. Drennen, United States Tax Court, 1979-1980. Adjunct Professor of Law: Pepperdine University School of Law, 1980—; University of San Diego School of Law, 1983-1987. Co-Author: "Corporate Compensation," 31 Major Tax Planning, 1981. Author: "Tax Consequences to Borrowers, Lenders and Investors," Ch. 28 Law of Distressed Real Estate, 1985. *Member:* State Bar of California; American Bar Association. **PRACTICE AREAS:** Tax; Business Law; Business Transactions.

**ROGER G. HALFHIDE,** born Rochester, Minnesota, May 28, 1954; admitted to bar, 1980, California; 1983, New York. *Education:* University of California, Davis (B.A., 1976); McGeorge School of Law, University of the Pacific (J.D. with distinction, 1979); New York University (LL.M., in Taxation, 1980). Lecturer, California State University at Long Beach, 1982. Adjunct Professor of Law, University of San Diego School of Law, 1985-1989. Lecturer of Law, University of California at Los Angeles Paralegal Program, 1985-1991. *Member:* State Bar of California; New York State Bar Association. **PRACTICE AREAS:** Tax; Pensions; Estate Planning.

**DAVID J. CAMEL,** born St. Louis, Missouri, July 9, 1957; admitted to bar, 1983, Texas; 1985, California. *Education:* University of California at Los Angeles (B.A., summa cum laude, 1979); Harvard University (J.D., 1983). Phi Beta Kappa. Law Clerk to Judge Arthur L. Nims III, U.S. Tax Court, 1983-1985. *Member:* State Bar of California; State Bar of Texas (Member, Tax Section). **PRACTICE AREAS:** Tax.

**M. KATHARINE DAVIDSON,** born Lubbock, Texas, January 22, 1952; admitted to bar, 1984, California; 1985, District of Columbia. *Education:* University of Southern California (B.A., cum laude, 1974); Loyola Marymount University (J.D., 1984, St. Thomas More Law Honor Society). Managing Editor, Loyola of Los Angeles Law Review, 1983-1984. Law Clerk to Judge Mary Ann Cohen, U.S. Tax Court, 1984-1985. *Member:* Los Angeles County (Member: Section on Taxation, Chair, 1994-1995; Tax Procedure and Litigation Committee) and American (Member, Section on

*(This Listing Continued)*

Taxation) Bar Associations; State Bar of California (Member, Section on Taxation). **PRACTICE AREAS:** Tax.

### OF COUNSEL

**THOMAS N. LAWSON,** born Lincoln, Nebraska, March 24, 1952; admitted to bar, 1977, Nebraska; 1980, California. *Education:* University of Nebraska at Lincoln (B.S., with high distinction, 1974; J.D., with distinction, 1976); New York University (LL.M., in Taxation, 1978). Beta Gamma Sigma; Phi Eta Sigma; Order of the Coif; Delta Theta Phi. Assistant Editor, Nebraska Law Review, 1975-1976. Instructor, New York University School of Law, Graduate Tax Program, 1978-1979. *Member:* Los Angeles County, Nebraska State and American (Member, Corporate Tax Committee, Section of Taxation) Bar Associations; The State Bar of California. **PRACTICE AREAS:** Tax.

REFERENCE: City National Bank (Los Angeles, Calif.)

## WEINSTEIN & EISEN

A PROFESSIONAL CORPORATION

Established in 1992

1925 CENTURY PARK EAST
SUITE 1150
LOS ANGELES, CALIFORNIA 90067-2712
Telephone: 310-203-9393
Fax: 310-203-8110

*Bankruptcy, Insolvency, Reorganization and Creditors Rights.*

**DAVID R. WEINSTEIN,** born Glen Cove, New York, June 20, 1952; admitted to bar, 1978, California. *Education:* Syracuse University (B.S., with honors, 1974); University of Southern California (J.D., 1978). Beta Gamma Sigma; Phi Kappa Phi. *Member:* San Fernando Valley, Century City, Beverly Hills and Los Angeles County Bar Associations; State Bar of California.

**DEBORAH H. EISEN,** born Kansas City, Missouri, 1955; admitted to bar, 1983, California. *Education:* Brown University; University of California at Berkeley (B.A., 1978); Cornell University (J.D., 1982). Phi Beta Kappa. Associate, 1980-1981 and Note Editor, 1981-1982, Cornell Law Review. Law Clerk to the Hon. Robert E. Coyle, U.S. District Court, Eastern District of California, 1982-1983. *Member:* Los Angeles County Bar Association (Member, Commercial Law and Bankruptcy Section); Financial Lawyers Conference.

**HOWARD S. LEVINE,** born New York, N.Y., November 20, 1959; admitted to bar, 1988, California. *Education:* Brooklyn College (B.A., 1981); Cardozo School of Law (J.D., cum laude, 1988). Moot Court Honors. Extern to the Honorable Carol B. Amon, Eastern District of New York, 1987. *Member:* Century City and Los Angeles County (Member, Sections on: Commercial Law and Bankruptcy and Litigation) Bar Associations; State Bar of California; Financial Lawyers Conference; Los Angeles Bankruptcy Forum.

**BRUCE S. SCHILDKRAUT,** born New York, New York, January 21, 1963; admitted to bar, 1988, Pennsylvania, California and U.S. District Court, Eastern District of Pennsylvania; 1989, U.S. District Court, Central District of California and U.S. Court of Appeals, Third Circuit; 1994, U.S. District Court, Eastern District of California. *Education:* Muhlenberg College (B.A., 1983); Temple University School of Law (J.D., 1986). Law Clerk to the Honorable Lisa Hill Fenning, 1986-1987 and to the Honorable Robert L. Eisen, 1987-1988, Bankruptcy Judges for the Central District of California. *Member:* Pennsylvania and American Bar Associations; State Bar of California; Commercial Law League. [U.S. Army, 2960-1963, (E-3)]

**C. JOHN MELISSINOS,** born Rochester, New York, August 27, 1964; admitted to bar, 1990, California; 1991, U.S. District Court, Central, Southern and Eastern Districts of California. *Education:* Cornell University (B.A., cum laude, in history, 1986); University of California at Los Angeles (J.D., 1989).

CAA1280B

# PROFESSIONAL BIOGRAPHIES

CALIFORNIA—LOS ANGELES

## WEINSTOCK, FEINBERG, MINDEL & KLINE
12400 WILSHIRE BOULEVARD, 4TH FLOOR
LOS ANGELES, CALIFORNIA 90025-1023
Telephone: 310-447-8675
Facsimile: 310-447-8678

*General Civil Litigation, Family Law.*

### MEMBERS OF FIRM

**IRWIN FEINBERG,** born Los Angeles, California, November 14, 1954; admitted to bar, 1979, California; 1980, U.S. District Court, Central, Southern and Northern Districts of California. *Education:* University of California at Los Angeles (B.A., 1976); University of California at Davis (J.D., 1979). Law Clerk to the Hon. Bertram D. Janes, California Court of Appeals, Third Appellate District, 1978-1979. *Member:* Los Angeles County and American Bar Associations; State Bar of California (Member, Commission to Study the Assimilation of New Lawyers into the Profession, 1979); California Young Lawyers Association; Commercial Law League of America.

**BRUCE J. WEINSTOCK,** born Los Angeles, California, February 17, 1951; admitted to bar, 1977, California. *Education:* University of Colorado at Boulder (B.A., 1974); Tulane University of Louisiana (J.D., 1977). *Member:* Los Angeles County and American Bar Associations; State Bar of California. *PRACTICE AREAS:* Business Law; Real Estate; Entertainment Law; Civil Practice.

**STEVEN A. MINDEL,** born Phoenix, Arizona, January 25, 1959; admitted to bar, 1985, California, U.S. District Court, Central District of California and U.S. Court of Appeals, Ninth Circuit. *Education:* University of California at Los Angeles (B.A., magna cum laude, 1981); University of Southern California (J.D., 1985). Member: Board of Directors, Los Angeles Free Clinic, 1995-1996; Legal Advisory Board Los Angeles Free Clinic, 1993-1996. Past President and Member, Board of Directors, American Gemological Society, Southern California Guild, 1990-1996. *Member:* Los Angeles County Bar Association (Member, Family Law Section); State Bar of California (Member, Family Law Section). *PRACTICE AREAS:* Family Law; General Civil Litigation.

**JEREMY B. KLINE,** born Los Angeles, California, March 8, 1961; admitted to bar, 1985, California, U.S. District Court, Central District of California and U.S. Court of Appeals, Ninth Circuit. *Education:* University of California at Los Angeles (B.A., cum laude, 1982); University of Southern California Law Center (J.D., 1985). Phi Alpha Delta. *Member:* Los Angeles County (Member, Real Property Section) and American (Member, Law Practice Management Section) Bar Associations; State Bar of California. *PRACTICE AREAS:* General Civil Litigation; Family Law.

### ASSOCIATES

**MARITONI ACOSTA,** born Quezon City, Philippines, April 30, 1969; admitted to bar, 1995, California. *Education:* University of California at Los Angeles (B.A., Political Sciences, 1991); Loyola Marymount University (J.D., 1994). *Member:* Los Angeles County Bar Association. *PRACTICE AREAS:* General Civil Litigation; Family Law.

**LINDA FENTON,** born Los Angeles, California, August 27, 1960; admitted to bar, 1987, California and U.S. District Court, Central District of California. *Education:* University of California at Berkeley (B.A., 1984); Whittier College (J.D., 1986). *Member:* State Bar of California. *PRACTICE AREAS:* General Civil Litigation; Construction Defect; Personal Injury.

## WEINSTOCK, MANION, REISMAN, SHORE & NEUMANN
A LAW CORPORATION
*Established in 1959*
SUITE 800, 1888 CENTURY PARK EAST (CENTURY CITY)
LOS ANGELES, CALIFORNIA 90067
Telephone: 310-553-8844
Los Angeles: 213-879-4481
Fax: 310-553-5165

*Estate Planning, Trust and Probate, Taxation, Corporate, Partnership, Real Property, General Business Law, Civil and Trust Litigation.*

**BRIAN G. MANION** (Retired).

*(This Listing Continued)*

**HAROLD WEINSTOCK,** born Stamford, Connecticut, November 30, 1925; admitted to bar, 1950, Connecticut; 1951, Illinois; 1953, U.S. Tax Court; 1955, U.S. Supreme Court; 1958, California. *Education:* New York University (B.S., 1947); Harvard University (J.D., 1950). Recipient, Arthur K. Marshall Award for outstanding contribution in Trust and Estate Law, Los Angeles County Bar Association, 1996. Listed in The Best Lawyers in America. Author: *Planning an Estate A Guidebook of Principles and Techniques,* Clerk, Boardman & Callaghan, 4th edition 1995 (Supplemented annually); "Grats, Gruts and Grits," 51 New York University of Federal Taxation, 16-1; "Factors to Consider in Selecting a Trustee," UCLA Estate Planning Institute 193, 1991; "Why Exempt Interstate Commerce?," 19 George Washington Law Review 613; "Buy-Sell Agreements," 105 Trusts and Estates, 338; "Considerations in Designating the Beneficiaries Under A Life Insurance Policy," 105 Trusts and Estates, 679; "How to Avoid Probate— A Tax Analysis," 26 Journal of Taxation 38; "Charitable Gifts and Trusts," 30 Journal of Taxation 238. Co-Author, "Accumulation Trusts and Charitable Remainder Trusts," 23 U.S.C. Tax Institute 501; "The A B C's of Generation Skipping Trusts," 52 Taxes 68; "Trusts: Planning For College Education of Children," 1 UCLA Estate Planning Institute 59; "Beyond Freezes: Planning to Reduce the Taxable Estate," 16 Miami University Institute on Estate Planning 500; "The Marital Deduction: Beyond The Basics," 35 U.S.C. Tax Institute 1000; "Private Lead Trusts and Life Estate-Remainder Interest Purchases," UCLA Estate Planning Institute 409, 1983; "Irrevocable Insurance Trusts," 10 Estate Planning 258; "Nontaxable Grantor and Beneficiary Powers," 43 N.Y.U. Inst. on Fed. Tax. 51-1; "Sales and Purchases of Remainder Interests and Grantor Income Trusts," 45 N.Y.U Inst. on Fed. Tax. 28-1; "The Marital Deduction: A Planning Update," 41 U.S.C. 18-1. Attorney, Securities and Exchange Commission, 1950-1952. Special Attorney, Office of Chief Counsel, Internal Revenue Service, 1952-1956. *Member:* Beverly Hills (Chairman, Probate and Trust Committee, 1967-1968), Los Angeles County and American Bar Associations; The State Bar of California. Fellow, American College of Trust and Estate Counsel. (Certified Specialist, Taxation Law and Probate, Estate Planning and Trust Law, The State Bar of California Board of Legal Specialization). *PRACTICE AREAS:* Estate Planning Law; Probate Law; Taxation Law.

**LOUIS A. REISMAN,** born Chicago, Illinois, January 3, 1945; admitted to bar, 1970, Illinois; 1972, California and U.S. District Court, Central District of California; 1980, U.S. Tax Court. *Education:* University of Illinois (B.S., with honors, 1967); Northwestern University (J.D., 1970). Phi Alpha Delta. President, Julius H. Miner Moot Court Board. Co-Author: "How to Handle Tax Aspects of Retirement Plan Disposition on Divorce," Prentice-Hall, 1978; "Employee Benefit Plans and Divorce: Type of Plan, Date of Retirement and Income Tax Consequences as Factors in Dispositions," 5 Community Property Journal, 179, 1979; "More Ways to Divide the Retirement Plan," California State Bar Family Law News, Vol. 3, No. 1. Author: "Pension Rules and Probate Practice - The New Rules and Aggravation," USC Probate and Trust Conference, 1987. Certified Public Accountant, Illinois, 1967 and California, 1973. Faculty Member, UCLA Extension, 1975—. *Member:* Beverly Hills, Los Angeles County and American Bar Associations; The State Bar of California. *PRACTICE AREAS:* Taxation Law; Business Law; Estate Planning Law.

**SUSSAN H. SHORE,** born Alingsas, Sweden, August 18, 1952; admitted to bar, 1976, California; 1977, U.S. Tax Court and U.S. District Court, Central District of California; 1991, U.S. Supreme Court. *Education:* University of California at Los Angeles (B.A., cum laude, 1973) Loyola University (J.D., 1976). Listed in The Best Lawyers in America. Co-Author: "Outright NonCharitable Gifts," California Will Drafting Practice, Third Ed. California Continuing Education of the Bar. "Grantor Income Trusts - A New Tool to Save Estate Taxes," Trust & Tax Forum - TSA, 1985; "Recent Developments in Tax Practice," Continuing Education of the Bar, 1984, 1985. Faculty Member, Estate Planning, UCLA Extension 1982—. Member: Taxation Subcommittee of CEB Joint Advisory Committee, 1986—; Planning Committee for USC Probate and Trust Conference; Beverly Hills Estate Planning Council. *Member:* Beverly Hills (Chairman, Probate and Trust Committee, 1985-1986), Los Angeles County (Chairman, Trusts and Estates Section, 1994-1995) and American (Member, Real Property, Probate and Trust Law Section) Bar Associations; The State Bar of California. Fellow, American College of Trust and Estate Counsel. (Certified Specialist, Probate, Estate Planning and Trust Law, The State Bar of California Board of Legal Specialization). *PRACTICE AREAS:* Estate and Trust Administration; Estate Planning Law; Probate Litigation; Pre Marital Planning.

**MARTIN A. NEUMANN,** born Toronto, Ontario, Canada, January 29, 1957; admitted to bar, 1981, California. *Education:* University of California

*(This Listing Continued)*

CAA1281B

## WEINSTOCK, MANION, REISMAN, SHORE & NEUMANN, A LAW CORPORATION, Los Angeles—Continued

at Los Angeles (B.A., summa cum laude, 1978; J.D., 1981). Phi Beta Kappa. Author: "The Generation-Skipping Transfer Tax - Two Years Later--Coping with Technical Corrections," 47 NYU Inst. on Federal Taxation. Co-Author: "Outright NonCharitable Gifts," California Will Drafting Practice, Third Ed., California Continuing Education of the Bar. Speaker, "Estate Planning for Larger Estates," USC Tax Institute, 1990. "Estate Freezes Outside of Chapter 14" 52nd New York Institute on Federal Taxation. Adjunct Professor of Law, University of San Diego School of Law, 1984-1986. Faculty Member, Beginning and Advanced Estate Planning, UCLA Extension, 1987—. *Member:* Beverly Hills and Century City (Chairman, Estate Planning Section, 1990-1991) Bar Associations; State Bar of California. **PRACTICE AREAS:** Taxation Law; Estate Planning Law; Business Law.

**MARC L. SALLUS,** born Washington, D.C., September 14, 1954; admitted to bar, 1979, California. *Education:* Claremont Men's College (B.A., cum laude, 1976); Hastings College of the Law, University of California (J.D., 1979). Order of the Coif. Member, Thurston Society. Research Editor, Hastings International and Comparative Law Review (Special Edition-Japan), 1978-1979. Co-Author: Will Contest Chapter, CEB's Decedents Estate Practice, Vol. 3. Member, CEB Probate/Estate Planning Advisory Subcommittee. *Member:* Los Angeles County (Member: Executive Committee, 1986-1988; Board of Trustees, 1986-1988; Barristers, President, 1987-1988; Chairperson, Committee on the ABA, 1993-1995; Chairperson, Committee on the State Bar, 1992-1993; Member: Litigation Section; Executive Committee, 1987-1990) Beverly Hills (Member: Probate Section; Executive Committee, 1986—) , American (Chairperson, ABA Center on Children and the Law Advisory Board, 1985-1986, 1988-1990; Family Law Section; Council, 1988-1990, Chair, Task Force on Children Needs and Juvenile Justice Committee, 1990-1993) and Mexican American (Member: Board of Trustees, 1993-1996 ; Historian, 1995-1996; Treasurer, 1997—) Bar Associations. **PRACTICE AREAS:** Civil Litigation; Probate; Trust Litigation.

**ROBERT E. STRAUSS,** born Modesto, California, February 17, 1964; admitted to bar, 1990, California, U.S. Tax Court and U.S. District Court, Central District of California. *Education:* Harvard University (A.B., magna cum laude, 1986); University of California at Los Angeles (J.D.,1990). *Member:* Los Angeles County Bar Association; State Bar of California. **PRACTICE AREAS:** Corporate; Business; Tax; Estate Planning.

**SUSAN ABRAHAM,** born Brooklyn, New York, March 12, 1957; admitted to bar, 1986, California; 1987, U.S. District Court, Central District of California. *Education:* Indiana University (B.S., with highest distinction, 1979); University of Denver (M.S., 1980); University of California at Los Angeles (J.D., 1986). Order of the Coif. Distinguished Advocate, Moot Court Competition. Recipient, American Jurisprudence Awards for Wills and Trusts and Legal Professions. Co-Author: "Transfers to Noncitizen Spouses Significantly Affected by RRA '89," The Journal of Taxation, May, 1990. *Member:* Los Angeles County and American Bar Associations; State Bar of California. **PRACTICE AREAS:** Estate Planning and Probate Law.

---

**GORDON H. EINSTEIN,** born Los Angeles, California, August 6, 1969; admitted to bar, 1995, California. *Education:* Brandeis University (B.A., 1991); University of Southern California (J.D., 1995). Recipient, American Jurisprudence Awards. *Member:* State Bar of California. **LANGUAGES:** German. **PRACTICE AREAS:** General Practice; Business Law; Corporate Law.

### OF COUNSEL

**GARY M. BOROFSKY,** born Chicago, Illinois, May 28, 1944; admitted to bar, 1971, California and U.S. District Court, Central District of California; U.S. Tax Court. *Education:* University of California at Los Angeles (B.S., 1966; M.S., 1967; J.D., 1970). Beta Gamma Sigma. Co-Author: "How to Handle the Deduction for Amortization of Customer Lists," Prentice Hall Tax Ideas Service, April, 1979. *Member:* Beverly Hills (Member, Committees on: Probate and Trust Law, 1971—; Taxation, 1971—; Chairman, 1976-1977, Law Practice Management Committee); Los Angeles County and American (Member, Section on Taxation) Bar Associations; The State Bar of California. (Certified Specialist, Taxation Law, The State Bar of California Board of Legal Specialization) (Also Member, Borofsky & Solarz, Los Angeles, California). **PRACTICE AREAS:** Corporate; Business; Tax; Estate Planning; Probate/Trusts.

*(This Listing Continued)*

**M. NEIL SOLARZ,** born Los Angeles, California, December 30, 1952; admitted to bar, 1977, California; 1979, U.S. Court of Appeals, Ninth Circuit. *Education:* University of California at Los Angeles (B.A., magna cum laude, 1974); University of San Francisco (J.D., magna cum laude, 1977). Phi Beta Kappa; Pi Gamma Mu. Member, McAuliffe Honor Society. *Member:* State Bar of California. (Certified specialist, Estate Planning, Trust and Probate Law, The State Bar of California Board of Legal Specialization) (Also Member, Borofsky & Solarz, Los Angeles, California). **PRACTICE AREAS:** Estate Planning; Probate/Trusts; Corporate; Business; Tax.

REFERENCES: City National Bank (Century City); Wells Fargo Bank (Beverly Hills Main Office); Northern Trust Bank of California; Sanwa Bank California; Bank of America (Century City).

---

## WEISMAN & ROSEN

Established in 1989

1900 AVENUE OF THE STARS, SUITE 1800
**LOS ANGELES, CALIFORNIA 90067**
Telephone: 310-788-7000
Fax: 310-788-7010

*Business Litigation.*

**FIRM PROFILE:** *The Weisman & Rosen Law Firm is a law firm which concentrates on representing clients in sophisticated and complex business litigation.*

*The firm currently is comprised of 8 lawyers, all of whom are litigators. The Weisman & Rosen Law Firm's attorneys have developed a particular expertise in the following specialized areas of litigation: securities, directors and officers, financial institutions, defense contractors, insurance coverage, partnership, class action, business tort and real estate litigation in federal and state trial and appellate courts.*

**MARK L. WEISMAN,** born Duluth, Minnesota, June 8, 1944; admitted to bar, 1970, California and U.S. District Court, Northern, Central and Southern Districts of California; 1977, U.S. Court of Appeals, 9th Circuit. *Education:* University of Southern California (B.A., 1966; J.D., 1969). Member, 1967-1968 and Note and Comment Editor, 1968-1969, Southern California Law Review. Author: "The Financial Responsibility Laws vs. Liability Insurance Cancellation," 41 Southern California Law Review 367, 1968. Law Clerk to Judge David W. Williams, U.S. District Court, Central District of California, 1969-1970. Judge Pro Tem: Small Claims, Beverly Hills, 1977-1979, Civil Trials, Los Angeles Municipal Court, 1978-1979 and Los Angeles Superior Court, West District, 1987-1990. *Member:* Beverly Hills and Los Angeles County (Member, Los Angeles Superior Courts Committee, 1976-1978) Bar Associations; The State Bar of California. **LANGUAGES:** Spanish. **PRACTICE AREAS:** Business Litigation; Intellectual Property; Financial Institutions; Real Estate; Environmental.

**PETER K. ROSEN,** born Toronto, Canada, December 13, 1954; admitted to bar, 1978, California. *Education:* Occidental College, University of California at Los Angeles (B.A., 1975); University of Southern California (M.P.A., 1978; J.D., 1978). Author: "Linking the Office With a Local Area Network" (CA Lawyer, November, 1991); "To Make the Best Use of Computerized Litigation Support, You Need To Know What's Available," (CA Lawyer, February 1991); "Computer-Assisted Legal Research Can Make Short Work of a Tough Job--If You Know Where To Look," (Ca Lawyer, August 1990); "A Review of Litigation Support Programs," (CaliGrams, August 1989); "A Look at Retrieval, Abstracting and Indexing Programs," (CA Lawyer, April 1990); "Confessions of a PC Junkie," (CA Lawyer, October 1990). Member, Southern California Law Review, 1977-1978. *Member:* Los Angeles County and American Bar Associations; State Bar of California. **REPORTED CASES:** Nicolet, Inc. v. Superior Court (Insurance Co. of North America) 188 Cal. App.3d 28 (Cal. Ap. 1d 1986); Estate of Linnick 171 Cal. App. 3d 752 (Cal. Ap. 2 Dist. 1985); Blue Chip Properties v. Permanent Rent Control Bd. of City of Santa Monica, 170 Cal. App.3d 648 (Cal. Ap. 2 Dist. 1985); Santa Monica Pines, Ltd. v. Rent Control Bd. of City of Santa Monica, 35 Cal.3d 858 (Cal. 1984); Williams v. Hartford Ins. Co., 147 Ca. App.3d 893 (Cal.Ap. 2 Dist. 1983); ACC v. Baker, 22F. 3d 880 (9th Cir. 1994); Modzelewski v. RTC 14 F.3d 1374 (9th Cir. 1994), Cohen v. RTC, 61 F.3d 725 (9th Cir. 1995)); In re Consolidated Pinnacle West Securities Litigation 51 F.3d 194 (9th Cir. 1995); Keating v. National Union, 995 F. 2d 154 (9th Cir. 1993); RTC v. Liebert, 871 F. Supp. 370 (C.D. Cal. 1994); RTC v. Blasdell 154 F.R.D. 675 (D.Az. 1993); ACC v. Baker, 758 F.Supp. 1340 (C.D. Ca. 1991); FDIC v. Baker, 1991 WL 329757, (C.D. Ca. 1991); FDIC v. Israel, 739 F. Supp. 1411 (C.D. 1990); FDIC v. Baker, 739 F. Supp 1401 (C.D. Ca. 1990); FSLIC v. Israel, 686 F. Supp. 819 (C.D.Ca. 1988); Aetna. v. Dannenfeldt 778 F. Supp.. 484 (D. Az.

*(This Listing Continued)*

1991); RTC v. Wood 870 F. Supp. 797 (W.D. Tn. 1994); RTC v. Blasdell, 1994 WL 583131 (D. Az. 1994); McAllister v. FDIC, 87 F.3d 762 (5th Cir. 1996); FDIC v. Davidson, 92 F.3d 1503 (9th Cir. 1996). *PRACTICE AREAS:* Directors & Officers Litigation; Securities Litigation; Financial Institutions Litigation; Insurance Coverage; General Litigation. *Email:* prosen@earthlink.net

**DANA E. WEISMAN,** born Abilene, Texas, October 21, 1956; admitted to bar, 1980, California and U.S. District Court, Central and Southern Districts of California; 1981, U.S. Court of Appeals, Ninth Circuit. *Education:* Texas Tech University (B.B.A. in Accounting, 1977); University of Texas (J.D., 1980). Author: "Income and Gift Tax Consequences of Nonbusiness Interest-Free Loans: Looking A Gift Horse in the Mouth," 58 Taxes-The Tax Magazine 675-82, 1980. *Member:* Beverly Hills and Los Angeles County Bar Associations; The State Bar of California. *LANGUAGES:* Spanish. *PRACTICE AREAS:* State and Federal Court Litigation; Intellectual Property and Entertainment; Unfair Competition; Real Estate; Corporate Law; Entertainment.

**MARK P. LYNCH,** born Kansas City, Missouri, March 2, 1955; admitted to bar, 1986, New Mexico; 1988, California and U.S. District Court, Central District of California; 1994, U.S. District Court, Southern District of California; 1995, Arizona. *Education:* Miami University of Ohio; University of New Mexico; University of California at San Diego (B.A., magna cum laude 1978); Southwestern University (J.D., 1986). Law Clerk to Honorable Thomas A. Donnelly, New Mexico Court of Appeals, 1986-1987. Extern to the Honorable Robert M. Takasugi, U.S. District Court, Central District of California, 1986. *Member:* State Bar of California; State Bar of New Mexico; American Bar Association (Member, Litigation Section). *PRACTICE AREAS:* Business Litigation; Construction Defect; Financial Institutions; Insurance Coverage; Real Estate Litigation.

### ASSOCIATES

**JERI DYE LYNCH,** born Encino, California, January 7, 1960; admitted to bar, 1986, California, U.S. District Court, Central, Southern and Northern Districts of California and U.S. Court of Appeals for the Ninth and Federal Circuits. *Education:* University of Southern California (B.A., cum laude, 1981); Southwestern University School of Law (J.D., magna cum laude, 1986). Recipient, American Jurisprudence Award in Wills and Trust and Professional Responsibility. Member, 1984-1986 and Note and Comment Editor, 1985-1986, Southwestern Law Review. Author: Article, "Can Government Be Held Liable For the Savings & Loan Crisis?" National Law Journal, December 3, 1990. Extern to Hon. Eugene Wright, U.S. Court of Appeals, Ninth Circuit, 1985. *Member:* Los Angeles County (Member: Litigation Section; Animal Rights Committee) and American Bar Associations; State Bar of California. *LANGUAGES:* French and Spanish. *PRACTICE AREAS:* General Civil Litigation; Business Litigation; Insurance Coverage Litigation; Defense of Savings & Loan Executives; Professional Liability; Securities Litigation.

**BRAD S. KANE,** born Hollywood, California, March 19, 1965; admitted to bar, 1990, California; 1991, Alaska and U.S. District Court, District of Alaska; 1994, U.S. District Court, Central and Southern Districts of California; 1995, U.S. District Court, Northern District of California, District of Arizona and U.S. Court of Appeals, Fifth and Ninth Circuits. *Education:* University of California at Los Angeles (B.A., magna cum laude, Phi Beta Kappa, 1987); Hastings College of Law, University of California (J.D., 1990). Articles Editor, Hastings International & Comparative Law Review. Law Clerk to Chief Justice Jay A. Rabinowitz, Alaska Supreme Court, 1991 and Alaska Superior Court Judges Richard Savell and Jay Hedges, 1990-1991. Extern to U.S. District Court Judge Stanley A. Weigei, 1990. Lecturer, Real Property Law and Civil Procedure, University of Alaska at Fairbanks, 1992-1994. *PRACTICE AREAS:* Business Litigation; Appellate Practice.

**KENNETH G. RUTTENBERG,** born Los Angeles, California, April 26, 1967; admitted to bar, 1993, California and U.S. District Court, Central District of California. *Education:* University of California at San Diego (B.A., 1989); Loyola University of Los Angeles (J.D., 1993). Member, Loyola of Los Angeles Law Review, 1992-1993. *Member:* State Bar of California; Association of Business Trial Lawyers. *PRACTICE AREAS:* Civil Litigation; Business Litigation.

**LAWRENCE J. WALDINGER,** born New York, N.Y., July 21, 1968; admitted to bar, 1994, California and U.S. District Court, Central District of California. *Education:* Tufts University (B.A., cum laude, 1990); George Washington University (J.D., 1994). *PRACTICE AREAS:* Business Litigation; Corporate; Transactional Law.

## DAVID WEISS
**2551 COLORADO BOULEVARD**
**LOS ANGELES, CALIFORNIA 90041**
Telephone: 213-254-5020
Telecopier: 213-254-4538

*Technology, Patent, Trademark, and Copyright Law, Unfair Competition and Intellectual Property Law.*

**DAVID WEISS,** born New York, N.Y., January 31, 1935; admitted to bar, 1965, California; registered to practice before U.S. Patent and Trademark Office. *Education:* University of California at Los Angeles (B.S.,Engr., 1957; M.S.,Engr., 1959; J.D., 1964). Phi Alpha Delta. Legal and Patent Counsel, Bell & Howell Company, Pasadena, California, 1968-1983. *Member:* Los Angeles County Bar Association; State Bar of California (Member, Intellectual Property Section); Los Angeles Intellectual Property Law Association; American Electronics Association (Member, Los Angeles Lawyers Committee); Institute of Electrical and Electronics Engineers.

## WALTER S. WEISS
**12424 WILSHIRE BOULEVARD, NINTH FLOOR**
**LOS ANGELES, CALIFORNIA 90025**
Telephone: 310-207-6679
Fax: 310-207-6830

*Litigation Practice including Professional Negligence, Securities and Insurance Coverage Law.*

**WALTER S. WEISS,** born Newark, New Jersey, March 12, 1929; admitted to bar, 1952, District of Columbia; 1956, New Jersey and U.S. Supreme Court; 1961, California. *Education:* Rutgers University (A.B., 1949; LL.B., 1952). Trial Attorney, Office of the Regional Counsel, Internal Revenue Service, 1957-1962. Assistant U.S. Attorney, Chief Tax Division, Central District of California, 1962-1963. Author: "Tax Aspects of Sports and Entertainment Law," Counseling Professional Athletes and Entertainers-3D, Practicing Law Institute, New York, 1971; "Federal Tax Reform - The Need for Change in the Financing of Political Campaigns," Proceedings of Sixty-First National Tax Conference, National Tax Association, 1968; "Do Taxpayers Have Constitutional Rights?" Taxes, The Tax Magazine, August, 1968; "Special Tax Problems of Creators of Literary, Musical and Artistic Compositions," The 19th Annual Tax Forum, Title Insurance and Trust Company, 1967; "Special Agents Need Not Advise a Taxpayer of His Constitutional Rights," The Journal of Taxation, July, 1966; "Self-Incrimination and Income Tax Investigations," Taxes, October, 1964. Co-Author: "Tax Refunds Through Class Actions?" Los Angeles County Bar Bulletin, November, 1970; Chairman, California Continuing Education of the Bar Panels in Southern California and Hawaii, "Attorneys' Malpractice-Prevention and Current Aspects," February, 1973; "Attorneys' Malpractice-Errors and Omissions Update," June, 1974; Panel Member, California Continuing Education of the Bar Panel "Federal Tax Procedure for General Practitioners," September, 1968; "Tax Problems of Closely-Held Corporations and Their Shareholders," April, May, 1974; "Fundamentals of Civil Litigation During Trial, 1985, 1989, 1991, 1995; Panel Member, General Practice Section of the State Bar of California and the Errors and Omissions Prevention Committee of the Los Angeles County Bar Association Panel, "Lawyer Liability in the 1990's." Arbitrator: National Association of Securities Dealers, 1974—; Pacific Stock Exchange, 1977—. Chairman, State of California Advisory Council on Economic Development, 1983-1987. Judge Pro Tem, Los Angeles Municipal Court, 1996—. *Member:* Beverly Hills, Los Angeles County and American Bar Associations; The State Bar of California (Member, Executive Committee, General Practice Section, 1988-1989); Conference of Insurance Counsel (President, 1980; Vice-President and Member, Board of Directors, Attorneys Insurance Mutual Risk Retention Group, Ltd.; Chairman Investment Committee, 1992-1993). Fellow, American College of Trial Lawyers. [Capt., U.S. Air Force, JAG Dept., 1953-1956]

## LAW OFFICES OF
## DAVID J. WEISS
**LOS ANGELES, CALIFORNIA**

(See Santa Monica)

*Medical, Dental, Legal, Professional Liability, General Products Liability. General Civil and Trial Practice in all State and Federal Courts.*

## WEISS & HUMPHRIES
*A PROFESSIONAL CORPORATION*
**2049 CENTURY PARK EAST, SUITE 880**
**LOS ANGELES, CALIFORNIA 90067-3110**
Telephone: 310-843-2800; 714-548-4700
Facsimile: 310-843-2820
Email: weiss@weisslaw.com

*Newport Beach, California Office:* 610 Newport Center Drive, Suite 1010, 92658-7920. Telephone: 714-548-4700.

*Health Care, Business, Corporation, Commercial, Real Property.*

**MARK F. WEISS,** born January 8, 1954; admitted to bar, 1979, California and U.S. Tax Court. *Education:* University of California at Irvine (B.A., 1976); University of Southern California (J.D., 1979). Phi Alpha Delta. Author: "Kickbacks: Extracting a Prize for Your Right to Treat Patients," Bulletin of the California Society of Anesthesiologists, May-June, 1994; "Specialists and Managed Care: Strategies for Maximizing Opportunity," Hispanic Physician, Vol. V, 1995; "Does your Hospital's MSO Owe You a Fiduciary Duty?" Los Angeles County Medical Association Physician Magazine, September 18, 1995; "Assign of the Times: The Prohibition Against the Reassignment of Medicare and Medi-Cal Claims," Bulletin of the California Society of Anesthesiologists, September-October, 1995; "Beware of 'Standard' Contract Provisions," Los Angeles County Medical Association Physician Magazine, November 6, 1995. Co-Author, With Robin J. Humphries, "Sure I'll Agree to Arbitrate. 'I Just Don't Want to Waive Any of My Rights (And Other Fairy Tales)'," Bulletin of the California Society of Anesthesiologists, January-February, 1996; "Physician Recruiting Packages," Los Angeles County Medical Association Physician Magazine, June 17, 1996. "Physician Recruiting Packages," Los Angeles County Medical Association Physician Magazine, June 17, 1996; "Antifraud Aspects of the Health Insurance Portability & Accountability Act of 1996," Los Angeles County Medical Association Physician Magazine, October 7, 1996. Adjunct Professor, Taxation, American College of Law, 1982. Judge Pro-Tem, Beverly Hills Municipal Court, 1990—. *Member:* Beverly Hills, Los Angeles County (Treasurer, Executive Committee, Health Care Law Section) and American (Member, Health Law Forum and Section on Taxation) Bar Associations; The State Bar of California; National Health Lawyers Association; California Society for Healthcare Attorneys. *PRACTICE AREAS:* Healthcare; Corporate; Real Property; Business Law.

**ROBIN J. HUMPHRIES,** born Newport Beach, California, March 10, 1956; admitted to bar, 1984, California and U.S. District Court, Central District of California. *Education:* University of California, San Diego (B.A., cum laude, 1978); University of Southern California (J.D., 1984). Author: "Recent Developments in Directors' and Officers' Liability Insurance," Matthew Bender Health Care Law Newsletter, July, 1986; "Physician Recruiting Packages," Los Angeles County Medical Association Physician Magazine, June 17, 1996. Co-Author, with Mark F. Weiss: "Specialists and Managed Care: Strategies for Maximizing Opportunity," Hispanic Physician, Vol. V, 1995; "Does Your Hospital's MSO Owe You a Fiduciary Duty?" Los Angeles County Medical Association Physician Magazine, September 18, 1995; "Assign of the Times: The Prohibition Against the Reassignment of Medicare and Medi-Cal Claims," Bulletin of the California Society of Anesthesiologists, September-October, 1995; "Beware of 'Standard' Contract Provisions," Los Angeles County Medical Association Physician Magazine, November 6, 1995; "Sure I'll Agree to Arbitrate. 'I Just Don't Want to Waive Any of My Rights (And Other Fairy Tales)'," Bulletin of the California Society of Anesthesiologists, January-February, 1996. "Antifraud Aspects of the Health Insurance Portability & Accountability Act of 1996," Los Angeles, County Medical Association Physician Magazine, October 7, 1996. *Member:* Beverly Hills Bar Association; State Bar of California; Women Lawyers Association of Los Angeles; National Health Lawyers Association. *PRACTICE AREAS:* Corporate Law; Health Care Law.

## WEISS LAW CORPORATION
**1901 AVENUE OF THE STARS, 20TH FLOOR**
**LOS ANGELES, CALIFORNIA 90067**
Telephone: 310-282-8600
Fax: 310-785-0010

*Real Estate, Corporate, Bankruptcy, Civil Litigation, Estate Planning, Tax, Business and Commercial.*

**SAMUEL H. WEISS,** born Elizabeth, New Jersey, October 4, 1955; admitted to bar, 1978, California; U.S. Supreme Court, U.S. Court of Appeals, Ninth Circuit, U.S. District Court, Central, Eastern, Northern and Southern Districts of California and U.S. Tax Court. *Education:* University of California at Los Angeles (B.A., summa cum laude, 1975; M.A., J.D., 1978). Departmental Scholar in Economics. Phi Beta Kappa; Omicron Delta Epsilon; Pi Gamma Mu. John M. Olin Foundation Fellowship. *Member:* Beverly Hills and Los Angeles County Bar Associations; State Bar of California (Member, Business Law Section); Los Angeles Bankruptcy Forum; Financial Lawyers Conference. *LANGUAGES:* French.

## ROBERT E. WEISS
*INCORPORATED*
**LOS ANGELES, CALIFORNIA**
(See Covina)

*Real Estate, Corporation and mortgage Law.*

## WEISS, SCOLNEY, SPEES, DANKER & SHINDERMAN
**1875 CENTURY PARK EAST, SUITE 800**
**LOS ANGELES, CALIFORNIA 90067-4104**
Telephone: 310-785-1313
Fax: 310-785-1301

*General Civil and Trial Practice, Bankruptcy, Corporate, Tax, Business and Commercial Law.*

FIRM PROFILE: Weiss, Scolney, Spees, Danker & Shinderman is a general practice law firm which specializes in bankruptcy-related matters, including representation of debtors and creditors in title 11 proceedings and structuring work-outs for troubled businesses. The firm's practice also encompasses all aspects of business, commercial and securities litigation as well as tax, corporate and transactional matters.

**MICHAEL H. WEISS,** born Philadelphia, Pennsylvania, January 8, 1951; admitted to bar, 1982, California, U.S. District Court, Central, Eastern, Northern and Southern Districts of California. *Education:* New York University (B.A., magna cum laude, 1975); University of San Francisco (J.D., cum laude, 1982). Member, McAuliffe Honor Society. Law Clerk to the Hon. Barry Russell, Bankruptcy Judge, Central District of California, 1982-1983. Author: "Copyright Licensees and Bankruptcy," Los Angeles Lawyer, April, 1993. *Member:* Los Angeles County Bar Association (Member, Commercial Law and Bankruptcy Section); State Bar of California. *PRACTICE AREAS:* Bankruptcy Law.

**SHERRY D. SPEES,** born Philadelphia, Pennsylvania, November 11, 1956; admitted to bar, 1981 Pennsylvania; 1985, U.S. Tax Court; 1986, New York; 1987, California and U.S. District Court, Central and Southern Districts of California. *Education:* University of Pennsylvania (B.A., magna cum laude, 1977); Temple University (J.D., 1981); New York University (LL.M., Tax, 1983). Author: "Treatment of Federal Tax Claims In Bankruptcy," Tax Ideas, 1991. *Member:* State Bar of California. *PRACTICE AREAS:* Tax Law; Bankruptcy Law; Corporate Law.

**PETER N. SCOLNEY,** born Los Angeles, California, January 22, 1948; admitted to bar, 1979, California and U.S. District Court, Central District of California; 1981, U.S. Court of Appeals, Ninth Circuit; 1992, U.S. District Court, Southern District of California. *Education:* University of California at Los Angeles (B.A., 1969); California State University, Northridge (M.A., 1972); University of Southern California (M.Leg.S., 1977); Loyola University of Los Angeles (J.D., cum laude, 1979). Phi Sigma Tau. Associate Editor, Loyola of Los Angeles International and Comparative Law Annual, 1978-1979. *Member:* Los Angeles County and American Bar Associations; State Bar of California (Member, Executive Committee, Litigation Section). *PRACTICE AREAS:* Litigation.

**ASHLEIGH A. DANKER,** born Detroit, Michigan, July 31, 1963; admitted to bar, 1988, California, U.S. District Court, Central, Northern, Eastern and Southern Districts of California and U.S. Court of Appeals, Ninth Circuit. *Education:* Duke University (B.A., magna cum laude, 1985); University of Southern California (J.D., 1988). Recipient, American Jurisprudence Awards in Bankruptcy, Professional Responsibility and Insurance Law. *Member:* Los Angeles County Bar Association; State Bar of California; American Bar Association; Financial Lawyers Conference. *PRACTICE AREAS:* Bankruptcy Law.

*(This Listing Continued)*

**MARK SHINDERMAN,** born Queens, N.Y., May 22, 1963; admitted to bar, 1988, California and U.S. District Court, Eastern, Northern and Central Districts of California; 1989, U.S. District Court, Southern District of California. *Education:* Georgetown University (B.S.B.A., summa cum laude, 1985); Harvard Law School (J.D., cum laude, 1988). Beta Gamma Sigma; Phi Sigma Pi. Scholarship Recipient. Member, Financial Lawyers Conference. Author: "Copyright Licensees and Bankruptcy," Los Angeles Lawyer, April, 1993. *Member:* State Bar of California; Los Angeles County Business Association (Member, Bankruptcy Subcommittee, Commercial and Business Law Section). *PRACTICE AREAS:* Bankruptcy Law; Civil Litigation.

**LAURA J. MELTZER,** born New York, N.Y., June 7, 1956; admitted to bar, 1981, Pennsylvania and U.S. District Court, Eastern District of Pennsylvania; 1986, U.S. Court of Appeals, Third Circuit; 1989, New York; 1991, California. *Education:* University of New Hampshire (B.A., magna cum laude, 1978); Temple University (J.D., cum laude, 1981). Phi Beta Kappa. Law Clerk for the Hon. Abraham J. Gafni, Philadelphia Court of Common Pleas, 1981-1982. *Member:* Philadelphia and Pennsylvania Bar Associations; State Bar of California. *PRACTICE AREAS:* Litigation; Civil Trials & Appeals; Negligence Law; Personal Injury Law; Products Liability Law.

---

## LAW OFFICES OF
## RICHARD WEISSMAN, INC.
*A PROFESSIONAL CORPORATION*

SUITE 255
5959 TOPANGA CANYON BOULEVARD (WOODLAND HILLS)
**LOS ANGELES, CALIFORNIA 91367**
Telephone: 818-226-5434
Fax: 818-226-9105
Email: RichW7616@aol.com

*Receiverships.*

**FIRM PROFILE:** *Expertise in commercial and residential property management, operation of automobile dealerships, automotive service, wholesale and retail parts sales, luxury suites hotels, franchised and non-franchised motels and mobile home parks; jewelry wholesale and retail stores, possession of and selling collateral under institutional and private secured loans, food markets, the sale of real properties and ongoing businesses under partition actions, completed construction of housing and condominium projects, and domestic animals; liquor stores, restaurants, cocktail lounges, retail operations of hardware stores, a lumber yard, banquet facilities, fast food outlets, manufacturing and distribution of women's garments; manufacturing equipment, gasoline stations, public storage facilities, sale of liquor licenses, securities regulatory enforcement, complex real estate fraud actions; bulk vending manufacture and wholesale distribution and collection agencies.*

**RICHARD WEISSMAN,** born 1947; admitted to bar, 1972, California. *Education:* University of California (A.B., 1969); Loyola University of Los Angeles (J.D., 1972). Author, "A Small Right to Privacy," Century City Bar Journal, 1976. *PRACTICE AREAS:* Receivership Law; Real Estate Law; Corporate Law; Commercial Law; Litigation.

**CAROL A. WEISSMAN,** born Whittier, California, March 8, 1949; admitted to bar, 1976, California; 1977, U.S. District Court, Central District of California. *Education:* University of California at Los Angeles (B.S., 1971); Loyola Marymount University (J.D., 1976). *Member:* State Bar of California.

---

## WEISSMANN, WOLFF, BERGMAN,
## COLEMAN & SILVERMAN

**LOS ANGELES, CALIFORNIA**

(See Beverly Hills)

*General Civil, Trial and Appellate Practice in all Courts. Entertainment, Motion Picture, Television, Cable, Copyright, Real Estate, Corporate and Securities Law, Taxation, Estate Planning and Probate.*

---

## WELTER AND GREENE

SUITE 817
1880 CENTURY PARK EAST
**LOS ANGELES, CALIFORNIA 90067**
Telephone: 310-552-5252
Fax: 310-552-1006

*Business and Corporate Litigation and Transactions, Real Estate and Probate.*

**GERALD G. WELTER,** born 1940; admitted to bar, 1966, California. *Education:* University of Wisconsin-Madison (B.S., 1962); University of California School of Law (LL.B., 1965). *Member:* State Bar of California. *PRACTICE AREAS:* Business Litigation; Real Estate; Probate.

**RICHARD J. GREENE,** born New York, N.Y., 1947; admitted to bar, 1975, California. *Education:* California State University at Northridge (B.S., 1969); Southwestern University School of Law (J.D., 1975). *Member:* State Bar of California. *PRACTICE AREAS:* Business Law; Corporate; Real Estate Law.

---

## LAW OFFICES OF MARK J. WERKSMAN

601 WEST FIFTH STREET, TWELFTH FLOOR
**LOS ANGELES, CALIFORNIA 90071**
Telephone: 213-688-0460
Fax: 213-624-1942

*Criminal Litigation in all State and Federal Courts.*

**MARK J. WERKSMAN,** born New York, N.Y., October 19, 1959; admitted to bar, 1985, California and U.S. District Court, Central District of California; 1987, U.S. Court of Appeals, Ninth Circuit. *Education:* Yale University (B.A., 1981); University of Southern California (J.D., 1985). Recipient: First Place, Hale Moot Court Honors Competition, 1984; Honorable Mention, John Traynor Moot Court Competition, 1994; American Jurisprudence Award in Contracts, 1991, 1992; Corpus Juris Secundum Award in Contracts. Author: "Juvenile Court For Beginners," Los Angeles Lawyer, April, 1987. Deputy District Attorney, Los Angeles County, 1986-1988. Assistant U.S. Attorney, Criminal Division, Central District of California, 1988-1991. *Member:* State Bar of California (Executive Committee, Criminal Law Section, Term, 1991-1994); Federal and American Bar Associations; National Association of Criminal Defense Attorneys; California Attorneys for Criminal Justice.

### ASSOCIATE

**DONNA TRYFMAN,** born New York, N.Y., March 22, 1967; admitted to bar, 1995, California and U.S. District Court, Central District of California. *Education:* Brandeis University (B.A., 1989); University of Laverne School of Law (J.D., 1994). Honorable Mention - John Traynor Moot Court Competition, 1994. Recipient: American Jurisprudence Award in Contracts, 1991, 1992; Corpus Juris Secundum. *Member:* Los Angeles County and American Bar Associations; Women Lawyers Association. **LANGUAGES:** Spanish, Hebrew. *PRACTICE AREAS:* Criminal Defense.

---

## WESIERSKI & ZUREK

**LOS ANGELES, CALIFORNIA**

(See Irvine)

*General Civil Litigation, Insurance Bad Faith, Defense and Coverage, Appellate Practice, Insurance Defense, Products Liability, Professional Liability, Representation of Employers and Employees, Premises Liability, Real Property (Land Subsidence), Toxic Torts and Intellectual Property.*

---

## WEWER LAW FIRM

*Established in 1979*

777 SOUTH FIGUEROA STREET, SUITE 3700
**LOS ANGELES, CALIFORNIA 90017**
Telephone: 213-622-7021
Toll-free: 888-449-2700
Fax: 213-622-8781
Email: wewerlaw@ixi.net

*Helena, Montana Office:* 21 North Last Chance Gulch. P.O. Box 555. 59624. Telephone: 406-449-2700. Fax: 406-449-0942.

*Washington, D.C. Office:* 4401 Connecticut Avenue, N.W. Suite 292A. 20008. Telephone: 202-393-9575. Fax: 202-363-5672.

*(This Listing Continued)*

**WEWER LAW FIRM,** Los Angeles—Continued

Nonprofit Organizations, Postal, Tax, Corporate and Election Law, Administrative and Legislative Practice.

FIRM PROFILE: Wewer Law Firm has expertise in all aspects of the creation, management, and regulation of nonprofit organizations. The firm focuses on the interplay among the various federal and state agencies which regulate its clients, with particular attention to nonprofit laws dealing with corporate, tax, postal, election and lobby matters, ERISA plans, and charitable solicitation regulations. Attorneys in the firm have unique expertise with nonprofit postal appellate practice and choice of entity decisions for most U.S. jurisdictions. Clients of the firm include public charities, private foundations, grassroots activists, trade associations, labor organizations, VEBAs, public interest litigation firms, supporting organizations, title-holding corporations, political action committees, candidates for public office, ballot measure committees, public accountancy firms, and issue-oriented businesses. The firm also advises clients on media relations and grassroots lobby strategies.

### MEMBERS OF FIRM

**WILLIAM WEWER,** born San Diego, California, May 27, 1947; admitted to bar, 1977, District of Columbia and U.S. Court of Appeals for the District of Columbia Circuit; 1980, California and U.S. Court of Appeals, Ninth Circuit; 1981, U.S. District Court, District of Columbia; 1982, U.S. Supreme Court and U.S. District Court, Northern District of California; 1990, Colorado; 1994, Montana; U.S. District Court, Central District of California. *Education:* Pomona College (B.A., with honors, 1970); George Washington University (J.D., with high honors, 1977). Pi Sigma Alpha; Order of the Coif. Author: *Exempt Organizations and Charitable Activities,* NBI, 1996; "Choice of Tax-Exempt Organizations," NBI, 1996; "Recent Federal Actions Affecting Long Distance Telecommunications: A Survey of Issues Concerning the Microwave Specialized Common Carrier Industry," 43 George Washington Law Review 878, 1975. Faculty Member, CLE and CPE, Nonprofit Organization Law. *Member:* District of Columbia Bar; State Bar of California; State Bar of Montana; American Bar Associations (Member, Exempt Organizations Subcommittee). **SPECIAL AGENCIES:** U.S. Postal Service; Internal Revenue Service; all state charitable solicitation regulatory agencies. **PRACTICE AREAS:** Nonprofit & Charitable Organizations; Postal Law. *Email:* wewerlaw@ixi.net

### COUNSEL

**STEWART MOLLRICH,** born 1952; admitted to bar, 1979, California. *Education:* University of Southern California (B.A., 1974); Pepperdine University (J.D., 1979). Member, American Association of Political Consultants, 1988—. *Member:* State Bar of California. **PRACTICE AREAS:** Election Law; Legislation. *Email:* wewerlaw@ixi.net

(For Complete Biographical Data on other Personnel, see Professional Biographies at Helena, Montana and Washington, D.C.)

---

## LAW OFFICES OF DAVID S. WHITE

**10960 WILSHIRE BOULEVARD, SUITE 1225**
**LOS ANGELES, CALIFORNIA 90024**
Telephone: 301-479-4222
Telecopier: 301-479-3008

Business, Real Estate, Entertainment and Family Law. General Civil Trial and Appellate Practice in all State and Federal Courts.

**DAVID S. WHITE,** born Brookline, Massachusetts, January 16, 1950; admitted to bar, 1977, California. *Education:* Clark University (A.B., 1971); University of California at Davis (J.D., 1977). Phi Kappa Phi National Honor Society. First Place, U.C. Davis Environmental Law Moot Court Competition, 1976. Member: National Moot Court Team, 1976; Moot Court Honors Board, 1977. Recipient, State Bar Pro Bono Commendation, 1983-1984. Author: "Business Tort Remedies," "Consumer Protection Remedies," Association of Business Trial Lawyers (Seventh Annual Seminar), "Remedies in Business Litigation," 1980; "Demeanor in the Courtroom," Association of Business Trial Lawyers (Eighth Annual Seminar); "Techniques of Persuasion," 1981. Member, Panel of Arbitrators, Commercial Panel, American Arbitration Association. *Member:* Beverly Hills (Arbitrator, Mandatory Fee Arbitration Program, 1982—), Los Angeles County (Member: Ethics Committee, 1984-1985; Superior Courts Committee, 1984-1985; Arbitrator, Mandatory Fee Arbitration Program, 1982—) and American Bar Associations; State Bar of California; Association of Business Trial Lawyers (Member, Board of Governors, 1982-1984; Chairperson, Ninth

*(This Listing Continued)*

---

Annual Seminar on "Business Torts", 1982). (Also Of Counsel to Jacobson, Sanders & Bordy, LLP, Beverly Hills). **PRACTICE AREAS:** Real Estate; Business and Entertainment Litigation; Alternate Dispute Resolution; Arbitration.

### ASSOCIATES

**JOHN R. WINANDY,** born Concord, Massachusetts, February 7, 1964; admitted to bar, 1989, California. *Education:* Columbia University (B.A., 1986); University of Southern California (J.D., 1989). *Member:* State Bar of California. **PRACTICE AREAS:** Real Estate; Business and Entertainment Litigation; Alternative Dispute Resolution; Arbitration.

REPRESENTATIVE CLIENTS: Mar International Records, Inc.; Union Home Loan, Inc.; Disco Azteca; Amtec Audiotext, Inc.; Amlon Publishing Group, Inc.
REFERENCE: California Trust Deed Brokers Association; Bank of America.

---

## WHITE & CASE

**633 WEST FIFTH STREET, SUITE 1900**
**LOS ANGELES, CALIFORNIA 90071-2007**
Telephone: 213-620-7700
Telex: 277823 WHCS UR
Facsimile: 213-687-0758; 213-617-2205; 213-617-0376
Additional information on White & Case and our lawyers is available on our home page
URL: http://www.whitecase.com/

*New York, New York:* Telephone: 212-819-8200. Facsimile: 212-354-8113.
*Miami, Florida:* Telephone: 305-371-2700. Facsimile: 305-358-5744; 305-358-5745.
*Washington, D.C.:* Telephone: 202-626-3600. Facsimile: 202-639-9355.
*Brussels, Belgium:* Telephone: (32-2) 647-05-89. Facsimile: (32-2) 647-16-75.
*Budapest, Hungary:* Telephone: (36-1) 269-0550. Facsimile: (36-1) 269-1199.
*Helsinki, Finland:* Telephone: (358-9) 631-100. Facsimile: (358-9) 179-477.
*Istanbul, Turkey:* Telephone: (90-212) 275-75-33; (90-212) 275-68-98. Facsimile: (90-212) 275-75-43.
*Ankara, Turkey:* Telephone: (90-312) 446-2180. Facsimile: (90-312) 446-9871.
*London, England:* Telephone: (44-171) 726-6361. Facsimile: (44-171) 726-4314; (44-171) 726-8558.
*Moscow, Russia:* Telephone: (7-095) 961-2112. Satelite Telephone: (7-501) 961-2112. Facsimile: (7-095) 961-2121. Satelite Facsimile: (7-501) 961-2121.
*Paris, France:* Telephone: (33) 01-42-60-34-05. Facsimile: (33) 01-42-60-82-46.
*Prague, Czech Republic:* Telephone: (42-2) 2481-1796. Facsimile: (42-2) 232-5522; (42-2) 232-5585.
*Stockholm, Sweden:* Telephone: (46-8) 679-80-30. Facsimile: (46-8) 611-21-22.
*Warsaw, Poland:* Telephone: (48-22) 625-33-33; (48-22) 622-67-67; (48-39) 12-19-06. Facsimile: (48-22) 628-22-28.
*Almaty, Kazakhstan:* Telephone: (7-3272) 50-74-91/2; (7-3272) 50-78-71. Facsimile: (7-3272) 50-74-93.
*Tashkent, Republic of Uzbekistan:* Telephone: (7-3712) 32-00-59; (7-3712) 32-01-49. Satellite Telephone: (7-3712) 40-61-18; (7-3712) 40-61-24. (7-3712) 40-61-32. Facsimile: (7-3712) 40-61-81.
*Bangkok, Thailand:* White & Case (Thailand) Limited. Telephone: (662) 236-6154/7. Facsimile: (662) 237-6771.
*Bombay, India:* Liaison Office, (91-22) 282-6300/01/02/03. Facsimile: (91-22) 282-6305.
*Hanoi, Vietnam:* Representative Office, Telephone: (84-4) 822-7575. Facsimile: (84-4) 822-7297.
*Hong Kong:* Telephone: (852) 2822-8700. Facsimile: (852) 2845-9070.
*Singapore, Republic of Singapore:* Telephone: (65) 225-6000. Facsimile: (65) 225-6009.
*Tokyo, Japan:* White & Case Gaikokuho Jimu Bengoshi Jimusho. Telephone: (81-3) 3239-4300. Facsimile: (81-3) 3239-4330.
*Jeddah, Saudi Arabia:* Law Office of Hassan Mahassni, Telephone: (966-2) 665-4353. Facsimile: (966-2) 669-2996.
*Riyadh, Saudi Arabia:* Law Office of Hassan Mahassni, Telephone: (966-1) 464-4006; (966-1) 462-1626. Facsimile: (966-1) 465-1348.
*Johannesburg, Republic of South Africa:* Telephone: 27 (11) 333-1584. Facsimile: 27 (11) 333-0310.
*Mexico City, Mexico:* Telephone: (52-5) 540-9600; (52-5) 520-4770. Facsimile: (52-5) 520-4656; (52-5) 520-7262; (52-5) 520-1271; (52-5) 540-9698; (52-5) 540-9699.
*Jakarta, Indonesia Office:* Telephone: (62-21) 231-1965; (62-21) 381-8805. Facsimile: (62-21) 231-1778.

*(This Listing Continued)*

*General Practice.*

### PARTNERS

**C. RANDOLPH FISHBURN,** born Tucson, Arizona, June 16, 1956; admitted to bar, 1981, California; 1990, New York. *Education:* University of Southern California (A.B., 1978); Hastings College of the Law, University of California (J.D., 1981). *Member:* Los Angeles County Bar Association; State Bar of California; Association of Business Trial Lawyers. *Email:* FISHBRA@LA.WHITECASE.COM

**BURTON H. FOHRMAN,** born Chicago, Illinois, July 9, 1939; admitted to bar, 1964, California. *Education:* University of Southern California (A.B., 1960); University of California at Los Angeles (J.D., 1963). *Member:* The State Bar of California; American College of Real Estate Lawyers. *Email:* FOHRMBU@LA.WHITECASE.COM

**BRIAN L. HOLMAN,** born Los Angeles, California, September 26, 1955; admitted to bar, 1980, California. *Education:* University of Southern California (B.S., 1977); Harvard Law School (J.D., 1980). *Member:* Los Angeles County, Federal and American Bar Associations; State Bar of California; American Bankruptcy Institute. *Email:* HOLMABR@LA.WHITECASE.COM

**NEAL S. MILLARD,** born Dallas, Texas, June 6, 1947; admitted to bar, 1972, California; 1990, New York. *Education:* University of California, Los Angeles (A.B., 1969); University of Chicago (J.D., 1972). Adjunct Professor of Law, U.S.C. Law Center. *Member:* Los Angeles County (Trustee, 1985-1987), New York State and American Bar Associations; State Bar of California. *Email:* MILLANE@LA.WHITECASE.COM

**NEIL W. RUST,** born Haslemere, Surrey, England, August 14, 1957; admitted to bar, 1987, California. *Education:* University of London (B.Sc., 1978; LL.B., 1985); University of Pennsylvania (J.D., 1987). *Member:* American Bar Association. *Email:* RUSTNEI@LA.WHITECASE.COM

**RICHARD K. SMITH, JR.,** born Pittsburgh, Pennsylvania, April 13, 1955; admitted to bar, 1981, California. *Education:* University of Illinois (B.A., 1977; J.D., 1980). *Member:* State Bar of California; American Bar Association. *Email:* SMITHRI@LA.WHITECASE.COM

**JOHN A. STURGEON,** born Hollywood, California, January 23, 1936; admitted to bar, 1963, California. *Education:* Stanford University (A.B., 1957; J.D., 1962). *Member:* Los Angeles County Bar Association; The State Bar of California; Association of Business Trial Lawyers. Fellow: American College of Trial Lawyers; American Bar Foundation. *Email:* STURGJO@LA.WHITECASE.COM

**TRAVERS D. WOOD,** born Los Angeles, California, November 1, 1943; admitted to bar, 1970, California. *Education:* University of California, Los Angeles (B.A., 1966); University of Southern California (J.D., 1969). *Member:* Los Angeles County and American Bar Associations; State Bar of California; The Association of Business Trial Lawyers; International Association of Defense Counsel. *Email:* WOODTRA@LA.WHITECASE.COM

**DANIEL J. WOODS,** born Brooklyn, New York, November 12, 1952; admitted to bar, 1977, California. *Education:* University of Southern California (A.B., 1974; J.D., 1977). *Member:* Los Angeles County and American Bar Associations; State Bar of California. *Email:* WOODSDA@LA.WHITECASE.COM

### PARTNER OF COUNSEL

**JAY H. GRODIN,** born Los Angeles, California, May 29, 1944; admitted to bar, 1970, California; 1989, New York. *Education:* University of Southern California (B.S., 1966); Boalt Hall School of Law, University of California, Berkeley (J.D., 1969). *Email:* GRODIJA@LA.WHITECASE.COM

### COUNSEL

**BRYAN A. MERRYMAN,** born New York City, N.Y., February 4, 1962; admitted to bar, 1988, California; U.S. District Court, Northern, Central, Eastern and Southern Districts of California; U.S. Court of Appeals, Ninth Circuit. *Education:* Kenyon College (B.A., 1984); University of Pennsylvania (J.D., 1987). *Email:* MERRYBR@LA.WHITECASE.COM

### ASSOCIATES

**DAVID H. BATE,** born Clovis, New Mexico, July 8, 1957; admitted to bar, 1982, Colorado; 1988, California. *Education:* Claremont Men's College (B.A., 1979); University of California, Los Angeles (J.D., 1982). *Email:* BATEDAV@LA.WHITECASE.COM

*(This Listing Continued)*

**JAMES R. CAIRNS,** born Los Angeles, California, April 24, 1959; admitted to bar, 1988, California. *Education:* University of San Diego (B.A., 1981); University of California, Los Angeles (J.D., 1988). *Email:* CAIRNJA@LA.WHITECASE.COM

**JORDAN S. COHEN,** born Park Ridge, Illinois, August 11, 1966; admitted to bar, 1991, California. *Education:* UCLA (B.A., 1988); Vanderbilt University (J.D., 1991). *Member:* Los Angeles County and American Bar Associations; Barristers. *Email:* COHENJO@LA.WHITECASE.COM

**JAMES R. COWAN,** born Sacramento, California, September 20, 1964; admitted to bar, 1992, California. *Education:* Harvard University (A.B., 1986); Oxford University (M.S., 1988); Hastings College of the Law (J.D., 1992). *Email:* COWANJA@LA.WHITECASE.COM

**SUSAN J. DE WITT,** born Riverside, California, April 7, 1961; admitted to bar, 1987, California. *Education:* University of California (B.S., 1983; B.S., 1984); Georgetown University (J.D., 1987). *Email:* DEWITSU@LA.WHITECASE.COM

**JOHN D. EARLY,** born Schenectady, New York, July 6, 1968; admitted to bar, 1993, California. *Education:* University of Notre Dame (B.A., 1990); University of California, Los Angeles (J.D., 1993). *Email:* EARLYJO@LA.WHITECASE.COM

**AMBER N. HARTGENS,** born New York, New York, April 20, 1967; admitted to bar, 1995, California. *Education:* Columbia University (B.A., 1989); Boalt Hall School of Law, University of California (J.D., 1994). *Email:* HARTGAM@LA.WHITECASE.COM

**CHRISTOPHER W. KELLY,** born Los Angeles, CA, June 15, 1963; admitted to bar, 1992, California. *Education:* California State (B.A., 1989); Loyola Law School (J.D., 1992). *Member:* State Bar of California. *Email:* KELLYCH@LA.WHITECASE.COM

**MATTHEW P. LEWIS,** born Springfield, Illinois, July 6, 1965; admitted to bar, 1991, California. *Education:* Occidental College (A.B., 1987); Loyola University (J.D., 1991). *Email:* LEWISMA@LA.WHITECASE.COM

**PHILIP L. MALONEY,** born Boston, Massachusetts, May 22, 1963; admitted to bar, 1990, California. *Education:* Tufts University (B.A., 1985); Stanford University (J.D., 1990). *Email:* MALONPH@LA.WHITECASE.COM

**STEVEN L. MILLER,** born Salinas, California, November 25, 1964; admitted to bar, 1989, California; 1992, Colorado. *Education:* University of California, Irvine (B.A., 1986); Pepperdine University School of Law (J.D., 1989). *Email:* MILLEST@LA.WHITECASE.COM

**RACHEL CHARLES O'BRYAN,** born Lima, Ohio, March 23, 1967; admitted to bar, 1995, New York (Not admitted in California). *Education:* Brown University (B.A., 1989); University of Michigan (J.D., 1994). *Member:* American Bar Association. *Email:* OBRYARA@LA.WHITECASE.COM

**JACKSON K. PEK,** born New York, N.Y., September 23, 1970; admitted to bar, 1995, California. *Education:* The Wharton School, University of Pennsylvania (B.S., 1992); New York University (J.D., 1995). *Email:* PEKJACK@LA.WHITECASE.COM

**CAROLE C. PETERSON,** born Santa Monica, California, August 17, 1969; admitted to bar, 1994, California. *Education:* University of Southern California, Los Angeles (B.A., 1991; J.D., 1994). *Email:* PETERCA@LA.WHITECASE.COM

**JOHN W. PETERSON,** born Royal Oak, Michigan, August 7, 1967; admitted to bar, 1995, California. *Education:* University of Southern California (B.S., 1989; J.D., 1995). *Email:* PETERJO@LA.WHITECASE.COM

**JOHN E. ROSENBAUM,** born New York, New York, October 2, 1958; admitted to bar, 1995, California. *Education:* The Wharton School, University of Pennsylvania (B.A.; B.S., 1980); New York University (M.B.A., 1984); University of San Francisco (J.D., 1994). *Email:* ROSENJO@LA.WHITECASE.COM

**RENEE M. RUBIN,** born New York, N.Y., August 21, 1965; admitted to bar, 1992, California. *Education:* State University of New York, Binghamton (B.S., 1987); Stanford University (J.D., 1992). *Email:* RUBINRE@LA.WHITECASE.COM

**ROBERT L. SKINNER,** born Washington, D.C., January 6, 1963; admitted to bar, 1990, California. *Education:* University of Southern California (B.S., 1985; J.D., 1990). *Email:* SKINNRO@LA.WHITECASE.COM

*(This Listing Continued)*

## WHITE & CASE, Los Angeles—Continued

**STEVEN W. TURNBULL,** born Idaho Falls, Idaho, August 21, 1960; admitted to bar, 1989, California. *Education:* Brigham Young University (B.S., 1985); University of Washington (J.D., 1989). *Email:* TURNBST@LA.WHITECASE.COM

**GARY L. URWIN,** born Toledo, Ohio, January 6, 1955; admitted to bar, 1982, California. *Education:* Oberlin College (B.A., 1977); University of California (J.D., 1982). *Email:* URWINGA@LA.WHITECASE.COM

**TED S. WARD,** born Ft. Belvoir, VA, November 4, 1962; admitted to bar, 1989, California. *Education:* University of Colorado (B.S., 1984); University of California at Los Angeles (J.D., 1989). *Member:* Beverly Hills, Los Angeles County and American Bar Associations. *Email:* WARDTED@LA.WHITECASE.COM

**ROBERT L. WILKERSON,** born 1961; admitted to bar, 1989, California. *Education:* University of California, San Diego (B.A., 1984); Boalt Hall School of Law, University of California (J.D., 1989). *Email:* WILKERO@LA.WHITECASE.COM

**MARK A.H. YOUNG,** born Melbourne, Australia, June 23, 1969; admitted to bar, 1995, California. *Education:* University of California at Los Angeles (B.A., 1991); U.S.C. (J.D., 1995). *Email:* YOUNGMA@LA.WHITECASE.COM

(For biographical data as to other locations, see Professional Biographies at New York, New York; Miami, Florida; Washington, D.C.; Brussels, Belgium; Budapest, Hungary; Helsinki, Finland; Istanbul, Turkey; Ankara, Turkey; London, England; Moscow, Russia; Paris, France; Prague, Czech Republic; Stockholm, Sweden; Warsaw, Poland; Almaty, Kazakhstan; Tashkent, Republic of Uzbekistan; Bangkok, Thailand; Hanoi, Vietnam; Hong Kong; Singapore, Republic of Singapore; Tokyo, Japan; Jeddah and Riyadh, Saudi Arabia; Johannesburg, Republic of South Africa; Mexico City, Mexico)

## WHITE O'CONNOR CURRY & AVANZADO LLP

10900 WILSHIRE BOULEVARD
SUITE 1100
LOS ANGELES, CALIFORNIA 90024-3959
Telephone: 310-443-0222
Fax: 310-443-0233
Email: whiteo.com

*General Civil and Trial Practice in all States and Federal Courts.*

**ANDREW M. WHITE,** born Dayton, Ohio, December 19, 1947; admitted to bar, 1974, California; 1977, U.S. Supreme Court. *Education:* Yale University (B.A., cum laude, 1969); Stanford University (J.D., 1974). Adjunct Instructor, Loyola Law School, 1978-1979. Author: "Candid Camcorder: Legal Restrictions on Use of Surreptitiously Recorded Videos," ABA Entertainment and Sports Lawyer (Winter 1992); "In Defense of Poetic License: Why Created Quotations Deserve Constitutional Protection," Los Angeles Lawyer (April 1990); "Work Product Issues for Corporate Counsel," ALI-ABA Seminar for Corporate Counsel (November 1988). *Member:* Beverly Hills, Los Angeles County and American Bar Associations; State Bar of California. *PRACTICE AREAS:* Civil Litigation; Entertainment.

**MICHAEL J. O'CONNOR,** born San Mateo, California, September 28, 1954; admitted to bar, 1979, California and U.S. District Court, Central, Eastern and Northern Districts of California. *Education:* University of California at San Diego; University of California at Berkeley (A.B., 1976); University of California at Los Angeles (J.D., 1979). *Member:* Los Angeles County Bar Association; The State Bar of California. *PRACTICE AREAS:* Civil Litigation; Insurance Law.

**JAMES E. CURRY,** born Munich, Germany, September 7, 1958; admitted to bar, 1984, California. *Education:* Stanford University (B.A., with distinction, 1981); University of Chicago (J.D., 1984). *Member:* Los Angeles County and American Bar Associations; State Bar of California. *PRACTICE AREAS:* Civil Litigation.

**MELVIN N.A. AVANZADO,** born Manila, Philippines, April 24, 1962; admitted to bar, 1988, California. *Education:* University of California, Los Angeles (B.S., 1984); University of Notre Dame (J.D., cum laude, 1988). Member, Barristers National Mock Trial Team. Recipient, William T. Kirby Award for Excellence in Legal Writing. *Member:* Los Angeles County and Beverly Hills Bar Associations; State Bar of California. LAN-

*(This Listing Continued)*

**GUAGES:** Tagalog. *PRACTICE AREAS:* Civil Litigation; Entertainment; Sports Law.

**JOHN M. GATTI,** born Rockville Centre, New York, June 23, 1963; admitted to bar, 1988, California, U.S. District Court, Central, Northern and Southern Districts of California and U.S. Court of Appeals, Ninth Circuit. *Education:* University of Southern California (B.S., magna cum laude, 1985; J.D., 1988). Beta Gamma Sigma. Member, Hale Moot Court Honors Program. Member, Blackstonians Law Society, 1983-1985. *Member:* Los Angeles County and Beverly Hills Bar Associations; State Bar of California. *PRACTICE AREAS:* Civil Litigation; Entertainment Litigation; Entertainment Law.

---

**JONATHAN H. ANSCHELL,** born Calgary, Alberta, Canada, March 27, 1968; admitted to bar, 1992, California; 1993, U.S. District Court, Central and Southern Districts of California and U.S. Court of Appeals, Ninth Circuit. *Education:* University of Toronto (B.A., with high distinction, 1989; LL.B., 1992). Associate Editor, University of Toronto Law Review, 1991. Recipient, Borden and Elliot Award for Excellence in Moot Court. Co-Author: "You Must Remember This—Oral Agreements and the Motion Picture Industry," 25 University of West Los Angeles Law Review 155, 1994. *Member:* Los Angeles County Bar Association; State Bar of California. *PRACTICE AREAS:* Civil Litigation; Media Law; Entertainment Law.

**DAVID E. FINK,** born Chicago, Illinois, April 9, 1966; admitted to bar, 1993, California. *Education:* University of California at Berkeley (B.A., 1988); Hastings College of the Law, University of California (J.D., 1993). Phi Delta Phi. *Member:* State Bar of California. *PRACTICE AREAS:* Business; Entertainment Litigation.

**HOLLY J. SADLON,** born Perth Amboy, New Jersey, March 23, 1969; admitted to bar, 1994, California. *Education:* Rutgers College (B.A., 1991); University of California at Los Angeles (J.D., 1994). Phi Delta Phi (Vice Magistrate, 1993-1994). Recipient, American Jurisprudence Award in Constitutional Criminal Procedure. Editor, UCLA Law Review, 1993-1994. *Member:* State Bar of California. *PRACTICE AREAS:* Civil Litigation.

**LEE S. BRENNER,** born Waukesha, Wisconsin, March 18, 1970; admitted to bar, 1995, California. *Education:* University of Wisconsin-Madison (B.S., with distinction, 1992); Hastings College of the Law, University of California (J.D., cum laude, 1995). *Member:* State Bar of California. *PRACTICE AREAS:* Litigation.

**RANDALL L. MURPHY,** born Lincoln, Nebraska, September 29, 1954; admitted to bar, 1989, Connecticut; 1990, New York; 1993, California. *Education:* University of Nebraska (B.A., 1985); Yale Law School (J.D., 1989). *Member:* The Association of the Bar of the City of New York; American Indian Bar Association; New York State Bar Association; State Bar of California.

**JAMES W. IREY,** born San Diego, California, September 18, 1964; admitted to bar, 1991, California. *Education:* Southern Oregon State College (B.S., cum laude, 1986); Hastings College of the Law, University of California (J.D., 1990). Member, Moot Court. Note Editor, Hastings International and Comparative Law Review, 1989-1990. *PRACTICE AREAS:* General Commercial Litigation.

## WHITMAN BREED ABBOTT & MORGAN

633 WEST FIFTH STREET
LOS ANGELES, CALIFORNIA 90071
Telephone: 213-896-2400
Cable Address: "Whitsom LSA"
Telex: 68-6157 (WU)
Telecopier: 213-896-2450
URL: http://www.financelaw.com

*New York, New York Office:* 200 Park Avenue. Telephone: 212-351-3000.
*Greenwich, Connecticut Office:* 100 Field Point Road. Telephone: 203-869-3800.
*Sacramento, California Office:* Senator Hotel Building, 1121 L Street. Telephone: 916-441-4242.
*Newark, New Jersey Office:* One Gateway Center. Telephone: 201-621-2230.
*Palm Beach, Florida Office:* 220 Sunrise Avenue. Telephone: 407-832-5458.
*London, England Office:* 11 Waterloo Place. Telephone: 71-839-3226. Telex: 917881.
*Tokyo, Japan Office:* Suite 450, New Otemachi Building, 2-2-1 Otemachi, Chiyoda-Ku, Tokyo 100. Telephone: 81-3-3242-1289.

*(This Listing Continued)*

*Associated with:* Tyan & Associes, 22, La Sagesse Street-Rmeil, Beirut, Lebanon. Telephone: 337968. Fax: 200969. Telex: 43928.

*General Practice including International Commercial Law.*

### RESIDENT PARTNERS

**CHRISTOPHER A. BURROWS,** born Glendale, California, 1958; admitted to bar, 1983, California. *Education:* Pomona College (B.A., 1980); Loyola Law School (J.D., cum laude, 1983). Member, St. Thomas More Honor Society. *Member:* Pasadena, Los Angeles County (Member, Section on Labor Law) and American (Member, Section of Labor and Employment Law, Committee on Labor Arbitration and the Law of Collective Bargaining Agreements) Bar Associations. **PRACTICE AREAS:** Labor and Employment Law.

**FRANCIS W. COSTELLO,** born Cambridge, Massachusetts, 1946; admitted to bar, 1974, New York; 1977, California. *Education:* Columbia University (B.A., 1968; J.D., 1973). Executive Editor, Columbia Journal of Transnational Law, 1972-1973. *Member:* Los Angeles County Bar Association; The State Bar of California. **PRACTICE AREAS:** Business Law; Corporate Law; International Law; Pacific Rim Trade.

**JOSEPH P. DAILEY,** born Scranton, Pennsylvania, 1944; admitted to bar, 1970, New York; 1975, U.S. Court of Appeals, 2nd Circuit (Not admitted in California). *Education:* Georgetown University (A.B., 1966; J.D., 1969). Member, Georgetown Law Journal, 1968-1969. **PRACTICE AREAS:** Litigation.

**RICHARD A. EASTMAN,** born Quincy, Massachusetts, 1937; admitted to bar, 1966, California; 1985, New York; 1987, Japan (Gaikokuho-Jimu-Bengoshi) (Foreign Legal Counsellor). *Education:* Harvard University (B.A., cum laude, 1959; LL.B., cum laude, 1965). Author: "Tax Aspects of Doing Business in Japan" in *Current Legal Aspects of Doing Business in the Far East* (ABA, 1972); "Allocation of Risk in Construction Contracts," *International Business Lawyer,* July/August, 1984; "The FIDIC Red Book Fourth Edition," *Construction Lawyer,* November, 1989; Chapter 4, "Joint Venturing In the Far East" in *Business Opportunities in the Far East* (Dow Jones-Irwin (1990). *Member:* State Bar of California; American, Inter Pacific and International Bar Associations; Second Tokyo Bar Association; Japan Federation of Bar Associations; American Arbitration Association. Fellow, Chartered Institute of Arbitrators. **LANGUAGES:** Japanese.

**JAMES C. HUGHES,** born New York, N.Y., 1954; admitted to bar, 1983, California. *Education:* St. John's University (B.A., magna cum laude, 1976); St. John's Graduate School of Arts & Sciences (M.A., 1978); Loyola Law School, Los Angeles (J.D., 1981). *Member:* Los Angeles County (Member, Real Property Section) and American (Member, Real Property Section) Bar Associations; State Bar of California; American Planning Association; Urban Land Institute.. **PRACTICE AREAS:** Real Estate; Commercial Real Estate Development; Shopping Center Development; Residential Real Estate Development; Land Use.

**ROBERT L. IVEY,** born Americus, Georgia, 1941; admitted to bar, 1967, Virginia; 1970, California. *Education:* Davidson College (B.A., 1964); University of Virginia (LL.B., 1967). Managing Board, Notes Editor, Virginia Journal of International Law, 1966-1967. Author: "Claim Certification" (November 1991) and "Qui Tau Lawsuits" (September 1989), Government Contractor Briefing Papers (Federal Publications). Co-author: "Payment Delay Claims," Proving and Pricing Construction Claims, Wiley Construction Law Library (John Wiley & Sons 1990). *Member:* Los Angeles County, Federal and American (Member, Sections on: Public Contracts; International Law; Litigation; Forum on the Construction Industry) Bar Associations; State Bar of California; Association of Business Trial Lawyers. [Capt., U.S. Army, 1968-1970]. **PRACTICE AREAS:** Construction Litigation; Business Litigation.

**GEROLD W. LIBBY,** born New York, N.Y., 1942; admitted to bar, 1969, New York; 1978, California. *Education:* Yale University (B.A., 1965); New York University (J.D., 1969). *Member:* Los Angeles County and American (Chair, Section of International Law and Practice, 1991-1992; Delegate, House of Delegates, 1994—) Bar Associations; The State Bar of California. **PRACTICE AREAS:** Business Law; Corporate Law; Project Finance; International Law.

**MAITA DEAL PROUT,** born Pomona, California, 1950; admitted to bar, 1981, California; 1982, U.S. District Court, Central District of California; 1987, U.S. District Court, Eastern, Northern and Southern Districts of California; 1991, Hawaii. *Education:* University of California at Los Angeles (B.A., 1973; J.D., 1981). *Member:* Los Angeles County Bar Association (Program Chair, Commercial Law Committee of Commercial Law and Bankruptcy Section, 1993-1996; Vice Chair, 1997—); State Bar of California (Member, Debtor/Creditor Relations and Bankruptcy Committee, 1986-1990); Financial Lawyers Conference; Women Lawyers of Los Angeles. **PRACTICE AREAS:** Bankruptcy; Commercial Law; Debtor and Creditor; Secured Transactions.

**MARK S. SHIPOW,** born Los Angeles, California, 1954; admitted to bar, 1979, California. *Education:* University of California at Los Angeles (B.A., cum laude, 1976); University of California at Los Angeles School of Law (J.D., 1979). Author: "Litigation Costs in the U.S.," September 1992, *Liberty & Justice,* Japan Federation of Bar Associations; Speaker, "Real Estate Workouts, A Comprehensive Approach," October 1992. Extern To Hon. Justice James C. Cobey, California Court of Appeal, Second Appellate District, 1978. Member, Town Hall Los Angeles. *Member:* Los Angeles County and American Bar Associations; The State Bar of California; Association of Business Trial Lawyers. **PRACTICE AREAS:** Business Litigation; Intellectual Property Infringement; Complex Commercial Litigation.

**RICHARD T. WILLIAMS,** born Evergreen Park, Illinois, 1945; admitted to bar, 1972, California. *Education:* Stanford University (A.B., 1967; M.B.A., 1972; J.D., 1972). Managing Editor, Stanford Journal of International Studies, 1970-1971. Contributing Editor, Oil and Gas Price Regulation Analyst, 1978-1982. Chairman, Energy Law Committee, Los Angeles County Bar Association, 1980-1982. *Member:* State Bar of California; American Bar Association; Association of Business Trial Lawyers. **PRACTICE AREAS:** Antitrust; Business Litigation; Intellectual Property Litigation.

**PAUL C. WORKMAN,** born Los Angeles, California, 1954; admitted to bar, 1980, California. *Education:* University of California at Berkeley (A.B., 1976); Loyola University of Los Angeles (J.D., 1980). *Member:* Los Angeles County Bar Association; The State Bar of California. **PRACTICE AREAS:** Business Litigation.

### RESIDENT ASSOCIATES

**ALEX R. BAGHDASSARIAN,** born Beirut, Lebanon, 1963; admitted to bar, 1989, California and U.S. District Court, Central District of California. *Education:* University of Chicago (B.A., 1985); University of Southern California (J.D. , 1989). Phi Delta Phi. Author, "Time Limits at Trial: Cutting the Case Down to Size," ABTL Report, 1992. Co-Author: "Tactical Disqualification of Attorneys," ABTL Report, 1993. *Member:* Los Angeles County (Member, Litigation Section) and American Bar Associations; State Bar of California (Member, Litigation Section). **LANGUAGES:** Armenian, French and Arabic.

**DONALD M. CLARY,** born Fresno, California, 1953; admitted to bar, 1979, California. *Education:* California State University at Northridge; University of California at Los Angeles (B.A., magna cum laude, 1975); Loyola Marymount University (J.D., 1979). Pi Gamma Mu. *Member:* State Bar of California; American Bar Association.

**VITO A. COSTANZO,** born Worcester, Massachusetts, 1962; admitted to bar, 1987, California; 1989, U.S. District Court, Southern District of California. *Education:* University of California at Los Angeles (B.A., 1984); Loyola University of Los Angeles (J.D., 1987). Recipient, Fletcher Jones Scholarship for Achievement in Trial Advocacy. Author: "Defamation: A Case of Mistaken Identity," Loyola Entertainment Law Journal, Vol. 7, 1987. *Member:* Los Angeles County Bar Association; State Bar of California.

**ROGER B. COVEN,** born Stamford, Connecticut, 1947; admitted to bar, 1979, Massachusetts; 1979, District of Columbia; 1988, California. *Education:* Tufts University (B.A., 1969); Suffolk University (J.D., 1979). Member, 1977-1979 and Comment Editor, 1978-1979, Suffolk University Law Review. Staff Counsel, Federal Energy Regulatory Commission, 1979-1983. *Member:* State Bar of California; The District of Columbia Bar; Federal Energy (Treasurer, 1986-1987) and American Bar Associations.

**DANIEL W. LEE,** born Seoul, Korea; admitted to bar, 1985, Hawaii and U.S. District Court, District of Hawaii; 1986, District of Columbia; 1987, California and U.S. District Court, Central District of California. *Education:* Yonsei University, Seoul, Korea (B.A., 1976); Michigan State University (M.A., 1980); University of San Francisco (J.D., 1983). Speaker: "North American Trade Issues for the '90's," Korea Foreign Trade Association, 1993; "Doing Business With Korea," State Bar of California, 1992; "Doing Business With Korea," Los Angeles County Bar Association, 1992; "South Korea: An Emerging Source of Real Estate Capital," Asian Real Estate Association, 1990; "A Guide to Real Estate Acquisition, Development and Construction in California for Korean Corporations," Federations of Korean Industries, 1988. *Member:* Los Angeles County and American (Member, International Law Section) Bar Associations; State Bar of Cali-

*(This Listing Continued)*

## CALIFORNIA—LOS ANGELES

**WHITMAN BREED ABBOTT & MORGAN,** Los Angeles—*Continued*

fornia; The District of Columbia Bar (Member, Sections on: International Law; Intellectual Property); State Bar of Hawaii. **LANGUAGES:** Korean.

**JASON J. LIBERMAN,** born Van Nuys, California, 1967; admitted to bar, 1993, California; 1994, U.S. District Court, Northern, Southern, Eastern and Central Districts of California. *Education:* University of Southern California (B.S., 1991); Pepperdine University School of Law (J.D., 1993). Member, Moot Court. *Member:* Beverly Hills, Los Angeles County and Century City Bar Associations; State Bar of California.

**TOBY ROSE MALLEN,** born Japan, 1955; admitted to bar, 1980, California, U.S. District Court, Central District of California and U.S. Court of Appeals, Ninth Circuit. *Education:* University of California at Berkeley (A.B., 1977); University of California at Los Angeles (J.D., 1980).

**PAUL S. MARKS,** born Providence, Rhode Island, 1960; admitted to bar, 1988, California. *Education:* Brown University (A.B., 1983); University of Southern California (J.D., 1988). Phi Delta Phi. Editor, Hale Moot Court Honors Competition, 1987-1988. *Member:* Los Angeles County Bar Association; State Bar of California.

**ANN BRIDGET MCCARTHY,** born New York, N.Y., 1955; admitted to bar, 1990, California and U.S. District Court, Central District of California. *Education:* California State University (B.A., 1980); Southwestern University (J.D., cum laude, 1990). Staff Member, 1988-1989, Chief Note and Comment Editor, 1989-1990, Southwestern University Law Review. *Member:* State Bar of California.

**TASHA D. NGUYEN,** born Saigon, Vietnam, 1963; admitted to bar, 1986, California. *Education:* University of Southern California (A.B., 1983); Harvard University (J.D., 1986). *Member:* State Bar of California; American Bar Association.

**JACK S. SHOLKOFF,** born Los Angeles, California, 1964; admitted to bar, 1989, California, U.S. District Court, Central and Eastern Districts of California and U.S. Court of Appeals, Ninth Circuit; 1994, New Jersey. *Education:* Tufts University (B.A., magna cum laude in History, 1986); University of Southern California (J.D., 1989). Phi Alpha Delta. Executive Articles Editor, Computer/Law Journal 1988-1989; Major Tax Planning, 1988-1989. Author: "Breaking the Mold: Forging A New Standard for Protection of Computer Software," 8 Computer Law Journal 1198. *Member:* Los Angeles County Bar Association; State Bar of California (Member, Section of Labor and Employment Law).

**DOUGLAS K. SIMPSON,** born Walnut Creek, California, 1956; admitted to bar, 1985, California. *Education:* University of California, Irvine (B.A., 1981); University of San Francisco (J.D., 1985). Member, University of San Francisco Law Review, 1983-1984. *Member:* State Bar of California.

**ALAN J. WATSON,** born Wynnewood, Pennsylvania, 1968; admitted to bar, 1995, California. *Education:* University of California, Irvine (B.A., 1990); De Paul University (J.D., 1994). *Member:* State Bar of California.

(For Biographical data on Firm Members and Counsel, see New York, New York Professional Biographies)

## *LAW OFFICES OF VALERIE C. WHITWORTH*

*Established in 1988*

**10850 WILSHIRE BOULEVARD, SUITE 819**
**LOS ANGELES, CALIFORNIA 90024-4305**
*Telephone: 310-446-5836*
*Fax: 310-446-5838*

*Complex Business Litigation, Entertainment, Transactional, Bankruptcy, Appellate Law.*

**VALERIE C. WHITWORTH,** admitted to bar, 1980, California. *Education:* University of California at Berkeley (B.A., 1974); University of California at Los Angeles (M.B.A., 1979); University of California School of Law at Los Angeles (J.D., 1979). County Deputy District Attorney, Los Angeles, 1980-1983. *Member:* State Bar of California; Beverly Hills Bar Association; John M. Langston Bar Association; National Association of Female Executives, Women Incorporated.

CAA1290B

## MARTINDALE-HUBBELL LAW DIRECTORY 1997

## *WICKWIRE GAVIN LLP*

*35TH FLOOR*
*777 SOUTH FIGUEROA STREET*
**LOS ANGELES, CALIFORNIA 90017-5831**
*Telephone: 213-688-9500*
*Telecopier: 213-627-6342*
*Email: wgca@wickwire.com*

*Vienna, Virginia Office:* Wickwire Gavin, P.C., International Gateway, 8100 Boone Boulevard, Suite 700. Telephone: 703-790-8750. Telecopier: 703-448-1801.

*Washington, D.C. Office:* Wickwire Gavin, P.C., Two Lafayette Centre, Suite 450, 1133 21st Street, N.W. Telephone: 202-887-5200. Cable Address: "WireGG". FAX: 202-223-0120.

*Madison, Wisconsin Office:* Wickwire Gavin, P.C., Suite 300, 2 East Gilman Street, P.O. Box 1683. Telephone: 608-257-5335. Fax: 608-257-2029.

*Greenbelt, Maryland Office:* Wickwire Gavin, P.C., Suite 220, 6411 Ivy Lane. Telephone: 301-441-9420.

*Minneapolis, Minnesota Office:* Wickwire Gavin, P.A., 4700 Norwest Center, 90 South Seventh Street. Telephone: 612-347-0408. Telecopier: 612-673-0720.

*General Civil, Administrative and Legislative Practice before all Federal and Local Courts, Departments, Agencies and the Congress. Construction, Public Contract, Fidelity and Surety, Federal Grant, Environmental, Bankruptcy, Corporate and Commercial Syndication.*

*FIRM PROFILE: Wickwire Gavin LLP is affiliated with the national law firm of Wickwire Gavin, P.C. Founded in 1974, Wickwire Gavin, P.C. quickly became recognized as a prominent force in the areas of construction claims and government contract litigation. The firm has grown into a diverse organization with attorneys who advise and assist clients in a variety of practice areas, in both the domestic and international arenas. The nearly 40 Wickwire Gavin attorneys, with offices in Virginia, Wisconsin, Washington, D.C., Minnesota and California are committed to establishing long-standing client relationships. Our goals continue to include small-firm attention to client needs with the provision of large-firm depth of legal experience and the competitive rates of a mid-size firm.*

**DAVID P. DAPPER,** born La Canada, CA., July 19, 1953; admitted to bar, 1978, California; 1980, U.S. Court of Federal Claims. *Education:* University of California at Los Angeles (A.B., 1975); University of Southern California (J.D., 1978). Chairman, Executive Board, Hale Moot Court Honors Program, 1977-1978. Co-Author: *Fifty State Construction Lien and Bond Law,* Vol. III, Wiley, 1995. *Member:* American Bar Association (Torts and Insurance Practice Section, Fidelity and Surety Committee; Litigation Section, Construction Law Subsection; Forum on the Construction Industry, Chair, Contract Documents Division, 1991-1993). **PRACTICE AREAS:** Construction; Public Agency; Fidelity and Surety Law. **Email:** ddapper@wickwire.com

**JOSEPH G. MCGUINNESS,** born Brooklyn, NY., January 15, 1958; admitted to bar, 1984, California. *Education:* Loyola Marymount University (J.D., 1984). Co-Author: *Fifty State Construction Lien and Bond Law,* Vol. III, Wiley, 1995. Member: Trial Advocacy Team. *Member:* American Bar Association (Litigation Section, Construction Law Subsection); Associated General Contractors (Legal Advisory Committee, Construction Forms Subcommittee). **PRACTICE AREAS:** Construction and General Business Litigation. **Email:** jmcguinness@wickwire.com

### *ASSOCIATES*

**KAYHAN M. FATEMI,** born Kansas City, MO., July 13, 1964; admitted to bar, 1993, California. *Education:* University of California, Los Angeles (B.A., 1987); Pepperdine University (J.D., cum laude, 1993). Recipient, American Jurisprudence Awards in Corporations, Securities Regulation and International Business Transactions. Extern for Honorable Lisa Hill Fenning, Bankruptcy Court, Central District, Fall, 1992; Extern for Honorable Presiding Justice Mildred Lillie, California Court of Appeals, Second District, Summer, 1991; Extern to the Securities and Exchange Commission, Enforcement Division, Spring, 1993. Co-Author: *Fifty-State Construction Lien and Bond Law,* Vol. III, Wiley, 1995. **Email:** kfatemi@wickwire.com

**ELIZABETH M. LASCHEID,** born Los Angeles, CA., September 5, 1955; admitted to bar, 1991, California; 1992, Pennsylvania. *Education:* Loyola Marymount University (B.A., magna cum laude, 1987); Loyola University Law School (J.D., 1991). Alpha Sigma Nu, Phi Delta Phi. *Member:* Wilshire (Board of Governors), Los Angeles County and American Bar Associations; National Association of Women in Construction; California

*(This Listing Continued)*

Chinese American Construction Association. *PRACTICE AREAS:* Commercial; Corporate; Construction Law; Litigation. *Email:* elascheid@wickwire.com

**JODI M. LEWIS,** born New York, NY., May 25, 1961; admitted to bar, 1987, California;. *Education:* University of California at Santa Barbara; California State University at Northridge (B.A., 1983); Loyola University, Los Angeles (J.D., 1987). Member, Entertainment Law Journal, 1986-1987. *Member:* American Bar Association; California Trial Lawyers Association; The Association of Trial Lawyers of America. *PRACTICE AREAS:* Litigation; Construction and Business Law. *Email:* jlewis@wickwire.com

(For Biographical data on other Personnel, see Vienna, Virginia, Washington, D.C., Greenbelt, Maryland, Minneapolis, Minnesota and Madison, Wisconsin, Professional Biographies)

## LAW OFFICES OF
## JAMES S. WIEDERSCHALL
### LOS ANGELES, CALIFORNIA
(See Woodland Hills)

*Complex State and Federal Litigation, including Bad Faith, Insurance Coverage, Surety and Fidelity, Commercial, Construction Defects, Discrimination, and Public Entities. Trial and Appellate.*

## ARNOLD F. WILLIAMS
### 800 WILSHIRE BOULEVARD
### 12TH FLOOR
### LOS ANGELES, CALIFORNIA 90017
Telephone: 213-688-7523
Fax: 213-688-2771
Email: arnofwms@netcom.com

*Wills, Trusts and Estate Planning, Probate, Charitable Tax Planning and Elder Law.*

FIRM PROFILE: Mr. Williams law practice consists only of the above areas. He believes that proper estate planning consists of taking care of people and their families, passing on their values, goals and property to the next generation with dignity and love, without unnecessary taxes and fees.

Upon request, Mr. Williams has presented private seminars on estate planning and planned giving, and continues to teach seminars to insurance and financial professionals on estate planning.

**ARNOLD F. WILLIAMS,** born San Diego, California, December 24, 1955; admitted to bar, 1987, California and U.S. District Court, Eastern District of California. *Education:* Stanford University (A.B. in Classics, with honors in Humanities, 1979); University of Southern California (M.B.A., 1984); University of California at Los Angeles School of Law (J.D., 1987). *Member:* Los Angeles County (Member, Sections on: Trusts and Estates) and American (Member, Sections on: Business Law; General Practice; Intellectual Property; Real Property, Probate and Trust Law; Taxation) Bar Associations; State Bar of California (Member, Sections on: Business Law; Law Practice Management; Estate Planning and Probate; General Practice; Taxation); National Network of Estate Planning Attorneys; National Academy of Elder Law Attorneys.

## LAW OFFICES OF
## NORMA J. WILLIAMS
### 600 WILSHIRE BOULEVARD, NINTH FLOOR
### LOS ANGELES, CALIFORNIA 90017-3212
Telephone: 213-975-1845
Facsimile: 213-975-1833

*Real Estate Transactions and Real Estate Litigation.*

FIRM PROFILE: Law Offices of Norma J. Williams is a growing law firm whose practice emphasizes representation of sophisticated public and private entities involved in real estate transactions including lenders, commercial, industrial and residential developers and parties to sale and lease transactions. The firm also handles commercial lending matters and litigation related to real estate finance. Founded in 1985 by its principal, Norma J. Williams, the firm has consistently provided first quality representation and individualized attention to its clients. The firm has worked on highly sophisticated transactions in representation solely by the firm and on a joint venture basis with other law firms.

**NORMA J. WILLIAMS,** born Brooklyn, New York, September 19, 1952; admitted to bar, 1977, California. *Education:* Wesleyan University (B.A., magna cum laude, 1974); University of California, Berkeley, Boalt Hall School of Law (J.D., 1977). Phi Beta Kappa. Author: "A Comparison of the Treatment of Real Estate Interests Under FIRREA and the Bankruptcy Law," 11 California Real Property Law Journal 22, Summer, 1993; "Real Estate Issues Under the 1994 Bankruptcy Reform Act," 25 Real Estate Review, Volume 3, 58, Fall, 1995; "Mixed Collateral Foreclosures," A Real Property Law Reporter 113, May, 1996. *Member:* Los Angeles County Bar Association (Member, Executive Committee, Real Property Law Section, 1993—); State Bar of California (Member, Executive Committee, Real Property Law Section, 1990-1993; Adviser, 1993-1995; Adviser Emeritus, 1995-1996; Chair, Secured Transactions Law Reform Committee, 1992-1996; Member, Joint Committee on Legal Opinions, 1992—; Co-chairperson, Real Estate Finance Subsection, 1988-1990); Women Lawyers Association of Los Angeles (Board Member, 1991-1992); Financial Lawyers Conference. *PRACTICE AREAS:* Real Estate; Bankruptcy Law; Commercial Law.

### OF COUNSEL

**VAHAN SAROIANS,** born Tehran, Iran, August 27, 1967; admitted to bar, 1994, California. *Education:* California State University, Northridge (B.S., 1989); Loyola University of Los Angeles (J.D., 1993). Licensed Realtor, California, 1989. *Member:* Los Angeles County Bar Association; The Armenian Bar Association. *PRACTICE AREAS:* Real Estate; Lending; Bankruptcy.

## WILLIAMS AND BALLAS
### 1800 CENTURY PARK EAST, SUITE 510
### LOS ANGELES, CALIFORNIA 90067
Telephone: 310-557-8383
Fax: 310-557-8380

San Francisco, California Office: 160 Sansome Street, Suite 1200. Telephone: 415-296-9904. Fax: 415-981-0898.

*Estate Planning, Tax Planning, Probate and Corporate Law.*

FIRM PROFILE: The firm of Williams and Ballas is involved in tax and estate planning, administration and the representation of small to medium sized businesses. In addition, the firm handles all matters relating to probate, estates, trusts and federal and state gift and death taxes. The firm has several attorneys that are of counsel that have expertise in banking and real estate law. Mr. Williams and Mr. Ballas specialize in federal and state estate planning, income tax planning, non-qualified deferred compensation plans and life and disability insurance planning. The firm represents clients in tax litigation before the IRS, Franchise Tax Board, State Board of Equalization and other tax agencies. The law firm is listed in the Bar Register of Preeminent Lawyers.

### MEMBERS OF FIRM

**LAWRENCE D. WILLIAMS,** born Los Angeles, California, May 11, 1938; admitted to bar, 1964, California. *Education:* University of Redlands; California State University, Long Beach (B.A., summa cum laude, 1960); University of California, Los Angeles, School of Law (J.D., 1963). Alpha Kappa Psi Scholar. Member, Blue Key. *Member:* Santa Monica, Los Angeles County and American Bar Associations; The State Bar of California. (Certified Specialist, Estate Planning, Trust and Probate Law, The State Bar of California Board of Legal Specialization) (Also Of Counsel, Weisz & Associates, P.C., Philadelphia, Pennsylvania). *PRACTICE AREAS:* Estate Planning Law; Tax Planning Law; Corporate Law.

**STEPHEN B. BALLAS,** born Los Angeles, California, June 4, 1954; admitted to bar, 1979, California. *Education:* University of California at Los Angeles (B.A., 1975); University of Southern California (M.B.A., 1978; J.D., 1978). Phi Beta Kappa; Phi Gamma Mu. Certified Public Accountant, California. *Member:* State Bar of California; American Bar Association (Member, Sections of: Taxation; Real Property, Probate and Trust Law). (Certified Specialist, Taxation Law, The State Bar of California Board of Legal Specialization). *PRACTICE AREAS:* Tax Law; Estate Planning Law; Probate.

### OF COUNSEL

**STANLEY P. GRAHAM,** born Sharon, Pennsylvania, July 13, 1943; admitted to bar, 1970, California. *Education:* University of Arizona (B.A., 1966); University of California at Los Angeles (J.D., 1969). Author: "Collateral Tax Issues related to Equity Participation Mortgages," Real Estate

*(This Listing Continued)*

*WILLIAMS AND BALLAS, Los Angeles—Continued*

Finance Law Journal, Winter 1986. Lecturer: The 22nd Annual Mid-American Tax Conference, 1983; California Society of Certified Public Accountants, 1987-1988. Certified Public Accountant, California, 1974. *Member:* Century City (Chairman, Tax Section, 1987-1989), Los Angeles County (Member, Sections on: Taxation; Probate and Trust Law) and American (Member, Sections on: Taxation; Real Property, Probate and Trust Law) Bar Associations; State Bar of California (Member, Sections on: Taxation; Estate Planning, Trust and Probate Law Sections); American Institute of Certified Public Accountants. *PRACTICE AREAS:* Tax Law; Estate Planning Law.

ASSOCIATES

**MELISSA HAMILTON,** born Selma, Alabama, July 16, 1966; admitted to bar, 1992, New York; 1995, California. *Education:* University of Alabama (B.A., with honors, 1988); Columbia University (J.D., 1991). Moot Court Editor, Journal of Law and the Arts. *Member:* New York State and American (Member, Real Property, Probate and Trust Law Section) Bar Associations; State Bar of California. *PRACTICE AREAS:* Estate Planning.

## WILLIAMS, BERGES & SANFORD

Established in 1975

SUITE 511, 10850 RIVERSIDE DRIVE
**LOS ANGELES, CALIFORNIA 91602**
*Telephone: 818-769-6622*
*Fax: 818-769-9632*
*Email: wbs1@lawnt.com*

*General Civil and Trial Practice. Negligence, Products Liability, Probate, Malpractice and Insurance Law.*

FIRM PROFILE: *William, Berges & Sanford is a state-wide, civil litigation and insurance defense firm founded in 1975. The firm specializes in insurance defense law including negligence, construction defect, product liability, bad faith and all forms of casualty cases, as well as alternative dispute resolution.*

*The firms' attorneys have experience in all aspects of litigation, arbitration, mediation and administrative proceedings, including substantial experience in successfully trying cases.*

MEMBERS OF FIRM

**RONALD A. BERGES,** born Los Angeles, California, September 30, 1945; admitted to bar, 1972, California. *Education:* California State University at Long Beach (B.A., 1968); Loyola University at Los Angeles (J.D., 1971). Recipient: American Jurisprudence Award in Criminal Law, 1969; American Trial Lawyers Association Award for Environmental Law Legal Essay Contest, 1971. Attorney, Office of the City Attorney of Los Angeles, 1969-1974. *Member:* State Bar of California; Southern California Defense Attorneys Association. *PRACTICE AREAS:* Negligence; Products Liability; Probate; Insurance; Mediation; Arbitration.

**THOMAS C. SANFORD,** born Philadelphia, Pennsylvania, December 4, 1947; admitted to bar, 1975, California. *Education:* California State University at Los Angeles (B.S., 1970); Southwestern University (J.D., 1975). *Member:* State Bar of California; Southern California Defense Attorneys' Association. *PRACTICE AREAS:* Negligence; Products Liability; Medical Malpractice; Insurance; Arbitration.

ASSOCIATES

**STEPHEN M. KALPAKIAN,** born Montebello, California, May 8, 1960; admitted to bar, 1990, California. *Education:* Whittier College (B.S., 1982); Loyola Law School, Los Angeles (J.D., 1990). *Member:* Los Angeles County Bar Association; State Bar of California; Southern California Defense Attorneys Association.

**PAUL J. SKITZKI,** born Richmond, Virginia, May 5, 1963; admitted to bar, 1990, California. *Education:* University of Arizona (B.A., 1986); Creighton University (J.D., 1989). *Member:* Los Angeles County and American Bar Associations; State Bar of California.

REPRESENTATIVE CORPORATE CLIENTS: Acceptance Insurance Co.; Berkley Risk Services, Inc.; Carolina Casualty Co.; CenCal Insurance Services; Central National Insurance Co.; Columbia Insurance Co.; The Empire Insurance Cos.; GEICO Insurance Co.; Guaranty National Cos.; Home Insurance Co.; IPS Corp.; Jonnell Agnew & Associates; Malone Service Co.; Mid Valley Cab, Inc.; National Indemnity Insurance Co.; Precision Risk Management, Inc.; Protective National Insurance Co.; Risk Administrative Services; Seguros Interamericana; State Auto Insurance Cos.; United Southern Assurance; United States Fidelity & Guaranty Co.; William Spawr Racing Stable.
REFERENCE: Wells Fargo Bank (Toluca Lake Branch).

## WILLIAMS & KILKOWSKI

Established in 1989

22ND FLOOR, 2121 AVENUE OF THE STARS
**LOS ANGELES, CALIFORNIA 90067**
*Telephone: 310-282-8995*
*Facsimile: 310-282-8930*

*Civil Litigation. Bankruptcy, Secured Transactions, Corporate, Business, Real Estate and Entertainment Law.*

**LEE D. WILLIAMS,** born Enid, Oklahoma, September 2, 1950; admitted to bar, 1977, California. *Education:* University of California at Santa Barbara (B.A., with high honors, 1973); University of California School of Law at Los Angeles (J.D., 1977). Member, UCLA Law Review, 1975-1977. Extern-Clerk to Hon. Joseph T. Sneed, U.S. Court of Appeals, Ninth Circuit, Winter, 1976. Member, Board of Trustees, Children's Institute International, 1981—. Vice President, Treasurer, Children's Institute International, 1994—. Participant, Public Counsel's Volunteer Legal Services Project, 1977-1979. Member, Board of Directors, Santa Susan Repertory Company. *Member:* State Bar of California.

**JAMES M. KILKOWSKI,** born Baltimore, Maryland, March 20, 1947; admitted to bar, 1982, California; 1983, U.S. District Court, Central District of California; 1988, U.S. District Court, Eastern District of California. *Education:* Harvard University (A.B., with honors, 1969); University of Minnesota (Ph.D., 1976); Boalt Hall School of Law, University of California (J.D., 1982). Licensed Psychologist, California, 1977; Member, Panel of Arbitrators, American Arbitration Association. *Member:* Century City Bar Association; State Bar of California (Member, Real Estate and Business Sections). *REPORTED CASES:* Abeytas v. Superior Court (1993) 17 Cal. App. 4th 1037.

REFERENCE: Santa Monica Bank.

## WILLIAMS WOOLLEY COGSWELL NAKAZAWA & RUSSELL

**LOS ANGELES, CALIFORNIA**

(See Long Beach)

*Commercial Transactions and Litigation, Maritime Law, Transportation and International Law, Immigration Law, Personal Injury and Product Liability Litigation.*

## WILLIAMSON, RALEIGH & DOHERTY

A LAW CORPORATION

801 SOUTH GRAND AVENUE, 11TH FLOOR
**LOS ANGELES, CALIFORNIA 90017**
*Telephone: 213-629-3480*
*Facsimile: 213-688-0057*

*General Civil Litigation in all State and Federal Courts, Insurance Defense, Business Litigation, Products Liability, Construction Defect, Professional Malpractice, Insurance Coverage, Catastrophe and Land Subsidence Losses, Insurance Fraud, Premise Liability, Governmental/Municipality Defense, Environmental Liability.*

FIRM PROFILE: *Williamson, Raleigh & Doherty is a group of experienced attorneys who were former principals and trial counsel for other insurance defense firms and/or large corporations. Each had a desire to develop a small firm designed as a response to the growing need for personalized quality service often lost in a large firm environment. The firm is handling all types of litigation for its clients from the simple to the complex.*

**JOHN J. DOHERTY,** born Los Angeles, California, April 4, 1946; admitted to bar, 1976, California and U.S. District Court, Central, Northern and Southern Districts of California. *Education:* University of Southern California; Loyola University of Los Angeles (J.D., 1975). Arbitrator, Los Angeles Superior Court, 1981—. *Member:* Los Angeles County Bar Association; The State Bar of California (Probation Monitor and Fee Arbitrator, 1986—); Association of Southern California Defense Counsel; Defense Research Institute. [With USN, 1967-1969; Served with USMC in Vietnam,

*(This Listing Continued)*

1968]. *PRACTICE AREAS:* Insurance Defense; Bad Faith; Professional Malpractice; Products Liability; Business Litigation; Toxic Torts; Hotel Security; Construction Defect.

**JOHN K. RALEIGH,** born Washington, D.C., April 8, 1961; admitted to bar, 1988, California and U.S. District Court, Central District of California; U.S. Court of Appeals, Ninth Circuit. *Education:* University of Southern California (B.A., cum laude, 1984); Loyola Marymount University (J.D., 1987). Phi Alpha Delta; Blackstonian. Executive Editor, Loyola International and Comparative Law Journal, 1985-1987. Law Clerk, Justice Leon Thompson, U.S. Court of Appeals, 1987. Arbitrator, Mediator and Settlement Officer, Los Angeles Superior Court. *Member:* Los Angeles County Bar Association; State Bar of California; Association of Southern California Defense Counsel; Risk Management Society; Defense Research Institute. *PRACTICE AREAS:* Insurance Defense; Professional Malpractice; Construction Defect; Products Liability; Insurance Coverage; Insurance Fraud; Catastrophe and Land Subsidence Losses; Governmental/Municipality; Business Litigation.

**MARCUS R. WILLIAMSON,** born Norfolk, Virginia, July 13, 1941; admitted to bar, 1976, California; 1977, U.S. District Court, Southern and Central Districts of California. *Education:* Lafayette College (B.A., 1963); Kent State University (M.A., Psychology, 1966); Emory University Medical School (M.S., Neuroanatomy, 1972); Mercer University (J.D., 1975). Psi Chi. Member, Mercer University Law Review, 1974-1975. Arbitrator, Los Angeles Superior Court. *Member:* State Bar of California; Association of Southern California Defense Counsel. *PRACTICE AREAS:* Insurance Defense; Business Litigation; Products Liability; Construction Defect; Professional Malpractice.

---

**JEFFREY S. BRETOI,** born Montebello, California, January 5, 1962; admitted to bar, 1988, California and U.S. Court of Appeals, Ninth Circuit. *Education:* Fullerton College; Western State University College of Law (J.D., 1987); Graduate Studies, University of Southern California Law School. Recipient, American Jurisprudence Awards in Real Estate and Federal Income Tax. Arbitrator, Los Angeles Superior Court. *Member:* State Bar of California. *PRACTICE AREAS:* Insurance Defense; Governmental; Municipal; Business Litigation; Construction Defect.

**PAUL F. SULLIVAN,** born New York, N.Y., January 24, 1965; admitted to bar, 1990, California; 1991, U.S. District Court, Eastern and Northern Districts of California. *Education:* San Diego State (B.S., 1986); McGeorge School of Law (J.D., 1990). Moot Court and Trial Advocacy Program, McGeorge School of Law; Legal Aid, McGeorge School for Community Legal Services. *Member:* San Joaquin County and Los Angeles County Bar Associations. *PRACTICE AREAS:* Insurance Defense; Professional Malpractice; Intellectual Property; Business Litigation; Construction Defect.

### OF COUNSEL

**JAMES T. CATLOW,** born Pasadena, California, August 31, 1948; admitted to bar, 1974, California and U.S. District Court, Southern District of California; 1978, U.S. District Court, Central District of California. *Education:* University of California at Los Angeles (B.A., with honors in Speech, 1970); University of San Diego (J.D., cum laude, 1974). Phi Alpha Delta. Member, Arbitration Panel of Orange County Special Arbitration Plan, 1979—. *Member:* State Bar of California; Orange County Trial Lawyers Association; Association of Southern California Defense Counsel; The Association of Trial Lawyers of America. *PRACTICE AREAS:* Insurance Coverage; Bad Faith; Complex Litigation; Construction Defect; Professional Malpractice; Products Liability; Maritime Matters; Catastrophe and Land Subsidence Losses.

---

## DANIEL H. WILLICK

*1999 AVENUE OF THE STARS*
*TWENTY-SEVENTH FLOOR*
**LOS ANGELES, CALIFORNIA 90067**
*Telephone: 310-286-0485*
*Facsimile: 310-286-0487*

*General Civil Litigation Practice in all State and Federal Courts. Health Care Law. Administrative Law.*

**DANIEL H. WILLICK,** born St. Louis, Missouri, September 4, 1942; admitted to bar, 1973, California; 1982, District of Columbia. *Education:* University of California, Los Angeles (A.B., with highest honors, 1964; J.D., 1973); University of Chicago (A.M., 1966; Ph.D., 1968). Phi Beta

*(This Listing Continued)*

Kappa; Order of the Coif. Russell Sage Foundation Resident in Law and Social Science, University of California, Los Angeles School of Law, 1970-1972. Co-author: "Attacks on Medical Staff Self-Governance Intensify," Vol. 37, No. 8 Southern California Psychiatrist, April, 1989. Adjunct Professor of Law, Loyola Law School, Los Angeles, 1977-1978. Lecturer, 1993-1996, Assistant Clinical Professor, 1996—, U.C.L.A. School of Medicine, Los Angeles. Member, Board of Directors, 1981-1994 and Vice President, 1983-1989, Constitutional Rights Foundation. *Member:* Los Angeles County and American Bar Associations; The District of Columbia Bar; State Bar of California. (Also of Counsel Pircher, Nichols & Meeks).

### ASSOCIATE

**MARC I. WILLICK,** born Santa Barbara, California, July 20, 1968; admitted to bar, 1994, California. *Education:* University of California at San Diego (B.A., 1991); Loyola Law School, Los Angeles (J.D., 1994). Volunteer Staff, The Center for Conflict Resolution, Loyola Law School. *Member:* Los Angeles County and American Bar Associations; State Bar of California.

---

## ANDREW RUSSELL WILLING

*PROMENADE WEST*
*880 WEST FIRST STREET*
*SUITE 302*
**LOS ANGELES, CALIFORNIA 90012**
*Telephone: 213-626-6600*
*Facsimile: 213-626-0488*

*Criminal Defense in State and Federal Courts. Appellate Practice. Municipal Law. Land Use. Administrative Law (Emphasizing Medical License Defense).*

**ANDREW RUSSELL WILLING,** born Mt. Vernon, New York, January 21, 1941; admitted to bar, 1966, New York; 1969, U.S. Court of Appeals, Second Circuit and U.S. District Court, Southern District of New York; 1971, U.S. Court of Appeals, Ninth Circuit; 1972, California and U.S. District Court, Central District of California; 1975, U.S. District Court, Southern District of California. *Education:* Amherst College (B.A., cum laude, 1962); Harvard University (J.D., 1965). Recipient, California State Assembly Resolution of Commendation by Hon. Richard Alatorre, 1981. Law Clerk to Honorable Richard H. Levet, U.S. District Judge, Southern District of New York, 1965-1966. Author: "Protection By Law Enforcement: The Emerging Constitutional Right," 35 Rutgers Law Review 1-99, 1982. Associate Professor of Law, Southwestern University School of Law, Los Angeles, California, 1977-1982. Guest Speaker, McGeorge School of Law, Symposium on Victims' Rights in California, "Public Safety: A New Constitutional Right," April, 1992. Assistant U.S. Attorney, Central District of California, 1970-1972. Assistant District Attorney and Chief, Special Prosecutions, City and County of San Francisco, 1976. Member, Federal Indigent Defense Panel, Central District of California, 1985—. *Member:* Los Angeles County (Member, Sections on: Government Law; Criminal Justice) New York State and American (Member, Sections on: Criminal Justice; Judicial Administration; Antitrust) Bar Associations; The State Bar of California; Selden Society; Association of Former Assistant United States Attorneys. [E.4, USAR, 4th and 78th JAGD, 1965-1971]. *LANGUAGES:* Spanish.

REFERENCE: Wells Fargo Bank (Pasadena Main Office).

---

## WILLSEY LAW OFFICES

*OWNED BY A PROFESSIONAL CORPORATION*

**LOS ANGELES, CALIFORNIA**

(See Pasadena)

*General Civil Practice. Taxation Law, Family Law including Dissolutions, Paternity, Cohabitation, Spousal Support, Prenuptials and District Attorney Enforcement, Real Estate, Bankruptcy.*

## LAW OFFICES OF ROBERT D. WILNER
601 WEST 5TH STREET, ROOM 203
**LOS ANGELES, CALIFORNIA 90071-2000**
Telephone: 213-624-4223

*Probate and Estate Planning, Trusts and Wills.*

**ROBERT D. WILNER,** born Detroit, Michigan, March 14, 1936; admitted to bar, 1964, California. *Education:* Los Angeles City College (A.A., 1959); Southwestern University School of Law (LL.B., 1963). (Certified Specialist, Estate Planning, Trust and Probate Law, The State Bar of California Board of Legal Specialization).

---

## WILNER, KLEIN & SIEGEL
A PROFESSIONAL CORPORATION
**LOS ANGELES, CALIFORNIA**
(See Beverly Hills)

*General Civil and Trial Practice in all State and Federal Courts. Admiralty and General Maritime Law. Real Property, Corporate, Community Association Law, Insurance, Federal Employers Liability Act and Professional Liability Law.*

---

## WILSON, ELSER, MOSKOWITZ, EDELMAN & DICKER
SUITE 2700
1055 WEST SEVENTH STREET
**LOS ANGELES, CALIFORNIA 90017**
Telephone: 213-624-3044
Telex: 17-0722
Facsimile: 213-624-8060

*New York, N.Y. Office:* 150 East 42nd Street, 10017. Telephone: 212-490-3000. Telex: 177679. Facsimile: 212-490-3038; 212-557-7810.
*San Francisco, California Office:* 650 California Street, 94108. Telephone: 415-433-0990. Telex: 16-0768. Facsimile: 415-434-1370.
*Washington, D.C. Office:* The Colorado Building, Fifth Floor, 1341 "G" Street, N.W., 20005. Telephone: 202-626-7660. Telex: 89453. Facsimile: 202-628-3606.
*Newark, New Jersey Office:* Two Gateway Center, 07102. Telephone: 201-624-0800. Telex: 6853589. Facsimile: 201-624-0808.
*Philadelphia, Pennsylvania Office:* The Curtis Center, Independence Square West, 19106. Telephone: 215-627-6900. Telex: 6711203. Facsimile: 215-627-2665.
*Baltimore, Maryland Office:* 250 West Pratt Street, 21201. Telephone: 410-539-1800. Telex: 19-8280. Facsimile: 410-539-1820.
*Miami, Florida Office:* International Place, 100 Southeast Second Street, 33131. Telephone: 305-374-4400. Telex: 810845940. Facsimile: 305-579-0261.
*Chicago, Illinois Office:* 120 N. LaSalle Street, 26th Floor, 60602. Telephone: 312-704-0550. Telex: 1561590. Facsimile: 312-704-1552.
*White Plains, N.Y. Office:* 925 Westchester Avenue, 10604. Telephone: 914-946-7200. Facsimile: 914-946-7897.
*Dallas, Texas Office:* 5000 Renaissance Tower, 1201 Elm Street, 75270. Telephone: 214-698-8000. Facsimile: 214-698-1101.
*Albany, New York Office:* One Steuben Place. Telephone: 518-449-8893. Fax: 518-449-8927.
*London, England Office:* 141 Fenchurch Street, EC3M 6BL. Telephone: 01-623-6723. Telex: 885741. Facsimile: 01-626-9774.
*Tokyo, Japan Office:* AIU Building, 1-3 Marunouchi 1-chome, Chiyoda-Ku, 100. Telephone: 011-813-216-6551. Facsimile: 011-(813) 3216-6965.
*Affiliate Office in Paris, France:* Honig Buffat Mettetal. 21 rue Clément Marot, 75008. Telephone: 33 (1) 44.43.88.88. Fax: 33 (1) 44.43.88.77.
*Affiliate Offices in Germany:* Munich, Germany: Bach, Langheid Dallmayr Pacellistrasse 8, 80333. Telephone: (49) 89 296 259. Facsimile: (49) 89 290 4756.
*Cologne, Germany:* Bach, Langheid Dallmayr Wilhelm-Waldeyer-Strasse 14, 50937. Telephone: (49) 221 944 027 0. Facsimile: (49) 221 944 027 8.
*Frankfurt/Main, Germany:* Bach, Langheid Dallmayr Schutzenstrasse 4, 60313. Telephone: (49) 69 920 740 0. Facsimile: (49) 69 920 740 40.
*Wiesbaden, Germany:* Bach, Langheid Dallmayr Robert-Koch, Ste. 6. Telephone(49) 611 56 42 38. Facsimile: (49) 611 564232.

*(This Listing Continued)*

CAA1294B

---

*General Insurance and Reinsurance Practice and Litigation. Commercial, Corporate and Securities Law. Domestic and International Property and Casualty Insurance and Reinsurance. Products and Professional Liability, Toxic Tort Defense, Environmental Impairment Liability, Medical and Hospital Malpractice, Municipal and Public Officials Liability, Trusts and Estates. Aviation, Marine and Inland Marine. Securities and Fiduciary Liability and General Subrogation.*

**FIRM PROFILE:** Wilson, Elser, Moskowitz, Edelman & Dicker is a full service international law firm, ranking among the largest law firms in the United States with offices in twelve major cities in the United States. We have provided our clients with a full range of expert and innovative legal services for more than a quarter of a century. Our dramatic growth during this period has been a response to the emerging needs of existing clients and addition of new ones. Initially, ours was an insurance-related practice and we maintain a preeminent position with regard to all aspects of insurance law and the insurance/reinsurance industry serving insureds, brokers, insurers and reinsurers. As our clients have matured and broadened in scope, so have our services and expertise and we have expanded into the general corporate law, including creditors' rights and bankruptcy, trusts and estates and real estate transactions and regulatory work.

### RESIDENT PARTNERS

**PATRICK M. KELLY,** born Pasadena, California, April 4, 1943; admitted to bar, 1970, California. *Education:* Pomona College (B.A., 1966); Loyola University of Los Angeles (J.D., 1969). Phi Delta Phi (Magister, 1968-1969). Member, St. Thomas More Society. Author: "Practical Approaches to Punitive Damages Cases," 1981; "Closing the Case," 1983; "Litigation and Liability," Ski Area Management, 1984. Co-author: "Closing the Case: Resolving Multi-Party Suits Through Good-Faith Settlements," Business Insurance, October 31, 1983; "Updated Approaches to Punitive Damages," California Lawyer, December, 1984; "Good Faith Settlements: Overcoming New Obstacles," Los Angeles County Bar Trial Lawyers Newsletter, February/March, 1985. Contributor, "Civil Procedure Before Trial," 1978. Lecturer: Presenting Evidence, 1986, Construction Claims and Disputes for Owners and Contractors, 1983-1986, Construction Disputes for Auditors and Engineers and Civil Discovery, 1976 Association of Business Trial Lawyers. Contributor, "Insurance Litigation," California Judges Association, 1989 Trial Practice, Los Angeles County Bar Association, 1975. Member, Panel of Arbitrators, American Arbitration Association. *Member:* Los Angeles County (Trustee, 1978-1980, 1985—; President, 1990-1991; President-Elect, 1989-1990; Senior Vice President, 1988-1989; Vice President and Treasurer, 1987-1988; Chair: Editorial Board and Editorial Advisory Committee, Los Angeles Lawyer, 1977-1978; Attorneys Errors and Omissions Committee, 1986-1987; Legislative Committee, 1980-1981; Los Angeles Delegation to State Bar Conference of Delegates; Legislative Activity Committee, 1982-1984; Member, Judicial Appointments Committee, 1980-1985; Vice Chairman, 1984-1985, Trial Lawyers Section; Fast Track Committee, 1988-1989; Chair, Litigation Section, 1987-1988) and American (Member, Sections on: Litigation; Tort and Insurance Practice) Bar Associations; The State Bar of California (Member: Executive Committee of the Conference of Delegates, 1981-1984; Editorial Board, California Lawyer, 1981—; Chair, Public Affairs Committee, 1979-1980); Association of Southern California Defense Counsel (Chancery, 1986—); National Association of Railroad Trial Counsel; Association of Business Trial Lawyers; Defense Research Institute; American Society for Testing and Materials; Los Angeles County Bar Foundation (Director, 1984—; Secretary, 1987-1988); American Bar Foundation. (Partner in Charge- Los Angeles).

**JONATHON F. SHER,** born Los Angeles, California, April 28, 1949; admitted to bar, 1973, California; U.S. Court of Appeals, Ninth Circuit; U.S. District Court, Central, Southern, Northern and Eastern Districts of California. *Education:* University of California at Santa Barbara (B.A., 1970); University of Southern California (J.D., 1973). *Member:* Los Angeles County Bar Association; Wilshire Bar Association (Member, Board of Governors, 1986—).

**ROBERT M. YOUNG, JR.,** born St. Louis, Missouri, April 24, 1948; admitted to bar, 1974, California and U.S. District Court, Northern District of California; 1977, U.S. District Court, Central District of California; 1987, U.S. District Court, Southern District of California. *Education:* University of California at Los Angeles (B.S., Engineering, 1970); Hastings College of Law, University of California (J.D., 1974). Lecturer and Co-author: "Representing Architects, Engineers and other Design Professionals," California Continuing Education of the Bar, 1986. Member, National Panel of Construction Industry Arbitration, American Arbitration Association. *Member:* Los Angeles County and American (Member, Section on Litigation) Bar Associations; The State Bar of California; National Society

*(This Listing Continued)*

of Professional Engineers; California Society of Professional Engineers; Association of Southern California Defense Counsel.

**L. VICTOR BILGER, JR.,** born Oklahoma City, Oklahoma, December 8, 1945; admitted to bar, 1978, California. *Education:* Harvey Mudd College (B.S., Engineering, 1967); Loyola Law School, Los Angeles (J.D., 1978). *Member:* The State Bar of California; Defense Research Institute.

**STEVEN R. PARMINTER,** born Whittier, California, November 26, 1953; admitted to bar, 1979, California; U.S. District Court, Central and Eastern Districts of California; U.S. Court of Appeals, Ninth Circuit. *Education:* Whittier College (B.A., 1975); Loyola Law School, Los Angeles (J.D., 1979). Member, 1978-1979, Contributing Author, 1979, Loyola International and Comparative Law Annual. *Member:* Los Angeles County Bar Association (Member, Litigation Section); The State Bar of California.

**OTIS D. WRIGHT, II,** born Tuskegee, Alabama, July 31, 1944; admitted to bar, 1980, California; 1981, U.S. District Court, Central District of California; 1984, U.S. District Court, Eastern District of California; 1985, U.S. Court of Appeals, Ninth Circuit; 1986, U.S. Supreme Court. *Education:* California State University at Los Angeles (B.S. Bus. Adm., 1976); Southwestern University School of Law (J.D., 1980). Member, Moot Court. Deputy Attorney General, 1980-1983. *Member:* Los Angeles County (Member, Executive Committee, Litigation Section) and American Bar Associations; Langston Bar Association; The State Bar of California; Southern California Defense Counsel; The Association of Trial Lawyers of America; California Trial Lawyers Association.

**VINCENT P. D'ANGELO,** born New York, N.Y., July 8, 1953; admitted to bar, 1980, California and U.S. District Court, Central District of California. *Education:* Fordham University (B.S.B.A., 1975); Loyola University of Los Angeles (J.D., 1980). Arbitrator, Los Angeles County Judicial Arbitration Program. *Member:* Los Angeles County and American (Member, Section on Tort and Insurance Practice) Bar Associations; The State Bar of California.

**JAMES A. STANKOWSKI,** born Schenectady, New York, July 19, 1957; admitted to bar, 1982, California. *Education:* Fordham University (B.A. in Political Science, 1979); Pepperdine University (J.D., cum laude, 1982). Recipient, American Jurisprudence Awards, Contracts and Torts. *Member:* Los Angeles County Bar Association; The State Bar of California.

**MARTIN K. DENISTON,** born Pasadena, California, June 10, 1956; admitted to bar, 1982, California, U.S. District Court, Central, Southern, Northern and Eastern Districts of California and U.S. Court of Appeals, Ninth Circuit. *Education:* University of California at Santa Barbara (B.A., with honors, 1978); Pepperdine University (J.D., 1982). Staff Member, 1980-1981 and Literary Editor, 1981-1982, Pepperdine University Law Review. Member: Moot Court Board, 1981-1982; ABA National Moot Court Team, 1981. Author: "Hubbard v. Boelt: The Fireman's Rule Extended," 9 Pepperdine Law Review 1977, 1981. Executive Committee Member, Los Angeles County Bar Association Barristers, 1987-1990. Operating Committee Member, Dispute Resolution Services, Inc., 1987-1990. Chair, Dispute Resolution Services Municipal Court Programs Subcommittee, 1989-1990. Chair of Barristers Landlord-Tenant Settlement Officer Program, 1987-1989. Member, Attorneys Errors and Omissions Prevention Committee, 1989-1995. Volunteer Judge pro tem. Volunteer Attorney for Public Counsel. *Member:* Los Angeles County and American (Member: Tort and Insurance Practice Section; National Legal Malpractice Data Center) Bar Associations; State Bar of California. *LANGUAGES:* Spanish.

**ROLAND L. COLEMAN, JR.,** born Los Angeles, California, December 28, 1949; admitted to bar, 1974, California. *Education:* Claremont McKenna College; University of Southern California (B.A., Philosophy, 1971); Loyola University of Los Angeles (J.D., 1974). Lecturer: "How to Defend a Personal Injury Case," California Continuing Education of the Bar, 1993; Products Liability: "Who to Depose and What you Can Get," Los Angeles Trial Lawyers Association, 1993; Interstate Conferences concerning Government Tort Liability, 1979-1986. Deputy Trial Attorney for the City Attorney of Los Angeles, 1974-1975. Trial and Supervising Attorney for the State of California Department of Transportation, 1975-1986. Member, State of California Department of Transportation Tort Committee regarding Risk Management, 1984-1986. *Member:* Los Angeles County Bar Association (Litigation Section Executive Committee, 1988-1991; Co-Chair, Program Committee for Litigation Section, 1988-1989; Trustee, 1990-1992; Judicial Evaluation Committee, 1988-1989; Steering Committee for Los Angeles County Bar Association Inn of Court, 1990-1992; Master in Litigation Section Inn of Court, 1991—); State Bar of California (Commissioner of Judicial Nominations Evaluation Commission, 1991-1993; Legal Services Section, Employment Law Section, 1992—); John M. Langston Bar Association (Vice President, 1989; President, 1990). *PRACTICE AREAS:* Prod-

*(This Listing Continued)*

uct Liability; Government Tort Liability; Employment Law; Civil Rights Litigation; Construction Law; General Liability.

**JACK A. JANOV,** born Los Angeles, California, June 5, 1954; admitted to bar, 1982, California; 1983, U.S. District Court, Central District of California. *Education:* California State University at Northridge (B.A., 1977); Loyola Law School, Los Angeles (J.D. 1982). Recipient, American Board of Trial Advocates Award. First Place, Loyola Trial Advocacy Competition, 1981. *Member:* Los Angeles County and American Bar Associations; State Bar of California.

**GEORGE A. PISANO,** born San Pedro, California, October 7, 1957; admitted to bar, 1983, California and U.S. District Court, Central and Southern Districts of District of California. *Education:* Loyola Marymount University (B.A., 1979); University of California at Davis (J.D., 1982). *Member:* Los Angeles County Bar Association; State Bar of California. *LANGUAGES:* Italian.

**STEPHEN R. KNAPP,** born Washington, D.C., December 3, 1941; admitted to bar, 1968, New York; 1970, California and U.S. District Court, Northern District of New York; U.S. District Court, Central and Southern Districts of California; U.S. Court of Appeals, Ninth Circuit. *Education:* Cornell University (B.A., 1965; J.D., 1968). Phi Delta Phi. Author: "The Nature of Procedural Due Process as Between the University and the Student," The College Counsel, Vol. III, No. 1, 1968. Winner, Warren's Weed New York Real Property Award, 1968. *Member:* Century City, Los Angeles County (Member, Sections on: Intellectual Property and Unfair Competition; Real Property Litigation; Pre-Judgment Remedies; Business and Corporations; Commercial Law and Bankruptcy) and New York State Bar Associations; State Bar of California. (Resident). *REPORTED CASES:* Merchants Home Delivery Service, Inc. vs. Reliance Group Holdings Inc., et al. *PRACTICE AREAS:* Business Law; Corporate Law; Commercial Law; Real Estate Law; Securities Law; Entertainment Law; Copyright Law; Trademark Law; Contract Law.

**FREDRIC W. TRESTER,** born Chicago, Illinois, November 20, 1954; admitted to bar, 1980, California. *Education:* University of Arizona (B.A., 1976); University of Santa Clara School of Law (J.D., cum laude, 1980). Licensed Real Estate Broker, California, 1984. Judge Pro Tem Los Angeles Superior Court. Arbitrator, Los Angeles Superior and Municipal Courts. *Member:* Los Angeles County Bar Association; State Bar of California; Association of Defense Counsel. *PRACTICE AREAS:* Construction Law; Real Estate Law; Products Liability.

**E. PAUL DOUGHERTY, JR.,** born Baltimore, Maryland, November 20, 1956; admitted to bar, 1981, New Jersey and U.S. District Court, District of New Jersey; 1982, New York and U.S. District Court, Southern and Eastern Districts of New York (Not admitted in California). *Education:* Georgetown University (B.S.B.A., cum laude, 1978); Villanova University (J.D., 1981). *Member:* The Association of the Bar of the City of New York; American Bar Association (Member, Section on Tort and Insurance Practice). (Resident, Tokyo, Japan Office; see Tokyo Listing for Biography).

**MARK K. WORTHGE,** born Sacramento, California, July 31, 1957; admitted to bar, 1985, California. *Education:* University of California at Los Angeles (B.S., with honors, 1979); University of West Los Angeles School of Law (J.D., 1985). Registered Professional Engineer, California, 1979. *Member:* State Bar of California.

*RESIDENT ASSOCIATES*

Robert M. Anderson; Jonathan C. Balfus; Bradley R. Blamires; Vernon A. Fagin; Terry Lees Higham; Jordan T. Jones; Herbert P. Kunowski; Robert A. Latham III; Jeffrey M. Lenkov; Janice S. Lucas; Vincent A. McGonagle; Carey B. Moorehead; Michael D. Payne; Lorne M. Pollock; Denise Kabakow Rasmussen; William S. Roberts; Gary E. Tavetian.

(For additional Biographical data, see Professional Biographies at New York, New York.)

# WILSON, KENNA & BORYS, LLP

A Limited Liability Partnership including Professional Corporations

*Established in 1984*

**THIRD FLOOR, 11075 SANTA MONICA BOULEVARD**
**LOS ANGELES, CALIFORNIA 90025-3556**
Telephone: 310-478-4285
FAX: 310-478-4351
Email: WKBLAW@AOL.COM

*Professional Malpractice, Errors and Omissions, Product Liability, General Liability, Insurance Coverage, Bad Faith, Surety, Casualty and Fidelity Law. General Litigation in all State and Federal Courts.*

## MEMBERS OF FIRM

**LAWRENCE BORYS, (PROFESSIONAL CORPORATION),** born Winnipeg, Manitoba, Canada, April 25, 1950; admitted to bar, 1974, California. *Education:* University of California at Los Angeles (A.B., 1971); University of California School of Law (J.D., 1974). Member, Moot Court. *Member:* State Bar of California; Federation of Insurance and Corporate Counsel (FICC); Southern California Defense Counsel; Defense Research Institute.

**TIMOTHY W. KENNA, (PROFESSIONAL CORPORATION),** born Orange, California, March 10, 1949; admitted to bar, 1975, California. *Education:* University of California at Santa Barbara (B.A., with honors, 1971); University of San Francisco (J.D., 1975). California State Scholar. Recipient, American Jurisprudence Awards in Administrative Law and Corporations. Assistant Editor, University of San Francisco Law Review, 1974. Author: "The Patient-Physician Relationship: Present Law and Trends for the Future Implied in Cobbs v. Grant," 8 University of San Francisco Law Review 320, 1973. *Member:* Los Angeles County (Member, Sections on: Litigation; Business and Corporate Law) and American (Member, Tort and Insurance Practice Section) Bar Associations; State Bar of California; American Board of Trial Advocates; Defense Research Institute; Southern California Defense Counsel.

**GARTH GOLDBERG,** born Los Angeles, California, November 8, 1957; admitted to bar, 1983, California; 1984, U.S. District Court, Central District of California. *Education:* University of California at Berkeley (B.A., with distinction, Physics, 1980); University of California at Davis (J.D., 1983). *Member:* Los Angeles County Bar Association; State Bar of California.

**CHRISTOPHER A. KANJO,** born Los Angeles, California, March 31, 1960; admitted to bar, 1987, California and U.S. District Court, Central District of California. *Education:* University of California at Riverside (B.A., 1982); University of Southern California Law Center (J.D., 1986). Phi Alpha Delta. *Member:* Beverly Hills and Los Angeles County Bar Associations; State Bar of California.

**JEFFREY C. BURT,** born Patchogue, New York, October 31, 1959; admitted to bar, 1986, California; 1989, U.S. District Court, Central District of California. *Education:* University of California at Los Angeles (B.A., 1981); Loyola Marymount University (J.D., 1986). *Member:* Beverly Hills, Century City and Los Angeles County Bar Associations; State Bar of California. *REPORTED CASES:* Montrose Chemical vs. Superior Court (1993) 6 Cal 4th 287; Montrose Chemical vs. Admiral Insurance (1995) 10 Cal 4th 645. *PRACTICE AREAS:* Insurance Coverage Litigation.

## ASSOCIATES

**RONALD W. ITO,** born Santa Monica, California, January 16, 1960; admitted to bar, 1986, California; 1987, U.S. District Court, Central District of California. *Education:* University of California at Irvine (A.B., 1982); Hastings College of the Law, University of California (J.D., 1986). Phi Beta Kappa. Member, Hastings Law Journal, 1985-1986. *Member:* Los Angeles County Bar Association; State Bar of California.

**ARTURO T. SALINAS,** born Los Angeles, California, August 4, 1961; admitted to bar, 1988, California and U.S. District Court, Central District of California. *Education:* Loyola Marymount University (B.A., 1984); Loyola Law School (J.D., 1987). Scott Moot Court Honors. Federal Extern to the Hon. Robert M. Takasugi. *Member:* Los Angeles County and American Bar Associations; State Bar of California. *LANGUAGES:* Spanish.

**BRIAN S. NELSON,** born Seattle, Washington, May 21, 1962; admitted to bar, 1988, California; 1989, U.S. District Court, Central District of California. *Education:* Washington State University (B.A., 1984); Pepperdine University (J.D., 1988). Delta Theta Phi (Vice-Dean, 1987-1988). Co-author, "Implied Assumption of Risk Redux: Confusion and Contradic-

*(This Listing Continued)*

tion," Declarations, page 24, Summer, 1994. *Member:* Los Angeles County and American Bar Associations; State Bar of California. *REPORTED CASES:* Pacific Estates v. American Speciality Ins. 13 CA4th, 561, 17 CR2d 434 (1993); Santa Patricia v. Murrissette Construction, 231 CA3d 113, 282 CR2d 209 (1991). *PRACTICE AREAS:* Insurance Defense; Construction Defect; Personal Injury.

**SYLVIA ANNE DYAL,** born Washington, D.C., March 15, 1958; admitted to bar, 1989, California. *Education:* University of California at Davis (B.A., 1980); University of San Francisco (J.D., 1988). *Member,* U.S. Northern District Court Historical Society; Member, Queen's Bench, 1989-1990. *Member:* Los Angeles County Bar Association.

**LISA K. GARNER,** born Los Angeles, California; admitted to bar, 1991, California and U.S. District Court, Central District of California; 1994, District of Columbia. *Education:* Trinity College; University of California at Los Angeles (B.A., cum laude, honors in History, 1988); Loyola Law School (J.D., 1991). Chief Notes and Comments Editor, Loyola Entertainment Law Journal, 1990-1991. Federal Extern to the Honorable David V. Kenyon. *Member:* Los Angeles County Bar Association.

**CHARLES N. HARGRAVES,** born Framingham, Massachusetts, October 8, 1964; admitted to bar, 1989, California and U.S. District Court, Central District of California. *Education:* Colby College (B.A., 1986); Pepperdine University (J.D., 1989). Recipient, American Jurisprudence Award for Contract Law. *Member:* State Bar of California.

**NANCY J. WENGER,** born Los Angeles, California, February 18, 1965; admitted to bar, 1990, California and U.S. District Court, Eastern District of California; 1991, Nevada. *Education:* University of California at Berkeley (B.A., 1987); University of California at Davis (J.D., 1990). Judicial Clerk, Justice Robert Rose, Nevada Supreme Court, 1990-1991. *Member:* Los Angeles County and American Bar Associations; State Bar of California.

**JOSHUA M. SABLE,** born Boston, Massachusetts, November 22, 1968; admitted to bar, 1993, Massachusetts; 1994, California and U.S. District Court, Central District of California. *Education:* Tufts University (B.A., 1990); University of California School of Law at Los Angeles (J.D., 1993).

**SHENNE J. HAHN,** born Los Angeles, California, November 22, 1968; admitted to bar, 1994, California. *Education:* University of California at Los Angeles (B.A., 1991); University of Southern California (J.D., 1994). Judicial Extern, Honorable Gary Taylor, U.S. District Court, Central District of California. *Member:* Los Angeles County Bar Association; Korean American Bar Association.

**KRISTIN M. KUBEC,** born San Jose, California, January 4, 1966; admitted to bar, 1991, California; 1992, Colorado. *Education:* University of California at Santa Barbara (B.A., 1988); McGeorge School of Law (J.D., 1991). Oral Finalist, Moot Court, 1989. *Member:* Los Angeles County, Colorado and American Bar Associations; State Bar of California.

**YVONNE JANET LIM,** born Chicago, Illinois, March 20, 1966; admitted to bar, 1994, California. *Education:* Brown University (B.A., 1988); University of California School of Law, Los Angeles (J.D., 1993). Assistant Managing Editor, Women's Law Journal, 1991-1992. Legal Extern to Hon. Ronald S.W. Lew, 1991. *LANGUAGES:* Korean.

## OF COUNSEL

**ROBERT L. WILSON, (PROFESSIONAL CORPORATION),** born Detroit, Michigan, February 22, 1931; admitted to bar, 1959, California and U.S. District Court, Southern District of California. *Education:* University of California at Los Angeles (A.B., 1953; J.D., 1958). Phi Delta Phi. *Member:* Los Angeles County and American (Member, Section of Insurance, Negligence and Compensation Law) Bar Associations; The State Bar of California; Association of Southern California Defense Counsel (Director and Secretary-Treasurer, 1967-1968); American Board of Trial Advocates; American Society of Hospital Attorneys; Excess and Surplus Lines Claims Association; Los Angeles Copyright Society. Fellow, American College of Trial Lawyers.

REPRESENTATIVE CLIENTS: Admiral Insurance Co.; Agricultural Excess and Surplus Insurance Co.; American States Insurance Company; American Bonding; American Family Insurance Group; Baxter Corp.; Baxter Bentley Laboratories; Baxter Healthcare Corp.; Bay Harbor Hospital, Inc.; CIGNA Companies; Claims Control Corp.; Cravens, Dargan & Co.; Employers Reinsurance Corp.; Fireman's Fund Insurance Companies; Firemen's Insurance Company of Washington D.C.; The Gainsco Companies; General Reinsurance Corporation; Genstar Management Co.; Great American Insurance Companies; Hull Pine Top; Investors Insurance Co.; Fred S. James & Co., Inc.; Jefferson Insurance; John Deere Insurance Company; Kemper Insurance Group; Lawyers Surety Corporation; Media Professionals, Inc./E&O Professionals; National Security Fire & Casualty; New England Life Insurance Co.; Northwestern National Insurance Co.; Old Republic Surety Company; Penn-America Insurance

*(This Listing Continued)*

## PROFESSIONAL BIOGRAPHIES

Co.; Prudential Reinsurance Co.; Public Service Mutual Insurance Co.; Safeco Insurance Companies; SCM Corporation; Scott-Wetzel Services Inc.; Special Risk Insurance Services; Statewide Adjusters of Omaha; Stonewall Insurance Co.; Toplis & Harding; U.S. Liability Insurance Co.; UTICA Mutual Insurance Company; Warwick Group; W.R.G. Claims Management Services; Zenith Insurance Company; Zurich American Insurance Cos.; Western Surety Co.

### WINN & FIELDS
1801 CENTURY PARK EAST, SUITE 1150
**LOS ANGELES, CALIFORNIA 90067**
*Telephone: 310-772-0800*
*Fax: 310-552-4760*

*Estate Planning including Charitable Gift and Tax Planning. General Business Law.*

**ROSS E. WINN,** born Los Angeles, California, April 15, 1954; admitted to bar, 1983, California and U.S. Tax Court. *Education:* University of California at Los Angeles (B.A., 1976); University of Southern California (M.B.T., 1979); Loyola Law School (J.D., 1983). Certified Public Accountant, California, 1984. Member, Board of Trustees, 1985— and Chairperson, 1993-1994, Los Angeles Family Housing Corporation. Member, Board of Directors, Southern California Institute of Architecture, 1986—. Vice President, California Association of Attorney-Certified Public Accountants, Inc., 1988—. *Member:* Beverly Hills, Los Angeles County (Member, Taxation Section) and American Bar Associations; State Bar of California; American Institute of Certified Public Accountants.

**STACEY B. FIELDS,** born Los Angeles, California, January 15, 1960; admitted to bar, 1987, California, U.S. Tax Court, U.S. Court of Appeals, Ninth Circuit and U.S. District Court, Central and Southern Districts of California. *Education:* University of Southern California (B.S., Finance, 1982); Pepperdine Law School (J.D., 1986); Georgetown University Law Center (LL.M. in Taxation, 1987). Phi Delta Phi. Extern to Federal District Court Judge James Ideman, 1984. *Member:* Los Angeles County (Member, Taxation Section) and American Bar Associations; State Bar of California.

### WINTROUB & FRIDKIS
A Partnership including a Professional Corporation
1875 CENTURY PARK EAST, 20TH FLOOR
**LOS ANGELES, CALIFORNIA 90067**
*Telephone: 310-277-0440*
*Telecopier: 310-277-7994*

*Civil Trial and Appellate Practice. Arbitration, Mediation, Corporation, Business, Government Contracts, Real Property, Secured Financing, Title Insurance, Taxation, Probate, Insurance, Estate Planning.*

**DAVID L. WINTROUB,** born Omaha, Nebraska, May 1, 1941; admitted to bar, 1967, California. *Education:* University of Nebraska (B.S., 1963); University of Michigan (LL.B., 1966). *Member:* Beverly Hills (Member, Committees on: Probate and Trust Law, 1970—) and Los Angeles County (Member, Probate and Trust Section) Bar Associations; The State Bar of California (Member, Taxation Committee, 1977—). **PRACTICE AREAS:** Estate Planning; Probate; Taxation; Real Estate.

**CLIFF FRIDKIS, (P.C.),** born New York, N.Y., January 26, 1947; admitted to bar, 1974, California; 1981, U.S. Supreme Court. *Education:* Pennsylvania State University (B.A., 1968); George Washington University (J.D., with honors, 1974). Order of the Coif. Managing Editor, George Washington Law Review, 1973-1974. Co-Author: "Securities and Exchange Commission: Coping with Institutional Membership and Anticompetitive Practices," 41 George Washington University Law Review 841, 1973; "Radiation and the Environment," Federal Environmental Law, West Publishing Company, 1974. Judge Pro Tem, Los Angeles Municipal Court, 1981-1990. *Member:* Century City and Los Angeles County (Member, Bioethics Committee, 1993—) Bar Associations; The State Bar of California (Member, Committee on the Administration of Justice, 1986-1989); Association of Business Trial Lawyers. **REPORTED CASES:** Crawford vs. Board of Education (1980) 113 Cal. App. 3d 633; Paul vs. State Farm Fire & Casualty Co. (1987) 193 Cal. App. 3d 223. **PRACTICE AREAS:** Civil Litigation.

## CALIFORNIA—LOS ANGELES

### WISE, WIEZOREK, TIMMONS & WISE
A PROFESSIONAL CORPORATION
**LOS ANGELES, CALIFORNIA**
(See Long Beach)

*General Civil and Trial Practice in State and Federal Courts. Corporation, International Business, Insurance, Real Property, Immigration, Estate Planning, Probate and Tax Law.*

### ERNEST ALLEN WISH
A PROFESSIONAL LAW CORPORATION
2121 AVENUE OF THE STARS, 22ND FLOOR
**LOS ANGELES, CALIFORNIA 90067-5010**
*Telephone: 310-277-0785*
*Fax: 310-203-0599*

*Business, Entertainment, Sports, Real Estate Litigation.*

**ERNEST ALLEN WISH,** born Los Angeles, California, June 7, 1951; admitted to bar, 1976, California, U.S. District Court, Southern, Central, Eastern and Northern Districts of California and U.S. Supreme Court. *Education:* University of California at Los Angeles (B.A., summa cum laude, with highest departmental honors, 1973); Hastings College of Law, University of California (J.D., 1976). Phi Beta Kappa; Pi Gamma Mu. Editorial Associate, Hastings Law Journal, 1975-1976. Faculty Member, University of West Los Angeles School of Law. Judge Pro Tempore, Los Angeles Municipal Court, 1981—. *Member:* Beverly Hills, Century City, San Fernando Valley and Los Angeles County Bar Associations; State Bar of California (Member, Section on Business Law); Association of Real Estate Attorneys; The Association of Trial Lawyers of America.

### WITTER AND HARPOLE
**LOS ANGELES, CALIFORNIA**
(See Pasadena)

*Federal and State Tax. Estate Planning, Tax Litigation, Trust and Probate Law.*

### LAW OFFICES OF HERBERT WOLAS
1875 CENTURY PARK EAST, SUITE 2000
**LOS ANGELES, CALIFORNIA 90067**
*Telephone: 310-277-0408*
*Fax: 310-282-0843*

*Chapter 11 Reorganizations, Bankruptcy, Insolvency, Creditor-Debtor Relations, Commercial Law and Business Related Matters.*

**HERBERT WOLAS,** born Bronx, New York, June 27, 1933; admitted to bar, 1961, California. *Education:* University of California at Los Angeles (A.A., 1953; B.A., 1954; J.D., 1960). *Member:* Beverly Hills and Los Angeles County (Member, Sections on Commercial Law; Bankruptcy) Bar Associations; State Bar of California. **REPORTED CASES:** Union Bank v. Wolas, Trustee, 112 S.Ct. 632. **PRACTICE AREAS:** Bankruptcy; Insolvency; Reorganization; Commercial Litigation; Restructuring; Negotiated Settlements.

### WOLF, RIFKIN & SHAPIRO, LLP
A Partnership including a Professional Corporation
11400 WEST OLYMPIC BOULEVARD
NINTH FLOOR
**LOS ANGELES, CALIFORNIA 90064-1565**
*Telephone: 310-478-4100*
*FAX: 310-479-1422*

*General Civil Practice in State and Federal Courts. Trials and Appeals. Corporate, Real Estate, Community Associations, Entertainment, Taxation, Estate Planning and Probate, Construction, Products Liability and Related Litigation Matters.*

(This Listing Continued)

CAA1297B

## WOLF, RIFKIN & SHAPIRO, LLP, Los Angeles—Continued

FIRM PROFILE: Wolf, Rifkin & Shapiro, LLP was founded in 1977. Our Attorneys, who are graduates of prestigious law schools from throughout the country, specialize in a variety of legal disciplines. We have assembled a highly effective team by selecting and developing associates who complement each partner's expertise. As a result we are able to provide our clients with the finest possible legal services, while efficiently managing the costs of those services. As our firm has grown, we have achieved our goal of providing top quality representation while maintaining small firm economics and commitment. Our clientele includes individuals and community associations, as well as businesses ranging from fledgling firms to Fortune 500 companies. Wolf, Rifkin & Shapiro offers comprehensive, high quality legal representation.

### MEMBERS OF FIRM

**MICHAEL WOLF, (A PROFESSIONAL CORPORATION),** born New York, N.Y., March 30, 1952; admitted to bar, 1976, California; 1977, U.S. Tax Court; 1978, U.S. District Court, Central District of California. *Education:* University of California at Los Angeles (B.A., 1973; J.D., 1976). Recipient, Prentice Hall Tax Award. *Member:* Century City and Los Angeles County Bar Associations; State Bar of California. **PRACTICE AREAS:** Entertainment Law; Corporate Law.

**DANIEL C. SHAPIRO,** born Los Angeles, California, February 6, 1954; admitted to bar, 1979, California; 1980, U.S. District Court, Central District of California. *Education:* University of California at Los Angeles (B.A., 1976); Southwestern University School of Law (J.D., 1979). Member, Community Associations Institute. *Member:* Westwood, Santa Monica, Los Angeles County and American (H-2 Committee of the Real Property, Probate and Trust Law Section) Bar Associations; State Bar of California. **PRACTICE AREAS:** Community Association Law; Real Estate.

**ROY G. RIFKIN,** born Brooklyn, New York, February 25, 1953; admitted to bar, 1978, New York and California; 1979, U.S. District Court, Central District of California and U.S. Court of Appeals, Ninth Circuit; 1992, U.S. District Court, Southern District of California. *Education:* Cornell University (A.B., 1974); University of Pennsylvania (J.D., 1977). Recipient, Nathan Burkan Memorial Award. Adjunct Professor of Law, Trial Advocacy Program, University of Iowa Law School, 1984. Panel of Commercial Arbitrators, American Arbitration Association. *Member:* Century City and Los Angeles County Bar Associations; State Bar of California. **PRACTICE AREAS:** Civil Litigation; Real Estate; Entertainment Law.

**MICHAEL T. SCHULMAN,** born Washington, D.C., July 27, 1955; admitted to bar, 1980, California and U.S. District Court, Central District of California. *Education:* University of Virginia (B.A., with high distinction, 1977); Columbia University (J.D., 1980). Phi Delta Phi. *Member:* Century City and Los Angeles County Bar Associations; The State Bar of California (Business Law Section). **PRACTICE AREAS:** Corporate Law; Securities; Entertainment Law.

**LESLIE STEVEN MARKS,** born Chicago, Illinois, November 5, 1955; admitted to bar, 1980, California; 1981, U.S. District Court, Central District of California; 1982, U.S. Court of Appeals, Ninth Circuit. *Education:* University of California at Los Angeles (B.A., summa cum laude, 1976); Loyola University of Los Angeles (J.D., 1980). Phi Beta Kappa; Phi Alpha Delta. Author: "Condominium Association Directors at Risk - Suggestions for Avoiding Personal Tort Liability," Los Angeles Lawyer, 5th Annual Real Estate Edition, 1990. *Member:* Los Angeles County Bar Association; State Bar of California. **PRACTICE AREAS:** Civil Litigation; Construction Litigation; Entertainment Litigation; Real Estate Litigation.

**ALLAN M. ROSENTHAL,** born Winnipeg, Manitoba, Canada, July 5, 1946; admitted to bar, 1973, California; 1976, U.S. District Court, Central District of California; 1980, U.S. Supreme Court; 1985, U.S. District Court, Eastern District of California. *Education:* University of California at Los Angeles (A.B., 1968); Loyola University of Los Angeles (J.D., 1972). *Member:* Los Angeles County Bar Association; State Bar of California; Association of Southern California Defense Counsel. **PRACTICE AREAS:** Products Liability Law; Civil Litigation.

**MINDY SHEPS,** born Hackensack, New Jersey, October 11, 1953; admitted to bar, 1982, New York; 1985, California. *Education:* Rutgers University (B.S.W., with honors, 1976; J.D., 1981). Teaching Assistant, Rutgers School of Law, Legal Writing, 1980. Law Clerk to Hon. Lawrence A. Whipple, U.S. District Judge, Newark, N.J., 1981. *Member:* Beverly Hills, Century City (Real Estate Sections) and Los Angeles County (Member,

*(This Listing Continued)*

Real Property Section) Bar Associations; State Bar of California. **PRACTICE AREAS:** Real Estate.

**NORMAN S. WISNICKI,** born Brooklyn, New York, June 9, 1953; admitted to bar, 1980, California; 1981, U.S. District Court, Central District of California. *Education:* Yeshiva University (B.A., 1975); Brooklyn Law School; Loyola University of Los Angeles (J.D., cum laude, 1980). Recipient, American Jurisprudence Award. *Member:* Beverly Hills and Los Angeles County Bar Associations; State Bar of California; Los Angeles Trial Lawyers Association. **PRACTICE AREAS:** Civil Litigation; Construction Litigation; Business and Commercial Litigation; Real Estate Litigation.

**BARRY T. MITIDIERE,** born Wantagh, New York, January 14, 1953; admitted to bar, 1979, California and U.S. District Court, Central District of California. *Education:* University of California at Los Angeles (B.A., 1975); Loyola University of Los Angeles (J.D., 1978). Phi Alpha Delta. Political Science Honor Society. Editor, California Escrow Update Monthly Newsletter. Member, Escrow Institute of California, 1990—. Real Estate Broker, California, 1978. *Member:* Beverly Hills (Member, Sections on: Real Estate Law; Bankruptcy Law; Litigation) and Federal (Member, Bankruptcy Law Section) Bar Associations; State Bar of California (Member, Real Property Law Section). **PRACTICE AREAS:** Civil Litigation; Real Estate; Business Law; Bankruptcy Law.

**MARC E. ROHATINER,** born Los Angeles, California, September 9, 1953; admitted to bar, 1978, California and U.S. District Court, Central District of California; U.S. Court of Appeals, Ninth Circuit. *Education:* University of California at Los Angeles (B.A., summa cum laude, 1975; J.D., 1978). Phi Beta Kappa. Member, UCLA-Alaska Law Review, 1976-1977. Member, Panel of Arbitrators, American Arbitration Association. *Member:* Los Angeles County Bar Association (Member, Sections on: Litigation; Real Estate); State Bar of California.

**CHARLES H. BAREN,** born New York, N.Y., November 8, 1962; admitted to bar, 1988, California and U.S. District Court, Central District of California. *Education:* University of California at Los Angeles (B.A., 1984); Loyola University of Los Angeles (J.D., 1987). Author: "Protecting News Sources: Playboy Extends Publisher's Rights," 6 Loyola Ent. Law Journal, 1986. *Member:* Century City, Santa Monica and Los Angeles County Bar Associations; State Bar of California. **PRACTICE AREAS:** Community Associations Law; Civil Litigation.

**MICHAEL W. RABKIN,** born Los Angeles, California, September 7, 1962; admitted to bar, 1988, California, U.S. District Court, Central District of California and U.S. Court of Appeals, Ninth Circuit. *Education:* University of California at Los Angeles (B.A., 1984); University of Southern California (J.D., 1988). Phi Alpha Delta. Recipient, American Jurisprudence Award in Land Use Planning. *Member:* Los Angeles County (Member: Real Estate Section; Artists and the Law Committee) and American (Member, Homeowners and Community Associations, H-6, Committee) Bar Associations; State Bar of California. **PRACTICE AREAS:** Community Association Law; Real Estate; Business Law.

### ASSOCIATES

**ANDREW S. GELB,** born New York, N.Y., April 24, 1956; admitted to bar, 1981, California and U.S. District Court, Central District of California; 1983, U.S. Court of Appeals, Ninth Circuit; 1987, U.S. Court of Appeals, Sixth Circuit and U.S. District Court, Northern District of California; 1988, U.S. District Court, Eastern District of California. *Education:* California State University, Fresno (B.S., summa cum laude, 1978); University of California at Los Angeles (J.D., 1981). Blue Key. *Member:* Los Angeles County (Member, Sections on: Labor and Employment Law; Litigation), Century City and American (Member, Sections on: Business Law; Litigation; Labor and Employment Law) Bar Associations; State Bar of California (Member, Labor and Employment Law and Intellectual Property Sections). **PRACTICE AREAS:** Intellectual Property Law; Employment Law; Litigation; Business Law.

**MATTHEW L. GRODE,** born Queens, New York, March 27, 1962; admitted to bar, 1986, California; 1987, U.S. District Court, Central District of California. *Education:* State University of New York at Albany (B.S., cum laude, 1983); Pepperdine University (J.D., 1986). Recipient, American Jurisprudence Award in Criminal Procedure. *Member:* Los Angeles County and American Bar Associations; State Bar of California. **PRACTICE AREAS:** Real Estate; Construction Litigation; Civil Litigation; Products Liability Law.

**MATTHEW FLADELL,** born New York, New York, April 24, 1955; admitted to bar, 1982, British Columbia; 1993, California. *Education:* Simon Fraser University (B.A., 1977); University of British Columbia

*(This Listing Continued)*

## PROFESSIONAL BIOGRAPHIES

## CALIFORNIA—LOS ANGELES

(LL.B., 1981). *Member:* Beverly Hills, Los Angeles County and Canadian Bar Associations. *PRACTICE AREAS:* Entertainment Law; Business Law.

**STEVEN A. SILVER,** born Los Angeles, California, October 1, 1956; admitted to bar, 1989, California and U.S. District Court, Central District of California; U.S. Court of Appeals, Ninth Circuit. *Education:* California State University (B.A., 1979); Southwestern University (J.D., 1989). *Member:* Santa Monica, Century City and Los Angeles County Bar Associations; State Bar of California. *PRACTICE AREAS:* Products Liability Law; Civil Litigation.

**MARK J. ROSENBAUM,** born Los Angeles, California, July 30, 1968; admitted to bar, 1994, California and U.S. District Court, Central District of California. *Education:* Yeshiva University (B.S., 1991); Loyola University of Los Angeles (J.D., 1993). *Member:* State Bar of California. *PRACTICE AREAS:* Community Association Law; Civil Litigation.

**KELLY MARIE ALLEGRA,** born Santa Monica, California, July 21, 1967; admitted to bar, 1994, California and U.S. District Court, Central District of California. *Education:* University of Southern California (B.S., 1989; J.D., 1993; M. of Real Estate Development, 1993). Hale Moot Court Honors Program. *Member:* State Bar of California. *PRACTICE AREAS:* Community Association Law; Real Estate.

**RICHARD S. GRANT,** born Toledo, Ohio, September 16, 1960; admitted to bar, 1986, California. *Education:* University of Wisconsin (B.A., 1983; J.D., cum laude, 1986).

**KARIN E. FREEMAN,** born Fort Lee, Virginia, January 13, 1970; admitted to bar, 1996, California. *Education:* University of California at Los Angeles (B.A., 1992); University of Southern California (J.D., 1995). *Member:* Beverly Hills Bar Association. *PRACTICE AREAS:* Real Estate; Bankruptcy; Community Association.

**LORI A. VAN OOSTERHOUT,** born Tucson, Arizona, April 11, 1960; admitted to bar, 1991, California. *Education:* University of Arizona (B.S., with honors, 1983); University of California School of Law, Davis (J.D., 1991). Editor, University of California Davis Law Review, 1991. Member, Moot Court Board. *Member:* Los Angeles County Bar Association; State Bar of California. *LANGUAGES:* French. *PRACTICE AREAS:* Real Estate Litigation; Business Litigation.

**PAUL W. WINDUST,** born Orange, California, January 20, 1968; admitted to bar, 1993, California, U.S. District Court, Central District of California and U.S. Court of Appeals, Ninth Circuit; 1996, U.S. District Court, Northern District of California. *Education:* University of Southern California (B.S., 1990; J.D., 1993). *PRACTICE AREAS:* Commercial Litigation.

**DANIEL NG,** born Hong Kong, April 19, 1960; admitted to bar, 1995, California. *Education:* University of California at Berkeley (A.B., highest honor, 1983); Massachusetts Institute of Technology (M. Arch., 1986); University of California, Berkeley, Boalt Hall School of Law (J.D., 1995). *Member:* Beverly Hills, Los Angeles County and American Bar Associations. *LANGUAGES:* Cantonese, Mandarin. *PRACTICE AREAS:* Litigation.

**LAURA S. BLINT,** born Glasgow, Scotland; admitted to bar, 1996, California. *Education:* University of California, Santa Barbara (B.A., 1992); University of Southern California (J.D., 1996). Recipient, Douglas Simon Memorial Scholarship. *Member:* State Bar of California. *PRACTICE AREAS:* Community Association Law.

*OF COUNSEL*

**GERALD LLOYD FRIEDMAN,** born New York, N.Y., May 22, 1938; admitted to bar, 1963, California. *Education:* Colgate University (A.B., 1959); Cornell Law School (J.D., 1962). Phi Alpha Delta. Instructor, San Fernando University College of Law, 1970-1977 and Mid-Valley College of Law, 1977-1979. *Member:* Beverly Hills and Los Angeles County Bar Associations; State Bar of California. (Certified Specialist, Family Law, The State Bar of California Board of Legal Specialization). *PRACTICE AREAS:* Matrimonial Law; Business Law.

**JEFFREY R. LIEBSTER,** born Brooklyn, New York, December 8, 1954; admitted to bar, 1981, California and U.S. District Court, Central District of California. *Education:* University of Michigan (B.A., Journalism, with high distinction, 1976; J.D., 1980). Licensed Real Estate Broker, California, 1982. Certified Player Agent, Major League Baseball Players Association, 1988—. *Member:* Los Angeles County (Member, Real Property Section) and American Bar Associations; State Bar of California. *PRACTICE AREAS:* Commercial Law; Real Estate Law; Labor Law.

*(This Listing Continued)*

**DENISE M. PARGA,** born New York, N.Y., December 15, 1951; admitted to bar, 1982, California and U.S. District Court, Central, Northern, Southern and Eastern Districts of California. *Education:* New York University (B.A., 1973); University of Texas (J.D., with honors, 1982). Managing Editor, Texas Law Review, 1981-1982. Judge Pro Tempore, Santa Monica Small Claims Court, 1992—. Judicial Arbitrator, Van Nuys Superior Court, 1993. *Member:* Los Angeles County Bar Association; State Bar of California; Association of Business Trial Lawyers (Member, Newsletter Committee); Women Lawyers Association (Member, Trials Committee). *PRACTICE AREAS:* Construction Litigation; Civil Litigation.

---

## WOLFLICK & SIMPSON
### LOS ANGELES, CALIFORNIA

(See Glendale)

*Labor, Employment Law.*

---

## BERNARD P. WOLFSDORF
*A PROFESSIONAL CORPORATION*

Established in 1986

17383 SUNSET BOULEVARD, SUITE 120 (PACIFIC PALISADES)
**LOS ANGELES, CALIFORNIA 90272**
Telephone: 310-573-4242
FAX: 310-573-5093
Email: visalaw@wolfsdorf.com
URL: http://ilw.com/wolfsdorf

*Specializes in the exclusive practice of Immigration and Nationality Law, with an emphasis on Business and Entertainment related Immigration Matters. Asylum/Refugee, Deportation, Family-Based Immigration, Nationality and Appellate Matters are also handled.*

**BERNARD P. WOLFSDORF,** born Durban, South Africa, October 10, 1954; admitted to bar, 1978, South Africa; 1981, Massachusetts; 1983, California. *Education:* University of Natal, South Africa (B.A., 1975; LL.B., 1978); Suffolk University. Author: "DV Lotteries - A Mad or Rational Way to Allocate Immigrant Visas in the Nineties," AILA National Conference Handbook, 1996; "Alternate State Chargeability Applicability in the DV - 1 Lottery," AILA National Conference Handbook 1995; "Consular Processing," AILA National Conference Handbook, 1993; "Processing Artists and Entertainers," AILA California Conference Handbook, 1992. Presentations: "J-1 Waiver for Physicians," AILA Workshop, San Francisco, California, 1994: "Citizenship and Naturalization," AILA National Conference, Atlanta, Georgia, 1995; "Diversity Immigrants," AILA National Conference, San Francisco, California, 1994; "Processing Artists and Entertainers, Part II," AILA Workshop, San Francisco, California, 1993; "Consular Processing," AILA National Conference, Toronto, Canada, 1993; "Consular Processing," AILA California Conference, Pasadena, California, 1993; "The Chinese Student Protection Act," University of California, Los Angeles, California, 1993; "Immigration of Physicians and Waivers," Los Angeles County Bar, California, 1993; "Processing Artists and Entertainers," AILA Winter Conference, 1992; "Immigration Act of 1990," AILA National Conference, 1991. Moderator: "North American Consulates," AILA Visa Conference, Los Angeles, California, 1993. Lecturer: Commercial Law, Natal Technikon, South Africa, 1978-1979. *Member:* Los Angeles County Bar Association (Member, Executive Committee, Immigration Law Section); American Immigration Lawyers Association (Co-Chair, California Service Center Liaison, 1996-1997; Chair, Artists and Entertainers Committee, 1994-1996; Chair, State Department Liason, 1993-1994; Co-Chair, Western U.S. Region Liaison, 1992-1993; Chair, Southern California Chapter, 1991-1992). (Certified Specialist, Immigration and Nationality Law, The State Bar of California Board of Legal Specialization). *Email:* visalaw@wolfsdorf.com

**MICHELE A. BUCHANAN,** born Appleton, Wisconsin, September 5, 1963; admitted to bar, 1992, California. *Education:* University of Wisconsin-Madison (B.A., 1985); University of West Los Angeles (J.D., 1991). Author: "Non-Traditional H-1B's and TN's, Emerging Issues in Immigration Law," AILA California Conference, 1994; "An Overview of Recent Changes in Immigration Law Affecting Health Care Human Resource Administrators," AHHRA News, 1996; "DV Lotteries - A Mad or Rational

*(This Listing Continued)*

## BERNARD P. WOLFSDORF A PROFESSIONAL CORPORATION, Los Angeles—Continued

Way to Allocate Immigrant Visas in the Nineties," AILA Immigration & Nationality Law Handbook, 1996. *Member:* Los Angeles County Bar Association (Member, Immigration Section); American Immigration Lawyers Association (Acting Chair, Southern California Chapter, 1996-1997). *LANGUAGES:* Mandarin Chinese. *PRACTICE AREAS:* Immigration and Naturalization. *Email:* mbuchanan@wolfsdorf.com

**C. DANIEL LEVY,** born Lima, Peru, August 25, 1953; admitted to bar, 1986, New York and California. *Education:* Columbia University (B.A., 1975; M.A., 1977; M.Phil., 1979; J.D., 1985). Author: "Naturalization Handbook," Clark, Boardman, Callaghan; "Document Fraud Proceedings: An Update," 72 Interpreter Releases, 1113, August 21, 1995; "A Practitioner's Guide to Section 274C, Parts One and Two," 94-6 and 94-7 Immigration Briefings, June-July 1994; "The Family in Immigration and Nationality Law, Parts I and II," 92-9 and 92-10 Immigration Briefings, September/October 1992; "An Outline of Immigration Law," 25 Clearinghouse Review 1442, March 1992; "Exclusion Grounds Under the Immigration Act of 1990," Parts I and II, 91-8 and 91-9 Immigration Briefings, August-September 1991. *Member:* American Immigration Lawyers Association (Co-Chair, Employer Sanctions and Verification Committee). *LANGUAGES:* Spanish, French, German, Hebrew. *PRACTICE AREAS:* Immigration and Nationality Law. *Email:* dlevy@wolfsdorf.com

**STEPHEN M. DEWAR,** born South Africa, March 12, 1957; admitted to bar, 1981, South Africa (Not admitted in California). *Education:* University of Natal, South Africa (BPROC, 1980). General Counsel, Toyota, South Africa Manufacturing, 1986-1990. *PRACTICE AREAS:* Immigration Law. *Email:* sdewar@wolfsdorf.com

**MICHAEL S. GREENBAUM,** born Johannesburg, South Africa, February 9, 1955; admitted to bar, 1982, South Africa (Not admitted in California). *Education:* University of Natal, Durban, South Africa (B.A., 1976; LL.B., 1979); University of Nevada, Las Vegas (B.Sc, Hotel Administration, 1988). Member, Law Student Council, University of Natal, Durban, 1978. Tutor, Introduction to South African Law, University of Natal, Durban, 1979. *PRACTICE AREAS:* Immigration Law. *Email:* mgreenbaum@wolfsdorf.com

**MITCHELL BERENSON,** born Los Angeles, California, February 26, 1965; admitted to bar, 1991, South Africa; 1996, California. *Education:* University of the Witwatersrand, Johannesburg, South Africa (B.A., 1986; LL.B., 1988; Higher Diploma in Company Law, 1991). Member, Law Student Council, 1987-1988. Vice-Chairperson: Johannesburg Association of Candidate Attorneys, 1989-1990; Transvaal Law Society, 1991-1994. *PRACTICE AREAS:* Immigration Law. *Email:* mberenson@wolfsdorf.com

---

## J. KIRK WOOD
### LOS ANGELES, CALIFORNIA
(See Santa Monica)

General Civil Trial and Appellate Practice in all Courts. Unfair Competition, Trade Secrets, Real Estate, Business and Technology Litigation. Trademark and Copyright Litigation. Mining Litigation.

---

## WOOLLACOTT JANNOL & WOOLLACOTT
A Partnership including Professional Corporations

*1875 CENTURY PARK EAST, SUITE 1400*
**LOS ANGELES, CALIFORNIA 90067**
*Telephone: 310-277-5504*
*Telecopier: 310-552-7552*

General and Complex Business, Real Estate and Construction Litigation in Federal and State Courts and Arbitration, General Business and Real Estate Transactions, Corporate and Partnership Law.

### MEMBERS OF FIRM

**JAY A. WOOLLACOTT (A LAW CORP.),** born Pasadena, California, September 4, 1954; admitted to bar, 1978, California; U.S. District Court, Central and Northern Districts of California; U.S. Court of Appeals, Federal Circuit and U.S. Court of Appeals, Ninth Circuit. *Education:* Loyola University of Los Angeles (B.A., magna cum laude, 1975); University of California at Los Angeles (J.D., 1978). Co-Author, "Land Development

*(This Listing Continued)*

and Environmental Control in the California Supreme Court," 27 University of California at Los Angeles Law Review 859, 1980. Judge Pro Tem, Los Angeles Municipal Court, 1983—. *PRACTICE AREAS:* Business Litigation; Commercial Litigation; Corporate Law; Real Property Law.

**MARTIN B. JANNOL (A PROF. CORP.),** born Los Angeles, California, July 5, 1955; admitted to bar, 1980, California; U.S. District Court, Central District of California. *Education:* Pomona College (B.A., 1977); Southwestern University (J.D., 1980). *PRACTICE AREAS:* General Business and Real Estate Transactions; Corporate Law; Franchising; Real Property Law.

**CYNTHIA A. R. WOOLLACOTT,** born San Diego, California, December 14, 1958; admitted to bar, 1983, California; U.S. District Court, Central, Southern and Northern Districts of California; U.S. Court of Appeals, Ninth Circuit. *Education:* University of California at Berkeley (B.S., 1980); University of California at Los Angeles (J.D., 1983). Member, Moot Court. Member, U.C.L.A. Law Review, 1982-1983; Editor, U.C.L.A.-Alaska Law Review, 1982-1983. Author: "Evaluating Video Evidence," Los Angeles Lawyer, October 1991. Judge Pro Tem, Los Angeles Municipal Court. State Bar and National Futures Association Arbitrator. *PRACTICE AREAS:* Business Litigation; Commercial Litigation; Complex Litigation.

### ASSOCIATES

**JANET L. KARKANEN,** born Livingston, Montana, February 27, 1963; admitted to bar, 1992, California; U.S. District Court, Central District of California. *Education:* Colorado State University (B.A., 1986); Hastings College of the Law, University of California, San Francisco (J.D., 1992). Editor-in-Chief, Hastings Communications and Entertainment Law Journal, 1991-1992. Author, "The Struggle over Performing Rights to Music: BMI and ASCAP vs. Cable Television," 14 Hastings Comm/Ent L.J. 47 (1991), republished in Entertainment, Publishing and the Arts Handbook, Clark, Boardman, Callaghan (1992). *PRACTICE AREAS:* Business Litigation; Intellectual Property Law.

---

## WRIGHT, ROBINSON, OSTHIMER & TATUM
*SUITE 1800*
*888 SOUTH FIGUEROA STREET*
**LOS ANGELES, CALIFORNIA 90017**
*Telephone: 213-488-0503*
*Telefax: 213-624-3755*

*Richmond, Virginia Office:* Suite 400, 411 East Franklin Street. Telephone: 804-783-1100.
*San Francisco, California Office:* Suite 1800, 44 Montgomery Street. Telephone: 415-391-7111.
*Washington, D.C. Office:* Suite 920, 5335 Wisconsin Avenue, N.W. Telephone: 202-244-4668. Telefax: 202-244-5135.
*Norfolk, Virginia Office:* 1600 Nationsbank Center, One Commercial Place. Telephone: 757-623-0035. Telefax: 757-623-4160.

General Civil and Trial Practice. Products Liability, Construction, Corporate, Insurance and Environmental Law.

### RESIDENT PRINCIPALS

**FRANKLIN M. TATUM, III,** born Hattiesburg, Mississippi, July 4, 1946; admitted to bar, 1973, Virginia; 1994, California. *Education:* Baylor University; Texas Christian University (B.A., cum laude, 1969); Vanderbilt University (J.D., 1972). Order of the Coif. Articles Editor, Vanderbilt Law Review, 1971-1972. *Member:* Richmond, Virginia and American Bar Associations; Virginia State Bar. (Also at Richmond, Virginia Office). *PRACTICE AREAS:* Products Liability Law.

**PAUL H. BURLEIGH,** born Dublin, Ireland, March 17, 1956; admitted to bar, 1983, California; 1984, U.S. District Court for the Central District of California; 1990, U.S. District Court, Southern District of California; 1991, U.S. District Court, Eastern and Northern Districts of California. *Education:* California State University at Northridge (B.A., 1980); Pepperdine University (J.D., 1983). *Member:* State Bar of California; American Bar Association; Association of Southern California Defense Counsel; Defense Research Institute (Member, Subcommittee on Agriculture, Construction, Mining and Industrial Equipment). *PRACTICE AREAS:* Products Liability Law; Toxic Torts; Insurance Defense Law; Personal Injury Law; Wrongful Death Litigation.

**KENNETH G. KATEL,** born Oak Park, Illinois, November 17, 1953; admitted to bar, 1979, California. *Education:* University of Illinois (B.A.,

*(This Listing Continued)*

1975, James Scholar); University of San Diego (J.D., 1979). Phi Kappa Phi. James Scholar. Member: Appellate Moot Court Board; National Moot Court Team. Instructor, Legal Research and Writing, Univ. San Diego, 1979. *Member:* State Bar of California; American Bar Association. *PRACTICE AREAS:* Litigation.

**MICHAEL J. BELCHER,** born Los Angeles, California, December 17, 1942; admitted to bar, 1970, California. *Education:* Loyola University of Los Angeles (B.A., 1965); Loyola University of Los Angeles School of Law (J.D., 1969). Student Legal Writing Instructor, Loyola University of Los Angeles School of Law, 1968-1969. President, St. Thomas More Law Society, 1968-1969. Member, Board of Governors, Loyola Law School Alumni Association, 1971-1973. *Member:* Los Angeles County Bar Association; The State Bar of California; Italian-American Lawyers Association; Association of Business Trial Lawyers. *PRACTICE AREAS:* Insurance Bad Faith; Insurance Coverage; Employment Law; Product Liability; Commercial Litigation.

**NANCY E. FITZHUGH,** born New York, N.Y., March 16, 1955; admitted to bar, 1980, New York; 1990, California. *Education:* Williams College (B.A., cum laude, 1976); Hofstra University (J.D., 1979). Associate Editor, Hofstra Law Review, 1978-1979. *Member:* Los Angeles County, New York State and American Bar Associations; Women's Lawyers Association of Los Angeles; California Women Lawyers. *PRACTICE AREAS:* Commercial; Commercial Litigation; General Civil; Pharmaceutical/Device; Workers Compensation.

**ROBERT A. RICH,** born Pittsburgh, Pennsylvania, October 8, 1955; admitted to bar, 1981, District of Columbia; 1984, U.S. District Court for the District of Columbia; 1989, California. *Education:* University of Maryland (B.S., 1977; J.D., 1980). *Member:* Beverly Hills, Los Angeles County and American Bar Associations; District of Columbia Bar; State Bar of California; The Association of Trial Lawyers of America. *PRACTICE AREAS:* Asbestos Litigation; Business Law; Translational Law; Personal Injury Law; Aviation Litigation; Communications Law; Labor Litigation.

**ARTHUR I. WILLNER,** born Brooklyn, New York, May 23, 1955; admitted to bar, 1982, New York; 1985, California. *Education:* Columbia University (B.A., 1976); St. Johns University (J.D., 1981). *Member:* New York State and American (Member: Section of Litigation; Air and Space Law Committee) Bar Associations; State Bar of California. *PRACTICE AREAS:* Products Liability Litigation; Insurance Defense Litigation; Aviation Law.

**DAVID V. ROSE,** born Muncie, Indiana, December 10, 1954; admitted to bar, 1983, California; 1984, U.S. District Court, Central and Southern Districts of California. *Education:* Murray State University (B.S., 1976); University of Virginia (J.D., 1983). Chairman, Natural Resources Commission. Judge Pro Tem, Probation Monitor. *Member:* Los Angeles County Bar Association. *PRACTICE AREAS:* Insurance Coverage Litigation; Commercial Litigation.

*RESIDENT ASSOCIATES*

**BRIAN S. INAMINE,** born Los Angeles, California, November 29, 1956; admitted to bar, 1985, California; 1986, U.S. District Court, Central District of California; 1987, U.S. District Court, Southern District of California. *Education:* University of Hawaii (B.A., 1979); University of Southern California (J.D., 1984). *Member:* Los Angeles County and American Bar Associations; State Bar of California. *PRACTICE AREAS:* Insurance Coverage Law; Products Liability Law.

**ROBERT G. HARRISON,** born Berkeley, California, April 2, 1959; admitted to bar, 1985, California, U.S. Supreme Court, and U.S. District Court, Northern District of California; 1986, U.S. Court of Appeals, Ninth Circuit; 1988, U.S. District Court, Central District of California. *Education:* University of the Pacific (B.A., with honors, 1981); Hastings College of Law, University of California (J.D., 1984). Member, 1982-1983 and Editor, 1983-1984, Hastings Law Journal. *Member:* State Bar of California. *PRACTICE AREAS:* Insurance Defense Litigation and Appeals; Public Entity Liability Law; Aviation Law.

**COLIN J. GIBSON,** born Nyack, New York, September 18, 1959; admitted to bar, 1991, New Jersey; 1993, California. *Education:* American University (B.S., 1981); Loyola Marymount University (J.D., 1990). *PRACTICE AREAS:* Negligence; Products Liability; Business/Contracts.

**TAYLOR L. CLARK,** born Philadelphia, Pennsylvania, March 20, 1965; admitted to bar, 1994, California. *Education:* University of Alaska, Anchorage (B.B.A., 1990); Pepperdine University School of Law (J.D., cum laude, 1993; M.I.B., 1995); University of Paris II (LL.M., in European Intellectual Property and Antitrust Law, 1995). Recipient, American Jurisprudence

*(This Listing Continued)*

Award, Federal Courts, 1993. Editor, Pepperdine Law Review, 1992-1993. Author: 20 Pepp. L. Rev. California Supreme Court Survey. *LANGUAGES:* French. *PRACTICE AREAS:* Business Litigation; Intellectual Property/Antitrust; Employment Law.

(For Complete Biographical Data on Personnel at San Francisco, Washington, D.C. and Richmond, Virginia see Professional Biographies at those locations)

## *WYNNE SPIEGEL ITKIN*

*A LAW CORPORATION*

*1901 AVENUE OF THE STARS, SUITE 1600*
**LOS ANGELES, CALIFORNIA 90067-6080**
*Telephone: 310-551-1015*
*Fax: 310-551-3059*

*Practice Limited to Bankruptcy Law, Insolvency Law and Business Reorganization.*

**RICHARD L. WYNNE,** born Brooklyn, New York, November 6, 1957; admitted to bar, 1982, New Jersey; 1983, New York; 1985, California; U.S. District Court, District of New Jersey, Southern and Eastern Districts of New York, Southern, Central and Northern Districts of California and U.S. Court of Appeals, Second and Ninth Circuit; U.S. Supreme Court. *Education:* Indiana University (B.A., with distinction, 1979); Columbia University (J.D., 1982); Parker School of Foreign and Comparative Law (1983). Editor, California Bankruptcy Journal. Author: "Coin of the Realm: Multinational Insolvency," Los Angeles Lawyer, October, 1996; "Qualified Retirement Plans and the Debtor Participant," California Bankruptcy Journal, 1993; "LBO's Legal Binding Obligations or Looting Business Opportunities," Norton's Bankruptcy Law Adviser, 1991. Speaker: "Mediation in Bankruptcy," Turn Around Managers Association, April, 1996; "Getting Paid in Chapter 11," Southern California, American Bankruptcy Institute, March, 1996; "Musical Chairs and Ethical Battles: Changing Firms, Multiple Roles and Disinterestedness," 2nd Annual Women Insolvency Professionals Workshop, March 1996; "Mediation in Bankruptcy," Federal Bar Association, October 1995; "Reconcilable Differences: Mediation and Arbitration in Bankruptcy Courts," Los Angeles County Bar Association, April 1995; "Current Developments in Chapter 11," American Bankruptcy Institute, Third Annual Bankruptcy Battleground West, March 1995; "The New Federalism in Multinational Insolvencies," National Conference of Bankruptcy Judges, 1994 (American Bar Association Business Bankruptcy Committee Program); "Some Faith, Some Credit: Recent Developments in Multinational Insolvencies," Commercial Insolvency in the Americas Symposium, Spring 1994; "Real Estate Workouts & Insolvency: The Debtor Perspective," Executive Enterprises, Inc. Seminar, San Diego, CA, Spring 1994; "Reversal of Fortune: Fraudulent Conveyance Laws," Los Angeles County Bar Association, Spring 1994; "Pending Chapter 11 Legislation," Los Angeles County Bar Association, 1993; "Sex, Lies and Bankruptcy," American Bar Association Annual Meeting, 1993; "Intro to Chapter 11," Los Angeles County Bar Association, 1992; "Bankruptcy Litigation," American Bar Association, Litigation Section Annual Meeting, 1991; "LBO's: Legal Binding Obligations or Looting Business Opportunities," and "Pending Chapter 11 Legislation: SB 540," Los Angeles County Bar Association, Fall 1993, Federal Bar Association, October, 1995. Mediator, U.S. Bankruptcy Court, Central District of California. *Member:* Century City, Beverly Hills, Los Angeles County (Chairman, Bankruptcy Committee, 1996) and American (Co-Chairman, Programs; Litigation Section; Bankruptcy and Insolvency Committee) Bar Associations; American Bankruptcy Institute; Los Angeles Bankruptcy Forum; Financial Lawyers Conference. (Certified Specialist, Business Bankruptcy Law, American Bankruptcy Board of Certification).

**BENNETT L. SPIEGEL,** born Bronx, New York, February 13, 1959; admitted to bar, 1985, Connecticut, New York and District of Columbia; 1986, New Jersey; 1987, California; U.S. District Court, Districts of Connecticut, New Jersey, Southern and Eastern Districts of New York, District of Columbia, Central, Northern, Southern and Eastern Districts of California; U.S. Court of Appeals, Second, Ninth and District of Columbia Circuits. *Education:* Rutgers College, Rutgers University (B.A., with highest honors, 1980); Yale School of Management (M.P.P.M., 1983); Yale Law School (J.D., 1984). Law Clerk, United States District Judge M. Joseph Blumenfeld, United States District Court, District of Connecticut, 1984-1985. *Member:* The Association of the Bar of the City of New York; Beverly Hills, Century City, Los Angeles County, New York State, Federal and American Bar Associations; State Bar of California; District of Columbia Bar; Financial Lawyers Conference; American Bankruptcy Institute.

*(This Listing Continued)*

CAA1301B

**WYNNE SPIEGEL ITKIN,** A LAW CORPORATION, Los Angeles—Continued

**ROBBIN L. ITKIN,** born Los Angeles, California, August 7, 1959; admitted to bar, 1984, California and U.S. District Court, Central and Northern Districts of California and U.S. Court of Appeals, Ninth Circuit. *Education:* University of California, Los Angeles (B.A., magna cum laude, 1981); University of Southern California (J.D., 1984). Author: "The Bankruptcy Mirage-Springing and Vanishing Guarantees," ABA Business Law Section, Spring Meeting, 1995; "Spring Forward or Fall Back: The Enforceability of Springback Provisions on the Bankruptcy Clock," presented at the ABA Business Law Section Spring Meeting, 1993 and at the Los Angeles Financial Lawyers Conference, September 1993 (speaker). Co-Author: "Advanced Chapter 11 Bankruptcy Practice," Professional Education Systems, Inc., 1987; "Misappropriation of Computer Services-The Need to Enforce Civil Liability," IV Computer/Law Journal 401 (1983). Panelist: "Negotiating and Drafting Bankruptcy Deterrents In Workout Agreements," ABA Business Law Section, Spring Meeting, 1995. Moderator and primary organizer of: An Interactive Workshop Specially Designed For The Woman Bankruptcy Lawyer, November, 1994. Bankruptcy Court for the Central District of California Mediation Panel. Board Member, Los Angeles Bankruptcy Forum. President and Board Member, City of Hope Inner Circle. *Member:* Century City, Beverly Hills, Federal and American Bar Associations; State Bar of California; Women Lawyers Association of Los Angeles; National Association of Women Lawyers; California Women Lawyers; Financial Lawyers Conference (Member, Board of Governors); Commercial Law League of America; Women's Progress Alliance (a Founding Member).

**EVE JAFFE,** born Brooklyn, New York, December 28, 1963; admitted to bar, 1989, California. *Education:* San Francisco State University (B.A., cum laude, 1986); University of Southern California (J.D., 1989). Panelist, Recent Developments in Bankruptcy Law, Young Lawyer's Division, American Bar Association Annual Meeting, 1992. *Member:* Beverly Hills, Century City, Los Angeles County and American Bar Associations; Women Lawyer's Association of Los Angeles.

**CHRISTOPHER W. COMBS,** born Santa Monica, California, March 24, 1962; admitted to bar, 1990, California, U.S. District Court, Northern, Southern and Central Districts of California and U.S. Court of Appeals, Ninth Circuit. *Education:* Harvard University (A.B., magna cum laude, 1984); Stanford University (J.D., with Distinction, 1990). Phi Beta Kappa. Stanford Law Review. Law Clerk to the Honorable Thelton E. Henderson, United States District Court, Northern District of California. *LANGUAGES:* French and German. *PRACTICE AREAS:* Bankruptcy.

**STUART J. WALD,** born Brooklyn, New York, December 25, 1966; admitted to bar, 1994, California, U.S. Court of Appeals, Ninth Circuit and U.S. District Court, Northern, Central and Eastern Districts of California. *Education:* University of California at Berkeley (B.A., 1989); Tulane University School of Law (J.D., 1993). Phi Alpha Theta; Federalist Society; MENSA Society. Member, Tulane Constitutional Law Moot Court Team (Craven Invitational Champions, 1993). Law Clerk, Hon. Arthur S. Weisbrodt, U.S. Bankruptcy Court, Northern District of California, 1993-1994. President, Tulane Jewish Law Students 1991-1993. *Member:* Century City, Los Angeles County (Member, Moot Court Committee), American and Federal Bar Associations.

**HAYLEY E. RAMER,** born New York, N.Y., May 20, 1969; admitted to bar, 1994, Pennsylvania; 1995, New Jersey; 1996, California and U.S. District Court, Central District of California. *Education:* Brandeis University (B.A., cum laude, 1991); Rutgers School of Law, Camden (J.D., 1994). Member, Moot Court Advisory Board, 1993-1994. *Member:* Pennsylvania, New Jersey State and American Bar Associations; Women Lawyers Association of Los Angeles; National Association of Women lawyers; California Women Lawyers. *PRACTICE AREAS:* Bankruptcy.

**JACQUELINE H. SLOAN,** born Chicago, Illinois, May 17, 1968; admitted to bar, 1995, California and U.S. District Court, Central District of California. *Education:* Harvard University (B.A., magna cum laude, 1990); Southwestern University School of Law (J.D., summa cum laude, 1995). Member, Southwestern Law Review. Outstanding Woman Law Graduate, National Association of Women Lawyers, 1995. Law Clerk to The Honorable Lisa Hill Fenning, United States Bankruptcy Court, Central District of California. Author: Comment, "Extending Rape Shield Protection to Sexual Harassment Actions: New Federal Rule of Evidence 412 Undermines *Meri-*

*(This Listing Continued)*

*tor Savings Bank v. Vinson,"* 25 Southwestern Law Review 363 (1996). *Member:* State Bar of California; American Bar Association; Women Lawyer's Association of Los Angeles; National Association of Women Lawyers.

---

# GERALD M. YAROSLOW

SUITE 950, CENTURY CITY NORTH BUILDING
10100 SANTA MONICA BOULEVARD
**LOS ANGELES, CALIFORNIA 90067-4013**
Telephone: 310-277-8863
Fax: 310-556-3847

*Estate Planning, Estate and Trust Administration, Probate, Estate and Trust Dispute Resolution.*

**GERALD M. YAROSLOW,** born New York, N.Y., May 10, 1947; admitted to bar, 1976, California; 1986, U.S. Tax Court. *Education:* University of Pennsylvania (A.B., cum laude, 1969); Columbia University (M.A., 1973); University of Southern California (J.D., 1976). Phi Alpha Delta; Pi Gamma Mu. Member, 1974-1976 and Note and Article Editor, 1975-1976, Southern California Law Review. Lecturer: University of Southern California Institute on Federal Taxation, "Marital Deduction: Developments and Problems," 1986; California Continuing Education of the Bar, "Fundamentals of Estate Administration," 1981, 1982, 1983 and "Tax and Non-Tax Aspects of Property Co-Ownership," 1985. *Member:* Beverly Hills (Chairperson, Probate, Trust and Estate Planning Committee, 1982-1983), Century City (Co-Chairperson, Trusts and Estates Section, 1991—; Member, Board of Governors, 1994—); Los Angeles County and American Bar Associations; Beverly Hills Estate Planning Council (President, 1991-1992; Member, Executive Board, 1987-1992). Fellow, American College of Trust and Estate Counsel. Certified Specialist, Probate, Estate Planning and Trust Law, The State Bar of California Board of Legal Specialization.

---

# LAW OFFICES OF
# GREGORY A. YATES

A PROFESSIONAL CORPORATION

**LOS ANGELES, CALIFORNIA**

(See Beverly Hills)

*Personal Injury and Products Liability, Civil Litigation, Trial Practice.*

---

# GERALD T. YOSHIDA

**LOS ANGELES, CALIFORNIA**

(See Santa Monica)

*General Civil Practice. Construction, Business Litigation, Corporate, Insurance and Real Estate Law.*

---

# YOUNG, HENRIE, HUMPHRIES & MASON

**LOS ANGELES, CALIFORNIA**

(See Pomona)

*General Civil and Trial Practice, Business and Corporate Law, Estate Planning, Probate, Trust, Real Estate and Personal Injury.*

---

# YOUNG & THOMPSON

**LOS ANGELES, CALIFORNIA**

(See Arlington, Virginia)

*U.S. and International Patent, Trademark, Copyright and Unfair Competition Law and Related Licensing and Litigation.*

## YOUNGMAN, HUNGATE & LEOPOLD
*A PROFESSIONAL CORPORATION*
**LOS ANGELES, CALIFORNIA**
(See Leopold, Petrich & Smith)

---

## YUKEVICH & SONNETT
601 SOUTH FIGUEROA STREET
SEVENTEENTH FLOOR
**LOS ANGELES, CALIFORNIA 90017**
Telephone: 213-362-7777
Telecopier: 213-362-7788

*Litigation and Products Liability.*

FIRM PROFILE: Yukevich & Sonnett was founded in January, 1995 by James J. Yukevich and Anthony E. Sonnett, both former partners of a well known New York based firm which specialized in insurance defense and products liability litigation. Located in downtown Los Angeles, the office has convenient access to all Southern California courts.

Mr. Yukevich served four years as an Assistant District Attorney in the Homicide and Major Offense Bureaus of the Bronx County District Attorney's Office, entered private practice, specializing in complex products liability and general liability matters. After twelve years of practice, Mr. Yukevich accepted a special assignment as Assistant General Counsel of Honda North America. After the successful completion of that assignment Mr. Yukevich returned to private practice as the managing partner of the Los Angeles office of Lester Schwab Katz & Dwyer. One of Mr. Yukevich's more well known trials was the successful defense of Moore v. Honda: a major products liability case in San Francisco Superior Court which lasted nearly six months and encompassed over 15,000 pages of trial record. (Defense verdict April 1, 1993.) Moore was the first jury trial to test the design and warnings of Honda's currently marketed 4-wheeled all-terrain vehicles. The case involved important legal issues, including the definition of defect under Barker v. Lull and the admissibility of computer generated accident reconstruction animation. It also involved many complex technical issues relating to dynamic stability of vehicles, warnings and rollover protection systems (ROPS). Mr. Yukevich is a frequent lecturer on products liability and defense litigation issues.

Mr Sonnett specializes in products liability and general liability defense, and also has significant experience in both corporate and real estate litigation, including contract disputes, U.C.C. Article 9 actions, franchise rights, and real and personal property foreclosures. Mr. Sonnett joined the New York office of Lester Schwab Katz & Dwyer in 1986 and was made a partner in 1991. He was also on special assignment with Honda North America from May, 1991 to November, 1992. As Managing Counsel of Honda's legal department, he was responsible for the day-to-day management of a majority of Honda's products liability cases.

The Varied experience of Mr. Yukevich and Mr. Sonnett have provided them with a wide range of expertise in a number of areas in addition to complex product liability defense, such as case management, coordination and defense of multiple product litigation, national discovery coordination, alternative dispute resolution (mediation and arbitration), crisis management, jury research, products liability prevention and computerized litigation support. In addition, they have been involved in trials not just in New York and California, but in numerous other jurisdictions throughout the United States.

### MEMBERS OF FIRM

**JAMES J. YUKEVICH,** born Pittsburgh, Pennsylvania, February 1, 1953; admitted to bar, 1978, Massachusetts; 1979, New York; 1982, U.S. District Court, Southern and Eastern Districts of New York; 1986, U.S. District Court, District of Massachusetts, U.S. District Court, Northern District of New York and U.S. Court of Appeals for the District of Columbia Circuit; 1988, U.S. District Court, Western District of New York; 1990, U.S. Supreme Court; 1992, California. *Education:* Boston College (B.A., 1975; J.D., 1978). Adjunct Professor, Juvenile Law, Boston College, 1977-1978. Assistant District Attorney, Bronx County, Major Offense/Homicide Bureau, 1978-1982. Member, American Boat and Yacht Club Council, 1987—. Member, American Association of Automotive Medicine, 1987—. Assistant General Counsel, Honda North America, 1991-1992. *Member:* Boston, New York State and American Bar Associations; Southern California Defense Counsel; The Association of Trial Lawyers of America; New York State Trial Lawyers Association; Society of Automotive Engineers;

*(This Listing Continued)*

Federation of Insurance and Corporate Counsel. **PRACTICE AREAS:** Products Liability Defense; Personal Injury Defense.

**ANTHONY E. SONNETT,** born New York, N.Y., April 13, 1960; admitted to bar, 1986, New York; 1987, U.S. District Court, Southern and Eastern Districts of New York; 1993, California; 1995, U.S. District Court, Central and Southern Districts of California. *Education:* Vassar College (B.A., 1982); Hofstra University (J.D., 1985). Member, Hofstra University Law Review, 1983-1985. Law Fellow, Hofstra University, 1983-1985. Author: "Discovery and the Deposition in Products Liability Litigation," International Legal Strategy, May, 1993. Managing Counsel, Honda North America, 1991-1992. *Member:* State Bar of California; New York State and American Bar Associations; Defense Research Institute. **PRACTICE AREAS:** Products Liability Defense; Personal Injury Defense; Commercial Litigation.

### ASSOCIATES

**H. DAVID HENRY,** born Paradise, California, February 8, 1962; admitted to bar, 1987, California; 1988, U.S. District Court, Central and Southern Districts of California; 1992, U.S. Court of Appeal, Ninth Circuit and U.S. Supreme Court. *Education:* University of Southern California (A.B., magna cum laude, 1984; J.D., with honors, 1987). Phi Beta Kappa. Member, Editorial Board: Major Tax Planning; Computer Law Journal. Author: "Handling Complex Discovery," ABA-ALI, 1991; "Warning and Instruction Liability," ILS, 1996. Member, Inns of Court, 1989-1991. *Member:* American Bar Association; Legion Lex - University of Southern California. **PRACTICE AREAS:** Products Liability; Business Litigation.

**ALEXANDER G. CALFO,** born Denver, Colorado, August 20, 1964; admitted to bar, 1991, California. *Education:* Marquette University (B.A., 1986); Loyola University, Rome Center of Liberal Arts; Creighton University (J.D., 1990). Phi Delta Phi. Member, International Moot Court Board. *Member:* Los Angeles County (Member, Litigation Committee on Pretrial Practice and Discovery, Barristers Moot Court Committee, Inn of Court), American and Federal Bar Associations; American Judicature Society; Defense Research Institute. **REPORTED CASES:** Rinauro v.Honda Motor Co. (1995) 31 Cal. App. 4th 506, 37 Cal. Rptr. 2d 181. **PRACTICE AREAS:** Products Liability; Civil Litigation.

**SARAH M. MAKOWSKY,** born Sellersburg, Indiana, February 21, 1966; admitted to bar, 1991, California. *Education:* University of Kent, Canterbury, England; Indiana University at Bloomington (B.A., with distinction, 1987); Loyola Law School (J.D., 1991). Phi Beta Kappa. Author: "A Punitive Damages Primer: An Overview of Past and Upcoming U.S. Supreme Court Decisions and Some Advice on How Japanese Companies Can Cope," International Legal Strategy, March, 1994. *Member:* Los Angeles County Bar Association; State Bar of California. **PRACTICE AREAS:** Products Liability Defense; Personal Injury Defense.

**KIMBERLY A. SMITH,** born Los Angeles, California, May 7, 1966; admitted to bar, 1991, Pennsylvania; 1995, California and U.S. District Court, Central District of California. *Education:* University of California, Berkeley (B.A., 1987); Syracuse University (J.D., magna cum laude, 1991). Recipient, American Jurisprudence Award in Civil Procedure. *Member:* State Bar of California. **PRACTICE AREAS:** Products Liability Defense; Personal Injury Defense; Employment Law.

**ABDALLA J. INNABI,** born Amman, Jordan, August 6, 1967; admitted to bar, 1994, California; 1996, U.S. District Court, Central District of California. *Education:* University of California at Irvine (B.A., 1990); Quinnipiac College (J.D., 1994). Editorial Board Member, Moot Court Honor Society. *Member:* Los Angeles Bar Association. **LANGUAGES:** Arabic.

---

## ZAMORA & HOFFMEIER
*A PROFESSIONAL CORPORATION*
520 SOUTH GRAND AVENUE, SUITE 675
**LOS ANGELES, CALIFORNIA 90071**
Telephone: 213-488-9411
Fax: 213-488-9418

*Corporate, Bankruptcy, Real Estate, Commercial Transactions, Business Litigation, Land Use, Employment and Public Law.*

**ANTHONY N.R. ZAMORA,** born Los Angeles, California, March 4, 1961; admitted to bar, 1990, California. *Education:* Harvard University (A.B., 1982); University of Southern California (J.D., 1990). Articles Editor, Southern California Law Review. Author: "The Century Freeway Consent Decree," Southern California Law, Rev., 1989-1990, Vol. 60. No. 6., September 1989. Commissioner, City of Los Angeles Planning Commis-

*(This Listing Continued)*

**ZAMORA & HOFFMEIER,** A PROFESSIONAL CORPORATION, Los Angeles—Continued

sion. Member, Editorial Board, *Los Angeles Lawyer*. *Member:* Los Angeles County and American Bar Associations; State Bar of California; Mexican-American Bar Association. **LANGUAGES:** Spanish. **PRACTICE AREAS:** Corporate; Commercial Transactions; Litigation; Real Estate.

**NANCY HOFFMEIER ZAMORA,** born Cambridge, Illinois, February 28, 1960; admitted to bar, 1988, California; 1991, District of Columbia. *Education:* Harvard University (A.B., cum laude, 1982); University of California at Los Angeles (J.D., 1988). Editor, UCLA Law Review, 1987-1988. Author: "New Financing Strategy for Rapid Transit: Model Legislation Authorizing the Use of Benefit Assessments to Fund the Los Angeles Metro Rail," UCLA Law Rev., 1987-1988, Vol. 35, No. 3. Commissioner, City of Los Angeles Building and Safety Commission. Member, Board of Directors, NOW Legal Defense and Education Fund. *Member:* Los Angeles County (Member, Board of Trustees) and American Bar Associations; State Bar of California; California Women Lawyers; Women Lawyers Association of Los Angeles (President). **PRACTICE AREAS:** Bankruptcy; Real Estate; Land Use; Litigation.

---

## GARRETT J. ZELEN

Established in 1980

**12100 WILSHIRE BOULEVARD, SUITE 1500
LOS ANGELES, CALIFORNIA 90025**
Telephone: 310-820-0077
FAX: 310-820-1205

*Criminal Trial, Appellate, Forfeiture, and Juvenile Practice State and Federal Courts.*

**FIRM PROFILE:** *Firm has a national practice in the areas of criminal and forfeiture law.*

**GARRETT J. ZELEN,** born Los Angeles, California, February 2, 1952; admitted to bar, 1978, California; 1979, U.S. District Court, Central District of California and U.S. Court of Appeals, Ninth Circuit; 1983, U.S. Supreme Court; 1986, U.S. District Court, Northern and Southern Districts of California; 1990, U.S. District Court, Eastern District of California; U.S. Court of Appeals, Eleventh and Sixth Circuits. *Education:* University of California at Santa Cruz (B.A., 1974); Loyola University, Los Angeles (J.D., 1978). *Member:* Beverly Hills (Past President, Criminal Law Section, 1986-1987), Los Angeles County and American Bar Associations; State Bar of California (Member, Criminal Law Section); National Association of Criminal Defense Lawyers; California Attorneys for Criminal Justice; Criminal Courts Bar Association; California Public Defenders Association. (Certified Specialist, Criminal Law, The State Bar of California Board of Legal Specialization). **PRACTICE AREAS:** Criminal Trial (State and Federal); Appellate Law; Forfeiture Law; Juvenile Law.

REFERENCE: Santa Monica Bank, West Los Angeles Branch.

---

## ZELLE & LARSON

Established in 1988

**OPPENHEIMER TOWER
10990 WILSHIRE BOULEVARD
LOS ANGELES, CALIFORNIA 90024**
Telephone: 310-478-7877
Telecopier: 310-478-5420

*Minneapolis, Minnesota Office:* 33 South Sixth Street, City Center, Suite 4400. Telephone: 612-339-2020.
*Waltham, Massachusetts Office:* 3 University Office Park, 95 Sawyer Road, Suite 500. Telephone: 617-891-7020.
*Dallas, Texas Office:* 1201 Main Street, Suite 3000. Telephone: 214-742-3000.
*San Francisco, California Office:* One Market Plaza, Steuart Street Tower, 15th Floor. Telephone: 415-978-9788.
*Miami, Florida Office:* 200 South Biscayne Boulevard, Suite 4670. Telephone: 305-373-5000.

*Trials and Appeals in all Federal and State Courts. Insurance Law, Environmental Law, International Litigation, Antitrust, Corporate, Securities, Reinsurance, Alternative Dispute Resolution, Equine Law, Employment, Intellectual Property and Product Liability.*

*(This Listing Continued)*

### MEMBERS OF FIRM

**BRYAN M. BARBER,** born Elyria, Ohio, February 12, 1959; admitted to bar, 1985, California and U.S. District Court, Northern, Eastern and Central Districts of California. *Education:* Miami University (B.A., 1981); University of Virginia (J.D., 1984). Pi Mu Epsilon. *Member:* Bar Association of San Francisco; State Bar of California; American Bar Association; Barristers Club of San Francisco. **PRACTICE AREAS:** Litigation; Insurance Coverage; Environmental Law; Product Liability.

**RICHARD J. STONE,** born Chicago, Illinois, 1945; admitted to bar, 1971, California and U.S. District Court, Central District of California; 1977, U.S. District Court, Northern District of California and U.S. Court of Appeals for the District of Columbia Circuit; 1986, U.S. Court of Appeals for the Federal Circuit; 1987, U.S. Court of Appeals, Ninth Circuit; 1994, Oregon and U.S. District Court, Southern District of California. *Education:* University of Chicago (B.A., 1967); University of California at Los Angeles (J.D., 1970). Editor-in-Chief, UCLA Law Review, 1969-1970. Assistant to the Secretary, U.S. Department of Energy, 1979-1980. Deputy Assistant General Counsel for Intelligence, International and Investigative Programs, U.S. Department of Defense, 1978-1979. General Counsel and Staff Director, Study and Report by the Special Advisor to the Los Angeles Board of Police Commissioners on the Civil Disorder in Los Angeles, 1992. *Member:* Los Angeles County (Trustee, 1986-1988; Chair, Antitrust Section, 1987-1988; Chair, Federal Courts Practices and Procedures Committee, 1987-1988) and American Bar Associations; State Bar of California; Association of Business Trial Lawyers. Fellow, American Bar Foundation.

### COUNSEL

**ELIZABETH D. LEAR,** born Woodland, California, July 4, 1958; admitted to bar, 1986, California, U.S. District Court, Northern District of California and U.S. Court of Appeals, Ninth Circuit; 1988, District of Columbia; 1990, U.S. District Court, Central District of California; 1994, U.S. District Court, Southern District of California. *Education:* University of California at Berkeley (B.S., 1979); Stanford University (M.B.A., 1981); Boalt Hall School of Law, University of California (J.D., 1985). *Member:* Bar Association of San Francisco; State Bar of California; American Bar Association; Association of Business Trial Lawyers. **PRACTICE AREAS:** Litigation.

### RESIDENT ASSOCIATES

**JENNIFER A. CHMURA,** born Pensacola, Florida, August 26, 1967; admitted to bar, 1992, California; 1993, U.S. District Court, Northern, Central, Eastern and Southern Districts of California and U.S. Court of Appeals, Ninth Circuit. *Education:* University of Chicago (B.A., with honors, 1989); Hastings College of the Law, University of California, San Francisco (J.D., 1992). Phi Delta Phi. Recipient, Hastings 1066 Foundation Award for Distinguished Service to the Law School, 1992. First Place Winner, I.H. Prinzmetal Writing Competition, 1992. Senior Executive Editor, Hastings Comm/Ent Law Journal, 1992. Author: "Liability and Regulation of Municipal Solid Waste Landfills," 26 Beverly Hills Bar Assoc. L.J., 154, Fall 1992. **PRACTICE AREAS:** Environmental Litigation; Environmental Insurance Coverage; Civil Litigation.

**DESIREE DE LISLE,** born Lubbock, Texas, February 7, 1969; admitted to bar, 1995, California. *Education:* University of Notre Dame (B.A., with honors, 1991); Southern Methodist University (J.D., 1995). **PRACTICE AREAS:** Insurance Coverage; Environmental.

**RENÉ I. GAMBOA, IV,** born San Francisco, California, May 8, 1963; admitted to bar, 1988, California, U.S. District Court, Northern District of California and U.S. Court of Appeals, Ninth Circuit. *Education:* University of San Francisco (B.A., cum laude, 1985; J.D., 1988). Phi Alpha Theta; Alpha Sigma Nu. Recipient, American Jurisprudence Award, Legal Theory. *Member:* Bar Association of San Francisco; State Bar of California; American Bar Association. **LANGUAGES:** Spanish. **PRACTICE AREAS:** Insurance Defense; Civil Litigation.

**CRAIG C. HUNTER,** born Chicago, Illinois, August 22, 1946; admitted to bar, 1976, California and U.S. District Court, Central District of California; 1977, U.S. Court of Appeals, Ninth Circuit. *Education:* The Principia College (B.A., 1968); McGeorge School of Law (J.D., 1972). Comment Editor, Pacific Law Journal, 1975-1976. Clerk, Hon. Clarke Stephens, California Court of Appeals, Second District, 1976-1977. *Member:* Los Angeles County Bar Association; State Bar of California. **PRACTICE AREAS:** Litigation; Securities; Insurance Coverage Litigation.

**DEVERA L. PETAK,** born Paterson, New Jersey, October 22, 1953; admitted to bar, 1980, California; 1981, U.S. District Court, Central District of California; 1992, U.S. District Court, Eastern and Northern Dis-

*(This Listing Continued)*

# PROFESSIONAL BIOGRAPHIES

CALIFORNIA—LOS ANGELES

tricts of California. *Education:* California State College, Stanislaus (B.A., 1975); University of Southern California (M.A., 1977; M.A., 1978); Western State University (J.D., 1979). Recipient: American Jurisprudence Awards in Evidence, I and II; Remedies. Member, Moot Court. Member, Western State Law Review, 1978-1979. Faculty Member, The Rutter Group, Inc., Los Angeles, California, 1986-1987. *Member:* Los Angeles County and American Bar Associations; The State Bar of California; Southern California Defense Lawyers Association; Medical-Legal Society. *PRACTICE AREAS:* Insurance Coverage; Medical Malpractice; Bad Faith Litigation.

**STEVPHEN A. WATSON,** born 1959; admitted to bar, 1988, California and U.S. District Court, Central and Southern Districts of California; 1992, U.S. District Court, Northern and Eastern Districts of California and U.S. Court of Appeals, Ninth Circuit. *Education:* University of Illinois (B.S., 1984); University of San Diego (J.D., cum laude, 1988). Phi Delta Phi. Author: Comment, "Haskel v. Sup. Ct.," International Insurance Law Review, 1995; Comment, "Montrose v. Admiral," International Insurance Law Review, 1995. *Member:* Hennepin County (Founder and Chair, Insurance Committee, 1995) and American (Member: TIPS and Coverage) Bar Associations; American Inns of Court.

(For Complete Biographical Data on all Personnel, see Minneapolis, Minnesota Professional Biographies.)

---

## ZEMANEK & MILLS

*A PROFESSIONAL CORPORATION*

11845 WEST OLYMPIC BOULEVARD, SUITE 625
**LOS ANGELES, CALIFORNIA 90064**
Telephone: 310-473-8100
Fax: 310-445-3166

*Business, Real Estate and Construction Litigation. State and Federal Civil Trial and Appellate Practice, Creditors' Rights, Trade Secrets, Corporate and Partnership Law.*

**JOHN D. ZEMANEK,** born Wasco, California, June 1, 1951; admitted to bar, 1977, California. *Education:* Pomona College (B.A., magna cum laude, 1973); Boalt Hall School of Law, University of California (J.D., 1977). Phi Beta Kappa. **REPORTED CASES:** Joffe v. United California Bank, 141 Cal.App.3d 541, 190 Cal.Rptr.443 (1983). *PRACTICE AREAS:* Real Estate, Business and Construction Litigation (Trials and Appeals); Real Property Financing; Secured Transactions.

**STEPHAN A. MILLS,** born Geneva, Illinois, July 1, 1955; admitted to bar, 1980, California. *Education:* University of California at Irvine (B.A., cum laude, 1977); University of California at Los Angeles (J.D., 1980). Member, Moot Court Honors Program. *PRACTICE AREAS:* Real Estate, Business and Construction Litigation (Trials and Appeals); Secured Transactions.

---

## ZEUTZIUS & LaBRAN

**LOS ANGELES, CALIFORNIA**

(See Pasadena)

*General Civil and Trial Practice in State and Federal Courts. Criminal, Personal Injury, Corporate, Real Property, Business, Commercial, Collections, Contract and Family Law. Trials and Appeals. Probate and Estate Planning.*

---

## ZEVNIK HORTON GUIBORD & McGOVERN, P.C.

333 SOUTH GRAND AVENUE
TWENTY FIRST FLOOR
**LOS ANGELES, CALIFORNIA 90071**
Telephone: 213-437-5200
Telefax: 213-437-5222

*Chicago, Illinois Office:* Thirty Third Floor, 77 West Wacker Drive.
Telephone: 312-977-2500. Fax: 312-977-2560.
*Washington, D.C. Office:* Ninth Floor, 1299 Pennsylvania Avenue, N.W.
Telephone: 202-824-0950. Fax: 202-824-0955.
*New York, N.Y. Office:* 745 Fifth Avenue, Twenty-Fifth Floor. Telephone: 212-935-2735. Telefax: 212-935-0614.

*Palo Alto, California Office:* 5 Palo Alto Square, 3000 El Camino Real.
Telephone: 415-842-5900. Facsimile: 415-855-9226.
*London, England Office:* 4 Kings Bench Walk, Temple, London, EC4Y 7DL. Telephone: 071-353-0478. Facsimile: 071-583-3549.
*Norfolk, Virginia Office:* Main Street Tower, 300 Main Street, 13th Floor.
Telephone: 757-624-3480. Fax: 757-624-3479.

*Commercial Litigation, Environmental Law, Insurance Coverage, Toxic Tort Litigation, International Law, Practice before State and Federal Courts and Administrative Tribunals.*

**PAUL ANTON ZEVNIK,** born Ashland, Wisconsin, November 2, 1950; admitted to bar, 1977, California; 1978, District of Columbia, U.S. District Court for the District of Columbia, U.S. Court of Appeals for the District of Columbia Circuit and U.S. District Court, Northern District of California; 1980, U.S. Court of Appeals, Ninth Circuit and U.S. Tax Court; 1981, U.S. Supreme Court and U.S. Claims Court; 1984, U.S. Court of Appeals for the Federal Circuit; 1985, Pennsylvania. *Education:* Harvard University (A.B., magna cum laude, 1972; A.M., 1972; J.D., cum laude, 1976). Author: "Federal Product Liability Legislation," American Bar Association, 1986; "When an Underlying Carrier Goes Broke: Recent Trends in 'Drop Down' Coverage," Coverage, ABA Committee on Insurance Coverage Litigation, Vol. 1, 1989. Faculty, Management of Mass Tort Litigation, Practising Law Institute, 1983. Fellow, Joint Center for Urban Studies, Harvard University and Massachusetts Institute of Technology, 1976. *Member:* The District of Columbia Bar; State Bar of California; Pennsylvania and Federal Communications Bar Associations. *PRACTICE AREAS:* Insurance Coverage; Environmental Law; Toxic Tort Litigation.

**MICHEL YVES HORTON,** born Washington, D.C., October 22, 1951; admitted to bar, 1984, California and District of Columbia. *Education:* Virginia Commonwealth University (B.S., cum laude, 1978); College of William & Mary (J.D., 1981). Kappa Tau Alpha. Author: "Bad Faith Insurance Litigation and Insurance Broker Liability," Practising Law Institute, Vol. 231; "The Impact of Antitrust and RICO Treble Damage Theories on the Insurance Industry," ABA National Institute, 1986; "The Status of the Unlimited Duty to Defend Under Pre-1966 CGL Policies," ABA National Institute, 1986; "When an Underlying Carrier Goes Broke: Recent Trends in 'Drop Down' Coverage," Coverage, Vol. 1, 1989, ABA Committee on Insurance Coverage Litigation. *Member:* The District of Columbia Bar; State Bar of California. *PRACTICE AREAS:* Insurance Coverage; Commercial Litigation.

**BARBARA B. GUIBORD,** born White Plains, New York, June 14, 1951; admitted to bar, 1977, New York; 1979, U.S. District Court, Western District of New York; 1983, U.S. District Court, Northern District of Illinois and Illinois (Not admitted in California). *Education:* Connecticut College (B.A., cum laude, 1973); Fordham University (J.D., 1976). Writing and Research Editor, Fordham University Urban Law Journal, Vol. IV, 1975-1976. Author: Note, "The New Equal Protection: Substantive Due Process Resurrected Under a New Name?" 3 Fordham Law Journal 311, 1975. Adjunct Professor of Environmental Law, Rachel Carson College of Environmental Studies, State University of New York at Buffalo, September, 1983 to December, 1983. Presenter: "The New Hazardous Solid Waste Amendments of 1984," Hofstra Law School Environmental Symposium, 1985; "Title III SARA: Community Right to Know," Ibidem, 1987; "Lender Liability Under Environmental Law," Continuing Legal Education Satellite Network, Inc., Springfield, Illinois, 1988 and 1989; "Environmental Auditing," Ibidem, 1988; "Siting Issues Surrounding Medical Waste Treatment and Disposal Facilities," Environmental Symposium sponsored by Katten, Muchin & Zavis, Chicago, 1990; "Environmental Aspects of Doing a Deal," American Bar Association, 1990; "Managing Risk--Anticipating Liability---Structuring the Deal," Continuing Legal Education Satellite Network, Inc., Springfield, Illinois, 1990. Associate General Counsel, New York State Department of Environmental Conservation, 1980-1983. *Member:* Chicago, Erie County (Chairperson, Environmental Law Committee, 1979-1980), Illinois State, New York State (Member, Environmental Law Section) and American (Member, Committee on Land and Natural Resources, 1988-1992) Bar Associations. *LANGUAGES:* French. *PRACTICE AREAS:* Environmental Law; Insurance Coverage.

**PATRICK MICHAEL McGOVERN,** born Yeovil, Somerset, England, June 9, 1955; admitted to bar, 1982, England and Wales (Solicitor of the Supreme Court); 1986, New York; 1987, U.S. District Court, Southern District of New York; 1991, U.S. District Court, Eastern District of New York (Not admitted in California). *Education:* University of Sheffield, England (LL.B., with Honors, 1976; M.A., 1978); College of Law, Guildford, England (Solicitors Final Qualifying Exam, 1979). *Member:* Law Society of

*(This Listing Continued)*                                                                            *(This Listing Continued)*

**ZEVNIK HORTON GUIBORD & McGOVERN, P.C., Los Angeles—Continued**

England and Wales. LANGUAGES: French. PRACTICE AREAS: International Law; Insurance Coverage; Commercial Litigation.

**JOSEPH G. HOMSY,** born New York, N.Y., February 27, 1945; admitted to bar, 1978, New York and U.S. District Court, Southern District of New York; 1988, Illinois (Not admitted in California). *Education:* University of Pennsylvania (B.A., 1966); New England School of Law (J.D., 1977). Author: "The Scope of Private Cost-Recovery Actions under CERCLA §107 (a) (4) (B) And Allocation Among Potentially Responsible Parties," *Hazardous Waste Litigation*, Practicing Law Institute, 1988; "Environmental Reporting Required by the Securities and Exchange Commission," BNA Environment Report, 1991. *Member:* American Bar Association (Member, Sections on: Environmental Law; Litigation); American Association of Corporate Counsel; Environmental Law Institute (Associate Representative, 1984-1987). [Capt., USAF, 1967-1971]. PRACTICE AREAS: Environmental Law.

**JOHN W. ROBERTS,** admitted to bar, 1982, Illinois (Not admitted in California). *Education:* Lake Forest College (B.A., 1979); Harvard University (J.D., cum laude, 1982). Phi Beta Kappa. REPORTED CASES: Monsanto Company in Hines v. Vulcan, 658 F.Supp. 651 (N.D. Ill. 1988); Inland Steel Company in Inland Steel v. Koppers Company, 498 N.E.2d 1247 (Ind. App. 1986). PRACTICE AREAS: Commercial Litigation; Compensation and Liability; Environmental; Construction.

**JOHN K. CROSSMAN,** born Miami, Florida, June 28, 1962; admitted to bar, 1987, Connecticut and New York; 1988, U.S. District Court, Southern and Eastern District of New York; 1993, U.S. Court of Appeals, Second Circuit (Not admitted in California). *Education:* Tufts University (B.S., cum laude, 1984); Boston University (J.D., 1987). *Member:* Association of the Bar of the City of New York (Computer Law Committee); American Bar Association; New York Patent, Trademark and Copyright Law Association.

**JONATHAN L. OSBORNE,** born Ft. Thomas, Kentucky, July 4, 1961; admitted to bar, 1986, Kentucky and U.S. District Court, Eastern and Western Districts of Kentucky; 1996, District of Columbia (Not admitted in California). *Education:* Georgetown College (B.A., 1983); University of Louisville (J.D., 1986). Member and Vice-President, Moot Court Board, 1985-1986. *Member:* Kentucky and American Bar Associations; The Association of Trial Lawyers of America. PRACTICE AREAS: Insurance Coverage; Commercial Litigation.

---

**K. ERIC ADAIR,** born Petaluma, California, April 17, 1962; admitted to bar, 1990, California. *Education:* Brigham Young University (B.A., 1987; J.D., 1990). Moot Court National Team; Order of the Barristers. LANGUAGES: Spanish. PRACTICE AREAS: Environmental Insurance Coverage; General Litigation.

**KRISTEN C. BOLING,** born Atlanta, Georgia, October 28, 1967; admitted to bar, 1992, California and U.S. District Court, Central District of California; 1994, U.S. Court of Appeals, Ninth Circuit; 1995, District of Columbia. *Education:* Harvard University (A.B., cum laude, 1989); Vanderbilt University (J.D., 1992). Vanderbilt Moot Court, Semi-Finalist, 1990-1991; Associate Problem Editor, 1991-1992. Vanderbilt A.B.A. National Moot Court Team (Chief Oralist, 1991-1992). Complex Litigation Inn of Court, Los Angeles, 1995. LANGUAGES: French.

**DAVID S. COX,** born Lawrence, Massachusetts, January 16, 1968; admitted to bar, 1995, California. *Education:* Princeton University (B.A., 1990); University of California, Los Angeles (J.D., 1995).

**CAROL A. CROTTA,** born Los Angeles, California, May 25, 1956; admitted to bar, 1995, California. *Education:* Yale University (B.A., cum laude, 1978); University of California at Los Angeles (J.D., 1995). LANGUAGES: Italian. PRACTICE AREAS: Environmental Insurance; General Litigation.

**MARK B. HARTZLER,** born Oakland, California, May 14, 1963; admitted to bar, 1994, California. *Education:* University of Arizona (B.A., magna cum laude, 1990); University of Texas at Austin (J.D., 1993). Article and Notes Editor, Texas International Law Journal; Director, Legal Research Board. Author: "National Security Export Controls on Data Encryption - How They Limit U.S. Competitiveness," Texas International Law Journal, Vol. 29, Number 3, Summer 1994. [U.S. Air Force, 1983-1989]. LANGUAGES: Arabic. PRACTICE AREAS: Insurance Coverage; General Civil Litigation.

*(This Listing Continued)*

**NICK P. KARAPETIAN,** born Lyon, France, August 1, 1968; admitted to bar, 1994, California. *Education:* California State University, Northridge (B.S., 1991); Loyola University (J.D., 1994). *Member:* State Bar of California. PRACTICE AREAS: Commercial Litigation; Environmental.

**STEVEN E. KNOTT,** born Columbia, South Carolina, January 3, 1961; admitted to bar, 1990, California; 1991, U.S. Court of Appeals, Ninth Circuit. *Education:* University of California at Berkeley (A.B., 1983); University of California School of Law, Davis (J.D., 1990). Order of the Barristers. Member, Moot Court Board. Recipient, American Jurisprudence Award in Appellate Advocacy. *Member:* Los Angeles County Bar Association; State Bar of California. [Capt., USMC, 1983-1987]. PRACTICE AREAS: Environmental Law; Insurance Coverage.

**JASON B. KOMORSKY,** born Los Angeles, California, October 8, 1964; admitted to bar, 1991, California and U.S. District Court, Central, Northern and Southern Districts of California; U.S. Court of Appeals, Ninth Circuit. *Education:* University of California at Berkeley (B.A., 1986); University of California, Hastings College of the Law (J.D., 1991). Phi Alpha Delta. Author: Cover Article, Los Angeles Lawyer, Nov. 1993 "Taking the Fifth in Civil Litigation". *Member:* State Bar of California. PRACTICE AREAS: Environmental; Securities; Insurance Coverage; Antitrust; General Business.

**CHARLES J. MALARET,** born San Francisco, California, April 17, 1964; admitted to bar, 1989, California. *Education:* University of San Francisco (B.A., 1986); University of California at Davis (J.D., 1989). Member, Moot Court Board. Recipient, American Jurisprudence Award. *Member:* State Bar of California. PRACTICE AREAS: Litigation; Insurance; Environmental.

**MEREDITH (MIMI) NEWTON,** born Abington, Pennsylvania, March 25, 1962; admitted to bar, 1989, District of Columbia; 1994, California; 1996, U.S. District Court, Central District of California. *Education:* University of Pennsylvania (B.A., cum laude, 1985); Georgetown University (J.D., 1989). Editor, International Environmental Law Journal. *Member:* State Bar of California (Member, Environmental Law Section). PRACTICE AREAS: Environmental; Insurance.

**DAWN S. PITTMAN,** born San Francisco, California; admitted to bar, 1995, California. *Education:* University of California at Berkeley (B.A., 1992); University of California at Los Angeles (J.D., 1995). PRACTICE AREAS: Insurance Coverage Litigation; Environmental.

---

## ZIDE & O'BIECUNAS

*Established in 1929*

**SUITE 403, 1300 WEST OLYMPIC BOULEVARD**
**LOS ANGELES, CALIFORNIA 90015**
*Telephone: 213-487-7550*
*Fax: 213-382-6095*
*Email: leoatzano@aol.com*

Mailing Address: P.O. Box 15363, Del Valle Station

*Ventura, California Office:* 101 South Victoria Avenue. Telephone: 805-642-2426. Fax: 805-642-8881.

*Commercial, Insolvency, Business and Construction Law.*

FIRM PROFILE: *The law firm of Zide & O'Biecunas continues a tradition of quality Business and commercial representation in Southern California that spans more than 30 years.*

*Offering corporate general counsel and commercial representation, the firm's clients are a diverse group of local, regional and national companies.*

*Zide & O'Biecunas specializes in meeting the legal needs of both small and large businesses. Our objective is to establish a long term relationship, seeking not only to solve existing legal problems, but also to prevent future legal problems from occurring.*

**THOMAS ZIDE,** born Los Angeles, California, January 1, 1935; admitted to bar, 1960, California; 1973, U.S. Court of Appeals, Ninth Circuit; 1974, U.S. Supreme Court. *Education:* California State University at Los Angeles (B.A., 1956); University of Southern California. Judge Pro Tem, Los Angeles Municipal Court, 1970. *Member:* Los Angeles County Bar Association; State Bar of California; Financial Lawyers Conference; Commercial Law League of America (Member, Board of Governors, 1980-1983; Recording Secretary, 1986-1987; Secretary, Fund for Public Education, 1983-1985; President, 1985; Chair; Member, Creditor's Rights Section, 1994-1995). PRACTICE AREAS: Commercial Collection; Insolvency; Business.

*(This Listing Continued)*

**LEO G. O'BIECUNAS, JR.,** born Los Angeles, California, July 16, 1957; admitted to bar, 1981, California; 1988, U.S. Supreme Court. *Education:* Southwestern University (J.D., 1981). Board Certified Creditors' Rights Specialist, CLLA Academy of Commercial and Bankruptcy Law Specialists. *Member:* Los Angeles County, Ventura County and American Bar Associations; State Bar of California; Commercial Law League of America (Chairman, Western Region Members Association, 1993-1994; Member, Executive Council, 1985-1993; Executive Council, Young Members Section, 1989-1991); Los Angeles Bankruptcy Forum (Member, Board of Governors, 1983-1990); Financial Lawyers. *PRACTICE AREAS:* Commercial Collection; Construction Law.

*ASSOCIATES*

**DOUGLAS M. KAYE,** born Minneapolis, Minnesota, April 17, 1961; admitted to bar, 1988, California and U.S. District Court, Central, Eastern and Southern Districts of California; 1993, U.S. Supreme Court. *Education:* University of Minnesota (B.A., Economics, 1983); Southwestern University School of Law (J.D., 1987). *Member:* Los Angeles County and American Bar Associations; State Bar of California. *PRACTICE AREAS:* Commercial Collection; Retail Collection; Insolvency.

**NATHAN SWEDLOW,** born 1928; admitted to bar, 1971, California. *Education:* Van Norman University (J.D., 1969). Real Estate Broker, California, 1960. *Member:* Los Angeles County Bar Association; State Bar of California.

## ZIFFREN, BRITTENHAM, BRANCA & FISCHER

THIRTY SECOND FLOOR, 2121 AVENUE OF THE STARS
LOS ANGELES, CALIFORNIA 90067
Telephone: 310-552-3388
Fax: 310-553-7068; 553-1648
*Entertainment and Tax Law.*

FIRM PROFILE: *Ziffren, Brittenham, Branca & Fischer is a leading transactional entertainment law firm, providing innovative and strategic advice to its domestic and international clientele. Founded in 1979, the Firm represents the highest caliber clients, both talent and corporate, in the motion picture, television, music and interactive fields.*

*MEMBERS OF FIRM*

**KENNETH ZIFFREN,** born Chicago, Illinois, June 24, 1940; admitted to bar, 1967, California. *Education:* Northwestern University (B.A., 1962); University of California at Los Angeles (J.D., 1965). Phi Delta Phi; Order of the Coif. Editor-in-Chief, UCLA Law Review, 1965. Law Clerk to Chief Justice Warren, 1965-1966. Recipient: The American Jewish Committee Learned Hand Award, 1995; UCLA School of Law Alumnus of the Year Award for Professional Achievement, 1995. *Member:* Beverly Hills, Los Angeles County and American Bar Associations; State Bar of California; Los Angeles Copyright Society (President, 1977-1978). *PRACTICE AREAS:* Entertainment Law.

**HARRY M. BRITTENHAM,** born Port Huron, Michigan, September 6, 1941; admitted to bar, 1971, California. *Education:* United States Air Force Academy (B.S., 1963); University of California at Los Angeles (J.D., 1970). Articles Editor, U.C.L.A. Law Review, 1969-1970. *Member:* The State Bar of California. [Capt., USAF, 1963-1967]. *PRACTICE AREAS:* Entertainment Law.

**JOHN G. BRANCA,** born Bronxville, New York, December 11, 1950; admitted to bar, 1975, California. *Education:* Occidental College (A.B., cum laude, 1972); University of California at Los Angeles (J.D., 1975). Phi Alpha Delta; Sigma Tau Sigma. Editor-in-Chief, UCLA-Alaska Law Review, 1974-1975. Recipient, Bancroft-Whitney American Jurisprudence Award, 1974-1975. Author: Comment, "Bar Association Fee Schedules and Suggested Alternatives: Reflections on a Sherman Exemption that Doesn't Exist," 3 UCLA-Alaska Law Review 207-54, 1974; "Dischargeability of Financial Obligations in Divorce: The Support Obligation and the Division of Marital Property," 9 (ABA) Family Quarterly 405-34, 1975; "Enforceability of Charitable Pledges: A Matter Which Deserves Some Consideration," 10 Journal of the Beverly Hills Bar Association 34-35, 1976; "Antenuptial Agreements in California: An Examination of the Current Law and In re Marriage of Dawley," 11 University of San Francisco Law Review 317-344, 1977; "A Practitioner's Guide to the Wages of Sin: Marvin v. Marvin," 52 Los Angeles Bar Journal 502-507, April, 1977; "Attorney Fee Schedules and Legal Advertising: The Implications of Goldfarb," 24 UCLA Law Review 475-522, 1977. *Member:* Beverly Hills (Member, Entertain-

*(This Listing Continued)*

ment Law Section) and American (Member, Section of Patent, Trademark and Copyright Law) Bar Associations; State Bar of California. *PRACTICE AREAS:* Entertainment Law.

**SAMUEL N. FISCHER,** born San Diego, California, April 23, 1956; admitted to bar, 1982, California. *Education:* Brown University (B.A., magna cum laude, 1978); University of California at Los Angeles (J.D., 1982). Phi Beta Kappa; Order of the Coif. Articles Editor, 1980-1981 and Editor-in-Chief, 1981-1982, Federal Communications Law Journal. Extern to Justice Frank Richardson, California Supreme Court, 1980. *Member:* State Bar of California. *PRACTICE AREAS:* Entertainment Law.

**PAUL L. BRINDZE,** born Detroit, Michigan, January 3, 1945; admitted to bar, 1974, California. *Education:* University of California at Los Angeles (B.A., cum laude, 1971; J.D., 1974). Phi Alpha Delta. *Member:* Beverly Hills and American (Member, Section of Patent, Trademark and Copyright Law) Bar Associations; State Bar of California. [1st Lt., U.S. Army, 1964-1968]. *PRACTICE AREAS:* Entertainment Law.

**R. DENNIS LUDERER,** born New York, N.Y., September 13, 1945; admitted to bar, 1975, California. *Education:* Boston College (A.B., 1967); University of San Diego (J.D., 1974); New York University (LL.M. in Taxation, 1975). Phi Delta Phi. Notes and Comments Editor, San Diego Law Review, 1973-1974. *Member:* Beverly Hills and Los Angeles County Bar Associations; State Bar of California. *PRACTICE AREAS:* Tax Law.

**DAVID NOCHIMSON,** born Paterson, New Jersey, June 19, 1943; admitted to bar, 1970, New York; 1977, California. *Education:* Yale University (B.A., cum laude, 1965); Columbia University (LL.B., cum laude, 1968); Australian National University, Canberra, Australia (LL.M., 1970). Harlan Fiske Stone Scholar. Fulbright Scholar, Canberra, Australia, 1968-1969. Member, Board of Editors, Columbia Journal of Transnational Law, 1967-1968. Editor, The Entertainment and Sports Lawyer, 1982-1989. Author: "A New Legal Approach to Foreign Investment," Australian Law Journal, March, 1969. Member, Advisory Committee, 1979— and Coordinator, 1980-1981, UCLA Entertainment Symposium. *Member:* Beverly Hills, American (Member, Forum Committee on the Entertainment and Sports Industries, 1980—, Chairman, 1989-1992) and International (Vice Chairman, Intellectual Property, Entertainment and Communications Committee, 1989-1992) Bar Associations; State Bar of California. *PRACTICE AREAS:* Entertainment Law.

**GARY S. STIFFELMAN,** born Kansas City, Missouri, August 8, 1952; admitted to bar, 1979, California. *Education:* Washington University; Kansas University (B.S., 1974); University of Southern California (M.F.A., 1976); University of California at Los Angeles (J.D., 1979). Order of the Coif. Chief Comment Editor, UCLA Law Review, 1978-1979. Recipient, First Prize, UCLA Nathan Burkan Memorial Competition, 1978. Author: "Community Property and the Right of Publicity: Fame and/or Fortune?" UCLA Law Review, Vol. 25, p. 1095, 1978. Member, Advisory Committee UCLA Entertainment Symposium, 1977-1996. *Member:* State Bar of California. *PRACTICE AREAS:* Entertainment Law.

**CLIFFORD W. GILBERT-LURIE,** born Detroit, Michigan, September 30, 1954; admitted to bar, 1979, California. *Education:* University of California at Los Angeles (A.B., summa cum laude, 1976); Boalt Hall School of Law, University of California (J.D., 1979). Phi Beta Kappa; Order of the Coif. Associate Editor, California Law Review, 1978-1979. *Member:* State Bar of California. *PRACTICE AREAS:* Entertainment Law.

**KATHLEEN HALLBERG,** born Los Angeles, California, June 26, 1951; admitted to bar, 1976, California. *Education:* University of California at Davis (B.A., 1972); Hastings College of Law, University of California (J.D., 1976). *Member:* State Bar of California. *PRACTICE AREAS:* Entertainment Law.

**JAMIE YOUNG,** born New York, N.Y., February 6, 1956; admitted to bar, 1982, New York; 1987, California. *Education:* Washington University (B.A., summa cum laude, 1977); New York University (J.D., 1981). Phi Beta Kappa. *Member:* Beverly Hills, New York State and American Bar Associations; State Bar of California. *PRACTICE AREAS:* Entertainment Law.

**MITCHELL C. TENZER,** born New York, N.Y., October 26, 1953; admitted to bar, 1980, New York; 1992, California. *Education:* Johns Hopkins University (B.A., summa cum laude, 1975) Phi Beta Kappa; Harvard University (J.D., 1979). *PRACTICE AREAS:* Entertainment Law.

**KENNETH A. AUGUST,** born Bridgeport, Connecticut, February 15, 1947; admitted to bar, 1993, California. *Education:* Stanford University (B.A., History, 1968); Columbia University (J.D., 1974). National Merit Scholar, Stanford University. Harlan Fiske Stone Scholar, Columbia Uni-

*(This Listing Continued)*

## ZIFFREN, BRITTENHAM, BRANCA & FISCHER, Los Angeles—Continued

versity. Articles Editor, Columbia Human Rights Law Review. *Member:* Beverly Hills and American Bar Associations; State Bar of California. *PRACTICE AREAS:* Entertainment Transactions.

**STEVEN H. BURKOW,** born Pasadena, California, March 4, 1955; admitted to bar, 1978, California. *Education:* Swarthmore College; Pomona College (A.B., magna cum laude, 1975); University of California at Los Angeles (J.D., 1978). Phi Beta Kappa. Member, Board of Judges, UCLA Moot Court Honors Program, 1977-1978. Member, University of California at Los Angeles Law Review, 1977-1978. *Member:* Beverly Hills, Los Angeles County and American Bar Associations; State Bar of California. *PRACTICE AREAS:* Entertainment Law.

**DAVID LANDE,** born Philadelphia, Pennsylvania, January 18, 1967; admitted to bar, 1994, California. *Education:* University of Pennsylvania (B.A., cum laude, 1989; J.D., 1994). *PRACTICE AREAS:* Entertainment Law.

**JAMEY COHEN,** born New Orleans, Louisiana, July 30, 1956; admitted to bar, 1990, California. *Education:* Stanford University (A.B., with distinction, 1978); Harvard University (J.D., cum laude, 1989). Phi Beta Kappa. *PRACTICE AREAS:* Entertainment Law.

### LEGAL SUPPORT PERSONNEL
#### PARALEGALS

**KAREN W. LANGFORD,** born Albany, New York, July 25, 1957. *Education:* University of California, Los Angeles (1975-1979). Member: National Paralegal Association; National Academy of Recording, Arts and Sciences. *PRACTICE AREAS:* Entertainment Law.

**PENNY SCHULER LAMBERT,** born New York, February 23, 1954. *Education:* State University of New York at New Paltz (1972); University of Miami (B.A., cum laude, 1974); Southwestern University School of Law (1977); University of California (Paralegal Certification, 1978). Member, University of California at Los Angeles Paralegal Association. *Member:* Beverly Hills Bar Association. *PRACTICE AREAS:* Entertainment Law.

**ALICIA WINFIELD,** born Los Angeles, California, April 20, 1962. *Education:* Middle Tennessee State (B.S., 1984).

**GLORIA D. GOLDSTEIN,** born Los Angeles, California, January 26, 1952. *Education:* University of California at Los Angeles (B.A., 1973); University of Los Angeles College of Law (Paralegal Certification, 1975). *PRACTICE AREAS:* Entertainment Law.

---

## ZIMMERMANN, KOOMER & CONNOLLY LLP

10960 WILSHIRE BOULEVARD, SUITE 1225
**LOS ANGELES, CALIFORNIA 90024**
Telephone: 310-231-6565
Fax: 310-231-6566

*Representation and Counseling in the areas of Business and Real Estate Litigation, Employment Law, Torts and Equine Law.*

### MEMBERS OF FIRM

**SCOTT Z. ZIMMERMANN,** born Milwaukee, Wisconsin, March 27, 1953; admitted to bar, 1977, California. *Education:* University of California at Irvine (A.B., 1974); University of California at Los Angeles (J.D., 1977). Law Clerk to Associate Justice Clarke E. Stephens, California Court of Appeal, Second Judicial District, Fifth Division, 1977-1978. *PRACTICE AREAS:* Business Litigation; Torts; Equine Law.

**MICHAEL D. KOOMER,** born New York, N.Y., July 10, 1942; admitted to bar, 1969, California. *Education:* University of California at Los Angeles (A.B., 1964), Phi Beta Kappa; University of Southern California (J.D., 1968). Order of the Coif. Note and Comment Editor, University of Southern California Law Review, 1967-1968. *PRACTICE AREAS:* Employment Law; Business Litigation.

**JOHN G. CONNOLLY,** born Portsmouth, New Hampshire, November 23, 1959; admitted to bar, 1984, California. *Education:* Brandeis University (B.A., cum laude, 1981); University of California at Los Angeles (J.D., 1984). Member, Moot Court Honors Program. Staff Member, 1981-1983

*(This Listing Continued)*

---

and Articles Editor, 1983-1984, UCLA Journal of Environmental Law and Policy. *PRACTICE AREAS:* Business Litigation; Real Estate; Labor Litigation.

---

## STUART D. ZIMRING

Established in 1991
12650 RIVERSIDE DRIVE (NORTH HOLLYWOOD)
**LOS ANGELES, CALIFORNIA 91607-3492**
Telephone: 818-755-4848
Fax: 818-508-0181

*Estate Planning, Trust and Probate Law, Elder Law, Business and Banking, Real Estate, Condominiums and Homeowners Associations.*

*FIRM PROFILE:* The Law Offices of Stuart D. Zimring is a broad based, general civil practice firm. We have a full-service estate and life planning practice capable of providing virtually all the estate planning needs of our clients. We work closely with each client's accountant, insurance advisor, stockbroker, pension and profit sharing plan administrator or other financial advisor. In addition, we have expertise in the developing area of elder law, a growing subspecialty of estate planning. The firm represents individuals, business organizations and institutions as plaintiffs and defendants in business, real estate, construction and other civil litigation. The firm has over twenty five years of experience in the formation, operation and dissolution of for-profit and non-profit business entities, including corporations, partnerships and sole proprietorships. Members of the firm have over two decades of both transactional and litigation experience in real estate. We also represent institutional and private lenders in negotiating, structuring and documenting loan transactions. Incidental to our real estate practice, the firm has become experienced in environmental issues and the way in which they impact leases, loans, sales and other real property transactions, and each party thereto. We pride ourselves on our ability to provide our clients with high quality, personalized service.

**STUART D. ZIMRING,** born Los Angeles, California, December 12, 1946; admitted to bar, 1972, California and U.S. District Court, Central District of California; 1974, U.S. District Court, Northern District of California; 1994, U.S. Supreme Court. *Education:* University of California at Los Angeles (B.A., 1968); University of California School of Law (J.D., 1971). Lecturer in Law, Los Angeles Community College, 1973-1983. Member, Board of Directors of Bet Tzedek Jewish Legal Services, 1976-1988. Member, Los Angeles Superior Court Probate Volunteer Panel. Member: Beverly Hills Estate Counselors Forum; San Fernando Valley Estate Counselor's Forum. President, National Academy of Elder Law Attorneys, Southern California Chapter, 1996-1997. Vice-President, Organization for the Needs of the Elderly (O.N.E.), 1995—. *Member:* San Fernando Valley and Los Angeles County Bar Associations; State Bar of California; National Academy of Elder Law Attorneys; Southern California Council of Elder Law Attorneys; Beverly Hills and San Fernando Valley Estate Counselors Forum. (Certified Specialist, Estate Planning, Probate and Trust Law, The State Bar of California Board of Legal Specialization). *PRACTICE AREAS:* Estate Planning; Probate and Trust; Real Estate Law; Business; Elder Law.

### ASSOCIATE

**DENA L. KLOTZ,** born Los Angeles, California, December 21, 1968; admitted to bar, 1994, California. *Education:* University of California at Los Angeles (B.A., 1991); Pepperdine University (J.D., 1994). *Member:* San Fernando Valley and Los Angeles County Bar Associations; State Bar of California; San Fernando Valley Estate Counselors Forum. *PRACTICE AREAS:* Estate Planning; Probate and Trust; Real Estate Law; Business; Elder Law.

REPRESENTATIVE CLIENTS: TransWorld Bank; Cytec Industries Inc.; Huntington Palisades Property Owners Association; Buff, Smith & Hensman, Architects, Inc.; Leslie's Poolmart, Inc.
REFERENCE: TransWorld Bank.

---

## ZOLLA AND MEYER

A Partnership including a Professional Corporation
SUITE 1020, 2029 CENTURY PARK EAST
**LOS ANGELES, CALIFORNIA 90067**
Telephone: 310-277-0725
Facsimile: 310-277-3784
Email: *familylaw@zmlaw.com*
URL: *http://www.zmlaw.com/familylaw*

*Family Law.*

*(This Listing Continued)*

*FIRM PROFILE: The firm concentrates its practice exclusively in the area of family law. The firm represents marital and non-marital partners in complex marital dissolution proceedings, valuation and division of property, child custody and visitation disputes, Prenuptial Agreements and contested paternity and adoption proceedings. The firm's clients include professionals, business executives and prominent persons in the fields of sports and entertainment. Partners and associates participate in continuing legal education seminars and professional association activities. The partners of the firm publish extensively and lecture frequently on family law topics.*

### MEMBERS OF FIRM

**MARSHALL S. ZOLLA, (A P.C.),** born Chicago, Illinois, February 4, 1939; admitted to bar, 1964, California. *Education:* University of California, Los Angeles (A.B., cum laude, 1960); Boalt Hall School of Law, University of California, Berkeley (J.D., 1963). Member, Moot Court Board. Editorial Consultant and Commentator, California Family Law Monthly, Published by Matthew Bender & Company; Practice Consultant, California Family Law Trial Guide, Published by Matthew Bender & Company; Co-Author: "Promises, Promises: Enforcement of a Prenuptial Agreement in California May Founder on Three Conflicting Standards of Law," Los Angeles Lawyer, December, 1995; Co-Author: "Qualified Medical Child Support Orders (QMSCO's)," Beverly Hills Bar Association, 1995;Co-Author: "The Perpetuation of Shattered Hearts: The Disturbing Conflict Between Dependency Court and Family Law Jurisdiction," Los Angeles Lawyer, July/August, 1993; Co-Author: "Guideline Child Support: How to Get 'Off' the Mandatory Guideline," Beverly Hills Bar Association Family Law Workshop, 1993; Co-Author: "The Diversity of Child Custody Proceedings in California," Los Angeles County Bar Association Family Law Symposium Reference Book, 1993; Co-Author: "Child Custody Proceedings Other Than in Marital Dissolution Actions," Los Angeles County Bar Association Family Law Symposium Reference Book, 1991, 1992; Editorial Consultant, California Marital Settlement Agreement, Cal. Draft Master Series, Published by Matthew Bender & Co., 1990; Author: "When Parents Change Their Minds," California State Bar Journal, January 1985; Author: "Evaluation, Division and Proof of Retirement Plan Benefits Incident to a Marital Dissolution Proceeding," Beverly Hills Bar Association Eleventh Annual Family Law Symposium, 1985; Editorial Consultant, California Legal Systems, Domestic Relations, Published by Matthew Bender & Company, 1983; Author: "Tax Implications of Living Together: Close Encounters of the Uncertain Kind," Beverly Hills Bar Journal, Spring, 1981 (Reprinted by the Continuing Education of the Bar, Advanced Family Law Series, "Solving the Problems of Unmarried Couples," 1982) Author: "Prenuptial Agreements and Freedom of Contract in California," California State Bar Journal, January, 1981; Co-Author: "Report of the Family Law Mediation Program of the Los Angeles County Superior Court," Beverly Hills Bar Association Journal, Spring, 1980; Panelist: Beverly Hills Bar Association Family Law Symposium, 1979, 1980, 1981, 1984, 1987, 1989, 1991, 1992, 1993, 1995; Beverly Hills Bar Association Citizens Law School, 1991, 1993. Chairperson, Family Law Mediation Program, Los Angeles Superior Court, West District, 1978-1980. *Member:* Beverly Hills (Chairman, Family Law Section, 1982-1983; Member, Board of Governors, 1983-1984) and Los Angeles County (Member, Sections on: Family Law; Real Property) Bar Associations; State Bar of California (Member, Family Law Section); Association of Business Trial Lawyers. (Certified Specialist, Family Law, The State Bar of California Board of Legal Specialization). *PRACTICE AREAS:* Family Law.

**LISA HELFEND MEYER,** born Los Angeles, California, October 11, 1957; admitted to bar, 1982, California. *Education:* University of California, Los Angeles (B.A., 1979); Pepperdine University, School of Law; Loyola Law School, Los Angeles (J.D., 1982). Phi Delta Phi. Recipient, American Jurisprudence Award in Contracts. Honors Moot Court. Co-Author: "Promises, Promises: Enforcement of a Prenuptial Agreement in California May Founder on Three Conflicting Standards of Law," Los Angeles Lawyer, December, 1995; Co-Author: Practical Tips for Obtaining Discovery from Third Party Privately Held Corporations," Los Angeles County Bar Association, Family Law News & Review, Spring, 1995; Co-Author: "The Perpetuation of Shattered Hearts: The Disturbing Conflict Between Dependency Court and Family Law Jurisdiction," Los Angeles Lawyer, July/August 1993; "Guideline Child Support: How to Get 'Off' the Mandatory Guideline," Beverly Hills Bar Association Family Law Workshop, 1993; "The Diversity of Child Custody Proceedings in California," Los Angeles County Bar Association Family Law Symposium Reference Book, 1993; "Child Custody Proceedings Other Than in Marital Dissolution Actions," Los Angeles County Bar Association Family Law Symposium Reference Book, 1991, 1992. *Member:* Beverly Hills, Century City and Los Angeles County Bar Associations; State Bar of California. (Certified Specialist, Family Law,

*(This Listing Continued)*

The State Bar of California Board of Legal Specialization). *LANGUAGES:* Spanish. *PRACTICE AREAS:* Family Law.

### ASSOCIATES

**DOREEN MARIE OLSON,** born Santa Ana, California, August 19, 1966; admitted to bar, 1993, California. *Education:* University of California, Los Angeles (B.A., 1989); Whittier College School of Law (J.D., 1992). Co-Author: "Practical Tips for Obtaining Discovery from Third Party Privately Held Corporations," Los Angeles County Bar Association Family Law News & Review, Spring, 1995. Research Consultant, Beverly Hills Bar Association Family Law Workshop, "Guideline Child Support: How to Get 'Off' the Mandatory Guideline," 1993. *Member:* Beverly Hills and Los Angeles County Bar Associations; State Bar of California. *LANGUAGES:* Spanish. *PRACTICE AREAS:* Family Law.

**DANA LOWY,** born Los Angeles, California, June 4, 1961; admitted to bar, 1992, California and U.S. District Court, Central District of California. *Education:* University of California at Santa Barbara (B.A., 1984); Southwestern University School of Law (J.D., summa cum laude, 1992). Member, Moot Court Honors Program; Intramural Moot Court Competition. Listed National Dean's List. Recipient, American Jurisprudence Book Awards: Legal Research and Writing, Evidence, Remedies, Wills and Trusts. Managing Editor, Southwestern University Law Review. *Member:* Beverly Hills and Los Angeles County Bar Associations; State Bar of California; Women Lawyers Association of Los Angeles. *PRACTICE AREAS:* Family Law.

**GREGORY M. MARSH,** born Los Angeles, California, March 21, 1968; admitted to bar, 1994, California. *Education:* University of California at Los Angeles (B.A., 1991); Loyola Marymount University (J.D., 1994). Recipient, American Jurisprudence Awards in Corporations. *Member:* Beverly Hills and Los Angeles County Bar Associations; State Bar of California. *PRACTICE AREAS:* Family Law.

REFERENCE: Bank of California, Beverly Hills.

---

## GEORGE S. ZUGSMITH
### A PROFESSIONAL CORPORATION
### LOS ANGELES, CALIFORNIA
(See Long Beach)

*Family Law, Child Support, Spousal Support, Divorce, Custody and Visitation.*

---

## LAW OFFICES OF
## ROSALINE L. ZUKERMAN
Established in 1981

*1888 CENTURY PARK EAST*
*SUITE 1100*
**LOS ANGELES, CALIFORNIA 90067**
Telephone: 310-277-5277
Fax: 310-277-5276

*Family, Business, Corporate and Real Estate Law. Criminal Defense, Litigation.*

*FIRM PROFILE: A substantial portion of the practice of the firm is devoted to family law, including marital dissolution processings, co-habitation, antenuptial and partnership agreements, child custody, visitation, paternity and adoption. Members of the firm assist throughout the Los Angeles County as volunteer mediators, recognizing the value of those services.*

**ROSALINE L. ZUKERMAN,** born Cleveland, Ohio, October 4, 1930; admitted to bar, 1981, California; 1982, U.S. Court of Appeals, Ninth Circuit and U.S. District Court, Central District of California; 1989, U.S. District Court, Southern District of California. *Education:* University of Illinois (B.A., Psychology, summa cum laude, 1952); University of Iowa (M.A., 1974); Southwestern University School of Law (J.D., 1980). Law Clerk, Los Angeles District Attorney Career Criminal Unit, 1978-1980. Volunteer Attorney, Bet Tzedek Legal Services, 1981-1983. School Board Member, Rock Island, Illinois, 1971-1974. Board Member, Los Angeles Free Clinic, 1979-1985. Commissioner, Los Angeles City Library Commission, 1982-1984. Volunteer Mediator, Santa Monica Family Court, 1984—. Commissioner ProTem, Beverly Hills and West Los Angeles Municipal Court, 1984—. Special Consultant, "Tax Crimes - Corporate Liability," Tax Management Inc., B.N.A., 1983. *Member:* Beverly Hills, Los Angeles County (Member, Sections on: Family Law; Business; Real Estate; Minors

*(This Listing Continued)*

## LAW OFFICES OF ROSALINE L. ZUKERMAN, Los Angeles—Continued

Panel Planning Committee) and American (Member, Current Legislation Committee, Section of Real Property, Probate and Trust Law, 1987-1989) Bar Associations; State Bar of California (Member, Education Committee, Business Law Section, 1990—); Womens Lawyers Association of Los Angeles (Member, Hollywood Woman's Political Committee). *PRACTICE AREAS:* Family Law; Real Estate; Business Law; Criminal Law.

### ASSOCIATES

**DEBORAH L. GRABOFF,** born Los Angeles, California, December 6, 1957; admitted to bar, 1983, California. *Education:* University of California at Los Angeles (B.A., cum laude 1979); Loyola Marymount University School of Law (J.D., 1983). Volunteer Attorney, Harriet Buhai Family Law Center, 1991-1992. *Member:* Beverly Hills and Los Angeles County Bar Associations; The State Bar of California. *PRACTICE AREAS:* Family Law; Civil Litigation.

**SHARON MARAVALLI,** born New York, N.Y., June 24, 1953; admitted to bar, 1994, California. *Education:* State University of New York at Buffalo (B.A., 1975); Southwestern University School of Law (J.D., 1993). *PRACTICE AREAS:* Family Law; Civil Litigation.

**DEBORAH DAVIS,** born New York, N.Y., March 19, 1957; admitted to bar, 1985, New Jersey; 1995, California. *Education:* University of Maryland, College Park (B.S., 1978); Brooklyn Law School (J.D., 1981). Omicron Delta Kappa. Recipient, Honors Program Bryd Prize. Certified Mediator, Los Angeles Center for Dispute Resolution. *Member:* Beverly Hills, Los Angeles County and New Jersey State Bar Associations; State Bar of California. *PRACTICE AREAS:* Family Law; Commercial Litigation; Real Estate.

**RACHEL S. JACOBY,** born Suffern, New York, March 7, 1969; admitted to bar, 1993, New Jersey; 1995, New York; 1996, California. *Education:* Stern College for Women (B.S., magna cum laude, 1989); Benjamin N. Cardoza School of Law (J.D., 1993). Recipient, Carl C. Icahn Children's Rights Scholarship. Volunteer Attorney, Bet Tzedek Legal Services, 1994-1995. Law Clerk, Legal Aid Society, Juvenile Rights Division, 1992. Law Clerk, Ohel Family Services, 1991. *Member:* Los Angeles County, New York State and American Bar Associations; State Bar of California.

### OF COUNSEL

**CAROL PERRIN,** born New York, N.Y., March 14, 1952; admitted to bar, 1977, Florida; 1979, California. *Education:* State University of New York at Binghamton, (B.A., 1983); Western New England College School of Law (J.D., 1977); New York University (LL.M. Taxation, 19 78). Recipient, Moot Court Award. Chairperson, Examining Committee, California Board of Medical Assurance Acupuncture, 1982-1985. *Member:* Beverly Hills, Los Angeles County and American (Member, Taxation Section) Bar Associations; The State Bar of California; The Florida Bar (Member, Tax Section); California Women Lawyers; Los Angeles Women Lawyers. (Also practicing individually and Of Counsel, Tilles, Webb, Kulla & Grant, A Law Corporation). *PRACTICE AREAS:* Estate Planning; Tax Law; Probate; General Business; Real Estate Law.

### LEGAL SUPPORT PERSONNEL

**ROBERT C. MUDD,** born Laredo, Texas, August 19, 1963. *Education:* University of Houston (B.A., 1985); Pepperdine University (M.B.A., 1989); Thurgood Marshall School of Law (J.D., 1993). Phi Alpha Delta. Recipient, American Jurisprudence Award, Contract Law, 1992. (Law Clerk). *LANGUAGES:* Spanish. *PRACTICE AREAS:* Family Law.

---

## THE LAW OFFICES OF HELEN E. ZUKIN

11755 WILSHIRE BOULEVARD, SUITE 1400
LOS ANGELES, CALIFORNIA 90025-1520
Telephone: 310-477-5455
Facsimile: 310-477-8531

*Civil Litigation, specializing in Products Liability, Complex Personal Injury, Property Damage Litigation and Toxic Exposure Matters.*

**HELEN E. ZUKIN,** born January 7, 1958; admitted to bar, 1985, California. *Education:* University of California at Santa Cruz (B.A., 1980); Loyola Law School (J.D., 1984). Board of Governors, Consumer Attorneys Association of Los Angeles, 1995. Commissioner for the State Bar of California Commission on Judicial Nominees Evaluation. *Member:* State Bar of California; Consumer Attorneys of California; The Association of Trial Lawyers of America.

---

## GERMINO, RUNTE, AMARAL, JORDAN, CARPENTER & MacKAY

A PROFESSIONAL LAW CORPORATION
1120 WEST I STREET, SUITE B
P.O. BOX 591
LOS BANOS, CALIFORNIA 93635
Telephone: 209-826-5024
Fax: 209-826-3164

Palo Alto, California Office: 2500 El Camino Real, Suite 210. Telephone: 415-857-9211. Fax: 415-852-9256.

*General Civil and Trial Practice in State and Federal Courts. Personal Injury, Probate, Water Rights, Corporation, Taxation, Agricultural, Condemnation, Family and Corporate Law.*

**D. OLIVER GERMINO** (1903-1972).

**JOHN O. GERMINO,** born Los Banos, California, March 6, 1936; admitted to bar, 1962, California. *Education:* Stanford University (A.B., 1959; J.D., 1962). *PRACTICE AREAS:* Civil Litigation.

**DONALD O. GERMINO,** born Los Banos, California, October 1, 1939; admitted to bar, 1965, California. *Education:* University of Southern California (A.B., 1961); University of California at Berkeley (J.D., 1964). *PRACTICE AREAS:* Transactional; Civil Litigation; Estate Planning; Probate.

**JOHN A. RUNTE,** born Milwaukee, Wisconsin, May 18, 1938; admitted to bar, 1973, California. *Education:* Marquette University (B.S., 1961); University of Santa Clara (J.D., 1973). *PRACTICE AREAS:* Real Property; Trusts; Commercial Transactions; Taxation; Probate.

**EDWARD M. AMARAL,** born San Francisco, California, April 1, 1953; admitted to bar, 1980, California. *Education:* Modesto Junior College (A.S., 1973); California Polytechnic State University (B.S., 1976); Loyola University of Los Angeles (J.D., 1979). *PRACTICE AREAS:* Real Estate Law; Agricultural Law; Probate and Estate Planning; Elder Care Law; Business Law.

**J. SCOTT JORDAN,** born Tracy, California, May 14, 1954; admitted to bar, 1979, California. *Education:* University of Santa Clara (B.S., 1976; J.D., 1979). *PRACTICE AREAS:* Family Law; Bankruptcy; Transactional; Litigation.

**GLENN C. CARPENTER,** born Denver, Colorado, September 30, 1955; admitted to bar, 1981, California. *Education:* University of Colorado (B.A., with distinction, 1977); Stanford University (J.D., 1980). *PRACTICE AREAS:* Business Law; Real Property Law; Probate and Estate Planning; Trust Administration.

**NORMAN E. MACKAY,** born Oakland, California, October 31, 1943; admitted to bar, 1975, California and U.S. District Court, Northern District of California; 1977, U.S. District Court, Southern District of California. *Education:* Stanford University (B.A., 1965); University of Santa Clara (J.D., 1975). *PRACTICE AREAS:* Business Litigation; Real Estate Transactions; Toxic or Hazardous Materials Litigation.

**SUSAN R. F. SOLOMON,** born Philadelphia, Pennsylvania, October 29, 1947; admitted to bar, 1980, California. *Education:* University of Pennsylvania (B.A., 1968) Bryn Mawr College and University of Hawaii (M.S.W., 1975); University of Santa Clara (J.D., magna cum laude, 1980). *PRACTICE AREAS:* Real Property Law; Civil Litigation; Appellate Practice.

**PAUL J. MCDONALD,** born Milwaukee, Wisconsin, March 11, 1955; admitted to bar, 1989, California. *Education:* University of Wisconsin-Milwaukee (B.S., 1978); San Francisco Law School (J.D., 1989).

*(This Listing Continued)*

## LINNEMAN, BURGESS, TELLES, VAN ATTA & VIERRA

Established in 1932

654 K STREET
P.O. BOX 1364
**LOS BANOS, CALIFORNIA 93635**
Telephone: 209-826-4911
FAX: 209-826-4766
Email: 1btvv@aol.com

*Merced, California Office:* 312 West 19th Street, P.O. Box 2263. Telephone: 209-723-2137. Fax: 209-723-0899.

*Dos Palos, California Office:* 1820 Marguerite Street, P.O. Box 156. Telephone: 209-392-2141. Fax: 209-392-3964. E-Mail: drathmann@aol.com

*General Civil and Trial Practice. Water District and Rights Law. Real Property, Probate, Negligence, Products Liability, Agricultural Law and Personal Injury.*

### MEMBERS OF FIRM

**EUGENE J. VIERRA,** born Gustine, California, July 25, 1935; admitted to bar, 1996, California. *Education:* University of California at Davis (A.B., 1959); Troy State College; Hastings College of Law, University of California (LL.B., 1965). *Member:* Merced County Bar Association; State Bar of California. **LANGUAGES:** Portuguese. **PRACTICE AREAS:** Agricultural Law; Probate Law; Personal Injury Law.

**ALFRED L. WHITEHURST,** born Dos Palos, California, March 29, 1958; admitted to bar, 1984, California. *Education:* University of Puget Sound; University of Santa Clara (B.A., magna cum laude, 1979; J.D., 1983). *Member:* Merced County and American Bar Associations; State Bar of California. **PRACTICE AREAS:** Personal Injury; Product Liability; Criminal Law; Real Property.

---

## DAVID G. BICKNELL

15951 LOS GATOS BOULEVARD, SUITE 1A
P.O. BOX 536
**LOS GATOS, CALIFORNIA 95031-0536**
Telephone: 408-358-4900
Facsimile: 408-356-2638

*Real Estate and Construction Litigation.*

**DAVID G. BICKNELL,** born Reno, Nevada, May 6, 1951; admitted to bar, 1979, California and U.S. Court of Appeals, Ninth Circuit; 1980, U.S. District Court, Central, Eastern and Northern Districts of California; U.S. Court of Federal Claims. *Education:* California State University at San Jose (B.A., 1976); Santa Clara University (J.D., 1979). City Commissioner for San Jose, January-June, 1989. *Member:* Santa Clara County and American Bar Associations; State Bar of California; Santa Clara County Trial Lawyers Association. **PRACTICE AREAS:** Real Property; Construction Litigation.

---

## DEMPSTER, SELIGMANN & RAINERI

LA CAÑADA BUILDING
3 1/2 NORTH SANTA CRUZ AVENUE, SUITE A
**LOS GATOS, CALIFORNIA 95030**
Telephone: 408-399-7766
Fax: 408-399-7767
Email: Joe@Southbaylaw.com
URL: http://www.Southbaylaw.com

*Litigation, Personal Injury, Land Use, Construction Law, Real Estate, Business, Products Liability and Other Civil Matters.*

### MEMBERS OF FIRM

**J. ROBERT DEMPSTER** (Retired 1985).

**WILLIAM R. SELIGMANN,** born Davenport, Iowa, October 10, 1956; admitted to bar, 1983, California and U.S. District Court, Northern District of California. *Education:* University of California at Santa Barbara (B.A., 1979); University of Santa Clara (J.D., 1982). Author, "Blew v. Horner: The Case of the Phantom Employer," CAAA-MENTS, Vol. 10, p.14, Oct. 1987. Listed in Who's Who in American Law. City Attorney of Campbell 1985—. Pro Tem Judge, Municipal Court, 1990—. *Member:* Santa Clara County Bar Association; The Association of Trial Lawyers of America; National Institute of Municipal Law Officers.,. **PRACTICE AREAS:** Land Use; Public Entity Law; Personal Injury; Eminent Domain; Construction Law; Civil Litigation.

**JOSEPH RAINERI,** admitted to bar, 1988, California and U.S. District Court, Northern District of California. *Education:* Arizona State University (B.S., 1984); University of Santa Clara (J.D., 1987). *Member:* Santa Clara County (Member, Arbitration Panel) and American Bar Associations; The Association of Trial Lawyers of America. **PRACTICE AREAS:** Personal Injury; Products Liability; Construction Law; Business Litigation; Real Estate; Municipal Law; Civil Litigation.

### LEGAL SUPPORT PERSONNEL

**BRENDA L. BREON** (Paralegal).

**SHARON KAHLE** (Legal Assistant).

REPRESENTATIVE CLIENTS: City of Campbell; Photo Drive-Up, Inc.; Santa Clara Methodist Retirement Foundation; Assoc. of Bay Area Governments; Cushman Construction; Data Glass Co.; R.W. Construction; Orchids Enterprise, Inc.; Courtesy Limousine; Best Dry Wall.

---

## ROGER W. POYNER

16450 LOS GATOS BOULEVARD, SUITE 216
**LOS GATOS, CALIFORNIA 95032**
Telephone: 408-358-1900
FAX: 408-358-1225

*Monterey, California Office:* 232 Madison Street, The Panetta Building. Telephone: 408-649-3131. FAX: 408-649-1934.

*Trust Law, Estate Planning and Probate.*

**ROGER W. POYNER,** born 1935; admitted to bar, 1966, California. *Education:* University of California (A.B.); Lincoln College of Law (J.D.). County Supervisor, Monterey County Fourth District, 1973-1977. Counsel, Association of Monterey Bay Area Governments (AMBAG), 1978—. *Member:* Santa Clara County (Member, Executive Committee, Estate Planning, Trust and Probate Law Section, 1983—) and American (Member, Real Property, Probate and Trust Law, 1972—) Bar Associations; State Bar of California (Member, Estate Planning, Trust and Probate Law, 1974—). (Certified Specialist, Probate, Estate Planning and Trust Law, The State Bar of California Board of Legal Specialization). **PRACTICE AREAS:** Probate; Estate Planning Law; Trust Law.

---

## MASON J. SACKS, INC.

A PROFESSIONAL LAW CORPORATION

SUITE 101, 16615 LARK AVENUE
**LOS GATOS, CALIFORNIA 95030**
Telephone: 408-358-4400
Fax: 408-358-2487

*Trusts, Estate Planning, Estate and Trust Administration, Probate, and Disputed Inheritance Matters.*

**MASON J. SACKS,** born Johnstown, Pennsylvania, May 29, 1951; admitted to bar, 1974, California and U.S. District Court, Northern District of California; 1976, U.S. Tax Court; 1978, U.S. Court of Appeals, Ninth Circuit; 1979, U.S. Supreme Court. *Education:* Stanford University (A.B., with great distinction, 1971); Harvard Law School (J.D., cum laude, 1974). Author: Books: "Modern Tax Planning Checklists," Warren, Gorham & Lamont, Inc., 1977; "Doctor's and Dentist's Concise Guide to Tax and Estate Planning Opportunities," Prentice-Hall, Inc., 1979; "Federal Tax Deductions," Warren, Gorham & Lamont, Inc., 1983; *Articles:* "A Practitioner's Guide to Depreciation Under the ADR System," Income Tax Techniques, Matthew Bender & Co., Inc., 1977; "Professional Corporations: Protecting Corporate Status for Federal Income Tax Purposes," The Review of Taxation of Individuals, Vol. 2, No. 1, Winter 1978; "An Estate Planning Tool: Severance and Re-Creation of Joint Tenancies," The Practical Lawyer, Vol. 24, No. 5, July 1978; "Inter Vivos and Testamentary Trusts," Estate Planning for the General Practitioner, California Continuing Education of the Bar, 1979; "Who Can Be The Trustee?," In Brief, Vol. 20, No. 1, Spring 1983; "Some Recurring Questions Concerning The Use of Trusts," In Brief, Vol. 23, No. 2, Fall 1986; "Living Trust Holds Number of Real Advantages Over Will," The Business Journal, Vol. 5, No. 28, November 1987. *Member:* Santa Clara County (Chairman, Tax Law Section, 1979) and American (Member, Section on Real Property, Probate & Trust Law) Bar Associa-

*(This Listing Continued)*

MASON J. SACKS, INC. A PROFESSIONAL LAW CORPORATION, Los Gatos—Continued

tions; The State Bar of California (Member, Estate Planning, Trust and Probate Law Section). *PRACTICE AREAS:* Contested Trusts and Estates; Will Contests; Probate; Living Trust Law; Beneficiary Rights Disputes.

---

## SWEENEY, MASON & WILSON

A PROFESSIONAL LAW CORPORATION

Established in 1989

983 UNIVERSITY AVENUE, SUITE 104C

**LOS GATOS, CALIFORNIA 95030**

Telephone: 408-356-3000

Fax: 408-354-8839

*Business and Corporate Law and Litigation, Labor and Employment Law, Wage and Hour Law, Prevailing Wage Law, Construction, Insurance and Real Estate.*

**JOSEPH M. SWEENEY,** born Livermore, California, November 2, 1952; admitted to bar, 1977, California and U.S. District Court, Northern and Southern Districts of California. *Education:* University of Notre Dame, Indiana (B.B.A., 1974); University of San Francisco (J.D., magna cum laude, 1977). Member, McAuliffe Law Honor Society. Member: Associated General Contractors, Inc.; American Subcontractors Association; Construction Financial Managers Association. *Member:* Santa Clara County Bar Association; The State Bar of California (Member, Section on Real Property, Construction subsection). *LANGUAGES:* Spanish. *PRACTICE AREAS:* Construction Law; Real Estate Law; Business Litigation.

**ROGER M. MASON,** born Buffalo, New York, January 10, 1956; admitted to bar, 1983, California, U.S. District Court, Northern, Eastern, Southern and Central Districts of California and U.S. Court of Appeals, Ninth Circuit. *Education:* State University of New York at Fredonia (B.A., magna cum laude, 1978); University of San Francisco (J.D., 1982). Author: "Drug Testing in the Workplace, Can an Employer Afford Not To?" In Brief, Volume 24, No. 1. Co-Author: "Lowest Responsible Bidder," Executive Enterprises Publications Co. Inc., 1985. Member, City of San Jose Advisory Committee on Prevailing Wages, 1988. *Member:* Santa Clara County and American Bar Associations; State Bar of California. *PRACTICE AREAS:* Labor and Employment Law; Wage and Hour Law; Prevailing Wage Litigation.

**KURT E. WILSON,** born San Francisco, California, September 10, 1959; admitted to bar, 1985, California and U.S. District Court, Northern, Southern and Central Districts of California; U.S. Court of Appeals, Sixth Circuit. *Education:* University of California at Berkeley (B.A., 1981); Hastings College of the Law, University of California (J.D., magna cum laude, 1985). Author: "Raising and Lowering the Stakes in Contract Litigation: The Tort of Bad Faith Denial of Contract," Bad Faith Law Reporter, April 1991. Instructor, Trial Advocacy, Santa Clara School of Law, 1990-1992. *Member:* Santa Clara County and American Bar Associations; State Bar of California; American Electronics Association; International Trade Counsel, Santa Clara Chapter. *PRACTICE AREAS:* Business Litigation.

**BRADLEY D. BOSOMWORTH,** born Toronto Ontario, Canada, October 1, 1962; admitted to bar, 1988, California. *Education:* University of Oregon (B.S., 1984); University of Santa Clara (J.D., magna cum laude, 1987). Recipient, American Jurisprudence Award for Evidence. Member, Construction Financial Managers Association. President, Shasta/Hanchett Park Neighborhood Association, 1991. Member: City of San Jose Guadalupe Gardens Advisory Committee, 1991-1993; City of San Jose Midtown Specific Plan Task Force, 1991. Director, Los Gatos Chamber of Commerce, 1994-1995. *Member:* Santa Clara County Bar Association (Member, Business Section); State Bar of California. *PRACTICE AREAS:* Business Law; Corporate Law; Real Estate Law.

**ALLAN JAMES MANZAGOL,** born Palo Alto, California, April 22, 1967; admitted to bar, 1993, California and U.S. District Court, Northern, Southern and Central Districts of California. *Education:* University of California at Santa Barbara (B.A., cum laude, 1989); Santa Clara University (J.D., 1993). Golden Key Honor Society. Business Editor, Santa Clara Law Review, 1992-1993. Vice President, Criminal Law Society, 1991-1992. Member, Construction Industry Forum, 1992-1993 and Litigation Section, 1991-1992, American Bar Association. Member, Santa Clara County Advisory Commission on Consumer Affairs. *Member:* Santa Clara County Bar

*(This Listing Continued)*

Association; American Subcontractors Association. *PRACTICE AREAS:* Business Litigation; Construction Law; Landlord-Tenant Law.

REPRESENTATIVE CLIENTS: ABM Industries; Alameda and Contra Costa Counties Chapter, PHCC; Ampco Parking Services, Inc.; Associated Builders & Contractors, Inc.; CDK Contracting, Inc.; Contra Costa Chapter, NECA; County of Santa Clara; Dan Caputo Co.; Fujitsu America, Inc.; Fujitsu Network Transmission Systems, Inc.; Fujitsu Computer Products of America; Galletti & Sons, Inc.; Gilroy Unified School District; Green Valley Disposal Co., Inc.; Guadalupe Rubbish Disposal Co., Inc.; Houston Wire & Cable Co.; Hyundai Electronics America; Jack and Cohen Builders, Inc.; J.T. Thorpe and Son, Inc.; McCandless Construction Corp.; Oki Semiconductor, Inc.; DeSilva Gates; Pacific States Industries, Inc.; Maxim Company, Inc.; Santa Clara District; Scientific Custom Metal Products International; SMACNA; Sierra Lumber Co.; Sobrato Development Cos.; South Bay Construction and Development Co.; Stallion Technologies, Inc.; Toda Construction of California, Inc.

---

## MICHAEL COLLINS

**LOS OSOS, CALIFORNIA**

(See San Luis Obispo)

*Real Estate and Business Law, Probate, Guardianship, Conservatorship, Estate Planning and Elder Law.*

---

## GEORGE, GALLO & SULLIVAN

A LAW CORPORATION

Established in 1976

2238 BAYVIEW HEIGHTS DRIVE

P.O. BOX 6129

**LOS OSOS, CALIFORNIA 93402**

Telephone: 805-528-3351

Telecopier: 805-528-5598

Email: jgeorgeggs@aol.com

San Luis Obispo, California Office: 694 Santa Rosa, P.O. Box 12710. Telephone: 805-544-3351. Facsimile: 805-528-5598.

*Probate, Estate Planning and Trust Administration, Business and Corporate Transactions, Taxation, Real Property and Construction, Civil Litigation.*

(For Personnel and Biographical Data, see Professional Biographies, San Luis Obispo, California)

---

## DOWLING, AARON & KEELER

INCORPORATED

**MADERA, CALIFORNIA**

(See Fresno)

*Civil Trial and Appellate Practice, State and Federal Courts. Corporation, Banking, Creditor' Rights, Bankruptcy, Securities, Real Estate, Estate Planning, Probate, Taxation, Pension, Agricultural, Administrative, Government, Health Care, Insurance, Labor and Employment, Family Law and Sports Law.*

---

## KIMBLE, MacMICHAEL & UPTON

A PROFESSIONAL CORPORATION

**MADERA, CALIFORNIA**

(See Fresno)

*Civil, Trial and Appellate Practice in all Courts with Emphasis in Business, Construction and Environmental Litigation, Real Estate, Bank Securities, Lender and Creditors Rights, Bankruptcy, Secured Lending, Banking, Federal and State Income, Gift and Estate Tax, Securities, Antitrust, Corporation and Probate and Estate Planning, Patent, Trademark and Copyright, Water Rights, Environmental Law, Employee Benefits Law, Products Liability Defense, ERISA Litigation, Employment Defense, Administrative and Health Care Law.*

## LANG, RICHERT & PATCH

A PROFESSIONAL CORPORATION

### MADERA, CALIFORNIA

(See Fresno)

*General Civil and Trial Practice in all Courts. Appeals. Business, Community Property, Corporation, Bankruptcy, Insolvency, Construction, Real Property, Probate and Estate Planning, Trusts, Personal Injury and Insurance Law.*

---

## LINN, LINDLEY & BLATE

A PROFESSIONAL ASSOCIATION

### MADERA, CALIFORNIA

(See Oakhurst)

*General Civil and Trial Practice including Personal Injury, Probate and Estate Planning, Corporate, Business, Taxation, Natural Resources Law, Banking Litigation, Criminal Law and Family Law.*

---

## MORTIMER AND OAKLEY

110 NORTH D STREET
### MADERA, CALIFORNIA 93638
Telephone: 209-674-8712
Fax: 209-674-4160

*General Practice.*

**STEVEN R. MORTIMER,** born Berkeley, California, January 3, 1946; admitted to bar, 1972, California. *Education:* University of California at Berkeley (B.A., 1967); California School of Law, University of Davis (J.D., 1972). **PRACTICE AREAS:** Domestic Relations; Collections; Landlord Tenant; Probate and Estate Planning; Real Property; Guardianship and Conservatorship.

**JAMES E. OAKLEY,** born Long Beach, California, February 11, 1953; admitted to bar, 1977, California and U.S. District Court, Central and Eastern Districts of California. *Education:* University of California, at Los Angeles (B.A., 1974); Pepperdine University (J.D., 1976). Member, Law Review, Pepperdine University. City Council Member, City of Madera, 1984-1986. Mayor, City of Madera, 1985-1986. Justice Court Judge, Madera County, 1986-1988. **PRACTICE AREAS:** Family Law; General Litigation; Estate Planning/Probate; Real Property Law; Probate.

**ERIC WYATT,** born Visalia, California, June 28, 1966; admitted to bar, 1992, California. *Education:* University of California, at Davis (B.A., 1988); University of Santa Clara (J.D., 1992). **PRACTICE AREAS:** Criminal Defense; Civil Litigation; Family Law.

---

## STAMMER, McKNIGHT, BARNUM & BAILEY

### MADERA, CALIFORNIA

(See Fresno)

*General Civil and Trial Practice. Insurance, Water Rights Law.*

---

## WILD, CARTER & TIPTON

A PROFESSIONAL CORPORATION

### MADERA, CALIFORNIA

(See Fresno)

*General Civil, Trial and Appellate Practice, Business, Real Estate, Corporation, Construction, Banking, Environmental, Agriculture, Insurance, Trademark, Probate and Estate Planning, Oil and Gas, Taxation, Bankruptcy and Employment Law.*

---

## JAMES E. BIAVA

Established in 1970

22526 PACIFIC COAST HIGHWAY
### MALIBU, CALIFORNIA 90265
Telephone: 310-456-3330

*General Civil Practice. Trust, Probate, Real Estate, Corporation and Business Law.*

**JAMES E. BIAVA,** born Trinidad, Colorado, November 26, 1931; admitted to bar, 1960, California and District of Columbia. *Education:* Wharton School, University of Pennsylvania (B.S., 1954); Harvard University (LL.B., 1959). Beta Alpha Psi; Beta Gamma Sigma. Assistant U.S. Attorney, 1960-1964. *Member:* The State Bar of California (Member, Sub Committee to Propose Legislation, 1978-1981; President, Los Angeles Estate Planning Council, 1982). [Lt. Col., USAFR, 1954-1956]

REFERENCE: Bank of America National Trust & Savings Assn., Malibu, California.

---

## CHALEFF & ENGLISH

### MALIBU, CALIFORNIA

(See Santa Monica)

*Criminal and Juvenile Law Practice.*

---

## FRYE & HSIEH LLP

A Partnership including A Professional Corporation

23955 PACIFIC COAST HIGHWAY
SUITE A201
### MALIBU, CALIFORNIA 90265
Telephone: 310-456-0800
Fax: 310-456-0808

Los Angeles, California Office: 626 Wilshire Boulevard, Suite 800. Telephone: 310-820-5545.

*General Civil and Trial Practice in all Courts. Corporation, Business, State, Federal and International Taxation, Estate Planning, Real Estate, Securities, Administrative, Professional Liability, Negligence Law and Government Finance.*

**DOUGLAS J. FRYE, (PROFESSIONAL CORPORATION),** born Rochester, New York, August 13, 1948; admitted to bar, 1975, New Jersey and U.S. District Court, District of New Jersey; 1976, Pennsylvania; 1977, U.S. Tax Court; 1978, California; 1980, New York. *Education:* Ithaca College (B.S., 1970); Syracuse University (J.D., 1974); New York University (LL.M., in Taxation, 1977). Author: "How to Handle the Split-up of A Professional Corporation," Prentice-Hall Professional Corporation Guide, 1976; "The Tax Benefit Role: Revisited," Los Angeles Lawyer Magazine, February, 1984. Contributor, Annual Report on Recent Developments, State Bar Tax Section, 1980. Speaker and Contributor, Employee Benefits and Executive Compensation Conference, Beverly Hills Bar Association, 1983. *Member:* Los Angeles County (Member, Subcommittee on Corporate and Executive Tax, Tax Section, 1979-1980) and American (Member, Tax Section, Committee on Closely Held Corporations, Corporate Tax Subcommittee, 1979-1981) Bar Associations; State Bar of California (Member, Subcommittee on Corporation Taxation, 1980-1981; Project Editor, California Taxation Annual Report on Recent Developments, 1980, Taxation Section). **PRACTICE AREAS:** Corporations; Business; Taxation; Estate Planning; Health Care.

**STEWART HSIEH,** born Los Angeles, California, April 5, 1953; admitted to bar, 1988, California; 1991, U.S. District Court, Central District of California. *Education:* California State University (B.S., 1975); Southwestern University School of Law (J.D., 1978). Phi Delta Phi. Member, Medical Board of California, Division of Allied Health Professions, 1992-1994; Division of Licensing, 1994—; Board Secretary; California State Treasurer's Housing Finance Advisory Committee, 1995—. *Member:* Los Angeles County Bar Association (Co-Chair, Senior Outreach Committee, 1990-1993); State Bar of California; National Association of Bond Lawyers. **PRACTICE AREAS:** Business Transactions; Estate Planning; Probate; Corporations.

## LAW OFFICES OF
## TODD M. SLOAN

**22601 PACIFIC COAST HIGHWAY, SUITE 240**
**MALIBU, CALIFORNIA 90265**
Telephone: 310-456-7900
Facsimile: 310-317-6266

*General Litigation, Unfair Competition Law, Banking Litigation.*

**TODD M. SLOAN,** born Pennsylvania, 1939; admitted to bar, 1972, California. *Education:* University of Pennsylvania (B.A., cum laude, 1961); University of Virginia (J.D., 1972). Instructor, Conflicts of Law, Western State University College of Law, 1974-1975. Adjunct Professor, Trial Practice and Conflict of Laws, Pepperdine University College of Law, 1989—. Author: "Trade Secrets: Real Toads in a Conceptual Garden," 1 Western State University Law Review 133, 1973; "Trade Secrets: 1973; Was it a Very Good Year?" 2 Western State University Law Review 1, 1974; "Millions for Defense and Not One Cent for Tribute-Defending Trade Secret Litigation," Monograph of Papers on Intellectual Property, Section of Patent, Trademark and Copyright Law, American Bar Association. *Member:* Los Angeles County and American Bar Associations; State Bar of California. **LANGUAGES:** Spanish. **PRACTICE AREAS:** General Litigation; Unfair Competition Law; Banking Regulatory Litigation.

### ASSOCIATE

**JULIA L. BIRKEL,** born Palo Alto, California, October 11, 1957; admitted to bar, 1984, California; 1985, U.S. District Court, Southern, Northern, Eastern and Central Districts of California. *Education:* Stanford University (A.B., 1979); University of California at Los Angeles (J.D., 1984). Mass Media Institute, Stanford University, 1990. *Member:* American Bar Association; State Bar of California. **PRACTICE AREAS:** Civil Litigation.

## LAW OFFICES OF DAVID S. BAUMWOHL

*A PROFESSIONAL CORPORATION*
*Established in 1980*
**THE MAMMOTH MALL, SUITE 220**
**P.O. BOX 1188**
**MAMMOTH LAKES, CALIFORNIA 93546**
Telephone: 619-934-2000
Fax: 619-934-2600
Email: MAMMOTHLAW@QNET.COM

*General Business, Real Estate and Litigation.*

**DAVID S. BAUMWOHL,** born Los Angeles, California, June 5, 1955; admitted to bar, 1980, California. *Education:* California State University-Northridge (B.S., 1977); McGeorge School of Law, University of the Pacific (J.D., 1980). Real Estate Broker, California, 1985. *Member:* State Bar of California (Member: Real Property Section, 1980; Employment/Labor Section, 1993). **PRACTICE AREAS:** Real Property (Transaction and Litigation); Business (Transaction and Litigation); General Litigation.

REPRESENTATIVE CLIENTS: Mammoth Mountain Ski Area; Dempsey Construction Corp.; Southern Mono Hospital District; Minaret Sports; George Mee Memorial Hospital; Southern Inyo County Local Hospital District; Intrawest Corp.

## LAW OFFICES OF MICHAEL BERGER

**4 OAK TREE PLACE**
**P.O. BOX 1768**
**MAMMOTH LAKES, CALIFORNIA 93546**
Telephone: 619-934-6215
Fax: 619-934-4063

*Criminal and Civil Litigation.*

**MICHAEL BERGER,** born Santa Barbara, California, March 3, 1948; admitted to bar, 1973, California. *Education:* University of California at Santa Barbara (B.A., Political Science, with highest honors, 1970); University of California at Davis (J.D., 1973). Member, Board of Trustees, Mammoth Unified School District, 1988-1992. Listed in Marquis Who's Who in American Law (9th Edition). *Member:* Mono County (Chairman, Local Rules Committee, 1989; President, 1994—) and American (Member, Litigation Division) Bar Associations; State Bar of California; Association of Trial Lawyers of America; National Association of Criminal Defense Lawyers; California Public Defenders Association (Penal Code Section 1524

*(This Listing Continued)*

Special Master, 1989—). (Certified by the National Board of Trial Advocacy in Civil Litigation). **LANGUAGES:** Spanish. **PRACTICE AREAS:** Civil Litigation; Criminal Law.

### ASSOCIATE

**ROBERT S. HANNA,** born Orange, New Jersey, September 1, 1964; admitted to bar, 1992, California; 1994, U.S. District Court, Eastern District of California. *Education:* Texas Christian University (B.S., summa cum laude, 1986); University of California at Berkeley (M.S., 1988); Hastings College of the Law, University of California (J.D., 1992). *Member:* Mono County Bar Association. **PRACTICE AREAS:** Civil Litigation; Criminal Law.

REPRESENTATIVE CLIENTS: Century Motors; Chalfont Press; Inyo County Counsel; Taff Electric; William C. Taylor Company; Graphic Conclusions; Montgomery Securities.
REFERENCES: Bank of America; Mammoth Unified School District; Parks, Palmer, Turner & Yemenidjian.

## LIEBERSBACH, MOHUN, CARNEY & REED

**SHERWIN PROFESSIONAL PLAZA, 2ND FLOOR**
**OLD MAMMOTH ROAD**
**P.O. BOX 3337**
**MAMMOTH LAKES, CALIFORNIA 93546**
Telephone: 619-934-4558
Facsimile: 619-934-2530

*General Civil Practice in State Courts, Trials and Appeals, Real Estate, Condominium/Homeowners' Association, Criminal Defense, Negligence, Commercial and Business Law, Land Use Development Law, Environmental Law, Public and Administrative Law.*

**RICHARD W. LIEBERSBACH,** born Glendale, California, October 22, 1952; admitted to bar, 1977, California; 1983, U.S. District Court, Central District of California; 1987, U.S. District Court, Eastern District of California. *Education:* University of Southern California (B.A., 1974); Loyola University of Los Angeles (J.D., 1977). Phi Beta Kappa. Recipient: American Jurisprudence Award in Partnerships/Agency and in Criminal Law. *Member:* Loyola Law Review; St. Thomas Moore Law Society. Judge Pro Tem, Mono County Justice Court, 1987—. Patent Board Member and Chairman, Southern Mono Hospital District, 1988-1995. Board Member, Paramedics' Joint Power Association, 1988-1995. Member, Airport Advisory Commission, 1991—. *Member:* Mono County Bar; American Bar Association; Blackstonian. **PRACTICE AREAS:** Real Estate Litigation; Land Use Development Law; Condominium and Homeowners Association; Business Law; Corporate Law.

**GERALD FITZGIBBON MOHUN, JR.,** born San Francisco, California, April 14, 1956; admitted to bar, 1983, California and U.S. District Court, Northern District of California; 1987, U.S. District Court, Eastern District of California; 1993, Nevada. *Education:* University of California at Santa Barbara (B.A., 1979); Hastings College of the Law, University of California (J.D., 1983). Contributor: CEB Action Guide, "Laying a Foundation to Introduce Evidence." Town of Mammoth Lakes Park and Recreation Commission (Commissioner, 1989—; Chairman, 1990-1992). Judge Pro Tem, Mono County Justice Court, 1990—. Member, Board of Directors, Mammoth Lakes Chamber of Commerce, 1992-1993. *Member:* Mono County and American (Member, Litigation Section) Bar Associations. **PRACTICE AREAS:** Civil Litigation; Criminal Law; Tort and Insurance Law.

**R. MARK CARNEY,** born Chicago, Illinois, April 16, 1958; admitted to bar, 1985, California; 1986, U.S. District Court, Central District of California. *Education:* University of Notre Dame (B.A., 1980; J.D., 1984). Associate Editor, Notre Dame Law Review; Volume 59, Issues 1 and 5. President, Mono County Bar Association, 1996. Co-Founder and Chairman, Legal Advice and Referral Clinic, 1990-1995. Member, General Plan Advisory Committee, Town of Mammoth Lakes. **LANGUAGES:** Spanish. **PRACTICE AREAS:** Commercial and Real Estate Litigation and Transactions; Land Use Development Law; Education Law.

**JAMES S. REED,** born Ely, Nevada, January 23, 1938; admitted to bar, 1966, California; U.S. District Court, Eastern District of California; U.S. Court of Appeals, Ninth Circuit. *Education:* San Diego State University (B.A., 1961); Hastings College of Law, University of California (J.D., 1966). Order of the Coif; Thurston Society; Law Journal. *Member,* Moot Court Board. Recipient, American Jurisprudence Award in Constitutional Law. Chief Counsel, Assembly Judiciary Committee, California Legislature (1967-1971). General Practice, Sacramento, (1971-1985). Executive Direc-

*(This Listing Continued)*

tor, Governors Commission on Retail Credit Installment Rates (1982). Executive Director, Consumer Federation of California. Instructor, Environmental Law, University of California at Davis, Department of Environmental Sciences, 1974-1979. Professor of Constitutional Law, Lincoln Law School, Sacramento, California, 1977-1985. County Counsel, County of Mono 1985-1996. Member: Governing Board, Tahoe Regional Planning Agency (1981-1989); Senate Select Committee on Consumer Credit; Senate Select Committee on No-Fault Automobile Insurance; Assembly Select Committee on CEQA; State Bar Committee on Administration of Justice; State Bar Committee on the Environment. Author: "The Legal Profession on Trial: Group Legal services" 2 Loyola (LA) Rev. 12 (1969); "Legislating For The Consumer: An Insider's View of the Consumer Legal Remedies Act" 2 Pac. L.J. 1 (1971). *Member:* Mono County Bar Association. *PRACTICE AREAS:* Public Land Law (10%); Environmental Law (20%); Public Law (60%).

REPRESENTATIVE CLIENTS: Anheuser-Busch, Inc.; Chicago Title Co.; Inyo-Mono Title Co.; Lodestar Development Co.; Mammoth Unified School District; The Town of Mammoth Lakes; 1849 Condominiums Owners' Association; Red's Meadow Resort and Pack Station; Mountainback Condominium Owners' Association; Triad Engineering; Mammoth Times; Bank of America; Convict Lake Resort, Inc; Running Springs Bottling, Inc.; Mammoth Equestrian Center; Esis Insurance Services Co.; Mammoth Towing; Wave Rave Snowboard Shop.

## ANDERSEN, KELEHER & SPATA
*1332 PARK VIEW AVENUE, SUITE 102*
*MANHATTAN BEACH, CALIFORNIA 90266*
*Telephone: 310-546-6662*
*Fax: 310-546-5707*

*General Civil Litigation and Trial Practice, Eminent Domain, Inverse Condemnation, Land Use, Zoning, Environmental and Mobile Home Park Law, Real Property Litigation, General Liability and Insurance Law.*

### MEMBERS OF FIRM

**G. STEVEN ANDERSEN,** born Inglewood, California, August 3, 1942; admitted to bar, 1982, California. *Education:* University of California at Los Angeles (A.B., 1964); Loyola University (M.Ed., 1974); Loyola Law School (J.D., 1982). Mayor, City of Hawthorne, 1983; 1991-1993. Member, Hawthorne City Council, 1983—. Member, Hawthorne Redevelopment Agency, 1983—. *Member:* Los Angeles County Bar Association (Member, The Condemnation and Land Valuation Committee, 1988—); State Bar of California (Member: Real Property Section; Condemnation Subcommittee).

**JAMES F. KELEHER,** born Chicago, Illinois, June 30, 1950; admitted to bar, 1982, California. *Education:* Northern Illinois University (B.S., 1972); Loyola Law School (J.D., 1982). Service and Industry Member, Western Mobilehome Association, 1991—. *Member:* State Bar of California (Member, Litigation Section, 1983—). *REPORTED CASES:* Tenants Association of Park Santa Anita vs. Beverly Southers, et al. (1990) 222 CA 3d 1293, 272 CR 361.

**MICHAEL C. SPATA,** born New York, N.Y., October 11, 1951; admitted to bar, 1977, California; 1988, Wisconsin. *Education:* University of Maryland (B.A., 1973); Western State University (J.D., 1976); University of San Diego (LL.M., 1990). Instructor, University of California at San Diego Extension, Development Law & Procedures, 1983-1991. Assistant Professor, Western State University, Real Property, Contracts, Environmental Law, 1982-1987. Author: "Conducting Discovery in Land Use, CEQA, Inverse Condemnation and Eminent Domain Litigation," 5 Cal. Environmental Law Rptr. 159 (1993); "A Practical Approach to the Deductibility of a Charitable Contribution for a Qualified Conservation Easement," 22 Real Estate Law Journal 132 (1993); "Redevelopment Law and Its Relationship to Environmental, Land Use, Eminent Domain and Inverse Condemnation Law," 5 Cal. Environmental Law Rptr. 194 (1992). *Member:* San Diego County (Chairman, Eminent Domain Section, 1985) and American (Member, Sections on: Natural Resources, Urban, State and Local Government) Bar Associations; State Bar of California (Member: Real Property Section; Condemnation Subcommittee).

**DENNIS NEIL JONES,** born Portland, Oregon, May 12, 1954; admitted to bar, 1984, California and Nevada; U.S. Court of Appeals, Ninth Circuit; U.S. District Court, Central District of California and U.S. District Court, District of Nevada. *Education:* University of Southern California (B.A., cum laude, 1976; Certificate in Judicial Administration, 1978; M.P.A., summa cum laude, 1979); University of San Diego (J.D., 1983). Co-Author: "Multiple Punitive Damage Awards for a Single Course of Wrongful Conduct: The Need for a National Policy to Protect Due Process," 43 Alabama L. Rev. 1, 1991. Author: "The Independent Medical

*(This Listing Continued)*

Exam: A Lawyer's Perspective," Medical Legal Reporter, Vol. 3, No. 3., March, 1989; "Sewing Up the 'Deep-Pocket' Proposition 51 Offers Hope," Insurance Journal, March 17, 1986. *Member:* State Bar of California; State Bar of Nevada. *REPORTED CASES:* Valentino v. Elliott SAV-ON-GAS, Inc., (1988) 201 Cal. App. 3d 692; People ex rel Goramendi v. American Autoplan, Inc., (1993) 20 Cal. App. 4th 710; Adler v. Western Home Insurance Co., 878 F.Supp. 1329 (C.D. Cal. 1995).

### OF COUNSEL

**ROBERT C. LITTLEJOHN,** born Los Angeles, California, April 26, 1949; admitted to bar, 1978, California. *Education:* University of California at Los Angeles (B.A., 1971); Southwestern University (J.D., 1977). *Member:* Los Angeles County and American Bar Associations; State Bar of California.

REPRESENTATIVE CLIENTS: Calprop Corporation; City of Palmdale (Special Counsel); American States Insurance Co.; Insurance Company of North America.

## CHRISTOPHER D. CARICO
*1141 HIGHLAND AVENUE, SUITE 201*
*MANHATTAN BEACH, CALIFORNIA 90266*
*Telephone: 310-545-8199*
*Fax: 310-546-8540*

*Estate Planning, Trust, Probate and Elder Law.*

*FIRM PROFILE: The Law Office of Christopher D. Carico serves the South Bay with a full range of estate planning and administration services, including preparation of Trusts, Wills and Powers of Attorney, funding of Trusts, representation of Trustees and Executors, post-death Trust and Probate Administration, Trust and Probate Litigation and preparation of estate and gift tax returns. The firm also counsels older individuals and their families with respect to the preservation of resources in the event of long-term illness or incapacity.*

**CHRISTOPHER D. CARICO,** born El Centro, California, January 10, 1961; admitted to bar, 1988, California; 1993, U.S. District Court, Central District of California. *Education:* University of California at Berkeley; Occidental College (A.B., 1983); Loyola Law School (J.D., cum laude, 1987). *Member:* State Bar of California (Member, Estate Planning, Trust and Probate Law Section); South Bay Bar Association. (Certified Specialist, Estate Planning, Trust and Probate Law, The State Bar of California Board of Legal Specialization). *PRACTICE AREAS:* Estate Planning; Trusts and Estates; Probate; Elder Law.

## LAW OFFICES OF
## DANIEL V. DuROSS
*Established in 1941*
*1001 SIXTH STREET*
*SUITE 150*
*MANHATTAN BEACH, CALIFORNIA 90266-6750*
*Telephone: 310-374-3336*
*Fax: 310-318-3832*
*Email: DeweyDur@aol.com*

*Probate and Estate Planning.*

**DANIEL V. DUROSS,** born Los Angeles, California, February 20, 1947; admitted to bar, 1976, California; 1985, U.S. District Court, Central District of California. *Education:* Loyola University (B.A., 1969); Southwestern (J.D., 1974). *Member:* Los Angeles County Bar; South Bay Bar; State Bar of California; Irish-American Bar Association. *PRACTICE AREAS:* Wills and Trusts; Probate; Estate Planning; Elder Law.

### ASSOCIATE

**KAYSIE A. FITZPATRICK,** born Dallas, Texas, May 9, 1967; admitted to bar, 1993, California. *Education:* University of California at Berkeley (B.A., 1989); McGeorge School of Law (J.D., 1993). *Member:* South Bay Bar Association; State Bar of California. *PRACTICE AREAS:* Estate Planning; Probate; Elder Law.

## LAW OFFICE OF
## IRA M. FIERBERG
1334 PARK VIEW AVENUE, SUITE 100
**MANHATTAN BEACH, CALIFORNIA 90266**
Telephone: 310-546-8181
Fax: 310-546-8180
Email: tiburon27@aol.com

*Personal Injury, including Vehicular, Slip and Fall, Major Bodily Injury, Dog Bites, Wrongful Death. General Civil Litigation in all State and Federal Courts, Trial, Business Litigation, Sports Law, Motor Racing Sports Representation and Motor Racing Consulting.*

**IRA M. FIERBERG,** born Los Angeles, California, April 3, 1962; admitted to bar, 1989, California. *Education:* University of California at Los Angeles (B.A., 1984); Loyola Law School (J.D., 1988). Phi Alpha Delta. Member: Ward & Jampol, 1989-1991; Mannis, Barbakow & Lerner, 1991-1993. *Member:* Beverly Hills, Los Angeles County and American Bar Associations; State Bar of California.

## KENNETH L. HARVEY
818 MANHATTAN BEACH BOULEVARD
**MANHATTAN BEACH, CALIFORNIA 90266**
Telephone: 310-545-6445; 376-1857
FAX: 310-376-9008
Email: kharvey333@aol.com

*General Civil Trial. Family and Real Estate Law.*

**KENNETH L. HARVEY,** born Martinez, California, December 17, 1947; admitted to bar, 1973, California. *Education:* University of California at Davis (B.S., 1970); University of Santa Clara (J.D., 1973). Phi Alpha Delta. *Member:* South Bay and Los Angeles County Bar Associations; State Bar of California.

## REBACK, HULBERT, McANDREWS & KJAR, LLP
1230 ROSECRANS AVENUE
SUITE 450
**MANHATTAN BEACH, CALIFORNIA 90266**
Telephone: 310-297-9900
Facsimile: 310-297-9800

*Civil Litigation Defense, Insurance Defense, Professional Liability, Personal Injury, Product Liability, Business Litigation, Real Estate, Commercial Litigation, Risk Management, Loss Prevention, Mediation, Legal and Medical Malpractice.*

**ROBERT C. REBACK,** born Los Angeles, California, September 17, 1943; admitted to bar, 1973, California. *Education:* University of California, Los Angeles (B.S., 1965); University of California School of Law, Los Angeles (J.D., 1971). Adjunct Professor of Law, University of West Los Angeles, 1975-1981. Author and Lecturer: *"Calculation, Proof and Disproof of Damages in Personal Injury Cases,"* California Continuing Education of the Bar, 1988; *"The Practical Effects of Proposition 51,"* California Continuing Education of the Bar, 1989; *"Closing Argument Presented by Master Trial Lawyers,"* American Board of Trial Advocates Annual Convention, 1994. Invited Lecturer: Annual California State Judges' Annual College, 1994. Lecturer: University of Southern California School of Medicine, 1988—. Settlement Officer, Los Angeles County, Superior Court, 1988—. *Member:* Los Angeles County and American Bar Associations; State Bar of California; Association of Southern California Defense Counsel.

**GREGORY M. HULBERT,** born Los Angeles, California, February 11, 1957; admitted to bar, 1983, California. *Education:* California State University, Northridge (B.A., cum laude, 1980); Loyola Law School; Loyola Marymount University, Los Angeles (J.D., 1983). Author: "Name of the Game," Verdict Magazine, Spring 1993. Court Appointed: Arbitrator, 1992—; Settlement Officer, 1990—, Los Angeles County Superior Court. Member, Ethics Committee Bayshores Medical Group, 1996—. *Member:* State Bar of California; American Bar Association; Association of Southern California Defense Counsel (Chairman, Amicus Committee, 1995); American Board of Trial Advocates.

**THOMAS F. McANDREWS,** born New York, N.Y., March 19, 1954; admitted to bar, 1985, California. *Education:* University of Santa Clara

*(This Listing Continued)*

CAA1316B

---

(B.S., 1976); Loyola Law School; Loyola Marymount University, Los Angeles (J.D., 1984). Invited Lecturer: Real Estate Sales, The Prudential/Jon Douglas Co. Court Appointed: Arbitrator, 1993—; Settlement Officer, 1993—, Los Angeles County Superior Court. *Member:* Los Angeles County and American Bar Associations; State Bar of California; Association of Southern California Defense Counsel.

**JAMES J. KJAR,** born Los Angeles, California, March 15, 1955; admitted to bar, 1980, California. *Education:* University of Southern California (B.S., 1977); Loyola Law School, Loyola Marymount University (J.D., 1980). Author and Presenter: *"Cross-Examination of a Medical Expert at Trial,"* Los Angeles Trial Lawyers Association (LATLA) Annual Symposium, October 1989; *"Common Mistakes of Plaintiff Personal Injury Lawyers at Trial,"* California Trial Lawyers Association Annual Symposium, September 1990; *"Mock Trial of a Personal Injury Case,"* LATLA Annual Symposium, September 1991; *"Cross-examination of Plaintiff's Economist Expert at Trial,"* LATLA Annual Symposium, September 1992; *"Medical Malpractice Litigation: The Defense Perspective,"* California Trial Lawyers Annual Convention, 1994; *"Courtroom Conduct: Tactics, Ethics, Contempt, and Common Sense,"* California Continuing Education of the Bar, June 1994; *"Techniques in Taking the Deposition of a Plaintiff,"* Los Angeles Trial Lawyers Association, March 1995. Co-Author: *"Selection & Presentation of Expert Witnesses at Trial,"* James Publishing, in press, 1996; *"Current Issues in HMO Litigation,"* July 1996. Co-Editor, California Law Digest, Best's Directory of Recommended Insurance Attorneys, A.M. Best Company, Inc., 1992. Lecturer: University of Southern California School of Medicine, 1988—; Loma Linda University School of Medicine, 1988; University of California at Los Angeles School of Dentistry, 1992. Settlement Officer, 1988—; Arbitrator, 1994—, Los Angeles County Superior Court. Guest Speaker: Annual Convention of International College of Surgeons, October, 1993; Los Angeles Trial Lawyers MCLE Credit Seminar, January 1994. Lecturer: *Persuasive Presentation of Damages* presented at Los Angeles Trial Lawyers Association Annual Damages Symposium, June 1993. Featured in Los Angeles Daily Journal *Litigator Profile* December, 1993. *Member:* Los Angeles County and American Bar Associations; State Bar of California; Association of Southern California Defense Counsel (Board of Directors, 1991-1993).

---

**JIN N. LEW,** born Lubbock, Texas, November 16, 1962; admitted to bar, 1988, California. *Education:* University of California at Los Angeles (B.A., 1985); Loyola Marymount University (J.D., 1988). Author and Presenter: *"Roles of Minorities in the Legal Profession,"* Southwestern School of Law; *"Sexual Harassment and the Emergency Room,"* National Board of Directors for Janzen, Johnson & Rockwell Emergency Medical Group, 1996. *Member:* State Bar of California; Korean-American Bar Association; Association of Southern California Defense Counsel.

**DONNA P. HULBERT,** born East St. Louis, Illinois, February 21, 1959; admitted to bar, 1984, California. *Education:* University of California, Irvine (B.A., magna cum laude, 1981); University of California, Los Angeles (J.D., 1984). Phi Beta Kappa. *Member:* Los Angeles County Bar Association; State Bar of California.

**TERI E. MANKO,** born Los Angeles, California, December 17, 1963; admitted to bar, 1992, California. *Education:* University of California at Berkeley (B.A., 1985); Southwestern University School of Law (J.D., 1992). Psi Chi; Moot Court Honors Program. Judicial Extern to the Honorable Terry J. Hatter, Jr., U.S. District Court for the Central District of California, 1991. Participant: Jerome Prince Invitational Evidence Competition, 1991; J. Braxton Craven Jr. Moot Court Competition, 1992. Best Brief Finalist, Intramural Moot Court Competition, 1990. Listed in, "Who's Who Among American Law Students," 1990-1991; 1991-1992. *Member:* Los Angeles County Bar Association; State Bar of California.

**RUSSELL D. KINNIER,** born Minot, North Dakota, October 23, 1964; admitted to bar, 1993, California. *Education:* University of Maryland (B.A., magna cum laude, 1990); Southwestern University; American University (J.D., 1993). Recipient, American Jurisprudence Book Award in Constitutional Criminal Procedure. *Member:* Los Angeles County (Member, Litigation Section) and American Bar Associations; State Bar of California. [Signals Intelligence, U.S. Army, 1983-1987]

**DAVID M. FERRANTE,** born New Orleans, Louisiana, June 22, 1964; admitted to bar, 1991, California; 1992, U.S. District Court, Central District of California. *Education:* Louisiana State University (B.A., 1986); Loyola University, New Orleans (J.D., 1990). Moot Court Board (1989). Senior Representative to Student Bar Association. *Member:* Los Angeles County

*(This Listing Continued)*

Bar Association; State Bar of California; Association of Southern California Defense Lawyers.

**MARCUS J. BRADLEY,** born Drexel Hill, Pennsylvania, March 24, 1962; admitted to bar, 1994, California. *Education:* University of California at Davis (B.A., 1991); Loyola Law School, University of San Francisco (J.D., 1994). *Member:* State Bar of California.

**ELLIOT S. BLUT,** born Las Vegas, Nevada, September 13, 1967; admitted to bar, 1992, California. *Education:* Dartmouth College; University of California, San Diego (B.A., 1989); Hastings College of the Law, University of California (J.D., 1992). Volunteer, Barristers Pro Bono Domestic Violence Project, Los Angeles County Bar Association. *Member:* Los Angeles County Bar Association; State Bar of California.

**PATRICK E. STOCKALPER,** born San Diego, California, May 10, 1962; admitted to bar, 1991, California and U.S. District Court, Southern District of California. *Education:* University of California at Irvine (B.A. Political Science, 1985); University of San Diego (J.D., 1991). *Member:* State Bar of California.

**MICHAEL B. HORROW,** born Philadelphia, Pennsylvania, December 21, 1966; admitted to bar, 1992, California. *Education:* Pennsylvania State University (B.S., 1989); California Western School of Law (J.D., 1992). Recipient, American Jurisprudence Award in Trial Practice, 1991. Member, Advocacy Honors Board Trial Team, 1991-1992. *Member:* Los Angeles County Bar Association; State Bar of California; Association of Southern California Defense Counsel.

**NANCY A. LUKE,** born Los Angeles, California, May 15, 1957; admitted to bar, 1983, California. *Education:* Lee College; University of Tennessee (B.A., with highest honors, 1980); Loyola Marymount University, Los Angeles (J.D., 1983). Phi Alpha Delta; Phi Kappa Phi; Phi Sigma Alpha. Jessup International Moot Court. Member, Barristers Child Abuse Committee, 1983—. *Member:* Los Angeles County Bar Association; State Bar of California; Association of California Cremationists; Orangebelt Funeral Directors' Association.

**ETHAN PARITZKY,** born Minneapolis, Minnesota, February 12, 1968; admitted to bar, 1995, California. *Education:* University of Pennsylvania (B.A., 1990); University of Southern California (J.D., 1994); University of Southern California School of International Relations (M.A., 1994). *Member:* Los Angeles (Member, International Law Section) and American Bar Associations; State Bar of California (Member, International Law Section). *PRACTICE AREAS:* Business Transactions.

## SIMON & SIMON, LTD.
*1500 ROSECRANS AVENUE*
*SUITE 360*
**MANHATTAN BEACH, CALIFORNIA 90266**
Telephone: 310-536-9393
Fax: 310-536-9351

Hawthorne, California Office: 4477 W. 118th Street, Suite 101. Telephone: 319-973-0474.

*General Civil Litigation, Family Law, Real Property, Probate, Estate Planning, Personal Injury, Business.*

*FIRM PROFILE:* Simon & Simon is a full service law firm who represents both plaintiffs and defendants, businesses and individuals in a wide variety of civil cases. The practice consists of General Civil Litigation with emphasis on Family Law, Real Property, Estate Planning, Personal Injury, Business matters in all state and federal courts. The firm takes pride in providing our clients with individual service intended to produce as effective a solution to the problem as circumstances will permit at a fair price.

**DAVID E. SIMON,** born Vallejo, California, April 1, 1943; admitted to bar, 1969, California. *Education:* University of California at Los Angeles (B.S., 1965); University of Southern California (J.D., 1968). *PRACTICE AREAS:* Estate Planning; Wills; Trusts; Probate; Civil Litigation; Real Property.

**CAROL BREMER SIMON,** born Indianapolis, Indiana, August 3, 1951; admitted to bar, 1981, California. *Education:* American River Junior College (A.A.,1973); California State University at Sacramento (B.A., 1974); McGeorge School of Law, University of the Pacific (J.D., 1981). *Member:* California State Bar. (Certified Specialist, Family Law, The State Bar of California Board of Legal Specialization). *PRACTICE AREAS:* Family Law.

## STEINBERG BARNESS GLASGOW & FOSTER LLP
*1334 PARK VIEW AVENUE, SUITE 100*
**MANHATTAN BEACH, CALIFORNIA 90266**
Telephone: 310-546-5838
Telecopier: 310-546-5630
Email: SGBF@ix.netcom.com

*General Business Practice, Corporation, Real Estate, Estate Planning, Trust and Probate Law, Civil Litigation, Bankruptcy, Creditor's Rights and Commercial Law.*

*FIRM PROFILE:* Steinberg Barness Glasgow & Foster is engaged in the practice of law domestically and internationally, with offices in New York and Los Angeles, California.

*The practice of the firm includes federal and state general civil litigation, trials and appeals, arbitrations, general corporate and commercial law, bankruptcy and creditors' rights, banking law, regulatory law, taxation, business immigration, probate, trusts and estates, domestic relations law and real estate and international business litigation and transactions. The firm is also experienced in counseling United States entities and individuals, as well as foreign clients, with respect to international transactions, both in the United States and abroad, including project development and financing and joint venture, technology transfer, distributorship, agency and licensing agreements. The firm engages in the practice of law in English, Spanish, Portuguese, French and Hebrew.*

### MEMBERS OF FIRM

**ALEX STEINBERG,** born Port Townsend, Washington, December 8, 1933; admitted to bar, 1961, California. *Education:* University of California at Los Angeles (B.A., 1955); University of Southern California (J.D., 1960). Phi Alpha Delta; Order of the Coif. Associate Editor, USC Law Review, 1959-1960. *Member:* South Bay, Los Angeles County (Member, Probate and Trust Law Section) and American Bar Associations; The State Bar of California (Member, Estate Planning, Trust and Probate Law Section; Real Property Section). *PRACTICE AREAS:* General Business; Real Property; Estate Planning; Trusts and Probate Administration.

**DANIEL I. BARNESS,** born Los Angeles, California, February 9, 1955; admitted to bar, 1982, California and U.S. Court of Appeals, Ninth Circuit; 1985, New York. *Education:* University of California at Berkeley (B.A., 1977); Hastings College of the Law, University of California (J.D., 1982). Author: "How To Become A Notary Public," Duane-Reed Publication, 1984. Mediator, U.S. Bankruptcy Court, Central District of California. *Member:* Santa Clara County and Los Angeles County Bar Associations; State Bar of California (Member, Business Law Section); Financial Lawyers Conference; American Judicature Society; Los Angeles Bankruptcy Forum. *LANGUAGES:* French, Spanish and Hebrew. *PRACTICE AREAS:* Bankruptcy Law; Creditors Rights Law; Commercial Law; Business Law.

**DONNA GLASGOW,** born New York, N.Y., August 23, 1951; admitted to bar, 1978, New York, U.S. District Court, Southern District of New York and U.S. Court of Appeals, District of Columbia Circuit; 1979, U.S. District Court, Eastern District of New York; 1984, U.S. Supreme Court; 1986, U.S. Court of Appeals, Second Circuit (Not admitted in California). *Education:* University of Chicago and Clark University (B.A., 1972); New York University; Rutgers Law School (J.D., 1977). Co-Author: "Export Controls: Extraterritorial Conflict-The Dilemma of the Host Country Employee," 19 Case Western Reserve Journal of International Law 303, 1987. *Member:* The Association of the Bar of the City of New York; New York State (Charter Member, International Law and Practice Law Section) and American Bar Associations; New York Women's Bar Association. (Also Of Counsel to Kevorkian & Partners, New York, New York). *LANGUAGES:* French. *PRACTICE AREAS:* Commercial and Real Estate Transactions; Litigation; Real Estate Foreclosures; Domestic Relations; Probate; Trusts and Estates; International Transactions; Business Immigration.

**DOUGLAS B. FOSTER,** born Edwards, California, July 5, 1959; admitted to bar, 1987, California and U.S. District Court, Central District of California. *Education:* College of William & Mary (B.A., 1982); Loyola Law School of Los Angeles (J.D., 1986). Editor, Loyola of Los Angeles International and Comparative Law Journal, 1985-1986. Author: "Recent Developments in U.S. Trademark, Copyright and Semiconductor Chip Anticounterfeiting Laws," 8 Loyola of Los Angeles International and Comparative Law Journal 649, 1986. *Member:* South Bay, Los Angeles County and American Bar Associations; State Bar of California. *PRACTICE AREAS:* Civil Litigation; General Business Practice.

*(This Listing Continued)*

CALIFORNIA—MANHATTAN BEACH • MARTINDALE-HUBBELL LAW DIRECTORY 1997

**STEINBERG BARNESS GLASGOW & FOSTER LLP,**
*Manhattan Beach—Continued*

**JORDAN G. BARNESS,** born Los Angeles, California, February 26, 1957; admitted to bar, 1984, California and U.S. District Court, Central and Northern Districts of California; 1985, New York; 1986, U.S. District Court, Southern and Eastern Districts of New York; 1987, U.S. District Court, Southern District of California. *Education:* University of California at Berkeley (B.A., 1979); Southwestern University School of Law (J.D., 1983). Phi Alpha Delta. Co-Author: "Export Controls: Extraterritorial Conflict-The Dilemma of the Host Country Employee," 19 Case Western Reserve Journal of International Law 303, 1987; "La Regulacion de la Importacion y Exportacion en los Estados Unidos," (The Regulation of Imports and Exports in the United States), Dirigencia, December, 1985. *Member:* Association of the Bar of the City of New York; New York State (Charter Member, International Law and Practice Section), American, Inter-American and International Bar Associations. **LANGUAGES:** Portuguese, Spanish, French and Hebrew. **PRACTICE AREAS:** Corporate; Entertainment; Real Estate Law.

**PAUL J. LAURIN,** born Honolulu, Hawaii, June 8, 1962; admitted to bar, 1988, California. *Education:* University of California at Berkeley (B.A., 1985); Hastings College of the Law, University of California (J.D., 1988). *Member:* Los Angeles County and American Bar Associations; State Bar of California. **PRACTICE AREAS:** Bankruptcy Law; Creditors Rights Law; Commercial Law; Entertainment Law.

**SHANNON M. FOLEY,** born Henderson, Nevada, May 25, 1960; admitted to bar, 1986, California and U.S. District Court, Central District of California; 1987, U.S. Court of Appeals, Ninth Circuit; 1988, Nevada and U.S. District Court, District of Nevada. *Education:* Arizona State University (B.S., magna cum laude, 1982); George Washington University National Law Center (J.D., with honors, 1986). Associate: McKenna, Conner & Cuneo, 1986-1989; Burkley, Moore, Greenberg & Lyman, 1989-1990. Member, Feinstein for Governor Campaign, 1990. *Member:* Los Angeles County and American Bar Associations; The State Bar of California; Women Lawyers Association of Los Angeles; South Bay Bar Association of Business Trial Lawyers. **PRACTICE AREAS:** Business Litigation.

**RICHARD L. WEINER,** born Tucson, Arizona, January 27, 1960; admitted to bar, 1986, California; U.S. District Court, Central and Southern Districts of California; U.S. Court of Appeals, Ninth Circuit. *Education:* University of Arizona (B.A., 1982); California Western School of Law (J.D., 1985). Staff Writer, 1983-1984 and Notes and Comments Editor, 1984-1985, California Western International Law Journal. Author: Comment, "Limited Armed Conflict Causing Physical Damage to Neutral Countries Questions of Liability?" 15 Calif. W. Int'l. L.J. 161 (1985). Judge Pro Tem, Beverly Hills Municipal Court. *Member:* Los Angeles County (Member: Litigation Section; Business Law Section) and American Bar Associations; State Bar of California; Association of Business Trial Lawyers. **PRACTICE AREAS:** Business Litigation; Entertainment Litigation.

**WILLIAM R. (RANDY) KIRKPATRICK,** born Houston, Texas, December 17, 1947; admitted to bar, 1974, California; 1980, U.S. District Court, Central District of California and U.S. Supreme Court. *Education:* Wesleyan University (B.A., 1969); University of Southern California (J.D., 1973); Master's Degree, Real Estate Development, 1988); University of California at Los Angeles (M.B.A., 1979). Licensed Real Estate Broker, California, 1981. Deputy County Counsel, Office of Los Angeles County Counsel, 1974-1977. *Member:* State Bar of California. **PRACTICE AREAS:** Real Estate; General Business Practice.

**JEFFREY MICHAEL LEE,** born Pittsburg, Pennsylvania, May 19, 1966; admitted to bar, 1996, California and U.S. District Court, Central District of California. *Education:* University of California at Berkley (B.A., high honors and distinction, 1988; J.D., 1996). Member, California Law Review. **PRACTICE AREAS:** Estates and Trusts; Commercial Law.

OF COUNSEL

**ROANLD D. HARARI,** born Forest Hills, May 31, 1957; admitted to bar, 1982, New York and U.S. District Court, Southern and Eastern Districts of New York (Not admitted in California). *Education:* Columbia University (A.B., magna cum laude, 1978; J.D., 1981). **LANGUAGES:** Spanish.

REPRESENTATIVE CLIENTS: Bay Loan Investment Bank; BB&T Leasing Corporation; Gold & Associates (Real estate development); Laique, Inc.; Leigh Aerosystems; Pacific Relocation Consultants; Paramount Interests (Real estate investment); Precision Dynamics Corporation; Prime Electro; Raison Pure International, Inc.; Redondo Shores Shopping Center; Republic Bank California N.A.; Republic Factors; Thomas C. Major & Associates (Real estate investment); Thrifty Corporation; Trans International Management Corporation; Univision Television Group, Inc.; Western Land & Development Company (general partner).

*(This Listing Continued)*

---

## ROBERT S. VALENTINE

*1334 PARK VIEW AVENUE, SUITE 100*
*P.O. BOX 8*
**MANHATTAN BEACH, CALIFORNIA 90267-0008**
Telephone: 310-545-6565
Fax: 310-546-8151

*Probate, Estate Planning, Real Estate and Personal Injury Practice.*

**ROBERT S. VALENTINE,** born Utica, New York, December 16, 1938; admitted to bar, 1967, California and U.S. District Court, Central District of California; 1977, U.S. District Court, Southern District of California; 1993, District of Columbia Court of Appeals; 1994, New York. *Education:* University of California at Los Angeles (B.A., 1963); Loyola University of Los Angeles (J.D., 1966). Student Teaching Fellow, Loyola Law School, 1964-1966. Member, Planning Commission, City of Manhattan Beach, 1976. Judge Pro Tem, South Bay, 1986—. *Member:* Los Angeles County, South Bay (Member, Board of Directors, 1980-1981), Inglewood District (Member, Board of Trustees, 1971-1979; 1st Vice-President, 1976; President, 1977), New York State and American Bar Associations; The State Bar of California; California Trial Lawyers Association. (Also Of Counsel to Law Offices of A.B. Chettle, Jr., Redondo Beach, California).

REFERENCE: Wells Fargo Bank, California.

---

## H. ANDREW WASMUND

*Established in 1976*

*1334 PARK VIEW AVENUE, SUITE 100*
**MANHATTAN BEACH, CALIFORNIA 90266**
Telephone: 310-545-3243
Fax: 310-545-4782

*General Civil and Criminal Litigation with emphasis in Federal Court. Arbitration and Mediation, Family Law, Personal Injury.*

**H. ANDREW WASMUND,** born Long Beach, California, August 31, 1946; admitted to bar, 1972, California, U.S. District Court, Central District of California and U.S. Court of Appeals, Ninth Circuit. *Education:* University of California at Los Angeles (A.B.); Loyola University of Los Angeles (J.D., 1972). Phi Alpha Delta. St. Thomas More Law Honor Society. Member, Loyola Law Review, 1972. Author: "Use and Abuse of Congressional Franking Privilege," 5 Loy. (L.A.) L. Rev., 1972. Law Clerk to the Honorable Albert Lee Stephens, United States District Court, Central District of California. Panel of Arbitrators of American Arbitration Association, Los Angeles Superior Court and Los Angeles County Bar Association. *Member:* Los Angeles County and Federal Bar Associations; State Bar of California.

---

## NEUMILLER & BEARDSLEE

*A PROFESSIONAL CORPORATION*

**MANTECA, CALIFORNIA**

(See Stockton)

*General Civil Practice and Litigation in all State and Federal Courts. Real Property, Condominium, Land Use, Natural Resources, Environmental, Water and Water Rights, Mining, Agricultural, Corporation, Partnership, Business Planning, Securities, Creditor's Rights in Bankruptcy, Taxation, Employee Benefits, Insurance, Administrative, Health Care, Governmental and Legislative, Trusts, Estate Planning, Probate and Municipal Law.*

## LAW OFFICE OF
## ELIZABETH BRANDON-BROWN
**8055 WEST MANCHESTER AVENUE, SUITE 405**
**MARINA DEL REY, CALIFORNIA 90293**
Telephone: 310-302-0035

*Securities and Corporate Law.*

**ELIZABETH BRANDON-BROWN,** born Hamilton, Ontario, Canada, June 12, 1948; admitted to bar, 1991, Florida; 1992, District of Columbia, 1995, California. *Education:* University of Florida (B.S., 1969); Columbus School of Law, Catholic University (J.D., 1991). Recipient, National Association of Areas Business Publications Award for series on Venture Capital, 1981. Author: ABA Newsletter, Network 2nd, "Facsimiles Can Breach Confidentiality", 1993; "E-Mail Snoops May Breach Confidentiality", 1993; "Knock, Knock - It's the Government Calling", 1994. *Member:* The Florida Bar; District of Columbia Bar; State Bar of California (Sections on: Business Law and Intellectual Property). (Also Of Counsel to Sanchez & Amador, LLP at Los Angeles). *PRACTICE AREAS:* Securities; Corporate; Business Law.

---

## MAGASINN & MAGASINN
*A LAW CORPORATION*
Established in 1968
**4640 ADMIRALITY WAY, SUITE 402**
**MARINA DEL REY, CALIFORNIA 90292**
Telephone: 310-301-3545
Telecopier: 310-301-0035

*Specializing in Taxation, Estate Planning, Probate, Trusts, Charitable Organizations, Real Estate, Business, Corporate and Partnership Law and Business Secession Planning.*

FIRM PROFILE: *Magasinn & Magasinn, A Law Corporation, specializes in matters of Taxation, Estate Planning, Probate, Trusts, Charitable Organizations, Real Estate, Business, Corporate and Partnership Law and Business Succession Planning.*

**JONATHAN M. FELDMAN,** born Los Angeles, California, March 21, 1954; admitted to bar, 1981, California and U.S. Tax Court. *Education:* University of California at Los Angeles (B.A., magna cum laude, 1976); University of San Francisco (J.D., 1981). Phi Gamma Mu. Recipient, American Jurisprudence Award in Wills and Trusts. *PRACTICE AREAS:* Business Law; Real Estate.

**ARNOLD W. MAGASINN,** born Los Angeles, California, September 25, 1935; admitted to bar, 1967, California and U.S. Tax Court. *Education:* University of California at Los Angeles (B.S., 1958); University of San Fernando Valley (LL.B., 1966). Certified Public Accountant, California, 1959. Lecturer, The American College, Bryn Mawr, Pennsylvania, 1978-1985. President, Los Angeles Estate Counselors Forum, 1980. Commodore, Del Rey Yacht Club, 1994. *Member:* Beverly Hills (Member: Taxation Committee, 1972—; Probate Committee, 1972—; Corporations Committee, 1972—); Los Angeles County (Member, Taxation Section) and American Bar Associations; California Association of Attorneys-Certified Public Accountants (President, 1972); American Association of Attorneys-Certified Public Accountants (President, 1979); American Institute of Certified Public Accountants; California Society of Certified Public Accountants. (Certified Specialist, Taxation Law, The State Bar of California Board of Legal Specialization). *PRACTICE AREAS:* Business Law; Taxation Law; Trust and Estate Planning.

**VICKI FISHER MAGASINN,** born Los Angeles, California, October 2, 1949; admitted to bar, 1977, California. *Education:* University of California at Los Angeles (B.A., cum laude, 1971); Southwestern University School of Law (J.D., with honors, 1977). Outstanding Advocate, Moot Court Competition. Recipient, American Jurisprudence Awards in Trusts, Business Organizations. President, Beverly Hills Estate Counselor's Forum, 1986. Instructor, "Corporate Organizations," U.C.L.A. Legal Assistant Training Program, 1985-1991. Lecturer: American Bar Association, 1987; California State University at Los Angeles, "To Probate or Not to Probate," 1987, 1990; California C.P.A. Foundation Annual Tax Accounting Conference, 1983-1985; American Society of Pension Actuaries, Business Techniques Seminar, 1985, 1986. Author: "Weighing Funded Living Trust Advantages and Disadvantages," Warren, Gorham & Lamont, 1989. *Member:* Beverly Hills Bar Association (Member, Probate and Trust Section). (Certified Specialist, Estate Planning, Trust and Probate Law, The State Bar of

*(This Listing Continued)*

California Board of Legal Specialization). *PRACTICE AREAS:* Estate Planning; Trusts; Probate; Business.

---

**MICHAEL L. MAGASINN,** born Los Angeles, California, March 28, 1965; admitted to bar, 1995, California. *Education:* California State University, Northridge (B.S., 1991); Southwestern University School of Law (J.D., 1995). *Member:* State Bar of California. *PRACTICE AREAS:* Estate Planning; Probate; Business Law.

---

## ALLEN, POLGAR, PROIETTI & FAGALDE
A Partnership including a Professional Corporation
**5079 HIGHWAY 140**
**P.O. BOX 1907**
**MARIPOSA, CALIFORNIA 95338**
Telephone: 209-966-3007
Fax: 209-742-6353

Merced, California Office: 1640 "N" Street, Suite 200. P.O. Box 2184. Telephone: 209-723-4372. Fax: 209-723-7397.

*General Civil and Criminal Trial Practice. Personal Injury, Wrongful Termination, Family Law, Corporation, Business, Condemnation, Taxation, Estate Planning, Probate, Real Property, Bankruptcy and Creditors' Rights Law.*

**F. DANA WALTON,** born 1950; admitted to bar, 1979, California. *Education:* California State University, Fresno; Humphreys College (J.D.). *Member:* Mariposa County Bar Association; State Bar of California. (Resident). *PRACTICE AREAS:* Probate; Trusts; Estate Planning; Family Law; Civil Litigation.

A list of Representative Clients will be Furnished upon Request.

(For Complete Biographical Data on all Personnel, See Professional Biographies, Merced, California)

---

## LINN, LINDLEY & BLATE
*A PROFESSIONAL ASSOCIATION*
**MARIPOSA, CALIFORNIA**
(See Oakhurst)

*General Civil and Trial Practice including Personal Injury, Probate and Estate Planning, Corporate, Business, Taxation, Natural Resources Law, Banking Litigation, Criminal Law and Family Law.*

---

## BRAY AND BRAY
**736 FERRY STREET**
**MARTINEZ, CALIFORNIA 94553**
Telephone: 510-228-2550
FAX: 510-370-8558

*Estate Planning, Probate, Trust Administration and Litigation, Conservatorships and Guardianships.*

**A. F. BRAY, JR.,** born San Francisco, California, November 24, 1918; admitted to bar, 1949, California; 1960, U.S. Supreme Court. *Education:* Stanford University (A.B., 1940); University of Southern California (J.D., 1949). Delta Theta Phi. Chairman, City of Martinez Recreation Commission, 1949-1955. *Member:* Contra Costa County Bar Association (President, 1964); State Bar of California (Chairman, Committee on Adoption, 1965-1966). [Lieut., U.S.N.R., 1942-1946]. *PRACTICE AREAS:* Estate Planning; Probate Law; Guardianship and Conservatorship.

**OLIVER W. BRAY,** born San Francisco, California, November 15, 1954; admitted to bar, 1985, California. *Education:* California State University at Sacramento (B.S., 1977); John F. Kennedy University (J.D, 1985). Ex-Officio Regent, John F. Kennedy University, 1989-1996. President, John F. Kennedy University Alumni Association, 1989-1996. *Member:* Contra Costa County Bar Association; State Bar of California. *PRACTICE AREAS:* Probate Law; Estate Planning; Trust Administration; Trust Litigation; Guardianship and Conservatorship.

## RICHARD J. BREITWIESER
736 FERRY STREET
MARTINEZ, CALIFORNIA 94553
Telephone: 510-838-8430
Fax: 510-370-8558

*Court appearances for out of area attorneys. Family Law, Interstate Support (URESA, UCCJA), Civil Litigation, Business, Estate Planning, Probate and Taxation Law. Guardianship and Conservatorship.*

**RICHARD J. BREITWIESER,** born Buffalo, New York, August 30, 1934; admitted to bar, 1966, California. *Education:* Canisius College (B.S., 1957); Hastings College of Law, University of California (J.D., 1965); Golden Gate University (M.S. in Taxation, 1978). Phi Alpha Delta. Instructor in Taxation, John F. Kennedy University Law School, 1974-1979. *Member:* Contra Costa County Bar Association (President, 1978); The State Bar of California; California Trial Lawyers Association; Alameda-Contra Costa Trial Lawyers Association (Director, 1976-1979). *PRACTICE AREAS:* Family Law; Uniform Child Custody Jurisdiction Act; Civil Litigation; Business Law; Estate Planning and Probate Law; Taxation Law; Uniform Transfers to Minors Act.

---

## BERNARD F. CUMMINS
917 LAS JUNTAS STREET
P.O. BOX 351
MARTINEZ, CALIFORNIA 94553
Telephone: 510-228-3001
Fax: 510-228-6825

*General Civil, Trial and Appellate Practice in all Courts. Business, Probate, Real Property and Condemnation Law.*

**BERNARD F. CUMMINS,** born Oakland, California, August 7, 1931; admitted to bar, 1961, California. *Education:* St. Marys College of California (A.B., 1957); University of San Francisco (LL.B., 1960). Judge Pro Tempore, Contra Costa County Superior Court, 1994—. Member, Board of Trustees, Contra Costa Legal Services Foundation, 1975-1987. *Member:* Contra Costa County (President, 1976; Member, Criminal Conflicts Program, 1985-1988; Chairman, 1987-1988) and American Bar Associations; The State Bar of California. [With USN, 1951-1955]. *REPORTED CASES:* Los Angeles Metropolitan Transit Authority v. Public Utilities Commission (1963) 59 Cal. 2d 863; People v. Estrada (1965) 234 Cal..App.2d 136; 11 ALR 3d 1307; Pleasant Hill v. First Baptist Church (1969) 1 Cal. App. 3d 384; Estate of Wochos (1972) 23 Cal.App.3d 47; Titus v. Superior Court (1972) 23 Cal.App.3d 792.

---

## GORDON, DeFRAGA, WATROUS & PEZZAGLIA
A LAW CORPORATION
611 LAS JUNTAS STREET
P.O. BOX 630
MARTINEZ, CALIFORNIA 94553
Telephone: 510-228-1400
Fax: 510-228-3644

*Civil and Trial Practice before all Federal, State and Local Courts and Administrative Agencies, Business, Corporate, Real Property and Land Use Matters, Landslide and Soil Subsidence, Inverse Condemnation and Municipal Law, Civil Rights, Environmental, Air Pollution and Toxic Torts, Estate Planning and Probate Law, Insurance Defense.*

**ALLAN DEFRAGA,** born Concord, California, January 24, 1941; admitted to bar, 1966, California. *Education:* Stanford University (A.B., 1962); Hastings College of Law, University of California (LL.B., 1965). Member, City of Martinez Parking Commission, 1981-1986. *Member:* Contra Costa County Bar Association; The State Bar of California. *PRACTICE AREAS:* Personal Injury Law; Real Property Law; Probate Law.

**THOMAS A. WATROUS,** born Riverside, California, July 8, 1938; admitted to bar, 1964, California; 1987, U.S. Supreme Court. *Education:* University of California at Riverside and University of California at Berkeley (A.B., 1960); Boalt Hall School of Law, University of California (J.D., 1963). Deputy and Assistant District Attorney, Contra Costa County, 1967-1973. Hearing Officer, Contra Costa County Retirement Board, 1976—. *Member:* Contra Costa County Bar Association; The State Bar of

*(This Listing Continued)*

California. [Capt., U.S. Marine Corps, 1964-1966]. *PRACTICE AREAS:* Personal Injury Law; Business Litigation; Civil Rights Law.

**JAMES A. PEZZAGLIA,** born Fairfield, California, March 6, 1941; admitted to bar, 1968, California. *Education:* University of California at Berkeley (B.S., 1964); San Jose State College (M.B.A., 1967); Hastings College of Law, University of California (J.D., 1967). Phi Delta Phi. Deputy District Attorney, Contra Costa County, 1968-1970. Member, Contra Costa Council Hazardous Waste Committee, 1984—. *Member:* Contra Costa County Bar Association; The State Bar of California. *PRACTICE AREAS:* Administrative Law; Environmental Law; Estate Planning Law.

**TIMOTHY JOHN RYAN,** born Oakland, California, July 24, 1952; admitted to bar, 1978, California. *Education:* University of Santa Clara (B.S., 1974); Lincoln University (J.D., 1978). *Member:* Contra Costa County Bar Association; The State Bar of California (Member, State Bar Litigation Section); Association of Defense Counsel; Community Associations Institute; East Bay Adjusters Association. *PRACTICE AREAS:* Tort Litigation; Landslide Law; Homeowner Association Law; Inverse Condemnation Law; Insurance Defense Law.

**PETER D. LANGLEY,** born Milwaukee, Wisconsin, August 30, 1944; admitted to bar, 1972, California; 1983, U.S. Supreme Court. *Education:* University of Wisconsin (B.S., 1968); George Washington University (J.D., 1972). Legislative Assistant, Office of Senator Gaylord Nelson, Washington, D.C., 1971-1972. City Councilman, City of Martinez, 1984-1988. Chairman, Water Task Force Contra Costa Council, 1989—. Member, Board of Directors, Contra Costa Council, 1990—. *Member:* Contra Costa County Bar Association; The State Bar of California. *PRACTICE AREAS:* Real Property Law; Family Law; Business Law; Homeowner Association Law; Public Entity Defense; Estate Planning.

**RICHARD S. BRUNO,** born San Francisco, California, March 16, 1955; admitted to bar, 1984, California. *Education:* St. Mary's College (B.S., 1977); Armstrong College (J.D., 1983). Planning Commissioner, City of Martinez, California, 1985-1988. *Member:* Contra Costa County Bar Association; The State Bar of California; Barristers Association; The Association of Trial Lawyers of America; California Trial Lawyers Association. *PRACTICE AREAS:* Land Use Litigation; Real Property Law; Personal Injury Law.

**BRUCE C. PALTENGHI,** born South Bend, Indiana, September 23, 1950; admitted to bar, 1978, California. *Education:* California State University at Fresno (B.A., cum laude, 1973); San Mateo Law School (J.D., Valedictorian, 1978). Blue Key. Author: "Superfund Amendments and the Metal Casting Industry," Modern Casting, Feb.-March, 1987; "Where EPA Regulations Are Taking The Foundry Industry," Modern Casting, February 1990. Commissioner, City of Lafayette Crime Prevention Commission, 1983-1988. President, California Cast Metals Association, 1980-1981. *Member:* Contra Costa County Bar Association; State Bar of California (Member Sections on: Estate Planning; Probate and Trust; Business Law; Environmental Law). *PRACTICE AREAS:* Probate and Estate Administration; Environmental Law; Toxic Torts; Estate Planning Law; Administration Law; Business Law.

---

**GREGORY D. RUEB,** born Anchorage, Alaska, February 26, 1966; admitted to bar, 1991, California; U.S. District Court, Northern District of California and U.S. Court of Appeals, Ninth Circuit. *Education:* University of Pacific (B.S., 1988); McGeorge School of Law (J.D., 1991). Alpha Chi Sigma. Deputy District Attorney, Contra Costa County, 1991-1992. *Member:* Contra Costa County and American Bar Associations; State Bar of California; The Association of Trial Lawyers of America. *PRACTICE AREAS:* General Litigation and Trial Practice; Criminal Law; Personal Injury; Medical Malpractice; Environmental Law.

REPRESENTATIVE CLIENTS: Acme Fill Corp.; Lippow Development Co.; Plant Maintenance, Inc.; County of Contra Costa; City of Concord; City of El Cerrito; City of San Pablo; City of Hercules; City of Pleasant Hill; City of Brentwood; Winton Jones Contractors, Inc.; Delta Tech., Inc.; Clean Bay, Inc.; Concord Crane and Rigging; Contra Costa County Taxpayers Assn.; East Bay Sanitary Co.; Contra Costa County Municipal Risk Management Authority; TOSCO Refining Company; TOSCO Corp. Pacific Steel Casting Co.; Chemical and Pigment Co.; Power Systems Testing, Inc.; Hospital Building & Equipment; Gregg Industries, Inc.; IT Corporation; Suntree Homeowners Association; Hilltop Village Owners Association; East Bay Regional Park District; Rose Trucking; Bay Area Training Corp.; KTI.

## SANDERS, DODSON, RIVES & COX
### MARTINEZ, CALIFORNIA
(See Pittsburg)

*Personal Injury, Products Liability, Construction Defects, Eminent Domain, Tax, Estate Planning, Probate, Living Trusts, General Business.*

---

## LEANNE SCHLEGEL
### 736 FERRY STREET
### MARTINEZ, CALIFORNIA 94553
Telephone: 510-228-6225
Fax: 510-228-5663

*Family Law including Custody and Visitation, Business, Corporations, Non-Profit Organizations.*

**LEANNE SCHLEGEL,** born Sacramento, California, November 28, 1942; admitted to bar, 1993, California. *Education:* California State University (B.A., 1976); John F. Kennedy University (J.D., 1993). *Member:* Contra Costa County Bar Association.

---

## TURNER, HUGUET & ADAMS
### Established in 1961
### 924 MAIN STREET
### P.O. BOX 110
### MARTINEZ, CALIFORNIA 94553
Telephone: 510-228-3433
Fax: 510-228-3596

*General Civil and Trial Practice. Property and Casualty Insurance, Probate, Trusts, Estate Planning, Real Estate, Business, Municipal, Environmental, Land Use and Corporation Law.*

### MEMBERS OF FIRM

**MAURICE E. HUGUET, JR.,** born Oakland, California, November 6, 1936; admitted to bar, 1962, California. *Education:* University of California at Berkeley (A.B., 1958); Hastings College of the Law, University of California (LL.B., 1961). Phi Delta Phi. Assistant Publications Editor, Hastings Law Journal, 1960-1961. City Attorney, City of Clayton, 1964—. *Member:* Contra Costa County Bar Association; The State Bar of California (Public Law, Estate Planning and Probate Sections). **PRACTICE AREAS:** Probate; Trusts; Estate Planning; Municipal; Real Estate; Business Law.

**JONATHAN DANIEL ADAMS,** born Los Angeles, California, August 9, 1943; admitted to bar, 1976, California and U.S. District Court, Northern and Eastern Districts of California; 1984, U.S. Court of Appeals, Ninth Circuit. *Education:* California State University at Los Angeles (B.S., 1966); McGeorge School of Law, University of the Pacific (J.D., 1976). Assistant City Attorney, City of Clayton. *Member:* Contra Costa County and American Bar Associations; The State Bar of California (Real Property Section). [Captain, USAF, 1966-1971]. **REPORTED CASES:** Moore v. R.G. Industries Inc., 789 F2d 1326. **PRACTICE AREAS:** Real Estate Litigation; Construction Litigation; Environmental Law; Insurance Coverage; Personal Injury.

---

## LEONARD D. WEILER
### A PROFESSIONAL CORPORATION
### MARTINEZ, CALIFORNIA
(See San Ramon)

*Family Law, Related Civil Litigation and Estate Planning.*

---

## WILLIS & LAWRENCE
### Established in 1971
### 615 GREEN STREET
### P.O. BOX 830 (COURT STATION)
### MARTINEZ, CALIFORNIA 94553
Telephone: 510-229-1230
Fax: 510-229-1232

*Criminal Trial Practice. Family, (Interstate Support-RURESA, UCCJA), Civil Litigation, Juvenile, Business, Personal Injury and Negligence Law.*

**STUART W. WILLIS,** born Santa Cruz, California, April 25, 1943; admitted to bar, 1971, California and U.S. District Court, Northern District of California. *Education:* University of California at Berkeley (A.B., 1967); Boalt Hall School of Law, University of California (J.D., 1970). Phi Beta Kappa. Judge Pro Tem, Superior, Juvenile and Municipal Courts, Contra Costa County, 1975—. Professor, Criminal Trial Practice, John F. Kennedy School of Law, 1981—. Inquest Hearing Officer, Contra Costa County, 1979—. *Member:* Contra Costa County Bar Association; State Bar of California. **PRACTICE AREAS:** Criminal Trial; Family; Civil Litigation; Juvenile (Criminal).

**JUDITH E. LAWRENCE,** born Richmond, California, April 24, 1948; admitted to bar, 1989, California and U.S. District Court, Northern District of California. *Education:* University of California at Berkeley (A.B., 1978); Golden Gate University (J.D., 1981). Judge Pro Tem, Superior, Juvenile and Municipal Courts, Contra Costa County, 1994—. *Member:* Contra Costa County Bar Association; State Bar of California. **PRACTICE AREAS:** Family; Civil Litigation; Juvenile (Dependency).

---

## RICH, FUIDGE, MORRIS & IVERSON, INC.
### Established in 1909
### 1129 D STREET
### P.O. BOX "A"
### MARYSVILLE, CALIFORNIA 95901
Telephone: 916-742-7371
Fax: 916-742-5982

*General Civil and Trial Practice. Corporation, Water Rights, Insurance, Real Estate, Crop Damage, Estate Planning, Family and Probate Law. Medical and Legal Malpractice, Personal Injury, Employment Law, Criminal Law, Alternative Dispute Resolution.*

**FIRM PROFILE:** Founded by W.P. Rich in 1909, Mr. Rich served twenty-five years as President of the State Senate, while building the foundation of the law firm. Rich, Fuidge, Morris, & Iverson represent clients in three primary areas of law: Civil Litigation, Corporate and Business Law, and Family Law (focusing on dissolution, custody, adoption, servatorships and probate).

*Practicing in Northern California, our firm has ready access to many county seats. Our size and focus and personal attention, combined with our experience and abilities allow us to provide the most cost-effective, result-oriented representation available.*

**WILLIAM P. RICH** (1880-1965).

**RICHARD H. FUIDGE** (1906-1976).

**CHESTER MORRIS,** born Chicago, Illinois, November 21, 1932; admitted to bar, 1962, California. *Education:* Modesto Junior College (A.A., 1957); University of California at Berkeley; Hastings College of Law, University of California (J.D., 1961). Phi Delta Phi. Associate Editor, Hastings Law Journal, 1959-60. *Member:* Yuba-Sutter (President, 1970) and American Bar Associations; The State Bar of California; Northern California Association of Defense Counsel (Director, 1982—; President, 1990); American Board of Trial Advocates (President, Sacramento Valley Chapter, 1988). **PRACTICE AREAS:** General Tort & Insurance Litigation; Business Litigation; Medical & Legal Malpractice; Crop Damage Cases; Alternative Dispute Resolution.

**ROLAND K. IVERSON, JR.,** born Fort Stanton, New Mexico, July 4, 1942; admitted to bar, 1970, California. *Education:* University of California (B.A., 1965); Hastings College of Law, University of California (J.D., 1968). *Member:* Yuba-Sutter Bar Association; The State Bar of California; Northern California Association of Defense Counsel. [Captain, U.S. Marine Corps, 1968-1971]. **PRACTICE AREAS:** Construction Law; Personal Injury; Products Liability (Plaintiff and Defendant); Medical Malpractice.

**DAVID R. LANE,** born San Jose, California, July 29, 1947; admitted to bar, 1973, California. *Education:* Chico State College (B.A., 1970); Univer-

*(This Listing Continued)*

**RICH, FUIDGE, MORRIS & IVERSON, INC.,** Marysville—Continued

sity of California at Davis (J.D., 1973). *Member:* Yuba-Sutter and American Bar Associations; The State Bar of California; Northern California Association of Defense Counsel. (Certified Specialist, Family Law, The State Bar of California Board of Legal Specialization). *PRACTICE AREAS:* Civil Litigation; Criminal Law; Family Law.

**BRANT J. BORDSEN,** born Stockton, California, August 9, 1955; admitted to bar, 1981, California. *Education:* University of California at Davis (B.S., 1977); McGeorge School of Law, University of the Pacific (J.D., 1981). Phi Delta Phi. *Member:* State Bar of California; Northern California Association of Defense Counsel. *PRACTICE AREAS:* Civil Litigation; Landlord/Tenant; Bankruptcy; Land Use Planning; Municipal Law.

**STEPHEN W. BERRIER,** born Fort Dix, New Jersey, March 28, 1956; admitted to bar, 1984, California. *Education:* Yuba College; University of California at Davis (B.S., 1977); McGeorge School of Law (J.D., 1984). *Member:* Yuba-Sutter Bar Association; State Bar of California; Northern California Association of Defense Counsel. *PRACTICE AREAS:* Insurance Defense; Personal Injury; Insurance Coverage; General Litigation.

**JILL CERUDA HALL,** born San Francisco, California; June 17, 1964; admitted to bar, 1991, California. *Education:* University of California at Berkeley (B.A., 1986); University of California at Davis (J.D., 1990). Member, Board Senior Honor Society. *Member:* Yuba-Sutter Bar Association. *LANGUAGES:* Spanish. *PRACTICE AREAS:* Domestic Relations; Civil Litigation and Practice; Immigration.

GENERAL COUNSEL: City of Yuba City; Yuba-Sutter Mosquito Abatement District; Hi and Dry Warehouse, Inc.; Linda Fire Protection District; Yuba County Water District; City of Live Oak; Sunset Moulding Co.; Wheeler Cadillac Oldsmobile; City of Gridley; Plumas Brophy Fire Protection District; Loma Rica-Browns Valley Community Services District; Bank of America N.T & S.A.; Yuba River Lumber Co., Inc.
LOCAL COUNSEL: American Insurance Group; California State Automobile Assn.; General Accident Fire and Life Assurance Corp., Ltd.; Lumbermens Mutual Casualty Co.; State Farm Insurance Cos.; Government Employees Insurance Co.; Allstate Insurance Co.; Kemper Insurance Group; Naumes of Oregon, Inc.; Gulf Stream, Inc.

## ARNOLD, WHITE & DURKEE

*A PROFESSIONAL CORPORATION*

**155 LINFIELD DRIVE**
**MENLO PARK, CALIFORNIA 94025-3741**
Telephone: 415-614-4500
Facsimile: 415-614-4599
Email: info@awd.com
URL: http://www.awd.com

*Houston, Texas Office:* 750 Bering Drive, 77057-2198; P.O. Box 4433, 77210-4433. Telephone: 713-787-1400. Facsimile: 713-789-2679. Telex: 79-0924.
*Austin, Texas Office:* 1900 One American Center, 600 Congress Avenue, 78701-3248. Telephone: 512-418-3000. Facsimile: 512-474-7577.
*Arlington, Virginia Office:* 2001 Jefferson Davis Highway, Suite 401, 22202-3604. Telephone: 703-415-1720. Facsimile: 703-415-1728.
*Chicago, Illinois Office:* 800 Quaker Tower, 321 North Clark Street, 60610-4714. Telephone: 312-744-0090. Facsimile: 312-755-4489.
*Minneapolis, Minnesota Office:* 4850 First Bank Place, 601 Second Avenue South, 55402-4320. Telephone: 612-321-2800. Facsimile: 612-321-9600.

*Intellectual Property including Patent, Trademark, Copyright, Trade Secret, Unfair Competition, Licensing and Related Government Agency Proceedings, Antitrust and International Trade Matters. Trials and Appeals in Federal and State Courts.*

**GERALD P. DODSON,** born Pittsburgh, Pennsylvania, September 15, 1947; admitted to bar, 1972, Pennsylvania; 1977, District of Columbia; 1989, California. *Education:* Lafayette College (B.S.M.E., 1969); University of Maryland, Baltimore (J.D., 1972); George Washington University (LL.M., 1977). Assistant County Solicitor, Allegheny County, Pennsylvania, 1972-1975. Staff Attorney, U.S. Department of the Interior, 1976-1978. Counsel, U.S. House of Representatives, Subcommittee on Health and Environment, 1979-1988. *Member:* Bar Association of San Francisco; The District of Columbia Bar; Federal Circuit Bar Association; Peninsula Intellectual Property Law Association; San Francisco Intellectual Property Law Association. *Email:* jdodson@awd.com

*(This Listing Continued)*

**GLENN W. RHODES,** born Kansas City, Missouri, July 20, 1956; admitted to bar, 1985, Texas; 1995, California. *Education:* William Jewell College (B.A. in Chemistry, magna cum laude, 1982); University of Houston (J.D., cum laude, 1985). Phi Delta Phi. Member, Order of the Barons. Adjunct Professor, University of Houston Law Center, 1986-1987. *Member:* Houston Bar Association; State Bar of Texas; Federal Circuit and Federal Bar Associations; San Francisco Intellectual Property Law Association; Peninsula Intellectual Property Law Association. *Email:* grhodes@awd.com

**DAVID L. BILSKER,** born Miami, Florida, June 29, 1962; admitted to bar, 1990, Florida; 1991, California. *Education:* Columbia University (B.S.Ch.E., 1984); University of Miami (M.S., Bio. Med. E., 1986); University of Florida (J.D., with honors, 1990). Phi Kappa Phi; Order of the Coif. Research Editor, Florida Law Review, 1989-1990. *Member:* Bar Association of San Francisco; San Francisco Intellectual Property Law Association; Peninsula Intellectual Property Law Association. *Email:* dbilsker@awd.com

**JAMES F. VALENTINE,** born Cincinnati, Ohio, December 22, 1961; admitted to bar, 1990, California. *Education:* The Ohio State University (B.S.E.E., 1984); Loyola University (J.D., 1990). Order of the Coif; Tau Beta Pi; Eta Kappa Nu. *Member:* Los Angeles County and Santa Clara County Bar Associations; San Francisco Intellectual Property Law Association; Peninsula Intellectual Property Law Association. *Email:* jvalentine@awd.com

**MARK K. DICKSON,** born Pueblo, Colorado, May 25, 1955; admitted to bar, 1988, Texas; 1989, District of Columbia; 1990, California. *Education:* University of Southern Colorado (B.S., with special distinction, 1977); Washington State University (Ph.D., 1982); University of Houston (J.D., 1988). Sigma Xi. Law Clerk to Honorable Pauline Newman, Judge, U.S. Court of Appeals, Federal Circuit, 1989-1990. *Member:* Bar Association of San Francisco; State Bar of Texas; The District of Columbia Bar; Federal Circuit Bar Association; San Francisco Intellectual Property Law Association; Peninsula Intellectual Property Law Association. *Email:* mdickson@awd.com

**THOMAS C. MAVRAKAKIS,** born New York, N.Y., November 28, 1964; admitted to bar, 1994, Texas; 1995, California. *Education:* Polytechnic University (B.S.E.E., 1989); St. John's University School of Law (J.D., cum laude, 1994). Eta Kappa Nu. *Member:* State Bar of Texas; San Francisco Intellectual Property Law Association; Peninsula Intellectual Property Law Association. *Email:* tmavrakakis@awd.com

**EMILY A. EVANS,** born New York, N.Y., September 4, 1960; admitted to bar, 1992, New York; 1993, California. *Education:* Barnard College (A.B., in Biology, 1979); Columbia University School of Engineering & Applied Science (B.S.Ch.E., 1980); The Rockefeller University (Ph.D., in Cell Biology, 1986); Fordham University (J.D., cum laude, 1991). Staff Member, Fordham Law Review, 1990-1991. *Member:* Bar Association of San Francisco; Peninsula Intellectual Property Law Association. *Email:* eevans@awd.com

**ERICA D. WILSON,** born San Diego, California, February 12, 1962; admitted to bar, 1992, California; not registered to practice before U.S. Patent and Trademark Office. *Education:* University of California at San Diego (B.S.C.E., 1983); Hastings College of the Law, University of California at San Francisco (J.D., magna cum laude, 1992). Order of the Coif. *Email:* ewilson@awd.com

**KAREN J. KRAMER,** born Bronx, New York, January 8, 1964; admitted to bar, 1989, New York (Not admitted in California). *Education:* Duke University (A.B., 1985); Washington University School of Law (J.D., 1988). Member, 1986-1987, Notes and Comments Editor, 1987, Washington University Law Quarterly. Judicial Extern to the Honorable Joseph J. Simeone, Missouri Court of Appeals, St. Louis, 1987. *Email:* kkramer@awd.com

**JOHN R. MOORE,** born Cleveland, Ohio, May 18, 1964; admitted to bar, 1993, New York (Not admitted in California). *Education:* University of North Carolina at Chapel Hill (B.S. in Chemistry, 1986; J.D., with honors, 1992); University of Illinois at Champaign-Urbana (M.S. in Biochemistry, 1988). Order of the Coif. Staff Member, North Carolina Journal of International Law and Commercial Regulation, 1991-1992. *Email:* jmoore@awd.com

**CHUN-POK "ROGER" LEUNG,** born Hong Kong, December 10, 1961; admitted to bar, 1995, California; not registered to practice before U.S. Patent and Trademark Office. *Education:* University of Arkansas (B.S.M.E., 1982); George Institute of Technology (Ph.D., 1988); Boalt Hall School of Law, University of California, Berkeley (J.D., 1995). Tau Beta Pi; Pi Tau

*(This Listing Continued)*

Sigma. Member, Asian Law Journal, 1992-1995. Articles Editor, High Technology Law Journal, 1993-1994. Executive Editor, California Law Review, 1994-1995. *Member:* Orange County Bar Association. **LANGUAGES:** Cantonese Chinese, Mandarin Chinese. **Email:** rleung@awd.com

**DAVID WEST,** born Springfield, Illinois, December 27, 1959; admitted to bar, 1996, California; not registered to practice before U.S. Patent and Trademark Office. *Education:* San Jose University (B.A. in Biochemistry, 1993); Stanford Law School (J.D., 1996. **Email:** dwest@awd.com

**DANIEL T. SHVODIAN,** born Teaneck, New Jersey, November 27, 1965; admitted to bar, 1996, California; not registered to practice before U.S. Patent and Trademark Office. *Education:* Bucknell University (B.S.E.E., magna cum laude, 1987); University of Maryland (M.S.E.E., 1990); University of Virginia (J.D., 1996). Tau Beta Pi. Member, 1994-1996, Articles Review Board, 1995-1996, Virginia Journal of International Law. **Email:** dshvodian@awd.com

All Attorneys resident in the Palo Alto, California Office are Members of the American Bar Association, American Intellectual Property Law Association and The State Bar of California and are registered to practice before U.S. Patent and Trademark Office unless otherwise indicated.

(For a complete list of attorneys, see professional biographies at Houston, Texas)

---

## BERGESON, ELIOPOULOS, GRADY & GRAY

**MENLO PARK, CALIFORNIA**

(See San Jose)

*Intellectual Property, Antitrust and Construction.*

---

## JEFFERY L. BOYARSKY

**SUITE 200, 800 OAK GROVE AVENUE**
**MENLO PARK, CALIFORNIA 94025**
Telephone: 415-325-7000

*Criminal and Civil Trial Practice in all Courts. Misdemeanor and Felony, Criminal Appeals, Juvenile, Guardianship and Conservatorship Law.*

**JEFFERY L. BOYARSKY,** born Berkeley, California, March 24, 1947; admitted to bar, 1972, California. *Education:* University of California at Berkeley (A.B., 1968); University of San Francisco (J.D., 1971). Member, Moot Court Board. Instructor of Business Law: Golden Gate University, 1978-1979; College of San Mateo, 1980-1982. Superior Court Mental Health Hearings Officer, 1984—. *Member:* San Mateo County Bar Association (Member: Board of Directors, 1982-1983; Client Relations Committee, 1981-1987; Private Defender Committee, 1981-1982; Conference of Delegates to State Bar Convention, 1988); State Bar of California (Member, State Bar Standing Committee on Fee Arbitration, 1985-1988); California Public Defenders Association.

---

## BURNS, DOANE, SWECKER & MATHIS, L.L.P.

**BUILDING 4, SUITE 160**
**3000 SAND HILL ROAD**
**MENLO PARK, CALIFORNIA 94025**
Telephone: 415-854-7400
Facsimile: 415-854-8275
Email: burnsdoane.com

*Alexandria, Virginia Office:* Suite 100, 699 Prince Street, 22314, P.O. Box 1404, 22313. Telephone: 703-836-6620. Facsimile: 703-836-2021; 836-7356; 836-3503; Group 4: 703-836-0028.

*Research Triangle Park, North Carolina Office:* P.O. Box 14846, Research Triangle Park, 27709-4846, 1009 Slatter Road, Suite 210, Durham, 27703. Telephone: 919-941-9240. Facsimile: 919-941-1515.

*Patent, Trademark, Copyright, Trade, Unfair Competition and Related, Antitrust Law. Litigation. Practice before State and Federal Courts and U.S. International and Administrative Agencies.*

**RALPH L. FREELAND, JR.,** born Lovell, Oklahoma, December 17, 1917; admitted to bar, 1947, District of Columbia; 1948, California; registered to practice before U.S. Patent and Trademark Office. *Education:* Stanford University (B.A., 1939; M.E., 1941); Stanford University and George Washington University (J.D., 1947). *Member:* State Bar of California (Chairman, Conference on Patent, Trademark & Copyright Law, 1974); District of Columbia Bar; American Bar Association; American Intellectual Property Law Association; San Francisco Patent and Trademark Law Association (SFIPLA) (President, 1969-1970). **Email:** ralphf@burnsdoane.com

**JAMES W. PETERSON,** born Washington, D.C., March 30, 1944; admitted to bar, 1972, Maryland; 1973-1982, U.S. Court of Customs and Patent Appeals; 1974, Delaware; 1976, U.S. Supreme Court; 1981, California; 1984, U.S. Court of Appeals for the Federal Circuit; registered to practice before U.S. Patent and Trademark Office. *Education:* University of Maryland (B.S.M.E., 1966); Catholic University of America (J.D., 1972). *Member:* Palo Alto, San Mateo County and American (Member, Patent, Trademark and Copyright Section) Bar Associations; Licensing Executive Society; American Intellectual Property Law Association; San Francisco Patent and Trademark Law Association; Peninsula Patent Law Association. **Email:** jamesp@burnsdoane.com

**ROBERT E. KREBS,** born Saginaw, Michigan, July 25, 1943; admitted to bar, 1969, Colorado; 1971, Utah; 1973, California; registered to practice before U.S. Patent and Trademark Office. *Education:* University of Colorado at Boulder (B.S., 1966; J.D., 1969); University of California at Berkeley (M.B.A., 1976); California State University at San Jose (M.S., 1981). Pi Tau Sigma. Lecturer, Legal and Political Environment of Business: San Francisco State University, 1982-1983; University of Utah, 1983-1984; California State University at San Jose, 1985; University of Santa Clara, 1989. Member, Panel of Arbitrators, American Arbitration Association. *Member:* State Bar of California (Member, Intellectual Property Section); San Francisco Patent and Trademark Law Association. (Also Of Counsel, Pezzola & Reinke, A Professional Corporation). **Email:** robertk@burnsdoane.com

**T. GENE DILLAHUNTY,** born Granite, Oklahoma, October 2, 1942; admitted to bar, 1969, Virginia; 1970-1982, U.S. Court of Customs and Patent Appeals; 1975, Ohio; 1971, Canadian Patent Office; 1977, U.S. Supreme Court; 1982, U.S. Court of Appeals for the Federal Circuit; registered to practice before U.S. Patent and Trademark Office (Not admitted in California). *Education:* Oklahoma State University (B.S.Ch.E., 1965); George Washington University (J.D., 1969). Lecturer, Patent Law for Scientists and Engineers, The Center for Professional Advancement, 1980-1996. *Member:* Virginia State Bar; American Bar Association; American Intellectual Property Law Association; Peninsula Patent Law Association; San Francisco Intellectual Property Law Association; Licensing Executive Society. **Email:** gened@burnsdoane.com

**WILLIAM H. BENZ,** born September 15, 1942; admitted to bar, 1971, California; registered to practice before U.S. Patent and Trademark Office. *Education:* Allegheny College (B.S. in Chemistry, 1964); Case-Western Reserve University (M.S. in Physical Chemistry, 1966); University of San Francisco (J.D., 1971). Phi Delta Phi. *Member:* State Bar of California; American Bar Association; Peninsula Patent Law Association (President, 1989); San Francisco Patent and Trademark Law Association (President, 1986). **Email:** billb@burnsdoane.com

**GERALD F. SWISS,** born Franklin, New Jersey, September 6, 1953; admitted to bar, 1981, California, U.S. District Court, Northern District of California and U.S. Court of Appeals, Ninth Circuit; 1983, New Jersey; registered to practice before U.S. Patent and Trademark Office. *Education:* University of Notre Dame (B.S., cum laude, 1975); University of Chicago (M.S., 1976); Seton Hall University (J.D., cum laude, 1981). *Member:* State Bar of California; New Jersey State and American Bar Associations; American Intellectual Property Law Association; San Francisco Intellectual Property Law Association; Peninsula Intellectual Property Law Association. **Email:** geralds@burnsdoane.com

### ASSOCIATES

**MICHAEL J. URE,** born Salt Lake City, Utah, November 11, 1960; admitted to bar, 1990, Virginia and U.S. Court of Appeals, Fourth Circuit; 1993, California; registered to practice before U.S. Patent and Trademark Office. *Education:* Brigham Young University (B.S.E.E., 1985); George Mason University School of Law (J.D., 1990). *Member:* Virginia State Bar; State Bar of California. **LANGUAGES:** Mandarin Chinese. **Email:** mikeu@burnsdoane.com

**LESLIE A. MOOI,** born Weston, Ontario, Canada, May 4, 1959; admitted to bar, 1990, Ontario; 1992, California; registered to practice before U.S. Patent and Trademark Office. *Education:* University of Toronto (B.Sc., 1982; M.Sc., 1985; LL.B., 1988). *Member:* State Bar of California; Ameri-

*(This Listing Continued)*

## BURNS, DOANE, SWECKER & MATHIS, L.L.P., Menlo Park—Continued

can Bar Association; San Francisco Intellectual Property Law Association; Law Society of Upper Canada; Patent and Trademark Institute of Canada. *Email:* lesliem@burnsdoane.com

**EARL A. BRIGHT II,** born Gastonia, North Carolina, September 16, 1965; admitted to bar, 1993, California; registered to practice before U.S. Patent and Trademark Office. *Education:* University of Oklahoma (B.S.M.E., 1987); University of Oklahoma College of Law (J.D., with distinction, 1993). Pi Tau Sigma; Phi Delta Phi. Order of Barristers. Member, Philip C. Jessup International Law Moot Court Team. Member, American Indian Law Review. Member, American Society of Mechanical Engineers, 1986—. *Member:* Federal Circuit and American Bar Associations; State Bar of California; American Intellectual Property Law Association; San Francisco Intellectual Property Law Association; Peninsula Intellectual Property Law Association. *Email:* earlb@burnsdoane.com

**CHARLES H. JEW,** born Hong Kong, August 18, 1956; admitted to bar, 1985, California; registered to practice before U.S. Patent and Trademark Office. *Education:* Columbia University (B.A., Chemistry, 1978; B.S.Ch.E., 1980; M.S.Ch.E., 1982); New York University (J.D., 1985). Author: "Nuclear Energy," *Annual Survey of American Law* Issue 4 (1984) NY University. *Member:* State Bar of California; American Chemical Society; San Francisco Intellectual Property Law Association; Peninsula Intellectual Property Law Association. *Email:* charlesj@burnsdoane.com

**LESLIE J. BOLEY,** born North Kansas City, Missouri, December 3, 1967; admitted to bar, 1996, California. *Education:* University of California at Berkeley (B.A., 1990); Chicago-Kent College of Law, IIT (J.D., 1995). Phi Alpha Delta. *Member:* State Bar of California; American Intellectual Property Law Association.

### LEGAL SUPPORT PERSONNEL

**SUSAN E. HEMINGER,** born Berwyn, Illinois, August 8, 1958; registered to practice before U.S. Patent and Trademark Office. *Education:* University of Illinois (B.S.E.E., 1981). *Email:* sueh@burnsdoane.com

(For complete biographical data on all personnel, see Professional Biographies at Alexandria, Virginia)

## CLAPP, MORONEY, BELLAGAMBA, DAVIS AND VUCINICH

*4400 BOHANNON DRIVE, SUITE 100*
**MENLO PARK, CALIFORNIA 94025**
Telephone: 415-327-1300
Fax: 415-327-3707

*Pleasanton, California Office:* 6140 Stoneridge Mall Road, Suite 545. Telephone: 510-734-0990. Fax: 510-734-0888.

*San Francisco, California Office:* One Sansome Street, Suite 1900. Telephone: 415-398-6045. Fax: 415-327-3707.

*General Insurance Law and Civil Trial Practice. Casualty Insurance (Automobile and Fire), Aviation, Professional Liability, Medical and Legal Malpractice Law. Real Estate and Insurance Liability (Agent Errors and Omissions), Construction Litigation, Environmental and Toxic Tort, Products Liability Law, Employment Discrimination, Wrongful Termination, Discrimination Law (Sex and Housing) Insurance Coverage, Declaratory Relief and Bad Faith Litigation.*

### MEMBERS OF FIRM

**DUANE E. CLAPP, JR.,** born New York, N.Y., October 28, 1943; admitted to bar, 1969, California. *Education:* Stanford University (A.B., 1965); Hastings College of Law, University of California (J.D., 1968). Member, Faculty, Hastings Civil College of Advocacy, 1982-1983. Direct-Elect, Defense Counsel Trial Academy, 1988-1989. *Member:* Santa Clara and San Mateo County and American (Member, Committee on Insurance, Negligence and Compensation Law, 1979-1980) Bar Associations; The State Bar of California; Association of Defense Counsel; International Association of Insurance Counsel; Defense Research and Trial Lawyers Association.

**CARL J. MORONEY,** born San Mateo, California, June 10, 1942; admitted to bar, 1968, California. *Education:* University of Notre Dame (B.A., 1964); University of San Francisco School of Law (J.D., 1967). *Member:* San Mateo County, Santa Clara County and American Bar Associations; State Bar of California; Association of Defense Counsel; International

*(This Listing Continued)*

Association of Insurance Counsel; Defense Research and Trial Lawyers Association. [Capt., U.S. Marine Corps, 1967-1971]

**ROBERT A. BELLAGAMBA,** born San Francisco, California, June 24, 1947; admitted to bar, 1973, California. *Education:* University of California at Davis (B.A., 1969); University of San Francisco (J.D., 1973). Member: McAuliffe Law Honor Society; Faculty, Hastings Civil College of Advocacy, 1982. *Member:* San Mateo County, Santa Clara County and American Bar Associations; State Bar of California; Association of Defense Counsel (Member, Board of Directors, 1989-1990); Defense Research and Trial Lawyers Association; International Association of Insurance Counsel.

**TIMOTHY C. DAVIS,** born Altoona, Pennsylvania, January 18, 1946; admitted to bar, 1974, California. *Education:* University of Virginia (B.A., 1968; J.D., 1974). *Member:* Santa Clara County, San Mateo County and American Bar Associations; State Bar of California; Association of Defense Counsel; Defense Research and Trial Lawyers Association. [1st Lt., U.S. Army, 1968-1971]

**JEFFREY M. VUCINICH,** born San Francisco, California, August 22, 1950; admitted to bar, 1975, California. *Education:* Stanford University (B.S., cum laude, 1972); University of San Francisco (J.D., 1975). *Member:* Santa Clara County, San Mateo County and American Bar Associations; State Bar of California; Association of Defense Counsel; Defense Research and Trial Lawyers Association.

**CHRISTOPHER W. WOOD,** born Philadelphia, Pennsylvania, April 17, 1952; admitted to bar, 1979, New Hampshire; 1984, California. *Education:* University of Pennsylvania (B.A., cum laude, 1975); Franklin Pierce Law Center (J.D., 1978). Representative to New Hampshire House of Representatives, 1980-1982. *Member:* Santa Clara County, San Mateo County and New Hampshire Bar Associations; State Bar of California.

**GREGORY J. SEBASTINELLI,** born San Francisco, California, August 31, 1957; admitted to bar, 1982, California. *Education:* University of San Francisco (B.S., 1979; J.D., 1982). Phi Alpha Delta. *Member:* Bar Association of San Francisco; Alameda County, San Mateo County and American Bar Associations; The State Bar of California.

**MARK O'CONNOR,** born Syracuse, New York, October 18, 1960; admitted to bar, 1986, California. *Education:* Marquette University (B.A., 1982); Santa Clara University (J.D., 1986). Phi Alpha Theta. Winner, Moot Court Competition in Insurance Bad Faith. *Member:* Santa Clara and San Mateo County Bar Associations; State Bar of California.

**P. CHRISTIAN SCHELEY,** born San Francisco, California, June 14, 1961; admitted to bar, 1986, California. *Education:* University of California at Berkeley (B.A., with high honors, 1983); McGeorge School of Law, University of the Pacific (J.D., 1986). Order of the Coif. Traynor Honor Society. Staff Member, Pacific Law Journal, 1984-1985. *Member:* San Mateo County and American Bar Associations; State Bar of California.

**DONALD L. SULLIVAN,** born San Francisco, California, June 27, 1961; admitted to bar, 1987, California. *Education:* University of California at San Diego (B.A., 1984); Santa Clara University (J.D., 1987).

**GREGORY C. SIMONIAN,** born Fresno, California, October 11, 1959; admitted to bar, 1987, California. *Education:* California State University at Fresno (B.S., 1982); Santa Clara University (J.D., 1985).

**JANE A. CORNING,** born Chicago, Illinois, November 27, 1956; admitted to bar, 1982, California. *Education:* University of the Pacific (B.A., with honors, 1979); Institute of European Studies, Vienna, Austria; McGeorge School of Law, University of the Pacific (J.D., 1982).

### ASSOCIATES

| | |
|---|---|
| Seth E. Watkins | Norman C. Escover |
| Timothy L. Yoshida | Steven M. Cvitanovic |
| Terilynn T. Perez | James S. Thielmann |
| Bruce N. Furukawa | Julie E. Bonnel |
| Andrew R. Pollack | Mary Kaela Kozlovsky |
| L. Theodore Scheley, III | Dawson G. Crawford |
| Marc H. Baer | Jessica L. Grant |
| Tracy C. Neistadt | Robert Shatzko |
| Merrilee Hague | Mark L. Weaver |
| Robert L. Rosenthal | Paul V. Lankford |
| Carol J. Stair | Daniela Davidian |
| Patricia Anna Kantor | Matthew A. Schenone |

REPRESENTATIVE CLIENTS: Central Mutual Insurance Co.; CIGNA; California Casualty Indemnity Exchange; Farmers Insurance Group; American States Insurance Co.; Interstate National Corp.; State Farm Mutual Automobile Insurance Co.; The Travelers Insurance Co.; Continental National American Group; Kemper Group; Insurance Company of the West; Crawford & Co.; Albertsons,

*(This Listing Continued)*

Inc.; American Hardware Mutual; Chubb Group; Grain Dealers Mutual; Republic Claims Services; U-Haul International; Underwriters Adjusting Co.; Argonaut Ins., Co.; Firemens Fund Insurance Co.; State Farm Fire & Casualty Co.; Wausau Ins. Co.; Black & Bland Ins. Adj.; Allianz Insurance Co.; American Star Insurance Co.; Grange Insurance; Gulf Insurance Group; Hartford Insurance Group; Industrial Indemnity; Liberty Mutual Insurance; Orion Group; Residence Mutual; Truck Insurance Exchange; Universal Underwriters Insurance Co.; Western Mutual Insurance Co.; Walgreens.

## CODDINGTON, HICKS & DANFORTH

### A PROFESSIONAL CORPORATION

### MENLO PARK, CALIFORNIA

(See Redwood City)

*Insurance, Aviation, Business, Tort and Products Liability Law. General Civil and Trial Practice in all State and Federal Courts.*

## GEORGE S. COLE

*Established in 1982*

### 793 NASH AVENUE
### MENLO PARK, CALIFORNIA 94025

Telephone: 415-322-7760
Fax: 415-322-6117
Email: gscdlawyer@aol.com

*Computer Law and Intellectual Property.*

**FIRM PROFILE:** *Providing legal assistance sensitive to business concerns for expanding software and computer technology businesses.*

**GEORGE S. COLE,** born 1955; admitted to bar, 1981, California. *Education:* Stanford University (A.B., with Honors and Distinction); University of Michigan (J.D. cum laude, 1981); Stanford University (M.S., C.S., 1987). Teaching Fellow, Computer-related Courses, Stanford University. Consultant, Apple Computer and Xerox PARC. Arbitrator, American Arbitration Association. *Member:* State Bar of California. **PRACTICE AREAS:** Computer Law; Intellectual Property.

## COOLEY GODWARD LLP

### 3000 SAND HILL ROAD, BUILDING 3, SUITE 230
### MENLO PARK, CALIFORNIA 94025

Telephone: 415-843-5000
Telex: 380816 COOLEY PA
Fax: 415-854-2691
Email: webmaster@cooley.com
URL: http://www.cooley.com

*San Francisco, California Office:* 20th Floor, One Maritime Plaza. Telephone: 415-693-2000. Telex: 380815 COOLEY SFO Fax: 415-951-3698 or 415-951-3699.
*Palo Alto, California Office:* Five Palo Alto Square, 3000 El Camino Real. Telephone: 415-843-5000. Telex: 380816 COOLEY PA Fax: 415-857-0663.
*San Diego, California Office:* 4365 Executive Drive, Suite 1100. Telephone: 619-550-6000. Fax: 619-453-3555.
*Boulder, Colorado Office:* 2595 Canyon Boulevard, Suite 250. Telephone: 303-546-4000. Fax: 303-546-4099.
*Denver, Colorado Office:* One Tabor Center, 1200 17th Street, Suite 2100. Telephone: 303-606-4800. Fax: 303-606-4899.

*General Practice.*

**FIRM PROFILE:** Cooley Godward LLP's practice emphasizes the representation of entrepreneurial growth companies - often in high technology fields - and venture capital investors in those companies. The firm provides the full range of legal services including securities law, patent, copyright, licensing and other intellectual property expertise, assistance with mergers, acquisitions and corporate partnering transactions, finance, litigation, tax, real estate, employment and other specialties.

### MEMBERS OF FIRM

**CRAIG E. DAUCHY,** born San Diego, California, March 3, 1949; admitted to bar, 1975, California. *Education:* Yale University (B.A., magna cum laude, 1971); Stanford University (M.B.A., 1975; J.D., 1975). Order of the Coif. **PRACTICE AREAS:** Venture Capital Law; Emerging Company Law. *Email:* DAUCHYCE@COOLEY.COM

*(This Listing Continued)*

**ERIC C. JENSEN,** born Denver, Colorado, June 6, 1962; admitted to bar, 1988, California; 1989, Colorado. *Education:* Stanford University (A.B., with distinction and honors, 1984); University of California at Los Angeles (J.D., 1988). Order of the Coif. Editor, UCLA Law Review, 1987-1988. **PRACTICE AREAS:** Corporate and Securities Law; Venture Capital Law. *Email:* JENSENEC@COOLEY.COM

**DAVID R. LEE,** born Hartford, Connecticut, March 31, 1957; admitted to bar, 1987, California. *Education:* University of California at Berkeley (A.B., with highest honors, 1980); Georgetown University (J.D., 1986). Phi Beta Kappa. **PRACTICE AREAS:** Emerging Growth Companies; Corporate Law; Computer Law. *Email:* LEEDR@COOLEY.COM

**MARK P. TANOURY,** born Zanesville, Ohio, November 18, 1954; admitted to bar, 1982, California. *Education:* Ohio State University (B.S., summa cum laude, 1977); University of California at Berkeley (M.B.A., 1978); University of Michigan (J.D., magna cum laude, 1982). Order of the Coif. Member, University of Michigan Law Review, 1980-1982. Certified Public Accountant, Ohio, 1980. **PRACTICE AREAS:** Corporate Law; Partnerships; Venture Capital Law. *Email:* TANOURYMP@COOLEY.COM

### SPECIAL COUNSEL

**JOHN E. CUMMERFORD,** born Queens, New York, June 21, 1958; admitted to bar, 1984, New York; 1992, California. *Education:* Arizona State University (B.A., 1980); Universidad de Sonora; Columbia University (J.D., 1983). Attorney: IBM Corp., 1983-1992; Integrated Systems Solutions Corp., 1992-1993. *Member:* The Association of the Bar of the City of New York (Member, Computer Law Committee 1990-1991); Computer Law Association. **LANGUAGES:** Spanish. **PRACTICE AREAS:** Technology Law; Corporate. *Email:* CUMMERFORDJE@COOLEY.COM

### ASSOCIATES

**STEPHANIE A. ANAGNOSTOU,** born Burlingame, California, July 8, 1967; admitted to bar, 1994, California. *Education:* University of California at Los Angeles (B.A., 1989); University of San Francisco (J.D., cum laude, 1994). Recipient, American Jurisprudence Award. **PRACTICE AREAS:** Corporate and Securities; Mergers and Acquisitions; Emerging Growth Companies; Venture Capital. *Email:* ANAGNOSTOUSA@COOLEY.COM

**JOHN A. DADO,** born Santa Rosa, California, August 20, 1962; admitted to bar, 1990, California. *Education:* University of California at Berkeley (B.S., 1984); University of California at Los Angeles (J.D., 1990). Order of the Coif. Law Clerk to Judge John G. Davies, U.S. District Court, Los Angeles, 1990-1991. **PRACTICE AREAS:** Venture Capital; Emerging Companies. *Email:* DADOJA@COOLEY.COM

**CATHERINE A. DRING,** born San Diego, California, May 14, 1963; admitted to bar, 1991, California. *Education:* University of California at San Diego (B.S., 1986); University of Southern California (J.D., 1991). **PRACTICE AREAS:** Corporate Law; Emerging Companies. *Email:* DRINGCA@COOLEY.COM

**LAWRENCE J. FASSLER,** born Alexandra, Virginia, March 8, 1960; admitted to bar, 1991, New York; 1996, California. *Education:* University of California, Berkeley (B.S., 1981); Columbia Law School (J.D., 1991); Columbia Graduate School of Business (M.B.A., 1991). Articles Editor, Journal of Transnational Law. Author, "The Italian Penal Procedure Code: An Adversarial System of Criminal Procedure in Continental Europe," 29 Columbia Journal of Transnational Law 245, 1991. **LANGUAGES:** Italian, French. **PRACTICE AREAS:** Corporate; Mergers and Acquisitions; Securities; Partnerships; Licensing. *Email:* FASSLERLJ@COOLEY.COM

**MATTHEW P. FISHER,** born Providence, Rhode Island, December 12, 1962; admitted to bar, 1990, New York (Not admitted in California). *Education:* Yale University (B.A., 1985); Georgetown University (J.D., 1989). **PRACTICE AREAS:** Mergers and Acquisitions; Leveraged Buyouts; Venture Capital. *Email:* FISHERMP@COOLEY.COM

**JAMES F. FULTON, JR.,** born Queens, New York, November 21, 1966; admitted to bar, 1995, California. *Education:* Georgetown University (B.S.F.S., cum laude, 1989; J.D., cum laude, 1995). Member, Walter Chandler AIC, 1993-1994. *Member:* American Bar Association. **PRACTICE AREAS:** General Corporate; Venture Capital; Securities Regulation. *Email:* FULTONJF@COOLEY.COM

**VINCENT P. PANGRAZIO,** born Orange, California, July 15, 1963; admitted to bar, 1993, California. *Education:* Loyola Marymount University (B.S.E.E., 1985); Loyola University of Los Angeles (J.D., 1993). Tau Beta Pi; Alpha Sigma Nu; Order of the Coif. Staff Member, 1991-1992 and

*(This Listing Continued)*

CALIFORNIA—MENLO PARK — MARTINDALE-HUBBELL LAW DIRECTORY 1997

**COOLEY GODWARD LLP,** Menlo Park—Continued

Articles Editor, 1992-1993, Loyola of Los Angeles Law Review. Professional Electrical Engineer, California, 1989. *PRACTICE AREAS:* Securities; Emerging Growth Companies; Licensing. *Email:* PANGRAZIOVP@COOLEY.COM

**ERIKA F. ROTTENBERG,** born Smithtown, New York, June 26, 1962; admitted to bar, 1992, California. *Education:* State University of New York at Genesco (B.S., 1984); Boalt Hall School of Law, University of California, Berkeley (J.D., 1992). Author, "The Americans with Disabilities Act: Erosion of Collective Rights?" Industrial Relations Law Journal, 1993. *PRACTICE AREAS:* Employer-Employee Relations; Labor Law. *Email:* ROTTENBERGEF@COOLEY.COM

**MARK G. SENEKER,** born Washington, District of Columbia, November 30, 1968; admitted to bar, 1994, California. *Education:* Cornell University (B.A., 1991); University of California at Los Angeles (J.D., 1994). *PRACTICE AREAS:* Venture Capital; Emerging Companies; Corporate Law. *Email:* SENEKERMG@COOLEY.COM

### LEGAL SUPPORT PERSONNEL
### ADMINISTRATOR

**SUSAN Y. CHEN-WONG.** *Education:* University of California, Berkeley (B.A., 1987). Instructor, St. Mary's Paralegal Studies Program, 1992-1993. Advisory Board Member, St. Mary's College and University of San Francisco Paralegal Studies Programs, 1991—. *Member:* San Francisco Association of Legal Assistants (President, 1991-1992); Legal Assistant Management Association; Association of Legal Administrators. *LANGUAGES:* Mandarin. *PRACTICE AREAS:* Recruitment and Hiring; Evaluation; Training; Budgeting; Workflow Coordination. *Email:* CHENWONGSY@COOLEY.COM

### SENIOR LEGAL ASSISTANTS

**BOBBI MILLIKEN,** *Member:* San Francisco Association of Legal Assistants. *PRACTICE AREAS:* Securities; Corporate Law; Venture Capital. *Email:* MILLIKENB@COOLEY.COM

(For Complete Biographical Data on Personnel at San Francisco, Palo Alto and San Diego, California and Boulder, Colorado, see Professional Biographies at those locations).

---

## CURTIS & DASCHBACH
**MENLO PARK, CALIFORNIA**

(See Thoits, Love, Hershberger & McLean, Palo Alto, California)

---

## DYER & WHITE
**SUITE 200, 800 OAK GROVE AVENUE**
**MENLO PARK, CALIFORNIA 94025**
Telephone: 415-325-7000
Fax: 415-325-3116

Civil and Trial Practice. Personal Injury, Products Liability, Professional Negligence, Labor and Employment Law, Securities, Trade Secret and Corporate Litigation.

### MEMBERS OF FIRM

**CHARLES A. DYER,** born Blairstown, Missouri, August 29, 1940; admitted to bar, 1971, California. *Education:* University of Missouri (B.J., 1962); Hastings College of the Law, University of California (J.D., 1970). State Bar Court Referee, 1982—. Judge Pro Tem: San Mateo County Superior Court; Santa Clara County Superior Court; San Mateo County Municipal Court. Member, Panel of Arbitrators, American Arbitration Association. *Member:* Palo Alto, Santa Clara County, San Mateo County and American Bar Associations; The State Bar of California; Consumer Attorneys of San Mateo County (Member, Board of Directors, 1978; Secretary, 1979; President, 1980); Consumer Attorneys of California (Member, Board of Governors, 1979-1981; Vice President, 1982); The Association of Trial Lawyers of America (State Committeeman, 1982); American Board of Trial Advocates; National Board of Trial Advocacy; Trial Lawyers for Public Justice (Founder); San Mateo County Legal Aid Society (Member, Board

*(This Listing Continued)*

CAA1326B

---

of Directors, 1992-1994); Association of Attorney-Mediators. [Capt., U.S.N.R., active duty, 1963-1967; U.S.N.R., 1967-1993]

**RAND N. WHITE,** born Oakland, California, March 1, 1950; admitted to bar, 1976, California. *Education:* Stanford University (B.A., with distinction, 1972; LL.B., 1976). Member, Stanford Law Review, 1974-1976. Co-Author: "The Preliminary Hearing in California; Adaptive Procedures in a Plea Bargain System of Criminal Justice," Vol. 28, No. 6, appearing July, 1976. President, San Mateo County Legal Aid Society, 1986, 1987. Member, Trial Court Delay Reduction Consortium. Judge Pro Tem, 1985—, and Arbitrator, 1984—, San Mateo County and Santa Clara County Superior and Municipal Courts. *Member:* Palo Alto, Santa Clara, San Mateo County (Delegate, State Bar Convention, 1982, 1985; Delegation Chair, 1988, 1989) and American Bar Associations; The State Bar of California (San Mateo County Representative, Trial Court Delay Reduction Consortium, 1989—); San Mateo County Trial Lawyers Association (Member, Board of Directors, 1984—; Secretary, 1988; Vice-President, 1990; President, 1991); Consumer Attorneys of California; The Association of Trial Lawyers of America.

---

## BORIS E. EFRON
*A PROFESSIONAL CORPORATION*
**3351 EL CAMINO REAL, SUITE 200 (ATHERTON)**
**MENLO PARK, CALIFORNIA 94027**
Telephone: 415-369-1900
Telecopier: 415-363-1117

*General Civil and Trial Practice in State and Federal Courts. Personal Injury, Insurance, Business Litigation and Construction Law.*

**BORIS E. EFRON,** born Lvov, Russia, October 27, 1948; admitted to bar, 1978, California and U.S. District Court, Northern District of California; 1982, U.S. District Court, Southern District of California. *Education:* Oregon State University (B.S., 1972); California Western School of Law (J.D., 1977). Phi Delta Phi. Vice President, Litigation, Western Temporary Services, Inc., 1979-1986. *Member:* Bar Association of San Francisco; San Mateo County Bar Association; State Bar of California; Consumer Attorneys of California; The Association of Trial Lawyers of America; Commercial Law League of America. *PRACTICE AREAS:* Personal Injury Law; Insurance Law; Business Law.

---

**KAREN M. PLATT,** born Brooklyn, New York, March 25, 1951; admitted to bar, 1984, Wisconsin; 1985, California. *Education:* University of Maryland (B.A., with high honors, 1972; M.A., 1974); University of Wisconsin (J.D., 1984). Phi Beta Kappa; Phi Kappa Phi. *Member:* Santa Clara County Bar Association; State Bar of California; State Bar of Wisconsin. *PRACTICE AREAS:* Personal Injury Law; Insurance Law; Real Estate Law.

**YANI D. SAKEL,** born Phoenixville, Pennsylvania, July 4, 1955; admitted to bar, 1989, California and U.S. District Court, Northern District of California. *Education:* San Jose City College (A.A., 1978); San Jose State University (B.A., 1980); University of Santa Clara (J.D., 1987). *Member:* Santa Clara County Bar Association (Barristers Board Member, 1989—); State Bar of California; Consumer Attorneys of California; The Association of Trial Lawyers of America. *LANGUAGES:* Greek. *PRACTICE AREAS:* Personal Injury Law; Insurance Law; Product Liability Law.

Languages: Russian, Greek and Korean.

REPRESENTATIVE CLIENTS: Dal Industries; Westcorp; Western Temporary Services, Inc.; The Travel Co.; Guzik Technical.

---

## ENTERPRISE LAW GROUP, INC.
**MENLO OAKS CORPORATE CENTER**
**4400 BOHANNON DRIVE, SUITE 280**
**MENLO PARK, CALIFORNIA 94025-1041**
Telephone: 415-462-4700
Facsimile: 415-462-4747
Email: info@enterpriselaw.com

*Business Transactional, Intellectual Property and Business Litigation, Practice Representing Domestic Technology Clients and Technology and Other Clients Headquartered Outside of the U.S.*

*(This Listing Continued)*

## PROFESSIONAL BIOGRAPHIES

*FIRM PROFILE: Enterprise Law Group, Inc. advises domestic and foreign entities in all primary areas of business law. Our clients range from start-ups and emerging growth companies to well-established publicly held companies, as well as their investors, founders and executives. Our clients' businesses reflect the entire spectrum of commerce in Silicon Valley: semiconductors, computer systems, computer hardware and software, telecommunications, biomedical technologies and products and venture capital, as well as other non-technology businesses.*

**WAYLAND M. BRILL,** born Ross, California, January 20, 1948; admitted to bar, 1977, California. *Education:* Stanford University (B.A., 1972); Hastings College of the Law, University of California (J.D., 1976). Member, The Executive Committee (TEC), an International Organization of CEO's. Past Co-Chair, International Committee: Silicon Valley Chapter, American Electronics Association. Past Trustee, San Jose Museum of Art. Past Chairman, San Jose Bank Attorneys Association. *Member:* Bar Association of San Francisco; Santa Clara County and American Bar Associations; State Bar of California. *PRACTICE AREAS:* General Business Law; Securities Law; International Transactions; Joint Ventures; Mergers and Acquisitions; Intellectual Property; Start-Ups.

**NELSON D. CRANDALL,** born Auburn, California, August 8, 1954; admitted to bar, 1979, California. *Education:* University of California at Irvine and University of California at Berkeley (A.B., with high honors, 1976); University of California at Davis (J.D., 1979). Phi Beta Kappa; Phi Delta Phi. Member, 1977-1978 and Articles Editor, 1978-1979, U.C. Davis Law Review. Co-Chair, Moot Court Board, 1978-1979. Reporter, "Report on Legal Opinions Concerning California Partnerships," Partnerships and Unincorporated Business Organizations Committee, Business Law Section, State Bar of California (to be published). Author: "Handling a Shareholder Buy-Out Involving a Closely Held California Corporation," 8 California Business Law Practitioner 1 (1993) and 8 California Business Law Practitioner (1969-1993); "Corporate Share Repurchases: Dealing With the Corporations Code Insolvency Tests," 6 California Business Law Practitioner 238 (1991); "Demystifying Partnership Allocations," 4 California Business Law Practitioner 1 (1989). Co-author: "Partnership Tax Issues," in Harroch, *Partnership and Joint Venture Agreements* (Law Journal Seminars Press, 1992). Contributor, "Guide to Organizing and Operating a Limited Liability Company in California," State Bar of California Business Law Section, Partnerships and Unincorporated Business Organizations Committee. Extern to Hon. Wiley W. Manuel, Associate Justice, California Supreme Court, Summer, 1978. Board of Directors, American Red Cross Santa Clara Valley Chapter, 1985-1992; American Red Cross Blood Services Central California Region, 1992-1994. Board of Trustees, Junior Statesmen Foundation, 1985—. Member, Rotary Club of San Jose, 1987-1994. Board of Directors, Hope Rehabilitation Services, 1985-1988. *Member:* Santa Clara County and American Bar Associations; State Bar of California (Member: Business Law Section; Partnerships and Unincorporated Business Organizations Committee). *PRACTICE AREAS:* Corporate Law; Partnership Law; Limited Liability Companies; Securities Law; Business Law; Technology Transfers; Financial Transactions.

**SHERWOOD M. SULLIVAN,** born Detroit, Michigan, February 16, 1932; admitted to bar, 1961, California; 1975, U.S. Supreme Court. *Education:* University of Texas at Austin (B.B.A., with honors, 1958; J.D., with honors, 1960). Order of the Coif; Phi Delta Phi; Beta Gamma Sigma; Phi Eta Sigma. Associate Editor, Texas Law Review, 1959-1960. Associate Professor of Law, University of Nebraska Law College, 1964-1967. President, The American Inns of Court, Santa Clara Inn, 1995-1996. *Member:* Bar Association of San Francisco; Santa Clara County and American (Member, Sections on: Antitrust Law, 1967—; Litigation, 1974—) Bar Associations; State Bar of California. *REPORTED CASES:* Shahvar v. Superior Court, 25 Cal. App. 4th 653, 30 Cal. Rptr. 2 597 (statements by attorney outside of court proceeding not privileged). *PRACTICE AREAS:* Litigation of Corporation and Shareholder and Partnership and Partner Relations; Commercial Litigation; Commercial Property Tax Litigation.

**WILLIAM B. WALKER,** born Knoxville, Tennessee, November 9, 1935; admitted to bar, 1964, Maryland; 1970, California. *Education:* University of Tennessee (B.SCh.E., 1958); Georgetown University (LL.B., 1964). Member, Association of University Technology Managers. *Member:* Maryland State and American Bar Association (Member, Intellectual Property Section); State Bar of California; Association of Intellectual Property Law; Licensing Executives Association; San Francisco Patent Law Association. *PRACTICE AREAS:* Patent Law; Trademark; Copyright; Unfair Competition; Licensing; Intellectual Property Law. *Email:* wwalker@enterpriselaw.com

*(This Listing Continued)*

### CALIFORNIA—MENLO PARK

*OF COUNSEL*

**WILLIAM D. SAUERS,** born Santa Cruz, California, June 18, 1926; admitted to bar, 1953, California. *Education:* Fresno State College (A.B., 1949); Stanford University (J.D., 1952). Phi Delta Phi. Director, 1968-1976, Advisory Director, 1976— and Chairman, 1973-1976, American Red Cross, Palo Alto Chapter. Director, 1969-1976 and Chairman, 1973-1976, Family Service Association. Secretary, Stanford-Mid Peninsula Urban Coalition, 1969-1972. Trustee, 1973-1990 and Chairman, 1984-1988, Menlo School and College. Director and President, San Jose Repertory Theatre, 1989-1991 and Director, Oregon Shakespeare Festival, 1989-1995. Chairman, The San Jose Shakespeare Festival, 1994—. *Member:* State Bar of California; American Bar Association (Member, Section of Taxation); National Association of College and University Attorneys. *LANGUAGES:* German. *PRACTICE AREAS:* Corporate Law; Business Law.

**THOMAS S. JORDAN, JR.,** born Panama City, Florida, September 3, 1933; admitted to bar, 1961, California; 1965, U.S. Tax Court; 1976, U.S. Supreme Court. *Education:* Princeton University (A.B., cum laude, 1955); Harvard University (J.D., 1960). Former General Counsel, American Land Conservancy, San Francisco, California. Member, Governor's Blue Ribbon Panel on a Unified Environmental Statute, 1994-1996. *Member:* State Bar of California (Member, Environmental Law Section). *PRACTICE AREAS:* Real Estate Law; Environmental Law.

**JOSEPH G. BECKFORD,** born Boston, Massachusetts, 1937; admitted to bar, 1962, District of Columbia; 1965, California. *Education:* Amherst College (B.A., 1959); Yale University (J.D., 1962); Harvard University (M.B.A., 1970). Author: *Bank Compliance Law,* Warren Gorham Lamont (1995); *Bank Holding Company Compliance Manual,* Matthew Bender (1986). *Member:* State Bar of California (Member: Business Law Section; Financial Institutions Committee, 1992-1995).

# ESSELSTEIN, WRIGHT, JONES & GREENBERG

*A PROFESSIONAL CORPORATION*

Established in 1963

750 MENLO AVENUE, SUITE 250
**MENLO PARK, CALIFORNIA 94025**
Telephone: 415-614-0160
Fax: 415-321-0198

*Estate Planning, Trust Administration and Probate, Family Law Mediation and Litigation, Local Government Law, Real Property and Business Law, General Trial Practice.*

**KINGSFORD F. JONES** (1941-1996).

**WILLIAM D. ESSELSTEIN,** born Palo Alto, California, November 2, 1938; admitted to bar, 1969, California. *Education:* Santa Clara University and United States Military Academy (B.S., 1961); Hastings College of Law, University of California (J.D., 1968). Judge Pro Tem, Superior Court, San Mateo County. Member, Judicial Arbitration Panels, U.S. District Court, Northern District of California and Superior and Municipal Courts, San Mateo County. Member, Board of Trustees, Los Lomitas School District, 1974-1979. Director, Legal Aid Society, San Mateo County, 1976-1981. *Member:* Palo Alto, Santa Clara County and American (Member, Urban, State and Local Government Law Sections) Bar Associations; San Mateo County Trial Lawyers Association (Director, 1982-1983). [Capt., U.S. Army, 1961-1965]. *PRACTICE AREAS:* Local Government; Commercial Law; Civil Litigation.

**TIMOTHY C. WRIGHT,** born San Bernardino, California, November 30, 1940; admitted to bar, 1970, California. *Education:* San Diego State College (B.A., 1963); California Western University (J.D., 1967). Judge Pro Tem, Superior Court, San Mateo County. Member, Judges and Attorney Resolution Service (J.A.R.S.) Member, Legal Aid Society of San Mateo County, Board of Directors, 1972-1983, and President, 1980-1982. *Member:* San Mateo County (Director, 1986-1989; President, 1990) and American (Member: Family Law Section; Litigation Section) Bar Associations. (Certified Specialist, Family Law, The State Bar of California Board of Legal Specialization). *PRACTICE AREAS:* Family Law; Civil Litigation.

**DIANE STEIN GREENBERG,** born New York, N.Y., 1947; admitted to bar, 1971, New York; 1972, District of Columbia; 1974, California; 1980, U.S. Supreme Court. *Education:* Bryn Mawr College; Barnard College (B.A., 1968); New York University (J.D., 1971). Assistant to the Under Secretary of the Interior, 1980-1981. Assistant Legislative Counsel, U.S.

*(This Listing Continued)*

**ESSELSTEIN, WRIGHT, JONES & GREENBERG,** A PROFESSIONAL CORPORATION, Menlo Park—*Continued*

Department of Interior, 1977-1980. Trustee, Trust for Hidden Villa. Member, Planned Giving Council, Packard Children's Hospital and Jewish Community Endowment Fund. *Member:* San Mateo (Chair, Employment Law Section, 1990) and Santa Clara County Bar Associations. **PRACTICE AREAS:** Estate Planning, Trust and Probate Law.

---

**SUSAN D. FLAX,** born Toledo, Ohio, July 4, 1946; admitted to bar, 1984, California and U.S. District Court, Northern District of California. *Education:* St. Mary's College, Notre Dame (B.A., 1968); Golden Gate University School of Law (J.D., 1983). Research Attorney, Superior Court, San Mateo County, 1983-1985. *Member:* Palo Alto and San Mateo County (Co-Chair, Family Law Section, 1994) Bar Associations. **PRACTICE AREAS:** Family Law; Mediation.

**GOLNAR YAZDI MOGHIMI,** born Tehran, Iran, August 31, 1966; admitted to bar, 1992, California and U.S. District Court, Northern District of California. *Education:* Universite de Haute Bretagne, Rennes, France; University of California at Santa Barbara (B.A., with honors, 1988); Santa Clara University (J.D., 1992). *Member:* San Mateo County Bar Association (Member, Probate and Estate Planning Section). **LANGUAGES:** Farsi and French. **PRACTICE AREAS:** Estate Planning, Trust and Probate Law..

REFERENCES: Wells Fargo Bank, Bank of America, University National Bank & Trust Co., all in Menlo Park, and Trust Departments of same in Palo Alto and San Mateo.

---

## ROBIN D. FAISANT
*Established in 1958*
1550 EL CAMINO REAL, SUITE 220
**MENLO PARK, CALIFORNIA 94025**
Telephone: 415-328-6333
Telecopier: 415-324-1031

*Litigation in State and Federal Courts. Business, Land Use Law. Municipal, Planning and Zoning Law. Estate Planning, Wills, Trusts and Probate Law.*

**ROBIN D. FAISANT,** born New Jersey, March 5, 1931; admitted to bar, 1958, California; 1971, U.S. Supreme Court. *Education:* University of Idaho (B.A., 1952); Stanford University (J.D., 1958). Delta Theta Phi. City Attorney: Los Altos Hills, California, 1958-1973; Belvedere, California, 1975-1976; San Carlos, California, 1977-1988; Atherton, California, 1981—. *Member:* Palo Alto, Santa Clara County and American Bar Associations; State Bar of California (Member, Estate Planning, Trust and Probate Law Section). **PRACTICE AREAS:** Estate Planning; Probate Law; Land Use Law.

---

## FISH & RICHARDSON P.C.
2200 SAND HILL ROAD
SUITE 100
**MENLO PARK, CALIFORNIA 94025**
Telephone: 415-322-5070
Fax: 415-854-0875
Email: info@fr.com
URL: http://www.fr.com

*Washington, D.C. Office:* 601 13th Street, N.W. Telephone: 202-783-5070. Fax: 202-783-2331.
*Houston, Texas Office:* One Riverway, Suite 1200. Telephone: 713-629-5070. Fax: 713-629-7811.
*Boston, Massachusetts Office:* 225 Franklin Street. Telephone: 617-542-5070. Fax: 617-542-8906. Telex: 200154.
*Minneapolis, Minnesota Office:* Fish & Richardson P.C., P.A., 60 South Sixth Street, Suite 3300. Telephone: 612-335-5070. Fax: 612-288-9696.
*La Jolla, California Office:* 4225 Executive Square, Suite 1400. Telephone: 619-678-5070. Fax: 619-678-5099.
*New York, N.Y. Office:* 45 Rockefeller Plaza, Suite 2800. Telephone: 212-765-5070. Fax: 212-258-2291.

*Intellectual Property Law: Trials, Transactions, Patents, Trademarks, Copyrights, Trade Secrets, Entertainment Law, Telecommunications Law, Drug and Medical Device and Antitrust Law.*

**FREDERICK P. FISH** (1855-1930).
*(This Listing Continued)*

**W.K. RICHARDSON** (1859-1951).

**JAMES H. A. POOLEY,** born 1948; admitted to bar, 1973, California. *Education:* Lafayette College (B.A., 1970); University of Paris; Columbia University (J.D., 1973). Special Master, California Superior Court and Federal Court, Northern District of California in Commercial and Intellectual Property Disputes. Author, *Trade Secrets: A Guide To Protecting Proprietary Business Information,* McGraw/Hill 1982; Amacon 1989 (also published in Japanese in 1991 by Chukei Publishing Co.). Chair, National Trade Secrets Law Institute. Former Chairman, Lawyers Committee, American Electronics Association. **PRACTICE AREAS:** Intellectual Property; Litigation; Trade Secrets. *Email:* pooley@fr.com

**HANS R. TROESCH,** born 1949; admitted to bar, 1982, California; registered to practice before U.S. Patent and Trademark Office. *Education:* University of Southern California (B.A., magna cum laude, 1970) Phi Beta Kappa; University of Michigan (M.S., Computer Science, 1974); Stanford University (J.D., 1982). **PRACTICE AREAS:** Intellectual Property; Patents; Copyrights; Trade Secrets. *Email:* troesch@fr.com

**JOHN E. GARTMAN,** born 1960; admitted to bar, 1986, Virginia; 1988, District of Columbia; 1991, California. *Education:* University of Texas (B.S.E.E., with highest honors, 1983; J.D., with honors, 1986). Law Clerk to the Honorable Giles S. Rich, U.S. Court of Appeals for the Federal Circuit, 1988-1990. Patents Contributing Editor, Federal Circuit Bar Journal. Author: "Infringement Under the Doctrine of Equivalents: Gazing Into the Crystal Ball," 3 Fed. Cir. Bar J. 299 (1993). **PRACTICE AREAS:** Intellectual Property; Litigation and Counseling. *Email:* gartman@fr.com

**JOHN R. SCHIFFHAUER,** born 1959; admitted to bar, 1986, New York; 1989, Massachusetts; 1995, California; registered to practice before U.S. Patent and Trademark Office. *Education:* Massachusetts Institute of Technology (S.B., 1981; S.M., 1982); Albany Law School of Union University (J.D., 1985). Committee Chair, AIPLA Chemical Practice Committee, Legislative Reporter Subcommittee, 1989-1991. Committee Chair, AIPLA Chemical Practice Committee, Continuing Legal Education Subcommittee, 1991-1992. **PRACTICE AREAS:** Intellectual Property; Litigation; Patents; Trademarks. *Email:* schiffhauer@fr.com

**KARL BOZICEVIC,** born 1952; admitted to bar, 1978, Florida; 1979, District of Columbia; 1986, Ohio; 1989, California; registered to practice before U.S. Patent and Trademark Office. *Education:* Tulane University of Louisiana (B.S., Chemistry, 1974); Nova University (J.D., 1978); George Washington University (LL.M., Intellectual Property Law, 1985). Author: "A Landmark Decision on Patenting DNA in the U.S.," 3 Financial Times #57 (1994); "Patenting DNA - Obviousness Rejections," 74 J. Pat. & Tm. Office Soc'y 750 (1992); "Reversing *In re Ruscetta,*" 71 J. Pat. & Tm. Office Soc'y 814 (1989); "The Reverse Doctrine of Equivalents in the World of Reverse Transcriptease," 71 J. Pat. & Tm. Office Soc'y 353 (1989); "Contributory Infringement and the Molecular Biologist," 70 J. Pat. & Tm. Office Soc'y 237 (1988); "Distinguishing Products of Nature from Products Derived from Nature," 69 J. Pat. & Tm. Office Soc'y 415 (1987). **PRACTICE AREAS:** Medical Devices and Biotechnology; Cell and Molecular Biology; Biochemistry; Molecular Genetics; Biomedical Sciences; Intellectual Property; Patent Applications; Licensing Agreements. *Email:* bozicevic@fr.com

**JACK L. SLOBODIN,** born 1935; admitted to bar, 1963, California; registered to practice before U.S. Patent and Trademark Office. *Education:* Cornell University (B.S., 1957); University of California at Berkeley (LL.B., 1962). **PRACTICE AREAS:** Civil Litigation; Patent Law; Intellectual Property Law. *Email:* slobodin@fr.com

**WILLIAM J. EGAN, III,** born 1947; admitted to bar, 1975, Louisiana; 1976, California; 1977, Texas; registered to practice before U.S. Patent and Trademark Office. *Education:* Louisiana State University and A. and M. College (B.S.E.E., 1970); Tulane University (J.D., 1975). **PRACTICE AREAS:** Intellectual Property; Patents; Trademarks; Copyrights; Trade Secrets; Litigation. *Email:* egan@fr.com

**REGINALD J. SUYAT,** born 1946; admitted to bar, 1976, Virginia; 1979, California; registered to practice before U.S. Patent and Trademark Office. *Education:* University of Washington (B.S., 1968); Stanford University (M.S., 1972); Georgetown University (J.D., 1976). **PRACTICE AREAS:** Intellectual Property. *Email:* suyat@fr.com

**JODI L. SUTTON,** born 1961; admitted to bar, 1986, Utah; 1988, Washington; 1991, California. *Education:* University of California, Irvine; Stanford University (B.A., with distinction, 1983); University of Utah (J.D., 1986) William H. Leary Scholar. Judicial Clerk, Honorable Judith M. Billings, Utah State Court of Appeals, 1987-1988. **PRACTICE AREAS:** Intellectual Property; Litigation. *Email:* jsutton@fr.com

*(This Listing Continued)*

## OF COUNSEL

**MARK A. LEMLEY,** born 1966; admitted to bar, 1991, California; registered to practice before U.S. Patent and Trademark Office. *Education:* Stanford University (A.B., with distinction, 1988); Boalt Hall School of Law, University of California at Berkeley (J.D., 1991). Order of the Coif. Law Clerk to Hon. Judge, Dorothy W. Nelson, U.S. Court of Appeals, Ninth Circuit, 1991-1992. Assistant Professor of Law, University of Texas at Austin, 1994—. *PRACTICE AREAS:* Intellectual Property; Antitrust. *Email:* lemley@fr.com

**ROGER S. BOROVOY,** born 1935; admitted to bar, 1960, Massachusetts; 1961, California; registered to practice before U.S. Patent and Trademark Office. *Education:* Massachusetts Institute of Technology (B.S., 1956); Harvard Law School (LL.B., 1959). Patent Counsel with Fairchild Camera and Instrument Corporation, Mountain View, California, 1963-1974. Vice President, General Counsel and Secretary of Intel Corporation, Santa Clara, California, 1974-1983. Vice President, Sevin Rosen Management Company, Sunnyvale, California, 1983-1987. Lecturer, Patent Law, Stanford Law School, 1991—. *PRACTICE AREAS:* Intellectual Property; Patent. *Email:* borovoy@fr.com

---

**FRANK E. SCHERKENBACH,** born 1963; admitted to bar, 1990, California. *Education:* Stanford University (B.S., with distinction, 1986; A.B., with distinction, 1986) Phi Beta Kappa; Harvard University (J.D., 1989). Judicial Clerk, Honorable H. Robert Mayer, United States Court of Appeals for the Federal Circuit, 1989-1991. *PRACTICE AREAS:* Intellectual Property; Litigation. *Email:* scherkenbach@fr.com

**SHELLEY K. WESSELS,** born 1959; admitted to bar, 1991, California. *Education:* University of Oklahoma (B.A., with general honors, 1980) Phi Beta Kappa; Phillips University (M.Div., summa cum laude, 1983); Stanford Law School (J.D., 1989). Judicial Clerk, Honorable Betty B. Fletcher, United States Court of Appeals for the Ninth Circuit. *PRACTICE AREAS:* Intellectual Property; Litigation. *Email:* wessels@fr.com

**WAYNE P. SOBON,** born 1962; admitted to bar, 1992, California; registered to practice before U.S. Patent and Trademark Office. *Education:* Stanford University (B.A.,B.S., with honors, 1985); Walter A. Haas School of Business, University of California (M.B.A., 1992); Boalt Hall School of Law, University of California (J.D., 1992). *LANGUAGES:* German. *PRACTICE AREAS:* Intellectual Property; Patents. *Email:* sobon@fr.com

**HOWARD G. POLLACK,** born 1966; admitted to bar, 1992, California. *Education:* Stanford University (A.B., 1988, B.S., 1988); Georgetown University (J.D., cum laude, 1992). *PRACTICE AREAS:* Intellectual Property; Litigation; Patents; Computer Science. *Email:* pollack@fr.com

**DAVID M. SHAW,** born 1966; admitted to bar, 1992, New York; registered to practice before U.S. Patent and Trademark Office (Not admitted in California). *Education:* North Carolina State University (B.S.Ch.E, summa cum laude, 1987); Duke University (J.D., 1992). Order of the Coif. Law Clerk to Honorable Raymond C. Clevenger, III, U.S. Court of Appeals for the Federal Circuit, 1992-1994. *PRACTICE AREAS:* Intellectual Property; Patents; Litigation. *Email:* shaw@fr.com

**DAVID J. GOREN,** admitted to bar, 1994, California; registered to practice before U.S. Patent and Trademark Office. *Education:* University of California at Berkeley (B.A., 1989); Georgetown University Law Center (J.D., 1994). *PRACTICE AREAS:* Intellectual Property; Patents; Trademarks. *Email:* goren@fr.com

**DAVID M. BARKAN,** born 1965; admitted to bar, 1992, California. *Education:* Harvard University (A.B., Government, magna cum laude, 1987); Boalt Hall School of Law, University of California, Berkeley (J.D., 1992). Order of the Coif. Law Clerk to Hon. Fern M. Smith, U.S. District Court for the Northern District of California, 1992-1993. *PRACTICE AREAS:* Patent Litigation. *Email:* barkan@fr.com

**MARK D. KIRKLAND,** born 1962; admitted to bar, 1994, California; registered to practice before U.S. Patent and Trademark Office. *Education:* University of Notre Dame (B.S.E.E., 1984); Santa Clara University (J.D., 1994). *PRACTICE AREAS:* Patent; Technology Licensing; Trademark; Copyright. *Email:* kirkland@fr.com

**TIMOTHY A. PORTER,** born 1965; admitted to bar, 1993, California. *Education:* Princeton University (A.B., Chemistry, magna cum laude, 1987); Yale University (M.S., Organic Chemistry, 1990); Boalt Hall School of Law (J.D., 1993). Judicial Clerk to the Honorable H. Robert Mayer, U.S. Court of Appeals, Federal Circuit, 1993-1995. *PRACTICE AREAS:* Patent Prosecution and Litigation. *Email:* porter@fr.com

*(This Listing Continued)*

**AUDREY M. SUGIMURA,** born 1968; admitted to bar, 1994, California; registered to practice before U.S. Patent and Trademark Office. *Education:* University of California, Berkeley (B.A., Computer Science and Oriental Languages, 1991); Georgetown University (J.D., 1994). Phi Beta Kappa. *PRACTICE AREAS:* Patent Prosecution. *Email:* sugimura@fr.com

**MARK D. WIECZOREK,** born 1965; (admission pending). registered to practice before U.S. Patent and Trademark Office. *Education:* California Institute of Technology (B.S., Applied Physics, 1987); Johns Hopkins University (M.A., Physics, 1989; Ph.D., Experimental Physics, 1992); George Washington University (J.D., 1995). *Email:* wieczorek@fr.com

REFERENCE: First National Bank of Boston, Boston, Massachusetts.

(For Biographical Data on Personnel at Washington, D.C., Boston, Massachusetts, Minneapolis, Minnesota, Houston, Texas, La Jolla, California and New York, N.Y., see Professional Biographies at those locations)

---

## JOHN M. GREGORY

1550 EL CAMINO REAL, SUITE 220
MENLO PARK, CALIFORNIA 94025-4111
Telephone: 415-328-6335
Facsmile: 415-324-1031

*Litigation in State and Federal Courts.*

**JOHN M. GREGORY,** born Portland, Oregon, June 9, 1947; admitted to bar, 1973, California. *Education:* Stanford University (B.A, 1968); University of Santa Clara (J.D., magna cum laude, 1973). Associate, 1973-1980 and Partner, 1980-1984, Chickering & Gregory, San Francisco, California. Instructor, Federal Practice Program, U.S. District Court, Northern District of California, 1985-1989. *Member:* San Mateo County Bar Association; The State Bar of California. [1st Lt., U.S. Army, 1968-1970]. *PRACTICE AREAS:* Products Liability Law (40%); Insurance Law (40%); Legal Malpractice Law (20%).

COUNSEL FOR: Plant Insulation Company.

---

## HOWREY & SIMON

301 RAVENSWOOD AVENUE
MENLO PARK, CALIFORNIA 94025
Telephone: 415-463-8100
Fax: 415-463-8400

*Washington, D.C. Office:* 1299 Pennsylvania Avenue, N.W., 20004-2402. Telephone: 202-783-0800. Fax: 202-383-6610.

*Los Angeles, California Office:* Suite 1400, 550 South Hope Street, 90071-2604. Telephone: 213-892-1800. Fax: 213-892-2300.

*General and Trial Practice including Antitrust, Commercial Litigation, Corporate and Transactional, Environmental, Government Contracts, Insurance Coverage, Intellectual Property, International Trade, Products Liability, Securities Litigation, Supreme Court and Appellate and White Collar Criminal Defense.*

### MEMBERS OF FIRM

**WILLIAM S. COATS,** born Fresno, California, March 31, 1950; admitted to bar, 1980, California. *Education:* University of San Francisco (A.B., 1972); Hastings College of Law, University of California (J.D., 1980). Thurston Society. Member, Moot Court Board. Co-Chair, Copyright Committee, California State Bar, Intellectual Property Section, 1994. *PRACTICE AREAS:* Intellectual Property; Licensing; General Litigation; Bankruptcy.

**STEPHEN J. ROSENMAN,** born Philadelphia, Pennsylvania, October 1, 1955; admitted to bar, 1980, District of Columbia; 1994, California; U.S. Court of Appeals for the Federal Circuit; registered to practice before U.S. Patent and Trademark Office. *Education:* Massachusetts Institute of Technology (B.S.E.E., 1977); George Washington University (J.D., 1980). *Member:* The District of Columbia Bar; State Bar of California; American Bar Association; American Intellectual Property Law Association; The International Trade Commission Trial Lawyers Association (Member, Executive Steering Committee, 1992-1995). *PRACTICE AREAS:* International Trade; Intellectual Property. *Email:* rosenmans@howrey.com

**ROBERT P. TAYLOR,** born Douglas, Arizona, May 6, 1939; admitted to bar, 1970, California. *Education:* University of Arizona (B.S.E.E., 1961); Georgetown University (J.D., 1969).

**EDWIN H. WHEELER,** born Knoxville, Tennessee, July 20, 1957; admitted to bar, 1983, District of Columbia (Not admitted in California). *Ed-*

*(This Listing Continued)*

**HOWREY & SIMON, Menlo Park—Continued**

*ucation:* Vanderbilt University (B.A., magna cum laude, 1979); University of Chicago (J.D., 1983). Phi Beta Kappa; Phi Delta Phi. *Member:* The District of Columbia Bar. **PRACTICE AREAS:** Antitrust; Complex Litigation; Intellectual Property. *Email:* wheelere@howrey.com

### RESIDENT ASSOCIATES

**EVANGELINA ALMIRANTEARENA,** born Fresno, California, July 15, 1963; admitted to bar, 1988, California and U.S. District Court, Northern District of California; 1993, U.S. Court of Appeals, Fourth Circuit. *Education:* Stanford University (B.A., with honors, 1985); Boalt Hall School of Law, University of California (J.D., 1988). **LANGUAGES:** Spanish. **PRACTICE AREAS:** Antitrust; Criminal Litigation.

**N. THANE BAUZ,** born Hinsdale, Illinois, August 4, 1963; admitted to bar, 1991, Illinois; 1993, U.S. Court of Appeals for the Federal Circuit; 1994, Washington and U.S. District Court, Western District of Washington (Not admitted in California). *Education:* Illinois Institute of Technology (B.S.M.E., with highest honors, 1986; J.D., 1991); George Washington University (LL.M., with highest honors, 1992). Tau Beta Pi; Pi Tau Sigma. Law Clerk to the Honorable Wilson Cowen, U.S. Court of Appeals for the Federal Circuit, 1992-1993. Author: "Reanimating U.S. Patent Reexamination: Recommendations for Change Based Upon a Comparative Study of German Law," 27 Creighton Law Review 945 (1994) *Member:* American Intellectual Property Law Association; Institute of Electrical and Electronics Engineers. **PRACTICE AREAS:** Intellectual Property Litigation; Patent Prosecution.

**CHRISTOPHER KELLEY,** born Santa Monica, California, June 9, 1963; admitted to bar, 1993, California. *Education:* Massachusetts Institute of Technology (B.S.E.E., 1987); University of California at Los Angeles (J.D., 1993).

---

## JORGENSON, SIEGEL, McCLURE & FLEGEL

*Established in 1961*

SUITE 210
1100 ALMA STREET
**MENLO PARK, CALIFORNIA 94025-3392**
Telephone: 415-324-9300
Fax: 415-324-0227

*General Civil and Trial Practice, Estate Planning, Probate and Trust Administration, Business, Real Property, Land Use and Municipal Law.*

### MEMBERS OF FIRM

**JOHN D. JORGENSON,** born San Francisco, California, October 16, 1925; admitted to bar, 1951, California. *Education:* Stanford University (A.B., 1947; LL.B., 1950). City Attorney, Menlo Park, 1961-1985. *Member:* San Mateo County Bar Association; The State Bar of California. **PRACTICE AREAS:** Estate Planning; Probate and Trust Administration.

**MARVIN S. SIEGEL,** born Fargo, North Dakota, April 10, 1936; admitted to bar, 1962, California. *Education:* University of Michigan (B.A., 1958); Stanford University (J.D., 1961). *Member:* Palo Alto Area, San Mateo County and American Bar Associations; The State Bar of California. **PRACTICE AREAS:** Business Law; Estate Planning; Probate and Trust Administration. *Email:* Mplaw@ix.netcom.com

**WILLIAM L. McCLURE,** born Palo Alto, California, November 17, 1952; admitted to bar, 1978, California. *Education:* University of California at Davis (B.A., 1974); Santa Clara University (J.D., magna cum laude, 1978). City Attorney of Menlo Park, 1993—. *Member:* Palo Alto Area and San Mateo County Bar Associations; The State Bar of California. **PRACTICE AREAS:** Real Estate Law; Land Use Law; Business Law; Municipal Law.

**JOHN L. FLEGEL,** born San Mateo, California, May 30, 1948; admitted to bar, 1973, California. *Education:* Claremont Men's College (B.A., 1970); Santa Clara University (J.D., 1973). *Member:* San Mateo County Bar Association; The State Bar of California. **PRACTICE AREAS:** Litigation; Civil and Business Law.

**MARGARET A. SLOAN,** born Jasper, Alabama, December 1, 1943; admitted to bar, 1979, California and U.S. District Court, Northern District of. *Education:* Duke University (B.A., 1965); Northwestern University (M.A.T., 1966); Stanford University (J.D., 1979). City Attorney, Los Altos

*(This Listing Continued)*

---

Hills (1990—) and Portola Valley, (1996—). *Member:* San Mateo and Santa Clara County Bar Associations; The State Bar of California. **PRACTICE AREAS:** Real Estate Law; Land Use Law; Municipal Law.

### ASSOCIATES

**DAN K. SIEGEL,** born Stanford, California, July 19, 1967; admitted to bar, 1992, California. *Education:* University of California at Berkeley (A.B., with honors, 1989); Cornell University (J.D., 1992). Member, Moot Court Board. *Member:* Palo Alto Area, San Mateo and American Bar Associations; The State Bar of California.

COUNSEL FOR: City of Menlo Park; Town of Los Altos Hills; Town of Portola Valley.
REFERENCE: Mid-Peninsula Bank (Palo Alto).

---

## LAW OFFICES OF ROBERT P. KAHN

*A PROFESSIONAL CORPORATION*

*Established in 1980*

3351 EL CAMINO REAL, SUITE 200 (ATHERTON)
**MENLO PARK, CALIFORNIA 94027**
Telephone: 415-369-1900
Telecopier: 415-363-1117

*General Civil and Business and Construction Law, Trial Practice in all State and Federal Courts, Personal Injury, Insurance, Landslide and Subsidence, Products Liability Law, and Public Entity Defense Law. Elder Rights Law.*

**ROBERT P. KAHN, (P.C.),** born Norfolk, Virginia, January 31, 1945; admitted to bar, 1969, Virginia; 1972, California. *Education:* College of William & Mary (B.A., 1966); Marshall-Wythe School of Law, College of William & Mary (J.D., 1969). Phi Delta Phi. Chairman, Moot Court Board. Member, William & Mary Law Review, 1968-1969. *Member:* San Mateo County and Monterey County Bar Associations; State Bar of California; California Trial Lawyers Association; Defense Research Institute; Association of Defense Counsel; San Mateo County Trial Lawyers Association. [Lt., U.S. Navy, JAGC, 1969-1973]. **PRACTICE AREAS:** Personal Injury; Insurance Defense; Real Estate Litigation; Elder Abuse.

---

**CATHERINE A. HOHENWARTER,** born Utica, New York, June 22, 1963; admitted to bar, 1990, California; 1991, Idaho. *Education:* Middlebury College (B.A., cum laude, 1985); University of Idaho (J.D., 1990). Case Note Editor, University of Idaho Law Review, 1989-1990. *Member:* Bar Association of San Francisco; San Mateo and American Bar Associations; State Bar of California. **PRACTICE AREAS:** Personal Injury; Insurance Defense; Real Estate Litigation; Elder Abuse.

REPRESENTATIVE CLIENTS: United Adjusters, Inc.; City of Fremont; Oakland Housing Authority; Lucky Stores, Inc.; American Stores, Inc.; Allegheny Intl.; HGHB Architects; Taco Bell.

---

## LAW OFFICE OF DENNIS LAWRENCE KENNELLY

1030 CURTIS STREET, SUITE 200
**MENLO PARK, CALIFORNIA 94025-4501**
Telephone: 415-853-1291
Fax: 415-328-4715

*Employment Law and General Civil Trial Practice.*

**DENNIS LAWRENCE KENNELLY,** born 1948; admitted to bar, 1973, Iowa; 1974, Hawaii; 1975, California. *Education:* Holy Cross College (A.B. cum laude, 1970); Duke University (J.D., 1973). *Member:* California State Bar; American Bar Association.

---

## KURT A. LATTA

*Established in 1975*

750 MENLO AVENUE, SUITE 250
**MENLO PARK, CALIFORNIA 94025**
Telephone: 415-324-0622
Fax: 415-322-8485

*Business Practice (excluding Litigation) with emphasis on Transactions and Securities Law.*

*(This Listing Continued)*

**KURT A. LATTA,** born St. Louis, Missouri, March 16, 1943; admitted to bar, 1969, California and U.S. District Court, Northern District of California; 1970, U.S. Tax Court. *Education:* Princeton University (A.B., 1965); Stanford University (LL.B., 1968). *Member:* Palo Alto and Santa Clara County (Member: Tax Committee; Business Law Section) Bar Associations; State Bar of California (Member, Business Law Section). *PRACTICE AREAS:* Business Transactions; Real Estate; Taxation.

---

## LITTLER, MENDELSON, FASTIFF, TICHY & MATHIASON

*A PROFESSIONAL CORPORATION*

Established in 1942

750 MENLO AVENUE, SUITE 300
**MENLO PARK, CALIFORNIA 94025**
Telephone: 415-326-5732
Facsimile: 415-326-1351
URL: http://www.littler.com

*Offices located in:* California -- Bakersfield, Fresno, Long Beach, Los Angeles, Oakland, Sacramento, San Diego, San Francisco, San Jose, Santa Maria, Santa Rosa and Stockton; Denver, Colorado; Washington, D.C.; Atlanta, Georgia; Baltimore, Maryland; Reno and Las Vegas, Nevada (a partnership with the Law Offices of Hicks & Walt); Morristown, New Jersey; New York, New York; and Dallas and Houston, Texas.

*FIRM PROFILE: Littler, Mendelson, Fastiff, Tichy & Mathiason is the largest law firm in the United States engaged exclusively in the practice of employment and labor law. The firm has over 250 attorneys in 23 offices nationwide who represent and advise management in all the major sub-specialities of employment and labor law including: wage and hour law; NLRB cases and collective bargaining; workers' compensation; sex, race, and age discrimination; wrongful termination; unemployment benefits; workplace violence; substance abuse; employee privacy rights; occupational safety and health; the ADA; ERISA, employee benefits, tax issues; and immigration.*

### RESIDENT ATTORNEY

**J. RICHARD THESING,** born Los Angeles, California, July 1, 1939; admitted to bar, 1967, California. *Education:* Loyola University of Los Angeles (B.S., 1961); California State College at Los Angeles (M.A., 1963); Stanford University (LL.B., 1963). (Also at San Francisco, California Office).

**ALAN B. CARLSON,** born Oakland, California, November 7, 1946; admitted to bar, 1972, California. *Education:* University of California at Santa Barbara (B.A., 1968); University of California School of Law at Davis (J.D., 1972). Order of the Coif. Editor-in-Chief, University of California at Davis Law Review, 1971-1972. (Also at San Jose, California Office).

**BRIAN T. MCMILLAN,** born San Francisco, California, March 23, 1957; admitted to bar, 1983, California. *Education:* University of California at Davis (B.A., with honors, 1980); University of Santa Clara (J.D., 1983).

**DENNIS M. BROWN,** born San Jose, California, January 10, 1960; admitted to bar, 1986, California. *Education:* University of California at Berkeley (B.A., 1983); Santa Clara University (J.D., 1986).

---

**MARLENE S. KLEINMAN,** born Boston, Massachusetts, September 27, 1966; admitted to bar, 1991, California. *Education:* University of California at Berkeley (B.A., 1988); University of Minnesota (J.D., cum laude, 1991).

**MICHELLE L. BUCEK,** born Grand Forks, North Dakota, May 24, 1967; admitted to bar, 1995, California. *Education:* California State University (B.S., magna cum laude, 1989); University of Minnesota (J.D., magna cum laude, 1995).

(For biographical data on personnel at other locations, see Professional Biographies at those cities).

---

## ROBERT E. MILLER, INC.

*A PROFESSIONAL CORPORATION*

1550 EL CAMINO REAL, SUITE 220
**MENLO PARK, CALIFORNIA 94025-4111**
Telephone: 415-326-6135
Fax: 415-324-1031
Email: 73532.77@compuserve.com

Business Law.

*FIRM PROFILE: Bob Miller provides corporate, commercial, contracts and intellectual property law services to a select number of privately held California corporations, particularly technology and professional services businesses.*

**ROBERT E. MILLER,** born Glen Ridge, New Jersey, July 13, 1947; admitted to bar, 1972, Pennsylvania; 1974, California. *Education:* Johns Hopkins University (B.A., 1969); University of Texas at Austin School of Law (J.D., 1972). *Member:* State Bar of California (Member, Section on: Business Law). *PRACTICE AREAS:* Business Law. *Email:* 73532.77@compuserve.com

REPRESENTATIVE CLIENTS: Aeroground, Inc.; Hussmann Corp.; International Scientific Products; Space Power, Inc.; Tiburon Systems, Inc.; Walt & Company Communications, Inc.; Western Multiplex Corp.; Z-Tech Sales, Inc.

---

## BRIAN W. NEWCOMB

770 MENLO AVENUE, SUITE 101
**MENLO PARK, CALIFORNIA 94025**
Telephone: 415-322-7780
Telefax: 415-327-0619

*General Civil and Trial Practice. Business Litigation, Construction, Real Estate and Mechanics Lien Law.*

**BRIAN W. NEWCOMB,** born Little Rock, Arkansas, April 4, 1947; admitted to bar, 1973, California; 1974, U.S. District Court, Northern District of California; 1985, U.S. District Court, Eastern District of California; 1986, U.S. Court of Appeals, Ninth Circuit. *Education:* University of New Mexico (B.A., 1969); Hastings College of the Law, University of California (J.D., 1972). *Member:* Palo Alto and San Mateo County Bar Associations; San Francisco Trial Lawyers Association; American Arbitration Association; Consumer Attorneys of San Francisco County; Consumer Attorneys of San Mateo County.

---

## O'REILLY & COLLINS

*A PROFESSIONAL CORPORATION*

Established in 1987

2500 SAND HILL ROAD, SUITE 201
**MENLO PARK, CALIFORNIA 94025**
Telephone: 415-854-7700
Fax: 415-854-8350

*Civil Trial Practice. Plaintiff Personal Injury, Aviation, Products Liability, Medical and Legal Malpractice, Bad Faith and Consumer Fraud Law.*

*FIRM PROFILE: After 12 years of partnership with Bruce Walkup in San Francisco, Terry O'Reilly decided to establish a firm in the Silicon Valley and invited Jim Collins to join him, in a practice strictly limited to trying cases for the plaintiff. Although the firm has specialized in the trial of aviation and products liability matters, a broad range of cases are now active, ranging from libel to business fraud. The members of the firm regularly lecture at professional and legal seminars and act as arbitrators and mediators. The firm restricts its practice to cases involving catastrophic injuries, but maintains a preference for unusual liability issues. In 1991, the firm settled the largest single personal injury case paid in the United States for $31.2 million (Paboojian v. Piper, et al, Santa Clara County Superior Court Case No. 654490).*

**TERRY O'REILLY,** born Farnborough, Hampshire, England, April 12, 1945; admitted to bar, 1970, California. *Education:* Loyola University of Los Angeles (B.A., 1966); Boalt Hall School of Law, University of California (J.D., 1969). Alpha Sigma Nu. Director, Boalt Hall Alumni Association, 1981-1985. Author: "Ethics and Experts," 59 SMU Journal of Air Law and Commerce 113, 1993. ENE Evaluator, U.S. District Court, Northern District of California. *Member:* San Mateo County Bar Association (Director, 1993—); State Bar of California; San Francisco (Director, 1977-1979; 1986-1993); Consumer Attorneys of California (Director, 1996—); The Association of Trial Lawyers of America (Diplomate); American Board of

*(This Listing Continued)*

## O'REILLY & COLLINS, A PROFESSIONAL CORPORATION, Menlo Park—Continued

Professional Liability Lawyers (Trustee, 1989—; Chairman, 9th Circuit, 1992—); Consumer Attorneys of San Mateo County. (Board Certified, Civil Trial Specialist, National Board of Trial Advocacy). *PRACTICE AREAS:* Plaintiff Personal Injury; Aviation; Products Liability; Medical Malpractice; Legal Malpractice; Bad Faith; Consumer Fraud.

**JAMES P. COLLINS,** born San Francisco, California, September 6, 1952; admitted to bar, 1980, California and U.S. District Court, Northern District of California. *Education:* University of California at Berkeley (B.S., 1975); University of San Francisco (J.D., 1980). *Member:* State Bar of California; American Bar Association (Member, Litigation Section); consumer Attorneys of California; San Francisco Trial Lawyers Association; San Mateo County Trial Lawyers Association; Santa Clara County Trial Lawyers Association; The Association of Trial Lawyers of America. *PRACTICE AREAS:* Plaintiff Personal Injury; Aviation; Products Liability; Medical Malpractice; Legal Malpractice; Bad Faith; Consumer Fraud.

**JAMES P. TESSIER,** born Milwaukee, Wisconsin, April 19, 1962; admitted to bar, 1988, California, U.S. District Court, Northern District of California and U.S. Court of Appeals, Ninth Circuit. *Education:* University of Wisconsin-Madison (B.B.A., with distinction, 1984); Boalt Hall School of Law, University of California (J.D., 1988). *PRACTICE AREAS:* Plaintiff Personal Injury; Aviation; Products Liability; Medical Malpractice; Legal Malpractice; Bad Faith; Consumer Fraud.

**MICHAEL DANKO,** born Middletown, Connecticut; admitted to bar, 1983, California. *Education:* Dartmouth College (A.B., magna cum laude, 1980); University of Virginia School of Law (J.D., 1983). Instrument Pilot. Formerly with: Brown & Wood; Sheppard, Mullin, Richert & Hampton; Severson & Werson. *PRACTICE AREAS:* Personal Injury/Wrongful Death; Business Litigation; Aviation Litigation; Environmental Litigation; Insurance Bad Faith.

---

# ORRICK, HERRINGTON & SUTCLIFFE LLP

*Established in 1863*

**1020 MARSH ROAD**
**MENLO PARK, CALIFORNIA 94025**

*Telephone:* 415-833-7800
*Telecopier:* 415-614-7401
*URL:* http://www.orrick.com

*San Francisco, California Office:* Old Federal Reserve Bank Building, 400 Sansome Street. Telephone: 415-392-1122. Telecopier: 415-773-5759.
*Los Angeles, California Office:* 777 South Figueroa Street. Telephone: 213-629-2020. Telecopier: 213-612-2499.
*New York, New York Office:* 666 Fifth Avenue. Telephone: 212-506-5000. Telecopier: 212-506-5151.
*Sacramento, California Office:* 400 Capitol Mall. Telephone: 916-447-9200. Telecopier: 916-329-4900.
*Singapore Office:* 10 Collyer Quay, #23-08 Ocean Building, Singapore. Telephone: 011-65-538-6116. Telecopier: 011-65-538-0606.
*Washington, D.C. Office:* Washington Harbour, 3050 K Street, N.W. Telephone: 202-339-8400. Telecopier: 202-339-8500.

*General Practice, including Corporate and Municipal Finance, Domestic and International Commercial Law, Banking and Commercial Finance, Project Finance, Structured Finance, Mergers and Acquisitions, Commercial Litigation, Insurance, Insurance Insolvency, White Collar Criminal Defense, Tax, Employee Benefits and Personal Estates, Antitrust, Distribution, and Trade Regulation, Intellectual Property, Real Estate, Environmental and Energy, Labor and Employment Law and Bankruptcy.*

### MEMBERS OF FIRM

**W. REECE BADER,** born Portland, Oregon, 1941; admitted to bar, 1967, District of Columbia; 1969, California. *Education:* Williams College (B.A., 1963); Duke University (J.D., 1966). Member, Duke Law Journal, 1965-1966. Author: "Annual Survey of Broker-Dealer Litigation," in Securities Industry Association (SIA), Compliance and Legal Seminar, 1986-1995. Editor: "Annual Survey of Broker-Dealer Litigation," in Securities Industry Association, Compliance And Legal Seminar, 1990-1993. Editor, Securities News, ABA Section of Litigation, 1993-1994. Law Clerk to Hon. Warren E. Burger, U.S. Court of Appeals, District of Columbia Circuit, 1966-68. Member, Committee on Rules of Practice and Procedure, 1987-

*(This Listing Continued)*

1970, and Advisory Committee on Civil Rules, 1982-1987, U.S. Judicial Conference; NASD National Arbitration and Mediation Committee. *Member:* State Bar of California; District of Columbia Bar; American Bar Association (Co-Chair, Securities Litigation Committee, Section on Litigation). *PRACTICE AREAS:* Securities; Commodities Law; Environmental Law.

**G. HOPKINS GUY, III,** born Roanoke, Virginia, April 9, 1957; admitted to bar, 1982, Virginia; 1986, California; 1992, registered to practice before U.S. Patent and Trademark Office. *Education:* University of Virginia (B.S., 1979); University of Richmond (J.D., 1982). *Member:* State Bar of California; Virginia State Bar; American Bar Association. *PRACTICE AREAS:* Intellectual Property Litigation; Patent and Trade Secret Litigation.

**LYNNE C. HERMLE,** born New Haven, Connecticut, 1956; admitted to bar, 1981, California. *Education:* University of California at Santa Barbara (B.A., magna cum laude, 1978); Hastings College of the Law, University of California (J.D., 1981). Senior Research Editor, Hastings Law Journal, 1980-1981. Author: "A Balanced Approach to Affirmative Action Plan Discovery in Title VII Suits," 32 Hastings Law Journal 1013, 1981; "The Employment Tort: What to Do About It When You Hear About It," American Bar Association National Institute on Employer-Employee Tort Liability, 1987; "EAPs: An Expert Roundtable on Problems, Solutions," published in Employment Relations Today (Autumn, 1991); "Fuller: An Intolerable Burden on Employers?" CPER, October 1995. Co-Author: "Sexual Harassment in the Workplace: A Guide to the Law," 4th ed., 1994. Faculty Member, National Institute of Trial Advocacy, 1990—. Commissioner, San Francisco Relocation Appeals Board. *Member:* State Bar of California; American Bar Association (Member, Section of Labor and Employment Law). *PRACTICE AREAS:* Employment and General Litigation.

**TERRENCE P. MCMAHON,** born Pasadena, California, 1950; admitted to bar, 1976, California and U.S. District Court, Northern District of California. *Education:* University of Santa Clara (B.S.C., 1972; J.D., cum laude, 1976). Member of Faculty, Hastings Center for Trial and Appellate Advocacy, 1983—. Judge Pro Tem, Santa Clara Superior Court, 1986—. Member, Santa Clara County Superior Court Panel of Arbitrators, 1984—. *Member:* Santa Clara and American Bar Associations; Association of Defense Counsel of Northern California; California Trial Lawyers Association (Member, Defense Lawyers Section). *PRACTICE AREAS:* Intellectual Property Litigation.

**CHRISTOPHER R. OTTENWELLER,** born Fort Wayne, Indiana, 1948; admitted to bar, 1977, California; 1978, District of Columbia. *Education:* University of Pennsylvania (B.A., magna cum laude, 1971); Georgetown University Law Center (J.D., 1976). Executive Editor, *Georgetown Law Journal*, 1975-1976. Law Clerk to Hon. Robert J. Kelleher, U.S. District Court, Central District of California, 1976-1977. *PRACTICE AREAS:* Intellectual Property Litigation.

**JON B. STREETER,** born Seattle, Washington, 1956; admitted to bar, 1981, California. *Education:* Stanford University (A.B., 1978); Boalt Hall School of Law, University of California (J.D., 1981). Law Clerk to Hon. Harry T. Edwards, U.S. Court of Appeals, District of Columbia Circuit, 1982-1983. *Member:* State Bar of California. *PRACTICE AREAS:* Intellectual Property Litigation.

**GARY E. WEISS,** born Ridgewood, New Jersey, 1957; admitted to bar, 1984, New York; 1986, California. *Education:* Cornell University (B.A., 1979); Columbia University (J.D., 1983). Harlan Fiske Stone Honor Competition, 1981-1982. Winner, Thomas E. Dewey Prize for Outstanding Written Advocacy, 1982. Member, Columbia Human Rights Law Review, 1982-1983. Recipient, Bar Association of San Francisco's Volunteer Legal Services Program's Outstanding Pro Bono Lawyer Award, 1989. *Member:* State Bar of California. *PRACTICE AREAS:* Securities and Intellectual Property Litigation.

### ASSOCIATES

**DAVID J. ANDERMAN,** born New York, New York, 1969; admitted to bar, 1994, California. *Education:* University of Pennsylvania (B.A., cum laude, 1991; J.D., 1994). Executive Editor, University of Pennsylvania Law Review. Author: "Title III at a Crossroads: The Ordinary Course of Business in the Home, the Consent of Children, and Parental Wiretapping," 141 University of Pennsylvania Law Review 2261, 1993.

**CARL W. CHAMBERLIN,** born Alexandria, Virginia, 1958; admitted to bar, 1985, California. *Education:* Stanford University (A.B., with distinction and honors, 1980); Hastings College of the Law, University of California (J.D., magna cum laude, 1985). Thurston Honor Society; Order of the Coif; Milton D. Green Scholar. Member, 1983-1984 and Editor, 1984-1985, Hastings Law Journal. Co-author: "Recent Developments in State Antitrust

*(This Listing Continued)*

Law," International Litigation (June 1995); "Rule 30(b)(6): Procedure and Strategy," 13 San Francisco Barrister Law Journal 10 (1994). Author: "Punitive Damages in California: The Drunken Driver," Hastings Law Journal, 1985. Faculty, National Institute of Trial Advocacy, 1993—. Instructor, Continuing Education of the Bar. Recipient, Wiley W. Manuel Pro Bono Services Award. *Member:* State Bar of California.

**ERIN FARRELL,** born Redondo Beach, California, 1967; admitted to bar, 1993, California. *Education:* University of Virginia (B.A., 1989); Boalt Hall School of Law, University of California (J.D., 1993). *Member:* State Bar of California.

**KENNETH J. HALPERN,** born Manhasset, New York, 1966; admitted to bar, 1995, Florida; 1996, California. *Education:* Brown University (B.A., 1988); Harvard University (J.D., cum laude, 1995).

**LESLIE Y. KIMBALL,** born Walnut Creek, California, 1959; admitted to bar, 1987, California. *Education:* California State University, Chico (B.A., 1981); University of San Francisco (J.D., cum laude, 1987). *Member:* State Bar of California.

**WENDY KOSANOVICH,** born Indianapolis, Indiana, 1962; admitted to bar, 1996, California. *Education:* Randolph-Macon Woman's College (B.A., 1984); San Francisco State University (M.A., 1990); University of San Francisco School of Law (J.D., 1996).

**AMY L. LANDERS,** born Erie, Pennsylvania, 1960; admitted to bar, 1994, California. *Education:* Rochester Institute of Technology (B.F.A., 1982); Hastings College of the Law, University of California (J.D., magna cum laude, 1993). Order of the Coif; Thurston Society. Author: "The Current State of Moral Rights Protection for Visual Artists in the United States," 15 Hastings COMM/ENT Law Journal 165, Fall, 1992. Extern to Hon. J.P. Vukasin, Jr., U.S. District Court, Northern District of California, 1992. Law Clerk to Hon. Oliver W. Wagner, U.S. District Court, Eastern District of California, 1993-1994. *Member:* State Bar of California.

**JOSEPH C. LIBURT,** born Huntington, New York, 1965; admitted to bar, 1991, California; 1993, U.S. District Court, Northern District of California. *Education:* Deep Springs College; Haverford College (B.A., 1987); Boalt Hall School of Law (J.D., 1991). Law Clerk to Hon. D. Brook Bartlett, U.S. District Court, Western District of Missouri, 1991-1993. *Member:* State Bar of California.

**SEAN A. LINCOLN,** born Fredericksburg, Virginia, 1963; admitted to bar, 1988, California, U.S. District Court, Northern District of California and U.S. Court of Appeals, Ninth Circuit. *Education:* New College (University of South Florida) (B.A., 1985); Harvard University Law School (J.D., cum laude, 1988).

**ALEXANDRA MCCLURE,** born Los Angeles, California, 1969; admitted to bar, 1996, California. *Education:* California Polytechnic State University, San Luis Obispo (B.A., 1991); Santa Clara University (J.D., 1995). Associate Editor, *Santa Clara Law Review.*.

**PETER C. MCMAHON,** born Washington, D.C., February 11, 1964; admitted to bar, 1992, California. *Education:* University of Maryland (B.A., 1986); Catholic University (J.D., 1992). *Member:* State Bar of California (Labor and Employment Section).

**MATTHEW H. POPPE,** born San Francisco, California, 1968; admitted to bar, 1995, California. *Education:* Stanford University (A.B., with honors, 1990); University of Chicago (J.D., with high honors, 1994). Phi Beta Kappa; Order of the Coif. Staff Member, University of Chicago Law Review. Author: "Defining the Scope of the Equal Protection Clause with Respect to Welfare Waiting Periods," 61 U.Chi.L. Rev. 291. *LANGUAGES:* French.

**EVE T. SALTMAN,** born Washington, D.C., 1964; admitted to bar, 1990, California. *Education:* Cornell University (B.A., magna cum laude, with distinction in all subjects, 1986); Georgetown University Law Center (J.D., cum laude, 1990). Phi Beta Kappa; Phi Kappa Phi. Recipient, Wiley W. Manuel Pro Bono Award, 1992; Outstanding Volunteer in Public Service, 1992. Author: "What's In A Name: The *Dilution Solution 'Expands Trademark Protection, but What Will it Do to the Registration Process?" The Recorder, Intellectual Property Supplement, Summer, 1986. Co-author:* with Jeffrey S. White, "Problem Counsel, Problem Witnesses". *Member:* State Bar of California.

**SHELLEY J. SANDUSKY,** born Seattle, Washington, 1966; admitted to bar, 1991, California. *Education:* Stanford University (A.B., honors and distinction, 1988); Boalt Hall School of Law, University of California, Berkeley (J.D., 1991). Phi Beta Kappa. Member, Moot Court Board. Law

*(This Listing Continued)*

Clerk to the Honorable Lawrence T. Lydick, U.S. District Court, Central District of California. *Member:* State Bar of California.

**GRAEME ELLIS SHARPE,** born London, England, 1966; admitted to bar, 1991, California. *Education:* Carleton College (B.A., 1987); University of Michigan (J.D., 1991). Note Editor, 1989-1990 and Associate Editor, 1988-1989, Michigan Law Review. *Member:* Bar Association of San Francisco; State Bar of California; American Bar Association.

**ERIC L. WESENBERG,** born Palo Alto, California, 1960; admitted to bar, 1987, Illinois; 1989, California. *Education:* University of California at Santa Barbara (B.A., cum laude, 1982); George Washington University (J.D., magna cum laude, 1987). *Member:* Palo Alto and American (Property Law Committee of the ABA Tort and Insurance Practice Section) Bar Associations; State Bar of California.

**THOMAS H. ZELLERBACH,** born San Francisco, California, 1949; admitted to bar, 1991, California. *Education:* Colorado College (B.A., 1971); University of Pennsylvania (J.D., cum laude, 1991). Senior Editor, Journal of Int'l. Business Law, 1990-91. Co-author: "Prosecution Aids Recovery in Trade-Secrets Theft," The National Law Journal (October 23, 1995). Extern to Hon. William Schwarzer, U.S. District Court, Northern District of California, 1989. *Member:* State Bar of California; American Bar Association (Member, Sections on: Intellectual Property Law; Litigation; Committee on Unfair Competition-Trade Identity, 1993-1996).

## LOS ANGELES, CALIFORNIA
### MEMBERS OF FIRM

| | |
|---|---|
| Alan G. Benjamin | W. Douglas Kari |
| William W. Bothwell | Michael A. McAndrews |
| Lori A. Bowman | Richard C. Mendelson |
| William B. Campbell | Lawrence Peitzman |
| Eugene J. Carron | Gary D. Samson |
| Robert E. Freitas | Larry D. Sobel |
| Earl A. Glick | Payne L. Templeton |
| Todd E. Gordinier | Paul A. Webber |
| Greg Harrington | Howard J. Weg |

### OF COUNSEL

| | |
|---|---|
| Jeffrey S. Allen | Mary H. Neale |
| John P. Kreis | Michael E. Silver |

### ASSOCIATES

| | |
|---|---|
| Ella L. Brown | Lisa Girand Mann |
| Diana K. Chuang | Paul T. Martin |
| Christopher L. Davis | Antonio D. Martini |
| Andrew D. Garelick | Bradley Scott Miller |
| Margaret H. Gillespie | Melanie Murakami |
| Owen P. Gross | William W. Oxley |
| Brett L. Healy | Luan Phan |
| Victor Hsu | Georgiana Rosenkranz |
| Alisa Jardine | Christopher S. Ruhland |
| Julie E. Knipstein | John P. Sharkey |
| Linda S. Koffman | David B. Shemano |
| Scott G. Lawson | Bridgette M. Smith |
| Victoria A. Levin | Winnie Tsien |
| Douglas E. Love | Bradley S. White |

## NEW YORK, NEW YORK
### MEMBERS OF FIRM

| | |
|---|---|
| Paul B. Abramson | F. Susan Gottlieb |
| Charles W. Bradley | William A. Gray |
| Bradford S. Breen | Arnold Gulkowitz |
| Peter R. Bucci | Eileen B. Heitzler |
| Charles N. Burger | Robyn A. Huffman |
| Colman J. Burke | Laurence Bryan Isaacson |
| Fred C. Byers, Jr. | Robert M. Isackson |
| Richard Chirls | John J. Keohane |
| Katharine I. Crost | Alan M. Knoll |
| Bruce S. Cybul | Peter J. Korda |
| Duncan N. Darrow | Jeffrey A. Lenobel |
| Michael Delikat | Herbert J. Levine |
| Edward M. De Sear | Carl F. Lyon, Jr. |
| Rubi Finkelstein | Daniel A. Mathews |
| Robert A. Fippinger | Sam Scott Miller |
| Lawrence B. Fisher | Kathleen H. Moriarty |
| Adam W. Glass | Barbara Moses |
| Lawrence B. Goodwin | David Z. Nirenberg |

*(This Listing Continued)*

## ORRICK, HERRINGTON & SUTCLIFFE LLP, Menlo Park—Continued

### NEW YORK, NEW YORK
### MEMBERS OF FIRM (Continued)

Joshua E. Raff
Jill L. Rosenberg
Stephen K. Sawyier
Albert Simons, III
Louis H. Singer
Michael Voldstad
Richard Weidman
Neil T. Wolk

### SPECIAL COUNSEL

Donald J. Robinson

### OF COUNSEL

Stanley L. Amberg
Thomas Barr, IV
Susan L. Barry
Michael E. Emrich
William H. Horton, Jr.
John A. MacKerron
Robert B. Michel
Martin R. Miller
Amy Moskowitz
Richard H. Nicholls

### ASSOCIATES

Craig T. Beazer
Jonathan K. Bender
Thomas J. Benison
Leon J. Bijou
Colette Bonnard
Patti Lynn Boss
Eric R. Bothwell
Whitney R. Bradshaw
Karen M. Braun
Jarrett D. Bruhn
Juliet F. Buck
Benjamin C. Burkhart
Lawton M. Camp
Anthony Carabba, Jr.
Michael B. Carlinsky
Jennifer M. Clapp
Joseph M. Cohen
Caterina A. Conti
Robert A. Cote
Kyle W. Drefke
Joseph Evall
Marguerite J. Felsenfeld
Jeffrey J. Fessler
John D. Giansello, III
Michael A. Gilbert
Howard M. Goldwasser
Meryl A. Griff
Tzvi Hirshaut
Kiran J. Kamboj
René A. Kathawala
Joseph T. Kennedy
Jaemin Kim
Steven L. Kopp
Diane Krebs
Kenneth R. Linsk
Christopher Locke
Jonathan B. Lurvey
Michael D. Maline
Joseph E. Maloney
David A. Marple
Edward Mayfield
Lisa K. McClelland
Thomas N. McManus
James H. McQuade
Aimee B. Meltzer
Ronald Millet
Bradford E. Monks
Christopher J. Moore
C. Rochelle Moorehead
P. Quinn Moss
Bryan Jay Neilinger
William O'Brien
John F. Olsen
Edwin Gerard Oswald
Scott M. Pasternack
Marc J. Pensabene
Sheryl Lynn Pereira
Gail Pflederer
Nanci Prado
Ruth D. Raisfeld
Marlene Watts Reed
Marni J. Roder
Ira G. Rosenstein
Sidney M. Ruthenberg
Hooman Sabeti-Rahmati
David J. Sack
Al B. Sawyers
Martin L. Schmelkin
Patricia A. Seddon
William C. Seligman
Ronit Setton
Katherine A. Simmons
Corey A. Tessler
David M. Traitel
Sandra L. Tsang
Robert A. Villani
Steven I. Weinberger
Bradley E. Wolf
Michael J. Zeidel

### SACRAMENTO, CALIFORNIA
### MEMBERS OF FIRM

R. Michael Bacon
Norman C. Hile
Perry E. Israel
Cynthia J. Larsen
Marc A. Levinson
Timothy J. Long
John R. Myers
Cynthia L. Remmers

### SPECIAL COUNSEL

William E. Donovan

### OF COUNSEL

E. Randolph Hooks
Iain Mickle

### ASSOCIATES

Jennifer P. Brown
Jordon Lee Burch
James T. Cahalan
Virginia M. Christianson
John P. Cook
William T. Darden
Stephen L. Davis
Edward P. Dudensing
Lynn T. Ernce
Eric J. Glassman
Kelcie M. Gosling
Trish Higgins
Christopher E. Krueger
Constance L. LeLouis
Kim Mueller
Charles W. Nugent
Andrew W. Stroud
Susan R. Thompson
Margaret Carew Toledo
Thomas J. Welsh

### SAN FRANCISCO, CALIFORNIA
### MEMBERS OF FIRM

John E. Aguirre
William F. Alderman
Ralph H. Baxter, Jr.
Elaine R. Bayus
Daniel R. Bedford
Michael J. Bettinger
Steven A. Brick
Frederick Brown
Charles Cardall
Thomas Y. Coleman
Mary A. Collins
Dean E. Criddle
Roger L. Davis
Stanley J. Dirks
William M. Doyle
Raymond G. Ellis
Robert P. Feyer
Carlo S. Fowler
David S. Fries
Richard A. Gilbert
Robert J. Gloistein
Richard E. V. Harris
Richard D. Harroch
Gary A. Herrmann
Patricia K. Hershey
Richard I. Hiscocks
William L. Hoisington
Leslie P. Jay
John H. Kanberg
Lawrence T. Kane
Dana M. Ketcham
John H. Knox
Geoffrey P. Leonard
Mark R. Levie
Michael H. Liever
Peter Lillevand
Dora Mao
John E. McInerney, III
Michael R. Meyers
Thomas C. Mitchell
William G. Murray, Jr.
Noel W. Nellis
M. J. Pritchett
Greg R. Riddle
Marie B. Riehle
William L. Riley
Paul J. Sax
John F. Seegal
Thomas R. Shearer, Jr.
Gary R. Siniscalco
Richard V. Smith
Stephen A. Spitz
Alan Talkington
Ralph C. Walker
Jeffrey S. White
Kenneth G. Whyburn
Jeffrey D. Wohl
George G. Wolf
Cameron W. Wolfe, Jr.
George A. Yuhas

### OF COUNSEL

Bruce S. Klafter
Philip C. Morgan
Catherine K. O'Connell
Douglas C. Sands
Samuel A. Sperry
Timothy P. Walker

### ASSOCIATES

Melody A. Barker
Pamela H. Bennett
Gregory D. Bibbes
Scott D. Blickenstaff
Paul C. Borden
Kerry Anne Bresnahan
Jessica L. Cahen
David Malcolm Carson
David J. Castillo
Kevin Shih-Chun Chou
Brett E. Cooper
Robert E. Curry, II
Mark Davis
Kirsten J. Day
Ana Marie del Rio
Mary Patricia Dooley
Scott D. Elliott
Gabriela Franco
David K. Gillis
Carlos E. Gonzalez
Mary Elizabeth Grant
Maria Gray
Dolph M. Hellman
Mats F. Hellsten
Tanya Herrera
Lynne T. Hirata
Laura A. Izon
Stephen J. Jackson, Jr.
Andrew P. Johnson
Daniel Judge
Susan R. Kelley
Hera Lie Kim
Thomas P. Klein
William J. Kramer
Kathleen Hughes Leak
Nancy M. Lee
Gary Louie
Ashley E. Lowe
Steven C. Malvey
Douglas D. Mandell
Karen L. Marangi
George P. Miller
James W. Miller Jr.
Genevieve M. Moore

(This Listing Continued)

## PROFESSIONAL BIOGRAPHIES

Adam J. Gutride
John M. Hartenstein
Lowell D. Ness
Mark F. Parcella

ASSOCIATES (Continued)

Anthony B. Pearsall
David C. Ritchey
Peter E. Root
Christian J. Rowley
Paul I. Rubin
Dave A. Sanchez
Michelle W. Sexton
Usha Rengachary Smerdon
David Sobul
Lawrence N. Tonomura
Adrienne Diamant Weil
Stephen E. Whittaker

SINGAPORE
MEMBER OF FIRM

William R. Campbell

ASSOCIATES

Kenneth S. Aboud
M. Tamara Box
Nicholas Chan Kei Cheong
Bruce R. Schulberg
David Z. Vance
Eleanor Wong

WASHINGTON, D.C.
MEMBERS OF FIRM

Cameron L. Cowan
Felicia B. Graham
Keith W. Kriebel
Lorraine S. McGowen
Paul Weiffenbach

RESIDENT OF COUNSEL

David S. Katz
Dianne Loennig Stoddard

ASSOCIATES

Michele E. Beasley
Mark S. Dola
Michael H. Freedman
Rohit H. Kirpalani
Douglas Madsen
Thomas D. Salus
Adam B. Tankel

---

# PENNIE & EDMONDS LLP

*Established in 1884*
**2730 SAND HILL ROAD**
**MENLO PARK, CALIFORNIA 94025**
Telephone: 415-854-3660
Fax: 415-854-3694
Email: pennie.com
URL: http://www.pennie.com

*New York, N.Y. Office:* 1155 Avenue of the Americas. Telephone: 212-790-9090. Telex: (WUI) 66141-Pennie. Cable Address: "Penangold." Facsimile: GII/GII/GIII (212) 869-9741; GIII (212) 869-8864.
*Washington, D.C. Office:* 1667 K Street, N.W., Suite 1000. Telephone: 202-496-4400. Facsimile: 202-496-4444.

Intellectual Property and Technology Litigation including Patent, Trademark, Trade Secrets, Copyright and Unfair Competition Causes, Computer and Communication Law and Related Government Agency Proceedings, Licensing, Arbitration and International Trade Matters. Trials and Appeals in all Federal and State Courts.

## RESIDENT PARTNERS

**JON R. STARK,** born Washington, D.C., September 17, 1951; admitted to bar, 1982, California, U.S. District Court, Northern District of California and U.S. Court of Appeals, Ninth Circuit; 1983, Colorado, U.S. District Court, District of Colorado and U.S. Court of Appeals for the Federal Circuit; 1986, U.S. Supreme Court; 1987, District of Columbia; 1989, New York; 1991, U.S. District Court, Southern District of California; 1995, U.S. District Court, Central District of California; 1996, U.S. District Court, District of Arizona; registered to practice before the U.S. Patent and Trademark Office. *Education:* University of New Mexico (B.S., magna cum laude, Mathematics and Physics, 1973; M.A., Mathematics, 1977); University of Illinois (graduate study in Astrophysics, 1973-1974); Stanford Law School (J.D., 1982). Phi Beta Kappa. Member of Technical Staff, Sandia National Laboratories, 1977-1979; Regional Patent Counsel, Hewlett-Packard Company, 1980-1987. *PRACTICE AREAS:* Intellectual Property; Litigation. *Email:* starkj@pennie.com

**PAUL R. DE STEFANO,** born Philadelphia, Pennsylvania, September 16, 1950; admitted to bar, 1975, California; 1976, Alaska; 1980, District of Columbia. *Education:* Dickinson College, University of Vienna (B.A., Philosophy, with high honors, 1971); University of Southern California (J.D., with honors, 1974); Johns Hopkins University, School of Advanced International Studies (1981-1982). Adjunct Professor, Dickinson School of Law, 1988. LANGUAGES: German and French. *PRACTICE AREAS:* Intellectual Property; International Transactional Work related to the Biological Sciences. *Email:* destafanop@pennie.com

**ALBERT P. HALLUIN,** born Washington, D.C., November 8, 1939; admitted to bar, 1970, Maryland; 1985, New York; 1991, California; registered to practice before U.S. Patent and Trademark Office. *Education:* Louisiana State University and A. and M. College (B.A., Chemistry/Biochemistry, 1964); University of Baltimore (J.D., 1969). *PRACTICE AREAS:* Intellectual Property. *Email:* halluin@pennie.com

## RESIDENT COUNSEL

**CHARLES F. HOYNG,** born Dayton, Ohio, January 11, 1950; admitted to bar, 1989, California, U.S. District Court, Northern District of California and U.S. Court of Appeals, Ninth Circuit; registered to practice before U.S. Patent and Trademark Office. *Education:* Miami University (B.S., Chemistry, 1972); Massachusetts Institute of Technology (Ph.D., Organic Chemistry, 1976); Boalt Hall School of Law, University of California, Berkeley (J.D., 1989). Member, 1986-1989 and Topics Editor, 1988-1989, High Technology Law Journal. *PRACTICE AREAS:* Licensing; Intellectual Property. *Email:* hoyngc@pennie.com

**SARALYNN MANDELL,** born Glenns Falls, New York, April 2, 1956; admitted to bar, 1984, California; 1986, Washington; registered to practice before U.S. Patent and Trademark Office. *Education:* University of California, Los Angeles (B.A., Biology, cum laude, 1977); University of Washington (M.S., Plant Physiology and Biochemistry, 1981); University of Puget Sound School of Law (J.D., cum laude, 1984). *PRACTICE AREAS:* Intellectual Property; Biotechnology. *Email:* mandels@pennie.com

## RESIDENT ASSOCIATES

**THOMAS D. KOHLER,** born Syracuse, New York, May 7, 1961; admitted to bar, 1990, New York and Connecticut; registered to practice before U.S. Patent and Trademark Office (Not admitted in California). *Education:* Clarkson University (B.S., Mechanical Engineering, 1983); Marshall-Wythe School of Law, College of William & Mary (J.D., 1988); London School of Economics and Political Science (LL.M., European Law, Merit, 1989). *PRACTICE AREAS:* Intellectual Property; Medical and Mechanical Patents; Patent Litigation. *Email:* kohlert@pennie.com

**WARREN S. HEIT,** born Boston, Massachusetts, January 16, 1965; admitted to bar, 1990, Connecticut; 1991, New York; 1993, California; registered to practice before U.S. Patent and Trademark Office. *Education:* Tufts University (B.S., Electrical Engineering, magna cum laude, 1986); Fordham University (J.D., 1990). Eta Kappa Nu. *PRACTICE AREAS:* Intellectual Property. *Email:* heitw@pennie.com

**MICHAEL J. LYONS,** born Seattle, Washington, December 19, 1966; admitted to bar, 1993, New York (Not admitted in California). *Education:* Pennsylvania State University (B.S., Physics, 1989); Georgetown University (J.D., 1992). Phi Beta Kappa. *PRACTICE AREAS:* Intellectual Property. *Email:* lyonsm@pennie.com

**BERNARD H. CHAO,** born Stillwater, Oklahoma, December 8, 1965; admitted to bar, 1990, California; registered to practice before U.S. Patent and Trademark Office. *Education:* Purdue University (B.S., Electrical Engineering, 1987); Duke University (J.D., 1990). *PRACTICE AREAS:* Intellectual Property; Litigation. *Email:* choab@pennie.com

**FREDERICK F. HADIDI,** born Lexington, Kentucky, July 26, 1967; admitted to bar, 1992, California. *Education:* Cornell University (B.S., Electrical Engineering, 1989); Stanford University (J.D., 1992). Tau Beta Pi; Eta Kappa Nu. *PRACTICE AREAS:* Intellectual Property; Patent Prosecution; Patent Litigation. *Email:* hadidif@pennie.com

**VICTOR K. LEE,** born Hong Kong, September 10, 1958; admitted to bar, 1996, New York; registered to practice before U.S. Patent and Trademark Office (Not admitted in California). *Education:* Eastern Washington University (B.Sc., Biology, 1979); University of Washington (Ph.D., Experimental Pathology, 1985); Brooklyn Law School (J.D., 1995). LANGUAGES: Chinese. *PRACTICE AREAS:* Biotechnology Patent Law; Intellectual Property. *Email:* leev@pennie.com

**LANCE K. ISHIMOTO,** born Hollywood, California, May 11, 1959; admitted to bar, 1994, California. *Education:* University of California at Los Angeles (B.A., Microbiology, 1982; Ph.D., Microbiology, 1988); Stanford University (J.D., 1994). *PRACTICE AREAS:* Intellectual Property. *Email:* lkishimoto@pennie.com

*(This Listing Continued)*

### PENNIE & EDMONDS LLP, Menlo Park—Continued

**MARK R. SCADINA**, born San Jose, California, May 2, 1969; admitted to bar, 1994, California and U.S. District Court, Northern District of California; 1995, U.S. Court of Appeals, Ninth Circuit, U.S. District Court, Southern and Central Districts of California; registered to practice before U.S. Patent and Trademark Office. *Education:* Santa Clara University (B.S., Electrical Engineering, magna cum laude, 1991); Boalt Hall School of Law, University of California (J.D., 1994). Tau Beta Pi. *PRACTICE AREAS:* Intellectual Property, Patent Litigation and Prosecution. *Email:* scadinam@pennie.com

**WILLIAM L. WANG,** born Princeton, New Jersey, August 17, 1965; admitted to bar, 1994, California; U.S. District Court, Northern District of California, U.S. Court of Appeals, Ninth Circuit; registered to practice before U.S. Patent and Trademark Office. *Education:* University of California at Santa Barbara (B.S., Electrical Engineering, high honors, 1988; B.A., Business Economics, highest honors, 1988); Boalt Hall School of Law, University of California (J.D., 1994). *PRACTICE AREAS:* Intellectual Property; Patent Prosecution; Patent Litigation. *Email:* wangw@pennie.com

**DANIEL M. BECKER,** born East Orange, New Jersey, May 18, 1959; admitted to bar, 1995, California; registered to practice before U.S. Patent and Trademark Office. *Education:* Harvard College (B.A., magna cum laude, 1980); Stanford University School of Medicine (M.D., 1987); Stanford Law School (J.D., 1995). Phi Beta Kappa (Harvard College Chapter, 1980). Recipient: President's Writing Award, San Francisco Intellectual Property Law Association, 1995; Leukemia Society Special Fellowship (1990-1991; Host: M.I.T.); Sandoz Research Institute Postdoctoral Research Award (1990, Host: M.I.T.); American Cancer Society Postdoctoral Fellowship (1988-1989; Host: Wistar Institute); Research Honors Award for Distinguished Research in Molecular and Cellular Genetics (Stanford Medical School, 1987); Gina Finzi Memorial Summer Fellowship, Lupus Foundation of America (1984; Host: Stanford Medical School); Stanford Alumni Medical Student Scholarship (Stanford Medical School, 1983); Medical Student Research Fellowship, Pharmaceutical Manufacturers' Association Foundation (1982; Host: Harvard Medical School); John Harvard Scholarship (Harvard College 1979, 1980); Detur Prize (Harvard College 1978); National Science Foundation Summer Research Fellowship (Host: The Jackson Laboratory, 1978); Edwards Whitaker Prize (Harvard College, 1977); National Science Foundation High School Summer Studentship (1975; Host: Colorado School of Mines); National Merit Semifinalist, 1975. Judicial Extern to Judge Vaughn R. Walker, U.S. District Court, Northern District of California, 1994. *PRACTICE AREAS:* Intellectual Property; Patent Law. *Email:* dbecker@pennie.com

**BRIAN J. DAIUTO,** born Cleveland, Ohio, May 7, 1964; admitted to bar, 1995, California; 1996, U.S. Court of Appeals, Ninth Circuit, U.S. District Court, Northern, Central and Southern Districts of California and U.S. District Court, District of Arizona; registered to practice before U.S. Patent and Trademark Office. *Education:* University of Akron (B.S., Electrical Engineering, summa cum laude, 1987); Stanford University (M.S., Electrical Engineering, 1989); University of California, Berkeley (J.D., 1995). General Electric Foundation Fellowship. *PRACTICE AREAS:* Intellectual Property; Patent Prosecution; Patent Litigation. *Email:* daiutob@pennie.com

**KATHLEEN FOWLER,** born Yonkers, New York, March 19, 1960; admitted to bar, 1995, California. *Education:* Cornell University (B.S., Biology, 1982); University of California, Berkeley (Ph.D., Molecular Biology, 1990); Stanford University School of Medicine, Department of Biochemistry (postdoctoral Fellow, 1990-1992); University of California, Hastings College of the Law (J.D., 1995). *PRACTICE AREAS:* Patent Prosecution; Opinion Work; Intellectual Property; Biotechnology. *Email:* kfowler@pennie.com

**ANN M. CAVIANI PEASE,** born Iron Mountain, Michigan, February 27, 1963; admitted to bar, 1995, California. *Education:* University of Wisconsin, Madison (B.S., Chemistry, with honors, 1985); University of California, Berkeley (Ph.D., Biophysical Chemistry, 1990); Stanford Law School (J.D., 1995). *PRACTICE AREAS:* Intellectual Property. *Email:* peasea@pennie.com

**VICKI L. HUNTWORK,** born Miami, Florida, February 6, 1965; admitted to bar, 1991, California. *Education:* University of Miami (B.S., Biology, with General Honors, 1987); University of North Carolina School of Law, Chapel Hill (J.D., with High Honors, 1991). *PRACTICE AREAS:* Intellectual Property; Corporate. *Email:* huntworkv@pennie.com

(This Listing Continued)

**JUNG-HUA KUO,** born Kaohsiung, Taiwan, January 7, 1970; (admission pending). *Education:* Massachusetts Institute of Technology (B.S., Mechanical Engineering; M.S., Mechanical Engineering, 1993); University of California, Boalt Hall School of Law (J.D., 1996). Tau Beta Pi; Pi Tau Sigma. *LANGUAGES:* Chinese (Mandarin). *PRACTICE AREAS:* Intellectual Property. *Email:* kuoj@pennie.com

**JEFFERY J. MCDOW,** born Grand Forks, British Columbia, Canada, January 24, 1968; (admission pending). *Education:* Walla Walla College (B.S., Electrical Engineering, 1991); Stanford University (M.S., Electrical Engineering, 1993); Harvard University (J.D., 1996). *PRACTICE AREAS:* Intellectual Property. *Email:* mcdowj@pennie.com

**DANIEL E. VAUGHAN,** born Pittsburgh, Pennsylvania, April 21, 1962; (admission pending). *Education:* University of Pittsburgh (B.S., Computer Science, cum laude, 1985); Johns Hopkins University (M.S., Computer Science, 1991); New York University (J.D., 1996). *PRACTICE AREAS:* Intellectual Property. *Email:* vaughand@pennie.com

**BRADLEY A. GREENWALD,** born Gary, Indiana, August 22, 1962; admitted to bar, 1993, California. *Education:* University of Iowa (B.A., Physics and Philosophy, with honors and high distinction, 1985); University of Wisconsin (M.A., Philosophy, 1987); Harvard Law School (J.D., cum laude, 1993). *PRACTICE AREAS:* Intellectual Property. *Email:* greenwaldb@pennie.com

(For Complete personnel and biographical data, see New York, New York Professional Biographies).

---

## PEZZOLA & REINKE

*A PROFESSIONAL CORPORATION*
BUILDING 4
3000 SAND HILL ROAD, SUITE 160
**MENLO PARK, CALIFORNIA 94025**
*Telephone: 415-854-8797*

*Oakland, California Office:* Suite 1300, Lake Merritt Plaza, 1999 Harrison Street, 94612, Telephone: 510-273-8750. Fax: 510-834-7440.
*San Francisco, California Office:* 650 California Street, 32nd Floor, 94111. Telephone: 415-989-9710.

Corporate, Partnership, Emerging Growth Companies, Health Care, Mergers and Acquisitions, State and Federal Securities Law, Computer Law, Venture Capital, Intellectual Property, Real Estate, Nonprofit Representation and State, Federal and International Taxation.

(For Complete Biographical Data on all Personnel see Professional Biographies at Oakland, California)

---

## PILLSBURY MADISON & SUTRO LLP

2700 SAND HILL ROAD
**MENLO PARK, CALIFORNIA 94025-7020**
*Telephone: 415-233-4500*
*FAX: 415-233-4545*

*Costa Mesa, California Office:* Plaza Tower, Suite 1100, 600 Anton Boulevard, 92626. Telephone: 714-436-6800. Fax: 714-662-6999.
*Los Angeles, California Office:* Citicorp Plaza, 725 South Figueroa Street, Suite 1200, 90017. Telephone: 213-488-7100. Fax: 213-629-1033.
*New York, New York Office:* 520 Madison Avenue, 40th Floor, 10022. Telephone: 212-328-4810. Fax: 212-328-4824.
*Sacramento, California Office:* 400 Capitol Mall, Suite 1700, 95814. Telephone: 916-329-4700. Fax: 916-441-3583.
*San Diego, California Office:* 101 West Broadway, Suite 1800, 92101. Telephone: 619-234-5000. Fax: 619-236-1995.
*San Francisco, California Office:* 235 Montgomery Street, 94104. Telephone: 415-983-1000. Fax: 415-983-1200.
*Washington, D. C. Office:* 1100 New York Avenue, N.W., Ninth Floor, 20005. Telephone: 202-861-3000. Fax: 202-822-0944. 1050 Connecticut Avenue, N.W., Suite 1200, 20036-5303. Telephone: 202-887-0300. Fax: 202-296-7605.
*Hong Kong Office:* 6/F Asia Pacific Finance Tower, Citibank Plaza, 3 Garden Road, Central. Telephone: 011-852-2509-7100. Fax: 011-852-2509-7188.
*Tokyo, Japan Office:* Pillsbury Madison & Sutro, Gaikokuho Jimu Bengoshi Jimusho, 5th Floor, Samon Eleven Building, 3-1, Samon-cho, Shinjuku-ku, Tokyo 160 Japan. Telephone: 800-729-9830; 011-813-3354-3531. Fax: 011-813-3354-3534.

(This Listing Continued)

General Civil Practice and Litigation in all State and Federal Courts. Business: Banking and Corporate Finance; Commercial Transactions/Energy; Corporate, Securities and Technologies; Creditors' Rights and Bankruptcy; Employee Benefits; Employment and Labor Relations; Environment, Health & Safety; Estate Planning; Finance and Commercial Transactions; Food and Beverage Regulation; Health Care; Political Law; Real Estate; Tax (domestic and international); and Telecommunications. Litigation: Alternative Dispute Resolution; Antitrust/Trade Regulation; Appellate; Banking/Financial Institutions; Commercial Disputes; Construction/Real Estate; Creditors' Rights, Bankruptcy and Insurance Insolvency; Energy Matters; Employment/Equal Opportunity; Environmental/Land Use; ERISA; Insurance; Intellectual Property; Maritime/Admiralty; Media/Entertainment/Sports; Securities; Tort/Product Liability; and White Collar Defense. Intellectual Property: Aesthetic Design & Trade Dress Protection; Biotechnology; Computer Law; Copyright Law; Intellectual Property Audits and Strategic Planning; International Trade Commission; Licensing and Technology Transfer; Procurement of Property Rights; Patent Prosecution; Trade Secrets and Unfair Competition; Trademark Law; Interference Practice; Mechanical/Biomed/Aeronautical; and Physics/Optics.

FIRM PROFILE: Founded in 1874, Pillsbury Madison & Sutro LLP has grown to become one of the largest law firms in the United States, with more than 560 attorneys and expertise in virtually every area of the law. With offices in seven California cities, New York, Washington, D.C., and two offices in Asia, Hong Kong and Tokyo, the firm combines a strong domestic practice with a dynamic presence in the rapidly changing international markets. The firm's corporate expertise encompasses all aspects of business law and covers the full range of legal needs. Our litigation practice is conducted by trial lawyers who have handled landmark cases in the federal and state courts. Our intellectual property practices focuses on litigation, patent and trademark prosecution, licensing and copyright protection. Pillsbury attorneys also work in other legal areas where technology interacts with law, including international trade, environmental protection and food and drug regulation. The firm's clients range from large national and international corporations to start-up companies, the U.S. and foreign governments to universities to individuals. The Cushman Darby & Cushman Intellectual Property Group of Pillsbury Madison & Sutro LLP has practiced intellectual property law since 1892, concentrating on United States and international patent, trademark, copyright and unfair competition law, other technology-associated matters, and related litigation in all courts and administrative agencies. Our patent attorneys have degrees in technical disciplines, and a number hold advanced degrees. Many have practical experience as engineers, microbiologists, physicists, computer experts and chemists.

### MEMBERS OF FIRM

**JAMES P. CLOUGH,** born Amsterdam, New York, April 29, 1950; admitted to bar, 1976, New York; 1979, District of Columbia; 1981, California. *Education:* Siena College (B.S., 1972); Albany Law School of Union University (J.D., 1976); New York University (LL.M., 1979). **Email:** clough_jp@pillsburylaw.com

**JORGE A. DEL CALVO,** born Habana, Cuba, October 13, 1955; admitted to bar, 1982, California. *Education:* Stanford University (B.A., 1976); University of California at Los Angeles (M.A., 1978); Harvard University (M.P.P., 1981); Harvard Law School (J.D., 1981)); University of Philippines, Diliman, Quezon City, Philippines. **Email:** delcalvo_ja@pillsburylaw.com

**F. KINSEY HAFFNER,** born San Francisco, California, February 20, 1948; admitted to bar, 1974, California. *Education:* Stanford University (B.A., 1971); Stanford Law School (J.D., 1974). **Email:** haffner_fk@pillsburylaw.com

**KATHARINE A. MARTIN,** born Womborne, England, November 1, 1962; admitted to bar, 1987, California. *Education:* University of California, Berkeley (B.A., 1984); McGeorge School of Law (J.D., 1987). **Email:** martin_k@pillsburylaw.com

**LYNN L. MILLER,** born Los Angeles, California, April 18, 1950; admitted to bar, 1974, California. *Education:* University of California at Berkeley (B.A., 1971); University of California at Los Angeles Law School (J.D., 1974). **Email:** miller_ll@pillsburylaw.com

**JONATHAN M. OCKER,** born Sterling, Illinois, April 1, 1953; admitted to bar, 1978, Illinois; 1983, California. *Education:* University of Wisconsin (B.A., 1975); Washington University (J.D., 1978). **Email:** ocker_jm@pillsburylaw.com

**MARINA H. PARK,** born Pasadena, California, November 6, 1956; admitted to bar, 1982, California. *Education:* University of California at

*(This Listing Continued)*

Berkeley (B.A., 1978); University of Michigan (J.D., 1982). **Email:** park_mh@pillsburylaw.com

**SCOTT T. SMITH,** born San Francisco, California, February 14, 1954; admitted to bar, 1981, California. *Education:* Colorado College (B.A., 1976); Boalt Hall School of Law, University of California (J.D., 1981). **Email:** smith_st@pillsburylaw.com

**MICHAEL J. SULLIVAN,** born Albany, New York, May 19, 1959; admitted to bar, 1984, California. *Education:* Williams College (B.A., 1981); University of Michigan (J.D., 1984). **Email:** sullivan_mj@pillsburylaw.com

**ALLISON M. LEOPOLD TILLEY,** born Berkeley, California, November 18, 1963; admitted to bar, 1988, California. *Education:* University of California at Davis (B.A., 1985); Boalt Hall School of Law, University of California (J.D., 1988). **Email:** tilley_am@pillsburylaw.com

**GEORGIA K. VAN ZANTEN,** born Portland, Oregon, January 13, 1943; admitted to bar, 1984, California. *Education:* Washington State University (B.A., 1964); Santa Clara University School of Law (J.D., 1984). **Email:** vanzanten_gk@pillsburylaw.com

**WAYNE M. WHITLOCK,** born Worland, Wyoming, May 25, 1955; admitted to bar, 1983, Colorado; 1987, California. *Education:* Utah State University (B.S., 1980); J. Rueben Clark Law School Brigham Young University (J.D., 1983). **Email:** whitlock_wm@pillsburylaw.com

**DEBRA L. ZUMWALT,** born Phoenix, Arizona, November 15, 1955; admitted to bar, 1979, California. *Education:* Arizona State University (B.S., 1976); Stanford University (J.D., 1979). **Email:** zumwalt_dl@pillsburylaw.com

### OF COUNSEL

**KENNETH A. MANASTER,** born Chicago, Illinois, June 6, 1942; admitted to bar, 1967, Illinois; 1974, California. *Education:* Harvard University (A.B., 1963); Harvard Law School (J.D., 1966). **Email:** manaster_ka@pillsburylaw.com

### SENIOR COUNSEL

**SUSAN R. MENDELSOHN,** born Washington, Pennsylvania, January 2, 1946; admitted to bar, 1980, California. *Education:* Pennsylvania State University (B.S., 1967); University of San Francisco (J.D., 1980). **Email:** mendelsoh_sr@pillsburylaw.com

**BARBARA R. SHUFRO,** born Boston, Massachusetts, August 5, 1957; admitted to bar, 1983, Massachusetts; 1987, California. *Education:* Hampshire College (B.A., 1980); Northeastern University (J.D., 1983); Georgetown University (LL.M., 1985). **Email:** shufro_br@pillsburylaw.com

**JOHN S. WESOLOWSKI,** born China Lake, California, October 21, 1948; admitted to bar, 1986, California. *Education:* University of California at Santa Barbara (B.A., 1970); Santa Clara University (J.D., 1986). **Email:** wesolowsk_js@pillsburylaw.com

### ASSOCIATES

Melissa A. Burke  
L. William Caraccio (Resident)  
Patricia L. Cotton  
Patrick H. Dunkley  
Adam T. Ettinger  
Davina K. Kaile  
Michael D. Lee  
Christine F. Nakagawa  
Betsy G. Stauffer  
John E. Wood  

(For biographical data on San Diego, Los Angeles, Sacramento, San Jose, Costa Mesa and San Francisco, CA, Washington, DC and Tokyo, Japan, New York, NY and Hong Kong personnel, see Professional Biographies at each of those cities).

---

## GEORGE B. RICHARDSON
*750 MENLO AVENUE, SUITE 250*  
**MENLO PARK, CALIFORNIA 94025**  
Telephone: 415-614-0160  
Fax: 415-321-0198  
Email: DissoLawGR@aol.com

*Litigation and Mediation Involving Family Law, Dissolution and Post-Dissolution Matters.*

**GEORGE B. RICHARDSON,** born Plainfield, New Jersey, January 22, 1947; admitted to bar, 1972, California. *Education:* Princeton University (B.A., cum laude, 1969); Stanford University (J.D., 1972). *Member:* Palo Alto (Member, Family Law Section), Santa Clara (Member, Family Law Section) and San Mateo County (Member, Family Law Section) Bar Asso-

*(This Listing Continued)*

## GEORGE B. RICHARDSON, Menlo Park—Continued

ciations; Association of Certified Family Law Specialists. (Certified Specialist, Family Law, The State Bar of California, Board of Legal Specialization). *PRACTICE AREAS:* Family Law; Pre-Marital Law; Dissolution; Post-Dissolution Matters.

---

## ROBERTSON, ALEXANDER, LUTHER, ESSELSTEIN, SHIELLS & WRIGHT

*A PROFESSIONAL CORPORATION*

**MENLO PARK, CALIFORNIA**

(See Esselstein, Wright, Jones & Greenberg, A Professional Corporation)

---

## SCHACHTER, KRISTOFF, ORENSTEIN & BERKOWITZ, L.L.P.

90 MIDDLEFIELD ROAD, SUITE 201
**MENLO PARK, CALIFORNIA 94025**
Telephone: 415-473-1400
Telecopier: 415-463-0346

*San Francisco, California Office:* 505 Montgomery Street, 14th Floor. Telephone: 415-391-3333. Telecopier: 415-392-6589.

*Sacramento, California Office:* 980 9th Street, Suite 1760. Telephone: 916-442-3333. Telecopier: 916-442-2348.

Labor Relations and Employment Law and Litigation on Behalf of Employers. Legislative Law.

FIRM PROFILE: Schachter, Kristoff, Orenstein & Berkowitz is a labor and employment law firm representing employers in a broad range of industries throughout the United States. The Firm's practice encompasses all aspects of the employer-employee relationship. It specializes in employment litigation involving wrongful discharge, discrimination, sexual harassment, drug and alcohol testing, and wage/hour disputes. Members of the Firm are also heavily involved in representing unionized employers in collective bargaining, arbitrations, strikes and contract administration; advising non-union employers on dealing with union organizational activity; and counseling employers regarding employee discipline and termination, privacy issues, employment agreements, substance abuse, wage and hour, and safety and health matters; unfair competition; ERISA; and workers' compensation.

The Firm emphasizes preventive counseling and provides a broad range of employment law seminars and management training programs to help clients avoid the expense of litigation and to achieve their human resource goals.

(For Complete Biographical Data, see San Francisco, California)

---

## LAW OFFICES OF JOHN C. SHAFFER, JR.

*A PROFESSIONAL LAW CORPORATION*

Established in 1984

750 MENLO AVENUE, SUITE 250
**MENLO PARK, CALIFORNIA 94025**
Telephone: 415-324-0622
Fax: 415-321-0198

Civil Trial Practice. Labor Employment Law Issues including Discrimination, Sexual Harassment and Wrongful Termination from Employment, Business and Personal Injury Litigation, Insurance Bad Faith and Coverage Issues.

**JOHN C. SHAFFER, JR.,** born San Mateo, California, October 5, 1943; admitted to bar, 1969, California. *Education:* Occidental College (A.B., with Departmental Honors, 1965); Boalt Hall School of Law, University of California (J.D., 1968). Author, "Fired Employees: Psychological Reactions to Termination," The Recorder, San Francisco, 1985. Panelist, "How to Handle Commercial Bad Faith Cases," Continuing Education of the Bar, Palo Alto, San Jose and Monterey, California, 1985. Arbitrator, San Mateo County Superior Court, 1987—. *Member:* Santa Clara (Arbitrator, Fee Dispute, 1983—) and San Mateo Bar Associations; State Bar of California; Consumer Attorneys of California. *PRACTICE AREAS:* Labor and Employment; Personal Injury; Insurance Law.

---

## VENTURE LAW GROUP

*Established in 1993*

2800 SAND HILL ROAD
**MENLO PARK, CALIFORNIA 94025**
Telephone: 415-854-4488
Fax: 415-854-1121
URL: http://www.venlaw.com

*Kirkland, Washington Office:* 4750 Carillan Point, 7th Floor. Telephone: 206-739-8700. Fax: 206-739-8750.

Securities Law, Mergers and Acquisitions, Intellectual Property, Complex Corporate Transactions and Relationships.

FIRM PROFILE: Venture Law Group specializes in representing deal-intensive growth companies both public and private and investment firms that support these companies.

### DIRECTORS

**ELIAS J. BLAWIE,** born Berkeley, California, October 30, 1958; admitted to bar, 1983, California. *Education:* University of California at Berkeley (A.B., with great distinction, 1979; M.B.A., 1982); Boalt Hall School of Law, University of California at Berkeley (J.D., 1983). Phi Beta Kappa. *Member:* State Bar of California. *PRACTICE AREAS:* Corporate Law; Securities.

**JAMES LEE BROCK,** born Phoenix, Arizona, April 19, 1962; admitted to bar, 1987, California. *Education:* Claremont McKenna College (B.A., with honors, 1983); University of Chicago (J.D., with honors, 1986). Order of the Coif. James M. Olin Fellow. Topics and Comments Editor, University of Chicago Law Review, 1985-1986. Law Clerk, Hon. Patrick E. Higginbotham, U.S. Court of Appeals for the Fifth Circuit, 1987-1988. *Member:* State Bar of California. *PRACTICE AREAS:* Corporate Law; Securities; Mergers; Acquisitions.

**CATHRYN S. CHINN,** born Lawrence, Kansas, January 30, 1957; admitted to bar, 1984, California. *Education:* Stanford University (B.A., with distinction and departmental honors, 1979; J.D., 1984). Phi Beta Kappa. *Member:* State Bar of California; American Bar Association. *PRACTICE AREAS:* Corporate Law; Securities.

**WILLIAM W. ERICSON,** born Washington, D.C., July 3, 1958; admitted to bar, 1990, New York; 1991, California. *Education:* Georgetown University (B.S.F.S., 1982); Cornell University (Certificate in Asian Studies, 1983); Northwestern University (J.D., 1988). Member, Editorial Board, 1986-1987 and Articles Editor, 1987-1988, Northwestern Journal of International Law and Business. (Resident at Kirkland, Washington Office). *LANGUAGES:* Japanese. *PRACTICE AREAS:* Business Transactions.

**JOSHUA L. GREEN,** born Los Angeles, California, March 11, 1956; admitted to bar, 1980, California. *Education:* University of California at Los Angeles (B.A., magna cum laude, 1977; J.D., 1980). Member, UCLA Law Review, 1978-1980. Member, Committee on Federal Regulation of Securities, American Bar Association. *PRACTICE AREAS:* General Securities Law; Emerging Growth Companies Law; Venture Capital Law.

**MICHAEL W. HALL,** born Willimantic, Connecticut, March 8, 1948; admitted to bar, 1982, California. *Education:* California State College, Sonoma (B.A., with honors, 1970); Boalt Hall School of Law, University of California at Berkeley (J.D., 1982). *Member:* State Bar of California (Member, Business Law Section); American Bar Association (Member, Section on Corporation, Banking and Business Law). *PRACTICE AREAS:* Corporate Law; Securities.

**CRAIG W. JOHNSON,** born Pasadena, California, December 28, 1946; admitted to bar, 1974, California. *Education:* Yale University (B.A., magna cum laude, 1968); Stanford Law School (J.D., 1974). Recipient, Lawrence S. Fletcher Award, 1973-1974. Member, Stanford Law School Board of Visitors, 1974-1977. *Member:* State Bar of California. *PRACTICE AREAS:* Corporate Law; Securities.

**DONALD M. KELLER, JR.,** born Norfolk, Virginia, September 23, 1957; admitted to bar, 1982, Massachusetts; 1985, California. *Education:* Dartmouth College (A.B., 1979); Boston College (J.D., 1982). Alpha Sigma Nu; Order of the Coif. Member, Boston College Law Review, 1981-1982. *PRACTICE AREAS:* Corporate Law; Securities.

**MARK A. MEDEARIS,** born Albuquerque, New Mexico, April 6, 1954; admitted to bar, 1979, Colorado; 1982, California. *Education:* University of Colorado (B.S., with special honors, 1975); Stanford University (M.S., 1976; J.D., 1979). Tau Beta Pi. Associate Editor, Stanford Law Review, 1978-1979. Co-Author: Counseling the Board on Pre-Bid Defensive Plan-

*(This Listing Continued)*

ning, University of California Securities Law Institute, 1991. *Member:* Colorado and American (Member, Sections on: Corporation, Banking and Business Law; Science and Technology) Bar Associations; State Bar of California. *PRACTICE AREAS:* Corporate Law; Securities; Intellectual Property.

**TAE HEA NAHM,** born Seoul, Korea, February 28, 1960; admitted to bar, 1985, California and U.S. District Court, Northern District of California. *Education:* Harvard College (A.B., magna cum laude, 1982); University of Chicago (J.D., 1985). Phi Beta Kappa. *Member:* State Bar of California. *LANGUAGES:* Korean. *PRACTICE AREAS:* Corporate Law; Securities.

**JOSHUA W. R. PICKUS,** born Walnut Creek, California, March 30, 1961; admitted to bar, 1986, California. *Education:* Princeton University (A.B., 1983); University of Chicago (J.D., cum laude, 1986). Champion, Hinton Moot Court Competition, 1985. Law Clerk to Judge (now Justice ) Anthony M. Kennedy, U.S. Court of Appeals, Ninth Circuit, 1987. *PRACTICE AREAS:* Corporate Law; Securities; Intellectual Property.

**CRAIG E. SHERMAN,** born Granada Hills, California, July 22, 1963; admitted to bar, 1990, New York; 1995, Washington (Not admitted in California). *Education:* Institut d'Etudes Politiques, Paris, France (certificat d'études politiques, 1983); Stanford University (A.B., with honors, 1985; M.A., 1985); Harvard University (J.D., cum laude, 1989). Articles Editor, Harvard Human Rights Yearbook, 1988-1989. (Resident at Kirkland Washington Office). *LANGUAGES:* French, Italian, Spanish, Korean. *PRACTICE AREAS:* Corporate Finance; Securities.

**JEFFREY Y. SUTO,** born Los Angeles, California, December 3, 1961; admitted to bar, 1988, California. *Education:* Stanford University (A.B., 1983); University of California at Los Angeles (J.D., 1988). Recipient, American Jurisprudence Award for: Contracts; Patent Law. *PRACTICE AREAS:* Securities Law; General Corporate Law; Venture Capital Law.

**STEVEN J. TONSFELDT,** born Boone, Iowa, July 27, 1960; admitted to bar, 1987, California. *Education:* University of Iowa (B.B.A., with highest distinction, 1982); Boalt Hall School of Law, University of California at Berkeley (J.D., 1987). Graduate Student Instructor, Haas School of Business, University of California at Berkeley, 1985-1986. Certified Public Accountant, Colorado, 1984. *Member:* American Institute of Certified Public Accountants. *PRACTICE AREAS:* General Corporate Law; Securities Law; Banking Law. *Email:* stonsfeldt@brobeck.com

**MARK B. WEEKS,** born Redwood City, California, March 17, 1961; admitted to bar, 1987, California. *Education:* Williams College (B.A., 1983); Santa Clara University (J.D., 1987). Co-Chairman, Santa Clara Moot Court Competition, 1986-1987. Articles Editor, Santa Clara Computer and High Technology Law Journal, 1986-1987. *Member:* State Bar of California. *LANGUAGES:* Japanese. *PRACTICE AREAS:* Corporate Law; Securities; Intellectual Property.

**MARK WINDFELD-HANSEN,** born Lancaster, Pennsylvania, September 28, 1956; admitted to bar, 1983, New York; 1984, California. *Education:* Amherst College (B.A., summa cum laude, 1978); Yale Law School (J.D., 1982). Phi Beta Kappa. Co-Author: "State Taxation of Pass-Through Entities", Tax Management, Inc. *PRACTICE AREAS:* Tax.

**ROBERT V. W. ZIPP,** born Nürnberg, West Germany, December 10, 1962; admitted to bar, 1988, Texas; 1994, California. *Education:* Texas A & M University (B.A., with honors, 1985); Duke University (J.D., with honors, 1988). Senior Editor, Alaska Law Review, 1986-1988. *PRACTICE AREAS:* Corporation Law. *Email:* rzipp@venlaw.com

### SENIOR ATTORNEYS

**JOHN V. BAUTISTA,** born Mountain View, California, July 7, 1966; admitted to bar, 1991, California. *Education:* University of California at Los Angeles (B.A., 1988); Harvard University (J.D., 1991). Phi Beta Kappa. Recipient, UCLA Division Honors. Elected City Council Member, City of Cupertino, November, 1993. *Member:* State Bar of California. *LANGUAGES:* French and Spanish. *PRACTICE AREAS:* Corporate Law; Securities.

**EDGAR B. "CHIP" CALE,** born Upper Darby, Pennsylvania, September 9, 1963; admitted to bar, 1992, California. *Education:* University of Pennsylvania (B.A., 1985); Boalt Hall School of Law (J.D., 1991). Notes and Comment Editor, High Technology Law Journal (1990-1991). *Member:* Palo Alto and American (Member, Section on Business Law) Bar Associations. *PRACTICE AREAS:* Corporate Law; Securities Law.

**PETER COHN,** born Erie, Pennsylvania, May 7, 1956; admitted to bar, 1982, California; 1983, New York. *Education:* University of California at Berkeley (B.S., with highest honors, 1978); Boalt Hall School of Law, University of California (J.D., 1981). Phi Beta Kappa; Beta Alpha Psi; Beta Gamma Sigma. Articles Editor, California Law Review, 1980-1981. Member, Industrial Relations Law Journal, 1978-1979. Law Clerk to Judge Robert W. Sweet, U.S. District Court, Southern District of New York, 1981-1982. *Member:* American Bar Association (Member, Section of Business Law, Committees on Small Business and Federal Regulation of Securities). *PRACTICE AREAS:* Securities; Mergers and Acquisitions; Venture Capital; Corporate.

**RENÉE RAIMONDI DEMING,** born Sacramento, California, June 17, 1953; admitted to bar, 1981, California; 1982, U.S. Tax Court. *Education:* Stanford University (A.B., 1975); University of California at Davis (J.D., 1981). Volume Editor, University of Davis Law Review, 1980-1981. *Member:* State Bar of California. *PRACTICE AREAS:* Tax; Employee Benefits.

**ELIZABETH F. ENAYATI,** born San Jose, California, December 30, 1960; admitted to bar, 1989, California; 1990, Massachusetts; registered to practice before U.S. Patent and Trademark Office. *Education:* University of Santa Clara (B.S., 1980); Leavy School of Business, University of Santa Clara (M.B.A., 1989); University of Santa Clara (J.D., 1989). Co-Author: *1991 Licensing Law Handbook.* .

**SONYA F. ERICKSON,** born Vancouver, Washington, July 8, 1965; admitted to bar, 1990, California. *Education:* Pepperdine University (B.A./B.S., cum laude, 1987); University of Washington (J.D., 1990). Recipient, American Jurisprudence Award. *Member:* Orange County (Business Section, 1992-1993) and Santa Clara County Bar Associations. (Resident at Kirkland, Washington Office). *PRACTICE AREAS:* Securities/Corporate Finance; Licensing; General Corporate.

**JON E. GAVENMAN,** born Stanford, California, June 15, 1967; admitted to bar, 1991, California. *Education:* Pomona College (B.A., 1988); University of California, Hastings College of Law (J.D., 1991). Member, Mortar Board, 1987-1988. Recipient, Arvid Pierre Zetterberg, Jr. Award, 1985. Executive Editor, Hastings Constitutional Law Q. Author: Case Comment, "Florida v. Riley: The Descent of Fourth Amendment Protections in Aerial Surveillance Cases," 17 Hast. Const. L.Q. 725 (1990). *Member:* State Bar of California. *PRACTICE AREAS:* Corporate Law; Securities.

**MICHAEL A. MORRISSEY,** born Peoria, Illinois, August 27, 1964; admitted to bar, 1992, California. *Education:* Stanford University (B.A., with distinction, 1986; M.S., 1987); University of California Boalt Hall School of Law (J.D., 1990). Order of the Coif. Member, 1988-1989 and Associate Editor, 1989-1990, California Law Review. Member, High Technology Law Journal, 1988. Clerkship, U.S. District Court, 1990-1991. *Member:* State Bar of California. *PRACTICE AREAS:* Corporate Law; Securities.

**DAVID C. LEE,** born Hong Kong, March 13, 1963; admitted to bar, 1991, California, U.S. District Court, Northern District of California and U.S. Court of Appeals, Ninth Circuit. *Education:* University of California at Berkeley (B.A., summa cum laude, 1987); Stanford University (J.D., 1990). Phi Beta Kappa. *Member:* State Bar of California (Member, Sections on: Business, Intellectual Property and International Law); Asian American Bar Association. *LANGUAGES:* Cantonese. *PRACTICE AREAS:* Corporate Law; Securities; Intellectual Property Law.

**STANLEY F. PIERSON,** born São Paulo, Brazil, June 21, 1959; admitted to bar, 1985, California and U.S. District Court, Northern District of California. *Education:* Stanford University (B.A., 1981); University of California at Los Angeles (J.D, 1985). *LANGUAGES:* French and Portuguese. *PRACTICE AREAS:* Corporate; Securities.

**PATRICK G. REUTENS,** born December 29, 1958; admitted to bar, 1991, California. *Education:* University of Western Australia (B.Sc., with first class honors, 1979); University of Chicago (Ph.D., 1986); Yale University (J.D., 1991). *Member:* State Bar of California. *PRACTICE AREAS:* Intellectual Property; Technology Development and Transfer.

**EDMUND S. RUFFIN, JR.,** born Richmond, Virginia, January 11, 1962; admitted to bar, 1990, New York; 1992, California. *Education:* University of Texas (B.A., 1984); College of William & Mary (M.B.A., 1989; J.D., 1989). *Member:* State Bar of California; New York State and American Bar Associations. *PRACTICE AREAS:* Corporate Law; Mergers and Acquisitions; Securities.

**MARK L. SILVERMAN,** born Oakland, California, August 18, 1964; admitted to bar, 1991, California and New York. *Education:* University of California at Berkeley (B.A., 1986); University of California School of Law (J.D., 1990).

**GLEN R. VAN LIGTEN,** born Burlingame, California, October 22, 1963; admitted to bar, 1990, California and U.S. District Court, Central

*(This Listing Continued)*

**VENTURE LAW GROUP, Menlo Park—Continued**

District of California. *Education:* University of California at Davis (B.S., 1985); University of California, Hastings College of the Law, (J.D., cum laude, 1990). *PRACTICE AREAS:* Securities Law; Corporate Law; Venture Capital Law; Intellectual Property Law. *Email:* gvenligten@venlaw.com

### ATTORNEYS

**PATRICK R. BARRY,** born Santa Clara, California, December 16, 1966; admitted to bar, 1995, California. *Education:* Columbia College (B.A., 1990); University of California, Hastings College of the Law (J.D., 1995). Thurston Society. Senior Staff Member, Hastings Law Journal. Recipient, Milton D. Green Award. Author: "Software Copyrights as Loan Collateral: Evaluating Reform Proposals," Hastings Law Journal, Vol. 46, January 1995. *PRACTICE AREAS:* Corporate; Securities.

**STEVE J. BOOM,** born Morristown, New Jersey, July 12, 1968; admitted to bar, 1994, California; 1995, District of Columbia. *Education:* Stanford University (B.S., 1990); Harvard University (J.D., 1994). Phi Beta Kappa; Tau Beta Pi. Author: "The European Union After the "Maastricht" Decision," 43 Am.J.C.L., 177, 1995. *LANGUAGES:* French, German and Spanish. *PRACTICE AREAS:* Corporate; Securities; Technology. *Email:* sboom@venlaw.com

**ARNOLD E. BROWN, II,** born Teaneck, New Jersey, March 19, 1967; admitted to bar, 1993, California. *Education:* Harvard University (B.A., 1989); Boalt Hall School of Law (J.D., 1993). I Member: San Francisco Bar Association. *PRACTICE AREAS:* Corporate and Securities; Entertainment Transactions.

**CAROLYN M. BRUGUERA,** born Champaign, Illinois, March 4, 1966; admitted to bar, 1993, California. *Education:* Harvard University (A.B., 1988); University of California, Boalt Hall School of Law (J.D., 1993). High Technology Law Journal, 1992-1993.

**BROOKE CAMPBELL,** born Dayton, Ohio, December 2, 1970; (admission pending). *Education:* University of Norte Dame (B.A., 1991); Yale Law School (J.D., 1996). *PRACTICE AREAS:* Mergers and Acquisitions; Venture Capital Financing; Securities. *Email:* bcampbell@venlaw.com

**AMY L. CUSTALOW,** born Richmond, Virginia, June 8, 1968; admitted to bar, 1994, California. *Education:* Duke University (B.A., cum laude, 1990); Stanford University (J.D., 1994). Member, Environmental Law Journal, 1992-1993. *Member:* State Bar of California.

**LAUREL FINCH,** born La Jolla, California, November 11, 1956; admitted to bar, 1994, Arizona (Not admitted in California). *Education:* Stanford University (B.A., 1978; J.D., 1992). Order of the Coif. Law Clerk to Judge Joseph T. Sneed, U.S. Court of Appeals, Ninth Circuit, 1992-1993. *PRACTICE AREAS:* Corporate Transactions; Securities Law; Private and Public Company Representation. *Email:* lfinch@venlaw.com

**ROBERT C. FOURR,** born Los Angeles, California, October 7, 1947; admitted to bar, 1975, Pennsylvania; 1979, California. *Education:* Stanford University (A.B., 1969; J.D., 1975). Recipient, Lockheed Leadership Scholarship. Note Editor, Stanford Law Review, Vol. 27, 1972-1975. Law Clerk to the Honorable Alfred L. Luongo, U.S. District Court, Eastern District of Pennsylvania, 1975-1977. Lecturer, Trial Advocacy, Stanford Law School, 1990-1992. Instructor, U.S. District Court, Federal Practice Program, 1985-1991. Mediator, Arbitrator and Early Neutral Evaluator, Alternative Dispute Resolution Program, U.S. District Court, Northern District of California, 1993—. Arbitrator, Marin County Superior Court, 1994—. Senior Counsel, Stanford University, 1987-1994. Assistant U.S. Attorney, U.S. Department of Justice, San Francisco, California, 1983-1987; Philadelphia, Pennsylvania, 1977-1979. *Member:* State Bar of California; Pennsylvania Bar Association. *LANGUAGES:* German. *PRACTICE AREAS:* Intellectual Property.

**LAURA A. GORDON,** born Oakland, California, September 18, 1967; admitted to bar, 1992, California. *Education:* University of California, Berkeley (B.A., 1989); Stanford University (J.D., 1992). Phi Beta Kappa. *Member:* State Bar of California. *PRACTICE AREAS:* Corporate Law; Securities.

**SHARON HENDRICKS,** born Jersey City, New Jersey, November 12, 1964; admitted to bar, 1992, California. *Education:* Duke University (A.B., 1986); University of Chicago School of Law (J.D., with honors, 1991). Symposium Editor, University of Chicago Legal Forum, 1990-1991. Recipient: Richard and Dorothy Merrill Tax Fellowship, 1991. Law Clerk to the Honorable W. Eugene Davis and the Honorable John M. Duhe, U.S. Court of Appeals, Fifth Circuit. *Member:* State Bar of California. *PRACTICE AREAS:* Corporate Law; Securities.

**DAVID M. JARGIELLO,** born Erie, Pennsylvania, March 16, 1960; admitted to bar, 1989, California. *Education:* Case Western Reserve University (B.A., magna cum laude, 1982); Stanford University (M.S., 1986); University of California at Berkeley (J.D., 1989). *Member:* State Bar of California. *PRACTICE AREAS:* Corporate Law; Securities.

**FRANCES JOHNSTON,** born April 26, 1957; admitted to bar, 1994, California. *Education:* Stanford University (B.A., 1980); University of California at Los Angeles (M.B.A., 1986); Stanford Law School (J.D., 1994). Phi Beta Kappa. *PRACTICE AREAS:* Corporations; Securities.

**SANJAY K. KHARE,** born Westwood, New Jersey, July 13, 1967; admitted to bar, 1995, California. *Education:* University of Chicago (B.A., 1989); Stanford University (J.D., 1995). *PRACTICE AREAS:* Corporate; Securities.

**EDWARD Y. KIM,** born Seattle, Washington, May 11, 1967; admitted to bar, 1995, California. *Education:* Bowdoin College (A.B., magna cum laude, 1988); University of Michigan (J.D., cum laude, 1995). *Member:* State Bar of California. *PRACTICE AREAS:* Corporate; Securities.

**JASON M. LEMKIN,** born Boston, Massachusetts, December 18, 1969; admitted to bar, 1996, California. *Education:* Harvard University (B.A., 1991); Boalt Hall School of Law, University of California (J.D., 1996). Order of the Coif. California Law Review, 1995-1996. Managing Editor, Ecology Law Quarterly. Author: A Proposal for the New Organizational Sentencing Guidelines. 84 Cal. L. Rev. 307 (1996). *PRACTICE AREAS:* Corporate; Securities Law. *Email:* jlemkin@venlaw.com

**JOHN P. MCINTIRE,** born Palos Verdes, California, March 18, 1969; admitted to bar, 1994, California. *Education:* Claremont McKenna College (B.A., summa cum laude, 1991); Yale University (J.D., 1994). *PRACTICE AREAS:* Corporate Law. *Email:* jmcintire@venlaw.com

**KEITH A. MILLER,** born Los Angeles, California, September 28, 1964; admitted to bar, 1993, California. *Education:* Brigham Young University (B.A., 1989); University of Chicago (J.D., 1993). Phi Delta Phi. Outstanding Chemistry Graduate, Brigham Young University. *LANGUAGES:* Japanese. *PRACTICE AREAS:* Corporate Securities; Technology Licensing. *Email:* kmiller@venlaw.com

**CHARLES L. MOORE,** born St. Louis, Missouri, January 27, 1966; admitted to bar, 1996, California. *Education:* U.S. Naval Academy (B.S., 1989); Boat Hall School of Law, University of California (J.D., 1996). Executive Editor, Berkeley Technology Law Journal. *Member:* State Bar of California. [Lieutenant U.S. Navy 1985-1993]. *PRACTICE AREAS:* Corporate Law; Securities Law; Venture Capital Transactions; Technology Transactions. *Email:* cmoore@venlaw.com

**KARA DIANE PALMER,** born Boulder, Colorado, May 29, 1967; admitted to bar, 1993, California. *Education:* University of California at Berkeley (B.A., with honors, 1989); Boalt Hall School of Law, University of California (J.D., 1993). (Resident at Kirkland, Washington Office). *PRACTICE AREAS:* Business and Technology; General Corporate Practice.

**SCOTT P. POTTER,** born Los Angeles, California, August 13, 1968; admitted to bar, 1995, California. *Education:* University of California at Berkeley (B.A., 1991); Boalt Hall School of Law, University of California at Berkeley (J.D., 1994). Recipient, American Jurisprudence Awards: Corporations; Research and Writing. *PRACTICE AREAS:* Securities; General Corporate; Venture Capital.

**JOHN W. ROBERTSON,** born Cleveland, Ohio, January 23, 1968; admitted to bar, 1995, Washington (Not admitted in California). *Education:* Duke University (A.B., magna cum laude, 1990); University of Virginia (J.D., 1994). (Resident at Kirkland, Washington Office). *LANGUAGES:* Mandarin. *PRACTICE AREAS:* Securities; Mergers and Acquisitions; Venture Capital; International Commercial Transactions.

**JOHN H. SELLERS,** born Bangor, Maine, April 21, 1966; admitted to bar, 1994, California. *Education:* Stanford University (A.B., with honors and distinction, 1988); University of Chicago (J.D., with honors, 1994). Comment Editor, Law Review. Senior Legislative Assistant to U.S. Representative Tom Campbell (CA), 1989-1991. *PRACTICE AREAS:* Corporate; Securities.

**CARL L. SPATARO, JR.,** born Harrison, Pennsylvania, March 12, 1959; admitted to bar, 1996, California. *Education:* United States Naval Academy (B.S., 1981); Vanderbilt University (M.B.A., 1993); Stanford University (J.D., 1996). Order of the Coif. [1st Lieutenant, U.S. Marine Corps].

*(This Listing Continued)*

**PRACTICE AREAS:** Corporate Finance; Licensing. **Email:** cspataro@venlaw.com

**THOMAS H. TOBIASON,** born Landstuhl, Germany, May 14, 1966; admitted to bar, 1992, California. *Education:* Brown University (A.B., magna cum laude, 1988); University of Michigan Law School (J.D., magna cum laude, 1992). Phi Beta Kappa. Order of the Coif. Contributing Editor, Michigan Law Review. Author: "The New Legal Puritanism of Catharine MacKinnon", 54 Ohio State Law Journal, 1375 (1993). **PRACTICE AREAS:** Corporate; Securities. **Email:** ttobiason@venlaw.com

**CHRISTINE A. TOMOMATSU,** born March 6, 1954; admitted to bar, 1990, California. *Education:* University of Utah (B.A., magna cum laude, 1976); University of California, Hastings College of the Law (J.D., cum laude, 1990).

**HEAYOON J. WOO,** born Seoul, Korea, September 23, 1964; admitted to bar, 1992, New York; 1994, California. *Education:* Harvard University (B.A., magna cum laude, 1987); Stanford University (J.D., 1991). Member, International Law, Journal, 1988-1989. Author: "Selected Securities Law Issues After the Merger Agreement is Signed", Handling Mergers and Acquisitions In A High Tech Environment, PLI 1996. *Member:* State Bar of California; American Bar Association. **LANGUAGES:** Korean. **PRACTICE AREAS:** Corporate Securities; Intellectual Property Licensing.

**DEANN K. WRIGHT,** born Decatur, Illinois, 1961; admitted to bar, 1992, California. *Education:* University of Wisconsin at Madison (B.S., Biochemistry, 1984); Hastings College of the Law, University of California (J.D., 1992). Hastings International and Comparative Law Journal. **PRACTICE AREAS:** Corporate Law; Biotechnology; Emerging Growth Companies.

**MITCHELL STANTON ZUKLIE,** born New Haven, Connecticut, April 27, 1969; admitted to bar, 1996, California. *Education:* Bowdoin College (A.B., 1991); Boalt Hall School of Law, University of California (J.D., 1996). California Law Review, Editor and Chief, 1995-1996. **PRACTICE AREAS:** Corporate Law; Securities.

*OF COUNSEL*

**RICHARD E. MONROE,** born Flint, Michigan, July 2, 1943; admitted to bar, 1974, Washington and U.S. District Court, Western District of Washington (Not admitted in California). *Education:* University of Michigan (B.A., 1964; M.A., 1966); Stanford University (J.D., 1974). Phi Beta Kappa. Lecturer on Contracts, Bar Review Associates of Washington, 1976-1989. Author: "Law Firm Agreements," Washington State Bar News, 1988. *Member:* King County, Washington State (Member, Sections on: Corporation, Banking and Business Law; Taxation; Real Property, Probate and Trust Law) and American (Member, Banking and Business Law and Taxation Sections) Bar Associations. (Resident at Kirkland, Washington Office).

REPRESENTATIVE CLIENTS: AirSoft; AccelGraphics; Adeza Biomedical Corporation; Alex. Brown & Sons, Incorporated; Alliance Semiconductor Corporation; Applied Micro Circuits; Aspect Telecommunications; Balance Pharmaceuticals; Baxter Healthcare; Cardima, Inc.; Celtrix Pharmaceuticals; Chiron; Collagen; Conceptus; Connect; Connective Therapeutics; Cowen & Company; Creative Technology Ltd.; Dolch American Instruments, Inc.; FiberStars; Fractal Design; General Surgical Innovations; Goldman Sachs & Co.; Gupta Corporation; Hambrecht & Quist Incorporated; IC Works; ISOCOR; InnerDyne, Inc.; Intel Corporation; KeraVision; Landec; Laserscope; Lattitude Communications; Lectus; Lipomatrix; Manzinita Software; MasPar Computer Corporation; Metra Biosystems; Morgan Stanley & Co., Incorporated; Motorola; Mycotech; NeoMagic Corporation; Oceania; Oclassen Pharmaceuticals; OnStream Networks; Oracle Corporation; Paradigm Health Corporation; Park Scientific; Persistence Software; Preview Media; Prograft Medical; Prudential Securities; Quality Semiconductor; Raster Graphics; ReSound; Retix; RiboGene; Risk Management Solutions; Samsung; SciClone Pharmaceuticals; Sherpa; StrataCom; Synaptics; Sync Research; Target Therapeutics; Visioneer; Visual EDGE Technology; Wearnes; Yahoo; Xylan.

# WEIL, GOTSHAL & MANGES LLP

A Limited Liability Partnership including Professional Corporations

Silicon Valley Office

**2882 SAND HILL ROAD, SUITE 280**
**MENLO PARK, CALIFORNIA 94025-7022**
*Telephone: 415-926-6200*
*Telecopier: 415-854-3713*

*New York, N.Y. Office:* 767 Fifth Avenue. Telephone: 212-310-8000. Cable Address: "Wegoma". Telex: 424281; 423144. Telecopier: 212-310-8007.
*Dallas, Texas Office:* 100 Crescent Court, Suite 1300. Telephone: 214-746-7700. Fax: 214-746-7777.

*Houston, Texas Office:* 700 Louisiana Street, Suite 1600. Telephone: 713-546-5000. Telecopier: 713-224-9511.
*Miami, Florida Office:* 701 Brickell Avenue, Suite 2100. Telephone: 305-577-3100. Telecopier: 305-374-7159.
*Washington, D.C. Office:* 1615 L Street, N.W., Suite 700. Telephone: 202-682-7000. Telecopier: 202-857-0939; 857-0940. Telex: 440045.
*Brussels, Belgium Office:* 81 avenue Louise, Box 9-10, 1050 Brussels. Telephone: 011-32-2-543-7460. Telecopier: 011-32-2-543-7489.
*Budapest, Hungary Office:* Bank Center, Granite Tower, H-1944 Budapest. Telephone: 011 36 1 302-9100. Fax: 011 36 1 302-9110.
*London, England Office:* 99 Bishopsgate, London EC2M 3XD. Telephone: 44-171-426-1000. Telecopier: 44-171-426-0990.
*Prague, Czechoslovakia Office:* Charles Bridge Center, Krizovnicke nam. 1, 110 00 Prague 1, Czech Republic. Telephone: 011-42-2-24-09-73-00. Telecopier: 011-42-2-24-09-73-10.
*Warsaw, Poland Office:* ul. Zlota 44/46, 00-120 Warsaw. Telephone: 011-48-22-622-1300. Telecopier: 011-48-22-622-1301.

*General Practice.*

*RESIDENT PARTNERS*

**ROBERT BARR,** born Washington, D.C., September 15, 1947; admitted to bar, 1974, California; registered to practice before U.S. Patent and Trademark Office. *Education:* Massachusetts Institute of Technology (S.B.E.E., 1970; S.B., Political Science, 1970); Boston University (J.D., cum laude, 1973). Law Associate, University of California Law School, Boalt Hall, Berkeley, California, 1973-1975. Adjunct Professor of Law, Hastings College of the Law, San Francisco, California, 1994-1997. Author: "Design Patents Revisited: Icons as Statutory Subject Matter," The Computer Lawyer, June 1992; "Software Protection and Licensing," Practicing Law Institute Handbook on Technology Licensing and Litigation, 1992. *Member:* Santa Clara County Bar Association; State Bar of California; American Intellectual Property Association; Peninsula Intellectual Property Law Association. **PRACTICE AREAS:** Intellectual Property.

**JARED BOBROW,** born Seattle, Washington, 1962; admitted to bar, 1988, California. *Education:* University of Washington (B.A., magna cum laude, 1983); Columbia University (J.D., 1986). Member and Senior Revising Editor, Columbia Law Review, 1984-86. Author: Note, "Antitrust Immunity For State Agencies: A Proposed Standard," Columbia Law Review, 1985. Law Clerk to Hon. Charles P. Sifton, U.S. District Court, Eastern District of New York, 1986-87. *Member:* State Bar of California. **PRACTICE AREAS:** Intellectual Property Litigation. **Email:** jared.bobrow@weil.com

**DOUGLAS K. DERWIN,** born Hollywood, California, August 28, 1957; admitted to bar, 1983, California. *Education:* University of California at Los Angeles (B.A., summa cum laude, 1980); Harvard University (J.D., cum laude, 1983). Phi Beta Kappa. Regents Scholar. Author: "Licensing Software Created Under 'Clean Room' Conditions," *Computer Software* 1989, P.L.I., 1989; "Educating the Judge in a High-Tech Copyright Case," VI *Computer Law Strategist*, No. 1, May, 1989; "NEC v. Intel: The Scope of Copyright Protection for Functional Works," *Computer Lawyer*, March, 1989; "Using 'Clean Room' Design Procedures to Reduce the Legal Risk Involved in the Creation of Functionally Compatible Products," *Digest of Papers*, 34th IEEE Computer Society International Conference, March, 1989. Co-author: "Microcode Copyright Infringement," *Computer Lawyer*, April, 1987; "Copyright Infringement of the 'Look and Feel' of an Operating System By its Own Applications Program," *Computer Lawyer*, January, 1987; "The Impact of the Uniform Trade Secret Act on California Trade Secret Law," *Computer Lawyer*, March, 1985; "Microcomputer Software Marketing Agreement Disputes," *P.L.I.*, 1985; "Copyright in the 'Look and Feel' of Computer Software," *Computer Lawyer*, February, 1985; "Tying Hardware to Software: The Data General Decision," 220 *Information Age*, Vol. 6, No. 4. *Member:* State Bar of California. (Resident). **PRACTICE AREAS:** Intellectual Property Law and Litigation; Commercial Litigation.

**MATTHEW D. POWERS,** born San Francisco, California, July 7, 1959; admitted to bar, 1982, California and U.S. District Court, Northern District of California; 1983, U.S. District Court, Central District of California and U.S. Court of Appeals, Ninth Circuit; 1985, U.S. District Court, Eastern District of California; 1986, U.S. Court of Appeals, Federal Circuit; 1988, U.S. Supreme Court; 1990, U.S. Court of International Trade and U.S. District Court, Southern District of Texas; 1991, U.S. District Court, Northern District of Indiana and U.S. Court of Appeals, Second, Fifth and Seventh Circuits. *Education:* Northwestern University (B.S., 1979); Harvard University (J.D., cum laude, 1982). Author: "Analyzing the Federal Circuits' Record on Injections," *National Law Journal* June 1, 1992; "International Intellectual Property Developments in 1991: A Year of Transfor-

*(This Listing Continued)*

**WEIL, GOTSHAL & MANGES LLP, Menlo Park—**
*Continued*

mation and Evolution," 4 *Journal of Proprietary Rights* 7 (February 1992); "Japanese Intellectual Property Law: Past, Present and Future," *J. Propriety Rights* (March, 1991). Member, ICC Commission on Intellectual and Industrial Property, 1990. Chairman, International Patent Law Subcommittee, 1989, American Bar Association. Co-Editor-in-Chief: The Journal of Propriety Rights; Editorial Board, International Litigation Quarterly, 1991. *Member:* State Bar of California. (Resident). *PRACTICE AREAS:* Intellectual Property Law; International Litigation. *Email:* matthew.powers@weil.com

### RESIDENT ASSOCIATES

**STEVEN S. CHERENSKY,** born Perth Amboy, New Jersey, March 27, 1958; admitted to bar, 1993, California and U.S. District Court, Northern District of California; 1994, U.S. District Court, Central District of California. *Education:* Johns Hopkins University (B.S.E., with honors, 1980); University of Michigan (M.S., 1982); University of California, Boalt Hall School of Law (J.D., 1993).

**BARRY M. EISLER,** born Newark, New Jersey, January 16, 1964; admitted to bar, 1989, Pennsylvania; 1991, District of Columbia (Not admitted in California). *Education:* Cornell University (B.A., 1986; J.D., 1989).

**ANDREW L. FILLER,** born New York, N.Y., December 1, 1966; admitted to bar, 1995, California. *Education:* Cornell University (B.S.M.E., 1989); University of San Francisco (J.D., magna cum laude, 1995).

**LAURA A. HANDLEY,** born Syracuse, New York, July 31, 1963; admitted to bar, 1991, Massachusetts; 1993, U.S. Court of Appeals, Federal Circuit; 1994, California. *Education:* St. Lawrence University (B.S., magna cum laude, 1985); Harvard Law School (J.D., cum laude, 1991).

**JASON D. KIPNIS,** born Skokie, Illinois, February 14, 1967; admitted to bar, 1993, California, U.S. District Court, Northern District of California and U.S. Court of Appeals, Ninth Circuit. *Education:* Massachusetts Institute of Technology (B.S. and M.S., 1988); Stanford Law School (J.D., 1993).

**DENNIS Y. LEE,** born Seoul, Korea, January 5, 1964; admitted to bar, 1993, California, U.S. District Court, Northern District of California and U.S. Court of Appeals, Ninth Circuit; registered to practice before Patent and Trademark Office. *Education:* University of Michigan (B.S.E.E., 1986); University of Iowa, College of Law (J.D., with honors, 1993).

**PATRICK P. NGUYEN,** born Saigon, Vietnam, September 15, 1966; admitted to bar, 1991, California and U.S. District Court, Northern and Central Districts of California. *Education:* University of California, Irvine (B.S., 1988); University of California School of Law (J.D., 1991).

**ELIZABETH H. RADER,** born Cambridge, Massachusetts, April 7, 1965; admitted to bar, 1993, New York; 1995, District of Columbia; U.S. District Court, Southern and Eastern Districts of New York; U.S. Court of Appeals, Federal Circuit; registered to practice before U.S. Patent and Trademark Office (Not admitted in California). *Education:* Bryn Mawr College (A.B., cum laude, 1987); University of Minnesota (J.D., cum laude, 1992).

**ARIEL REICH,** born Brussels, Belgium, November 4, 1961; admitted to bar, 1993, California. *Education:* University of Toronto (B.Sc. in Mathematics and Physics, with high distinction, 1983); University of California, Berkeley (Ph.D. in Physics, 1988); Columbia Law School (J.D., 1993).

**EDWARD REINES,** born New York, N.Y., 1963; admitted to bar, 1988, California. *Education:* State University of New York at Albany (B.A., with honors, 1985); Columbia University (J.D., 1988).

**ROBERT L. RISBERG, JR.,** born Milwaukee, Wisconsin, January 21, 1957; admitted to bar, 1990, Wisconsin; 1991, California; registered to practice before U.S. Patent and Trademark Office. *Education:* University of Wisconsin (B.S.E.E., 1987; J.D., 1990).

**PAUL M. SARACENI,** born Hartford, Connecticut, September 25, 1964; admitted to bar, 1992, Texas; 1995, California; registered to practice before U.S. Patent and Trademark Office. *Education:* Bucknell University (B.S., Engineering, 1986); Rensselaer Polytechnic Institute (M.B.A., 1989); University of North Carolina (J.D., 1992).

**DANIEL R. SIEGEL,** born St. Louis, Missouri, April 20, 1958; admitted to bar, 1984, California. *Education:* Brown University (B.S., Computer Science, 1980); Stanford University; Columbia University (J.D., 1983).

*(This Listing Continued)*

**ANNE M. VANBUSKIRK,** born Naperville, Illinois, September 4, 1965; admitted to bar, 1995, California. *Education:* Southern Methodist University (B.S.E.E., 1988); University of Texas (J.D., 1995).

**PETER A. WENZEL,** born Walnut Creek, California, September 6, 1965; admitted to bar, 1992, California. *Education:* University of California at Davis (B.A., 1988); University of Santa Clara (J.D., 1992).

**JACK YANG,** born Syracuse, New York, August 3, 1967; admitted to bar, 1992, California and U.S. Court of Appeals, Ninth Circuit. *Education:* Bates College (B.S., 1989).

(For complete biographical data on New York, New York, Dallas, Texas, Houston, Texas, Miami, Florida, Washington, D.C., Brussels, Belgium, Budapest, Hungary, London, England, Prague, Czech Republic and Warsaw, Poland, see Professional Biographies at those locations)

## ALLEN, POLGAR, PROIETTI & FAGALDE

A Partnership including a Professional Corporation

*1640 "N" STREET, SUITE 200*
*P.O. BOX 2184*
**MERCED, CALIFORNIA 95344**
*Telephone: 209-723-4372*
*Fax: 209-723-7397*

*Mariposa, California Office:* 5079 Highway 140. P.O. Box 1907. Telephone: 209-966-3007. Fax: 209-742-6353.

*General Civil and Criminal Trial Practice. Personal Injury, Wrongful Termination, Family Law, Corporation, Business, Condemnation, Taxation, Estate Planning, Probate, Real Property, Bankruptcy and Creditors' Rights Law.*

### MEMBERS OF FIRM

**TERRY L. ALLEN, (P.C.),** born Myrtle Point, Oregon, March 3, 1938; admitted to bar, 1964, California. *Education:* Portland State University; San Francisco Law School (J.D., 1963). *Member:* Merced County Bar Association; State Bar of California; California Trial Lawyers Association; The Association of Trial Lawyers of America. *PRACTICE AREAS:* Personal Injury Law; Business Litigation and Criminal Law.

**GARY B. POLGAR,** born New York, N.Y., June 12, 1949; admitted to bar, 1974, California. *Education:* University of California at Berkeley (B.A., with distinction, 1970); Hastings College of the Law, University of California (J.D., 1973). *Member:* Merced County Bar Association; State Bar of California (Member, Business Section); Central California Bankruptcy Association. *PRACTICE AREAS:* Creditor, Debtor and Trustee Bankruptcy Law; Commercial Law; Real Estate Law.

**DONALD J. PROIETTI,** born Oakland, California, July 6, 1954; admitted to bar, 1979, California. *Education:* University of Arizona (B.A., 1976); Western State University (J.D., with honors, 1979). Phi Alpha Delta. Recipient, American Jurisprudence Award in Contracts. *Member:* Merced County Bar Association; State Bar of California; California Trial Lawyers Association. *PRACTICE AREAS:* Personal Injury Law; Civil Law; Business Litigation; Probate Litigation.

**MICHAEL A. FAGALDE,** born San Jose, California, August 22, 1953; admitted to bar, 1983, California. *Education:* San Jose State University (B.S., with distinction, 1975); University of Santa Clara (J.D., 1983). Member, Personnel Board for Santa Clara County Office on Education, 1983. *Member:* Merced County Bar Association (Secretary and Treasurer, 1994); State Bar of California (Member, Criminal Law Section); California Attorneys for Criminal Justice. *PRACTICE AREAS:* Criminal Law; Employment Law; Family Law.

**JEFFREY S. KAUFMAN,** born Savannah, Georgia, June 10, 1960; admitted to bar, 1986, California. *Education:* University of California at Berkeley (B.A., with honors, 1978); Hastings College of the Law, University of California (J.D., 1985). *Member:* Merced County Bar Association; State Bar of California (Member, Sections on: Litigation; Real Property). *PRACTICE AREAS:* Real Property Law; Business Transactions; Business Litigation.

**F. DANA WALTON,** born 1950; admitted to bar, 1979, California. *Education:* California State University, Fresno; Humphreys College (J.D.). *Member:* Mariposa County Bar Association; State Bar of California. (Resident, Mariposa Office). *PRACTICE AREAS:* Probate; Trusts; Estate Planning; Family Law; Civil Litigation.

**BRIAN L. MCCABE,** born Redding, California, June 10, 1961; admitted to bar, 1989, California; 1991, District of Columbia, U.S. Court of Appeals, Ninth Circuit and Federal Circuit, U.S. District Court, Northern,

*(This Listing Continued)*

Eastern, Central and Southern Districts of California; 1995, U.S. Supreme Court. *Education:* University of California at Davis (B.S., 1985); Whittier College School of Law (J.D., 1989). *Member:* Merced County and American Bar Associations; State Bar of California; District of Columbia Bar; California Young Lawyers Association. **PRACTICE AREAS:** Family Law; Labor Law; Civil Litigation.

**PAUL C. LO,** born Laos, February 15, 1968; admitted to bar, 1994, California. *Education:* University of California at Davis (B.A., 1991); University of California at Los Angeles (J.D., 1994). Member, Moot Court. *Member:* Merced County and American Bar Associations; State Bar of California. **LANGUAGES:** Hmong. **PRACTICE AREAS:** Personal Injury; Criminal Defense; General Civil Litigation.

A list of Representative Clients will be Furnished upon Request.

## BRUNN & FLYNN
### A PROFESSIONAL CORPORATION
### MERCED, CALIFORNIA
(See Modesto)

*Insurance Defense, Civil Defense. General Civil Trial Practice. Real Estate, Construction Law, Probate, Trust, Estate Planning, Corporate, Family and Workers Compensation Law, Personal Injury. Trials in all Courts.*

## CANELO, HANSEN, WILSON, WALLACE & PADRON
### PROFESSIONAL CORPORATION
*Established in 1959*
548 WEST 21ST STREET
P.O. BOX 2165
**MERCED, CALIFORNIA 95344-0165**
Telephone: 209-383-0720
Fax: 209-383-4213

*General Trial and Appellate Practice. Personal Injury, Workers Compensation, Business, Real Property, Partnership, Probate and Family Law.*

**ADOLPH B. CANELO, III,** born San Francisco, California, June 19, 1925; admitted to bar, 1954, California. *Education:* University of San Francisco (LL.B., 1950); University of Santa Clara. *Member:* Merced County Bar Association (President, 1959); State Bar of California; Consumer Attorneys of California; Law Science Institute. [United States Army Air Corps, 1943-1945]. **PRACTICE AREAS:** Personal Injury Law; Products Liability Law; Malpractice Law.

**RONALD W. HANSEN,** born Newman, California, October 19, 1947; admitted to bar, 1972, California. *Education:* University of Santa Clara (B.A., 1969; J.D., cum laude, 1972). Phi Alpha Delta. Member, Santa Clara Law Review, 1972. State Bar Court Hearing Referee, 1980—. *Member:* Merced County (President, 1981) and American Bar Associations; State Bar of California; Consumer Attorneys of California; Merced Estate Planning Council (President, 1978). **REPORTED CASES:** Irwin v. Irwin, G9 CA 3d 317 (1977); Segoviano v. Housing Authority, 143 CA3d 162 (1983). **PRACTICE AREAS:** Personal Injury Law; Probate Law; Business Litigation.

**CHARLES RAYBURN WILSON,** born Bloomington, Illinois, January 5, 1945; admitted to bar, 1970, Wisconsin; 1971, U.S. Court of Military Appeals; 1974, California. *Education:* University of Wisconsin (B.S., 1967; J.D., 1970). State Bar Court, Hearing Referee, 1980-1990. *Member:* Merced County (President, 1984) and American Bar Associations; State Bar of California; State Bar of Wisconsin (inactive); Consumer Attorneys of California; The Association of Trial Lawyers of America; California Applicant's Attorney Association. [Capt., USAF, Judge Advocate, 1970-1974]. **REPORTED CASES:** Mullen v. Glens Falls Insurance Co., 73 CA 3d 163 (1977); In re Marriage of Spengler, 5 CA 4th 288 (1992). **PRACTICE AREAS:** Personal Injury Law; Probate Law; Civil Litigation.

**JAMES H. WILSON,** born Oswego, New York, August 24, 1943; admitted to bar, 1973, California. *Education:* Union University (B.A., 1965); University of Santa Clara (J.D., 1972). Member, Santa Clara Law Review, 1971-1972. Author: "Long Hair and the Judicial Clippers," Santa Clara Lawyer, 1972. *Member:* Merced County Bar Association; State Bar of California; Consumer Attorneys of California. [LTJG, U.S. Navy, 1965-1968].

*(This Listing Continued)*

**REPORTED CASES:** Elston v. City of Turlock, 38 C3d 227 (1985); Mendez v. Superior Court, 206 CA3 557 (1988); Baker v. Walker & Walker, 133 CA3 746 (1982). **PRACTICE AREAS:** Personal Injury Law; Workers Compensation Law; General Civil Litigation; Family Law.

**RICKEY D. WALLACE,** born San Jose, California, December 23, 1951; admitted to bar, 1977, California. *Education:* University of Santa Clara (B.S., 1974); McGeorge College of Law (J.D., 1977). Author: Chapter 38, "Deposition of Expert Witnesses," 3 Weiner, *Innovations in Pain Management.* *Member:* Merced County Bar Association; State Bar of California; Consumer Attorneys of California. **REPORTED CASES:** Buhlert Trucking v. WCAB (1988) 199 CA 3d 1530. **PRACTICE AREAS:** Personal Injury; General Civil Litigation.

**JAMES P. PADRON,** born Tulare, California, September 15, 1948; admitted to bar, 1984, California. *Education:* College of the Sequoias (A.A., 1969); California State University at Fresno (B.A., 1979); Hastings College of the Law, University of California (J.D., 1984). *Member:* Merced County Bar Association; State Bar of California; Consumer Attorneys of California. **LANGUAGES:** Spanish. **PRACTICE AREAS:** Personal Injury Law; Workers Compensation Law; Family Law.

**SHELLY A. SEYMOUR,** born Dubuque, Iowa, September 24, 1960; admitted to bar, 1986, Iowa; 1989, California. *Education:* Loras College (B.A., magna cum laude, 1983); University of Iowa (J.D., with distinction, 1986). Delta Epsilon Sigma. *Member:* Merced County, Iowa State and American Bar Associations; State Bar of California. **PRACTICE AREAS:** Family Law.

### LEGAL SUPPORT PERSONNEL

**JANICE FARIAS** (Paralegal).

**DEBRA CRISP** (Paralegal).

## FLANAGAN, MASON, ROBBINS, GNASS & CORMAN
*Established in 1976*
3351 NORTH "M" STREET, SUITE 100
P.O. BOX 2067
**MERCED, CALIFORNIA 95344-0067**
Telephone: 209-383-9334
Fax: 209-383-9386
Email: FMRGC@cell2000.com

*General Civil and Trial Practice. Real Estate, Business, Corporation, Family, Personal Injury, Estate Planning and Probate Law. Tax, Labor, Municipal, Water, Eminent Domain, Land Use/Zoning.*

### MEMBERS OF FIRM

**HUGH M. FLANAGAN,** born Indianapolis, Indiana, May 22, 1939; admitted to bar, 1971, California, U.S. Supreme Court, U.S. Court of Military Appeals and U.S. District Court, Central District of California; U.S. District Court, Eastern District of California and U.S. Tax Court; registered to practice before U.S. Patent and Trademark Office. *Education:* Purdue University (B.S.M.E., 1961); Michigan State University (M.S.E.E., 1966); Loyola University of Los Angeles (J.D., 1970). Phi Alpha Delta. *Member:* Merced County Bar Association (President, 1983); State Bar of California. [Capt., JAGC, USNR (ret.)]. **PRACTICE AREAS:** Real Estate Law; Business Law; Landlord-Tenant Law.

**MICHAEL L. MASON,** born Fullerton, California, April 19, 1944; admitted to bar, 1969, Oklahoma; 1970, U.S. Court of Military Appeals; 1974, California; U.S. District Court, Eastern District of California. *Education:* Whittier College (B.A., 1966); University of Oklahoma (J.D., 1969). Phi Alpha Delta. *Member:* Merced County Bar Association (President, 1985); State Bar of California. [Capt., JAGC, U.S. Army, 1970-1975]. **PRACTICE AREAS:** Personal Injury Law; Civil Litigation.

**KENNETH M. ROBBINS,** born McKinney, Texas, July 22, 1950; admitted to bar, 1976, California; 1981, U.S. Tax Court; U.S. District Court, Eastern District of California. *Education:* University of California at Davis (B.A., 1972); Pepperdine University (J.D., 1976). Recipient, American Jurisprudence Award. *Member:* Merced County Bar Association; State Bar of California; Judge Advocates Association. [CDR, JAGC, USNR, 1977]. **PRACTICE AREAS:** Tax; Business; Agriculture; Water Law.

**WILLIAM E. GNASS,** born Plattsburgh, New York, July 14, 1942; admitted to bar, 1972, California; 1976, Florida. *Education:* University of Georgia (B.S., 1963); University of San Diego (J.D., 1971). City Attorney,

*(This Listing Continued)*

## FLANAGAN, MASON, ROBBINS, GNASS & CORMAN, Merced—Continued

Wintergarden, Florida, 1979-1981. Merced County Counsel, 1982-1986. President, Greater Merced Chamber of Commerce, 1994-1995. *Member:* Merced County Bar Association; State Bar of California. **SPECIAL AGENCIES:** City of Waterford, City of Turlock, Madera Civil Service Commission. **REPORTED CASES:** Merced County Taxpayers' Association, et. al. v. County of Merced, et al., 218 Cal. App. 3d 396. **PRACTICE AREAS:** Land Use including CEQA; Municipal Law including Public Financing; Eminent Domain Law; Air and Water Quality.

**GERALD W. CORMAN,** born Moscow, Idaho, January 23, 1948; admitted to bar, 1974, California; 1975, U.S. District Court, Eastern District of California. *Education:* University of Washington (B.A., 1970); Willamette University (J.D., 1974). Note Editor, Willamette Law Review, 1973-1974. *Member:* Merced County Bar Association (Secretary/Treasurer, 1975-1976; President, 1990; Family Law Committee Chairman, 1990-1995); State Bar of California (Member, Family Law Section; Delegate, State Bar Convention, 1989-1990). **PRACTICE AREAS:** Family Law.

**CORBETT J. BROWNING,** born Dos Palos, California, August 4, 1962; admitted to bar, 1989, California. *Education:* Merced College (A.A., 1982); Westmont College (B.A., 1985); West Virginia University (J.D., 1989). *Member:* Merced County and American Bar Associations; State Bar of California. **PRACTICE AREAS:** Employment Law; Municipal Law; Civil Litigation.

**PHILIP R. GOLDEN,** born Palo Alto, California, November 21, 1958; admitted to bar, 1985, California and U.S. District Court, Northern District of California; 1986, U.S. Tax Court; 1990, U.S. District Court, Eastern District of California. *Education:* Stanford University (A.B., 1981); University of Santa Clara (J.D., 1984); University of Miami (LL.M., Estate Planning, 1985). Author: "Deferred Annuities - Ownership and Beneficiary Designation Issues," Estate Planning, Trust and Probate News, Vol. 14, No. 4, 1994. *Member:* Merced County Bar Association; State Bar of California (Member, Estate Planning Committee, 1990—); Merced Estate Planning Council (President, 1992). (Certified Specialist, Estate Planning, Trust and Probate Law, The State Bar of California Board of Legal Specialization). **PRACTICE AREAS:** Estate Planning; Trusts and Estates; Business Law.

### ASSOCIATES

**SHARON E. WILLIAMS,** born Merced, California, April 14, 1966; admitted to bar, 1994, California and U.S. District Court, Eastern District of California. *Education:* Arizona State University (B.S., cum laude, 1991); University of the Pacific, McGeorge School of Law (J.D., 1994). Phi Alpha Delta. *Member:* Merced County Bar Association; State Bar of California. **PRACTICE AREAS:** Land Use; Corporate; Municipal; Trusts; Taxation.

### LEGAL SUPPORT PERSONNEL

**KAREN SPINARDI** (Paralegal).

**BETH BRUSH** (Paralegal).

**JUDY A. CAMPBELL** (Legal Assistant).

**CARMELINA MCKEE** (Legal Assistant).

SPECIAL COUNSEL: Merced County; Madera County Civil Service Commission; City of Turlock.
REPRESENTATIVE CLIENTS: Merced Irrigation District; San Luis Canal Co.; El Nido Irrigation District; Gustine Drainage District; San Luis Canal Co.; Courtesy Oldsmobile; Isenberg Motors; Flanagan Almonds; California Independent Almonds; Richwood Meat; Imberi Construction; Trans County Title Co.; Commercial Construction Co., Inc.; Merced Screw Products; Foundation for Medical Care, Merced; Circle "N" Farms, Inc.; Rieke Brothers Inc.; Bucanhan Enterprises; City of Waterford.

## KIMBLE, MacMICHAEL & UPTON
### A PROFESSIONAL CORPORATION
### MERCED, CALIFORNIA
(See Fresno)

Civil, Trial and Appellate Practice in all Courts with Emphasis in Business, Construction and Environmental Litigation, Real Estate, Bank Securities, Lender and Creditors Rights, Bankruptcy, Secured Lending, Banking, Federal and State Income, Gift and Estate Tax, Securities, Antitrust, Corporation and Probate and Estate Planning, Patent, Trademark and Copyright, Water Rights, Environmental Law, Employee Benefits Law, Products Liability Defense, ERISA Litigation, Employment Defense, Administrative and Health Care Law.

*(This Listing Continued)*

## KEITH C. KING
510 WEST 21ST STREET
MERCED, CALIFORNIA 95340
Telephone: 209-722-5746
Fax: 209-725-0803

Estate Planning, Trust and Probate Law, Elder Law, Medi-Cal Planning, Real Estate and Business Law, Probate Litigation.

**KEITH C. KING,** born Long Beach, California, June 23, 1931; admitted to bar, 1961, California and U.S. District Court, Northern District of California; 1967, U.S. District Court, Eastern District of California. *Education:* University of California at Berkeley (B.A., 1957); Boalt Hall School of Law, University of California (J.D., 1960). Probate Rules Committee, Merced Probate Court. *Member:* Merced County Bar Association (President, 1968-1969); The State Bar of California, (Estate Planning, Trust and Probate Law Section); National Academy of Elder Law Attorneys. [Lt., USNR, 1952-1956, Naval Aviator]. (Certified Specialist, Estate Planning, Trust and Probate Law, The State Bar of California Board of Legal Specialization). **PRACTICE AREAS:** Estate Planning and Probate; Trusts; Business Law; Conservatorships; Will Contests; Medi-Cal Planning; Elder Law.

REFERENCES: Bank of America; Wells Fargo Bank.

## LANG, RICHERT & PATCH
### MERCED, CALIFORNIA
(See Fresno)

General Civil and Trial Practice in all Courts. Appeals. Business, Corporation, Bankruptcy, Insolvency, Construction, Real Property, Probate and Estate Planning, Trusts, Personal Injury and Insurance Law.

## LINNEMAN, BURGESS, TELLES, VAN ATTA & VIERRA
Established in 1932
312 WEST 19TH STREET
P.O. BOX 2263
MERCED, CALIFORNIA 95344
Telephone: 209-723-2137
FAX: 209-723-0899

*Dos Palos, California Office:* 1820 Marguerite Street, P.O. Box 156. Telephone: 209-392-2141. Fax: 209-392-3964. E-Mail: drathmann@aol.com

*Los Banos, California Office:* 654 K Street, P.O. Box 1364. Telephone: 209-826-4911. FAX: 209-826-4766. E-Mail: 1btvv@aol.com

General Civil and Trial Practice. Water District and Rights Law. Real Property, Probate, Negligence, Products Liability, Agricultural Law and Personal Injury.

### MEMBERS OF FIRM

**JAMES E. LINNEMAN,** born Merced, California, December 8, 1933; admitted to bar, 1960, California. *Education:* Stanford University (B.A., 1955; J.D., 1959). Order of the Coif. Public Defender, Merced County, 1962-1963. *Member:* Merced County Bar Association; The State Bar of California; Consumer Attorneys of California. **PRACTICE AREAS:** Personal Injury Litigation; Agricultural Law; Real Property Law.

**JEFFREY A. NELSON,** born Fresno, California, October 12, 1951; admitted to bar, 1977, California and U.S. District Court, Northern District of California; 1982, U.S. District Court, Central District of California; 1984, U.S. District Court, Southern District of California; 1985, U.S. Supreme Court. *Education:* University of Washington (B.A., 1973); Hastings College of the Law, University of California (J.D., 1976). *Member:* Merced County Bar Association; State Bar of California; Consumer Attorneys of California. **PRACTICE AREAS:** Personal Injury Litigation; Insurance Law; Criminal Law.

REPRESENTATIVE CLIENTS: Panoche Water District; Panoche Drainage District; San Luis Water District; Redfern Ranches, Inc.; Westside Produce; Telles Transport, Inc.; Spain Air; John F. Bennett Ranch; San Joaquin Valley

*(This Listing Continued)*

Dairymen; Lower San Joaquin Levee District; Berkeley Farms; Parreira & Co.; Koda Farms; Tavares Farms/Veal; Tavares Family Trust; San Luis & Delta-Mendota Water Authority.
REFERENCE: The Bank of America National Trust and Savings Assn.

## CASEY A. OLIVER
2040 M STREET, SUITE C
**MERCED, CALIFORNIA 95340**
Telephone: 209-725-0770

*Personal Injury, Juvenile Law, Insurance Disputes and Family Law.*

**CASEY A. OLIVER,** born Birmingham, Alabama, March 6, 1962; admitted to bar, 1989, California and U.S. District Court, Eastern District of California. *Education:* California State College, Stanislaus; San Joaquin College of Law (J.D., 1989). Top Oral Advocate Finalist, Moot Court, 1986. President, Student Bar Association, 1987-1988. *Member:* Merced County Bar Association; State Bar of California; The Association of Trial Lawyers of America; Consumer Attorneys of California; California Attorneys for Criminal Justice. **PRACTICE AREAS:** Personal Injury, Juvenile Law and Family Law; Insurance Disputes.

## WILLIAM P. (PAT) QUIGLEY
Established in 1971
650 WEST 20TH STREET
P.O. BOX 1229
**MERCED, CALIFORNIA 95341**
Telephone: 209-383-4444
Fax: 209-383-5989

*General Trial Practice. Business, Real Estate, Estate Planning, Probate.*

**WILLIAM P. (PAT) QUIGLEY,** born Oakland, California, November 9, 1937; admitted to bar, 1965, California, U.S. District Court, Northern and Eastern Districts of California and U.S. Court of Appeals, Ninth Circuit. *Education:* University of California at Berkeley (A.B., 1959; LL.B., 1964). Phi Delta Phi. Member, Merced City Council, 1971-1979. Mayor, City of Merced, 1975-1979. International Director, Lyons Club International, 1996-1998. *Member:* Merced County Bar Association (President, 1974); State Bar of California (Referee, State Bar Court, 1979—).

REPRESENTATIVE CLIENTS: Wainwright Development Co.; Black Rascal Estates; Riggs Ambulance Service; Riggs Communications; Merced Transportation; Isenberg Motors; Ron Smith Buick; Pierre Perrett Farming; Yosemite Motels; Farnsworth Farming.
REFERENCE: Wells Fargo Bank (Merced Branch).

## SILVEIRA, MATTOS & LEWIS
530 WEST 21ST STREET
P.O. BOX 2287
**MERCED, CALIFORNIA 95344-0287**
Telephone: 209-722-3815
Fax: 209-722-5957

*General Civil and Trial Practice. Personal Injury Defense, Insurance, Real Property and Real Estate Law.*

**F.A. SILVEIRA** (1907-1989).

**WELDON J. MATTOS, JR.,** born Gustine, California, October 1, 1948; admitted to bar, 1973, California and U.S. District Court, Eastern District of California. *Education:* University of California at Santa Barbara (A.B., 1970); University of California at Davis (J.D., 1973). *Member:* Merced County Bar Association; The State Bar of California; Northern California Association of Defense Counsel (Member, Board of Directors, 1988-1989); Defense Research Institute; American Board of Trial Advocates (Chapter Officer, San Joaquin Valley, 1994—). **PRACTICE AREAS:** Personal Injury; Business; Probate; Mediation Services.

**THOMAS E. LEWIS,** born San Jose, California, February 16, 1955; admitted to bar, 1982, California. *Education:* University of California at Davis (B.A., 1977); McGeorge School of Law, University of the Pacific (J.D., 1982). *Member:* Merced County Bar Association; The State Bar of California; Northern California Association of Defense Counsel; Defense Research Institute. **PRACTICE AREAS:** Litigation; Real Estate; Business Law.

**KATHLEEN CRIST,** born Chicago, Illinois, August 22, 1964; admitted to bar, 1990, California, U.S. District Court, Northern District of California and U.S. Court of Appeals, Ninth Circuit; 1992, U.S. District Court, Eastern District of California. *Education:* Elmhurst College (B.S., with honors, 1986); University of San Francisco; Loyola University (J.D., 1989). Member, Barrister's Club. *Member:* State Bar of California; American Bar Association. **LANGUAGES:** German. **REPORTED CASES:** Koch v. Hankins. **PRACTICE AREAS:** Securities Litigation; General Law; Commercial Litigation.

*(This Listing Continued)*

### PARALEGALS
**LINDA M. PRUETT,** CLA
**KRISTINE R. KELLEY,** CLA
**RHONDA M. AMEZCUA**

TRIAL COUNSEL FOR: Allied Insurance Group; California Casualty; California State Automobile Assn.; Inter-Insurance Bureau; CNA Insurance Co.; County of Merced (Self-Insurance Program); Grange Insurance Co.; Homestead Insurance; Ryder Truck Rental; Safeco Title Insurance Co.; Shelter Insurance Co.; Star Insurance Co.; State Farm Fire & Casualty Co.; State Farm Mutual Automobile Insurance Co.; Transamerica; Travelers/Aetna Property & Casualty Corp.; United Pacific Reliance Insurance Co.

## JULIE E. FURMAN STODOLKA
800 W. 20TH STREET, SUITE C-1
**MERCED, CALIFORNIA 95348**
Telephone: 209-725-2025
Fax: 209-725-2620

*Bankruptcy Law, Real Estate and Tax Workouts.*

**JULIE E. FURMAN STODOLKA,** born Port Washington, Wisconsin, March 31, 1949; admitted to bar, 1987, California. *Education:* Cornell University (A.B., 1971); University of California at Berkeley (M.A., 1973); University of California at Los Angeles (J.D., 1987). UCLA Law Review. Law Clerk to Honorable Joseph W. Hedrick, Jr., U.S. Bankruptcy Judge, Eastern District of California, Modesto Division, 1988-1991. *Member:* Central California Bankruptcy Association (Member, Board of Directors, 1992-1995). **PRACTICE AREAS:** Bankruptcy Law; Real Estate; Tax Workouts.

## TENENBAUM, LAMPE & FROMSON
2005 "O" STREET
**MERCED, CALIFORNIA 95340**
Telephone: 209-384-7887
Fax: 209-384-5865

*General Civil and Criminal Trial Practice in State and Federal Courts. Negligence, Criminal and Family Law. Business Litigation.*

### MEMBERS OF FIRM

**SAMUEL S. TENENBAUM,** born Lodz, Poland, July 4, 1945; admitted to bar, 1971, California. *Education:* University of California at Los Angeles (A.B., 1967); University of Santa Clara (J.D., 1970). Phi Alpha Delta. Deputy District Attorney, Merced County, 1971-1974. *Member:* Merced County Bar Association (President, 1978); State Bar of California; California Attorneys for Criminal Justice. **PRACTICE AREAS:** Trial; Criminal Law; Family Law.

**CHRISTOPHER W. LAMPE,** born Bronx, New York, August 14, 1950; admitted to bar, 1975, California. *Education:* University of California at Santa Barbara and University of California at Berkeley (A.B., 1972); Hastings College of Law, University of California (J.D., 1975). Winner, Moot Court Award, 1974. Author: "Landowner Liability," California Trial Lawyers Association, Forum, December, 1987. *Member:* Merced County Bar Association (President, 1992; Member, 1979— and Chairman, 1982, Family Law Committee); State Bar of California; California Trial Lawyers Association (President, Merced Chapter, 1990). **PRACTICE AREAS:** Civil Trials; Negligence Law; Business Law.

**PAUL D. FROMSON,** born Los Angeles, California, December 3, 1946; admitted to bar, 1975, California. *Education:* California State University at Long Beach (B.A., 1969); California Western University (J.D., 1974). Instructor, Law of Evidence, Merced College, 1976-1981. Adjunct Professor, Humphrey's College of Law, Paralegal Program - Criminal Law, 1989—. Deputy District Attorney, Merced County, 1976-1979. Member, Judicial Council Advisory Council on Court Profiles, 1990. *Member:* Merced County Bar Association (President, 1989); State Bar of California; California Attorneys for Criminal Justice (Member: Board of Governors, 1988—; Executive Board Committee; Fundraising Chair, 1991; Membership Chair, 1990—). **PRACTICE AREAS:** Trial; Criminal Law; Family Law.

## WILD, CARTER & TIPTON
*A PROFESSIONAL CORPORATION*

**MERCED, CALIFORNIA**

(See Fresno)

*General Civil, Trial and Appellate Practice, Business, Real Estate, Corporation, Construction, Banking, Environmental, Agriculture, Insurance, Trademark, Probate and Estate Planning, Oil and Gas, Taxation, Bankruptcy and Employment Law.*

---

## CHURCH & ASSOCIATES
BAY VIEW FEDERAL BANK BUILDING
475 EL CAMINO REAL, SUITE 300
**MILLBRAE, CALIFORNIA 94030**
Telephone: 415-697-2400

*General Civil and Trial Practice. Business, Corporate, Real Property, Probate, Estate Planning, Personal Injury and Family Law.*

(For Complete Biographical Data on all Personnel, See Professional Biograhies at Mark M. Church, Millbrae, California)

---

## COREY, LUZAICH, MANOS & PLISKA LLP
700 EL CAMINO REAL
P.O. BOX 669
**MILLBRAE, CALIFORNIA 94030**
Telephone: 415-871-5666
Fax: 415-871-4144

*General Civil and Criminal Trial Practice. Probate, Estate Planning, Business, Corporate, Personal Injury, Negligence, Real Estate and Municipal Law.*

**GEORGE R. COREY,** born Arnold, Pennsylvania, June 28, 1933; admitted to bar, 1964, California and U.S. District Court, Northern District of California. *Education:* University of Michigan (B.A., 1956); Hastings College of Law, University of California (LL.B., 1963). Member, Board of Directors: Center for Independence of Disabled, 1983-1994; United Bay Area Crusade, 1977. Chairman, Peninsula Bank of Commerce, 1982—. City Council Member, San Bruno, 1968-1975. Mayor, San Bruno, 1972-1973. Chairman: North San Mateo County Council of Cities, 1973; Local Agency Formation Commission, 1973-1975. Superior Court Judge Pro Tem, 1980—. *Member:* North San Mateo County (President, 1970) and San Mateo County (Member, Board of Directors, 1971-1972) Bar Associations; State Bar of California; San Mateo County Trial Lawyers Association (President, 1973). **PRACTICE AREAS:** Business Litigation; Municipal Law; Civil Litigation.

**STEVAN N. LUZAICH,** born San Mateo, California, March 22, 1950; admitted to bar, 1975, California and U.S. District Court, Northern District of California. *Education:* University of California at Berkeley (A.B., 1972); Hastings College of Law, University of California (J.D., 1975). Instructor: Real Estate Law and Practice, College of San Mateo, 1981; San Mateo County Adult Education Program, 1989-1990. Member, 1979-1992 and Chairman, 1982, 1986 and 1990, Millbrae Planning Commission. Judge Pro Tem, Superior Court, 1990—. *Member:* North San Mateo County and San Mateo County Bar Associations; State Bar of California (Member, Probate and Business Law Section); San Mateo County Trial Lawyers Association. **PRACTICE AREAS:** Probate; Commercial Law; Real Estate; Elder Law.

**JEFFREY D. MANOS,** born Burlingame, California, October 22, 1955; admitted to bar, 1981, California and U.S. District Court, Northern District of California; 1985, U.S. Court of Appeals, Ninth Circuit. *Education:* University of San Francisco (B.A., magna cum laude, 1978); Hastings College of Law, University of California (J.D., 1981). Member, Editorial Board, Comment Law Journal, 1980-1981. *Member:* North San Mateo County (President, 1989) and San Mateo County Bar Associations; State Bar of California; San Mateo County Trial Lawyers Association; California Trial Lawyers Association; Barristers Club of San Mateo County (President, 1990). **PRACTICE AREAS:** Civil Practice; Personal Injury; Business Litigation.

**EDWARD W. PLISKA,** born Rockville, Connecticut, April 13, 1935; admitted to bar, 1965, California, U.S. District Court, Northern and Southern Districts of California and U.S. Court of Appeals, Ninth Circuit. *Edu-*

*(This Listing Continued)*

*cation:* Princeton University (A.B., 1956); University of Connecticut (LL.B., 1964). Recipient: American Jurisprudence Award for Municipal Corporations; National Judicial Education Award, 1986. Listed in: Who's Who in California; Who's Who in the World. Author: "Cults: Bias in the Courts?" *Court Review*, Fall 1983; Praxis, 1983. Executive Editor, *Court Review*, Published by National Center for State Courts, 1981-1988. Instructor, Criminal Law and Constitutional Law, San Mateo Law School, 1971-1976. Municipal Court Judge, San Mateo County, 1973-1986. Deputy District Attorney, 1965-1971 and Chief Trial Deputy, 1970-1971, San Mateo County District Attorney's Office. Deputy District Attorney, Santa Barbara County, 1965. First Vice President, 1985-1986, Second Vice President, 1984-1985 and Secretary, 1983-1984, American Judges Association. World Chairperson, Free Press - Fair Trial Committee, World Judges Association, 1982. Speaker, Conference of National District Attorneys Association, 1975-1976. Trustee, Belmont Elementary School District, 1987-1991. Host: "Justice Forum, TV Show, 1973-1978; "Legal Currents," TV Show, 1990. Private Judge, Litigation Cases, 1986—. *Member:* San Mateo County Bar Association; State Bar of California; California Attorneys for Criminal Justice; National Association of Criminal Defense Lawyers. **PRACTICE AREAS:** Criminal Law; Civil Litigation.

**DARIO B. DEGHETALDI,** born San Francisco, October 19, 1950; admitted to bar, 1986, California, U.S. District Court, Northern District of California and U.S. Court of Appeals, Ninth Circuit. *Education:* Stanford University (B.A., 1972); Hastings College of the Law, University of California (J.D., 1986). Adjunct Professor, Cañada College, 1988-1997. *Member:* North San Mateo County and San Mateo County Bar Associations; State Bar of California; Consumer Attorneys of California; Consumer Attorneys of San Mateo County (Director, 1996-1997). **PRACTICE AREAS:** Business Litigation; Real Estate Litigation; Municipal Law; Civil Appeals and Writs.

**LETICIA G. TOLEDO,** born Northridge, California, May 16, 1961; admitted to bar, 1989, California. *Education:* St. Mary's College of California (B.A., 1983); Hastings College of the Law, University of California (J.D., 1986). Member, Latina Mentor Program Advisory Counsel, 1995—. Member, 1993—and Chair, 1993, Conference of Delegates. Board of Directors, San Mateo Legal Aid Society, 1994—; Treasurer, 1996. *Member:* San Mateo County Bar Association (Member, Estate Planning and Probate Section, 1991—; Member, 1993—and Chair, 1993, Women Lawyers Section Executive Board); State Bar of California (Member, Committee on Professional Responsibility and Conduct, 1991-1994). **LANGUAGES:** Spanish. **PRACTICE AREAS:** Estate Planning; Probate Administration; Trust Administration; Guardianship and Conservatorship.

---

## DONAHUE, GALLAGHER, WOODS & WOOD
*Established in 1918*

SHELTER POINT
591 REDWOOD HIGHWAY, SUITE 1200
**MILL VALLEY, CALIFORNIA 94941**
Telephone: 415-381-4161
Facsimile: 415-381-7515

*Oakland, California Office:* 300 Lakeside Drive, Suite 1900. Telephone: 415-451-0544. Facsimile: 415-832-1486.
*Walnut Creek, California Office:* 1646 North California Boulevard, Suite 310. Telephone: 510-746-7770. Facsimile: 510-746-7776.

*General Civil and Trial Practice in all State and Federal Courts. Corporate, Real Property, Intellectual Property, Insurance, Immigration, Labor and Employment, Tax, Probate and Estate Planning Law.*

*FIRM PROFILE: Founded in Oakland in 1918, the firm presently has 35 attorneys and 10 legal assistants serving clients nationwide from strategically located offices in Oakland, Walnut Creek and Marin County. Our diverse practice and locations, combined with our extensive use of voice and data-communication networks, reflect our commitment to being accessible and able to quickly meet our clients' requirements in a complex and fast-paced business environment. Throughout our 78 years of practicing law, our goal has always been to provide our clients with the highest quality of service in the most cost-effective manner. To achieve this end, we carefully staff all projects matching client objectives with the professional skills and experience of our practitioners. Whether we are retained for one project or to handle a company's on-going legal needs, we strive to develop a close working relationship with our clients so that we can more fully assist them with their legal needs. Our philosophy is to be sensitive and responsive to our clients' expectations regarding our services*

*(This Listing Continued)*

and fees, and make every attempt to meet specific requests regarding their level of involvement in the matter, billing preferences and particular service requirements. Ultimately, we seek what we believe is the only true measure of our success-that is, a satisfied client.

### MEMBERS OF FIRM

**ERIC W. DONEY,** born Lynwood, California, February 2, 1952; admitted to bar, 1977, California; 1978, U.S. Tax Court. *Education:* University of California, Davis (B.A., magna cum laude, 1973); Hastings College of the Law, University of California (J.D., 1977). *Member:* Alameda County Bar Association; State Bar of California. **PRACTICE AREAS:** Computer Law; Computer Software; Copyright. *Email:* Eric@donahue.com

**JONATHAN G. WONG,** born Santa Monica, California, January 27, 1959; admitted to bar, 1983, California. *Education:* Pomona College (B.A., 1979); University of California, Davis (J.D., 1982). Editor, University of California, Davis Law Review, 1981-1982. *Member:* Alameda County Bar Association; The State Bar of California. **LANGUAGES:** French, German, Spanish and Mandarin Chinese. **PRACTICE AREAS:** Litigation; Immigration and Nationality Law; Employment Law. *Email:* Jonathan@donahue.com

### ASSOCIATES

**ROBYN RENÉE NEWCOMB,** born San Francisco, California, September 19, 1966; admitted to bar, 1993, California. *Education:* University of California at Berkeley (B.A., 1989); University of San Francisco (J.D., 1993). *Member:* Alameda County Bar Association; State Bar of California. *Email:* RobRob@donahue.com

**JONATHAN N. OSDER,** born Los Angeles, California, May 20, 1967; admitted to bar, 1994, California. *Education:* University of California at Berkeley (B.A., 1989); University of San Francisco (J.D., 1994). Comments Editor, University of San Francisco Law Review, 1994. *Member:* Alameda County Bar Association; State Bar of California. **LANGUAGES:** Spanish. *Email:* Jon@donahue.com

**JONAS W. KANT,** born Los Angeles, California, April 12, 1965; admitted to bar, 1996, New York (Not admitted in California). *Education:* University of California at Davis (B.A., 1989); Benjamin N. Cardozo School of Law (J.D., 1995). *Member:* The Association of the Bar of the City of New York; New York State Bar Association.

(For complete biographical data on all personnel, see Professional Biographies at Oakland, California)

## ROBERT A. HELMENSTINE
591 REDWOOD HIGHWAY
MILL VALLEY, CALIFORNIA 94941
Telephone: 415-388-7181
Fax: 415-383-2074

*General Practice with special emphasis on Civil Litigation, Business Contracts, Torts, Construction, Environmental, Personal Injury and Property Damage.*

**ROBERT A. HELMENSTINE,** born Viroqua, Wisconsin, October 2, 1939; admitted to bar, 1967, California. *Education:* University of Wisconsin (B.S.M.E., 1962; B.B.A., 1963); Hastings College of Law, University of California (J.D., 1967). *Member:* Marin County Bar Association; State Bar of California; Northern California Association of Defense Counsel; Association of Defense Trial Attorneys; National Board of Trial Advocacy.

## VALERIE ANSEL KARPMAN
103 EAST BLITHEDALE AVENUE
MILL VALLEY, CALIFORNIA 94941
Telephone: 415-381-8887
Facsimile: 415-381-8888

*Civil Litigation in all Courts. Business Litigation, Personal Injury, Professional Liability, Products Liability, Insurance Bad Faith Litigation, Women's Health Litigation.*

**VALERIE ANSEL KARPMAN,** born New York, N.Y., December 9, 1943; admitted to bar, 1976, California. *Education:* Queens College of the City University of New York (B.A., 1963); Golden Gate College (J.D., with honors, 1976). Author: Case Comment, Golden Gate Law Review, Fall, 1974. *Member:* Bar Association of San Francisco; State Bar of California; American Bar Association (Member, Litigation Section); San Francisco

*(This Listing Continued)*

Trial Lawyers Association (Member, Board of Directors, 1988-1989); California Trial Lawyers Association; The Association of Trial Lawyers of America.

## NIELSEN, MERKSAMER, PARRINELLO, MUELLER & NAYLOR, LLP
A Partnership including a Professional Corporation
591 REDWOOD HIGHWAY, BUILDING 4000
MILL VALLEY, CALIFORNIA 94941
Telephone: 415-389-6800
Email: nmpmn@aol.com

*San Francisco, California Office:* 120 Montgomery Street, Suite 1055, 94104. Telephone: 415-389-6800.

*Sacramento, California Office:* One City Centre, 770 L Street, Suite 800, 95814. Telephone: 916-446-6752.

*Government, Administrative, Constitutional, Civil Rights, Election and Legislative Law. Civil Trial and Appellate Practice in all State and Federal Courts.*

REPRESENTATIVE CLIENTS: The Irvine Co.; The Southland Corp.; ARCO; Pacific Gas and Electric Co.; California Medical Assn.; Pfizer, Inc.; Philip Morris; R.J. Reynolds; Merck & Co., Inc.; Pacific Enterprises; Kraft, Inc.; Southern Pacific Co.; Sunkist Growers; Fluor Corp.; California Governor Pete Wilson; California Association of Health Facilities; California Council for Environmental & Economic Balance; California Housing Council; California Unitary Tax Council; California Correctional Peace Officers Assn.; California Professional Firefighters; WMX Technologies; California Cable Television Assn.; Los Angeles County Metropolitan Transportation Authority; Hemacare Corp.; California Republican Party; Circus Circus Enterprises, Inc.; 3M Company; Apple Computer, Inc.; Thomas J. Lipton Co.; Addus Healthcare; Merrill Lynch, Inc.; Wells Fargo Bank; Oracle Corporation.

(For Complete Biographical Data on all Personnel see Professional Biographies at San Francisco, California)

## SUSAN RABIN
219 EAST BLITHEDALE AVENUE, SUITE 4
MILL VALLEY, CALIFORNIA 94941-2033
Telephone: 415-381-5252
Fax: 415-381-5222

*Entertainment, Business, Copyright and Trademark Law.*

**SUSAN RABIN,** born Chicago, Illinois, January 5, 1941; admitted to bar, 1986, California; 1989, U.S. District Court, Northern District of California. *Education:* Northwestern University (B.S., 1962; M.A., 1967); Golden Gate University (J.D., 1984). Author, "Moral Rights and the Realistic Limits of Artistic Control," 14 Golden Gate 447, 1984. Instructor: Entertainment and Arts Law, Golden Gate University Law School, 1990; Golden Gate University, 1991—; University of San Francisco Law School, 1990—; Monterey College of the Law, 1996—; College for Recording Arts, 1992-1994. Lecturer: California Lawyers for the Arts; Northern California Songwriters Association; N.A.I.R.D. Member, Board of Governors (Elected) National Academy of Recording Arts and Sciences, San Francisco Chapter, 1993—; Faculty: Hastings College of Advocacy, 1994, 1995, 1996. *Member:* Bar Association of San Francisco (Chair, Sports and Entertainment Law Section, 1992—); American Bar Association (Member, Forum Committee on Sports and Entertainment Law, 1983—).

## ROBB & ROSS
A Partnership including Professional Corporations
591 REDWOOD HIGHWAY, SUITE 2250
MILL VALLEY, CALIFORNIA 94941
Telephone: 415-332-3831
Fax: 415-383-2074

*Estates and Trusts, General Business and Real Estate.*

**JOSEPH W. ROBB, JR.,** born San Francisco, California, November 3, 1926; admitted to bar, 1952, California. *Education:* University of California (B.A., 1947); Hastings College of the Law, University of California (J.D., 1951). *Member:* Bar Association of San Francisco; Marin County and American Bar Associations; State Bar of California. **PRACTICE AREAS:** Business Organization; Estate Planning.

**STERLING L. ROSS,** born Evanston, Illinois, January 7, 1946; admitted to bar, 1972, California. *Education:* Stanford University (B.A., 1968); University of Michigan (J.D., 1971). Author: *California Will Drafting Sup-*

*(This Listing Continued)*

**ROBB & ROSS, Mill Valley—Continued**

plement, Chapter 23, Special Needs Trusts, Continuing Education of the Bar, 1995; "Recent Developments in the Litigation Special Needs Trust," Civil Litigation Reporter, California Continuing Education of the Bar, June 1994; "Sheltering Zebley Retroactive SSI Benefits in Trust," Clearinghouse Review (National Clearinghouse for Legal Services, Inc.), Vol. 5, Number 10, February 1992; "The Special Needs Trust and Its Use in Estate Planning for Families With Disabled Children," Estate Planning for the Aging or Incapacitated Client, Practicing Law Institute, 1986. Lecturer: "Public Benefit Planning for the Elderly and Disabled," 1990 USC Probate and Trust Conference, University of Southern California Law Center, October 1990; "The Special Needs Trust and Future Care Planning for Persons with Mental Disabilities," Government Law Center, Albany Law School and the New York State Office of Mental Health, September 1992. *Member:* State Bar of California (Estate Planning, Trust and Probate Section; Chair, Estate Planning, Trust and Probate Law Advisory Commission for the Board of Legal Specialization); Fellow, American College of Trusts and Estates Counsel. (Certified Specialist, Estate Planning, Trust and Probate Law, The State Bar of California Board of Legal Specialization). *PRACTICE AREAS:* Estate Planning; Trust Law; Probate Law; Business Law.

**ALAN J. TITUS,** born San Francisco, California, March 19, 1956; admitted to bar, 1983, California. *Education:* University of California at Berkeley (A.B., 1978); University of California School of Law at Davis (J.D., 1983). *Member:* Bar Association of San Francisco; State Bar of California. *PRACTICE AREAS:* Business Law; Real Estate; Estate Planning and Probate Law; Business Litigation.

**PHILIP A. ROBB,** born San Francisco, California, September 13, 1962; admitted to bar, 1990, California. *Education:* University of California at Berkley (B.A., 1985); Golden Gate University (J.D., 1989). *Member:* Bar Association of San Francisco; Marin County and American Bar Associations; State Bar of California (Member; Estate Planning, Trust and Probate Section; Business Law Section). *PRACTICE AREAS:* Business Law; Estate Planning and Probate Law.

---

## SKJERVEN, MORRILL, MacPHERSON, FRANKLIN & FRIEL LLP

### MILPITAS, CALIFORNIA

(See San Jose)

*Intellectual Property Law, including Patents, Trademarks, Copyrights, Mask Works, Unfair Competition, Trade Secrets and Licensing; Litigation in Federal and State Courts; Corporate, Commercial and General Business Law; and International and Government Contracts Law.*

---

## THOMAS J. BORCHARD, INC.

*A PROFESSIONAL CORPORATION*

25909 PALA, SUITE 380

### MISSION VIEJO, CALIFORNIA 92691

*Telephone:* 714-457-9505
*Facsimile:* 714-457-1666

*Vista, California Office:* 510 Escondido Avenue, Suite E. Telephone: 619-758-3500. Fax: 619-758-0545.

*Saginaw, Michigan Office:* 2604 West Genesee.

*Business and Real Estate Practice, including Corporate, Partnerships, Estate Planning, Real Property and Construction Law. Civil Trial and Appellate Litigation.*

**THOMAS J. BORCHARD,** born Saginaw, Michigan, December 13, 1954; admitted to bar, 1982, Michigan and California, U.S. District Court, Central and Southern Districts of California, U.S. District Court, Eastern District of Michigan, U.S. Court of Appeals, Ninth Circuit and U.S. Tax Court. *Education:* Michigan State University (B.A., 1977); Thomas M. Cooley Law School (J.D., 1981); University of San Diego. *Member:* State Bar of Michigan; State Bar of California; Orange County Trial Lawyers Association. *PRACTICE AREAS:* Business; Real Estate Litigation; Civil Litigation; Intellectual Property Litigation.

*(This Listing Continued)*

CAA1348B

---

**DAVID S. NICHOL,** born Cleveland, Ohio, April 28, 1962; admitted to bar, 1992, California and U.S. District Court, Central District of California. *Education:* Kent State University (B.S.); Thomas M. Cooley Law School (J.D.). *Member:* State Bar of California. *PRACTICE AREAS:* Real Estate; Business Litigation; Environmental Hazard Litigation Matters; Intellectual Property Litigation.

**MAUREEN E. BAUR,** born Inglewood, California, October 30, 1963; admitted to bar, 1994, California. *Education:* University of California, Irvine (B.A., 1988); Western State University (J.D., 1994). *Member:* Orange County Bar Association; State Bar of California; Orange County Barristers Association. *PRACTICE AREAS:* Business Litigation.

**ANNA M. CAMARENA,** born San Bernardino, California, February 26, 1958; admitted to bar, 1994, California. *Education:* Sonoma State University; Ventura College of Law (J.D., 1994). *PRACTICE AREAS:* Business Transactional; Estate Planning; Family Law; Business Litigation.

**NANCY CHRISTINE GREEN,** born Los Angeles, California, December 25, 1967; admitted to bar, 1994, California and U.S. District Court, Central District of California. *Education:* California State University, Long Beach (B.S., 1989; M.B.A., 1990); Western State University College of Law (J.D., 1994). Member, 1987-1989, and President, 1988, C.S.U.L.B. Law Society. *Member:* Orange County Bar Association (Member: Executive Committee; Law Management Section); State Bar of California; The Association of Trial Lawyers of America; Orange County Barristers. *LANGUAGES:* Spanish. *PRACTICE AREAS:* Business Litigation; Corporate Litigation/Transaction; Civil Transaction/Litigation.

### OF COUNSEL

**CHARLES B. FLOOD, III,** born Omaha, Nebraska, October 17, 1934; admitted to bar, 1966, California, U.S. District Court, Southern, Central and Eastern Districts of California and U.S. Court of Appeals, Ninth Circuit. *Education:* Fresno State College; Humphries College (J.D., 1966). *Member:* Northern San Diego County Bar Association; State Bar of California. (Resident, Vista, California Office). *PRACTICE AREAS:* Business; Real Estate; Probate; Civil Litigation.

**J. LEE BOOTHBY,** born Washington, D.C.; admitted to bar, 1979, District of Columbia; 1992, California and U.S. Court of Appeals, Ninth Circuit. *Education:* University of Tennessee at Knoxville (B.A., 1975; J.D., 1979). Assistant Editor, Law Review. Author: "Comparative Bad Faith," Thomas Jefferson Law Review, Vol 18 #2, Spring 1996; "Juvenile's Right to Trial by Jury," Tennessee Law Review, Spring 1979. *Member:* State Bar of California; District of Columbia Bar. *LANGUAGES:* Greek. *PRACTICE AREAS:* General Civil Litigation.

REPRESENTATIVE CLIENTS: American Investment Group; Star Motors; Rogerson Aircraft Corporation; Iliff Thorn & Co. Real Estate Brokerage; Pacific Southwest District, Missouri Synod Lutheran Church; Elliott Construction; McCarthy Construction; Frank Gonzales & Associates; Spectrum Enterprises, Inc.; Frank Gonzales & Associates, Architects; Sundance Spas; Westar Nutrition, Inc.; Casha Resources Home Health Services; Platecorp (Plating Operation); Reppel Steel, Inc.; Metropolitan Steel, Inc.; Alternative Building Systems, Inc.; Ruby's Restaurant; Lindora Medical Clinics; Martin Investigative Services.

---

## LAW OFFICES OF JOHN ROBERTS BOYD

*Established in 1971*

LOS ALTOS PLAZA

26691 PLAZA DRIVE, SUITE 250

### MISSION VIEJO, CALIFORNIA 92691

*Telephone:* 714-582-8188
*Telecopier:* 714-582-5902

*Civil and Real Estate Litigation, Family Law, Wills, Trusts and Probate Related Matters.*

**JOHN ROBERTS BOYD,** born Los Angeles, California, April 6, 1937; admitted to bar, 1971, California. *Education:* California State College of Los Angeles (B.S., 1961); Southwestern University (J.D., 1969). Licensed Real Estate Broker, California, 1964. *Member:* Orange County and South Orange County (President, 1977) Bar Associations; State Bar of California; California Trial Lawyers Association; The Association of Trial Lawyers of America.

*(This Listing Continued)*

**SHANNON ROBERTS BOYD,** born Pasadena, California, July 21, 1965; admitted to bar, 1994, California. *Education:* The University of Southern California (B.S., 1987); Thomas Jefferson University (J.D., 1993). *Member:* Orange County, South Orange County and American Bar Associations; State Bar of California; California Trial Lawyers Association. *PRACTICE AREAS:* Real Estate; Probate; Wills; Trusts and Estates.

REFERENCES: Bank of America; Sanwa Bank; ABKO Corp., Wichita, Kansas; Cambridge-Lee Industries, Inc., Boston, Mass., Lloviel Corp., Edina, Minn.

## THE BUCKLEY FIRM, P.C.
*Established in 1977*
SUITE 200, 26522 LA ALAMEDA
**MISSION VIEJO, CALIFORNIA 92691**
Telephone: 714-348-8300
Facsimile: 714-348-8310
Email: TBF__law@ix.netcom.com
Email: 73321.331@compuserve.com

*Real Estate, Commercial and Business Litigation. Creditor Bankruptcy, Title Insurance Litigation, Real Estate Foreclosures and Related Litigation; Construction Defect and Employment Litigation.*

FIRM PROFILE: The Buckley firm strategy is to combine its collective resources with those of the client to achieve positive results. We have integrated our staff of attorneys, paralegals, support and administrative personnel to work together as a team.

It is the firm's mission to improve the legal affairs of those we serve with a commitment to excellence in all we do.

Our goal is to offer quality services, to set community standards, and to exceed our clients' expectations in a caring, convenient, cost-effective and accessible manner.

To accomplish our mission and be recognized as a leader in providing quality services, we work hard and we encourage continuing education.

**LAWRENCE J. BUCKLEY,** born Chicago, Illinois, December 18, 1951; admitted to bar, 1976, California; 1977, U.S. District Court, Central District of California; 1978, U.S. District Court, Southern District of California; 1983, U.S. District Court, Eastern and Northern Districts of California; 1987, Arizona, U.S. District Court, District of Arizona and U.S. Court of Appeals, Ninth Circuit; 1988, Colorado, Texas and U.S. District Court, Northern, Southern and Western Districts of Texas; 1994, U.S. District Court, Eastern District of Texas and U.S. Supreme Court. *Education:* University of Illinois; Southern Illinois University (B.A., 1973); Pepperdine University (J.D., 1976). *Member:* Orange County and American Bar Associations; State Bar of California; State Bar of Arizona; State Bar of Texas; State Bar of Colorado; Orange County Bankruptcy Forum; Mortgage Bankers Association of America. (Also Of Counsel, Lieberman, Dodge, Sendrow & Gerding, Ltd., Phoenix, Arizona). *PRACTICE AREAS:* Real Estate, Commercial and Business Litigation; Creditor Representation; Bankruptcy and Insolvency Litigation; Foreclosures.

**JOHN THOMAS CALLAN,** born San Francisco, California, December 11, 1955; admitted to bar, 1991, California, U.S. District Court, Central District of California and U.S. Court of Appeals, Ninth Circuit; 1993, U.S., District Court Eastern and Southern Districts of California; 1995, Arizona; 1996, U.S. District Court, District of Arizona. *Education:* University of San Francisco (B.S., 1982); University of Notre Dame (M.B.A., 1984); University of Southern California (J.D., 1991). Recipient, American Jurisprudence Award. *Member:* Orange County and American Bar Associations; State Bar of California; State Bar of Arizona. (Also Of Counsel to Lieberman, Dodge, Sendrow & Gerding, Ltd., Phoenix, Arizona). *PRACTICE AREAS:* Real Estate Transactions and Litigation; Business Litigation.

**JEFFREY W. GRIFFITH,** born Los Angeles, April 18, 1950; admitted to bar, 1975, Texas; 1976, California; 1977, U.S. District Court, Central District of California; 1980, U.S. Tax Court; 1981, U.S. Court of Appeals, Ninth Circuit. *Education:* Claremont McKenna College; University of California at Los Angeles (B.A., cum laude, 1971; J.D., 1974). Pi Sigma Alpha; Phi Alpha Delta. Senior Briefing Attorney, Chief Justice, Texas Fifth Court of Appeals, 1976-1977. Financial Lawyers Conference. *Member:* Los Angeles County, Orange County, Dallas County and Federal Bar Associations; State Bar of California (Member, House of Delegates, 1980); State Bar of Texas; Los Angeles County Barristers (Member, Executive Committee, 1979-1980; Chairman, Stress and the Practice of Law Committee, 1978-1979; Chairman, Speaker Program, 1979-1980); Financial Lawyers Confer-

*(This Listing Continued)*

ence. *PRACTICE AREAS:* Business Litigation; Bankruptcy Law; Real Estate Law; Creditor's Rights; Anti Competitive Practices.

**STEPHEN J. KANE,** born Bowling Green, Ohio, April 6, 1967; admitted to bar, 1993, California and U.S. District Court, Southern District of California; 1996, U.S. District Court, Northern District of California. *Education:* Arizona State University (B.S., 1990); University of San Diego, School of Law (J.D., 1993). *PRACTICE AREAS:* Construction; Real Estate; Business; Commercial Litigation.

**JOHN W. KLEIN,** born West Berlin, Germany, December 16, 1956; admitted to bar, 1986, Virginia and U.S. Court of Appeals, Fourth Circuit; 1987, California ; 1988, District of Columbia, U.S. Court of Appeals for the District of Columbia Circuit and U.S. Court of Appeals, Ninth Circuit; 1989, U.S. District Court, Southern District of California and U.S. Supreme Court; 1990, U.S. District Court, Central District of California; 1992, Minnesota Supreme Court; 1994, Washington, Texas and U.S. District Court, District of Arizona; 1996, U.S. District Court, Northern and Eastern Districts of California. *Education:* Columbia University (B.A., Pol. Sc., 1980); George Washington University (J.D., 1983). *Member:* Orange County and American Bar Associations; Virginia State Bar; State Bar of California; State Bar of Texas; The District of Columbia Bar; Washington State Bar Association. *LANGUAGES:* German. *PRACTICE AREAS:* Real Estate; Commercial and Business Litigation; Bankruptcy; Insolvency.

**PAULA SCOTLAND,** born Michigan, June 11, 1949; admitted to bar, 1987, California; 1996, U.S. District Court, Central, Southern, Eastern and Northern Districts of California. *Education:* Michigan State University (B.S., cum laude, 1971); Phi Kappa Phi, Loyola Marymount University (J.D., 1987). Recipient, American Jurisprudence Book Award in Bankruptcy. *Member:* Orange County Bar Association (Member, Commercial and Bankruptcy Section). *REPORTED CASES:* In Re Thomas K. Morgan, 149 B.R. 147 (9th Cir. BAP (Cal.), Jan 12, 1993). *PRACTICE AREAS:* Bankruptcy Law.

**EDGAR C. SMITH, III,** born Philadelphia, Pennsylvania, July 10, 1957; admitted to bar, 1986, California and U.S. District Court, Central District of California; 1989, U.S. District Court, Northern, Southern and Eastern Districts of California; 1994, U.S. District Court, District of Nevada. *Education:* La Salle University (B.A., 1979); Southwestern University School of Law (J.D., 1986). *Member:* State Bar of California; State Bar of Nevada; American Bar Association. *PRACTICE AREAS:* Business Commercial and Real Estate Litigation; Bankruptcy.

**ADAM H. SPRINGEL,** born Cleveland, Ohio, September 28, 1968; admitted to bar, 1993, California; 1994, U.S. District Court, Central and Southern Districts of California; 1996, U.S. District Court, Northern and Eastern Districts of California and U.S. District Court, District of Arizona. *Education:* University of Michigan (B.A., 1990); Institute of Economic and Political Studies, Cambridge, England (1989); University of San Diego (J.D., 1993). *Member:* Orange County and American Bar Associations; State Bar of California; Building Industry Association. *PRACTICE AREAS:* Construction, Real Estate and Business Litigation.

### OF COUNSEL

**TIMOTHY D. CARLYLE,** born Orange, California, 1948; admitted to bar, 1974, California. *Education:* University of California, Santa Barbara (B.A. in Political Science, with high honors, 1970); Hastings College of the Law, University of California (J.D., 1974). Member, Laguna Beach Unified School District Board of Education. *Member:* Orange County and American Bar Associations; State Bar of California. (Also Of Counsel, Lieberman, Dodge, Sendrow & Gerding, Ltd., Phoenix, Arizona). *PRACTICE AREAS:* Real Estate; Business Law; Finance.

**JONATHAN C. CAVETT,** born Los Angeles, California, May 12, 1940; admitted to bar, 1977, California. *Education:* California State University at Northridge (B.A., 1973); University of San Fernando Valley (J.D., 1977). *Member:* Los Angeles and Orange County Bar Associations; State Bar of California. (Also Practicing Individually). *PRACTICE AREAS:* Real Estate Litigation; Title Insurance; Intellectual Property; Construction Law; Mortgage Banking Defense.

REPRESENTATIVE CLIENTS: Alliance Insurance Group; Associates Financial Services Co, Inc.; Banc One Corporation; Bank One Arizona; Banc One Texas; Barclays American Mortgage Corporation; Beal Bank; Benefit Land Title Insurance Company; Berkeley Federal Savings; Broadway Federal Savings and Loan Association; Capstead Centennial Properties, Inc.; Chicago Title Insurance Co. Citizens Thrift and Loan Association; Coast Federal Bank; Crossland Mortgage Corporation; Eastern Savings Bank; Eastman Kodak Company; EMC Mortgage Corporation; Fairbanks Capital Corporation; Fidelity National Title Insurance Company; First American Title Insurance Company; First Interstate Bank of Arizona; First Savings Bank; Ford Consumer Finance Company; Glendale Federal Bank; Great Financial Mortgage; Greentree Mort-

*(This Listing Continued)*

CAA1349B

**THE BUCKLEY FIRM, P.C., Mission Viejo**—*Continued*

gage Company; Hamilton Financial Services; Hancock Savings Bank; Home Insurance Company; Home Savings of America; Interpacific Asset Management Co.; Investors Title Insurance Company of Southern California; ITT Consumer Financial Corporation; Long Beach Mortgage; Main Street Mortgage Company; Matrix Financial Services; M&I Thunderbird Bank; Motorola, Inc.; Mountain States Mortgage Center; Nations Bank Mortgage Corporation; National Pacific Mortgage Corporation; Option One Mortgage Corporation; PHH Asset Management; Platte Mortgage Corporation; Risk Enterprise Management; Security Pacific Financial Services; Security National Planners; The Sherwin-Williams Company; Stewart Title Company; Transamerica Financial Services; United Special Services; Westfall & Co.; West Starr Mortgage Corporation. Reference: Bank of California.

---

## FAUST & FAUST
SUITE 200
27281 LAS RAMBLAS
**MISSION VIEJO, CALIFORNIA 92691**
Telephone: 714-582-3540
Fax: 714-582-5300

*Orange, California Office:* 500 North State College Boulevard, Suite 780. Telephone: 714-582-3540.

*Custody Support, Family, Personal Injury Law, Probate and Estates.*

### MEMBERS OF FIRM

**ROBERT V. FAUST** (1921-1988).

**ROBERT V. FAUST, II,** born Orange, California, January 24, 1951; admitted to bar, 1978, California, U.S. Supreme Court and U.S. District Court, Central and Southern Districts of California. *Education:* California State University at Fullerton (B.A., 1973); California State University at San Diego; Western State University (J.D., 1977). Judge Pro Tem, Orange County Superior Court. Member: Orange County Bar Association; State Bar of California.

---

## ASKEW & ARCHBOLD
**MODESTO, CALIFORNIA**
(See Stockton)

*Providing Litigation and Appellate Services in State and Federal Courts and Counseling which emphasizes Business, Commercial, Agricultural, Food Processing, Lender Liability, Environmental, Toxics, Water, Employment, Wage, Patent, Trademark, Copyright, Insurance Coverage, Insurance Defense and Personal Injury Issues.*

---

## BORTON, PETRINI & CONRON
THE TURNER BUILDING
900 "H" STREET, SUITE D
**MODESTO, CALIFORNIA 95354**
Telephone: 209-576-1701
Fax: 209-527-9753
Email: bpcmod@bpclaw.com

*Bakersfield, California Office:* The Borton, Petrini & Conron Building, 1600 Truxtun Avenue, P.O. Box 2026. Telephone: 805-322-3051. Fax: 805-322-4628. Email: bpcbak@bpclaw.com.

*San Luis Obispo, California Office:* 1114 Marsh Street. Telephone: 805-541-4340. Fax: 805-541-4558. Email: bpcslo@bpclaw.com.

*Visalia, California Office:* 206 South Mooney Boulevard, P.O. Box 1028. Telephone: 209-627-5600. Fax: 209-627-4309. Email: bpcvis@bpclaw.com.

*Fresno, California Office:* T. W. Patterson Building, 2014 Tulare Street, Suite 830. Telephone: 209-268-0117. Fax: 209-237-7995. Email: bpcfrs@bpclaw.com.

*Sacramento, California Office:* 2233 Watt Avenue, Suite 290. Telephone: 916-484-3555. Fax: 916-484-3550. Email: bpcsac@bpclaw.com.

*Santa Barbara, California Office:* 211 East Victoria Street, Suite D. Telephone: 805-564-2404. Fax: 805-564-2176. Email: bpcsb@bpclaw.com.

*Los Angeles, California Office:* 707 Wilshire Boulevard, Suite 5100. Telephone: 213-624-2869. Fax: 213-489-3930. Email: bpcla@bpclaw.com.

*San Diego, California Office:* John Burnham Building, 610 West Ash Street, 9th Floor. Telephone: 619-232-2424. Fax: 619-531-0794. Email: bpcsd@bpclaw.com.

*(This Listing Continued)*

*Newport Beach, California Office:* 4675 MacArthur Court, Suite 1150. Telephone: 714-752-2333. Fax: 714-752-2854. Email: bpcnb@bpclaw.com.

*San Francisco, California Office:* 111 Pine Street, Suite 730. Telephone: 415-981-4415. Fax: 415-391-5538. Email: bpcsf@bpclaw.com.

*Redding, California Office:* 280 Hemsted Drive, Suite 100. Telephone: 916-222-1530. Fax: 916-222-4498. Email: bpcred@bpclaw.com.

*San Bernardino, California Office:* 290 North "D" Street, Suite 500. Telephone: 909-381-0527. Fax: 909-381-0658. Email: bpcsbdo@bpclaw.com.

*San Jose, California Office:* 2 North Second Street. Telephone: 408-298-3997. Fax: 408-298-3365. Email: bpcsj@bpclaw.com.

*Ventura, California Office:* 1000 Hill Road, Suite 310. Telephone: 805-650-9994. Fax: 805-650-7125. Email: bpcvta@bpclaw.com.

*Santa Rosa, California Office:* 50 Santa Rosa Avenue, Suite 300. Telephone: 707-527-9477. Fax: 707-527-9488. Email: bpcsr@bpclaw.com.

*Commercial/Real Estate Litigation, Insurance Law, General Civil Trial and Appellate Practice in State and Federal Courts, Personal Injury and Casualty Defense Litigation, Insurance Bad Faith and Coverage, Labor and Employment, Toxic Torts, Real Estate, Land Use Planning, Zoning, Municipal, Professional Errors and Omissions, Healthcare Provider Malpractice Defense, Products Liability, Oil and Gas, Water, Natural Resources, Environmental, Public Entity, Administrative, Agricultural, Banking, Contracts, Corporations, Partnerships, Taxation, Creditor's Remedies, Bankruptcy, Probate, Estate Planning, Family Law.*

**FIRM PROFILE:** *Founded by Fred E. Borton in 1899, the firm offers high quality legal services in all of the practice areas described above through its California network of sixteen regional offices. Our mission is to handle each file as if we were the client. We are responsive to the clients' need for communication, cost effectiveness and prompt evaluation.*

### MEMBERS OF FIRM

**BRADLEY A. POST,** born Yuba City, California, February 11, 1959; admitted to bar, 1986, California. *Education:* University of the Pacific (B.A., 1981); McGeorge School of Law (J.D., 1986). *Member:* Stanislaus County, San Joaquin County and American Bar Associations; The State Bar of California; Association of Defense Counsel, Northern California; Mid-Valley Claims Association. **PRACTICE AREAS:** Agricultural Litigation; Civil Rights Violations; Public Entity Law; Products and Premises Liability.

**MICHAEL J. MACKO,** born Centralia, Washington, June 30, 1959; admitted to bar, 1986, California. *Education:* University of California at Santa Barbara (B.A., 1981); Whittier College School of Law (J.D., 1985). Phi Alpha Delta. *Member:* Contra Costa County, Stanislaus County, San Joaquin County and American Bar Associations; The State Bar of California; Modesto Claims Association; Mid-Valley Claims Association. **PRACTICE AREAS:** Bankruptcy; Personal Injury; Public Entity Defense; Products Liability; Employment Law; Construction Defect.

**SAMUEL L. PHILLIPS,** born Modesto, California, February 2, 1960; admitted to bar, 1987, California. *Education:* University of San Francisco (B.A., 1982; J.D., 1985). Alpha Sigma Nu. Member, Jesuit Honor Society. *Member:* Stanislaus County, San Joaquin County and American Bar Associations; The State Bar of California; Association of Defense Counsel; Modesto Claims Association; Mid-Valley Claims Association. **LANGUAGES:** Spanish. **PRACTICE AREAS:** Civil Litigation; Agricultural Law; Construction Law.

(For a Complete Listing of Personnel and Representative Clients, please refer to our Bakersfield listing).

---

## RICHARD DOUGLAS BREW
A PROFESSIONAL LAW CORPORATION
SUITE 350 / JUDGE FRANK C. DAMRELL BUILDING
1601 I STREET
**MODESTO, CALIFORNIA 95354-1110**
Telephone: 209-572-3157
Telefax: 209-572-4641
Email: interleg.com

*Sophisticated Business, Financial, and Transactional Legal Service.*

**RICHARD DOUGLAS BREW,** born Los Angeles, California, January 1, 1947; admitted to bar, 1972, California and U.S. Court of Appeals, Ninth Circuit; 1975, U.S. Supreme Court; 1976, District of Columbia and U.S. Court of Appeals for the District of Columbia. *Education:* University of

*(This Listing Continued)*

California at Los Angeles (B.A., 1968); Pepperdine University School of Business and Management (M.B.A., summa cum laude, 1977); Loyola University School of Law (J.D., with honors, 1971); Cambridge University, Cambridge, England (LL.M., with honors, 1979). *Member:* State Bar of California; District of Columbia Bar; International Trademark Association. *PRACTICE AREAS:* Business; Corporation and Corporate Financing; International Business; Real Estate; Taxation; Trademark and Copyright.

REPRESENTATIVE CLIENTS: Ace Lathing, Inc.; The ARC of Stanislaus County (Association for Retarded Citizens); Bambacigno Steel Co., Inc.; Brush Creek Mining and Development Co., Inc.; Cranbrook Equity Investment Corporation; Delta Horseshoe Co., Inc.; Hi-Tec Sports, plc; Hi-Tec Sports International Ltd.; Hi-Tec Sports, USA, Inc.; Jack McCoy Enterprises, Inc.; McHenry Medical Group, Inc.; Medical Surgical Associates; Modesto Executive Air Charter and Skytrek Aviation; Resource Development; Saab-Scania Combitech; SavMax Foods, Inc.; Sierra Internal Medicine Medical Group, Inc.; Stanislaus County Library Foundation; Staveley Inc.; The Women's Auxiliary - A Modesto Community Connection.

## BRUNN & FLYNN

*A PROFESSIONAL CORPORATION*

928 12TH STREET
P.O. BOX 3366
**MODESTO, CALIFORNIA 95353**
*Telephone: 209-521-2133*
*Fax: 209-521-7584*
Email: brunnfly@ix.netcom.com

*Insurance Defense, Civil Defense. General Civil Trial Practice. Real Estate, Construction Law, Probate, Trust, Estate Planning, Corporate, Family and Workers Compensation Law, Personal Injury. Trials in all Courts.*

FIRM PROFILE: Brunn & Flynn, founded in 1963 by Charles K. Brunn, is actively engaged in the practice of law in state, federal and appellate courts throughout California. The attorneys and legal staff are dedicated to excellence in the practice of law.

**CHARLES K. BRUNN,** born San Francisco, California, December 3, 1931; admitted to bar, 1957, California, U.S. District Court, Eastern and Northern Districts of California, U.S. Court of Appeals, Ninth Circuit and U.S. Supreme Court. *Education:* University of San Francisco (B.S., 1954; J.D., 1957). Phi Alpha Delta. *Member:* Stanislaus County Bar Association; The State Bar of California (Member, Board of Directors); Association of Defense Counsel, Northern California; Mid-Valley Claims Association; American Board of Trial Advocates (Rank, Advocate); Association of Attorney Mediators.

**TIMOTHY T. FLYNN,** born Placerville, California, August 29, 1949; admitted to bar, 1976, California, U.S. District Court, Northern, Southern and Eastern Districts of California, U.S. Court of Appeals, Ninth Circuit, U.S. Supreme Court; 1981, U.S. Court of Military Appeals. *Education:* University of California at Davis (B.A., 1971); University of San Francisco (J.D., 1975). *Member:* Stanislaus County Bar Association; The State Bar of California; Association of Defense Counsel, Northern California; Mid-Valley Claims Association. [Commander, U.S. Naval Reserve]

**GERALD E. BRUNN,** born San Francisco, California, April 26, 1957; admitted to bar, 1982, California, U.S. District Court, Eastern and Central Districts of California; 1987, U.S. Court of Appeals, Ninth Circuit, U.S. Supreme Court. *Education:* University of San Francisco (B.A., cum laude, 1979; J.D., 1982). *Member:* Stanislaus County Bar Association; State Bar of California; Association of Defense Counsel, Northern California; Mid-Valley Claims Association. [Major, U.S. Army Reserve]

**ROGER S. MATZKIND,** born Los Angeles, California, March 28, 1953; admitted to bar, 1977, California, U.S. District Court, Central and Eastern Districts of California. *Education:* San Jose State University (B.A., with distinction, Political Science, 1974); Southwestern University (J.D., 1977). Former Assistant Professor of Law U.S. Military Academy, West Point. *Member:* Stanislaus County Bar Association; State Bar of California Association of Defense Counsel, Northern California; Mid-Valley Claims Association; Former Member, California District Attorney's Association. [Lieutenant Colonel, U.S. Army Reserve]

---

**MICHAEL G. DONOVAN,** born Boston, Massachusetts, October 4, 1950; admitted to bar, 1992, California, U.S. District Court, Northern District of California, U.S. Court of Appeals Ninth Circuit. *Education:* California State University, Sacramento (B.A., 1976); John F. Kennedy University (J.D., 1991). *Member:* Stanislaus County Bar Association; The State Bar of California; California Young Lawyers Association.

*(This Listing Continued)*

**ANDREW N. ESHOO,** born San Francisco, California, September 28, 1947; admitted to bar, 1984, California and U.S. District Court, Eastern and Northern Districts of California. *Education:* University of California at Berkeley (B.A., 1974); Humphreys College (J.D., 1983). *Member:* Stanislaus County Bar Association; State Bar of California. [1st. Lt., U.S. Army, 1965-1969]. **REPORTED CASES:** Pacific Gas & Electric Co. v. County of Stanislaus, 35 Cal.App.4th 908, review granted 9/28/95.

REPRESENTATIVE CLIENTS: Allied Dealers Insurance Co.; All-Cal Equipment, Inc.; Andreini & Company Insurance; Associated Claims Management Services; Bearden Realty, Inc.; Campbell Taggart, Inc.; Carpenter Claim Services; Circle K Corporation; City of Merced; County of Merced; County of Mariposa; County of Tuolumne; Duarte Nurseries; Freese & Gianelli Claim Adjusters; Hussmann Corp.; K-Mart Corp.; Kemper Group; Mines Engineering & Equipment Co.; Modesto Irrigation District; Mother Lode Plastics, Inc.; Mullen Trucking, Ltd.; Oakdale Irrigation District; Quik Stop Markets; Save Mart; Sign Designs, Inc.; Valley Slurry Seal Company; Viking Insurance Co.; Wausau Insurance Co.; Weyerhauser; Zurich of Canada; Yosemite Community College District; Colonial Insurance Co.; State Farm Fire & Casualty; State Farm Mutual Automobile Insurance Co.; Fireman's Fund Insurance Co.; Travelers Insurance Co.; Hartford Insurance Co.; Royal Insurance Co.; Industrial Indemnity Co.; CNA Insurance Cos.; CIGNA Insurance Co.; Zurich-American Insurance Co.; General Accident Group; Crawford & Co.; Oregon Mutual Insurance Co.; GAB Business Services; Basic Resources, Inc.; George Reed, Inc.; International Paper Co.; Home Insurance Co.; ACWA-Joint Powers Insurance Authority; Boudreau Corp.; Crum & Forster; Federated Insurance; Grange Insurance Association; Keenan and Associates; May Company Department Stores, Inc.; Pacific Gas & Electric Co.; Payless Shoe Source; Superior National Insurance Co.; Toastmaster, Inc.; Vanliner Insurance Co.; Western Atlas International, Inc.; Westside Irrigation District; USAA Insurance.

## CARDOZO & CARDOZO

1101 SYLVAN AVENUE, #B-4
**MODESTO, CALIFORNIA 95350**
*Telephone: 209-571-3600*
*FAX: 209-571-1553*

*Civil and Trial Practice, Insurance Defense, F.E.L.A., Personal Injury, Labor-/Employment Law and Sexual Harassment.*

### MEMBERS OF FIRM

**A. A. CARDOZO, JR.,** born Modesto, California, November 14, 1936; admitted to bar, 1961, California. *Education:* Stanford University (A.B., 1958); Hastings College of Law, University of California (J.D., 1961). *Member:* Stanislaus County Bar Association; State Bar of California; Association of Defense Counsel; American Board of Trial Advocates; National Association of Railroad Trial Counsel. *PRACTICE AREAS:* Insurance Defense; Personal Injury; Railroad Law; Medical Malpractice; Employment Litigation.

**RICHARD A. CARDOZO,** born Modesto, California, October 8, 1950; admitted to bar, 1976, California. *Education:* California State College, Turlock (B.A., 1973); Western State University (J.D., 1975). Judge Pro Tem, Stanislaus County Superior and Municipal Courts. *Member:* Stanislaus County Bar Association; The State Bar of California; California Association of Defense Counsel; American Arbitration Association (Mediator/Arbitrator). *PRACTICE AREAS:* General Civil Litigation; Insurance Defense Law; Personal Injury Law.

### LEGAL SUPPORT PERSONNEL

**PATRICIA BOWERS**

REPRESENTATIVE CLIENTS: California State Automobile Association (CSAA); Santa Fe Railway Co.; City of Riverbank.

## COLAW & AUGUSTINE

717 16TH STREET, SUITE 3
**MODESTO, CALIFORNIA 95354**
*Telephone: 209-549-0933*
*Fax: 209-549-2357*

*Commercial Collections, Creditors, Bankruptcy, Estate Planning, Business Law, Personal Injury, Family Law, Taxation Law and Civil Trial Practice.*

**CURTIS D. COLAW,** born Champaign, Illinois, January 8, 1960; admitted to bar, 1987, California and U.S. District Court, Eastern and Northern Districts of California. *Education:* California State University at Fresno (B.S., 1984); McGeorge School of Law, University of the Pacific (J.D., 1987). Recipient, American Jurisprudence Awards in Estate and Gift Tax and Sales. Special Projects Editor, Owen's California Forms and Procedure, 1986-1987. *Member:* Stanislaus County Bar Association; State Bar of Cali-

*(This Listing Continued)*

*COLAW & AUGUSTINE, Modesto—Continued*

fornia. PRACTICE AREAS: Collections; Business Law; Family Law; Civil Litigation.

**RODNEY A. AUGUSTINE,** born Stockton, California; July 26, 1960; admitted to bar, 1987, California and U.S. District Court, Eastern and Northern Districts of California; U.S. Tax Court. *Education:* University of California at Davis (B.A., 1982); McGeorge School of Law (J.D., 1987; L.L.M., 1990). Moot Court Honors Board. Estate Planning Council, Stanislaus County. *Member:* American Bar Association; State Bar of California. PRACTICE AREAS: Estate Planning; Business Law; Tax; Civil Litigation.

REPRESENTATIVE CLIENTS: American Shared Hospital Services; Cure Care, Inc.; Major-Sysco Corporation; Central Valley Dairymen; Mountain View Feed & Seed; C.W. Brower, Inc.; Youngs Market; California Milk Market; McMann Trucking; Golden Arm Breeding Service.

## CRABTREE, SCHMIDT, ZEFF, JACOBS & FARRAR

*Established in 1936*

**1100 14TH STREET, SECOND FLOOR**
P.O. BOX 3307
**MODESTO, CALIFORNIA 95353**
Telephone: 209-522-5231
Fax: 209-526-0632

*General Civil and Criminal Trial Practice. Probate, Estate Planning, Insurance, Real Property, Commercial Law, Secured Transactions, Bankruptcy (Debtor and Creditor), Banking, Insurance Defense, Family Law, Adoptions and Corporation Law.*

*FIRM PROFILE: Our firm's history dates back to 1936 when Les Cleary and William Zeff formed Cleary and Zeff. Both respected leaders in the legal community, Les Cleary was a co-founder of The American College of Trial Lawyers and William Zeff was appointed as a Stanislaus County Superior Court Judge in 1965.*

*Throughout our 50 plus year history and various name changes, for such reasons as the appointment of Edward Dean Price to the Federal Bench.*

### MEMBERS OF FIRM

**ROBERT W. CRABTREE,** born Modesto, California, June 30, 1940; admitted to bar, 1967, California. *Education:* University of California at Berkeley (B.S., 1962); Hastings College of Law, University of California (LL.B., 1966). Order of the Coif. Member, Thurston Society (President, 1966). Member of Staff, 1964-1966 and Research Editor, 1966, Hastings Law Journal. Chairman, Stanislaus County Air Pollution Control Hearing Board, 1970-1976. *Member:* Stanislaus County (President, 1977) and American Bar Associations; The State Bar of California; Association of Defense Counsel of Northern California. PRACTICE AREAS: Probate; Estate Planning; Corporate; Business Transactions.

**WALTER J. SCHMIDT,** born Modesto, California, February 20, 1946; admitted to bar, 1971, California. *Education:* University of California (A.B., 1967); Hastings College of Law, University of California (J.D., 1970). Member, Lawyer Representative to the Ninth Circuit Judicial Conference, 1990-1993. *Member:* Stanislaus County and American Bar Associations; The State Bar of California (Member, 1976-1978, 1982-1985 and Chairman, 1984-1985, Advisory Committee for Continuing Education of the Bar; Member, 1985-1989 and Chairman, 1988-1989, Governing Committee on Continuing Education of the Bar; Member, State Bar Task Force on Lawyer Education, 1989; Member, State Bar Standing Committee on MCLE, 1990-1993). PRACTICE AREAS: Agricultural Law; Commercial; Banking; Bankruptcy (Creditor); Business.

**THOMAS D. ZEFF,** born Modesto, California, June 29, 1951; admitted to bar, 1976, California. *Education:* University of Oregon (B.S., 1973); Hastings College of Law, University of California (J.D., 1976). *Member:* Stanislaus County and American Bar Associations; The State Bar of California; Association of Defense Counsel of Northern California (Director, 1982-1983); Defense Research Institute; American Board of Trial Advocates. PRACTICE AREAS: Insurance Defense; Civil Litigation.

**NAN COHAN JACOBS,** born Indianapolis, Indiana, April 9, 1951; admitted to bar, 1977, Indiana and Ohio; 1981, California. *Education:* Indiana University (A.B., 1973; J.D., 1977). Note and Development Editor, Indiana Law Review, 1976-1977. Law Clerk to Hon. August Pryatel, Court of Appeals of Ohio, Eighth Appellate District, 1977-1979. Attorney, Ches-

*(This Listing Continued)*

CAA1352B

sie System, 1979-1980. Outstanding Woman of Stanislaus County, Stanislaus County Commission for Women, 1994. *Member:* Stanislaus County and American Bar Associations; The State Bar of California (Member, Adoption Committee, 1990—); Stanislaus County Women Lawyers (Member, Board of Directors; Chair, Continuing Legal Education, 1993-1994). PRACTICE AREAS: Business; Commercial; Banking; Bankruptcy (Creditor); Real Estate; Agriculture; Family Law; Adoptions.

**E. DANIEL FARRAR,** born San Jose, California, May 2, 1964; admitted to bar, 1991, California; U.S. Court of Appeals, Ninth Circuit; U.S. District Court, Northern and Eastern Districts of California. *Education:* Westmont College (B.A., 1986); University of Wyoming School of Law (J.D., 1991). *Member:* Stanislaus County Bar Association; State Bar of California; Mid-Valley Claims Association; Association of Defense Counsel. PRACTICE AREAS: Insurance Defense; Civil Litigation.

### ASSOCIATE

**HELEN M. CALVERLEY,** born Royal Oak, Michigan, May 21, 1964; admitted to bar, 1991, California. *Education:* Michigan State University (B.A., 1987); University of Detroit (J.D., 1990). *Member:* Stanislaus County and American Bar Associations; State Bar of California. PRACTICE AREAS: Business Law; Employment Litigation; Health Care.

TRIAL ATTORNEYS FOR: Chevron USA; Employers Self Insurance Service; Great American Insurance Co.; Kemper Insurance Co.; Keenan & Associates; United Pacific Reliance Insurance Co.; City of Modesto; County of Stanislaus; California Insurance Guarantee Association; State Farm Fire & Casualty; Concord General Corp.; National Chiropractic Mutual Insurance Co.; Nationwide Insurance Co.; Occidental Fire & Casualty; State Farm Mutual Insurance Co.; Western Mutual Insurance Co.
LOCAL COUNSEL FOR: Hahn Property Management Corp.; Heritage Ford; Alfred Matthews, Inc.; National Can Co.; WestAmerica Bank; Central Valley Production Credit Assn.; Varco Pruden; GCH Insurance Services, Inc.; Modesto City Schools; Christian Salvesen; Modesto Banking Co.; CBC Steel Buildings, Sierra Bay Farm Credit Services; Cal-Almond.
REFERENCE: WestAmerica Bank.

## CURTIS & ARATA

*A PROFESSIONAL CORPORATION*

*Established in 1953*

**1300 K STREET, SECOND FLOOR**
P.O. BOX 3030
**MODESTO, CALIFORNIA 95353**
Telephone: 209-521-1800
Fax: 209-572-3501

*General Civil, Trial and Appellate Practice. Corporation, Business, Real Property, Tax, Bankruptcy, Insurance and Insurance Defense, Estate Planning, Probate, Trusts, Family Law, Workers' Compensation Defense, Personal Injury, Employment Law, Environmental Law, Products Liability, Guardianships, Conservatorships and Adoptions.*

*FIRM PROFILE: Curtis & Arata is a full-service law firm providing counsel and trial advocacy to businesses, individuals and governmental entities in the San Joaquin Valley. As one of the area's oldest and most experienced firms, Curtis & Arata continues a tradition of maintaining the highest professional and ethical standards while providing quality legal services. The firm seeks to reach legal solutions that are prudent, practical and appropriate through the use of experienced counsel, skilled negotiators and, when necessary, expert trial practitioners. Curtis & Arata's team of attorneys is supported by a trained paralegal staff and the latest computerized research tools.*

**A. A. CARDOZO** (1910-1985).

**RALPH S. CURTIS,** born Albany, New York, January 16, 1948; admitted to bar, 1974, California. *Education:* St. Mary's College of California (B.A., cum laude, 1970); University of California at Davis (J.D., 1974). *Member:* Stanislaus County Bar Association (Secretary and Chair, Bench-Bar Committee); State Bar of California; California Association of Defense Counsel (Board of Directors, 1991- 1992); Defense Research Institute; California Trial Lawyers Association. (Firm President). PRACTICE AREAS: General Civil Litigation; Insurance Defense Law; Personal Injury Law; Employment Law; Professional Liability.

**GEORGE S. ARATA,** born Stockton, California, July 26, 1950; admitted to bar, 1976, California. *Education:* University of the Pacific (B.A., 1972); Western State University (J.D., 1975). Nu Beta Epsilon. *Member:* Stanislaus County and American Bar Associations; State Bar of California; California Association of Defense Counsel. PRACTICE AREAS: Insurance Defense Law; Workers Compensation Law; Personal Injury Law.

*(This Listing Continued)*

# PROFESSIONAL BIOGRAPHIES

# CALIFORNIA—MODESTO

**D. LEE HEDGEPETH,** born San Fernando, California, May 15, 1953; admitted to bar, 1979, California. *Education:* California State University, Stanislaus (B.A., 1975); University of the Pacific, McGeorge School of Law (J.D., 1979). *Member:* Stanislaus County Bar Association; State Bar of California; California Association of Defense Counsel (Board of Directors). **PRACTICE AREAS:** Insurance Defense Law; Workers Compensation Defense; General Civil Litigation.

**MICHAEL B. IJAMS,** born Modesto, California, June 25, 1952; admitted to bar, 1978, California. *Education:* University of California at Davis (A.B., 1974; J.D., 1978). *Member:* Stanislaus County Bar Association; State Bar of California (Member, Business Law and Real Property Sections). **PRACTICE AREAS:** Business Law; Civil Litigation; Insurance Defense Law; Employment Law.

**EDGAR H. HAYDEN, JR.,** born Elizabeth City, North Carolina, June 19, 1945; admitted to bar, 1971, California. *Education:* Ventura College (A.A., 1965); California Western University (B.A., 1967); University of San Diego (J.D., 1970). Member, University of San Diego Law Review, 1969-1970. Deputy in Charge, Consumer Fraud and Environmental Protection Unit, 1982-1985. *Member:* Stanislaus County Bar Association (Member, Board of Directors, 1982-1985); State Bar of California; Association of Defense Counsel of Northern California. **PRACTICE AREAS:** Insurance Defense; Subrogation; Collections; Personal Injury; Products Liability; Environmental; Torts.

**HUGH E. BRERETON,** born San Antonio, Texas, September 2, 1943; admitted to bar, 1974, California. *Education:* University of San Francisco; University of California at Berkeley (B.A., 1966); University of the Pacific, McGeorge School of Law (J.D., 1974). *Member:* Stanislaus County Bar Association (President, 1985); State Bar of California. **PRACTICE AREAS:** Family Law; Probate Law.

---

Erik R. Anderson
Jonathan A. Carlson
Terri L. Cipponeri
Richard J. Sordello, Jr.
Ross W. Lee
Jack M. Jacobson
Ted M. Cabral
Sabrina Tourtlotte
Judy A. Betker
Andrew S. Mendlin
Kimberly W. Ringer

REPRESENTATIVE CLIENTS: Sears; General Motors Co.; Save Mart Supermarkets; Raley's Supermarkets; Mallard's Restaurants; Davis-Lay, Inc.; Gottschalks; MTC Distributing; American Chevrolet-GEO; Doctors Medical Center; Rogers Jewelers; California State Automobile Association; St. Paul Fire and Marine Insurance Co.; State Farm Mutual Insurance Co.; Allstate Insurance Co.; Carolina Casualty Group; John Deere Insurance Co.; ESIS, Inc.; Allied Group Insurance Co.; Wilshire Insurance Co.; Clarendon Insurance Co.; Houston General Insurance Group; Gulf Insurance Co.; California Insurance Group; Northbrook Insurance Co.; Acclamation Insurance Management Services; General Accident; Modesto City Schools; Yosemite Community College District; County of Stanislaus; City of Ceres; City of Turlock.
REFERENCE: Modesto Banking Company (Main Branch-Modesto).

## DAMRELL, NELSON, SCHRIMP, PALLIOS & LADINE

*A PROFESSIONAL CORPORATION*

Established in 1968

*1601 I STREET, FIFTH FLOOR*
**MODESTO, CALIFORNIA 95354**
Telephone: 209-526-3500
Fax: 209-526-3534
Email: dnsp1@ix.netcom.com

*Sacramento, California Office:* Suite 200, 1100 K Street. Telephone: 916-447-2909. Fax: 916-447-0552.

*Oakdale, California Office:* 703 West "F" Street, P.O. Drawer C. Telephone: 209-848-3500. Fax: 209-848-3400.

*Civil Trial and Appellate Practice in all State and Federal Courts. General Business Practice, Complex Business Litigation, Government, Administrative and Legislative Practice, Business Planning and Dissolution, Personal Injury and Insurance Law, Corporate, Environmental, Resource Recovery, Water and Agricultural Law, Land Use, Real Estate Development, Zoning and Construction Law, Healthcare and Hospital Law, Taxation, Estate Planning and Probate and Trust Administration.*

FIRM PROFILE: *The firm's attorneys practice before all levels of federal and California courts with particular emphasis on civil litigation, including complex and business litigation, as well as commercial law, general business, real estate law, environmental law, governmental law, and probate. The firm also has extensive experience representing clients before the U.S. Congress and the California Legislature, as well as before federal, state, and local government boards and agencies.*

**FRANK C. DAMRELL** (1898-1988).

**FRANK C. DAMRELL, JR.,** born Modesto, California, July 6, 1938; admitted to bar, 1965, California and U.S. District Court, Eastern and Northern Districts of California; 1979, U.S. Supreme Court; 1980, U.S. District Court, Central District of California. *Education:* University of Santa Clara and University of California at Berkeley (B.A., 1961); Yale University (LL.B., 1964). Deputy Attorney General, California, 1965-1966. Deputy District Attorney, Stanislaus County, 1966-1968. Member, 1973-1980 and Chairman, 1975-1980, Consumer Advisory Council, State of California. Member: Board of Regents, Santa Clara University, 1986-1994; Board of Visitors, Santa Clara University Law School, 1983-1994. *Member:* Stanislaus County, American and Federal Bar Associations; State Bar of California. **PRACTICE AREAS:** Complex Litigation; Business Litigation; Government Law; Administrative Law.

**DUANE L. NELSON,** born Modesto, California, March 19, 1942; admitted to bar, 1967, California; 1979, U.S. District Courts, Northern, Central and Eastern Districts of California; 1981, U.S. Supreme Court. *Education:* University of California at Berkeley (B.A., 1964); Hastings College of the Law, University of California (J.D., 1967). Member, Thurston Society. Member, Editorial Board, Hastings Law Journal, 1966-1967. Author: "Mental Distress from Collection Activities," 17 Hastings Law Journal 369, 1965. *Member:* Stanislaus County and American Bar Associations; State Bar of California; Consumer Attorneys of California; Stanislaus County Trial Lawyers Association; The Association of Trial Lawyers of America. **PRACTICE AREAS:** Civil Litigation; Personal Injury Law.

**ROGER M. SCHRIMP,** born Stockton, California, May 26, 1941; admitted to bar, 1966, California; 1967, U.S. District Courts, Northern, Central and Eastern Districts of California; 1978, U.S. Tax Court and U.S. Supreme Court; 1981, U.S. Claims Court. *Education:* University of California (A.B., with honors, 1963); Boalt Hall School of Law, University of California (J.D., 1966); McGeorge School of Law, University of the Pacific (LL.M. in Taxation, 1982). Phi Alpha Delta. Appointed by Gov. Pete Wilson to Board of Governors, California Community Colleges, July 1996. Chairman of the Board, Oak Valley Community Bank. President, Boy Scouts of America, Area III, Western Region. *Member:* Stanislaus County (President, 1993) and American (Member, Committee on Agriculture, Section of Taxation) Bar Associations; State Bar of California; The Association of Trial Lawyers of America; California Trial Lawyers Association; American Judicature Society; Lawyer-Pilots Bar Association; Northern California Association of Defense Counsel; Defense Research Institute; National Association of Eagle Scouts. **PRACTICE AREAS:** Business Law; Real Estate Law; Complex Business Litigation.

**STEVEN G. PALLIOS,** born Modesto, California, January 4, 1950; admitted to bar, 1975, California; 1976, U.S. District Court, Central District of California; 1977, U.S. District Court, Eastern District of California; 1986, U.S. Tax Court. *Education:* California State University at Fresno (B.S., summa cum laude, 1972); University of California at Los Angeles (J.D., 1975); McGeorge School of Law, University of the Pacific (LL.M. in Taxation, 1985). Phi Kappa Phi; Beta Gamma Sigma. Member, University of California at Los Angeles Law Review, 1973-1975. *Member:* Stanislaus County Bar Association; State Bar of California. **PRACTICE AREAS:** Real Estate Law; Corporation Law; Estate Planning Law.

**WRAY F. LADINE,** born San Jose, California, December 15, 1950; admitted to bar, 1976, California, U.S. District Court, Northern District of California and U.S. Court of Appeals, Ninth Circuit; 1982; U.S. District Court, Eastern District of California; 1986, U.S. Supreme Court; 1989, U.S. District Court, Central District of California. *Education:* University of California at Los Angeles (B.A., 1972); Southwestern University (J.D., 1976). Chief Deputy District Attorney, 1983-1986. *Member:* Stanislaus County Bar Association (President, 1990); State Bar of California; National Health Lawyers Association. **PRACTICE AREAS:** Administrative Law; Civil Litigation; Alcoholic Beverage Licensing Law.

**MATTHEW O. PACHER,** born New York, New York, May 3, 1954; admitted to bar, 1983, California; 1984, U.S. District Court, Eastern District of California; 1993, U.S. Court of Appeals, Ninth Circuit. *Education:* Herbert H. Lehman College of the City University of New York (B.A., cum laude, 1976); University of North Carolina (M.A., 1980); McGeorge School of the Law, University of the Pacific (J.D., 1983). *Member:* Stanislaus

*(This Listing Continued)*

*DAMRELL, NELSON, SCHRIMP, PALLIOS & LADINE, A PROFESSIONAL CORPORATION, Modesto—Continued*

County and American Bar Associations; State Bar of California. *PRACTICE AREAS:* Civil Litigation; Real Estate Law; Corporation Law.

**FRED A. SILVA,** born Azores, Portugal, December 11, 1958; admitted to bar, 1987, California and U.S. District Court, Eastern and Northern Districts of California. *Education:* University of the Pacific (B.A., cum laude, 1982); University of California at Davis (J.D., 1986). Phi Kappa Phi; Omicron Delta Epsilon. *Member:* Stanislaus County (Member, Board of Directors, 1991—; President, 1994-1995) and American (Member, Corporation, Banking and Business Law Section) Bar Associations; State Bar of California (Member, Business Law Section). *LANGUAGES:* Portuguese. *PRACTICE AREAS:* Complex Litigation; Business Litigation.

---

**CRAIG W. HUNTER,** born Oakland, California, November 1, 1955; admitted to bar, 1980, California. *Education:* San Francisco State University (B.A., 1977); University of California at Berkeley (J.D., 1980). *Member:* Stanislaus County Bar Association (Member, Board of Directors, 1996—); State Bar of California (Member, Real Estate Section). *PRACTICE AREAS:* Real Estate; Workouts; Banking.

**JOHN K. PELTIER,** born Vancouver, British Columbia, 1953; admitted to bar, 1988, British Columbia; 1991, California. *Education:* University of British Columbia (B.A., 1984; LL.B., 1987). Author: "Microcomputer Hardware," Continuing Legal Education Society of British Columbia, 1991. *Member:* Stanislaus County (Member, Board of Directors, 1994-1995) and American Bar Associations; State Bar of California; California Trial Lawyers Association; The Association of Trial Lawyers of America. *PRACTICE AREAS:* Civil Litigation; Complex Litigation.

**BRIAN J. BARTOW,** born Queens, New York, January 14, 1955; admitted to bar, 1989, California, and U.S. District Court, Northern District of California. *Education:* Defense Language Institute (German, 1976); City University of New York, Queensborough Community College (A.A.S., 1983); University of California at Riverside (A.B., 1986); University of California at Davis (J.D., 1989). Registered Nurse: New York, 1983; California, 1984. Chairman, Board of Directors, 1992-1993 and Counsel, 1994—, Miracle Mission. *Member:* Stanislaus County Bar Association; State Bar of California; National Academy of Elder Law Attorneys; California Trial Lawyers Association. [with U.S. Army, Military Police, 1975-1978]. *PRACTICE AREAS:* Healthcare and Hospital Law; Litigation; Business Law.

**JEFFEREY A. WOOTEN,** born Fresno, California, November 16, 1963; admitted to bar, 1991, California and U.S. District Court, Northern District of California. *Education:* University of California at Berkeley (B.A., 1985); University of California at Davis (J.D., 1991). Phi Beta Kappa. *Member:* Stanislaus County Bar Association; State Bar of California. *PRACTICE AREAS:* Business Law; Real Estate; Business Litigation; Personal Injury.

**C. KELLEY EVANS,** born Banbury, England, November 6, 1964; admitted to bar, 1990, California, U.S. District Court, Northern, Central and Eastern Districts of California and U.S. Court of Appeals, Ninth Circuit. *Education:* Oxford University, Oxford, England (B.A., honors, 1987; M.A., 1992); University of California at Davis (J.D., 1990). Recipient: American Jurisprudence Award in Criminal Procedure; BNA Law Student Award; U.C. Davis Distinguished Scholar; Member, U.C. Davis Law Review, 1989-1990. *Member:* Stanislaus County, Sacramento County and American Bar Associations; State Bar of California; Barristers' Club of Sacramento (President, 1994). *LANGUAGES:* French, German and Welsh. *PRACTICE AREAS:* Labor and Employment Law; Business Litigation; Probate and Trust Administration and Litigation.

**WENDELIN Z. WARWICK,** born Los Angeles, California, September 14, 1962; admitted to bar, 1991, California. *Education:* University of California, Santa Barbara (B.A., with great distinction, 1984); McGeorge School of Law (J.D., valedictorian, 1991). Order of the Coif; Traynor Society. Recipient: American Jurisprudence Awards: Decedents, Estates and Trusts and Advanced Torts. Certified Public Accountant, California, 1988. *Member:* Stanislaus County and American Bar Associations; State Bar of California (Member: Corporate and Business Law Sections, 1991—; Antitrust Section, 1993; Employment Law Section, 1995); American Association of Attorney-Certified Public Accountants, Inc. *PRACTICE AREAS:* Business and Corporation.

**LISA L. GILLISPIE,** born Carbondale, Illinois, December 22, 1968; admitted to bar, 1993, California, U.S. District Court, Eastern, Central and Northern Districts of California and U.S. Court of Appeals, Ninth Circuit. *Education:* University of California, Santa Barbara (B.A., cum laude, 1989); Boston University (J.D., 1993). Order of Omega. Recipient: Gold & Silver Congressional Medals of Honors; Second Place NE Region, ACTL National Moot Court Competition; Best Team, Best Brief, 1992 Albers Honors Moot Court Competition; 1992 American Jurisprudence Award for Excellence in Moot Court Competition; Best Brief, 1991 Stone Moot Court Competition. National Finalist, ACTL National Moot Court Competition. Treasurer, Criminal Justice Society. Member, International Law Society. Extern for Presiding Justice Hollis G. Best, Court of Appeals, Fifth Appellate District, Fresno, California, Summer 1991. Member, Board of Directors and Vice President, Income Development, American Cancer Society, Stanislaus County Chapter. Member, Stanislaus County Domestic Violence Coordinating Council. *Member:* Stanislaus County Bar Association (Member, Board of Directors); Stanislaus County Women Lawyers Association. *LANGUAGES:* German. *PRACTICE AREAS:* Business Litigation; Securities Litigation; Complex Litigation.

**AMY E. ELLIOTT,** born Turlock, California, June 27, 1970; admitted to bar, 1996, California and U.S. District Court, Eastern District of California. *Education:* University of California (B.A., with distinction, 1992); The Ohio State University (J.D., 1995). Member, 1992-1995 and Vice-President, 1994, Student Health Care Law Association. Author: "Managed Care and Arbitration: Will Consumers Suffer if the Two are Combined?" 10 Ohio State Journal on Dispute Resolution 418, 1995. *Member:* Stanislaus County Bar Association; State Bar of California; Stanislaus County Women's Lawyers Association. *PRACTICE AREAS:* Business Litigation; Insurance Defense.

**KRISTINE L. BURKS,** born Los Gatos, California, August 17, 1967; admitted to bar, 1996, California. *Education:* California State University, Chico (B.S., 1990; B.A., 1990); Golden Gate University (J.D., honors, 1995). Member, 1993-1994 and Associate Editor, 1994-1995, Law Review. Recipient: Joseph R. Rensch Scholarship, 1993-1994; Merit Scholarship, 1994-1995; Sherbourne-Thompson Scholarship, 1995; Outstanding Editor Award, 1994-1995. American Jurisprudence Award, Corporations; Writing and Research. Judicial Extern: U.S. Court of Appeals, Ninth Circuit, 1995; San Francisco Superior Court, Law and Motion Department, Summer 1993. Author: "Redefining Parenthood: Child Custody and Visitation When Non-Traditional Dissolve," 24 Golden Gate U.L.Rev. 223, 1994. *Member:* Stanislaus County Bar Association; Stanislaus County Women Lawyers Association. *PRACTICE AREAS:* Business Litigation; Commercial Litigation; Antitrust.

**MICHELLE LUISA CHRISTIAN,** born Turlock, California, June 29, 1971; admitted to bar, 1996, California. *Education:* University of California, Los Angeles (B.A., Political Science, 1993); University of Hastings College of Law (J.D., 1996). *Member:* Stanislaus County Bar Association; State Bar of California.

*OF COUNSEL*

**SURENDRA J. SOOD, M.D.,** born Punjab, India, June 2, 1945; admitted to bar, 1995, California. *Education:* School of Medicine, M.S. University Baroda, India (M.D., 1969); Humphreys College (J.D., 1994). *Member:* State Bar of California. *LANGUAGES:* Hindi and Punjabi. *PRACTICE AREAS:* Personal Injury.

**CRESSEY H. NAKAGAWA,** born Chicago, Illinois, September 12, 1943; admitted to bar, 1969, California, U.S. District Court, Northern District of California and U.S. Court of Appeals, Ninth Circuit; 1971, U.S. District Court, Eastern District of California; 1981, U.S. Supreme Court; 1985, U.S. Tax Court and U.S. Court of Appeals, District of Columbia Circuit. *Education:* Stanford University (B.A., 1965); Hastings College of Law, University of California (J.D., 1968). National President, Japanese American Citizens League, 1988-1994. Member, Steering Committee, San Francisco 2000. *Member:* Bar Association of San Francisco; State Bar of California; American Bar Association. (Also Member, Eber & Nakagawa, San Francisco).

REPRESENTATIVE CLIENTS: Wineries: E & J Gallo Winery; Bronco Wine Co. Agriculture: American Fruit Juice Assn.; S. Martinelli & Co.; Besnier America; Welch Foods; Tree Top, Inc.; Dairy Feed Manufacturing Council; California Grain and Feed Association; Pik'd Rite; The DiMare Co.; Tri Valley Growers; A.L. Gilbert Co.; Farmer's Warehouse; Amerine Systems, Inc.; Sparrowk Livestock. Financial: Bank of America; Union Bank; Chicago Title; Bay View Federal Bank. Real Estate Development/Construction: Morrison Homes; The Luckey Co.; Morrison-Knudsen Company, Inc.; Horn Construction; Cen-Cal Wallboard; Kiewit Pacific Co.; Huff Construction Co.; Arco Insulation; Brunk Insulation; Boese Construction Co. Industrial/Transportation/Energy: Gallo Glass Co.; W.R. Grace Co.; Atlantic Richfield Co.; The Coastal Corp.; Pep

*(This Listing Continued)*

Boys, Inc.; Fleetwood Enterprises, Inc.; Ogden Corp.; Massey Ferguson Co.; Stockton Terminal and Eastern Railroad; Norfolk Southern Corp.; Turlock Irrigation District; Ward-Schmid, Inc. *Healthcare:* National Medical Enterprises, Inc.; California Association of Hospitals and Health Systems; California Ambulatory Surgery Association; Doctors Medical Center (Modesto); Doctors Hospital (Manteca); Oak Valley Hospital (Oakdale).

## GIANELLI & FORES
*A PROFESSIONAL LAW CORPORATION*

Established in 1972

1014 16TH STREET
P.O. BOX 3212
**MODESTO, CALIFORNIA 95353**
Telephone: 209-521-6260
Telecopier: 209-521-5971

*Business and Corporate Planning, Estate Planning, Probate and Trusts, Bankruptcy (Creditor), Commercial, Debt Collection, Civil Litigation, Personal Injury and Negligence, Construction, Taxation, Discrimination Defense, Adoption, Guardianships, Conservatorships and Juvenile Dependency.*

**LOUIS F. GIANELLI,** born Stockton, California, April 16, 1928; admitted to bar, 1972, California. *Education:* University of Nevada; University of California at Berkeley (B.S., 1950); Humphreys College (J.D., 1972). Author: "Treating Children Equally: Estate Planning for the Family Business or Farm," Probate and Property, January/February, 1988. California Probate Referee, 1968—. *Member:* American Bar Association. **PRACTICE AREAS:** Estate Planning, Probate and Trusts; Business and Corporate Planning.

**MICHAEL L. GIANELLI,** born Stockton, California, August 5, 1951; admitted to bar, 1976, California. *Education:* University of California at Irvine (B.A., 1973); McGeorge School of Law, University of the Pacific (J.D., 1976). Instructor, Business Law and Estate Planning, Modesto Junior College, 1980—. *Member:* California Trial Lawyers Association; Stanislaus County Estate Planning Council. (Certified Specialist, Probate, Estate Planning and Trust Law, The State Bar of California Board of Legal Specialization). **PRACTICE AREAS:** Bankruptcy (Creditor); Commercial; Debt Collection; Civil Litigation; Estate Planning, Probate and Trusts.

**ROBERT P. FORES,** born Sonora, California, July 29, 1958; admitted to bar, 1985, California. *Education:* University of California at Berkeley (A.B., 1980); McGeorge School of Law, University of the Pacific (J.D., 1985). *Member:* Stanislaus County Bar Association, (Member, Board of Directors). **PRACTICE AREAS:** Civil Litigation; Debt Collection; Personal Injury and Negligence; Construction.

**DAVID L. GIANELLI,** born Modesto, California, May 21, 1960; admitted to bar, 1985, California; 1986, U.S. Tax Court. *Education:* University of California at San Diego (B.A., 1982); McGeorge School of Law, University of the Pacific (J.D., 1985); LL.M. in Taxation, 1986). *Member:* Stanislaus County Estate Planning Council. (Certified Specialist, Probate, Estate Planning and Trust Law, The State Bar of California Board of Legal Specialization). **PRACTICE AREAS:** Estate Planning, Probate and Trusts; Business and Corporate Planning; Taxation.

**LISA B. WILLIAMS,** born Walnut Creek, California, June 23, 1963; admitted to bar, 1989, California. *Education:* San Francisco State University; University of California, Davis (B.S in Human Development, 1985); University of California School of Law, Davis (J.D., 1989). *Member:* Contra Costa County Bar Association; State Bar of California. **PRACTICE AREAS:** Litigation.

All Attorneys are Members of The Stanislaus County Bar Association.

REPRESENTATIVE CLIENTS: Aderholt Specialty Company, Inc.; Alfred Matthews, Inc. (Cadillac, Oldsmobile, Pontiac and BMW); Braden Farms; California-Arizona Watermelon Association; Clark Equipment Credit Corp.; Dave Wilson Nursery, Inc.; Delta Brands; Don Miller Sales; Evans Communications; Ferry Morse Seed Company; Freese and Gianelli Claim Services; Hughson Chemical; Keckler Medical Co., Inc.; Market Wholesale Grocers; Martin Optical Service, Inc.; May Transfer & Storage; Memorial Hospitals Association; Mid State Tire Warehouse, Inc.; Modesto Banking Co.; Pacific Southwest Container, Inc.; Paul Oil Company, Inc.; Phillips Electric Company; Royal Robbins, Inc.; Save Mart Supermarkets; Sierra Beverage; Sierra Pacific Lumber Co.; Sonora Community Hospital; Stanislaus County Medical Society; Stanislaus Surgery Center, Inc.; Thomas Equipment Rental Co.; Volk International, Inc.

## *ISRAELS, BRINK & GRIFFITH*
*A PROFESSIONAL LAW CORPORATION*

Established in 1988

1500 J STREET
P.O. BOX 1637
**MODESTO, CALIFORNIA 95353**
Telephone: 209-572-1130
Fax: 209-572-1134
Email: ibg@Sonnet.com
URL: http://www.sonnet.com:80/modesto/ibg/

San Francisco, California Office: 353 Sacramento Street, Suite 1500, 94111. Telephone: 415-576-1130. Fax: 415-362-1776.

*Civil Practice including Business Litigation, Real Estate Law, Estate Planning, Elder Rights, Guardianships and Conservatorships, Trusts and Probate Matters, Agribusiness Law, Health Care, Bankruptcy, Creditor Representation, Administrative Law, Trademark Law, Business Acquisition and Sale, Zoning, Commercial Law and Assistance to General Counsel, including local litigation referral and establishment of business area location.*

*FIRM PROFILE: The firm provides quality legal services, effective practical solutions and fair billing practices. When necessary, the firm refers to recognized outside counsel with continued involvement to assure cost-effective results and continued responsiveness to the client's needs.*

**SIDNEY A. ISRAELS,** born Modesto, California, May 3, 1943; admitted to bar, 1971, California. *Education:* University of California at Berkeley (A.B., 1965); University of California at Los Angeles (J.D., 1970). Instructor, Real Property Law and Practice, Yosemite College District, 1980—. Author: "How to Write a Valid Contract," 1983; "Real Estate Law Update," 1983, 1984, California Depository for Continuing Education. Panelist, California State Bar Program, 1985, 1986. Panelist, "Lender Liability and Hazardous Waste," California State Bar Real Property Section, 1988. Moderator, "From Rags to Riches," State Bar of California, 1989. *Member:* State Bar of California (Member, Commercial and Industrial Real Estate Subsection, 1988-1989; Member, Vice Chair, Advisor Executive Committee, State Real Property Section, 1989-1993).

**KARIN SMITH BRINK,** born Monterey, California, May 31, 1963; admitted to bar, 1990, California and U.S. District Court, Eastern District of California. *Education:* University of Southern California (A.B., International Relations, 1985; A.B., Political Science, 1985); McGeorge School of Law, University of the Pacific (J.D., 1990). Phi Delta Phi. *Member:* American Society of International Law, 1985-1990; Pacific International Law Society, 1986-1990; Business Law Forum, 1986-1988. Staff Writer, Owens Treatise on California Procedure, 1987-1988. Co-Chair, Womens Financial and Estate Planning Seminar. *Member:* State Bar of California (Member, Estate Planning and Elder Law Sections); American Bar Association; Stanislaus Estate Planning Counsel; Stanislaus County Womens Legal Association. **PRACTICE AREAS:** Estate Planning; Elder Rights; Guardianships; Conservatorships; Trusts and Probate Matters; Trademark Asset Preservation.

**DAVID R. GRIFFITH,** born Petaluma, California, July 10, 1965; admitted to bar, 1994, California and U.S. District Court, Eastern District of California. *Education:* Modesto Junior College (A.A., 1989); Northwestern California School of Law (J.D., 1993). Co-Chair, Bankruptcy Reform Act of 1994, "What Every Creditor Needs to Know." *Member:* Stanislaus County Bar Association; State Bar of California (Member, Litigation and Business Law Sections); California Trial Lawyers Association. **PRACTICE AREAS:** Complex Business Litigation; Civil Litigation; Bankruptcy (Creditor).

REPRESENTATIVE CLIENTS: 1524 McHenry Investors-PV Financial; Booker Lawlor Architect; Brentwood Estates; California Escrow Association; Coldwell Banker - Vinson Chase Realtor; Del Monte Corporation; Downey Park Professional Group; Empire Fire District; Empire Fire Protection District; Union Safe Deposit Bank; Inland Investment; Showcase Auto Plaza; Central California Downs Syndome Non Profit Foundation; National Medical Enterprises, Inc.; NCB Geldria of The Netherlands; North American, Inc.; Modesto Radiology; JLL/Turbo Productions; First Consumer's Mtg.; National Hospital; North Modesto Industrial Park; C. J. Brayton Construction; Crocco Vineyards, Inc.; Suns Modesto Radiology; Silva Dairy, Inc.; Southern Pacific Transportation Company, Inc.; Stanislaus Orthopedic and Sports Medicine; Stewart Title of Central California; Stewart Title of Modesto; Stockton Terminal and Eastern Railroad; The Prudential Stone Real Estate; Yusemite Meat & Locker Service Inc.

CAA1355B

## JACOBSON, HANSEN, NAJARIAN & FLEWALLEN

*A PROFESSIONAL CORPORATION*

**MODESTO, CALIFORNIA**

(See Fresno)

*Civil Litigation emphasizing Insurance Defense.*

---

## JONES, COCHRANE, HOLLENBACK, NELSON & ZUMWALT

Established in 1896

819 TENTH STREET
P.O. BOX 3209
**MODESTO, CALIFORNIA 95353**
Telephone: 209-577-6100
Fax: 209-577-1038

*General Civil and Trial Practice. Family, Domestic Relations, Business, Corporate, Real Estate, Estate Planning, Probate, Trust, Personal Injury, Insurance Law, Agricultural and Bankruptcy Law, Workers Compensation.*

### MEMBERS OF FIRM

**JACK R. JONES,** born Modesto, California, April 5, 1928; admitted to bar, 1952, California, U.S. District Court, Eastern District of California and U.S. Court of Appeals, Ninth Circuit. *Education:* Stanford University (B.A., with distinction, 1949; J.D., 1951). *Member:* Stanislaus County Bar Association; State Bar of California. (Certified Specialist, Probate, Trust and Estate Planning Law, The State Bar of California Board of Legal Specialization). **PRACTICE AREAS:** Estate Planning; Probate; Transactional Business Law.

**KENNETH C. COCHRANE,** born Berkeley, California, January 3, 1948; admitted to bar, 1972, California, U.S. District Court, Northern District of California and U.S. Court of Appeals, Ninth Circuit; 1975, U.S. District Court, Eastern District of California. *Education:* University of California at Davis (B.S., 1969); Hastings College of Law, University of California (J.D., 1972). Lecturer, Family Law, Continuing Education of the Bar, 1989—. *Member:* Stanislaus County Bar Association (President, 1984); State Bar of California (Member, Family Law Section); Stanislaus County Criminal Defense Bar (President, 1979); Association of Certified Family Law Specialists; California Trial Lawyers Association (Chairman, Speakers Bureau, Stanislaus County Chapter, 1982-1985). (Certified Specialist, Family Law, The State Bar of California Board of Legal Specialization). **PRACTICE AREAS:** Family Law.

**JOHN J. HOLLENBACK, JR.,** born Council Bluffs, Iowa, July 27, 1950; admitted to bar, 1975, California. *Education:* California State University at Sacramento (B.A., 1971; M.A., 1972); University of Texas (J.D., with honors, 1975). Recipient, American Jurisprudence Award in Civil Procedure. Edited, *Digest of California Labor Law,* California Chamber of Commerce, Sacramento, 1973, 1974 and 1975 Editions. Judge Pro Tem, Stanislaus County Superior Court, 1994-1995. *Member:* Stanislaus County Bar Association; State Bar of California. (Certified Specialist, Family Law, The State Bar of California Board of Legal Specialization). **PRACTICE AREAS:** Family Law; Business Litigation; Civil Litigation; Writs and Appeals.

**GARY C. NELSON,** born Modesto, California, November 15, 1958; admitted to bar, 1986, California, U.S. District Court, Northern and Eastern Districts of California and U.S. Court of Appeals, Ninth Circuit. *Education:* California State University, Stanislaus (B.A., 1982); McGeorge School of Law, University of the Pacific (J.D., with distinction, 1985). Order of the Coif. Member, Traynor Society. Recipient, American Jurisprudence Award, Family Law. Judge Pro Tem, Stanislaus County Superior Court, 1994-1995. *Member:* Stanislaus County (Board of Directors, 1991-1992) and American Bar Associations; State Bar of California; California Applicant's Attorneys Association; California Trial Lawyers Association. **PRACTICE AREAS:** Personal Injury; Workers' Compensation; Family Law.

**FRANK T. ZUMWALT,** born Oakdale, California, July 10, 1960; admitted to bar, 1987, California. *Education:* California State University at Chico (B.A., cum laude, 1982; Phi Kappa Phi); University of the Pacific, McGeorge School of Law (J.D., with distinction, 1987). Order of the Coif. *Member:* Moot Court Honors Board; Traynor Society. Arbitrator,

Stanislaus County, 1991-1995. *Member:* Stanislaus County and American Bar Associations; State Bar of California; California Consumers Attorneys.
**PRACTICE AREAS:** Personal Injury Law; Insurance Law; Civil Litigation.

REFERENCES: Union Safe Deposit Bank.

*(This Listing Continued)*

---

## MARK A. KANAI

*A PROFESSIONAL CORPORATION*

Established in 1972

1101-15TH STREET
P.O. BOX 791
**MODESTO, CALIFORNIA 95353**
Telephone: 209-527-3650
Facsimile: 209-527-5518

*Business, Corporate, Estate Planning, Probate, Elder Law, Real Estate and Communications Law.*

**MARK A. KANAI,** born Colorado Springs, Colorado, December 3, 1945; admitted to bar, 1971, California and U.S. District Court, Northern District of California; 1975, U.S. District Court, Eastern District of California. *Education:* University of California at Berkeley (A.B., 1967); Boalt Hall School of Law, University of California (J.D., 1970). President, Stanislaus County Estate Planning Council, 1986-1987. Member, Advisory Board, Salvation Army, Modesto, California. Chairman, Unified Air Pollution Control Northern District Hearing Board, San Joaquin Valley, California. *Member:* Stanislaus County Bar Association; State Bar of California (Member, Sections on: Business; Estates and Trusts).

---

## LAMB & MICHAEL

*A PROFESSIONAL CORPORATION*

Established in 1952

1314 G STREET
**MODESTO, CALIFORNIA 95354**
Telephone: 209-578-4111
Fax: 209-578-4969

*Representation of Collection agencies, manufacturers, insurance companies and other enterprises in the collection of money, credit reporting and collection practices. Suits in all California Courts and creditor representation in bankruptcy.*

FIRM PROFILE: *The firm was founded by Jack B. Lamb in 1952, and incorporated in 1985. The practice has included the representation of regional collection clients continuously since 1957. Case processing is heavily automated, and operates in all State Courts and bankruptcy districts within the State of California.*

**JACK B. LAMB** (1924-1992).

**WILLIAM H. MICHAEL,** born South Bend, Indiana, December 16, 1947; admitted to bar, 1973, Colorado; 1976, California. *Education:* Indiana University (A.B., with departmental honors in Economics, 1970; J.D., 1973). *Member:* Stanislaus County and Colorado Bar Associations; State Bar of California; Commercial Law League of America. **PRACTICE AREAS:** Collections.

**LINDA S. LEONG,** born Hong Kong, July 14, 1957; admitted to bar, 1991, California. *Education:* Modesto Junior College; Humphreys College (J.D., 1991). *Member:* State Bar of California; American Bar Association; California Trial Lawyers Association. **LANGUAGES:** Cantonese. **PRACTICE AREAS:** Commercial Law; Civil Trial Practice.

REPRESENTATIVE CLIENTS: Delta Collection Service; Stanislaus Credit Control Service, Inc.

---

## MARDEROSIAN, SWANSON & OREN

**MODESTO, CALIFORNIA**

(See Fresno)

*Insurance Defense including Products Liability Defense, Insurance Bad Faith Defense and Personal Injury Law.*

## MAYALL, HURLEY, KNUTSEN, SMITH & GREEN

*A PROFESSIONAL CORPORATION*

**MODESTO, CALIFORNIA**

(See Stockton)

*General Civil and Trial Practice in all State and Federal Courts. Insurance, Personal Injury, Business, Corporate Real Estate, Taxation, Estate Planning and Probate Law, Environmental, Construction.*

---

## MAYOL & BARRINGER

1324 "J" STREET
P.O. BOX 3049
**MODESTO, CALIFORNIA 95353**
Telephone: 209-544-9555
Fax: 209-544-9875

*General Civil Litigation, Real Estate, Business, Personal Injury, Employment and Construction Law.*

### MEMBERS OF FIRM

**JAMES D. MAYOL,** born Oakland, California, October 1, 1957; admitted to bar, 1984, California. *Education:* University of the Pacific (B.A., 1980); McGeorge School of Law, University of the Pacific (J.D., with distinction, 1984). Phi Delta Phi. Member, Traynor Honor Society. President, Modesto Chamber of Commerce, 1994. Secretary/General Counsel, Pacific Southwest Container, Inc. *Member:* Stanislaus County Bar Association; State Bar of California. *PRACTICE AREAS:* Employment Law; Civil Litigation; Construction Law; Real Estate; Business Law.

**BART W. BARRINGER,** born Oakdale, California, April 30, 1957; admitted to bar, 1985, Oregon and U.S. District Court, District of Oregon; 1986, California and U.S. District Court, Southern District of California; 1988, U.S. District Court, Eastern District of California. *Education:* Pacific University (B.A., 1980); McGeorge School of Law, University of the Pacific (J.D., 1984). *Member:* Stanislaus County and American Bar Associations; Oregon State Bar; State Bar of California; The Association of Trial Lawyers of America; California Trial Lawyers Association. *PRACTICE AREAS:* Civil Litigation; Real Estate Law; Business Transactions.

**CARL E. COMBS,** born Modesto, California, March 8, 1960; admitted to bar, 1990, California and U.S. District Court, Eastern and Northern Districts of California. *Education:* Brigham Young University (B.A., 1985); University of Arizona (J.D., 1989). Phi Alpha Delta. Member, Pacific Law Journal, 1987. *Member:* Stanislaus County and American Bar Associations; State Bar of California. *LANGUAGES:* Spanish. *PRACTICE AREAS:* Business Law; Civil Litigation; Insurance Law.

REPRESENTATIVE CLIENTS: Beard's Quality Nut Co.; Burns Refuse Service; Chicago Title Co.; Ferry Morse Seed Co.; Food 4 Less of Modesto; Franco Construction; Freese & Gianelli, Inc., Claim Services; Gilton Solid Waste Management; Gould Medical Foundation; Manufacturers Council of the Central Valley; Memorial Hospitals Assoc.; Modesto Chamber of Commerce; Pacific Southwest Container, Inc.; Roadrunner Manufacturing; SavMax Foods; Stewart Title of Modesto; The Salvation Army; Transamerica Title Insurance Co.; M. Van Vliet & Sons, Inc.; Oakdale Ag & Turf; Save Mart Supermarkets; SoleCon Plumbing & Piping, Inc.

---

## McALLISTER & McALLISTER

CITY MALL BUILDING
SUITE 32, 948 11TH STREET
**MODESTO, CALIFORNIA 95354**
Telephone: 209-575-4844
FAX: 209-575-0240

*Civil and Criminal Trial Practice, Estate Planning and Probate Law, Business Law, Alcoholic Beverage Control Practice, Equine Law.*

### MEMBERS OF FIRM

**KIRK W. MCALLISTER,** born San Francisco, California, April 18, 1944; admitted to bar, 1970, California; U.S. District Court, Eastern District of California. *Education:* Stanford University (B.A., 1966); University of Southern California (J.D., 1969). *Member:* Stanislaus County, San Joaquin County, Tuolumne County and American Bar Associations; State Bar of California (Member, Committee for Legal History, 1984-1987); Consumer Attorneys of California; California Attorneys For Criminal Justice; Stanislaus County Criminal Courts Bar Association (President, 1990-1992).

*(This Listing Continued)*

[Captain, U.S. Army, 1970-1972]. (Certified Specialist, Criminal Law, The State Bar of California Board of Legal Specialization). *PRACTICE AREAS:* Criminal Law; Equine Law.

**JANE E. MCALLISTER,** born Staten Island, New York, November 28, 1961; admitted to bar, 1988, California and U.S. District Court, Northern and Eastern District of California; U.S. Court of Appeals, Ninth Circuit. *Education:* Stanford University (B.A., Humanities, with honors, 1983); Humphrey's College (J.D., 1988). *Member:* Stanislaus County and American (Member, Estate Planning Law Section) Bar Associations; State Bar of California; California Women Lawyers; Stanislaus County Estate Planning Council. *LANGUAGES:* French and Italian. *PRACTICE AREAS:* Estate Planning Law; Business Law; Alcoholic Beverage Control Law.

REPRESENTATIVE CLIENTS: Peace Officers Research Association of California (PORAC).

---

## McCORMICK, BARSTOW, SHEPPARD, WAYTE & CARRUTH LLP

CENTRE PLAZA OFFICE TOWER
1150 NINTH STREET, SUITE 1510
**MODESTO, CALIFORNIA 95354**
Telephone: 209-524-1100
Fax: 209-524-1188

*Fresno, California Office:* Five River Park Place East, 93-720-1501.
Telephone: 209-433-1300. Mailing Address: P.O. Box 28912, 93729-8912.

*General Civil and Trial Practice. Agricultural and Water Law, Banking Law, Bankruptcy and Reorganization, Civil Rights Litigation, Civil Practice, Commodities Law, Condemnation Law, Construction Law, Corporate Law, Employment Law, Environmental Law, Estate Planning, Family Law, Franchise Law, Health Care Law, Insurance Law Legal Malpractice, Medical Malpractice, Municipal Law, Probate, Public Entity, Real Estate Agent Malpractice, Real Estate Law, Securities and Taxation Law.*

**MATTHEW K. HAWKINS,** born Melbourne, Florida, February 22, 1962; admitted to bar, 1987, California; 1989, U.S. Court of Appeals, Ninth Circuit. *Education:* Brigham Young University (B.A., 1984; J.D., 1987); Regent's College, London, England, 1987. Member: Brigham Young University Board of Advocates; Jessup International Moot Court Team. *Member:* Stanislaus County, Fresno County and American Bar Associations; State Bar of California; Fresno County Young Lawyer's Association (Member, Board of Directors, 1990-1991). *LANGUAGES:* Spanish.

### ASSOCIATE

**JOHN M. DUNN,** born Lawton, Oklahoma, August 8, 1968; admitted to bar, 1993, California. *Education:* University of Notre Dame (B.A., 1990); Notre Dame Law School (J.D., 1993). Staff Member, 1991-1992 and Editor, 1992-1993, Journal of College and University Law. *Member:* Fresno County Bar Association; Fresno County Young Lawyers Association.

GENERAL COUNSEL FOR: ValliWide Bank; Bank of Stockton; ValliCorp.; Kings River State Bank; Deniz Packing Incorporated; Setton Pistachio of Terra Bella, Inc.; Farmers Firebaugh Ginning Company; TVK Containers, Inc.; Ranchwood Homes; Granville Homes; Trend Homes; McCaffrey Development LP: Diversified Development; Piccolo's Franchising Corp.; California State University Fresno Foundation; Central California Blood Center; Valley Children's Hospital; O.P.C. Farms.
LOCAL COUNSEL FOR: Helena Chemical Co.; Patriot Homes; Wilbur-Ellis (Chemicals); Setton International Foods, Inc.; Fruehauf Corp.; U S Homes; Dentel; Stewart Enterprises; Santa Ana and Fresno Land Co.
TRIAL COUNSEL FOR: Aetna Life and Casualty Co.; Allstate Insurance Co.; American States Insurance Co.; Colonial Penn; CNA; Crum & Forster Insurance CSE Insurance Group; The Dentist's Insurance Co.;Farmer's Insurance Group; Fireman's Fund Insurance Co.; Hartford Accident & Indemnity Co.; Industrial Indemnity; Insurance Company of the West; Kemper Insurance Group; Maryland Casualty Co.; Nationwide Ins. Co.; Nobel Insurance Co.; Northland Insurance Co.; Oregon Mutual Insurance Co.; Pioneer Life Insurance Co.; Prudential Property & Casualty Ins. Co.; Republic Insurance Co.; The Travelers Insurance Co.; State Farm Fire & Casualty Co.; Special District Risk Management Authority; County of Fresno; FMA Corp.; Chicago Title Insurance Co.; First American Title Insurance Company; GS Roofing Product Company, Inc.; U-Haul International Corporation; Save Mart Supermarkets, Inc.; California Bankers Association; California State Automobile Assn.; American International Group; Lawyers Mutual Insurance Co.; St. Agnes Hospital; Norcal Ins. Co.; Physicians & Surgeons Ins. Co.; CAMICO; American Sentinal Ins. Co.; Zurich American; Reliance Ins. Co.; Mercury Ins. Co.; CIGNA.

(For complete biographical data on all Personnel, see Professional Biographies at Fresno, California)

CALIFORNIA—MODESTO                    MARTINDALE-HUBBELL LAW DIRECTORY 1997

## MITCHELL & VANCE

Established in 1975

SUITE G, 821 THIRTEENTH STREET
P.O. BOX 3166
**MODESTO, CALIFORNIA 95353**
Telephone: 209-524-9331
Fax: 209-524-5501
Email: DVANCEESQ@aol.com

*Estate Planning, Probate and Trust Administration, General Civil and Trial Practice, Elder Care, Real Estate, Personal Injury and Business.*

### MEMBERS OF FIRM

**WILLIAM R. MITCHELL** (Retired).

**DONALD L. VANCE,** born Los Angeles, California, December 18, 1943; admitted to bar, 1974, California. *Education:* University of California at Berkeley (A.B., 1966); Hastings College of Law, University of California (J.D., 1974). Member of Staff, Hastings Law Journal, 1973-1974. Member, 1975-1983 and Vice Chairman, 1979-1983, Board of Building Appeals, City of Modesto, California. Member, Board of Directors, 1983—, President, 1985-1986, Y.M.C.A. *Member:* Stanislaus County Bar Association; State Bar of California; Stanislaus County Estate Planning Council (President, 1993-1994). [Lt., U.S. Naval Reserve, 1968-1980]

REFERENCES: Bank of America National Trust and Savings Assn., Modesto Main; Union Safe Deposit; First Interstate Bank, Modesto Main.

## NEUMILLER & BEARDSLEE

A PROFESSIONAL CORPORATION

611 THIRTEENTH STREET
**MODESTO, CALIFORNIA 95354-2435**
Telephone: 209-577-8200
Fax: 209-577-4910

Stockton, California Office: 5th Floor, Waterfront Office Towers II, 509 West Weber Avenue, P.O. Box 20, 95201-3020. Telephone: 209-948-8200. Fax: 209-948-4910.

*General Civil Practice and Litigation in all State and Federal Courts. Real Property, Condominium, Land Use, Natural Resources, Environmental, Water and Water Rights, Mining, Agricultural, Corporation, Partnership, Business Planning, Securities, Creditor's Rights in Bankruptcy, Taxation, Employee Benefits, Insurance, Administrative, Health Care, Governmental and Legislative, Trusts, Estate Planning, Probate and Municipal Law.*

| | |
|---|---|
| *Thomas J. Shephard, Sr.* | *Steven A. Herum* |
| *Robert C. Morrison* | *Michael J. Dyer* |
| *James R. Dyke* | *Jeanne Marie Zolezzi* |
| | *Thomas H. Terpstra* |

| | |
|---|---|
| *Clifford W. Stevens* | *Matthew I. Friedrich* |
| *Karna E. Harrigfeld* | *Patrick M. McGrath* |

COUNSEL FOR: Apache Plastics, Inc. (plastic pipes); Brown-Sand, Inc. (sand and gravel); Building Material Distributors; California Pet Food, Inc. (distributor); Roman Catholic Bishop of Stockton; Delicato Vineyards (winery and vineyards); Delta Container Corporation; DeYoung Memorial Chapel; Doctors Medical Center of Modesto; Eckert Cold Storage (food processor); ECRI, Inc. (automobile leasing and rentals); Farmland Management Services (agriculture); The Fillmore Co., LLS (software consultants); Forward, Inc. (waste disposal); Holt Bros. (heavy equipment); John Kautz Farms (agriculture; vineyards, winery); Libbey-Owens-Ford Glass Co.; Morada Distribution, Inc. (warehousing and trucking); Montgomery Ward & Co., Incorporated; O'Connor Woods (housing and assisted living for seniors); NUSS Farms (row crops and farming); Oakwood Lake Resorts (recreational facilities); Pacific Steel and Supply; PacWest Telecomm, Incorporated (telecommunications); Paragon Family Services (funeral homes); Professional Apartment Management (real estate management and operation); Barton Co. (agriculture); St. Joseph's Regional Health Systems and Medical Center; OMNI Health Plan, Inc.; Santa Fe Aggregates, Inc. (sand and gravel); Sebastiani Vineyards; Sierra Lumber Manufacturers (lumber); Stanislaus Food Products (food processor); Strategic Products Corporation (telecommunications); Sunset Disposal Corporation; Tandy Corporation; The McCarty Company (agribusiness); Teichert Aggregate (sand and gravel); Tracy Material Recovery and Solid Waste Transfer, Inc. (recycling and waste collection); Ukiah Broadcasting Corporation (radio broadcasting); Union Safe Deposit Bank; University of the Pacific; Vita Bran, LIC (horse feed); Yosemite Medical Clinic.
REAL ESTATE DEVELOPERS: A.G. Spanos Land Company, Inc.; Anderson Homes; Bright Development; Building Industry Association of Central California; Building Industry Association of the Delta; Building Industry Association of Kings/Tulare County; Carey Development Company; Crown View Corporation (home builders); Franco Construction; The Grupe Cos.; J.C. Williams Company; Kaufman & Broad; Central California; LeBaron Ranches; Morrison Homes; The Patmon Company; Raymus Development and Sales; SCM Corporate Group (home builders); Surland Development Company; Trimark Communities, Inc.
PUBLIC AGENCIES: Alpine County; Bear Valley Water District; City of Hughson; City of Manteca (personnel Matters); City of Newman (special water counsel); City of Ripon; County of Stanislaus (special counsel, eminent domain); Marina County Water District; Modesto Irrigation District (special counsel municipal water); Mokelumne River Water & Power Authority; Reclamation District 800; Reclamation District 1608; Rock Creek Water District; San Joaquin County Council of Governments (regional transportation planning); San Joaquin Regional Rail Commission (passenger rail service); Solano County Water Agency; Stanislaus County Area Association of Governments (regional transportation planning) Stockton-East Water District; The Westside Irrigation District; Turlock Irrigation District; Woodbridge Sanitary District.
INSURANCE CLIENTS: Equitable Life Assurance; Metropolitan Life Insurance Co.

(For complete biographical data on all personnel, see Professional Biographies at Stockton, California)

## NORMOYLE & NEWMAN

A PROFESSIONAL LAW CORPORATION

Established in 1988

801-10TH STREET, FIFTH FLOOR, SUITE 1
**MODESTO, CALIFORNIA 95354**
Telephone: 209-521-9521
Telecopier: 209-521-4968

*General Business Practice. Civil Trial and Appellate Practice. Real Estate Development and Zoning, Real Estate and Business Transactions, Corporation, Construction, Administrative, Environmental, Solid Waste, Toxic and Hazardous Waste, Resource Recovery, Government and Legislative Law, Estate Planning and Probate.*

**MICHAEL C. NORMOYLE,** born Neenah, Wisconsin, July 10, 1948; admitted to bar, 1976, New York and U.S. District Court, Western District of New York; 1978, U.S. Court of Appeals, Second Circuit; 1980, U.S. Supreme Court; 1981, California and U.S. District Court, Northern District of California; 1982, U.S. District Court, Eastern District of California; 1985, U.S. Court of Appeals, Ninth Circuit. *Education:* University of the Pacific (B.A., magna cum laude, 1970); Cornell University (J.D., 1975). Recipient, Lawyer Advocate of the Year Award, United States Small Business Administration. *Member:* Stanislaus County, New York State and American Bar Associations; State Bar of California. **SPECIAL AGENCIES:** State Water Resources Control Board (SWRCB); Regional Water Quality Control Boards (RWQCBs); San Joaquin Valley Unified Air Pollution Control District (SJVUAPCD); California Integrated Waste Management Board (CIWMB); Board of Supervisors, City Councils and Planning Commissions in Stanislaus, San Joaquin, Merced, Tuolumne, Calaveras and surrounding Counties. **PRACTICE AREAS:** Civil Litigation; Environmental Law; Business Transactions.

**RUSSELL A. NEWMAN,** born Spokane, Washington, September 13, 1951; admitted to bar, 1978, California and U.S. District Court, Northern District of California; 1981, U.S. District Court, Eastern District of California. *Education:* Stanford University (B.A., with distinction, 1973); Hastings College of Law, University of California (J.D., 1978). Member, Board of Trustees, California State University, Stanislaus Foundation. *Member:* Stanislaus County Bar Association; State Bar of California. **SPECIAL AGENCIES:** Board of Supervisors, City Councils Planning Commissions, LAFCO, for Stanislaus, San Joaquin, Merced, Tuolumne, Calaveras and surrounding counties. School Boards on developer fee issues. **PRACTICE AREAS:** Real Estate Transactions; Business Transactions; Land Use; Zoning and Development Law.

**WYLIE P. CASHMAN,** born Chambersburg, Pennsylvania, February 8, 1947; admitted to bar, 1981, California and U.S. District Court, Central, Eastern and Northern Districts of California. *Education:* Concordia Senior College (B.A., 1970); Christ Seminary (M.Div., 1974); University of Santa Clara (M.B.A., 1979; J.D., cum laude, 1980). *Member:* Stanislaus County and American Bar Associations; State Bar of California. **PRACTICE AREAS:** Civil Litigation; Real Estate Transactions; Business Transactions; Construction Law.

**JOHN T. RESSO,** born Modesto, California, April 16, 1966; admitted to bar, 1991, California. *Education:* University of California at Berkeley (B.A., 1988); Santa Clara University (J.D., 1991). *Member:* Stanislaus County Bar Association; State Bar of California; Stanislaus County Estate Planning Council. **PRACTICE AREAS:** Civil Litigation; Business Transactions; Real Estate Law; Estate Planning; Probate.

*(This Listing Continued)*     *(This Listing Continued)*

# PROFESSIONAL BIOGRAPHIES
## CALIFORNIA—MODESTO

**GEORGE A. PETRULAKIS,** born Modesto, California, February 2, 1963; admitted to bar, 1991, California. *Education:* Harvard University (A.B., cum laude, 1987); University of California, Los Angeles (J.D., 1991). *Member:* Stanislaus County and American Bar Associations; State Bar of California (City of Modesto General Plan Steering committee, 1992-1995); Building Industry Association of Central California (Secretary-Treasurer, 1995-1997; Board of Directors, 1994—; Legislative Committee, 1993—); California Building Industry Association (Legal Action Committee; Select Conferences on Industry Litigation); Modesto Chamber of Commerce Land Use Committee (Chairman, 1997—); Urban Land Institute. **SPECIAL AGENCIES:** Board of Supervisors, City Councils, Planning Commissions, LAFCO, School Boards on developer fee issues; Property Tax Assessment Appeals Boards; Emergency Medical Services Agencies; County Committees on School District Organization; Community Services Districts, Irrigation Districts and other special districts in Stanislaus, San Joaquin, Merced, Tuolumne and surrounding counties. **REPORTED CASES:** Save Stanislaus Area Farm Economy vs. Board of Supervisors (1993) 13 Cal.App.4th 191, 16 Cal.Rept.2d 408. **PRACTICE AREAS:** Zoning, Planning and Land Use; Subdivisions; Real Estate Law; Property Rights; Emergency Medical Services Law.

**MICHAEL S. WARDA,** born Skokie, Illinois, November 22, 1967; admitted to bar, 1995, California. *Education:* California State University at Stanislaus (B.A., 1990); Humphrey's College of Law (J.D., 1994). *Member:* Stanislaus County Bar Association; State Bar of California. **PRACTICE AREAS:** Land Use; Real Estate Law; Business Transactions; Governmental Relations.

### LEGAL SUPPORT PERSONNEL

**DAVID O. ROMANO,** born Modesto, California, May 17, 1961. *Education:* University of California at Berkeley; University of Wyoming (B.S. in Civil Engineering, 1984). Registered Civil Engineer, California, 1987. *Member:* National Society of Professional Engineers; California Society of Professional Engineers; American Planning Association. **PRACTICE AREAS:** Subdivisions; Zoning, Planning and Land Use.

REPRESENTATIVE CLIENTS: *Energy/Environmental/Natural Resources:* United American Energy Co.; Modesto Energy Limited Partnership; Rudy Bonzi, Inc.; WHF Environmental Consultants, Inc.; Geological Technics; PolyRecycling, Inc.; Aquatic Bio Enhancement Systems, Inc.; HKM Environmental, Inc.; Global Labs; McCulloch Environmental Equipment Sales. *Real Estate Development/Home Building/Construction:* Diablo Grande Ltd. Partnership; Nineveh, Inc.; PMZ Realty Co.; Resource Development; Inland Developers LLC; Morrison Homes; Self-Help Enterprises; Cen Cal Homes; Arambel & Rose Development Co.; McRoy-Wilbur Communities, Inc.; Village One Group; Crossroads Village Group; Oski Construction; Crown View Corp.; Swan Construction, Inc.; The Waterstone Group; Building Industry Association of Central California (BIACC); Zagaris Management Services, Inc.; Creative Golf Courses, Inc.; Turlock Golf and Country Club; Kimball Hill Holmes California, Inc.; Lowe Development Co.; Ranchwood Homes Corp.; Oakwood Builders, Inc. *Commercial:* InnCall, Inc.; K & M Industries, Inc.; United Pallet Services; American Medical Response; 911 Emergency Services, Inc.; Directline Technologies, Inc.; National Home Business Assn.; Modesto Livestock Commission; Stanislaus Dairy Herd Improvement Assn.; Mohler Brothers; 1524 McHenry Investors - Pacific Valley Financial; California Equity Management Group, Inc.; Ambeck Mortgage Associates. *Government:* Yosemite Community College District; Western Hills Water District; Central California Irrigation District; Gustine Unified School District.
REFERENCE: WestAmerica Bank.

---

## RALPH C. OGDEN, III
*1535 J STREET, SUITE A*
*P.O. BOX 1867*
**MODESTO, CALIFORNIA 95353**
Telephone: 209-524-4466
Fax: 209-524-1660

*Collections, Real Estate and Business Transactions, Environmental and Hazardous Waste Law, Corporate Law, Wills/Trusts/Estate Planning and Probate.*

**RALPH C. OGDEN, III,** born Farmington, New Mexico, May 5, 1953; admitted to bar, 1979, California. *Education:* Pepperdine University (B.A., 1976); McGeorge College of the Law, University of the Pacific (J.D., 1979). *Member:* Stanislaus County and American Bar Associations; State Bar of California.

---

## DANIEL F. QUINN
**MODESTO, CALIFORNIA**
(See Stockton)
*General Civil and Trial Practice, Construction Law, Insurance Law.*

---

## STEPHEN RINGHOFF
*1500 J. STREET*
*P.O. BOX 3009*
**MODESTO, CALIFORNIA 95354**
Telephone: 209-527-5360
Fax: 209-527-1727
Email: ringhoff@S2.Sonnet.com

*Personal Injury, Commercial Litigation.*

**STEPHEN RINGHOFF,** born Pasadena, California, December 19, 1944; admitted to bar, 1975, California. *Education:* American River; Humphrey's College of Law (J.D., 1975).

---

## STOCKTON & SADLER
Established in 1952
*1034 TWELFTH STREET*
*P.O. BOX 3153*
**MODESTO, CALIFORNIA 95353**
Telephone: 209-523-6416
Fax: 209-523-2315

*Civil Trial and Appellate Practice. Agriculture, Business, Corporate, Estate Planning, Probate, Partnerships, Real Estate, Personal Injury.*

**FIRM PROFILE:** Stockton & Sadler and it's predecessors have been active in legal representation in the Central Valley since 1952. It is a small firm devoted to personalized legal service and enjoys a reputation for excellence and timely responsiveness to the needs of its clients. The firm practice encompasses a broad range of litigation involving agricultural, real estate, personal injury, property damage, business and financial concerns. In addition the attorneys perform extensive services in business planning including corporate, partnership and real estate and in trusts, estate planning and probate matters.

### MEMBERS OF FIRM

**CLEVELAND J. STOCKTON,** born New Orleans, Louisiana, May 11, 1920; admitted to bar, 1949, California. *Education:* Tulane University of Louisiana and Northwestern University (B.A., 1941); Harvard University (LL.B., 1944); University of San Francisco (LL.M., 1951). *Member:* Stanislaus County (President, 1958-1959) and American Bar Associations; State Bar of California; The Association of Trial Lawyers of America. **REPORTED CASES:** Riddle vs Leushner (1959) 51 Cal 2nd 574; Estate of Neilson (1962) 57 Cal 2nd 733; Sunset-Sterneau vs Bonzi (1964) 60 Cal 2nd 834; Sanders Construction Co., Inc. vs San Joaquin First Federal Savings and Loan Association (1982) 136 Cal App. 3rd 387; Quigley vs Pet (1984) 162 Cal. App. 3rd 877. **PRACTICE AREAS:** Trials; Banking Law; Personal Injury Law; Estate Planning Law; Corporate Law; Real Property; Construction Law.

**JAMES L. SADLER,** born Magna, Utah, April 6, 1946; admitted to bar, 1973, Utah; 1979, Idaho and California. *Education:* University of Utah (B.S., cum laude, 1970; J.D., 1973). *Member:* Stanislaus County, Salt Lake County, Seventh District and American Bar Associations; Utah State Bar; Idaho State Bar; The State Bar of California; Idaho Trial Lawyers Association; California Trial Lawyers Association. **PRACTICE AREAS:** Trials; Crop Damage Law; Real Property Law; Personal Injury Law; Negligence Law.

### ASSOCIATES

**KAREN TALL SADLER,** born Rigby, Idaho, September 3, 1947; admitted to bar, 1978, Utah; 1979, Idaho, 1981, California. *Education:* University of Utah (B.S., 1970; J.D., 1977). *Member:* Salt Lake County, Stanislaus County and American Bar Associations; Utah State Bar; Idaho State Bar; The California State Bar.

REPRESENTATIVE CLIENTS: Dan Mellis Liquors; American Lumber Co.; American Distributing Co.; Tro-Pic-Kal Mfg. Co.; Paul M. Zagaris Realtor, Inc.; Pete Pappas Broadcasting Co.; Bright Development; B & H Manufacturing Co.; Stone Real Estate Co.; Lyons Investments; Mapes Ranch; Turlock Dairy

*(This Listing Continued)*

STOCKTON & SADLER, Modesto—Continued

& Refrigeration; Zagaris Management Services, Inc.; Metromedia; Gagos Properties; Union Safe Deposit Bank; Major Sysco; Overholtzer Church Furniture, Inc.; Bearden Real Estate; Transworld Financial; Greystone Block; Stone Cheney Construction; CLS Investments; Phil Overholtzer Construction, Inc.; Rawe Development; Dompe Supply Company; Harman Mgt. Corporation-Kentucky Fried Chicken; Builder's Choice; Prudential Real Estate; Liberty Development Company.
REFERENCE: Union Safe Deposit Bank.

## STRAUSS, NEIBAUER, ANDERSON & RAMIREZ

A PROFESSIONAL CORPORATION
Established in 1967
620 12TH STREET
**MODESTO, CALIFORNIA 95354**
Telephone: 209-526-2211
Fax: 209-526-0244

*Civil and Criminal Trial Practice. Negligence, Products Liability, Workers Compensation, Corporate and Probate Law. Bankruptcy and Family Law.*

**DOUGLAS L. NEIBAUER,** born Billings, Montana, February 3, 1940; admitted to bar, 1964, Montana; 1967, U.S. District Court, Eastern District of Montana; 1969, California and U.S. District Court, Eastern District of California; 1971, U.S. District Court, Northern District of California; 1974, U.S. District Court, Central District of California. *Education:* University of Montana (B.S., Business, 1963; LL.B., 1964). Law Clerk, Montana Supreme Court, Judge Wesley Castles, 1964. *Member:* State Bar of California; State Bar of Montana; American Bar Association; California Trial Lawyers Association (Recognized experience as a Trial Lawyer); The Association of Trial Lawyers of America. [Capt., USAF, JAG, 1964-1967]. (Member of California Trial Lawyers Association, with recognized experience in the field of Trial Lawyer). **PRACTICE AREAS:** Civil Trial; Corporate Law; Probate.

**THOMAS L. ANDERSON,** born Provo, Utah, May 14, 1945; admitted to bar, 1974, California and U.S. District Court, Eastern District of California. *Education:* Brigham Young University (B.A., with honors, 1969); University of Utah (J.D., 1972). Blue Key. Instructor, Business Law, Modesto Junior College, 1975-1977. Judge Pro Tem, Modesto Municipal Court, 1989—. *Member:* State Bar of California; American Bar Association; California Trial Lawyers Association (Vice-President, Local Chapter, 1985 ); The Association of Trial Lawyers of America. (Member of California Trial Lawyers Association, with recognized experience in the fields of Trial Lawyer, General Personal Injury and Workers' Compensation). **PRACTICE AREAS:** Negligence; Products Liability; Workers Compensation; Civil Trial.

**MINA RAMIREZ,** born Vallejo, California, September 12, 1956; admitted to bar, 1985, California and U.S. District Court, Northern and Eastern Districts of California. *Education:* University of California at Santa Cruz (B.A., 1979); University of Madrid, Spain; Boalt Hall School of Law, University of California (J.D., 1983). Phi Alpha Delta. President, Stanislaus County Women's Shelter, 1986-1987. Vice-President, Stanislaus County Big Brothers Big Sisters Association, 1986-1987. *Member:* Stanislaus County Bar Association; State Bar of California (Chairman, Legal Services and Social Events Committee, 1987-1988); The Association of Trial Lawyers of America; California Public Defenders Association; California Trial Lawyers Association (Recognized as an experienced Trial Lawyer in the fields of General Personal Injury, Workers Compensation and Family Law); Stanislaus County Hispanic Bar Association. (Member of California Trial Lawyers Association, with recognized experience in the fields of General Personal Injury, Workers' Compensation and Family Law). **LANGUAGES:** Spanish. **PRACTICE AREAS:** Civil Trial; Negligence; Products Liability; Medical Malpractice; Sexual Harassment.

**RANDALL EDWARD STRAUSS,** born Modesto, California, July 10, 1966; admitted to bar, 1993, California; 1994, U.S. District Court, Eastern District of California and U.S. Court of Appeals, Ninth Circuit. *Education:* University of California at Berkeley (B.A., 1988); Boalt Hall School of Law, University of California (J.D., 1993). **PRACTICE AREAS:** Civil Litigation; Business Law; Environmental Law.

**GEORGE P. HARRIS,** born Chicago, Illinois, October 20, 1951; admitted to bar, 1978, Illinois; 1990, California and Nevada. *Education:* Princeton University (A.B., 1973); Suffolk University (J.D., cum laude, 1978).

*(This Listing Continued)*

Member, Suffolk University Law Review, 1976-1977. **PRACTICE AREAS:** Civil Litigation.

**JORGE MASTACHE,** born Tijuana, Mexico, January 20, 1959; admitted to bar, 1990, California and U.S. District Court, Northern District of California. *Education:* University of California, Berkeley (B.A., 1982); Hastings College of Law (J.D., 1990). [Capt., USMC, 1982-1989]. **LANGUAGES:** Spanish. **PRACTICE AREAS:** Workers Compensation.

*OF COUNSEL*

**ALAN H. STRAUSS,** born Albany, New York, June 10, 1932; admitted to bar, 1956, New York; 1959, Colorado; 1962, California; 1967 U.S. District Court, Eastern District of California and U.S. Court of Appeals, Ninth Circuit. *Education:* University of Michigan (B.A., 1953); Harvard University (LL.B., 1956). Lecturer, Legal Considerations in Contracting and the Uniform Commercial Code: California Association of Public Purchasing Officers, 1965; Purchasing Agents Association of Northern California at the University of the Pacific, 1964. Instructor, Economics, Modesto Junior College, 1965-1966. President, Congregation Beth Shalom, 1968 and 1984-1986. Judge Pro Tem, Modesto Municipal Court, 1984—. *Member:* State Bar of California; American Bar Association; The Association of Trial Lawyers of America; California Trial Lawyers Association (Recognized as an experienced Trial Lawyer in the Fields of Family Law and Criminal Defense); California Attorneys for Criminal Justice. [1st Lt., USAF, JAG, 1957-1960]. (Member of California Trial Lawyers Association, with recognized experience in the fields of Family Law and Criminal Defense - Misdemeanor). **PRACTICE AREAS:** Family Law; Civil Trial; Criminal Trial; Bankruptcy.

## TRIMBUR DAVIS ECHOLS & BOYD

A PROFESSIONAL CORPORATION
SUITE ONE, 1301 "L" STREET
P.O. BOX 3464
**MODESTO, CALIFORNIA 95353-3464**
Telephone: 209-521-2040
Fax: 209-521-2634

*General Civil Trial Practice. Personal Injury and Insurance Defense, Elder, Probate, Real Estate, Employment Law and Corporation Law.*

**KEVIN L. CLARK** (1950-1994).

**JOHN M. TRIMBUR,** born San Francisco, California, December 9, 1920; admitted to bar, 1948, California and U.S. Court of Appeals, Ninth Circuit. *Education:* University of San Francisco (B.S., 1942; J.D., 1948). Alpha Sigma Nu; Phi Alpha Delta. *Member:* Stanislaus County (President, 1966-1967) and American Bar Associations; State Bar of California; Association of Defense Counsel of Northern California (Director, 1975-1976); American Judicature Society. **PRACTICE AREAS:** Estate Planning; Probate.

**GARY S. DAVIS,** born San Francisco, California, November 29, 1939; admitted to bar, 1965, California; 1979, U.S. Supreme Court. *Education:* Menlo College (A.A., 1959); University of Arizona (B.S., 1961); Hastings College of Law, University of California (J.D., 1964). *Member:* Stanislaus County Bar Association; State Bar of California; The Association of Trial Lawyers of America; American Board of Trial Advocates (President, San Joaquin Chapter, 1984-1986; National Director, 1991—); Association of Defense Counsel of Northern California (Director, 1985-1987 and 1987-1989); California Trial Lawyers Association. **PRACTICE AREAS:** Civil Litigation; Personal Injury; Insurance Defense; Employment Law.

**PAUL E. ECHOLS,** born Marysville, California, December 21, 1960; admitted to bar, 1989, California, U.S. District Court, Northern District of California and U.S. Court of Appeals, Ninth Circuit. *Education:* Chabot College (A.A., 1982); California State University at Hayward (B.A., Pol. Science, 1985); University of the Pacific, McGeorge School of Law (J.D., 1989). *Member:* Stanislaus County and American Bar Associations; Association of Defense Counsel of Northern California. **PRACTICE AREAS:** Corporate; Business Law; Business Litigation; Real Estate; Civil Litigation; Insurance Defense.

**KATHERINE R. BOYD,** born Memphis, Tennessee, June 3, 1960; admitted to bar, 1989, California, U.S. District Court, Northern District of California and U.S. Court of Appeals, Ninth Circuit; 1990, Tennessee; 1996, U.S. Supreme Court. *Education:* Memphis State University (B.S., cum laude, 1982); Cecil B. Humphreys School of Law, Memphis State University (J.D., 1989). Gamma Beta Phi; Kappa Delta Phi; Alpha Lambda Delta;

*(This Listing Continued)*

Phi Alpha Delta. Member, Golden Key National Honor Society. Member, Mortar Board National Honor Society. Recipient, American Jurisprudence Award in Criminal Procedure, 1988. *Member:* Stanislaus County and American Bar Associations; State Bar of California; Association of Defense Counsel of Northern California; Defense Research Institute; Stanislaus County Women Lawyers Association (Secretary, 1994). **PRACTICE AREAS:** Civil Litigation; Personal Injury; Insurance Defense; Employment Law.

**BARBARA L. OCHSNER,** born Walla Walla, Washington, April 1, 1959; admitted to bar, 1990, California and U.S. District Court, Eastern District of California. *Education:* Walla Walla College (B.S., 1982); University of the Pacific, McGeorge School of Law (J.D., 1990). Recipient, American Jurisprudence Award, Insurance Law, 1988, Family Law, 1990. *Member:* Stanislaus County and American Bar Associations; State Bar of California. **PRACTICE AREAS:** Insurance Coverage; Insurance Defense; Personal Injury; Employment Law.

DEFENSE COUNSEL FOR: County of Stanislaus; County of Merced.
TRIAL COUNSEL FOR: Aetna Casualty and Surety Company; Allstate Insurance Company; Amex Insurance Company; California Insurance Group; Civil Service Employees Insurance Co. (CSE); County of Merced; County of Stanislaus; Crusaders Insurance Company; Employers National Insurance; ESIS, Inc.; Financial Indemnity; Fremont Insurance; General Mills Restaurants; Grange Insurance Association; Helene Curtis, Inc.; Houston General Insurance Co.; John Deere Insurance Co.; Northbrook Property and Casualty Insurance; Regis Corporation; RLI Insurance Co.; State Farm Fire & Casualty Company; State Farm Mutual Insurance Company; Tri-State Insurance Company; Truck Insurance Exchange.
LOCAL COUNSEL FOR: Central California Floor Covering Outlet (dba Georgia Carpet Outlet; House of Carpets; Kaeslner and Associates Architects; Mattice Enterprises; Modesto Banking Company; Modesto Junk Company; North American Technical Services; Randik Paper Co.; Valley Sporting Goods; Westside Hulling.
REFERENCES: Modesto Banking Co.; Bank of America; Pacific Valley National Bank.

## ALVAREZ-GLASMAN & COLVIN
**200 EAST BEVERLY BOULEVARD, 2ND FLOOR**
**MONTEBELLO, CALIFORNIA 90640**
Telephone: 213-727-0870
Fax: 213-727-0878

*Sole Practice Public Agency, Land Use, Redevelopment, Litigation and Bankruptcy.*

### MEMBERS OF FIRM

**ARNOLD M. ALVAREZ-GLASMAN,** born Los Angeles, California, September 13, 1953; admitted to bar, 1978, California and U.S. District Court, Central District of California. *Education:* California State Polytechnic University (B.A., 1975); University of Loyola, Los Angeles (J.D., 1978). Pomona City Attorney and General Counsel to Redevelopment Agency, 1989—. South Gate City Attorney and General Counsel to Redevelopment Agency, 1993—. City of Montebello City Council Member, 1985—. Mayor of Montebello, 1987-1988 and 1991-1992. *Member:* State Bar of California; Los Angeles County City Attorneys Association. **PRACTICE AREAS:** Municipal Law; Redevelopment Law; Public Agency Law; Real Estate Law.

**ROGER A. COLVIN,** born Santa Monica, California, March 15, 1948; admitted to bar, 1976, California. *Education:* University of Southern California (B.A., 1973); University of San Fernando Valley (J.D., 1976). *Member:* State Bar of California. **PRACTICE AREAS:** Municipal Law; Tort Defense Litigation; Real Estate.

### ASSOCIATES

**SCOTT S. WIDITOR,** born Pittsfield, Massachusetts, September 29, 1956; admitted to bar, 1987, California, U.S. District Court, Central District of California and U.S. Court of Appeals, Ninth Circuit. *Education:* Berkshire Community College (A.S., summa cum laude, 1980); Williams College (B.A., cum laude, 1982); University of California School of Law (J.D., 1986). Co-Author: "California Public Agency Practice," Chapters 60 and 61, Matthew Bender, 1988; "Civil Procedure Before Trial, C.E.B., 1991 Supplement. *Member:* State Bar of California. **PRACTICE AREAS:** Municipal Litigation; Real Estate Litigation; Tort Litigation; Business Litigation.

**RICHARD L. ADAMS,** Member, Montebello Planning Commission, 1986—. Member, Montebello Unified School District Personnel Commission, 1984-1990. *Member:* State Bar of California. **PRACTICE AREAS:** Land Use, Zoning and Planning; Transactional Contracts; Personnel Matters; Estate Planning; Family Law.

*(This Listing Continued)*

**GREGORY A. DOCIMO,** born San Gabriel, California, December 11, 1956; admitted to bar, 1982, California and U.S. District Court, Central District of California. *Education:* Loyola Marymount University (B.A., cum laude, 1978; J.D., 1981). *Member:* Los Angeles County, Orange County and American Bar Associations; The State Bar of California; Association of Southern California Defense Counsel. **PRACTICE AREAS:** Municipal Tort Liability Defense; Insurance Defense (Personal Injury); Construction Defect Defense; Products Liability Defense.

**MARTHA E. ROMERO,** born Los Angeles, California, August 15, 1957; admitted to bar, 1987, California; 1988, U.S. District Court, Central District of California. *Education:* University of California at Los Angeles (B.A., 1979); Hardin-Simmons University (M.A., 1982); Loyola Marymount University (J.D., 1986). Scott Moot Court. Recipient, Alumni Association Award, 1986. Student Body Vice-President, Loyola Law School, 1984-1985. Author: State of California Treasurer and Tax Collector Bankruptcy Manual, 1991. Arbitrator, Los Angeles Superior and Municipal Courts. *Member:* Los Angeles (Chair, Governmental Law Committee, 1992-1993) and Mexican-American (President, 1993) Bar Associations; State Bar of California. **REPORTED CASES:** 17 CAL App. 4th 1240 Mann v. Board of Retirement. **PRACTICE AREAS:** Bankruptcy Creditor; Municipal Law; Municipal Taxation.

## YVONNE A. ASCHER
**2100 GARDEN ROAD, SUITE C307**
**MONTEREY, CALIFORNIA 93940**
Telephone: 408-641-9019
Fax: 408-641-9018

*Estate Planning, Estate Administration, Trusts, Long Term Care and Medicaid Planning.*

**YVONNE A. ASCHER,** born Fairfield, California, August 15, 1958; admitted to bar, 1985, California. *Education:* University of Antioch West (B.A., 1980); Monterey College of Law (J.D., 1985); Golden Gate University (LL.M., Tax, 1991). *Member:* Monterey and American Bar Associations (Member, Committee on Special Problems of the Aged and Persons Under Disability, 1987-1989); State Bar of California. (Certified Specialist, Estate Planning, Trust and Probate Law, The State Bar of California Board of Legal Specialization).

## BOHNEN, ROSENTHAL & DUSENBURY
**555 ABREGO STREET, SECOND FLOOR**
**P.O. BOX 1111**
**MONTEREY, CALIFORNIA 93942-1111**
Telephone: 408-649-5551
Fax: 408-649-0272

*Business and Civil Litigation, Insurance Defense, Personal Injury, Family Law, Business, Corporation, Real Property, Taxation, Estate Planning and Probate, Creditor's Rights, Environmental and Employment Law.*

### MEMBERS OF FIRM

**THOMAS P. BOHNEN,** born St. Paul, Minnesota, July 26, 1943; admitted to bar, 1969, California. *Education:* Seattle University (B.S., 1965); University of San Francisco (J.D., 1968); New York University. Phi Alpha Delta. Member, Moot Court Board. *Member:* Monterey County and American Bar Associations; The State Bar of California (Member, Executive Committee, Taxation Section, 1978-1982). (Certified Specialist, Taxation Law, The State Bar of California Board of Legal Specialization). **PRACTICE AREAS:** Taxation; Estate Planning; Wills; Trusts; Probate.

**ROBERT E. ROSENTHAL,** born San Mateo, California, December 19, 1949; admitted to bar, 1975, California. *Education:* California State University at Chico (B.A., 1972); University of the Pacific, McGeorge School of the Law (J.D., 1975). California State Finalist, Moot Court Competition. *Member:* Monterey County and American Bar Associations; The State Bar of California. **PRACTICE AREAS:** Business and Civil Litigation; Personal Injury; Insurance Defense; Contract Negotiation. **Email:** bobthal@aol.com

**DOUGLAS K. DUSENBURY,** born Anthony, Kansas, March 8, 1943; admitted to bar, 1968, Kansas and U.S. District Court, District of Kansas; 1978, California. *Education:* Kansas State University (B.A., 1965); University of Kansas (J.D., 1968). Blue Key. Member, Kansas Law Review. *Member:* Kansas and American Bar Associations; State Bar of California. **PRACTICE AREAS:** Business and Civil Litigation; Personal Injury; Family Law.

*(This Listing Continued)*

## BOHNEN, ROSENTHAL & DUSENBURY, Monterey—Continued

### OF COUNSEL

**ROGER D. BOLGARD,** born St. Louis, Missouri, March 9, 1939; admitted to bar, 1976, California. *Education:* Princeton University (A.B., 1961); Lincoln University at San Jose (J.D., 1976). Member, Panel of Arbitrators: American Arbitration Association; Arbitration and Mediation Association, Inc.; Asia/Pacific Center for the Resolution of International Business Disputes. *Member:* San Mateo County and Monterey County Bar Associations; State Bar of California (Member, International Law Section). (Also of Counsel to Jackson, Mittlesteadt, Miller & Dugoni in Redwood). **PRACTICE AREAS:** Business Law; Construction Law; Partnership; Corporations Law; Business Litigation; Estate Planning Law.

**HARRY FINKLE,** born Paterson, New Jersey, July 20, 1948; admitted to bar, 1972, California and District of Columbia. *Education:* University of California at Santa Barbara (B.A., cum laude, 1968); Hastings College of Law, University of California and University of California at Berkeley (J.D., 1971). Member, Hastings Law Journal, 1968-1969. Faculty Member, American Society for Industrial Security, 1981—. Co-Editor, California School Law Digest, 1986—. *Member:* Fresno County and American (Member, Section on Labor Relations and Employment Law) Bar Associations; State Bar of California (Member, Law Office Management Committee, 1982-1985); District of Columbia Bar. **PRACTICE AREAS:** Labor and Employment; Litigation.

REPRESENTATIVE CLIENTS: KMST Television (CBS); Quail Lodge; Carmel Valley Golf and Country Club; Pacific Grove Municipal Golf Links; Carmel Valley Disposal; Monterey Peninsula Chamber of Commerce; Castlerock Estates, Inc. (Markham Ranch Residential Development); KBOQ Radio; Millcrest Products, Inc.
LOCAL COUNSEL FOR: Sanwa Bank California; Retlaw Broadcasting; Access Technology, Inc.; Vintners International, Beneficial California, Inc.; Carriage House Fruit.
REFERENCES: 1st National Bank of Monterey County.

---

## WILLIAM A. BRANDWEIN
### A PROFESSIONAL LAW CORPORATION
*Established in 1969*

215 WEST FRANKLIN STREET
P.O. BOX LAW
**MONTEREY, CALIFORNIA 93942**
Telephone: 408-372-3266
Fax: 408-372-0812

Columbus, Ohio Office: 42 East Gay Street, 11th Floor. Telephone: 614-461-1352. Fax: 614-221-0816.

*Tax Law, Individual, Corporate and Estate Taxation. Civil and Criminal Tax Litigation, Probate and Estate Planning.*

**WILLIAM A. BRANDWEIN,** born Chicago, Illinois, May 25, 1936; admitted to bar, 1967, Illinois, U.S. District Court, Northern District of Illinois; 1969, Ohio and U.S. District Court, Southern District of Ohio; 1970, U.S. Tax Court; 1971, U.S. Supreme Court; 1985, California; 1987, U.S. District Court, Northern District of California. *Education:* University of Illinois; DePaul University (J.D., 1967). Certified Public Accountant, Illinois, 1958. Author: "Stock and Debt Basis in Subchapter S Corporations," Taxation for Accountants, January, 1969. Member, Advisory Committee, IRS Central Regional Council, 1988-1989. Board of Visitors, Capital University Law School Masters in Taxation Program, 1987—. *Member:* Monterey County, Columbus (Chairman: Committee on Taxation, 1973-1976), Illinois State, Ohio State and American (Member: Section on Taxation; Committee on Sub S Corporations, 1969-1974; Committee on Capital Gains and Basis, 1975-1987; Committee on Corporations, 1979-1992; Committee on Attorneys in Small Law Firms, 1986—; Committee on Estates and Gifts, 1992—) Bar Associations; State Bar of California (Section of Taxation: Executive Committee, 1992-1995; Chairman, Nonmetropolitan Communities Committee, 1992-1993); American Institute of Certified Public Accountants. (Certified Specialist, Taxation Law, The State Bar of California Board of Legal Specialization). **PRACTICE AREAS:** Civil and Criminal Tax Litigation; Estate Planning.

---

## CALL & BOYNS

500 CAMINO EL ESTERO, SUITE 200
**MONTEREY, CALIFORNIA 93940**
Telephone: 408-649-3218
FAX: 408-649-4705

*Real Estate and Business Transactions, Civil Litigation and Appeals, Probate and Estate Planning.*

### MEMBERS OF FIRM

**SARA B. BOYNS,** born Long Beach, California, October 20, 1957; admitted to bar, 1988, California. *Education:* University of Utah (B.S., cum laude, 1980); Monterey College of Law (J.D., 1987). Phi Kappa Phi. *Member:* Monterey County Bar Association; State Bar of California; Monterey County Women Lawyers Association. **PRACTICE AREAS:** Business Litigation; Civil Litigation; Civil Appeals; Employment Litigation; Estate Planning.

**BRIAN D. CALL,** born Palo Alto, California, July 9, 1955; admitted to bar, 1981, California. *Education:* Lewis and Clark College (B.A., 1978); Southwestern University (J.D., cum laude, 1981). *Member:* Monterey County Bar Association; State Bar of California. **PRACTICE AREAS:** Business Transactions; Real Estate Transactions; Business Litigation.

REPRESENTATIVE CLIENTS: Inns-By-The-Sea; Carmel Candy & Confections, Inc.; Mangold Property Management, Harris Court Partners; Hidden Hills North Homeowners Association; Pebble Beach Financial Services; Chamisal Tennis Club; Sierra Instruments; Big Sur Land Trust.

---

## DAVIS & SCHROEDER, P.C.
*Established in 1978*

4TH FLOOR, PROFESSIONAL BUILDING
215 WEST FRANKLIN STREET
POST OFFICE BOX 3080
**MONTEREY, CALIFORNIA 93942-3080**
Telephone: 408-649-1122
FAX: 408-649-0566
URL: http://www.iplawyers.com

*Internet, Computer and High Technology Law, Estate Planning, Probate, Real Property, Business and Computer Litigation, Corporation, Tax Law and Patent, Trademark, Trade Secret, and Copyright Law.*

**G. GERVAISE DAVIS III,** born Marshalltown, Iowa, November 18, 1932; admitted to bar, 1958, District of Columbia; 1959, California; 1961, U.S. Tax Court; 1966, U.S. Supreme Court. *Education:* Georgetown University School of Foreign Service (B.S., 1954); Georgetown Law Center (J.D., 1958). Delta Theta Phi. Member, Board of Editors, Georgetown Law Journal, 1958. Author: "Software Protection: Practical and Legal Steps to Protect and Market Computer Programs," Van Nostrand Reinhold, New York City, 1985; "The Digital Dilemma: Coping With Copyright In A Digital World," The Computer Law Association Bulletin, Vol. 8, No. 1, 1992; "Clone Wars: The Empire Strikes Back," The Computer Lawyer, Vol. 5, No. 5, May, 1988; "Computer Software—: The Final Frontier: Clones, Compatibility and Copyright," The Computer Lawyer Vol. II, No. 6, June, 1985. Speaker: "Computer Law," USC Computer Conferences, May, 1985, 1986 and 1989. Speaker, PLI Computer Law Institutes, NYC, 1983, 1984, 1985, 1986, 1987, 1988, 1989, 1991, 1992. Chairman, CLA Fall Computer Conference, San Francisco, 1987. Invited Speaker: CLA European Computer Law Conference, Amsterdam, 1988; International Federation of Computer Law Associations Conference, Munich, Germany, 1990, Stockholm, Sweden, 1992, Bath, England, 1994, Brussels, Belgium 1996; Computer and Telecommunications Law Conference, Sao Paolo, Brazil, 1996. Adjunct Professor, Intellectual Property Law, Monterey College of Law, 1987—. Law Clerk, Hon. Judge Stanley N. Barnes, U.S. 9th Circuit Court of Appeals, 1958-1959. Member and Past President, Monterey Peninsula Unified School District, Board of Education, Monterey, California, 1963-1978. *Member:* Bar Association of San Francisco; Santa Clara County, Monterey County and American (Member, Sections on: Science and Technology; Patent, Trademark and Copyright Law; Business Law) Bar Associations; State Bar of California; The District of Columbia Bar; Computer Law Association (Member, Board of Directors, 1986-1994, 1995—). **PRACTICE AREAS:** Computer Law; Intellectual Property Law and Litigation; General Business Law.

**GEORGE L. SCHROEDER,** born Reedley, California, December 4, 1931; admitted to bar, 1959, California; 1979, U.S. Supreme Court. *Education:* University of California (A.B., 1953); Boalt Hall School of Law, Uni-

*(This Listing Continued)*

versity of California (J.D., 1958). Phi Delta Phi. Member, 1976-1981 and Chairman, 1978-1980, Monterey City Planning Commission. American Arbitration Association. *Member:* Monterey County and American (Member, Real Property, Probate and Trust Law Section) Bar Associations; State Bar of California (Member, Estate Planning, Trust and Probate Section). *PRACTICE AREAS:* Estate Planning Law; Probate Law; Real Property Law.

**JOHN D. LAUGHTON,** born Carmel, California, April 11, 1948; admitted to bar, 1978, California. *Education:* University of California at Berkeley (B.A., 1971); Hastings College of Law, University of California (J.D., 1978). Member, Del Rey Oaks Planning Commission, 1986-1992. *Member:* Monterey County and American Bar Associations; State Bar of California (Member, Sections on: Business; Real Property and Environmental Law). *PRACTICE AREAS:* Real Estate Law; General Business Law.

**ROBERT T. DAUNT,** born Stuttgart, Germany, February 23, 1949; admitted to bar, 1977, Michigan and Ohio; 1981, California. *Education:* University of Michigan (B.A., 1971); University of Toledo (J.D., 1976). Member, Board of Editors, University of Toledo Law Review, 1975-1976. Author: "Warranties and Mass Distributed Software," Santa Clara Computer and High-Technology Law Journal, Vol. 1, No. 2, 1985; "When Statutory Maximum Interest Rate Becomes Usury: Interest Formulas," 6 University of Toledo Law Review 541, 1975. *Member:* Monterey County and American Bar Associations; State Bar of Michigan; State Bar of California; Computer Law Association. *PRACTICE AREAS:* Computer Law; Intellectual Property Law; Corporate Law.

---

**CATHERINE MCCAULEY-LIBERT,** born Salinas, California, April 28, 1954; admitted to bar, 1990, California. *Education:* University of California at Berkeley (A.B., cum laude, 1977); University of San Francisco, School of Law; Monterey College of Law (J.D., cum laude, 1990). Regent's Fellow at University of California, Irvine, 1977-1978. *Member:* Monterey County and American Bar Associations; Monterey County Women Lawyers; California Women Lawyers; Computer Law Association; California Women for Agriculture. *PRACTICE AREAS:* Trademark and Copyright Law.

**ERIC BAKRI BOUSTANI,** born Berkeley, California, July 25, 1969; admitted to bar, 1996, California. *Education:* San Francisco State University (B.S., 1993); Santa Clara University (J.D., 1996). *PRACTICE AREAS:* Intellectual Property; Litigation. *Email:* eric@iplawyers.com

REPRESENTATIVE CLIENTS: Acuity Software, Inc.; ALEMBIC, Inc.; Arkenstone, Inc.; Atari Games Corp.; Brosis Innovations, Inc.; Central Valley Seeds; Daniels & House Construction Co.; DeltaPoint, Inc.; Mobileparks West (Mobile Home Park Developer); MetaWare Inc.; Monterey Bay Aquarium Research; Monterey City Disposal Service; Monterey Peninsula Golf Foundation; Network Intelligence; Newman Consulting; Packard Humanities Institute, a Non-Profit Foundation; Post Harvest Technologies, Inc.
REFERENCE: First National Bank of Central California, Monterey, California.

## *DEWAR AND ROCKWOOD*

*A PROFESSIONAL CORPORATION*
587 HARTNELL STREET
P.O. BOX 1027
**MONTEREY, CALIFORNIA 93940**
Telephone: 408-373-4463; 800-200-8515
Fax: 408-373-2566

*General Civil and Trial Practice in all Courts. Personal Injury, Government Tort Claims, Family, Real Property and Mortgage Law, Business, Estate Planning and Probate Law.*

**RODERICK L. DEWAR,** born Oakland, California, August 28, 1929; admitted to bar, 1955, California. *Education:* Stanford University (A.B., 1952; LL.B., 1954). Phi Delta Phi. *Member:* Monterey County and American Bar Associations; State Bar of California. *PRACTICE AREAS:* Real Property Law; Mortgage Law; Wills Law; Probate Law; Estate Planning Law; Business Law.

**TERRY G. ROCKWOOD,** born Monterey, California, November 15, 1946; admitted to bar, 1974, California. *Education:* University of California at Berkeley (B.A., 1971); University of San Francisco (J.D., 1974). *Member:* Monterey County Bar Association; State Bar of California (Member, Board of Directors, Lawyers Referral Service of Monterey County, 1982-1986); California Trial Lawyers Association; Monterey County Trial Lawyers Association (President, 1990-1991); American Trial Lawyers Association.

*(This Listing Continued)*

---

LANGUAGES: Spanish. *PRACTICE AREAS:* General Civil Litigation; Personal Injury Law; Insurance Law; Family Law.

**BRIAN C. MCCOY,** born Glendale, California, August 16, 1953; admitted to bar, 1978, California. *Education:* University od California (B.A., 1975); Loyola University of Los Angeles (J.D., 1978. *Member:* Monterey County Bar Association; State Bar of California. *PRACTICE AREAS:* Personal Injury; Family; Real Property; General Civil Litigation.

REPRESENTATIVE CLIENTS: C. L. Frost Roofing; Ross Roofing; Fidelity Moving and Storage; Key Property Management; Heritage Real Estate; Management Application; Red's Donuts; Consolidated Van Lines.

## *DUFFY & GUENTHER*

419 WEBSTER STREET
**MONTEREY, CALIFORNIA 93940**
Telephone: 408-649-5100
Fax: 408-649-5102
Email: dglaw@mbay.net

*Commercial Litigation, Bankruptcy, Secured Transactions, Commercial Law and Business Reorganization.*

### MEMBERS OF FIRM

**THOMAS R. DUFFY,** born Jacksonville, California, December 25, 1949; admitted to bar, 1971, California; 1989, U.S. Supreme Court. *Education:* Dartmouth College; Stanford University (A.B., 1971); University of Southern California; Boalt Hall School of Law, University of California (J.D., 1975). Selected for the University of Southern California Law Review. Charter Member, Board of Editors, Industrial Relations Law Quarterly. *Member:* Monterey County and Santa Clara County Bar Associations; State Bar of California. *PRACTICE AREAS:* Commercial and Real Estate Litigation; Creditor's Remedies in Insolvency Matters; Real Property and Commercial Transactions.

**RALPH P. GUENTHER,** born Hollywood, California, April 14, 1961; admitted to bar, 1986, California, U.S. District Court, Northern District of California and U.S. Court of Appeals, 9th Circuit. *Education:* California State University at Northridge (B.S., cum laude, 1983); University of California at Davis (J.D., 1986). Member, Committee of Lawyer Representatives, U.S. Bankruptcy Court, Northern District of California, 1994—. *Member:* Monterey County (Executive Director, 1991) and Santa Clara County Bar Associations; State Bar of California; Monterey County Barristers (President, 1991). *PRACTICE AREAS:* Creditor's Remedies; Bankruptcy; Commercial and Real Estate Litigation; Real Property and Commercial Transactions.

---

**JOHN E. KESECKER,** born Greenbree, California, January 24, 1967; admitted to bar, 1993, California. *Education:* California Polytechnic State University (B.S., 1990); University of the Pacific, McGeorge School of Law (J.D., with great distinction, 1993). Member, Order of the Coif. Member, Traynor Society. Member, Pacific Law Journal, 1991 and Assistant Editor, 1993. Member, Transnational Lawyer, 1992. *Member:* Monterey County Bar Association; Monterey COunty Barristers.

REPRESENTATIVE CLIENTS: Bank of Salinas; Commercial Real Estate Service, Inc.; City of Salines; City of Medesto; First National Bank of Central California; County of Stanislaus.

## *FENTON & KELLER*

2801 MONTEREY-SALINAS HIGHWAY
P.O. BOX 791
**MONTEREY, CALIFORNIA 93942-0791**
Telephone: 408-373-1241
Telecopier: 408-373-7219

*Salinas, California Office:* 132 West Gabilan Street. Telephone: 408-757-8937. Facsimile: 408-574-0621.

*General Civil, Trial and Appellate Practice in State and Federal Courts, Administrative, Agribusiness, Commercial, Corporation, Insurance, Land Use Planning, Probate, Real Estate, Taxation, Trust and Estates Law.*

### MEMBERS OF FIRM

**J. HAMPTON HOGE** (1899-1977).

**LEWIS L. FENTON,** born Palo Alto, California, August 20, 1925; admitted to bar, 1951, California. *Education:* Stanford University (B.A., 1948; LL.B., 1950). Phi Delta Phi. First Recipient, Chief Justice Phil Gibson

*(This Listing Continued)*

CAA1363B

**FENTON & KELLER, Monterey—Continued**

Award for Community Service. President, Stanford Alumni Association, 1966-1967. Member, Board of Visitors, Stanford Law School, 1963-1965. Faculty Member, Center for Trial and Appellate Advocacy, Hastings College of Law, 1980—. *Member:* Monterey County (President, 1963) and Santa Clara County Bar Associations; American Society of Hospital Attorneys; California Medical-Legal Committee (President); National Association of Railroad Trial Counsel; International Association of Defense Counsel; Association of Defense Counsel of Northern California (President, 1969); Advocate, American Board of Trial Advocates. Fellow: American College of Trial Lawyers; International Academy of Trial Lawyers. (Also Member, Hoge, Fenton, Jones & Appel, Inc., San Jose, California) (Certified as a Civil Trial Advocate by the National Board of Trial Advocacy).

**CHARLES R. KELLER,** born Champaign, Illinois, April 12, 1940; admitted to bar, 1966, California. *Education:* Stanford University (B.A., 1962; LL.B., 1965). Member and Revising Editor, Stanford Law Review, 1964-1965. Arbitrator, American Arbitration Association. *Member:* Monterey County Bar Association (President, 1973-1974); American Board of Trial Advocates; California Trial Lawyers Association.

**GERALD V. BARRON, III,** born San Francisco, California, September 8, 1945; admitted to bar, 1972, California. *Education:* University of San Francisco (B.A., 1969; J.D., 1972). Secretary, McAuliffe Scholastic Honor Society, 1970-1971. Law Clerk to Presiding Justice G. Brown, California Court of Appeals, Fifth District, 1972-1973. Co-Author, Recent Developments in Torts Practice, California Continuing Education of the Bar, 1983-1992. Adjunct Professor of Law, Monterey College of Law, 1983-1987. Lecturer, California Continuing Education of the Bar, 1983—. *Member:* Monterey County Bar Association; American Board of Trial Advocates; California Medical-Legal Committee; California Trial Lawyers Association; Experimental Test Pilots Association (Member, Legal Committee, 1980-1981); Lawyer Pilots Bar Association.

**NOLAN M. KENNEDY,** born Birmingham, Alabama, October 26, 1943; admitted to bar, 1973, California. *Education:* Baylor University (B.A., 1965); Hastings College of the Law, University of California (J.D., 1973). Order of the Coif. Thurston Society. Managing Editor, Hastings Law Journal, 1972-1973. Contributing Author, Chapter 6 "Options," California Real Property Sales Transactions, Second Ed., California Continuing Education of the Bar, 1993. *Member:* Monterey County Bar Association.

**RONALD F. SCHOLL,** born Chicago, Illinois, February 27, 1942; admitted to bar, 1974, California. *Education:* University of Texas (B.S., Engr., 1963); Northwestern University (M.S., Engr., 1966); Loyola University of Los Angeles (J.D., 1974). Member, St. Thomas More Law Honor Society. *Member:* Monterey County Bar Association; Northern California Association of Defense Counsel.

**THOMAS H. JAMISON,** born Fresno, California, December 29, 1947; admitted to bar, 1975, Oregon; 1976, California. *Education:* Williams College (B.A., cum laude, 1970); Hastings College of the Law, University of California (J.D., 1975). Order of the Coif. Member, Thurston Society. Member, 1973-1974 and Associate Articles Editor, 1974-1975, Hastings Law Journal. Law Clerk to Ralph M. Holman, Associate Justice, Supreme Court of Oregon, 1975-1976. Contributing Author, Chapter 6 "Options", California Real Property Sales Transactions, Second Ed., California Continuing Education of the Bar, 1993. Panel Member, Real Property Law, Section Presentation on Conversion of Agricultural Land Development, California State Bar Convention, 1990. *Member:* Monterey County Bar Association; Oregon State Bar.

**SUSAN M. DAUPHINÉ,** born Los Angeles, California, March 5, 1944; admitted to bar, 1969, Massachusetts; 1976, California. *Education:* Stanford University (B.A., with distinction, 1965); Columbia University (J.D., 1968). Attorney Adviser, Department of Health, Education & Welfare, Boston, 1968-1969. Speaker, CEB Fundamentals of Real Property, 1990. Member, Board of Directors, Lyceum of Monterey Peninsula, 1978-1984. Commissioner, Monterey County Commission on Status Women, 1976-1980. *Member:* Monterey County (President, 1992-1993; Treasurer, 1986-1988; Member: Executive Committee, 1979-1980, 1986-1991; Education Committee, 1984, 1985; Chairman, 1991—) and Massachusetts Bar Associations; State Bar of California (Delegate, 1978-1980, 1987, 1989, 1990, 1991; Chair, Monterey Delegation to Conference of Delegates, 1989, 1990); Association of Defense Counsel of Northern California.

**LARRY E. HAYES,** born Lawton, Oklahoma, January 12, 1946; admitted to bar, 1980, California, U.S. District Court, Northern and Central Districts of California and U.S. Court of Appeals, Ninth Circuit. *Education:* California Lutheran College (B.S., 1974); University of Santa Clara (J.D., magna cum laude, 1980). *Member:* Monterey County Bar Association (Treasurer, 1985; Executive Committee, 1984 and 1986); Association of Defense Counsel of Northern California.

**NANCY P. TOSTEVIN,** born San Bernardino, California, August 31, 1938; admitted to bar, 1978, California. *Education:* Stanford University (B.A., with distinction, 1961); University of Santa Clara (J.D., summa cum laude, 1978). *Member:* Monterey County Bar Association; Association of Defense Counsel of Northern California; California Medical-Legal Committee.

**MARK H. JOHNSON,** born Grants Pass, Oregon, June 12, 1956; admitted to bar, 1981, California. *Education:* Harvard College (B.A., 1978); Hastings College of the Law, University of California (J.D., 1981). Order of the Coif; Thurston Society. Member and Note and Comment Editor, Hastings Constitutional Law Quarterly, 1979-1981. *Member:* Monterey County Bar Association. (Certified Specialist, Estate Planning, Trust and Probate Law, The State Bar of California Board of Legal Specialization).

**MARK A. CAMERON,** born El Paso, Texas, April 9, 1957; admitted to bar, 1983, California. *Education:* California State University at San Bernardino (B.A., with honors, 1980); Hastings College of the Law, University of California (J.D., magna cum laude, 1983). Order of the Coif; Thurston Honor Society. Moot Court Board. *Member:* Monterey County Bar Association.

**JOHN S. BRIDGES,** born Eugene, Oregon, November 6, 1958; admitted to bar, 1985, California. *Education:* Montana State University (B.S., with highest honors, 1980); King Hall School of Law-University of California at Davis (J.D., 1985). *Member:* Monterey County Bar Association.

**FRANCES R. GAVER,** born Lexington, Kentucky, March 13, 1929; admitted to bar, 1986, California. *Education:* Wellesley College (B.A., 1950); University of Pittsburgh (M.A. 1968); Monterey College of Law (J.D., 1986). Phi Beta Kappa. Board of Trustees, 1972-1981 and President of the Board, 1974-1976, Carmel Unified School District. *Member:* Monterey County Bar Association. (Certified Specialist, Estate Planning, Trust and Probate Law, The State Bar of California Board of Legal Specialization).

**DENNIS G. MCCARTHY,** born Santa Cruz, California, December 11, 1951; admitted to bar, 1985, California. *Education:* San Jose State University (B.A., summa cum laude, 1975); Columbia University (M.A., 1979); New York University (J.D., 1984). Note and Comment Editor, Review of Law and Social Change, 1983-1984. Contributing Author: "Damages in a Wrongful Discharge Context: An Overview", Damages and Trial Techniques Course Book, Defense Research Institute Inc., 1984; "Principles Governing the Award of Costs and Expenses Under Attorneys' Fee Statues", Court Award of Attorneys' Fees: Litigating Antitrust, Civil Rights, Public Interest and Securities Cases," Practicing Law Institute, 1987. *Member:* Monterey County Bar Association; Association of Defense Counsel of Northern California.

**DANIEL F. ARCHER,** born Altus, Oklahoma, January 23, 1963; admitted to bar, 1989, California. *Education:* California State University at Sacramento (B.S., 1985); Santa Clara University (J.D., 1988). National Order of the Barristers. Business Editor, Santa Clara University Law Review, 1987-1988. Law Clerk to Presiding Justice Nat Agliano, California Court of Appeal, Sixth District, 1987-1988. *Member:* Monterey County Bar Association.

**JACQUELINE P. MCMANUS,** born Los Angeles, California, August 2, 1961; admitted to bar, 1986, California. *Education:* University of San Diego (B.A., with honors, 1983; J.D., 1986). *Member:* Monterey County and San Diego County Bar Associations; Industrial Relations Research Association.

**DONALD FORREST LEACH,** born Syracuse, New York, December 12, 1959; admitted to bar, 1991, California; 1992, District of Columbia. *Education:* St. Lawrence University (B.A., 1982); Georgetown University (J.D., 1986; M.B.A., 1986). *Member:* Monterey County Bar Association. **Email:** Carmeleach@aol.com

**DAVID C. SWEIGERT,** born July 14, 1953; admitted to bar, 1991, California. *Education:* California State University at Sacramento (B.A., 1977); University of California at Davis (J.D., 1991). Order of the Coif. *Member:* Monterey County Bar Association.

**LORIE A. KRUSE,** born Ogden, Utah, July 19, 1965; admitted to bar, 1993, California. *Education:* University of California at Davis (B.A., 1987); Santa Clara University (J.D., cum laude, 1993). Phi Delta Phi (Charter

*(This Listing Continued)*

Member). National Order of the Barristers. Member, Santa Clara Trial Team. Member, Santa Clara County Inns of Court, 1992-1993.

**LONNIE TRUAX,** born Neptune, New Jersey, April 3, 1949; admitted to bar, 1994, California. *Education:* Syracuse University (B.S., 1972); Santa Clara University (J.D., summa cum laude, 1994). *Member:* Monterey County Bar Association.

**VIRGINIA H. LAUDERDALE,** born New York, N.Y., 1960; admitted to bar, 1986, Illinois; 1987, California; 1989, District of Columbia. *Education:* Amherst College (B.A., 1981); New York University School of Law (J.D., 1986). Adjunct Professor, Business Organization, Moterey College of Law, 1995—. Associate Graham & James (Sacramento) 1991-1993; Associate, Luce, Forward, Hamilton & Scripps (San Diego) 1987-1988. Deputy Public Defender, San Diego County, 1989-1990. *Member:* Monterey County, Sacramento County and Yolo County Bar Associations. **PRACTICE AREAS:** Corporate Law; Securities Law; Real Estate Law.

**CHRISTOPHER E. PANETTA,** born San Jose, California, May 12, 1963; admitted to bar, 1994, California and U.S. District Court, Central District of California. *Education:* University of California, Berkeley (B.A., with high distinction, 1985); University of California School of Law at Los Angeles (J.D., 1994). Phi Beta Kappa. Recipient, American Jurisprudence Award in Constitutional Law. *Member:* Monterey County Bar Association; State Bar of California. **PRACTICE AREAS:** General Litigation; Employment Litigation.

REPRESENTATIVE CLIENTS: Community Hospital of the Monterey Peninsula; Crown Packing; Del Monte Realty Co.; First National Bank of Central California; McDonald Development Co.; Mission Packing; Monterey Bay Aquarium; Pebble Beach Company; Shamrock Seed Co.; Kaiser Foundation Health Plan, Inc.
LOCAL COUNSEL FOR: American Medical International, Inc.; California Insurance Group; California State Automobile Assn.; Cigna Cos.; County of Monterey; Epic Healthcare; Mobile Exploration and Producing U.S., Inc.; Norcal Mutual Insurance Co.; Pacific Gas & Electric Co.; Program Beta Hospital Risk Management Authority; Safeway, Inc.; Southern Pacific Transportation Co.; Texaco; Wells Fargo Bank.

## SEAN FLAVIN

500 CAMINO EL ESTERO, SUITE 200
P.O. BOX 2229
**MONTEREY, CALIFORNIA 93942-2229**
Telephone: 408-372-7535
Fax: 408-372-2425

*General Civil Practice, Corporations and Partnerships, Estate Planning, Probate and Real Property Law, State and Local Taxation.*

**SEAN FLAVIN,** born Chicago, Illinois, January 8, 1924; admitted to bar, 1950, District of Columbia; 1952, California. *Education:* Stanford University (A.B., 1947); Harvard University (LL.B., cum laude, 1950). Author: "Estate Planning and Proposition 13," California Continuing Education of the Bar, Estate Planning California Probate Reporter, June, 1984. Co-Author: "Taxing California Property," Clark Boardman Callaghan, 3 ed., 1991. *Member:* Monterey County Bar Association; The State Bar of California (Member, Committee on Property, Sales and Local Taxes); District of Columbia Bar. **PRACTICE AREAS:** Estate Planning; Probate Law; Real Estate Law; Corporate Law; Partnership Law; Taxation Law.

## DENNIS W. FOX

2100 GARDEN ROAD, SUITE H
**MONTEREY, CALIFORNIA 93940**
Telephone: 408-646-9898
Telecopier: 408-646-0720
Email: dwfox@redshift.com

*Estate Planning, Probate, Trust Administration, Estate Litigation.*

**DENNIS W. FOX,** born Los Angeles, California, October 28, 1946; admitted to bar, 1974, California and U.S. District Court, Central District of California; 1978, U.S. District Court, Northern District of California. *Education:* University of California at Santa Barbara (B.A., 1968); Southwestern University School of Law (J.D., cum laude, 1974). *Member:* Monterey County Bar Association; State Bar of California (Member, Estate Planning, Trust and Probate Section, 1978-1992). (Certified Specialist, Estate Planning, Trust and Probate Law, The State Bar of California Board of Legal Specialization). **REPORTED CASES:** Estate of Stevenson, 14 Cal. Rptr.

*(This Listing Continued)*

2d 250. **PRACTICE AREAS:** Living Trusts; Estate Planning; Trust Administration; Probate.

REPRESENTATIVE CLIENTS: Ralph Knox Foundation; Ng Foundation.
REFERENCES: Comerica Bank; First National Bank; Bank of America Trust.

## GRUNSKY, EBEY, FARRAR & HOWELL

*A PROFESSIONAL CORPORATION*

**MONTEREY, CALIFORNIA**

(See Watsonville)

*General Civil and Trial Practice. Probate, Corporate, Creditor and Bankruptcy, Insurance, Insurance Coverage, Real Estate and Landslide and Subsidence Law, Criminal Law, Construction Law and Litigation, Medical Malpractice, Estate and Trust Litigation, Court Appointed and Private Arbitration and Mediation and Governmental Agency.*

## HARRAY, MASUDA & LINKER

80 GARDEN COURT, SUITE 260
**MONTEREY, CALIFORNIA 93940**
Telephone: 408-373-3101
Fax: 408-373-6712

*Civil Litigation and Appellate Practice in all State and Federal Courts. Casualty, Insurance, Public Entity, Employment, Medical and Professional Malpractice.*

*FIRM PROFILE: Harray, Masuda and Linker is actively involved in California litigation with trial experience from 1968. Members provide expertise in Civil Litigation and Appellate Practice in all State and Federal Courts including, but not limited to, Casualty, Building Construction, Insurance, Professional Malpractice, Medical, Banking, Public Entity and Employment Law; firm also provides Mediation and Arbitration services. Richard K. Harray, Michael M. Masuda, Stan Lee Linker.*

**RICHARD K. HARRAY,** born Turlock, California, May 16, 1942; admitted to bar, 1968, California. *Education:* Northwestern University (A.B., 1964); Stanford University School of Law (LL.B., 1967). *Member:* Monterey County Bar Association; The State Bar of California; Northern California Association of Defense Counsel (Member, Board of Directors, 1975-1977); International Association of Defense Counsel; American Board of Trial Advocates. **LANGUAGES:** French and Spanish. **PRACTICE AREAS:** General Insurance Including Casualty and Malpractice; Employment Law; Personal Injury; Property Damage; Products Liability; Medical Malpractice.

**MICHAEL P. MASUDA,** born Billings, Montana, September 25, 1956; admitted to bar, 1981, North Dakota and Minnesota; 1987, California. *Education:* University of North Dakota (B.A., 1978; J.D., with distinction, 1981); University of California at Berkeley (M.A., 1984). Adjunct Professor of Law, Constitutional Law, Monterey College of Law, 1987—. *Member:* Monterey County and American Bar Associations; State Bar of California; Northern Association of Defense Counsel. **PRACTICE AREAS:** General Insurance Including Casualty and Malpractice; Employment Law; Personal Injury; Property Damage; Products Liability; Medical Malpractice.

**STAN L. LINKER,** born Salinas, California, March 8, 1949; admitted to bar, 1974, California; 1981, U.S. District Court, Northern District of California; 1985, U.S. District Court, Central District of California and U.S. Supreme Court. *Education:* Hartnell Junior College (A.A., 1969); California State University at Fresno (B.A., 1971); University of the Pacific (J.D., 1974). Member, Moot Court Honors Board, 1973-1974. *Member:* Monterey County (Member, Executive Committee, 1980; Treasurer, 1983) and American Bar Associations; State Bar of California; Monterey County Trial Lawyers Association (President, 1985-1986). **PRACTICE AREAS:** General Insurance Including Casualty and Malpractice; Employment Law; Personal Injury; Property Damage; Products Liability; Medical Malpractice.

REPRESENTATIVE CLIENTS: The Travelers/Aetna; The Doctors' Company/CHIC; Program Beta; CNA; DPIC; Sequoia Insurance Co.; Midstate Ins. Co.; County of Monterey; Cities of Monterey, Pacific Grove & Seaside.

CAA1365B

## HEISINGER, BUCK, MORRIS & ROSE
MONTEREY, CALIFORNIA
(See Carmel)

*General Civil and Trial Practice. Corporations and Partnerships. Real Estate. Estate Planning, Probate, Trusts and Estates.*

---

## Horan, Lloyd, Karachale, Dyer, Schwartz, Law & Cook

*Incorporated*
*Established in 1960*

**499 VAN BUREN STREET**
**P.O. BOX 3350**
**MONTEREY, CALIFORNIA 93942-3350**
Telephone: 408-373-4131
FAX: 408-373-8302

*General Civil and Trial Practice. Corporation, Taxation, Employee Benefit, Real Estate, Personal Injury, Professional Negligence, Wrongful Termination, Condemnation, Land Use, Environmental, Commercial, Trusts, Estate Planning, Probate, Trust and Estate Litigation.*

*FIRM PROFILE: The law firm originated in 1960 when Laurence P. Horan joined former State Senator Fredrick S. Farr in the practice of law in Carmel. The firm relocated to Monterey in 1971 and continues to represent clients in a general civil and trial practice throughout Northern and Central California.*

**LAURENCE P. HORAN**, born Oakland, California, June 23, 1929; admitted to bar, 1955, California; U.S. District Court, Northern District of California; U.S. Court of Appeals, Ninth Circuit; 1973, U.S. Supreme Court; 1985, U.S. Tax Court. *Education:* University of California at Berkeley (A.B., 1952); Boalt Hall School of Law, University of California (J.D., 1955). Phi Delta Phi. Trustee, 1969— and Chairman of the Board, 1975-1976, Monterey Institute of International Studies. Doctor of Human letters Honoris Causa. *Member:* Monterey County and American (Chairman, 9th Circuit, 1977 and Member, Committee on Condemnation, Zoning and Property Use, Litigation Section, 1975—; Member, Committee on Products, General Liability and Consumer Law, Insurance, Negligence and Compensation Law Section, 1977—) Bar Associations; The State Bar of California; California Trial Lawyers Association (President, Monterey County Chapter, 1975-1977); The Association of Trial Lawyers of America. Diplomate, National Board of Trial Advocacy. Fellow, American College of Trial Lawyers. *LANGUAGES:* Spanish. *PRACTICE AREAS:* Civil Litigation; Professional Negligence Law; Eminent Domain Law.

**FRANCIS P. LLOYD**, born Montreal, Canada, January 11, 1935; admitted to bar, 1960, California; 1973, U.S. Supreme Court. *Education:* Stanford University and University of California at Berkeley (A.B., 1956); Boalt Hall School of Law, University of California (J.D., 1959). Phi Delta Phi. Director, Big Sur Land Trust, (1994—). *Member:* Bar Association of San Francisco; Monterey County and American (Member, Committee on Estate and Trust Litigation, Real Estate, Probate and Trust Law Section) Bar Associations; The State Bar of California (Member, Section on: Estate Planning, Trust and Probate). (Certified Specialist, Estate Planning, Trust and Probate Law, The State Bar of California Board of Legal Specialization). *PRACTICE AREAS:* Trust Law; Estate Planning Law; Probate Law; Estate Law; Estate and Trust Litigation.

**ANTHONY T. KARACHALE**, born Eureka, California, March 7, 1939; admitted to bar, 1965, California; 1976, U.S. Tax Court. *Education:* Stanford University (A.B., 1962; LL.B., 1964); Boston University (LL.M., in Taxation, 1970). Author: "Did The OTEY Case Survive the Tax Reform Act of 1984?" Vol 12, No. 2 California State Bar Tax Section News. Co-editor: "Review of Selected Code Legislation," California Continuing Education of the Bar, 1963. Co-Author: "Installment Sales," 5 Taxation for Lawyers 270. Lecturer, Golden Gate University Center for Tax Studies, 1972-1977. Instructor, Federal Income Taxation, Monterey College of Law, 1977—. Member, American Society of Pension Actuaries Department of Labor Enforcement Committee, 1995—. *Member:* Monterey County and American (Member, Committee on Professional Service Corporations, Section of Taxation, 1978-1980) Bar Associations; The State Bar of California. (Certified Specialist, Taxation Law, The State Bar of California Board of Legal Specialization).

*(This Listing Continued)*

CAA1366B

**DENNIS M. LAW**, born Los Angeles, California, November 15, 1944; admitted to bar, 1970, California; 1981, U.S. District Court, Northern District of California. *Education:* Stanford University (A.B., Economics, with honors, 1966); University of California at Los Angeles (J.D., 1969). Recipient, American Jurisprudence Award, Torts. Professor, Monterey College of Law, 1976-1986. *Member:* State Bar of California. *PRACTICE AREAS:* Civil, Commercial and Real Estate Litigation; Real Property Transactions.

**GARY D. SCHWARTZ**, born Quincy, Illinois, March 2, 1944; admitted to bar, 1973, California; 1975, U.S. District Court, Central District of California; 1976, Illinois; 1984, U.S. Tax Court. *Education:* Indiana University (B.S., cum laude, 1967); Loyola University of Los Angeles (J.D., magna cum laude, 1973); Golden Gate University (LL.M., Taxation, cum laude, 1986). Beta Gamma Sigma. Member, St. Thomas More Honor Law Society. Instructor: Banking Law, American Institute of Banking, 1977-1978 and Golden Gate University M.S. Taxation Program, 1987—. Associate, O'Melveny & Myers, Los Angeles, California, 1973-1976. *Member:* The State Bar of California; Illinois State and American (Member, Sections on: Taxation; Corporation, Banking and Business Law; Real Property, Probate and Trust Law) Bar Associations. [Capt., USAF, 1972]. (Certified Specialist, Taxation Law, The State Bar of California Board of Legal Specialization). *PRACTICE AREAS:* Estate Planning; Taxation; International Tax; Probate and Trust Law; Business; Corporate; Partnerships; Limited Liability Company; Real Estate Law.

**JAMES J. COOK**, born New Jersey, July 31, 1948; admitted to bar, 1973, Pennsylvania and U.S. Court of Military Appeals; 1976, California and U.S. District Court, Northern District of California. *Education:* East Stroudsburg University (B.A., 1970); Dickinson School of Law (J.D., 1973). Listed in, Who's Who in American Colleges and Universities. *Member:* Monterey County Bar Association; State Bar of California. [Capt., U.S. Army, 1973-1976]. *PRACTICE AREAS:* Personal Injury; Business Litigation.

**STEPHEN W. DYER**, born San Francisco, California, June 25, 1946; admitted to bar, 1974, California; 1985, U.S. Court of Appeals, Ninth Circuit. *Education:* University of California at Berkeley (A.B., 1968); University of San Francisco (J.D., cum laude, 1974). Comments Editor, University of San Francisco Law Review, 1973-1974. Author: "Judicial Foreclosure After the Revised Enforcement of Judgments Act," VI Continuing Education of the Bar, Real Property Law Reporter 53. Instructor, Real Estate Secured Transactions, Monterey College of Law, 1977—. *Member:* Monterey County (President, 1991) and American Bar Associations; The State Bar of California (Member, and Chairperson, (1984-1985) Real Property Law Section; Member (1988-1992) and Chair (1992), Resolutions Committee of the Conference of Delegates); California Continuing Education of the Bar Real Property Law Institute (Member, Planning Committee, 1983—); American College of Real Estate Lawyers. [Lt., USNR, 1968-1971]

**MARK A. BLUM**, born San Francisco, California, February 12, 1954; admitted to bar, 1986, California, U.S. Court of Appeals, Ninth Circuit and U.S. District Court, Northern District of California. *Education:* San Francisco State University (B.A., magna cum laude, 1982); Hastings College of the Law, University of California (J.D., 1986). Instructor, Moot Court Board, Hastings College of the Law, 1985-1986. *Member:* Monterey County and American Bar Associations; State Bar of California (Member, Real Property, Public Law Section). *PRACTICE AREAS:* Land Use; Planning; Zoning; Subdivision; Inverse Condemnation.

---

**MARK A. O'CONNOR**, born Sacramento, California, June 1, 1959; admitted to bar, 1990, California and U.S. District Court, Northern and Eastern Districts of California. *Education:* University of Pacific (B.S., 1980); McGeorge School of Law (J.D., with distinction, 1990). Order of the Coif. Member, Traynor Honor Society. Recipient, American Jurisprudence Award in Insurance Law. Instructor, Monterey College of Law, 1995—. *Member:* Monterey County and American Bar Associations; State Bar of California. *PRACTICE AREAS:* Civil Litigation; Insurance Law.

**SONIA S. SHARMA**, born India, July 30, 1969; admitted to bar, 1994, California, U.S. District Court, Northern District of California and U.S. Court of Appeals, Ninth Circuit. *Education:* California State University at Fullerton (B.A., highest honors, 1991); Hastings College of Law (J.D., 1994); Golden Gate University (LL.M. in Taxation, with high honors, 1995). Instructor, Moot Court Board, Hastings College of Law, 1992-1994. Licensed Real Estate Broker, California. *Member:* Monterey County, Santa Clara County and American (Member, Young Lawyers Section) Bar Associations; State Bar of California (Member, Sections on: Business Law; Estate Planning and Probate; Real Property Law; Taxation). *PRACTICE*

*(This Listing Continued)*

*AREAS:* Taxation; Estate Planning; Probate and Trust Law; Business Law; Corporate Law; Partnership; Real Estate.

**ROBERT E. ARNOLD, III,** born Denver, Colorado, November 21, 1962; admitted to bar, 1996, California; 1997, U.S. District Court, Northern District of California and U.S. Court of Appeals, Ninth Circuit. *Education:* Dartmouth College; University of Michigan (B.A., Economics, 1988); Golden Gate University School of Law (J.D., with highest honors, 1996). Recipient: Criminal Law Award for Academic Excellence; American Jurisprudence Awards: Civil Procedure, Writing and Research, Criminal Procedure, Corporations, Community Property, Evidence, Insurance Law and Securities Regulation. Associate Editor, Golden Gate University Law Review, 1995-1996. Author: Board of Natural Resources v. Brown: New York Grows Roots in Washington, Golden Gate University Ninth Circuit Review, Spring 1995. Member, Golden Gate University Moot Court Board. *PRACTICE AREAS:* Business Transactions; Corporate Law; Securities Law; Real Estate; Civil Litigation.

*OF COUNSEL*

**WILLIAM C. MARSH,** born Los Angeles, California, July 17, 1930; admitted to bar, 1959, California. *Education:* University of California (B.S., 1952); Hastings College of the Law, University of California (LL.B., 1958). Deputy District Attorney, Monterey County, (1959-1962). City Attorney, Monterey, (1952-1990). Agency Counsel, Monterey-Salinas Transit Joint Powers Agency, (1975—). *Member:* State Bar of California; American Arbitration Association.

**ROBERT C. CLIFFORD,** born Berkeley, California, January 5, 1926; admitted to bar, 1952, California. *Education:* Stanford University (A.B., 1949; LL.B., 1951). Author: "California Insurance Disputes" and "California Uninsured Motorist Law," Michie-Butterworth Legal Publishers, Parker Publications Div., 1991; "Qualifying and Attacking Expert Witnesses," James Publishing, 1988. *Member:* Monterey County and American Bar Associations; State Bar of California.

Language: Spanish.

REPRESENTATIVE CLIENTS: Monterey Institute of International Studies; California State University; Naval Postgraduate School Foundation; Lawyers Mutual Insurance Co.; First American Title Insurance Co.; Mercury Insurance Co.; Ackerley Communications, Inc./KCBA TV, Inc.; Northern California Golf Association; Poppy Hills Golf Club; Forest Golf Properties; Chateau Julien Winery; San Saba Vineyards; Fresh Western Marketing, Inc.; Anthony Pools-/Anthony Industries; Stahl Motor Co.; Victory Toyota; El Sur Ranch; Northtree Ranch; Fish Ranch; Wenwest, Inc.; H-Y-H Corp.; Rreef Management Company; Bay View Hotels; Mesiti-Miller Engineering; WWD Engineering; The Chapman Foundation; Harvestland Express.
REFERENCES: Wells Fargo Bank; Bank of America National Trust & Savings Assn.; First National Bank of Monterey; Monterey County Bank.

## HUDSON, MARTIN, FERRANTE & STREET

*Established in 1907*

**490 CALLE PRINCIPAL**
**P.O. BOX 112**
**MONTEREY, CALIFORNIA 93940**
Telephone: 408-375-3151
Telecopier: 408-375-0131
Email: hmfs@aol.com

*General Civil and Trial Practice. Banking, Real Property, Commercial, Cable and Communications, Corporation, Construction, Personal Injury, Estate Planning, and Probate Law.*

**W. G. HUDSON** (1877-1954).

**CARMEL MARTIN** (1879-1965).

**PETER J. FERRANTE** (1903-1975).

**WILLIAM L. HUDSON** (1907-1982).

**WEBSTER STREET** (1898-1984).

*OF COUNSEL*

**JOHN F. MARTIN,** born Monterey, California, June 15, 1916; admitted to bar, 1940, California. *Education:* University of California (A.B., 1937; LL.B., 1940). Phi Delta Phi. City Attorney, Monterey, 1944. Member, Executive Board, Monterey Bay Area Council Boy Scouts of America, 1942—. *Member:* Monterey County and American Bar Associations; The State Bar of California. Fellow, American College of Trust and Estate Counsel. *PRACTICE AREAS:* Estate Planning; Probate; Elder Law.

*(This Listing Continued)*

*MEMBERS OF FIRM*

**CARMEL MARTIN, JR.,** born Monterey, California, June 7, 1920; admitted to bar, 1950, California. *Education:* University of California (B.S., 1942); Stanford University (LL.B., 1949). Phi Delta Phi. Member, City Council, Monterey, 1952-1954. *Member:* Monterey County and American Bar Associations; The State Bar of California. *PRACTICE AREAS:* Estate Planning; Probate; Real Property Law.

**PETER J. CONIGLIO,** born Monterey, California, May 6, 1929; admitted to bar, 1956, California. *Education:* University of Santa Clara (B.S., 1951); University of San Francisco (LL.B., 1956). Member, City Council, Monterey, 1971-1973. Mayor, City of Monterey, 1973-1977. *Member:* Monterey County Bar Association (Secretary, 1959); The State Bar of California. *PRACTICE AREAS:* Estate Planning; Family Law; Business Litigation.

**GERALD B. DALTON,** born San Francisco, California, October 16, 1931; admitted to bar, 1960, California. *Education:* University of San Francisco (B.S., 1953; LL.B., 1959). Phi Alpha Delta. *Member:* Monterey County and American Bar Associations; The State Bar of California (Chairman, Committee on Continuing Legal Education of the Bar, 1974-1975; Member, Board of Legal Specialization, 1974-1976). *PRACTICE AREAS:* Real Property Law; Corporations; Partnerships; Estate Planning.

**MICHAEL A. ALBOV,** born Carmel, California, April 11, 1949; admitted to bar, 1976, California. *Education:* University of California at Santa Cruz (B.A., 1972); University of California at Davis (J.D., 1976). *Member:* Monterey County and American Bar Associations; The State Bar of California. *PRACTICE AREAS:* Real Property Law; Environmental Law; Maritime Law; Administrative Law.

**PETER R. WILLIAMS,** born Fort Campbell, Kentucky, May 8, 1949; admitted to bar, 1985, California. *Education:* Monterey College of Law (J.D., 1985). Licensed Real Estate Broker; Board President, Monterey County Legal Services Corporation. *Member:* Monterey County Bar Association; The State Bar of California. *PRACTICE AREAS:* Real Property Law; Construction Law; Negligence Litigation.

**ANNA M. FRESKA,** born Warsaw, Poland, February 10, 1961; admitted to bar, 1991, California. *Education:* Amherst College (B.A., 1983); Monterey Institute of International Studies (M.A., 1987); University of Tübingen, Germany (1980-1981); Santa Clara School of Law (J.D., 1990). *Member:* The State Bar of California. *LANGUAGES:* Polish, English and German.

REPRESENTATIVE CLIENTS: CTB-McMillan/McGraw-Hill; California American Water Co., Monterey; Monterey Peninsula TV Cable; Western Communications; Granite Construction Co., Inc.; Tynan Lumber Co., Inc.; M. J. Murphy Lumber Co., Inc.; Fisherman's Wharf Property Owners Association.
REFERENCES: Bank of America National Trust & Savings Assn. (Monterey and Pacific Grove Offices); Wells Fargo Bank (Monterey Branch).

## ROBERT J. KOONTZ

**631 ABREGO STREET**
**MONTEREY, CALIFORNIA 93940**
Telephone: 408-644-9232
Fax: 408-644-9405

*Estate Planning, Probate, Conservatorship Law, Business, Real Property and Civil Practice.*

**ROBERT J. KOONTZ,** born Omaha, Nebraska, August 23, 1947; admitted to bar, 1976, California; 1978, U.S. District Court, Northern District of California. *Education:* University of California at Berkeley (B.A., 1970); University of Oregon (M.B.A., 1972); Hastings College of Law, University of California (J.D., 1976). Deputy District Attorney, Monterey County, 1977-1978. *Member:* Monterey County and American Bar Associations; The State Bar of California. [1st Lt., USAF, 1972-1973]

## LARIVIERE, GRUBMAN & PAYNE

*Established in 1993*

**4 JUSTIN COURT**
**P.O. BOX 3140**
**MONTEREY, CALIFORNIA 93942**
Telephone: 408-649-8800
Facsimile: 408-649-8835

*San Jose, California Office:* 160 West Santa Clara Street, Suite 1400.

*(This Listing Continued)*

CALIFORNIA—MONTEREY

## LARIVIERE, GRUBMAN & PAYNE, Monterey—Continued

Patent, Trademark, Trade Secrets, Trade Dress, Copyright and Multi-National High Technology Law. Commercial, Industrial, Agricultural and Aerospace/defense Contracts and Licensing and related Litigation. Due Diligence Studies, Validity and Patentability Searches and Opinions.

FIRM PROFILE: *The firm is technology based. It offers counseling and litigation services in obtaining, enforcing and integrating all forms of protection for most technologies, including electrical, electro-mechanical, mechanical, electronic, communications and computer systems, and in prudent, practical, business-oriented solutions to problems encouraged by clients of all sizes which design, manufacture or market products or services in most technology-oriented businesses.*

### MEMBERS OF FIRM

**F. DAVID LARIVIERE,** born Los Angeles, California, August 28, 1939; admitted to bar, 1973, California and U.S. District Court, Northern and Central Districts of California; 1978, U.S. Supreme Court; 1983, U.S. Court of Appeals, Federal Circuit; registered to practice before U.S. and Canadian Patent and Trademark Offices. *Education:* Stanford University (B.S.E.E., 1963); University of Santa Clara (J.D., 1972). Adjunct Professor, Intellectual Property Law, Monterey College of Law, 1987—. *Member:* Monterey County and Santa Clara County Bar Associations; State Bar of California (Vice Chair, Intellectual Property Section); Licensing Executives Society. *PRACTICE AREAS:* Patents, Trademarks and Copyrights; Contracts and Licensing; Business; Intellectual Property Interface; Litigation Support.

**ROBERT W. PAYNE,** born Springfield, Missouri, December 21, 1950; admitted to bar, 1976, California and Idaho. *Education:* Stanford University (B.A., 1972); University of California (J.D., 1975); University of London (LL.M. in International Law, 1978). Law Clerk, Hon. Allan G. Sheppard, Idaho Supreme Court, 1975-1977. Assistant Editor, New Matter Magazine. *Member:* Monterey County, Santa Clara County, San Mateo County and American (Member, Sections on: Intellectual Property; Litigation) Bar Associations; State Bar of California (Member, Intellectual Property Section). *PRACTICE AREAS:* Intellectual Property; Business Litigation; Licensing.

### OF COUNSEL

**RONALD E. GRUBMAN,** born Philadelphia, Pennsylvania, July 9, 1943; admitted to bar, 1974, California, U.S. District Court, Northern District of California, U.S. Court of Appeals, Ninth and Federal Circuits and U.S. Supreme Court; registered to practice before the U.S. Patent and Trademark Office. *Education:* Drexel University (B.S., in Physics); University of California at San Diego (M.S. and Ph.D., in Physics); Stanford University Law School (J.D., 1974). *PRACTICE AREAS:* Business; Intellectual Property Interface; Licensing; Due Diligence.

### ASSOCIATES

**P. FRANCOIS DE VILLIERS,** born Pretoria, South Africa, March 7, 1967; admitted to bar, 1995, Supreme Court of South Africa; 1996, California. *Education:* University of the Witwatersrand (B.S.M.E., 1988); University of South Africa (J.D. equivalent, 1993). Articles of Clerkship, South Africa, 1993. *Member:* Monterey County Bar Association; State Bar of California (Member, Intellectual Property Section); Law Society of Transvaal. *LANGUAGES:* Afrikaans. *PRACTICE AREAS:* Patent, International and Domestic; Trademarks; Copyrights.

**VICTOR FLORES,** born Artesia, New Mexico, March 6, 1943; admitted to bar, 1982, Arizona and U.S. District Court, District of Arizona; registered to practice before U.S. Patent and Trademark Office (Not admitted in California). *Education:* New Mexico State University (B.S.E.E., 1971); University of Denver (J.D., 1979). *Member:* State Bar of Arizona; American Intellectual Property Association (Member, Intellectual Property Section). *LANGUAGES:* Spanish. *PRACTICE AREAS:* Patents; Trademarks; Copyrights; Licensing.

### LEGAL SUPPORT PERSONNEL

### PATENT AGENTS

**NOEL BAILEY HAMMOND,** born Indianapolis, Indiana, February 12, 1928. registered to practice before U.S. and Canadian Patent and Trademark Offices. *Education:* U.S. Armed Forces Institute (1947); The George Washington University Extension School (1950-1954); Capital Radio Engineering Institute, Washington, D.C. (1948-1950); University of California at Los Angeles (1955). *Member:* Institute of Radio Engineers; Los Angeles, Orange County and San Diego Patent Law Associations. [U.S. Army, 1946-

*(This Listing Continued)*

CAA1368B

MARTINDALE-HUBBELL LAW DIRECTORY 1997

1948, T4]. *LANGUAGES:* Spanish. *PRACTICE AREAS:* Patent preparation and prosecution in the fields of: Microwave; Semiconductor; MASER and LASER Technologies; Communication Systems/Satellites; Computer Hardware/Software; Electronic/Electrical; Mechanical/Electromechanical Technologies; Patent Litigation Support.

**HOWARD E. MORTON,** born Santa Monica, California, August 20, 1946. registered to practice before U.S. Patent and Trademark Office. *Education:* Humboldt State University (B.S., Fisheries, 1976); Naval Postgraduate School (M.S., Information Systems, 1984). [U.S. Navy, 1965-1969; 1976-1992, LCDR (Ret.)]. *PRACTICE AREAS:* Patent preparation and prosecution in the fields of: Computer/Hardware/Software; Medical and Biological Technologies; Food Processing, Packaging and Storage Technologies; Mechanical/Electromechanical Technologies; Weapons Systems; Patent Litigation Support.

REPRESENTATIVE CLIENTS: Asymetrix Corp.; Fresh Valley Technology/Albert Fisher; PF Magic, Inc.; Seagate Technology; Sierra On-line; Exatron Automatic Test Equipment; Perkin-Elmer; Smith & Hook; Sierra Instruments; Advanced Micro Devices.

---

## BRUCE LINDSEY
### MONTEREY, CALIFORNIA
(See Salinas)

*Bankruptcy, Commercial and Insolvency Law.*

---

## ANTHONY LOMBARDO & ASSOCIATES
### MONTEREY, CALIFORNIA
(See Salinas)

*Real Estate Acquisitions and Development, Civil Trial and Litigation.*

---

## JAY B. LONG
*500 CAMINO EL ESTERO, SUITE 200*
**MONTEREY, CALIFORNIA 93940**
Telephone: 408-649-3877; Fax: 408-649-4705
Email: jayblong@ix.netcom.com

*Long Beach, California Office:* Greater Los Angeles World Trade Center, One World Trade Center, Suite 800, 90831-0800. Telephone: 310-983-8146. Fax: 310-983-8199.

Environmental and Energy Law, including Regulatory and Legislative Matters; Insurance Coverage Law; Construction and Design Law; Sports, Sponsorship and Event Law; Advertising, Marketing and Distribution Law; Select Business, Real Estate, other Civil Litigation and Trial Practice in all State and Federal Courts; Alternate Dispute Resolution.

(For complete Biographical Data on all Personnel, see Professional Biographies at Long Beach)

---

## LOW, BALL & LYNCH
*A PROFESSIONAL CORPORATION*
*10 RAGSDALE DRIVE, SUITE 175*
**MONTEREY, CALIFORNIA 93940**
Telephone: 408-655-8822
Fax: 408-655-8881

*Redwood City, California Office:* 10 Twin Dolphin Drive, Suite B-500, 94065. Telephone: 415-591-8822. Fax: 415-591-8884.
*San Francisco, California Office:* 601 California Street, Suite 2100, 94108. Telephone: 415-981-6630.

General Civil and Trial Practice, Insurance, Environmental Law, Land Use, Real Estate, Corporate, Professional Malpractice, Products Liability, Securities, Commercial Litigation and Appellate Practice.

**SARAH J. BOUHABEN,** born Oakland, California, January 21, 1962; admitted to bar, 1990, California, U.S. District Court, Northern District of California and U.S. Court of Appeals, Ninth Circuit. *Education:* Golden

*(This Listing Continued)*

# PROFESSIONAL BIOGRAPHIES

## CALIFORNIA—MONTEREY

Gate University (B.A., cum laude, 1983); Santa Clara University (J.D., 1990). *Member:* Monterey County and Santa Clara County Bar Associations; State Bar of California; Women Lawyers Association.

REPRESENTATIVE CLIENTS: Allianz Insurance Co.; American International Group; Amica Mutual Insurance Co.; Atlantic Cos.; Balboa Insurance Co.; Bay Area Rapid Transit District (BARTD); California State Automobile Assn.; Carl Warren & Co.; Certain Underwriters at Lloyds; Crum & Forster; Flagstar Corp.; GAB Business Services; Gallagher-Basset Insurance Co.; Gay & Taylor, Inc.; Hartford Insurance Co.; Highlands Insurance Co.; Industrial Indemnity; McGraw Insurance Services; National Union Insurance Cos.; Northbrook Insurance Co.; Northland Insurance Co.; Ohio Casualty Insurance Co.; Pacific Coast Building Products; Scottsdale Insurance Co.; Star Insurance Co.; USX Corp.; Western Heritage Insurance Co.; Zimmer Manufacturing Co.

## *LOZANO SMITH*
## *SMITH WOLIVER & BEHRENS*

*A PROFESSIONAL CORPORATION*

Established in 1988

BUILDING A, SUITE 200
ONE HARRIS COURT
**MONTEREY, CALIFORNIA 93940**
Telephone: 408-646-1501
Fax: 408-646-1801

*Fresno, California Office:* 2444 Main Street, Suite 260. Telephone: 209-445-1352. Fax: 209-233-5013.

*San Rafael, California Office:* 1010 B Street, Suite 200. Telephone: 415-459-3008; 800-648-3435. Fax: 415-456-3826.

*San Luis Obispo, California Office:* 987 Osos Street. Telephone: 805-549-9541. Fax: 805-549-0740.

Education, Labor and Employment, Civil Rights and Disability, Local Government, Land Use, Eminent Domain, Public Finance, Business and Insurance Litigation.

FIRM PROFILE: *Lozano Smith Smith Woliver & Behrens is a law firm specializing in labor, public agency, private employment and business law. The firm began the practice of law on January 1, 1988, and has offices in Fresno, San Rafael, Monterey ans San Luis Obispo.*

*Lozano Smith Smith Woliver & Behrens emphasizes representation of public agencies in all areas, private sector employment and business law and litigation. The firm's attorneys have special expertise in representing school districts, cities and other public agencies and business.*

**LOUIS T. LOZANO,** born Fresno, California, September 18, 1948; admitted to bar, 1975, California; 1976, U.S. District Court, Northern and Eastern Districts of California and U.S. Court of Appeals, Ninth Circuit. *Education:* University of California at Berkeley (B.A., 1970); Boalt Hall School of Law, University of California (J.D., 1975). Law Clerk, Contra Costa County Superior Court. Author: "Grossmont: A Victory for School Districts," California School Boards, Vol. 44, No., Fall 1985. Senior Deputy County Counsel for Schools, Fresno County, 1975-1980. President, Schools Legal Defense Association, 1987-1988, 1990-1991, 1992-1993. *Member:* Fresno County and Monterey County Bar Associations; State Bar of California. (Resident). *LANGUAGES:* French and Armenian. *REPORTED CASES:* Trend v. Central Unified School Dist (1990) 220 Cal. App. 3d 102; N. State v. Pittsburg Unified School Dist. (1990) 220 Cal. App. 3d 1418; San Francisco Unified S.D. v. Superior Court (1981) 116 Cal. App. 3d 231. *PRACTICE AREAS:* Public Facilities Finance; Labor Relations; Employment; Education Law. *Email:* lou@lozanom.mhs.compuserve.com

**ELLEN M. JAHN,** born Chicago, Illinois, February 26, 1953; admitted to bar, 1988, California; 1989, U.S. District Court, Eastern District of California. *Education:* Illinois State University; Indiana University (B.S., with distinction, 1977); San Joaquin College of Law (J.D., with high honors, 1988). Fourth Place, Roger Traynor State Moot Court Tournament. Adjunct Professor, Contracts, Legal Research and Writing, San Joaquin College of Law, 1988-1994. Member, San Joaquin College of Law Faculty Committee, 1993-1994. *Member:* Fresno County Bar Association; State Bar of California; Fresno County Women Lawyers. (Resident). *REPORTED CASES:* Belanger v. Madera, Unified School District 963 F. 2d 248 (9th Cir, 1992). *PRACTICE AREAS:* Personnel; Employment Discrimination; Collective Bargaining; Federal Litigation. *Email:* emj@lozanom.mhs.compuserve.com

*(This Listing Continued)*

**HAROLD M. FREIMAN,** born Brooklyn, New York, August 19, 1964; admitted to bar, 1990, California and U.S. District Court, Northern District of California; 1991, U.S. Court of Appeals, Ninth Circuit; 1993, U.S. District Court, Eastern District of California. *Education:* University of California at Berkeley (A.B., 1987); Columbia University (J.D., 1990). Harlan Fiske Stone Scholar. Member, Columbia Human Rights Law Review, 1988-1990. Law Clerk to Justice Lloyd Doggett, Texas Supreme Court, 1991-1992. Author: "Some Get a Little and Some Get None: When is Process Due Through Fair Hearings Under P.L. 96-272," 20 Columbia Human Rights Law Review 343 (1989). Co-Author: "Standards for Interoperability and the Copyright Protection of Computer Programs", in 365 Intellectual Property/Antitrust 1993, 891 (P.L.I. 1993). *Member:* State Bar of California; American Bar Association. (Resident). *PRACTICE AREAS:* Litigation; Education Law. *Email:* harold@lozanom.mhs.compuserve.com

**CHRISTOPHER D. KEELER,** born La Jolla, California, November 10, 1966; admitted to bar, 1994, California. *Education:* Stanford University (B.A., 1991); Brigham Young University (J.D., cum laude, 1994). Member, Law Review, 1993-1994. Author: Casenote BYU Education and Law Journal, Spring, 1994. *Member:* American Bar Association; The State Bar of California. (Resident). *LANGUAGES:* Spanish. *PRACTICE AREAS:* Education Law; Construction Law; Public Entity Law. *Email:* chris@lozanom.mhs.compuserve.com

**KAREN SEGAR SALTY,** born Detroit, Michigan, May 5, 1961; admitted to bar, 1994, California. *Education:* Tulane University of Louisiana (B.A., 1983); University of San Francisco (J.D., 1993). (Resident). *LANGUAGES:* French. *Email:* karen@lozanom.mhs.compuserve.com

*OF COUNSEL*

**PAUL R. DELAY,** born Beresford, South Dakota, November 12, 1919; admitted to bar, 1949, District of Columbia; 1965, California. *Education:* University of Notre Dame (A.B., 1941); Georgetown University (LL.B., 1949). *Member:* State Bar of California (Panelist); District of Columbia Bar. (Resident). *REPORTED CASES:* Monterey County Deputy Sheriff's Association v. County of Monterey (1979) 23 Cal. 3d 296; CSEA v. King City Unified School District (1981) 116 Cal. App. 3d 695; MPUSD v. Certificated Employees Council (1974) 42 Cal. App. 3d 328; Sheehan v. Eldridge (1970) 5 Cal. App. 3d 77. *PRACTICE AREAS:* Government Law; Litigation. *Email:* paul@lozanom.mhs.compuserve.com

**JUDD L. JORDAN,** born Glendale, California, December 27, 1950; admitted to bar, 1976, California; 1977, U.S. District Court, Central and Northern Districts of California; 1978, U.S. Court of Appeals, Ninth Circuit; 1982, U.S. Supreme Court; 1991, U.S. District Court, Eastern District of California. *Education:* University of California, Berkeley (B.A., 1973); University of California, Los Angeles (J.D., 1976). Comment Editor, UCLA Law Review, 1975-1976. *Member:* American Bar Association; The State Bar of California; American Institute of Mining, Metallurgical and Petroleum Engineers (Chairman, Southern California Mining Section, 1990-1991). (Resident). *PRACTICE AREAS:* Litigation. *Email:* judd@lozanom.mhs.compuserve.com

(For complete biographical data on all personnel see Professional Biographies at Fresno, California)

## *TERRY M. MALLERY*

*215 WEST FRANKLIN STREET, FIFTH FLOOR*
**MONTEREY, CALIFORNIA 93940**
Telephone: 408-655-2020
Fax: 408-655-2030
Email: tmallery@mbay.net

*Business and Real Estate Transactions, including Corporations, Partnerships and Leases, Business and Real Estate Sales and Exchanges, Tax Collection Defense, Mediation of Business Disputes.*

**TERRY M. MALLERY,** born Pasadena, California, September 18, 1947; admitted to bar, 1979, California and U.S. District Court, Northern District of California; 1980, U.S. Tax Court. *Education:* California State University at Chico (B.S., Act., 1976); McGeorge School of Law (J.D., 1979). Member, National Moot Court Team, 2nd in nation, 1978. Instructor, Paralegal Certification Program, 1989-1990. Real Estate Broker, California, 1981, 1990. *Member:* Monterey County Bar Association; State Bar of California (Member, Business and Real Property Sections). [1st Lt., U.S.A.R., 1967-1970]

CAA1369B

## TERRANCE K. McCLEEREY

457 WEBSTER STREET
**MONTEREY, CALIFORNIA 93940**
Telephone: 408-373-0933
Fax: 408-373-3172

*Criminal Law, Military Criminal Law, D.U.I./D.W.I. Defense, Personal Injury and Family Law.*

**TERRANCE K. MCCLEEREY,** born Ansley, Nebraska, September 22, 1937; admitted to bar, 1963, Iowa; 1964, U.S. Court of Military Appeals; 1967, U.S. Supreme Court; 1970, California, U.S. District Court, Northern District of California and U.S. Court of Appeals, Ninth Circuit. *Education:* Iowa State University (B.S., 1960); State University of Iowa (J.D., with distinction, 1963). Phi Delta Phi. *Member:* Monterey County Bar Association; State Bar of California; California Attorneys for Criminal Justice; California Public Defenders Association; Association of United States Army. *PRACTICE AREAS:* Criminal Law; Military Criminal Law; Personal Injury; Family Law.

## C. MICHEAL McCLURE

631 ABREGO STREET
P.O. BOX 3315
**MONTEREY, CALIFORNIA 93942-3315**
Telephone: 408-649-6161
Fax: 408-649-1384
Email: CMM3315@AOL.COM

*General Civil Trial Practice. Real Property, Business, Family and Personal Injury Law.*

**C. MICHEAL MCCLURE,** born New Brighton, Pennsylvania, July 7, 1943; admitted to bar, 1969, California; 1976, U.S. District Court, Northern District of California and U.S. Court of Appeals, Ninth Circuit. *Education:* Chaffey College and California State College at Los Angeles (B.A., 1965); Loyola University of Los Angeles (J.D., 1968). Phi Delta Phi. Member, Monterey County Airport Land Use Planning Commission, 1978-1988. *Member:* Monterey County (President-Elect, 1978; President, 1979) and American Bar Associations; State Bar of California; Consumer Attorneys of California (President, Monterey County Chapter, 1977-1982). *LANGUAGES:* Spanish.

REPRESENTATIVE CLIENTS: Carmel Marina Corp.; Portable Site Services Corp.; Pacific Valley Disposal Corp.; Neal Road Lanfill Corp.; Jolon Road Landfill Corp.; Bayfire Sprinklers, Inc.; Monterey Peninsula Engineering, Inc. REFERENCE: First National Bank of Monterey County.

## JAMES H. NEWHOUSE

631 ABREGO STREET
**MONTEREY, CALIFORNIA 93940**
Telephone: 408-655-2000
FAX: 408-649-1384

*Criminal Law and Appeals.*

**JAMES H. NEWHOUSE,** born New York, N.Y., November 22, 1938; admitted to bar, 1966, California. *Education:* University of California at Santa Barbara (B.A., with honors, 1961); Boalt Hall School of Law, University of California (J.D., 1965). Order of the Coif. Member, California Law Review, 1964-1965. Author: "Search and Seizure of Automobiles," 51 California Law Review 907, 1963; "Juvenile Due Process in the German Republic, England & California," 4 California Western Law Review 35, 1968. *Member:* State Bar of California; California Attorneys for Criminal Justice (Member: Board of Governors, 1973—; Education Committee, 1977—; Chairman, Bail Reform Committee, 1973-1974). (Certified Specialist, Criminal Law, The State Bar of California Board of Legal Specialization).

## NOLAND, HAMERLY, ETIENNE & HOSS

A PROFESSIONAL CORPORATION
HERITAGE HARBOR
99 PACIFIC STREET
BUILDING 200, SUITE C
**MONTEREY, CALIFORNIA 93940**
Telephone: 408-373-4427
Fax: 408-373-4797

Salinas, California Office: Civic Center Building, 333 Salinas Street. Telephones: 408-424-1414; 372-7525. Fax: 408-424-1975.
King City, California Office: 104 South Vanderhurst, Suite D, 93930. Telephone: 408-386-1080. Fax: 408-386-1083.

*Business and Commercial Litigation. Construction Litigation. General Business, Corporation, Probate, Estate Planning, Real Property, Land Use, Administrative Law, Tax Law and Family Law.*

(For Personnel and Biographical Data, see Professional Biographies, Salinas, California)

## ONTIVEROS & KREEFT

**MONTEREY, CALIFORNIA**
(See Salinas)

*General Civil and Appellate Practice in State and Federal Courts, Public Agency Law, Employment Law, Insurance Defense with Emphasis on Personal Injury, Automobile, Premises Liability, Products Liability and Construction Litigation, Insurance Coverage.*

## JOSEPH R. PANETTA

THE PANETTA BUILDING
MADISON AT PACIFIC
P.O. BOX 1709
**MONTEREY, CALIFORNIA 93940**
Telephone: 408-646-0916

*Civil and Criminal Trial Practice. Real Property, Probate, Business, Construction, Family and Personal Injury Law. State and Federal Taxation.*

**JOSEPH R. PANETTA,** born Sheridan, Wyoming, August 2, 1933; admitted to bar, 1959, California. *Education:* University of Santa Clara (B.S., magna cum laude, 1955; J.D., 1958). Alpha Sigma Nu. Deputy District Attorney, Monterey County, 1962-1969. Assistant District Attorney, 1969-1971. *Member:* Monterey County Bar Association (Member, Executive Committee, 1975, 1978; Treasurer, 1978); State Bar of California; California Trial Lawyers Association. *LANGUAGES:* Italian.

ASSOCIATES

**DENNIS E. POWELL,** born Portland, Oregon, July 10, 1946; admitted to bar, 1976, California. *Education:* Lewis & Clark College (B.A., 1972; J.D., 1975). *Member:* Monterey County Bar Association; State Bar of California.

## A. DAVID PARNIE

SUITE I, 2100 GARDEN ROAD
**MONTEREY, CALIFORNIA 93940**
Telephone: 408-649-4802
Fax: 408-649-1306

*General Litigation, Family and Business Law.*

**A. DAVID PARNIE,** born New York, N.Y., September 23, 1939; admitted to bar, 1965, California. *Education:* Bowdoin College (A.B., 1961); Stanford University (LL.B., 1964). Order of the Coif. Member, 1963-1964 and Chairman, 1964, Board of Revisors, Stanford Law Review. *Member:* Monterey County Bar Association (President, 1977); The State Bar of California. [Lieut., USNR, 1965-1968]. *PRACTICE AREAS:* General Litigation; Family; Business.

## DANIEL I. REITH

*457 WEBSTER STREET*
**MONTEREY, CALIFORNIA 93940-3220**
*Telephone: 408-372-6999*
*FAX: 408-373-3172*

*General Civil Practice, including Family Law, Personal Injury, Civil Litigation, Probate and Trust.*

**DANIEL I. REITH,** born Sacramento, California, February 28, 1939; admitted to bar, 1965, California. *Education:* Dartmouth College (A.B., cum laude, 1961); Boalt Hall School of Law, University of California (LL.B., 1964). Order of the Coif. Associate Editor, California Law Review, 1963-1964. Author: "Jurisdiction Over Parent Corporations," Corporate Practice Commentator, August, 1964; "Contractual Exculpation From Tort Liability in California," Personal Injury Annual, Matthew Bender and Company, 1964; "California Debt Collection Practice," California Continuing Education of the Bar, 1974 and 1976 Supplements. President, Legal Aid Society of Monterey County, 1974. *Member:* Monterey County Bar Association (President, 1975); State Bar of California (Bar Court Referee, 1973-1989; Fee Arbitration Panelist, 1984—); Association of California Family Law Specialists. (Certified Specialist, Family Law, The State Bar of California Board of Legal Specialization). *PRACTICE AREAS:* Family Law; Personal Injury; Civil Litigation.

## LAW OFFICES OF
## WILLIAM H. SOSKIN

*Established in 1978*

*SUITE F, 2100 GARDEN ROAD*
**MONTEREY, CALIFORNIA 93940**
*Telephone: 408-649-8006*

*Corporate, Business, Taxation, Real Estate, Estate Planning and Probate Law.*

**WILLIAM H. SOSKIN,** born New York, N.Y., September 23, 1942; admitted to bar, 1969, California and U.S. District Court, Northern District of California; 1976, U.S. Tax Court. *Education:* Antioch College (B.A., 1965); University of Chicago (J.D., 1968). Certified Public Accountant, California, 1976. Associate Professor, Accounting, Economics, University of the Pacific, 1968-1969. Professor, Economics, American College of Switzerland, 1969-1970. Lecturer, Estate Planning, Monterey College of Law, 1982-1983. Deputy Public Defender, Monterey County, 1972-1975. Associate, Kaplan, Livingston, Berkowitz & Selvin, Paris, France Office, 1970-1971. *Member:* Monterey County Bar Association; The State Bar of California; California Society of Certified Public Accountants.

## SPIERING, SWARTZ & KENNEDY

*Established in 1975*

*550 HARTNELL STREET*
**MONTEREY, CALIFORNIA 93940-2890**
*Telephone: 408-373-3235; 800-624-9911*
*Facsimile: 408-373-8211*

*General Civil Trial and Appellate Practice. Personal Injury, Real Property, Administrative Law, Banking Law and Employment Law.*

FIRM PROFILE: *The law firm of Spiering, Swartz & Kennedy was formed in 1975. Since that time, it has continually served local businesses and individuals throughout Monterey, Santa Cruz and San Benito Counties. The attorneys have an active trial practice. They specialize in business litigation, real estate litigation and personal injury, representing businesses, injured parties, and insurance companies.*

### MEMBERS OF FIRM

**JAMES F. SPIERING,** born San Francisco, California, April 17, 1948; admitted to bar, 1974, California. *Education:* University of Oregon (B.A., 1970); University of San Francisco (J.D., 1973). Instructor, Remedies, Monterey College of Law, 1980-1987. *Member:* Monterey County and Los Angeles County Bar Associations; State Bar of California; California Trial Lawyers Association (President, Monterey County Chapter, 1986-1987). *PRACTICE AREAS:* Personal Injury; Civil Litigation.

**ANDREW H. SWARTZ,** born Pittsburgh, Pennsylvania, August 29, 1948; admitted to bar, 1973, California. *Education:* University of Pittsburgh (B.A., 1970); University of Santa Clara (J.D., 1973). Comments Editor, Santa Clara Law Review, 1973-1973. Author: "An Employer's Right of *(This Listing Continued)*

Freedom of Speech During a Union Organizational Campaign," Santa Clara Law Review, Vol. 12, pg. 580, 1973. *Member:* Monterey County Bar Association; State Bar of California (Member, Standing Committee on Professional Responsibility and Conduct, 1979; Vice-Chairman, 1981-1982; Chairman, 1982-1983); California Trial Lawyers Association. *PRACTICE AREAS:* Civil Litigation; Banking Litigation; Personal Injury; Employment Law.

**MICHELE C. KENNEDY,** born Iowa City, Iowa, April 9, 1951; admitted to bar, 1982, California. *Education:* University of California at Berkeley (B.A., 1975); Monterey Institute of International Studies (M.A., 1981); Hastings College of the Law, University of California (J.D., 1981). Note Editor, Hastings International and Comparative Law Review, 1980-1981. Extern, Justice Poche, California Court of Appeal, 1980-1981. Instructor on Remedies, Monterey College of Law, 1986-1987. *Member:* Monterey County and Los Angeles County Bar Associations; State Bar of California; Monterey County Trial Lawyers Association. *LANGUAGES:* Spanish, German and Italian. *PRACTICE AREAS:* Personal Injury; Civil Litigation.

REPRESENTATIVE CLIENTS: First National Bank of Central California; Universal Underwriters; Castroville Cold Storage, Ltd.; Household Credit Services, Inc.; American Western Banker, Inc.; Butts Pontiac-Cadillac; Boulevard Communications d.b.a. Monterey Jaguar-Rolls Royce-Ferrari; Coast Counties Glass, Inc.
REFERENCE: First National Bank of Central California (Monterey Branch).

## THOMPSON & HUBBARD

*A LAW CORPORATION*

*Established in 1963*

*AGUAJITO BUILDING*
*400 CAMINO AGUAJITO*
**MONTEREY, CALIFORNIA 93940**
*Telephone: 408-372-7571*
*Fax: 408-372-1700*

*General Civil, Trial and Appellate Practice in State and Federal Courts. Corporation, General Business, Real Property, Land Use, Construction, Estate Planning, Probate, Conservatorships and Trusts, Personal Injury, Product Liability, Domestic, Administrative and Taxation Law.*

**RALPH W. THOMPSON,** born Cuyahoga Falls, Ohio, August 6, 1919; admitted to bar, 1948, California. *Education:* Colgate University (A.B., 1941); Stanford University (LL.B., 1948). Phi Delta Phi. *Member:* Monterey County Bar Association (President, 1951-1952). *PRACTICE AREAS:* Litigation; General Business; Real Property; Estate Planning; Probate.

**DONALD G. HUBBARD,** born Watsonville, California, December 12, 1934; admitted to bar, 1962, California. *Education:* San Jose State University (B.A., 1956); University of California at Berkeley, Boalt Hall (LL.B., 1961). Phi Delta Phi; Order of the Coif. Managing Editor, California Law Review, 1960-1961. *Member:* Monterey County Bar Association (President, 1967). *PRACTICE AREAS:* Real Property; Land Use; General Business; Administrative Law and Estate Planning.

**TIMOTHY J. WALSH,** born Springfield, Massachusetts, May 22, 1951; admitted to bar, 1984, California. *Education:* College of the Holy Cross (B.A., cum laude, 1973); University of Santa Clara (J.D., 1984). *Member:* Santa Cruz County and Monterey County Bar Associations; California Trial Lawyers Association. *PRACTICE AREAS:* Litigation; Family Law.

**ALEXANDER F. HUBBARD,** born Carmel, California, November 10, 1965; admitted to bar, 1991, California. *Education:* University of California at Irvine (B.A., cum laude, 1987); Hastings College of Law, University of California (J.D., 1991). *Member:* Monterey County Bar Association. *PRACTICE AREAS:* Litigation; Real Property; General Business; Estate Planning; Probate.

REPRESENTATIVE CLIENTS: The Cannery Row Co.; Armstrong Ranch; Foursome Development Co.; John Gardiner's Tennis Ranch; Surfside Enterprises Inc.; Sea Products Co.; Fremont Bank; The Sardine Factory; Carmel Board of Realtors; U.S. Freezer Co.; Consolidated Factors; Kings Plaza Shopping Center; Gill Properties.
REFERENCES: Bank of America National Trust & Savings Assn.; First National Bank of The Central Coast; Wells Fargo Bank.

## THE THOMPSON LAW FIRM
*580 CALLE PRINCIPAL, FIRST FLOOR*
**MONTEREY, CALIFORNIA 93940-2818**
Telephone: 408-646-1224
Fax: 408-646-1225

*General Civil and Trial Practice, Arbitration and Mediation Services.*

FIRM PROFILE: The Thompson Law Office is a high tech law boutique in the historic Miller Adobe (circa 1874). Mr. Thompson co-founded the original firm, Thomas, Panetta & Thompson in 1971. Donald A. Thomas was appointed Municipal Court Judge in 1972 and former Presidential Chief of Staff Leon E. Panetta was a partner until his election to Congress in 1976. Mr. Thompson was the managing partner through dissolution of Murphy, Thompson & Gunter LLP in 1996. Mr. Thompson is committed to professional excellence, the highest ethical standards, dedication to his clients and community service.

**RALPH W. THOMPSON, III,** born Glendale, California, April 22, 1942; admitted to bar, 1968, California. *Education:* Loma Linda University (B.A., 1964); California Western School of Law (J.D., 1967). Adjunct Professor, Political Science and Constitutional Law, Golden Gate University, Monterey, 1971-1987. Deputy District Attorney, Monterey County, 1968-1971. Member, Panel of Arbitrators, American Arbitration Association. President, Legal Services for Seniors, 1993-1995. *Member:* Monterey County Bar Association (President, 1995); State Bar of California (Member, Litigation Section; Chairman, Jury Instructions Subsection, 1984-1986); Consumer Attorneys of California (Member, Board of Governors, 1984-1990; Recognized Experience as a Trial Lawyer and in the fields of General Personal Injury, Products Liability, Professional Negligence, Insurance Bad Faith and Public Entity Liability); The Association of Trial Lawyers of America; Monterey County Trial Lawyers Association (President, 1984-1985). *PRACTICE AREAS:* Business; Commercial Litigation; Personal Injury; Wrongful Death; Sexual Harassment; Discrimination; Arbitration and Mediation Services.

## GEORGE R. WALKER
*5TH FLOOR, PROFESSIONAL BUILDING*
*215 WEST FRANKLIN STREET*
*P.O. BOX LAW*
**MONTEREY, CALIFORNIA 93942**
Telephone: 408-649-1100
Fax: 408-649-6805

*Civil Practice. Estate Planning, Probate, Trust and Real Property Law.*

**GEORGE R. WALKER,** born Columbus, Ohio, April 9, 1928; admitted to bar, 1952, Ohio, 1955, California, U.S. District Court, Northern District of California and U.S. Court of Appeals, Ninth Circuit. *Education:* The Ohio State University (B.S., 1950; J.D., cum laude, 1952). Phi Delta Phi; Order of the Coif. Member, Editorial Staff, The Ohio State University Law Journal, 1950-1951. Member, State Bar Committee on Continuing Education of The Bar, 1962-1968. *Member:* Monterey County (President, 1958-1959) and American Bar Associations; The State Bar of California. [1st Lieut., J.A.G.C., 1952-1954]. *PRACTICE AREAS:* Estate Planning; Probate; Trusts; Real Property Law.

### ASSOCIATES

**UTE M. ISBILL,** born Bayreuth, Germany, July 22, 1959; admitted to bar, 1993, California. *Education:* Hartnell College; Monterey Peninsula College; Monterey College of Law (J.D., 1992). Recipient, West Publishing Company Award for Outstanding Scholarship, Monterey College of Law, 1989-1990, 1990-1991 and 1991-1992. Certified Senior Escrow Officer, California, 1989-1992. Member, California Escrow Association, 1980-1992. *Member:* Monterey County Bar Association; State Bar of California. *PRACTICE AREAS:* Estate Planning; Probate; Trusts; Real Property Law.

**KATHLEEN LLEWELLYN,** born Alameda, California, July 8, 1949; admitted to bar, 1992, California, U.S. District Court, Northern District of California and U.S. Court of Appeals, Ninth Circuit. *Education:* St. Mary's College of California (B.A. in Management, 1983); Monterey College of Law (J.D., 1992). Director: American Red Cross, Monterey Chapter, 1992-1994; Central Coast Light Keepers Association, 1992—. *Member:* Monterey County and American Bar Associations; State Bar of California. *PRACTICE AREAS:* Estate Planning; Probate; Trusts; Real Property Law.

*(This Listing Continued)*

REPRESENTATIVE CLIENTS: The Carmel Foundation, Carmel, California; A.F. Victor Foundation, Carmel, California; Robert Louis Stevenson School, Pebble Beach, California; The Mildred Hitchcock Huff Charitable Trust; C & E Farms, Inc.
REFERENCES: Wells Fargo Bank, Monterey and Carmel, California; Monterey County Bank.

## LAW OFFICES OF
## CHARLES G. WARNER
*2340 GARDEN ROAD, SUITE 208*
**MONTEREY, CALIFORNIA 93940**
Telephone: 408-375-0203
Facsimile: 408-375-4159

*Civil Litigation.*

**CHARLES G. WARNER,** born San Diego, California, December 27, 1941; admitted to bar, 1966, California; 1975, U.S. Supreme Court. *Education:* Stanford University (A.B., 1963); Boalt Hall School of Law, University of California (LL.B., 1966). Faculty: Hastings College of Trial and Appellate Advocacy, 1982; U.S. District Court, Federal Practice Program, 1987—. Faculty Member, Monterey College of Law, 1993—. *Member:* Monterey County (President, 1987) and American Bar Associations; The State Bar of California; The Association of Trial Lawyers of America; California Trial Lawyers Association (Member, Board of Governors, 1978, 1979); American Board of Trial Advocates. Certified as a Civil Trial Advocate by the National Board of Trial Advocacy.

## LAW OFFICES OF
## ROBERT R. WELLINGTON
*857 CASS STREET, SUITE D*
**MONTEREY, CALIFORNIA 93940**
Telephone: 408-373-8733
Facsimile: 408-373-7106
Email: robwlaw@aol.com

*Municipal and Administrative Law, Public Employment and Personnel, General Civil, Trial and Appellate Practice. Real Property, Condemnation, Land Use and Construction Law.*

**ROBERT R. WELLINGTON,** born Crawford, Nebraska, December 28, 1940; admitted to bar, 1966, California. *Education:* Stanford University (B.A., 1963); Hastings College of Law, University of California (LL.B., 1966). Phi Alpha Delta. Associate Editor, Hastings Law Journal, 1965-1966. Attorney: Monterey Regional Water Pollution Control Agency, 1972—; Monterey Regional Waste Management District, 1973—; Monterey Community Human Services Project-Joint Powers Agency, 1975—; Carmel Area Wastewater District, 1984—; Pebble Beach Community Services District, 1988—. Diablo Canyon Independent Safety Committee, 1990—. City Attorney: Del Rey Oaks, California, 1974—; City of Marina, California, 1975—. *Member:* Monterey County Bar Association; State Bar of California.

### ASSOCIATES

**KENNETH D. BUCHERT,** born Cincinnati, Ohio, August 18, 1937; admitted to bar, 1987, California. *Education:* University of Cincinnati (B.S., 1960); Duquesne University (M.Ed., 1970); Monterey College of Law (J.D., 1987). Assistant City Attorney: Del Rey Oaks, 1987—; Marina, 1987—. *Member:* Monterey County and American Bar Associations; State Bar of California. [Lt. Col., U.S. Army, 1960-1982]. *PRACTICE AREAS:* Municipal and Administrative Law; Public Employment and Personnel Law.

**ROBERT W. RATHIE,** born Oakland, California, July 6, 1950; admitted to bar, 1994, California. *Education:* Chico State University (B.A., 1972); Monterey College of Law (J.D., 1993). *Member:* Monterey County and American Bar Associations; State Bar of California. *PRACTICE AREAS:* Municipal Law; Administrative Law; Personnel Policies; Real Property.

REFERENCE: First National Bank, Monterey Main Branch.

## WIEBEN & WIEBEN

444 PEARL STREET, SUITE C
**MONTEREY, CALIFORNIA 93940**
Telephone: 408-375-0577
Fax: 408-375-0580

*A General Civil Trial Practice, Specializing in Complex Family Law Litigation and Mediation; Personal Injury, Medical Malpractice, Municipal and Employment Law.*

### MEMBERS OF FIRM

**JOHN S. WIEBEN,** born Boulder, Colorado, February 28, 1947; admitted to bar, 1973, California. *Education:* University of California at Davis (A.B., 1970); University of California School of Law at Davis (J.D., 1973). Phi Beta Kappa. Adjunct Professor: Lone Mountain College, 1975; Monterey College of Law, 1985-1987. Member, Board of Directors, Legal Aid Society of San Mateo County, 1976-1978. *Member:* Monterey County Bar Association (Chairman, Family Law Committee, 1981-1982); State Bar of California. (Certified Specialist, Family Law, The State Bar of California Board of Legal Specialization). **PRACTICE AREAS:** Family Law.

**PAMELA SHEA WIEBEN,** born Concord, New Hampshire, August 14, 1948; admitted to bar, 1974, Michigan; 1993, California. *Education:* Smith College (B.A., cum laude, 1970); University of Michigan (J.D., 1973). Instructor, I.C.L.E. "Advocacy Workshop" Programs, 1983-1989. City Attorney, City of Birmingham, Michigan, 1988-1993. *Member:* Monterey County Bar Association; State Bar of Michigan; State Bar of California; International Association of Defense Counsel. **PRACTICE AREAS:** Personal Injury Law; Civil Litigation; Employment Law.

## ZERBE, BUCK & LEWIS

PROFESSIONAL LAW CORPORATION
400 CAMINO EL ESTERO
**MONTEREY, CALIFORNIA 93940**
Telephone: 408-646-1733
Fax: 408-646-8484

*Business, Real Property, Estate Planning, Taxation, Family, Civil Litigation, Personal Injury, Partnership, Corporation, Probate, Trademark and Copyright Law.*

**GWENDOLEN S. BUCK,** born New York, N.Y., December 18, 1942; admitted to bar, 1976, California. *Member:* Monterey County Bar Association (President-Elect, 1996 and President, 1997); State Bar of California. **PRACTICE AREAS:** Family Law; Civil Litigation; Personal Injury Law; Intellectual Property Law; Trademark Law and Copyright Law.

**ROSE-EVE K. LEWIS,** born New York, N.Y., February 26, 1949; admitted to bar, 1980, California. *Education:* Chatham College (B.A., 1970); Institut des Hautes Etudes Internationales, Geneva, Switzerland; Columbia University (M.I.A., 1972); Institute of Comparative Law, Paris, France; Hastings College of the Law, University of California (J.D., 1980). Intern, United States Senate, Office of Senator Jacob K. Javits, 1966-1967. *Member:* Monterey County and American Bar Associations; State Bar of California. **LANGUAGES:** French. **PRACTICE AREAS:** Real Estate Law; Business Law; Partnership Law; Corporation Law.

**THOMAS E. MALLETT,** born Stockton, California, December 6, 1958; admitted to bar, 1984, California; 1985, U.S. Tax Court. *Education:* University of California at Davis (B.S., with high honors, 1981; J.D., 1984). Order of the Coif. *Member:* Monterey County and American (Member, Section of Taxation) Bar Associations; The State Bar of California (Member, Taxation Section). (Certified Specialist, Taxation Law, The State Bar of California Board of Legal Specialization). **PRACTICE AREAS:** Taxation; Estate Planning.

**JO MARIE OMETER,** born Columbus, Ohio, February 10, 1946; admitted to bar, 1972, California and U.S. District Court, Northern District of California. *Education:* The Ohio State University (B.A., 1968); University of San Francisco (J.D., 1972). Phi Alpha Delta. Law Clerk, Superior Court, San Mateo County, 1972-1973. Instructor, Wills and Trusts, Monterey College of Law, 1977. *Member:* Monterey County Bar Association (Member, Executive Committee, 1978); The State Bar of California (Member, Estate Planning, Trust and Probate Section; Liaison Committee Member, 1987; Delegate, 1992 and 1993). (Certified Specialist, Probate, Estate Planning and Trust Law, The State Bar of California Board of Legal Specialization). **PRACTICE AREAS:** Probate; Estate Planning; Conservatorships and Trusts.

*(This Listing Continued)*

### OF COUNSEL

**CARL ZERBE,** born Indianapolis, Indiana, January 6, 1946; admitted to bar, 1971, California. *Education:* DePauw University (B.A., 1968); Stanford University (J.D., 1971). Phi Beta Kappa. Adjunct Professor, Law and Real Property, Monterey College of Law, 1985-1988. *Member:* Monterey County Bar Association; State Bar of California. **PRACTICE AREAS:** Estate Planning Law; Business Law; Real Estate Law; Partnership Law; Corporation Law.

## FALK, VESTAL & FISH, L.L.P.

16590 OAK VIEW CIRCLE
**MORGAN HILL, CALIFORNIA 95037**
Telephone: 408-778-3624
Fax: 408-776-0426
Pager: 408-683-1839
Cellular: 408-781-3145
Email: Rcfpatlaw@aol.com

*Dallas, Texas Office:* Plaza of the Americas, 700 North Pearl, Suite 970.
Telephone: 214-954-4400.

*Matters of Intellectual Property and Trade Regulation. Patent, Trademark and Copyright Prosecution and Trial Practice. Trade Secret Protection. Related matters of Antitrust Law and Deceptive Trade Practices.*

**RONALD C. FISH,** born Grand Rapids, Michigan, September 21, 1947; admitted to bar, 1977, California, Arizona, U.S. District Court, Northern, Southern Central and Eastern; Districts of California and U.S. Court of Appeals, Ninth Circuit; U.S. Court of Appeals, Federal Circuit; 1992, Texas; registered to practice before U.S. Patent and Trademark Office. *Education:* Northwestern University (B.S.E.E., with distinction, 1970); Hastings College of the Law, University of California (J.D., 1977). Order of the Coif. Member: Thurston Society. Law Review, 1978-1979. Extern, to Justice William C. Clark, California Supreme Court. Former Chair, Orange County Bar Bulletin. Former Chair of Orange County Corporate Law Section. Contributing Author, Review of Federal Circuit Cases, American Intellectual Property Cases. *Member:* Santa Clara County and America Intellectual Property Law. **PRACTICE AREAS:** Intellectual Property Law.

REFERENCE: Provident Bank, Dallas, Texas.

(For Complete Biographical Information, see Professional Biographies at Dallas, Texas)

## LAW OFFICES OF C. RANDALL COOK

780 PINEY WAY
**MORRO BAY, CALIFORNIA 93442-1926**
Telephone: 805-772-4431
FAX: 805-772-5134

*General Civil and Trial Practice, Personal Injury, Real Property, Business Law, Probate and Trusts, Unlawful Detainers and Creditors and Debtors Rights.*

**C. RANDALL COOK,** born Pomona, California, February 26, 1954; admitted to bar, 1980, California; U.S. District Court, Central District of California; U.S. Court of Appeals, Ninth Circuit; 1987, U.S. Supreme Court; 1991, Hawaii and U.S. District Court, District of Hawaii; 1992, Oregon. *Education:* Harvey Mudd College; University of California at Irvine (B.A., cum laude, 1976, Phi Beta Kappa); Hastings College of the Law, University of California (J.D., 1979). Deputy County Counsel, County of Los Angeles, 1980-1983. Staff Attorney, Pacific Enterprises, Los Angeles, 1983-1985. Referee and Arbitrator, State Bar Court, 1984-1985. Judge Pro Tem and Arbitrator, San Luis Obispo Superior Court, 1985—. Instructor: University of California, Torts, 1987; California Polytechnic University, Torts, 1990. *Member:* San Luis Obispo County and American Bar Associations; State Bar of California; American Judicature Society. **PRACTICE AREAS:** Civil Litigation - Plaintiff and Defendant; Personal Injury; General Real Property; General Business/Corporate; Probate and Estates/Wills; General Civil.

## GEORGE, GALLO & SULLIVAN

A LAW CORPORATION

**MORRO BAY, CALIFORNIA**

(See San Luis Obispo)

*Probate, Estate Planning and Trust Administration, Business and Corporate Transactions, Taxation, Real Property and Construction, Civil Litigation.*

---

## OGLE & MERZON

A Partnership including a Professional Corporation

Established in 1953

770 MORRO BAY BOULEVARD
P.O. BOX 720
**MORRO BAY, CALIFORNIA 93443-0720**
Telephone: 805-772-7353
Fax: 805-772-7713

San Luis Obispo, California Office: P.O. Box 1855, 93406. Telephone: 805-543-0295.

*General Civil and Trial Practice. Real Property, Business Law, Probate, Estate Planning, Trusts, Negligence, Condemnation, Family Law and Creditors Rights.*

**CHARLES E. OGLE, (A PROFESSIONAL CORPORATION),** born St. Louis, Missouri, January 3, 1925; admitted to bar, 1952, California; U.S. Court of Appeals, Ninth Circuit; U.S. Supreme Court; U.S. District Court, Northern, Central and Southern Districts of California. *Education:* Washington University; Southwestern University (LL.B., 1952). *Member:* San Luis Obispo County (President, 1968-1969) and American Bar Associations; State Bar of California; The Association of Trial Lawyers of America. **PRACTICE AREAS:** Condemnation Law; Business Litigation; Probate Estate Planning and Administration.

**JAMES B. MERZON,** born Fresno, California, August 3, 1942; admitted to bar, 1969, California. *Education:* Fresno State College (B.A., 1964); University of California at Los Angeles (J.D., 1968). Member, Moot Court Honors Program. Judge Pro Tem, Superior Court, 1975—. *Member:* San Luis Obispo County (President, 1985) and American Bar Associations; The State Bar of California. **PRACTICE AREAS:** Real Estate Law; Business Litigation; Probate Estate Planning and Administration.

**CHARLES G. KIRSCHNER,** born San Diego, California, March 28, 1956; admitted to bar, 1984, California. *Education:* University of California at Davis (B.S., 1978); University of Santa Clara (M.B.A., 1984; J.D., 1984). *Member:* San Luis Obispo County Bar Association; The State Bar of California. **PRACTICE AREAS:** Family Law; Civil Litigation.

**CHARLES PATRICK OGLE,** born San Luis Obispo, California, July 22, 1956; admitted to bar, 1982, California. *Education:* University of California at Berkeley (A.B., 1978); University of San Francisco (J.D., 1982). *Member:* State Bar of California. **PRACTICE AREAS:** Real Property Law; Estate Planning; Creditors Rights.

REPRESENTATIVE CLIENTS: Coldwell Banker Liberty Real Estate and Mortgage; Madonna Plaza Shopping Center; Merzon Industries; Summit Hills Development; Vault Corp.; Westlake Village; Great American Fish Co.; Grad II Restaurants, Inc.
REFERENCES: Bank of America National Trust & Savings Assn.

---

## J. NORMAN BAKER

SAN ANTONIO CENTER
2570 EL CAMINO REAL WEST, SUITE 504
**MOUNTAIN VIEW, CALIFORNIA 94040**
Telephone: 415-941-0604
Fax: 415-941-4697

*General Civil and Trial Practice. Family Law, Personal Injury, Real Property, Business Litigation and Arbitration.*

**J. NORMAN BAKER,** born New Waterford, Nova Scotia, Canada, December 3, 1933; admitted to bar, 1963, Massachusetts; 1965, California. *Education:* University of Pennsylvania (A.B., 1955); Boston College (LL.B., 1963). Member, Boston College Law Review, 1962-1963. Superior Court Judge Pro Tem, Family and Civil Court, Santa Clara County. Santa Clara County Superior Court Arbitrator. *Member:* Santa Clara County (Member,
*(This Listing Continued)*

Family Law Section) and Massachusetts Bar Associations; The State Bar of California (Member, Family Law Section); The Association of Trial Lawyers of America. [Lt., USNR, 1956-1964; active duty, 1956-1959]. (Certified Specialist, Family Law, The State Bar of California Board of Legal Specialization). **REPORTED CASES:** In Re Marriage of Hug 154 Cal. App. 3rd 780 (1984).

REFERENCE: Bank of the West (Los Altos Branch).

---

## BURRISS & MONAHAN

A PROFESSIONAL CORPORATION

Established in 1969

OLD MILL OFFICE CENTER
SUITE 160, 201 SAN ANTONIO CIRCLE
**MOUNTAIN VIEW, CALIFORNIA 94040**
Telephone: 415-948-7127
Fax: 415-941-6709

*General Practice. Civil Litigation, Corporate, Copyright/Trademark, Securities, Business, Employment Law, Taxation, Exempt Organizations, Real Estate, Bankruptcy, Estate Planning, Probate, Family and Pension Law, Toxic Substances, Legislative Advocacy, Marketing Communications.*

**RICHARD S. BURRISS,** born Jersey City, New Jersey, February 14, 1940; admitted to bar, 1967, California; 1983, U.S. Supreme Court and U.S. Tax Court. *Education:* Lehigh University (B.S., 1962); University of Maryland; University of Santa Clara (J.D., 1966). Judge Pro Tem, Santa Clara County Superior Court, 1984—. Author: "Use of Another's Name or Likeness," Copy Magazine, Feb. 1992. *Member:* Santa Clara County Bar Association; The State Bar of California (Member, Section on Business Law). **PRACTICE AREAS:** Business Law; Business Litigation; Intellectual Property; Marketing Communications.

**SUSAN HOWIE BURRISS,** born Danbury, Connecticut, November 5, 1942; admitted to bar, 1979, California and U.S. District Court, Northern District of California; 1980, U.S. Tax Court. *Education:* George Mason University (B.A., 1976); University of Santa Clara (J.D., 1979). *Member:* Palo Alto Area, Santa Cruz County, Santa Clara County (Member, Sections on: Probate/Estate Planning; Business Law; Tax) and American (Member, Sections on: Taxation, Real Property, Probate and Trust Law) Bar Associations; The State Bar of California (Member, Sections on: Business Law; Estate Planning and Probate; Taxation). **LANGUAGES:** French. **PRACTICE AREAS:** Estate Planning; Probate; Tax; Civil Litigation.

**WILLIAM J. MONAHAN,** born Long Beach, California, October 26, 1957; admitted to bar, 1983, California and U.S. District Court, Northern District of California; 1986, U.S. Court of Appeals, Ninth Circuit. *Education:* Foothill College (A.A., 1977); University of California at Santa Barbara (B.A., 1979); University of Santa Clara (J.D., 1983). Real Estate Broker, California, 1990. *Member:* Santa Clara County Bar Association; State Bar of California. **PRACTICE AREAS:** Civil Litigation; Business Litigation; Civil Appeals; Commercial Law; Real Property; Marketing Communications.

**ALAN T. FOSTER,** born Long Beach, California, August 18, 1952; admitted to bar, 1978, California. *Education:* California Polytechnic State University, San Luis Obispo (B.S., 1974); Loyola Law School of Los Angeles (J.D., 1977). Registered Lobbyist. *Member:* Palo Alto Area and Santa Clara County (Member, Sections on Business Law, High Technology, Real Estate and Environmental Law) Bar Associations; State Bar of California (Member, Sections on: Business Law; Intellectual Property; Environmental; Real Estate Law). **PRACTICE AREAS:** Business Law; Intellectual Property; Mergers and Acquisitions; Nonprofit Corporations; Real Estate; Environmental Law; Government Law.

**STEPHANIE A. CASPER,** born San Francisco, California, March 17, 1967; admitted to bar, 1993, California. *Education:* University of California at Berkley (B.A., 1989); Santa Clara University, School of Law (J.D., 1993). *Member:* Santa Clara County Bar Association; State Bar of California. **PRACTICE AREAS:** Business Law; Business Litigation; Labor Law.

## GENERAL COUNSEL ASSOCIATES
*1891 LANDINGS DRIVE*
*MOUNTAIN VIEW, CALIFORNIA 94043*
*Telephone: 415-428-3900*
*Fax: 415-428-3901*

**FIRM PROFILE:** *General Counsel Associates LLP provides a broad range of legal service to emerging growth companies, particularly in the high technology sector, and to venture capital investors in such companies. The GCA includes corporate and securities law; copyright, licensing and other intellectual property matters; litigation; real estate, land use and environmental law; tax commercial lending and leasing; and employment law and executive compensation.*

### PARTNERS

**DEBORAH CHURTON AIKINS,** born El Paso, Texas, May 31, 1954; admitted to bar, 1984, California. *Education:* University of California at Berkeley (B.A., 1975); Hastings College of the Law, University of California, San Francisco (J.D., 1984). Order of the Coif. Member, Thurston Honor Society. *Member:* Santa Clara County Bar Association (Member, Real Property Section); State Bar of California (Member, Real Property Section). **PRACTICE AREAS:** Real Estate; Land Use.

**DOUGLAS B. AIKINS,** born San Diego, California, October 10, 1950; admitted to bar, 1978, California. *Education:* University of Oklahoma (B.A., 1972; M.A., 1974); University of San Francisco (J.D., 1977). Deputy City Attorney, City of Cupertino, 1978-1979. Assistant City Attorney, City of Sunnyvale, 1979-1986. Redevelopment Counsel, East Palo Alto Redevelopment Agency, 1987-1992. *Member:* Santa Clara County Bar Association; The State Bar of California. **SPECIAL AGENCIES:** Redevelopment Agencies; City Councils and Planning Commissions; U.S. Army Corps of Engineers; California Fish & Game Commission; LAFCO's; U.S. Fish & Wildlife Service. **PRACTICE AREAS:** Land Use Law; Redevelopment Law; California Environmental Law; Municipal Law. *Email:* dbaikins@gcounsel.com

**ALISA J. BAKER,** born Orange, New Jersey, August 5, 1957; admitted to bar, 1984, District of Columbia; 1985, California; 1986, U.S. Tax Court. *Education:* University of Pennsylvania (B.A., cum laude, 1979; M.A., English, with distinction, 1979; M.S.Ed., 1980); Georgetown University (J.D., cum laude, 1984). Teaching Fellow, Stanford Law School, 1984-1985. Staff Member, 1981-1982 and Associate Editor, 1982-1983, Georgetown Law Journal. *Member:* Santa Clara County Bar Association; State Bar of California (Member Sections on: Business Law; Intellectual Property); The District of Columbia Bar. **PRACTICE AREAS:** Corporate Law; Multimedia Law; Technology Licensing; Intellectual Property; Executive Compensation.

**BETSY E. BAYHA,** born New York, N.Y., February 12, 1951; admitted to bar, 1977, California. *Education:* Oakland University (B.A., magna cum laude, 1972); The Ohio State University (M.A., 1973); Harvard University (J.D., 1977). *Member:* American Bar Association (Member, Sections on: Corporation, Banking and Business Law; Intellectual Property; Antitrust); The State Bar of California; Computer Law Association. **PRACTICE AREAS:** Corporate Law; Technology Licensing; Technology Transfers; Intellectual Property; Business Law.

**PAUL C. GRAFFAGNINO,** born Hartford, Connecticut, March 9, 1958; admitted to bar, 1983, District of Columbia; 1987, California. *Education:* Williams College (B.A. in Political Economy, cum laude, 1980); Georgetown University (J.D., cum laude, 1983). Staff Member, 1981-1982 and Articles and Notes Editor, 1982-1983, American Criminal Law Review. *Member:* Santa Clara County Bar Association (Member, Business Law Section); State Bar of California (Member, Business Law Section); The District of Columbia Bar. **PRACTICE AREAS:** Corporate; Securities; Venture Capital; Corporate Finance. *Email:* pgraff@gcounsel.com

**JOHN W. HOLLINGSWORTH,** born Hollywood, California, September 8, 1958; admitted to bar, 1984, California. *Education:* University of California at Irvine (B.A., 1980); Hastings College of the Law, University of California, San Francisco (J.D., 1983). Associate Managing Editor, Hastings Law Journal, 1982-1983. *Member:* Santa Clara County Bar Association; State Bar of California. **PRACTICE AREAS:** Corporate Law; Technology Licensing; Technology Transfers; Multimedia Law; Commercial Law.

**ROBERT W. LUCKINBILL,** born Paris, Tennessee, August 12, 1962; admitted to bar, 1987, California and U.S. District Court, Northern District of California; 1993, U.S. District Court, Southern, Eastern and Central Districts of California and U.S. Court of Appeals, Ninth Circuit. *Educa-*
*(This Listing Continued)*

*tion:* California State University, Stanislaus (B.A., cum laude, 1983); Santa Clara University (J.D., magna cum laude, 1987). *Member:* Palo Alto Area, Santa Clara County and American Bar Associations; State Bar of California (Member, Sections on: Litigation; Business Law). **PRACTICE AREAS:** Business Law; Employment Litigation; Intellectual Property.

**JOHN B. MONTGOMERY,** born New York, N.Y., August 28, 1957; admitted to bar, 1985, California. *Education:* Stanford University (A.B., 1980); Northwestern School of Law of Lewis and Clark College (J.D., 1984). Member, Moot Court Board. Member, City of Palo Alto Public Art Commission, 1988-1994. *Member:* State Bar of California. **PRACTICE AREAS:** Corporate Law; Securities; Venture Capital; Business Law.

**ANNE L. NEETER,** born Almelo, The Netherlands, September 2, 1950; admitted to bar, 1978, Minnesota; 1980, Illinois; 1984, California. *Education:* Leiden University, Netherlands (J.D. and LL.M., 1975); Cornell University (J.D., 1978). *Member:* Santa Clara County (Member, Executive Committee of the High Technology Law Section) and American (Member, Sections on: Corporation, Banking and Business Law; Science and Technology; Antitrust) Bar Associations; State Bar of California; Computer Law Association. **LANGUAGES:** Dutch and German. **PRACTICE AREAS:** Computer Law; Multimedia Law; Commercial Law; Equipment Finance and Leasing; Corporate Law; Securities. *Email:* aneeter@gcounsel.com

**CLIFFORD S. ROBBINS,** born St. Louis, Missouri, November 25, 1956; admitted to bar, 1982, District of Columbia; 1992, California. *Education:* University of Texas (B.A., summa cum laude, 1978); Harvard University (J.D., 1982). Phi Beta Kappa. *Member:* The District of Columbia Bar; State Bar of California. **PRACTICE AREAS:** Corporate Law; Venture Capital; Corporate Finance; Technology Licensing; Technology Transfers. *Email:* crobbins@gcounsel.com

**ELIZABETH ROTH,** born New York, N.Y., March 16, 1946; admitted to bar, 1982, California. *Education:* Cornell University (B.A., 1967); University of Washington (M.A., 1968; Ph.D., 1972); Duke University School of Law (J.D., 1982). Associate Editor, Litigation News, ABA Section of Litigation, 1988—. *Member:* Santa Clara County and American Bar Associations; State Bar of California. **PRACTICE AREAS:** Employment Litigation. *Email:* eroth@gcounsel.com

**ROGER ROYSE,** born Mandan, North Dakota, September 18, 1959; admitted to bar, 1984, North Dakota and Minnesota; 1985, South Dakota; 1990, New York; 1991, California. *Education:* University of North Dakota (B.A., 1981; J.D., 1984); New York University (LL.M., 1989). Certified Public Accountant, North Dakota, 1981. Author: "RRA '93 Limits Application of Portfolio Interest Exemption," 79 Journal of Taxation, 1993. *Member:* Santa Clara County and American Bar Associations; State Bar of California. **PRACTICE AREAS:** Taxation. *Email:* rroyse@gcounsel.com

**ROBERT H. SLOSS,** born Highland Park, Illinois, September 6, 1954; admitted to bar, 1979, California. *Education:* Stanford University (A.B., 1975; B.S., 1976); Hastings College of Law, University of California (J.D., 1979). Order of the Coif. Member, Thurston Honor Society. Author: "Taking a Business Approach to Intellectual Property Litigation," *New Matter,* Winter, 1993; "Trademark Parody: A Plea for Consistency in Analysis," *New Matter,* Winter, 1995. *Member:* State Bar of California; American Bar Association (Member, Intellectual Property Law Section); American Intellectual Property Law Association. **PRACTICE AREAS:** Business; Employment; Intellectual Property Litigation. *Email:* rsloss@gcounsel.com

**SAMUEL L. WRIGHT, III,** born Palo Alto, California, June 14, 1955; admitted to bar, 1984, California. *Education:* Williams College (B.A., 1977); University of Kent, England; Hastings College of the Law, University of California (J.D., 1984). Licensed Real Estate Broker, California, 1990—. Extern, Hon. Stanley Mosk, California Supreme Court, 1984. *Member:* Santa Clara County and American Bar Associations; State Bar of California. **PRACTICE AREAS:** Real Estate. *Email:* swright@gcounsel.com

### OF COUNSEL

**VIVIAN METZGER CLAUSING,** born Redondo Beach, California, January 4, 1962; admitted to bar, 1987, California. *Education:* Stanford University (B.A., honors in English, 1984); University of California, Los Angeles (J.D., 1987). Co-Advocacy Chairman, Moot Court Honors Program, 1987. Articles Editor, California Real Property Law Journal. Author: "The California Underground Storage Tank Cleanup Fund - New Opportunities and Requirements for Owners and Operators of Underground Storage Tanks," California Real Property Law Journal, Winter, 1992. *Member:* State Bar of California (Member, Real Estate and Environmental Law Sections; American Bar Association (Environmental/Real Estate Section).
*(This Listing Continued)*

## GENERAL COUNSEL ASSOCIATES, Mountain View—Continued

**PRACTICE AREAS:** Environmental; Real Estate Law. **Email:** vclausing@igc.apc.org

**NAOMI A. VARGAS,** born Fresno, California, September 8, 1954; admitted to bar, 1980, California. *Education:* University of California, San Diego (B.A., with honors, 1977); University of California, Boalt Hall School of Law (J.D., 1980); New York University (LL.M. in Taxation, 1984). Law Clerk to Presiding Justice Clinton W. White, California District Court of Appeal, 1980-1981. *Member:* Bar Association of San Francisco; State Bar of California (Member: Personal Income Tax Committee, Taxation Section, 1984-1987; Real Property, Probate and Trust Law Section; Banking and Business Law Section); American Bar Association (Member, Taxation Section); Association of Women in Commercial Real Estate; San Francisco Area Women Tax Lawyers. **PRACTICE AREAS:** Real Estate; Land Use.

---

## LUCE & QUILLINAN

Established in 1974

444 CASTRO STREET, SUITE 900
MOUNTAIN VIEW, CALIFORNIA 94041-2073
Telephone: 415-969-4000
FAX: 415-969-6953

*Business and Commercial Transactions, Estate and Tax Planning, Probate Estate and Trust Administration, Conservatorships, Guardianships, Tax, Real Estate, Land Use and Development and Environmental Law, Contracts, Business Entity Structuring and Tax Planning and Securities. Litigation and Appellate Practice with emphasis in the areas of Estate and Trust Litigation, Commercial Disputes, Trade Secrets, Employer Defense, Personal Injury, Construction and Insurance Matters. Arbitration, Mediation and Special Master Services. Preventive Law Counseling to Businesses.*

*FIRM PROFILE: Established in 1974, Luce & Quillinan is a full service business law firm, providing prompt and cost competitive services to all its clients. The Firm's areas of practice are allocated among its members by specialty to assure clients' practical, proficient and personal advice and service. Firm attorneys are active in community and local and state bar matters and committees and some lecture and publish in respective areas of specialty.*

### MEMBERS OF FIRM

**JAMES G. LUCE,** born Dayton, Ohio, February 23, 1945; admitted to bar, 1974, California; 1978, U.S. Court of Appeals, Ninth Circuit. *Education:* Yale University (B.A., 1966); University of Santa Clara (J.D., magna cum laude, 1974). Judge Pro Tem, 1985—; Special Master, 1992—, Santa Clara County, Superior Court. Board Member, Commission for Advanced California Paralegal Specialization, Inc. Fellow, National Center for Preventive Law. [Capt., USAF, Special Investigations, 1967-1971]. **REPORTED CASES:** Stephenson v. Calpine Conifers II, 652 F. 2d 808 (1981) (9th Circuit); Bank of America v. Salinas Nissan, Inc., 207 Cal. App. 3d 260 (Sixth Dist., 1989); In Re Hoffmeister I, 161 Cal. App. 3d 1163 (First Dist., 1984); In Re Hoffmeister II, 191 Cal. App. 3d 351 (First Dist., 1987). **PRACTICE AREAS:** General Business; Corporate and Real Estate Litigation; Arbitration.

**JAMES V. QUILLINAN,** born San Francisco, California, November 9, 1948; admitted to bar, 1974, California. *Education:* Stanford University (B.A., 1970); University of Santa Clara (J.D., 1974). Chairman, State Bar Executive Committee, Estate Planning, Trust and Probate Law Section, 1989-1990. Chair, California State Bar, Council of Section Chairs, 1991-1992. Member, State Bar Estate Planning, Trust and Probate Law Advisory Commission for Specialization, 1993-1996. Fellow, American College of Probate Counsel. (Certified Specialist, Estate Planning, Trust and Probate Law, The State Bar of California Board of Legal Specialization). **PRACTICE AREAS:** Estate Planning Law; Probate Administration Law; Conservatorship and Guardianship; Trust Administration Law and related Litigation.

**MELISSA C. JOHNSON,** born Sioux Falls, South Dakota, September 19, 1952; admitted to bar, 1987, California; 1988, U.S. District Court, Eastern, Northern and Southern Districts of California. *Education:* University of Kansas (B.G.S., 1975); Faculty of Law, Salzburg University, Austria (Certificate in International Legal Studies and in East/West Law and Relations, 1985); McGeorge School of Law, University of the Pacific (J.D., 1986). *Member:* Santa Clara County and Palo Alto Area Bar Associations (PAABA, (Co-Chair, Womens Lawyers Committee; Financial Women's

*(This Listing Continued)*

---

Association of San Francisco. **PRACTICE AREAS:** Civil, Commercial and Trust Litigation; Administrative Law.

### ASSOCIATE

**SALLY F. BERRY,** born Denver, Colorado; admitted to bar, 1989, California. *Education:* University of Denver (B.A., 1960); Santa Clara University (J.D., 1989). *Member:* Palo Alto Area and Santa Clara County Bar Associations. **PRACTICE AREAS:** Estate Planning Law; Probate Administration Law; Conservatorship and Guardianship; Trust Administration Law.

All Firm Members and Associates are Members of the State Bar of California.

A List of Representative Clients will be Furnished upon Request.

---

## MORGAN & POSILIPPO

444 CASTRO STREET, SUITE 900
MOUNTAIN VIEW, CALIFORNIA 94041-2073
Telephone: 415-969-4000
Fax: 415-969-6953

*General Civil Trial Practice including Business Law, Construction Contract Law, Insurance Litigation, Tax Planning Law, Estate Planning, Torts and Personal Injury.*

**MICHAEL R. MORGAN,** born Sacramento, California, October 10, 1941; admitted to bar, 1972, California, U.S. District Court, Northern District of California and U.S. Tax Court. *Education:* San Francisco State University (B.A., 1968); University of San Francisco (J.D., 1972). Beta Alpha Psi. *Member:* Santa Clara County Bar Association; AICPA; California Association of Certified Public Accountants. **PRACTICE AREAS:** Business Law; Tax Planning Law; Estate Planning.

**RICHARD POSILIPPO,** born Yonkers, New York, August 18, 1943; admitted to bar, 1969, California, U.S. District Court, Northern District of California and U.S. Court of Appeals, Ninth Circuit; 1975, U.S. District Court, Southern District of California; 1980, U.S. Tax Court. *Education:* University of Santa Clara (B.A., 1965); Boalt Hall School of Law, University of California (J.D., 1968). Member, Moot Court Board. Co-Author: with R. Donald Chapman, "Has Gideon's Trumpet Blown for Misdemeanants," 1967. *Member:* Palo Alto Area (Chairman, Community Relations Committee, 1976), Santa Clara County, San Mateo County and American Bar Associations; Association of Defense Counsel. **PRACTICE AREAS:** Construction Contract Law; Insurance Litigation; Personal Injury; Torts.

---

## SKJERVEN, MORRILL, MACPHERSON, FRANKLIN & FRIEL LLP

MOUNTAIN VIEW, CALIFORNIA

(See San Jose)

*Intellectual Property Law, including Patents, Trademarks, Copyrights, Mask Works, Unfair Competition, Trade Secrets and Licensing; Litigation in Federal and State Courts; Corporate, Commercial and General Business Law; and International and Government Contracts Law.*

---

## WHITMORE JOHNSON & BOLANOS

Established in 1991

2570 WEST EL CAMINO REAL, SUITE 600
MOUNTAIN VIEW, CALIFORNIA 94040
Telephone: 415-941-9333; 800-585-4529
Fax: 415-941-9476

*Labor and Employment Law.*

### MEMBERS OF FIRM

**RICHARD S. WHITMORE,** born Los Angeles, California, October 21, 1942; admitted to bar, 1967, California and U.S. Court of Appeals, Ninth Circuit; U.S. District Court, Northern District of California; 1985, U.S. Supreme Court; 1987, U.S., District Court, Eastern and Southern District of California. *Education:* Stanford University (B.A., 1964; J.D., 1967). Author: "Model Law Enforcement Contract: A Management Perspective," published by Labor Relations Information System, Portland, Oregon, 1992; "Model Firefighters Contact: A Management Perspective," published by Labor Relations System, Portland, Oregon, 1994; "Skelly v. State Personnel

*(This Listing Continued)*

Board: A Ten Year Perspective," California Public Employee Relations (CPER), No. 66., 1985; Co-Author, "Public Employees Do Not Have Right to Strike," League of California Cities, Employee Relations Service, 1987. Contributing Author: *California Public Sector Labor Relations,* Matthew Bender and State Bar of California, 1989; Administrative Mandamus, Continuing Education of the Bar (CEB), University of California, 1989. Contributing Editor, *Municipal Law Handbook,* League of California Cities, 1993. Contributing Author, Western Cities Magazine. Guest Lecturer, Stanford Law School, Santa Clara University School of Law, League of California Cities, Southern California Public Labor Relations Council. President, Sunnyvale-Cupertino Bar Association, 1974. Assistant City Attorney, Sunnyvale, CA, 1972-1974. *Member:* Palo Alto, Santa Clara County and American Bar Associations; State Bar of California. **REPORTED CASES:** Sunnydale Public Safety Officers Assoc. v. City of Sunnydale (1976) 55 Cal.App. 3d 732; Vernon Firefighters v. City of Vernon (1980) (107 Cal.App.3f 802; ULAC v. City of Salinas (1981) 654 F.2d 557; Relyea v. Ventura County Fire Protection District (1992) 2 Cal. App. 4th 875; Gauthier v. City of Red Bluff (1995) 34 Cal.App. 4th 1441. **PRACTICE AREAS:** Labor and Employment Law (90%); Municipal Law (10%).

**JANICE E. JOHNSON,** born Oakland, California, November 20, 1949; admitted to bar, 1981, California and U.S. District Court, Northern District of California; 1982, U.S. District Court, Southern District of California and U.S. Court of Appeals, Ninth Circuit. *Education:* University of California at Santa Barbara and San Francisco State University (B.A., 1973); Hastings College of Law, University of California (J.D., 1981). Order of The Coif; Thurston Society. Co-Editor-in-Chief, California Public Sector Labor Relations, Matthew Bender and State Bar of California, 1989. Co-Author: "What City Officials Need to Know About Workforce Reductions," Western City Magazine, February 1993. *Member:* State Bar of California (Member, Sections on: Employment and Labor Section); American Bar Association (Member, Section on: Labor Law). **LANGUAGES:** Spanish. **PRACTICE AREAS:** Labor and Employment Law (90%); Municipal Law (5%); Education Law (5%).

**RICHARD C. BOLANOS,** born San Francisco, California, October 29, 1955; admitted to bar, 1983, California and U.S. District Court, Northern District of California, 1986, U.S. District Court, Eastern District of California; 1992, U.S. Court of Appeals, Ninth Circuit. *Education:* San Francisco State University (B.A., 1977); California State University at San Jose (M.S., 1980); University of Santa Clara (J.D., 1983). *Member:* State Bar of California; American Bar Association. **REPORTED CASES:** Barner v. City of Novato (9th Cir. 1994) 17 F.3d 1256; Zazueta v. San Benito County (1995) 38 Cal.App.4th 106. **PRACTICE AREAS:** Labor and Employment Law (100%).

**CYNTHIA O'NEILL,** born Newport Beach, California, August 7, 1959; admitted to bar, 1987, California; U.S. Court of Appeals, Ninth Circuit; U.S. District Court, Eastern, Northern and Southern Districts of California. *Education:* University of California at Berkeley (B.A., 1981); University of Santa Clara (J.D., 1987). Managing Editor, Santa Clara Law Review, 1986-1987. Author: "Pregnancy Discrimination Act," Santa Clara Law Review, Vol. 25:2-3. League of California Cities Attorneys Continuing Education Seminar on Personnel Issues, "The Nature of the Public Employee/Employer Relationship-The Myers-Milias-Brown Act; How A Municipal Employer's Duty To Bargin In Good Faith Impacts The Employment Relationship," 1990. San Pablo, City Attorney, 1991. POST Instructor, investigation of sexual harassment complaints, 1993. *Member:* Santa County Bar Association; State Bar of California. **PRACTICE AREAS:** Labor and Employment Law (100%).

### ASSOCIATES

**KATHRYN J. BURKE,** born Neenah, Wisconsin, May 28, 1950; admitted to bar, 1976, California and U.S. District Court, Northern District of California; 1990, U.S. District Court, Central District of California; 1992, U.S. Court of Appeals, Ninth Circuit. *Education:* University of Wisconsin-Madison (B.A., 1972); Boalt Hall School of Law, University of California, Berkeley (J.D., 1976). Phi Beta Kappa. Note and Comment Editor, California Law Review, 1975-1976. *Member:* State Bar of California. **REPORTED CASES:** Relyea v. Ventura County Fire Protection District (1992) 2 Cal. App. 4th 875; Zuzueta V. San Benito County (1995) 38 Cal.App. 4th 106; Gauthier v. City of Red Bluff (1995) 34 Cal.App. 4th 1441; Barner v. City of Novato (1994) 17 F.3d 1256. **PRACTICE AREAS:** Labor and Employment Law (100%).

**NANCY J. CLARK,** born Cameron, Missouri, August 9, 1959; admitted to bar, 1992, California and U.S. District Court, Southern and Eastern Districts of California and U.S. Court of Appeals, Ninth Circuit. *Education:* University of Iowa (B.B.A, 1983); Hastings College of the Law (J.D., 1991).

*(This Listing Continued)*

Author: "Sexual Harassment Investigations and the Attorney-Client Privilege," California Public Employee Relations (CPER), Vol. 121, 1996. *Member:* State Bar of California. **PRACTICE AREAS:** Labor and Employment Law (100%).

**CHRISTOPHER H. ALONZI,** born Los Angeles, California, December 26, 1964; admitted to bar, 1992, California; 1993, U.S. District Court, Central, Northern and Eastern Districts of California and U.S. Court of Appeals, Ninth Circuit. *Education:* California State University-Northridge (B.A., magna cum laude, 1989); Hastings College of the Law (J.D., 1992). *Member:* San Mateo County Bar Association; State Bar of California (Member, Labor and Employment Law Section). **PRACTICE AREAS:** Labor and Employment (100%).

**SUSANNA L. MOULD,** born Palo Alto, California, November 5, 1958; admitted to bar, 1991, California, U.S. District Court, Northern District of California and U.S. Court of Appeals, Ninth Circuit; 1993, U.S. District Court, Eastern District of California. *Education:* University of California-Santa Barbara (B.A., with honors, 1980); California State University (M.A., 1985); Hastings College of the Law (J.D., 1991). Contributing Author: Municipal Law Handbook, League of California Cities, 1994. Certified Teacher: Secondary Education, California, 1985; Community College, 1985. *Member:* State Bar of California. **LANGUAGES:** Spanish. **PRACTICE AREAS:** Labor and Employment Law (100%).

**MAUREEN M. DUFFY,** born Hazelcrest, Illinois, April 14, 1959; admitted to bar, 1993, California; 1996, U.S. District Court, Eastern District of California. *Education:* University of Michigan and University of Iowa (B.G.S., with highest honors, 1981); University of Michigan Law School (J.D., 1993). Clerk, Honorable Peter Nowinski, U.S. District Court Eastern District of California, 1994-1995. *Member:* Palo Also and Santa Clara County Bar Associations; State Bar of California (Member, Labor and Employment Law Section). **LANGUAGES:** French and Swahili. **PRACTICE AREAS:** Labor and Employment Law (100%).

**JACK W. HUGHES,** born Los Gotos, California, September 5, 1970; admitted to bar, 1996, California, U.S. Court of Appeals, Ninth Circuit and U.S. District Court, Northern, Eastern and Southern Districts of California. *Education:* University of California-Davis (B.A., with honors, 1993); Duke University, School of Law (J.D., 1996). *Member:* State Bar of California. **PRACTICE AREAS:** Labor and Employment Law (100%).

---

## ARNOLD DAVID BREYER

*Established in 1974*

*112 SISKIYOU AVENUE*

*P.O. BOX 201*

### MOUNT SHASTA, CALIFORNIA 96067
*Telephone: 916-926-3134*
*Fax: 916-926-8607*

Redding, California Office: 1721 Court Street. Telephone: 916-244-3690. Fax: 916-244-0923.

*Practice Limited to Personal Injury and Family Law.*

**ARNOLD DAVID BREYER,** born Chicago, Illinois, February 20, 1942; admitted to bar, 1967, Illinois and U.S. District Court, Northern District of Illinois; 1970, California and U.S. District Court, Northern District of California; 1971, U.S. Court of Appeals, 9th Circuit; 1994, U.S. District Court, Eastern District of California. *Education:* University of Illinois (B.A., 1963); Roosevelt University; Loyola University of Los Angeles (J.D., 1967). Phi Alpha Delta. Lecturer, Lawyers' Mutual Family Law Continuing Legal Education Program. Member, Board of Directors, Legal Services of Northern California. *Member:* Siskiyou County (President, 1980-1981), Shasta-Trinity Counties (member, Family Law Section) and American (Member, Family Law Section) Bar Associations; State Bar of California (Member, Family Law Section); California Trial Lawyers Association; The Association of Trial Lawyers of America; Association of Certified Family Law Specialists. (Certified Specialist, Family Law, The State Bar of California Board of Legal Specialization).

## THE LAW OFFICE OF DANIEL CHESTER

*1001 2ND STREET, SUITE 345*
**NAPA, CALIFORNIA 94559**
Telephone: 707-257-5378
Fax: 707-257-5399
Email: ChesterDK@AOL.COM

*Civil Litigation, Construction Law, Real Estate Litigation, Business Law, Evictions, Estate Planning, Living Trusts and Wills.*

**DANIEL CHESTER,** born Bellflower, California, June 9, 1959; admitted to bar, 1989, California, U.S. District Court, Northern District of California and U.S. Court of Appeals, Ninth Circuit. *Education:* California State University at Sacramento (B.A., 1984); University of San Francisco (J.D.,1988). *Member:* Napa County Bar Association; State Bar of California. *PRACTICE AREAS:* Civil Litigation; Construction Law; Real Estate Litigation; Business Law; Evictions; Estate Planning; Living Trusts and Wills.

---

## COOMBS & DUNLAP

*Established in 1876*
*1211 DIVISION STREET*
**NAPA, CALIFORNIA 94559**
Telephone: 707-252-9100
Fax: 707-252-8516

*St. Helena, California Office:* 1110 Adams Street. Telephone: 707-963-5202; 944-8779.

*General Civil, Trial and Appellate Practice, all State and Federal Courts. Business, Real Property, Municipal, Personal Injury, Family, Estate Planning and Probate Law.*

**FRANK L. COOMBS** (1853-1934).

**NATHAN F. COOMBS** (1881-1973).

**FRANK L. DUNLAP** (1913-1984).

### MEMBERS OF FIRM

**MALCOLM A. MACKENZIE,** born Los Angeles, California, August 6, 1945; admitted to bar, 1971, California. *Education:* Stanford University (A.B., with honors, 1967); Boalt Hall School of Law, University of California (J.D., 1970). Deputy City Attorney of Napa, 1971-1978. City Attorney of Napa, 1978-1981. City Attorney of Calistoga, 1990—. *Member:* Napa County Bar Association (President, 1982-1983); State Bar of California (Member, Family Law Section). (Certified Specialist, Family Law, The State Bar of California Board of Legal Specialization). *PRACTICE AREAS:* Civil Litigation; Family Law; Probate Law; Municipal Law.

**C. PRESTON SHACKELFORD,** born Virginia, January 30, 1948; admitted to bar, 1974, California. *Education:* Smith College and State University of New York (B.A., 1970); Boalt Hall School of Law, University of California (J.D., 1974). Deputy City Attorney of Napa, 1975-1981; Town Attorney of Yountville, 1980—. *Member:* Napa County Bar Association; State Bar of California (Member, Family Law Section); California Women Lawyers; Napa County Women Lawyers; Association of Certified Family Law Specialists. (Certified Specialist, Family Law, The State Bar of California Board of Legal Specialization). *PRACTICE AREAS:* Family Law; Municipal Law; Probate Law.

**DIANE M. PRICE,** born Pasadena, California, September 3, 1953; admitted to bar, 1979, California. *Education:* University of California at Berkeley (B.A., with honors, 1975); Hastings College of Law, University of California (J.D., 1979). Articles Editor, Hastings Law Journal, 1978-1979. Author: "Assessment of Civil Monetary Penalties for Water Pollution: A Proposal for Shifting the Burden of Proof Regarding Damages," 30 Hastings Law Journal 651, 1979. Deputy City Attorney of Napa, 1979-1981. City Attorney of St. Helena, 1988—. *Member:* Bar Association of San Francisco; Napa County Bar Association; State Bar of California (Member, Section on Litigation); California Women Lawyers; Napa County Women Lawyers; The Association of Trial Lawyers of America; Consumer Attorneys of California. *PRACTICE AREAS:* General Civil Litigation; Personal Injury Law; Municipal Law; Family Law.

**DIANE L. DILLON,** born Napa, California, October 17, 1952; admitted to bar, 1981, California. *Education:* University of California at Santa Barbara (B.A., with honors, 1975); University of California at Los Angeles *(This Listing Continued)*

(M.L.I.S., 1977); University of California at Davis (J.D., 1981). Phi Delta Phi. Member, Moot Court Board. Editor, The Advocate, 1980-1981. Member, University of California at Davis Law Review, 1980-1981. *Member:* Napa County Bar Association; State Bar of California (Member, Sections on: Tax Law and Estate Planning and Probate); California Women Lawyers; Napa County Women Lawyers; Estate and Financial Planning Council of Napa County. *PRACTICE AREAS:* Estate Planning Law; Probate Law.

**L. RANDOLPH SKIDMORE,** born Annapolis, Maryland, September 19, 1946; admitted to bar, 1976, California. *Education:* University of California at Berkeley (A.B., with honors, 1968); California Western School of Law (J.D., 1976). Phi Beta Kappa. Member, Board of Editors, California Western Law Review, 1975-1976. Author: "Nitrate Pollution and the California Environment Quality Act: The Appropriate Solution to A Neglected Problem," California Western Law Review, 1975. *Member:* Napa County Bar Association; State Bar of California (Member, Real Estate and Business Law Sections). *PRACTICE AREAS:* Business Law; Real Estate Law.

**CHARLES P. KUNTZ,** born Los Angeles, California, May 7, 1944; admitted to bar, 1970, California and New York; 1979, U.S. Supreme Court. *Education:* Stanford University (B.A., with honors, 1966; J.D., 1969); New York Law School (LL.M., 1971). *Member:* Napa County Bar Association; State Bar of California; Consumer Attorneys of California. *PRACTICE AREAS:* Civil Litigation; Personal Injury Law; Probate Law; Trust Law; Litigation.

**DONALD M. DAVIS,** born Detroit, Michigan, September 30, 1961; admitted to bar, 1993, California. *Education:* Wake Forest University (B.A., 1984); University of California at Davis (J.D., 1993). Member, National Trial Team, 1993. Editor, The Advocate, 1992-1993. *Member:* Napa County Bar Association; State Bar of California. *LANGUAGES:* Arabic, French. *PRACTICE AREAS:* Business Law; Real Estate Law; Civil Litigation; Municipal Law.

**RAFAEL RIOS, III,** born Zamora, Michoacan, Mexico, September 28, 1966; admitted to bar, 1994, California. *Education:* University of California School of Law, Davis (B.S., 1989); Santa Clara University Law School (J.D., 1994). Phi Delta Phi. *Member:* Napa County Bar Association; State Bar of California. *LANGUAGES:* Spanish. *PRACTICE AREAS:* General Practice.

### OF COUNSEL

**JUNE E. MORONEY,** born Houston, Texas, June 25, 1947; admitted to bar, 1975, California. *Education:* Stanford University (A.B., with honors, 1969); Hastings College of the Law, University of California, San Francisco (J.D., 1974). Member, Thurston Society. *Member:* State Bar of California; Napa County Women Lawyers. *LANGUAGES:* Spanish and Italian. *PRACTICE AREAS:* Civil Litigation; Appeals.

REPRESENTATIVE CLIENTS: City of St. Helena; Town of Yountville; City of Calistoga; Napa Sanitation District; Kont Rasmussen Winery; Manzanita Winery; Napa Vineyards, Inc.; Saintsbury; Snowden Vineyards; St. Helena Hospital; Napa Valley Family Medical Group, Inc.; California Council of the Blind; Adolescent Treatment Centers, Inc.; Napa Valley Special Games, Inc.; Vintage Ranch Properties; Tower Road Winery Co-Op; Havens Wine Cellars; Nova Wines, Inc.; Coldwell-Banker, Brokers of the Valley; Land Intermediary, Inc.; ZD Winery; Anderson's Conn Valley Vineyards; Corison Wines; Demptos Napa Cooperage.

---

## DAVID A. DIAMOND

*816 BROWN STREET*
**NAPA, CALIFORNIA 94559**
Telephone: 707-254-8100
Fax: 707-254-8147
Email: diamond@napanet.net
URL: http://www.trustwizard.com

*Estate Planning, Administration of Estates and Trusts, Estate and Gift Taxation, Inheritance Disputes, Business and Tax Planning, Family Partnerships, Charitable Trust Planning.*

**DAVID A. DIAMOND,** born Saugus, Massachusetts, April 21, 1959; admitted to bar, 1984, California. *Education:* University of Arizona (B.A., with high distinction, 1981); University of California at Davis (J.D., 1984). Phi Beta Kappa. Author: "Highlights of the New Trust Law," Estate Planning, Trust and Probate News, Spring, 1987. *Member:* Napa County and American (Member, Real Property, Probate and Trust Law Section) Bar Associations; State Bar of California. (Certified Specialist, Estate Planning, *(This Listing Continued)*

Trust and Probate Law, The State Bar of California Board of Legal Specialization). **PRACTICE AREAS:** Estate Planning, Trust and Probate Law; Estate and Gift Taxation.

---

## DICKENSON, PEATMAN & FOGARTY

*A PROFESSIONAL LAW CORPORATION*

Established in 1965

809 COOMBS STREET
**NAPA, CALIFORNIA 94559-2977**
Telephone: 707-252-7122
Telecopier: 707-255-6876

*General Civil and Trial Practice in all State and Federal Courts. Personal Injury, Real Estate, Alcohol Beverage Law and Related Trade Regulations, Land Use Planning and Local Government Law. Estate Planning and Probate Administration, Business, Corporate, Construction, Personal Taxation Law.*

**JOSEPH G. PEATMAN,** born Los Angeles, California, February 16, 1934; admitted to bar, 1959, California. *Education:* Stanford University (A.B., 1956; J.D., 1958). Member, Board of Visitors, Stanford Law School, 1978-1980. Member, Board of Trustees, 1962-1968; President, 1964-1966, Napa School District. Napa County Supervisor, 1969-1973. Member, Board of Trustees: Queen of the Valley Hospital, 1971-1986; Gasser Foundation, 1989—; The Center for Wine, Food and the Arts, 1992-1994. Director, Napa National Bank, 1994—. Judge Pro Tem, Napa Superior Court, 1985-1986. *Member:* Napa County Bar Association (President, 1963-1964); State Bar of California. **PRACTICE AREAS:** Land Use Law; Zoning Law; Real Estate Law. *Email:* JPeatman@aol.com

**DAVID W. MEYERS,** born Tasmania, Australia, July 19, 1942; admitted to bar, 1968, California. *Education:* University of Redlands (B.A., magna cum laude, 1964); University of California at Berkeley (J.D., 1967); University of Edinburgh, Edinburgh, Scotland (LL.M., 1968). Author: *The Human Body and the Law*, Edinburgh University Press, 1970 (1st ed.), Edinburgh University Press and Stanford University Press 1990 (2nd ed.); *Medico-Legal Implications of Death and Dying*, Lawyers Co-operative Publishing Co., 1981 and annual supplements 1982-1993. Co-Editor: *Comparative and Historical Essays in Scots Law: A Tribute to Professor Sir Thomas Smith, Q.C.*, Chapter, "Letting Doctor and Patient Decide - The Wisdom of Scots Law," London and Edinburgh, Butterworths, 1992; Chapter, "The Family and Life and Death Decisions," in Family Rights: Family Law and Medical Advance, Edinburgh University Press, 1990; Chapter, "Selective Non-Treatment of Handicapped Infants," in Issues in Human Reproduction, Hampshire, Gower Pub. Ltd., 1989; Chapter, "Parental Rights and Consent to Medical Treatment of Minors," in Pediatric Forensic Medicine & Pathology, London, Champan & Hall Ltd., 1989. Co-Author: "Parental Choice and Selective Non-Treatment of Deformed Newborn: A View from the Mid-Atlantic," The Journal of Medical Ethics, June, 1986; "The Contingent Fee in California Legal Practice," The Journal of the Law Society of Scotland, Vol. 30, 9, September 1985; "The Durable Power of Attorney for Health Care: A New Element of the Estate Planning Package," Estate Planning and California Probate Reporter, Vol. VI, No. 4, p. 73, February, 1985; "Legal Aspects of Withdrawing Nourishment From An Incurably Ill Patient," Arch Intern Med., Vol. 145, p. 125, January, 1985; "Using a Durable Power of Attorney for the Authorization of Withdrawal of Medical Care," Estate Planning, Vol. II, No. 5, p.282, September, 1984; "The Right to Die," International Academy of Estate and Trust Law Proceedings, July, 1984; "Informed Consent to Medical Treatment and the Incompetent Patient Under California's New Conservatorship Law," CTLA Forum, Vol. XI, No. 10, December, 1981; "Medico/Legal Aspects of Care for the Dying," 1980 Scots Law Times 193; "Time of Death —Medico-legal Considerations," 16 Am Jur Proof of Facts 2d. 87, August, 1978; "The California Natural Death Act: A Critical Appraisal," 52 Calif. State Bar Journal No. 4, July/August, 1977; Chapter, "Legal Aspects," The Dilemmas of Euthanasia, New York, Doubleday, 1975; "The Legal Aspects of Medical Euthanasia," Bioscience, August, 1973; "Organ Transplantation and the Law," XXI Impact of Science on Society, Paris, UNESCO, No. 3, 1971; "Problems of Sex Determination and Alteration," The Medico-Legal Journal, Vol. 36, No. 4, 1968. Adjunct Lecturer, Department of Medical Ethics, University of California at San Francisco Medical School, 1984-1987. Visiting Lecturer: University of Edinburgh School of Law, 1985; University of Aberdeen School of Law 1980, 1985 and 1988. Judge Pro Tem, Napa Superior Court, 1982—; Napa Municipal Court, 1986—. Member, Board of Trustees, 1987-1992 and Chairman, 1990-1992, Queen of the Valley Hospital. *Member:* Napa County Bar Association (President, 1986-1987); State Bar of California; Consumer Attorneys of California. **PRACTICE AREAS:**

*(This Listing Continued)*

Civil Litigation; Local Government Law; Environmental Law; Real Estate Law.

**C. RICHARD LEMON,** born Orange, California, May 30, 1943; admitted to bar, 1969, California. *Education:* University of California at Los Angeles (A.B., 1965); Boalt Hall School of Law, University of California (J.D., 1968). Blue Key. Lecturer, Vineyard Leases and Winery Finance and Acquisition, University of California. Chairman, Napa Valley Winery Financial Group. Member, Board of Directors: Beringer Wine Estates; Napa National Bancorp; Chamber Music in Napa Valley. *Member:* State Bar of California (Member: Section of Corporation, Banking and Business Law; Committee on Corporations of Business Law Section, 1977-1979; Argibusiness Committee, Business Law Section); American Bar Association. **PRACTICE AREAS:** Corporate Law; Real Estate Law; Tax Law.

**FRANCIS J. COLLIN, JR.,** born San Francisco, California, December 1, 1942; admitted to bar, 1967, California. *Education:* University of California at Berkeley (A.B., 1964; J.D., 1967). Phi Beta Kappa. Co-Author: "Drafting the Durable Power of Attorney: A Systems Approach," Shephards-McGraw Hill, 1987, 1991, 1994. Instructor, Estate Planning, Golden Gate University Graduate School of Tax, 1976-1979. Lecturer, California Continuing Education of the Bar, 1969, 1980, 1982, 1987 and 1990; Estate Planning For The Client Who Owns Agricultural Assets, AICPA, 1986; AICPA Ninth Estate Planning Conference, 1986. Member, Probate and Estate Planning Subcommittee of the California Continuing Education of the Bar Joint Advisory Committee, 1982-1996. *Member:* Napa County and American (Member: Real Property, Probate and Trust Law Section; Senior Associate Article Editor, Probate and Property Magazine, 1988-1994; Chairman, Committee on Special Problems of the Aged and Persons Under Disability, 1986-1988) Bar Associations; State Bar of California (Member, Estate Planning, Trust and Probate Section; Chair, Pre-Death, Estate Planning Committee, 1982-1985). Fellow and Regent, American College of Trust and Estate Counsel; Acamedician, International Academy of Estate and Trust Law. Certified Specialist, Probate, Estate Planning and Trust Law, California Board of Specialization. **PRACTICE AREAS:** Estate Law; Tax Planning Law; Trust Law; Estate Administration Law.

**DAVID B. GILBRETH,** born Los Angeles, California, June 28, 1947; admitted to bar, 1976, California. *Education:* University of California at Berkeley (B.A., 1970); University of Denver (J.D., 1975); New York University (LL.M., in Taxation, 1976). Member, Denver Journal of International Law & Policy, 1974-1975. *Member:* Bar Association of San Francisco; Napa County Bar Association; State Bar of California (Member, Sections on: Public Law; Taxation; Real Property). **PRACTICE AREAS:** Real Estate Law; Land Use Law; Tax Law.

**CHARLES H. DICKENSON,** born Napa, California, March 27, 1953; admitted to bar, 1978, California. *Education:* University of California at Berkeley (A.B., 1975); Hastings College of Law, University of California (J.D., 1978). Phi Delta Phi. Co-Author: Note, "The Effect of the 1976 Tax Reform Act on the Ownership of Professional Sports Franchises," COM-/ENT-a Journal of Communications and Entertainment Law, Vol. 1, No. 1, Fall 1977. Judge Pro Tem, Napa Municipal Court, 1986—. *Member:* Napa County Bar Association; State Bar of California; Consumer Attorneys of California. **PRACTICE AREAS:** Civil Litigation; Personal Injury Law.

**PAUL G. CAREY,** born Santa Monica, California, February 7, 1956; admitted to bar, 1982, California. *Education:* University of California at Los Angeles (B.A., summa cum laude, Phi Beta Kappa, 1979); Hastings College of Law; Boalt Hall School of Law, University of California (J.D., 1982). Recipient, Milton D. Greene Award, 1980. First Place, McBaine and Traynor Moot Court Competitions, 1981. *Member:* Napa County Bar Association; State Bar of California. **PRACTICE AREAS:** Civil Litigation; Personal Injury Law; Real Property Litigation.

**RICHARD P. MENDELSON,** born Jacksonville, Florida, September 14, 1953; admitted to bar, 1982, California. *Education:* Harvard University (B.A., magna cum laude, Phi Beta Kappa, 1975); Oxford University, Oxford, England (M.A., 1977); Stanford University (J.D., 1982). Author: "New Prohibition Attacks on Alcohol: Demon Rum and Ineffective Paternalism Revisited," Washington Legal Foundation Legal Backgrounder, Vol. 9, No. 27, August 12, 1994. "Product Standards for Wines Sold in the U.S., " 1993 General Assembly of the International Office of Wine, San Francisco; "Product Liability for Defective Alcoholic Beverages," 1989 General Assembly of the International Association of Wine Law, Germany; "Trade in Wine with Canada: A Case Study of Trade Deregulation," 7 International Tax & Business Lawyer 91-119 (Winter 1989). Co-Author: "U.S. Wine Law," 61 Bulletin de l'OIV, 351-380, May-June, 1980; "Geographic References on U.S. Wine Labels," Conference on Historic Appellations of Origin,

*(This Listing Continued)*

**DICKENSON, PEATMAN & FOGARTY,** A PROFESSIONAL LAW CORPORATION, Napa—Continued

Spain, 1987; "Preparation for the Uruguay Round-California Agriculture Barriers to Trade," for the California State World Trade Commission, June, 1987; "Dismantling Wine Subsidies," Wines & Vines, October 1986; "Appellations of Origin for Wine in the U.S.," Bolletino del CIDEAO No. 1, August, 1985. Visiting Professor at Université d'Aix-Marseille Law Faculty, Aix-en-Provence, France, Summer, 1986, 1988, 1990. Lecturer, Université de Bordeaux Law Faculty, 1988, 1991, 1993. Past President and Director, Stanford Club of Napa Valley. *Member:* Napa County and American (Member, Steering Committee on Alcoholic Beverages Practice) Bar Associations; State Bar of California; International Association of Wine Law (President, 1993-1995); Hospitaliers de Pomerol. *LANGUAGES:* French. *PRACTICE AREAS:* Alcohol Beverage Law; Land Use Planning.

**JOSEPH M. KEEBLER,** born Abington Township, Pennsylvania, May 14, 1942; admitted to bar, 1967, California. *Education:* University of Redlands (B.A., in Economics, cum laude, 1964); Boalt Hall School of Law; University of California (J.D., 1967). Author: "Effect of the Randone Decision on Attachment and Release of Attachment Bonds," Res Ipsa Loquitur (San Francisco Law School), Vol. IV, No. 4, April, 1972. Writ Research Clerk, First District Court of Appeals, 1967-1968. City Attorney, City of St. Helena, 1975-1987. Adjunct Professor, Construction Law, University of Santa Clara School of Law, 1984-1988. Member, Panel of Arbitrators, American Arbitration Association. Member, Board of Trustees: Queen of The Valley Hospital, 1993—; Justin Siena High School, 1996—; Napa Valley College Foundation (President, 1986-1988). *Member:* Napa County Bar Association (President, 1993); State Bar of California. *PRACTICE AREAS:* Real Property; Land Use Planning; Estate Planning; Wills and Trust; Litigation; Corporate; Business and Construction.

**CATHY A. ROCHE,** born Worcester, Massachusetts; admitted to bar, 1988, California. *Education:* California State University at San Bernardino (B.A., 1979); Ohio State University (M.S., 1982); Hastings College of Law, University of California (J.D., 1988). Member, Hastings Journal of Communications and Entertainment Law, 1987-1988. Author: "A Convenient Procedure for the Chlorination of Deactivated Anilines," Journal of Synthetic Organic Chemistry (1985) 669. *Member:* Napa County Bar Association; State Bar of California. *PRACTICE AREAS:* Land Use Law; Real Estate Law.

**JONATHAN P. DYER,** born Kansas City, Missouri, August 20, 1957; admitted to bar, 1989, California and U.S. District Court, Eastern District of California; 1990, U.S. District Court, Northern District of California; 1993, South Carolina and U.S. Court of Appeals, Fourth Circuit; 1994, U.S. District Court, District of South Carolina. *Education:* University of Maryland (B.A., cum laude, 1986); University of California at Davis (J.D., 1989). Executive Editor, University of California at Davis Law Review, 1988. *Member:* Napa County Bar Association; State Bar of California (Member, Litigation Section); South Carolina Bar. *LANGUAGES:* Russian. *PRACTICE AREAS:* Civil Litigation.

**JAMES W. TERRY,** born Oakland, California, November 4, 1949; admitted to bar, 1976, California. *Education:* University of California at Berkeley (A.B., with distinction, 1972); University of Santa Clara (J.D., magna cum laude, 1976); New York University (LL.M. in Trade Regulation, 1978). Recipient: Donald L. Brown Fellowship in Trade Regulation. Member, Board of Trustees, Queen of the Valley Hospital Foundation, 1990—. *Member:* Napa County Bar Association; State Bar of California (Member; Real Property and Business Sections). *LANGUAGES:* French. *PRACTICE AREAS:* Corporate; Business Law; Banking Law; Real Property; Estate Planning and Administration.

**KATHERINE OHLANDT,** born Venezuela, June 26, 1951; admitted to bar, 1991, California. *Education:* Stanford University (B.A., with distinction, 1973); University of Texas (J.D., with honors, 1990). Order of the Coif. Co-Author: "Gift-Giving Under Durable Powers of Attorney," Tax Management Estate, Gifts and Trusts Journal, Jan.-Feb., 1995. *Member:* Napa County and American (Member: Section of Real Property, Probate and Trust Law, 1991-1996; Marital Deduction Committee, 1993; Special Problems of Farmers and Ranchers Committee, 1993; Generation Skipping Transfers, 1996; Employee Benefit Planning, 1996) Bar Associations; State Bar of California. *PRACTICE AREAS:* Estate Planning; Business Succession; Trust Administration; Probate. *Email:* KOHLANDT@LANCN.COM

**STANLEY D. BLYTH,** born Minneapolis, Minnesota, October 30, 1958; admitted to bar, 1993, California, U.S. District Court, Eastern District of California; 1994, U.S. District Court, Southern and Northern Districts of California and U.S. Court of Appeals, Tenth Circuit. *Education:* Sonoma State University (B.A., with distinction, 1990); University of California at Davis (J.D., 1993). Moot Court Board, Jessup Moot Court Team. *Member:* Napa County Bar Association; State Bar of California (Member, Litigation Section). [U.S. Marine Corps, 1983-1987]. *PRACTICE AREAS:* Civil Litigation; Personal Injury; Taxation.

**LINDA EMERSON,** born Chateauroux, France, September 6, 1958; admitted to bar, 1993, California. *Education:* California State University, Fullerton (B.A., highest honors, 1990); University of California, Davis (J.D., 1993). *Member:* Napa County Bar Association; State Bar of California (Member: Section of Environmental Law; Section of Real Property Law; Section of Public Law). *PRACTICE AREAS:* Land Use Planning; Local Government Law.

**THOMAS F. CAREY,** born Napa, California, February 23, 1968; admitted to bar, 1995, California. *Education:* Stanford University (B.A., 1990); Duke University (J.D., 1995). *Member:* Napa County and American Bar Associations; State Bar of California. *PRACTICE AREAS:* Land Use Planning; Alcoholic Beverage Regulation.

**GRACE GOODMAN ROSS,** born Tucson, Arizona, February 6, 1958; admitted to bar, 1983, Arizona; 1993, Washington; 1996, California. *Education:* University of California at Irvine (B.A., in Social Ecology, 1978); University of Southern California (J.D., 1982). Author: "With This Ring," Brides Magazine, August, 1988. Instructor, Business Law, University of Phoenix, 1989-1990. Special Magistrate, Justice of the Peace Pro Tem, Special Superior Court Commissioner, Pima County, Arizona, 1990-1991. Intern, U.S. Department of the Interior, 1996. *Member:* State Bar of Arizona; Napa County Women Lawyers (Vice President, 1996). *LANGUAGES:* Spanish. *PRACTICE AREAS:* Estate Planning; Trust Administration; Land Use.

OF COUNSEL

**WALTER J. FOGARTY, JR.,** born Sacramento, California, April 27, 1939; admitted to bar, 1965, California. *Education:* University of California at Berkeley (B.S., 1961; J.D., 1964). Phi Delta Phi. Member, Board of Trustees, Tulocay Cemetery Association, 1979—. *Member:* Napa County (President, 1972-1973) and American (Member; Real Property, Probate and Trust Law Section) Bar Associations; State Bar of California. *PRACTICE AREAS:* Estate Planning; Estate Administration Law.

**HOWARD G. DICKENSON** (Retired).

REPRESENTATIVE CLIENTS: Anchor Brewing Co.; Beckstoffer Vineyards; Beringer Wine Estates Company; Cakebread Cellars; Charles Krug Winery; Chateau St. Jean; Chateau Souverain; Clos du Val Wine Co.; Codorniu Napa, Inc.; Domaine Carneros; Domaine Chandon; Hess Collection Winery; Meridian Cellars; Napa Garbage Service; Napa County Land Trust; Napa Ridge; Napa Valley Vintners Association; Napa Land Title Co.; Napa National Bank; Niebaum-Coppola; Queen of the Valley Hospital; Robert Mondavi Winery; Silver Oak Cellars; Silverado Country Club & Resort; Stone Products Corp.; Sutter Home Winery; Trefethen Vineyards and Winery; Tulocay Cemetery; Upper Valley Disposal Service; Village Outlets.
LOCAL COUNSEL FOR: Heublein Fine Wine Group; Meadowood Resort Hotel; Remy Martin; Seagram Classics Wine Co.; Sterling Vineyards.

## GAGEN, McCOY, McMAHON & ARMSTRONG

A PROFESSIONAL CORPORATION
1001 SECOND STREET, SUITE 315
NAPA, CALIFORNIA 94559
Telephone: 707-224-8396
FAX: 707-224-5817

*Danville, California Office:* 279 Front Street P.O. Box 218. Telephone 510-837-0585. Fax: 510-838-5985.

*Real Estate, Business, Estate Planning, Federal and State Income Taxation, General Civil and Criminal Trial Practice, Insurance, Probate, Family and Corporation Law, Wine Industry Regulatory Matters, Sales, Leases, Mergers and Acquisitions of Vineyards and Wineries.*

**ROBERT M. FANUCCI,** born San Francisco, California, February 21, 1956; admitted to bar, 1982, California. *Education:* San Francisco State University (B.A., Political Science, 1978); Golden Gate University (J.D., with honors, 1982); New York University (LL.M., Taxation, 1989). Member, Golden Gate Law Review, 1981-1982. Author: "The Proper Treatment of Bad Debt Loss Involving Intra Family Loans," 11 Golden Gate Law Review, 1981. "§1031 Exchanges in Real Estate Subdivisions", CCIM Northern California, April-May 1990. Board of Directors, Napa Valley

*(This Listing Continued)*

Family Homes, 1991—. Planning Commissioner, City of St. Helena. Instructor, Income Tax and Financial Planning, University of California, Berkeley, Graduate School of Finance, 1986-1990. . *Member:* Napa and American Bar Associations; Bar Association of San Francisco (Member, Tax Section); State Bar of California. *LANGUAGES:* Italian. *PRACTICE AREAS:* Tax Law; Business Law; Real Estate Law; Estate Planning Law; Tax Law; Winery and Business Law.

**STEPHEN T. BUEHL,** born St. Louis, Missouri, February 11, 1947; admitted to bar, 1974, California. *Education:* Yale University (B.A., 1968); Stanford Law School (J.D., 1971). Chief Deputy Secretary of Agriculture and Services Agency, State of California, 1975-1977. Special Counsel and Executive Assistant to Chief Justice of California, San Francisco, 1977-1986. *Member:* Napa County and American Bar Associations; State Bar of California. (Resident). *PRACTICE AREAS:* Commercial Litigation; Business Law; Land Use Law; Wine Industry Regulatory Matters.

REPRESENTATIVE CLIENTS: Security Pacific National Bank; Tri-Valley Bank; Bank of San Ramon Valley; Mission-Valley Bancorp; Coldwell Banker; Shell Chemical Co.; East Bay Regional Park District; Hayden, Inc.; Merrill Lynch Relocation Management, Inc.; Provimi, Inc.; Transamerica Title Insurance Co.; First American Title Co.; Title Insurance & Trust.

(For personnel and biographical data, see professional biographies at Danville, California.)

## GAW, VAN MALE, SMITH, MYERS & MIROGLIO

*A PROFESSIONAL LAW CORPORATION*

Established in 1974

944 MAIN STREET
NAPA, CALIFORNIA 94559-3045
Telephone: 707-252-9000
Telecopier: 707-252-0792
URL: http://www.gvmsmm.com

Fairfield, California Office: Corporate Plaza. 1261 Travis Boulevard, Suite 350. Telephone: 707-425-1250. Fax: 707-425-1255.

*General Civil Trial Practice in all State and Federal Courts. Land Use, Planning and Local Government Law, Business and Corporate Law, Real Estate, Estate Planning and Probate Administration, Elder Law, Family Law, Criminal Law, Corporate and Personal Taxation, Pension and Profit Sharing, Agricultural Law, Alcohol Beverage Law and Personal Injury.*

**DAVID B. GAW,** born Berkeley, California, June 2, 1945; admitted to bar, 1971, Colorado; 1972, California. *Education:* University of Colorado (A.B., 1967); Hastings College of Law, University of California (J.D., 1971). Order of the Coif; Phi Delta Phi. Member, Thurston Society. Board of Directors (Chairman, 1991-1994), The Vintage Bank. *Member:* Napa County (President, 1994; Chairman, Estate Planning, Probate and Trust Law Section, 1982-1986), Solano County and American Bar Associations; State Bar of California (Member, Estate Planning and Probate Section); National Academy of Elder Law Attorneys. (Certified Specialist, Probate, Estate Planning and Trust Law, State Bar of California, Board of Legal Specialization; Certified as an Elder Law Attorney by the National Elder Law Foundation). *PRACTICE AREAS:* Estate Planning Law; Trust and Probate Law; Elder Law.

**NICHOLAS R. VAN MALE,** born Denver, Colorado, May 21, 1938; admitted to bar, 1971, Colorado and California. *Education:* University of California at Berkeley (A.B., 1962); University of California at Davis (J.D., 1970). Deputy District Attorney, Napa County, 1971-1973. *Member:* Napa County (President, 1986; Chairman, Criminal Law Section, 1982-1984) and American Bar Associations; State Bar of California. [Capt., USNR Ret.]. *PRACTICE AREAS:* Civil Litigation; Family Law; Land Use Planning Law.

**WYMAN G. SMITH, III,** born Sacramento, California, April 3, 1950; admitted to bar, 1976, California. *Education:* University of Colorado (B.A., 1972); McGeorge School of Law, University of the Pacific (J.D., 1976). Member, Traynor Society. *Member:* Napa County (Member, Real Estate and Corporate Sections), Solano County and American (Member, Business Law Section) Bar Associations; State Bar of California (Member, Real Property Law and Business Law Sections). *PRACTICE AREAS:* Business; Corporate; Real Estate Transactions.

**BRUCE A. MYERS,** born Oakland, California, November 3, 1951; admitted to bar, 1981, California and District of Columbia; 1982, U.S. Tax Court. *Education:* University of California at Berkeley (B.S., 1974); California State University at Chico (M.B.A., 1975); McGeorge School of Law, University of the Pacific (J.D., 1981; LL.M., 1984). Certified Public Accountant, 1980. *Member:* Napa County (Member, Real Estate and Corporate Sections) and American Bar Associations; State Bar of California (Member, Business Law Section); California Society of Certified Public Accountants; American Institute of Certified Public Accountants. *PRACTICE AREAS:* Taxation Law; Business Transactions; Pension Law; Profit Sharing Law.

**BRUCE A. MIROGLIO,** born St. Helena, California, September 13, 1957; admitted to bar, 1982, California. *Education:* University of California at Santa Barbara (B.A., 1979); McGeorge School of Law, University of the Pacific (J.D., 1982). Deputy District Attorney, Solano County, 1983-1984. *Member:* Napa County Bar Association; State Bar of California. *REPORTED CASES:* Vianna v. Doctors' Management Company (1994) 27 Cal.App.4th 1186. *PRACTICE AREAS:* Civil Litigation; Personal Injury Law; Medical Malpractice Defense; Probate Litigation; Employment Litigation; Wrongful Termination.

**JOYCE L. ELLIOTT,** born Fremont, California, May 12, 1959; admitted to bar, 1988, California. *Education:* California State University at Chico (B.S., 1981); University of San Francisco (J.D., 1988). Member, University of San Francisco Law Review, 1986-1987. *Member:* Solano County and Napa County (Member, Board of Directors, 1996-1997) Bar Associations; State Bar of California (Member, Family Law Section); Napa County Women Lawyer's Association. *PRACTICE AREAS:* Family Law.

**KELLY JAYNE BERRYMAN,** born Evanston, Illinois, September 30, 1965; admitted to bar, 1990, California. *Education:* Northwestern University (B.A., 1987); Hastings College of the Law, University of California (J.D., cum laude, 1990). Order of the Coif. Thurston Society. American Jurisprudence Award in Real Property. Member, Hastings Law Review, 1989-1990. *Member:* Napa County Bar Association (Member, Board of Directors, 1995-1996); State Bar of California; Napa County Women Lawyer's Association (President, 1993). *PRACTICE AREAS:* Business Transactions; Real Estate Transactions; Secured Finance; Commercial Leasing.

**CHRISTINE L. CRAIG,** born San Leandro, California, December 19, 1965; admitted to bar, 1992, California. *Education:* University of California at Berkeley (B.A., 1987); Santa Clara University (J.D., 1991; M.B.A., 1992). *Member:* Napa County Bar Association; State Bar of California (Member, Estate Planning, Trust and Probate Section); Napa County Women Lawyers Association. *PRACTICE AREAS:* Trust Administration; Probate; Estate Planning.

**ROBYN L. BALDWIN,** born Santa Maria, California, November 3, 1965; admitted to bar, 1993, California and U.S. District Court, Northern District of California. *Education:* University of California, San Diego (B.A., 1987); University of California Hastings College of the Law (J.D., 1992). Member, Hastings International and Comparative Law Journal, 1990-1991. *Member:* Sonoma County and American (Member, Steering Committee) Bar Associations; Association of Defense Counsel of Northern California; Sonoma County Young Lawyers Association; Sonoma County Women in Law; California Women Lawyers; Redwood Empire Trial Lawyers Association. *PRACTICE AREAS:* Litigation; Employment; Environmental; Trademark; Copyright.

**RHONDA LEE SAVITCH,** born Los Angeles, California, July 17, 1952; admitted to bar, 1993, California, U.S. District Court, Northern District of California and U.S. Court of Appeals, Ninth Circuit. *Education:* University of California, Berkeley (A.B., linguistics distinction, 1975); Hastings College of the Law, University of California (J.D., cum laude, 1993). Note Editor, Hastings Constitutional Law Quarterly, 1993. *Member:* Bar Association of San Francisco; Napa County Bar Association; State Bar of California; Napa County Women Lawyers Association; International Society of Wine Lawyers; Society of Wine Educators. *LANGUAGES:* French and Italian. *PRACTICE AREAS:* Civil Litigation; Land Use; Insurance Coverage; Bad Faith Litigation. *Email:* rsavitch@gvmsmm.com

REPRESENTATIVE CLIENTS: The Vintage Bank; The Doctor's Company; Eldex Laboratories, Inc.; Browns Valley Shopping Center; Diablo Timber; S. Anderson Vineyards; Cassayre-Forni Cellars; Heitz Wine Cellars; Robert Pecota Winery; Stags Leap Wine Cellars; ZD Wines; Duetto Wine Company, Ltd.; Napa Valley Vineyard Engineering; Ed Barwick Chrysler-Plymouth; Kastner Pontiac-Oldsmobile-GMC; Zumwalt Ford; Royce Instruments, Inc.; Bay-Tec Engineering; Chuadhary & Associates, Civil Engineers; Heide & Williams General Engineering; Mahorney, Alfonso & Associates, Civil Engineers; Ramondin, U.S.A., Inc.; North Bay Plywood; Ellis Construction Company; Skylark Wholesale Nursery; Michael W. Brooks & Associates; Jack Neal & Son Inc.; Indian Harvest Specialtifoods; Real Restaurants; Gerhard's Napa Valley Sausage; Coldwell Banker Brokers of the Valley; Crown Realty; Napa Land Title Company; Napa Valley Country Club; Silverado Country

*(This Listing Continued)*

**GAW, VAN MALE, SMITH, MYERS & MIROGLIO,** A PROFESSIONAL LAW CORPORATION, Napa—Continued

Club; Allen & Benedict, Inc.
LOCAL COUNSEL FOR: Wells Fargo Bank.
REFERENCE: The Vintage Bank.

(For additional biographical data, see Professional Biographies at Fairfield)

## JAMES V. JONES

1564 FIRST STREET
**NAPA, CALIFORNIA 94559**
Telephone: 707-252-8644
Fax: 707-252-0852

*General Civil and Criminal Trial Practice. Probate, Real Property, Family, Personal Injury, Municipal and Corporate Law.*

**JAMES V. JONES,** born Brooklyn, New York, June 26, 1939; admitted to bar, 1967, California. *Education:* Napa Junior College (A.A., 1959); University of California at Berkeley (A.B., 1961); Hastings College of Law, University of California (J.D., 1967). Chairman, Moot Court. Councilman, 1972-1976; Vice-Mayor, 1975-1976, City of Napa. Commissioner, Napa Community Redevelopment Agency, 1972-1976. Member, North Bay Regional Criminal Justice Board, 1973-1976. Judge Pro Tem, Napa County Superior and Municipal Courts, 1979—. Member, Napa County Law Library Commission, 1980-1987, 1992. *Member:* Napa County Bar Association (President, 1978); State Bar of California; Consumer Attorneys of California; The Association of Trial Lawyers of America. **LANGUAGES:** Spanish. **REPORTED CASES:** Roads v. Superior Court 275 Cal. App. 2d 593; People v. Mentzer 163 Cal. App. 3d 482.

A List of Clients Will Be Furnished Upon Request.
REFERENCE: Napa National Bank.

## BEVERLY SAXON LEONARD

Established in 1993

1001 2ND STREET, SUITE 345
**NAPA, CALIFORNIA 94559**
Telephone: 707-257-5378
Facsimile: 707-257-5399
Email: bsleonard@aol.com

*Civil Trial Practice, Business, Family, Land Use, Environmental and Employment Law.*

**BEVERLY SAXON LEONARD,** born San Francisco, California, March 3; admitted to bar, 1991, California. *Education:* Sonoma State University (B.A., 1984); San Francisco State University; Golden Gate University (J.D., 1990). Editor, Ninth Circuit Survey, vol. 21, Golden Gate University Law Review, 1989-1990. Author: "National Audubon Society v. Department of Water: The Ninth Circuit Disallows Federal Common Law Nuisance Claim for Mono Lake Water and Air Pollution," 20 Golden Gate University Law Review 209. Chairman, Napa City Planning Commission, 1985; 1991-1996. President, Napa County Legal Assistance. Member, Napa County Family Violence Prevention Council, 1995—. *Member:* State Bar of California; American Bar Association; Napa County Women Lawyers; Napa County Bar Association.

### ASSOCIATE

**KIM H. JORDAN**

## MURPHY, LOGAN, BARDWELL & LOOMIS

A PROFESSIONAL CORPORATION

2350 FIRST STREET
P.O. BOX 5540
**NAPA, CALIFORNIA 94581-0540**
Telephone: 707-257-8100
Fax: 707-257-6479

*General Civil and Trial Practice. Real Estate, Construction, Land Use, Taxation, Business, Corporate, Commercial, Family, Personal Injury, Bankruptcy, Labor, Criminal, Estate Planning and Probate Law.*

**J. MICHAEL MURPHY,** born Lander, Wyoming, November 7, 1950; admitted to bar, 1977, California and U.S. Court of Appeals, Ninth Circuit. *Education:* University of California at Davis (A.B., 1973); McGeorge
*(This Listing Continued)*

School of Law, University of the Pacific (J.D., 1977). Recipient, Certificate of Merit Institute for Administrative Justice, University of the Pacific. Lecturer, Construction Law, Napa Valley College, 1984-1986. Member, Board of Directors, Napa County Legal Assistance Agency, 1979-1980. Member, Legal Advisory Committee, Associated General Contractors, Inc., 1984—. *Member:* Napa County Bar Association; State Bar of California. **PRACTICE AREAS:** General Civil Litigation; Real Estate Law; Business Law; Personal Injury Law; Construction Law.

**DONALD J. LOGAN,** born Glendale, California, April 21, 1954; admitted to bar, 1981, California. *Education:* Pacific Union College (B.S., 1977); University of San Diego (J.D., 1980). Recipient, Ralph Gano Miller Award for Tax Studies, University of San Diego. Lecturer, Real Estate Law, Napa Valley College, 1983-1987. Member, Board of Trustees, Pacific Union College, 1986—; Member, Board of Directors, St. Helena Hospital, 1993—. *Member:* Napa County Bar Association; State Bar of California. **PRACTICE AREAS:** Real Estate Law; Tax Law; Business Law; Estate Planning.

**PAUL A. BARDWELL,** born Ipswich, England, March 13, 1951; admitted to bar, 1976, California; 1978, U.S. District Court, Northern District of California. *Education:* University of San Francisco (B.A., 1973); McGeorge School of Law, University of the Pacific (J.D., 1976). Instructor, Business Law, Napa Valley College, 1977-1990. *Member:* Napa County Bar Association (Member, Family Law Section; Vice President, 1996-1997); State Bar of California (Member, Family Law Section). **PRACTICE AREAS:** Family Law; Personal Injury Law.

**PAUL LOOMIS,** born Napa, California, September 25, 1954; admitted to bar, 1983, California and U.S. District Court, Northern District of California; 1989, U.S. District Court, Eastern District of California. *Education:* Humboldt State University; University of California at Santa Barbara (B.A., 1979); Loyola University of Los Angeles (J.D., 1983). *Member:* Napa County Bar Association; State Bar of California; Consumer Attorneys of California. **PRACTICE AREAS:** Construction Litigation; Personal Injury; Commercial Torts; Insurance Law.

**KELLY A. LANN,** born Burlingame, California, September 23, 1966; admitted to bar, 1993, California; 1994, U.S. District Court, Northern District of California. *Education:* University of California at Davis (A.B., 1988); Washington University (J.D., 1992). Phi Delta Phi. Member, Order of Barristers. Recipient, Dean's Book Award. *Member:* Napa County Bar Association; State Bar of California. **PRACTICE AREAS:** Family Law; Civil Litigation.

## JAMES D. RENDLEMAN

3273 CLAREMONT WAY #206
**NAPA, CALIFORNIA 94558**
Telephone: 707-258-6234
Fax: 707-258-6264

*Labor and Employment Law, Corporate and Business, Insurance Defense, Insurance Coverage, Tax.*

**JAMES D. RENDLEMAN,** born Columbia, South Carolina, October 1, 1956; admitted to bar, 1985, California; 1986, U.S. District Court, Northern, Southern, Eastern and Central Districts of California. *Education:* University of North Carolina (B.S., 1977); Golden Gate University (M.B.A., 1980; M.P.A., 1981); Whittier College School of Law (J.D., 1985); University of San Diego School of Law (LL.M., 1986). Delta Theta Phi. Member, Moot Court. Recipient: American Jurisprudence Award for Legal Skills; Napa Valley Grand Jury, 1992-1993. *Member:* Napa County Bar Association (Board of Directors, 1993-1994). [Lt. Col., U.S.A.F. Reserve, Active Duty, 1977-1986]. **LANGUAGES:** German. **PRACTICE AREAS:** Labor Law; Business Law; General Litigation; Political and Community Affairs.

REPRESENTATIVE CLIENTS: A list of representative clients will be furnished upon request.

## ZELLER, HOFF & ZELLER, INC.

Established in 1952

929 RANDOLPH STREET
**NAPA, CALIFORNIA 94559-2997**
Telephone: 707-252-6633
FAX: 707-252-9204

*General Civil and Trial Practice. Probate, Wills, Trusts, Estate Planning and Administration, Construction, Real Property, Corporate, Family Law. Commercial and Banking, Municipal Law, Insurance Law, Negligence, Personal Injury, Tort Law, Real Property and Governmental Entity Litigation.*

*(This Listing Continued)*

**ROBERT H. ZELLER,** born Napa, California, November 4, 1924; admitted to bar, 1952, California. *Education:* University of California (A.B., 1950); Hastings College of Law, University of California (J.D., 1951). City Attorney, City of St. Helena, 1959-1975. *Member:* Napa County Bar Association (President, 1962-1963); State Bar of California. **PRACTICE AREAS:** Estate Planning; Probate Law; Living Trusts and Wills; Corporate Law; Real Estate Transactions.

**PAUL M. HOFF,** born Culver City, California, September 27, 1946; admitted to bar, 1972, California. *Education:* University of California at Santa Barbara (B.A., 1968); Hastings College of the Law, University of California (J.D., 1971). Member, Panel of Arbitrators, American Arbitration Association. *Member:* Napa County (Secretary, 1980) and American (Member, Section of Tort and Insurance Practice) Bar Associations; State Bar of California. **REPORTED CASES:** Mavroudis vs. Superior Court (1980) 102 Cal.App.3d 594; Molien vs. Kaiser Foundation Hospitals (1980) 27 Cal.3d 916; Dinong vs. Superior Court (1980) 102 Cal.App.3d 845. **PRACTICE AREAS:** Civil Litigation; Personal Injury; Governmental Affairs; Real Property Litigation.

**CATHY A. ZELLER,** born San Francisco, California, September 21, 1952; admitted to bar, 1982, California. *Education:* University of California at Berkeley (A.B., 1974); San Francisco Law School (J.D., 1980). President, Napa Valley Cal Alumni. Member, Napa Valley Family Violence Prevention Council. *Member:* Napa County Bar Association; State Bar of California; Napa County Women Lawyers (Member, Board of Directors). **PRACTICE AREAS:** Estate Planning; Probate; Guardianships; Conservatorship; Business and Corporations; Family Law.

REPRESENTATIVE CLIENTS: Shafer Vineyards; Joseph Phelps Vineyards; Napa Electric Co.; Napa Valley Unified School District; County of Napa; Nestle USA; Piover's Services; Walkenhorst's; Vyborny Vineyard Mgt.; Oakville Grocery; Wight Vineyard Mgt.; Colonial Saddle Shop; Volcani Cucina Co.; Durilon Brake Co.; Shelter Creek Homeowners Association; China Epicure, LLC.
REFERENCE: Westamerica Bank.

---

## WELEBIR & McCUNE

A PROFESSIONAL LAW CORPORATION

### NEEDLES, CALIFORNIA

(See Redlands)

*Practice limited to Catastrophic Personal Injury and Wrongful Death, Products Liability, Aviation, Railroad and Toxic Torts. Class Actions related to Defective Products and Mass Torts.*

---

## BERLINER LAW OFFICES

224 MAIN STREET
### NEVADA CITY, CALIFORNIA 95959
Telephone: 916-265-5585
Fax: 916-478-0303
Email: berlinlw@nccn.net

*General Civil Practice emphasizing Corporate Law and Civil Litigation, Taxation.*

**HAROLD A. BERLINER,** born San Francisco, California, June 24, 1923; admitted to bar, 1951, California; 1964, U.S. Supreme Court. *Education:* University of San Francisco; University of Notre Dame (J.D., cum laude, 1945). Member, Notre Dame Lawyer, 1944-1945. City Attorney, Nevada City, 1955-1957. District Attorney, Nevada County, 1957-1973. Director, The California Supreme Court Historical Society, 1990—. *Member:* State Bar of California; American Bar Association.

**ERIC L. BERLINER,** born Nevada City, California, January 3, 1963; admitted to bar, 1991, Idaho and U.S. District Court, District of Idaho; 1992, U.S. Court of Appeals, Ninth Circuit; 1994, California. *Education:* Gonzaga University (B.A., 1985); University of San Francisco (J.D., 1991). Recipient, American Jurisprudence Award in Secured Transactions and Partnership Taxation. Member, Governing Counsel of Idaho Corporate and Securities Section, 1992-1994. Member, Idaho LLC Drafting Task Force and Idaho RUPA Task Force. *Member:* American Bar Association.

*(This Listing Continued)*

---

### ASSOCIATE

**LAWRENCE D. SANDERS,** born Queens, New York, May 28, 1967; admitted to bar, 1994, California and U.S. District Court, Eastern District of California. *Education:* University of Chicago (B.A., 1989); University of Oregon (J.D., 1994).

REPRESENTATIVE CLIENTS: Boise Cascade Corporation; Coast to Coast; BancTexas; Roman Catholic Diocese of Boise; Alumet Corporation; Pechiney Corporation; Monotype Digital.

---

## NANCI G. CLINCH

A PROFESSIONAL CORPORATION

Established in 1982

SUITE 204, 401 SPRING STREET
### NEVADA CITY, CALIFORNIA 95959
Telephone: 916-265-8690
Fax: 916-265-8694

*Family Law.*

**NANCI G. CLINCH,** born Nevada City, California, May 21, 1950; admitted to bar, 1977, California; 1981, U.S. District Court, Eastern District of California and U.S. Court of Appeals, Ninth Circuit; 1989, U.S. Supreme Court. *Education:* University of Arizona (B.A., 1973); University of San Diego (J.D., December, 1976). Member, 1981-1988 and Secretary, 1986-1988, Board of Directors, Legal Services of Northern California. Commissioner, Commission on Judicial Nominees Evaluation of the State Bar of California, 1986-1988. Commission Member, "2020 Vision: A Plan for the Future of California's Courts." Delegate, ABA House of Delegates, representing the State Bar of California, 1992-1996. *Member:* Nevada County Bar Association (President, 1988 and 1989); State Bar of California (Member, Board of Governors, District One, 1989-1991; Vice President, 1990-1991); California Women Lawyers; Foundation of the State Bar (Treasurer, 1990-1992; Chair, Scholarship Committee, 1991-1996). (Certified Specialist, Family Law, The State Bar of California Board of Legal Specializations).

---

## LAW OFFICES OF
## CHARLES R. FARRAR, JR.

### NEVADA CITY, CALIFORNIA

(See Grass Valley)

*Business and Commercial Transactions and Agreements. General Civil and Trial and Appellate Practice, Easements and Real Property Law, Land Use and Environmental Law (C.E.Q.A.), Computer Law, Administrative and Municipal Law and Mediation Law.*

---

## STEPHEN A. MUNKELT

Established in 1983

107 COURT STREET
### NEVADA CITY, CALIFORNIA 95959
Telephone: 916-265-8508
Fax: 916-265-0881
Email: smunk@gv.net

*Civil and Criminal Litigation, and Family Law.*

**STEPHEN A. MUNKELT,** born San Diego, California, December 12, 1950; admitted to bar, 1978, California and U.S. District Court, Southern, Central and Eastern Districts of California; 1989, U.S. Court of Appeals, Ninth Circuit. *Education:* University of California at Santa Barbara (B.A., 1973); University of San Diego (J.D., 1977). *Member:* Nevada County Bar Association; California Attorneys for Criminal Justice; National Association of Criminal Defense Lawyers. **REPORTED CASES:** People v. Aldridge (1984) 35 Cal. 3d 473; People v. Schroeder (1991) 227 Cal. App. 3d 784. **PRACTICE AREAS:** Criminal Defense Law; Civil Litigation; Personal Injury-Plaintiff.

## OLESON LAW CORPORATION

11931 WILLOW VALLEY ROAD
**NEVADA CITY, CALIFORNIA 95959**
Telephone: 916-478-0415
Fax: 916-478-0184
Email: olelaw@oro.net

*San Francisco, California Office:* 601 California Street, Suite 800. Telephone: 415-392-0415. Fax: 415-392-0372.

*General Civil Litigation emphasizing Insurance Coverage, Environmental, Real Estate, Business and Construction Litigation.*

**RAYMOND C. OLESON,** born Casper, Wyoming, March 1, 1950; admitted to bar, 1976, California. *Education:* Stanford University (A.B., with distinction, 1972); Northwestern University (J.D., cum laude, 1976). Notes and Comments Editor, Journal of Criminal Law and Criminology, 1975-1976. *Member:* Bar Association of San Francisco; Los Angeles County and Nevada County Bar Associations. **REPORTED CASES:** CNA Casualty v. Seaboard Surety 176 Cal. App. 3d 598 (1986); Lunsford v. American Guarantee and Liability, 18 F.3d 653 (9th Cir. 1994).

---

## RICH, FUIDGE, MORRIS & IVERSON, INC.

**NEVADA CITY, CALIFORNIA**

(See Marysville)

*General Civil and Trial Practice. Corporation, Water Rights, Insurance, Real Estate, Crop Damage, Estate Planning, Family and Probate Law. Medical and Legal Malpractice, Personal Injury, Employment Law, Criminal Law, Alternative Dispute Resolution.*

---

## TERRY A. ROACH

14137 BANNER MOUNTAIN LOOKOUT ROAD
P.O. BOX 1558
**NEVADA CITY, CALIFORNIA 95959**
Telephone: 916-265-2475
FAX: 916-265-3198
Email: terryr@treehouse.org

*Real Property, Land Use, Environmental, Business Law, Estate Planning and Probate, Computer Law, General Civil Trial and Appellate Practice and Alternative Dispute Resolution.*

**TERRY A. ROACH,** born Beloit, Kansas, April 28, 1938; admitted to bar, 1966, California. *Education:* Stanford University (A.B., 1961); Hastings College of Law, University of California (LL.B., 1965). *Member:* Nevada County and American Bar Associations; State Bar of California.

A List of Representative Clients and References will be furnished upon request.

---

## SHINE, COMPTON & NELDER-ADAMS

**NEVADA CITY, CALIFORNIA**

(See Grass Valley)

*General Civil and Real Estate Litigation, environmental, Land Use, Family Law, Estate Planning/Probate, Business Law, Employment, Government and Public Agency Law and Personal Injury.*

---

## SPILLER, McPROUD & KRAEMER

505 COYOTE STREET, SUITE A
**NEVADA CITY, CALIFORNIA 95959**
Telephone: 916-265-5831
Telecopier: 916-265-5836
URL: http://www.SMBK.COM

*General Civil Trial Practice. Real Property, Land Use and Environmental Law, Commercial Litigation, Probate, Administrative, Corporate, Mediation and Arbitration.*

**FIRM PROFILE:** The law firm began in 1977 with its offices in Nevada City, the county seat of Nevada County, just over one hour's drive from Sacramento. The firm's specialization and the expertise of its attorneys, balanced between litigation and transactional work, has allowed the firm to provide the highest quality legal services and effective practical solutions for our clients. We value each client relationship and recognize that their success will directly result in the success of our firm.

**STEVEN T. SPILLER,** born Baton Rouge, Louisiana, August 7, 1946; admitted to bar, 1976, California; 1984, U.S. Court of Appeals, Ninth Circuit; 1987, U.S. Supreme Court and U.S. District Court, Northern and Eastern Districts of California. *Education:* American College of Switzerland, Leysin, Switzerland and Occidental College (B.A., 1972); Louisiana State University (J.D., 1975). *Member:* State Bar of California; American Bar Association. [U.S. Army, 1967-1970]. **REPORTED CASES:** Moylan v. Dykes, 181 Cal.App. 3d. 561 (1986). **PRACTICE AREAS:** Commercial Litigation; Real Property; Business Transactions.

**CLARENCE H. McPROUD,** born Whittier, California, July 6, 1954; admitted to bar, 1979, California and U.S. District Court, Eastern District of California. *Education:* University of California at Davis (B.S., with highest honors, 1976); King Hall School of Law, University of California at Davis (J.D., 1979). Phi Kappa Phi. Former Trustee, Nevada County Board of Law Library. *Member:* State Bar of California. **REPORTED CASES:** Neighborhood Action Group v. County of Calaveras, 156 Cal. App. 3d. 1176 (1984). **PRACTICE AREAS:** Property Law; Probate and Estate Planning; Business Law. **Email:** mcproud@nccn.net

**HOLLY KRAEMER,** born Mt. Vernon, New York, October 30, 1944; admitted to bar, 1984, California and U.S. District Court, Eastern District of California. *Education:* University of California at Santa Barbara (B.A., 1980); University of Utah (J.D., 1984). Author: "Motions to Strike," California Civil Procedure Before Trial, 3d Ed., Continuing Education of the Bar (1990). Consultant: Bancroft-Whitney, California Civil Practice (1992) "Format of Court Papers" and "Submission of Agreed Case." *Member:* State Bar of California. **LANGUAGES:** French. **PRACTICE AREAS:** Business and Real Estate Transactions; General Civil Litigation.

REPRESENTATIVE CLIENTS: Boys Town USA (Father Flangan's Boy's Home); Sierra Nevada Memorial Hospital; Newmont Explorations, Ltd.; DANA Commercial Credit Corp.; Toyota Motor Sales, U.S.A., Inc.; Nevada City Winery; Thermo Ecotek Corp.; Graham-Patten Systems, Inc.; Midwest Cooling Towers; Evergreen Teller Services; Fidelity National Title Insurance Company.

---

## KARL J. SCHNETZ

671 NEWCASTLE ROAD, SUITE 1
P.O. BOX 291
**NEW CASTLE, CALIFORNIA 95658**
Telephone: 916-663-1100
Fax: 916-663-2602

*Personal Injury, Civil Litigation, Insurance Law, Real Estate, Contracts and Criminal Law.*

**KARL J. SCHNETZ,** admitted to bar, 1977, California. *Education:* California State University, Sacramento (A.B., 1957); Lincoln University (J.D., 1976). *Member:* State Bar of California. **LANGUAGES:** Spanish, German and French. **PRACTICE AREAS:** Personal Injury; Civil Litigation; Insurance Law; Real Estate; Contracts; Criminal Law.

---

## LAW OFFICES OF JOHN R. ALCORN

Established in 1980

500 NEWPORT CENTER DRIVE, SUITE 300
**NEWPORT BEACH, CALIFORNIA 92660**
Telephone: 714-721-1100
Fax: 714-721-9700

*U.S. Immigration and Nationality Law.*

**JOHN R. ALCORN,** born Waukegan, Illinois, May 20, 1949; admitted to bar, 1975, District of Columbia; 1980, California and U.S. District Court, Central District of California; 1987, U.S. Court of Appeals, Ninth Circuit. *Education:* Stanford University (B.A., 1970); University of Santa Clara (J.D., 1973). *Member:* District of Columbia Bar; State Bar of California. [Capt., U.S. Marine Corps., 1974-1977]. (Certified Specialist, Immigration and Nationality Law, The State Bar of California Board of Legal Specialization). **LANGUAGES:** German. **PRACTICE AREAS:** Deportation; Asylum; Immigration; U.S. Work Visas; Appeals; U.S. Permanent Residents.

*(This Listing Continued)*

## PROFESSIONAL BIOGRAPHIES

## CALIFORNIA—NEWPORT BEACH

*LEGAL SUPPORT PERSONNEL*

**Denise Pierce** (Paralegal)  **Amy L. Gettys** (Legal Assistant)

REPRESENTATIVE CLIENTS: Fluor Daniel, Inc.; Litton Industries, Inc.; Transamerica Corporation; Pacific Mutual Life Insurance; Mercedes-Benz Advanced Design of North America; Meridien Hotels.

## ALLEN AND FLATT INCORPORATED
Established in 1974

SUITE 370, 4400 MACARTHUR BOULEVARD
**NEWPORT BEACH, CALIFORNIA 92660**
Telephone: 714-752-7474
FAX: 714-752-1645

*General Civil Trial and Appellate Practice. Personal Injury, Products Liability, Insurance Coverage, Insurance Defense, Negligence, Bad Faith and Business Litigation. Trials in all State and Federal Courts.*

FIRM PROFILE: *The practice was established in 1974 and has been located in Newport Beach since inception. Since 1990 the firm has successfully concluded by settlement or jury verdict four separate cases resulting in recoveries in excess of $1,000,000 each. The firm has a number of reported cases including Afuso v. U.S.F.G. (1985) 169 Cal. App. 3d 859, 215 Cal. Rptr. 490, Westfield Insurance Co. v. DeSimone (1988) 201 Cal.App.3d 598, 247 Cal. Rptr. 291 and Brookview v. Heltzer Enterprises (1990) 218 Cal. App. 3d 502, 267 Cal. Rptr. 76.*

**ROBERT F. ALLEN, JR.,** born Knoxville, Tennessee, May 10, 1949; admitted to bar, 1974, California and U.S. District Court, Central District of California; 1985, U.S. Supreme Court. *Education:* University of California at Irvine (B.S., Economics, cum laude, 1971); University of the Pacific, McGeorge School of Law (J.D., 1974). Judge Pro Tem, Orange County Superior Court, 1980—. Arbitrator: Orange County Superior Court, 1979—. Member, Panel of Arbitrators, American Arbitration Association. *Member:* Orange County and American Bar Associations; State Bar of California; The Association of Trial Lawyers of America; Consumer Attorneys of California; Consumer Attorneys Association of Los Angeles; Orange County Trial Lawyers Association; Association of Southern California Defense Counsel; The Association of Trial Lawyers of America. **PRACTICE AREAS:** Civil Trial Practice; Appellate Practice; Personal Injury Law; Products Liability Law; Insurance Coverage.

**JOHN C. FLATT,** born Takoma Park, Maryland, February 3, 1944; admitted to bar, 1970, Maryland; 1976, California; 1977, U.S. District Court, Central District of California and U.S. Tax Court. *Education:* University of Richmond (B.A., 1966); University of Baltimore (J.D., 1969). *Member:* Orange County Bar Association (Member, Business and Real Estate Sections); State Bar of California. **PRACTICE AREAS:** Negligence Law; Business Litigation; Insurance Coverage.

---

**JAMES E. BALLIDIS,** born San Francisco, California, October 17, 1955; admitted to bar, 1985, California; 1990, U.S. District Court, Central District of California. *Education:* California State University (B.S., 1982); Southwestern University (J.D., 1985). Editor, Engineering Magazine, 1985. Member, Hastings Advanced Advocacy Program, 1991. *Member:* Orange County and American Bar Associations; State Bar of California; Consumer Attorneys Association of California; Consumer Attorneys of Los Angeles; Orange County Trial Lawyers Association; Association of Trial Lawyers of America. **PRACTICE AREAS:** Civil Trial Practice; Appellate Practice; Personal Injury Law; Products Liability Law; Negligence Law.

**SUZANNE BOYER LESLIE,** born Inglewood, California, May 1, 1962; admitted to bar, 1987, California; 1990, U.S. District Court, Central District of California. *Education:* California State University (B.A., 1983); Western State University (J.D., 1986). Delta Theta Phi. *Member:* Orange County and American Bar Associations; State Bar of California; Consumer Attorneys of California; Association of Trial Lawyers of America. **PRACTICE AREAS:** Civil Trial Practice; Personal Injury Law; Negligence Law.

**JOHN A. EL-FARRA,** born Hollywood, California, October 29, 1969; admitted to bar, 1995, California and U.S. District Court, Central District of California. *Education:* University of California at Santa Barbara (B.A., 1992); Southwestern University (J.D., magna cum laude, 1995). Editor, Notes and Comments, Southwestern University Law Review, 1994-1995. *Member:* Orange County, Los Angeles County (Member, Litigation Sec-

*(This Listing Continued)*

tion) and American Bar Associations; State Bar of California. **PRACTICE AREAS:** Civil Trial Practice; Personal Injury Law; Product Liability Law; Negligence Law.

REFERENCE: Bank of America, Newport Beach.

## ALVARADO, SMITH, VILLA & SANCHEZ
*A PROFESSIONAL CORPORATION*

SUITE 800
4695 MACARTHUR COURT
P.O. BOX 8677
**NEWPORT BEACH, CALIFORNIA 92658-8677**
Telephone: 714-955-1433
Fax: 714-955-1704
URL: http://www.Alvarado-Smith.com

Los Angeles, California Office, 611 West Sixth Street, Suite 2650. Telephone: 213-229-2554. Fax: 213-617-8966.

*Sophisticated Business Transactions and Complex Litigation.*

FIRM PROFILE: *Alvarado, Smith, Villa & Sanchez is a diversified law firm made up of highly-skilled and experienced attorneys, representing clients engaged in sophisticated business transactions and complex litigation. The firm maintains offices in Newport Beach and Los Angeles and is well-positioned to service clients throughout the entire Southern California region.*

*The Firm's transactional department represents numerous real estate developers, corporate clients, governmental entities, financial institutions and mortgage lenders in connection with all aspects of commercial and residential real estate matters, loan originations, documentation and loan portfolio management. The Firm also represents various real estate developers, investors and manufacturers relative to transactions in Mexico. In addition, the Firm's litigation department has extensive experience handling routine and complex litigation matters pertaining to general commercial disputes, franchise, employment, construction defect litigation and financial institution actions, including director and officer professional liability, loan defaults, and foreclosure actions.*

*The Firm has achieved additional prominence through the extensive involvement of the Firm's attorneys in civic and philanthropic activities throughout Southern California.*

**RAYMOND G. ALVARADO** (See Los Angeles Office).

**RUBEN A. SMITH,** born Guadalajara, Jalisco, Mexico, 1957; admitted to bar, 1985, California. *Education:* University of Southern California (B.S., 1979; M.P.A., 1982); Yale Law School (J.D., 1984). Managing Editor, Yale Journal on Regulation, 1982-1984. *Member:* Orange County, Hispanic Bar Association (Past President, 1994); State Bar of California; Southern California Edison Advisory Board; Orange County Economic Development Consortium Board; Hispanic Chamber of Commerce Board. **LANGUAGES:** Spanish. **PRACTICE AREAS:** Real Estate; Commercial and Financial Transactions; U.S./Mexico Transactions.

**MAURICE SANCHEZ,** born Orange, California, June 6, 1956; admitted to bar, 1981, California and U.S. District Court, Central District of California; 1982, U.S. District Court, Southern District of California. *Education:* University of California at Irvine (B.A., 1978); Boalt Hall School of Law, University of California at Berkeley (J.D., 1981). Co-Director, James Patterson McBaine Moot Court Honors Competition, 1981. Member, Moot Court Board. Judicial Extern to Hon. Matthew O. Tobriner, California Supreme Court, 1980. *Member:* Orange County (Member, Business Litigation Section) and Orange County Hispanic Bar Associations (Trustee, 1988, 1990; President, 1989); State Bar of California. **LANGUAGES:** Spanish. **PRACTICE AREAS:** Automotive Franchise; Labor and Employment; General Business Litigation.

**FERNANDO VILLA** (See Los Angeles Office).

**JOHN M. SORICH,** admitted to bar, 1986, California; 1988, U.S. District Court, Central, Southern, and Northern Districts of California. *Education:* Harvard University (B.A., 1982); Suffolk University (J.D., 1986); Loyola University. **PRACTICE AREAS:** Secured Transaction Litigation; Business Litigation; Environmental Litigation; Construction Defect Litigation.

**BARBARA L. TANG,** admitted to bar, 1988, California. *Education:* University of California at Berkeley (B.A., 1980); Loyola of Los Angeles (J.D., 1988). Staff Member and Editor, Loyola of Los Angeles Law Review, 1986-1988. **PRACTICE AREAS:** Public Utilities; Corporate.

*(This Listing Continued)*

CAA1385B

CALIFORNIA—NEWPORT BEACH                                    MARTINDALE-HUBBELL LAW DIRECTORY 1997

**ALVARADO, SMITH, VILLA & SANCHEZ, A PROFESSIONAL CORPORATION, Newport Beach—Continued**

RAÚL F. SALINAS (See Los Angeles Office).

J. MICHELLE HICKEY (See Los Angeles Office).

**JOHN B. CARMICHAEL, III,** admitted to bar, 1982, California and U.S. District Court, Southern District of California; U.S. District Court, Central District of California. *Education:* University of Southern California (B.S., 1978; J.D., 1982). *PRACTICE AREAS:* Mortgage Banking; Real Estate Transactions and Lending; Commercial Corporate Law.

**FRANCES Q. JETT** (See Los Angeles Office).

**SUSAN BADE HULL** (See Los Angeles Office).

**CHRISTOPHER M. LEO,** admitted to bar, 1993, California. *Education:* University of California, Los Angeles (B.A., Economics/Business, 1989); Gonzaga University School of Law (J.D., cum laude, 1992); Georgetown University Law Center (LL.M., International and Comparative Law, 1993). *PRACTICE AREAS:* General Corporate; International.

**AMY TOBOCO DIBB,** admitted to bar, 1990, California and U.S. District Court, Southern and Northern Districts of California; 1994, U.S. Court of Appeals, Ninth Circuit. *Education:* University of Denver (B.A., 1986); Loyola University (J.D., 1990). *PRACTICE AREAS:* Business Litigation; Civil Litigation; Commercial Litigation.

**STEVEN M. LAWRENCE** (See Los Angeles Office).

**ROBERT W. BROWN, JR.** (See Los Angeles Office).

**STEVEN C. YUNG** (See Los Angeles Office).

**THOMAS A. ZEIGLER,** born Orange, California, March 4, 1960; admitted to bar, 1989, California and U.S. District Court, Central District of California; 1991, U.S. District Court, Southern District of California. *Education:* University of California at Los Angeles; University of California at Irvine; California State Polytechnic University (B.S., 1984); Northwestern School of Law, Lewis & Clark College (J.D., 1988). *PRACTICE AREAS:* Corporate/Business; Public Utilities; Intellectual Property.

**ROGER E. BORG,** born Salt Lake City, Utah, November 6, 1956; admitted to bar, 1985, California and U.S. District Court, Central, Northern and Southern Districts of California; 1989, U.S. Court of Appeals, Ninth Circuit; 1994, U.S. District Court, Eastern District of California and U.S. District Court, District of Arizona. *Education:* Brigham Young University (B.A., summa cum laude and high honors, 1981); University of California at Los Angeles (J.D., 1984). *LANGUAGES:* Italian. *PRACTICE AREAS:* Litigation.

REPRESENTATIVE CLIENTS: Arco; Bank of America; Chevron U.S.A. Products Company; CIGNA; City of San Diego; CRS Sirrine, Inc.; EMC Mortgage; FDIC; Fujitsu Business Communications; Honda North America, Inc.; Long Beach Bank; Mazda Motor of America, Inc.; Mission Viejo Company; Nissan Motor Corporation in U.S.A.; Pacific Equity Funding, Inc.; The Presley Companies; Southern California Edison; STV Engineering; Taco Bell Corporation; Union Bank; Univision Television Group; Unocal; Volvo Cars of North America; Wells Fargo Bank.

(For Complete Biographical Data on additional personnel, please see Professional Biographies at Los Angeles, California)

## ASHWORTH & MORAN
*18 CORPORATE PLAZA, SUITE 114*
**NEWPORT BEACH, CALIFORNIA 92660**
Telephone: 714-720-1477
Fax: 714-720-1478

Laguna Niguel, California Office: 28202 Cabot Road, Suite 300. Telephone: 714-365-5776. Fax: 714-365-5720.

*General Civil, Trial and Appellate Practice. State and Federal Courts, Corporation, Business and Real Estate Law, Estate Planning.*

**MARK S. ASHWORTH,** born Provo, Utah, April 20, 1951; admitted to bar, 1978, California; 1982, U.S. District Court, Northern and Southern Districts of California and U.S. Appeals Court, Ninth Circuit. *Education:* Brigham Young University (B.S., 1972); Western State University (J.D., 1978). Listed in, Who's Who in California, 1986. Arbitrator, 1992—; Judge Pro Tem, 1992—, Orange County Superior Court. *Member:* Orange County and American Bar Associations; State Bar of California (Member, Litigation Section). *PRACTICE AREAS:* Professional Liability; General Civil

*(This Listing Continued)*

CAA1386B

Litigation; Insurance Defense; Chiropractic Malpractice Law; Medical Malpractice Law; Legal Malpractice Law; Personal Injury; Insurance Litigation.

(For biographical data of firm other personnel, See Professional Biographies at Laguna Niguel, California)

## BALDIKOSKI, CHARLES & KANE
*4695 MACARTHUR COURT, SUITE 860*
**NEWPORT BEACH, CALIFORNIA 92660**
Telephone: 714-852-8868
Facsimile: 714-852-9878

*General Business, Corporate, Business Finance, and Real Property Law and Transactions.*

**THOMAS H. BALDIKOSKI** (1937-1993).

**BRUCE H. CHARLES,** born Los Angeles, California, December 16, 1951; admitted to bar, 1977, California; 1978, U.S. District Court, Central District of California. *Education:* University of Southern California (B.A., cum laude, 1974); Waseda University, Tokyo, Japan; University of California at Los Angeles (J.D., 1977). *Member:* Orange County Bar Association; State Bar of California.

**STEPHEN M. KANE,** born Olean, New York, August 6, 1956; admitted to bar, 1982, California. *Education:* Stanford University (B.A., 1978); University of Southern California (MBA, 1982; J.D., 1982). *Member:* Orange County Bar Association; State Bar of California.

## BALFOUR MacDONALD MIJUSKOVIC & OLMSTED
*A PROFESSIONAL CORPORATION*
**NEWPORT BEACH, CALIFORNIA**
(See Costa Mesa)

*Corporate and Business Practice. Estate and Trust Planning and Administration. Litigation in all Federal and State Courts. Mergers and Acquisitions. Real Property.*

## BALOG & RASCH
*1601 DOVE STREET, SUITE 184*
**NEWPORT BEACH, CALIFORNIA 92660**
Telephone: 714-851-2500
Fax: 714-851-2520

*Sports, Transactions, Estate Planning, Probate, Corporate, Family and Real Property Law.*

### MEMBERS OF FIRM

**TIMOTHY A. BALOG,** born Cleveland, Ohio, July 30, 1962; admitted to bar, 1994, California. *Education:* Cleveland State University (B.B.A., 1984; M.B.A., 1987); Western State University College of Law (J.D., 1992). *Member:* Orange County Bar Association; State Bar of California. *PRACTICE AREAS:* Sports Law; Estate Planning; Probate; Corporate; Family Law; Real Property.

**ROBERT M. RASCH,** born Santa Monica, California, April 21, 1953; admitted to bar, 1978, California. *Education:* University of Southern California (B.S., 1975); Loyola University Law School (J.D., 1977). Certified Public Accountant, California, 1983. *PRACTICE AREAS:* Estate Planning; Business Law; Tax Planning; Non-Profit Tax Law; Corporate Law; Family Law; Trust Administration; Probate Administration; Real Property.

## BARGER & WOLEN
*19800 MACARTHUR BOULEVARD, SUITE 800 (IRVINE)*
**NEWPORT BEACH, CALIFORNIA 92715**
Telephone: 714-757-2800
FAX: 714-752-6313
Email: barwol@ix.netcom.com

Los Angeles, California Office: 515 South Flower Street, 34th Floor, 90071. Telephone: 213-680-2800. Cable Address: "Barwol". Facsimile: 213-614-7399.

*(This Listing Continued)*

# PROFESSIONAL BIOGRAPHIES

# CALIFORNIA—NEWPORT BEACH

*San Francisco, California Office:* 47th Floor, 101 California Street, 94111. Telephone: 415-434-2800. FAX: 415-434-2533.

*New York, N.Y. Office:* 100 Park Avenue, 23rd Floor, 10017. Telephone: 212-557-2800. FAX: 212-213-1199.

*Sacramento, California Office:* 925 "L" Street, Suite 1100, 95814. Telephone: 916-448-2800. FAX: 916-442-5961.

*General Civil Practice. Banking, Municipal, Tax, Corporation, Securities, Real Property, Construction, Family, Estate Planning, Probate, Business and Bankruptcy Law. Trial and Appeals.*

## MEMBERS OF FIRM

**DON R. ADKINSON,** born Santa Ana, California, June 14, 1928; admitted to bar, 1956, California. *Education:* Pomona College (B.A., 1950); Boalt Hall School of Law, University of California (LL.B., 1956). Phi Delta Phi. Deputy District Attorney, 1956-1960. Member, Newport Beach Planning Commission, 1968-1972. *Member:* Orange County Bar Association; State Bar of California. (Resident). **PRACTICE AREAS:** Real Property Law; Estate Planning Law; Probate Law; Municipal Law.

**DENNIS W. HARWOOD,** born Orange, California, October 8, 1938; admitted to bar, 1965, California. *Education:* Pomona College (B.A., 1960); University of Southern California (LL.B., 1964). Phi Delta Phi. Member, Editorial Board, University of Southern California Law Review, 1963-1964. Member, Board of Trustees, Orange County Law Library, 1977-1986 (President, 1979-1980) Vice Chairman, Fountain Valley Planning Commission. Councilman, City of Fountain Valley, 1967-1968. *Member:* Orange County (Director, 1972-1978) and American Bar Associations; State Bar of California. (Resident). **PRACTICE AREAS:** Real Property Law; Corporate Law; Securities Law.

**JOHN M. MEINDL,** born Regensburg, Germany, February 1, 1944; admitted to bar, 1972, California and U.S. District Court, Central, Eastern, Northern and Southern Districts of California; 1979, U.S. Supreme Court; 1984, U.S. Court of Appeals, Ninth Circuit. *Education:* University of California at Berkeley (B.A., 1966); University of Sussex, England and University of Surrey, England (M.Sc., 1968); Loyola University of Los Angeles (J.D., 1971). *Member:* Orange County and American Bar Associations; State Bar of California; American Society of International Law. (Resident). **LANGUAGES:** German. **PRACTICE AREAS:** Real Property Law; Construction Law; Business Law.

**EDWIN A. OSTER,** born French Camp, California, December 6, 1950; admitted to bar, 1976, California and U.S. District Court Central District of California; 1978, U.S. Court of Appeals, Ninth Circuit; 1981, U.S. District Court, Northern and Southern Districts of California; 1982, U.S. District Court, Eastern District of California. *Education:* Stanford University (B.A., 1972); University of California at Davis (J.D., 1976). Instructor, Legal Research and Writing, University of California at Davis School of Law, 1975-1976. Law & Motion Judge Pro Tem, Orange County Superior Court, 1989—. Arbitrator, Orange County Superior Court, 1991—. CEB Panelist, "Enforcement of Judgments," 1984. CEB Moderator, "How to Handle Nonmedical Professional Liability Claims," 1985. CEB Moderator, "How to Win Post-Trial Motions and Enforce Judgments," 1986; CEB Moderator, "Enforcement of Civil Money Judgements," 1992, 1995 CEB Moderator, "Introduction to Creditor's Remedies and Debtor's Rights," 1993. *Member:* Los Angeles County, Orange County and American Bar Associations; State Bar of California. (Resident). **PRACTICE AREAS:** Business Litigation; Insurance Coverage; ERISA; Professional Liability.

## ASSOCIATES

**ERIC M. CROWE,** born Miami, Florida, July 23, 1951; admitted to bar, 1988, California. *Education:* Lindenwood College; George Washington University (B.A., 1975); Lincoln University (J.D., 1987). Editor, Lincoln University Law School Law Review/Whites Inn Chronicles. *Member:* Marin County and Orange County Bar Associations; State Bar of California.

**J. RONALD IGNATUK,** born Ridley Park, Pennsylvania, June 26, 1953; admitted to bar, 1990, California; U.S. Court of Appeals, 9th Circuit; U.S. District Court, Northern, Central, Eastern and Southern Districts. *Education:* Pennsylvania State University (B.A., 1986); Loyola Law School at Los Angeles (J.D., 1990). Order of the Coif. *Member:* Orange County and American Bar Associations; State Bar of California. (Resident).

**ROBERT K. RENNER,** born West Lafayette, Indiana, December 6, 1965; admitted to bar, 1991, California, U.S. District Court, Central and Southern Districts of California and U.S. Court of Appeals, Ninth Circuit; 1992, U.S. District Court, Northern and Eastern Districts of California and

*(This Listing Continued)*

U.S. Court of Appeals, Seventh Circuit. *Education:* University of Illinois at Urbana-Champaign (B.S., 1988); University of California at Los Angeles (J.D., 1991). Teaching Assistant, Legal Research and Writing, 1989-1990. Participant, Moot Court Honors Program, 1990. Judicial Extern to the Honorable John G. Davies, U.S. District Court, Central District of California, 1990. *Member:* Orange County and American Bar Associations; State Bar of California. (Resident).

REFERENCES: Bank of America (Los Angeles Main Office); Security Pacific National Bank (Los Angeles Main Office).

(For Complete Biographical Data on all Personnel, see Professional Biographies at Los Angeles).

## BARTON, KLUGMAN & OETTING

A Partnership of Professional Corporations

SUITE 700, 4400 MACARTHUR BOULEVARD
P.O. BOX 2350
**NEWPORT BEACH, CALIFORNIA 92660**
Telephone: 714-752-7551
Telecopier: 714-752-0288

*Los Angeles, California Office:* 37th Floor, 333 South Grand Avenue, 90071-1599. Telephone: 213-621-4000. Telecopier: 213-625-1832.

*General Civil and Trial Practice. Taxation, Corporation, Banking, Probate and Trust Law. Antitrust, Corporate Securities, Real Property, Environmental, Oil and Gas, Labor and International Business Law. Professional Liability Defense, Insurance Coverage, Directors and Officers Insurance Defense and Coverage.*

FIRM PROFILE: *Barton, Klugman & Oetting is a full service law partnership with offices in Los Angeles and Orange Counties. Our attorneys are trained at a wide variety of law schools, including Boalt Hall, Cornell, Harvard, Hastings, Illinois, Michigan, Northwestern, UCLA, USC and Wisconsin. The Firm has engaged in a diversified general civil law practice for over 30 years and has developed a reputation for high quality, responsive legal work.*

### COUNSEL TO FIRM

**†ROBERT M. BARTON,** born Jacksonville, Florida, April 4, 1922; admitted to bar, 1945, California. *Education:* University of Kansas (A.B., 1942); University of Michigan (J.D., 1944). Phi Delta Phi. Member, Board of Editors, Michigan Law Review, 1944. Author: "Terminating an Interest in a Close Corporation," published by New York University, 1974; "Trusts: Some Nontestamentary Uses," Trust & Estates, January, 1981, Lecturer, "Tax Highlights of 1975," 1975 at New York University Tax Institute; Title Insurance and Trust Tax Forum, 1981. Special Assistant to the Attorney General of the U.S., 1954-1965. *Member:* Los Angeles County (Member, Board of Trustees, 1949; 1960-1963), Orange County and American Bar Associations; State Bar of California (Secretary, Committee on Rules of Professional Conduct, 1953-1959; Chairman, Committee on Bar Examiners, 1967-1968); Chancery Club; American Law Institute (Life Member). **PRACTICE AREAS:** Business Law; Taxation; Estate Planning; Estate Administration.

†Denotes a lawyer whose Professional Corporation is a member of the partnership or is Counsel to the Firm

(For Complete Biographical data on all Personnel, see Los Angeles, California Professional Biographies).

## THOMAS A. BERNAUER

A PROFESSIONAL CORPORATION

500 NEWPORT CENTER DRIVE, SUITE 950
**NEWPORT BEACH, CALIFORNIA 92660**
Telephone: 714-720-1313
Fax: 714-720-7457

*Practice Limited to Family Law, Custody, Division of Property, Spouse Support, Child Support.*

FIRM PROFILE: *I began practicing in Orange County in January, 1968 joining the firm of Harwood, Heffernan, Soden & Corfman. Said firm being the third oldest firm in Newport Beach at said date and time. Robert L. Corfman became an Orange County Superior Court Judge, retired and is now deceased. Mark A. Soden became an Orange County Superior Court Judge and is now retired. The firm name became Harwood, Adkinson & Bernauer. The founding partner of the firm Donald D. Harwood passed on in 1985 and I decided to establish my sole practice of law and continue to specialize in family law com-*

*(This Listing Continued)*

CAA1387B

**THOMAS A. BERNAUER** *A PROFESSIONAL CORPORATION,*
Newport Beach—Continued

*mencing January 1, 1986 which I maintain at the present date. In August 1980, I was a member of the first group of California family lawyers to be certified as a Specialist in Family Law. I have lectured for the Continuing Education of the Bar on the subjects of community property, division of community property and child custody. I have lectured for and on behalf of The National Business Institute, Inc., on the subject of the Effective Family Law Practice in California. I was asked to and have been participating in the Judge Pro Tem program in Orange County Superior Court since 1980. I maintain a specialty practice for those clients who wish individual, high quality legal work and full and complete representation performed promptly. It is my primary goal to provide for each individual client exceptional, personal and excellent representation.*

**THOMAS A. BERNAUER,** born Culver City, California, September 4, 1942; admitted to bar, 1968, California and U.S. District Court, Central District of California; 1979, U.S. Supreme Court. *Education:* University of Southern California (B.A., 1964; J.D., 1967). Listed in International and National Who's Who. *Member:* Orange County and American Bar Associations; State Bar of California. Fellow, American Academy of Matrimonial Lawyers. [With U.S. Army]. (Certified Specialist, Family Law, The State Bar of California Board of Legal Specialization).

*LEGAL SUPPORT PERSONNEL*

**MICHAEL MINICK** (Secretary).

## BIDNA & KEYS

A PROFESSIONAL LAW CORPORATION

Established in 1986

5120 CAMPUS DRIVE

**NEWPORT BEACH, CALIFORNIA 92660**

Telephone: 714-752-7030

Telecopier: 714-752-8770

*Business, Commercial, Financial and Real Estate Transactions and Litigation. Creditor-Debtor Relations. Business Bankruptcy and Insolvency Law.*

**HOWARD M. BIDNA,** born Los Angeles, California, May 1, 1953; admitted to bar, 1978, California, U.S. District Court, Central, Southern, Eastern and Northern Districts of California and U.S. Court of Appeals, Ninth Circuit. *Education:* University of California, Irvine (B.A., magna cum laude, 1975); University of California, Los Angeles (J.D., 1978). Phi Beta Kappa. Member, UCLA Law Review, 1977-1978. Lecturer, 1986 and Moderator, 1988, Creditors Remedies and Debtors Rights. Lecturer: Business Law Practice: Annual Recent Developments Program, 1995; Recent Developments in Civil (Business) Litigation, 1985, 1986, 1987, 1988, 1989, 1990, 1991, 1992, 1993, 1994, 1995 and 1996; Preparing and Implementing a Successful Discovery Plan, 1985; Effective Pleading Practice, 1984, California Continuing Education of the Bar; Orange County Escrow Association, 1985; Trial Court Delay Reduction Program, Stanford Bar Institute, 1988; Bankruptcy Trial Workshop, Orange County Bankruptcy Forum, 1989. Member, Bankruptcy Court Mediation Panel, Central District of California. Judge Pro Tem, Orange County Superior Court. *Member:* Orange County Bar Association (Member, Business Litigation Section); State Bar of California; Orange County Bankruptcy Forum.

**RICHARD D. KEYS,** born Swickley, Pennsylvania, April 23, 1957; admitted to bar, 1982, California, U.S. District Court, Central, Southern, Eastern and Northern Districts of California and U.S. Court of Appeals, Ninth Circuit. *Education:* University of California, Riverside (B.A., magna cum laude, 1979); University of California, Berkeley (J.D., 1982). Member, California Law Review, 1980-1982. Lecturer, Preparing and Implementing a Successful Discovery Plan, 1991, California Continuing Education of the Bar. *Member:* Orange County and American (Member: Business Litigation Section; Litigation Section) Bar Associations; State Bar of California; Orange County Bankruptcy Form. *PRACTICE AREAS:* Business Litigation.

**HARVEY M. MOORE,** born Los Angeles, California, December 23, 1955; admitted to bar, 1981, California, U.S. District Court, Central, Southern, Eastern and Northern Districts of California and U.S. Court of Appeals, Ninth Circuit. *Education:* University of California, Berkeley (A.B., 1977); University of California, Los Angeles (J.D., 1981; M.B.A.). Beta Gamma Sigma. Order of the Coif. Recipient: American Jurisprudence Award in Real Property Law; Edward W. Carter Fellowship. Lecturer,

*(This Listing Continued)*

When Bankruptcy and Family Law Collide, State Bar of California, 1994. *Member:* Orange County Bar Association (Member, Commercial Law and Bankruptcy Section); State Bar of California; Orange County Bankruptcy Forum (Treasurer, 1988-1989; Founding Member, 1988; Member, Board of Directors, 1988-1989).

**JON A. LONGERBONE,** born Minneapolis, Minnesota, March 19, 1949; admitted to bar, 1979, California; 1980, U.S. District Court, Central District of California and U.S. Court of Appeals, Ninth Circuit; 1982, U.S. District Court, Eastern and Northern Districts of California. *Education:* University of California at Los Angeles; California State University at Northridge (B.A., magna cum laude, 1976); Hastings College of Law, University of California (J.D., 1979). Associate Editor, Hastings Law Journal, Vols. 29 and 30, 1978-1979. Judge Protem, Los Angeles Municipal Court, 1986—. *Member:* Los Angeles County, Orange County and American (Member, Sections of: Trial Lawyers; Litigation) Bar Associations; State Bar of California; Association of Business Trial Lawyers. [With USAF, 1968-1972]. *PRACTICE AREAS:* Business Litigation.

REFERENCE: The Bank of California (Newport Beach Branch).

## CHRISTOPHER L. BLANK

4695 MACARTHUR COURT, SUITE 1200

**NEWPORT BEACH, CALIFORNIA 92660**

Telephone: 714-250-4600

Facsimile: 714-250-4604

Email: clblank@aol.com

*Business Law, Business Litigation, Bankruptcy, Equipment Finance and Leasing, Commercial Law.*

**CHRISTOPHER L. BLANK,** born Sacramento, California, 1957; admitted to bar, 1984, California; 1985, District of Columbia, U.S. Court of Appeals, Ninth Circuit and U.S. District Court, Central, Northern, Southern and Eastern Districts of California; 1994, U.S. Supreme Court. *Education:* University of California, Irvine (B.S., Biological Science, 1979; M.S., Administration, 1981); George Washington University (J.D., 1984). Member, Board of Editors, California Bankruptcy Journal, 1989-1991. Member, Financial Lawyers Conference, 1985—. Member: Orange County Bankruptcy Forum, 1988—; Los Angeles Bankruptcy Forum 1989—. *Member:* Orange County (Chairperson, Commercial Law and Bankruptcy Section, 1991-1992) and American Bar Associations; State Bar of California. *PRACTICE AREAS:* Business Litigation; Business Law.

## RICHARD W. BONNER

A PROFESSIONAL CORPORATION

Established in 1983

(Formerly Crosby, Gary & Bonner)

SUITE 200, 1300 DOVE STREET

**NEWPORT BEACH, CALIFORNIA 92660**

Telephone: 714-752-8266

Fax: 714-752-7967

*Criminal Trial Practice.*

**RICHARD W. BONNER,** born Lynn, Massachusetts, January 8, 1947; admitted to bar, 1974, California; 1980, U.S. Supreme Court. *Education:* California State University at Fullerton (B.A., 1968); Pepperdine University (J.D., 1974). Member, Pepperdine Law Review, 1973-1974. Member of Faculty, Orange County College of Trial Advocacy. Deputy Public Defender, Orange County, 1975-1979. Chairman, Samuel Adams Society, 1990. *Member:* Newport Harbor and Orange County Bar Associations; State Bar of California; Orange County Trial Lawyers Association; California Trial Lawyers Association.

REFERENCE: Bank of America, Newport Beach.

## BORTON, PETRINI & CONRON

4675 MACARTHUR COURT, SUITE 1150
**NEWPORT BEACH, CALIFORNIA 92660**
Telephone: 714-752-2333
Fax: 714-752-2854
Email: bpcnb@bpclaw.com

*Bakersfield, California Office:* The Borton, Petrini & Conron Building, 1600 Truxtun Avenue, P.O. Box 2026. Telephone: 805-322-3051. Fax: 805-322-4628. Email: bpcbak@bpclaw.com.

*San Luis Obispo, California Office:* 1114 Marsh Street. Telephone: 805-541-4340. Fax: 805-541-4558. Email: bpcslo@bpclaw.com.

*Visalia, California Office:* 206 South Mooney Boulevard, P.O. Box 1028. Telephone: 209-627-5600. Fax: 209-627-4309. Email: bpcvis@bpclaw.com.

*Fresno, California Office:* T. W. Patterson Building, 2014 Tulare Street, Suite 830. Telephone: 209-268-0117. Fax: 209-237-7995. Email: bpcfrs@bpclaw.com.

*Sacramento, California Office:* 2233 Watt Avenue, Suite 290. Telephone: 916-484-3555. Fax: 916-484-3550. Email: bpcsac@bpclaw.com.

*Santa Barbara, California Office:* 211 East Victoria Street, Suite D. Telephone: 805-564-2404. Fax: 805-564-2176. Email: bpcsb@bpclaw.com

*Los Angeles, California Office:* 707 Wilshire Boulevard, Suite 5100. Telephone: 213-624-2869. Fax: 213-489-3930. Email: bpcla@bpclaw.com.

*San Diego, California Office:* John Burnham Building, 610 West Ash Street, 9th Floor. Telephone: 619-232-2424. Fax: 619-531-0794. Email: bpcsd@bpclaw.com.

*Modesto, California Office:* The Turner Building, 900 "H" Street, Suite D. Telephone: 209-576-1701. Fax: 209-527-9753. Email: bpcmod@bpclaw.com.

*San Francisco, California Office:* 111 Pine Street, Suite 730. Telephone: 415-981-4415. Fax: 415-391-5538. Email: bpcsf@bpclaw.com.

*Redding, California Office:* 280 Hemsted Drive, Suite 100. Telephone: 916-222-1530. Fax: 916-222-4498. Email: bpcred@bpclaw.com.

*San Bernardino, California Office:* 290 North "D" Street, Suite 500. Telephone: 909-381-0527. Fax: 909-381-0658. Email: bpcsbdo@bpclaw.com.

*San Jose, California Office:* 2 North Second Street. Telephone: 408-298-3997. Fax: 408-298-3365. Email: bpcsj@bpclaw.com.

*Ventura, California Office:* 1000 Hill Road, Suite 310. Telephone: 805-650-9994. Fax: 805-650-7125. Email: bpcvta@bpclaw.com.

*Santa Rosa, California Office:* 50 Santa Rosa Avenue, Suite 300. Telephone: 707-527-9477. Fax: 707-527-9488. Email: bpcsr@bpclaw.com.

*Commercial/Real Estate Litigation, Insurance Law, General Civil Trial and Appellate Practice in State and Federal Courts, Personal Injury and Casualty Defense Litigation, Insurance Bad Faith and Coverage, Labor and Employment, Toxic Torts, Real Estate, Land Use Planning, Zoning, Municipal, Professional Errors and Omissions, Healthcare Provider Malpractice Defense, Products Liability, Oil and Gas, Water, Natural Resources, Environmental, Public Entity, Administrative, Agricultural, Banking, Contracts, Corporations, Partnerships, Taxation, Creditor's Remedies, Bankruptcy, Probate, Estate Planning, Family Law.*

FIRM PROFILE: Founded by Fred E. Borton in 1899, the firm offers high quality legal services in all of the practice areas described above through its California network of sixteen regional offices. Our mission is to handle each file as if we were the client. We are responsive to the clients' need for communication, cost effectiveness and prompt evaluation.

### MEMBERS OF FIRM

**WILLIAM H. CANTRELL,** born Santa Monica, California, January 8, 1952; admitted to bar, 1976, California; 1978, Alaska. *Education:* California State College at Bakersfield (B.S., 1973); University of California at Los Angeles (J.D., 1976). Editor-in-Chief, California Defense Journal, 1989—. Author: "Mary Carter Agreements: An Unfair Agreement to Paint Over the Truth," Verdict Legal Journal, Spring, 1984. *Member:* Orange County and Alaska Bar Associations; The State Bar of California; Association of Southern California Defense Counsel. **PRACTICE AREAS:** Casualty Litigation; Commercial Litigation; Employment Law; Professional Liability; Environmental Law.

**PHILLIP B. GREER,** born Long Beach, California, February 1, 1953; admitted to bar, 1980, California. *Education:* University of California at Los Angeles (B.A., 1976); Southwestern University (J.D., 1979). *Member:* Orange County Bar Association; State Bar of California; American Subcontractors Association. **PRACTICE AREAS:** Business Litigation; Construction Litigation.

**MICHAEL F. LONG,** born Pocatello, Idaho, December 8, 1958; admitted to bar, 1984, Illinois; 1988, California. *Education:* Arizona State University (B.S., cum laude, 1981); John Marshall Law School (J.D., 1984). *Member:* Illinois State and American Bar Associations; State Bar of California. [with U.S. Marine Corps, 1985-1988; Judge Advocate]. **PRACTICE AREAS:** Construction Defect and Accidents; Professional Malpractice; Commerical Litigation.

### ASSOCIATES

**DONALD A. DIEBOLD,** born Amityville, New York, November 19, 1963; admitted to bar, 1990, California. *Education:* Duke University (B.S., 1986); Washington University (J.D., 1990; (.B.A., 1991). *Member:* Orange County and American Bar Associations; State Bar of California. **PRACTICE AREAS:** Construction Defect; Personal Injury; General Liability Defense.

**PAUL T. MCBRIDE,** born Grand Rapids, Michigan, August 2, 1956; admitted to bar, 1981, Pennsylvania; 1993, California. *Education:* University of Michigan at Ann Arbor (B.A., 1978); Cornell University (J.D., 1981). *Member:* Pennsylvania Bar Association; State Bar of California. [U.S. Marine Corps 1983-1993, Judge Advocate; U.S. Marine Corps Reserves, 1993—, Major]. **PRACTICE AREAS:** Casualty Defense; Construction Defects.

**CARI S. BAUM,** born Council Bluffs, Iowa, February 27, 1961; admitted to bar, 1990, California. *Education:* University of California at Riverside (B.A., Psychology, 1983; B.S., Administrative Studies, 1983); Southwestern University School of Law (J.D., 1990). *Member:* State Bar of California. **PRACTICE AREAS:** Insurance Defense.

**CAROLYN M. KERN,** born Macomb, Illinois, August 6, 1962; admitted to bar, 1994, California. *Education:* Bradley University (B.S., 1984); Western State University (J.D., 1993). Member, Young Lawyers Division & Forum Committee on the Construction Industry, 1993—. *Member:* Orange County and American Bar Associations; State Bar of California. **PRACTICE AREAS:** Construction Defect Litigation.

(For a Complete Listing of Personnel and Representative Clients, please refer to our Bakersfield listing).

---

## PETER C. BRADFORD

SUITE 1250, 610 NEWPORT CENTER DRIVE
**NEWPORT BEACH, CALIFORNIA 92660**
Telephone: 714-640-1800
FAX: 714-721-9923

*Estate Planning, Trust and Probate Law.*

**PETER C. BRADFORD,** born Los Angeles, California, July 7, 1935; admitted to bar, 1961, California. *Education:* Stanford University (A.B., 1958; LL.B., 1960); Harvard University (M.B.A., with distinction, 1962). Phi Delta Phi. Member, Stanford Law Review, 1958-1959. Associate, 1962-1967 and Partner, 1967-1969, Musick, Peeler & Garrett, Los Angeles. *Member:* Orange County and American Bar Associations; State Bar of California. (Certified Specialist, Estate Planning, Trust and Probate Law, The State Bar of California Board of Legal Specialization). **LANGUAGES:** French.

REFERENCES: Wells Fargo Bank; Bank of America, Trust Department.

---

## BRAGG, SHORT, SEROTA & KULUVA

4695 MACARTHUR COURT, SUITE 530
**NEWPORT BEACH, CALIFORNIA 92660-1860**
Telephone: 714-442-4800
Fax: 714-442-4816

*San Francisco, California Office:* Bragg & Dziesinski, Two Embarcadero Center, Suite 1400. Telephone: 415-954-1850. Fax: 415-434-2179.
*Los Angeles, California Office:* 801 South Figueroa Street, Suite 2100. Telephone: 213-612-5335. Fax: 213-612-5712.

*Insurance Defense Practice.*

**ROBERT A. BRAGG,** born San Francisco, California, November 18, 1951; admitted to bar, 1981, California and U.S. District Court, Northern District of California; 1983, U.S. Court of Appeals, Ninth Circuit; 1986, U.S. District Court, Eastern District of California. *Education:* University of

*(This Listing Continued)*

### BRAGG, SHORT, SEROTA & KULUVA, Newport Beach—Continued

San Francisco (B.A., cum laude, 1974); San Francisco Law School (J.D., 1980). Arbitrator, San Francisco County Superior Court. *Member:* Bar Association of San Francisco; Contra Costa County, Alameda County, San Mateo County and American Bar Associations; The State Bar of California (Member, Litigation Section); Defense Research Institute; National Institute for Trial Advocacy.

**PATRICIA D. SHORT,** born Fullerton, California, November 26, 1952; admitted to bar, 1979, California. *Education:* Fullerton College (A.A., 1973); University of Southern California (B.S., 1976); Pepperdine University (J.D., 1979). *Member:* Orange County Bar Association; State Bar of California (Former Delegate State Bar Conference; Member, Litigation Section); Lawyers Club of Los Angeles County (Former Member, Board of Governors; Resolutions Committee); The Association of Trial Lawyers of America; Defense Research Institute; Los Angeles Trial Lawyers Association; Association of Southern California Defense Counsel.

**LORI D. SEROTA,** born Oak Harbor, Washington, December 9, 1958; admitted to bar, 1984, California; 1985, U.S. District Court, Central District of California. *Education:* University of Southern California (B.A., 1981); Southwestern University School of Law (J.D., 1984). Arbitrator, Los Angeles County Superior and Municipal Courts. Member, Initial Defense Experiment (IDEX). *Member:* Orange County and American Bar Associations; State Bar of California; Association of Southern California Defense Counsel; Defense Research Institute.

#### ASSOCIATES

**CODY DALE LUND,** born St. Cloud, Minnesota, November 6, 1961; admitted to bar, 1988, California; 1990, U.S. District Court, Central District of California. *Education:* Cerritos College (A.A., 1984); Western State University College of Law (J.D., 1987). *Member:* Orange County Bar Association; State Bar of California; American Criminal Justice Association.

**MARVIN A. MARTINEZ,** born Gary, Indiana, May 18, 1946; admitted to bar, 1979, California; 1982, U.S. District Court, Central District of California and U.S. Court of Appeals, Ninth Circuit. *Education:* Purdue University (B.S., 1971); Western State University (J.D., 1978). *Member:* Orange County Barristers (Treasurer, 1988-1989). [U.S. Marine Corps., 1966-1972]

(Association of California House Counsel)

---

### JOHN H. BRAINERD
4100 NEWPORT PLACE, SUITE 800
**NEWPORT BEACH, CALIFORNIA 92660**
Telephone: 714-252-2824
Facsimile: 714-863-0164

*Business, Estate and Individual Tax and Transaction Planning and Related Matters. Drafting of Legal Documents. Related Court and Administrative Tax Representation. Business Acquisitions and Dispositions.*

**JOHN H. BRAINERD,** born Los Angeles, CA, July 21, 1943; admitted to bar, 1970, California and U.S. Tax Court. *Education:* University of California at Los Angeles (B.A., 1966); University of Southern California (J.D., 1969); New York University (LL.M. in Taxation, 1972). Certified Public Accountant, CA, 1974. Phi Delta Phi. Instructor, Master of Business Taxation: University of Southern California, 1968; Golden Gate University, 1989-1993. Author and Lecturer for California Society of C.P.A.'s. *Member:* Los Angeles, Orange County and American (Member, Sections on: Taxation; Estate Planning, Trust and Probate; Real Property Law) Bar Associations; California Society of C.P.A.'S.

---

### STEVEN E. BRIGGS
2700 NEWPORT BOULEVARD, SUITE 172
**NEWPORT BEACH, CALIFORNIA 92663**
Telephone: 714-673-7410

*Family Law and Related Litigation.*

**STEVEN E. BRIGGS,** born San Diego, California, August 18, 1942; admitted to bar, 1971, California and U.S. District Court, Central District of California; 1973, U.S. Supreme Court. *Education:* University of San Diego (B.S., 1964; J.D., magna cum laude, 1970). Editor, San Diego Law Review, 1970. *Member:* State Bar of California; Fellow, American Academy of Matrimonial Lawyers. [Capt., USMC, 1964-1967]. (Certified Specialist, Family Law, The State Bar of California Board of Legal Specialization). **PRACTICE AREAS:** Family Law.

*(This Listing Continued)*

---

### BROBECK, PHLEGER & HARRISON LLP
A Partnership including a Professional Corporation
4675 MACARTHUR COURT, SUITE 1000
**NEWPORT BEACH, CALIFORNIA 92660**
Telephone: 714-752-7535
Facsimile: 714-752-7522

*San Francisco, California Office:* Spear Street Tower, One Market. Telephone: 415-442-0900. Facsimile: 415-442-1010.
*Palo Alto, California Office:* Two Embarcadero Place, 2200 Geng Road. Telephone: 415-424-0160. Facsimile: 415-496-2885.
*Los Angeles, California Office:* 550 South Hope Street. Telephone: 213-489-4060. Facsimile: 213-745-3345.
*San Diego, California Office:* 550 West C Street, Suite 1300. Telephone: 619-234-1966. Facsimile: 619-236-1403.
*Austin, Texas Office:* Brobeck, Phleger & Harrison LLP, 301 Congress Avenue, Suite 1200. Telephone: 512-477-5495. Facsimile: 512-477-5813.
*Denver, Colorado Office:* Brobeck, Phleger & Harrison LLP, 1125 Seventeenth Street, 25th Floor. Telephone: 303-293-0760. Facsimile: 303-299-8819.
*New York, N.Y. Office:* Brobeck, Phleger & Harrison LLP, 1633 Broadway, 47th Floor. Telephone: 212-581-1600. Facsimile: 212-586-7878.
*Brobeck Hale and Dorr International Office:*
*London, England Office:* Veritas House, 125 Finsbury Pavement, London EC2A 1NQ. Telephone: 44 071 638 6688. Facsimile: 44 071 638 5888.

*General Practice, including Business and Technology, Litigation, Securities Litigation, Technology Litigation, Environmental Litigation, Product Liability Litigation, Labor Law, Financial Services and Insolvency (including Bankruptcy and Loan Workout), Real Estate, and Tax/Estate Planning.*

#### MANAGING PARTNER

**BRUCE R. HALLETT,** born Covina, California, February 2, 1956; admitted to bar, 1981, California. *Education:* University of California, Irvine (B.A., magna cum laude, with highest departmental honors in English, 1978); University of California, Los Angeles (J.D., 1981). *Member:* Orange County (Member, Business Section) and American (Member, Corporation, Banking and Business Law Section) Bar Associations; The State Bar of California. **PRACTICE AREAS:** Corporate Finance and Securities Law. **Email:** bhallett@brobeck.com

#### RESIDENT PARTNERS

**R. PATRICK ARRINGTON,** born Duncan, Oklahoma, July 28, 1942; admitted to bar, 1968, California. *Education:* University of New Mexico (B.A., magna cum laude, 1964); Harvard University (LL.B., 1967). Phi Kappa Phi; Phi Alpha Theta. Member, Business Section, State Bar of California. Member, Section of Corporation, Banking and Business Law, American Bar Association. *Member:* Orange County Bar Association. **PRACTICE AREAS:** Corporate Securities. **Email:** parrington@brobeck.com

**ROGER M. COHEN,** born Palo Alto, California, March 30, 1956; admitted to bar, 1981, California. *Education:* American College of Switzerland (A.A., 1975); University of California at San Diego (B.A., summa cum laude, 1978); University of California at Berkeley (J.D., 1981). Member, International Society of Hospitality Consultants; Director, Association for Corporate Growth. **PRACTICE AREAS:** Corporate Finance; Leverage Buyouts; Banking. **Email:** rcohen@brobeck.com

**RICHARD A. FINK,** born Chicago, Illinois, February 8, 1955; admitted to bar, 1981, California. *Education:* Indiana University (B.A., 1977); Northwestern University (J.D., 1980). **PRACTICE AREAS:** General Corporate Law; Securities Law; Venture Capital Law. **Email:** rfink@brobeck.com

**LAURA B. HUNTER,** born St. Paul, Minnesota, May 26, 1960; admitted to bar, 1987, California. *Education:* University of San Diego (B.B.A., magna cum laude, 1982); University of California at Davis (J.D., 1987). Beta Gamma Sigma. Editor, University of California at Davis Law Review, 1986-1987. Author: Comment, "Structure and Price: Striking a Delicate Balance in Tender Offer Negotiations," 20 University of California at Davis Law Review 987, Summer, 1987. Member: Business Law Section, Los Angeles County Bar Association, 1987-1989; Business Law Section, 1987-1989. *Member:* Orange County Bar Association. **PRACTICE AREAS:** Venture Capital; Corporate and Securities Law; Mergers and Acquisitions. **Email:** lhunter@brobeck.com

*(This Listing Continued)*

**PROFESSIONAL BIOGRAPHIES**  CALIFORNIA—NEWPORT BEACH

**KATHLENE W. LOWE,** born San Diego, California, December 1, 1949; admitted to bar, 1976, Utah and U.S. District Court, District of Utah; 1980, U.S. Court of Appeals, Tenth Circuit; 1989, California; 1990, U.S. District Court, Northern, Southern, Eastern and Central Districts of California and U.S. Court of Appeals, Ninth Circuit. *Education:* University of Utah (B.A., magna cum laude, 1971; M.A., 1973; J.D., 1976). Member, 1974-1976 and Comment Editor, 1975-1976, University of Utah Law Review. Editorial Staff, Journal of Contemporary Laws, 1974-1975. *Member:* Utah State Bar. **PRACTICE AREAS:** Employment Law; Commercial and Real Property Litigation. *Email:* klowe@brobeck.com

**FREDERIC ALPORT RANDALL, JR.,** born Detroit, Michigan, November 16, 1956; admitted to bar, 1984, California; 1985, Washington. *Education:* University of Michigan (B.A., with distinction, 1978); University of San Francisco (J.D., cum laude, 1984). Topics Editor, University of San Francisco Law Review, 1983-1984. **PRACTICE AREAS:** General Corporate Law; Securities Law; Venture Capital Law. *Email:* frandall@brobeck.com

**GABRIELLE M. WIRTH,** born Walnut Creek, California, June 8, 1957; admitted to bar, 1982, California. *Education:* University of California at Berkeley (B.A., 1978); University of California at Davis (J.D., 1982). Member, University of California at Davis Law Review, 1981-1982. **PRACTICE AREAS:** Labor Law; Employment Litigation; Insurance Coverage Litigation; Unfair Competition. *Email:* gwirth@brobeck.com

*OF COUNSEL*

**JEFFREY S. ROVNER,** born Washington, D.C., July 6, 1957; admitted to bar, 1982, California. *Education:* University of Maryland (B.S., 1979); George Washington University National Law Center (J.D., cum laude, 1982). George Washington Law Review, 1980-1982. Author, Note, Mama Rag, Inc. v. United States," 49 George Washington Law Review 623, 1981. *Member:* Orange County Bar Association. **PRACTICE AREAS:** Corporate Finance; Municipal Finance; Real Estate.

*ASSOCIATES*

*Jonathan F. Atzen; Richard J. Babcock; John S. Baker; Ellen S. Bancroft; James S. Brennan; Susan N. Cayley; Kevin D. DeBré; Scott S. Draeker; Ethan D. Feffer; R. Scott Feldmann; Dana E. Frost; Lisa Schechter Goon; Neel Grover; Anita Gruettke; Elizabeth T. Hall; Lee J. Leslie; Gregory T. May; Barbara J. Miller; Daniel E. Roston; Matthew V. Waterman; Greg T. Williams.*

All Members and Associates of the Firm are Members of the State Bar of California and the American Bar Association.
Brobeck, Phleger & Harrison and Brobeck Hale and Dorr International have a joint venture office in London, England.

---

## *BROKER & O'KEEFE*

*PROFESSIONAL CORPORATION*

*4695 MACARTHUR COURT*
*SUITE 1200*
**NEWPORT BEACH, CALIFORNIA 92660**
*Telephone: 714-222-2000*
*Fax: 714-222-2022*
*Email: chpter11@aol.com*
*URL: http://wwwbroker-okeefe.com*

Bankruptcy and Insolvency Law, Corporate Reorganizations and Related Commercial Litigation.

FIRM PROFILE: *The firm limits its practice to bankruptcy and insolvency law, workouts and related commercial litigation in all state and federal courts. Broker & O'Keefe's professional experience in the bankruptcy field includes the reorganization of in excess of $500,000,000 in diverse business assets through the Chapter 11 process and the successful representation of the interests of financial institutions, municipalities, suppliers and other creditors holding secured and unsecured claims in insolvency matters. The firm's experience in the bankruptcy area is complemented by a demonstrated expertise in complex commercial and financial litigation matters. References from satisfied clients are available upon request.*

**JEFFREY W. BROKER,** born Los Angeles, California, August 23, 1947; admitted to bar, 1972, California; 1991, District of Columbia. *Education:* University of California at Los Angeles (A.B., 1969; J.D., 1972). Author: "The Practical Aspects of Claim and Delivery," 51 Los Angeles Bar Journal 121, 1975. Co-Author: "Serving on the Creditors' Committee," "Non-Bankruptcy Workouts," "Out of Court Arrangements" and "Alternatives to Insolvency Proceedings: Can They Really Happen?" and panelist on

*(This Listing Continued)*

Practicing Law Institute Programs on Business Loan Workouts, 1983-1987. Panelist, California Continuing Education of the Bar programs on: Handling Debt Collection Matters; Commercial Law; Attachments, Claim and Delivery and Receiverships; The New Enforcement of Judgments Law; The Enforcement of Judgments Law - One Year After Its Effective Date; Bankruptcy Practice After the 1984 Code Amendments; Fundamentals of Bankruptcy; Introduction to Bankruptcy. Practicing Law Institute National programs on Business Loan Workouts, 1983-1987. Orange County Bankruptcy Forum programs on Pre-trial Preparation In Bankruptcy Adversary Proceedings and Unveiling the Secrets of Valuation and Interest Rates. Association of Insolvency Accountants, Valuation Conference, Program on Cash Collateral Valuation Issues. *Panel Member:* United States Bankruptcy Court, Central District of California, Bankruptcy Mediation Program, 1995—. *Member:* Los Angeles County, Orange County and American (Member, Business Bankruptcy Committee and Business Law Section, 1982—) Bar Associations; The State Bar of California; District of Columbia Bar; American Bankruptcy Institute; Financial Lawyers Conference; Orange County Bankruptcy Forum (Member, Board of Directors, 1989—; President, 1992); California Bankruptcy Forum (Member, Board of Directors, 1990—; Treasurer, 1994-1995; Secretary, 1995-1996; Vice President, 1996-1997; Co-Chair, Statewide Conference, 1994). *Email:* JWBroker@aol.com

**SEAN A. O'KEEFE,** born Providence, Rhode Island, July 9, 1958; admitted to bar, 1984, New York; 1986, California. *Education:* Dartmouth College (B.A., 1980); Fordham University (J.D., 1983). Author: "Adequate Protection After United Savings v. Timbers of Inwood Forest," 16 Cal. Bankr. J. 8 (1988); "Post-Petition Perfection of Assignment of Rent Clauses Under 11 U.S.C. §546(b): A Creative Illusion," 17 Cal. Bankr. J. 123 (1989). Speaker: 1990 Annual Conference of the California Bankruptcy Forum, "Converting Rents, Rates and Revenues Into Cash Collateral: New Challenges to an Old Alchemy;" Orange County Bankruptcy Forum, "What Price Justice: Is There an Exception to The Absolute Priority Rule?" February, 1993. Panelist, National Business Institute Seminar: "How to Protect Secured Interests in Bankruptcy in California," August, 1993. *Member:* Orange County (Member, Commercial Law and Bankruptcy Section; Program Chairman, 1990' Chairman, 1991; Member, Board of Directors, 1994) and New York State Bar Associations; State Bar of California; Orange County Bankruptcy Forum. *Email:* SAOKeefr@aol.com

---

**LAUREN B. LESSLER,** born New York, N.Y., November 25, 1965; admitted to bar, 1993, California. *Education:* University of California at Los Angeles (B.A., 1987); University of Southern California Law Center (J.D., 1993). Phi Delta Phi. Judicial Extern to the Honorable William J. Lasarow, United States Bankruptcy Judge, 1992. Certified Public Accountant, California, 1990. *Member:* Orange County (Member, Commercial Law and Bankruptcy Section) and American Bar Associations; State Bar of California; Orange County Bankruptcy Forum; American Institute of Certified Public Accountants. *Email:* LLessler@aol.com

**DAVID D. PIPER,** born Newport Beach, California, July 28, 1968; admitted to bar, 1995, California. *Education:* University of California at Berkeley (B.A., 1991); University of the Pacific, McGeorge School of Law (J.D., with distinction, 1995). Phi Delta Phi. Judicial Extern to the Honorable Lynne Riddle, U.S. Bankruptcy Judge, 1994. *Member:* Orange County (Member, Commercial Law and Bankruptcy Section; Bankruptcy Forum) and American Bar Associations; State Bar of California.

---

## *BRUCK & PERRY*

*A PROFESSIONAL CORPORATION*

*Established in 1978*

*500 NEWPORT CENTER DRIVE*
**NEWPORT BEACH, CALIFORNIA 92660**
*Telephone: 714-719-6000*
*Telecopier: 714-719-6040*

*Corporate, Securities, Finance, Mergers and Acquisitions, Domestic and International Commercial Transactions, Real Estate and Civil Litigation in all State and Federal Courts including Business, Securities, Commercial Insurance, and Legal Malpractice Defense.*

**RICHARD H. BRUCK,** born Brooklyn, New York, March 2, 1948; admitted to bar, 1972, California and U.S. District Court, Central District of California. *Education:* University of California at Los Angeles (B.A., cum laude, 1969; J.D., 1972). Adjunct Professor of Business Law, Califor-

*(This Listing Continued)*

**BRUCK & PERRY,** A PROFESSIONAL CORPORATION, Newport Beach—Continued

nia State University at Long Beach, 1974-1979. Author: "Investment Contracts: To Qualify or Not To Qualify?" L.A. Bar Bull., Vol. 49, No. 5, March, 1974. Panelist, California Continuing Education of the Bar: "Organizing and Advising Limited Liability Companies," 1994; "California Limited Liability Companies, Beyond the Basics," 1995. Arbitrator, American Arbitration Association. *Member:* State Bar of California; American Bar Association. **PRACTICE AREAS:** Corporate Law; Securities Law; Commercial Transactions.

**DAVID J. PERRY,** born Pasadena, California, May 8, 1950; admitted to bar, 1976, California and U.S. District Court, Southern District of California. *Education:* California State University at Long Beach (B.S., cum laude, 1972; M.B.A., 1973); Southwestern University (J.D., 1976). Phi Kappa Phi. Member, Southwestern University Law Review, 1975-1976. *Member:* State Bar of California. **PRACTICE AREAS:** Real Estate Law; Finance Law; Commercial Transactions.

**KAREN NICOLAI WINNETT,** born Long Beach, California, November 2, 1953; admitted to bar, 1979, California, U.S. District Court, Central District of California and U.S. Court of Appeals, Ninth Circuit. *Education:* California State University at Long Beach (B.A., 1975; M.S., 1976); University of Southern California (J.D., 1979). Phi Kappa Phi; Omicron Delta Epsilon. *Member:* State Bar of California. **PRACTICE AREAS:** Corporate Law; Securities Law; Commercial Transactions.

**PAUL C. NYQUIST,** born Utica, New York, August 24, 1945; admitted to bar, 1972, California and U.S. District Court, Eastern and Central Districts of California; 1981, U.S. Court of Appeals, Ninth Circuit. *Education:* University of Southern California (B.A., cum laude, 1968); University of California at Los Angeles (J.D., 1971). Sigma Chi. *Member:* Orange County Bar Association; State Bar of California. **PRACTICE AREAS:** Business and Commercial Litigation; Employment Law; Insurance Defense; Legal Malpractice Defense.

**DANIEL K. DONAHUE,** born Omaha, Nebraska, April 6, 1954; admitted to bar, 1980, Nebraska; 1986, California. *Education:* Creighton University (B.A., 1977; J.D., 1980). Omicron Delta Epsilon. Staff Attorney, U.S. Securities and Exchange Commission, 1980-1986. Member, NASD Panel of Arbitrators. *Member:* American Bar Association; The State Bar of California; State Bar of Nebraska. **PRACTICE AREAS:** Corporate Law; Securities Law; Commercial Transactions.

**TIMOTHY CARL AIRES,** born Bristol, Pennsylvania, April 21, 1962; admitted to bar, 1988, California. *Education:* San Diego State University (B.S., 1985); McGeorge School of Law, University of the Pacific (J.D., 1988). *Member:* Orange County (Member, Creditor's Rights Section) and American Bar Associations; State Bar of California; Commercial Law League of America. **PRACTICE AREAS:** Commercial Litigation; Creditor's Rights; Enforcement of Judgments.

**TERESA TORMEY FINEMAN,** born Fullerton, California, May 21, 1964; admitted to bar, 1989, California. *Education:* University of California at Davis (B.A., 1986); Pepperdine University (J.D., cum laude, 1989). Member, 1987-1988 and Managing Editor, 1988-1989, Pepperdine Law Review. *Member:* State Bar of California; American Bar Association. **PRACTICE AREAS:** Corporate Law; Securities Law; Commercial Transactions.

**RICK L. RAYNSFORD,** born Auburn, California, November 12, 1956; admitted to bar, 1982, California and U.S. District Court, Eastern District of California. *Education:* University of California at Davis (B.A., 1978); McGeorge School of Law (J.D., 1982). Member, Traynor Society. Graduate, Academy of Dispute Resolution. *Member:* Sacramento County Bar Association; State Bar of California. **PRACTICE AREAS:** Mediation; Business Litigation; Wrongful Termination; Real Estate Litigation; Trade Secrets; Unfair Competition.

**KEVIN W. KIRSCH,** born Los Angeles, California, November 21, 1967; admitted to bar, 1993, California. *Education:* University of California at Berkeley (B.A., 1989); Loyola Marymount University (J.D., 1993). *Member:* State Bar of California. **PRACTICE AREAS:** Business and Commercial Litigation; Creditor's Rights and Enforcement of Judgments; Construction Defect; Insurance Defense; Employment Law.

**DANA M. ZEIGLER,** born Akron, Ohio, February 5, 1964; admitted to bar, 1989, California. *Education:* University of California, San Diego (B.A.,

*(This Listing Continued)*

magna cum laude, 1986); University of Hasting College of Law (J.D., 1989). *Member:* State Bar of California. **PRACTICE AREAS:** Securities Law; Corporate Law.

# BUCHALTER, NEMER, FIELDS & YOUNGER

A PROFESSIONAL CORPORATION

Established in 1949

SUITE 1450, 620 NEWPORT CENTER DRIVE
**NEWPORT BEACH, CALIFORNIA 92660**
Telephone: 714-760-1121
Fax: 714-720-0182
Email: buchalter@earthlink.net
URL: http://www.buchalter.com

*Los Angeles, California Office:* 24th Floor, 601 South Figueroa Street. Telephone: 213-891-0700. Fax: 213-896-0400.

*New York, New York Office:* 15th Floor, 605 Third Avenue. Telephone: 212-490-8600. Fax: 212-490-6022.

*San Francisco, California Office:* 29th Floor, 333 Market Street. Telephone: 415-227-0900. Fax: 415-227-0770.

**FIRM PROFILE:** *Buchalter, Nemer, Fields & Younger was founded in 1949 by Irwin R. Buchalter, who passed away in 1994, Murray M. Fields, who is still with the firm, and Jerry Nemer, who passed away in 1980. The firm's legal practice encompasses every major area of business law including Commercial, Corporate, Environmental, Banking, Finance, Intellectual Property, Entertainment, Real Property, Probate, Insurance, Securities, Taxation, Labor, Reorganization, Bankruptcy, International Business Law, Alternate Dispute Resolution, and General Civil and Trial Practice in all State and Federal Courts.*

**CLIFFORD JOHN MEYER,** born South Bend, Indiana, July 24, 1932; admitted to bar, 1961, California. *Education:* Harvard University (A.B., 1954; LL.B., 1960). *Member:* Orange County and American Bar Associations; State Bar of California; Association of Business Trial Lawyers; Financial Lawyers Conference. **PRACTICE AREAS:** Financial Institutions; General Business Litigation. *Email:* cmeyer.bnfy@mcimail.com

**DEBRA SOLLE HEALY,** born St. Paul, Minnesota, September 29, 1954; admitted to bar, 1979, California; 1984, Oregon. *Education:* California State Polytechnic University (B.A., magna cum laude, 1976); Loyola University of Los Angeles (J.D., 1979). *Member:* Los Angeles County Bar Association (Treasurer, Prejudgment Remedies Section, 1992-1993; Member, Trial Lawyers Section); State Bar of California; Oregon State Bar; Association of Business Trial Lawyers; Financial Lawyers Conference. **PRACTICE AREAS:** Bank & Finance Litigation. *Email:* dhealy.bnfy@mcimail.com

**KIRK S. RENSE,** born Los Angeles, California, June 10, 1947; admitted to bar, 1980, California. *Education:* California State University, Los Angeles (B.A., 1969); University of South ern California (J.D., 1980). *Member:* Los Angeles County and Orange County Bar Associations; State Bar of California; Los Angeles Bankruptcy Forum; Orange County Bankruptcy Forum. **PRACTICE AREAS:** Creditor and Trustee Representation; Receivership Administration; Financial Litigation. *Email:* krense.bnfy@mcimail.com

---

**LORI S. ROSS,** born Culver City, California, August 23, 1961; admitted to bar, 1986, California; 1987, U.S. District Court, Central District of California; 1989, U.S. District Court, Northern and Eastern Districts of California. *Education:* University of California, Berkeley (A.B., 1983); University of York, England; University of California, Los Angeles (J.D., 1986). *Member:* State Bar of California; American Bar Association; Financial Lawyers Conference. **LANGUAGES:** French. **PRACTICE AREAS:** Insolvency. *Email:* lross.bnfy@mcimail.com

**MARK M. SCOTT,** born Nashville, Tennessee, June 13, 1963; admitted to bar, 1988, California and U.S. District Court, Central District of California. *Education:* Arizona State University (B.S., summa cum laude, 1985); University of Southern California (J.D., 1988). *Member:* Los Angeles County Bar Association (Member, Litigation and Prejudgment Remedies Section); State Bar of California; Association of Business Trial Lawyers.

*(This Listing Continued)*

**PRACTICE AREAS:** Financial Institutions Litigation. **Email:** mscott.bnfy@mcimail.com

REFERENCES: City National Bank; Wells Fargo Bank; Metrobank.

(For complete biographical data on all personnel, see Professional Biographies at New York, New York, Los Angeles and San Francisco)

---

## BUXBAUM & CHAKMAK

*A LAW CORPORATION*

Established in 1971

5160 CAMPUS DRIVE
**NEWPORT BEACH, CALIFORNIA 92660**
Telephone: 714-833-3107
Fax: 714-833-2466

Claremont, California Office: 414 Yale Avenue. Telephone: 909-621-4707. Fax: 909-621-7112.

*Business, Commercial, Banking, Insurance (Coverage and Defense), Corporate, Real Estate, Bankruptcy (Creditors' Rights), Estate Planning, Administrative Law, and Family Law. Trials in all State and Federal Courts.*

**DAVID A. BUXBAUM,** born Long Beach, California; admitted to bar, 1970, California and U.S. District Court, Central District of California; 1976, U.S. Supreme Court. *Education:* Occidental College (B.A., 1966); University of California at Los Angeles (J.D., 1969). Licensed Real Estate Broker, California, 1982. *Member:* Los Angeles County and American Bar Associations; State Bar of California. **PRACTICE AREAS:** Corporate; Business Banking; Estate Planning; Commercial; Real Estate.

**JOHN CHAKMAK,** born Fresno, California, August 17, 1945; admitted to bar, 1971, California and U.S. District Court, Central District of California; 1977, U.S. Court of Appeals, Ninth Circuit; 1988, U.S. District Court, Southern District of California; 1990, U.S. District Court, Eastern District of California. *Education:* Stanford University (B.A., 1967); University of California at Los Angeles (J.D., 1970). Member, Moot Court. Licensed Real Estate Broker, California, 1982. Judge Pro Tem, 1984— and Court Appointed Arbitrator, 1980-1986, Orange County Superior Court. *Member:* Orange County Bar Association (Member, Client Relations Committee, 1976-1981); State Bar of California (Member, Litigation Section). **PRACTICE AREAS:** Civil Litigation; Insurance; Commercial; Banking.

**CHARLES L. ZETTERBERG,** born Pomona, California, October 15, 1943; admitted to bar, 1971, California and U.S. District Court, Central District of California, 1976, U.S. Court of Appeals, Ninth Circuit; 1988, U.S. District Court, Southern District of California. *Education:* Wesleyan University (B.A., with honors, 1965); Columbia University (LL.B., 1968). Law Clerk to Hon. Leonard P. Moore, United States Circuit Judge, 2nd Circuit, 1968-1969. *Member:* Los Angeles County Bar Association; State Bar of California. **PRACTICE AREAS:** Civil Litigation; Insurance; Real Estate; Business.

**BETTY O. YAMASHIRO,** born Honolulu, Hawaii; admitted to bar, 1985, California; 1986, U.S. District Court, Central District of California and U.S. Court of Appeals, Ninth Circuit. *Education:* University of Hawaii, (B.Ed.); University of Illinois (M.A.); Western State University College of Law (J.D., cum laude, 1985). Recipient, American Jurisprudence Awards in Torts, Evidence, Real Property, Remedies and Professional Responsibility. Member and Planning Editor, Western State University Law Review, 1982-1983. President, 1992-1993, Orange County Japanese-American Lawyers' Association. *Member:* Orange County (Assistant Co-Chairman, Minority Issues Committee, 1993-1994; Member, Long Range Planning Committee, 1993-1994 and Commercial Law and Bankruptcy Sections) and Los Angeles County Bar Associations; State Bar of California; Orange County Bankruptcy Forum. **PRACTICE AREAS:** Banking; Bankruptcy; Creditors Rights; Civil Litigation.

---

**JOHN P. HOWLAND,** born New York, N.Y., June 23, 1941; admitted to bar, 1967, New York; 1989, California; 1991, U.S. District Court, Central District of California. *Education:* Dartmouth College (B.A., 1963); University of Pennsylvania (LL.B., 1966). Member, Moot Court Finals. Small Claims Court Arbitrator, New York City, 1970-1974. Member, Law Committee, National Consumer Finance Association, 1984-1986. *Member:* Los Angeles County and American Bar Associations; State Bar of California. **PRACTICE AREAS:** Estate Planning; Corporate; Business; Bankruptcy (Creditor's Rights).

*(This Listing Continued)*

---

**JOAN PENFIL,** born Cleveland, Ohio, July 13, 1938; admitted to bar, 1985, California; 1986, U.S. District Court, Central District of California and U.S. Court of Appeals, Ninth Circuit. *Education:* University of Michigan (B.A., cum laude, 1960); Wayne State University (M.A., 1964); Western State University (J.D., cum laude, 1984). Recipient: Corpus Juris Secundum Award; American Jurisprudence Award; Foundation Press Award. Editor, Western State University Law Review, 1984-1985. *Member:* Orange County Bar Association; State Bar of California. **PRACTICE AREAS:** Family Law.

---

## CALL, CLAYTON & JENSEN

*A PROFESSIONAL CORPORATION*

Established in 1981

SUITE 700, 610 NEWPORT CENTER DRIVE
**NEWPORT BEACH, CALIFORNIA 92660**
Telephone: 714-717-3000
FAX: 714-717-3100
Email: ccj@ix.netcom.com

*Business and Real Estate Litigation, State and Federal Courts. Corporate, Securities and Real Estate Matters.*

FIRM PROFILE: Call, Clayton & Jensen is one of California's premiere "boutique" (small size/high quality) law firms. The firm handles sophisticated business and real estate litigation matters, as well as sophisticated corporate/securities and real estate transactional matters. The firm also handles "conflict referrals" from prominent law firms--respecting the relationship between the referring firm and the client.

The firm has a well established reputation for excellence and efficiency; and a history, since its founding in 1981, of achieving superb results for its clients. Its attorneys have preeminent skills, exceptional academic credentials and backgrounds with prominent firms.

The firm serves clients in a wide variety of businesses, including: real estate, banking, lending and finance, manufacturing, technology, education, healthcare, transportation, retailing, insurance and data processing.

The firm provides a broad range of litigation expertise involving general business, commercial and real estate matters. The firm's extensive litigation experience includes, among other things, disputes involving: real estate transactions; commercial contracts; banking; employment and wrongful discharge (including discrimination, A.D.A. and related claims); construction; real estate developer and broker liability; mortgages and deeds of trust; private and judicial foreclosures; receiverships; mechanic's liens; subsidence; titles and title insurance; co-ownership and joint ventures; partnership and corporate disputes and dissolutions; unfair competition and wrongful solicitation; intellectual property, technology, trade names, trademarks and trade secrets; creditor bankruptcy representation; lender and professional liability; legal malpractice defense; insurance coverage and bad faith; architects and engineers; civil RICO liability; securities litigation; tax and tax fraud; administrative agencies; antitrust; franchise terminations; products liability; environmental litigation; and a variety of other civil disputes.

The firm handles litigation throughout California. It practices in both state and federal courts, at all trial and appellate levels, and also handles arbitrations, mediations and similar proceedings. The firm also acts as co-counsel and local counsel with other firms, including out-of-state and foreign firms.

The firm also handles a wide variety of corporate/securities and real estate transactional matters.

**WAYNE W. CALL,** born Logan, Utah, July 21, 1947; admitted to bar, 1973, California; U.S. District Court, Northern, Central and Southern Districts of California and U.S. Court of Appeals Ninth Circuit. *Education:* Utah State University (B.A., cum laude, 1971); University of Utah (J.D., third in class, 1973). Phi Kappa Phi; Order of the Coif. Member and Articles Editor, Utah Law Review, 1971-1973. Gibson, Dunn & Crutcher, Los Angeles and Newport Beach, California, 1973-1981. *Member:* Los Angeles County and Orange County Bar Associations; State Bar of California. **PRACTICE AREAS:** Litigation.

**L. WHITNEY CLAYTON, III,** born Salt Lake City, Utah, February 24, 1950; admitted to bar, 1978, California, U.S. Court of Appeals, Ninth Circuit and U.S. District Court, Central District of California; 1980, U.S. District Court, Northern District of California. *Education:* University of Utah (B.A., 1974); McGeorge School of Law, University of the Pacific (J.D., 1978). *Member:* Los Angeles County and Orange County Bar Associations; State Bar of California. **LANGUAGES:** Spanish. **PRACTICE AREAS:** Litigation.

*(This Listing Continued)*

CAA1393B

## CALL, CLAYTON & JENSEN, A PROFESSIONAL CORPORATION, Newport Beach—Continued

**JON E. JENSEN,** born Salt Lake City, Utah, March 30, 1947; admitted to bar, 1975, California. *Education:* Dartmouth College, Brigham Young University (B.A., 1971); Stanford University (M.B.A., 1975; J.D., 1975). Order of the Coif. Associate, O'Melveny & Myers, Los Angeles, California, 1975-1980. Associate, 1980-1983 and Partner, 1983-1984, Drummy Garrett King & Harrison, Costa Mesa, California. *Member:* State Bar of California. **PRACTICE AREAS:** Corporate Law; Securities Law.

**TROY L. TATE,** born Salt Lake City, Utah, June 26, 1956; admitted to bar, 1982, California; 1983, U.S. Court of Appeals Ninth Circuit and U.S. District Court, Central, Northern, Eastern and Southern Districts of California. *Education:* University of Utah (B.A., 1979); University of California at Los Angeles School of Law (J.D., 1982). Phi Beta Kappa; Phi Kappa Phi; Order of the Coif. Member, UCLA Law Review, 1980-1981. Associate, Gibson, Dunn & Crutcher, Newport Beach, California, 1982-1987. *Member:* State Bar of California. **PRACTICE AREAS:** Litigation.

**SETH L. LIEBMAN,** born New York, N.Y., December 25, 1960; admitted to bar, 1985, California; 1989, U.S. District Court, Central District of California; 1994, U.S. District Court, Southern District of California; 1995, U.S. District Court, Northern District of California. *Education:* University of Georgia (B.B.A., magna cum laude, 1982); University of Texas at Austin (J.D., 1985). Order of the Coif. Recipient, Best Brief. Associate, O'Melveny & Myers, Los Angeles, California, 1985. Special Counsel for Judicial Selection, U.S. Department of Justice, Washington, D.C., 1985-1988. *Member:* State Bar of California. **LANGUAGES:** Spanish and French. **REPORTED CASES:** Mansour v. Superior Court, 38 Cal. App. 4th 1750 (1995); Barber v. Rancho Mortgage Investment Corp., 26 Cal. App. 4th 1819 (1994). **PRACTICE AREAS:** Litigation.

---

**MICHAEL R. OVERLY,** born Hanover, Pennsylvania, September 9, 1960; admitted to bar, 1989, California and U.S. District Court, Central and Northern Districts of California. *Education:* Texas A. & M. University (B.S., 1982; M.S., 1984); Loyola University of Los Angeles (J.D., cum laude, 1989). Phi Alpha Delta; Eta Kappa Nu; Phi Alpha Phi; Order of the Coif; St. Thomas More Honor Society. Recipient: American Jurisprudence Awards, Evidence, Corporations and Trial Advocacy. Articles Editor, Loyola Los Angeles Law Review, 1988-1989. Author: "E-Mail Trouble," Los Angeles Daily Journal, California Law Business (June 24, 1966); "Admissibility of Electronic Documents," Los Angeles Lawyer Magazine (June, 1966); "An Attorney's Guide to E-Mail Security," Los Angeles Daily Journal, California Law Business (November 20, 1995); "New California Statue Imposes Sanctions for Frivolous Lawsuits," Orange County Business Journal (February 20, 1995); West's California Criminal Law, authored chapter on larceny and embezzlement (West Publishing, 1995); "Hidden Liability: Implied Warranties Under The Uniform Commercial Code," U.C.C. Bulletin (Fall 1992); Note, "Boyle v. United Technologies Corp.: The Turning Point For The Government Contractor Defense?" 21 Loy. L.A.L.Rev. 935, 1988; "Private Confidentiality Agreements v. the Public's Right to Access--A Nationwide Debate," 2 State Legis. F. (June 1992). Contributor: "Handling Expert Witnesses in California Courts," C.E.B. Action Guide (Spring 1992); "Confidentiality Agreements and the First Amendment: The Right to Say Nothing," California Litigation, Vol. 5, No. 1, Fall, 1991. *Member:* State Bar of California. **PRACTICE AREAS:** Litigation.

**MARYAM SHOKRAI,** born Tehran, Iran, June 26, 1963; admitted to bar, 1990, California and U.S. District Court, Central District of California. *Education:* University of California at Irvine (B.A., cum laude, 1983); Monterey Institute of International Studies; Institut Catholique; University of California at Los Angeles (J.D., 1990). Phi Beta Kappa. Extern to Hon. Alicemarie H. Stotler, U.S. District Court, Central District of California. *Member:* State Bar of California. **LANGUAGES:** Farsi, French. **PRACTICE AREAS:** Litigation.

**JEFFREY A. BLACKIE,** born Pasadena, California, July 25, 1960; admitted to bar, 1990, California; 1991, U.S. Court of Appeals, Ninth Circuit; 1993, U.S. District Court, Central District of California; 1994, U.S. District Court, Southern District of California. *Education:* University of California at Berkeley (B.A., 1983); University of California, Hastings College of Law (J.D., magna cum laude, 1990). Order of the Coif. Recipient: American Jurisprudence Awards, Real Property, Legal Writing and Research; Milton D. Green Citation; Thurston Society Award; 1066 Foundation Scholarship. Senior Research Editor, Hastings Law Journal, 1989-1990. Author: Note, "Conservation Easements and the Doctrine of Changed Conditions", 40

*(This Listing Continued)*

CAA1394B

Hast. L.J. 1187 (1989). Law Clerk to the Honorable Melvin R. Brunetti, U.S. Court of Appeals, Ninth Circuit, 1990-1991. Associate, Gibson, Dunn & Crutcher, Irvine, California, 1991-1993. *Member:* State Bar of California. **PRACTICE AREAS:** Litigation.

*OF COUNSEL*

**PETER N. KALIONZES,** born Los Angeles, California, December 30, 1945; admitted to bar, 1974, California and U.S. District Court, Central District of California; 1977, U.S. Court of Appeals, Ninth Circuit. *Education:* University of Southern California (B.A., 1968); Pepperdine University (J.D., 1974). Recipient, Law Review Editorial Board Scholarship Award. Editorial Board, The Pepperdine Law Review, 1973-1974. Author: "Infant Pain and Suffering," Pepperdine Law Review, 1973. *Member:* Orange County Bar Association (Member, Real Estate Section); State Bar of California. [U.S. Army Reserve, 1970-1976]. **PRACTICE AREAS:** Residential Real Estate Development, Sale and Financing; General Corporate Business Matters; Construction Defect Litigation.

---

## CALLAHAN & ASSOCIATES
### 5120 CAMPUS DRIVE
### NEWPORT BEACH, CALIFORNIA 92660
*Telephone:* 714-476-2898
*Facsimile:* 714-752-8770

*FIRM PROFILE: The Firm handles commercial, business and commercial real estate disputes in all forums, including arbitration and workout negotiations. The attorneys comprising the Firm have had extensive trial and mediation experience, representing both creditors and debtors in bankruptcy and other civil litigation proceedings. In all matters, the Firm strives to provide legal services in an efficient and economic manner and endeavors to tailor its services to meet the particular needs of each client.*

**REBECCA CALLAHAN,** born Fresno, California, August 4, 1952; admitted to bar, 1982, California; U.S. District Court, Central, Southern and Northern Districts of California; U.S. Court of Appeals, Ninth Circuit. *Education:* University of Southern California (B.A., cum laude, 1974); Boalt Hall School of Law, University of California (J.D., 1982). Member, 1980-1982 and Notes and Comments Editor, 1981-1982, Ecology Law Quarterly. *Author* : "What Do Bankruptcy and Family Law Have in Common?....A Lot!" Business Law News, p.13 (Summer, 1994); "Police Power Exception to the Automatic Stay: What Is Its Scope When Applied To Postpetition Governmental Action Against Property of the Estate," 18 Cal. Bankr. J. 261, 1990. *Lecturer:* "A Bankruptcy Trial Program," Orange County Bankruptcy Forum (panelist, May, 1989); "Bankruptcy Appellate Practice," Orange County Bankruptcy Forum (program coordinator, January, 1990); "Alternative Dispute Resolution," Orange County Bankruptcy Forum (moderator, April, 1991); "Fast Attack: Capitalizing On the Supreme Court's Expanded View of The Availability of Summary Judgment Under F.R.C.P. 56," Orange County Bar Association, Commercial Section Meeting (Speaker, May, 1991); "Bankruptcy Evidence I: Overcoming Evidentiary Roadblocks," Orange County Bankruptcy Forum (panelist, June, 1992); "Basic Federal Practice," CEB (panelist, November, 1992); "Bankruptcy Tips For the General Practitioner," Business Law Section of the State Bar of California (program chair and panelist, October, 1993); "Fundamentals of Civil Litigation Before Trial," CEB (panelist, October, 1993); "Bankruptcy Issues For State Trial Judges 1993," American Bankruptcy Institute (panelist, November, 1993); "When Bankruptcy and Family Law Collide—Two Negatives May Equal A Positive," Orange County Bankruptcy Forum (panelist, March, 1994); "The New Value Defense in Preference Actions," Orange County Bar Association, Commercial Law and Bankruptcy Section (moderator, June, 1994); "Trial and Appellate Procedures in the Bankruptcy Court: An Overview for the State Court Litigator," Business Law Section of the State Bar of California (Program chair and panelist, September, 1994); "Fundamentals of Bankruptcy," The Rutter Group (panelist, September, 1994); "Bankruptcy Litigation: A Workshop in Trial Strategy and Technique," Orange County Bankruptcy Forum (program chair and panelist, November, 1995); "Getting Paid What You Are Worth," Business Law Section of the State Bar of California (Panelist, October, 1996). *Member:* Orange County, Federal and American Bar Associations; State Bar of California (Member: Bankruptcy Court Long Range Planning Implementation Committee, 1994-1995; Debtor/Creditor Relations and Bankruptcy Committee, Business Law Section, 1991-1994; Program Chair, 1993, 1994); Orange County Bankruptcy Forum (Director, 1994-1995; Co-Chair, Special Projects Committee, 1994-1995); California Women Lawyers Association; American Bankruptcy Institute; Bankruptcy Mediation Panel for the Central District of California, Appointee, 1995-1996; Peter M. Elliott Inn of

*(This Listing Continued)*

Court (Master, 1995-1996). *PRACTICE AREAS:* Insolvency; Business Litigation; Bankruptcy Litigation; Appellate Practice.

### ASSOCIATE

**KATHERINE T. CORRIGAN,** born Oakland, California, March 27, 1962; admitted to bar, 1987, California; U.S. District Court, Central and Southern Districts of California. *Education:* University of California at Irvine (B.A., 1984); Pepperdine University School of Law (J.D., 1987); University of London (International Law Studies, 1986). Contributor, "Bankruptcy Litigation: A Workshop in Trial Strategy and Technique," Orange County Bankruptcy Forum, November, 1995. Deputy District Attorney, Orange County Harbor Municipal Court Branch Office, 1989-1995. Narcotic Enforcement Team Asset Forfeiture Unit, 1994-1995. Associate, Ramsay, Johnson & Klunder, 1987-1989. Judge ProTem, O.C. Harbor Municipal Court, 1996—. *Member:* Orange County, Federal (Member, Orange County Chapter) and American Bar Associations; State Bar of California; Orange County Bankruptcy Forum; National Institute For Trial Advocacy; Robert A. Banyard American Inn of Court. *LANGUAGES:* French. *PRACTICE AREAS:* Bankruptcy; Commercial Real Estate; Business Litigation; Appellate Practice.

### LEGAL SUPPORT PERSONNEL

**SANDRA A. THOMPSON,** born Detroit, Michigan, October 23, 1943. *Education:* Central Michigan University (A.A., 1963); University of California at Irvine (Paralegal Extension Courses, Advanced Bankruptcy, 1994). *Member:* Orange County Paralegal Association; Orange County Bankruptcy Forum. (Paralegal).

---

## KRISTIN M. CANO

Established in 1984

ONE CORPORATE PLAZA
**NEWPORT BEACH, CALIFORNIA 92660**
Telephone: 714-759-1505
FAX: 714-640-9535
Email: KristinCanoLawOffice@internetMCI.com

*Corporate Securities, Business, Corporate, Corporate Finance, Securities Regulation, Securities Litigation, Mergers and Acquisitions, Venture Capital, and Commodities Law. Partnership, Contract, Class Actions Law. Complex and Multi District Litigation, and State and Federal Government Contracts.*

**KRISTIN M. CANO,** born McKeesport, Pennsylvania, October 27, 1951; admitted to bar, 1978, California and U.S. District Court, Central District of California; 1984, U.S. District Court, Northern and Southern Districts of California; 1988, U.S. Supreme Court; 1992, U.S. Court of Appeals, Ninth Circuit. *Education:* Pennsylvania State University (B.S. in Biochemistry, 1973); George Washington University (M.S. in Forensic Science, 1975); Southwestern University (J.D., 1978); Georgetown University (LL.M. in Securities Regulation, 1984). Member: Southwestern University Law Review, 1977-1978; Orange Coast Venture Group, 1986-1990. Listed: Who's Who of Emerging Leaders in America; Who's Who in American Law. Member, Leadership Tomorrow Class of 1994. National Board of the Acting Company, New York, N.Y., 1995-1996. *Member:* Orange County Bar Association; State Bar of California; Balboa Bay Club.

---

## CAPRETZ & RADCLIFFE

Established in 1970

5000 BIRCH STREET, WEST TOWER
SUITE 2500
**NEWPORT BEACH, CALIFORNIA 92660-2139**
Telephone: 714-724-3000
Fax: 714-757-2635
Email: CRLAWYERS@AOL.CON
URL: http://www.CAPRETZ.com

*General Civil and Trial Practice, State and Federal Courts, Business, International, Medical, Product Liability, Mass Tort Litigation, Corporate and Construction Law.*

**JAMES T. CAPRETZ,** born New Orleans, Louisiana, February 24, 1939; admitted to bar, 1963, Louisiana; 1967, U.S. District Court, Eastern District of Louisiana; 1969, California and U.S. District Court, Central District of California; 1973, U.S. Supreme Court; 1986, U.S. Court of Appeals, 10th Circuit; 1987, U.S. District Court, Western District of Pennsylvania. *Education:* Loyola University (B.B.A., 1961; LL.B., 1963). Co-Editor, Loyola Law Review, 1962-1963. Judge Pro Tem, Orange County Superior Court, 1983—. Member, Arbitration Panel, Orange County Superior Court, 1978—. Mediator with, ProMediate, a division of Capretz & Radcliffe, specializing in complex multi-party disputes and Real Estate Arbitration and Mediation Services (REAMS), a firm specializing in real estate disputes. National Association of Securities Dealers (Board of Arbitrators). *Member:* Orange County (Chairman, International Law Committee, 1978-1979) and Louisiana State Bar Associations; State Bar of California (Special Master, 1989—). *PRACTICE AREAS:* International Law; Commercial Litigation; Medical Product Liability; Mediation.

**RICHARD J. RADCLIFFE,** born Lodi, California, April 8, 1966; admitted to bar, 1991, California and U.S. District Court, Central District of California; 1992, U.S. District Court, Eastern, Southern and Northern Districts of California. *Education:* Biola University (B.S., summa cum laude, 1988); Loyola Law School (J.D., 1991). Recipient, American Jurisprudence Award in Trial Advocacy. Member, Loyola of Los Angeles Law Review, 1990-1991. Who's Who Among Rising Young Americans. Who's Who Among Students in American Universities. Adjunct Faculty, Pacific Christian College, Master of Business Administration Program, 1995—. *Member:* Orange County Bar Association; State Bar of California. *PRACTICE AREAS:* Business Litigation; Construction Law; Corporate Law; Real Property; Medical Product Liability.

### ASSOCIATES

**PETER A. MARTIN,** born Arcadia, California, August 11, 1963; admitted to bar, 1993, California and U.S. District Court, Central District of California. *Education:* Azusa Pacific University (B.A., cum laude, 1985); Fuller Theological Seminary (M.A., 1989); Western State University (J.D., 1993). Recipient, Distinguished Achievement Award. *Member:* Orange County Bar Association; State Bar of California; Orange County Barristers. *LANGUAGES:* Spanish and German. *PRACTICE AREAS:* Construction Defect; Business Litigation; Medical Product Liability.

### OF COUNSEL

**WILLIAM B. LAWLESS,** born Buffalo, New York, 1922; admitted to bar, 1946, New York; 1972, District of Columbia; 1976, Massachusetts (Not admitted in California). *Education:* University of Notre Dame (J.D., with distinction, 1944); University of Buffalo (A.B., 1949); Harvard University (LL.M., 1950). Editor-in-Chief, Notre Dame Law Review, 1943-1944. Justice, New York Supreme Court, 1960-1968. Dean: Notre Dame Law School, 1968-1971; National Judicial College, 1987-1990. Visiting Scholar, Wolfson College, Cambridge University, England, 1990-1991. President, Judges Mediation Network, 1992—. Member, National Advisory Board, Martindale-Hubbell, 1990—. Fellow, American College of Trial Lawyers. (Also Of Counsel to Lawless & Lawless, Barnstable, Massachusetts).

### LEGAL SUPPORT PERSONNEL

**ROSANNA S. BERTHEOLA,** born Fort Carson, Colorado, March 30, 1956. *Education:* University of Georgia (B.A., 1978); University of California at Irvine (Certificate of Legal Assistantship). *Member:* Orange County Paralegal Association. *PRACTICE AREAS:* Civil Litigation; Trial Preparation; Administrator, ProMediate and REAMS.

---

## STEVEN CASSELBERRY

ONE NEWPORT PLACE
1301 DOVE STREET, SUITE 940
**NEWPORT BEACH, CALIFORNIA 92660-2473**
Telephone: 714-476-9999
Fax: 714-476-0175
Email: steve@speed.net

*Financial Institutions, Mortgage Banking, Bankruptcy and Foreclosure, Business and Commercial Litigation, Real Estate, Commercial Financing and General Civil Trial in all State and Federal Courts.*

**STEVEN CASSELBERRY,** born Santa Monica, California, August 28, 1950; admitted to bar, 1977, California. *Education:* University of California at Los Angeles (B.A., 1972); American University (J.D., 1976). Phi Delta Phi. Administrative Editor, American University Law Review, 1975-1976. *Member:* Orange County and American Bar Associations; State Bar of California; Community Bankers of Southern California; California Trustees Association. *PRACTICE AREAS:* Banking Law; Litigation; Bankruptcy Law; Commercial Law; Real Estate (Property) Law; Title Insurance Law.

*(This Listing Continued)*

### STEVEN CASSELBERRY, Newport Beach—Continued

#### OF COUNSEL

**RICHARD A. HARVEY,** born Bremerton, Washington, July 23, 1944; admitted to bar, 1974, California. *Education:* California State University, Long Beach (B.S., cum laude, 1971); University of California Hastings College of Law (J.D., 1974). *Member:* Orange County and American Bar Association; State Bar of California. **PRACTICE AREAS:** Real Estate Law; Commercial Law; Litigation; Contractor's Law.

REPRESENTATIVE CLIENTS: AccuBanc Mortgage Corp.; Amresco Financial, Inc.; California State Bank; Central Pacific Bank; Cerritos Valley Bank; Champion Fence, Inc.; Cushman & Wakefield, Inc.; Davis Partners Incorporated; El Camino National Bank; First Bank & Trust; First National Bank of Portsmouth; First Valley National Bank; Forest City Development, Inc.; Golden Pacific Bank; Hawthorne Savings & Loan Assn.; Huntington National Bank; Inland Empire National Bank; Landmark Bank; Life Savings Bank; Omni Bank; Pacific Business Bank; Panel Concepts, Inc.; Pioneer Savings and Loan Association; Queen City Bank; Redlands Centennial Bank.

---

## CHANDLER & VATAVE
### 3 CORPORATE PLAZA DRIVE
### SUITE 204
### NEWPORT BEACH, CALIFORNIA 92660
Telephone: 714-721-0580
Facsimile: 714-721-0981

*Business and Employment Law with related Civil Litigation including Contracts, Real and Personal Properties, Wrongful Termination and related Tort actions.*

#### MEMBERS OF FIRM

**LINDA HART CHANDLER,** born Springfield, Massachusetts, May 13, 1938; admitted to bar, 1974, California and U.S. District Court, Central District of California; 1981, U.S. Supreme Court. *Education:* University of Pennsylvania (B.A., with honors, 1960); Western State University College of Law (J.D., magna cum laude, 1974). Nu Beta Epsilon. Recipient, American Jurisprudence Award in Real Property. Re write and Associate Editor, Western State University Law Review, 1973-1974. *Member:* Orange County Bar Association (Member, Ethics Committee, 1993—); State Bar of California (Member, Business Litigation Section); National Employment Lawyers Association; Orange County Women Lawyers. **PRACTICE AREAS:** Business Law; Employment Law; Related Civil Litigation.

**SUNIL LEWIS VATAVE,** born England, October 7, 1968; admitted to bar, 1995, California and U.S. District Court, Central District of California. *Education:* University of California at Irvine (B.A., 1991); Whittier College School of Law (J.D., 1994). *Member:* Orange County Bar Association; State Bar of California (Member, Business Law Section); Indo-American Bar Association; National Employment Lawyers Association. **PRACTICE AREAS:** Busines Torts; NASD Arbitration; Employment Litigation; Civil Litigation.

#### LEGAL SUPPORT PERSONNEL

**LORI M. MORENO** (Legal Assistant).

A list of References will be furnished upon request.

---

## COLLEEN M. CLAIRE
### SUITE 1, 3800 PACIFIC COAST HIGHWAY (CORONA DEL MAR)
### NEWPORT BEACH, CALIFORNIA 92625
Telephone: 714-675-0755
Fax: 714-675-7536

*Estate Planning, Probate, Trusts and Taxation Law.*

**COLLEEN M. CLAIRE,** born November 18, 1931; admitted to bar, 1957, California. *Education:* University of Southern California (B.S., 1952; LL.B., 1955). Beta Gamma Sigma. *Member:* Orange County (Chairman, 1969, 1971, 1972 and 1973 and Vice Chair, 1970, Probate and Trust Law Section; Member, Board of Directors and Liaison between the Board and Probate Section, 1973-1977) and American (Member, Section of Real Property, Probate and Trust Law) Bar Associations; State Bar of California (Member, Executive Committee, 1977-1982, Chair, 1980 and Advisor to Executive Committee, 1983-1985, Section of Estate Planning, Trust and Probate Law); American College of Trust and Estate Counsel; International Academy of Estate and Trust Law; Orange Coast Estate Planning Council.

---

## IVAN P. COHEN
### 1301 DOVE STREET, SUITE 670
### NEWPORT BEACH, CALIFORNIA 92660
Telephone: 714-851-8494
Facsimile: 714-851-8499
714-660-1462

*Johannesburg, South Africa Office:* 1, 14th Street, Corner Louis Botha Avenue, Orange Grove, 2192. Telephone: 011-2711-485-2270. Facsimile: 011-2711-485-1453.

*Domestic and International, Commercial and Consumer Collections Law, Corporate Finance and Business Law, General Civil Practice and Litigation in all State and Federal Courts.*

*FIRM PROFILE:* Ivan Cohen an Irvine based law firm with international practice provides legal services to his clients.

Mr. Cohen has built a reputation on legal skill, personalized client service and dedication to handling every case with the same energy and determination.

**IVAN P. COHEN,** born Johannesburg, South Africa, February 7, 1952; admitted to bar, 1979, South Africa; 1984, California. *Education:* University of Witwatersrand (Bachelor of Law, 1977; J.D., 1979). *Member:* Orange County and American Bar Associations; State Bar of California; Law Society of the Transvaal. **LANGUAGES:** Dutch and Afrikaans.

REPRESENTATIVE CLIENTS: Available Upon Request.
REFERENCE: Wells Fargo Bank, Irvine, California.

---

## COLLINS, COLLINS, MUIR & TRAVER
### Established in 1964
### 333 BAYSIDE DRIVE
### NEWPORT BEACH, CALIFORNIA 92660
Telephone: 714-723-6284
Fax: 714-723-7701

*Pasadena, California Office:* Suite 300, 265 North Euclid, 91101. Telephone 818-793-1163. Fax: 818-793-5982.

*Casualty, Products Liability, Construction, Malpractice Insurance, Employment Termination, Sexual Abuse, and Personal Injury Law. General Trial Practice.*

*FIRM PROFILE:* The firm of Collins, Collins, Muir and Traver is the successor to Collins & Collins established in 1964. The firm has 30 years of trial practice in the Southern California area.

*The practice emphasizes casualty defense, with focus on product liability, construction, architects and engineers, malpractice, public entity liability, automobile liability and insurance matters involving personal injury and property damage.*

*The firm has extensive experience in dealing with a wide variety of clients, as many of our cases require communication with adjusters, investigators, risk managers, claims representatives, in-house counsel, self insured parties, as well as expert witnesses of all disciplines.*

(For Complete Biographical Data on all Personnel, see Professional Biographies at Pasadena, California)

---

## COX BUCHANAN PADMORE & SHAKARCHY
### 840 NEWPORT CENTER DRIVE, SUITE 700
### NEWPORT BEACH, CALIFORNIA 92660-6310
Telephone: 714-720-9100
Fax: 714-720-1508
Email: cbpssocal@aol.com

*Palo Alto Office:* 755 Page Mill Road, Suite A280. Telephone: 415-424-0600. Fax: 415-493-9408.
*Denver, Colorado Office:* 1775 Sherman Street, Suite 2500. Telephone: 303-839-9191. Fax: 303-839-9318.
*New York, New York Office:* 630 Third Avenue. Telephone: 212-953-6633. Fax: 212-576-1614.

*Trial and Appellate Practice in State and Federal Courts. Corporation, Contracts, Business, International Business Transactions and Natural Resources Law.*

(This Listing Continued)

FIRM PROFILE: Cox Buchanan Padmore & Shakarchy founded in 1971 by Jonathan C.S. Cox, is dedicated to providing legal services of the highest quality in a timely manner. The firm represents local, national and international clients which involve the firm in complex commercial litigation and international business transactions. The firms attorneys are admitted to practice in various state and federal courts, thereby offering its clients the personal attention and relationship of the small sized firm, and providing the extensive litigation experience, credibility and geographic versatility of a large national firm.

**VICKI MAROLT BUCHANAN,** born Aspen, Colorado, September 15, 1949; admitted to bar, 1984, Colorado, U.S. District Court, District of Colorado and U.S. Court of Appeals, Tenth Circuit; 1986, U.S. District Court, Northern District of California; 1988, U.S. Supreme Court; 1991, California, Texas, U.S. District Court, Central District of California, U.S. Court of Appeals, Fifth and Ninth Circuits; 1992, U.S. District Court, Southern District of Texas, 1994, New York; 1995, U.S. District Court, Eastern District of California; 1996, U.S. District Court, Southern District of California and U.S. Court of Appeals, Second Circuit. *Education:* University of Colorado at Boulder (B.S., 1971); University of Denver (J.D., 1983). **PRACTICE AREAS:** Complex Commercial Litigation; Insurance Bad Faith; Creditor Bankruptcy; Appellate Advocacy.

## CUMMINS & WHITE, LLP

Limited Liability Partnership, including Professional Corporation

2424 S.E. BRISTOL STREET, SUITE 300
P.O. BOX 2513
**NEWPORT BEACH, CALIFORNIA 92660-0757**
Telephone: 714-852-1800
Telecopier: 714-852-8510

*Los Angeles, California Office:* 865 South Figueroa Street, 24th Floor. Telephone: 213-614-1000. Telecopier: 213-614-0500.

*Affiliated Taipei, Taiwan Office:* Chang & Associates, No. 12 Jen-Ai Road, Section 2, Seventh Floor, Taipei, Taiwan, Republic of China. Telephone: (02) 341-4602. Fax: (02) 321-6388.

*General Practice.*

(For biographical data on all firm personnel, see Professional Biographies at Los Angeles, California).

## LAW OFFICES OF
## RANDY D. CURRY

660 NEWPORT CENTER DRIVE, SUITE 950
**NEWPORT BEACH, CALIFORNIA 92660**
Telephone: 714-760-3836
Fax: 714-644-0840

*Insurance Bad Faith.*

**RANDY D. CURRY,** born Upland, California, September 24, 1953; admitted to bar, 1985, California. *Education:* University of La Verne (B.A.,1975; M.S.,1977; J.D., 1984). Articles Editor, Journal of Juvenile Law, 1983-1984. Author: "The Employment Contract with the Minor under California Civil Code Section 36," 7 Journal of Juvenile Law 93, 1983. *Member:* State Bar of California; The Association of Trial Lawyers of America; California Trial Lawyers Association; Los Angeles Trial Lawyers Association.

## C D DALY LAW CORPORATION

Established in 1982

500 NEWPORT CENTER DRIVE, SUITE 630
**NEWPORT BEACH, CALIFORNIA 92660**
Telephone: 714-644-9083
FAX: 714-720-3790

*Business, Real Estate Law and Related Litigation.*

**CHARLES DION DALY,** born Eureka, California, February 26, 1940; admitted to bar, 1970, California. *Education:* Stanford University (B.A., 1961); Hastings College of Law, University of California (J.D., 1969). Order of the Coif. Member, Thurston Society. Associate Editor, Hastings Law Journal, 1968-1969. Author: "Eminent Domain: The California Compatibility Requirement and the Corporate Utility Condemnor," 20 Hastings Law Journal 597, 1969. Senior Partner: Duryea, Malcolm & Daly, 1973-1979;

*(This Listing Continued)*

Malcolm & Daly, 1979-1982, Newport Beach, California. *Member:* Orange County and American Bar Associations; The State Bar of California.

### LEGAL SUPPORT PERSONNEL

**JOJO NGHIEM** (Legal Assistant).

REPRESENTATIVE CLIENTS: Charterhouse Investment Co.; Grubb & Ellis Co.; Western Realco; New England Mutual Life Insurance Co.; Pacific Midwest Mortgage, Inc.; California Business Interiors, Inc.; Baxter Travenol Laboratories; Copley R.E. Advisors; R.B. Allen Group, Inc.; Langdon Rieder Corporation; Resco; Zeno Table Company, Inc.

## STANTON W. DAVIES, II

2700 NEWPORT BOULEVARD, SUITE 172
**NEWPORT BEACH, CALIFORNIA 92663**
Telephone: 714-723-9000

*Practice Limited to Family Law. Divorce, Property Settlement, Support Issues.*

**STANTON W. DAVIES, II,** born Oakland, California, February 23, 1946; admitted to bar, 1972, California; U.S. Supreme Court. *Education:* University of Southern California (B.S., 1967); California Western School of Law (J.D., 1971). *Member:* Orange County (Member, Family Law Section) and American (Member, Family Law Section) Bar Associations; State Bar of California. **PRACTICE AREAS:** Family Law.

### LEGAL SUPPORT PERSONNEL

**SHEILA ELLIS** (Secretary).

REFERENCE: Union Bank.

## DAVIS, PUNELLI, KEATHLEY & WILLARD

Established in 1971

610 NEWPORT CENTER DRIVE, SUITE 1000
P.O. BOX 7920
**NEWPORT BEACH, CALIFORNIA 92658-7920**
Telephone: 714-640-0700
Telecopier: 714-640-0714

*San Diego, California Office:* 501 West Broadway, Suite 900, 92101. Telephone: 619-558-2581.

*Real Estate and Mortgage Banking, Corporate, Partnership, Construction, Commercial, Bankruptcy, Business Litigation, Creditor's Rights Law, Environmental Law. Including Trial and Appellate Practice in all State and Federal Courts.*

### MEMBERS OF FIRM

**ROBERT E. WILLARD,** born Bronxville, New York, December 13, 1929; admitted to bar, 1959, California. *Education:* State College of Washington (B.A., 1954); Harvard University (J.D., 1958). Co-Author: "The Limits of Advocacy: A Proposal For the Tort of Malicious Defense in Civil Litigation," Vol. 35, Hastings Law Journal, July, 1984. Law Clerk to U.S. District Judge William C. Mathes, 1958-1959. *Member:* Orange County and American Bar Associations; State Bar of California; The Association of Trial Lawyers of America; American Judicature Society. **PRACTICE AREAS:** Business Litigation; Construction; Real Estate; Environmental Law.

**S. ERIC DAVIS,** born New York, N.Y., October 10, 1942; admitted to bar, 1968, California. *Education:* Rutgers University (A.B., summa cum laude, 1964); University of Michigan (J.D., 1967). Phi Beta Kappa. *Member:* Orange County and American Bar Associations; State Bar of California. **PRACTICE AREAS:** Bankruptcy; Corporate; Real Estate Transactions.

**FRANK PUNELLI, JR.,** born Des Moines, Iowa, April 28, 1943; admitted to bar, 1967, Iowa; 1970, California. *Education:* University of Iowa (B.A., 1965); University of Iowa (J.D., 1967). Phi Delta Phi. Law Clerk to Hon. Robert L. Larson, Justice, Iowa Supreme Court, 1967-1969. *Member:* Orange County (Member, Sections on Business Litigation and Real Property) and Iowa State Bar Associations; State Bar of California (Member, Real Property, Environmental and Litigation Sections); California Trial Lawyers Association; The Association of Trial Lawyers of America. **PRACTICE AREAS:** Business Litigation; Real Estate Transactions; Mortgage Banking; Environmental Law.

**H. JAMES KEATHLEY,** born Havre de Grace, Maryland, February 16, 1955; admitted to bar, 1983, California. *Education:* Chapman College (B.A., 1977); Western State University (J.D., 1981). *Member:* Orange

*(This Listing Continued)*

## DAVIS, PUNELLI, KEATHLEY & WILLARD, Newport Beach—Continued

County and American Bar Associations; State Bar of California. *PRACTICE AREAS:* Business Litigation.

**ERIC G. ANDERSON,** born San Bernadino, California, July 15, 1961; admitted to bar, 1989, California; U.S. District Court, Central District of California; 1991, District of Columbia; U.S. Court of Appeals, Ninth Circuit. *Education:* California State Polytechnic University, Pomona (B.S., 1983); University of Southern California (J.D., 1989). Editor, Hale Honors Moot Court Executive Board, University of Southern California, 1988-1989. *Member:* State Bar of California. *PRACTICE AREAS:* Business Litigation.

**KATHERINE D. KEATHLEY,** born Lansing, Michigan, September 22, 1959; admitted to bar, 1990, California. *Education:* Western State University (J.D., 1990). *Member:* Orange County Bar Association; State Bar of California. *PRACTICE AREAS:* Business Litigation.

### OF COUNSEL

**LEWIS K. UHLER,** born Alhambra, California, November 22, 1933; admitted to bar, 1958, California. *Education:* Yale University (B.A., 1955); University of California (LL.B., 1958). Phi Delta Phi. President and Co-Founder, National Tax Limitation Committee, 1979—. Chairman, Governor's Tax Reduction Task Force, 1972-1973. Assistant Secretary, Human Relations Agency, 1971. Director, Economic Opportunity Office, State of California, 1970. Member, California Law Revision Commission, 1968-1970. *Member:* Los Angeles County and American Bar Associations; State Bar of California. *PRACTICE AREAS:* Governmental Affairs; International Law.

---

## DOSS & PAGE

A Partnership including a Professional Corporation

**SUITE 590, 4695 MACARTHUR COURT**
**NEWPORT BEACH, CALIFORNIA 92660**
Telephone: 714-752-5370
Fax: 714-752-2521

*Banking, Corporate, Title Insurance, Business, Real Estate and Civil Litigation.*

**DENNIS H. DOSS, (A PROFESSIONAL CORPORATION),** born Kenosha, Wisconsin, 1952; admitted to bar, 1978, California and U.S. District Court, Southern District of California. *Education:* California State University at Northridge (B.A., 1974); California Western University (J.D., 1978). *Member:* Orange County Bar Association (Member, Financial Services Section); State Bar of California.

**GREGORY S. PAGE,** born Long Beach, California, August 30, 1956; admitted to bar, 1986, California. *Education:* California State University at Long Beach (B.S., 1981); Southwestern University (J.D., 1984). *Member:* Orange (Member, Sections on: Real Property; Title Insurance) and Los Angeles County (Member, Sections on: Real Property; Title Insurance) Bar Associations; State Bar of California.

### ASSOCIATE

**DANIEL A. NASSIE,** born Ukiah, California, November 14, 1952; admitted to bar, 1990, California. *Education:* California State University (B.A., 1976); Cal-Northern School of Law (J.D., 1989). *Member:* Orange County and American Bar Associations; State Bar of California.

REPRESENTATIVE CLIENTS: Bankers Trust Company; Budget Finance Company; Century 21 Beachside; Chicago Title Insurance Company; Coast Security Mortgage; Commonwealth Land Title Insurance Company; Fidelity National Title Insurance Company; First Alliance Mortgage Company; First American Title Insurance Company; Fleet Mortgage; Fleet National Bank; Freedom Escrow; Fremont Investment & Loan; Goodrich & Pennington; Hamilton Materials; I.D.C. Italdesign California, Inc; Lawyers Title Insurance Company; Mariners Escrow Corporation; Meridian Medical, Inc.; Mesa Loans Services, Inc.; Nationscapital Corporation; One Stop Mortgage; Option One Mortgage Corporation; Quality Mortgage USA, Inc.; R.C. Temme Corporation; Temple Inland Mortgage Corporation; Title West Mortgage; Transnation Title Insurance Company.

---

## DRUMMOND & DUCKWORTH

**4590 MACARTHUR BOULEVARD, SUITE 500**
**NEWPORT BEACH, CALIFORNIA 92660**
Telephone: 714-724-1255
Fax: 714-724-1139
Email: patent_lawyer@msn.com

*Patent, Trademark, Copyright and Unfair Competition Law, Litigation.*

**WILLIAM H. DRUMMOND,** born Kansas City, Missouri, 1931; admitted to bar, 1961, Missouri, Illinois and U.S. District Court, Northern District of Illinois; 1962, U.S. District Court, Western District of Missouri; 1962-1982, U.S. Court of Customs and Patent Appeals, 1964, Arizona and U.S. District Court of Arizona; 1967, U.S. Court of Appeals, Ninth Circuit; 1968, U.S. Court of Appeals, Seventh Circuit; 1983, California, U.S. District Court, Central and Southern District of California and U.S. Court of Appeals, Federal Circuit, registered to practice before U.S. Patent and Trademark Office and Canadian Patent Office. *Education:* University of Missouri (B.S.Ch.E., 1956; J.D., 1961). Phi Alpha Delta. *Member:* State Bar of California; State Bar of Arizona; Missouri Bar; Illinois State Bar Association; American Intellectual Property Law Association. *PRACTICE AREAS:* Patent, Trademark, Copyright and Unfair Competition Law; Litigation. *Email:* patent_lawyer@msn.com

**DAVID G. DUCKWORTH,** born Santa Monica, California, November 20, 1966; admitted to bar, 1993, California and U.S. District Court, Central and Southern Districts of California; registered to practice before U.S. Patent and Trademark Office. *Education:* University of Santa Clara (B.S.M.E., 1988); Loyola Law School (J.D., 1993). Member, Inn of Court. *Member:* American Bar Association (Member, Intellectual Property and Space Law Sections); American Society of Mechanical Engineers; Intellectual Property Law Association. *PRACTICE AREAS:* Patent; Trademark; Unfair Competition; Related Litigation.

---

## DRUMMY KING WHITE & GIRE

*A PROFESSIONAL CORPORATION*

**NEWPORT BEACH, CALIFORNIA**

(See Costa Mesa)

*General Civil Practice, Litigation in all State and Federal Courts. Trial and Appellate Practice, Business, Real Estate, Public and Private Works Construction Law, Financial Institution Liability, Labor Law Matters, Commercial Litigation, Corporate Mergers and Acquisitions, Partnerships, Joint Ventures, Licensing, Securities Offerings, Sale and Leasings of Real Property.*

---

## LAW OFFICES OF DON M. DRYSDALE

Established in 1987

**SUITE 700**
**610 NEWPORT CENTER DRIVE**
**NEWPORT BEACH, CALIFORNIA 92660-6442**
Telephone: 714-760-9677
Fax: 714-760-9551
Email: 75722.164@compuserve.com

*Franchise Law, Business, Corporate Law and International Domestic and Regulatory Compliance.*

**DON M. DRYSDALE,** born Orange, California, February 13, 1947; admitted to bar, 1976, California and U.S. District Court, Central District of California; 1981, U.S. District Court, Southern District of California. *Education:* Ventura College (A.A., 1966); California State University at Northridge (B.A., 1968); University of California at Los Angeles (J.D., 1976). Member, University of California at Los Angeles Law Review, 1974-1976. Author: "California Franchise Law Undergoes A Minor Face-Lift," Franchise Legal Digest, November/December, 1988; "Mediation: an Alternative to Litigation," Franchise Legal Digest, January/February, 1990; "International Franchising" Asia-Pacific Law Journal, Spring, 1990. Advisory Commissioner to California Senate on Franchise Matters, 1986-1988. Member, Franchise Development Task Force, established by the President Pro Tem, California Senate, 1984-1986. President, Franchise Arbitration and Mediation, Inc., 1989—. *Member:* Orange County (Member, Business Law Section, 1989—) and American (Member, Forum on Franchising, 1986—) Bar Associations; State Bar of California (Chairman, Franchise Law Com-

*(This Listing Continued)*

mittee, 1990; Member, Business Court Committee, 1992-1995); California Franchise Association (Director of Membership, 1994-1995); International Franchise Association (Member, Legal-Legislative Committee, 1986—); Asia-Pacific Lawyers Association (Chairman, Business Law Committee, 1989-1993). [Flight Officer, U.S. Navy, 1969-1972; Cmdr., USNR, Ret.]

### LEGAL SUPPORT PERSONNEL

**IRENE E. REYNOLDS** (Paralegal).

**TIFFANY L. MILBY** (Paralegal).

**MICHELLE K. DRYSDALE** (Secretary).

REPRESENTATIVE CLIENTS: The Prudential Real Estate Affiliates, Inc.; Caffe Tazza; Surf City Squeeze; Budget Blinds; Dyno-Rod USA; New Horizons Computer Learning Centers; Fred Sands Affiliates; J.C. Nichols Co.; Great Earth Vitamin Stores; ISU International; Color Me Mine; Met-Rx Juice Cafe; The Ding King; Naut-A-Care Marine Services; Juice Safari; Grubb & Ellis; JC Java; First Internet Alliance; Hair Replacement Centers; Bonjour Bagels; Kelly's Coffee and Fudge; Auto Service 2000; E-Z Take Out Burger.
REFERENCES: Union Bank; International Franchise Assn.

---

## JOHN A. DUNCAN

A PROFESSIONAL CORPORATION

**NEWPORT BEACH, CALIFORNIA**

(See Orange)

*Estate and Trust Litigation. Probate Litigation, Conservatorship Litigation, Estate Planning, Estate and Trust Law, Estate and Trust Professional Negligence Litigation, Legal Malpractice Litigation and Consulting in these fields.*

---

## EADINGTON, MERHAB & EADINGTON

A PROFESSIONAL CORPORATION

Established in 1969

SUITE 600, SOUTH TOWER
3501 JAMBOREE ROAD
P.O. BOX 9408
**NEWPORT BEACH, CALIFORNIA 92658-9408**
Telephone: 714-854-5000
Telecopier: 714-854-5138

*General Business, Corporate and Partnership, State and Federal Securities, Finance, Real Estate and Commercial, Employment, Taxation, Business and Commercial Litigation in all State and Federal Courts, Trust and Estate Planning and Probate and Trust Litigation.*

FIRM PROFILE: *Eadington, Merhab & Eadington is a full service, business law firm established in 1969 and incorporated under its present name in the mid-1970's. The firm has extensive expertise representing businesses (especially closely held middle market and emerging growth companies) in all phases of transactional and business litigation matters.*

**GEORGE EADINGTON,** born Fullerton, California, July 4, 1950; admitted to bar, 1976, California. *Education:* University of Santa Clara (B.S., 1972; J.D., magna cum laude, 1976). Member: Orange County (Member, Sections of Business and Corporate Law) and American Bar Associations; The State Bar of California.

**MARLA MERHAB ROBINSON,** born Fullerton, California, October 7, 1960; admitted to bar, 1987, California. *Education:* University of San Diego (B.B.A., 1982); Western State University College of Law (J.D., 1987). Recipient, American Jurisprudence Award. *Member:* Orange County (Member, Labor Law Section) Bar Association; State Bar of California.
**PRACTICE AREAS:** Labor and Employment; General Corporate Matters; Business Litigation.

**DEBRA L. KLEVATT,** born Los Angeles, California, March 15, 1967; admitted to bar, 1993, California. *Education:* California State University, Fullerton (B.A., summa cum laude, 1989); Loyola Law School (J.D., 1993). Phi Kappa Phi. Kappa Tau Alpha. Golden Key. Chief Note & Comment Editor, 1991-1993 and Editorial Staff Member, 1991-1992, Loyola Entertainment Law Journal. Author: Note, "Public Television and the Government's Perpetuation of a Bipartite System: The Democratic and Republican Parties," 12 Loy. L.A. Ent. L.J. 509 (1992). *Member:* Stanislaus County, Orange County and American Bar Associations. **PRACTICE AREAS:** Business; Corporate; Employment Law; Civil Litigation.

REPRESENTATIVE CLIENTS: American Computer Hardware Corp.; Ashton Mining, Ltd. (Australia); Bristol Fiberlite Industries; Casanova, Pendrill Publicidad, Inc.; Compel Corp.; Crevier Motors, Inc.; Crown Bolt, Inc.; DSW Distri-

*(This Listing Continued)*

---

bution Centers, Inc.; The Eadington Cos.; Florasense by Endar; General Agency Insurance Development Services, Inc.; Homestead House; Independent Forge Co.; Marbella Golf & Country Golf Club; Rand Technology, Inc.
REFERENCE: Orange National Bank.

---

## EDWARDS, SOOY & BYRON

A PROFESSIONAL CORPORATION

Established in 1986

660 NEWPORT CENTER DRIVE, SUITE 465
**NEWPORT BEACH, CALIFORNIA 92660**
Telephone: 714-717-5000
Fax: 714-717-5001
URL: http://sdclaw.com/ews

*San Diego, California Office:* 101 West Broadway, Ninth Floor, 92101. Telephone: 619-231-1500. Fax: 619-231-1588.

*Civil Litigation and Trial Practice in all State and Federal Courts with emphasis on Commercial, Governmental, Insurance and Professional Liability Defense in all Fields. Architect and Engineering Defense, Accountant Liability, Legal and Medical Defense, Municipal Corporations and Related Issues, Land Use Law, Real Estate and Construction, Delay Damage Claims, Heavy Construction Claims, Insurance Coverage, Bad Faith Litigation, Products Liability, Torts and Negligence, Wrongful Death Law, Securities Arbitration, Wrongful Termination, Employment Law.*

REPRESENTATIVE CLIENTS: Design Professionals Insurance Co.; Allstate Insurance Co. (Brea Branch, San Diego Branch and North County Branch); Shand Morahan Co.; Transamerica Insurance Group; 20th Century Insurance Company; Boy Scouts of America; Ryder Truck Rental, Inc.; U-Haul International, Inc.; Budget Rent-A-Car; Camico; CNA; Millar Elevator Service Company; Schindler Elevator Corporation; Hyster Corporation; Crawford & Company; Chilcote, Inc.; Tucker, Sadler & Associates; A.I.A.; SGPA Planning & Architecture; Mega Foods, Inc.; Wausau Insurance; Wawanesa Insurance; CIGNA Insurance; American Eagle Insurance.

(For complete biographical data on all personnel, see Professional Biographies at San Diego, California)

---

## JONATHAN R. ELLOWITZ

ONE CORPORATE PLAZA, SUITE 110
**NEWPORT BEACH, CALIFORNIA 92660**
Telephone: 714-640-8441
Telefax: 714-640-9009

*Small Business and Bankruptcy Law.*

**JONATHAN R. ELLOWITZ,** born Washington, D.C., May 1, 1957; admitted to bar, 1979, California. *Education:* University of California (B.A., 1969); Southwestern University School of Law (J.D., 1978). *Member:* Orange County Bar Association; State Bar of California. (Certified Specialist, Personal Injury and Small Business Bankruptcy Law, The State Bar of California, Board of Legal Specialization).

---

## LAW OFFICE OF
## THOMAS J. FEELEY, P.C.

**NEWPORT BEACH, CALIFORNIA**

(See Los Angeles)

*General Civil and Municipal Law.*

---

## FISHER & PHILLIPS

A Partnership including Professional Corporations and Associations

4675 MACARTHUR COURT, SUITE 550
**NEWPORT BEACH, CALIFORNIA 92660**
Telephone: 714-851-2424
Telecopier: 714-851-0152

*Atlanta, Georgia Office:* 1500 Resurgens Plaza, 945 East Paces Ferry Road, N.E., 30326. Telephone: 404-231-1400. Telecopier: 404-240-4249. Telex: 54-2331.
*Fort Lauderdale, Florida Office:* Suite 2300 NationsBank Tower, One Financial Plaza, 33394. Telephone: 954-525-4800. Telecopier: 954-525-8739.
*Redwood City, California Office:* Suite 345, Three Lagoon Drive, 94065. Telephone: 415-592-6160. Telecopier: 415-592-6385.

*(This Listing Continued)*

## FISHER & PHILLIPS, Newport Beach—Continued

*New Orleans, Louisiana Office:* 3710 Place St. Charles, 201 St. Charles Avenue, 70170. Telephone: 504-522-3303. Telecopier: 504-529-3850.

FIRM PROFILE: *Fisher & Phillips, a national law firm founded in 1943, practices labor and employment law exclusively, representing management. The firm offers preventive advice and litigation defense in such areas as airline and railway law, alternative dispute resolution, business immigration, collective bargaining and arbitration, reductions in force, compensation, disability, employment discrimination, leave statutes, labor/employee relations, mergers, acquisitions, and closings, non-compete and confidentiality agreements, OSHA, pensions and benefits, personnel policies, privacy/workplace monitoring, security, sexual harassment, training, wage-hour, whistleblower claims, and wrongful discharge litigation.*

### RESIDENT MEMBERS

**ROBERT J. BEKKEN,** born Kalamazoo, Michigan, May 15, 1951; admitted to bar, 1976, Georgia; 1991, California. *Education:* Albion College (B.A., 1973); Emory University (J.D., 1976). Phi Delta Phi; Omicron Delta Kappa; Omicron Delta Epsilon. Member, Moot Court Society. Author: "Preventing Drug and Alcohol Abuse in Your Dealership (1991)." *Member:* Orange County and American Bar Associations; State Bar of Georgia; State Bar of California. **PRACTICE AREAS:** Labor (Management) Laws; Employment Law; Wrongful Discharge Law.

**JAMES J. MCDONALD, JR.,** born Cincinnati, Ohio, February 15, 1960; admitted to bar, 1984, Georgia; 1990, California. *Education:* New College of the University of South Florida (B.A., 1981); Georgetown University (J.D., cum laude, 1984). Member, Editorial Advisory Board, Employee Relations Journal, 1994—. Editor, *Mental and Emotional Injuries in Employment Litigation,* 1994. Author: "Avoiding 'Junk Science' in Sexual Harassment Litigation," 21 Employee Relations Law Journal 51, 1995; "Mental Disabilities Under the ADA: A Management Rights Approach," 20 Employee Relations Law Journal 541, 1995; "The Relevance of Childhood Sexual Abuse in Sexual Harassment Cases," 20 Employee Relations Law Journal 221, 1994; "The Role of Forensic Psychiatry In the Defense of Sexual Harassment Cases," 20 Journal of Psychiatry & Law 5, 1992; "Airline Employee Slowdowns and Sickouts as Unlawful Self Help: A Legal and Statistical Analysis," 55 Journal of Air Law and Commerce 349, 1989; "Airline Management Prerogative In the Deregulation Era," 52 Journal of Air Law and Commerce 869, 1987. *Member:* Orange County and American Bar Associations; State Bar of California; State Bar of Georgia; American Psychological Association (Division 41); American College of Forensic Psychiatry. **PRACTICE AREAS:** Labor (Management) Laws; Employment Law; Wrongful Discharge Law.

**KARL R. LINDEGREN,** born Waimea, Kauai, Hawaii, April 8, 1960; admitted to bar, 1986, California. *Education:* University of Southern California (A.B., magna cum laude, 1982; J.D., 1986). Phi Beta Kappa. Member, Southern California Law Review, 1984-1986. *Member:* Orange County and American Bar Associations; State Bar of California.

**ROBERT V. SCHNITZ,** born Oklahoma City, Oklahoma, August 28, 1962; admitted to bar, 1988, Georgia; 1991, California. *Education:* Northwestern University (B.A., 1984); Loyola University of Chicago (J.D., 1988). Wagner Labor Law Moot Court Competition, First Place, 1988. *Member:* Orange County and American Bar Associations; State Bar of California; State Bar of Georgia.

### RESIDENT ASSOCIATES

**GEORGIA V. INGRAM,** born Biddeford, Maine, September 27, 1958; admitted to bar, 1988, California. *Education:* Duke University (B.A., 1980); University of San Diego (J.D., cum laude, 1988). Lead Articles Editor, San Diego Law Review. Judicial Externship, Judge J. Clifford Wallace, U.S. Court of Appeals, Ninth Circuit, 1987. *Member:* Orange County and American Bar Associations; State Bar of California.

**ROBERT YONOWITZ,** born Bloomfield, New Jersey, September 5, 1962; admitted to bar, 1987, California. *Education:* Rutgers University (B.A., summa cum laude, 1984); National Law Center, George Washington University (J.D., with honors, 1987). Pi Sigma Alpha; Phi Alpha Delta. Henry Rutgers Scholar. Recipient, Board of Trustees Scholarship. Member, The George Washington Law Review. Internship, U.S. Senate Judiciary Committee Subcommittee on Courts. *Member:* Orange County and American Bar Associations; State Bar of California.

**JOHN M. POLSON,** born Des Moines, Iowa, June 15, 1965; admitted to bar, 1991, California. *Education:* University of South Florida (B.S.,
*(This Listing Continued)*

1987); Loyola Law School (J.D., 1991). *Member:* Orange County and American Bar Associations; State Bar of California.

**LYNE A. RICHARDSON,** born Los Angeles, California, 1964; admitted to bar, 1989, California; U.S. District Court, Central District of California. *Education:* University of Southern California (B.S., cum laude, 1985); Loyola Law School (J.D., 1989). President, Phi Delta Phi, 1988-1989. Recipient, American Jurisprudence Award in Contracts. Managing Editor, Loyola Entertainment Law Journal, 1988-1989. *Member:* Los Angeles and American Bar Associations; State Bar of California; Women Lawyers Association of Los Angeles.

**CYNTHIA WALKER LANE,** born Milwaukee, Wisconsin, April 30, 1954; admitted to bar, 1987, California. *Education:* University of Wisconsin, Milwaukee (B.A., 1976); Pepperdine University (J.D., 1987). Faculty, Loyola University, Continuing Education, Personnel and Industrial Relations Division, 1989-1994. *Member:* State Bar of California.

**JEFFREY B. FREID,** born Los Angeles, California, October 29, 1968; admitted to bar, 1993, California. *Education:* University of Texas (B.B.A., with honors, 1990); Loyola Law School (J.D., 1993). Member, Entertainment Law Journal, 1992-1993. *Member:* Orange County and American Bar Associations; State Bar of California.

**WARREN LEE NELSON,** born Louisville, Kentucky, May 3, 1947; admitted to bar, 1995, Wisconsin; 1996, California. *Education:* University of California at Santa Cruz (B.A., 1969); University of Sussex (M.A., 1971); University of Oregon (M.S.I.R., 1978); University of Wisconsin (J.D., 1994). *Member:* Orange County and American Bar Associations; State Bar of California; State Bar of Wisconsin.

**ANNE M. TERRA,** born Sacramento, California, January 9, 1966; admitted to bar, 1994, California. *Education:* University of California at Santa Barbara (B.A., with high honors, 1988); University of San Diego (J.D., cum laude, 1994). *Member:* Orange County and American Bar Associations; State Bar of California.

**CHRISTOPHER C. HOFFMAN,** born Eugene, Oregon, July 16, 1969; admitted to bar, 1995, California. *Education:* Santa Clara University (B.S., 1992); University of San Diego (J.D., magna cum laude, 1994). Member, San Diego Law Review, 1993-1994. *Member:* Orange County and American Bar Associations; State Bar of California.

**NANCY E. MCALLISTER,** born Livonia, Michigan, June 30, 1967; admitted to bar, 1994, California. *Education:* University of West Florida (B.A., magna cum laude, 1988); Loyola Law School (J.D., 1994). Certified Public Accountant, California, 1990. *Member:* Orange County and American Bar Associations; State Bar of California.

**MICHELLE M. CASEY,** born Wiesbaden, Germany, January 31, 1971; admitted to bar, 1996, California. *Education:* Cornell University (B.S., 1993); George Washington University Law School (J.D., with honors, 1996). *Member:* Orange County and American Bar Associations; State Bar of California.

**CHRISTINA T. NGUYEN,** born Saigon, Vietnam, April 26, 1971; admitted to bar, 1996, California. *Education:* University of Southern California, Los Angeles (B.S., 1993); University of California at Berkeley (J.D., magna cum laude, 1996). Phi Beta Kappa; Phi Kappa Phi. Associate Editor, Asian Law Journal and the Berkeley Women's Law Journal. President Asian Pacific American Law Students Association, 1995-1996. *Member:* Orange County and American Bar Associations; State Bar of California.

REPRESENTATIVE CLIENTS: Airborne Freight Corp.; Alaska International Industries, Inc.; Behr Process Corp.; Marie Callender Pie Shops, Inc.; Centex Cement; Chevron Land and Development Co.; Equifax, Inc.; Fleming Cos.; The Home Depot Co.; Hyatt Corp.; The M. W. Kellogg Co.; Manchester Tank & Equipment Co.; Motor Car Dealers Association of Orange County; New Car Dealers Association of San Diego; California Motor Car Dealers Association; National Automobile Dealers Assn.; National Association of Convenience Stores; Siemens Energy & Automation, Inc.; Textron, Inc.; Treasure Chest Advertising Co.; Universal Underwriters Group; Waste Management, Inc.; Wetterau, Incorporated; Wheelabrator Technologies Inc.; Yellow Freight System, Inc.

## JACK A. FLEISCHLI

1300 DOVE STREET, SUITE 200
**NEWPORT BEACH, CALIFORNIA 92660**
*Telephone: 714-660-7200*
*Fax: 714-660-0308*

*Constuction Defects, Real Estate and Business Litigation.*

**JACK A. FLEISCHLI,** born 1949; admitted to bar, 1975, California. *Education:* University of California at Santa Barbara (B.A., 1971); Pepperdine University (J.D., 1975). *Member:* Orange County Bar Association; State Bar of California.

## GARDNER AND QUAN
### INCORPORATED
*Established in 1975*

5000 BIRCH STREET, SUITE 4400
**NEWPORT BEACH, CALIFORNIA 92660**
*Telephone: 714-851-9025*
*FAX: 714-752-7132*

*Federal, State and International Taxation, General Business, Corporations, Pension and Profit Sharing. Estate Planning, Probate, Real Property, Health Care, Securities, ERISA and Tax Litigation.*

**DAVID H. GARDNER,** born Whittier, California, September 20, 1946; admitted to bar, 1973, California and U.S. District Court, Central District of California. *Education:* University of California, Riverside (B.A., 1968); University of California at Los Angeles (J.D., 1973). *Member:* Orange County and American Bar Associations; State Bar of California. **PRACTICE AREAS:** Taxation.

**JUDY A. QUAN,** born Los Angeles, California, October 23, 1955; admitted to bar, 1981, California. *Education:* Santa Clara University (B.S., summa cum laude, 1977); University of California at Los Angeles (J.D., 1980). Distinguished Advocate Moot Court Honors Program, 1980. *Member:* Orange County Bar Association (Chair, Business and Corporate Law Section, 1992); State Bar of California. **PRACTICE AREAS:** Business Corporations.

**SHANNON GALLAGHER,** born Lynwood, California, September 20, 1957; admitted to bar, 1982, California. *Education:* Long Beach City College (A.A., 1977); Santa Clara University (B.S.C., 1979); Loyola Law School (J.D., 1982); New York University (LL.M., Taxation, 1987). Member: St. Thomas More Law Honor Society; Moot Court Honors Board. Instructor, Golden Gate University, Graduate Tax Program, 1989—. *Member:* State Bar of California. **PRACTICE AREAS:** Taxation.

REPRESENTATIVE CLIENTS: Ringler Associates, Incorporated; Otto Laboratories; Redeye, Inc.; Winrich Capital Management, Inc.; Concordia Homes, Inc.; First Byte; Van Daele Development Corp.
REFERENCE: First Interstate Bank.

## GEIGER & WEBER
*Established in 1991*

WESTERLY PLACE
1500 QUAIL STREET, SUITE 200
**NEWPORT BEACH, CALIFORNIA 92660**
*Telephone: 714-756-0100*
*Facsimile: 714-756-0137*

*Real Estate, Franchise, Corporate and General Business; Litigation in areas of Franchise, Real Estate, Business and ERISA; Tax, Probate and Estate Planning.*

FIRM PROFILE: Geiger & Weber offers our clients the personal attention and accessibility of a small firm with reasonable fees, combined with the quality of experience and expertise that is usually available only from a larger firm. We believe this is an unusual combination that can work to the great advantage of clients of all sizes, from the individual to the large corporation.

**PAUL J. GEIGER,** born Glendale, California, October 1, 1949; admitted to bar, 1975, California and U.S. District Court, Southern and Central Districts of California. *Education:* Loyola University (B.B.A., 1972); St. John's College (1969-1970); Loyola Law School (J.D., 1975). Member, National Association of Corporate Real Estate Executives (NACORE), 1980-1985. Phi Alpha Delta. *Member:* Los Angeles County, Orange County and

*(This Listing Continued)*

American Bar Associations. **PRACTICE AREAS:** Real Estate; General Business; Franchise.

**MARC LINDSEY WEBER,** born St. Louis, Missouri, August 4, 1953; admitted to bar, 1978, California; 1979, U.S. Tax Court and U.S. Court of Appeals, Ninth Circuit; 1982, U.S. District Court, Southern District of California. *Education:* University of California at Irvine (B.A., 1975); Golden Gate University (M.S., 1985); University of California at Los Angeles (J.D., 1978). *Member:* Orange County Bar Association; The State Bar of California. **PRACTICE AREAS:** Real Estate; Franchise; Taxation.

### ASSOCIATE

**NICOLA J. TRIGG,** born Elmsworth, England, 1961; admitted to bar, 1990, California. *Education:* University of Birmingham, England (LL.B., with honors, 1984); Guildford College of Law, England (Solicitors Qualifying Examinations, 1985). Director, British American Chamber of Commerce, Orange County, 1991. *Member:* State Bar of California; Law Society of England and Wales. **PRACTICE AREAS:** Real Estate; Corporate Law; Business Law; Finance; Contracts; Immigration and Naturalization.

REPRESENTATIVE CLIENTS: Flagstar, Inc.; Denny's, Inc.; Marie Callender's; Carl Karcher Enterprises, Inc.; Winchell's Donut Houses Operating Company, L.P.; Home Depot U.S.A., Inc.; The Von's Companies, Inc.; Del Taco, Inc.; Arby's, Inc.

## MICHAEL J. GENOVESE
*Established in 1977*

2123 SAN JOAQUIN HILLS ROAD
**NEWPORT BEACH, CALIFORNIA 92660**
*Telephone: 714-729-8000*
*FAX: 714-729-1580*

*General Business, Real Estate, Corporate, Partnership and Taxation Law.*

**MICHAEL J. GENOVESE,** born Long Beach, California, September 24, 1948; admitted to bar, 1976, California; 1977, U.S. Tax Court; 1978, U.S. District Court, Central District of California. *Education:* Northern Arizona University (B.S., 1972); Western State University (J.D., 1976). *Member:* State Bar of California (Member, Business and Real Property Sections); Orange County and American (Member, Taxation Section) Bar Associations.

## GIBSON, DUNN & CRUTCHER LLP

**NEWPORT BEACH, CALIFORNIA**

(See Irvine)

*General Civil, Trial and Appellate Practice, State and Federal Courts. Antitrust Law. Specialized Criminal Defense. General Corporation, Securities, Administrative, Labor, Taxation, Estate Planning, Probate and Trust, International Business, Entertainment, Commercial, Insolvency, Bankruptcy and Reorganization, Natural Resources, Oil and Gas, Environmental Energy, Municipal and Public Utility Law.*

## PHILIP JOHN GOLD
*Established in 1977*

1301 DOVE STREET, SUITE 440
**NEWPORT BEACH, CALIFORNIA 92660**
*Telephone: 714-752-0800*
*Fax: 714-752-0313*

*Practice Limited To Probate, Estate Planning, Guardianship, Conservatorship, Wills, Trusts and Elder Law.*

**PHILIP JOHN GOLD,** born Fullerton, California, July 12, 1929; admitted to bar, 1977, California and U.S. District Court, Central District of California. *Education:* University of California (B.S., 1951); Pepperdine University School of Law (J.D., 1976). Lecturer: California Continuing Education of the Bar, "Planning For Aging & Incapacity," 1987, 1989, 1991 and 1993; "Fundamentals of Estate Planning, 1989; Handling a Descendant's Estate, 1991; Drafting Wills and Related Documents, 1992. *Member:* Orange County (Chairman, Legislative Committee, 1982-1984; Member, Estate Planning, Probate and Trust and Real Property Sections) and American Bar Associations; The State Bar of California.

REFERENCE: Union Bank (Sunny Hills Branch).

## GOOD, WILDMAN, HEGNESS & WALLEY

A Partnership including Professional Corporations

*Established in 1979*

5000 CAMPUS DRIVE
**NEWPORT BEACH, CALIFORNIA 92660**
Telephone: 714-955-1100
Fax: 714-833-0633

General Civil Litigation and Commercial Trial Practice, Real Estate, Acquisition, Development and Financing, Construction, Commercial Landlord-Tenant, Business and Commercial Transactions, Securities, Taxation, Estate Planning, Probate and Trusts, Intellectual Property and Licensing, Family Law, Labor and Employment Law, Alternative Dispute Resolution and White Collar Criminal Defense.

### MEMBERS OF FIRM

**THOMAS J. O'KEEFE, (A PROFESSIONAL CORPORATION),** born Detroit, Michigan, November 11, 1936; admitted to bar, 1962, California, U.S. District Court, Southern District of California and U.S. Tax Court; 1975, U.S. Supreme Court; 1983, U.S. District Court, Central District of California. *Education:* Loyola University (B.B.A., 1958); Stanford University (J.D., 1961). Phi Delta Phi; Alpha Sigma Nu. Outstanding Senior, Stanford Law School, 1961. Member, Stanford Law School Moot Court Board, 1960-1961. Vice President, Stanford Law Association, 1960-1961. Planning Commissioner, 1964-1965, Councilman, 1966-1978 and Mayor, 1974-1975, City of San Clemente. *Member:* Orange County Bar Association (Member, Committee on Taxation, 1966—; Director, 1970-1976); State Bar of California; Orange County Barristers (President, 1967-1969). (Certified Specialist, Taxation Law, The State Bar of California Board of Legal Specialization). **PRACTICE AREAS:** Estate Planning Law; Wills Law; Trusts Law; Probate Law; Taxation Law; Business Transactions; Real Estate Law.

**JOHN A. STILLMAN,** born Minneapolis, Minnesota, December 20, 1940; admitted to bar, 1969, California and U.S. District Court, Central and Southern Districts of California. *Education:* San Francisco State University (B.A., 1965); University of Southern California (J.D., 1968). Deputy District Attorney, Los Angeles County, 1969-1984. Special Assistant United States Attorney, Central District of California, 1982-1984. *Member:* State Bar of California. **PRACTICE AREAS:** Business; Real Estate; Litigation; White Collar Criminal.

**THOMAS E. WALLEY,** born Burbank, California, July 1, 1944; admitted to bar, 1970, California; U.S. District Court, Central District of California. *Education:* University of Southern California (B.A., cum laude, 1966; J.D., 1969). Phi Delta Phi. Recipient of Carl M. Franklin Award. Deputy District Attorney, County of Orange, 1970-1973. *Member:* State Bar of California (Member, Business and Real Estate Sections). **PRACTICE AREAS:** Civil Litigation; Family Law; Construction.

**PAUL C. HEGNESS, A PROFESSIONAL CORPORATION,** born Van Nuys, California, April 23, 1947; admitted to bar, 1973, California. *Education:* University of Arizona (B.S. in B.A., 1969; J.D., 1972). Phi Delta Phi. Director: Koll Real Estate Group; Walter Foster Publishing. Partner, Irvine Meadows Amphitheatre. Member: County of Orange Real Estate Advisory Committee, 1986-1987; Orange County Privatization Committee, 1991-1992. *Member:* Orange County and American Bar Associations; State Bar of California. **PRACTICE AREAS:** Business Transactions.

**ROBERT W. DYESS, JR.,** born Memphis, Tennessee, January 4, 1950; admitted to bar, 1975, Arizona; 1978, California. *Education:* Vanderbilt University (B.E., cum laude, 1972); University of Arizona (J.D., with high distinction, 1975); New York University (LL.M., in Taxation, 1978). Order of the Coif. Executive Vice-President and General Counsel, L'Abri Properties, 1986-1993. *Member:* State Bar of California. (Certified Specialist, Taxation Law, The State Bar of California Board of Legal Specialization). **PRACTICE AREAS:** Taxation; Real Estate; Business; Estate Planning.

**GARY A. DAPELO, (A PROFESSIONAL CORPORATION),** born June 28, 1952; admitted to bar, 1980, California; U.S. District Court, Central District of California. *Education:* University of California at Irvine (B.A., 1977); Western State University (J.D., 1980). *Member:* Orange County and American (Member, Sections on: Real Property; Business Litigation) Bar Associations; State Bar of California; The Association of Trial Lawyers of America. [U.S. Marine Corps, 1971-1973]. **PRACTICE AREAS:** Business Litigation; Wrongful Termination; Real Estate Litigation; Intellectual Property Litigation.

*(This Listing Continued)*

**RICHARD L. SEIDE,** born Santa Monica, California, March 10, 1954; admitted to bar, 1980, California, U.S. District Court, Central District of California and U.S. Court of Appeals, Ninth Circuit. *Education:* University of Southern California (B.S., magna cum laude, 1976; J.D., 1980). Judge Pro Tempore, Los Angeles Municipal Court, 1987—. *Member:* Orange County Bar Association (Member, Real Property Section). **PRACTICE AREAS:** Commercial Landlord/Tenant Law; Leases and Leasing; Receivership Law; Civil Litigation.

**RONALD K. BROWN, JR., (A PROFESSIONAL CORPORATION),** born Long Beach, California, October 1, 1956; admitted to bar, 1981, California and U.S. District Court, Central District of California. *Education:* California State University at Long Beach (B.A., 1978); Western State University College of Law (J.D., cum laude, 1981). Member, Western State University Law Review, 1979-1980. *Member:* Orange County and American Bar Associations; State Bar of California. **PRACTICE AREAS:** Landlord-Tenant Transaction and Litigation; General Business Litigation.

**KRISTINE A. THAGARD,** born Lynwood, California, March 4, 1957; admitted to bar, 1980, California, U.S. District Court, Central, Northern and Southern Districts of California and U.S. Court of Appeals, Ninth Circuit. *Education:* Menlo College (B.S., cum laude, 1977); University of Southern California (J.D., 1980). *Member:* State Bar of California. **PRACTICE AREAS:** Civil Litigation; Construction Defect Litigation; Wrongful Termination; Real Estate.

**HEIDI STILB LEWIS,** born Tucson, Arizona, June 11, 1954; admitted to bar, 1981, California. *Education:* University of Denver; University of Arizona (B.A., 1976); Western State University (J.D., 1980). Phi Alpha Delta. Recipient, Donald Wright Competition Moot Court Award, 1980. *Member:* Orange County Bar Association (Member, Construction Law Section); State Bar of California. **LANGUAGES:** Spanish. **PRACTICE AREAS:** Civil Litigation.

**NANCY E. RANEY,** born Los Angeles, California, February 24, 1958; admitted to bar, 1983, California; 1984, U.S. District Court, Central District of California and U.S. Court of Appeals, Ninth Circuit. *Education:* Stanford University (B.A., 1980); Loyola Law School (J.D., 1983). Member, 1981-1982 and Ninth Circuit Editor, 1982-1983, Loyola of Los Angeles Law Review. Extern for the Honorable Laughlin E. Waters, U.S. District Judge, Central District of California, 1981. **PRACTICE AREAS:** Civil Litigation.

**PAUL W. WILDMAN** (1924-1983).

REPRESENTATIVE CLIENTS: Upon Request.

---

## JAMES R. GORMAN

4041 MCARTHUR BOULEVARD, SUITE 400
**NEWPORT BEACH, CALIFORNIA 92660-2554**
Telephone: 714-752-2266
Fax: 714-756-0625

*Business Litigation, General and Civil Litigation, Estate Planning.*

**JAMES R. GORMAN,** born Philadelphia, Pennsylvania, May 12, 1944; admitted to bar, 1976, California and U.S. District Court, Southern District of California; 1977, U.S. District Court, Central District of California; 1978, U.S. District Court, Eastern District of California. *Education:* Pennsylvania State University (B.S., 1966); University of San Diego (J.D., 1975). Adjunct Professor, Irvine School of Law, 1977-1978. *Member:* Orange County Bar Association (Business Litigation Section); State Bar of California. [U.S. Navy 1966-1973 - LCDR Retired]. (Also Of Counsel, Barnes, Crosby & FitzGerald). **PRACTICE AREAS:** Business Litigation; General and Civil Litigation; Estate Planning.

REFERENCES: Marine National Bank; National Bank of Southern California.

---

## GREENBAUM & KATZ

An Association including a Professional Corporation

359 SAN MIGUEL DRIVE
**NEWPORT BEACH, CALIFORNIA 92660**
Telephone: 714-760-1400
Fax: 714-760-1300
URL: http://www.collectionlaw.com

*Collection, Enforcement of Judgments, Mechanics Liens, Construction Payment Law.*

*(This Listing Continued)*

*FIRM PROFILE: Mr. Greenbaum and Mr. Katz restrict their practice to commercial collection cases such as sales, notes, judgments, mechanics liens and related cases accepted on contingent or hourly fees.*

**MARTIN B. GREENBAUM, (P.C.),** born Cheyenne, Wyoming, March 11, 1945; admitted to bar, 1969, California; 1993, Colorado; U.S. District Court, Central, Eastern and Southern Districts of California. *Education:* University of California at Los Angeles (B.A., 1966; J.D., 1969). Deputy District Attorney, Los Angeles County, 1970-1974. Instructor: California Continuing Education of the Bar, Enforcement of Judgments, 1987-1994. Extension Instructor-Course, "Obtaining and Enforcing Money Judgments," University of California at Los Angeles, University of California at Irvine, University of California at Santa Barbara, University of California at Riverside and University of California at San Diego. Extension Instructor, Mechanics Liens and Construction Payment Remedies, University of California at Irvine. Speaker, "Get Your Money Fast," Seminars, 1985-1990. Author: Bad Debt Danger Signals; What Good is Winning; The Fastest Way to Collect; Where Have all the Debtors Gone-Skip Tracing, publisher: Get Your Money Fast Publishers, 1987. *Member:* Orange County (Chairman, Creditors Rights Section, 1992-1993) and American Bar Associations; State Bar of California. **PRACTICE AREAS:** Collections; Mechanics Lien Law; Enforcement of Judgement Law; Construction Collection.

**STUART A. KATZ,** born South Bend, Indiana, November 1, 1957; admitted to bar, 1985, California; 1995, Colorado; U.S. District Court, Northern, Central, Southern and Eastern Districts of California. *Education:* Indiana University (B.A., with distinction, 1980; M.B.A., 1984; J.D., 1984). Phi Beta Kappa. *Member:* Orange County Bar Association (Chairman, Creditors Rights Section, 1994); State Bar of California. **PRACTICE AREAS:** Collections; Creditors Rights; Enforcement of Judgments; Construction Remedies; Commercial Litigation.

---

*MELISSA J. FOX,* born Anaheim, California, February 12, 1968; admitted to bar, 1993, California. *Education:* Brandeis University (B.A., 1989); Tulane University of Louisiana (J.D., 1992). *Member:* State Bar of California. **LANGUAGES:** Hebrew. **PRACTICE AREAS:** Collections; Probate; Trusts and Estates; Criminal Law.

## THEODORE M. HANKIN
SUITE 900, ONE NEWPORT PLACE
**NEWPORT BEACH, CALIFORNIA 92660**
Telephone: 714-752-8840
FAX: 714-851-1732

*Corporate, Business, Tax, Probate and Estate Planning Law. Civil Litigation, Business Transactions, Banking, Real Estate, Partnership.*

**THEODORE M. HANKIN,** born Los Angeles, California, October 7, 1952; admitted to bar, 1977, California and U.S. District Court, Northern District of California; 1981, U.S. District Court, Eastern and Central District of California; 1985, U.S. District Court, Southern District of California. *Education:* University of California at Los Angeles (B.A., cum laude, 1974); Hastings College of the Law, University of California (J.D., 1977). Certified Public Accountant, California, 1978. *Member:* Orange County and American Bar Associations; State Bar of California; American Association of Attorney —Certified Public Accountants; American Institute of Certified Public Accountants; California Society of Certified Public Accountants.

## MARK C. HARGAN
1300 DOVE STREET, SUITE 200
**NEWPORT BEACH, CALIFORNIA 92660**
Telephone: 714-851-1229
Fax: 714-851-5014

*Construction Litigation, Civil Litigation, Business, Corporate, Real Estate Law, Bankruptcy, Insolvency and Creditor's Rights.*

**MARK C. HARGAN,** born Indianapolis, Indiana, April 2, 1951; admitted to bar, 1978, California; 1979, U.S. District Court, Central and Southern Districts of California; 1980, U.S. District Court, Northern District of California. *Education:* Menlo School of Business Administration (B.S., 1973); Western State University College of Law (J.D., 1978). Member: Engineering Contractors Association; Associated General Contractors. *Member:* Orange County (Member, Business Litigation, Real Estate, Commer-

*(This Listing Continued)*

cial and Bankruptcy and Construction Law Sections) and American Bar Associations; State Bar of California. **REPORTED CASES:** National Marble Co. v. Bricklayers and Allied Craftsmen (1986) 184 Cal. App. 3d 1057.

## HARLE, JANICS & KANNEN
1300 DOVE STREET, SUITE 200
**NEWPORT BEACH, CALIFORNIA 92660**
Telephone: 714-756-2170
Fax: 714-756-2171

*Community Association Law, Real Estate, General Corporate, Civil Litigation.*

*FIRM PROFILE: Harle, Janics & Kannen is recognized as one of the premier law firms providing legal services to community associations. In addition to its community association representation, the firm's practice also includes general real estate, corporate, business and civil litigation matters. The firm is committed to the highest standards of professional excellence in the delivery of legal services.*

**JAKOB S. HARLE,** born Lynwood, California, January 17, 1962; admitted to bar, 1987, California; 1988, U.S. District Court, Central District of California. *Education:* University of California, Los Angeles (B.A., magna cum laude, 1984; J.D., 1987). Member, 1985-1986 and Managing Editor, 1986-1987, UCLA Law Review. Author: "Challenging Rent Control: Strategies for Attack," 34 UCLA Law Review 149 (1986). *Member:* Orange County and Los Angeles County Bar Associations; State Bar of California; Community Associations Institute; California Association of Community Managers. **LANGUAGES:** German. **PRACTICE AREAS:** Community Association Law; Real Estate; General Corporate.

**KATHLEEN A. JANICS,** born Los Angeles, California, February 15, 1961; admitted to bar, 1990, California. *Education:* University of Southern California (B.S., 1983; M.S., cum laude, 1985); University of San Diego (J.D., cum laude, 1990). Member, Journal of Contemporary Legal Issues, 1989-1990. *Member:* Los Angeles County Bar Association; State Bar of California; Community Associations Institute; California Association of Community Managers. **PRACTICE AREAS:** Community Association Law; Real Estate; General Corporate.

**KAREN A. KANNEN,** born Bricktown, New Jersey, March 26, 1963; admitted to bar, 1990, California and U.S. District Court, Southern District of California; 1995, Colorado and U.S. District Court, Central District of California. *Education:* Cornell University (B.S., 1985); University of San Diego (J.D., cum laude, 1990). Member, University of San Diego Law Review, 1988-1990. *Member:* Los Angeles County Bar Association; State Bar of California; Community Associations Institute; California Association of Community Managers. **PRACTICE AREAS:** Civil Litigation; Community Association Law; Real Estate; General Corporate.

## HARWOOD, ADKINSON & MEINDL
**NEWPORT BEACH, CALIFORNIA**
(See Barger & Wolen)

## LAW OFFICES OF
## ROBERT C. HAWKINS
110 NEWPORT CENTER DRIVE
SUITE 200
**NEWPORT BEACH, CALIFORNIA 92260**
Telephone: 714-650-5550
FAX: 714-650-1181
Email: rhawkins@earthlink.net

*Water Law, Municipal Law, Condemnation/Land Use and Environmental Law.*

**ROBERT C. HAWKINS,** born Chula Vista, California, September 3, 1951; admitted to bar, 1987, Oregon; 1989, California and U.S. District Court, Southern District of California; 1990, U.S. District Court, Northern District of California; 1992, U.S. Court of Appeals, Ninth Circuit; 1994, U.S. District Court, Central District of California. *Education:* San Diego State University (B.A., 1974); University of California at Davis (M.A.,

*(This Listing Continued)*

**LAW OFFICES OF ROBERT C. HAWKINS,** Newport Beach—Continued

1982); University of Oregon (J.D., 1987). Recipient: American Jurisprudence Award in Jurisprudence; Wiley W. Manuel Award (1990-1993). Law Clerk to Hon. James A. Redden, U.S. District Court, District of Oregon, 1987-1989. Author: "MWD's Integrated Resources Planning Process-Smoke & Mirrors, or the Real Thing?" Shepard's California Water Law and Policy Reporter, January, 1995. Co-Author: "The New Age Land Grab: Habitat Protection as the Politically Correct (and Cheap) Taking of Private Property," Shepard's California Water Law and Policy Reporter, August, 1994; "Safe Drinking Water Act Reauthorization: In the Eye of the Storm," ABA Natural Resources & Environment Magazine (Summer 1994). *Member:* Orange County and American (Member, Sections on: Litigation; Natural Resources and Environmental Law) Bar Associations; State Bar of California (Member, Litigation Section); State Bar of Oregon.

REPRESENTATIVE CLIENTS: Pomona Valley Protective Association; West End Consolidated Water Company; Diamond Brothers Inc.; Wilhelm Family Trust.

---

## THOMAS W. HENDERSON
5030 CAMPUS DRIVE
NEWPORT BEACH, CALIFORNIA 92660
*Telephone: 714-252-8544*
*Fax: 714-252-8548*

General Civil and Trial Practice. Probate, Estate Planning and Personal Injury Law.

**THOMAS W. HENDERSON,** born Los Angeles, California, June 17, 1934; admitted to bar, 1961, California. *Education:* Pomona College (B.A., 1956); University of California at Los Angeles (LL.B., 1960). Phi Delta Phi. Judge Pro Tem and Arbitrator, Superior Court of California, 1979—. *Member:* Orange County and American Bar Associations; The State Bar of California; California Trial Lawyers Association; Orange County Trial Lawyers Association; The Association of Trial Lawyers of America. (Certified Specialist, Probate, Estate Planning, Trust Law, The State Bar of California Board of Legal Specialization).

REFERENCE: Bank of America, Westcliff Branch, Newport Beach.

---

## HESTON & HESTON
4041 MACARTHUR BOULEVARD
SUITE 400
NEWPORT BEACH, CALIFORNIA 92660
*Telephone: 714-222-1041*
*FAX: 714-222-1043*

Bankruptcy Law, Family Law, Probate, Wills and Estate Planning.

**RICHARD G. HESTON,** born Cedar Rapids, Iowa, January 10, 1954; admitted to bar, 1979, California; 1980, U.S. District Court, Central District of California; 1982, U.S. Court of Appeals, Ninth Circuit; 1985, U.S. Tax Court; 1996, U.S. District Court, Southern District of California. *Education:* University of California at Irvine (B.A., 1976); Southwestern University School of Law (J.D., 1979). Commissioner, Personal and Small Business Bankruptcy Law Advisory Commission, Board of Legal Specialization of the State of California, 1993-1996; Chair, 1996-1997. Member, Board of Directors, American Board of Bankruptcy Certification, 1996-1988. Member, Orange County Bankruptcy Forum. *Member:* Orange County Bar Association; State Bar of California. (Certified Specialist, Family Law, The State Bar of California Board of Legal Specialization; Certified Specialist, Consumer Bankruptcy Law, American Bankruptcy Board of Certification). *REPORTED CASES:* In re Kullgren, 109 B.R. 949 (Bankruptcy C.D.Cal 1990); In re Marriage of McCann, 27 Cal.App 4th 102 (1996). *PRACTICE AREAS:* Family Law; Bankruptcy Law.

**HALLI B. HESTON,** born Los Angeles, California, January 24, 1955; admitted to bar, 1979, California; 1984, U.S. District Court, Central District of California. *Education:* University of California at Irvine (B.A., 1976); Southwestern University School of Law (J.D., 1979). Member, Orange County Bankruptcy Forum. *Member:* Orange County Bar Association. (Certified Specialist, Personal and Small Business Bankruptcy Law, The State Bar of California Board of Legal Specialization). *PRACTICE AREAS:* Bankruptcy Law; Probate; Wills; Estate Planning.

---

## HOAG & OVERHOLT
5030 CAMPUS DRIVE
NEWPORT BEACH, CALIFORNIA 92660
*Telephone: 714-955-2260*

Los Angeles, California Office: Suite 1902, Wilshire Financial Tower. Telephone: 213-386-7848. Fax: 213-386-0194.

Probate and Trust Law. Federal and State Taxation. General Civil Practice.

### MEMBERS OF FIRM

**HALLACK W. HOAG,** born Newton, Kansas, December 5, 1905; admitted to bar, 1932, California. *Education:* University of Paris, 1926, University of Montpellier (Diplome, 1927); Indiana University (A.B., 1928); Yale University Law School (LL.B., 1931). Phi Delta Phi. Trustee, Los Angeles Bar Association, 1938-1940. President, 1951-1956; Member, Board of Directors, 1937-1972, Legal Aid Foundation. *Member:* Los Angeles County and American Bar Associations; The State Bar of California. *PRACTICE AREAS:* Probate; Trust Law; Tax.

**DAVID G. OVERHOLT,** born Los Angeles, California, January 25, 1935; admitted to bar, 1961, California. *Education:* Yale University (B.A., 1956); Stanford University (J.D., 1959). Phi Alpha Delta. Member, Board of Managers, Hollywood Wilshire Y.M.C.A., 1967—. Member, Board of Directors, Goodwill Industries of Southern California, 1976-1988. Director, Hollywood Presbyterian Medical Center Foundation, 1979—. Member, Board of Directors and Trustee, McKinley Home For Boys Foundation, 1978-1988. *Member:* Wilshire, Los Angeles County and American Bar Associations; The State Bar of California; Lawyers Club of Los Angeles; American Judicature Society. [With U.S. Air Force, 1959-1965]. *PRACTICE AREAS:* Probate; Trust Administration; Tax.

REFERENCE: Bank of America (Fashion Island Branch).

(For Complete Biographical Data on all Personnel, See Professional Biographies at Los Angeles, California)

---

## HOWARD & ASSOCIATES, P.C.
Established in 1977
ONE CORPORATE PLAZA
NEWPORT BEACH, CALIFORNIA 92660
*Telephone: 714-759-1477*
*FAX: 714-640-9009*

Business and Real Estate Litigation, Securities and Investment Fraud.

**JEFFREY M. HOWARD,** born December 4, 1946; admitted to bar, 1974, California and U.S. District Court, Central District of California; 1976, U.S. District Court, Southern District of California and U.S. Court of Appeals, Ninth Circuit. *Education:* Colgate University (B.A., 1969); Hastings College of Law (J.D.). *Member:* Orange County (Business Litigation Section; Real Estate Law Section) and Federal Bar Associations; State Bar of California (Business Litigation Section; Real Estate Law Section). *REPORTED CASES:* Hadley v. Krepel, 167 Cal.App. 3d 677 (1985). *PRACTICE AREAS:* Business Litigation; Securities and Investment Fraud; Real Estate Litigation; Complex Litigation.

### LEGAL SUPPORT PERSONNEL

**LINDA BURLEIGH,** born San Diego, California, October 27, 1948. *Member:* Association of Legal Administrators (Secretary/Board of Directors, 1986-1987; Vice President/Board of Directors, 1987-1988). (Legal Administrator).

REPRESENTATIVE CLIENTS: Interport International, Inc.; Pacific Snax Corporation; Travelmax International, Inc.

## HOWARD, RICE, NEMEROVSKI, CANADY, FALK & RABKIN

*A PROFESSIONAL CORPORATION*

Established in 1964

**610 NEWPORT CENTER DRIVE**
**SUITE 450**
**NEWPORT BEACH, CALIFORNIA 92660-6435**

Telephone: 714-721-6900
Telecopier: 714-721-6910
URL: http://www.hrice.com

*San Francisco, California Office:* 7th Floor, Three Embarcadero Center, 94111. Telephone: 415-434-1600. Telecopy: 415-399-3041.

General Practice including Trial and Appellate Litigation. General Corporate; Finance; Securities; Mergers and Acquisitions; Administrative; Municipal; Public Utility; Banking; Constitutional; Entertainment; Estate Planning; International Business; Real Estate, Land Use and Environmental; Bankruptcy and Reorganization; Trade Secret; Intellectual Property; Taxation; Trade Regulation Law; Alternative Dispute Resolution including Arbitration, Mediation and Early Neutral Evaluation.

**ROBERT E. GOODING, JR.,** born Wheeling, West Virginia, August 3, 1944; admitted to bar, 1969, Illinois; 1972, California. *Education:* Northwestern University (B.S., magna cum laude, 1966); University of Michigan (J.D., summa cum laude, 1969). Order of the Coif. Article Editor, Michigan Law Review, 1968-1969. Law Clerk to Justice Walter V. Schaefer, Illinois Supreme Court, 1969-1970 and Justice Harry A. Blackmun, U.S. Supreme Court, 1970-1971. *Member:* American Bar Association (Co-Chair, Pretrial Practice and Discovery Committee). **PRACTICE AREAS:** Trials and Appellate Practice; Securities and Antitrust Litigation; Business Litigation; Professional Responsibility Litigation.

**FAY E. MORISSEAU,** born Houston, Texas, July 16, 1951; admitted to bar, 1978, Texas; 1992, California; registered to practice before U.S. Patent and Trademark Office. *Education:* University of Oklahoma (B.S., with distinction, 1973); University of Houston (J.D., magna cum laude, 1978). Order of the Barons; Phi Eta Sigma; Pi Epsilon Tau; Tau Beta Pi. *Member:* Houston Intellectual Property Association; American Intellectual Property Association; Computer Law Association. **PRACTICE AREAS:** Intellectual Property Litigation and Counseling; Business and Commercial Litigation.

**MARTHA K. GOODING,** born Los Angeles, California, November 2, 1954; admitted to bar, 1981, California; 1983, U.S. District Court, Northern District of California; 1984, U.S. Court of Appeals for the D.C. Circuit and U.S. Tax Court; 1990, U.S. District Court, Central District of California. *Education:* California State University at Long Beach (B.A., with highest honors, 1978); Boalt Hall School of Law, University of California (J.D., 1981). Phi Beta Kappa; Order of the Coif. Law Clerk to Judge Aubrey E. Robinson, Jr., U.S. District Court, District of Columbia, 1981-1983. *Member:* American Bar Association (Co-Chair, Litigation Section ADR Committee; Litigation Section, Council Member, Dispute Resolution Section; Litigation Section Liaison with Dispute Resolution Section). **PRACTICE AREAS:** Business Litigation; Securities Litigation; Arbitration; Alternative Dispute Resolution.

**WILLIAM C. ROOKLIDGE,** born Portland, Oregon, August 10, 1957; admitted to bar, 1985, Oregon; 1988, California; registered to practice before the U.S. Patent and Trademark Office. *Education:* University of Portland (B.S.M.E., 1979); Lewis & Clark College (J.D., 1984); George Washington University (LL.M. in Patent and Trade Regulation Law, 1985). Recipient: 1993 John Marshall Law School Gerard Rose Memorial Award; 1988 Patent and Trademark Office Soc. Joseph Rossman Memorial Award; 1987 AIPLA Robert C. Watson Award. Author: "Willful Patent Infringement in the U.S.," Patent World, 1993; "The On Sale and Public Use Bars to Patentability: The Policies Reexamined," 1 Fed. Cir. B.J. 7, 1991; "Application of the On-Sale Bar to Activities Performed Before Reduction to Practice," JPTOS, 1990; "The Federal Circuit, Assignor Estoppel, and the Progeny of *Lear v. Adkins*," JPTOS, 1988; "License Validity Challenges and The Obligation to Pay Accrued Royalties," *Lear v. Adkins* Revisited," 1986-1987. Co-Author: "Vacating Patent Invalidity Judgment Upon Appellate Determinations of Noninfringement," JPTOS, 1990; "Reduction to Practice, Experimental Use, and the On Sale and Public Use Bars to Patentability," 63 St. Johns L. Rev. 1, 1988. Law Clerk to Judge Helen W. Nies, U. S. Court of Appeals for the Federal Circuit, 1985-1987. *Member:* American Bar Association (Member, Section on: Litigation; Intellectual Property

*(This Listing Continued)*

Law; Chair, Committee on Inequitable Conduct); American Intellectual Property Law Association (Vice Chair, Section on Litigation); Orange County Patent Law Association (President, 1993-1994). **PRACTICE AREAS:** Intellectual Property Litigation and Counselling.

**MATTHEW FRANCIS WEIL,** born Los Angeles, California, October 17, 1961; admitted to bar, 1992, California. *Education:* University of California at Davis (A.B., 1985); Columbia University (M.A., 1988); Boalt Hall, University of California, Berkeley (J.D., 1991). Phi Beta Kappa; Order of the Coif. Executive Editor, Ecology Law Quarterly. Author, "Protecting Employees' Fetuses From Workplace Hazards: *Johnston Controls* Narros the Options," 14 Berkeley Journal of Employment and Labor Law, 142 (1993). Law Clerk, Hon. Mary M. Schroeder, U.S. Court of Appeals, Ninth Circuit, 1991-1992. **LANGUAGES:** Russian. **PRACTICE AREAS:** Litigation; Intellectual Property.

**STACY J. MAY,** born Davenport, Iowa, June 25, 1965; admitted to bar, 1993, Arizona (Not admitted in California). *Education:* University of Iowa (B.B.A., with distinction and special honors, 1987; J.D., with distinction, 1993). Beta Gamma Sigma; Phi Eta Sigma. Member and Associate Editor, Iowa Law Review, 1992-1993. Contributor: Nichols on Eminent Domain, Mathew Bender; Arizona Legal Forms, West Publishing Co., Supp. 1993. *Member:* State Bar of Arizona. **PRACTICE AREAS:** Commercial Litigation.

**ERIC P. DAMON,** born Weymouth, Massachusetts, June 17, 1965; admitted to bar, 1995, California. *Education:* Tufts University (B.S.E., magna cum laude, 1987); University of Southern California (J.D., 1994). Hale Moot Court Honors Competition. *Member:* State Bar of California.

**LEE M. GORDON,** born West Nyack, New York, March 31, 1969; admitted to bar, 1994, California. *Education:* University of California at Los Angeles (B.A., summa cum laude, 1990); Harvard Law School (J.D., cum laude, 1994). Phi Beta Kappa.

**STEVEN S. BAIK,** born Seoul, Korea, June 18, 1968; admitted to bar, 1996, California. *Education:* California Polytechnic State University (B.S.E.E., magna cum laude, 1990); Stanford University (M.S.E.E., 1991); Hastings College of the Law, University of California, San Francisco (J.D., 1996). Eta Kappa Nu; Tau beta Pi. Senior Symposium Editor, Hastings Communications & Entertainment Law Journal. **PRACTICE AREAS:** Patents; Copyright; Trademark; General Litigation.

## KIM R. HUBBARD

**1301 DOVE STREET**
**SUITE 440**
**NEWPORT BEACH, CALIFORNIA 92660**

Telephone: 714-752-0800
Fax: 714-752-0313

*Probate Law, Conservatorship Law, Elder Law.*

**KIM R. HUBBARD,** born Albuquerque, New Mexico, July 24, 1953; admitted to bar, 1979, California, U.S. Court of Appeals, Ninth Circuit and U.S. District Court, Central District of California. *Education:* College of the Desert; University of California at Irvine; Irvine University (B.S.L., 1973; J.D., 1977); Western State University. Instructor, Business Law, National University, Irvine, California, 1985-1986. *Member:* Orange County Bar Association (Member, Sections on: Estate Planning, Probate and Trusts; Elder Law); State Bar of California; National Association of Elder Law Attorneys. **PRACTICE AREAS:** Probate Law; Conservatorship Law; Elder Law.

## IRELL & MANELLA LLP

A Law Partnership including Professional Corporations

Established in 1941

**SUITE 500, 840 NEWPORT CENTER DRIVE**
**NEWPORT BEACH, CALIFORNIA 92660-6324**

Telephone: 714-760-0991
Telecopier: 714-760-0721

*Los Angeles, California Offices:* Suite 900, 1800 Avenue of the Stars, 90067-4276. Telephone: 310-277-1010. Cable Address: "Irella LSA". Telecopier: 310-203-7199 and Suite 3300, 333 South Hope Street, 90071-3042. Telephone: 213-620-1555. Telecopier: 213-229-0515.

*(This Listing Continued)*

## IRELL & MANELLA LLP, Newport Beach—Continued

*General Civil Practice and Litigation in all State and Federal Courts and Arbitration Tribunals. Administrative, Antitrust, Aviation, Computer, Corporate, Corporate Securities and Finance, Mergers and Acquisitions, Election and Redistricting, Entertainment, Estate Planning, Trusts and Probate, Federal, State and Local Taxation, First Amendment and Media, International Business and Taxation, Insolvency, Bankruptcy, Reorganization and Creditors Rights, Insurance, Labor Relations, Wrongful Termination and Discrimination, Pension and Profit Sharing, Real Estate, Real Estate Finance, Banking and Secured Transactions Law. Patent, Trademark and Copyright Law. Intellectual Property and Trade Secrets. High Technology Litigation, Including Intellectual Property, Trade Secrets and Unfair Competition Litigation. Selected Criminal Defense.*

### RESIDENT MEMBERS

**SCOTT D. BASKIN, (P.C.),** born New York, N.Y., October 24, 1953; admitted to bar, 1978, California. *Education:* Stanford University (B.A., 1975); Yale University (J.D., 1978). Editor, Yale Law Journal, 1977-1978. Author: "Let the Buyer Beware: the Pre-Sale Examination Strategy," Computer Litigation Journal, 1995; "Practicalities of Using Experts in Civil Litigation," 1990; "The Use of Experts in Civil Actions," Preparing and Examining Expert Witnesses in Civil Litigation, 1987; "The Use of Experts in Non-Medical Malpractice Actions," Nonmedical Professional Malpractice, 1985. Co-author: "The Internal Corporate Investigation: Ad Hoc 'Search and Destroy' or Routine Record Retention Programs," The Internal Corporate Investigation 209, 1980. Assistant in Instruction, Constitutional Law, Yale Law School, 1977-1978. Law Clerk to Hon. Herbert Y.C. Choy, U.S. Court of Appeals, Ninth Circuit, 1978-1979. *Member:* State Bar of California; American Bar Association.

**FRANK A. CAPUT,** born Los Angeles, California, August 22, 1940; admitted to bar, 1966, California. *Education:* University of Southern California (B.S. cum laude, 1962); Harvard University (LL.B., 1965). *Member:* Los Angeles County and American Bar Associations; State Bar of California.

**MICHAEL G. ERMER,** born St. Louis, Missouri, May 20, 1958; admitted to bar, 1983, California. *Education:* Washington University (A.B., with honors, 1979); Harvard University (J.D., cum laude, 1983). Legal Methods Instructor, Harvard Law School, 1982. *Member:* Orange County and American (Member, Sections of Litigation, Tort and Insurance Practice, and National Resources, Energy and Environmental Law) Bar Associations; State Bar of California.

**JOHN C. FOSSUM, (P.C.),** born Minneapolis, Minnesota, May 20, 1941; admitted to bar, 1967, California. *Education:* University of California at Berkeley (B.A., 1963; LL.B., 1966). Order of the Coif. Book Review Editor, California Law Review, 1965-1966. *Member:* State Bar of California.

**ANDRA BARMASH GREENE,** born Chicago, Illinois, March 11, 1957; admitted to bar, 1981, District of Columbia; 1986, California. *Education:* Brown University (B.A., magna cum laude, 1978); Harvard University (J.D., 1981); Georgetown University. Phi Beta Kappa. Law Clerk to Judge Catherine B. Kelly, D.C. Court of Appeals, 1981-1982. Author: "Everybody's Doing It-But Who Should Be? Standing to Make a Disqualification Motion Based on an Attorney's Representation of a Client with Interests Adverse to Those of a Former Client," 6 University of Puget Sound Law Review 205, Spring, 1983. Co-Editor: "The Woman Advocate: Excelling in the 90's" (1995). *Member:* State Bar of California; The District of Columbia Bar; Orange County (Member, Judicial Nominations Committee) and American (Member, Section on Litigation; Chair, Committee on Program Evaluation and Utilization, 1992-1995; Co-Chair, 1993 Conference on the Woman Advocate) Bar Associations; Orange County Women Lawyers Association.

**THOMAS W. JOHNSON, JR.,** born Indianapolis, Indiana, October 18, 1941; admitted to bar, 1969, Indiana; 1970, California. *Education:* Indiana University (B.S., 1963; J.D., summa cum laude, 1969). Editor-in-Chief, Indiana Legal Forum, 1967-1968. Law Clerk to Chief Justice Donald H. Hunter, Indiana Supreme Court, 1968-1969. Co-Author: "California Practice Guide: Insurance Litigation" (The Rutter Group, 1995); "California Liability Insurance Practice: Claims & Litigation" (California Continuing Education of the Bar, 1992). *Member:* Orange County (Member, Insurance Law Section) and American (Chair, Insurance Coverage Litigation Committee of the Tort and Insurance Practice Section, 1995-1996) Bar Associations; State Bar of California (Member, Business Law Section; Member, 1978-1980 and Chairman, 1979-1980, Committee on Group Insurance Programs).

*(This Listing Continued)*

**KYLE S. KAWAKAMI,** born New York, N.Y., November 7, 1959; admitted to bar, 1986, California and U.S. Tax Court. *Education:* University of California at San Diego (B.A., magna cum laude, 1981); Stanford University (J.D., with distinction, 1986). Extern to the Honorable William A. Norris, United States Court of Appeal for the Ninth Circuit, 1985. Law Clerk to the Honorable Richard A. Gadbois, Jr., United States District Court, Central District of California, 1986-1987. *Member:* State Bar of California.

**RICHARD J. MCNEIL,** born Los Angeles, California, September 24, 1959; admitted to bar, 1984, California. *Education:* Yale University (B.A., 1981); Boalt Hall School of Law, University of California, Berkeley (J.D., 1984). Member, California Law Review, 1982-1984. Author: "Proposition 65, Asbestos and the Real Estate Industry," 6 California Real Property Journal 29, (Spring, 1988). Speeches: California Environmental Trial Academy, San Diego, California, May 31-June 2, 1996 (Co-Chair); "Swimming Toward A Safe Harbor,": EPA's Lender Liability Rule, State Bar Of California Environmental Subsection Of The Real Property Section, San Diego, California, November 13, 1993; "Environmental Regulations And Financing Transactions: Their Impact On Lenders, Borrowers And Regulators: EPA's Lender Liability Rule," State Bar Of California Environmental Subsection Of The Real Property Section, Irvine, California, June 4, 1993; "Environmental Concerns In Real Estate Transactions: The Developer's Perspective," CEB Presentation, Los Angeles, California, October 31, 1992; "Requirements For Publicly Owned Treatment Works," Executive Enterprises Water Quality Regulation Course, San Francisco, California, May 15, 1990; "Current Developments In Environmental Law," Environmental And Energy Council, Orange County Chamber of Commerce, Santa Ana, California, May 11, 1989; "Asbestos Abatement," Hazardous Materials and Water Pollution Subcommittee of the Environmental Law Section of the Los Angeles County Bar Association, Los Angeles, California, April 14, 1988; "Environmental Issues For Lenders," Pension and Real Estate Advisors Winter Meeting, Los Angeles, California, February 11, 1988. Law Clerk, Chief Judge Aubrey E. Robinson, U.S. District Court, District of Columbia, 1984-1985. *Member:* Orange County (Member, Environmental Law Section) and American (Member, Section of Natural Resources, Energy and Environmental Law) Bar Associations; State Bar of California (Member, Executive Committee, Environmental Law Section).

**LAYN R. PHILLIPS,** born Oklahoma City, Oklahoma, January 2, 1952; admitted to bar, 1977, Oklahoma; 1978, District of Columbia; 1981, California. *Education:* University of Tulsa (B.S., Economics, 1974; J.D., 1977); Georgetown University Law School (1978-1979). Recipient: Wall Street Journal Award for Outstanding Economics Graduate, 1974; Robert Butler Award for Outstanding Legal Writing, 1977. Managing Editor, Georgetown University Law Journal, 1978-1979. Trial Attorney, Federal Trade Commission, 1977-1980. Assistant United States Attorney, Central District of California, 1980-1983; United States Attorney, Northern District of Oklahoma, 1984-1987; United States District Judge, Western District of Oklahoma, 1987-1991; Named, United States Junior Chamber of Commerce, One of Ten Outstanding Young Americans, 1989. *Member:* Oklahoma and American (Member: Committee on Environmental Litigation; Committee on White Collar Crime) Bar Associations; The District of Columbia Bar; State Bar of California; State Bar of Texas; American Inn of Court XXIV (President, 1989-1990); American Inn of Court CV (President, 1990-1991); Orange County Federal Bar Association (Board of Directors, 1995-1996).

**ANTHONY W. PIEROTTI,** born Hawthorne, California, December 20, 1960; admitted to bar, 1987, California; 1988, U.S. Tax Court. *Education:* California State University at Long Beach (B.S., 1984); University of California at Davis (J.D., 1987). Order of the Coif; Phi Kappa Phi; Beta Gamma Sigma. Editor, University of California at Davis Law Review, 1986-1987. *Member:* State Bar of California.

**RICHARD M. SHERMAN, JR.,(P.C.),** born Denver, Colorado, June 20, 1947; admitted to bar, 1974, U.S. District Court, Central District of California; 1975, California; 1983, U.S. District Court, Southern District of California; 1985, U.S. District Court, Eastern District of California; 1987, U.S. Supreme Court and U.S. Court of Appeals, Ninth Circuit. *Education:* Claremont Men's College (B.A., cum laude, 1969); Occidental College (M.A., 1971); University of California at Berkeley (J.D., 1974). Exec. V.P. and General Counsel, The William Lyon Companies, 1989-1994. Co-author: "A Summary of American Airport Access Law," 1985 and "A Survey of Recent Development in United States Aviation Law," 1986, each presented to the International Bar Association. Member, Panel of Arbitrators, American Arbitration Association. *Member:* Orange County, Federal (Founding Member, Orange County Chapter), American (Member: Section of Litigation; Forum Committee on Air and Space Law) and International

*(This Listing Continued)*

(Member, Section on Business Law, Committee on Aeronautical Law) Bar Associations; State Bar of California.

### RESIDENT OF COUNSEL

**ROBERT W. STEDMAN, (P.C.),** born Sturgeon Bay, Wisconsin, April 22, 1938; admitted to bar, 1967, California. *Education:* University of Wisconsin (B.B.A., 1960); University of California at Berkeley (LL.B., 1966). Order of the Coif; Beta Gamma Sigma. Article Editor, California Law Review, 1965-1966. *Member:* State Bar of California; American Bar Association.

### RESIDENT ASSOCIATES

**LEIGH TAYLOR COMBS,** born Whittier, California, May 2, 1972; admitted to bar, 1994, California. *Education:* California State University, Los Angeles (B.A., 1990); University of Southern California (J.D., 1994). Golden Key Honor Society; Phi Kappa Phi Honor Society. National Dean's List. Honors Program Graduate. Honors at Entrance. CSULA Early Entrance Program. Delta Zeta Scholarship. Delta Zeta Highest Junior GPA.

**STEVEN W. HOPKINS,** born Redlands, California, July 11, 1967; admitted to bar, 1996, California. *Education:* University of Utah (B.S., 1990); University of Chicago (J.D./M.B.A., 1995). Comment Editor, University of Chicago Law Review. Author: "Is God a Preferred Creditor Tithing as an Avoidable Transfer in Chapter 7 Bankruptcies," 62 Chicago Law Review 1139, Summer 1995. *LANGUAGES:* Japanese. *Email:* shopkins@irell.com

**FRANCINE J. LIPMAN,** born St. Louis, Missouri, March 6, 1959; admitted to bar, 1994, California. *Education:* University of California-Santa Barbara (B.A., 1981); University of California-Davis (J.D., 1993); San Diego State University (M.B.A., 1989); New York University School of Law (LL.M. in Taxation, 1994). Beta Gamma Sigma; Order of the Coif. National Association of Women Lawyers Outstanding Woman Law Graduate, U. C. Davis, 1993. Recipient, Tax Law Review Scholarship. Member, 1991-1992, and Editor-in-Chief, 1992-1993, U.C. Davis Law Review. Graduate Editor, Tax Law Review, 1993-1994. Co-Author: "Will the Final Regulations Under IRC Section 469 (c) (7) Renew Taxpayer Interest in Real Estate?" Real Estate Law Journal, Fall 1996; "Will Changes to the Passive Income Rules Renew Interest in Real Estate?" Journal of Property Management, May/June 1996; "Passive Loss Rules for Real Estate Professionals," Los Angeles Lawyer, January 1996. Author: "Improving the Principal Residence Disaster Relief Provisions," Tax Notes, February 6, 1995. Co-Author: "The Earned Income Tax Credit: Too Difficult for the Targeted Taxpayers?" Tax Notes, November 9, 1992; "Recent Proposals to Redesign the EITC: A Reply to an Economist's Response," Tax Notes, February 28, 1994.

**MARC S. MAISTER,** born Johannesburg, South Africa, December 1, 1964; admitted to bar, 1991, California and U.S. District Court, Central District of California; 1995, U.S. Supreme Court. *Education:* University of Witwatersrand, Johannesburg, South Africa (B.Comm., 1987); Boalt Hall, University of California at Berkeley (J.D., 1991). Order of the Coif. Author: "Trigger of Coverage--A Contract Approach," published by the American Bar Association in "The Brief," Spring 1996, Vol. 25, No. 3 and at Mealey's Emerging Insurance Battles Conference, February, 1996. *Member:* Orange County (Member and Vive Chairperson, Insurance Law Section) and American (Tort and Insurance Practice Section) Bar Associations. *LANGUAGES:* English and Afrikaans.

**JOHN M. NAKASHIMA,** born Los Angeles, California, September 10, 1954; admitted to bar, 1987, California. *Education:* California State University at Long Beach (B.A., with high distinction, 1976; B.S., with distinction, 1978; M.B.A., 1983); University of Southern California (J.D., 1987). *Member:* State Bar of California; American Bar Association.

**ELIZABETH K. PENFIL,** born Silver Spring, Maryland, July 14, 1966; admitted to bar, 1995, California. *Education:* Wellesley College (A.B., Art History and Architectural History, 1987); University of Southern California (J.D., 1995). Order of the Coif. Southern California Law Review. Southern California Review of Law and Women's Studies. University of Southern California Law Center, Lawyering Skills Instructor, 1994-1995.

**NOAH B. SALAMON,** born Nashville, Tennessee, May 4, 1971; admitted to bar, 1996, California. *Education:* Swarthmore College (B.A., Philosophy, with distinction, 1993); University of Chicago (J.D., with honors, 1996). Tony Patiño Fellow. Member, The University of Chicago Law Review. Comment Editor, The University of Chicago Law School Roundtable.

**MARY-CHRISTINE (M.C.) SUNGAILA,** born Mountain View, California, December 1, 1967; admitted to bar, 1991, California, U.S. District Court, Central District of California and U.S. Court of Appeals, Ninth Circuit; 1985, U.S. Supreme Court and U.S. District Court, Southern District of California. *Education:* Stanford University (B.A., with distinction and honors in Humanities, 1988); University of California at Los Angeles, (J.D., 1991). Recipient: Stanford University Undergraduate Research Grant, 1987-1988; American Jurisprudence Award in Torts; UCLA University Fellowship for Academic Excellence, 1989-1990 and 1990-1991. Member, Moot Court Honors Program, 1989-1990. Publications: Bibliography, *The Woman Advocate: Excelling in the 90's,* (Prentice Hall Law & Business, 1995); "Taking the Gendered Realities of Female Offenders into Account: Downward Departures for Coercion and Duress," 8 Fed. Sent. R. 1 (1995). Extern to the Honorable Dorothy W. Nelson, U.S. Court of Appeals, Ninth Circuit. Law Clerk to the Honorable Alicemarie H. Stotler, U.S. District Court, Central District of California, 1991-1992. Law Clerk to the Honorable Ferdinand F. Fernandez, U.S. Court of Appeals, Ninth Circuit, 1993-1994. *Member:* Orange County (Member, Gender Equity Committee) and American (Newsletter Editor, The Woman Advocate Committee of the Section of Litigation, 1996—) Bar Associations; State Bar of California (Member, Litigation Section, Technology Committee, 1992-1994); Orange County Women Lawyers.

(For Complete Biographical Data on all Personnel, see Professional Biographies at Los Angeles).

---

## LAW OFFICES OF KELLY S. JOHNSON

160 NEWPORT CENTER DRIVE, SUITE 110
**NEWPORT BEACH, CALIFORNIA 92660**
Telephone: 714-729-8014
Fax: 714-729-8050

*Bankruptcy, Debtor Rights, Business and Real Estate Litigation.*

**KELLY S. JOHNSON,** born Iowa City, Iowa, November 15, 1960; admitted to bar, 1988, California and U.S. District Court, Central District of California. *Education:* University of Southern California (B.S., 1983); Pepperdine University (J.D., 1986). *Member:* Orange County Bar Association; State Bar of California (Member, Business Law and Real Property Law Sections); Orange County Bankruptcy Forum. (Also Of Counsel at Feldsott Lee & Feinberg).

---

## JONES, DAY, REAVIS & POGUE

**NEWPORT BEACH, CALIFORNIA**

(See Irvine)

*General Practice.*

---

## KELEGIAN & THOMAS

4685 MACARTHUR COURT, SUITE 400
**NEWPORT BEACH, CALIFORNIA 92660**
Telephone: 714-553-1200
Fax: 714-553-1013
Email: KelThomLaw@aol.com

*Civil Litigation, Insurance Defense, Personal Injury, Premises Liability, Products Liability, Construction Defect, Insurance Law, Automobile Liability, Business Torts and Disputes, Landlord Tort Liability, Copyright and Trademark Infringement, Fraudulent (S.I.U.) Claims.*

**MARK A. KELEGIAN,** born Milwaukee, Wisconsin, October 13, 1960; admitted to bar, 1987, California; U.S. Court of Appeals, Ninth Circuit. *Education:* University of San Diego, School of Law (B.A., with honors, 1982; J.D., 1986). Recipient, Best Brief Award, Appellate Moot Court Competition. Co-Author: Bancroft-Whitney's California Premises Liability: Law and Practice; "How Do You Plead", March 14, 1995, Los Angeles Daily Journal and San Francisco Daily Journal. Lecturer: Western State University College of Law, Settlement Negotiations; Civil Procedure; Legal Writing and Corporations. *Member:* Orange County and Los Angeles County Bar Associations; State Bar of California; Association of Southern California Defense Counsel; Armenian Bar Association; Defense Research Institute. **PRACTICE AREAS:** Premises Liability; Products Liability; Construction Defect; Fraudulent (S.I.U.) Claims; Civil Litigation; Business Litigation.

*(This Listing Continued)*

## KELEGIAN & THOMAS, Newport Beach—Continued

**MICHAEL PAUL THOMAS,** born Maywood, California, October 13, 1956; admitted to bar, 1986, California, U.S. Court of Appeals, Ninth Circuit, U.S. District Court, Northern, Central and Southern Districts of California and U.S. Supreme Court. *Education:* Cypress College (A.A., cum laude, 1979); California State University at Fullerton (B.A., cum laude, 1981); Boalt Hall School of Law, University of California (J.D., 1984). Phi Delta Phi. Associate Editor, Ecology Law Quarterly and Industrial Relations Law Journal, 1983-1984. Author: "Equitable Discretion Under the Federal Water Pollution Control Act: Weinberger v. Romero-Barcelo," Ecology Law Quarterly, Vol. II, No. 1, 1983. Columnist, Los Angeles Daily Journal, 1990—. Co-Author: Bancroft-Whitney's California Civil Practice: Procedure (Five Volumes). Co-Author: Bancroft-Whitney's California Premises Liability: Law and Practice. Adjunct Professor, Civil Litigation, Civil Procedure, Research and Writing, Western State University College of Law, 1991—. Instructor, Legal Writing, Whitter Law School, 1996—. Instructor, Civil Litigation, Research and Writing, Corporations, Rancho Santiago College, 1989-1991. MCLE Lecturer on "Law and Motion," The Rutter Group (1996). Judge Pro-Tem, Los Angeles County Municipal Court, 1992. *Member:* Orange County (Member, Resolutions Committee), Los Angeles and American (Member, Litigation Section) Bar Associations; State Bar of California; Defense Research Institute; Association of Southern California Defense Counsel. *REPORTED CASES:* Radcliff v. Landau (1991) 883 F.2d 1481; Elder v. Rice (1994) 21 Cal.App. 4th 1604. *PRACTICE AREAS:* Civil Litigation; Premises Liability Law; Insurance Law; Appellate Law.

**JOSEPH P. GALLO,** born Long Beach, California, July 29, 1965; admitted to bar, 1994, California. *Education:* Occidental College (A.B., 1987); Whittier College Law School (J.D., 1993). Moot Court Competitor & Law Review Editor. *PRACTICE AREAS:* Construction Defect; Premises Liability.

**BRUCE A. THOMASON,** born Los Angeles, California, October 31, 1961; admitted to bar, 1989, California. *Education:* University of California at Santa Cruz; University of California at Berkeley (A.B., 1984); University of Notre Dame (J.D., 1987). *Member:* Orange County (Member, Construction Section) and Los Angeles County Bar Associations; State Bar of California. *PRACTICE AREAS:* Construction Defect Litigation; General Civil Litigation.

**STEVEN M. HEPPS,** born San Francisco, California, July 3, 1961; admitted to bar, 1987, California. *Education:* University of Southern California (B.A., 1983); Pepperdine University (J.D., 1986). *Member:* Orange County Bar Association; State Bar of California. *PRACTICE AREAS:* Civil Litigation; Construction Defect; Insurance Defense; Personal Injury; Product Liability.

**JAMES P. HABEL,** born Springfield, Massachusetts, May 13, 1962; admitted to bar, 1988, Massachusetts; 1989, Connecticut and California. *Education:* Springfield College (B.S., magna cum laude, 1984); Boston College Law School (J.D., 1988). Judge Pro-Tem, Los Angeles Municipal Court, 1995. *PRACTICE AREAS:* Personal Injury Defense; Civil Litigation.

**JERI E. TABBACK,** born Glendale, California, April 22, 1954; admitted to bar, 1992, California and U.S. District Court, Central, Northern, Southern and Eastern Districts of California; 1993, U.S. Court of Appeals, Ninth Circuit. *Education:* Western State University (B.S.L., 1990; J.D., with honors, 1991). Recipient: Presidents Achievement Award Scholarship; American Jurisprudence Award, Constitutional Law, Evidence; Second Place Moot Court Best Brief. Law Review Editor-in-Chief, 1991. Moot Court Advisory Board. Author: "Opening Statements" in Federal Litigation Guide (MB), 1993. *Member:* Orange County Bar Association. *PRACTICE AREAS:* General Liability Defense; Insurance Bad Faith; Civil Rights Defense.

**DEAN H. MCVAY,** born Hastings, Michigan, October 26, 1963; admitted to bar, 1990, California; 1991, District of Columbia and U.S. District Court, Central District of California. *Education:* University of Michigan (B.A., with distinction, 1987); Vanderbilt Universit y (J.D., 1990). Phi Alpha Delta. Pi Sigma Alpha. Moot Court Director and Adjunct Professor of Appellate Advocacy, Western State School of Law, 1995—. Adjunct Professor, Appellate Advocacy, University of La Verne School of Law, 1997—. *Member:* Orange County, Long Beach and American Bar Associations; The State Bar of California; Association of Southern California Defense Counsel. *PRACTICE AREAS:* General Liability Defense; Fraudulent (S.I.U.) Claims; Construction Defects.

*(This Listing Continued)*

**ERIK R. MUSURLIAN,** born Whittier, California, February 11, 1969; admitted to bar, 1995, California. *Education:* University of California at San Diego (B.S. political science, 1991); University of San Diego, School of Law (J.D., 1995). *Member:* Los Angeles County, Orange County and Armenian Bar Associations. *PRACTICE AREAS:* Civil Litigation; Construction Defect; Premises Liability.

**WILLIAM N. VILLARD,** born White Plains, New York, October 13, 1967; admitted to bar, 1994, California. *Education:* Wake Forest University (B.S., Health and Sports Science, 1989); California Western School of Law (J.D., 1993); University of San Diego Law School (LL.M., in Taxation, 1997). *Member:* Orange County Bar Association; State Bar of California. *PRACTICE AREAS:* Civil Litigation; Premises Liability Law; Construction Defect.

REPRESENTATIVE CLIENTS: Farmers Insurance Group of Companies; Scottsdale Insurance Company; CalFarm Insurance; VIK Brothers Insurance Group; Special District Risk Management Authority; National Casualty Insurance; Pacific National Insurance Company; Northwestern National Casualty Company; General Accident Insurance Company; Team Rehab Inc.; Tri-Star International, Inc.; Economy Mail Service, Inc.; Cater Craft Foods, Inc.; NAFTA Distributors; Ocean 11 Casino, Inc.; Sun Plastic, Inc.; Clover Industries.

## DONN KEMBLE
SUITE 6000, 4000 MACARTHUR BOULEVARD
**NEWPORT BEACH, CALIFORNIA 92660**
Telephone: 714-833-3335
Fax: 714-752-8170

*General Trial and Appellate Practice in all Courts, Business, Corporation, Estate Planning, Real Estate and Taxation Law.*

**DONN KEMBLE,** born Belleville, Illinois, June 23, 1928; admitted to bar, 1959, California. *Education:* University of Illinois and University of California at Los Angeles (B.S., 1955); University of California at Los Angeles (J.D., 1958). Phi Delta Phi. Certified Public Accountant, California, 1959. *Member:* Orange County and American (Member, Sections on: Taxation; Corporation, Banking and Business Law) Bar Associations; The State Bar of California (Member, Committee on Taxation, 1973-1975); California Society of Certified Public Accountants; American Institute of Certified Public Accountants. *LANGUAGES:* German.

## KESTER & QUINLAN
1470 JAMBOREE ROAD, SUITE 200
**NEWPORT BEACH, CALIFORNIA 92660**
Telephone: 714-759-7760
FAX: 714-760-8156
Email: F.E.Quinlan@aol.com

*Business Litigation, Banking, Real Estate, Taxation, Insurance Defense, Medical Malpractice, Environmental Law, Estate and Business Planning.*

*FIRM PROFILE: Kester and Quinlan provides high quality representation to financial institutions and other business entities. It has broad experience evaluating fraudulent activities and can perform in dept data based on research by computer.*

**FRANCIS E. QUINLAN,** born Sumter, South Carolina, July, 28, 1948; admitted to bar, 1979, California; 1984, U.S. District Court, Northern, Central, Eastern and Southern Districts of California and U.S. Claims Court; 1994, Colorado. *Education:* University of Wisconsin-Madison (B.A., 1970); Southwestern University School of Law (J.D., 1978); Boston University (LL.M., Taxation, 1981). Lecturer, Bank Operations and Financial Fraud Prevention. Member of the Board: University of Irvine, School of Social Ecology Associates; Marine Corps University Foundation. President, Marine Corps Reserve Officers Association, Orange County Chapter. California, Society of Former Special Agents of the FBI. *Member:* Orange County and Colorado Bar Associations; State Bar of California. [Colonel, U.S. Marine Corps Reserve, 1969—]. *SPECIAL AGENCIES:* Federal Bureau of Investigation, 1979-1982. *PRACTICE AREAS:* Banking; Commercial Litigation; Taxation; Estate Planning; White Collar Crime (Civil and Criminal). *Email:* F.E.Quinlan@aol.com

**STEVEN L. KESTER,** born Ames, Iowa, February 24, 1950; admitted to bar, 1978, California; 1979, U.S. District Court, Central District of California. *Education:* California State University at Northridge (B.A., 1974); University of California, Davis (M.A., 1975); Southwestern University (J.D., 1978). Deputy District Attorney, Orange County District Attorney's Office, 1979-1982. *Member:* Los Angeles County, Orange County and American Bar Associations; Japanese-American Bar Association; The State

*(This Listing Continued)*

Bar of California; California District Attorneys Association; Peter M. Elliott Inn of Court. [U.S. Marine Coprs, 1968-1971]. *PRACTICE AREAS:* Banking; Business Law; Environmental Law; Real Estate.

**DALE K. QUINLAN,** born Montgomery, Alabama, November 23, 1950; admitted to bar, 1982, Florida; 1988, California. *Education:* United States Naval Academy (B.S., 1972); University of Florida (M.B.A., 1982; J.D., 1982). Member: The Order of Barristers; Moot Court Board. Chairman, Appellate Advocacy Board of Editors, 1981. *Member:* The Florida Bar (Member, Professional Stress Committee, 1983—); American Bar Association (Member, Science and Technology Section); The State Bar of California. The Association of Trial Lawyers of America. [With U.S. Navy, 1968-1978]

REPRESENTATIVE CLIENTS: World Savings and Loan Association; Golden West Savings Association; National Bank of Southern California; Liberty Bank; National Bank of California; Quiksilver, U.S.A.

## KIMBALL, TIREY & ST. JOHN

1600 DOVE STREET, SUITE 450
**NEWPORT BEACH, CALIFORNIA 92660**
Telephone: 714-476-5585; 800-564-6611
Fax: 714-476-5580
Email: ktsud@evict-collect.com
URL: http://www.evict-collect.com/~ktsud

*San Diego, California Office:* 1202 Kettner Boulevard, Fifth Floor, 92101. Telephone: 619-234-1690; 800-338-6039. Fax: 619-237-0457.
*San Mateo, California Office:* 1900 South Norfolk Street, Suite 320, 94403. Telephone: 415-525-1690; 800-525-1690. Fax: 415-525-2120.

*Residential and Commercial Landlord/Tenant Law, Collections, Real Estate, Business, Banking and Finance Litigation.*

FIRM PROFILE: *Kimball, Tirey & St. John is the preeminent landlord/tenant law firm in California, with offices in San Diego, Newport Beach and the San Francisco Bay Area. The firm's offices are fully staffed with twenty-three attorneys and fifty three staff members. In addition to practicing residential and commercial landlord/tenant law, the firm operates a full service collection division. The firm's commercial division represents clients in general real estate and business litigation and in labor law issues. Other divisions of practice include the representation of homeowner associations, mobile home park owners and financial institutions. The firm has trained and certified mediators and emphasizes the practice of "preventive law" with its clientele.*

**THEODORE C. KIMBALL,** born Lincoln, Nebraska, September 20, 1951; admitted to bar, 1977, California. *Education:* Arizona State University at Tempe (B.S., 1973); Western State University (J.D., 1977). Editor-in-Chief, Law Review. *Member:* State Bar of California (Member, Real Property Section); California Apartment Association; Resident Relations Foundation of San Diego. *PRACTICE AREAS:* Landlord/Tenant Law (85%, 600).

**PATRICIA H. TIREY,** born Hamilton, Bermuda, June 21, 1957; admitted to bar, 1983, California. *Education:* University of California (B.A., English); University of San Diego (J.D., 1983). Order of the Barrister; Moot Court Board. Instructor, California Department of Real Estate, 1992—. Judge Pro Tempore, Northern Judicial District, 1989-1992. *Member:* State Bar of California; American Bar Association; California Women Lawyers. *PRACTICE AREAS:* Landlord/Tenant Law.

**WENDY ST. JOHN,** born Waterville, Maine, January 23, 1958; admitted to bar, 1983, California. *Education:* University of Michigan (B.A., 1979); University of San Diego (J.D., 1983). Judge Pro Tem, Commissioner Pro Tem, 1988-1993. *Member:* San Diego County Bar Association (Chair, Civil Municipal Court Committee, 1995—); State Bar of California; San Diego Trial Lawyers Association. *PRACTICE AREAS:* Landlord/Tenant Law.

**ROBERT C. THORN,** born Albany, Georgia, March 4, 1955; admitted to bar, 1981, California and U.S. District Court, Southern District of California. *Education:* San Diego State University (B.A., 1977); California Western School of Law (J.D., 1980). Pi Alpha Delta. Author: "ADA Compliance, The Continuing Cunundrum," Visions Magazine, Nov. 1994. *Member:* San Diego County Bar Association. *PRACTICE AREAS:* Landlord/Tenant; Real Estate.

**HELAINE S. ASHTON,** born Chicago, Illinois, January 29, 1953; admitted to bar, 1988, California; 1990, U.S. District Court, Central District of California. *Education:* Western State University (B.S.L., 1985; J.D., 1987). *Member:* State Bar of California (Member, Real Estate Section);

*(This Listing Continued)*

Apartment Association-Greater Inland Empire (Director, 1995—). (Managing Partner, Newport Beach Office). *PRACTICE AREAS:* Landlord/Tenant.

**LINDA C. FRITZ,** born Evanston, Illinois, March 17, 1952; admitted to bar, 1983, California and U.S. District Court, Southern District of California. *Education:* Southern Illinois University; Western State University (B.S.L., 1981; J.D., 1982). Member, Law Review. Adjunct Professor, ADR, California Western School of Law, San Diego, 1994-1995. Member, Board of Directors, SPIDR, 1993-1994. *Member:* North County Bar Association (Founding Co-Chair, 1991-1992); San Diego County Apartment Association (Member, Board of Directors, 1994-1995); American Arbitration Association. *LANGUAGES:* Spanish. *PRACTICE AREAS:* Real Estate Litigation; Business Litigation.

**MARK A. BRODY,** born Detroit, Michigan, December 7, 1949; admitted to bar, 1976, California; U.S. District Court, Southern District of California. *Education:* University of Michigan (B.A., 1971); Detroit College of Law and University of San Diego (J.D., 1975). Judge Pro Tem. Member: San Diego County Municipal Court; Arbitration Panel, San Diego County Superior Court. *Member:* San Diego County and American Bar Associations; State Bar of California (Member, Business Law Section). (Resident, San Diego Office). *PRACTICE AREAS:* Real Estate; Business Law; Civil Litigation; Employment.

## KING & ASSOCIATES

620 NEWPORT CENTER DRIVE, SUITE 1425
P.O. BOX 10071
**NEWPORT BEACH, CALIFORNIA 92658**
Telephone: 714-644-1355
Facsimile: 714-644-1366

*Civil Trials, Banking and Commercial Litigation, Receivership, Business, Construction and Real Estate Litigation, Creditor's Rights in Bankruptcy.*

**RAYMOND KING,** born Vernon, Texas, August 3, 1955; admitted to bar, 1980, California; 1981, U.S. District Court, Central, Eastern, Northern and Southern Districts of California and U.S. Court of Appeals, Ninth Circuit. *Education:* University of California, Irvine (B.A., cum laude, 1977); University of California, Davis (J.D., 1980). Member, University of California, Davis Law Review, 1979-1980. *Member:* Orange County and Los Angeles County Bar Associations; State Bar of California (Member, Sections on: Litigation; Business Law). *PRACTICE AREAS:* Civil Trials; Banking Litigation; Commercial Litigation; Business; Construction; Commercial Collection; Real Estate; Bankruptcy; Federal Court Litigation.

## KNECHT & HANSEN

A Partnership of Professional Corporations

*Established in 1986*

SUITE 900, 1301 DOVE STREET
**NEWPORT BEACH, CALIFORNIA 92660**
Telephone: 714-851-8070
FAX: 714-851-1732

*General Business Practice. Banking, Corporate, Commercial and Real Estate Law.*

### MEMBERS OF FIRM

**RICHARD E. KNECHT, (P.C.),** born Brooklyn, New York, December 12, 1948; admitted to bar, 1973, California. *Education:* University of California (B.A., 1970); California Western University (J.D., with honors, 1973). Note and Comments Editor, California Western Law Review, 1972-1973. California Regents Scholar and California State Scholar, University of California. Staff Attorney, Honors Program, Federal Deposit Insurance Corporation, Washington, D.C., 1973-1975. *Member:* Orange County (Corporate Law Section) and American (Member, Corporation, Banking and Business Law Section) Bar Associations; The State Bar of California. *PRACTICE AREAS:* Banking Law; Corporate Law; Real Estate Law.

**LOREN P. HANSEN, (P.C.),** born Los Angeles, California, March 20, 1950; admitted to bar, 1979, California. *Education:* University of California at Los Angeles (B.A., 1971; M.A., 1973); Loyola Law School (J.D., 1979). Commercial and Trust Examiner, California State Banking Department, 1974-1979. Counsel, California State Banking Department, 1980-1983. *Member:* Orange County and American (Member, Corporation, Banking

*(This Listing Continued)*

CAA1409B

**KNECHT & HANSEN,** Newport Beach—*Continued*

and Business Law Section) Bar Associations; The State Bar of California.
**PRACTICE AREAS:** Banking Law; Securities Law; Corporate Law.

REPRESENTATIVE CLIENTS: Marine National Bank; Corporate Bank; Rancho Santa Fe National Bank; Huntington National Bank; Monarch Bank; Bank of Yorba Linda; Bank of Santa Maria; Dana Niguel Bank, N.A.; Garfield Bank; Harbor Bank; Merchants National Bank of Sacramento; National Bank of Southern California; American Independent Bank; Sun Country Bank.

# KNOBBE, MARTENS, OLSON & BEAR, LLP

A Limited Liability Partnership including Professional Corporations

Established in 1962

620 NEWPORT CENTER DRIVE, 16TH FLOOR
**NEWPORT BEACH, CALIFORNIA 92660**
Telephone: 714-760-0404
Fax: 714-760-9502

*San Diego, California Office:* 501 West Broadway, Suite 1400. Telephone: 619-235-8550. Fax: 619-235-0176.

*Riverside, California Office:* 3801 University Avenue, Suite 710. Telephone: 909-781-9231. Fax: 909-781-4507.

*Intellectual Property Law including Patent, Trademark, Copyright, Unfair Competition, Trade Secret, Licensing, Computer Law, Antitrust Law, and related litigation.*

**LOUIS J. KNOBBE, (P.C.),** born Iowa, 1932; admitted to bar, 1960, California; 1961, U.S. Court of Customs and Patent Appeals; 1963, U.S. Supreme Court; registered to practice before U.S. Patent and Trademark Office. *Education:* Iowa State University (B.S.E.E., 1953) Tau Beta Pi; Eta Kappa Nu; Phi Kappa Phi; Loyola Law School, Los Angeles (J.D., 1959). Author: "Supplement to Attorney's Guide to Trade Secrets," 1979; 1981, 1983, California Continuing Education of the Bar. Co-Author: "Using Intellectual Property Rights to Protect Domestic Markets," Advanced Business Law Series Program Material, January/February, 1986. Speaker and Author: "Patenting Computer Software," Remarks delivered at the 1991 Pacific Rim Computer Law Conference, February 1991 and paper published in the conference proceedings. Author: "The First Ten Years: The Federal Circuit and Patent Prosecution," published in New Matter, Summer, 1992. Adjunct Professor, Intellectual Property, University of San Diego School of Law. *Member:* Orange County (Program Chairman, 1975), San Diego County, Riverside County and American Bar Associations; American Intellectual Property Law Association; Orange County Patent Law Association; International Bar Association; Institute for the Advancement of Engineering; American Electronics Association (Chair-Legal Committee of Orange County). *Email:* lknobbe@kmob.com

**DON W. MARTENS, (P.C.),** born Wisconsin, 1934; admitted to bar, 1964, California and U.S. Supreme Court; registered to practice before U.S. Patent and Trademark Office. *Education:* University of Wisconsin (B.S. Petroleum Eng., with honors, 1957) Tau Beta Pi; George Washington University (J.D., with honors, 1963). Order of the Coif; Patent Editor, George Washington University Law Review, 1962-1963. Adjunct Professor, Loyola Law School, 1984-1985. Member, State of California Judicial Council, 1988-1990. Delegate, Ninth Circuit Judicial Conference, 1986-1988, 1996—. Advisory Committee to Court of Appeals for the Federal Circuit. National Inventors Hall of Fame Foundation, Board of Directors, 1995—. *Member:* Orange County Bar Association (President, 1975); The State Bar of California (Vice President, 1986-1987; Board of Governors, 1985-1987; Executive Committee, 1976-1979; Chairman, Intellectual Property Law Section, 1977); Los Angeles Intellectual Property Law Association (President, 1988); Orange County Patent Law Association (President, 1984); American Intellectual Property Law Association (President, 1995-1996). *Email:* dmartens@kmob.com

**GORDON H. OLSON, (P.C.),** born North Dakota, 1933; admitted to bar, 1962, Connecticut; 1964, District of Columbia; 1967, California; registered to practice before U.S. Patent and Trademark Office. *Education:* North Dakota State University (B.S.M.E. 1955) Tau Beta Pi; Pi Tau Sigma; George Washington University (J.D., 1961). *Member:* Orange County Bar Association; Orange County Patent Law Association. *Email:* golson@kmob.com

**JAMES B. BEAR,** born Austin, Minnesota, 1941; admitted to bar, 1969, California; registered to practice before U.S. Patent and Trademark Office. *Education:* University of California at Los Angeles (B.S.E.E., 1965; J.D., 1968). *Member:* Orange County Bar Association (Member, Board of Directors, 1971-1979; President, 1983); Orange County Barristers Club (President, 1973-1974). *Email:* jbear@kmob.com

**DARRELL L. OLSON, (P.C.),** born Winfield, Illinois, 1952; admitted to bar, 1977, California; registered to practice before U.S. Patent and Trademark Office. *Education:* Wabash College (B.A., Chemistry, magna cum laude, 1974) Phi Beta Kappa; George Washington University Law School (J.D., with high honors, 1977). Order of the Coif. *Member:* Orange County and Federal (President, Orange County Chapter, 1991) Bar Associations; Orange County Patent Law Association (President, 1986); Peter Elliott Inns of Court (Master in Charge, 1991); International Trademark Association (Member, Projects Editorial Committee). *Email:* dolson@kmob.com

**WILLIAM B. BUNKER,** born Las Vegas, Nevada, 1951; admitted to bar, 1978, California; registered to practice before U.S. Patent and Trademark Office. *Education:* California State Polytechnic University Pomona (B.S., Aerospace Eng., with honors, 1975) Tau Beta Pi; Brigham Young University (J.D., cum laude, 1978). Author: "Ashton-Tate 'Out-Foxed' by Copyright Application Form," California Republic, February, 1991; "Drafting Representations and Warranties in Contracts Involving Intellectual Property," California Business Law Practitioners, Vol. VII, No. 4, Fall, 1992. Author: Monthly Intellectual Property Column, Los Angeles Daily Journal. Adjunct Professor, Intellectual Property Law, University of San Diego School of Law, 1987-1994. *Member:* Orange County, San Diego County and Riverside Bar Associations. *Email:* wbunker@kmob.com

**WILLIAM H. NIEMAN,** born St. Louis, Missouri, 1942; admitted to bar, 1980, California; registered to practice before U.S. Patent and Trademark Office. *Education:* Washington University (B.S.E.E., 1964) Eta Kappa Nu; Arizona State University (M.B.A., 1970); University of San Diego (J.D., cum laude, 1980). Author: "Officer & Director Liability for Patent Infringement: Managing the Risks," Issues & Solutions Vol. 1, No. 1, April, 1990. *Member:* Orange County and Riverside County Bar Associations; Orange County Patent Law Association. *Email:* wnieman@kmob.com

**LOWELL ANDERSON,** born Lexington, Nebraska, 1950; admitted to bar, 1982, California; registered to practice before the U.S. Patent and Trademark Office. *Education:* University of Nebraska at Lincoln (B.S.M.E., 1972); University of Michigan (M.S.M.E., 1977); Hastings College of the Law, University of California (J.D., 1982). Pi Tau Sigma; Sigma Tau. Member, Southwestern Law Review, 1979-1980. Managing Editor, Hastings Constitutional Law Quarterly, 1981-1982. Editor, "New Matter," California State Bar Intellectual Property Law Section, 1986-1988; Chair, 1992-1993. Author: Case Comments, New Matter 1986-1994. *Member:* Orange County and American (Member, Intellectual Property Law Section), Bar Associations. *Email:* landerson@kmob.com

**ARTHUR S. ROSE,** born Washington, D.C., 1951; admitted to bar, 1981, District of Columbia; 1983, California; registered to practice before U.S. Patent and Trademark Office. *Education:* University of California at Los Angeles (B.S. in Engineering, with concentration in Electronics, 1974); George Washington University (J.D., with honors, 1981). Law Clerk to the Honorable Judge Colaianni, United States Court of Claims, 1981-1982. Co-Author: "Should Experimental Use End Upon Reduction to Practice? Two Divergent Views," New Matter, Vol. 15, No. 2, Summer, 1990. *Member:* Orange County and American Bar Associations; Orange County Patent Law Association; The Licensing Executives Society (U.S.A. and Canada; Chairman, Orange County Chapter); American Electronics Association (AEA). *Email:* arose@kmob.com

**JAMES F. LESNIAK,** born Detroit, Michigan, 1943; admitted to bar, 1969, Delaware; 1970, Michigan; 1984, California; registered to practice before U.S. Patent and Trademark Office. *Education:* University of Michigan (B.S.Chem., 1965; J.D., 1968). Sigma Phi Epsilon. *Member:* Orange County and American Bar Associations; Orange County Patent Law Association; Association of Business Trial Lawyers. *Email:* jlesniak@kmob.com

**JERRY T. SEWELL,** born Tuscumbia, Missouri, 1949; admitted to bar, 1980, Louisiana; 1984, California; registered to practice before U.S. Patent and Trademark Office. *Education:* University of Missouri at Rolla (B.S.E.E., 1971) Phi Kappa Phi; Tau Beta Pi; Eta Kappa Nu; University of Minnesota (M.S.E.E., 1980; J.D., 1980). Professional Electrical Engineer: Minnesota, 1977; Louisiana, 1981. *Member:* Orange County Bar Association; National Society of Professional Engineers; Institute Electrical and Electronics Engineers. *Email:* jsewell@kmob.com

**JOHN B. SGANGA, JR.,** born Brooklyn, New York, 1960; admitted to bar, 1984, California; registered to practice before the U.S. Patent and Trademark Office. *Education:* Lafayette College (B.S.M.E., summa cum

*(This Listing Continued)*

laude, 1981) Phi Beta Kappa; Tau Beta Pi; Pi Tau Sigma; New York University (J.D., 1984). Recipient, 1990 Patent Office Society Rossman Memorial Award. Author: "Direct Molding Statutes: Patent Weapons But Are They Constitutional?" JPTOS, Vol. 71, No. 1, 1989. *Member:* Orange County Bar Association (Member, Board of Directors, 1992-1996); Orange County Barristers (President, 1992); American Society of Mechanical Engineers; Orange County Patent Law Association; Lexion Lex Inn of Court. *Email:* jsganga@kmob.com

**EDWARD A. SCHLATTER,** born Toledo, Ohio, 1959; admitted to bar, 1985, California; 1986, Ohio; registered to practice before the U.S. Patent and Trademark Office. *Education:* Georgia Institute of Technology (B.S.I.E., with highest honors, 1982); University of Michigan (J.D., 1985). Alpha Pi Mu; Phi Kappa Phi; Pi Eta Sigma. Co-Editor, New Matter, 1994. *Member:* California State Bar Intellectual Property Section; Orange County Bar Association (Executive Committee, O.C. Delegation to State Bar Conference); Orange County Patent Law Association. *Email:* eschlatter@kmob.com

**W. GERARD VON HOFFMANN, III,** born San Francisco, California, 1956; admitted to bar, 1984, California; 1986, registered to practice before U.S. Patent and Trademark Office. *Education:* Occidental College (A.B., Chemistry, 1978); University of San Diego (J.D., cum laude, 1983). Phi Alpha Delta. Co-Author: "Reduction to Practice, Experimental Use and the On Sale and Public Use Bars to Patentability," 63 St. Johns L. Rev. 1, 1988. Law Clerk to the Honorable Helen W. Nies, Circuit Judge, United States Court of Appeals for the Federal Circuit, 1984-1986. *Member:* Orange County and American (Member, Section on Patent, Trademark and Copyright Law) Bar Associations; American Intellectual Property Law Association; Orange County Patent Law Association. *Email:* gvonhoffmann@kmob.com

**JOSEPH R. RE,** born Brooklyn, New York, 1960; admitted to bar, 1986, New York, California and U.S. Supreme Court; registered to practice before the U.S. Patent and Trademark Office. *Education:* Rutgers University (B.S., in Civil Engineering, 1982); St. John's University (J.D., 1985). Recipient: 1993 Patent and Trademark Office Society Rossman Memorial Award. Notes and Comments Editor, St. John's Law Review, 1984-1985. Author: "Federal Circuit Jurisdiction over Appeals From District Court Patent Decisions," AIPLA Quarterly Journal, Vol. 16, No. 2, 1988; "Parallel Prosecution: Effect of Patent Prosecution on Concurrent Litigation," 73 JPTOS 965 (1991); "Using Rule 30 (b) (6) for Corporate Depositions," 3 Prac. Lit. 83 (No. 4, 1992). Co-Author: "Vacating Patent Invalidity Judgments Upon Appellate Determination of Noninfringement," 72 JPTOS 780, 1990; "Brief Writing and Oral Argument (Oceana Pubs. 7th ed. 1993). Law Clerk to Hon. Howard T. Markey, Chief Judge, U.S. Court of Appeals for the Federal Circuit, 1985-1987. *Member:* Orange County and American Bar Associations; American Intellectual Property Law Association (Member, Amicus Brief Committee); Orange County Patent Law Association. *Email:* jre@kmob.com

**CATHERINE J. HOLLAND,** born Omaha, Nebraska, 1962; admitted to bar, 1987, California. *Education:* University of Notre Dame (B.A., English, 1983); University of San Francisco (J.D., 1987). Author: "What is a Copyright?" Orange County Business Journal, November, 1993. *Member:* Orange County (Chair, O.C. Delegation to California Conference of Delegates, 1996) and American Bar Associations; International Trademark Association; Orange County Patent Law Association (President, 1996-1997). *Email:* cholland@kmob.com

**KAREN J. VOGEL,** born Los Angeles, California, 1958; admitted to bar, 1984, District of Columbia (Not admitted in California). *Education:* University of California at Davis (B.A., History, 1980), Phi Beta Kappa; George Washington University (J.D., with honors, 1984). Member, George Washington Journal of International Law and Economics, 1982-1983. Co-Author: Book 3, *Unfair Import Competition: Section 337 of the Tariff Act of 1930 as Amended by the Trade Act of 1974,* in Law and Practice of United States Regulation of International Trade (C. Johnston, Jr. ed., 1987). *Member:* Orange County and Federal Bar Associations. *Email:* kvogel@kmob.com

**ANDREW H. SIMPSON,** born Birkenhead, England, 1948; admitted to bar, 1991, California; registered to practice before the U.S. Patent and Trademark Office. *Education:* University of Salford (B.S., Applied Chemistry, honors, 1972); Loyola Law School, Los Angeles (J.D., 1990). *Member:* American Intellectual Property Law Association; Licensing Executives Society; AIPPI; European Communities Trade Mark Association; International Bar Association; FICPI; The Institute of Trademark Agents; Orange County Patent Law Association; Royal Society of Chemistry. *Email:* asimpson@kmob.com

*(This Listing Continued)*

**JEFFREY L. VAN HOOSEAR,** born Coldwater, Michigan, 1960; admitted to bar, 1986, Illinois, 1990, California. *Education:* Beloit College (B.A., Government, cum laude, 1983), Phi Beta Kappa. Recipient, Martha Peterson Award; Boston University (J.D., 1986). *Member:* Chicago, Orange County and American Bar Associations; International Trademark Association; Orange County Patent Law Association. *Email:* jvanhoosear@kmob.com

**DANIEL E. ALTMAN,** born Chicago, Illinois, 1958; admitted to bar, 1989, California; registered to practice before U.S. Patent and Trademark Office. *Education:* University of Illinois at Urbana-Champaign (B.S., Biochem., with distinction, 1980); University of California at Los Angeles (M.A., Biology, 1985); Boalt Hall School of Law, University of California, Berkeley (J.D., 1989). Legislative/Case Editor, High Technology Law Journal. Judicial Extern to the Hon. Terry Hatter, U.S. District Court, 1988. Adjunct Professor of Law, USD School of Law. *Member:* Orange County and American Bar Associations; Orange County Patent Law Association. *Email:* daltman@kmob.com

**ERNEST A. BEUTLER, JR.,** born Chicago, Illinois, 1933; admitted to bar, 1961, Michigan; 1992, California, registered to practice before U.S. Patent and Trademark Office. *Education:* Northwestern University (B.S.M.E., 1956); George Washington University (LL.B., 1960). *Member:* State Bar of Michigan; American Bar Association; American Intellectual Property Law Association. *Email:* ebeutler@kmob.com

**MARGUERITE L. GUNN,** born Norfolk, Virginia, 1960; admitted to bar, 1987, Illinois; 1989, California. *Education:* University of Illinois at Urbana-Champaign (B.S. in Accounting, 1984); IIT Chicago-Kent College of Law (J.D., with high honors, 1987). Order of the Coif. Certified Public Accountant, Illinois, 1984. *Member:* Orange County, Federal and American Bar Associations. *Email:* mgunn@kmob.com

**STEPHEN C. JENSEN,** born Fullerton, California, 1963; admitted to bar, 1990, California; registered to practice before U.S. Patent and Trademark Office. *Education:* Brigham Young University (B.S.E.E., magna cum laude, 1987); University of California at Los Angeles (J.D., 1990). Phi Kappa Phi; Order of the Coif. Co-Author: "Amendments to the Rules of Civil Procedure," New Matter, Winter, 1991. Co-Author: "Common Sense, Simplicity and Experimental Use Negation of the Public Use and on Sale Bars to Patentability," The John Marshall Law Review, Vol. 29, No. 1, Fall, 1995. *Member:* Federal Circuit and American Bar Associations; Orange County Patent Law Association. *LANGUAGES:* Dutch. *Email:* sjensen@kmob.com

**VITO A. CANUSO III,** born Philadelphia, Pennsylvania, 1958; admitted to bar, 1990, California; registered to practice before U.S. Patent and Trademark Office. *Education:* Villanova University (B.S.M.E., 1980); University of Notre Dame (M.S., Environmental Health Engineering, 1983); University of San Diego (J.D., 1990). Licensed Professional Engineer, Pennsylvania. *Member:* Orange County and American Bar Associations; Orange County Patent Law Association; Orange County Barristers (President, 1996-1997). *Email:* vcanuso@kmob.com

**WILLIAM H. SHREVE,** born Los Angeles, California, 1963; admitted to bar, 1990, California, registered to practice before U.S. Patent and Trademark Office. *Education:* University of California at Irvine (B.S.M.E., 1985); George Washington University (J.D., with honors, 1990). Co-Author: "Amendments to the Rules of Civil Procedure," New Matter, Winter, 1991. *Member:* Orange County Patent Law Association; American Intellectual Property Law Association. *Email:* wshreve@kmob.com

**LYNDA J. ZADRA-SYMES,** born London, England, 1962; admitted to bar, 1989, England and Wales; 1991, California. *Education:* Leicester Polytechnic, Leicester (LL.B., 1988); Inns of Court, London (Barrister, 1989). *Member:* Inner Temple Inn of Court; International Bar Association; American Intellectual Property Law Association (AIPPI); Orange County Patent Law Association; British American Chamber of Commerce. *LANGUAGES:* French, German. *Email:* ljs@kmob.com

**STEVEN J. NATAUPSKY,** born New York, N.Y., 1966; admitted to bar, 1991, California, registered to practice before U.S. Patent and Trademark Office. *Education:* Tufts University (B.S.E.S., 1988), Tau Beta Pi; New York University (J.D., 1991). *Member:* Orange County Bar Association; Orange County Patent Law Association. *Email:* snataupsky@kmob.com

**PAUL A. STEWART,** born Huntington, New York, 1965; admitted to bar, 1991, California. *Education:* Pomona College (B.A., Math., magna cum laude, 1987) Phi Beta Kappa; University of Virginia (J.D., 1990). Order of the Coif. Law Clerk to Honorable James Browning, Circuit Judge, U.S. Court of Appeals, Ninth Circuit. *Email:* pstewart@kmob.com

*(This Listing Continued)*

## KNOBBE, MARTENS, OLSON & BEAR, LLP, Newport Beach—Continued

**JOSEPH F. JENNINGS,** born Philadelphia, Pennsylvania, 1962; admitted to bar, 1990, California. *Education:* Drexel University (B.S., Chem.E., 1985); University of Notre Dame (J.D., cum laude, 1989). Phi Eta Sigma. Member and Note Editor, Notre Dame Law Review. *Member:* Orange County and American Bar Associations; Orange County Patent Law Association. *Email:* jjennings@kmob.com

**CRAIG S. SUMMERS,** born Whittier, California, January 20, 1956; admitted to bar, 1983, California; registered to practice before U.S. Patent and Trademark Office. *Education:* University of Southern California (B.S., Mech.Engr., 1979); Loyola Law School (J.D., 1983). Recipient, American Jurisprudence Award in Conflicts of Law, 1981. Co-Author: "California Laws and Intellectual Property; Inventions, Copyrights and Unfair Competition," California Continuing Education of the Bar, 1985. Author: "Remedies for Patent Infringement in the Federal Circuit - A Survey of the First Six Years," IDEA Journal of Law and Technology, Vol. 29, 1989. *Member:* American Bar Association (Member, Intellectual Property Law Section, Chair, Special Committee on Government Relations and Implementation of Section Resolutions, 1995—); American Intellectual Property Law Association. *Email:* csummers@kmob.com

**BRENTON R. BABCOCK,** born Inglewood, California, 1964; admitted to bar, 1992, California. *Education:* University of California, Los Angeles (B.S.M.E., cum laude, 1988; M.S.M.E., 1988) Tau Beta Pi; Georgetown University (M.B.A., 1992; J.D., 1992). Member and Business Editor, American Criminal Law Review, 1990-1992. Legal Intern to the Honorable Glenn L. Archer, Jr., United States Court of Appeals for the Federal Circuit, 1990-1991. *Member:* Federal Circuit and American Bar Associations; American Intellectual Property Law Association; Orange County Patent Law Association; Christian Legal Society; American Society of Mechanical Engineers; Society of Manufacturing Engineers. *Email:* bbabcock@kmob.com

**DIANE M. REED,** born Alexandria, Virginia, 1962; admitted to bar, 1990, California. *Education:* University of Michigan (B.S., 1984); University of San Diego (J.D., cum laude, 1990). Author, "Use of 'Like/Love'Slogans in Advertising: Is the Trademark Owners Protected?" San Diego Law Review, Volume 26, Number 1. *Member:* Orange County Bar Association; American Intellectual Property Law Association; Orange County Patent Law Association. *Email:* dreed@kmob.com

**JOHNATHAN A. BARNEY,** born Coronado, California, 1965; admitted to bar, 1993, California; registered to practice before Patent and Trademark Office. *Education:* Virginia Polytechnic Institute and State University (B.S.M.E., cum laude, 1987); University of Michigan (J.D., cum laude, 1993). *Member:* Orange County Bar Association; Orange County Patent Law Association; Orange County Barristers (Board of Directors); Legion Lex. *Email:* jbarney@kmob.com

**JOHN R. KING,** born Twin Falls, Idaho, 1960; admitted to bar, 1993, California, registered to practice before U.S. Patent and Trademark Office. *Education:* Brigham Young University (B.S.E.E., cum laude, with honors, 1986) Phi Kappa Eta; Eta Kappa Nu; Tau Beta Phi; Phi Delta Phi; University of Texas at Austin (J.D., with honors, 1993). *Member:* Orange County and American Bar Associations; American Intellectual Property Law Association; Orange County Patent Law Association. *Email:* jking@kmob.com

**RONALD J. SCHOENBAUM,** born Lockbourne, AFB, Ohio, 1965; admitted to bar, 1993, California; registered to practice before U.S. Patent and Trademark Office. *Education:* Tulane University (B.S.E.E., summa cum laude, 1987); Cornell University (M.S.E.E., 1988); University of Florida (J.D., with honors, 1993). *Member:* Orange County Patent Law Association; American Electronics Association. *Email:* rschoenbaum@kmob.com

**RICHARD C. GILMORE,** born Grand Junction, Colorado, 1965; admitted to bar, 1993, California, registered to practice before U.S. Patent and Trademark Office. *Education:* University of Utah (B.S.M.E., 1990; Tau Beta Pi; Pi Tau Sigma; J.D., 1993). Member, Utah Law Review. Note and Comment Editor, Journal of Contemporary Law. *Member:* American Intellectual Property Law Association; Orange County Patent Law Association. *Email:* rgilmore@kmob.com

**JOHN P. GIEZENTANNER,** born Los Angeles, California, September 30, 1964; admitted to bar, 1994, California; registered to practice before U.S. Patent and Trademark Office. *Education:* University of California, Irvine (B.S., Biology and Chemistry, cum laude, 1989); Harvard Law School (J.D., cum laude, 1994). Phi Beta Kappa. *Email:* jgiezentanner@kmob.com

**ADEEL S. AKHTAR,** born Halifax, Nova Scotia, Canada, February 1, 1970; admitted to bar, 1994, California. *Education:* Dalhousie University (B.Sc., Physics, 1991); Harvard University (J.D., cum laude, 1994). *Member:* Orange County Bar Association; Orange County IPA. *LANGUAGES:* French, Urdu, Arabic. *Email:* aakhtar@kmob.com

**FREDERICK S. BERRETTA,** born New York, N.Y., December 29, 1957; admitted to bar, 1989, California; registered to practice before U.S. Patent and Trademark Office. *Education:* Massachusetts Institute of Technology (B.S.M.E., 1979; M.S.M.E., 1980); Harvard Law School (J.D., cum laude, 1989). Author: "Section 998 Offers to Compromise," Civil Litigation Reporter, Vol. 15, Dec. 1993. *Member:* American Intellectual Property Law Association; Orange County Patent Law Association. *Email:* fberretta@kmob.com

**CHRISTOPHER A. COLVIN,** born Bethesda, Maryland, April 27, 1966; admitted to bar, 1995, California; registered to practice before U.S. Patent and Trademark Office. *Education:* Princeton University (B.S.A.E., 1988); George Washington University (J.D., 1995). Member, George Washington Journal of International Law and Economics. Moot Court Board. *LANGUAGES:* French. *Email:* ccolvin@kmob.com

**JAMES T. HAGLER,** born Whittier, California, August 14, 1965; admitted to bar, 1995, California. *Education:* U.S. Naval Academy (B.S.E.E., 1987); University of San Diego (J.D., cum laude, 1995). San Diego Law Review. *Member:* Orange County Bar Association; Orange County Barristers; Orange County Patent Law Association. [Lt., U.S. Navy, 1987-1992] *Email:* jhagler@kmob.com

**STEPHEN M. LOBBIN,** born Columbia, Maryland, January 28, 1970; admitted to bar, 1995, California. *Education:* University of Virginia (B.S.E.E., with high honors, 1991); University of California at Los Angeles (J.D., 1995). Tau Beta Pi, Eta Kappa Nu, Phi Alpha Delta. Member, UCLA Law Review, 1993-1995. Comment, UCLA Entertainment Law Review, Vol. 2, Issue 1, Winter, 1995. *Email:* slobbin@kmob.com

**DOUGLAS G. MUEHLHAUSER,** born Inglewood, California, November 1, 1960; admitted to bar, 1995, California. *Education:* University of California, San Diego (B.A., Computer Science, 1983); Pepperdine University (M.B.A., 1990); University of San Diego Law School (J.D., 1995). *Email:* dmuehlhauser@kmob.com

**DAVID N. WEISS,** born Elizabeth, New Jersey, April 24, 1958; admitted to bar, 1994, New Jersey and New York; 1995, California. *Education:* University of California, Los Angeles (B.S.E.E., 1979); Rutgers School of Law (J.D., 1994). Member, University of California, Los Angeles Honor Society. *Email:* dweiss@kmob.com

**LORI L. YAMATO,** born Lompoc, California, May 28, 1970; admitted to bar, 1995, California. *Education:* University of Southern California (B.S.E.E., magna cum laude, 1992); University of Michigan (J.D., cum laude, 1995). Phi Kappa Phi, Tau Beta Pi. *Email:* lyamato@kmob.com

**GLENN R. SMITH,** born Fort Collins, Colorado, October 15, 1951; admitted to bar, 1992, California; registered to practice before U.S. Patent and Trademark Office. *Education:* Colorado State University (B.S.E.E., 1973); University of California, Irvine (M.S.E.E., 1979); California State University at Fullerton (M.B.A., 1985); University of California at Los Angeles (J.D., 1992). *Email:* gsmith@kmob.com

**ANN A. BYUN,** admitted to bar, 1992, California. *Education:* University of Southern California (B.S., Biomedical Engineering, 1989); Loyola Law School of Los Angeles (J.D., 1992). *Member:* Los Angeles County and Orange County Bar Associations. *Email:* abyun@kmob.com

**STACEY R. HALPERN,** born Syracuse, New York, January 10, 1964; admitted to bar, 1993, California. *Education:* University of Rhode Island (B.A., 1985); McGeorge School of Law, University of the Pacific (J.D., with great distinction, 1993); The George Washington University Law School, Washington, D.C. (LL.M. in Intellectual Property, 1996). Class Valedictorian. Order of the Coif. Recipient, American Jurisprudence Awards: Contracts; Civil Procedure; Real Property; and Decedents' Estates and Trusts. Extern, Judge Randall R. Rader, U.S. Court of Appeals for the Federal Circuit, 1995-1996. *Member:* American Intellectual Property Law Association. *Email:* shapern@kmob.com

**R. SCOTT WEIDE,** born Pittsburg, Kansas, August 10, 1965; admitted to bar, 1991, California; 1992, U.S. District Court, Central and Eastern Districts of California; 1993, U.S. Court of Appeals for the Federal Circuit; 1994, Nevada and U.S. District Court, District of Nevada; registered to

*(This Listing Continued)*

## PROFESSIONAL BIOGRAPHIES

## CALIFORNIA—NEWPORT BEACH

practice before U.S. Patent and Trademark Office. *Education:* University of Nebraska at Lincoln (B.S. in Mechanical Engineering, 1988); Creighton University (J.D., summa cum laude, 1991). Tau Beta Pi; Pi Tau Sigma. Recipient, American Jurisprudence Award in Torts II, Civil Procedure and Conflicts of Law. Member, American Society of Mechanical Engineers, 1988—. *Email:* rweide@kmob.com

**MICHAEL K. FRIEDLAND,** born Redlands, California, November 11, 1966; admitted to bar, 1991, California; 1995, U.S. Supreme Court; registered to practice before U.S. Patent and Trademark Office. *Education:* University of California at Berkeley (B.A., with honors and distinction, 1988); Harvard University (J.D., 1991). Recipient, Judge Liebman Scholarship. Managing Editor, Harvard Journal of Law & Technology. Member: Pacific Legal Foundation, 1996—; Federalist Society, 1996—. Co-Author: "Copyrighting Look and Feel," 3 Harvard Journal of Law & Technology 195, 1990. Traffic Commissioner, City of Redlands, 1983-1984. *Member:* Orange County Bar Association. **LANGUAGES:** Spanish and Russian. *Email:* mfriedland@kmob.com

**STEPHEN C. BEUERLE,** born Royal Oak, Michigan, March 16, 1970; admitted to bar, 1996, California. *Education:* University of Michigan (B.S.M.E., 1992); The John Marshall Law School (J.D., 1995). Tau Beta Pi. Registered Patent Attorney, 1996. *Member:* Orange County Bar Association; Orange County Patent Law Association; Intellectual Property Law Association of Chicago.

**JOHN C. WILSON,** born La Mirada, California, September 14, 1971; admitted to bar, 1996, California. *Education:* University of California, San Diego (B.A., 1993); George Washington University Law School (J.D., 1996). Delta Theta Phi. Executive Managing Editor, AIPLA Quarterly Journal. *Member:* American Intellectual Property Law Association. *Email:* jcw@kmob.com

**JOSEPH J. BASISTA,** born Waverly, New York, August 15, 1966; admitted to bar, 1997, California. *Education:* Union College (B.S.M.E., 1988); George Washington Law School (J.D., 1996). Phi Delta Phi. Executive Managing Editor, AIPLA Quarterly Journal. *Member:* American Intellectual Property Law Association. [LTJG, U.S. Navy 1988-1992] *Email:* jjb@kmob.com

**LEE W. HENDERSON,** born Bartlesville, Oklahoma, December 25, 1955; admitted to bar, 1996, California. *Education:* The Ohio State University (B.S.E.E., 1977; M.Sc., 1980; Ph.D., 1983); Capital University (J.D., magna cum laude, 1996). *Member:* American Bar Association; Institute of Electrical and Electronics Engineers (Senior Member, 1977—). *Email:* lwh@kmob.com

**CHAD W. MILLER,** born Great Falls, Montana, November 19, 1968; admitted to bar, 1996, California. *Education:* University of Nevada (B.S.E.E., 1992); Northwestern School of Law of Lewis and Clark College (J.D., 1996). Tau Beta Pi. Member, Northwestern School of Law Law Review.

**LENA A. BASILE,** born New York, N.Y.; admitted to bar, 1996, California. *Education:* Hunter College (B.A., summa cum laude, 1984); Columbia University (Ph.D., Chemistry, 1990); University of Houston Law Center (J.D., cum laude, 1996).

REPRESENTATIVE CLIENTS: ASM America, Phoenix; AST Research Inc., Irvine; Advanced Surgical Intervention, Inc.; San Clemente; Air Industries, Garden Grove; Applied Magnetics Corporation, Santa Barbara; Archive Corporation, Costa Mesa; Beckman Instruments, Inc., Fullerton; Bird Products Corp., Palm Springs; Carl's Jr., Anaheim; Chem-tronics, San Diego; Comprehensive Care Corporation, St. Louis; Computer Automation, Richardson, TX; Computer Products Plus, Inc., Huntington Beach; Daystar of California aka Off Shore Sportswear, Santa Ana; Excellon, Torrance; Interstate Electronics Corp., Anaheim; Interstate Engineering, Division of Figgie International, Inc., Anaheim; Life Support Products, Irvine; Litton Industries, Woodland Hills; Micro Motors, Santa Ana; Mitsubishi Electric American, Inc.; Cypress; Morehouse Industries, Inc., Fullerton; The National Institutes of Health; Department of Health and Human Services, Bethesda, MD; Oakley, Inc., Irvine; Pacific Outlook Sportswear, Inc., Anaheim; Pacific Scientific Company, Newport Beach; Panel Concepts L.P. div. of Standard Pacific, Santa Ana; Personal Computer Products, San Diego; Pfizer, New York City; Quiksilver, Inc., Costa Mesa; Stanford University, Palo Alto; State of the Art, Inc., Irvine; Stein/Brief, Dana Point; Technology Marketing, Inc., Irvine; Techniclone International Corp., Santa Ana; Textron, Cherry Rivet Division, Santa Ana; Tolco, Corona; United Can Co., La Mirada; Verteq Inc., Anaheim.

(For other Personnel and Biographical data, see Professional Biographies at San Diego and Riverside)

---

## BETTY L. KOONTZ

*Established in 1980*

SUITE 320, 5 CIVIC PLAZA
**NEWPORT BEACH, CALIFORNIA 92660-5915**
Telephone: 714-721-8730
Facsimile: 714-720-1232

*Practice limited to Estate Planning, Probate and Trust Law.*

**BETTY L. KOONTZ,** born Santa Rosa, California, July 11, 1930; admitted to bar, 1980, California. *Education:* Pepperdine University (B.A., 1951); Whittier College School of Law (J.D., cum laude, 1980). Articles Editor, Whittier Law Review, 1978-1979. Consulting Editor, "Trust Administration," California Continuing Education of the Bar, 1986. Author: "California Decedent Estate Practice," Vol. 3, California Continuing Education of the Bar, 1988 Supplement. Lecturer for California Continuing Education of the Bar: "Tax & Nontax Aspects of Co-Ownership of Property," 1985; "Revocable Trusts-Drafting, Implementing & Administering," (Moderator) 1986; "How to Plan an Estate," 1987; "How to Draft Wills & Other Estate Planning Instruments," (Moderator) 1988; "Drafting Wills & Related Estate Planning Documents," 1990; "How to Administer a Decedent's Estate, 1991; Estate Planning & Administration Practice, 11th Annual Recent Developments, 1996; Fundamentals of Decedent Estate Practice, 1995. Lecturer for Orange County Bar Association/Rutter Group: "Alternatives to Probate," 1985; "Basic Training Series: Probate," 1986; "Alternatives to Probate," 1987. *Member:* Orange County (Chairman, 1984, Estate Planning, Probate and Trust Section) and American (Member, Section of Real Property, Probate and Trust Law) Bar Associations; The State Bar of California; Orange County Women Lawyers; California Women Lawyers; Orange Coast Estate Planning Council. Fellow, American College of Trust and Estate Counsel. (Certified Specialist, Estate Planning, Trust and Probate Law, The State Bar of California Board of Legal Specialization).

REFERENCE: Glendale Federal Bank.

---

## LATHAM & WATKINS

**NEWPORT BEACH, CALIFORNIA**

(See Costa Mesa)
*General Practice.*

---

## JOHN C. LAUTSCH

A PROFESSIONAL CORPORATION

*Established in 1986*

1200 QUAIL STREET, SUITE 140
**NEWPORT BEACH, CALIFORNIA 92660**
Telephone: 714-955-9095
Telefax: 714-955-2978

*Business Litigation and Appeals, Trade Secret and Copyrights, General Business and Corporate, Estate Planning.*

**JOHN C. LAUTSCH,** admitted to bar, 1972, California. *Education:* Stanford University (B.S., 1961); University of California, Davis (J.D., 1972). Pi Sigma Alpha. Editor, Bulletin of Law, Science and Technology, American Bar Association, 1988-1990. Author: "American Standard Handbook of Software Business Law," Prentice Hall, 1986. Consultant to U.S. Congress to assess the impact of Computerization 1983-1984. *Member:* Orange County Bar Association (Founding Chairman, Appellate Law Section); State Bar of California.

---

## C. STEPHEN LAWRENCE

4675 MACARTHUR COURT
SUITE 670
**NEWPORT BEACH, CALIFORNIA 92660**
Telephone: 714-250-4550
Fax: 714-833-0976

*Food, Drug and Medical Device Law.*

**C. STEPHEN LAWRENCE,** born Long Branch, New Jersey, January 13, 1948; admitted to bar, 1984, Virginia; 1986, District of Columbia; 1992,

*(This Listing Continued)*

CAA1413B

**C. STEPHEN LAWRENCE**, Newport Beach—Continued

California. *Education:* University of Maine (B.A., 1972); Catholic University School of Law (J.D., 1984). Member, Catholic University of America Law Review, 1983-1984. Author: "George Washington University V. Weintraub: Implied Warranty of Habitability as a (Ceremonial?) Sword," 33 Catholic University Law Review 1137, 1984; "In re Goldberg: Standards for Imposing Concurrent Reciprocal Bar Discipline," 33 Catholic University Law Review 1165, 1984; "FDA Inspection of Clinical Research Sponsors and Investigators: Avoiding the Pitfalls," 22 Drug Information Journal 207, 1988. Co-Author: "FDA Will Regulate Bovine Interferon as an Animal Drug," 3 Genetic Engineering News 1, 1983; "A New Era for Clinical Studies of Medical Devices," Medical Device and Diagnostics Industries, May 1994; "GMP's and ISO 9000: Beware the Differences," Regulatory Affairs Focus, March 1996, At 8. Investigator and Consumer Safety Officer, Food and Drug Administration, 1972-1983. *Member:* District of Columbia Bar; Virginia, Federal (Co-Chairperson, Food and Drug Committee, 1986-1989; Chairperson, Food and Drug Committee, 1995—) and American (Member, Sections on: Administrative Law; Science and Technology) Bar Associations; Virginia State Bar; State Bar of California. (Partner, Hogan & Hartson L.L.P.). *PRACTICE AREAS:* Food, Drug and Medical Device Law.

---

## DOUGLAS C. LIECHTY

SUITE 520 NEWPORT FINANCIAL PLAZA
500 NEWPORT CENTER DRIVE
**NEWPORT BEACH, CALIFORNIA 92660-7005**
*Telephone: 714-644-8600*
*Fax: 714-759-6832*

*Family, Civil Litigation, Personal Injury Law and Mediation.*

**DOUGLAS C. LIECHTY,** born Silverton, Oregon, November 13, 1934; admitted to bar, 1961, California. *Education:* University of Oregon (B.A., 1956); Hastings College of the Law, University of California (J.D., 1960). Judge Pro Tempore, Orange County Superior Court, 1971—. Arbitrator, Orange County Superior Court, 1978—. *Member:* Orange County Bar Association (Member, Sections on Family Law and Mediation and Alternative Dispute Resolution); The State Bar of California (Member, Section on Family Law); California Trial Lawyers Association.

LEGAL SUPPORT PERSONNEL

*Rosemary K. Buchan* (Legal Assistant)

REPRESENTATIVE CLIENTS: Church Engineering, Inc.; The Hill Partnership, Inc.

---

## MAHER, LEE & GODDARD, LLP

**NEWPORT BEACH, CALIFORNIA**
(See Newport Beach)

*General Civil and Business Practice. Environmental Law, Employment Law, Insurance Coverage, Trial and Appellate Practice.*

---

## MARIO W. MAINERO, JR., INC.

*Established in 1988*

SUITE 201, 5160 BIRCH STREET
**NEWPORT BEACH, CALIFORNIA 92660**
*Telephone: 714-851-7763*
*FAX: 714-851-8188 (7765)*
*Email: mwmlaw@aol.com*

*Business, Real Estate and Probate Litigation, Civil Trial.*

**MARIO W. MAINERO, JR.,** born Youngstown, Ohio, January 10, 1955; admitted to bar, 1980, California; 1981, U.S. District Court, Central District of California; 1982, U.S. District Court, Southern District of California, U.S. Court of Appeals, Ninth Circuit and U.S. Tax Court; 1984, U.S. Supreme Court. *Education:* Claremont Men's College (B.A., 1975); University of New Mexico (M.A., 1977; J.D., magna cum laude, 1980). Phi Kappa Phi; Delta Theta Phi; Order of the Coif. Instructor, Legal Research, University of California at Irvine Paralegal Program, 1985. Adjunct Professor of Law, Chapman University, 1994—. *Member:* The State Bar of California;

*(This Listing Continued)*

---

fornia; American Bar Association. **LANGUAGES:** Italian. *REPORTED CASES:* Spellis v. Lawn, 200 Cal. App. 3d 1075, 246 Cal. Rptr. 385 (1988).

**JAN A. ZEMANEK,** born Blythe, California, February 19, 1964; admitted to bar, 1993, California, U.S. District Court, Central District of California and U.S. Court of Appeals, Ninth Circuit. *Education:* University of California at Irvine (B.S., 1987; M.B.A., 1990); University of Southern California Law Center (J.D., 1993). *Member:* State Bar of California. *LANGUAGES:* Czech.

REPRESENTATIVE CLIENTS: Attyah Development Corp.; U.S. Mortgage; Mamey Family Trust; Orange Coast Title; Capital Vest Property Management, Inc.

---

## JEFFREY R. MATSEN & ASSOCIATES

**NEWPORT BEACH, CALIFORNIA**
(See Santa Ana)

*Taxation and General Practice. Business, Corporation, International Law, Commercial, Partnership, Securities, Taxation, Real Estate, Probate, Trusts, Estate Planning and Civil Litigation.*

---

## JAMES E. McCORMICK III

4100 NEWPORT PLACE, SUITE 455
**NEWPORT BEACH, CALIFORNIA 92660-2437**
*Telephone: 714-252-8100*
*Fax: 714-252-8300*

*Corporate and Corporate Securities, Limited liability Company Practice, Mergers and Acquisitions, Real Estate, Real Estate Leasing Practice, International Business, Venture Capital and Finance.*

**JAMES (KIMO) E. MCCORMICK, III,** born Honolulu, Hawaii, October 30, 1948; admitted to bar, 1974, California. *Education:* Stanford University (A.B., 1970); Georgetown University (J.D., 1974). Associate Editor, American Criminal Law Review, 1972-1974. *Member:* Orange County, Los Angeles County and American Bar Associations; The State Bar of California.

---

## McDERMOTT & TRAYNER

PROFESSIONAL LAW CORPORATION

*Established in 1981*

ONE NEWPORT PLACE
1301 DOVE STREET, SUITE 1050
**NEWPORT BEACH, CALIFORNIA 92660**
*Telephone: 714-851-0441*
*Telecopier: 714-851-1735*

*Pasadena, California Office:* 225 South Lake Avenue, Suite 410. Telephone: 818-792-8242. Telecopier: 818-449-2458.

*Health Care, Hospital, Corporate and Administrative Law and Civil Litigation.*

FIRM PROFILE: McDermott & Trayner was founded in 1981 by Ronald G. Trayner and John A. McDermott. The firm opened and has continued to maintain two fully-staffed offices, in Pasadena and Newport Beach. The firm primarily provides legal services to large organizations as well as smaller firms and individuals engaged in the business of health care. The main areas of practice include corporate organizational and operating matters, joint venture formation and syndication under federal and state securities laws, mergers and acquisitions, charitable organization and partnership tax matters, real estate and construction matters, government bond financing, and general contract, business and commercial matters. The firm also provides litigation services covering commercial disputes, bankruptcy, government investigations, and collection matters as well as specialized legal services involving the licensing and regulation of health care providers and facilities, public and private reimbursement of health care services, patient management issues and hospital-physician relationships and disciplinary matters.

**JOHN A. MCDERMOTT, II,** born Midland, Texas, November 1, 1943; admitted to bar, 1970, California. *Education:* University of Notre Dame (B.B.A., 1966); University of California at Los Angeles (J.D., 1969). Co-author: "Comprehensive Health Planning and Procedures: The California Experience," 11 University of San Diego Law Review 353, 1974. Member, Executive Board, Moot Court Honors Program, UCLA, 1968-1969.

*(This Listing Continued)*

# PROFESSIONAL BIOGRAPHIES

## CALIFORNIA—NEWPORT BEACH

*Member:* The State Bar of California; California Society for Healthcare Attorneys. *PRACTICE AREAS:* Health Care; Capital Financing; Commercial Transactions; Real Estate Law; Civil Litigation.

**RONALD G. TRAYNER,** born Los Angeles, California, December 6, 1942; admitted to bar, 1968, California and U.S. District Court, Central District of California. *Education:* Occidental College (A.B., 1964); Stanford University (J.D., 1967). Member, Moot Court Board, 1967-1968. *Member:* American Bar Association; The State Bar of California; American Academy of Hospital Attorneys. (Resident, Pasadena Office). *PRACTICE AREAS:* Healthcare; Corporate; Contracts; Medical Staff. *Email:* McDandT@aol.com

**ERIC E. JOHNSON,** born Tampa, Florida, October 7, 1955; admitted to bar, 1980, California and U.S. District Court, Central District of California. *Education:* University of Redlands (B.A., in Political Science, with distinction, 1976); Willamette University (J.D., 1980). Omicron Delta Kappa. Member, The Order of The Barristers. Member, Willamette University Law Review, 1979-1980. *Member:* American Bar Association; The State Bar of California; California Society for Health Care Attorneys. *PRACTICE AREAS:* Medicare Reimbursement; Medicare Fraud and Abuse; Hospital and Medical Practice Acquisitions; Medical Staff Issues and Service Agreements.

**VICTOR C. IRELAND,** born Newport Beach, California, August 24, 1954; admitted to bar, 1981, California; 1982, U.S. District Court, Central District of California. *Education:* California State University at Fullerton (B.A., 1978); University of San Diego (J.D., 1981). *Member:* Orange County Bar Association; The State Bar of California. *PRACTICE AREAS:* Health Care Law; Tax; Corporate; Securities.

**RALPH J. MORGAN,** born Blue Island, Illinois, March 10, 1943; admitted to bar, 1970, California. *Education:* University of California at Berkeley (A.B., 1966); University of California at Los Angeles (J.D., 1969). Member, University of California at Los Angeles Law Review, 1967-1969. *Member:* The State Bar of California. *PRACTICE AREAS:* Civil Litigation; Corporate; Municipal Law; Real Estate Law.

### OF COUNSEL

**THOMAS M. COLLINS,** born Los Angeles, California, August 26, 1934; admitted to bar, 1962, California; 1973, U.S. Supreme Court. *Education:* University of Santa Clara (B.S., 1956); Stanford University (LL.B., 1961). Phi Delta Phi; Alpha Sigma Nu. Professional Organizations: President, American Academy of Healthcare Attorneys, 1990-1991; Chairman, Finance Committee, 1989-1990; Member, Board of Directors, 1984-1992. Member, Committee on Legal Services of Catholic Health Association of U.S., 1980-1985; Board of Regents, Santa Clara University, 1980-1990. Member: State Bar of California; American Academy of Hospital Attorneys. Author: "Legal Aspects of Pollution Control," Hospitals, Journal of the American Hospital Association, Oct. 1972; "Opening Up the Subject of the Closed-Staff Speciality Department," Trustee, July, 1977; "Nonphysician Practitioners in the Hospital." Trustee, November, 1981; "The For Profit/Not for Profit Debate: Issues and Responses," Colloquium II, Catholic Health Association of the U.S., 1982; "Trustees and Personal Liability: The Good News," Trustee, September, 1988. Contributor: "Contracts for Professional Services," Aspen Systems: Hospital Contracts Manual. (Resident, Pasadena Office). *PRACTICE AREAS:* Healthcare; Business Law. *Email:* McDandT@aol.com

---

**MICHAEL A. MC DERMOTT,** born Midland, Texas, April 20, 1949; admitted to bar, 1975, California and U.S. District Court, Northern District of California. *Education:* Notre Dame University (B.S., in Geology, 1971); Hastings College of Law, University of California (J.D., 1975). *Member:* The State Bar of California. *LANGUAGES:* French. *PRACTICE AREAS:* Charitable Trust Law; Nonprofit Corporate; Tax; Pension Plans; Civil Litigation.

REPRESENTATIVE CLIENTS: Adventist Health System-West; Beverly Hospital; Glendale Adventist Medical Center; Hoag Memorial Hospital-Presbyterian; Huntington Memorial Hospital; Methodist Hospital of Southern California; Providence St. Joseph Medical Center; Sierra View Local Hospital District; White Memorial Medical Center; South Coast Medical Center; Southern California Healthcare Systems.

## McDERMOTT, WILL & EMERY
A Partnership including Professional Corporations
*Established in 1934*
1301 DOVE STREET, SUITE 500
**NEWPORT BEACH, CALIFORNIA 92660-2444**
Telephone: 714-851-0633
Facsimile: 714-851-9348
URL: http://www.mwe.com

*Chicago, Illinois Office:* 227 West Monroe Street. Telephone: 312-372-2000. Facsimile: 312-984-7700.

*Boston, Massachusetts Office:* 75 State Street, Suite 1700. Telephone: 617-345-5000. Facsimile: 617-345-5077.

*Miami, Florida Office:* 201 South Biscayne Boulevard. Telephone: 305-358-3500. Facsimile: 305-347-6500.

*Washington, D.C. Office:* 1850 K Street, N.W. Telephone: 202-887-8000. Facsimile: 202-778-8087.

*Los Angeles, California Office:* 2049 Century Park East. Telephone: 310-277-4110. Facsimile: 310-277-4730.

*New York, N.Y. Office:* 50 Rockefeller Plaza. Telephone: 212-547-5508. Facsimile: 212-547-5444.

*St. Petersburg, Russia Office:* AOZT McDermott, Will & Emery, Griboyedova Canal 36, 191023 St. Petersburg, Russia. Telephone: (7) (812) 310-52-44; 310-55-44; 310-59-44; 850-20-45. Facsimile: (7) (812) 310-54-46; 325-84-50.

*Vilnius, Lithuania Office:* Smetonos 6, 2600 Vilnius, Lithuania. Telephone: 370 2 61-43-08. Facsimile: 370 2 22-79-55.

General Practice (including Corporate, Employee Benefits, Estate Planning, Health, Litigation and Tax Law).

FIRM PROFILE: McDermott, Will & Emery is an international law firm founded in 1934. Originally a Chicago tax law practice, the firm has established a full-service presence in seven domestic and three international offices with more than 600 attorneys. Clients include large corporations and individuals as well as small and medium-sized businesses. The firm represents a wide range of industrial, financial and commercial enterprises, both publicly and privately held. Firm attorneys represent clients in every state as well as numerous foreign jurisdictions.

The firm is organized by legal specialization: corporate, employee benefits, estate planning, health law, legislative/government regulation, international, litigation and tax. Many firm attorneys also practice interdepartmentally distinguishing us from many other large law firms.

### MEMBERS OF FIRM

**THOMAS K. BROWN,** born April 15, 1950; admitted to bar, 1978, California. *Education:* University of Santa Clara (B.A., 1972; J.D., summa cum laude, 1978). Associate Editor, Santa Clara Law Review, 1977-1978. *Member:* Orange County Bar Assn.; State Bar of California. *PRACTICE AREAS:* Corporate Law; Real Estate.

**JILL M. DRAFFIN,** born June 1, 1953; admitted to bar, 1978, California and U.S. District Court, Northern District of California. *Education:* University of California at Santa Barbara (B.A., 1975); Hastings College of the Law, University of California (J.D., 1978). Chair, OCBA Financial Practice Section, 1993-1994. *Member:* Orange County Bar Assn.; State Bar of California; Orange County Women Lawyers; California Women Lawyers. *PRACTICE AREAS:* Finance; Real Estate; Banks and Banking.

**PAUL B. GEORGE,** born March 8, 1947; admitted to bar, 1973, California; U.S. District Court, Central, Northern and Southern Districts of California. *Education:* University of Oregon (B.S., with honors, 1969); University of San Francisco (J.D., 1972). Phi Alpha Delta. Instructor: The Hastings College of Law, University of California, 1986-1991; Federal Bar Assn., Bankruptcy Seminar Panelist on trying cases in Bankruptcy Court and Complex Litigation. Lecturer, Demonstrative Evidence and Trial of Short Causes Matters, California Continuing Education of the Bar. *Member:* Orange County Bar Assn.; State Bar of California; American Inns of Court/Peter M. Elliott Inn of Court (Master of the Bench).

**PETER D. HOLBROOK,** born May 31, 1956; admitted to bar, 1982, California. *Education:* Boston College (B.S., magna cum laude, 1978) Beta Gamma Sigma; Villanova University (J.D., 1982). Member, 1980-1981 and Editor, 1981-1982, Villanova Law Review. *PRACTICE AREAS:* Civil Rights; Labor and Employment; Unfair Competition.

**STEVEN N. HOLLAND,** born Whittier, California, May 29, 1961; admitted to bar, 1987, California, U.S. District Court, Central District of California and U.S. Court of Appeals, Ninth Circuit; 1989, U.S. District Court,

*(This Listing Continued)*

# CALIFORNIA—NEWPORT BEACH

**McDERMOTT, WILL & EMERY,** Newport Beach—
*Continued*

Southern District of California. *Education:* University of California at Los Angeles (B.A., 1983); Loyola Law School, Los Angeles (J.D., 1987). Member, St. Thomas More Law Honor Society, 1985-1987. **PRACTICE AREAS:** Commercial Litigation.

**JOHN B. MILES,** born October 4, 1943; admitted to bar, 1973, California. *Education:* Duke University (B.A., 1966); Rutgers University (J.D., summa cum laude, 1973). Editor in Chief, Rutgers Law Journal, 1972-1973. *Member:* Orange County Bar Assn.; State Bar of California. **PRACTICE AREAS:** Corporate Law; Real Estate.

**GREGORY W. PRESTON,** born Cleveland, Ohio, August 19, 1955; admitted to bar, 1982, California. *Education:* Colgate University (B.A., 1977); Southwestern University (J.D., cum laude, 1982); New York University (LL.M. in Corporate and Securities Law, 1983). Lead Articles Editor, Southwestern University Law Review, 1980-1982. *Member:* Orange County and American Bar Assns.; State Bar of California. **PRACTICE AREAS:** General Corporate Law; Securities Law; Mergers and Acquisitions; Corporate Finance; Venture Capital Law; Partnership and Syndication Law.

**STUART W. PRICE,** born January 20, 1962; admitted to bar, 1986, California. *Education:* University of California at Santa Barbara (B.A., with high honors, 1983); University of California at Los Angeles (J.D., 1986). Phi Beta Kappa. Member: Moot Court Honors Program; Peter M. Elliott Inns of Court. *Member:* Orange County Bar Assn.; State Bar of California.

**BERNARD E. SCHNEIDER,** born June 23, 1946; admitted to bar, 1973, California and U.S. District Court, Central District of California. *Education:* Whittier College (B.A., 1968); University of Southern California (J.D., 1973). *Member:* Orange County and American Bar Assns.; State Bar of California. **PRACTICE AREAS:** Corporate Law; Banks and Banking; Real Property.

**MICHAEL SCHULMAN,** born July 6, 1951; admitted to bar, 1978, California; 1982, U.S. Supreme Court. *Education:* University of California at Berkeley (B.A., 1974); University of Santa Clara (J.D., 1977). Adjunct Assistant Professor of Law: University of California Law Center, 1979-1981; U.C. Riverside, 1984-1989. Member: Orange County Charitable Giving Council; Board of Directors, University of California, Irvine, Foundation. *Member:* Orange County Estate Planning Council. [With U.S. Coast Guard Reserve, 1969-1975]. **PRACTICE AREAS:** Trusts and Estates; Taxation; Charitable Organizations.

**JOSEPH E. THOMAS,** born Atlantic City, New Jersey, June 4, 1955; admitted to bar, 1981, California; 1982, U.S. District Court, Central District of California and U.S. Court of Appeals, Ninth Circuit; 1984, U.S. District Court, Southern District of California. *Education:* Lehigh University (B.A., cum laude, 1977); Pepperdine University (J.D., cum laude, 1981). Phi Delta Phi. Recipient, American Jurisprudence Award for Contracts and Evidence. Member, 1979-1980 and Articles Editor, 1980-1981, Pepperdine Law Review. Author: "Gibson, Dunn & Crutcher v. Superior Court: The Attorneys Right to Cross-Explain Indemnification From Opposing Counsel," 7 Pepperdine Law Review 171, 1979. Federal Judicial Extern Clerk to Judge Hatter, Federal District Court, 1980. *Member:* Los Angeles County and Orange County (Member, Business Litigation Section, 1988—) Bar Assns.; The Barristers, Orange County, California. **PRACTICE AREAS:** Securities; Real Estate; General Business Litigation.

**J. RUSSELL TYLER, JR.,** born Nürnberg, Germany, June 8, 1959; admitted to bar, 1987, California and U.S. District Court, Central District of California. *Education:* University of Utah (B.A., B.S., magna cum laude, 1983; J.D., 1986). Phi Beta Kappa; Phi Kappa Phi. William H. Leary Scholar, 1983-1984. Member, University of Utah Law Review, 1984-1986. Co-Author: "Common Law of Access in Surface Use and Mining," University of Kentucky College of Law, Journal of Mineral Law and Policy, Vol. 1, 1985-1986. *Member:* Orange County Bar Assn. (Member, Sections on: Real Estate; Business Litigation). **LANGUAGES:** Spanish. **PRACTICE AREAS:** Lender Liability Securities; Litigation; Real Property Litigation.

---

**ANNE HELLER DUNCAN,** born November 29, 1955; admitted to bar, 1986, California. *Education:* Univ. of California at Santa Barbara (B.A., 1977); Univ. of California at Irvine (M.B.A., 1984); Univ. of San Diego (J.D., cum laude, 1986). *Member:* State Bar of California.

**MARTIN P. FLORMAN,** born July 30, 1963; admitted to bar, 1989, California. *Education:* UCLA (B.A., 1986); Southwestern Univ. (J.D., 1989). *Member:* Orange County Bar Assn.

*(This Listing Continued)*

**GEORGE L. HAMPTON IV,** born June 7, 1964; admitted to bar, 1989, California; 1990, U.S. District Court, Northern, Central, Eastern and Southern Districts of California. *Education:* Rice Univ. (B.A., cum laude, 1986); Univ. of Texas (J.D., 1989). *Member:* Orange County and American Bar Assns.; State Bar of California.

**ROBERT I. NEWTON,** born May 29, 1965; admitted to bar, 1990, California. *Education:* Univ. of Texas (B.B.A., with highest honors, 1987; J.D., with honors, 1990).

**RENÉE M. RAITHEL,** born September 21, 1968; admitted to bar, 1993, California. *Education:* Univ. of Southern California (B.A., Economics, 1989); Oxford Univ., Oxford, England, Truman Scholar; New York Univ. (J.D., 1992). *Member:* State Bar of California; Peter M. Elliott Inns of Court; American Society on Aging Business Forum.

**TAMBRA L. RAUSH,** born July 23, 1966; admitted to bar, 1991, California. *Education:* Univ. California at San Diego (B.A., 1988); Univ. of San Diego (J.D., 1991). *Member:* Riverside County (Member, Civil Litigation Section) and American (Member, Civil Litigation Section) Bar Assns.; State Bar of California.

(For Biographical data on all firm personnel, see Professional Biographies listings at other office locations)

---

## JEFFREY B. McMILLEN

ONE NEWPORT PLACE
1301 DOVE STREET, SUITE 670
**NEWPORT BEACH, CALIFORNIA 92660-2468**
Telephone: 714-660-0119
Fax: 714-660-1462

*Consumer Law, Criminal Law, Family Law, Bankruptcy, Business and Real Estate Litigation.*

**JEFFREY B. MCMILLEN,** born Los Angeles, California, January 15, 1965; admitted to bar, 1992, California. *Education:* California State University at Fullerton (B.S., 1988); Western State University College of Law (J.D., 1992). Instructor, University of California at Irvine, 1994—. *Member:* Orange County Bar Association; Orange County Barristers; Legal Aid Society of Orange County. **PRACTICE AREAS:** Consumer Law (35%, 50); Criminal Law (20%, 20); Family Law (10%, 10); Bankruptcy (10%, 10); Business (10%, 10); Real Estate Litigation (10%, 10).

---

## ROBERT A. MERRING

369 SAN MIGUEL DRIVE
SUITE 305
**NEWPORT BEACH, CALIFORNIA 92660**
Telephone: 714-760-6655
Fax: 714-760-9292
Email: rmerring@counsel.com

*Business, Commercial and Real Property Litigation. Alternative Dispute Resolution. Intellectual Property, Trade Regulation. Bankruptcy and Debtor-Creditor Rights, Real Property and Transactional Matters.*

**ROBERT A. MERRING,** born October 5, 1951; admitted to bar, 1977, California; 1978, U.S. District Court, Central District of California; 1980, U.S. District Court, Southern and Eastern Districts of California and U.S. Court of Appeals, Ninth Circuit; 1983, U.S. District Court, Northern District of California; 1987, U.S. Supreme Court; 1989, Colorado. *Education:* Ohio Wesleyan University; Stanford University (A.B., with distinction and departmental honors in Political Science, 1973); Columbia Law School (J.D., with honors in International and Foreign Law, 1977). Member, 1975-1977, and Administrative Editor, 1976-1977, Columbia Journal of Transnational Law. Pepperdine University Institute of Dispute Resolution, Certificate in Mediation, 1996. *Member:* Orange County and American Bar Associations; State Bar of California; American Arbitration Association (Member and Panel of Arbitrators, 1993—); Association of Business Trial Lawyers; Orange County Bankruptcy Forum. **PRACTICE AREAS:** Business; Commercial; Real Property Litigation; Alternative Dispute Resolution; Intellectual Property.

## PROFESSIONAL BIOGRAPHIES

CALIFORNIA—NEWPORT BEACH

### WENDY J. MICKELSON

5120 CAMPUS DRIVE
**NEWPORT BEACH, CALIFORNIA 92660**
Telephone: 714-724-1872
Fax: 714-752-8770

*Family Law.*

**WENDY J. MICKELSON,** born Hempstead, New York, September 21, 1949; admitted to bar, 1980, California; U.S. District Court, Central and Eastern Districts of California. *Education:* California State College at Sonoma (B.A., 1974); Western State University (J.D., 1980). Phi Alpha Delta. Author and Editor, Western State University Law Review, 1979-1980. Instructor, Golden Gate University. *Member:* Orange County Bar Association (Board of Directors, Delegate and Officer Conference of Delegates State Bar Convention; Chairperson, Law Day and Community Outreach Committees; Ethics Committee; Homeless Task Force; Member, Sections on: Business Litigation; Commercial Law and Bankruptcy; Family Law); State Bar of California; Inns of Court; Orange County Bar Foundation (Member, Board of Trustees). *PRACTICE AREAS:* Family Law.

---

### MILLAR, HODGES & BEMIS

Established in 1979

ONE NEWPORT PLACE, SUITE 900
1301 DOVE STREET
**NEWPORT BEACH, CALIFORNIA 92660-2448**
Telephone: 714-752-7722
FAX: 714-752-6131

*General Trial and Appellate Practice in all Courts. Business, Corporation, Estate Planning, Real Estate and Taxation Law.*

#### MEMBERS OF FIRM

**RICHARD W. MILLAR, JR.,** born Los Angeles, California, May 11, 1938; admitted to bar, 1967, California; 1971, U.S. Supreme Court. *Education:* Occidental College; University of San Francisco (LL.B., 1966). Member, Editorial Staff, U.S.F. Law Review, 1965-1966. Deputy District Attorney, Los Angeles County, 1967. *Member:* Orange County (Chairman, Business Litigation Section, 1981; Chairman, Judiciary Committee, 1988-1990. Member, Sections: of Real Estate and Appellate Law) and American (Member: Section of Litigation; House of Delegates, 1990—) Bar Associations; The State Bar of California; Family Law Section Committee on Property Division (South), 1981-1982). Fellow, American Bar Foundation. *REPORTED CASES:* Shearer v. Superior Court (1977) 70 Cal.App.3d 424, 138 Cal.Rptr. 824; Canal-Randolph Anaheim, Inc. v. Moore (1978) 78 Cal.App.3d 477, 143 Cal.Rptr. 789, 144 Cal.Rptr. 474; Canal-Randolph Anaheim, Inc. v. Wilkoski (1980) 103 Cal.App.3d 282, 163 CalRptr. 30; Askew v. Askew (1994) 22 Cal.App.4th 942, 28 Cal.Rptr.2d 284. *PRACTICE AREAS:* Business Litigation; Real Estate Litigation.

**KENNETH R. HODGES,** born Los Angeles, California, June 16, 1940; admitted to bar, 1966, California. *Education:* Whittier College (B.A., 1962); University of California at Los Angeles (LL.B., 1965). *Member:* Orange County and American Bar Associations; The State Bar of California. *PRACTICE AREAS:* Real Estate Law; Real Estate Litigation; Business Litigation.

**LARRY R. BEMIS,** born Los Angeles, California, August 1, 1944; admitted to bar, 1972, California; 1973, U.S. Tax Court. *Education:* University of Southern California (B.S., 1966); Southwestern University (J.D., cum laude, 1972). Phi Delta Phi. Member, Southwestern University Law Review, 1970-1972. *Author:* "Personal Corporate Guaranty Losses: A Business Or Non-Business Bad Debt," 3 Southwestern Law Review, 135, 1971; "Children of Dissolved Marriages: A Disputed Tax Deduction," 4 Southwestern University Law Review, 101, 1972. Co-Author, "Checklist for the Evaluation of the 100% Penalty Case," Orange County Bar Journal, Vol. 4, No. 2, Summer, 1977. Revenue Agent and Appellate Conferee, Office of the Regional Commissioner, Internal Revenue Service, 1967-1972. *Member:* Orange County (Member, Sections on: Taxation; Probate) Bar Association; The State Bar of California. *PRACTICE AREAS:* Taxation Law; Estate Planning Law; Corporate Law.

*(This Listing Continued)*

---

*ASSOCIATES*

**DAVID A. ST.CLAIR,** born Los Angeles, California, August 10, 1968; admitted to bar, 1993, California. *Education:* University of California-Riverside (B.S., 1990); Western State University (J.D., cum laude, 1992). Member, Western State Law Review, 1991-1992. Judicial Extern to Justice Henry T. Moore, Jr., California Court of Appeal, Fourth District, Division 3, 1992. *Member:* Orange County and American Bar Associations; State Bar of California.

REPRESENTATIVE CLIENTS: Bomel Construction Co., Inc.; Bowe Co; Chicago Title Insurance Co. (formally known as Safeco Title Insurance Co.); Commonwealth Title Insurance Co.; Corporate National Bank; F.M. Tarbell Co.; Family Fitness Centers; Kelly-Wright Hardwoods, Inc.; Marine National Bank; Production Supply Co.; Royal Paper Box Company of California; Pioneer Bank; Stroud's; Ticor Title Insurance Co.; Transamerica Title Insurance Co.; Turnstone Corp.
REFERENCE: Manufacturers Bank, Newport Beach, California.

---

### JOHN ANDREW MILLER

SOUTH TOWER, SUITE 600
3501 JAMBOREE ROAD
**NEWPORT BEACH, CALIFORNIA 92660**
Telephone: 714-725-6311
Fax: 714-725-6340

*Employment Law for Employers and Executives. Corporate and Transactional Law.*

**JOHN ANDREW MILLER,** born Los Angeles, California, December 12, 1940; admitted to bar, 1966, California, U.S. District Court, Central District of California and U.S. Court of Appeals, Ninth Circuit. *Education:* Dartmouth College (A.B., 1962); University of Southern California (LL.B., 1965). Member, Southern California Law Review, 1964-1965. *Member:* Los Angeles County (Member: Business and Corporations Law Section; Executive Committee, 1975-1978), Orange County and American (Member, Business Law Section) Bar Associations; The State Bar of California. *PRACTICE AREAS:* Employment Law; Business Transactions; Business Litigation; Corporate and Partnership Formation.

---

### FRANK B. MYERS

SUITE 720, 4400 MACARTHUR BOULEVARD
**NEWPORT BEACH, CALIFORNIA 92660**
Telephone: 714-752-2001
Facsimile: 714-955-3670

*International Business Law, Mining and Ore Processing Facilities Development, Natural Resource Development, Engineering, Construction, Electronics and General Business and Corporate Law.*

**FRANK B. MYERS,** born Chicago, Illinois, April 4, 1941; admitted to bar, 1966, California and U.S. District Court, Southern District of California; 1974, U.S. Supreme Court. *Education:* Claremont Mens College (B.A., 1962); Loyola University of Los Angeles (LL.B., 1965). Alpha Sigma Nu; Phi Alpha Delta. Member, St. Thomas More Law Honor Society. Author: "Mining Projects", Chapter 8, Construction Project Form Book, John Wiley & Sons, Inc. 1994. Adjunct Professor, Western State University, College of Law, 1994—. Teaching Fellow, Loyola University of Los Angeles, 1965-1966. Director and General Counsel, Fluor Constructors, Inc., 1983-1985. General Counsel, Fluor Mining and Metals, Inc., 1979-1983. Member, Legal Advisory Committee, Associated General Contractors of California, 1984-1985, 1992-1993. Director, Center for International Commercial Arbitration, 1986—. Director, The Newport Foundation, 1994—. *Member:* Los Angeles County, Orange County and American Bar Associations; American Institute of Mining, Metallurgical and Petroleum Engineers. [Capt., U.S. Army, 1965-1967]

---

### NEWMEYER & DILLION

Established in 1984

NORTH TOWER, SUITE 6000
3501 JAMBOREE ROAD
**NEWPORT BEACH, CALIFORNIA 92660**
Telephone: 714-854-7000
Telecopier: 714-854-7099

*Real Estate, Real Estate Finance, Corporate, Bankruptcy, Partnerships, General Civil Litigation.*

*(This Listing Continued)*

## NEWMEYER & DILLION, Newport Beach—Continued

*FIRM PROFILE: Newmeyer & Dillion, originally formed in 1984, is comprised of creative highly motivated business attorneys. The firm represents clients which include international, national and local financial institutions, real estate development companies, manufacturers and service organizations, as well as individuals. The firm takes pride in its ability to provide excellent service to its clients and is dedicated to achieving the results desired by clients through teamwork and hard work. Newmeyer & Dillion is dedicated to assisting its clients in pursuit of success. By making that commitment and dealing with clients with the highest degree of honesty and professional integrity, the future of the firm and the welfare of its clients may be assured. The firm is a member of The Bar Register Preeminent Lawyer.*

### MEMBERS OF FIRM

**THOMAS F. NEWMEYER,** born Los Angeles, California, June 24, 1953; admitted to bar, 1978, California; 1980, U.S. District Court, Central and Southern Districts of California and U.S. Court of Appeals, Ninth Circuit; 1986, U.S. District Court, Eastern District of California; 1987, U.S. Supreme Court. *Education:* San Diego State University (B.S., with highest honors, 1975); Loyola University of Los Angeles (J.D., cum laude, 1978). Note and Comment Editor, Loyola Law Review, 1977-1978. Scott Moot Court Champion, 1977. Member, St. Thomas More Law Honor Society. *Member:* Orange County Bar Association; State Bar of California. **PRACTICE AREAS:** Litigation involving Business; Unfair Competition; Trade Secrets; Partnership Dissolutions; Wrongful Termination; Employment Discrimination.

**GREGORY L. DILLION,** born Lima, Ohio, June 21, 1954; admitted to bar, 1980, California, U.S. District Court, Central and Northern Districts of California and U.S Court of Appeals, Ninth Circuit; 1981, U.S. District Court, Southern and Eastern Districts of California; 1986, U.S. Supreme Court. *Education:* Cornell University (B.A., with distinction, 1977); University of Texas (J.D., with honors, 1980). Phi Kappa Phi. Recipient, American Jurisprudence Award in Torts. *Member:* Orange County Bar Association; State Bar of California. **PRACTICE AREAS:** Litigation involving Real Estate; Lender Liability; Construction and Insurance Coverage.

**JOHN A. O'HARA,** born Arlington, Virginia, June 7, 1960; admitted to bar, 1985, California; 1986, District of Columbia; 1987, U.S. District Court, Central District of California; 1989, U.S. District Court, Eastern, Northern and Southern Districts of California and U.S. Court of Appeals, Ninth Circuit; 1990, U.S. Supreme Court. *Education:* University of California at Irvine (B.A., 1982); Catholic University of America (J.D., 1985). Co-author: "Four Practical Tips, Defenses and Strategies for Developers in Construction Defect Litigation," Shepard's California Construction Law Reporter, Vol. 4, No. 8, October, 1994. *Member:* Orange County Bar Association; State Bar of California. **PRACTICE AREAS:** Litigation involving Construction; Real Estate; Insurance Coverage; Business Litigation.

**MADISON S. SPACH JR.,** born Durham, North Carolina, November 30, 1951; admitted to bar, 1980, California and U.S. District Court, Northern, Southern and Central Districts of California. *Education:* Duke University (B.A., magna cum laude, 1974; J.D., 1980); University of North Carolina (M.A., Slavic Languages and Literatures, 1977). Hardt Cup Intramural Moot Court Competition Co-Champion, 1978. Member: National Moot Court Competition Team, 1978-1979, 1979-1980; Moot Court Board, 1978-1980. President, Duke International Law Society, 1977-1978. Associate Editors' Program, Law and Contemporary Problems, 1979-1980. Author: Forward to "Human Rights and Dissent," 43 Law and Contemporary Problems 254, 1979. *Member:* Orange County Bar Association; State Bar of California. **PRACTICE AREAS:** Bankruptcy; Litigation involving Real Estate Development and Construction.

**JOHN E. POPE,** born Glendale, California, December 8, 1942; admitted to bar, 1977, California. *Education:* University of California at Berkeley (B.S., Industrial Engineering, 1965); University of Southern California (M.B.A., Marketing, 1967); University of California at Los Angeles School of Law (J.D., 1977). Order of the Coif. Member, UCLA Law Review, 1975-1977. *Member:* Orange County and American Bar Associations; State Bar of California. **PRACTICE AREAS:** Real Estate Law.

**MICHAEL S. CUCCHISSI,** born August 29, 1953; admitted to bar, 1978, California. *Education:* Massachusetts Institute of Technology (S.B., 1975); University of Pennsylvania (J.D., cum laude, 1978). Associate Editor, 1976-1977 and Comment Editor, 1977-1978, University of Pennsylvania Law Review. Law Clerk to the Honorable Samuel P. King, Chief Judge, U.S. District Court, District of Hawaii, 1978-1979. **PRACTICE AREAS:** Real Estate Law.

*(This Listing Continued)*

CAA1418B

**CRAIG A. CALLAHAN,** born Danville, Illinois, June 8, 1959; admitted to bar, 1986, California; 1987, U.S. District Court, Central District of California. *Education:* University of California at Los Angeles (B.A., summa cum laude, 1981); University of California at Davis (J.D., 1986). Phi Beta Kappa; Order of the Coif. *Member:* State Bar of California. **PRACTICE AREAS:** Construction Litigation; Insurance Litigation; General Business Litigation.

### ASSOCIATES

**GENE M. WITKIN,** born Johannesburg, South Africa, 1965; admitted to bar, 1990, California and U.S. District Court, Central and Southern Districts of California; 1991, U.S. District Court, Southern District of California. *Education:* University of California at Irvine (B.A., cum laude, 1987); University of California at Los Angeles (J.D., 1990). Phi Beta Kappa; Phi Eta Sigma; Moot Court. Editor, 1989-1990: Federal Communications Law Journal; Environmental Law Journal. *Member:* Orange County Bar Association (Co-Chairman, Insurance Section); State Bar of California. **PRACTICE AREAS:** Litigation involving Insurance Coverage; Business; Construction; Bankruptcy.

**TIMOTHY S. MENTER,** born Washington, D. C., May 22, 1961; admitted to bar, 1987, California and U.S. District Court, Southern District of California; 1993, District of Columbia, U.S. Court of Appeals, Fourth, Ninth and District of Columbia Circuits, U.S. District Court, District of Columbia, U.S. District Court, Southern District of California, U.S. District Court, District of Maryland and U.S. Supreme Court; 1995, Maryland and U.S. District Court, Central District of California. *Education:* Virginia Polytechnic Institute (B.A., 1984); Washington & Lee University (J.D., 1987); George Washington University (LL.M., Environmental Law, 1993). Author: "CERCLA and the Duty to Defend: How Will 'Suit' be Interpreted in CGL Policies?" 6 Environmental Claims Journal 155, 1993-1994. *Member:* Orange County Bar Association; The District of Columbia Bar; State Bar of California. **PRACTICE AREAS:** Environmental Law; Insurance Law.

**R. BRAD SEVIER,** born Glendale, California, July 6, 1963; admitted to bar, 1989, California. *Education:* University of California, Santa Barbara (B.A. in Business Economics, 1986); Loyola Law School (J.D., 1989). *Member:* State Bar of California; American Bar Association. **PRACTICE AREAS:** Real Estate Law; Finance; General Business Law.

**SANDRA SCHAEFFER,** born New York, New York, April 4, 1966; admitted to bar, 1991, California and U.S. District Court, Central District of California; 1993, Arizona. *Education:* Arizona State University (B.S., 1988); University of San Diego (J.D., cum laude, 1991). *Member:* Orange County Bar Association; State Bar of California. **PRACTICE AREAS:** Business Litigation.

**INGRID M. CAUSEY,** born Los Angeles, California, April 6, 1968; admitted to bar, 1993, California and U.S. District Court, Central District of California. *Education:* University College, London, England (1989); Vassar College (B.A., 1990); University of Southern California (J.D., 1993). *Member:* Orange County Bar Association; State Bar of California.

**JOSEPH A. FERRENTINO,** born Los Angeles, California, February 11, 1967; admitted to bar, 1992, California. *Education:* California State Polytechnic University (B.A., 1989); Loyola University of Los Angeles (J.D., 1992). Member, St. Thomas Moore Honor Society. *Member:* State Bar of California. **PRACTICE AREAS:** Business Litigation; Construction Litigation; Insurance.

**MICHAEL G. DIBB,** born Long Beach, California, February 18, 1964; admitted to bar, 1991, California. *Education:* Loyola Marymount University (B.A., cum laude, 1986; J.D., 1991). Alpha Sigma Nu; Phi Alpha Theta. Candidate, Rhodes Scholar. *Member:* Orange County Bar Association (Executive Committee, 1995—; Insurance and Construction Sections); American Bar Association; State Bar of California. **PRACTICE AREAS:** Insurance; Construction; Business Litigation.

**DWIGHT C. HIRSH,** born Mountain View, California, May 16, 1969; admitted to bar, 1994, California. *Education:* Santa Clara University (B.A., 1991); McGeorge School of Law (J.D., 1994). Legislative Review Staff Writer, 1992; Coment Staff Writer, 1992-1993, Managing Editor, 1993-1994, Pacific Law Journal. Author: Yee v. City of Escondino--A Rejection of The Ninth Circuit's Unique Physical Takings Theory Opens the Gate for Mobile Home Park Owners' Regulatory Taking Claims, Pacific Law Journal, Vol. No. 3, 1681 (1993). *Member:* Orange County Bar Association; Orange County Trial Lawyers Association; Orange County Barristers. **PRACTICE AREAS:** Construction Litigation; Business Litigation; Insurance Coverage.

*(This Listing Continued)*

**DEBRA B. BRANSE,** born Los Angeles, California, November 6, 1969; admitted to bar, 1995, California and U.S. District Court, Southern District of California. *Education:* University of California at Berkeley (B.A., 1991); University of Michigan (J.D., 1994). Phi Beta Kappa. *Member:* State Bar of California.

**MICHAEL PAUL HUTCHINS,** born Ironton, Missouri, February 14, 1962; admitted to bar, 1995, California and U.S. District Court, District of California. *Education:* Villanova University (B.C.E., 1984); University of Minnesota (J.D., 1993). Chi Epsilon. Author: "Emergency Preparedness and Response," The Environmental Handbook for the Precious Metals Industry, Gemini Industries, 1996; "California Supreme Court Affirms Broad Insurance Carrier Responsibilities Under Standard Firm CGL Policies," The Law Report, 1995. Professional Engineer, Washington, 1990 and California, 1995. *Member:* Orange County Bar Association (Member, Construction Law Section); State Bar of California (Member, Sections on: Environmental Law and Litigations); American Society of Civil Engineers (Member, Professional Practices Committee); International Conference of Building Officials. *PRACTICE AREAS:* Construction Law; Environmental Law; Products Liability; Public Works; Insurance.

REPRESENTATIVE CLIENTS: The Irvine Co.; Standard Pacific Corp.; McDonnell Douglas Corporation; McDonnell Douglas Realty Company; First Health International; Urban West; Presley Homes; Catellus; William Lyon Homes; California Pacific Homes; Citimark, Inc.; Coast Federal Bank; California Federal Bank; Jason International; Western Financial Savings Bank; Chicago Title; Willis Corroon Corp.
REFERENCE: Marine National Bank.

---

## FRANK NICHOLAS
*A LAW CORPORATION*
Established in 1978

*610 NEWPORT CENTER DRIVE, SUITE 1010*
**NEWPORT BEACH, CALIFORNIA 92660-6419**
Telephone: 714-760-6760

*General Civil Trial Practice, Plaintiff's Personal Injury, Medical Malpractice, Legal Malpractice, Products Liability, Negligence and Tort Law, Insurance Bad Faith, Insurance Coverage, Wrongful Employment Termination and Discrimination.*

**FRANK NICHOLAS,** born Bronx, New York, June 22, 1950; admitted to bar, 1977, California; 1980, District of Columbia; 1983, New York; 1981, U.S. Supreme Court and U.S. District Court, Central, Northern and Southern Districts of California. *Education:* State University of New York (B.S., magna cum laude, 1972); University of Southern California (J.D., 1977). Semi-Finalist, University of Southern California Moot Court Honors Oral Advocacy Competition. Recipient, Best Appellate Brief Award in Moot Court Honors Competition. Author: "Comparative Liability Among Joint Tortfeasors: The Aftermath of *Li vs. Yellow Cab Co.*," University of West Los Angeles Law Review, 1976. *Member:* Orange County, New York State and American Bar Associations; State Bar of California; The District of Columbia Bar; The Association of Trial Lawyers of America; California Trial Lawyers Association; Orange County Trial Lawyers Association.

REFERENCES: Bank of America; Union Bank; California Federal Savings and Loan; American States Savings and Loan.

---

## OBEGI & BREWER, P.C.
Established in 1981

*SUITE 350*
*4041 MACARTHUR BOULEVARD*
**NEWPORT BEACH, CALIFORNIA 92660**
Telephone: 714-833-7824
Fax: 714-833-3133

*Estate Planning, Trust, Probate and Tax Law.*

**FIRM PROFILE:** *The firm emphasizes practice in estate planning, trust, probate, and related tax matters for high wealth individuals and families. The firm's clients, while predominately from the Orange Coast area, come from throughout California.*

**BURLEIGH J. BREWER,** born Mineral Wells, Texas, May 6, 1942; admitted to bar, 1967, California and U.S. District Court, Southern, Central and Northern Districts of California; 1973, U.S. Supreme Court; 1975, U.S. Tax Court. *Education:* University of Southern California (B.S. in Finance, 1964; M.B. in Business Taxation, 1975); Loyola University of Los Angeles (J.D., 1967). Phi Delta Phi; Alpha Sigma Nu; Beta Gamma Sigma.

*(This Listing Continued)*

---

Student Teaching Fellow, Loyola University, 1965-1967. Comment Editor, Loyola Law Review, 1967. Lecturer, Real Estate Practice, University of Southern California Law Center, 1978. *Member:* Orange County (Member, Sections on: Taxation; Estate Planning and Probate) and American (Member, Taxation Committee) Bar Associations; State Bar of California. [Lt., JAGC, USNR, 1968-1971]. *PRACTICE AREAS:* Estate Planning; Trust Law; Probate; Tax Law.

**JOSEPH C. OBEGI,** born Van Nuys, California, October 20, 1945; admitted to bar, 1971, California and U.S. District Court, Central District of California. *Education:* University of Southern California (B.S. in Finance, 1967; J.D., 1970). Author: "Estate Planning in Light of Carryover Basis," Tax and Probate Forum Journal, 1977; "Handling Conflict of Interest Problems in Estate Planning," Community Property Journal, 1987. President, Newport Beach-Irvine Estate Planning Council, 1978. Member: Planning Committee, University of Southern California Trust and Probate Conference, 1985—; Endowment Committee, Orange County Performing Arts Center; Endowment and Planned Gifts Committee, Hoag Hospital Foundation. *Member:* Los Angeles County (Member, Probate and Trust Law Section), Orange County (Member, Probate and Trust Law Section) and American (Member, Real Property, Probate and Trust Law Section) Bar Associations; State Bar of California. Fellow, American College of Trust and Estate Counsel. *PRACTICE AREAS:* Estate Planning; Trust Law; Probate; Tax Law.

---

## PHILIP N. OFFICER
*1300 DOVE STREET, SUITE 200*
**NEWPORT BEACH, CALIFORNIA 92660**
Telephone: 714-261-8322

*Construction Law, Products Liability, Contracts, Criminal Law, Personal Injury.*

**PHILIP N. OFFICER,** born Albuquerque, New Mexico, September 7, 1938; admitted to bar, 1970, California. *Education:* San Francisco City College (A.A., with honors, 1963); University of California at Berkeley (B.S., 1965) Beta Gamma Sigma; Boalt Hall School of Law, University of California (J.D., 1969). Deputy District Attorney, 1970-1983. *Member:* Kern County Bar Association; The State Bar of California; California Trial Lawyers Association. [U.S. Navy, 1956-1959]. *PRACTICE AREAS:* Construction Law (60%); Products Liability (5%); Contracts (10%); Criminal Law (10%); Personal Injury (15%).

---

## O'MELVENY & MYERS LLP
Established in 1885

*610 NEWPORT CENTER DRIVE*
**NEWPORT BEACH, CALIFORNIA 92660-6429**
Telephone: 714-760-9600
Cable Address: "Moms"
Facsimile: 714-669-6994
Email: ommifo@omm.com

*Los Angeles, California Office:* 400 South Hope Street, 90071-2899. Telephone: 213-669-6000. Cable Address: "Moms". Facsimile: 213-669-6407. E-mail: omminfo@omm.com.
*Century City, California Office:* 1999 Avenue of the Stars, 90067-6035. Telephone: 310-553-6700. Facsimile: 310-246-6779.
*San Francisco, California Office:* Embarcadero Center West Tower, 275 Battery Street, 94111-3305. Telephone: 415-984-8700. Facsimile: 415-984-8701.
*New York, New York Office:* Citicorp Center, 153 East 53rd Street, 10022-4611. Floor. Telephone: 212-326-2000. Facsimile: 212-326-2061.
*Washington, D.C. Office:* 555 13th Street, N.W., 20004-1109. Telephone: 202-383-5300. Cable Address: "Moms". Facsimile: 202-383-5414.
*London, England Office:* 10 Finsbury Square, London, EC2A 1LA. Telephone: 0171-256-8451. Facsimile: 0171-638-8205.
*Tokyo, Japan Office:* Sanbancho KB-6 Building, 6 Sanbancho, Chiyoda-ku, Tokyo 102, Japan. Telephone: 03-3239-2800. Facsimile: 03-3239-2432.
*Hong Kong Office:* Suite 1905, Peregrine Tower, Lippo Centre, 89 Queensway, Central, Hong Kong. Telephone: 852-2523-8266. Facsimile: 852-2522-1760.
*Shanghai, People's Republic of China Office:* Shanghai International Trade Centre, Suite 2011, 2200 Yan An Road West, Shanghai, 200335, PRC. Telephone: 86-21-6219-5363. Facsimile: 86-21-6275-4949.

*(This Listing Continued)*

## O'MELVENY & MYERS LLP, Newport Beach—Continued

General Civil Litigation, Appellate Practice, and Criminal Trials Practice in all State and Federal Courts. Administrative; Antitrust; Banking; Bankruptcy; Commercial; Communications; Construction; Corporation and Corporate Financing; Environmental; Immigration and Naturalization; Insurance Coverage Defense; Intellectual Property; International Business; Labor and Employment; Employment Benefits; Media and Entertainment; Municipal, Municipal Zoning, and Municipal Finance; Natural Resources; Oil and Gas; Patent, Trademark, Copyright, and Unfair Competition; Probate, Trusts, and Estate Planning; Public Utilities; Real Estate; Securities; and Tax Law.

FIRM PROFILE: O'Melveny & Myers LLP, founded over 110 years ago on January 2, 1885, is the oldest law firm in Los Angeles. Since that time, we have grown from two attorneys in two rooms specializing in the local concerns of a frontier community to a firm of more than 500 lawyers involved in matters of regional, national and global concern.

Initially, the growth of our firm paralleled the growth of Los Angeles. Under founder Henry O'Melveny, the firm benefited from the first great California land and population booms that transformed a small outpost into one of the nation's most important cities. Our practice kept pace with the region's growth, and the early decades of the century saw O'Melveny attorneys working on behalf of clients in the aircraft, oil, motion picture and utility sectors. In the post World War II period, leadership passed to John O'Melveny, who presided over the development of the modern firm until 1970. The ensuing years have seen a dramatic acceleration of our practice on both the national and international fronts: today O'Melveny ranks as one of the largest law firms in the world.

Each of our ten offices - Los Angeles, Century City, Newport Beach, San Francisco, Washington, D.C., New York, Tokyo, London, Hong Kong and Shanghai - is specifically located both to provide service affecting a particular region and to contribute important strengths and specializations to the firm as a whole.

Office to office collaborations are the norm, with attorneys on different coasts and different continents working together to structure complex transactions and to resolve important controversies.

Among our lawyers are many who have distinguished themselves through their leadership at the Bar or in public service. Our ranks include former Executive Branch and Capitol Hill policy makers; some of the nation's leading litigators and labor lawyers; recognized experts in public finance, financial institutions, corporate, securities, entertainment, real estate, bankruptcy, constitutional and tax law; and the nation's foremost practitioners in representations concerning Europe, Latin America, and the Pacific Rim. This combination of highly skilled lawyers and a strategic presence in key economic centers enables O'Melveny to offer our clients the highest level of legal service and consultation.

### MEMBERS OF FIRM

**DOUGLAS W. ABENDROTH,** born Seattle, Washington, December 9, 1952; admitted to bar, 1982, California and U.S. District Court, Central District of California; 1983, U.S. District Court, Southern, Northern and Eastern Districts of California and U.S. Court of Appeals, Ninth Circuit; 1995, U.S. District Court, District of Arizona. *Education:* University of California at Los Angeles (B.A., magna cum laude, 1976); Loyola Law School of Los Angeles (J.D., magna cum laude, 1982). Member, St. Thomas More Law Honor Society. Staff Member, 1980-1981 and Chief Note and Comment Editor, 1981-1982, Loyola of Los Angeles Law Review. Author: Comment, "Religious Meetings on Public School Property: The Constitutional Dimensions of Church-State Neutrality," 15 Loyola of Los Angeles Law Review 103, 1981. *Member:* Orange County (Member, Business Litigation Section), Federal Bar (Orange County) and American Bar Associations; Orange County Bar Foundation (Director, 1993-1994); Orange County Federal Bar Association (Director, 1994-1995).

**WILLIAM G. ADAMS,** born Dallas, Oregon, July 26, 1939; admitted to bar, 1969, California; 1983, Conseil Juridique, France. *Education:* Stanford University (A.B., 1963); University of Utah (J.D., 1968). Order of the Coif; Phi Kappa Phi; Phi Delta Phi. Editor-in-Chief, Utah Law Review, 1967-1968. Member, Committee on Non Profit Corporations and Unincorporated Associations, State Bar of California, 1988-1992. *Member:* Los Angeles County and American Bar Associations. *LANGUAGES:* French. *PRACTICE AREAS:* Corporate Securities; International Law. *Email:* wadams@omm.com

**RUSSELL G. ALLEN,** born Ottumwa, Iowa, November 7, 1946; admitted to bar, 1971, California. *Education:* Grinnell College (B.A., 1968); Stanford University (J.D., 1971). Order of the Coif. Member, Board of Editors, Stanford Law Review, 1969-1971. Member, Board of Visitors, Stanford Law School, 1993-1996. Fellow, American College of Trust and Estate

*(This Listing Continued)*

Counsel. [Capt., U.S. Air Force, JAGC, 1971-1975]. (Certified Specialist, Probate, Estate Planning and Trust Law, The State Bar of California Board of Legal Specialization). *Email:* rallen@omm.com

**JERRY W. CARLTON,** born Stamford, Texas, November 17, 1941; admitted to bar, 1968, California. *Education:* North Texas State University (B.B.A., 1964); University of Texas (LL.B., 1967). *Member:* Orange County and American Bar Associations. *PRACTICE AREAS:* Taxation.

**CORMAC J. CARNEY,** born Detroit, Michigan, May 6, 1959; admitted to bar, 1987, California; 1991, Illinois. *Education:* University of California at Los Angeles (B.A., 1983); Harvard University (J.D., 1987).

**KAREN K. DREYFUS,** born Palo Alto, California, April 3, 1961; admitted to bar, 1987, California. *Education:* Cornell University (B.A., 1982); Hastings College of the Law, University of California (J.D., cum laude, 1987). Order of the Coif. Member, Thurston Society. Member, 1985-1986 and Note Editor, 1986-1987, Hastings Law Journal. *Member:* Orange County and American Bar Associations. *PRACTICE AREAS:* Corporate Law. *Email:* kdreyfus@omm.com

**STEVEN L. EDWARDS,** born New York, N.Y., September 9, 1947; admitted to bar, 1973, California and U.S. District Court, Central District of California. *Education:* Lehigh University (B.A., with high honors, 1969) Phi Beta Kappa; New York University (J.D., 1973). Root-Tilden Scholar. Editor, New NYU Law Review, 1972-1973. Licensed Real Estate Broker, California, 1981. Member, Real Property Law Section, California State Bar. *Member:* National Association of Review Appraisers and Mortgage Underwriters. *PRACTICE AREAS:* Real Estate. *Email:* sedwards@omm.com

**PATRICIA FROBES,** born Salt Lake City, Utah, March 12, 1947; admitted to bar, 1978, California. *Education:* Antioch College (B.A., 1970); University of Utah (J.D., 1978). Order of the Coif. Note and Comment Editor, Utah Law Review, 1977-1978. Graduate Research Fellow and Leary Scholar, University of Utah. Law Clerk to Hon. Chief Judge Aldon Anderson, U.S. District Court, District of Utah, 1978-1979. Chair, Real Property Law Section, Executive Committee, 1989 and Co-Chair, Joint Committee on Anti-Deficiency Laws, State Bar of California. Chair, Real Estate and Natural Resources Department. *Member:* American College of Real Estate Lawyers. (Also at Los Angeles Office). *Email:* pfrobes@omm.com

**PAMELA C. GRAY,** born Salt Lake City, Utah, August 6, 1944; admitted to bar, 1976, California. *Education:* Wellesley College (B.A., 1966); Loyola University School of Law, Los Angeles (J.D., 1976). Alpha Sigma Nu. Member, St. Thomas More Law Honor Society, 1974-1976. Member, Jessup Moot Court Honors Board, 1975-1976. *Member:* Los Angeles County (Officer, Death and Gift Tax Subsection, 1983-1985; Chair, Foreign Tax Subsection of the Tax Section, 1987-1990) and American Bar Associations. (Also at Los Angeles Office). *Email:* pgray@omm.com

**TODD A. GREEN,** born New York, New York, November 9, 1967; admitted to bar, 1995, California and U.S. District Court, Southern and Central Districts of California. *Education:* Princeton University (A.B., 1990); Columbia University School of Law (J.D., 1994). Harlan Fiske Stone Scholar. *Member:* Orange County Bar Association (Business Litigation Section).

**CATHERINE BURCHAM HAGEN,** born Long Beach, California, June 6, 1943; admitted to bar, 1978, California and U.S. District Court, Central District of California; U.S. Court of Appeals, Ninth Circuit; 1987, U.S. Supreme Court. *Education:* Occidental College (B.A., magna cum laude, 1964); Loyola University of Los Angeles (J.D., summa cum laude, 1978). Phi Beta Kappa (Mortar Board, 1964). Staff Member, 1976-1977 and Ninth Circuit Editor, 1977-1978, Loyola of Los Angeles Law Review. Chair, 1990 Southern California Labor Law Symposium. *Member:* Los Angeles County and American (Member, Labor and Employment Law Section) Bar Associations. *PRACTICE AREAS:* Labor and Employment; Sexual Harassment and Disability Discrimination.

**THEODORE C. HAMILTON,** born San Rafael, California, February 14, 1956; admitted to bar, 1983, California. *Education:* Stanford University (A.B., with distinction, 1978; J.D., 1983). Book Review Editor, Stanford Journal of International Law, 1982-1983. *Email:* thamilton@omm.com

**JOSEPH J. HERRON,** born Lake City, Minnesota, October 29, 1954; admitted to bar, 1980, California and U.S. District Court, Central District of California. *Education:* California State University at Fullerton and University of California at Berkeley (B.S., 1977) Phi Beta Kappa; Beta Alpha Psi; Stanford University (J.D., 1980). Order of the Coif.

**WAYNE JACOBSEN,** born Landstuhl, Germany, January 25, 1956; admitted to bar, 1982, California; 1983, U.S. District Court, Central District of California; 1989, U.S. Tax Court. *Education:* San Francisco State

*(This Listing Continued)*

University; University of California at Los Angeles (A.B., magna cum laude, 1979); University of Southern California (J.D., 1982). Member, Order of the Coif. Member, 1980-1981 and Notes and Articles Editor, 1981-1982, Southern California Law Review. Author: "Withdrawal Liability for Double-Breasted Construction Employees Under the Multiemployer Pension Plan Amendments Act of 1982," 54 Southern California Law Review, 1981. PRACTICE AREAS: ERISA; Employee Benefits. Email: wjacobsen@omm.com

PHILLIP R. KAPLAN, born Downey, California, April 25, 1951; admitted to bar, 1977, California and U.S. District Court, Central District of California. Education: Yale College (B.A., 1973); University of Southern California (J.D., 1977). Order of the Coif. Staff Member, University of Southern California Law Review, 1975-1977. Author: "A Critique of the Penalty Limitation on Liquidated Damages," 50 Southern California Law Review 1055, 1977. Law Clerk to Hon. David W. Williams, U.S. District Court, Central District of California, 1977. Member: Orange County and American Bar Associations. Email: pkaplan@omm.com

DAVID A. KRINSKY, born August 7, 1948; admitted to bar, 1973, California. Education: University of Southern California (B.A., 1969; J.D., 1973); Rutgers University (M.A., 1970). Member, Southern California Law Review, 1972-1973. PRACTICE AREAS: Corporate Law; Securities Law; Business Law. Email: dkrinsky@omm.com

LOWELL C. MARTINDALE, JR., born Little Rock, Arkansas, August 25, 1940; admitted to bar, 1969, California. Education: California State College at Long Beach (B.A., 1962); University of Southern California (J.D., 1969). Phi Alpha Delta. Comment Editor, Southern California Law Review, 1968-1969. Author: "Testing the Limits of State Power to Alter Contracts by Eminent Domain," The National Law Journal (May 22, 1995). Member: Los Angeles County (Member, Real Property Section), Orange County (Member, Real Property Section) and American Bar Associations.

SCOTT A. MEYERHOFF, born Chicago, Illinois, April 14, 1958; admitted to bar, 1984, California and U.S. District Court, Central District of California. Education: California State University at Northridge (B.S., magna cum laude, 1981); Loyola Marymount University (J.D., cum laude, 1984). Alpha Sigma Nu. Member, St. Thomas More Law Society. Recipient, American Society of Writers on Legal Subjects Award, 1984. Staff Member, 1982-1983 and Editor-in-Chief, 1983-1984, Loyola of Los Angeles Law Review. Member: Los Angeles County (Real Property Section), Orange County (Real Property Section) and American Bar Associations.

PAUL E. MOSLEY, born Phoenix, Arizona, December 28, 1959; admitted to bar, 1986, California and U.S. District Court, Central District of California. Education: Brigham Young University (B.A., magna cum laude, 1982; B.S., 1982; J.D., magna cum laude, 1986). Order of the Coif. Member, 1984-1985 and Lead Articles Editor, 1985-1986, Brigham Young University Law Review. Member: American Bar Association (Section of Natural Resources, Energy and Environmental Law); Environmental Law Institute. LANGUAGES: Spanish. Email: pmosley@omm.com

STEPHEN P. PEPE, born Paterson, New Jersey, October 30, 1943; admitted to bar, 1969, California. Education: Montclair State College (B.A., 1965); Duke University (J.D., 1968). Editor, Duke Law Journal, 1967-1968. Co-Author: "Avoiding and Defending Wrongful Discharge Claims," Clark Boardman Callaghan, 1987; "Designing an Effective Fair-Hiring and Terminations Compliance Program," 9 Corporate Compliance Series, Clark Boardman Callaghan, 1993. Co-Editor "O'Melveny & Myers Guide to Acquiring and Managing a U.S. Business" Eurostudy Publ. Co. 1992 (and IPC Japanese Edition); California Employment Law Letter, 1990-1995. Co-Author: "Privacy in the Workplace," Employers Group, 1992; "Defamation in the Workplace," L. Smith & Co. 1993. Board of Visitors, Duke Law School, 1992-1996; Board of Trustees, Montclair State College Foundation. Member: Los Angeles County and American (Management Co-Chair, Labor and Employment Law Section, Committee on Individual Rights and Responsibilities, 1982-1985) Bar Associations; American Hospital Association (Member, Labor Advisory Committee, 1975-1990; Chair, Employers Group Legal Committee, 1988-1993); I.I.R.A. (President, 1991-1993); O'Melveny & Myers (Chair, Labor and Employment Law Department, 1989-1992). PRACTICE AREAS: Labor and Employment. Email: spepe@omm.com

FRANK L. RUGANI, born California, May 3, 1948; admitted to bar, 1978, California. Education: Occidental College (A.B., with honors, 1970); University of California at Davis (J.D., 1978). Participant, Roger Traynor Moot Court Competition, 1978. Thomas J. Watson Fellow, 1970. Member, University of California at Davis Law Review, 1977-1978. Clerk-Extern, Judge Philip C. Wilkins, U.S. District Court, Eastern District of California,

*(This Listing Continued)*

1977-1978. Co-Author: "Counselling on Vacation-Property Time Sharing," California Lawyer, February 1982; "Analysis of the Regulations of the Department of Real Estate, State of California, Regulating Real Property Time Share Sales," Time Sharing Industry Review, December 1981/January 1982; "Time-sharing of Real Property," Real Property News, Fall, 1980. Member: Los Angeles County and American Bar Associations. Email: frugani@omm.com

JAMES V. SELNA, born Santa Clara, California, February 22, 1945; admitted to bar, 1971, California. Education: Stanford University (A.B. with distinction, 1967); Stanford University (J.D., 1970). Phi Beta Kappa; Order of the Coif. Article and Book Review Editor, Stanford Law Review, 1969-1970. Member: State Bar of California (Member, Standing Committee on Federal Courts, 1982-1985; Executive Committee, Litigation Section, 1986-1989; Executive Committee, Antitrust Section, 1992-1995, and Advisor, 1995—); Los Angeles County (Member, Executive Committee, Antitrust Law Section, 1981-1983), Orange County and American Bar Associations; Orange County Federal Bar Association (Director, 1991-1993). PRACTICE AREAS: Antitrust; Complex Commercial Litigation. Email: jselna@omm.com

GARY J. SINGER, born Los Angeles, California, October 8, 1952; admitted to bar, 1977, California. Education: University of California at Irvine (B.A., magna cum laude, 1974); Loyola of Los Angeles (J.D., cum laude, 1977). Alpha Sigma Nu; Phi Beta Kappa. Member, St. Thomas More Law Honor Society. Editor-in-Chief, Loyola of Los Angeles Law Review, 1976-1977. Author: Case Note, "Gordon v. New York Stock Exchange," 9 Loyola of Los Angeles Law Review 226, 1975. Member: Orange County and American Bar Associations. PRACTICE AREAS: Corporate; Securities; Mergers and Acquisitions. Email: gsinger@omm.com

STEPHANIE I. SPLANE, born Bakersfield, California, April 13, 1956; admitted to bar, 1986, California; 1995, District of Columbia and New York. Education: University of Redlands (B.A., summa cum laude, 1977); University of California, Irvine (Ph.D., 1981); Yale University (J.D., 1984). Phi Beta Kappa. Note Editor, Yale Law Journal, 1983-1984. Law Clerk for Patricia M. Wald, U.S. Court of Appeals, District of Columbia Circuit, 1984. Author: Note, "Tort Liability of the Mentally Ill in Negligence Actions," 93 Yale Law Journal 153, 1983. PRACTICE AREAS: Banking; Securities; General Corporate Law; Mergers and Acquisitions.

THOMAS E. WOLFE, born Jacksonville, Florida, July 1, 1952; admitted to bar, 1981, California and U.S. District Court, Central District of California. Education: University of California (A.B., 1976); Loyola Marymount University (J.D., magna cum laude, 1981). Alpha Sigma Nu. Staff Member, 1979-1980 and Managing Editor, 1980-1981, Loyola Law Review. Member, St. Thomas More Law Honor Society, 1979-1981. Extern for the Honorable Wm. Matthew Byrne, Jr., U.S. District Judge, Central District of California, 1981. PRACTICE AREAS: Corporate Law. Email: twolfe@omm.com

MICHAEL G. YODER, born Lynwood, California, November 12, 1953; admitted to bar, 1978, California. Education: University of Southern California (A.B., 1975); Stanford University (J.D., 1978). Phi Beta Kappa; Order of the Coif; First Year Honor. Member: Orange County (Chair-Elect, Business Litigation Section, 1996) and American (Litigation Section, Business Torts Committee, 1992-1995; Co-Chair, Fraud Subcommittee, and Chair, California Region, 1996—) Bar Associations. PRACTICE AREAS: Complex Business Litigation; Land Use Litigation; Business Torts; Trade Secrets.

## OF COUNSEL

BARTON BEEK, born Pasadena, California, January 23, 1924; admitted to bar, 1955, California. Education: California Institute of Technology (B.S., 1944); Stanford University (M.B.A., 1948); Loyola University (LL.B., 1955). Member: Los Angeles County and American Bar Associations. PRACTICE AREAS: Corporate Finance; Mergers and Acquisitions; Emerging hi-tech companies.

## SPECIAL COUNSEL

KEVIN RAY BAKER, born Kirksville, Missouri, July 1, 1961; admitted to bar, 1989, California, U.S. District Court, Central District of California and U.S. Court of Appeals, Ninth Circuit. Education: Claremont McKenna College (B.A., cum laude, with honors in Economics and Accounting, 1984); Harvard University Law School (J.D., cum laude, 1989). Omicron Delta Epsilon. Certified Public Accountant, Texas, 1986. Member: Orange County (Member, Business Law Section) and American (Member, Business Law and Taxation Sections) Bar Associations; Texas Society of Certified Public Accountants; American Institute of Certified Public Accountants; National Association of Accountants; Christian Legal Society. PRACTICE

*(This Listing Continued)*

## O'MELVENY & MYERS LLP, Newport Beach—Continued

AREAS: Mergers and Acquisitions; Securities Offerings; Franchise Law and General Corporate Matters.

**GEORGE C. DEMOS,** born La Mesa, California, October 5, 1962; admitted to bar, 1989, California, U.S. District Court, Central District of California and U.S. Court of Appeals, Ninth Circuit. *Education:* University of California at San Diego (B.A., cum laude, Departmental honors, with highest Distinction, 1984); University of Southern California (J.D., 1989). Order of the Coif; Alpha Beta Psi; Beta Gamma Sigma. *Member:* Los Angeles County (Tax Section) and American Bar Associations. **PRACTICE AREAS:** Health Care.

**BRETT J. WILLIAMSON,** born Newport Beach, California, October 12, 1963; admitted to bar, 1989, California, U.S. Court of Appeals, Ninth Circuit and U.S. District Court, Central District of California; 1990, U.S. District Court, Northern, Southern and Eastern Districts of California. *Education:* University of California at Irvine (B.A., with honors, 1986); University of Southern California (J.D., 1989). Order of the Coif. Recipient, American Jurisprudence Awards in Constitutional Law II and Local Government Law. Staff Member, 1987-1988 and Articles Editor, 1988-1989, Southern California Law Review. Author: "Constitutional Privacy After Bowers v. Hardwick: Rethinking the Second Death of Substantive Due Process," 62 Southern California Law Review 1297, March/May, 1989. *Member:* Orange County and American (Member, Litigation Section) Bar Associations. **PRACTICE AREAS:** Litigation.

All Members and Associates are Members of The State Bar of California and the Orange County Bar Association.

(For Complete Personnel and Biographical Data see Professional Biographies at Los Angeles, California.)

## PAONE, CALLAHAN, McHOLM & WINTON
### NEWPORT BEACH, CALIFORNIA
(See Irvine)

Real Property, Land Use, Environmental, Partnership, Business and Commercial Law, Banking, Business, Redevelopment and Family Law Litigation. General Civil Trial and Appellate Practice, State and Federal Courts.

## JAMES M. PARKER
4695 MACARTHUR COURT, SUITE 1290
NEWPORT BEACH, CALIFORNIA 92660
Telephone: 714-752-2408
Fax: 714-752-2464

General Civil, Trial and Appellate Practice, State and Federal Courts. General Corporate, Real Estate, Commercial, Land Use and Administrative.

**JAMES M. PARKER,** born Los Angeles, California, February 11, 1934; admitted to bar, 1966, California and U.S. District Court, Central District of California; 1976, U.S. Court of Appeals, Ninth Circuit; 1978, U.S. District Court, Southern District of California and U.S. Supreme Court. *Education:* Loyola University of Los Angeles (B.S., 1957); Southwestern University (J.D., 1966). Phi Alpha Delta. Member, Moot Court, 1962. Author: "General Plans in California: A Description: Some Tips and A Prognosis," Orange County Bar Journal, Winter, 1975; "Real Estate Brokerage Reforms Need Reforming," Orange County Lawyer, April, 1988. Instructor, Real Estate Law, California Community College, 1968-1989. Panelist: Disclosure Dilemma in the Real Estate Brokerage Industry, Real Estate Law Section, State Bar of California, 1987; Real Estate Brokerage Practice, Continuing Education of the Bar, 1991 and 1995. Assistant Counsel, American Hawaiian Land Co., 1966. Vice President, Division Counsel, Occidental Land Inc., 1970-1974. Member, City of Newport Beach Planning Commission, 1973-1975. President, Newport Harbor Area Chamber of Commerce, 1976. Advocate, Catholic Diocese of Orange Marital Tribunal, 1971-1992. Settlement Conference Judge Pro Tem, Orange County Superior Court, 1979—. Member, Superior Court Arbitration Panel, 1982—. Arbitrator, Orange County Bar Association Mandatory Fee Arbitration Committee, 1992—. *Member:* Orange County Bar Association (Member, Real Estate Law Section, 1993—); State Bar of California (Member, Real Estate Sec-

*(This Listing Continued)*

tion). **PRACTICE AREAS:** Real Estate; Corporate Law; Construction Defects; Litigation.

REPRESENTATIVE CLIENTS: The East Orange County Association of Realtors; Waterfront Homes, Inc.; Coast Newport Properties; Sanwa Bank Trust Dept.; Lifescapes, International, Inc.

## PAUL, HASTINGS, JANOFSKY & WALKER LLP
### NEWPORT BEACH, CALIFORNIA
(See Costa Mesa)
*General Practice*

## LAW OFFICES OF MARSHALL M. PEARLMAN
A PROFESSIONAL CORPORATION
SUITE 600, SOUTH TOWER
3501 JAMBOREE ROAD
NEWPORT BEACH, CALIFORNIA 92660
Telephone: 714-854-0890
Facsimile: 714-854-0891
Email: 75671.1771@compuserve.com

Litigation: Environmental, Toxic Tort, Product Liability, General Business, Due Diligence: Environmental.

**MARSHALL M. PEARLMAN,** born Jersey City, New Jersey, May 9, 1936; admitted to bar, 1967, New York; 1968, U.S. District Court, Southern and Eastern Districts of New York; 1981, California, U.S. District Court, Central, Southern, Northern and Eastern Districts of California and U.S. Court of Appeals, Ninth Circuit. *Education:* Fairleigh Dickinson University (B.A., 1960); New York Law School. *Member:* Orange County, New York State and American Bar Associations; The State Bar of California.

REPRESENTATIVE CLIENTS: Uniroyal Chemical Co., Inc.; Cooper Tire & Rubber Co.; Chevron Chemical Co.; Valent U.S.A. Corp.; Amana Refrigeration, Inc.

## PEDERSEN & BLACK
A PROFESSIONAL LAW CORPORATION
1300 DOVE STREET, SUITE 200
NEWPORT BEACH, CALIFORNIA 92660
Telephone: 714-263-9955
Fax: 714-263-0575

Business Litigation, Trials and Appeals, Insurance Coverage and Bad Faith Litigation, Construction Defect Litigation, Entertainment Law, General Corporate, Business Entity Formation.

**NEIL PEDERSEN,** born Hollywood, California, May 24, 1957; admitted to bar, 1989, California and U.S. District Court, Northern, Southern, Central and Eastern Districts of California. *Education:* Western State University (B.S., 1986; J.D., magna cum laude, 1988). Editor-in-Chief, Western State University Law Review, 1988. Co-Valedictorian, 1988. Author: "Representing an Insured: Avoiding Insurer Reimbursement Actions," O.C. Lawyer, October, 1994; "Effective Closing Argument," Western State University Law Review, May 1990. Judicial Extern to Justice Edward J. Wallin, California Court of Appeal, Fourth District, Division Three, 1987. Member, Adjunct Faculty, Legal Writing, Western State University College of Law, 1989-1990. *Member:* Los Angeles County and Orange County (Member, Sections on: Business Litigation; Insurance Law; Executive Committee, 1994—, Program Chair, 1995, Section Co-Chair, 1996, Insurance Law Section; Arbitrator, Mandatory Fee Arbitration Program) Bar Associations; State Bar of California. Legion Lex Inns of Court (Barrister, 1994-1996).

**WILLIAM A. BLACK,** born Pontiac, Michigan, December 24, 1957; admitted to bar, 1990, California and U.S. District Court, Central District of California. *Education:* University of Wisconsin (B.S., Communication, 1980); Regent University (M.A., Communication, 1982); Western State University (J.D., magna cum laude, 1989). Recipient, First Place-Team, Third Place-Oralist, Moot Court Competition, 1988. Listed in Who's Who in American Universities, 1988-1989. Member, 1987-1989 and Preliminary

*(This Listing Continued)*

Editor, 1987-1988, Western State University Law Review. Author: "Ingersoll v. Palmer, Sobriety Checkpoints in California take the Long Way Home," Western State University Law Review, 1988. Adjunct Faculty, Legal Writing, Western State University College of Law, 1990-1997. *Member:* Los Angeles County and Orange County Member, Business Litigation Section) Bar Associations; State Bar of California.

REPRESENTATIVE CLIENTS: the Bailey Group; QuantumLink Corp.; Far West Caster Corp.; Future Communities, Inc.; Video Pioneers Corp.; Surgin, Inc.; Economic Computer Solutions, Inc.; Schetne Drywall, Inc.; Petrofsky Center for Rehabilitation and Research, Inc.; Prima Royale Enterprises; Artists in Christian Testimony, Inc.

## DONALD PETERS

*A LAW CORPORATION*

1300 DOVE STREET, SUITE 200

**NEWPORT BEACH, CALIFORNIA 92660**

Telephone: 714-955-3818

Fax: 714-955-1341

*General Civil Trial Practice. Personal Injury, Medical Malpractice, Elder Law, Elder Abuse, Estate Planning, Estate Supervision, Public Entity Liability, Maritime, Aviation and Insurance Law.*

**DONALD PETERS,** born Jacksonville, Florida, September 28, 1932; admitted to bar, 1965, California and U.S. District Court, Southern District of California. *Education:* University of Notre Dame (B.S.C., 1955); Southwestern University (J.D., 1964). Assistant Trust Officer, Bank of America, 1957-1960. Executive Assistant to the Executive Officer, 1962-1965 and Judge Pro Tem, 1976-1977, Probate Attorney, 1965-1966, Los Angeles County Superior Court; Judge Pro Tem, 1994—, Orange County Superior Court. Listed: Who's Who in American Law; Who's Who in California. Markhams Negligence Counsel. Member, Board of Directors, Beverly Hospital, Montebello, California, 1966—; Treasurer, 1967-1974; Second Vice President, 1991-1994. Instrument Rated Private Pilot. *Member:* Orange County Bar Association; State Bar of California. [LTJG, USNR, 1955-1957]

## THOMAS L. POWELL

3501 JAMBOREE ROAD, SUITE 6000

**NEWPORT BEACH, CALIFORNIA 92660**

Telephone: 714-721-7287

Fax: 714-721-7388

*Real Estate Development, Subdivisions, Real Estate Transactions, Land Use and Redevelopment.*

**THOMAS L. POWELL,** admitted to bar, 1974, California. *Education:* Whittier College (B.A., magna cum laude, 1971); University of Southern California (J.D., 1974). Order of the Coif. Semi-Finalist, University of Southern California Hale Moot Court Honors Program, 1973. Co-Recipient, Best Appellate Brief, 1973. Member, University of Southern California Law Review, 1972-1974. Member, California Department of Real Estate; Commissioner's Subdivision Advisory Committee, 1991-1995. Panelist: Building Industry Association, Proper Mapping of Subdivisions, 1991; Lecturer: California Department of Real Estate. Condominiums and Planned Developments, 1990. *Member:* State Bar of California.

REPRESENTATIVE CLIENTS: Bramalia California, Inc.; California Pacific Homes, Inc.; Catellus Residential Group; Ford Leasing Development Co.; Koll Real Estate Group; ; Presley Homes; The Irvine Company.

## PAUL W. RAYMOND

SUITE 950

1301 DOVE STREET

**NEWPORT BEACH, CALIFORNIA 92660-2473**

Telephone: 714-476-2197

Fax: 714-955-2886

*Federal and State Taxation. Civil and Criminal Tax Litigation and Tax Controversy.*

**PAUL W. RAYMOND,** born Los Angeles, California, June 1, 1953; admitted to bar, 1983, California, U.S. District Court, Central, Eastern, Northern and Southern Districts of California, U.S. Court of Appeals, Ninth Circuit and U.S. Tax Court; 1991, U.S. Court of Federal Claims. *Education:* University of California at Santa Barbara (B.A., 1976); Western State University (J.D., 1980). Author: "100% Penalty Collection In Community Property States", IRS Practice & Policy Bulletin, Tax Management, Inc., Vol. 3, No. 9 (June 11, 1993). Adjunct Professor of Law, Taxation, Western State University, 1992—. Co-Founder and President, Orange County Tax Forum, 1990—. *Member:* Los Angeles County, Orange County and American (Member, Section on Taxation; Chair, Committee on Employment Taxes; Co-Chairman, Section 6672 Task Force) Bar Associations; State Bar of California (Member, Section on Taxation). **PRACTICE AREAS:** Taxation-Civil and Criminal, Federal and State.

*(This Listing Continued)*

## REMER, DiVINCENZO & GRIFFITH

*A PROFESSIONAL CORPORATION*

Established in 1951

2121 EAST PACIFIC COAST HIGHWAY, SUITE 280 (CORONA DEL MAR)

**NEWPORT BEACH, CALIFORNIA 92625**

Telephone: 714-759-0781

Fax: 714-759-0788

*General Trial and Appellate Practice in all State and Federal Courts. General Business, Agri-Business, Corporation, Real Property, Estate Planning, Trust, Probate, Negligence, Taxation, Complex Litigation, Products Liability and Insurance Law.*

**MAX HURWITZ** (1914-1974).

**ROBERT R. HURWITZ** (1921-1990).

**FRANKLIN I. REMER,** born New York, N.Y., June 7, 1929; admitted to bar, 1951, New York; 1958, California and U.S. District Court, Central District of California. *Education:* Brooklyn College and Long Beach State College; Brooklyn Law School (LL.B., 1951). Judge Pro Tem, Orange County Superior Court, 1976—. Member, Orange County Fair Board, 1966-1970. Professor of Law, Pepperdine University School of Law, 1968-1970. Member, Federal Court Indigent Criminal Defense Panel, 1971—. *Member:* Orange County (Member, Superior Court Arbitration Panel, 1976—) and American Bar Associations; State Bar of California (Chairman, Local Administrative Committee, 1972-1974); California Trial Lawyers Association; Orange County Trial Lawyers Association. [Capt., JAGC, USAR, 1951-1955]. **PRACTICE AREAS:** Litigation; Personal Injury.

**JOSEPH P. DiVINCENZO,** born Cleveland, Ohio, June 26, 1950; admitted to bar, 1975, California and U.S. District Court, Central District of California. *Education:* University of Southern California (B.A., cum laude, 1972); Law School of the Aristotelian University and Institute of Public International Law, University of Thessaloniki, Thessaloniki, Greece (Graduate, Special Session, 1974); University of Southern California Law Center (J.D., 1975). *Member:* Orange County (Member, Sections on: International Law; Business Litigation) and American (Member, Section of Litigation) Bar Associations; State Bar of California; Orange County Trial Lawyers Association; California Trial Lawyers Association. **PRACTICE AREAS:** Personal Injury; Corporate; Litigation.

**DWIGHT J. GRIFFITH,** born Beverly Hills, California, August 3, 1950; admitted to bar, 1975, California and U.S. District Court, Central District of California. *Education:* University of Southern California (B.A., cum laude, 1972); University of Southern California, Gould School of Law (J.D., 1975). Editor, Honors Moot Court Executive Board, Gould School of Law, 1974-1975. *Member:* State Bar of California; American Bar Association. **PRACTICE AREAS:** Estate Planning; Trust; Transactional.

**KATHLEEN A. CARTER,** born Des Moines, Iowa, August 3, 1961; admitted to bar, 1990, California. *Education:* University of Iowa (B.A., 1983; J.D., 1988). Donald Bruce Johnson Scholar. Instructor, Introduction to Law, University of Iowa, College of Business Administration, 1986-1987. *Member:* Orange County (Member, Estate Planning Section), Los Angeles County and American Bar Associations.

**GINA L. GENOVA,** born Pensacola, Florida, September 24, 1967; admitted to bar, 1992, California and U.S. District Court, Central District of California; 1993, U.S. District Court, Northern District of California. *Education:* University of California, Los Angeles (B.A., 1989); McGeorge School of Law (J.D., 1992). Phi Delta Phi. *Member:* Orange County Bar Association; State Bar of California; Orange County Barristers; Orange County Women Lawyers Association.

REFERENCES: First American Trust Co., Newport Beach; Sanna Trust, Newport Beach; Northern Trust, Newport Beach, California; Bank of Newport, Newport Beach.

## ROBERTS AND QUIOGUE

A LAW CORPORATION

Established in 1983

660 NEWPORT CENTER DRIVE, SUITE 710
P.O. BOX 8569
**NEWPORT BEACH, CALIFORNIA 92658**
Telephone: 714-640-6200
Facsimile: 714-640-1206

*Intellectual Property Law, Patent, Trademark and Trade Secret and Related Matters.*

**MANUEL QUIOGUE,** born Philippines, October 11, 1949; admitted to bar, 1976, Illinois; 1977, U.S. District Court, Northern District of Illinois; 1979, California; 1981, U.S. District Court, Central District of California; 1984, U.S. District Court, Southern District of California; 1986, U.S. District Court, Northern District of California; registered to practice before U.S. Patent and Trademark Office. *Education:* University of Michigan (B.S.E.E., with honors, 1971); George Washington University (J.D., with honors, 1976). Eta Kappa Nu. *Member:* Orange County, Illinois State and American Bar Associations; State Bar of California; American Intellectual Property Law Association; Los Angeles Patent Law Association; Orange County Patent Law Association. **PRACTICE AREAS:** Patent; Trademark; Intellectual Property.

**LARRY K. ROBERTS,** born Decatur, Illinois, August 10, 1949; admitted to bar, 1976, California; 1977, U.S. District Court, Central District of California; 1984, U.S. District Court, Southern District of California; 1986, U.S. District Court, Northern District of California; registered to practice before U.S. Patent and Trademark Office. *Education:* University of Illinois (B.S.E.E., 1971); University of California at Los Angeles (M.S., 1975); Loyola University of Los Angeles (J.D., 1976). Eta Kappa Nu; Sigma Tau. *Member:* Orange County and American Bar Associations; Los Angeles Patent Law Association; Orange County Patent Law Association. **PRACTICE AREAS:** Patent; Trademark; Intellectual Property.

---

## ROBINSON, PHILLIPS & CALCAGNIE

**NEWPORT BEACH, CALIFORNIA**

(See Laguna Niguel)

*Automobile Product Liability Litigation, Toxic Tort, Corporate Fraud, Serious Injury and Death Cases.*

---

## THE RUDOLPH LAW GROUP

A PROFESSIONAL CORPORATION

**NEWPORT BEACH, CALIFORNIA**

(See Costa Mesa)

*General Trial and Appellate Practice in State and Federal Courts, including General Business and Commercial Litigation, Real Estate Litigation, Product Liability, Intellectual Property, Trade Secrets and Unfair Competition, Environmental, Employment and Partnership, Corporate and Trust Disputes.*

---

## RUTAN & TUCKER, LLP

**NEWPORT BEACH, CALIFORNIA**

(See Costa Mesa)

*General Civil and Trial Practice in all State and Federal Courts. Municipal Law, Real Estate, Corporate, Securities, Employment and Labor Relations (Management and Public Sector), Taxation, Estate Planning, Trust and Probate, Environmental and Land Use Law, Municipal Finance, Water Rights, Education Law, Bankruptcy and Creditors Rights.*

CAA1424B

---

## RYNN & JANOWSKY

Established in 1985

4100 NEWPORT PLACE DRIVE, SUITE 700
**NEWPORT BEACH, CALIFORNIA 92660**
Telephone: 714-752-2911
Telecopier: 714-752-0953

*Employment Law, Agricultural Law and Commercial Law.*

MEMBERS OF FIRM

**LEWIS P. JANOWSKY,** born Newark, New Jersey, February 8, 1951; admitted to bar, 1977, Illinois; 1980, California. *Education:* State University of New York at Buffalo (B.A., magna cum laude, 1974, Phi Beta Kappa); Illinois Institute of Technology, Chicago-Kent College of Law (J.D., 1977). Assistant State's Attorney, Cook County, Illinois, 1977-1980. Senior Counsel, Western Growers Association, 1980-1985. *Member:* Orange County (Chairperson, Labor Law Section, 1986) and American Bar Associations; State Bar of California (Member, Employment Law Section); Agricultural Law Association. **PRACTICE AREAS:** Employment Law; Agricultural Law.

**PATRICIA J. RYNN,** born San Bernardino, California, November 25, 1955; admitted to bar, 1980, California, U.S. District Court, Central, Eastern, Southern and Northern Districts of California, U.S. District Court, District of Arizona and U.S. Court of Appeals, Ninth Circuit. *Education:* San Diego State University (B.A., magna cum laude, 1976; M.A., Public Administration, 1977); University of San Diego (J.D., 1979). Author: "Injunctive Relief Under the 1984 Trust Amendment to Perishable Agricultural Commodities Act: A Necessary Means of Trust Enforcement," 23 U.C.D. L. Rev. 625-636 (1990). Senior Counsel, Western Growers Association, 1980-1985. Lecturer, "Current Issues in Employment Law," CEB, 1991. *Member:* Orange County and American Bar Associations; The State Bar of California (Chair, Agri Business Committee, Business Law Section, 1991-1992); American Agricultural Law Association, (Member, Board of Directors, 1991-1994). **PRACTICE AREAS:** Agricultural Law; Employment Law.

---

**RANDAL JASON READ,** born Avenal, California, June 16, 1957; admitted to bar, 1985, California. *Education:* California State University at Fresno (B.A., 1980); Pepperdine University (J.D., 1984); University of Exeter, London, England (LL.M., International Business Law, 1989). Phi Alpha Delta. *Member:* Orange County Bar Association; The State Bar of California; The Association of Trial Lawyers of America.

**LOIS E. RUBIN,** born Los Angeles, California, March 19, 1954; admitted to bar, 1980, California; U.S. District Court, Central District of California. *Education:* University of California at Irvine (B.A., 1975); Loyola University of Los Angeles Law School (J.D., 1979). *Member:* Orange County Bar Association (Member, Family Law Section); State Bar of California. (Certified Specialist, Family Law, The State Bar of California Board of Legal Specialization).

**BARTHOLOMEW M. BOTTA,** born Belleville, New Jersey, November 24, 1968; admitted to bar, 1993, California and U.S. District Court, Central and Eastern Districts of California. *Education:* Seton Hall University (B.A., cum laude, 1990); Washburn University of Topeka (J.D., cum laude, 1993). Phi Delta Phi. Recipient, Tax Law Proficiency Certificate, 1993. Member, Washburn Law Journal, 1991-1993. *Member:* State Bar of California.

REPRESENTATIVE CLIENTS: All Fresh Produce Distributors; Sam Andrews' Sons; George Arakelian Farms, Inc.; Asociacion Agricola Local "Janitzio y Anexos"; Bertuccio Farms; Cal Fruit; Carlsbad Produce, Inc.; Cedimar S.A.; Citizens Thrift and Loan Assn.; Earl Manufacturing Company, Inc.; Food Products International, Inc.; G & K Distributing, Inc.; Gerawan Co., Inc.; High Low Nursery, Inc.; J.C.'s Sunny Winter, Inc.; Jefferson Management Group; Kavanaugh Transportation; Kamprath Seed Company, Inc.; Kirk Produce, Inc.; L & J Packing, Inc.; Lawndale Orthopaedic Group; Moore Farming International, Inc.; Meyer Tomatoes; Rancho dos Palmas, Inc.; Royal Packing Co.; Seacoast Distributing, Inc.; Souza Brothers Packing Co.; Tom Lange Inc.; Union Agricola Regional de Productores de Fresa y Hortalizas del Valle de Zamora; United Agribusiness League; United Customs Brokers, Ltd.; Sam Wong & Sons, Inc.

PROFESSIONAL BIOGRAPHIES  CALIFORNIA—NEWPORT BEACH

## MARTIN J. SABLE

1300 DOVE STREET, SUITE 200
**NEWPORT BEACH, CALIFORNIA 92660-2416**
Telephone: 714-474-2380
Facsimile: 714-474-1516
Email: 71271.1656@compuserve.com

*Civil Litigation, Personal Injury, Corporate Law, Business.*

**MARTIN J. SABLE,** born New York, N.Y., 1953; admitted to bar, 1979, California and U.S. District Court, Central District of California; 1982, U.S. Court of Appeals for the Federal Circuit. *Education:* George Washington University (B.A., 1975); Western State University (J.D., 1979). Management Analyst Assistant, The Executive Office of the President, The Office of Management and Budget, Washington, D.C., 1973-1974. Trademark Attorney, U.S. Department of Commerce, Patent and Trademark Office, 1980-1982. *Member:* Orange County Bar Association; State Bar of California. **PRACTICE AREAS:** Civil Litigation; Personal Injury; Corporate Law; Business Law; Construction Defects.

## SALTZBURG, RAY & BERGMAN, LLP

**NEWPORT BEACH, CALIFORNIA**

(See Los Angeles)

*Commercial Litigation, Bankruptcy, Federal and State Court Receiverships, Real Estate, Financial Institutions, Commercial Transactions and Financing, Mortgage Banking, Entertainment Industry, Insurance Defense, Probate and Estate Planning.*

## IRA M. SALZMAN

**NEWPORT BEACH, CALIFORNIA**

(See Pasadena)

*General Civil Litigation in all State and Federal Courts with emphasis on the Defense of Professional Negligence, Personal Injury and Public Safety Employees, General Wrongful Termination, Criminal Defense in State and Federal Courts.*

## JOHN R. SCHILLING

A PROFESSIONAL CORPORATION

Established in 1985

4675 MACARTHUR COURT
SUITE 590, TOWER ONE
**NEWPORT BEACH, CALIFORNIA 92660-1839**
Telephone: 714-833-8833
Fax: 714-833-3883

*Practice Limited to Family Law.*

**JOHN R. SCHILLING,** born Huntington Park, California, November 27, 1942; admitted to bar, 1968, California. *Education:* University of California at Santa Barbara (B.A., 1964); University of California at Los Angeles (J.D., 1967). Chief Research Attorney, Court of Appeals, Fourth District, Division Two, California, 1967-1969. Trustee, Santa Ana Unified School District, 1971-1975. *Member:* Orange County Bar Association; State Bar of California. Fellow: American Academy of Matrimonial Lawyers; Robert A. Banyard Inn of Court (Master Bencher). (Certified Specialist, Family Law, The State Bar of California Board of Legal Specialization).

REFERENCES: Union Bank (Airport Branch); City National Bank (Newport Beach); Bank of America (Newport Beach).

## ROGER H. SCHNAPP

A PROFESSIONAL CORPORATION

Established in 1984

4041 MACARTHUR BOULEVARD, SUITE 160
**NEWPORT BEACH, CALIFORNIA 92660-2513**
Telephone: 714-752-0491
Fax: 714-752-1102
Email: RHS@SCHNAPP.COM
URL: HTTP://WWW.SCHNAPP.COM

*Employment Law. Government Relations.*

**ROGER H. SCHNAPP,** born New York, N.Y., March 17, 1946; admitted to bar, 1970, New York and U.S. Court of Appeals, Second Circuit; 1974, U.S. Supreme Court; 1975, U.S. District Court, Southern District of New York; 1976, U.S. Court of Appeals, Fourth and Sixth Circuits; 1977, U.S. Court of Appeals, Seventh Circuit; 1980, U.S. District Court, Northern District of California and U.S. Court of Appeals, Eighth Circuit; 1982, California and U.S. District Court, Central District of California; 1984, U.S. Court of Appeals, Ninth Circuit and U.S. District Court, Eastern and Southern Districts of California. *Education:* Cornell University (B.S., 1966); University of Michigan; Harvard University (J.D., 1969). Editor-in-Chief, Industrial and Labor Relations Forum, 1964-1966. Member, Secretary of Labor's Business Research Advisory Council. *Member:* Orange County Bar Association; New York State Bar; State Bar of California.

## RICHARD J. SCHWARZSTEIN

SECOND FLOOR, REDSTONE PLAZA
1300 DOVE STREET
**NEWPORT BEACH, CALIFORNIA 92660**
Telephone: 714-752-9152
Fax: 714-752-0651

*Corporation, Securities, Real Property, International Business and Computer Law.*

**RICHARD J. SCHWARZSTEIN,** born Yonkers, New York, July 6, 1934; admitted to bar, 1960, New York; 1961, U.S. District Court, Southern and Eastern Districts of New York and U.S. Court of Appeals, Second Circuit; 1974, California; 1976, U.S. District Court, Central District of California. *Education:* Columbia University (A.B., 1956); Harvard Law School (J.D., 1959). Listed in: Who's Who in the World, 9th Edition and Who's Who in American Law, 9th Edition. Author: "Computers, Computer Law and You," Orange County Bar Journal Vol. 2, p. 700, 1975. Associate and Partner, Delson & Gordon, New York City, 1962-1974. Counsel, Economic Development Corporation of Orange County, 1976-1986. Member, Board of Directors, 1976—; Chairman, 1986-1987; Vice Chairman, 1988-1993, World Trade Center Association of Orange County. Member, Board of Directors, Santa Ana Economic Development Corporation, 1990-1995. Member, National Panel of Arbitrators, American Arbitration Association. Member and Board of Directors, 1978—; President, 1993-1994; Chairman, 1994-1995, Orange County Philharmonic County Society. *Member:* Orange County (Member, Corporate and International Law Sections; Chairman, International Section, 1980—), New York State, American (Member, Sections on: Corporation, Banking and Business Law; International Law; Science and Technology; Member, Committee on Computers, Section on Economics of Law Practice, 1979—) and International Bar Associations; State Bar of California (Member, Executive Committee: Section on Economics of Law Practice, 1976-1979; International Law Practice Committee, 1986-1987); The Association of the Bar of the City of New York (Member, Committee on Bankruptcy and Corporate Reorganization, 1965-1969).

## SCOTT, REILLY & WHITEHEAD

1301 DOVE STREET, SUITE 1000
**NEWPORT BEACH, CALIFORNIA 92660**
Telephone: 714-222-0166
Facsimile: 714-222-0113
URL: http://www.employerlaw.com

*FIRM PROFILE: The firm represents private and public employers in Labor and Employment Law matters, including state and federal employment litigation, alternative dispute resolution, arbitration, wrongful discharge, discrimination, harassment, wage/hour, reductions-in-force and labor relations. The firm advises management on workplace compliance, policy development and preventive practices.*

(This Listing Continued)

## SCOTT, REILLY & WHITEHEAD, Newport Beach—Continued

**R. CRAIG SCOTT,** born Salt Lake City, Utah, January 23, 1953; admitted to bar, 1978, California; U.S. District Court, Central, Southern, Eastern and Northern Districts of California; U.S. Court of Appeals, Seventh and Ninth Circuits; U.S. Supreme Court. *Education:* University of Utah (B.S., magna cum laude, 1975; J.D., 1978). Order of the Coif. Member, 1976-1977 and Articles Editor, 1977-1978, Utah Law Review. City Council, 1991-1996 and Mayor, 1994, City of Laguna Hills, California. Previous Employment: Sheppard, Mullin, Richter & Hampton, Los Angeles and Newport Beach, California, 1978-1990; Pettis, Tester, Kruse & Krinsky, Irvine, California, 1990-1993. *Member:* Orange County (Member, Labor Law Section) and American (Member, Labor Law Section) Bar Associations; State Bar of California.

**THOMAS H. REILLY,** born Pompton Plains, New Jersey, June 19, 1957; admitted to bar, 1983, California; U.S. District Court, Central and Southern Districts of California and U.S. Court of Appeals, Ninth Circuit. *Education:* Yale University (B.A., 1979); University of Southern California (J.D., 1983). Member, 1981-1982 and Articles Editor, 1982-1983, Southern California Law Review. Previous Employment: O'Melveny & Myers, Los Angeles and Newport Beach, California, 1983-1995. *Member:* Orange County (Member, Labor Law Section) and American (Member, Labor Law Section) Bar Associations; State Bar of California.

**NANCY RADER WHITEHEAD,** born Fontana, California, October 21, 1957; admitted to bar, 1982, California; U.S. District Court, Central, Southern and Northern Districts of California and U.S. Court of Appeals, Ninth Circuit. *Education:* California State Polytechnic University (B.A., magna cum laude, 1979); University of Southern California (J.D., 1982). Phi Alpha Theta. Member, Southern California Law Review, 1980-1981. Author: "Evaluating Prosecutorial Vindictiveness Claims in Non-Plea-Bargained Cases," 55 Southern California Law Review, 1982. Previous Employment: Stradling, Yocca, Carlson & Rauth, Newport Beach, California, 1982-1987; Corbett & Steelman, Irvine, California, 1987-1993. *Member:* Orange County Bar Association (Member, Business Litigation Section); Orange County Women Lawyers Association; California Women Lawyers; State Bar of California.

---

**DIANE DESFOR STALDER,** born Long Beach, California, June 15, 1955; admitted to bar, 1991, California; U.S. District Court, Central, Southern, Eastern and Northern Districts of California and U.S. Court of Appeals, Ninth Circuit. *Education:* University of Southern California (B.A., 1977; J.D., 1991). Phi Beta Kappa. Member, Computer Law and Major Tax Planning Journal, 1990-1991. Previous Employment: Paul, Hastings, Janofsky & Walker, Costa Mesa, California, 1991-1995. *Member:* Orange County Bar Association (Member, Labor Law Section); State Bar of California.

**PAMELA L. WHITESIDES,** born Santa Barbara, California, December 28, 1946; admitted to bar, 1991, California; U.S. District Court, Central District of California and U.S. Court of Appeals, Ninth Circuit. *Education:* University of Southern California (B.S., 1970; J.D., 1991). Order of the Coif; Phi Kappa Phi. Member, Southern California Law Review, 1989-1990. Founding Member, USC Review of Law and Women's Studies. Law Clerk to Honorable Judge Linda H. McLaughlin, U.S. District Court, Central District of California, 1993. Previous Employment: Paul, Hastings, Janofsky & Walker, Costa Mesa, California, 1991-1993. *Member:* Orange County (Member, Labor Law Section) and American (Member, Labor Law Section) Bar Associations; State Bar of California.

REPRESENTATIVE CLIENTS: Alcon Surgical; Allergan, Inc.; Amplicon, Inc.; Area Trade Bindery; City of Newport Beach; City of Torrance; County Sanitation Districts, Orange County; Farmers Insurance Group; Los Angeles Unified School District; Polar Air Cargo; Printronix; Shea Homes; Sterling Homes; Wet Seal/Contempo Casuals; Women's Medical Group of Irvine.

CAA1426B

---

# THE LAW OFFICES OF ROBERT K. SCOTT

*A PROFESSIONAL CORPORATION*

660 NEWPORT CENTER DRIVE, SUITE 950
**NEWPORT BEACH, CALIFORNIA 92660**
Telephone: 714-644-1301
Fax: 714-644-0840
URL: http://www.robertkscott.com

*San Francisco, California Office:* 100 Van Ness Avenue, 19th Floor, 94102. Telephone: 415-437-0673.

*Associate Office:* Mart & DeVries, Sacramento, California

Practice limited to Plaintiffs Insurance Bad Faith, Automobile Insurance, Fire Insurance, Commercial Liability Insurance, Homeowners Insurance, Accident and Health Insurance. Catastrophic Personal Injury, Wrongful Death, Wrongful Termination, Lender's Liability and Consumer Law, Litigation.

**ROBERT K. SCOTT,** born Glendale, California, December 7, 1949; admitted to bar, 1975, California; 1980, U.S. Supreme Court. *Education:* United States International University (B.A., 1971); California Western School of Law (J.D., 1975). Member, Editorial Board, California Western International Law Journal, 1974-1975. Teaching Assistant, Legal Research and Writing Course, California Western School of Law, 1974-1975. Rutter Group Lecturer, Insurance Bad Faith, 1989—. Member, State Bar Court-California State Bar, 1980-1990. Los Angeles County Superior Court Arbitrator, 1982—. Judge Pro Tem, Los Angeles Municipal Court, 1982-1995. Member, Board of Trustees, California Western School of Law, 1990—; Chairman, Nominating Committee; Member, Executive Committee. Member and Vice Chairman, Board of Trustees, Irvine Medical Center Hospital, Irvine, California, 1990—. *Member:* Los Angeles County, Orange County and American (Member, Tort and Insurance Practice Section, Member, Life Insurance Law Committee, Member, Policy Sub-Committee; Member, and Vice-Chair, Health Insurance Law Committee); State Bar of California (Member, Committee on Group Insurance Programs, 1987— and Chairman, 1990; Member, Commission on Professional Liability Insurance, 1986); The Association of Trial Lawyers of America; consumer Attorneys of Los Angeles; Consumer Attorneys of California (Board Member, 1986—; Member, Political Action Committee, 1984—; Board Member, 1985-1988 and President, 1988, Inland Chapter).

---

**DAVID I. LIPSKY,** born New York, N.Y., October 31, 1939; admitted to bar, 1972, California and U.S. District Courts, Central, Northern and Eastern Districts of California. *Education:* California State University at Los Angeles (B.A., 1961; M.A., 1965); Loyola University (J.D., 1971). St. Thomas More Law Honor Society. *Member:* State Bar of California; California Trial Lawyers Association; consumer Attorneys of California.

**D. SCOTT MOHNEY,** born Pomona, California, March 8, 1953; admitted to bar, 1986, California; 1987, U.S. District Court, Central District of California. *Education:* California State University at Los Angeles; California State University at Long Beach; University of La Verne (J.D., 1985). *Member:* State Bar of California; Consumer Attorneys of California.

**JOHN C. MCCARTY,** born Montebello, California, September 14, 1963; admitted to bar, 1988, California. *Education:* Long Beach State University (B.A., 1985); Western State University (J.D., 1988). Delta Theta Phi (Vice Dean, Master Scholar, 1986). Member, Honors Moot Court. Recipient, American Jurisprudence Award for Civil Procedure. Listed in: Outstanding Young Men of America; Who's Who in American Universities and Colleges. Instructor, DOW Program-Student Writing Program, Western State College of Law, 1986-1987. *Member:* State Bar of California.

**RHONDA R. HARRIS,** born San Jose, California, September 25, 1966; admitted to bar, 1993, California. *Education:* California Polytechnic State University (B.A., 1988); Santa Clara University (J.D., 1992). *Member:* State Bar of California.

**MARY T. RAHMES,** born Dallas, Texas, December 18, 1956; admitted to bar, 1985, California and U.S. District Court, Central District of California. *Education:* Michigan State University (B.A., cum laude, 1979); California Western School of Law (J.D., 1982). Instructor, Legal Research and Writing, California Western School of Law, 1980-1981. Arbitrator, San Bernadino County Superior Court Panel of Arbitrators. *Member:* The State Bar of California; Association of Southern California Defense Counsel.

**CHRISTIAN J. GARRIS,** born Palo Alto, California, December 21, 1968; admitted to bar, 1994, California. *Education:* Claremont McKenna

*(This Listing Continued)*

College (B.A., 1991); Santa Clara University (J.D., 1994). Author: "Bosnia and The Limitations of International Law," 34 Santa Clara L. Rev. 1039 (1994). Articles Editor, Santa Clara Law Review, 1993-1994. *Member:* State Bar of California.

### OF COUNSEL

**WILLIAM M. SHERNOFF, (P.C.),** born Chicago, Illinois, October 26, 1937; admitted to bar, 1962, Wisconsin; 1966, California. *Education:* University of Miami (B.B.A., 1959); University of Wisconsin (J.D., 1962). Co-Author: Legal Treatise, "Insurance Bad Faith Litigation," published by Matthew Bender, 1984; "How to Make Insurance Companies Pay Your Claims and What to do if They Don't," Hastings House, 1990. Author: "Payment Refused," published by Richardson & Steirman, 1986. *Member:* State Bar of California; Los Angeles Trial Lawyers Association (Trial Lawyer of the Year, 1975); California Trial Lawyers Association (President, 1981); The Association of Trial Lawyers of America. (Also Member, Shernoff, Bidart & Darras, Claremont, California).

**JAMES A. ROBERTS,** born San Diego, California, May 2, 1950; admitted to bar, 1976, California and U.S. District Court, Northern District of California; 1979, U.S. Court of Appeals, Ninth Circuit; 1980, U.S. Supreme Court. *Education:* Claremont Mens College (B.S., magna cum laude, 1972); Hastings College of the Law, University of California (J.D., 1976). Author: "Insurance Coverage for Intentional Acts," cover article, Barclay's California Law Monthly, November, 1988; "Garvey v. State Farm: The Dawning of a New Era," feature article, Insurance Litigation Reporter, Summer, 1990. Lecturer, Insurance Coverage and Bad Faith, California Trial Lawyers Association, San Diego Trial Lawyers Association, 1985—. Faculty, Hastings College of Advocacy, 1980-1983. Member, California Judge's Association, 1994. *Member:* San Diego County Bar Association; State Bar of California; San Diego Trial Lawyers Association.

---

## SEELY & RUSSELL
### Established in 1982
### SUITE 140, 4631 TELLER AVENUE
### NEWPORT BEACH, CALIFORNIA 92660
Telephone: 714-955-3575; 955-3570
FAX: 714-851-2722

*General Civil and Administrative Agency Practice. Business, Real Estate, Family Law, Business Litigation, Arbitration and Estate Planning.*

### MEMBERS OF FIRM

**HALL SEELY,** born San Francisco, California, October 1, 1936; admitted to bar, 1963, California and U.S. District Court, Southern and Central Districts of California. *Education:* Stanford University (B.A., 1958); Harvard Law School (LL.B., 1962). Pi Sigma Alpha. Instructor in Law, Western State University, Anaheim, California, 1971-1972. Lecturer, Arbitration Law, Family Law and Trial Practice, California Continuing Education of the Bar, 1981-1990. Member, Planning Commission, City of Newport Beach, 1973-1977. Member and Chairman, Parks, Beaches and Recreation Commission, City of Newport Beach, 1968-1972. *Member:* Orange County (Vice-President, 1979-1980, Secretary-Treasurer, 1978-1979, Director, 1977-1978 and Member, Administration of Justice Committee, 1989-1993; Member, Client Relations Committee, 1974-1996; Chairman, Bench and Bar Committee, 1977-1979) and American (Vice-Chairman, Committee on Public Relations, Section of General Practice, 1978-1980; Member, Sections on: Litigation; General Practice; Economics of Law Practice, 1986—) Bar Associations; State Bar of California (Member, Executive Committee, Legal Services Section, 1974-1977; Delegate, California State Bar Conference, 1984-1996). (Certified Specialist, Family Law, The State Bar of California Board of Legal Specialization). *PRACTICE AREAS:* Business Litigation; Closely Held Businesses; Family Law; Estate Planning; Estate Litigation.

**ANTHONY R. RUSSELL,** born York, Pennsylvania, January 17, 1947; admitted to bar, 1974, California; 1975, U.S. District Court, Southern and Central Districts of California. *Education:* York Junior College; Pennsylvania State University (B.S., summa cum laude 1972); University of San Diego (J.D., 1974). Phi Kappa Phi. Moot Court Best Oralist. Teaching Assistant, Business Law and Management, Pennsylvania State University, 1971-1972. *Member:* Orange County Bar Association; State Bar of California. [With USN, 1966-1970]. *PRACTICE AREAS:* Limited Liability Companies; Business Organization; Buying and Selling of Businesses; Corporate Contracts; Partnership and Commercial; Real Estate; Estate Planning.

---

## SELF & BHAMRE
### 4400 MACARTHUR BOULEVARD, SUITE 320
### NEWPORT BEACH, CALIFORNIA 92660
Telephone: 714-955-0230
Fax: 714-955-0240

*General Business Transactional and Litigation including Civil and Trial Practice, State and Federal Courts, Corporations, Contract, Transactional, Securities, Employment, Commercial, Professional Negligence, Taxation, Estate Planning, Probate and Trust Administration and Wills.*

*FIRM PROFILE:* Self & Bhamre, formed in March, 1993, is committed to providing sound, timely legal advice, for transactional and litigation matters, to our clients at a fair and reasonable cost. Our clients are primarily individuals and corporations involved in a broad range of businesses. Self & Bhamre utilizes the latest technology in its law practice.

**MICHAEL C. SELF,** born Los Angeles, California, July 2, 1958; admitted to bar, 1987, California. *Education:* University of California at Berkeley (B.S., 1980); McGeorge School of Law, University of the Pacific (J.D., with distinction, 1987). Member, Traynor Society. Certified Public Accountant, California, 1983. *Member:* The State Bar of California; American Bar Association (Member, Business Law Section); California Society of Certified Public Accountants. *PRACTICE AREAS:* Corporate Law; Contract; Commercial Law; Securities; Transactional.

**HEMA CHRISTINE BHAMRE,** born London, England, July 28, 1962; admitted to bar, 1987, California; 1988, U.S. District Court, Central District of California; 1995, U.S. District Court, Southern District of California. *Education:* University of California at Davis (B.A., 1984); McGeorge School of Law, University of the Pacific (J.D., 1987). Member: Traynor Moot Court Team; National Moot Court Team. *Member:* Orange County Bar Association; State Bar of California. *PRACTICE AREAS:* Civil Litigation; Professional Negligence; Employment Litigation.

---

**GEORGE D. STRAGGAS,** born Oakland, California, January 18, 1960; admitted to bar, 1987, California; 1988, U.S. District Court, Central District of California; 1990, U.S. District Court, Eastern District of California and U.S. Court of Appeals, Ninth Circuit. *Education:* University of California (A.B., 1983); McGeorge School of Law (J.D., 1987). *Member:* Los Angeles County Bar Association; State Bar of California. *PRACTICE AREAS:* Civil Litigation; Financial Services; Commercial Litigation.

### OF COUNSEL

**CRAIG C. ALEXANDER,** born Pasadena, California, June 23, 1952; admitted to bar, 1977, California; 1978, U.S. Tax Court. *Education:* University of San Diego and Northern Arizona University (B.S., in Accountancy, magna cum laude, 1974); Hastings College of Law, University of California (J.D., 1977). Phi Kappa Phi; Beta Gamma Sigma; Kappa Sigma. Panelist, "Estate Planning for Owners of Closely Held Businesses," Continuing Education of the Bar Program, 1984; "Fundamentals of Estate Planning," CEB, 1991; "Will Drafting," CEB 1992; "Using Trusts," CEB 1993. Instructor on: Employee Benefits, University of Southern California College of Continuing Education, 1985; Pension and Profit Sharing Plans, University of California, Irvine Extension, 1985-1988. *Member:* Orange County Bar Association; (Member, Probate and Trust Law Section; Delegate, State Bar Conference of Delegates, 1986-1994; Arbitrator, Mandatory Fee Arbitration, 1986-1992); State Bar of California (Member: Estate Planning Section ; Taxation Section); Orange Coast Estate Planning Council. *PRACTICE AREAS:* Estate Planning; Probate; Estate Administration; Pension and Profit Sharing Plans; Taxation.

---

## SEVERSON & WERSON
### A PROFESSIONAL CORPORATION
### 4675 MACARTHUR COURT, SUITE 370
### NEWPORT BEACH, CALIFORNIA 92660
Telephone: 714-442-7110
Facsimile: 714-442-7118

*San Francisco, California Office:* Twenty-Fifth Floor, 1 Embarcadero Center. Telephone: 415-398-3344. Telecopier: 415-956-0439.

*General Civil Practice in State and Federal Courts and Administrative Agencies, Appeals, Commercial and Consumer Lending Transactions, Work-outs and Bankruptcy, Construction, Professional Liability, Environmental, Insurance, Publishing, Employment Relations, Real Estate, Securities, Franchising, Corporate, Tax, Estate Planning and Probate.*

*(This Listing Continued)*

## CALIFORNIA—NEWPORT BEACH

**SEVERSON & WERSON, A PROFESSIONAL CORPORATION,**
Newport Beach—Continued

FIRM PROFILE: When Severson & Werson was founded in 1945 it provided litigation services to financial institutions. The firm has expanded both its areas of expertise and the industries it serves. In addition to major financial institutions, the firm represents construction companies, design professionals, development companies, insurance companies, manufacturers, franchise and service organizations, and a wide variety of corporations and substantial individuals. The firm's philosophy is to provide cost effective approaches to legal matters, including alternative arrangements to customary hourly rates.

**LORAINE P. EBER,** born Washington, D.C., September 29, 1955; admitted to bar, 1981, California and U.S. District Court, Northern District of California; 1982, Illinois and U.S. District Court, Northern District of Illinois. *Education:* Pennsylvania State University; San Francisco State University (B.A., 1978); Hastings College of Law, University of California (J.D., 1981). Member: Order of the Coif; Thurston Society. Recipient, Milton Green Citation, First Year Section Award. Member of Staff, Hastings Law Journal, 1980-1981. Author: "The Battered Wife's Dilemma: To Kill or to be Killed," 32 Hastings Law Journal 895, 1981. *Member:* Illinois State and American Bar Associations; State Bar of California. *Email:* lpe@severson.com

**CAROLYN POWELL,** born Santa Barbara, California, January 5, 1968; admitted to bar, 1992, California, U.S. District Court, Northern and Eastern Districts of California and U.S. Court of Appeals, Ninth Circuit. *Education:* University of California, Berkeley (B.A., with honors, 1989); Boalt Hall School of Law, University of California (J.D., 1992). Phi Beta Kappa. Member, Golden Key Honor Society. *Member:* Orange County Bar Association (Business Litigation Section); Financial Women International. **LANGUAGES:** French, German. **PRACTICE AREAS:** Auto Finance Defense; Professional Malpractice; Insurance Defense; Insurance Coverage. *Email:* cp@severson.com

**KIMBERLY D. TAYLOR,** born Greenwich, Connecticut, July 1, 1967; admitted to bar, 1992, California and U.S. District Court, Central District of California; 1993, U.S. District Court, Southern District of California. *Education:* University of Connecticut (B.S., summa cum laude, 1985; J.D., with honors, 1992). Phi Kappa Phi. Recipient, American Jurisprudence Award for Commercial Law, 1991. *Member:* Orange County Bar Association (Member, Creditor's Rights Committee); Financial Women International. **PRACTICE AREAS:** Business Litigation; Automobile Finance Law; Creditor's Rights. *Email:* kdt@severson.com

References furnished upon request.

(For complete biographical data on all personnel, See Professional Biographies at San Francisco)

---

### SIMS, MORROW & MANNING

A Partnership including a Professional Corporation

*Established in 1984*

**450 NEWPORT CENTER DRIVE, SUITE 250**
**NEWPORT BEACH, CALIFORNIA 92660-7612**
Telephone: 714-721-8101
Fax: 714-721-8661

Insurance, Personal Injury, Railroad, Legal Malpractice, Products and Premises Liability, Construction, Business, Insurance Agent Broker Law, General Civil Litigation.

#### MEMBERS OF FIRM

**WAYNE R. SIMS (A PROFESSIONAL CORPORATION),** born Los Angeles, California, May 26, 1941; admitted to bar, 1966, California; 1969, U.S. District Court, Central District of California; 1971, U.S. District Court, Northern District of California. *Education:* Occidental College (B.A., 1963); Boalt Hall School of Law, University of California (J.D., 1966). *Member:* Los Angeles County and Orange County Bar Associations; State Bar of California; Association of Southern California Defense Counsel; National Association of Railroad Trial Counsel (Vice President, Pacific Region, 1988-1989; National Treasurer, 1992—); American Board of Trial Advocates. [With U.S. Army, Office of the Judge Advocate General, 1967-1968]. **PRACTICE AREAS:** Insurance Defense Law; Railroad Law; Legal Malpractice Law.

**PATRICK JOHN MANNING,** born San Bernardino, California, September 21, 1953; admitted to bar, 1985, California and U.S. District Court, Central and Southern Districts of California; 1986, U.S. Court of Appeals, Ninth Circuit. *Education:* Lewis and Clark College (B.S., 1979; J.D., 1982). Managing Editor, Environmental Law, 1982. Author: "The Implication Doctrine Under the Federal Water Pollution Control Act Amendments of 1972," Environmental Law, 1982. Judicial Clerk, Oregon Court of Appeals, 1983-1984. *Member:* Orange County Bar Association; State Bar of California. **PRACTICE AREAS:** Insurance Defense Law; Legal Malpractice Law.

**WILLIAM D. MORROW,** born Lynwood, California, December 24, 1954; admitted to bar, 1982, California and U.S. District Court, Central and Southern Districts of California. *Education:* Claremont Men's College (B.A., 1977); Pepperdine University School of Law (J.D., 1981); Oxford University, England (Public International Law, 1980). *Member:* Orange County Bar Association (Member: Insurance Advisory Committee; Insurance, Construction and Real Estate Sections); State Bar of California; Association of Southern California Defense Counsel. **PRACTICE AREAS:** Construction Defect Litigation; Land Subsidence.

---

**DAVID A. SPROWL,** born Indianapolis, Indiana, April 10, 1954; admitted to bar, 1979, California; 1983, U.S. District Court, Northern, Eastern and Southern Districts of California; 1997, U.S. District Court, Central District of California. *Education:* Pepperdine University (B.A., 1976); Pepperdine University School of Law (J.D., 1979). Principal Member, Technical Committee of Fire Investigation. National Fire Protection Association, 1993—. *Member:* Orange County Bar Association; State Bar of California.

**RALPH F. POPELAR, JR.,** born San Diego, California, September 30, 1952; admitted to bar, 1983, California, U.S. District Court, Central District of California and U.S. Court of Appeals, Ninth Circuit. *Education:* California State University, Northridge (B.A., 1974); University of La Verne College (J.D., 1977). *Member:* Orange County Bar Association; State Bar of California.

**SELIM MOUNEDJI,** born Algiers, Algeria, December 12, 1959; admitted to bar, 1994, California. *Education:* University of Southern California (B.S., 1983; M.S., 1985); Loyola Law School of Los Angeles (J.D., 1994). Phi Delta Phi. St. Thomas Moore Honor Society. Recipient, American Jurisprudence Awards of Excellence in Evidence, Trusts and Wills. Articles Editor, 1993; Staff Member, 1992, Loyola of Los Angeles Law Review. *Member:* State Bar of California. **LANGUAGES:** French and Arabic.

**LEONARD T. FINK,** born Brooklyn, New York, September 29, 1967; admitted to bar, 1994, California. *Education:* Arizona State University (B.S. in Accounting, 1989); Institute of International and Corporation Law, London, England (Summer, 1991); University of San Diego (J.D., 1993). Member, Appellate Moot Court Board, University of San Diego, 1992-1993. *Member:* State Bar of California.

**MICHAEL E. MURPHY,** born Panorama City, California, July 3, 1968; admitted to bar, 1994, California and U.S. District Court, Central District of California. *Education:* Pepperdine University (B.S., 1991; J.D., 1994). Judicial Extern, Justice Armand Arasian, California Supreme Court, 1993. *Member:* Ventura County Bar Association; State Bar of California.

**CHRISTOPHER A. WHITE,** born Van Nuys, California, March 18, 1964; admitted to bar, 1991, California and U.S. District Court, Central District of California. *Education:* University of California at Berkeley (B.A., with honors in Political Science, 1987); Loyola of Los Angeles (J.D., 1990). Dean's Award Winner. *Member:* Orange County and American Bar Associations; State Bar of California; Association of Southern California Defense Counsel. (Resident).

**ANDERSON M. SIMMONS,** born Quantico, Virginia, November 10, 1963; admitted to bar, 1995, California and U.S. District Court, Central District of California. *Education:* Institute of Electronic Science at Texas A&M University (Certification, 1983); University of Texas at Austin (B.A., 1989); Case Western Reserve University, Cleveland, Ohio (J.D., cum laude, 1995). First Place Winner of 1995 California Bankruptcy Journal Joseph Bernfeld Writing Competition. *Member:* State Bar of California.

**THOMAS W. OVERTON,** born Greenwich, Connecticut, July 21, 1966; admitted to bar, 1995, California, U.S. District Court, Central District of California and U.S. Court of Appeals, Ninth Circuit. *Education:* University of Southern California (B.A., English, departmental honors, 1992); University of California at Los Angeles (J.D., 1995). Executive Editor, UCLA Law Review (1994-1995); Staff, 1993-1994. Author: Comment, "Lawyers, Lightbulbs and Dead Snakes: The Lawyer Joke as Societal Text," 42 UCLA L. Rev. 1069 (1995). *Member:* State Bar of California.

*(This Listing Continued)*

## PROFESSIONAL BIOGRAPHIES

CALIFORNIA—NEWPORT BEACH

REPRESENTATIVE CLIENTS: Golden Eagle Insurance Co.; Southern Pacific Transportation Co.; National Railroad Passenger Corp. aka Amtrak; Union Pacific Railroad; Atchison Topeka & Santa Fe Railway; Maryland Casualty Co.; Amerisure, Inc.; Lawyers Mutual Insurance Co.; Travelers Insurance Co.; Reliance Insurance Co.; Carl Warrne & Co.

### ALTON J. SMITH
*A PROFESSIONAL CORPORATION*

Established in 1987

610 NEWPORT CENTER DRIVE, SUITE 700
**NEWPORT BEACH, CALIFORNIA 92660**
Telephone: 714-760-8800
Fax: 714-760-9204

*General Civil and Trial Practice. Medical Malpractice, Insurance, Bad Faith Litigation, Personal Injury, and Products Liability.*

**ALTON J. SMITH,** born Phoenix, Arizona, October 25, 1948; admitted to bar, 1978, California and U.S. District Court, Southern District of California; 1982, U.S. District Court, Central District of California. *Education:* University of the Pacific (B.A., 1972); Western State University (J.D., 1978). Master Bencher, American Inns of Court Foundation. *Member:* Orange County and American Bar Associations; State Bar of California; California Trial Lawyers Association; Orange County Trial Lawyers Association (Board Member, 1988-1990); The Association of Trial Lawyers of America; American Board of Trial Advocates.

*LEGAL SUPPORT PERSONNEL*
**LESLIE BONING** (Paralegal).

### STEVEN L. STERN
610 NEWPORT CENTER DRIVE, SUITE 1000
**NEWPORT BEACH, CALIFORNIA 92660**
Telephone: 714-640-9193
Fax: 714-640-0714

*General Business, Corporate and Partnership, Finance, Real Estate and Commercial Employment, Business and Commercial Litigation in all State and Federal Courts, Probate and Trust Litigation, Employment Law and Creditor's Rights.*

**STEVEN L. STERN,** born New York, N.Y., August 17, 1943; admitted to bar, 1969, California, U.S. Tax Court and U.S. Court of Military Appeals; 1985, District of Columbia. *Education:* Stanford University (B.A., with great distinction, 1965); Harvard University (J.D., magna cum laude, 1968). Phi Beta Kappa. *Member:* Los Angeles County and Orange County (Member, Executive Committee, Real Estate Law Section, 1992—) Bar Associations; The State Bar of California; The District of Columbia Bar. [1st Lt., U.S. Army Reserve, 1969]. *LANGUAGES:* German. **PRACTICE AREAS:** Business; Real Estate Litigation; Construction Law.

REPRESENTATIVE CLIENTS: Allergan Inc.; Commercial Coolins Inc.; Coast Sign Bio Play Inc.; Taget Express Inc.; Lee Jennings Enterprises Inc.; QCP Construction Inc.; Artesa Fabrics Inc.; Black Flys Eyewear LLC; Hot Lava Magazine; ILSI America Inc.; Newport Orthopedic Inc.

### EDWARD H. STONE, P.C.
270 NEWPORT CENTER DRIVE
**NEWPORT BEACH, CALIFORNIA 92660-7535**
Telephone: 714-640-2812
Fax: 714-640-9951

*Estate Planning, Probate and Business Planning.*

**EDWARD H. STONE,** born Chicago, Illinois, July 20, 1939; admitted to bar, 1967, Illinois; 1968, U.S. District Court, Northern District of Illinois and U.S. Tax Court; 1970, California; 1974, U.S. District Court, Southern District of California. *Education:* University of Illinois (B.S. in Accounting, 1961); John Marshall Law School (J.D., 1965). Phi Alpha Delta (President, Alumni Chapter, 1975-1976). Internal Revenue Service, Income Tax, Organized Crime and Estate Tax Divisions, 1962-1971. President, Jewish Family Services of Orange County, 1975. Vice President and Director, Jewish Community Foundation of Orange County, 1985-1993; Director, Jewish Home For Aging, Orange County (Heritage Pointe) 1992-1994. Member, The Wellness Community, Orange County, 1994. *Member:* Orange County (Chairman and Co-Chairman, Continuing Education of the Bar, 1975-1994; Director, 1977-1982; Vice-Chairman, 1976-1977 and

*(This Listing Continued)*

Chairman, 1977-1978, Estate Planning, Probate and Trust Law Section; Chair, Real Property & Probate for State Bar Convention, 1992—; CEB Joint Advisory Committee, Probate & Estate Planning Subcommittee, 1991—) and American (Member, Section on: Income Tax; Real Property, Probate and Trust Law) Bar Associations; State Bar of California (Member, Section on Estate Planning). (Certified Specialist, Probate, Estate Planning and Trust Law, The State Bar of California Board of Legal Specialization).
**REPORTED CASES:** Estate of Pittman, 104 CAL. APP. 3d 288.

### STRADLING, YOCCA, CARLSON & RAUTH
*A PROFESSIONAL CORPORATION*

660 NEWPORT CENTER DRIVE, SUITE 1600
**NEWPORT BEACH, CALIFORNIA 92660-6441**
Telephone: 714-725-4000
Facsimile: 714-725-4100

Mailing Address: P.O. Box 7680, 92658-7680

*San Francisco, California Office:* 44 Montgomery Street, Suite 2950, 94104-4803. Telephone: 415-765-9180. Facsimile: 415-765-9187.

*General Business, Corporate and Partnership, Corporate Securities, Finance, Taxation, Real Estate and Real Estate Finance, Banking, Commercial, Labor, Administrative, Estate Planning, Trusts, Probate, ERISA, Municipal, Municipal Finance, Water Law and Redevelopment Law. General Civil Practice and Litigation in all State and Federal Courts.*

**FRITZ R. STRADLING,** born Green Bay, Wisconsin, November 14, 1926; admitted to bar, 1950, Wisconsin; 1954, California; 1970, U.S. Supreme Court. *Education:* University of Wisconsin (B.B.A., 1948; LL.B., 1950). Phi Delta Phi. *Member:* Orange County and American Bar Associations; State Bar of Wisconsin; The State Bar of California; California Association of Bond Lawyers.

**NICK E. YOCCA,** born Windber, Pennsylvania, December 9, 1929; admitted to bar, 1959, California. *Education:* University of Pittsburgh (A.B., 1951); University of Michigan (J.D., with distinction, 1958). Order of the Coif. Assistant Editor, Michigan Law Review, 1957-1958. *Member:* Los Angeles County, Orange County and American Bar Associations; The State Bar of California; American Judicature Society.

**C. CRAIG CARLSON,** born Grand Island, Nebraska, September 5, 1942; admitted to bar, 1969, California; 1970, U.S. Tax Court. *Education:* University of Southern California (B.S., cum laude, 1964; J.D., 1968). Beta Gamma Sigma. Certified Public Accountant, California, 1969. *Member:* Orange County and American Bar Associations; The State Bar of California.

**WILLIAM R. RAUTH III,** born New York, N.Y., March 9, 1944; admitted to bar, 1970, California. *Education:* University of California at Santa Barbara (A.B., with honors, 1966); University of California at Berkeley (J.D., 1969). Order of the Coif. *Member:* Orange County and American Bar Associations; The State Bar of California.

**K. C. SCHAAF,** born Glenwood Springs, Colorado, February 17, 1948; admitted to bar, 1973, California. *Education:* University of Colorado at Boulder (B.S.E., with special honors, 1970); Stanford University (J.D., 1973). *Member:* Orange County (Member, Corporate Law Section) and American Bar Associations; The State Bar of California.

**RICHARD C. GOODMAN,** born New York, N.Y., August 7, 1945; admitted to bar, 1971, California. *Education:* University of California at Berkeley (B.A., 1967); University of California at Los Angeles (J.D., 1970). Member, University of California at Los Angeles Law Review, 1969-1970. Author: "Privacy and Political Freedom: Application of the Fourth Amendment to National Security Investigations," 17 U.C.L.A. Law Review, 1205-50, 1970. *Member:* Orange County, Federal and American Bar Associations; The State Bar of California.

**JOHN J. MURPHY,** born Buffalo, New York, March 10, 1944; admitted to bar, 1970, California. *Education:* Canisius College (B.S., 1966); Loyola University, Rome, Italy; University of Virginia (LL.B., 1969). *Member:* Orange County Bar Association; The State Bar of California.

**THOMAS P. CLARK, JR.,** born New York, N.Y., September 16, 1943; admitted to bar, 1973, California. *Education:* University of Notre Dame (A.B., 1965); University of Missouri-Kansas City (J.D., 1973). Phi Kappa Phi. Member, Bench and Robe. Member, University of Missouri-Kansas City Law Review, 1972-1973. Editor-in-Chief, The Urban Lawyer, 1972-1973. Author: "Strategies for Metropolitan Stabilization," University of Missouri-Kansas City Law Review, Vol. 41, 1972; "First Amendment: Con-

*(This Listing Continued)*

CAA1429B

## STRADLING, YOCCA, CARLSON & RAUTH, A PROFESSIONAL CORPORATION, Newport Beach—Continued

gressional Investigation and the Speech or Debate Clause," University of Missouri-Kansas City Law Review, Vol. 40, 1971; "Growth Control in California: Prospects for Local Implementation of Timing and Sequential Control of Residential Development," 5 Pacific Law Journal 570, 1974; "The Relationship of Just Compensation to the Land Use Regulatory Power: An Analysis and Proposal," Symposium-Land Use Planning and Control, Pepperdine Law Review, Vol. 2, 1974. *Member:* Orange County Bar Association; The State Bar of California. [Capt., U.S. Marine Corps, 1966-1970]

**BEN A. FRYDMAN,** born Stuttgart, Germany, January 12, 1947; admitted to bar, 1973, California. *Education:* University of California at Los Angeles (A.B., cum laude, 1968); Harvard University (J.D., cum laude, 1973). Phi Beta Kappa. *Member:* Orange County and American Bar Associations; The State Bar of California.

**DAVID R. MCEWEN,** born Greeley, Colorado, January 19, 1946; admitted to bar, 1975, California. *Education:* University of California at Los Angeles (B.A., 1968); Loyola University of Los Angeles (J.D., cum laude, 1975). Member of Staff, Loyola of Los Angeles Law Review, 1974-1975. Author: "Land-Use Controls, Externalities and the Municipal Affairs Doctrine; A Border Conflict," 8 Loyola Law Review 432, 1975. City Attorney: City of Lynwood, 1981-1984; City of Lancaster, 1987—. *Member:* Orange County Bar Association; The State Bar of California.

**PAUL L. GALE,** born Los Angeles, California, November 13, 1950; admitted to bar, 1975, California; 1976, U.S. District Court, Central District of California; 1977, U.S. District Court, Southern District of California; 1979, U.S. District Court, Northern District of California and U.S. Court of Appeals, Ninth Circuit; 1983, U.S. Supreme Court; 1991, U.S. District Court, Eastern District of California; 1996, U.S. Court of Appeals, Federal Circuit. *Education:* University of California at Los Angeles (A.B., magna cum laude, 1972; J.D., 1975). Phi Beta Kappa. Member, U.C.L.A. Law Review, 1974-1975. Extern, Law Clerk to the Honorable Harold H. Greene, Chief Judge, District of Columbia Superior Court, 1974. Delegate, 1990 State Bar Convention. Judge Pro Tem, Orange County Superior Court, 1986—. Pro Tem Settlement Judge, Orange County Superior Court, 1991—. Member, Panel of Arbitrators, American Arbitration Association. *Member:* Orange County (Elected, Board of Directors, 1992-1994; Member, Business Litigation Section, Chairman, Law and Motion Committee, 1986; Member, Resolutions Committee), Federal and American Bar Associations; The State Bar of California.

**RUDOLPH C. SHEPARD,** born Philadelphia, Pennsylvania, August 14, 1941; admitted to bar, 1970, California. *Education:* University of Southern California (B.S., 1963; M.A., 1966); University of California School of Law at Los Angeles (J.D., 1967). Certified Public Accountant, California, 1969. *Member:* Orange County Bar Association; The State Bar of California; American Institute of Certified Public Accountants; California Society of Certified Public Accountants.

**ROBERT J. KANE,** born New York, N.Y., December 3, 1946; admitted to bar, 1972, California; 1973, U.S. District Court, Central District of California; 1978, U.S. Court of Appeals, Ninth Circuit; 1979, U.S. Supreme Court. *Education:* St. John's University (B.A., 1968); New York University (J.D., 1971). Member, Board of Editors, New York University Law Review, 1970-1971. *Member:* Orange County (Member, Labor Law Section) and American (Member, Labor and Employment Law Section) Bar Associations; The State Bar of California.

**BRUCE C. STUART,** born Pasadena, California, January 18, 1952; admitted to bar, 1976, California; 1977, U.S. District Court, Central District of California. *Education:* Dartmouth College (A.B., cum laude, 1973); University of California at Los Angeles (J.D., 1976). *Member:* Orange County and American (Member, Sections on: Corporation, Banking and Business Law; Real Property, Probate and Trust Law) Bar Associations; The State Bar of California (Member, Real Property Section).

**E. KURT YEAGER,** born Boston, Massachusetts, December 12, 1953; admitted to bar, 1978, California. *Education:* University of California at Davis (A.B., with highest honors, 1975); University of California at Berkeley, Boalt Hall School of Law (J.D., 1978). Member and Associate Editor, Ecology Law Quarterly, 1975-1978. City Attorney, City of Lynwood, California, 1984-1987. *Member:* Orange County Bar Association; The State Bar of California (Member, Public Law Section); National Association of Bond Lawyers.

**ROBERT J. WHALEN,** born Boston, Massachusetts, September 10, 1953; admitted to bar, 1978, California. *Education:* Harvard University (A.B., cum laude, 1975); Boalt Hall School of Law, University of California (J.D., 1978). Executive Editor, Ecology Law Quarterly, 1977-1978. Law Clerk to Hon. Edward J. Schwartz, U.S. District Judge, Southern District of California, 1978-1979. Member, Board of Directors, Boalt Hall Alumni Association and Laguna Beach Education Foundation. *Member:* Orange County and American Bar Associations; The State Bar of California (Member, Legal Services Section); National Association of Bond Lawyers; Orange County Bar Foundation (Member, Board of Directors).

**ROBERT E. RICH,** born New York, N.Y., August 24, 1950; admitted to bar, 1975, California; 1976, U.S. District Court, Central District of California; 1977, U.S. Court of Appeals, Ninth Circuit. *Education:* University of California at Los Angeles (B.A., magna cum laude, 1972; J.D., 1975). Phi Beta Kappa. Member, University of California at Los Angeles Law Review, 1973-1975. Member, Moot Court Honors Program, University of California at Los Angeles, 1973-1975. *Member:* Orange County (Member, Business Law Section) and American (Member, Business Law and Intellectual Property Law Sections) Bar Associations; The State Bar of California (Member, Business Law Section).

**RANDALL J. SHERMAN,** born Warren, Ohio, October 22, 1954; admitted to bar, 1979, California, U.S. District Court, Central District of California and U.S. Court of Appeals, Ninth Circuit; 1983, U.S. Supreme Court. *Education:* University of California at Irvine and University of California at Los Angeles (B.A., cum laude, 1976); University of Southern California (J.D., 1979). Order of the Coif. Member, Southern California Law Review, 1977-1979. *Member:* Orange County (Member, Business Litigation Section) and American (Member, Litigation Section) Bar Associations; The State Bar of California (Member, Litigation Section).

**BRUCE FEUCHTER,** born Santa Monica, California, January 1, 1953; admitted to bar, 1979, California. *Education:* University of California at Berkeley (B.A., 1975; M.B.A., 1979); Hastings College of the Law, University of California (J.D., 1979). Phi Alpha Phi; Order of the Coif. Member, Thurston Society. Editor and Author: "The United States Domestic International Sales Corporation: An Analysis of its Objectives and Effects," Hastings International and Comparative Law Review, Inaugural Issue, Spring, 1977. *Member:* Orange County and American Bar Associations; The State Bar of California.

**MARK J. HUEBSCH,** born Los Angeles, California, May 9, 1951; admitted to bar, 1975, California; 1977, U.S. District Court, Central District of California. *Education:* University of Southern California (A.B., magna cum laude, 1972) Phi Beta Kappa; University of California at Los Angeles (J.D., 1975). Deputy City Attorney, 1978-1979 and Assistant City Attorney, 1980-1981, Costa Mesa. *Member:* The State Bar of California; American Bar Association; National Association of Housing and Redevelopment Officials.

**DAVID G. CASNOCHA** (Resident, San Francisco Office).

**KAREN A. ELLIS,** born Hedgesville, West Virginia, July 18, 1938; admitted to bar, 1980, District of Columbia; 1987, California. *Education:* George Mason University (B.A., with honors, 1971); University of Virginia (M.A., 1978); Catholic University of America (J.D., 1979). *Member:* State Bar of California (Member, Public Law Section); American Bar Association (Member, Committee on Affordable Housing and Community Development Law); Orange County Womens Bar Association; National Association of Bond Lawyers.

**BRUCE D. MAY,** born Oakland, California, October 21, 1954; admitted to bar, 1979, California; 1980, U.S. District Court, Central District of California and U.S. Court of Appeals, Ninth Circuit; 1985, U.S. District Court, Southern District of California. *Education:* University of California at Berkeley (A.B., 1976); University of California at Los Angeles (J.D., 1979). Judge Pro Tem, Los Angeles Municipal Court, 1984—. Author: "Early Retirement Incentives and Age Discrimination in Employment," Labor & Employment Law News, Vol. 5, No. 2, 1986. Co-author: "Labor Relations Column," Personnel Journal , 1984—; "Employee Termination Handbook," John Wiley & Sons, N.Y., 1986. Instructor, University of California Extension, Wrongful Termination of Employment, 1987. *Member:* Los Angeles County, Orange County and American (Member, Section on Labor and Employment Law) Bar Associations; State Bar of California (Member, Labor and Employment Law Section). **REPORTED CASES:** Todd Shipyards v. City of Los Angeles (1982) 130 Cal. App. 3d 222, 181 Cal. App. 3d 222, 181 Cal. Rptr. 652, hrng. denied; Santos v. Todd Pacific Shipyards Corporation, 585 F.Supp. 482 (C.D. Cal. 1984) Todd Pacific Shipyards Corporation, 81 L.A. 1095 (1983) (E. Jones, Arb.).

**ANDREW F. PUZDER,** born Cleveland, Ohio, July 11, 1950; admitted to bar, 1978, Missouri, U.S. Court of Appeals, Eighth Circuit and U.S. Dis-

*(This Listing Continued)*

trict Court, Eastern and Western Districts of Missouri; 1980, U.S. Court of Appeals, Ninth Circuit; 1982, Nevada and U.S. District Court, District of Nevada; 1983, U.S. Supreme Court 1990, California; 1992, U.S. District Court, Central District of California. *Education:* Cleveland State University (B.A., 1975); Washington University (J.D., 1978). Phi Alpha Theta. Editor, Washington University Law Quarterly, 1977-1978. *Member:* The Missouri Bar; State Bar of Nevada; State Bar of California.

**DONALD J. HAMMAN,** born Downey, California, November 5, 1955; admitted to bar, 1980, California; 1982, U.S. District Court, Central District of California; 1985, U.S. District Court, Southern District of California; 1990, U.S. Court of Appeals, Ninth Circuit and U.S. District Court, Eastern District of California. *Education:* University of California at Santa Barbara (B.A., with high honors, 1977); Hastings College of Law, University of California (J.D., 1980). Order of the Coif. Member, Thurston Society. *Member:* Orange County (Member, Business Litigation, Toxics and Environmental Law and Real Estate Law Sections) and Federal Bar Associations; The State Bar of California (Member, Litigation, Real Estate and Environmental Sections).

**JOHN J. SWIGART, JR.,** born Los Angeles, California, July 29, 1947; admitted to bar, 1980, California. *Education:* Princeton University (B.A., 1969); Boston University (M.S.B.A., 1977); Hastings College of Law, University of California (J.D., 1980). Member, Communications/Entertainment Law Review, 1978-1979. *Member:* Orange County Bar Association (Member, Section on: Estate Planning, Probate and Trust Law); State Bar of California (Member, Section on: Estate Planning, Probate and Trust Law); Orange Coast Estate Planning Council. [Lt. U.S. Navy, 1970-1977]. (Certified Specialist, Probate, Estate Planning and Trust Law, The State Bar of California Board of Legal Specialization).

**CELESTE STAHL BRADY,** born Cincinnati, Ohio, June 5, 1955; admitted to bar, 1980, California and U.S. District Court, Southern District of California. *Education:* San Diego State University (B.S., Public Admin., magna cum laude, 1977); University of San Diego (J.D., 1980). Phi Kappa Phi; Mortar Board. *Member:* Orange County and American (Member, Public Law Section) Bar Associations; The State Bar of California (Member, Public Law Section); Orange County City Attorneys Association; National Association of Housing and Redevelopment Officials; Community Redevelopment Agencies Association.

**CHRISTOPHER J. KILPATRICK,** born Lynwood, California, January 8, 1957; admitted to bar, 1982, California. *Education:* University of California at Irvine (B.A., summa cum laude, 1979); University of California at Los Angeles (J.D., 1982). Member, Moot Court. Member, UCLA-Alaska Law Review, 1981-1982. *Member:* Orange County Bar Association (Member, Corporate Law Section); State Bar of California.

**DOUGLAS S. BROWN,** born Pittsburgh, Pennsylvania, August 8, 1957; admitted to bar, 1983, New York; 1985, California. *Education:* Princeton University (A.B., 1979); Columbia University (J.D., 1982).

**JULIE McCOY AKINS,** born Dallas, Texas, August 14, 1958; admitted to bar, 1983, Texas; 1987, California and U.S. District Court, Central District of California. *Education:* Baylor University (B.A., cum laude, 1980); Southern Methodist University (J.D., 1983). Order of the Coif. Member, Jessup Moot Court Team, 1981-1983. Notes and Comments Editor, Journal of Air Law and Commerce, 1982-1983. *Member:* Orange County and Federal (Director and Officer, Orange County Chapter) Bar Associations; State Bar of California; California Women Lawyers; Orange County Women Lawyers; Peter M. Elliott Inn of Court.

**LAWRENCE B. COHN,** born New York, N.Y., November 2, 1949; admitted to bar, 1984, California. *Education:* University of California at Santa Cruz (A.B., 1971); University of Oregon (M.A., 1972); Loyola Marymount University (J.D., magna cum laude, 1984). Member: St. Thomas More Law Honor Society. Member, 1982-1983 and Articles Editor, 1983-1984, Loyola Law Review. *Member:* Orange County and American Bar Associations; The State Bar of California; Licensing Executives Society.

**STEPHEN T. FREEMAN,** born Detroit, Michigan, September 12, 1958; admitted to bar, 1984, Michigan; 1987, California. *Education:* University of Michigan at Dearborn (B.B.A., 1980); University of Detroit (J.D., summa cum laude, 1984). Alpha Sigma Nu. Member, 1982-1984 and Managing Editor, 1983-1984, University of Detroit Law Review. Recipient, Best Brief Award, National Moot Court Competition. Adjunct Lecturer, Corporate Tax, Masters in Tax Program, Golden Gate University. Author: "Equity Expansion Act of 1993," S.B. 1175, introduced June 29, 1993. *Member:* Los Angeles County, Orange County (Member, Tax Section) and American (Member, Tax Section) Bar Associations; State Bar of Michigan; State Bar of California (Member, Tax Section).

*(This Listing Continued)*

**CAROL L. LEW,** born Los Angeles, California, January 3, 1962; admitted to bar, 1986, California. *Education:* California State University at Northridge (B.A., summa cum laude, 1983); Hastings College of the Law, University of California (J.D., magna cum laude, 19 86). Order of the Coif. Member, Thurston Society. Note Editor, Constitutional Law Quarterly, 1985-1986. *Member:* The State Bar of California (Co-Chair, Income/Other Taxes Committee of Taxation Section, 1994-1996); American Bar Association (Secretary, Tax Section, Tax-exempt Financing Committee, 1993-1995, Chair, Task Force on Change in Use, Tax Section, Tax-exempt Financing Committee, 1995-1997); National Association of Bond Lawyers.

**MICHAEL E. FLYNN,** born Munich, Germany, May 30, 1960; admitted to bar, 1985, California; 1988, U.S. District Court, Central District of California. *Education:* University of Notre Dame (B.B.A., 1982); Loyola Law School, Los Angeles (J.D., 1985). St. Thomas More Law Honor Society (President, 1984-1985). Editor, Loyola of Los Angeles International and Comparative Law Journal, 1984-1985. *Member:* Orange County, Los Angeles County and American (Member, Business Law Section) Bar Associations; State Bar of California.

**JULIE M. PORTER,** born Los Angeles, California, September 15, 1959; admitted to bar, 1985, California; 1986, U.S. District Court, Central and Southern Districts of California. *Education:* Loyola Marymount University, Loyola University of Los Angeles (B.S., magna cum laude, 1981; J.D., cum laude, 1985). St. Thomas More Honor Society. Member, Loyola Law School National Trial Advocacy Team. Staff Member, Loyola International and Comparative Law Review, 1984-1985. American Bar Association, Ninth Circuit Governor, Law Student Division Representative, 1984-1985. *Member:* Orange County Bar Association (Member, Employment Law Section); State Bar of California.

**GARY A. PEMBERTON,** born San Diego, California, September 26, 1955; admitted to bar, 1986, California and U.S. District Court, Southern, Northern and Central Districts of California; U.S. Court of Appeals, Federal Circuit. *Education:* University of California at Los Angeles (B.A., 1977); Princeton Theological Seminary (M.Div., 1981); University of California, Berkeley (J.D., 1986). Member, Pi Gamma Mu National Social Science Honor Society. *Member:* Orange County Bar Association (Member, Business Litigation Section); The State Bar of California.

**DENISE HARBAUGH HERING,** born Wellington, Kansas, September 5, 1950; admitted to bar, 1987, California. *Education:* Stephens Womens College (A.A., 1970); University of Missouri (B.S., 1972); University of San Diego (J.D., 1987). Member, University of San Diego School of Law Review, 1986-1987. Author: "Must the Foreign Sovereign Immunity Act Bar International Human Rights Claims?" 26 University of San Diego Law Review 3, 1985. *Member:* Orange County and American Bar Association; The State Bar of California (Member, Public Law Section); National Association of Bond Lawyers.

**JON E. GOETZ,** born Los Angeles, California, October 4, 1960; admitted to bar, 1987, California. *Education:* University of California at San Diego (B.A., magna cum laude, 1982); Harvard University (J.D., cum laude, 1987). Author: "Direct Democracy in Land Use Planning: The State Response to Eastlake," 19 Pacific L.J. 793, 1988; 20 Land Use and Environment L. Rev. 203, 1989. *Member:* The State Bar of California (Member, Sections of: Public Law; Real Property); American Bar Association (Member, Sections of: State and Local Government; Affordable Housing).

**RUSSELL A. MILLER** (Resident, San Francisco Office).

**MICHAEL A. ZABLOCKI,** born Brooklyn, New York, June 14, 1944; admitted to bar, 1969, Maryland and U.S. District Court, District of Maryland; 1976, California. *Education:* City University of New York (B.A., 1965); University of California at Los Angeles (M.P.H., 1975); George Washington University (J.D., 1968). Phi Delta Phi. Corporations Counsel, 1977-1980 and Senior Corporations Counsel, 1980-1985, California Department of Corporations, Health Care Service Plan Division. *Member:* State Bar of California; American Bar Association; National Health Lawyers Association; California Society for Healthcare Attorneys.

**NEILA R. BERNSTEIN,** born Liberty, New York, June 23, 1955; admitted to bar, 1980, California, U.S. District Court, Central District of California and U.S. Court of Appeals, Ninth Circuit. *Education:* University of California at Los Angeles (B.A., summa cum laude, 1977) Phi Beta Kappa; University of California at Los Angeles School of Law (J.D., 1980). Associate Editor, U.C.L.A. Law Review, 1979-1980. Author: "Voluntary Affirmative Action after United Steelworkers of America v. Weber," 27 U.C.L.A. Law Review 501, 1980. *Member:* Orange County Bar Association; The State Bar of California.

*(This Listing Continued)*

## STRADLING, YOCCA, CARLSON & RAUTH, A PROFESSIONAL CORPORATION, Newport Beach—Continued

**NICHOLAS J. YOCCA,** born Ann Arbor, Michigan, September 8, 1957; admitted to bar, 1986, California, U.S. District Court, Central District of California and U.S. Court of Appeals, Ninth Circuit. *Education:* Harvard University (A.B., 1983); University of San Diego (J.D., 1985). Licensed Real Estate Broker, California, 1989. *Member:* Orange County and American Bar Associations; State Bar of California.

**J. MICHAEL VAUGHN,** born New Orleans, Louisiana, January 22, 1961; admitted to bar, 1987, California. *Education:* Arizona State University (B.S., cum laude, 1983); University of Southern California (J.D., 1987). Beta Gamma Sigma; Phi Alpha Delta. Recipient, American Jurisprudence Awards in Business Organizations and Bankruptcy. *Member:* Orange County (Member, Business and Corporate Law Section) and American Bar Associations; The State Bar of California.

**JOHN D. IRELAND,** born Ft. Leavenworth, Kansas, November 7, 1962; admitted to bar, 1988, California; U.S. District Court, Central and Northern Districts of California. *Education:* University of California at Los Angeles (B.A., 1984; J.D., 1988). Phi Beta Kappa. *Member:* Orange County (Member, Business Litigation Section) and American Bar Associations; The State Bar of California.

**DAVID H. MANN,** born Sacramento, California, November 12, 1960; admitted to bar, 1988, California and U.S. District Court, Southern District of California; 1990, U.S. District Court, Central District of California and U.S. Court of Appeals, Ninth Circuit. *Education:* California State University at Sacramento (B.S., 1983); Hastings College of the Law, University of California (J.D., 1988). Chief Articles Editor, Hastings International & Comparative Law Review, 1987-1988. Certified Public Accountant, California, 1985. Author: "Hold That Thought - Extending The Legislator's Privilege," Los Angeles Daily Journal, August 2, 1995; "Standards Are Applied to Local Government Self-Insurance Pools," Los Angeles Daily Journal, October 19, 1994; "Why Special Assessments Aren't So Special Anymore," State Bar of California Public Law Journal, Spring 1994; "Property 'Charges' in Localities Escape Prop. 13 Requirements," Los Angeles Daily Journal, March 21, 1994. *Member:* Orange County Bar Association (Member, Sections on: Appellate Law; Environmental Law); The State Bar of California (Member, Public Law and Litigation Sections).

**DOUGLAS J. EVERTZ,** born Torrance, California, October 12, 1960; admitted to bar, 1986, California and U.S. District Court, Central and Southern Districts of California. *Education:* University of San Diego (B.A., 1982); McGeorge School of Law, University of the Pacific (J.D., with distinction, 1985). Member, Traynor Honor Society. Member and Staff Writer, Pacific Law Journal, 1984-1985. Author: Comment, "Two-Tiered Tender Offers and the Poison Pill: The Propriety of a Potent Takeover Defense," 17 Pacific Law Journal 891, 1986. Judge Pro Tem, Orange County Municipal Court, Harbor Judicial District, 1993—. *Member:* Orange County Bar Association (Member, Sections on: Environmental Law; Business Litigation); The State Bar of California (Member, Sections on: Environmental Law; Public Law).

**SEAN TIERNEY** (Resident, San Francisco Office).

**DARRYL S. GIBSON,** born Santa Monica, California, May 27, 1964; admitted to bar, 1989, California, U.S. District Court, Central District of California and U.S. Court of Appeals, Ninth Circuit. *Education:* University of Southern California (B.S., 1986; J.D., 1989). Editor, Hale Moot Court Board, 1988-1989. *Member:* Orange County and American Bar Associations; The State Bar of California.

**JEE HI PARK,** born Seoul, Korea, December 23, 1961; admitted to bar, 1990, California. *Education:* Barnard College (B.A., cum laude, 1984); Manhattan School of Music (M.M., 1986); Hastings College of the Law, University of California (J.D., 1989).

**RICHARD T. NEEDHAM,** born Long Beach, California, December 18, 1964; admitted to bar, 1990, California. *Education:* University of California, Berkeley (B.S., Business Administration, 1987); Loyola Law School (J.D., 1990). Delta Sigma Pi. Licensed Real Estate Broker. *Member:* Orange County (Member, Real Estate Section) and American Bar Associations; State Bar of California. *LANGUAGES:* German.

**ROBERT CRAIG WALLACE,** born Santa Paula, California, January 22, 1965; admitted to bar, 1990, California, U.S. District Court, Central District of California and U.S. Court of Appeals, Ninth Circuit. *Education:* Concordia University, Irvine (B.A., summa cum laude, valedictorian, 1987); University of Southern California (J.D., 1990). Participant, Hale Moot Court Competition, 1988-1989. President, Concordia University Alumni Association. *Member:* Orange County (Member, Business Litigation Section), Federal and American Bar Associations; State Bar of California (Member, Litigation and Public Law Sections).

**JOHN F. CANNON,** born Fullerton, California, May 1, 1964; admitted to bar, 1990, California and U.S. District Court, Central, Southern and Northern Districts of California; U.S. Court of Appeals, Ninth Circuit. *Education:* Loyola Marymount University (B.A., Business, 1986; B.A. History, 1986); Loyola Law School (J.D., 1990). Law Clerk to Senior U.S. District Court Judge Francis C. Whelan, Central District of California, 1990-1991. *Member:* Orange County, Federal and American Bar Associations; State Bar of California.

**DAVID A. HOFFER,** born Groton, Connecticut, August 28, 1963; admitted to bar, 1988, California. *Education:* Stanford University (A.B., 1985); Boalt Hall School of Law, University of California (J.D., 1988). Order of the Coif. Assistant U.S. Attorney, 1990-1995. *Member:* Orange County and Federal Bar Associations; State Bar of California.

**DOUGLAS P. FEICK,** born Cleveland, Ohio, February 18, 1965; admitted to bar, 1991, California. *Education:* Miami University (B.S., 1987); University of Southern California (J.D., 1991). Phi Delta Phi. Staff Member, 1989-1990, and Editor, 1990-1991, Computer/Law and Major Tax Planning Journals. *Member:* Orange County Bar Association; American Bar Association (Member, Sections on: Business Law; Intellectual Property; Science and Technology); State Bar of California (Member, Sections on: Business Law; Intellectual Property).

**MARK L. SKAIST,** born Los Angeles, California, November 8, 1965; admitted to bar, 1991, California. *Education:* University of California at Los Angeles (B.A., 1988); Loyola Law School (J.D., 1991). Order of the Coif. Member, Alpha Sigma Nu Honor Society. Member, St. Thomas More Honor Society. Member, 1989-1990 and Editor, 1990-1991, Loyola of Los Angeles Law Review. *Member:* Orange County Bar Association; State Bar of California (Member, Sections on: Business Law; Intellectual Property).

**JEFFREY B. COYNE,** born Redondo Beach, California, June 20, 1966; admitted to bar, 1991, California. *Education:* Duke University (A.B., 1988); University of Southern California (J.D., 1991). Staff Member, 1989-1990 and Editor, 1990-1991, Major Tax Planning Journal; Computer Law Journal. *Member:* Orange County Bar Association; State Bar of California.

**JOHN E. WOODHEAD, IV,** born Riverside, California, January 6, 1960; admitted to bar, 1992, California. *Education:* University of California at Los Angeles (B.S., 1987); Loyola Law School (J.D., 1991).

**MATTHEW P. THULLEN,** born Baton Rouge, Louisiana, December 29, 1962; admitted to bar, 1993, California. *Education:* University of Michigan (B.A., cum laude, with distinction, 1986; J.D., cum laude, 1992); University of Southern California (M.A., 1989). *Member:* State Bar of California.

**ANDREA LEVITAN REEVES,** born Manhasset, New York, October 27, 1967; admitted to bar, 1993, New York, New Jersey and U.S. District Court, Southern District of New York; 1994, California; U.S. District Court, Central, Northern, Southern and Eastern Districts of California and U.S. Court of Appeals, Ninth and Federal Circuits. *Education:* Cornell University (B.S., 1989); University of Pennsylvania (J.D., 1992). Member, University of Pennsylvania Comparative Labor Law Journal. *Member:* Orange County Bar Association; State Bar of California.

**JOHN DAVID VAUGHAN,** born Flint, Michigan, October 21, 1964; admitted to bar, 1993, California. *Education:* Harvard University (A.B., cum laude, 1987); University of Southern California (J.D., 1993). Extern to Hon. Alex Kozinski, U.S. Court of Appeals for the Ninth Circuit, Pasadena, California, 1992. *Member:* State Bar of California.

**STEVEN M. HANLE,** born Key West, Florida, April 9, 1963; admitted to bar, 1993, California, U.S. Court of Appeals, Ninth Circuit and U.S. District Court, Central, Northern and Southern Districts of California. *Education:* University of California, Los Angeles (B.S., 1986); Loyola Law School, Los Angeles (J.D., 1993). Member: St. Thomas More Law Honor Society; Loyola of Los Angeles Law Review, 1991-1992. Extern to Judge Gary L. Taylor, U.S. District Court, Central District of California, 1992. *Member:* Orange County and Federal Bar Associations; State Bar of California.

**MICHAEL HENNESSEY MULROY,** born Buffalo, New York, March 17, 1966; admitted to bar, 1993, California. *Education:* University of Chicago (B.A., 1988); University of California, Los Angeles (J.D., 1993). *Member:* Orange County Bar Association; State Bar of California.

*(This Listing Continued)*

**MARY ANNE WAGNER,** born Arlington, Virginia, July 24, 1965; admitted to bar, 1993, California. *Education:* San Diego State University (A.B., with distinction, 1987); University of California, Hastings College of the Law (J.D., magna cum laude, 1993). Phi Eta Sigma; Order of the Coif. Member, Thurston Society. Member, 1991-1992 and Executive Articles Editor, 1992-1993, Hastings International and Comparative Law Review. Recipient, American Jurisprudence Awards in Real Property I & II and Trial Advocacy I. Author: "Canadian Rape Shield Statutes," Hastings International and Comparative Law Review, Vol. 16, P. 637. *Member:* Orange County and American Bar Associations; State Bar of California.

**MATTHEW MCQUEEN,** born Pasadena, California, June 19, 1967; admitted to bar, 1993, New Mexico and California; 1994, Texas. *Education:* Williams College (B.A., cum laude, 1989); University of Michigan (J.D., cum laude, 1992; M.S., Natural Resources Policy, 1993). Law Clerk to the Honorable Bruce D. Black, New Mexico Court of Appeals, 1993-1994.

**HOLLY A. ELLIS,** born Houston, Texas, September 8, 1963; admitted to bar, 1993, California, U.S. District Court, Central District of California and U.S. Court of Appeals, Ninth Circuit. *Education:* University of California, Santa Barbara (B.A., with honors, 1989); University of Southern California (J.D., 1993). Member, Hale Moot Court Honors Program. *Member:* State Bar of California.

**WILLIAM E. GARRETT,** born Los Angeles, California, February 8, 1965; admitted to bar, 1993, California. *Education:* University of Pennsylvania (B.S., 1987); Hastings College of the Law (J.D., 1993). *Member:* Orange County Bar Association; The State Bar of California.

**CHRISTOPHER D. IVEY,** born Anaheim, California, July 31, 1968; admitted to bar, 1994, California. *Education:* California State University at Long Beach (B.S., Finance, cum laude, 1990); University of San Diego (J.D., magna cum laude, 1994). Order of the Coif. Member, San Diego Law Review, 1992-1994. *Member:* Orange County Bar Association; State Bar of California. *LANGUAGES:* Spanish.

**H. LEE KOLODNY,** born Los Angeles, California, July 27, 1967; admitted to bar, 1994, California, U.S. District Court, Central District of California and U.S. Court of Appeals, Ninth Circuit. *Education:* Loyola Marymount University (B.B.A., 1989); University of Southern California (M.B.A., 1990; J.D., 1994). Recipient, American Jurisprudence Award in Trial Advocacy.

**GERALD J. RAMIZA,** born Paterson, New Jersey, February 12, 1966; admitted to bar, 1994, California. *Education:* University of Pennsylvania (B.S., 1988); University of California, Davis (J.D., 1994).

**DANIEL GLASSMAN,** born Philadelphia, Pennsylvania, April 7, 1970; admitted to bar, 1995, California, U.S. District Court, Central District of California and U.S. Court of Appeals, Ninth and Federal Circuits. *Education:* Bucknell University (B.S., 1992); University of Southern California (J.D., 1995). Hale Moot Court Honors Program. *Member:* Orange County Bar Association.

**DAVID E. OUTWATER,** born Los Angeles, California, February 23, 1970; admitted to bar, 1995, California. *Education:* California Polytechnic University (B.S., 1992); University of California, Davis (J.D., 1995). Phi Kappa Phi; Order of the Coif. Staff Editor, U.C. Davis Law Review. *Member:* Orange County Bar Association; State Bar of California; Constitutional Rights Foundation.

**JOY HEUSER OTSUKI,** born Los Angeles, California, April 8, 1961; admitted to bar, 1996, California. *Education:* University of California, Santa Barbara (B.A., 1984); Loyola Law School (J.D., 1995). Member, St. Thomas More Honor Society. Recipient, American Jurisprudence Award. Certified Public Accountant, 1989.

**NUMAN J. SIDDIQI,** born Rampur, India, March 2, 1972; admitted to bar, 1995, California. *Education:* University of California, Davis (B.A., with highest honors, 1992); Boalt Hall School of Law, University of California (J.D., 1995). Phi Beta Kappa; Phi Kappa Phi. *Member:* Orange County Bar Association; The State Bar of California. *LANGUAGES:* Hindi/Urdu.

**DAVID E. LAFITTE,** born New Orleans, Louisiana, June 9, 1964; admitted to bar, 1991, California. *Education:* University of Colorado (B.A., 1987); Tulane University (J.D., cum laude, 1991). *Member:* State Bar of California.

**TERI N. HOLLANDER,** born Los Angeles, California, April 4, 1968; admitted to bar, 1996, California. *Education:* Bryn Mawr College (A.B., 1988); American Graduate School of International Management (M.I.M., 1989); Loyola Law School (J.D., cum laude, 1995). Order of the Coif; Phi Delta Phi. Member, St. Thomas More Law Honor Society. Author: "Enjoining Unauthorized Biographies and Docudramas," 16 Loy. of LA Ent. L.J. 133 (1995). *LANGUAGES:* German, French, Italian.

**MARC G. ALCSER,** born Detroit, Michigan, December 21, 1969; admitted to bar, 1996, California. *Education:* University of Southern California (B.S., cum laude, 1991); University of California, Davis (J.D., 1996). Phi Delta Phi. Member, 1994-1996 and Senior Research Editor, 1995-1996, UC Davis Law Review. Author: "The Howey Test: A Common Ground for the Common Enterprise Theory," 29 UC Davis L. Rev. 1217 (Summer 1996). *Member:* The State Bar of California.

**RYAN E. DAVIS,** born Inglewood, California, August 23, 1969; admitted to bar, 1996, California. *Education:* University of California at Los Angeles (B.A., magna cum laude, 1991); University of Southern California (J.D., 1996; M.B.A., 1996). Beta Gamma Sigma. *Member:* The State Bar of California.

**BRENT N. TRIFF,** born Long Beach, California, March 22, 1970; admitted to bar, 1996, California. *Education:* University of Queensland, Australia; University of California at Santa Barbara (B.A., 1992); University of San Diego (J.D., cum laude, 1996). Order of the Coif. Executive Editor, San Diego Law Review, 1995-1996. Recipient, Best Orator Award, 1995 St. Thomas More Constitutional Law Moot Court Competition. Author: "Should a Non-Designing Manufacturer Be Held Strictly Liable For a Design Defect? An Approach for California," 33 San Diego L.Rev. 385 (1996). *Member:* The State Bar of California.

**MICHELE MCCORMICK TROYAN,** born Los Angeles, California, May 9, 1971; admitted to bar, 1996, California. *Education:* Loyola Marymount University (B.S., 1993; J.D., cum laude, 1996). Order of the Coif; Phi Delta Phi. Member, St. Thomas More Law Honor Society. Justice, Scott Moot Court Honors Board.

**GARY J. VYNEMAN,** born Kewanee, Illinois, March 11, 1959; admitted to bar, 1993, Illinois; 1994, California; 1996, U.S. Tax Court. *Education:* University of Illinois (B.S.G.E., 1981); Whittier College (J.D., cum laude, 1992); New York University (LL.M. in Taxation, 1994). Member, 1989-1991 and Executive Editor, 1991-1992, Whittier Law Review. Author, "Irreconcilable Differences: The Role of Mitigating Circumstances in Capital Publishment Sentencing Schemes," Whittier Law Review, Vol. 13:3. *Member:* Los Angeles County (Tax Section), Orange County (Tax Section) and American (Tax Section) Bar Associations; The State Bar of California. *PRACTICE AREAS:* Taxation.

**THOMAS M. WILLIAMS,** born Rahway, New Jersey, June 15, 1969; admitted to bar, 1996, California. *Education:* Trinity College (B.A., 1991); University of Southern California (J.D., 1996).

## OF COUNSEL

**JOHN E. BRECKENRIDGE,** born Los Angeles, California, March 10, 1934; admitted to bar, 1959, California. *Education:* Yale University (B.A., 1955); University of California at Berkeley (LL.B., 1958). Order of the Coif; Phi Delta Phi. Orange County Resident Partner, Kindel & Anderson, 1966-1979. *Member:* Orange County Bar Association; The State Bar of California.

**RENA C. STONE,** born Los Angeles, California, May 6, 1953; admitted to bar, 1978, California. *Education:* University of California at Los Angeles (B.A., 1975); Loyola University of Los Angeles (J.D., 1978). *Member:* Orange County (Member, Estate Planning, Probate and Trust Law Section) and American (Member, Real Property, Probate and Trust Law Section) Bar Associations; The State Bar of California.

**DOUGLAS J. ROVENS,** born San Francisco, California, August 3, 1956; admitted to bar, 1982, California and U.S. District Court, Central District of California; 1983, U.S. Court of Appeals, Ninth Circuit; 1984, U.S. Tax Court; 1985, U.S. District Court, Southern District of California; 1990, U.S. Court of Appeals, Tenth Circuit; 1991, U.S. District Court, Northern District of California; 1996, U.S. Court of Appeals, Federal Circuit. *Education:* University of California at Santa Barbara (B.A., 1978); Southwestern University (J.D., magna cum laude, 1982). Executive Editor, Southwestern University Law Review, 1981-1982. Recipient, American Jurisprudence Awards in Constitutional Law, Torts, Wills and Trusts and Civil Procedure. Author: "Religious Tax Exemptions: A Challenge to Walz v. Tax Commission," Southwestern University Law Review, Vol. 13, No. 1 (1982). Clerk, Hon. Joseph Reichmann, U.S. Magistrate Judge, 1982. Member, National Association of Securities Dealers, Inc., Arbitration Panel.

**ROBERT J. MATTHEWS,** born Los Angeles, California, September 19, 1955; admitted to bar, 1981, California, U.S. District Court, Central District of California and U.S. Court of Appeals, Ninth Circuit. *Education:* University of Southern California (B.S., magna cum laude, 1977); Univer-

*(This Listing Continued)*

CALIFORNIA—NEWPORT BEACH

**STRADLING, YOCCA, CARLSON & RAUTH,** A PROFESSIONAL CORPORATION, Newport Beach—Continued

sity of Virginia (J.D., 1980). *Member:* Orange County (Member, Real Property and Business Law Sections) and Los Angeles County (Member, Real Property Section, 1983-1993) Bar Associations; The State Bar of California.

(For complete Biographical Data on Personnel at San Francisco, California, see Professional Biographies at that location)

## LAWRENCE TAYLOR
### NEWPORT BEACH, CALIFORNIA
(See Long Beach)
*Criminal Defense practice limited to Drunk Driving Defense.*

## THROCKMORTON, BECKSTROM, OAKES & TOMASSIAN LLP
### NEWPORT BEACH, CALIFORNIA
(See Pasadena)

Construction (claims and defects), Real Estate, Insurance, Business, Commercial and Medical Legal Law. General Civil Litigation, Defense of Religious Institutions. All aspects of Trial and Appellate Work.

## JOHN W. TULAC
### NEWPORT BEACH, CALIFORNIA
(See Claremont)

International Business Law, International Trade Law, General Business and Corporate Law, Foreign Investment in the United States, International Arbitration, Mediation and Litigation, Business Litigation. Professional Mediator and Arbitrator.

## TUVERSON & HILLYARD
A Limited Liability Partnership, including Professional Corporations
**4675 MACARTHUR COURT, SUITE 650**
**NEWPORT BEACH, CALIFORNIA 92660**
Telephone: 714-752-7855
Fax: 714-752-5437

*Los Angeles, California Office:* 12400 Wilshire Boulevard, Suite 900, Los Angeles, California 90025. Telephones: 310-826-7855; 625-1234. Fax: 310-826-8738.

*Palm Springs, California Office:* 1800 Tahquitz Canyon Way, Palm Springs, California 92263. Telephone: 619-322-7855. Fax: 619-322-5121.

*San Diego, California Office:* 4365 Executive Drive, Suite 700, San Diego, California 92121. Telephone: 619-452-7855. Fax: 619-452-2153.

General Civil and Trial Practice in all State and Federal Courts. Medical and Legal Malpractice Defense, Public Entity and Insurance Defense.

(For personnel, representative clients and biographical data, see professional biographies at Los Angeles, California.)

## RONALD K. VAN WERT
A PROFESSIONAL CORPORATION
Established in 1977
**ONE NEWPORT PLACE**
**SUITE 900, 1301 DOVE STREET**
**NEWPORT BEACH, CALIFORNIA 92660**
Telephone: 714-752-7964

Federal and State Business Tax Litigation, including Criminal Tax Litigation, Estate Planning and Corporate.

**RONALD K. VAN WERT,** born Inglewood, California, September 25, 1943; admitted to bar, 1969, California; 1971, U.S. Court of Military Appeals; 1976, U.S. Tax Court; 1978, U.S. Court of Appeals, Ninth Circuit

*(This Listing Continued)*

CAA1434B

MARTINDALE-HUBBELL LAW DIRECTORY 1997

and U.S. Supreme Court; 1982, U.S. Court of Federal Claims; 1993, U.S. Court of Appeals for the Federal Circuit; U.S. District Court, Central, Southern, Northern and Eastern Districts of California. *Education:* University of California at Santa Barbara (B.A., 1965); Hastings College of the Law, University of California (J.D., 1968); George Washington University (LL.M. in Taxation, 1970). Author: "Miranda and the Military," 19 Hastings Law Review 1441, 1968; "Donruss and the Accumulated Earnings Tax," 28 Tax Law Review 171, 1970; "Tax Frauds and the Government's Right of Access to Taxpayer's Books and Records," 5 Pepperdine Law Review No. 2, 1978. Adjunct Professor of Law: Loyola University, 1973-1975; Pepperdine University, 1975-1979. Professorial Lecturer, Golden Gate University, 1981-1991. *Member:* Orange County and American (Member: Section on Taxation; Committee on Federal Sentencing Guidelines) Bar Associations; State Bar of California. (Certified Specialist, Taxation Law, The State Bar of California Board of Legal Specialization).

REPRESENTATIVE CLIENTS: El Toro Materials, Inc.; ARV Housing Group; Steve P. Rados, Inc.; Urological Consultants Medical Group, Inc.

## JEFFREY M. VERDON, P.C.
Established in 1995
**2801 W. PACIFIC COAST HIGHWAY, SUITE 380**
**NEWPORT BEACH, CALIFORNIA 92663**
Telephone: 714-631-3500; 800-521-0464
Fax: 714-631-0355
Email: jmvstaff@earthlink.net

*Advanced Asset Protection Strategies, Advanced Estate Planning Strategies and International Trusts.*

FIRM PROFILE: *Firm specializes in sophisticated estate planning strategies for high net worth/high income individuals and closely-held businesses. Special emphasis on the use of Advanced Asset Protection planning strategies in estate planning, including the foreign Asset Protection Trust, family limited partnerships, and limited liability companies for the protection of assets. Mr. Verdon lectures extensively to professional organizations and national and international financial conferences on the use of Advanced Asset Protection techniques and sophisticated estate planning strategies.*

**JEFFREY M. VERDON,** born Miami, Florida, July 24, 1954; admitted to bar, 1978, California. *Education:* Woodland University (B.S.L., 1974; J.D., 1974); Boston University (LL.M., in taxation 1979). Author: "S Corporations - A Wolf In Sheep's Clothing - S Corporations v. Family Partnerships - The Proper Way To Own Your Mobilehome Park," WMA Reporter, March, 1990; "Why You Should Consider Asset Protection," Sonoma County Physician, Vol. 41, No. 1, Jan/Feb., 1990; "How You Can Insulate Your Assets From Liability Lawsuits and Unintended Creditors," 1989. Instructor, Business Law, Brooks College, 1977-1978. CEB Course Lecturer, Asset Protection, State Bar of California. Fellow and Senator, Isle of Man-based Offshore Institute. *Member:* Beverly Hills (Member, Sections on: Income Tax; Probate/Trust; Corporate), Orange County (Member, Sections on: Estate Planning and Taxation) and American (Member, Section of Taxation) Bar Associations; State Bar of California.

*LEGAL SUPPORT PERSONNEL*

**CHERYL FIORENZA** (Senior Paralegal).

**TERRI O'BRIEN** (Chief of Staff).

## MICHAEL V. VOLLMER
**4340 CAMPUS DRIVE, SUITE 100**
**NEWPORT BEACH, CALIFORNIA 92660-1892**
Telephone: 714-852-0833
Fax: 714-852-8731
Email: mvollmer@aol.com

*Practice limited to Estate Planning, Probate, Trust and Taxation Law.*

**MICHAEL V. VOLLMER,** born Oakland, California, March 7, 1945; admitted to bar, 1972, California; 1973, U.S. District Court, Central District of California; 1977, U.S. Tax Court. *Education:* University of California at Los Angeles (B.A., 1966); Loyola University of Los Angeles (J.D., cum laude, 1972). Phi Alpha Delta. Author: "Legislated Ethics: Comply or Die (Legislated Ethics in California and Beyond: How to Protect Your Clients, Their Beneficiaries, and Yourself as Drafter," 14th Annual Southern California Tax and Estate Planning Forum, 10-20-94; "Legislated Ethics: What You Don't Know (About Assembly Bill 21) Will Hurt You," Estate Planning, Trust & Probate News, Sept., 1993; "Drafting Solutions to the

*(This Listing Continued)*

1989 Changes in the California Probate Code," 13th Annual Program, Estate Planning, Trust and Probate Law Section, State Bar of California, 1989; "Lifetime Funding Considerations in Administering Revocable Trusts," Tenth Annual UCLA-CEB Estate Planning Institute, May 1988; "Proposition 13: Revised and Revisited (An Analysis of AB 1488)," 6 Orange County Bar Journal 387, Winter, 1979. Quarterly Author: "Mike's Minutiae" California Trusts and Estates Quarterly. Co-Draftsman: "Death Taxes: Completing the Forms and Computing the Taxes," California Continuing Education of the Bar, June, 1979. *Member:* Orange County (Director, 1984, Chairman, 1980, Vice-Chairman, 1979 and Secretary, 1978, Estate Planning, Probate and Trust Law Section) and American (Member, Section of Real Property, Probate and Trust Law) Bar Associations; State Bar of California (Chair, 1993-1994; Vice Chair, 1992-1993; Advisor, 1991-1992; Member, 1988-1990; Executive Committee, Estate Planning, Trust and Probate Law Section; Editor, Estate Planning, Trust and Probate News, 1990-1991). Fellow, American College of Trust and Estate Counsel. *PRACTICE AREAS:* Estate Planning Law; Probate Law; Trust Law.

REFERENCES: Bank of America NT&SA (Newport Beach, California); First American Trust Co. (Newport Beach, California).

## VOSS, COOK & THEL

A Partnership including Law Corporations
Established in 1978
SUITE 700, 840 NEWPORT CENTER DRIVE
**NEWPORT BEACH, CALIFORNIA 92660**
Telephone: 714-720-0300
Telecopier: 714-720-1508
Email: VossCook@aol.com

*Real Estate, Construction, Land Use, Partnerships, Federal and State Taxation, Financial Institutions, Mortgage Banking, Secured Financing, Commercial, General Business, Corporations, Securities Syndications, Bankruptcy, Advertising and Estate Planning Law. General Civil and Trial Practice in all State and Federal Courts.*

FIRM PROFILE: *Voss, Cook & Thel was founded in 1978 and, over the years, has established itself as one of the most respected law firms based in Orange County. The Firm is a full service commercial/busines/litigation law firm with the principal areas of practice including corporate, real estate, taxation, litigation, financial institutions and bankruptcy. The Firm prides itself in the high level pf partner involvement with each matter, a strong emphasis on client responsiveness and a genuine desire to serve the clients' needs within the clients' budget.*

### MEMBERS OF FIRM

**BRUCE V. COOK, P.C.,** born Berkeley, California, May 4, 1947; admitted to bar, 1975, California. *Education:* Brigham Young University (B.S., 1972); University of Utah (J.D., 1975). Order of the Coif. Comment Editor, Utah Law Review, 1974-1975. *Member:* Orange County and American Bar Associations; State Bar of California. *PRACTICE AREAS:* Construction Law; Real Estate Development Law; Commercial Leasing; Business Law; Property Management.

**JAMES G. DAMON III,** born Los Angeles, California, December 5, 1957; admitted to bar, 1984, California; 1985, Connecticut. *Education:* Johns Hopkins University (B.A., 1980); Loyola Law School at Los Angeles (J.D., 1984). Law Clerk for the Hon. Warren W. Eginton, U.S. District Court, District of Connecticut, 1985-1986. *Member:* Orange County, Los Angeles County and American Bar Associations; State Bar of California. *PRACTICE AREAS:* Litigation; Complex Litigation; Lender Liability; Directors and Officers Liability; Landlord and Tenant Law.

**EDWARD L. LAIRD,** born Waverly, Iowa, September 18, 1955; admitted to bar, 1982, California. *Education:* University of California at Irvine (B.S., with honors, 1979); Pepperdine University (J.D., 1981). *Member:* Orange County Bar Association (Member, Business Litigation and Construction Law Sections); State Bar of California; Orange County College of Trial Advocacy; Association of General Contractors (Member, Legal Advisory Committee). *PRACTICE AREAS:* Litigation; Construction Law; Mechanics Lien Law; Insurance Coverage/Bad Faith Law; Commercial Law; Bankruptcy; Adversary Proceedings.

**DAVID A. LURKER,** born Akron, Ohio, May 5, 1954; admitted to bar, 1979, California. *Education:* California State University at Long Beach (B.A., magna cum laude, 1976); McGeorge School of Law, University of the Pacific (J.D., with distinction, 1979). Best Appellant's Brief, Roger J. Traynor Moot Court Competition, 1979. *Member:* Orange County Bar Association; State Bar of California (Member, Real Property Law Section, Condominium, Cooperative Housing and Subdivision Committee). *PRACTICE AREAS:* Real Estate (Property) Law; Commercial Leasing; Construction Law; Real Estate Development Law.

*(This Listing Continued)*

**M. EDWARD MISHOW,** born St. Louis, Missouri, October 28, 1955; admitted to bar, 1981, California. *Education:* Washington University at St. Louis (B.S.B.A., with highest honors, 1978); Harvard University (J.D., 1981). Beta Gamma Sigma. Co-Author, "Representative Tax Shelter Investment Opportunities in the United States of America," presented at the International Tax Planning Association Conference in Brussels, May, 1983. *Member:* State Bar of California. *PRACTICE AREAS:* Individual and Corporate Tax Planning; Taxation (Local, Personal Property, State, Federal or International) Law; Federal Income, Estate and Gift Taxation Law; Partnership Law.

**ALBERT J. THEL, JR.,** born Baltimore, Maryland, September 30, 1949; admitted to bar, 1978, California; 1980, District of Columbia. *Education:* University of Virginia (B.A., 1971; J.D., 1978). *Member:* State Bar of California; The District of Columbia Bar. [Capt., U.S. Army, 1971-1975]. *PRACTICE AREAS:* Real Estate (Property) Law; Corporate Law; Corporate (Corporation) Financing Law; Secured Transactions; Business Acquisitions.

### ASSOCIATES

**MARC REICH,** born New York, N.Y., February 23, 1965; admitted to bar, 1992, California and U.S. District Court, Central and Southern Districts of California. *Education:* State University of New York at Albany (B.S., 1986); University of California at Davis (J.D., 1991). Moot Court Board. Recipient, American Jurisprudence Award, Evidence and Moot Court Competition. Law Clerk to Justice Warren Matthews, Alaska Supreme Court, 1991-1992. *Member:* State Bar of California; American Bar Association.

**MARC S. STRECKER,** born New Orleans, Louisiana, February 22, 1963; admitted to bar, 1989, California. *Education:* University of Chicago (A.B., with honors, 1985); University of Michigan (J.D., 1988). National Merit Scholar. Yee Scholar. *Member:* Orange County and Los Angeles County Bar Associations; State Bar of California (Member, Litigation Section); Association of Business Trial Lawyers. *PRACTICE AREAS:* General and Complex Business Litigation; Estate Litigation; Real Property Law; Foreclosures; Partition of Real Property; Commercial Lease Disputes; Partnership Disputes; Contract Litigation; Construction Defect and Mechanic's Lien Litigation; Antitrust; Insurance Bad Faith Litigation.

**MAXY RUSH OTUTEYE,** born Cleveland, Ohio, June 3, 1949; admitted to bar, 1995, California. *Education:* Harvard University (B.A., 1971); University of California (M.S., 1979); Boalt Hall School of Law (J.D., 1995). *PRACTICE AREAS:* Corporate; Real Estate; Financial.

**BABAK SAMINI,** born Tehran, Iran, October 27, 1970; admitted to bar, 1995, California; 1996, U.S. District Court, Central District of California. *Education:* University of Southern California (B.A., 1992); The Ohio State University (J.D., 1995). Editor in Chief, The Ohio State Journal on Dispute Resolution. *Member:* Orange County Bar Association. *PRACTICE AREAS:* Corporate; Federal Taxation; Real Estate.

### OF COUNSEL

**LORI WINDER LIVINGSTON,** born Los Angeles, California, December 23, 1953; admitted to bar, 1980, California; 1984, U.S. Tax Court. *Education:* University of California at Irvine (B.A., cum laude, 1975); Pepperdine University (J.D., 1979); University of Miami at Miami, Florida (L.L.M., Tax and Estate Planning 1980). *Member:* Orange County and American Bar Associations; The State Bar of California (Member and former President, Tax Section and Member, Estate Planning Section). *PRACTICE AREAS:* Estate Planning; Probate and Trust Administration; Conservatorship Law; Elder Care Law; Wills Contests; Charitable Trusts and Foundations.

REPRESENTATIVE CLIENTS: America Kuk Dong; American Zettler, Inc.; Bay Meadows Racetrack; Beauchamp Enterprises; Birtcher Enterprises; CCL Holdings; Celeritas Technologies; CT Realty Corporation; ELS Educational Services, Inc.; Farmers Market, Inc.; FJS, Inc.; Innovations in Composites, Inc.; Los Alisos Development Company; MBK Construction; MBK Real Estate Ltd.; Mitsui & Co., Ltd.; Near Cal Corp.; Pacific Southwest Mortgage Services; PM Realty Advisors; Southern California Bank; Sun Cal Companies; The Equitable Real Estate Investment Management Inc.; USLIFE Real Estate Services Corp.

# THE WALKER LAW FIRM
A PROFESSIONAL CORPORATION
Established in 1979

SUITE 450
1301 DOVE STREET
NEWPORT BEACH, CALIFORNIA 92660-2464
Telephone: 714-752-2522
Telecopier: 714-752-0439
Email: JWALKER208@AOL.COM

Civil Litigation in all State and Federal Courts. Employment Litigation for Employers, Commercial U.D.'s and Appeals, Real Property, Business, Partnership and Corporate Law and Bankruptcy; Arbitration and Mediation Representation.

FIRM PROFILE: The Walker Law Firm began in Orange County in 1979 as a civil litigation and general business practice, and has developed into a multi-service firm with the individual attorneys providing a wide range of legal services in the State and Federal Courts in the areas of real property, business, partnership and corporate law, employment law, and bankruptcy.

**JOSEPH A. WALKER,** born Waukegan, Illinois, April 20, 1945; admitted to bar, 1970, California and U.S. District Court, Central District of California; 1975, U.S. District Court, Southern District of California. *Education:* University of Illinois (B.A., 1967); George Washington University (M.B.A., 1974); University of Southern California (J.D., 1970). Phi Delta Phi. Lecturer: What Business Lawyers Need to Know About the Law of Evidence, California Continuing Education of the Bar, 1977-1981. Panel Member, United States Bankruptcy Court, Central District of California, Bankruptcy Mediation Program, 1995—. *Member:* Orange County (Fee Arbitration Panel Member, 1992—) and American Bar Associations; State Bar of California (Chairman, Group and Pre-paid Legal Services Committee, 1978-1979; Member, Executive Committee, Legal Services Section, 1980-1982; Member, Committee on Mandatory Fee Arbitration, 1996—). [Capt., JAG, U.S.A.F., 1970-1974]. *PRACTICE AREAS:* Business and Real Property Litigation; Business Law; Employment Law; Bankruptcy.

### OF COUNSEL

**DUFF S. MCEVERS,** born Los Angeles, California, April 21, 1954; admitted to bar, 1981, California and U.S. District Court, Central District of California; 1988, U.S. Court of Appeals, Ninth Circuit; 1993, U.S. District Court, Southern District of California. *Education:* University of Southern California (A.B., cum laude, 1976); Western State University at San Diego (J.D., 1980). Nu Beta Epsilon. Skull & Dagger. Law Review. Jessup Moot Court. *Member:* Orange County Bar Association; The State Bar of California (Member, Section on International Law, 1985-1996). *PRACTICE AREAS:* International Law; Litigation; Business Law.

**DAVID T. SANFORD,** born Philadelphia, Pennsylvania, June 15, 1957; admitted to bar, 1990, California; 1995, U.S. District Court, Central District of California. *Education:* University of Southern California at Los Angeles (B.A., 1980); Western State University at Fullerton (J.D., 1990). *Member:* Orange County Bar Association; State Bar of California. *LANGUAGES:* Spanish and French. *PRACTICE AREAS:* Business and Real Property Litigation; Corporations; Real Estate; Business and Transactional Law; Civil Litigation.

**KARYN S. NEUE,** born Neptune, New Jersey, April 6, 1967; admitted to bar, 1995, California and U.S. District Court, Central District of California. *Education:* University of California at Irvine (B.A., cum laude, 1990); University of Southern California (J.D., 1995). Member, Moot Court. *Member:* State Bar of California. *PRACTICE AREAS:* Business Litigation; Corporations; Bankruptcy; Wills; Trusts.

REFERENCE: Marine National Bank.

# WENTWORTH & PAOLI, P.C.
Established in 1963

4631 TELLER AVENUE, SUITE 100
NEWPORT BEACH, CALIFORNIA 92660
Telephone: 714-752-7711
Fax: 714-752-8339

*Practice Limited to Personal Injury, including Wrongful Death, Professional Liability and Products Liability Litigation, Business and Estate Fraud, Fire Loss and Human Rights Violations.*

(This Listing Continued)

FIRM PROFILE: Wentworth & Paoli, P.C., Trial Lawyers, is a member of the Bar Register of Preeminent Lawyers was founded in 1963. the firm offers extensive knowledge in personal injury and professional malpractice. Specializing in complex litigation and technical discovery issues. Over 50% of the firms early cases were referrals from other lawyers. Mr. Wentworth's experience has been recognized by the California Trial Lawyers, and he is a Certified Civil Trial Specialist and a member of ABOTA. The firm handles cases as far north as Santa Barbara and as far south as San Diego.

**THEODORE S. WENTWORTH,** born Brooklyn, New York, July 18, 1938; admitted to bar, 1963, California, U.S. District Court, Northern District of California, U.S. Court of Appeals, Ninth Circuit and California Supreme Court; 1979, U.S. District Court, Central District of California; 1985, U.S. Supreme Court. *Education:* American River College; Hastings College of Law, University of California (J.D., 1962). Phi Alpha Delta. Judge Pro-Tem: Municipal Court (Attorney's Panel), 1968-1972; Orange County Superior Court (Attorney's Panel), 1974—. Partner, Hunt, Liljestrom & Wentworth, 1967-1978. Judge Pro Tem, Municipal Court, Newport Harbor, 1989. *Member:* Orange County Bar Association (Member, Ethics Committee, 1966-1971; Chairman, Committee on Administration of Justice, 1969-1971; Member: Judiciary Committee, 1972-1975; Board of Directors, 1972-1975); The State Bar of California; California Trial Lawyers Association (Recognized as an experienced Trial Lawyer in the fields of Trial Law, General Personal Injury, Professional Negligence, Products Liability, Appellate Law, Motion, Public Entity Liability and Insurance Bad Faith) and Member, Board of Governors, 1968-1970; President, Orange County Chapter, 1967-1968); The Association of Trial Lawyers of America; Lawyer-Pilots Bar Association. Certified as a Civil Trial Advocate by the National Board of Trial Advocates; American Board of Trial Advocates. (Member of California Trial Lawyers Association, with recognized experience in the fields of Trial Lawyer, General Personal Injury, Professional Negligence, Product Liability, Appellate Law and Motion, Public Entity Liability and Insurance Bad Faith). *PRACTICE AREAS:* Personal Injury; Wrongful Death; Products Liability; Professional Malpractice; Business Fraud; Fire Loss; Human Rights.

**WILLIAM M. DELLI PAOLI,** born Detroit, Michigan, May 18, 1954; admitted to bar, 1993, California, U.S. Court of Appeals, Ninth Circuit and U.S. District Court, Central, Northern and Southern Districts of California. *Education:* California State University (B.A., Economics, 1985); Whittier College School of Law (J.D., 1991). Phi Delta Phi. Extern Law Clerk to the Honorable Alex Kozinski, U.S. Circuit Court of Appeals, 1991. Editor, Law Review, Whittier College School of Law. Vice Chair, Moot Court Honors Board. Member, J. Ruben Clark Honor Society. *Member:* Orange County (Member, Sections on: Insurance Law; Appellate Law) and American Bar Associations; State Bar of California (Member, Sections on: Litigation; General and Solo Practice); Orange County Trial Lawyers Association; The Association of Trial Lawyers of America; California Trial Lawyers Association. [U.S. Marine Corp., 1971-1975]. *PRACTICE AREAS:* Personal Injury; Wrongful Death; Products Liability; Insurance Bad Faith; Civil Appeals; Professional Malpractice; Business Fraud; Fire Loss; Environmental Issues; Construction Defects; Human Rights.

**NANCY MORSE KNIGHT,** born Boston, Massachusetts, March 7, 1931; admitted to bar, 1974, California. *Education:* Smith College (B.A., cum laude, 1952); University of California at Los Angeles (J.D., 1974). Phi Beta Kappa. Judge Pro Tem, Attorneys Panel, Orange County Superior Court, 1989—. *Member:* Orange County Bar Association; State Bar of California; Orange County Trial Lawyers Association; The Association of Trial Lawyers of America. *PRACTICE AREAS:* Personal Injury; Wrongful Death; Professional Negligence; Products Liability; Business Fraud; Human Rights.

**COURT BRYANT PURDY,** born Boston, Massachusetts, March 14, 1969; admitted to bar, 1995, California. *Education:* University of Colorado at Boulder (B.A., 1991); University of San Diego (J.D., 1995). State Bar of California Writing Competition Finalist, 1994. Author: Purdy, C. Kibel, P.S. (1995, February 13) Exporting Environmental Ignorance. Legal Times, p. 47; Kibel, P.S. Klinski, S (1994, December) Rapping at the Courthouse Door: Judicial Access for Environmental Advocates in the U.S. and Germany. Journal of Environmental Law and Practice, 5, 59-76. Contributing Researcher and Editor: Court Bryant Purdy; Purdy C., Loundberry, D. (1993-1994) California Intergrated Waste Management and Recycling Board. California Regulatory Law Reporter, 13 (4); 14(5-6); Purdy, C. (1993-1994) Osteopathic Medical Board of California. California Regulatory Law Reporter, 13 (4); 14 (5-6). *Member:* Marin County and American

(This Listing Continued)

Bar Associations; The Bar Association of San Fransisco (Member: Environmental Law Section; Litigation Section); State Bar of California. *PRACTICE AREAS:* Personal Injury; Environmental.

REFERENCE: Wells Fargo Bank, Newport Beach, Calif.

## LAW OFFICES OF
## HARRY E. WESTOVER & ASSOCIATES

*901 DOVER DRIVE, SUITE 100*
**NEWPORT BEACH, CALIFORNIA 92660**
*Telephone: 714-646-7200*
*Fax: 714-646-7665*

*Probate and Trust Litigation and Administration, Estate Planning, Probate and Trust Law.*

**HARRY E. WESTOVER,** born Hollywood, California, November 11, 1931; admitted to bar, 1957, California. *Education:* University of Arizona (B.S. in M.E., 1954); University of California at Los Angeles (J.D., 1957). Phi Delta Phi. *Member:* Orange County and American Bar Associations; The State Bar of California. Fellow, American College of Trust and Estate Counsel. (Certified Specialist, Estate Planning, Trust and Probate Law, The State Bar of California Board of Legal Specialization). *PRACTICE AREAS:* Probate Law; Probate Litigation; Estate Planning Law; Trust Law.

*ASSOCIATES*

**PIERRE E. AUW,** born Pasadena, California, April 16, 1929; admitted to bar, 1964, California. *Education:* Pasadena City College; Southwestern University. Judge Pro Tem, Orange County Superior Court, Probate, 1988-1989. *Member:* Long Beach, Los Angeles County and Orange County Bar Associations; State Bar of California; The Association of Trial Lawyers of America. (Certified Specialist, Estate Planning, Trust and Probate Law, The State Bar of California Board of Legal Specialization). *PRACTICE AREAS:* Trust Law; Probate Law; Estate Planning Law.

**BARRETT E. WESTOVER,** born Newport Beach, California, August 16, 1963; admitted to bar, 1991, California. *Education:* University of Southern California (B.A. in Political Science, 1986); Western State University (J.D., 1990). Chi Phi (President, 1985-1986). *Member:* Orange County Bar Association; State Bar of California. *PRACTICE AREAS:* General Civil Litigation; Probate Litigation; Probate Administration; Estate Planning; Trust Law.

**ALYSSA C. WESTOVER,** born Newport Beach, California, April 21, 1966; admitted to bar, 1991, California. *Education:* University of Southern California (B.S., 1988); Pepperdine University (J.D., 1991). Phi Alpha Delta. Editor, Pepperdine Law Review, 1990-1991. *Member:* Orange County Bar Association; State Bar of California. *PRACTICE AREAS:* General Civil Litigation; Probate Litigation; Probate Administration; Estate Planning and Trust Law.

REPRESENTATIVE CLIENTS: First American Trust Co.; Northern Trust Bank of California, N.A.

## WHITE & ROSEMAN

*1201 DOVE STREET, SUITE 480*
**NEWPORT BEACH, CALIFORNIA 92660**
*Telephone: 714-622-6100*
*Fax: 714-852-2141*

*Bankruptcy, Sexual Harassment, Discrimination, Wrongful Termination, Personal Injury*

*MEMBERS OF FIRM*

**BRUCE DAVID WHITE,** born Lincoln, Nebraska, November 13, 1948; admitted to bar, 1973, Nebraska, U.S. District Court, District of Nebraska; 1978, U.S. District Court, Eastern District of Missouri, U.S. Court of Appeals, 8th Circuit; 1980, U.S. Supreme Court; 1985, California, U.S. District Court, Southern District of California; 1990, U.S. District Court, Central District of California. *Education:* University of Nebraska (B.S., 1970; J.D., 1973). Assistant U.S. Attorney, Eastern District of Missouri, 1978-1984. *Member:* Orange County Bar Association (Member, Bankruptcy Forum, 1991—); California State Bar; Nebraska State Bar Association. *PRACTICE AREAS:* Bankruptcy.

**LESLIE R. ROSEMAN,** born Elyria, Ohio, September 23, 1949; admitted to bar, 1990, California; 1991, U.S. District Court, Central District of California. *Education:* Ohio State University (B.S., 1971); California State University at Fullerton (M.S., 1977); Western State University (J.D., 1989). *Member:* Orange County Bar Association; State Bar of California; Orange County Women Lawyers Association; California Employment Lawyer's Association. *PRACTICE AREAS:* Sexual Harassment; Discrimination; Wrongful Termination; Personal Injury.

REFERENCE: Glendale Federal.

## WINTHROP COUCHOT PROFESSIONAL CORPORATION

*Established in 1995*

*3 CIVIC PLAZA, SUITE 280*
**NEWPORT BEACH, CALIFORNIA 92660**
*Telephone: 714-720-4100*
*Fax: 714-720-4111*

*Bankruptcy, Insolvency, Corporate Reorganization and Commercial Litigation.*

*FIRM PROFILE: Winthrop Couchot was established in 1995. The Firm specializes in bankruptcy, insolvency, business reorganizations, debtor/creditor matters and related litigation including real estate. The Firm provides workout and bankruptcy representation to businesses in a variety of fields including, aerospace, apparel, architecture, automotive dealerships, computer equipment and software, construction, electronics, energy, engineering, entertainment, equipment leasing, government, healthcare providers, hotels and motels, manufacturing, radio, restaurants, retailing and transportation. Members of the firm have confirmed plans of reorganization in over forty cases in the past five years.*

**MARC J. WINTHROP,** born Philadelphia, Pennsylvania, 1948; admitted to bar, 1974, California. *Education:* University of California at Los Angeles (A.B., 1969; J.D., 1974). Order of the Coif. Member, University of California at Los Angeles Law Review, 1972-1974. Author: "Toward a Less than Absolute Priority Rule for Small Business Reorganizations; Reforming the New Value Exception," 18 California Bankruptcy Journal 59, January 1990. "Marshalling Under the Bankruptcy Code," Financial Lawyers Conference, 1987. "Debtor in Possession Financing and Cash Collateral," Continuing Education of the Bar, 1988. Co-Author: "Post Confirmation Issues: When A Confirmed Plan Doesn't Go According to Plan," Financial Lawyers Conference, 1989. Lecturer: "Practice Under the Bankruptcy Code," California Continuing Education of the Bar, 1983; "Enforcement of Judgments," California Continuing Education of the Bar, 1984; Fundamentals of Bankruptcy, California Continuing Education of the Bar, 1986. Moderator, "Bankruptcy Practice After the 1984 Code Amendments," California Continuing Education of the Bar, 1985; Moderator, Introduction to Bankruptcy Practice, California Continuing Education of the Bar, 1987. Lecturer, "Representing Creditors Before and During Bankruptcy," California Continuing Education of the Bar, 1988. Co-Moderator, "Selected Issues in Bankruptcy Practice," California Continuing Education of the Bar, 1989. "Counseling Creditors of Distressed Business Before and During Bankruptcy; Loan Workouts and Chapter 11 Proceedings," California Continuing Education of the Bar, 1988. Co-Moderator, "Selected Issues in Bankruptcy and Reorganization" (Advanced Course), California Continuing Education of the Bar, 1989 and 1991. Moderator/Panelist, "Current Developments in Bankruptcy," Continuing Education of the Bar, 1992-1996. Speaker/Panelist, "Negotiating Debt Restructuring," Turnaround Management Association Conference, 1993. Panelist, "Bailing Out the Sinking Partnership," Financial Lawyers Conference, 1992. Panelist, "Bankruptcy Appeals," Orange County Bankruptcy Forum, 1990; Panelist, "The Chapter 11 Plan Confirmation Process," Orange County Bankruptcy Forum, 1990 and 1995. Panelist, "Roadmap Through the Reorganization Process," Orange County Bar Association, 1996. Instructor: Bankruptcy Practice for Paralegals, University of Southern California Extension 1985, University of California at Irvine Extension and University of California at San Diego, 1986. *Member:* Board of Governors, Financial Lawyers Conference, ABA (Business Bankruptcy Committee). *PRACTICE AREAS:* Bankruptcy Reorganization; Commercial Bankruptcy; Workouts.

**PAUL J. COUCHOT,** born Fremont, California, December 25, 1961; admitted to bar, 1987, California and U.S. District Court, Central and Southern Districts of California. *Education:* University of California at Santa Barbara (B.A., 1984); University of California at Davis (J.D., 1987). Panelist, "Current Developments in Bankruptcy," California Continuing Education of the Bar, 1995. *Member:* State Bar of California; Orange County Bankruptcy Forum. *TRANSACTIONS:* Rusty Pelican Restau-

*(This Listing Continued)*

## CALIFORNIA—NEWPORT BEACH

*WINTHROP COUCHOT PROFESSIONAL CORPORATION, Newport Beach—Continued*

rants; Sherwood Shutter Corporation; Chen-Tech Industries, Inc.; Baldwin Park Town Center; Rancho Mirage Bob Hope Associates; Multi Family Partners; Parkridge Associates; Sunrise Growers, Inc.; BHI Dover VII; BHI Dover Fund XVII; Long Beach Airport Business Park. **PRACTICE AREAS:** Bankruptcy Law; Reorganization.

**ROBERT W. PITTS,** born Calgary, Alberta, February 19, 1963; admitted to bar, 1989, California and U.S. District Court, Central District of California; 1990, U.S. District Court, Northern, Southern and Eastern Districts of California; 1991, U.S. Court of Appeals, Ninth Circuit. *Education:* Arizona State University (B.Sc., 1985); The National Law Center, George Washington University (J.D., 1988). Phi Alpha Delta; Gold Key. Panelist: "Roadmap Through the Reorganization Process," Orange County Bar Association, 1996. *Member:* Orange County and American Bar Associations; State Bar of California; Orange County Bankruptcy Forum; Financial Lawyers Conference; Orange County Barristers; American Bankruptcy Institute. **TRANSACTIONS:** Debtor-Go Vacations America, Inc., and Go Vacations California, Inc.; Debtor-La Jolla Building Associates, A California Limited Partnership; Trustee-Glen Ivy Resorts, Inc., and Affiliated Entities; Debtor-Besteel Industries, Inc.; Debtor-Pleion Corporation; Debtor-Statordyne Corporation; Debtor-Five Brothers, Inc.; Debtor-Achievement Dynamics, Inc. **PRACTICE AREAS:** Reorganization; Bankruptcy Law; Corporate Insolvency Law.

---

**RICHARD H. GOLUBOW,** born Brooklyn, New York, March 3, 1964; admitted to bar, 1992, California. *Education:* State University of New York at Albany (B.S., cum laude, 1985); Southwestern University School of Law (J.D., 1992). Recipient, American Jurisprudence Award in Civil Procedure. Extern Law Clerk to the Hon. John J. Wilson, U.S. Bankruptcy Court, Central District, California, 1992. Law Clerk to the Hon. John J. Wilson, U.S. Bankruptcy Court, Central District, California, 1992-1994. Publications: "Bankruptcy's Effect on Environmental Claims: Should Involuntary Environmental Creditors be Entitled to Non-Dischargeable Super-Priority Creditor Status," 3 Univ. Miami L. Rev. 100 (1993). *Member:* Orange County Bar Association; State Bar of California; Orange County Bankruptcy Forum; Financial Lawyers Conference. **TRANSACTIONS:** Tam's Stationers, Inc.; BHI Dover XI; BHI Dover Fund IVII; Sunrise Growers, Inc. **PRACTICE AREAS:** Bankruptcy Law; Corporate Reorganization; Workouts.

**DORIT GOOSSENS,** born Inglewood, California, November 21, 1968; admitted to bar, 1994, California and U.S. District Court, Central District of California. *Education:* Biola University (B.S. magna cum laude, 1991); Southwestern University School of Law (J.D., 1994). Recipient, Excellent Achievement Award in Intellectual Property. Extern to Justice Miriam Vogel, California Court of Appeals 2nd District, 1992. Extern to the Honorable Kathleen P. March, U.S. Bankruptcy Court, Central District of California, 1994. Relief Law Clerk to the Honorable Ernest M. Robles, U.S. Bankruptcy Court, Central District of California, 1994-1995. *Member:* State Bar of California; Women Lawyers Association of Los Angeles.

**PETER LIANIDES,** born San Francisco, California, August 11, 1965; admitted to bar, 1992, California and U.S. District Court, Central District of California. *Education:* University of California at Santa Cruz (B.A., with highest honors, 1987); University of California at Santa Barbara (M.A., 1988); Santa Clara University (M.B.A., Beta Gamma Sigma, 1992; J.D., 1992). Extern Law Clerk to the Hon. John J. Wilson, U.S. Bankruptcy Court, Central District of California, 1992-1993. Law Clerk to the Hon. John J. Wilson, U.S. Bankruptcy Court, Central District of California, 1994-1996. *Member:* State Bar of California; Orange County Bankruptcy Forum.

---

### WITTER AND HARPOLE
*610 NEWPORT CENTER DRIVE, SUITE 1050*
**NEWPORT BEACH, CALIFORNIA 92660**
*Telephone: 714-644-7600*
*Fax: 714-759-1014*

*Pasadena, California Office:* Wells Fargo Building, 350 W. Colorado Boulevard, Suite 400. Telephone: 213-624-1311; 818-440-1111. FAX: 213-620-0430.

*(This Listing Continued)*

CAA1438B

---

## MARTINDALE-HUBBELL LAW DIRECTORY 1997

Federal and State Tax, Tax Litigation, Estate Planning, Trust and Probate Law.

(For complete biographical data on all personnel, see Professional Biographies at Los Angeles)

---

### WOLF & PFEIFER
*A LAW CORPORATION*
*500 NEWPORT CENTER DRIVE*
*SUITE 800*
**NEWPORT BEACH, CALIFORNIA 92660**
*Telephone: 714-720-9200*
*Fax: 714-720-9250*
*URL: http://www.wolfpfeifer.com*

*Real Estate Finance and Mortgage Banking (Residential and Commercial/Multi-Family), Regulatory Compliance, Multistate Licensing, Corporate and Loan Origination/Servicing Matters, Securitization and Secondary Marketing (MBS/CMBS), Federal and State Court Litigation including Complex and Class Action Defense Litigation, Default Servicing (Residential and Commercial/Multifamily), Mortgage Fraud Resolution, Foreclosures, Deeds-in-Lieu, Bankruptcy Representation (Freddie Mac Approved), REO Management and Evictions.*

**ALAN S. WOLF,** born Jersey City, New Jersey, January 5, 1955; admitted to bar, 1980, California; 1981, U.S. District Court, Northern, Eastern, Central and Southern Districts of California. *Education:* Dartmouth College (B.A., cum laude, 1977); Southwestern University School of Law (J.D., 1980). Author: "Multiple Bankruptcy Filing Abuse," US Network News, September/October 1996; "Your Attorney is Your Partner," Servicing Management, June 1996; "The Effect of Forced Loan Modification on Foreclosures," California Trustee's Association, Winter 1996; "Peter's Decision Hits Chapter 13's," Servicing Management, November 1995; "Another Take On The Peter's Decision," Servicing Management, October 1995; "Bankruptcy Update" (A Review of Proposed Fannie Mae Procedures Regarding Bankruptcy), US Network News, Spring 1995; "Bankruptcy Fraud, A Growing Problem," US Network News, Spring 1994. Speaker: "Legal Issues Panel," 1996 Western States Loan Servicing Conference, August 1996; "It's the Law," 1996 Mortgage Bankers Association of America (MBA) Loss Mitigation Seminar, April 1996; "Bankruptcy Panel," California Trustee's Association Educational Seminar, October 1995; "Bankruptcy Session," Mortgage Bankers Association of the Carolina's Risk Management/Foreclosure Workshop, August 1995; "Free Legal Advice," 1994 MBA National Servicing Conference, June 1994; "Bankruptcy Issues," Freddie Mac, California Counsel Meeting, October 1994; "Legal Issues," MBA Multifamily Servicing & Asset Management Conference, June 1993; "Bankruptcy Panel," MBA National Servicing Conference, May 1992. Member: Mortgage Bankers Association of America; California Mortgage Bankers Association (Chairperson, Legal Issues Committee, 1994-1995); U.S. Foreclosure Network (Member, Board of Directors, 1990-1995; Chair, Bankruptcy Committee, 1995); College of Mortgage Attorneys. *Member:* Orange County and American Bar Associations; State Bar of California; American Bankruptcy Institute. **PRACTICE AREAS:** Mortgage Banking; Creditors Rights in Bankruptcy Proceedings; Real Estate Law. **Email:** ASW@Wolf Pfeifer.com

**MICHAEL R. PFEIFER,** born Denver, Colorado, January 6, 1950; admitted to bar, 1976, California; 1977, U.S. District Court, Central District of California; 1980, U.S. District Court, Northern District of California, U.S. Court of Appeals, Ninth Circuit and U.S. Supreme Court. *Education:* London School of Economics and Political Science (1971); Claremont Men's College (B.A., magna cum laude, 1972); Cornell University Law School (J.D., 1975). Recipient, Nathan Rothstein Prize. Managing Editor, Cornell International Law Journal, 1974-1975. Real Estate Broker, California, 1984—. Author: "Legal Fiction," (Misapplication of Class Action Remedies to Mortgage Banking Regulations), Mortgage Banking Magazine, November 1996; "Legal Effects of Securitization on Loan Servicing," Mortgage Finance, March/April 1996; "Sharing Secrets" (An Examination of Servicing Liability Risks), Mortgage Banking Magazine, December 1995; "Commercial/Multi-Family Lines," US Network News, Summer 1995; "A Legal Safety Net," Mortgage Banking, June, February, 1995; "Buying Servicing Rights? Beware!," Servicing Management, December 1994; "Applying Fair Lending Principles and Practices to Commercial Loans," Mortgage Finance, October 1994. Contributing Author: The Handbook of Commercial Mortgage-Backed Securities edited by Frank Fabozzi; "The Legal Issues of Problem Collections in California," National Business Institute Program. Speaker: "Case Law/Class Action Development," California Mortgage

*(This Listing Continued)*

Bankers Association (CMBA) Regulatory Conference, November 1996; "Legal Issues in Mortgage Fraud," CMBA Legal Issues Seminar, November 1996; "Document Review and Legal Issues," Mortgage Bankers Association (MBA) Commercial Multi-Family Conference, June 1996; "Getting Business Done Between Now and the Year 2000," CMBA meeting of the Commercial Real Estate Division, May 1996; "Outsourcing Panel" MBA Legal Issues Seminar, March 1996; "Perceived Conflicts of Interest in Servicers," Real Estate Capital Resources Association (RECRA) Winter Conference, March 1996; "Legal Issues," USFN National Default Servicing Seminar and Round Table, Chicago, Illinois, July 1995; "Criminal and Regulatory Liability: Has Limiting Exposure For Officers and Directors Become The Impossible Dream?," Orange County Bar Association, Corporate Counsel Section, May 1994; "Perspectives on Receivers," Financial Institutions and Services, Orange County Bar Association, May 1993. Judge Pro Tem, Orange County Superior Court, 1984—. Delegate to the State Bar Convention, 1992-1994. Vice-Chairman, Commercial/Multi-Family Division, 1995 and Member, Legal Issues Committee, U.S. Foreclosure Network, 1995. Member, Legal Issues Committee, U.S. Foreclosure Network. Member: Mortgage Bankers Association of America; Commercial Real Estate Secondary Market and Securitization Association; California Mortgage Bankers Association of America. *Member:* Orange County (Member, Sections on: Business Litigation; Commercial Law; Bankruptcy; Chairman, Financial Practice, 1995) and American (Member, Sections on: Business Law; Litigation) Bar Associations; State Bar of California (Member, Sections on: Real Estate; Business Law). *PRACTICE AREAS:* Real Estate; Commercial and Bankruptcy Litigation; Mortgage Servicing and Secondary Market Transactions; Mortgage-Backed Securities; Creditor Rights. *Email:* MRP@WolfPfeifer.com

**MELISSA L. RICHARDS,** born 1963; admitted to bar, 1989, California and U.S. District Court, Central, Northern and Southern Districts of California. *Education:* University of California at Davis (B.S., 1985); University of San Francisco (J.D., 1988). Speaker: California Mortgage Bankers Association's Annual Regulatory, Legislative and Compliance Conferences, 1991-1996. Panel Moderator, "Protecting Your Assets," Financial Women International, April 1996. Member: Mortgage Bankers Association of America; California Mortgage Bankers Association; Western League of Savings Associations; The California Association of Thrift and Loan Companies; Loan Service Managers Association; The National Association of Real Estate Owned Brokers; Financial Women International. *PRACTICE AREAS:* Regulatory Compliance; Lending Transactions.

**JANICE L. CELOTTI,** admitted to bar, 1978, California and U.S. District Court, Central and Eastern Districts of California; 1979, U.S. District Court, Southern District of California; 1980, U.S. District Court, Northern District of California and U.S. Court of Appeals, Ninth Circuit. *Education:* University of California at Los Angeles (B.A., summa cum laude, 1975; J.D., 1978). Member, UCLA Law Review. Speaker, "Civil Procedure and Commercial Law," California Professional Continuing Education of the Bar (CEB), 1996. *Member:* Orange County Bar Association; State Bar of California; Financial Lawyers' Conference; Orange County Bankruptcy Forum. *PRACTICE AREAS:* Creditors Rights Litigation (Commercial/Multi-Family and Residential).

**DONALD R. DAVIDSON, III,** born Syracuse, New York, July 17, 1946; admitted to bar, 1972, Nevada and U.S. District Court, District of Nevada; 1987, California and U.S. District Court, Southern District of California. *Education:* Dartmouth College (B.A., 1968); George Washington University (J.D., 1971). Author: "Lender's Aftershock--Loss of Insurance Proceeds," California Trustee's Newsletter, Fall 1995; "California Bilingual Loan Documents May Create Enforcement Problems," US Network News, Summer 1995; "Legislative Update," REOMAC Newsletter, March 1995; "Boston Harbor, Safety Net or Gill Net for Borrowers," REOMAC Newsletter, January 1995. *Member:* Orange County Bar Association; State Bar of California; State Bar of Nevada. *PRACTICE AREAS:* Mortgage Banking; Real Estate Litigation; Unlawful Detainers.

---

**ROLAND P. REYNOLDS,** born West Covina, California, April 5, 1965; admitted to bar, 1990, California, U.S. District Court, Northern, Central, Eastern and Southern Districts of California; U.S. Court of Appeals, Ninth Circuit. *Education:* Dartmouth College (A.B., 1987); McGeorge School of Law (J.D., with distinction, 1990). Order of the Coif. Assistant Editor, Pacific Law Journal. Editor in Chief, Dartmouth Review, 1986-1987. Real Estate Broker, California, 1991. Author: "Danger From the Fair Debt Collection Practices Act," CTA Newsletter, Summer 1995; "Borrowers in Distress Attract a New Industry," CTA Newsletter, Spring 1995; "Companies Pitch Payment Relief," Servicing Management Magazine,

*(This Listing Continued)*

April 1955; "Boston Harbor, Safety Net or Gill Net for Borrowers," REOMAC Update newsletter, January 1995; "The Legality of Optical Storage", Mortgage Finance Magazine, January 1994; "Electronic Mortgage Talk," Mortgage Banking Magazine, August 1993. Member: U.S. Foreclosure Network (Vice-Chair, USFN Publications Committee, 1995); California Mortgage Bankers Association; Southern California Mortgage Bankers Association; Orange County Mortgage Bankers Association. *Member:* Orange County and American Bar Associations; State Bar of California. *PRACTICE AREAS:* Mortgage Banking; Real Estate and Commercial Litigation; Creditors' Rights. *Email:* RPR@WolfPfeifer.com

**DONNA L. LA PORTE,** born Montebello, California, November 13, 1950; admitted to bar, 1979, Utah and U.S. District Court, District of Utah; 1980, California and U.S. District Court, Central, Southern, Northern and Eastern Districts of California. *Education:* University of Utah (B.A., Phi Beta Kappa, 1976; J.D., 1979). Speaker, "Bankruptcy Fraud Panel," Independent Bankers Roundtable, June 1996. Member, Orange County Bankruptcy Forum; Southern California Mortage Bankers Association. *Member:* Orange County Bar Association; State Bar of California; Utah State Bar. *PRACTICE AREAS:* Secured Real Property Creditor Rights.

**C. ROBERT SIMPSON,** born Los Angeles, California, July 16, 1957; admitted to bar, 1984, Utah, U.S. District Court, District of Utah; 1995, California; 1996, U.S. District Court, Eastern, Central, Southern and Northern Districts of California. *Education:* University of California at Los Angeles (B.A., cum laude, 1981); Duke University (J.D., 1984). Author, "Getting Snake Bit by Fraud," Mortgage Banking Magazine, December 1996. Member, Mortgage Bankers Association of America. *Member:* Orange County and American Bar Associations; State Bar of California; Utah State Bar; Orange County Barristers Association. *PRACTICE AREAS:* Mortgage Fraud.

**DIANE WEIFENBACH,** born Carrington, North Dakota, August 21, 1959; admitted to bar, 1992, California and U.S. District Court, Central District of California; 1993, U.S. District Court, Eastern District of California. *Education:* Western State University (B.S., 1991; J.D., cum laude, 1992). Production Editor, Law Review. Speaker, "Bankruptcy for the California Attorney," Orange County Bar Association Seminar, 1995. *Member:* Orange County Bar Association; State Bar of California. *PRACTICE AREAS:* Secured Real Property Creditor Rights.

**JAMES F. LEWIN,** born New York, New York, June 22, 1957; admitted to bar, 1989, California and U.S. District Court, Eastern, Central and Southern Districts of California. *Education:* University of Colorado at Boulder (B.A., 1982); Southwestern University School of Law (J.D., 1986). Member, Los Angeles Bankruptcy Forum. *Member:* Los Angeles County Bar Association; State Bar of California. *PRACTICE AREAS:* Secured Real Property Creditor Rights.

*OF COUNSEL*

**KAY VIRGINIA GUSTAFSON,** born Omaha, Nebraska, May 28, 1952; admitted to bar, 1977, California. *Education:* Stanford University (A.B., Phi Beta Kappa, 1973; J.D., 1977). Author: "Compliance with the Fair Debt Collection Practices Act," Mortgage Finance Magazine, September 1995; "Reducing the Risk of Fair Lending Violations," Mortgage Finance Magazine, October 1994; "Fraud Begins at Home...Or at Least With the Loan Application," Orange County Lawyer, August 1992; "Ain't Got No Home," Orange County Lawyer, August 1991; Column, "Regulatory Notes," Orange County Association of Mortgage Bankers Newsletter, 1991-1994. Speaker: "Fair Debt Collection Practices Act," Loan Servicing Conference, September 1995; "Fair Debt Collection Practices Act," California Mortgage Bankers Association, July 1995; "A Primer in the Secondary Mortgage Market," Orange County Bar Association Financial Practice Section, January 1994; "Legal Issues," Wholesale Roundtable, January 1992. Regular Speaker on Loan Fraud and Regulatory Issues for Orange County Mortgage Banking Industry Trade Groups. Member, Orange County Association of Mortgage Professionals. *Member:* Orange County Bar Association (Member, Section on: Financial Practice (Chairperson, 1996); Business and Corporate Law (Vice-Chairperson, 1996); Pro Bono Committee) State Bar of California. *PRACTICE AREAS:* Mortgage Banking; Regulatory Matters; Real Estate; General Business Transactions. *Email:* KVG@WolfPfeifer.com

*LEGAL SUPPORT PERSONNEL*

**DONA M. HARMAN** (Director of Client Relations).

(Representative Client List Furnished Upon Request)

## YOUNG & AMUNDSEN

*Established in 1993*

620 NEWPORT CENTER DRIVE, SUITE 420
**NEWPORT BEACH, CALIFORNIA 92660**
Telephone: 714-640-4400
Fax: 714-717-4862

Construction and Real Estate Litigation, Real Estate, Bankruptcy, Broker Liability, Subsidence Law. General Litigation in all Courts, Trade and Customs Law.

FIRM PROFILE: Young & Amundsen maintains its primary focus on the trial of business, construction and real estate lawsuits. In the last two years, its attorneys have tried 15 cases to judgment or verdict. Young, Amundsen & Dial prides itself on a high success rate derived from intelligent trial preparation performed within the client's budget rather than unproductive, unfocused pretrial skirmishes. The philosophy is to provide the highest level of service in the business litigation arena and to take cases to trial without reservation when it serves the best interests our clients. The law firm is listed in the Bar Register Preeminent Directory of lawyers.

*MEMBERS OF FIRM*

**STEVEN R. YOUNG,** born Los Angeles, California, June 30, 1954; admitted to bar, 1980, California; 1981, U.S. District Court, Central and Northern Districts of California and U.S. Court of Appeals, Ninth Circuit; 1986, U.S. District Court, Southern District of California; 1987, U.S. Tax Court; 1991, Washington. *Education:* University of Utah (B.A., cum laude, 1977); Pepperdine University (J.D., 1980). Phi Delta Phi. Literary Editor, Clinical Law Reporter, Pepperdine University School of Law, 1979-1980. Author: "Can a Jury Consultant Help Your Case?" Orange County Lawyer, June 1996, pg 27. Panelist: "Evidence in Bankruptcy Court", sponsored by the Orange County Bankruptcy Forum, June 1992; "Real Estate Found", The Orange County Bar Association, April 1996; Bevadry Law in California", The National Business Institute. Contributor: "A Bankruptcy Trial Workshop," sponsored by the Orange County and Los Angeles County Bankruptcy Forums and The Commercial Law and Bankruptcy Section of the Los Angeles County Bar Association, May 1989. Moderator: "Foreclosures In The 90's: Nuts, Bolts, Screws & Cranks," sponsored by the Real Property Section of the Orange County Bar Association, Nov. 1993; "Real Estate Contracts: A Primer," sponsored by the Real Property Section of the Orange County Bar Association, June, 1994. Lecturer, "Landlord/Tenant Law, Recent Developments and Trial Strategies," presented by Orange County Bar Association, Nov. 1994. *Member:* Orange County (Member, Sections on: Construction Law; Business Litigation; Executive Committee of Real Property Law Section; Past Co-Chair, Construction Law Section), Los Angeles County and American (Member, Sections on: Litigation) Bar Associations; State Bar of California (Member: Litigation Section; Real Property Section); State Bar of Washington; Washington State Trial Lawyers Association; The Association of Trial Lawyers of America. *PRACTICE AREAS:* Trials; Real Estate Law; Construction Disputes. *Email:* sryoung@kaiwan.com

**ROLAND J. AMUNDSEN,** born Bakersfield, California, October 11, 1953; admitted to bar, 1987, California; 1988, U.S. District Court, Central and Southern Districts of California. *Education:* California State University at Long Beach (B.A., 1981); Western State University, college of Law, at Fullerton (J.D., 1987). Who's Who in Law Schools of America. *Member:* Orange County (Member, Sections on: Business Litigation; Construction and Real Property) and Los Angeles County Member, Sections on: Real Property, Taxation and Construction) Bar Associations; State Bar of California (Member, Sections on: Litigation; Real Property). *PRACTICE AREAS:* General; Real Estate; Construction Litigation; General Tort Law.

REPRESENTATIVE CLIENTS: Mitsui/SBD America Fund; New London Oil Inc.; Waterfront Homes; SBD Properties; The Dalebout Association.

## GUY W. MURRAY

671 WEST TEFFT STREET, SUITE 9
P.O. BOX 180
**NIPOMO, CALIFORNIA 93444**
Telephone: 805-929-7150
Fax: 805-929-7151
Email: NIPOMOLAW@AOL.COM

General Civil Trial Practice in all State and Federal Courts, Civil Litigation, Casualty Defense, Real Estate and Construction Law.

*(This Listing Continued)*

**GUY W. MURRAY,** born Salt Lake City, Utah, January 25, 1954; admitted to bar, 1987, California and U.S. District Court, Central District of California. *Education:* Brigham Young University (B.A., 1983); Whittier College (J.D., 1986). *Member:* State Bar of California.

## LAW OFFICES OF RAND F. HARRIS

*A PROFESSIONAL CORPORATION*

**NORTH HOLLYWOOD, CALIFORNIA**

(See Los Angeles)

Family Law, Criminal Law, Personal Injury, Workers Compensation Defense, Business and Real Estate.

## F. BENTLEY MOONEY, JR.

*A LAW CORPORATION*

*Established in 1972*

4605 LANKERSHIM BOULEVARD, SUITE 718
**NORTH HOLLYWOOD, CALIFORNIA 91602**
Telephone: 818-769-4221
213-877-3902
FAX: 818-769-5002

Practice limited to Business Law, Estate Planning and Probate Law.

FIRM PROFILE: President and sole shareholder is F. Bentley Mooney, Jr.

Mr. Mooney began in 1972 as an associate with Clarke and Leary, a firm established in this city in 1938. In 1976, he became a partner (then Clarke, Leary & Mooney) and practiced as such until June 30, 1981. The partnership was then dissolved, Clarke and Leary continuing as a part-time law partnership and Mr. Mooney continuing as a sole practitioner.

He is the author of several books on business and estates law and many legal articles. His most recent book is Preserving Your Wealth (Probus 1993), a 450-page work on asset protection planning.

**F. BENTLEY MOONEY, JR.,** born Tulare, California, April 13, 1936; admitted to bar, 1972, California and U.S. District Court, Central District of California; 1975, U.S. Supreme Court. *Education:* University of San Fernando Valley (B.A., 1970; LL.B., 1972). *Member:* Los Angeles County (Member, 1972-1995; Chair, Law Office Management Section, 1984-1985; Vice-Chair, Attorney-Client Relations Committee, 1986-1987, Trustee, 1990-1991) and American Bar Associations; State Bar of California (Member, Executive Committee, Law Practice Management Section, 1983-1986; Conference of Bar Delegates, 1980—); Lawyers Club of Los Angeles County (Governor, 1986-1988, President, 1988-1989); Glendale Estate Planning Council (Co-Founder, Member and Director, 1970—; President, 1995—); Association of Business Trial Lawyers; Christian Legal Society; National Academy of Elder Law Attorneys. *PRACTICE AREAS:* Business Law; Estate Planning; Medicaid Eligibility Planning; Asset Protection.

## ROSATO & SAMUELS

*A PROFESSIONAL CORPORATION*

R & S PLAZA
11650 RIVERSIDE DRIVE
**NORTH HOLLYWOOD, CALIFORNIA 91602-1066**
Telephone: 818-753-9200
Telecopier: 818-766-2507

General Civil Trial and Appellate Practice in all Courts. Life, Health and Disability Insurance Claims and Defense including Managed Care and ERISA, Professional Liability, Errors and Omissions Insurance Coverage and Legal Malpractice, General and Commercial Property and Casualty Defense, Employment Law, Business Litigation, Commercial Litigation, Entertainment Litigation, Products Liability, Surplus Lines and Special Risk Insurance Defense, Real Estate Litigation, including the Representation of Brokers and Real Estate Agents, Property Law, Escrow and Title Matters, Structural Defense and Premises Liability, Partnership Disputes and Breaches of Fiduciary Duties as between partners.

*(This Listing Continued)*

**FIRM PROFILE:** Rosato & Samuels is a litigation specialty insurance defense firm, dedicated to client satisfaction. The firm specializes in all manner of health litigation, including managed care, ERISA, "bad faith", life and disability claims and defense, professional liability, errors and omissions, legal malpractice, EMPLOYMENT LAW, products liability and general and commercial casualty and property litigation.

**RALPH L. ROSATO,** born Los Angeles, California, October 24, 1948; admitted to bar, 1974, California. *Education:* Loyola Marymount University (B.A., 1970); University of California at Los Angeles (J.D., 1974). Lecturer: USC Institute for Law and Psychiatry, 1975-1984; Los Angeles County Bar, Juvenile Courts, 1983. Judge Pro Tem, Los Angeles Superior Court, 1981. Member, Los Angeles Public Defender's Office, 1974-1978. *Member:* Los Angeles County and American Bar Associations; State Bar of California; Italian-American Lawyers Association; California Attorneys for Criminal Justice. **PRACTICE AREAS:** Commercial Litigation; Prosecution Insurance Defense Law; Bad Faith Law.

**CARY S. SAMUELS,** born Los Angeles, California, October 30, 1948; admitted to bar, 1974, California. *Education:* University of California at Los Angeles (B.A., magna cum laude, 1970); Southwestern University (J.D., 1974). Member, Southwestern University Law Review, 1972-1973. *Member:* State Bar of California. **PRACTICE AREAS:** Commercial Litigation; Prosecution Insurance Defense Law; Bad Faith Law.

**ELLEN B. KAMON,** born New York, N.Y., May 4, 1951; admitted to bar, 1982, California. *Education:* University of California at Los Angeles (A.B., cum laude, 1972; M.A., 1974 and M.A., 1976); San Fernando Valley College of Law (J.D., 1981). *Member:* Los Angeles County Bar Association; State Bar of California. **PRACTICE AREAS:** Commercial Litigation; Prosecution Insurance Defense Law; Bad Faith Law.

**MICHAEL B. MAGLOFF,** born New York, N.Y., April 24, 1940; admitted to bar, 1966, California and U.S. District Court, Central District of California. *Education:* Brandeis University (B.A., cum laude, 1962); Boalt Hall School of Law, University of California (LL.B., 1965). Arbitrator, Los Angeles County Municipal and Superior Courts. *Member:* Los Angeles County and American Bar Associations; The State Bar of California. **PRACTICE AREAS:** Commercial Litigation; Prosecution Insurance Defense Law; Bad Faith Law.

---

## PHILLIP SCHLOSBERG

A PROFESSIONAL CORPORATION
12650 RIVERSIDE DRIVE
**NORTH HOLLYWOOD, CALIFORNIA 91607-3492**
Telephone: 818-755-4848
Fax: 818-760-2583

*Real Property, Business Litigation, Domestic Relations Law and Personal Injury.*

**PHILLIP SCHLOSBERG,** born San Francisco, California, January 1, 1946; admitted to bar, 1971, California. *Education:* University of California (B.A.); University of Hastings College of Law (J.D.).

---

## WILLIAMS, BERGES & SANFORD

**NORTH HOLLYWOOD, CALIFORNIA**

(See Los Angeles)

*General Civil and Trial Practice. Negligence, Products Liability, Probate, Malpractice and Insurance Law.*

---

## STUART D. ZIMRING

**NORTH HOLLYWOOD, CALIFORNIA**

(See Los Angeles)

*Estate Planning, Trust and Probate Law, Elder Law, Business and Banking, Real Estate, Condominiums and Homeowners Associations.*

---

## PAUL H. MILLER

**NORWALK, CALIFORNIA**

(See Santa Fe Springs)

*Probate, Estate Planning and Trust, Real Estate and Corporate Law.*

---

## ROBERT E. MITCHELL

13915 SOUTH SAN ANTONIO DRIVE
P.O. BOX 365
**NORWALK, CALIFORNIA 90650**
Telephone: 310-863-8736
Fax: 310-868-7266

*Corporate, Estate Planning, Real Estate and Business Litigation Law.*

**ROBERT E. MITCHELL,** born Los Angeles, California, February 4, 1928; admitted to bar, 1956, California. *Education:* University of Southern California (B.S., 1952; LL.B., 1956). Phi Delta Phi; Blue Key. Member, Skull and Dagger. Appointed by Governor Reagan and Retained by Governor Brown as Member and Chairman of the State Benefits & Services Advisory Board, 1968-1979. Member, 1981-1987 and Chairman, 1984-1987, Recombinant DNA Advisory Committee of the National Institute of Health, 1981-1987. Member, Acquired Immunodeficiency Syndrome Advisory Committee of the National Institute of Health, 1987-1990. *Member:* Los Angeles County and American Bar Associations; Southeast Bar Association; State Bar of California (Former Member, Child Custody and Adoption Committee). [Corporal, U.S. Army, 1946-1948]. **PRACTICE AREAS:** Corporate Law; Estate Planning; Real Estate Law; Business Litigation.

REPRESENTATIVE CLIENTS: Dunn-Edwards Corp.; LeFiell Manufacturing Co.

---

## CHARLES R. WELDON

SUITE 104 SOUTHEAST LAW CENTER
12749 NORWALK BOULEVARD
P.O. BOX 1110
**NORWALK, CALIFORNIA 90651**
Telephone: 310-864-3737
FAX: 310-863-9962

*General Civil and Trial Practice in all State and Federal Courts. Personal Injury, Products Liability, Medical and Legal Malpractice and Negligence Law.*

**CHARLES R. WELDON,** born Pauls Valley, Oklahoma, January 11, 1933; admitted to bar, 1957, California. *Education:* Long Beach State College (B.A., 1954); University of Southern California (J.D., 1957). Co-Author: *Trial Lawyers Ready Reference to Evidence Code of California,* 1968; *Courtroom Ready Reference for Plaintiff's Attorneys,* 1968; *Ready Reference to Class Actions,* 1971. Co-founder, Southeast Law Center, 1969. Member, Board of Directors, Norwalk Community Hospital, 1976-1979. Councilman, City of Paramount, 1978-1990. *Member:* Los Angeles County, Orange County, Southeast District (Member, Board of Directors, 1966-1971; President, 1972) and American Bar Associations; State Bar of California; Los Angeles Trial Lawyers Association; California Trial Lawyers Association; The Association of Trial Lawyers of America; American Board of Trial Advocates; Long Beach Trial Association. **PRACTICE AREAS:** Personal Injury; Medical Malpractice; Legal Malpractice; Product Liability.

---

**JERRY D. TURNER,** born Smithville, Tennessee, December 2, 1937; admitted to bar, 1972, California. *Education:* South Macomb Community College; Cerritos College; Southwestern University (J.D., 1971). *Member:* Los Angeles County Bar Association; State Bar of California; California Trial Lawyers Association; The Association of Trial Lawyers of America; Los Angeles Trial Lawyers Association. **PRACTICE AREAS:** Personal Injury; Medical Malpractice; Legal Malpractice; Product Liability.

**E. NEAL DALEY,** born Sacramento, California, August 7, 1951; admitted to bar, 1976, California. *Education:* University of California at Davis (B.A., 1972); Pepperdine University (J.D., 1976). Recipient, Award for Excellence in Real Property at Pepperdine University. *Member:* Los Angeles County, Orange County, Southeast District and American Bar Associations; State Bar of California. **PRACTICE AREAS:** Personal Injury; Medi-

*(This Listing Continued)*

CHARLES R. WELDON, Norwalk—Continued

cal Malpractice; Legal Malpractice; Product Liability; Workers Compensation.

**PAUL R. DIXON,** born Los Angeles, California, May 3, 1953; admitted to bar, 1978, California. *Education:* Whittier College (B.A., 1975); California Western School of Law (J.D., 1978). *Member:* Los Angeles County and Southeast District Bar Associations; State Bar of California. **PRACTICE AREAS:** Personal Injury; Medical Malpractice; Legal Malpractice; Product Liability; Workers Compensation.

**PAUL D. BRAU,** born Auburn, California, February 20, 1952; admitted to bar, 1977, California. *Education:* University of California at Davis (B.A., 1974); Pepperdine University (J.D., cum laude, 1977). *Member:* Los Angeles County and Southeast District Bar Associations; State Bar of California. **PRACTICE AREAS:** Personal Injury; Medical Malpractice; Legal Malpractice; Products Liability; Workers Compensation.

**LAILA HAVRE JACOBSMA,** born Los Angeles, California, August 5, 1958; admitted to bar, 1993, California. *Education:* Rio Hondo College; Western State University (B.S.L., 1989; J.D., 1990). *Member:* Los Angeles County, Orange County and Southeast Bar Associations; State Bar of California; Los Angeles Trial Lawyers Association; Orange County Trial Lawyers Association; California Trial Lawyers Association; Women's Lawyer Association of Los Angeles. **PRACTICE AREAS:** Personal Injury Law; Medical Malpractice; Legal Malpractice; Product Liability Law; Workers' Compensation.

---

## BERGER, KAHN, SHAFTON, MOSS, FIGLER, SIMON & GLADSTONE

A Professional Corporation including a Professional Corporation

SUITE 304
1701 NOVATO BOULEVARD
**NOVATO, CALIFORNIA 94947**
Telephone: 415-899-1770
Telecopier: 415-899-1769

*Los Angeles, California Office:* 4215 Glencoe Avenue (Marina L.C. Del Rey), 90292-5634. Telephone: 310-821-9000. Telecopier: 310-578-6178.

*Irvine, California Office:* Suite 650, 2 Park Plaza, 92614. Telephone: 714-474-1880. Telecopier: 714-474-7265.

*San Diego, California Office:* 402 W. Broadway, Suite 400, 92101. Telephone: 619-236-8602. Telecopier: 619-236-0812.

*Bend, Oregon Office:* P.O. Box 1407, 97709. Telephone: 541-388-1400. Telecopier: 541-388-4731.

General Civil and Trial Practice in all State and Federal Courts. Corporation, Real Estate, Music and Entertainment Law and Intellectual Property, Labor and Insurance Law.

(For complete biographical data on all personnel, see Professional Biographies at Los Angeles)

---

## PALMER, JONES, HAWKINS & STRONG

Established in 1951

SUITE 200, 7665 REDWOOD BOULEVARD
**NOVATO, CALIFORNIA 94948**
Telephone: 415-892-1616
Fax: 415-897-5316
Email: LawPalmer@AOL.COM

*Santa Rosa, California Office:* 50 Santa Rosa Avenue, 95404. Telephone: 707-576-7182. Fax: 707-578-3943.

General Civil and Trial Practice. Construction Law and Litigation, Business, Corporations, Partnerships, Real Estate, Mobilehome Park Law, Landlord Representation, Bankruptcy, Trusts, Wills, Probate, Insurance Defense, and Family Law.

**FIRM PROFILE:** Since Clark Palmer established his general practice in Novato in 1952, our firm has expanded to offer a full range of legal services to North Bay businesses and individuals. By choice, our firm has remained small in order to provide legal services in a cost effective and result-oriented manner at a quality equal to or exceeding those offered by large firms. We attend to the individual needs of our clients and counsel them so that they are informed, active participants in the management of their legal concerns.

(This Listing Continued)

CAA1442B

---

**CLARK M. PALMER,** born New York, N.Y., November 17, 1924; admitted to bar, 1951, California. *Education:* Stanford University (A.B., 1948; LL.B., 1950). Phi Alpha Delta. City Attorney, City of Novato, 1960-1979. *Member:* Marin County Bar Association; State Bar of California. **PRACTICE AREAS:** Estate Planning; Probate Law.

**DAVID PRICE JONES,** born Berkeley, California, January 20, 1935; admitted to bar, 1962, California. *Education:* University of California at Berkeley (B.A., 1957); Boalt Hall School of Law, University of California (J.D., 1961). Mayor, Novato, California, 1974-1975. *Member:* Marin County Bar Association (Director, 1974-1975); State Bar of California. **PRACTICE AREAS:** Business Law; Corporate Law; Estate Planning; Probate Law; Real Estate Law; Real Estate and Business Litigation.

**BRUCE M. PALMER,** born Palo Alto, California, June 25, 1948; admitted to bar, 1976, California. *Education:* Stanford University (A.B., 1970); Hastings College of Law, University of California (J.D., 1976). Member: Order of the Coif; Thurston Society. Member, Hastings Law Journal, 1974-1975. *Member:* Marin County and American Bar Associations; State Bar of California. **PRACTICE AREAS:** Real Estate Law; Business Law; Mobilehome Park Law.

**LAURA TRACY HAWKINS,** born Oakland, California, April 6, 1951; admitted to bar, 1986, California and U.S. District Court, Central, Eastern, Western, Southern and Northern Districts of California. *Education:* University of California at Berkeley (B.A., 1973); Secondary Teaching Credential, 1974); Empire College School of Law (J.D., 1986). *Member:* Sonoma County and Marin County Bar Associations; State Bar of California; Sonoma County Women in Law; Marin County Women Lawyers Association. **PRACTICE AREAS:** Family Law; Bankruptcy Law.

**KENNETH F. STRONG,** born Berkeley, California, January 13, 1952; admitted to bar, 1979, California. *Education:* University of California at Santa Barbara (B.A., 1975); Hastings College of the Law, University of California (J.D., 1979). Outside General Counsel, Harding Lawson Associates. *Member:* Bar Association of San Francisco; Marin County and American (Member, Sections Forum on Construction Industry and Natural Resources, Energy and Environmental Law) Bar Associations. **PRACTICE AREAS:** Litigation; Construction Law; Environmental Law.

**E. MARK ZUNINO,** born Oakland, California, December 22, 1960; admitted to bar, 1987, California and U.S. Court of Appeals, Ninth Circuit. *Education:* University of California at Berkeley (A.B., 1983); University of San Francisco (J.D., 1987). *Member:* Bar Association of San Francisco; Marin County and American Bar Associations; State Bar of California. **PRACTICE AREAS:** Construction Law; Insurance Law; Construction Litigation.

REPRESENTATIVE CLIENTS: Harding Lawson Associates; R.C. Roberts; Redwood Insurance; Atlantic Mutual Insurance Company; DeAnza Associates; Carlsberg Management; Treadwell & Rollo, Inc.
REFERENCES: Westamerica Bank (Novato Office); Bank of America (Novato Office).

---

## GEORGE J. SILVESTRI, JR.

365 BEL MARIN KEYS BOULEVARD, SUITE 102
**NOVATO, CALIFORNIA 94949-5654**
Telephone: 415-883-8800
Fax: 415-883-8818

General Civil, Municipal, Real Estate, Land Use, Personal Injury, Landslide and Subsidence, Redevelopment, Environmental, Business, Legislative, Probate, Mediation, Arbitration and Appeals.

**GEORGE J. SILVESTRI, JR.,** born San Francisco, California, 1941; admitted to bar, 1969, California; 1977, U.S. Supreme Court. *Education:* St. Mary's College of California (B.A., 1963); Hastings College of Law, University of California (J.D., 1968). Deputy Marin County Counsel, 1969-1974. City Attorney and Redevelopment Agency Counsel, City of Brisbane, 1976-1984. Member, Board of Directors, The National Italian American Foundation, Washington, D.C. *Member:* Marin County Bar Association; State Bar of California; Marin Council Boy Scouts; Rotary Club of Novato.

## DAMRELL, NELSON, SCHRIMP, PALLIOS & LADINE

*A PROFESSIONAL CORPORATION*
Established in 1968

703 WEST "F" STREET
P.O. DRAWER C
**OAKDALE, CALIFORNIA 95361**
Telephone: 209-848-3500
Fax: 209-848-3400
Email: dnsp1@ix.netcom.com

*Modesto, California Office:* 1601 I Street, Fifth Floor. Telephone: 209-526-3500. Fax: 209-526-3534.
*Sacramento, California Office:* Suite 200, 1100 K Street. Telephone: 916-447-2909. Fax: 916-447-0552.

Civil Trial and Appellate Practice in all State and Federal Courts, General Business Practice, Complex Business Litigation, Government, Administrative and Legislative Practice, Business Planning and Dissolution, Personal Injury and Insurance Law, Corporate, Environmental, Resource Recovery, Water and Agricultural Law, Land Use, Real Estate Development, Zoning and Construction Law, Health Care and Hospital Law, Taxation, Estate Planning and Probate and Trust Administration.

*FIRM PROFILE:* The firm's attorneys practice before all levels of federal and California courts with particular emphasis on civil litigation, including complex and business litigation, as well as commercial law, general business, real estate law, environmental law, governmental law, and probate. The firm also has extensive experience representing clients before the U.S. Congress and the California Legislature, as well as before federal, state, and local government boards and agencies.

**ROGER M. SCHRIMP,** born Stockton, California, May 26, 1941; admitted to bar, 1966, California; 1967, U.S. District Courts, Northern, Central and Eastern Districts of California; 1978, U.S. Tax Court and U.S. Supreme Court; 1981, U.S. Claims Court. *Education:* University of California (A.B., with honors, 1963); Boalt Hall School of Law, University of California (J.D., 1966); McGeorge School of Law, University of the Pacific (LL.M. in Taxation, 1982). Phi Alpha Delta. Appointed by Gov. Pete Wilson to Board of governors, California Community Colleges, July 1996. Chairman of the Board, Oak Valley Community Bank. President, Boy Scouts of America, Areas III, Western Region. *Member:* Stanislaus County (President, 1993) and American (Member, Committee on Agriculture, Section of Taxation) Bar Associations; State Bar of California; The Association of Trial Lawyers of America; California Trial Lawyers Association; American Judicature Society; Lawyer-Pilots Bar Association; Northern California Association of Defense Counsel; Defense Research Institute; National Association of Eagle Scouts. *PRACTICE AREAS:* Business Law; Real Estate Law; Complex Business Litigation.

**FRED A. SILVA,** born Azores, Portugal, December 11, 1958; admitted to bar, 1987, California and U.S. District Court, Eastern and Northern Districts of California. *Education:* University of the Pacific (B.A., cum laude, 1982); University of California at Davis (J.D., 1986). Phi Kappa Phi; Omicron Delta Epsilon. *Member:* Stanislaus County (Member, Board of Directors, 1991—; President, 1994-1995) and American (Member, Corporation, Banking and Business Law Section) Bar Associations; State Bar of California (Member, Business Law Section). *LANGUAGES:* Portuguese. *PRACTICE AREAS:* Business Litigation; Complex Litigation.

(For Biographical Data, see Professional Biographies at Modesto, California).

---

## STOCKTON & SADLER

**OAKDALE, CALIFORNIA**

(See Modesto)

Civil Trial and Appellate Practice. Agriculture, Business, Corporate, Estate Planning, Probate, Partnerships, Real Estate, Personal Injury.

---

## LINN, LINDLEY & BLATE

*A PROFESSIONAL ASSOCIATION*

YOSEMITE BANK BUILDING
40061 49 HIGHWAY, SUITE 101
P.O. BOX 2347
**OAKHURST, CALIFORNIA 93644**
Telephone: 209-683-7333; 209-642-2555
FAX: 209-683-3634

General Civil and Trial Practice including Personal Injury, Probate and Estate Planning, Corporate, Business, Taxation, Natural Resources Law, Banking Litigation, Criminal Law and Family Law.

**DAVID A. LINN,** born Pittsburgh, Pennsylvania, August 8, 1948; admitted to bar, 1976, California; 1977, U.S. District Court, Central District of California; 1982, U.S. District Court, Eastern District of California and U.S. Claims Court; 1992, U.S. Court of Appeals for the Federal Circuit and U.S. Supreme Court. *Education:* Purdue University (B.S., 1970); California State University (M.B.A., 1986); Pepperdine University (J.D., 1976). Phi Alpha Delta. Chairman, Oakhurst Park Committee, 1984; Eastern Madera County Man of the Year, 1989. Judge Pro-Tem Madera Superior Court, 1988—. *Member:* Madera County (President, 1991) and Mariposa County Bar Associations; State Bar of California; Federal Circuit Bar Association. [CDR. USNR, Active 1970-1973, Reserve 1970—]. *REPORTED CASES:* LDG Timber Enterprises Incorporated v. United States U.S. Claims Court Reporter, 8 Cl. Ct. 445 (1985). *PRACTICE AREAS:* Personal Injury Litigation; Banking Litigation; Natural Resources Law; Business Litigation; Criminal Law.

**ROBERT B. LINDLEY,** born Orange, California, February 28, 1950; admitted to bar, 1976, California and U.S. District Court, Central District of California; 1980, U.S. District Court, Eastern District of California; 1991, U.S. Tax Court. *Education:* Stanford University (B.A., with honors, 1972); University of California at Los Angeles (J.D., 1975); University of San Diego (LL.M., Tax, 1990). Instructor, Business Law, Fresno City College, 1980. Judge Pro Tem, Bass Lake Municipal Court, 1984, 1985, 1991. *Member:* Madera County (Treasurer, 1992; President, 1994) Bar Associations; State Bar of California (Member, Taxation and Estate Planning Sections). *PRACTICE AREAS:* Probate and Estate Administration; Estate Planning; Taxation; Corporate; Real Estate.

**GARY T. BLATE,** born Santa Monica, California, November 11, 1950; admitted to bar, 1979, California and U.S. District Court, Central District of California; 1989, U.S. District Court, Eastern District of California. *Education:* University of California at Los Angeles (B.A., 1974); Western State University (J.D., 1978). Author: Western State Law Review, Spring 1988. *Member:* Orange County and Eastern Madera County Bar Associations. [U.S. Army, 1970-1972, Specialist]. *REPORTED CASES:* Duckett v. Pistoresi Ambulance Service, Inc., 19 Cal. App. 4th 1525-Cal Rptr 2d Nov. 1993. *PRACTICE AREAS:* Personal Injury; Business and Collections; Family; Criminal.

**JOHN P. LALONDE,** born Charleston, South Carolina, December 9, 1953; admitted to bar, 1995, California and U.S. District Court, Eastern District of California. *Education:* Michigan State University (B.S., Psychology with high honors, 1977); California State University (Masters in Social Work, MSW, 1981); Empire College School of Law (J.D., cum laude, 1995). Licensed Clinical Social Worker (L.C.S.W., 1984). *Member:* Sonoma County and Eastern Madera County Bar Associations; State Bar of California. *PRACTICE AREAS:* Family Law; Juvenile Court; Criminal; Business Litigation; Mediation.

REPRESENTATIVE CLIENTS: Yosemite Bank; L.D.G. Timber, Inc.; H & L Lumber Co., Inc.; Disabled Veterans of America; Interwest Corp., Salt Lake City, Utah; Golden Oak Bank, Oakhurst, Calif.; Madera Newspapers Incorporated; Suburban Propane of Morristown, New Jersey; J.R. Forest Products, Inc.; Butler Logging, Inc.

## AIKEN, KRAMER & CUMMINGS
INCORPORATED
*Established in 1896*

SUITE 550 ORDWAY BUILDING
ONE KAISER PLAZA
**OAKLAND, CALIFORNIA 94612**
Telephone: 510-834-6800
Fax: 510-834-9017
Email: aikenkrame@aol.com

*General Business and Real Estate, Transactional Practice, General Civil Litigation Practice, Corporate, Commercial, Environmental, Employment, Construction, Insurance, Intellectual Property, Estate Planning, Probate and Tax.*

**BENJ. R. AIKEN** (1879-1955).

**BAUER E. KRAMER** (Retired).

**BENJ. R. AIKEN, JR.** (Retired).

**FRED V. CUMMINGS** (Retired).

**JOHN A. HARKAVY,** born New York, N.Y., January 4, 1943; admitted to bar, 1967, California, U.S. District Court, Northern District of California, U.S. Court of Appeals, Ninth Circuit and U.S. Tax Court. *Education:* Bucknell University (A.B., 1964); University of California at Berkeley (J.D., 1967). Phi Sigma Alpha; Phi Delta Phi. Recipient, American Jurisprudence Awards for Corporations, Real Property, Secured Transactions and Security Law. Expert Witness, Legal Malpractice Involving Business Transactions. *Member:* Alameda County and American (Member, State and Local Taxes Committee of the Section of Taxation, 1980-1983) Bar Associations. [Capt., U.S. Army Artillery, 1967-1969]. **REPORTED CASES:** Beamer v. Franchise Tax Board, 19 Cal 3d 467, 138 Cal Rptr. 199, 563 P2d 238 (1977). **PRACTICE AREAS:** Transactional Matters; Business Acquisitions; Real Estate; Solid Waste; Municipal Solid Waste; Environmental; Expert witness for Legal Malpractice Actions.

**ELIZABETH M. ENGH,** born Los Angeles, California, March 21, 1952; admitted to bar, 1978, California. *Education:* University of California at Los Angeles (B.A., cum laude, 1973); Boalt Hall School of Law, University of California at Berkeley (J.D., 1977). *Member:* Alameda County Bar Association (Past Chairperson, Estate Planning Committee; Member, Section on Estate Planning, Trust and Probate Law). (Certified Specialist, Probate, Estate Planning and Trust Law, State Bar of California Board of Legal Specialization). **PRACTICE AREAS:** Estate Planning; Probate; Trust.

**MATTHEW F. GRAHAM,** born San Francisco, March 30, 1956; admitted to bar, 1980, California. *Education:* University of San Francisco (B.A., magna cum laude, 1977; J.D., 1980). Alpha Sigma Nu. *Member:* Alameda County and San Francisco Bar Associations; State Bar of California. **PRACTICE AREAS:** Litigation; Construction Law; Labor and Employment.

**STEVEN J. CRAMER,** born Oakland, California, April 3, 1958; admitted to bar, 1983, California. *Education:* University of Santa Clara (B.S., cum laude, 1980); University of California at Los Angeles (J.D., 1983). Order of the Coif. *Member:* Alameda County Bar Association. **PRACTICE AREAS:** Real Estate; Transactional Matters.

**RICHARD A. SIPOS,** born Van Nuys, California, July 22, 1961; admitted to bar, 1986, California. *Education:* University of California at Los Angeles (B.A., cum laude, 1983); Santa Clara University (J.D., 1986). Research Editor, Santa Clara Law Review, 1985-1986. Author: "California's 'New' Newsman's Shield Law and the Criminal Defendant's Right to Fair Trial," 26 Santa Clara L. Rev. 219 (1986); "Preventative Measures in the Lateral Hiring Process to Avoid Disqualification," 1 Legal Malpractice Report 4 (1991). *Member:* Alameda County Bar Association; State Bar of California. **PRACTICE AREAS:** Business Law; Construction Law; Professional Malpractice; Insurance Litigation.

### OF COUNSEL

**RUSSELL L. BARLOW,** born Oakland, California, March 20, 1936; admitted to bar, 1961, California. *Education:* Stanford University (A.B., 1957); University of California at Berkeley (LL.B., 1960). Phi Delta Phi. *Member:* Alameda County and American Bar Associations.

**BRUCE G. HEROLD,** born New York, N.Y., June 28, 1938; admitted to bar, 1968, California. *Education:* Cornell University (A.B., 1958); Hastings College of Law, University of California (J.D., 1967). Law Clerk, Presiding Judge, Alameda County Superior Court, 1969-1970. Deputy District Attorney, 1970-1972. *Member:* Alameda County and American Bar Associ-

*(This Listing Continued)*

ations. [Lt. Col., USAFR, Ret.]. **PRACTICE AREAS:** Litigation; Construction Law; Family Law.

**MICHAEL A. COAN,** born Washington, D.C., August 19, 1951; admitted to bar, 1976, California. *Education:* University of Notre Dame (B.S., magna cum laude, 1973); Boalt Hall School of Law (J.D., 1976). **PRACTICE AREAS:** Estate Planning; Trusts; Probate; Nonprofit Corporations.

---

**ELLEN SUZANNE WYATT,** born Chicago, Illinois, January 28, 1943; admitted to bar, 1979, California. *Education:* California Western University (B.A., magna cum laude, 1964); Hastings College of Law, University of California (J.D., 1979). *Member:* Alameda County and American Bar Associations.

**MICHAEL S. TREPPA,** born Royal Oak, Michigan, March 8, 1964; admitted to bar, 1989, California. *Education:* University of California at Santa Barbara (B.A., 1986); Golden Gate University (J.D., 1989). Editor-in-Chief, Golden Gate Law Review, 1988-1989. Recipient, American Jurisprudence Award, Constitutional Law. Author: "The Education for All Handicapped Children Act: Trends and Problems with the 'Related Services' Provision," Vol. 18 G.G. L. Rev. 427, 1988. *Member:* Alameda County and American Bar Associations; The State Bar of California.

REPRESENTATIVE CLIENTS: The Customer Company (owner and operator of CHEAPER! stores throughout California); J.A. Jones Construction Company (general contractor); Harding Associates, Inc. (environmental engineers/consultants); McCaulou's, Inc. (department stores); United Security Products, Inc. (safety and security devices); Total Scan (owner and operator of MRI scanner); Jatco Incorporated and Master Plastics, Incorporated (plastics manufacturing); Ralph Garrow, Inc. and Condiotti Enterprises, Inc. (developers and contractors specializing in residential subdivisions); Winton Jones Contractor, Inc.; Masonry Services, Inc.; L&D Scaffold, Inc.; Hillhouse, Inc.; Carey Bros., (general or speciality contractors); Timco Distributors, Inc.; Grant J. Hunt Company (produce distributors); Morse-Starrett Products Co.; Price Pump Co. and Bay Area Industrial Filtration, Inc. (manufacturing); Wastech Incorporated, Wastech Services, Ltd.; Norcal Waste Services, Inc.; Nortech Waste, LLC (waste management); East Bay Tire Company (distributor of commercial tires); Genius Inc. and Appintec Corp. (developers and distributors of specialized software); The Gifted Line (manufacturers of gift products and licensor of antique ephemera); Lassen Electronics (manufacturer of electronic products). Reference: Union Bank of California.

---

## ALLSWANG, SMITH & WALSH
7700 EDGEWATER DRIVE, SUITE 215
**OAKLAND, CALIFORNIA 94621**
Telephone: 510-567-1010
Fax: 510-567-1020

*San Francisco, California Office:* 180 Montgomery Street, Suite 2000, 94104. Telephone: 415-291-8844. Fax: 415-291-8855.

*Civil Litigation specifically utilizing Alternative Dispute Resolution in the following areas: Construction, Land Use, Commercial, Environmental, Real Estate Errors and Omissions, Products Liability, Professional Liability, Premises Liability, Insurance Defense, Insurance Fraud, Bad-Faith Defense and Insurance Coverage.*

FIRM PROFILE: *Allswang, Smith & Walsh is one of California's largest women-owned litigation firms, with a civil practice emphasizing dispute resolution on behalf of corporations, insurance carriers and public entities. The firm is traditional in its dedication to quality representation and results-oriented services but innovative in response to its clients' needs, including close monitoring of litigation, alternative fee arrangements and budgeting.*

**DAVID ALLSWANG,** born St. Paul, Minnesota, April 30, 1940; admitted to bar, 1977, California. *Education:* University of California at Berkeley (A.B., 1962; M.A., 1963); University of San Francisco (J.D., 1977). Member, McAuliffe Law Honor Society. Instructor, Hastings College of Law, 1979-1981. Member: National Panel of Arbitrators, American Arbitration Association; Panel of Arbitrators, San Francisco Superior Court. *Member:* Bar Association of San Francisco; Bar Association of Alameda; Contra Costa County and American (Member, Sections on: Litigation; Torts and Insurance Practice); Bar Associations; State Bar of California; Association of Defense Counsel of Northern California; Defense Research Institute.

**ANNE SCHMITZ,** born Chicago, Illinois, September 29, 1961; admitted to bar, 1993, California. *Education:* University of California, Davis (A.B., 1986); McGeorge School of Law (J.D., 1993). Staff Writer, Pacific Law Journal, 1991-1992. Symposium Editor, 1992-1993. Recipient, Outstanding Student Achievement Award. *Member:* State Bar of California.

*(This Listing Continued)*

REPRESENTATIVE CLIENTS: State Farm Mutual Automobile Insurance Co.; State Farm Fire & Casualty Co.; Pacific Gas & Electric Company; City and County of San Francisco; Port of San Francisco; Lloyds of London; Maxon Young & Associates, Inc.; Dollar Rent-a-Car; Cosdel International; Bechtel; Alameda Contra Costa Transit District.

## ANTHONY & CARLSON

*1999 HARRISON STREET, SUITE 1750*
**OAKLAND, CALIFORNIA 94612**
Telephone: 510-835-8400
Fax: 510-835-5566

*General Civil Trial Practice, Professional Negligence, Insurance Bad Faith, Wrongful Termination/Discrimination, Commercial Litigation.*

### MEMBERS OF FIRM

**STEVEN R. ANTHONY,** born Oakland, California, September 23, 1940; admitted to bar, 1966, California. *Education:* Arizona State University (B.A., 1962); Hastings College of Law, University of California (LL.B., 1965). Phi Delta Phi. Law Clerk to Shirley Hufstedler and John Aiso, Appellate Department, Los Angeles Superior Court, 1965-1966. *Member:* Alameda County Bar Association; The State Bar of California; National Association of Railroad Trial Counsel; American Board of Trial Advocates; Association of Defense Counsel of Northern California; Arbitrator and Mediator, Alameda County. *PRACTICE AREAS:* Civil Trial Law; Insurance Law; Medical Liability Defense Law; Wrongful Termination; Legal Malpractice.

**RICHARD H. CARLSON,** born Los Angeles, California, June 27, 1941; admitted to bar, 1967, California. *Education:* University of California at Berkeley (A.B., 1963); Hastings College of Law, University of California (LL.B., 1966). Phi Delta Phi. Law Clerk to Hon. Jesse W. Curtis, Jr., U.S. District Court, Central District of California, 1966-1967. With Hoberg, Finger, Brown & Abramson, 1967-1981. Superior Court Judge, Pro-Tem (Jury Trials), 1990—. *Member:* Bar Association of San Francisco; The State Bar of California (Member, Committee on Administration of Justice, 1972-1978; Lecturer, Panelist and Consulting Author, Committee on Continuing Education, 1976—); Lawyers Club of San Francisco; San Francisco Trial Lawyers Association; California Trial Lawyers Association (Recognized experience in the fields of Trial Lawyer, Professional Negligence, Products Liability and General Personal Injury); The Association of Trial Lawyers of America; American Board of Trial Advocates. *REPORTED CASES:* Morris vs. County of Marin (1977) 18 Cal 3d 901; Sunseri vs. Camperos DeValle (1986) 185 Cal App 3d 559.

### ASSOCIATES

**BARBARA L. VANKOLL,** born Burlingame, California, May 17, 1964; admitted to bar, 1993, California. *Education:* St. Mary's College of California (B.S., Nursing, 1988); University of San Francisco (J.D., 1993). Registered Nurse, California, 1988. Judicial Extern to Justice Jerome Smith, California Court of Appeal, 1993,. *PRACTICE AREAS:* Medical Malpractice; Personal Injury Law.

### OF COUNSEL

**JANE L. TRIGERO,** born Reno, Nevada, February 26, 1952; admitted to bar, 1980, Nevada; 1981, U.S. District Court, Northern District of California; 1982, California; 1987, U.S. District Court, Eastern District of California. *Education:* University of Nevada; University of California at Davis (B.S., with honors, 1974); Mayo Clinic, University of Minnesota (R.D., with highest honors, 1975); University of San Francisco (J.D., 1980). Law Clerk to the Hon. Noel E. Manoukian, Supreme Court, State of Nevada, 1979. Law Clerk to the Hon. John E. Gabrielli, District Court, State of Nevada, 1980. Lecturer: University of San Francisco McLAren Hall, 1988-1993. *Member:* Bar Association of San Francisco; State Bar of California; State Bar of Nevada; National Employment Lawyers Association. *PRACTICE AREAS:* Labor and Employment; Civil Trial Practice.

## DAVID W. BARRON

*6250 MERCED AVENUE*
**OAKLAND, CALIFORNIA 94611**
Telephone: 510-339-7330
Fax: 510-339-7337
Email: 71722.3454@compuserve.com

*Real Estate, Real Estate Finance and Commercial Leasing Law.*

**DAVID W. BARRON,** born San Francisco, California, May 14, 1953; admitted to bar, 1979, California. *Education:* University of California at
*(This Listing Continued)*

Berkeley (B.A., 1975); Boalt Hall School of Law, University of California at Berkeley (J.D., 1979). Author: "Help for the Commercial Tenant Negotiating a Lease," Real Estate Review, Summer, 1988; "Making Sense Out Of Casualty Provisions in Commercial Leases," Real Estate Review, Winter, 1992; "Simplifying Lease Calculations," The Practical Real Estate Lawyer, May, 1993; "The Small-Store Tenant's Guide to Shopping Center Leases," Real Estate Review, Winter, 1995. Lecturer: National Business Institute, 1993. *PRACTICE AREAS:* Real Estate Law; Financing Law; General Business Law.

## BECHERER BEERS MURPHY KANNETT & SCHWEITZER

**OAKLAND, CALIFORNIA**
(See Emeryville)

*Civil Trial and Litigation.*

## ROBERT J. BELES

*#1 KAISER PLAZA, SUITE 1750*
**OAKLAND, CALIFORNIA 94612**
Telephone: 510-836-0100
FAX: 510-832-3690

*Criminal Trials in State and Federal Courts.*

**ROBERT J. BELES,** born Milwaukee, Wisconsin, April 17, 1942; admitted to bar, 1968, California. *Education:* Ohio University (A.B., 1964); Hastings College of the Law, University of California (J.D., 1967). Assistant Public Defender, County of Alameda, 1968-1979. *Member:* Alameda County Bar Association; State Bar of California; California Attorney's for Criminal Justice; National Association of Criminal Defense Lawyers. (Certified Specialist, Criminal Law, The State Bar of California Board of Legal Specialization).

## BELL, ROSENBERG & HUGHES LLP

*1300 CLAY STREET, SUITE 1000*
*P.O. BOX 70220, STATION "D"*
**OAKLAND, CALIFORNIA 94612-0220**
Telephone: 510-832-8585
Fax: 510-839-6925

*General Civil and Trial Practice. Business, Estate Planning, Taxation, Probate, Construction Litigation and Real Estate Law.*

### MEMBERS OF FIRM

**ROBERT ROSENBERG,** born Rochester, New York, December 18, 1932; admitted to bar, 1957, California. *Education:* Stanford University (A.B., 1954; LL.B., 1956). Phi Alpha Delta. Law Clerk to Hon. Jesse Carter and Raymond E. Peters, Justices, California Supreme Court, 1958-1960. Member, Board of Trustees, Orinda Union School District, 1969-1977. *Member:* Alameda County Bar Association; The State Bar of California. (Certified Specialist, Estate Planning, Trust and Probate Law, The State Bar of California Board of Legal Specialization). *PRACTICE AREAS:* Estate Planning Law; Probate Law.

**ROGER M. HUGHES,** born Bakersfield, California, August 20, 1946; admitted to bar, 1972, California. *Education:* University of the Pacific (B.A., 1969); Hastings College of the Law, University of California (J.D., 1972). Co-Author: California Construction Law, National Business Institute. Presenter, "Dispute Avoidance Through Partnering," International Commerce Commission's Paris Conference, 1995. Presenter, "Dispute Resolution During Project Administration; International Commerce Commission's Brussels Conference, Fall 1995. *Member:* Advisory Board and Standard Form Subcommittee, California Associated General Contractors, 1985—; Mediation and Arbitration Services, American Arbitrators Association Large Complex Construction Case (LCCP). Member, Panel of Arbitrators, American Arbitration Association. *Member:* Alameda County and American Bar Associations; The State Bar of California. *PRACTICE AREAS:* Construction Law; Mediation and Arbitration.

**JAMES C. NELSON,** born Hammond, Indiana, November 6, 1941; admitted to bar, 1967, Indiana; 1970, California. *Education:* Northwestern University (B.A., 1964); Indiana University (J.D., 1967). Deputy District Attorney, Contra Costa County, 1970-1984. *Member:* Indiana State and
*(This Listing Continued)*

## BELL, ROSENBERG & HUGHES LLP, Oakland—Continued

American Bar Associations; The State Bar of California. [Lt., U.S. Navy, 1967-1970]. *PRACTICE AREAS:* Business Law; Business and Real Estate Litigation.

**CATHERINE M. FISHER,** born Milwaukee, Wisconsin, December 27, 1955; admitted to bar, 1980, Wisconsin; 1985, California. *Education:* Northwestern University (B.A., with departmental honors, 1977); University of Wisconsin-Madison (J.D., 1980). *Member:* Alameda County Bar Association; State Bar of Wisconsin; The State Bar of California. *PRACTICE AREAS:* Business Law; Real Estate Law.

**JOHN H. BANISTER,** born Berkeley, California, February 11, 1956; admitted to bar, 1981, California. *Education:* Claremont Men's College (B.A., 1978); Pepperdine University (J.D., 1981). Clerkship with Justice John C. Brand, 1980. *Member:* Alameda County and American (Member, Section of Litigation) Bar Associations; The State Bar of California (Member, Section of Civil Litigation). *PRACTICE AREAS:* Construction Law; Business Litigation; Environmental Law.

**ROLAND NIKLES,** born Switzerland, January 11, 1955; admitted to bar, 1983, Washington; 1987, California. *Education:* University of Washington (B.A., 1977); University of Puget Sound (J.D., 1983). *Member:* Washington State Bar Association; State Bar of California. *LANGUAGES:* German. *PRACTICE AREAS:* Construction Law; Business and Real Estate Litigation.

### OF COUNSEL

**HOWARD H. BELL,** born Schenectady, New York, August 19, 1924; admitted to bar, 1951, California. *Education:* Syracuse University (A.B., 1946); Stanford University (LL.B., 1950). Delta Theta Phi; Phi Beta Kappa. *Member:* Alameda County and American Bar Associations; The State Bar of California. *PRACTICE AREAS:* Business Law; Real Estate Law.

### RETIRED MEMBER

**JAMES DUNLAVEY,** admitted to bar, 1955, California. *Education:* Cornell College (B.A., 1953); Boalt Hall School of Law, University of California (J.D., 1955). *Member:* The State Bar of California.

### ASSOCIATES

**TERESA JENKINS MAIN,** born San Francisco, California, February 28, 1953; admitted to bar, 1985, California. *Education:* College of Martin (A.A., 1973); Stanford University (B.A., with honors, 1975); University of Santa Clara (J.D., magna cum laude, 1985). Phi Beta Kappa. Recipient: Best Team and Best Brief Awards, Leo A. Huard Moot Court Competition; American Jurisprudence Awards in Trusts and Estates and Advanced Corporations. *Member:* Bar Association of San Francisco; State Bar of California; American Bar Association. *PRACTICE AREAS:* Estate Planning; Probate; Litigation.

**HOWARD G. CURTIS, II,** born Pasadena, California, April 18, 1947; admitted to bar, 1977, California; 1989, U.S. Supreme Court, U.S. Court of Appeals, Federal Circuit and U.S. Claims Court. *Education:* U.S. Military Academy (B.S., 1969); University of San Diego (J.D., 1977). Author: "Academic Researchers and The First Amendment: Constitutional Protection For Their Confidential Sources?" 14 San Diego L. Rev. 876 (1977). Chief Counsel: Oakland Army Base, California, 1990-1992; Contract Law Division Head Quarters, Department of the Army, 1988-1992. *Member:* Federal Bar Association (Member, Government Contracts Section); State Bar of California. [Lt. Col., U.S. Army JAG Corps., Active Duty, 1969-1992]. *PRACTICE AREAS:* Government Contracts.

**JENNIFER M. FERGUSSON,** born Berkeley, California, February 18, 1968; admitted to bar, 1993, California. *Education:* Oregon State University (B.S., 1990); Hastings College of the Law, University of California (J.D., 1993). Project Editor, Constitutional Law Quarterly, Hastings College of the Law, University of California. *Member:* State Bar of California.

**JOHN A. RUSSO,** born Brooklyn, New York, February 6, 1959; admitted to bar, 1985, Missouri; 1987, California and U.S. District Court, Northern District of California. *Education:* Yale University (B.A., cum laude, 1982); New York University (J.D., 1985). Director, Roger J. Traynor Moot Court Competition, 1994. Recipient, Clarke Prize for Best Senior Thesis in Comparative Government, 1985. Editor: CYLA Quarterly, 1994-1995; CYLA Conference 611, 1992-1993; "Managing The Client's Expectations," Chapter 4, Insurance Settlement Handbook, James Publishing, 1994. Instructor, Torts Law, St. Louis Community College, Spring, 1987. Co-Chairman, Campaign Services Committee, Oakland/Berkeley Rainbow Coalition, 1987-1988. Member: City of Oakland Environmental Affairs Commission, 1992-1994; Oakland City Council, 1995—. *Member:* State Bar of California; The Missouri Bar; California Trial Lawyers Association; California Young Lawyers Association (Member, Board of Directors, 1989-1991); Alameda County Barristers Club (Vice-President and Member, Board of Directors, 1989-1991). *LANGUAGES:* Spanish and Italian. *PRACTICE AREAS:* Construction Law; Commercial Real Estate; Professional Malpractice; Personal Injury.

COUNSEL FOR: Longs Drug Stores Corporation; Morrison Homes, a division of George Wimpey, Inc.; Lathrop Construction Associates, Inc.; The Golden Rain Foundation of Rossmoor, Walnut Creek; The California State Parks Foundation; O.C. Jones & Co.; Roederer U.S., Inc.; Prometheus Development Co., Inc.; C. Overaa and Co.; Principal Mutual Life Insurance Company; Physics International Co; Moraga Country Club Homeowners Association; Oakland Society for Prevention of Cruelty to Animals; Palo Alto Medical Foundation; Judson Steel Corp; Hysol, a division of Dexter Corp; Children's Hospital Medical Center Foundation; California State Parks Foundation.

---

## BENNETT, SAMUELSEN, REYNOLDS AND ALLARD

*A PROFESSIONAL CORPORATION*

Established in 1979

1951 WEBSTER STREET, SUITE 200
**OAKLAND, CALIFORNIA 94612**
Telephone: 510-444-7688; 510-987-8001
Fax: 510-444-5849

*General Civil Trial and Appellate Practice in all State and Federal Courts. Casualty Insurance, Personal Injury, Insurance Coverage, Construction and Landslide/Subsidence Law.*

**BRYANT M. BENNETT** (Retired).

**DAVID J. SAMUELSEN,** born Berkeley, California, July 6, 1950; admitted to bar, 1976, California. *Education:* University of California at Berkeley (B.A., 1972); University of San Francisco (J.D., 1976). Phi Beta Kappa. Staff Member, 1975; Assistant Comments Editor, 1976, University of San Francisco Law Review. Author: Comment, "Employee or Independent Contractor: The Need for a Reassessment of the Standard Used Under California Workmen's Compensation," 10 University of San Francisco Law Review 133, 1975. *Member:* Alameda County and American Bar Associations; The State Bar of California; Association of Defense Counsel; Defense Research Institute. *PRACTICE AREAS:* Litigation; Insurance Defense Law; Insurance Law.

**RICHARD L. REYNOLDS,** born Petaluma, California, June 24, 1952; admitted to bar, 1977, California. *Education:* University of San Francisco (B.A., 1974; J.D., magna cum laude, 1977). Member, McAuliffe Law Honor Society (Vice President, 1977). *Member:* Alameda County Bar Association; The State Bar of California; Association of Defense Counsel. *PRACTICE AREAS:* Litigation; Landslide Law; Subsidence Law; Public Entity Defense Law.

**ANTHONY J. ALLARD,** born Oakland, California, November 28, 1950; admitted to bar, 1977, California. *Education:* California State University at San Diego (B.A., 1973); Golden Gate University (J.D., 1976). *Member:* Alameda County Bar Association; The State Bar of California; California District Attorneys' Association; Association of Defense Counsel. *PRACTICE AREAS:* Litigation; Landslide Law; Subsidence Law; Construction Law.

**JOHN G. COWPERTHWAITE,** born San Anselmo, California, June 10, 1953; admitted to bar, 1980, California. *Education:* University of Puget Sound (B.A., 1975); University of San Francisco (J.D., 1980). Author: Comment, "Admiralty Jurisdiction and the FMLA: The Maritime Lien on Houseboats," 14 University of San Francisco Law Review 641, 1980. *Member:* Bar Association of San Francisco; Alameda County Bar Association (Delegate, State Bar Convention, 1985); The State Bar of California; Association of Defense Counsel. *PRACTICE AREAS:* Litigation; Surety Law; Construction Law.

---

**ROGER BLAKE HOHNSBEEN,** born Palo Alto, California, June 12, 1959; admitted to bar, 1985, California; 1987, District of Columbia (inactive) and Hawaii (inactive). *Education:* University of California at Santa Barbara (B.A., with honors, 1981); University of Kent, Canterbury, England; George Washington University (J.D., 1985). Member, George Washington Law Review, 1984-1985. Author: Note, "Fourth Amendment and

*(This Listing Continued)*

Posse Comitatus Act Restrictions on Military Involvement in Civil Law Enforcement," 54 Geo. Wash. L. Rev. 404, 1986. *Member:* State Bar of California; Hawaii State Bar Association.

**DON HENRY SCHAEFER,** born Oakland, California, April 26, 1960; admitted to bar, 1989, California. *Education:* Golden Gate University (B.S., 1985, summa cum laude); University of San Francisco (J.D., 1989). Associate Professor, Paralegal Certificate Program, Cal-State Hayward, Fall, 1990. *Member:* Alameda County Bar Association. *PRACTICE AREAS:* Insurance Defense.

**THOMAS S. GELINI,** born San Francisco, California, November 24, 1966; admitted to bar, 1991, California. *Education:* University of California, Berkeley (B.A., 1988); University of San Francisco (J.D., 1991). *Member:* Alameda County Bar Association; State Bar of California. *PRACTICE AREAS:* Litigation; Insurance Defense Law.

**FREDERICK W. GATT,** born San Francisco, California, November 2, 1958; admitted to bar, 1987, California. *Education:* University of San Francisco (B.A., 1980; J.D., 1983). *Member:* Alameda County Bar Association; State Bar of California; The Association of Trial Lawyers of America. *PRACTICE AREAS:* Insurance Defense; Products Liability; Civil Litigation.

**RODNEY IAN HEADINGTON,** born Berkeley, California, September 27, 1961; admitted to bar, 1988, California. *Education:* University of the Pacific (B.A., in Biology, 1983); University of Southern California (J.D., 1987). *Member:* Alameda County and American Bar Associations; State Bar of California. *LANGUAGES:* French. *PRACTICE AREAS:* Products Liability; Insurance Defense; Toxic Tort Litigation.

**CANDACE SMITH-DABNEY,** born East St. Louis, Illinois, August 10, 1964; admitted to bar, 1993, Pennsylvania; 1995, California. *Education:* California State University, Northridge (B.A., 1987); Arizona State University (J.D., 1992). *Member:* American Bar Association; State Bar of California; Charles Houston Bar Association; Association of Black Lawyers. *PRACTICE AREAS:* Civil Litigation; Insurance Defense.

REPRESENTATIVE CLIENTS: Allstate Insurance Co.; California State Automobile Assn.; The Continental Insurance Cos.; County of Alameda; Underwriters Adjusting Co.; Pacific Insurance Co.; Transamerica Insurance Group; The Travelers; California Insurance Guarantee Assn.; Western Surety; Leaseway Transportation Corp.; Dresser Industries; City of Hayward; Chubb-Pacific Insurance Group; Federal Insurance Co.; Wausau Insurance Cos.; Alliance Shippers; National Service Industries, Inc.; Deere & Co.; State of California; County of Contra Costa; Employers Mutual Casualty Co.; Budget Rent A Car; Iveco Trucks of North America, Inc.; Fiat Auto U.S.A., Inc.

---

## BERRY & BERRY
*A PROFESSIONAL CORPORATION*
Established in 1976
1300 CLAY STREET, NINTH FLOOR
P.O. BOX 70250, STATION D
**OAKLAND, CALIFORNIA 94520**
Telephone: 510-835-8330
Fax: 510-835-5117

Civil Litigation. Casualty Insurance Law. Professional Liability, Personal Injury, Torts, Products Liability, Asbestos and Toxic Tort Defense, and Pharmaceutical and Medical Device Liability Law.

FIRM PROFILE: Berry & Berry specializes in product liability, toxic tort, professional malpractice, bad faith, automobile, and other civil matters, with particular emphasis in complex medical issues and pharmaceutical and medical device litigation.

**SAMUEL H. BERRY** (1904-1990).

**PHILLIP S. BERRY,** born Berkeley, California, January 30, 1937; admitted to bar, 1962, California. *Education:* Stanford University (A.B., 1958); Stanford Law School (J.D., 1961). Recipient, John Muir Award, 1978. Member, 1974-1986 and Vice Chairman, 1977-1986, California State Board of Forestry. National President, Sierra Club, 1969-1971 and 1991-1992. *Member:* Alameda County and American Bar Associations; The State Bar of California.

**CAROLYN COLLINS,** born San Francisco, California, May 31, 1953; admitted to bar, 1978, California. *Education:* University of California at Berkeley (B.A., 1975); University of San Francisco (J.D., 1978). *Member:* San Francisco Bar Association; State Bar of California; Defense Research Institute. *LANGUAGES:* Spanish.

*(This Listing Continued)*

---

**LEONARDO J. VACCHINA,** born Reno, Nevada, July 1, 1946; admitted to bar, 1974, California. *Education:* University of San Francisco (B.A., 1967); Hastings College of Law, University of California (J.D., 1974). *Member:* State Bar of California.

**PETER R. GILBERT,** born Visalia, California, September 22, 1947; admitted to bar, 1974, California. *Education:* University of Nevada (B.A., 1970); Golden Gate University (J.D., 1974). *Member:* State Bar of California.

**LYNNE P. BLAIR,** born San Francisco, California, May 12, 1959; admitted to bar, 1983, California. *Education:* University of California at Berkeley (B.A., 1980); Hastings College of Law, University of California (J.D., 1983). Member, Queens Bench. *Member:* San Francisco Bar Association; State Bar of California.

---

**EVANTHIA SPANOS,** born Stockton, California, May 23, 1957; admitted to bar, 1983, California. *Education:* University of California at Los Angeles (B.A., magna cum laude, 1979); Hastings College of Law, University of California (J.D., 1983). *Member:* State Bar of California.

**GREGORY D. MERONEK,** born Chicago, Illinois, September 21, 1956; admitted to bar, 1981, District of Columbia; 1982, California. *Education:* University of Illinois (B.A., 1978); Georgetown University (J.D., 1981). *Member:* Napa County Bar Association; The State Bar of California; The District of Columbia Bar.

**ELLEN D. BERRIS,** born Minneapolis, Minnesota, January 19, 1963; admitted to bar, 1988, California. *Education:* University of Florida (B.S., with honors, 1985); University of San Francisco (J.D., 1988). *Member:* State Bar of California; American Bar Association.

**LAURA PRZETAK,** born San Francisco, California, December 8, 1957; admitted to bar, 1985, California and U.S. District Court, Northern District of California. *Education:* University of California at Berkeley (A.B., 1979); University of San Francisco School of Law (J.D., 1984). Barristers Club. Queen's Bench. *Member:* Bar Association of San Francisco; State Bar of California; Association of Defense Counsel; California Women Lawyers; Defense Research Institute. *PRACTICE AREAS:* Insurance Defense.

REPRESENTATIVE CLIENTS: Parke-Davis; Warner-Lambert; Pacific Gas & Electric; American Optical; GTE-Sylvania; St. Paul Insurance Co.; Fireman's Fund Insurance Co.; American International Underwriters; Lloyd's of London; Celina Insurance Group; Underwriters Adjusting Co.; American Indemnity; Canal Insurance Group; Hawkeye Insurance Co.; Voluntary Plan Administrators; Executive Life Insurance Co.; Biomet, Inc.; Hyatt, Inc.

---

## BJORK, LAWRENCE, POESCHL & KOHN
THE ROSS HOUSE
483 NINTH STREET
**OAKLAND, CALIFORNIA 94607**
Telephone: 510-832-8134
FAX: 510-832-0461
Email: home@bjorklaw.com

General Civil Litigation. Trials, Business and Construction Litigation, Insurance Coverage and Defense, Professional and Products Liability Litigation, Employment Law.

### MEMBERS OF FIRM

**ROBERT D. BJORK, JR.,** born Evanston, Illinois, September 29, 1946; admitted to bar, 1974, Louisiana; 1977, U.S. Supreme Court; 1983, California. *Education:* University of Wisconsin (B.B.A., 1968); Tulane University (J.D., 1974). Member, Tulane University Law Review, 1973-1974. *Member:* Alameda County, Louisiana State and American Bar Associations; State Bar of California. *PRACTICE AREAS:* Admiralty Law; Drug and Medical Device Litigation; Products Liability Law; Toxic Torts.

**ROBERT K. LAWRENCE,** born Birmingham, Alabama, April 7, 1953; admitted to bar, 1978, California. *Education:* University of Santa Clara (B.S., 1975; J.D., 1978). *Member:* Bar Association of San Francisco; Alameda County Bar Association; State Bar of California; Defense Research Institute; American Academy of Hospital Attorneys; California Society for Healthcare Attorneys. *PRACTICE AREAS:* Medical Malpractice Law; Hospital Law; Commercial Litigation; Employment Law; Insurance Defense; Drug and Medical Device Litigation.

**THOMAS F. POESCHL, JR.,** born San Francisco, California, February 6, 1957; admitted to bar, 1986, California. *Education:* St. Mary's College (B.A., 1978); University of San Francisco (J.D., 1983). Comments Editor, University of San Francisco Law Review, 1982-1983. Extern, U.S.

*(This Listing Continued)*

## BJORK, LAWRENCE, POESCHL & KOHN, Oakland—Continued

District Court, Northern District of California, 1982. *Member:* San Francisco, Alameda County, San Mateo County and American Bar Associations; State Bar of California. **PRACTICE AREAS:** Insurance Defense Law; Landlord and Tenant Law; Lemon Law; Insurance Coverage; Automobile Design Liability.

**DORINE RUIZ KOHN,** born San Francisco, California, February 28, 1943; admitted to bar, 1975, California and U.S. District Court, Northern District of California. *Education:* San Francisco State University (B.A., 1964); University of San Francisco (M.A., 1968; J.D., 1974). Member: American Arbitration Association, National Panel of Arbitrators, 1981—. *Member:* Alameda County and American Bar Associations; State Bar of California (Member, Litigation Section Education Committee); California Women Lawyers; Defense Research Institute; La Raza Alameda-Contra County Costa Lawyers Association; Women Lawyers of Alameda County; Alameda-Contra Costa County Trial Lawyers Association. **LANGUAGES:** Spanish and French. **PRACTICE AREAS:** Premises Liability; Medical and Professional Liability Defense; Employment; Products Liability; Construction Defects; Commercial Litigation; Alternative Dispute Resolution.

### ASSOCIATES

**ELIZABETH K. RYAN,** born San Rafael, California, March 1, 1959; admitted to bar, 1984, California. *Education:* University of California at San Diego (B.A., 1981); Hastings College of Law, University of California (J.D., 1984). Order of the Coif. *Member:* Alameda County Bar Association; The State Bar of California. **PRACTICE AREAS:** Drug and Medical Device Litigation; Fraud Law; Medical Malpractice Law; Medical Contract Staffing Law; Risk Management.

**MARK P. EPSTEIN,** born Boston, Massachusetts, September 15, 1959; admitted to bar, 1990, California; 1992, District of Columbia. *Education:* University of Vermont (B.A., 1981); National Law Center, George Washington University (J.D., 1989). *Member:* Alameda County and American Bar Associations; State Bar of California; District of Columbia Bar; California Society for Healthcare Attorneys. **PRACTICE AREAS:** Appellate Law; Automobile Law; Construction Defect Litigation; Defense of Legal and Medical Malpractice; Products Liability Law.

**PATRICIA H. PERRY,** born New Haven, Connecticut, February 26, 1964; admitted to bar, 1989, California and U.S. District Court, Southern District of California. *Education:* Rutgers University (B.A., with high honors, 1986); National Law Center, George Washington University (J.D., 1989). Phi Beta Kappa; Phi Delta Phi. Henry Rutgers Scholar. Author: Comment, "A New Tort in California: Negligent Infliction of Emotional Distress (For Married Couples Only)," Hastings L.J. 447, 1990. *Member:* Bar Association of San Francisco; San Diego County and American Bar Associations. **PRACTICE AREAS:** Arson and Insurance Fraud Defense Law; Hospital Law; Medical Malpractice Law; Products Liability Law; Professional Liability Law.

**SUSAN J. SHERRILL,** born White Plains, New York, September 24, 1964; admitted to bar, 1989, California; U.S. District Court, Northern District of California. *Education:* California State University at Fullerton (B.A., 1986); McGeorge School of Law, University of the Pacific (J.D., 1989). *Member:* Contra Costa County and Alameda County Bar Associations; State Bar of California. **PRACTICE AREAS:** Insurance Defense Law; Toxic Torts; Medical Malpractice Law.

**LILLY M. OMID,** born Berkeley, California, January 16, 1966; admitted to bar, 1992, California. *Education:* Occidental College (A.B., 1988); McGeorge School of Law, University of the Pacific (J.D., 1992). Moot Court Best Oral Advocate. Member, Order of Barristers. *Member:* Alameda County Bar Association; State Bar of California. **LANGUAGES:** French. **PRACTICE AREAS:** Premises Liability; Lemon Law; Landlord and Tenant Law; Insurance Defense Law.

REPRESENTATIVE CLIENTS: Altana, Inc.; Carlsen Subaru-Volvo, Inc.; Catholic Healthcare West; Colonial Insurance Company of California; Colorspot Nurseries; Dunn-Edwards Paint; Farmers Insurance Group; Guardian Foundation; Owens-Corning Fiberglas; Pacific Telesis; The Rockbestos Co.; St. Mary's Hospital and Medical Center; Truck Insurance Exchange; Union Tank Car Co.

---

## EDWARD L. BLUM

*1999 HARRISON STREET, SUITE 1333*
**OAKLAND, CALIFORNIA 94612**
Telephone: 510-452-4400
Fax: 510-452-4406

*Real Estate and Commercial Litigation.*

**EDWARD L. BLUM,** born Oakland, California, July 4, 1946; admitted to bar, 1972, California, U.S. District Court, Northern District of California and U.S. District Court, Eastern District of California. *Education:* University of California at Berkeley (B.A., 1968); University of California at Davis (J.D., 1971). *Member:* Bar Association of San Francisco; Alameda County Bar Association (Member, Real Property Section); State Bar of California (Member, Litigation Section); Alameda/Contra Costa Trial Lawyers Association; California Trial Lawyers Association. **PRACTICE AREAS:** Real Estate Law; Commercial Litigation.

### ASSOCIATE

**ANNE TREMAINE,** born Long Island, New York, December 24, 1938; admitted to bar, 1987, California, U.S. District Court, Central and Northern Districts of California. *Education:* University of Michigan School of Architecture and Design (B.S., 1960); Southwestern University School of Law (J.D., 1985). *Member:* Bar Association of San Francisco; Alameda County Bar Association; State Bar of California. **LANGUAGES:** French, German. **PRACTICE AREAS:** Real Estate; Civil Litigation.

---

## LAW OFFICES OF LORIN B. BLUM

*1939 HARRISON STREET, SUITE 618*
**OAKLAND, CALIFORNIA 94612-3533**
Telephone: 510-465-3927
Fax: 510-465-4222
Email: lbblum@ix.netcom.com

*Walnut Creek, California Office:* 1850 Mt. Diablo Boulevard, Suite 605, 94596. Telephone: 510-933-6125.

*Family Law.*

**LORIN B. BLUM,** born Oakland, California, April 6, 1938; admitted to bar, 1963, California. *Education:* University of California at Berkeley (B.A., 1959); Hastings College of Law, University of California (LL.B., 1962). *Member:* Alameda County and Contra Costa County Bar Associations; The State Bar of California. (Certified Specialist, Family Law, The State Bar of California Board of Legal Specialization). **PRACTICE AREAS:** Family Law.

### ASSOCIATES

**SHARON M. BRAZ,** born Washington, D.C., November 18, 1946; admitted to bar, 1987, California. *Education:* University of California at Berkeley; University of California at San Francisco (B.S., 1969); San Francisco Law School (J.D., 1987). *Member:* Alameda County and Contra Costa County Bar Associations; State Bar of California. (Certified Specialist, Family Law, The State Bar of California Board of Legal Specialization). **PRACTICE AREAS:** Family Law; Family Law Mediation.

### LEGAL SUPPORT PERSONNEL

*Sandra L. Kellum*
*Stephanie Snyder*

---

## BOORNAZIAN, JENSEN & GARTHE

*A PROFESSIONAL CORPORATION*
*1800 HARRISON STREET, 25TH FLOOR*
*P.O. BOX 12925*
**OAKLAND, CALIFORNIA 94604**
Telephone: 510-834-4350
Telecopier: 510-839-1897

*Walnut Creek, California Office:* Suite 550, 2121 North California Boulevard. Telephone: 510-934-8400. Telecopier: 510-934-3635.

*Insurance, Trial, Appellate Practice and General Business. Legal, Medical, Dental, Real Estate Malpractice and Products Liability Law.*

(This Listing Continued)

## PROFESSIONAL BIOGRAPHIES

**DAVID J. GARTHE,** born Minneapolis, Minnesota, July 28, 1946; admitted to bar, 1972, California. *Education:* University of California at Davis (B.A., 1968); University of California School of Law at Davis (J.D., 1971). Order of the Coif. Member, University of California at Davis Law Review, 1969-1970. *Member:* Alameda County Bar Association; State Bar of California; Association of Defense Counsel of Northern California (Member, Board of Directors). *PRACTICE AREAS:* Insurance Coverage; Personal Injury; Products Litigation.

**ANDREW R. ADLER,** born Philadelphia, Pennsylvania, February 20, 1948; admitted to bar, 1973, California. *Education:* University of California (B.A., 1970); Boalt Hall School of Law, University of California (J.D., 1973). *Member:* Alameda County Bar Association; State Bar of California. (Resident, Walnut Creek Office). *PRACTICE AREAS:* Professional Malpractice; Business; Real Estate Litigation; General Business.

**CHARLES I. EISNER,** born Los Angeles, California, April 14, 1949; admitted to bar, 1974, California. *Education:* University of California at Riverside (B.A., with high honors, 1970); Hastings College of Law, University of California (J.D., 1974). Phi Beta Kappa; Omicron Delta Epsilon. *Member:* Alameda County Bar Association; State Bar of California; Association of Defense Counsel of Northern California. *PRACTICE AREAS:* Insurance Coverage; Wrongful Termination; Personal Injury Litigation.

**GREGORY J. ROCKWELL,** born Oakland, California, May 25, 1951; admitted to bar, 1975, California. *Education:* University of San Francisco (B.A., 1973; J.D., 1975). Member, McAuliffe Law Honor Society. Assistant Editor, University of San Francisco Law Review, 1974-1975. Author: Comment, "Inadequate Representation of Counsel in Criminal Cases: The Need for a New Approach," 9 U.S.F.L. Rev. 166, 1974. *Member:* Alameda County Bar Association; State Bar of California; San Francisco Lawyers Club; Association of Defense Counsel of Northern California. *PRACTICE AREAS:* Medical Malpractice; Personal Injury; Products and Public Entity Litigation.

**ROBERT G. CROW,** born Salinas, California, January 12, 1949; admitted to bar, 1974, California. *Education:* University of California at Berkeley (B.A., 1971); Hastings College of Law, University of California (J.D., 1974). Order of the Coif. Editor, Hastings College of Law, University of California Law Review, 1972-1974. *Member:* Alameda County Bar Association; The State Bar of California; Association of Defense Counsel of Northern California. *PRACTICE AREAS:* Toxic Tort; Environmental; Public Entity Litigation.

**WILLIAM T. MULVIHILL,** born San Francisco, California, November 24, 1950; admitted to bar, 1977, California; 1983, U.S. Court of Appeals, Ninth Circuit. *Education:* University of San Francisco (B.A., 1972); Golden Gate University (J.D., 1977). Faculty Member, Personal Injury Litigation, Hastings College of Advocacy, Hastings Center for Trial & Appellate Advocacy, 1988-1989. Arbitrator: San Francisco Superior Court, 1988—; Contra Costa Superior Court, 1989—. *Member:* Alameda County Bar Association; State Bar of California; Defense Research Institute; Association of Defense Counsel of Northern California. *PRACTICE AREAS:* Personal Injury; Products; Psychological Injury; Medical Malpractice Litigation.

**ROBERT B. LUECK,** born San Diego, California, February 6, 1953; admitted to bar, 1978, California. *Education:* University of Southern California (B.A., cum laude, 1975); McGeorge College of the Law, University of the Pacific (J.D., with distinction, 1978). Member, Traynor Society. *Member:* Contra Costa County and American Bar Associations; State Bar of California; Association of Defense Counsel of Northern California. (Resident, Walnut Creek Office). *PRACTICE AREAS:* Building Industry Litigation; Construction Defect Claims; Construction Disputes; Job Site Injuries; Insurance Coverage Matters.

**GAIL C. TRABISH,** born New York, N.Y., November 2, 1955; admitted to bar, 1980, Virginia; 1981, District of Columbia; 1982, California. *Education:* Georgetown University (B.S.B.A., 1976); Catholic University (J.D., 1980). *Member:* Alameda County Bar Association; State Bar of California; Virginia State Bar; The District of Columbia Bar. *PRACTICE AREAS:* Personal Injury; Public Entity Litigation.

**KATHLEEN E. HEGEN,** born Palo Alto, California, November 14, 1946; admitted to bar, 1982, California. *Education:* University of California at Berkeley (B.A., 1970); University of Santa Clara (J.D., 1982). *Member:* Alameda County Bar Association (Foundation President, 1996); State Bar of California; Association of Defense Counsel of Northern California. *PRACTICE AREAS:* Insurance Coverage Litigation.

**DAVID R. SIDRAN,** born Farmington, Massachusetts, July 23, 1961; admitted to bar, 1985, California. *Education:* University of California at

*(This Listing Continued)*

Santa Cruz (B.A., 1982); McGeorge School of Law, University of the Pacific (J.D., 1985). Order of the Coif. Member, Traynor Society. Staff Writer, "Selected Review of 1982 California Legislation," Pacific Law Journal. *Member:* Contra Costa County Bar Association; State Bar of California. (Resident, Walnut Creek Office). *PRACTICE AREAS:* Personal Injury; Products; Building Industry Litigation; Construction Disputes; Insurance Coverage Matters.

**BRUCE H. WINKELMAN,** born Los Angeles, California, September 7, 1961; admitted to bar, 1986, California. *Education:* University of California at Berkeley (A.B., 1983); University of San Diego (J.D., 1986). Author: "Insurance Coverage Issues in Toxic Tort and Environmental Pollution Cases," C.P.C.U. Journal, June, 1988. *Member:* Alameda County and American Bar Associations; State Bar of California. *PRACTICE AREAS:* Toxic Tort; Environmental; Insurance Coverage Litigation.

**COLETTE F. STONE,** born Los Angeles, California, October 31, 1962; admitted to bar, 1987, California. *Education:* University of California at Los Angeles (B.A., 1984); McGeorge School of Law, University of the Pacific (J.D., 1987). Order of the Barristers. *Member:* Contra Costa County Bar Association; State Bar of California; Association of Defense Counsel of Northern California. (Resident, Walnut Creek Office). *LANGUAGES:* French. *PRACTICE AREAS:* Building Industry Litigation; Construction Defect Claims; Construction Disputes; Job Site Injuries; Insurance Coverage Matters; Real Estate Litigation.

**ALAN E. SWERDLOW,** born Chicago, Illinois, May 8, 1961; admitted to bar, 1987, California. *Education:* University of California at Berkeley (A.B., 1984); McGeorge School of Law, University of the Pacific (J.D., 1987). Editor, Pacific Law Journal, 1986-1987. *Member:* Alameda County and American Bar Associations; State Bar of California. *PRACTICE AREAS:* Personal Injury; Insurance Coverage.

---

Steven G. Lanum
Paul G. Minoletti
Marjorie J. Heinrich (Resident, Walnut Creek Office)
Kathy M. Katano-Lee
Paul A. Giacoletti
Dennis P. Fitzsimons
Joan M. Saupé (Resident, Walnut Creek Office)
Jacqueline Jordan Leung
Janice Amenta
Benjamin T. Reyes, II

Jonathan Talbot Rodriguez (Resident, Walnut Creek Office)
Kristin L. Jenny (Resident, Walnut Creek Office)
Kelly T. Nugent
Christopher T. Bates
Brenda M. Lillington (Resident, Walnut Creek Office)
Jordan A. Rodman
John S. Huster
Jennifer E. McEneaney (Resident, Walnut Creek Office)

### OF COUNSEL

**ROBERT E. JENSEN,** born Chicago, Illinois, March 3, 1931; admitted to bar, 1971, California; 1974, U.S. Supreme Court. *Education:* University of California at Berkeley (B.A., 1957); Golden Gate College (J.D., 1970). Member, Golden Gate College Law Review, 1970. *PRACTICE AREAS:* Personal Injury; Products Litigation; Medical Malpractice; Psychiatric Injury and Brain Damage.

REPRESENTATIVE CLIENTS: Admiral Insurance Company; Affiliated FM Insurance Company; American International Group; American Reinsurance; American States Insurance Company; California Compensation Insurance Company; Carl Warren Company; The CIGNA Group; City of Albany; City of Fremont; City of Hayward; City of Vallejo; CNA Insurance Companies; Corning Glass; County of Alameda; County of Solano; East Bay Municipal Utility District; Employers Reinsurance; Fireman's Fund Insurance Companies; Fremont Insurance Company; Fremont Unified School District; General Reinsurance Company; Guaranty National Insurance Company; Harley-Davidson, Inc.; Industrial Indemnity Insurance Company; Kemper Insurance Companies; Market Center Administrators, Inc.; Mervyn's; Price Costco, Inc.; NACCO Materials Handling Group, Inc.; North American Specialty Insurance Company; Reliance National Risk Specialists; Royal Insurance Company; Seibels Bruce Group, Inc; State Farm Fire and Casualty Company; Sunbeam Household Products; Travelers Indemnity Company; Wausau Insurance Company; Wausau Insurance Company; United Capitol Insurance Company; Universal Underwriters Group; U.S. Elevator Corporation; Valley Insurance Company.

## BRANSON, FITZGERALD & HOWARD

A PROFESSIONAL CORPORATION

**OAKLAND, CALIFORNIA**

(See Redwood City)

*Insurance, Professional Liability, Civil Litigation. Construction, Products Liability, Insurance Defense, Medical and Other Professional Liability, Landslide and Subsidence, Personal Injury, Wrongful Death, Real Estate, Probate and Business Law. General, Civil and Trial Practice.*

---

## BRODY & SATZ

405 FOURTEENTH STREET, SUITE 1100
**OAKLAND, CALIFORNIA 94612**
Telephone: 510-763-0600
Telex: WUI 650-250-5965
MCI MAIL: 250-5965
FAX: 510-763-0668

*Civil and Trial Practice. Business, Business Formation, Operation and Dissolution, Commercial Practice, Commercial and Retail Leases, Tax, Bankruptcy, Real Property, Estate Planning, Probate.*

### MEMBERS OF FIRM

**RICHARD B. SATZ,** born Dayton, Ohio, October 6, 1945; admitted to bar, 1972, New York; 1973, California and U.S. District Court, Northern, Eastern and Southern Districts of California. *Education:* Princeton University (A.B., 1967); Yale Law School (LL.B., 1970). *Member:* State Bar of California; New York State Bar Association. **PRACTICE AREAS:** Commercial Litigation; Real Property Litigation; Bankruptcy; Employer and Employee Representation. *Email:* RSATZ@AOL.COM

**MARY M. RUDSER,** born East Chicago, Indiana, April 29, 1948; admitted to bar, 1981, New York and U.S. District Court, Southern and Eastern District of New York; 1983, U.S. Tax Court; 1985, California and U.S. District Court, Northern District of California. *Education:* Carleton College (B.A., 1970); University of Maryland (M.L.S., 1971); Boston College (J.D., magna cum laude, 1980); New York University (LL.M. in Taxation, 1984). Managing Editor, Boston College Editorial Board, American Journal of Law and Medicine, 1979-1980. *Member:* State Bar of California; New York State Bar Association. **PRACTICE AREAS:** Estate Planning; Probate; Tax; Business; Real Estate.

---

## PRISCILLA CAMP

THE ARLINGTON
492 NINTH STREET, SUITE 300
**OAKLAND, CALIFORNIA 94607**
Telephone: 510-465-3885
Fax: 510-839-9800

*Elder Law, including Powers of Attorney, Probate, Conservatorship and Medi-Cal Eligibility for Nursing Home Patients.*

**PRISCILLA CAMP,** born New Haven, Connecticut, March 12, 1941; admitted to bar, 1978, California. *Education:* University of Kansas (B.S., 1963; M.S., 1966); Golden Gate University (J.D., 1977). Recipient, State Bar President's Pro Bono Award for District 3, 1990. Author: *California Elder Law*, 1993 and *California Durable Powers of Attorney*, 1996, California Continuing Education Of The Bar (CEB). Columnist, "The Senior Partner," Bulletin of the Alameda County Bar Association. *Member:* Alameda County Bar Association (Chair: Community Services Committee, 1985-1986; Elder Law Committee, Estate Planning, Probate and Trust Section, 1989-1991; Conservatorship and Guardianship Committee, Estate Planning, Probate and Trust Section, 1994-1995); State Bar of California (Member, 1990-1994 and Chair, 1994, Interest on Lawyer Trust Accounts Commission, IOLTA); California Women Lawyers (Secretary, 1981); Women Lawyers of Alameda County (President, 1985). **PRACTICE AREAS:** Elder Law; Conservatorship; Probate; Long Term Care.

---

## MARIAN C. CHAPMAN

1939 HARRISON STREET, SUITE 290
**OAKLAND, CALIFORNIA 94612-3532**
Telephone: 510-444-0599
Fax: 510-238-5100

**FIRM PROFILE:** *Litigation and mediation of family law matters including complex property divisions, post judgement modifications of support and/or child custody orders.*

**MARIAN C. CHAPMAN,** born Washington, D.C., December 19, 1945; admitted to bar, 1976, California and U.S. District Court, Northern District of California. *Education:* University of California at Berkeley (A.B., 1968); University of Santa Clara (J.D., cum laude, 1976). Professor of Family Law, New College of California School of Law, 1983-1986. Participant, Alameda County Bar Association Joint Training Program re Child Custody Mediation, 1984. Lecturer, Family Court Services sponsored Family Law Lecture Series, Alameda County Superior Court, 1985. Mediation Trainer, Administrative Office of the Courts, Judicial Council. Member, Alameda County Women Lawyers Board of Governors, 1982-1984. Consultant, Statewide Office of Family Court Service, 1996-1997. Editorial Consultant, California Family Law Monthly, 1985-1986. Judge, Pro Tempore, Alameda and Contra Costa County Family Law Departments. Special Master and Referee, Alameda County. *Member:* State Bar of California (Member, Family Law Section); Alameda County Family Law Association (Board Member, 1989 —); California Women Lawyers (Member, Board of Governors, 1982-1983); Academy of Family Mediators; Association of Family and Conciliation Courts. **PRACTICE AREAS:** Family Law; Mediation.

---

## CHILVERS & TAYLOR, P.C.

2030 FRANKLIN STREET, FIFTH FLOOR
**OAKLAND, CALIFORNIA 94612**
Telephone: 510-444-7744
Fax: 510-444-4713

*Antitrust, Complex Business and Commercial Litigation and Health Care Industry Litigation, including Trials, Appeals, Mediation, Arbitration and Private Judging.*

**FIRM PROFILE:** *The firm focuses on all areas of business litigation with particular emphasis on competitive business practice issues and on disputes involving the health care industry.*

**ROBERT M. CHILVERS,** born Long Beach, California, October 23, 1942; admitted to bar, 1975, California; 1980, U.S. Supreme Court. *Education:* University of California at Berkeley (A.B., 1972); Harvard University (J.D., 1975). Recipient: California State Bar Commendation for Outstanding Contributions to the Delivery of Voluntary Legal Services. Member of Faculty: National Institute for Trial Advocacy, 1986—; Stanford School of Law Advocacy Skills Workshop, 1994—; Hastings Center for Trial and Appellate Advocacy, 1983-1989; University of San Francisco School of Law Intensive Advocacy Program, 1994—; Emory Law School Trial Techniques Program, 1984-1990; Widener School of Law Trial Advocacy Institute, 1993-1994; Cardozo School of Law Intensive Trial Advocacy Program, 1993—. Partner, Brobeck, Phleger & Harrison, 1982-1993. Special Master, U.S. District Court, 1994—. Member, Board of Trustees, 1985-1989 and Chairman, 1987-1988, Mill Valley School District. [USMC (1964-1971)]

**WILLIAM "ZAK" TAYLOR,** born Milwaukee, Wisconsin, January 26, 1948; admitted to bar, 1976, California; 1980, U.S. Supreme Court. *Education:* Yale University (B.A., magna cum laude, 1970); Harvard University (J.D., cum laude, 1976). Editor-in-Chief, Harvard Civil Rights-Civil Liberties Law Review, 1975-1976. Recipient: Jean Waldman Child Advocacy Award, 1988; Award of Merit, 1984. Law Clerk to the Hon. Shirley M. Hufstedler, U.S. Court of Appeals for the Ninth Circuit, 1976-1977. Co-Author: "California Antitrust Law," Antitrust and Trade Regulation Law Section of the State Bar of California, 1991. Contributing Editor, CEB California Business Law Reporter, 1995-1996. Partner, Brobeck, Phleger & Harrison, 1983-1995. Member, Board of Directors, 1986-1987 and Chair, Antitrust Section, 1987, Chair, Federal Courts Section, 1994—, Bar Association of San Francisco. ADR Neutral, National Health Lawyers Association.

*(This Listing Continued)*

**LEILA CLARK-RIDDELL,** born San Mateo, California, April 11, 1965; admitted to bar, 1993, California. *Education:* University of California at Berkeley (B.A., with highest distinction, 1987); Harvard University (J.D., cum laude, 1993). Phi Beta Kappa. *Member:* Bar Association of San Francisco; State Bar of California.

REPRESENTATIVE CLIENTS: General Motors Corp.; Saatchi & Saatchi Advertising, Inc, N.A.; United Broadcasting Company; Omni Healthcare, Inc.; San Francisco IPA; Health Net; Marin IPA; Santa Clara IPA; Prudential Health Plan of California; Merisel FAB, Inc.; QuadraMed Corporation.

## COOPER, MARGOLIN & BIATCH
1970 BROADWAY, SUITE 940
**OAKLAND, CALIFORNIA 94612-2263**
Telephone: 510-451-4114
Facsimile: 510-451-4115

*Real Estate Law and Lease Negotiations, Business Planning, Business Finance and Sales, Corporate and Partnership Law and Syndications, Architect and Construction Law, Estate and Tax Planning, Probate and Related Civil Litigation.*

FIRM PROFILE: *Cooper, Margolin & Biatch is a small law firm dedicated to providing personal service and high quality legal services to its clients. The firm traces it roots back to the solo practice established by Mr. Cooper in 1974; it adopted its present name in 1986. The firm's practice is oriented to providing legal services to professionals, small business entities and small business owners.*

### MEMBERS OF FIRM

**THOMAS E. COOPER,** born Berkeley, California, June 14, 1945; admitted to bar, 1970, California. *Education:* University of California at Berkeley (A.B., 1966); Boalt Hall School of Law, University of California (J.D., 1969). Phi Beta Kappa. *Member:* Alameda County and American Bar Associations; State Bar of California. **PRACTICE AREAS:** Real Estate Law; Business Law.

**SANFORD H. MARGOLIN,** born Los Angeles, California, November 22, 1953; admitted to bar, 1979, California. *Education:* University of California at Berkeley (A.B. in Political Science, 1975); Boalt Hall School of Law, University of California (J.D., 1979). *Member:* Alameda County Bar Association; State Bar of California (Member, Real Property Law Section). **PRACTICE AREAS:** Real Estate and Business Law; Probate and Related Civil Litigation.

**JOEL A. BIATCH,** born Los Angeles, California, August 20, 1956; admitted to bar, 1983, California, U.S. District Court, Northern District of California and U.S. Court of Appeals, Ninth Circuit; 1984, U.S. Tax Court. *Education:* University of California at Santa Cruz (A.B., 1978); Boalt Hall School of Law, University of California (J.D., 1982). *Member:* Alameda County, American and International Bar Association; State Bar of California (Member, Business Law and Estate Planning Sections). **PRACTICE AREAS:** Business Law; Architect Law; Estate Planning.

### OF COUNSEL

**ERIC P. GOLD,** born New York, N.Y., May 31, 1945; admitted to bar, 1971, California. *Education:* University of Chicago (B.A. in Political Science, 1967); Boalt Hall School of Law, University of California (J.D., 1971). *Member:* Alameda County Bar Association; State Bar of California.

**FREDERICK C. HERTZ,** born St. Paul, Minnesota, August 30, 1952; admitted to bar, 1981, California; 1983, U.S. District Court, Northern District of California. *Education:* University of Minnesota (B.A., 1975); University of Texas; Boalt Hall School of Law, University of California (J.D., 1981). *Member:* San Francisco and Alameda County Bar Associations; State Bar of California; Bay Area Lawyers for Individual Freedom (Member, Board of Directors, 1985—). **PRACTICE AREAS:** Real Estate Transactions; Litigation; Land Use Administrative Proceedings.

REPRESENTATIVE CLIENTS: Applied Optics, Inc.; El Cerrito Plaza; E Sherick Homsey Dodge and Davis; E-Fax Communications, Inc.; Lifetime Security Partners; N-Viro International Corporation; Reaction Supply Corporation; Remainder Equity Deeds Corporation; Rosenblum Cellars, Inc.; Wholesale Jewelers Exchange, Ltd.
REFERENCES: Bank of California; Rooney, Ida, Nolt & Ahern, Certified Public Accountants.

## CORBETT & KANE
*A PROFESSIONAL CORPORATION*
Established in 1976
2000 POWELL STREET, SUITE 1450 (EMERYVILLE)
**OAKLAND, CALIFORNIA 94608**
Telephone: 510-547-2434
Fax: 510-658-5014
Email: attorney@cklaw.com
URL: http://www.cklaw.com

*San Francisco, California Office:* Citicorp Center, One Sansome Street, Suite 1900. Telephone: 415-956-4100.

*Labor Relations, Employment Law and Litigation.*

FIRM PROFILE: *Corbett & Kane is a San Francisco Bay Area labor and employment law firm. The firm's practice focuses on counseling and advising public and private sector employers in employee relations and employment law compliance matters and in representing clients in negotiations involving government agencies and unions, in litigation before state and federal courts and government agencies, in arbitration and in mediation. Corbett & Kane is a women-owned law firm. The firm is the Northern California representative of LABNET, Labor Attorneys for Business Network, a nationwide organization of labor and employment law specialty firms. Member firms share information and resources on legal and practice-related issues. LABNET has member firms in California, Colorado, Florida, Illinois, Massachusetts, New York, Ohio, Oregon, Tennessee, Texas and Washington, D.C.*

**JUDITH DROZ KEYES,** born Pittsburgh, Pennsylvania, January 16, 1946; admitted to bar, 1975, California. *Education:* Pennsylvania State University (B.S., with distinction, 1966); University of Missouri (M.A., 1970); Boalt Hall School of Law, University of California (J.D., 1975). Order of the Coif. Membership Editor, California Law Review, 1974-1975. Judicial Extern to Judge Stanley Weigel, U.S. District Court, Northern District of California, 1974. Visiting Associate Professor, Suffolk University Law School, 1986-1987. Early Neutral Evaluator, U.S. District Court, Northern District of California, 1988—. Attorney, National Labor Relations Board, 1975-1976. *Member:* Bar Association of San Francisco (Vice-Chair, Executive Committee, Labor and Employment Law Section); Alameda County (President-Elect, 1996; Delegate, California State Bar, 1990—) and American (Member, Sections on: Labor and Employment Law; Law Practice Management; International Law) Bar Associations; American Academy of Attorney-Mediators (Northern California Chapter); Society for Professionals in Dispute Resolution. **PRACTICE AREAS:** Labor and Employment Law.

**MARY MALONEY ROBERTS,** born Oakland, California, December 7, 1952; admitted to bar, 1981, California. *Education:* University of Hawaii (B.Ed., 1975); Hastings College of Law, University of California (J.D., 1981). Member, Moot Court Board, 1980-1981. Judicial Extern to Judge Joseph R. Grodin, California Court of Appeal, First Appellate District, 1980. *Member:* Bar Association of San Francisco (Member, Labor and Employment Law Section); State Bar of California (Member, Labor and Employment Law Section); American Bar Association (Member, Equal Employment Opportunity Committee; Section of Labor and Employment Law); California Women Lawyers; San Francisco Trial Lawyers Association; Alameda Trial Lawyers Association. **PRACTICE AREAS:** Labor and Employment Law.

**SHARON J. GRODIN,** born Berkeley, California, June 13, 1956; admitted to bar, 1983, California. *Education:* Brown University (B.A., 1977); Penn State University; Temple University (J.D., 1982). Associate Research Editor, Temple Law Quarterly, 1980-1982. Associate Editor, 1990-1992, Editorial Board, California Labor & Employment Law Quarterly, 1992—. *Member:* Bar Association of San Francisco (Member, Labor and Employment Law Section); State Bar of California (Executive Committee of Labor and Employment Law Section; Delegate, 1992—); American Bar Association (Member, Sections of: Labor and Employment Law; Litigation, Corporate Counsel Committee). **PRACTICE AREAS:** Labor and Employment Law.

**TIM J. EMERT,** born Eau Claire, Wisconsin, September 3, 1949; admitted to bar, 1983, California. *Education:* University of Wisconsin-Madison (B.A., 1974); San Francisco State University (M.S., 1979); Hasting College of Law University of California (J.D., 1983). **PRACTICE AREAS:** Labor and Employment Law.

**DENISE M. DEROSE,** born San Jose, California, May 19, 1951; admitted to bar, 1985, California. *Education:* University of Santa Clara (B.A., 1973; J.D., magna cum laude, 1985). Editor-in-Chief, Santa Clara Law Re-

*(This Listing Continued)*

*CORBETT & KANE, A PROFESSIONAL CORPORATION,*
  *Oakland—Continued*

view, Volume 25, Symposium Issue, 1985. Articles Editor, Santa Clara Law Review, Volume 25, 1985. Author: Casenote, "In re Reed," 33 California 3d 914, 663, p.2d 216, 191 California Reporter 658, 1983; "Adult Incest Survivors and the Statute of Limitations: The Delayed Discovery Rule and Long Term Damages," 25:1 Santa Clara Law Review, 1985. *Member:* Santa Clara County Bar Association (Vice Chairperson and Co-Chairperson, Committee on Gay and Lesbian Concerns, 1993-1994); State Bar of California (Member, Section of Labor and Employment Law). *PRACTICE AREAS:* Labor and Employment Law.

*IAN P. FELLERMAN,* born New York, New York, June 23, 1960; admitted to bar, 1985, California. *Education:* University of California at San Diego (B.A., 1982); University of California at Davis (J.D., 1985). Member, Moot Court and Trial Practice Honors Board. *Member:* Bar Association of San Francisco (Member, Labor and Employment Law Section); Alameda County and American (Member, Section of Labor and Employment Law) Bar Associations; State Bar of California (Member, Section on Labor and Employment Law). *PRACTICE AREAS:* Labor and Employment Law.

*DOUGLAS N. FREIFELD,* born Los Angeles, California, September 16, 1953; admitted to bar, 1984, California. *Education:* Stanford University (A.B., with distinction, 1980); Columbia University School of Law (J.D., 1984).

*DOUGLAS J. FARMER,* born Upland, California, January 23, 1960; admitted to bar, 1989, California and U.S. District Court, Northern and Central Districts of California; 1990, U.S. District Court, Eastern District of California; 1991, U.S. District Court, District of Hawaii and U.S. District Court, Southern District of California. *Education:* Harvard University (A.B., magna cum laude, 1982; J.D., 1986).

*PHILIP OBBARD,* born Ann Arbor, Michigan, June 26, 1960; admitted to bar, 1986, Delaware; 1987, Pennsylvania; 1988, California. *Education:* Haverford College (B.A., 1982); Georgetown University (J.D., 1986).

*JOAN PUGH NEWMAN,* born Los Angeles, California, November 29, 1959; admitted to bar, 1990, California. *Education:* Stanford University (B.A., with distinction, 1981; M.A., 1983); University of California at Los Angeles (J.D., 1990).

*MATTHEW H. BURROWS,* born Washington, D.C., November 18, 1968; admitted to bar, 1994, California and U.S. District Court, Northern District of California. *Education:* University of California, Santa Barbara (B.A. in Sociology, 1990); Hastings College of the Law, University of California, San Francisco (J.D., 1994).

*WILLIAM L. KASLEY,* born Peoria, Illinois, September 1, 1951; admitted to bar, 1976, Illinois; 1988, California. *Education:* Bradley University (B.S., summa cum laude, 1973); University of Illinois (J.D., with honors, 1976).

REPRESENTATIVE CLIENTS: AC Transit; Alameda County Superior Court; Barr Rosenberg Investment Management, Inc.; Bass Tickets; Bay Area Rapid Transit; City of Berkeley; Blue Cross of California; Blue Shield (California Physicians' Service); Brown and Caldwell; California Academy of Sciences; California Credit Union League; California Pacific Medical Center; Central Contra Costa Sanitary District; Charles Schwab & Co., Inc.; Davies Medical Center; Dey Laboratories; Domaine Chandon; F.A.O. Schwarz; Fuller O'Brien Corp.; FWB, Inc.; City of Hayward; LucasArts Entertainment Company; Lucasfilm Ltd.; MCI Telecommunications; NEC Electronics, Inc.; Pacific Gas and Electric Co.; The Permanente Medical Group, Inc.; The Quaker Oats Company; The Regents of the University of California; Sandia National Laboratories; County of Santa Clara; Southwest Airlines; State Bar of California; Summit Medical Center; Tele-Communications, Inc.; University of the Pacific; Viacom International Inc.; Watsonville Community Hospital.

---

## CRESSWELL, CAKE & ECHEGUREN

*A PROFESSIONAL CORPORATION*

*270 GRAND AVENUE*
**OAKLAND, CALIFORNIA 94610-0266**
*Telephone: 510-444-1735*
*Fax: 510-444-6923*

*Mailing Address:* P.O. Box 10266, Oakland, California 94610-0266

*General Civil and Trial Practice. Casualty Insurance, Insurance Coverage and Professional Liability Law.*

(This Listing Continued)

CAA1452B

---

*RONALD D. ECHEGUREN,* born Berkeley, California, October 25, 1951; admitted to bar, 1977, California. *Education:* University of California at Berkeley (A.B., 1973); Hastings College of Law, University of California (J.D., 1977). Phi Alpha Delta. Note and Comment Editor, Hastings Law Quarterly, 1976-1977. *Member:* Alameda County and American Bar Associations; The State Bar of California; Association of Defense Counsel of Northern California; Defense Research Institute.

*G. DENNIS RODGERS,* born San Diego, California, May 23, 1952; admitted to bar, 1983, California. *Education:* University of California at Santa Barbara (B.A., 1980); Hastings College of Law, University of California (J.D., 1983). Phi Beta Kappa. *Member:* Alameda County and American Bar Associations; The State Bar of California; Association of Defense Counsel of Northern California.

*EDWARD R. KARP,* born Mamaroneck, New York, May 11, 1955; admitted to bar, 1983, California. *Education:* University of Wisconsin-Madison (B.A., 1977); Golden Gate University (J.D, 1982). Extern, Justice Betty Barry-Deal, Third District Court of Appeal, 1982. *Member:* Alameda County and American Bar Associations; State Bar of California; Association of Defense Counsel of Northern California.

*ANDREW F. NOBLE,* born Edinburgh, Scotland, January 23, 1962; admitted to bar, 1988, California. *Education:* University of Michigan; Indiana University (B.A., 1984); Hastings College of the Law, University of California (J.D., 1988). *Member:* Alameda County and American Bar Associations; State Bar of California. *PRACTICE AREAS:* General Civil Litigation; Products Liability Law; Toxic Torts.

*GRETA L. KAPLAN,* born San Francisco, California, February 1, 1961; admitted to bar, 1991, California. *Education:* University of California at Berkeley (A.B., 1985; M.A., 1988); University of California at Los Angeles School of Law (J.D., 1991). Editor-In-Chief, UCLA Journal of Environmental Law and Policy, 1990-1991. *Member:* State Bar of California. *PRACTICE AREAS:* Civil Litigation.

REPRESENTATIVE CLIENTS: Employers Reinsurance Corporation; Ohio Casualty Group; Media/Professional Insurance, Inc.; MGIC; CIGNA; Farmers Insurance Group; Transamerica Insurance Group; Motors Insurance Group; Arkansas Best Corporation; Country-Wide Insurance Co.; Gallagher Bassett Services; Insurance Corporation of America; National American Insurance; Harleysville Mutual Ins.; Interstate National Corporation; Underwriters of Lloyds of London; Cal Union; Truck Insurance Exchange; Safeco Companies.

---

## CROSBY, HEAFEY, ROACH & MAY

*PROFESSIONAL CORPORATION*

*Established in 1900*

*1999 HARRISON STREET*
**OAKLAND, CALIFORNIA 94612-3573**
*Telephone: 510-763-2000*
*FAX: 510-273-8832*

*San Francisco, California Office:* One Market Plaza Spear Street Tower, Suite 1800. Telephone: 415-543-8700. FAX: 415-391-8269.

*Los Angeles, California Office:* 700 South Flower Street, Suite 2200. Telephone: 213-896-8000. FAX: 213-896-8080.

*Santa Rosa, California Office:* 1330 N. Dutton. Telephone: 707-523-2433. FAX: 707-546-1360.

*General Civil Practice and Litigation in all State and Federal Courts. Litigation: Product Liability; Pharmaceutical and Medical Device; Insurance Coverage and Claims; Business Litigation; Labor and Employment; Intellectual Property; Environmental/Toxic Tort; Property, Land Use and Condemnation; Construction; Professional Liability; Antitrust; Appellate; Bankruptcy and Creditors' Rights; Media and First Amendment Rights; Health Care; Property Tax. Business: Real Estate; General Corporate and Partnership; Commercial Transactions; Mergers and Acquisitions, Trust and Estate Planning; Tax; Finance and Banking; Securities.*

*FIRM PROFILE: Our nearly 200 lawyers in offices located in Oakland, Los Angeles, San Francisco and Santa Rosa, California provide quality legal services in virtually every area of civil law. Our corporate attorneys offer clients an extensive range of expertise in every facet of legal representation for businesses and the people who run them. Our trial lawyers, with particular expertise in product liability, insurance, and business litigation, are among the most experienced in the nation. Our jury trial experience is exceptionally strong, especially for a large law firm. Our litigation philosophy is one our clients appreciate: We staff cases leanly and are aggressive in our approach, yet realistic and responsive to our clients' best interests by resolving disputes through alternative means whenever possible. Our local, national and international clients range from Fortune 500 companies to start-up companies to individuals.*

(This Listing Continued)

## PROFESSIONAL BIOGRAPHIES

**SCOTT D. BAKER,** born Omaha, Nebraska, April 30, 1953; admitted to bar, 1979, California. *Education:* Brown University (A.B., 1975); Hastings College of the Law, University of California (J.D., 1978). Member, Order of the Coif; Thurston Society. Director and Legal Counsel, Scleroderma Research Foundation, Santa Barbara, California, 1987—. *Member:* Bar Association of San Francisco; American Bar Association (Member, Litigation Section). **PRACTICE AREAS:** Business Litigation; Intellectual Property Litigation. *Email:* sdb@chrm.com

**KATHY M. BANKE,** born Glendale, California, March 1, 1953; admitted to bar, 1979, California. *Education:* California State University at Sacramento (B.A., 1974); University of Colorado (J.D., 1979). Order of the Coif. *Member:* Alameda County and Federal Bar Associations; California Academy of Appellate Lawyers. (Certified Specialist, Appellate Law, The State Bar of California Board of Legal Specialization). **PRACTICE AREAS:** Appellate. *Email:* kmb@chrm.com

**STEPHEN G. BLITCH,** born Dayton, Ohio, May 25, 1947; admitted to bar, 1976, California. *Education:* University of California at Berkeley (A.B., Architecture, 1972); Master of City and Regional Planning, College of Environmental Design, 1977); Boalt Hall School of Law, University of California at Berkeley (J.D., 1976). *Member:* Alameda County and American Bar Associations; Defense Research Institute. **PRACTICE AREAS:** Civil Litigation; Business Litigation; Product Liability; State and Local Government Law. *Email:* sgb@chrm.com

**DOUGLAS G. BOVEN,** born Holland, Michigan, August 11, 1943; admitted to bar, 1970, California. *Education:* University of Michigan (B.S.E., 1966; J.D., 1969). Tau Beta Pi. Arbitrator, Federal and Superior Court Panel of Arbitrators, 1980—. Panelist, Superior Court Early Settlement Program, 1987—. Mediator, Bankruptcy Dispute Resolution, 1994—. *Member:* Bar Association of San Francisco (Member, Commercial Law and Bankruptcy Section; Arbitrator, Fee Disputes Committee, 1983—); Alameda County, Sonoma County and American (Member, Business Bankruptcy, Chapter 11 and Secured Creditors Committees) Bar Associations; American Bankruptcy Institute; Bay Area Bankruptcy Forum; Commercial Law League of America. **PRACTICE AREAS:** Finance and Commercial Law; Reorganization and Workouts; Creditor and Debtors Rights; Bankruptcy; Secured Transactions; Commercial Litigation. *Email:* dgb@chrm.com

**TIMOTHY N. BROWN,** born Tallahassee, Florida, November 26, 1942; admitted to bar, 1968, California. *Education:* Harvard University (A.B., cum laude, 1964; LL.B., cum laude, 1967). *Member:* Bar Association of San Francisco (Member, Sections on: Real Estate and Environmental Law); American Bar Association (Chair Committee on Public/Private Partnerships Section of Real Property, Probate and Trust Law); American College of Real Estate Lawyers. **PRACTICE AREAS:** Real Estate; Environmental Law. *Email:* tnb@chrm.com

**RICHARD A. BRUZZONE,** born San Francisco, California, September 17, 1955; admitted to bar, 1982, California. *Education:* Stanford University (B.S., 1978); Santa Clara University (M.B.A.; J.D., 1982). *Member:* Alameda County and American Bar Associations. **PRACTICE AREAS:** Real Estate. *Email:* rab@chrm.com

**MIKE C. BUCKLEY,** born Atlanta, Georgia, September 1, 1944; admitted to bar, 1970, California. *Education:* University of California at Berkeley (A.B., 1966); Boalt Hall School of Law, University of California at Berkeley (J.D., 1969). Arbitrator, U.S. District Court Panel (1978—). Resolution Advocate, U.S. Bankruptcy Court Panel, 1994—. *Member:* Bar Association of San Francisco; Alameda County, Contra Costa County and American (Member, Bankruptcy and Commercial Law Sections) Bar Associations; American Bankruptcy Institute; Bay Area Bankruptcy Forum (Director, 1993—). **PRACTICE AREAS:** Bankruptcy; Creditor and Debtor Rights; Secured Transactions. *Email:* mcb@chrm.com

**BOYD E. BURNISON,** born Arnolds Park, Iowa, December 12, 1934; admitted to bar, 1962, California; 1971, U.S. Supreme Court. *Education:* Iowa State University (B.Sc., 1957); Boalt Hall School of Law, University of California at Berkeley (J.D., 1961). *Member:* Bar Association of San Francisco (Member, Labor Law Section), Alameda County (Member, Labor Relations Law Committee; Director, 1981-1985; President, 1984) and American (Member, Labor and Employment Law Section) Bar Associations. Life Fellow, American Bar Foundation. **PRACTICE AREAS:** Labor and Employment.

**PHILIP L. BUSH,** born Oakland, California, October 25, 1949; admitted to bar, 1974, California. *Education:* Stanford University (B.A., 1971); Hastings College of the Law, University of California (J.D., 1974). Order of *(This Listing Continued)*

the Coif. Associate Articles Editor, Hastings Law Journal, 1973-1974. *Member:* Alameda County and American Bar Associations. **PRACTICE AREAS:** Business; Real Estate Finance and Acquisitions; Securities Regulation; Corporate and Partnership. *Email:* plb@chrm.com

**JOHN E. CARNE,** born Lincoln, Nebraska, May 1, 1946; admitted to bar, 1972, California. *Education:* University of California at Riverside (B.A., 1968); Boalt Hall School of Law, University of California at Berkeley (J.D., 1972). Lecturer, University of California at Berkeley, Graduate School of Journalism, 1987-1990. *Member:* Alameda County and American (Member, Sections of Litigation and Communication Law and Property Taxation) Bar Associations. **PRACTICE AREAS:** Media; Business Litigation; Property Taxation; Land Use and Condemnation Litigation. *Email:* jec@chrm.com

**BRAD A. CHAMBERLAIN,** born Escondido, California, December 5, 1954; admitted to bar, 1987, California; 1993, Nevada. *Education:* San Diego State University (B.A., 1978); Hastings College of Law, University of California (J.D., 1987). **PRACTICE AREAS:** Business Law; Corporate Law. *Email:* bac@chrm.com

**EUN-HEE CHANG,** born Seoul, Korea, August 22, 1955; admitted to bar, 1985, Massachusetts; 1991, California. *Education:* Harvard-Radcliffe College (A.B., summa cum laude, 1977); Harvard University (A.M., 1981); Harvard Law School (J.D., cum laude, 1985). Editor, Harvard Law Review, 1983-1985. **PRACTICE AREAS:** Real Estate. *Email:* ehc@chrm.com

**HECTOR J. CHINCHILLA,** born San Francisco, California, August 29, 1953; admitted to bar, 1986, California. *Education:* University of California at Berkeley (A.B., 1983); Hastings College of the Law, University of California (J.D., 1986). Wiley Manuel Law Scholar. Commissioner and Vice President, San Francisco Planning Commission, 1996—. Commissioner, 1982-1987 and President, 1985-1986, San Francisco Residential Rent Stabilization and Arbitration Board. *Member:* Bar Association of San Francisco; Alameda County and American Bar Associations; San Francisco La Raza Lawyers Association (Past President); Hispanic National Bar Association (Past Regional President). **PRACTICE AREAS:** Business; Real Estate; Land Use; Commercial Litigation. *Email:* hjc@chrm.com

**BRUCE E. COPELAND,** born San Mateo, California, March 28, 1961; admitted to bar, 1986, California. *Education:* University of California at Berkeley (A.B., 1983); University of San Francisco (J.D., cum laude, 1986). *Member:* Alameda County and American (Member, Sections on: Litigation and Torts and Insurance) Bar Associations. **PRACTICE AREAS:** Insurance and Environmental Coverage; Commercial Litigation. *Email:* bec@chrm.com

**COLLEEN T. DAVIES,** born Sacramento, California, October 22, 1958; admitted to bar, 1983, California. *Education:* University of California at Davis (B.A., 1980); Santa Clara University (J.D., 1983). Phi Beta Kappa. Comments Editor, Santa Clara Law Review, 1982-1983. *Member:* Alameda County and American Bar Associations; Association of Business Trial Lawyers (Board of Governors); Queen's Bench (Member, Judicial Appointments Committee); Defense Research Institute; California Women Lawyers and Association of Northern California Defense Counsel. **PRACTICE AREAS:** Product Liability; Pharmaceutical Liability; Commercial Litigation. *Email:* ctd@chrm.com

**PETER W. DAVIS,** born Portland, Oregon, May 2, 1942; admitted to bar, 1970, California. *Education:* University of Oregon (B.S., 1965); Hastings College of Law, University of California (J.D., 1969). Order of the Coif. Issue Editor, Hastings Law Journal, 1968-1969. Chair, Ninth Circuit Advisory Committee on Rules of Practice and Procedure. Member, Board of Directors, 1986— and Treasurer, 1988—, First District Appellate Project. Past President and Member, California Academy of Appellate Lawyers. Member, American Academy of Appellate Lawyers. *Member:* Alameda County and American (Member, Section of Litigation) Bar Associations. (Certified Specialist, Appellate Law, The State Bar of California Board of Legal Specialization). **PRACTICE AREAS:** Appellate. *Email:* pwd@chrm.com

**MICHAEL E. DELEHUNT,** born San Francisco, California, June 27, 1948; admitted to bar, 1976, California. *Education:* St. Mary's College (A.B., 1970); Hastings College of the Law, University of California (J.D., 1976). *Member:* Bar Association of San Francisco; Alameda County and American (Member, Litigation Tort Insurance Sections) Bar Associations. **PRACTICE AREAS:** Commercial; Land Use; Environmental and Insurance Litigation. *Email:* med@chrm.com

**CHARLES W. DENNY,** born Fayette, Missouri, December 1, 1934; admitted to bar, 1959, Missouri; 1962, California. *Education:* University of *(This Listing Continued)*

**CROSBY, HEAFEY, ROACH & MAY**, PROFESSIONAL CORPORATION, Oakland—Continued

Missouri (A.B., 1956; LL.B., 1958). *Member:* Alameda County and American (Member, Section of International Law and Practice) Bar Associations; The Missouri Bar; Asia-Pacific Lawyers Association; Inter-Pacific Bar Association; International Bar Association. *PRACTICE AREAS:* Real Estate; Corporate; Domestic and International Transactions. *Email:* cwd@chrm.com

**JOHN E. DITTOE,** born San Francisco, California, June 20, 1954; admitted to bar, 1979, California. *Education:* University of California at Berkeley (B.S., 1976); Hastings College of the Law, University of California (J.D., 1979). Associate Editor, Hastings Law Journal, 1978-1979. *Member:* Bar Association of San Francisco; Alameda County Bar Association; Association of Defense Counsel, Northern California; Defense Research Institute. *PRACTICE AREAS:* Health Care; Insurance; Toxic Tort; Business Litigation. *Email:* jed@chrm.com

**WILLIAM A. DURGIN,** born Pawtucket, Rhode Island, January 7, 1955; admitted to bar, 1984, California. *Education:* College of the Holy Cross (A.B., 1979); Santa Clara University (J.D., 1984). *Member:* Alameda County Bar Association. *PRACTICE AREAS:* Real Estate. *Email:* wad@chrm.com

**BETTE B. EPSTEIN,** born Orange, California, July 23, 1944; admitted to bar, 1986, California. *Education:* University of Southern California (B.S., 1965); California State University at Hayward (M.S., 1979); University of San Francisco (J.D., magna cum laude, 1986). Member, McAuliffe Law Honor Society. *Member:* Alameda County Bar Association (Co-Chair, Probate Litigation Committee). *PRACTICE AREAS:* Trust & Estate Litigation; Contested Conservatorships; Representation of Regional Centers. *Email:* bbe@chrm.com

**PAUL D. FOGEL,** born Santa Monica, California, September 19, 1949; admitted to bar, 1976, California. *Education:* University of California at Berkeley (A.B., 1971); Université de Paris, Paris, France; University of California at Los Angeles School of Law (J.D., 1976). Fulbright Fellow in American Law, Université de Paris II, Faculté de Droit, Paris, France, 1979-1980. Visiting Lecturer, Boalt Hall, Appellate Advocacy Program, 1991—. Supervising Senior Attorney, Staff of Chief Justice Bird, California Supreme Court, 1983-1987. *Member:* Alameda County Bar Association; Bar Association of San Francisco. California Academy of Appellate Lawyers; Union Internationale des Avocates. (Certified Specialist, Appellate Law, The State Bar of California Board of Legal Specialization). *LANGUAGES:* French. *PRACTICE AREAS:* Appellate. *Email:* pdf@chrm.com

**THOMAS M. FREEMAN,** born Huntsville, Alabama, April 14, 1954; admitted to bar, 1983, California. *Education:* University of California at Berkeley (A.B., 1979); Hastings College of the Law, University of California (J.D., 1983). Senior Research Editor, Hastings Constitutional Law Quarterly, 1982-1983. Co-Chair International Insurance Coverage Litigation Sub Committee of the American Bar Association. *Member:* Alameda County and American Bar Associations; Defense Research Institute. *PRACTICE AREAS:* Civil Litigation; Products Liability; Insurance Coverage. *Email:* tmf@chrm.com

**JOAN M. HARATANI,** born Redwood City, California, August 2, 1957; admitted to bar, 1985, California. *Education:* St. John's College (B.A., 1979); University of California at Davis (J.D., 1984). Member, Law Review, 1984. Advisory Committee Member, ABA Conference on Minority Partners in Majority Law Firms. Executive Committee Member, Law Practice Management Committee, State Bar of California. *Member:* National Asian Pacific American Bar Association; Asian Bar Association of Northern California; Defense Research Institute (Member, Sections on: Pharmaceutical and Medical Device Litigation. *PRACTICE AREAS:* Pharmaceutical and Medical Device Litigation; Product Liability. *Email:* jmh@chrm.com

**EDWIN A. HEAFEY, JR.,** born Oakland, California, November 1, 1930; admitted to bar, 1955, California. *Education:* Santa Clara University (B.S., 1952); Stanford University (LL.B., 1955). Author: "California Trial Objections," (CEB 4th Edition, 1996). Instructor, Trial Practice, Boalt Hall School of Law, University of California, 1963-1978. *Member:* Bar Association of San Francisco; Alameda County and American Bar Associations. Fellow, American College of Trial Lawyers (certified Trial Specialist); past national president, American Board of Trial Advocates; International Society of Barristers; past fellow, Stanford and Georgetown Law Schools. Best Lawyers in America, 1987-1996. *PRACTICE AREAS:* Civil Litigation. *Email:* eahj@chrm.com

**EZRA HENDON,** born Brooklyn, New York, September 15, 1936; admitted to bar, 1967, District of Columbia; 1968, California. *Education:* University of Michigan (B.A., 1958; J.D., 1966); University of Iowa (M.A., 1960). Adjunct Professor, Prison Law, University of San Francisco, 1977. Director, Moot Court Program, Stanford University, 1979-1980. *Member:* Alameda County Bar Association. (Certified Specialist, Appellate Law, The State Bar of California Board of Legal Specialization). *PRACTICE AREAS:* Appellate. *Email:* ezh@chrm.com

**B. CLYDE HUTCHINSON, III,** born Yuma, Colorado, November 14, 1941; admitted to bar, 1966, California. *Education:* University of Colorado (B.A., 1962); Boalt Hall School of Law, University of California at Berkeley (J.D., 1965). *Member:* Bar Association of San Francisco; Alameda County and American (Member, Sections of Tort and Insurance Practice and Litigation) Bar Associations; National Association of Railroad Trial Counsel (President, 1988-1989). *PRACTICE AREAS:* Transportation Law; Toxic Tort; Products Liability. *Email:* bch@chrm.com

**NED N. ISOKAWA,** born Topaz, Utah, October 14, 1944; admitted to bar, 1975, California. *Education:* University of California at Berkeley (B.S.E.E., 1966) Boalt Hall School of Law, University of California at Berkeley (J.D., 1975). *Member:* Alameda County and American Bar Associations; Bar Association of San Francisco (Member, Committee on Minority Employment); Asian-American Bar Association of the Greater Bay Area (Member, Board of Directors, 1987-1992; President, 1993). *PRACTICE AREAS:* Complex Litigation; Intellectual Property; Environmental; Toxic Tort. *Email:* nni@chrm.com

**HOWARD A. JANSSEN,** born Modesto, California, June 1, 1943; admitted to bar, 1970, California. *Education:* University of California at Davis (B.A., 1966); Hastings College of the Law, University of California (J.D., 1970). Associate Professor of Law, Hastings College of the Law, 1980-1989. Member, Board of Directors, Hastings Center for Trial and Appellate Advocacy, 1982-1990. *Member:* Alameda County and American Bar Associations. *PRACTICE AREAS:* Litigation; Employment; Business; Insurance Coverage and Claims; Products Liability. *Email:* haj@chrm.com

**JACQUELINE M. JAUREGUI,** born Oakland, California, September 13, 1952; admitted to bar, 1980, California. *Education:* San Francisco State University (B.A., magna cum laude, 1977); Hastings College of Law, University of California (J.D., 1980). Order of the Coif. Note Editor, Hastings International and Comparative Law Review, 1979-1980. *Member:* Alameda County Bar Association; California Women Lawyers; Women Lawyers of Alameda County. *PRACTICE AREAS:* Complex Civil Litigation; Insurance Coverage; Employment. *Email:* jmj@chrm.com

**GARY A. JEFFREY,** born Chicago, Illinois, October 1, 1952; admitted to bar, 1986, California. *Education:* Loyola University (B.S., 1974); Ohio State University (M.S., 1978); University of San Francisco (J.D., with honors, 1986). *Member:* Alameda County Bar Association; The State Bar of California. *PRACTICE AREAS:* Business Litigation; Products Liability. *Email:* gaj@chrm.com

**CRAIG S. J. JOHNS,** born San Diego, California, April 29, 1961; admitted to bar, 1988, California. *Education:* University of California at Los Angeles (B.A., 1983); University of California at Davis (J.D., 1988). Chairman, California Regional Water Quality Control Board, San Francisco Bay Region. Member, San Francisco Bay Conservation and Development Commission. Member, American Bar Association, Natural Resources, Energy and Environmental Law Section, Section Liaison to Real Property Probate and Trust Law Section. *PRACTICE AREAS:* Environmental. *Email:* csjj@chrm.com

**KENNETH F. JOHNSON,** born Fort Bragg, California, June 10, 1938; admitted to bar, 1970, California. *Education:* University of California at Berkeley (B.S., Civil Engineering, 1962); Hastings College of the Law, University of California (J.D., 1969). Order of the Coif. Note and Comment Editor, 1968-1969, Hastings Law Journal. *Member:* Bar Association of San Francisco; Alameda County, Contra Costa County and American (Member, Sections on: Litigation and Tort and Insurance Practice) Bar Associations; Association of Business Trial Lawyers; Association of Trial Lawyers of America; Association of Defense Counsel. *PRACTICE AREAS:* Construction; Product Liability; Insurance; Business; Civil Litigation; Alternative Dispute Resolution. *Email:* kfj@chrm.com

**JOHN M. KEMP,** born Mexico, Missouri, February 14, 1945; admitted to bar, 1974, California. *Education:* University of Missouri (B.A., 1967); University of San Francisco (J.D., cum laude, 1974); New York University (LL.M. in Taxation, 1975). Member, McAuliffe Honor Society. Managing

*(This Listing Continued)*

Editor: University of San Francisco Law Review, 1973-1974; Graduate Editor, Tax Law Review, 1974-1975. Law Clerk (Extern): The Honorable James R. Browning, Chief Judge, U.S. Court of Appeals, Ninth Circuit, 1974. Adjunct Professor, Golden Gate University School of Law, 1987-1991. Author, Subchapters: Reclassification of Debt as a Second Class of Stock, 7 U.S.F. Law Rev. 542, 1973. *Member:* Bar Association of San Francisco; Alameda County and American Bar Associations. **PRACTICE AREAS:** Complex Tax Planning; Tax Exempt Entities; Mergers and Acquisitions; Corporate and Partnership Law; Tax Litigation. **Email:** jmk@chrm.com

**JOHN MCD. KERN,** born Omaha, Nebraska, November 28, 1946; admitted to bar, 1973, District of Columbia; 1980, California. *Education:* Creighton University (B.A., 1970); The National Law Center, George Washington University (J.D., cum laude, 1973). Author: "AIDS Litigation For the Primary Care Physician," *Medical management of AIDS*, Sande and Volberding Eds., W.B. Saunders; Harcourt Brace Jovanovich, 1992; "A Survey of Transfusion Associated AIDS Litigation: 1984 through 1993," Transfusion 1994;34:484-91. Assistant U.S. Attorney: District of Columbia, 1973-1978; Northern District of California, 1978-1981. *Member:* Bar Association of San Francisco; Alameda County and American Bar Associations; The District of Columbia Bar. Advocate, American Board of Trials Advocates, American Inns of Court. **PRACTICE AREAS:** Civil Litigation. **Email:** jmck@chrm.com

**STEVEN M. KOHN,** born Chicago, Illinois, June 19, 1942; admitted to bar, 1974, California. *Education:* University of California at Los Angeles (A.B., 1965; M.B.A., 1967); University of San Francisco (J.D., 1974). Member, McAuliffe Law Honor Society. Co-Author: "Practical Considerations for Preparing a Market Share Case," *Defending Drug and Medical Device Cases,* Defense Research Institute, Chicago, Illinois. Author: "Memory Experts in Drug and Device Cases," *R.X. for the Defense: The Newsletter of the DRI* Drug and Medical Device Committee, Spring, 1993; "Memory Experts Can Debunk Recollection of Absent Product," Leader's Product Liability Law and Strategy, April 1994. Member, International Association of Defense Counsel. *Member:* Bar Association of San Francisco; Alameda County and American Bar Associations; Defense Research Institute. **PRACTICE AREAS:** Civil Litigation; Product Liability; Environmental; Insurance Coverage; Commercial Litigation. **Email:** smk@chrm.com

**F. RONALD LAUPHEIMER,** born Baltimore, Maryland, August 13, 1945; admitted to bar, 1973, California; 1977, U.S. Supreme Court; U.S. Court of Appeals, District of Columbia and Ninth Circuits. *Education:* Washington & Lee University (B.S., 1966); University of San Francisco (J.D., 1973). Member, McAuliffe Law Honor Society. *Member:* Bar Association of San Francisco; Alameda County and American (Member, Sections of Litigation and Tort and Insurance) Bar Associations; Barristers Club of San Francisco (Board of Directors, 1977-1978; Treasurer, 1978). **PRACTICE AREAS:** Complex Civil Litigation; Toxic Tort Law; Environmental Law. **Email:** frl@chrm.com

**MICHAEL J. LOEB,** born Evanston, Illinois, June 28, 1947; admitted to bar, 1974, California. *Education:* Cornell University (B.A., 1969); Hastings College of the Law, University of California (J.D., 1974). Order of the Coif. Member: Panel of Arbitrators, American Arbitration Association; Mediation and Early Neutral Evaluation Panelist, U.S. District Court, Northern District of California. *Member:* Bar Association of San Francisco (Member, Labor and Employment Law Section); Alameda County (President, 1993) and American (Member, Sections of Labor and Employment Law, Individual Rights and Responsibilities) Bar Associations. **PRACTICE AREAS:** Labor; Employment; Employment Benefits; Alternative Dispute Resolution. **Email:** mjl@chrm.com

**JOSEPH P. MASCOVICH,** born Martinez, California, May 11, 1954; admitted to bar, 1980, Oregon; 1982, California. *Education:* University of California at Berkeley (A.B., 1977); Hastings College of the Law, University of California (J.D., 1980). Order of the Coif. Articles Editor, Hastings Law Journal, 1979-1980. Co-Author, Chapter on Petitions for Rehearing, California Civil Appellate Practice 3rd ed., 1996. Author: "The Impact of the Lucas Court on California Tort Law", Winter, 1992, California Litigation. Co-author, Chapter, "Appellate Issues", California Complex Litigation Manual, Parker & Sons, 1990. *Member:* Alameda County Bar Association; Oregon State Bar. **PRACTICE AREAS:** Appellate. **Email:** jpm@chrm.com

**LOUISE M. MCCABE,** born Bakersfield, California, October 10, 1957; admitted to bar, 1983, California. *Education:* University of California at Los Angeles (B.A., 1979); University of Santa Clara (M.B.A. 1983; J.D., 1983). Alpha Kappa Delta. *Member:* Bar Association of San Francisco; Alameda County and American (Member, Section of Taxation) Bar Associations. **PRACTICE AREAS:** Commercial Litigation; Professional Liability; Property Tax Litigation; Insurance and Environmental Coverage. **Email:** lmm@chrm.com

**JOHN L. MCDONNELL, JR.,** born Oakland, California, December 12, 1937; admitted to bar, 1964, California. *Education:* St. Patrick's Seminary (A.B., 1960); University of Notre Dame; University of San Francisco (J.D., 1963). Phi Delta Phi. *Member:* Alameda County (Chairman, Probate Committee, 1980-1990; Chair, Estate Planning, Trust and Probate Law Section, 1990-1991) and American (Member, House of Delegates, 1989—) Bar Associations. Fellow, American College of Trust and Estate Counsel (State Chair, 1991-1996). Academician, The International Academy of Estate and Trust Law. (Certified Specialist, Probate, Estate Planning and Trust Law, The State Bar of California Board of Legal Specialization). **PRACTICE AREAS:** Estate Planning Law; Administration of Trust and Estates; Fiduciary Asset Management; Trust and Estate Litigation. **Email:** jlm@chrm.com

**STEPHEN A. MCFEELY,** born Renton, Washington, June 18, 1947; admitted to bar, 1972, California. *Education:* St. Mary's College (B.S., 1969); Hastings College of the Law, University of California (J.D., 1972). Note and Comment Editor, Hastings Law Journal, 1971-1972. Formerly Adjunct Professor, Hastings Law School. Author of Several Chapters in *Trial Practice: Civil Procedure During Trial,* 1995. *Member:* Alameda County and American Bar Associations. (Managing Partner). **PRACTICE AREAS:** Business Disputes; Insurance Bad Faith. **Email:** sam@chrm.com

**MICHELE BALLARD MILLER,** born New York, N.Y., July 14, 1954; admitted to bar, 1982, California. *Education:* University of Michigan (B.A., 1978); Hastings College of the Law, University of California (J.D., 1982). *Member:* Bar Association of San Francisco; American Bar Association (Member, Sections on: Labor and Employment Law; Litigation). **PRACTICE AREAS:** Labor and Employment Law; Litigation. **Email:** mbm@chrm.com

**RANDALL D. MORRISON,** born Helena, Montana, August 6, 1946; admitted to bar, 1972, California. *Education:* University of Washington, Arts and Science Honors College (B.A., cum laude, 1967); Boalt Hall School of Law, University of California at Berkeley (J.D., 1972). *Member:* Bar Association of San Francisco; Alameda County and American Bar Associations. **PRACTICE AREAS:** Commercial Litigation; Environmental Litigation. **Email:** rdm@chrm.com

**RONALD L. MUROV,** born Ukiah, California, July 16, 1946; admitted to bar, 1974, California. *Education:* University of the Pacific (B.A., 1969); University of California at Los Angeles School of Law (J.D., 1974). Order of the Coif. *Member:* Bar Association of San Francisco; Alameda County Bar Association. **PRACTICE AREAS:** Civil Litigation with emphasis on Business Torts; Finance Securities Litigation. **Email:** rlm@chrm.com

**JACK R. NELSON,** born Minneapolis, Minnesota, July 6, 1958; admitted to bar, 1983, California. *Education:* University of Minnesota (B.S., 1980); Boalt Hall School of Law, University of California at Berkeley (J.D., 1983). Phi Beta Kappa; Beta Gamma Sigma. Comments Editor, Ecology Law Quarterly, 1982-1983. *Member:* Bar Association of San Francisco; Alameda County and American Bar Associations. **PRACTICE AREAS:** Insurance and Commercial Litigation. **Email:** jrn@chrm.com

**LAWRANCE W. NILE** (1957-1994).

**ALBERT B. NORRIS, JR.,** born Portland, Oregon, November 8, 1935; admitted to bar, 1964, California. *Education:* University of Southern California (B.S., 1957); University of California at Los Angeles School of Law (LL.B., 1963). *Member:* Alameda County Bar Association; American Board of Trial Advocates; Association of Defense Counsel, Northern California (Member, Board of Directors, 1977-1979). Fellow, American College of Trial Lawyers. **PRACTICE AREAS:** Toxic Tort; Environmental. **Email:** abn@chrm.com

**MARY C. OPPEDAHL,** born Duluth, Minnesota, September 5, 1946; admitted to bar, 1983, California. *Education:* Holy Names College (B.A., 1968); St. Louis University (M.S.W., 1976); University of San Francisco (J.D., 1983). *Member:* Bar Association of San Francisco; Alameda County Bar Association. **PRACTICE AREAS:** Professional Liability; Insurance Litigation; Products Liability Litigation. **Email:** mco@chrm.com

**BETTY J. ORVELL,** born Lancaster, Pennsylvania, September 21, 1942; admitted to bar, 1986, California, U.S. District Court, Northern District of California and U.S. Court of Appeals, Ninth Circuit; 1991, U.S. Tax Court. *Education:* Tufts University (B.A., cum laude, 1964); University of Pennsylvania (M.A., 1984); Hastings College of the Law, University of California (J.D., magna cum laude, 1986). Thurston Society; Order of the Coif.

*(This Listing Continued)*

**CROSBY, HEAFEY, ROACH & MAY,** *PROFESSIONAL CORPORATION,* Oakland—*Continued*

Technical Editor, Hastings Law Journal, 1985-1986. Member, Executive Committee, State Bar of California Estate Planning, Trust and Probate Law Section. *Member:* Alameda County (Vice-Chair, Estate Planning, Trust and Probate law Section) and American (Real Property, Probate and Trust Law Section) Bar Associations; California Women Lawyers. (Certified Specialist, Probate, Estate Planning and Trust Law, The State Bar of California Board of Legal Specialization). *PRACTICE AREAS:* Trusts and Estates; Estate Planning for Employee Benefits. *Email:* bjo@chrm.com

**DAVID V. OTTERSON,** born Merced, California, October 4, 1953; admitted to bar, 1980, California. *Education:* California State University at Chico (B.A., 1977); Hastings College of the Law, University of California (J.D., 1980). Articles Editor, Hastings Law Journal, 1979-1980. Co-Author: "Business Buy-Out Agreements," (CEB, 1991); "Sales & Leases in California Commercial Law Practice," (CEB, 1993). *Member:* Alameda County and American (Sections on Business and Antitrust) Bar Associations. *PRACTICE AREAS:* Corporate Finance; Mergers and Acquisitions; Domestic and International Product Distribution; Technology Licensing. *Email:* dvo@chrm.com

**KURT C. PETERSON,** born Salem, New Jersey, March 31, 1953; admitted to bar, 1978, California. *Education:* Stanford University (B.A., 1975); Hastings College of the Law, University of California (J.D., 1978). Law Clerk to The Honorable Robert F. Kane, California Court of Appeals, First Appellate District, 1978. *Member:* Bar Association of San Francisco; Los Angeles, Alameda County, Beverly Hills and American (Litigation Section, Legal Malpractice Subcommittee, Vice Chair, 1989-1993) Bar Associations; Association of Defense Counsel; California Society for Healthcare Attorneys; Association of Business Trial Lawyers. (Resident, Los Angeles Office). *PRACTICE AREAS:* Commercial Litigation with special emphasis on Professional Liability; Securities; Insurance; Entertainment. *Email:* kcp@chrm.com

**THOMAS J. QUINLAN,** born Aberdeen, Maryland, June 12, 1952; admitted to bar, 1985, California. *Education:* Santa Clara University (B.S., 1974); University of San Francisco (J.D., 1 985). *Member:* American Bar Association (Member, Antitrust and Intellectual Property Sections); National Health Lawyers Association; American Academy of Hospital Attorneys. *PRACTICE AREAS:* Mergers and Acquisitions; Corporate Finance; Health; Intellectual Property. *Email:* tjq@chrm.com

**JOHN A. REDING,** born Orange, California, May 26, 1944; admitted to bar, 1970, California; U.S. Supreme Court; U.S. Claims Court. *Education:* University of California at Berkeley (A.B., 1966) Boalt Hall School of Law, University of California at Berkeley (J.D., 1969). *Member:* Bar Associations of San Francisco; Alameda County and American (Member, Section on Litigation, Intellectual Property and Natural Resources, Energy and Environmental Law and Committees on Business Torts, International Law, Trial Practice and Torts and Insurance) Bar Associations; State Bar of California (Member, Litigation Section); American Intellectual Property Law Association; Association of Business Trial Lawyers. *LANGUAGES:* German. *PRACTICE AREAS:* Commercial Litigation; Environmental Litigation; Toxic Tort Litigation; Intellectual Property Litigation. *Email:* jar@chrm.com

**SEAN M. RHATIGAN,** born Huntington, New York, April 22, 1954; admitted to bar, 1980, California and U.S. Tax Court; 1983, U.S. Court of Federal Claims. *Education:* Stanford University (B.A., with honors, 1976); University of California (M.B.A., 1979); Boalt Hall School of Law, University of California at Berkeley (J.D., 1979). *Member:* Alameda County Bar Association. *PRACTICE AREAS:* Income Tax; Corporate and Partnership; Mergers & Acquisitions. *Email:* smr@chrm.com

**MARGARET R. ROISMAN,** born Barnesville, Ohio, December 1, 1945; admitted to bar, 1982, California. *Education:* Oberlin College (B.A., magna cum laude, 1967); Boalt Hall School of Law, University of California (J.D., 1982). Phi Beta Kappa. Order of the Coif. Associate Editor, California Law Review, 1981-1982. *Member:* Alameda County and American (Member, Section on Real Property, Probate and Trust Law) Bar Associations. (Certified Specialist, Probate, Estate Planning and Trust Law, The State Bar of California Board of Legal Specialization). *PRACTICE AREAS:* Estate Planning; Probate and Trust Administration. *Email:* mrr@chrm.com

**RONALD V. ROSEQUIST,** born San Francisco, California, May 1, 1941; admitted to bar, 1970, California. *Education:* Occidental College (B.A., 1962); Hastings College of the Law, University of California (J.D.,

1969). *Member:* Alameda County and American Bar Associations. *PRACTICE AREAS:* Mergers & Acquisitions; Corporate. *Email:* rvr@chrm.com

**STEPHEN H. SCHADLICH,** born San Francisco, California, March 17, 1936; admitted to bar, 1964, California. *Education:* University of California (B.S., 1958); Boalt Hall School of Law, University of California at Berkeley (J.D., 1963). *Member:* Alameda County (President, 1989) and American Bar Associations; National Association of College and University Attorneys. Life Fellow, American Bar Association. *PRACTICE AREAS:* Higher Education; Corporate; Business. *Email:* shs@chrm.com

**WILLIAM W. SCHOFIELD, JR.,** born Newark, New Jersey, August 13, 1948; admitted to bar, 1974, California. *Education:* University of California at Berkeley (A.B., 1970); Hastings College of the Law, University of California (J.D., 1974). Order of the Coif. Associate Articles Editor, Hastings Law Journal, 1973-1974. *Member:* Alameda County and American Bar Associations. *PRACTICE AREAS:* General Litigation. *Email:* wws@chrm.com

**GREGORY E. SCHOPF,** born Portland, Oregon, February 9, 1949; admitted to bar, 1986, California. *Education:* University of Portland (B.A., 1971); Hastings College of the Law, University of California (J.D., 1985). *Member:* Alameda County (Member, Trial Practice Section) and American (Member, Tort and Insurance Practice Section) Bar Associations; Association of Defense Counsel; Association of Business Trial Lawyers. *PRACTICE AREAS:* General Civil Litigation; Insurance Coverage Disputes. *Email:* ges@chrm.com

**STEPHEN G. SCHREY,** born Pomona, California, October 9, 1948; admitted to bar, 1974, California. *Education:* Santa Clara University (B.A., 1970); University of San Francisco (J.D., 1 974). Associate Editor, University of San Francisco Law Review, 1973-1974. Co-author: "California Trial Techniques," Parker, 1991; "Current Trends and Developments in Environmental Coverage Litigation," *Insurance, Excess and Reinsurance Coverage Disputes* , PLI, 1992; "Special Problems in Hazardous Waste Litigation," *Insurance, Excess and Reinsurance Coverage Disputes,* PLI, 1994. *Member:* Bar Association of San Francisco; Alameda County, Contra Costa County and American (Member, Litigation Section; Co-Chair, Joint Task Force on Complex Insurance Coverage Litigation) Bar Associations; Defense Research Institute. *PRACTICE AREAS:* Insurance Coverage and Claims Litigation. *Email:* sgs@chrm.com

**CHARLES H. SEAMAN,** born Visalia, California, May 17, 1952; admitted to bar, 1978, California. *Education:* University of California at Berkeley (A.B., 1975); Hastings College of the Law, University of California (J.D., 1978). *Member:* Bar Association of San Francisco; Alameda County and American Bar Associations. *PRACTICE AREAS:* Real Estate. *Email:* chs@chrm.com

**KENNETH M. SEEGER,** born New York, N.Y., August 15, 1955; admitted to bar, 1988, California. *Education:* State University of New York at Stony Brook (B.A., 1979); Temple University (J.D., 1988). *Member:* Bar Association of San Francisco; Alameda County Bar Association. *PRACTICE AREAS:* Insurance; Product Liability; Business Litigation. *Email:* kms@chrm.com

**EMBER L. SHINN,** born Kahului, Hawaii, November 5, 1950; admitted to bar, 1978, California. *Education:* University of Hawaii (B.A., 1972); McGeorge School of Law, University of the Pacific (J.D., 1976). *Member:* Bar Association of San Francisco (Member, Labor and Employment Law Section); Alameda County Bar Association; Asian American Bar Association. *PRACTICE AREAS:* Employment Litigation; Labor; Education. *Email:* els@chrm.com

**BOYD C. SLEETH,** born Los Angeles, California, May 25, 1952; admitted to bar, 1982, California. *Education:* Immaculate Heart College (B.A., 1975); Hastings College of the Law, University of California (J.D. 1982). Order of the Coif. Co-author, "Insurance Law Handbook", Parker & Son, 1992. *Member:* Alameda County Bar Association. *PRACTICE AREAS:* Commercial and Insurance Litigation. *Email:* bcs@chrm.com

**WALTER E. THOMAS,** born Indonesia, April 7, 1948; admitted to bar, 1972, California. *Education:* Harvard University (A.B., 1969). Stanford University School of Law (J.D., 1972). Order of the Coif. *Member:* Alameda County and American Bar Associations. *PRACTICE AREAS:* Business; Corporate. *Email:* wet@chrm.com

**MORGAN W. TOVEY,** born Pocatello, Idaho, January 1, 1963; admitted to bar, 1988, California. *Education:* University of California at Davis (A.B., with high honors, 1985); University of California at Los Angeles (J.D., 1988). Law Clerk to the Honorable Charles A. Legge, U.S. District

*(This Listing Continued)*

Court, Northern District of California, 1988-1989. *PRACTICE AREAS:* Intellectual Property; Business Litigation. *Email:* mwt@chrm.com

**MARSHALL CLARK WALLACE,** born Oakland, California, April 20, 1959; admitted to bar, 1987, California and District of Columbia. *Education:* Princeton University (B.S., summa cum laude, 1981); University of California at Berkeley (M.B.A., 1986); Boalt Hall School of Law, University of California at Berkeley (J.D., 1986). Phi Beta Kappa. *PRACTICE AREAS:* Business and Insurance Litigation. *Email:* mcw@chrm.com

**ERIC G. WALLIS,** born Astoria, New York, January 8, 1950; admitted to bar, 1975, California. *Education:* University of the Pacific (A.B., magna cum laude, 1972); Hastings College of the Law, University of California (J.D., 1975). Editorial Associate, Hastings Law Journal, 1974-1975. Author, "California Civil Procedure Before Trial," CEB, 1988 Supplement. Securities Arbitrator, NASD and AAA. *Member:* Alameda County and American (Member, Section of Litigation) Bar Associations. *PRACTICE AREAS:* Commercial Litigation with emphasis in Securities; Products Liability. *Email:* egw@chrm.com

**WILLIAM D. WICK,** born Dayton, Ohio, August 18, 1949; admitted to bar, 1974, California. *Education:* Northwestern University (B.A., 1971); Georgetown University (J.D., 1974). Adjunct Professor, Environmental Law, Golden Gate University School of Law, 1981—. Co-editor, "Cleanup of Hazardous Substances," California Environmental Law and Land Use Practice, Matthew-Bender, 1995. Attorney, U.S. Environmental Agency, 1978-1991. Hazardous Waste Branch Chief, Region 9 Office of Regional Counsel, 1985-1991. *Member:* Bar Association of San Francisco; Alameda County and American Bar Associations. *PRACTICE AREAS:* Environmental. *Email:* wdw@chrmc.com

**JAMES T. WILSON,** born Newport, Rhode Island, December 23, 1946; admitted to bar, 1977, California. *Education:* Stanford University (B.A., 1969); Boalt Hall School of Law, University of California at Berkeley (J.D., 1977). *Member:* Alameda County and American Bar Associations; Association of Defense Counsel. *PRACTICE AREAS:* Environmental; Toxics Litigation; Insurance and Commercial Litigation. *Email:* jtw@chrm.com

**MALCOLM B. WITTENBERG,** born Worcester, Massachusetts, June 24, 1946; admitted to bar, 1972, Virginia; 1974, District of Columbia; 1976, California; registered to practice before U.S. Patent and Trademark Office. *Education:* Worcester Polytechnic Institute (B.S., with distinction, 1968); The National Law Center, George Washington University (J.D., with honors, 1972). Law Clerk to Hon. Phillip B. Baldwin, Associate Judge, U.S. Court of Customs and Patent Appeals, 1974-1976. *PRACTICE AREAS:* Patent, Trademark and Copyright Litigation; Prosecution and Counseling. *Email:* mbw@chrm.com

**JAMES M. WOOD,** born Oakland, California, March 22, 1948; admitted to bar, 1973, California. *Education:* St. Mary's College (B.A., 1970); University of San Francisco (J.D., 1973). *Member:* Alameda County and American (Member, Section of Litigation) Bar Associations; Association of Defense Counsel, Northern California; The Association of Trial Lawyers of America (Associate); California Trial Lawyers Association (Associate); American Academy of Hospital Attorneys; Defense Research Institute Trial Lawyers Association; American Society for Pharmacy Law; National Health Lawyers Association. *PRACTICE AREAS:* Products Liability Law; Pharmaceutical and Medical Device Litigation. *Email:* jmw@chrm.com

---

Jennifer Beckett
Susan P. Beneville
Marc R. Benson
Stephanie L. Berman
J. David Bickham
Steven J. Boranian
Anthony M. Bova
SusanBeth Bowden
Thomas E. Brinley
Duffy Carolan
Avalyn Y. Castillo
Kevin D. Caton
Laura Jane Coles
Darren K. Cottriel
Birgit A. Dachtera
David E. Durant
Barry N. Endick
W. Manning Evans
Alan S. Feiler
Gregg M. Ficks
Jennifer S. Fluet
Kerry McInerney Freeman
Todd Grant Gattoni
Stephanie A. Gleason
Jeffrey Goss
Samantha L. Hardaway
Terence N. Hawley
Helen S. Haynes
Lisa V. Heilbron
Carolyn E. Henel
Adaline Hilgard
John J. Horton
Tiffanie K. Kalmbach
Genevieve S. Katz
Jo Saxe Kerlinsky
Nathan P. Koenig

*(This Listing Continued)*

---

*(Continued)*

Jane Kow
Peter Laufenberg
Jacques B. LeBoeuf
Vera Marcus McEntee
Scott C. McKnight
Peter C. Meier
Tanda L. Neundorf
Robert A. Olson
Garth A. Osterman
William R. Overend
John P. Phillips
Toni A. Ragozzino
Shelagh K. Redding
James Daniel Riley, Jr.
Darren P. Roach
Jonathan C. Rolnick
Pamela G. H. Rupright
Robin J. Samuel
Pamela A. Schock
Jennifer A. Shy
John Lynn Smith
Randall J. Sperring
Walter M. Stella
Kristine De Serpa Stone
Adam H. Tachner
Robert A. Trodella, Jr.
Philip L. Tudor
Lindsey A. Urbina
Sonja S. Weissman
Leslie M. Yuki

*OF COUNSEL*

**MCKNIGHT BRUNN,** born Salt Lake City, Utah, April 17, 1919; admitted to bar, 1950, California. *Education:* University of Chicago (Ph.B., 1946; J.D., 1949). *Member:* Alameda County (Member, Probate Committee; Chair, Legislation Committee) and American Bar Associations.

**ANDRE L. DE BAUBIGNY,** born Cannes, France, July 2, 1932; admitted to bar, 1959, California. *Education:* Stanford University (B.A., 1953; LL.B., 1958). *Member:* Bar Association of San Francisco; Alameda County and American Bar Associations.

**JAMES N. DAWE,** born Los Angeles, California, August 8, 1943; admitted to bar, 1969, California. *Education:* University of San Francisco (A.B., 1965; J.D., 1968). National Merit Scholar. Visiting Fellow, St. Anthony's College, Oxford University, 1991-1992 (European Integration). Member, Business Law Section, State Bar of California. Member, National Panel of Arbitrators (Commercial), American Arbitration Association. *Member:* Bar Association of San Francisco; Contra Costa County and American (Member, Sections on: Tax; Business Law; Antitrust Law) Bar Associations. *Email:* jnd@chrm.com

**RICHARD J. HEAFEY,** born Oakland, California, August 3, 1935; admitted to bar, 1962, California. *Education:* Santa Clara University (B.S., 1958); University of Michigan (LL.B., 1961). Adjunct Professor, University of San Francisco Law School, Ethics and Product Liability. Co-Author, "Product Liability: Winning Strategies and Tactics," Law Journal Seminars Press, 1994. *Member:* Alameda County and American Bar Associations; Federation of Insurance & Corporate Counsel. *PRACTICE AREAS:* Product Liability; Pharmaceutical and Medical Device Litigation. *Email:* rjh@chrm.com

**JAY R. MARTIN,** born Birmingham, Alabama, August 12, 1928; admitted to bar, 1953, California. *Education:* University of California at Berkeley (B.S., 1949) Boalt Hall School of Law, University of California at Berkeley (LL.B., 1952). *Member:* Bar Association of San Francisco; Federal, American and International Bar Associations; The Association of Trial Lawyers of America; American Board of Trial Advocates. *Email:* jrm@chrm.com

**JOHN D. RASKIN,** born Los Angeles, California, August 25, 1947; admitted to bar, 1973, California. *Education:* Stanford University (B.A., 1968); Harvard University (J.D., 1973). Author, "Paying Tax on the Death of the First Spouse: Revisiting a Strategy of Generosity," CEB *Estate Planning and California Probate Reporter* Vol. 16, No. 5, April, 1995. *Member:* Alameda County and Contra Costa County Bar Associations; State Bar of California. (Certified Specialist, Estate Planning, Trust and Probate Law State Bar of California Board of Legal Specialization). *Email:* jraskin@chrm.com

**NORMAN K. TUTTLE II,** born Watsonville, California, October 30, 1935; admitted to bar, 1964, California. *Education:* University of California at Berkeley (A.B., 1957); Boalt Hall School of Law, University of California at Berkeley (LL.B., 1963). *Member:* Alameda County and American Bar Associations. *Email:* nkt@chrm.com

**ROBERT M. WINOKUR,** born New York, New York, October 28, 1924; admitted to bar, 1949, New York; 1955, California. *Education:* College of the City of New York (B.S.S., magna cum laude, 1947); Columbia University Law School (J.D., 1949). Phi Beta Kappa. Editor, Columbia Law Review, 1948-1949. *Member:* Bar Association of San Francisco (Chairman, Tax Committee, 1970); Alameda County and American Bar Associations; American Law Institute. *Email:* rmw@chrm.com

*(This Listing Continued)*

CAA1457B

## CROSBY, HEAFEY, ROACH & MAY, PROFESSIONAL CORPORATION, Oakland—Continued

**EUGENE K. YAMAMOTO,** born Bellflower, California, June 3, 1957; admitted to bar, 1983, California. *Education:* Loyola Marymount University (B.A., cum laude, 1978; M.B.A., magna cum laude, 1980) Hastings College of the Law, University of California (J.D., 1983). Author: "Rejection of a Mortgagee's Leasehold Collateral Lender Bankruptcy Code 365—Another Trap," 5 *Norton Bankruptcy Law Advisor* 8, May 1988; "Lease Termination Workouts," 14 *CEB Real Property Law Reporter* 116, April 1991; "Real Estate Workouts: Problems and Solutions," 14 *CEB Real Property Law Reporter* July 1991; "Protecting a Lender's Interest in Rents: Receivership is the Safest Option," *CEB Real Property Law Reporter,* July 1991. Adjunct Professor, "Creditor's Rights," Golden Gate University Law School, Spring 1989—. Instructor, Building Owners and Managers Institute (BOMI), Certification Class entitled "Law for Property Managers," 1988. Lecturer: "The ABC's of Workouts," California State Bar, Real Property Section, July and October, 1990; "Mortgage Foreclosure and Related Issues," Lorman Business Center Seminar, April 1994. *Member:* Bar Association of San Francisco (Member, Sections on Real Property, Business, Commercial and Bankruptcy); State Bar of California; Asian American Bar Association; Commercial Law League of America; American Bankruptcy Institute; Bay Area Bankruptcy Forum (Director); California Bankruptcy Forum. *Email:* eky@chrm.com

All Members and Associates of the firm are members of The State Bar of California.

REPRESENTATIVE CLIENTS: AirTouch Communications; Allstate Insurance Company; Chevron Corporation; The Coca-Cola Company; Dai-Tokyo Fire & Marine Co., Ltd.; Farmers Insurance Group of Companies; First USA Bank; ITT Hartford; Mills College, Northern Telecom Inc.; Oakland-Alameda County Coliseum, Inc.; Pacific Telesis Group; Pfizer Inc.; Sofamor Danek Group, Inc.; Summit Medical Center; Tele-Communications, Inc.; United States Surgical Corp.; Wells Fargo Bank; Valent USA Inc.; Westinghouse Electric Corporation; WMX Technologies, Inc.; The Yasuda Fire & Marine Insurance Company; Yokohama Tire Corporation.

(For Complete Biographical Data on all Personnel at Los Angeles, San Francisco and Santa Rosa, see Professional Biographies at those Locations)

## CULLEY * GOODWIN
OAKLAND, CALIFORNIA
(See Livermore)
*Business Law and Family Law.*

## GARRETT C. DAILEY
Established in 1977
519 - 17TH STREET, 7TH FLOOR
**OAKLAND, CALIFORNIA 94612**
Telephone: 510-465-3920
Fax: 510-465-7348
Email: BriefCase@aol.com
*Practice Limited to Family Law.*

**GARRETT C. DAILEY,** born Bethesda, Maryland, March 22, 1947; admitted to bar, 1977, California. *Education:* University of California at Los Angeles (A.B., 1969); Arizona State University (M.A., 1974); University of California School of Law at Davis (J.D., 1977). Phi Kappa Phi. Editor, University of California at Davis Law Review, 1976-1977. Co-Author: "Attorney's BriefCase California Family Law," Attorney's BriefCase: California Evidence, Civil and Criminal; Attorney's BriefCase: Children and the Law 1989—; Lawgic: Marital Settlement Agreements. Lecturer: Marital Property, University of California at Davis School of Law, 1988-1990; Legal, Tax and Valuation Aspects of Marital Dissolutions, Golden Gate University, Graduate School of Taxation, 1986—. Panelist: Family Law, Attorney's BriefCase, 1989—; American Bar Association, 1993—; State Bar of California, 1991—; Continuing Education of the Bar, 1980-1988; Norton Family Law Systems, 1990. Judge Pro-Tem, Superior Court, 1991 —. *Member:* Alameda County, Contra Costa County, Los Angeles County and American Bar Associations; The State Bar of California; Association of Family and Conciliation Courts. Fellow, American Academy of Matrimonial Lawyers. [Capt., USAF, 1969-1974]. (Certified Specialist, Family Law, The State Bar of California Board of Legal Specialization).

REFERENCE: Wells Fargo Bank (Oakland City Center Office).

## DANG & TRACHUK
SUITE 2360, ORDWAY BUILDING
ONE KAISER PLAZA
**OAKLAND, CALIFORNIA 94612**
Telephone: 510-832-8700
Fax: 510-836-2595

*General Civil Trial and Appellate Practice. Government, Business, Personal Injury, Real Property, Land Use, Products Liability, Insurance, Environmental and Construction Law.*

### MEMBERS OF FIRM

**DOUGLAS Y. DANG,** born Sacramento, California, July 23, 1942; admitted to bar, 1969, California. *Education:* University of California at Berkeley (A.B., 1963); Hastings College of Law, University of California (J.D., 1969). City Attorney of San Mateo, 1980-1984. Assistant to the City Attorney of Oakland, 1974-1979. Assistant General Counsel of the Bay Area Air Pollution Control District, 1973-1974. *Member:* Alameda County and San Mateo County Bar Associations; State Bar of California. **PRACTICE AREAS:** Municipal and Public Entity Defense; Environmental Law.

**THOMAS J. TRACHUK,** born Jersey City, New Jersey, November 10, 1950; admitted to bar, 1979, California. *Education:* State University of New York at Albany (B.A., 1973); Lincoln University Law School (J.D., 1979). Research Editor, Lincoln Law Review, 1978-1979. *Member:* Bar Association of San Francisco; Alameda County Bar Association; State Bar of California; Association of Defense Counsel. **PRACTICE AREAS:** Insurance and Public Entity Tort Defense; Employment Discrimination; Civil Rights Law.

REPRESENTATIVE CLIENTS: City of Alameda; City of Livermore; City of San Mateo; City of Hayward; City of San Bruno; San Francisco Redevelopment Agency; City of Emeryville; County of Monterey; Livermore Unified School District; Oakland Unified School District; County of Alameda; Alamo Rent-A-Car, Inc.; Cable Oakland; Emergency Physicians Medical Group; Insurance Associates of Northern California; Calcorp Insurance Agency, Inc.; Lundeen & Associates; Anchor Container Services; A.C. Transit; East Bay Municipal Utility District; Hartford Insurance Company; TransAmerica Insurance Group.

## DIGARDI & CAMPBELL
Established in 1931
SUITE 600 TRANS PACIFIC CENTRE
1000 BROADWAY
**OAKLAND, CALIFORNIA 94607**
Telephone: 510-832-5409; 832-5406

*Civil Litigation including Personal Injury and Wrongful Death Claims in the Fields of Admiralty, Aviation, Motor Vehicle, Railroad, Premises, Government Tort, Products Liability and Work Related Accidents and Injuries. Professional Negligence.*

FIRM PROFILE: *Founded in 1931 as Nichols & Richard. In 1954 after Mr. Richard departed, formed Nichols, Williams, Morgan & Digardi. The firm later achieved the distinction of all named partners becoming Fellows in the American College of Trial Lawyers. In 1978, Nichols, Williams and Morgan retired to form Digardi & Campbell.*

Mr. Digardi was lead attorney in over 350 Jury Trials in the State and Federal Courts.

### MEMBERS OF FIRM

**JESSE NICHOLS** (1899-1985).

**EDWARD M. DIGARDI,** born Oakland, California, March 14, 1919; admitted to bar, 1947, California. *Education:* University of California (A.B., 1940); Hastings College of Law (J.D., 1947). Order of the Coif. Lecturer and Writer, Continuing Education of The Bar, 1961—. Lecturer in Law, Boalt Hall, University of California, 1964-1981. Member of Faculty, Hastings College Center for Trial Advocacy, 1988—. Lawyer Representative, Northern District of California for the Ninth Circuit Judicial Conference, 1976-1979. Chairman, Northern District of California for the Ninth Circuit Judicial Conference, 1978-1979. Judge, Trial Practice Course, Hastings College of Law, University of California, 1979—. *Member:* Alameda County, Contra Costa County and American Bar Associations; The State

*(This Listing Continued)*

Bar of California. Diplomate, American Board of Trial Advocates; Fellow, American College of Trial Lawyers; International Society of Air Safety Investigators. *PRACTICE AREAS:* Admiralty; Aviation; Railroad; Products Liability; Work Related Accidents and Injuries.

**JOSEPH W. CAMPBELL,** born Glen Ridge, New Jersey, June 9, 1948; admitted to bar, 1972, California. *Education:* Dartmouth College (A.B., 1969); Boalt Hall School of Law, University of California (J.D., 1972). Phi Beta Kappa. *Member:* Alameda County and Contra Costa County Bar Associations; The State Bar of California; Alameda-Contra Costa County Trial Lawyers Association; The Association of Trial Lawyers of America; Lawyers Club of Alameda County; California Trial Lawyer's Association. [Capt. USAF, Reserve, JAG, 1973-1981]. *PRACTICE AREAS:* Motor Vehicle; Civil Litigation; Personal Injury; Wrongful Death; Claims and Government Torts; Professional Negligence.

REFERENCE: First Interstate Bank, Central Office, Oakland, Calif.

## DONAHUE, GALLAGHER, WOODS & WOOD

*Established in 1918*
*300 LAKESIDE DRIVE*
*SUITE 1900*
**OAKLAND, CALIFORNIA 94612-3570**
*Telephone: 510-451-0544*
*Facsimile: 510-832-1486*

*Mill Valley, California Office:* Shelter Point, 591 Redwood Highway, Suite 1200. Telephone: 415-381-4161. Facsimile: 415-381-7515.
*Walnut Creek, California Office:* 1646 North California Boulevard, Suite 310. Telephone: 510-746-7770. Facsimile: 510-746-7776.

*General Civil and Trial Practice in all State and Federal Courts. Corporate, Real Property, Intellectual Property, Insurance, Immigration, Labor and Employment, Tax, Probate and Estate Planning Law.*

FIRM PROFILE: *Founded in Oakland in 1918, the firm presently has 35 attorneys and 10 legal assistants serving clients nationwide from strategically located offices in Oakland, Walnut Creek and Marin County. Our diverse practice and locations, combined with our extensive use of voice and data-communication networks, reflect our commitment to being accessible and able to quickly meet our clients' requirements in a complex and fast-paced business environment. Throughout our 78 years of practicing law, our goal has always been to provide our clients with the highest quality of service in the most cost-effective manner. To achieve this end, we carefully staff all projects matching client objectives with the professional skills and experience of our practitioners. Whether we are retained for one project or to handle a company's on-going legal needs, we strive to develop a close working relationship with our clients so that we can more fully assist them with their legal needs. Our philosophy is to be sensitive and responsive to our clients' expectations regarding our services and fees, and make every attempt to meet specific requests regarding their level of involvement in the matter, billing preferences and particular service requirements. Ultimately, we seek what we believe is the only true measure of our success-that is, a satisfied client.*

### MEMBERS OF FIRM

**WILLIAM H. DONAHUE** (1871-1948).

**JAMES E. GALLAGHER** (1911-1981).

**BRUCE D. GILLIES,** born Watertown, New York, March 12, 1935; admitted to bar, 1963, California. *Education:* Stanford University (A.B., 1959); University of California, Berkeley (J.D., 1962). *Member:* Alameda County Bar Association; The State Bar of California. *PRACTICE AREAS:* Business Law; Employee Benefit Law. *Email:* Bruce@donahue.com

**ROBERT N. WOOD,** born Chicago, Illinois, June 24, 1937; admitted to bar, 1963, California. *Education:* Northwestern University (B.S., 1959); University of California, Berkeley (J.D., 1962). *Member:* Alameda County Bar Association; The State Bar of California. *PRACTICE AREAS:* Complex Litigation; Business Torts; Dealer and Distributor Terminations. *Email:* Bob@donahue.com

**WILFRID F. ROBERGE, JR.,** born Los Angeles, California, November 28, 1939; admitted to bar, 1965, California; 1975, U.S. Tax Court. *Education:* University of California, Riverside (A.B., 1961); Stanford University (J.D., 1964). *Member:* Alameda County Bar Association; The State Bar of California. (Certified Specialist, Estate Planning, Trust and Probate Law, The State Bar of California Board of Legal Specialization). *PRACTICE AREAS:* Estate Planning; Probate, Trust Law. *Email:* Wil@donahue.com

*(This Listing Continued)*

**HARRISON S. ROBINSON,** born San Francisco, California, March 10, 1942; admitted to bar, 1966, California. *Education:* College of Wooster and University of California, Berkeley (A.B., 1962); Hastings College of the Law, University of California (J.D., 1966). *Member:* Alameda County and American Bar Associations; The State Bar of California. *PRACTICE AREAS:* Complex Commercial Real Estate; Real Estate Finance; Business Law. *Email:* Harry@donahue.com

**ANDREW W. LAFRENZ,** born Oakland, California, September 18, 1947; admitted to bar, 1972, California. *Education:* Dartmouth College (A.B., magna cum laude, 1969); Stanford University (J.D., 1972). Phi Beta Kappa. *Member:* Alameda County and American Bar Associations; The State Bar of California. *PRACTICE AREAS:* Litigation; Insurance Defense; Real Estate; Environmental; Commercial Law. *Email:* Andy@donahue.com

**GEORGE J. BARRON,** born Oakland, California, June 18, 1947; admitted to bar, 1972, California. *Education:* University of San Francisco (B.A., 1969); University of California at Los Angeles (J.D., 1972). Alpha Sigma Nu. Member, University of California at Los Angeles Law Review, 1970-1972. *Member:* Alameda County Bar Association; The State Bar of California. *PRACTICE AREAS:* Employment Law; Insurance Defense Law; Labor (Management or Employees) Law. *Email:* George@donahue.com

**LAWRENCE K. ROCKWELL,** born Boston, Massachusetts, January 3, 1953; admitted to bar, 1976, California. *Education:* University of California, Berkeley (A.B., B.S., 1973); Hastings College of the Law, University of California (J.D., 1976). Phi Beta Kappa. Member, Hastings Constitutional Law Quarterly, 1974-1976. *Member:* Alameda County and American Bar Associations; The State Bar of California. *PRACTICE AREAS:* Litigation; Complex Computer Law; Commercial Law. *Email:* Larry@donahue.com

**ERIC W. DONEY,** born Lynwood, California, February 2, 1952; admitted to bar, 1977, California; 1978, U.S. Tax Court. *Education:* University of California, Davis (B.A., magna cum laude, 1973); Hastings College of Law, University of California (J.D., 1977). *Member:* Alameda County Bar Association; State Bar of California. *PRACTICE AREAS:* Computer Law; Computer Software; Copyright. *Email:* Eric@donahue.com

**THOMAS L. HANAVAN,** born Buffalo, New York, March 20, 1952; admitted to bar, 1978, California. *Education:* College of the Holy Cross (A.B., 1974); University of Santa Clara (J.D., cum laude, 1978). Managing Editor, Santa Clara Law Review, 1977-1978. *Member:* Alameda County Bar Association; The State Bar of California; International Council of Shopping Centers; Oakland Metropolitan Chamber of Commerce (Director). *PRACTICE AREAS:* Complex Commercial Real Estate; Environmental Law; Commercial Leasing. *Email:* Tom@donahue.com

**GAIL PREBIL CLARK,** born Fargo, North Dakota, November 28, 1947; admitted to bar, 1981, California. *Education:* University of Santa Clara (B.A., magna cum laude, 1969); Hastings College of the Law, University of California (J.D., 1981). Member, 1979-1981 and Associate Managing Editor, 1980-1981, Hastings Law Journal. *Member:* Alameda County and American Bar Associations; The State Bar of California. *LANGUAGES:* French. *PRACTICE AREAS:* Corporate Law; Securities; Computer Software. *Email:* Gail@donahue.com

**JOHN J. COPPINGER,** born Colorado Springs, Colorado, September 13, 1955; admitted to bar, 1981, California. *Education:* University of Santa Clara (B.S., 1977; J.D., 1981). *Member:* Alameda County Bar Association; The State Bar of California. *PRACTICE AREAS:* Complex Commercial Real Estate; Development and Land Use Law; Real Estate Finance. *Email:* John@donahue.com

**MICHAEL J. DALTON,** born New York, N.Y., December 4, 1954; admitted to bar, 1984, California. *Education:* University of California, Berkeley (A.B., summa cum laude, 1977; M.A. 1979; J.D., 1984). Supreme Court Editor, California Law Review, 1983-1984. *Member:* Alameda County Bar Association; The State Bar of California. *LANGUAGES:* French, German and Italian. *PRACTICE AREAS:* Buying and Selling of Businesses; Corporate Law; Trademark Law. *Email:* MichaelD@donahue.com

**WILLIAM R. HILL,** born San Pedro, California, September 5, 1955; admitted to bar, 1984, California. *Education:* University of California, Berkeley (B.A., 1978; J.D., 1984); Stanford University (M.A., 1981). *Member:* Alameda County Bar Association; The State Bar of California. *PRACTICE AREAS:* Litigation; Intellectual Property Law; Employment Law. *Email:* Rock@donahue.com

*(This Listing Continued)*

**DONAHUE, GALLAGHER, WOODS & WOOD, Oakland—**
*Continued*

**JONATHAN G. WONG,** born Santa Monica, California, January 27, 1959; admitted to bar, 1983, California. *Education:* Pomona College (B.A., 1979); University of California, Davis (J.D., 1982). Editor, University of California, Davis Law Review, 1981-1982. *Member:* Alameda County Bar Association (Director); The State Bar of California. *LANGUAGES:* French, German, Spanish and Mandarin Chinese. *PRACTICE AREAS:* Litigation; Immigration and Nationality Law; Employment Law. *Email:* Jonathan@donahue.com

### ASSOCIATES

**DOUGLAS A. CROSBY,** born Redwood City, California, December 30, 1960; admitted to bar, 1987, California. *Education:* Stanford University (B.A., 1983); Santa Clara University (J.D., 1987). Articles Editor, Santa Clara Law Review, 1986-1987. *Member:* Alameda County Bar Association; The State Bar of California. *PRACTICE AREAS:* Real Estate; Commercial Leasing; Computer Law. *Email:* Doug@donahue.com

**A. CLIFFORD ALLEN,** born Independence, Missouri, January 12, 1956; admitted to bar, 1984, California; 1985, U.S. Tax Court. *Education:* University of California at Berkeley (B.A., with honors, 1978); Hastings College of the Law, University of California (J.D., cum laude, 1984). Author: "Advising Clients on Tax Shelter Investments," California Business Law Reporter (C.E.B. 1986); "Ethical Considerations and Professional Liability," California Wills and Trusts (1991); "Why Software Support Companies Face Unexpected Exposure," Computer Law Strategist (May 1993). *Member:* Alameda County Bar Association; State Bar of California (Member, Intellectual Property Section). *PRACTICE AREAS:* Litigation; Computer Software Law; Employment Law; Trade Secrets Law. *Email:* Cliff@donahue.com

**SUSANNE T. DOLGOFF,** born San Francisco, California, March 2, 1964; admitted to bar, 1989, California. *Education:* University of California at Los Angeles (B.A., cum laude, 1986); Santa Clara University (J.D., 1989). Alpha Lambda Delta. Instructor, Intellectual Property, University of California, Extension. *Member:* Alameda County and American Bar Associations; State Bar of California. *PRACTICE AREAS:* High Technology Law; Computer Law. *Email:* Susanne@donahue.com

**GERALD J. KARCZEWSKI,** born Chicago, Illinois, December 14, 1962; admitted to bar, 1989, California. *Education:* St. Mary's College (B.S., 1985); University of San Diego (J.D., magna cum laude, 1989). Member, San Diego Law Review, 1988-1989. *Member:* Alameda County Bar Association; State Bar of California. *PRACTICE AREAS:* Litigation; Intellectual Property. *Email:* Gerry@donahue.com

**JEANNE M. KLUCZNIK,** born Providence, Rhode Island, December 8, 1965; admitted to bar, 1993, California. *Education:* University of California, Berkeley (B.A., 1987); Boalt Hall School of Law (J.D., 1992). Phi Beta Kappa. Instructor, Intellectual Property, University of California, Extension. *Member:* Alameda County Bar Association; State Bar of California (Member, Sections on: Intellectual Property and Business Law). *Email:* Jeanne@donahue.com

**DAVID B. SULLIVAN,** born San Francisco, California, October 13, 1967; admitted to bar, 1992, California. *Education:* University of San Francisco (B.A., 1989); Hastings College of the Law (J.D., 1992). Member, St. Thomas More Society, 1990-1991. Articles Editor, Hastings Int'l and Comp. L. Rev, 1991-1992. Author: Note, "Abandoning the Rule of Noninquiry in International Extradition," 15 Hastings Int'l and Comp. L. Rev. 111-33 (1991). *Member:* Alameda County Bar Association; State Bar of California. *Email:* Dave@donahue.com

**ROBYN RENÉE NEWCOMB,** born San Francisco, California, September 19, 1966; admitted to bar, 1993, California. *Education:* University of California at Berkeley (B.A., 1989); University of San Francisco (J.D., 1993). *Member:* Alameda County Bar Association; State Bar of California. *Email:* RobRob@donahue.com

**JULIE E. HOFER,** born Bryant, South Dakota, July 30, 1955; admitted to bar, 1982, Alaska; 1991, California. *Education:* South Dakota State University (B.A., with highest honors, 1979); University of Minnesota (J.D., cum laude, 1982). Phi Kappa Phi. *Member:* State Bar of California. *Email:* Julie@donahue.com

**JONATHAN N. OSDER,** born Los Angeles, California, May 20, 1967; admitted to bar, 1994, California. *Education:* University of California at Berkeley (B.A., 1989); University of San Francisco (J.D., 1994). Comments Editor, University of San Francisco Law Review, 1994. *Member:* Alameda County Bar Association; State Bar of California. *LANGUAGES:* Spanish. *Email:* Jon@donahue.com

**PAUL J. MORI,** born San Francisco, California, September 3, 1966; admitted to bar, 1993, California, U.S. District Court, Northern District of California and U.S. Court of Appeals, Ninth Circuit. *Education:* University of California at Los Angeles (B.A., 1988); University of San Francisco (J.D., 1992). *Member:* Alameda County Bar Association; State Bar of California (Member, Section on Intellectual Property). *LANGUAGES:* Italian. *Email:* Paul@donahue.com

**JASON A. GELLER,** born San Francisco, California, December 9, 1966; admitted to bar, 1993, California. *Education:* University of California (B.A., with honors, 1989); Gonzaga University (J.D., 1993). Phi Delta Phi. Recipient, American Jurisprudence Award in Legal Writing, Gonzaga University. Member, Northern California Human Resources Council, 1994. *Member:* San Francisco (Member, Labor Employment Law Section) and Alameda County Bar Associations; State Bar of California. *LANGUAGES:* Spanish. *Email:* Jason@donahue.com

**BARTON L. JACKA,** born Henderson, Nevada, March 20, 1965; admitted to bar, 1991, California; 1994, U.S. District Court, Eastern District of California; 1995, U.S. District Court, Northern District of California. *Education:* St. Mary's College of California (B.A., summa cum laude, 1987); Boalt Hall School of Law, University of California (J.D., 1990). Judicial Clerk to Justice Anthony Scariano, Illinois Appellate Court, First District, 1990-1991. *Member:* American Bar Association (Member, Section on Litigation); State Bar of California. *PRACTICE AREAS:* Commercial Litigation; Employment Law; Intellectual Property. *Email:* Barton@donahue.com

**CAROL B. O'NEILL,** born New York, New York, November 14, 1950; admitted to bar, 1979, California. *Education:* Smith College (B.A., 1972); Hastings College of the Law (J.D., 1979). *Member:* Contra Costa County Bar Association; State Bar of California; Diablo Valley Estate Planning Council. (Resident, Walnut Creek Office). *PRACTICE AREAS:* Trusts and Estates; Real Property. *Email:* Carol@donahue.com

**JONAS W. KANT,** born Los Angeles, California, April 12, 1965; admitted to bar, 1996, New York (Not admitted in California). *Education:* University of California at Davis (B.A., 1989); Benjamin N. Cardozo School of Law (J.D., 1995). *Member:* The Association of the Bar of the City of New York; New York State Bar Association.

**STEPHEN C. GUSTAFSON,** born New Bedford, Massachusetts, March 7, 1966; admitted to bar, 1992, California; U.S. District Court, Northern District of California and U.S. Court of Appeals, Ninth Circuit. *Education:* University of California at Davis (B.A., with honors, 1988); University of San Francisco (J.D., 1992). University of San Francisco Law Review. *Member:* Alameda County Bar Association; State Bar of California.

**LEONID M. ZILBERMAN,** born Bendery, Russia, April 22, 1968; admitted to bar, 1996, California and U.S. District Court, Northern District of California. *Education:* University of California at Santa Barbara (B.A., 1990); Santa Clara University (J.D., 1995). Phi Theta Phi; National Order of Barristers; Chair: Honors Moot Court Board. Recipient: American Jurisprudence Awards in Criminal Procedure, Constitutional Law, Legal Research and Writing. *Member:* Alameda County, Santa Clara County and American Bar Associations; State Bar of California. *LANGUAGES:* Russian. *PRACTICE AREAS:* Litigation.

### OF COUNSEL

**JOSEPH A. WOODS, JR.,** born Decatur, Alabama, March 24, 1925; admitted to bar, 1950, California. *Education:* University of California, Berkeley (A.B., 1947; J.D., 1949). Phi Beta Kappa; Order of the Coif. Associate Editor, California Law Review, 1949. Senior Associate Special Counsel, Committee on the Judiciary of the House of Representatives, 1974. *Member:* Alameda County (President, 1975) and American (Member, House of Delegates, 1982-1990) Bar Associations; The State Bar of California; American Judicature Society. Fellow, American Bar Foundation. [Lieut. (j.g.), U.S. Naval Reserve, 1944-1946] *Email:* Joe@donahue.com

### TAX COUNSEL

**DONALD H. READ,** born New York, N.Y., November 28, 1942; admitted to bar, 1969, California; 1970, U.S. Tax Court; 1972, New York; 1976, Hawaii; 1979, U.S. Claims Court; 1988, Washington. *Education:* Deep Springs College; Cornell University; University of California, Berkeley (B.A., 1964); Columbia University (J.D., cum laude, 1968); New York University (LL.M. in Taxation, 1972). Adjunct Professor, Tax Procedure, University of San Francisco Law School, 1985. Attorney-Advisor, Office of

*(This Listing Continued)*

Tax Legislative Counsel, Department of the Treasury, Washington, D.C., 1974-1976. *Member:* Alameda County, Santa Clara County and American Bar Associations; The State Bar of California. (Certified Specialist, Taxation Law, The State Bar of California Board of Legal Specialization) (Also Counsel to Lakin, Spears, Palo Alto, CA). *PRACTICE AREAS:* Taxation; Partnership Law; Business Law. *Email:* 445-4292@mcimail.com

REPRESENTATIVE CLIENTS: Adobe Systems, Inc.; Advantage Communications, Inc.; Albertson's, Inc.; Aldus Corp.; American Stores Properties, Inc.; Autodesk, Inc.; Berkeley Farms; Business Software Alliance; Computer Learning Centers, Inc.; Crawford & Company; Decision Development Corporation; Deep Ocean Engineering, Inc.; ERM West; General American Life Insurance Co.; Geoworks; Grateful Dead Merchandising, Inc,; The Great-West Life & Annuity Insurance Company; Hancock Fabrics, Inc.; Hotwired; Intelligent Graphics Corp.; Intuit; Jacuzzi Inc.; Lucas Arts Entertainment; Lucky Stores, Inc.; Mason-McDuffie Real Estate, Inc.; Melrose Lumber & Supply; Microsoft Corporation; Minnesota Mutual Life Insurance Co.; Pacific Software Services, Inc.; Public Storage Management, Inc.; R.B. Matheson Trucking, Inc.; Safeco Life Insurance Co.; San Joaquin Delta College; Stenograph Corporation; Stern Property Company; Summit Medical Center; Total Clearance, Inc.; Unisys Corporation; Unisys Financial Corporation; Wholesale Finance Corp.
REFERENCE: Bank of California (Oakland Main Office).

## ERICKSEN, ARBUTHNOT, KILDUFF, DAY & LINDSTROM, INC.

*Established in 1950*

*530 WATER STREET*
*PORT BUILDING, SUITE 720*
**OAKLAND, CALIFORNIA 94607-3746**
*Telephone: 510-832-7770*
*Fax: 510-832-0102*

*San Francisco, California Office:* 260 California Street, Suite 1100. Telephone: 415-362-7126. Fax: 415-362-6401.
*Sacramento, California Office:* 100 Howe Avenue, Suite 240N. Telephone: 916-483-5181. Fax: 916-483-7558.
*Fresno, California Office:* 2440 West Shaw Avenue, Suite 101. Telephone: 209-449-2600. Fax: 209-449-2603.
*San Jose, California Office:* 152 North Third Street, Suite 700. Telephone: 408-286-0880. Fax: 408-286-0337.
*Walnut Creek, California Office:* 2700 Ygnacio Valley Road, Suite 280. Telephone: 510-947-1702. Fax: 510-947-4921.
*Riverside, California Office:* 1770 Iowa Avenue, Suite 210. Telephone: 909-682-3246. Fax: 909-682-4013.
*Los Angeles, California Office:* 835 Wilshire Boulevard, Suite 500. Telephone: 213-489-4411. Fax: 213-489-4332.

*General Civil, Trial and Appellate Practice in all State and Federal Courts. Insurance and Liability Defense, Environmental and Toxic Tort.*

FIRM PROFILE: Ericksen, Arbuthnot, Kilduff, Day & Lindstrom is a statewide, civil litigation and insurance defense firm founded in 1950. This multiple office approach ensures uniform procedures and capabilities for both out-of-state and California-based clients. Experienced attorneys, backed by a well-trained paralegal staff, handle cases involving liability defense and insurance coverage and general civil litigation.

**LOIS A. LINDSTROM**, born Orange, New Jersey, April 17, 1948; admitted to bar, 1983, California. *Education:* University of Wisconsin-Madison (B.A., 1970); Golden Gate University (J.D., 1983). *Member:* Bar Association of San Francisco; Contra Costa and American Bar Associations; The State Bar of California. *PRACTICE AREAS:* Professional Liability; Product Liability Defense; Construction Defense; Discrimination; Harassment; Wrongful Termination; Personal Injury.

**WILLIAM G. HOBACK**, born Washington, D.C., August 3, 1944; admitted to bar, 1979, California. *Education:* Sacramento City College (A.A., 1969); California State University at Sacramento; Lincoln University (LL.B., 1979). *Member:* The State Bar of California; Northern California Association of Defense Counsel. *PRACTICE AREAS:* Products Liability; Declaratory Relief; Errors and Omission; Discrimination; Wrongful Termination.

**KENDALL A. LAYNE**, born Palo Alto, California, June 23, 1953; admitted to bar, 1981, California, U.S. District Court, Northern District of California and U.S. Court of Appeals, Ninth Circuit. *Education:* University of California at Santa Cruz (B.A., with honors in Environmental Planning and Psychology, 1977); Stanford University (J.D., 1981). Private Pilot, ASEL, California, 1979. *Member:* Bar Association of San Francisco; Contra Costa and American Bar Associations; State Bar of California; Maritime Law Association of the United States. *PRACTICE AREAS:* Product Lia-

*(This Listing Continued)*

bility Defense; Professional Malpractice Defense; Wrongful Death Defense; Insurance Defense; Admiralty.

**DEREK R. LONGSTAFF**, born Scottsdale, Arizona, October 14, 1965; admitted to bar, 1990, California and U.S. District Court, Northern District of California; 1992, Arizona. *Education:* Arizona State University (B.S., 1987); McGeorge School of Law, University of the Pacific (J.D., 1990). Member, Moot Court Honors Board. *Member:* Santa Clara County, San Francisco County and Alameda County Bar Associations.

**PAMELA R. PETERS**, born Akron, Ohio, December 5, 1953; admitted to bar, 1992, California. *Education:* Miami University (B.S., 1976); San Francisco State University; Golden Gate University (J.D., 1991). *PRACTICE AREAS:* Personal Injury; Asbestos; General Civil.

**JOHN V. MEJIA**, born Ensenada, Mexico, June 24, 1966; admitted to bar, 1993, California. *Education:* University of California, Berkeley (B.A., 1989); University of San Francisco (J.D., 1992). *Member:* Bar Association of San Francisco; Alameda County and American Bar Associations; State Bar of California. *LANGUAGES:* Spanish.

**GREGORY A. MASE**, born Portland, Oregon, March 23, 1963; admitted to bar, 1993, California. *Education:* University of California, Santa Cruz; University of California, Berkeley (B.A., 1986); Hastings College of Law, University of California (J.D., 1992). *PRACTICE AREAS:* Insurance Defense.

REPRESENTATIVE CLIENTS: AIG Companies; Alexsis Risk Management Co.; Allegiance Insurance Co.; Argonaut Insurance Co.; Atlantic Cos.; Bridgestone/Firestone Tire & Rubber Co.; Carl Warren & Co.; CIGNA; CNA Insurance Co.; Crawford & Co.; Dominos' Pizza; Explorer Insurance Co.; Financial Indemnity Co.; First State Management Co.; Foremost Insurance Co.; Freightliner Corp.; GAB Business Services; Goodyear Tire and Rubber Co.; Hartford Insurance Co.; HFIC Management Co.; Homes Insurance Co.; Kentucky Fried Chicken; Long's Drug Stores; Montgomery Elevator Co.; National Union Insurance Co.; Otis Elevator Co.; Professional Risk Management Co.; State Farm Insurance Co.; Time Oil Corp.; Toplis & Harding; United Technologies, Inc.; Utica Insurance Co.; Volvo-GM Corp.; Western Heritage Insurance Co.; Wheeled Coach Industries; Worldwide Insurance Co.; York Claim Service.

*(For biographical data on other personnel, see Professional Biographies at other office locations)*

## ERICKSON, BEASLEY, HEWITT & WILSON

*491 NINTH STREET*
**OAKLAND, CALIFORNIA 94607**
*Telephone: 510-839-3448*
*Fax: 510-839-1622*

*Civil Litigation and Appellate Practice.*

FIRM PROFILE: *A minority-owned law firm established in 1978, our firm is made up of lawyers who are recognized throughout Northern California for expertise and trial skills in the following areas of law: Eminent Domain, Inverse Condemnation, Environmental, Civil Rights, Employment, Wrongful Discharge, Personal Injury, Medical Malpractice, and Professional Liability Litigation. Our clients include public entities and individuals.*

**JOHN H. ERICKSON**, born Grants Pass, Oregon, June 10, 1937; admitted to bar, 1969, California and U.S. District Court, Northern District of California; 1977, U.S. Court of Appeals, Ninth Circuit; 1984, U.S. Court of Appeals for the Federal Circuit; 1985, U.S. District Court, Eastern District of California; 1987, U.S. Supreme Court. *Education:* Yale University (B.A., 1959); University of California at Berkeley (M.A., 1961; J.D., 1968). *Member:* Alameda County Bar Association; State Bar of California; International Right of Way Association.

**ALICE M. BEASLEY**, born Tuskegee, Alabama, April 27, 1945; admitted to bar, 1973, California and U.S. District Court, Northern District of California; 1977, U.S. Court of Appeals, Ninth Circuit; 1988, U.S. Supreme Court. *Education:* Marygrove College (B.A., 1966); University of California at Berkeley (J.D., 1973). Member, California Law Review, 1972-1973. Lecturer: Practicing Law Institute: Federal Civil Practice, April 1978; Public Interest on a Fee Award Basis, October, 1978; Federal Civil Rights Litigation-1982, January, 1982; Section 1983 Civil Rights Litigation and Attorneys' Fees, 1988; League of California Cities Annual Conference: "If You Had a Brother, Would He Like Cheese and Other Recent Developments in Eminent Domain Law," October, 1992; State Bar Annual Meeting, Real Property Law Section; "Give Me Liberty or Give Me Bucks;" Inverse and Direct Condemnation in the Context of Property Development, October 1992; ABA Litigation Section Annual Fall Meeting: "The Art and Science of Settling Litigation," November, 1992. Publications: Condemnation Power: Both Sword and Shield When Dealing with Contaminated Real Property, CEB Real Property Reporter, May 1993. Visiting Lecturer, Boalt

*(This Listing Continued)*

**ERICKSON, BEASLEY, HEWITT & WILSON,** Oakland—
*Continued*

Hall School of Law, University of California at Berkeley, Spring, 1984. Board Member, NAACP Legal Defense and Educational Fund, Inc., 1983—. *Member:* Bar Association of San Francisco (Board Member, 1987-1988; Judiciary Committee, 1986-1987, 1989-1991, Chair 1990); State Bar of California (Member, Committee on Condemnation, 1990-1991, Vice-Chair, 1991; Judicial Nominees Evaluation Committee, 1992—); American Bar Association (Co-Chair, Subcommittee on Wrongful Discharge, 1983-1985); Charles Houston Bar Association; Black Women Lawyers Association.

**HENRY S. HEWITT,** born Los Angeles, California, June 21, 1943; admitted to bar, 1967, California and U.S. District Court, Northern District of California; 1971, U.S. Court of Appeals, Ninth Circuit; 1988, U.S. Supreme Court; 1990, U.S. Claims Court. *Education:* Occidental College (B.A., 1964); University of Chicago (J.D., 1967). Clerk to Judge George B. Harris, U.S. District Court, Northern District of California, 1967-1968. Adjunct Professor, University of San Francisco School of Law, 1989-1992. *Member:* Bar Association of San Francisco; Alameda County Bar Association; State Bar of California (Co-Chair, EEO Sub-Committee, Labor Committee of the State Bar, 1983-1984); California Employment Lawyers Association.

**EDWIN J. WILSON, JR.,** born Cleveland, Ohio, December 14, 1943; admitted to bar, 1971, California, U.S. District Court, Northern District of California and U.S. Court of Appeals, Ninth Circuit; 1980, U.S. District Court, Southern District of California; 1990, U.S. District Court, Central District of California. *Education:* University of California at Berkeley (B.A., 1966; J.D., 1970). Lecturer: Practicing Law Institute, Product Design Liability Panel, 1982; CEB: Approaching a Personal Injury Case, 1993; Compelling, Opposing and Enforcing Discovery in State Courts, 1991, 1993; Preparing a Case for Trial (Last 100 Days), 1994. Publications: Product Design Litigation, Practicing Law Institute, 1982; Section 1983 Civil Rights Litigation and Attorneys Fees, 1988; CEB California Procedure Before Trial, 1993. Faculty Member, Hastings College of Trial Advocacy, 1977, 1979. *Member:* Alameda County and American Bar Associations; State Bar of California; Fellow, American Bar Foundation; Charles Houston Bar Association.

**BRENDA AGUILAR-GUERRERO,** born Concord, California, June 25, 1964; admitted to bar, 1990, California, U.S. District Court, Northern District of California and U.S. Court of Appeals, Ninth Circuit. *Education:* University of California at Berkeley (B.A., 1987); University of California, Los Angeles (J.D., 1990). *Member:* Bar Association of San Francisco; State Bar of California; La Raza Lawyers Association; Barrister Club of San Francisco. *LANGUAGES:* Spanish.

**BEATRICE LIU,** born South Bend, Indiana, October 16, 1965; admitted to bar, 1993, California; 1996, U.S. District Court, Northern District of California. *Education:* University of California at Berkeley (B.A., 1988); University of California at Davis (J.D., 1992). *Member:* State Bar of California.

**MARGARET E. MOORE,** born Washington, D.C., August 31, 1966; admitted to bar, 1972, California; 1995, U.S. District Court, Northern District of California. *Education:* University of North Carolina at Chapel Hill (B.A., 1988); University of San Francisco (J.D., cum laude, 1992). *Member:* State Bar of California.

**SHARON J. PERSONS,** born Shirley, Massachusetts, August 13, 1961; admitted to bar, 1996, California. *Education:* Columbia University (B.A., magna cum laude); Stanford University (J.D., 1996). *Member:* American Bar Association; National Lawyers Guild; Bay Area Lawyers for Individual Freedom.

## FITZGERALD, ABBOTT & BEARDSLEY LLP
A Partnership including Professional Corporations
*Established in 1883*
1221 BROADWAY, 21ST FLOOR
P.O. BOX 12867
**OAKLAND, CALIFORNIA 94602-2867**
Telephone: 510-451-3300
Telecopy: 510-451-1527

*General Corporate, Business and Trial Practice. Banking, Taxation, Estate Planning, Probate, Trust and Estate Administration, Litigation, Securities Industry Litigation, Commercial Law, Real Estate Construction Law, Family and Elder law, Labor and Employment Law, Land Use Planning and Environmental Law.*

**FIRM PROFILE:** Founded in 1883, Fitzgerald, Abbott & Beardsley LLP is one of the oldest law firms in continuous existence in California. The firm's practice reflects the diversity of its clients and their legal needs. Dedicated to excellence, the Firm serves its clientele by achieving a balance between the traditional one-to-one relationship of attorney and client and the exigencies of complex disputes and transactions, which are often handled by a team of attorneys selected to provide the breadth of expertise required.

*MEMBERS OF FIRM*

**ROBERT M. FITZGERALD** (1858-1934).

**CARL H. ABBOTT** (1867-1933).

**CHARLES A. BEARDSLEY** (1882-1963).

**JAMES C. SOPER, (INC.),** born Billings, Montana, January 15, 1929; admitted to bar, 1954, California; 1970, U.S. Supreme Court. *Education:* Stanford University (A.B., 1951; J.D., 1953). Phi Delta Phi. Member, Panel of Arbitrators, American Arbitration Association, 1963—. *Member:* Alameda County (Director, 1968-1971) and American Bar Associations; The State Bar of California (Member, 1972-1976 and Chairman, 1973, Governing Committee, Continuing Education of the Bar); Fellow, American Bar Foundation. **PRACTICE AREAS:** Corporate and Business Law; Estate Planning, Trust and Estate Administration.

**PHILIP M. JELLEY, (INC.),** born Troy, New York, February 29, 1932; admitted to bar, 1956, California; 1971, U.S. Supreme Court. *Education:* U.S. Naval Academy; Stanford University (J.D., 1956). *Member:* Alameda County and American Bar Associations; The State Bar of California. (Certified Specialist, Taxation Law, The State Bar of California Board of Legal Specialization). **PRACTICE AREAS:** Business and Real Estate Law; Nonprofit and Charitable Organizations; Ranch and Water Law.

**GERALD C. SMITH,** born Columbus, Ohio, April 11, 1940; admitted to bar, 1965, California. *Education:* University of Notre Dame (B.A., 1961); Boalt Hall School of Law, University of California (J.D., 1964). *Member:* Alameda County and American (Member, Section on Taxation) Bar Associations; The State Bar of California (Member, Business Law Section). **PRACTICE AREAS:** Commercial Law; Corporate Law; Business Litigation.

**LAWRENCE R. SHEPP,** born Bridgeport, Connecticut, May 14, 1939; admitted to bar, 1965, California. *Education:* Stanford University (A.B., 1961); Boalt Hall School of Law, University of California (J.D., 1964). Phi Delta Phi. *Member:* Alameda County Bar Association (Director, 1974-1975); State Bar of California. [J.A.G., U.S. Air Force, active duty, 1965-1968]. **PRACTICE AREAS:** Estate Planning; Estate and Probate Litigation; Real Estate; Construction Law and Litigation.

**RICHARD T. WHITE,** born Oakland, California, December 14, 1947; admitted to bar, 1973, California; 1979, U.S. Supreme Court; 1991, U.S. Tax Court. *Education:* University of Innsbruck, Innsbruck, Austria (1967-1968) and University of Notre Dame (B.A., 1970); University of San Francisco (J.D., 1973). Member, McAuliffe Scholastic Honor Society. *Member:* Alameda County Bar Association; State Bar of California (Member, Litigation and Antitrust Sections). **PRACTICE AREAS:** Business and Environmental Litigation; Employment Disputes; Antitrust and Competitive Business Practices.

**MICHAEL P. WALSH,** born Oakland, California, January 6, 1949; admitted to bar, 1974, California; 1979, U.S. Supreme Court. *Education:* University of California at Berkeley (B.A., 1971); University of San Francisco (J.D., 1974). Deputy District Attorney, Alameda County, 1974-1979. *Member:* Alameda County Bar Association; The State Bar of California; California Trial Lawyers Association. **PRACTICE AREAS:** Litigation involving Securities, Real Estate, Contract and Employment Disputes.

*(This Listing Continued)*

**J. BRITTAIN HABEGGER,** born Oakland, California, June 7, 1947; admitted to bar, 1973, California and U.S. District Court, Northern District of California. *Education:* University of Oregon (A.B., 1969); Hastings College of the Law, University of California (J.D., 1973). Phi Delta Phi. Member, Moot Court Board, 1972-1973. *Member:* Alameda County and American (Member, Sections on: Litigation; Economics of Law Practice) Bar Associations; State Bar of California. *PRACTICE AREAS:* Business Law; Business Litigation; Estate and Probate Litigation.

**VIRGINIA PALMER,** born Portland, Oregon, November 8, 1950; admitted to bar, 1981, California and U.S. District Court, Northern District of California; 1984, U.S. District Court, Central District of California. *Education:* San Francisco State University (B.A., 1975); Golden Gate University (J.D., 1980). *Member:* Alameda County Bar Association (Member, Committees on: Arbitration, Probate, Trust and Estate Planning). (Certified Specialist, Family Law, The State Bar of California Board of Legal Specialization). *PRACTICE AREAS:* Family and Elder Law; Estate Planning; Probate; Conservatorships and Trust Related Litigation.

**TIMOTHY H. SMALLSREED,** born Derby, Connecticut, December 12, 1946; admitted to bar, 1978, California and U.S. District Court, Northern District of California. *Education:* Pomona College (B.A., 1969); Maxwell School, Syracuse University (M.P.A., 1972); Golden Gate University (M.B.A. in Taxation, 1978; J.D., 1977). *Member:* Alameda County Bar Association; State Bar of California. *PRACTICE AREAS:* Corporate and Business Law; Estate Planning, Trust and Estate Administration; Probate Law.

**STEPHEN M. JUDSON,** born Berkeley, California, June 1, 1960; admitted to bar, 1985, California and U.S. District Court, Northern District of California. *Education:* Stanford University (A.B., with Departmental Honors, 1982); University of San Francisco (J.D., 1985). Phi Delta Phi. Co-Director, Moot Court Board (Advanced Competitions), 1984-1985. Roger J. Traynor Advocacy Team, 1984. Extern Clerk to Honorable Ira A. Brown, Jr., San Francisco Superior Court, 1984. *Member:* Bar Association of San Francisco; Alameda County and American Bar Associations; State Bar of California. *PRACTICE AREAS:* Business Law; Business Litigation; Commercial Law; Commercial Litigation; Bankruptcy Litigation; Probate Litigation.

**STEPHEN M. WILLIAMS,** born Havre de Grace, Maryland, July 18, 1957; admitted to bar, 1985, California and U.S. District Court, Northern and Central Districts of California; 1986, U.S. Court of Appeals, Ninth Circuit. *Education:* Montana State University (B.A., with honors, 1981); University of San Francisco School of Law (J.D., 1985). Recipient, American Jurisprudence Awards in: Administrative Law; Criminal Procedure. Interim General Counsel, University of San Francisco, 1989-1990 and 1994. *Member:* Bar Association of San Francisco; Alameda County and American (Student Liaison to General Practice Section, 1984-1985; Member: Young Lawyers Division-Northern California, Membership Chairman, 1987-1993) Bar Associations. *REPORTED CASES:* Kennedy Cabot & Co. v. National Assn. of Securities Dealers, Inc. 41 Cal App. 4th 1167. *PRACTICE AREAS:* College and University Law; General Civil Litigation; Securities Litigation; Environmental Law; Labor and Employment Law.

**JONATHAN W. REDDING,** born Ridgewood, New Jersey, July 7, 1954; admitted to bar, 1987, California, U.S. District Court, Northern District of California and U.S. Court of Appeals, Ninth Circuit. *Education:* University of California at Santa Cruz (B.A., 1976); Golden Gate University (M.P.A., 1979); Hastings College of the Law, University of California (J.D., cum laude, 1987). Member, Thurston Society. Recipient, American Jurisprudence Awards in Professional Responsibility and Comparative Law. Extern-Clerk, Office of Staff Attorneys, U.S. Court of Appeals, Ninth Circuit, 1987. *Member:* State Bar of California (Member, Real Property and Environmental Law Sections). *PRACTICE AREAS:* Environmental Law; Land Use Planning; Hazardous Waste and Environmental Law.

**BETH E. ASPEDON,** born Webster City, Iowa, June 24, 1958; admitted to bar, 1986, California. *Education:* University of Denver (B.A., cum laude, 1980); Cornell University (J.D., 1984). Member, Moot Court Board, 1984. Research Editor, Cornell International Law Journal, 1983-1984. Law Clerk, Chief Magistrate Jean F. Dwyer, United States District Court, District of Columbia, 1984-1985. *Member:* Bar Association of San Francisco; Alameda County Bar Association; The State Bar of California. *PRACTICE AREAS:* Labor and Employment Law.

**KRISTIN A. PACE,** born Tacoma, Washington, February 16, 1963; admitted to bar, 1988, California; 1989, U.S. Tax Court. *Education:* California Polytechnic State University at San Luis Obispo (B.A., cum laude, 1985); University of San Francisco (J.D., with honors, 1988); New York University (LL.M., 1989). Phi Kappa Phi; Phi Alpha Delta. Recipient, American Jurisprudence Awards: Evidence; Corporate Tax. Recipient, Wallace Scholarship. Adjunct Professor, Graduate Tax Program, Golden Gate University. *Member:* Alameda County and American Bar Associations; State Bar of California. *PRACTICE AREAS:* Tax Law; Corporate Law; Estate Planning; Trust Administration; Elder Law.

**MICHAEL M.K. SEBREE,** born San Francisco, California, March 29, 1964; admitted to bar, 1989, California and U.S. District Court, Northern District of California. *Education:* Pepperdine University; California Polytechnic State University at San Luis Obispo (B.A., 1986); University of Washington (J.D., 1989). Editor, Washington Law Review, 1988-1989. Member, University of Washington International Law Society, 1988. Author: "One Century of Constitutional Home Rule: A Progress Report?" 64 Washington Law Review 155. *Member:* Alameda County and American (Member, Business Law Section) Bar Associations; State Bar of California. *PRACTICE AREAS:* Corporate; Real Estate; Commercial.

**ANTONIA L. MORE,** born Cincinnati, Ohio, September 19, 1959; admitted to bar, 1989, California, U.S. District Court, Northern and Central Districts of California and U.S. Court of Appeals, Ninth Circuit. *Education:* Grinnell College (B.A., 1981); Leningrad State University, Leningrad, U.S.S.R, 1985; Hastings College of the Law, University of California (J.D., 1989). Executive Editor, Hastings Constitutional Law Quarterly, 1988-1989. *Member:* Alameda County Bar Association; State Bar of California (Member, Sections on: Litigation; Intellectual Property). *LANGUAGES:* Russian and French. *PRACTICE AREAS:* Securities Litigation; NYSE and NASD Arbitration; Unfair Trade Practices; Noncompetition and Nonsolicitation Agreements; Trade secrets.

### ASSOCIATES

**SARAH ROBERTSON MCCUAIG,** born Jacksonville, Florida, April 26, 1965; admitted to bar, 1989, California, U.S. District Court, Northern, Eastern and Central Districts of California. *Education:* Wellesley College (B.A., 1986); Tulane University of Law (J.D., cum laude, 1989). Member, 1987-1989 and Notes and Comments Editor, 1988-1989, Tulane Law Review. *Member:* State Bar of California. *PRACTICE AREAS:* labor and Employment Law.

**PHILIP E. DRYSDALE,** born Mount Vernon, New York, June 8, 1953; admitted to bar, 1990, California and U.S. District Court, Northern District of California; 1991, U.S. Court of Appeals, Ninth Circuit; 1995, U.S. District Court, Eastern, Central and Southern Districts of California. *Education:* Harvard College (A.B., cum laude, 1975); Columbia University School of Journalism; Tulane University of Law (J.D., 1990). Senior Fellow, Legal Writing and Research, 1989-1990. *Member:* Bar Association of San Francisco; Alameda County and American Bar Associations; State Bar of California; Charles Houston Bar Association. *PRACTICE AREAS:* Labor and Employment Law; Litigation.

**KRISTEN THALL PETERS,** born Concord, California, June 1, 1967; admitted to bar, 1992, California; 1994, U.S. District Court, Eastern District of California; 1995, U.S. District Court, Northern District of California. *Education:* University of California at Berkeley (B.A., 1989); Santa Clara University (J.D., 1992). Phi Delta Phi. Author, "Clean Air Act Amendments of 1990," Legislative Note, Santa Clara Computer and High Technology Law Journal, 1992. *Member:* Alameda County Bar Association; State Bar of California (Member, Environmental Law Section, 1992—). [French]. *PRACTICE AREAS:* Environmental Litigation; Regulatory Compliance; Land Use.

**JAY M. GOLDMAN,** born Chicago, Illinois, June 7, 1956; admitted to bar, 1993, California, U.S. District Court, Northern District of California and U.S. Court of Appeals, Ninth Circuit; 1994, U.S. District Court, Eastern, Central and Southern Districts of California. *Education:* San Francisco State University (B.A., magna cum laude, 1985); Hastings College of the Law, University of California (J.D., 1993). Extern Clerk to the Honorable Court, Northern District of California. *Member:* Bar Association of San Francisco; Alameda County Bar Association; State Bar of California. *PRACTICE AREAS:* Business and Commercial Litigation; Securities Litigation; Products Liability; Premises Liability.

**CARLO C. MORMORUNNI,** born San Francisco, California, November 18, 1968; admitted to bar, 1994, California. *Education:* University of Virginia (B.A., 1990); University of San Francisco (J.D., cum laude, 1994). McAuliffe Honor Society. Member, University of San Francisco Law Review. Associate Director, Moot Court Board. Recipient, American Jurisprudence Award in Contracts. Extern Clerk to the Honorable Ming W. Chin, California Court of Appeal, 1994. *Member:* Alameda County and

*(This Listing Continued)*

**FITZGERALD, ABBOTT & BEARDSLEY LLP,** Oakland—
*Continued*

American Bar Associations. *LANGUAGES:* Italian. *PRACTICE AREAS:* Commercial Law; Corporate Law; Estate Planning; Business Litigation.

**MICHAEL S. WARD,** born Norwood, Massachusetts, November 20, 1967; admitted to bar, 1995, California. *Education:* Stanford University (B.A., 1990); University of California, Boalt Hall School of Law (J.D., 1995). Recipient, Commendation for Excellence in Appellate Advocacy, 1993. Member, Moot Court Board, 1994-1995. Co Editor-in-Chief, Berkeley Journal of Employment and Labor Law, 1994-1995. Extern Clerk, Hon. James Perley, California Court of Appeals, 1993. *PRACTICE AREAS:* Employment and Labor Law; Litigation.

**JEAN BUO-LIN CHEN FUNG,** born San Jose, California, December 8, 1969; admitted to bar, 1995, California. *Education:* Stanford University (B.S., A.B., 1992); Boalt Hall School of Law (J.D., 1995). Executive Editor, Ecology Law Quarterly, 1994-1995. Articles Editor, High Technology Law Journal, 1993-1994. Author, "KFC Western Inc. v. Meghrig: The Merits and Implications of Awarding Restitution to Citizen Plaintiffs Under RCRA §6972 (9)(1)(B)," 22 Ecology L.Q. 785, (1996). *Member:* State Bar of California. *LANGUAGES:* Cantonese. *PRACTICE AREAS:* Environmental Law; Hazardous Waste.

**FATIMA MICHON BRUNSON,** born Oakland, California, August 18, 1970; admitted to bar, 1996, California. *Education:* University of California at Los Angeles (B.A., cum laude, 1992); Boalt Hall School of Law (J.D., 1996). Member, Moot Court Board. *Member:* Alameda County Financial Mediation Project. *PRACTICE AREAS:* Family Law; Probate Administration; Estate Planning.

ATTORNEYS FOR: Betts Spring Co.; Bigge Crane & Rigging Corp.; The Clorox Company; Coastcom; Graduate Theological Union; Melrose Ford; Peterson Tractor Co.; The Nell J. Redfield Foundation; Redfield Land Co.; Serra Shopping Center; Sunset View Cemetery Assn.; The L. J. Skaggs and Mary C. Skaggs Foundation; Church Divinity School; Peter Hartdegen Co.; The Port of Oakland; Bar X Ranch; The University of San Francisco; Stevenson Properties; Napa County; Napa County Flood Control District; Dermody Properties; Brighton Pacific Property Management; Boardwalk Investments Property Management; Atlas Heating and Air Conditioning; Norton Packaging; Val Strough Auto Dealerships; California Optical Leather, Inc.
LOCAL COUNSEL FOR: Exxon Corp.; Volvo White Truck Credit Co.; General Electric Capital Corp.; National Medical Care, Inc.; VW Credit, Inc.; Jeras Corp.; PaineWebber, Inc.; Prudential Securities, Inc.; Sutro & Co., Inc.

---

## FLEHR, HOHBACH, TEST, ALBRITTON & HERBERT

### OAKLAND, CALIFORNIA

(See San Francisco)

*Patent, Trademark, Copyright, Unfair Competition, Trade Secrets, Biotechnology, Genetic Engineering, Electronics and Computer Law. Trials.*

---

## JEREMY L. FRIEDMAN

2801 SYLHOWE ROAD
### OAKLAND, CALIFORNIA 94602
Telephone: 510-530-9060
Fax: 510-530-9087

*Civil Trial and Appellate Practice. Civil Rights Litigation, Attorneys' Fees Litigation and Qui Tam False Claims Act Prosecutions.*

**JEREMY L. FRIEDMAN,** born Chicago Heights, Illinois, August 3, 1961; admitted to bar, 1988, Illinois; 1989, California; U.S. District Court, Northern District of Illinois, U.S. District Court, Northern District of California, U.S. Supreme Court. *Education:* Brown University (A.B., magna cum laude, 1984); University of Chicago (J.D., cum laude, 1987). Order of the Coif. Member, University of Chicago Law Review. Law Clerk, Honorable James B. Moran, U.S. District Court, Northern District of Illinois, 1987-1989. Author: California Employment Law Reporter (CELR); "New Punitive Damage Liability for Employers Under the Civil Rights Act of 1991." Adjunct Professor, New College of California, School of Law, 1994-1995. Associate: Law Offices of Thomas Steel, 1989-1990; Saperstein, Goldstein, Demchak & Baller, 1990-1995. *Member:* National Lawyers Guild.

---

## GASSETT, PERRY & FRANK

ONE KAISER PLAZA, SUITE 1330
### OAKLAND, CALIFORNIA 94612
Telephone: 510-645-1487
Fax: 510-763-7284

*San Jose, California Office:* 210 North Fourth Street, Suite 400. Telephone: 408-295-7034. Telecopier: 408-295-5799.
*Santa Cruz, California Office:* 55 River Street, Suite 200. Telephone: 408-425-5023. Fax: 408-427-3159.

*General Civil and Trial Practice in all State and Federal Courts. Insurance and Workers Compensation Law.*

### RESIDENT MEMBERS

**RONALD VALENCIA,** born Castro Valley, California, August 22, 1957; admitted to bar, 1983, California. *Education:* University of California at Berkeley (A.B. in Political Science, 1979); Hastings College of Law, University of California (J.D., 1983). *Member:* Santa Clara County and American Bar Associations; The State Bar of California; Santa Clara County Barristers Club. *PRACTICE AREAS:* Workers' Compensation Defense; Employment Litigation.

**THOMAS A. WILBERDING,** born Oakland, California, June 7, 1960; admitted to bar, 1985, California. *Education:* University of California at Berkeley (A.B., 1982); University of The Pacific, McGeorge School of Law (J.D., 1985). *Member:* Santa Clara County Bar Association; The State Bar of California. *PRACTICE AREAS:* Workers' Compensation Defense; Employment Litigation.

**ROBIN Y. TREMBATH,** born Fremont, California, May 12, 1960; admitted to bar, 1985, California. *Education:* University of California at Davis (B.A., with honors, 1982); University of California, Hastings College of Law (J.D., 1985). *Member:* Santa Clara County Bar Association; Contra Costa County Bar Association; The State Bar of California; Defense Research Institute. *PRACTICE AREAS:* Personal Injury Defense; Legal Malpractice Defense.

**SEAN W. MORRISROE,** born Alameda, California, March 10, 1960; admitted to bar, 1983, California. *Education:* California State University at Hayward (B.S, cum laude, 1980); University of San Francisco (J.D., 1983). *Member:* Alameda County Bar Association; The State Bar of California. [Capt., U.S. Army, JAGC, 1984-1987]. *PRACTICE AREAS:* General Civil Litigation; Trial Practice.

### RESIDENT ASSOCIATES

**DEAN A. TOMPKINS,** born Oakland, California, February 23, 1966; admitted to bar, 1991, California. *Education:* University of California at Santa Barbara (B.A., 1988); Golden Gate University (J.D., cum laude, 1991). *Member:* Bar Association of San Francisco; State Bar of California; American Bar Association. *PRACTICE AREAS:* Workers' Compensation Defense.

**BRUCE A. BERMAN,** born Chicago, Illinois, March 6, 1963; admitted to bar, 1994, California, U.S. District Court, Northern District of California and U.S. Court of Appeals, Ninth Circuit. *Education:* University of California, Los Angeles (B.A., Psych., 1985); McGeorge School of Law (J.D., 1994). Phi Alpha Delta (Clair Engle Chapter, 1992-1994). Staff Writer, 1992 and Associate Articles Editor, 1993-1994, Pacific Law Journal. *PRACTICE AREAS:* General Civil Litigation; Insurance Defense; Defense of Self Insureds.

**DANIEL J. BAN,** born San Francisco, California, December 23, 1967; admitted to bar, 1994, California. *Education:* University of California at Berkeley (B.A., 1990); University of California at Davis (J.D., 1994). *PRACTICE AREAS:* Workers Compensation.

**STEVEN M. LEEB,** born Queens, New York, June 25, 1969; admitted to bar, 1995, California. *Education:* University of California at Irvine (B.A., 1991); University of California at Davis (J.D., 1995). *PRACTICE AREAS:* Workers' Compensation Defense.

(For complete biographical data on personnel at San Jose and Santa Cruz, California, see Professional Biographies at those locations)

## GENERAL COUNSEL SERVICES

A PROFESSIONAL LAW CORPORATION

**725 WASHINGTON STREET, 2ND FLOOR**
**OAKLAND, CALIFORNIA 94607**
Telephone: 510-891-0620
Fax: 510-836-3331
Email: dhicks@astsoft.com
URL: http://www.genlaw.com

*Beverly Hills, California Office:* 9606 Santa Monica Boulevard, Third Floor, 90210.

*Business, Labor, Governmental Regulation, Insurance, Unfair Competition, Trade Secrets, Negligence, First Amendment Litigation, Defamation, Food, Drug and Cosmetic Law. State and Federal Litigation Court.*

**DAVID HICKS,** admitted to bar, 1972, California and U.S. District Court, Eastern District of California; 1979, U.S. Supreme Court; 1982, U.S. District Court, Northern District of California; 1986, New York; U.S. District Court, District of Maine. *Education:* California State University at San Jose (B.A., Humanities honors, 1969); University of California at Davis (J.D., 1972). Judge, Pro Tem Superior Court, Alameda, Contra Costa and Solano Counties, 1979—. Arbitrator, U.S. District Court, Northern District of California, 1987—. President, Alameda-Contra Costa Trial Lawyers Association, 1992-1993.

*ASSOCIATE COUNSEL*

**DANIEL E. BEHRENDT, ESQ.,** admitted to bar, 1995, California. *Education:* University of California at Berkeley (B.A., 1992); University of California at Davis (J.D., 1995). Author, "Computer Software Copyright Law In The People's Republic of China," Journal of International Law and Policy Vol. 2, No.1, University of California at Davis. **PRACTICE AREAS:** Business Litigation; Employment/Labor.

*OF COUNSEL*

**CHRISTOPHER P. VALLE-RIESTRA, ESQ.,** admitted to bar, 1983, California. *Education:* University of California at Santa Cruz (B.A., 1978); Boalt Hall School of Law, University of California (J.D., 1983). Member, Alameda-Contra Costa Fee Arbitration Committee. **PRACTICE AREAS:** Commercial Collection; Business Litigation; General Practice; Bankruptcy Law; Probate; Judgement Enforcement.

---

## WILLIAM D. GIBBS

Established in 1986

**169 14TH STREET**
**P.O. BOX 1917**
**OAKLAND, CALIFORNIA 94604-1917**
Telephone: 510-893-2270

*Practice Limited to Personal Injury, Negligence, Business Tort and Professional Negligence Actions.*

**WILLIAM D. GIBBS,** born Topeka, Kansas, November 10, 1938; admitted to bar, 1964, California; U.S. Court of Appeals, Ninth Circuit; U.S. District Court, Northern, Eastern and Central Districts of California. *Education:* San Francisco State University (B.A., 1960); Hastings College of the Law, University of California (J.D., 1963). Author: "General Procedures for Avoiding Malpractice," California Attorneys Practice, Ch. 42, Matthew Bender, 1986-1992; "Settlement, A Practical Approach," Negotiating Favorable Personal Injury Settlement, California Continuing Education of the Bar, 1986. Lecturer, Continuing Education of the Bar, 1982—. President, Barristers Club of Alameda County, 1969-1970. *Member:* Alameda County Bar Association (Member, Board of Directors, 1974-1976); State Bar of California (Member, Board of Directors, California Barristers Association, 1971-1974); Lawyers Club of Alameda County (President, 1970-1971; Board of Directors, 1991—); Alameda-Contra Costa County Trial Lawyers Association (Member, Board of Governors, 1974-1978; 1982—; President, 1988); Consumer Attorneys of California.

---

## GILLIN, JACOBSON, ELLIS, LARSEN & DOYLE

**OAKLAND, CALIFORNIA**

(See Orinda)

*Civil Trial Practice including Intellectual Property Litigation, Commercial Torts, Products Liability, Personal Injury and Wrongful Death.*

---

## JAMES T. GIVEN

**5825 MARGARIDO DRIVE**
**OAKLAND, CALIFORNIA 94618**
Telephone: 510-655-6749
Email: jtg@fwpa.com

*General Business.*

**JAMES T. GIVEN,** born Gary, Indiana, April 2, 1954; admitted to bar, 1979, California. *Education:* Indiana University (A.B., 1976); University of California at Berkeley (J.D., 1979). Phi Beta Kappa; Order of the Coif. *Member:* State Bar of California. (Also Special Counsel to Fenwick & West LLP, Palo, Alto, California). **PRACTICE AREAS:** Intellectual Property (40%); Business Law (40%); Real Estate (20%).

---

## GOLDBERG, STINNETT, MEYERS & DAVIS

A PROFESSIONAL CORPORATION

**OAKLAND, CALIFORNIA**

(See San Francisco)

*Bankruptcy, Business Reorganization and Creditors Rights Law.*

---

## GORDON & GODDARD, L.L.P.

**ONE KAISER PLAZA, SUITE 2360**
**OAKLAND, CALIFORNIA 94612**
Telephone: 510-836-2400
Fax: 510-836-2595

*General Civil and Trial Practice, Business Litigation, Unfair Competition, Real Estate, Construction, Employment, Intellectual Property, Trademark, Product Liability, Insurance, Malpractice, Probate and Property Tax Litigation.*

*MEMBERS OF FIRM*

**PAUL M. GORDON,** born Los Angeles, California, July 9, 1952; admitted to bar, 1977, California. *Education:* University of California, Berkeley (B.A., 1974); Boalt Hall, University of California, Berkeley (J.D., 1977). Associate Editor, Industrial Relations Law Journal, 1976. Recipient, First Prize, McBaine Moot Court Competition, 1976. Judicial Extern to Judge Charles B. Renfrew, U.S. District Court, Northern District of California, 1976. Law Clerk to Judge William H. Orrick, U.S. District Court, Northern District of California, 1977-1978. *Member:* Alameda County Bar Association; State Bar of California; Bar Association of San Francisco.

**WENDELL H. GODDARD,** born Detroit, Michigan, March 5, 1945; admitted to bar, 1975, California and New York. *Education:* Yale University (B.A., 1968); Boalt Hall, University of California, Berkeley (J.D., 1972). Associate Editor, California Law Review, 1972. Recipient, Second Prize, American Bar Association Essay Contest in Family Law, 1972. Law Clerk to Judge Whitman Knapp, U.S. District Court, Southern District of New York, 1972-1974. *Member:* Alameda County and American Bar Associations; State Bar of California; State Bar of New York; Bar Association of San Francisco.

## GRAVES & ALLEN
*Established in 1975*

**2101 WEBSTER STREET, SUITE 1746**
**OAKLAND, CALIFORNIA 94612**
Telephone: 510-839-8777
Telecopier: 510-839-5192
Email: jallenlaw@aol.com

Mailing Address: P.O. Box 30817, Oakland, CA 94604-6917

*Civil and Trial Practice. Real Estate and Business.*

**JEFFREY ALLEN,** born Chicago, Illinois, December 13, 1948; admitted to bar, 1973, California, U.S. District Court, District of California and U.S. Court of Appeals, 9th Circuit; 1974, U.S. District Court, Eastern District of California; 1977, U.S. Supreme Court and U.S. District Court, Central District of California. *Education:* University of California at Berkeley (B.A., 1970) Phi Beta Kappa; University of California, Boalt Hall. California Law Review (Special Projects Editor, 1973); Founding Member, Environmental Law Quarterly, 1972. Member, Panel of Civil Arbitrators, Alameda County Superior Court; Panel of Arbitrators, American Arbitration Association; State Bar's Special Masters Panel, Alameda County. Author: Comment, "Pretrial Release Under California Penal Code Section 853.6: An Examination of Citation Release," 60 California Law Review 1339, 1972; "Computers and the Litigator," 7 The American Journal of Trial Advocacy 493, 1984; reprinted at 34 Defense Law Journal 183, 1985. Lecturer, St. Mary's College (Paralegal Program). Teaching Assistant, University of California, Berkeley, Political Science Department, 1970-1973. *Member:* Alameda County (Former Vice-Chair, Committee on Continuing Education; Member, Mediators Panel) and American (Former Chair, Real Property Committee, General Practice Section: Former Chair, Subcommittee on the Use of Computers in Real Estate Transactions; Former Member, Program Board of General Practice Section, 1996—; Advocacy Coordinator and Member, Section Counsel, General Practice Section) Bar Associations; State Bar of California (Member, Real Estate Section). *PRACTICE AREAS:* Real Estate; Bankruptcy; Litigation; Receiverships; General Practice.

---

## GWILLIAM, IVARY, CHIOSSO, CAVALLI & BREWER
*A PROFESSIONAL CORPORATION*

**1999 HARRISON STREET, SUITE 1600**
**OAKLAND, CALIFORNIA 94612-3528**
Telephone: 510-832-5411
Fax: 510-832-1918
Email: Info@GICCB.com

Mailing Address: P.O. Box 2079, 94604-2079

*Practice Limited to Personal Injury, Products Liability, Negligence, Medical Malpractice, Legal Malpractice, Wrongful Termination, Employment Discrimination, Bad Faith and Insurance Litigation.*

**FIRM PROFILE:** *Gwilliam, Ivary, Chiosso, Cavalli & Brewer specializes soley in representing people who have been seriously injured or otherwise victimized by the wrongful conduct of others. The firm has had its roots in Oakland for more than thirty years and all of the partners have been in the personal injury field for 15 years or more. The firm's practice has evolved to primarily handling more serious and complex cases in the consumer law and personal injury fields. The firm has achieved the highest standing in the legal community due to high ethical standards and outstanding results achieved for its clients. Testimony to the firm's reputation is the fact that many cases are referred to the firm by other lawyers. Gwilliam, Ivary, Chiosso, Cavalli & Brewer is committed to providing the best possible representation to its clients and in so doing, it hopes to contribute to a safer and more just community.*

**J. GARY GWILLIAM,** born Ogden, Utah, May 18, 1937; admitted to bar, 1963, California. *Education:* Pomona College (B.A., 1959); Boalt Hall, University of California (LL.B., 1962). Phi Delta Phi. Member, Boalt Hall Moot Court Board, 1961-1962. Faculty Member, Hastings College of Trial Advocacy, 1981—. Member, Panel of Arbitrators, American Arbitration Association. Nominated Trial Lawyer of the Year 1995 and 1996, Trial Lawyers for Public Justice. *Member:* The State Bar of California; American Bar Association; Alameda County Lawyers Club (Lawyer of the Year, 1985-1986); California Trial Lawyers Association (now Consumer Attorneys of California) (President, 1988; Parliamentarian, 1986; Chairman, Political Action Committee, 1986; Chairman, Long Range Planning Committee, 1990-1994; Member, Board of Governors, 1983—; Sustaining Member; recognized experience as a Trial Lawyer and in the Fields of Products Liability, General Personal Injury and Professional Negligence); The Association of Trial Lawyers of America; Alameda-Contra Costa County Trial Lawyers Association (President, 1974-1975; Member, Board of Governors, 1970—); American Board of Trial Advocates (Advocate, 1976). Certified as a Civil Trial Advocate by the National Board of Trial Advocacy, 1982. *PRACTICE AREAS:* General Personal Injury; Products Liability; Medical and Legal Negligence; Wrongful Termination; Employment Discrimination; Insurance Bad Faith.

**ERIC H. IVARY,** born Oakland, California, September 15, 1946; admitted to bar, 1972, California. *Education:* St. Mary's College of California (B.A., 1968); University of Santa Clara (J.D., 1971). Phi Alpha Delta. Member, Panel of Arbitrators, American Arbitration Association. Principal Author: Winning at Arbitration, Bancroft Whitney, 1992. Alameda County Lawyers' Club Lawyer of the Year, 1995. CTLA recognition of experience in areas of Insurance Bad Faith, General Personal Injury, Products Liability, Trial Law and Professional Negligence. *Member:* Alameda County Bar Association; State Bar of California; Alameda-Contra Costa Trial Lawyers Association (Member, Board of Governors, 1977—; President, 1990); Consumer Attorneys of California; The Association of Trial Lawyers of America; American Board of Trial Advocates; American Inns of Court, 1996—. *PRACTICE AREAS:* Negligence; Insurance Bad Faith; Products Liability.

**JAMES R. CHIOSSO,** born San Francisco, California, July 13, 1942; admitted to bar, 1975, California. *Education:* University of San Francisco (B.A., 1964); Lincoln University (J.D., 1972). *Member:* Alameda County and Federal Bar Associations; State Bar of California; Alameda-Contra Costa Trial Lawyers Association; Consumer Attorneys of California; American Board of Trial Advocates (Associate); The Association of Trial Lawyers of America; Italian-American Bar Association; Trial Lawyers for Public Justice (Nominated for Trail Lawyer of the Year, 1996). *PRACTICE AREAS:* Trials; Personal Injury; Product Liability; Governmental Torts; Employment Discrimination.

**STEVEN R. CAVALLI,** born San Francisco, California, September 23, 1948; admitted to bar, 1981, California; 1984, U.S. Supreme Court. *Education:* University of California at Berkeley (B.A., 1971); San Francisco Law School (J.D., 1981). Judge Pro Tempore, Santa Clara, Alameda and Contra Costa Counties. *Member:* Alameda County Bar Association; State Bar of California. Alameda-Contra Costa County Trial Lawyers Association; Consumer Attorneys of California; Italian-American Bar Association; Trial Lawyers for Public Justice. *PRACTICE AREAS:* Product Liability; Construction Accidents; Highway Design.

**STEVEN J. BREWER,** born San Francisco, California, October 22, 1954; admitted to bar, 1980, California. *Education:* University of California at Berkeley (B.A., 1976); Lincoln University (J.D., 1980). Judge Pro Tempore, Santa Clara and Alameda Counties. *Member:* San Francisco and Alameda County Bar Associations; State Bar of California; Alameda-Contra Costa Trial Lawyers Association; Consumer Attorneys of California; The Association of Trial Lawyers of America; National Spinal Cord Injury Association. *PRACTICE AREAS:* General Negligence; Professional Malpractice; Product Liability; Construction Accidents.

---

**MARGUERITE E. MEADE,** born Berkeley, California, March 18, 1957; admitted to bar, 1988, California; 1989, U.S. District Court, Eastern, Northern and Southern Districts of California and U.S. Court of Appeals, Ninth Circuit; 1990, U.S. Court of Appeals, Sixth Circuit. *Education:* University of California at Berkeley (B.A., 1980); Hastings College of the Law, University of California (J.D., 1988). *Member:* Alameda County Bar Association; State Bar of California; Consumer Attorneys of California; Alameda-Contra Costa Trial Lawyers Association; The Association of Trial Lawyers of America. *PRACTICE AREAS:* Personal Injury; Insurance Bad Faith; Employment Discrimination; Governmental Torts.

**STEVEN A. REAVES,** born Berkeley, California, December 11, 1951; admitted to bar, 1979, California and U.S. District Court, Eastern District of California; 1980, U.S. Court of Appeals, Federal Circuit; 1986, U.S. District Court, Northern District of California. *Education:* California State University (B.A., cum laude, Political Science, 1974); Lincoln University (J.D., 1979). *Member:* Alameda County, Contra Costa County and American Bar Associations; State Bar of California; Consumer Attorneys of California; Alameda and Contra Costa Trial Lawyers Association; The Association of Trial Lawyers of America. *PRACTICE AREAS:* Personal Injury; Insurance Bad Faith; Wrongful Termination.

*(This Listing Continued)*

**MOLLY HARRINGTON,** born Torrance, California, February 27, 1968; admitted to bar, 1996, California. *Education:* Georgetown University (B.A., 1990); University of Southern California Law Center (J.D., 1995). *Member:* Alameda County Bar Association; State Bar of California; Consumer Attorneys of California; Alameda-Contra Costa Trial Lawyers Association; The Association of Trial Lawyers of America; Trial Lawyers for Public Justice. *LANGUAGES:* Spanish. *PRACTICE AREAS:* Personal Injury; Employment Discrimination; Bad Faith.

REFERENCE: Civic Bank of Commerce, Oakland, California.

## HAIMS, JOHNSON, MacGOWAN & McINERNEY

Established in 1976

490 GRAND AVENUE
**OAKLAND, CALIFORNIA 94610**
Telephone: 510-835-0500
Facsimile: 510-835-2833

*General Civil and Trial Practice. Professional Liability, Products Liability, Aviation, Corporation, Casualty Insurance, Fire Insurance, Marine and Inland Marine Insurance, Life Insurance and Accident and Health Insurance Law.*

FIRM PROFILE: *Haims, Johnson, MacGowan & McInerney is an innovative and resourceful San Francisco Bay Area firm which specializes in the defense of policyholders and self insureds against suits asserting automobile, premises, product, employment, landlord tenant, construction defect and health law liabilities. We also represent the direct interests of insurers in rendering coverage opinions and practical advice on everything from toxic tort issues through sexual harassment claims to the detection and exposure of fraudulent claims. Our reputation for delivering practical, accurate legal advice and opinions which will survive judicial muster is convincingly proven by the referenced representative clients, alongside whom we have victoriously fought.*

### MEMBERS OF FIRM

**ARNOLD B. HAIMS,** born New York, N.Y., June 19, 1931; admitted to bar, 1960, California. *Education:* Stanford University (A.B., 1953; LL.B., 1959). *Member:* Alameda County and American Bar Associations; The State Bar of California; Association of Defense Counsel of Northern California; National Association of Railroad Trial Counsel; International Association of Insurance Counsel. [Capt., USMCR]. *PRACTICE AREAS:* Insurance Defense Law; Insurance Coverage; Civil Trial; Railway Law.

**GARY R. JOHNSON,** born Seattle, Washington, June 20, 1943; admitted to bar, 1969, California. *Education:* Pacific University and University of California at Berkeley (A.B., 1965); Hastings College of Law, University of California (J.D., 1968). Recipient, 1996 Lawyer of the Year, Alameda County Lawyers Club. Deputy District Attorney, Alameda County, 1971-1974. Member, Board of Directors, Alameda County Lawyers' Club, 1975-1979. *Member:* Alameda County and American Bar Associations; The State Bar of California; Association of Defense Counsel, Northern California (Director, 1988-1989); Defense Research Institute; American Board of Trial Advocates. *PRACTICE AREAS:* Insurance Defense Law; Insurance Law; Litigation Defense; Tort Law; Bad Faith Law.

**CLYDE L. MACGOWAN,** born Eureka, California, March 17, 1934; admitted to bar, 1964, California. *Education:* University of California at Berkeley (A.B., 1955); Hastings College of Law, University of California (J.D., 1963). Deputy District Attorney, Alameda County, 1963-1966. *Member:* Alameda County and American Bar Associations; The State Bar of California; Association of Defense Counsel of Northern California; American Board of Trial Advocates. [Col., USAFR; Vice-Commander, 349 MAS, Travis AFB, 1981-1987]. *PRACTICE AREAS:* Automobile Negligence; Uninsured Motorist; Products Liability Law; Insurance Fraud; Insurance Defense Law.

**THOMAS MCINERNEY,** born San Francisco, California, July 11, 1926; admitted to bar, 1956, California. *Education:* College of the Pacific and University of Santa Clara (B.S.C., 1949); Hastings College of Law, University of California (LL.B., 1953). *Member:* Alameda County and American Bar Associations; The State Bar of California; Association of Defense Counsel of Northern California (Director, 1976). *PRACTICE AREAS:* Insurance Defense Law; Civil Defense; Alternative Dispute Resolution.

**LAWRENCE A. BAKER,** born Berkeley, California, July 22, 1948; admitted to bar, 1978, California, U.S. District Court, Northern District of California and U.S. Court of Appeals, Ninth Circuit; 1981, U.S. District

*(This Listing Continued)*

Court, Central District of California; 1988, U.S. District Court, Eastern District of California. *Education:* University of California at Berkeley (B.A., 1970); San Francisco Law School (J.D., 1978). *Member:* Alameda County Bar Association; The State Bar of California; Association of Defense Counsel, Northern California. *PRACTICE AREAS:* Insurance; Personal Injury Defense; Bad Faith Law; Construction Litigation; Appellate Practice.

**RANDY M. MARMOR,** born Brooklyn, New York, November 5, 1948; admitted to bar, 1974, New York and U.S. District Court, Southern and Eastern Districts of New York; 1977, California and U.S. District Court, Northern District of California. *Education:* Syracuse University (B.A., 1970); Georgetown University (J.D., 1973); Golden Gate University (LL.M. in Taxation, with honors, 1983). *Member:* New York State Bar Association; The State Bar of California. *PRACTICE AREAS:* Insurance Coverage; Bad Faith Law; Construction Defect Litigation; Accident and Personal Injury; Landlord and Tenant.

**JOHN K. KIRBY,** born Quincy, Massachusetts, January 4, 1947; admitted to bar, 1980, Massachusetts; 1982, California. *Education:* Middlebury College (A.B., with honors in History, 1968); University of San Francisco (J.D., 1980). Member, Moot Court Board. Recipient, American Jurisprudence Awards in Wills and Trusts and Family Law. *Member:* Alameda County and Massachusetts Bar Associations; The State Bar of California. [1st Lt., U.S. Army, 1970-1972]. *PRACTICE AREAS:* Litigation Defense; Environmental Insurance Litigation; Trial Practice; Insurance Coverage.

**ROBERT J. FRASSETTO,** born Salinas, California, July 21, 1956; admitted to bar, 1982, California. *Education:* University of California at Los Angeles (B.A., 1979); University of Santa Clara (J.D., 1982); Magdalen College, Oxford University. Recipient, American Jurisprudence Award in Torts. Comments Editor, Santa Clara Law Review, 1981-1982. *Member:* Alameda County Bar Association; The State Bar of California. *PRACTICE AREAS:* Insurance Defense Law; Products Liability Law; Fire Loss Litigation; Toxic Exposure; Alternative Dispute Resolution.

**CAROLINE N. VALENTINO,** born Concord, California, October 3, 1956; admitted to bar, 1985, California and U.S. District Court, Northern District of California. *Education:* California Polytechnic State University (B.A., cum laude, 1978); Golden Gate University (J.D., 1983). *Member:* Alameda County Bar Association; State Bar of California; Bay Area Lawyers for the Arts. *LANGUAGES:* German. *PRACTICE AREAS:* General Civil Litigation; Insurance Defense; Bad Faith Law; Health, Disability and Life Insurance Law and Coverage; Personal Injury Defense; Fraud Law.

**DIANNE D. PEEBLES,** born Santa Barbara, California, December 28, 1960; admitted to bar, 1987, California. *Education:* University of California at Berkeley (A.B., 1983); Golden Gate University (J.D., 1986). *Member:* State Bar of California; Alameda County Bar Association; Association of Defense Counsel of Northern California; Northern California Fraud Investigators Association. *PRACTICE AREAS:* Insurance Defense Law; Automobile Negligence; Uninsured Motorist; Insurance Fraud; Construction Law.

### ASSOCIATES

**JOSEPH Y. AHN,** born Seoul, Korea, March 3, 1961; admitted to bar, 1989, California and U.S. District Court, Northern District of California. *Education:* University of California at Berkeley (B.A., 1983); Hastings College of the Law, University of California (J.D., 1987). *Member:* Alameda County Bar Association. *LANGUAGES:* Korean. *PRACTICE AREAS:* Insurance Defense Law; Insurance Coverage; Litigation.

**EDWARD D. BALDWIN,** born Shreveport, Louisiana, March 28, 1961; admitted to bar, 1992, California. *Education:* U.S. Naval Academy (B.S., 1983); Golden Gate University (J.D., 1992). Recipient, American Jurisprudence Award in Professional Responsibility, 1992. *Member:* Alameda County Bar Association; State Bar of California; Association of Defense Counsel of Northern California. [Lt., U.S. Navy, 1983-1988]. *PRACTICE AREAS:* Personal Injury Law; Environmental Insurance Litigation; Construction Defect Litigation.

**MARC P. BOURET,** born San Mateo, California, January 20, 1953; admitted to bar, 1978, California and U.S. District Court, Northern District of California; 1979, U.S. Court of Appeals, Ninth Circuit and U.S. Tax Court; 1987, U.S. Supreme Court. *Education:* University of the Pacific (B.A., with honors, 1975); St. Mary's College (M.B.A., 1980); California Western School of Law (J.D., 1978). Member, 1976-1977 and Topics Editor, 1977-1978, California Western Law Review. Recipient: Distinguished Service Award, Alameda County Bar Association, 1993; American Jurisprudence Award, Criminal and Labor Law. Author: "The California Going and Coming Rule: A Plea for Legislative Clarification," 15 California West-

*(This Listing Continued)*

### HAIMS, JOHNSON, MacGOWAN & McINERNEY, Oakland—Continued

ern Law Review 601, 1979; "A Defense Primer on Temporomandibular Joint (TMJ) Injury," 34 For The Defense 11, 1992; "Temporomandibular Joint (TMJ) Disorder Emerging Criteria for Defense Counsel," 60 Defense Counsel Journal 534, 1993. *Member:* Contra Costa County, Alameda County (Member, Board of Directors, 1994—; Vice President, 1996-1997) and American Bar Associations; State Bar of California; Association of Defense Counsel of Northern California; Defense Research Institute. *PRACTICE AREAS:* Civil Litigation; Insurance Defense; Negligence; Torts; Products Liability.

**ANNE M. MICHAELS**, born Springfield, Massachusetts, February 22, 1960; admitted to bar, 1988, California, U.S. District Court, Northern and Eastern Districts of California and U.S. Court of Appeals, Ninth Circuit. *Education:* Simmons College (B.A., 1983); Golden Gate University (J.D., 1988). Member, Volunteers in Parole Program, 1989-1990. *Member:* Alameda County and American Bar Associations; State Bar of California. *LANGUAGES:* Spanish. *PRACTICE AREAS:* Insurance Defense Litigation; Landlord/Tenant Litigation; Construction Law.

**MICHELLE DIANE PERRY**, born Alexandria, Virginia, January 1, 1965; admitted to bar, 1993, California, U.S. District Court, Northern District of California and U.S. Court of Appeals, Ninth Circuit. *Education:* University of California at Santa Barbara; California Polytechnic State University (San Luis Obispo); University of San Francisco (B.S., 1996); Monterey College of Law (J.D., 1993). Delta Theta Phi. Recipient: MCL Board of Directors' Scholarship, 1990, 1991 and 1992; Stephen F. Cook Memorial Scholarship, 1993. Real Estate License, California, 1984-1987. Contributing Author, "Evidence Discovery and Trial Practice," Foundation for Paralegal Association, 1989. Visiting Professor, Civil Litigation, University of California at Santa Cruz, California, 1992—. *Member:* Monterey County, Alameda County and American Bar Associations; State Bar of California; Barristers Club; Women Lawyers of Alameda County (Member, 1994—; President-Elect, 1996-1997; Board Member, 1994—). *PRACTICE AREAS:* Insurance Defense; Insurance Coverage.

**EDWARD C. SCHROEDER, JR.,** born Santa Monica, California, July 26, 1958; admitted to bar, 1990, California. *Education:* University of California at Los Angeles (B.A., 1980); University of San Francisco (J.D., 1989). *Member:* Alameda County Bar Association; State Bar of California. *PRACTICE AREAS:* Insurance Defense.

REPRESENTATIVE CLIENTS: Aetna Casualty & Surety Company; Aetna Life & Casualty Company; American National Property & Casualty Company; California Insurance Group; California State Automobile Association; Georgia-Pacific Corporation Gjerde Construction Company; Golden Eagle Insurance Company; John Hancock Mutual Life Insurance Company; John Hancock Property and Casualty Holding Company; Kaiser Gypsum Company, Inc. Kaiser Cement Corporation; K&K Insurance Agency, Inc.; Ladbroke, Inc.; Metropolitan Property and Liability Insurance Company; Mutual Of Omaha; Nationwide Insurance Company; New York Life Insurance Company; Pacific Racing Association; Southern Pacific Transportation Company; St. Paul Fire and Marine Insurance Company; State Farm Mutual Automobile Insurance Company; State Farm Fire & Casualty Company; Transamerica Insurance Group; Unigard Insurance Group.

---

## HARDIN, COOK, LOPER, ENGEL & BERGEZ

*1999 HARRISON STREET, 18TH FLOOR*
**OAKLAND, CALIFORNIA 94612-3541**
Telephone: 510-444-3131
Telecopier: 510-839-7940

*General Civil and Trial Practice. Insurance, Environmental, Toxic Torts, Estate Planning and Administration, Labor Relations, Corporation and Family Law.*

### MEMBERS OF FIRM

**J. MARCUS HARDIN** (1905-1993).

**L. S. FLETCHER** (1905-1964).

**HERMAN COOK** (1914-1982).

**JOHN C. LOPER,** born Great Falls, Montana, May 3, 1923; admitted to bar, 1950, California. *Education:* University of California (A.B., 1944; J.D., 1949). Deputy District Attorney, Alameda County, 1949-1952. *Member:* Alameda County (President, 1974) and American Bar Associations; The State Bar of California (Member, Executive Committee of Conference of Delegates, 1977-1980; Vice President, 1980); International Association of

*(This Listing Continued)*

Defense Counsel; American Board of Trial Advocates. [Lt., (j.g.) U.S. Navy, 1943-1946]. (Partner Emeritus). *PRACTICE AREAS:* Estate Planning; Administration.

**BARRIE ENGEL,** born Detroit, Michigan, June 16, 1937; admitted to bar, 1963, California. *Education:* University of California at Berkeley (A.B., 1959; J.D., 1962). Phi Delta Phi; Order of the Coif. *Member:* Alameda County and American Bar Associations; The State Bar of California. *PRACTICE AREAS:* Business Law; Corporate Law; Estate Planning Law.

**RAYMOND J. BERGEZ,** born San Francisco, California, August 27, 1938; admitted to bar, 1964, California. *Education:* University of California at Berkeley (A.B., 1960); Boalt Hall School of Law, University of California (J.D., 1963). *Member:* Alameda County and American Bar Associations; The State Bar of California; National Association of Railroad Trial Counsel; Defense Research Institute; Association of Defense Counsel of Northern California (Member, Board of Directors, 1982-1983). *PRACTICE AREAS:* Civil Litigation; Toxic Torts; Products Liability Law.

**GEORGE S. PEYTON, JR.,** born Dallas, Texas, July 18, 1938; admitted to bar, 1966, California. *Education:* Princeton University (A.B., 1960); Boalt Hall School of Law, University of California (J.D., 1965). City Attorney, City of Piedmont, 1971—. *Member:* Alameda County and American Bar Associations; The State Bar of California. *PRACTICE AREAS:* Estate Administration Law; Estate Planning Law; Municipal Law.

**RALPH A. LOMBARDI,** born Vallejo, California, August 22, 1945; admitted to bar, 1971, California. *Education:* University of California at Berkeley (A.B., 1967); Boalt Hall School of Law, University of California (J.D., 1970). Pi Sigma Alpha. Deputy City Attorney, City of Piedmont, 1974—. *Member:* Alameda County and American Bar Associations; The State Bar of California; Association of Defense Counsel of Northern California; Defense Research Institute (Member, Board of Directors); International Association of Insurance Counsel; American Board of Trial Advocates. Fellow, American College of Trial Lawyers. *PRACTICE AREAS:* Products Liability Law; Insurance Law; Civil Litigation.

**SANDRA F. WAGNER,** born Cincinnati, Ohio, January 8, 1943; admitted to bar, 1971, California. *Education:* Stanford University (A.B., 1965); Loyola University of Los Angeles (J.D., 1970). *Member:* Alameda County and American (Member, Family Law Section) Bar Associations; The State Bar of California. *PRACTICE AREAS:* Family Law.

**WILLARD L. ALLOWAY,** born Merced, California, August 14, 1946; admitted to bar, 1972, California. *Education:* University of California at Berkeley (A.B., 1968); Boalt Hall School of Law, University of California (J.D., 1972). Pi Sigma Alpha. Member, Moot Court Board. *Member:* Alameda County and American Bar Associations; The State Bar of California; Association of Defense Counsel of Northern California; National Association of Railroad Trial Counsel. *PRACTICE AREAS:* Civil Trials; Toxic Torts; Governmental Liability.

**GENNARO A. FILICE, III,** born Berkeley, California, August 28, 1949; admitted to bar, 1974, California. *Education:* University of California at Berkeley (A.B., 1971); Hastings College of Law, University of California (J.D., 1974). *Member:* Alameda County and American Bar Associations; The State Bar of California; Defense Research Institute; Association of Defense Counsel of Northern California. *PRACTICE AREAS:* Products Liability Law; Toxic Substances Law; Environmental Law.

**STEPHEN MCKAE,** born Pasadena, California, June 11, 1947; admitted to bar, 1975, California; 1981, U.S. Supreme Court. *Education:* Stanford University (B.A., with distinction, 1969); Hastings College of Law, University of California (J.D., 1975). *Member:* Bar Association of San Francisco (Member, Labor Relations Law Section); The State Bar of California; American Bar Association (Member, Sections on: Labor Relations Law; Natural Resources, Energy and Environmental Law); Defense Research Institute. *LANGUAGES:* French. *PRACTICE AREAS:* Civil Litigation; Labor Law; Environmental Law.

**BRUCE P. LOPER,** born Berkeley, California, September 28, 1950; admitted to bar, 1975, California. *Education:* Dartmouth College (B.A., cum laude, 1972); University of California at Davis (J.D., 1975). Deputy District Attorney, Alameda County, 1976-1979. Deputy City Attorney, City of Piedmont, 1980—. *Member:* Alameda County and American Bar Associations; The State Bar of California; Association of Defense Counsel of Northern California; Defense Research Institute; International Association of Insurance Counsel. *PRACTICE AREAS:* Civil Litigation; Insurance Law.

**BRUCE E. MCLEOD,** born San Mateo, California, April 28, 1949; admitted to bar, 1976, California. *Education:* Brigham Young University

*(This Listing Continued)*

(B.S., 1973; J.D., 1976). Member, National Moot Court Team. Deputy District Attorney, Alameda County, 1977-1980. *Member:* Alameda County and American Bar Associations; The State Bar of California; Association of Defense Counsel of Northern California. **PRACTICE AREAS:** Civil Trials; Products Liability Law; Toxic Substances Law.

**EUGENE BROWN, JR.,** born Los Angeles, California, December 4, 1947; admitted to bar, 1978, California. *Education:* University of California at Berkeley (A.B., 1970); University of San Francisco (J.D., 1977). *Member:* San Francisco, Alameda County and American Bar Associations; The State Bar of California; Association of Defense Counsel of Northern California; Defense Research Institute. **PRACTICE AREAS:** Products/Toxic Tort Liability; Governmental Tort Liability Law; Civil Trials.

**LINDA C. ROODHOUSE,** born Jacksonville, Illinois, January 30, 1943; admitted to bar, 1980, California. *Education:* Carleton College (B.A., 1965); Northwestern University (M.A.T., 1966); McGeorge School of Law, University of the Pacific (J.D., 1980). Deputy City Attorney, City of Piedmont, 1981—. *Member:* Alameda County and American Bar Associations; The State Bar of California. (Certified Specialist, Estate Planning, Trust & Probate Law, The State Bar of California, Board of Legal Specialization). **PRACTICE AREAS:** Estate Planning Law; Estate Administration Law; Municipal Law.

**MATTHEW S. CONANT,** born Los Angeles, California, February 10, 1955; admitted to bar, 1980, California. *Education:* University of California at San Diego (B.A., 1976); Hastings College of Law, University of California (J.D., 1980). *Member:* Alameda County and American Bar Associations; The State Bar of California; Association of Defense Counsel of Northern California. **PRACTICE AREAS:** Personal Injury Law; Products Liability Law; Insurance Defense Law.

**CHRIS P. LAVDIOTIS,** born San Francisco, California, July 24, 1952; admitted to bar, 1980, California. *Education:* University of California at Berkeley (B.A., 1975); Hastings College of Law, University of California (J.D., 1980). *Member:* Bar Association of San Francisco; Alameda County and American Bar Associations; The State Bar of California; Association of Defense Counsel of Northern California. **PRACTICE AREAS:** Products Liability Law; Civil Trials; Insurance Defense Law.

**ROBERT D. EASSA,** born San Francisco, California, November 6, 1953; admitted to bar, 1983, California. *Education:* San Francisco State University (B.A., 1976); San Francisco State University School of Business (M.B.A., 1978); Hastings College of Law, University of California (J.D., 1982). *Member:* Bar Association of San Francisco; Alameda County and American Bar Associations; The State Bar of California; Barristers Club of San Francisco; Association of Defense Counsel of Northern California. **PRACTICE AREAS:** Products Liability Law; Insurance Defense Law; Civil Litigation.

**PETER O. GLAESSNER,** born St. Louis, Missouri, September 2, 1955; admitted to bar, 1980, California. *Education:* University of California at Los Angeles (B.A., magna cum laude, 1977); University of San Diego (J.D., magna cum laude, 1980). Instructor, Insurance Education Association, 1988—. Research Attorney, California Court of Appeal, Fourth District, 1980-1982. *Member:* Alameda County and American (Member, Torts and Insurance Practice Section) Bar Associations; State Bar of California; Association of Defense Counsel of Northern California; Defense Research Institute. **PRACTICE AREAS:** Insurance Law and Litigation; Professional Liability.

**NICHOLAS D. KAYHAN,** born San Francisco, California, October 11, 1957; admitted to bar, 1987, California. *Education:* University of California at Berkeley (B.A., 1979); Hastings College of the Law, University of California (J.D., 1987). Legal Extern, The Honorable John P. Vukasin, U.S. District Court, Northern District of California, Spring, 1987. *Member:* Alameda County and American Bar Associations; State Bar of California; Association of Defense Counsel of Northern California. **PRACTICE AREAS:** Products Liability Law; Civil Litigation; Toxic Substances Law.

**JOHN A. DE PASQUALE,** born Trenton, New Jersey, April 7, 1962; admitted to bar, 1987, California. *Education:* State University of New York at Albany (B.A., magna cum laude, 1984); Villanova University (J.D., 1987). Pi Sigma Alpha; Phi Delta Phi. *Member:* Alameda County and American Bar Associations; State Bar of California; Association of Defense Counsel of Northern California. **PRACTICE AREAS:** Products Liability Law; Toxic Substances Law; Civil Litigation.

**PETER A. STROTZ,** born San Francisco, California, August 3, 1960; admitted to bar, 1987, California; 1988, U.S. District Court, Northern District of California. *Education:* University of California at Berkeley (A.B., 1983); Pepperdine University; University of San Francisco (J.D., 1987).

*(This Listing Continued)*

Winner: 1985 Advocate of the Year; John Brennan Mock Trial Competition, 1987. *Member:* Bar Association of San Francisco; Alameda County and American (Member, Sections on: Tort; Products Liability) Bar Associations; State Bar of California. **LANGUAGES:** German and Swiss German. **PRACTICE AREAS:** Civil Defense Litigation; Toxic Torts; Product Liability Law.

**AMBER L. KELLY,** born Oakland, California, November 18, 1959; admitted to bar, 1984, California. *Education:* California State University at Hayward (B.A., 1980); University of San Francisco (J.D., 1983). Member, University of San Francisco Law Review, 1981-1982. *Member:* San Francisco, Alameda County and American Bar Associations; The State Bar of California; Black American Law Students Association; Association of Defense Counsel of Northern California. **PRACTICE AREAS:** Civil Litigation; Toxic Torts; Governmental Liability.

**ELSA M. BALDWIN,** born February 4, 1957; admitted to bar, 1990, Oregon and California. *Education:* Pomona College (B.A., cum laude, 1979); Hastings College of Law (J.D., cum laude, 1989). *Member:* Alameda County and American Bar Associations; State Bar of California. **PRACTICE AREAS:** Environmental Law; Civil Litigation; Labor Law.

**MARSHALL A. JOHNSON,** born Martinez, California, November 21, 1954; admitted to bar, 1983, California. *Education:* University of California at Berkeley (B.A., 1977); McGeorge School of Law, University of the Pacific (J.D., 1983). *Member:* Bar Association of San Francisco; Contra Costa County Bar Association; The State Bar of California. **PRACTICE AREAS:** Civil Trial Law; Insurance Defense Law; Toxic Substances Law.

**DIANE R. STANTON,** born San Antonio, Texas, November 17, 1960; admitted to bar, 1989, California, U.S. District Court, Northern District of California and U.S. Court of Appeals, Ninth Circuit. *Education:* University of California (B.A., with distinction, 1982; M.A., 1983); Hastings College of the Law, University of California (J.D., 1989). *Member:* The State Bar California. **PRACTICE AREAS:** Products Liability Law; Civil Litigation.

**JENNIFER M. WALKER,** born Hong Kong, April 1, 1960; admitted to bar, 1985, California. *Education:* University of California at Berkeley (B.A., 1981); Hastings College of the Law, University of California (J.D., 1984). *Member:* Los Angeles County, Alameda County and American Bar Associations; State Bar of California. **PRACTICE AREAS:** Toxic Substances Law; Civil Litigation; Products Liability Law.

**MARGARET L. KOTZEBUE,** born Palo Alto, California, November 17, 1963; admitted to bar, 1990, California and U.S. District Court, Northern District of California. *Education:* University of California at Davis (A.B., 1985); Hastings College of the Law, University of California (J.D., 1990). *Member:* Alameda Bar Association; State Bar of California. **PRACTICE AREAS:** Insurance Law; Products Liability Law; Civil Litigation.

**AMEE A. MIKACICH,** born Sacramento, California, March 13, 1962; admitted to bar, 1989, California. *Education:* University of California at Berkeley (B.A., 1984); San Francisco Law School (J.D., 1989). *Member:* State Bar of California. **PRACTICE AREAS:** Product Liability Law; Civil Litigation; Toxic Torts.

**TIMOTHY J. MCCAFFERY,** born Reno, Nevada, May 4, 1966; admitted to bar, 1991, California. *Education:* St. Mary's College of California (B.S., 1988); University of San Francisco (J.D., 1991). Phi Delta Phi. *Member:* Alameda County and American Bar Associations; State Bar of California. **PRACTICE AREAS:** Products Liability; Civil Litigation; Insurance Law.

**STEPHEN J. VALEN,** born Orange, California, December 5, 1962; admitted to bar, 1990, California, U.S. District Court, Northern District of California and U.S. Court of Appeals, Ninth Circuit. *Education:* University of California at Berkeley (A.B., 1986); University of Michigan (J.D., 1989). Associate and Notes Editor, Michigan Journal of International Law, 1987-1989. *Member:* Bar Association of San Francisco; Alameda County (Member, Litigation Section) and American Bar Associations; State Bar of California. **PRACTICE AREAS:** Civil Litigation; Toxic Substances; Product Liability.

**TROY D. MCMAHAN,** born Rapid City, South Dakota, April 22, 1964; admitted to bar, 1990, California, U.S. District Court, Northern District of California and U.S. Court of Appeals, Ninth Circuit; 1991, U.S. District Court, Central District of California. *Education:* University of Idaho (B.S. Finance, 1987); University of Utah (J.D., 1990). Leary Scholar, 1989. Note and Comment Editor and Staff Member, University of Utah, Journal of Contemporary Law, 1989-1990. *Member:* Bar Association of San Francisco; Alameda County and American Bar Associations; State Bar of

*(This Listing Continued)*

CAA1469B

### HARDIN, COOK, LOPER, ENGEL & BERGEZ,
*Oakland—Continued*

California. **PRACTICE AREAS:** Asbestos Litigation; General Civil Litigation.

**GAYLYNN RENEE KIRN,** born San Luis Obispo, California, April 25, 1967; admitted to bar, 1992, California, U.S. Court of Appeals, Ninth Circuit and U.S. District Court, Northern District of California. *Education:* University of California (B.A., 1989); McGeorge University of the Pacific (J.D., 1992). *Member:* Alameda County Bar Association; State Bar of California. **PRACTICE AREAS:** Products Liability; Civil Litigation; Insurance Law.

**RICHARD V. NORMINGTON III,** born Madison, Wisconsin, July 25, 1954; admitted to bar, 1983, Texas; 1987, California. *Education:* Pomona College (B.A., 1976); University of California at Los Angeles (M.P.H., 1980; J.D., 1983). *Member:* State Bar of Texas; State Bar of California. **PRACTICE AREAS:** Civil Litigation; Toxic Substance; Environmental Law.

**LISA M. BROWN,** born Billings, Montana, April 21, 1968; admitted to bar, 1993, California. *Education:* Rocky Mountain College; University of California at Berkeley (B.A., 1989); University of Minnesota (J.D., 1993); San Francisco State University. *Member:* Alameda County Bar Association; State Bar of California. **PRACTICE AREAS:** Civil Litigation; Products Liability; Toxic Torts.

**JASON J. CURLIANO,** born San Francisco, California, April 2, 1964; admitted to bar, 1993, California. *Education:* University of California at Davis (B.A., 1989); McGeorge School of Law (J.D., 1993). Member, Traynor Honor Society. *Member:* State Bar of California. **PRACTICE AREAS:** Workplace Sexual Harassment and Discrimination; Personal Injury Torts Defense; Products Liability Defense.

**RACHEL L. BARACK,** born Bethesda, Maryland, December 26, 1969; admitted to bar, 1994, California and U.S. District Court, Northern District of California. *Education:* University of California at Santa Barbara (B.A., 1991); Hastings College of the Law, University of California (J.D., 1994). Phi Delta Phi. Senior Products Editor, Hastings Constitutional Law Quarterly, 1993-1994. *Member:* State Bar of California. **PRACTICE AREAS:** Products Liability; Civil Litigation.

**LYNN S. SAMUELS,** born Houston, Texas, February 6, 1956; admitted to bar, 1981, Texas; 1990, California. *Education:* Duke University (B.A., 1978); University of Texas (J.D., 1981). *Member:* State Bar of California. **PRACTICE AREAS:** Insurance Litigation; Coverage Analysis and Litigation; Commercial Litigation.

**GARY S. ALEXANDER,** born Scottsdale, Arizona, September 26, 1966; admitted to bar, 1993, California and U.S. District Court, Northern District of California; 1994, U.S. Court of Appeals, Ninth Circuit. *Education:* Harvard University (A.B., 1988); University of San Francisco (J.D., 1993). McAuliffe Honor Society. Member, Law Review. Author: "When The Client Harasses The Attorney," 28 USF L. Rev. 715. Adjunct Professor, Legal Research and Writing, John F. Kennedy University, 1995—. *Member:* State Bar of California. **REPORTED CASES:** Medina v. Hillshore Partners 40 Cal App 4th 477. **PRACTICE AREAS:** Civil Litigation; Environmental Law; Product Liability.

**JAMES S. KNOPF,** born Washington, D.C., September 29, 1967; admitted to bar, 1995, California. *Education:* Dartmouth College (B.A., 1989); Cornell University (J.D., 1995). *Member:* State Bar of California. **PRACTICE AREAS:** Civil Litigation; Products Liability; Environmental Law.

**JONATHAN M. COHEN,** born Schenectady, New York, May 7, 1968; admitted to bar, 1993, California. *Education:* Washington University (B.A., 1990); Hastings College of the Law, University of California (J.D., 1993). Externship, Hon. Ming Chin. *Member:* State Bar of California. **PRACTICE AREAS:** Personal Injury; Products Liability; Insurance Defense.

OF COUNSEL

**RONALD A. WAGNER,** born Oakland, California, June 19, 1934; admitted to bar, 1960, California. *Education:* Stanford University (A.B., 1956; LL.B., 1959). Phi Beta Kappa. *Member:* Alameda County and American (Member, Section of Family Law) Bar Associations; The State Bar of California. (Certified Specialist, Family Law, The State Bar of California Board of Legal Specialization).

**RACHEL K. ANGRESS,** born Oakland, California, April 4, 1969; admitted to bar, 1994, California and U.S. District Court, Northern District

*(This Listing Continued)*

of California. *Education:* California State University, Sacramento (B.S., 1991); Hastings College of the Law, University of California (J.D., 1994). Phi Kappa Phi; Golden Key; Moot Court Board. Assistant Note Editor, Hastings International and Comparative Law Review, 1993-1994. *Member:* State Bar of California. **PRACTICE AREAS:** Family Law.

REPRESENTATIVE CLIENTS: Alexander & Alexander, Inc.; Bay Area Rapid Transit District; Bay Cities Joint Powers Ins. Authority; Bell Industries; Broadway Motors, Inc.; Brunswick Corporation; California Casualty Indemnity Insurance Exchange; Chevron Corp.; City of Piedmont; Coregis; Crum & Forster; Cumis Insurance Co.; Cuna Mutual Insurance Society; Diamond Shamrock; Dow Chemical Co.; DowElanco; East Bay Heart Surgery; Employers Reinsurance Corp.; Fireman's Fund Insurance Cos.; Hartford Insurance Co.; Hertz Corp.; Home Indemnity Co.; ICI Americas, Inc.; INA/CIGNA; Industrial Indemnity; Kaiser Foundation Health Plan, Inc.; Kaiser Foundation Hospitals; Kansa General Insurance Co.; Lloyds of London; Long's Drug Stores California; Los Angeles Raiders Football Team; Makita, USA, Inc.; Marriott Corp.; Maxus Energy Corp.; Mazda Motor of America, Inc.; Nissan Motor Corporation in USA; Oakland Scavenger Company; Peralta Junior College District; PPG Ind. Inc.; Rhone-Poulenc, Inc.; Rohm and Haas; Santa Fe Southern Pacific Corp.; S.C. Johnson, Inc.; Sherwin Williams Paint Co.; Solano-Napa Counties Electrical Workers Pension and Health and Welfare Trusts and the Alameda County Electrical Workers Pension Trust; Studios Architecture; Subaru of America, Inc.; The Permanente Medical Group, Inc.; Tokio Marine and Fire Insurance Co., Ltd; Unocal Corp.; Waste Management, Inc.; Weyerhaeuser Co.; Zeneca, Inc.

---

## CONSTANCE M. HOSEMANN
2101 WEBSTER STREET, SUITE 1760
**OAKLAND, CALIFORNIA 94612**
Telephone: 510-444-4941
Facsimile: 510-465-5985

*Estate Planning.*

FIRM PROFILE: *My entire client base is from my volunteer activities. I understand how 501(c)(3) organizations work. I understand their needs and understand the people who support these organizations.*

**CONSTANCE M. HOSEMANN,** born East Liverpool, Ohio, February 20, 1938; admitted to bar, 1990, California. *Education:* Ohio University (B.S., 1959); Golden Gate University (J..D, 1980). Member, United Methodist Church, Oakland California (Chair, Board of Trustees. *Member:* Alameda County and American Bar Associations. **PRACTICE AREAS:** Estate Planning.

---

## HOYT, MILLER & ANGSTADT
A PROFESSIONAL CORPORATION
915 FINANCIAL CENTER BUILDING
405 FOURTEENTH STREET
**OAKLAND, CALIFORNIA 94612**
Telephone: 510-893-0990
Fax: 510-930-7595

Walnut Creek, California Office: 1910 Olympic Boulevard, Suite 220.
Telephone: 510-930-9255. Fax: 510-930-7595.

*Labor Relations and Employment Law. Employee Benefits, Equal Employment Opportunity, OSHA and Public Employment Relations. Unlawful Termination, Business and Corporation Law.*

Ralph B. Hoyt
David Miller
Eric P. Angstadt

(For Complete biographical Data on all Personnel, see Professional Biographies at Walnut Creek, California)

---

## JOHNSTON, HORTON & ROBERTS
SUITE 1500, 1901 HARRISON STREET
**OAKLAND, CALIFORNIA 94612**
Telephone: 510-452-2133
Fax: 510-452-2280

*Federal and State Tax Law. Litigation, Estate Planning, Probate, General Business and Corporate Law.*

MEMBERS OF FIRM

**V. JUDSON KLEIN** (1933-1976).

**J. RICHARD JOHNSTON,** born Los Angeles, California, April 22, 1915; admitted to bar, 1939, California. *Education:* University of California

*(This Listing Continued)*

at Los Angeles (A.B., 1936); University of California (J.D., 1939). Order of the Coif. Instructor, Hastings College of The Law, San Francisco, 1948-1951. Lecturer, University of California School of Law, 1963-1964. Attorney, National Labor Relations Board, Washington, D.C., 1940; General Counsel's Office, U.S. Treasury Department, Washington, D.C. and Honolulu, Hawaii, 1941-1943. Special Attorney, Penal Division, Chief Counsel's Office, Bureau of Internal Revenue, San Francisco, 1946-1951. Member, 1961-1973 and President, 1968-1970, School Board, Lafayette School District. President, Boalt Hall Alumni Association, 1971-1972. *Member:* Alameda County and American (Member, Taxation Section) Bar Associations; State Bar of California (Member, Taxation Section: Member, 1951— and Chairman, 1962-1963, Bay Area Section on Taxation; Member, 1964-1968 and Chairman, 1968-1969, Committee on Taxation; Member, Taxation Advisory Commission, 1971-1976); Western Regional Bar Association (Member, 1967— and Chairman, 1969-1970, Revenue Service Liaison Committee); American College Tax Counsel. (Certified Specialist, Taxation Law, The State Bar of California Board of Legal Specialization). *PRACTICE AREAS:* Federal Tax Law; State Tax Law; Litigation; Probate; Estate Planning.

**NEIL F. HORTON,** born Chicago, Illinois, June 23, 1937; admitted to bar, 1962, California. *Education:* Grinnell College (B.A., 1958); Harvard University (LL.B., 1961). Law Clerk to Hon. Wm. T. Sweigert, U.S. District Court, Northern District of California, 1962-1964. Member, Tax Law Advisory Commission. *Member:* Alameda County (Director, 1981-1986 and President, 1985) and American (Member, Taxation Section; Member, Committee on Civil and Criminal Penalties, 1972-1973 and 1975—) Bar Associations; State Bar of California (Member, Taxation Section; Member, 1988-1991 and Chair, 1991, Commission of Judicial Nominees Evaluation). (Certified Specialist, Taxation Law and Probate, Estate Planning and Trust Law, The State Bar of California Board of Legal Specialization). *PRACTICE AREAS:* Federal Tax Law; State Tax Law; Litigation; Probate; Estate Planning.

**JAMES G. ROBERTS,** born Frankfurt, Germany, August 15, 1949; admitted to bar, 1979, California. *Education:* Brown University (A.B., with honors, 1972); Boalt Hall School of Law, University of California (J.D., 1979); Golden Gate University (L.L.M., taxation, 1992). Associate Editor, California Law Review, 1977-1979. Court Law Clerk, U.S. Court of Appeals, Ninth Circuit, 1979-1981. Author: "People v. Pettingill: The Independent State Ground Debate in California," 67 California Law Review 768 (1979). *Member:* Alameda County and American (Member, Taxation Section) Bar Associations; State Bar of California (Member, Taxation Section). *PRACTICE AREAS:* Business Law; Corporate Law.

*ASSOCIATES*

**MARGARET M. HAND,** born Los Angeles, California, May 13, 1960; admitted to bar, 1993, California. *Education:* University of California at San Diego (B.A., with honors, 1989); Boalt Hall School of Law, University of California (J.D., 1993). *Member:* Alameda County and American Bar Associations; State Bar of California. *PRACTICE AREAS:* Federal Tax Law; State Tax Law; Litigation; Probate; Estate Planning.

## MARJORY A. KAPLAN

THE ORDWAY BUILDING
ONE KAISER PLAZA, SUITE 1725
**OAKLAND, CALIFORNIA 94612-3612**
Telephone: 510-763-5611
Fax: 510-763-3430

*Family Law. Adoption and Guardianship.*

**MARJORY A. KAPLAN,** born Pittsburgh, Pennsylvania, February 21, 1948; admitted to bar, 1974, California and U.S. District Court, Northern District of California. *Education:* Chatham College (B.A., 1969); Hastings College of the Law, University of California (J.D., 1974). Phi Beta Kappa. Lecturer, Administrative Law, New College of the Law, 1974-1977. President, Board of Directors, Battered Women's Alternatives, 1982-1983. Member, Volunteer Legal Service Panel, 1986—. Member, Superior Court Committee of Domestic Violence, Death Review Subcommittee, 1995. *Member:* Alameda County Bar Association; State Bar of California; Alameda County Family Law Association (Board of Directors, 1990—). *PRACTICE AREAS:* Family Law; Adoption/Guardianship Law.

## KAY & MERKLE

OAKLAND, CALIFORNIA

(See San Francisco)

*Taxation, Entertainment, Professional Sports, Real Property, Business Litigation, Estate Planning and Probate Law.*

## KAZAN, McCLAIN, EDISES, SIMON & ABRAMS

A PROFESSIONAL LAW CORPORATION
Established in 1974
171 TWELFTH STREET, SUITE 300
**OAKLAND, CALIFORNIA 94607**
Telephone: 510-465-7728; 893-7211
TDD: (510) 763-8808
Fax: 510-835-4913
Email: postmaster@kmes.com

*Environmental and Industrial Disease Law, Asbestos Litigation, Catastrophic Injuries, Plaintiffs' Class Action Litigation, Workers Compensation, Longshore and Harborworkers' Litigation, Medical Malpractice, Medical Products Liability, Personal Injury and Federal Tort Law. Trials in all State and Federal Courts.*

**STEVEN KAZAN,** born New York, N.Y., September 1, 1942; admitted to bar, 1967, New York; 1969, U.S. Court of Appeals, Ninth Circuit; 1970, California and U.S. District Court, Northern District of California; 1971, U.S. Supreme Court; 1979, U.S. District Court, Eastern District of California; 1994, U.S. Court of Appeals, Third Circuit. *Education:* Brandeis University (A.B., 1963); Harvard University (LL.B., 1966). Assistant to General Counsel, Interstate Commerce Commission, Washington, D.C., 1967-1969. Assistant United States Attorney, Northern District of California, 1969-1971. Member, Asbestos Litigation Group, 1975—. *Member:* Alameda County, New York State and Federal Bar Associations; State Bar of California; Consumer Attorneys of California (Member, Board of Governors, 1980—; Parliamentarian, 1989; Vice-President, North, 1990; Recognized experience in the fields of Trial Lawyer, Professional Negligence, General Personal Injury and Products Liability Law); The Association of Trial Lawyers of America; Alameda-Contra Costa Trial Lawyers Association (Member, Board of Governors, 1975-1983; President, 1980). *TRANSACTIONS:* Plaintiffs' Class Counsel: Ahearn v. Fibreboard. Creditors Committees for: H.K. Porter; Celotex and Amatex. *Email:* kazan@kmes.com

**DAVID M. McCLAIN,** born Pasadena, California, August 20, 1947; admitted to bar, 1972, California and U.S. District Court, Northern District of California; 1981, U.S. District Court, Central District of California. *Education:* University of California at Los Angeles (B.A., 1969); Hastings College of Law, University of California (J.D., 1972). Member, Thurston Society. *Member:* The Bar Association of San Francisco (Member, Committee on Fee Disputes, 1978-1980); Alameda County Bar Association; State Bar of California; Consumer Attorneys of California (Sustaining Member); Alameda-Contra Costa Trial Lawyers Association (Member, Board of Governors, 1987—; Treasurer, 1993; Secretary, 1994; President Elect, 1995; President, 1996); California Attorneys for Criminal Justice; National Lawyers Guild; The Association of Trial Lawyers of America; Asbestos Litigation Group. *Email:* mcclain@kmes.com

**VICTORIA EDISES,** born Sacramento, California, November 11, 1951; admitted to bar, 1977, California and U.S. District Court, Northern District of California; 1991, U.S. Supreme Court. *Education:* University of California at Los Angeles (B.A., cum laude, 1973); Golden Gate University (J.D., 1977). Author: "EMF: Perhaps Tomorrow's Tort But Not Yet Today's," Environmental Law, Autumn, 1995. *Member:* State Bar of California; Alameda County Bar Association; Alameda-Contra Costa Trial Lawyers Association; Consumer Attorneys of California; California Applicants Attorney's Association. *REPORTED CASES:* General Foundry Service v. WCAB (Jackson), 42 Cal. 3d 331 (1986); Lustig v. Todd Shipyards Corp., 20 BRBS 207 (1988), aff'd 881 F.2d 593 (9th Cir. 1989); Baptist v. John's-Manville Corp., 137 Cal.App.3d 903 (1980); Berkebile v. Johns-Manville Corp. 144 Cal.App.3d 940 (1983); Steele v. Chevron, Inc., 219 Cal.App.3d

*(This Listing Continued)*

**KAZAN, McCLAIN, EDISES, SIMON & ABRAMS,** A
*PROFESSIONAL LAW CORPORATION, Oakland—Continued*

1265 (1990); Force v. Kaiser Aluminum and Chemical Corporation, 938 F.2d 981 (9th Cir. 1989).

**AARON H. SIMON,** born Cincinnati, Ohio, January 23, 1948; admitted to bar, 1975, California. *Education:* University of Cincinnati (B.A., with high honors, 1970); University of California at Los Angeles (J.D., 1975). Member, UCLA Law Review, 1974-1975. Author: "Draft Law: A Selective Bibliography," Law Library Journal, Vol. 64, No. 3, 1971. Co-Author: "Liver Failure Associated with Halothane," Medico-Legal Annual, 1977. *Member:* Alameda County Bar Association; State Bar of California; Alameda-Contra Costa Trial Lawyers Association (Member, Board of Governors, 1991—); Los Angeles Trial Lawyers Association (Member, Board of Governors, 1978-1984); Consumer Attorneys of California; The Association of Trial Lawyers of America.

**DENISE ABRAMS,** born Philadelphia, Pennsylvania, June 4, 1950; admitted to bar, 1986, California and U.S. District Court, Northern District of California. *Education:* University of Rhode Island (B.A., 1972); University of Maryland (M.A., 1975; Ph.D., 1983); Boalt Hall School of Law, University of California (J.D., 1986). *Member:* State Bar of California; American Bar Association; Alameda-Contra Costa Trial Lawyers Association (Board Member, 1990); Consumer Attorneys of California; The Association of Trial Lawyers of America; National Lawyers Guild; Trial Lawyers for Public Justice; Board Member, Santa Clara County Committee on Occupational Safety and Health (Chair, 1991—).

---

**FRANCIS E. FERNANDEZ,** born El Salvador, January 29, 1948; admitted to bar, 1975, California and U.S. District Court, Northern District of California. *Education:* San Francisco State University (B.S., 1971); Boalt Hall School of Law , University of California (J.D., 1975). Member, California Law Review. *Member:* State Bar of California (Member, Legal Services Trust Fund Commission, 1990-1994); Consumer Attorneys of California; Alameda-Contra Costa Trial Lawyers Association. *LANGUAGES:* Spanish.

**ANNE MICHELLE BURR,** born Whitefish Bay, Wisconsin, October 28, 1963; admitted to bar, 1992, California, U.S. District Court, Northern District of California and U.S Court of Appeals, Ninth Circuit. *Education:* University of California at Berkeley (B.S., 1985); Golden Gate University School of Law (J.D., with highest honors, 1991). Recipient, American Jurisprudence Award for Writing and Research, Constitutional Law and Criminal Procedure. *Member:* State Bar of California; Consumer Attorneys of California; Alameda-Contra Costa Trial Lawyers Association; Trial Lawyers for Public Justice.

**DIANNA J. LYONS,** born Reedley, California, September 27, 1945; admitted to bar, 1977, California and U.S. District Court, Northern, Southern, Central and Eastern Districts of California; 1984, U.S. Supreme Court; 1986, U.S. Court of Appeals, Ninth Circuit. *Education:* California State University, Stanislaus (B.A., 1966); California School of Law, Davis, University (J.D., 1977). Recipient, American Jurisprudence Award, Labor Law. *Member:* State Bar of California; Consumer Attorneys of California; Alameda-Contra Costa Trial Lawyers Association (Member, AFL-CIO Lawyers Coordinating Committee). *LANGUAGES:* Spanish.

**FRANCES C. SCHREIBERG,** born Cincinnati, Ohio, September 14, 1946; admitted to bar, 1972, New York; 1973, California; U.S. District Court, Northern District of California and District of South Dakota. *Education:* Northwestern University (B.A., 1968); New York University School of Law (J.D., 1972). Legal Professor: Juvenile Law, Supervised Criminal Law Clinic, University of San Francisco School of Law, Fall 1975 to Spring 1978. Labor Representative: Cal/OSHA Advisory Committee, 1989-1991; Cal/OSHA Advisory Committees for Asbestos, Lead, Ergonomics, Fall Protection, Injury and Illness Prevention Programs and ReBar Caps, 1984—. Co-Chair, Northern California Worksafe, 1984—. *Member:* State Bar of California (Member, Labor and Employment Law Section); National Lawyers Guild (Member, Labor Committee and Toxics Committee); Consumer Attorneys of California; Alameda-Contra Costa Trial Lawyers Association (Member, AFL-CIO Lawyers Coordinating Committee). *REPORTED CASES:* In Re Garcia 41 C.A. 3d 997 116 Cal. Rptr. 503 (1974); Henning v Division of Occupational Safety & Health 219 CA 3d 747, 268 Cal Rptr. 476 (1990); Agricultural Labor Relations Bd. v. California Coastal Farms, Inc. 31 CAL. 3d 469 (1982). *PRACTICE AREAS:* Occupational Safety and Health; Construction Accidents; Litigation; Toxic Torts.

*(This Listing Continued)*

**SIMONA A. FARRISE,** born Chicago, Illinois, November 14, 1965; admitted to bar, 1994, California. *Education:* DePaul University (B.S., Accounting, 1990); Golden Gate University (J.D., 1993). Recipient: DePaul University Dean's Award for Academic Excellence; Merit Scholar, Golden Gate University; Diana Richmond Scholarship; American Jurisprudence Award for Constitutional Law. *Member:* Charles Houston and Alameda County Bar Associations; State Bar of California; Alameda-Contra Costa Trial Lawyers Association; Consumer Attorneys of California; Trial Lawyers for Public Justice. *PRACTICE AREAS:* Personal Injury; Toxic Torts.

**RONALD J. SHINGLER,** born San Francisco, California, January 22, 1958; admitted to bar, 1989, California and U.S. District Court, Northern District of California. *Education:* California State University (B.A., in Criminal Justice and Communications, 1980); Golden Gate University (J.D., 1989). Author: "Antitrust Law and the Sports Relocation Rules," Golden Gate University Law Review, 1988. *Member:* Alameda County Bar Association; State Bar of California; Consumer Attorneys of California. *PRACTICE AREAS:* Asbestos Litigation (100%, 25).

**SUSAN S. OCHI,** born Ehime, Japan, October 14, 1962; admitted to bar, 1991, California; U.S. Court of Appeals, Ninth Circuit. *Education:* University of California at Berkeley (A.B., 1985); University of San Francisco (J.D., 1990). Recipient, American Jurisprudence Award, Research and Writing, 1987. *Member:* State Bar of California.

**TERRY GROSS,** born New York, N.Y., September 14, 1949; admitted to bar, 1989, California; U.S District Court, Northern District of California. *Education:* Queens College (B.A., 1971); University of California, Los Angeles (J.D., 1988). Extern, Judge Marilyn Hall Patel, 1988. Board Member, Berkeley Dispute Resolutions. *Member:* Alameda County Bar Association; State Bar of California; Alameda-Contra Costa Trial Lawyers Association.

*LEGAL SUPPORT PERSONNEL*

**ELIZABETH C. JOHNSON,** born Jamestown, New York, December 23, 1952. *Education:* College of William & Mary in Virginia (B.A., 1974); California State University (M.B.A., in Finance, 1989). English Instructor, Freshman Comp and Research Writing, City College of Philadelphia, 1975. Member, Association of Legal Administrators, 1989—; Golden Gate Chapter and East Bay Chapter, 1991—. (Director of Administration and Finance). *LANGUAGES:* German.

REFERENCE: Union Bank (Oakland Main Branch).

---

# JOHN M. KELSON

*SUITE 1340, ORDWAY BUILDING*

*ONE KAISER PLAZA*

**OAKLAND, CALIFORNIA 94612**

Telephone: 510-465-1326

Telecopier: 510-465-0871

*General Civil Trial and Appellate Practice.*

**JOHN M. KELSON,** born Detroit, Michigan, January 18, 1944; admitted to bar, 1971, Michigan; 1977, California and District of Columbia. *Education:* University of Michigan (A.B., with distinction, 1965); Harvard University (J.D., 1971). Author: "State Responsibility and the Abnormally Dangerous Activity," Harvard International Law Journal, Spring, 1972; "Sales Commission Agreements in the Oil Industry," Harvard Legal Commentary, Spring, 1970. Trial Attorney, U.S. Department of Justice, General Litigation Section, Civil Division, 1971-1977. *Member:* Bar Association of San Francisco; Alameda County Bar Association; State Bar of California.

REPRESENTATIVE CLIENTS: Bankers National Life Insurance Co.; California Couriers, Inc.; J.E.M. Restaurant Management Corp.; KMG International; Levi Strauss & Co.; Nationwide Mutual Insurance Co.; NEBI Leasing, Inc.; Petroleum Recycling Corp.; Jack B. Taylor & Associates; Valley Decorating Co.
REFERENCE: Civic Bank of Commerce.

## KENNEDY, GONG, MITCHELL & COMBS, LLP

1970 BROADWAY, 12TH FLOOR
**OAKLAND, CALIFORNIA 94612**
Telephone: 510-272-0433
Telecopier: 510-272-0579
Email: kgmc@hooked.net

*Real Estate, Land Use and Environmental Law, Construction, Financial Institutions, Bankruptcy, Public Finance, Redevelopment, Technology, Transfer, Business Trial and Appellate Practice.*

### MEMBERS OF FIRM

**MELVIN L. KENNEDY,** born Chicago, Illinois, August 27, 1940; admitted to bar, 1973, California, U.S. Court of Appeals, Ninth Circuit and U.S. District Court, Northern and Eastern Districts of California. *Education:* Morehouse College; Georgia Institute of Technology (B.S., with honors in Industrial Management and Computer Sciences, 1969); Stanford University (J.D., 1973). Beta Gamma Sigma. Assistant Director, San Francisco Lawyers Committee for Urban Affairs, 1976-1977. Contributing Editor to "Attorney's Guide to Damages" (CEB, 1984). Member, Committee for Protection of Human Subjects and standards review board Alta Bates/Herrick Hospitals. *Member:* Bar Association of San Francisco; Alameda County and American (Member, Sections on: Litigation; Tort and Insurance Practice and Economics of Law Practice) ) Bar Associations; State Bar of California; National Bar Associations; Charles Houston Bar Association.

**RAYMOND G. GONG,** born Richmond, California, January 25, 1948; admitted to bar, 1973, California and U.S. District Court, Northern District of California. *Education:* Stanford University (B.A., 1973); Boalt Hall School of Law, University of California at Berkeley (J.D., 1973); Golden Gate University (LL.M., Taxation, 1984). Chief Counsel, Pacific District of the Economic Regulatory Administration, U.S. Department of Energy, 1980-1984. *Contributor to A Lawyer's Manual on Community Based Economic Development,* published by the National Housing and Economic Development Law Project. *Member:* Alameda County Bar Association (Co-Chair State Bar Delegation); State Bar of California (Member, Environment Committee); Asian American Bar Association of the Greater Bay Area (President, 1983).

**WENDALL A. MITCHELL,** born Peru, Indiana, August 19, 1959; admitted to bar, 1985, California and U.S. District Court, Northern District of California. *Education:* Brandeis University (A.B., 1981); University of California at Berkeley (J.D., 1984). Earl Warren Scholar. Recipient, NAACP Legal Defense Fund, John W. Davis Award for excellence in Legal Scholarship. President and Director, Oakland Development Council, 1993-1994. Director, Lincoln Child Care Center, 1993—. Member, Oakland Chamber of Commerce, Planning and Construction Committee. *Member:* Alameda County, Contra Costa County and American Bar Associations (Member, Section on Natural Resources, Energy and Environmental Law); State Bar of California (Member, Sections on: Environmental Law and Real Property); National Bar Association (Member, Commercial Law Section); Charles Houston Bar Association; Rotary Club of Oakland.

**ROY A. COMBS,** born Rangoon, Union Of Burma, October 3, 1959; admitted to bar, 1986, California and U.S. District Court, Northern District of California; 1987, U.S. District Court, Eastern District of California; 1988, U.S. Court of Appeals, Ninth Circuit; 1991, U.S. Supreme Court. *Education:* University of California at Berkeley (B.A., 1982; J.D., 1985). *Member:* Alameda County and American (Member, Tort and Insurance Practice Section, Sections on: Natural Resources, Energy and Environmental Law; Forum Committee on Construction and Section on: Litigation) Bar Associations; State Bar of California; National Bar Association; Charles Houston Bar Association.

**JO-LYNNE Q. LEE,** born Cleveland, Ohio, November 15, 1949; admitted to bar, 1974, New York and U.S. District Court, Southern District of New York; 1978, California and U.S. District Court, Northern District of California. *Education:* Brooklyn College of the City University of New York (B.A., magna cum laude, 1969), Phi Beta Kappa; Columbia University (LL.B., 1974). Co-Author: *Pre-Trial Delay,* National Center for State Courts, 1976. *Member:* Alameda County Bar Association; State Bar of California; Asian-American Bar Association of the Greater Bay Area; American Bar Association.

**ERIC R. DEWALT,** born Memphis, Tennessee, October 14, 1949; admitted to bar, 1988, California; 1989, U.S. District Court, Northern District of California and U.S. Court of Appeals, Ninth Circuit. *Education:* University of Tennessee (B.A., 1972); Memphis State University (B.B.A.,

*(This Listing Continued)*

1985); University of San Francisco (J.D., 1988). Member, University of San Francisco Law Review, 1987-1988. Student Extern to Justice Allen E. Broussard, Supreme Court of California. *Member:* Alameda County and American Bar Associations; State Bar of California; National Bar Association; Charles Houston Bar Association.

### OF COUNSEL

**JOSEPH J. BRECHER,** born June 28, 1941; admitted to bar, 1966, New York; 1968, California; 1973, U.S. Supreme Court, U.S. Court of Appeals, Second, Ninth, Tenth and District of Columbia Circuits and U.S. District Court, Northern, Central and Eastern Districts of California. *Education:* Amherst College (B.A., cum laude, 1962), New York University (J.D., 1966). Instructor, Golden Gate University School of Law; Lecturer, Environmental Law for the American Bar Institute. Co-Author, *"Environmental Law Handbook,"* California Continuing Education of the Bar, (1970); Author: "The Public Interest and Intimidation Suits: A New Approach," 28 Santa Clara L. Rev. 105 (1988); "Venue in Conservation Cases: A Potential Pitfall for Environmental Lawyers," 2 Ecology Law Quarterly 91 (1972); "Federal Regulatory Statutes and Indian Self-Determination: Some Problems and Proposed Legislative Solutions," 19 Ariz. L. Rev. 285 (1977). Board of Trustees, California Indian Legal Services. City Attorney, City of Point Arena, 1993—. *Member:* Alameda County Bar Association. **LANGUAGES:** Spanish. **PRACTICE AREAS:** Environmental Law; Land Use Law; Consumer Law; High Technology Law.

REPRESENTATIVE CLIENTS: Alameda County Transportation Authority; Bank of America; Chevron Corp; Chevron Products, Inc.; City of Oakland; Del Monte Corp.; Frito-Lay, Inc.; Kaiser Foundation Hospital; Metropolitan Life Insurance Co.; Pacific Gas & Electric Company; Purina Mills, Inc.; San Francisco Bay Area Rapid Transit District; Selection Meilland; Shell Oil Company; Wells Fargo Bank; University of California/Lawrence Livermore Laboratory.

---

## EDWARD A. KENT, JR.

**OAKLAND, CALIFORNIA**

(See Palo Alto)

*Bankruptcy and Insolvency Law.*

---

## KING, SHAPIRO, MITTELMAN & BUCHMAN

**OAKLAND, CALIFORNIA**

(See Shapiro, Mittelman & Buchman, LLP, Walnut Creek)

---

## KNOX RICKSEN, LLP

LAKE MERRITT PLAZA
SUITE 1700, 1999 HARRISON STREET
**OAKLAND, CALIFORNIA 94612**
Telephone: 510-893-1000
Fax: 510-446-1946

*Fairfield, Solano County, California Office:* Corporate Plaza, Suite 300, 1261 Travis Boulevard, 94533. Telephone: 707-426-3313 . Fax: 707-426-0426.

*San Jose, Santa Clara County, California Office:* 100 Park Center Plaza, Suite 560, 95113. Telephone: 408-295-2828. Fax: 408-295-6868.

*General Civil and Trial Practice. Corporate, Real Estate, Land Use, Zoning and Urban Development and Environmental Law, Mergers and Acquisitions, Taxation, Probate, Trusts and Estate Planning, Conservatorships, Insurance and Medical Liability Defense, Energy Law, Public Utility and Regulatory Law.*

### MEMBERS OF FIRM

**WALLACE W. KNOX** (1905-1982).

**MARSHALL RICKSEN** (1908-1975).

**JOHN C. RICKSEN,** born Berkeley, California, November 20, 1931; admitted to bar, 1960, California. *Education:* University of California at Berkeley (A.B., 1953); Hastings College of Law, University of California (LL.B., 1959). Phi Delta Phi. Member, Hastings Law Journal, 1957-1959. *Member:* Alameda County and American Bar Associations; The State Bar

*(This Listing Continued)*

**KNOX RICKSEN, LLP,** Oakland—*Continued*

of California. *PRACTICE AREAS:* Estate Planning; Probate, Trust and Tax Law.

**RUPERT H. RICKSEN,** born Berkeley, California, November 20, 1931; admitted to bar, 1960, California. *Education:* University of California at Berkeley (A.B., 1953); Hastings College of Law, University of California (LL.B., 1959). Phi Delta Phi. Member, Thurston Honor Society. Member, Hastings Law Journal, 1957-1959. Arbitrator and Mediator, Alameda and Contra Costa Counties. *Member:* Alameda County Bar Association; The State Bar of California; Association of Defense Counsel of Northern California; American Arbitration Association; Center for Mediation. *PRACTICE AREAS:* Civil Trial; Insurance; Medical Liability Defense; Asbestos Litigation; Mediation; Arbitration; Products Liability.

**WILLIAM C. ROBBINS, III,** born Oakland, California, December 16, 1941; admitted to bar, 1966, California. *Education:* Yale University (B.A., magna cum laude, 1963); Boalt Hall School of Law, University of California (LL.B., 1966). Phi Delta Phi. *Member:* Alameda County and Solano County Bar Associations; The State Bar of California. (Also at Fairfield Office). *PRACTICE AREAS:* Real Estate Law; Zoning, Land Use Planning and Estate Planning.

**ROBERT G. ALLEN,** born Stockton, California, January 28, 1946; admitted to bar, 1971, California; 1972, U.S. Tax Court. *Education:* California State University, San Jose (A.B., 1967); University of Uppsala, Uppsala, Sweden; Hastings College of Law, University of California (J.D., 1970). Arbitrator, Business Panel, Alameda County Superior Court, 1982—. *Member:* Alameda County Bar Association; The State Bar of California. *PRACTICE AREAS:* Corporate; Real Estate and Probate Law.

**THOMAS A. PALMER,** born Akron, Ohio, March 9, 1942; admitted to bar, 1966, California. *Education:* University of California at Berkeley (B.A., with great distinction, 1963); Boalt Hall School of Law, University of California (LL.B., 1966). Phi Delta Phi; Phi Beta Kappa. State Bar Disciplinary Officer, 1982-1983. *Member:* Alameda County Bar Association (Fee Arbitrator, 1980-1985); The State Bar of California. [Capt., USAR]. *REPORTED CASES:* Lowell v. Mothers Cake & Cookie Co. 79 Cal. App. 3d 13. *PRACTICE AREAS:* Corporate; Securities; Mergers and Acquisitions; Business; Commercial and Real Estate Law; Civil Litigation.

**RICHARD G. LOGAN, JR.,** born Oakland, California, September 28, 1954; admitted to bar, 1979, California. *Education:* University of California at Berkeley (A.B., 1976); Hastings College of Law, University of California (J.D., 1979). Phi Delta Phi. *Member:* Alameda County Bar Association (Fee Arbitrator, 1984—); The State Bar of California. *PRACTICE AREAS:* Business and Commercial Litigation.

**JEFFREY A. HARPER,** born Oakland, California, January 11, 1947; admitted to bar, 1978, California. *Education:* University of California at Berkeley (B.A., 1968); Hastings College of Law, University of California (J.D., 1978). Arbitrator, Napa, Contra Costa and Solano Counties. *Member:* Alameda, Contra Costa and Solano County Bar Associations; State Bar of California; Association of Defense Counsel of Northern California; American Arbitration Association Center for Mediation (Mediator). [USAR, 1969-1975]. *PRACTICE AREAS:* Civil Trial and Insurance Defense.

**THOMAS E. FRAYSSE,** born San Francisco, California, March 13, 1956; admitted to bar, 1982, California. *Education:* University of California at Berkeley (B.A., 1978); McGeorge School of Law, University of the Pacific (J.D., 1982). Arbitrator, Alameda County. Judge Pro Tempore, Alameda County Municipal Court. *Member:* Alameda County Bar Association; State Bar of California; Association of Defense Counsel of Northern California; Northern California Fraud Investigators Association; Defense Research Institute. *PRACTICE AREAS:* Civil Trial; Insurance Defense and Asbestos Litigation.

**KENNETH G. HECHT, JR.,** born Evanston, Illinois, July 7, 1942; admitted to bar, 1969, Illinois; 1970, California. *Education:* University of the Pacific (B.A., 1964); University of Caen, France; Chicago-Kent College of Law (J.D., 1969). *Member:* Alameda County Bar Association; State Bar of California. *PRACTICE AREAS:* Real Estate; Employee Relocation; Corporate and Insurance.

**MARK L. CEDERBORG,** born Oakland, California, September 20, 1951; admitted to bar, 1979, California; 1980, Washington. *Education:* Seattle Pacific College (B.A., 1973); McGeorge School of Law, University of the Pacific (J.D., 1979). *Member:* Alameda County and Washington State Bar Associations; The State Bar of California. *PRACTICE AREAS:* Estate Planning; Probate and Trust Law; Conservatorships; Civil Trial Law and Asbestos Land Probate Litigation.

**GREGORY D. PIKE,** born New York, N.Y., April 13, 1960; admitted to bar, 1986, California; U.S. Court of Appeals, Ninth Circuit and U.S. District Court, Northern District of California. *Education:* University of California at Berkeley (B.S., 1982); Willamette University, College of Law (J.D., 1986). Omicron Delta Epsilon. Member, 1984-1985 and Senior Articles Editor, 1985-1986, Willamette Law Review. Judge Pro Tempore, Alameda County Municipal Court. Arbitrator, Alameda County. *Member:* Alameda County Bar Association; State Bar of California; The Association of Defense Counsel of Northern California; Northern California Fraud Investigators Association. *PRACTICE AREAS:* Civil Trial and Insurance Defense.

**THOMAS V. BRET,** born Los Angeles, California, September 18, 1949; admitted to bar, 1977, California; 1978, U.S. Tax Court. *Education:* University of San Francisco (B.S., 1971); Golden Gate University (J.D., 1977). Certified Public Accountant, California, 1977. Certified Financial Planner, College for Financial Planning of Denver, 1984. *Member:* Alameda County Bar Association; State Bar of California; California Society of Certified Public Accountants. *PRACTICE AREAS:* Taxation; Estate Planning and Probate, Trust Law.

**ANDREW J. SKAFF,** born Sioux Falls, South Dakota, August 30, 1945; admitted to bar, 1971, California; 1974, U.S. Supreme Court; 1975, U.S. Court of Appeals, Ninth and District of Columbia Circuits. *Education:* Miami University (B.S., 1967); University of Toledo (J.D., 1970). *Member:* Alameda County Bar Association; Los Angeles County Bar Association; The State Bar of California; Association of Transportation Practitioners; Conference of California Public Utility Counsel. *PRACTICE AREAS:* Energy Law; Regulatory Law; Public Utility Law; Business Litigation.

**KENNETH A. DREYFUSS,** born Stockton, California, March 9, 1952; admitted to bar, 1979, California. *Education:* University of California at Berkeley; Brandeis University (B.A., 1975); University of San Francisco (J.D., 1978). *Member:* Alameda County Bar Association; State Bar of California; Bar of the Supreme Court. *PRACTICE AREAS:* Civil Trial and Insurance Defense.

**HUBERT LENCZOWSKI,** born Berkeley, California, 1954; admitted to bar, 1981, California. *Education:* Harvard University (A.B., cum laude, 1975); Columbia University, School of International Affairs (M.I.A., 1977); Hastings College of Law, University of California (J.D., 1980). Clerk for the Honorable William P. Clark, Associate Justice, Supreme Court of California, 1980. *Member:* State Bar of California; American Bar Association. *LANGUAGES:* French. *PRACTICE AREAS:* Corporate; Securities; Business; Commercial; Real Estate; Trademark Law.

**KENNETH J. McCARTHY,** born San Francisco, California, June 25, 1957; admitted to bar, 1985, California. *Education:* San Jose State University (B.A., 1979); Lincoln University (J.D., 1984). *Member:* State Bar of California; Association of Defense Counsel of Nothern California; Defense Research Institute; American Association for the Advancement of Sciences; New York Academy of Sciences. *PRACTICE AREAS:* Civil Trial; Insurance Defense; Asbestos Litigation; Products Liability.

**R. PATRICK SNOOK,** born Oakland, California, December 30, 1958; admitted to bar, 1987, California. *Education:* University of California at Santa Cruz (B.A., with honors, 1984); Hastings College of the Law, University of California (J.D., 1987). *Member:* Solano County Bar Association; State Bar of California; Northern California Fraud Investigators Association; The Association of Defense Counsel of Northern California. *PRACTICE AREAS:* Civil Trial; Insurance Defense; Insurance Coverage.

**MARK C. SKILLING,** born Denver, Colorado, February 2, 1960; admitted to bar, 1986, California. *Education:* Colorado College (B.A., 1982); McGeorge School of Law (J.D., 1986); Golden Gate Law School (LL.M., 1994). Member, Contra Costa County Arbitrator's Panel. Judge Pro Tem, Alameda County Municipal Court. *Member:* Contra Costa County and American Bar Associations; The State Bar of California. *REPORTED CASES:* Rios v. Wagner, 4 Cal.App. 4th 608; Perez v. Smith 19 Cal.App. 4th 1595. *PRACTICE AREAS:* Civil Trial; Insurance Defense; Construction; Taxation and Appellate.

**JOHN S. BOAT,** born Jackson, Mississippi, July 19, 1967; admitted to bar, 1992, California. *Education:* Southern Methodist University (B.B.A., 1989); McGeorge School of Law (J.D., with distinction, 1992). Order of the Coif. Trainer Honor Society. Comment Writer, Pacific Law Journal. *Member:* Alameda County Bar Association; State Bar of California. *PRACTICE AREAS:* Corporate, Business, Zoning and Real Estate.

*(This Listing Continued)*

## ASSOCIATES

**JAMES T. GOTCH,** born Omaha, Nebraska, September 12, 1961; admitted to bar, 1986, California and U.S. District Court, Northern District of California. *Education:* University of Santa Clara (B.A., 1983; J.D., 1986); Creighton University. Honors Moot Court Board, 1985-1986; Semi-finalist Moot Court Competition, 1984. *Member:* Solano County Bar Association; State Bar of California. (Resident, San Jose Office). *PRACTICE AREAS:* Civil Trial Law; Insurance Defense Law; Dental Liability Defense Law.

**THOMAS H. LEMMON,** born Marin County, California, June 29, 1957; admitted to bar, 1985, California. *Education:* University of California at Berkeley (B.A., 1980); Western State University (J.D., 1984). Judge Pro-Tem, Alameda County Municipal Court. *Member:* State Bar of California; Northern California Fraud Investigators Association. *PRACTICE AREAS:* Civil Trial and Insurance Defense.

**TIMOTHY CASS MCKENZIE,** born Tulsa, Oklahoma, April 2, 1963; admitted to bar, 1992, California and U.S. Court of Appeals, Ninth Circuit. *Education:* University of Oklahoma (B.A., 1987); University of San Francisco (J.D., 1992). *Member:* Alameda County Bar Association; State Bar of California. *PRACTICE AREAS:* Civil Trial Construction and Insurance Defense.

**CHRISTINE A. CARRINGER,** born Atwater, California, April 10, 1954; admitted to bar, 1987, California and U.S. District Court, Eastern District of California. *Education:* Pennsylvania State University (B.A., 1974); McGeorge School of Law, University of the Pacific (J.D., 1987). Recipient, American Jurisprudence Award. *Member:* Solano County Bar Association; The State Bar of California; Solano County Women Lawyers; Association of Defense Counsel of Northern California. *PRACTICE AREAS:* Civil Trial; Insurance Defense.

**KAREN L. PETERSON,** born Santa Rosa, California, November 16, 1955; admitted to bar, 1988, California; U.S. District Court, Eastern, Northern and Southern Districts of California and U.S. Court of Appeals, Ninth Circuit. *Education:* University of California at Berkeley (A.B., 1985); University of San Francisco (J.D., 1988). Recipient, Comment of the Year Award, University of San Francisco, 1988. Member, University of San Francisco Law Review, 1986-1988. *Member:* Bar Association of San Francisco; State Bar of California. *PRACTICE AREAS:* Regulatory Law; Public Utility Law; Business Litigation.

**DENNIS EARL RAGLIN,** born Walnut Creek, California, May 13, 1970; admitted to bar, 1995, California. *Education:* University of California, Riverside (B.A., 1992); University of California, Davis (J.D., 1995). Phi Delta Phi. Roger J. Traynor, Moot Court Competition. Order of the Barrister. *Member:* Solano County and Sacramento County Bar Associations; State Bar of California. *PRACTICE AREAS:* Insurance Defense.

**CHRISTOPHER P. SWENSON,** born Concord, California, March 31, 1968; admitted to bar, 1994, California; 1996, New York; Illinois. *Education:* University of California at Berkley (A.B., 1990); Pepperdine University School of Law (J.D., cum laude, 1994). Pepperdine Law Review, 1992-1993. Extern, National Labor Relations Board, San Francisco, California, 1994. *Member:* Alameda County and American Bar Associations; State Bar of California (Member, Business Law Section). *PRACTICE AREAS:* Corporate Law; Business Transactions; Real Estate; Business Litigation.

**NICOLE BROWN YUEN,** born Berkeley, California, January 20, 1971; admitted to bar, 1996, California. *Education:* California Polytechnic State University (B.A., 1993); University of San Francisco (J.D., cum laude, 1996). Phi Alpha Delta. Member, University of San Francisco Law Review, 1994-1996.

**JENNIFER L. SIPES,** born Media, Pennsylvania, September 8, 1965; admitted to bar, 1992, California, U.S. District Court, Northern District of California. *Education:* University of California, Santa Barbara (B.A., 1988); University of Pacific, McGeorge (J.D., 1992). Omicron Delta Epsilon. *Member:* Contra Costa County Bar Association (Womans' and Real Estate Section); State Bar of California. *PRACTICE AREAS:* Business; Real Estate; Civil Litigation.

REPRESENTATIVE CLIENTS: Alameda Reuse and Redevelopment Authority; Albay Construction Co.; American Home Food Products Corp.; American Protective Services, Inc.; AM&S Trucking Co.; Asian Micro Sources, Inc.; Bay Alarm Co.; Bay Area Physical Therapy; Central Garden & Pet Co.; C.I.M. Industries, Inc.; Citibank; City of Brentwood; City of Pleasanton; Coldwell Banker Relocation Services, Inc.; Color Spot Nurseries; Combustion Engineering, Inc.; Conway Western Express; Devcon Corp.; East Bay Municipal Utility District; Electric Clearinghouse, Inc.; Electro-Test, Inc.; Embarcadero Physical Therapy, Inc.; Emerald Packaging Co.; Glidden Paint Company; Grant Laboratories, Inc.; Hoffman, Lewis, Mandelbaum, Mooney & Ashley; James River Corp.; J.T. Thorpe & Son, Inc.; Kaiser Foundation Hospitals; Kaiser Sand & Gravel; Levine-Fricke, Inc.; MacKay & Somps, Civil Engineers; Markstein Beverage Co.; Mason-McDuffie; Mother's Cake & Cookie Co.; Natural Gas Clearinghouse; New York Mercantile Exchange; Peralta Community College District; Permanente Medical Group; Power Star Products; Pump Repair Service Co.; Repro-Media, Inc.; Preservation Capital Corp.; Sea Tel, Inc; Seattle Systems; Scotts Restaurants; Sprint Spectrum, L.P.; Syar Industries Inc.; Technicolor, Inc.; The Beaver Foundation; Trauma Records; Washington Energy Gas Marketing Company.

REPRESENTATIVE INSURANCE CLIENTS: Allstate Insurance Co.; Automobile Club of Southern California; California State Automobile Assn.; Inter-Insurance Bureau; Cigna; Crum & Forster; Fireman's Fund Insurance Co.; Forum Insurance Co.; Grange Insurance Co.; Liberty Mutual Insurance Co.; Safeco Insurance Co.; Unigard Insurance Group.

---

## LAW OFFICES OF
## LYNN ANDERSON KOLLER

*JACK LONDON PARK BUILDING*
*SUITE 200*
*520 THIRD STREET*
**OAKLAND, CALIFORNIA 94607**
*Telephone: 510-893-5550*
*Fax: 510-893-5688*

*Tucson, Arizona Office:* Number 35, 810 North Camino Santiago. 85745. Telephone: 520-884-9044. Fax: 520-623-3003.

*Bankruptcy and Reorganization. General Civil Trial and Appellate Practice in all State and Federal Courts. Real Estate and Commercial Business Law. Civil Litigation.*

**LYNN ANDERSON KOLLER,** born Oakland, California, May 27, 1942; admitted to bar, 1969, California; 1972, U.S. Supreme Court. *Education:* Contra Costa College (A.A., 1963); San Jose State College (A.B., 1965); Boalt Hall School of Law, University of California (J.D., 1968). Listed in Best Lawyers in America. *Member:* Bar Association of San Francisco; Alameda County and American Bar Associations; The State Bar of California.

---

## KORNFIELD, PAUL & BUPP

*A PROFESSIONAL CORPORATION*
*Established in 1986*
*SUITE 800, LAKE MERRITT PLAZA*
*1999 HARRISON STREET*
**OAKLAND, CALIFORNIA 94612**
*Telephone: 510-763-1000*
*Fax: 510-273-8669*

*Bankruptcy and Reorganization. General Civil Trial and Appellate Practice in all State and Federal Courts. Commercial, Business, Construction, Banking, Probate and Corporate Law.*

FIRM PROFILE: *Kornfield, Paul & Bupp was established in 1986 by a merger of sole proprietorships. The firm was formed for the purpose of providing services in the bankruptcy and commercial litigation areas. A "full service" bankruptcy firm, the members represent debtors under all chapters of the code, creditors (secured and unsecured), creditors' committees and bankruptcy trustees, primarily in the Northern District of California. Litigation includes all bankruptcy related litigation, together with general commercial and real property litigation in local federal and state courts. The firm also provides services in alternative dispute resolution, with an emphasis on mediation.*

**IRVING J. KORNFIELD,** born Oakland, California, May 15, 1936; admitted to bar, 1963, California; 1975, U.S. Supreme Court, U.S. District Court, Northern, Eastern, Central and Southern Districts of California and U.S. Court of Appeals, Ninth Circuit. *Education:* University of California at Berkeley (B.S., 1958); Boalt Hall School of Law, University of California (J.D., 1962). Phi Beta Kappa; Order of the Coif; Phi Delta Phi. Lecturer in Bankruptcy, St. Mary's College Paralegal Program, 1983 and 1986; Member, Advisory Committee, 1988—. Member, Committee of Lawyers' Representatives, U.S. Bankruptcy Court, Northern District of California, 1988-1991. Listed in Best Lawyers in America, 1985-1996. Resolution Advocate, Bankruptcy Court for the Northern District of California, 1994—. *Member:* Bar Association of San Francisco (Member, Bankruptcy and Commercial Law Section); Alameda County (Member, Fee Arbitration Committee) and American Bar Associations; State Bar of California; California Bankruptcy Forum; Bay Area Bankruptcy Forum; American Bankruptcy Institute; National Association of Bankruptcy Trustees. Board Certified, Consumer Bankruptcy Law and Business Bankruptcy Law,

*(This Listing Continued)*

KORNFIELD, PAUL & BUPP, A PROFESSIONAL CORPORATION, Oakland—Continued

American Bankruptcy Board of Certification. *PRACTICE AREAS:* Bankruptcy Practice; Bankruptcy Law; Bankruptcy and Commercial Litigation.

**AARON PAUL,** born Wilmington, Delaware, June 30, 1934; admitted to bar, 1963, California and U.S. Court of Appeals, Ninth Circuit; 1974, U.S. Supreme Court and U.S. District Court, Northern and Central Districts of California. *Education:* University of Delaware (B.S., 1957); Hastings College of the Law, University of California (J.D., 1962). Member, Hastings Law Journal, 1960-1961. Lecturer, League of California Cities Continuing Education Seminars. *Member:* Bar Association of San Francisco (Member, Bankruptcy and Commercial Law Section); Alameda County Bar Association; State Bar of California; American Bankruptcy Institute; Northeast Bankruptcy Law Institute; Western Mountain Bankruptcy Law Institute; Norton Bankruptcy Litigation Institute; California Bankruptcy Forum; Bay Area Bankruptcy Forum. [With U.S. Army, 1956-1958]. *PRACTICE AREAS:* Bankruptcy Practice; Commercial Litigation.

**C. RANDALL BUPP,** born San Bernardino, California, January 30, 1950; admitted to bar, 1975, California and U.S. District Court, Northern and Eastern Districts of California; U.S. Court of Appeals, Ninth Circuit. *Education:* Cornell University (B.A., 1971); Hastings College of Law, University of California (J.D., 1975). Faculty Member, John F. Kennedy School of Law, 1981-1984. *Member:* Alameda County Bar Association; State Bar of California; Bar Association of San Francisco; Bay Area Bankruptcy Forum; American Bankruptcy Institute. *PRACTICE AREAS:* Bankruptcy Practice; Commercial Litigation; Financial Institution Representation Law.

**MERRIDITH A. SCHNEIDER,** born St. Louis, Missouri, July 8, 1952; admitted to bar, 1980, California and U.S. District Court, Northern and Eastern Districts of California. *Education:* University of Missouri; Indiana University (B.A., with honors, 1976); Golden Gate University (J.D., 1979). Mediation Training, ADRP, Inc. and Pepperdine University. *Member:* Bar Association of San Francisco; Alameda County Bar Association (Member: Fee Arbitration Committee; Client Conciliation Committee; ADR Section; Commercial Law and Bankruptcy Section); State Bar of California; California Bankruptcy Forum; Bay Area Bankruptcy Forum; American Bankruptcy Institute; Society of Professionals in Dispute Resolution; Northern District of California Bankruptcy Dispute Resolution Panel (Resolution Advocate). *LANGUAGES:* French. *PRACTICE AREAS:* Bankruptcy Practice; Reorganization Law; Business Law; Commercial Mediation.

**ERIC A. NYBERG,** born Oakland, California, September 3, 1958; admitted to bar, 1987, California, U.S. Court of Appeals, Ninth Circuit and U.S. District Court, Northern District of California; 1988, U.S. District Court, Eastern District of California; 1991, U.S. District Court, Southern District of California; 1992, U.S. District Court, Central District of California. *Education:* California State University at Hayward; St. Mary's College; San Francisco Law School (J.D., 1987). Author: "Bankruptcy Reform Act of 1994," Westland Review's Quick Guide to Foreclosure Law, 1995 Pacific 60. Mediator, Bankruptcy Dispute Resolution Program, United States Bankruptcy Court for the Northern District of California, 1994—. *Member:* Bar Association of San Francisco; Alameda County (Vice-Chair, Bankruptcy and Commercial Law Section, 1996) and American Bar Associations; State Bar of California; American Bankruptcy Institute; National Association of Bankruptcy Trustees; California Bankruptcy Forum; Bay Area Bankruptcy Forum. *PRACTICE AREAS:* Bankruptcy Practice; Bankruptcy and Commercial Litigation; Probate.

---

**CHARLES D. NOVACK,** born New York, New York, November 27, 1958; admitted to bar, 1984, New York; 1987, California. *Education:* Duke University; Rutgers College (B.A., with honors, 1980); University of California, Hastings College of the Law (J.D., cum laude, 1983). Phi Alpha Theta. Member, Hastings Law Journal, 1983. Legal Research and Writing Instructor, Hastings College of the Law, 1990-1994. Law Clerk to the Honorable Randall J. Newsome, U.S. Bankruptcy Court, 1991-1993. *Member:* Bar Association of San Francisco; Alameda County and New York State Bar Associations; State Bar of California. *PRACTICE AREAS:* Bankruptcy Practice; Bankruptcy Litigation; Commercial Litigation.

**CHRIS D. KUHNER,** born Oakland, California, February 15, 1968; admitted to bar, 1995, California. *Education:* University of California at Los Angeles (B.A., 1991); University of San Francisco (J.D., 1994). *Member:* Bar Association of San Francisco (Member, Bankruptcy and Commercial Law Section); Alameda County Bar Association (Member, Commercial

*(This Listing Continued)*

Law Section); State Bar of California; Barrister Club of San Diego (Member, Bankruptcy and Commercial Law Section). *LANGUAGES:* Spanish. *PRACTICE AREAS:* Bankruptcy; Commercial.

**GARETH M. CHOW,** born Boulder, Colorado, July 16, 1965; admitted to bar, 1994, California and U.S. District Court, Northern District of California. *Education:* University of California at Davis (B.S.; B.A., 1988); Santa Clara University (J.D., 1992; M.B.A., 1992). Law Clerk to the Honorable Arthur Weissbrodt, U.S. Bankruptcy Court, 1992-1995. *Member:* Bar Association of San Francisco (Member: Bankruptcy and Commercial Law Section; Barristers Club); Alameda County Bar Association (Member: Commercial Law Section; Barristers Club); State Bar of California. *PRACTICE AREAS:* Bankruptcy Practice; Business Law; Commercial Law; Real Estate Law.

REPRESENTATIVE CLIENTS: Admiral Insurance Co. (Cherry Hill, NJ); Kwik-Kopy Corp.; Magnolia Federal Bank; Sutter Mortgage Corp. (Walnut Creek, CA); Better Homes Realty, Inc. (Walnut Creek, CA); Civic Bank of Commerce (Oakland); Specialty Foods (Richmond, CA); City of Oakland (Oakland, CA); Sunnyside Nurseries, Inc.; The San Francisco Spiders.
REFERENCES: Sutter Mortgage Corp. (Walnut Creek, CA); Civic Bank of Commerce (Oakland); Admiral Insurance Co.; Kwik-Kopy Corp.

---

## SALLY J. LAIDLAW

405-14TH STREET, SUITE 710
OAKLAND, CALIFORNIA 94612-2706
Telephone: 510-891-3969
Fax: 510-891-3971

*Family Law.*

**SALLY J. LAIDLAW,** born Boise, Idaho, May 12, 1937; admitted to bar, 1970, California. *Education:* Swarthmore College; Idaho State College (A.B., high honors, 1959); University of California, Berkeley (J.D., 1969). Phi Sigma Alpha. Advisor, Principles of the Law of Family Dissolution, The American Law Institute. *Member:* Alameda County Bar Association (Chair: Legislation Committee, 1978; Board of Directors, 1979-1980); State Bar of California; Alameda County Democratic Lawyers (President, 1978); Lawyers Alliance for World Security; Women Lawyers of Alameda County. (Certified Specialist, Family Law, The State Bar of California Board of Legal Specialization). *PRACTICE AREAS:* Family Law.

---

## WAYNE A. LAMPERT

180 GRANT AVENUE, SUITE 1250
OAKLAND, CALIFORNIA 94612
Telephone: 510-834-0500
Fax: 810-835-1311

*Business and Corporate Law.*

**WAYNE A. LAMPERT,** born Midland, Texas, December 19, 1956; admitted to bar, 1984, Texas; 1989, California. *Education:* Washington University; University of Texas at Austin (B.A., with honors, 1979; M.B.A., 1984; J.D., 1984). *Member:* Alameda County and American Bar Associations; State Bar of Texas; State Bar of California; Fort Worth/Tarrant County Young Lawyers Association. *PRACTICE AREAS:* Business Representation; Real Property.

---

## LARSON & BURNHAM

A PROFESSIONAL CORPORATION

1901 HARRISON STREET, 11TH FLOOR
P.O. BOX 119
OAKLAND, CALIFORNIA 94604
Telephone: 510-444-6800
Fax: 510-835-6666

*General Civil and Trial Practice. Construction, Environmental, Insurance, Professional Liability, Tax, Estate Planning and Probate.*

FIRM PROFILE: *Larson & Burnham, formerly Moore, Clifford, Wolfe, Larson & Trutner, has provided general civil litigation and other services in Northern California for more than 75 years. Our office in Oakland is within a short distance of all San Francisco Bay Area courthouses. We are conveniently located for appearances in Alameda, Contra Costa, San Francisco, San Mateo, Santa Clara and Marin Counties as well as the U.S. District Court for the Northern District of California. We also regularly appear in Sacramento, Solano, Napa, Sonoma, San Joaquin and other state and federal courts in Northern and Southern California.*

*(This Listing Continued)*

**A. HUBBARD MOFFITT, JR.** (1908-1969).

**HOWARD S. RODE** (1907-1973).

**ARTHUR JAY MOORE, JR.** (1918-1984).

**DAVID O. LARSON,** born Modesto, California, September 9, 1935; admitted to bar, 1961, California. *Education:* Menlo College (A.A., 1955); Stanford University (B.A., 1957; LL.B., 1960). *Member:* Alameda County and American (Member, Sections on: Torts and Insurance Practice; Excess/Surplus; Litigation) Bar Associations; The State Bar of California; Alameda-Contra Costa Trial Lawyers Association; Association of Defense Counsel of Northern California; Defense Research Institute; International Association of Defense Counsel; American Board of Trial Advocates. Fellow: American Bar Foundation; International Academy of Trial Lawyers; American College of Trial Lawyers. *Email:* dlarson@larson-burnham.com

**CLARK J. BURNHAM,** born Berkeley, California, April 26, 1942; admitted to bar, 1968, California. *Education:* University of California at Berkeley (B.A., 1964); University of California at Los Angeles (J.D., 1967). Phi Delta Phi. *Member:* Alameda County Bar Association; The State Bar of California; National Health Lawyers Association. [Capt., U.S. Army, 1967-1969] *Email:* cburnham@larson-burnham.com

**GREGORY D. BROWN,** born Cowell, California, February 23, 1949; admitted to bar, 1975, California. *Education:* University of California at Berkeley (B.A., 1971); Golden Gate University (J.D., 1975). *Member:* Alameda County Bar Association; The State Bar of California; Northern California Association of Defense Counsel. *Email:* gbrown@larson-burnham.com

**GEORGE J. ZISER,** born Berkeley, California, February 10, 1947; admitted to bar, 1972, California. *Education:* University of California at Davis (A.B., 1968); Boalt Hall School of Law, University of California (J.D., 1971). Member, Moot Court Board, 1971-1972. *Member:* Contra Costa County, Alameda County and American Bar Associations; The State Bar of California. [Lt., JAGC, U.S. Navy, 1972-1975] *Email:* gziser@larson-burnham.com

**ROBERT J. LYMAN,** born New York, N.Y., May 3, 1948; admitted to bar, 1974, Arizona; 1977, U.S. Supreme Court; 1979, California. *Education:* Arizona State University (B.A., 1971; J.D., 1974). Arbitrator, Alameda County Superior Court, 1985—. *Member:* Alameda County and American Bar Associations; The State Bar of California; State Bar of Arizona; Association of Defense Counsel of Northern California; Alameda Contra Costa Trial Lawyers Association; Defense Research Institute. *Email:* rlyman@larson-burnham.com

**ERIC R. HAAS,** born Berkeley, California, October 2, 1951; admitted to bar, 1977, California. *Education:* Stanford University (B.A., 1973); Hastings College of Law, University of California (J.D., 1976). *Member:* Alameda County Bar Association; The State Bar of California. *Email:* ehaas@larson-burnham.com

**SCOTT C. FINCH,** born Berkeley, California, June 7, 1953; admitted to bar, 1978, California. *Education:* California Polytechnic State University (B.A., summa cum laude, 1975); McGeorge College of the Law, University of the Pacific (J.D., with distinction, 1978). *Member:* Alameda County Bar Association; The State Bar of California. *Email:* sfinch@larson-burnham.com

**STEVEN M. MARDEN,** born Portsmouth, Virginia, August 1, 1952; admitted to bar, 1978, California. *Education:* University of California at Santa Barbara (B.A., 1974); McGeorge College of the Law, University of the Pacific (J.D., 1978). Phi Alpha Delta. *Member:* Alameda County and Santa Clara County Bar Associations; The State Bar of California; Association of Defense Counsel. *Email:* smarden@larson-burnham.com

**RALPH A. ZAPPALA,** born Philadelphia, Pennsylvania, October 27, 1954; admitted to bar, 1981, California; 1988, U.S. Supreme Court. *Education:* Frostburg State College; Golden Gate University; San Francisco State University (B.A., 1976); International Law, Salzburg, Austria, 1979; McGeorge School of Law, University of the Pacific (J.D., 1981). *Member:* Alameda County and Alameda-Contra Costa County Bar Associations; The State Bar of California; The Association of Trial Lawyers of America; Federation of Insurance and Corporate Counsel. *Email:* rzappala@larson-burnham.com

**PETER DIXON,** born Merced, California, September 4, 1941; admitted to bar, 1966, California. *Education:* Stanford University (A.B., 1963); Hastings College of Law, University of California (LL.B., 1966). Phi Delta Phi. *Member:* Bar Association of San Francisco; Alameda County Bar Association; The State Bar of California; American Board of Trial Advocates; Association of Defense Counsel of Northern California. [Capt., JAGC, United States Army, 1967-1971] *Email:* pdixon@larson-burnham.com

**MONICA DELL'OSSO,** born Oakland, California, March 28, 1949; admitted to bar, 1982, California. *Education:* St. Mary-of-the-Woods College (B.A., summa cum laude, 1971); Boalt Hall School of Law, University of California (J.D., 1981); University of Virginia (Ph.D., 1989). Fellow, American College of Trust and Estate Counsel. *Member:* Alameda County (Estate Planning, Trust and Probate Law Section) and San Francisco County Bar Associations; The State Bar of California (Member, Executive Committee of Estate Planning, Trust and Probate Law Section). (Certified Specialist, Probate, Estate Planning and Trust Law, The State Bar of California Board of Legal Specialization). *Email:* mdell'osso@larson-burnham.com

**JEFFREY G. BAIREY,** born Sacramento, California, July 5, 1957; admitted to bar, 1983, California. *Education:* California Polytechnic State University; University of California at Berkeley (A.B., 1979); Hastings College of Law, University of California (J.D., 1983). *Member:* Alameda County Bar Association; The State Bar of California. *Email:* jbairey@larson-burnham.com

**SUSAN FELDSTED HALMAN,** born Santa Barbara, California, July 7, 1957; admitted to bar, 1983, California. *Education:* Duke University (B.S.N., 1979); University of Santa Clara (J.D., 1983). Associate Editor, Santa Clara Law Review, 1982-1983. Registered Nurse, California, 1979. *Member:* Alameda County Bar Association; The State Bar of California; Association of Defense Counsel of Northern California (Director, 1991-1993). *Email:* shalman@larson-burnham.com

**PATRICK K. M. MCCARTHY,** born Huntington, New York, May 4, 1948; admitted to bar, 1983, California. *Education:* University of California at Berkeley (B.A., 1975); San Francisco Law School (J.D., 1982). Chairman, William Tyler Moot Court, 1981-1982. *Member:* Alameda County Bar Association (Member, Board of Directors, 1988-1989); The State Bar of California; Barristers Club of Alameda County (President, 1988). *Email:* pmccarthy@larson-burnham.com

**GARY R. SELVIN,** born Waltham, Massachusetts, January 3, 1957; admitted to bar, 1983, California. *Education:* Occidental College (A.B., 1978); Hastings College of the Law, University of California (J.D., 1983). *Member:* Alameda County Bar Association; The State Bar of California; Association of Defense Counsel of Northern California. *Email:* gselvin@larson-burnham.com

**H. WAYNE GOODROE,** born Oswego, New York, May 25, 1943; admitted to bar, 1975, California; 1978, U.S. Supreme Court. *Education:* United States Naval Academy (B.S., 1965); California Western Law School (J.D., 1974). Phi Alpha Delta. Member, City of Oakland Citizens' Complaint Board, 1982. Commissioner, Port of Oakland Board of Port Commissioners, 1982-1987. *Member:* Alameda County and American Bar Associations; The State Bar of California. [With U.S. Navy, 1965-1971; Capt., USNR, 1971—] *Email:* hgoodroe@larson-burnham.com

**ROBERT A. FORD,** born Fort Worth, Texas, April 11, 1943; admitted to bar, 1968, Colorado; 1973, California; 1984, U.S. Supreme Court. *Education:* Texas Tech University (B.B.A., 1965); University of Colorado at Boulder (J.D., 1968). Phi Alpha Delta. Instructor, Personal Injury Litigation, St. Mary's College, 1982—. Arbitrator, San Francisco Superior Court, 1985—. Hearing Officer, San Francisco Retirement Board, 1986-1990. Member, Panel of Arbitrators, American Arbitration Association. *Member:* Bar Association of San Francisco; Alameda County and Colorado Bar Associations; The State Bar of California; California Trial Lawyers Association. [LCDR, JAGC, U.S. Navy, 1969-1973] *Email:* rford@larson-burnham.com

**DAVID R. PINELLI,** born San Francisco, California, August 4, 1952; admitted to bar, 1985, California. *Education:* University of San Francisco (B.S., 1975); San Francisco Law School (J.D., 1984). *Member:* Alameda County Bar Association; The State Bar of California. *Email:* dpinelli@larson-burnham.com

**MICHAEL R. REYNOLDS,** born Alameda, California, April 25, 1954; admitted to bar, 1981, California; 1994, U.S. Supreme Court. *Education:* California State University at Sonoma (B.A., 1977); San Francisco Law School (J.D., 1981). Recipient, American Jurisprudence Award for Corporations, 1980. Arbitrator, Alameda County Superior Court. *Member:* Bar Association of San Francisco; Alameda County and American Bar Associations; The State Bar of California; Association of Defense Counsel of Northern California; Defense Research Institute. *Email:* mreynolds@larson-burnham.com

*(This Listing Continued)*

**LARSON & BURNHAM, A PROFESSIONAL CORPORATION, Oakland—Continued**

**JAMES L. WRAITH,** born San Francisco, California, July 20, 1958; admitted to bar, 1983, California and U.S. District Court, Northern and Eastern Districts of California. *Education:* University of California at Berkeley (B.S., 1980); Hastings College of Law, University of California (J.D., 1983). *Member:* Alameda County Bar Association; The State Bar of California; Association of Defense Counsel. *Email:* jwraith@larson-burnham.com

**RICHARD J. FINN,** born New York, N.Y., January 9, 1952; admitted to bar, 1981, California. *Education:* New York University (B.A., Urban Studies; B.A: Politics, 1974); University of San Francisco (J.D., 1981). *Member:* Alameda County Bar Association; The State Bar of California; American Bar Association. *Email:* rfinn@larson-burnham.com

**JOHN J. VERBER,** born San Francisco, California, May 9, 1958; admitted to bar, 1989, California. *Education:* University of San Francisco (B.S., 1980; J.D., 1988); University of Texas at Houston (M.P.H., 1982). *Member:* The State Bar of California. *Email:* jverber@larson-burnham.com

**CATHY L. ARIAS,** born Torrance, California, May 22, 1964; admitted to bar, 1989, California. *Education:* University of California at Davis (B.A., 1986; J.D., 1989). *Member:* Alameda County and American Bar Associations; State Bar of California; California Young Lawyers Association. *Email:* carias@larson-burnham.com

**THOMAS M. DOWNEY,** born South Bend, Indiana, December 15, 1963; admitted to bar, 1989, California. *Education:* Ohio State University (B.A., 1986); University of Toledo (J.D., 1989). Recipient, American Jurisprudence Award, Legal Research and Writing. *Member:* Alameda County Bar Association; The State Bar of California. *Email:* tdowney@larson-burnham.com

**MICHAEL K. JOHNSON,** born Grand Haven, Michigan, March 18, 1961; admitted to bar, 1987, California. *Education:* Stanford University (B.A., 1983); Hastings College of the Law, University of California (J.D., 1987). *Member:* Alameda County Bar Association (Member, Litigation Section); The State Bar of California. *Email:* mjohnson@larson-burnham.com

---

**JOHN P. BEVAN,** born Pocatello, Idaho, February 2, 1954; admitted to bar, 1994, California. *Education:* University of Idaho (B.Arch., 1978); University of San Francisco (J.D., 199 4). Architect: Washington State, 1980; California, 1986. *Member:* State Bar of California. *Email:* jbevan@larson-burnham.com

**TARA D. BODDEN,** born New York, N.Y., June 15, 1967; admitted to bar, 1994, California. *Education:* Georgetown University (A.B., 1989); Sussex University, Brighton, England (M.A., 1991); Santa Clara University (J.D., 1994). *Member:* State Bar of California. *Email:* tbodden@larson-burnham.com

**CARYN BORTNICK,** born Kansas City, Missouri, November 20, 1956; admitted to bar, 1985, California; 1987, U.S. District Court, Northern and Eastern Districts of California; 1988, U.S., District Court, Southern District of California; 1989, U.S. Court of Appeals, Ninth Circuit; 1990, U.S. District Court, Central District of California. *Education:* Bradley University (B.A., 1980); Southwestern University School of Law (J.D., 1985). Recipient, American Jurisprudence Award, Insurance; Exceptional Achievement Health Care Provider's Law. *Member:* Bar Association of San Francisco; The State Bar of California; American Bar Association; Lawyers Club of San Francisco. *REPORTED CASES:* Industrial Indemnity v. Superior Court (1989), 209 Cal. App. 3d 1093. *Email:* cbortnick@larson-burnham.com

**PAUL D. CALEO,** born Melbourne, Victoria, Australia, January 25, 1962; admitted to bar, 1986, Victoria, Australia; 1991, California. *Education:* University of Melbourne (B.A., 1984; LL.B., 1984). Barrister and Solicitor of Supreme Court of Victoria, Victoria, Australia, 1986. *Member:* Alameda County Bar Association; The State Bar of California; Law Institute of Victoria. *Email:* pcaleo@larson-burnham.com

**JOHN D. COLOMBO,** born Bronx, New York, October 7, 1960; admitted to bar, 1990, California. *Education:* Arizona State University (B.S., 1987); Pepperdine University (J.D., 1990). Margaret M. Brock Scholarship. Moot Court Vice Chair, Honor Board, Pepperdine. *Member:* State Bar of California. *Email:* jcolombo@larson-burnham.com

*(This Listing Continued)*

**VERA C. DE MARTINI,** born San Francisco, California; admitted to bar, 1991, California. *Education:* University of Bordeaux, France; University of California, Davis (B.A., 1974); University of San Francisco (J.D., cum laude, 1991). Member, McAuliffe Honor Society. *Member:* Bar Association of San Francisco; Alameda County and American Bar Associations; The State Bar of California; The Association of Trial Lawyers of America. *LANGUAGES:* French. *Email:* vdemartini@larson-burnham.com

**MATTHEW G. DUDLEY,** born Seattle, Washington, September 13, 1969; admitted to bar, 1995, California. *Education:* University of Montana (B.A., 1992); Hastings College of the Law, University of California (J.D., 1995). *Member:* State Bar of California. *Email:* mdudley@larson-burnham.com

**PAMELA FASTIFF ELLMAN,** born San Francisco, California, December 16, 1964; admitted to bar, 1993, California. *Education:* Wellesley College (B.A., 1987); University of California Hastings College of the Law (J.D., 1992). Executive Editor, Hastings Constitutional Law Quarterly, 1992. *Member:* State Bar of California. *LANGUAGES:* French. *Email:* pellman@larson-burnham.com

**SUSAN E. FIRTCH,** born San Diego, California, May 30, 1955; admitted to bar, 1991, California. *Education:* San Diego State University (B.A., 1977); University of California School of Law, Davis (J.D., 1991). Recipient, American Jurisprudence Award for Debtor-Creditor Law. *Member:* Alameda County Bar Association; The State Bar of California. *Email:* sfirtch@larson-burnham.com

**DOUGLAS S. FREE,** born Boston, Massachusetts, September 25, 1963; admitted to bar, 1991, California. *Education:* Boston College (B.A., 1988); Santa Clara University (J.D., 1991). Comments Editor, Santa Clara University Computer and High Technology Law Journal, 1990-1991. *Member:* Alameda County and American Bar Associations; The State Bar of California. *Email:* dfree@larson-burnham.com

**BETH S. FREEDMAN,** born Boston, Massachusetts, August 2, 1968; admitted to bar, 1993, California. *Education:* University of California at Santa Clara (B.A., in English, cum laude, 1990); Santa Clara University (J.D., 1993). Recipient, American Jurisprudence Awards in Pleading and Civil Procedure and Family Law. Extern to the Honorable Judge D. Lowell Jensen, U.S. District Court, Northern District of California, 1992. *Member:* The State Bar of California. *Email:* bfreedman@larson-burnham.com

**ALISON F. GREENE,** born Mountain View, California, December 28, 1964; admitted to bar, 1990, California, U.S. District Court, Northern District of California and U.S. Court of Appeals, Ninth Circuit. *Education:* University of California at Davis (B.A., 1986); Hastings College of the Law, University of California (J.D., 1990). Judicial Extern to the Honorable William Channell, First District Court of Appeals, 1989. *Member:* Marin County Bar Association; State Bar of California; The Association of Defense Counsel. *LANGUAGES:* Hebrew. *Email:* agreene@larson-burnham.com

**ANNE COBBLEDICK GRITZER,** born Oakland, California, August 5, 1951; admitted to bar, 1993, Texas; 1994, California. *Education:* University of Texas, San Antonio (B.A., 1989); St. Mary's University School of Law (J.D., 1993). *Member:* State Bar of California. *Email:* agritzer@larson-burnham.com

**AYESHA Z. HASSAN,** born Chicago, Illinois, November 3, 1965; admitted to bar, 1990, California. *Education:* University of Chicago (B.A., 1987); University of San Diego (J.D., 1990). Phi Alpha Delta. *Member:* San Diego County Bar Association; The State Bar of California; San Diego Defense Lawyers; Barristers Club. *LANGUAGES:* French and URDU. *Email:* ahassan@larson-burnham.com

**JAMES F. HODGKINS,** born Oakland, California, October 6, 1961; admitted to bar, 1989, California. *Education:* University of California at Santa Barbara (B.A., 1984); McGeorge School of Law (J.D., 1989). Phi Delta Phi. *Member:* Alameda County and American Bar Associations; The State Bar of California; Bay Area Lawyers for Individual Freedom. *Email:* jhodgkins@larson-burnham.com

**NANCY E. HOOTEN,** born Sacramento, California, February 11, 1961; admitted to bar, 1989, California; 1990, Oregon; 1991, Washington. *Education:* California State University, Sacramento (B.S., 1985); McGeorge School of Law, University of the Pacific (J.D., 1988). *Member:* Alameda County (Member, Estate Planning, Trust and Probate Law Section), Washington State and American Bar Associations; The State Bar of California; Oregon State Bar. *Email:* nhooten@larson-burnham.com

**JULIE JARDINE,** born San Leandro, California, December 13, 1968; admitted to bar, 1995, California. *Education:* University of California at

*(This Listing Continued)*

Santa Barbara (B.A., 1992); University of San Diego (J.D., 1995). Phi Alpha Delta. *Member:* State Bar of California. *Email:* jjardine@larson-burnham.com

**JULIE HWANG KIM,** born Inchon, Korea, April 22, 1967; admitted to bar, 1995, California. *Education:* University of California, Davis (B.A., 1990); Santa Clara University (J.D., 1994). Associate Editor, Santa Clara Law Review, 1993-1994. *Member:* State Bar of California. *Email:* jkim@larson-burnham.com

**PETER LEO LAGASSE,** born Los Angeles, California, August 25, 1967; admitted to bar, 1995, California. *Education:* Southern Methodist University (B.S., 1989); Loyola Marymount University (J.D., 1993). *Member:* Alameda County Bar Association; Bar Association of San Francisco; State Bar of California. *Email:* plagasse@larson-burnham.com

**FRANK C. LIUZZI,** born San Francisco, California, January 11, 1966; admitted to bar, 1992, California. *Education:* Santa Clara University (B.S., 1988); University of San Francisco (J.D., 1991). *Member:* The State Bar of California. *Email:* fliuzzi@larson-burnham.com

**PELAYO ANTONIO LLAMAS, JR.,** born New Orleans, Louisiana, July 4, 1963; admitted to bar, 1992, California. *Education:* University of California at Berkeley (A.B., 1986); Santa Clara University (J.D., 1992). *Member:* State Bar of California. *Email:* pllamas@larson-burnham.com

**JOANNA MACQUEEN,** born London, England, September 20, 1957; admitted to bar, 1992, California. *Education:* Royal College of Music (B.A., 1978); University of San Francisco (J.D., 1991). *Member:* Bar Association of San Francisco; State Bar of California. *Email:* jmacqueen@larson-burnham.com

**RANDOLPH G. MCCALLA,** born San Jose, California, February 4, 1967; admitted to bar, 1995, California, U.S. District Court, Northern District of California and U.S. Court of Appeals, 9th Circuit. *Education:* University of California at Berkeley (B.A., 1989); University of California at Davis (J.D., 1995). Phi Delta Phi. Editor, University of California at Davis Law Review, 1994-1995. Extern to the Honorable Judge Melvin Brunetti, U.S. Court of Appeals, 9th Circuit, 1994. *Member:* State Bar of California. *Email:* rmccalla@larson-burnham.com

**MICHAEL T. MCKEEMAN,** born San Francisco, California, April 3, 1968; admitted to bar, 1994, California. *Education:* University of California, Berkeley (B.S., with high honors, 1991); Santa Clara University (J.D., magna cum laude, 1994). Phi Beta Kappa. Recipient: American Jurisprudence Award for Community Property; Emery Law Scholarship. *Member:* Alameda County Bar Association; The State Bar of California. *Email:* mmckeeman@larson-burnham.com

**STEVEN A. NIELSEN,** born San Diego, California, February 1, 1962; admitted to bar, 1988, California. *Education:* Chico State University (B.A., 1983); Santa Clara School of Law; Boalt Hall School of Law, University of California (J.D., 1987). Recipient: American Jurisprudence Award in Torts; Boalt Hall Prosser Prize in Finance and Accounting. Associate Editor, "Boalt Hall International Tax and Business Lawyer." *Member:* Alameda County Bar Association; The State Bar of California. *Email:* snielsen@larson-burnham.com

**GUSTAVO PEÑA,** born Hayward, California, September 30, 1966; admitted to bar, 1993, California and U.S. District Court, Northern District of California. *Education:* San Francisco State University (B.A., 1990); Hastings College of Law, University of California (J.D., 1993). Recipient, Moot Court Award, Best Oralist Argument. *Member:* The State Bar of California. *LANGUAGES:* Spanish. *Email:* gpena@larson-burnham.com

**NOREEN N. QUAN,** born Taipei, Taiwan, October 16, 1968; admitted to bar, 1994, California. *Education:* University of California, Berkeley (B.A., 1990); Santa Clara University (J.D., 1994). Recipient, Law Faculty Scholarship. Member, Santa Clara Inn, American Inns of Court, 1993-1994. *Member:* State Bar of California. *Email:* nquan@larson-burnham.com

**JAMES J. ROSATI,** born Sacramento, California, September 22, 1961; admitted to bar, 1989, California. *Education:* University of California at Santa Barbara (B.A., cum laude, 1984); Hastings College of the Law, University of California (J.D., 1989). Member, COMM/ENT, Hastings Journal of Communications and Entertainment Law, 1987-1988. *Member:* Bar Association of San Francisco; Alameda County Bar Association; The State Bar of California. *Email:* jrosati@larson-burnham.com

**STEPHEN Q. ROWELL,** born Tuskegee, Alabama, October 21, 1954; admitted to bar, 1981, California and U.S. District Court, Northern District of California. *Education:* University of California, Berkeley (A.B.,

*(This Listing Continued)*

1976); Hastings College of the Law, University of California (J.D., 1979). Contributing Author: "Insurance Law and Practice," 1986. *Member:* Alameda County Bar Association; The State Bar of California; Association of Defense Counsel of Northern California. *Email:* srowell@larson-burnham.com

**WALTER C. RUNDIN, III,** born Chicago, Illinois, February 12, 1949; admitted to bar, 1976, California and U.S. District Court, Northern District of California. *Education:* Loyola University; University of California, Berkeley (A.B., 1971); Hastings College of the Law, University of California (J.D., 1976). *Member:* Alameda County Bar Association; The State Bar of California. *Email:* wrundin@larson-burnham.com

**BRYAN K. STAINFIELD,** born Eugene, Oregon, October 19, 1960; admitted to bar, 1986, California. *Education:* University of California at San Diego (B.A., 1982); McGeorge School of Law, University of the Pacific (J.D., 1986). Member, California District Attorneys Association, 1987-1991. *Member:* The State Bar of California; Association of Defense Counsel of Northern California. *Email:* bstainfield@larson-burnham.com

**ANJALI TALWAR,** born India, 1966; admitted to bar, 1990, California. *Education:* University of California at Santa Barbara (B.A., 1987); Santa Clara University (J.D., 1990). Recipient, Faculty Law Scholarship, 1987, 1988 and 1989. Member, Honor Moot Court Board, 1989-1990. *Member:* Alameda County Bar Association; The State Bar of California. *Email:* atalwar@larson-burnham.com

**DARRELL T. THOMPSON,** born Walnut Creek, California, September 1, 1964; admitted to bar, 1992, California. *Education:* Brigham Young University (B.A., 1989); University of California at Davis (J.D., 1992). *Member:* State Bar of California. *LANGUAGES:* Spanish. *Email:* dthompson@larson-burnham.com

**SHAWN A. TOLIVER,** born London, England, January 31, 1961; admitted to bar, 1990, California. *Education:* Oral Roberts University (B.S., 1985); McGeorge School of Law, University of the Pacific (J.D., 1990). *Member:* Alameda County Bar Association; The State Bar of California; Pacific International Law Society. *Email:* stoliver@larson-burnham.com

**JEDEDIAH WAKEFIELD,** born San Luis Obispo, California, August 21, 1969; admitted to bar, 1995, California and U.S. District Court, Northern District of California. *Education:* University of California at Santa Barbara (B.A., 1992); Santa Clara University (J.D., cum laude, 1995). Phi Beta Kappa. *Member:* State Bar of California. *Email:* jwakefield@larson-burnham.com

**DAVID H. WATERS,** born Redwood City, California, April 5, 1951; admitted to bar, 1977, California and U.S. District Court, Northern District of California; 1980, U.S. District Court, Eastern District of California; 1983, U.S. District Court, Southern District of California. *Education:* University of California at Berkeley (A.B., with distinction, 1973); Hastings College of Law, University of California (J.D., 1977). Member: Order of the Coif; Thurston Society. *Member:* Bar Association of San Francisco; The State Bar of California. *Email:* dwaters@larson-burnham.com

**DAVID S. WEBSTER,** born Ramey A.F.B., Puerto Rico, July 2, 1965; admitted to bar, 1991, California and U.S. District Court, Northern District of California. *Education:* California State University, Chico (B.S., 1987); University of San Francisco (J.D., 1991). Recipient, American Jurisprudence Award in Constitutional Law I, 1989. *Member:* The State Bar of California. *Email:* dwebster@larson-burnham.com

**BRADLEY M. ZAMCZYK,** born Harvey, Illinois, June 12, 1963; admitted to bar, 1990, California. *Education:* University of California at Berkeley (B.A., 1985); Santa Clara University ( J.D., 1990). Recipient, School of Law Merit Scholarship. *Member:* Alameda County Bar Association; The State Bar of California. *Email:* bzamczyk@larson-burnham.com

**BARRY ZOLLER,** born Los Angeles, California, January 11, 1966; admitted to bar, 1992, California. *Education:* University of California at Berkeley (B.A., 1989); Santa Clara University (J.D., 1992). Moot Court Board, Santa Clara University. Recipient, American Jurisprudence Award in Insurance Law. *Member:* State Bar of California. *Email:* bzoller@larson-burnham.com

## OF COUNSEL

**JAMES H. RIGGS,** born Melrose, Massachusetts, October 21, 1924; admitted to bar, 1952, California. *Education:* University of California at Berkeley (A.B., 1949); Boalt Hall School of Law, University of California (LL.B., 1951). *Member:* Alameda County (Member, Estate Planning, Trust and Probate Law Section) and American (Member, Section on Real Property, Probate and Trust Law) Bar Associations; The State Bar of California

*(This Listing Continued)*

**LARSON & BURNHAM, A PROFESSIONAL CORPORATION,**
Oakland—Continued

(Chairman, Client Security Fund Committee, 1978). (Formerly a Member of Koford, McLeod & Riggs, Oakland, California); (Certified Specialist, Probate, Estate Planning and Trust Law, The State Bar of California Board of Legal Specialization. *Email:* jriggs@larson-burnham.com

GENERAL COUNSEL: Chan Miller Smith, Inc.; Goodwill Industries of the Greater East Bay, Inc.; Higgins Lumber Co.; Bay Point Control; Marina Heating & Air Conditioning; Folger Graphics; Wholesale Building Supply Co.
LOCAL COUNSEL: American Hardware Mutual; Argonaut Insurance Co.; Atlantic Mutual Insurance Co.; Cal Accountants Mutual Insurance Co.; Canadian Indemnity; Chrysler Insurance Co.; CNA Insurance Cos.; Cigna/INA; Cooper Industries, Inc.; Donaldson Co., Inc.; Farmers Insurance Group; Goodyear Tire & Rubber Co.; Home Insurance Co.; Lexington Insurance; OUM; PLCM; Scott Wetzel Services, Inc.; Shell Oil Co.; State Farm Fire & Casualty Company; Thomas Industries, Inc.; The Travelers Insurance Cos.; U.S. Fidelity & Guaranty Co.; Zenith Insurance Co.
REPRESENTATIVE COUNSEL: City of Alameda; County of Alameda; City of Livermore; Berkeley Unified School District; City of Oakland Housing Authority.

---

## LEMPRES & WULFSBERG

PROFESSIONAL CORPORATION

KAISER CENTER
24TH FLOOR, 300 LAKESIDE DRIVE
**OAKLAND, CALIFORNIA 94612**
Telephone: 510-835-9100
Telecopier: 510-451-2170

*San Francisco, California Office:* 1 Maritime Plaza, Suite 1600, 94111.

*General Civil and Trial Practice. Construction, Environmental, Insurance Coverage, Products Liability, Professional Liability, Real Estate, Corporate, Merger and Acquisition, Taxation, Estate Planning and Probate, Bankruptcy, Insolvency and Creditor's Rights Law.*

**DANIEL N. LEMPRES** (May 31, 1931 - March 19, 1987).

**H. JAMES WULFSBERG,** born Long Beach, California, May 24, 1944; admitted to bar, 1970, California. *Education:* University of Southern California (A.B., 1966); Boalt Hall, University of California (J.D., 1969). Phi Beta Kappa. *Member:* The Bar Association of San Francisco; Alameda County and American (Member: Forum Committee on the Construction Industry, 1980—; Public Contract Law Section; Tort and Insurance Law Section) Bar Associations; State Bar of California. Fellow, American College of Construction Lawyers (Member, Board of Governors, 1989-1992). *PRACTICE AREAS:* Construction Law; Insurance Coverage Law; Professional Liability Law.

**CHARLES W. REESE, JR.,** born San Antonio, Texas, June 21, 1944; admitted to bar, 1970, California; 1975, U.S. Supreme Court. *Education:* Washington & Lee University (B.A., cum laude, 1966); University of California at Berkeley (J.D., 1969). *Member:* Bar Association of San Francisco; Alameda County and American (Member, Forum Committee on the Construction Industry and Sections on: Corporations, Banking and Business Law; Real Property, Probate and Trust Law; Natural Resources Law; Taxation) Bar Associations; State Bar of California. *PRACTICE AREAS:* Environmental Law; Real Estate Law; Mergers and Acquisitions Law.

**PETER H. FERRIS,** born Ithaca, New York, May 25, 1950; admitted to bar, 1976, California. *Education:* Cornell University (B.A., cum laude, 1972); Boston University (J.D., cum laude, 1976). Editor, Boston University Law Review, 1974-1976. *Member:* Bar Association of San Francisco; Alameda County and American Bar Associations; State Bar of California; Defense Research Institute. *PRACTICE AREAS:* Insurance Coverage Law; Environmental Law; Professional Liability Law; Products Liability Law.

**JEFFREY A. SYKES,** born Columbus, Ohio, August 6, 1952; admitted to bar, 1977, California. *Education:* Kent State University (B.A., summa cum laude, 1974); The Ohio State University (J.D., cum laude, 1977). Trained Attorney Mediator. *Member:* Alameda County and American (Member: Litigation Section; Forum Committee, Construction Industry, 1981—) Bar Associations; State Bar of California; Association of Attorney Mediators. *PRACTICE AREAS:* Construction Law; Real Estate Law; Insurance Law; Surety Litigation.

**TIMOTHY A. COLVIG,** born Woodland, California, May 15, 1957; admitted to bar, 1984, California. *Education:* University of California at Davis (B.S., 1979); Boalt Hall School of Law, University of California

*(This Listing Continued)*

(J.D., 1984). Contributing Author: "Construction Contracts and Litigation 87," Practising Institute, 1987; "Construction Contracts and Litigation 1989," Practicing Institute, 1989; "Construction Subcontracting: A Legal Guide for Industry Professionals," John Wiley & Sons, Inc., 1991; "1992 Wiley Construction Law Update," John Wiley & Sons, Inc., 1992; "1996 Wiley Construction Law Update," John Wiley & Sons, Inc., 1996. *Member:* Alameda County and American Bar Associations; State Bar of California. *REPORTED CASES:* In re Foodsource, Inc., 130 B.R. 549 (N.D. Cal. 1991). *PRACTICE AREAS:* Environmental Law; Professional Liability Law; Insurance Coverage Law; Construction Law.

**ERIC J. FIRSTMAN,** born Santa Monica, California, September 4, 1957; admitted to bar, 1983, California. *Education:* University of California at Los Angeles (B.A., 1980); Hastings College of the Law, University of California (J.D., 1983). Co-Author: "Forms of Jury Instruction, Chapters on Construction Contracts, Real Property Sales, Common Counts for Indebtedness, Debt Collection, Torts," Matthew Bender & Company, 1989; "Mens-Rea: State of Mind Defenses in Criminal and Civil Fraud," Practicing Law Institute, November, 1985. Lecturer and Co-Author: "Construction Contracting for Public Entities," Lorman Educational Services Inc., 1995—; "Construction Liens in California", Lorman Educational Services, Inc. 1994—. Research Assistant, Wang, "Post-Chiarella Developments in Rule 10b-5," 15 Rev. Sec. Reg. 956, 1982. *Member:* Alameda County, Contra Costa County and American (Member, Sections on: Construction Law and Litigation) Bar Associations; The State Bar of California;. *PRACTICE AREAS:* Construction Law; Real Property Litigation.

**GREGORY R. AKER,** born Hackensack, New Jersey, July 7, 1953; admitted to bar, 1982, California and U.S. District Court, Northern, Southern, Eastern and Central Districts of California; U.S. Court of Appeals, Ninth Circuit. *Education:* University of Michigan (B.A., with honors, 1977); Hastings College of Law, University of California (J.D., cum laude, 1982). Member, Thurston Society. *Member:* Bar Association of San Francisco; Alameda County and American Bar Associations; State Bar of California (Member, Litigation Section). *PRACTICE AREAS:* Business and Commercial Litigation; Banking Law; Construction Law; Real Estate; Insurance Law.

**MATTHEW D. LEMPRES,** born San Francisco, California, February 19, 1957; admitted to bar, 1984, California. *Education:* Stanford University (A.B., 1979); University of California at Berkeley (M.B.A., 1984); Hastings College of Law, University of California (J.D., 1984). Contributing Author, *California Closely Held Corporations, Tax Planning and Practice Guide,* Matthew Bender & Company, Inc., 1987; *Alternative Dispute Resolution in the Construction Industry,* John Wiley & Sons, Inc., 1991. *Member:* The Bar Association of San Francisco; Alameda County and American Bar Associations; State Bar of California (Member, Business Law and Real Property Sections). *PRACTICE AREAS:* Business Law; Corporate Law; Real Estate Law.

**MARK A. STUMP,** born Galion, Ohio, October 15, 1956; admitted to bar, 1982, California. *Education:* Miami University (B.A., 1978); Boalt Hall School of Law, University of California (J.D., 1982). Phi Beta Kappa. *Member:* Alameda County and American Bar Associations; The State Bar of California. *REPORTED CASES:* Fireman's Fund Ins. Co. v Fibreboard Corp. (1986) 182 Cal. App. 3d 462: Guardino v. Santa Clara County Local Transportation Authority (1995) 11 Cal. 4th 462. *PRACTICE AREAS:* Insurance Coverage Law; Construction Litigation; Legal Malpractice.

**MOLLY J. BAIER,** born Walnut Creek, California, September 14, 1958; admitted to bar, 1984, California; 1986, U.S. District Court, Eastern and Northern Districts of California; 1987, U.S. Court of Appeals, Ninth Circuit. *Education:* Cornell College (B.A., magna cum laude, 1980); University of California at Davis (J.D., 1983). Phi Beta Kappa; Pi Sigma Alpha. Law Clerk, Ninth Circuit Bankruptcy Appellate Panels, U.S. Bankruptcy Court, Southern District of California, Honorable James W. Meyers, Chief Judge, 1985-1986. Deutsche Akademische Austauschdienst, Young Lawyer's Exchange Program, West Germany, 1983-1984. Faculty Member, Pacific Bankruptcy Law Institute, 1991-1995. *Member:* Bar Association of San Francisco (Member, Rules Committee, Bankruptcy Section, 1987; Chair, Region 17 US Trustee Guidelines Committee, 1990; Chair, Barristers' Club, Commercial Law and Bankruptcy Committee, 1991; Delegate, State Bar Conference of Delegates, 1991-1993); State Bar of California; American Bar Association; Bay Area Bankruptcy Forum (Director, 1996). (Certified Specialist, Business Bankruptcy Law, American Bankruptcy Board of Certification). *LANGUAGES:* German, Spanish. *REPORTED CASES:* Corman c. Morgan (In re Morgan), 197 B.R. 892 (N.D. Cal. 1996). *PRACTICE AREAS:* Bankruptcy; Creditors' Rights; Real Estate; Commercial Litigation.

*(This Listing Continued)*

**DAVID A. ROSENTHAL,** born New York, N.Y., February 16, 1960; admitted to bar, 1985, California. *Education:* Stanford University (A.B., 1982); Boalt Hall School of Law, University of California (J.D., 1985). *Member:* Bar Association of San Francisco; Alameda County and American Bar Associations; State Bar of California. *PRACTICE AREAS:* Corporate Law; Commercial Law; Real Estate Law; Estate Planning and Probate Law.

---

**CHARLES A. COBB,** born Richland, Washington, June 18, 1951; admitted to bar, 1978, California. *Education:* University of Oregon (B.B.A., 1973); Boalt Hall School of Law, University of California (J.D., 1978). Certified Public Accountant, California, 1975. *Member:* Alameda County and American Bar Associations; State Bar of California. *PRACTICE AREAS:* Real Estate Law; Corporate Law; Taxation Law.

**DAVID W. GINN,** born San Diego, California, June 1, 1959; admitted to bar, 1986, California, U.S. District Court, Northern District of California and U.S. Court of Appeals, Ninth Circuit. *Education:* University of California at Berkeley (B.A., 1981); Hastings College of Law, University of California (J.D., 1986). Instructor, Hastings College of Law Moot Court Appellate Advocacy Program, 1985-1986. Lecturer, Construction Liens in California, 1994-1996; Overview of California False Claims Act, 1996. *Member:* Alameda County and American Bar Associations; State Bar of California; International Council of Shopping Centers.

**MARK W. KELLEY,** born Portland, Oregon, August 22, 1955; admitted to bar, 1983, California, U.S. District Court, Northern District of California and U.S. Court of Appeals, Ninth Circuit; 1984, U.S. District Court, Southern and Eastern Districts of California. *Education:* Reed College (B.A., 1978); University of Oregon (J.D., 1983). Recipient, International Academy of Trial Lawyers Outstanding Advocate Award, 1983. *Member:* State Bar of California; American Bar Association. *PRACTICE AREAS:* Construction Law; Commercial Litigation; Alternative Dispute Resolution.

**TERRI ANN KIM,** born Los Angeles, California, June 10, 1947; admitted to bar, 1984, California. *Education:* University of California at Berkeley (B.A., 1968); Golden Gate University (J.D., 1983). *Member:* Alameda County and American Bar Associations; State Bar of California; Asian-American Bar Association; Women Lawyers of Alameda County. *PRACTICE AREAS:* Commercial Litigation; Construction Litigation.

**PAULETTE G. ANDREWS,** born Palo Alto, California, November 7, 1958; admitted to bar, 1989, California. *Education:* St. Mary's College of California (B.A., cum laude, 1984); Hastings College of the Law, University of California (J.D., 1988). *Member:* Alameda County Bar Association; State Bar of California; National Association of Women in Construction (Vice President, Contra County Chapter, 1995-1996). *LANGUAGES:* Spanish. *PRACTICE AREAS:* Litigation.

**STEPHEN L. CALI,** born Syracuse, New York, May 20, 1959; admitted to bar, 1988, California. *Education:* University of California at Berkeley (B.A., 1981); Golden Gate University (J.D., 1987). *Member:* Bar Association of San Francisco; Alameda County and American Bar Associations; State Bar of California. *PRACTICE AREAS:* Commercial; Construction; Legal Malpractice; Personal Injury; Property Damage; Civil Litigation.

**CAMERON C. WARD,** born Edmonton, Alberta, Canada, April 13, 1952; admitted to bar, 1976, Alberta; 1989, California. *Education:* University of Alberta (B.A., 1974; LL.B., 1975). *Member:* State Bar of California; American Bar Association. *PRACTICE AREAS:* Construction Litigation; General Litigation.

**WILLIAM L. DARBY,** born Winona, Minnesota, January 22, 1960; admitted to bar, 1988, California; U.S. Court of Appeals, Ninth Circuit; U.S. District Court, Northern, Southern and Eastern Districts of California. *Education:* Carleton College (B.A., cum laude, 1983); University of Minnesota (J.D., cum laude, 1987). *Member:* State Bar of California. *PRACTICE AREAS:* Construction Litigation.

**GILLIAN SMALL, G.M.,** born Georgetown, Guyana, South America, January 25, 1959; admitted to bar, 1992, California. *Education:* University of Akron (B.A., 1981); California State University, Hayward (M.P.A., 1987); University of California, Hastings College of the Law (J.D., 1992). Alpha Lambda Delta; Sigma Delta Pi, University of Akron. Hastings Law Journal, Note Editor; Charles Hamilton Houston Award-Frederick Douglas Moot Court Competition; Sadie T.M. Alexander Law Scholarship. *Member:* State Bar of California; Charles Houston Bar Association. *LANGUAGES:* Spanish. *PRACTICE AREAS:* Commercial Litigation; Insurance Coverage Litigation; Environmental Litigation.

*(This Listing Continued)*

## OF COUNSEL

**ROBERT L. HUGHES,** born Visalia, California, February 2, 1926; admitted to bar, 1958, California. *Education:* University of California at Berkeley (B.A., 1948); Hastings College of Law, University of California (LL.B., 1957). Contributing Editor, Dischargeability of Debt and Exemptions, Norton Bankruptcy Law and Practice, 1981. Author: "Chapter 13's Potential for Abuse," 58 North Carolina Law Review 831, 1980; "Code Exemptions: Far-reaching Achievement," 28 DePaul Law Review 1025, 1979; Contributions to CEB and PLI Course Books. Adjunct Lecturer: University of San Francisco, 1973-1974; Federal Judicial Center, 1974-1981. U.S. Bankruptcy Judge, Northern District of California, 1968-1984. Chief Judge, Ninth Circuit Bankruptcy Appellate Panels, 1979-1983. President, National Conference of Bankruptcy Judges, 1980-1981. Fellow, American College of Bankruptcy. *Member:* Bar Association of San Francisco; Alameda County and American Bar Associations; State Bar of California. Fellow, American Bar Foundation. *PRACTICE AREAS:* Bankruptcy Law; Insolvency Law; Creditors' Rights Law.

**BARBARA SUZANNE FARLEY,** born Salt Lake City, Utah, December 13, 1949; admitted to bar, 1976, California. *Education:* Mills College (B.A., with honors, 1972); Hastings College of Law, University of California (J.D., 1976). Recipient, Editorial Scholarship Award. Managing Editor, Hastings Constitutional Law Quarterly, 1976. Author: "Mary Carter/Sliding Scale Settlements and the Good Faith Standard," California Continuing Education of the Bar, Vol. VII, No. 7, October, 1985. National Business Institute Speaker, Estate Administration, June 1993. Extern Clerk to Justice Mathew O. Tobriner, California Supreme Court, 1975. Arbitrator: U.S. District Court, Northern District of California, 1981—; San Francisco Superior Court, 1985. Judge Pro Tem, San Francisco Municipal Court, 1984—. Probation Monitor, State Bar of California, 1990—. *Member:* Bar Association of San Francisco; Alameda County Bar Association; State Bar of California; San Francisco Trial Lawyers Association; California Trial Lawyers Association. *PRACTICE AREAS:* Business Litigation; Trust Law; Estates Law; Property Tax; Proposition 13.

**DIANNE K. BARRY,** born San Francisco, California, December 5, 1944; admitted to bar, 1971, California. *Education:* San Jose State University (B.A., 1968); University of San Francisco (J.D., 1970). Member: Board of Directors, 1977-1979, Environmental Law and Land Use Committee, 1976-1980, and Secretary and Treasurer, 1979, Order of Barristers. Delegate, State Bar Conference of Delegates, 1977-1986. *Member:* Bar Association of San Francisco (Member, Board of Directors, 1984-1986); State Bar of California. (Resident, San Francisco Office). *REPORTED CASES:* City and County of San Francisco v. Pace (1976) 60 Cal.App.3d 906; Pacello v. City and County of San Francisco, 85 Cal.App.3d 637; Russ Building Partnership v. City and County of San Francisco, 44 Cal.App.3d 839; Brydon v. East Bay Municipal Utility District (1994) 24 Cal.App.4th 178. *PRACTICE AREAS:* Construction Law; Public Entity Law; Public Contract Law.

REPRESENTATIVE CLIENTS: Brown and Caldwell; Certain Underwriters at Lloyd's of London; County of Alameda; County of Sonoma; East Bay Municipal Utility District; Eaton Corp.; Encon Group, Inc.; Evanston Insurance Co.; Ferma Corp; Fluor-Daniel Inc.; Fluor Constructors, Inc.; Hanson Industries; Hobart Corp.; Hyster-Yale Materials Handling Corp.; Kaiser Cement Corp.; Lassen Community College District; Longs Drug Stores; National Energy Production Co.; O'Brien Kreitzberg & Assoc.; Pacific Lightweight Products Co.; Port Costa Materials Co., Inc.; Richmond Unified School District; Shand Morahan & Co., Inc.; SCM Chemicals; City of Union City; United Enterprises; URS Engineers; VPS Companies; Vulcan-Hart Corporation; Westlake Development Co.; Zurn Industries.
REFERENCES: Mowat Mackie & Anderson; Union Bank.

---

## LEON & LEON
*2101 WEBSTER STREET, SUITE 1570*
**OAKLAND, CALIFORNIA 94612**
Telephone: 510-208-6600
Facsimile: 510-451-1010
Email: jleon@a.crl.com

*General Litigation Practice.*

FIRM PROFILE: *Leon & Leon was formed in 1993 by Heller, Ehrman and Morrison & Foerster alumni to offer sophisticated litigation representation at modest rates. The firm strives to provide efficient and attentive service with creative problem-solving including all forms of alternative dispute resolution. Recent representative engagements include lead defense counsel in several multimillion-dollar construction defects suits, products liability suits involving medical devices and other high-tech products and a wide variety of real estate,*

*(This Listing Continued)*

## LEON & LEON, Oakland—Continued

wrongful termination, environmental, insurance and unfair competition disputes.

**JEFFREY A. LEON,** born Warren, Ohio, July 28, 1956; admitted to bar, 1981, District of Columbia; 1982, California. *Education:* University of Virginia (B.A., with highest honors, 1978; J.D., 1981). Phi Beta Kappa; Order of the Coif. Virginia Law Review, 1979-1981. Author: "Contribution for Antitrust Co-defendants," 66 Virginia Law Review 797, 1980. Law Clerk to Hon. Norma Holloway Johnson, U.S. District Court, District of Columbia, 1981-1983. **PRACTICE AREAS:** Construction; Real Estate; Financial Institutions; Product Liability; Insurance; Intellectual Property and Environmental Matters.

**DEBORAH L. LEON,** born Richmond, Virginia, July 12, 1957; admitted to bar, 1982, California; 1984, District of Columbia. *Education:* University of Virginia (B.A., with high distinction, 1979; J.D., 1982). Phi Beta Kappa; Order of the Coif. Virginia Law Review, 1981-1982. **PRACTICE AREAS:** Civil Litigation; Insurance.

### OF COUNSEL

**JOHN C. MCCUTCHEN,** born Bethesda, Maryland, April 8, 1952; admitted to bar, 1977, District of Columbia; 1978, California. *Education:* Tulane University (B.A., cum laude, 1973); Catholic University of America (J.D., 1977). Author: "Standing to Sue in Federal Courts," Tulane University Law Review, 1977. **PRACTICE AREAS:** Construction Litigation; General Civil Litigation; Corporate Transactions.

REPRESENTATIVE CLIENTS: Circuit City Stores, Inc.; Albert Fisher, Inc.; Travelers Insurance Co.; Canandaigua Wine Company, Inc.; Pacesetter, Inc.; All West Coach Lines, Inc.; Prins Recycling Corp.; The Southern California & Arizona Glazier Pension Trust; Thermo Power, Inc.; Fireman's Fund Insurance Co.; Stratford Homes, Inc.; Siemens Corp.

---

## ANTHONY S. LEUNG

436 14TH STREET, SUITE 503
OAKLAND, CALIFORNIA 94612
Telephone: 510-452-9111

*Real Property.*

**ANTHONY S. LEUNG,** born Taosham, China, June 12, 1945; admitted to bar, 1987, California. *Education:* Seattle Pacific University (B.S., 1969); California State University at Fullerton (M.A., Chemistry, 1974); John F. Kennedy University (J.D., 1985). Student Representative, California State University at Fullerton Department of Chemistry, 1974. *Member:* State Bar of California. **LANGUAGES:** Cantonese, Mandarin.

---

## THOMAS G. LEWELLYN

2030 FRANKLIN STREET, 5TH FLOOR
OAKLAND, CALIFORNIA 94612
Telephone: 510-444-7530
Fax: 510-444-5027
Email: lewellyn@ccnet.com

*Personal Injury, Professional Negligence, Wrongful Termination, Legal Malpractice, Americans with Disabilities Act Law.*

**THOMAS G. LEWELLYN,** born San Francisco, California, November 15, 1951; admitted to bar, 1983, California and U.S. District Court, Northern District of California. *Education:* University of California at Berkeley (B.A., 1975); San Francisco Law School (J.D., 1983). Judge Pro Tempore, Superior Court, Santa Clara County, 1989-1993. Arbitrator, Superior Court, Santa Clara County, 1989-1993. Board Member, Santa Clara County Barristers Club, 1985-1986. Founding Board Member, Alameda County Barristers Club, 1984-1985. *Member:* Santa Clara County and Alameda County Bar Associations; State Bar of California; The Association of Trial Lawyers of America; Consumer Attorneys of California; Alameda County Trial Lawyers Association. **PRACTICE AREAS:** Personal Injury.

CAA1482B

---

## LICCARDO, ROSSI, STURGES & McNEIL

*A PROFESSIONAL LAW CORPORATION*

1999 HARRISON, SUITE 1300
OAKLAND, CALIFORNIA 94612
Telephone: 510-273-8740
Fax: 510-832-4432

San Jose, California Office: 1960 The Alameda, Suite 200. Telephone: 408-244-4570. Fax: 408-244-3294.

*General Trial and Appellate Practice. Personal Injury, Products Liability, Corporate, Real Property, Tort, Business, Condemnation, Tax, Estate Planning and Probate Law.*

**MARTHA LOUISE CARON** (Resident).

---

Deborah T. Bjonerud (Resident)    Daniel A. Hershkowitz (Resident)

---

A List of Clients will be furnished upon request.
REFERENCES: Pacific Western Bank; Plaza Bank.

(For Complete Biographical Data on all Personnel, see Professional Biographies at San Jose, California)

---

## LITTLER, MENDELSON, FASTIFF, TICHY & MATHIASON

*A PROFESSIONAL CORPORATION*

Established in 1942

1300 CLAY STREET, SUITE 1020
OAKLAND, CALIFORNIA 94612
Telephone: 510-873-8650
Facsimile: 510-873-8656
URL: http://www.littler.com

*Offices located in:* California -- Bakersfield, Fresno, Long Beach, Los Angeles, Menlo Park, Sacramento, San Diego, San Francisco, San Jose, Santa Maria, Santa Rosa and Stockton; Denver, Colorado; Washington, D.C.; Atlanta, Georgia; Baltimore, Maryland; Reno and Las Vegas, Nevada (a partnership with the Law Offices of Hicks & Walt); Morristown, New Jersey; New York, New York; and Dallas and Houston, Texas.

FIRM PROFILE: *Littler, Mendelson, Fastiff, Tichy & Mathiason is the largest law firm in the United States engaged exclusively in the practice of employment and labor law. The firm has over 250 attorneys in 23 offices nationwide who represent and advise management in all the major sub-specialities of employment and labor law including: wage and hour law; NLRB cases and collective bargaining; workers' compensation; sex, race, and age discrimination; wrongful termination; unemployment benefits; workplace violence; substance abuse; employee privacy rights; occupational safety and health; the ADA; ERISA, employee benefits, tax issues; and immigration.*

**CYNTHIA E. MAXWELL,** born Shreveport, Louisiana, September 4, 1958; admitted to bar, 1984, California. *Education:* Brown University (A.B., magna cum laude, 1980); University of California at Los Angeles (J.D., 1984). Phi Beta Kappa.

**THEODORA R. LEE,** born Dallas, Texas, July 22, 1962; admitted to bar, 1987, California. *Education:* Spelman College (B.A., cum laude, 1984); University of Texas at Austin (J.D., 1987).

---

**KEVIN A. MARKS,** born Neptune, New Jersey, February 17, 1967; admitted to bar, 1993, Pennsylvania and New Jersey (Not admitted in California). *Education:* Lafayette College (A.B., cum laude, 1989); Villanova University (J.D., 1993).

(For biographical data on personnel at other locations, see Professional Biographies at those cities).

## BARBARA D. LITTWIN

*1999 HARRISON STREET, SUITE 1300*
**OAKLAND, CALIFORNIA 94612**
*Telephone: 510-893-9736*
*Email: BDLITTWIN@AOL.COM*

*Family Law, Custody, Wills, General Practice.*

**BARBARA D. LITTWIN,** born New Haven, Connecticut, May 7, 1947; admitted to bar, 1972, California; 1975, U.S. District Court, Northern District of California. *Education:* Wellesley College (B.A., 1968); Hastings College of the Law, University of California (J.D., 1972). *Member:* Alameda County Bar Association; State Bar of California; Alameda County Women Lawyers; California Women Lawyers; Alameda County Bar Foundation (Board, 1991-1993, President, 1992). **PRACTICE AREAS:** Family Law; Custody Law; Wills.

---

## LAW OFFICES OF
## DOUGLAS E. LORD

*1999 HARRISON STREET, SUITE 2700*
**OAKLAND, CALIFORNIA 94612**
*Telephone: 510-834-8210*
*Fax: 510-273-8632*

*Plaintiff's Insurance Bad Faith, Insurance Coverage Litigation.*

**DOUGLAS E. LORD,** born Los Angeles, California, April 8, 1936; admitted to bar, 1964, California. *Education:* Stanford University (A.B., 1957); University of California Boalt Hall School of Law (J.D., 1963). *Member:* State Bar of California; Alameda/Contra Costa Trial Lawyers Association; Association of Trial Lawyers of America; Consumers Attorneys of California. **PRACTICE AREAS:** Plaintiffs Insurance Bad Faith; Insurance Coverage Litigation.

---

## LAW OFFICES OF
## WILLIAM P. LUCKE

*Established in 1972*

*3824 GRAND AVENUE*
**OAKLAND, CALIFORNIA 94610-1004**
*Telephone: 510-284-7881*
*Fax: 510-284-7886*

Piedmont, California Office: 536 Magnolia Avenue, 94611. Telephone: 510-652-5185. Fax: 510-652-5175.

*Civil and Business Litigation, Insurance, Environmental Law, Product Liability and Professional Negligence.*

**WILLIAM P. LUCKE,** born Oakland, California, December 8, 1942; admitted to bar, 1972, California, U.S. District Court, Northern District of California and U.S. Court of Appeals, 9th Circuit; 1977, U.S. Supreme Court; 1988, U.S. District Court, Eastern District of California; 1992, Colorado. *Education:* University of San Francisco (A.B., with honors, 1964); Hastings College of Law, University of California; Golden Gate College School of Law (J.D., 1971). Pi Sigma Alpha; Sigma Iota Sigma. *Member:* Bar Association of San Francisco; Alameda County, Contra Costa County (Member: Insurance Sections; Lawyers Assistance Program; Professional Stress, Drug and Alcohol Abuse Committee, 1981—) and American Bar Associations; State Bar of California; Association of Defense Counsel of Northern California; Defense Research Institute. **PRACTICE AREAS:** Civil and Business Litigation; Insurance and Environmental Law; Personal Injury; Product Liability and Professional Negligence; Employment Litigation.

REFERENCE: Wells Fargo Bank, Lafayette, CA.

---

## MARION'S INN

A Law Partnership
*Established in 1989*

*1611 TELEGRAPH AVENUE, SUITE 707*
**OAKLAND, CALIFORNIA 94612**
*Telephone: 510-451-6770*
*Fax: 510-451-1711*
*Email: marions@marionsinn.com*
*URL: www.marionsinn.com*

*Appellate Advocacy, Products Liability, Unfair Competition, Insurance Coverage, Professional Liability Defense, Employment, Real Estate, Construction and General Business Litigation.*

**PARTNERS**

Kennedy P. Richardson          Sam Walker
Mark A. Palley

**ASSOCIATES**

Albert Lee          Yvonne M. Pierrou

---

## MARLIN & SALTZMAN

*A PROFESSIONAL LAW CORPORATION*

*1999 HARRISON STREET, SUITE 990*
**OAKLAND, CALIFORNIA 94612**
*Telephone: 510-208-9400*
*Fax: 510-208-9410*

Woodland Hills, California Office: Westhills Plaza, 20700 Ventura Boulevard, Suite 227, 91364. Telephone: 818-702-0600. Fax: 818-702-6555.
Orange, California Office: 701 Parker Street, Suite 8800. Telephone: 714-541-1066. Fax: 714-542-4184.
San Diego, California Office: 750 "B" Street, Suite 1925. Telephone: 619-235-0600. Fax: 619-235-0675.

*Practice limited to Insurance Defense, Insurance Coverage and Bad Faith Litigation.*

(For complete biographical data on all personnel, see Professional Biographies at Orange, California)

---

## MARSHALL, AKAWIE & LaPIETRA

*PROFESSIONAL CORPORATION*

*ONE KAISER PLAZA, SUITE 1340*
**OAKLAND, CALIFORNIA 94612**
*Telephone: 510-874-7200*
*Telecopier: 510-874-7219*

Walnut Creek, California Office: 1981 North Broadway, Suite 330, 94596. Telephone: 510-947-4347. Telecopier: 510-947-6636.

*Real Property, Corporate Law, General Business, Real Estate and Business Litigation, Financing, Partnerships, Securities, Taxation and Estate Planning.*

**FIRM PROFILE:** The attorneys at our firm have many years experience in handling business and real estate matters. We are able to find creative and practical solutions to difficult problems, and to protect our clients' interests in tough negotiations. We care about our clients and value their long-term business and referrals.

**EDWARD T. MARSHALL,** born Detroit, Michigan, September 2, 1948; admitted to bar, 1976, California. *Education:* University of Michigan (B.A., with high honors, 1970); Boalt Hall School of Law, University of California (J.D., 1976). Order of the Coif. Articles Editor, California Law Review, 1975-1976. Real Estate Broker, California, 1980-1996. Author, "Down to Earth: Practice Tips for Real Property Lawyers," CEB Real Property Law Reporter, 1987-1996. Member, Rotary Club. *Member:* Alameda County Bar Association; State Bar of California (Member, Sections on: Real Property Law; Business Law). **PRACTICE AREAS:** Real Estate Law; Corporate and Business Law.

**ALICE L. AKAWIE,** born Los Angeles, California, October 1, 1954; admitted to bar, 1979, California and U.S. District Court, Northern District of California. *Education:* University of California at Los Angeles and University of California at Berkeley (A.B., 1975); Hastings College of Law, University of California (J.D., 1979). Member, Thurston Society. Author,

*(This Listing Continued)*

## MARSHALL, AKAWIE & LAPIETRA, PROFESSIONAL CORPORATION, Oakland—Continued

"Down To Earth-Practice Tips for Real Property Lawyers," CEB Real Property Law Reporter, 1989-1996. Co-Author, California Real Property Sales Transactions, 2d Edition, CEB, 1993. *Member:* Alameda County Bar Association; State Bar of California (Member, Real Property Law Section); Commercial Real Estate Women, San Francisco (President, 1992). National Network of Commercial Real Estate Women (Director of Communications, 1995). *PRACTICE AREAS:* Real Estate Law; Financing Law.

**LAUREN M. LAPIETRA,** born Sacramento, California, January 11, 1958; admitted to bar, 1983, California and U.S. District Court, Northern District of California. *Education:* University of California at Berkeley (A.B., with high honors, 1980); Boalt Hall School of Law, University of California (J.D., 1983). Phi Beta Kappa. Author, "Implications of the Integration Doctrine for the Financing of Real Estate Ventures Through the Formation of Loan and Equity Limited Partnerships," Real Estate Securities Journal, Vol. 4, No. 2, Spring, 1983. Author, "Down to Earth-Practice Tips for Real Property Lawyers," CEB Real Property Law Reporter, 1989-1996; Co-Author, California Real Property Sales Transactions, 2d Edition, CEB, 1993. *Member:* Alameda County Bar Association; State Bar of California. *PRACTICE AREAS:* Real Estate Law; Corporations; General Business Law.

### OF COUNSEL

**BRUCE G. PETERSON,** born Oakland, California, May 2, 1941; admitted to bar, 1977, California and U.S. District Court, Northern District of California; 1983, U.S. Tax Court. *Education:* University of California at Berkeley (B.S., 1963; M.B.A., 1967); Golden Gate University (J.D., with highest honors, 1976); New York University (LL.M., 1977). Adjunct Professor: Taxation of Partner and Partnerships, Golden Gate University School of Law, 1993—. Instructor: Tax Aspects of Real Estate Transactions, University of California Extension, 1985-1993; Legal Aspects of Real Estate, Merritt College, 1987-1993. Civil Engineer, California, 1973. *Member:* Alameda County and American Bar Associations; State Bar of California. *PRACTICE AREAS:* Taxation Law; Real Estate Law; General Business Law.

**GREGORY S. NERLAND,** born Stockton, California, January 29, 1965; admitted to bar, 1989, California, U.S. District Court, Northern District of California and U.S. Court of Appeals, 9th Circuit. *Education:* Dartmouth College (A.B., with honors, 1986); Hastings College of the Law, University of California (J.D., cum laude, 1989). Order of the Coif. Member, Thurston Society. *Member:* Contra Costa and American Bar Associations. (Resident, Walnut Creek Office). *PRACTICE AREAS:* Litigation; Business Law; Insurance Law.

REPRESENTATIVE CLIENTS: Argenta LLC's; Bradford Properties, Inc.; Dewey Land Company; Harbor Bay Realty; Invespar, Inc.; Intgra Health International; Lender Service Bureau; Maxim Property Management; Oakland Association of Realtors; Ophma Property Management; P.I.C., Inc.; Oliver & Company; The Prometheus Companies; Sequoia Equities, Inc.; Southern Alameda County Association of Realtors; Vintage & Jacinto Mortgage; West Contra Costa Association of Realtors.

## McDONOUGH, HOLLAND & ALLEN

*A PROFESSIONAL CORPORATION*

*Established in 1953*

**1999 HARRISON STREET, SUITE 1300**
**OAKLAND, CALIFORNIA 94612**
Telephone: 510-273-8780
Fax: 510-839-9104

*Sacramento, California Office:* 9th Floor, 555 Capitol Mall. Telephone: 916-444-3900. Fax: 916-444-8334.

*Yuba City, California Office:* 422 Century Park Drive, Suite A, P.O. Box 776. Telephone: 916-674-9761. Fax: 916-671-0990.

General Civil, Trial and Appellate Litigation, Local Government, Redevelopment, Construction, Eminent Domain, Employment, Environmental, Land Use, Health Care, International, Water, Toxics.

**NATALIE E. WEST,** born Greenwich, Connecticut, March 11, 1947; admitted to bar, 1974, California. *Education:* Smith College (A.B., 1968); Boalt Hall School of Law, University of California, Berkeley (J.D., 1973). City Attorney: City of Novato, 1985-1992; City of Berkeley, 1980-1985. Counsel for California Fair Political Practices Commission, Sacramento, 1975-1979. President, City Attorney's Department, League of California Cities, 1986-1987. Board of Directors, League of California Cities, 1996—. *Member:* Alameda County Bar Association; State Bar of California. *PRACTICE AREAS:* Public Agency Law; Land Use Law; Litigation. *Email:* natalie_west@mha.com

**CRAIG LABADIE,** born San Mateo, California, June 30, 1955; admitted to bar, 1981, California. *Education:* University of California at Berkeley (B.S., 1977); University of California at Davis (J.D., 1981). Order of the Coif. Editor, University of California at Davis Law Review, 1980-1981. Law Clerk to Associate Justice Stanley Mosk, California Supreme Court, 1981-1982. Member, Public Law Section, State Bar of California, 1989-1992. Chair, State Bar CEB, Joint Advisory Committee, 1994-1995. *PRACTICE AREAS:* Municipal Law; Land Use Law; Environmental Law. *Email:* craig_labadie@mha.com

**MICHELLE MARCHETTA KENYON,** born Los Angeles, California, May 12, 1957; admitted to bar, 1987, California and U.S. District Court, Eastern District of California. *Education:* University of California at Los Angeles; University of California at Berkeley (B.A., 1980); University of California at Davis (J.D., 1986). Law Clerk to the Hon. Raul A. Ramirez, U.S. District Court, Eastern District, 1987. *Member:* State Bar of California. *PRACTICE AREAS:* Public Law; Land Use; Litigation. *Email:* michelle_kenyon@mhalaw.com

---

**PAUL C. ANDERSON,** born Pasadena, California, December 28, 1964; admitted to bar, 1989, California; U.S. District Court, Northern and Central Districts of California; U.S. Court of Appeals, Ninth Circuit. *Education:* University of Notre Dame (B.A., 1986); Loyola University of Los Angeles (J.D., 1989). *Member:* Los Angeles County and American Bar Associations; The State Bar of California. *PRACTICE AREAS:* Real Estate Law; Land Use Law; Municipal Law. *Email:* paul_anderson@mhalaw.com

**MICHELLE RUDD,** born Culver City, California, December 5, 1963; admitted to bar, 1995, California. *Education:* Stanford University (B.S.C.E., 1985); University of California, Berkeley (Masters in City Planning, 1994; J.D., 1994). *Member:* State Bar of California. *PRACTICE AREAS:* Municipal Law. *Email:* michelle_rudd@mhalaw.com

REPRESENTATIVE CLIENTS: City of Hercules; Town of Moraga; City of Livermore; Stanislaus County; Emeryville Redevelopment Agency; Alameda Contra Costa Transit District; City of Mill Valley; City of Brentwood; City of Pacifica.

(For Complete Biographical Data on all Personnel, see Professional Biographies at Sacramento)

## McGUINESS & NORTHRIDGE

**1939 HARRISON STREET, 7TH FLOOR**
**OAKLAND, CALIFORNIA 94612**
Telephone: 510-273-8870
Fax: 510-273-8830

General Civil and Trial Practice. Family Law and Plaintiff Class Actions, Securities Litigation.

### MEMBERS OF FIRM

**ROBERT D. MCGUINESS,** admitted to bar, 1975, California. *Education:* University of Santa Clara (B.A., 1972); University of California at Los Angeles (J.D., 1975). Judge Pro Tem, Alameda County Superior Court, 1993—. Research Attorney, Sonoma County Superior Court, 1976-1977. *Member:* Alameda County Bar Association; The State Bar of California; California Trial Lawyers Association; Alameda-Contra Costa Trial Lawyers.

**YOLANDA N. NORTHRIDGE,** admitted to bar, 1979, California. *Education:* Holy Names College (B.A., 1967); Claremont Graduate School (M.A., 1974); University of San Diego (J.D., 1978). Lead Articles Editor, San Diego Law Review, 1977-1978. Judge Pro Tem, Alameda County Superior Court, 1992—. Chair, Alameda County Family Law Association, 1991-1996. *Member:* Alameda County (Member, Board of Directors, 1990-1991) Bar Association; The State Bar of California.

*(This Listing Continued)*

## McINERNEY & DILLON
*PROFESSIONAL CORPORATION*
Established in 1954
18TH FLOOR ORDWAY BUILDING
ONE KAISER PLAZA
**OAKLAND, CALIFORNIA 94612-3610**
Telephone: 510-465-7100
Facsimile: 510-465-8556

*Construction Law, Government and Public Contract Law, Administrative Law (including practice before Boards of Contract Appeals). Civil Litigation, Environmental Law, Employment Law, Corporation, Real Property, Estate Planning and Probate Law. Business and Commercial Trial Practice. Tax Planning and Tax Litigation.*

**WILLIAM H. McINERNEY,** born Los Angeles, California, October 5, 1924; admitted to bar, 1951, California, U.S. District Court, Northern District of California and U.S. Court of Appeals, Ninth Circuit; 1959, U.S. Supreme Court; 1982, U.S. Claims Court. *Education:* University of Santa Clara (B.S., cum laude, 1947); Boalt Hall School of Law, University of California (J.D., 1950). Member and Chairman, California Associated General Contractors Legal Advisory Committee, 1976. President, University of Santa Clara Alumni Association, 1962-1963. Regent, St. Ignatius High School, 1982—. Member and Chairman, Board of Directors, Hanna Home for Boys, 1975-1985. Member, California Public Works Contract Arbitration Panel. *Member:* Alameda County, Federal and American Bar Associations; State Bar of California (Member, Public Contract Law Section, Forum Committee on the Construction Industry); The Association of Trial Lawyers of America; American Arbitration Association (Member, Construction Industry Advisory Committee). **PRACTICE AREAS:** Construction Law.

**TIMOTHY F. WINCHESTER,** born Los Angeles, California, June 14, 1947; admitted to bar, 1972, California; 1976, U.S. District Court, Northern District of California; 1979, U.S. District Court, Eastern District of California. *Education:* University of California at Santa Barbara (A.B., 1969); University of California at Berkeley (J.D., 1972). Assistant Regional Counsel, U.S. Department of Housing and Urban Development, San Francisco, California, 1973-1976. *Member:* Alameda County Bar Association; State Bar of California.

**ROBERT L. LESLIE,** born Adak, Alaska, February 24, 1947; admitted to bar, 1974, California and U.S. District Court, Northern District of California; 1975, U.S. Tax Court and U.S. Court of Appeals, Ninth Circuit; 1979, District of Columbia; 1980, U.S. Supreme Court; 1982, U.S. Claims Court and U.S. Court of Appeals for the Federal Circuit. *Education:* United States Military Academy (B.S., 1969); Hastings College of Law, University of California (J.D., 1974). Registered Engineer-in-Training, Pennsylvania, 1969; California, 1974. Senior Trial Attorney, Contract Appeals, Department of Army, 1974-1980. Arbitrator, California Public Works Contract. Member, Associated General Contractors of California Legal Advisory Committee, 1987—. *Member:* National Panel of Arbitrators; Large Complex Construction Case Panel, American Arbitration Association. *Member:* State Bar of California; The District of Columbia Bar; Federal (Member, Committees on: Board of Contract Appeals, 1975—; Government Contracts, 1975—) and American (Member: Public Contract Law Section; Forum Committee on the Construction Industry) Bar Associations. [U.S. Army, 1969-1980; Col., U.S. Army Reserve, 1980—]

**WILLIAM H. McINERNEY, JR.,** born Oakland, California, April 1, 1952; admitted to bar, 1980, California and U.S. District Court, Northern District of California; 1984, U.S. Claims Court. *Education:* University of Santa Clara (B.S., 1974); University of Notre Dame (M.B.A., 1976); McGeorge College of the Law, University of the Pacific (J.D., 1980). Co-Author: Architect and Engineer Liability: Claims Against Design Professionals, 1988-1995 Supplement. Member, California Associated General Contractors Legal Advisory Committee, 1985-1995. Member, Board of Directors, 1980-1987 and President, 1985-1986, Bay Area Notre Dame Alumni Club. Member, Board of Directors, Hanna Boys Center, 1986-1995. *Member:* State Bar of California. [Maj., U.S. Army Reserve, 1974-1994]

**MICHAEL E. LONDON,** born San Francisco, California, March 15, 1951; admitted to bar, 1981, California; 1982, U.S. District Court, Northern, Eastern and Central Districts of California; 1984, U.S. Claims Court; 1985, U.S. Court of Appeals, Ninth Circuit. *Education:* University of Santa Clara (B.S.C.E., 1973); Stanford University (M.S.C.E., 1974); University of Santa Clara (J.D., 1981). Registered Engineer-in-Training, California, 1973. Co-author: Landslide and Subsidence Liability Supplement Continuing Education of the Bar, September, 1993. Consulting Associate Professor, Civil Engineering, Stanford University. Member, Construction Panel, National Panel of Arbitrators, American Arbitration Association. *Member:* State Bar of California (Member, Real Property Section).

---

**FRANKLIN H. YAP,** born Kingston, Jamaica, July 17, 1955; admitted to bar, 1982, California and U.S. District Court, Northern District of California. *Education:* McMaster University (B.Engr., 1977); Hastings College of Law, University of California (J.D., 1982). Licensed Professional Engineer, California, 1981. Co-Author: Architect and Engineer Liability: Claims Against Design Professionals, 1988-1992 Supplement. Extern, California Court of Appeals, District One, 1982. Member, Construction Panel of Arbitrators, American Arbitration Association. *Member:* State Bar of California; American Society of Civil Engineers.

**TIMOTHY L. McINERNEY,** born Oakland, California, September 6, 1961; admitted to bar, 1986, California; U.S. District Court, Northern and Eastern Districts of California; U.S. Claims Court. *Education:* University of Santa Clara (B.S., Civil Engineering, 1983); McGeorge School of Law (J.D., 1986). Registered Engineer-in-Training, California, 1983. *Member:* State Bar of California.

**CHARLES E. TOOMBS,** born Berkeley, California, June 29, 1951; admitted to bar, 1984, California and U.S. District Court, Northern District of California. *Education:* University of California at Berkeley (B.A., 1974); University of San Francisco (J.D., 1984); New York University (LL.M. in Taxation, 1987). Co-Author: "Tax Aspects of California Partnerships," 1989-1995 Supplement, California Continuing Education of the Bar. Contributing Author, "Selecting and Forming the Appropriate Entity," Business Starup Manual, California Continuing Education of the Bar. Consultant, Business Buy-Out Agreement, 2nd Edition, California Continuing Education of the Bar. *Member:* Alameda County Bar Association (Member, Taxation Section); State Bar of California. **PRACTICE AREAS:** Tax; Corporate Law; Real Estate.

**EAMONN P. CONLON,** born Kansas City, Missouri, February 12, 1961; admitted to bar, 1984, Ireland; 1987, California; 1988, U.S. District Court, Northern, Southern and Eastern Districts of California and U.S. Claims Court; 1990, U.S. Court of Appeals, Ninth and Federal Circuits and U.S. District Court, Central District of California; 1993, U.S. Supreme Court. *Education:* National University of Ireland (B.C.L. Honors, 1981; LL.M. Honors, 1983); Law School of The Honorable Society of Kings Inns, Ireland (Barrister-at-Law Honors, 1983). The Honorable Society of Kings Inns (Council, 1984-1986). *Member:* Alameda County and American (Member: Litigation Section; Forum Committee on the Construction Industry) Bar Associations; State Bar of California (Member, Sections on: International Law; Litigation). **PRACTICE AREAS:** Construction; Bankruptcy; Unfair Competition.

**WILLIAM A. BARRETT,** born San Francisco, California, August 25, 1941; admitted to bar, 1969, California and U.S. Court of Appeals, Ninth Circuit; 1978, U.S. Supreme Court; 1982, U.S. Claims Court. *Education:* University of San Francisco (B.S., 1964); Golden Gate University (J.D., 1968). Registered Contract Advisor, certified by the Sports Law Institute, University of Wisconsin Law School. Deputy City Attorney, City and County of San Francisco, 1969-1988. *Member:* San Francisco Bar Association (Member, Sports and Entertainment Law Section); State Bar of California (Member, Sections on: Litigation; Taxation and Business Law); Sport Lawyers Association. **PRACTICE AREAS:** Construction; Business Litigation; Athlete Representation.

**JEWELL J. HARGLEROAD,** born Auburn, California, June 1, 1958; admitted to bar, 1987, California; U.S. District Court, Northern and Eastern Districts of California; U.S. Court of Appeals, Ninth Circuit; 1993, U.S. Supreme Court. *Education:* University of California at Santa Cruz (B.A., 1981); University of San Francisco (J.D., 1987). Recipient, American Jurisprudence Award, Trusts and Estates. Member, University of San Francisco Law Review, 1986-1987. Author: Comment, "Punitive Damages: The Burden of Proof Required by Procedural Due Process," 22 University of San Francisco Law Review 99 (1987). Judicial Extern, California Supreme Court. *Member:* American Bar Association; State Bar of California. **LANGUAGES:** Spanish. **PRACTICE AREAS:** Business; Construction and Commercial Litigation; Constitutional; Political and Election Law.

**CAROL KNIGHT WATSON,** born Winnsboro, Texas, February 7, 1948; admitted to bar, 1987, California. *Education:* University of North Texas (B.A., 1969); University of California, Hastings College of Law (J.D., 1987). *Member:* Bar Association of San Francisco; Alameda County and

*(This Listing Continued)*

McINERNEY & DILLON, PROFESSIONAL CORPORATION,
Oakland—Continued

American (Member, Construction Forum) Bar Associations; State Bar of California. PRACTICE AREAS: Construction and Real Estate Litigation; Commercial Litigation.

QUINLAN S. TOM, born San Francisco, California, February 6, 1963; admitted to bar, 1989, California, U.S. District Court, Northern District of California and U.S. Court of Appeals, Ninth Circuit; 1990, U.S. District Court, Southern and Eastern Districts of California. Education: University of California at Davis (A.B., 1986); Hastings College of the Law, University of California (J.D., 1989). Member: State Bar of California; San Francisco Bar Association; Asian American Bar Association.

REPRESENTATIVE CLIENTS: Abbett Electric Co.; Alameda County Water District; Anderson Pacific Engineering Construction, Inc.; Anderson, Rowe & Buckley; N.L. Barnes Construction Co., Inc.; Black & Veatch; Corey Delta, Inc.; Corporate Travel; Dillingham Construction N.A., Inc.; Gallagher & Burke, Inc.; Granite Construction Company; Hanna Boys Center; Holy Names College; Impact Fastening Systems, Inc.; Independent Construction Co.; JWP West; Kiewit-Pacific Co.; Lamberson Koster & Co.; M.G.C. Co.; MJB Pipeline, Inc.; McGuire & Hester Co.; Modesto Irrigation District; Mountain Cascade Inc.; Natkin & Co.; J.V.; Oakland National Engraving Co.; Homer J. Olsen, Inc.; Pacific Mechanical Corp.; RGW Construction, Inc.; Rosendin Electric, Inc.; James E. Roberts-Ohbayashi Corp.; Scott Company of California; S&Q Corporation; Swinerton & Walberg Co.; Underground Construction Co., Inc.; Union Sanitary District; William P. Young, Inc.; University of California at Berkeley Foundation; J.W. McClenahan Co.; Power Engineering Contractors, Inc.

## McLEMORE, COLLINS & TOSCHI

200 WEBSTER STREET, SUITE 200
OAKLAND, CALIFORNIA 94607
Telephone: 510-835-3400
FAX: 510-835-7800

*General Civil Practice in all State and Federal Courts; Casualty Defense.*

GEORGE D. MCLEMORE, born Oakland, California, October 5, 1950; admitted to bar, 1978, California. Education: University of California at Santa Cruz (B.A., 1973); Golden Gate University (J.D., 1977). Member: Contra Costa County Bar Association; State Bar of California; Association of Defense Council of Northern California. PRACTICE AREAS: Casualty Defense.

WAYNE M. COLLINS, born San Francisco, California, April 20, 1945; admitted to bar, 1973, California. Education: University of California at Berkeley (B.A., 1968); Golden Gate University (J.D., 1973). Member: Alameda County Bar Association; State Bar of California; Association of Defense Council of Northern California. PRACTICE AREAS: Casualty Defense; General Civil Litigation; Construction Law.

STEVEN C. TOSCHI, born San Jose, California, September 2, 1961; admitted to bar, 1986, California. Education: University of California at Santa Cruz (B.A., 1983); McGeorge School of Law, University of the Pacific (J.D., 1986). Member: State Bar of California. PRACTICE AREAS: Casualty Defense.

GREGORY MICHAEL DOYLE, born Oakland, California, July 20, 1952; admitted to bar, 1980, California. Education: University of California at Berkeley (B.A., 1974); University of San Francisco (J.D., 1979). Member: Alameda County and American (Member, Tort and Insurance Practice Section) Bar Associations; The State Bar of California; Northern California Association of Defense Counsel; Saint Thomas More Society of San Francisco. PRACTICE AREAS: Insurance Defense; Litigation Defense; Construction Law (Defects).

IRENE TAKAHASHI, born San Francisco, California; admitted to bar, 1977, California and U.S. District Court, Northern District of California; 1978, U.S. District Court, Southern District of California; 1979, U.S. Court of Appeals, Ninth Circuit. Education: University of California at Berkeley (B.A., 1972); University of California at Davis (J.D., 1976). Deputy District Attorney, Alameda County, 1977-1978. Assistant U.S. Attorney, Southern District of California, 1978-1979. Deputy District Attorney, Contra Costa County, 1982-1988. Judge of the Municipal Court, Contra Costa County, 1988-1990. PRACTICE AREAS: Litigation Defense.

*(This Listing Continued)*

CAA1486B

JOEL P. FRANCIOSA, born New York, N.Y., January 30, 1950; admitted to bar, 1993, California. Education: St. Mary's College of California (B.A., 1972); John F. Kennedy University (J.D., 1992). Member: San Francisco and Alameda County Bar Associations. PRACTICE AREAS: Casualty Defense.

ALVIN D. HUNTER, born San Diego, California, January 31, 1954; admitted to bar, 1994, California. Education: University of California at San Diego (B.A., cum laude, 1976); Boalt Hall School of Law, University of California (J.D., 1979). Member: Alameda and San Francisco County Bar Association; State Bar of California. PRACTICE AREAS: Casualty Defense.

REBECCA WEISMAN, born Cincinnati, Ohio, December 1, 1963; admitted to bar, 1994, California. Education: Brandeis University (B.A., 1985); Golden Gate University (J.D., 1994). Editor, Women's Law Forum, Golden Gate University Law Review, 1993-1994. Author: "Reforms in Medical Device Regulation: An Examination of the Silicone Gel Breast Implant Debacle," Golden Gate University Law Review, 1993. Member: State Bar of California. PRACTICE AREAS: Insurance Defense.

CATHYE E. LEONARD, born Oakland, California, August 2, 1956; admitted to bar, 1995, California. Education: University of California (B.A., 1983); Golden Gate University (J.D., 1993). Member: State Bar of California; American Bar Association. PRACTICE AREAS: Insurance Defense.

REPRESENTATIVE CLIENTS: California State Auto Association; State Farm Insurance Co.; Farmers Insurance Group.

## McNAMARA, HOUSTON, DODGE, McCLURE & NEY

OAKLAND, CALIFORNIA
(See Walnut Creek)

*General Civil Trial Practice in all State and Federal Courts. Corporation, Insurance and Professional Liability Law, Municipal, Corporate, Real Estate and Education Litigation Practice.*

## DAVID J. MEADOWS

679 ARIMO AVENUE
OAKLAND, CALIFORNIA 94610
Telephone: 510-451-6410
Fax: 510-451-2651
Email: djmeadows@aol.com

*Mediation & ADR Services.*

DAVID J. MEADOWS, born Paris, France, January 24, 1953; admitted to bar, 1979, California; U.S. District Court, Northern District of California; U.S. Supreme Court. Education: Tufts University (B.A., 1974); Boalt Hall School of Law, University of California (J.D., 1979). Order of the Coif. Associate Editor, 1977-1978 and Executive Editor, 1978-1979, California Law Review. Author: Note, "The Involuntary Commitment of Minors: Where to Draw the Line on Parental Authority," 66 California Law Review 443, 1978. Law Clerk to Honorable Edward T. Gignoux, Chief, U.S. District Judge, District of Maine, 1979-1980. Member: Alameda County Bar Association; State Bar of California; Bar Association of San Francisco.

## MILLER, STARR & REGALIA

A PROFESSIONAL LAW CORPORATION
SUITE 1575, ORDWAY BUILDING
ONE KAISER PLAZA
OAKLAND, CALIFORNIA 94612
Telephone: 510-465-3800
Email: msr@msandr.com

*Walnut Creek, California Office:* 1331 North California Boulevard, Fifth Floor, P.O. Box 8177. Telephone: 510-935-9400.
*Sacramento, California Office:* 455 Capitol Mall, Suite 604. Telephone: 916-443-6700.

*(This Listing Continued)*

## PROFESSIONAL BIOGRAPHIES

*General Civil and Trial Practice. Real Estate, Zoning and Land Use, Environmental, Taxation, Securities, Commercial and Real Estate Finance, General Corporate, Bankruptcy, Reorganizations and Creditors Rights, Intellectual Property, Trusts, Title Insurance Practice.*

**VICTOR HARRIS,** born Los Angeles, California, December 25, 1946; admitted to bar, 1972, California; 1977, U.S. Supreme Court and U.S. District Court, Northern, Eastern and Southern Districts of California. *Education:* University of California at Berkeley (B.S., summa cum laude, 1968); Harvard University (J.D., cum laude, 1972). Phi Beta Kappa. Author: Comment, "Intervention in HEW Welfare Conformity Proceedings," 6 Harvard Civil Rights-Civil Liberties Law Review, 559 (1971). *Member:* Alameda County Bar Association; State Bar of California (Member, Business Law Section, Financial Institutions Committee); United Association of Equipment Leasing (Member, Board of Directors, 1996—). (Also at Walnut Creek Office). *PRACTICE AREAS:* Commercial Litigation; Commercial Transactions; Equipment Financing; Financial Institutions. *Email:* vh@msandr.com

**JAMES A. TIEMSTRA,** born Ridgewood, New Jersey, July 21, 1955; admitted to bar, 1980, California, U.S. District Court, Northern, Eastern, Central and Southern Districts of California, District of Arizona and District of Hawaii and U.S. Court of Appeals, Ninth Circuit. *Education:* Lawrence University (B.A., magna cum laude, 1977); Golden Gate University (J.D., 1980). Notes and Comments Editor, Golden Gate University Law Review, 1980. *Member:* Bar Association of San Francisco (Member, Commercial Law and Bankruptcy Section); American Bar Association (Member, Corporations, Banking and Business Law Section); American Bankruptcy Institute; Past President and Founding Director, Bay Area Bankruptcy Forum. (Certified in Business Bankruptcy Law by the American Bankruptcy Board of Certification). *PRACTICE AREAS:* Bankruptcy Law. *Email:* jat@msandr.com

**LEWIS J. SOFFER,** born Chicago, Illinois, April 14, 1949; admitted to bar, 1978, California. *Education:* Stanford University (B.A., with honors, 1971); University of California at Berkeley (M.B.A., 1978); Boalt Hall School of Law, University of California (J.D., 1978). *Member:* Alameda County Bar Association. *PRACTICE AREAS:* Real Estate Litigation; Title Insurance; Secured Lending; Financial Institutions. *Email:* ljs@msandr.com

**JOHN H. WUNSCH,** born Pomona, California, May 13, 1958; admitted to bar, 1983, Washington; 1988, California. *Education:* University of Washington (B.A. History, 1980); University of Washington School of Law (J.D., 1983). *Member:* Bar Association of San Francisco (Member, Bankruptcy and Commercial Law and Bankruptcy Section); Bay Area Bankruptcy Forum; American Bankruptcy Institute; California Mortgage Bankers Association; Building Owners and Managers Association. *PRACTICE AREAS:* Bankruptcy Law. *Email:* jhw@msandr.com

---

**Leslie E. Orr**

REPRESENTATIVE CLIENTS: Bank of the West; Hewlett Packard; Prometheus Development; First American Title Insurance Co.; Weyerhaeuser Co.

(For complete biographical data on all personnel, see Professional Biographies at Walnut Creek, California)

---

## MORTON, LULOFS & ALLEN

*A PROFESSIONAL LAW CORPORATION*

Established in 1977

ORDWAY BUILDING
ONE KAISER PLAZA, SUITE 801
**OAKLAND, CALIFORNIA 94612**
Telephone: 510-444-5521
Fax: 510-444-8263
Email: rmorton@ix.netcom.com

*Insurance Defense, Insurance Coverage and Bad Faith Litigation, Products Liability, Construction, Civil Trial, Real Estate.*

**WILLIAM R. MORTON,** born Sioux City, Iowa, April 16, 1944; admitted to bar, 1968, California. *Education:* University of Idaho (B.S., 1966; J.D., 1968). National Coordinating Counsel for Sunrise Medical, Inc. *Member:* Northern California Association of Defense Counsel; Federation of Insurance and Corporate Counsel; Defense Research Institute. *REPORTED CASES:* Tarasoff v. Regents of U.C. (1976) 17 Cal. 3d 425.

*(This Listing Continued)*

---

*PRACTICE AREAS:* ... Litigation.

**LARRY E. LULOFS,** ... bar, 1979, California. *Education:* ... 1971); University of California ... cisco (J.D., 1979). *Member:* ... California Association of ... *PRACTICE AREAS:* Civil ... Real Estate.

**ROGER F. ALLEN,** born ... ted to bar, 1977, California. ... 1968; M.A., 1971); Golden G... Gate Law Review, 1976-1... Costa County Bar Associa... fense Counsel. *PRACTIC*... sonal Injury; Mediation; ...

**G. GEOFFREY WOO**... ted to bar, 1983, Californ... sity, Pomona (B.A., w... 1983). *Member:* Alam... Association of Defense ... struction Law; Insuranc...

**TYLER G. OLPIN,** b... ted to bar, 1991, Californ... (B.A., with high honors ... 1985); University of Califor... Phi Beta Kappa. *Member:* ... California Association of D... ance Coverage; Civil Trial; Co...

**LISA S. KLOTCHMAN,** ... 1964; admitted to bar, 1990, Ca... at Berkeley (B.A., 1986); Univers... and Co-Chair, Committees on: Scho... Queen's Bench. *Member:* Bar Associa... County and American Bar Associations. ... *TICE AREAS:* Civil Rights; Civil Trial; Ins... jury.

**MICHAEL G. DINI,** born Burlingame, Californ... admitted to bar, 1992, California. *Education:* Univers... Davis (B.A., 1988); Santa Clara University (J.D., 1992). R... can Jurisprudence Award in Commercial Transactions. *Mem*... County Bar Association; Sonoma County Young Lawyers As... California Young Lawyers Association. *SPECIAL AGENCIES:* ... States General Accounting Office. *PRACTICE AREAS:* Civil Trial; In... ance Defense.

REPRESENTATIVE CLIENTS: Maryland Insurance Group; Unigard Insurance Group; Sunrise Medical, Inc. (principal subsidiaries Guardian Products, Inc. and Quickie Designs); State Farm Mutual Automobile Insurance Company; California State Automobile Association; California Insurance Guarantee Association; Horace Mann Insurance Company; Agency Rent-A-Car of Solon, Ohio; American States Insurance Company; Medmarc Insurance Company.

---

## PETER S. MYERS

4100-10 REDWOOD ROAD #331
**OAKLAND, CALIFORNIA 94619**
Telephone: 510-530-1593
Fax: 510-530-5272
Email: CBCG2@AOL.COM

*Business Law.*

**PETER S. MYERS,** born Utica, New York, June 16, 1960; admitted to bar, 1984, California. *Education:* The American University (B.A., 1981); University of California, Hastings College of the Law (J.D., 1984). Adjunct Faculty, Hastings College of Law, 1988-1990. Member, Board of Directors, Barristers' Club of San Francisco, 1993-1994. *PRACTICE AREAS:* Civil Practice; Business Law; Real Estate; Corporations.

MARTINDALE-HUBBELL LAW DIRECTORY 1997

*Education:* University of California at Berkeley (A.B., with highest honors, 1978) Regents Scholar; California State Scholar; McGeorge School of Law, University of the Pacific (J.D., 1983). Editor, *The Trial Notebook* and *The Postgraduate Course on Trial Practice,* California Trial Lawyers Association, 1982. Member, Academy of Rail Labor Attorneys, 1990-1991. Member, Association of Defense Counsel of Northern California. Lifetime Member, United Transportation Union, 1971—. *Member:* Alameda County Bar Association; Bar Association of San Francisco (Litigation Section) The State Bar of California (Litigation Section); California Trial Lawyers Association; San Francisco Trial Lawyers Association.

**GARY A. HALL,** born Syracuse, New York, October 31, 1946; admitted to bar, 1975, Virginia and District of Columbia; 1985, California. *Education:* Syracuse University; George Washington University (J.D., 1974). Instructor: J.F. Kennedy School of Law, 1989-1991; St. Mary's College, 1987-1990. Clinical Instructor, Boalt Hall School of Law, University of California, 1989-1990. *Member:* Bar Association of San Francisco; Alameda, Charles Houston, National and American Bar Associations. [1st Lt., U.S. Marine Corps]. *PRACTICE AREAS:* Litigation; Labor and Employment; White Collar Crime Defense.

**CHARLES E. FINBERG,** born Brooklyn, New York, February 24, 1951; admitted to bar, 1984, Vermont; 1986, U.S. District Court, District of Vermont; 1991, U.S. Court of Appeals, Second Circuit; 1992, California and U.S. District Court, Northern District of California; 1993, U.S. District Court, Eastern District of California and U.S. Court of Appeals, Ninth Circuit. *Education:* Harvard University (B.A., cum laude, 1973); Cornell University (J.D., cum laude, 1984). Member, Cornell Law Review, 1982-1984. Law Clerk, Hon. Ernest W. Gibson, III, Vermont Supreme Court, 1984-1985. *Member:* Bar Association of San Francisco; Chittenden County, Vermont and American Bar Associations; State Bar of California. (Certified as a Civil Trial Advocate by the National Institute of Trial Advocacy). *PRACTICE AREAS:* Accidents; Personal Injury; Insurance Defense; Litigation; Labor and Employment; Discrimination; Commercial Litigation.

**JAN A. GRUEN,** born Los Angeles, California, December 2, 1959; admitted to bar, 1987, California, U.S. District Court, Northern District of California and U.S. Court of Appeals, Ninth Circuit; 1988, U.S. District Court, Eastern District of California. *Education:* University of California at Santa Barbara (B.A., 1981); Hastings College of the Law, University of California (J.D., 1987). Member, Moot Court Board. Moot Court Instructor, Hastings College of the Law, 1986-1987. *Member:* State Bar of California. *LANGUAGES:* Spanish. *PRACTICE AREAS:* Construction Defect Litigation; Personal Injury Litigation; Business Litigation.

**JONATHAN C. TERRY,** born Salt Lake City, Utah, December 27, 1962; admitted to bar, 1993, California and U.S. District Court, Central District of California; 1994, U.S. District Court, Northern District of California. *Education:* Brigham Young University (B.A., 1987); University of San Diego School of Law (J.D., 1990). *Member:* San Francisco Bar Association (Member, Real Property Section); State Bar of California; J. Reuben Clark Law Society (Board Member, Northern California Chapter). *LANGUAGES:* Fijian. *PRACTICE AREAS:* Construction Defect Litigation; Real Estate Litigation; Tort Claims Defense; Business; Intellectual Property Litigation.

**DAVID M. MILLER,** born Burbank, California, July 28, 1966; admitted to bar, 1992, California, U.S. District Court, Northern District of California and U.S. Court of Appeals, Ninth Circuit; 1995, U.S. District Court, Central District of California. *Education:* University of California at Berkeley (B.A., 1988); University of The Pacific, McGeorge School of Law (J.D., 1992). Phi Delta Phi. Recipient: Emil Gampert Award for Trial Advocacy. *PRACTICE AREAS:* Construction Defect Litigation; Labor and Employment. *Email:* dmmiller@nevinlaw.com

---

## *PEZZOLA & REINKE*

*A PROFESSIONAL CORPORATION*

*Established in 1989*

**SUITE 1300, LAKE MERRITT PLAZA**
**1999 HARRISON STREET**
**OAKLAND, CALIFORNIA 94612**
*Telephone: 510-273-8750*
*Telecopier: 510-834-7440*

*San Francisco, California Office:* 650 California Street, 32nd Floor, 94111. Telephone: 415-989-9710.

*(This Listing Continued)*

---

CALIFORNIA—OAKLAND

**NEAL & ASSOCIATES**
MONTCLAIR VILLAGE
6200 ANTIOCH STREET, SUITE 202
P.O. BOX 13314, 500
OAKLAND, CALIFORNIA 94661-0314
Telephone: 510-339-023
FAX: 510-339-6672
URL: http://seamless.com/hd
n/hdn.html

Companies, Wills, Trusts, Estates, Copyrights, and Trademarks.

Newly Acquired

Oregon, December 2, 1946; admitted, District of Columbia and U.S. District Court, 1986, U.S. District Court, Central District. *Education:* Stanford University (A.B.); University of California (J.D., 1973). Phi Beta Kappa. Jurisprudence Award in Antitrust. Author, Computer Law Journal, Winter, 1980; Legal Automation News, February, 1982; "Sources of Law and Facts," ABA Legal [...], 1982; "Read My Lips: Documentary [...]," SF/LA Daily Journal, November 30, [...]on of San Francisco; Alameda County, Los Angeles (Member, Committee on Law Relating to Technology Section, 1978—) Bar Associations; the District of Columbia Bar. *LANGUAGES:* German, Spanish. *PRACTICE AREAS:* Wills, Trusts and Estates; Bankruptcy Law; Computer Law.

**[...]ERT,** born Chicago, Illinois, December 14, 1960; admitted, California, U.S. District Court, Northern District of [...], Court of Appeals, 9th Circuit. *Education:* University of [...] 1983); University of San Francisco (J.D., cum laude, [...]; McAuliffe Honor Society. Recipient, American Jurisprudence [...] Civil Procedure. Staff Member, University of San Francisco [...] 1985-1987. Teaching Assistant, University of San Francisco [...] Program, 1986. Judicial Extern, Chief Justice Malcolm M. [...] Associate Justice, Marcus M. Kaufman, California Supreme [...]. *Member:* Bar Association of San Francisco; State Bar of California, American Bar Association. (Also Of Counsel to Methven & Associates, Berkeley, California). *PRACTICE AREAS:* Litigation; Real Estate; Business Law.

**STEVEN S. MIYAKE,** born Chicago, Illinois, September 9, 1950; admitted to bar, 1984, California and U.S. District Court, Northern District of California. *Education:* University of California at Santa Cruz (B.A., with honors from Board of Politics, 1978); Hastings College of the Law, University of California (J.D., 1983). Judicial Extern, Associate Justice Betty Barry-Deal, California Court of Appeals, First District, Division Three. Pro Bono Attorney with Alameda County Volunteer Legal Services Corporation. *Member:* Alameda County Bar Association; State Bar of California.

REPRESENTATIVE CLIENTS: *High Technology Clients:* Data Directors, Inc.; Mathematical Sciences Research Institute; Vision Network Systems, Inc.; CAD Masters, Inc. *Lenders:* Sears Consumer Financial Corporation; Bogman, Inc.; San Francisco Federal Savings; Recovery Asset Group, Ltd. *Franchise Law Clients:* Papyrus Franchise Corporation; Alpha Graphics of Walnut Creek, Fremont and Hayward, California; Byte Industries, Inc.

---

## NEVIN & HALL LLP

*180 GRAND AVENUE, SUITE 950*
**OAKLAND, CALIFORNIA 94612**
*Telephone: 510-873-8600*
*Fax: 510-873-8601*

*San Francisco, California Office:* 507 Polk Street, Suite 300. Telephone: 415-834-1777. Fax: 415-834-1774.

*Washington, D.C. Office:* 2021 L Street N.W., Suite 300. Telephone: 202-887-0945. Fax: 202-887-0968.

*Insurance Defense and Coverage, Construction, Railroad, Securities, Real Estate, Business and Commercial Litigation.*

**JEFFREY G. NEVIN,** born Tracy, California, February 12, 1953; admitted to bar, 1984, California; 1985, U.S. District Court, Northern District of California; U.S. Tax Court; 1988, U.S. District Court, Eastern District of California; 1990, U.S. District Court, Central District of California.

*(This Listing Continued)*

CAA1488B

Menlo Park, California Office: 3000 Sand Hill Road, Building 4, Suite 160, 94025. Telephone: 415-854-8797.

*Corporate, Partnership, Emerging Growth Companies, Health Care, Mergers and Acquisitions, State and Federal Securities Law, Computer Law, Venture Capital, Intellectual Property, Real Estate, Nonprofit Representation and State, Federal and International Taxation.*

**STEPHEN P. PEZZOLA**, born Berkeley, California, September 14, 1956; admitted to bar, 1981, California. *Education:* University of California at Berkeley (B.S., with highest honors, 1978); Boalt Hall School of Law, University of California (J.D., 1981). Phi Beta Kappa. Co-Author: Chapter 1, "Corporate Housekeeping," Counseling California Corporations, California Continuing Eduction of the Bar, 1990. Lecturer: "Negotiating the Sale of Businesses," California Continuing Education of the Bar (1990). Consultant: "Drafting Agreements for the Sale of Businesses," California Continuing Education of the Bar, 1988; *Member:* Bar Association of San Francisco; Alameda County Bar Association; State Bar of California. **PRACTICE AREAS:** Business Planning; Corporate Law; Venture Capital Law; Healthcare Law; Non-Profit Representation; Mergers and Acquisitions.

**DONALD C. REINKE**, born Inglewood, California, January 16, 1957; admitted to bar, 1983, California. *Education:* Pomona College (B.A., cum laude, 1980) Phi Beta Kappa; University of California, Los Angeles (J.D., 1983). Member: UCLA Law Review, 1981-1983; UCLA-Alaska Law Review, 1981. Author: Casenote, "Educational Malpractice," UCLA-Alaska Law Review, Vol. 11, No. 1, 1983. Recipient, American Jurisprudence Award - Constitutional Law. Consultant: Advising California Corporations - "Mergers and Acquisitions," California Continuing Education of the Bar, 1990. Equity Compensation for Emerging Growth Companies CEB *California Business Law Practitioner,* Fall, 1995. Board Member, San Francisco Renaissance Entrepreneurship Center, 1989-1993; 1996—; Board Secretary 1991-1993. *Member:* Bar Association of San Francisco; Alameda County and American Bar Associations; State Bar of California. **PRACTICE AREAS:** Corporate; Business Planning; Venture Capital Law; Mergers and Acquisitions; State and Federal Securities Law; Health Care Law; Intellectual Property; Compensation Structuring.

**THOMAS A. MAIER**, born Chicago, Illinois, March 23, 1955; admitted to bar, 1979, California. *Education:* Southern Illinois University (B.A., 1976); University of California at Berkeley (J.D., 1979); New York University (LL.M., 1980). Adjunct Lecturer, School of Accounting and Tax and The School of Law, Golden Gate University. *Member:* Bar Association of San Francisco; American Bar Association; State Bar of California; International Fiscal Association. (Certified Specialist, Taxation Law, The State Bar of California Board of Legal Specialization).

**THOMAS C. ARMSTRONG**, born Augusta, Georgia, May 30, 1959; admitted to bar, 1985, Massachusetts; 1989, California. *Education:* Pomona College (B.A., 1981); Hastings College of the Law, University of California (J.D., 1984). Note and Comment Editor, Hastings Journal of Communication and Entertainment Law, 1983-1984. *Member:* State Bar of California; Massachusetts Bar Association.

**BRUCE D. WHITLEY**, born New York, N.Y., January 22, 1960; admitted to bar, 1987, California and U.S. District Court, Northern District of California; 1989, U.S. Tax Court. *Education:* University of California at Berkeley (B.S., 1982); Hastings College of the Law, University of California (J.D., 1987). Director, Moot Court Board. Associate Managing Editor, Hastings International and Comparative Law Review, 1986-1987. Certified Public Accountant, California, 1984. Co-Author: "Qualified Personal Residence Trusts (QPRTS) in Drafting California Irrevocable Living Trusts," (CEB 2d ed 1995); "Qualified Personal Residence Trust Under the New IRC 2702 Regulations," Sample Language and Comments," 13 CEB Estate Planning and Probate Reporter 157 (1992); "Drafting the Qualified Personal Residence Trust: Sample Language and Comments," 14 CEB Estate Planning and Probate Reporter 1 (1992). *Member:* Alameda County Bar Association.

**BRUCE P. JOHNSON**, born Sacramento, California, August 11, 1963; admitted to bar, 1988, California. *Education:* Duke University (B.A., magna cum laude, 1985); University of California at Los Angeles (J.D., 1988). Recipient, American Jurisprudence Award in Civil Procedure. *Member:* Bar Association of San Francisco (Member, Business Section); State Bar of California. **PRACTICE AREAS:** Public and Private Securities Law; Corporate Law; Venture Capital Law; Mergers and Acquisitions.

**GIZELLE A. BARANY**, born Oakland, California, March 21, 1958; admitted to bar, 1990, California. *Education:* University of California at Berkeley (A.B., 1980); Boalt Hall School of Law, University of California (J.D., 1990). *Member:* State Bar of California.

*(This Listing Continued)*

**JEREMY E. WENOKUR**, born Detroit, Michigan, November 18, 1967; admitted to bar, 1992, Michigan; 1993, Utah; 1996, California. *Education:* University of Utah (B.S., 1989); University of Michigan (J.D., 1992); New York University (LL.M., Taxation, 1994). Omicron Delta Epsilon. *Member:* State Bar of Michigan; Utah State Bar. **PRACTICE AREAS:** Federal Taxation.

*OF COUNSEL*

**ROBERT E. KREBS**, born Saginaw, Michigan, July 25, 1943; admitted to bar, 1969, Colorado; 1971, Utah; 1973, California; registered to practice before U.S. Patent and Trademark Office. *Education:* University of Colorado at Boulder (B.S., 1966; J.D., 1969); University of California at Berkeley (M.B.A., 1976); California State University at San Jose (M.S., 1981). Pi Tau Sigma. Lecturer, Legal and Political Environment of Business: San Francisco State University, 1982-1983; University of Utah, 1983-1984; California State University at San Jose, 1985; University of Santa Clara, 1989. Member, Panel of Arbitrators, American Arbitration Association. *Member:* State Bar of California (Member, Intellectual Property Section); San Francisco Patent and Trademark Law Association. (Also Member, Burns, Doane, Swecker & Mathis, L.L.P., Menlo Park).

*LEGAL SUPPORT PERSONNEL*

**LORETTA H. HINTZ**, born Portland, Oregon, March 18, 1962. *Education:* Vassar College (B.A., 1984). (Corporate Paralegal).

**MARY A. FITZPATRICK**, born Boston, Massachusetts, November 30, 1951. *Education:* Ohio University (B.S., Journalism, 1974). (Corporate Paralegal).

**GAYLE F. DETILLION** (Corporate and Securities Paralegal).

REPRESENTATIVE CLIENTS: Auntie Pasta, Inc.; Autohaus Automotive, Inc.; Bridge End Multimedia; Burr, Egan, Deleage & Co.; California Medical Association; California Private Investment Corp.; Cancer Center Medical Group; DSP Communications, Inc.; DSP Group, Inc.; Golden Gate Transit Amalgamated Ret. Fund; Intracellular Diagnostics; Medlogic Global Corp.; Mid-West Microelectronics, Inc.; Mountain Cablevision; Pacific American Institute; Pacific Capital Partners; Plynetics; Primed Management Consulting ; Radiation Oncology Corp.; Salesian Society; Software Sundicate; Summit Bank; TA Engineering; Tom Sawyer Software; U.S. Electricar, Inc.; U.S. Ice Ventures; Vertisoft Systems, Inc.; Wise Communications, Inc.

---

# *PLAGEMAN & ASSOCIATES*

*1999 HARRISON, SUITE 2700*
**OAKLAND, CALIFORNIA 94612**
*Telephone: 510-273-8553*
*Fax: 510-273-8559*

*Real Estate, Land Use, Construction, General Litigation, General Corporate, Estate Planning and Estate Administration.*

**WILLIAM H. PLAGEMAN**, born San Francisco, California, June 13, 1943; admitted to bar, 1969, California; 1978, U.S. Tax Court. *Education:* University of California (B.A., 1965); Boalt Hall School of Law, University of California (J.D., 1968). Member, 1981-1984 and Advisor, 1984-1986, Executive Committee, Estate Planning, Trust and Probate Law Section and Member, Real Property Section, State Bar of California. Chairman of the Board, Better Business Bureau, 1992-1993. Vice President, Bay Area Tumor Institute. *Member:* Alameda County and American (Member, Sections on: Real Property, Probate and Trust Law; Economics of Law Practice) Bar Associations; San Francisco Estate Planning Council; National Association of Estate Planning Councils. Fellow, American College of Trust and Estate Counsel. **PRACTICE AREAS:** Land Use; Real Estate; Estate Planning; Estate and Trust Administration.

**RICHARD W. LUND**, born Vallejo, California, April 23, 1960; admitted to bar, 1985, California. *Education:* University of California at Berkeley (B.S., Mechanical Engineering, 1982); Hastings College of the Law, University of California (J.D., 1985). Tau Beta Pi; Order of the Coif. Member, Hastings Law Journal, 1984-1985. Engineer-in-Training, California, 1982. Member: Oakland Chamber of Commerce Planning and Construction Committee; Oakland Rotary Club. *Member:* State Bar of California (Member, Real Property Section; Subsection on Construction Law). **PRACTICE AREAS:** Real Estate and Construction Litigation; Environmental and Land Use Law.

**LILLIAN F. HAMRICK**, born San Angelo, Texas, March 5, 1960; admitted to bar, 1989, California, U.S. District Court, Northern District of California and U.S. Court of Appeals, Ninth Circuit. *Education:* Yale College (B.A., 1982); University of California at Berkeley (M.A., 1989); Boalt Hall School of Law, University of California at Berkeley (J.D., 1989). Edi-

*(This Listing Continued)*

### PLAGEMAN & ASSOCIATES, Oakland—Continued

tor-in-Chief, Berkeley Women's Law Journal, 1988-1989. Co-Author with Nancy L. Murray, "Assignment and Subletting in Commercial Leases: The Impact of the New Civil Code Sections," 13 Real Property Law Reporter 65, 1990. *Member:* Alameda County and American Bar Associations; State Bar of California. **PRACTICE AREAS:** Real Estate; Land Use; Corporate Law.

**PAULA J. GALLEANO,** born Madera, California, October 21, 1952; admitted to bar, 1980, District of Columbia; 1987, California. *Education:* University of Redlands; University of California at Davis (B.A., 1974); Catholic University of America (J.D., 1980). Editor, "Fundamentals of Municipal Bond Law," National Association of Bond Lawyers, 1983 and 1984. *Member:* Bar Association of San Francisco; The District of Columbia Bar; American Bar Association. **PRACTICE AREAS:** Real Estate; Land Use; Corporate; Environmental; Municipal Finance.

**SARA MANN,** born St. Louis, Missouri, January 15, 1969; admitted to bar, 1995, California. *Education:* University of California, Berkeley (B.A., English, 1991); University of California, Los Angeles (J.D., 1995). *Member:* State Bar of California. **PRACTICE AREAS:** Real Estate; Land Use; Estate Planning. *Email:* SMann@ix.netcom.com

**TIMOTHY A. DEWITT,** born Berkeley, California, November 25, 1964; admitted to bar, 1990, California; 1992, District of Columbia (inactive). *Education:* University of California, Berkeley (B.S., with high honors, 1985); Walter A. Haas School of Business (M.B.A., 1990); Boalt Hall School of Law, University of California (J.D., 1990). Phi Beta Kappa; Beta Gamma Sigma. Associate Editor, University of California Law Review, 1989-1990. *Member:* State Bar of California.

**MAUREEN A. KELLY,** born San Francisco, California, September 12, 1967; admitted to bar, 1992, California. *Education:* University of California, Davis (B.A., 1989); Hastings College of the Law (J.D., 1992). Member Hastings Constitutional Law Quarterly, 1990-1992. *Member:* San Francisco Bar Association; State Bar of California. **PRACTICE AREAS:** Estate Planning.

### LEGAL SUPPORT PERSONNEL

**DEBRA J. MILLER,** born Detroit, Michigan, January 19, 1965. *Education:* St. Louis University, Honors Program; University of California at Berkeley (B.A., 1987); University of Maryland School of Law. (Paralegal). **PRACTICE AREAS:** Estate Planning; Estate and Trust Administration; Land Use.

REPRESENTATIVE CLIENTS: Better Business Bureau; Kaiser Aluminum; Kaiser Center, Inc.; Pinole Point Properties, Inc.; Rigging International; S. H. Cowell Foundation.

---

## LAW OFFICES OF
## MARK D. PONIATOWSKI

Established in 1989

THE LEIMERT-OLD BUILDING
456 EIGHTH STREET
OAKLAND, CALIFORNIA 94607
Telephone: 510-881-8700
Fax: 510-881-8702

*Castro Valley, California Office:* 2811 Castro Valley Boulevard, Suite 208, 94546.

*Real Estate and Business Litigation; Real Estate and Business Transactions; Creditors Rights.*

FIRM PROFILE: *Mark D. Poniatowski founded the firm after 6 years of industrial finance/leasing experience with Clark Equipment Credit Corporation and CIT Leasing Corporation; and 2 years with Crosby, Heafey, Roach & May, Oakland, CA. The firm, consisting of Mr. Poniatowski and associate attorney, paralegal and secretarial support staff, prides itself on responsive, quality, results oriented representation. The firm generally represents business clients of all sizes and professional individuals seeking an alternative to large firm representation.*

**MARK D. PONIATOWSKI,** born Detroit, Michigan, June 18, 1957; admitted to bar, 1986, California. *Education:* University of Michigan (B.B.A., with distinction, 1979); University of Santa Clara (J.D., 1985). Instructor, Credit Law, Credit Managers Association of California, 1993. Board of Directors, Castro Valley Rotary Club, 1990-1992. *Member:* Alameda County Bar Association (Member, Bankruptcy and Real Estate Sec-

*(This Listing Continued)*

tions) State Bar of California (Member, Business Law and Real Estate Sections).

REPRESENTATIVE CLIENTS: Caterpillar Financial Services Corporation; Deutsche Financial Service; U.S. Amada Leasing, Ltd.; Matsco Financial Corporation; Pacific Union Investment Corporation; Filesafe, Inc.; Amalco Metals, Inc.; Tenco Tractor, Inc.; 24 Hour Fitness, Inc.

---

## DANIEL F. QUINN

OAKLAND, CALIFORNIA

(See Stockton)

*General Civil and Trial Practice, Construction Law, Insurance Law.*

---

## RANDICK & O'DEA

Established in 1971

1800 HARRISON STREET, SUITE 2350
OAKLAND, CALIFORNIA 94612
Telephone: 510-836-3555
Telecopier: 510-834-4748

*General Civil and Trial Practice. Corporate, Antitrust, Commercial and Petroleum Marketing Practices, Environmental, Litigation and Franchise Law.*

FIRM PROFILE: *Since its founding in 1971, the firm has engaged in a general, civil and commercial litigation practice throughout Northern California. The civil practice emphasizes commercial transactions, business planning, estate planning and probate. The commercial litigation practice emphasizes trade regulation, franchise, environmental, retail petroleum marketing, and other forms of complex litigation, in both state and federal courts. The litigation services provided include both primary representation, and service as local counsel.*

### MEMBERS OF FIRM

**ROBERT A. RANDICK, JR.,** born Pueblo, Colorado, July 2, 1943; admitted to bar, 1970, California. *Education:* Pomona College (B.A., 1965); University of Stockholm, Sweden; University of San Francisco (J.D., 1969). Phi Alpha Delta. Member, Board of Counselors, University of San Francisco School of Law, 1981—. *Member:* Alameda County and American (Member, Section on Antitrust Law) Bar Associations; State Bar of California. **REPORTED CASES:** Estate of Toy, 72 Cal. App. 3d 392; David K. Lindemuth Co. v. Shannon Financial Corp. 637 F Supp. 991; 660 F Supp. 261. **PRACTICE AREAS:** Antitrust Litigation; Franchise Litigation; Commercial Law; Real Estate Litigation; General Business Planning Law.

**BRIAN M. O'DEA,** born San Francisco, California, October 31, 1944; admitted to bar, 1970, California. *Education:* St. Mary's College (B.A., 1966); University of San Francisco (J.D., 1969). *Member:* Alameda County (Chairman, Fee Arbitration Committee, 1982-1984; Member, Board of Directors, 1985-1987) and American Bar Associations; State Bar of California. **REPORTED CASES:** Gerdlund v. Electronic Dispensers International, 190 Cal. App. 3d 263. **PRACTICE AREAS:** Business Litigation; Petroleum Marketing Practices Law.

**BERNARD F. ROSE,** born Syracuse, New York, April 17, 1943; admitted to bar, 1985, California. *Education:* Syracuse University (B.S., 1964); Florida State University (Ph.D., 1973); John F. Kennedy University (J.D., 1985). *Member:* Contra Costa County and American Bar Associations; State Bar of California. **PRACTICE AREAS:** Environmental Law; Business Litigation; Petroleum Marketing Practices Law.

### ASSOCIATES

**JULIE ROSE,** born Cresco, Iowa, November 22, 1952; admitted to bar, 1988, California. *Education:* Lawrence University (B.A., 1975); John F. Kennedy University (J.D., 1988). Recipient, West Horn Book Award for Scholastic Achievement. *Member:* State Bar of California. **PRACTICE AREAS:** Environmental Law; Business Litigation; Petroleum Marketing Practices Law.

**WILLIAM J. TRINKLE,** born Los Angeles, California, July 29, 1950; admitted to bar, 1981, California. *Education:* University of San Francisco (B.A., 1972); McGeorge School of Law, University of the Pacific (J.D., 1981). Phi Alpha Delta (Treasurer, 1980-1981). Member, Trial Advocacy Competition Team. *Member:* Alameda County Bar Association; State Bar of California. **PRACTICE AREAS:** Business Law; Franchise Litigation; Commercial Litigation.

*(This Listing Continued)*

## OF COUNSEL

**LISA ROBINSON SWANSON,** born Boston, Massachusetts, September 19, 1958; admitted to bar, 1985, Massachusetts; 1986, California. *Education:* Harvard University (A.B., magna cum laude, 1980; J.D., cum laude, 1985). Phi Beta Kappa. *LANGUAGES:* French. *PRACTICE AREAS:* Litigation; General Transactional.

REPRESENTATIVE CLIENTS: Seven-Up Bottling Company of San Francisco; David K. Lindemuth Co., Inc.; Hammon, Jensen, Wallen & Associates; Lange Trucking, Inc.; Total Information Management Corp.; Bell Carter Foods, Inc.; Navlets, Inc.; Woodard Industries; Broadway Motors Ford; General Foundry Service Corp.; Veronica Foods Co.; Cherry Payments Systems, Inc.

## RANKIN, SPROAT, MIRES, TRAPANI & REISER

*A PROFESSIONAL CORPORATION*

Established in 1946

**SUITE 1616, 1800 HARRISON STREET**
**OAKLAND, CALIFORNIA 94612**
Telephone: 510-465-3922
Fax: 510-452-3006
Email: rankin@best.com
URL: http://www.rankinlaw.com

*General Civil and Trial Practice in all State and Federal Courts. Insurance Defense, Medical, Legal and other Professional Liability, Toxic Tort Litigation. Commercial, Business and Employment Law.*

FIRM PROFILE: *The firm was founded in 1946 and initially specialized in the representation of public carriers. The firm went on to become recognized in the areas of medical and legal malpractice defense. The firm now has further expanded its practice to include toxic tort general commercial litigation as well as labor and employment law. Trial experience has been our hallmark. We bring the benefits of this experience to each of our clients. The firm's philosophy is concise: a commitment to legal excellence, a close relationship with clients and responsiveness to each client's needs.*

**JOSEPH F. RANKIN** (-1977).

**PATRICK T. RANKIN** (1943-1990).

**RONALD G. SPROAT,** born Portland, Oregon, January 26, 1934; admitted to bar, 1964, California. *Education:* University of California at Berkeley (B.S., 1958) Boalt Hall School of Law, University of California (LL.B., 1963). *Member:* Alameda County Bar Association; State Bar of California; Association of Defense Counsel of Northern California; Defense Research and Trial Lawyers Association; American Board of Trial Advocates; American College of Trial Lawyers. *PRACTICE AREAS:* Medical Law; Legal Malpractice; General Insurance Defense; Products Liability Law; Commercial Litigation. *Email:* Sproat@best.com

**GEOFFREY A. MIRES,** born San Antonio, Texas, September 10, 1954; admitted to bar, 1981, California. *Education:* University of California at Berkeley (B.A., 1976); Golden Gate University (J.D., 1980). Legal Writing and Research Instructor, 1979-1980. *Member:* Alameda County and American Bar Associations; State Bar of California; Association of Defense Counsel of Northern California. *PRACTICE AREAS:* Medical Law; Legal Malpractice; General Insurance Defense; Products Liability Law; Commercial Litigation. *Email:* Mires@best.com

**THOMAS A. TRAPANI,** born Fulton, New York, May 9, 1956; admitted to bar, 1981, California. *Education:* University of California at Los Angeles (B.A., summa cum laude, 1978); University of California at Davis (J.D., 1981). Phi Beta Kappa. *Member:* Bar Association of San Francisco; Alameda County Bar Association; State Bar of California. *PRACTICE AREAS:* Medical Law; Legal Malpractice; General Insurance Defense; Products Liability Law; Commercial Law; Environmental Law; Toxic Tort Litigation. *Email:* Trapani@best.com

**MICHAEL J. REISER,** born Garden Grove, California, July 16, 1961; admitted to bar, 1986, Colorado; 1988, California. *Education:* University of California at Berkeley; University of Colorado at Boulder (B.S., magna cum laude, 1983; J.D., 1986). Beta Gamma Sigma. Recipient, American Jurisprudence Award in Criminal Law. Lecturer, Business Law, University of Colorado School of Business, 1987. *Member:* Boulder, Alameda County, Colorado and American Bar Associations; State Bar of California. *PRACTICE AREAS:* Medical Law; Legal Malpractice; General Insurance Defense; Products Liability Law; Commercial Litigation; Employment Law. *Email:* Reiser@best.com

*(This Listing Continued)*

**DAVID T. SHUEY,** born Concord, California, October 25, 1966; admitted to bar, 1992, California and U.S. Court of Appeals, Ninth Circuit. *Education:* Stanford University (B.A., 1989); Santa Clara University School of Law (J.D., 1992).

**G. TRENT MORROW,** born Lakewood, Ohio, January 17, 1966; admitted to bar, 1993, California. *Education:* University of California (B.S., 1989); McGeorge School of Law, University of the Pacific (J.D., 1993).

**EUGENE G. ASHLEY,** born Palo Alto, California, May 14, 1967; admitted to bar, 1994, California. *Education:* University of California at Santa Barbara (B.A., 1989); McGeorge School of Law (J.D., 1994).

**KEVIN R. MINTZ,** born Castro Valley, California, June 14, 1964; admitted to bar, 1994, California; U.S. District Court, Northern District of California; U.S. Court of Appeals, Ninth Circuit. *Education:* University of California (B.A., 1991); University of California, Boalt Hall School of Law (J.D., 1994). Phi Beta Kappa; Phi Alpha Theta. *Member:* State Bar of California.

**MARIBEL DELGADO OSBORNE,** born Tijuana, Mexico, February 5, 1969; admitted to bar, 1996, California. *Education:* Stanford University (B.A., 1992); Boalt Hall School of Law, University of California (J.D., 1995). *Member:* State Bar of California. *LANGUAGES:* Spanish.

## LEGAL SUPPORT PERSONNEL

**JENNIFER L. RANKIN.** *Education:* University of California at Berkeley (B.A., 1973); Holy Names College (Teaching Creditation, 1974); University of San Francisco/Lone Mountain College (M.A. in Legal Studies, 1975). Phi Beta Kappa. (Administrator).

**BETTY E. EVANS,** born Evanston, Illinois, September 11, 1941. *Education:* Chabot College (A.A., 1980); St. Mary's College (Paralegal Cert., 1992). Registered Nurse, California, 1992. (Nurse Paralegal).

**SUE PERATA,** born Oakland, California, November 1, 1952. *Education:* St. Mary's College (Paralegal Cert., 1991). Respiratory Care Practitioner, 1985. (Medical Paralegal).

**TRISH J. FUZESY,** born Alameda, California, May 13, 1957. *Education:* University of California at Berkeley (A.B., 1980) St. Mary's College (Paralegal Cert., 1992). (Paralegal).

**SALLY J. ATTIA,** born Summerside, Prince Edward Island, Canada, October 1, 1944. *Education:* California State University (Paralegal Certificate, 1990). (Medical Paralegal).

REPRESENTATIVE CLIENTS: Medical Insurance Exchange of California; Fremont Indemnity; Farmers' Insurance Group; Lawyers' Mutual Insurance Co.; Ryder Truck Rental; Alta Bates Medical Center; Eureka Chemical Co.; San Francisco Elevator Co.; Tremco; The Earth Grains Co.; Security U.S.A.; Empire Fire & Marine; Summit Medical Center; Micro/Resources, Inc.; San Francisco Bar Pilots; Allied Digital Technologies, Inc.
REFERENCE: Union Bank.

## WILLIAM A. RESNECK

**2201 BROADWAY, SUITE 803**
**OAKLAND, CALIFORNIA 94612**
Telephone: 510-465-6505
Fax: 510-763-3674

*General Civil Litigation, Personal Injury, Legal Malpractice, Workers Compensation and Arbitration.*

**WILLIAM A. RESNECK,** admitted to bar, 1971, California. *Education:* Oberlin College (B.A., with honors, Economics, 1967); Indiana University School of Law (J.D., magna cum laude, 1970). Order of the Coif. Note and Comment Editor, Indiana Law Journal, 1969-1970. Professor, St. Mary's College Paralegal Program, 1980-1985. Part-time Deputy City Attorney, City of Berkeley, 1985-1987. Hearing Officer, San Francisco County Civil Service Commission, 1979—. Arbitrator and Early Neutral Evaluator: United States District Court, Northern District of California; Alameda County Superior Court; Contra Costa County Superior Court; Marin County Superior Court; American Arbitration Association. *Member:* State Bar of California; Alameda/Contra Costa Trial Lawyers Association. *PRACTICE AREAS:* Civil Trial; Personal Injury; Legal Malpractice; Workers Compensation; Arbitration.

## RIFKIND & FUERCH

OAKLAND, CALIFORNIA

(See Hayward)

General Civil and Trial Practice. Insurance, Insurance Defense, Real Estate, Transportation Law, Fire Insurance, Products Liability, Automobile, Professional Liability, Landslide and Subsidence, Construction, Business, Municipal and Education Law.

---

## DENNIS K. ROTHHAAR

ONE KAISER PLAZA, SUITE 1725
OAKLAND, CALIFORNIA 94612-3612
Telephone: 510-763-5611
Fax: 510-763-3430

Family Law.

**DENNIS K. ROTHHAAR,** born Ft. Wayne, Indiana, June 8, 1944; admitted to bar, 1972, California; U.S. District Court, Northern District of California and U.S. Court of Appeals, Ninth Circuit. *Education:* Stanford University (A.B., 1966); Harvard University (J.D., 1972). Judge Pro Tem: Oakland-Piedmont-Emeryville Municipal Court, 1977-1988; Alameda Superior Court, 1980—; San Francisco Superior Court, 1986-1988. Member, Board of Directors, Legal Aid Society, Alameda County, 1983—; President, 1993-1995. *Member:* Alameda County Bar Association (Chair, Lawyer Referral Service Committee, 1979-1981; Member, Board of Directors, 1982-1984); State Bar of California (Member, Family Law Section); Alameda County Family Law Association (Member, Board of Directors, 1990—; Chair, 1991-1992). (Certified Specialist, Family Law, The State Bar of California Board of Legal Specialization).

---

## RYAN, ANDRADA & LIFTER

A PROFESSIONAL CORPORATION

TENTH FLOOR, KAISER CENTER BUILDING
300 LAKESIDE DRIVE, SUITE 1045
OAKLAND, CALIFORNIA 94612-3536
Telephone: 510-763-6510
Fax: 510-763-3921

General Civil and Trial Practice. Insurance Defense and Coverage Law.

**JOSEPH D. RYAN, JR.,** born Toledo, Ohio, January 26, 1946; admitted to bar, 1974, California; U.S. District Court, Northern, Central and Eastern Districts of California; U.S. Court of Appeals, Ninth Circuit. *Education:* Harvard University (B.A., 1968); Hastings College of the Law, University of California (J.D., 1974). Order of the Coif. *Member:* Alameda County Bar Association; The State Bar of California; Association of Defense Counsel of Northern California; American Board of Trial Advocates. **PRACTICE AREAS:** Civil Trial; Construction Defect Litigation; Insurance Coverage; Insurance Defense Law; Landslide and Subsidence Litigation.

**J. RANDALL ANDRADA,** born Oakland, California, February 11, 1951; admitted to bar, 1976, California; U.S. District Court, Northern and Eastern Districts of California. *Education:* St. Mary's College of California (B.A., cum laude, 1973); Hastings College of the Law, University of California (J.D., 1976). *Member:* Alameda County Bar Association; The State Bar of California; Alameda County Lawyers Club (Member, Board of Directors, 1984-1986); Association of Defense Counsel of Northern California (Member, Board of Directors, 1994-1995); American Board of Trial Advocates. **PRACTICE AREAS:** Civil Trial; Insurance Defense Law; Malpractice Defense; Sexual Abuse Litigation; Premises Liability.

**JILL J. LIFTER,** born Kittery, Maine, January 29, 1962; admitted to bar, 1985, California; U.S. District Court, Northern and Eastern Districts of California. *Education:* University of California, Los Angeles (B.A., cum laude, 1982); University of Southern California (J.D., 1985). Phi Alpha Delta. *Member:* The State Bar of California (Member, Litigation Section); Association of Defense Counsel of Northern California. **PRACTICE AREAS:** Civil Trial; Construction Defect Litigation; Insurance Coverage; Insurance Defense Law; Landslide and Subsidence Litigation.

**JOLIE KRAKAUER,** born New York, New York, September 25, 1956; admitted to bar, 1984, California; U.S. District Court, Northern District of California. *Education:* University of California, Santa Cruz (B.A., 1978); Hastings College of the Law, University of California (J.D., 1984). *Member:* The State Bar of California; American Bar Association.

**GLENN GOULD,** born Glen Cove, New York, February 28, 1962; admitted to bar, 1989, California; U.S. District Court, Northern District of California; U.S. Court of Appeals, Ninth Circuit; U.S. Supreme Court. *Education:* Washington University, St. Louis, Missouri (B.A., 1984); Benjamin N. Cardozo School of Law, New York, NY (J.D., 1988). *Member:* The State Bar of California; American Bar Association.

**MICHAEL J. DALEY,** born Neptune, New Jersey, August 8, 1964; admitted to bar, 1990, Georgia and U.S. District Court, Northern District of Georgia; 1991, California; U.S. District Court, Northern District of California and U.S. Court of Appeals, Eleventh Circuit. *Education:* University of California, Berkeley (A.B., 1987); University of Georgia (J.D., cum laude, 1990). The Order of Barristers. *Member:* State Bar of Georgia; The State Bar of California.

**CHARLES E. KALLGREN,** born Berkeley, California, November 11, 1964; admitted to bar, 1991, California; U.S. District Court, Northern District of California; U.S. Court of Appeals, Ninth Circuit; U.S. Supreme Court. *Education:* Pomona College (B.A., 1987); Hastings College of the Law, University of California (J.D., 1991). *Member:* The State Bar of California; American Bar Association.

**RHONDA D. SHELTON,** born Stayton, Oregon, August 1, 1962; admitted to bar, 1991, California; 1992, Oregon; U.S. District Court, Northern District of California and District of Oregon. *Education:* Oregon State University (B.S., 1984); Hastings College of the Law, University of California (J.D., 1991). *Member:* Oregon State Bar; State Bar of California; American Bar Association.

**LORA VAIL FRENCH,** born Northridge, California, April 25, 1968; admitted to bar, 1993, California; U.S. District Court, Northern District of California. *Education:* University of California, Riverside (B.A., Phi Beta Kappa, cum laude, 1990); University of San Francisco, California (J.D., McAuliffe Honor Society, cum laude, 1993). *Member:* State Bar of California; American Bar Association.

**VIKKI L. BARRON,** born Los Angeles, California, April 30, 1966; admitted to bar, 1993, California; U.S. District Court, Northern District of California. *Education:* University of California, Berkeley (B.A., 1989); University of San Francisco, California (J.D., 1993). *Member:* State Bar of California; San Francisco La Raza Lawyers Association.

**BRUCE A. MCINTOSH,** born San Gabriel, California, March 22, 1959; admitted to bar, 1994, California and U.S. District Court, Northern, Southern, Eastern and Central Districts of California. *Education:* Westmont College, Santa Barbara, California (B.A., Omicron Delta Kappa, cum laude, 1981); University of Colorado, Colorado Springs, Colorado (M.B.A., Beta Gamma Sigma, 1991); Hastings College of Law, University of California (J.D., 1994). *Member:* State Bar of California. [Capt., USAF, 1982-1991]

**MICHAEL J. THOMAS,** born Santa Clara, California, March 7, 1966; admitted to bar, 1994, California; U.S. District Court, Northern District of California. *Education:* California Polytechnic State University, San Luis Obispo (B.S.M.E., 1989); University of California, Hastings College of the Law (J.D., 1994). Recipient, American Jurisprudence Award. Associate Editor, Hastings Law Journal, 1993-1994. *Member:* The State Bar of California.

**LAURA E. OZAK,** born Detroit, Michigan, July 2, 1958; admitted to bar, 1994, California; U.S. District Court, Northern District of California. *Education:* University of Michigan; Eastern Michigan University (B.S.N., 1982); Golden Gate University (J.D., 1994). Recipient: American Jurisprudence Award, Civil Procedure I; "The Labor and Employment Law Student Achievement Award for Academic Excellence." *Member:* State Bar of California (Member, Labor and Employment Section); American Bar Association (Member: Health Law Forum; Tort and Insurance Practice Section; Labor and Employment Law Section); The American Association of Nurse Attorneys.

REPRESENTATIVE CLIENTS: Alameda Contra Costa County Transit District; Gallagher & Burk (General Contractors); Fireman's Fund Insurance Company; Liberty Mutual Insurance Group; Safeway Stores, Inc.; Truck Insurance Exchange; Alameda County (Highland General Hospital); Contra Costa County; Kmart Corporation; MSI Insurance Company; United National Group; Reliance Insurance Company; Alamo Rent-A-Car; McBail Company (General Contractors); Financial Pacific Insurance Co.; Crawford and Company; CNA Insurance Companies; Caldwell International Inc.; Alta Bates Medical Center.

*(This Listing Continued)*

## SAPERSTEIN, GOLDSTEIN, DEMCHAK & BALLER

*A PROFESSIONAL CORPORATION*
**1300 CLAY STREET, 11TH FLOOR**
**OAKLAND, CALIFORNIA 94612**
Telephone: 510-763-9800
Email: info@saperstein.com

*Civil Trial and Appellate Practice. Class Actions, Employment and Environmental Litigation, Attorneys' Fees Litigation; False Claims Act Prosecutions.*

**BARRY GOLDSTEIN,** born New York City, June 9, 1945; admitted to bar, 1971, New York; 1977, District of Columbia; 1989, California. *Education:* Harvard University (B.A., cum laude, 1967); Columbia University (J.D., cum laude, 1970); University of Cambridge (Diploma in Criminology, 1971). Editor, Columbia Law Review, 1969-1970. James Kent Scholar, 1970. Co-Editor, Schlei & Grossman's Employment Discrimination Law, Third Edition. Lecturer on Law, Harvard Law School, 1985-1986. Assistant Counsel, NAACP Legal Defense & Educational Fund, Inc., 1971-1987. Director, Washington Office of the NAACP Legal Defense & Educational Fund, Inc., 1988-1989. *Member:* New York State and American (Co-Chairman, EEO Committee, Labor and Employment Law Section, 1986-1991) Bar Associations; The District of Columbia Bar; State Bar of California. *PRACTICE AREAS:* Litigation; Employment Law.

**TERESA DEMCHAK,** born Canton, Ohio, July 5, 1947; admitted to bar, 1976, Ohio, U.S. District Court, Southern and Northern Districts of Ohio and U.S. District Court, Eastern District of Missouri; 1986, California, U.S. District Court, Eastern, Northern and Central Districts of California and U.S. Court of Appeals, Sixth and Ninth Circuits. *Education:* Cleveland State University (B.A., 1970); Case Western Reserve University (M.S.S.A., 1972); Cleveland Marshall College of Law (J.D., 1976). Cooperating Counsel, NAACP, 1976-1980; Assistant General Counsel, NAACP, 1980-1982; Staff Attorney, National Center for Youth Law, 1983-1990. *Member:* State Bar of California (Member, Labor and Employment Litigation Sections). *PRACTICE AREAS:* Litigation; Employment Law.

**MORRIS J. BALLER,** born Pasadena, California, July 17, 1944; admitted to bar, 1970, California; 1975, U.S. Supreme Court. *Education:* Harvard University (B.A., with high honors, 1966; J.D. with honors, 1970). Adjunct Professor, University of San Francisco Law School, 1978-1979; Hastings College of Law, 1979-1980. Director, National Employment Law Project, Inc., 1974-1985. Mexican American Legal Defense & Education Fund, Senior Vice President, 1980-1985. Member, Lawyers Committee for Civil Rights of the San Francisco Bay Area. Member, Ninth Circuit Judicial Conference Lawyer Delegate for the Northern District of California. *LANGUAGES:* French. *PRACTICE AREAS:* Litigation; Employment Law.

*OF COUNSEL*

**GUY T. SAPERSTEIN,** born Chicago, Illinois, June 20, 1943; admitted to bar, 1969, Colorado; 1970, California; U.S. District Court, District of Colorado; U.S. District Court, Northern, Eastern and Central Districts of California; U.S. Court of Appeals, Ninth and Tenth Circuit ; U.S. Supreme Court. *Education:* University of California at Berkeley (A.B., 1966; J.D., 1969). Recipient, Reginald Heber Smith Fellowship in Law, 1969-1971. *Member:* State Bar of California; American Bar Association (Member, Labor and Employment Law Section); California Trial Lawyers Association. *PRACTICE AREAS:* Litigation; Employment Law; False Claims Act.

---

**MICHELLE ALEXANDER,** born Chicago, Illinois, October 7, 1967; admitted to bar, 1995, California. *Education:* Vanderbilt University (B.A., 1989); Stanford Law School (J.D., 1992). Order of the Coif. Law Clerk: Honorable Abner Mikva, U.S. Court of Appeals, District of Columbia, 1992-1993; Honorable Harry A. Blackmun, U.S. Supreme Court, 1993-1994. *Member:* State Bar of California (Member, Labor and Employment Section); Berkley Community Law Center (Board of Directors). *PRACTICE AREAS:* Civil Rights.

**DAVID BORGEN,** born New York, New York, January 20, 1952; admitted to bar, 1981, California and U.S. District Court, Northern District of California; 1984, U.S. District Court, Eastern District of California; 1988, U.S. District Court, Central District of California; U.S. Court of Appeals, Ninth Circuit. *Education:* Rutgers University (B.A., highest honors, 1974); University of Iowa (M.A., 1975); Hastings College of Law (J.D., 1981). Phi Beta Kappa. Member, Thurston Society. Order of the Coif. Lecturer, Legal Writing and Research, Hastings College of Law, 1985-1990.

District Counsel, Communications Workers of America, AFL-CIO, Burlingame, CA, 1983-1990. *Member:* State Bar of California (Member, Labor and Employment Section); National Lawyers Guild (Treasurer, 1990-1992); American Arbitration Association (San Francisco, Member, Employment Advisory Committee, 1993-1994); Bay Area Community Law Foundation (President, 1989-1994).

**LINDA M. DARDARIAN,** born Oakland, California, May 7, 1960; admitted to bar, 1987, California, U.S. District Court, Northern District of California and U.S. Court of Appeals, Ninth Circuit; 1992, U.S. District Court, Central District of California, U.S. District Court, District of Minnesota and U.S. Supreme Court; 1995, U.S. District Court, Eastern District of California. *Education:* California State University, Chico (B.A., magna cum laude, 1983); Boalt Hall School of Law, University of California (J.D., 1987). Notes and Comments Editor, Berkeley Women's Law Journal, 1985-1987. *Member:* Alameda County Bar Association; State Bar of California (Member, Labor and Employment and Litigation Sections). *PRACTICE AREAS:* Litigation; Employment Law.

**JOLLEE C. FABER,** born Los Angeles, California, October 31, 1965; admitted to bar, 1992, California and U.S. District Court, Central District of California; 1993, U.S. District Court, Northern District of California. *Education:* University of California at Berkeley (B.A., 1987); University of California at Los Angeles (J.D., 1992). Phi Beta Kappa. Author: "Expanding Title IX of the Education Amendments of 1972 to Prohibit Student to Student Sexual Harassment," 2 UCLA Women's Law Journal 85, 1992.

**LAUREL E. FLETCHER,** born San Francisco, California, April 5, 1963; admitted to bar, 1991, California; U.S. District Court, Northern District of California; U.S. Court of Appeals, Ninth Circuit; 1995, U.S. District Court, Central District of California. *Education:* Brandeis University (B.A., summa cum laude, 1986); Harvard University (J.D., cum laude, 1990). Phi Beta Kappa. Law Clerk to the Honorable Charles A. Legge, U.S. District Court, Northern District of California, 1990-1991. Co-Author: "Time for Justice, The Case for International Prosecutions of Rape and Gender-Based Violence in the Former Yugoslavia," 9 Berkeley Women's L.J. 77, 1994. *PRACTICE AREAS:* Litigation; Employment Law.

**SUSAN GUBERMAN-GARCIA,** born New York, New York, June 17, 1947; admitted to bar, 1975, California and U.S. District Court, Central and Northern Districts of California. *Education:* University of California, Los Angeles; University of San Fernando Valley College of Law (J.D., 1974). *Member:* The State Bar of California.

**CHRISTOPHER J. KELLER,** born Minneapolis, Minnesota, March 12, 1964; admitted to bar, 1995, California; U.S. District Court, Northern District of California; U.S. Court of Appeals, Ninth Circuit. *Education:* St. Olaf College (B.A., 1986); Yale University (MAR, 1989); University of Minnesota (J.D., 1995). Recipient of the Steven M. Block Prize for Scholarship in Civil Rights and Civil Liberties. Article Editor, Journal of Law and Inequality. Author, A Case Comment on Baehr v. Levin, Journal of Law and Inequality, Volume 12, No. 2, 1994. Co-Author: Legal Update on Affirmative Action, University of San Francisco Law School Journal of Law and Social Challenges, Volume I, No. 1, 1996. *Member:* San Francisco (Member, Committee on Sexual Orientation) and American Bar Associations; State Bar of California (Member, Labor and Employment Law Section); Bay Area Lawyers for Individual Freedom (BALIF); Foundation for the Robert Mapplethorpe AIDS Research Laboratory (Cambridge, MA). *PRACTICE AREAS:* Litigation; Employment Law; False Claims Act.

**JACK W. LEE,** born Stockton, California, October 20, 1951; admitted to bar, 1976, California, U.S. District Court, Northern and Eastern Districts of California and U.S. Court of Appeals, Ninth Circuit. *Education:* University of California, Berkeley (B.A., 1973); University of California, Hastings College of Law, San Francisco (J.D., 1976). Phi Beta Kappa.

**KRISTINE A. POPLAWSKI,** born Holyoke, Massachusetts, February 2, 1950; admitted to bar, 1976, Illinois, U.S. District Court, Southern, Central and Northern Districts of Illinois and U.S. Court of Appeals, Fifth, Seventh, Ninth and District of Columbia Circuits; 1992, California, U.S. District Court, Northern and Eastern Districts of California. *Education:* Boston University (B.A., 1972) Suffolk University (J.D., 1976). *LANGUAGES:* Spanish.

**MICHAEL A. SCARLETT,** born Daytona Beach, Florida, March 17, 1954; admitted to bar, 1994, California. *Education:* Florida A & M University (B.S., 1976); University of San Francisco (J.D., 1994). Law Clerk to the Hon. Cecil F. Poole, U.S. Court of Appeals, Ninth Circuit, 1995-1996. *Member:* State Bar of California.

**DEBRA A. SMITH,** born Riverdale, Maryland, August 20, 1953; admitted to bar, 1981, Texas; U.S. District Court, Southern and Northern

*(This Listing Continued)*

### SAPERSTEIN, GOLDSTEIN, DEMCHAK & BALLER, A PROFESSIONAL CORPORATION, Oakland—Continued

Districts of Texas; U.S. Courts of Appeals, Fifth and Tenth Circuits; 1990, California, U.S. District Court, Northern District of California. *Education:* Mount Holyoke College (B.A., magna cum laude, 1975); Stanford University (M.A., 1977); Northeastern University School of Law (J.D., 1980). *Member:* State Bar of California (Litigation and Employment Sections). *LANGUAGES:* Spanish. *PRACTICE AREAS:* Litigation; Employment Law.

**ROBERTA L. STEELE,** born Pittsburgh, Pennsylvania, September 3, 1954; admitted to bar, 1993, Ohio; 1994, U.S. District Court, Northern District of Ohio and U.S. Court of Appeals, Sixth Circuit (Not admitted in California). *Education:* University of Massachusetts (B.A., summa cum laude, 1990); Case Western Reserve University (J.D., 1993). Editor, Case Western Reserve Law Review, 1992-1993. Author: "All Things Not Being Equal: The Case for Race Separate Schools," 43 Case Western Reserve Law Review 591, 1993. *Member:* Cleveland, Ohio State and American Bar Associations. *PRACTICE AREAS:* Litigation.

---

## LAW OFFICES OF
## ERIC P. SCHNURMACHER

A PROFESSIONAL CORPORATION

CENTRAL BUILDING
436 FOURTEENTH STREET
**OAKLAND, CALIFORNIA 94612**
Telephone: 510-836-3534; 839-3990

*General Civil and Trial Practice. Business, Personal Injury, Family and Probate Law.*

**ERIC P. SCHNURMACHER,** born Manila, Philippine Islands, January 8, 1929; admitted to bar, 1956, California; 1962, U.S. Supreme Court and U.S. Court of Military Appeals. *Education:* University of California at Berkeley (A.B., 1950); Boalt Hall School of Law, University of California (J.D., 1956). Phi Delta Phi. Deputy District Attorney, Alameda County, California, 1956-1964. Councilman, 1964-1968 and Mayor, 1968-1970, City of Piedmont, California. Member, Alameda County Mayors' Conference, 1968-1970. Member, National Panel of Arbitrators, American Arbitration Association. Member, Governor's Advisory Committee, Project, Safer California, 1974; Attorney Generals Volunteer Advisory Council, 1974-1976. Municipal Court Judge (Pro Tem), Oakland-Piedmont Judicial District, 1977—. Member, Alameda County Superior Court Bench-Bar Liaison Committee, 1985—. *Member:* Alameda County and American Bar Associations; State Bar of California; Alameda-Contra Costa County Trial Lawyers Association (President, 1984-1985; Member, Board of Governors, 1984); California Trial Lawyers Association; The Association of Trial Lawyers of America. [Lt. Col., J.A.G.C., U.S. Army Reserve, (Retired)]. *LANGUAGES:* Spanish. *PRACTICE AREAS:* Civil Trial Practice; Business Law; Personal Injury; Family Law; Probate Litigation.

---

**ELAINE ERCOLINI,** born Vallejo, California, April 23, 1959; admitted to bar, 1987, California, U.S. District Court, Northern District of California and U.S. Court of Appeals, Ninth Circuit. *Education:* University of California at Berkeley (A.B., 1982); Hastings College the Law, University of California (J.D., 1987). Member: Bar Association of San Francisco, 1987-1990; San Francisco Trial Lawyers Association, 1988-1990; California Public Defenders, 1989; Criminal Trial Lawyers Association of Northern California, 1988-1989. *Member:* Alameda County and American Bar Associations; State Bar of California; American Civil Liberties Union; National Lawyers Guild. *PRACTICE AREAS:* Litigation.

---

## SANDRA L. SCHWEITZER

5826 FREMONT STREET
**OAKLAND, CALIFORNIA 94608**
Telephone: 510-652-8151
Fax: 510-547-1008

*Family Law, including Divorce and Custody.*

**SANDRA L. SCHWEITZER,** born San Jose, California, November 16, 1952; admitted to bar, 1980, Maryland and District of Columbia; 1981, U.S. District Court, District of Maryland and U.S. Court of Appeals,
*(This Listing Continued)*

Fourth Circuit; 1987, U.S. Supreme Court, U.S. District Court for the District of Columbia, U.S. Court of Appeals for the District of Columbia Circuit and U.S. Court of Appeals for the Federal Circuit; 1994, California, U.S. District Court, Northern District of California and U.S. Court of Appeals, Ninth Circuit. *Education:* Cornell University (B.S.N., with distinction, 1974); Georgetown University (J.D., cum laude, 1979). Sigma Theta Tau. Regional Finalist White House Fellowship Program, 1987. Recipient, Lawyers' Co-op Publishing Company American Jurisprudence Award for Commercial Law, 1979. Registered Nurse License: Texas, 1974; Maryland, 1975; California, 1994. Adjunct Professor, Legal Aspects of Implementing Public Health Care Programs, George Washington University Medical School, 1988-1994. *Member:* State Bar of California; District of Columbia Bar; San Francisco, Alameda County, Maryland State and American Bar Associations; Women Lawyers of Alameda County Bar Association. [U.S. Army, 1972-1976, Capt., Army Nurse Corps]. *LANGUAGES:* French. *PRACTICE AREAS:* Family Law.

---

## STALEY, JOBSON & WETHERELL

A PROFESSIONAL CORPORATION

**OAKLAND, CALIFORNIA**

(See Pleasanton)

*Practice limited to Family Law and related areas.*

---

## JOHN O. STANSBURY

5TH FLOOR, 2030 FRANKLIN STREET
**OAKLAND, CALIFORNIA 94612**
Telephone: 510-444-4022
Fax: 510-444-3667

*General Civil and Trial Practice. Tort, Business, Real Estate, Partnership and Commercial Collection Law.*

**JOHN O. STANSBURY,** born Cheyenne, Wyoming, January 10, 1942; admitted to bar, 1969, California. *Education:* University of California at Santa Barbara (B.A., 1964); Boalt Hall School of Law, University of California (J.D., 1968). Vice-Chairman, Boalt Hall Moot Court Board, 1967-1968. President, The Growing Mind, 1971-1986. Member: Alameda County Charter Review Commission, 1974-1977; Board of Directors, 1974-1976 and President, 1975-1976, Oakland Citizens Committee for Urban Renewal; President's Commission on White House Fellowships, Regional Finalist, 1976. Incorporating Director and Member, Board of Directors, Commonweal, 1976-1988. Judge Pro Tem, Oakland-Piedmont Municipal Court, 1979. Chairman, Special Committee to Revise Constitution and Canons, Episcopal Diocese of California, 1979-1982. *Member:* Alameda County and American (Member, Section on Litigation) Bar Associations; State Bar of California (Member, Section on Litigation). *PRACTICE AREAS:* Commercial and Business Litigation.

COUNSEL FOR: Nissan Motor Acceptance Corp.; Hyundai Motor Finance Co.; Commonwealth Insurance Services; Pension Dynamics Corp.; Knockout Sportswear; Northern Automotive Corp.; Roberts & Associates, Inc.; Delta Excavating, Inc.; Red River Land Co.; National Medical Services, Inc.; Reininga Corp.; Florafax International, Inc.; Oakland Land Co.; American Management Group, Inc.; Mid-Com Communications, Inc.; Peregren Management Group, Inc.; Bannatyne Gallery; Mitsubishi Motors Credit of America.

---

## STARK, WELLS, RAHL, SCHWARTZ & SCHIEFFER

LAKE MERRITT PLAZA
1999 HARRISON STREET, SUITE 1300
**OAKLAND, CALIFORNIA 94612**
Telephone: 510-834-2200
Telecopier: 510-763-5121

*General Civil Trial and Appellate Practice. Business, Commercial, Real Estate, Estate Planning and Probate.*

### MEMBERS OF FIRM

**HERBERT L. BREED** (1878-1967).

**GEORGE F. DUNKER, JR.** (1937-1986).

**BESTOR ROBINSON** (1898-1987).

**FRANKLIN C. STARK** (1915-1989).

*(This Listing Continued)*

**MERRILL J. SCHWARTZ,** born Chicago, Illinois, November 18, 1941; admitted to bar, 1966, California. *Education:* Northern Illinois University (A.B., with honors, 1963); Northwestern University (J.D., cum laude, 1966). Order of the Coif. Editor, Northwestern University Law Review, 1965-1966. Affiliate Member, Oakland Board of Realtors. Member: Board of Directors, Alameda County Legal Aid Society, 1985—; Board of Directors, Alameda County Y.M.C.A., 1987—; Board of Directors, Piedmont Council, Boy Scouts of America. Member, Executives Association of Oakland. *Member:* Alameda County and American Bar Associations; The State Bar of California. *PRACTICE AREAS:* Real Estate; Estate Planning; Probate; Commercial Transactions.

**JOSEPH H. SCHIEFFER,** born Stamford, Connecticut, May 17, 1951; admitted to bar, 1976, California and U.S. District Court, Northern District of California; 1983, U.S. District Court, Eastern District of California. *Education:* University of San Francisco (B.A., 1973); Hastings College of Law, University of California (J.D., 1976). Order of the Coif. Member, Thurston Society. Member, Board of Directors and Secretary, Proctor Avenue Neighbors, 1992—. *Member:* Alameda County (Member, 1984-1988, and Chairman, 1986-1987, Race Judicata Committee) and American Bar Associations; The State Bar of California. *PRACTICE AREAS:* Real Estate Transactions; Real Estate Litigation; Business Transactions; Business Litigation.

**MAY LEE TONG,** born Los Angeles, California, June 25, 1947; admitted to bar, 1983, California; 1987, Hawaii. *Education:* Pomona College (B.A., 1970); Golden Gate University (J.D., with highest honors, 1983). Member, Golden Gate Law Review. Law Clerk to Judge Lawrence K. Karlton, U.S. District Court, Eastern District of California, 1984-1986. Law Clerk to Associate Justice Cruz Reynoso, California Supreme Court, 1986-1987. *Member:* State Bar of California; Hawaii State and American Bar Associations. *LANGUAGES:* Chinese, Mandarin and Cantonese. *PRACTICE AREAS:* Civil Litigation; Estate Planning; Trust.

*OF COUNSEL*

**JOHN F. WELLS,** born Jamestown, North Dakota, December 24, 1926; admitted to bar, 1952, California; 1965, U.S. Supreme Court. *Education:* Jamestown College (B.S., 1949); Stanford University (LL.B., 1952). Order of the Coif; Phi Delta Phi. President, Stanford Law Review, 1951-1952. Instructor, San Francisco Law School, 1954-1959. *Member:* Alameda County (Director, 1968-1969) and American Bar Associations; The State Bar of California.

**RICHARD H. RAHL,** born Los Angeles, California, January 18, 1934; admitted to bar, 1962, California; 1967, U.S. Supreme Court. *Education:* University of California at Berkeley (A.B., 1955); Boalt Hall School of Law, University of California (LL.B., 1961). Order of the Coif; Phi Delta Phi. Member, Board of Editors, California Law Review, 1960-1961. *Member:* Alameda County and American Bar Associations; The State Bar of California; Estate Planning Council of The East Bay. Fellow, American College of Trust and Estate Counsel. [Capt., U.S.A.F.R., 1955-1958]. (Certified Specialist, Estate Planning, Trust and Probate Law, California Board of Legal Specialization).

REFERENCE: Wells Fargo Bank (Oakland City Center Branch).

## HARVEY W. STEIN

A PROFESSIONAL CORPORATION

Established in 1975

SUITE 600 TRANSPACIFIC CENTRE
1000 BROADWAY
**OAKLAND, CALIFORNIA 94607**
Telephone: 510-763-6233
Fax: 510-832-1717

*Civil and Trial Practice. Business, Corporate, Petroleum Marketing Practices, Real Estate, Estate Planning, Trust and Probate Law.*

**HARVEY W. STEIN,** born Philadelphia, Pennsylvania, March 30, 1943; admitted to bar, 1969, California and U.S. Court of Appeals, Ninth Circuit; 1974, U.S. Supreme Court, U.S. Tax Court and U.S. District Court, Southern, Central, Northern and Eastern Districts of California. *Education:* University of California at Los Angeles (A.B., 1965); Hastings College of Law, University of California (J.D., 1968). Phi Alpha Delta. Member, Panel of

*(This Listing Continued)*

Arbitrators, American Arbitration Association. Contributor, CEB Counseling California Corporations, 1990. *Member:* Alameda County and American Bar Associations; State Bar of California.

## MIRIAM STEINBOCK

1 KAISER PLAZA, SUITE 1725
**OAKLAND, CALIFORNIA 94612-3612**
Telephone: 510-763-5611
FAX: 510-763-3430

*Family Law.*

**MIRIAM STEINBOCK,** born New York, N.Y., November 28, 1941; admitted to bar, 1972, California and U.S. District Court, Northern District of California. *Education:* Smith College (A.B., 1963); Stanford University; Harvard University (J.D., 1971). Phi Beta Kappa. *Member:* State Bar of California (Member, Family Law Section); Alameda County Family Law Association (Member, Governing Board, 1988-1990). (Certified Specialist, Family Law, The State Bar of California Board of Legal Specialization).

## STRICKLAND & HAAPALA

Established in 1979

SUITE 800, PARK PLAZA BUILDING
1939 HARRISON STREET
**OAKLAND, CALIFORNIA 94612**
Telephone: 510-763-2324
Fax: 510-273-8534

*General Civil and Trial Practice in all State and Federal Courts. Casualty Insurance Law.*

*PARTNERS OF FIRM*

**WILLIAM R. STRICKLAND,** born Rochester, Minnesota, August 9, 1942; admitted to bar, 1969, California. *Education:* San Jose State College (A.B., with distinction, 1965); Hastings College of Law, University of California (J.D., 1968). *Member:* Alameda County (President, 1986) and American Bar Associations; State Bar of California; Association of Defense Counsel of Northern California (Director, 1984-1987; President, 1990); Defense Research Institute. *PRACTICE AREAS:* Personal Injury; Construction Defect; Roof Industry Liability; Medical Negligence; Legal Negligence; Sexual Harassment; Mediation.

**JOHN E. HAAPALA,** born Hibbing, Minnesota, December 22, 1939; admitted to bar, 1969, California. *Education:* University of California at Berkeley (A.B., 1964); Hastings College of Law, University of California (J.D., 1968). Arbitrator, Superior Court Arbitrator's Panel. Member, Panel of Arbitrators, American Arbitration Association. *Member:* Alameda County and American Bar Associations; State Bar of California; Association of Defense Counsel. *PRACTICE AREAS:* Commercial Litigation; Personal Injury.

**CHRISTOPHER M. HARNETT, JR.,** born Temple, Texas, June 12, 1945; admitted to bar, 1974, California. *Education:* University of California at Berkeley (B.A., 1967); University of San Francisco (J.D., 1973). Member, McAuliffe Law Honor Society. Attorney, San Joaquin County Public Defender's Office, 1974-1979. Judge Pro Tem, State of California, Office of Administrative Hearings. *Member:* State Bar of California; Association of Defense Counsel. [LTJG, U.S. Navy, 1967-1970]. *PRACTICE AREAS:* Products Liability; Employer Liability; Public Entity Liability; Insurance Defense; Administrative Law.

**CHARLES J. MAGUIRE, JR.,** born Weymouth, Massachusetts, April 7, 1951; admitted to bar, 1981, California. *Education:* Gettysburg College (B.A., 1973); San Francisco Law School (J.D., 1981). *Member:* Alameda County and American Bar Associations; State Bar of California; Association of Defense Counsel. *PRACTICE AREAS:* Construction Defect; Toxic Claims; Environmental Claims; Intellectual Property.

**CLYDE A. THOMPSON,** born San Francisco, California, November 3, 1946; admitted to bar, 1976, California. *Education:* San Francisco State University (B.A., 1968); Lincoln University (J.D., 1976). Member, Lincoln University Law Review, 1975-1976. *Member:* Alameda County Bar Association; State Bar of California; Association of Defense Counsel. [Lt., U.S. Navy, 1968-1971]. *PRACTICE AREAS:* Public Entity; Construction Injuries; Premises Liability; Business Torts; Contracts; Employment Claims.

**JUDITH B. ALTURA,** born Brooklyn, New York, February 17, 1945; admitted to bar, 1981, California. *Education:* Brooklyn College of the City

*(This Listing Continued)*

STRICKLAND & HAAPALA, Oakland—Continued

University of New York (B.A., cum laude, 1969); University of San Francisco (J.D., 1981). *Member:* Alameda County, Contra Costa County and American Bar Associations; State Bar of California; Association of Defense Counsel. *PRACTICE AREAS:* Auto Medical Fraud; Personal Injury; Premises Liability; Products Liability.

REPRESENTATIVE CLIENTS: Aetna Insurance Co.; Allstate Insurance Co.; California State Automobile Assn.; County of Alameda; City of Oakland; The Farmers Insurance Group of Companies; Harco Insurance Co.; John Glenn Adjusters and Administrators, Inc.; Republic Insurance; Sisters of Providence Hospital; Transamerica Insurance Co.; Travelers Insurance Co.

## MICHAEL R. SULLIVAN

2100 EMCARCADERO, SUITE 100
**OAKLAND, CALIFORNIA 94606**
Telephone: 510-535-2580
Facsimile: 510-535-2579
Email: msulli5559@aol.com

*Construction.*

**MICHAEL R. SULLIVAN,** born Oakland, California, June 3, 1950; admitted to bar, 1990, California. *Education:* University of California (B.A., 1973); Golden Gate University (J.D., 1990). Licensed, California State Contractors 1975—. *Member:* Alameda County Bar Association; State Bar of California; National Roofing Contractors Association.

REFERENCES: Available Upon Request.

## ERNEST M. THAYER

A PROFESSIONAL CORPORATION
LAKE MERRITT PLAZA, SUITE 1300
1999 HARRISON STREET
**OAKLAND, CALIFORNIA 94612**
Telephone: 510-874-4122
Telecopier: 510-834-7440

*Civil Trial and Appellate Practice. Insurance, Products Liability, Malpractice, Consumer and Business Litigation.*

**ERNEST M. THAYER,** born Nashville, Tennessee, November 10, 1930; admitted to bar, 1961, California; 1978, U.S. Supreme Court. *Education:* DePauw University (A.B., 1953); Harvard University (LL.B., 1959). Arbitrator: San Francisco Superior Court, 1979—; U.S. District Court, 1981—. *Member:* Bar Association of San Francisco (Arbitrator: Committee on Fee Disputes, 1967—; Ethics Committee, 1981—); The State Bar of California (Referee, State Bar Court of California, 1980-1984; Presiding Referee, 1985-1989; Arbitrator, 1990—); American Bar Association (Member, Litigation Section); Association of Defense Counsel of Northern California; American Judicature Society; California Trial Lawyers Association; The Association of Trial Lawyers of America; California Academy of Appellate Lawyers.

## LAW OFFICES OF
## CHARLES A. TRIAY

Established in 1977
1 KAISER PLAZA, SUITE 2360
**OAKLAND, CALIFORNIA 94612**
Telephone: 510-832-8700
Fax: 510-836-2595

*Probate Litigation, Probate Administration and Estate Planning.*

FIRM PROFILE: Mr. Triay concentrates on probate litigation, including Will contests, oral promises to make a Will, step-child inheritance claims and spousal rights re estates.

**CHARLES A. TRIAY,** born Seattle, Washington, May 23, 1950; admitted to bar, 1977, California and U.S. District Court, Central District of California. *Education:* University of California at Berkeley (A.B., 1972); University of San Diego (J.D., 1977). *Member:* Alameda County Bar Association (Member, Probate Section); State Bar of California; Consumer Attorneys of California. (Certified Specialist, Estate Planning, Trust and Pro-

*(This Listing Continued)*

bate Law, The State Bar of California Board of Legal Specialization). *PRACTICE AREAS:* Probate Litigation; Probate and Trust Administration; Estate Planning.

## LAW OFFICES OF
## HERMAN A. TRUTNER

ORDWAY BUILDING
ONE KAISER PLAZA, SUITE 1545
**OAKLAND, CALIFORNIA 94612**
Telephone: 510-287-5222
FAX: 510-763-5010

*Business, Estate Planning, Trust, Probate and Related Litigation.*

**HERMAN A. TRUTNER,** born Oakland, California, June 14, 1928; admitted to bar, 1965, California. *Education:* University of California at Berkeley (B.S., 1953); San Francisco Law School (LL.B., 1964). *Member:* Alameda County and American Bar Associations; The State Bar of California. (Certified Specialist, Estate Planning, Trust and Probate Law, The State Bar of California Board of Legal Specialization). *PRACTICE AREAS:* Probate; Estate Planning; Trust Law; Trust Litigation; Conservatorships.

**SHARON A. ISENHOUR,** born Atascadero, California, March 9, 1944; admitted to bar, 1992, California. *Education:* San Francisco Law School (J.D., 1990). Adjunct Professor, Paralegal Program in Taxation, Wills and Trusts, St. Mary's College. *Member:* Alameda County and American Bar Associations; The State Bar of California. *PRACTICE AREAS:* Probate; Trust Administration; Conservatorships; Estate Planning; Probate Litigation.

ASSOCIATES

**CYNTHIA DE NEVERS TRUTNER,** born Marin County, California, September 28, 1960; admitted to bar, 1989, California. *Education:* University of California at Berkeley (B.A., 1982); Hastings College of the Law, University of California (J.D., 1989). *Member:* Alameda County and American Bar Associations; The State Bar of California. *PRACTICE AREAS:* Probate; Trust Administration; Conservatorships; Estate Planning.

## LAW OFFICES OF PAUL F. UTRECHT

OAKLAND, CALIFORNIA
(See San Francisco)
*Civil Litigation, Probate Litigation, and Appeals.*

## VAN BLOIS, KNOWLES, SCHWARTZ &
## BASKIN

SUITE 2245 ORDWAY BUILDING
ONE KAISER PLAZA
**OAKLAND, CALIFORNIA 94612**
Telephone: 510-444-1906
Contra Costa County 510-947-1055
Fax: 510-444-1294

*Plaintiffs Trial Practice in fields of Product Liability, Highway Design, Construction Accidents, Airplane Crash Litigation, Railroad Accidents, Medical Malpractice, Bad Faith, Employment, Negligence Law and Class Actions regarding Fraudulent Sales and Truth in Lending.*

MEMBERS OF FIRM

**R. LEWIS VAN BLOIS,** born Warren, Pennsylvania, June 27, 1939; admitted to bar, 1966, California; 1974, U.S. Supreme Court. *Education:* George Washington University (B.A., 1961); University of Vienna, Austria; Boalt Hall School of Law, University of California (J.D., 1965). Faculty, National Institute for Trial Advocacy, 1984-1985. Arbitrator, Alameda County Superior Court, 1971—. Member, Panel of Arbitrators, American Arbitration Association. *Member:* Alameda County, Southern Alameda County, Contra Costa County and American Bar Associations; State Bar of California; The Association of Trial Lawyers of America; Pennsylvania Trial Lawyers Association; California Trial Lawyers Association (Member, Board of Governors, 1977-1979); Alameda-Contra Costa County Trial

*(This Listing Continued)*

Lawyers Association (Member, Board of Governors, 1971—; President, 1977-1978); California Trial Lawyers Association (Recognized experience as a Trial Lawyer and in the fields of Products Liability, Professional Negligence, Public Entity Liability and General Personal Injury Law). Certified as a Civil Trial Advocate by the National Board of Trial Advocacy. *PRACTICE AREAS:* Personal Injury; Product Liability; Highway Design; Construction Accidents; Medical Malpractice; Class Actions.

*THOMAS C. KNOWLES,* born New York, N.Y., April 22, 1942; admitted to bar, 1967, California. *Education:* Williams College (A.B., 1964); Hastings College of Law, University of California (J.D., 1967). *Member:* Alameda County Bar Association; State Bar of California; California Trial Lawyers Association (Recognized Experience as a Trial Lawyer and in the fields of Products Liability and General Personal Injury Law); Alameda-Contra Costa Trial Lawyers Association (Member, Board of Governors, 1985-1990). *PRACTICE AREAS:* Personal Injury Law; Products Liability Law; Medical Malpractice Law; Highway Design Law; Construction Accidents.

*ELLEN R. SCHWARTZ,* born New York, N.Y., April 5, 1953; admitted to bar, 1980, California. *Education:* State University of New York at Binghamton (B.A., 1976); John F. Kennedy University (J.D., 1980). Associate Professor, Paralegal Courses in Paralegal Certificate Program, Department of Continuing Education, California State University at Hayward, 1984-1987. *Member:* Alameda County Bar Association; State Bar of California. *PRACTICE AREAS:* Accident and Personal Injury; Medical Malpractice Law; Public Entity Law; Professional Malpractice Law; Class Actions.

*RICHARD J. BASKIN,* born Hayward, California, December 20, 1952; admitted to bar, 1983, California. *Education:* University of California at Santa Barbara (B.A., with honors, 1977); George August University, Gottingen, West Germany; University of San Francisco (J.D., 1981). Deputy District Attorney, San Joaquin County, 1984-1987. *Member:* Alameda County and Southern Alameda County Bar Associations; State Bar of California; California Trial Lawyers Association (Member, Board of Governors, 1993—); Alameda-Contra Costa Trial Lawyers Association (Member, Board of Governors, 1990—; Education Chair, 1991—). *LANGUAGES:* German. *PRACTICE AREAS:* Personal Injury; Wrongful Death; Products Liability; Construction Accidents; Class Actions.

*OF COUNSEL*

*CHARLES E. FARNSWORTH,* born Singapore, July 31, 1938; admitted to bar, 1969, California; 1986, U.S. Supreme Court. *Education:* University of Kansas (B.S., 1960); Stanford University (LL.B., 1966). Superior Court Arbitrator and Mediator, Alameda County, 1983—. Member, Panel of Arbitrators, American Arbitration Association. *Member:* State Bar of California; Alameda-Contra Costa Trial Lawyers Association (Education Chairman, 1986-1988). *LANGUAGES:* Spanish. *PRACTICE AREAS:* Employment Law; Personal Injury Law.

---

## VAN BOURG, WEINBERG, ROGER & ROSENFELD

*180 GRAND AVENUE, SUITE 1400*
**OAKLAND, CALIFORNIA 94612-3741**
*Telephone: 510-839-6600*
*Fax: 510-891-0400*

*Labor Relations and Workers Compensation Law.*

*STANFORD L. GELBMAN* (1932-1992).

*VICTOR J. VAN BOURG,* born New York, N.Y., March 19, 1931; admitted to bar, 1956, California, U.S. Court of Appeals, Ninth Circuit and U.S. District Court, Northern District of California; 1957, U.S. District Court, Southern District of California; 1962, U.S. Supreme Court. *Education:* University of California at Berkeley (B.A., 1953); Boalt Hall School of Law, University of California (LL.B., 1956). *PRACTICE AREAS:* Labor Law.

*STEWART WEINBERG,* born Chicago, Illinois, April 1, 1936; admitted to bar, 1961, California, U.S. Court of Appeals, Ninth Circuit and U.S. District Court, Northern District of California; 1963, U.S. District Court, Southern District of California; 1969, U.S. District Court, Eastern District of California; 1985, U.S. Supreme Court. *Education:* University of California at Berkeley (A.B., with honors, 1957); Boalt Hall School of Law, University of California (J.D., 1960). *PRACTICE AREAS:* Labor Law.

*(This Listing Continued)*

*MICHAEL B. ROGER,* born San Francisco, California, December 22, 1941; admitted to bar, 1967, California, U.S. District Court, Northern, Eastern and Southern Districts of California, U.S. Court of Appeals, Ninth Circuit, U.S. Claims Court and U.S. Supreme Court. *Education:* Reed College; University of California at Berkeley (B.A., 1964); Hastings College of Law, University of California (J.D., 1967). *PRACTICE AREAS:* Labor Law.

*DAVID A. ROSENFELD,* born Jackson, Michigan, March 10, 1945; admitted to bar, 1973, California, U.S. District Court, Northern, Central, Eastern and Southern Districts of California, U.S. Court of Appeals, Ninth Circuit, U.S. Supreme Court; 1983, U.S. Court of Appeals for the Federal Circuit. *Education:* Brown University (B.A., 1966); Boalt Hall School of Law, University of California (J.D., 1973). *PRACTICE AREAS:* Labor Law.

*WILLIAM A. SOKOL,* born Cleveland, Ohio, February 20, 1946; admitted to bar, 1976, California, U.S. Court of Appeals, Ninth Circuit and U.S. District Court, Northern, Central and Eastern Districts of California; 1980, U.S. Supreme Court. *Education:* University of Wisconsin (B.A., 1968); University of California at Berkeley (M.A., 1972); Yale Law School; Boalt Hall School of Law, University of California (J.D., 1976). *LANGUAGES:* Spanish. *PRACTICE AREAS:* Labor Law.

*VINCENT A. HARRINGTON, JR.,* born Boston, Massachusetts, December 24, 1947; admitted to bar, 1974, Massachusetts; 1976, California; 1978, U.S. District Court, Northern and Eastern Districts of California; 1980, U.S. Court of Appeals, Ninth Circuit. *Education:* Boston College (B.A., cum laude, 1969); Cornell University (J.D., 1973). *PRACTICE AREAS:* Labor Law.

*W. DANIEL BOONE,* born Boston, Massachusetts, March 9, 1943; admitted to bar, 1968, Virginia, District of Columbia and U.S. District Court, Northern District of Virginia; 1970, California, U.S. District Court, Northern, Eastern and Southern Districts of California and U.S. Court of Appeals, Ninth Circuit. *Education:* Amherst College (B.A., cum laude in Philosophy, 1965); Georgetown University (J.D., 1968). *PRACTICE AREAS:* Labor Law.

*PAUL D. SUPTON,* born New York, N.Y., January 7, 1940; admitted to bar, 1976, California. *Education:* City College of New York (B.S., magna cum laude, 1961); New York University (M.A., 1968); Stanford University (J.D., 1976). *PRACTICE AREAS:* Labor Law.

*BLYTHE MICKELSON,* born Los Angeles, California, February 9, 1954; admitted to bar, 1980, California; 1982, U.S. Court of Appeals, Ninth Circuit and U.S. District Court, Northern, Eastern and Southern Districts of California. *Education:* Stanford University (B.A., with distinction, 1976); Boalt Hall School of Law, University of California (J.D., 1980). *PRACTICE AREAS:* Labor Law.

*BARRY E. HINKLE,* born Gettysburg, Pennsylvania, April 11, 1947; admitted to bar, 1976, California and U.S. District Court, Northern District of California; 1977, U.S. District Court, Eastern District of California and U.S. Court of Appeals, Ninth Circuit; 1980, U.S. Supreme Court. *Education:* Fullerton College (A.A., 1971); University of California at Berkeley (B.A., 1973); Hastings College of the Law, University of California (J.D., 1976). *PRACTICE AREAS:* Labor Law.

*JAMES RUTKOWSKI,* born Eric, Pennsylvania, February 26, 1944; admitted to bar, 1971, Arizona; 1973, U.S. Court of Appeals, Ninth Circuit; 1978, California; 1979, U.S. Supreme Court. *Education:* Gannon College (A.A., 1964); St. Bonaventure University (B.A., 1966); Arizona State University (J.D., 1971). *PRACTICE AREAS:* Labor Law.

*SANDRA RAE BENSON,* born San Francisco, California, July 15, 1949; admitted to bar, 1985, California, U.S. Court of Appeals, Ninth Circuit and U.S. District Court, Northern and Southern Districts of California. *Education:* University of California at Berkeley (B.A., 1982); Hastings College of the Law, University of California; Boalt Hall School of Law, University of California (J.D., 1985). *PRACTICE AREAS:* Labor Law.

*JAMES G. VARGA,* born Buffalo, New York, October 1, 1949; admitted to bar, 1979, California, U.S. District Court, Central District of California and U.S. Court of Appeals, Ninth Circuit. *Education:* State University of New York at Buffalo (B.A., 1973); Glendale University College of Law (J.D., 1977). Editor-in-Chief, Glendale Law Review, 1977-1978. *Member:* National Lawyers Guild (Member, Labor Committee; Treasurer, 1987).

*CHRISTIAN L. RAISNER,* born New Britain, Pennsylvania, July 31, 1940; admitted to bar, 1985, Wisconsin and U.S. District Court, Eastern and Western Districts of Wisconsin; 1988, California, U.S. District Court,

*(This Listing Continued)*

### VAN BOURG, WEINBERG, ROGER & ROSENFELD,
Oakland—Continued

Eastern and Northern Districts of California and U.S. Court of Appeals, Ninth Circuit. *Education:* University of Illinois (B.A., 1979; M.A., 1981); Northwestern University (J.D., 1985). *PRACTICE AREAS:* Labor Law.

**JAMES J. WESSER,** born Los Angeles, California, January 11, 1948; admitted to bar, 1989, California, U.S. District Court, Northern District of California and U.S. Court of Appeals, Ninth Circuit. *Education:* University of California at Los Angeles (B.A., 1971); Golden Gate University (J.D., 1988); New York University (LL.M., 1989).

**AMY D. MARTIN,** born Fresno, California, April 1, 1964; admitted to bar, 1990, California and U.S. District Court, Northern District of California. *Education:* University of San Francisco (B.A., 1987); McGeorge School of Law, University of the Pacific (J.D., with great distinction, 1990). *PRACTICE AREAS:* Labor Law; Employment Law.

**THEODORE FRANKLIN,** born Passaic, New Jersey, May 20, 1949; admitted to bar, 1993, California and U.S. District Court, Northern District of California. *Education:* Harvard College; Hastings College of the Law (J.D., cum laude, 1993). *PRACTICE AREAS:* Labor.

---

### VENERUSO & MONCHARSH

A Partnership of Professional Corporations

Established in 1987

440 GRAND AVENUE, SUITE 360
**OAKLAND, CALIFORNIA 94610-5012**
Telephone: 510-433-0390
Fax: 510-433-0389

*Professional Malpractice Defense including Medical, Podiatric and Legal, Real Estate Litigation, Family, Sports Liability and Equine Law. General Liability Insurance Defense. Land Use.*

**DONNA M. VENERUSO, (P.C.),** born St. Louis, Missouri, October 1, 1944; admitted to bar, 1974, California. *Education:* Syracuse University (A.B., 1966); University of San Francisco (J.D., magna cum laude, 1974). Psi Chi. *Member:* Bar Association of San Francisco; Alameda County Bar Association; State Bar of California. *PRACTICE AREAS:* Family; Insurance Defense; Sports Liability.

**LEILA H. MONCHARSH, (P.C.),** born San Francisco, California, October 15, 1950; admitted to bar, 1977, California. *Education:* University of St. Andrews, Scotland; University of California at Santa Cruz (A.B., 1973); University of San Francisco (J.D., 1976). Deputy District Attorney: San Francisco County, 1978-1979; San Joaquin County, 1979-1982. *Member:* Bar Association of San Francisco; Alameda County and American Bar Associations; State Bar of California. *PRACTICE AREAS:* Insurance Defense; Product Liability; Medical; Equine Law; Land Use.

---

**DAVID G. HYSINGER,** born Falls Church, Virginia, November 23, 1965; admitted to bar, 1992, California. *Education:* University of California at Berkeley (A.B., with honors, general academic citation, 1987); University of San Francisco (J.D., 1991; M.B.A., 1993). *Member:* State Bar of California. *LANGUAGES:* French. *PRACTICE AREAS:* Professional Malpractice Defense; General Liability Insurance Defense.

REPRESENTATIVE CLIENTS: Fremont Indemnity Co.; PICA; Interstate National; Physicians Interindemnity Trust; Continental Insurance Co.; O.U.M.; Pioneer Claims Management, Inc.; First Mercury Syndicate; Jefferson Insurance Group; NAHA.

---

### WALD & BENDES

1999 HARRISON STREET, SUITE 1300
**OAKLAND, CALIFORNIA 94612**
Telephone: 510-444-0560
Fax: 510-273-8707

*General Civil and Trial Practice. Personal Injury, Real Property, Business, Family Law, Corporations.*

**MICHAEL E. WALD,** born Chicago, Illinois, August 2, 1938; admitted to bar, 1964, California, U.S. District Court, Northern District of California and U.S. Court of Appeals, Ninth Circuit; 1971, U.S. Supreme Court. *Education:* University of Colorado at Boulder (B.A., 1960); University of

*(This Listing Continued)*

California at Berkeley (J.D., 1963). Phi Sigma Alpha. Listed in: Naifeh & White's, "The Best Lawyers in America". Assistant Professor, John F. Kennedy School of Law, 1975—. Legislative Intern, California State Assembly, 1963-1964. Disciplinary Hearing Officer, State Bar of California, 1970-1989. Panelist, Continuing Education of the Bar: Family Law, Evidence. *Member:* Contra Costa County and Alameda County Bar Associations; State Bar of California; California Trial Lawyers Association; Alameda-Contra Costa County Trial Lawyers Association. *PRACTICE AREAS:* Personal Injury; Family Law.

**CHARLES N. BENDES,** born New York, N.Y., July 21, 1951; admitted to bar, 1976, California and U.S. District Court, Northern District of California; 1977, U.S. Court of Appeals, Ninth Circuit. *Education:* Antioch College (BA., 1973); University of Santa Clara (J.D., summa cum laude, 1976). Instructor of Law, John F. Kennedy University School of Law, Walnut Creek, California, 1982-1985. Panelist, Continuing Education of the Bar, Recent Developments in Torts, 1986-1989 and How to Avoid and Survive Attorneys' Fees Disputes, 1993 and 1994. *Member:* Alameda County Bar Association (Member: Fee Arbitration Executive Committee; Pro Bono Legal Services Committee; Chair, Community Services Committee, 1993); State Bar of California (Member, Sections on: Business Law; Real Estate). *REPORTED CASES:* Roffinella v. Sherinian 179 Cal App 3d 230 (1986). *PRACTICE AREAS:* Real Estate Law and Litigation; Corporate and Business Law and Litigation; Probate Litigation. *Email:* cnb@aol.com

---

### WENDEL, ROSEN, BLACK & DEAN, LLP

Established in 1909

TWENTY-FOURTH FLOOR
1111 BROADWAY
**OAKLAND, CALIFORNIA 94607**
Telephone: 510-834-6600
Facsimile: 510-834-1928
Email: info@wendel.com

*General Civil and Trial Practice. Real Property. Commercial. Taxation. Construction. Business. Securities. Corporate. Franchise. Pension and Profit Sharing. Bankruptcy. Estate Planning and Probate. Public Finance. Land Use and Environmental. Secured Transactions. Public Agency Law. Intellectual Property.*

#### MEMBERS OF FIRM

**C. GREGG ANKENMAN,** born 1960; admitted to bar, 1988, California. *Education:* Brigham Young University (B.A., 1984); Boalt Hall School of Law, University of California at Berkeley (J.D., 1988). Consulting Author: "Handling Real Property Sales Transactions," California Continuing Education of the Bar, 1992. Consultant: *Office Leasing, Drafting & Negotiating the Lease,* Continuing Education of the Bar, 1996. *LANGUAGES:* Spanish. *PRACTICE AREAS:* Real Estate Law; Business Law.

**MARK S. BOSTICK,** born 1953; admitted to bar, 1983, California. *Education:* University of California at Berkeley (A.B., 1978); University of San Francisco (J.D., 1983). *PRACTICE AREAS:* Bankruptcy Law; Commercial Litigation.

**MICHAEL P. CARBONE,** born 1942; admitted to bar, 1966, California. *Education:* University of San Francisco (B.S., 1966; J.D., 1966). Member, McAuliffe Law Honor Society. Author and Lecturer, California Continuing Education of the Bar, 1971—. Contributing Author, *Drafting & Negotiating the Lease,* Continuing Education of the Bar, 1996. Member, International Council of Shopping Centers, 1981—. Member, Panel of Arbitrators, American Arbitration Association. *Member:* California Business Properties Association (Member, Board of Directors). *PRACTICE AREAS:* Commercial Leasing; Real Property Development; Alternative Dispute Resolution.

**MICHAEL D. COOPER,** born 1943; admitted to bar, 1969, California. *Education:* San Francisco State University (B.A., 1965); University of San Francisco (J.D., 1968). Faculty Member, Pacific Bankruptcy Law Institute, 1992. Lawyer Representatives of the U.S. Bankruptcy Court for the Northern District of California, 1990-1993; Rules Subcommittee to Revise Bankruptcy for the Northern District, 1991-1992. Chair, Personal and Small Business Bankruptcy Advisory Commission, State Bar of California. Member, Bar Association of San Francisco. *PRACTICE AREAS:* Bankruptcy Law; Reorganization Law; Business Workouts Law.

**MICHAEL A. DEAN,** born 1942; admitted to bar, 1967, California. *Education:* San Jose State College (B.A., 1964); Boalt Hall School of Law, University of California (J.D., 1967). Co-Author, Commercial Real Prop-

*(This Listing Continued)*

erty Lease Practice, California Continuing Education of The Bar, 1976; Supplement, 1992. Contributing Author: *Office Leasing, Drafting & Negotiating the Lease*, Continuing Education of the Bar, 1996; "California Real Property Sales Transactions," California Continuing Education of the Bar, 1981, 1982 and 1984 Supplement to "Ground Lease Practice," California Continuing Education of the Bar, 1988. Author: California Continuing Education of the Bar, California Real Property Law Journal, ICSC Law Library Construction Issues. Co-Author, "Selected Issues in Build To Suit Leases," ICSC Law Library Construction Issues, 1995. Member, Planning Committee, Annual Real Property Institute, California Continuing Education of the Bar, 1983—. Member, Board of Directors, Oakland Convention Center Management, Inc., 1987—. Lecturer on Real Property Law: California Continuing Education of the Bar, State Bar Real Property Law Section, International Council of Shopping Centers, 1976—. *Member:* American College of Real Estate Lawyers. **PRACTICE AREAS:** Real Property Law; Business Law; Franchise Law.

**DAVID GOLDMAN,** born 1952; admitted to bar, 1977, California. *Education:* Michigan State University (B.A., with honors, 1974); Hastings College of Law, University of California (J.D., 1977). Author, "Confusing a Lender with a Vendor under §580b: Has Legislative Intent and Public Policy Been Subverted?" California Real Property Journal, Vol. 12, No. 2, Spring, 1994. Chair, Trial Practice Section, Alameda County Bar Association, 1996. Deputy City Attorney, City and County of San Francisco, 1977-1981. **PRACTICE AREAS:** Employment Litigation; Real Property Litigation; Business Litigation.

**CHARLES A. HANSEN,** born 1951; admitted to bar, 1977, California; 1978, U.S. Court of Appeals, Ninth Circuit; 1981, U.S. Supreme Court; 1992, U.S. District Court, Northern District of Texas. *Education:* University of California at Los Angeles (B.A., summa cum laude, 1973); Boalt Hall School of Law, University of California (J.D., 1977). Phi Beta Kappa. Recipient, American Jurisprudence Award. Author: "Making a Claim Under Title Insurance Policy," Continuing Education of the Bar 1992. Co-Author, "Cases and Materials on Real Estate Transactions," Boalt Hall Course Materials. Lecturer in Law, Boalt Hall School of Law, University of California, Berkeley, 1986—. **PRACTICE AREAS:** Real Estate Litigation and Appeals; Commercial and Secured Transactions.

**LES A. HAUSRATH,** born 1947; admitted to bar, 1973, California. *Education:* University of California (B.A., with distinction, 1969); Boalt Hall School of Law, University of California at Berkeley (J.D., 1973). Phi Beta Kappa. Lecturer: Land Subsidence Law, California Continuing Education of the Bar, 1988, 1990. Author: "In with a Roar, Out with a Meow: A Review of the Legislative and Developments in the California Environmental Quality Act in 1993," California Real Property Journal, 1994; "Slip Sliding Away: An Analysis of Governmental Agency Liability in Landslide and Other Damage Actions Involving Natural Conditions of Public Land," California Real Property Journal, 1992. Chairman, Executive Committee, Real Property Section, State Bar of California, 1996. **PRACTICE AREAS:** Real Property Litigation; Land Use; Eminent Domain; Government Agency Law; Land Subsidence Litigation.

**WILLIAM E. HORWICH,** born 1942; admitted to bar, 1969, California. *Education:* Princeton University (A.B., 1964); London School of Economics; Centre de Recherche d'Urbanisme, Paris, France; Yale University (LL.B., 1968). Phi Beta Kappa. Vice President, French-American Chamber of Commerce, 1986-1996. **PRACTICE AREAS:** Corporate; Securities.

**HOWARD W. LIND,** born 1953; admitted to bar, 1978, California. *Education:* University of California at Davis (A.B., 1975); Hastings College of Law, University of California (J.D., 1978). Consultant, *Office Leasing, Drafting & Negotiating the Lease* , Continuing Education of the Bar, 1996. Author: "A Real Estate Attorney's Guide to California Usury Laaws," *CEB Real Property Law Reporter,* Vol. 18, No. 7, October 1995. Lecturer, Real Property Law, California Continuing Education of the Bar, 1984—. **PRACTICE AREAS:** Real Property Law.

**BRUCE LYMBURN,** born 1953; admitted to bar, 1982, California. *Education:* University of California at Santa Cruz (A.B., 1979); Boalt Hall School of Law, University of California (J.D., 1982). Member, 1979-1980 and Associate Editor, 1980-1981, Ecology Law Quarterly. **PRACTICE AREAS:** Real Estate Transaction Law; Business Law.

**DEANNA DOWN LYON,** born 1947; admitted to bar, 1972, California. *Education:* California State College at Fullerton (B.A., with honors, 1969); Boalt Hall School of Law, University of California (J.D., 1972). Phi Kappa Phi. Co-Author: "California Decedent Estate Practice," California Continuing Education of the Bar, 1986, 1987 and 1988 Supplements. Lecturer on Estate Planning and Probate, California Continuing Education of the Bar, 1985—. Judge Pro Tem, Alameda County Superior Court, 1986—. (Certified Specialist, Estate Planning, Trust and Probate Law, The State Bar of California Board of Legal Specialization). **PRACTICE AREAS:** Estate Planning Law; Probate Law; Trust Law.

**DONALD A. MCISAAC,** born 1953; admitted to bar, 1978, California. *Education:* University of California at Berkeley (A.B., 1975); Boalt Hall School of Law, University of California (J.D., 1978). Phi Beta Kappa. Consultant, *Office Leasing, Drafting & Negotiating the Lease*, Continuing Education of the Bar, 1996. Author: "Handling Public Works Remedies (Stop Notices and Payment Bonds)," California Continuing Education of the Bar (CEB), 3rd Ed., 1993; "Can Construction Bond Claimants Sue Sureties for Bad Faith?" California Construction Law Reporter, Shepard's Sept. 1991; "Handling Unlawful Detainers," CEB, 3d. Ed. 1993. Lecturer, Continuing Education of the Bar, Continuing Legal Education International, 1987—. Judge Pro Tem, Oakland-Piedmont Municipal Court, 1984—. Chair, "Advanced Symposium on Commercial Leases," CLE Int'l., 1993. **PRACTICE AREAS:** Construction Law; Real Property Law; Business Litigation.

**STEVEN M. MORGER,** born 1959; admitted to bar, 1984, California, U.S. District Court, Northern District of California; 1985, U.S. District Court, Central District of California; 1986, U.S. District Court, Eastern District of California; 1988, U.S. District Court, Southern District of California and U.S. Court of Appeals, Ninth Circuit; 1991, U.S. District Court, Northern District of Texas. *Education:* University of California at Berkeley (B.S., 1981); Boalt Hall School of Law, University of California (J.D., 1984). Federal Practice Program, Certificated, 1986. Lecturer in Law, Boalt Hall School of Law, University of California, Berkeley, 1996—. **PRACTICE AREAS:** Real Estate and Secured Transactions Litigation.

**CHRISTINE K. NOMA,** born 1957; admitted to bar, 1982, California. *Education:* University of California at Berkeley (B.S., with honors, 1979); Hastings College of the Law, University of California (J.D., 1982). Judge pro tem, Alameda County Municipal Court; Superior Court Settlement Panel, 1991—. Alameda County Bar Foundation, 1990-1993. Director, Legal Assistance for Seniors, 1994. Director, Legal Assistance for Seniors, 1994. Commissioner, Judicial Nominee Evaluation, The State Bar of California, 1992-1993. **PRACTICE AREAS:** Environmental Law; Employment Law; Insurance Law.

**DAVID L. PREISS,** born 1955; admitted to bar, 1982, California. *Education:* Williams College (B.A., magna cum laude, 1977); University of California, Davis (J.D., 1982). Phi Beta Kappa. Co-author: *California Subdivision Map Act Practice*, Continuing Education of the Bar. Contributing author, *Office Leasing, Drafting & negotiating the Lease*, Continuing Education of the Bar, 1996. **PRACTICE AREAS:** Land Use Law; Real Estate Law; Franchise Law.

**DANIEL RAPAPORT,** born 1950; admitted to bar, 1975, California and U.S. Court of Appeals, Ninth Circuit. *Education:* University of California at Berkeley (B.A., 1972); University of California at Davis (J.D., 1975). Arbitrator: Marin County Superior Court, 1980—. Settlement Facilitator, San Francisco Superior Court, 1988. Superior Court Judge Pro Tem, 1990—. Member, Committee on Administration of Justice, State Bar of California. **PRACTICE AREAS:** Business Litigation; Banking Law; Creditors Rights Law; Insurance Law.

**GILLIAN M. ROSS,** born 1946; admitted to bar, 1986, California. *Education:* University of Cincinnati (B.A., 1969); Connecticut College (M.A., 1971); Hastings College of the Law (J.D., 1986). Consultant, *Office Leasing, Drafting & negotiating the Lease*, Continuing Education of the Bar, 1996. First Vice President, California Women Lawyers, 1996. *Member:* Women Lawyers of Alameda County (Past-President). **PRACTICE AREAS:** Commercial Law; Business Litigation; Employment Law.

**WALTER R. TURNER,** born 1951; admitted to bar, 1978, California. *Education:* Southern Illinois University (B.A., 1973); Pepperdine University (J.D., cum laude, 1977); New York University (LL.M., in Taxation, 1978). Wallace Scholar, Member, Pepperdine University Law Review, 1976-1977. Co-Author, Annual Supplement to "Commercial Real Property Lease Practice," California Continuing Education of the Bar. Lecturer on Taxation, California Continuing Education of the Bar, 1984—. (Certified Specialist, Taxation Law, The State Bar of California Board of Legal Specialization). **PRACTICE AREAS:** Income Tax Law; Business Law.

**R. ZACHARY WASSERMAN,** born 1947; admitted to bar, 1972, California; 1973, U.S. District Court, Northern District of California. *Education:* University of California at Santa Cruz (B.A., Regents Scholar, 1969); Stanford University (J.D., 1972). Commissioner, Oakland Board of Port Commissioners, 1987-1990. Managing Editor, California Real Property Journal; Director, 1995, Oakland Chamber of Commerce, 1993—. Member, Urban Land Institute. Chair, Northern California Manufacturing Exten-

*(This Listing Continued)*

## WENDEL, ROSEN, BLACK & DEAN, LLP, Oakland—Continued

sion Center, 1995—. *PRACTICE AREAS:* Real Estate Law; Science and Technology Law.

**RICHARD P. WAXMAN,** born 1952; admitted to bar, 1984, California. *Education:* University of California at Berkeley (B.A., 1974); Hastings College of Law, University of California (J.D., 1978). Panelist, Continuing Education of the Bar. Consultant, Continuing Education of the Bar. *PRACTICE AREAS:* Business and Real Estate Law; Commercial Law; Franchise Law.

**DAVID I. WENDEL,** born 1921; admitted to bar, 1949, California. *Education:* University of California at Berkeley (A.B., 1942); Harvard University (J.D., cum laude, 1948). Phi Beta Kappa. Counsel, Oakland Chamber of Commerce (Chairman, 1985-1987). *PRACTICE AREAS:* Business Law; Securities Law; Real Property Law.

**TIMOTHY S. WILLIAMS,** born 1955; admitted to bar, 1980, California. *Education:* Stanford University (B.A., 1977); Boalt Hall School of Law, University of California (J.D., 1980). Consultant, *Office Leasing, Drafting & Negotiating the Lease,* Continuing Education of the Bar, 1996. Co-Author: "California's New Legislation Regarding Use Restrictions in Commercial Leases: Can Commercial Landlords Just Say No?," California Real Property Journal, Summer, 1992. *PRACTICE AREAS:* Real Property Law; Construction Law.

**RICHARD E. WINNIE,** born 1947; admitted to bar, 1975, California; 1986, U.S. Supreme Court. *Education:* California State University at Humboldt (A.B., magna cum laude, 1969); University of California at Berkeley (M.A., magna cum laude, 1971); University of San Francisco (J.D., 1975). Author: "Abatement of Civil Nuisances," National Institute of Municipal Law Officers, Fort Worth, 1985; "Regulation of Video Games," League of California Cities, San Diego, 1982. City Attorney, Oakland, California, 1981-1987. Member, California Districts Security Advisory Commission, 1987—. President, Bay Area City Attorneys Association, 1982-1983. President, Community Alliance for Syndicated Housing, Inc., Oakland, CA, 1989—. Member, Legal Advocacy Committee, League of California Cities, 1984-1986. Member, Oakland Housing Authority Board of Commissioners. *Member:* National Institute of Municipal Law Officers (State Chair, 1985-1986 and 1986-1987). *PRACTICE AREAS:* Municipal Law; Public Finance; Land Use Law.

**JEFFREY C. WURMS,** born 1959; admitted to bar, 1984, New Jersey and Pennsylvania; 1986, California and U.S. District Court, Northern District of California. *Education:* Georgetown University (A.B., cum laude, 1981); Rutgers University Law School (J.D., 1984). Author: "Limitations on Use of the California Homestead Exemption in Bankruptcy Cases: The Case for Following In re Pladson," California Bankruptcy Journal, Vol. 21, No. 4, page 323 (1993). *LANGUAGES:* Dutch. *REPORTED CASES:* In re Pladson, 154 B.R. 305 (N.D.Cal. 1993); In re Bair Island Marina & Office Center, 116 B.R. 180 (Bankr. N.D. Cal. 1990). *PRACTICE AREAS:* Bankruptcy.

### OF COUNSEL

**STANLEY P. HÉBERT,** admitted to bar, 1950, Wisconsin; 1968, U.S. Supreme Court; 1976, California; 1979, District of Columbia; U.S. District Court, Northern District of California, Middle District of Georgia and Eastern District of Wisconsin; U.S. Court of Appeals, 9th Circuit. *Education:* University of Wisconsin (Ph.B., 1947); Marquette University (J.D., 1950). Port Attorney and General Counsel, Port of Oakland, Oakland, California, 1977-1996. Member: Holy Names College, Board of Regents; Marcus Foster Educational Institute Board; National Catholic Conference for Interracial Justice Board. *Member:* Charles Houston Bar Association. *PRACTICE AREAS:* Public Finance; Transportation Law (ports and airports); International Trade Concerns; General Business.

### ASSOCIATES

**ELIZABETH BERKE-DREYFUSS,** born 1953; admitted to bar, 1984, California. *Education:* Ohio State University (B.A., 1976); Lone Mountain College (M.A., 1978); University of San Francisco Law School (J.D., magna cum laude, 1984). Phi Kappa Phi. Member, McAuliffe Honor Society. Recipient, American Jurisprudence Awards for Criminal Law, Criminal Procedure and Constitutional Law. *PRACTICE AREAS:* Bankruptcy.

**JOAN M. CAMBRAY,** born 1956; admitted to bar, 1989, California, U.S. District Court, Northern, Central and Eastern Districts of California and U.S. Court of Appeals, Ninth Circuit. *Education:* Oakland University (B.S.N., magna cum laude, 1984); University of Detroit; University of San Diego (J.D., summa cum laude, 1989). Sigma Theta Tau. Recipient: International Trial Lawyers Award for Trial Advocacy; American Jurisprudence Awards for: Real Property; Civil Procedure; Corporations; Administrative Law; Professional Responsibility; UCCII. Registered Nurse: Michigan, 1984; California, 1987. *PRACTICE AREAS:* Litigation.

**THIELE R. DUNAWAY,** born 1952; admitted to bar, 1987, California, U.S. District Court, Northern District of California and U.S. Court of Appeals, Ninth Circuit; 1988, U.S. District Court, Eastern District of California; 1990, U.S. District Court, Southern District of California; 1991, U.S. District Court, Central District of California. *Education:* Augustana College (A.B., cum laude, 1974); Boalt Hall School of Law, University of California (J.D., 1987). Phi Beta Kappa. *Member:* San Francisco Women Lawyers Alliance; Air and Waste Management Association. *PRACTICE AREAS:* Environmental Law; Real Property Secured Transactions; Litigation.

**BARBARA FINKLE,** born 1953; admitted to bar, 1984, California and U.S. District Court, Northern District of California. *Education:* University of California at Berkeley (A.B., 1976); University of California at Riverside (teaching credential, 1977); Golden Gate University (J.D., 1984). *PRACTICE AREAS:* Corporate; General Business; Securities; Real Estate.

**TRACY GREEN,** born 1957; admitted to bar, 1984, California and U.S. District Court, Northern District of California; 1985, U.S. District Court, Eastern District of California; 1989, U.S. Supreme Court. *Education:* University of Denver, Alpha Lambda Delta; University of California at Santa Cruz (B.A., 1979); University of San Francisco (J.D., 1984). Adjunct Professor, Introductory Bankruptcy and Advanced Chapter 11 Reorganization, University of San Francisco, School of Law, 1991—. *Member:* Bay Area Bankruptcy Forum. *REPORTED CASES:* In re Seawinds, Ltd. v. Xtra, Inc., 91 B.R. 88 (Bankr. N.D. Cal. 1988). *PRACTICE AREAS:* Bankruptcy Law; Commercial Reorganization.

**ANDREW N. JACOBSON,** born 1960; admitted to bar, 1991, California. *Education:* University of California at Davis; California Polytechnic State University at San Luis Obispo (B. Arch., 1984); Boalt Hall School of Law, University of California (J.D., 1991). Licensed Architect, California, 1987. *PRACTICE AREAS:* Real Property Law; Land Use Law.

**KAREN BROWN KEPLER,** born 1960; admitted to bar, 1991, California, U.S. District Court, Central District of California and U.S. Court of Appeals, Ninth Circuit. *Education:* University of California at Los Angeles (B.A., 1987); University of California Law School (J.D., 1990). Editor, UCLA Law Review. Special Projects Editor, National Black Law Journal. *PRACTICE AREAS:* Litigation.

**LAURA K. MEYER,** born 1960; admitted to bar, 1988, California. *Education:* University of California at Berkeley (B.A., 1982); Hastings College of the Law, University of California (J.D., 1988). Associate Articles Editor, Comm/Ent, Hasting Journal of Communications and Entertainment Law, 1987-1988. *PRACTICE AREAS:* Litigation.

**MICHAEL ERIC OLMSTEAD,** born 1960; admitted to bar, 1987, California. *Education:* Weber State College (B.S., with distinction, 1983); University of Utah (J.D., 1987). Member, Moot Court Board. Member, Committee for Governmental Relations, Oakland Metropolitan Chamber of Commerce. *PRACTICE AREAS:* Litigation; Construction Law; Labor Law.

**BERTHA A. ONTIVEROS,** born 1953; admitted to bar, 1982, California. *Education:* Yale University (B.A., 1975); University California Boalt Hall School of Law (J.D. ,1979). Chief of Staff, California Assembly Member Johan Klehs, Chair of the Assembly Revenue and Taxation Committee, 1989-1992. Executive Director, Bernal Heights Community Foundation, 1984-1985. President, Latino Connection, 1993—. *Member:* La Raza Lawyers Association (East Bay, President, 1985). *LANGUAGES:* Spanish. *PRACTICE AREAS:* Real Estate Law; Public Agency Law.

**JOHN G. PRICE,** born 1959; admitted to bar, 1985, California. *Education:* University of Wisconsin (B.A., with honors, 1982); Hastings College of the Law, University of California (J.D., cum laude, 1985). Order of the Coif. Thurston Society. *PRACTICE AREAS:* Business Law; Securities; Intellectual Property Law.

**JUDITH Y. TANG,** born 1970; admitted to bar, 1995, California. *Education:* University of California at Berkeley (B.S., with high honors, 1992); Hastings College of the Law, University of California (J.D., 1995). Recipient: American Jurisprudence Award; Asian American Bar Association Scholarship Award, 1994 *Member:* Asian American Bar Association. *LANGUAGES:* Cantonese. *PRACTICE AREAS:* Corporate and General Business Law.

*(This Listing Continued)*

**LUCINDA H. YOUNG,** born 1956; admitted to bar, 1982, Florida; 1990, California. *Education:* University of Florida (B.S., Economics, magna cum laude, 1978; J.D., 1982; LL.M., Taxation, 1989). Beta Gamma Sigma; Phi Kappa Phi. *Member:* San Francisco Bay Area Women Tax Lawyers. *PRACTICE AREAS:* Estate Planning; Taxation; Probate.

All Members of the firm are members of the State Bar of California, the Alameda County Bar Association and committees. In addition, some attorneys are members of the National Bar Association, the Bar Association of San Francisco, the Charles Houston Bar Association, the Asian American Bar Association, the American Bar Association, the Bar Association of Santa Clara, the Queen's Bench, and the Women Lawyers of Alameda County.

REPRESENTATIVE CLIENTS: Alameda County (Surplus Property Authority); Blackhawk Corporation; Big "O" Tires; City of Hayward (Land Use); City of Oakland; City of Fremont (Cable television); Crescent Jewelers; Del Monte Corporation; East Bay Regional Park District; 24 Hour Fitness; Fidelity Mutual Life Insurance Company; Friedman's Jewelers; Gannett; Gray & Reynolds; Gray Line of San Francisco; Harris Theater Group; Hexcel Corporation; Lakeview Club, Inc.; Lark Creek Inn; Lincoln Property Co.; Livermore Valley Tennis Club; Montclair Better Homes Realty; Motel 6; Northwest Lodging, Inc.; Oakland Chamber of Commerce; Oakland Football Marketing Association; Oakland Hills Tennis Club; One Market Restaurant; Pacific Steel Casting Co.; The Pasha Group; Peerless Coffee Co.; The Prudential Insurance Company of America; Rabo Bank Nederland; Regional Medical Systems; Renaissance Rialto Theaters; Reunion Resource Company; Riverbank America; San Francisco Public Utilities Commission; Save Mart Supermarkets; SavMax Foods; Spanish Speaking Unity Council; Telecare Corp. (Psychiatric Hospitals).

## WILEY PRICE & RADULOVICH

*1300 CLAY STREET, SUITE 600*
**OAKLAND, CALIFORNIA 94612**
*Telephone: 510-466-6336*
*Fax: 510-466-6337*
*Email: wprlaw.com*
*URL: http://www.wprlaw.com*

*Labor and Employment Law and Litigation.*

*FIRM PROFILE: The attorneys and staff at Wiley Price & Radulovich specialize exclusively in representing public and private sector management in labor and employment law and litigation and alternative dispute resolution. Our many years of experience in providing effective representation to Bay Area and Northern California public and private sector employers and our client loyalty led us to believe that we are providing the experience counsel that management needs and that we are offering our services in efficient and cost-effective ways. Our clients tell us they especially value our ability to communicate effectively with them. We believe that our firm's commitment to a diverse and supportive work environment with an emphasis on teamwork, assists us in understanding our clients' needs and in providing solutions to their employment problems. We are a women owned and managed law firm.*

**JOSEPH E. WILEY,** born Indianapolis, Indiana, September 30, 1951; admitted to bar, 1978, California. *Education:* Michigan State University (B.A., magna cum laude, 1972); University of Wisconsin (M.S., 1975); University of Santa Clara (J.D., magna cum laude, 1978). Phi Alpha Delta. Attorney, National Labor Relations Board, 1978-1980. Early Neutral Evaluator U.S. District Court, Northern District of California. *Member:* Bar Association of San Francisco (Member, Labor and Employment Law Section); Alameda County Bar Association; American Bar Association (Member, Committee on Practice and Procedure Before the National Labor Relations Board, Section of Labor and Employment Law); Associated General Contractors of California (Member, Legal Advisory Committee). *PRACTICE AREAS:* Labor and Employment; Collective Bargaining; Public Sector Employment Law; Public Sector Labor Relations; Labor Arbitration. **Email:** jwiley@wprlaw.com

**SUZANNE I. PRICE,** born Sacramento, California, December 7, 1959; admitted to bar, 1985, California. *Education:* Mills College (B.A., with honors, 1981); University of San Francisco (J.D., 1985). Judicial Extern to the Honorable Robert H. Schnacke, U.S. District Court, Northern District of California, 1984. *Member:* Bar Association of San Francisco (Member, Labor and Employment Law Section); American Bar Association (Member, Section on Labor and Employment Law; Government and Public Sector Lawyers Division); State Bar of California (Member, Labor and Employment Law Section). *PRACTICE AREAS:* Labor and Employment; Affirmative Action; Public Sector Labor Relations; Employment Discrimination; Age Discrimination in Employment.

**MONNA R. RADULOVICH,** born San Francisco, California, August 26, 1960; admitted to bar, 1985, California. *Education:* University of California at Santa Barbara (B.A., with high honors, 1982); Boalt Hall School of Law, University of California (J.D., 1985). Phi Beta Kappa. *Member:* Bar Association of Francisco (Member, Labor and Employment Law Section); State Bar of California (Member, Labor and Employment Law Section); American Bar Association; California Women Lawyers. *PRACTICE AREAS:* Labor and Employment; Employment Litigation; Personnel Policies; Wage and Hour Law; Employment Disability Discrimination. **Email:** mradulovich@wprlaw.com

**ELIZABETH S. SYGER,** born Miami, Florida, April 30, 1959; admitted to bar, 1984, Florida; 1996, California. *Education:* University of North Carolina at Chapel Hill (B.A., 1981); University of Florida (J.D., with honors, 1984). Phi Delta Phi. Staff Attorney and Hearing Officer, Florida Public Employees Relations Commission, 1984-1985. *Member:* The Florida Bar (Member, Labor and Employment Law Section); Florida Association of Women Lawyers. *PRACTICE AREAS:* Labor and Employment; Sexual Harassment Law; Employment Litigation.

## ZACKLER & ASSOCIATES

*3824 GRAND AVENUE, SUITE 100*
**OAKLAND, CALIFORNIA 94610**
*Telephone: 510-834-4400*
*Fax: 510-834-9185*

*Business Law (Domestic and International Transactions); Food & Drug Regulatory Matters (Federal and State Agencies); Consumer Products, Packaging and Labeling, Trademarks, Technology Licensing, Advertising Review and Customs Law.*

**ALLAN I. ZACKLER,** admitted to bar, 1972, Illinois; 1974, California. *Education:* University of Illinois (B.A., cum laude, 1968); Northwestern University School of Law (J.D., 1972). Senior Editor, Northwestern University Law Review, 1971-1972. *Member:* American Bar Association (Member, Food & Drug Law Section); Food & Drug Law Institute. *PRACTICE AREAS:* Marketing Law; Food, Drug and Cosmetic Law; Commercial Law; Advertising Law; Trade Regulations.

### ASSOCIATES

**GEORGIA H. BURKE,** admitted to bar, 1983, District of Columbia; 1986, U.S. Court of International Trade; 1991, California. *Education:* Manhattanville College (B.A., senior honors, 1969); University of Southern California; Georgetown University Law Center (J.D., magna cum laude, 1983). Editor, Law & Policy in International Business, 1981-1983. *LANGUAGES:* Japanese. *PRACTICE AREAS:* Food, Drug and Cosmetic Law; International Sales; Customs Law; Trademarks; Administrative Law.

REPRESENTATIVE CLIENTS: California Walnut Commission; Clorox Co.; &W Co.; Del Monte Foods; Dole Packaged Foods Co.; Dreyer's Grand Ice Cream Co.; Guernsey Dell, Inc.; ; Kagome U.S.A., Inc.; Monnens-Addis Design Group, Inc.; Nestle, Inc.; S. Martinelli & Co.; Safeway Inc.; Sealright Co., Inc.; Shasta/National Beverage, Inc.; Sunkist Growers, Inc.; Turtle Mountain, Inc.

## HARRIS ZIMMERMAN

*Established in 1951*

*SUITE 710, 1330 BROADWAY*
**OAKLAND, CALIFORNIA 94612**
*Telephone: 510-465-0828*
*Fax: 510-465-2041*
*Email: hzimerman@ix.netcom.com*

*Patent, Trademark, Unfair Competition and Trade Secrets Law. Trials.*

**HARRIS ZIMMERMAN,** born Omaha, Nebraska, November 29, 1919; admitted to bar, 1951, California; 1967, U.S. Supreme Court; registered to practice before U.S. Patent and Trademark Office. *Education:* Illinois Institute of Technology (B.S., 1941); Golden Gate College (J.D., 1951). Member, National Panel of Arbitrators (Patent) American Arbitration Association. *Member:* Alameda County and American (Member, Patent, Trademark and Copyright Law Section) Bar Associations; The State Bar of California; San Francisco Patent Law Association; American Intellectual Property Law Association. *PRACTICE AREAS:* Intellectual Property Litigation; Counseling; Mediation; Arbitration; Patent Litigation.

### ASSOCIATES

**MICHAEL J. CRONEN,** born Monterey Park, California, February 8, 1958; admitted to bar, 1987, California, U.S. Court of Appeals, Federal Circuit and U.S. District Court, Northern and Central Districts of California. *Education:* California State University at Los Angeles (B.A., with honors, 1983); Hastings College of the Law, University of California (J.D., 1987). Extern Clerk to Justice Jerome Smith, Second Appellate District,

*(This Listing Continued)*

## HARRIS ZIMMERMAN, Oakland—Continued

California Court of Appeal, 1986. Associate Professor, Intellectual Property Law, California State University Hayward, 1993—. Instructor, Intellectual Property Law, Saint Mary's College, 1996—. *Member:* Alameda County and American (Member, Patent, Trademark and Copyright Law Section) Bar Associations; The State Bar of California; American Intellectual Property Law Association; San Francisco Patent and Trademark Law Association; The Association of Trial Lawyers of America. **REPORTED CASES:** Fraige v. American National Watermattress, 996 F.2d 295 (Fed.-Cir. 1993). **PRACTICE AREAS:** Intellectual Property Litigation; Counseling.

REPRESENTATIVE CLIENTS: Berkeley Medevices; Blue Cross of California; California Optical Leather; Clyde Robin Seed Co.; DaMert Company; Imtec Products, Inc.; Lyon's Restaurants, Inc.; Novalek, Inc.; Nulaid Foods; Saag's, Inc.; Selectone Corp.; Surgijet, Inc.; Unenco; Unicare Insurance Company; Unisec, Inc.; United Lighting; Vinyl Products Manufacturing, Inc.; WellPoint Health Networks Inc.

## FEIST, VETTER, KNAUF AND LOY

*A PROFESSIONAL CORPORATION*

Established in 1968

SUITE 300, 810 MISSION AVENUE
P.O. BOX 240

**OCEANSIDE, CALIFORNIA 92049-0240**

Telephone: 619-722-1914
Telecopier: 619-721-8943

*General Civil Trial Practice. Corporate, Real Property, Personal Injury, Estate Planning and Probate Law, Condominium Law.*

**RAYMOND F. FEIST** (1916-1988).

**NORMAN L. VETTER,** born San Diego, California, March 14, 1930; admitted to bar, 1958, California. *Education:* San Diego State College (A.B., 1952); University of California School of Law (J.D., 1957). Phi Delta Phi. *Member:* San Diego County and American Bar Associations; The State Bar of California; The Association of Trial Lawyers of America. **PRACTICE AREAS:** Personal Injury Law; Real Estate; Probate; Trust Law.

**ROBERT C. KNAUF** (1920-1979).

**JOHN I. LOY** (Retired).

**RAYMOND F. FEIST, JR.,** born Coronado, California, June 27, 1946; admitted to bar, 1975, California. *Education:* University of California at Santa Barbara (B.A., 1968); California Western School of Law (J.D., 1975). Phi Delta Phi. *Member:* North San Diego County, San Diego County and American Bar Associations; The State Bar of California. **PRACTICE AREAS:** Corporate Law; Business Law; Probate; Trust Law.

**ALAN H. BURSON,** born Spokane, Washington, February 25, 1946; admitted to bar, 1974, California. *Education:* University of Washington (B.A., 1969); University of San Diego (J.D., 1974). *Member:* North San Diego County Bar Association; The State Bar of California. **PRACTICE AREAS:** Homeowners Association Law; Real Estate; Litigation; Collections.

**HENRY R. HAGUE,** born The Hague, Holland, April 9, 1945; admitted to bar, 1973, California. *Education:* Williams College (B.A., 1967); University of San Diego (J.D., 1971). *Member:* North San Diego County and San Diego County Bar Associations; State Bar of California. **PRACTICE AREAS:** Business Law; Real Estate; Community Association Law.

**LISA FRAZEE MORGOSH,** born Oceanside, California, October 29, 1961; admitted to bar, 1989, California. *Education:* University of California at San Diego (B.A., 1984); University of San Diego (J.D., 1989). *Member:* Northern San Diego County and San Diego County Bar Association; State Bar of California. **PRACTICE AREAS:** Homeowners Association; Collections.

**JAY J. BROWN,** born Los Angeles, California, November 12, 1963; admitted to bar, 1990, California. *Education:* University of California at San Diego (B.A., 1986); California Western School of Law (J.D., 1990). California Western Law Review/International Law Journal, Managing Editor 1990. *Member:* North San Diego County and San Diego County Bar Associations; State Bar of California. **PRACTICE AREAS:** Homeowners Association; Collection; Real Estate.

REFERENCE: Bank of America National Trust & Savings Assn. (Oceanside Branch Office).

## GORE, GROSSE, GREENMAN & LACY

*A Partnership including a Professional Law Corporation*

Established in 1951

900 PIER VIEW WAY
P.O. BOX 299

**OCEANSIDE, CALIFORNIA 92049-0299**

Telephone: 619-722-1234
FAX: 619-722-5860

*Civil Litigation. Estate Planning, Probate, Business, Personal Injury, Real Estate, Corporation and Domestic Law.*

**KENNETH L. GREENMAN, JR., (A P.L.C.),** born Inglewood, California, September 13, 1943; admitted to bar, 1972, California and U.S. Court of Appeals, Fifth Circuit; 1973, U.S. District Court, Southern District of California; 1976, U.S. Court of Appeals, Seventh Circuit; 1977, U.S. District Court, Central District of California; 1978 U.S. Supreme Court and U.S. Court of Appeals, Ninth Circuit. *Education:* University of Southern California (B.S. in Finance, 1965); California Western School of Law, (J.D., magna cum laude, 1971). Phi Alpha Delta (President, 1969-1970). Member, 1969-1971 and Editor-in-Chief, 1970-1971, California Western Law Review. Recipient, American Jurisprudence Awards in Corporations, Wills and Conflict of Laws. Attorney, U.S. Department of Justice, Honor Law Graduate Program, 1971-1972; Deputy City Attorney, City of San Diego, CA 0002-1973. Member, Board of Directors, 1990-1993; Vice-President, 1993, San Diego County Bar Association; Elder, La Jolla Presbyterian Church 1981-1984; San Diego County Bar Foundation, 1991—; Member, Board of Directors, 1994—; President, 1996-1997; Trustee, California Western School of Law, 1994—. *Member:* San Diego County and North San Diego County Bar Associations; State Bar of California. **PRACTICE AREAS:** Civil Litigation; Commercial Law; Real Estate Law; Personal Injury Law; Probate Law; Trust Law; Wills Law.

**JANET BLEDSOE LACY,** born Riverside, California, June 15, 1948; admitted to bar, 1974, California. *Education:* California State University at San Diego (B.A., 1971); California Western School of Law (J.D., 1974). Judge Pro Tem Panel, Vista Superior Court, North County Judicial District, 1978—. Member, Oceanside Planning Commission, 1976-1978. Member, Board of Directors, Women's Resource Center, 1974—. Member, Board of Trustees, Oceanside Unified School District, 1993—. President, Board of Trustees, Oceanside Unified School District, 1994—. Winner, Lawyer's Club North County, 1995; Madge Bradley Award; Winner, First Annual Community Relation Award, City of Oceanside, 1995. *Member:* North San Diego County (Chair, Family Law Section, 1990-1993) and San Diego County Bar Associations; State Bar of California. **PRACTICE AREAS:** Family Law.

**MICHAEL L. KLEIN,** born Brooklyn, New York, October 17, 1952; admitted to bar, 1978, California; 1981, U.S. District Court, Central District of California; 1983, U.S. District Court, Southern District of California. *Education:* University of California at Los Angeles (A.B., 1974); Loyola Law School (J.D., 1977). Presiding Officer, Manufactured Home Fair Practices Commission, City of Oceanside, 1984-1987. Chairman of the Board, Casa de Amparo, 1987. Board Member, 1984—; Judge Advocate Oceanside Yacht Club, 1992-1994 and 1996-1997. *Member:* San Diego County Bar Association; North County Bar Association; State Bar of California. **REPORTED CASES:** Stecks v. Young, 38 Cal. App. 4th/365. **PRACTICE AREAS:** Civil Litigation; Bankruptcy Law; Business Law; Personal Injury Law.

**J. DELENE ST. JOHN,** born Union City, Tennessee, May 13, 1949; admitted to bar, 1987, California. *Education:* University of West Florida (B.S., Social Work, 1980); Western State University (J.D., 1985). Member, U.S. District Court, Southern District of California Superior Court Judge Pro Tem Panel, 1992. President and Board Member, Lawyers Club, 1989-1992. Member, Legal Panel for Women's Resource Center. *Member:* North San Diego (Member, Broad of Director, 1995) and San Diego County Bar Associations. **PRACTICE AREAS:** Family Law and Mediation.

**COLLEEN C. O'HARRA,** born Orange, California, April 9, 1937; admitted to bar, 1978, California. *Education:* Chapman College (B.A., cum laude, 1959); Western State University College of Law (J.D., 1978). Nu Beta Epsilon. Recipient, American Jurisprudence Award for Corporations. Member, Lawyers Club of San Diego, 1980-1994; President, Oceanside Chamber of Commerce, 1986—; Superior Court Judge Pro Tem and Arbitrator, 1981-1994; Member, Planning Commission, City of Oceanside,

*(This Listing Continued)*

## PROFESSIONAL BIOGRAPHIES

CALIFORNIA—ONTARIO

1978-1982; Member, Oceanside City Council, 1992—. Deputy Mayor, Oceanside, 1994—. Member, Board of Directors: Women's Resource Center, 1974—; North County Concert Association, 1987—. *Member:* North San Diego County Bar Association (Member, Board of Directors, 1983-1986;Treasurer, 1985, 1986 and 1991; Member, Family Law Section Chair 1982-1984); San Diego County Bar Association; State Bar of California. *PRACTICE AREAS:* Probate Law; Estate Planning Law.

**KAREN M. HEFFRON,** born Baraboo, Wisconsin, June 10, 1956; admitted to bar, 1984, California and U.S. District Court, Southern District of California. *Education:* University of Minnesota (B.S, 1978); Western State University (J.D., 1983). Judge Protem Superior Court, North San Diego County, Branch Family Law Division, 1992—. Director, North San Diego County Bar Association, 1993—, and Lawyer Referral Service, 1988—. *Member:* North San Diego County and San Diego County (Director, 1996—) Bar Associations; State Bar of California; Lawyers Club of San Diego (Vice President, Northern County Chapter, 1986-1987; Secretary, Northern County Chapter, 1987-1988; Judicial Evaluations Committee, 1989). (Certified Specialist, Family Law, The State Bar of California Board of Legal Specialization). *PRACTICE AREAS:* Family Law.

REPRESENTATIVE CLIENTS: Bank of America; Britannica Motors; Alexander Moving and Storage; La Jolla Bank and Trust Co.; Machine Industries, Inc.; Murray Bridge Corp.; Russell W. Grosse Development Co.; Union Bank; Weseloh Chevrolet.

## LAW OFFICES OF JAMES B. PANTHER

2424 VISTA WAY, THIRD FLOOR
**OCEANSIDE, CALIFORNIA 92054**
Telephone: 619-722-6895
Fax: 619-754-5132

*Business Law with an Emphasis in Real Estate, Mortgage Banking and Commercial Transactions and Consumer Credit Laws.*

**JAMES B. PANTHER,** born 1942; admitted to bar, 1973, California. *Education:* University of Washington (B.A., 1965) Seattle University (M.B.A., 1968); California Western School of Law (J.D., 1972). *Member:* State Bar of California. *PRACTICE AREAS:* Real Estate; Finance; Business Law; Banking.

## BEST BEST & KRIEGER LLP

A California Limited Liability Partnership including Professional Corporations

*Established in 1987*

800 NORTH HAVEN, SUITE 120
**ONTARIO, CALIFORNIA 91764**
Telephone: 909-989-8584
Fax: 909-944-1441

*Riverside, California Office:* 400 Mission Square, 3750 University Avenue, P.O. Box: 1028. Telephone: 909-686-1450. Fax: 909-686-3083; 909-682-4612.

*Rancho Mirage, California Office:* Hope Square Professional Centre, 39700 Bob Hope Drive, Suite 312, P.O. Box: 1555. Telephone: 619-568-2611. Fax: 619-340-6698; 619-341-7039.

*San Diego, California Office:* 402 West Broadway, 13th Floor. Telephone: 619-525-1300. Fax: 619-233-6118.

*Victorville, California Office:* High Desert Corporate Pointe Building, 14350 Civic Drive, Suite 270. Telephone: 619-245-4127. Fax: 619-245-6437.

*General Civil and Trial Practice. Corporation, Water Rights, Probate, Trusts and Estate Planning, Real Estate, Municipal, Bankruptcy Litigation, Environmental Law and Toxic Waste.*

### RESIDENT PARTNERS

Meredith A. Jury, (P.C.)          Stephen P. Deitsch
Wynne S. Furth                    Peter M. Barmack
                Dennis M. Cota

### RESIDENT ASSOCIATES

Kevin K. Randolph                 Sonia Rubio Carvalho
Richard T. Egger                  Karen M. Lewis
                Jeffrey T. Melching

REPRESENTATIVE CLIENTS: Torno America; City of Claremont; City of Fontana; Fontana Redevelopment Agency; Arcadia Redevelopment Agency; Marcus and Millichap Real Estate Brokers; Principal Mutual Life Insurance Co.;

*(This Listing Continued)*

Upland Bank; Chevron Land and Development; California Steel Pressure Pipe; Pasadena Fair Oaks Project Area Committee; Pacific Agricultural Holdings; Pitzer College; Casa Colina Hospital; California Tubular Products Company; Maury Microwave Corp.; Chem Lab Products, Inc.; Keystone Automotive Industries, Inc.; City of San Bernardino; Michael E. Steppe, DVM.

(For Complete Personnel and Biographical Data, see Professional Biographies at Riverside, California)

## COVINGTON & CROWE

*Established in 1968*

1131 WEST SIXTH STREET
P.O. BOX 1515
**ONTARIO, CALIFORNIA 91762**
Telephone: 909-983-9393
Fax: 909-391-6762
Email: covcrowe@ix.netcom.com

*General Civil and Trial Practice. Corporations, Municipal, Real Estate, Estate Planning, Trust, Probate, Family, Labor Law, Criminal Defense, Bankruptcy, Creditor's Rights and Water Rights Law.*

FIRM PROFILE: *Unfailing dependability, integrity, close professional attention, and personal concern are the principles which govern the basic philosophy at Covington & Crowe.*

*Built on a widely recognized reputation for competence and effective representation, Covington & Crowe has grown with the region, offering uncompromising dedication to high standards and to client satisfaction.*

*Business Law and Litigation form the firm's two broadest areas of practice.*

*Clients receive a special benefit from the collective resources of the firm's diversified knowledge, skill and experience.*

*This collective resource is also the foundation of the firm's noted ability to render highly effective personal attention to the client's needs and goals.*

### MEMBERS OF FIRM

**HAROLD A. BAILIN** (1930-1988).

**SAMUEL P. CROWE,** born Ashville, Alabama, February 17, 1935; admitted to bar, 1961, California. *Education:* University of California at Los Angeles (B.A., 1957); University of Southern California (J.D., 1960). Member: Ontario City Planning Commission, 1962-1964; Ontario City Council, 1964-1972. City Attorney: City of Ontario, 1975—; City of Rancho Cucamonga, 1977-1982. Assistant City Attorney, City of Rancho Cucamonga, 1982-1985. Airport Commission, Ontario International Airport, 1964-1972. Ontario Community Hospital Advisory Board, 1984-1985. *Member:* Western San Bernardino County, San Bernardino County and American Bar Associations; The State Bar of California (Chairman: Committee on the Economics of the Practice of Law, 1975-1976; Commission to Study Assimilation of New Lawyers Into the Profession, 1978-1981). (Certified Specialist, Taxation Law, The State Bar of California Board of Legal Specialization). *PRACTICE AREAS:* Corporations Law; Partnerships Law; Estate Planning Law.

**GEORGE W. PORTER,** born Manila, Philippine Islands, August 22, 1930; admitted to bar, 1959, California. *Education:* University of Redlands (A.B., 1952); University of California at Berkeley (J.D., 1958). Phi Alpha Delta. Co-Author: "Law of Arrest, Search and Seizure," pub. by Legal Book Store, 1966. Adjunct Professor of Law, La Verne University Law School, 1981-1985, 1990-1994. Listed in "The Best Lawyers in America," 1989-1990, 1994, by Naifeh and Smith, Woodward/White, Inc., 3rd ed., 1989. *Member:* Western San Bernardino County (President, 1968), San Bernardino County (President, 1973) and American Bar Associations; The State Bar of California (Member, Executive Committee, 1973-1976; Vice Chairman, 1975-1976); "Independent Inquiries and Review Panel, Legal Specialization", California Trial Lawyers Association; Association of Business Trial Attorneys of Los Angeles; California Attorneys for Criminal Justice (President, 1975-1976). (Certified Specialist, Criminal Law, The State Bar of California Board of Legal Specialization). *REPORTED CASES:* Progress Bulletin Pub Co. v. Superior Court 29 CA3 815, 105 Cal.Rptr. 873. *PRACTICE AREAS:* Criminal Defense Law; Business Litigation; Professional Disciplinary Hearings.

**ROBERT E. DOUGHERTY,** born Honolulu, Hawaii, December 30, 1937; admitted to bar, 1968, California. *Education:* University of California at Los Angeles (B.S., 1959; J.D., 1967). Phi Alpha Delta; Order of the Coif. Assistant City Attorney: City of Ontario, 1975—; Rancho Cucamonga, 1977-1982. City Attorney, City of Rancho Cucamonga, 1982-1985. *Member:* Western San Bernardino County (President, 1974-1975), San Bernardino County and American Bar Associations; The State Bar of California.

*(This Listing Continued)*

CAA1503B

## COVINGTON & CROWE, Ontario—Continued

**PRACTICE AREAS:** Municipal Law; General Civil Litigation; Water Rights Law.

**DONALD G. HASLAM,** born Provo, Utah, February 16, 1942; admitted to bar, 1970, California. *Education:* University of California at Berkeley (A.B., 1966); Boalt Hall School of Law, University of California (J.D., 1969). Associate Editor, Family Law News, 1981-1988. Adjunct Professor, La Verne University, 1984. Member, Family Law Advisory Commission Board of Legal Specialization, 1990-1993. *Member:* San Bernardino and Western San Bernardino County Bar Associations; The State Bar of California. (Certified Specialist, Family Law, The State Bar of California Board of Legal Specialization).

**ROBERT F. SCHAUER,** born Fargo, North Dakota, July 27, 1945; admitted to bar, 1971, California. *Education:* University of California at Davis (A.B., 1967; J.D., 1970). Staff Member, 1968-1969, and Issue Editor, 1969-1970, University of California at Davis Law Review. Author: "Unionization of Farm Labor," University of California at Davis Law Review, Vol. 2, 1970. *Member:* San Bernardino County and Western San Bernardino County Bar Associations; The State Bar of California. **PRACTICE AREAS:** Construction and Commercial Litigation; Deferred Compensation Plans; General Corporate; Business.

**EDWARD A. HOPSON,** born Detroit, Michigan, January 27, 1947; admitted to bar, 1972, California. *Education:* Pomona College (B.A., 1969); University of Southern California (J.D., 1972). Order of the Coif. Staff Member, 1970-1971, and Executive Editor, 1971-1972, University of Southern California Law Review. Author: "Courts, Corrections and the Eighth Amendment," 44 Southern California Law Review, 1060 (1971). Assistant City Attorney, City of Rancho Cucamonga, 1977-1985. *Member:* Western San Bernardino County Bar Association; The State Bar of California. **PRACTICE AREAS:** Real Property Law; Real Estate Development Law; Real Estate Finance Law.

**STEPHEN R. WADE,** born Long Beach, California, June 28, 1951; admitted to bar, 1978, California. *Education:* University of California at Santa Barbara (B.A., 1973); University of California at Los Angeles (J.D., 1977). President, University of California at Los Angeles Student Bar Association, 1975-1976. *Member:* Western San Bernardino County and San Bernardino County Bar Associations; The State Bar of California; American Bankruptcy Institute; Inland Empire Bankruptcy Forum (President, 1993). **PRACTICE AREAS:** Bankruptcy Law; Creditor's Rights Law.

**JETTE R. ANDERSON,** born Glendale, California, January 5, 1944; admitted to bar, 1978, California; U.S. District Court, Central District of California. *Education:* University of Redlands (B.A., magna cum laude, 1975); Pepperdine University School of Law (J.D., 1978). Pi Gamma Mu; Phi Alpha Delta (Vice-Justice, 1976-1977). *Member:* San Bernardino County and Western San Bernardino County Bar Associations; The State Bar of California (Member, Real Property, Probate and Estate Planning Sections); Estate Planning Council, Pomona Valley, Inc. **PRACTICE AREAS:** Real Property Law; Management Employee Relations Law; General Business Law; Probate Law; Estate Planning Law; Trust Administration.

**AUDREY A. PERRI,** born Oxnard, California, February 2, 1936; admitted to bar, 1976, California; U.S. District Court, Central District of California. *Education:* University of Redlands (B.A., 1958); University of LaVerne Law School (J.D., 1976). Articles Editor, Journal of Juvenile Law, University of LaVerne Law School Law Review, 1975-1976. Deputy District Attorney, 1976-1981. Recipient: University of LaVerne Law School Distinguished Alumnus of the Year (1993); San Bernardino County Commission on the Status of Women (Woman of the Year 1993). Commissioner of the State Bar of California Legal Services Trust Fund Commission, 1992-1994. *Member:* Commission on Judicial Nominees Evaluation, 1995—; Legal Services Trust Fund Commission, 1992-1994. Panelist, Family Law, Continuing Legal Education (CEB), 1989—. *Member:* Western San Bernardino County (Board of Directors, 1992—), San Bernardino County (Member, Judicial Evaluation Committee, 1987-1994; Board of Directors, 1981-1986; Chair: Resolutions - Legislation Committee, 1979-1980, 1983-1984; Bench Bar Committee, 1980-1985) and American (Member, Family Law Section) Bar Associations; State Bar of California (Member, Executive Committee, 1985-1988; Vice Chair, 1987-1988); East West Family Law Council; Inland Counties Women at Law (President, 1980-1981); California Women Lawyers (Member, Board of Directors, 1980-1983; First Vice-President, 1983-1984; Chair: Legislation Committee, 1982-1983). (Certified Specialist, Family Law, The State Bar of California Board of Legal Specialization). **PRACTICE AREAS:** Family Law.

*(This Listing Continued)*

CAA1504B

**TRACY L. TIBBALS,** born San Francisco, California, May 25, 1945; admitted to bar, 1974, California and U.S. District Court, Central District of California; 1978, District of Columbia; 1979, U.S. Claims Court; 1979-1982, U.S. Court of Customs and Patent Appeals; 1982, U.S. Court of Appeals for the Federal Circuit. *Education:* University of California at Riverside (B.A., 1967); California Western School of Law (J.D., 1974); Georgetown University. Phi Delta Phi. Member, Order of the Barristers. Member, Editorial Board, California Western International Law Journal, 1972-1974. Author: Comment, "Border Broadcasting Dilemma," California Western International Law Journal, 1974. *Member:* Riverside County, San Bernardino County, Western San Bernardino County (President, 1985-1986) and American (Member, Sections on: Administrative Law; International Law; Real Property, Probate and Trust Law; Litigation) Bar Associations; The State Bar of California; The District of Columbia Bar. **LANGUAGES:** German and Spanish. **PRACTICE AREAS:** Civil Litigation.

**MELANIE FISCH,** born Los Angeles, California, April 18, 1950; admitted to bar, 1985, California. *Education:* University of California at Riverside (B.A., 1976); University of Santa Clara (J.D., cum laude, 1985). Comments Editor, University of Santa Clara Law Review, 1984-1985. *Member:* Los Angeles County, Western San Bernardino County and San Bernardino County Bar Associations; State Bar of California; Inland Counties Women at Law. **PRACTICE AREAS:** Civil Litigation.

**ROBERT H. REEDER,** born Arcadia, California, February 6, 1961; admitted to bar, 1986, California and U.S. District Court, Central District of California. *Education:* University of California at Davis (B.A., 1983); University of Southern California (J.D., 1986). *Member:* San Bernardino County Bar Association; State Bar of California. **PRACTICE AREAS:** Business Law.

**R. DOUG DONESKY,** born Lacombe, Alberta, Canada, August 9, 1960; admitted to bar, 1987, California and U.S. District Court, Central District of California. *Education:* Pacific Union College (B.S., 1982); University of California at Davis (J.D., 1987). Recipient, American Jurisprudence Award in Negotiations. *Member:* San Bernardino County Bar Association; State Bar of California. **PRACTICE AREAS:** Civil Litigation; Real Estate Litigation.

**TAMMY S. JAGER,** born Fontana, California, November 4, 1963; admitted to bar, 1989, California. *Education:* California State University (B.A., 1986); University of La Verne (J.D., 1989). Delta Theta Phi (Tribune, 1987-1988; Dean, 1988-1989; District Chancellor, 1989). Member, Journal of Juvenile Law, Law Review, 1987-1988. Recipient, American Jurisprudence Award in: Torts, Introduction to Law, Constitutional Law, Family Law and Children and the Law. *Member:* West End San Bernardino, San Bernardino and American Bar Associations; State Bar of California. **PRACTICE AREAS:** Civil Litigation; Construction Law; Business Law.

### ASSOCIATES

**HOWARD S. BORENSTEIN,** born Los Angeles, California, May 29, 1959; admitted to bar, 1985, California, U.S. Court of Appeals, Ninth Circuit, U.S. District Court, Central District of California and U.S. Tax Court. *Education:* California State University at Northridge (B.S., 1982); Southwestern University (J.D., 1985). Certified Public Accountant, California, 1987. *Member:* Los Angeles County, San Bernardino County and American (Member, Taxation Section) Bar Associations; State Bar of California (Member, Taxation Section); California Society of Certified Public Accountants; American Institute of Certified Public Accountants. **PRACTICE AREAS:** Taxation Law; Tax Controversy; Business Law.

**DENISE MATTHEY,** born Dumont, New Jersey, April 3, 1945; admitted to bar, 1990, California and U.S. District Court, Central District of California. *Education:* University of Redlands (B.S. in B.A., 1987); University of San Diego (J.D., 1990). Member, Inland County Legal Services. Legal Aid Secretary, West End. *Member:* Western San Bernardino County and San Bernardino County Bar Associations; State Bar of California (Member, IOLTA Commission); California Women Lawyers; East/West Family Law Council. **PRACTICE AREAS:** Family Law.

**KATRINA WEST,** born Chicopee, Massachusetts, June 27, 1963; admitted to bar, 1990, California and U.S. District Court, Central District of California; 1991, U.S. District Court, Eastern District of California. *Education:* Bryn Mawr College (A.B., 1986); University of California School of Law (J.D., 1990). Author: "Best Intentions: The Education and Killing of Edmund Perry," National Black Journal, Vol. 11 No. 2, Summer 1989. Member: Inland Valley Professionals, 1992-1993; Special Legal Committee, NAACP, San Bernardino Chapter, 1993; Inns of Court, San Bernardino Chapter, 1992-1994 and Resolutions Committee, 1994. *Member:* Western

*(This Listing Continued)*

# PROFESSIONAL BIOGRAPHIES

## CALIFORNIA—ONTARIO

San Bernardino County, San Bernardino County (Member, Resolutions Committee, San Bernardino Chapter, 1994), Riverside County and American (Member, Sections On: Family Law; Litigation) Bar Associations; State Bar of California (Member, Calendar Coordinating Committee, 1995—); American Business Women's Association (Co-Chair, Programs, 1993-1994 and Vice-President, 1994—, Upland Chapter); East-West Family Law Council; African American Attorneys of the Inland Empire. *PRACTICE AREAS:* Family Law.

RICHARD R. MUIR, born Grand Rapids, Michigan, June 14, 1958; admitted to bar, 1988, California, U.S. District Court, Central and Southern Districts of California and U.S. Tax Court. *Education:* Albion College (B.A., 1980); University of San Diego (J.D., 1988; LL.M. in Tax, 1991). *Member:* Western San Bernardino County Bar Association; State Bar of California; American Institute of Certified Public Accountants; California Society of Certified Public Accountants. *PRACTICE AREAS:* Business Law; Estate and Succession Planning; Taxation; ERISA; Qualified Domestic Relations Orders (QDRO's).

KIMBERLY A. ROHN, born Shawnee, Oklahoma, October 30, 1958; admitted to bar, 1991, California, U.S. District Court, Central District of California and U.S. Tax Court. *Education:* Central Washington University (B.A. in Law and Justice, 1980); University of La Verne (J.D., 1990). *Member:* San Bernardino County and American Bar Associations; State Bar of California. *PRACTICE AREAS:* Business Law; Corporate Law; Municipal Law.

J. MICHAEL KALER, born Mayfield, Kentucky, April 23, 1959; admitted to bar, 1992, California, U.S. District Court, Central, Southern, Northern and Eastern Districts of California and U.S. Court of Appeals, Ninth Circuit. *Education:* Murray State University (B.S., 1980); Kent State University (M.A., 1984); National University (M.B.A., 1987); University of San Diego (J.D., 1991). National Merit Scholar. Winner: Alumni Moot Court Competition, 1990, 1991; Best Brief, Alumni Moot Court Competition, 1990, 1991; Constitutional Law Moot Court Competition, 1991. Member, San Diego Law Review, 1991. Deputy City Attorney, City of Ontario, 1992—. *Member:* Western San Bernardino County and San Bernardino County Bar Associations; State Bar of California. *PRACTICE AREAS:* Business Litigation; Civil Litigation; Trial Practice; Municipal Law.

ERIC S. VAIL, born San Diego, California, July 21, 1966; admitted to bar, 1992, California. *Education:* California State Polytechnic University (B.A., summa cum laude, 1989); McGeorge School of Law (J.D., 1992). Phi Kappa Phi. *Member:* San Bernadino County Bar Association; State Bar of California. *PRACTICE AREAS:* Municipal Law; Civil Litigation.

---

## *GASSNER & GASSNER*

A PROFESSIONAL CORPORATION

Established in 1979

**337 NORTH VINEYARD AVENUE, SUITE 205**
**ONTARIO, CALIFORNIA 91764**
Telephone: 909-983-1352
Fax: 909-391-0096

*Family, Juvenile, Interstate Custody and Related Litigation. Appellate Practice.*

FIRM PROFILE: *Established 1979, specializing in Family Law, Juvenile Court matters and Guardianships, Conservatorships and Probate. Interstate Custody matters are frequently handled, as are appellate proceedings.*

LAWRENCE M. GASSNER, born New York, N.Y., October 30, 1932; admitted to bar, 1966, California and U.S. District Court, Central and Southern Districts of California. *Education:* Carnegie Mellon University (B.S., 1954; M.S., 1955); Loyola University of Los Angeles (J.D., 1965). Instructor, Environmental Law and Procedure, LaVerne Law School, 1974-1976. President, 1986-1987, Program Chair, 1984-1986 and Co-Chair, 1989-1990, East-West Family Law Council. County Liaison, California Continuing Education of the Bar, 1986-1988. Panelist, California Continuing Education of the Bar, Family Law Advisory Committee, 1989—. *Member:* West End San Bernardino County and American (Member, Family Law Section) Bar Associations; State Bar of California (Member: Family Law Section, Executive Committee, 1987-1993, Vice-Chair, Family Law Section, 1989-1990; Family Law Advisory Commission, Board of Legal Specialization, 1992—, and Chair, Family Law Advisory Commission, 1995-1996). (Certified Specialist, Family Law, The State Bar of California

*(This Listing Continued)*

Board of Legal Specialization). *PRACTICE AREAS:* Family Law; Interstate Custody; Probate; Appeals.

BEVERLY J. GASSNER, born Homestead, Pennsylvania, June 20, 1931; admitted to bar, 1977, California and U.S. District Court, Central District of California. *Education:* Carnegie Mellon University (B.S., 1953); Claremont Graduate School (M.A., 1968); University of La Verne (J.D., magna cum laude, 1977). President, East-West Family Law Council, 1988-1989. Member, State Bar Executive Committee, 1994—. *Member:* San Bernardino County (Director, 1983-1984), Western San Bernardino County (Trustee, 1989) and American (Member and Chair, Domestic Violence Committee, 1989, Family Law Section) Bar Associations; State Bar of California (Member, Executive Committee, 1983-1987, 1994— and Chair, Custody Committee South, Family Law Section, 1988-1990. Member, Commission on Minimum Continuing Legal Education; California Women Lawyers. (Certified Specialist, Family Law, The State Bar of California Board of Legal Specialization). *PRACTICE AREAS:* Family Law.

---

## *HEMER, BARKUS & CLARK*

**3401 CENTRE LAKE DRIVE, SUITE 400**
**ONTARIO, CALIFORNIA 91764**
Telephone: 909-467-0660
Fax: 909-390-3628

Glendale, California Office: 550 N. Brand, Suite 1800, 91202-6002.
Telephone: 818-241-8999. Fax: 818-241-2014.

*Civil Trial and Appellate Practice. Medical and Legal Professional Liability, Products Liability, Negligence and Insurance Law.*

FIRM PROFILE: *Mr. Hemer first started working for Allstate Insurance Company when he attended Claims School and worked in their house counsel firm. Thereafter, he was general counsel for the Financial Indemnity Company, another auto carrier, for five years before forming the firm of Bolton & Hemer. The latter firm was in existence until 1983. The present firm was established in 1984 and is dedicated to the aggressive defense of civil litigation.*

*We have found that very early contact with the insured and the claims representative is conductive to establishing a good working relationship. The insured is contacted shortly after assignment, and is urged to work with counsel in successful defense of the litigation. Every effort is used to work with the claims personnel to bring about the earliest resolution to litigation.*

REPRESENTATIVE CLIENTS: The Doctors Co.; Southern California Physicians Insurance Exchange; Physicians Interindemnity; Hartford Insurance Group; Home Insurance; Kaiser Foundation Health Plan, Inc.; Professional Underwriters Liability Insurance Co.
REFERENCE: One Central Bank, Glendale, California.

(For complete Biographies on all Personnel, See Professional Biographies at Glendale)

---

## *KINKLE, RODIGER AND SPRIGGS*

PROFESSIONAL CORPORATION

**ONTARIO, CALIFORNIA**

(See Riverside)

*General Trial Practice. Negligence, Malpractice, Products Liability, Construction and Insurance Law.*

---

## *McCLAUGHERTY & ASSOCIATES*

**3350 SHELBY STREET**
**SUITE 200**
**ONTARIO, CALIFORNIA 91764**
Telephone: 909-944-2505

Pasadena, California Office: 301 North Lake Avenue, Suite 800, 91101.
Telephone: 818-449-7522. FAX: 818-583-9187.

*Insurance Defense, General Civil Trial in all State and Federal Court.*

JAY S. McCLAUGHERTY, born Los Angeles, California, March 1, 1952; admitted to bar, 1981, California and U.S. District Court, Southern, Central and Eastern Districts of California; 1983, U.S. District Court, Eastern District of California; 1989, U.S. District Court, Central District of California. *Education:* Pacific Lutheran University (B.A., magna cum laude, 1974); University of San Diego (J.D., 1979). Co-Chairman of Seminars for Southern California Defense Counsel, 1995 and 1996; Seminar Lecturer, Topic, Arbitrations, Las Vegas Seminar, Los Angeles Trial Lawyers, 1992;

*(This Listing Continued)*

CAA1505B

## McCLAUGHERTY & ASSOCIATES, Ontario—Continued

Seminar Moderator: Topic, Taking & Defending Expert Depositions, Southern California Defense Counsel Seminar, May 1995; Topic, Claims and Defense Perspectives on Handling a Litigated File, Southern California Defense Counsel Seminar, July 1995. Appointed to Board of Directors, Southern California Defense Counsel, 1997. Judge Pro Tem, Los Angeles Municipal Court. Settlement Officer, Los Angeles County Superior Court. Mediator, Los Angeles Superior Court. *Member:* State Bar of California (Member, Litigation and Law Practice Management Sections); Association of Southern California Defense Counsel; Defense Research Institute. *LANGUAGES:* Norwegian. *REPORTED CASES:* Valdez v. Smith (1985) 166 Cal. App. 3d 723; Holmes v. Roth (1992) 11 Cal. App. 4th 931. *PRACTICE AREAS:* High Exposure Personal Injury; Insurance Defense.

### ASSOCIATES

**ROBERT E. HENKE,** born Alliance, Ohio, August 23, 1963; admitted to bar, 1990, California; 1991,U.S. District Court, Central District of California; 1995, U.S. District Court, Southern and Eastern Districts of California. *Education:* The Ohio State University (B.A., 1985; J.D., 1990). Order of the Coif. Staff Member (1988-1989) and Managing Editor, 1989-1990, Ohio State Law Journal. Author: "Ohio's View of the Pollution Exclusion Clause: Is There Still Ambiguity?" 50 Ohio State Law Journal 983, 1989. *Member:* State Bar of California; Association of Southern California Defense Counsel; Defense Research Institute. *PRACTICE AREAS:* Insurance Defense.

**JEFFREY B. SMITH,** born Santa Monica, California, December 19, 1965; admitted to bar, 1991, California. *Education:* University of Southern California (A.B. in Sociology, 1988); McGeorge School of Law, University of the Pacific (J.D., 1991). *Member:* American Bar Association. *PRACTICE AREAS:* Insurance Defense Litigation.

**ANASTASIA SWIATEK HOYT,** born Pomona, California, April 15, 1964; admitted to bar, 1992, California and U.S. District Court, Central District of California. *Education:* University of Southern California at Los Angeles (B.A., 1985); Pepperdine University (J.D., 1992). Phi Alpha Delta. Recipient, American Jurisprudence Awards in Insurance Law and Family Law. Literary Editor and Staff Member, Pepperdine Law Review, 1990-1992. *Member:* San Fernando Valley and American Bar Associations; State Bar of California. *PRACTICE AREAS:* Insurance Defense.

---

## REID & HELLYER

*A PROFESSIONAL CORPORATION*

**ONTARIO, CALIFORNIA**

(See Riverside)

*General Civil and Trial Practice in all State and Federal Courts. Administrative, Bankruptcy, Commercial, Communications, Constitutional, Construction, Corporate, Environmental, Ethics and Professional Responsibility, Estate Planning, Eminent Domain and Water Rights Law, Government, High Technology, Insurance, Intellectual Property, Labor and Employment Law, Litigation, Malpractice, Military, Personal Injury, Probate, Real Property, Torts, Zoning and Municipal.*

---

## JOHN SCHESSLER

Established in 1970

*218 WEST E STREET*

**ONTARIO, CALIFORNIA 91762**

Telephone: 909-986-2095

Fax: 909-391-0058

*Corporation, Probate, Trust, Taxation and Real Estate Law.*

**JOHN SCHESSLER,** born Columbia, South Carolina, September 5, 1928; admitted to bar, 1949, South Carolina; 1955, Kansas and U.S. Tax Court; 1962, California and U.S. District Court, Central District of California. *Education:* University of South Carolina (A.B., 1948; J.D., 1949); New York University (LL.M. in Taxation, 1954). Instructor: La Verne College Law Center, 1975-1978; 1980-1983; Taxation Law, San Bernardino State College, 1979-1980. Trial Attorney, Office of Regional Counsel, Internal Revenue Service, Los Angeles, 1958-1966. *Member:* Western San Bernardino; San Bernardino County, Federal and American Bar Associations; State Bar of California. [1st Lt., JAGC, U.S. Air Force, 1950-1953].

REFERENCE: PFF Bank, Ontario CA.; Wella Fargo Bank, Ontario CA.

---

## AGAPAY, LEVYN & HALLING

*A PROFESSIONAL CORPORATION*

Established in 1974

*ONE CITY BOULEVARD WEST, SUITE 835*

**ORANGE, CALIFORNIA 92668**

Telephone: 714-634-1744

Fax: 714-634-0417

Los Angeles, California Office: Fourth Floor, 10801 National Boulevard, 90064. Telephone: 310-470-1700. Fax: 310-470-2602.

*General Civil Practice. Real Estate, Construction, Corporation, Computer Law, Business, Banking, Unfair Competition, Taxation, Commercial Law and Related Litigation and Risk Management.*

(For Complete Biographical Personnel, See Professional Biographies at Los Angeles, California)

---

## AGREN & WERNER LLP

*SUITE 1210*

*333 CITY BOULEVARD, WEST*

**ORANGE, CALIFORNIA 92868**

Telephone: 714-634-8999

Fax: 714-634-2704

*Business Litigation, Insolvency, Corporate Law, Real Estate, Taxation, Estate Planning and Probate.*

### MEMBERS OF FIRM

**LEE G. WERNER,** born Chicago, Illinois, April 16, 1953; admitted to bar, 1977, Illinois, U.S. District Court, Northern District of Illinois and U.S. Court of Appeals, Seventh Circuit; 1978, California; 1979, U.S. District Court, Central and Southern Districts of California and U.S. Court of Appeals, Ninth Circuit. *Education:* Lewis University (B.A., summa cum laude, 1974); Loyola University of Chicago (J.D., 1977). Delta Epsilon Sigma. Member, Loyola Law Journal, 1976-1977. Author: Comment," Alyeska Pipeline Service, Co. v. Wilderness Society, The Private Attorney General Theory is No Longer Available to Shift the Cost of Attorneys' Fees from the Victorious Litigant to the Losing Party," 7 Loyola Law Journal, 277, 1976. Staff Attorney, Division of Enforcement of U.S. Securities and Exchange Commission, Chicago Regional Office, 1977-1979. *Member:* Illinois State Bar Association; The State Bar of California. *PRACTICE AREAS:* Real Estate; Business Litigation; Corporate Law.

**CARL F. AGREN,** born Long Beach, California, October 1, 1944; admitted to bar, 1971, California and U.S. District Court, Northern District of California; 1972, U.S. District Court, Central District of California. *Education:* California State University at Long Beach (B.S., cum laude, 1965); Loyola University (J.D., 1970). Lecturer, Lawyers Use of Financial Statements in Litigation, California Continuing Legal Education, 1982-1983. Judge Pro Tempore, Orange County, California, 1977—. *Member:* Orange County (Member, Commercial Law and Bankruptcy Section) and American Bar Associations; State Bar of California; California Society of Certified Public Accountants; American Institute of Certified Public Accountants; American Association of Attorney-Certified Public Accountants; California Trial Lawyers Association; Association of Trial Lawyers of America; Los Angeles Trial Lawyers Association. *PRACTICE AREAS:* Business Litigation; Corporate Law; Insolvency; Taxation; Estate Planning; Probate.

---

## ALVARADO, SMITH, VILLA & SANCHEZ

*A PROFESSIONAL CORPORATION*

**ORANGE, CALIFORNIA**

(See Newport Beach)

*Sophisticated Business Transactions and Complex Litigation.*

## ASTOR & PHILLIPS

A PROFESSIONAL LAW CORPORATION

Established in 1963

333 CITY BOULEVARD WEST, 17TH FLOOR
**ORANGE, CALIFORNIA 92668-2924**
Telephone: 714-634-8050
Facsimile: 714-634-8469

*Los Angeles, California Office:* 800 Wilshire Boulevard, Fifteenth Floor. Telephone: 213-680-9212.

*Business, Real Estate, Corporate, Estate Planning, Probate, Taxation, Solid Waste Management/Environmental Law. General Trial Practice in Business, Real Estate, Eminent Domain, Commercial Law, and Trust Litigation, Governmental Affairs, Family Law.*

(For complete Biographical Data on all personnel, see Professional Biographies at Los Angeles, California)

---

## JAMES K. BATCHELOR

A PROFESSIONAL CORPORATION

765 SOUTH THE CITY DRIVE
SUITE 270
**ORANGE, CALIFORNIA 92668**
Telephone: 714-750-8388; 714-542-2333
Fax: 714-750-8002

*Practice limited to Family Law.*

**JAMES K. BATCHELOR,** born Long Beach, California, October 4, 1934; admitted to bar, 1960, California; 1968, U.S. Supreme Court. *Education:* California State College at Long Beach (A.B., 1956); Hastings College of the Law, University of California (J.D., 1959). Phi Delta Phi. Instructor on Family Law, Santa Ana College, 1982-1983. Deputy District Attorney, Orange County, 1960-1962. President, Orange County Barristers, 1962-1964. Vice President, California State Barristers, 1966. Listed in *Best Lawyers in America*, 1989-1990, 1991-1992, 1993-1994, 1995-1996, 1997-1998. California Continuing Education of the Bar (CEB), 1975-1985. *Member:* Orange County (Chairman, Family Law Section, 1968-1971) and American (Member, Family Law Section) Bar Associations; The State Bar of California (Member, 1971-1976 and Chairman, 1976, Family Law Committee; Advisor, Family Law Section, 1976-1978); Family Law Judge Pro-tem, 1974—). Certified Fellow, American Academy of Matrimonial Lawyers (President, 1988-1989, Southern California Chapter). (Certified Specialist, Family Law, The State Bar of California Board of Legal Specialization).

REFERENCE: Wells Fargo Bank

---

## WILLIAM P. BENNETT, A P.L.C.

Established in 1979

333 CITY BOULEVARD WEST, SUITE 1810
**ORANGE, CALIFORNIA 92668**
Telephone: 714-978-3293
FAX: 714-634-3688

*Family Law, Real Estate and General Civil Litigation.*

**WILLIAM P. BENNETT,** born Inglewood, California, August 28, 1938; admitted to bar, 1964, California. *Education:* Compton College (A.A., 1959); California State University at Long Bea ch (B.A., 1961); University of Southern California (J.D., 1964). Phi Delta Phi; Order of the Coif; Blue Key. Law Review Editor, Chairman, Moot Court. Member, Editorial Board, 1962-1964 and Articles Editor, 1963-1964, Southern California Law Review. Licensed Real Estate Broker, California, 1979—. Instructor, Business and Real Estate Law, California State University at Long Beach, 1965-1985. Judge Pro Tem Panel, 1975-1977; Mediator Panel, 1978-1985; Arbitrator Panel, 1989—; Los Angeles County Superior Court, Long Beach. *Member:* Long Beach (Member, Board of Governors, 1970-1971; 1973-1974; 1975-1976) and Orange County Bar Associations; The State Bar of California; Barristers Club of Long Beach (President, 1971); Christian Legal Society. [U.S.M.C. 1959-1965, 1st Lieutenant]. **PRACTICE AREAS:** Family Law; Real Property Law; General Civil Litigation.

*(This Listing Continued)*

---

OF COUNSEL

**KELLY A. BENNETT,** born Orange, California, March 2, 1965; admitted to bar, 1991, California and U.S. District Court, Central District of California. *Education:* Pepperdine University (B.S., 1987; J.D., 1990). Mediator/Arbitrator, Christian Conciliation Service. *Member:* Orange County Bar Association; State Bar of California; Christian Legal Society. **PRACTICE AREAS:** Business Litigation; Construction Litigation; Corporations; Contracts.

LEGAL SUPPORT PERSONNEL

**ANDREA D. EVERAGE** (Paralegal).

---

## CHARLES E. BERGSTROM

Established in 1976

770 THE CITY DRIVE
SUITE 8000
**ORANGE, CALIFORNIA 92668-4956**
Telephone: 714-750-0400
Fax: 714-740-1412

*Family Law and Juvenile Dependency. Abandonment.*

**CHARLES E. BERGSTROM,** born Pasadena, California, April 7, 1942; admitted to bar, 1974, California and Wisconsin. *Education:* Western State University (B.S.L., 1971; J.D., 1973). Panel Attorney, Orange County Juvenile Court, 1984—. *Member:* Orange County Bar Association; State Bar of California. (Certified Specialist, Family Law, The State Bar of California Board of Legal Specialization).

LEGAL SUPPORT PERSONNEL

**KIMBERLY M. MARRUJO,** born Escondido, California, January 16, 1959. *Education:* Rancho Santiago College (A.S., 1993). Phi Theta Kappa. (Paralegal). **PRACTICE AREAS:** Legal Writing; Client Contact; Calendaring; Full Office Supervision.

---

## BARRY I. BESSER

333 CITY BOULEVARD WEST
SUITE 1700
**ORANGE, CALIFORNIA 92668**
Telephone: 714-978-1788
Fax: 714-938-3252

*Family Law, Custody, Visitation Support, Criminal Law, Juvenile Criminal Law, Civil Litigation, Personal Injury, Auto, Slip and Fall.*

**BARRY I. BESSER,** born Los Angeles, California, June 21, 1952; admitted to bar, 1979, California. *Education:* California State University at Northridge (B.S., 1974); Western State University (J.D., 1977). Nu Beta Epsilon. *Member:* Orange County Bar Association; (Member, Board of Directors, 1988-1989; Delegate to State Bar Convention and Chairman, Family Law Section to that Convention, 1989—); State Bar of California; Orange County Trial Lawyers Association (Member, Board of Directors, 1992-1995); Orange County Barristers (Past President, 1989). **PRACTICE AREAS:** Personal Injury Law; Family Law; Criminal Defense.

---

## DOROTHEA C.R. BLAINE, P.C.

**ORANGE, CALIFORNIA**

(See Santa Ana)

*Family Law, Probate, Estate Planning, Personal Injury, Guardianship, Conservatorship, Civil Litigation.*

---

## LAW OFFICES OF DAVID B. BLOOM

A PROFESSIONAL CORPORATION

**ORANGE, CALIFORNIA**

(See Los Angeles)

*General Civil Practice, Litigation, Insurance, Personal Injury, Bankruptcy, Creditors Rights, Probate, Real Property, Banking and Entertainment Law.*

## ROBERT D. CHATTERTON
*1400 BANK OF AMERICA TOWER*
*ONE CITY BOULEVARD WEST*
**ORANGE, CALIFORNIA 92668**
*Telephone: 714-547-8484*
*Facsimile: 714-634-2153*

*Criminal and Juvenile.*

**ROBERT D. CHATTERTON,** born Ann Arbor, Michigan, January 31, 1939; admitted to bar, 1969, California. *Education:* Orange Coast College, California State University at Long Beach; University of California at Los Angeles (B.A., 1965); Loyola University of Los Angeles (J.D., 1968). Phi Delta Phi. Associate Editor, Loyola Law Review, 1967-1968. Member of Faculty, College of Trial Advocacy, Pepperdine University School of Law, 1976-1986. Deputy District Attorney, Orange County, 1969-1981. Member, District Attorney Homicide Unit, 1973-1980. Member, Board of Directors, Orange County Association of Deputy District Attorneys, 1979. State Bar Court Referee, 1982. Chairman, Magistrate Selection Panel, U.S. District Court, Central District of California, 1984-1985. Member: Federal Indigent Defense Panel, 1988-1989; Orange County Superior Court Homicide Conflict Panel, 1990-1995. *Member:* Orange County (Member, Judicial Evaluation Committee, 1982; Chairman, Judiciary Committee, 1984-1986; Member: Board of Directors, 1985-1987; Criminal Law Section) and Federal (Member, Board of Directors, 1987-1989) Bar Associations; The State Bar of California. [With USAF, 1957-1961]

---

## BERT COOK
*333 CITY BOULEVARD WEST*
*SUITE 1700*
**ORANGE, CALIFORNIA 92868**
*Telephone: 714-938-3239*
*Facsimile: 714-938-3249*

*Practice Exclusive to Real Estate Law, Residential, Transactional, Litigation, Financing, Contracts, Leases, Foreclosures, Escrow, Title Claims, Mediation and Arbitration.*

**BERT COOK,** born Cleveland, Ohio, December 26, 1941; admitted to bar, 1986, California. *Education:* Kent State University (B.S., 1965); Western State University (J.D., 1984). Delta Theta Phi. Recipient, American Jurisprudence Awards in Constitutional Law and Evidence. Licensed Real Estate Broker, California, 1979. Graduate Instructor, California Association of Realtors, 1994. Certified Real Estate Instructor, California Community Colleges, 1986. Instructor, Business Law, Legal Aspects of Real Estate: Coastline Community College, 1986—; Rancho Santiago College, 1987—. Member: Irvine Toastmasters, 1994-1996, Saddleback Toastmasters, 1986-1994. Partner in National Partners in Homeownership Strategy. *Member:* Orange County Bar Associations; State Bar of California.

REPRESENTATIVE CLIENTS: Century 21 Independent Offices.

---

## DONOVAN & DRAHEIM
*A PROFESSIONAL CORPORATION*
*Established in 1987*
*500 NORTH STATE COLLEGE BOULEVARD, SUITE 500*
**ORANGE, CALIFORNIA 92868**
*Telephone: 714-938-0123*
*Fax: 714-938-0603*

San Diego, California Office: 402 W. Broadway, Suite 400. Telephone: 619-531-1919. Fax: 619-531-7911.

*Civil Trial Practice before all State and Federal Courts. Insurance Defense, Construction Defect, Products Liability, Premises Liability, Architect, Real Estate Agent and Engineering Malpractice, Automobile Liability and Insurance Coverage.*

*FIRM PROFILE: Donovan and Draheim specializes in the defense of civil litigation in both State and Federal Courts. The firm's main office in Orange, California and branch office in San Diego, allow access to all Orange County, Riverside County, San Diego County and Southern Los Angeles County courts without extensive difficulty or delay.*

*The firm was founded as Donovan and Quilligan in 1987 and reorganized to its present structure in 1994 by founding partner Gary N. Donovan.*

*(This Listing Continued)*

---

**GARY N. DONOVAN,** born New York, N.Y., February 25, 1955; admitted to bar, 1982, California; 1983, U.S. District Court, Central District of California; 1985, U.S. District Court, Northern, Eastern and Southern Districts of California and U.S. Court of Appeals, Ninth Circuit; 1987, U.S. Supreme Court. *Education:* Fordham University (B.A., Econ., 1977); Southwestern University (J.D., 1981). Licensed Pilot. *Member:* Orange County and American Bar Associations; State Bar of California; Association of Southern California Defense Counsel. **PRACTICE AREAS:** Products Liability; Construction Liability; Premises Liability; Automobile Law; Professional, Architect and Real Estate Agent Malpractice.

**JENNIFER E. DRAHEIM,** born Inglewood, California, March 31, 1961; admitted to bar, 1985, Ohio; 1987, California; 1989, U.S. District Court, Central District of California. *Education:* University of California at Irvine (B.A., 1982); University of Toledo (J.D., 1985). Delta Theta Phi. *Member:* Orange County, Ohio State and American Bar Associations; State Bar of California; Association of Southern California Defense Counsel. **PRACTICE AREAS:** Insurance Defense; Products Liability; Premises Liability; Construction Liability.

REPRESENTATIVE CLIENTS: Century-National Insurance; Crawford & Company Risk Management Services; Del Taco, Inc.; Fireman's Fund; Gallagher-Bassett Services; General Accident Insurance Company; Northbrook Insurance; Pacific National Insurance; Pepsico Food Service, Inc.; Taco Bell Corp.; Western Heritage Insurance; Western Mutual Insurance Companies.

---

## JOHN A. DUNCAN
*A PROFESSIONAL CORPORATION*
*Established in 1967*
*333 CITY BOULEVARD WEST, SUITE 1420*
**ORANGE, CALIFORNIA 92668-2924**
*Telephone: 714-935-9800*
*FAX: 714-939-1485*

*Estate and Trust Litigation. Probate Litigation, Conservatorship Litigation, Estate Planning, Estate and Trust Law, Estate and Trust Professional Negligence Litigation, Legal Malpractice Litigation and Consulting in these fields.*

*FIRM PROFILE: John A. Duncan specializes in high profile estate and trust litigation. Mr. Duncan provides aggressive representation to a "results oriented" clientele. He possesses outstanding skills, top credentials and substantial litigation experience. His goal is to do whatever it takes for the successful resolution of his client's cases. Mr. Duncan is listed in the Martindale-Hubbell Bar Register of Preeminent Lawyers under Probate, Trusts and Estate Planning Law.*

**JOHN A. DUNCAN,** born Seattle, Washington, May 5, 1937; admitted to bar, 1964, California; 1973, U.S. Tax Court and U.S. Supreme Court. *Education:* University of Washington (B.A., 1960); Hastings College of the Law, University of California (J.D., 1963). Phi Delta Phi. Author: "No Contest Clauses - A Current Overview," Estate Planning, Trust and Probate News, Fall, 1990, Vol. 10, No. 4. Lecturer: Estates and Trusts, Disputes and Resolution and Litigation, California Continuing Education of the Bar, 1991, 1994. *Member:* Orange County (Member and Chair, 1996, Estate Planning, Probate and Trust Law Section; Member, Section on Business Litigation) and American Bar Associations; State Bar of California (Member, Sections on: Estate Planning, Probate and Trust Law Litigation); Orange County Trial Lawyers Association. Fellow, American College of Trust and Estate Counsel. (Certified Specialist, Probate, Estate Planning and Trust Law, The State Bar of California Board of Legal Specialization). **PRACTICE AREAS:** Estate and Trust Litigation; Legal Malpractice Litigation and consulting in these fields.

REFERENCE: First American Trust Co., Newport Beach, California.

---

## ELLIOT, LAMB, LEIBL & SNYDER
*Established in 1988*
*333 SOUTH ANITA STREET, SUITE 660*
**ORANGE, CALIFORNIA 92668**
*Telephone: 714-978-6255*
*Fax: 714-978-9087*

Encino Office: 16501 Ventura Boulevard, Suite 301, 91436. Telephone: 818-380-0123; 310-553-5767. Facsimile: 818-380-0124.

Redlands, California Office: 101 East Redlands Boulevard, Suite 285, 92373. Telephone: 909-792-8861. Fax: 909-798-6997.

*Civil Litigation. Insurance Defense and Medical Malpractice Defense.*

*(This Listing Continued)*

FIRM PROFILE: Our law firm which specializes in the defense of professional malpractice actions against health care providers. Our cases include all types of medical malpractice, including claims involving psychiatric care, birth injuries, disputes concerning medical staff privileges and representation of physicians before the Medical Board of California. We are active in both the state and federal courts, which matters pending throughout the counties of Los Angeles, Riverside, San Bernardino and Orange. We deal primarily with complex, high damage potential cases, involving claims of brain damage, paralysis and wrongful death allegedly due to medical negligence.

**MICHAEL V. LAMB,** born Fairfield, Iowa, December 23, 1952; admitted to bar, 1979, California; 1985, U.S. District Court, Central District of California. *Education:* University of Michigan (B.A., 1975); Rutgers University; Pepperdine University (J.D., 1978). *Member:* Los Angeles County and American Bar Associations; State Bar of California. **PRACTICE AREAS:** Insurance Defense; Medical Malpractice Defense.

**MICHAEL R. SNYDER,** born Downey, California, July 10, 1958; admitted to bar, 1984, California; U.S. District Court, Central District of California. *Education:* California State University at Long Beach (B.A., 1980); Western State University (J.D., 1983). *Member:* State Bar of California; American Bar Association. **PRACTICE AREAS:** Insurance Defense; Medical Malpractice Defense.

**LOREN S. LEIBL,** born Pasadena, California, July 11, 1953; admitted to bar, 1983, California and U.S. District Court, Central District of California; U.S. Court of Appeals, Ninth Circuit. *Education:* California State University at Long Beach (B.A., 1979); Southwestern University (J.D., 1983). Recipient: American Jurisprudence Award in Torts; Southwestern University Award in Torts and Legal Communication Skills. *Member:* Los Angeles County and American Bar Associations; State Bar of California. **PRACTICE AREAS:** Insurance Defense; Medical Malpractice Defense.

**D. SCOTT ELLIOT,** born Cleveland, Ohio, September 3, 1952; admitted to bar, 1977, California; 1979, U.S. District Court, Central District of California; U.S. Court of Appeals, Ninth Circuit. *Education:* California State University at Northridge (B.A., cum laude, 1974); Southwestern University (J.D., 1977). Recipient, American Jurisprudence Award in Constitutional Law. *Member:* State Bar of California; Association of Southern California Defense Counsel. **PRACTICE AREAS:** Insurance Defense; Medical Malpractice Defense.

**REBECCA J. HOGUE,** born Huntington Park, California, July 20, 1954; admitted to bar, 1984, California and U.S. District Court, Central District of California. *Education:* University of California at Irvine (B.A., 1976); Western State University (J.D., cum laude, 1983). Member, Western State University Law Review, 1982-1983. Recipient: Corpus Juris Secundum Award; American Jurisprudence Awards in Torts, Evidence, Criminal Law and Community Property. *Member:* State Bar of California. **PRACTICE AREAS:** Insurance Defense; Medical Malpractice Defense.

---

**DAVID R. CALDERON,** born Hollywood, California, December 24, 1964; admitted to bar, 1992, California and U.S. District Court, Central District of California. *Education:* California State Polytechnic University (B.A., 1988); Pepperdine University (J.D., 1991). Phi Delta Phi. President, Hispanic Law Students Association, 1990-1991. *Member:* Orange County and American Bar Associations; State Bar of California. **LANGUAGES:** Spanish. **PRACTICE AREAS:** Insurance Defense; Medical Malpractice Defense.

REPRESENTATIVE CLIENTS: The Doctors Co.; Southern California Physicians Insurance Exchange; Fremont Indemnity Co.; National Auto & Casualty Insurance Co.

(For Complete Biographical Data on Personnel, see Professional Biographies at Encino)

---

## FABOZZI, THIERBACH & CALEY

3111 NORTH TUSTIN AVENUE, SUITE 200
**ORANGE, CALIFORNIA 92665**
Telephone: 714-637-3385
FAX: 714-637-3489

*Banking, Commercial, Bankruptcy, Real Estate, General Business and Civil Litigation in all State and Federal Courts.*

FIRM PROFILE: The principals of our firm have a combined experience of nearly 40 years in the areas of business and banking law. Our firm represents clients in every aspect of civil litigation before all California state and federal courts, including real estate, creditor's rights, business litigation and bank-

(This Listing Continued)

ruptcy. We offer the expertise and attention of a specialist with the resources of a large firm. Our clients appreciate our efficient and timely services, with competitive rates. Currently our clients are national and local financial institutions and businesses for which we provide a wide range of services covering all aspects of commercial law and lender liability issues. The law firm is listed in the Martindale-Hubbell Bar Register of Preeminent Lawyers, under Banking Law and Bankruptcy Law.

**DENNIS F. FABOZZI,** born Bethlehem, Pennsylvania, April 1, 1952; admitted to bar, 1977, California and U.S. District Court, Central District of California. *Education:* Arizona State University (B.S., 1974); Loyola University (J.D., 1977). *Member:* Orange County (Member, Commercial and Bankruptcy Sections) and American (Member, Section of Litigation) Bar Associations; State Bar of California. **PRACTICE AREAS:** Banking Law; Bankruptcy Law; Business Litigation.

**MARLENE L. THIERBACH,** born Phoenix, Arizona, November 3, 1951; admitted to bar, 1986, California; 1987, U.S. District Court, Central and Southern Districts of California; 1988, U.S. District Court, Eastern and Northern Districts of California. *Education:* California State University at Fullerton (B.A., magna cum laude, 1982); Loyola Law School (J.D., 1986). Phi Kappa Phi; Phi Delta Phi. Author: "Lender Liability: Should Lenders be Required to Continue to Advance Credit to Marginal Borrowers?" 15 Western State University Law Review No. 2, 1988. Law Clerk to Hon. Edward J. Wallin, Justice of the Court of Appeal, Fourth Appellate District, Division III, Santa Ana, California, 1985-1986. *Member:* Orange County (Member, Sections on: Business Litigation, Business and Corporate Law), Riverside and American Bar Associations; State Bar of California; Orange County Women Lawyers; Inland Empire Bankruptcy Forum; Financial Women International. (Also Member, Robert Morris & Associates). **PRACTICE AREAS:** Banking Law; Bankruptcy Law; Business Litigation.

**REBECCA A. CALEY,** born Whittier, California, May 9, 1962; admitted to bar, 1987, California; 1988, U.S. District Court, Central, Southern and Northern Districts of California. *Education:* California State University at Fullerton (B.A., 1984); Loyola Marymount University (J.D., 1987). Member, Scott Moot Honors Board; Scott Moot Court State Team. Third Place Brief, CYLA-Roger J. Traynor Moot Court Competition. *Member:* Orange County and American Bar Associations; State Bar of California; Financial Women International. **PRACTICE AREAS:** Banking Law; Bankruptcy Law; Business Litigation.

### ASSOCIATES

**JIMA IKEGAWA,** born Pasadena, California, November 24, 1967; admitted to bar, 1994, California. *Education:* University of California at Davis (B.S., 1990); McGeorge School of Law (J.D., with distinction, 1994). Recipient, American Jurisprudence Award in Constitutional Law and Transnational Law. Staff Writer, 1992-1993; Comment Editor, 1993-1994, Law Review. Author: Comment, "NAFTA: How Will It Affect U.S. Environmental Regulations?" 6 Transnational Lawyer 225 (1993). *Member:* Orange County (Member, Business Litigation Section) and Asian American Bar Associations; State Bar of California.

**BRUCE T. BAUER,** born Fort Wayne, Indiana, February 7, 1964; admitted to bar, 1990, California and U.S. District Court, Central District of California. *Education:* California State University at Long Beach (B.S., with honors, 1987); Loyola Law School (J.D., 1990). Phi Alpha Delta. Law Clerk to Bankruptcy Judge Alan M. Ahart. *Member:* Orange County (Member, Business Section) and American Bar Associations; State Bar of California; Orange County Bankruptcy Forum. (Also Member, Robert Morris & Associates). **LANGUAGES:** Spanish. **PRACTICE AREAS:** Banking Litigation; Commercial Litigation; Business Law; Business Insurance; Bankruptcy.

REPRESENTATIVE CLIENTS: Allianz Insurance Company; Allied Bancorp; Bank of the Desert; California Center Bank; California State Bank; California United Bank; Citibank; Citicorp Mortgage, Inc.; Corporate Bank; Foote, Cone & Belding; Foote, Cone & Belding; Fleet Morgage Group; Hanmi Bank; Leader Federal Bank for Savings; Mercedes-Benz Credit Corporation; Mercedes-Benz of North America; Nara Bank; National Bank of Southern California; Norwest Mortgage; Orange National Bank; Pacific Inland Bank; Pacific National Bank; S.B.S. Trust Deed Network; Security Pacific National Trust Company; Tokai Bank; U.S. Bancorp; Wells Fargo Bank.

## GILBERT, KELLY, CROWLEY & JENNETT

SUITE 310 NEXUS FINANCIAL CENTER
721 SOUTH PARKER STREET
**ORANGE, CALIFORNIA 92668-4702**
Telephone: 714-541-5000
Fax: 714-541-0670

*Los Angeles, California Office:* 1200 Wilshire Boulevard. Telephone: 213-580-7000. Fax: 213-580-7100.

*Riverside County Office:* 3801 University Avenue, Suite 700, Riverside, California. Telephone: 909-276-4000. Fax: 909-276-4100.

*San Diego, California Office:* 501 West Broadway, Suite 1260 Koll Center. Telephone: 619-687-3000. Fax: 619-687-3100.

*General Civil and Trial Practice in all State and Federal Courts. Appellate Practice. Corporation and Insurance Law.*

### RESIDENT PARTNERS

**JEFFREY L. CRAFTS,** born Long Beach, California, June 22, 1952; admitted to bar, 1978, California. *Education:* Loyola University of Los Angeles (B.A., 1974; J.D., 1977). *Member:* Los Angeles County, Orange County and American Bar Associations; State Bar of California; The Association of Trial Lawyers of America; Association of Southern California Defense Counsel; Defense Research Institute; Orange County Trial Lawyers Association; American Board of Trial Advocates, ABOTA (Eligible). **PRACTICE AREAS:** Insurance Defense; Construction Defect; Employment Law.

**STEPHEN S. GRANDE,** born Los Angeles, California, August 25, 1956; admitted to bar, 1981, California. *Education:* University of Arizona (B.A., 1978); Southwestern University (J.D., 1981). Delta Theta Phi. Recipient, American Jurisprudence Awards in Insurance Law and Corporations, 1980-1981. *Member:* Los Angeles County, Orange County and American (Tort and Insurance Practice Section) Bar Associations; State Bar of California; Association of Southern California Defense Counsel; International Association of Special Investigators in Insurance Fraud Prevention. **PRACTICE AREAS:** Insurance Defense; Business Litigation; Construction Defect; Employment Law.

**ALBERT P. DIROCCO, JR.,** born Long Beach, California, September 28, 1958; admitted to bar, 1984, California. *Education:* University of California at Davis (B.A., 1980); Loyola Marymount University (J.D., 1984). *Member:* Los Angeles County and American Bar Associations; State Bar of California; Association of Southern California Defense Counsel.

**JENNIFER M. DAMON,** born Redwood City, California, October 13, 1959; admitted to bar, 1984, California and U.S. District Court, Central District of California; 1985, Connecticut; 1986, U.S. District Court, District of Connecticut. *Education:* University of California at Los Angeles (B.A., 1981); Loyola University of Los Angeles (J.D., 1984). *Member:* Los Angeles County and Connecticut Bar Associations; State Bar of California.

### RESIDENT ASSOCIATES

**GEOFFREY S. MORRIS,** born Orange, California, September 30, 1964; admitted to bar, 1991, California and U.S. District Court, Central District of California. *Education:* University of Southern California (A.B., 1987); University of the Pacific, McGeorge School of Law (J.D., 1991). *Member:* Orange County Bar Association; State Bar of California. **PRACTICE AREAS:** Employment Law; Insurance Defense; Business Defense.

**MARY CATHERINE REID,** born West Covina, California, October 10, 1960; admitted to bar, 1991, California. *Education:* University of California at Los Angeles (B.A., 1982); California State University at Los Angeles (M.A., 1986); University of San Diego (J.D., 1991). *Member:* Orange County and American (Real Property, Probate and Trust Sections) Bar Associations; State Bar of California. **PRACTICE AREAS:** Corporate Law; Employment Law; Estate Planning; Business Planning.

**ERIC W. THORSON,** born Omaha, Nebraska, March 28, 1963; admitted to bar, 1991, California; 1993, Colorado. *Education:* Hastings College (B.A., with distinction, 1985); University of Colorado at Boulder (J.D., 1989). *Member:* Colorado Bar Association; State Bar of California; Colorado Defense Lawyers Association. **PRACTICE AREAS:** Insurance Defense.

REPRESENTATIVE CLIENTS: Automobile Club of Southern California; Allstate Insurance Co.; 20th Century Insurance Co.; National Automobile & Casualty Insurance Co.; Colonial Insurance Company of California.

(For complete biographical data on all personnel, see Professional Biographies at Los Angeles, California)

CAA1510B

## JAMES J. GUZIAK

A PROFESSIONAL CORPORATION
333 CITY BOULEVARD WEST, SUITE 1700
**ORANGE, CALIFORNIA 92668**
Telephone: 714-938-3282
Facsmile: 714-938-3284

*Civil Litigation with emphasis on Wrongful Termination and Employment Discrimination.*

**JAMES J. GUZIAK,** born 1953; admitted to bar, 1978, Wisconsin; 1979, California. *Education:* University of Wisconsin-Madison (B.A.; J.D.).

## HAGENBAUGH & MURPHY

A Partnership including Professional Corporations
Established in 1954
701 SOUTH PARKER STREET, SUITE 8200
**ORANGE, CALIFORNIA 92668**
Telephone: 714-835-5406
Fax: 714-835-5949

*Glendale, California Office:* 700 North Central Avenue, Suite 500. Telephone: 818-240-2600. Fax: 818-240-1253. E-mail: hmurphy@interserv.com.

*San Bernardino, California Office:* 301 Vanderbilt Way, Suite 220. Telephone: 909-884-5331. FAX: 909-889-1250.

*General Civil and Trial Practice in all State and Federal Courts. Insurance, Casualty, Life, Health, Accident and Disability Insurance, Malpractice, Employment Law, Business Litigation (including Commercial and Advertising Disputes) and General Tort Litigation*

### MEMBERS OF FIRM

**NEIL R. GUNNY,** born Los Angeles, California, February 10, 1951; admitted to bar, 1977, California; 1979, U.S. District Court, Central District of California; 1983, U.S. Court of Appeals, Ninth Circuit. *Education:* University of California at Los Angeles (B.A., 1973); University of Santa Clara (J.D., summa cum laude, 1977). *Member:* State Bar of California; Association of Southern California Defense Counsel (Committee Chairman, 1991-1994); Community Associations Institute. **PRACTICE AREAS:** Appraisal Malpractice; Homeowners Association Litigation; General Tort Litigation.

**DANIEL A. LEIPOLD,** born Chicago, Illinois, December 22, 1947; admitted to bar, 1977, California. *Education:* St. Mary's College (B.A., 1970); Western State University (J.D., 1977). Author: *Law & Motion Manual,* Orange County Bar Association, 1980. *Member:* Orange County and American Bar Associations; The State Bar of California; Association of Southern California Defense Counsel. **PRACTICE AREAS:** Serious Injury Cases; Malpractice Defense; First Amendment Defense; Elder Abuse Defense; Slapp Suit Defense.

**ROBERT F. DONOHUE,** born Philadelphia, Pennsylvania, April 9, 1951; admitted to bar, 1983, California. *Education:* Western Michigan University (B.A., 1973); University of Toledo (J.D., 1983). *Member:* State Bar of California; State Bar of Arizona. **PRACTICE AREAS:** Civil Rights Defense; Serious Bicycle Accident; Accounting Malpractice; Partnership; Business Litigation.

**ALAN H. BOON,** born Los Angeles, California, July 2, 1954; admitted to bar, 1983, California; 1986, U.S. District Court, Central, Eastern, Northern and Southern Districts of California. *Education:* University of California at Berkeley (B.A., with distinction, 1976); Loyola Marymount University (J.D., cum laude, 1983). Member, St. Thomas More Law Honor Society. *Member:* State Bar of California; Association of Southern California Defense Counsel.

---

**DAVID M. CHUTE,** born Kansas City, Missouri, May 6, 1963; admitted to bar, 1988, California; 1989, U.S. District Court, Central District of California. *Education:* University of California at Irvine (B.A., 1985); Loyola Marymount University (J.D., 1988). *Member:* State Bar of California.

**CATHY L. SHIPE,** born California, November 20, 1960; admitted to bar, 1991, California. *Education:* National University (B.B.A., cum laude, 1982; M.B.A., 1985); California Western School of Law (J.D., magna cum laude, 1991). Phi Alpha Delta. Notes and Comments Editor, California

*(This Listing Continued)*

Western Law Review/International Law Journal, 1990-1991. Recipient: American Jurisprudence Awards: Contracts and Trial Practice; National Telecommunications Law Moot Court Competition; First Place Oral Argument, Best Brief Award. *Member:* Los Angeles County Bar Association; State Bar of California; Association of Southern California Defense Counsel.

**HOWARD J. HIRSCH,** born New York, N.Y., April 19, 1964; admitted to bar, 1995, California and U.S. District Court, Central District of California. *Education:* University of Arizona (B.F.A., 1987); University of Southern California; Western State University, College of Law (J.D., 1994). Delta Theta Phi (Vice Dean). Associate Planning Editor, 1992-1993 and Lead Articles/Planning Editor, 1993-1994, Western State University Law Review. *Member:* Orange County Bar Association; State Bar of California.

(For Complete Personnel and Biographical data, see Professional Biographies at Glendale).

## HARRINGTON, FOXX, DUBROW & CANTER

SUITE 1020, 1100 TOWN AND COUNTRY ROAD
**ORANGE, CALIFORNIA 92668**
*Telephone: 714-973-4595*
*Facsimile: 714-973-7923*

*Los Angeles, California Office:* Thirtieth Floor, 611 West Sixth. Telephone: 213-489-3222. Facsimile: 213-623-7929.
*San Diego, California Office:* Suite 1150, 401 West A Street. Telephone: 619-233-5553. Fax: 619-233-0005.
*San Francisco, California Office:* 444 Market Street, Suite, 3050. Telephone: 415-288-6600. Facsimile: 415-288-6618.

*General Civil and Trial Practice in all State and Federal Courts and before Federal and State Administrative Agencies. Real Estate, Corporation, Business, Estate Planning, Trust, Probate, Medical, Products Liability, Health and Insurance Law.*

### MEMBERS OF FIRM

**DAVID H. CANTER,** born Plainfield, New Jersey, June 4, 1937; admitted to bar, 1965, California. *Education:* Purdue University (B.S., 1959); University of Southern California (J.D., 1964). Phi Alpha Delta. Member, Board of Editors, University of Southern California Law Review, 1963-1964. *Member:* Los Angeles County Bar Association (Member, Trial Lawyers Section); The State Bar of California; Association of Southern California Defense Counsel; Defense Research Institute; American Society of Agricultural Engineers. *PRACTICE AREAS:* Products Liability Law; Toxic Torts Law; Medical Malpractice Law.

**EDWARD R. LEONARD,** born San Diego, California, January 13, 1953; admitted to bar, 1978, California. *Education:* San Diego State University (B.A., cum laude, 1974); University of San Diego (J.D., 1978). *Member:* The State Bar of California; American Bar Association; Association of Southern California Defense Counsel. *PRACTICE AREAS:* Personal Injury Defense Law; Product Liability Law; Professional Negligence Law; Construction Defects Law.

### ASSOCIATES

**PETER A. SCHNEIDER,** born New York, N.Y., June 14, 1959; admitted to bar, 1984, California, U.S. District Court, Central District of California and U.S. Court of Appeals, Ninth Circuit; 1992, U.S. District Court, Southern District of California and U.S. Supreme Court. *Education:* University of California at Riverside (B.A., 1981); University of San Diego (J.D., 1984). Phi Alpha Delta. Author of Opinions: "Burgess v. Superior Court (1992) 2 Cal 4th 1062, 9 Cal Rptr. 2nd 615; Coon vs Nicola (1993) 17 Cal App. 4th 1225. Torts Instructor, First Year Instructional Program, University of San Diego School of Law, 1983-1984. *Member:* Orange County Bar Association; The State Bar of California; Association of Southern California Defense Counsel.

**MARK W. EISENBERG,** born New York, N.Y., March 22, 1965; admitted to bar, 1992, California; 1993, U.S. District Court, Northern and Central Districts of California. *Education:* State University of New York at Albany (B.A., 1987); California Western School of Law (J.D., 1992). *Member:* State Bar of California. *PRACTICE AREAS:* Civil Litigation.

**BRAD M. ELDER,** born Fullerton, California, May 9, 1967; admitted to bar, 1994, California. *Education:* California State University at Fullerton (B.A., 1990); Western State University (J.D., 1994). Recipient, American

*(This Listing Continued)*

Jurisprudence Award in Professional Responsibility. *Member:* State Bar of California. *PRACTICE AREAS:* Civil Defense Litigation.

REPRESENTATIVE CLIENTS: *Insurance:* Associated International Insurance Co.; The Canada Life Assurance Co.; Canadian Insurance Company of California; CIGNA; Clarendon Insurance Co.; Commercial Underwriters Insurance Co.; Commerical Union Insurance Companies; Crum and Forster; John Deere Insurance Co.; Discovery Re; Dorsey, Nevin & Associates; Employers Self Insurance Service; ESIS International; Farm Bureau Insurance Group; Farmers Insurance Group; Gerling-Konzern; John Hancock Property and Casualty Co.; Gerald J. Sullivan & Associates; Harco Insurance Co.; Industrial Indemnity Insurance Co.; Insurance Company of North America; Liberty Mutual Insurance Co.; Metropolitan Property & Liability Insurance Co.; MMI (Multi-Systems Agency); Pharmacists Mutual Companies; The Robert Plan; Royal Insurance Co; State Farm Fire and Casualty Co.; State Farm Insurance Companies; TCO Insurance Services; Topa Insurance Co.; Transamerica Insurance; Truck Insurance Exchange; Unigard Mutual Insurance Co.; United Companies Life Insurance Co.; The Yasuda Claims Services, Inc.; The Yasuda Fire and Marine Insurance Co. *Health:* Children's Hospital and Health Center of Los Angeles; Children's Hospital of Orange County; Daniel Freeman Hospital; Gallatin Medical Clinic; Health West Inc.; Henry Mayo Memorial Hospital; Huntington Memorial Hospital; Scripps Memorial Hospital; Sharp Cabrillo Hospital; Sharp Healthcare; Sharp Memorial Hospital; St. Mary's Desert Valley Hospital; United Western Medical Centers; Victor Valley Community Hospital. *Manufacturing:* Alamo Group; AGIE USA, Inc.; AGIE Losonne; Altec, Inc.; Applied Power Inc.; B & M Machine Works, Inc.; Butler Manufacturing Co.; Cannon Equipment Co.; Cincinnati Milacron Inc.; Clark Equipment Co.; Cummins Engine Company, Inc.; Cummins West, Inc.; Deere & Co.; ELOX Corporation; Ford Motor Co.; Freightliner Corporation; Fuji Seiko Co., Ltd.; Fuji Seisakusho Co., Ltd.; Gametime, Inc.; Harsco; H.C. Muddox Company; IMI Group, Inc.; Iowa Industrial Hydraulics, Inc.; Iwatani International Corporation; Jaguar; Kartridg Pak, Inc.; Kelley Company, Inc.; Kerr Manufacturing Co.; Mack Trucks, Inc.; The Melroe Company; Mitsubishi Electric Corp.; Navistar International Transportation Corp.; Nissan Motor Corporation U.S.A.; Plasti-Kote, Inc.; The Raymond Corporation; Rexworks Inc.; Savage Arms, Inc.; Sturm Ruger & Company, Inc.; Sybron; Taylor Machine Works, Inc.; Toyota Motor Sales, U.S.A., Inc.; TRW Inc.; Van Dorn Company; VME Americas, Inc.; Walterscheid; Wheeler Manufacturing Company; Yale Security Inc.; Zimmer, Inc. *Business:* Angeles Metal Systems; Bank of America; Brownline, Inc.; Calgary Flames; City of Coronado; Dart Industries Inc.; Fedco, Inc.; Federal Deposit Insurance Corp.; Hussman Refrigeration Co.; Kraft General Foods Inc.; Nestle USA, Inc.; The Newhall Land and Farming Co.; Nissan Motor Acceptance Corp.; Oscar Mayer Corp.; Phillip Morris Companies Inc.; Premark International, Inc.; Resolution Trust Corp.; Santa Monica College District; Schneider National, Inc.; Sears Roebuck & Company; Vanencia Company.

## HILLSINGER AND COSTANZO

PROFESSIONAL CORPORATION
*Established in 1973*

701 SOUTH PARKER STREET, SUITE 6000
**ORANGE, CALIFORNIA 92868-4741**
*Telephone: 714-542-6241*
*Telecopier: 714-667-6806*

*Los Angeles, California Office:* 12th Floor, 3055 Wilshire Boulevard. Telephone: 310-388-9441. Telecopier: 310-388-1592.
*Rancho Cucamonga, California Office:* 10737 Laurel Street, Suite 110 - Main Floor. Telephone: 909-483-6200. Telecopier: 909-483-6277.
*Santa Barbara, California Office:* 220 East Figueroa Street. Telephone: 805-966-3986. Telecopier: 805-965-3798.

*General Civil and Appellate Trial Practice in all State and Federal Courts. Insurance, Corporation, Commercial, Business, Medical and Professional Malpractice, Product Liability, Aviation, Asbestos, Toxic Tort, Bad Faith, Insurance Coverage, Declaratory Relief, Wrongful Termination, Vehicular, Property Damage, General Liability Cases.*

(For personnel and biographical data, see Biographical Card, Los Angeles, California).

## HOLDEN & FERGUS

500 N. STATE COLLEGE BOULEVARD
SUITE 780
**ORANGE, CALIFORNIA 92868-1607**
*Telephone: 714-939-6776*
*Fax: 714-939-6840*

*Corporate (Profit and Non-Profit), Estate Planning, Trust and Probate Law, Real Estate Transactions and Brokerage, Construction Law, Civil Litigation, Trials in all Courts.*

**DANIEL W. HOLDEN,** born Anaheim, California, May 1, 1934; admitted to bar, 1959, California. *Education:* University of California at Berkeley (B.S., 1955); Loyola University (J.D., cum laude, 1958). Phi Delta Phi; Alpha Sigma Nu. Recipient: Aggeler Award for Superior Scholarship, Loyola Law School, 1958. State Inheritance Tax Referee, 1971-1976. *Member:* Or-

*(This Listing Continued)*

## HOLDEN & FERGUS, Orange—Continued

ange County Bar Association (Member, Board of Directors, 1978-1981; Chairman, Estate Planning, Trust and Probate Section, 1979; Member, Real Estate Section); State Bar of California.

**DONALD E. FERGUS, JR.,** born Fullerton, California, July 27, 1951; admitted to bar, 1979, California. *Education:* University of California at Irvine (B.A., 1974); California Western School of Law (J.D., 1978). *Member:* Orange County (Member, Estate Planning, Trust and Probate Law, Elder Law, and Business and Corporate Law Sections) Bar Association; State Bar of California (Member, Estate Planning, Trust and Probate Law Sections). (Certified Specialist, Estate Planning, Trust and Probate Law, The State Bar of California Board of Legal Specialization).

REPRESENTATIVE CLIENTS: Le Vecke Corporation; The Roman Catholic Bishop of Orange, a corporation sole; Catholic Charities of Orange County; Excel Distributing, Inc.; Junckers Hardwood, Inc.; J M G Security System, Inc.; B.T.L. Technologies, Inc.; Etchandy Farms; Penhall Company.
REFERENCES: California State Bank; Northern Trust.

---

# HOLLINS, SCHECHTER & FEINSTEIN

*A PROFESSIONAL CORPORATION*

Established in 1981

12TH FLOOR, 505 SOUTH MAIN STREET
P.O. BOX 11021
**ORANGE, CALIFORNIA 92856**
Telephone: 714-558-9119
Fax: 714-558-9091

*San Diego, California Office:* 12526 High Bluff Drive, Suite 300, 92130. Telephone: 619-792-3502.
*Moreno Valley, California Office:* 22690 Cactus Avenue, Suite 240, 92553. Telephone: 909-247-2903.
*Palm Springs, California Office:* 1111 Tahquitz Canyon Way, Suite 121, 92262. Telephone: 619-416-0288.

*General, Civil and Trial Practice in all State and Federal Courts. Personal Injury Defense, Insurance Law, Construction Defect, Product Liability, Governmental Entity, Professional Liability, Director and Officers Liability, Workers Compensation, Wrongful Termination, Lender Liability, Employment Law, Real Estate Litigation and Business Litigation.*

**ANDREW S. HOLLINS,** born Brooklyn, New York, July 22, 1951; admitted to bar, 1978, California; 1981, U.S. District Court, Southern District of California; 1983, U.S. District Court, Central District of California; 1986, U.S. District Court, Northern District of California; 1992, U.S. Claims Court. *Education:* University of Tennessee (B.S., 1973); Woodland University, Mid Valley College of Law (J.D., 1978). Research Editor, Woodland University, Mid Valley College of Law, 1977-1978. *Member:* State Bar of California; Association of Southern California Defense Counsel; Defense Research Institute; The Association of Trial Lawyers of America; ABOTA. *PRACTICE AREAS:* Insurance Law; Governmental Entity Law; Products Liability Law.

**BRUCE LEE SCHECHTER,** born Chicago, Illinois, March 14, 1956; admitted to bar, 1981, California; 1983, U.S. District Court, Central District of California; 1986, Utah and U.S. District Court, District of Utah. *Education:* Arizona State University (B.S., criminal justice, 1978); California Western School of Law (J.D., 1981). Member: Moot Court Board, Donald Wright Competition; National Moot Court. Member, 1980 and Semifinalist, 1981, National Trial Practice. *Member:* State Bar of California; Utah State Bar. *PRACTICE AREAS:* Personal Injury Defense Law; Products Liability Law; Construction Defect.

**THOMAS M. CONDAS,** born Salt Lake City, Utah, October 24, 1957; admitted to bar, 1984, California; 1985, Utah and U.S. District Court, District of Utah; 1986, U.S. District Court, Central and Southern Districts of California and U.S. Court of Appeals, Ninth Circuit. *Education:* University of Utah (B.S., 1981); Western State University (J.D., 1983). Delta Theta Phi. *Member:* Orange County and American Bar Associations; State Bar of California; Utah State Bar. *PRACTICE AREAS:* Personal Injury Defense Law; Construction Law; Products Liability Law; Worker's Compensation; Subrogation; Uninsured Motorist/Underinsured Motorist.

**KENNETH E. GERTZ,** born Chicago, Illinois, June 15, 1958; admitted to bar, 1986, California and U.S. District Court, Central and Southern Districts of California; 1992, U.S. Claims Court. *Education:* University of California at Irvine (B.A., 1981); De Paul University (J.D., 1986). Assistant Editor, ASILS International Law Journal, 1985-1986. Author: Book Review, "Transnational Terrorism," by Edward F. Mickolus, 56 Revue Internationale de Droit Penal 394; Book Review, "Documents on the Laws of War," edited by Adam Roberts and Richard Guelff, 56 Revue Internationale de Droit Penal 365. *Member:* Orange County and American Bar Associations; State Bar of California; The Association of Trial Lawyers of America. *PRACTICE AREAS:* Insurance Law; Personal Injury Defense Law; Products Liability Law; Governmental Entity Law; Business Litigation.

**JACK H. SNYDER,** born Pasadena, California, July 22, 1958; admitted to bar, 1983, California; 1984, U.S. District Court, Central District of California. *Education:* University of California at Irvine (B.A., cum laude, 1980); University of California at Davis (J.D., 1983). Member, University of California at Davis Law Review, 1982-1983. *Member:* Orange County and American Bar Associations; State Bar of California. *PRACTICE AREAS:* Personal Injury Defense Law; Products Liability Law; Insurance Law; Uninsured Motorist/Underinsured Motorist Practice; Legal Malpractice Defense.

**KENNETH C. JONES,** born Pico Rivera, California, February 21, 1962; admitted to bar, 1987, California and U.S. District Court, Central District of California; 1991, U.S. Supreme Court and U.S. District Court, Northern District of Texas; 1993, U.S. District Court, Northern District of California; 1994, U.S. Court of Appeals, Ninth Circuit. *Education:* Whittier College (B.A., 1984; J.D., magna cum laude, 1987). Member: Moot Court Honors Board; Whittier Law Review, 1985-1987. Author: "Kendall v. Ernest Pestana, Inc., Commercial Lease Assignments," 9 Whittier Law Review 93, 1987. *Member:* Orange County (Member: Business Litigation; Insurance Law) and American (Member, Insurance Litigation Subcommittee) Bar Associations; State Bar of California (Member, Community Associations Institute). *REPORTED CASES:* Baker v. Mid-Century Insurance Company (1993), 20 Cal. App. 4th, 921. *PRACTICE AREAS:* Business Litigation; Real Estate Litigation; Insurance Coverage Law; Community Association Law.

**THOMAS L. HYATT,** born Newport Beach, California, October 20, 1959; admitted to bar, 1991, California, U.S. District Court, Central District of California and U.S. Court of Appeals, Ninth Circuit. *Education:* University of Nevada (B.S., cum laude, 1982); Southwestern University School of Law (J.D., cum laude, 1990). Recipient, American Jurisprudence Awards: Torts I; Real Property; Civil Procedure I; Civil Procedure II. Listed in Who's Who in American Colleges and Universities. *Member:* Orange County and American Bar Associations; State Bar of California. *PRACTICE AREAS:* Personal Injury Defense; Products Liability; Construction Defect; Insurance Law.

---

**BRYAN R. BUSH,** born Kalamazoo, Michigan, July 10, 1962; admitted to bar, 1988, Michigan and California. *Education:* University of California at Irvine; Hope College (A.B., 1984); Pepperdine University (J.D., 1987). Pi Sigma Alpha. Recipient, American Jurisprudence Award in Workers Compensation. Member, Alumni Board, Hope College, 1992—. *Member:* Orange County Bar Association; State Bar of Michigan; State Bar of California; Christian Legal Society. *PRACTICE AREAS:* Civil Litigation; Products Liability; Subrogation.

**MARY ANN SCHILLER,** born Gardena, California, May 22, 1960; admitted to bar, 1987, California. *Education:* University of California at Santa Barbara (B.A., with honors, 1982); University of Santa Clara (J.D., 1986). *Member:* Orange County Bar Association; State Bar of California. *PRACTICE AREAS:* Uninsured Motorists Law; General Civil Litigation.

**JOY L. KRIKORIAN,** born Fresno, California, April 17, 1953; admitted to bar, 1984, California and U.S. District Court, Central District of California. *Education:* California State University at Fresno (B.A., 1978); McGeorge School of Law, University of the Pacific (J.D., 1983). *Member:* State Bar of California; Orange County Workers' Compensation Defense Association. *PRACTICE AREAS:* Workers' Compensation Defense; Insurance Defense.

**ROBERT M. DENICHILO,** born New York, N.Y., July 6, 1967; admitted to bar, 1993, California and U.S. District Court, Central District of California. *Education:* University of California at Irvine (B.A., 1989); Loyola Law School (J.D., 1993). Judicial extern for the Hon. Gary L. Taylor, U.S. District Court, Central District of California. *Member:* Orange County Bar Association; State Bar of California. *LANGUAGES:* Italian. *PRACTICE AREAS:* Insurance Bad Faith; Business Litigation; Insurance Coverage.

**ELLIOTT J. BLOCK,** born Ardsley, New York, March 2, 1961; admitted to bar, 1990, California and U.S. District Court, Central District of

*(This Listing Continued)*

California. *Education:* Cornell University (B.S., 1985); Loyola Marymount University; Illinois Institute of Technology (J.D., 1990). Phi Alpha Delta. Judicial extern, Hon. Judge Robin L. Riblet, U.S. Bankruptcy Court, Central District of California. *Member:* Orange County, Los Angeles and American Bar Associations; State Bar of California. *PRACTICE AREAS:* Litigation; Transactional; Business Law; Insurance Law.

**WENDY ALINE MITCHELL,** born Mountain View, California, June 3, 1965; admitted to bar, 1992, California and U.S. District Court, Southern District of California. *Education:* University of Southern California (B.A., 1988); Cambridge University (Certificate, International Law, 1990); Western State University (J.D., 1991). Member, 1990 and Associate Director, 1991, Warren J. Ferguson Honors Moot Court. Recipient, Fellowship in Trial Advocacy, American Board of Trial Advocates, 1992. *Member:* State Bar of California; American Bar Association; Orange County Barristers; California Young Lawyers Association. *LANGUAGES:* French and German. *PRACTICE AREAS:* Premises Liability; Insurance Defense; Construction Defect; Bad Faith; Medical Malpractice.

**MEKA MOORE,** born Los Angeles, California; admitted to bar, 1995, California and U.S. District Court, Central District of California. *Education:* San Diego State University (B.S., 1992); Southwestern University School of Law (J.D., 1995). Recipient: Chancellors Award of Distinction. *Member:* Los Angeles Bar Association; State Bar of California. *PRACTICE AREAS:* Insurance Law; Personal Injury Defense.

**ERIC M. SCHIFFER,** born Washington, D.C., December 2, 1970; admitted to bar, 1995, California; U.S. District Court, Central District of California; 1996, U.S. District Court, Northern District of California; U.S. Court of Appeals, Ninth Circuit. *Education:* University of California, Irvine (B.A., cum laude, 1992); Southwestern University School of Law (J.D., 1995). Delta Theta Phi. Phi Beta Kappa. Regents Scholar. Member, Humanities Honors Program and Campus Wide Honors Program, University of California, Irvine. Oralist and Writer, Moot Court Honors Program. Recipient: American Jurisprudence Book Award, Legal Research and Writing 2 (Appellate Advocacy); Exceptional Achievement Award, Law and Literature; Dean's Merit Scholarship, Southwestern University. *Member:* Orange County Bar Association; State Bar of California. *LANGUAGES:* Spanish. *PRACTICE AREAS:* General Practice; Civil Practice; Business Law; Insurance.

**TANJA DARROW-MEANS,** born Castro Valley, California, October 27, 1968; admitted to bar, 1994, California. *Education:* University of California at Los Angeles (B.A., 1990); Whittier College School of Law (J.D., 1994). Phi Alpha Delta. President, Black Law Students Association. Associate Justice, Moot Court Honors Board. Semifinalist, Frederick Douglas Moot Court Competition, 1994. Recipient: Thurgood Marshall Award for Best Brief, 1994; National Bar Association Scholarship Award, 1993; Los Angeles Bench & Bar Academic Scholarship, 1992-1994; Best Oral Advocate, Best Brief and Best Overall, Moot Court Internal Competition, 1993. *Member:* State Bar of California; Association of Trial Lawyers of America. *PRACTICE AREAS:* Business Litigation; Insurance Law.

**DAO-MARY DO,** born Saigon, Vietnam, October 27, 1969; admitted to bar, 1996, California. *Education:* University of California, Irvine (B.A., 1991) Southwestern University (J.D., 1995). *Member:* State Bar of California (Member, Litigation Section, 1996); Orange County, American, Vietnamese, Asian American and Southern California Fraud Associations. *LANGUAGES:* Vietnamese. *PRACTICE AREAS:* Personal Injury Defense; Insurance; Business Law; Real Estate; Construction Defect.

**JODIE P. FILKINS,** born Los Angeles, California, November 21, 1968; admitted to bar, 1994, California. *Education:* University of California, Riverside (B.A., 1990); Whittier Law School (J.D., 1994). Member, Chancellor's Committee, University of California, Riverside. Recipient: American Jurisprudence Awards; American Bar Association Award. *Member:* Los Angeles, Orange County and American Bar Associations; Association of Trial Lawyers of America. *PRACTICE AREAS:* Uninsured Motorist Law; Workers Compensation; Subrogation; Construction Defect; Civil Litigation.

**RICHARD T. COLLINS,** born Minneola, New York, July 7, 1966; admitted to bar, 1993, California. *Education:* University of California at Davis (A.B., 1988); Whittier College School of Law (J.D., 1993). Member, Southern California Fraud Investigators Association, 1996. *Member:* Los Angeles County Bar Association; State Bar of California. *PRACTICE AREAS:* Insurance Bad Faith; Insurance Coverage; General Civil Litigation.

*(This Listing Continued)*

*OF COUNSEL*

**MARC J. FEINSTEIN,** born Bronx, New York, August 5, 1954; admitted to bar, 1981, California and U.S. District Court, Eastern District of California; 1982, New Jersey; 1983, U.S. District Court, Central District of California; 1987, U.S. District Court, Southern District of California and U.S. Court of Appeals, Ninth Circuit; 1988, U.S. District Court, Northern District of California. *Education:* Wharton School, University of Pennsylvania (B.S., 1976); McGeorge School of Law, University of the Pacific (J.D., 1981). Moot Court Honors in Oral Advocacy. *Member:* Orange County (Member, Business Litigation and Law Practice Management Sections ) and American (Member, Torts and Insurance Practice Section) Bar Associations; State Bar of California (Member, Business Law, Law Practice Management and Litigation Sections). *PRACTICE AREAS:* Insurance Law; Business Litigation; Professional Liability Law.

REPRESENTATIVE CLIENTS: Acceptance Risk Managers; Admiral Insurance Co.; American Drug Store, Inc.; American States Insurance Co.; Colonial Penn Insurance Co.; Commercial Union Insurance Cos.; Farmers Insurance Group; Home Base d.b.a. Waban; Hull & Company, Inc.; Investors Insurance Group; John Hancock Insurance Co.; K&K Insurance Group, Inc.; Lexington Insurance Company; Mercury Insurance Company; Prudential-LMI Commercial Insurance Co.; St. Paul Fire and Marine Insurance Co.; Teachers Insurance Co.; The Regents of the University of California; U.S. Rentals; UniCare Insurance Co.; Uniguard Insurance Co.; Utica Mutual Insurance Co.; Vista Paint.

---

# RICHARD E. HOLMES

ONE CITY BOULEVARD WEST

SUITE 410

**ORANGE, CALIFORNIA 92868-3605**

Telephone: 714-978-3311

Fax: 714-978-3425

Email: semlohr@aol.com

*Civil Practice including: Real Estate, Landlord/Tenant, Business, Credit, Probate and Collections.*

**RICHARD E. HOLMES,** born Greenwich, Connecticut, June 7, 1947; admitted to bar, 1976, California; 1979, U.S. District Court, Central District of California. *Education:* Southern Connecticut State University (B.A., 1970); Western State University (J.D.., 1976). *Member:* Orange County Bar Association (Member, Real Estate Section); State Bar of California. *PRACTICE AREAS:* Real Estate Law; Landlord and Tenant Law; Business; Credit; Probate; Collections.

---

# KAYAJANIAN & BREWSAUGH

**ORANGE, CALIFORNIA**

(See Irvine)

*Personal Injury, Business Law, Civil Litigation, Family Law, Construction.*

---

# KEGEL, TOBIN & TRUCE

*A PROFESSIONAL CORPORATION*

**ORANGE, CALIFORNIA**

(See Long Beach)

*Workers Compensation, Longshore and Harborworkers, Public Employment, Retirement Law. Insurance Law, Third Party Subrogation.*

---

# KEGEL, TOBIN & TRUCE

*A PROFESSIONAL CORPORATION*

**ORANGE, CALIFORNIA**

(See Rancho Cucamonga)

*Workers Compensation, Longshore and Harborworkers, Public Employment, Retirement Law. Insurance Law, Third Party Subrogation.*

## KOSSLER & HAMBY LLP

3111 NORTH TUSTIN, SUITE 235
**ORANGE, CALIFORNIA 92665-1753**
Telephone: 714-282-8050
Fax: 714-282-8867
Email: kosslerhamby@earthlink.net
URL: http://www.kosslerhamby.com

*Business, Transaction, Litigation, Personal Injury.*

FIRM PROFILE: *Kossler & Hamby LLP serves business and corporate clients and is one of the primary firms in southern California which emphasizes solving legal problems involving the moving and storage industry. The firm also serves as corporate counsel, provides counsel regarding the buying and selling of businesses and the drafting of contracts. The firm's attorneys also represent businesses and individuals in civil litigation before both California and federal courts.*

**RICHARD J. KOSSLER, II,** born Tripoli, Libya, Africa, June 4, 1954; admitted to bar, 1981, California and U.S. District Court, Central District of California. *Education:* Orange Coast College (A.A., 1975); California State University at Fullerton (B.S., 1977); Western State University (J.D., 1980). Omicron Delta Epsilon. *Member:* Orange County and American Bar Associations; State Bar of California; Transportation Lawyers Association; Los Angeles Trial Lawyers; California Moving & Storage Association. **PRACTICE AREAS:** Commercial Transactions (30%, 30); Transportation Law (30%, 30); Business Litigation (20%, 20); Personal Injury Litigation (20%, 20). **Email:** kosslerhamby@earthlink.net

**BRUCE W. HAMBY,** born Independence, Missouri, November 2, 1964; admitted to bar, 1991, California and U.S. District Court, Central District of California; 1992, U.S. Court of Appeals, Ninth Circuit; 1994, U.S. Supreme Court; 1995, U.S. District Court, Northern District of Illinois. *Education:* U.S. Military Academy, West Point, N.Y.; University of Missouri-Columbia (B.S., 1986); University of Illinois, Champaign-Urbana (J.D., 1990). Beta Alpha Psi. Certified Public Accountant, Missouri, 1991; Illinois, 1988. Author: "Recent Decisions: Franchise Tax Board of California v. Alcan Aluminum Limited," Illinois Bar Journal, Vol 78, no. 12, Dec. 1990. Alternate, Orange County Republican Party Central Committee, Seventy-First Assembly, District, 1997—. *Member:* Orange County (Member, Appellate Practice and Insurance Sections) and American Bar Associations; State Bar of California; California Association of Consumer Attorneys; Orange County Trial Lawyer Association. **REPORTED CASES:** Jennings v. Marralle (1994) 8 Cal. 4th 121. **PRACTICE AREAS:** Business Litigation (15%, 20); Commercial Litigation (15%, 20); Personal Injury (20%, 20); Civil Appeals (6%, 20); ERISA (5%, 20). **Email:** kosslerhamby@earthlink.net

REPRESENTATIVE CLIENTS: Anaheim Market Place; Apace Moving Systems, Inc.; Arrow Flooring Contractors, Inc.; Confidante Management, Inc.; Convention Connection, Inc.; Direct Container Line, Inc.; EDN Insurance Services, Inc.; Global Moving Systems, Inc.; Global Relocation System, Inc.; Global Van Lines, Inc.; Global Worldwide, Inc.; GVL Equipment Company; GVL, Inc.; J & V Cartage Systems, Inc.; Laidlaw Carriers, Inc.; Lyon Van Lines, Inc.; Merit Moving Systems, Inc.; Munters Moisture Control Services, Inc.; Rensom Medical Equipment, Inc.; Sunset West Financial, Inc.; Tri-Valley, Inc.; Urban Futures, Inc.; Urban Futures Bond Administration, Inc.; Urban Futures Planning, Inc.; Western Federal Credit Union.

## LANDAU, OMAHANA & KOPKA, LTD.

*Established in 1987*

500 NORTH STATE COLLEGE BOULEVARD
SUITE 1260
**ORANGE, CALIFORNIA 92668-1638**
Telephone: 714-836-9630
Fax: 715-836-4401

*Chicago, Illinois Office:* 222 North La Salle Street, Suite 200, 60601-1005. Telephone: 312-630-9630. Fax: 312-630-9001.
*Lisle, Illinois Office:* 1001 Warrenville Road, Suite 255, 60532-1393. Telephone: 708-434-9630. Fax: 708-434-9644.
*Vernon Hills, Illinois Office:* 850 North Milwaukee, Suite 880, 60061-1553. Telephone: 708-918-4700. Fax: 708-918-4719.
*Belleville, Illinois Office:* 23 South First Street, 62220-2029. Telephone: 618-746-9540. Fax: 618-746-9541.
*St. Louis, Missouri Office:* 7912 Bonhomme Avenue, Suite 400, 63105-1912. Telephone: 314-726-2310. Fax: 314-726-2360.
*Merrillville, Indiana Office:* 8585 Broadway Street, Suite 480, 46410-7001. Telephone: 219-769-9630.

*Dallas, Texas Office:* 5430 LBJ Freeway, Suite 980, 75240-6248. Telephone: 972-503-0100. Fax: 972-503-0110.
*Carmel, Indiana Office:* 11611 North Meridian Street, Suite 706, 46032-4542. Telephone: 317-846-6700. Fax: 317-846-6701.
*South Bend, Indiana Office:* 100 East Wayne Street, Suite 455, 46601-2353. Telephone: 219-288-3270. Fax: 219-288-3280.
*Southfield, Michigan Office:* 26877 Northwestern Highway, Suite 408, 48037-8418. Telephone: 810-208-8400. Fax: 810-208-8410.

FIRM PROFILE: *The firm concentrates in the defense of insurance companies, corporations and self-insureds in the areas of product and manufacturers' liability, hospitals', physicians' and health care providers' professional liability, legal, accountants' and real estate brokers' professional liability, property, environmental, toxic tort, employment and workers compensation litigation and the direct representation of clients in corporate and transactional matters.*

**MARILYN L. BONETATI,** born Los Angeles, California, September 29, 1948; admitted to bar, 1985, California. *Education:* University of Southern California (B.S., 1969); Western State University (J.D., 1985). Research Director, Moot Court; Best Brief Award, Moot Court. Recipient, American Jurisprudence Awards. Managing Editor, Western State University Law Review, 1984-1985. Associate Professor, Southern California College of Law, 1986. *Member:* Orange County Bar Association (Section: Real Estate); State Bar of California; Society of Automotive Engineers. **PRACTICE AREAS:** Professional E & O Defense; Products Liability Defense; Auto Defense; Construction.

---

**DIETER ZACHER,** born Inglewood, California, August 26, 1965; admitted to bar, 1993, California. *Education:* University of California at Santa Barbara (B.A., 1987); Western State University (J.D., 1992). *Member:* State Bar of California; Japan American Society; William P. Gray Inns of Court. **LANGUAGES:** German. **REPORTED CASES:** Gernter v. VW Credit Cal. App. 4th. **PRACTICE AREAS:** Insurance; Torts; Medical Malpractice.

**SCOTT K. KUBIS,** born San Diego, California, December 1, 1962; admitted to bar, 1990, California. *Education:* California State University at San Diego (B.A., 1985); University of San Diego (J.D., magna cum laude, 1990). Phi Alpha Delta. Member, Law Review. *Member:* Los Angeles County Bar Association; State Bar of California. **PRACTICE AREAS:** Insurance Defense; Construction Defense; Medical Malpractice.

**GLENN L. SILVERII,** born Barstow, California, April 15, 1953; admitted to bar, 1979, California, U.S. Court of Appeals, Ninth Circuit and U.S. District Court, Southern and Central Districts of California. *Education:* California State University at Northridge (B.A., 1975); Southwestern University (J.D., 1979). Author: "Commercial Arbitration-Safeguards Needed," 4 CEB California Business Law Reporter. *Member:* Orange County and Los Angeles County Bar Associations; State Bar of California.

**DANIEL A. REED,** born Los Angeles, California, June 1, 1961; admitted to bar, 1990, California. *Education:* University of California at Los Angeles (B.A., 1984); Southwestern University (J.D., 1989).

**J. RODNEY DEBIASO,** born Norfolk, Virginia, August 24, 1949; admitted to bar, 1981, California and U.S. District Court, Central District of California. *Education:* University of Virginia (B.A., 1971); Western State University (J.D., cum laude, 1981). Editor, Western State Law Review, 1980-1981. Recipient: American Jurisprudence Award in Civil Procedure, Constitutional Law and Uniform Commercial Code; Corpus Juris Secundum Award. *Member:* Long Beach and Los Angeles County Bar Associations; State Bar of California; Association of Southern California Defense Counsel.

**DAVID G. BEBB,** born Inglewood, California, September 18, 1964; admitted to bar, 1989, California. *Education:* University of California at Davis (B.A., 1986); University of San Diego School of Law (J.D., 1989). *Member:* Orange County and American Bar Associations; State Bar of California. **PRACTICE AREAS:** Professional Liability; Construction Defects; Directors and Officers Liability; Personal Injury.

**JACOB M. WIESEL,** born Dallas, Texas, May 1, 1950; admitted to bar, 1984, New York and U.S. District Court, Eastern and Southern Districts of New York; 1987, California; 1988, U.S. District Court, Central District of California. *Education:* Columbia University (B.A., 1980); Brooklyn Law School, New York (J.D., 1983). Phi Beta Kappa. *Member:* State Bar of California. **PRACTICE AREAS:** Civil Tort Litigation.

REPRESENTATIVE INSURANCE COMPANY CLIENTS: A.I. Management & Professional Liability; Alembic Group; Andover Companies; The ARDI Exchange; Bankers & Shippers Insurance Company; CIGNA; CNA Insurance

*(This Listing Continued)*

Companies; Christian Brothers; Chubb Group of Insurance; Colonial Penn Group; Coronet Insurance Company; Crawford & Co.; Crum & Forster; Employers Mutual Companies; Equipment Insurance Managers; ERIC Group, Inc.; Federated Insurance; Fireman's Fund Insurance Company; First State Management Group; GAB Business Services, Inc.; Gallagher Bassett Services; Gay & Taylor; General Accident Insurance; Golden Rule Insurance Company; Guaranty National Insurance Company; Gulf Insurance Group; Home Base; Home Insurance Company; Houston General Insurance Company; Illinois Insurance Guaranty Fund; Illinois State Medical Insurance Services, Inc.; Laidlaw; Legion Insurance Company; Lexington Insurance Company; Lindsey Morden Claim Services, Inc.; Lloyd's of London; MASCO; Merchant's Home Delivery; National American Insurance Company; National Union Fire Insurance Company; Nationwide Insurance Company; Northland Insurance Company; Northwestern National Insurance Company; Paradigm Insurance Company; Preferred Physicians; PST Van Lines; Republic Insurance Company; Scott Wetzel Services, Inc.; Sentry Insurance Company; State Farm Insurance Companies; Sumitomo Marine & Fire Insurance; Tokio Marine Management, Inc.; Trammell Crow; TransAmerica Insurance Group; Travelers Insurance Company; VASA Insurance Company; Willis Corroon; Yasuda Fire & Marine Insurance Company of America; Zurich Insurance Company.

## JAMES W. LUNDQUIST, INC.
850 EAST CHAPMAN AVENUE, SUITE A
**ORANGE, CALIFORNIA 92866**
Telephone: 714-997-2394
Fax: 714-532-3996

*Business Litigation, Real Estate Litigation, Transactional.*

**JAMES W. LUNDQUIST,** born Los Angeles, California, August 27, 1942; admitted to bar, 1972, California. *Education:* California State University, Fullerton (B.A., 1968); University of California (J.D., 1971). Adjunct Professor, Western State University, 1976-1986. *Member:* Orange County and American Bar Associations; State Bar of California. [U.S. Army, 1963-1966, NCO]. *PRACTICE AREAS:* Business Litigation; Real Estate Litigation; Landlord and Tenant Law; Contracts; Civil Litigation.

### OF COUNSEL

**PAULA C. MATOS,** born Evanston, Illinois, October 31, 1943; admitted to bar, 1980, California. *Education:* Arizona State University (B.A., 1965); California State University at Fullerton (M.S., 1971); Western State University (J.D., 1980). Phi Alpha Delta. Recipient, American Jurisprudence Awards in Trusts, Contracts, Evidence and Wills. *Member:* The State Bar of California. (Certified Specialist, Probate, Estate Planning and Trust Law, The State Bar of California Board of Legal Specialization); (Also Practicing Individually in Laguna Hills, California). *PRACTICE AREAS:* Probate Law; Estate Planning Law; Trust Law.

## MARLIN & SALTZMAN
A PROFESSIONAL LAW CORPORATION
701 SOUTH PARKER STREET, SUITE 8800
**ORANGE, CALIFORNIA 92868-4720**
Telephone: 714-541-1066
Fax: 714-542-4184

*Woodland Hills, California Office:* Westhills Plaza, 20700 Ventura Boulevard, Suite 227, 91364. Telephone: 818-702-0600. Fax: 818-702-6555.

*San Diego, California Office:* 750 "B" Street Suite 1925. Telephone: 619-235-0600. Fax: 619-235-0675.

*Oakland, California Office:* 1999 Harrison Street, Suite 990. Telephone: 510-208-9400. Fax: 510-208-9410.

*Practice limited to Insurance Defense, Insurance Coverage and Bad Faith Litigation.*

**LOUIS M. MARLIN,** born Los Angeles, California, June 7, 1947; admitted to bar, 1972, California. *Education:* University of California at Irvine (B.A., 1969); Hastings College of the Law, University of California (J.D., 1972). *Member:* Los Angeles County Bar Association; State Bar of California; Association of Southern California Defense Counsel. *LANGUAGES:* French. *REPORTED CASES:* Christensen v. Superior Court, California Supreme Court 53 Cal 3rd 868. *PRACTICE AREAS:* Insurance Defense Law; Professional Malpractice Law; Construction Defect Law.

**STANLEY D. SALTZMAN,** born Montreal, Canada, November 15, 1952; admitted to bar, 1979, California. *Education:* McGill University (D.C.S., 1972); University of Montreal (LL.L., 1977); Southwestern University (J.D., 1979). Recipient, American Jurisprudence Award in Civil Procedure. *Member:* Los Angeles County and American Bar Associations; Association of Southern California Defense Counsel. *LANGUAGES:*

*(This Listing Continued)*

French, Italian. *REPORTED CASES:* Christensen v. California Supreme Court 53 Cal 3rd 868. *PRACTICE AREAS:* Insurance Defense Law; Professional Malpractice Law; Construction Defect Law.

---

Kathy Carter
Christy L. Conner
Lynne A. Pearson
Toni L. Kern
Scott A. Marriott
William C. Gibson
Alan S. Lazar

Craig Pynes
Katy M. Gronowski
John Hollingshead
Jeffrey R. Vincent
Marilynn J. Winters
Daniel J. Yauger
Thomas F. Hozduk (Resident, Woodland Hills Office)

---

## MINYARD AND MORRIS
Established in 1978
ONE CITY BOULEVARD WEST, 11TH FLOOR, SUITE 1100
**ORANGE, CALIFORNIA 92868**
Telephone: 714-937-1020
Facsimile: 714-978-6060

*Practice Limited to Family Law.*

**MARK E. MINYARD,** born McAlester, Oklahoma, June 19, 1951; admitted to bar, 1976, California. *Education:* California State University at Fullerton (B.A., with honors, 1973); Loyola University of Los Angeles Law School (J.D., 1976). Phi Alpha Delta. Judge Pro Tem, Orange County Superior Court. Lecturer: Dividing Property on Dissolution of Marriage, 1984; Family Law Litigation and Enforcement of Orders, 1984; Family Law Litigation, 1985; Dividing Property on Dissolution, May, 1990; Valuing Assets in Dissolutions, 1991; Spousal and Child Support, California Education of the Bar, 1993. *Member:* Orange County (Member, Executive Committee, Family Law Section, 1984; 1994-1996) and American Bar Associations; State Bar of California. (Certified Specialist, Family Law, The State Bar of California Board of Legal Specialization). *PRACTICE AREAS:* Family Law.

**MICHAEL A. MORRIS,** born Winston Salem, North Carolina, October 8, 1953; admitted to bar, 1982, California. *Education:* University of California at Los Angeles (B.A., 1976); Western State University (J.D., 1979). Lecturer: Fundamentals of Family Law, 1993, Child Custody and Visitation in California, 1995, State Bar of California; Recent Development in Family Law, California Education of the Bar, 1996. Judge Pro Tem, Orange County Superior Court. *Member:* Orange County Bar Association; State Bar of California. (Certified Specialist, Family Law, The State Bar of California Board of Legal Specialization). *PRACTICE AREAS:* Family Law.

**JACQUELINE A. WHISNANT,** born Burbank, California, December 11, 1960; admitted to bar, 1987, California; 1988, U.S. District Court, Central District of Los Angeles. *Education:* California State University at Northridge (B.A., 1984); Loyola Law School of Los Angeles (J.D., 1987). Member, Philip C. Jessup International Moot Court Honors Program. Judge Pro Tem, Orange County Superior Court. Author: " Division of Community Property: How Many Bites of the Apple Do The Parties Really Get?", Orange County Lawyer, August 1996. Lecturer: Recent Developments in Family Law, California Education of the Bar, 1996. *Member:* Orange County Bar Association (Member: Family Law Section; Women Lawyers Association); State Bar of California. (Certified Specialist, Family Law, The State Bar of California Board of Legal Specialization). *PRACTICE AREAS:* Family Law.

**LONNIE K. SEIDE,** born Huntington, New York, March 15, 1959; admitted to bar, 1985, Massachusetts; 1986, New York; 1989, U.S. Tax Court; 1990, U.S. District Court, Eastern and Southern Districts of New York and U.S. Court of Appeals, Second Circuit; 1991, U.S. Supreme Court; 1992, California. *Education:* Northeastern University (B.S., with honors, 1982); St. John's University (J.D., 1985). Judge Pro Tem, Orange County Superior Court. Co-Author: "The Genesis and Development of Enhanced Earning Capacity," American Conference Institute, 1991; "Preparation of Expert Forensic Accountant for Trial," Nassau Academy of Law, 1991. Lecturer: All You Ever Wanted to Know About Child Support, Orange County Barristers, 1996. *Member:* Orange County Bar Association (Director at Large, Board of Directors, Family Law Section, 1977; Chair, Publication Committee, Family Law Section, 1995-1997); State Bar of California. (Certified Specialist, Family Law, The State Bar of California Board of Legal Specialization). *REPORTED CASES:* Paulsen, et. al. v. County of

*(This Listing Continued)*

CAA1515B

*MINYARD AND MORRIS, Orange—Continued*

Nassau, et. al., 925 F 2d 65 (2d Cir. 1991). **PRACTICE AREAS:** Family Law.

**RICK C. LAL,** born Ranchi, India, May 9, 1965; admitted to bar, 1991, California, U.S. District Court, Central, Northern and Southern Districts of California; 1992, U.S. District Court, Eastern District of California. *Education:* University of California at Riverside; California State Polytechnic University (B.A., cum laude, 1987); University of California School of Law at Davis (J.D., 1991). Phi Delta Phi (President, 1989-1990). Senior Research Editor, University of California Davis Law Review, 1990-1991. Editor in Chief, Law Practice Management Journal. Author: "The Evidence Code § 1043 Pitfall; Pitching Pitchess to a Divorce Court" Family Law News, Spring, 1996; "Binding Arbitration: Just How Binding Is It In The Real World?", Los Angeles Daily Journal, May 21, 1993 at 7 and San Francisco Daily Journal, May 21, 1993 at 5; "What Johnny Didn't Learn In College: The Conflict Over Where Students May Vote," Beverly Hills Bar Association Journal, Vol. 26, No. 1, Winter 1992; *Member:* San Bernardino County, Riverside County and American Bar Associations; State Bar of California (Chair, Executive Committee, Law Practice Management and Technology Section 1996-1997); The Association of Trial Lawyers of America; California Trial Lawyers Association. (Certified Specialist, Family Law, The State Bar of California Board of Legal Specialization). **LANGUAGES:** Hindi. **PRACTICE AREAS:** Family Law.

**KENNETH T. DEMMERLE,** born Long Beach, California, July 27, 1965; admitted to bar, 1992, California. *Education:* University of California at Irvine (B.A., 1987); Loyola University of Los Angeles (J.D., 1991). *Member:* Orange County Bar Association (Member, Family Law Section). **PRACTICE AREAS:** Family Law.

## MORRIS, POLICH & PURDY

Established in 1969

**500 NORTH STATE COLLEGE BOULEVARD, 11TH FLOOR**
**ORANGE, CALIFORNIA 92666**
*Telephone: 714-939-1100*
*Facsimile: 714-939-9261*

*Los Angeles, California Office:* 1055 West Seventh Street, Suite 2400. Telephone: 213-891-9100. Facsimile: 213-488-1178.

*San Diego, California Office:* 501 W. Broadway, Suite 500. Telephone: 619-557-0404. Facsimile: 619-557-0460.

*General Civil Trial and Appellate Practice in all State and Federal Courts. Construction Law, Insurance Law Environmental Law, Products Liability Professional Liability, Architect and Engineer Liability, Government Tort Liability, Police Civil Liability, Pharmaceutical and Medical Device Liability, Toxic Tort Litigation and Commercial Litigation.*

### MEMBERS OF FIRM

**GARY L. HOFFMAN,** born Orange, California, April 30, 1959; admitted to bar, 1985, California. *Education:* Loyola Marymount University (B.A., 1981); University of San Diego (J.D., 1984).

**RANDALL F. KOENIG,** born Glendale, California, January 18, 1954; admitted to bar, 1981, California. *Education:* University of Southern California (B.A., magna cum laude, 1976); University of San Diego (J.D., 1979). Phi Beta Kappa. Notes and Comments Editor, San Diego Law Review.

**JOHN P. MILLER,** born Springfield, Illinois, July 22, 1945; admitted to bar, 1971, California; 1977, U.S. Supreme Court. *Education:* Loyola University of Los Angeles (B.A., 1967; J.D., 1970).

**STEVEN C. MILLER,** born Bloomington, Illinois, November 10, 1956; admitted to bar, 1984, California. *Education:* California State University at Long Beach (B.A. in Political Science, cum laude, 1980) Loyola Law School (J.D., 1983).

### ASSOCIATES

**WILLIAM M. BETLEY,** born Warwick, Rhode Island, December 9, 1954; admitted to bar, 1984, California. *Education:* University of Rhode Island (B.A., 1977); Southwestern University (J.D., 1983).

**KAY ANN CONNELLY,** born Newport Beach, California, May 30, 1966; admitted to bar, 1991, California. *Education:* University of the Pacific, Stockton (B.A., 1988); McGeorge School of Law (J.D., 1991).

*(This Listing Continued)*

**STEPHEN J. MCGREEVY,** born Hartford, Connecticut, July 2, 1969; admitted to bar, 1994, California. *Education:* Loyola Marymount University (B.A., 1991); USD (J.D., 1994).

**DANIEL J. MCNAMEE,** admitted to bar, 1994, California. *Education:* University of San Diego (B.A., 1989; J.D., 1994).

**THIERRY R. MONTOYA,** born Montreal, Quebec, Canada, November 24, 1960; admitted to bar, 1992, California. *Education:* University of California at Riverside (B.A., 1982); University of Notre Dame (J.D., 1991).

**KRISTEN KAY NELSON,** born San Diego, California, February 6, 1968; admitted to bar, 1993, California. *Education:* University of California at Santa Barbara (B.A., 1989); University of California School of Law, Los Angeles (J.D., 1993).

**CARLOS A. PRIETTO, III,** born Lynwood, California, June 16, 1968; admitted to bar, 1993, California. *Education:* Loyola Marymount University (B.A., 1990); Santa Clara University (J.D., 1993).

**PAUL S. SIENSKI,** born Honolulu, Hawaii, January 20, 1958; admitted to bar, 1989, California. *Education:* U.C. Santa Barbara (B.A., 1981); McGeorge School of Law (J.D., 1989).

## LOUIS M. NIVEN

*A PROFESSIONAL LAW CORPORATION*

Established in 1960

**333 CITY BOULEVARD WEST, SUITE 1605**
**ORANGE, CALIFORNIA 92868-2924**
*Telephone: 714-978-7887*
*Fax: 714-978-7330*
*Email: louniv@earthlink.net*

*Family Law, Personal Injury, General Civil and Criminal Trial Practice, Business, Corporate, Probate, Real Estate Law and Sports/Entertainment Law.*

**LOUIS M. NIVEN,** born Birmingham, Alabama, December 21, 1933; admitted to bar, 1960, California and U.S. District Court, Central District of California; 1976, U.S. Court of Appeals, Ninth Circuit and U.S. Supreme Court. *Education:* Florida State College; University of Alabama; Birmingham-Southern College (B.A., 1956); Tulane University of Louisiana; University of California at Los Angeles (J.D., 1960). Phi Alpha Delta. Professor of Law, American College of Law, 1992. Panel Chair, California State Bar Fee Arbitration Department, 1983—. Orange County Supreme Court Arbitrator, 1983—. *Member:* Orange County (Member, Section on Family Law) and American Bar Associations; State Bar of California (Member, Family Law Section); Orange County Trial Lawyers Association; California Trial Lawyers Association. (Certified Specialist, Family Law, The State Bar of California Board of Legal Specialization). **REPORTED CASES:** Uva v. Evans, 83 CA 3d 356 (1978). **PRACTICE AREAS:** Family Law; Personal Injury; General Civil and Criminal Trial Practice; Business; Corporate; Malpractice; Probate; Real Estate Law.

**LESLIE L. NIVEN,** born Long Beach, California, May 31, 1964; admitted to bar, 1995, California; U.S. District Court, Central District of California; U.S. Court of Appeals, Ninth Circuit. *Education:* Rancho Santiago College (A.A., 1986); California State University at Fullerton; Western State University (B.S.L., 1991); American College of Law (J.D., 1992). *Member:* Orange County and American Bar Associations; Orange County Barristers. **PRACTICE AREAS:** Personal Injury; General Civil Litigation; Sports/Entertainment Law; Family Law.

### LEGAL SUPPORT PERSONNEL

**LYNDA S. TEUBEN,** born San Diego, California, October 10, 1963. *Education:* Golden West College (A.A., 1987); Santa Ana College (Legal Assistant Certification, 1983).

## GERALD J. PHILLIPS

**ONE CITY BOULEVARD WEST, SUITE 1400**
**ORANGE, CALIFORNIA 92668**
*Telephone: 714-978-0325*

*Family Law.*

**GERALD J. PHILLIPS,** born Westwood, Massachusetts, December 18, 1940; admitted to bar, 1965, Massachusetts; 1966, U.S. Court of Military Appeals; 1968, California. *Education:* Boston College (A.B., 1962); Boston University (LL.B., 1965). CEB Lecturer, "Negotiating Marital Settlements,"

*(This Listing Continued)*

1983, 1985; "Joint Ownership of Marital and Non-Marital Property," 1982. Judge Pro Tem, Orange County Superior Court, 1975—. *Member:* Orange County (Chairman, Family Law Section, 1984; Member, Executive Committee, 1986-1987; Member, Board of Directors, 1985, 1986, 1987) and Massachusetts Bar Associations; State Bar of California. [With USMC, Judge Advocate, 1966-1968]. (Certified Specialist, Family Law, The State Bar of California Board of Legal Specialization).

## WILMA E. PRESLEY

A PROFESSIONAL CORPORATION

*Established in 1979*

333 CITY BOULEVARD WEST
SUITE 1420
ORANGE, CALIFORNIA 92868-2924
Telephone: 714-939-1420
Fax: 714-939-1485

*Family Law Practice, including Child Custody, Child and Spousal Support, Community Property Evaluation and Division. Interstate Custody (U.C.C.-J.A.), Post Dissolution Modifications, Juvenile Law and International Family Law.*

FIRM PROFILE: *There will be times in your life when you will urgently need a trusted ally. These are the times when W. Presley and her Associates can provide a most important service - this considerate and competent representative has been in practice since December, 1977. Her firm believes that cooperation, not combat, spells success.*

**WILMA E. PRESLEY,** born San Diego, California, December 30, 1936; admitted to bar, 1977, California; 1978, U.S. District Court, Central District of California. *Education:* Western State University (B.S., 1975; J.D., 1977). Member, Western State University Law Review, 1976-1977. Professor, Legal Research, 1980, Family Law, 1981, Western State University. Charter Member, Women in Business, Orange County. *Member:* Orange County (Member, Family Law Section), American (Member, Family Law Section) and International (Member, Family Law Section) Bar Associations. (Certified Specialist, Family Law, The State Bar of California Board of Legal Specialization).

## MICHAEL J. QUIGLEY

1420 EAST CHAPMAN AVENUE
ORANGE, CALIFORNIA 92666
Telephone: 714-633-4921
Fax: 714-633-8014

*Civil and Insurance Litigation. Criminal, Probate, Business, Corporate and Family Law. Bankruptcy.*

**MICHAEL J. QUIGLEY,** born New York, N.Y., August 9, 1930; admitted to bar, 1964, California; 1981, U.S. Tax Court. *Education:* United States Merchant Marine Academy (B.S., 1953); New York Law School (LL.B., 1961). Phi Delta Phi. President, Family Services Association, Orange County, 1976-1980. Member, Board of Directors, United Way, Orange County, 1981-1985. Presiding Judge, B.P.O.E. Lodge 1475, 1988—. *Member:* Orange County and American Bar Associations; State Bar of California. [LCDR, USNR, active duty, 1954-1959]. **PRACTICE AREAS:** Business Law.

## RUS, MILIBAND, WILLIAMS & SMITH

ORANGE, CALIFORNIA

(See Irvine)

*General Civil and Trial Practice. Complex Commercial Litigation, Bankruptcy, Insolvency, Corporate Reorganization and Creditors Rights.*

## BRIAN G. SAYLIN

625 THE CITY DRIVE SOUTH, SUITE 355
ORANGE, CALIFORNIA 92668-4986
Telephone: 714-750-3200
Fax: 714-750-6250

*Appellate, Family and Matrimonial Law.*

**BRIAN G. SAYLIN,** born Los Angeles, California, November 4, 1942; admitted to bar, 1968, California. *Education:* University of Southern California (B.S., 1964; J.D., 1967). Phi Alpha Delta. Instructor, Western State University College of Law, 1977. Lecturer, Continuing Education of the Bar Appellate Practice in Family Law Proceedings, 1992, 1993, 1994. CEB Panelist, How to Handle a Marital Dissolution, 1996. *Member:* Orange County Bar Association (Member, Sections on: Appellate Law; Family Law); State Bar of California (Member, Family Law Section); American Academy of Matrimonial Lawyers (Certified Fellow). (Certified Specialist, Family Law, The State Bar of California Board of Legal Specialization).

## STUTZ, GALLAGHER, ARTIANO, SHINOFF & HOLTZ

A PROFESSIONAL CORPORATION

ORANGE, CALIFORNIA

(See San Diego)

*General Civil Trial Practice with Special Emphasis in Product Liability, Employment, Environmental, Professional Liability, Construction Defect Litigation, Public Entity, Commercial Litigation, Insurance Coverage, Defense of the Hospitality Industry and Medical Providers.*

## TESTA & ASSOCIATES

A Partnership including a Professional Corporation

765 THE CITY DRIVE
SUITE 405
ORANGE, CALIFORNIA 92668
Telephone: 714-748-8030
Facsimile: 714-748-1045

*Vista, California Office:* Vista Corporate Center, 1800 Thibodo Road, Suite 300, P.O. Box 1720. Telephone: 619-599-9565. Facsimile: 619-599-9571.

*General Civil and Trial Practice. Insurance, Medical Malpractice, Personal Injury, Construction, Business Disputes, Employment and Real Estate Law.*

REPRESENTATIVE CLIENTS: Farmers Insurance Exchange; Truck Insurance Exchange; Fire Insurance Exchange; Reliance Insurance; Lusardi Construction Co.; Tri-Electric Supply; Amoco Oil; Mercury Finance Co.
REFERENCE: Grossmont Bank (Vista Branch), Dunn & Bradstreet.

(For complete biographical data on all personnel, see Professional Biographies at Vista, California)

## DIRK VAN TATENHOVE

SUITE 355
625 THE CITY DRIVE SOUTH
ORANGE, CALIFORNIA 92668
Telephone: 714-750-3500
Fax: 714-750-6250

*Probate Administration, Will Contests, Probate and Trust Litigation, Conservatorship and Guardianship Law.*

**DIRK VAN TATENHOVE,** born Orange, California, April 1, 1947; admitted to bar, 1975, California; 1976, U.S. District Court, Central District of California. *Education:* California State University at Los Angeles (B.A., 1972); University of Santa Clara (J.D., 1975). Law Review Comments Editor, University of Santa Clara School of Law, Law Review, 1975. *Member:* Orange County Bar Association (Member, Executive Committee, 1995-1996 and Seminar Chair, 1996, Estate Planning, Probate and Trust Law Section); State Bar of California. **REPORTED CASES:** Estate of Claffey (1989) 209 Cal. App, 3d254.

# WALSWORTH, FRANKLIN, BEVINS & McCALL

*1 CITY BOULEVARD WEST, SUITE 308*
**ORANGE, CALIFORNIA 92668**
*Telephone: 714-634-2522*
*LAW-FAX: 714-634-0686*

*San Francisco, California Office:* 580 California Street, Suite 1335. Telephone: 415-781-7072. Fax: 415-391-6258.

*Santa Barbara, California Office:* 4520 Via Esperanza. Telephone: 805-569-3100 Fax: 805-569-1906.

*Houston, Texas Office:* 2425 West Loop South, Suite 200. Telephone: 713-787-9009. Fax: 713-787-9010.

*Business, Construction and Development, Real Estate, Corporate, Banking, Creditors Rights, Employment, Insurance Coverage, Products Liability, Environmental, General Appellate, Federal and State Trial Practice. Municipal Law.*

**JEFFREY P. WALSWORTH,** born King City, California, June 26, 1953; admitted to bar, 1977, California. *Education:* Santa Ana College (A.A., 1973); Western State University (B.S.L., 1975; J.D., 1977). Member, Moot Court. Member, Western State University Law Review, 1976-1977. Licensed Real Estate Broker, California, 1978. *Member:* State Bar of California.

**FERDIE F. FRANKLIN,** born Lynwood, California, October 19, 1947; admitted to bar, 1974, California and U.S. District Court, Central, Southern and Northern Districts of California; U.S. Court of Appeals, Ninth Circuit. *Education:* Pepperdine University (B.A., 1969); California State University at Long Beach (M.A., 1971); Loyola University (J.D., 1974). Boss of the Year, Orange County Legal Secretaries Association, 1982-1983. *Member:* Orange County Bar Association; Orange County Trial Lawyers Association; California Trial Lawyers Association; Association of Trial Lawyers of America.

**RONALD H. BEVINS, JR.,** born Fullerton, California, March 20, 1958; admitted to bar, 1983, California; 1984, U.S. District Court, Central District of California. *Education:* Loyola Marymount University (B.A., 1980; J.D., 1983). Alpha Sigma Nu. *Member:* Orange County Bar Association (Member, Sections on: Business Litigation; Insurance); State Bar of California.

**MICHAEL T. MCCALL,** born Los Angeles, California, August 4, 1954; admitted to bar, 1983, California. *Education:* University of Southern California (A.B., cum laude, 1976); California Western School of Law (J.D., 1983). Recipient: Senior Student Athlete Academic Award; Academic Achievement Award, Medical Malpractice. *Member:* Orange County (Member, Toxic Torts Section) and American Bar Associations; State Bar of California.

**NOEL EDLIN,** born Washington, D.C., May 14, 1956; admitted to bar, 1982, California; 1985, U.S. District Court, Northern District of California. *Education:* University of Hawaii (B.A., 1979); University of California, Hastings College of the Law (J.D., 1982). Managing Editor, Hastings Communications and Entertainment Law Journal, 1981-1982. Deputy District Attorney, Sacramento District Attorneys Office, 1982-1983. Assistant District Attorney, San Francisco, 1983-1985. Panelist, American Arbitration Association, August 1991. Faculty, Hastings College of Trial and Appellate Advocacy, 1987—. General Counsel and Secretary for National Council on Crime and Delinquency, 1989—. *Member:* San Francisco Bar Association; State Bar of California; Charles Houston Bar Association. (Resident, San Francisco Office).

**LAWRENCE E. DUFFY, JR.,** born Orange, California, June 6, 1956; admitted to bar, 1982, California; 1983, U.S. District Court, Central and Southern Districts of California. *Education:* Loyola Marymount University (B.A., 1979); Loyola Law School (J.D., 1982). *Member:* Orange County Bar Association; State Bar of California.

**JAMES A. ANTON,** born Rochester, Pennsylvania, May 1, 1962; admitted to bar, 1989, California; U.S. District Court, Central, Southern, Eastern and Northern Districts of California. *Education:* University of California at Irvine (B.A., 1985); Western State University (J.D., 1989). Recipient, American Jurisprudence Award in Civil Procedure, 1987. Member: Jessop International Moot Court Competition, 1989; International Law Society; Knights of Columbus. *Member:* Orange County Bar Association; The State Bar of California. **REPORTED CASES:** City of San Diego v. U.S. Gypsum, 30 Cal. App. 4th 575, 35 Cal. rptr. 2d 876 (1994). **PRAC-**

*(This Listing Continued)*

**TICE AREAS:** Business Litigation; Construction Litigation; Environmental Litigation.

**INGRID K. CAMPAGNE,** born Los Angeles, California, September 1, 1967; admitted to bar, 1992, California. *Education:* University of California at Berkeley (B.A., 1989); Loyola Law School, Los Angeles (J.D., 1992). Articles Editor, Loyola Law Review, 1992. Recipient, American Jurisprudence Award, Trial Advocacy, 1992. Author: Barnes v. Glen Theatre; Is The Court Stripping Away First Amendment Protections to Reveal A New Standard, Loyola Law Review, December, 1992. *Member:* State Bar of California. (Resident, San Francisco Office). **LANGUAGES:** German. **PRACTICE AREAS:** Environmental Litigation; Business Litigation.

**ROBERT M. CHANNEL,** born Pasadena, California, November 26, 1955; admitted to bar, 1983, California. *Education:* University of California at Irvine (B.A., 1977); University of California at Davis (J.D., 1983). *Member:* State Bar of California. (Resident, San Francisco Office).

**NICHOLAS A. CIPITI,** born Cleveland, Ohio, March, 1, 1955; admitted to bar, 1981, California. *Education:* Loyola Marymount University of Los Angeles (B.A., 1977); Loyola Law School (J.D., 1981). Recipient, American Jurisprudence Award in Civil Procedure. Staff Member, 1979-1980 and Editor, 1980-1981, Loyola University of Los Angeles Law Review. Member, St. Thomas More Law Honor Society. Co-Author: Ninth Circuit Labor Law Survey, Vol. XIII, No. 2. *Member:* State Bar of California; American Bar Association.

**SHARON L. CLISHAM,** born San Francisco, California, April 3, 1961; admitted to bar, 1992, California. *Education:* Newcomb College (B.A., 1982); Tulane University (M.A., 1983); University of California, Hastings College of the Law (J.D., 1992). *Member:* State Bar of California; American Bar Association. (Resident, San Francisco Office). **PRACTICE AREAS:** Environmental Law.

**RICHARD M. HILLS,** born Las Vegas, Nevada, February 18, 1956; admitted to bar, 1987, California; 1988, U.S. District Court, Northern District of California; 1990, U.S. District Court, Eastern and Southern Districts of California. *Education:* University of California at San Diego (B.A., cum laude, 1980); University of California at Los Angeles (J.D., 1983). Distinguished Advocate, Moot Court Honors Competition. Instructor, Universite de Paris II, International Law Department, 1983-1984. Mayor of San Francisco's Representative, Airport Community Roundtable. *Member:* State Bar of California; French-American Chamber of Commerce of San Francisco (Member, Public Affairs Committee). (Resident, San Francisco Office). **LANGUAGES:** French.

**SANDRA G. KENNEDY,** born Chicago, Illinois, April 17, 1958; admitted to bar, 1983, California, U.S. District Court, Central District of California and U.S. Court of Appeals, Ninth Circuit. *Education:* Loyola Marymount University (B.A., 1980); Loyola Law School of Los Angeles (J.D., 1983). Phi Alpha Delta. Recipient: Bureau of National Affairs Law Week Award; American Jurisprudence Award for Remedies. *Member:* South Bay, Los Angeles County and Orange County Bar Associations; State Bar of California; Association of Business Trial Lawyers; Orange County Women's Lawyers Association.

**RANDALL J. LEE,** born San Francisco, California, September 3, 1962; admitted to bar, 1989, California and U.S. District Court, Northern District of California. *Education:* Pepperdine University (B.A., 1984); Santa Clara University School of Law (J.D., 1987). *Member:* State Bar of California; Asian-American Bar Association; Asian Business Association; San Francisco Chamber of Commerce. Research Fellow, Kokusai Kirisutokyoo Daigaku, 1987-1988. (Resident, San Francisco Office). **LANGUAGES:** Chinese (Toisanese) and Japanese.

**KEVIN PEGAN,** born Orange, California, June 18, 1956; admitted to bar, 1985, California and U.S. District Court, Central and Southern Districts of California. *Education:* California State University at Long Beach (B.A., 1982); University of Santa Clara (J.D., 1985). Extern Law Clerk to the Honorable Edward J. Wallin, Associate Justice, California Court of Appeal, 4th Appellate District, 1984. *Member:* State Bar of California.

**ALLAN W. RUGGLES,** born Glens Falls, New York, August 9, 1952; admitted to bar, 1984, New York; 1991, California. *Education:* St. Michael's College (B.A., 1974); Vermont Law School (J.D., 1983). *Member:* California State Bar Association; Los Angeles County, Orange County (Member, Bankruptcy Forum) and American Bar Associations. **PRACTICE AREAS:** Creditor Bankruptcy Representation; Civil Litigation.

**LAURIE E. SHERWOOD,** born Los Angeles, California, January 20, 1957; admitted to bar, 1991, California; U.S. District Court, Central District of California and U.S. Court of Appeals, Ninth Circuit. *Education:*

*(This Listing Continued)*

Loyola Marymount University (B.S., 1979); Mount St. Mary's College (M.S., 1985); University of California, Hastings College of the Law (J.D., 1991). Executive Editor, Hastings International and Comparative Law Review, 1990-1991. Extern to U.S. Magistrate Judge Claudia Wilken, Northern District of California, 1991. Author: "The Child Care Tax Credit: An Investment in the Future," Hastings International and Comparative Law Review, Volume 14, Issue 1. *Member:* Los Angeles County and American Bar Associations; State Bar of California. *PRACTICE AREAS:* Litigation; Police Civil Liability Law.

**CINDY R. HUGHES,** born Newport Beach, California, 1957; admitted to bar, 1987, California. *Education:* California State University, Long Beach (B.S., with distinction, 1980); University of Southern California (M.B.T., 1987; J.D., 1987). Beta Gamma Sigma; Phi Alpha Delta. Staff Editor, The Computer Law Journal and Major Tax Planning, 1985-1986. Certified Public Accountant, California, 1983. *Member:* Orange County Bar Association; State Bar of California.

**STEPHEN M. NICHOLS,** born Los Angeles, California, 1956; admitted to bar, 1981, California; U.S. District Court, Central and Southern Districts of California and U.S. District Court, District of Hawaii. *Education:* Santa Clara University (B.S., 1978); Loyola Law School (J.D., 1981). *Member:* State Bar of California. *PRACTICE AREAS:* Trial Law; Commercial Law; Banking Law; Personal Injury; Construction Defects.

**CYRIAN B. TABUENA,** born San Francisco, California, July 15, 1957; admitted to bar, 1983, California and U.S. District Court, Northern District of California; 1984, U.S. Court of Appeals, Ninth Circuit. *Education:* San Francisco State University (B.A., cum laude, 1979); University of California, Hastings College of the Law (J.D., 1983). Lecturer, Constitutional Law, San Francisco State University, 1986. *Member:* Bar Association of San Francisco; State Bar of California; American Bar Association (Member, ABA/YLD Minorities In The Legal Profession, 1987); Filipino Bar Association of Northern California (President, 1985-1986); Defense Research Institute. (Resident, San Francisco Office). *PRACTICE AREAS:* Mass Torts; Products Liability Law; Litigation; Environmental Law; Creditor Bankruptcy.

**MARY A. WATSON,** born Bridgeport, Connecticut, January 20, 1965; admitted to bar, 1992, California. *Education:* Vassar College (B.A., 1987); Pepperdine University (J.D., cum laude, 1992). Pepperdine Law Review, 1992. *Member:* Orange County Bar Association. *LANGUAGES:* Spanish.

**ALISA A. SHORAGO,** born Miami, Florida, 1967; admitted to bar, 1993, California. *Education:* University of California, Los Angeles (B.A., 1989); Hastings College of the Law, University of California (J.D., 1992). Recipient, American Jurisprudence Award in Legal Writing and Research, 1990. Chief Articles Editor, Hastings International and Comparative Law Review, 1991-1992. Law Clerk to the Hon. Stephen Bistline, Associate Justice (retired), Idaho Supreme Court, 1992-1993. *Member:* Orange County Bar Association; State Bar of California.

**DEIDRE F. COHEN,** born Culver City, California, 1967; admitted to bar, 1993, California; U.S. District Court, Central District of California. *Education:* Stanford University (B.A., 1989); College of William & Mary, Marshall-Wythe School of Law (J.D., 1993). Member, William & Mary Law School Moot Court Bar, 1992-1993. *Member:* State Bar of California; Sports Lawyers Association.

**DEMETRIUS D. SHELTON,** born Bernice, Louisiana, 1965; admitted to bar, 1994, California; U.S. District Court, Northern District of California and U.S. Court of Appeals, Ninth Circuit. *Education:* University of California, Los Angeles (B.A., 1987); University of California, Davis School of Law (J.D., 1993). Member, Board of Directors, Young Lawyer's Chair. *Member:* Alameda County Bar Association; State Bar of California; Charles Houston Bar Association.

**JENNIFER A. JOHNSON,** born Abington, Pennsylvania, 1968; admitted to bar, 1993, Louisiana; 1994, Pennsylvania; 1995, California; U.S. District Court, Northern District of California and U.S. Court of Appeals, Ninth Circuit. *Education:* University of Delaware (B.S., cum laude, 1990); Paul M. Hebert Law Center, Louisiana State University (J.D., 1993). Semifinalist, Flory Trial Competition, 1992. *Member:* Bar Association of San Francisco; State Bar of California; Louisiana State Bar Association.

**MARK J. MULKERIN,** born Springfield, Minnesota, September 29, 1965; admitted to bar, 1993, California; U.S. District Court, Central District of California. *Education:* Stanford University (B.A., 1984); London School of Economics; Loyola University of Los Angeles (J.D., 1993). Editor, International and Comparative Law Journal, 1992-1993. *Member:* Los Angeles and Orange County Bar Associations; State Bar of California; Southern California Defense Counsel. *LANGUAGES:* Spanish and French.

*(This Listing Continued)*

*PRACTICE AREAS:* Business Litigation; Construction Defects; Insurance Coverage.

**JOHN S. MURRAY,** born Bismarck, North Dakota, March 15, 1956; admitted to bar, 1981, California; U.S., District Court, Central, Southern and Northern Districts of California; U.S. Court of Appeals, Ninth Circuit. *Education:* University of Washington (B.A., 1978); University of Southern California (J.D., 1981). *Member:* South Bay and Los Angeles County (Member, Litigation and Construction Sections) Bar Associations; State Bar of California. *PRACTICE AREAS:* Business and Real Estate Litigation; Construction Law.

**ALLYSON B. FOX,** born New Iberia, Louisiana, July 24, 1967; admitted to bar, 1993, Louisiana; 1994, Texas; U.S. District Court, Southern District of Texas; U.S. District Court, Western District of Louisiana. *Education:* University of Southern Louisiana (B.S., 1989); Louisiana State University (J.D., 1993). Phi Delta Phi. *Member:* Louisiana State and American Bar Associations; State Bar of Texas; Texas Trial Lawyers Association; The Association of Trial Lawyers of America. (Resident, Houston Office). *PRACTICE AREAS:* Personal Injury Litigation; Civil Trial Law.

## BRUCE S. WEINER
*333 CITY BOULEVARD WEST, SUITE 1700*
**ORANGE, CALIFORNIA 92668**
*Telephone: 714-938-3216*
*FAX: 714-938-3217*

*Real Estate, Bankruptcy, Civil Litigation, General Business.*

**BRUCE S. WEINER,** born Culver City, California, March 14, 1952; admitted to bar, 1977, California and U.S. Supreme Court; 1978, U.S. District Court, District of California. *Education:* University of Southern California (B.S., cum laude, 1974); Southwestern University (J.D., 1977). Member, Southwestern University Law Review, 1977-1978. Licensed Real Estate Broker, California, 1987. Author: "An Anomalous Result: Daniel v. Louisiana and the Doctrine of Nonretroactivity," Southwestern Law Review, Summer, 1977. *Member:* Orange County and American Bar Associations; State Bar of California (Member, Real Property and Litigation Sections). *PRACTICE AREAS:* Real Estate Law; Bankruptcy; Civil Litigation; General Business.

## WOODRUFF, SPRADLIN & SMART
*A PROFESSIONAL CORPORATION*
Established in 1976

*SUITE 7000, 701 SOUTH PARKER STREET*
**ORANGE, CALIFORNIA 92868-4720**
*Telephone: 714-558-7000*
*Facsimile: 714-835-7787*

*General Civil and Trial Practice in State and Federal Courts. Administrative, Municipal, Water Rights, Public Utilities, Waste Water, Solid Waste, Environmental, Hazardous Waste, Transportation, School, Zoning, Real Estate Law and Liability Defense.*

*FIRM PROFILE: Woodruff, Spradlin & Smart has, since 1976, had an extensive public law practice on a statewide basis with emphasis in providing all general counsel and special counsel services to various forms of local government agencies as well as advising and representing the private sector in transactions and litigation involving public agencies. Subject areas of expertise include liability defense, municipal, environmental, transportation, water, wastewater, schools, redevelopment, public finance, and political law.*

*An aggressive litigation group within the firm has established a premier reputation as advocates with a highly successful public agency defense practice.*

*The many highly experienced and qualified attorneys within the firm have been recognized in leadership roles in numerous state and national organizations. The firm takes pride in developing close working relationships with every client and ensures that all firm members maintain the highest quality of expertise by continuous training and education.*

*The unique qualifications of both the transactional and litigation attorneys have been proven in appearances in all state and federal trial and appellate courts as well as in legislative, regulatory and administrative proceedings before Federal, State and local government agencies.*

**THOMAS L. WOODRUFF,** born Rochester, New York, January 4, 1939; admitted to bar, 1966, California; 1977, U.S. Supreme Court. *Education:* Michigan State University (B.A., 1960); Hastings College of Law, Uni-

*(This Listing Continued)*

**WOODRUFF, SPRADLIN & SMART,** A PROFESSIONAL CORPORATION, Orange—Continued

versity of California (J.D., 1965). President, Michigan State University Alumni Club of Southern California, 1969-1970. Deputy City Attorney, Inglewood, 1966-1967. Assistant City Attorney, Newport Beach, 1967-1969. City Attorney, Fountain Valley, 1969-1982. City Councilman, Tustin, 1972-1974. General Counsel: County Sanitation Districts of Orange County, 1975—; South Coast Water District, 1976—; Midway City Sanitary District, 1986—; San Diego Area Wastewater Management District, 1993—. Judge Pro Tempore, Orange County Superior Court, 1978—. Arbitrator, State of California Public Works Contracts Administration, 1979—. *Member:* Orange County Bar Association; State Bar of California; National Institute of Municipal Law Officers; Orange County City Attorneys Association (President, 1976). *PRACTICE AREAS:* Water Law; Sanitation Law; Environmental Law.

**DANIEL K. SPRADLIN,** born Los Angeles, California, December 26, 1953; admitted to bar, 1978, California. *Education:* Citrus College (A.A., 1973); University of California at Los Angeles (B.A., cum laude, 1975); Pepperdine University School of Law (J.D., 1978). Omicron Delta Epsilon; Pi Gamma Mu. Member, Pepperdine University Law Review, 1977-1978. Recipient, American Jurisprudence Award in Contracts. Author: "Mens REA, Due Process and the Burden of Sanity or Insanity," Pepperdine University School of Law, Law Review, Vol. 5, No. 1, 1977; "Enslavement in the Twentieth Century: The Right of Parents to Retain their Children's Earnings," Pepperdine University School of Law, Law Review, Vol. 5, No. 3, 1978. *Member:* Orange County Bar Association; State Bar of California; Association of Southern California Defense Counsel. *PRACTICE AREAS:* Litigation; Liability Defense Law; Environmental Law.

**KENNARD R. SMART, JR.,** born Lakewood, Ohio, June 14, 1944; admitted to bar, 1971, California and U.S. Supreme Court. *Education:* University of California at Los Angeles (B.A., 1966); Hastings College of Law, University of California (J.D., 1970). Assistant City Attorney, City of Orange, 1971-1972. Deputy County Counsel, Orange, 1972-1977. General Counsel: Orange County Transportation Authority, 1991—; Orange County Transit District, 1977—; Riverside Transit Agency, 1977—; Regional Center of Orange County, 1991—. *Member:* Orange County Bar Association; State Bar of California. *PRACTICE AREAS:* Transportation Law.

**LOIS E. JEFFREY,** born San Francisco, California, February 10, 1943; admitted to bar, 1979, California. *Education:* University of California, Berkeley (B.A., 1964); Columbia University (M.A., 1965); Western State University College of Law (J.D., cum laude, 1978). Recipient, American Jurisprudence Award in Torts, Corporations, Evidence and Constitutional Law. Member Editor, Western State University Law Review, 1977-1978. Author: "An Implied Right of Action Under the FTC Act," "The Mono Lake Decision-What it Means for Southern California," Orange County Bar Bulletin, September, 1983. City Attorney, Laguna Hills, 1991—. City Attorney, Tustin, 1994—. General Counsel: Los Alamitos County Water District, 1988—. San Diego Area Wastewater Management District, 1993—. Member, Panel of Arbitrators, American Arbitration Association. *Member:* Orange County Bar Association; State Bar of California. *PRACTICE AREAS:* Land Use Law; Water Law; Municipal Law.

**THOMAS F. NIXON,** born North Hollywood, California, July 8, 1954; admitted to bar, 1984, California. *Education:* University of California at Santa Barbara (B.A., with honors, 1976); Loyola University of Los Angeles (J.D., 1984). Member, St. Thomas More Law Honor Society. *Member:* Orange County Bar Association; State Bar of California. *PRACTICE AREAS:* Environmental Law; Hazardous Materials Law; Litigation.

**JOHN R. SHAW,** born San Francisco, California, March 18, 1944; admitted to bar, 1971, California. *Education:* University of California at Berkeley (B.A., 1966); Hastings College of Law, University of California (J.D., 1970). City Attorney, Garden Grove, 1992—. Deputy City Attorney, City of South San Francisco, 1972-1973. Assistant City Attorney, Walnut Creek, 1973-1977. City Attorney, Pittsburg, 1977-1984; San Juan Capistrano, 1984-1991. Instructor, Land Use Law and Administrative Law, Lincoln Law School, 1980-1982. *Member:* Orange County Bar Association; State Bar of California. [First Lieutenant, JAGC, Army Reserves, 1968-1974]. *PRACTICE AREAS:* Municipal Law; Sanitation Law; Land Use Law.

**CRAIG G. FARRINGTON,** born Rochester, New York, September 7, 1961; admitted to bar, 1986, California. *Education:* University of California at Irvine (B.A., 1983); Pepperdine University (J.D., 1986). *Member:* State Bar of California. *PRACTICE AREAS:* Litigation.

*(This Listing Continued)*

**TERRY C. ANDRUS,** born Fort Myers, Florida, May 14, 1944; admitted to bar, 1973, California. *Education:* University of Michigan (A.B., 1967); Loyola University of Los Angeles (J.D., 1973); University of Southern California at Los Angeles (M.S.L.S., 1970). Member, 1991-1995, Deputy, 1973-1983, 1984-1991, Orange County Counsel. General Counsel: Orange County Fire Authority. *Member:* Orange County and American Bar Associations. *PRACTICE AREAS:* Employment Law; Governmental Law.

**M. LOIS BOBAK,** born San Pedro, California, January 10, 1961; admitted to bar, 1987, California. *Education:* University of California at Irvine (B.A., cum laude, 1983); McGeorge School of the Law, University of the Pacific (J.D., with distinction, 1986). Order of the Coif. Member, Traynor Honor Society. Assistant City Attorney: Mission Viejo, 1988-1992; Dana Point, 1989-1991; Cypress, 1989-1992. *Member:* State Bar of California. *PRACTICE AREAS:* Municipal Law; Writs and Appeals.

**JOHN E. CAVANAUGH,** born Cedar Rapids, Iowa, April 15, 1954; admitted to bar, 1986, California and U.S. District Court, Central District of California. *Education:* University of Southern California (B.A., 1977); Southwestern University School of Law (J.D., 1983). City Attorney, Cypress, 1994—. Author: "An Overview of First Amendment and Adult Entertainment," League of California Cities, Spring Conference, 1994. Lecturer, Graduate Center for Public Policy and Administration/California State University, Long Beach - Redevelopment Law, 1991-1993. *Member:* Orange County and American Bar Associations; State Bar of California; Orange County City Attorneys Association. *LANGUAGES:* French and German. *PRACTICE AREAS:* Municipal Law; Redevelopment.

**BETTY C. BURNETT,** born Santa Rosa, California, September 11, 1959; admitted to bar, 1988, California. *Education:* California State University at San Bernardino (B.A., 1981); Loyola Marymount University (J.D., 1988). General Counsel, San Diego Solid Waste Management Authority, 1994—. *Member:* Orange County, Los Angeles County and American Bar Associations; State Bar of California; Orange County Barristers; Los Angeles Women Lawyers Association. *PRACTICE AREAS:* Environmental Law; Hazardous Materials Law.

**ALAN R. WATTS,** born Wichita, Kansas, December 17, 1935; admitted to bar, 1961, California; 1970, U.S. Supreme Court. *Education:* San Jose State College (B.A., 1957); University of California at Los Angeles (J.D., 1960). Deputy City Prosecutor, Pasadena, 1961-1962. Deputy City Attorney, 1962-1967, Assistant City Attorney, 1967-1973 and City Attorney, 1973-1976, Anaheim. General Counsel, Chino Basin Municipal Water District. Chairman, Legal Section of the American Public Power Association, 1975. Member, Panel of Arbitrators, American Arbitration Association. *Member:* Orange County Bar Association; State Bar of California (Member, Public Works Contract Arbitration Committee, 1979—); Orange County City Attorneys Association (President, 1975). *PRACTICE AREAS:* Public Utilities Law; Administrative Law; Municipal Law.

---

**MARY E. BINNING,** born Los Angeles, California, February 19, 1959; admitted to bar, 1992, California. *Education:* Georgetown University (B.S., 1981); California State University at Long Beach (M.B.A., 1988); University of San Diego (J.D., cum laude, 1991). Recipient, American Jurisprudence Awards in Contracts, Trusts and Estates. Co-author: "Invocations at School Board Meetings: Still Constitutional After All These Years," Inquiry & Analysis, National School Boards Assn., March 1994. *Member:* Orange County Bar Association; State Bar of California; Orange County City Attorneys Association. *LANGUAGES:* French, German. *PRACTICE AREAS:* Municipal Law.

**RODELL R. FICK,** born Los Angeles, California, January 17, 1943; admitted to bar, 1987, California; 1988, U.S. District Court, Southern and Central Districts of California; 1992, U.S. District Court, Eastern District of California and U.S. Court of Appeals, Ninth Circuit; 1993, U.S. Supreme Court. *Education:* California State University at Los Angeles (B.S., 1973); University of Southern California (M.P.A., 1977); Loyola Law School, Los Angeles (J.D., 1986). Phi Alpha Delta (Ford Chapter, 1984-1986). Contributing Editor, "California Peace Officers' Association Model Firearms Policy". Lecturer: Foundation for Continuing Legal Education in Corrections Seminar, "Legal Update on Peace Officers' Bill of Rights and Civil Liability Issues for Probation Managers," 1991; California Peace Officers Association Seminar, "Canine Liability Issues," 1991; California Probation, Parole and Correctional Association Seminar, "Managing and Surviving Litigation," 1991; California Probation Manager's Association, "Sexual Harassment Seminar," 1991; California Probation, Parole and Corrections Association Seminar, "Guns, Dogs--What's Next?" 1992;

*(This Listing Continued)*

California Peace Officers' Association, "Pursuit Driving Liability Issues," 1994. Member, Legal Advisor Committee, California Peace Officers Association. *Member:* Los Angeles County and Federal Bar Associations; State Bar of California. *SPECIAL AGENCIES:* Appointed: California Peace Officer Standards and Training, Advisory Committee for Development of "Police Pursuit Guidelines," 1994. *PRACTICE AREAS:* Police Misconduct Liability Defense; Civil Rights; Municipal and Administrative Law; Litigation.

JOSEPH W. FORBATH, born Newport Beach, California, March 6, 1964; admitted to bar, 1990, California; 1991, U.S. District Court, Central District of California. *Education:* University of California at Santa Barbara (B.A., 1986); Loyola Law School (J.D., 1990). St. Thomas Moore Law Honor Society. Staff Member, International Law Journal, 1989-1990. *Member:* Orange County and American Bar Associations; State Bar of California. *LANGUAGES:* Spanish. *PRACTICE AREAS:* Personal Injury Defense; Business Litigation.

MAGDALENA LONA-WIANT, born Los Angeles, California, August 3, 1950; admitted to bar, 1982, California. *Education:* California State University at Los Angeles (B.A., 1979); Western State University (J.D., with scholastic merit, 1981); University of San Diego (Post-graduate diploma, Tax, 1983); LL.M., Taxation, 1987). Recipient, American Jurisprudence Award. Casenote and Article Editor, Western State Law Review, 1980-1981. Author: "Curlendar v. Bio-Science Laboratories, The Pricing of Nonexistence?" Western State University Law Review, 1980. *Member:* Orange County Bar Association; State Bar of California. *LANGUAGES:* Spanish. *PRACTICE AREAS:* Litigation; Liability Defense.

JASON E. RESNICK, born Los Angeles, California, March 12, 1970; admitted to bar, 1995, California; 1996, U.S. District Court, Central District of California. *Education:* University of California, Irvine (B.A., 1992); University of the Pacific, McGeorge School of Law (J.D., 1995). *Member:* Orange County and American Bar Associations; American Trial Lawyers of America. *PRACTICE AREAS:* Litigation.

DANIE I. SPENCE, born Redwood City, California, July 8, 1957; admitted to bar, 1984, California. *Education:* Loyola Marymount University (B.A., summa cum laude, 1979; J.D., magna cum laude, 1984). Alpha Sigma Nu. Member, National Jesuit Honor Society. Member, St. Thomas More Law Honor Society. Recipient, American Jurisprudence Award in Constitutional Law. Senior Attorney, Section Chief, 1990, Staff Attorney, 1988-1989, Federal Deposit Insurance Corporation. *Member:* Orange County (Member, Estate Planning and Probate Section) and American Bar Associations; The State Bar of California. *PRACTICE AREAS:* Banking Law; Real Estate Transactions.

REPRESENTATIVE CLIENTS: City of Tustin; City of Laguna Hills; City of Garden Grove; City of Cypress; Orange County Transportation Authority; City of Riverside; City of San Bernardino; City of Anaheim; County Sanitation Districts of Orange County; Riverside Transit Agency; Public Cable Television Authority; South Coast Water District; San Diego Solid Waste Management Authority; Midway City Sanitary District; San Diego Area Wastewater Management District; Southern California Public Power Authority; Power Agency of California; Orange County Fire Authority; Regional Center of Orange County.
REFERENCE: Union Bank.

---

## JOHN K. YORK

SUITE 1400
ONE CITY BOULEVARD WEST
ORANGE, CALIFORNIA 92668
Telephone: 714-547-8484
Facsimile: 714-634-2153

*General Civil and Trial Practice. Family, Probate and Insurance Law.*

JOHN K. YORK, born Salem, Oregon, June 22, 1947; admitted to bar, 1972, California; 1973, U.S. District Court, Central District of California. *Education:* University of California at Berkeley (B.A., 1969); University of California at Davis (J.D., 1972). Phi Delta Phi. Teaching Assistant, Legal Research and Writing, University of California School of Law, 1971-1972. *Member:* Orange County Bar Association (President, Family Law Section, 1990); State Bar of California (Delegate, State Bar Convention, 1986-1988).

## LAW OFFICES OF BARRY BALAMUTH

3 ALTARINDA, SUITE 210
ORINDA, CALIFORNIA 94563
Telephone: 510-254-1234
Fax: 510-254-0778
Email: info@balamuth.com
URL: http://www.balamuth.com

*Practice Limited to Personal Injury, Professional Malpractice (Legal, Medical and Accounting).*

BARRY BALAMUTH, born Chicago, Illinois, December 10, 1945; admitted to bar, 1972, California, U.S. District Court, Northern, Eastern and Southern Districts of California, U.S. Supreme Court and U.S. Court of Appeals, Ninth Circuit. *Education:* University of California at Davis and University of California at Berkeley (B.S., 1967); Hastings College of the Law, University of California (J.D., 1971). Order of the Coif; Phi Delta Phi. Member, Thurston Honor Society. *Member:* Alameda County and Contra Costa County Bar Associations; State Bar of California; Consumer Attorneys of California; The Association of Trial Lawyers of America; Alameda-Contra Costa Trial Lawyers Association (Member, Board of Governors, 1979-1981 and 1990—); Northern California Lawyers and Judges Association (Director, 1991—). *PRACTICE AREAS:* Professional Negligence (Legal, Medical and Accounting Law); Personal Injury Law.

---

KELLY BALAMUTH, born San Francisco, California, December 22, 1968; admitted to bar, 1994, California, U.S. District Court, Northern District of California and U.S. Court of Appeals, Ninth Circuit. *Education:* University of California at Davis (B.A., 1991); University of California School of Law, Davis (J.D., 1994). Research Editor, University of California, Davis Law Review, 1993-1994. *Member:* Contra Costa County Bar Association; State Bar of California; Consumer Attorneys of California; Alameda-Contra Costa Trial Lawyers Association. *PRACTICE AREAS:* Personal Injury; Attorney Negligence; Medical Negligence. *Email:* kelly@balamuth.com

---

## GILLIN, JACOBSON, ELLIS, LARSEN & DOYLE

Established in 1972
2 THEATRE SQUARE
SUITE 230
ORINDA, CALIFORNIA 94563
Telephone: 510-258-0800
Fax: 510-848-0266
Email: lawfirm@gjeld.com

*San Francisco Office:* One Sutter Street, 10th Floor. Telephone: 415-986-4777.

*Civil Trial Practice including Intellectual Property Litigation, Commercial Torts, Products Liability, Personal Injury and Wrongful Death.*

FIRM PROFILE: Founded in 1972, the law firm practices exclusively in the field of Civil Trial Practice. The firm has achieved numerous multi-million dollar verdicts and settlements for its business and individual clients. The partners have lectured and written extensively in the field of Civil Trial Practice. Engaged in all facets of Civil Litigation, the firm is listed in the Martindale-Hubbell Bar Registry of Preeminent Lawyers.

ANDREW R. GILLIN, born Los Angeles, California, December 25, 1943; admitted to bar, 1970, California, U.S. District Court, Northern District of California and U.S. Court of Appeals, Ninth Circuit. *Education:* University of California at Berkeley (A.B., 1965); University of Chicago (J.D., 1968). Writer, Lecturer and panelist on Civil Litigation Strategy and Tactics for California Continuing Education of the Bar, California State Bar Association Education Institute, California Trial Lawyers Association. *Member:* Bar Association of San Francisco; Alameda County and American Bar Associations; State Bar of California; The Association of Trial Lawyers of America; Association of Business Trial Lawyers of Northern California; Sustaining Member, California Trial Lawyers Association; San Francisco Intellectual Property Law Association. *PRACTICE AREAS:* Civil Litigation; Trials and Appeals; Intellectual Property Litigation; Commercial Torts; Plaintiff's Personal Injury.

*(This Listing Continued)*

## GILLIN, JACOBSON, ELLIS, LARSEN & DOYLE,
Orinda—Continued

RALPH L. JACOBSON, born Kansas City, Missouri, December 5, 1945; admitted to bar, 1970, California, Georgia, U.S. District Court, Northern District of California, U.S. Court of Appeals, Ninth Circuit and U.S. Supreme Court. *Education:* Washington University (B.A., magna cum laude, 1966); Stanford University (J.D., 1969). Co-Author: "Litigation in the Fast Lane", California Continuing Education of the Bar, February, 1988; "California Government Tort Liability Practice", California Continuing Education of the Bar, 1992. *Member:* Alameda County Bar Association; State Bar of California; San Francisco Intellectual Property Law Association. *PRACTICE AREAS:* Civil Trials; Intellectual Property Litigation; Commercial Torts; Plaintiff's Personal Injury.

LUKE ELLIS, born Los Angeles, California, January 3, 1951; admitted to bar, 1976, California, U.S. District Court, Northern District of California and U.S. Court of Appeals, Ninth Circuit. *Education:* Antioch College (B.A., 1972); Boalt Hall School of Law, University of California at Berkeley (J.D., 1975). Consultant, California Continuing Education of the Bar, California Trial Objections, Third Edition (1995). Lecturer: Trial Practice, and Evidence. *Member:* Alameda County Bar Association; State Bar of California; San Francisco Intellectual Property Law Association; Association of Business Trial Lawyers of Northern California; San Francisco Patent Law Association. *PRACTICE AREAS:* Civil Trials; Intellectual Property Litigation; Commercial Torts; Plaintiff's Personal Injury.

JAMES PAUL LARSEN, born Berkeley, California, April 4, 1959; admitted to bar, 1987, California and U.S. District Court, Northern District of California. *Education:* University of California at Berkeley (B.A., 1982); University of Oregon (J.D., 1986). *Member:* Alameda and Contra Costa Counties Bar Associations; State Bar of California; Association of Business Trial Lawyers of Northern California; Sustaining Member, Consumer Attorneys of California; San Francisco Intellectual Property Law Association; The Association of Trial Lawyers of America; Almeda Contra Costa Trial Lawyers Association. *PRACTICE AREAS:* Civil Litigation; Trials and Appeals; Plaintiff's Personal Injury; Intellectual Property Litigation; Commercial Torts.

RICHARD P. DOYLE, JR., born San Francisco, California, August 23, 1958; admitted to bar, 1983, California; 1985, U.S. Court of Appeals for the Federal Circuit; 1986, U.S. District Court, Northern, Eastern, Central and Southern Districts of California. *Education:* Creighton University (B.S., Chemistry, 1980); University of San Francisco (J.D., 1983). Pi Mu Epsilon; Phi Delta Pi. Technical Law Clerk to the Honorable Giles S. Rich, Federal Circuit, 1983-1985. *Member:* The State Bar of California (Member, Patent, Trademark and Copyright Law Section); American Bar Association; American Intellectual Property Law Association; San Francisco Intellectual Property Law Association (President). *PRACTICE AREAS:* Intellectual Property; Litigation; Licensing and Protection; Prosecution.

SUSAN HUNT, born Ontario, Canada, April 3, 1963; admitted to bar, 1992, California, U.S. District Court, Northern District of California and U.S. Court of Appeals, Ninth Circuit; 1996, Ontario. *Education:* University of Winnipeg (B.A., 1986); University of Manitoba (L.L.B., 1990). Law Review Editor, University of Manitoba, 1987-1990. *Member:* Alameda County and American (Member Committee on Intellectual Property Litigation) Bar Associations; State Bar of California (Member, Patent, Trademark and Copyright Section); Association of Business Trial Lawyers of Northern California; Consumer Attorneys of California; San Francisco Intellectual Property Law Association; Law Society of Upper Canada. *PRACTICE AREAS:* Civil Litigation and Trials; Intellectual Property Litigation; Commercial Torts; Plaintiff's Personal Injury.

MITCHELL S. ROSENFELD, born Baltimore, Maryland, June 1, 1966; admitted to bar, 1992, California, U.S. Court of Appeals for the Federal Circuit, U.S. Court of Appeals, Ninth Circuit, U.S. District Court, Northern, Eastern, Central and Southern District of California; registered to practice before U.S. Patent and Trademark Office. *Education:* Duke University (B.S., Physics, cum laude, 1988); George Washington University (J.D., 1992). *Member:* San Francisco Intellectual Property Law Association; *Member:* American Bar Association (Member, Intellectual Property Section); The State Bar of California (Member, Patent, Trademark and Copyright Law Section). *PRACTICE AREAS:* Intellectual Property Litigation; Licensing and Prosecution.

CATHERINE T. DOYLE, born San Francisco, California, February 25, 1967; admitted to bar, 1993, California, U.S. District Court, Northern District of California and U.S. Court of Appeals, Ninth Circuit. *Education:* Marquette University (B.A., 1989); University of San Francisco (J.D.,

*(This Listing Continued)*

1993). Research Assistant to Professor J. Thomas McCarthy, January, 1992 to May, 1993. *Member:* State Bar of California; San Francisco Patent and Trademark Law Association. *LANGUAGES:* French and Italian. *PRACTICE AREAS:* Trademark and Copyright Law.

## EDGAR J. LANA
A PROFESSIONAL CORPORATION
Established in 1969
18 ORINDA WAY
P.O. BOX 2180
**ORINDA, CALIFORNIA 94563**
Telephone: 510-253-1010
Fax: 510-253-1742

*General Commercial and Civil Practice. Litigation. Creditors Rights, Bankruptcy, Corporate, Real Property, Landlord and Tenant, Real Estate, Wills, Trust and Probate.*

EDGAR J. LANA, born Whittier, California, March 26, 1942; admitted to bar, 1969, California and U.S. District Court, Northern District of California; 1972, U.S. Supreme Court; 1975, U.S. Claims Court; 1976, U.S. District Court, Eastern District of California; 1982, U.S. District Court, Central District of California; 1983, U.S. District Court, Southern District of California. *Education:* University of California at Los Angeles (B.A., 1965); Hastings College of the Law, University of California (J.D., 1968). Member, Oakland Law Forum, 1969-1985. *Member:* Bar Association of San Francisco; Alameda County (Member, Business Law, Debtor-Creditor Relations Committee), Contra Costa County, Oakland County and American Bar Associations; State Bar of California; Commercial Law League of America; California Trial Lawyers Association. *PRACTICE AREAS:* Collection Law.

REPRESENTATIVE CLIENTS: Montgomery Ward Credit Corp.; ITT Consumer Financial Services Corp.; John Breuner Co.; Avco Financial Services; Beacon Oil Co.; Buehrer, Inc.; General Electric Capital Corp.; S & H Truck Lines, Inc.; LKL Industries, Inc.; Gimbels; Spiral Binding, Inc.; Kay Jewelers; Austin-Laws, Inc.; Orinda Computerware, Inc.; Tri Valley Computer Co.; Conference Claimants Endowment Board of the California Annual Conference of the Methodist Church; Ford Motor Credit Co.

## PEREZ & McNABB
A PROFESSIONAL CORPORATION
140 BROOKWOOD ROAD, 2ND FLOOR
**ORINDA, CALIFORNIA 94563**
Telephone: 510-254-6100
Fax: 510-254-0653

*Business and Real Estate Litigation in State and Federal Courts, Computer Disputes and Construction Claims. General Corporate, Real Estate and Commercial Law. Federal and State Income Taxation.*

RICHARD L. PEREZ, born Los Angeles, California, November 17, 1946; admitted to bar, 1972, California; 1974, U.S. District Court, Northern District of California and U.S. Court of Appeals, Ninth Circuit; 1982, U.S. District Court, Eastern District of California; 1984, U.S. District Court, Northern District of Texas. *Education:* University of California at Los Angeles (B.A., 1968); Boalt Hall School of Law, University of California (J.D., 1971). Associate Editor, California Law Review, 1970-1971. Author: "Slander Of Title By Improper Recording Of Notice Of Default," 28 Am. Jur. Trials, 229. Member, Board of Advisors: Computer Litigation Reporter, 1983-1985; Boalt Hall High Technology Law Journal, 1985—. *Member:* Alameda County, Contra Costa County and American Bar Associations; State Bar of California. *REPORTED CASES:* Consolidated Data Terminals v. Applied Digital Data Systems (9th Cir. 1983) 708 F. 2d 385; Glovatorium v. NCR Corporation (9th cir. 1992) 684 F2d 658. *PRACTICE AREAS:* Computer Law; Real Estate Law; Business Litigation.

SANDRA J. MCNABB, born Tacoma, Washington, February 12, 1952; admitted to bar, 1977, California and U.S. District Court, Northern District of California. *Education:* Washington State University; University of Washington (B.A., 1974); Stanford University (J.D., 1977). Alpha Lambda Delta; Phi Beta Kappa. Co-Author: "The Law Behind Today's Construction Contracts," Deskbook of Construction Contract Law--With Forms, Hohns, et al., 1981; "Arbitration: It May Not Be As Desirable For Customer As Vendor," Computer Law Reporter, Vol. 3, No. 1, July, 1984. *Member:* San Mateo County, Contra Costa County and American Bar Associations; State Bar of California. *REPORTED CASES:* Schmidt v. Foun-

*(This Listing Continued)*

dation Health (1995) 35 Cal. App. 4th 1702; NCR ad. Hayes (9th Cir. 1995). *PRACTICE AREAS:* Business Litigation; Construction; Computer Law.

**JEFFREY A. MILLER,** born San Francisco, California, July 2, 1950; admitted to bar, 1979, California; 1980, Nevada; 1981, U.S. Supreme Court; 1983, U.S. District Court, Northern District of California; 1990, U.S. Court of Appeals Ninth Circuit. *Education:* San Francisco State University (B.A., magna cum laude, 1972); University of California at Los Angeles; University of California at Berkeley (J.D., 1979). Member: Panel of Arbitrators, American Arbitration Association. *Member:* Alameda County, Contra Costa County and American Bar Associations; State Bar of California.

**MARJORIE A. WALLACE,** born Neenah, Wisconsin, July 27, 1952; admitted to bar, 1976, California; 1992, U.S. District Court, Northern District of California; 1994, U.S. District Court, Eastern District of Michigan and U.S. Court of Appeals, Ninth Circuit. *Education:* University of California at Los Angeles (B.A., 1973); University of Pittsburgh (M.S.I.S., 1986); Hastings College of the Law, University of California (J.D., 1976); Yale Law School (LL.M., 1980). Author: "Commercial Unfairness and Economic Inefficiency As Exemplified by Unfair Allocations of Risk in Computer Contracts," 6 Journal of Law and Commerce 59-105, 1986; "E-Mail and Employee Privacy: What's the Law?" Information Protection Advisor, Vol. 3, No. 1, January 1994; "The Pros and Cons of Arbitration and Mediation," International Business & Technology Protection, Vol. 3, No. 8, August 1994; "The Need for Precision in Arbitration Agreements," International Business & Technology Protection, Vol. 3, No. 12, December 1994; "Mandatory Arbitration for Employment Disputes," Contra Costa Lawyer, June 1995; Surfing Intellectual Property 101," Contra Costa Lawyer, June 1996. Associate Professor: Law, Contracts and Remedies, Duquesne University School of Law, 1981-1984. Assistant Professor: Law, Contracts and Commercial Transactions, Washburn University School of Law, 1980-1981. Instructor, Legal Research and Writing, University of Puget Sound, 1977-1979. *Member:* San Francisco and Contra Costa County Bar Associations; State Bar of California; California Women Lawyers; Contra Costa Council. *PRACTICE AREAS:* Computer Law; Business Litigation; Technology Licensing.

**RICHARD G. THOMAS,** born Oakland, California, July 6, 1948; admitted to bar, 1975, California. *Education:* University of California at Santa Barbara (B.A., 1970); University of San Francisco (J.D., 1974); New York University (LL.M. in Taxation, 1975). Member, University of San Francisco Law Review, 1973-1974. *Member:* Contra Costa County Bar Association; State Bar of California. (California Specialist, Taxation, California Board of Legal Specialization). *LANGUAGES:* Russian. *PRACTICE AREAS:* Taxation; Real Estate; Corporate Law.

**HAROLD P. SELAN,** born Chicago, Illinois, June 15, 1956; admitted to bar, 1982, California. *Education:* University of California at Berkeley (B.A., 1979, Phi Beta Kappa); Hastings College of the Law (J.D., 1982). Writer and Note Editor, Hastings Constitutional Law Quarterly, 1980-1982. Judicial Extern to Presiding Justice Thomas Caldecott and Justice Preston Devine, California Court of Appeals, First Appellate District, 1981. Author: "Interpreting RICO's Pattern of Racketeering Activity Requirement After Sedima: Separate Schemes, Episodes or Related Acts," 24 California Western Law Review 1. Instructor: Legal Writing and Research, 1989-1996; Moot Court, 1992 and 1996, Hastings College of the Law.

REPRESENTATIVE CLIENTS: Alliance Savings & Loan Association; Altmann Construction; Beaver Insurance Co., Inc.; Blickman Turkus, Inc.; Capitol Growth Investors; Commonwealth Financial Corp.; Cooper Industries; Cushman & Wakefield; Digitex Computers, a Hong Kong Corp.; DNB Commercial Properties; East Bay Regional Park District; The Glovatorium; Hollywood Federal Savings & Loan Assn.; Insurance Company of America, Texas; KLS Logistics Service, Inc.; Mason McDuffie Real Estate; MDS-Quantel, Inc.; Mr. Penguin Tuxedo Rental & Sales, Inc., Texas; Mohawk Data Sciences, Inc.; Morrow & Co., Inc.; Nationwide Real Estate Register, Inc.; NCR Corp.; Pacifica Computers, Ltd., a Hong Kong Corp.; Plus Financial, Inc.; Redwood Theatres, Inc.; Royal LePage; R.W. Lynch Co., Inc.; Wang Laboratories.

## LAW OFFICES OF LAURIE J. ROBERTSON

23 ALTARINDA ROAD, SUITE 215
**ORINDA, CALIFORNIA 94563**
Telephone: 510-254-6721
Toll Free: 888-254-6721
Fax: 510-254-4787
Email: laurie@ljrlaw.com
URL: http://www.ljrlaw.com

*General Civil and Trial Practice, Business and Family Law.*

**LAURIE J. ROBERTSON,** born Berkeley, California, May 18, 1956; admitted to bar, 1984, California and U.S. District Court, Northern District of California; 1989, U.S. Court of Appeals, Ninth Circuit. *Education:* University of California, Berkeley (A.B., 1979); University of San Francisco (J.D., cum laude, 1984). Vice Magister, 1983-1984, Province President, 1988-1992 and Recipient, Balfour Scholarship Award, 1983 and Outstanding Province President Award, 1991, Phi Delta Phi. Recipient, American Jurisprudence Award, Constitutional Law. Senior Staff Member, University of San Francisco Law Review, 1984. *Member:* Contra Costa County Bar Association; State Bar of California; Daughters of California Pioneers.

## HENDREN LAW OFFICES

19 NELSON AVENUE
P.O. BOX 1822
**OROVILLE, CALIFORNIA 95965**
Telephone: 916-533-0661
Fax: 916-533-3956

*Civil Trial and Appellate Practice, Aviation Law, Banking Litigation, Real Property, Business, Corporation and Partnership Law, Unfair Competition and Labor Law.*

**ED W. HENDREN,** born Fort Sill, Oklahoma, May 18, 1938; admitted to bar, 1976, California. *Education:* U.S. Military Academy (B.S., 1962); University of Freiburg, Germany and American University (M.A., 1968); Stanford University (J.D., 1976). *Member:* Santa Clara County, Butte County and American Bar Associations; The State Bar of California. *PRACTICE AREAS:* Civil Trial and Appellate Practice; Aviation Law; Banking Litigation; Real Property; Business; Corporation and Partnership Law; Unfair Competition; Labor Law.

REPRESENTATIVE CLIENTS: Utility Workers Union of America; Bank of America; Bank of the West; Louisiana Pacific Corporation; State Federal Savings of Lubbock, Texas; New West Federal Savings; Accent Software, Inc.; Hobbie Chevrolet-Cadillac-Toyota; Chemtec Ag Chemicals, Inc.
REFERENCE: Butte Community Bank.

## LEONARD & LYDE

A Partnership including Professional Corporations

Established in 1963

1453 HUNTOON STREET
**OROVILLE, CALIFORNIA 95965**
Telephone: 916-533-2662
Fax: 916-533-3843

Chico, California Office: 1600 Humboldt Road, Suite 1. Telephone: 916-345-3494. Fax: 916-345-0460.

*General Civil and Trial Practice. Medical Law, Business, Probate, Insurance.*

(For Complete Biographical Data on all Personnel, See Professional Biographies at Chico).

## PETERS, FULLER, RUSH, FARNSWORTH & HABIB

**OROVILLE, CALIFORNIA**

(See Chico)

*General Civil and Trial Practice in all State and Federal Courts. Insurance Defense, Real Property. Estate Planning and Administration, Business and Commercial Law, Workers Compensation.*

## PRICE, BROWN & HALSEY
### OROVILLE, CALIFORNIA
(See Chico)

*General Civil and Trial Practice, Business, Insurance and Public Entity Defense, Real Property, and Probate Law.*

---

## ARNOLD, BACK, MATHEWS, WOJKOWSKI & ZIRBEL
Established in 1990

**2901 NORTH VENTURA ROAD, SUITE 240**
**OXNARD, CALIFORNIA 93030**
Telephone: 805-988-9886
Fax: 805-988-1937

Westlake Village, California Office: 100 North Westlake Boulevard, Suite 201, 91362. Telephone: 805-371-8800. Fax: 805-495-6212.

*Civil Litigation, Real Property, Corporations, Construction, Land Use, Estate Planning, Business, Commercial, Taxation, Mergers and Acquisitions, Administrative, Municipal and Governmental Law, Environmental, Solid and Liquid Waste, Water Rights, Probate and Trust, Homeowners' Associations.*

### MEMBERS OF FIRM

**GARY D. ARNOLD,** born Los Angeles, California, July 20, 1951; admitted to bar, 1976, California; 1977, U.S. District Courts, Central, Northern, Southern and Eastern Districts of California; 1978, U.S. Court of Appeals, Ninth Circuit; 1983, U.S. Supreme Court; 1987, U.S. Tax Court. *Education:* University of Southern California (B.S., 1973; J.D., 1976). Order of the Coif. Law Clerk, California Supreme Court, 1976. *Member:* Ventura County Bar Association; The State Bar of California. **PRACTICE AREAS:** Real Estate; Business Law; Banking and Finance; Creditor Rights; Appellate Law.

**BRIAN J. BACK,** born Chicago, Illinois, June 19, 1950; admitted to bar, 1977, California. *Education:* Claremont Men's College (B.A., 1972); University of Santa Clara (J.D., 1977). Chairman of Board, Los Robles Regional Medical Center, 1989-1990. *Member:* Ventura County Bar Association; The State Bar of California (Co-Chairman, Sub-committee on Landlord/Tenant Law, 1985-1990; Member, Executive Committee, Real Estate Section, 1990-1993, Vice Chair, 1992-1993). **PRACTICE AREAS:** General Civil Litigation; Landlord/Tenant Law; Construction Law and Disputes.

**JOHN M. MATHEWS,** born Los Angeles, California, May 14, 1948; admitted to bar, 1973, California. *Education:* Brigham Young University (B.A., 1970); UCLA (J.D., 1973). *Member:* Ventura County Bar Association (Member, Real Property Section, Chairman, 1987-1989). [1st Lieut., USAR, 1973-1981]. **PRACTICE AREAS:** Water Law; Public Agency Law; Land Use and Development; Liquid and Solid Waste; Environmental Law.

**JAMES WOJKOWSKI,** born Beverly, Massachusetts, March 19, 1948; admitted to bar, 1975, California and U.S. District Court, Central District of California; 1982, U.S. Tax Court. *Education:* California State University at San Diego (B.S., 1971); University of Santa Clara (J.D., magna cum laude, 1975). Phi Alpha Delta. *Member:* Ventura County, Los Angeles County and American (Member, Taxation Section) Bar Associations. **PRACTICE AREAS:** Taxation; Estate Planning; Probate and Trust Law; Real Estate and Business Law.

**DAVID R. WORLEY,** born Bakersfield, California, May 19, 1954; admitted to bar, 1981, California; 1982, U.S. District Court, Central District of California and U.S. Court of Appeals, Ninth Circuit. *Education:* United States Military Academy at West Point; California State College at Bakersfield (B.A., with honors, 1977); Loyola University of Los Angeles (J.D., 1981). Ventura County Deputy District Attorney, 1981-1984. **PRACTICE AREAS:** Business and Environmental Litigation; Oil and Gas Litigation; Probate and Trust Litigation; Construction Defects; Arbitration and Mediation.

**MARK A. ZIRBEL,** born Manhattan Beach, California, May 20, 1950; admitted to bar, 1975, California. *Education:* University of California at Los Angeles (B.A., cum laude, 1972); Northwestern School of Law, Lewis and Clark College (J.D., 1975). Assistant County Counsel, County of Ventura, 1976-1979. **PRACTICE AREAS:** Liquid and Solid Waste; Public Agency Law; Environmental Law; Land Use.

*(This Listing Continued)*

---

**WAYNE K. BALDWIN,** born Oldham, England, April 22, 1960; admitted to bar, 1988, California. *Education:* University of California at Santa Barbara (B. A., with honors, 1985); Brigham Young University (J.D., 1988). Note and Comment Editor, Brigham Young University Journal of Public Law, 1987-1988. *Member:* Los Angeles County, Ventura County and East County (Vice-President) Bar Associations. **PRACTICE AREAS:** Business; Construction and Real Estate Litigation; Broker Defense; Business and Commercial Transactions.

### ASSOCIATES

Denise B. Rothwell          Ellen S. Rosenberg
                            (Not admitted in CA)

### OF COUNSEL

Kathleen J. Back

REPRESENTATIVE CLIENTS: Shell Oil Company; Ventura Regional Sanitation District; Pleasant Valley County Water District; Triunfo Sanitation District; Oceanview Municipal Water District; Los Robles Bank; The Travelers Companies; Mittag Farms; Thornhill Ranches; Pacific Sod; The Haaland Group; NL Industries, Inc.; California Lutheran University; Los Robles Regional Medical Center; National Diagnostic Services; DCN Wireless; First American Title Insurance Company; State Ready Mix; JLS Concrete Pumping; Avex, Inc.; CNM Paving; Forest Construction Co.; Maulhardt Industrial Park; Axtive Software Corporation; Clothestime; Ladin Lincoln/Mercury; Times Square Shopping Center.

---

## EDWARD R. BROWN
**2521 CABRILLO WAY**
**OXNARD, CALIFORNIA 93030-8405**
Telephone: 805-981-9645
Fax: 805-981-9655

*Business and Real Estate Law. Civil Trial and Appellate Practice. Arbitration/Mediation.*

**EDWARD R. BROWN,** born Spokane, Washington, October 11, 1920; admitted to bar, 1964, California and U.S. District Court, Southern and Central Districts of California; 1973, U.S. Court of Appeals, Ninth Circuit and U.S. Supreme Court. *Education:* University of California at Berkeley (A.B., 1942); Loyola Marymount University (J.D., 1963). Phi Alpha Delta. Arbitrator, Los Angeles and Ventura County Superior Municipal Court. Member, Panel of Arbitrators, American Arbitration Association. *Member:* San Fernando Valley (President, 1975) and Ventura County Bar Associations; The State Bar of California; Los Angeles Trial Lawyers Association; Consumer Attorneys of California. [With U.S. Navy, 1942-1946; 1951-1952]

REFERENCE: Union Bank of California.

---

## KENNETH G. EADE
**143 SOUTH B STREET**
**OXNARD, CALIFORNIA 93030**
Telephone: 805-487-0403
Fax: 805-483-7634

*Corporate, Securities Law and Public/Private Offerings.*

**KENNETH G. EADE,** born Encino, California, December 29, 1957; admitted to bar, 1980, California; 1981, U.S. District Court, Central District of California; 1989, U.S. Court of Appeals, Ninth Circuit. *Education:* California State University at Northridge (B.A., cum laude, 1977); Southwestern University (J.D., 1980). Instructor, Law Update in Real Estate, Pierce College, 1981-1982. *Member:* Ventura County Bar Association; State Bar of California. **LANGUAGES:** French.

REPRESENTATIVE CLIENTS: Health Tek Holdings, Inc.; Ag Armeno Mines & Minerals; Champion Financial Corp.; Allied Fasteners of Texas, Inc.; Bert M. Dahl Trust; Internet Broadcast Systems.

## ENGLAND & COHEN

Established in 1992

300 ESPLANADE DRIVE
FINANCIAL PLAZA TOWER, SUITE 380
OXNARD, CALIFORNIA 93030

Telephone: 805-983-8181; California Toll Free: 800-675-6166
FAX: 805-983-8813

General Civil and Trial Practice, General Business, Commercial, Corporate, Real Property Transactions and Development, Tax, Probate, Trusts and Estate Planning.

FIRM PROFILE: The firm of England & Cohen was established in 1992. Its partners and associate counsel provide general and highly specialized legal services for a varied clientele, with emphasis in civil litigation, estate planning and Probate Code matters and real property use and development.

### MEMBERS OF FIRM

**ROBERT B. ENGLAND,** born Vermillion, South Dakota, August 4, 1943; admitted to bar, 1979, California; 1980, U.S. Tax Court. *Education:* California State University at Northridge (B.S., 1972); New York University (M.B.A., with distinction, 1975); Fordham University (J.D., 1979). Certified Public Accountant, New York, 1977. Member: Ventura County and American Bar Associations; State Bar of California; New York State Society of Certified Public Accountants; American Institute of Certified Public Accountants. [USMC, 1961-1965]. (Certified Specialist, Estate Planning, Trust and Probate Law, State Bar of California Board of Legal Specialization). *PRACTICE AREAS:* Taxation; Estate Planning; Probate and Trusts; Business and Real Estate Transactions.

**RANDALL A. COHEN,** born Los Angeles, California, October 4, 1955; admitted to bar, 1986, California. *Education:* University of California at Santa Barbara (B.S., 1978); Pepperdine University (J.D., magna cum laude, 1986). Licensed Real Estate Broker, California, 1982. Author: "Proposition 8: California Law After In Re Lance W. and People v. Castro," Pepperdine Law Review, Vol. 12, Issue 4, 1985. Member: Ventura County Bar Association; State Bar of California. *PRACTICE AREAS:* General Business; Civil Litigation; Real Property Use and Development.

### OF COUNSEL

**STANLEY E. COHEN,** born Newark, New Jersey, March 29, 1931; admitted to bar, 1958, California. *Education:* University of Illinois (B.A., 1952); University of California at Los Angeles (J.D., 1957). Phi Alpha Delta. Deputy District Attorney, Ventura County, 1958-1961. Member, Board of Trustees, Ventura County Law Library, 1960. President, Ventura County Economic Development Association, 1970-1971. Member: Ventura County Bar Association (President, 1971); State Bar of California. [1st Lt., USAF, 1952-1954]. *PRACTICE AREAS:* Real Property; Commercial; Land Use and Development.

REPRESENTATIVE CLIENTS: Strathmore Homes; Channel Islands National Bank; Martin V. Smith and Associates; Morrison Entity.

---

## ENGLAND, WHITFIELD, SCHRÖEDER & TREDWAY, L.L.P.

Established in 1960

300 ESPLANADE DRIVE, 6TH FLOOR
OXNARD, CALIFORNIA 93030

Telephone: 805-485-9627
Ventura: 647-8237
Southern California Toll Free: 800-255-3485
Fax: 805-983-0297
URL: http://www.tsurf.com/ewst/

Thousand Oaks, California Office: Rolling Oaks Office Center, 351 Rolling Oaks Drive. Telephone: Southern California Toll Free: 800-255-3485.

Employment and Labor Law, Banking, Commercial, Corporate, Taxation, Land Use, Environmental, Real Property, Bankruptcy, Insolvency, Personal Injury, Construction, Trusts, Wills and Estate Planning Law. General Trial and Appellate Practice. Probate.

### MEMBERS OF FIRM

**THEODORE J. ENGLAND,** born Boston, Massachusetts, January 29, 1942; admitted to bar, 1967, California. *Education:* University of California at Santa Barbara (B.A., 1963); Boalt Hall, University of California (LL.B., 1966). Phi Delta Phi; Order of the Coif. Member, Board of Editors, California Law Review, 1965-1966. Member, Board of Trustees, Ventura County Law Library, 1972-1980. *Member:* Ventura County (Secretary, 1976) and American Bar Associations; State Bar of California. (Certified Specialist, Taxation Law, The State Bar of California Board of Legal Specialization). *PRACTICE AREAS:* Taxation Law; Real Property Law; Pension/Profit Sharing Law.

**ANSON M. WHITFIELD,** born Milwaukee, Wisconsin, June 8, 1931; admitted to bar, 1963, California. *Education:* Northwestern University (B.S., 1953); University of Hawaii; University of California at Berkeley (LL.B., 1962). Member, Board of Editors, California Law Review, 1961-1962. Counsel, The Port of Hueneme. *Member:* Ventura County Bar Association (Secretary-Treasurer, 1972); State Bar of California. [Lt., U.S.N.R., 1953-1957]. *PRACTICE AREAS:* Real Property Leasing Law; Business Litigation; Bankruptcy Law; Business Law.

**ROBERT W. SCHRÖEDER,** born Davenport, Iowa, September 15, 1946; admitted to bar, 1973, California. *Education:* University of California at Los Angeles (B.A., 1969); Loyola University of Los Angeles (J.D., 1973). Board Member, Legal Affairs Committee, California Association of Realtors. Seminar Panelist, Real Estate Broker Practice, Continuing Education of the Bar, 1991 and 1995. *Member:* Ventura County Bar Association; State Bar of California. *PRACTICE AREAS:* Real Property Law; Commercial Law; Business Litigation; Automotive Franchises and Dealerships.

**DAVID W. TREDWAY,** born Fresno, California, January 31, 1949; admitted to bar, 1974, California. *Education:* University of California at Santa Barbara (B.S.E.E., 1971); Loyola University of Los Angeles (J.D., 1974). Eta Kappa Nu; Delta Sigma Rho; Tau Kappa Alpha. Member, Loyola Law Review Staff, 1973-1974. Author: "Rent Withholding Won't Work: The Need for a More Realistic Rehabilitation Policy," 7 Loyola of Los Angeles Law Review 66. *Member:* Ventura County Bar Association; State Bar of California. *PRACTICE AREAS:* Civil Litigation; Construction Law; Land Use Law; Development Law.

**ROBERT A. MCSORLEY,** born Washington, D.C., June 23, 1945; admitted to bar, 1971, Washington; 1972, U.S. Court of Military Appeals; 1973, Texas; 1975, California; 1976, U.S. Supreme Court. *Education:* University of Washington and University of California at Los Angeles (A.B., 1968); University of Washington (J.D., 1971). *Member:* Ventura County, Washington State Bar Associations; State Bar of Texas; State Bar of California. [Capt., U.S. Army, JAGC, 1972-1976]. *PRACTICE AREAS:* Business Law; Real Estate; Personal Injury Litigation; Labor and Employment; Government Employment; Military Employment.

**STUART A. COMIS,** born Los Angeles, California, September 25, 1954; admitted to bar, 1978, California. *Education:* University of California at Los Angeles (B.S., magna cum laude, 1974); University of California at Davis (J.D., 1978). Phi Beta Kappa. Order of the Coif. Recipient, American Jurisprudence Awards. Member, Board of Trustees, 1989-1996 and President, 1991 and 1996, Ventura County Law Library. *Member:* Ventura County Bar Association; State Bar of California. *PRACTICE AREAS:* Real Property Law; Business Law.

**MITCHEL B. KAHN,** born Los Angeles, California, June 2, 1946; admitted to bar, 1972, California. *Education:* California State University at Northridge (B.S., 1969); Loyola Marymount University (J.D., 1971). Phi Alpha Delta. Lecturer, Consumer Law, Glendale University School of Law, 1977-1978. Assistant City Attorney, Beverly Hills, 1972-1979. City Attorney, Simi Valley, 1979-1983. Member, League of California Cities, City Attorney Department and National Institute of Municipal Law Officers, 1979-1983. President, 1983 and Treasurer/Secretary, 1982, Tri-Counties Government Attorney Association. Board Member: Building Industry Association, 1985-1988; Ventura County Economic Development Association, 1994—. *Member:* Ventura County Bar Association (Board Member, 1995—); State Bar of California. *PRACTICE AREAS:* Land Use; Real Estate; Commercial Law; Business Law.

**MARK A. NELSON,** born Bakersfield, California, November 6, 1954; admitted to bar, 1981, California, U.S. District Court, Central and Southern District of California and U.S. Court of Appeals, Ninth Circuit. *Education:* University of California at Los Angeles (B.A., 1977); University of Southern California (J.D., 1981). Member, Moot Court Honors Program, 1979-1980. *Member:* Ventura County Bar Association (Member, Board of Directors, 1988-1990; Chairman, Real Property Section, 1986); State Bar of California. *PRACTICE AREAS:* Business Litigation; Real Property Law; Family Law.

**ERIC J. KANANEN,** born Kansas City, Missouri, October 4, 1956; admitted to bar, 1983, California. *Education:* California Lutheran College (B.A., summa cum laude, 1978); University of California at Davis (J.D.,

*(This Listing Continued)*

## ENGLAND, WHITFIELD, SCHRÖEDER & TREDWAY, L.L.P., Oxnard—Continued

1983). *Member:* Ventura County Bar Association; State Bar of California. *PRACTICE AREAS:* Civil Litigation; Construction Law; Environmental Law; Real Property Law.

*MARY E. SCHRÖEDER,* born Denver, Colorado, December 21, 1948; admitted to bar, 1974, California. *Education:* California State University at Long Beach (B.A., cum laude, 1970); Loyola University of Los Angeles (J.D., cum laude, 1974). Member, Loyola University of Los Angeles Law Review, 1972-1973. *Member:* Ventura County Bar Association; State Bar of California. *LANGUAGES:* German. *PRACTICE AREAS:* Civil Litigation; Employment Law and Litigation; Probate.

*OSCAR C. GONZALEZ,* born Ventura, California, April 19, 1959; admitted to bar, 1988, California. *Education:* California State University at Northridge (B.A., 1983); University of California at Davis (J.D., 1988). *Member:* Ventura County Bar Association; State Bar of California (Member, Executive Committee, Estate Planning, Trust & Probate Law Section, 1994-1995). *PRACTICE AREAS:* Civil Litigation; Real Property; Estate Planning; Probate.

*STEVEN K. PERRIN,* born Orange, California, January 13, 1964; admitted to bar, 1989, California; 1990, U.S. District Court, Central District of California. *Education:* Bucknell University (B.A., 1986); McGeorge School of Law, University of the Pacific (J.D., with distinction, 1989). Order of the Coif; The Traynor Society. Member, National Moot Program. Oral Finalist, National Moot Court Team. Recipient, American Jurisprudence Awards in Advanced Criminal Procedure and Land Use Planning. Member, Pacific Law Journal. Professor of law at the Southern California Institute of Law. *Member:* Ventura County Bar Association; State Bar of California. *PRACTICE AREAS:* Business Law; Civil Litigation; Personal Injury; Environmental Torts.

*ANDREW S. HUGHES,* born Los Angeles, California, August 19, 1965; admitted to bar, 1990, California and U.S. District Court, Central District of California. *Education:* University of California (B.A., 1987); Santa Clara University (M.B.A., 1990 ; J.D., 1990). American Jurisprudence Award in Constitutional Law I. Senior Comments Editor, Law Review, 1989-1990. Author, "Education Lost: The Homeless Children's Right to Education", 30 Santa Clara Law Review, 829, 1990. *Member:* Ventura County Bar Association; State Bar of California. *PRACTICE AREAS:* Business Litigation; Real Property Law.

*MADISON M. CHRISTIAN,* born Salt Lake City, Utah, May 15, 1963; admitted to bar, 1990, California and U.S. District Court, Central District of California. *Education:* University of Utah (B.S., cum laude, 1987); McGeorge School of Law (J.D., 1990). Member, Order of the Barristers, McGeorge Chapter, National Moot Court Team. *Member:* Ventura County Bar Association; State Bar of California.

*KURT EDWARD KANANEN,* born Coral Gables, Florida, March 22, 1959; admitted to bar, 1991, California and U.S. District Court, Central District of California. *Education:* University of California at Berkeley; University of San Diego (B.A., cum laude, 1981); Loyola Law School (J.D., 1991). *Member:* Ventura County Bar Association; State Bar of California. *PRACTICE AREAS:* Business Law; Business Litigation; Real Property Law.

### ASSOCIATES

*WILLIAM J. KESATIE,* born Dayton, Ohio, August 1, 1961; admitted to bar, 1987, California; 1988, U.S. District Court, Northern, Southern, Central and Eastern Districts of California. *Education:* Wright State University; California Lutheran College (B.A., with honors, 1984); Loyola Marymount University (J.D., 1987). Adjunct Professor, Pre-Law Studies, California Lutheran University. *Member:* Ventura County Bar Association; State Bar of California. *PRACTICE AREAS:* General Business Law; Business Litigation; Bankruptcy; Debtor-Creditor Relations.

*MELISSA E. COHEN,* born Hollywood, California, July 12, 1962; admitted to bar, 1987, California; 1988, U.S. District Court, Central District of California. *Education:* University of California at Davis (B.A., cum laude, 1983); University of Southern California School of Law (J.D., 1986). Phi Alpha Delta. Staff Editor, Journal of Law and Environment, University of Southern California. *Member:* Ventura County Bar Association; State Bar of California. *LANGUAGES:* Spanish.

*LINDA KATHRYN ASH,* born Grosse Pointe, Michigan; admitted to bar, 1994, California. *Education:* Arizona State University (B.S., summa cum laude, 1986); University of San Diego (J.D., 1994). Phi Alpha Delta.

*(This Listing Continued)*

Recipient, American Jurisprudence Award in Business Planning. *Member:* Ventura County Bar Association; State Bar of California. *PRACTICE AREAS:* Business Law; Copyrights; Trademarks.

*MARK T. BARNEY,* born Los Angeles, California, July 6, 1963; admitted to bar, 1989, California; 1993, Colorado. *Education:* University of California at Santa Barbara (B.A., 1986); Santa Clara University (J.D., 1989). *Member:* State Bar of California; Colorado Bar Association. *PRACTICE AREAS:* Corporate Law; Business Law.

REPRESENTATIVE CLIENTS: Dah Chong Hong (Honda, Toyota, Mazda, Lexus, Acura, Saturn automobile dealerships); Steve Thomas BMW; Vreeland Cadillac, Inc.; PAC Foundries; Williamette Industries; Westlake North Property Owner's Association; Oxnard Harbor Association of Realtors; Conejo Valley Association of Realtors; Martin V. Smith & Associates; The Port of Hueneme; Janss Corp.; Viola, Inc. (General Contracting); Santa Clara Chemical Co.; Nakamura Berry Growers; Power-One, Inc.; John Taft Electric Co.; Rodgers Mortgage Co.; Seneca Resources Corp. (oil and gas); Manufacturing Technology, Inc.; Oxnard Vegetable Exchange, Inc.; Cal-Sun Produce Co.; E.J. Harrison & Sons, Inc.; Waste Management of California, Inc.; Ventura Pacific Capital Company.

## LAW OFFICES OF HIEPLER & HIEPLER

A Professional Partnership

*500 ESPLANADE DRIVE, SUITE 1550*
**OXNARD, CALIFORNIA 93030**
*Telephone: 805-988-5833*
*Facsimile: 805-988-5828*

*General Civil Trial Practice. Bad Faith Insurance Practices, HMO and Healthcare, Personal Injury, Construction and Employment Law, Medical Malpractice.*

FIRM PROFILE: *Hiepler & Hiepler assists clients in obtaining medical treatments which are wrongfully denied by their HMOs and insurance companies. Mark Hiepler's work as a patient advocate has been showcased in three successful verdicts of Fox V. Healthnet 89.3 million (The largest verdict for bad faith denial of medical care in U.S. history); Ching v. Gaines 3 Million (The largest verdict for medical malpractice in history of Ventura County); and deMeurers v. Healthnet 1.4 million (The largest published arbitration verdict for denial of healthcare in U.S. history). All of these verdicts have received national attention for their impact on the medical-HMO industry. In addition to health care and bad faith insurance practices, Mr. Hiepler's trial work extends into the areas of personal injury, construction defect, employment and contract.*

*Mark Hiepler has been featured in a number of publications such as Time Magazine, Newsweek Magazine, U.S. News & World Report Magazine, Wallstreet Journal, USA Today and featured on the television programs "20/20", 60 Minutes, Nightline, among others.*

### MEMBERS OF FIRM

*MARK O. HIEPLER,* born Inglewood, California, December 25, 1961; admitted to bar, 1988, California and U.S. District Court, Central, Eastern and Southern Districts of California; 1991, District of Columbia. *Education:* Point Loma College (B.A., magna cum laude, 1984); Regent's College, London England (International Law Study, 1987); Pepperdine University (J.D., 1988). Margaret Martin Brock Public Service Scholar. Member: Moot Court Honor Board; F. Lee Bailey National Moot Court. Recipient, American Jurisprudence Award in Trial Practice. President, Ventura County Barristers Association, 1993-1994. Member, Board of Directors, American College of Quality Assurance. Member, Advisory Board, Media Fellowship Inc. Honorary Chairperson, Margaret Martin Brock Scholars. Member, Board of Directors, Ventura County Economic Development Association. Advisor to Board of Directors of MADD. Member, Board of Visitors and President's Executive Association, Pepperdine University. The President's Builders, Point Loma Nazarene College. High School Sunday School Teacher, First Lutheran Church. Voted *"Top 10 National Trial Lawyers of the Year 1994"* by Trial Lawyers for Public Justice, Wash., D.C. Featured as "Nation's Top 10 Largest Verdicts of the Year 1993" by National Law Journal. Voted one of California's *"Top 100 Most Interesting and Influential Healthcare Leaders,"* 1996, by California Medicine, an independent health industry magazine. Voted One of California's "Top 100 Most Interesting and Influential Healthcare Leaders" or 1996 by California Medicine, an Independent Health Industry Magazine. *Member:* Los Angeles County, Ventura County and American Bar Associations; District of Columbia Bar. *REPORTED CASES:* Fox v. Health Net; deMeurers v. Health Net; Ching v. Gaines. *PRACTICE AREAS:* Bad Faith Insurance Practices; HMO and Healthcare Practices; Personal Injury; Construction; Defect Law; Medical Malpractice.

*(This Listing Continued)*

**MICHELLE R. HIEPLER,** born Scottsbluff, Nebraska, October 9, 1963; admitted to bar, 1989, California, U.S. District Court, Central District of California and U.S. Court of Appeals, Ninth Circuit; 1993, Colorado. *Education:* University of Colorado (B.S., Journalism, cum laude, 1986); Pepperdine University School of Law (J.D., cum laude, 1989). Member, Moot Court. Recipient: American Jurisprudence Awards. Editor, Pepperdine Law Review, 1988-1989. Author: "California Supreme Court Survey," 15 Pepperdine Law Review, 1989. Associate General Counsel, Pepperdine University. *Member:* Los Angeles County, Colorado and American Bar Associations; State Bar of California; National Association of College and University Attorneys. **PRACTICE AREAS:** General Civil Litigation; Employment Law.

### ASSOCIATES

**JAMES D. MCGINLEY,** born Pasadena, California, April 8, 1959; admitted to bar, 1992, California and U.S. District Court, Central District of California. *Education:* California State University at Long Beach (B.A., 1981); Pepperdine University School of Law (J.D., 1991). Phi Delta Phi. California Survey Editor, Pepperdine Law Review, 1990-1991. Author: "Thing v. La Chusa: A Guarantee With a Price," Pepperdine Law Review, 17:2; "Summary of Death Penalty Law III," Pepperdine Law Review, 17:2. Member, Pepperdine University Alumni Board. Expert Legal Analysis Quoted in *The American Lawyer,* Bureau of National Affairs, *Health Law Reporter,* and *The Wall Street Journal.* . [Maj., U.S. Marine, 1981— ]. **PRACTICE AREAS:** General Civil Litigation.

**DARCI D. TEOBALDI,** born Albuquerque, New Mexico, December 15, 1966; admitted to bar, 1992, California and U.S. District Court, Central District of California. *Education:* San Diego State University (B.S., 1988); Pepperdine University School of Law (J.D., 1992). Certificate: Institute for Dispute Resolution; Pepperdine University School of Law, 1988. *Member:* Los Angeles and Ventura County Bar Associations; State Bar of California. **PRACTICE AREAS:** General Civil Litigation; Health Care Law; Dispute Resolution.

---

## *LAWLER, BONHAM & WALSH*

*Established in 1980*

*300 ESPLANADE DRIVE, SUITE, 1900*
*P.O. BOX 5527*
**OXNARD, CALIFORNIA 93031**
*Telephone: 805-485-8921*
*MCI Fax: 805-485-3766*
*Email: LBW@INTERNETMCI.COM*

*General Civil Trial Practice in all State and Federal Courts. Municipal and School Representation. Personnel, Community Redevelopment, Land Use, Environmental and Toxic Tort Law. Products Liability, Casualty (Defense), General Insurance, Civil Rights, Security Law, Police Defense, Premises Liability and Commercial Transactions.*

*FIRM PROFILE: Mr. Lawler, Mr. Bonham & Mr. Walsh began practicing together in 1980. Messrs. Lawler, Bonham, Walsh and Ellis have a combined past experience in civil trial litigation totalling over 40 years. Ms. Carol A. Woo became a partner in 1994. Korman Dorsey Ellis joined the firm as a partner in 1996. This firm, consisting of 7 attorneys, specializes in civil litigation. The firm encourages participation in continuing legal education seminars, professional association activities and civic affairs for all staff. The Firm is Listed in Martindale-Hubbell's Bar Register of Preeminent Lawyers under Commercial Litigation and Insurance Defense. Located between Santa Barbara and Los Angeles counties.*

### MEMBERS OF FIRM

**BYRON J. LAWLER,** born Los Angeles, California, April 2, 1936; admitted to bar, 1964, California. *Education:* University of California at Los Angeles (B.A., 1958; J.D., 1964). Phi Delta Phi. *Member:* Ventura County and American Bar Associations; The State Bar of California; Association of Southern California Defense Counsel; American Board of Trial Advocates (President, Santa Barbara, Ventura, San Luis Obispo Chapter, 1983). [Lieut., U.S. Navy, 1958-1961]. **PRACTICE AREAS:** Civil Rights Law; Discrimination Law; Environmental Law; International Business Transactions Law.

**TERRENCE J. BONHAM,** born Richmond, California, June 8, 1938; admitted to bar, 1964, California and U.S. Court of Military Appeals. *Education:* Saint Mary's College of California (A.B., 1960); Hastings College of Law, University of California (J.D., 1963). Member, Ventura County Arbitration Panel, 1979— . *Member:* Ventura, Ventura County (Member, 1990— and Director, 1971, Executive Board) and American (Member, Section on Tort and Insurance Practice) Bar Associations; The State Bar of California; Association of Southern California Defense Counsel; American Board of Trial Advocates (President, Santa Barbara, Ventura, San Luis Obispo Chapter, 1985; Director, National Board, 1991— ). [Capt., U.S. Army, 1964-1968]. **PRACTICE AREAS:** Products Liability Law; Administrative Law; Legal Malpractice; Arbitration.

**HENRY J. WALSH,** born Brooklyn, New York, November 12, 1943; admitted to bar, 1971, California. *Education:* Stanford University (B.A., 1965); Loyola University of Los Angeles (J.D., 1970). Arbitrator, Ventura County Arbitration Panel, 1979— . *Member:* Ventura County Bar Association; The State Bar of California; American Board of Trial Advocates; Association of Southern California Defense Counsel. **PRACTICE AREAS:** Automobile Law; Intentional Torts; General Civil Litigation; Arbitration.

**CAROL A. WOO,** born San Francisco, California, March 21, 1955; admitted to bar, 1986, California. *Education:* University of California at Berkeley (B.A., 1977); Lone Mountain College (M.A., 1978); Pepperdine University (J.D., 1985). Member, Pepperdine University Law Review, 1984-1985. Author: "Antitrust and California's New Preferred Provider Organization Legislation: A New Alternative in Health Care Cost Containment," 12 Pepperdine L.Rev. 121 (1984); "California Supreme Court Survey: August 1984-November 1984," 12 Pepperdine L.Rev. 789 (1985). *Member:* Ventura County and American Bar Associations; State Bar of California; Southern California Defense Counsel. **REPORTED CASES:** Cottle v. Superior Court, 1992, 30 A 4th 1367, 5 C.R. 2d 882. **PRACTICE AREAS:** Environmental Law; Municipal Law; School Law; Insurance Law; Commercial Transactions.

**KORMAN DORSEY ELLIS,** born Chicago, Illinois, July 15, 1934; admitted to bar, 1965, California. *Education:* California State College at Los Angeles (B.A., 1960); University of Southern California (J.D., 1965); National College of Advocacy and Medi-Legal Institute (1975). Phi Alpha Delta. Finalist, National Moot Court Competition, 1963. Member of Faculty, Ventura College of Law, Advanced Torts and Insurance Law. Judge Pro Tempore and Arbitrator, Superior Court, 1972— . *Member:* Santa Barbara Bar Association (Chairman, Civil Trial Lawyers Section, 1976-1977); State Bar of California; Association of Southern California Defense Counsel; Diplomate, American Board of Trial Advocates (Member, Board of Directors, 1980-1990); Defense Research Institute. **REPORTED CASES:** Anderson v. Chancellor Western 53 CA.3d, 235; Lehto v. City of Oxnard 171 CA.3d, 285; Truhitte v. French Hospital 128 CA.3d, 332; Constantinescu v. Conejo Valley Unified School District 16 CA.4th, 1466; Joyce v. Simi Valley Unified School District 6 CA.4th, 80; 8 CA.4th 1188; Morelli v. Superior Court 262 CA.2d, 262. **PRACTICE AREAS:** Civil Practice; Government Tort Liability Law; Insurance Law; Municipal Law; School Law.

### ASSOCIATES

**RICHARD A SHIMMEL,** born Norfolk, Virginia, August 14, 1954; admitted to bar, 1988, California. *Education:* Western State University (B.S.L., magna cum laude, 1986); Western State University College of Law (J.D., summa cum laude, Valedictorian, 1987). Instructor, Oxnard Community College Paralegal Program, 1989-1990. *Member:* Ventura County Bar Association; State Bar of California; Ventura Trial Lawyers Association; Association of Southern California Defense Counsel. **PRACTICE AREAS:** Civil Litigation; Government Tort Liability; Construction Defect; Products Liability; Insurance Law.

**MAUREEN M. HOUSKA,** born Burbank, California, June 30, 1965; admitted to bar, 1990, California and U.S. District Court, Central District of California; 1993, U.S. District Court, Northern District of California and U.S. Court of Appeals, 9th Circuit. *Education:* University of Notre Dame (B.B.A., 1987); Loyola Law School (J.D., 1990). *Member:* State Bar of California; Southern California Defense Counsel. **PRACTICE AREAS:** Civil Litigation; Premises Liability; Security Guard Law; Police Defense.

REPRESENTATIVE CLIENTS: Allied Insurance Group; Allstate Insurance Co.; Cal Farm Ins.; Casitas Municipal Water District; City of Camarillo; City of Fillmore; City of Oxnard; City of Port Hueneme; City of Simi Valley; City of Thousand Oaks; Conejo Valley Unified School; County of Ventura; Oak Park School; Ocean View School District; Oxnard High School; Prudential Property and Casualty Co.; Rio School District; Santa Barbara Area Joint Powers Insurance Authority; Southern California Joint Powers Insurance Authority; Ventura County Community College District; Ventura Regional Sanitation District; Ventura, Simi Valley and Oxnard Unified School Districts; Weyerhaeuser; Stauffer Information Systems; Rushing Minerals; Ventura Unified School District, LMI; Division of Vik Bros.; Kinko's Service Corp.; Cigna; Brock Hills/Paseo del Mar; Deerfield Homeowners Association; Fairfield II Homeowners Association; Malibu Bay Owners Association; Palm Colony Homeowners Association; Seaview Hills Homeowners Association (Phase II); West Hills Homeowners Association; American States Ins. Co.; California Insurance Group; City of Ojai; Statewide Adjusters; Industrial Indemnity; Insurance Company of the West; Crawford and Co.; Carl Warren and Co.; United Pacific/Reliance; Royal Insur-

*(This Listing Continued)*

*LAWLER, BONHAM & WALSH, Oxnard—Continued*

ance; St. Paul Fire & Marine Insurance Co.; South Coast Area Transit; Ventura County Schools Self-Funding Authority; Crum & Forester Insurance Services; Santa Paula Unified School District; City of Agoura Hills; City of Moor Park; Hueneme School District; Ventura Unified School District; Cregis Insurance Co.

---

## *LOWTHORP, RICHARDS, McMILLAN, MILLER, CONWAY & TEMPLEMAN*

*A PROFESSIONAL CORPORATION*

Established in 1969

*300 ESPLANADE DRIVE, SUITE 850*
*P.O. BOX 5167*
**OXNARD, CALIFORNIA 93031**
Telephone: 805-981-8555
FAX: 805-983-1967

*Real Estate, Agricultural, Taxation, Estate Planning, Probate, Zoning, Condemnation, Domestic, Insurance, Products Liability, Securities, Bankruptcy, Construction Law, Business and Personal Injury Law. General Civil Litigation.*

FIRM PROFILE: *The firm is listed in Martindale-Hubbell Bar Register of Preeminent Lawyers.*

**CARL F. LOWTHORP, JR.** (1933-1992).

**RICHARD A. RICHARDS,** born Prosser, Washington, October 3, 1934; admitted to bar, 1962, California. *Education:* University of Washington (B.A., 1956); University of California at Los Angeles (J.D., 1962). Phi Delta Phi. Director, 1967-1969 and President, 1969, Ventura County Legal Aid Association. *Member:* Ventura County and American Bar Associations; State Bar of California (Referee, State Bar Court, 1982-1990). [Capt., USAF, 1956-1959]. **PRACTICE AREAS:** Real Estate Law; Business Law; Probate Law; Trust Law; Estate Planning.

**ROBERT C. McMILLAN,** born Los Angeles, California, January 15, 1940; admitted to bar, 1971, California. *Education:* Occidental College (B.A., 1961); California Western University (J.D., 1970). Phi Delta Phi. Editor-in-Chief, California Western University Law Review, 1969-1970. *Member:* Ventura County (Member, Executive Committee, 1983-1984) and American Bar Associations; State Bar of California. [Lt., USNR, 1962-1967]. **PRACTICE AREAS:** Estate Planning Law; Probate Law; Real Estate Law; Agriculture Law.

**PAUL A. MILLER,** born Oxnard, California, January 15, 1947; admitted to bar, 1974, California. *Education:* Loyola University of Los Angeles (B.S., 1969); University of San Diego (J.D., 1973). Phi Delta Phi. *Member:* Ventura County (Member, Board of Directors, 1989-1991) and American Bar Associations; State Bar of California. **PRACTICE AREAS:** Domestic Relations Law; Construction Law; Business Law.

**CHARLES J. CONWAY, JR.,** born Oxnard, California, December 23, 1946; admitted to bar, 1973, California. *Education:* University of Santa Clara (B.A., 1969); University of California at Davis School of Law (J.D., 1972). *Member:* Ventura County and American Bar Associations; State Bar of California. **PRACTICE AREAS:** Real Estate Law; Probate Law; Estate Planning Law.

**ALAN R. TEMPLEMAN,** born Newark, New Jersey, October 17, 1941; admitted to bar, 1972, California. *Education:* Ohio University (B.A., cum laude, 1963); University of California at Los Angeles (J.D., 1971). Arbitrator: New York Stock Exchange; Ventura County Superior Court. *Member:* Ventura County and American Bar Associations; State Bar of California; Ventura County Trial Lawyers Association (President, 1984); California Trial Lawyers Association; American Board of Trial Advocates. [Lieut. Comdr., USNR, 1963-1968]. **PRACTICE AREAS:** Securities Litigation; Civil Trials; Personal Injury; Products Liability Litigation.

**PATRICK T. LOUGHMAN,** born Santa Monica, California, March 17, 1956; admitted to bar, 1982, California. *Education:* Thomas Aquinas College; Loyola Marymount University (B.A., 1978); Loyola Law School (J.D., 1982). *Member:* Ventura County (Co-Chairman, Bankruptcy/Commercial Law Section, 1992) and American Bar Associations; State Bar of California. **REPORTED CASES:** Karrin v. Ocean-Aire Mobile Home Estates (1991) 1 Cal.App.4th, 1066; Hurst Concrete Products, Inc. v. Lane (In Re Lane) (Ninth Circuit 1992) 980 F2d 601. **PRACTICE AREAS:** Business Litigation; Bankruptcy Law; Real Property Law; Probate; Trusts.

*(This Listing Continued)*

**GLENN J. CAMPBELL,** born Brooklyn, New York, January 3, 1952; admitted to bar, 1983, California. *Education:* Canal Zone College, La Boca, Canal Zone; Florida State University (B.S., cum laude, 1977); Pepperdine University (J.D., 1983). Pi Gamma Mu; Phi Delta Phi. Recipient, American Jurisprudence Award for Criminal Law. Business Manager, National Conference of Law Reviews, Inc., 1981-1982. Arbitrator: New York Stock Exchange; Ventura County Superior County Court. *Member:* Ventura County and American Bar Associations; State Bar of California; Ventura County Trial Lawyers Association (Member, Board of Directors, and Secretary/Treasurer, 1987-1989); California Trial Lawyers Association; Ventura County Barristers (President, 1988). [Sgt., U.S. Army, 1969-1972; California ARNG, 1979-1981]. **PRACTICE AREAS:** Civil Trials.

**JOHN Q. MASTELLER,** born Madison, Wisconsin, September 19, 1953; admitted to bar, 1982, Missouri; 1983, Illinois and U.S. District Court, Eastern District of Missouri; 1987, U.S. Court of Appeals, Eighth Circuit; 1990, California; 1991, U.S. District Court, Central District of California; 1996, U.S. Supreme Court. *Education:* University of Notre Dame (A.B., 1975); Drake University (M.B.A., 1978); St. Louis University (J.D., 1982). Phi Alpha Delta. Note and Comment Editor, St. Louis University Law Journal, 1981-1982. Law Clerk to Hon. Carl R. Gaertner, Missouri Court of Appeals, 1982-1983. *Member:* Ventura County Bar Association; State Bar of California; The Missouri Bar; The Illinois Bar; Ventura County Trial Lawyers Association. **PRACTICE AREAS:** Business Law; Real Estate; Probate Law.

**E.P. MICHAEL KARCIS,** born Seattle, Washington, February 26, 1961; admitted to bar, 1989, California. *Education:* Claremont McKenna College; Mars Hill College (B.A., 1985); Boston University (J.D., 1988). Ventura County Barristers (President, 1992). *Member:* State Bar of California; Ventura County Trial Lawyers Association; California Trial Lawyers Association. **PRACTICE AREAS:** Civil Trials.

**GREGORY J. RAMIREZ,** born Ventura, California, June 8, 1959; admitted to bar, 1990, California; 1991, U.S. District Court, Central District of California and U.S. Court of Appeal, Ninth Circuit. *Education:* University of Southern California (B.S., 1981); University of California at Los Angeles (J.D., 1990). Judicial Extern to the Honorable Justice Arthur Gilbert, California Court of Appeal, Second District, Div. Six, 1989. Member, Board of Directors, Oxnard Chamber of Commerce. *Member:* Ventura County (Member, Board of Directors) and Federal Bar Associations; State Bar of California; Ventura County Trial Lawyer's Association; The Association of Trial Lawyers of America. **PRACTICE AREAS:** Civil Trials; Products Liability; Employment Discrimination.

*LEGAL SUPPORT PERSONNEL*

**ELIZABETH T. LADIANA, CLA,** born Geneva, New York, January 22, 1954. *Education:* University of California at Santa Barbara (Certificate in Legal Assistantship, 1984); State University of New York at Farmingdale. Phi Theta Kappa. *Member:* National Association of Legal Assistants; Ventura County Association of Legal Assistants.

REPRESENTATIVE CLIENTS: Pleasant Valley Mutual Water Co.; Friedrich Ranches, Inc.; Deardorff Jackson Co.; Pacific Coast Plastering; AGRX, Inc.; Terry Farms; Hurst Concrete Products; Chase Bros. Dairy; Dullam Nursery; Gene Jackson Farms, Inc.; Triple J & G Ranches Ltd.; Rio Lindo Properties (Real Estate Developers); Westside Strawberry Farms, Inc.; Southern California Builders; Weber Motor Co. (Lincoln-Mercury/Mazda Nissan/Infiniti Dealer); Hagle Lumber Co.; MacElhenny, Levy & Co.; Hamer Motors, Inc. (Toyota Dealer); Kirby Oldsmobile-Jeep; American Interstate Millworks; Corning Glass; In Vitro; Las Posas Country Club; Laurin Publishing Co.; Bel-Air Flower Growers and Shippers, Inc.; Alert Management; Oasis Technology, Inc.; Network Digital Publishing, Inc.
REFERENCES: Ventura County National Bank; Bank of A. Levy.

---

## *IRWIN R. (ROB) MILLER*

*300 ESPLANADE DRIVE, 19TH FLOOR*
**OXNARD, CALIFORNIA 93030**
Telephone: 805-485-2700
Fax: 805-485-2751

*General Civil and Trial Practice in State and Federal Courts. Real Estate, Family, Negligence and Malpractice Law.*

**IRWIN R. (ROB) MILLER,** born Mt. Vernon, New York, May 19, 1942; admitted to bar, 1969, California. *Education:* Los Angeles Valley College and Woodbury College (B.B.A., 1964); University of Cincinnati (J.D., 1968). Author: "Constitutional Problems Inherent in the Admissibility of Prior Record Conviction Evidence for the Purpose of Impeaching the Creditability of the Defendant Witness," 37 University of Cincinnati Law Review 168. Member, Board of Editors, University of Cincinnati Law Re-

*(This Listing Continued)*

view, 1967-1968. *Member:* Hollywood (Member, Board of Governors, 1974-1980; President, 1977-1978), Los Angeles County and Ventura County Bar Associations; The State Bar of California (Member, Committee on Maintenance of Professional Competency, 1978-1983); American Trial Lawyers Association. *REPORTED CASES:* Dibene v. Waste Management, Inc., Los Angeles Superior Court Case No. NWCO29341 (1993). Personal injury below knee amputation jury trial verdict $4,268,000 motorcycle v. truck accident. *PRACTICE AREAS:* Personal Injury Law; Domestic Relations Law; Real Estate; Tort Law; Professional Liability Law.

## *NORDMAN, CORMANY, HAIR & COMPTON*

Established in 1939

1000 TOWN CENTER DRIVE, SIXTH FLOOR
P.O. BOX 9100
**OXNARD, CALIFORNIA 93031-9100**
Telephone: 805-485-1000
Ventura: 805-656-3304
Telecopier: 805-988-8387
805-988-7790

*Westlake Village, California Office:* 920 Hampshire Road, Suite A-17, 91361. Telephone: 805-497-2795.

General Civil Litigation in all State and Federal Courts. Environmental and Hazardous Waste, Employment, Banking and Finance, Real Estate, Securities, Municipal and Special Districts, Creditors' Rights and Insolvency, Insurance Coverage, Commercial and Business, Corporation, Condemnation, Oil and Gas, Probate and Estate Planning, Taxation, Intellectual Property, Entertainment Litigation, Civil Service, Administrative Law, Education, State and Federal Appellate Practice.

**BEN E. NORDMAN** Founder (1913-1985).

### MEMBERS OF FIRM

**WILLIAM H. HAIR,** born Santa Paula, California, January 5, 1933; admitted to bar, 1960, California; 1981, U.S. Supreme Court. *Education:* California State Polytechnic College; Ventura College; University of California, Hastings College of the Law (J.D., 1959). Phi Alpha Delta. Deputy District Attorney, County of Ventura, 1960-1962. City Attorney, City of Port Hueneme, 1963-1975. Secretary, Camarillo Protection District, 1962-1971. Board of Trustees and Secretary, 1973—, Chairman, 1989—, Ojai Valley School. Member, Board of Trustees, Hastings 1066 Foundation, 1975-1982 (Secretary, 1978). Board of Trustees, Ventura County Maritime Museum, 1992—. *Member:* Ventura County Bar Association (Trustee, 1972; President, 1980); State Bar of California (Member, Commission on Judicial Nominees Evaluation, 1982). *PRACTICE AREAS:* Land Use Law; Condemnation Litigation; Administrative Law.

**ROBERT L. COMPTON,** born Corvallis, Oregon, September 29, 1931; admitted to bar, 1962, California; 1981, U.S. Supreme Court. *Education:* Oregon State University (B.S. in Mechanical Engineering, 1953); University of California, Boalt Hall School of Law (LL.B., 1961). Phi Delta Phi; Phi Kappa Phi; Tau Beta Pi. Author: "The Right to the Subjacent Support of Oil and Gas," 49 California Law Review 354, 1961. Director, United Fund, 1968-1971. Assistant U.S. Attorney, 1962. *Member:* Ventura County and American Bar Associations; State Bar of California (Member, Committee on Rules and Procedures of Court, 1980-1982). (Also at Westlake Village Office). *PRACTICE AREAS:* Civil Law; Business Litigation; Construction Law; Business Law; Oil and Gas Law.

**MARC L. CHARNEY,** born Chicago, Illinois, June 3, 1941; admitted to bar, 1968, California and U.S. District Court, Central District of California; 1981, U.S. Supreme Court. *Education:* El Camino College and University of California at Los Angeles (A.B., 1964); University of California School of Law at Los Angeles (J.D., 1967). Phi Alpha Delta. City Attorney, Port Hueneme, 1973-1975. Agency Attorney, Redevelopment Agency, City of San Buenaventura, 1978—. Vice President and Director, United Way of Ventura County, 1979-1986. Director, 1990— and President, 1993-1994, Ventura County Economic Development Association. President, Ventura County Division, American Heart Association, 1993-1994. Director, Greater Oxnard Economic Development Corporation, 1994—. *Member:* Ventura County (Member, Real Estate Section) and Los Angeles County Bar Associations; State Bar of California (Member, Real Estate Section). *PRACTICE AREAS:* Land Use Law; Environmental Regulation Law; Redevelopment Law; Real Estate Development Law.

*(This Listing Continued)*

**RONALD H. GILL,** born Chicago, Illinois, September 10, 1940; admitted to bar, 1966, California and U.S. District Court, Central District of California. *Education:* University of California at Los Angeles (A.B., with honors, 1962); University of California, Boalt Hall School of Law (J.D., 1965). Ventura County Deputy District Attorney, 1966-1968. *Member:* Ventura County and Los Angeles County Bar Associations; State Bar of California. *PRACTICE AREAS:* Business and Real Estate Litigation; Commercial Law; Banking Law; Creditors Rights Law; Bankruptcy Law.

**LARRY L. HINES,** born Wilmington, California, August 13, 1939; admitted to bar, 1970, California and U.S. District Court, Central District of California; 1972, U.S. Court of Federal Claims; 1978, U.S. Court of Appeals, Ninth Circuit; 1979, U.S. Supreme Court; 1983, U.S. Court of Appeals for the Federal Circuit. *Education:* Humboldt State College (B.A., with distinction, 1963; M.A., 1964); University of California at Berkeley; Willamette University (J.D., 1969). Author, 245 page training manual, *Employment Law for Private Businesses - How to Reduce Risks of Employee Lawsuits*; Council on Education in Management, articles entitled: "How to Properly Investigate Sexual Harassment Claims," "Drug Testing: The Battle of Safety vs. Privacy" and "Compliance with CAL/OSHA's Injury Prevention Program." *Member:* Ventura County, Los Angeles County and American Bar Associations; State Bar of California; Ventura County Trial Lawyers Association; The Association of Trial Lawyers of America. *PRACTICE AREAS:* Complex Civil Business Litigation; Labor/Employment Law; Trust/Will Contests; Administrative Law.

**KENNETH M. HIGH, JR.,** born San Fernando, California, October 28, 1946; admitted to bar, 1971, California and U.S. District Court, Central District of California. *Education:* University of California at Berkeley (A.B., 1968); University of California School of Law at Los Angeles (J.D., 1971). California Real Estate Broker Licensee. *Member:* Ventura County and Los Angeles County Bar Associations; State Bar of California; Ventura County Taxpayer Association (Director and President, 1994—). *PRACTICE AREAS:* Real Property Sales, Leasing, Financing and Development and Business Organization.

**MICHAEL C. O'BRIEN,** born Ventura, California, June 4, 1947; admitted to bar, 1973, California and U.S. District Court, Central District of California; U.S. Court of Federal Claims. *Education:* Seattle University (B.A., cum laude, 1969); Loyola University of Los Angeles (J.D., 1973). Member, Loyola University Law Review, 1972-1973. Graduate, National Institute for Trial Advocacy, Advanced Professional Training Program, 1983. Member, Editorial Board, "California Real Estate Reporter," Matthew Bender & Co., 1987-1991. Member, Board of Directors, United Way of Ventura County, 1993—. *Member:* Ventura County Bar Association (Secretary-Treasurer, 1983; Executive Committee, 1983-1984); State Bar of California; Ventura County Trial Lawyers Association (Second Vice-President, 1982; President, 1983; Member, Board of Directors, 1979-1984). *PRACTICE AREAS:* General Civil Litigation with emphasis on real estate related matters.

**LAURA K. MCAVOY,** born Van Nuys, California, December 11, 1947; admitted to bar, 1974, California and U.S. District Court, Central District of California; 1975, U.S. Court of Appeals, Ninth Circuit; 1992, U.S. District Court, Eastern District of California. *Education:* University of California at Los Angeles (B.A., magna cum laude, 1970); University of California School of Law at Los Angeles (J.D., 1973). Phi Beta Kappa. Member, University of California at Los Angeles Law Review, 1972-1973. Law Clerk, U.S. Court of Appeals, Ninth Circuit, 1974-1975. Director, 1986-1993 and President, 1988-1990, United Way of Ventura County. Director and Treasurer, Ventura County Community Foundation, 1988—. Director, Livingston Memorial Visiting Nurse Association, 1986—. *Member:* Ventura County Bar Association (Member, Business Law Section; Director, 1989-1991); State Bar of California (Member, Business Section); American Association of Petroleum Landmen. *PRACTICE AREAS:* General Corporate Law; Business Law; Banking Law; Oil and Gas Law; Agricultural Law.

**RANDALL H. GEORGE,** born Santa Monica, California, October 21, 1953; admitted to bar, 1978, California; 1982, U.S. District Court, Central District of California. *Education:* University of California at Davis (B.A., with highest honors, 1975); University of California School of Law, Davis (J.D., 1978); University of Southern California (M.B.T., Business Taxation, 1993). Phi Beta Kappa; Phi Delta Phi; Beta Gamma Sigma. Member, Moot Court Honors Program. Deputy District Attorney for Ventura County, 1978-1980. *Member:* Ventura County and American Bar Associations; State Bar of California. *PRACTICE AREAS:* Corporate, General Business and Taxation Law; Banking Law.

**JANET ANNE REESE,** born Fullerton, California, August 11, 1953; admitted to bar, 1978, California. *Education:* Whittier College (B.A., 1975);

*(This Listing Continued)*

CAA1529B

## NORDMAN, CORMANY, HAIR & COMPTON, Oxnard—Continued

Loyola University of Los Angeles (J.D., 1978). *Member:* Ventura County Bar Association (Member, Executive Committee, Probate and Estate Planning Section, 1984—; Co-Chairman, Probate and Estate Planning Section, 1992—); State Bar of California; Women Lawyers of Ventura County (Member, Board of Directors, 1982-1984). (Also at Westlake Village Office). *PRACTICE AREAS:* Estate Planning; Probate; Trust Administration and Litigation.

**PAUL W. KURZEKA,** born Minneapolis, Minnesota, October 17, 1952; admitted to bar, 1982, California; U.S. District Court, Central District of California and U.S. Court of Appeals, Ninth Circuit. *Education:* University of Nevada (B.S., with honors, 1979); Pepperdine University School of Law (J.D., with distinction, 1982). *Member:* Ventura County Bar Association (Member, Steering Committee, Real Estate Section, 1987-1990 and 1992—); State Bar of California. *PRACTICE AREAS:* General Business Law; Real Estate Transactions.

**ANTHONY H. TREMBLEY,** born San Francisco, California, July 17, 1956; admitted to bar, 1983, California; 1984, U.S. District Court, Central District of California and U.S. Court of Appeals, Ninth Circuit. *Education:* Trinity College, Dublin, Ireland; University of California at Davis (B.A., with highest honors, 1978); University of California School of Law, Davis (J.D., 1983). Phi Kappa Phi. Editor, University of California at Davis Law Review, 1982-1983. Author: "Alone Against The State: Lassiter v. Department of Social Services," 15 University of California at Davis Law Review 1123, 1982. California Legislature, Assembly Fellow, 1978-1979. *Member:* Ventura County Bar Association (Member, Steering Committee, Environmental Law Section); State Bar of California. *PRACTICE AREAS:* Municipal Law; Administrative Law; Land Use Law; Environmental Regulation Law; Business Law.

**JONATHAN FRASER LIGHT,** born Sherman Oaks, California, February 13, 1957; admitted to bar, 1981, California, U.S. District Court, Central District of California and U.S. Court of Appeals, Ninth Circuit. *Education:* University of California at Los Angeles (B.A., magna cum laude, 1978); University of California School of Law at Los Angeles (J.D., 1981); National Institute for Trial Advocacy (Graduate, National Session, 1986). Phi Alpha Delta. Staff Member, U.C.L.A. Law Review, Vol. 28, 1980-1981. Executive Board Member and Legal Counsel, Ventura County Boy Scout Council, 1987—(President, 1993—). Board Chairman, Medical Resource Foundation, 1993—. *Member:* Ventura County Bar Association; State Bar of California. *PRACTICE AREAS:* Employment; Employer Labor Litigation; Real Estate Litigation; Business Litigation.

**KENT M. KELLEGREW,** born Glendale, California, May, 30, 1953; admitted to bar, 1981, California. *Education:* California State University at Northridge (B.A., magna cum laude, 1975); University of Tel Aviv, Israel; Southwestern University School of Law (J.D., 1980). Ventura County Deputy District Attorney, 1983-1985. Judicial Attorney, California District Court of Appeal, Division 6, 1982-1983. *Member:* Ventura County and Los Angeles County Bar Associations; State Bar of California. (Also at Westlake Village Office). *PRACTICE AREAS:* Civil Litigation; Business Law.

**WILLIAM E. WINFIELD,** born Port Hueneme, California, May 17, 1958; admitted to bar, 1985, California; 1986, U.S. District Court, Central and Eastern Districts of California; 1989, U.S. District Court, Northern and Southern Districts of California and U.S. Court of Appeals, Ninth Circuit; 1990, U.S. Supreme Court. *Education:* Brigham Young University (B.A., 1982); University of Utah (J.D., 1985). Member: University of Utah Law Review, 1984-1985; Journal of Contemporary Law and Policy, 1983-1984. Author: "Rejection of Non-Residential Leases of Real Property in Bankruptcy: What Happens to the Mortgagee's Security Interest?" 17 Pepperdine Law Review 429, 1990. Member, Board of Governors, Goodwill Industries of Southern California. *Member:* Ventura County Bar Association (Chairman, Bankruptcy Section); State Bar of California (Member, Real Property Section); American Association of Petroleum Landmen; California Bankruptcy Forum. *LANGUAGES:* Dutch. *PRACTICE AREAS:* Bankruptcy Law; Creditors Rights Law; Commercial Law.

**GERALD M. ETCHINGHAM,** born Chicago, Illinois, February 19, 1958; admitted to bar, 1986, California, U.S. Court of Appeals, Ninth Circuit and U.S. District Court, Central and Eastern Districts of California. *Education:* Augustana College (B.A., 1980); University of California, Hastings College of the Law (J.D., 1985). Certified Public Accountant, Illinois, 1982. 1995-1996 Bankruptcy Mediation Panel Member for the U.S. Bankruptcy Court for the Central District of California. Panel Member of Arbitration Re: Superior and Municipal Courts Ventura County Judicial District and Santa Barbara County Mobile Home Rent Control Ordinance. *Member:* Ventura County Bar Association; State Bar of California; California Bankruptcy Forum. *PRACTICE AREAS:* Creditors Rights and Insolvency; Environmental Litigation; General Civil and Business Litigation; Non-Profit Organization Law.

**CHRIS K. KITASAKI,** born Ann Arbor, Michigan, March 19, 1956; admitted to bar, 1983, California. *Education:* University of California at Irvine (B.S., 1978); University of San Francisco (J.D., 1983); Georgetown University (LL.M., Taxation, 1986). Member, University of San Francisco Law Review, 1982-1983. Attorney, Division of Corporation Finance, Securities and Exchange Commission, 1983-1986. *Member:* Ventura County Bar Association; State Bar of California. *PRACTICE AREAS:* Corporate Securities Law; General Business Law.

**SCOTT B. SAMSKY,** born Minneapolis, Minnesota, October 19, 1956; admitted to bar, 1981, California, U.S. Court of Appeals, Ninth Circuit and U.S. District Court, Central District of California; 1983, U.S. Tax Court. *Education:* University of Minnesota (B.S., Acct., 1978); University of California School of Law at Los Angeles (J.D., 1981). Beta Gamma Sigma; Beta Alpha Psi. Member, Ventura County Community Foundation, Technical Advisory Committee. Member, Board of Directors, Boys and Girls Club of Camarillo, 1993—. *Member:* Ventura County Bar Association (Member, Sections on: Taxation; Probate and Estate Planning); State Bar of California. *PRACTICE AREAS:* Estate Planning; Taxation and Business Law.

**GUY C. PARVEX, JR.,** born Reno, Nevada, January 11, 1959; admitted to bar, 1989, California and U.S. District Court, Central District of California. *Education:* University of California at Santa Barbara (B.A., with high honors and distinction, 1985); University of California, Hastings College of the Law (J.D., 1988). Phi Delta Phi. Board of Directors, Ventura Boys and Girls Club. *Member:* Ventura County Bar Association (President, Barristers of Ventura County, 1993); State Bar of California. *PRACTICE AREAS:* Family Law; Civil Litigation.

**ROBERT J. LENT,** born Cambridge, Ohio, June 1, 1955; admitted to bar, 1985, California, U.S. District Court, Southern, Central, Eastern and Northern Districts of California and U.S. Court of Appeals, Ninth Circuit. *Education:* American University, Washington D.C. (B.A., magna cum laude, 1979); University of California at Los Angeles (M.A., Pol.S., 1981); University of California, Hastings College of the Law (J.D., 1985). Phi Kappa Phi; Phi Sigma Alpha. Rotary International Graduate Scholarship, University of Exeter, England, 1981-1982. Externship for the Honorable David V. Kenyon, U.S. District Court, Central District of California, 1984. *Member:* Los Angeles County and Ventura County Bar Associations; State Bar of California. (Also at Westlake Village Office). *PRACTICE AREAS:* Business Litigation; Intellectual Property including Copyright; Trademark; Unfair Competition; Trade Secrets.

**SUSAN WESTEEN NOVATT,** born Asheville, North Carolina, February 11, 1958; admitted to bar, 1984, Washington; 1985, California. *Education:* Oberlin College (A.B., 1979); Duke University (J.D., 1983); New York University (LL.M. in Taxation, 1984). *Member:* Ventura County, Los Angeles County and Washington State Bar Associations; State Bar of California. *PRACTICE AREAS:* Taxation.

### OF COUNSEL

**RALPH L. CORMANY,** born Beloit, Wisconsin, March 12, 1921; admitted to bar, 1950, Missouri; 1960, California. *Education:* Loras College (B.A., 1942); University of Missouri at Kansas City (LL.B., 1950). Director, Ventura County Public Facilities Corp., 1975—. President, Ventura County Economic Development Association, 1975-1976. President, American Association of Petroleum Landmen, 1960. Member: Outer Continental Shelf Advisory Committee to Secretary of Interior, 1984-1986. President, Rancheros Visitadores, 1978-1980. *Member:* Ventura County (President, 1976-1977) and American Bar Associations; The Missouri Bar; State Bar of California (Member, Administrative Committee, 1968-1973). [Major, U.S. Marine Corps, 1942-1946; 1950-1951]. *PRACTICE AREAS:* Real Estate Law; Oil and Gas Transactions.

**JOHN A. SLEZAK,** born Philadelphia, Pennsylvania, October 5, 1949; admitted to bar, 1974, California and U.S. District Court, Central District of California; 1978, U.S. Supreme Court; 1980, U.S Court of Appeals, Ninth Circuit. *Education:* Claremont McKenna College (B.A., magna cum laude, 1970); Vanderbilt University (J.D., 1974); Loyola Marymount University (M.A. in Environmental Science, 1994). Adjunct Professor, Environmental Law, Pepperdine University School of Law. Member, California Regional Water Quality Control Board, Los Angeles Region. *Member:* Ventura County and Los Angeles County Bar Associations; State Bar of

*(This Listing Continued)*

California. *PRACTICE AREAS:* Civil Business Litigation; Environmental Law; Election Law.

## ASSOCIATES

**SUSAN M. SEEMILLER,** born Portland, Maine, June 22, 1959; admitted to bar, 1990, California; 1991, U.S. Court of Appeals, Tenth Circuit; 1993, U.S. District Court, Central and Eastern Districts of California and U.S. Court of Appeals, Ninth Circuit. *Education:* Westbrook College (B.S., summa cum laude, 1987); Pepperdine University (J.D., magna cum laude, 1990). Member, 1988-1989 and Editor in Chief, 1989-1990, Pepperdine Law Review. Author: Note, "Thompson v. Oklahoma: Debating the Constitutionality of Juvenile Executions," 16 Pepperdine L. Rev. 737 (1989). Law Clerk, Honorable Ruggero J. Aldisert, U.S. Court of Appeals, Third Circuit, 1990-1992. *Member:* State Bar of California. *PRACTICE AREAS:* Civil Litigation and Appeals.

**JOHN M. ANDERSEN,** born Los Angeles, California, March 15, 1963; admitted to bar, 1992, California and U.S. District Court, Central District of California. *Education:* University of California at Los Angeles (B.A., 1986); University of California, Hastings College of the Law (J.D., 1992). Member, Hastings Communications and Entertainment Law Journal, 1990-1992. *Member:* Ventura County Bar Association; State Bar of California. (Also at Westlake Village Office). *PRACTICE AREAS:* Estate Planning; Taxation; Business Law; Civil Litigation.

**LAUREL A. MCLAUGHLIN,** born Pittsburgh, Pennsylvania, May 26, 1967; admitted to bar, 1992, California and U.S. District Court, Central District of California. *Education:* University of Santa Clara (B.S., 1989); Pepperdine University (J.D., magna cum laude, 1992). Member, Pepperdine Law Review, 1990-1992. *Member:* Ventura County and Los Angeles County Bar Associations; State Bar of California. *PRACTICE AREAS:* Civil Litigation.

**GLENN J. DICKINSON,** born Champaign, Illinois, September 4, 1959; admitted to bar, 1992, California; 1993, U.S. District Court, Central District of California; 1994, U.S. Court of Appeals, Ninth Circuit. *Education:* University of Maryland (B.A.; B.S., 1987); University of Cincinnati (J.D., 1991). Recipient: Dr. William L. Dornett Prize, 1991; Arthur Russell Morgan Fellow, Urban Morgan Institute for Human Rights, 1988-1991. Articles Editor, 1989-1990 and Managing Editor, 1990-1991, Human Rights Quarterly. Lead Articles Editor, University of Cincinnati Law Review, 1990-1991. Law Clerk to the Hon. Ruggero J. Aldisert, U.S. Court of Appeals, Third Circuit, 1991-1993. Author: "The Supreme Court's Narrow Reading of the Public Interest Served by the Freedom of Information Act," 59 U. Cinn. L. Rev. 191 (1990) (Student note). Co-Author: Statistical Evidence of Racial Disparities in Death Sentencing: A Critical Analysis of McCleskey v. Kemp, in *Statistics and Human Rights: Getting the Record Straight,* (Richard P. Claude and Tom Jabine eds. 1991); *The Year of the Lie: Censorship and Disinformation in the People's Republic of China,* 1989. *Member:* State Bar of California.

**NANCY MILLER,** born Glendale, California, July 6, 1945; admitted to bar, 1989, California, U.S. Court of Appeals, Ninth Circuit, U.S. District Court, Central District of California. *Education:* Immaculate Heart College (B.A., 1967); Loyola University of Los Angeles (J.D., 1989). Phi Delta Phi. Recipient, American Jurisprudence Award in Trial Advocacy. *Member:* Ventura County, Santa Barbara County and American Bar Associations; State Bar of California (Member, Public Law/Labor and Employment Law Sections); California Women Lawyers. *PRACTICE AREAS:* Education; Public Agency Law.

REPRESENTATIVE CLIENTS: Berry Petroleum Company; Real Estate Investment Trust of California; Amgen; Kmart Corp.; Saticoy Lemon Association; The Procter & Gamble Paper Products Co.; Halliburton Services; Schlumberger; The Prudential Insurance Company of America; Laguna Pacific Development; Ojai Valley Sanitary District; Carpinteria Sanitary District; Channel Islands Beach Community Services District; Oxnard Union High School District; Pleasant Valley School District; Redevelopment Agency of the City of San Buenaventura; City of San Buenaventura; Ventura Association of Realtors; Hertel Homes, Inc.; McGrath Industrial Park; Rancheros Visitadores; Mike Wallace Ford; Camarillo Community Bank; Saticoy Foods; Ventura Coastal Corp.; Ventura Pacific Company; Southland Sod; Chicago Title Insurance Company; Standard Pacific of Ventura County; First Interstate Bank of California; Ventura County National Bank; First National Bank of Ventura; Great Western Bank.

## PAMELA J. PRIVETT
A PROFESSIONAL LAW CORPORATION

Established in 1994

300 ESPLANADE DRIVE, SUITE 1865
OXNARD, CALIFORNIA 93030
Telephone: 805-981-3611
Fax: 805-981-3616
Email: pjplaw@aol.com

*Real Estate, Real Estate Financing, Acquisitions/Dispositions.*

**PAMELA J. PRIVETT,** born Long Beach, California, December 5, 1957; admitted to bar, 1985, California. *Education:* Scripps College (B.A., 1980); George Washington University National Law Center (J.D., with honors, 1985). *Member:* Los Angeles County, Ventura County and American Bar Associations; California Women Lawyers. *PRACTICE AREAS:* Real Estate; Secured Financing.

## RICHARD A. REGNIER

Established in 1965

301 NORTH A STREET
P.O. BOX 5505
OXNARD, CALIFORNIA 93031
Telephone: 805-483-7040
Fax: 805-486-7393

*Civil Trial Practice. Tort and Business Litigation. Trials in all Courts. Arbitrations, Administrative Law, Criminal Law.*

**RICHARD A. REGNIER,** born Portland, Oregon, August 23, 1931; admitted to bar, 1963, California; 1968, U.S. Supreme Court. *Education:* Harvard University and United States Military Academy (B.S., 1955); Boalt Hall School of Law, University of California (LL.B., 1962). Deputy District Attorney, Ventura County, 1963-1965. Ventura County Superior Court Judge Pro Tem, 1971—; Arbitrator, 1966—. President, Ventura County Legal Aid Association, 1968. Partner, Ferguson, Regnier & Paterson, 1965-1990. *Member:* Ventura County and American Bar Associations; State Bar of California (Member: Group Insurance Committee, 1973-1976; Committee of Bar Examiners, Site Review Team, 1994); Consumer Attorneys of California; The Association of Trial Lawyers of America; Ventura County Trial Lawyers Association (President, 1970-1971; 1986-1987); American Judicature Society; American Board of Trial Advocates; American Inns of Court (Ventura County Chapter). [Capt., U.S. Air Force, 1955-1959]. (Certified as a Civil Trial Advocate by the National Board of Trial Advocacy). *REPORTED CASES:* Adduddel vs Board of Administration, 8 Cal. App. 3d 243; Linvill vs Perello, 189 Cal. App. 3d 195.

REPRESENTATIVE CLIENTS: Honda of Oxnard; Thomas Aquinas College; Oxnard College; Oxnard Federal Credit Union; Laubacher Insurance Agency; LucaSystems (soft water plants); Fire Electric; Custom Printing; Growers Fresh Marketing; Ocean Technology Systems.
REFERENCES: Ventura County National Bank; Oxnard Police Officer's Association.

## LAW OFFICES OF GLEN M. REISER

300 ESPLANADE DRIVE, SUITE 2030
OXNARD, CALIFORNIA 93030
Telephone: 805-988-0826
Fax: 805-983-6146

*Environmental Matters including CCQA, Wetlands, Soil and Ground Water Issues, and Regulation, Real Property Litigation, Land Use, Public Agency Litigation, Business and Employment and Civil Appellate Litigation.*

**GLEN M. REISER,** born San Andreas, California, October 15, 1953; admitted to bar, 1978, California; 1981, U.S. Court of Appeals, Ninth Circuit; 1982, U.S. Supreme Court. *Education:* United States Military Academy and University of California at Santa Barbara (B.A., with high honors, 1975); University of California at Los Angeles (J.D., 1978). Graduate, National Institute for Trial Advocacy, National Session, 1981. Author: "Effective Petitions for Review in the California Supreme Court: A Survival Guide," 151 Santa Barbara County Bar Assn., October, 1993. Lecturer on Environmental Law, Pepperdine University School of Law, 1992-1994. Lead Defense Counsel, Oxnard Dunes Litigation, 1987-1992. Special Prosecutor, McGrath Lake Oil Spill, 1994. *Member:* Ventura County Bar Association; The State Bar of California (Member, Committee on Administration of Justice, 1991-1992). *REPORTED CASES:* Lundquist v. Reusser, 7 Cal.

*(This Listing Continued)*

## LAW OFFICES OF GLEN M. REISER, Oxnard—
Continued

4th 1193; Burch v. George, 7 Cal. 4th 246; McKinney v. Board of Trustees, 31 Cal. 3d 79; Bradbury v. Superior Court, 49 Cal. App. 4th 1108; Ramos v. Estrada 8 Cal. App. 4th 1070; Cottle v. Superior Court, 3 Cal. App. 4th 1367; Guild Mortgage v. Heller, 193 Cal. App. 3d 1505; Roskamp Manley v. Davin Development, 184 Cal. App. 3d 513; Citizens to Preserve the Ojai v. County of Ventura, 179 Cal. App. 3d 421; New v. Consolidated Rock Products, 171 Cal. App. 3d 681; Powell v. Goldsmith, 152 Cal. App. 3d 746; In re Marriage of Lister, 152 Cal. App. 3d 411; Higgins v. Del Faro, 123 Cal. App. 3d 558; Trent Meredith v. City of Oxnard, 114 Cal. App. 3d 317. **PRACTICE AREAS:** Environmental Litigation; Complex Real Property Litigation; Public Agency Litigation; Condemnation; Land Use; Civil Appellate Practice.

### OF COUNSEL

**CAROLYN OH TAKETA,** born 1967; admitted to bar, 1992, California; 1993, U.S. District Court, Central District of California. *Education:* Pomona College (B.A., cum laude, 1989); Boalt Hall School of Law University of California at Berkeley (J.D., 1992). Author: "Questioning The Cultural and Gender-Bases Assumptions of the Adversary System: Voices of Asian-American Law Students," 7 Berkeley Women's Journal, 125. **LANGUAGES:** Korean. **PRACTICE AREAS:** Business Litigation; Employment Law.

REPRESENTATIVE CLIENTS: Ag Land Service; Calleguas Municipal Water District; Casitas Municipal Water District; Channel Islands Business Center Owners' Association; County of Ventura; First American Title Insurance Company; First Exchange Corporation; GTE California, Inc.; K.E. Curtis Construction Company; The Newhall Land and Farming Company; Southdown, Inc.; Bobby Unser; Ventura County District Attorney's Office.

---

## WENNERGREN & SHAIN
PROFESSIONAL LAW CORPORATION

*300 ESPLANADE DRIVE, SUITE 1180*
**OXNARD, CALIFORNIA 93030**
*Telephone: 805-983-2800; 988-0610*
*Telecopier: 805-988-1422*
*Email: WSPLC@AOL.COM*

Business and Entertainment Law, Personal Injury and Civil Litigation.

**DAVID L. SHAIN,** born New York, N.Y., March 10, 1953; admitted to bar, 1978, District of Columbia; 1980, New York and U.S. District Court, Eastern and Southern Districts of New York; 1983, California; 1985, U.S. District Court, Central District of California; U.S. Court of Appeals, 9th Circuit. *Education:* State University of New York at Albany (B.A., 1974); Georgetown University Law Center (J.D., 1978). Instructor, Business Law, Elizabeth Seton College, Yonkers N.Y., 1981-1982. Temporary Judge, Ventura County Municipal Court, 1989. Chair, Pro Bono Committee, 1997. Settlement Officer, Ventura County Superior Court, 1993. *Member:* Ventura County (President, 1996) and New York State Bar Associations; State Bar of California; The District of Columbia Bar. **PRACTICE AREAS:** Business Litigation; Personal Injury; Criminal Defense.

**KENNETH H. WENNERGREN,** born Logan, Utah, November 16, 1950; admitted to bar, 1979, California; 1981, U.S. Tax Court. *Education:* University of California at Santa Barbara (B.A., with high honors, 1974); University of California at Los Angeles (J.D., 1978). Author: "Nonretirement Fringe Benefits of Professional Corporations," Chapter 5, California Professional Corporations, California Continuing Education of the Bar, Fourth Edition, 1987. *Member:* State Bar of California. **PRACTICE AREAS:** Entertainment Law; Business and Estate Planning; Taxation.

### OF COUNSEL

**DAVID B. SHEA,** born Glendale, California, January 20, 1962; admitted to bar, 1990, California. *Education:* Grossmont College; Ventura College of Law (J.D., 1989). *Member:* Ventura County and San Diego County Bar Associations; California Trial Lawyers Association. **PRACTICE AREAS:** Estate Planning; Real Estate Law; Business Law.

REPRESENTATIVE CLIENTS: Delta Music Inc.; Bend-Pak, Inc.; Senior System Technology, Inc.; Neversoft Entertainment, Inc.; Aspen Enterprises, Inc.; The Tires Pros; Magnecomp Corporation; Abel Automatics, Inc.; Creative Images; Gaiser Tool Company; Mundo Musical, LLC; Grupo Modelo; Concrete Records; MVS Productions; Western Electronic; Components Corporation.

---

## LAW OFFICES OF
## ALAN E. WISOTSKY

*Established in 1983*

*1000 TOWN CENTER DRIVE*
*SUITE 200*
**OXNARD, CALIFORNIA 93030**
*Telephone: 805-278-0920*
*Fax: 805-278-0289*

Insurance and Self-Insured Defense and Civil Trial Practice. General, Automobile, Product, Public Entity and Police Misconduct Litigation.

FIRM PROFILE: The firm is listed in Martindale-Hubbell Bar Register of Preeminent Lawyers.

**ALAN E. WISOTSKY,** born Brooklyn, New York, June 14, 1948; admitted to bar, 1975, California; 1976, U.S. District Court, Central District of California; 1988, U.S. Court of Appeals, Ninth Circuit; 1996, U.S. Supreme Court. *Education:* California State University at Los Angeles (B.S., 1970); Southwestern University (J.D., 1975). Special Counsel to Ventura County Sheriff's Department, Oxnard Police Department and Port Hueneme Police Department. *Member:* Ventura County Bar Association; State Bar of California; Association of Southern California Defense Counsel; American Board of Trial Advocates.

### ASSOCIATES

**BRIAN P. KEIGHRON**

**JEFFREY B. HELD**

**PHILIP ERICKSON**

REPRESENTATIVE CLIENTS: Will be furnished upon request.

---

## LAW OFFICES OF
## NANCY A. AIMOLA

*515 ROCKAWAY BEACH AVENUE*
**PACIFICA, CALIFORNIA 94044-3228**
*Telephone: 415-355-4720*
*Fax: 415-355-8943*

Civil Trial and Appellate Practice. Business Litigation, Bankruptcy Trusteeship, Receivership, Real Estate, Construction, Discrimination and Personal Injury Law.

**NANCY A. AIMOLA,** born Quincy, Massachusetts, October 16, 1949; admitted to bar, 1975, California and U.S. District Court, Northern District of California; 1980, U.S. Court of Appeals, Ninth Circuit. *Education:* University of California at Santa Cruz; University of California at Berkeley (B.A., 1971); Hastings College of Law, University of California (J.D., 1975). Phi Beta Kappa. Recipient, David Snodgrass Moot Court Writing Award. Instructor, San Francisco Law School, 1981-1982. *Member:* State Bar of California.

---

## ARMEN L. GEORGE

*80 DRIFTWOOD CIRCLE*
**PACIFICA, CALIFORNIA 94044**
*Telephone: 415-355-9314*
*Fax: 415-355-9315*

Civil and Business Litigation, Civil Appeals, Real Property and Contract Law.

**ARMEN L. GEORGE,** born Sacramento, California, September 25, 1959; admitted to bar, 1986, California and U.S. District Court, Northern District of California; 1989, U.S. District Court, Eastern District of California. *Education:* University of California at Davis (B.A., Economics, 1981); University of San Francisco Law School (J.D., 1985). *Member:* State Bar of California (Member, Section on: Litigation and Employment Law). **REPORTED CASES:** Dafonte v. Up-Right, Inc. (1992) 2 Cal. 4th 593; Hunter v. Up-Right, Inc. (1993) 6 Cal. 4th 1174. **PRACTICE AREAS:** Civil; Business Litigation; Civil Appeals; Personal Injury; Real Property; Contract.

## WILLIAM A. SAMPSON II & ASSOCIATES
*15332 ANTIOCH STREET, SUITE 525*
**PACIFIC PALISADES, CALIFORNIA 90272**
*Telephone: 310-472-1839*
*Fax: 310-472-8670*

Civil Trial Practice in all State and Federal Courts. Personal Injury, Products Liability, Medical Malpractice, Aviation and Admiralty Law. Criminal Law.

**WILLIAM A. SAMPSON, II,** born Los Angeles, California, March 12, 1935; admitted to bar, 1961, California; 1964, U.S. Supreme Court. *Education:* Stanford University (B.A., 1957; J.D., 1960). Phi Delta Phi. Member, National Board of Arbitrators, American Arbitration Association, 1965-1973. *Member:* Beverly Hills, Santa Monica and Los Angeles County Bar Associations; The State Bar of California; California Trial Lawyers Association; The Association of Trial Lawyers of America; American Board of Trial Advocates. [Capt., U.S. Air Force, 1961-1963]. *LANGUAGES:* Spanish (Written and Oral). *PRACTICE AREAS:* Traumatic Injury; Bad Faith; Strict Liability; Professional Negligence; Criminal Law.

---

## SNYDER & PECSOK
*Established in 1959*
*SUITE 309, 881 ALMA REAL DRIVE*
**PACIFIC PALISADES, CALIFORNIA 90272-3773**
*Telephone: 310-454-1388*
*Telecopier: 310-459-9720*
*Email: WILLIAMHSNYDER76300.632@COMPUSERVE.COM*

Family Law, Probate, Estate Planning, Trusts, Real Estate.

### MEMBERS OF FIRM

**WILLIAM HENRI SNYDER,** born West Chester, Pennsylvania, March 14, 1931; admitted to bar, 1959, California. *Education:* Franklin & Marshall College (B.S., 1953); University of California at Los Angeles (J.D., 1958). Phi Alpha Delta. *Member:* Los Angeles County, Santa Monica (Member, Board of Directors, 1972-1978; Secretary, 1972-1973; President, 1976-1977) Beverly Hills, and American Bar Associations; State Bar of California (Member, Sections on: Business Law; Estate Planning, Trust and Probate). (Certified Specialist, Estate Planning, Trust and Probate Law, The State Bar of California Board of Legal Specialization). *PRACTICE AREAS:* Probate, Estate Planning and Trust Law; Residential Real Property.

**MARILYN S. PECSOK,** born Cleveland, Ohio, April 8, 1940; admitted to bar, 1983, California. *Education:* Tulane University; Case Western Reserve University (B.B.A., magna cum laude, 1962); University of California at Los Angeles (J.D., 1983). Beta Gamma Sigma. Albert James Award for highest scholarship in Banking and Finance. Licensed Real Estate Broker, California, 1980. Member, Citizens Advisory Commission, XXIII Olympiad, 1983-1984. Member, Board of Directors, UCLA Law Alumni Association, 1986-1988. *Member:* Beverly Hills, Santa Monica (Chairman, Family Law Section) and Los Angeles County (Member, Family Law Section) Bar Associations; State Bar of California (Member, Family Law Section). *PRACTICE AREAS:* Family Law.

REFERENCES: Bank of America; Santa Monica Bank; Wells Fargo Bank.

---

## BERMAN & WEISS
*73-710 FRED WARING DRIVE, SUITE 100*
**PALM DESERT, CALIFORNIA 92260**
*Telephone: 619-773-6677*
*Fax: 619-346-7779*
*Email: rw1224@aol.com*
*URL: http://www.lawinfo.com/law/ca/berman.html*

*Encino, California Office:* 16055 Ventura Boulevard, Suite 900, 91436. Telephone: 818-986-8000. Facsimile: 818-986-3162.

*Palm Springs, California Office:* 1111 Tahquitz Canyon Way, Suite 203, 92262. Telephone: 619-327-1777. Fax: 619-346-7779.

Personal Injury, Products Liability, Medical and Legal Malpractice, Insurance and Bad Faith Law, Aviation Law, Construction Accidents.

*FIRM PROFILE:* Achieved first California verdict in an AIDS-related blood transfusion case resulting in a $3.1 million verdict versus defendant doctors and hospital with a confidential settlement with the blood bank. Successfully represented 35 plaintiffs in the Palomar fire litigation, resulting in a seven figure verdict. Settlements and verdicts in excess of sixty million dollars, including the largest compensation settlement ($3.74 million present value) in California history. Recognized by the California Trial Lawyers Association as experienced Trial Lawyers. Charter member of the International Society of Primerus Law Firms. The Law firm is listed in the Martindale-Hubbell Bar Register of Preeminent Lawyers under Personal Injury and Medical Malpractice.

### MEMBERS OF FIRM

**RICHARD B. WEISS,** born Schenectady, New York, September 26, 1954; admitted to bar, 1982, California; 1983, U.S. District Court, Central District of California and U.S. Court of Appeals, Ninth Circuit. *Education:* University of Dayton (B.A., 1976); Northrop University (J.D., cum laude, 1981). Phi Delta Phi. Editor-in-Chief, Northrop University Law Review. Recipient, California Trial Lawyers Association Presidential Award for 1988. Speaker: "Handling Third-Party Liens," NME Medical Care Conference, December 1990; "Big Case: Small Firm; Handling Complex Litigation with Limited Resources," Kentucky Academy of Trial Attorneys, May 1991; "Motorcycle Accident Litigation," Los Angeles Trial Lawyers Association, April 1991; "Winning the Tough Liability Case Through Accident Reconstruction," California Trial Lawyers Association Litigation Techniques Seminar, March 1992; "Expediting Access to Life Saving Therapies for AIDS, Cancer and Alzheimer's Patients," April 1992; "How to Present Special Damages Without High Priced Experts," California Trial Lawyers Association Litigation Techniques Seminar, June 1992; Arguing the Intangibles: Pain, Suffering and Emotional Distress," California Trial Lawyers Association Litigation Techniques Seminar, July 1992; "Persuasive Presentation of Damages at Arbitration," California Trial Lawyers Association Litigation Techniques Seminar, July 1992; October 1993, "Winning The Construction Accident Case With Your Investigation," Annual Conference; November 1994, "Building a Successful Attorney Network," International Society of Primerus Attorneys Annual Convention. Author: "Big Case: Small Firm," Kentucky Trial Academy of Trial Attorneys, May 1992; California Litigation Techniques, "Arguing the Law of Damages: BAJI Brought to Life," May 1993; California Litigation Techniques," Complex Litigation for the Small Firm, October, 1993; National Association of Investigations; "Voir Dire: Magic or Mathematics?" Orange County Trial Lawyers Association, October 1996. *Member:* State Bar of California; The Association of Trial Lawyers of America; California Trial Lawyers Association (Member, Board of Governors, 1990—; Chair/Moderator, Damages Seminar, July 1992; State Chair, "Complex Litigation for the Small Firm," Litigation Techniques Seminar, October 1993; Chair: Legislative Review Sub-Committee, 1991—; Mandatory Continuing Legal Education Program Committee, 1992—; Mandatory Continuing Legal Education Standing Committees on Program and Syllabus; Member, Amicus Curiae Committee); Palm Springs Trial Lawyers Association (President, 1991-1992); Orange County Trial Lawyers Association (Chair/Moderator, Modern Voir Dire Techniques, October 1996). *PRACTICE AREAS:* Construction Accident Law; Product Liability Law; Personal Injury Law; Medical Malpractice Law.

**MARTIN M. BERMAN,** born Los Angeles, California, December 24, 1934; admitted to bar, 1963, California. *Education:* University of Southern California (B.S.Ch.E., 1957; LL.B., 1962). Speaker: "Litigation Involving Blood Transfusions," Association of Trial Lawyers of America National College of Advocacy, October 1991; "Standard of Care for Blood Banks in AIDS Litigation," Association of Trial Lawyers of America National Trial Advocacy Seminar, July 1992; "Liability of Blood Banks: Post Elisa," Association of Trial Lawyers of America Trial Advocacy Seminar, July 1992. *Member:* Los Angeles County Bar Association; State Bar of California; Los Angeles Trial Lawyers Association; California Trial Lawyers Association; The Association of Trial Lawyers of America (Vice-Chairman; Chairman, AIDS Litigation Section). *PRACTICE AREAS:* Medical Malpractice Law; Products Liability Law; Personal Injury Law; Aviation Law.

---

## DONALD M. BOLAS
*44712 MONTEREY AVENUE*
**PALM DESERT, CALIFORNIA 92260**
*Telephone: 619-568-0675*

Family Law, Workers Compensation, Personal Injury.

**DONALD M. BOLAS,** born Northampton, Pennsylvania, May 8, 1942; admitted to bar, 1967, Pennsylvania; 1968, District of Columbia and U.S. Court of Appeals for the District of Columbia Circuit; 1971, California and U.S. Supreme Court; 1971, U.S. Court of Military Appeals. *Education:* The Citadel (B.A., 1964); Dickinson School of Law (J.D., 1967); George Washington University Law Center (LL.M., 1974). Phi Alpha Delta. Author:

*(This Listing Continued)*

## DONALD M. BOLAS, Palm Desert—Continued

"Eugenic Sterilization in California: An Anachronism in 1973?", California Trial Lawyers Association Journal, Fall 1974 at 71; "No-Fault Divorce: Born In The Soviet Union?", 14 Journal of Family Law 31. Attorney, Office of the General Counsel, Federal Communications Commission, 1972-1974. *Member:* The District of Columbia Bar; Desert and Pennsylvania Bar Associations; State Bar of California; Consumer Attorneys of California; California Applicant Attorneys Association. [Capt., Judge Advocate General's Department, USAF, 1968-1971]. *LANGUAGES:* Czech.

## LAW OFFICES OF VIRGINIA S. CRISTE

74-075 EL PASEO, SUITE A-14
**PALM DESERT, CALIFORNIA 92260**
Telephone: 619-776-1770
Fax: 619-776-1775

*Family Law and Bankruptcy Reorganization.*

**VIRGINIA S. CRISTE,** born Chicago, Illinois, February 7, 1944; admitted to bar, 1969, District of Columbia; 1971, Maryland and U.S. District Court, District of Maryland; 1976, Pennsylvania; 1977, California; 1978, U.S. District Court, Middle District of Pennsylvania; 1980, U.S. District Court, Central District of California and U.S. Court of Appeals, Ninth Circuit. *Education:* Mt. Holyoke College (B.A., 1966); George Washington University (J.D., 1969). *Member:* Desert (President, 1995-1996), Maryland State and Pennsylvania Bar Associations; State Bar of California; District of Columbia Bar. *LANGUAGES:* Spanish, French and German. *PRACTICE AREAS:* Family Law; Bankruptcy Law.

## CRISTE, PIPPIN & GOLDS

SUITE 200
73-550 ALESSANDRO DRIVE
**PALM DESERT, CALIFORNIA 92260**
Telephone: 619-862-1111
Fax: 619-776-4197
Email: cpgca@aol.com

*Civil Litigation and Business Law Practice, including Real Estate and Business Transactions, Bankruptcy, Business Reorganizations, Real Property and Construction Litigation. Trial, Appellate and Extraordinary Writ Practice.*

FIRM PROFILE: *Transactional/Litigation focused on business, commercial and real estate law. The firm takes pride in being listed in the Martindale-Hubbell Bar Register of Preeminent Lawyers.*

### MEMBERS OF FIRM

**MICHAEL A. CRISTE,** born 1943; admitted to bar, 1979, California. *Education:* University of Maryland (B.S.C.E., cum laude, 1973); University of Maryland (M.B.A., 1974) Dickinson School of Law (J.D., 1979). *Member:* State Bar of California. *PRACTICE AREAS:* Business Law; Real Estate. *Email:* cpgca@aol.com

**ROBERT L. PIPPIN,** born 1941; admitted to bar, 1967, California. *Education:* State University of San Diego (B.A., 1964); University of California, Boalt Hall School of Law (J.D., 1967). *Member:* State Bar of California. *PRACTICE AREAS:* Civil Litigation; Bankruptcy Law; Business Law; Construction Law. *Email:* cpgca@aol.com

**IRWIN L. GOLDS,** born Fort Ord, California, March 18, 1956; admitted to bar, 1981, California. *Education:* University of California at Los Angeles (B.A., 1978); Hastings College of Law, University of California (J.D., 1981). Associate Executive Editor, Comment Communications and Entertainment Law Journal, 1980-1981. *Member:* Desert and Riverside County Bar Associations; The State Bar of California. *PRACTICE AREAS:* Real Estate Law; Business Law. *Email:* cpgca@aol.com

### ASSOCIATES

**MARIE A. BOCHNEWICH,** born San Diego, California, July 26, 1961; admitted to bar, 1993, California. *Education:* San Diego State University (B.S., Bus. Adm., 1985); California Western School of Law (J.D., cum laude, 1993). Staff Editor, California Western Law Review, 1992-1993. Judicial Extern to the Honorable David R. Thompson, 9th Circuit Court of Appeals, 1993. *Member:* Desert Bar Association; State Bar of California. *PRACTICE AREAS:* Civil Litigation. *Email:* cpgca@aol.com

## STEVEN J. DEDINA

74-090 EL PASEO, SECOND FLOOR
**PALM DESERT, CALIFORNIA 92260**
Telephone: 619-320-2500
Fax: 619-341-3635

*Real Estate, Business Law and General Civil Litigation.*

**STEVEN J. DEDINA,** born San Francisco, California, May 22, 1967; admitted to bar, 1993, California. *Education:* Chapman College (B.S., B.A., 1990); University of San Francisco (J.D., 1993). *Member:* State Bar of California. *PRACTICE AREAS:* Real Estate; Business Law; Civil Litigation.

## FIORE, WALKER, RACOBS & POWERS

A PROFESSIONAL LAW CORPORATION
74-361 HIGHWAY III, SUITE 1
**PALM DESERT, CALIFORNIA 92261-4250**
Telephone: 619-776-6511
Fax: 619-776-6517

*Irvine, California Office:* Koll Center Irvine. 18400 Von Karmen, Suite 600. 92612-1514. Telephone: 714-955-0560. Fax: 714-955-2894.

*Riverside, California Office:* 6670 Alessandro, Suite B. Telephone: 909-789-8100. Fax: 909-789-8105.

*Community Association, Real Property, Civil Litigation, Construction and Business.*

FIRM PROFILE: *Fiore, Walker, Racobs & Powers, A Professional Law Corporation, has been in existence since August, 1972, and has established the practice of law in the fields of community association law, real property and civil litigation.*

*Our mission is to: Provide quality legal services to our clients; set a positive example for the legal profession; contribute to the continuing success of community associations through education, legislation and legal services.*

**PETER E. RACOBS,** born Lucerne Valley, California, November 4, 1957; admitted to bar, 1983, California. *Education:* University of California at Riverside (B.A., 1979); University of California at Davis (J.D., 1983). Member, Moot Court Board. *Member:* Orange County and American Bar Associations; The State Bar of California; Orange County Barristers.

**MARGARET G. WANGLER,** born Missoula, Montana, March 24, 1950; admitted to bar, 1986, Michigan; 1988 California. *Education:* University of Iowa (B.A., 1976); Thomas M. Cooley Law School (J.D., cum laude, 1986).

(For Complete Biographical Data on all Personnel, see Professional Biographies at Irvine, California)

## DAVID M. FRANKLIN

74-075 EL PASEO, SUITE A-6
**PALM DESERT, CALIFORNIA 92261-3253**
Telephone: 619-568-1585

*Practice limited to Family Law and Business Litigation.*

**DAVID M. FRANKLIN,** born New York, N.Y., November 21, 1940; admitted to bar, 1975, California. *Education:* Western State University (B.S., 1972; J.D., 1975); California Judicial College. Judge Pro Tem, Superior Court, Indio, California, 1990-1996. Family Law Commissioner, Indio Superior Court, 1986-1990. Fellow, American Academy of Matrimonial Lawyers. *Member:* Desert (Member, Section on Family Law) and American (Member, Section on Family Law) Bar Associations; State Bar of California; Association of Family and Conciliation Courts; Association of Certified Family Law Specialists; California Judges Association (Member, Family Law Committee, 1988-1990). [With USMC, 1958-1968; USMCR, 1968-1986]. (Certified Specialist, Family Law, The State Bar of California Board of Legal Specialization).

## GALTON & HELM

SUITE 377
73-290 EL PASEO
**PALM DESERT, CALIFORNIA 92260**
Telephone: 619-776-5600
Fax: 619-776-5602

*Los Angeles, California Office:* 500 South Grand Avenue, Suite 1200. 213-629-8800. Fax: 213-629-0037.

*Civil Litigation Practice in State and Federal Courts. Insurance Defense. (Life, Accident and Health, Bad Faith Defense, Professional Negligence, Reinsurance Law and ERISA).*

*FIRM PROFILE: The firm of Galton & Helm is engaged in a specialized legal practice involving life, accident and health, and disability insurance law, including the representation of insurers in "bad faith" and ERISA litigation. The firm's practice also includes the representation of insurance brokers and other professionals in professional negligence litigation. All attorneys in the firm are active in professional and civil endeavors related to our clients' interest. The firm of Galton & Helm maintains a commitment to provide the highest quality of legal service to its clients, at rates which are fair. Listed in Best's Directory of Recommended Insurance Attorneys, The Insurance Bar, Hines Insurance Counsel and American Insurance Attorneys.*

### MEMBERS OF FIRM

**DANIEL W. MAGUIRE,** born New York, N.Y., August 31, 1960; admitted to bar, 1985, California. *Education:* University of Notre Dame (B.A., 1981); Pepperdine University (J.D., cum laude, 1985). Student Director, Clinical Law, National Moot Court Team. *Member:* Wilshire, Los Angeles County (Member, Appellate Courts Committee, 1986—) and American Bar Associations; State Bar of California; Supreme Court of The United States; Los Angeles Public Counsel. **PRACTICE AREAS:** Civil Litigation.

REPRESENTATIVE CLIENTS: A.I.G. Life Insurance Co.; Aetna Life Insurance Co.; Alexander & Alexander; American Home Assurance Co.; American General Group; American Republic Insurance Co.; Amex Life Assurance Co.; Banner Life Insurance Co.; Benefit Trust Life Insurance Co.; Blue Cross of California; Celtic Life Insurance Co.; CIGNA Cos.; Cologne Life Reinsurance Co.; Fidelity Mutual Life Insurance Co.; General Americans Life Insurance Co.; Great American Reserve Insurance Co.; The Guardian Life Insurance Company of America; Hartford Life and Accident Insurance Co.; Home Insurance Co.; J.C. Penney Life Insurance Co.; Lone Star Life Insurance Co.; Massachusetts Casualty Insurance Co.; The Mutual Benefit Life Insurance Co. of New Jersey; Mutual of Omaha Insurance Co.; The Paul Revere Life Insurance Co.; Provident Life and Accident Insurance Co.; Royal Maccabees Life Insurance Co.; Sovereign Life Insurance Co.; State Farm Life Insurance Co.; Standard Insurance Co.; Standard Security Life Insurance Company of New York; Transport Life Insurance Co.; United American Insurance Co.; United Insurance Cos.; U.S. Life Insurance Co.

(For complete biographical data on all personnel, see Professional Biographies at Los Angeles, California)

## DALE S. GRIBOW

A PROFESSIONAL CORPORATION
43-585 MONTEREY AVENUE
**PALM DESERT, CALIFORNIA 92260**
Telephone: 619-341-4411
Fax: 619-773-3636

*Los Angeles (Century City), California Office:* 1925 Century Park East, Suite 2250. Telephone: 310-273-DALE. Fax: 310-203-0140.

*Civil and Criminal Litigation, General Business and Real Estate Law, Personal Injury, Medical and Legal Malpractice, Estate Planning and Airplane Accidents.*

**DALE S. GRIBOW,** born Chicago, Illinois, June 18, 1943; admitted to bar, 1969, California; 1974, U.S. District Court, Central District of California; 1977, U.S. Supreme Court; 1983, U.S. Tax Court. *Education:* University of Southern California (B.A., 1965); Loyola University of Los Angeles (J.D., 1968); University of Southern California and University of California at Los Angeles. Phi Alpha Delta; Blue Key. Legion Lex. Recipient: "Man of the Year Award, American Biological Institute, 1990, 1993, City of Hope, 1992. Author: "Facts of Law," Los Angeles Herald Examiner and Santa Monica Evening Outlook, 1988; "One Toke Away," Single Life Magazine, 1975; "You and the Law," weekly legal column, Los Angeles Herald Examiner and Santa Monica Evening Outlook. "Accidentally-Yours", Weekly Legal Column, Century City News and Beverly Hills Today, 1991. Guest Lecturer on Law: University of West Los Angeles, 1977-1979. Invited Guest Lecturer, California Trial Lawyers Association Convention, 1990.

*(This Listing Continued)*

Member: Faculty and Guest Lecturer, International College of Surgeons, 1989—; Co-Chair, Symposium to Doctors and Attorney's Update on the Management of Back Pain and Back Injury, 1993. Listed in "Who's Who in American Law." Radio Talk Show Host "Accidentally-Yours," 1991-1992. Legal Analyst, O.J. Simpson Trial, KESQ (ABC-TV). *Member:* Beverly Hills, Desert, Century City, San Fernando Valley, Riverside, Los Angeles County (Member, Litigation Section) and American (Member, Litigation and Tort Sections) Bar Associations; State Bar of California; The Association of Trial lawyers of America; California Trial Lawyers Association (Presidents Club; Recipient, Outstanding Achievement Award, 1990 and 1991); Los Angeles Trial Lawyers Association; San Fernando Valley Criminal Courts Bar Association; Los Angeles Criminal Courts Bar Association; California Attorneys for Criminal Justice; National Network of Estate Planning Attorneys. **LANGUAGES:** Spanish.

## HEALEY & HEALEY

Established in 1970
74075 EL PASEO AVENUE, SUITE A-15
P.O. BOX 3366
**PALM DESERT, CALIFORNIA 92261-3366**
Telephone: 619-341-8366
Fax: 619-341-4967
Email: LAWDJH@AOL.COM

*Estate Planning, Probate, Wills and Trusts, Elder Law, Real Estate, Personal Injury and General Business.*

### MEMBERS OF FIRM

**JAMES P. HEALEY,** born San Francisco, California, August 27, 1911; admitted to bar, 1936, California; 1957, U.S. Supreme Court and U.S. Court of Military Appeals. *Education:* University of California at Berkeley (B.S., 1933); Hastings College of Law, University of California (J.D., 1936). Phi Delta Phi. *Member:* Desert, Riverside County and American Bar Associations; State Bar of California. [Col., U.S. Army, Ret., 1943-1967]. **PRACTICE AREAS:** Estate Planning; Probate; Wills and Trusts.

**DENNIS J. HEALEY,** born Hollywood, California, July 4, 1944; admitted to bar, 1969, Texas; 1970, California; 1977, U.S. Tax Court and U.S. Court of Customs and Patent Appeals. *Education:* University of Texas (B.A., 1966); St. Mary's University (J.D., 1969). Phi Delta Phi. President, Desert Estate Planning Council, 1980-1981. President, Palm Desert Rotary, 1983-1984. *Member:* Desert (Member, Board of Trustees, 1975-1976; Treasurer, 1976-1977; Secretary, 1977-1978; President, 1979-1980), Riverside County and American Bar Associations; State Bar of Texas; State Bar of California. **PRACTICE AREAS:** Probate and Estate Planning; Wills and Trusts; Elder Law; Real Estate; Personal Injury Law.

### ASSOCIATES

**ROBERT H. STEMPLER,** born New York, N.Y., December 27, 1962; admitted to bar, 1992, California. *Education:* Claremont McKenna College (B.A., 1984); McGeorge School of Law (J.D., 1992). Member, McGeorge Federalist Society (President, 1991-1992). Certified Public Accountant, California, 1987. Author, Co-Author and Editor, Selected Chapters: "An Attorney's Guide To Planning For Long Term Care In California," Legal Center for the Elderly and Disabled, 1992; "Costa Rica: A Nirvana For Export Manufacturers?" Transnational Lawyer, 1991. *Member:* American Bar Association; State Bar of California. **PRACTICE AREAS:** Estate Planning; Civil Litigation; Wrongful Termination.

## HINCHY, WITTE, WOOD, ANDERSON & HODGES

A LAW CORPORATION
Established in 1965
74-010 EL PASEO, SUITE 200
**PALM DESERT, CALIFORNIA 92260**
Telephone: 619-779-8569
Fax: 619-568-6175

*Rancho Bernardo, California Office:* 11440 West Bernardo Court, Suite 280. Telephone: 619-487-7948; 586-7696. FAX: 619-487-2177.
*Irvine, California Office:* 2030 Main Street, Suite 1300. Telephone: 714-260-4710. FAX: 714-260-4711.
*San Diego, California Office:* 525 B Street, Suite 1500. Telephone: 619-239-1901. FAX: 619-696-0555.

*(This Listing Continued)*

**HINCHY, WITTE, WOOD, ANDERSON & HODGES,** A LAW CORPORATION, Palm Desert—Continued

General Civil Litigation, General Commercial, including Corporations, Limited Liability Companies, Partnerships and Taxation; Real Estate, Estate Planning and Probate; Financial Institutions, Mortgage Banking, Collection, Bankruptcy, Family Law, Labor Relations and Employment Law and Related Litigation, Agricultural Labor Relations, Employee Stock Ownership Plans (ESOPs), ERISA, Pension and Profit Sharing, Employee Benefits Law and Litigation.

Gayle F. Anderson

REFERENCE: Scripps Bank.

(For complete Biographical Data on all Personnel see Professional Biographies at San Diego, California)

---

## JEAN ANN HIRSCHI

74-075 EL PASEO, SUITE A-5
**PALM DESERT, CALIFORNIA 92260**
Telephone: 619-568-5661
Fax: 619-568-5668

*Estate Planning and Probate.*

**JEAN ANN HIRSCHI,** born Wichita Falls, Texas, June 25, 1931; admitted to bar, 1958, California. *Education:* University of California at Los Angeles (B.A., 1954; J.D., 1957). Recipient, Golden Plate Award, American Academy of Achievement, 1970. *Member:* Desert (Member, Board of Trustees, 1971-1975; President, 1974-1975) Bar Association; State Bar of California. **PRACTICE AREAS:** Estate Planning; Wills; Trusts; Probate; Conservatorship.

---

## MARC S. HOMME

A PROFESSIONAL LAW CORPORATION

Established in 1977

74-361 HIGHWAY 111, SUITE 1
**PALM DESERT, CALIFORNIA 92260**
Telephone: 760-568-5694
Facsimile: 760-568-1324

General Civil and Trial Practice. Business, Construction and Commercial Litigation. Banking, Real Estate, Estate Planning, Corporate and Partnership Law. Business and Commercial Litigation.

**MARC S. HOMME,** born Bismarck, North Dakota, October 7, 1949; admitted to bar, 1974, California and U.S. District Court, Central District of California; 1975, U.S. District Court, Southern District of California; 1979, U.S. Supreme Court; Interstate Commerce Commission. *Education:* College of the Desert; University of Colorado at Boulder (B.A., with distinction, 1971); Loyola Law School (J.D., 1974). Phi Beta Kappa. Instructor: Business Law, College of the Desert, 1983; Paralegal Course, Chapman College, 1984. Member: Interstate Commerce Commission, 1979; Advisory Board, California State University, San Bernardino. *Member:* Desert Bar Association; State Bar of California; Desert Contractors Association (Member, Board of Directors).

REPRESENTATIVE CLIENTS: Mark Avriette Drywall; Breeze Air Conditioning; RPM Graphics; Cove Electric; Palm Desert National Bank; Prentice Hall; Affiliated Construction; System Electric; Hayhoe Construction; C.A. Rasmussen, Inc.; C & M Building Materials; Dependable Roofing; 1st Bank; Mercedes Benz of North America; A.C. Houston Lumber; Vectra Bank; Champion Mitsubishi; E.G. Williams Development Corporation; Guy Evans, Inc.; California Turf; Sunterrace Development; Costa Mesa Mitsubishi.
REFERENCES: Palm Desert National Bank; System Electric; Cove Electric; Champion Mitsubishi; 1st Bank; Affiliated Construction; California Turf.

---

## RICHARD C. HOUGHTON

74-075 EL PASEO, SUITE A14
**PALM DESERT, CALIFORNIA 92260**
Telephone: 619-773-4044
Fax: 619-776-1775
Email: houghtonr@earthlink.net

*Family Law.*

**RICHARD C. HOUGHTON,** born Philadelphia, Pennsylvania, March 22, 1947; admitted to bar, 1974, Massachusetts; 1975, Oregon; 1985, California. *Education:* University of Oregon (B.A., 1969; J.D., 1973). *Member:* Desert (Member, Family Law Committee), Riverside County (Member, Section on Family Law) and Massachusetts Bar Associations; Oregon State Bar; The State Bar of California (Member, Section on Family Law). (Certified Specialist, Family Law, The State Bar of California Board of Legal Specialization). **LANGUAGES:** Italian. **PRACTICE AREAS:** Family Law; Civil Litigation.

---

## NADINE K. QUINN

74-361 HIGHWAY 111, SUITE 1
**PALM DESERT, CALIFORNIA 92260**
Telephone: 619-346-0445
Fax: 619-341-7374

*Estate Planning, Probate, Probate Administration, Estate Administration, Family Trusts and Contested Trusts and Estates.*

**NADINE K. QUINN,** born Little Falls, New York, October 6, 1937; admitted to bar, 1989, California. *Education:* California State University (B.A., 1982; M.A., 1984); Western State University (J.D., President's Scholar, 1988). Member: Advisory Board, Desert CPA/Law Forum, 1994—; Desert Estate Planning Council, 1994, 1996. *Member:* Riverside, Desert and American Bar Associations; State Bar of California (Member, Estate Planning, Trust and Probate Law Section). **PRACTICE AREAS:** Estate Planning; Probate; Probate Administration; Estate Administration; Family Trusts; Contested Trusts and Estates.

---

## QUINN EMANUEL URQUHART & OLIVER, LLP

74-090 EL PASEO, SUITE 101
**PALM DESERT, CALIFORNIA 92260**
Telephone: 619-340-2276
Telecopier: 619-346-1368

Los Angeles, California Office: 865 South Figueroa Street, 10th Floor. Telephone: 213-624-7707. Telecopier: 213-624-0643.

Business Litigation and Trial Practice, including Antitrust; Banking; Construction; Copyright, Trademark and Patent Litigation; Employment; ERISA; Government Contracts; Health Care; Intellectual Property; Product Liability; Real Estate; Securities; Unfair Competition; White Collar Crime.

### MEMBERS OF FIRM

**JOHN B. QUINN,** born Ft. Belvoir, Virginia, June 20, 1951; admitted to bar, 1978, New York; 1979, California. *Education:* Claremont Men's College (B.A., magna cum laude, 1973); Harvard University (J.D., cum laude, 1976). Editor, Harvard Law Review, 1974-1976. Knox Fellow, Harvard University, 1976-1977. Instructor in Law, J. Reuben Clark School of Law, 1977. Lecturer on Federal Practice, California Continuing Education of the Bar. Associate, Cravath, Swaine & Moore, New York, NY, 1976-1979. General Counsel, Academy of Motion Picture Arts and Sciences, 1987—. Named "One of the Top 3 Trial Lawyers of Choice by General Counsel in California" by California Law Business, 1994. Named "One of the Top 15 Litigators in California" by The Los Angeles Daily Journal, 1995. Selected as "One of the Top 45 Lawyers Under the Age of 45 in the United States" by The American Lawyer, 1995. *Member:* Los Angeles County (Member, Federal Courts and Practices Committee) and American (Member, Sections on: Corporation, Banking and Business Law; Litigation; Patent, Trademark and Copyright Law; Member, Forum Committees on: Health Law; Construction Industry) Bar Associations; State Bar of California (Member, Committee on Federal Courts). (Also at Los Angeles Office). *REPORTED CASES:* Ficalora v. Lockheed Corp., 193 Cal. App. 3d 489 (1987); America's Cup Properties, Inc. v. America's Cup Club, Inc., 8 U.S.P.Q. 2d (BNA) 2025 (1988); Academy of Motion Picture Arts and Sciences v. Creative House Promotions, Inc., 944 F.2d 1446 (9th Cir. 1991)

*(This Listing Continued)*

and 728 F. Supp. 1442 (C.D. Cal. 1989); Cinemateca Uruguaya v. Academy of Motion Picture Arts and Sciences, 826 F.Supp.323 (C.D. Cal. 1993). *PRACTICE AREAS:* Employment; Intellectual Property; Unfair Competition; Real Estate; General Commercial Litigation; General Trial Practice. *Email:* jquinn05@counsel.com

DAVID W. QUINTO, born New York, New York, June 11, 1955; admitted to bar, 1982, California; 1983, Arizona. *Education:* Amherst College (B.A., magna cum laude, 1977); Harvard University (J.D., 1982). *Member:* Los Angeles County and American Bar Associations; State Bar of California; State Bar of Arizona; Los Angeles Intellectual Property Lawyers. (Also at Los Angeles Office). *LANGUAGES:* Spanish. *REPORTED CASES:* Quinto v. Legal Times of Washington, Inc., 506 F. Supp. 554 and 511 F. Supp. 579 (1981); Ficalora v. Lockheed Corp., 193 Cal. App. 3d 489 (1987); America's Cup Properties, Inc. v. America's Cup Club, Inc., 8 U.S.P.Q. 2d (BNA) 2025 (1988); Academy of Motion Picture Arts and Sciences v. Creative House Promotions, Inc., 944 F.2d 1446 (9th Cir. 1991) and 728 F. Supp. 1442 (C.D. Cal. 1989); Cinemateca Uruguaya v. Academy of Motion Pictures Arts and Sciences, 826 F.Supp. 323 (C.D. Cal. 1993); Florentine Art Studio v. Vedet K Corp., 891 F. Supp. 532 (C.D. Cal. 1995). *PRACTICE AREAS:* Copyright and Trademark; Real Property Litigation.

### ASSOCIATES

HAROLD W. HOPP, born Takoma Park, Maryland, March 25, 1960; admitted to bar, 1986, California. *Education:* Pacific Union College (B.S., 1983); University of Southern California (J.D., 1986). Staff Editor, 1984-1985, Articles Editor, 1985-1986, Southern California Law Review. *Member:* Desert and American Bar Associations; State Bar of California. (Resident).

SAMUEL BROOKS SHEPHERD, born New Haven, Connecticut, January 25, 1966; admitted to bar, 1992, California. *Education:* Bowdoin College (B.A., summa cum laude, 1988); University of Chicago (J.D., M.B.A., 1992). Phi Beta Kappa. Recipient: University of Chicago Business Fellow; Jefferson Davis Award; James Bowdoin Cup; Pray English Prize; Nixon Class of 1868 Prize; James Bowdoin Collection Scholar; Shakespeare Prize. *Member:* State Bar of California. (Also at Los Angeles Office).

REPRESENTATIVE CLIENTS: Academy of Motion Picture Arts and Sciences; Avery Dennison; Bank of America; California Institute of Technology; Computer Sciences Corp.; Countrywide Credit; Federal Home Mortgage Corp.; General Motors Corporation; GranCare, Inc.; H.F. Ahmanson & Co.; Hughes Aircraft Company; Johnson Controls, Inc.; Litton Industries, Inc.; Lockheed Martin Corp.; Lewis Homes; Maguire Thomas Partners; Marriott Corp.; Mattel, Inc.; Northrop Grumman Corp.; The Parsons Corporation; Sizzler International, Inc.; Teledyne, Inc.; Texaco, Inc.; Ticket Master, Inc.; Toyota Motor Sales, U.S.A., Inc.; TRW, Inc.; WMX Technologies, Inc.
REFERENCE: Bank of California.

(For complete biographical data on all personnel, see Professional Biographies at Los Angeles)

---

## SHERNOFF, BIDART & DARRAS

A Partnership including Professional Corporations

**73-111 EL PASEO, SUITE 208
PALM DESERT, CALIFORNIA 92260**
Telephone: 619-568-9944

Claremont, California Office: 600 South Indian Hill Boulevard. Telephone: 909-621-4935. Fax: 909-625-6915.
Laguna Beach, California Office: 130 Cleo Street. Telephone: 714-494-6714. Fax: 714-497-0825.

*Practice Limited to Plaintiff's Insurance Bad Faith, Automobile Insurance, Fire Insurance, Commercial Liability Insurance, Homeowners Insurance, Accident and Health Insurance, Catastrophic Personal Injury, Wrongful Death, Wrongful Termination, Lender's Liability and Consumer Law Litigation.*

### MEMBER OF FIRM

WILLIAM M. SHERNOFF, (P.C.), born Chicago, Illinois, October 26, 1937; admitted to bar, 1962, Wisconsin; 1966, California. *Education:* University of Miami (B.B.A., 1959); University of Wisconsin (J.D., 1962). Co-Author: Legal Treatise, "Insurance Bad Faith Litigation," published by Matthew Bender, 1984; "How to Make Insurance Companies Pay Your Claims and What to do if They Don't," Hastings House, 1990. Author: "Payment Refused," published by Richardson & Steirman, 1986. *Member:* State Bar of California; Los Angeles Trial Lawyers Association (Trial Law-
*(This Listing Continued)*

---

yer of the Year, 1975); California Trial Lawyers Association (President, 1981); The Association of Trial Lawyers of America.

(For complete Biographical Data on all personnel, see Professional Biographies at Claremont, California).

---

## JAMES H. STEIN

**75-585 DEMPSEY DRIVE
PALM DESERT, CALIFORNIA 92211**
Telephone: 619-346-7773
Fax: 619-346-9812

*General Civil Litigation, Corporate, Real Estate, Probate and Estate Planning.*

JAMES H. STEIN, born Kansas City, Missouri, July 28, 1948; admitted to bar, 1974, Missouri and U.S. District Court, Western District of Missouri; 1976, California. *Education:* University of Missouri at Columbia (B.S., 1971); University of Missouri at Kansas City (J.D., 1974). *Member:* The Missouri Bar; State Bar of California; Desert Bar Association. [With U.S. Air Force, 1967-1973]

---

## THOMPSON & COLEGATE

**74-303 HIGHWAY III, SUITE 2-B
PALM DESERT, CALIFORNIA 92260**
Telephone: 619-773-1998
Fax: 619-773-9078

Riverside, California Office: 3610 Fourteenth Street, P.O. Box 1299, 92502. Telephone, 909-682-5550. Fax: 909-781-4012.

*General Civil and Trial Practice, Personal Injury Defense, Business Litigation, Construction, Medical Malpractice, Products Liability, Corporate, Estate Planning, Wills and Trusts, Probate, Insurance, Real Estate, Commercial, Education, Employment Law and Appellate Practice, Media-First Amendment Law and Bankruptcy.*

(For complete biographical data on all personnel, see Professional Biographies at Riverside)

---

## LAW OFFICE OF
## STEVEN J. WEINBERG

*Established in 1988*

**42-580 CAROLINE COURT, SUITE A
PALM DESERT, CALIFORNIA 92211**
Telephone: 619-346-0227
Facsimile: 619-346-8573

*Practice Limited to General Civil and Trial Practice in all State and Federal Courts. Aviation, Insurance, Medical Malpractice, Personal Injury, Products Liability, Negligence Law, Business Fraud.*

FIRM PROFILE: *The firm was founded in 1988, after Steven Weinberg terminated his association with his partner of the prior 11 years. The firm serves the entire State representing primarily victims of medical negligence. In addition to Mr. Weinberg, the firm is staffed by a paralegal and full time nurse consultant. Steven Weinberg is active in the California Trial Lawyers Association and the Western Trial Lawyers Association serving as an officer in both of those organizations. The firm encourages continuing professional education and development and is active in civic and community affairs with particular interest in youth sports activities.*

STEVEN J. WEINBERG, born Casa Grande, Arizona, July 3, 1950; admitted to bar, 1975, California. *Education:* University of California (B.A., 1972); Pepperdine University (J.D., 1975). Professor of Law, Civil Procedure, Cabrillo Pacific College of Law, 1975. *Member:* The State Bar of California; Los Angeles Trial Lawyers Association; California Trial Lawyers Association (Recognized expertise in the fields of Trial Law, General Personal Injury, Products Liability and Professional Negligence; Member, Board of Governors, 1981-1996; Financial Secretary, 1990-1991); The Association of Trial Lawyers of America (State Delegate, 1985-1987); Lawyer-Pilots Bar Association; Western Trial Lawyers Association (Member, Board of Governors, 1985-1988; Parliamentarian, 1989; Secretary, 1991; President, 1992; American Board of Trial Advocates (Associate). *LANGUAGES:* Spanish. *PRACTICE AREAS:* Medical Malpractice; Major Injury Tort Litigation.

## WILLIAMS AND BALLAS
### PALM DESERT, CALIFORNIA
(See Los Angeles)

*Estate Planning, Tax Planning, Probate and Corporate Law.*

---

## THOMAS T. ANDERSON, P.C.
### PALM SPRINGS, CALIFORNIA
(See Indio)

*Negligence Law, Highway Safety, Products Liability, Insurance Bad Faith, Legal Malpractice and Consumer Fraud.*

---

## BERMAN & WEISS
### 1111 TAHQUITZ CANYON WAY, SUITE 203
### PALM SPRINGS, CALIFORNIA 92262
Telephone: 619-773-6677
Fax: 619-327-1646
Email: rw1224@aol.com
URL: http://www.lawinfo.com//law/ca/berman.html

Encino, California Office: 16055 Ventura Boulevard, Suite 900, 91436.
Telephone: 818-986-8000. Facsimile: 818-986-3162.

Palm Desert, California Office: 74-040 Highway III, Suite L-204, 92260.
Telephone: 619-773-6677. Facsimile: 619-346-7779.

*Personal Injury, Products Liability, Medical and Legal Malpractice, Insurance and Bad Faith Law, Aviation Law, Construction Accidents.*

FIRM PROFILE: *Achieved first California verdict in an AIDS-related blood transfusion case resulting in a $3.1 million verdict versus defendant doctors and hospital with a confidential settlement with the blood bank. Successfully represented 35 plaintiffs in the Palomar fire litigation, resulting in a seven figure verdict. Settlements and verdicts in excess of sixty million dollars, including the largest compensation settlement ($3.74 million present value) in California history. Recognized by the California Trial Lawyers Association as experienced Trial Lawyers. Charter member of the International Society of Primerus Law Firms. The Law firm is listed in the Martindale-Hubbell Bar Register of Preeminent Lawyers under Personal Injury and Medical Malpractice.*

### MEMBERS OF FIRM

**RICHARD B. WEISS,** born Schenectady, New York, September 26, 1954; admitted to bar, 1982, California; 1983, U.S. District Court, Central District of California and U.S. Court of Appeals, Ninth Circuit. *Education:* University of Dayton (B.A., 1976); Northrop University (J.D., cum laude, 1981). Phi Delta Phi. Editor-in-Chief, Northrop University Law Review. Recipient, California Trial Lawyers Association Presidential Award for 1988. Speaker: "Handling Third-Party Liens," NME medical care Conference, December 1990; "Big Case: Small Firm; Handling Complex Litigation with Limited Resources," Kentucky Academy of Trial Attorneys, May 1991; "Motorcycle Accident Litigation," Los Angeles Trial Lawyers Association, April 1991; "Winning the Tough Liability Case Through Accident Reconstruction," California Trial Lawyers Association Litigation Techniques Seminar, March 1992; "Expediting Access to Life Saving Therapies for AIDS, Cancer and Alzheimer's Patients," April 1992; "How to Present Special Damages Without High Priced Experts," California Trial Lawyers Association Litigation Techniques Seminar, June 1992; Arguing the Intangibles: Pain, Suffering and Emotional Distress," California Trial Lawyers Association Litigation Techniques Seminar, July 1992; "Persuasive Presentation of Damages at Arbitration," California Trial Lawyers Association Litigation Techniques Seminar, July 1992; October 1993 "Winning The Construction Accident Case With Your Investigation," National Association of Investigators Annual Conference; November 1994 "Building a Successful Attorney Network," International Society of Primerus Attorneys Annual Convention. Author: "Big Case: Small Firm," Kentucky Trial Academy of Trial Attorneys, May 1992; California Litigation Techniques, "Arguing the Law of Damages: BAJI Brought to Life," May 1993. California Litigation Techniques," Complex Litigation for the Small Firm, October 1993; National Association of Investigators; "Voir Dire: Magic or Mathematics?" Orange County Trial Lawyers Association, October 1996. Member: State Bar of California; The Association of Trial Lawyers of America; California Trial Lawyers Association (Member, Board of Governors, 1990—; Chair/Moderator, Damages Seminar, July 1992; State Chair, "Complex Litigation for the Small Firm," Litigation Techniques Seminar, October 1993; Chair: Legislative Review Sub-Committee, 1991—; Mandatory Continuing Legal Education Program Committee, 1992—; Mandatory Continuing Legal Education Standing Committees on Program and Syllabus; Member, Amicus Curiae Committee); Palm Springs Trial Lawyers Association (President, 1991-1992); Orange County Trial Lawyers Association (Chair/Moderator, Modern Voir Dire Techniques, October 1996). *PRACTICE AREAS:* Construction Accident Law; Product Liability Law; Personal Injury Law; Medical Malpractice Law.

**MARTIN M. BERMAN,** born Los Angeles, California, December 24, 1934; admitted to bar, 1963, California. *Education:* University of Southern California (B.S.Ch.E., 1957; LL.B., 1962). Speaker: "Litigation Involving Blood Transfusions," Association of Trial Lawyers of America National College of Advocacy, October 1991; "Standard of Care for Blood Banks in AIDS Litigation," Association of Trial Lawyers of America National Trial Advocacy Seminar, July 1992; "Liability of Blood Banks: Post Elisa," Association of Trial Lawyers of America Trial Advocacy Seminar, July 1992. *Member:* Los Angeles County Bar Association; State Bar of California; Los Angeles Trial Lawyers Association; California Trial Lawyers Association; The Association of Trial Lawyers of America (Vice Chairman; Chairman, AIDS Litigation Section). *PRACTICE AREAS:* Medical Malpractice Law; Products Liability Law; Personal Injury Law; Aviation Law.

---

## LEONARD A. BOCK
### SUITE C-3
### 1900 TAHQUITZ CANYON WAY
### PALM SPRINGS, CALIFORNIA 92262-7024
Telephone: 619-325-9686

*General Civil Trial Practice. Business, Corporation, Real Estate, Probate, Family, Construction and Condominium Law.*

**LEONARD A. BOCK,** born Trenton, New Jersey, September 23, 1919; admitted to bar, 1951, California; 1953, U.S. District Court, Central District of California; 1965, U.S. District Court, Southern District of California. *Education:* University of California at Berkeley (A.B., 1940); New York University (J.D., 1948). *Member:* State Bar of California.

REPRESENTATIVE CLIENTS: Radio Stations KCMJ and KPSL; Palm Springs Lite Magazine; Whitewater Rock & Supply; Master Pools & Supplies; Frank Properties, Ltd and Palm Springs Opera Guild; Desert Publications, Inc.
REFERENCES: First Trust Bank; Bank of America National Trust and Savings Assn.

---

## GLEN R. BRADAK
*Established in 1968*
### 193 SOUTH CIVIC DRIVE, SUITE 6
### PALM SPRINGS, CALIFORNIA 92262
Telephone: 619-323-2648
Fax: 619-323-4755

*Criminal Law, D.U.I., White Collar Crime, Assault and Battery, Felonies and Misdemeanors.*

**GLEN R. BRADAK,** born Kemmerer, Wyoming, October 10, 1937; admitted to bar, 1962, Utah; 1964, California and U.S. District Court, Central District of California and District of Utah. *Education:* University of Utah (J.D., 1962). *Member:* Desert and Utah State Bar Associations; State Bar of California.

---

## ANTHONY C. CARONNA, P.C.
### PALM SPRINGS, CALIFORNIA
(See Rancho Mirage)

*Practice limited to General Civil and Trial Practice in all State and Federal Courts. Aviation, Insurance, Malpractice, Personal Injury, Products Liability, Negligence, Workers' Compensation.*

*(This Listing Continued)*

## LAW OFFICE OF BYRON G. CORNELIUS
### 225 SOUTH CIVIC DRIVE
### SUITE 1-3
### PALM SPRINGS, CALIFORNIA 92262
Telephone: 619-327-8119
Fax: 619-864-1285

General Civil and Trial Practice in all State and Federal Courts. Business Litigation, Personal Injury, Contract Law, and Probate.

FIRM PROFILE: Byron G. Cornelius would not disagree with the old notion about an ounce of prevention being worth a pound of cure in legal matters. Waiting until legal problems get out of hand before getting a lawyer's help is obviously not the answer. Mr. Cornelius has opened his practice to the citizens and businesses of Canada and is listed in the Martindale-Hubbell Canadian Law Directory.

**BYRON G. CORNELIUS,** born Tallahassee, Florida, November 8, 1951; admitted to bar, 1983, California; New South Wales, Australia. *Education:* Grossmont Community (A.A., 1980); Western State University at San Diego (J.D., 1982); University of Technology, Sidney, Australia, (Diploma in Legal Practice). *Member:* Riverside County Bar Association; State Bar of California; Association of Trial Lawyers of America.

REPRESENTATIVE CLIENTS: Dollsville Dolls & Bearsville Bears; Audio Village; Palm Spring Village Apartments; Desert Sunshine Reality; Desert Empire Mortgage Corporation.

---

## RUSSELL L. DAVIS
### PALM SPRINGS, CALIFORNIA
(See Indian Wells)

Federal and State Taxation, Tax Litigation and Tax Controversies, Estate Planning, Probate and Probate Litigation.

---

## DAUN ALINE DE VORE
### P.O. BOX 8987
### PALM SPRINGS, CALIFORNIA 92262
Telephone: 619-773-2257
Fax: 619-325-2732

Public and Private International Law. Litigation. State and Federal Appeals.

FIRM PROFILE: See International Law Directory for Comprehensive Biography.

**DAUN ALINE DE VORE,** born Fort Worth, Texas, August 1; admitted to bar, 1981, California; 1988, U.S. Court of International Trade and U.S. Court of Appeals, Ninth Circuit; U.S. Court of Appeals for the Federal Circuit; 1990, U.S. Court of Veterans Appeals. *Education:* University of Paris IV (Sorbonne), (Troisième Année License); University of California (B.A., magna cum laude, Philosophy, 1977); University of San Francisco (J.D., 1981); Harvard University (M.P.A., International Affairs and Security, 1983); Hastings School of Advanced Advocacy (Graduate, 1991); Oxford University. Member, International Institute of Strategic Studies (I.I.S.S.), London. *Member:* American Bar Association (Chair, International Law Committee, 1992—; Standing Committee Liaison to Foreign and International Bars, General Practice Section, 1992-1994; Chair, Asia/Pacific Subcommittee of the International Services Committee, International Law Section, 1990); State Bar of California;.

---

## C L FARRELL
### PALM SPRINGS, CALIFORNIA
(See Redlands)

Probate, Conservatorships, Guardianships, General Civil Trial Practice.

---

## FITZGERALD & ASSOCIATES
### 3001 TAHQUITZ CANYON WAY, SUITE 105
### PALM SPRINGS, CALIFORNIA 92262
Telephone: 619-325-5055
FAX: 619-327-9262

Employment Law, Wrongful Termination, Discrimination in all Courts.

FIRM PROFILE: FitzGerald & Associates represents businesses, employers and individuals in employment law, wrongful discharge and discrimination cases, from all aspects of counselling to jury trials. The Law firm takes pride in its listing in the Martindale-Hubbell Bar Register of Preeminent Lawyers. The firm is listed under Labor and Employment.

**JOHN E. FITZGERALD, III,** born Cambridge, Massachusetts, January 12, 1945; admitted to bar, 1975, Pennsylvania; 1978, New York; 1983, California; 1985, U.S. District Court, Central District of California and U.S. Court of Appeals, Ninth Circuit; 1991, U.S. Supreme Court. *Education:* United States Military Academy (B.S., Civil Eng., 1969); Wharton School and University of Pennsylvania Law School (J.D., M.P.A., 1975). Winner, American Bar Association Legal Essay Contest, 1975. Author: "How Employers Can Avoid Wrongful Discharge Lawsuits," 1988; "Federal & State Laws Affecting Employment Terminations," 1992; "Summary of Employment Law," 1993; Summary of Employers Questions and Answers," 1996, "California Employment Law- 1996", all published in The Public Record. Lecturer: CEB and CTLA, Seminars, 1990—. Judge Pro Tem, Palm Springs Municipal Court, 1984—. Member, Board of Governors and Vice Chairman, Desert Hospital Foundation, 1988—. Trustee, Freedoms Foundation at Valley Forge, 1987—. Member, Panel of Arbitrators, American Arbitration Association. *Member:* Desert (Trustee) and American (Member, Labor Law Committee) Bar Associations; The State Bar of California; The Association of Trial Lawyers of America; National Employment Lawyers Association. [Capt., U.S. Army, 1969-1972]. **PRACTICE AREAS:** Employment and Discrimination Law; Wrongful Discharge; Litigation.

---

**MORTON GOLLIN,** born Cleveland, Ohio; admitted to bar, 1949, Wisconsin; 1987, California. *Education:* University of Wisconsin (J.D., 1948).

REPRESENTATIVE CLIENTS: Armtec Defense Products; Desert Hospital; Association of California Hospital Districts; Eldorado Country Club; Palm Springs Savings Bank; Denny's; Desert Sun; Stratamerica, Inc.; Fantasy Springs Casino; KPSI; KWXY; KFRG; Smoke Tree Ranch.
REFERENCE: Palm Desert National Bank.

---

## FLETCHER & PATTON
### PALM SPRINGS, CALIFORNIA
(See Carlsbad)

Criminal Defense Litigation in all State and Federal Courts, Felonies and Misdemeanors, Drug Crimes, Violent Crimes, Theft, Sex Crimes, D.U.I. and Administrative Hearings.

---

## FURNESS, MIDDLEBROOK, KAISER & HIGGINS
### A PROFESSIONAL CORPORATION
### 3001 EAST TAHQUITZ CANYON WAY, SUITE 109
### PALM SPRINGS, CALIFORNIA 92262
Telephone: 619-322-0806
Fax: 619-322-8979

*San Bernardino, California Office:* 1411 North "D" Street, P.O. Box 1319. Telephone: 909-888-5751. Fax: 909-888-7360.

General Civil and Trial Practice. Personal Injury, Insurance and Government Law, Workers Compensation Subrogation, General Business and Construction Law.

**MICHAEL R. KAISER,** born Oxnard, California, December 1, 1951; admitted to bar, 1977, California, U.S. District Court, Central and Southern Districts of California and U.S. Tax Court. *Education:* Loma Linda University (B.S., 1973); University of San Diego (J.D., 1977). Recipient, American Jurisprudence Awards in Torts and Family Law. Member, San Diego Law Review, 1976-1977. Adjunct Professor of Trusts, Loma Linda School of Law, 1978. *Member:* Riverside County Bar Association; State Bar of California; Association of Southern California Defense Counsel. (Resi-

*(This Listing Continued)*

**FURNESS, MIDDLEBROOK, KAISER & HIGGINS,** A PROFESSIONAL CORPORATION, Palm Springs—Continued

dent). *PRACTICE AREAS:* Insurance Defense; Civil Trial; Business Litigation; Homeowners Association; Tort Litigation.

**JEFFREY MARK YOSS,** born Cape Town, South Africa, September 15, 1955; admitted to bar, 1992, California and Oregon; 1995, District of Columbia. *Education:* University of Cape Town (B.Sc.), in Computer Science, 1979; B.A., in Economics, with honors, 1982); Loyola Law School (J.D., 1990). Author: "A Study of Poverty Among the 'Coloured' Community: A General Analysis and a Case Study of Worcester," Second Carnegie Inquiry into Poverty and Development in Southern Africa, 1984. *Member:* District of Columbia Bar; State Bar of California; Oregon State Bar; Association of Southern California Defense Counsel. (Resident). *LANGUAGES:* Afrikaans. *PRACTICE AREAS:* Insurance Defense.

**SANDRA A. SHOUPE-GORGA,** born Cleveland, Ohio, April 20, 1951; admitted to bar, 1995, California and U.S. District Court, Central District of California. *Education:* Cleveland Institute of Art (B.F.A., 1976); Kent State University, Kent, Ohio (M.F.A., 1978); Cleveland State University, Cleveland Marshall College of Law (J.D., 1991). *Member:* Riverside County Bar Association; State Bar of California; Desert Bar Association; Association of Southern California Defense Counsel. (Resident). *PRACTICE AREAS:* Insurance Defense.

For complete client listing, see San Bernardino listing.

(For complete biographical data on all personnel, see Professional Biographies at San Bernardino, California)

## MARK D. GERSHENSON
400 SOUTH FARRELL DRIVE, SUITE B-203
**PALM SPRINGS, CALIFORNIA 92262**
Telephone: 619-322-0555
Fax: 619-322-3395

*Complex Business and Commercial Litigation in all States and Federal Courts; Family, Matrimonial Law and Marital Dissolutions.*

**MARK D. GERSHENSON,** born New York, N.Y., May 15, 1953; admitted to bar, 1979, Georgia; 1980, California and U.S. District Court, Northern District of Georgia; 1982, U.S. District Court, Central District of California; 1984, U.S. District Court, Northern District of California; 1990, U.S. District Court, Eastern District of California. *Education:* Brandeis University (B.A., 1974); Emory University (J.D., 1979). Commissioner, Palm Springs, Regional Airport. *Member:* Los Angeles County and Desert Bar Associations; State Bar of California; State Bar of Georgia.

## JOSEPH A. GIBBS
901 E. TAHQUITZ CANYON WAY, SUITE C-203
**PALM SPRINGS, CALIFORNIA 92262**
Telephone: 619-320-9111
Fax: 619-320-6392

*Indian Wells, California Office:* 74900 Highway 111, Suite 211. Telephone: 619-779-1790. Fax: 619-779-1780.

*Civil Litigation, Real Estate, Business, Commercial, Corporate and Partnership Law.*

*FIRM PROFILE: Articles written by the Palm Desert Newspaper, "It is critically important that a lawyer have complete knowledge of all aspects of his client's business", says Joe Gibbs. Whether its planning a car dealership expansion or inspecting the progress of a bib lettuce crop, a hands on approach and the knowledge gained with it is the foundation for good sound legal advice. Joe Gibbs of Indian Wells is the youngest member of the Board of Directors that Eisenhower Medical Center has ever had. He is one of the most experienced and ethical trial attorneys in the desert. Why write a story about him? Well, because whether you know the legal profession or not, he can serve as a sort of benchmark for selecting attorneys. He's a good example of a good example.*

**JOSEPH A. GIBBS,** born Los Angeles, California, November 24, 1951; admitted to bar, 1978, California and U.S. District Court, Southern District of California; 1983, U.S. Court of Appeals, Ninth Circuit; 1988, U.S. Supreme Court. *Education:* Loyola University of Chicago; University of San Diego (B.A., 1974); Western State University (J.D., 1977). Deputy District Attorney, Riverside County, 1979-1981. Member, Schlecht, Shevlin and *(This Listing Continued)*

Shoenberger, A Law Corporation, 1981-1993. Judge Pro Tem, Riverside Superior Court and Municipal Courts, 1981—. Member, Rent Review Commission, 1986-1988 and Chairman and Hearing Officer, 1986-1987, City of Palm Desert. Member, Board of Trustees: Eisenhower Medical Center; Palm Springs Bank Advisory Board; Riverside County District Attorney Advisory Board; Palm Desert High School Foundation. *Member:* Desert (President, 1988-1989; Board of Trustees, 1986-1990) and Riverside County Bar Associations; State Bar of California (Special Master); California Trial Lawyers Association; Palm Springs Trial Lawyers Association; The Association of Trial Lawyers of America. *PRACTICE AREAS:* Civil Litigation; Real Estate; Business; Commercial.

### ASSOCIATE

**GREGORY R. OLESON,** born Boston, Massachusetts, August 4, 1967; admitted to bar, 1993, California. *Education:* Elmira College (B.A., 1989); Marquette University (J.D., 1993). *Member:* Desert County Bar Association; State Bar of California. *PRACTICE AREAS:* Civil Litigation; Real Estate; Business Litigation.

REPRESENTATIVE CLIENTS: Carl Karcher; Fury Investments, Inc.; Heathman Inc.; Desert Orthopedic Group; Outdoor Media Group, A California Corp.; Palm Springs Motors, Inc.; Sleep N' Den, Inc.; Wells Fargo Bank; Independent Credit Card Assn.; Remax Realty; Valley Fair Management Corp.; Golden Acre Farms, Inc.

## HILL WALKER
1111 TAHQUITZ CANYON WAY, SUITE 117
**PALM SPRINGS, CALIFORNIA 92262**
Telephone: 619-864-9800
Fax: 619-864-9816

*Business, Commercial, Corporate, Partnership, Estate Planning and Probate, Conservatorship and Guardianship, Real Estate, Environmental, Land Use and Zoning, Bankruptcy, Indian Law.*

**ELAINE E. HILL,** born Sacramento, California, March 30, 1944; admitted to bar, 1986, Colorado; 1990, California. *Education:* Stanford University (B.A., 1967); University of Colorado (M.P.A., 1977); University of Denver (J.D., 1985). Member, Order of St. Ives. Recipient: American Jurisprudence Award in Constitutional Law, Legal Profession and Future Interests; West Publishing Co. Awards, 1983-1985; Corpus Juris Secundum Award 1985-1986; University of Denver College of Law Faculty Award, 1985-1986. Member, Eisenhower Medical Center Planned Gifts Committee, 1992—. *Member:* Desert, Riverside, Colorado and American Bar Associations; State Bar of California; California Women Lawyers; Colorado Women's Bar Association (Secretary, 1989-1990); Women's Forum of Colorado (Board Member and Vice President, 1983-1985); Denver Alliance of Professional Women (Board Member, 1989-1990); Desert Alliance of Professional Women (Founding President, 1992-1993; Desert Estate Planning Council, Board Member, 1993—). (Certified Specialist, Estate Planning, Trust and Probate Law The State Bar of California Board of Legal Specialization). *PRACTICE AREAS:* Estate Planning; Trust Planning; Probate; Corporate Law; Indian Land Law.

**SHARYL WALKER,** born Troy, New York, April 6, 1957; admitted to bar, 1983, Maine; 1985, California. *Education:* Colgate University (B.A., magna cum laude, 1979); Cornell University (M.B.A., 1983; J.D., 1983). Phi Beta Kappa. Editor-in-Chief, Cornell Law Review, 1981-1982. Author: "Judicial Abstention and Exclusive Federal Jurisdiction: A Reconciliation," 67 Cornell L. Rev. 219, 1982. Law Clerk to Chief Judge Samuel P. King, U.S. District Court, District of Hawaii, 1983-1984. Board Member: Desert Facilities Corporation, 1993—; Desert Alliance of Professional Women, 1992—. *Member:* Desert and American Bar Associations; The State Bar of California. *PRACTICE AREAS:* Business Law; Corporate Law; Real Estate; Land Use; Environmental Law; Indian Lands.

REPRESENTATIVE CLIENTS: Agua Caliente Band of Cahuilla Indians; Desert Adventures, Inc.; Eisenhower Medical Center; Kaiser Ventures Inc.; Mine Reclamation Corp.

CAA1540B

## IVES, KIRWAN & DIBBLE

*A PROFESSIONAL CORPORATION*

Established in 1939

777 TAHQUITZ WAY
SUITE 23
**PALM SPRINGS, CALIFORNIA 92262**
Telephone: 619-778-2611
FAX: 619-778-2612

*Los Angeles Office:* The Biltmore Court, Fourth Floor, 520 South Grand Avenue. Telephone: 213-627-0113. FAX: 213-627-1547.
*Ventura-Santa Barbara Office:* 5210 Carpinteria Avenue, P.O. Box 360, Carpinteria, California. Telephone: 805-684-7641. FAX: 805-684-9649.
*Orange-San Diego County Office:* 101 Pacifica, Suite 250, Irvine, California. Telephone: 714-450-8900. FAX: 714-450-8908.
*San Bernardino-Riverside Office:* 777 Tahquitz Way, Suite 23, Palm Springs, California. Telephone: 619-778-2611. FAX: 619-778-2612.

*FIRM PROFILE:* Ives, Kirwan & Dibble specializes in general civil litigation in both State and Federal Courts. For many years we have practiced in the traditional area of general liability defense, including but not limited to products liability, premises liability, professional liability, auto liability, truckers liability, cargo loss and damage, fire loss and damage, construction defect litigation, general negligence, international torts, insurance coverage (primary, excess, and reinsurance), and workers' compensation. In more recent years, our practice has grown in several developing areas such as business torts, directors and officers' errors and omissions, trademark and copyright infringement, business transactional work and litigation, wrongful termination, legal malpractice, child abuse, insurance bad faith, toxic torts, environmental pollution litigation, Americans with Disabilities Act claims, and municipal liability and Federal civil rights litigation.

**STEPHEN A. BOST,** born Hampton, Virginia, April 16, 1955; admitted to bar, 1981, California and U.S. District Court, Central District of California; 1988, U.S. Court of Appeals, Ninth Circuit; 1989, U.S. Supreme Court. *Education:* Christopher Newport College of the College of William & Mary (B.S., 1977); Southwestern University (J.D., 1980). Delta Theta Phi. *Member:* Los Angeles County and American Bar Associations; State Bar of California; Association of Southern California Defense Counsel.

**STEVEN B. KOTULAK,** born Philadelphia, Pennsylvania, February 21, 1959; admitted to bar, 1985, California, U.S. District Court, Central District of California and U.S. Court of Appeals, Ninth Circuit. *Education:* Lafayette College; Trenton State College (B.S., 1981); Southwestern University (J.D., 1985). *Member:* Los Angeles County and American Bar Associations; State Bar of California; The Association of Trial Lawyers of America; California Trial Lawyers Association.

MAJOR INSURANCE COMPANY CLIENTS: Acceptance Insurance Companies; Allianz Insurance Company; Allianz Underwriters Insurance Company; American International Group, Inc.; American Mutual Insurance Company; American States Insurance Company; Amica Mutual Insurance Company; The Canadian Insurance Company of California; Citation Insurance Group; The Chubb Group of Insurance Companies; California Insurance Guaranty Association; First State Insurance Company; Government Employees Insurance Company; Harbor Insurance Company; The Hartford Specialty Company; Home & Automobile Insurance Company; Houston General Insurance Company; Industrial Fire & Casualty; Industrial Indemnity Company; Industrial Underwriters, Inc.; Jefferson Insurance Group; Monticello Insurance Co.; National Indemnity Company; National Union Fire Insurance Company; Planet Insurance Company; Preferred Risk Mutual Insurance Company; Prudential-LMI Mutual Insurance Company; Reliance Insurance Company; Safeco Insurance Company; Stonewall Insurance Company; Tokio Marine & Fire Insurance Company; Transport Insurance Company; Union Bankers Insurance Company; Utica Mutual Insurance Company; Westchester Specialty Group.

(For Complete Biographical Data on all Personnel see Professional Biographies at Los Angeles, California)

## RONALD W. JOHNSON

**PALM SPRINGS, CALIFORNIA**

(See Indian Wells)

*Family Law, Divorce, Child and Spousal Support, Child Custody Disputes, Premarital and Separation Agreements, Living Arrangement Agreements.*

## MICHAEL S. KAHN

Established in 1979

777 EAST TAHQUITZ CANYON WAY, SUITE 200
P.O. BOX 2286
**PALM SPRINGS, CALIFORNIA 92263-2286**
Telephone: 619-320-5656
Fax: 619-320-5659

*Probate, Estate Planning, Real Estate, Trust, Corporate and Business Law.*

**MICHAEL S. KAHN,** born Rome, New York, May 6, 1946; admitted to bar, 1972, California and U.S. Court of Appeals, Ninth Circuit; 1975, U.S. Tax Court. *Education:* State University of New York at Buffalo (B.S. in Accounting, 1968); Hastings College of Law, University of California (J.D., 1971). Certified Public Accountant, California 1974. Airport Commissioner, City of Palm Springs, 1982-1988. Convention Center Commissioner, City of Palm Springs, 1992-1994. Member, Desert Hospital Authority, 1988-1990. Director, Boys Club of Palm Springs, 1988-1990. *Member:* State Bar of California; California Society of Certified Public Accountants.

## KINKLE, RODIGER AND SPRIGGS

PROFESSIONAL CORPORATION

**PALM SPRINGS, CALIFORNIA**

(See Riverside)

*General Trial Practice. Negligence, Malpractice, Products Liability, Construction and Insurance Law.*

## KNAPP, PETERSEN & CLARKE

*A PROFESSIONAL CORPORATION*

960 EAST TAHQUITZ CANYON WAY, SUITE 101
**PALM SPRINGS, CALIFORNIA 92262**
Telephone: 619-325-8500
Telecopier: 619-325-2454

*Glendale, California Office:* 500 North Brand Boulevard, 20th Floor. Telephone: 818-547-5000; 213-245-9400. FAX: 818-547-5329.

*General Civil, Trial and Appellate Practice in all State and Federal Courts, Arbitration Tribunals and Administrative Agencies. General Insurance, Professional Liability, Product Liability, Environmental, Corporate and General Business, State, Federal and Local Taxation, Real Estate, Escrow Errors and Omissions Defense, Construction and Land Use, Construction Defect Litigation, Estate Planning, Probate, Labor and Employment, Administrative and Regulatory Insurance Law and Title Banking.*

**NANCY MENZIES VAESSEN,** born Everett, Washington, July 29, 1946; admitted to bar, 1975, California, U.S. District Court, Central District of California and U.S. Court of Appeals, Ninth Circuit; 1984, U.S. District Court, Northern District of California. *Education:* Everett Junior College (A.A., 1966); Eastern Washington State College (B.A., cum laude, 1970); Loyola Law School, Los Angeles (J.D., 1975). Member, Products Liability Committee, National Spa and Pool Institute, 1984-1988. *Member:* Desert and Riverside County Bar Associations. (Resident).

**JOHN J. HIGGINS,** born Lompoc, California, September 30, 1959; admitted to bar, 1987, California. *Education:* Oakland University (A.S., 1980); Michigan State University (B.A., 1983); University of London, London, England; Pepperdine University (J.D., 1987). First Place Gray's Inn-International Moot Court Competition, London, England, 1985. Recipient, American Jurisprudence Award in Insurance Law. *Member:* Association of Southern California Defense Counsel.

**WILLIAM J. ROHR,** born San Diego, California, July 1, 1945; admitted to bar, 1976, California; 1977, U.S. District Court, Central District of California; 1983, U.S. Court of Appeals, Ninth Circuit. *Education:* Cerritos College (A.A., 1973); Western State University (B.S.L., 1975; J.D., 1976). *Member:* Los Angeles County, Orange County and American Bar Associations; State Bar of California; Lawyers Club of Los Angeles County; Southern California Defense Counsel Association. [Sgt., USAR, 1965-1971]. (Resident).

**CATHERINE A. GAYER,** admitted to bar, 1991, California. *Education:* L.A. Pierce Junior College (A.A., 1984); San Diego State University (B.S., 1987); Northern Illinois University (J.D., 1990). *Member:* Desert Bar Association. (Resident).

*(This Listing Continued)*

KNAPP, PETERSEN & CLARKE, A PROFESSIONAL CORPORATION, Palm Springs—Continued

**DEBBIE S. HARRIS SHERMAN,** born Los Angeles, California, May 26, 1961; admitted to bar, 1995, California and U.S. District Court, Central District of California. *Education:* University of Southern California (B.A., cum laude, 1983); University of Madrid, Madrid, Spain; Western State University (J.D., 1994). Recipient, American Jurisprudence Award, Legal Writing II. Charter Member, Western State University Tax Law Society. *Member:* Desert Bar Association. (Resident). *LANGUAGES:* Spanish.

All attorneys are admitted to the State Bar of California unless otherwise noted.

(For Complete Biographical Data on all Personnel see Professional Biographies at Glendale, California).

## WILLIAM STEELE LEDGER
Established in 1971
193 SOUTH CIVIC DRIVE, SUITE 6
**PALM SPRINGS, CALIFORNIA 92262**
Telephone: 619-320-6691
Fax: 619-323-4755

*Practice Limited to Criminal Defense, D.U.I., White Collar Crime, Drug Cases and Felonies.*

**WILLIAM STEELE LEDGER,** born Los Angeles, California, August 25, 1939; admitted to bar, 1971, California and U.S. District Court, Central District of California. *Education:* University of Southern California; Pepperdine University (J.D., cum laude, 1970). Riverside County Deputy Public Defender, 1974-1976. *Member:* Desert Bar Association; California Attorneys for Criminal Justice; National Association of Criminal Defense Lawyers; California Public Defenders Association.

REFERENCE: Wells Fargo Bank.

## KIPP IAN LYONS
400 SOUTH FARRELL DRIVE, SUITE B 200-2
**PALM SPRINGS, CALIFORNIA 92262-7964**
Telephone: 619-320-1213
Facsimile: 619-320-2466

*Real Estate, Business, Estate Planning, Probate and Corporate Law.*

**KIPP IAN LYONS,** born Los Angeles, California, December 23, 1956; admitted to bar, 1982, California; 1985, Washington. *Education:* University of California at Irvine (B.A., 1979); Loyola University of Los Angeles (J.D., 1982). Member, Loyola of Los Angeles Law Review, 1981-1982. Member, Board of Directors, Agua Caliente Development Authority, a subsidiary of The Agua Caliente Band of Cahuilla Indians. *Member:* Desert (Member, Board of Trustees, 1992—), Riverside County and Washington State (Member, Sections on: Business; Taxation; Real Estate) Bar Associations; The State Bar of California (Member, Sections on: Business; Taxation; Real Estate). *PRACTICE AREAS:* Real Estate; Business Law; Estate Planning; Probate; Corporate Law.

REPRESENTATIVE CLIENTS: Fey's Canyon Realtors; Palm Springs Hotel & Hospitality Association, Inc.; Fanny's Fabrics (Canada).

## LAW OFFICES OF
## GUY MANNING
**PALM SPRINGS, CALIFORNIA**
(See Rancho Mirage)

*Criminal Defense Trial Practice, Juvenile Criminal Defense, Personal Injury, Wrongful Death, Professional Liability Law.*

## DOUGLAS MARTIN
A LAW CORPORATION
**PALM SPRINGS, CALIFORNIA**
(See Indian Wells)

*Estate Planning, Probate, Real Estate, Corporate, Taxation and Business Law.*

## LEE R. MOHR
A PROFESSIONAL LAW CORPORATION
SUITE 121, 1111 EAST TAHQUITZ CANYON WAY
**PALM SPRINGS, CALIFORNIA 92262**
Telephone: 619-325-1711
Fax: 619-322-4171

*Family Law.*

**LEE R. MOHR,** born Maywood, California, December 24, 1943; admitted to bar, 1970, California and U.S. District Court, Central District of California; 1978, U.S. Supreme Court. *Education:* University of California at Davis (B.A., 1966); Hastings College of Law, University of California (LL.B., 1969). *Member:* Desert (President, 1977-1978; Chairman, Family Law Committee, 1988-1990), Riverside County, Los Angeles County and American Bar Associations; The State Bar of California. *PRACTICE AREAS:* Family Law.

## QUINN EMANUEL URQUHART & OLIVER, LLP
**PALM SPRINGS, CALIFORNIA**
(See Palm Desert)

*Business Litigation and Trial Practice, including Antitrust; Banking; Construction; Copyright, Trademark and Patent Litigation; Employment; ERISA; Government Contracts; Health Care; Intellectual Property; Product Liability; Real Estate; Securities; Unfair Competition; White Collar Crime.*

## REID & HELLYER
A PROFESSIONAL CORPORATION
**PALM SPRINGS, CALIFORNIA**
(See Riverside)

*General Civil and Trial Practice in all State and Federal Courts. Administrative, Bankruptcy, Commercial, Communications, Constitutional, Construction, Corporate, Environmental, Ethics and Professional Responsibility, Estate Planning, Eminent Domain and Water Rights Law, Government, High Technology, Insurance, Intellectual Property, Labor and Employment Law, Litigation, Malpractice, Military, Personal Injury, Probate, Real Property, Torts, Zoning and Municipal.*

## LAW OFFICES OF
## RICHARD JAMES RYDER
1111 EAST TAHQUITZ CANYON WAY
SUITE 121
**PALM SPRINGS, CALIFORNIA 92262**
Telephone: 619-327-2999
Fax: 619-327-9838

*Family Law.*

**RICHARD JAMES RYDER,** born Miami, Florida, June 18, 1945; admitted to bar, 1977, California, U.S. District Court, Southern and Central Districts of California and California Supreme Court; 1993, U.S. Supreme Court. *Education:* University of Florida (B.A., 1968); Western State University (J.D., 1976). Recipient: American Jurisprudence Award. Arbitrator, Riverside County, California, Attorney-Client Fee Disputes. Judge Pro Tem, Riverside, San Bernardino Superior Court, California. *Member:* California State Bar; Desert Bar Association (Chairman, Family Law Section, 1995-1996). [Lt., USN, 1968-1976]. (Certified Specialist, Family Law, California Board of Legal Specialization).

## IRA M. SALZMAN
**PALM SPRINGS, CALIFORNIA**

(See Pasadena)

*General Civil Litigation in all State and Federal Courts with emphasis on the Defense of Professional Negligence, Personal Injury and Public Safety Employees, General Wrongful Termination, Criminal Defense in State and Federal Courts.*

---

## LAW OFFICES OF
## HOWARD L. SANGER
Established in 1987

SUITE B-102, 400 SOUTH FARRELL DRIVE
**PALM SPRINGS, CALIFORNIA 92262**
Telephone: 619-320-7421
Fax: 619-320-0351
Email: @smlaw.ccmail.compuserve.com

*Corporate, Taxation, Planning and Tax Controversy, Probate, Estate Planning Real Property Law, Business Planning, Business Litigation in State and Federal Courts.*

**HOWARD L. SANGER,** born Los Angeles, California, May 5, 1942; admitted to bar, 1968, California and Kansas; 1971, U.S. Tax Court. *Education:* University of California at Berkeley (B.A., 1964); University of California at Los Angeles (J.D., 1967); New York University (LL.M., in Taxation, 1970). Author: "Dangers in Estate Planning: Recent Cases," San Fernando Valley Bar Assoc. Bulletin, May, 1982; "Good News (for a Change) for Professional Corporations," The Bottom Line, March, 1982. Co-Author: "Do Not Permit Deductible Employee Contributions Under Corporate Retirement Plans," Taxes--The Tax Magazine, May, 1982. Adjunct Faculty Member, Golden Gate University Graduate Tax Program, 1978. Speaker: Estate Planning Conference for California Society of C.P.A.'s, 1988-1995; "Final Partnership," §704 (b) Regulations for California CPA Foundation, 1990 and 1991 Programs. Lecturer: "Divorce is a Tax & Accounting Exercise," 31st Annual Meeting, American Association of Attorney-Certified Public Accountants, 1995; Practical Estate Planning for Wealthy Clients, California C.P.A. Foundation, 1988; Divorce Tax Accounting, 1988-1995; Tax Accounting Conference, California Society of C.P.A.'s. President, San Fernando Valley Estate Planning Council, 1975-1976. *Member:* Beverly Hills Bar Association (President, Probate Committee, 1978-1979); State Bar of California (Member, Taxation Section). [Capt., U.S. Army, 1967-1969]. (Certified Specialist, Taxation Law, The State Bar of California Board of Legal Specialization). **PRACTICE AREAS:** Taxation Law; Estate Planning Law; Probate Law.

### ASSOCIATES

**CHRISTOPHER S. MANES,** born Chicago, Illinois, May 24, 1957; admitted to bar, 1993, California. *Education:* University of California at Los Angeles (B.A., summa cum laude, 1979); University of Wisconsin (M.A., 1980); University of Oregon; Boalt Hall School of Law, University of California (J.D., 1992). Phi Beta Kappa. Speaker: Community Property Conference for California Society of Certified Public Accountants, 1993, 1994; "Avoiding the Residency Tax Trap," Desert CPA/Law Forum. *Member:* Desert Bar Association; State Bar of California. **PRACTICE AREAS:** Business Litigation.

---

## GARY C. SCHEROTTER
A LAW CORPORATION
Established in 1977

HERITAGE SQUARE
SUITE C-203, 901 EAST TAHQUITZ CANYON WAY
P.O. BOX 2224
**PALM SPRINGS, CALIFORNIA 92262**
Telephone: 619-320-7111
Fax: 619-320-6392
Email: GARSCH@AOL.COM

*Practice Limited to Criminal and Constitutional Law in all State Courts. Trials.*

**GARY C. SCHEROTTER,** born El Paso, Texas, July 23, 1939; admitted to bar, 1965, California and U.S. District Court, Northern District of California; 1972, U.S. Supreme Court and U.S. District Court, Southern District of California; 1973, U.S. District Court, Central District of California. *Education:* University of Denver (B.A., 1960); Hastings College of the Law, University of California (J.D., 1963). Phi Alpha Delta. Chief Trial Deputy District Attorney, County of Riverside, 1967-1972. Member: Palm Springs Airport Commission, 1972-1976; Criminal Law Advisory Commission, California Board of Legal Specialization, 1974-1980. *Member:* Desert Bar Association (Secretary, 1973; Vice President, 1974 and President, 1975-1976); State Bar of California; California Attorneys for Criminal Justice (Board Member, 1981-1984). (Certified Specialist, Criminal Law, The State Bar of California Board of Legal Specialization). **LANGUAGES:** Spanish. **PRACTICE AREAS:** Criminal Defense.

REFERENCE: Palm Desert National Bank.

---

## SCHLECHT, SHEVLIN & SHOENBERGER
A LAW CORPORATION
Established in 1951

SUITE 100, 801 EAST TAHQUITZ CANYON WAY
P.O. BOX 2744
**PALM SPRINGS, CALIFORNIA 92263-2744**
Telephone: 619-320-7161
Facsimile: 619-323-1758; 619-325-4623

*Real Estate, Corporate and General Business Law, Estate Planning, Probate and Trust Administration, Probate Litigation, Family Law, General Trial Practice in all State and Federal Courts.*

FIRM PROFILE: The Schlecht, Shevlin and Shoenberger firm has been providing legal services to clients since 1951. The firm lawyers and staff are dedicated to providing high quality service on a timely and cost effective basis. The law firm believes that the client comes first. The law firm takes pride in listing in Martindale-Hubbell Bar Register of Preeminent Lawyers. The firm is also listed in the Martindale-Hubbell Canadian and International Law Directories and welcomes foreign clients.

**JAMES M. SCHLECHT,** born Bowdle, South Dakota, September 18, 1927; admitted to bar, 1955, California. *Education:* University of Southern California (B.S., 1951; LL.B., 1954). Phi Delta Phi; Blue Key. Member, Board of Editors, University of Southern California Law Review, 1953-1954. Deputy City Attorney, Los Angeles, 1955-1956. Deputy District Attorney, Riverside County, Palm Springs Office, 1956-1957. Member: Palm Springs Unified School Board, 1965-1969 and President, 1969; Board of Directors, Convention and Visitors Bureau, 1969; City Council, City of Palm Springs, 1972-1976. *Member:* Desert (President, 1962-1963) and American Bar Associations; The State Bar of California. **PRACTICE AREAS:** Real Estate Law; General Business Law.

**JOHN C. SHEVLIN,** born Oklahoma City, Oklahoma, June 2, 1943; admitted to bar, 1969, California; 1979, U.S. Supreme Court and U.S. Court of Appeals, Ninth Circuit. *Education:* Dartmouth College (B.A., 1965); Stanford University (LL.B., 1968). Member, Moot Court Board. Research Attorney, California Fourth District Court of Appeals, Division Two, 1969-1971. Judge Pro Tem, Riverside Municipal Court, 1978-1986. *Member:* Desert, Riverside County and American Bar Associations; The State Bar of California. (Certified Specialist, Estate Planning, Trust and Probate Law, The State Bar of California Board of Legal Specialization). **PRACTICE AREAS:** Estate Planning and Administration Law; Probate Litigation; General Business Law.

**JON A. SHOENBERGER,** born Billings, Montana, March 5, 1943; admitted to bar, 1967, California. *Education:* University of California at Berkeley (B.A., 1964); University of California at Los Angeles (J.D., 1967). Moot Court Honors Program, 1966-1967. Deputy Attorney General, State of California, 1967-1968. Judge Pro Tem, Riverside Superior and Municipal Courts, 1980-1993. *Member:* Desert (President, 1980-1981), Riverside County and American Bar Associations; The State Bar of California; California Trial Lawyers Association. (Certified Specialist, Family Law, The State Bar of California Board of Legal Specialization). **PRACTICE AREAS:** Civil Litigation; Family Law.

**DANIEL T. JOHNSON,** born Blythe, California, July 14, 1954; admitted to bar, 1980, California. *Education:* University of California at Los Angeles (B.A., magna cum laude, 1976); University of Southern California (M.B.A., 1980; J.D., 1980). Phi Beta Kappa; Phi Alpha Delta. Member, City of Palm Springs Economic Development Commission, 1989-1992. *Member:* Desert (Member, Board of Trustees, 1993-1995), Riverside

*(This Listing Continued)*

### SCHLECHT, SHEVLIN & SHOENBERGER, A LAW CORPORATION, Palm Springs—Continued

County and American Bar Associations; The State Bar of California. *PRACTICE AREAS:* Real Estate Law; General Business Law.

---

**DAVID DARRIN,** born San Diego, California, January 13, 1963; admitted to bar, 1992, California. *Education:* Southwestern Community College (A.A., 1984); University of California, Santa Barbara (B.A., high honors, 1986); University of California, Davis (J.D., 1992). Co-Chair, Moot Court Board. *PRACTICE AREAS:* Civil Litigation; Real Estate Transactions; Probate; Business; Corporate.

**ELIZABETH A. DREIER,** born New Jersey, October 26, 1961; admitted to bar, 1988, California. *Education:* University of California at Davis (B.A., 1983; J.D., 1988). *Member:* Desert, Riverside County and American Bar Associations; State Bar of California. *PRACTICE AREAS:* Civil Litigation; Family.

#### OF COUNSEL

**DONALD B. McNELLEY,** born Birmingham, Alabama, January 25, 1934; admitted to bar, 1970, California and U.S. District Court, Central District of California; 1976, U.S. Supreme Court. *Education:* University of Alabama (B.A., 1955); University of Southern California (J.D., 1969). Phi Alpha Delta. Member, Corporate Law Department Committee, State Bar of California, 1982-1984. Member, Executive Committee, (1986, 1987), Compliance and Legal Division, Securities Industry Association. Member, Arbitration Panels: New York Stock Exchange; Pacific Stock Exchange; National Association of Securities Dealers; American Arbitration Association. *Member:* Desert Bar, Los Angeles County (Member: Executive Committee, Corporate Law Department Section, 1980-1986; Business and Corporations Law Section), American (Member, Committee on Federal Regulation of Securities) and Public Investor Arbitration Bar Associations. [1st. Lt., USAF, 1955-1958]. *PRACTICE AREAS:* Corporate and Securities Law; Customer/Broker Dispute Resolution; Broker/Dealer Regulation Law; General Business Law; Estate Planning; Elder Law.

**ALLEN O. PERRIER** (Retired).

REPRESENTATIVE CLIENTS: Falcon Lake Properties; Bank of California; Palm Desert National Bank; Palm Springs Motors; Plaza Motors; Federal Deposit Insurance Corp.; KESQ-TV; KPSI Radio; Outdoor Resorts of America; The Escrow Connection; Wells Fargo Bank; Canyon Country Club; Waste Management Co.
REFERENCES: Griffin Financial Services; Bank of California (Palm Springs, Calif.).

---

## ROBERT A. SCHLESINGER
### A LAW CORPORATION
*Established in 1956*
**383 SOUTH PALM CANYON DRIVE**
P.O. BOX 2268
**PALM SPRINGS, CALIFORNIA 92262-2268**
Telephone: 619-325-2076
FAX: 619-325-2070

*Practice Limited to Estate Planning, Trust, Probate Law and Related Litigation.*

**ROBERT A. SCHLESINGER,** born Orange, New Jersey, July 16, 1927; admitted to bar, 1953, California; 1960, U.S. Supreme Court; 1974, U.S. Tax Court. *Education:* University of California at Los Angeles (B.S., 1948); University of Southern California (J.D., 1953). Phi Delta Phi. Author: "Testamentary Guardianships for Minors and Incompetents," California Will Drafting, Continuing Education of the Bar, 1964 (Revised, 1989); "California Indian Lease," California Continuing Education of the Bar, 1966; "Leases," California Decedent's Estate Administration, Continuing Education of the Bar, 1965 (Revised, 1992); "California Fiduciary and Attorney Compensation in Decedent's Estates Subject to Estate Administration," Fourth Annual USC Probate and Trust Conference, 1978. Member, Board of Editors, Southern California Law Review, 1952-1953. Associate, Irving M. Walker, Los Angeles, 1953-1955. Member, Board of Trustees, 1958-1977, President, 1960-1962, Palm Springs Desert Museum. Member, Board of Trustees, Palm Springs Unified School District, 1960. Member, 1976-1982, and Chairman, 1974-1975, Palm Springs Library. Member, 1978-1986, Chairman, 1978, and President, 1980—, Desert Hospital Authority. Member, 1977— and Founding President, 1977, Desert Estate Planning

*(This Listing Continued)*

---

Council. Panelist, Trust Administration, California Continuing Education of the Bar, 1979. Moderator, California Inheritance Tax Law Update, 1981 and Panelist, Estate Administration Program, 1982, Panelist, Will Drafting, 1992; California Continuing Education of the Bar. Member: California Continuing Education of the Bar Joint Advisory Committee on Probate, Trust and Estate Planning, 1981—; Institutional Review Board, Eisenhower Medical Center, 1988-1990. *Member:* Desert (President, 1959-1960), Riverside County and American Bar Associations; The State Bar of California (Member, Executive Committee, Estate Planning, Probate and Trust Law, 1983-1987); International Academy of Estate and Trust Law. Fellow, American College of Trust and Estate Counsel. (Certified Specialist, Probate, Estate Planning and Trust Law, The State Bar of California Board of Legal Specialization). *PRACTICE AREAS:* Estate Planning; Trusts; Probate; Related Litigation.

REPRESENTATIVE CLIENTS: Irene W. & Guy L. Anderson Children's Foundation; Ednah Root Foundation; Frederick Loewe Foundation.
REFERENCE: Bank of America (Palm Springs).

---

## RICHARD L. SCOTT
**PALM SPRINGS, CALIFORNIA**
(See San Bernardino)

*Civil Trials, Products Liability, Real Property, Personal Injury Law, Insurance Defense.*

---

## THE LAW OFFICES OF WILLIAM J. SIMON
**PALM SPRINGS, CALIFORNIA**
(See Riverside)

*Bankruptcy and Insolvency Law.*

---

## SLOVAK & BARON
**1900 EAST TAHQUITZ CANYON WAY, SUITE B-1**
**PALM SPRINGS, CALIFORNIA 92262**
Telephone: 619-322-2275
Fax: 619-322-2107

*Civil Litigation with emphasis in the following areas: Business and Commercial Law, Real Estate, Fraud and Business Torts, Construction Defects, Public Law, Estate, Trusts & Conservatorships, Personal Injury, Products Liability and Bad Faith, Discrimination and Wrongful Termination. General Practice in Land Use, Zoning and Governmental Affairs, Agricultural Law, Labor Law. Trial Practice in all State and Federal Courts.*

**THOMAS S. SLOVAK,** born El Centro, California, December 30, 1948; admitted to bar, 1974, California. *Education:* California State Polytechnic College (Pomona) (B.A., with honors, 1971); University of Southern California (J.D., 1974). Arbitrator, American Arbitration Association. *Member:* Desert (Member, Board of Directors, 1981-1985; President, 1986-1987; Chairman, Civil Courts/Litigation Section 1983-1985; Fee Arbitration Panel, 1983—), Riverside County (Member, Superior Court Settlement Panel, 1981-1990) and American Bar Associations; State Bar of California; The Association of Trial Lawyers of America. *PRACTICE AREAS:* Business Law; Fraud; Business Torts; Real Estate; Construction Defect Litigation; Estate, Trust and Conservatorship Litigation; Personal Injury; Products Liability; Labor Law Litigation; Agricultural and Labor Law.

**DAVID L. BARON,** born Chicago, Illinois, June 15, 1955; admitted to bar, 1982, California. *Education:* University of California at Berkeley (B.A., 1977); Hastings College of the Law, University of California (J.D., 1982). Judge Pro Tempore, Riverside County Municipal Court, 1986-1991. Chairman, Palm Springs Economic Development Committee, 1988-1991. Member, Riverside County Superior Court Arbitration Panel, 1988—. *Member:* Desert (Member, Fee Arbitration Panel, 1989) and American Bar Associations; State Bar of California; The Association of Trial Lawyers of America. *PRACTICE AREAS:* Business Law; Construction Defect; Litigation; Business Torts; Commercial; Real Estate; Employment and Public Law Litigation; Land Use; Zoning and Governmental Affairs.

*(This Listing Continued)*

## ASSOCIATES

**L. JOANE GARCIA-COLSON,** born Montrose, Colorado, November 25, 1960; admitted to bar, 1991, New York and California. *Education:* Loretto Heights College (B.F.A., 1984); University of Denver (J.D., 1990). Order of St. Ives. Rabb Foundation Scholar. Recipient, Hoffman Cup Award; American Jurisprudence Awards, Post Trial Procedure and Trial Tactics. Co-Editor-in-Chief, Transportation Law Journal University of Denver. Member, Trial Team, University of Denver, 1988-1990. Member, Actors Equity Association, 1985—. Comment, Through The Looking Glass Head v. Lithonia, Scrutiny on The Underlying Bases of An Expert Opinion, 67 D.U.L. Rev. 587 (1990). Student, Gerry Spence's Trial Lawyers College, 1996. *Member:* Desert, New York State and American Bar Associations; State Bar of California; The Association of Trial Lawyers of America. **PRACTICE AREAS:** Civil Litigation; Employment and Discrimination Litigation; Sexual Harassment Litigation; Family Law; Construction Defect Litigation; Business Litigation; Commercial Litigation; Real Estate Disputes; Personal Injury.

**PETER M. BOCHNEWICH,** born Yonkers, New York, September 19, 1959; admitted to bar, 1992, California and U.S. District Court, Southern and Central Districts of California; 1996, U.S. District Court, Central District of California. *Education:* Central Connecticut State University (B.S., 1981); California Western School of Law (J.D., 1992). *Member:* Riverside County and Desert Bar Associations; State Bar of California. **PRACTICE AREAS:** Civil Litigation; Business Litigation; Products Liability; Construction Defects; Medical Malpractice; California Medical Board Disciplinary Procedures.

REPRESENTATIVE CLIENTS: Abbott & Cobb, Inc.; Adobe Plaza; Alamo Ranch Co.; Arrowhead Lakes Owners Association; The Honorable Walter T.H. Annenberg; The Bob Hope Cultural Center/The McCallum Theater for the Performing Arts; Bristol Construction, Inc.; Builders Supply; Chelsea GCA Realty Inc.; Christopher Mills, Architects; City of Blyth; City of Indian Wells; City of Rancho Mirage; Crystal Chrysler; Culligan Water; Desert Asphalt; Desert Adventures; Desert Medical Plaza; Desert Surgery Center; Diamond Pontiac; Dunphy Construction; Energy Unlimited, Inc.; Fairway Outdoor Advertising Co.; Flying Buttress Engineers; I.W. Construction Co.; James Cioffi Architects; Hugh Kaptor, Architects; Kassinger Construction Co.; KESQ T.V.; Kuykendall, Inc.; Little League Baseball, Inc. (International); Maineiro, Smith & Associates; Martin Communications; McCarthy Western Constructors; The Oasis Group; Palm Springs Suns; Pyramid Medical, Inc.; Realty World; Sanborn Webb Engineering; Savoire-Faire; Suncrest Country Club; Tacmir Corporation; Temple Construction Company; TKD Associates, Inc.; Valley Fair Management; The Vintage Club;

---

## LAW OFFICES OF RICK M. STEIN

*Established in 1991*

**400 SOUTH FARRELL DRIVE
SUITE B-203
PALM SPRINGS, CALIFORNIA 92262**

Telephone: 619-325-5990
Facsimile: 619-325-6265

*General Civil Trial and Appellate Practice in all State and Federal Courts, Unfair Competition, Securities and Antitrust Litigation, Receivership and Real Property Law.*

**RICK M. STEIN,** born Memphis, Tennessee, August 18, 1943; admitted to bar, 1968, Texas; 1969, California; 1981, U.S. Supreme Court. *Education:* University of Virginia (B.A., 1965); University of Texas (LL.B., 1968). Hildebrand Moot Court Spring Competition. Legal Research Board. Author: "Some Observations on the Close Corporation Exemption Under the Corporate Securities Law of 1968," Los Angeles Bar Bulletin, May 1970. Instructor, Securities Regulation, University of West Los Angeles School of Law, 1976. Arbitrator, Business Cases, Los Angeles County Superior Court, 1978-1982. Member: Sigelman & Stein, Beverly Hills, California, 1970-1984; Sanger & Stein, Palm Springs, California, 1987-1991. *Member:* State Bar of California. **REPORTED CASES:** Phonetele, Inc. v. PUC, 11 Cal.3d 125, 113 Cal.Rptr. 16, 520 P.2d 400 (1974), en banc; DCD Programs, Ltd., et al. v. Leighton, 833 F2d 183 (9th Cir. 1987); Phonetele, Inc. v. AT&T, 664 F2d 716 (9th Cir. 1981); Phonetele, Inc. v. AT&T, 889 F2d 224 (9th Cir. 1981), cert. denied.; Hydrotech Systems v. Oasis Waterpark, 52 Cal.3d 988, 277 Cal.Rptr. 517, 803 P2d 370 (1991), en banc.

---

## IRA N. TUCK

**PALM SPRINGS, CALIFORNIA**

(See Yucca Valley)

*Estate Planning, Wills, Trusts and Probate and Conservatorship.*

---

## TUVERSON & HILLYARD

A Limited Liability Partnership, including Professional Corporations

**1800 TAHQUITZ CANYON WAY
PALM SPRINGS, CALIFORNIA 92262**

Telephone: 619-322-7855
Fax: 619-322-5121

*Los Angeles, California Office:* 12400 Wilshire Boulevard, Suite 900, Los Angeles, California 90025. Telephones: 310-826-7855; 625-1234. Fax: 310-826-8738.

*Newport Beach, California Office:* 4675 MacArthur Court, Suite 650, Newport Beach, California 82660. Telephone: 714-752-7855. Fax: 714-752-5437.

*San Diego, California Office:* 4365 Executive Drive, Suite 700, San Diego, California 92121. Telephone: 619-452-7855. Fax: 619-452-2153.

*General Civil and Trial Practice in all State and Federal Courts. Medical and Legal Malpractice Defense, Public Entity and Insurance Defense.*

(For personnel, representative clients and biographical data, see professional biographies at Los Angeles, California)

---

## VAN HULLE & PREVOST

**PALM SPRINGS, CALIFORNIA**

(See San Bernardino)

*General Civil Trial Practice in all Courts. Appellate Practice. Insurance, Malpractice and Products Liability Law.*

---

## WELEBIR & McCUNE

*A PROFESSIONAL LAW CORPORATION*

**PALM SPRINGS, CALIFORNIA**

(See Redlands)

*Practice limited to Catastrophic Personal Injury and Wrongful Death, Products Liability, Aviation, Railroad and Toxic Torts. Class Actions related to Defective Products and Mass Torts.*

---

## MICHAEL ZITOMER

**225 SOUTH CIVIC DRIVE, SUITE 2-14
PALM SPRINGS, CALIFORNIA 92262-7201**

Telephone: 619-320-6443
Fax: 619-323-1699

*Personal Injury, Civil Litigation, Real Estate Law.*

**MICHAEL ZITOMER,** born Milwaukee, Wisconsin, May 20, 1947; admitted to bar, 1972, California; 1976, U.S. District Court, Central District of California. *Education:* University of Michigan (B.A., 1969); University Southern California (J.D., 1972). President, Desert Bar Association, 1992-1993. *Member:* Desert Bar Association; State Bar of California; California Trial Lawyers Association. **PRACTICE AREAS:** Personal Injury Law; Civil Litigation; Real Estate Law.

## DAVID LAURENCE ACH

525 UNIVERSITY AVENUE, SUITE 702
**PALO ALTO, CALIFORNIA 94301**
Telephone: 415-321-4411
Fax: 415-326-0758
Email: achfamily@aol.com

*Estate Planning, Trusts and Wills, Probate, Estate Administration and Tax.*

**DAVID LAURENCE ACH,** born Cincinnati, Ohio, July 18, 1947; admitted to bar, 1977, California; 1984, U.S. Tax Court. *Education:* Harvard University (B.A., cum laude, 1969); University of California at Davis (J.D., 1977). Member, Honors Moot Court Board, 1976-1977. *Member:* Santa Clara County Bar Association (Member, Estate Planning, Probate and Trust Section); State Bar of California (Member, Estate Planning, Trust and Probate Law Section). **PRACTICE AREAS:** Estate Planning Law; Estate Administration Law; Probate Litigation.

## ALEXANDER & HANSON

Established in 1989

2600 EL CAMINO REAL, SUITE 110
**PALO ALTO, CALIFORNIA 94306**
Telephone: 415-812-8181

*General Business Practice. Civil Litigation and Appeals in all Federal and State Courts. Corporation, Securities, Employment, Real Estate, Environmental, Construction Defect, Trade Secret and Unfair Competition Law.*

FIRM PROFILE: *Alexander & Hanson is engaged in the general practice of business law and business litigation including structuring, organizing, financing and advising corporations and partnerships, securities, real estate, real estate development, toxic waste claims, construction, employment, trade secrets and unfair competition, and all aspects of business litigation.*

**DANIEL ALEXANDER,** born Marysville, California, April 3, 1948; admitted to bar, 1979, California. *Education:* University of California at Berkeley (B.A., 1972); University of San Francisco (J.D., cum laude, 1979). *Member:* Santa Clara County Bar Association (Member: Business Litigation Section; Labor Section, Executive Committee, 1988-1989); The State Bar of California. **PRACTICE AREAS:** Litigation; Civil Trial; Employment Law; Environmental Liability Law; Construction Defect Litigation.

**GORDON N. HANSON,** born St. Paul, Minnesota, June 21, 1950; admitted to bar, 1985, California. *Education:* United States Coast Guard Academy (B.S., with highest honors, 1972); Boalt Hall School of Law, University of California (J.D., 1985). *Member:* Palo Alto Area, Santa Clara County (Member, Real Property Section) and American Bar Associations; The State Bar of California. [LCDR, USCG 1972-1982; CAPT., USCGR 1982-1986]. **PRACTICE AREAS:** Business Law; Corporate Law; Partnership Law; Real Estate; Estate Planning.

## KAREN TIETJEN ALLEN

285 HAMILTON AVENUE, SUITE 400
**PALO ALTO, CALIFORNIA 94301**
Telephone: 415-327-7300
Fax: 415-327-7370

*Immigration and Nationality Law.*

**KAREN TIETJEN ALLEN,** born Mt. Kisco, New York, August 20, 1961; admitted to bar, 1988, California, U.S. District Court, Northern District of California and U.S. Court of Appeals, Ninth Circuit. *Education:* University of Santa Clara (B.S., cum laude, 1983); Hastings College of the Law, University of California (J.D., 1988). Phi Sigma Iota, Foreign Language Honor Society. First Place Brief, David E. Snodgrass Moot Court Competition for Outstanding Appellate Advocacy, 1988. Author: "Family Based Immigration: Approving Relationships, Documentation, Chargeability, and Priority Dates," *Key Issues in Immigration Law,* American Immigration Lawyers Association, 1992; "Employment Creation Visas," Foreign Investment in the U.S.—A Tool for Immigration, State Bar of California, Section Education Institute. Editor, *Emerging Issues in Immigration Law,* American Immigration Lawyers Association, 1994. Guest Lecturer: Immigration and Nationality Law, Lincoln Law School, 1991. Speaker: Immigrant Investor Visas, State Bar of California, Section Education Institute, 1995; Business Immigration Roundtable, American Immigration Lawyers Association Annual Conference, 1994; Immigration Consequences of Mergers and Acquisitions, American Immigration Lawyers Association Califor-

*(This Listing Continued)*

nia Conference, 1990; L-1 Intra-Company Transferee Visas, Santa Clara County Bar Association, 1990; Immigration Law in the 90's, Santa Clara University Kronick Conference, 1992. *Member:* Santa Clara County Bar Association (Chair, Immigration Law Section, 1990-1992); American Immigration Lawyers Association, Santa Clara Valley Chapter (Chair, 1994-1995; Chair-Elect, 1993-1994; Co-Chair, Immigration and Naturalization Service of California Service Center Liaison Committee, 1995-1996; Chair, Chapter Committee on Unauthorized Practice of Law, 1989-1990; Chair, Chapter Educational Committee, 1991-1992); State Bar of California. (Certified Specialist, Immigration and Nationality Law, The State Bar of California Board of Legal Specialization). **PRACTICE AREAS:** Immigration and Naturalization.

## AUFMUTH, FOX, WEED & LeBLANC

*A PROFESSIONAL CORPORATION*

Established in 1988

314 LYTTON AVENUE, SUITE 200
**PALO ALTO, CALIFORNIA 94301**
Telephone: 415-322-7100
Fax: 415-322-6635

*Real Estate, Partnerships, Taxation and Estate Planning and Family Tax Law.*

**LAWRENCE A. AUFMUTH,** born Cleveland, Ohio, July 8, 1944; admitted to bar, 1970, California. *Education:* Brown University (A.B., 1966); Stanford University (J.D., 1969). Member, Board of Editors, Stanford University Law Review, 1968-1969. (Certified Specialist, Taxation Law, The State Bar of California Board of Legal Specialization). **PRACTICE AREAS:** Taxation; Partnerships; Estate Planning.

**HARRY L. FOX,** born Glen Ridge, New Jersey, April 29, 1956; admitted to bar, 1983, California. *Education:* University of California at Santa Cruz (A.B., with honors, 1979); Harvard University (J.D., cum laude, 1983). **PRACTICE AREAS:** Taxation; Real Estate; Partnerships.

**MICHAEL H. WEED,** born Pittsburgh, Pennsylvania, July 12, 1954; admitted to bar, 1984, California. *Education:* Brown University (B.A., 1976); Duke University (J.D., with high honors, 1984). Order of the Coif. Member, Duke Law Journal, 1982-1983. **PRACTICE AREAS:** Real Estate.

**JOAN A. LeBLANC,** born San Francisco, California, February 7, 1953; admitted to bar, 1982, California. *Education:* University of California at Santa Barbara (B.A., 1975); Hastings College of the Law, University of California (J.D., 1982). (Certified Specialist, Probate, Estate Planning and Trust Law, The State Bar of California Board of Legal Specialization). **PRACTICE AREAS:** Estate Planning.

## BAKER & McKENZIE

660 HANSEN WAY
P.O. BOX 60309
**PALO ALTO, CALIFORNIA 94304-0309**
Telephone: (415) 856-2400
Intn'l. Dialing: (1-415) 856-2400
Facsimile: (1-415) 856-9299

*Associated Offices of Baker & McKenzie in:* Almaty, Amsterdam, Bangkok, Barcelona, Beijing, Berlin, Bogotá, Brasília, Brussels, Budapest, Buenos Aires, Cairo, Caracas, Chicago, Dallas, Frankfurt, Geneva, Hanoi, Ho Chi Minh City, Hong Kong, Juárez, Kiev, Lausanne, London, Madrid, Manila, Melbourne, México City, Miami, Milan, Monterrey, Moscow, Münich, New York, Paris, Prague, Rio de Janeiro, Riyadh, Rome, St. Petersburg, San Diego, San Francisco, Santiago, São Paulo, Singapore, Stockholm, Sydney, Taipei, Tijuana, Tokyo, Toronto, Valencia, Warsaw, Washington, D.C. and Zürich.

*Correspondent Law Firm:* Hadiputranto, Hadinoto & Partners, Jakarta.

*International and Domestic Practice. Administrative Taxation, Banking, Business and Civil Litigation and Arbitration, Commercial Transactions, Corporate and Securities, Customs Control, Employment Discrimination, Estate Planning, Immigration Law, Insurance, Legislative Practice, Mining and Natural Resources, Oil and Gas, Patent, Trademark and Copyright, Pension and Profit Sharing, Probate, Professional Liability, Publishing, Real Estate and Zoning Regulation, Taxation, Trade and Financing, Trade Regulation, Trust.*

*(This Listing Continued)*

## MEMBERS OF FIRM

**MAURICE S. EMMER,** born Oklahoma City, Oklahoma, June 26, 1947; admitted to bar, 1978, Illinois; 1987, California; 1991, New York. *Education:* University of Pennsylvania (B.S., 1969); University of Chicago (J.D., 1978). *Member:* State Bar of California; American Bar Association (Member, Section on Taxation); American Institute of Certified Public Accountants; International Fiscal Association. *PRACTICE AREAS:* Taxation.

**TOD L. GAMLEN,** born San Francisco, California, September 23, 1951; admitted to bar, 1978, California, U.S. District Court, Northern District of California and U.S. Court of Appeals, Ninth Circuit; 1984, U.S. District Court, Eastern District of California; 1986, U.S. District Court, Southern District of California; 1991, U.S. District Court, Central District of California. *Education:* Stanford University (B.S.C.E., 1973); Georgetown University (J.D., 1978). Tau Beta Pi. Member, National Moot Court Team. *Member:* Bar Association of San Francisco; Santa Clara County and American (Member, Sections on: Litigation; Antitrust; Corporation, Banking and Business Law) Bar Associations. *PRACTICE AREAS:* Commercial Litigation; Computers and Technology; Intellectual Property Law.

**JOHN C. KLOTSCHE,** born Milwaukee, Wisconsin, June 18, 1942; admitted to bar, 1967, Wisconsin; 1968, Illinois and U.S. District Court, Northern District of Illinois; 1969, U.S. Tax Court; 1970, U.S. Court of Appeals, 7th Circuit; 1972, U.S. Court of Appeals, 6th Circuit; 1987, Texas and U.S. Supreme Court; 1989, U.S. Court of Appeals, 5th Circuit; 1990, U.S. District Court, Northern District of Texas (Not admitted in California). *Education:* University of Arizona (B.S., 1964); University of Wisconsin (J.D., 1967). Order of the Coif. Law Clerk to Chief Judge, Wisconsin Supreme Court, 1967-1968. *Member:* State Bar of Wisconsin; Illinois State and American (Member, Tax Section) Bar Associations; State Bar of Texas.

**MICHAEL J. MADDA,** born Chicago, Illinois, March 23, 1945; admitted to bar, 1969, Illinois; 1970, U.S. District Court, Northern District of Illinois; 1974, U.S. Court of Appeals, Seventh Circuit; 1975, U.S. Supreme Court; 1989, California. *Education:* Georgetown University (A.B., 1966); Northwestern University (J.D., cum laude, 1969). Order of the Coif. Member, Board of Editors, Northwestern University Law Review, 1967-1969. Chairman, Writing Competition, Northwestern University, 1969. Law Clerk to Judge Edwin A. Robson, Chief Judge, U.S. District Court, Northern District of Illinois, 1969-1970. *Member:* Illinois State and American (Member, Sections on: International Law and Practice; Business Law) Bar Associations; State Bar of California. *PRACTICE AREAS:* Taxation.

**SUSAN H. NYCUM,** born Pittsburgh, Pennsylvania; admitted to bar, 1962, Pennsylvania; 1974, California. *Education:* Ohio Wesleyan (A.B., 1956); Stanford Law School; Duquesne University (J.D., 1960). Phi Beta Kappa; Delta Sigma Rho; Pi Sigma Alpha; Mortar Board. *Member:* American (Chairman, Science and Technology Section, 1979-1980; Counsel Member, 1987-1991) and International (Member, Section on Business Law; Chair, Committee on Software Protection, 1986; Chair, Committee on Computer Abuse, 1990—); Computer Law Association (President, 1986-1988); National Conference of Lawyers and Scientists. *PRACTICE AREAS:* Computers and Technology; Intellectual Property Law; Arbitration and Dispute Resolution.

**JOHN M. PETERSON, JR.,** born Evergreen Park, Illinois, June 15, 1951; admitted to bar, 1977, Illinois and U.S. District Court, Northern District of Illinois and U.S. Tax Court; 1981, California and U.S. District Court, Northern District of California. *Education:* University of Notre Dame (B.B.A., 1973); Harvard Law School (J.D., cum laude, 1977). Teacher, Corporate Taxation, John Marshall Law School, Tax LL.M. Program, 1980-1981. *Member:* American Bar Association (Member, Section on Taxation, Affiliated and Related Corporations Committee, 1977—; Subcommittee Chairman, 1980-1988; Committee Vice-Chair, 1988-1990; Committee Chair, 1991-1992); State Bar of California. *PRACTICE AREAS:* Taxation.

**J. PAT POWERS,** born San Luis Obispo, California, July 25, 1945; admitted to bar, 1974, California; 1981, U.S. Tax Court. *Education:* University of California at Berkeley (B.A., 1970); Boalt Hall School of Law, University of California (J.D., 1974). Order of the Coif. Associate Editor, California Law Review, 1973-1974. *Member:* Bar Association of San Francisco; State Bar of California; American Bar Association (Member: Section on Taxation, Committee on Foreign Activities of U.S. Taxpayers, 1979—; Committee on State and Local Taxes, 1989—). *PRACTICE AREAS:* Taxation.

**ANDRÉ M. SALTOUN,** born Bagdad, Iraq, January 21, 1930; admitted to bar, 1960, Wisconsin and Illinois; 1978, California. *Education:* University of North Carolina (B.A., 1950); University of Wisconsin (J.D., 1960). Order of the Coif. Managing Editor, Wisconsin Law Review, 1959-1960. *PRACTICE AREAS:* Taxation; Trade (International).

**GARY D. SPRAGUE,** born Stockton, California, August 4, 1955; admitted to bar, 1981, California. *Education:* Stanford University (B.A., in Pol. Sc., with distinction, 1977); Trinity College, Dublin, Ireland; Harvard University (J.D., cum laude, 1981). Phi Beta Kappa. *Member:* Bar Association of San Francisco; State Bar of California; American Bar Association (Member, Section on Taxation); International Fiscal Association (USA Branch). *PRACTICE AREAS:* Taxation; Executive Transfers.

## LOCAL PARTNER

**ROBIN L. FILION,** born McMinnville, Oregon, April 19, 1951; admitted to bar, 1985, California; U.S. District Court, Northern, Central, Southern and Eastern Districts of California; U.S. Court of Appeals, Ninth Circuit; U.S. Supreme Court. *Education:* University of California at Berkeley (B.S., 1978; M.S. 1980); Hastings College of the Law, University of California (J.D., 1985). [With U.S. Army, 1972-1975]. *PRACTICE AREAS:* Securities and Financial Products; Intellectual Property Law; Computers and Technology; Commercial Litigation; Civil Litigation.

## ASSOCIATES

**JON M. APPLETON,** born East Lansing, Michigan, March 19, 1963; admitted to bar, 1990, California. *Education:* University of Southern California (B.A., cum laude, 1985; J.D., with honors, 1989; M.A., 1989); University of Frankfurt (LL.M., summa cum laude, 1995). *Member:* State Bar of California. *LANGUAGES:* German.

**MICHAEL BUMBACA,** born Toronto, Ontario, Canada, April 9, 1959; admitted to bar, 1985, Ontario; 1990, New York; 1994, California. *Education:* York University; University of Ottawa (LL.B., 1983); New York University (LL.M., Corporate, 1987; LL.M., Tax, 1988). *Member:* State Bar of California. *LANGUAGES:* Italian. *PRACTICE AREAS:* Taxation.

**ROBIN A. CHESLER,** born Freeport, The Bahamas, September 24, 1964; admitted to bar, 1989, California; 1990, U.S. Tax Court. *Education:* Harvard University (B.A., magna cum laude, 1986); Boalt Hall School of Law, University of California (J.D., 1989). *Member:* State Bar of California; American Bar Association (Member, Section on Taxation). *PRACTICE AREAS:* Taxation.

**BRIAN GEOGHEGAN,** born Dublin, Ireland, April 3, 1955; admitted to bar, 1985, California and U.S. District Court, Northern District of California; 1986, U.S. Court of Appeals, Ninth Circuit. *Education:* Queens College of the City University of New York (B.A., 1982); University of California, Boalt Hall School of Law (J.D., 1985). *Member:* State Bar of California. *PRACTICE AREAS:* Intellectual Property Law.

**STEWART R. LIPELES,** born Orlando, Florida, July 15, 1966; admitted to bar, 1992, Illinois and U.S. Court of Appeals, Fifth Circuit; 1993, U.S. Tax Court and U.S. District Court, Nothern District of Illinois (Not admitted in California). *Education:* Rice University (B.A., cum laude, 1989); University of Chicago (J.D., with honors, 1992). Adjunct Professor of Law, IIT/Chicago Kent, College of Law, 1994-1996. Law Clerk to the Honorable E. Grady Jolly, U.S. Court of Appeals, Fifth Circuit, 1992-1993. *PRACTICE AREAS:* Taxation.

**OWEN P. MARTIKAN,** born Binghamton, New York, August 31, 1965; admitted to bar, 1990, Texas; 1995, California. *Education:* Yale University (B.A., 1987); University of Texas (J.D., 1990). *Member:* Dallas Bar Association; State Bar of Texas; State Bar of California. *LANGUAGES:* German and French. *PRACTICE AREAS:* Taxation.

**LOUISE C. OBER,** born Stamford, Connecticut, February 16, 1959; admitted to bar, 1987, California. *Education:* Princeton University (B.A., summa cum laude, 1981); Harvard Law School (J.D., 1986). Phi Beta Kappa. Judicial Law Clerk to the Honorable Wm. Matthew Bryne, Jr., U.S. District Court, Central District of California, 1986-1987. *Member:* State Bar of California. *LANGUAGES:* Spanish. *PRACTICE AREAS:* Taxation.

**TAYLOR S. REID,** born Oakland, California, February 20, 1963; admitted to bar, 1993, Illinois (Not admitted in California). *Education:* University of California at Berkeley (B.A., 1986); University of Vienna (Dip., 1990); Northwestern University (J.D., cum laude, 1993). *LANGUAGES:* German. *PRACTICE AREAS:* Taxation.

**JAMES C. ROSS,** born Ottawa, Ontario, June 23, 1958; admitted to bar, 1985, Québec, Canada; 1987, California; 1993, New York. *Education:* McGill University (B.C.L., 1983; LL.B., 1984); Universite De Paris-II (Assas) (Licence en droit, 1981); New York University (LL.M., 1992). Contrib-

*(This Listing Continued)*

CALIFORNIA—PALO ALTO — MARTINDALE-HUBBELL LAW DIRECTORY 1997

**BAKER & McKENZIE, Palo Alto**—Continued

utor, Tax Planning International Review, 1987—. *Member:* State Bar of California (Member, Taxation Section). **PRACTICE AREAS:** Taxation.

**MICHELLE J. WACHS,** born Reading, Pennsylvania, April 28, 1966; admitted to bar, 1993, California. *Education:* Brown University (B.A., magna cum laude, 1986); Albright College; Harvard University (J.D., 1993). *Member:* State Bar of California. **PRACTICE AREAS:** Litigation (Intellectual Property, Securities).

**ANDREW D. ZEIF,** born New York, N.Y., January 24, 1962; admitted to bar, 1988, New York; 1995, Massachusetts (Not admitted in California). *Education:* University of Pennsylvania (B.A., cum laude, 1983); Fordham University (J.D., 1987). **PRACTICE AREAS:** Corporate and Partnership Law.

---

## BIALSON, BERGEN & SCHWAB

A Partnership of Professional Corporations

Established in 1977

300 STANFORD FINANCIAL SQUARE
2600 EL CAMINO REAL
**PALO ALTO, CALIFORNIA 94306**
Telephone: 415-857-9500
Fax: 415-494-2738
Email: bbs@bbslaw.com

*Business, Secured Transactions and Commercial Law, Real Property, Corporate, Creditor Representation, Estate Planning, Estate, Probate and Trust Administration, General Business Litigation and Trial Practice.*

### MEMBERS OF FIRM

**ANNETTE G. BIALSON, (INC.),** born Iran, December 22, 1946; admitted to bar, 1970, California. *Education:* Pennsylvania State University (B.S., with Distinction, 1967); Stanford University (J.D., 1970). Judge Pro Tem, Santa Clara County Superior Court, 1977-1979. Member, Santa Clara County Superior Court Arbitrators Association, 1978-1979. *Member:* Palo Alto, Santa Clara County (Trustee, 1976-1978) and American (Member, Sections on: Real Property, Probate and Trust Law; Business Law) Bar Associations; State Bar of California (Member, Sections on: Business Law; Estate Planning, Trust and Probate; Real Property). **PRACTICE AREAS:** Real Property Law; Business Law; Estate Planning Law. **Email:** abialson@bbslaw.com

**SEYMOUR BERGEN, (P.C.),** born Brooklyn, New York, September 15, 1923; admitted to bar, 1974, California. *Education:* City College of New York (B.B.A., 1950); University of Santa Clara (J.D., magna cum laude, 1974). *Member:* Palo Alto, Santa Clara County and American (Member, Section of Corporation, Banking and Business Law) Bar Associations; State Bar of California (Member, Section on Business Law). **PRACTICE AREAS:** Business Law; Corporate Law.

**LAWRENCE M. SCHWAB, (INC.),** born Denver, Colorado, April 25, 1953; admitted to bar, 1979, California. *Education:* Stanford University (A.B., 1975); London School of Economics and Political Science, London, England (M.Sc., in Econ., 1976); University of Santa Clara (M.B.A., 1978; J.D., 1978). Phi Alpha Delta. *Member:* Palo Alto, Santa Clara County (Trustee, 1991-1992) and American (Member, Sections on: Real Property, Probate and Trust Law; Member, Committee on International Business Transactions, International Law Section, 1977—) Bar Associations; State Bar of California (Member, Sections on: Business Law; Taxation; Estate Planning, Trust and Probate Law). **PRACTICE AREAS:** Business Law; Commercial Law; Creditor's Representation Law.

---

**KAREN A. KOEPPE,** born San Jose, California, March 11, 1958; admitted to bar, 1983, California. *Education:* San Jose State University (B.A., with distinction, 1980); University of Santa Clara (J.D., 1983). Associate Editor, Santa Clara Law Review, 1982-1983. Author: Comment, "The Rights of Unwed Fathers are Being Violated," Vol. 23:3 Santa Clara Law Review, 1983. *Member:* Santa Clara County Bar Association (Member, Business Law Section); State Bar of California. **PRACTICE AREAS:** Commercial Law; Probate; Trust Administration.

**KERRY A. KELLY,** born Bakersfield, California, October 21, 1959; admitted to bar, 1986, California. *Education:* Stanford University (B.A., 1981; M.A., 1982); University of Santa Clara (J.D., 1986). Selected to Moot Court Honors Board. Winner, Moot Court Competition. *Member:* Santa Clara County and Palo Alto Bar Associations; The State Bar of California. **LANGUAGES:** German. **PRACTICE AREAS:** Litigation; Real Property; Bankruptcy Law.

**ALLISON WALSH HURLEY,** born San Jose, California, February 21, 1958; admitted to bar, 1986, California. *Education:* University of California at Santa Barbara (B.A., cum laude, Chancellor's Scholar, 1980); University of San Francisco (J.D., 1986). Member, Moot Court Board, 1985-1986. *Member:* Santa Clara County Bar Association; State Bar of California. **PRACTICE AREAS:** Business Law; Corporation Law. **Email:** allison@bbslaw.com

**BRIAN E. DOUCETTE,** born Boston, Massachusetts, March 14, 1961; admitted to bar, 1994, California. *Education:* University of Massachusetts (B.A., 1984); Golden Gate University School of Law (J.D., 1994). Phi Alpha Delta. Member, Northern District Historical Society, 1994—. *Member:* Santa Clara County Bar Association; State Bar of California. **PRACTICE AREAS:** Business Litigation; Business Law.

---

## JAMES W. BLACKMAN

A PROFESSIONAL CORPORATION

2370 WATSON COURT, SUITE 200
**PALO ALTO, CALIFORNIA 94304**
Telephone: 415-843-1000

*Criminal Law and Litigation. Civil Litigation.*

**JAMES W. BLACKMAN,** born Brooklyn, New York, February 17, 1943; admitted to bar, 1969, California, U.S. District Court, Northern District of California and U.S. Court of Appeals, Ninth Circuit. *Education:* Menlo College (A.A., 1963); University of California at Los Angeles (A.B., 1965); Hastings College of Law, University of California (J.D., 1968). Deputy District Attorney, Ventura County, (1969-1972). *Member:* Palo Alto, Santa Clara County (Trustee, 1981-1982; Trustee, 1993—), San Mateo County and American Bar Associations; The State Bar of California; California Attorneys for Criminal Justice. (Certified Specialist, Criminal Law, The State Bar of California Board of Legal Specialization).

---

## BLAKELY, SOKOLOFF, TAYLOR & ZAFMAN, LLP

PALO ALTO, CALIFORNIA

(See Sunnyvale)

*Intellectual Property Law, including Patents, Trademarks, Copyrights, Related Prosecution and Litigation.*

---

## LAW OFFICES OF ANTHONY BOSKOVICH

Established in 1985

2155 PARK BOULEVARD
**PALO ALTO, CALIFORNIA 94306-1543**
Telephone: 415-323-0391
Fax: 415-323-0141
Email: 71750.2502@compuserve.com

*San Jose, California Office:* 941 West Hedding Street. Telephone: 408-296-4345.

*General Civil and Criminal Litigation, Civil and Criminal Appeals, Writs and Related Trial Court Matters, Civil Rights and Employment Law.*

**ANTHONY M. BOSKOVICH,** born San Jose, California, January 6, 1953; admitted to bar, 1985, California. *Education:* Williams College (B.A., cum laude, 1974); Yale University; Santa Clara University (J.D., cum laude, 1985). Licensed: Fire and Casualty Insurance Agent and Life and Disability Insurance Agent, California, 1978; Fire and Casualty Insurance Broker, California, 1983; National Association of Security Dealers, Series 6, 1987. Fee Arbitrator, Jail Infraction Hearing Officer, Judge Pro-Tem, Small Claims and Traffic Courts. *Member:* Santa Clara County (Member: Judiciary Committee; Individual Rights and Constitutional Law Committee; Chairman, Task Force on Citizen Review of Police Conduct; Chair, Appellate Courts Section, 1992; Treasurer, 1995; Trustee, 1996—) and American (Member: Tort and Insurance Practice Section; Law Practice Management; General Practice; Criminal Justice, 1987—) Bar Associations; State Bar of

*(This Listing Continued)*

*(This Listing Continued)*

CAA1548B

California; Society of Chartered Property and Casualty Underwriters; Santa Clara Valley Charter of CPCU (President, 1992-1993). *REPORTED CASES:* In re Mark Bettencourt, 20 Cal. Rptr. 2d 240; In re Babak S., 22 Cal. Rptr. 2d 893. *PRACTICE AREAS:* Litigation; Appellate Practice; Insurance Law; Civil Rights; Police Misconduct; Labor and Employment.

### LEGAL SUPPORT PERSONNEL

**VALARIE D. HUFF,** born Des Moines, Iowa, September 20, 1944. *Education:* University of California (B.A., 1966); Canada College (Paralegal Certificate with honors, 1983). Member, Victim Witness Program, 1978-1983 and Senior Adult Legal Assistance, 1985-1987, Northern Municipal Court. Member, Center for Domestic Violence Prevention, 1996. Executive Director, San Francisco Opera Guild, 1996. Member, San Francisco Association of Legal Assistants. (Paralegal).

## JANET L. BREWER
### 1755 EMBARCADERO ROAD, SUITE 110
### PALO ALTO, CALIFORNIA 94303
Telephone: 415-856-8286
Fax: 415-856-8296
Email: HiTekLawyr@aol.com

*Business and Corporate Law, Business Planning, Estate Planning, Probate and Probate Litigation, and High Technology Law.*

**JANET L. BREWER,** born Chicago, Illinois, December 1, 1949; admitted to bar, 1975, Colorado; 1977, California. *Education:* University of Wisconsin (B.A., 1971); University of Denver (J.D., 1975); Golden Gate University (M.B.A., 1982). Former General Counsel: Hills Bros. Coffee; Corvus Computer Systems. *Member:* Palo Alto, San Mateo County and Santa Clara County (Member, Executive Committee, Estate Planning, Trust and Probate Law Section) Bar Associations; State Bar of California. *LANGUAGES:* Russian and Spanish. *PRACTICE AREAS:* Estate Planning; Probate and Trust Litigation; Corporate Law; Software Licensing.

## BROBECK, PHLEGER & HARRISON LLP
A Partnership including a Professional Corporation
### TWO EMBARCADERO PLACE
### 2200 GENG ROAD
### PALO ALTO, CALIFORNIA 94303
Telephone: 415-424-0160
Facsimile: 415-496-2885

*San Francisco, California Office:* Spear Street Tower, One Market. Telephone: 415-442-0900. Facsimile: 415-442-0900.

*Los Angeles, California Office:* 550 South Hope Street. Telephone: 213-489-4060. Facsimile: 213-745-3345.

*San Diego, California Office:* 550 West C Street, Suite 1300. Telephone: 619-234-1966. Facsimile: 619-236-1403.

*Orange County, California Office:* 4675 MacArthur Court, Suite 1000, Newport Beach. Telephone: 714-752-7535. Facsimile: 714-752-7522.

*Austin, Texas Office:* Brobeck, Phleger & Harrison LLP, 301 Congress Avenue, Suite 1200. Telephone: 512-477-5495. Facsimile: 512-477-5813.

*Denver, Colorado Office:* Brobeck, Phleger & Harrison LLP, 1125 Seventeenth Street, 25th Floor. Telephone: 303-293-0760. Facsimile: 303-299-8819.

*New York, N.Y. Office:* Brobeck, Phleger & Harrison LLP, 1633 Broadway, 47th Floor. Telephone: 212-581-1600. Facsimile: 212-586-7878.

*Brobeck Hale and Dorr International Office:*
*London, England Office:* Veritas House, 125 Finsbury Pavement, London EC2A 1NQ. Telephone: 44 071 638 6688. Facsimile: 44 071 638 5888.

*General Practice, including Business and Technology, Litigation, Securities Litigation, Technology Litigation, Environmental Litigation, Product Liability Litigation, Labor Law, Financial Services and Insolvency (including Bankruptcy and Loan Workout), Real Estate, and Tax/Estate Planning.*

### MANAGING PARTNER

**THOMAS W. KELLERMAN,** born St. Louis, Missouri, September 11, 1955; admitted to bar, 1980, California. *Education:* Western Illinois University (B.Bus., with high honors, 1976); University of California at Los Angeles (J.D., 1980). Member, Education Committee, Business Law Section, State Bar of California, 1988-1993 and Chair, 1991-1993. *PRACTICE AREAS:* Emerging Growth Companies; Securities Law; Mergers and Acquisitions Law. *Email:* tkellerman@brobeck.com

*(This Listing Continued)*

### PARTNERS

**WILLIAM C. ANDERSON,** born Menomonie, Wisconsin, July 11, 1952; admitted to bar, 1977, California. *Education:* University of Wisconsin-Eau Claire (B.A., 1974); University of Minnesota (J.D., 1977). Staff Member, 1975-1976 and Board Member, 1976-1977, Minnesota Law Review. *PRACTICE AREAS:* Labor Law; Employment Law. *Email:* banderson@brobeck.com

**WILLIAM L. ANTHONY, JR.,** born Torrington, Connecticut, September 17, 1939; admitted to bar, 1966, Connecticut; 1967, Michigan; 1982, California; registered to practice before U.S. Patent and Trademark Office. *Education:* Worcester Polytechnic Institute (B.S., 1961); University of Connecticut (J.D., 1966). Co-Author: "Litigating the Validity and Infringement of Software Patents," 41 Washington and Lee Law Review 1307, 1985. *Member:* American Intellectual Property Law Association. *PRACTICE AREAS:* Patent Litigation. *Email:* banthony@brobeck.com

**THOMAS A. BEVILACQUA,** born Castro Valley, California, 1956; admitted to bar, 1981, California. *Education:* University of California at Berkeley (B.S., 1978); Hastings College of Law, University of California (J.D., 1981). Phi Beta Kappa. Order of the Coif. Associate Editor, Hastings Law Journal, 1980-1981. *PRACTICE AREAS:* Corporate Law. *Email:* tbevilacqua@brobeck.com

**MICHAEL J. CASEY,** born New York, N.Y., November 14, 1962; admitted to bar, 1987, California. *Education:* University of California at Berkeley (A.B., with distinction, 1984); University of California at Los Angeles (J.D., 1987). *PRACTICE AREAS:* Corporate Law. *Email:* mcasey@brobeck.com

**GARI L. CHEEVER,** born Lincoln, Nebraska, March 22, 1957; admitted to bar, 1984, Colorado; 1987, California. *Education:* Arizona State University (B.S. and B.A., summa cum laude, 1980) Phi Beta Kappa; Stanford University (J.D., 1983). *PRACTICE AREAS:* General Corporate and Securities Law; Venture Capital Law. *Email:* gcheever@brobeck.com

**ROBERT DEBERARDINE,** born Brooklyn, New York, June 29, 1958; admitted to bar, 1983, California; 1988, New York; 1992, Texas; registered to practice before U.S. Patent and Trademark Office. *Education:* Lafayette (B.S. Chem. E., cum laude, 1980); Cornell (J.D., magna cum laude, 1983). Member: Intellectual Property Sections of American Bar Association, New York State Bar Association, State Bar of California; State Bar of Texas. *PRACTICE AREAS:* Patent, Trademark, Copyright, Trade Secrets and Related Litigation. *Email:* rdeberardine@brobeck.com

**S. JAMES DiBERNARDO,** born Hartford, Connecticut, October 15, 1946; admitted to bar, 1973, Rhode Island; 1977, California. *Education:* College of the Holy Cross (A.B., cum laude, 1967); Columbia University (J.D., with honors, 1973); Boston University (LL.M. in Taxation, 1977). *PRACTICE AREAS:* Executive Compensation; Research and Development Financing. *Email:* jdibernardo@brobeck.com

**J. STEPHAN DOLEZALEK,** born Friedberg, Hessen, West Germany, May 23, 1956; admitted to bar, 1982, Wisconsin; 1984, California. *Education:* University of Virginia (B.A., 1978; J.D., 1982). *LANGUAGES:* German. *PRACTICE AREAS:* General Corporate Law; Securities Law, Emerging Growth and Biotechnology Companies Law. *Email:* sdolezalek@brobeck.com

**DAVID M. FURBUSH,** born Palo Alto, California, March 25, 1954; admitted to bar, 1978, California. *Education:* Harvard University (B.A., cum laude, 1975; J.D., cum laude, 1978). *PRACTICE AREAS:* Securities Litigation; Intellectual Property Litigation. *Email:* dfurbush@brobeck.com

**NOEMI ESPINOSA HAYES,** born Philadelphia, Pennsylvania, November 24, 1958; admitted to bar, 1984, California; registered to practice before U.S. Patent and Trademark Office. *Education:* University of California at Santa Barbara; San Jose State University (B.S.Ch.E., 1981); Hastings College of the Law, University of California (J.D., 1984). Member, Intellectual Property Section, State Bar of California. *Member:* American Institute of Chemical Engineers; American Intellectual Property Law Association; Peninsula Intellectual Property Law Association. *PRACTICE AREAS:* Patent, Trademark, Copyright, Tradesecrets and related Litigation. *Email:* nespinosa@brobeck.com

**KAREN N. IKEDA,** born Redwood City, California, July 29, 1959; admitted to bar, 1987, California. *Education:* San Diego State University (B.S., summa cum laude, 1981); University of San Francisco (J.D., 1986). Judicial Extern to the Honorable Justice Joseph R. Grodin, California Supreme Court, January 1986-May, 1986. Member: American Bar Association, Intellectual Property, Science and Technology and Business Sections; California State Bar, Intellectual Property and Business Sections. *Member:*

*(This Listing Continued)*

## BROBECK, PHLEGER & HARRISON LLP, Palo Alto—Continued

Bar Association of San Francisco; Orange County Bar Association (Technology and Business Sections); United States Trademark Association. *PRACTICE AREAS:* Technology and Intellectual Property. *Email:* kikeda@brobeck.com

*MEREDITH NELSON LANDY,* born Baton Rouge, Louisiana, August 20, 1960; admitted to bar, 1988, California. *Education:* Mount Holyoke College; Louisiana State University and A. and M. College (B.A., 1983); Boalt Hall School of Law, University of California (J.D., 1988). Member, Moot Court Board, 1987-1988. Executive Editor, California Law Review, 1987-1988. Law Clerk to Presiding Justice Harry W. Low, California Court of Appeal. Author: "Quality Control for Indigent Defense Contracts," 76 California Law Review, Oct., 1988. Member, Antitrust Law Section, American Bar Association. *PRACTICE AREAS:* SEC. *Email:* mlandy@brobeck.com

*JOHN W. LARSON,* born Detroit, Michigan, June 24, 1935; admitted to bar, 1963, California. *Education:* Stanford University (B.A., with distinction, 1957); Stanford University Law School (LL.B., 1962). Order of the Coif. Member, Board of Editors, Stanford Law Review, 1961-1962. Assistant Secretary, United States Department of the Interior, 1971-1973. Counselor to the Chairman of the Cost of Living Council, 1973. Member, Board of Visitors, Stanford Law School, 1975-1977, 1985-1987, 1995-1997. Managing Partner Firmwide and Chairman of the Executive Committee, 1988 to 1992, Chairman, 1993-1996. *PRACTICE AREAS:* Securities Law; Mergers and Acquisitions Law; General Corporate Law. *Email:* jlarson@brobeck.com

*WARREN T. LAZAROW,* born Atlantic City, New Jersey, January 25, 1960; admitted to bar, 1988, New York; 1990, California. *Education:* Princeton University, Woodrow Wilson School (B.A., cum laude, 1982); Brooklyn Law School (J.D., 1986). Notes Editor, Brooklyn Law School Law Review, 1985-1986. Author: Note, "The SEC's Regulation of the Financial Press: The Legal Implications of the Misappropriation Theory," Brooklyn Law Review, Volume 52, 1986. Recipient, Morris Scholarship and American Jurisprudence Award in Civil Procedure. *Member:* New York State Bar Association. *LANGUAGES:* French and Hebrew. *PRACTICE AREAS:* Corporate and Securities Law; Venture Capital Law; Emerging Growth Companies Law; Intellectual Property Law. *Email:* wlazarow@brobeck.com

*GREGORY S. LEMMER,* born Saginaw, Michigan, August 24, 1960; admitted to bar, 1989, California; 1990, Wisconsin. *Education:* Michigan State University (B.A., with highest honors, 1982); Michigan State University (M.L.I.R., 1983); University of Wisconsin at Madison (J.D., 1989). Member, 1987-1989 and Associate Editor, 1988-1989, Wisconsin Law Review. *PRACTICE AREAS:* Labor and Employment. *Email:* glemmer@brobeck.com

*EDWARD M. LEONARD,* born New York, New York, November 29, 1941; admitted to bar, 1972, California. *Education:* Yale University (B.A., 1963); Stanford University (J.D., 1971). Order of the Coif. Member, Board of Editors, Stanford Law Review, 1970-1971. *PRACTICE AREAS:* Securities; Mergers and Acquisitions; Emerging Growth Companies; Venture Capital. *Email:* eleonard@brobeck.com

*THERESE A. MROZEK,* born Cleveland, Ohio, 1957; admitted to bar, 1985, Illinois; 1987, California. *Education:* University of California at Berkeley (B.S., cum laude, 1981); Northwestern University (J.D., cum laude, 1985). *PRACTICE AREAS:* Corporate Law; Emerging Companies and Venture Capital; Securities Law. *Email:* tmrozek@brobeck.com

*LUTHER KENT ORTON,* born Ames, Iowa, June 30, 1946; admitted to bar, 1972, California. *Education:* Northwestern University (B.S.I.E., 1969); Stanford University (J.D., 1972). Tau Beta Pi; Order of the Coif. *PRACTICE AREAS:* Trade Secret, Patent and Unfair Competition Litigation; General Commercial Litigation. *Email:* lorton@brobeck.com

*RONALD S. WYNN,* born Long Beach, California, February 14, 1955; admitted to bar, 1982, California. *Education:* University of California at Los Angeles (B.A., cum laude, 1978); University of California at Davis (J.D., 1982). *PRACTICE AREAS:* Intellectual Property and Antitrust Litigation. *Email:* rwynn@brobeck.com

*(This Listing Continued)*

### OF COUNSEL

*THOMAS H. CARLSON,* born Buffalo, New York, January 12, 1958; admitted to bar, 1985, California. *Education:* University of California at Berkeley (A.B., high honors, 1981); University of San Francisco (J.D., magna cum laude, 1985). Recipient, American Jurisprudence Awards for: Evidence, Corporations, Community Property. Member, McAuliffe Honor Society. *PRACTICE AREAS:* Civil Litigation. *Email:* tcarlson@brobeck.com

*ZAITUN POONJA,* born Nairobi, Kenya, March 21, 1953; admitted to bar, 1986, California. *Education:* Hollins College (B.A., with honors, 1974); Stanford University (J.D., 1986). *PRACTICE AREAS:* Corporate Tax; International Tax; Executive Compensation. *Email:* kpoonja@brobeck.com

### RESIDENT ASSOCIATES

*Craig Y. Allison; Charles F. Aragon* (admission pending).; *Mayao Armour* (admission pending).; *Charles K. Ashley II; Andrew Baw; Timothy S. Bergreen; Robert J. Blanch, Jr.* (Not admitted in CA); *Patricia G. Copeland; Jacqueline Cowden; Timothy R. Curry; Michael F. Cyran; Thomas P. Dennedy; Michael C. Doran; Amr A. El-Bayoumi; Helen G.F. Fields; Carol R. Freeman; Tamar Fruchtman; William P. Garvey; Hanna Casper George; Nora L. Gibson; Susan Giordano; Ahaviah D. Glaser* (admission pending).; *Scot A. Griffin; Rodrigo M. Guidero; Ramesh Hamadani; Daniel R. Hansen; Kimberley Erin Henningsen; Pamela B. Hiatt* (admission pending).; *Jeffrey P. Higgins; Franklin P. Huang; H. Richard Hukari; Gregory C. Jackson; Andrew B. Koslow; James N. Kramer; Peter C. Ku; Sara M. Kurlich; Lisa A. Laehy* (admission pending).; *Elaine Llewelyn; Taraneh Maghamé; Sharon E. Meieran; Margaret T. Miles; Patricia Montalvo; Benjamin P. Oelsner; Michael A. Plumleigh; Magan Ray; Christine L. Richardson; Melinda Collins Riechert; Christina Baker Robinson; Maura Roe; Anna A. Ruiz; Valerie L. Russell; Kevin A. Smith; Karen Y. Spencer; David W. Stevens; Andrew N. Thomases; Candace M. Tillman; Tomas C. Tovar; Peter Vaughan; Craig R. Venable; Roburt J. Waldow* (Not admitted in CA); *Craig E. Walker; Stephen G. Wanderer; Sarah H. Whittle; Elizabeth A. R. Yee.*

All Members and Associates of the Firm are Members of the State Bar of California and the American Bar Association.
Brobeck, Phleger & Harrison and Brobeck Hale and Dorr International have a joint venture office in London, England.

---

## BROOKS & RAUB, A.P.C.
721 COLORADO AVENUE, SUITE 101
PALO ALTO, CALIFORNIA 94303-3913
Telephone: 415-321-1400
Facsimile: 415-321-1450

*Bankruptcy and Business Reorganization, Commercial Insolvency and Related Litigation.*

*LINCOLN A. BROOKS,* born Cleveland, Ohio, May 25, 1942; admitted to bar, 1975, California. *Education:* Miami University (B.S., 1971); Santa Clara University (J.D., cum laude, 1974). *Member:* Bar Association of San Francisco; Palo Alto, Santa Clara County and American Bar Associations; State Bar of California. *PRACTICE AREAS:* Bankruptcy Law; Business Organization.

*L. DONALD RAUB, JR.,* born Wilkes-Barre, Pennsylvania, May 16, 1949; admitted to bar, 1983, California. *Education:* University of Pennsylvania (B.A., 1972; M.S., 1975); Hastings College of Law, University of California (J.D., magna cum laude, 1983). *Member:* Order of the Coif; Thurston Society. *Member:* Bar Association of San Francisco; State Bar of California; American Bar Association. *PRACTICE AREAS:* Bankruptcy Reorganization; Commercial Law; Bankruptcy; Insolvency; Workouts.

*DAVID S. CAPLAN,* born Fresno, California, November 25, 1948; admitted to bar, 1977, California and U.S. District Court, Northern District of California. *Education:* San Francisco State University (B.A., 1972); University of San Francisco (J.D., with honors, 1976). Member, McAuliffe Honor Society. Member, Panel of Commercial Arbitrators, American Arbitration Association. *Member:* State Bar of California. *PRACTICE AREAS:* Commercial Insolvency; Bankruptcy Reorganization.

PROFESSIONAL BIOGRAPHIES
CALIFORNIA—PALO ALTO

## BROWN & BAIN
### 1755 EMBARCADERO ROAD, SUITE 200
### PALO ALTO, CALIFORNIA 94306
Telephone: 415-856-9411
Telecopier: 415-856-6061

*Phoenix, Arizona Affiliated Office:* Brown & Bain, A Professional Association, 2901 North Central Avenue, P.O. Box 400. Telephone: 602-351-8000. Telecopier: 602-351-8516.

*Tucson, Arizona Affiliated Office:* Brown & Bain, A Professional Association. One South Church Avenue, Nineteenth Floor, P.O. Box 2265. Telephone: 602-798-7900 Telecopier: 602-798-7945.

*Administrative, Antitrust, Appellate, Banking, Bankruptcy, Bond, Commercial, Corporate, Employment, Environmental, Estate Planning and Probate, Litigation, Government, Health, Immigration, Insurance Coverage, Intellectual Property, International, Land Use, Licensing, Media, Natural Resources, Patent, Product Liability, Public Utility, Real Estate, Securities, Tax, Trademark and Water.*

FIRM PROFILE: Since its founding in 1960, Brown & Bain has developed a national reputation in high technology and complex litigation matters together with a regional reputation as a full service law firm. To meet clients' multistate needs, Brown & Bain has continued to grow and diversify through its offices in Phoenix and Tucson, Arizona and Palo Alto, California.

### RESIDENT PERSONNEL

**RICHARD H. HARVEY,** born Los Angeles, California, March 29, 1945; admitted to bar, 1975, California. *Education:* California State University at Los Angeles (B.S., in Finance with Highest Departmental Honors, 1971); University of Southern California (J.D., 1974). Beta Gamma Sigma. *Member:* The State Bar of California; American Bar Association (Member, Business Law Section). **PRACTICE AREAS:** Commercial; Corporate Securities; Mergers and Acquisitions; Intellectual Property; Licensing; Employment. *Email:* harvey@brains.com

**ERIC S. BEANE,** born New York, N.Y., October 27, 1971; (admission pending). *Education:* Cornell University (B.S., 1993); University of Pennsylvania (J.D., 1996). Recipient, H.H. Goldstein Memorial Prize. **PRACTICE AREAS:** General Litigation. *Email:* beane@brains.com

### COUNSEL

**LOIS W. ABRAHAM,** born San Francisco, California, November 17, 1933; admitted to bar, 1973, Arizona; 1978, California. *Education:* Stanford University (B.A., cum laude, 1955); Arizona State University (J.D., magna cum laude, 1973). Phi Beta Kappa. **PRACTICE AREAS:** Intellectual Property; Antitrust; General Litigation. *Email:* abraham@brains.com

**IAN C. BALLON,** born Montreal, Quebec, Canada, June 4, 1962; admitted to bar, 1986, Maryland; 1988, District of Columbia; 1989, California. *Education:* Tufts University (B.A., magna cum laude, 1983); George Washington University (J.D., with honors, 1986); Georgetown University (LL.M., International and Comparative Law, 1988). Member, 1984-1985, and Articles Editor, 1985-1986, The George Washington Journal of International Law and Economics. *Member:* American Bar Association (Computer Litigation Committee, Litigation, Science and Technology, and Intellectual Property Law Sections); World Forum of Silicon Valley. **PRACTICE AREAS:** Intellectual Property; Internet related Litigation; Strategic Counseling. *Email:* ballon@brains.com

**DOUGLAS CLARK NEILSSON,** born August 16, 1947; admitted to bar, 1973, California. *Education:* University of California at Los Angeles (B.A., 1970; J.D., 1973). Member, National Moot Court Team. Outstanding Advocate, Roscoe Pound Moot Court Competition, 1973. Chairman, Business Law Section, Santa Clara County Bar Association, 1989. **PRACTICE AREAS:** Commercial; Corporate; Securities; Mergers and Acquisitions; Equipment Leasing; Intellectual Property; Licensing. *Email:* neilsson@brains.com

**BERNARD PETRIE,** born Detroit, Michigan, September 9, 1925; admitted to bar, 1953, New York; 1955, California; 1961, U.S. Supreme Court. *Education:* Culver Military Academy (1943); United States Military Academy (B.S., 1946); University of Michigan (J.D., 1952). Order of the Coif. Associate Editor, Michigan Law Review, 1951-1952. Member, American Law Institute. Fellow, American College of Trial Lawyers. (Also practicing individually in San Francisco, California). **PRACTICE AREAS:** General Litigation; Media. *Email:* petrie@brains.com

(For complete biographical data on all personnel, see professional biographies at Phoenix, Arizona)

## BRYANT, CLOHAN, OTT, MAINES & BARUH
### 550 HAMILTON AVENUE, SUITE 220
### PALO ALTO, CALIFORNIA 94301
Telephone: 415-324-1606
Facsimile: 415-324-4613

*Corporation, Securities, Franchising, State and Federal Taxation, Sports and Real Estate Law. Estate Planning, Trusts and Probate. General Civil Trial Practice in all Courts. Administrative Law.*

### MEMBERS OF FIRM

**WILLIAM H. BRYANT,** born Presque Isle, Maine, October 8, 1940; admitted to bar, 1965, California. *Education:* University of California at Los Angeles (B.S., 1962); Stanford University (LL.B., 1965). Order of the Coif; Beta Gamma Sigma. Note Editor, Stanford Law Review, 1964-1965. *Member:* Palo Alto Bar Association. **PRACTICE AREAS:** Corporate; Securities (Private Placements); Real Estate; Mergers and Acquisitions.

**FRANK E. CLOHAN,** born Palo Alto, California, October 6, 1938; admitted to bar, 1967, California. *Education:* Stanford University (B.A., 1961); University of Santa Clara (J.D., 1966); New York University (LL.M., in Taxation, 1967). Phi Alpha Delta. Member, Taxation Section, American Bar Association. *Member:* Palo Alto Bar Association. **PRACTICE AREAS:** Taxation; Estate Planning; Corporate; Real Estate; Mergers and Acquisitions; Business Reorganizations.

**ROBERT L. MAINES,** born Tipton, Indiana, March 22, 1938; admitted to bar, 1967, California and Illinois. *Education:* Miami University (B.S.B.A., 1960, Omicron Delta Kappa); Stanford University (J.D., 1966, Order of the Coif). Member, Board of Editors, Stanford Law Review, 1964-1966. Partner, Petit & Martin, 1974-1995. *Member:* Bar Association of San Francisco; Santa Clara County and American (Member, Sections on: Litigation; Antitrust) Bar Associations; State Bar of California. **PRACTICE AREAS:** Business and Real Estate Litigation; Alternate Dispute Resolution.

**JUDITH M. OTT,** born Vancouver, Washington, February 2, 1943; admitted to bar, 1978, California. *Education:* University of Oregon (B.A., 1964); University of Santa Clara (J.D., summa cum laude, 1978). Member, Business Law Section, State Bar of California. *Member:* California Women Lawyers Association. **PRACTICE AREAS:** Franchising; Corporate Start-ups; Real Estate; Mergers and Acquisitions; Private Financing; Personal Tax and Estate Planning.

**JEFFREY A. BARUH,** born San Francisco, California, July 3, 1954; admitted to bar, 1979, California. *Education:* University of California at Los Angeles (B.A., cum laude, 1976, Pi Gamma Mu); University of San Francisco (J.D., 1979). **PRACTICE AREAS:** Real Estate Litigation; Business Litigation; Insurance Bad Faith; Construction Litigation; Lender Liability.

### ASSOCIATES

**ANDREW L. FAGAN,** born Seattle, Washington, September 13, 1959; admitted to bar, 1985, California and U.S. District Court, Northern District of California. *Education:* University of Washington (B.A., cum laude, 1981); Hastings College of the Law, University of California (J.D., 1985). Writer, 1983-1984 and Articles Editor, 1984-1985, Hastings Constitutional Law Quarterly. *Member:* Bar Association of San Francisco; Lawyers Club of San Francisco. **PRACTICE AREAS:** Manufacturers Representative Litigation; Business Litigation; Real Estate Litigation.

**MEREDITH L. FAHN,** born Bridgeton, New Jersey, April 4, 1963; admitted to bar, 1991, California and U.S. District Court, Northern District of California; 1992, U.S. Court of Appeals, Ninth Circuit. *Education:* University of Pennsylvania (B.A., 1987); Temple University School of Law (J.D., 1991). Moot Court. Staff Member, Temple International and Comparative Law Journal, Temple University, 1991. Author: Allegations of Child Sexual Abuse in Custody Disputes: Getting to the Truth of the Matter," ABA Family Law Quarterly, 1991; "Noncompliance with the Dowry Prohibition Act," 1961 (India); "A Society's Reactions to Imposed Law," Temple International and Comparative Law Journal, 1990. *Member:* Santa Clara County, San Mateo County, Palo Alto Area and American Bar Asso-

*(This Listing Continued)*

CAA1551B

**BRYANT, CLOHAN, OTT, MAINES & BARUH,** Palo Alto—Continued

ciations; State Bar of California. *PRACTICE AREAS:* Litigation; Business Law; Estate Disputes; Trials and Appeals.

All Attorneys except as noted in individual biographies are Members of the Santa Clara County and American Bar Associations and the State Bar of California.

## CARR, DeFILIPPO & FERRELL

Established in 1992

2225 EAST BAYSHORE ROAD, SUITE 200
**PALO ALTO, CALIFORNIA 94303**
Telephone: 415-812-3400
Fax: 415-812-3444

*Corporate and Securities, Employment Law, Intellectual Property (including Patent Prosecution and Litigation, Trademark, Copyright, Trade Secrets, and Unfair Competition), International Transactions, Licensing, Litigation (including Intellectual Property, Business Litigation and Insurance Coverage), Partnerships and Franchising, Real Estate, and Venture Financings and Placements.*

### MEMBERS OF FIRM

**BARRY A. CARR,** born New York, N.Y., 1958; admitted to bar, 1983, California. *Education:* University of California at Berkeley (B.A., Political Science, 1980); Columbia University School of Law (J.D., 1983). *Email:* carr@cdf.com

**STUART C. CLARK,** born Pietermaritzburg, South Africa, 1946; admitted to bar, 1972, South Africa; 1986, California. *Education:* University of Natal, South Africa (B.Comm., 1967) University of Natal Law School, South Africa (LL.B., 1969). *Email:* clark@cdf.com

**GARY A. DeFILIPPO,** born New York, N.Y., 1957; admitted to bar, 1982, California. *Education:* Stanford University (A.B., 1979); University of Southern California (J.D., 1982).

**JOHN S. FERRELL,** born Fairbanks, Alaska, 1957; admitted to bar, 1991, California; registered to practice before U.S. Patent and Trademark Office. *Education:* University of Texas (B.S.E.E., 1980); Texas A. & M. University (M.S.E.E., 1983); Santa Clara University (J.D., 1991). *Email:* jsferrell@cdf.com

**ROBERT J. YORIO,** born Albany, New York, 1951; admitted to bar, 1978, New York; 1980, California. *Education:* Syracuse University (B.A., 1973); Georgetown University Law Center (J.D., 1977).

### COUNSEL

**JAMES L. BERG,** born Iron Mountain, Michigan, 1953; admitted to bar, 1978, California. *Education:* University of Michigan (B.B.A., 1975); University of Michigan Law School (J.D., 1978).

**LISA A. GARONO,** born Austintown, Ohio, 1961; admitted to bar, 1987, Wisconsin; 1990, Illinois; 1992, California; registered to practice before U.S. Patent and Trademark Office. *Education:* John Carroll University (B.S., 1983); Ohio State University College of Law (J.D., 1987). *Email:* lgarono@cdf.com

**KEVIN A. GOODWIN,** born Teaneck, New Jersey, December 7, 1955; admitted to bar, 1982, California. *Education:* Claremont Men's College (B.A., summa cum laude, 1980); Columbia University (J.D., 1982).

**J. EPPA HITE, III,** born Richmond, Virginia, 1951; admitted to bar, 1981, California; registered to practice before U.S. Trademark and Patent Office. *Education:* University of Virginia (B.A., 1975; B.S.C.S., 1977); College of William & Mary (J.D., 1980). *Email:* eppa@cdf.com

**FRANCIS H. LEWIS,** born Milwaukee, Wisconsin, 1937; admitted to bar, 1974, California; registered to practice before U.S. Patent and Trademark Office. *Education:* Stanford University (Ph.D., 1964); University of San Francisco (J.D., 1974). *Email:* flewis@cdf.com

### ASSOCIATES

**KATHLEEN S. ANSARI,** born Astoria, Oregon, 1965; admitted to bar, 1995, California. *Education:* Pennsylvania State University (B.A., Mathematics, 1988; M.A., 1990); Santa Clara University (J.D., 1995). *Email:* kansari@cdf.com

**LLOYD E. DAKIN, JR.,** born Jennette, Pennsylvania, 1965; admitted to bar, 1994, Texas; registered to practice before U.S. Patent and Trade-

*(This Listing Continued)*

mark Office (Not admitted in California). *Education:* Pennsylvania State University (B.S.E.E., 1985); University of Texas (J.D., 1993). *Email:* lloyd@cdf.com

**LARRY E. HENNEMAN, JR.,** born Toledo, Ohio, 1961; (admission pending). *Education:* Lake Forest College (B.A., Physics, 1988); Wayne State University (J.D., 1994). *Email:* larry@cdf.com

**GREGORY J. KOERNER,** born Madison, Wisconsin, 1952; admitted to bar, 1995, California; registered to practice before U.S. Patent and Trademark Office. *Education:* Dominican College of San Rafael (B.A., 1977); The Union Institute, San Diego (B.S., 1994); California Western School of Law (J.D., 1994). *Email:* gkoerner@cdf.com

**JAMES W. LUCEY,** born San Francisco, California, 1965; admitted to bar, 1992, California. *Education:* University of San Francisco (B.S., Business, 1987; J.D., 1992).

**LEROY D. MAUNU,** born July 24, 1963; admitted to bar, 1993, Minnesota; registered to practice before U.S. Patent and Trademark Office (Not admitted in California). *Education:* Iowa State University (B.S., 1985); William Mitchel College of Law (J.D., cum laude, 1993). *PRACTICE AREAS:* Patent Prosecution; Software Licensing; Procurement.

**MARC A. SOKOL,** born Oakland, California, 1967; admitted to bar, 1992, California. *Education:* University of California at Davis (B.S.E.E., 1989); University of San Francisco (J.D., 1992).

### LEGAL SUPPORT PERSONNEL

### PATENT AGENT

**MARK A. WARDAS,** born Warsaw, Poland, 1954. Registered to practice before U.S. Patent and Trademark Office. University of California at San Diego (B.S., Bio-Engineering, 1982); Northwestern University (M.S., 1984). Patent Examiner, U.S. Patent and Trademark Office, 1994-1995.

REPRESENTATIVE CLIENTS: Apple; Cirrus Logic; Claris Corporation; CSX Transportation; GEC Plessy; Hobart; LSI Logic; A.T. Kearney; Octel Communications; Opti, Inc.; Philips North America; Polycom; Ricoh; Sega Enterprises; Seiko-Epson; SMOS; Software Publishing Corporation; Sun Microsystems Computer Company; Telernatics; Xilinx.

## COHEN & OSTLER

A PROFESSIONAL CORPORATION

Established in 1985

SUITE 410, 525 UNIVERSITY AVENUE
**PALO ALTO, CALIFORNIA 94301**
Telephone: 415-321-3835
Telecopier: 415-321-0171

*Corporate, Partnership, Securities, Finance, Venture Capital, Commercial, Federal, State, Local and International Taxation, Employee Benefits, Employment Law, Construction Law, Commercial and Civil Litigation, Antitrust, Trade Regulation and Unfair Competition, Estate Planning and Probate.*

**DAVID COHEN,** born Buffalo, New York, 1952; admitted to bar, 1978, California. *Education:* Brown University (B.A., magna cum laude, 1974); University of Michigan (J.D., cum laude, 1977). Phi Beta Kappa. Law Clerk to Hon. Louis C. McGregor, Michigan Court of Appeals, 1977-1978. *Member:* State Bar of California. *PRACTICE AREAS:* Corporate; Tax Law.

**MARK R. OSTLER,** born Oakland, California, 1952; admitted to bar, 1979, California. *Education:* Brigham Young University (B.A., magna cum laude, 1975; M.B.A., 1979; J.D., cum laude, 1979). Beta Gamma Sigma. Article Editor, Brigham Young University Law Review, 1978-1979. *Member:* State Bar of California; American Bar Association (Securities Regulation Subcommittee and Small Business Committee, Section of Business Law, 1983—). *PRACTICE AREAS:* Corporate Law.

**ANDREW R. KISLIK,** born Newark, New Jersey, 1954; admitted to bar, 1979, Minnesota; 1985, California. *Education:* Harvard University (A.B., cum laude, 1976; J.D., cum laude, 1979). Phi Beta Kappa. Note Editor, Harvard Law Review, 1978-1979. Law Clerk to Hon. Donald D. Alsop, U.S. District Court, Minnesota, 1979-1981. Author: "Court-Appointed Experts - Practical Implications for Software Copyright Actions," 5 The Computer Lawyer 11, 1988. *Member:* State Bar of California. *PRACTICE AREAS:* Civil Litigation; Commercial Litigation; Employment Law.

*(This Listing Continued)*

## OF COUNSEL

**HAL E. FORBES,** born Torrance, California, 1939; admitted to bar, 1969, California. *Education:* Stanford University (A.B., 1961); University of San Francisco (J.D., 1968). Certified Public Accountant, California, 1964. *Member:* State Bar of California (Member, Sections on: Probate, Estate Planning and Trust Law). **PRACTICE AREAS:** Estate Planning; Probate; Trust Administration; Estate Tax.

**G. KIP EDWARDS,** born Wichita, Kansas, 1947; admitted to bar, 1972, California. *Education:* University of Washington (B.A., 1968); Boalt Hall School of Law, University of California (J.D., 1971). Order of the Coif. Chief Research Editor, California Law Review, 1970-1971. Teaching Fellow, Stanford Law School, 1971-1972. Contributing Author: "Non-Price Predation," ABA Antitrust Section, Monograph Series, 1990. **PRACTICE AREAS:** Antitrust, Distribution and Trade Regulation Law; Trademark Litigation.

## SPECIAL COUNSEL

**DONALD A. SLICHTER,** born Milwaukee, Wisconsin, 1932; admitted to bar, 1962, California and U.S. District Court, Northern District of California. *Education:* Princeton University (A.B., 1954); University of Michigan (J.D., cum laude, 1961). Order of the Coif. Editor, Michigan Law Review, 1960-1961. *Member:* State Bar of California. **PRACTICE AREAS:** Corporate Law.

REPRESENTATIVE CLIENTS: Applied Materials, Inc.; Beeline Group, Inc.; BINDCO; Biolog, Inc.; Calogic; Crosspoint Venture Partners; Elcon Products International Co.; Enterprise Networking Systems; E&J Gallo Winery; Horton Image; Invest West Capital Corporation; LUNA Imaging, Inc.; Nortele; Pleasanton Garbage Service; South San Francisco Scavenger Co.; Specialty Solid Waste; Stanislaus Food Products; Taarcom, Inc.; Viking Freight, Inc.

---

# GEORGE S. COLE
## PALO ALTO, CALIFORNIA
(See Menlo Park)
*Computer Law and Intellectual Property.*

---

# COOLEY GODWARD LLP
**FIVE PALO ALTO SQUARE, 3000 EL CAMINO REAL**
**PALO ALTO, CALIFORNIA 94306**
Telephone: 415-843-5000
Telex: 380816 COOLEY PA
Fax: 415-857-0663
Email: webmaster@cooley.com
URL: http://www.cooley.com

*San Francisco, California Office:* 20th Floor, One Maritime Plaza. Telephone: 415-693-2000. Telex: 380815 COOLEY SFO Fax: 415-951-3698 or 415-951-3699.

*Menlo Park, California Office:* 3000 Sand Hill Road, Building 3, Suite 230. Telephone: 415-843-5000. Telex: 380816 COOLEY PA. Fax: 415-854-2691.

*San Diego, California Office:* 4365 Executive Drive, Suite 1100. Telephone: 619-550-6000. Fax: 619-453-3555.

*Boulder, Colorado Office:* 2595 Canyon Boulevard, Suite 250. Telephone: 303-546-4000. Fax: 303-546-4099.

*Denver, Colorado Office:* One Tabor Center, 1200 17th Street, Suite 2100. Telephone: 303-606-4800. Fax: 303-606-4899.

*General Practice.*

FIRM PROFILE: *Cooley Godward LLP's practice emphasizes the representation of entrepreneurial growth companies - often in high technology fields - and venture capital investors in those companies. The firm provides the full range of legal services including securities law, patent, copyright, licensing and other intellectual property expertise, assistance with mergers, acquisitions and corporate partnering transactions, finance, litigation, tax, real estate, employment and other specialties.*

## MEMBERS OF FIRM

**JAMES R. BATCHELDER,** born Pittsburgh, Pennsylvania, April 24, 1963; admitted to bar, 1988, California. *Education:* Franklin and Marshall College (B.A., 1985); University of California at Los Angeles (J.D., 1988). Phi Beta Kappa. **PRACTICE AREAS:** Technology Litigation. **Email:** BATCHELDERJR@COOLEY.COM

*(This Listing Continued)*

**LOIS K. BENES,** born Milwaukee, Wisconsin, May 4, 1953; admitted to bar, 1987, California. *Education:* Harvard College (A.B., cum laude, 1975); Boalt Hall School of Law, University of California, Berkeley (J.D., 1987). Associate Editor, 1984-1985, Managing Editor, 1985-1986 and Editor-in-Chief, 1986-1987, Industrial Relations Law Journal. **PRACTICE AREAS:** Employment and Labor Law. **Email:** BENESLK@COOLEY.COM

**LEE F. BENTON,** born Springfield, Ohio, February 18, 1944; admitted to bar, 1970, California. *Education:* Oberlin College (A.B., 1966); University of Chicago (J.D., 1969). Phi Beta Kappa; Order of the Coif. Executive Editor, University of Chicago Law Review, 1968-1969. Teaching Fellow, Stanford Law School, 1969-1970. Co-Author, "Venture Capital and Public Offering Negotiation," 2nd ed., Prentice-Hall Law and Business, 1992. **PRACTICE AREAS:** Mergers and Acquisitions; Business Law. **Email:** BENTONLF@COOLEY.COM

**ROBERT J. BRIGHAM,** born Redwood City, California, July 27, 1961; admitted to bar, 1988, California. *Education:* Amherst College (B.A., summa cum laude, 1985); Stanford University (J.D., with distinction, 1988). Phi Beta Kappa. **PRACTICE AREAS:** Emerging Growth Companies; Corporate Law; Securities. **Email:** BRIGHAMRJ@COOLEY.COM

**CRAIG HILL CASEBEER,** born Los Angeles, California, September 13, 1947; admitted to bar, 1973, California. *Education:* Stanford University (B.A., 1969); Boalt Hall School of Law, University of California, Berkeley (J.D., 1973). Order of the Coif. Note and Comment Editor, California Law Review, 1972-1973. Law Clerk to Judge Stanley A. Weigel, U.S. District Court, Northern District of California, 1973-1974. **Email:** CASEBEERCH@COOLEY.COM

**PAUL CHURCHILL,** born New York, N.Y., June 15, 1955; admitted to bar, 1986, California. *Education:* University of California at Berkeley (B.S., with highest honors, 1982); Boalt Hall School of Law, University of California, Berkeley (J.D., 1986). Phi Beta Kappa; Beta Gamma Sigma; Beta Alpha Psi. **Email:** CHIRCHILLP@COOLEY.COM

**RICHARD E. CLIMAN,** born New York, N.Y., July 19, 1953; admitted to bar, 1977, California. *Education:* Harvard College (A.B., cum laude, 1974); Harvard University (J.D., cum laude, 1977). Author: "Civil Liability Under the Credit-Regulation Provisions of the Securities Exchange Act of 1934," 63 Cornell Law Review 206, 1978. Co-Author with Gregg Alton: "Potential Securities Law Liabilities in the Sale of a Privately Held Business," 10 California Business Law Practitioner 1, 1995. *Member:* American Bar Association, Section of Business Law, Committee on Negotiated Acquisitions, Chairman, Editorial Subcommittee; Member, Executive Subcommittee. **Email:** CLIMANRE@COOLEY.COM

**JANET L. CULLUM,** born Burbank, California, November 9, 1948; admitted to bar, 1982, California. *Education:* California State University at Northridge (B.A., 1972); Boalt Hall School of Law, University of California, Berkeley (J.D., 1982). Order of the Coif. **PRACTICE AREAS:** Intellectual Property Law; Litigation. **Email:** CULLUMJL@COOLEY.COM

**BRIAN C. CUNNINGHAM,** born Sparta, Illinois, October 17, 1943; admitted to bar, 1971, New York; 1980, Missouri; 1982, California. *Education:* Washington University (B.S., 1965; J.D., 1970). Order of the Coif. Vice President, General Counsel and Corporate Secretary, Genentech, Inc., 1982-1989. Author: "Selected Problems in Licensing Biotechnology," Biotechnology Law Institute, (Co-Chairman), 1984, 1985 and 1987; "The Federal Food, Drug and Cosmetic Act: A Proposed Statutory Change," presentation at The National Academy of Sciences' Symposium on Biotechnology-Creating an Environment for Technological Growth, February, 1985. Co-Author with Catalina Valencia: "Employer/Employee Technology Contracts-Protecting Biotechnology," Employer-Employee Technology Contracts-Annual Fall Corporate Law Institute, Patent Resources Group, 1985; "Effects of the Legal Climate on Biotechnology," Law and Technology Conference, Stanford Law and Technology Association, 1986; "Review of Biotechnology in 1987," Biotechnology Law Institute (Co-Chairman) 1988. Co-Author: with Michael Traynor, "Emerging Product Liability Issues in Biotechnology," High Technology Law Journal, 1989. *Member:* Executive Advisory Board, High Technology Law Journal, University of California, Berkeley, 1986—; Board of Editors, The Journal of Proprietary Rights, 1988—. Adjunct Professor in Law, Santa Clara University Law School, 1993—. Member, American Law Institute. **PRACTICE AREAS:** Corporate and Securities Law; Life Sciences and Health Care Companies; Intellectual Property Law. **Email:** CUNNINGHAMB@COOLEY.COM

**JULIA LOEWY DAVIDSON,** born Burlingame, California, June 1, 1964; admitted to bar, 1988, California. *Education:* University of California

*(This Listing Continued)*

**COOLEY GODWARD LLP, Palo Alto—Continued**

at Davis (B.A., high honors, 1985); Harvard University (J.D., cum laude, 1988). Phi Beta Kappa. Notes Editor and Articles Editor, Harvard Journal on Legislation. *PRACTICE AREAS:* Mergers and Acquisitions; Securities. *Email:* DAVIDSONJL@COOLEY.COM

**LLOYD R. DAY, JR.,** born Summit, New Jersey, March 25, 1952; admitted to bar, 1979, California. *Education:* Williams College (B.A., cum laude, 1974); University of Chicago (J.D., cum laude, 1979). Phi Beta Kappa; Order of the Coif. Member, 1977-1978 and Associate Editor, 1978-1979, University of Chicago Law Review. Law Clerk to Chief Judge Irving R. Kaufman, U.S. Court of Appeals, 2nd Circuit, 1979-1980. *PRACTICE AREAS:* Technology Litigation. *Email:* DAYLR@COOLEY.COM

**STEPHEN W. FACKLER,** born Fort Wayne, Indiana, August 9, 1957; admitted to bar, 1984, California. *Education:* Harvard College (A.B., magna cum laude, 1979); St. John's College, University of Oxford (B.A., with honors, 1981); Stanford University (J.D., 1984). Phi Beta Kappa. *PRACTICE AREAS:* Employee Benefits; Executive Compensation; Trade Associations; Public Charities and Private Foundations. *Email:* FACKLERSW@COOLEY.COM

**WILLIAM S. FREEMAN,** born New York, N.Y., December 29, 1952; admitted to bar, 1978, California; 1979, District of Columbia. *Education:* Harvard University (A.B., summa cum laude, 1974; J.D., cum laude, 1978). Phi Beta Kappa. Editor, Harvard Law Review, 1977-1978. Trial Attorney, U.S. Department of Justice, 1978-1981. Member, ABA Securities Litigation Committee, Subcommittee on Accounting Issues, 1988—. *PRACTICE AREAS:* Securities Litigation; Accountant Liability. *Email:* FREEMANWS@COOLEY.COM

**JOHN W. GIRVIN, JR.,** admitted to bar, 1964, Virginia; 1968, Kentucky; 1994, California; registered to practice before U.S. Patent and Trademark Office. *Education:* University of Virginia (B.E.E., 1960); George Washington University (LL.B., 1964; LL.M., 1966). Order of the Coif. Counsel and Corporate Counsel, IBM Corporation, 1964-1993. *Email:* GIRVINJW@COOLEY.COM

**WILLIS E. HIGGINS,** born Pittsburgh, Pennsylvania, August 7, 1940; admitted to bar, 1966, Michigan; 1968, Vermont; 1976, Arizona; 1978, California; registered to practice before U.S. Patent and Trademark Office. *Education:* University of Pittsburgh (B.S. in Chem. Eng., 1962); University of Chicago (J.D., 1965). Author: "The Significance of Claim Preambles in Chemical Composition Claims," 49 Journal of the Patent Office Society 337, 1967. Patent Attorney: Dow Chemical Company, 1965-1967; International Business Machines Corporation, 1967-1973. Patent Attorney and Senior Patent Attorney, Motorola, Incorporated, 1974-1976. Patent Counsel and Director of Patents and Trademarks, National Semiconductor Corporation, 1976-1978. *Member:* Peninsula Patent Law Association (President, 1984-1985). *PRACTICE AREAS:* Electronics and Software Patent Prosecution; Strategic Counseling; Patent Litigation Support. *Email:* HIGGINSWE@COOLEY.COM

**MICHAEL R. JACOBSON,** born Boston, Massachusetts, August 24, 1954; admitted to bar, 1981, California. *Education:* Harvard College (A.B., 1975); Stanford University (J.D., 1981). Phi Beta Kappa; Order of the Coif. *PRACTICE AREAS:* Securities; Mergers and Acquisitions. *Email:* JACOBSONMR@COOLEY.COM

**RONALD L. JACOBSON,** born Los Angeles, California, July 30, 1929; admitted to bar, 1955, California. *Education:* University of California at Los Angeles (B.S., 1951; J.D., 1954). Order of the Coif. *PRACTICE AREAS:* Real Estate (Property) Law; Business Law. *Email:* JACOBSONRL@COOLEY.COM

**DANIEL JOHNSON, JR.,** born Vallejo, California, June 17, 1948; admitted to bar, 1973, California. *Education:* University of California at Berkeley (A.B., with honors, 1970); Yale University (J.D., 1973). *PRACTICE AREAS:* Commercial Litigation; Intellectual Property Litigation. *Email:* JOHNSOND@COOLEY.COM

**ROBERT L. JONES,** born Amityville, New York, August 9, 1954; admitted to bar, 1980, California. *Education:* Swarthmore College (B.A., with high honors, 1975); Stanford University (M.B.A., 1979; J.D., 1979). Phi Beta Kappa; Order of the Coif. Editor-in-Chief, Stanford Journal of International Studies, 1977-1978. Henry Ford II Scholar, 1979. *PRACTICE AREAS:* Securities; Licensing; Intellectual Property Law. *Email:* JONESRL@COOLEY.COM

**JAMES C. KITCH,** born Wichita, Kansas, June 20, 1947; admitted to bar, 1973, California. *Education:* Harvard College (A.B., 1969); Stanford University (J.D., 1972). Note Editor, Stanford Law Review, 1971-1972. Law Clerk to Judge John Paul Stevens, U.S. Court of Appeals, 7th Circuit, 1972-1973. *PRACTICE AREAS:* Corporate Law; Securities; Emerging Growth Companies; Mergers and Acquisitions. *Email:* KITCHJC@COOLEY.COM

**BARBARA A. KOSACZ,** born Pawtucket, Rhode Island, February 16, 1958; admitted to bar, 1988, California. *Education:* Stanford University (B.A., 1980); Boalt Hall School of Law, University of California, Berkeley (J.D., 1988). Senior Article Editor, High Technology Law Journal, 1987-1988. *PRACTICE AREAS:* Hi-tech Transactions; Emerging Growth Companies. *Email:* KOSACZBA@COOLEY.COM

**MARTIN L. LAGOD,** born Chattanooga, Tennessee, December 17, 1955; admitted to bar, 1981, Illinois; 1984, California. *Education:* University of North Carolina (B.A., with honors, 1977); Vanderbilt University (J.D., 1981). Phi Beta Kappa. Articles Editor, Vanderbilt Journal of Transnational Law, 1980-1981. *PRACTICE AREAS:* Patent, Copyrights, Trademark and General Intellectual Property Litigation and Counselling; Licensing; General Litigation; Securities Litigation. *Email:* LAGODML@COOLEY.COM

**DAVID M. MADRID,** born Los Angeles, California, March 25, 1958; admitted to bar, 1984, California. *Education:* Yale University (B.A., cum laude, 1980); Stanford University (J.D., 1984). Senior Editor, Stanford Journal of International Law, 1983-1984. *PRACTICE AREAS:* Intellectual Property Litigation. *Email:* MADRIDM@COOLEY.COM

**ANDREI M. MANOLIU,** born Bucharest, Romania, December 24, 1951; admitted to bar, 1982, California. *Education:* University of Bucharest, Romania; University of California at Berkeley (Ph.D., 1979); Stanford University (J.D., 1982). Order of the Coif. *Member:* American Physical Society. *PRACTICE AREAS:* Intellectual Property Law; Licensing; Securities. *Email:* MANOLIUAM@COOLEY.COM

**DEBORAH A. MARSHALL,** born Newark, New Jersey, November 9, 1954; admitted to bar, 1982, Massachusetts; 1986, California. *Education:* Columbia University (B.A., cum laude, 1979); Northeastern University (J.D., 1982); New York University (LL.M. in Taxation, 1985). *PRACTICE AREAS:* Securities; Intellectual Property Law. *Email:* MARSHALLDA@COOLEY.COM

**PAMELA J. MARTINSON,** born Minneapolis, Minnesota, February 4, 1959; admitted to bar, 1989, California; 1992, Colorado. *Education:* University of Denver (B.A., magna cum laude, 1980; M.B.A., 1983); Harvard University (J.D., 1989). Phi Beta Kappa. *PRACTICE AREAS:* Financial Institutions Law; Corporate Finance; Equipment Leasing. *Email:* MARTINSONPJ@COOLEY.COM

**HERBERT W. MCGUIRE,** born Chicago, Illinois, November 28, 1940; admitted to bar, 1966, California. *Education:* Purdue University (B.S., with distinction, 1962); Stanford University (J.D., 1965). *Member:* State Bar of California (Member, Sections on: Health Care; Competition); American Bar Association (Member, Sections on: Health Care; Antitrust); National Health Lawyers Association; California Health Lawyers Association; Foundation for Health Care (Member, Board of Directors). *Email:* MCGUIREHW@COOLEY.COM

**ALAN C. MENDELSON,** born San Francisco, California, March 27, 1948; admitted to bar, 1973, California. *Education:* University of California at Berkeley (B.A., with great distinction, 1969); Harvard University (J.D., cum laude, 1973). Phi Beta Kappa. Acting General Counsel, AMGEN, Inc., 1990-1991. *PRACTICE AREAS:* Corporate; Securities; Intellectual Property Law. *Email:* MENDELSONAC@COOLEY.COM

**WEBB B. MORROW, III,** born Kansas City, Missouri, January 24, 1948; admitted to bar, 1974, California. *Education:* Stanford University (B.A., 1970); Boalt Hall School of Law, University of California, Berkeley (J.D., 1974); New York University (LL.M., Taxation, 1980). (Certified Specialist, Taxation Law, The State Bar of California Board of Legal Specialization). *PRACTICE AREAS:* Taxation; Partnerships. *Email:* MORROWWB@COOLEY.COM

**STEPHEN C. NEAL,** born San Francisco, California, March 26, 1949; admitted to bar, 1973, Illinois; 1993, California. *Education:* Harvard College (A.B., 1970); Stanford University (J.D., 1973). Fellow, American College of Trial Lawyers. *PRACTICE AREAS:* Commercial Litigation; Civil; Criminal; Special Investigations; Contested Acquisitions. *Email:* NEALSC@COOLEY.COM

**RICHARD L. NEELEY,** born Raeford, North Carolina, March 1, 1948; admitted to bar, 1985, Virginia; 1986, California; registered to practice before U.S. Patent and Trademark Office. *Education:* Davidson College (B.S.,

*(This Listing Continued)*

1970); University of Illinois (Ph.D., 1977); George Washington University (J.D., 1985). *PRACTICE AREAS:* Patent Law. *Email:* NEELYRL@COOLEY.COM

**TIMOTHY G. PATTERSON,** born Riverside, California, February 22, 1954; admitted to bar, 1981, California. *Education:* Stanford University (B.A., 1976); Hastings College of the Law, University of California (J.D., 1981). Order of the Coif. Member, Thurston Society. Member, 1979-1980 and Associate Editor, 1980-1981, Hastings Law Journal. *PRACTICE AREAS:* Employee Benefit Law; ERISA. *Email:* PATTERSONTG@COOLEY.COM

**ANNE HARRIS PECK,** born Los Angeles, California, October 23, 1958; admitted to bar, 1986, California. *Education:* Georgetown University (B.S., 1980); Hastings College of the Law, University of California (J.D., 1986). *Member:* International Trademark Association. *PRACTICE AREAS:* Trademark, Copyright and Advertising. *Email:* PECKAH@COOLEY.COM

**MARK B. PITCHFORD,** born Washington, D.C., April 13, 1959; admitted to bar, 1984, California. *Education:* Stanford University (A.B., with distinction, 1981); University of Santa Clara (J.D., cum laude, 1984). *PRACTICE AREAS:* Commercial Litigation. *Email:* PITCHFORDMB@COOLEY.COM

**PATRICK A. POHLEN,** born Sheldon, Iowa, January 20, 1959; admitted to bar, 1985, New York; 1993, Missouri (Not admitted in California). *Education:* Iowa State University (B.S., Political Science, 1981); University of Iowa College of Law (J.D., 1984). Phi Beta Kappa. Instructor, University of Iowa, College of Business. *Member:* New York State Bar Association; The Missouri Bar. *LANGUAGES:* Spanish, Japanese. *PRACTICE AREAS:* General Corporate; Securities; Financings; Mergers and Acquisitions. *Email:* POHLENPA@COOLEY.COM

**ANNA B. POPE,** born Pittsburgh, Pennsylvania, February 22, 1953; admitted to bar, 1984, California. *Education:* University of California at Davis (B.A., 1981; J.D., 1984). Phi Beta Kappa. *PRACTICE AREAS:* Real Estate (Property) Law. *Email:* POPEAB@COOLEY.COM

**JEFFREY G. RANDALL,** born Glendale, California, May 24, 1962; admitted to bar, 1987, California and U.S. District Court, Northern District of California; 1988, U.S. District Court, Central District of California; 1992, U.S. District Court, Eastern District of California; 1993, U.S. Court of Appeals for the Federal Circuit; 1994, U.S. Court of Appeals, Ninth Circuit. *Education:* University of Oregon (B.S., French, 1984); University of California, Hastings College of the Law (J.D., 1987). *PRACTICE AREAS:* Intellectual Property Law. *Email:* RANDALLJG@COOLEY.COM

**DIANE WILKINS SAVAGE,** born Long Island, New York, March 5, 1950; admitted to bar, 1974, California. *Education:* Emory University (B.A., 1971); Boston College and Georgetown University (J.D., 1974). Phi Beta Kappa. Recipient, Presidential Scholarship. Author: *The Red Herring,* Technology Strategy, Financing & Investment, March, 1995, Editorial Commentary article written by Diane Wilkins Savage "Protecting Intellectual Property"; "The Cyber Criminal," California Law Business, March 20, 1995, Supplement to the Los Angeles Daily Journal and the San Francisco Daily Journal (article); "Law of the Lan," Santa Clara Computer and High Technology Law Journal, Volume 9, Number 1, March 1993, Santa Clara University, School of Law; Legal Times, Special Report, December 19, 1994, "Practicing Patents on the Foreign Stage". *Member:* Palo Alto and American Bar Associations; The State Bar of California. *PRACTICE AREAS:* Computer Law; Technology Licensing; Product Distribution Agreements; Intellectual Property Protection. *Email:* SAVAGEDW@COOLEY.COM

**GREGORY C. SMITH,** born Salt Lake City, Utah, January 16, 1963; admitted to bar, 1988, California. *Education:* Stanford University (B.A., with distinction, 1985); Columbia University (J.D., 1988). Phi Beta Kappa. Harlan Fiske Stone Scholar. *PRACTICE AREAS:* Corporate Finance; Mergers and Acquisitions; Emerging Growth Companies. *Email:* SMITHGC@COOLEY.COM

**MICHAEL STERN,** born Mansfield, Ohio, August 26, 1948; admitted to bar, 1983, California. *Education:* Columbia University (B.A., magna cum laude, 1970); Cambridge University, Cambridge, England (M.A., 1972); Yale University (Ph.D., 1976); Boalt Hall School of Law, University of California, Berkeley (J.D., 1983). Phi Beta Kappa. Writing Fellow, Yale. Kellett Fellow, Cambridge. Extern Law Clerk to Hon. Cecil F. Poole, U.S. Court of Appeals, Ninth Circuit, 1982. *Member:* The State Bar of California. *PRACTICE AREAS:* Intellectual Property Licensing and Protection; General Corporate Counselling. *Email:* STERNMD@COOLEY.COM

*(This Listing Continued)*

**DANIEL P. WESTMAN,** born Ann Arbor, Michigan, June 6, 1956; admitted to bar, 1982, Illinois and Wisconsin; 1983, California. *Education:* Stanford University (A.B., with distinction, 1978); University of Chicago (J.D., 1981). Author, Whistleblowing: The Law of Retaliatory Discharge, BNA Books (1991). Law Clerk to Chief Judge Barbara B. Crabb, U.S. District Court, Western District of Wisconsin, 1981-1982. *Member:* American Bar Association (Member, Labor and Employment Law Section). *PRACTICE AREAS:* Labor and Employment. *Email:* WESTMANDP@COOLEY.COM

**JOHN F. YOUNG,** born Pottstown, Pennsylvania, June 16, 1943; admitted to bar, 1971, Washington; 1976, California. *Education:* University of Washington (B.A., 1968; J.D., 1971). Associate Editor, Washington Law Review, 1970-1971. Law Clerk to Judge M. Oliver Koelsch, U.S. Court of Appeals, 9th Circuit, 1971-1973. Trial Attorney, 1973-1983, and Assistant Chief, 1984-1987, San Francisco Regional Office, Antitrust Division, U.S. Department of Justice. *PRACTICE AREAS:* Antitrust Law; Trade Secrets Law. *Email:* YOUNGJF@COOLEY.COM

*SPECIAL COUNSEL*

**ELISA CLOWES,** born Ventura, California, February 29, 1956; admitted to bar, 1982, California. *Education:* California State University at Long Beach (B.S., 1978); Boalt Hall School of Law, University of California, Berkeley (J.D., 1982). Member, Moot Court Board. Associate Editor, California Law Review. Certified Public Accountant, California, 1980. Lecturer, Golden Gate Law School, 1993-1994. *PRACTICE AREAS:* Employment Law. *Email:* CLOWESE@COOLEY.COM

**ANN HABERNIGG,** born Portland, Oregon, November 7, 1961; admitted to bar, 1987, California; 1989, Oregon. *Education:* Princeton University (A.B., cum laude, 1983); University of California, Lo s Angeles (J.D., 1986). *PRACTICE AREAS:* Equity Compensation; Employee Benefits. *Email:* HABERNIGGAE@COOLEY.COM

**JAMES R. JONES,** born St. Louis, Missouri, April 8, 1956; admitted to bar, 1982, California. *Education:* Harvard College (B.A., magna cum laude, 1978); Stanford University (M.B.A., 1982; J.D., 1982). *PRACTICE AREAS:* Corporate Law; Mergers and Acquisitions. *Email:* JONESJR@COOLEY.COM

**TOM M. MORAN,** born Dubuque, Iowa, May 8, 1942; admitted to bar, 1973, Texas; 1975, California. *Education:* Beloit College (B.S., 1964); Golden Gate University (J.D., 1973). *PRACTICE AREAS:* Intellectual Property Law; Patent Law (Biopharmaceuticals). *Email:* MORANTM@COOLEY.COM

**GARY H. RITCHEY,** born San Jose, California, January 9, 1952; admitted to bar, 1988, California. *Education:* Santa Clara University (B.S., magna cum laude, 1974); University of California at San Diego (Ph.D., 1978); Boalt Hall School of Law, University of California, Berkeley (J.D., 1988). *PRACTICE AREAS:* Technology Litigation; Litigation. *Email:* RITCHEYGH@COOLEY.COM

**DEIDRE LYNN SPARKS,** born Salinas, California, August 18, 1961; admitted to bar, 1987, California. *Education:* California State University at Fresno (B.S., 1984); University of California at Davis (J.D., 1987). Phi Kappa Phi; Order of the Coif. *PRACTICE AREAS:* Mergers and Acquisitions; Emerging Growth Companies. *Email:* SPARKSDL@COOLEY.COM

**GRETCHEN R. STROUD,** born Encino, California, June 14, 1961; admitted to bar, 1989, California. *Education:* University of Southern California (A.B., magna cum laude, 1982); University of California at Los Angeles; Stanford University (J.D., 1989). *PRACTICE AREAS:* Litigation. *Email:* STROUDGR@COOLEY.COM

**ANDREA H. VACHSS,** born Pasadena, California, May 12, 1950; admitted to bar, 1985, New York; 1989, California. *Education:* University of Connecticut (B.A., with honors, 1972); University of Pennsylvania (M.A., 1974); Fordham University (J.D., 1984). Member, Fordham Law Review. *PRACTICE AREAS:* Securities; Corporate; Business. *Email:* VACHSSA@COOLEY.COM

**CHRISTOPHER O. B. WRIGHT,** born Los Angeles, California, August 12, 1959; admitted to bar, 1986, California. *Education:* Stanford University (A.B., 1981); University of California, Berkeley (J.D., 1986). Managing Editor, High Technology Law Journal, 1985-1986. Author: Comment, "The National Cooperative Research Act of 1984: A New Antitrust Regime for Joint Research and Development Ventures," 1 High Technology Law Journal 133, 1986; "Computer Industry Faces Antitrust Issues," Computer Law Strategist, July, 1992; Co-Author, "Government Antitrust Review of High Technology Mergers," The Computer Lawyers, June, 1992; "Congress

*(This Listing Continued)*

## COOLEY GODWARD LLP, Palo Alto—Continued

Rewrites Joint Venture Law," The International Computer Lawyer, November 1993; "Antitrust Guidelines for Intellectual Property," Computer Law Strategist, September 1994. *Member:* State Bar of California; American Bar Association (Section of Antitrust Law). **PRACTICE AREAS:** Antitrust Law; Intellectual Property. **Email:** WRIGHTCOB@COOLEY.COM

### ASSOCIATES

**GREGG H. ALTON,** born Berkeley, California, March 4, 1966; admitted to bar, 1994, California. *Education:* University of California at Berkeley (B.A., 1989); Stanford University (J.D., 1994). **Email:** ALTONGH@COOLEY.COM

**KEVIN C. AUSTIN,** born Seattle, Washington, May 24, 1956; admitted to bar, 1993, California. *Education:* University of Washington; Seattle University (B.A., 1980); Stanford University (J.D., 1993). **PRACTICE AREAS:** Corporate Law; Corporate Finance; Foreign Corrupt Practices Law. **Email:** AUSTINKC@COOLEY.COM

**SUZANNE A. BARR,** born Los Angeles, California, October 14, 1966; admitted to bar, 1992, California; 1993, U.S. District Court, Northern District of California and U.S. Court of Appeals, Ninth Circuit. *Education:* Harvard College (A.B., magna cum laude, 1988); Harvard University (J.D., cum laude, 1991). *Member:* State Bar of California. **PRACTICE AREAS:** Securities Law; General Corporate Law. **Email:** BARRSA@COOLEY.COM

**ALEX H. BENN,** admitted to bar, 1995, California. *Education:* Brown University (B.A.); Stanford University (J.D.). **PRACTICE AREAS:** Intellectual Property; Software Licensing; Emerging Growth Companies. **Email:** BENNAH@COOLEY.COM

**LAURA A. BEREZIN,** born Chicago, Illinois, July 1, 1966; admitted to bar, 1992, California. *Education:* University of California at Berkeley (B.A., with high honors, 1988); University of Pennsylvania (J.D., 1992). Phi Beta Kappa. **PRACTICE AREAS:** Mergers and Acquisitions; Securities. **Email:** BEREZINLA@COOLEY.COM

**JUDITH E. BROWN,** born Toronto, Ontario, Canada, December 28, 1957; admitted to bar, 1996, California. *Education:* University of Toronto (B.Sc., M.A., Ph.D., 1992); Stanford University (J.D., with distinction, 1995). Managing Editor, Stanford Law and Policy Review, 1994-1995. **PRACTICE AREAS:** Intellectual Property; Corporate. **Email:** BROWNJE@COOLEY.COM

**TERRENCE J. CARROLL,** born Cleveland, Ohio, March 21, 1960; admitted to bar, 1994, California. *Education:* Cleveland State University (B.S., 1981); Santa Clara University (J.D., 1994). Editor-in-Chief, Santa Clara Computer & High Technology Law Journal, 1993-1994. **PRACTICE AREAS:** Patent; Copyright. **Email:** CARROLLTJ@COOLEY.COM

**SALVADOR A. CASENTE JR.,** born Morgan City, Louisiana, July 12, 1963; admitted to bar, 1989, California. *Education:* University of Virginia (B.A., with high distinction, 1985); Harvard University (J.D., cum laude, 1988); Stanford Graduate School of Business (M.S., 1994). Phi Beta Kappa; Pi Sigma Alpha. *Member:* State Bar of California. **Email:** CASENTESA@COOLEY.COM

**THEODORE A. CHEN,** born Atlanta, Georgia, October 17, 1969; admitted to bar, 1994, California. *Education:* Stanford University (B.S., 1991; J.D., 1994). **PRACTICE AREAS:** Patent; Licensing. **Email:** CHENTA@COOLEY.COM

**TROY F. CHRISTMAS,** born Chicago, Illinois, May 30, 1969; admitted to bar, 1995, California. *Education:* University of California, Berkeley (B.A., 1991); Stanford University (J.D., 1995). **Email:** CHRISTMASTF@COOLEY.COM

**PATRICIA LOUISE COX,** born Palo Alto, California, June 15, 1954; admitted to bar, 1988, California. *Education:* University of San Francisco (B.S., 1985); Stanford Law School (J.D., 1988). Queen's Bench, 1988-1989. *Member:* State Bar of California. **LANGUAGES:** Spanish. **PRACTICE AREAS:** General Corporate; Securities; Intellectual Property. **Email:** COXPL@COOLEY.COM

**LINDA DEMELIS,** born Mt. Vernon, New York, July 10, 1953; admitted to bar, 1994, California. *Education:* Radcliffe College (B.A., magna cum laude, 1975); Hastings College of Law, University of California (J.D., magna cum laude, 1994). Order of the Coif. Member, Thurston Society. Associate Notes Editor, Hastings Law Journal, 1993-1994. **PRACTICE AREAS:** Corporate Law; Securities Law. **Email:** DEMELISLM@COOLEY.COM

**SCOTT D. DEVEREAUX,** born Scranton, Pennsylvania, August 27, 1963; admitted to bar, 1989, California. *Education:* Bucknell University (B.A., 1985); Catholic University (J.D., 1989). *Member:* State Bar of California; National Association of Criminal Defense Lawyers. **PRACTICE AREAS:** Business Litigation; White Collar. **Email:** DEVEREAUXSD@COOLEY.COM

**TRACY FRIEDMAN DOBMEIER,** born Washington, District of Columbia, October 14, 1968; admitted to bar, 1994, California. *Education:* Princeton University (A.B., summa cum laude, 1990) Phi Beta Kappa; Boalt Hall School of Law, University of California, Berkeley (J.D., 1994). Member, California Law Review, 1993-1994. **PRACTICE AREAS:** Intellectual Property; Biotechnology Licensing. **Email:** DOBMEIERTF@COOLEY.COM

**CHUCK EBERTIN,** born Orange County, California, September 27, 1967; admitted to bar, 1992, California. *Education:* University of Southern California (B.S., cum laude, 1989); Northwestern University (J.D., cum laude, 1992). Articles Editor, Northwestern University Law Review, 1991-1992. **PRACTICE AREAS:** Patent Litigation; Contract Litigation; General Litigation. **Email:** EBERTINECP@COOLEY.COM

**DAVID T. EMERSON,** born Massachusetts, December 27, 1954; admitted to bar, 1993, California; 1995, Colorado. *Education:* Worcester Polytechnic Institute (B.S., 1975); Harvard University (M.Ed., 1989); Boalt Hall School of Law, University of California, Berkeley (J.D., 1993). **PRACTICE AREAS:** Business Law; Securities Law. **Email:** EMERSONDT@COOLEY.COM

**DAVID J. ESTRADA,** born San Mateo, California, March 28, 1968; admitted to bar, 1993, California. *Education:* University of California, Santa Barbara (B.A., 1990); Boalt Hall School of Law, University of California, Berkeley (J.D., 1993). **PRACTICE AREAS:** Intellectual Property Law. **Email:** ESTRADADJ@COOLEY.COM

**MELISSA A. FINOCCHIO,** born Salinas, California, February 2, 1964; admitted to bar, 1990, California. *Education:* Santa Clara University (B.A., 1986; J.D., 1990). Articles Editor, Santa Clara Computer and High Technology Law Journal. Member, San Francisco Bay Area Intellectual Property Inn of Courts. *Member:* Santa Clara County (Member, Intellectual Property Section) and American (Member, Intellectual Property Section) Bar Associations; State Bar of California (Member, Intellectual Property Section). **PRACTICE AREAS:** Patent Litigation; Intellectual Property Litigation; Commercial Litigation; Employment Litigation. **Email:** FINOCCHIO@COOLEY.COM

**JASON D. FIRTH,** born Murray, Utah, January 29, 1966; admitted to bar, 1993, Texas (Not admitted in California). *Education:* Brigham Young University (B.A., summa cum laude, 1990); Georgetown University (J.D., cum laude, 1993). Editor, Georgetown International Environmental Law Review. Member: Houston Intellectual Property Law Association, 1993-1995; American Intellectual Property Law Association, 1993-1995. *Member:* Houston Bar Association; State Bar of Texas; Houston Young Lawyers Association; International Trademark Association. **LANGUAGES:** Portuguese. **PRACTICE AREAS:** Trademark; Copyright; Licensing. **Email:** FIRTHJD@COOLEY.COM

**KEITH A. FLAUM,** born Brooklyn, New York, August 14, 1963; admitted to bar, 1989, California; 1993, Colorado. *Education:* University of California at Los Angeles (B.A., 1986); University of California at Davis (J.D., 1989). **PRACTICE AREAS:** Mergers and Acquisitions; Corporate Securities. **Email:** FLAUMKA@COOLEY.COM

**MOLLY BROWN FORSTALL,** born Bremerton, Washington, March 24, 1969; admitted to bar, 1994, California. *Education:* Stanford University (A.B., with distinction, 1991; J.D., with distinction, 1994). Phi Beta Kappa. **PRACTICE AREAS:** General Litigation; Employment. **Email:** FORSTALLMB@COOLEY.COM

**MICHELLE GREER GALLOWAY,** born Berkeley, California, December 28, 1964; admitted to bar, 1989, California. *Education:* Stanford University (B.A., with distinction, 1986; J.D., 1989). Topic Development Editor, Stanford Law Review, 1988-1989. **PRACTICE AREAS:** Intellectual Property; Technology Litigation; General Litigation. **Email:** GALLOWAYMG@COOLEY.COM

**ROBERT M. GALVIN,** born Anaheim, California, September 23, 1968; admitted to bar, 1994, California. *Education:* University of California at Los Angeles (B.A., 1990; J.D., 1993). Phi Beta Kappa. Order of the Coif. Articles Editor, UCLA Law Review, 1992-1993. Law Clerk to Judge

*(This Listing Continued)*

Stephen S. Trott, U.S. Court of Appeals, Ninth Circuit, 1993-1994. *PRACTICE AREAS:* Technology Litigation. *Email:* GALVINRM@COOLEY.COM

**KAREN A. GIBBS,** born Los Angeles, California, October 27, 1969; admitted to bar, 1995, California. *Education:* University of California, Santa Barbara (B.A./B.A., magna cum laude, 1991); Hastings College of the Law, University of California, San Francisco (J.D., 1995). Phi Beta Kappa. Moot Court Board, 1994-1995. Editor-in-Chief, Hastings Communications and Entertainment Law Journal, 1994-1995. Extern to U.S. Ninth Court of Appeals Judge Joseph T. Sneed, 1993. *PRACTICE AREAS:* General Business Litigation; Employment Law; Trademark and Copyright Law. *Email:* GIBBSKA@COOLEY.COM

**MICHELE K. GRANAADA,** born Brooklyn, New York; admitted to bar, 1985, Massachusetts; 1990, California. *Education:* State University of New York at Buffalo (B.A., magna cum laude, 1975); University of North Carolina (M.R.P., 1977); Georgetown University (J.D., 1985). Georgetown Law Journal, Member, 1983-1984, Editor, 1984-1985. *Email:* GRANAADA@COOLEY.COM

**BRADLEY A. HANDLER,** born Denver, Colorado, July 19, 1967; admitted to bar, 1995, California. *Education:* University of Pennsylvania (B.A., 1989); University of Pennsylvania, The Wharton School of Business (B.S.E., 1989); University of Virginia (J.D., 1995). Editorial Board, 1993-1994 and Managing Editor, 1994-1995, The Virginia Law Review. *PRACTICE AREAS:* Corporate Finance; Intellectual Property. *Email:* HANDLERBA@COOLEY.COM

**JUDITH A. HASKO,** born Waterbury, Connecticut, February 11, 1964; admitted to bar, 1995, California. *Education:* Vassar College (B.A., 1986); University of Wisconsin, Madison (J.D., 1994). Member, 1993, Articles Editor, 1994, Wisconsin Law Review. Author, 1995 Wisconsin Law Review 479. *Member:* State Bar of California; State Bar of Wisconsin. *PRACTICE AREAS:* Intellectual Property Licensing; Business Transactions; Corporate. *Email:* HASKOJA@COOLEY.COM

**LANA K. HAWKINS,** born Guntersville, Alabama, November 24, 1952; admitted to bar, 1988, Pennsylvania (inactive); 1991, District of Columbia (Not admitted in California). *Education:* University of Central Florida (B.A., summa cum laude, 1983); Georgetown University Law Center (J.D., 1988). *Member:* Bar Association of the District of Columbia; District of Columbia Bar; American Bar Association. *Email:* HAWKINSLK@COOLEY.COM

**MATTHEW B. HEMINGTON,** born San Jose, California, September 3, 1963; admitted to bar, 1990, California. *Education:* University of California at Berkeley (B.A., with high honors and distinction, 1985); University of California at Los Angeles (J.D., 1990). *PRACTICE AREAS:* Emerging Companies; Intellectual Property Law; Venture Capital. *Email:* HEMMINGTONMB@COOLEY.COM

**PAULA HOLM JENSEN,** born Seattle, Washington, September 30, 1964; admitted to bar, 1994, California. *Education:* Wesleyan University (B.A., 1986); Santa Clara University (J.D., 1994). *PRACTICE AREAS:* Corporate; Technology Licensing. *Email:* HOLMJENSENP@COOLEY.COM

**SUZANNE SAWOCHKA HOOPER,** born Cincinnati, Ohio, December 24, 1965; admitted to bar, 1991, California. *Education:* University of California, Santa Barbara (B.A., with high honors, 1988); Boalt Hall School of Law, University of California, Berkeley (J.D., 1991). Phi Beta Kappa. *Member:* American Bar Association. *PRACTICE AREAS:* Corporate Securities; Mergers and Acquisitions. *Email:* HOOPERSS@COOLEY.COM

**JEFFREY N. HYMAN,** born San Francisco, California, October 9, 1969; admitted to bar, 1994, California. *Education:* University of California at Santa Cruz (B.A., cum laude, 1991); Santa Clara University (J.D., cum laude, 1994). Member, Board of Directors, Santa Cruz County Metropolitan Transit District, 1990-1991. Judicial Extern to Judge James Ware, U.S. District Court, 1992. *PRACTICE AREAS:* Business Litigation; Securities Litigation; Real Estate Litigation. *Email:* HYMANJN@COOLEY.COM

**VIRAJ D. JHA,** born Boston, Massachusetts, September 26, 1970; admitted to bar, 1995, Massachusetts (Not admitted in California). *Education:* Brandeis University (B.A., Computer Science, cum laude, 1992); Boston College Law School (J.D., 1995). Spinnaker Software Corp., Cambridge, MA, 1991-1992. General Counsel, Reality Bytes, Inc., Cambridge, MA, 1995-1996. *Member:* Boston and Massachusetts Bar Associations. *LANGUAGES:* German. *PRACTICE AREAS:* Corporate; High Technology; Technology Licensing. *Email:* JHAVD@COOLEY.COM

*(This Listing Continued)*

**DAN S. JOHNSTON,** born Riverside, California, May 28, 1963; admitted to bar, 1994, California. *Education:* Humboldt State University (B.S., cum laude, 1986); Santa Clara University (J.D., 1994). Upsilon Pi Epsilon. Phi Alpha Delta. *PRACTICE AREAS:* Intellectual Property Licensing; Corporate Partnering; Corporate Law. *Email:* JOHNSTONDC@COOLEY.COM

**BARCLAY J. KAMB,** born Pasadena, California, May 30, 1958; admitted to bar, 1989, California. *Education:* Stanford University (B.S., Biology, 1983); Massachusetts Institute of Technology (Doctoral Program, 1983-1985) NSF Fellowship, 1983-1985; Boalt Hall School of Law, University of California, Berkeley (J.D., 1988). Associate Editor, California Law Review, 1987-1988. *PRACTICE AREAS:* Corporate Partnering; Intellectual Property Licensing; Business Law. *Email:* KAMB@COOLEY.COM

**ANTHONY R. KLEIN,** born Indianapolis, Indiana, August 29, 1964; admitted to bar, 1990, California. *Education:* Harvard College (A.B., magna cum laude, 1986); University of California at Los Angeles (J.D., 1990). Editor-in-Chief, Federal Communications Law Journal, Vol. 42. *Member:* Federal Communications Bar Association. *PRACTICE AREAS:* Information Technologies Licensing; Commercial Transactions. *Email:* KLEINAR@COOLEY.COM

**JUDITH LANDIS,** admitted to bar, 1994, New York (Not admitted in California). *Education:* University of California, Berkeley (A.B.); Columbia University School of Law (J.D., 1993). Harlan Fiske Stone Scholar. *PRACTICE AREAS:* Tax Law. *Email:* LANDISJA@COOLEY.COM

**T. GREGORY LANIER,** born San Jose, California, October 30, 1963; admitted to bar, 1988, California. *Education:* Santa Clara University (B.A., cum laude, 1985); Hastings College of the Law, University of California (J.D., 1988). *Member:* Defense Research Institute. *PRACTICE AREAS:* Securities; Mergers and Acquisitions; Business Litigation; Litigation. *Email:* LANIERTG@COOLEY.COM

**ELEONORA LEZNIK,** born Moscow, Russia, October 24, 1957; admitted to bar, 1995, California. *Education:* University of Houston (B.B.A., 1981; M.B.A., 1984); Stanford University (J.D., 1995). *LANGUAGES:* Russian. *PRACTICE AREAS:* Intellectual Property; Corporate Law. *Email:* LEZNIKE@COOLEY.COM

**DAVID M. LISI,** born Bridgeport, Connecticut, November 23, 1960; admitted to bar, 1991, California. *Education:* Yale University (B.A., 1983); Cornell University (J.D., 1991). Executive Editor, Moot Court Board, Cornell University. Founding Editor, Cornell Law and Public Policy Journal. *Member:* State Bar of California. *PRACTICE AREAS:* Securities Litigation; Technology Litigation. *Email:* LISIDM@COOLEY.COM

**JULIE C. LYTHCOTT-HAIMS,** born Lagos, Nigeria, November 28, 1967; admitted to bar, 1994, California. *Education:* Stanford University (A.B., 1989); Harvard University (J.D., 1994). *PRACTICE AREAS:* Intellectual Property Litigation; Trademark Prosecution. *Email:* LYTHCOTTJC@COOLEY.COM

**MATTHEW E. MARQUIS,** born San Rafael, California, August 7, 1965; admitted to bar, 1991, California. *Education:* University of California, Berkeley (B.A., with honors, 1987); Washington College of Law, The American University (J.D., cum laude, 1991). Author: "Doing Business Abroad: Recognizing and Avoiding the Hazards of the Foreign Corrupt Practices Act," International Lawyer Newsletter, 1993; "The Clinton Trade Agenda: Who Speaks for the Administration?" ABA International Trade Section Newsletter, 1993. Office of the President-Elect, Presidential Transition Team, Vetting Advisor, 1992-1993. *Member:* California Council on International Trade (Public Policy Committee; Commonwealth Club; World Affairs Council; German-American Business Council. *LANGUAGES:* German. *PRACTICE AREAS:* Information Technology; International Commercial. *Email:* MARQUISME@COOLEY.COM

**BARBARA J. MCGEOCH,** born Swartz Creek, Michigan, May 21, 1957; admitted to bar, 1992, California. *Education:* Michigan State University (B.A., cum laude, 1979); Georgetown University Law Center (J.D., cum laude, 1991). Author: "The American Voluntary Pension System: Can it Thrive Under a No-Reversion Rule?" Tax Lawyer, Vol. 43, No. 3. *PRACTICE AREAS:* Employee Benefits; Equity Compensation. *Email:* MCGEOCHBJ@COOLEY.COM

**GERALD T. MCLAUGHLIN,** born Philadelphia, Pennsylvania, November 25, 1963; admitted to bar, 1993, California. *Education:* University of Pennsylvania (B.A., Economics, cum laude, 1985); Temple University (J.D., magna cum laude, 1993). [Capt. USMC, 1985-1988]. *PRACTICE AREAS:* Business; Intellectual Property. *Email:* MCLAUGHLINGT@COOLEY.COM

*(This Listing Continued)*

CAA1557B

**COOLEY GODWARD LLP, Palo Alto—Continued**

**JOHN D. MENDLEIN,** born Miami, Florida, October 28, 1959; admitted to bar, 1993, California; registered to practice before U.S. Patent and Trademark Office. *Education:* University of Miami (B.S., 1982); University of California, Los Angeles (Ph.D., 1990); University of Leiden, Leiden, The Netherlands; Hastings College of the Law, University of California (J.D., 1993). *PRACTICE AREAS:* Intellectual Property Protection and Enforcement. *Email:* MENDLEINJD@COOLEY.COM

**WM. BRADFORD MIDDLEKAUFF,** born Cincinnati, Ohio, May 1, 1961; admitted to bar, 1994, California. *Education:* Brown University (A.B., 1983); Yale University (J.D., 1991). Law Clerk to Robert J. Ward, U.S. District Judge, Southern District of New York, 1991-1993. *PRACTICE AREAS:* Securities Offerings; Corporate Law. *Email:* MIDDLEKAUFFB@COOLEY.COM

**JANA R. MILLER,** born Fresno, California, May 28, 1959; admitted to bar, 1987, California. *Education:* University of California at Los Angeles (B.A., 1984); Loyola University of Los Angeles (J.D., 1987). *PRACTICE AREAS:* Business - Technology Licensing. *Email:* MILLERJR@COOLEY.COM

**DARREN B. MITCHELL,** born Montreal, Quebec, Canada, November 1, 1966; admitted to bar, 1995, California. *Education:* University of California, Los Angeles (B.S., summa cum laude, 1988); Harvard University (A.M., Chemistry, 1991); Stanford University (J.D., 1995). Phi Beta Kappa; Order of the Coif. *PRACTICE AREAS:* Patent Litigation. *Email:* MITCHELLDB@COOLEY.COM

**SHAWN N. MOLODOW,** born Phoenix, Arizona, November 20, 1965; admitted to bar, 1995, California. *Education:* Arizona State University (B.S., Engineering, magna cum laude, 1986; M.S., Engineering, 1990); Boalt Hall School of Law, University of California, Berkeley (J.D., 1995). Tau Beta Pi; Order of the Coif. Member, 1992-1995 and Executive Editor, 1993-1995, Boalt Hall High Technology Law Journal. *PRACTICE AREAS:* Intellectual Property Transactions; Corporate Law. *Email:* MOLODOWSN@COOLEY.COM

**DONALD J. MORRISSEY, JR.,** born Willimantic, Connecticut, January 30, 1966; admitted to bar, 1992, California. *Education:* University of Colorado (B.A., 1988); University of Southern California (J.D., 1992). Phi Beta Kappa; Order of the Coif. Member, University of Southern California Law Review. *PRACTICE AREAS:* Technology Licensing; Biotechnology; Emerging Growth Companies. *Email:* MORRISSEYDJ@COOLEY.COM

**TAHIR J. NAIM,** born Berkeley, California, June 28, 1961; admitted to bar, 1992, California. *Education:* Macalester College (B.A., 1987); Golden Gate University (J.D., 1992; LL.M., Tax, 1995). Adjunct Professor, Executive Compensation, Golden Gate University, 1995. *Member:* Alameda County and American (Member, Tax Section) Bar Associations. *PRACTICE AREAS:* Equity Compensation; ERISA/Qualified Plans; Federal Taxation. *Email:* NAIMTJ@COOLEY.COM

**JACKIE N. NAKAMURA,** born April 14, 1962; admitted to bar, 1990, California; registered to practice before U.S. Patent and Trademark Office. *Education:* Stanford University (B.S., with honors, 1984); University of California, Berkeley, Boalt Hall School of Law (J.D., 1990). Law Clerk to Judge Vaughn R. Walker, U.S. District Court, Northern District of California, 1990-1991. *PRACTICE AREAS:* American Intellectual Property Law. *Email:* NAKAMURA@COOLEY.COM

**GLENN GERARD NASH,** born St. John's, Newfoundland, 1964; admitted to bar, 1992, California. *Education:* Memorial University of Newfoundland (B.A., 1984); University of Saskatchewan (LL.B., 1988). Member, Canadian-American Chamber of Commerce, 1991—. World Affairs Council of Northern California, 1993—. Author: "Copyright Protection on the Global Information Infrastructure," The International Computer Lawyer (September 1994); Morph's Outpost on the Digital Frontier. *Member:* State Bar of California. *LANGUAGES:* French. *PRACTICE AREAS:* Intellectual Property; International Law. *Email:* NASHGG@COOLEY.COM

**KEITH C. NASHAWATY,** born Cambridge, MA., 1966; admitted to bar, 1991, California. *Education:* Stanford Univ. (A.B., with distinction, 1988; M.A., 1988); University of Chicago (J.D., 1991). Phi Beta Kappa. *PRACTICE AREAS:* Securities; Mergers and Acquisitions. *Email:* NASHAWATYKC@COOLEY.COM

**CRAIG P. OPPERMAN,** born Carnarvon, South Africa, September 9, 1962; admitted to bar, 1990, South Africa; 1993, California; 1990, South African Patent Office; registered to practice before U.S. Patent and Trademark Office. *Education:* University of Cape Town (B.Sc. in Engineering, 1984); University of South Africa (B.Proc., 1989). *Member:* Law Society of the Transvaal; South African Institute of Intellectual Property Law; South African Institute of Civil Engineers. *PRACTICE AREAS:* Patents; Intellectual Property Strategies; Licensing; Trade Secret; International Intellectual Property. *Email:* OPPERMANCP@COOLEY.COM

**LAURA M. OWEN,** born Chicago, Illinois, June 12, 1955; admitted to bar, 1994, California. *Education:* San Francisco State University (B.S., magna cum laude, 1985); Santa Clara University (J.D., magna cum laude, 1994). *PRACTICE AREAS:* Employment Claims; Labor Relations; Personnel Policies; Title VII Discrimination. *Email:* OWENLM@COOLEY.COM

**STEPHANIE J. PARR,** born Salt Lake City, Utah, June 20, 1965; admitted to bar, 1990, California; 1992, District of Columbia. *Education:* University of California at Berkeley (B.A., with honors, 1987); University of California at Los Angeles (J.D., 1990). *PRACTICE AREAS:* Securities; Emerging Growth Companies. *Email:* PARRSJ@COOLEY.COM

**MEHUL T. PATEL,** born Nairobi, Kenya, October 8, 1969; admitted to bar, 1995, California. *Education:* Brown University (A.B., magna cum laude, 1992); University of Virginia (J.D., 1995). *LANGUAGES:* Gujarati. *PRACTICE AREAS:* Corporate; Securities. *Email:* PATELMT@COOLEY.COM

**MARY-ALICE POMPUTIUS,** born Pittsburgh, Pennsylvania, October 6, 1965; admitted to bar, 1990, California. *Education:* Yale University (B.A., summa cum laude, 1987); Harvard University (J.D., cum laude, 1990). Phi Beta Kappa. *Email:* POMPUTIUSMA@COOLEY.COM

**KELVIN P. QUAN,** born San Francisco, California, October 7, 1957; admitted to bar, 1993, California. *Education:* Northwestern University (B.A., 1979); University of California at Berkeley (M.P.H., 1981); Hastings College of the Law, University of California, San Francisco (J.D., 1993). Public Interest Certificate. *member:* Bar Association of San Francisco; Asian American Bar Association. *PRACTICE AREAS:* Health Care Transactions. *Email:* QUANKP@COOLEY.COM

**RUTH REITMAN,** born Patchogue, New York, April 3, 1968; admitted to bar, 1994, California. *Education:* University of California, San Diego (B.A., magna cum laude, 1990); Santa Clara University (J.D., summa cum laude, 1994). Phi Beta Kappa. Recipient, American Jurisprudence Awards: Civil Procedure; Torts. Member, Santa Clara University Law Review, 1992-1994. Judicial Extern Law Clerk to the Honorable James Ware, U.S. District Court, 1994. *Member:* Santa Clara County Bar Association; State Bar of California (ADR and Federal Practice Section). *PRACTICE AREAS:* Civil Litigation; Business Securities. *Email:* REITMAN@COOLEY.COM

**MATTHEW F. ROBERTS,** born Sacramento, California, June 20, 1970; admitted to bar, 1995, California. *Education:* University of California, Los Angeles (B.A., 1992); Boalt Hall School of Law, University of California, Berkeley (J.D., 1995). Phi Beta Kappa. *Email:* ROBERTSMF@COOLEY.COM

**JULIE M. ROBINSON,** born Potsdam, New York, July 18, 1956; admitted to bar, 1991, California. *Education:* University of Rochester (B.A., 1978); Pepperdine University (J.D., summa cum laude, 1991). Valedictorian. *PRACTICE AREAS:* Corporate Law; Corporate Finance; Securities. *Email:* ROBINSONJM@COOLEY.COM

**RICARDO RODRIGUEZ,** born Los Angeles, California, September 28, 1969; admitted to bar, 1994, California. *Education:* Massachusetts Institute of Technology (B.S., 1991); Stanford University (J.D., 1994). *PRACTICE AREAS:* Intellectual Property Litigation. *Email:* RODRIGUEZR@COOLEY.COM

**STEPHEN N. ROSENFIELD,** born Chicago, Illinois, November 7, 1949; admitted to bar, 1992, California. *Education:* Hofstra University (B.S., cum laude, 1971); University of Southern California (M.F.A., 1984); Northeastern University (J.D., 1992). *Member:* Bar Association of San Francisco; State Bar of California; American Bar Association. *PRACTICE AREAS:* Corporate Finance; Emerging Growth Companies; General Corporate. *Email:* ROSENFIELDSN@COOLEY.COM

**GURJEEV K. SACHDEVA,** born Bombay, India, February 18, 1965; admitted to bar, 1993, California; registered to practice before U.S. Patent and Trademark Office. *Education:* Johns Hopkins University (B.A., 1987); Tulane University (J.D., cum laude, 1993). Member, Tulane Law Journal. *Member:* American Intellectual Property Law Association; San Francisco Intellectual Property Law Association; Peninsula Intellectual Property Law Association. *PRACTICE AREAS:* Patent Prosecution. *Email:* SACHDEVAGK@COOLEY.COM

*(This Listing Continued)*

**ERIC SCHLACHTER,** born Madison, Wisconsin, April 15, 1968; admitted to bar, 1994, California. *Education:* University of California at Los Angeles (B.A., summa cum laude, 1988; M.B.A., 1994; J.D., 1994). Phi Beta Kappa. Beta Gamma Sigma. Editor, UCLA Law Review, 1993-1994. Author, "Cyberspace, the Free Market and the Free Marketplace of Ideas," 16 Hastings COMM/ENT 87 (1993). Adjunct Professor in Cyberspace Law, University of San Francisco School of Law. **PRACTICE AREAS:** Cyberspace Law; Intellectual Property; Emerging Growth Companies. **Email:** SCHLACHTERE@COOLEY.COM

**JOANNE MARSHALL SHEA,** born Wichita Falls, Texas, April 17, 1966; admitted to bar, 1991, Maryland; 1993, District of Columbia; 1994, California. *Education:* University of Notre Dame (B.A., cum laude, with honors, 1988); Georgetown University (J.D., cum laude, with honors, 1991). Santa Clara County Inns of Court, 1995-1996. *Member:* Santa Clara County Bar Association; Maryland State and American Bar Associations; District of Columbia Bar. **PRACTICE AREAS:** Corporate; Securities. **Email:** SHEAJM@COOLEY.COM

**MYLES B. SILTON,** born New York, N.Y., August 17, 1959; admitted to bar, 1991, New York (Not admitted in California). *Education:* Cornell University (B.A., 1980); University of Pennsylvania (J.D., 1990). ATX Communications, 1992-1995. **PRACTICE AREAS:** Intellectual Property Licensing and Protection; General Corporate Counselling. **Email:** SILTONMB@COOLEY.COM

**MATTHEW W. SONSINI,** born Oakland, California, October 24, 1966; admitted to bar, 1992, California. *Education:* Dartmouth University (B.A., magna cum laude, 1988); Boalt Hall School of Law, University of California, Berkeley (J.D., 1992). **PRACTICE AREAS:** Emerging Growth Companies; Corporate Finance; Mergers and Acquisitions. **Email:** SONSINIMW@COOLEY.COM

**SEKSOM N. SURIYAPA,** born Bridgeport, Connecticut, March 30, 1966; admitted to bar, 1995, California. *Education:* Williams College (B.A., 1988); Stanford University (J.D., 1995). Editor-in-Chief, Stanford Law and Policy Review, 1993-1995. Special Assistant Deputy Director - General, Ministry of Finance (Thailand), 1990-1991. *Member:* American Bar Association. **LANGUAGES:** Thai. **PRACTICE AREAS:** Securities Law (Mergers and Acquisitions); Securities Law (Finances); General Corporate Law. **Email:** SURIYAPASN@COOLEY.COM

**JONATHAN H. TAKEI,** born Santa Clara, California, March 5, 1967; admitted to bar, 1994, California; registered to practice before U.S. Patent and Trademark Office. *Education:* University of California, Berkeley (B.A., 1989); Santa Clara University (J.D., 1994). Comments Editor, Santa Clara Computer & High Technology Law Journal, 1993-1994. Law Clerk to the Hon. James Ware, U.S. District Court, Northern District of California, 1995. *Member:* American Bar Association. **PRACTICE AREAS:** Litigation. **Email:** TAKEIJH@COOLEY.COM

**BARBARA E. TANZILLO,** born Mason City, Iowa, December 29, 1961; admitted to bar, 1993, California. *Education:* California State University (B.A., summa cum laude, 1990); Harvard University (J.D., 1993). Sigma Delta Chi, 1986-1992. Editor, Escape Magazine. **PRACTICE AREAS:** Employment Law; Labor Law; Intellectual Property Law. **Email:** TANZILLOBE@COOLEY.COM

**GREGORY C. TENHOFF,** born Austin, Minnesota, 1962; admitted to bar, 1991, California, U.S. District Court, Northern District of California and U.S. Court of Appeals, Ninth Circuit. *Education:* Mankato State University (B.S., summa cum laude, 1984); University of Southern California (J.D., 1991). Order of the Coif. Recipient: American Board of Trial Advocates Award for Excellence in Trial Preparation; American Jurisprudence Awards. Member, Southern California Law Review Staff, 1989-1990. Author: "Censoring the Public University Student Press: A Constitutional Challenge," 64 So. Cal. Law Review, 1991. *Member:* State Bar of California; Barrister's Club of San Francisco (Vice-Chair, Labor and Employment Law Committee, 1994, Chair, 1995). **Email:** TENHOFFGC@COOLEY.COM

**VICKI TING,** admitted to bar, 1995, California. *Education:* Stanford University (A.B., with distinction, 1992; J.D., 1995). Phi Beta Kappa. Moot Court Board. **LANGUAGES:** Mandarin. **PRACTICE AREAS:** Corporate; Securities. **Email:** TINGVW@COOLEY.COM

**WILLIAM S. VEATCH,** born Berkeley, California, August 18, 1961; admitted to bar, 1987, California. *Education:* University of Winnipeg (B.A., 1985), University of Manitoba, Faculty of Law (LL.B., 1985); Hastings College of the Law, University of California (J.D., 1987). **PRACTICE AREAS:** Equipment Leasing; Asset-Based Finance; General Corporate. **Email:** VEATCHWS@COOLEY.COM

*(This Listing Continued)*

**JULIE A. VEHRENKAMP,** born Rochester, Minnesota, January 22, 1959; admitted to bar, 1988, California. *Education:* Macalester College (B.A., cum laude, 1984); Hastings College of the Law, University of California (J.D., 1988). Omicron Delta Epsilon. **PRACTICE AREAS:** Employee Benefit Law. **Email:** VEHRENKAMPJA@COOLEY.COM

**ERIN M. VERNERIS,** born Paget, Bermuda, January 25, 1966; admitted to bar, 1995, California. *Education:* Syracuse University (B.S., 1987); Catholic University, Columbus School of Law (J.D., magna cum laude, 1995). **PRACTICE AREAS:** Employment Law; General Litigation. **Email:** VERNERISEM@COOLEY.COM

**LAURIE A. WEBB,** born Los Angeles, California, September 24, 1965; admitted to bar, 1994, California. *Education:* University of California at Berkeley (B.S., 1987); University of Michigan (J.D., 1993). Associate Editor, 1992-1993 and Contributing Editor, 1993, Michigan Journal of International Law. Coordinating Editor, Michigan Journal of Gender & Law, 1993. **PRACTICE AREAS:** Corporate Law. **Email:** WEBBLA@COOLEY.COM

**MICHAEL L. WEINER,** born Burlingame, California, May 10, 1968; admitted to bar, 1994, California. *Education:* University of Pennsylvania (B.S./B.A., 1990); University of California at Los Angeles (J.D., 1994). Phi Alpha Theta. Chief Comments Editor and Founding Editor, UCLA Entertainment Law Review, 1993-1994. Book Review Editor, Federal Communications Law Review, 1992-1993. **PRACTICE AREAS:** Corporate and Securities; Mergers and Acquisitions; Emerging Companies. **Email:** WEINERML@COOLEY.COM

**BRETT D. WHITE,** born Ithaca, New York, July 29, 1957; admitted to bar, 1991, California. *Education:* University of California, Berkeley (A.B., 1988); Harvard University (J.D., 1991). Phi Beta Kappa. Recipient, Perly Lionel Davis Award. **PRACTICE AREAS:** Securities; Corporate. **Email:** WHITEBD@COOLEY.COM

**LARA A. WILLIAMS,** born Ann Arbor, Michigan, February 26, 1968; admitted to bar, 1995, California. *Education:* Yale University (B.A., cum laude, 1989); Stanford University (J.D., with distinction, 1995). **Email:** WILLIAMSLA@COOLEY.COM

**KEVIN JAMES ZIMMER,** born San Diego, California, January 15, 1963; admitted to bar, 1991, California; registered to practice before the U.S. Patent and Trademark Office. *Education:* California State University, Los Angeles (B.S.E.E., with honors, 1985; M.S.E.E., 1988); University of Michigan Law School (J.D., 1991). Order of Omega. Hughes Aircraft Corporation Graduate Fellow; University of California Regents Scholar. *Member:* State Bar of California; Peninsula Intellectual Property Law Association; San Francisco Patent and Trademark Law Association; San Diego Venture Group. **PRACTICE AREAS:** Intellectual Property. **Email:** ZIMMERKJ@COOLEY.COM

## PATENT AGENTS

**MELYA J. HUGHES,** born Kingsbury, Middlesex, GB, January 3, 1964; registered to practice before U.S. Patent and Trademark Office. *Education:* University College, Cardiff, Wales (B.Sc., with honors, 1984); Biocenter of the University of Basel, Switzerland (Ph.D., 1988). *Member:* Peninsula Intellectual Property Law Association. **LANGUAGES:** German. **PRACTICE AREAS:** Patent Law. **Email:** HUGHESMJ@COOLEY.COM

## LEGAL SUPPORT PERSONNEL

### ADMINISTRATOR

**SUSAN Y. CHEN-WONG.** *Education:* University of California, Berkeley (B.A., 1987). Instructor, St. Mary's Paralegal Studies Program, 1992-1993. Advisory Board Member, St. Mary's College and University of San Francisco Paralegal Studies Programs, 1991—. *Member:* San Francisco Association of Legal Assistants (President, 1991-1992); Legal Assistant Management Association; Association of Legal Administrators. **LANGUAGES:** Mandarin. **PRACTICE AREAS:** Recruitment and Hiring; Evaluation; Training; Budgeting; Workflow Coordination. **Email:** CHENWONGSY@COOLEY.COM

### SECURITIES SPECIALIST

**LINDA M. RIGAS,** born San Francisco, California, April 16, 1958. *Education:* Paralegal Certificate (1978); University of San Francisco (B.S., 1980) Beta Gamma Sigma. *Member:* Bar Association of San Francisco; San Francisco Association of Legal Assistants (Director, 1992-1993). **PRACTICE AREAS:** Securities; Corporate Law. **Email:** RIGASLM@COOLEY.COM

*(This Listing Continued)*

## COOLEY GODWARD LLP, Palo Alto—Continued

### SENIOR LEGAL ASSISTANTS

**J. PAUL ARMSTRONG,** *Member:* SFLA. **PRACTICE AREAS:** Technology Law; Biotechnology. *Email:* ARMSTRONGJP@COOLEY.COM

**SUSAN P. BERMEL,** Member, International Trademark Association Education Committee. **PRACTICE AREAS:** Trademarks; Copyright.

**C. KIM MILLER,** born Clovis, New Mexico, May 13, 1964. *Education:* University of Santa Barbara (B.A., 1986); Santa Clara University Paralegal Certificate, 1987). *Member:* San Francisco Association of Legal Assistants. **PRACTICE AREAS:** Securities and Corporate Law. *Email:* MILLERCK@COOLEY.COM

**KARON PASOS,** *Member:* International Trademark Association (Education Committee); San Francisco Association of Paralegals. **PRACTICE AREAS:** Intellectual Property. *Email:* PASOSKP@COOLEY.COM

**ERIC J. STEINER,** born Las Vegas, Nevada, July 3, 1963. *Education:* University of California at Davis (A.B., 1985). *Member:* SFALA. **PRACTICE AREAS:** Securities; Corporate. *Email:* STEINEREJ@COOLEY.COM

**GARY A. THUNELL,** *Member:* International Trademark Association; San Francisco Association of Legal Assistants. **PRACTICE AREAS:** Trademark; Copyright. *Email:* THUNELLGA@COOLEY.COM

(For Complete Biographical Data on Personnel at San Francisco, Menlo Park and San Diego, California and Boulder, Colorado, see Professional Biographies at those locations).

---

## COX BUCHANAN PADMORE & SHAKARCHY

755 PAGE MILL ROAD, SUITE A280
**PALO ALTO, CALIFORNIA 94304**
Telephone: 415-424-0600
Telefax: 415-493-9408
*Email:* paoff@aol.com

*Denver, Colorado Office:* 1775 Sherman Street, Suite 2500. Telephone: 303-839-9191. Fax: 303-839-9318.

*Newport Beach, California Office:* 840 Newport Center Drive, Suite 700. Telephone: 714-720-9100. Fax: 714-720-1508.

*New York, New York Office:* 630 Third Avenue. Telephone: 212-953-6633. Fax: 212-576-1614.

Trial and Appellate Practice in State and Federal Courts. Corporation, Contracts and Business Law.

**FIRM PROFILE:** *Cox Buchanan Padmore Shakarchy, founded in 1971 by Jonathan C.S. Cox, is dedicated to providing legal services of the highest quality in a timely manner. The firm represents local, national and international clients which involve the firm in complex commercial litigation and international business transactions. The firms attorneys are admitted to practice in various state and federal courts, thereby offering its clients the personal attention and relationship of the small sized firm, and providing the extensive litigation experience, credibility and geographic versatility of a large national firm.*

**JONATHAN C. S. COX,** born Ipswich, Massachusetts, October 25, 1944; admitted to bar, 1971, Colorado; 1984, U.S. Tax Court; 1985, U.S. District Court, Northern District of California; 1988, Texas, U.S. Court of Appeals, Fifth Circuit, U.S. District Court, Southern District of Texas and U.S. Supreme Court; 1989, California and New York; U.S. District Court, District of Colorado; U.S. Court of Appeals, Second, Ninth and Tenth Circuit. *Education:* Stanford University (B.A., 1967); University of Denver (M.A., 1970; J.D., 1971). (Resident). **PRACTICE AREAS:** Commercial Litigation.

**VICKI MAROLT BUCHANAN,** born Aspen, Colorado, September 15, 1949; admitted to bar, 1984, Colorado, U.S. District Court, District of Colorado and U.S. Court of Appeals, Tenth Circuit; 1986, U.S. District Court, Northern District of California; 1988, U.S. Supreme Court; 1991, California, Texas, U.S. District Court, Central District of California, U.S. Court of Appeals, Fifth and Ninth Circuits; 1992, U.S. District Court, Southern District of Texas, 1994, New York; 1995, U.S. District Court, Eastern District of California; 1996, U.S. District Court, Southern District of California and U.S. Court of Appeals, Second Circuit. *Education:* University of Colorado at Boulder (B.S., 1971); University of Denver (J.D., 1983). (Resident, Newport Beach, California Office). **PRACTICE AREAS:** Complex Commercial

*(This Listing Continued)*

---

Litigation; Insurance Bad Faith; Creditor Bankruptcy; Appellate Advocacy.

### ASSOCIATES

**ANDREW F. PIERCE,** born Evanston, Illinois, January 4, 1956; admitted to bar, 1981, California and U.S. District Court, Northern District of California; 1988, U.S. District Court, Eastern District of California; 1993, U.S. District Court, Central District of California and U.S. Court of Appeals, Ninth Circuit. *Education:* Harvard University (A.B., magna cum laude, 1977); Boalt Hall School of Law, University of California (J.D., 1981).

(For Complete Biographical Data on other Personnel, See Professional Biographies at Denver, Colorado)

---

## CRIST, GRIFFITHS, SCHULZ & BIORN

*A PROFESSIONAL CORPORATION*

Established in 1927

550 HAMILTON AVENUE, SUITE 300
**PALO ALTO, CALIFORNIA 94301**
Telephone: 415-321-5000
Fax: 415-326-2404

*General Civil & Trial Practice, Estate Planning, Real Estate, Tax Corporate.*

**ROBERT E. SCHULZ,** born San Mateo, California, August 4, 1939; admitted to bar, 1966, California. *Education:* Stanford University (B.S., 1961; M.S., 1962; J.D., 1965). *Member:* State Bar of California; California Trial Lawyers Association.

**ROBERT A. BIORN,** born Minneapolis, Minnesota, January 19, 1941; admitted to bar, 1969, California. *Education:* University of Colorado (A.B., 1964); Hastings College of Law, University of California (J.D., 1968). *Member:* State Bar of California. (Certified Specialist, Probate, Estate Planning and Trust Law, The State Bar of California Board of Legal Specialization).

**KRISTOFER W. BIORN,** born Palo Alto, California, November 1, 1964; admitted to bar, 1992, California. *Education:* Duke University (A.B., 1987); Copenhagen University, Denmark; Hastings College of the Law, University of California (J.D., 1992). Extern Law Clerk to Hon. Eugene F. Lynch, 1992. *Member:* State Bar of California.

**MARK R. SHEPHERD,** born Pleasanton, California, March 26, 1953; admitted to bar, 1982, California. *Education:* San Francisco State University (B.A., magna cum laude, 1979); Golden Gate University (J.D., with honors, 1982; LL.M., Taxation, 1987). *Member:* State Bar of California. **REPORTED CASES:** Co-Counsel in Estate of Maria Cristofani, 97 TC 24 (1991, Acq. result only).

### OF COUNSEL

**JOHN R. GRIFFITHS,** born Santa Barbara, California, February 12, 1934; admitted to bar, 1961, California. *Education:* Stanford University (A.B., 1955; LL.B.-J.D., 1960). Phi Delta Phi. Special Master, Superior Court of California. *Member:* State Bar of California.

**FRANK LEE CRIST, SR.** (1898-1991).

REPRESENTATIVE CLIENTS: Wells Fargo Bank; Comerica Bank.

---

## DEHLINGER & ASSOCIATES

Established in 1989

350 CAMBRIDGE AVENUE, SUITE 250
**PALO ALTO, CALIFORNIA 94306-1546**
Telephone: 415-324-0880
Telecopier: 415-324-0960

*Patent Law.*

**FIRM PROFILE:** *Dehlinger & Associates specializes in patent protection for inventions in the fields of molecular biology, pharmaceutical and peptide chemistry, plant sciences, drug-delivery systems, instrumentation, materials science, and physics. Since its founding in 1989, the firm has developed a strong reputation for successfully prosecuting patent applications and for assisting clients with technology management issues.*

**PETER J. DEHLINGER,** born Pasadena, California, November 5, 1944; admitted to bar, 1982, Oregon and California; U.S. Court of Appeals, Federal Circuit; registered to practice before U.S. Patent and Trademark

*(This Listing Continued)*

Office. *Education:* University of Oregon (B.S., Physics, 1966); Stanford University (Ph.D., Biophysics, 1971); Lewis and Clark Northwestern School of Law (J.D., 1982). Author: " A Not-So-Radical Proposal for Selecting Radical Substitutions in Markush-Type Claims," J. Patent nad Trademark Office Soc., July 1992; "Design for an Invention Generator: An Alternative View of Nonobviousness," J. Patent and Trademark Soc., Jan 1994. *Member:* Bar Association of San Francisco; State Bar of California; Oregon State Bar Association; Oregon Patent Law Association; Peninsula Patent Law Association; San Francisco Patent Law Association. *PRACTICE AREAS:* Intellectual Property.

### ASSOCIATE

**CAROL STRATFORD,** born Los Angeles, California, March 9, 1952; admitted to bar, 1995, California; 1990, registered to practice before U.S. Patent and Trademark Office. *Education:* Stanford University (B.S., Biological Sciences, 1974; A.M., Biological Sciences, 1975); University of Michigan (Ph.D., Pharmacology, 1982); Santa Clara University School of Law (J.D., 1995). Sigma Xi. Phi Delta Phi. NIH Pre-Doctoral Fellow, 1977-1980. Recipient, Scottish Rite Dissertation Fellowship, 1980-1981. *Member:* State Bar of California; Peninsula Intellectual Property Law Association; Association of Science and Patent Professionals; American Association for the Advancement of Science. *PRACTICE AREAS:* Intellectual Property.

### LEGAL SUPPORT PERSONNEL

**VINCENT M. POWERS,** born 1961. *Education:* California Institute of Technology (B.S., in Chemistry, 1983); University of California at San Francisco (PhD., in Pharmaceutical Chemistry, 1986). Recipient, NIH NRSA Post-Doctoral Fellowship, University of California at Berkeley, 1989-1991. Registered to practice before U.S. Patent and Trademark Office. Member, American Chemical Society. (Patent Agent). *PRACTICE AREAS:* Patent Law.

**JUDY M. MOHR,** born Iowa City, Iowa, July 19, 1961. *Education:* Pepperdine University (B.S., Biology, 1983); University of Texas at Austin (Ph.D., Chemical Engineering, 1990). Registered to practice before U.S. Patent and Trademark Office. *Member:* Peninsula Intellectual Property Law Association. (Patent Agent). *PRACTICE AREAS:* Patent Law.

**CHARLES K. SHOLTZ,** born Prague, Czech Republic, January 6, 1960. *Education:* University of Michigan (B.S., Distinction, high honors in Cellular and Molecular Biology; B.S.E., cum laude, Engineering Science, 1983); Yale University (M.S., Physiology, 1985); Stanford University (Ph.D., Neuroscience, 1989); Massachusetts General Hospital; Harvard Medical School. Registered to practice before U.S. Patent and Trademark Office. *Member:* Society for Neuroscience; Biophysical Society. (Patent Agent). *LANGUAGES:* Czech. *PRACTICE AREAS:* Patent Law.

**SUSAN T. EVANS,** born San Francisco, California, October 11, 1961. *Education:* Smith College (B.A., cum laude in Chemistry, 1983); University of California at Davis (Ph.D, 1989). Registered to practice before U.S. Patent and Trademark Office. Phi Beta Kappa; Phi Lambda Upsilon; Sigma Xi. Recipient: American Chemical Society Award for Outstanding Work in Chemistry, 1983; Frances A. House Memorial Award for Best Record in Chemistry, 1983; Clorox Award for Outstanding Ph.D. Dissertation. Research Mentorship Program Fellow in Chemistry, 1984-1985. Member, American Chemical Society. (Patent Agent). *PRACTICE AREAS:* Patent Law.

**LEEANN GORTHEY,** born Dallas, Texas, April 15, 1957. *Education:* University of Texas at Arlington (B.S., summa cum laude, Chemistry, 1979); Stanford University (Ph.D., Organic Chemistry, 1984). Registered to practice before U.S. Patent and Trademark Office. Member: Association of Scientific and Patent Professionals; American Chemical Society. (Patent Agent). *PRACTICE AREAS:* Patent Law.

---

## DOTY & SUNDHEIM

Established in 1986

420 FLORENCE STREET
SUITE 200

**PALO ALTO, CALIFORNIA 94301**

Telephone: 415-327-0100
Fax: 415-327-0101; Modem: 415-327-1123
Email: attorney@dotysund.com

Corporate, Real Estate, Intellectual Property, Technology Contracts, Financing, Securities, Trade Secrets, and Computer Law, Employment Law.

(This Listing Continued)

---

**FIRM PROFILE:** Established in 1986, Doty & Sundheim has participated in the action and innovation of California's Silicon Valley. The firm has developed a vibrant business law practice with a reputation for enterprise, integrity and professionalism. Our practice includes business formation, technology licensing, business financing, real property development and leasing and contract drafting, review and negotiation of all types, both in the U.S. and internationally. In our practice, we strive to gain a full understanding of our clients' businesses in order better serve their needs and forge long-term professional relationships that they can rely on.

### MEMBERS OF FIRM

**STANLEY E. DOTY,** born Ponca City, Oklahoma, December 19, 1952; admitted to bar, 1978, California and U.S. District Court, Northern District of California. *Education:* Stanford University (B.A., Honors and Distinction, 1975); University of Michigan (J.D., 1978). *Member:* State Bar of California. *PRACTICE AREAS:* Technology Contracts; Multimedia; Business Formation; Commercial Contracts; Business Planning; Health Law.

**GEORGE M. SUNDHEIM, III,** born Chicago, Illinois, December 11, 1952; admitted to bar, 1981, California and U.S. District Court, Northern District of California. *Education:* Stanford University (B.A., Honors and Distinction, 1975); Northwestern University (J.D., 1980). Certified NFL Contract Advisor. State Farm Exceptional Student Post Graduate Fellowship. President, Palo Alto Bar Association, 1992. Recipient, California State Bar, Wiley W. Manuel Award for Pro Bono Legal Services, 1992. Trustee, Santa Clara Bar Association, 1992. Delegate: Soviet-U.S. Conference on the Law and Trade, Moscow, 1990; U.S./China Joint Session on Trade, Investment and Economic Law, Beijing, 1987. *PRACTICE AREAS:* Corporate Reorganization; Intellectual Property Licensing; Private Placements; Shareholder Agreements; Professional Sports Law.

### ASSOCIATES

**JARED A. SLOSBERG,** born Washington, D.C., February 26, 1969; admitted to bar, 1992, California. *Education:* Brandeis University (B.A., magna cum laude, 1989); Boalt Hall School of Law, University of California at Berkeley (J.D., 1992). Phi Beta Kappa. Order of the Coif. Justice Brandeis Merit Scholar. Recipient, American Jurisprudence Award. Editor-in-Chief, High Technology Law Journal, 1991-1992. Co-author, Smith & Slosberg, "Beware! Trade Secret Software May Be Patented by a Later Inventor," The Computer Lawyer, November, 1990. *LANGUAGES:* French. *PRACTICE AREAS:* Business Formation; Intellectual Property Licensing; Technology Contracts; Shareholder Agreements; Buying and Selling of Businesses.

**ANNETTE BARLOW,** born Santa Clara, California, March 25, 1968; admitted to bar, 1993, California; U.S. District Court, Northern District of California; 1996, District of Columbia. *Education:* University of California, Berkeley (B.A., with honors, 1990); Georgetown University (J.D., 1993). Executive Editor, Georgetown International Environmental Law Review, 1992-1993. *Member:* State Bar of California. *PRACTICE AREAS:* Business and Corporate Law; Contracts.

**REYNALDO A. DURÁN,** born San Salvador, El Salvador, November 3, 1962; admitted to bar, 1991, California. *Education:* Occidental College (A.B., 1984); University of California, Hastings College of the Law (J.D., 1991). *Member:* State Bar of California. *LANGUAGES:* Spanish. *PRACTICE AREAS:* Business and Corporate; Commercial Litigation.

---

## ENTERPRISE LAW GROUP, INC.

**PALO ALTO, CALIFORNIA**

(See Menlo Park)

---

## GEOFFREY C. ETNIRE

**PALO ALTO, CALIFORNIA**

(See Pleasanton)

Real Estate Transactions, Development and Land Use Issues.

# FENWICK & WEST LLP

*Established in 1972*

*TWO PALO ALTO SQUARE*
**PALO ALTO, CALIFORNIA 94306**
Telephone: 415-494-0600
Fax: 415-494-1417
URL: http://www.fenwick.com

*Washington, D.C. Office:* Suite 650, 1920 N Street, N.W. Telephone: 202-463-6300. Fax: 202-463-6520, 202-887-5143.

*San Francisco, California Office:* 100 Embarcadero, 3rd Floor. Telephone: 415-281-1330. Fax: 415-281-1350.

*General Practice. Corporate, Securities, International (Business, Trade and Customs, Trademark and Patent), Intellectual Property (Copyright, Trademark and Patent), Computer and High Technology Law, Biotechnology Law, Food and Drug Administration Law, Government Procurement, Litigation and Alternative Dispute Resolution, Antitrust and Trade Regulation, Tax, Estate Planning and Probate.*

## MEMBERS OF FIRM

**SALLY M. ABEL,** born Palo Alto, California, March 18, 1955; admitted to bar, 1984, California and U.S. District Court, Northern District of California. *Education:* University of California at Davis (B.A., summa cum laude, 1977); University of California at Los Angeles (J.D., 1984). **PRACTICE AREAS:** Trademark.

**ROBERTA CAIRNEY,** born Oakland, California, December 12, 1952; admitted to bar, 1979, California. *Education:* University of California at Santa Cruz (B.A., with honors, 1976); University of California, Hastings College of the Law (J.D., 1979). (Resident in San Francisco Office). **PRACTICE AREAS:** Intellectual Property Law; Trademark and Copyright Law; Media Law; Software Law; Entertainment Law.

**FREDERICK R. CHILTON, JR.,** born San Bernardino, California, February 6, 1945; admitted to bar, 1972, California. *Education:* Fresno State College (B.A., 1967); University of California, Hastings College of the Law (J.D., 1971); New York University (LL.M. in Taxation, 1973). Clerk to Judge Leo Irwin, United States Tax Court, Washington, D.C., 1973-1975. **PRACTICE AREAS:** Domestic and International Corporate Taxation.

**KENNETH B. CLARK,** born Los Angeles, California, October 13, 1954; admitted to bar, 1979, New York; 1980, California; 1990, U.S. Tax Court. *Education:* University of Redlands (B.A., summa cum laude, 1975); New York University (J.D., cum laude, 1978); University of California at Berkeley (M.B.A., 1987). **PRACTICE AREAS:** Litigation; Tax Litigation; Construction Law.

**TIMOTHY A. COVINGTON,** born Pasadena, California, January 17, 1958; admitted to bar, 1986, California and U.S. District Court, Northern District of California. *Education:* University of California at Berkeley (B.A., magna cum laude, 1981); University of California, Hastings College of Law (J.D., 1985). **PRACTICE AREAS:** Intellectual Property; Licensing Law.

**JACQUELINE A. DAUNT,** born Flint, Michigan, December 2, 1953; admitted to bar, 1978, California; 1979, Michigan. *Education:* University of Michigan (B.A., with honors, 1975; J.D., cum laude, 1978); University of Brussels, Brussels, Belgium. **PRACTICE AREAS:** Corporate.

**GORDON K. DAVIDSON,** born Port Chester, New York, July 30, 1948; admitted to bar, 1974, California. *Education:* Stanford University (B.S., Electrical Engineering, 1970; M.S., in Electrical Engineering, Computer Systems, 1971; J.D., 1974). Law Clerk to Judge Ben. C. Duniway, U.S. Court of Appeals, Ninth Circuit, 1974-1975. **PRACTICE AREAS:** Corporate.

**DENNIS R. DEBROECK,** born Denver, Colorado, October 11, 1951; admitted to bar, 1976, California. *Education:* University of Colorado (B.S., magna cum laude, 1973); University of California at Los Angeles (J.D., 1976). Order of the Coif. **PRACTICE AREAS:** Corporate.

**ROBERT B. DELLENBACH,** born Provo, Utah; admitted to bar, 1990, California. *Education:* University of Utah (B.A., summa cum laude, 1986); Stanford University (J.D., 1989). **PRACTICE AREAS:** Corporate.

**WILLIAM A. FENWICK,** born Curdsville, Kentucky, August 1, 1938; admitted to bar, 1968, New York; 1973, California; 1987, U.S. Tax Court. *Education:* Southern Illinois University (B.S., with honors, 1964); Vanderbilt University (LL.B., 1967). **PRACTICE AREAS:** Litigation; Intellectual Property.

*(This Listing Continued)*

**JOHN C. FOX,** born Fort Sill, Oklahoma, January 27, 1952; admitted to bar, 1976, District of Columbia; 1988, California. *Education:* Texas A & M University; University of California at Riverside (B.A., cum laude, 1973); George Washington University (J.D., 1976). **PRACTICE AREAS:** Employment and Labor.

**KATHRYN JEAN FRITZ,** born La Mesa, California, February 21, 1959; admitted to bar, 1986, New York and U.S. District Court, Southern and Eastern Districts of New York; 1990, California, U.S. District Court, Northern, Eastern and Central Districts of California and U.S. Court of Appeals, Ninth Circuit; 1993, U.S. Court of Appeals, Second Circuit. *Education:* University of California at Santa Barbara (B.A., magna cum laude, 1981); Georgetown University Law Center (J.D., cum laude, 1985). (Palo Alto and San Francisco Offices). **PRACTICE AREAS:** Intellectual Property Litigation; Trademark and Copyright Law; General Business Litigation.

**JAMES P. FULLER,** born Mineola, New York, August 27, 1942; admitted to bar, 1971, New York; 1977, California. *Education:* New York University (B.S., 1966; LL.M. in Taxation, 1974; Graduate Law School, 1974-1975); Fordham University (J.D., 1970);. **PRACTICE AREAS:** Taxation.

**JENNIFER L. FULLER,** born Bellflower, California, April 26, 1958; admitted to bar, 1987, California; 1990, U.S. Tax Court. *Education:* Whittier College (B.A., 1982); Loyola Law School of Los Angeles (J.D., 1985); Georgetown University Law Center (LL.M. in Taxation, 1988). **PRACTICE AREAS:** Taxation.

**JAMES C. GARAHAN,** born New York, N.Y., April 24, 1945; admitted to bar, 1980, California. *Education:* Haverford College (B.A., 1967); University of California at Berkeley (M.A., Mathematics, 1970); University of California at Berkeley, Boalt Hall School of Law (J.D., 1980). **PRACTICE AREAS:** Taxation.

**ROGER M. GOLDEN** (Resident in Washington, D.C. Office).

**FRED M. GREGURAS,** born Omaha, Nebraska, December 3, 1943; admitted to bar, 1976, Ohio; 1977, Nebraska; 1982, California. *Education:* University of Omaha (B.A., 1966); University of Nebraska at Omaha (M.S., Mathematics and Computer Science, 1968); University of Nebraska (J.D., 1975). **PRACTICE AREAS:** Corporate.

**GARRY S. GROSSMAN** (Resident in Washington, D.C. Office).

**DAVID L. HAYES,** born Amarillo, Texas, October 22, 1956; admitted to bar, 1986, California; registered to practice before U.S. Patent and Trademark Office. *Education:* Rice University (B.S., summa cum laude, Electrical Engineering, 1978) ; Stanford University (M.S.E.E., 1980); Harvard University (J.D., cum laude, 1984). Law Clerk to Honorable John Minor Wisdom, U.S. Court of Appeals for the Fifth Circuit, 1984-1985. **PRACTICE AREAS:** Intellectual Property.

**DAVID W. HEALY,** born Tokyo, Japan, May 15, 1954; admitted to bar, 1979, California and U.S. District Court, Northern District of California; 1981, U.S. District Court, Central District of California. *Education:* University of Santa Clara; University of California at Davis (B.A., cum laude, 1976); University of California, Hastings College of the Law (J.D., 1979). Clerk, California Supreme Court, 1979. **PRACTICE AREAS:** Corporate.

**BRUCE W. JENETT,** born Houston, Texas, May 24, 1946; admitted to bar, 1977, New York; 1979, California. *Education:* Princeton University (B.A., cum laude, 1969); Georgetown University Law Center (J.D., 1976). **PRACTICE AREAS:** Corporate.

**JOEL D. KELLMAN,** born New York, N.Y., December 8, 1942; admitted to bar, 1967, New York; 1972, California; 1984, Utah. *Education:* Harpur College (B.A., 1963); St. John's University (LL.B., 1966); New York University (LL.M. in Comparative and Foreign Law, 1968). **PRACTICE AREAS:** Corporate.

**C. KEVIN KELSO,** born Indianapolis, Indiana, August 14, 1954; admitted to bar, 1980, California. *Education:* University of Illinois (B.A., 1975); Harvard University (J.D., 1978). Law Clerk to Justice Anthony M. Kennedy, U.S. Court of Appeals, Ninth Circuit, 1978-1980. **PRACTICE AREAS:** Corporate Securities; Mergers and Acquisitions.

**PATRICIA NICELY KOPF,** born Rutherford, New Jersey, February 21, 1950; admitted to bar, 1975, New York; 1980, California. *Education:* Wellesley College (A.B., with high honors, 1971); Harvard Law School (J.D., 1974); New York University School of Law (LL.M. program in Intellectual Property Law). **PRACTICE AREAS:** Litigation; Employment and Labor Law.

*(This Listing Continued)*

**BARRY J. KRAMER,** born Baltimore, Maryland, February 12, 1958; admitted to bar, 1982, California. *Education:* University of Pennsylvania, Wharton School (B.S., 1978); Stanford University (J.D., 1982). *PRACTICE AREAS:* Corporate.

**MICHAEL M. LANDA** (Resident in Washington, D.C. Office).

**KENNETH A. LINHARES,** born San Francisco, California, August 11, 1955; admitted to bar, 1980, California. *Education:* University of Santa Clara (B.A., magna cum laude, 1977; J.D., summa cum laude, 1980). *PRACTICE AREAS:* Corporate.

**EDWIN N. LOWE,** born New York, N.Y., May 19, 1940; admitted to bar, 1967, California; 1968, New York. *Education:* Stanford University (B.A., 1963); University of California at Berkeley, Boalt Hall School of Law (J.D., 1966). *PRACTICE AREAS:* Corporate.

**PATRICIA M. LUCAS,** born San Francisco, California, May 9, 1954; admitted to bar, 1979, California. *Education:* Rice University (B.A., cum laude, 1976); University of California at Berkeley, Boalt Hall School of Law (J.D., 1979). *PRACTICE AREAS:* Litigation; Employment and Labor Law.

**BRUCE F. MACKLER** (Resident in Washington, D.C. Office).

**STUART P. MEYER,** born Long Island, New York, April 1, 1960; admitted to bar, 1988, California, U.S. District Court, Northern and Central Districts of California and Eastern District of Michigan and U.S. Court of Appeals, 9th Circuit; 1996, Vermont; registered to practice before the U.S. Patent and Trademark Office. *Education:* Carnegie Mellon University (B.S., Electrical Engineering, with full honors, 1982); Princeton University (M.S., Electrical Engineering/Computer Science, 1985); Yale University (J.D., 1988). *PRACTICE AREAS:* Intellectual Property.

**CHARLENE M. MORROW,** born Ventura, California, July 6, 1962; admitted to bar, 1988, California. *Education:* University of Southern California (A.B., summa cum laude, 1984); University of California at Berkeley, Boalt Hall School of Law (J.D., 1988). Law Clerk to Hon. William W Schwarzer, U.S. District Court, Northern District of California, 1988-1989. *PRACTICE AREAS:* Litigation.

**MARK S. OSTRAU,** born Atlanta, Georgia, November 26, 1960; admitted to bar, 1985, California and U.S. District Court, Northern District of California; 1990, U.S. Court of Appeals, Ninth Circuit. *Education:* Yale University (B.A., magna cum laude, 1982); Stanford University (J.D., 1985). *PRACTICE AREAS:* Corporate; Antitrust; Licensing Law.

**MICHAEL J. PATRICK,** born Cincinnati, Ohio, April 16, 1959; admitted to bar, 1984, California. *Education:* Wesleyan University (B.A., 1981); University of California at Los Angeles (J.D., 1984). *PRACTICE AREAS:* Corporate.

**EDWARD J. RADLO,** born Pawtucket, Rhode Island, March 7, 1946; admitted to bar, 1972, California; 1973, Rhode Island; registered to practice before U.S. Patent and Trademark Office and Canadian Patent Office. *Education:* Massachusetts Institute of Technology (B.S., Mathematics, 1967); Harvard University (J.D., 1972). Law Clerk, Supreme Court of Rhode Island, 1972-1973. *PRACTICE AREAS:* Intellectual Property; Patent Law.

**WALTER T. RAINERI,** born Coalinga, California, August 28, 1959; admitted to bar, 1987, California and U.S. Court of Appeals, Ninth and Federal Circuits, U.S. District Court, Northern and Southern Districts of California, U.S. Supreme Court, U.S. Court of Claims and U.S. Tax Court. *Education:* University of California at Berkeley (B.S., summa cum laude, 1982); Georgetown University Law Center (J.D., cum laude, 1987). *PRACTICE AREAS:* Taxation.

**I. JOEL RIFF,** born 1951; admitted to bar, 1983, Illinois; 1987, California. *Education:* University of Michigan (B.G.S., with distinction, 1972); De Paul University; University of Chicago (J.D., 1982). *PRACTICE AREAS:* Intellectual Property; Licensing Law.

**TIMOTHY K. ROAKE,** born Oakland, California, October 6, 1952; admitted to bar, 1981, California; 1983, Colorado; U.S. District Court, Northern, Central and Eastern Districts of California and District of Colorado; U.S. Court of Appeals, Ninth and Tenth Circuits. *Education:* University of California at Berkeley (B.A., 1976); University of California at Davis (J.D., 1981). Order of the Coif. *PRACTICE AREAS:* Business Litigation; including Securities and Trade Secret Litigation.

**EILEEN DUFFY ROBINETT,** born San Diego, California, June 18, 1964; admitted to bar, 1989, California. *Education:* Santa Clara University

*(This Listing Continued)*

(B.S., magna cum laude, 1986); University of California at Berkeley, Boalt Hall School of Law (J.D., 1989). *PRACTICE AREAS:* Corporate.

**PAUL H. ROSKOPH,** born Cleveland, Ohio, November 7, 1938; admitted to bar, 1963, Ohio; 1968, California; 1969, U.S. Tax Court. *Education:* The Ohio State University (B.S., 1960; J.D., 1963). *PRACTICE AREAS:* Taxation; Estate Planning.

**RONALD B. SCHROTENBOER,** born Ottawa, Ontario, Canada, July 31, 1956; admitted to bar, 1980, California. *Education:* Calvin College (B.A., with honors, 1977); University of Michigan (J.D., magna cum laude, 1980). *PRACTICE AREAS:* Domestic and International Corporate Taxation; California State Income and Sales Taxation.

**LAIRD H. SIMONS, III,** born Bryn Mawr, Pennsylvania, April 21, 1949; admitted to bar, 1974, California. *Education:* Haverford College (B.A., with honors, 1970); Harvard University (M.B.A., with distinction, 1974; J.D., 1974). *PRACTICE AREAS:* Corporate.

**DAVID W. SLABY,** born Evanston, Illinois, September 20, 1947; admitted to bar, 1976, Illinois; 1980, U.S. Supreme Court; 1981, California. *Education:* Gettysburg College; American University (B.S.B.A., magna cum laude, 1973); Boston University (J.D., 1976). *PRACTICE AREAS:* Litigation.

**ALBERT C. SMITH,** born New York, N.Y., March 30, 1937; admitted to bar, 1964, California, U.S. District Court, Northern District of California and U.S. Court of Appeals, Ninth Circuit; 1978, U.S. Supreme Court; 1980, U.S. Tax Court and U.S. District Court, Eastern District of California; 1982, U.S. Court of Appeals for the Federal Circuit. *Education:* Polytechnic University of New York (B.S., Electrical Engineering, 1958); Santa Clara University (J.D., 1963). *PRACTICE AREAS:* Intellectual Property; Patent Law.

**SCOTT P. SPECTOR,** born Chicago, Illinois, June 24, 1949; admitted to bar, 1975, Illinois; 1976, New York; 1990, California. *Education:* Tulane University of Louisiana (B.A., 1971; J.D., 1974); New York University (LL.M., Taxation, 1975). *PRACTICE AREAS:* Corporate.

**BLAKENEY STAFFORD,** born Somerville, New Jersey, April 25, 1942; admitted to bar, 1968, California; 1971, New York. *Education:* Princeton University (B.A., 1964); Stanford University (LL.B., 1967); New York University (LL.M. in Taxation, 1974).

**JOHN J. STEELE,** born Washington, D.C., May 29, 1960; admitted to bar, 1986, California. *Education:* Bucknell University (B.A., 1982); Georgetown University Law Center (J.D., 1985). *PRACTICE AREAS:* Litigation.

**CLAUDE M. STERN,** born Syracuse, New York, September 18, 1955; admitted to bar, 1980, California; U.S. Court of Appeals, Ninth Circuit; U.S. District Court, Northern, Eastern and Central Districts of California. *Education:* University of California at Los Angeles (B.A., magna cum laude, 1977); University of California, Hastings College of the Law (J.D., 1980). Order of the Coif. Law Clerk to the Honorable Jerome Farris, U.S. Court of Appeals, Ninth Circuit, 1980-1981. *PRACTICE AREAS:* Litigation; Intellectual Property Law.

**MARK C. STEVENS,** born San Jose, California, May 12, 1959; admitted to bar, 1983, California and U.S. District Court, Northern District of California. *Education:* University of Santa Clara (B.S., magna cum laude, 1979); Northwestern University (J.D., cum laude, 1983). (Palo Alto and San Francisco Offices). *PRACTICE AREAS:* Corporate; Licensing Law.

**GREG T. SUEOKA,** born Salt Lake City, Utah, 1963; admitted to bar, 1989, California; registered to practice before U.S. Patent and Trademark Office. *Education:* University of Utah (B.S., Political Science, 1984; B.S., Computer Science, 1985; J.D., 1988). *PRACTICE AREAS:* Intellectual Property; Patent Law.

**GAIL E. SUNIGA,** born Oakland, California, November 30, 1945; admitted to bar, 1982, California. *Education:* University of California at Berkeley (B.A., 1967); Santa Clara University, Leavy School of Business (M.B.A., with distinction, 1981); Santa Clara University School of Law (J.D., cum laude, 1982). *PRACTICE AREAS:* Corporate.

**HIROHISA TACHIBANA,** born Ashiya, Japan, 1956; admitted to bar, 1982, California. *Education:* Yale University (B.S./M.S., Engineering and Applied Science, magna cum laude, 1978); University of California, Hastings College of the Law (J.D., 1981); New York University (LL.M. in Taxation, 1982). *PRACTICE AREAS:* Intellectual Property; Licensing Law.

**JOHN T. WESTERMEIER, JR.** (Resident in Washington, D.C. Office).

*(This Listing Continued)*

**FENWICK & WEST LLP, Palo Alto—Continued**

MITCHELL ZIMMERMAN, born New York, N.Y., October 15, 1942; admitted to bar, 1979, California. *Education:* City College of the City University of New York (B.A., 1963); Princeton University (M.A., Politics, 1965); Stanford University (J.D., 1979).

*OF COUNSEL*

SUSAN A. DUNN, born Milwaukee, Wisconsin, June 11, 1957; admitted to bar, 1986, California. *Education:* Radcliffe College (B.A., magna cum laude, 1979); Stanford University (J.D., with distinction, 1986). Clerk to: the Honorable Joseph T. Sneed, U.S. Court of Appeals, Ninth Circuit; the Honorable Sandra Day O'Connor, U.S. Supreme Court. *PRACTICE AREAS:* Corporate.

SAVERY M. GRADOVILLE (Resident in Washington, D.C. Office).

JOHN W. KASTELIC, born St. Louis, Missouri, September 7, 1960; admitted to bar, 1985, New York; 1987, California. *Education:* Washington University (B.S., with honors, 1982); Georgetown University (J.D., cum laude, 1985). *PRACTICE AREAS:* Securities; Mergers and Acquisitions; General Corporate.

VALARIE L. McINROY, born Seattle, Washington, June 3, 1953; admitted to bar, 1978, California. *Education:* California State University at San Jose (B.A., with greatest distinction, 1975); University of Santa Clara (J.D., summa cum laude, 1978). *PRACTICE AREAS:* Corporate.

DAVID K. MICHAELS, born New York, N.Y., 1961; admitted to bar, 1987, New York; 1992, Massachusetts (Not admitted in California). *Education:* Hamilton College (B.A., magna cum laude, 1983); Cornell University (J.D., magna cum laude, 1986). *PRACTICE AREAS:* Securities; Mergers and Acquisitions; Venture Capital; General Corporate.

KATHERINE T. TALLMAN, born Margaretville, New York, September 15, 1947; admitted to bar, 1979, California. *Education:* William Smith College (B.A., cum laude, 1969); University of San Francisco (J.D., magna cum laude, 1979). Extern to Hon. Mathew O. Tobriner, Associate Justice, California Supreme Court, Summer, 1978 and Hon. Joseph T. Sneed, U.S. Court of Appeals, Ninth Circuit, Fall, 1978. *PRACTICE AREAS:* Corporate.

*SPECIAL COUNSEL*

CRAIG A. SELNESS, born July 5, 1955; admitted to bar, 1985, California; 1987, U.S. Court of Appeals, Ninth Circuit. *Education:* University of Minnesota (B.A., 1976); Bethel Theological Seminary (M.Div., 1979); University of Santa Clara (M.A., 1982); University of California at Berkeley, Boalt Hall School of Law (J.D., 1985). *PRACTICE AREAS:* Litigation; Employment and Labor Law.

JAMES T. GIVEN, admitted to bar, 1979, California. *Education:* Indiana University at Bloomington (A.B., 1976); University of California at Berkeley, Boalt Hall School of Law (J.D., 1979). (Also Practicing Individually in Oakland, California). *PRACTICE AREAS:* Corporate.

JOHN M. MASON, admitted to bar, 1974, District of Columbia (Not admitted in California). *Education:* Yale University (B.A., 1968); Washington & Lee University (J.D., 1973). *PRACTICE AREAS:* Litigation; Employment and Labor Law.

WILLIAM J. McCARREN, admitted to bar, 1967, Colorado; 1968, California. *Education:* St. Peter's College (B.A., magna cum laude, 1964); Stanford Law School (LL.B., 1967). (Also Member of Miller, McCarren & Helms, Denver, Colorado). *PRACTICE AREAS:* Litigation; Employment and Labor Law.

AMIR H. RAUBVOGEL, admitted to bar, 1991, California. *Education:* University of Toronto (B.A.Sc., with honors, 1986); Yale Law School (J.D., 1991). *PRACTICE AREAS:* Intellectual Property; Patent Law.

*ASSOCIATES*

SUSAN M. ALKEMA, born Ann Arbor, Michigan, April 28, 1966; admitted to bar, 1993, Illinois; 1995, California. *Education:* Northwestern University (B.A., 1988; J.D., cum laude, 1993). *PRACTICE AREAS:* Corporate.

PHYLLIS E. ANDES (Resident in Washington, D.C. Office).

BARTON W.S. BASSETT, admitted to bar, 1996, California. *Education:* University of California at Davis (B.A., 1992); University of California, Hastings College of the Law (J.D., magna cum laude, 1992). Order of the Coif. *PRACTICE AREAS:* Taxation.

HARRY BOADWEE, born 1959; admitted to bar, 1988, New York; 1994, California. *Education:* Stanford University (A.B.); Columbia University (J.D., 1987). *PRACTICE AREAS:* Corporate.

ELIZABETH K. BOHANNON, born Worcester, Massachusetts, January 27, 1962; admitted to bar, 1992, California. *Education:* Duke University (B.S., 1984); University of San Francisco School of Law (J.D., 1992). *PRACTICE AREAS:* Litigation; Employment and Labor Law.

KIMBERLY A. BOMAR, born Los Angeles, California, January 19, 1965; admitted to bar, 1993, California. *Education:* Dartmouth College (A.B., 1988); Stanford University (A.M., 1990; J.D., 1993). *PRACTICE AREAS:* Corporate.

TIMOTHY P. BOUDREAU, born New York, N.Y., January 26, 1965; admitted to bar, 1995, Arizona (Not admitted in California). *Education:* New York University (B.A., magna cum laude, 1987; J.D., cum laude, 1995). *PRACTICE AREAS:* Litigation.

MONA CHANDRA, born Atlanta, Georgia, July 1, 1968; admitted to bar, 1995, California. *Education:* University of Massachusetts (B.S., Electrical Engineering, with honors, 1990); University of Virginia School of Law (J.D., 1995). *PRACTICE AREAS:* Corporate.

G. CHIN CHAO, admitted to bar, 1996, California. *Education:* University of Illinois at Urbana-Champaign (B.S., 1992); Stanford University (M.S., 1993); Stanford Law School (J.D., 1996). *PRACTICE AREAS:* Corporate; Licensing Law.

LESLIE F. CHARD III, born Atlanta, Georgia, November 10, 1964; admitted to bar, 1992, Illinois; 1996, California. *Education:* Wesleyan University (B.A., Mathematics, Computer Science, 1987); University of Cincinnati (J.D., 1992). *PRACTICE AREAS:* Intellectual Property Law; Licensing Law.

ROBERT CHOW, admitted to bar, 1996, California. *Education:* University of California at Davis (B.S., 1986); University of California at Berkeley (M.S., 1989); University of California at Berkeley, Boalt Hall School of Law (J.D., 1996). *PRACTICE AREAS:* Corporate.

KAUI'ILANI CHUN, admitted to bar, 1996, California. *Education:* Brown University (B.S., 1989); Stanford University (M.B.A., 1996); Stanford Law School (J.D., 1996). *PRACTICE AREAS:* Corporate.

RODGER COLE, born Newport Beach, California, April 4, 1969; admitted to bar, 1995, California. *Education:* University of Redlands (B.A., 1991); Santa Clara University School of Law (J.D., magna cum laude, 1995). *PRACTICE AREAS:* Litigation.

WILLIAM F. COLGIN, JR., admitted to bar, 1992, Virginia (Not admitted in California). *Education:* University of Wyoming (B.A., 1987; M.A., 1989); University of Denver School of Law (J.D., 1992). *PRACTICE AREAS:* Litigation; Tax Litigation.

JEANINE M. CORR, born Oakland, California, September 30, 1965; admitted to bar, 1993, California. *Education:* Evergreen State College (B.A., 1987); University of San Francisco (J.D., 1993). *PRACTICE AREAS:* Corporate.

JOANN CORTI COVINGTON, born Waterbury, Connecticut, October 29, 1967; admitted to bar, 1993, California. *Education:* Clark University (B.A., summa cum laude, 1989); Harvard University (J.D., magna cum laude, 1993). *PRACTICE AREAS:* Litigation.

TYLER R. COZZENS, born Billings, Montana, February 21, 1968; admitted to bar, 1995, California. *Education:* Stanford University (B.S., Electrical Engineering, 1993; J.D., 1995). *PRACTICE AREAS:* Corporate.

DANIELLE C. CULLINANE, born Dallas, Texas, March 15, 1965; admitted to bar, 1995, California. *Education:* Stanford University (B.S., with distinction, 1987); University of California at Berkeley (M.S., 1992); Stanford Law School (J.D., 1995). *PRACTICE AREAS:* Corporate.

CATHERINE L. CURTISS, born Boston, Massachusetts, February 15, 1952; admitted to bar, 1989, California; 1991, U.S. Tax Court; 1992, U.S. Court of Federal Claims; 1994, U.S. Court of Appeals, Ninth Circuit. *Education:* Wittenberg University (B.A., cum laude, 1974); Middlebury College (M.A., 1976); Georgetown University (M.S.F.S., cum laude, 1976); Georgetown University Law Center (J.D., cum laude, 1988); New York University School of Law (LL.M. in Taxation, 1989). *PRACTICE AREAS:* Taxation.

GAY CROSTHWAIT DANFORTH, admitted to bar, 1985, California. *Education:* Wellesley College (B.A., 1981) Durant Scholar, Phi Beta Kappa; Columbia Law School (J.D., 1984). Law Clerk to Hon. Jack B. Weinstein, Eastern District of New York, 1984-1985. *PRACTICE AREAS:* Litigation; Labor and Employment Law.

*(This Listing Continued)*

**MARILYN TIKI DARE,** born Erie, Pennsylvania, April 14, 1966; admitted to bar, 1993, New York; 1994, District of Columbia; 1996, California. *Education:* Dartmouth College (B.A., cum laude, 1988); Duke University (J.D., 1992; M.A., 1992). *PRACTICE AREAS:* Intellectual Property; Copyright and Trademark.

**PAOLO M. (PAUL) DAU,** born Rome, Italy, 1953; admitted to bar, 1994, California. *Education:* McGill University (B.A., first class honors, 1973); University of Pittsburgh (Ph.D., 1980); University of California at Davis (J.D., 1992). Order of the Coif. Law Clerk to Hon. Warren M. Matthews, Alaska Supreme Court, 1992-1993. *PRACTICE AREAS:* Taxation.

**VALERIE M. DAWSON,** born Chambersburg, Pennsylvania, March 12, 1965; admitted to bar, 1993, California. *Education:* College of William & Mary (B.A., with high honors, 1987); University of Michigan (J.D., magna cum laude, 1992). Order of the Coif. *PRACTICE AREAS:* Litigation.

**VIRGINIA K. DEMARCHI,** admitted to bar, 1993, California. *Education:* Stanford University (B.A., with distinction, 1990); Harvard Law School (J.D., cum laude, 1993). *PRACTICE AREAS:* Litigation.

**RICHARD L. DICKSON,** admitted to bar, 1994, California. *Education:* Stanford University (B.A., with honor and distinction, 1990; J.D., 1994). *PRACTICE AREAS:* Corporate.

**JEFFERY L. DONOVAN,** born Quito, Ecuador, April 22, 1971; admitted to bar, 1995, California. *Education:* Brandeis University (B.A., summa cum laude, 1992); Stanford Law School (J.D., 1995). *PRACTICE AREAS:* Corporate Law; Securities.

**PATRICIA M. DOWNEY,** born Atlantic City, New Jersey, September 28, 1967; admitted to bar, 1992, California. *Education:* Catholic University of America (B.A., summa cum laude, 1989); Stanford Law School (J.D., with distinction, 1992). *PRACTICE AREAS:* Intellectual Property Litigation; Commercial Litigation.

**MICHAEL R. EGGER,** admitted to bar, 1991, California. *Education:* Queens College (B.A., magna cum laude, 1976); Eastman School of Music, University of Rochester (M.A., 1979); University of Dallas (M.B.A., 1986); University of California, Hastings College of the Law (J.D., 1991). (Palo Alto and San Francisco Offices). *PRACTICE AREAS:* Intellectual Property; Licensing Law.

**CONNIE L. ELLERBACH,** admitted to bar, 1990, California. *Education:* Iowa State University (B.A., 1984); University of Virginia (J.D., 1990). *PRACTICE AREAS:* Intellectual Property; Copyright and Trademark.

**WILLIAM P. FITZPATRICK,** born Montgomery, Alabama, December 25, 1966; admitted to bar, 1995, California. *Education:* Harvard College (B.A., magna cum laude, 1989); Columbia University School of Law (J.D., 1994). Law Clerk to Chief Judge, Myron H. Thompson, Middle District of Alabama. (Palo Alto and San Francisco Office). *PRACTICE AREAS:* Intellectual Property; Licensing Law.

**DAVID L. FORST,** born Los Angeles, California, December 26, 1967; admitted to bar, 1993, California. *Education:* Princeton University (A.B., cum laude, 1989); Stanford University (J.D., with distinction, 1992). *PRACTICE AREAS:* Taxation.

**VIRGINIA M. FOURNIER,** born Aurora, Colorado, March 17, 1963; admitted to bar, 1993, California. *Education:* University of Northern Colorado (B.A., magna cum laude, 1985); Santa Clara University (J.D., magna cum laude, 1993). *PRACTICE AREAS:* Intellectual Property Law; Licensing Law.

**ROBERT A. FREEDMAN,** born Boston, Massachusetts, January 31, 1966; admitted to bar, 1993, California. *Education:* Bowdoin College (A.B., summa cum laude, 1987); Stanford University (J.D., with distinction, 1993). *PRACTICE AREAS:* Corporate.

**ERIC D. FROTHINGHAM,** born Rye, New York; admitted to bar, 1995, California. *Education:* University of Vermont (B.A., magna cum laude, 1981); University of Oregon (M.S., 1989); Stanford Law School (J.D., with distinction, 1995). *PRACTICE AREAS:* Corporate.

**GARY E. GAMERMAN** (Resident in Washington, D.C. Office).

**RASHMI GARDE,** admitted to bar, 1995, California. *Education:* University of California at Berkeley (B.A., Computer Science, 1987); University of California at Berkeley, Boalt Hall School of Law (J.D., 1995). *PRACTICE AREAS:* Corporate.

**JAMES GIBBONS-SHAPIRO,** born Urbana, Illinois, February 18, 1969; admitted to bar, 1994, California. *Education:* Yale University (B.A., *(This Listing Continued)*

1991); University of California at Los Angeles (J.D., 1994). *PRACTICE AREAS:* Litigation.

**KIRSTEN M. HEATON,** (admission pending). *Education:* University of British Columbia (B.A., 1990); University of British Columbia, Faculty of Law (LL.B., 1995). Law Clerk to the Honorable Allan McEachern, Chief Justice of British Columbia, British Columbia Court of Appeal. *PRACTICE AREAS:* Litigation.

**RACHEL HERSEY,** admitted to bar, 1991, California. *Education:* City College of the City University of New York (B.S., Engineering, 1973); Harvard University (M.S., Computer Science, 1975; Ph.D., Computer Science, 1981); Stanford Law School (J.D., 1991). *PRACTICE AREAS:* Taxation.

**DOROTHY L. HINES,** born Darby, Pennsylvania, December 27, 1952; admitted to bar, 1995, California, U.S. District Court, Northern District of California and U.S. Court of Appeals, Ninth Circuit. *Education:* Chestnut Hill College (B.S., 1974); University of California, Hastings College of the Law (J.D., cum laude, 1995). Order of the Coif. Judicial Extern to Justice Marvin Baxter, California Supreme Court, 1995. Law Clerk to Honorable, Ronald M. Whyte, U.S. District Court, Northern District of California, 1995-1996. *PRACTICE AREAS:* Corporate.

**CHRISTINE LINH-CHAU HOANG,** admitted to bar, 1993, California. *Education:* Georgetown University (B.S., magna cum laude, 1990); University of California at Berkeley, Boalt Hall School of Law (J.D., 1993). *PRACTICE AREAS:* Intellectual Property; Copyright and Trademark.

**BRIAN M. HOFFMAN,** born San Francisco, California, November 29, 1968; admitted to bar, 1994, Illinois; 1995, Texas; registered to practice before U.S. Patent and Trademark Office (Not admitted in California). *Education:* Columbia University (B.S., 1991); Chicago-Kent College of Law (J.D., with high honors, 1994). Order of the Coif. *PRACTICE AREAS:* Intellectual Property; Patent Law.

**JOSEPHINE T. HUCKO,** admitted to bar, 1991, California. *Education:* University of Illinois, Urbana (B.S., with high honors, 1973); University of California at San Diego (M.S., 1977); Santa Clara University Leavy School of Business and Administration (M.B.A., with distinction, 1986); Santa Clara University School of Law (J.D., magna cum laude, 1991). *PRACTICE AREAS:* Corporate.

**TODD A. HUGE,** born Lincoln, Nebraska, January 8, 1963; admitted to bar, 1995, California. *Education:* Stanford University (B.S., 1987); University of California at Berkeley, Boalt Hall School of Law (J.D., 1995). *PRACTICE AREAS:* Litigation; Employment and Labor Law.

**BRIAN S. KELLY,** born 1968; admitted to bar, 1993, North Carolina (Not admitted in California). *Education:* University of Georgia (B.B.A., summa cum laude, 1990); Duke University (J.D., L.L.M., 1993). *PRACTICE AREAS:* Intellectual Property; Licensing Law.

**CHRISTINE L. KOPITZKE,** born Santa Barbara, California, 1952; admitted to bar, 1988, California, U.S. District Court, Northern District of California and U.S. Court of Appeals, Ninth Circuit. *Education:* University of California at Irvine; Pomona College (B.A., 1975); University of California at Berkeley, Boalt Hall School of Law (J.D., 1988). *PRACTICE AREAS:* Litigation; Intellectual Property Law.

**JANE KRANWINKLE,** born Pasadena, California, November 2, 1967; admitted to bar, 1994, California. *Education:* Stanford University (B.A., with distinction, 1990); University of Michigan (J.D., magna cum laude, 1993). Law Clerk to the Hon. Robert Boochever, U.S. Court of Appeals, Ninth Circuit. *PRACTICE AREAS:* Litigation.

**TIM J. LANE,** admitted to bar, 1993, California. *Education:* University of Texas at Austin (B.S., 1985); University of California at Berkeley (M.A., 1988); University of Iowa College of Law (J.D., with distinction, 1993); Georgia Tech (M.S., 1996). *PRACTICE AREAS:* Intellectual Property; Patent Law.

**MARK A. LEAHY,** born San Francisco, California, October 9, 1961; admitted to bar, 1990, California. *Education:* Stanford University (B.S., 1983); University of Chicago (M.B.A., 1989; J.D., 1989). *PRACTICE AREAS:* Corporate Law; Securities.

**MICHELLE K. LEE,** born Santa Clara, California, December 20, 1965; admitted to bar, 1992, California. *Education:* Massachusetts Institute of Technology (B.S., M.S., 1989); Stanford Law School (J.D., 1992). Law Clerk to the: Hon. Paul R. Michel, U.S. Court of Appeals for the Federal Circuit, 1993-1994; Hon. Vaughn R. Walker, U.S. District Court for the Northern District of California, 1992-1993. *PRACTICE AREAS:* Intellectual Property; Patent Law; Licensing Law.

*(This Listing Continued)*

### FENWICK & WEST LLP, Palo Alto—Continued

**TINA M. LESSANI,** admitted to bar, 1995, California. *Education:* Rice University (E.E., 1992); University of Michigan (J.D., 1994). PRACTICE AREAS: Intellectual Property; Patent Law.

**ANDREW LUH,** admitted to bar, 1996, California. *Education:* University of Virginia (B.A., with distinction, 1993); Stanford Law School (J.D., with distinction, 1996). Order of the Coif. PRACTICE AREAS: Corporate.

**CAROL L. MARTIN,** born New Ulm, Minnesota, January 3, 1966; admitted to bar, 1991, California; 1993, Minnesota. *Education:* Mankato State University (B.S., summa cum laude, 1987); Santa Clara University (J.D., magna cum laude, 1991). PRACTICE AREAS: Corporate; Healthcare; General Transactional Practice.

**MICHAEL J. MCADAM,** born New York, New York, November 24, 1967; admitted to bar, 1995, California. *Education:* Rutgers University (B.A., 1989); University of California at Los Angeles School of Law (J.D., 1995). PRACTICE AREAS: Corporate.

**SANDRA SMITH MCCOY,** admitted to bar, 1990, California. *Education:* University of California at Los Angeles (B.A., 1984); University of Southern California Law Center (J.D., 1989). PRACTICE AREAS: Litigation.

**DAVID C. MCINTYRE,** born Brooklyn, New York, July 14, 1962; admitted to bar, 1989, New York; 1990, U.S. District Court, Southern and Eastern Districts of New York; 1994, California and U.S. District Court, Southern District of California; 1995, U.S. District Court, Northern and Central Districts of California; registered to practice before U.S. Patent and Trademark Office. *Education:* Cornell University (B.S., 1984); Fordham University (J.D., 1988). Law Clerk to: Hon. William Timbers, U.S. Court of Appeals, Second Circuit, 1988-1989; Hon. Irma E. Gonzalez, U.S. District Court, Southern District of California, 1993-1994. PRACTICE AREAS: Intellectual Property Litigation; General Civil Litigation.

**JOHN T. MCNELIS,** born Huntington, New York, September 2, 1964; admitted to bar, 1992, Pennsylvania; 1993, District of Columbia and U.S. Court of Appeals for the Federal Circuit; 1995, California; registered to practice before U.S. Patent and Trademark Office. *Education:* University of Notre Dame (B.S.E.E., 1986); College of William & Mary (J.D., 1992). PRACTICE AREAS: Intellectual Property; Patent Law.

**E. PORTER MERRIMAN,** born Greenbrae, California, April 21, 1965; admitted to bar, 1993, California. *Education:* University of California at Santa Barbara (B.A, 1988); University of San Francisco School of Law (J.D., magna cum laude, 1993). (Palo Alto and San Francisco Offices). PRACTICE AREAS: Intellectual Property; Licensing Law.

**KELLY C. MULHOLLAND,** born Streator, Illinois, August 24, 1967; admitted to bar, 1992, Illinois; 1994, U.S. Tax Court (Not admitted in California). *Education:* University of Illinois (B.A., summa cum laude, 1989); Harvard University (J.D., cum laude, 1992). PRACTICE AREAS: Taxation.

**LISA D. NOBLE,** born St. Louis, Missouri, June 23, 1963; admitted to bar, 1994, California; registered to practice before U.S. Patent and Trademark Office. *Education:* Rice University (B.S., Electrical Engineering, 1985; M.S. Electrical Engineering, 1986); Stanford Law School (J.D., with distinction, 1994). PRACTICE AREAS: Intellectual Property Law; Licensing Law; Patent Law.

**JAMES K. OKAMOTO,** admitted to bar, 1996, California. *Education:* California Institute of Technology (B.S., with honors, 1988; M.S., 1989; Ph. D., 1993); Stanford Law School (J.D., 1996). PRACTICE AREAS: Intellectual Property; Patent Law.

**CARLTON X. OSBORNE,** born Washington, D.C., July 12, 1969; admitted to bar, 1995, California. *Education:* University of Pennsylvania (B.A., 1992); Stanford University (J.D., 1995). PRACTICE AREAS: Corporate.

**RAJIV P. PATEL,** born Morristown, New Jersey, May 20, 1967; admitted to bar, 1995, California; registered to practice before U.S. Patent and Trademark Office. *Education:* Rutgers University College of Engineering (B.S., Electrical Engineering, with high honors, 1989); Franklin Pierce Law Center (M.I.P., 1995; J.D., 1995). Intern to Chief Judge DiClerico, U.S. District Court, District of New Hampshire. PRACTICE AREAS: Intellectual Property; Patent Law.

**TRAM THI PHI,** born Saigon, Vietnam, September 10, 1970; admitted to bar, 1995, California. *Education:* San Jose State University (B.A., summa cum laude, 1992); University of California at Berkeley, Boalt Hall School of Law (J.D., 1995). PRACTICE AREAS: Corporate.

**JOHN F. PLATZ,** born Pasadena, California, December 1, 1960; admitted to bar, 1990, California and U.S. District Court, Northern District of California. *Education:* Stanford University (B.A., 1984; M.B.A.; J.D., 1989). PRACTICE AREAS: Corporate.

**MARK E. PORTER,** born Reno, Nevada, April 15, 1959; admitted to bar, 1988, California; 1990, U.S. District Court, Northern, Central, Eastern and Southern Districts of California and U.S. Court of Appeals, Ninth Circuit. *Education:* University of Southern California (B.A., 1981); University of California, Hastings College of the Law (J.D., 1988). Law Clerk to Hon. Lloyd King, Chief Judge, U.S. Bankruptcy Court, Northern District of California, 1988-1990. PRACTICE AREAS: Corporate; Securities; Bankruptcy.

**PATRICK E. PREMO,** born San Jose, California, March 13, 1967; admitted to bar, 1996, California and U.S. District Court, Northern District of California. *Education:* Santa Clara University (B.S., 1989; J.D., magna cum laude, 1996); University of Durham, England (M.A., 1990). PRACTICE AREAS: Litigation.

**JOHN G. RYAN,** admitted to bar, 1994, California. *Education:* University College, Dublin, Ireland (B.Sc., summa cum laude, 1977; M.Sc., 1978); University of California at Berkeley (Ph.D., 1984); Stanford Law School (J.D., 1994). PRACTICE AREAS: Taxation.

**ROBERT R. SACHS,** born Long Beach, California, March 3, 1965; admitted to bar, 1990, California. *Education:* University of California at San Diego (B.A., summa cum laude, 1987); Yale Law School (J.D., 1990). PRACTICE AREAS: Intellectual Property; Patent Law.

**MICHAEL A. SANDS,** born Santa Barbara, California, June 11, 1971; admitted to bar, 1995, California. *Education:* Tulane University (B.A., cum laude, 1992); Santa Clara University School of Law (J.D., summa cum laude, 1995). PRACTICE AREAS: Litigation.

**MELISSA H. SAYER,** born Havertown, Pennsylvania, October 27, 1966; admitted to bar, 1994, California. *Education:* Eckerd College (B.A., 1989); Santa Clara School of Law (J.D., summa cum laude, 1994). Extern to Judge David Allan Ezra, Federal District of Hawaii, 1993. PRACTICE AREAS: General Corporate; Securities.

**JEFFERSON F. SCHER,** born California, November 2, 1962; admitted to bar, 1991, California. *Education:* University of California at Berkeley (A.B., with high distinction, 1985); Stanford University (J.D., with distinction, 1989). Law Clerk to the Honorable A. Wallace Tashima, U.S. District Court for the Central District of California, 1989-1990. PRACTICE AREAS: Intellectual Property; Trademark; Copyright.

**JASON SCULLY,** admitted to bar, 1996, California. *Education:* University of California at Berkeley (B.A., with honors, 1993); University of California, Hastings College of the Law (J.D., cum laude, 1996). Order of the Coif. PRACTICE AREAS: Litigation; Intellectual Property; Licensing Law.

**JOHN J. SULLIVAN,** born Laguna Beach, California, September 11, 1963; admitted to bar, 1992, California. *Education:* Stanford University (B.A., 1985); University of California at Berkeley, Boalt Hall School of Law (J.D ., 1992). (Resident in San Francisco Office). PRACTICE AREAS: Intellectual Property; Licensing Law.

**SHAWNA M. SWANSON,** born Portland, Oregon, April 13, 1968; admitted to bar, 1993, California and U.S. District Court, Central and Northern Districts of California. *Education:* College of Idaho (B.A., summa cum laude, 1989); Harvard University (J.D., cum laude, 1993). PRACTICE AREAS: Litigation; Labor and Employment Law.

**MARK C. TERRANO,** born Cornwall, New York, November 28, 1967; admitted to bar, 1995, Florida; 1996, California; registered to practice before U.S. Patent and Trademark Office. *Education:* Rensselaer Polytechnic Institute (B.S., Electrical Engineering, 1989); Franklin Pierce Law Center (J.D., 1995). PRACTICE AREAS: Intellectual Property; Patent Law.

**CHRISTOPHER M. TOBIN,** born Yonkers, New York, 1964; admitted to bar, 1993, Pennsylvania; 1996, California. *Education:* Villanova University (B.S. Electrical Engineering, 1986; J.D., 1992). PRACTICE AREAS: Intellectual Property; Patent Law.

**LYNDA M. TWOMEY,** born Dublin, Ireland, February 19, 1968; admitted to bar, 1993, Ireland; 1994, California. *Education:* Trinity College, Ireland (LL.B., 1989). PRACTICE AREAS: General Corporate; Securities.

*(This Listing Continued)*

## PROFESSIONAL BIOGRAPHIES
### CALIFORNIA—PALO ALTO

**EDWARD M. URSCHEL,** born Bethesda, Maryland, June 26, 1963; admitted to bar, 1993, California. *Education:* University of California at Davis (B.A., 1985); University of California, Hastings College of the Law (J.D., 1993). *PRACTICE AREAS:* Corporate Law; Securities.

**JEFFREY R. VETTER,** born San Francisco, California, October 15, 1965; admitted to bar, 1990, California. *Education:* University of California at Berkeley (B.A., with honors, 1987); University of California, Hastings College of the Law (J.D., magna cum laude, 1990). Order of the Coif. *PRACTICE AREAS:* Corporate.

**ADAM W. WEGNER,** born Washington, D.C., September 5, 1965; admitted to bar, 1991, California; 1993, District of Columbia. *Education:* University of Pennsylvania (B.A., 1987); Georgetown University Law Center (J.D., cum laude, 1991). *PRACTICE AREAS:* General Corporate; Securities; Licensing.

**JEREMY S. WOODBURN,** admitted to bar, 1995, California. *Education:* Brandeis University (B.A., summa cum laude, 1991); Harvard Law School (J.D., cum laude, 1995). *PRACTICE AREAS:* Intellectual Property; Licensing Law.

**MOLLEE SUE OXMAN ZOKEN,** born Castro Valley, California, April 27, 1962; admitted to bar, 1989, California. *Education:* University of California at Berkeley (A.B., highest distinction, 1985); Stanford Business School (M.B.A., 1989) Stanford Law School (J.D., 1989). *PRACTICE AREAS:* Corporate.

---

## FERRARI, OLSEN, OTTOBONI & BEBB
### A PROFESSIONAL CORPORATION
*Established in 1981*
**550 HAMILTON AVENUE**
**PALO ALTO, CALIFORNIA 94301**
Telephone: 415-327-3233

San Jose, California Office: 333 West Santa Clara Street, Suite 700. Telephone: 408-280-0535.

*Corporation, Securities, Environmental and Health Law. State and Federal Taxation, Labor, Sports and Real Estate Law. Estate Planning, Trusts and Probate Law. General Civil Trial Practice in all Federal and State Courts. Administrative Law.*

**CLARENCE J. FERRARI, JR.,** born San Francisco, California, April 9, 1934; admitted to bar, 1960, California; 1961, U.S. Tax Court. *Education:* Stanford University (A.B., 1956; LL.B., 1959). Fellow, American College of Trust and Estate Counsel. (Certified Specialist, Taxation Law, The State Bar of California Board of Legal Specialization). *PRACTICE AREAS:* Federal and State Taxation; Estate Planning; Trusts and Estates; Tax Litigation.

**KENT E. OLSEN,** born Cleveland, Ohio, September 22, 1943; admitted to bar, 1968, California. *Education:* University of California at Berkeley (A.B., 1965); Hastings College of Law, University of California (J.D., 1968); New York University (LL.M. in Taxation, 1969). (Certified Specialist, Taxation Law, The State Bar of California Board of Legal Specialization). *PRACTICE AREAS:* Corporate Law; Estate and Family Tax Planning; Employee Benefits.

**JOHN M. OTTOBONI,** born Hayward, California, January 14, 1947; admitted to bar, 1972, California; 1975, U.S. Court of Appeals, Ninth Circuit; 1979, U.S. Supreme Court. *Education:* University of Santa Clara (B.A., magna cum laude, 1969); Boalt Hall School of Law, University of California (J.D., 1972). Member, Board of Trustees, University of Santa Clara. President, Alexian Brothers Hospital Foundation, 1993-1994. Fellow, American College of Trial Lawyers. *PRACTICE AREAS:* Business Litigation; Real Estate; Sports Law. *Email:* tstover107@aol.com

**RICHARD S. BEBB,** born Los Angeles, California, July 22, 1952; admitted to bar, 1977, California. *Education:* Stanford University (A.B., 1974); Hastings College of the Law, University of California (J.D., 1977). Member, Hastings Constitutional Law Quarterly, 1976-1977. *Member:* California Hospital Attorneys Association; California Health Lawyers Association; Santa Clara County Estate Planning Council. *PRACTICE AREAS:* Corporate Law; Business Law; Health Care; Estate Planning.

**JAMES J. ELLER,** born Chula Vista, California, April 29, 1952; admitted to bar, 1977, California; 1978, U.S. District Court, Northern District of California. *Education:* University of California at San Diego (B.A., 1974); University of Santa Clara (J.D., cum laude, 1977). Phi Alpha Delta (Secretary, 1977). Member, Real Estate Executive Committee, Santa Clara County Bar Association, 1985, 1986, 1989. *Member:* Association of South Bay Brokers. *LANGUAGES:* French. *PRACTICE AREAS:* Real Estate Law; Environmental Law.

### OF COUNSEL

**EDWARD M. ALVAREZ,** born San Jose, California, July 30, 1938; admitted to bar, 1966, California and U.S. Tax Court. *Education:* University of Santa Clara (B.Sc., 1960; LL.B., 1965). (Certified Specialist, Taxation Law, The State Bar of California Board of Legal Specialization). *PRACTICE AREAS:* State and Federal Taxation.

(For complete biographical data on all personnel, see Professional Biographies at San Jose, California)

---

## FINCH, MONTGOMERY & WRIGHT
**350 CAMBRIDGE AVENUE, SUITE 175**
**PALO ALTO, CALIFORNIA 94306**
Telephone: 415-327-0888
Fax: 415-327-5316

*Estate Planning and Probate, Trusts, Estate and Gift Tax and Nonprofit Organizations.*

### MEMBERS OF FIRM

**TOBY F. MONTGOMERY,** born Prescott, Arizona, June 22, 1939; admitted to bar, 1978, California. *Education:* Stanford University (B.A., with honors in Political Science, 1961; M.A., 1966; J.D., 1978). Co-Author: "Estate Planning Practice," California CEB, 1987; "California Durable Power of Attorney Handbook," California CEB, 1988, 1989, 1991, 1992, 1993. Member, Board of Directors: Hewlett-Packard Company Employee Scholarship Organization, 1985—. Lecturer: Stanford University Retirement Planning Seminars, 1982—; California Education of the Bar (Estate Planning), 1984—. *Member:* Palo Alto, Santa Clara County (Member, Executive Committee of Estate Planning and Probate Section, 1985—) and American Bar Associations; The State Bar of California. *PRACTICE AREAS:* Estate Planning; Gift and Estate Tax; Trusts and Wills; Probate, Estate and Trust Administration; Conservatorships.

**BARBARA P. WRIGHT,** born Appleton, Wisconsin, May 6, 1946; admitted to bar, 1983, California. *Education:* Stanford University (B.A., 1968; M.A., 1969); Loyola Law School, Los Angeles (J.D., 1983). Member, Loyola Law Review, 1982-1983. Co-Author: "California Durable Power of Attorney Handbook," California CEB, 1988, 1989, 1991, 1992, 1993. Member, Board of Directors, Albany International Corp., 1989—. *Member:* Santa Clara County and American Bar Associations; The State Bar of California. *PRACTICE AREAS:* Estate Planning; Nonprofit Organizations; Gift and Estate Tax; Trusts and Wills; Probate, Estate and Trust Administration.

**NATHAN C. FINCH** (1909-1990).

REPRESENTATIVE CLIENTS: The David and Lucile Packard Foundation; The Monterey Bay Aquarium Foundation; The Monterey Bay Aquarium Research Institute; The Packard Humanities Institute; The Stanford Theatre Foundation; The Center for Computer Assisted Research in the Humanities; Lucile Salter Packard Children's Hospital, Stanford; Lucile Packard Foundation for Children.
REFERENCE: Commercial Bank-California, Palo Alto, California; Cupertino National Bank & Trust, Palo Alto, California.

---

## FINNAN, FLEISCHUT & ASSOCIATES
**3030 HANSEN WAY, SUITE 120**
**PALO ALTO, CALIFORNIA 94304**
Telephone: 415-493-5790
FAX: 415-493-2641

*Immigration and Nationality Law.*

FIRM PROFILE: *The firm was founded in 1978 in Palo Alto and practices solely in the area of immigration and nationality law. The focus of Finnan, Fleischut & Associates has always been on work-related visas for individual and corporate clients in the electronics, biotechnology, and related high-technology industries, although the firm also does work with other businesses and in other areas of immigration law (naturalization, investment-based visas, political asylum, etc.). The firm's attorneys are active in the American Immigration Lawyers Association and have served as officers of AILA's San Francisco and Santa Clara Valley Chapters. The firm's attorneys are supported by paralegals, each of whom holds at least a B.A. degree. The firm files visa applications and labor certification applications at Immigration and Naturalization Service and U.S. Department of Labor offices throughout the United States.*

(This Listing Continued)

**FINNAN, FLEISCHUT & ASSOCIATES,** Palo Alto—
*Continued*

*MEMBERS OF FIRM*

**CHRISTOPHER J. FLEISCHUT,** born Philadelphia, Pennsylvania, January 1, 1955; admitted to bar, 1985, California; 1986, U.S. District Court, Northern District of California; 1987, U.S. Court of Appeals, Ninth Circuit. *Education:* Yale University (B.A., 1976); University of California, Berkeley (M.A., 1981); University of California, Hastings College of Law (J.D., 1985). *Member:* American Immigration Lawyers Association (Chair, Santa Clara Valley Chapter, 1990-1991). *LANGUAGES:* Russian, German. *PRACTICE AREAS:* Immigration and Nationality Law (100%).

**ROBERT (JACK) RIX,** born Oklahoma City, Oklahoma, August 24, 1953; admitted to bar, 1986, California, U.S. District Court, Northern District of California and U.S. Court of Appeals, Ninth Circuit. *Education:* University of Oklahoma (B.A., 1976); Golden Gate University (J.D., with highest honors, 1986). *Member:* Santa Clara County and American Bar Associations; State Bar of California; American Immigration Lawyers Association. *PRACTICE AREAS:* Immigration and Nationality Law (100%).

**MICHAEL E. GILL,** born Bryn Mawr, Pennsylvania, August 13, 1944; admitted to bar, 1977, California and U.S. District Court, Northern District of California. *Education:* University of Edinburgh; Villanova University (B.A. in History, 1966); University of California, Hastings College of Law (J.D., 1977). *Member:* State Bar of California; American Immigration Lawyers Association. *LANGUAGES:* Spanish, Nepali. *PRACTICE AREAS:* Immigration and Nationality Law (100%).

REPRESENTATIVE CLIENTS: Amdahl Corp.; Silicon Graphics, Inc.; Xilinx, Inc.; Zilog, Inc.; Xerox Corporation's Palo Alto Research Center; SRI International; Analog Devices, Inc.; Atari; Coherent, Inc.; Exar Corp.; Oral-B Laboratories; Quantum Corp.; Ross Systems, Inc.; Sola Visioncare; VLSI Technology; Zycad Corp.; Madge Networks, Inc.; Netscape Communications, Corp.; Rational Software Corp.

---

# FISH & NEAVE

Fish, Richardson & Neave, New York (1916-1969)

**525 UNIVERSITY AVENUE
SUITE 300
PALO ALTO, CALIFORNIA 94301**

*Telephone: 415-617-4000
Telecopier: 415-617-4090*

*New York, New York Office:* 1251 Avenue of the Americas. Telephone: 212-596-9000. Telex: 14-8367. Cable Address: Fishneave. Telecopier: 212-596-9090.

*Intellectual Property including Patent, Trademark, Trade Secret, Copyright and Unfair Competition, Unfair Trade Practice and Antitrust Law. Trials and Appeals in all Federal and State Courts and Governmental Administrative Agencies.*

*RESIDENT MEMBERS*

**EDWARD F. MULLOWNEY,** born New York, N.Y., 1943; admitted to bar, 1972, New York; 1990, California. *Education:* Stevens Institute of Technology (M.E., with honors, 1965; Master of Engineering, 1967); Columbia University (J.D., 1971). Tau Beta Pi. *Member:* The Association of the Bar of the City of New York (Member, Committee on Patents, 1986-1989); American Bar Association; New York Intellectual Property Law Association. *PRACTICE AREAS:* Intellectual Property.

**ROBERT J. GOLDMAN,** born Brooklyn, New York, 1954; admitted to bar, 1978, New York (Not admitted in California). *Education:* Columbia University (B.S., 1977; J.D., 1977). Co-author: "Monetary Remedies in Patent Cases," University of Houston Intellectual Property Program; "Evolution of the Inequitable Conduct Defense in Patent Litigation," Harvard Journal of Law and Technology. Adjunct Associate Professor of Law, Patents, Fordham University, 1995—. *Member:* The Association of the Bar of the City of New York; American Intellectual Property Law Association; New York Intellectual Property Law Association. *PRACTICE AREAS:* Intellectual Property.

**NORMAN H. BEAMER,** born Upper Darby, Pennsylvania, 1946; admitted to bar, 1979, New York; 1992, California. *Education:* Lehigh University (B.S., with honors, 1968); University of Illinois (M.S., 1973; M.B.A., 1975); University of Michigan (J.D., magna cum laude, 1978). Phi Beta Kappa; Tau Beta Pi; Sigma Iota Epsilon; Phi Eta Sigma. Recipient, American Jurisprudence Award. Member, Michigan Law Review, 1977-1978.

*(This Listing Continued)*

Co-author, "The New Court of Appeals for the Federal Circuit," 37 The Record of the Association of the Bar of the City of New York 732, December 1982. *Member:* American Bar Association; New York Intellectual Property Law Association. *PRACTICE AREAS:* Intellectual Property.

**MARK D. ROWLAND,** born Queens, New York, 1961; admitted to bar, 1987, New York; 1992, California. *Education:* University of Notre Dame (B.S.E.E., 1983); George Washington University (J.D., 1986). *PRACTICE AREAS:* Intellectual Property.

**EDWARD J. DEFRANCO,** born Brooklyn, New York, 1960; admitted to bar, 1987, New York; 1994, California. *Education:* Rensselaer Polytechnic Institute (B.S., 1982); Cornell University (J.D., 1986). *PRACTICE AREAS:* Intellectual Property.

*RESIDENT ASSOCIATES*

**VICKI S. VEENKER,** born Lafayette, Indiana, 1962; admitted to bar, 1988, Massachusetts; 1989, New York; 1992, California. *Education:* Indiana University (B.S., B.A., 1985); Georgetown University (J.D., 1988). *PRACTICE AREAS:* Intellectual Property.

**NICOLA A. PISANO,** born Staten Island, New York, 1959; admitted to bar, 1990, New York; 1990, California. *Education:* University of Notre Dame (B.S.M.E., 1980); Massachusetts Institute of Technology (M.S.N.E., 1982); Notre Dame Law School (J.D., 1989). *PRACTICE AREAS:* Intellectual Property.

**GABRIELLE E. HIGGINS,** born Brooklyn, New York, 1963; admitted to bar, 1989, Connecticut; 1990, New York; 1992, California. *Education:* College of the Holy Cross (B.A., 1985); Fordham University (J.D., 1989). *PRACTICE AREAS:* Intellectual Property.

**KEVIN P.B. JOHNSON,** born Chattanooga, Tennessee, 1966; admitted to bar, 1993, New York; 1995, California. *Education:* Cornell University (B.S.E.E., 1988); Hofstra University School of Law (J.D., 1992). *PRACTICE AREAS:* Intellectual Property.

**PETRINA S. HSI,** born London, England, 1968; admitted to bar, 1994, New York (Not admitted in California). *Education:* Johns Hopkins University (B.A., 1990); Boalt Hall School of Law, University of California (J.D., 1993). *PRACTICE AREAS:* Intellectual Property.

**DEREK MINIHANE,** born Boston, Massachusetts, 1969; admitted to bar, 1994, Massachusetts; 1995, New York (Not admitted in California). *Education:* Cornell University (B.S.E.E., 1991); The George Washington University National Law Center (J.D., 1994). *PRACTICE AREAS:* Intellectual Property.

**KURTIS D. MACFERRIN,** born Madrid, Spain, 1965; admitted to bar, 1995, California. *Education:* Occidental College (A.B., 1987); Harvard University (J.D., 1995). *PRACTICE AREAS:* Patent.

**ANN MARIE WHITLEY,** born Muskegon, Michigan, 1970; admitted to bar, 1996, New York (Not admitted in California). *Education:* Northwestern University (B.S.M.E., 1992); University of Michigan (J.D., 1995).

---

# FISH & RICHARDSON P.C.

**PALO ALTO, CALIFORNIA**

(See Menlo Park)

*Intellectual Property Law: Trials, Transactions, Patents, Trademarks, Copyrights, Trade Secrets, Entertainment Law, Telecommunications Law, Drug and Medical Device and Antitrust Law.*

---

# FLEHR, HOHBACH, TEST, ALBRITTON & HERBERT

**SUITE 200, 850 HANSEN WAY
PALO ALTO, CALIFORNIA 94304-1017**

*Telephone: 415-494-8700
Telefax: 415-494-8771*

*San Francisco, California Office:* Suite 3400, Four Embarcadero Center. Telephone: 415-781-1989.

*Patent, Trademark, Copyright, Unfair Competition, Trade Secrets, Biotechnology and Computer Law. Trials.*

FIRM PROFILE: *The firm was founded in 1947 by Paul D. Flehr, who commenced practicing law in 1927. The firm has an office in the heart of San Francisco's financial and commercial center as well as in Palo Alto, the center of*

*(This Listing Continued)*

California's "Silicon Valley." Its practice is intellectual property which includes litigation in Federal and State courts involving patents, trademarks, copyrights and trade secrets, the preparation and prosecution of patent and trademark matters in the United States and throughout the world, patent and trademark investigations and copyright matters. An international department is maintained which deals specifically with patent and trademark matters outside the United States. The firm's attorneys handle the major technical fields including mechanical and chemical engineering, electronics, computer and data storage systems and components, drilling and mining equipment, food processing and products, nuclear and other energy production, medical equipment and prostheses, pharmaceutical, diagnostics and therapeutics, biological and genetic engineering including patenting of genetically engineered plants and animals.

### RESIDENT ATTORNEYS

| Harold C. Hohbach | James A. Sheridan |
| Aldo J. Test | Gary S. Williams |
| Thomas O. Herbert | C. Michael Zimmerman |
| Edward S. Wright | Steven F. Caserza |
| | William S. Galliani |

### ASSOCIATES

| Janet Elizabeth Muller | R. Michael Ananian |
| Edward N. Bachand | David C. Ashby |
| | Maria S. Swiatek |

### OF COUNSEL

| Bertram I. Rowland | Julian Caplan |

(For complete Biographical Data on all Personnel, see Professional Biographies, San Francisco, California).

---

## FLICKER & KERIN
SUITE 460, 285 HAMILTON
P.O. BOX 840
PALO ALTO, CALIFORNIA 94302
Telephone: 415-321-0947
Fax: 415-326-9722

*Civil and Trial Practice. Family, Personal Injury, Negligence, Business, Corporate and Real Estate Law.*

### MEMBERS OF FIRM

**MICHAEL R. FLICKER,** born Long Branch, New Jersey, September 29, 1940; admitted to bar, 1966, California. *Education:* Yale University (B.S., 1962); Stanford University (LL.B., 1965). Order of the Coif. Member, 1963-1965 and Revising Editor, 1964-1965, Stanford Law Review. Law Clerk to Hon. Oliver D. Hamlin, Judge, U.S. Court of Appeals, Ninth Circuit, 1965-1966. *Member:* Palo Alto (President, 1980), Santa Clara County (Member, Executive Committee, 1981) and American (Member, Family Law Section) Bar Associations; State Bar of California. (Certified Specialist, Family Law, The State Bar of California Board of Legal Specialization). **PRACTICE AREAS:** Family Law.

**ANTHONY J. KERIN, III,** born Mineola, New York, June 29, 1951; admitted to bar, 1981, California. *Education:* San Francisco State University (B.A. cum laude, 1978); Hastings College of Law, University of California (J.D., 1981). Pi Sigma Alpha. Member, Political Science Honor Society. *Member:* Santa Clara County and Palo Alto Bar Associations; The State Bar of California. **PRACTICE AREAS:** Corporate Law; Business Law; Real Estate Law.

### ASSOCIATES

**RHESA C. RUBIN,** born Toronto, Ontario, Canada, May 23, 1958; admitted to bar, 1990, California, U.S. Court of Appeals, 9th Circuit and U.S. District Court, Northern District of California. *Education:* University of California (B.A., English, 1981); University of Rochester; Western State University (J.D., 1986). *Member:* Santa Clara County, Palo Alto and American (Member, Family Law Section) Bar Associations; Bar Association of San Francisco; State Bar of California. **PRACTICE AREAS:** Family Law.

**CHERI A. BELL,** born Oakland, California, February 10, 1968; admitted to bar, 1993, California. *Education:* University of California (B.A., Communication Studies, 1990); McGeorge School of Law (J.D., 1993). *Member:* Santa Clara County Bar Association (Member, Family Law Section, 1995—); State Bar of California. **PRACTICE AREAS:** Family Law.

---

## FRAGOMEN, DEL REY & BERNSEN, P.C.
525 UNIVERSITY AVENUE, SUITE 1450
PALO ALTO, CALIFORNIA 94301
Telephone: 415-323-7557
Facsimile: 415-323-5030
URL: http://www.fragomen.com

*New York, New York Office:* 515 Madison Avenue. Telephone: 212-688-8555. Facsimile: 212-319-5236; 212-758-7215.
*Washington, D.C. Office:* 1212 New York Avenue, N.W., Suite 850. Telephone: 202-223-5515. Facsimile: 202-371-2898.
*Coral Gables, Florida Office:* 890 South Dixie Highway. Telephone: 305-666-4655. Facsimile: 305-666-4467.
*Chicago, Illinois Office:* 300 South Wacker Drive, Suite 2900. Telephone: 312-263-6101. Facsimile: 312-431-0517.
*Los Angeles, California Office:* 11400 West Olympic Boulevard, Suite 1050. Telephone: 310-473-8700. Facsimile: 310-473-5383.
*San Francisco, California Office:* 88 Kearny Street, Suite 1300. Telephone: 415-986-1446. Facsimile: 415-986-7964.
*Stamford Connecticut Office:* Fragomen, Del Rey & Bernsen, 1177 High Ridge Road. Telephone: 203-321-1278. Facsimile: 203-321-1279.
*Short Hills, New Jersey Office:* Fragomen, Del Rey & Bernsen, 51 John F. Kennedy Parkway. Telephone: 201-564-5222. FAX: 201-564-5230.

*U.S. and Foreign Immigration and Nationality Law.*

**PETER H. LOEWY,** born New York, N.Y., October 2, 1955; admitted to bar, 1979, New Jersey; 1980, New York; 1981, Florida; 1984, California. *Education:* City College of the City University of New York (B.A., summa cum laude, 1976); Rutgers University (J.D., 1979). Phi Beta Kappa. Adjunct Professor of Law, Southwestern School of Law, 1989. *Member:* Practising Law Institute (Co-Chair, Annual Immigration Institute, 1993—). (Also at Los Angeles and San Francisco). **LANGUAGES:** French.

---

**FLORA HOUN HOFFMAN,** born Northampton, Massachusetts, April 8, 1965; admitted to bar, 1992, California, U.S. District Court, Northern District of California and U.S. Court of Appeals, Ninth Circuit. *Education:* Harvard University (B.A., cum laude, 1987); Boalt Hall School of Law, University of California (J.D., 1992). Associate Editor, California Law Review, 1990-1992. *Member:* Bar Association of San Francisco; Asian American Bar Association of Greater Bay Area; American Immigration Lawyers Association.

**BARBARA C. Y. LAAM,** born Hong Kong, January 8, 1953; admitted to bar, 1992, California. *Education:* Indiana University (B.A., with honors, 1978); Golden Gate University (J.D., 1991). *Member:* Bar Association of San Francisco; American Immigration Lawyers Association. **LANGUAGES:** Chinese (Cantonese and Mandarin).

**JIN YI PARK,** born Seoul, Korea, July 22, 1969; admitted to bar, 1995, California. *Education:* University of California (B.A., 1991); Santa Clara University (J.D., 1995). Editor, Santa Clara University Law Review. **LANGUAGES:** Korean.

(For complete biographical data on Personnel at New York, New York, Washington, D.C., Coral Gables, Florida, Chicago, Illinois, Los Angeles and San Francisco, California, Stamford, Connecticut and Short Hills, New Jersey, see Professional Biographies at those locations)

---

## FTHENAKIS & COLVIN
540 UNIVERSITY AVENUE, SUITE 300
PALO ALTO, CALIFORNIA 94301
Telephone: 415-326-1397
Telecopier: 415-326-3203

*General Civil and Trial Practice in all State and Federal Courts Including, Antitrust and Trade Regulation, Business Torts, Commercial Contracts, Construction and Real Property Disputes, Corporate Law, Director's and Officer's Liability, Distribution and Licensing, Environmental and Toxic Torts, Intellectual Property, Media Law, Product Distribution, Provisional Remedies, Real Estate Law, RICO, Sales and Leasing, Secured and Unsecured Lending, Securities Fraud, Securities Law, Suretyship, Trade Secrets, Corporate Transactions and Unfair Competition.*

(This Listing Continued)

## FTHENAKIS & COLVIN, Palo Alto—Continued

### MEMBERS OF FIRM

**BASIL P. FTHENAKIS,** born Long Island, New York, October 1, 1955; admitted to bar, 1979, California. *Education:* University of California at Davis (A.B., with honors in Economics, 1976); University of Santa Clara (J.D., 1979). Omicron Delta Epsilon. Author: "Terminating the Price-Cutting Distributor: What's Next?" 8 CEB California Business Law Reporter 52; "Discounts and Allowances ... Risky Business," The Channelmarker Letter Volume 2, Number 10, April 1991. *Member:* Santa Clara County, San Mateo County and American (Member: Section on Antitrust Law; Litigation and Business Torts Subcommittee, 1980-1985; Intellectual Property) Bar Associations; State Bar of California (Member, Section of Antitrust and Trade Regulation). *PRACTICE AREAS:* Antitrust; Business and Commercial Litigation; Intellectual Property; Securities; Corporate Transactions. *Email:* basil@fthcvn.com

**OLIVER P. COLVIN,** born Chicago, Illinois, July 13, 1962; admitted to bar, 1988, California. *Education:* University of California at Davis (B.A., Economics, 1985); University of Santa Clara (J.D., 1988); Georgetown University Law Center (LL.M., with distinction in securities regulation, 1990). Finalist, Moot Court Competition. Author: "A Dynamic Definition of and Prohibition Against Insider Trading," 31 Santa Clara Law Review 603, 1991; "A Constitutional Challenge to Rule 10b-5," 6 INSIGHTS: The Corporate & Securities Law Advisor No. 5, May 1992. *Member:* Santa Clara County and American (Member, Securities Law Section and Litigation) Bar Associations; State Bar of California; The District of Columbia Bar. *PRACTICE AREAS:* Business and Commercial Litigation; Intellectual Property; Securities; Construction; Real Property Disputes; Corporate Transactions. *Email:* oliver@fthcvn.com

---

# GERMINO, RUNTE, AMARAL, JORDAN, CARPENTER & MacKAY

*A PROFESSIONAL LAW CORPORATION*

2500 EL CAMINO REAL, SUITE 210
PALO ALTO, CALIFORNIA 94306
Telephone: 415-857-9211
Fax: 415-852-9256

*Los Banos, California Office:* 1120 West I Street, Suite B. Telephone: 209-826-5024. Fax: 209-826-3164.

General Civil and Trial Practice in State and Federal Courts. Personal Injury, Probate, Water Rights, Corporation, Taxation, Agricultural, Condemnation, Family and Corporate Law.

**D. OLIVER GERMINO** (1903-1972).

**JOHN O. GERMINO,** born Los Banos, California, March 6, 1936; admitted to bar, 1962, California. *Education:* Stanford University (A.B., 1959; J.D., 1962). *PRACTICE AREAS:* Civil Litigation.

**JOHN A. RUNTE,** born Milwaukee, Wisconsin, May 18, 1938; admitted to bar, 1973, California. *Education:* Marquette University (B.S., 1961); University of Santa Clara (J.D., 1973). (Certified Specialist, Taxation Law, The State Bar of California Board of Legal Specialization). *PRACTICE AREAS:* Real Property; Trusts; Commercial Transactions; Taxation; Probate.

**DONALD O. GERMINO,** born Los Banos, California, October 1, 1939; admitted to bar, 1965, California. *Education:* University of Southern California (A.B., 1961); University of California at Berkeley (J.D., 1964). City Attorney: Los Banos, 1970—; Dos Palos, 1980—. *PRACTICE AREAS:* Transactional; Civil Litigation; Estate Planning; Probate.

**EDWARD M. AMARAL,** born San Francisco, California, April 1, 1953; admitted to bar, 1980, California. *Education:* Modesto Junior College (A.S., 1973); California Polytechnic State University (B.S., 1976); Loyola University of Los Angeles (J.D., 1979). *PRACTICE AREAS:* Real Estate Law; Agricultural Law; Probate and Estate Planning; Elder Care Law; Business Law.

**J. SCOTT JORDAN,** born Tracy, California, May 14, 1954; admitted to bar, 1979, California. *Education:* University of Santa Clara (B.S., 1976; J.D., 1979). *PRACTICE AREAS:* Family Law; Bankruptcy; Transactional; Litigation.

**GLENN C. CARPENTER,** born Denver, Colorado, September 30, 1955; admitted to bar, 1981, California. *Education:* University of Colorado (B.A.,

*(This Listing Continued)*

---

with distinction, 1977); Stanford University (J.D., 1980). *PRACTICE AREAS:* Business Law; Real Property Law; Probate and Estate Planning; Trust Administration.

**NORMAN E. MacKAY,** born Oakland, California, October 31, 1943; admitted to bar, 1975, California and U.S. District Court, Northern District of California; 1977, U.S. District Court, Southern District of California. *Education:* Stanford University (B.A., 1965); University of Santa Clara (J.D., 1975). *PRACTICE AREAS:* Business Litigation; Real Estate Transactions; Toxic or Hazardous Materials Litigation.

**SUSAN R. F. SOLOMON,** born Philadelphia, Pennsylvania, October 29, 1947; admitted to bar, 1980, California. *Education:* University of Pennsylvania (B.A., 1968); Bryn Mawr College and University of Hawaii (M.S.W., 1975); University of Santa Clara (J.D., magna cum laude, 1980). *PRACTICE AREAS:* Real Property Law; Civil Litigation; Appellate Practice.

**PAUL J. McDONALD,** born Milwaukee, Wisconsin, March 11, 1955; admitted to bar, 1989, California. *Education:* University of Wisconsin-Milwaukee (B.S., 1978); San Francisco Law School (J.D., 1989).

---

# GIBSON, DUNN & CRUTCHER LLP

*Established in 1890*

525 UNIVERSITY AVENUE, SUITE 220
PALO ALTO, CALIFORNIA 94301
Telephone: 415-463-7300
Telecopier: 415-463-7333

*Los Angeles, California Office:* 333 South Grand Avenue. Telephone: 213-229-7000. Telex: 188171 GIBTRASK LSA (TRT), 674930 GIBTRASK LSA (WUT). Telecopier: 213-229-7520. Cable Address: GIBTRASK LOS ANGELES.

General Civil, Trial and Appellate Practice, State and Federal Courts. Antitrust Law, Specialized Criminal Defense. General Corporation, Securities, Administrative, Labor and Employment, Taxation, Estate Planning, Probate and Trust, International Business, Entertainment, Commercial, Insolvency, Bankruptcy and Reorganization, Natural Resources, Oil and Gas, Environmental Energy, Municipal and Public Utility Law.

*FIRM PROFILE:* Gibson, Dunn & Crutcher, originating in Los Angeles, has been providing legal services to clients since 1890. Today, the firm has grown to one of the largest law firms in the world with approximately 600 active attorneys in 15 offices situated in most of the world's important business centers. The firm has experts in virtually every area of the law, particularly those which relate to commercial transactions and disputes, and has more effective geographical coverage in the United States than any other major firm. The firm's lawyers and staff are dedicated to providing quality service on a timely and cost effective basis.

The Palo Alto office emphasizes the representation of high technology clients in the Silicon Valley and throughout the world, serving both established and emerging growth companies as well as venture capital firms. Lawyers in this office provide expertise in intellectual property protection, securities and corporate matters, litigation and labor.

### PARTNERS

**BRUCE L. GITELSON,** born June 4, 1941; admitted to bar, 1964, California. *Education:* Stanford University (B.A., 1963; J.D., 1964). Phi Beta Kappa; Order of the Coif. Articles Editor, Stanford Law Review, 1964. Instructor, Stanford Law School, 1964-1965, 1970, 1971. Adjunct Professor, Loyola University Law School, 1973-1979. Visiting Professor, Stanford Law School, 1979-1980. Lecturer in Law, Stanford Law School, 1980-1983. *Member:* American Bar Association. (Palo Alto and San Francisco Offices). *PRACTICE AREAS:* Business and Financial Planning for Entrepreneurs; Business and Financial Planning for Closely Held Businesses, Particularly High Technology; Corporations; Securities Regulation; International Business Organization and Finance. *Email:* gitelson@gdclaw.com

**DENIS R. SALMON,** born September 20, 1951; admitted to bar, 1976, California. *Education:* Hamline University (B.A., magna cum laude, 1973); University of Minnesota (J.D., magna cum laude, 1976). *Member:* American Bar Association (Member, Sections on: Litigation; Intellectual Property); American Intellectual Property Lawyers Association. *PRACTICE AREAS:* Patent, Trademark and Copyright; Litigation; Trade Secrets; Computers and Software; Antitrust. *Email:* dsalmon@gdclaw.com

**CHRISTOPHER J. MARTIN,** born July 22, 1951; admitted to bar, 1978, California. *Education:* Stanford University (A.B., 1973); University of California at Los Angeles (J.D., 1978). Phi Beta Kappa. (Palo Alto and San

*(This Listing Continued)*

Francisco Offices). *PRACTICE AREAS:* Labor and Employment Law. *Email:* cjmartin@gdclaw.com

**JONATHAN C. DICKEY,** born December 5, 1953; admitted to bar, 1979, California. *Education:* Harvard College (A.B., magna cum laude, 1976); University of Michigan (J.D., cum laude, 1979). Managing Editor, University of Michigan Journal of Law Reform, 1978-1979. *Member:* American Bar Association; American Electronics Association; Securities Industry Association. *PRACTICE AREAS:* Securities Litigation; Intellectual Property Litigation; Accountants' Liability. *Email:* jdickey@gdclaw.com

### OF COUNSEL

**SUSAN B. BURR,** born February 15, 1949; admitted to bar, 1982, Texas and California. *Education:* University of Texas (B.A., with honors, 1970; M.A., with honors, 1972; J.D., 1981). Order of the Coif. Associate Editor, University of Texas Law Review, 1981. *PRACTICE AREAS:* Labor and Employment Law. *Email:* sburr@gdclaw.com

### ASSOCIATES

**RIAZ A. KARAMALI,** born July 13, 1963; admitted to bar, 1988, California. *Education:* Rice University (B.A., 1985); Columbia University (J.D., 1988). Harlan Fiske Stone Scholar. *PRACTICE AREAS:* Corporate and Securities; New Enterprise Formation. *Email:* rkaramali@gdclaw.com

**H. MARK LYON,** born May 17, 1963; admitted to bar, 1992, California. *Education:* Michigan State University (B.S.E.E., 1985); Santa Clara University (J.D., summa cum laude, 1992). *PRACTICE AREAS:* Intellectual Property; Patent Litigation. *Email:* mlyon@gdclaw.com

**PAUL J. COLLINS,** born November 11, 1966; admitted to bar, 1993, New York (Not admitted in California). *Education:* University of Washington (B.A., magna cum laude, 1989); Georgetown University Law Center (J.D., cum laude, 1992). Executive Editor, The Tax Lawyer, 1991-1992. *PRACTICE AREAS:* Securities Litigation; Mergers and Acquisitions; Business Litigation; First Amendment Litigation. *Email:* pcollins@gdclaw.com

**TIMOTHY D. BLANTON,** born August 27, 1965; admitted to bar, 1993, California. *Education:* California Polytechnic State University (B.A., 1990); Santa Clara University (J.D., 1993). Editor-in-Chief, Santa Clara University Law Review. *PRACTICE AREAS:* Corporate Law; Intellectual Property. *Email:* tblanton@gdclaw.com

**LAURA C. ROCHE,** born November 20, 1965; admitted to bar, 1994, California. *Education:* Georgetown University School of Foreign Service (B.S.F.S., 1987); Georgetown University Law Center (J.D., cum laude, 1994). *Email:* lroche@gdclaw.com

Unless Otherwise Indicated All Members and Associates of the firm are members of The State Bar of California.

(For information on firm personnel, address and telephone information regarding the firm's offices located in Century City, Irvine, San Diego and San Francisco, California; Denver, Colorado; Washington, D.C.; New York, N.Y.; Dallas, Texas; Paris, France; London, England; Hong Kong and Jeddah and Riyadh, Saudi Arabia (Affiliated Offices), see professional biographies at Los Angeles, California)

---

## NORMAN H. GLICKMAN & ASSOCIATES

*A PROFESSIONAL CORPORATION*
SUITE A280
755 PAGE MILL ROAD
**PALO ALTO, CALIFORNIA 94304-9408**
Telephone: 415-857-1300
Fax: 415-493-9408

*Practice limited to International and Domestic Tax, Estate and Business Matters.*

**NORMAN H. GLICKMAN,** born Wichita, Kansas, April 16, 1940; admitted to bar, 1966, Colorado; 1967, California. *Education:* University of Michigan; University of Colorado at Boulder (B.A., 1962); University of California at Berkeley (J.D., 1966). Phi Beta Kappa; Order of the Coif; Woodrow Wilson Fellow, Philosophy. Co-Author: Chapter, "Income Tax and the Nonresident Alien," *International Estate Planning*, Matthew Bender, 1987. *Member:* Palo Alto (Tax Counsel, 1977-1984), Santa Clara County (Member, Client Relations and Professional Ethics Committee, 1974-1983), Colorado and American (Member: Advisory Committee on Estate and Gift Taxes; Sections on: Taxation; Real Property, Probate and Trust Law; Corporation, Banking and Business Law) Bar Associations;

*(This Listing Continued)*

State Bar of California. (Certified Specialist, Taxation Law, California Board of Specialization). *PRACTICE AREAS:* Business Law; Domestic and International Estate and Tax Planning; Asset Protection; Probate; Trust Administration.

---

**ROBIN P. JAMPLIS,** born Pasadena, California, March 17, 1952; admitted to bar, 1988, California. *Education:* University of Hawaii (B.A., with honors, 1984); Hastings College of the Law, University of California (J.D., cum laude, 1987). Phi Beta Kappa; Phi Kappa Phi; Order of the Coif. Member, Thurston Society. Recipient, Milton D. Green Award. *Member:* Santa Clara County Bar Association; State Bar of California; The International Tax Planning Association. *PRACTICE AREAS:* Domestic and International Estate and Tax Planning; Asset Protection; Probate; Trust Administration.

---

## GRAHAM & JAMES LLP

600 HANSEN WAY
**PALO ALTO, CALIFORNIA 94304**
Telephone: 415-856-6500
Telecopier: 415-856-3619
*Email:* dgross@gj.com
*URL:* http://www.gj.com

*Other offices located in:* San Francisco, Los Angeles, Orange County, Sacramento and Fresno, California; Seattle, Washington; Washington, D.C.; New York, New York; Milan, Italy; Beijing, China; Tokyo, Japan; London, England; Dusseldorf, Germany.

*Associated Offices:* Deacons Graham & James, Hong Kong, Sydney, Melbourne, Brisbane, Perth and Canberra, Australia.

*Affiliated Offices:* Deacons Graham & James, Hanoi and Ho Chi Minh City, Vietnam; Taipei, Taiwan and Bangkok, Thailand; In association with Dewi Soeharto & Rekan, Jakarta, Indonesia; Graham & James in affiliation with Taylor Joynson Garrett, London, England, Bucharest, Romania and Brussels, Belgium; Mishare M. Al-Ghazali & Partners, Safat, Kuwait; Law Firm of Salah Al-Hejailan, Jeddah and Riyadh, Saudi Arabia.

*General Practice, including Civil Litigation in State and Federal Courts, Corporation, Securities, Tax, Intellectual Property, Commercial, International Business, Bankruptcy.*

### MEMBERS OF FIRM

**DONALD R. DAVIS,** born Peoria, Illinois, 1940; admitted to bar, 1966, Illinois; 1969, New York; 1971, California. *Education:* Northwestern University (B.A., with highest distinction, 1962); Columbia University (LL.B., cum laude, 1965); University of Stockholm, Sweden (Master of Comparative Law, 1967). Phi Beta Kappa. Harlan Fiske Stone Scholar, 1962-1963 and International Fellow, 1964-1965, Columbia University. Articles Editor, Columbia Journal of Law and Social Problems, 1964-1965. Fulbright Fellow, University of Stockholm, Sweden, 1966-1967. Legislative Assistant, Congressman Sidney Yates, 1967-1968. Regent, Northwestern University, 1986-1989. Former Director and President, Santa Clara Valley World Trade Association. Former President and Director, Korean-American Chamber of Commerce of Northern California. Former President, Japan Society of Northern California. *Member:* Palo Alto, Santa Clara County (Chairman, Section on International Business Transactions, 1972-1974) and American Bar Associations. *PRACTICE AREAS:* International Business Law. *Email:* ddavis@gj.com

**JAMES E. EAKIN,** born Lynwood, California, November 20, 1951; admitted to bar, 1976, California; registered to practice before U.S. Patent and Trademark Office. *Education:* University of California at Berkeley (B.S.E.E., 1973); Hastings College of Law, University of California and University of California at Los Angeles (J.D., 1976). *Member:* The State Bar of California; American Bar Association. (Also practicing as Law Office of James E. Eakin, A Professional Corporation, Belmont). *PRACTICE AREAS:* Intellectual Property; Licensing Law & Litigation. *Email:* jeakin@gj.com

**CHRIS SCOTT GRAHAM,** born Berkeley, California, 1959; admitted to bar, 1984, California and U.S. District Court, Central, Eastern and Northern Districts of California and U.S. Court of Appeals, Ninth Circuit. *Education:* California State University at Chico (B.A., 1981); Foothill College; McGeorge School of the Law, University of the Pacific (J.D., cum laude, 1984). Alpha Gamma Sigma Honor Society. Lifetime Member, Traynor Honor Society. Assistant Managing Editor and Comment Staff Writer, Pacific Law Journal, 1983-1984. Author: "The California Dignitary Inter-

*(This Listing Continued)*

## GRAHAM & JAMES LLP, Palo Alto—Continued

est: Procedural Due Process and the Probationary Employee," 15, Pacific Law Journal 341, 1984. Member and Former Chairman, Board of Directors, San Jose Police Activities League, 1987-1995. Member, Board of Directors, Role Models In Action, 1989-1993. Santa Clara County Judge Pro Tem, 1988—. Barrister, American Inns of Courts, Santa Clara Chapter, 1989—. *Member:* Santa Clara County and American Bar Associations. *PRACTICE AREAS:* Litigation; Intellectual Property. *Email:* cgraham@gj.com

**LAWRENCE W. GRANATELLI,** born New York, N.Y., 1957; admitted to bar, 1984, California; registered to practice before U.S. Patent and Trademark Office. *Education:* State University of New York at Stony Brook (B.E., magna cum laude, 1979; M.S., 1981); Cornell University (J.D., 1984). Tau Beta Pi. *Member:* Santa Clara County Bar Association; Peninsula Intellectual Property Law Association; World Intellectual Property and Trade Forum. *PRACTICE AREAS:* Patent, Copyright and Trademark. *Email:* lgranatelli@gj.com

**DAVID F. GROSS,** born New York, N.Y., 1953; admitted to bar, 1978, California. *Education:* St. John's College (B.A., cum laude, 1974); Harvard University (J.D., magna cum laude, 1978). *Member:* Bar Association of San Francisco; American Bar Association (Member, Section of Litigation). *PRACTICE AREAS:* Intellectual Property; Commercial Litigation. *Email:* dgross@gj.com

**TIMOTHY T. HUBER,** born Niskayuna, New York, 1956; admitted to bar, 1981, California. *Education:* University of Tennessee at Knoxville (B.S., 1978); Duke University (J.D., 1981). Beta Gamma Sigma; Beta Alpha Psi; Phi Kappa Phi. *Member:* Santa Clara County and American Bar Associations; American Bankruptcy Institute; Bay Area Bankruptcy Forum. *PRACTICE AREAS:* Business Litigation; Creditors' Rights; Bankruptcy Litigation. *Email:* thuber@gj.com

**ALAN B. KALIN,** born Columbus, Ohio, 1953; admitted to bar, 1978, California. *Education:* University of Illinois (B.S., with high honors, 1974) Beta Gamma Sigma; Boalt Hall School of Law, University of California (J.D., 1978). Order of the Coif. Member, California Law Review, 1976-1978. Certified Public Accountant, Illinois, 1975. *Member:* American Bar Association. *PRACTICE AREAS:* Corporate and Securities Law; Mergers and Acquisitions. *Email:* akalin@gj.com

**MICHAEL H. KALKSTEIN,** born New York, N.Y., 1942; admitted to bar, 1968, California; U.S. Supreme Court and U.S. District Court, Northern, Central and Eastern Districts of California. *Education:* University of Pennsylvania (B.A., 1963); Boalt Hall School of Law, University of California (J.D., 1967). Member, John Marshall Pre-Law Society. Deputy District Attorney, Contra Costa County, 1968-1972. Member, Governor's Task Force on Agricultural Labor Relations, 1975. Member, City of San Jose, California Fine Arts Commission Arts 2020 Task Force, 1987-1988. Member, Board of Directors, The Cooper Companies, Inc. Member and President, Board of Trustees of Opera San Jose, 1992-1994; Member of President's Council of Silicon Valley Arts Fund, 1992-1994. *Member:* Bar Association of San Francisco; Santa Clara County, Alameda County and American Bar Associations. *PRACTICE AREAS:* Intellectual Property Litigation; Complex Business Litigation; Securities Litigation. *Email:* mkalkstein@gj.com

**RONALD S. LEMIEUX,** born Minneapolis, Minnesota, 1959; admitted to bar, 1985, California. *Education:* Stanford University (A.B., 1981); Hastings College of Law, University of California (J.D., 1985). 1066 Foundation Scholar. Member, 1983-1984 and Executive Articles Editor, 1984-1985, COMM/ENT-Hastings Journal of Communications and Entertainment Law. Legal Writing and Research Instructor, Hastings College of the Law, University of California, 1988-1990. *Member:* American Bar Association (Member, Sections on: Intellectual Property; Litigation); Japan Society of Northern California; World Affairs Council of Northern California. *PRACTICE AREAS:* Intellectual Property; Commercial Litigation. *Email:* rlemieux@gj.com

**RALPH M. PAIS,** born Binghamton, New York, 1948; admitted to bar, 1975, California. *Education:* Colorado College (B.A., 1970); University of Santa Clara (J.D., 1975). Co-Author: "Employee Participation in Corporate Decision Making: The Dutch Model," 15 The International Lawyer 3, 1981; "The Netherlands Works Councils Act," CCH Common Market Reports, No. 454, August, 1982. Consul for The Netherlands for Northern California, 1989—. *LANGUAGES:* Dutch. *PRACTICE AREAS:* International Business Transactions; Corporate and Commercial Transactions; Technology Licensing; Intellectual Property. *Email:* rpais@gj.com

*(This Listing Continued)*

**ROBERT E. PATTERSON,** born Los Angeles, California, 1942; admitted to bar, 1972, California. *Education:* University of California at Los Angeles (B.A., 1964); U.S. Navy Nuclear Power School, 1965; Stanford University (J.D., 1972); Graduate School of Business Executive Program, 1986). *PRACTICE AREAS:* Corporate Law; Venture Capital. *Email:* bpatterson@gj.com

**THOMAS R. RADCLIFFE,** born Klamath Falls, Oregon, 1953; admitted to bar, 1981, Washington and U.S. District Court, Western District of Washington; 1987, Oregon; 1989, California. *Education:* Lewis and Clark College (B.A., 1975); University of Oregon (J.D., 1980); University of Washington School of Law (LL.M. in Asian Law, 1984). Charles Dana Fellow. Author: "Exclusive Dealing Arrangements Under Japanese Antitrust Law: The Tōyō Seimaiki Case," 18 Law In Japan 76, 1986. Co-Author: "Checklist for Establishing Business Operations in Japan," Corporate Counsel's International Adviser, February 1991; "New Trade Secret Protection Law In Japan," International Computer Law Adviser, November 1991; "Accessing the Japanese Market: Legal Issues for U.S. Companies," Directors & Boards, Fall 1992; "Japan Invites Lawyers...Sort Of," Business Law Today, January/February 1994; "Good Market, Vietnam (End of Embargo Opens Beachhead to U.S. Business Ventures)," Business Law Today, September/October 1994. *Member:* Washington State Bar Association; Oregon State Bar; Japan Society of Northern California; Kaisha Society; World Intellectual Property and Trad Forum. *LANGUAGES:* Japanese. *PRACTICE AREAS:* Corporate Law; Technology Transfer. *Email:* tradcliffe@gj.com

**JOE C. SORENSON,** born Madison, Wisconsin, 1947; admitted to bar, 1979, California. *Education:* Oklahoma State University (B.S., 1970); Purdue University (M.S., 1971); Boalt Hall School of Law, University of California (J.D., 1979). *PRACTICE AREAS:* Corporate Law; Securities Law. *Email:* jsorenson@gj.com

### RESIDENT ASSOCIATES

*Michele Z. Allen; Douglas A. Carlen; Deborah M. Chang; W. Clay Deanhardt; David S. Elkins; U. P. Peter Eng; Jenny J. Kim; Brien B. Kirk; Jill F. Kopeikin; Laura A. Majerus; Thomas A. M'Guinness; Andrew Y. Piatnicia; Perpetua B. Tranlong; Harold T. Tsiang; Valerie M. Wagner.*

All Members and Associates Resident in California are Members of the State Bar of California except where otherwise indicated.

---

## GRANT & GORDON

*525 UNIVERSITY AVENUE, SUITE 1325*
**PALO ALTO, CALIFORNIA 94301**
Telephone: 415-614-3800
Fax: 415-614-3810

*Taxation, Estate Planning, Probate, Trust Administration, Charitable Giving.*

### MEMBERS OF FIRM

**ROBERT N. GRANT,** born Cairo, Illinois, December 23, 1945; admitted to bar, 1972, California. *Education:* Princeton University (B.A., cum laude, 1967); Stanford University (M.B.A., 1972; J.D., 1972). Member, Board of Governors, American National Red Cross, 1996—. *Member:* The State Bar of California; American Bar Associations; American College of Trusts and Estate Counsel. *PRACTICE AREAS:* Taxation; Estate Planning; Probate; Trust Administration; Charitable Giving.

**JUDITH V. GORDON,** born Lewiston, Maine, March 4, 1954; admitted to bar, 1978, California. *Education:* University of Florida (B.A., summa cum laude, 1975); Georgetown University (J.D., 1978); New York University (LL.M., in Taxation, 1981). Phi Beta Kappa. *Member:* Santa Clara and American Bar Associations; State Bar of California. (Certified Specialist, Probate, Estate Planning and Trust Law, The State Bar of California Board of Legal Specialization). *PRACTICE AREAS:* Probate; Estate Planning; Trust Administration; Taxation; Charitable Giving.

# GRAY CARY WARE & FREIDENRICH
*A PROFESSIONAL CORPORATION*

Gray Cary Established in 1927

Ware & Freidenrich Established in 1969

**400 HAMILTON AVENUE**
**PALO ALTO, CALIFORNIA 94301-1825**

Telephone: 415-328-6561

Telex: 348-372

Telecopier: 415-327-3699

Email: info@gcwf.com

URL: http://www.gcwf.com

*San Diego, California Office:* 401 B Street, Suite 1700. Telephone: 619-699-2700.

*San Diego/Golden Triangle, California Office:* 4365 Executive Drive, Suite 1600, 92121. Telephone: 619-677-1400. Fax: 619-677-1477.

*La Jolla, California Office:* 1200 Prospect Street, Suite 575. Telephone: 619-454-9101.

*El Centro, California Office:* 1224 State Street, P.O. Box 2890. Telephone: 619-353-6140.

General Civil and Trial Practice in all State and Federal Courts and Administrative Agencies. Admiralty, Agribusiness, Antitrust, Aviation, Banking, Bankruptcy and Insolvency, Business, Commercial, Computer Law, Compensation and Benefits, Condemnation, Construction, Copyright and Trademark, Corporation, Corporate Securities, Customs, Eminent Domain, Employment Counseling and Litigation, Environmental, Estate Planning, Family Law, Fidelity and Surety, Government Contracts, Hospital and Health Care, Immigration and Naturalization, Insurance, International Business and Litigation, Publishing, Labor, Land Use, Libel, Negligence, News Media, Pension and Profit Sharing, Privacy, Private Foundation, Probate, Products Liability, Professional Malpractice, Railroad, Real Property, Federal and State Securities, Taxation, Telecommunications, Trade Regulation, Unfair Competition, Wills and Trusts.

**PETER M. ASTIZ,** born San Francisco, California, January 24, 1958; admitted to bar, 1982, California. *Education:* University of California at Berkeley (B.S., with honors, 1979); University of San Francisco (J.D., cum laude, 1982). Member, McAuliffe Law Honor Society. Articles Editor, San Francisco Law Review, 1981-1982. *Member:* State Bar of California; American Bar Association; Barristers Club of San Francisco. **PRACTICE AREAS:** Corporate and Partnership Law; Mergers and Acquisitions; Securities and Financial Products.

**CYNTHIA BETH CARLSON,** born San Diego, California, September 2, 1959; admitted to bar, 1985, California. *Education:* University of California at Irvine (B.A., summa cum laude, Phi Beta Kappa, 1981); University of California at Davis (J.D., 1984). Order of the Coif; Phi Delta Phi (Magister, 1982-1983). Member, Moot Court. *Member:* Bar Association of San Francisco; Santa Clara County and American Bar Associations; The State Bar of California. **PRACTICE AREAS:** Employment Litigation and Counseling; Civil Business Litigation; Insurance Coverage and Bad Faith. *Email:* ccarlson@gcwf.com

**JOHN HOWARD CLOWES,** born Stockport, England, September 6, 1953; admitted to bar, 1982, California. *Education:* University of California at Santa Barbara (B.A., magna cum laude, 1976); Boalt Hall School of Law, University of California (J.D., 1982). *Member:* The State Bar of California; American Bar Association. *Email:* hclowes@gcwf.com

**LAWRENCE A. COGAN,** born Los Angeles, California, December 21, 1951; admitted to bar, 1984, California. *Education:* University of California at Berkeley (A.B., 1973); University of California at Davis (J.D., 1984). Phi Beta Kappa. *Member:* Bar Association of San Francisco; Santa Clara and American Bar Associations; The State Bar of California. **PRACTICE AREAS:** Environmental Law. *Email:* lcogan@gcwf.com

**STEVEN G. COHEN,** born Los Angeles, California, July 2, 1957; admitted to bar, 1983, California. *Education:* University of California at Santa Barbara; University of California at Irvine (B.A., cum laude, 1980); University of California at Davis (J.D., 1983). Order of the Coif. *Member:* Bar Association of San Francisco; Santa Clara Bar Association; The State Bar of California. **TRANSACTIONS:** Multi-million dollar administrative mandamus action; California Environmental Quality Act (CEQA) litigation for various commercial and residential real estate developers; Construction defect litigation; Mechanic's lien counseling and litigation; Commercial unlawful detainer actions for both landlords and tenants. **PRACTICE AREAS:** Real Estate and Construction Defect Litigation; Land Use and CEQA Litigation; Commercial Lease Dispute Litigation; Mechanics' Lien Litigation. *Email:* scohen@gcwf.com

**DAVID HENRY DOLKAS,** born Alhambra, California, July 6, 1956; admitted to bar, 1983, California, U.S. District Court, Southern District of California and U.S. Court of Appeals, Ninth Circuit. *Education:* Loyola Marymount University (B.A., 1978); University of San Diego (J.D., 1982). Adjunct Professor of Law, University of San Diego School of Law, 1989-1990. General Counsel, 1989, President, 1990, Otay Mesa Chamber of Commerce. *Member:* The State Bar of California; California Trial Lawyers Association; Southern California Defense Counsel Association. **PRACTICE AREAS:** Business Litigation (50%); Intellectual Property (25%); Personal Injury (25%). *Email:* ddolkas@gcwf.com

**IAN N. FEINBERG,** born San Francisco, California, September 17, 1954; admitted to bar, 1979, California. *Education:* Stanford University (A.B., with distinction, 1976); Stanford Law School (J.D., 1979). Phi Beta Kappa. Stanford Law Review, 1977-1978. *Member:* Bar Association of San Francisco; Palo Alto and American (Member, Sections on: Antitrust; Litigation) Bar Associations; The State Bar of California. **PRACTICE AREAS:** Intellectual Property Litigation; Antitrust Litigation; Distribution Litigation. *Email:* ifeinberg@gcwf.com

**MARK FOWLER,** born Albuquerque, New Mexico, April 14, 1961; admitted to bar, 1986, California. *Education:* University of California (A.B., with highest honors, 1983); Harvard Law School; Stanford University (J.D., 1986). Phi Beta Kappa. Alumni Scholar. *Member:* Santa Clara Bar Association; State Bar of California. **PRACTICE AREAS:** Commercial Litigation; Intellectual Property Litigation; ERISA Litigation; Real Estate Litigation. *Email:* mfowler@gcwf.com

**DIANE HOLT FRANKLE,** born Pittsburgh, Pennsylvania, May 18, 1953; admitted to bar, 1979, District of Columbia; 1980, Maryland; 1985, California. *Education:* College of Wooster (B.A., 1975); Georgetown University (J.D., magna cum laude, 1979). Phi Beta Kappa. Law Clerk to Senior District Judge R. Dorsey Watkins, U.S. District Court, District of Maryland, 1979-1981. *Member:* The District of Columbia Bar; The State Bar of California (Member, Corporations Committee, 1992-1995); American Bar Association (Member, Section of Corporation, Banking and Business Law and Committee on Negotiated Acquisitions). **PRACTICE AREAS:** Corporate and Securities; Mergers and Acquisitions. *Email:* dfrankle@gcwf.com

**THOMAS M. FRENCH,** born Athens, Ohio, December 14, 1941; admitted to bar, 1972, California. *Education:* St. Joseph's College and Butler University (B.S., 1963); Indiana University (J.D., cum laude, 1971). Editor-in-Chief, Indiana Law Review, 1970-1971. *Member:* Palo Alto, Santa Clara County and American Bar Associations; The State Bar of California. *Email:* tfrench@gcwf.com

**THOMAS W. FURLONG,** born Cleveland, Ohio, September 27, 1958; admitted to bar, 1987, California. *Education:* University of Chicago (A.B., cum laude, 1981); Northwestern University (J.D., 1986). Articles Editor, Northwestern Law Review, 1985-1986. *Member:* State Bar of California. **PRACTICE AREAS:** Securities; Intellectual Property. *Email:* tfurlong@gcwf.com

**GREGORY M. GALLO,** born Kenosha, Wisconsin, October 20, 1941; admitted to bar, 1969, District of Columbia; 1973, California. *Education:* University of Wisconsin (B.S., with honors, 1963); Harvard University (J.D., 1969). *Member:* Palo Alto, Santa Clara County and American (Member, Section on Corporation, Banking and Business Law) Bar Associations; The District of Columbia Bar; The State Bar of California. **TRANSACTIONS:** Synoptic Communications in merger with Wellfleet Communications to form Networks; General Magic Initial public offering; Network Peripherals and Microtech Research initial public offerings; Network General Corporation in acquisition of Progressive Computing, Inc.; Crystal Semicon debtor in acquisition of Pro Tools, Inc.; Protein Design Labs Inc. in equity sale of $75 million of equity and technology license to Corange International Ltd. **PRACTICE AREAS:** Corporate Securities; Mergers and Acquisitions; Venture Capital Financing; Technology Joint Ventures; Technology Licensing. *Email:* ggallo@gcwf.com

**PENNY HOWE GALLO,** born Fresno, California, December 29, 1945; admitted to bar, 1970, District of Columbia; 1973, California. *Education:* University of California at Berkeley (B.A., 1967); Harvard University (J.D., 1970). Phi Beta Kappa. *Member:* Palo Alto and American Bar Associations; The State Bar of California. **LANGUAGES:** French. **TRANSACTIONS:** Designed and implemented ESOP for national, privately held ESOP to buy out outside investors and retain employee ownership; Designed and qualified with IRS 401(k) plans for numerous public and private

*(This Listing Continued)*

**GRAY CARY WARE & FREIDENRICH, A PROFESSIONAL CORPORATION,** Palo Alto—*Continued*

companies; Represented plan fiduciaries in ERISA litigation and governmental investigations. *PRACTICE AREAS:* ERISA; Employee Benefits; Executive Compensation. *Email:* pgallo@gcwf.com

**HUGH GOODWIN, JR.,** born Fresno, California, June 22, 1959; admitted to bar, 1986, California. *Education:* University of California (B.S., magna cum laude, 1981; J.D., 1986). Phi Beta Kappa. Certified Public Accountant, California, 1983. *Member:* State Bar of California (Member, Taxation Section); American Bar Association (Member, Taxation Section); California Society of Certified Public Accountants. *Email:* hgoodwin@gcwf.com

**JOHN B. HALE,** born Ashland, Massachusetts, October 4, 1957; admitted to bar, 1982, Wisconsin and California. *Education:* Georgetown University (A.B., cum laude, 1979); University of Wisconsin (J.D., cum laude, 1982). *Email:* jhale@gcwf.com

**WILLIAM H. HOFFMAN,** born Milwaukee, Wisconsin, February 14, 1951; admitted to bar, 1989, California, U.S. District Court, Northern District of California and U.S. Court of Appeals, Ninth Circuit. *Education:* University of Wisconsin (B.A., with distinction, 1978); University of California at Los Angeles (M.B.A., 1980; J.D., 1989). Beta Gamma Sigma. Member, Financial Executives Institute, 1986—. *Member:* The State Bar of California (Member, Business Law Section). *PRACTICE AREAS:* Employee Benefits; Corporate Securities. *Email:* whoffman@gcwf.com

**RODRIGO J. HOWARD,** born New York, N.Y., 1955; admitted to bar, 1985, New York; 1996, California. *Education:* University of Arizona (B.A., with high distinction, 1977); University of Chicago (J.D., cum laude, 1982). Order of the Coif; Phi Beta Kappa; Phi Kappa Phi. Author: *Why Now, More Than Ever, PUHCA Should Be Repealed,* published in Electrical World (May 1996); *A More Flexible Approach: The SEC Is Easing Up On Investments By U.S. Public Utility Holding Companies,* published in Infrastructure Finance Magazine (August-September 1995); *Legal "Due Diligence" in U.S. Corporate Acquisitions,* published in Due Diligence for Corporate Acquisitions (AIJA 1996). *Member:* American Bar Association (Member: Sections of Business Law, 1987—; International Law and Practice, 1987—; Public Utilities, Communication and Transportation Law, 1996—). *LANGUAGES:* German. *PRACTICE AREAS:* Mergers and Acquisitions; General Corporate; Public Utilities. *Email:* rhoward@gcwf.com

**JOAN S. KATO,** born Lodz, Poland, November 20, 1945; admitted to bar, 1982, Illinois and U.S. District Court, Northern District of Illinois, including Trial Bar; 1986, U.S. Court of Appeals, Second Circuit; 1992, California and U.S. District Court, Northern District of California. *Education:* Washington University (A.B., Phi Beta Kappa, 1967); University of Chicago (M.A., 1969); University of Hawaii (J.D., 1982). Member, University of Hawaii Law Review, 1981-1982. Author: "Issues Regarding Loss Within The Meaning Of The D & O Policy," Practicing Law Institute, 1992; *Understanding And Working With The Japanese Business World,* Prentice-Hall, 1992. Assistant Professor, John Marshall Law School, 1988-1990. *Member:* State Bar of California; Illinois State and American (Member, Insurance Coverage Litigation Committee) Bar Associations. *PRACTICE AREAS:* Litigation. *Email:* jkato@gcwf.com

**MARGARET H. KAVALARIS,** born Rolling Hills, California, December 2, 1955; admitted to bar, 1981, California. *Education:* University of California at Berkeley (B.A., Prytanean Honor Society, 1977); University of San Francisco (J.D., 1980). *Member:* San Mateo County, Santa Clara County (Member, Business and Computer Law Sections) and American (Member, Sections on Business Law and Science and Technology) Bar Associations; State Bar of California (Member, Business Law Section); Queen's Bench. *PRACTICE AREAS:* Start-up Companies; Intellectual Property; Technology Transfer and Licensing; Business Transactions. *Email:* mkavalaris@gcwf.com

**JAMES M. KOSHLAND,** born Cambridge, Massachusetts, September 1, 1951; admitted to bar, 1978, California. *Education:* Haverford College (B.A., cum laude, 1973); Stanford University (J.D., 1978). Member, Board of Editors, Stanford Law Review, 1977-1978. Author: Note, "The Scope of the Program E1S Requirement: The Need for a Coherent Judicial Approach," 30 Stanford Law Review 767, 1978. *Member:* The State Bar of California (Member, Business Law Section). *PRACTICE AREAS:* Venture Capital (Retail and High Technology Start Ups); Intellectual Property; Mergers and Acquisitions; General Commercial. *Email:* jkoshland@gcwf.com

*(This Listing Continued)*

**ERIC J. LAPP,** born Frankfurt, Germany, June 2, 1948; admitted to bar, 1978, California. *Education:* American University (B.A., magna cum laude, 1970); Johns Hopkins School of Advanced International Studies (M.A., 1972); Georgetown University (J.D., 1978). International Economist, Office of the Special Representative for Trade Negotiations, Executive Office of the President, 1974-1978. *Member:* Bar Association of San Francisco; The State Bar of California; American Bar Association. *Email:* elapp@gcwf.com

**MARY LAVIGNE-BUTLER,** born Cleveland, Ohio, September 16, 1951; admitted to bar, 1985, Georgia; 1988, California. *Education:* Ohio University (B.G.S., cum laude, 1973); Michigan State University (M.L.I.R., 1976); Emory University; Rutgers University (J.D., 1985). *Member:* State Bar of Georgia; The State Bar of California; Santa Clara County and American Bar Associations. *PRACTICE AREAS:* Employment; ERISA. *Email:* mbutler@gcwf.com

**JEFFREY J. LEDERMAN,** born San Francisco, California, March 10, 1955; admitted to bar, 1982, California. *Education:* University of California, Davis (B.S., with honors, 1977; J.D., 1982). Phi Beta Kappa; Order of the Coif. *Member:* The State Bar of California (Member, UCC Committee); American Bar Association (Member, Section of Litigation). *PRACTICE AREAS:* Commercial Disputes; Real Estate and Construction Litigation; Insurance Coverage Disputes. *Email:* jlederman@gcwf.com

**PATRICK J. McGARAGHAN,** born Eureka, California, May 15, 1944; admitted to bar, 1970, California. *Education:* Stanford University (A.B., 1966); University of San Francisco (J.D., cum laude, 1969). Managing Editor, University of San Francisco Law Review, 1968-1969. Member, McAuliffe Law Honor Society. *Member:* Palo Alto Bar Association; The State Bar of California. *PRACTICE AREAS:* Real Estate Development; Environmental Compliance. *Email:* pmcgaraghan@gcwf.com

**MARVIN MEISEL,** born Los Angeles, California, July 8, 1941; admitted to bar, 1979, California. *Education:* University of California at Los Angeles (B.A., 1963); Stanford University (J.D., 1978). Phi Beta Kappa; Order of the Coif. *Member:* The State Bar of California; American Bar Association (Member, Section on Taxation). *SPECIAL AGENCIES:* Internal Revenue Service; California Franchise Tax Board; California State Board of Equalization. *PRACTICE AREAS:* Taxation; Estate Planning. *Email:* mmeisel@gcwf.com

**MARK F. RADCLIFFE,** born Dayton, Ohio, March 11, 1952; admitted to bar, 1982, California. *Education:* University of Michigan (B.S., Chem, magna cum laude, 1974); University of California at San Diego; Sorbonne University; Harvard University (J.D., 1981). Member, Scabbard & Blade. Author: "Recent U.S. Developments in Copyright Law Related to Computer Software," European Intellectual Property Law Review, Volume 2, 1986. Co-Author: "Intellectual Property Financing for High Technology Companies," UCC Law Journal, Summer, 1986. "Computer and Software Acquisitions under the UCC," 26th Annual UCC Institute (1993). Co-Author: *Multimedia Law Handbook* (1994). Law Clerk, Honorable Howard B. Turrentine, Chief Judge of Southern District of California, 1981-1982. *Member:* Bar Association of San Francisco; American Bar Association; American Intellectual Property Law Association; Licensing Executive Society; Computer Law Association (Member, Board of Directors). *Email:* mradcliffe@gcwf.com

**JONATHAN E. RATTNER,** born New York, N.Y., January 3, 1956; admitted to bar, 1982, New York and California. *Education:* Vanderbilt University (B.A., summa cum laude, 1978); Columbia University (J.D., 1981). Phi Beta Kappa; Phi Eta Sigma. Harlan Fiske Stone Scholar. Law Clerk, Hon. William P. Gray, United States District Court, Central District of California, 1981-1982. *Member:* Palo Alto Bar Association; The State Bar of California (Member, Real Property Law Section). *Email:* jrattner@gcwf.com

**ARTHUR C. RINSKY,** born Cincinnati, Ohio, July 10, 1944; admitted to bar, 1969, Florida; 1974, U.S. Tax Court; 1975, California. *Education:* University of Cincinnati (A.B., with honors, 1966); University of Michigan (J.D., cum laude, 1969); New York University (LL.M., in Taxation, 1974). Phi Beta Kappa; Phi Eta Sigma. *Member:* The State Bar of California; The Florida Bar; American Bar Association. (Certified Specialist, Taxation Law. California Board of Legal Specialization.). *Email:* arinsky@gcwf.com

**J. MARTIN ROBERTSON,** born Danville, Illinois, April 30, 1952; admitted to bar, 1978, Ohio; 1989, California. *Education:* Miami University (A.B., 1974); University of Cincinnati (J.D., 1978). Author: "The 'Lincoln Properties' Case: Shifting the Burden of Response," 8 Toxics Law Reporter, 1395 (May 11, 1994). Senior Trial Attorney, U.S. Department of the Navy, Office of the General Counsel, 1984-1992; Assistant Attorney General,

*(This Listing Continued)*

State of Ohio Attorney General's Office, Environmental Law Section, 1983-1984; Assistant District Counsel, U.S. Department of the Army, Corps of Engineers, Office of Counsel, 1980-1983. *Member:* Bar Association of San Francisco; State Bar of California; Federal and American Bar Associations. *PRACTICE AREAS:* Environmental Litigation and Compliance. *Email:* mrobertson@gcwf.com

**BRADLEY J. ROCK,** born Portland, Oregon, December 15, 1957; admitted to bar, 1985, California. *Education:* Princeton University (A.B., cum laude, 1980); Boalt Hall School of Law, University of California (J.D., 1985). Order of the Coif. *Member:* Moot Court Board; Ecology Law Quarterly, 1984-1985. *Member:* The State Bar of California. *Email:* brock@gcwf.com

**ROBERT T. RUSSELL,** born Hartford, Connecticut, June 22, 1949; admitted to bar, 1975, California. *Education:* University of Michigan (B.A., 1970); Hastings College of the Law, University of California (J.D., 1975). Member, Order of the Coif. Articles Editor, Hastings Law Journal, 1974-1975. Law Clerk, California Court of Appeals, 1975-1976. *Member:* Palo Alto, Santa Clara and American Bar Associations; The State Bar of California; Association of Trial Lawyers of America. *PRACTICE AREAS:* Insurance Coverage and Bad Faith Litigation; Policyholders' Insurance Coverage; Real Estate Litigation; Construction Litigation; Environmental Litigation. *Email:* rrussell@gcwf.com

**BRUCE E. SCHAEFFER,** born Brooklyn, New York, March 3, 1952; admitted to bar, 1977, Florida; 1979, California. *Education:* Columbia University (B.A., summa cum laude, 1974); Harvard Law School (J.D., cum laude, 1977). Phi Beta Kappa. Law Clerk, Hon. Norman C. Roettger, Jr., Judge of U.S. District Court, Southern District of Florida, 1977-1979. *Member:* Palo Alto and American (Member, Corporation, Banking and Business Law Section) Bar Associations; The State Bar of California (Member, Business Law Section); The Florida Bar. *Email:* bschaeffer@gcwf.com

**DANIEL K. SEUBERT,** born Seoul, Korea, December 11, 1960; admitted to bar, 1989, California. *Education:* University of Oregon (B.A., summa cum laude, 1984); University of Texas (J.D., 1989). Order of the Coif. *Member:* Santa Clara County and American Bar Associations; State Bar of California. *LANGUAGES:* Spanish and French. *PRACTICE AREAS:* Real Property; Commercial Law.

**JOHN R. SHUMAN, JR.,** born Brooklyn, New York, September 19, 1956; admitted to bar, 1981, California. *Education:* Dartmouth College (A.B., with distinction in History, 1978); Hastings College of Law, University of California (J.D., 1981). Order of the Coif. Member, Thurston Society. *Member:* The State Bar of California; American Bar Association. *PRACTICE AREAS:* Employment Law; Litigation. *Email:* jschuman@gcwf.com

**STACY SNOWMAN,** born Springfield, Massachusetts, June 14, 1954; admitted to bar, 1986, California. *Education:* Miami University (B.S., 1976); Hastings College of Law, University of California (J.D., 1986). Author: "Preemption of the Louisiana Software Enforcement Act (or Suffocation by Shrink-Wrap)," Volume 8 No. 2 Comm/Ent 163, 1986. *Member:* The State Bar of California. *PRACTICE AREAS:* Internet; Multimedia and Technology Licensing; Commercial Distribution (domestic and international); Intellectual Property Protection; Government Contracting. *Email:* ssnowman@gcwf.com

**JAY M. SPITZEN,** born Brooklyn, New York, January 18, 1950; admitted to bar, 1988, California and U.S. District Court, Northern District of California; 1989, U.S. Court of Appeals, Ninth Circuit. *Education:* Harvard University (A.B., summa cum laude, 1971; S.M., 1971; Ph.D., 1974; J.D., 1988). Phi Beta Kappa. Legal Intern to the Honorable Arlin M. Adams, United States Court of Appeals, Third Circuit, 1986. *Member:* The State Bar of California. *Email:* jspitzen@gcwf.com

**LILLIAN G. STENFELDT,** born Providence, Rhode Island, September 28, 1955; admitted to bar, 1981, Michigan; 1982, California; 1986, District of Columbia and U.S. Supreme Court. *Education:* Stanford University (B.A., 1976; M.A., 1977); University of Detroit (J.D., magna cum laude, 1980). Alpha Lambda Nu; Alpha Sigma Nu; Phi Alpha Delta (District Justice, 1981-1986). Member, Bankruptcy and Commercial Law Section, Bar Association of San Francisco. *Member:* Santa Clara County Bar Association. *PRACTICE AREAS:* General Business Law; Commercial Law; Bankruptcy Law. *Email:* lstenfeldt@gcwf.com

**DENNIS C. SULLIVAN,** born San Francisco, California, 1946; admitted to bar, 1972, California. *Education:* University of California at Berkeley (A.B., 1968); Boalt Hall School of Law, University of California (J.D., 1972). *PRACTICE AREAS:* Corporate Law; Securities Law. *Email:* dcsullivan@gcwf.com

*(This Listing Continued)*

**R. ALLYN TAYLOR,** born Salt Lake City, Utah, January 31, 1950; admitted to bar, 1977, New York; 1981, New Jersey; 1985, California; 1990, District of Columbia. *Education:* Stanford University (B.A., with honors, 1972); Columbia University (J.D., 1976). Harlan Fiske Stone Scholar. Member, Journal of Transnational Law, 1974-1975. Trial Attorney, U.S. Department of Justice, Antitrust Division (Honors Graduate Program, 1976-1978). Member, Computer Law Association, 1988-1989. *Member:* The State Bar of California (Co-Chair, Trademark Standing Committee of Intellectual Property Section); Trademark Association (Member, Proper Trademark Use Committee); Licensing Executives Society. *PRACTICE AREAS:* Intellectual Property; Trademark. *Email:* ataylor@gcwf.com

**CRAIG M. TIGHE,** born Mineola, New York, July 7, 1955; admitted to bar, 1981, California. *Education:* Wesleyan University (B.A., 1976); Stanford University (J.D., 1981). Article Editor, Stanford Journal of International Studies, 1979-1981. Author: "Secured Loans to Maquiladora Operations," The Secured Lender 52 (January-February 1993); "Surprised in Balance Sheets: Vanishing Assets and Materializing Liabilities," 7 Commercial Lending Review 63 (Spring 1992); "Fraudulent Conveyance Risk in Refinancing LBOs," 4 Banking Law Review 1 (Spring 1992); "LBO Lender Liability Under Shareholder Distribution Statutes," 1 Journal of Bankruptcy Law and Practice 365 (May-June 1992); "The Unjust Enrichment Doctrine: An Expanded Definition Threatens Rights of Secured Lenders," 25 Uniform Commercial Code Law Journal 203 (Fall 1992); "Hidden and Springing Liens: Challenges for the Lenders," 7 Commercial Lending Review 82 (Winter 1991-1992); "Protections for Lenders to Companies Using Licensed Trademarks," 5 Commercial Lending Review 53 (Fall 1990); "Bank Holding Company Act Limits on Debt/Equity Swaps," 4 Commercial Lending Review 57 (Summer, 1989); "Redefining Water Rights in California," 3 Stanford Environmental Law Annual 30 (1981); "Liquified Natural Gas Terminal Act of 1977: One Stop Siting as an Administrative End Run," 2 Stanford Environmental Law Annual 190 (1979). *PRACTICE AREAS:* Lending; Workouts; Leasing; Corporate. *Email:* ctighe@gcwf.com

**JEFFREY A. TRANT,** born San Francisco, California, March 22, 1951; admitted to bar, 1980, New York; 1981, California. *Education:* University of California at Davis (B.A., with high honors, 1974); Cornell University (J.D., cum laude, 1979). Law Clerk to Appellate Division, Fourth Department, New York Supreme Court, 1979-1980. *Member:* Palo Alto, American (Member, Real Property, Probate and Trust Law Section) and New York State Bar Associations; The State Bar of California. *Email:* jtrant@gcwf.com

**ELIZABETH H. WARD,** born New Orleans, Louisiana, May 28, 1958; admitted to bar, 1983, New York; 1990, California. *Education:* Tulane University (B.A., 1979); Vanderbilt University (J.D., 1982). *PRACTICE AREAS:* Commercial Law; Financial Institutions. *Email:* hward@gcwf.com

**RICHARD I. YANKWICH,** born Urbana, Illinois, February 25, 1955; admitted to bar, 1979, California. *Education:* Stanford University (A.B., with distinction, 1976); Duke University (J.D., 1979). *Member:* Palo Alto, Santa Clara County and American Bar Associations; The State Bar of California. *Email:* ryankwich@gcwf.com

**BARRY N. YOUNG,** born New Orleans, Louisiana, February 7, 1942; admitted to bar, 1975, Maryland and U.S. Patent and Trademark Office; 1978-1982, U.S. Court of Customs and Patent Appeals; 1980, U.S. Supreme Court; 1982, District of Columbia and U.S. Court of Appeals for the Federal Circuit; 1985, U.S. Court of Appeals, Fourth Circuit (Not admitted in California). *Education:* Louisiana State University (B.S.E.E., 1964; M.S.E.E., 1966); University of Maryland (J.D., 1975). Delta Theta Phi. Author: "Federal Circuit Patent Law Decisions - Infringement," AIPLA, 1985-1995. *Member:* The District of Columbia Bar; American Bar Association (Member, Sections on: Litigation; Patent, Trademark and Copyright Law); American Intellectual Property Law Association (Member, Federal Litigation Section). *REPORTED CASES:* In re Lowry 32 F.3d 1570 (Fed. Cir. 1994). *PRACTICE AREAS:* Patents and Intellectual Property (75%); Licensing (15%); Litigation (10%). *Email:* byoung@gcwf.com

**JAMES E. ANDERSON,** born Bedford, Indiana, September 13, 1964; admitted to bar, 1989, California. *Education:* Stanford University (B.A., 1986); Indiana University (J.D., cum laude, 1989). President, Indiana University Chapter, American Bar Association, 1988-1989. *Member:* Palo Alto and Santa Clara County Bar Associations; The State Bar of California (Member, Real Property Section). *PRACTICE AREAS:* Real Estate and Commercial Law. *Email:* janderson@gcwf.com

*(This Listing Continued)*

**GRAY CARY WARE & FREIDENRICH,** A PROFESSIONAL CORPORATION, Palo Alto—Continued

**JEFFREY D. BALL,** born Lansing, Michigan, December 2, 1968; admitted to bar, 1996, California. *Education:* Georgetown University (B.A., 1991); Santa Clara University (J.D., M.B.A., 1995). *Email:* jball@gcwf.com

**MARILYN M. BAUTISTA,** born Los Angeles, California, August 15, 1968; admitted to bar, 1993, California. *Education:* University of California at Los Angeles (B.A., magna cum laude, 1990); Boston College School of Law (J.D., magna cum laude, 1993). Phi Beta Kappa. Recipient, American Jurisprudence Award. Law Clerk, Hon. Leslie Tchaikovsky U.S. Bankruptcy Judge, 1993-1994. *Member:* San Francisco and (Member, Commercial Law and Bankruptcy Section) Santa Clara County (Member, Commercial Law and Bankruptcy Section) Bar Associations. *PRACTICE AREAS:* Bankruptcy; Commercial Lending; Commercial Litigation. *Email:* mbautista@gcwf.com

**MARCY BERKMAN,** born Chicago, Illinois, March 12, 1965; admitted to bar, 1991, California. *Education:* University of California at Berkeley (B.A., with high honors, 1987); Cornell University (J.D., 1990). Note Editor, Cornell International Law Journal. *Member:* Los Angeles County and American Bar Associations. *LANGUAGES:* Spanish and French. *PRACTICE AREAS:* Civil Litigation; Environmental Litigation; Business Litigation; Aviation Law. *Email:* mberkman@gcwf.com

**MARY ELIZABETH BERRY,** born Honolulu, Hawaii, March 17, 1963; admitted to bar, 1992, California. *Education:* Stanford University (B.A., 1985); Santa Clara University (J.D., 1991). *PRACTICE AREAS:* Litigation. *Email:* mberry@gcwf.com

**PAUL A. BLUMENSTEIN,** born Los Angeles, California, 1961; admitted to bar, 1988, California. *Education:* University of Rochester (B.A., cum laude, 1983); University of Michigan (J.D., cum laude, 1988). *Member:* State Bar of California; American Bar Association (Member, Business Law Section). *PRACTICE AREAS:* Corporate and Securities Law. *Email:* pblumenstein@gcwf.com

**LARRY J. BRADFISH,** born Tomahawk, Wisconsin, June 13, 1952; admitted to bar, 1988, California; 1989, District of Columbia. *Education:* University of Wisconsin (B.S., 1974); University of Arizona (M.S., 1979); Loyola Law School (J.D., 1988). Member, Loyola of Los Angeles Law Review, 1986-1988. Registered Geologist, Arizona, 1984; California, 1984. Comment, United States Strategic Mineral Policy, 21 Loy. L.A.L. Rev. 107, 1987. *Member:* State Bar of California; American Bar Association (Member, Natural Resource Section). *PRACTICE AREAS:* Environmental Law. *Email:* lbradfish@gcwf.com

**TODD SAMUEL BRECHER,** born Westfield, New Jersey, March 12, 1969; admitted to bar, 1994, Hawaii; 1996, California. *Education:* Yale University (B.A., magna cum laude, 1991); University of Boalt-Hall (J.D., 1994). Order of the Coif. *PRACTICE AREAS:* Corporate/Securities. *Email:* tbrecher@gcwf.com

**KATHLEEN K. BRYSKI,** born Camden, New Jersey, July 21, 1964; admitted to bar, 1995, California. *Education:* University of Massachusetts (B.B.A., 1986); Boalt Hall School of Law (J.D., 1995). Certified Public Accountant, Michigan, 1988—. *PRACTICE AREAS:* Commercial Law and Financial; Institutions Group. *Email:* kbryski@gcwf.com

**PAMELA B. BURKE,** born Brussels, Belgium, July 15, 1967; admitted to bar, 1994, New York; 1996, California. *Education:* Cornell University (B.A., 1989); George Washington University (J.D., 1993). *Email:* pburke@gcwf.com

**KELLY LYNN CANADY,** born Greenbrae, California, April 1, 1967; admitted to bar, 1994, California. *Education:* Cornell University (B.A., 1989); University of Iowa College of Law (J.D., 1994). Phi Delta Phi. Note and Comment Editor and Contemporary Studies Editor, Iowa Law Review, 1993-1994. *Member:* State Bar of California. *PRACTICE AREAS:* Corporate/Securities. *Email:* kcanady@gcwf.com

**HOPE A. CASE,** born Bar Harbor, Maine, July 11, 1966; admitted to bar, 1991, California. *Education:* Brigham Young University (B.S., cum laude, 1988; J.D., cum laude, 1991); University of Nevada. Phi Delta Phi; Order of the Barristers; American Inns of Court. Visiting Professor, University of Nevada, Summer, 1992. Law Clerk, Justice Thomas L. Steffen, Supreme Court of the State of Nevada, 1991-1992. *Member:* Santa Clara County and American Bar Associations; State Bar of California (Member, Litigation and Labor and Employment Sections). *PRACTICE AREAS:* Civil Litigation; Employment Law. *Email:* hcase@gcwf.com

*(This Listing Continued)*

**AMANDA CASTILLO,** born Fairbanks, Alaska, August 25, 1972; admitted to bar, 1996, California. *Education:* University of California, Los Angeles (B.A., 1993); Santa Clara University School of Law (J.D., cum laude, 1996). Moot Court Supervisor, 1996-1997. Santa Clara Inns of Court, Pupil, 1995-1996. Adjunct Faculty, Santa Clara University School of Law. *PRACTICE AREAS:* Commercial Litigation; Technology/Intellectual Property Litigation; General Litigation. *Email:* acastillo@gcwf.com

**KATHLEEN CATTANI,** born Tucson, Arizona, July 31, 1962; admitted to bar, 1993, California. *Education:* Brigham Young University (B.S., cum laude, 1985); University of Utah (M.S.W., 1989); Hastings College of Law (J.D., cum laude, 1993). Member, J. Reuben Clark Law Society. *Member:* San Diego County Bar Association (Member: Litigation Section; Labor and Employment Section). *Email:* kcattani@gcwf.com

**JULIA L. COCHRANE,** born Norfolk, Virginia, October 27, 1970; admitted to bar, 1995, California. *Education:* University of California at San Diego (Computer Science, 1992); University of Santa Clara (J.D., 1995). *PRACTICE AREAS:* Products, Technology, Multimedia Licensing; Copyright. *Email:* jcochrane@gcwf.com

**JANET M. CRAYCROFT,** born Mexico City, Mexico, August 20, 1961; admitted to bar, 1990, California. *Education:* Stanford University (A.B., 1983); Santa Clara University (J.D., 1990). Cap & Gown Honor Society. Phi Alpha Delta. Managing Editor, Santa Clara Law Review, 1989-1990. Member, 1991— and President, 1994-1995, Stanford Professional Women. *Member:* Santa Clara County (Trustee, 1994-1996; Chair, Federal Courts Section, 1995) and American Bar Associations; State Bar of California. *PRACTICE AREAS:* Intellectual Property Litigation. *Email:* jcraycroft@gcwf.com

**GARY L. DAHLBY,** born Denver, Colorado, May 26, 1956; admitted to bar, 1994, California and U.S. District Court, Northern District of California. *Education:* University of California, Davis (B.S., highest honors, 1978; J.D., 1994); Stanford University (M.B.A., 1982). Order of the Coif; Phi Delta Phi. *Member:* State Bar of California. *PRACTICE AREAS:* Intellectual Property; Technology Licensing. *Email:* gdahlby@gcwf.com

**M. ELIZABETH DAY,** born Redwood City, California, January 19, 1969; admitted to bar, 1995, California. *Education:* Dartmouth College (B.A., 1991); University of California (J.D./M.B.A., 1994). *Member:* Santa Clara County Bar Association; Santa Clara Inns of Court. *PRACTICE AREAS:* Intellectual Property; Commercial Litigation. *Email:* eday@gcwf.com

**ERIC H. DORF,** born Manhasset, New York, September 22, 1963; admitted to bar, 1988, California; 1989, U.S. District Court, Central District of California. *Education:* State University of New York at Albany (B.A., magna cum laude, 1985); George Washington University Law Center (J.D., with honors, 1988). Member, George Washington University Law Review, 1987-1988. *PRACTICE AREAS:* Commercial Litigation. *Email:* edorf@gcwf.com

**MAUREEN S. DORNEY,** born Englewood, New Jersey, August 10, 1957; admitted to bar, 1990, California. *Education:* University of California at Berkeley (A.B., 1979); Boalt Hall School of Law, University of California (J.D., 1990). Member, Editorial Board, Trademark Reporter. Author: Moore v. The Regents of the University of California: "Balancing the Need for Biotechnology Innovation Against the Right of Informed Consent," High Technology Law Journal, Volume 5:2, Fall 1990. *PRACTICE AREAS:* Technology Licensing; Intellectual Property Protection; Commercial Distribution. *Email:* mdorney@gcwf.com

**CHARLES M. DYKE,** born Florida, November 7, 1960; admitted to bar, 1992, Illinois; 1993, District of Columbia; 1995, U.S. Tax Court; 1996, California. *Education:* University of Maryland (B.S., 1985); DePaul University (J.D., 1992); Georgetown University Law Center (LL.M., 1995). Managing Editor of Lead Articles, DePaul Law Review, 1991-1992. *PRACTICE AREAS:* Employee Benefits; Taxation; ERISA. *Email:* cdyke@gcwf.com

**JOHN W. EASTERBROOK,** born Detroit, Michigan, November 19, 1950; admitted to bar, 1994, California. *Education:* Michigan State University (B.A., 1974); University of California, Berkeley (M.B.A., 1981); Santa Clara University (J.D., 1994). *PRACTICE AREAS:* Bankruptcy Litigation; Business Litigation; Commercial Loan Transaction. *Email:* jeasterbrook@gcwf.com

**RUSSELL S. ELMER,** born Denver, Colorado, July 20, 1964; admitted to bar, 1990, California and U.S. District Court, Northern District of California. *Education:* Stanford University (A.B., 1986); Boalt Hall School of Law, University of California (J.D., 1990). Member, 1989-1990 and Senior

*(This Listing Continued)*

Note and Comment Editor, 1990, California Law Review. *Member:* The State Bar of California. *PRACTICE AREAS:* General Civil Litigation; Employment Litigation. *Email:* relmer@gcwf.com

*MELANIE E. ERASMUS,* born Durban, South Africa, May 22, 1958; admitted to bar, 1996, California. *Education:* University of Natal, Durban South Africa (B.A., 1978); University of Witwatersrand, Johannesburg, South Africa (Human Resource Management Program, 1979); Santa Clara University (M.B.A., 1992); Stanford University (J.D., with distinction, 1995). Beta Gamma Sigma. *Email:* merasmus@gcwf.com

*JOHN M. FOGG,* born Oakland, California, September 11, 1968; admitted to bar, 1994, California. *Education:* Yale University (B.A., cum laude, 1991); Columbia University (J.D., 1994). *PRACTICE AREAS:* Corporate; Securities. *Email:* jfogg@gcwf.com

*BARBARA FRIEDRICH,* born Switzerland, March 5, 1965; admitted to bar, 1991, California. *Education:* University of California, Santa Barbara (Political Science, 1987); Santa Clara University (J.D., 1991). *PRACTICE AREAS:* Corporate and Securities. *Email:* bfriedrich@gcwf.com

*GILBERT GALLARDO,* born San Jose, California, July 18, 1965; admitted to bar, 1994, California. *Education:* Santa Clara University (B.S., 1987); University of California, Davis (J.D., 1994). *Member:* State Bar of California. *PRACTICE AREAS:* Corporate and Securities. *Email:* ggallardo@gcwf.com

*VANESSA R GONZALEZ,* born Manila, Philippines, May 13, 1970; admitted to bar, 1995, California. *Education:* Yale University (B.A., 1992); University of California, Los Angeles (J.D., 1995). *LANGUAGES:* Tagalog. *PRACTICE AREAS:* Real Estate Transaction. *Email:* vgonzalez@gcwf.com

*DAVID R. GRAHAM,* born Salisbury, Maryland, August 9, 1961; admitted to bar, 1991, California. *Education:* Georgia Institute of Technology (B.M.E., 1985); Stanford University; Cornell University (J.D., 1990). *PRACTICE AREAS:* Intellectual Property; Patents. *Email:* dgraham@gcwf.com

*CHRISTINA GROLL,* born Island Park, New York, February 10, 1968; admitted to bar, 1994, California. *Education:* Dartmouth College (B.A., 1989); Stanford University (J.D., 1994). *Email:* cgroll@gcwf.com

*WILMA (WOODY) GROWNEY,* born Montreal, Canada, April 17, 1971; admitted to bar, 1996, California. *Education:* Davidson College (B.A., 1993); Harvard University (J.D., 1996). *PRACTICE AREAS:* Intellectual Property Litigation. *Email:* wgrowney@gcwf.com

*MICHELLE R. HARBOTTLE,* born San Francisco, California, April 12, 1964; admitted to bar, 1991, California. *Education:* University of California, Berkeley (B.A., 1988); University of California, Davis (J.D., 1991). Member, California Lawyers for the Arts, 1992-1995. *Member:* San Francisco Bar Association; State Bar of California (Member, Intellectual Property Section); International Trademark Association; San Francisco La Raza Lawyers Association. *PRACTICE AREAS:* Domestic and International Trademark Counseling and Prosecution. *Email:* mharbottle@gcwf.com

*DANIEL ROSS HARRIS,* born Olean, New York, August 16, 1965; admitted to bar, 1992, Massachusetts and U.S. District Court, District of Massachusetts (Not admitted in California). *Education:* University of California at Santa Cruz (B.A., with honors, 1988); Washington College of Law of The American University (J.D., summa cum laude, 1992). Managing Editor, The American University Law Review, 1991-1992. Author: "Capital Sentencing After *Walton v. Arizona,* A Retreat From the 'Death is Different' Doctrine," Volume 40, The American University Law Review. *PRACTICE AREAS:* Litigation; Intellectual Property. *Email:* dharris@gcwf.com

*SHARON W. HAWKINS,* born Washington, D.C., May 1, 1969; admitted to bar, 1995, California. *Education:* University of Pennsylvania (B.A., 1991); University of California at Davis (J.D., 1995). History Honor Society. *PRACTICE AREAS:* Corporate/Securities. *Email:* shawkins@gcwf.com

*LINDA M. HAYES,* born San Francisco, California, August 30, 1947; admitted to bar, 1976, California. *Education:* University of California (B.A., 1973); University of Santa Clara (J.D., 1976); New York University (LL.M., Taxation, 1978). *PRACTICE AREAS:* Estate Planning; Probate. *Email:* lhayes@gcwf.com

*CHERYL K. HOUSE,* born Chicago, Illinois, June 5, 1966; admitted to bar, 1992, California and American Samoa. *Education:* Stanford University (A.B., 1988); Hastings College of Law, University of California (J.D., 1991). Order of the Coif. *PRACTICE AREAS:* Corporate. *Email:* chouse@gcwf.com

*DAVID ALAN HUBB,* born Palo Alto, California, August 17, 1963; admitted to bar, 1991, California. *Education:* Colorado College (B.A., 1986); University of California School of Law, Davis, (J.D., 1991). *Email:* dhubb@gcwf.com

*MARK HUPPIN,* born Spokane, Washington, May 26, 1970; admitted to bar, 1996, California. *Education:* University of California, Los Angeles (B.A., 1992); Stanford University (J.D., 1996). *PRACTICE AREAS:* Corporate/Securities. *Email:* mhuppin@gcwf.com

*CHRISTOPHER J. HURLEY,* born Nashua, New Hampshire, March 14, 1965; admitted to bar, 1993, California. *Education:* University of New Hampshire (B.A., magna cum laude, 1987); Boston University (M.B.A., 1993); Boston College (J.D., cum laude, 1993). Phi Beta Kappa; St. Thomas More Society. Staff Writer and Editor, Matthew Bender Uniform Commercial Code Reporter Digest, 1992-1993. *Member:* San Diego County Bar Association. *PRACTICE AREAS:* Corporate Law; Securities; Mergers and Acquisitions. *Email:* churley@gcwf.com

*JEFFREY R. II,* born Chicago, Illinois, October 8, 1963; admitted to bar, 1988, California. *Education:* University of Illinois (B.S., with highest honors, 1985); Boalt Hall School of Law (J.D., 1988). Beta Gamma Sigma; Beta Alpha Psi. Recipient, American Jurisprudence Award, Corporate Taxation. Certified Public Accountant, Illinois, 1985. *Email:* jii@gcwf.com

*ANDREW M. JACOBSON,* born Stanford, California, April 4, 1970; admitted to bar, 1996, California. *Education:* Pomona College (B.A., 1992); Boston University School of Law (J.D., cum laude, Business Organization and Finance Law, 1995); Boston University Graduate School of Management (M.B.A., 1995). *PRACTICE AREAS:* Corporate/Securities. *Email:* ajacobson@gcwf.com

*PAUL B. JOHNSON,* born Santa Clara, California, January 26, 1967; admitted to bar, 1996, California. *Education:* Brigham Young University (B.S., 1992; J.D./M.B.A., 1996). Articles Editor, Brigham Young University Law Review, 1995-1996. Member, J. Reuben Clark Law Society, 1996—. *Email:* pjohnson@gcwf.com

*LAWRENCE C. KING,* born Merced, California, December 10, 1962; admitted to bar, 1992, California, Commonwealth of the Northern Mariana Islands and U.S. District Court for the Northern Mariana Islands. *Education:* University of California at Berkeley (B.A., 1985); Hastings College of Law, University of California (J.D., 1991). *Member:* State Bar of California (Member, Business Law Section and Real Property Law Section) Bar Association of the Commonwealth of the Northern Mariana Islands. *PRACTICE AREAS:* Commercial Law; Financial Institutions. *Email:* lking@gcwf.com

*VICTORIA W-Y LEE,* born Hong Kong, August 17, 1968; admitted to bar, 1993, California. *Education:* University of California at Davis (A.B., 1990); University of California, King Hall (J.D., 1993). Phi Beta Kappa. Regents Scholar. Member, 1991-1992 and Senior Research Editor, 1992-1993, University of California at Davis Law Review. *Member:* San Mateo County (Member, Business Law Section), Santa Clara County and American (Member, Business Law Section) Bar Associations; State Bar of California (Member, Business Law Section). *Email:* vlee@gcwf.com

*GINGER L. LEVY,* born Minneapolis, Minnesota, November 2, 1962; admitted to bar, 1991, Pennsylvania; 1994, District of Columbia (Not admitted in California). *Education:* University of Pennsylvania (B.A., summa cum laude, 1985); Yale University (J.D., 1990). Phi Beta Kappa. Executive Editor, Yale Journal on Regulation. Clerk to Judge Barefoot Sanders, N.D. Texas. *PRACTICE AREAS:* Corporate and Securities. *Email:* glevy@gcwf.com

*TIMOTHY W. LOHSE,* born Stanford, California, May 29, 1967; admitted to bar, 1995, California; registered to practice before U.S. Patent and Trademark Office. *Education:* Tufts University (B.S.E.E., 1989); Golden Gate University School of Law (J.D., 1994). Phi Delta Phi. *PRACTICE AREAS:* Patent. *Email:* tlohse@gcwf.com

*CHARLES M. MILLER,* born Seattle, Washington, August 9, 1948; admitted to bar, 1990, California. *Education:* Western Washington University (B.A., 1970); University of San Francisco (J.D., magna cum laude, 1990). Author: "The First Amendment and the Navajo-Hopi Relocations Act", USF Law Review, Spring, 1990. *PRACTICE AREAS:* Environmental; Insurance; Native American. *Email:* cmiller@gcwf.com

*MARTIN H. MYERS,* born Cleveland, Ohio, September 10, 1962; admitted to bar, 1987, California, U.S. District Court, Northern District of California and U.S. Court of Appeals, Ninth Circuit. *Education:* Miami University (B.A., magna cum laude, 1984); University of Michigan (J.D., 1987). Phi Beta Kappa; Phi Kappa Phi. Member, Mortar Board. Recipient,

*(This Listing Continued)*

**GRAY CARY WARE & FREIDENRICH, A PROFESSIONAL CORPORATION, Palo Alto—Continued**

Writing and Advocacy Certificate of Honor. Director, University Michigan Unemployment Benefits Clinic, 1986-1987. *Member:* Bar Association of San Francisco; Santa Clara County Bar Association. *PRACTICE AREAS:* Insurance Litigation; Complex Commercial Litigation. *Email:* mmyers@gcwf.com

**NELS RAYMOND NELSEN,** born Oakland, California, April 23, 1962; admitted to bar, 1990, California. *Education:* Santa Clara University (B.S.C., cum laude, 1984; J.D., 1990). Beta Gamma Sigma; Phi Alpha Delta; American Inns of Court, 1989-1990. Certified Public Accountant, California, 1987—. *Member:* Santa Clara County and American Bar Associations; State Bar of California. *PRACTICE AREAS:* Insolvency Law; Bankruptcy; Corporate Reorganization. *Email:* nrnelsen@gcwf.com

**DENISE WOODSON OFRIA,** born Alva, Oklahoma, July 14, 1946; admitted to bar, 1983, Wisconsin and California; 1984, U.S. District Court, Northern District of California. *Education:* San Diego State University (B.S., 1970); University of Wisconsin (J.D., 1983). Author: 363-2d T.M., Age, Sex and Disability Discrimination in Employee Plans (BNA) 1994. Member, San Mateo County Retirement Board, 1986—. *Member:* American Bar Association (Member, Tax Section, Employee Benefits Committee, 1985-1990); State Bar of California. *PRACTICE AREAS:* Employee Benefits; Equity Compensation. *Email:* dwofria@gcwf.com

**L. SCOTT OLIVER,** born La Jolla, California, July 14, 1968; admitted to bar, 1994, California. *Education:* Harvard University (A.B., 1990); University of San Diego (J.D., 1994). *PRACTICE AREAS:* Litigation. *Email:* soliver@gcwf.com

**FRANK H. PAO,** born Boston, Massachusetts, July 26, 1968; admitted to bar, 1994, California. *Education:* University of California, Berkeley (B.S., 1991); Boalt Hall School of Law, University of California (J.D., 1994). Tau Beta Pi. *Member:* American Bar Association. *LANGUAGES:* Cantonese. *PRACTICE AREAS:* Technology Licensing (80%); Intellectual Property (20%). *Email:* fpao@gcwf.com

**PAMELA PASTI,** born Greenville, North Carolina, April 1, 1954; admitted to bar, 1995, California. *Education:* Cornell University (B.A., with distinction, 1975); University of California at Los Angeles (J.D., 1995). Member: Raven and Serpent. Member, Mortar Board. *LANGUAGES:* Japanese. *PRACTICE AREAS:* Corporate and Securities; Intellectual Property. *Email:* ppasti@gcwf.com

**JAMIE C. PAWLICZEK,** born Troy, New York, May 6, 1969; admitted to bar, 1995, New York; 1996, California. *Education:* University of Pennsylvania (B.A., 1991); Syracuse University College of Law (J.D., 1994). Member, Copyright Society of the USA, 1994—. *Member:* New York State Bar Association (Member, Entertainment Law Section). *PRACTICE AREAS:* Multimedia Law; Intellectual Property Law. *Email:* jpawliczek@gcwf.com

**DARREN J. PITTENGER,** born Phillipsburg, New Jersey, August 5, 1967; admitted to bar, 1993, California. *Education:* University of Arizona (B.A., 1990); University of California at Davis (J.D., 1993). Phi Delta Phi. Recipient, American Jurisprudence Award, Civil Procedure. *Email:* dpittenger@gcwf.com

**DAVID J. PLEWA,** born Detroit, Michigan, September 22, 1961; admitted to bar, 1987, California. *Education:* University of Michigan (B.B.A., with distinction, 1982; J.D., 1987). *Member:* State Bar of California; American Bar Association (Member, Taxation Section). *PRACTICE AREAS:* Tax. *Email:* dplewa@gcwf.com

**MARGARET M. POWERS,** born The Hague, The Netherlands, March 2, 1960; admitted to bar, 1986, California. *Education:* University of California at Berkeley (B.A., 1982); University of San Francisco School of Law (J.D., 1985). Phi Delta Phi. *Member:* Bar Association of San Francisco; American Bar Association. *PRACTICE AREAS:* Intellectual Property Law; Trademark Law. *Email:* mpowers@gcwf.com

**DOUGLAS J. RENERT,** born Oakland, California, December 21, 1967; admitted to bar, 1993, California. *Education:* Princeton University (A.B., cum laude, 1989); Boalt Hall School of Law (J.D., 1993). *LANGUAGES:* Spanish. *PRACTICE AREAS:* General Corporate; International Corporate. *Email:* drenert@gcwf.com

**WILLIAM A. RODONI,** born Los Angeles, California, August 9, 1970; admitted to bar, 1995, California. *Education:* Santa Clara University

*(This Listing Continued)*

(FNCE, 1992; J.D., magna cum laude, 1995). *PRACTICE AREAS:* Securities Transactions; General Corporate Law. *Email:* wrondoni@gcwf.com

**DIANNE B. SALESIN,** born Detroit, Michigan, 1963; admitted to bar, 1990, California. *Education:* University of Michigan (B.B.A., with high distinction, 1985; J.D., 1990). Certified Public Accountant, Illinois, 1985. *Member:* State Bar of California (Member, Business Law Section); American Bar Association. *PRACTICE AREAS:* General Corporate; Securities. *Email:* dsalesin@gcwf.com

**JASON SCHAUMBERG,** born San Francisco, California, May 3, 1967; admitted to bar, 1996, California. *Education:* Sonoma State University (B.A., Philosophy, 1991); University of California, Davis (J.D., 1996). Recipient: American Jurisprudence Awards, Criminal Law, Civil Procedure, Constitutional Law and Business Associations; Sacramento County Bar Association Business Law Division Scholarship. Senior Notes and Comments Editor, University of California Law Review. *PRACTICE AREAS:* Commercial Law; Bankruptcy; Real Estate. *Email:* jschaumberg@gcwf.com

**EILEEN EVANS SCHEFSKY,** born Youngstown, Ohio; admitted to bar, 1996, California. *Education:* University of California, Berkeley (B.A., 1990); University of California, Davis (J.D., 1996). Order of the Coif; Phi Kappa Phi. Executive Editor, University of California, Davis Law Review, 1995-1996. *Email:* eschefsky@gcwf.com

**JIM A. SCHEINMAN,** born Brooklyn, New York, October 27, 1966; admitted to bar, 1995, California. *Education:* Duke University (B.S., 1988); University of California, Davis School of Law (J.D., 1995). Phi Eta Sigma. Recipient, American Jurisprudence Award, Civil Procedure. Author: "Jewish Business Ethics," U.C. Davis International Law Review Journal, Spring 1995. *Member:* American Bar Association (Member, Business Division, 1994—). *LANGUAGES:* Hebrew. *PRACTICE AREAS:* Corporate Law; Securities. *Email:* jscheinman@gcwf.com

**WILLIAM R. SCHREIBER,** born Chicago, Illinois, June 7, 1965; admitted to bar, 1993, California. *Education:* University of California, Berkeley (B.S., 1988); Boalt Hall School of Law, University of California (J.D., 1993). Certified Public Accountant, California, 1990. *Member:* State Bar of California. *PRACTICE AREAS:* Securities; General Corporate. *Email:* wschreiber@gcwf.com

**MARY E. SHALLMAN,** born Minneapolis, Minnesota, January 2, 1958; admitted to bar, 1984, Minnesota; 1988, California. *Education:* Stanford University (A.B., with distinction and honors, 1980); University of Minnesota (M.A., 1984; J.D., cum laude, 1984). *Member:* State Bar of California; American Bar Association (Public Contract Law Section, 1988—). *PRACTICE AREAS:* Government Contracts. *Email:* mshallman@gcwf.com

**M. ANDREW SHERMAN,** born Montevideo, Uruguay, March 28, 1967; admitted to bar, 1992, California. *Education:* University of Southern California (B.S., 1989); McGeorge School of Law (J.D., 1992). Staff Writer, Transnational Law Journal. *Member:* San Francisco County and Santa Clara County Bar Associations. *LANGUAGES:* Spanish and French. *PRACTICE AREAS:* Technology-related Commercial Litigation; Intellectual Property Litigation. *Email:* asherman@gcwf.com

**SCOTT M. STANTON,** born Pocatello, Idaho, February 16, 1966; admitted to bar, 1993, California. *Education:* Stanford University (B.A., 1988); University of California, Davis (J.D., 1993). Research Editor, University of California Davis, Law Review. *PRACTICE AREAS:* Corporate. *Email:* sstanton@gcwf.com

**MARILYN N. TAKETA,** born Chicago, Illinois, February 18, 1943; admitted to bar, 1970, California. *Education:* Loyola University (B.S., honors Psychology, 1966); Stanford University (J.D., 1969); Golden Gate University (LL.M., 1980). *Member:* Santa Clara County Bar Association; State Bar of California. *PRACTICE AREAS:* Securities; Equity Compensation Plans; Estate Planning; General Corporate. *Email:* mtaketa@gcwf.com

**DON THORNBURGH,** born Birmingham, Alabama, November 26, 1969; admitted to bar, 1996, California. *Education:* Pomona College (B.A., 1992); University of California, Los Angeles (J.D., 1996). *PRACTICE AREAS:* Intellectual Property/Licensing. *Email:* dthornburgh@gcwf.com

**ANDREW PAUL VALENTINE,** born Washington, D.C., February 6, 1964; admitted to bar, 1992, California. *Education:* Bowdoin College (B.A., magna cum laude, 1986); Santa Clara University (J.D., 1992). Senior Comments Editor, Santa Clara Law Review, 1991-1992. Author, "Property Rights--The Effect of Nollan v. California Coastal Commission on Land Use Permits," Santa Clara Law Review, Vol. 32, Issue 4. *PRACTICE*

*(This Listing Continued)*

**AREAS:** Commercial Litigation; Intellectual Property Litigation. **Email:** avalentine@gcwf.com

**KAREN K. WILLIAMS,** born Sacramento, California, November 30, 1954; admitted to bar, 1985, California and U.S. District Court, Northern and Central Districts of California; 1986, U.S. Court of Appeals, Ninth Circuit. *Education:* University of California at Berkeley (B.A., with distinction, with honors in History, 1977); Hastings College of the Law, University of California (J.D., 1985). Extern to the Honorable Robert P. Aguilar, U.S. District Court, Northern District of California, 1985. Co-Author: "A Preliminary View of Injunctive Relief Based on Infringing Intermediate Copying: Some Reflections on the Recent *Sega* and *Atari* Decisions," *The Computer Lawyer,* December, 1995. Board and Program Co-Chair, Copyright Office Society, Northern California Branch, 1994—. *Member:* Santa Clara and San Francisco Bar Associations; Copyright Office Society (Board and Program Co-Chair, Northern California Branch, 1994—). **PRACTICE AREAS:** Intellectual Property Litigation; Licensing and Counselling; Copyright. **Email:** kkwilliams@gcwf.com

**KIRK ORLANDO WILLIAMS,** born New Orleans, Louisiana, July 7, 1969; admitted to bar, 1994, California. *Education:* Stanford University (B.A., 1991); New York University (J.D., 1994). **PRACTICE AREAS:** General Corporate (50%); Securities (50%). **Email:** kowilliams@gcwf.com

*OF COUNSEL*

**ADRIAN ARIMA,** born Waltham, Massachusetts, February 24, 1950; admitted to bar, 1975, California; 1980, U.S. Supreme Court. *Education:* Stanford University (B.A.M.S., 1972); Boalt Hall School of Law, University of California (J.D., 1975). Notes and Comments Editor, California Law Review, 1974-1975. Member, Board of Directors, Boalt Hall Alumni Association, 1978-1980. Member, Board of Directors, National Association of College and University Attorneys, 1993—. Extern Clerk, Chief Justice Donald Wright, California Supreme Court, 1975. **PRACTICE AREAS:** Licensing; Intellectual Property; Biotechnology. **Email:** aarima@gcwf.com

**ALBERT F. KNORP,** born San Francisco, California, July 31, 1935; admitted to bar, 1961, California. *Education:* Stanford University (A.B., 1957); University of Santa Clara (LL.B., 1960). *Member:* San Mateo County and American (Member, Business Law Section) Bar Associations; The State Bar of California (Member, Business Law Section). **PRACTICE AREAS:** Corporate Law; Business Transactions; Real Property Law. **Email:** aknorp@gcwf.com

**MARTA L. MORANDO,** born Portland, Oregon, June 20, 1952; admitted to bar, 1975, California. *Education:* University of the Pacific and University of California at Berkeley (A.B., magna cum laude, 1972); Boalt Hall School of Law, University of California (J.D., 1975). Phi Beta Kappa; Alpha Lambda Delta. *Member:* Palo Alto and American (Member, Corporation, Banking and Business Law Section) Bar Associations; The State Bar of California (Member, Committee on Partnerships and Unincorporated Associations, 1981-1984). **Email:** mmorando@gcwf.com

*RETIRED PARTNERS*

**JOHN FREIDENRICH,** born San Francisco, California, May 6, 1937; admitted to bar, 1964, California. *Education:* Stanford University (A.B., 1959; LL.B., 1963). Member, Board of Editors, Stanford Law Review, 1962-1963. *Member:* Palo Alto and American (Member, Sections on: Corporation, Banking and Business Law; Taxation) Bar Associations; The State Bar of California.

**LEONARD WARE,** born Everett, Washington, January 19, 1928; admitted to bar, 1953, Washington; 1956, California. *Education:* University of Washington; Syracuse University (LL.B., 1953). Phi Delta Phi. Assistant U.S. Attorney, Department of Justice, Western District of Washington, 1953-1955. Member, Palo Alto Planning Commission, 1965-1968. *Member:* Palo Alto, Santa Clara County, Washington State and American Bar Associations; The State Bar of California; California Trial Lawyers Association.

REPRESENTATIVE CLIENTS: 3 Com Corp.; Adobe Systems, Inc.; American Air Lines, Inc.; Anacomp Inc.; Anheuser-Busch; Automobile Club of Southern California; Blackman Flynn & Co.; Cessna Aircraft Co.; Chips and Technologies, Inc.; Citicorp; Consilium, Inc.; The Copley Press, Inc.; E.I. DuPont DeNemours & Co.; EMCON Associates; First Interstate Bank; Forward Landfill; General Atomics; General Dynamics Corp.; Gregory Group, Inc.; The Grupe Cos.; Harcourt General Corp.; Hitachi; Home Savings of America; Hyundai; Informix Corp.; John Hancock Mutual Life; Kaufman and Broad-South Bay, Inc.; King & Lyons; Kyocera; KLA Instruments Corp.; Lockheed Missiles & Space Division; The Lusk Co.; M.H. Golden Co.; Marine Engineering and Services, Inc.; Maxtor Corp.; McGraw Hill Broadcasting, Inc.; Merrill Lynch; Metaphor Computer Systems; NCR Corp.; Network General; NeXT, Inc.; Noble Broadcast Group; Pacific Bell; Peery/Arrillaga; Public Storage, Inc.; Pulte Home Corp.; Qualcomm; Ramada Inns; Regents of the University of California; Regis McKenna, Inc.; Renault & Handley; Robertson, Colman & Stephens; Ross Stores, Inc.; Safeway, Inc.; The Salk Institute; Samsung; San Diego Museum of Art; San Diego Blood Bank; San Diego Convention and Visitors Bureau; San Diego Employers Assn.; The Scripps Research Institute; Sea World, Inc.; Semiconductor Equipment and Materials Institute; Semiconductor Industry Assn. (SIA); Solar Turbines Inc.; Sony; Sutter Hill Ltd.; Synoptics Communications, Inc.; Systems Integrations, Inc.; Tab Products Co.; The Theodore Geisel Trust; Triad Systems Corp.; Union Bank; University of San Diego; Wells Fargo Bank, N.A.; Westgate Hotel; The Woodmont Cos.; Zoological Society of San Diego.

---

## HAGAN, SACA & HAGAN

LAW CORPORATION

350 CAMBRIDGE AVENUE, SUITE 150
**PALO ALTO, CALIFORNIA 94306**
Telephone: 415-322-8498
Fax: 415-322-8499

*San Francisco, California Office:* 350 Cambridge Avenue, Suite 150, 94306. Telephone: 415-322-8498. Fax: 415-322-8499.

*Business Transactions, Commercial Law, Civil and Business Litigation, Securities, Intellectual Property, Employment, Real Estate and Construction.*

**JAMES HAGAN,** admitted to bar, 1964, California. *Education:* University of Oklahoma (B.A., with distinction, 1957); Stanford University (J.D., 1964. *Member:* State Bar of California. [U.S.M.C., Jet Fighter Pilot, 1957-1962]. **PRACTICE AREAS:** Business Transactions; Corporations; Commercial Law; Real Estate Transactions; Securities Law.

**DIANA M. SACA,** born Sacramento, California, October 8, 1965; admitted to bar, 1991, California and U.S. District Court, Northern and Central Districts of California. *Education:* San Diego State University (B.A., Honor's Society, 1988); Santa Clara University (J.D., 1991). Associate Editor, Santa Clara Law Review. *Member:* Bar Association of San Francisco; State Bar of California; American Judicature Society. **PRACTICE AREAS:** Corporate; Commercial; Real Estate Litigation and Transactions.

**JENNIFER J. HAGAN,** admitted to bar, 1991, California. *Education:* California State University, Chico (B.A., 1985); Emerson College (M.A., 1988); Santa Clara University School of Law (J.D., 1991). Technical Editor, Santa Clara Computer and High Technology Law Journal, 1990-1991. Judicial Clerkship with the Honorable LaDoris H. Cordell, Superior Court Judge, Summer 1989. *Member:* Santa Clara County and American Bar Associations; State Bar of California. **PRACTICE AREAS:** Business Transactions; Corporations; Commercial Law; Real Estate Transactions; Securities Law.

**GEORGE M. SCHISLER, JR.,** born Corpus Christi, Texas, September 25, 1957; admitted to bar, 1982, California and U.S. District Court, Northern District of California; 1986, U.S. District Court, Eastern District of California; 1987, U.S. Court of Appeals, Ninth Circuit; 1992, U.S. District Court, Central District of California. *Education:* University of Edinburgh, Scotland; University of Pennsylvania (B.S., cum laude, 1979); University of Michigan (J.D., 1982). **PRACTICE AREAS:** Civil Litigation in all State and Federal Courts; Patent Law.

---

## HANNA & VAN ATTA

A Partnership of Professional Corporations
*Established in 1978*

525 UNIVERSITY AVENUE, SUITE 705
**PALO ALTO, CALIFORNIA 94301**
Telephone: 415-321-5700
Fax: 415-321-5639

*Real Estate Law, Land Use and Development, Purchase, Sale and Leasing of Real Estate, Real Estate Financing, Joint Ventures and Partnerships, Residential and Commercial Condominiums, Planned Developments and Common Interest Developments, Continuing Care Retirement Communities, Community Association Law, Local and State Permits, Hearings Before State and Local Government Land Use Agencies, FNMA and FHLMC Opinion Letters, Environmental Law, Arbitration and Mediation: Real Estate Disputes.*

FIRM PROFILE: *The firm serves the commercial Real Estate and Home Building Industries, Commercial and Residential Developers and Land Users throughout the State of California. The firm represents commercial lenders and borrowers in all aspects of real estate lending. It handles land use matters, such as subdivisions, zoning, use permits and other local land use matiers, before local San Francisco Bay Area government agencies. The firm provides expertise throughout California to homebuilders regarding the California Subdivided Land Sales Act and maintains contacts with the staff of the Depart-*

*(This Listing Continued)*

*HANNA & VAN ATTA, Palo Alto—Continued*

ment of Real Estate in Sacramento and Los Angeles. The firm has formed over 1,000 community and home owners associations. The firm is a member of the Community Association Institute and ECHO and represents many community associations.

**JOHN PAUL HANNA,** born New York, N.Y., July 12, 1932; admitted to bar, 1960, California and U.S. Tax Court. *Education:* Stanford University (B.A., 1954; J.D., 1959). Author: "Subdivisions: Conditions Imposed by Local Government," Santa Clara Lawyer, Spring, 1966, p. 172; "Compulsory Dedication of Subdivision Land May Be Illegal," California Builder, August, 1964; "Youth and the Law," first publication by Palo Alto Unified School District, July, 1962; "Teenagers and the Law," Ginn and Company, 1967; Comment, "Protecting Builders' Rights," The Voice of the Home Building Industry, December, 1964; "The Complete Layman's Guide to the Law," Prentice Hall, Spring, 1974; "California Condominium Handbook," Bancroft-Whitney Company, Summer, 1975; "Current Condominium Practice Problems," Pepperdine Law Review, Vol. 3, p. 5136, Symposium, 1976; "California Condominium Handbook II, Law and Practice, Residential and Commercial Common Interest Development," Bancroft-Whitney, 1986; "Homeowners Associations: A How-To Guide For Leadership and Effective Participation," Hanna Press, 1988; "Fannie-Mae Updates Her Guide for Condominiums and other Common Interest Developments," CEB Real Property Law Reporter, Vol. 16, No. 6, August, 1993. Visiting Lecturer in Law, Stanford Law School, 1981—. Member, Board of Visitors, Stanford Law School, 1983-1986. Lecturer on Common Interest Subdivisions CEB Continuing Legal Education California State Bar, 1990. *Member:* Palo Alto and American (Member, Real Property, Probate and Trust Law Section) Bar Associations; The State Bar of California (Member, Common Interest Subdivision Committee of the Real Property Law Section, 1980-1981); Home Builders Association of Northern California (Member, Department of Real Estate Committee, 1982—; Member, Board of Directors, South Bay Division); Department of Real Estate Homeowners Association Task Force; American College of Real Estate Lawyers; College of Community Associations Lawyers. *PRACTICE AREAS:* Real Estate (Property) Law; Land Use and Development Law; Community Association Law; Common Interest Community Law; Continuing Care Communities; Construction Defects; Construction Dispute Resolution.

**DAVID M. VAN ATTA,** born Berkeley, California, 1944; admitted to bar, 1944, California. *Education:* University of California at Berkeley (A.B., 1966); Hastings College of Law, University of California (J.D., 1969). Note and Comment Editor, Hastings Law Journal, 1968-1969. Author: "Current Income Taxation Issues Related to Real Property Development," First Annual Institute on Tax Planning for Real Property Transactions, California Continuing Education of the Bar, 1982; "What Every Developer's Successor Should Know," 6 Practical Real Estate Lawyer No. 3 (pt.1) and No. 4 (pt.2), 1990; "Using Letters of Credit as Credit Enhancement for Real Estate Loans," 5 The ACREL Papers 109, 1992; "Reciprocal Easements, Restrictive Covenants and Airspace Developments in Mixed Use Developments," *Planned Communities*, 7 The ACREL Papers 99, 1995; *Guide to California Subdivision Sales Law*, Supplement, California Continuing Education of the Bar, 1990-1996. Law Lecturer, University of California Extension, 1976-1987. Adjunct Professor, Real Property Secured Transactions, Golden Gate University School of Law, 1982-1983. Chairman, Condominium Cooperative Housing and Subdivision Committee, 1981-1983 and Vice-Chair, Executive Committee, 1982-1986, Real Property Law Section, State Bar of California. *Member:* Bar Association of San Francisco; American Bar Association (Member, Section of Real Property, Probate and Trust Law); American College of Real Estate Lawyers; Home Builders Association of Northern California (Chair, Department of Real Estate Committee); College of Community Associations Lawyers; Community Association Institute; Lambda Alpha International; Urban Land Institute (Member, District Council Executive Committee). *PRACTICE AREAS:* Real Estate (Property) Law; Land Use Development Law; Real Estate Finance; Real Estate Arbitration; Real Estate Mediation.

REPRESENTATIVE CLIENTS: American Dream Development; Bay Apartment Communities, Inc.; Bodega Harbour Homeowners Association; California Bararion Corp.; Calprop Corp.; The Castle Group; City of Alameda (base closure); Classic Communities, Inc.; DKB Homes; Diodati Development, Inc.; Rancho San Antonio Residential Housing Corp. (Continuing Care Retirement Community); G.T.E. Realty; Habitat for Humanity; Haseko Associates; Hayman Homes, Inc.; Kaufman and Broad; Lincoln Property Co.; Novato National Bank; ORIX USA Corporation; Pacific Peninsula Group; Peery-Arrillaga; Pinn Bros. Constr. Inc.; Rocky Ridge Properties Owners Association; SAP Technology, Inc.; Seaview Development; Silicon Graphics Computer Systems; Silicon Valley Bank; Sobrato Development Co.; Standard Pacific (Northern California); The Stratford Homeowners Association; Sunstream Homes; Union Bank; Vintage Properties Development Corp.

---

## HAVERSTOCK & ASSOCIATES
*260 SHERIDAN AVENUE, SUITE 420*
**PALO ALTO, CALIFORNIA 94306**
*Telephone: 415-833-0160*
*Facsimile: 415-833-0170*
*Email: tbh@crl.com*

*Patent, Trademark and Copyright Law, Trade Secrets, Unfair Competition, Technology, Licensing and Evaluation and related Trial and Appellate Litigation in State and Federal Courts and Alternative Dispute Resolution.*

**THOMAS B. HAVERSTOCK,** born St. Louis, Missouri, February 26, 1955; admitted to bar, 1985, California and U.S. District Court, Northern and Central Districts of California; 1991, U.S. Court of Appeals for the Federal Circuit; registered to practice before U.S. Patent and Trademark Office. *Education:* Purdue University (B.S.E.E., B.S., Math, 1978); University of Santa Clara (J.D., 1985). *Member:* Bar Association of San Francisco; Federal Circuit Bar Association; San Francisco Patent and Trademark Law Association. *PRACTICE AREAS:* Maskworks; Software; Electrical and Computer Patents.

---

**JONATHAN O. OWENS,** born Midwest City, Oklahoma, May 25, 1967; admitted to bar, 1993, California and U.S. District Court, Northern and Central Districts of California; registered to practice before U.S. Patent and Trademark Office. *Education:* Montana State University (B.S.E.E., 1989); Santa Clara University School of Law (J.D., 1993). Managing Editor, Santa Clara Computer and High Technology Law Journal. *PRACTICE AREAS:* Electrical and Mechanical Patents.

**DEREK J. WESTBERG,** born San Francisco, California, October 26, 1967; admitted to bar, 1995, California. *Education:* California Polytechnic State University (B.S., 1990); Golden Gate University (J.D., with highest honors, 1995). Associate Editor, Golden Gate University Law Review, 1994-1995. Author: "New Kids on the Block v. News American Publishing, Inc.: New Nominative Use Defense Increases the Likelihood of Confusion Surrounding the Fair Use Defense to Trademark Infringement," Golden Gate University Law Review. Member: The Institute of Electrical and Electronics Engineers, 1990—; San Francisco Intellectual Property Law Association, 1994. *PRACTICE AREAS:* Electronic Patents; Mechanical Patents; Trademarks.

---

## HAWKINS, BLICK & FITZPATRICK
*418 FLORENCE STREET*
**PALO ALTO, CALIFORNIA 94301**
*Telephone: 415-321-5656*
*Fax: 415-326-9636*

*San Jose, California Office:* 96 North Third Street, Suite 300. Telephone: 408-280-7111. Fax: 408-292-7868.

*Personal Injury Trial Practice.*

(For complete Biographical data on all personnel, see Professional Biographies at San Jose)

---

## HELLER EHRMAN WHITE & McAULIFFE
A Partnership including Professional Corporations
*Established in 1890*

*525 UNIVERSITY AVENUE, SUITE 1100*
**PALO ALTO, CALIFORNIA 94301-1908**
*Telephone: 415-324-7000*
*Facsimile: 415-324-0638*
*URL: http://www.hewm.com*

*Los Angeles, California Office:* 601 S. Figueroa Street. Telephone: 213-689-0200. Facsimile: 213-614-1868.
*San Francisco, California Office:* 333 Bush Street. Telephone: 415-772-6000. Facsimile: 415-772-6268. Cable Address: "Helpow". Telex: 340-895; 184-996.
*Seattle, Washington Office:* 6100 Columbia Center, 701 Fifth Avenue. Telephone: 206-447-0900. Facsimile: 206-447-0849.
*Portland, Oregon Office:* 200 S.W. Market Street, Suite 1750. Telephone: 503-227-7400. Facsimile: 503-241-0950.

*(This Listing Continued)*

*Anchorage, Alaska Office:* 1900 Bank of America Center, 550 West 7th Avenue. Telephone: 907-277-1900. Facsimile: 907-277-1920.
*Tacoma, Washington Office:* 1400 First Interstate Plaza, 1201 Pacific Avenue. Telephone: 206-572-6666. Facsimile: 206-572-6743.
*Washington, D.C. Office:* 815 Connecticut Avenue, N.W., Suite 200. Telephone: 202-785-4747. Facsimile: 202-785-8877.
*Hong Kong Office:* 1902A, 19/F, Peregrine Tower, Lippo Centre, 89 Queensway, Hong Kong. Telephone: (011) 852-2526-6381. Facsimile: (011) 852-2810-6242.
*Singapore Office:* 50 Raffles Place, 17-04 Shell Tower. Telephone: (011) 65 538-1756. Facsimile: (011) 65 538-1537.

*General Practice.*

MEMBERS OF FIRM

††**RICHARD H. ABRAMSON,** born New York, N.Y., March 11, 1956; admitted to bar, 1981, California. *Education:* Claremont McKenna College (B.A., 1978); University of California at Berkeley (J.D., 1981). Senior Articles Editor, California Law Review, 1980-1981. Law Clerk to the Hon. William H. Orrick, U.S. District Judge, Northern District of California, 1981-1982. *PRACTICE AREAS:* Intellectual Property Counseling and Litigation. *Email:* rabramson@hewm.com

††**PAUL ALEXANDER,** born Oklahoma City, Oklahoma, November 10, 1946; admitted to bar, 1972, California. *Education:* Westminster College (B.A., 1968); University of Michigan (J.D., 1971). Order of the Coif. Michigan Law Review, 1970-1971. *Member:* American College of Trial Lawyers. *PRACTICE AREAS:* Commercial Litigation. *Email:* palexander@hewm.com

††**DANIEL L. APPELMAN,** born Los Angeles, California, December, 29, 1944; admitted to bar, 1981, California. *Education:* San Francisco State University (B.A., 1964; M.A., 1971); University of California at Los Angeles (J.D., 1981); Temple University (Ph.D., 1983). *PRACTICE AREAS:* Intellectual Property. *Email:* dappelman@hewm.com

††**NORMAN J. BLEARS,** born Jamestown, New York, January 19, 1955; admitted to bar, 1980, California. *Education:* Denison University (B.A.,1977); Stanford University (J.D., 1980). Phi Beta Kappa. Law Clerk to Hon. William B. Enright, U.S. District Court, Southern District of California, 1980-1982. *PRACTICE AREAS:* Securities Litigation. *Email:* nblears@hewm.com

††**JOYCE M. CARTUN,** born Norfolk, Virginia, September 16, 1959; admitted to bar, 1989, California. *Education:* Stanford University (A.B., 1981); Hastings College of the Law (J.D., 1989). Hastings Law Journal, 1987-1989. *PRACTICE AREAS:* Securities and Corporate Governance Litigation; Complex Commercial Litigation. *Email:* jcartun@hewm.com

††**MICHAEL L. CHARLSON,** born Pittsburgh, Pennsylvania, September 1, 1958; admitted to bar, 1985, California. *Education:* Stanford University (B.S., 1981; M.S., 1981); University of California at Berkeley (J.D., 1985). Order of the Coif. California Law Review, 1983-1985. Law Clerk to Hon. William C. Canby, Jr., U.S. Court of Appeals for the Ninth Circuit, 1985-1986. *PRACTICE AREAS:* Securities Litigation; Financial Institutions Litigation; Appellate Litigation. *Email:* mcharlson@hewm.com

††**STEVEN R. FELDSTEIN,** born Modesto, California, February 25, 1948; admitted to bar, 1974, California. *Education:* Occidental College (B.A., 1970); University of California at Berkeley (J.D., 1973). Co-Author: "Settlement," Wrongful Employment Termination Partner (Practice, 1987); "Handling The Wrongful Discharge Action," Personal Injury Handbook (James Publishing, 1991). *PRACTICE AREAS:* Labor and Employment. *Email:* sfeldstein@hewm.com

††**STEPHEN C. FERRUOLO,** born Providence, Rhode Island, July 26, 1949; admitted to bar, 1992, California. *Education:* Wesleyan University (B.A., 1971); Oxford University (M.Phil., 1973); Princeton University (M.A., 1975; Ph.D., 1979); Stanford University (J.D., 1990). Rhodes Scholar. Danforth Fellow. Order of the Coif. Law Clerk to the Hon. Bruce M. Selya, U.S. Court of Appeals for the First Circuit, 1990-1991. *PRACTICE AREAS:* Corporate Securities. *Email:* sferruolo@hewm.com

††**NEIL W. FLANZRAICH,** born New York, N.Y., August 8, 1943; admitted to bar, 1969, New York; 1978, California. *Education:* Harvard College (A.B., magna cum laude, 1965); Harvard Law School (J.D., magna cum laude, 1968). Phi Beta Kappa. *PRACTICE AREAS:* Life Sciences/-Health Care includes: Corporate; Strategic Alliances; Transactional; Regulatory, Intellectual Property related to Pharmaceutical; Biotech; Medical Device Cos.; General Corporate and Transactional; Environmental; Insurance. *Email:* nflanzraich@hewm.com

*(This Listing Continued)*

††**ROBERT D. FRAM,** born New York, N.Y., May 21, 1955; admitted to bar, 1986, California; 1987, District of Columbia. *Education:* Princeton University (A.B., 1979); Harvard University (J.D., 1985). *PRACTICE AREAS:* Intellectual Property and Antitrust Litigation. *Email:* rfram@hewm.com

††**RICHARD FRIEDMAN,** born Buffalo, New York, December 21, 1962; admitted to bar, 1987, California. *Education:* University of Rochester (B.A., 1984); University of Chicago (J.D., 1987). University of Chicago Law Review, 1985-1987. *Email:* rfriedman@hewm.com

††**ROBERT T. HASLAM,** born Taunton, Massachusetts, May 4, 1946; admitted to bar, 1976, California. *Education:* Massachusetts Institute of Technology (B.S., 1968); Hastings College of the Law (J.D., 1976). Order of the Coif. Hastings Law Journal, 1974-1976. *PRACTICE AREAS:* Intellectual Property Litigation. *Email:* rhaslam@hewm.com

††**ROBERT B. HAWK,** born Dallas, Texas, January 31, 1958; admitted to bar, 1984, Texas; 1985, California. *Education:* University of Texas (B.A., 1980); Stanford University (J.D., 1983). Phi Beta Kappa; Order of the Coif. Law Clerk to Hon. Irving L. Goldberg, U.S. Court of Appeals, Fifth Circuit, 1983-1984. *PRACTICE AREAS:* Commercial, Antitrust and Trademark Litigation. *Email:* rhawk@hewm.com

††**CYNTHIA L. JACKSON,** born Houston, Texas, May 6, 1954; admitted to bar, 1979, Texas; 1980, California. *Education:* Stanford University (B.A., 1976); University of Texas (J.D., 1979). *PRACTICE AREAS:* Labor and Employment. *Email:* cjackson@hewm.com

††**ALAN M. KRUBINER,** born Bronx, New York, April 6, 1941; admitted to bar, 1975, California and U.S. District Court, Northern District of California; 1982, U.S. Court of Appeals, Federal Circuit; registered to practice before U.S. Patent and Trademark Office. *Education:* Queens College of the City University of New York (B.S., with honors in Chemistry, cum laude, 1961); University of California, Berkeley (Ph.D., 1965); Seton Hall University School of Law (J.D., cum laude, 1974). Phi Beta Kappa. Chair, Intellectual Property Section, State Bar of California, 1986-1987. *PRACTICE AREAS:* Patent Prosecution; Licensing; Intellectual Property Strategy. *Email:* akrubiner@hewm.com

††**EDWARD J. LYNCH,** born Indianapolis, Indiana, September 14, 1936; admitted to bar, 1968, District of Columbia; 1969, California; registered to practice before U.S. Patent and Trademark Office. *Education:* San Jose State University (B.S., 1963); Georgetown University; University of San Francisco (J.D., 1967). *Member:* District of Columbia Bar; American Intellectual Property Law Association; Los Angeles Intellectual Property Association. *PRACTICE AREAS:* Intellectual Property. *Email:* elynch@hewm.com

††**AUGUST J. MORETTI,** born Elmira, New York, August 18, 1950; admitted to bar, 1975, California; 1976, California. *Education:* Princeton University (B.A., 1972); Harvard University (J.D., 1975). *PRACTICE AREAS:* Corporate; Securities; Mergers and Acquisitions. *Email:* amoretti@hewm.com

††**SARAH A. O'DOWD,** born Manchester, New Hampshire, September 7, 1949; admitted to bar, 1978, California. *Education:* Immaculata College (A.B., 1971); Stanford University (M.A., 1973; J.D., 1977). (Office Managing Partner). *PRACTICE AREAS:* Corporate; Securities. *Email:* sodowd@hewm.com

††**RICHARD A. PEERS,** born Palo Alto, California, April 2, 1952; admitted to bar, 1979, California. *Education:* Stanford University (B.A., 1974); Harvard University (J.D., 1978). Law Clerk to Hon. Charles M. Merrill, U.S. States Court of Appeals, Ninth Circuit, 1978-1979. *PRACTICE AREAS:* Corporate; Securities; Mergers and Acquisitions. *Email:* rpeers@hewm.com

††**MATTHEW P. QUILTER,** born Birmingham, England, March 7, 1953; admitted to bar, 1982, California. *Education:* Princeton University (B.A., 1974); University of Pennsylvania (J.D., 1982). *PRACTICE AREAS:* Corporate; Technology Licensing; Venture Capital. *Email:* mquilter@hewm.com

††**GLENN A. SMITH,** born Oakland, California, July 11, 1946; admitted to bar, 1972, California; 1975, District of Columbia. *Education:* Pomona College (B.A., 1968); University of California at Berkeley (J.D., 1971); New York University (LL.M., Taxation, 1973). Tax Law Review, 1972-1973. Law Clerk to Hon. William M. Drennen, U.S. Tax Court, 1973-1975. (Also at San Francisco Office). *PRACTICE AREAS:* Federal Income Taxation; Tax Controversies. *Email:* gsmith@hewm.com

*(This Listing Continued)*

CAA1581B

## HELLER EHRMAN WHITE & MCAULIFFE, Palo Alto—Continued

††**KENT A. STORMER,** born Palo Alto, California, September 20, 1945; admitted to bar, 1970, California. *Education:* Stanford University (B.A., with honors, 1967); Stanford Law School (J.D., 1970). Author: "Selected Legal Aspects of a Dioxin Detoxification Project," *Detoxification,* Ann Arbor Science, 1982; "Environmental Health and Safety-Successful Evacuation of a dioxin Contaminated Hazardous Waste Site," *Chlorinated Dioxins and Dibenzofurans in the Total Environment,* Ann Arbor Science, 1985; "Juries Can Be Made to Understand," *National Law Journal,* 1989. Legal Advisor to U.S. Commissioner of Education, Washington, D.C., 1970-1973. Regional Attorney, Department of Health, Education and Welfare, San Francisco, California, 1973-1979. *Member:* Santa Clara County Bar Association; American Corporate Counsel Association. (Also at San Francisco Office). *LANGUAGES:* Spanish. *PRACTICE AREAS:* Environmental; Life Sciences. *Email:* kstormer@hewm.com

††**VANESSA WELLS,** born Palo Alto, California, August 30, 1959; admitted to bar, 1985, California. *Education:* Stanford University (A.B., 1981); University of Santa Clara (J.D., 1985). Santa Clara Law Review, 1984-1985. *PRACTICE AREAS:* Antitrust Litigation. *Email:* vwells@hewm.com

††**STANLEY YOUNG,** born Hollister, California, October 6, 1960; admitted to bar, 1985, California. *Education:* Stanford University (A.B., 1982; A.M., 1982); Harvard University (J.D., 1985). Phi Beta Kappa. Law Clerk to Hon. Charles M. Merrill, U.S. Court of Appeals, Ninth Circuit, 1985-1986. *PRACTICE AREAS:* Commercial Litigation and Intellectual Property. *Email:* syoung@hewm.com

### SPECIAL COUNSEL

**JOHN A. DHUEY,** born Casco, Wisconsin, July 26, 1942; admitted to bar, 1976, Illinois; 1980, California; registered to practice before U.S. Patent and Trademark Office. *Education:* University of Wisconsin, Madison (B.S., Ch.E., 1964); Northwestern University (M.S., Ch.E., 1968); Loyola University of Chicago (J.D., 1976). Tau Beta Pi. *Email:* jdhuey@hewm.com

**DEREK P. FREYBERG,** born Auckland, New Zealand, October 2, 1948; admitted to bar, 1982, California and U.S. District Court, Northern District of California; 1983, U.S. Court of Appeals, Federal Circuit; 1994, U.S. Supreme Court; registered to practice before U.S. Patent and Trademark Office. *Education:* Victoria University of Wellington, Wellington, New Zealand (B.S., 1968; M.Sc., 1969); University of Virginia (Ph.D., 1977); University of Santa Clara (J.D., 1982). DuPont Fellow, University of Virginia, 1973-1974. *Member:* American Chemical Society; Royal Society of Chemistry. *Member:* Federal Circuit Bar Association; American Intellectual Property Law Association; San Francisco Intellectual Law Association; Peninsula Intellectual Property Law Association. *LANGUAGES:* Japanese. *Email:* dfreyberg@hewm.com

**BETH M. GOLDMAN,** born Brooklyn, New York, January 22, 1952; admitted to bar, 1985, California. *Education:* State University of New York at Buffalo (B.A., 1972); University of California at Berkeley (Ph.D., 1980; J.D., 1984). Phi Beta Kappa. *Email:* bgoldman@hewm.com

**CHARLES M. HUNGERFORD,** born Emmett, Idaho, May 22, 1950; admitted to bar, 1976, California. *Education:* University of Arizona (B.A., cum laude, 1972); University of San Diego (J.D., 1975); George Washington University (LL.M., with highest honors, 1976). *Member:* American Corporate Council Association. *LANGUAGES:* French. *Email:* chungerford@hewm.com

**PAULA S. KASLER,** born Hartford, Connecticut, April 18, 1955; admitted to bar, 1983, California. *Education:* Cornell University (B.A., 1977); University of California, Boalt Hall School of Law (J.D., 1983). *LANGUAGES:* French. *Email:* pkasler@hewm.com

**LISA N. KAUFMAN,** born Jacksonville, Florida, September 7, 1953; admitted to bar, 1978, Florida; 1981, District of Columbia; 1985, Missouri (Not admitted in California). *Education:* Indiana University (B.A., with distinction, 1975); University of Florida College of Law (J.D., 1978). Phi Beta Kappa. Co-Author: Chapter 7, "Trademarks and Related Intellectual Property Rights," Franchise Law and Practice Manual of the Florida Bar. *Email:* lkaufman@hewm.com

**JULIE Y. MAR-SPINOLA,** born Portland, Oregon, July 2, 1956; admitted to bar, 1988, California; registered to practice before U.S. Patent and Trademark Office. *Education:* San Jose State University (B.A.Ch., 1984); Santa Clara University School of Law (J.D., 1987). *Email:* jmarspinola@hewm.com

**WILLIAM SCHMONSEES,** born Brooklyn, New York, February 11, 1947; admitted to bar, 1985, Pennsylvania; 1992, California; registered to practice before the U.S. Patent and Trademark Office. *Education:* Villanova University (B.S., 1968); Wayne State University (Ph.D., 1974); Delaware Law School of Widener University (J.D., 1984). *Member:* American Intellectual Property Law Association. *Email:* wschmonsees@hewm.com

**ANNE WILLIAMS,** born New York, N.Y., February 21, 1951; admitted to bar, 1976, Maryland; 1988, California. *Education:* American University/School of International Service (B.A., 1972); National Law Center, George Washington University (J.D., 1975). *Member:* American Corporate Counsel Association. *LANGUAGES:* French. *Email:* awilliams@hewm.com

### OF COUNSEL

**JULIAN N. STERN,** born New York, New York, October 13, 1924; admitted to bar, 1949, New York; 1954, District of Columbia; 1957, California. *Education:* New York University (B.S., 1946); Yale University (LL.B., 1949). Yale Law Journal, 1947-1949. *PRACTICE AREAS:* Corporate and Technology Licensing. *Email:* jstern@hewm.com

### ASSOCIATES

**E. J. FOURNIER,** born Holyoke, Massachusetts, August 8, 1966; admitted to bar, 1992, Illinois; 1993, U.S. District Court, Northern District of Illinois; 1996, California. *Education:* University of Chicago (B.A., with honors, 1988); University of Pennsylvania (J.D., 1992). *Member:* Chicago, Illinois State and American Bar Associations. *Email:* efournier@hewm.com

**ALI GHIASSI,** born Tehran, Iran, November 6, 1967; admitted to bar, 1992, California. *Education:* University of California at Santa Barbara (B.A., 1988); Pepperdine Law School (J.D., 1991); Georgetown University Law Center (LL.M., 1992). *LANGUAGES:* Farsi. *Email:* aghiassi@hewm.com

**R. RENEE GLOVER,** born Brooklyn, New York, August 27, 1961; admitted to bar, 1992, California. *Education:* Stanford University (B.A., 1982); Stanford University Law School (J.D., 1991). Planning Commissioner, City of East Palo Alto, 1995—. Chairperson, East Palo Alto Rent Stabilization Board, 1983-1985. *Member:* Bar Association of San Francisco; Charles Houston Bar Association. *LANGUAGES:* Spanish. *Email:* rglover@hewm.com

**KYLE GUSE,** born Portland, Oregon, December 7, 1963; admitted to bar, 1992, California. *Education:* California State University, Sacramento (B.S., 1986; M.B.A., 1988); Santa Clara University (J.D., cum laude, 1992). Member, Santa Clara Law Review, 1990-1992. Certified Public Accountant, California, 1989. *Email:* kguse@hewm.com

**LINDA G. HENRY,** born San Francisco, California, September 30, 1960; admitted to bar, 1991, California. *Education:* Wheaton College (B.A., 1982); Stanford Law School (J.D., 1991). *Email:* lhenry@hewm.com

**HOPE L. HUDSON,** born Buffalo, New York, October 27, 1965; admitted to bar, 1993, Pennsylvania; 1995, California. *Education:* Yale University (B.A., 1987); University of Pittsburgh (J.D., magna cum laude, 1992). Order of the Coif. *Email:* hhudson@hewm.com

**WILLIAM J. JAMES,** born Highland Park, Michigan, September 26, 1964; admitted to bar, 1994, California. *Education:* United States Naval Academy (B.S.M.E., 1986); Stanford Law School (J.D., 1994). Order of the Coif. *Member:* Santa Clara County Bar Association. *Email:* wjames@hewm.com

**JEFFREY P. JONES,** born San Diego, California, June 19, 1964; admitted to bar, 1993, California. *Education:* University of California at Berkeley (B.A., 1986); Georgetown University (M.A., 1987); McGeorge School of Law, University of the Pacific (J.D., with great distinction, 1993). Order of the Coif. Traynor Honor Society. Assistant Comment Editor, Pacific Law Journal. *Email:* jjones@hewm.com

**THOMAS P. MALISKA,** born Winchendon, Massachusetts, November 29, 1960; admitted to bar, 1990, California. *Education:* Stanford University (B.A., 1983; J.D., 1990). Phi Beta Kappa. Member, Stanford Journal of International Law, 1987-1989. Chair, Barrister's Club Intellectual Property Committee, 1995. Co-Chair, Digital Media Alliance, 1995. Chair, ABA Section 702 subcommittee on Protection of Database Architectures, 1995-1996. *Email:* tmaliska@hewm.com

**PRISCILLA H. MARK,** born Bethesda, Maryland, August 16, 1966; admitted to bar, 1996, California. *Education:* University of Massachusetts,

*(This Listing Continued)*

Amherst (B.S., 1988); University of California, Boalt Hall School of Law (J.D., 1996). *Email:* pmark@hewm.com

**SARAH E. MITCHELL,** born Nashville, Tennessee, November 20, 1969; admitted to bar, 1996, Massachusetts (Not admitted in California). *Education:* Harvard University (A.B., magna cum laude, 1991); University of Sussex (M.A., 1992); Harvard University (J.D., cum laude, 1995). Phi Beta Kappa. *Email:* smitchell@hewm.com

**SUZANNE K. ROTEN,** born Akron, Ohio, September 13, 1948; admitted to bar, 1990, California. *Education:* University of California at San Diego (B.A., 1970); University of California at Berkeley (M.L.S., 1978); University of California School of Law (J.D., 1990). Member, U.C.L.A. Law Review, 1988-1990. *Email:* sroten@hewm.com

**RANDALL B. SCHAI,** born Prince Albert, Saskatchewan, Canada, November 25, 1960; admitted to bar, 1992, Alberta (Not admitted in United States). *Education:* University of Saskatchewan (LL.B., with distinction, 1991). *Member:* Law Society of Alberta. *Email:* rschai@hewm.com

**JO-ANNE SINCLAIR,** born Ottawa, Ontario, June 28, 1961; admitted to bar, 1987, Saskatchewan; 1990, Ontario; 1996, California. *Education:* University of Regina (B.A., 1982); University of Saskatchewan (LL.B., 1986). *Member:* Canadian Bar Association. *Email:* jsinclair@hewm.com

**JONATHAN E. SINGER,** born New York, N.Y., October 24, 1965; admitted to bar, 1993, Illinois (Not admitted in California). *Education:* Dartmouth College (A.B., 1986); University of Chicago (J.D., with honors, 1992). *Email:* jsinger@hewm.com

**PETER F. STEWART,** born Providence, Rhode Island, January 10, 1969; admitted to bar, 1995, Massachusetts and New York (Not admitted in California). *Education:* Massachusetts Institute of Technology (B.S., 1991); Boston University (J.D., magna cum laude, 1994). Member, Boston University Legislative Services, 1992-1994. *Email:* pstewart@hewm.com

**NITIN SUBHEDAR,** born Warren, Michigan, January 7, 1968; admitted to bar, 1994, California. *Education:* University of Michigan (B.S.E., cum laude, 1990; J.D., cum laude, 1993). Law Clerk to Hon. Vaughn R. Walker, U.S. District Court, Northern District of California, 1993-1994. *Email:* nsubhedar@hewm.com

**PETER N. TOWNSHEND,** born Los Angeles, California, January 19, 1971; admitted to bar, 1996, California. *Education:* Yale University (B.A., with distinction, 1992); University of California, Boalt Hall School of Law, Berkeley (J.D., 1996); University of California, Haas School of Business, Berkeley (M.B.A., 1996). *LANGUAGES:* Japanese, French, Spanish. *Email:* ptownshend@hewm.com

**MICHELLE A. TRAVIS,** born Alexandria, Virginia, March 22, 1969; admitted to bar, 1995, California. *Education:* Cornell University (B.A., 1991); Stanford Law School (J.D., 1994). Executive Editor, Stanford Law Review. Author: "Psychological Health Tests for Violence-Prone Police Officers: Objectives, Shortcomings and Alternatives," 46 Stanford Law Review 1717 (1994). Co-Author: with John A. Martin, "Defending the Indigent During a War on Crime," 1 Cornell Journal of Law and Public Policy 69 (1992). Judicial Clerkship, Judge David M. Ebel, U.S. Court of Appeals for the Tenth Circuit. *Email:* mtravis@hewm.com

**CHRISTINA L. VAIL,** born Evanston, Illinois, September 17, 1969; admitted to bar, 1996, California. *Education:* Northwestern University (B.A., 1991); Santa Clara University School of Law (J.D., summa cum laude, 1996). *Email:* cvail@hewm.com

††Lawyer who is a stockholder and an employee of a professional corporation which is a member of the firm

Unless otherwise stated all members and associates resident in Palo Alto are members of the State Bar of California and the American Bar Association.

(For complete biographical data on Anchorage, Alaska, Los Angeles, California, San Francisco, California, Washington, D.C., Portland, Oregon, Seattle, Washington, Tacoma, Washington, Hong Kong and Singapore office personnel, see Professional Biographies at each of those cities)

## DAVID W. HETTIG
1755 EMBARCADERO ROAD, SUITE 110
**PALO ALTO, CALIFORNIA 94303**
Telephone: 415-856-2700
Fax: 415-856-2728
Email: DHETTIG@aol.com

*Estate Planning, Trust, Wills, Small Business, Tax, and Real Estate.*

**DAVID W. HETTIG,** born Salt Lake City, Utah, May 21, 1942; admitted to bar, 1977, California. *Education:* Stanford University (B.A., 1965); University of California at Los Angeles (M.A., 1966); University of North Carolina; University of San Francisco (J.D., cum laude, 1976). Member, McAuliffe Honor Society. *Member:* State Bar of California; Palo Alto Area, Santa Clara County and American (Member, Sections on: Taxation; Real Property, Probate and Trust Law) Bar Associations. *PRACTICE AREAS:* Estate Planning Law; Probate Law; Trusts Law; Real Estate Law; Tax Law.

## HICKMAN, BEYER & WEAVER, L.L.P.
Established in 1993
620 HANSEN WAY
**PALO ALTO, CALIFORNIA 94304**
Telephone: 415-493-6400
Fax: 415-493-6484

*Intellectual Property Law.*

FIRM PROFILE: *Hickman & Beyer is an intellectual property law firm with a varied domestic and international practice. Members of the firm are skilled in the preparation and prosecution of patent, trademark and copyright applications, the preparation of expert opinions concerning both the infringement and validity of U.S. patents, and in the negotiation and drafting of technology-related agreements in the areas of licensing, trade secrets, and technology sales. The firm also serves as patent co-counsel in litigation matters.*

### MEMBERS OF FIRM

**PAUL L. HICKMAN,** born 1953; admitted to bar, 1984, California; registered to practice before U.S. Patent and Trademark Office. *Education:* Stanford University (A.B., 1975); San Jose State University (B.S.E.E., 1985); Santa Clara University (J.D., 1983). Eta Kappa Nu. *Member:* Santa Clara and American Bar Associations; State Bar of California; World Intellectual Property and Trade Forum; Peninsula Intellectual Property Law Association; International Trademark Association; Licensing Executives Society; Institute for Electronic and Electrical Engineers; Association for Computing Machinery. *PRACTICE AREAS:* Intellectual Property Law; Patents.

**STEVE BEYER,** born 1959; admitted to bar, 1986, Colorado; 1987, California; registered to practice before U.S. Patent and Trademark Office. *Education:* University of Arizona (B.S., Mech. Engr., 1980); Stanford University (M.S., Electro Mech. Design, 1982); George Washington University (J.D., 1985). *Member:* Colorado and American Bar Associations; State Bar of California; San Francisco Patent and Trademark Law Association; World Intellectual Property and Trade Forum. *PRACTICE AREAS:* Intellectual Property Law; Patents.

**JEFFREY K. WEAVER,** born 1960; admitted to bar, 1986, California; registered to practice before U.S. Patent and Trademark Office. *Education:* Pennsylvania State University (B.S., with distinction, 1982); George Washington University (J.D., 1985); University of California, Berkeley (M.S., 1990). Tau Beta Pi. *Member:* State Bar of California; American Bar Association. *PRACTICE AREAS:* Intellectual Property Law; Patents.

### ASSOCIATES

**DAVID P. LENTINI,** born 1963; admitted to bar, 1993, California; registered to practice before U.S. Patent and Trademark Office. *Education:* University of Chicago (B.S., Chem., 1985); Harvard University (M.A., Chem., 1987); Hastings College of Law, University of California, San Francisco (J.D., 1993). Doctoral Fellow, Harvard University, 1985-1989. *Member:* State Bar of California; American Bar Association; Patent and Trademark Office Society; American Intellectual Property Law Association; American Chemical Society. *PRACTICE AREAS:* Intellectual Property Law; Patents.

**JOSEPH A. NGUYEN,** born 1965; admitted to bar, 1993, California; registered to practice before U.S. Patent and Trademark Office. *Education:* North Carolina State University (B.S.E.E., Computer Eng., 1990; B.S., Political Science, 1990); Boalt Hall School of Law, University of California,

*(This Listing Continued)*

**HICKMAN, BEYER & WEAVER, L.L.P., Palo Alto—**
*Continued*

Berkeley (J.D., 1993). Member, High Technology Law Journal, 1990-1991. *Member:* State Bar of California; American Bar Association; Peninsula Intellectual Property Law Association. **PRACTICE AREAS:** Intellectual Property Law; Patents.

**C. DOUGLASS THOMAS,** born 1962; admitted to bar, 1988, New Jersey and U.S. District Court, District of New Jersey; 1989, Pennsylvania and U.S. Court of Appeals for the Federal Circuit; 1990, District of Columbia; 1994, California; registered to practice before U.S. Patent and Trademark Office. *Education:* Pennsylvania State University (B.S.E.E., 1985); Dickinson School of Law (J.D., 1988); George Washington University (LL.M., in Intellectual Property, 1994). Eta Kappa Nu. Author: "Secret Prior Art - Get Your Priorities Straight!" Harvard Journal of Law and Technology, Volume 9, November 1, 1996; "Ownership of Inventions, Successful Patents and Patenting for Engineers and Scientists," IEEE Professional Communications Society, 1994. *Member:* The District of Columbia Bar; Pennsylvania, New Jersey State and American Bar Associations; State Bar of California; U.S. Patent Bar; American Intellectual Property Law Association (Member, Computer and Electronics Committee). (Patent Attorney). **PRACTICE AREAS:** Intellectual Property Law; Patents.

**JONATHAN SCOTT,** born 1961; admitted to bar, 1995, California; registered to practice before U.S. Patent and Trademark Office. *Education:* University of California at Los Angeles (Bachelor of Science in Electrical Engineering and Computer Science, 1983); University of San Francisco (J.D., 19 96). Former Software Engineer and Instructor, Teknowledge, Inc. Former Semiconductor Test Engineer, Megatest Corporation. *Member:* State Bar of California. **PRACTICE AREAS:** Patents; Trademarks; Copyrights; Trade Secrets; Intellectual Property.

**ALBERT PENILLA,** born 1969; admitted to bar, 1995, California. *Education:* University of California at Los Angeles (B.S.E.E, 1992); Arizona State University (J.D., 1995); Franklin Pierce Law Center. Clerk: O' Connor, Cavanagh, Anderson, Westover, Killinsworth & Beshears; Hughes Aircraft Company Patent Department. *Member:* Santa Clara County Bar Association; State Bar of California. **PRACTICE AREAS:** Patents; Trademarks; Intellectual Property Licensing; Intellectual Property.

**LEE VAN PELT,** born 1965; admitted to bar, 1993, California; registered to practice before U.S. Patent and Trademark Office. *Education:* University of Missouri, Rolla (B.S., summa cum laude, 1986); University of California, Boalt Hall School of Law (J.D., 1993). Order of the Coif. *Member:* State Bar of California; Peninsula Intellectual Property Law Association. **PRACTICE AREAS:** Patents.

**BEN H. BEDI,** born 1965; admitted to bar, 1994, California; registered to practice before the U.S. Patent and Trademark Office. *Education:* University of California, Davis (B.S., Chemical Engineering, 1988); Texas A & M University (M.S., Chemical Engineering, 1990); Santa Clara University School of Law; Chicago-Kent College of Law (J.D., 1993). Member, Annual Fund Scholarship, University of California. Co-Author: with R.W. Baker, "Process for Removal of Components from Liquids Batch Mode," U.S. Patent Serial No. 124,935, February 14, 1995, Patent No. 5,389,126; with A.M. Gadalla, "Effect of Composition and grain Size on Electrical Discharge Machining of BN-TiB2 composites," Journal of Materials Research, Vol. 6, No. 11, pp. 2457-2462, 1991; with A.M. Gadalla, "Machining of TiB2 and its Composites," Materials and Manufacturing Process, Vol. 6, No. 1, pp. 125-137, 1991. **PRACTICE AREAS:** Semiconductor Technology; Electrochemical Systems; Alloy Compositions; Metallurgical Cladding; Patents.

**JAMES E. AUSTIN,** born St. John's, Newfoundland, Canada, October 8, 1967; admitted to bar, 1993, California; registered to practice before U.S. Patent and Trademark Office. *Education:* McGill University (B.S., 1989; LL.B., 1993). *Member:* American Bar Association. **PRACTICE AREAS:** Patents.

### PATENT AGENTS

**JAMES R. RIEGEL.** *Education:* Santa Clara University (B.S.E.E., 1991). Registered to practice before U.S. Patent and Trademark Office. Specializes in Electrical, Electronic and Software Patents.

**BRIAN COLEMAN,** born 1967. *Education:* University of California at San Diego (B.S.E.E., 1990; M.S.E.E., 1991). Registered to practice before U.S. Patent and Trademark Office.

## IRVINE & COOPER
A Partnership of Professional Corporations
*Established in 1981*
635 BRYANT STREET
**PALO ALTO, CALIFORNIA 94301-2502**
Telephone: 415-328-3001
Fax: 415-328-2934

*Civil Trial Practice in all State and Federal Courts. Business Litigation, Personal Injury, Family Law, Securities, Insurance and Real Estate Litigation.*

### MEMBERS OF FIRM

**PERRY A. IRVINE, (P.C.),** born New York, N.Y., May 7, 1941; admitted to bar, 1966, California; 1979, U.S. Supreme Court. *Education:* Syracuse University (B.A., 1962); Georgetown University (J.D., 1966). Phi Delta Phi. *Member:* Palo Alto, Santa Clara County (Trustee, 1970; 1975-1978) and American (Member, Section of Antitrust Law) Bar Associations; State Bar of California (Member, Section of Business Law); The Association of Trial Lawyers of America. **PRACTICE AREAS:** Complex Litigation; Securities Litigation; Family Law; Personal Injury Law.

**DAVID L. COOPER, (P.C.),** born Nashville, Tennessee, December 9, 1950; admitted to bar, 1979, California; 1985, U.S. Supreme Court. *Education:* Boston University (B.A., cum laude, 1974); University of Santa Clara (J.D., 1979). *Member:* Palo Alto, Santa Clara and American (Member, Section of Litigation) Bar Associations; State Bar of California; Santa Clara County Trial Lawyers Association; The Association of Trial Lawyers of America. **PRACTICE AREAS:** Business Torts; Complex Litigation; Real Estate Litigation; Securities Litigation; Personal Injury Law.

## ROBERT B KAMANGAR
409 SHERMAN AVENUE, SUITE 212
**PALO ALTO, CALIFORNIA 94306**
Telephone: 415-327-2447
Facsimile: 415-327-2011

*Business Litigation, Wrongful Termination/Discrimination Litigation (Employee and Employer Representation), Employment Law, Family Law, Collections and Personal Injury.*

**ROBERT B KAMANGAR,** born Tehran, Iran, July 14, 1966; admitted to bar, 1992, California; 1993, U.S. District Court, Northern District of California. *Education:* University of California, Berkeley (B.A., 1988); University of San Diego (J.D., 1992). Formerly with Finch & Chavez. *Member:* Santa Clara County and Palo Alto Bar Associations; State Bar of California; Iranian Lawyers Association. **LANGUAGES:** Farsi. **PRACTICE AREAS:** Business Litigation; Real Estate Litigation; Wrongful Termination/Discrimination; Debt Collection; Family Law; Personal Injury.

## EDWARD A. KENT, JR.
2501 PARK BOULEVARD, SUITE 100
**PALO ALTO, CALIFORNIA 94306**
Telephone: 415-328-2089
Fax: 415-326-5430

*Bankruptcy and Insolvency Law.*

**EDWARD A. KENT, JR.,** born Oakland, California, September 8, 1938; admitted to bar, 1966, California, U.S. District Court, Northern District of California and U.S. Court of Appeals, Ninth Circuit; 1978, U.S. District Court, Eastern District of California. *Education:* Brown University (A.B., 1960); Stanford University (J.D., 1965). Author: "Basic Bankruptcy in California", National Business Institute, 1992; "How to Protect Secured Interests in Bankruptcy", National Business Institute, 1993; "Fundamentals of Bankruptcy Law and Procedure in California", National Business Institute, 1994. *Member:* Santa Clara, Palo Alto Area and Santa Clara County (Member, Executive Committee, Debtor/Creditor Committee) Bar Associations; Bar Association of San Francisco; State Bar of California; National Association of Bankruptcy Trustees; American Bankruptcy Institute; California Bankruptcy Forum. **REPORTED CASES:** Matter of Fondiller 707 F2d 441 9th Cir; Irizarry v. Schmidt 171BR874 (9th Cir BAP). **PRACTICE AREAS:** Bankruptcy; Insolvency.

REFERENCE: Bank of the West, Palo Alto, California.

## LAW OFFICES OF
## WILLIAM T. KEOGH

*Established in 1952*

SUITE 460, 285 HAMILTON AVENUE
P.O. BOX 840
**PALO ALTO, CALIFORNIA 94302**
Telephone: 415-321-0947
Fax: 415-326-9722

*Civil and Criminal Trial Practice. Family, Juvenile, Personal Injury, Estate Planning and Probate Law.*

**WILLIAM T. KEOGH,** born New York, N.Y.; admitted to bar, 1952, California. *Education:* Kansas State University (B.S. in Ch.E., 1942); Stanford University (LL.B., 1952). Judicial Officer, Ninth Judicial Circuit, 1959-1961. Associate Dean, Stanford Law School, 1961-1966; 1970-1977. Adjunct Professor of Law, Stanford Law School, 1977-1981. *Member:* State Bar of California; American Bar Association. [U.S. Army, JAGC, 1952-1961]

REFERENCE: Wells Fargo Bank.

## A. DUNCAN KING

SUITE 501, 2471 EAST BAYSHORE ROAD
**PALO ALTO, CALIFORNIA 94303**
Telephone: 800-255-3636; 415-494-6000
FAX: 415-494-3012
Email: adking@ix.netcom.com

*Tax Deferred Exchanges.*

FIRM PROFILE: *Mr. King is the President of Equity Exchange Corporation, a firm he founded in 1984 to accommodate tax deferred exchanges under Section 1031 of the Internal Revenue Code. The firm provides these services throughout the United States primarily to Fortune 500 companies and other users of large or complex exchanges of real and personal property, including oil and gas interests and a wide variety of equipment. Mr King limits his practice to consultation with counsel and tax advisors in connection with the business of Equity Exchange Corporation.*

**A. DUNCAN KING,** born Chicago, Illinois, April 29, 1937; admitted to bar, 1970, California. *Education:* Menlo School of Business Administration (B.S., 1963); Hastings College of the Law, University of California (J.D., 1969). Moot Court Judge, 1968-1969. *Member:* Palo Alto, Santa Clara County (Member, Real Property Section) and American (Member, Sections on: Corporation, Banking and Business Law; Real Property, Probate and Trust Law) Bar Associations; State Bar of California. *PRACTICE AREAS:* Tax Deferred Exchanges (100%).

REFERENCES: The Bank of California; Wells Fargo Bank.

## KOLISCH HARTWELL DICKINSON
## McCORMACK & HEUSER

*A PROFESSIONAL CORPORATION*

420 FLORENCE STREET
**PALO ALTO, CALIFORNIA 94301**
Telephone: 415-325-8673
Facsimile: 415-325-5076
Email: concepts@concepts-law.com

*Portland, Oregon Office:* 200 Pacific Building, 520 S.W. Yamhill Street. Telephone: 503-224-6655. Fax: 503-295-6679.
*Boise, Idaho Office:* 802 W. Bannock, Suite 403A. Telephone: 208-384-9166. Fax: 208-384-9169.

*Patent, Trademark and Unfair Competition Law. Trials.*

**JON M. DICKINSON,** born Bronxville, New York, April 12, 1938; admitted to bar, 1964, Oregon; registered to practice before U.S. Patent and Trademark Office (Not admitted in California). *Education:* Cornell University (B.E.E., 1964; LL.B., 1964). *Member:* Multnomah County and American Bar Associations; Oregon State Bar; American Patent Law Association; Oregon Patent Law Association (President, 1970-1972). *PRACTICE AREAS:* Patent, Trademark and Unfair Competition.

**JOHN M. McCORMACK,** born Palo Alto, California, April 13, 1944; admitted to bar, 1975, District of Columbia; 1989, California; registered to

*(This Listing Continued)*

practice before U.S. Patent and Trademark Office. *Education:* Oregon State University (B.S.M.E., 1967); American University (J.D., 1973). Recipient, American Jurisprudence Award. Examiner, U.S. Patent and Trademark Office, 1972-1973. *Member:* Bar Association of the District of Columbia; The District of Columbia Bar; American Bar Association; American Intellectual Property Law Association; Oregon Patent Law Association (President, 1982-1983). *LANGUAGES:* Spanish. *PRACTICE AREAS:* Patent, Trademark and Unfair Competition.

**PETER E. HEUSER,** born Milwaukee, Wisconsin, March 29, 1949; admitted to bar, 1976, Wisconsin and Illinois; 1981, Oregon; 1983, California; registered to practice before U.S. Patent and Trademark Office. *Education:* United States Merchant Marine Academy (B.S.M.E., 1971); University of Wisconsin (J.D., with honors, 1975). *Member:* Illinois State and American Bar Associations; Oregon State Bar; State Bar of Wisconsin; State Bar of California; American Intellectual Property Law Association; Oregon Patent Law Association (President, 1985-1986; 1987-1988). *PRACTICE AREAS:* Patent, Trademark and Unfair Competition.

**DAVID A. FANNING,** born Kermit, Texas, October 26, 1961; admitted to bar, 1988, Oregon; 1989, California; registered to practice before U.S. Patent and Trademark Office. *Education:* Brigham Young University (B.S., Physics, 1985); University of California, Hastings College of the Law (J.D., 1988). National First Place Winner, 1988 Giles Sutherland Rich Moot Court Competition (Patent Law). Note/Comment Editor, Hastings Constitutional Law Quarterly, 1987-1988. Extern, U.S. District Court for the Northern District of California, Aguilar, J., 1987. *Member:* Oregon State Bar (Member, Patent and Trademark Section); State Bar of California (Member, Intellectual Property Law Section); American Bar Association (Member, Section of Patent, Trademark and Copyright Law); American Intellectual Property Law Association; Oregon Patent Law Association. *PRACTICE AREAS:* Patent, Trademark and Unfair Competition.

**PIERRE C. VAN RYSSELBERGHE,** born Eugene, Oregon, July 11, 1958; admitted to bar, 1990, California; 1991, Oregon; registered to practice before U.S. Patent and Trademark Office. *Education:* Pomona College (B.A., Chemistry, 1980); Golden Gate University (J.D., with honors, 1990). *PRACTICE AREAS:* Patent, Trademark and Unfair Competition.

## LAKIN ● SPEARS

*Established in 1949*

285 HAMILTON AVENUE
P.O. BOX 240
**PALO ALTO, CALIFORNIA 94301**
Telephone: 415-328-7000

*Civil Trial Practice in all State and Federal Courts. Civil Appeals, Insurance, Family, Estate Planning, Probate, Real Property, Finance and Development, Corporation, Federal and State Taxation, Arbitration and Mediation Law.*

**EGERTON D. LAKIN** (1886-1968).

**ANDREW M. SPEARS** (1915-1988).

### MEMBERS OF FIRM

**GEORGE H. NORTON,** born Marietta, Ohio, November 21, 1930; admitted to bar, 1957, California. *Education:* Brown University (A.B., 1951); Stanford University (J.D., 1957). President, Palo Alto Bar Association, 1966-1967. Fellow, American Academy of Matrimonial Lawyers. (Certified Specialist, Family Law, The State Bar of California Board of Legal Specialization). *PRACTICE AREAS:* Family Law.

**FRANK A. SMALL,** born Brooklyn, New York, March 5, 1939; admitted to bar, 1965, California. *Education:* Dartmouth College (B.A., 1961); Stanford University (LL.B., 1964). President, Peninsula Industrial and Business Association, 1977 and 1978. *PRACTICE AREAS:* Real Estate Development and Finance.

**THOMAS J. CAHILL,** born San Francisco, California, August 26, 1942; admitted to bar, 1967, California. *Education:* University of San Francisco (B.A., 1964; J.D., 1967). *PRACTICE AREAS:* Civil Litigation.

**CAROL S. BOES,** born Lincoln, Nebraska, September 4, 1945; admitted to bar, 1980, California. *Education:* University of Nebraska; San Jose State University (B.A., 1974; M.U.P., 1976); Golden Gate University (J.D., 1980). *PRACTICE AREAS:* Land Use; Transactional Real Estate; Business Transactions.

**J. A. TONY VILLANUEVA,** born Chico, California, September 11, 1956; admitted to bar, 1981, California. *Education:* University of San Fran-

*(This Listing Continued)*

## LAKIN • SPEARS, Palo Alto—Continued

cisco (B.A., 1978); Hastings College of the Law, University of California (J.D., 1981). *PRACTICE AREAS:* Transactional Real Estate; Corporate and Business Transactions.

**RONALD A. VANDENBERG,** born National City, California, May 5, 1944; admitted to bar, 1973, California. *Education:* San Diego State University (B.A., 1966); California Western School of Law (J.D., 1969). Fellow, The American College of Trust and Estate Counsel. (Certified Specialist, Estate Planning, Trust and Probate Law, California Legal Board of Specialization). *PRACTICE AREAS:* Estate Planning; Estate and Trust Administration.

**MICHAEL G. DESMARAIS,** born Oakland, California, January 11, 1948; admitted to bar, 1973, California. *Education:* University of California at Davis (A.B., 1970); Hastings College of Law, University of California (J.D., 1973). Order of the Coif. (Certified Specialist, Estate Planning, Trust and Probate Law, California Legal Board of Specialization). *PRACTICE AREAS:* Estate Planning; Estate Administration and Estate Litigation.

**JESSICA F. ARNER,** born St. Louis, Missouri, February 3, 1953; admitted to bar, 1977, California. *Education:* Yale University (B.A., 1974); University of California at Davis (J.D., 1977). (Certified Specialist, Family Law, The State Bar of California Board of Legal Specialization). *PRACTICE AREAS:* Family Law.

**SHERROL L. CASSEDY,** born Furstenfeldbruk, Germany, June 26, 1956; admitted to bar, 1983, District of Columbia; 1985, California. *Education:* Stanford University (A.B., 1978); Georgetown University (J.D., magna cum laude, 1983). (Certified Specialist, Family Law, The State Bar of California Board of Legal Specialization). *PRACTICE AREAS:* Family Law.

**DANIEL R. MORRIS,** born Palo Alto, California, June 14, 1958; admitted to bar, 1985, California. *Education:* San Diego State University (B.S., 1981); University of San Francisco (J.D., 1985). *PRACTICE AREAS:* General Civil Litigation; Personal Injury and Construction Litigation.

**JENNIFER F. WALD,** born New Haven, Connecticut, January 4, 1965; admitted to bar, 1991, California. *Education:* Stanford University (B.A., 1987; J.D., 1991). *PRACTICE AREAS:* Family Law.

**LAURA L. REYNOLDS,** born Maracaibo, Venezuela, November 16, 1962; admitted to bar, 1991, California. *Education:* Brown University (A.B., International Relations, 1985); University of San Francisco (J.D., 1991). *Member:* State Bar of California. *LANGUAGES:* Spanish. *PRACTICE AREAS:* Family Law.

**JAMES P. CILLEY,** born Los Angeles, California, May 9, 1966; admitted to bar, 1993, California. *Education:* San Jose State University (B.S., 1990); McGeorge School of the Law, University of the Pacific (J.D., with distinction, 1993). *PRACTICE AREAS:* Litigation.

**ELLA J. DUNCANSON,** born New York, N.Y., September 18, 1969; admitted to bar, 1994, California. *Education:* University of California, Santa Barbara (B.A., 1991); California Western School of Law (J.D., 1994). *Member:* State Bar of California. *PRACTICE AREAS:* Estate Planning.

### OF COUNSEL

**DONALD H. READ,** born New York, N.Y., November 28, 1942; admitted to bar, 1969, California; 1972, New York; 1976, Hawaii; 1988, Washington. *Education:* University of California, Berkeley (B.A., 1964); Columbia University (J.D., cum laude, 1968); New York University (LL.M. in Taxation, 1972). (Certified Specialist, Taxation Law, The State Bar of California Board of Legal Specialization) (Also Counsel to Donahue, Gallagher, Thomas & Woods, Oakland, California and also practicing individually in Berkeley, California). *PRACTICE AREAS:* Tax Law.

**JOHN P. KELLY,** born Brookline, Massachusetts, October 20, 1933; admitted to bar, 1963, California. *Education:* University of Michigan (B.A., 1955); Boston College Law School (J.D., 1960). *PRACTICE AREAS:* Business Law.

**ROBERT L. BOUCHIER,** born Long Beach, California, January 6, 1946; admitted to bar, 1970, California; 1983, U.S. Tax Court. *Education:* Stanford University (A.B., with distinction, 1967; J.D., 1970). *PRACTICE AREAS:* Real Estate and Business.

All Attorneys are Members of The State Bar of California.

## McCUTCHEN, DOYLE, BROWN & ENERSEN
ONE EMBARCADERO PLACE
2100 GENG ROAD
**PALO ALTO, CALIFORNIA 94303-0913**
Telephone: 415-846-4000
Fax: 415-846-4086
*Email:* postmaster@mdbe.com
*URL:* http://www.mccutchen.com

*San Francisco, California Office:* Three Embarcadero Center, 94111-4066. Telephone: 415-393-2000. Facsimile: 415-393-2286 (G I, II, III) Telex: 340817 MACPAG SFO.

*Los Angeles, California Office:* 355 South Grand Avenue, Suite 4400, 90071-1560. Telephone: 213-680-6400. Facsimile: 213-680-6499.

*San Jose, California Office:* Market Post Tower, Suite 1500, 55 South Market Street, 95113-2327. Telephone: 408-947-8400. Facsimile: 408-947-4750. Telex: 910 250 2931 MACPAG SJ.

*Walnut Creek, California Office:* 1331 North California Boulevard, Post Office Box V, 94596-4502. Telephone: 510-937-8000. Facsimile: 510-975-5390.

*Washington, D.C. Office:* The Evening Star Building, Suite 800, 1101 Pennsylvania Avenue, N.W., 20004-2514. Telephone: 202-628-4900. Facsimile: 202-628-4912.

*Taipei, Taiwan Republic of China Office:* International Trade Building, Tenth Floor, 333 Keelung Road, Section 1, 110. Telephone: 886-2-723-5000. Facsimile: 886-2-757-6070.

*Affiliated Offices In:* Bangkok, Thailand; Beijing, China; Shanghai, China.

*General Practice.*

*FIRM PROFILE: Commercial litigation and business practice, including complex, securities and environmental litigation; environmental and natural resources; healthcare; intellectual property; biotechnology; antitrust and trade regulation; torts; product liability; insurance; maritime; agribusiness; white-collar crime; appellate; corporate; banking; finance; insolvency; real estate and land use; construction; tax and employee benefits; labor and employment; international trade law; estate planning and trusts; alternative dispute resolution.*

### MEMBERS OF FIRM

**CAROL K. DILLON,** born Honolulu, Hawaii, November 11, 1953; admitted to bar, 1982, California. *Education:* Stanford University (B.A., 1975); Boalt Hall School of Law, University of California (J.D., 1982). Managing Editor, California Law Review, 1982. Author: Supplement to "Guide to California Subdivision Sales Law," California Continuing Education of the Bar, 1984; "Damage as a Remedy for Temporary Regulatory Takings of Property: The Impact of First Lutheran," CEB Real Property Law Reporter, August, 1984. *PRACTICE AREAS:* Real Estate Law; Environmental Compliance Law. *Email:* cdillon@mdbe.com

**RONALD S. LAURIE,** born San Francisco, California, June 30, 1942; admitted to bar, 1969, California; registered to practice before U.S. Patent and Trademark Office. *Education:* University of California at Berkeley (B.S.I.E., 1964); University of San Francisco (J.D., 1968). Phi Delta Phi; Alpha Pi Mu. I.C.C.P Certificate in Data Processing, 1972. Co-Author: "Protection of Trade Secrets in Object Form Software: The Case for Reverse Engineering," The Computer Lawyer, July, 1984; "The Copyrightability of Microcode: Is it Hardware or Software or Both?" The Computer Lawyer, March 1985. Author: "The First Year's Experience Under the Chip Protection Act (Where Are the Pirates Now That We Need Them?)" The Computer Lawyer, February, 1986; "NEC v. Intel: Compatibility, Constraints and Choices—A Closer Look at the Scope of Copyright Protection in Microcode," The Computer Lawyer, October, 1986. Co-Author: "Beyond Microcode: Alloy v. Ultratek—The First Attempt to Extend Copyright Protection to Computer Hardware," The Computer Lawyer, April 1989; Co-Author: "A Bridge Over Troubled Waters? Software Patentability and the PTO's Proposed Guidelines," The Computer Lawyer, September/October, 1995. Lecturer, Stanford Law School (Computer Law) 1993. Co-editor: "International Intellectual Property," Prentice Hall Law & Business, 1992. Director, Computer Law Association, 1988—. *Member:* State Bar of California (Member, Executive Committee, Intellectual Property Section, 1990-1993); American and International Bar Associations; International Intellectual Property Law Association (Member, Executive Committee, 1988—); American Intellectual Property Law Association; Institute of Electrical and Electronics Engineers; Association for Computing Machinery. *Email:* rlaurie@mdbe.com

*(This Listing Continued)*

**PROFESSIONAL BIOGRAPHIES**                                                                                           CALIFORNIA—PALO ALTO

**DONALD M. LEVY JR.,** born Rochester, Minnesota, September 9, 1960; admitted to bar, 1987, Pennsylvania; 1988, District of Columbia and U.S. Court of Federal Claims; 1990, U.S. District Court for the District of Columbia; 1992, U.S. Supreme Court; 1995, California. *Education:* University of Wisconsin (B.A., with honors, 1982; M.A., 1984); George Washington University (J.D., with honors, 1987). Managing Editor, George Washington Law Review, 1986-1987. Judicial Clerk, U.S. Court of Federal Claims, Chambers of Judge L. Margolis, 1987-1988. *Member:* District of Columbia Bar; International Bar Association. *PRACTICE AREAS:* Corporate; Intellectual Property. *Email:* dlevy@mdbe.com

**GARY H. MOORE,** born Miami Beach, Florida, July 24, 1943; admitted to bar, 1971, California; 1976, U.S. Supreme Court. *Education:* Yale College (A.B., 1966); Harvard Law School (J.D., magna cum laude, 1969); Cambridge University, England (Dip. in Legal Studies, 1971). Teaching Assistant, University of Giessen, West Germany, 1970. Member, Harvard Law Review, 1968-1969. Co-Author: *Federal Litigation Guide,* Matthew Bender, 1985. Vice President and General Counsel, Next Computer, Inc., 1988-1992. *Member:* American Bar Association; American Intellectual Property Law Association. *PRACTICE AREAS:* Intellectual Property Law; Litigation; Licensing. *Email:* gmoore@mdbe.com

**WILLIAM J. NEWELL,** born Berkeley, California, August 27, 1957; admitted to bar, 1983, California. *Education:* Dartmouth College (A.B., cum laude, 1979); University of Michigan (J.D., 1983). *PRACTICE AREAS:* Corporate Law; Securities Law; Public Utilities Law. *Email:* wnewell@mdbe.com

**LYNN H. PASAHOW,** born Ft. Eustis, Virginia, March 13, 1947; admitted to bar, 1972, California. *Education:* Stanford University (B.A., 1969); University of California at Berkeley (J.D., 1972). Phi Beta Kappa; Order of the Coif. Clerk, Honorable A.J. Zirpoli, 1972-1973. Co-Author: *Civil Discovery and Mandatory Disclosure: A Guide to Efficient Practice,* Prentice Hall, Law & Business, Inc., 1994. Moderator, Lexis Counsel Connect National Patent Forum (1996—). *Member:* American Intellectual Property Law Association; Intellectual Property Owners Association. *PRACTICE AREAS:* Intellectual Property Litigation; Technology Litigation. *Email:* lpasahow@mdbe.com

**ULRICO S. ROSALES,** born Kansas City, Missouri, October 12, 1958; admitted to bar, 1984, Colorado; 1989, California. *Education:* Yale University (B.A., cum laude, 1980; J.D., 1983). Law Clerk to Hon. Zita L. Weinshienk, U.S. District Court, District of Colorado, 1984-1985. (Managing Partner, Palo Alto Office). *LANGUAGES:* Spanish. *PRACTICE AREAS:* Labor; Employment.

### COUNSEL

**SUSAN HERALD,** born Dayton, Ohio, July 6, 1946; admitted to bar, 1981, California; 1984, Texas. *Education:* University of California at Berkeley (B.A., 1971); Boalt Hall School of Law, University of California (J.D., 1981). Order of the Coif. Member: California Law Review, 1979-1981; Member, Ecology Law Quarterly, 1978-1979. Recipient: American Jurisprudence Award. Extern to Judge William W Schwarzer, U.S. District Court, Northern District, California, 1980. *PRACTICE AREAS:* Business; Real Estate Transactions. *Email:* sherald@mdbe.com

**SUSAN K. HOERGER,** born Preston, Idaho, September 21, 1944; admitted to bar, 1978, California. *Education:* University of Wisconsin (B.A., 1967; M.S., 1969); Hastings College of the Law (J.D., 1978). Articles Editor, Hastings Constitutional Law Quarterly (1997-1978). Extern to Justice John T. Racanelli, First District Appellate, California Court of Appeals, (1978). *PRACTICE AREAS:* Labor Law; Employment Law. *Email:* shoerger@mdbe.com

### ASSOCIATES

**RAJESH A. AJI,** born Bombay, India, September 3, 1962; admitted to bar, 1994, California and U.S. District Court, Central District of California. *Education:* Indian Institute of Technology, Bombay, India (B.Tech., 1985); University of Iowa, School of Engineering (M.S., 1987); Boalt Hall School of Law (J.D., 1994). Associate Editor, Ecology Law Quarterly, 1993—. *LANGUAGES:* Hindi, Urdu, Spanish. *PRACTICE AREAS:* Corporate; International Transactions; Licensing; Venture Capital Finance. *Email:* raji@mdbe.com

**MICHAEL D. HARTOGS,** born New York, N.Y., July 28, 1965; admitted to bar, 1992, California and U.S. District Court, Central and Northern Districts of California; registered to practice before U.S. Patent and Trademark Office. *Education:* University of Arizona (B.S., Engineering Physics, 1987); George Washington University (J.D., 1991). *PRACTICE AREAS:* Patent; Intellectual Property. *Email:* mhartogs@mdbe.com

*(This Listing Continued)*

**ANDREW KUMAMOTO,** born Berkeley, California, August 24, 1958; admitted to bar, 1995, California and U.S. Court of Appeals, Ninth Circuit; 1996, U.S. District Court, Southern, Central and Northern Districts of California and U.S. Court of Appeals for the Federal Circuit. *Education:* University of California, Los Angeles (B.S., Biochemistry, 1981; Ph.D., Molecular Biology, 1989); University of Southern California (J.D., 1995). *PRACTICE AREAS:* Biotechnology Patent Law. *Email:* akumamoto@mdbe.com

**ELAN Q.G. NGUYEN,** born Saigon, Vietnam, January 1, 1970; admitted to bar, 1995, California. *Education:* Stanford University (B.A., 1991); University of California at Boalt Hall (J.D., 1995). Articles Editor, Asian Law Journal, 1992-1993. Founder, Asian Community Immigration Clinic. *PRACTICE AREAS:* Corporate; Intellectual Property Transactions; Securities. *Email:* enguyen@mdbe.com

**CARISSA M. SMITH,** born Washington, D.C., March 21, 1963; admitted to bar, 1993, California. *Education:* University of Virginia (B.A., 1986); University of California Hastings (J.D., 1993). *Email:* cmsmith@mdbe.com

**PETER TONG,** born Hong Kong, December 17, 1956; admitted to bar, 1994, California; registered to practice before U.S. Patent and Trademark Office. *Education:* University of Hawaii (B.S.E.E., 1980); California Institute of Technology (M.S.E.E., 1981; Ph.D., 1985); Santa Clara University (M.B.A., 1992; J.D., 1994). Member, Santa Clara University Alumni Board, 1994—. "Les nouvelles," Volume XXIX, No. 1; Hewletlt Packard Journal Volume 43, No. 2; Microwave Journal Volume 31, No. 7; IEEE Transactions on Autennas and Propagation, Volume AP-35, No. 6. *LANGUAGES:* Cantonese, Mandarin. *PRACTICE AREAS:* Intellectual Property. *Email:* ptong@mdbe.com

**DR. JOSEPH YANG,** born Oklahoma City, Oklahoma, February 21, 1965; admitted to bar, 1996, California. *Education:* California Institute of Technology (Ph.D., 1991); Stanford Law School (J.D., 1996). Author: "Patenting Content: The Expanding Role of Patent Protection for Internet-Based Information Products," 17th Annual Computer Law Institute, USC, May 16-17, 1996; Seventh Annual Advanced Computer Law Seminar, University of Dayton School of Law, June 14, 1996. *PRACTICE AREAS:* Patent Law; Technology Licensing; Strategic Counseling. *Email:* jyang@mdbe.com

All Members and Associates are Members of The State Bar of California.

---

## METHVEN & ASSOCIATES
### PALO ALTO, CALIFORNIA
(See Berkeley)

*Computer, Multimedia and Telecommunications Law, Business Advising, Litigation and Arbitration, Copyright, Trademark and Trade Secret Law, Corporate, Partnership and Limited Liability Company Work, Business Leases.*

---

## JOHN E. MILLER
Established in 1987

*250 CAMBRIDGE AVENUE, SUITE 102*
**PALO ALTO, CALIFORNIA 94306-1504**
Telephone: 415-321-8886
Fax: 415-321-8998

*Family Law, Estate Planning and Probate.*

**JOHN E. MILLER,** born Los Angeles, California, December 17, 1939; admitted to bar, 1965, California. *Education:* Stanford University (B.A., 1961; LL.B., 1964). Phi Beta Kappa. Superior Court Judge, Family Court (pro tem), Santa Clara County, 1975—. *Member:* Palo Alto (President, 1975-1976) and Santa Clara County (Trustee, 1975-1976; 1988-1991) Bar Associations; State Bar of California. (Certified Specialist, Family Law, The State Bar of California Board of Legal Specialization). *LANGUAGES:* German. *REPORTED CASES:* In Re Marriage of Cademartori 119 Cal App 3rd 970. *PRACTICE AREAS:* Family Law; Wills and Probate.

### ASSOCIATES

**ANNALISA C WOOD,** born San Francisco, California; admitted to bar, 1987, California. *Education:* Stanford University (A.B., A.M., 1980); Santa Clara University (J.D., 1986). Fulbright Scholarship to teach English in Baden, Austria, 1980-1981. Law Clerk to Honorable William A. Ingram, North Federal District Court, 1987-1989. *LANGUAGES:* French and German. *PRACTICE AREAS:* Family Law.

*(This Listing Continued)*

JOHN E. MILLER, Palo Alto—Continued

**KERRE R. DUBINSKY,** born Lincoln, Nebraska, September 30, 1964; admitted to bar, 1991, California. *Education:* Stamford University (B.A., 1986); Santa Clara University (J.D., cum laude, 1991). *Member:* Santa Clara County Bar Association; State Bar of California,. **PRACTICE AREAS:** Family Law.

REFERENCE: Bank of the West.

## LINCOLN A. MITCHELL
SUITE 300, 550 HAMILTON AVENUE
**PALO ALTO, CALIFORNIA 94301**
Telephone: 415-321-5003
Fax: 415-326-2404

*Family Law. Civil and Trial Practice.*

**LINCOLN A. MITCHELL,** born Minneapolis, Minnesota, August 10, 1936; admitted to bar, 1964, California. *Education:* Dartmouth College (A.B., 1958); Stanford University (J.D., 1962). Phi Delta Phi. President, Family Service Mid-Peninsula, 1985-1987. Chairman, Palo Alto Community Drug Abuse Board, 1974-1975. Trustee, Golden Gate Chapter, American Red Cross, 1979-1980. Recipient, United Way Community Volunteer Award, 1987. *Member:* Palo Alto (President, 1979-1980), Santa Clara County (Trustee, 1974-1977, 1979-1980; Chairman, Client Relations and Professional Ethics Committee, 1975-1977) and American Bar Associations; State Bar of California (Member, Conference of Delegates, 1970-1979). (Certified Specialist, Family Law, The State Bar of California Board of Legal Specialization). **PRACTICE AREAS:** Family Law; Civil Trials.

## MITCHELL & MARKS
A PROFESSIONAL CORPORATION
525 UNIVERSITY AVENUE, SUITE 1425
**PALO ALTO, CALIFORNIA 94301-1903**
Telephone: 415-833-0280
Facsimile: 415-833-0299

General Civil, Trial and Appellate Practice in Federal State and Administrative Courts. Alternative Dispute Resolution including Mediation and Arbitration. Business Law including Forming and Counseling Corporations, Partnerships and Limited Liability Companies. Litigation including Real Property, Construction, Agent and Broker, Disclosure, Employment and Insurance Law.

**MARK T. MITCHELL,** born Stanford, California, August 19, 1963; admitted to bar, 1988, California, U.S. District Court, Northern District of California and U.S. Court of Appeals, Ninth Circuit. *Education:* University of the Pacific (B.A., with honors, 1985); Hastings College of the Law, University of California (J.D., 1988). Editor and Member, Hastings Constitutional Law Quarterly, 1986-1988. *Member:* Palo Alto Area, San Mateo County (Board Member, Lawyer Referral Service Committee, 1993), Santa Clara County and American Bar Associations; State Bar of California. **REPORTED CASES:** General American Life Insurance Co. v. Castonguay (9th Cir. 1993) 984 Fed.2d 1518. **PRACTICE AREAS:** Civil Practice; Appellate Practice; Administrative Courts; Alternative Dispute Resolution; Mediation; Arbitration; Business Law; Construction Law; Corporate Law; Environmental Law; Insurance Law; Personal Injury; Real Property; Technology and Science. *Email:* mtmlaw@aol.com

**E. DAVID MARKS,** born San Francisco, California, July 4, 1962; admitted to bar, 1988, California; U.S. District Court, Northern District of California. *Education:* Stanford University (A.B., with honors, 1984); Hastings College of the Law, University of California (J.D., 1988). Author: "Amending Your Association's Project Documents," ECHO, Vol. 20, #2, February, 1992; "A Primer: Mechanic's Liens, Stop Notices and Payment Bonds," 18 CEB Real Property Law Reporter 173, May, 1995. Member, Conference of Delegates, State Bar Convention, 1993. Chairperson: Conference of Delegates, Palo Alto Area Bar Association, 1994; Community Outreach Program, 1995-1996. *Member:* Palo Alto, Santa Clara County and American Bar Associations; The State Bar of California. **PRACTICE AREAS:** Real Estate; Homeowners Association Law; Construction Law; Labor and Employment; Business Litigation. *Email:* edmlaw@aol.com

*(This Listing Continued)*

**OWEN M. BYRD,** born New York, N.Y., December 30, 1962; admitted to bar, 1991, California; U.S. District Court, Northern District of California; U.S. Court of Appeals, Ninth Circuit. *Education:* Colorado College (B.A., honors, cum laude, 1985); University of Chicago (J.D., 1989). Phi Beta Kappa. Planning Commission, City of Palo Alto. *Member:* Palo Alto and Santa Clara County Bar Associations. **PRACTICE AREAS:** Land Use; Real Estate; Administrative Law; Environmental; Business Counseling.

## ELIZABETH R. MONNET
701 WELCH ROAD, SUITE 3320
**PALO ALTO, CALIFORNIA 94304**
Telephone: 415-833-1885
Fax: 415-833-1888

*Business and Corporate Law, Employment, Copyright, Trademark and International Law.*

**ELIZABETH R. MONNET,** born Weymouth, England, October 1, 1952; admitted to bar, 1974, England and Wales; 1978, California. *Education:* University of Nottingham, Nottingham, England (LL.B., honours, 1973); Inns of Court School of Law, London, England. Co-Author: "Exposing a Foreign Corporations' Worldwide Assets to Tax in California - Pitfalls Created by the California Unitary Tax System," San Francisco Bar Journal June/July 1989. Author of Series, "What Every British Business and Its American Lawyer Needs to Know," British American Chamber of Commerce Newsletter Company Law, August 1993; Employment Law, November 1993. President, Inns of Court Society of California, 1986-1988. *Member:* State Bar of California; San Francisco Lawyer's Club; American Arbitration Association (Member, Commercial Arbitration Panel).

## MORRISON & FOERSTER LLP
Established in 1883
755 PAGE MILL ROAD
**PALO ALTO, CALIFORNIA 94304-1018**
Telephone: 415-813-5600
Facsimile: 415-494-0792
URL: http://www.mofo.com

*Other offices located in:* San Francisco, Los Angeles, New York, Washington, D.C., London, Brussels, Hong Kong, Tokyo, Sacramento, Walnut Creek, Orange County and Denver.

FIRM PROFILE: *Morrison & Foerster is one of the world's largest international law firms with over 500 lawyers in 13 offices worldwide. The firm's legal practice encompasses every major area of commercial law, including corporate finance, project finance, institutional lending, financial services, real estate, environmental and land use planning, mining and natural resources, multimedia, intellectual property, energy, communications, computer technology, insurance, alternative dispute resolution, product liability, bankruptcy and workouts, estate planning, probate, trust administration, financial transactions, labor and employment, immigration, civil, criminal and securities litigation, entertainment and sports, food and beverage, health care, hotel and resort, antitrust, international business, international litigation and arbitration, trade regulation, transportation and tax.*

### MEMBERS OF FIRM

**GREGORY A. BONFIGLIO,** born May 30, 1952; admitted to bar, 1983, District of Columbia; 1984, Massachusetts; 1985, California. *Education:* Michigan State University (B.A., magna cum laude, 1975); University of Michigan Law School (J.D., magna cum laude, 1981). Order of the Coif. Law Clerk to Judge Howard F. Corcoran, U.S. District Court, District of Columbia, 1981-1982. **PRACTICE AREAS:** Labor and Employment; Alternative Dispute Resolution. *Email:* gbonfiglio@mofo.com

**MICHAEL M. CARLSON,** born July 29, 1955; admitted to bar, 1979, California. *Education:* Southern Methodist University (B.A., with highest honors, 1975); University of California, Berkeley, Boalt Hall School of Law (J.D., 1979). Phi Beta Kappa; Order of the Coif. **PRACTICE AREAS:** Intellectual Property Litigation. *Email:* mcarlson@mofo.com

**THOMAS E. CIOTTI,** born March 1, 1940; admitted to bar, 1965, California; registered to practice before U.S. Patent and Trademark Office. *Education:* University of Michigan (B.S.Ch.E., 1961); University of Michigan Law School (J.D., 1964). *Member:* State Bar of California (Chairman, Pa-

*(This Listing Continued)*

tent, Trademark and Copyright Section, 1981-1982); San Francisco Patent and Trademark Law Association (Member, Board of Directors, 1974-1979; President, 1978). **PRACTICE AREAS:** Intellectual Property. **Email:** tciotti@mofo.com

**STANLEY A. DOTEN,** born May 13, 1939; admitted to bar, 1965, California; 1984, Colorado. *Education:* Harvard College (A.B., 1961); Stanford Law School (LL.B., 1964). **Email:** sdoten@mofo.com

**LAURIE S. HANE,** born August 16, 1960; admitted to bar, 1984, California. *Education:* Knox College (B.A., magna cum laude, 1981); Northwestern University School of Law (J.D., 1984). Phi Beta Kappa; Order of the Coif. Law Clerk to Chief Judge Robert F. Peckham, U.S. District Court, Northern District of California, 1984-1985. **PRACTICE AREAS:** Commercial Litigation; Intellectual Property Litigation; Alternative Dispute Resolution. **Email:** lhane@mofo.com

**ALAN COPE JOHNSTON,** born March 4, 1946; admitted to bar, 1975, California; 1979, District of Columbia. *Education:* Yale University (A.B., cum laude, 1968); Harvard Law School (J.D., cum laude, 1975). **PRACTICE AREAS:** Intellectual Property Litigation; Securities Litigation; Alternative Dispute Resolution. **Email:** acjohnston@mofo.com

**KARL J. KRAMER,** born February 10, 1960; admitted to bar, 1987, Wisconsin and Illinois; 1988, California. *Education:* Lawrence University (B.A., cum laude, 1982); University of Wisconsin Law School (J.D., cum laude, 1987). Order of the Coif. **PRACTICE AREAS:** Commercial Litigation; Intellectual Property Litigation. **Email:** kkramer@mofo.com

**DON F. KUMAMOTO,** born December 1, 1955; admitted to bar, 1987, California. *Education:* University of California, Berkeley (B.S., with highest honors, 1976); Massachusetts Institute of Technology (Ph.D., 1981); University of California, Boalt Hall School of Law (J.D., 1987). Attorney, U.S. Department of Justice, Antitrust Division, 1995-1996. **PRACTICE AREAS:** Intellectual Property; General Litigation. **Email:** dkumamoto@mofo.com

**PHILIP J. LEVINE,** born October 19, 1957; admitted to bar, 1982, New Jersey; 1988, New York; 1989, California. *Education:* Johns Hopkins University (B.A., 1979); New York University School of Law (J.D., 1982). *Member:* Bar Association of San Francisco (Chairman, Housing Sub-Section, Real Property Section, 1991—); NACORE (Silicon Valley Chapter, Director and Executive Vice President, 1993—). **PRACTICE AREAS:** Real Estate. **Email:** plevine@mofo.com

**PAUL L. LION, III,** born March 2, 1957; admitted to bar, 1982, California. *Education:* University of California at Davis (B.A., with honors, 1979); Santa Clara University School of Law (J.D., magna cum laude, 1982); New York University (LL.M. in taxation, 1983). Phi Beta Kappa. Author: "California's Limited Liability Company Act Nearing Enactment," Vol. 1, No. 1, Journal of Limited Liability Companies, 1994. Co-Author: "Organization and Operation of the Limited Liability Company," Practicing Law Institute, 1994; "Organizing and Advising Limited Liability Companies," CEB Program Materials, 1994; "Tax Aspects of Limited Liability Companies," Practicing Law Institute, 1994; "Chapter 5, Converting Partnerships and Corporations to Limited Liability Companies," *Limited Liability Companies: Formation, Operation, and Conversion,* Wiley Publications, 1993; "Amendments to the California Revised Limited Partnership Act," Vol. 15, No. 1, Business Law News, State Bar of California, 1993; Organizing and Advising Partnerships and Joint Ventures, CEB Program Materials, 1993; "Partnership Tax Issues," in Partnership and Joint Venture Agreements (Law Journal Seminars Press, 1992). Visiting Lecturer in Law, University of Santa Clara School of Law, Income Tax, Advanced Federal Income Tax, Corporate Tax, and Business Planning, 1986—. Editorial Board, Business Law Today, ABA Publication, 1991—. Board of Advisors, Journal of Limited Liability Companies, Warren, Gorham & Lamont, 1994—. *Member:* Santa Clara County and American (Member, Taxation and Business Law Sections) Bar Associations; State Bar of California (Partnerships Committee Vice-Chair, 1990-1991, Chair, 1991-1992, Business Law Section). **PRACTICE AREAS:** Taxation Law; Estate Planning Law; Partnership Law; Business Law; Health Care Law. **Email:** plion@mofo.com

**JAMES F. MCCABE,** born September 6, 1954; admitted to bar, 1982, California. *Education:* Princeton University (A.B., cum laude, 1977); University of California, Berkeley, Boalt Hall School of Law (J.D., 1982). **PRACTICE AREAS:** Litigation. **Email:** jmccabe@mofo.com

**GLADYS H. MONROY,** born August 29, 1937; admitted to bar, 1986, California; registered to practice before U.S. Patent and Trademark Office. *Education:* Hunter College (A.B., Chemistry, 1957); New York University (M.S., Biology, 1968; Ph.D., Biochemistry, 1973); University of San Fran-

*(This Listing Continued)*

cisco School of Law (J.D., 1986). Member, Board of Governors, University of San Francisco Law Society. *Member:* San Francisco Patent and Trademark Law Association (Former Chair, Patent Committee); Peninsula Intellectual Property Law Association (Vice President, former Secretary, former Treasurer); American Intellectual Property Law Association (Co-Chair, Strategic Alliances Subcommittee). **PRACTICE AREAS:** Intellectual Property. **Email:** gmonroy@mofo.com

**MICHAEL C. PHILLIPS,** born September 11, 1950; admitted to bar, 1976, California; 1979, U.S. Tax Court. *Education:* Stanford University (B.A., 1972); University of California, Berkeley, Boalt Hall School of Law (J.D., 1976). **PRACTICE AREAS:** Corporate Finance; Multimedia. **Email:** mphillips@mofo.com

**STEPHEN J. SCHRADER,** born July 26, 1956; admitted to bar, 1982, California. *Education:* Northwestern University (B.A., 1978); Stanford Law School (J.D., 1982). Phi Beta Kappa. **PRACTICE AREAS:** Corporate Finance; Intellectual Property. **Email:** sschrader@mofo.com

**WILLIAM D. SHERMAN,** born November 11, 1942; admitted to bar, 1972, California. *Education:* Princeton University (B.A., 1964); University of California at Berkeley (M.B.A., 1972); University of California, Berkeley, Boalt Hall School of Law (J.D., 1972). Co-Author: Chapter 5, "State Securities Law Considerations of Raising Capital," Start-Up Companies-Planning, Financing and Operating the Successful Business, Law Journal Seminars-Press, New York, 1985. Lecturer, Graduate School of Business, University of California, Berkeley, 1976—. Member, National Advisory Board, The SEC Institute. **PRACTICE AREAS:** Business; Corporate Finance; Securities. **Email:** wsherman@mofo.com

**DEBRA A. SHETKA,** born July 29, 1958; admitted to bar, 1989, California; registered to practice before U.S. Patent and Trademark Office. *Education:* Macalester College (B.A., cum laude, with honors, 1980); University of Minnesota Law School (J.D., cum laude, 1987). Editor-in-Chief, Journal of Law and Inequality, 1986-1987. **PRACTICE AREAS:** Business; Patent. **Email:** dshetka@mofo.com

**STEPHEN M. TENNIS,** born May 27, 1942; admitted to bar, 1967, California. *Education:* Stanford University (A.B., with great distinction, 1965); Stanford Law School (LL.B., 1967). Order of the Coif. Law Clerk to: Judge Ben. C. Duniway, Ninth Circuit Court of Appeals, 1967-1968; Justice Thurgood Marshall, U.S. Supreme Court, 1968-1969. **PRACTICE AREAS:** Securities; Corporate Finance. **Email:** stennis@mofo.com

**RAYMOND L. WHEELER,** born February 10, 1945; admitted to bar, 1972, California. *Education:* University of Texas (B.A., 1967); Harvard Law School (J.D., magna cum laude, 1970). Phi Beta Kappa. Law Clerk, Judge Irving L. Goldberg, U.S. Court of Appeals, Fifth Circuit, 1970-1971. Member, National Advisory Board to Industrial Relations Law Journal, 1977—. Management Co-Chairman, Committee on Development of Law Under National Labor Relations Act, 1990-1993, and Council Member, 1995—, Section of Labor and Employment Law, American Bar Association. **PRACTICE AREAS:** Labor and Employment. **Email:** rwheeler@mofo.com

**PETER E. WILLIAMS III,** born September 10, 1961; admitted to bar, 1987, California. *Education:* University of California at Los Angeles (B.A., 1984); Santa Clara University School of Law (J.D., cum laude, 1987). **PRACTICE AREAS:** Corporate Finance; Intellectual Property. **Email:** pwilliams@mofo.com

**BRYAN J. WILSON,** born January 24, 1961; admitted to bar, 1988, California. *Education:* University of California at Berkeley (B.S., 1983); Stanford University Law School (J.D., 1988). **Email:** bwilson@mofo.com

**DAVID C. WILSON,** born March 10, 1954; admitted to bar, 1980, California. *Education:* University of California at Berkeley (B.A., Computer Sciences, 1976); Hastings College of the Law, University of California (J.D., 1979). Phi Beta Kappa. Editor-in-Chief, Hastings Constitutional Law Quarterly. With Office of the General Counsel, 1979-1981 and Counsel to Commissioner Bevis Longstreth, 1981-1983, Securities and Exchange Commission, Washington, D.C. **PRACTICE AREAS:** Corporate; Securities; Intellectual Property. **Email:** dcwilson@mofo.com

**THOMAS EARL WILSON,** born May 9, 1950; admitted to bar, 1976, California. *Education:* Stanford University (B.A., 1972); University of California, Davis (M.A., 1976); Stanford Law School (J.D., 1976). Phi Beta Kappa. Law Clerk to Hon. Edward J. Schwartz, Chief Judge, U.S. District Court, Southern District of California, 1976-1977. **PRACTICE AREAS:** Labor and Employment. **Email:** twilson@mofo.com

*(This Listing Continued)*

## MORRISON & FOERSTER LLP, Palo Alto—Continued

### OF COUNSEL

**DONALD CHISUM,** born May 5, 1944; admitted to bar, 1970, California; 1973, Washington. *Education:* Stanford University (A.B., 1966); Stanford Law School (LL.B., 1968). Phi Beta Kappa; Order of the Coif. Editor, Stanford Law Review, 1966-1967. Law Clerk to Judge Shirley M. Hufstedler, U.S. Court of Appeals, Ninth Circuit, 1968-1969. Author: Chisum, "Patents: A Treatise on the Law of Patentability, Validity and Infringement," 9 Vol., Matthew Bender, 1978—; Chisum and Jacobs, "Understanding Intellectual Property," 1992; Chisum," Intellectual Property," Matthew Bender Casebook, 1980; Chisum & Waldbaum," Acquiring and Protecting Intellectual Property Rights," Matthew Bender, Business Law Monograph, 1985—; Chisum, "1996 Patent Law Digest," Matthew Bender. Professor of Law at: University of Washington, 1974-1996; University of Santa Clara, 1997—. Director of Center for Advanced Study and Research on Intellectual Property, 1987-1996. Advisory Editorial Board to the Court of Appeals for the Federal Circuit Newsletter, 1986-1992. Chairman, Association of American Law Schools, Intellectual Property Law Section, 1987-1988. Recipient of the Jefferson Medal Award presented by the New Jersey Patent Law Association, May 12, 1989. *PRACTICE AREAS:* Patents; Intellectual Property. *Email:* dchisum@msn.com

**SUZANNE S. GRAESER,** born June 2, 1961; admitted to bar, 1987, California. *Education:* Claremont McKenna College (B.A., 1983); University of California, Davis School of Law (J.D., 1987). Member, University of California, Davis Law Review, 1986-1987. Director, Volunteer Income Tax Assistance (VITA) Program, 1986-1987. *PRACTICE AREAS:* Corporate Law; Business Law. *Email:* sgraeser@mofo.com

**JANET STONE HERMAN,** born March 19, 1959; admitted to bar, 1984, California. *Education:* University of California, Berkeley (B.S., 1981); University of California, Davis School of Law (J.D., 1984). Phi Beta Kappa. Managing Editor, U.C. Davis Law Review, 1983-1984. Co-Author: "Financing Methods for Small Businesses," California Closely Held Corporations, Vol. 1, Chapter 8, Matthew Bender & Company, 1991. Extern to Honorable Zerne P. Haning, III, Court of Appeals, First Appellate District, Summer 1983. *PRACTICE AREAS:* Corporate Law; Securities Law; Business Law. *Email:* jsherman@mofo.com

**ANTOINETTE F. KONSKI,** born August 10, 1960; admitted to bar, 1989, New York; 1993, California; registered to practice before U.S. Patent and Trademark Office. *Education:* University of Delaware (B.S., 1982); Fordham University School of Law (J.D., 1988). Author: "The Utility Rejection in Biotechnology & Pharmaceutical Prosecution Practice," JPTOS, 76 (11): 821-831, 1994. *PRACTICE AREAS:* Intellectual Property; Patent Prosecution. *Email:* akonski@mofo.com

**HARRY J. MACEY,** born September 15, 1952; admitted to bar, 1988, Pennsylvania; 1989, District of Columbia; 1992, California; registered to practice before the U.S. Patent and Trademark Office. *Education:* Tulane University (B.A., 1974); New Jersey Institute of Technology (B.S.M.E., summa cum laude, 1982); American University, Washington College of Law (J.D., 1988). *Email:* hmacey@mofo.com

**WILLIAM L. MYERS,** born March 30, 1958; admitted to bar, 1984, California. *Education:* University of Santa Clara (B.S.C., 1980); University of California, Hastings College of the Law (J.D., 1984). *Member:* Santa Clara County (Member, Real Property and Environmental Law Sections) and American (Member, Real Property Section) Bar Associations. *PRACTICE AREAS:* Real Estate Law; Environmental Law. *Email:* wmyers@mofo.com

**E. THOMAS WHEELOCK,** born April 9, 1947; admitted to bar, 1973, Texas; 1980, District of Columbia; registered to practice before U.S. Patent and Trademark Office (Not admitted in California). *Education:* University of Texas (B.S., 1970); University of Houston Law Center (J.D., 1973); George Washington University (LL.M., 1980). Technical Advisor, U.S. Court of Customs and Patent Appeals, Judge Phillip Baldwin, 1978-1980. *PRACTICE AREAS:* Intellectual Property. *Email:* ewheelock@mofo.com

### ASSOCIATES

**MANI ADELI,** born October 10, 1968; admitted to bar, 1995, California; registered to practice before U.S. Patent and Trademark Office. *Education:* University of California, Los Angeles (B.S., Electrical Engineering, magna cum laude, 1991); University of California, Los Angeles School of Law (J.D., 1994). Tau Beta Pi; Eta Kappa Nu. *Email:* madeli@mofo.com

**CORI M. ALLEN,** born April 27, 1965; admitted to bar, 1993, Massachusetts; 1994, California. *Education:* Princeton University (A.B., 1988); Cornell Law School (J.D., magna cum laude, 1992). Order of the Coif. Fulbright Scholar, 1992-1993. *Email:* cmallen@mofo.com

**LAURIE A. AXFORD,** born October 4, 1957; admitted to bar, 1992, California; registered to practice before U.S. Patent and Trademark Office. *Education:* San Diego State University (B.S., 1979; M.S., 1983); Western State University (J.D., 1992). Adjunct Faculty, Western State University, 1995. Director, San Diego Nucleic Acid Conference, 1992-1993. *Member:* San Diego Intellectual Property Law Association (President, 1996-1997); American Association for Clinical Chemistry. *Email:* laxford@mofo.com

**JUSTIN LEE BASTIAN,** born May 16, 1960; admitted to bar, 1992, California. *Education:* Brigham Young University (B.A., 1984; M.B.A., 1991); Brigham Young University, J. Reuben Clark Law School (J.D., magna cum laude, 1991). Managing Editor, International and Comparative Law Journal, 1990-1991. *LANGUAGES:* Mandarin. *Email:* jbastian@mofo.com

**HANS J. BRASSELER,** born May 22, 1966; admitted to bar, 1992, Belgium (Not admitted in the United States). *Education:* Catholic University of Louvain School of Law, Leuven, Belgium (Cand. Jur., 1987; Lic. Jur., magna cum laude, 1990); Duke University School of Law (LL.M., 1992). *LANGUAGES:* Dutch, German and French. *Email:* hbrasseler@mofo.com

**ALAN W. CANNON,** born September 11, 1956; admitted to bar, 1990, Virginia; registered to practice before U.S. Patent and Trademark Office (Not admitted in California). *Education:* McMurry College (B.S., 1980); Rensselaer Polytechnic Institute (M.S., Biomedical Engineering, 1984); George Mason University School of Law (J.D., 1990). Patent Examiner, 1984-1991. *Email:* acannon@mofo.com

**C. JEFFREY CHAR,** born October 16, 1963; admitted to bar, 1993, California. *Education:* Sophia University, Tokyo, Japan (B.S., cum laude, 1987); University of California, Berkeley, Boalt Hall School of Law (J.D., 1992). President, U.S.-Japan Legal Studies Institute, 1990-1991. *LANGUAGES:* Japanese. *Email:* jchar@mofo.com

**CHRISTOPHER S. DEWEES,** born January 2, 1964; admitted to bar, 1989, Arizona; 1990, California; 1995, District of Columbia. *Education:* Dartmouth College (A.B., 1986); Northwestern University School of Law (J.D., cum laude, 1989). Order of the Coif. *Email:* cdewees@mofo.com

**TYLER DYLAN,** born October 27, 1961; admitted to bar, 1992, California; registered to practice before U.S. Patent and Trademark Office. *Education:* McGill University (B.S., 1982); University of California, San Diego, Center for Molecular Genetics (Ph.D., 1989); University of California, Berkeley, Boalt Hall School of Law (J.D., 1992). California Biotechnology Research Development Fellow and National Institutes of Health Fellow. Visiting Researcher and Advisor, Indian Biotechnology Centre, New Delhi, India. Member, 1989-1991, and Associate Editor, 1990-1991, High Technology Law Journal, University of California, Berkeley. Special Advisor, Intellectual Property Law Reform Project, Jakarta, Indonesia, 1994-1995. *Member:* American Association for the Advancement of Science; American Chemical Society; American Intellectual Property Law Association; Peninsula Intellectual Property Law Association; San Francisco Patent and Trademark Law Association. *Email:* tdylan@mofo.com

**KEVIN A. FAULKNER,** born February 25, 1961; admitted to bar, 1986, Colorado; 1989, California. *Education:* Fort Hays State University (B.A., summa cum laude, 1983); University of Virginia School of Law (J.D., 1986). *Email:* kfaulkner@mofo.com

**HEIKE FISCHER,** born March 29, 1965; admitted to bar, 1994, Germany; 1996, California. *Education:* Albert-Ludwigs University, Freiburg (Referendarin, 1991); State of Baden-Wuerttemberg (Assessorin, 1994); University of California, Berkeley, Boalt Hall School of Law (LL.M., 1995). *LANGUAGES:* German. *Email:* hfischer@mofo.com

**CHRISTINE FITZPATRICK,** born November 30, 1963; admitted to bar, 1988, California. *Education:* University of Santa Clara (B.S., 1985); University of California, Hastings College of the Law (J.D., 1988). *Email:* cxfl@mofo.com

**STEPHAN GOECKELER,** born August 10, 1965; admitted to bar, 1993, Germany; 1996, California. *Education:* Staedtisches Gymnasium (Abitur., 1984); University of Heidelberg (First State Exam, 1990; Dr. Iur., 1990). *LANGUAGES:* German. *Email:* sgoeckeler@mofo.com

**JANA G. GOLD,** born June 16, 1960; admitted to bar, 1991, California. *Education:* University of California, Santa Cruz (B.A., with honors, 1984); University of California, Berkeley (M.A., 1988); University of California, Berkeley, Boalt Hall School of Law (J.D., 1991). Extern to Judge Robert F.

*(This Listing Continued)*

Peckham, U.S. District Court, Northern District of California, 1990. *Email:* jgold@mofo.com

**SU W. HWANG,** born December 23, 1966; admitted to bar, 1994, California. *Education:* Wesleyan University (B.A., 1988); Stanford Law School (J.D., 1994). Law Clerk to the Honorable Ronald M. Whyte, U.S. District Court, Northern District of California, 1994-1995. *Email:* shwang@mofo.com

**SHERMAN W. KAHN,** born July 1, 1963; admitted to bar, 1993, California. *Education:* University of California, Berkeley (B.A., highest honors, 1989); University of California, Berkeley, Boalt Hall School of Law (J.D., 1993). Law Clerk to Honorable Mariana R. Pfaelzer, U.S. District Court, Central District of California, 1993-1994. *Email:* skahn@mofo.com

**KENNETH A. KUWAYTI,** born December 16, 1964; admitted to bar, 1990, California; 1995, Ontario. *Education:* McGill University (B.A., highest honors, 1985); Stanford Law School (J.D., with distinction, 1989). Law Clerk, Justice G. V. La Forest, Supreme Court of Canada, 1990-1991. *Email:* kkuwayti@mofo.com

**SUSAN K. LEHNHARDT,** born January 8, 1959; admitted to bar, 1993, California and New York. *Education:* University of Delaware (B.A., 1981); State University of New York at Stony Brook (Ph.D., 1987); Fordham University School of Law (J.D., 1992). *Email:* slehnhardt@mofo.com

**JOSEPH T. LIN,** born April 6, 1965; admitted to bar, 1993, California; registered to practice before U.S. Patent and Trademark Office. *Education:* Cornell University (B.S., Electrical Engineering and Materials Science, with distinction, 1987); University of California, Los Angeles School of Law (J.D., 1993). *Email:* jlin@mofo.com

**CYNTHIA L. LOPEZ,** born March 4, 1969; admitted to bar, 1995, California. *Education:* Harvard-Radcliffe (B.A., cum laude, 1991); Harvard Law School (J.D., cum laude, 1995). *LANGUAGES:* Chinese and French. *Email:* cllopez@mofo.com

**JAMES M. MEENAGHAN,** born February 11, 1968; admitted to bar, 1993, California. *Education:* Boston University (B.A., cum laude, 1990); Georgetown University Law Center (J.D., 1993). *LANGUAGES:* Spanish. *Email:* jmeenaghan@mofo.com

**FREDDIE K. PARK,** born December 8, 1947; admitted to bar, 1990, Virginia; 1991, District of Columbia; 1993, California; registered to practice before the U.S. Patent and Trademark Office. *Education:* Texas Tech University (B.S., 1971); George Mason University School of Law (J.D., 1990). *LANGUAGES:* French. *Email:* fpark@mofo.com

**VALERIE R. PARK,** born July 31, 1962; admitted to bar, 1991, California. *Education:* University of California, Berkeley (A.B., with honors, 1985); Stanford Law School (J.D., 1991). *Email:* vpark@mofo.com

**DAHNA S. PASTERNAK,** born January 10, 1966; admitted to bar, 1995, California. *Education:* Stanford University (B.A.S., Biological Sciences and History, 1988); University of California, San Diego (M.S., Neuroscience, 1991); University of California, Berkeley, Boalt Hall School of Law (J.D., 1995). *Email:* dpastern@mofo.com

**JAMES C. PEACOCK III,** born March 4, 1966; (admission pending). registered to practice before U.S. Patent and Trademark Office. *Education:* University of Southern California (B.S., Biomedical Engineering, 1987); Santa Clara University School of Law (J.D., 1996). *Email:* jpeacock@mofo.com

**MARC J. PERNICK,** born November 10, 1967; admitted to bar, 1992, California. *Education:* Cooper Union (B.S.E., 1989); New York University School of Law (J.D., 1992). *Email:* mpernick@mofo.com

**SANDRA D. PETERSON,** born April 12, 1948; admitted to bar, 1992, California. *Education:* Stanford University (B.A., summa cum laude, 1970; M.A., 1974); Stanford Law School (J.D., 1992). Phi Beta Kappa. *Email:* speterson@mofo.com

**CATHERINE M. POLIZZI,** born August 20, 1954; admitted to bar, 1994, California; registered to practice before U.S. Patent and Trademark Office. *Education:* University of Mississippi (B.A., Chemistry, with distinction, 1976); University of California, Santa Barbara (M.A., Chemistry, 1978; Ph.D., Molecular Biology/Biochemistry, 1990); Stanford Law School (J.D., 1994). *PRACTICE AREAS:* Intellectual Property. *Email:* cpolizzi@mofo.com

**AKI Y. SHOJI,** born April 26, 1966; admitted to bar, 1994, California. *Education:* Sophia University (B.A., 1989); Stanford Law School (J.D., 1994). Senior Notes Editor, Stanford Journal of International Law. *LANGUAGES:* Japanese. *Email:* ashoji@mofo.com

*(This Listing Continued)*

**ERIC A. TATE,** born December 16, 1969; admitted to bar, 1995, California. *Education:* University of California, Berkeley (B.A., 1992); University of California, Berkeley, Boalt Hall School of Law (J.D., 1995). *Email:* etate@mofo.com

**ROBERT D. THOMAS,** born June 5, 1962; admitted to bar, 1993, California. *Education:* University of California, Los Angeles (B.A.; 1984); University of California Hastings College of the Law (J.D., magna cum laude, 1993). Order of the Coif. Thurston Society. Extern to Honorable Armand Arabian, California Supreme Court, Fall 1992. [Submarine Officer, U.S. Navy, 1986-1989] *Email:* rthomas@mofo.com

**CYNTHIA S. WEEKS,** born Alameda, California, 1963; admitted to bar, 1989, California. *Education:* University of California at Santa Barbara (B.A., 1985); Santa Clara University School of Law (J.D., 1989). Managing Editor, The Advocate, 1988-89. *Email:* cweeks@mofo.com

**GEOFFREY A. WEXLER,** born September 5, 1964; admitted to bar, 1993, California. *Education:* Stanford University (B.A., 1986); Columbia University School of Law (J.D., 1993). Production Editor, Columbia Journal of Law and Social Problems, 1992-1993. *Email:* gwexler@mofo.com

**ANNA ERICKSON WHITE,** born August 10, 1963; admitted to bar, 1992, California. *Education:* University of California, Berkeley (B.A., 1985); Stanford Law School (J.D., with distinction, 1992). *Email:* awhite@mofo.com

**MIRIAM WUGMEISTER,** born January 31, 1967; admitted to bar, 1992, Connecticut; 1993, New York; 1995, California. *Education:* Brandeis University (B.A., 1986); Boston University School of Law (J.D., magna cum laude, 1992). *Email:* mwugmeister@mofo.com

*LEGAL SUPPORT PERSONNEL*

**PAULA A. BORDEN,** born October 30, 1957. *Education:* University of Illinois (B.S., 1979); Columbia University (Ph.D., 1987). Alexander von Humboldt Fellowship, 1987-1989. (Legal Analyst). *LANGUAGES:* German.

**FRANK WU,** born Philadelphia, Pennsylvania, October 29, 1964. *Education:* University of Rochester (B.A., English, 1985); University of Wisconsin at Madison (M.S. in Bacteriology, 1991; Ph.D. in Bacteriology, 1995). Gamma Sigma Delta. (Legal Analyst).

**WILHELMUS J. WYTENBURG,** born September 19, 1964. *Education:* Queen's University (B.S., Chemistry, with honors, 1987); University of Cambridge, England (Ph.D., 1991). IBM Postdoctoral Fellowship, Stanford University, 1991-1992. Recipient: Commonwealth Scholarship, 1989-1991; Prince of Wales Prize, 1987; Society of Chemical Industry Merit Award, 1987; Chemical Institute of Canada Prize, 1986; Aldrich Chemical Company Scholarship, 1986; Cyanamid Canada Inc. Scholarship, 1986. *Member:* American Chemical Society. (Legal Analyst). *PRACTICE AREAS:* Patent; Intellectual Property; Chemistry. *Email:* wwytenburg@mofo.com

*PATENT AGENTS*

**DAVID L. BRADFUTE,** born October 16, 1964; registered to practice before U.S. Patent and Trademark Office. *Education:* Swarthmore College (B.A., 1987); Stanford University (M.S., 1992; Ph.D., 1994). Sigma Xi; Genetech Foundation ARCS Scholarship; Merck, Sharp and Dohme Graduate Research Fellowship. National Science Foundation Fellowship Honorable Mention, 1987. *PRACTICE AREAS:* Biotechnology; Patent; Intellectual Property. *Email:* bradfute@mofo.com

**SEAN M. BRENNAN,** born January 29, 1954; registered to practice before U.S. Patent and Trademark Office. *Education:* University of Delaware (B.A., high honors and degree with distinction, 1976); University of California, San Diego (Ph.D., 1982). Recipient: NIH predoctoral Fellowship; E.C. Anthony Fellowship; USPHS National Research Service Award; British Cancer Research Campaign Fellowship. Listed in: Who's Who in Science and Engineering; Who's Who in Medicine and Health Care. *Member:* American Association for the Advancement of Science; Association of Science and Patent Professionals; Peninsula Intellectual Property Law Association. (Patent Agent/Legal Analyst). *PRACTICE AREAS:* Patent; Intellectual Property; Biotechnology; Litigation Support. *Email:* sbrennan@mofo.com

**ROBERT K. CERPA,** born August 22, 1962; registered to practice before U.S. Patent and Trademark Office. *Education:* Harvard University (A.B., 1984); University of California (Ph.D., 1995). *Member:* American Association for the Advancement of Science. (Legal Analyst/Patent Agent). *LANGUAGES:* Spanish. *Email:* rcerpa@mofo.com

*(This Listing Continued)*

## MORRISON & FOERSTER LLP, Palo Alto—Continued

**PAUL F. SCHENCK,** born September 4, 1931; registered to practice before U.S. Patent and Trademark Office. *Education:* Technical University, Braunschweig (Diplom-Engineer, 1957). **LANGUAGES:** German. **PRACTICE AREAS:** Patent Applications (Electrical/Mechanical). **Email:** pschenck@mofo.com

**J. MICHAEL SCHIFF,** registered to practice before U.S. Patent and Trademark Office. *Education:* University of Toronto (M.B.A., 1994). Recipient: Hardi Cinader Graduate Student Prize, 1986, Department of Immunology, University of Toronto, 1986; Ontario Ministry of Health Scientist Development Award, 1986-1988. Assistant Editor, University of Toronto Faculty of Law Review, 1993-1994. **PRACTICE AREAS:** Biotechnology Patent Prosecution and Litigation; Portfolio Planning; Technology Transfer. **Email:** jmschiff@mofo.com

**LEE K. TAN,** born Penang, Malaysia, September 15, 1959; registered to practice before U.S. Patent and Trademark Office. *Education:* Wellesley College (B.A., magna cum laude, 1981); Columbia University (Ph.D., 1988); Post Doctoral Fellow, University of California, San Francisco (1988-1993). Sigma Xi. *Member:* American Association for the Advancement of Science. (Patent Agent). **LANGUAGES:** French and Malaysian.

(For biographical data on San Francisco, Los Angeles, Sacramento, Walnut Creek and Irvine, CA, New York, NY, Washington, DC, Denver, CO, London, England, Brussels, Belgium, Hong Kong and Tokyo, Japan see professional biographies at each of those cities.)

---

## MURRAY AND MURRAY
### A PROFESSIONAL CORPORATION
Established in 1975

SUITE 200, 3030 HANSEN WAY
**PALO ALTO, CALIFORNIA 94304**
Telephone: 415-852-9000
Telecopier: 415-852-9244

Insolvency, Bankruptcy, Business Reorganization, Creditors Rights, Secured Transactions and Commercial Law. Trial Practice.

**FIRM PROFILE:** *Murray & Murray is a professional law corporation specializing in Business Reorganization, Insolvency and Bankruptcy Law. The Firm was founded in 1975 in recognition of a growing need for such legal expertise in the greater Silicon Valley businesses community in the restructuring of their financial affairs both apart from and within Chapter 11 proceedings. The Firm also maintains a creditor practice, with a full litigation capacity, representing financial institutions, landlords, creditor committees and other clients in bankruptcy and commercial law matters. Since its founding, Murray & Murray has grown to become one of the largest independent law firms of its kind in the region. The Firm's members are predominantly long-time residents of the San Francisco Bay Area. With roots in the area and strong ties to the community, Murray & Murray is uniquely positioned to respond to its clients' needs.*

**DAVID S. MURRAY,** born San Francisco, California, January 8, 1943; admitted to bar, 1970, California. *Education:* University of Santa Clara (B.S.C., 1964); University of Santa Clara School of Law (J.D., 1969). Phi Alpha Delta. Comments Editor, Santa Clara Lawyer, 1968-1969. Author: "The Employer as the Agent of the Insurer in the Administration of the Group Insurance Plan," 8 Santa Clara Lawyer 242, 1968. Lecturer on Bankruptcy: Stanford University, 1988-1990; Santa Clara University, 1990; California Continuing Education of the Bar, 1994; Professional Law Courses, 1979; Santa Clara County Bar Association, 1979. Editorial Consultant, *The Bankruptcy System,* Mathew Bender, Publisher, 1983-1985. Judge Pro Tem, Santa Clara County Municipal Court, 1982-1985. National Chairman, Santa Clara University President's Club, 1984-1987. *Member:* Santa Clara University Board of Fellows (Secretary-Treasurer, 1991); Santa Clara University Law School Board of Visitors and Alumni Board (Treasurer, 1994). *Member:* Bar Association of San Francisco (Chairman, Commercial and Bankruptcy Law Section, 1975); Santa Clara County and American (Member: Business Bankruptcy Committee; Chapter 11 Subcommittee; Plan Process Task Force) Bar Associations; State Bar of California (Vice-Chairman, California State Bar Committee on Debtor and Creditor Relations, 1974-1975); Bay Area Bankruptcy Forum. **PRACTICE AREAS:** Business Workouts; Bankruptcy Reorganizations; Creditors Remedies.

**JOHN WALSHE MURRAY,** born San Francisco, California, September 6, 1952; admitted to bar, 1977, California. *Education:* University of California at Berkeley (B.A., 1974); Golden Gate University School of Law

*(This Listing Continued)*

(J.D., 1977). Editorial Consultant, *The Bankruptcy System,* Matthew Bender, Publisher, 1983-1984. Author: "Major Changes In Rules of Bankruptcy Procedure," 20 In Brief, Winter, 1983. Lecturer on Bankruptcy: California Continuing Education of the Bar, 1985-1995; Santa Clara County Bar Association, 1983-1995; The Association of Insolvency Accountants, 1996; Santa Clara University School of Law, 1996. Member, 1988-1991, and Chair, 1988, Committee of Lawyer Representatives for the United States Bankruptcy Court for the Northern District of California. Resolution Advocate, Bankruptcy Dispute Resolution Program for the United States Bankruptcy Court for the Northern District of California, 1994-1996. *Member:* Bar Association of San Francisco (Member, Commercial Law and Bankruptcy Section); Santa Clara County (Member, Executive Committee, Commercial Law and Bankruptcy Section, 1979-1996; Chairman, 1980-1981), San Mateo County and American (Member: Section of Corporation, Banking and Business Law; Business Bankruptcy Committee; Subcommittee on Chapter 11; General Practice Section, Bankruptcy Committee, 1984-1996) Bar Associations; State Bar of California (Member, Business Law Section); American Bankruptcy Institute, 1985-1995; Bay Area Bankruptcy Forum (Director, 1991-1994); National Association of Bankruptcy Trustees (1992-1996); Peninsula CPA-Bar Alliance (Chair, Bankruptcy Section, 1992-1996). **REPORTED CASES:** In re Swenor (N.D. Cal. 1978) 452 F.Supp. 673; In re Huang, (9th Cir. B.A.P. 1982) 23 B.R. 798. **PRACTICE AREAS:** Business Workouts; Bankruptcy Reorganizations; Creditors Remedies.

**CRAIG M. PRIM,** born Washington, D.C., December 24, 1952; admitted to bar, 1977, California. *Education:* University of Santa Clara (B.S., magna cum laude, 1974); University of California at Berkeley (J.D., 1977). Author: "Confirmation Of Plan Upon Acceptance By Creditors in Counseling Creditors of Distressed Business Before and During Bankruptcy: California Continuing Education of the Bar," 1988. Lecturer on Bankruptcy: California Continuing Education of the Bar; Bay Area Bankruptcy Forum, Association of Insolvency Accountants, Santa Clara County Bar Association. Resolution Advocate, Bankruptcy Dispute Resolution Program for the United States Bankruptcy Court for the Northern District of California, 1994-1995. *Member:* Bar Association of San Francisco (Member, Commercial Law and Bankruptcy Section); Santa Clara County Bar Association (Member, Commercial Law and Bankruptcy Section); The State Bar of California; Bay Area Bankruptcy Forum (Director, 1994-1997). **PRACTICE AREAS:** Business Workouts; Bankruptcy Reorganizations; Creditors Remedies.

**JANICE M. MURRAY,** born San Francisco, California, July 20, 1949; admitted to bar, 1981, California. *Education:* University of California at Berkeley (B.S., 1978); University of San Francisco School of Law (J.D., 1981). Lecturer on Bankruptcy: California State Bar, Bay Area Bankruptcy Forum, Santa Clara County Bar Association and Peninsula CPA/Bar Alliance. *Member:* Bar Association of San Francisco (Member, Commercial Law and Bankruptcy Section); Santa Clara County Bar Association (Member: Commercial Law and Bankruptcy Section; Women Lawyers Committee, Executive Board); State Bar of California (Member, Business Law Section); Palo Alto Area Bar Association (Chair, Women Lawyers Committee); Bay Area Bankruptcy Forum; Peninsula CPA/Bar Alliance; California Women Lawyers. **PRACTICE AREAS:** Business Workouts; Bankruptcy Reorganizations; Creditors Remedies.

**KENNETH T. LAW,** born Cleveland, Ohio, March 8, 1953; admitted to bar, 1983, California. *Education:* University of Santa Clara (B.S., cum laude, 1975; J.D., 1981). Member, Honors Moot Court Board, 1980-1981. Lecturer: Bankruptcy Litigation, Santa Clara County Bar Association, 1990-1996; Reclamation Litigation, Santa Clara County Bar Association, 1992; Bankruptcy Issues in Environmental Litigation, Santa Clara County Bar Association, 1994; Asset Protection Planning, California Continuing Education of the Bar, 1996; Fraudulent Conveyances, Santa Clara County Bar Association, 1996. Author: "Dischargeability of Environmental Liability in Bankruptcy," California Real Property Journal (Summer, 1996). *Member:* Santa Clara County Bar Association (Member, Executive Board of Bench/Bar Superior Court Liaison Committee, 1994-1996; Executive Committee, 1993-1996; Chairman, 1994-1996. Business Litigation Section; Member, Commercial Law and Bankruptcy Section); The State Bar of California; Bay Area Bankruptcy Forum. **PRACTICE AREAS:** Bankruptcy Litigation; Commercial Litigation; Creditors Remedies.

**PATRICK M. COSTELLO,** born New York, New York, January 11, 1958; admitted to bar, 1985, California and District of Columbia. *Education:* University of Chicago (B.A., 1980); University of California, Hastings College of the Law (J.D., 1984). Co-Author: "Technology Licensing: Protecting Licenses Against the Risk of the Licensors Insolvency," California Business Law Practitioner (Spring, 1988); "New Bankruptcy Code ¶365 (n):

*(This Listing Continued)*

Limited Comfort for the Technology Licensee," California Business Law Reporter (January, 1989); "Intellectual Property Licenses after Enactment of Special Legislation: Limited Security," Business Law News (Winter, 1989). *Member:* San Francisco, Santa Clara County and American Bar Associations. *PRACTICE AREAS:* Business Workouts; Bankruptcy Reorganizations; Creditors Remedies.

---

**STEPHEN T. O'NEILL,** born San Francisco, California, December 27, 1957; admitted to bar, 1984, California. *Education:* University of California at Los Angeles (B.A., 1980); Hastings College of Law (J.D., 1984). Phi Delta Phi. *Member:* Santa Clara County (Member, Commercial Law and Bankruptcy Section) Bar Association; State Bar of California; Bay Area Bankruptcy Forum. *PRACTICE AREAS:* Business Workouts; Bankruptcy Reorganizations; Creditors Remedies.

**ROBERT A. FRANKLIN,** born Los Angeles, California, April 28, 1954; admitted to bar, 1980, California. *Education:* University of Santa Clara (B.S., 1976); Southwestern University (J.D., 1979). Contributing Author: "Effective Introduction of Evidence in California," California Continuing Education of the Bar, 1990. Judge Pro Tem, Santa Clara County Municipal Court. *Member:* Santa Clara County Bar Association (Member, Executive Committee, Commercial Law and Bankruptcy Section); State Bar of California; Bay Area Bankruptcy Forum; California Trial Lawyers Association. *PRACTICE AREAS:* Commercial Litigation; Business Workouts; Bankruptcy Reorganizations; Creditors Remedies.

**MAUREEN COLLIGAN HARRISON,** born Wright-Patterson Air Force Base, Ohio, July 8, 1963; admitted to bar, 1992, California. *Education:* Santa Clara University (B.S., 1985; J.D., cum laude, 1992). Comment Editor, Santa Clara Law Review, 1991-1992. *Member:* Santa Clara County and Palo Alto Area Bar Associations; State Bar of California; Bay Area Bankruptcy Forum; Bay Area Women's Insolvency Network. *PRACTICE AREAS:* Business Workouts; Bankruptcy Reorganizations; Creditor Remedies.

**DAVID S. LEVIN,** born Chicago, Illinois, April 6, 1965; admitted to bar, 1991, California. *Education:* Northwestern University (B.A., with honors, 1987); University of Chicago (J.D., 1990). Law Clerk to The Honorable John L. Kane, Jr., U.S. District Judge, District of Colorado, 1990-1991. Member, Palo Alto Public Art Commission, 1996. *Member:* State Bar of California. *PRACTICE AREAS:* Commerical Litigation; Business Workouts; Creditors Remedies.

**GAYE NELL HECK,** born Kingsport, Tennessee, January 1, 1965; admitted to bar, 1990, Georgia; 1994, California. *Education:* Emory University (B.A., with honors, 1987; J.D., 1990). Law Clerk to the Honorable James R. Grube, U.S. Bankruptcy Judge, Northern District of California, 1994-1995. Co-Author: "Dischargeability of Environmental Liability in Bankruptcy," California Real Property Journal (Summer, 1996). *Member:* State Bar of Georgia; State Bar of California; American Bar Association. *PRACTICE AREAS:* Commercial Litigation; Creditors Remedies; Bankruptcy.

**BRADLEY N. RADERMAN,** born Los Angeles, California, March 23, 1970; admitted to bar, 1996, California. *Education:* University of Colorado (B.A., 1992); University of San Francisco (J.D., 1996). Moot Court, Best Brief. Editor, University of San Francisco Law Review, 1995-1996. Extern to the Honorable William D. Stein, California Court of Appeals. *PRACTICE AREAS:* Bankruptcy Reorganizations.

---

## NOLAN & ARMSTRONG
*Established in 1980*

**600 UNIVERSITY AVENUE**
**PALO ALTO, CALIFORNIA 94301**
*Telephone: 415-326-2980*
*Fax: 415-326-9704*

Criminal and Business Crimes Law. Trials and Appeals, Trade Secret and Juvenile Law.

FIRM PROFILE: *Nolan & Armstrong provides quality criminal defense in Silicon Valley. Both named partners are certified specialists in criminal law. The three partners in the firm have extensive experience in handling a wide variety of criminal matters, including criminal high tech trade secret and other business crimes, homicides, sex offenses, narcotics, drunk driving and misdemeanor charges. The firm serves Bay Area counties with a focus in Santa Clara and San Mateo counties. Its practice extends to State and Federal trial and*
*(This Listing Continued)*

appellate courts. All attorneys participate extensively in professional development programs.

### MEMBERS OF FIRM

**THOMAS J. NOLAN,** born Fresno, California, March 10, 1945; admitted to bar, 1971, California, U.S. District Court, Northern District of California and U.S. Court of Appeals, Ninth Circuit; 1977, U.S. Supreme Court; 1980, U.S. District Court, Central District of California and U.S. Court of Appeals, Tenth Circuit; 1983, U.S. District Court, Eastern District of California; 1984, U.S. Court of Appeals, District of Columbia Circuit. *Education:* California State University at Sacramento (B.A., 1967); University of California at Davis (J.D., 1970). Visiting Professor and Lecturer, 1987-1994 and Consulting Professor, 1995—, Stanford University School of Law. Lawyer Representative, Ninth Circuit Judicial Conference 1995—. *Member:* Palo Alto (Chairperson, Client Relations Committee, 1975-1977), Santa Clara County, San Mateo County (Chairperson, Private Defender Committee, 1977) and American (Member, Criminal Justice Section) Bar Associations; State Bar of California (Member: Criminal Law Executive Committee, 1985-1986; Criminal Law Advisory Commission, 1980-1985); California Attorneys for Criminal Justice (Member, Board of Governors, 1975; President, 1988); National Association of Criminal Defense Lawyers. Fellow, American College of Trial Lawyers. (Certified Specialist, Criminal Law, The State Bar of California Board of Legal Specialization). *PRACTICE AREAS:* Criminal Law; Business Crimes Law; Capital Litigation; High Technology Law; White Collar Criminal Defense.

**MICHAEL W. ARMSTRONG,** born Evanston, Illinois, June 17, 1948; admitted to bar, 1979, California and U.S. District Court, Northern District of California. *Education:* Stanford University (B.A., 1970); Northwestern University (J.D., 1979). Judge Pro Tem, San Mateo County, California. *Member:* Palo Alto Area (Member, Board of Trustees, 1996—), Santa Clara County (Member, Board of Trustees, 1992-1993) and San Mateo County Bar Associations; State Bar of California; California Attorneys for Criminal Justice; National Association of Criminal Defense Attorneys. (Certified Specialist, Criminal Law, The State Bar of California Board of Legal Specialization). *LANGUAGES:* Italian. *PRACTICE AREAS:* Criminal Law; Felonies; Misdemeanors; Juvenile Law.

**DANIEL L. BARTON,** born Minneapolis, Minnesota, July 18, 1961; admitted to bar, 1988, California, U.S. District Court, Northern District of California and U.S. Court of Appeals, Ninth Circuit. *Education:* Centro de Estudios Universitarios Colombo-Americano, Bogotá, Columbia; Brown University (B.S., magna cum laude, Phi Beta Kappa, 1983); Stanford University (J.D., 1988). Order of the Coif. Fulbright Scholar (University of Barcelona Law School, Spain) 1986-1987. *Member:* Palo Alto, San Mateo County and Santa Clara County Bar Associations; California Attorneys For Criminal Justice; California Public Defenders Association; National Lawyers Guild. *LANGUAGES:* Spanish and Catalan. *PRACTICE AREAS:* Criminal Law; Driving While Intoxicated (DWI); Felonies and Misdemeanors; Criminal Trial Practice.

### ASSOCIATE

**REBECCA LAIBSON,** born Philadelphia, Pennsylvania, June 27, 1969; admitted to bar, 1995, California; U.S. District Court, Northern District of California. *Education:* Wesleyan University (B.A., Phi Beta Kappa, 1991); Stanford University (J.D., 1995). Instructor, Legal Research and Writing, Boalt Hall School of Law, Fall 1995. *Member:* California Attorneys for Criminal Justice. *PRACTICE AREAS:* Criminal Law; Driving While Intoxicated; Felonies; Misdemeanors.

### LEGAL SUPPORT PERSONNEL

### LEGAL ASSISTANTS

**Lynn M. Memolo,** PLS, CCLS        **Marguerite Giuliano**

---

## PACKARD, PACKARD & JOHNSON
*A PROFESSIONAL CORPORATION*
*Established in 1979*

**260 SHERIDAN AVENUE, SUITE 208**
**PALO ALTO, CALIFORNIA 94306**
*Telephone: 415-327-3000*
*Fax: 415-327-0695*

Salt Lake City, Utah Office: 675 East 2100 South, Suite 350. Telephone: 801-485-6464. Fax: 801-485-3480.

*False Claims Act Prosecution, Class Actions, Complex Business Litigation (including Fraud, Insurance Bad Faith and Securities) and Personal Injury.*
*(This Listing Continued)*

## PACKARD, PACKARD & JOHNSON, A PROFESSIONAL CORPORATION, Palo Alto—Continued

*FIRM PROFILE:* Packard, Packard & Johnson is a multi-state law firm founded in 1979, has offices in Palo Alto, California and Salt Lake City, Utah. Firm attorneys are admitted to practice, variously, in California, Indiana, Texas and Utah. The firm devotes a significant percentage of its time to the prosecution of False Claims Act cases in which "whistle-blowers" pursue defense, medical and other government contractors for fraudulent claims made to the United States Government. In addition the firm's practice also emphasizes complex litigation and class actions involving the following areas of law: fraud, contractors, fiduciary relationships, business entities, insurance bad faith, securities, real property, environmental law, legal and medical malpractice, personal injury (especially paralysis and brain damage), wrongful death and product liability.

**RONALD D. PACKARD,** born Santa Monica, California, December 17, 1948; admitted to bar, 1976, California and U.S. District Court, Northern District of California; 1980, U.S. Tax Court; 1983, U.S. Supreme Court. *Education:* University of California at Riverside (B.A., cum laude, 1971; M.P.A., magna cum laude, 1972); University of California at Berkeley (M.B.A., 1976); Hastings College of Law, University of California (J.D., 1976). Member, Mountain View City Council, 1980-1985. Mayor, Mountain View, 1983-1984. *Member:* Santa Clara County and American Bar Associations; State Bar of California; Consumer Attorneys of California; The Association of Trial Lawyers of America. **PRACTICE AREAS:** Class Actions; False Claims Act; Complex Business Litigation.

**LON D. PACKARD,** born Boise, Idaho, August 7, 1951; admitted to bar, 1977, California and U.S. District Court, Central District of California; 1979, U.S. District Court, Northern and Eastern Districts of California; 1983, U.S. Supreme Court; 1993, Utah and U.S. District Court, District of Utah; 1996, U.S. District Court, Northern District of Texas. *Education:* Stanford University (B.A., 1974); Brigham Young University (J.D., cum laude, 1976). Member, Brigham Young University Law Review, 1975-1976. *Member:* State Bar of California; Utah State and American Bar Associations; Consumer Attorneys of California; The Association of Trial Lawyers of America. **LANGUAGES:** Spanish and Russian. **PRACTICE AREAS:** Class Actions; False Claims Act; Complex Business Litigation.

**VON G. PACKARD,** born Boise, Idaho, August 7, 1951; admitted to bar, 1977, California and U.S. District Court, Northern District of California; 1980, U.S. District Court, Eastern District of California; 1983, U.S. Supreme Court. *Education:* Stanford University (B.A., 1974); Brigham Young University (J.D., 1976). Member, Board of Advocates. *Member:* Santa Clara County and American Bar Associations; State Bar of California; The Association of Trial Lawyers of America; Consumer Attorneys of California. **LANGUAGES:** Spanish. **PRACTICE AREAS:** Class Actions; False Claims Act; Complex Business Litigation; Personal Injury.

**CRAIG H. JOHNSON,** born Pasadena, California, November 14, 1952; admitted to bar, 1979, California; U.S. District Court, Southern District of California; 1983, U.S. District Court, Central District of California; 1992, U.S. Supreme Court; 1995, Utah; U.S. District Court, Central District of Utah; 1996, U.S. District Court, Northern District of Texas. *Education:* Brigham Young University (B.A., 1976); University of the Pacific, McGeorge School of Law (J.D., 1979). Phi Delta Phi. Recipient: American Jurisprudence Award in Corporations: Securities Regulations; Awarded Lewis F. Powell Medallion for Excellence in Trial Advocacy by American College of Trial Lawyers. Western Winner, National Trial Advocacy Competition. Member, Traynor Honor Society. Staff Writer for "Legislative Review" of Pacific Law Journal, 1977. Author: "Criminal Procedure: Death Penalty," 9 Pacific Law Journal 439, 1978; "Career Criminals," 9 Pacific Law Journal 457, 1978. *Member:* American Bar Association; The State Bar of California; Utah State Bar; The Association of Trial Lawyers of America. **PRACTICE AREAS:** Class Actions; False Claims Act; Complex Business Litigation.

### OF COUNSEL

**CLARENCE BORNS,** born Chicago, Illinois, July 24, 1931; admitted to bar, 1956, Indiana (Not admitted in California). *Education:* University of Michigan (A.B., 1953); Northwestern University and Indiana University (LL.B., 1956). Phi Alpha Delta. President, Gary Industrial Foundation, 1969-1970. Member, Economic Development Commission of Gary, 1973-1975. *Member:* Lake County, Indiana State and American Bar Associations; The Association of Trial Lawyers of America; Indiana Trial Lawyers Association (Director, 1982-1985). (Certified as a Civil Trial Advocate by the National Board of Trial Advocacy). (Also Of Counsel to Spangler, Jennings & Dougherty, Merrillville, Indiana). **PRACTICE AREAS:** Personal Injury and Professional Malpractice.

---

## PENNIE & EDMONDS LLP
### PALO ALTO, CALIFORNIA
(See Menlo Park)

*Intellectual Property and Technology Litigation including Patent, Trademark, Trade Secrets, Copyright and Unfair Competition Causes, Computer and Communication Law and Related Government Agency Proceedings, Licensing, Arbitration and International Trade Matters. Trials and Appeals in all Federal and State Courts.*

---

## PETERS, PETERS & ELLINGSON
### A PROFESSIONAL CORPORATION
Established in 1968

550 LYTTON AVENUE, 3RD FLOOR
**PALO ALTO, CALIFORNIA 94301**
Telephone: 415-328-6770
Fax: 415-328-6776

*General Civil and Trial Practice. Family Law, Personal Injury, Wrongful Discharge, Real Property and Business Litigation, Architects' and Engineers' Liability.*

**COLIN PETERS,** born Palo Alto, California, March 23, 1919; admitted to bar, 1947, California. *Education:* San Jose State College (A.B., 1940); Stanford University (J.D., 1947). Order of the Coif. *Member:* Palo Alto and Santa Clara County Bar Associations; The State Bar of California; Santa Clara County Trial Lawyers Association. [Lieutenant, U.S. Naval Reserve, 1942-1946]. **PRACTICE AREAS:** Family Law; Business Litigation; Personal Injury.

**STEPHEN M. PETERS,** born Palo Alto, California, April 20, 1951; admitted to bar, 1976, California. *Education:* Harvard University (B.A., cum laude, 1973); Stanford University (J.D., 1976). *Member:* Palo Alto and Santa Clara Bar Associations; The State Bar of California. **LANGUAGES:** Spanish. **PRACTICE AREAS:** Personal Injury; Family Law; Construction Law; Wrongful Termination.

**PATRICIA ELLINGSON,** born Manitowoc, Wisconsin, August 23, 1940; admitted to bar, 1982, California. *Education:* Peninsula University (J.D., 1982). *Member:* The State Bar of California. **PRACTICE AREAS:** Family Law.

---

## PETERS, VERNY, JONES & BIKSA, L.L.P.
385 SHERMAN AVENUE
SUITE 6
**PALO ALTO, CALIFORNIA 94306-1840**
Telephone: 415-324-1677
Fax: 415-324-1678
Email: pvjb@patentsfo.com

*Intellectual Property Law, including Patent, Trademark, Copyright, Trade Secret and Unfair Competition Law. Trials in all Local Courts, all Federal Courts, and before the U.S. Patent and Trademark Office.*

### MEMBERS OF FIRM

**HOWARD M. PETERS,** born Beech Creek, Pennsylvania, October 13, 1940; admitted to bar, 1979, California; 1982, U.S. Court of Appeals for the Federal Circuit; 1978, registered to practice before U.S. Patent and Trademark Office. *Education:* Geneva College (B.S., magna cum laude, 1962); Stanford University (Ph.D., 1967); Santa Clara University (J.D., 1978). Sigma Xi. Patent Attorney, Syntex Corporation, 1980-1984. Editor, Understanding Chemical Patents, 2nd ed., The American Chemical Society, Washington, D.C., 1991. Recipient, Roger D. Middlekauff Award of the ACS-Division of Chemistry and The Law, 1991. *Member:* State Bar of California; American Bar Association; American Intellectual Property Law Association; Peninsula Intellectual Property Law Association; San Francisco Intellectual Property Law Association; American Chemical Society (Councilor, 1977-1983; Member, Patent Committee, 1979-1989; Founding Chairman, Division of Chemistry and the Law, 1979-1983; Councilor,

*(This Listing Continued)*

1985—; Inventure Place, 1996). *PRACTICE AREAS:* Patent, Trademark and Copyright Law. *Email:* hmpeters@patentsfo.com

**HANA VERNY,** born Pardubice, Czechoslovakia, February 13, 1938; admitted to bar, 1982, California; registered to practice before the U.S. Patent and Trademark Office. *Education:* Charles University (Ph.D., 1966); University of Connecticut (J.D., 1980). Scholar, Max Planck Institute, West Germany. Recipient, King Gustav 5th Research Institute Scholarship, Sweden. Member, Italian Society for Mass Spectrometry. *Member:* State Bar of California; American Bar Association; San Francisco Intellectual Property Law Association; Peninsula Intellectual Property Law Association; California Patent Law Association; American Intellectual Property Law Association; Licensing Executives Society. *LANGUAGES:* Czech, Russian and German. *PRACTICE AREAS:* Patent, Trademark and Copyright Law.

**ALLSTON L. JONES,** born Philadelphia, Pennsylvania, May 12, 1942; admitted to bar, 1977, California and U.S. District Court, Northern District of California; 1978, U.S. Court of Appeals, Ninth Circuit; 1981, U.S. Supreme Court; 1982, U.S. Court of Appeals for the Federal Circuit; registered to practice before U.S. Patent and Trademark Office. *Education:* Drexel University (B.S.E.E., 1964); Purdue University (M.S.E.E., 1966); Stanford University (Dr. SCI., 1971); Santa Clara University (J.D., 1977). Tau Beta Pi; Eta Kappa Nu. *Member:* State Bar of California (Member, Patent Section); American Bar Association (Member, Patent Section); Peninsula Intellectual Property Law Association; San Francisco Intellectual Property Law Association; Japan Society; Institute of Electrical and Electronics Engineers; American Intellectual Property Law Association. *PRACTICE AREAS:* Patent, Trademark and Copyright Law. *Email:* a__jones@patentsfo.com

**JANIS J. O. BIKSA,** born Saó Paulo, Brazil, May 10, 1954; admitted to bar, 1987, California and U.S. District Court, Northern District of California; 1992, U.S. Court of Appeals for the Federal Circuit; registered to practice before U.S. Patent and Trademark Office. *Education:* University of Southern California; University of California at Berkeley (B.S., Mechanical Engineering and Materials Science and Engineering, 1977); Golden Gate University; Santa Clara University (J.D., 1986). Recipient, American Jurisprudence Award for Civil Litigation. Licensed Professional Engineer in Mechanical Engineering, California, 1981. *Member:* Santa Clara County, San Mateo County and American Bar Associations; Peninsula Intellectual Property Law Association; San Francisco Intellectual Property Association; American Intellectual Property Law Association; American Society of Mechanical Engineers; Society of Automotive Engineers; American Society for Metals. (Also Of Counsel to Owen, Wickersham & Erickson, San Francisco). *LANGUAGES:* Latvian. *PRACTICE AREAS:* Patent, Trademark and Copyright Law. *Email:* jbiksa@patentsfo.com

## STEPHEN W. PLAYER LAW OFFICES
2600 EL CAMINO REAL, SUITE 410
**PALO ALTO, CALIFORNIA 94306**
Telephone: 415-494-9102
Fax: 415-856-8448

*General Business and Real Estate Practice with an emphasis on Land Use, Zoning and Administrative Law.*

**STEPHEN W. PLAYER,** born San Francisco, California, April 28, 1941; admitted to bar, 1967, California. *Education:* Stanford University (A.B., 1963); Hastings College of Law, University of California (LL.B., 1966). President, Stanford Mid-Peninsula Urban Coalition, 1980-1984. Member, Board of Directors, 1972-1978 and President of Board, 1974-1975, Palo Alto Y.M.C.A. President, Palo Alto Chamber of Commerce, 1993-1994. Member, Board of Directors, California Supreme Court Historical Society, 1994—. Member, Palo Alto Rotary Club, 1996—. *Member:* Palo Alto and Santa Clara County Bar Associations; State Bar of California.

REPRESENTATIVE CLIENTS: Peninsula Creamery; Channing House.

## KENNETH H. PROCHNOW
525 UNIVERSITY AVENUE, SUITE 702
**PALO ALTO, CALIFORNIA 94301-1906**
Telephone: 415-327-0400
Fax: 415-326-0758
Email: prochlaw@aol.com

*Civil Trial Practice in State and Federal Courts. Arbitration/ADR, Referral Litigation (Compensated and Cooperative). Litigation in the following areas: Commercial, Business, Banking, Real Estate, Securities, Consumer and Investment Fraud, Employment, Professional Liability (Non-Medical), Trade Secret, Elder Law and Bankruptcy.*

**KENNETH H. PROCHNOW,** born Milwaukee, Wisconsin, August 4, 1950; admitted to bar, 1978, New York; 1979, Minnesota; 1984, California. *Education:* Columbia University (B.A., 1972); New York University (J.D., 1976). Editor-in-Chief, New York University Law Review, 1975-1976. Law Clerk to Honorable Leonard I. Garth, U.S. Court of Appeals, Third Circuit, 1976-1977. *Member:* Palo Alto, Santa Clara County and American (Member, General Practice and Litigation Sections) Bar Associations; State Bar of California; National Institute for Trial Advocacy. *PRACTICE AREAS:* Civil Litigation; Civil Appeals; Alternative Dispute Resolution.

## CHRISTOPHER REAM
1717 EMBARCADERO ROAD
**PALO ALTO, CALIFORNIA 94303**
Telephone: 415-424-0821
Facsimile: 415-857-1288

*Business, Corporation and Securities Law. General Business and Civil Litigation.*

**CHRISTOPHER REAM,** born Somerville, New Jersey, October 31, 1942; admitted to bar, 1972, California. *Education:* Yale University (B.E. in Mechanical Engineering, 1964); Boalt Hall School of Law, University of California, Berkeley (J.D., 1971). Lecturer: "Fundamentals of Organizing and Advising Businesses," California Continuing Education of the Bar, 1982-1984; "Developments in California Corporate Law," The Rutter Group, 1988. Associate, Wilson, Sonsoni, Goodrich & Rosati, 1971-1976. Senior Partner, Ream, Roskoph & Buselle, 1976-1989. *Member:* Palo Alto Area (President, 1986) and American (Member, Section on Business Law) Bar Associations; The State Bar of California. [Lt., USNR, 1964-1968]. *PRACTICE AREAS:* Business Law; Corporations; Securities Law; Civil Litigation.

## REED & ROBINS LLP
285 HAMILTON AVENUE, SUITE 200
**PALO ALTO, CALIFORNIA 94301**
Telephone: 415-327-3400
Facsmilie: 415-327-3231

*Technology areas: Chemistry, Biotechnology and Biomedical Engineering, including Pharmaceuticals, Organic and Bio-Organic Chemistry, Polymer Science, Molecular Biology, Immunology and Genetics. Intellectual Property Law including Patent Preparation and Prosecution.*

### MEMBERS OF FIRM

**DIANNE E. REED,** born New York, N.Y., July 12, 1958; admitted to bar, 1984, California; registered to practice before U.S. Patent and Trademark Office. *Education:* Massachusetts Institute of Technology (S.B. Chemistry, 1979); University of California at Berkeley; Hastings College of the Law, University of California (J.D., 1984). Phi Lambda Upsilon. Associate Editor, Communications and Entertainment Law Journal, 1983-1984. *Member:* State Bar of California; American Bar Association; American Chemical Society; San Francisco Patent and Trademark Law Association; Peninsula Intellectual Property Law Association. *PRACTICE AREAS:* Patent Law; Strategic Counseling; Patent Preparation and Prosecution.

**ROBERTA L. ROBINS,** born New York, N.Y., January 4, 1953; admitted to bar, 1987, California; registered to practice before U.S. Patent and Trademark Office. *Education:* San Jose State University (B.A., Biological Sciences, with distinction, 1976); San Francisco State University; Hastings College of Law, University of California (J.D., cum laude, 1987). Member, Moot Court Board. Recipient, American Jurisprudence Awards for Academic Excellence. *Member:* State Bar of California; American Bar Association; American Intellectual Property Law Association; San Francisco Patent and Trademark Law Association; Peninsula Intellectual Property Law

*(This Listing Continued)*

## REED & ROBINS LLP, Palo Alto—Continued

Association. *PRACTICE AREAS:* Patent Law; Strategic Counseling; Patent Preparation and Prosecution.

### ASSOCIATES

**KENNETH BAROVSKY,** born St. Louis, Missouri, April 10, 1952; admitted to bar, 1993, California; registered to practice before U.S. Patent and Trademark Office. *Education:* University of California, San Diego (B.A., Chemistry, 1974; Ph.D., Physiology and Pharmacology, 1980); Santa Clara University (J.D., 1993). *Member:* State Bar of California; American Bar Association; American Intellectual Property Law Association; San Francisco Patent and Trademark Law Association; Peninsula Intellectual Property Law Association; American Society of Biochemistry and Molecular Biology. *PRACTICE AREAS:* Patent Law; Patent Preparation and Prosecution; Chemistry; Biotechnology; Biomedical Engineering.

**THOMAS P.G. MCCRACKEN,** born Berkeley, California, October 3, 1962; admitted to bar, 1994, California; registered to practice before U.S. Patent and Trademark Office. *Education:* University of California-San Diego (B.A. in microbiology, 1989); Santa Clara University (J.D., 1993). Member, Moot Court Board. National Quarter Finalist, G.S. Rich Moot Court Competition. Recipient, American Jurisprudence Award for Academic Excellence. *Member:* State Bar of California; San Francisco Patent and Trademark Law Association. *PRACTICE AREAS:* Patent Law; Patent Preparation and Prosecution; Biotechnology; Biomedical Engineering.

**SUSAN J. FRIEDMAN,** born New York, N.Y.; admitted to bar, 1002, Pennsylvania; 1995, California; registered to practice before U.S. Patent and Trademark Office. *Education:* Smith College (B.A., biochemistry, summa cum laude, 1962); Yale University (Ph.D., pharmacology, 1971); Georgetown University Law Center (J.D., 1992). Recipient, American Jurisprudence Award in Comparative Law. *Member:* Pennsylvania, Federal Circuit and American (Member, Sections on: IP Law; Science and Technology) Bar Associations; State Bar of California; The District of Columbia Bar; American Intellectual Property Law Association; Peninsula Intellectual Property Law Association; Bay Area Bioscience Center; American Association for the Advancement of Science. *PRACTICE AREAS:* Patent Law; Patent Preparation and Prosecution; Chemistry; Biotechnology.

### LEGAL SUPPORT PERSONNEL

**GAIL E. WARDWELL,** born Mountain View, California, October 25, 1953. *Education:* California State University, Long Beach (B.A., Mathematics, 1976); University of Colorado (Teacher Certificate, 1977). (Office Manager).

REPRESENTATIVE CLIENTS: ALZA Corporation; Avigen; Bristol-Myers Squibb Co.; Chiron Corporation; CIMA Labs; Ciba Corning Diagnostics Corp.; Cygnus, Inc.; Dow Dermatologics; Hewlett-Packard Company; Instrumentation Metrics, Inc.; Optical Senors Incorporated; SRI International; Stanford University; VIVUS, Inc.

---

## THOMAS D. REESE

285 HAMILTON AVENUE
P.O. BOX 240
**PALO ALTO, CALIFORNIA 94301**
Telephone: 415-328-7000
Fax: 415-329-8925
Email: thosreese@aol.com

Civil Litigation.

**THOMAS D. REESE,** born Chicago, Illinois, September 23, 1934; admitted to bar, 1961, California. *Education:* Occidental College (B.A., 1956); Fletcher School of Law and Diplomacy (M.A., 1957); Stanford University (J.D., 1960). *Member:* Palo Alto Bar Association (President, 1974-1995); State Bar of California. *PRACTICE AREAS:* Dispute Resolution; Mediation; Arbitration; Special Master/Referee.

---

## RITCHEY FISHER WHITMAN & KLEIN

A PROFESSIONAL CORPORATION
Established in 1965

(Formerly Blase, Valentine & Klein)
1717 EMBARCADERO ROAD
P.O. BOX 51050
**PALO ALTO, CALIFORNIA 94303**
Telephone: 415-857-1717
Telecopier: 415-857-1288
Email: rfwk@rfwklaw.com

General Civil and Trial Practice, Alternative Dispute Resolution including Arbitration, Mediation, and Mini-Trials. Corporation, Emerging Growth Companies, Taxation, Tax Exempt Organizations, Trade Secret, Unfair Competition, Intellectual Property, Real Property, Probate, Estate Planning, Construction, Professional Liability, Product Distribution, Employment, Health Care and Environmental Law.

FIRM PROFILE: The mission of Ritchey, Fisher, Whitman and Klein is to achieve the best possible outcome in the shortest possible time at a cost that results in excellent value to our clients. We have an excellent relationship with the local judiciary and with the American Arbitration Association. We thrive on the confidence of our colleagues in the legal community, who entrust us regularly with their own business disputes and with referrals of their clients.

The attorneys meet regularly to discuss current cases and transactions without charge to our clients. This results in constant cross-fertilization of ideas and expertise and enhances our flexibility and creativity. Our clients all have the benefit of our combined experience and expertise.

**GEORGE C. FISHER,** born Tacoma, Washington, May 1, 1943; admitted to bar, 1967, California. *Education:* Washington State University (B.A., 1965); Stanford University (LL.B., 1967). Phi Beta Kappa. Member, Board of Editors, Stanford Law Review, 1965-1967. President, Palo Alto Area Bar Association, 1981-1982. Judge Pro Tem and Special Master State and Federal Courts. Arbitrator and Mediator, American Arbitration Association. *PRACTICE AREAS:* Business Litigation; Partnerships; Construction; Real Estate; Technology Litigation. *Email:* gfisher@rfwklaw.com

**GILLIAN G. HAYS,** born Bedford, England, February 25, 1943; admitted to bar, 1969, California. *Education:* Oxford University, England (M.A., Jurisprudence, with honors, 1964). Municipal Court Judge, City of Taylor, Lake Village, Texas, 1979-1981. Presenter, "Estate Planning Strategies for Women," 1993; "Woman to Woman: A Financial Forum," 1993 and 1994. *PRACTICE AREAS:* Estate Planning; Probate; Trust Law. *Email:* ghays@rfwklaw.com

**JOHN G. HURSH,** born Minneapolis, Minnesota, March 27, 1950; admitted to bar, 1982, Montana; 1984, California. *Education:* University of Oregon (B.S., 1975); University of Montana (J.D., 1982). Member, University of Montana Law Review, 1981-1982. Law Clerk to the Honorable James R. Browning, Chief Judge, U.S. Court of Appeals, Ninth Circuit, 1982-1983; Judge Pro Tem, Santa Clara County Superior Court; Trustee Emeritus, University of Montana Foundation. *PRACTICE AREAS:* Real Estate; Construction Law; Employment Litigation. *Email:* jhursh@rfwklaw.com

**DAVID A. KAYS,** born St. Louis, Missouri, October 29, 1957; admitted to bar, 1985, California. *Education:* University of Massachusetts (B.A., cum laude, 1980); University of San Francisco (J.D., magna cum laude, 1985). Member, Law Review, 1982-1985. Extern for Justice Otto M. Kaus, California Supreme Court, Fall 1984. Judge Pro Tem, Santa Clara County Superior Court. Member, Mediator, City of Mountain View. *PRACTICE AREAS:* Business Litigation; Environmental Litigation. *Email:* dkays@rfwklaw.com

**TERENCE M. KELLY,** born Riverside, California, April 3, 1957; admitted to bar, 1984, California. *Education:* Stanford University (A.B., with distinction, 1979); Boalt Hall School of Law, University of California (J.D., 1983). Associate Editor, Ecology Law Quarterly, 1982-1983. Law Clerk to Justice John Code Mowbray, Supreme Court of Nevada, 1983-1984; Secretary, 1992 and Trustee, 1988-1991, Santa Clara County Bar Association. Santa Clara County Bar Association (Chair, Committee on Public Relations, 1990; Member, Executive Committee, 1991-1992). *PRACTICE AREAS:* Corporate Law; Business; Intellectual Property. *Email:* tkelly@rfwklaw.com

**LAWRENCE A. KLEIN,** born Tuckahoe, New York, May 21, 1938; admitted to bar, 1964, New York; 1967, California. *Education:* Cornell University (B.A., 1960); Harvard University (LL.B., magna cum laude, 1963).

*(This Listing Continued)*

## PROFESSIONAL BIOGRAPHIES

Recipient, Palo Alto Citizen of the Year, 1995. Member, Board of Editors, Harvard Law Review, 1961-1963. Special Counsel, Environmental Protection Agency, 1974. Member, Palo Alto City Council, 1981-1989; Mayor, 1984, 1989. **PRACTICE AREAS:** Corporate Law; Business; Taxation. **Email:** lklein@rfwklaw.com

**MARTHA C. LUEMERS,** born Bethesda, Maryland, December 5, 1954; admitted to bar, 1982, California. *Education:* Stanford University (A.B., with distinction, 1977; J.D., 1982); Universitaet Tuebingen, West Germany, Fulbright Scholar, 1977-1978. Phi Beta Kappa. Senior Note Editor, Stanford Law Review, 1981-1982. Law Clerk to the Hon. James R. Browning, Chief Judge, U.S. Court of Appeals for the Ninth Circuit, 1982-1983. Member, Panel of Arbitrators, American Arbitration Association. **Email:** mluemers@rfwklaw.com

**JEAN K. MCCOWN,** born Berkeley, California, October 5, 1949; admitted to bar, 1977, California. *Education:* University of Michigan (B.A., with high distinction, 1971); University of Wisconsin (M.A., 1973); Boalt Hall School of Law, University of California (J.D., 1977). Phi Beta Kappa. Articles Editor, Ecology Law Quarterly, 1976-1977. Member, Palo Alto Planning Commission, 1979-1987. Judge Pro Tem, Santa Clara Superior Court, 1992. Member, Palo Alto City Council, 1990—; Mayor, 1993. President, Palo Alto Bar Association, 1989-1990. **Email:** jmccown@rfwklaw.com

**CRAIG S. RITCHEY,** born Palo Alto, California, April 21, 1944; admitted to bar, 1970, California. *Education:* Stanford University (B.A., 1966); Hastings College of the Law (J.D., 1969). Order of the Coif. Member, Board of Editors, Hastings Law Journal, 1967-1969. White House Fellow and Special Assistant to Secretary of the Interior Cecil Andrus, 1978-1979. Chairman, National Public Lands Advisory Council, 1979-1980. Special Master, U.S. District Court, Northern District of California. Judge Pro Tem, Santa Clara Superior Court. Member, Panel of Arbitrators, American Arbitration Association. **Email:** critchey@rfwklaw.com

**KAREN E. WENTZEL,** born Lexington, Missouri, December 15, 1955; admitted to bar, 1983, California. *Education:* Colgate University (B.A., summa cum laude, 1978); Stanford University (J.D., 1983). Phi Beta Kappa. Note Editor, Stanford Law Review, 1982-1983. Law Clerk to Hon. Peter Stone, Santa Clara County Superior Court, 1983-1984. **PRACTICE AREAS:** Labor and Employment; Business Litigation. **Email:** kwentzel@rfwklaw.com

**PETER A. WHITMAN,** born Altadena, California, January 14, 1943; admitted to bar, 1969, California. *Education:* Stanford University (B.A., with distinction, 1965; LL.B., 1968). Member, Board of Editors, Stanford Law Review, 1966-1968. Law Clerk to Hon. Winslow Christian, California Court of Appeal, 1968-1969. Consultant: California Law Revision Commission, 1976; Henry J. Kaiser Family Foundation, 1982-1983. **PRACTICE AREAS:** Corporation; Health Care. **Email:** pwhitman@rfwklaw.com

---

**JENNIFER DEW,** born Kalamazoo, Michigan, May 5, 1964; admitted to bar, 1992, California. *Education:* Scripps college (B.A., 1987); University of San Francisco School of Law (J.D., 1992). **PRACTICE AREAS:** Business Litigation; Labor and Employment. **Email:** jdew@rfwklaw.com

**PAUL K. LAUHER,** born Elizabeth, New Jersey, October 22, 1961; admitted to bar, 1995, California. *Education:* University of Southern Mississippi (B.S.B.A., highest honors, 1990); Monterey Institute of International Studies (M.B.A., 1991); Santa Clara University (J.D., 1994). **PRACTICE AREAS:** Corporate Law. **Email:** plauher@rfwklaw.com

**STEPHEN M. MAURER,** born Lancaster, Pennsylvania, January 9, 1958; admitted to bar, 1982, Arizona; 1988, California. *Education:* Yale University (B.A., summa cum laude, 1979); Harvard University (J.D., 1982). **PRACTICE AREAS:** Business Litigation; Technology Litigation. **Email:** smaurer@rfwklaw.com

**ERIK J. OLSON,** born Sacramento, California, January 28, 1968; admitted to bar, 1994, California; 1996, District of Columbia. *Education:* Westmont College (B.A., summa cum laude, 1990); Stanford University (J.D., 1994). Phi Kappa Phi; Order of the Coif. Member, Board of Editors, Stanford Law Review, 1993-1994. Law Clerk, Judge Leonard I. Garth, U.S. Court of Appeals, Third Circuit, 1994-1995. Author: "No Room at the Inn" 46 Stanford Law Review 449, 1994. **Email:** eolson@rfwklaw.com

**PATRICIA A. WELCH,** born Boston, Massachusetts, November 15, 1959; admitted to bar, 1987, California. *Education:* Harvard University (A.B., cum laude, 1981); Boston College Law School (J.D., magna cum laude, 1986). **PRACTICE AREAS:** Business Litigation; Real Estate Litigation. **Email:** pwelch@rfwklaw.com

*(This Listing Continued)*

## CALIFORNIA—PALO ALTO

*OF COUNSEL*

**PAULA S. CROW,** born San Francisco, California, March 23, 1953; admitted to bar, 1980, California. *Education:* University of California at Berkeley (A.B., with highest honors, 1977); Boalt Hall School of Law, University of California (J.D., 1980). Phi Beta Kappa. **PRACTICE AREAS:** Technology and Real Estate Transactions. **Email:** pcrow@rfwklaw.com

**BYRON MELLBERG,** born Los Angeles, California, November 12, 1946; admitted to bar, 1974, California. *Education:* Stanford University (A.B., 1969); Hastings College of Law, University of California (J.D., 1974). Co-author: "Scope of Bargaining for Teachers in California's Public Schools," 18 Santa Clara Law Review 885, Fall, 1978. **PRACTICE AREAS:** Real Estate; Business. **Email:** bmellberg@rfwklaw.com

---

# LAW OFFICES OF
# WILLIAM D. ROSS

*A PROFESSIONAL CORPORATION*

*425 SHERMAN AVENUE, SUITE 310*
**PALO ALTO, CALIFORNIA 94306**
Telephone: 415-617-5678
Fax: 415-617-5680

Los Angeles, California Office: 520 South Grand Avenue, Suite 300.
Telephone: 213-892-1592. Telecopier: 213-892-1519.

*Civil Trial and Appellate Practice in State and Federal Courts. Business Litigation, Employment Rights, Land Use, Real Property, Environmental, Water Rights, Public Finance, State and Local Administrative Law.*

FIRM PROFILE: *Governmental, corporate and individual clients are assisted in the areas of local government, real estate development and real property title litigation. Governmental clients are advised and represented in administrative and litigation proceedings issues including employment rights, environmental compliance, real estate development, proceedings before Local Agency Formation Commission (LAFCO), formation, administration and dissolution of joint power authorities, public finance and administration of claims under the California Tort Claims Act.*

*The firm advises and represents developers and owners of residential, commercial and industrial properties and public entities in administrative and litigation proceedings in land use, California Environmental Quality Act (Public Resources Code §21000 et seq., "CEQA") compliance and LAFCO matters, The firm has been involved as lead counsel on several published appellate cases and trial court cases concerning land use and CEQA compliance issues. The firm also has extensive experience in obtaining land use entitlements from local, environmental, state and federal agencies. In connection with these matters, the firm has performed analyses of environmental documentation required under CEQA, including but not limited to, procedural notices, draft and final environmental impact reports.*

**WILLIAM D. ROSS,** born Cedar Rapids, Iowa, April 27, 1948; admitted to bar, 1975, California and U.S. District Court, Central District of California; 1978, U.S. Claims Court and U.S. District Court, Southern District of California; 1981, U.S. District Court, Eastern District of California; 1982, U.S. Court of Appeals, Tenth Circuit; 1983, U.S. Court of Appeals, Ninth Circuit, U.S. District Court, Northern District of California. *Education:* Stanford University (B.A., with honors in History, 1970); University of Santa Clara (J.D., 1974). Deputy County Counsel, County of Los Angeles, 1976-1981. Member, 1981-1989, and Chairman, 1986-1988, City of Pasadena Planning Commission. *Member:* Los Angeles County (Member, Sections on: Real Property; Environmental Law; Member, Committee on Municipal Courts, 1979-1980) and American (Member, Sections on: Natural Resources Law; Administrative Law and Regulatory Practice) Bar Associations. (Also at Los Angeles Office). **REPORTED CASES:** William S. Hart Union High School Dist. v. Regional Planning Commission, 226 Cal.App.3d 1612 (1991); Long Beach Unified School District v. State of California, 225 Cal.App.3d 155 (1990), Petition for Review denied February 28, 1991; City of Sacramento v. State of California, 50 Cal.3d 51, 266 Cal.Rptr. 139 (1990); American River Fire Protection Dist. v. Board of Supervisors, 211 Cal.App.3d 1076, 259 Cal.Rptr. 858 (1989); Carmel Valley Fire Protection Dist. v. State of California, 190 Cal.App.3d 521, 234 Cal.Rptr. 795 (1987); City of Anaheim v. State of California, et al., 189 Cal.App.3d 1478, 235 Cal.Rptr. 101 (1987); Division of Occupational Safety and Health v. State Board of Control, 189 Cal.App.3d 794, 234 Cal.Rptr. 661 (1987); County of Los Angeles, et al. v. State of California, et al.; City of Sonoma, et al. v. State of California, et al., 43 Cal.3d 46, 233 Cal.Rptr. 38 (1987); Las Virgenes Homeowners Federation, Inc., et al. v. County of Los Angeles,

*(This Listing Continued)*

CALIFORNIA—PALO ALTO

**LAW OFFICES OF WILLIAM D. ROSS** A PROFESSIONAL CORPORATION, Palo Alto—Continued

(Currey-Riach Company), Real Party-In-Interest), 177 Cal.App.3d 300, 223 Cal.Rptr. 18 (1986) (CEQA action); Rapid Transit Advocates v. Southern California Rapid Transit District, 752 F.2d 373 (9th Cir. 1985) (NEPA action); San Bernardino Valley Audobon Society v. County of San Bernardino, et al., (Gold. Mountain Memorial Park, Real Property-In-Interest), 155 Cal.App.3d 738, 202 Cal.Rptr. 424 (1984) (CEQA action). *PRACTICE AREAS:* Land Use; Municipal; Zoning; Real Estate.

**MYRA J. PRESTIDGE,** born San Francisco, California, April 25, 1956; admitted to bar, 1984, California and U.S. District Court, Northern District of California. *Education:* University of California at Santa Cruz (B.A., 1981); University of Santa Clara (J.D., 1984). Assistant and Senior Assistant City Attorney, City of Mountain View, 1990-1996. *Member:* San Mateo County and Santa Clara County Bar Associations; State Bar of California (Member, Sections on: Labor Law and Public Law. (Also at Los Angeles Office). REPORTED CASES: City of Redwood City V. Dalton Construction Company, 221 Cal.App.3d 1570 (1990).

## RUSSO & HALE

Established in 1985

401 FLORENCE STREET
**PALO ALTO, CALIFORNIA 94301**
Telephone: 415-327-9800
Fax: 415-327-3737
Email: info@computerlaw.com
URL: http://www.computerlaw.com

*Computer Law, Intellectual Property, Patent, Copyright, Trademark and Licensing Litigation, Commercial Litigation and General Business Litigation.*

### MEMBERS OF FIRM

**JACK RUSSO,** born Queens, New York, October 12, 1954; admitted to bar, 1980, California; 1981, New York; 1992, Washington, D.C.; 1994, Hawaii. *Education:* Brooklyn College of the City University of New York (M.A.-B.A., in Urban Management and Computer and Information Science, 1977); University of California at Los Angeles (J.D., 1980). Order of the Coif. Member: UCLA Law Review, 1979-1980; UCLA Moot Court. Co-Author, "Protection of Computer Software After the Copyright Act of 1980," Law & Business, 1981; "Pre-Trial and Discovery in a Software Marketing Dispute," Law and Business, 1982; "Copyright Law and Computer Software Disputes," Practising Law Institute, 1983; "Microcomputer Software Marketing Agreement Disputes," Practising Law Institute, 1985; "Copyright in the 'Look and Feel' of Computer Software," The Computer Lawyer, February, 1985. Co-Author: "The Impact of the Uniform Trade Secrets Act on California Trade Secret Law," Trade Secret Law Reporter, May, 1985; "Software Copyright Protection," 5 Software Publisher's Association News 3-4 (No. 1 January 1988); "Developments in Copyright Protection of Computer Software," 2 International Computer Law Adviser 9-12 (No. 4 January 1988); "Recent Developments in the Copyright Protection of the 'Look and Feel' of Computer Software: Apple Computer v. Microsoft and Hewlett-Packard," 6 Software Protection 1-15 (No. 10 March 1988); "Copyright Protection of Virtual Reality," ABA Science and Technology 1992; "New Frontiers: Copyright Protection in Virtual Reality Works," 15 The National Law Journal S1 (No. 6 October 12, 1992). Co-Author: "Software 'Look and Feel' Protection in the 1990's," 15 Hastings Communications and Entertainment Law Journal 571-603 (1993); "Virtual Reality-A Legal Overview" Chapter 19 in Computer Software, Clark Boardman, 1994; "Liability on the Internet," San Francisco Intellectual Property Association (March, 1995). Judge Pro Tem, Santa Clara Superior Court. Arbitrator, U.S. District Court, Northern District of California; Arbitrator, American Arbitration Association. *Member:* Hawaii State, New York State and American (Member, Sections on: Science and Technology; Patent, Trademark and Copyright Law) Bar Associations; State Bar of California; District of Columbia Bar; Copyright Society of the U.S.A.; International Trademark Association. *PRACTICE AREAS:* Civil Litigation; Intellectual Property Litigation; Computer Law; Licensing.

**TIMOTHY C. HALE,** born Dayton, Ohio, October 3, 1950; admitted to bar, 1984, California and U.S. District Court, Northern District of California; U.S. District Court, Western District of Texas. *Education:* Dartmouth College (B.A., summa cum laude, 1972); Stanford University (M.A., 1973; J.D., 1984). Phi Beta Kappa; Order of the Coif. Co-Author: "The Impact of the Uniform Trade Secrets Act on California Trade Secret Law," Trade Secret Law Reporter, May, 1985; "Software Copyright Protection," Computer

*(This Listing Continued)*

CAA1598B

---

MARTINDALE-HUBBELL LAW DIRECTORY 1997

Digest, February, 1988; "Trade Secrecy and Reverse Engineering," Minnesota State Bar Continuing Legal Education, April 1, 1987. *PRACTICE AREAS:* Civil Litigation; Intellectual Property Litigation; Computer Law; Trade Secrets. Email: THALE@computerlaw.com

**JOHN A.D. KELLEY,** born Portland, Oregon, April 7, 1955; admitted to bar, 1981, California. *Education:* Swarthmore College (B.A., High Honors in Humanities, 1977); Stanford University (J.D., 1981). Phi Beta Kappa. National Merit Scholar. Recipient, Brand Blanchard Prize. Topic Development Editor, Stanford Journal of International Law, 1979-1980. Author: "The Confines of Cosmopolitan Justice," 16 Stanford Journal of International Law 209 (1980); "Japan Gaining in Race to Build Brainy Computer," San Francisco Examiner, June 22, 1986; "Getting the Most from Your Computer," California Lawyer, March 1987; "A New Way to Communicate," California Lawyer, November 1987. *Member:* State Bar of California. *PRACTICE AREAS:* Civil Litigation; Intellectual Property Litigation; Computer Law.

## CHARLES G. SCHULZ

Established in 1969

517 BYRON STREET
P.O. BOX 1299
**PALO ALTO, CALIFORNIA 94302**
Telephone: 415-326-8080
Fax: 415-326-0825

*Estate Planning, Trust and Probate Law. General Civil Practice.*

**CHARLES G. SCHULZ,** born Brooklyn, New York, May 15, 1932; admitted to bar, 1958, California, U.S. District Court, Northern District of California; U.S. Court of Appeals, Ninth Circuit; 1995, U.S. Tax Court. *Education:* Cornell University (B.A., with Distinction and Honors, 1954); Harvard University (J.D., 1957). Phi Beta Kappa; Phi Kappa Phi. Law Clerk to Michael J. Roche, Chief Judge, U.S. District Court, Northern District of California, 1957-1959. Author, Annual Survey of California Laws on Probate, Trusts and Conservatorships, 1979—. Panelist, Estate Administration and Trusts, California Continuing Education of the Bar. *Member:* Palo Alto, Santa Clara County and American Bar Associations; The State Bar of California. Fellow, American College of Trust and Estate Counsel. *PRACTICE AREAS:* Estate Planning; Trusts; Conservatorships; Probate Law; Civil Trial.

REFERENCES: Wells Fargo Bank, Palo Alto; Bank of America National Trust & Savings Assn., Palo Alto, California.

## EARL NICHOLAS SELBY

Established in 1985

420 FLORENCE STREET, SUITE 200
**PALO ALTO, CALIFORNIA 94301**
Telephone: 415-323-0990
Fax: 415-325-9041
Email: nselby@well.com

*Public Utilities Law, Telecommunications, Cable Television, First Amendment and Administrative Law. General Civil and Trial Practice.*

**EARL NICHOLAS SELBY,** born Bryn Mawr, Pennsylvania, May 18, 1948; admitted to bar, 1977, California; 1980, District of Columbia. *Education:* Stanford University (B.A., with great distinction, 1970); Harvard University (J.D., cum laude, 1977). Law Clerk to Hon. Rose Elizabeth Bird, Chief Justice, California Supreme Court, 1978-1979. Lecturer, Telecommunications Regulation, California State University at Hayward, 1993-1994. Legal Advisor, Hon. Richard D. Gravelle, Commissioner, California Public Utilities Commission, 1980-1982. *Member:* State Bar of California; District of Columbia Bar; American Bar Association.

REPRESENTATIVE CLIENTS: Nextel Communications, Inc.; ICG Access Services, Inc (IntelCom Group U.S.A., Inc., Denver, CO); Bay Area Teleport; Linkatel of California, L.P. (San Diego, Calif.); Shared Telecommunication Systems, Inc. (Hayward, Calif.).

## LAW OFFICES OF
## JOHN C. SHAFFER, JR.
A PROFESSIONAL LAW CORPORATION

PALO ALTO, CALIFORNIA

(See Menlo Park)

*Civil Trial Practice. Labor Employment Law Issues including Discrimination, Sexual Harassment and Wrongful Termination from Employment. Business and Personal Injury Litigation, Insurance Bad Faith and Coverage Issues.*

---

## LAW OFFICES OF
## WAYNE A. SILVER

Established in 1984

409 SHERMAN AVENUE
SUITE 212
PALO ALTO, CALIFORNIA 94306
Telephone: 415-323-7100
Fax: 415-323-4154

*Bankruptcy and Litigation.*

**WAYNE A. SILVER,** born New York, N.Y., March 23, 1953; admitted to bar, 1983, California; 1984, U.S. Tax Court; 1987, U.S. Court of Appeals, Ninth Circuit; 1991, U.S. District Court, Eastern District of California; 1993, U.S. District Court, Northern District of Texas. *Education:* Wharton School, University of Pennsylvania (B.S., 1975); New York Law School; University of San Francisco (J.D., 1982). *Member:* Santa Clara County (Member, Debtor/Creditor Section) and Palo Alto Bar Associations; The Association of Trial Lawyers of America. (Certified Specialist, Bankruptcy Law, State Bar of California Board of Legal Specialization). **PRACTICE AREAS:** Bankruptcy; Bankruptcy Litigation.

---

## SKJERVEN, MORRILL, MacPHERSON,
## FRANKLIN & FRIEL LLP

PALO ALTO, CALIFORNIA

(See San Jose)

*Intellectual Property Law, including Patents, Trademarks, Copyrights, Mask Works, Unfair Competition, Trade Secrets and Licensing; Litigation in Federal and State Courts; Corporate, Commercial and General Business Law; and International and Government Contracts Law.*

---

## SLENKOVICH & FLANAGAN

525 UNIVERSITY AVENUE, SUITE 1420
PALO ALTO, CALIFORNIA 94301
Telephone: 415-688-6000
Facsimile: 415-688-6001
Email: info@SF-Law.com
URL: http://www.sf-law.com

Civil Litigation, Real Property Transactions, Business Litigation, Commercial Leasing, Securities, Alternative Dispute Resolution, including Arbitration, Mediation and Administrative Law, White Collar Criminal Defense.

FIRM PROFILE: *Slenkovich & Flanagan is a full-service business litigation firm. Our clients range from sole proprietorships to international corporations and include firms engage in high technology electronics and materials, real property transactions, design and construction, toxic waste assessment, internet-related technologies and remediation, commercial leasing, securities and syndications, franchising and licensing and retail sales. We offer our clients an extensive background in business, import/export transactions litigation and white collar criminal defense, which includes numerous bench and jury trials as well as appeals at both the state and federal levels. In addition the firm's members have extensive experience with informal and formal alternative dispute resolution including arbitration, mediation and administrative law.*

**KEITH SLENKOVICH,** born Seattle, Washington, June 21, 1961; admitted to bar, 1987, California, U.S. District Court, Northern District of California and U.S. Court of Appeals, Ninth Circuit; U.S. Supreme Court. *Education:* Colorado College (B.S., cum laude, Phi Beta Kappa, 1983); Boalt Hall School of Law, University of California (J.D., 1987). Seminar,

*(This Listing Continued)*

Real Property Insurance: Transactions and Development Claims and Coverage, Santa Clara County Bar Association. *Member:* Bar Association of San Francisco; Santa Clara County (Member, Real Property and Business Litigation Sections) and American Bar Associations; State Bar of California (Member, Real Property Section and Construction Subcommittee); American Arbitration Association. **LANGUAGES:** Spanish. **PRACTICE AREAS:** Real Estate; Construction; Intellectual Property; White Collar Criminal Defense; Commercial Litigation.

**MARK D. FLANAGAN,** born New York, N.Y., June 22, 1962; admitted to bar, 1987, California, U.S. District Court, Northern, Central and Eastern Districts of California and U.S. Court of Appeals, Ninth Circuit. *Education:* Boalt Hall School of Law, University of California at Los Angeles (B.A., magna cum laude, 1984); University of California at Berkeley (J.D., 1987). Phi Beta Kappa. Member, Moot Court Board. Editor, California Law Review, 1986-1987. Author: "Lateral Moves and the Quest for Clients: Tort Liability of Departing Attorneys for Taking Firm Clients," 75 California Law Review, 1809 (1987). Assistant U.S. Attorney, Criminal Division of the U.S. Attorney's Office in Los Angeles. *Member:* Palo Alto (Co-Chair, Program, 1996-1997), Santa Clara County and American Bar Associations; National Association of Criminal Defense Lawyers. **PRACTICE AREAS:** White Collar Criminal Defense; Business Litigation; Anti-Trust Litigation.

REPRESENTATIVE CLIENTS: Alexander Vineyards; Bay Area Records and Tapes; BayNet World, Inc.; Binaura Corporation; Concrete Solutions; Delta Products Corporation; DTS Trucking, Inc.; Epitaxi, Inc.; Eurotrade, Inc.; Excel Environmental, Inc.; Flowers In Suspension, Inc.; Kosich Construction/Real Estate; LASA Industries, Inc.; Mactivity, Inc.; McMurray Construction, Inc.; Marc Berry Construction, Inc.; Minagratex Corporation; Montalvo Design; NCP (Far East) Limited; Peripheral Technologies, Inc.; Pine Street Properties; Pro-Motions, Inc.; Provisions, Inc.; Reltronix, Inc.; Soma Broadcast, Inc.; Samitomo Construction America, Inc.; Sonic Images; Square Three Design; Sumicon California, Inc.; Sankee Restaurants; T.H.I.S. Design; Trans Texas Natural Gas Corporation; Ultra T Equipment, Inc.; Warner's Interiors.

---

## R. PATRICK SMITH

2600 EL CAMINO REAL
SUITE 618
PALO ALTO, CALIFORNIA 94306
Telephone: 415-494-8977
Fax: 415-494-8979
Email: esq@batnet.com

*Real Estate, Corporate, Business, Contracts, Estate Planning, Mediation.*

**R. PATRICK SMITH,** born Longmont, Colorado, February 14, 1940; admitted to bar, 1969, California. *Education:* University of Colorado (B.S., 1964); Hastings College of Law, University of California (J.D., 1968). *Member:* Palo Alto Area and Santa Clara County Bar Associations; State Bar of California. **PRACTICE AREAS:** Real Estate; Corporate; General Business; Estate Planning; Mediation.

---

## STANWOOD & PRICE

COURT HOUSE PLAZA
SUITE 300, 260 SHERIDAN AVENUE
PALO ALTO, CALIFORNIA 94306
Telephone: 415-321-1440
Fax: 415-321-4746

*General Civil and Trial Practice. Employment, Business, Trade Secrets, Probate, Trust and Estate Planning, Family, Real Property, Personal Injury and Civil Litigation.*

### MEMBERS OF FIRM

**DANIEL R. PRICE,** born Dayton, Ohio, March 17, 1947; admitted to bar, 1974, Ohio; 1977, California. *Education:* Northwestern University (B.S., Mechanical Engineering, 1970, Tau Beta Pi); Georgetown University (J.D., 1973). *Member:* Santa Clara County Bar Association; State Bar of California; California Trial Lawyers Association. **REPORTED CASES:** Parr v. Superior Court (1983) 139 CA3d 440. **PRACTICE AREAS:** Labor and Employment Law; Business Litigation; General Civil Litigation; Personal Injury. **Email:** priced@sourcesvc.com

**THOMAS R. STANWOOD,** born St. Louis, Missouri, March 6, 1948; admitted to bar, 1974, California; 1985, U.S. Tax Court. *Education:* Stanford University (B.A., 1970); Hastings College of the Law, University of California (J.D., 1974). *Member:* Palo Alto Area and Santa Clara County

*(This Listing Continued)*

STANWOOD & PRICE, Palo Alto—Continued

Bar Associations; State Bar of California. **PRACTICE AREAS:** Corporations & Partnerships; Family Law; Real Estate; Estate Planning. **Email:** stanshaw@aol.com

## LAW OFFICE OF
## JOTHAM S. STEIN

400 CAMBRIDGE AVENUE
**PALO ALTO, CALIFORNIA 94306**
Telephone: 415-327-1900
Fax: 415-327-2500
Email: jstein@jotham.com
URL: http://www.jotham.com

*Concentrating on representing employees, mid-level managers and executives in employment-and-business-related matters, including stock option compensation disputes, corporate squeeze outs and power plays, controversies involving usurpation of key players' technology and sexual harassment, breach of contract and wrongful termination cases. General Civil Litigation Practice, including contract disputes, unfair trade practices, business torts, consumer rights and securities law.*

**JOTHAM S. STEIN,** born Buffalo, New York, January 31, 1962; admitted to bar, 1991, California, U.S. District Court, Northern, Southern, Central and Eastern Districts of California, U.S. Court of Appeals, Ninth Circuit and U.S. Court of Federal Claims; 1992, U.S. Court of Appeals for the District of Columbia Circuit; 1993, District of Columbia. *Education:* Princeton University (A.B., 1984); Stanford University (J.D., 1991). Lecturer/Instructor, Legal Research and Writing, School of Law (Boalt Hall), University of California, 1993-1994. *Member:* Palo Alto Area; Santa Clara County and San Mateo County Bar Associations; State Bar of California; District of Columbia Bar. *LANGUAGES:* Spanish. **PRACTICE AREAS:** Litigation.

## LAW OFFICE OF
## PETER S. STERN

400 CAMBRIDGE AVENUE, SUITE A
**PALO ALTO, CALIFORNIA 94306**
Telephone: 415-326-2282
Fax: 415-326-1312
Email: pstern1939@aol.com

*Estate Planning and Administration, Elder Law.*

**PETER S. STERN,** born Philadelphia, Pennsylvania, December 19, 1939; admitted to bar, 1981, California and U.S. District Court, Northern District of California. *Education:* Institut d'Etudes Politiques, Paris, France (C.E.P, 1960); Denison University (B.A., 1961); Princeton University (M.A., 1963); Stanford University (J.D., 1981). *Member:* Palo Alto and Santa Clara County (Member, Board of Trustees, 1992-1994; Chairman, Estate Planning, Trust and Probate Section, 1993 ) Bar Associations; State Bar of California. *LANGUAGES:* French. **PRACTICE AREAS:** Estate Planning Law; Administration Law; Elder Law; Conservatorships; Incapacity Planning; Medi-Cal Planning.

## NANETTE SCHULZE STRINGER

430 COWPER STREET
**PALO ALTO, CALIFORNIA 94301**
Telephone: 415-617-4540
Fax: 415-617-4541

*Family Law and Family Law Mediation.*

**NANETTE SCHULZE STRINGER,** born Stuttgart, Germany, May 29, 1952; admitted to bar, 1978, California. *Education:* Radcliffe College (B.A., cum laude, 1974); Stanford University (J.D., 1978). *Member:* State Bar of California (Member, Family Law Section) (Certified Specialist, Family Law, The State Bar of California Board of Legal Specialization). *LANGUAGES:* French. **PRACTICE AREAS:** Family Law.

## TANKE & WILLEMSEN

*A PROFESSIONAL ASSOCIATION*
2501 PARK BOULEVARD
**PALO ALTO, CALIFORNIA 94306**
Telephone: 415-324-1468
Fax: 415-326-5430
Email: 75022.3105@compuserve.com

Belmont, California Office: 1523 Solana Drive, 94002. Telephone: 415-591-8627. Fax: 415-591-8635.

*Appellate Law, Civil and Criminal, and Civil Litigation.*

**TONY J. TANKE,** born 1951; admitted to bar, 1975, California. *Education:* University of Wisconsin (B.A.); University of Minnesota Law School (J.D., magna cum laude, 1975). Order of the Coif. Editor, Minnesota Law Review. Law Clerk, Justice Fallon Kelly, Minnesota Supreme Court, 1975-1976 and Judge William W. Schwarzer, U.S. District Court, Northern District of California, 1976-1977. Senior Judicial Staff Attorney, California Supreme Court, Chief Justice Malcolm M. Lucas, 1989-1994. Adjunct Professor: Commercial Law, University of San Francisco School of Law; Law and Religion, Graduate Theological Union, Berkeley. **PRACTICE AREAS:** Litigation (60%); Appellate Practice (40%).

**MICHAEL A. WILLEMSEN,** born Grand Rapids, Michigan, September 2, 1937; admitted to bar, 1963, California, U.S. District Court, Northern and Central Districts of California and U.S. Court of Appeals, 9th Circuit; 1991, U.S. Supreme Court. *Education:* Stanford University (B.A., 1959; M.A., 1959; LL.B., summa cum laude, 1962). Phi Beta Kappa; Order of the Coif. President, Stanford Law Review, 1961-1962. Assistant Professor, University of Washington, 1968-1969. Research Attorney, California Supreme Court, 1969-1991. *Member:* State Bar of California (Member, Committee on the Appellate Courts, 1985-1987); California Academy of Appellate Lawyers. **PRACTICE AREAS:** Appellate Practice (85%, 15); Law and Motion Practice (15%, 2).

## THOITS, LOVE, HERSHBERGER & McLEAN

*A PROFESSIONAL CORPORATION*
Established in 1949
245 LYTTON AVENUE, SUITE 300
**PALO ALTO, CALIFORNIA 94301-1426**
Telephone: 415-327-4200
Telecopier: 415-325-5572

*General Civil Practice in State and Federal Courts, Trial and Appeals. Corporate, Partnership, Commercial, Securities, Real Estate, Environmental, Estate Planning, Probate, Taxation, Pension and Profit Sharing, Employee Benefits, Employment, Computer and High Technology Law.*

*FIRM PROFILE: Established in 1949, Thoits, Love, Hershberger & McLean is one of Palo Alto's oldest law firms. Areas of practice are allocated among the members of the firm to fulfill its policy of proficient, efficient and prompt personalized service. Members of the firm and its associates are active in the Palo Alto and Santa Clara county bar associations and on committees of the State Bar. Many of the firm's attorneys have lectured at seminars for members of the Bar and other professionals.*

**JOHN E. LEHMAN** (1919-1982).

**DIANA BERGHAUSEN,** born Milwaukee, Wisconsin, October 14, 1948; admitted to bar, 1978, California. *Education:* Marquette University (B.A., 1970); Colorado State University; University of San Francisco (J.D., cum laude, 1978). Panelist, "Preparing For, Taking and Using Depositions," 1990, "Current Issues in Employment Law," 1991, "Recent Developments in Employment Law," 1992, 1993, 1994, 1995, 1996, California Continuing Education of the Bar. *Member:* Palo Alto, (President 1992-1993; Executive Board Member), Santa Clara County (Executive Board Member: Business Litigation Section, 1983-1985; Committee on Women Lawyers, 1983-1985) and American Bar Associations; The State Bar of California; California Women Lawyers Association. **PRACTICE AREAS:** Business Litigation; Employment Law; Insurance Bad Faith.

**TERRENCE P. CONNER,** born Seattle, Washington, September 19, 1954; admitted to bar, 1979, California. *Education:* University of Santa Clara (B.S., cum laude, 1976; J.D., 1979). *Member:* Palo Alto and American (Member, Section on Corporation, Banking and Business Law) Bar

*(This Listing Continued)*

Associations; The State Bar of California (Member, Sections on: Business Law; Intellectual Property Law and International Law). *PRACTICE AREAS:* Corporate Law; Commercial Law; Intellectual Property and Licensing.

**MICHAEL CURTIS,** born San Mateo, California, July 14, 1947; admitted to bar, 1972, California. *Education:* Menlo College (B.S., cum laude, 1969); Hastings College of the Law (J.D., 1972). *Member:* San Mateo, Palo Alto Area and American Bar Associations; State Bar of California. *PRACTICE AREAS:* Probate; Estate Planning; Trust Administration; Real Property; Business Law.

**STEPHEN A. DENNIS,** born Santa Cruz, California, November 11, 1957; admitted to bar, 1983, California, U.S. District Court, Northern District of California and U.S. Court of Appeals, Ninth Circuit; U.S. Tax Court. *Education:* University of San Diego (B.A., magna cum laude, 1979); University of Santa Clara (J.D., magna cum laude, 1983). Recipient, American Jurisprudence Award in Constitutional Law and Remedies. *Member:* Palo Alto, Santa Clara County and American (Member, Section of Taxation) Bar Associations; The State Bar of California (Member, Section on Taxation). *PRACTICE AREAS:* Taxation Law; Pensions Law; Corporate Law.

**STEPHEN C. GERRISH,** born Hollywood, California, October 24, 1948; admitted to bar, 1974, California and U.S. District Court, Northern District of California. *Education:* Willamette University (B.A., 1970; J.D., 1974). Member, Board of Editors, Williamette Law Journal, 1973-1974. Author: "Implied Warranties of Habitability in Rental Agreements," 9 Willamette Law Journal 164, 1973. Panelist, "Drafting Pleadings," 1984, "Trying A Wrongful Discharge Case," 1986 and "Current Issues in Employment Law," 1989, 1990, California Continuing Education of the Bar. Community Mediator, Los Altos Mediation Program. *Member:* Palo Alto (President, 1983-1984), Santa Clara County and American (Member, Section on Litigation) Bar Associations; The State Bar of California (Member, Section on Alternative Dispute Resolution). *PRACTICE AREAS:* Business Litigation; Real Estate Litigation; Construction Litigation; Employment Law; Alternative Dispute Resolution.

**J. RONALD HERSHBERGER,** born Klamath Falls, Oregon, May 22, 1934; admitted to bar, 1961, Oregon; 1963, California, U.S. District Court, Northern District of California and U.S. Court of Appeals, Ninth Circuit; 1979, U.S. Tax Court. *Education:* University of Oregon (B.A., 1957); Willamette University (J.D., with honors, 1961). Phi Delta Phi. Associate Editor, Willamette Law Journal, 1961. Author: "Trespassing Children: Oregon Adopts a New View," 1 Willamette Law Journal, 379, 1960. Panelist, "Administering the Simple Estate," 1983; "Handling Problems in Trust Administration," 1984; "Using California Trusts," 1988; "Fundamentals of Estate Planning," 1989; "Drafting Wills," 1990. Consultant, Vol. 3, "California Decedent Estate Practice," 1988, California Continuing Education of the Bar. Law Clerk to Justice B. Rey Schauer, California Supreme Court, 1961-1963. *Member:* Palo Alto and American Bar Associations; The State Bar of California (Member, Estate Planning, Trust and Probate Law Section). (Certified Specialist, Estate Planning, Trust and Probate Law, The State Bar of California Board of Legal Specialization). *PRACTICE AREAS:* Probate; Estate Planning; Trust Law.

**THOMAS B. JACOB,** born Lansing, Michigan, May 14, 1951; admitted to bar, 1978, California; 1988, Massachusetts. *Education:* Brown University (A.B., 1973); Hastings College of the Law, University of California (J.D., 1978); Harvard University (M.P.A., 1987). Order of the Coif; Thurston Society. Member, 1976-1977 and Editor, 1977-1978, Hastings Law Journal. Real Estate Broker, California, 1989—. *Member:* Palo Alto Area, San Mateo County, Santa Clara County and American (Member, Real Property, Probate and Trust Law Section) Bar Associations; The State Bar of California (Member, Sections on: Real Property Law; Business Law); The Urban Land Institute. *PRACTICE AREAS:* Real Estate Law.

**WILLIAM J. MCLEAN III,** born Detroit, Michigan, July 12, 1937; admitted to bar, 1966, California. *Education:* San Jose State College (B.S., 1959); The University of California, Hastings College of the Law (J.D., 1966). Deputy District Attorney, Alameda County, 1967-1968. Panelist, CLE Programs: Punitive Damages, Jury Instructions, Wrongful Termination, Remedies for Breach of Contract, Legal Ethics, Hastings College of Trial Advocacy. *Member:* Palo Alto, Alameda County and American Bar Associations; The State Bar of California; American Board of Trial Advocates (Advocate); International Society of Barristers. *PRACTICE AREAS:* Business Litigation; Wrongful Termination Law and Legal Malpractice.

**BRUCE H. MUNRO,** born Teaneck, New Jersey, June 2, 1938; admitted to bar, 1966, California; U.S. District Court, Northern and Eastern Districts of California; U.S. Court of Appeals, Ninth Circuit; U.S. Supreme Court. *Education:* Colgate University (A.B., 1960); University of California, Hastings College of the Law (J.D., 1966). Order of the Coif; Phi Alpha Delta; Thurston Society. Staff Writer, Hastings Law Journal, 1964-1965. Author: "Employment Termination-Silicon Valley Style," The Thoits Law Letter, August, 1989. *Member:* Santa Clara County, San Mateo County and American Bar Associations; The State Bar of California. *PRACTICE AREAS:* Business Litigation; Real Estate Litigation; Employment Law.

**PAUL E. RICE,** born San Mateo, California, August 18, 1948; admitted to bar, 1974, California; 1983, U.S. Tax Court. *Education:* University of Michigan (B.A., 1970); University of San Diego (J.D., cum laude, 1974); New York University (LL.M., in Taxation, 1979). *Member:* Palo Alto, Santa Clara County (Trustee, 1988-1989; Of Counsel, 1989) and American (Member, Section on Litigation) Bar Associations; The State Bar of California (Member, Section on Litigation). *PRACTICE AREAS:* Business Litigation; Real Estate Litigation; Bankruptcy Litigation.

**WARREN R. THOITS,** born Palo Alto, California, May 26, 1922; admitted to bar, 1949, California. *Education:* Stanford University (A.B., 1943; J.D., 1948). *Member:* Palo Alto and American Bar Associations; The State Bar of California (Member, Business Law Section). *PRACTICE AREAS:* Real Estate; Probate Law.

---

**JUDY KOONG BAETH,** born Los Angeles, California, May 26, 1966; admitted to bar, 1993, California. *Education:* Stanford University (A.B., with distinction, 1988); University of California, Hastings College of Law (J.D., 1993). Recipient, American Jurisprudence Award in Legal Writing and Research and in Corporations Law. Extern to the Honorable Fern M. Smith, Judge of the U.S. District Court, Northern District of California, 1992. *Member:* Palo Alto, Santa Clara County and American Bar Associations; State Bar of California. *PRACTICE AREAS:* Taxation; Corporate Law.

**JAMES R. BARNETT,** born Carmi, Illinois, October 16, 1964; admitted to bar, 1990, California. *Education:* Reed College (B.A., 1987); Santa Clara University (J.D., 1990). Recipient, American Jurisprudence Award in Constitutional Law. *Member:* Palo Alto, Santa Clara and American Bar Associations; The State Bar of California. *PRACTICE AREAS:* Corporate Law; Commercial Law; Intellectual Property and Licensing Law.

**LYNN HOWELL DUBOIS,** born Santa Fe, New Mexico, October 7, 1954; admitted to bar, 1994, California. *Education:* Smith College (A.B., summa cum laude, 1991); Stanford University Law School (J.D., 1994). Phi Beta Kappa. First Group Scholar. Symposium Editor, Stanford Law & Policy Review, 1993-1994. Extern to the Honorable Edward A. Panelli, California Supreme Court, 1993. *Member:* Palo Alto, Santa Clara County and American Bar Associations; The State Bar of California. *PRACTICE AREAS:* ERISA; Employee Benefits; Employment Counselling.

**RICHARD L. EHRMAN,** born Palo Alto, California, February 17, 1965; admitted to bar, 1991, California. *Education:* University of California at San Diego (B.A., 1988); University of San Diego (J.D., cum laude, 1991). Recipient, American Jurisprudence Award in Evidence and Torts. *Member:* Palo Alto, Santa Clara County and American Bar Associations; The State Bar of California. *PRACTICE AREAS:* Estate Planning; Trust Litigation; Probate Litigation.

**KENNETH H. HOROWITZ,** born Burlingame, California, April 14, 1962; admitted to bar, 1988, California. *Education:* University of California at Berkeley (B.A., 1984); Golden Gate University (M.S., Taxation, 1987; J.D., with honors, 1988). *Member:* Palo Alto, San Mateo County and American Bar Associations; State Bar of California. *PRACTICE AREAS:* Probate; Estate Planning; Trust Administration; Real Property; Business Law.

**JONATHAN M. SKILES,** born Modesto, California, March 6, 1962; admitted to bar, 1995, California. *Education:* California State University, Stanislaus (B.A., cum laude, 1986); University of Santa Clara (J.D., magna cum laude, 1995). *Member:* Palo Alto, Santa Clara County and American Bar Associations; State Bar of California. *PRACTICE AREAS:* Business Litigation.

**JEFFREY A. SNYDER,** born East Orange, New Jersey, October 27, 1962; admitted to bar, 1990, California, U.S. District Court, Northern and Central Districts of California and U.S. Court of Appeals, Ninth Circuit. *Education:* University of California at San Diego (B.A., 1986); University of San Diego (J.D., cum laude, 1990). Extern Law Clerk to Justice Nares, Fourth District Court of Appeal, San Diego California. *Member:* Palo Alto (President, 1996-1997), Santa Clara County and American Bar Associa-

*(This Listing Continued)*

THOITS, LOVE, HERSHBERGER & McLEAN, A PROFESSIONAL CORPORATION, Palo Alto—Continued

tions; The State Bar of California. *PRACTICE AREAS:* Business Litigation; Real Estate Litigation; Appeals and Writs; Employment Law.

REPRESENTATIVE CLIENTS: CPS Advanced Infusion Systems, Inc. (I.V. and Nutritional Supply Services) FMC Corporation; Guckenheimer Enterprises, Inc. (Food Services); Marriott Corporation (Entertainment); Mid-Peninsula Bank; Northern Telecom, Inc.; Pacific Western Systems, Inc. (semi-conductor test equipment manufacturer); Spectra-Physics Lasers, Inc. (Lasers); Stellar Homes, Inc. (home builders); Virtual World Entertainment Group, Inc. (entertainment software publisher).

## TOMLINSON ZISKO MOROSOLI & MASER LLP

Established in 1983

200 PAGE MILL ROAD, SECOND FLOOR
**PALO ALTO, CALIFORNIA 94306**
Telephone: 415-325-8666
Facsimile: 415-324-1808

*General Business, Business Litigation, Construction, Corporate Finance, Environmental Litigation, Intellectual Property, Labor and Employment, Mergers and Acquisitions, Secured Lending, Securities, Taxation, Trusts and Estates.*

### MEMBERS OF FIRM

**TIMOTHY TOMLINSON,** born Los Angeles, California, February 14, 1950; admitted to bar, 1976, California. *Education:* Stanford University (B.A., 1972; M.B.A., 1976; J.D., 1976). Order of the Coif. Member and Note Editor, Stanford Law Review, 1974-1976. *Member:* State Bar of California. *PRACTICE AREAS:* Corporate Finance and Acquisitions; Business Transactions.

**WILLIAM E. ZISKO,** born Los Angeles, California, December 13, 1952; admitted to bar, 1978, California. *Education:* San Diego State University (B.S., 1975); Boalt Hall School of Law, University of California (J.D., 1978). Order of the Coif. Member, Industrial Relations Law Journal, 1976-1978. *Member:* State Bar of California. *PRACTICE AREAS:* Corporate Finance and Acquisitions; Business Transactions. *Email:* wez@tzmm.com

**EUGENE B. MOROSOLI, JR.,** born San Francisco, California, August 5, 1930; admitted to bar, 1955, California. *Education:* University of San Francisco; University of California at Berkeley (B.A., 1952); Boalt Hall School of Law, University of California (J.D., 1955). Phi Delta Phi. Member, 1969-1973 and Chairman, 1970-1971, City of Millbrae Planning Commission. Partner, Bacigalupi, Elkus, Salinger & Rosenberg, San Francisco, California, 1971-1974. Of Counsel, Hession and Creedon, San Mateo, California, 1981-1984. Special Discovery Referee, San Mateo County Superior Court. Arbitrator, Construction and Employment Disputes. *Member:* Bar Association of San Francisco; State Bar of California (Labor and Employment Law Section). *PRACTICE AREAS:* Labor Law; Arbitration. *Email:* ebm@tzmm.com

**THOMAS F. MASER,** born St. Paul, Minnesota, July 15, 1942; admitted to bar, 1978, California. *Education:* San Jose State University (B.A., 1968); Boalt Hall School of Law, University of California (J.D., 1978). Partner, Anderson & Maser, San Jose, California, 1978-1985. *Member:* Santa Clara County and American (Member, Construction Law Section) Bar Associations; State Bar of California. *PRACTICE AREAS:* Real Estate Law; Construction Law; Construction Litigation. *Email:* tfm@tzmm.com

**JAMES R. BUSSELLE,** born Cheyenne, Wyoming, April 25, 1946; admitted to bar, 1977, California. *Education:* United States Air Force Academy (B.S. in International Studies/Aeronautics, with honors, 1968); Fletcher School of Law and Diplomacy (M.A. in International Affairs, 1969); University of California, Davis School of Law (J.D., 1977). Order of the Coif. Editor-in-Chief, University of California, Davis Law Review, 1976-1977. *Member:* Santa Clara County Bar Association; State Bar of California. [Capt., U.S. Air Force, 1968-1974]. *PRACTICE AREAS:* Intellectual Property; Litigation.

**POLLY A. DINKEL,** born Hamburg, Pennsylvania, March 12, 1955; admitted to bar, 1981, California. *Education:* Pennsylvania State University (B.A., with highest distinction, 1977); Hastings College of Law, University of California (J.D., 1981). Phi Beta Kappa; Order of the Coif. Member, Editorial Board, Hastings Constitutional Law Quarterly, 1980-1981. Extern to Associate Justice Frank K. Richardson, California Supreme Court,

*(This Listing Continued)*

CAA1602B

1980. Adjunct Professor of Law, Hastings College of the Law, 1986. *Member:* State Bar of California (Member, Business Law and Intellectual Property Sections); Computer Law Association; American Electronics Association. *PRACTICE AREAS:* Intellectual Property; Business Transactions. *Email:* pad@tzmm.com

**RICHARD D. JUDKINS,** born St. Louis, Missouri, March 6, 1947; admitted to bar, 1976, New York; 1982, California; 1992, Missouri. *Education:* The Principia College (B.A., with honors, 1968); Columbia University (J.D., 1975). Partner, Holtzmann, Wise & Shepard, Palo Alto, California, 1982-1990. *Member:* State Bar of California. *PRACTICE AREAS:* Corporate Finance and Acquisitions; Securities. *Email:* rdj@tzmm.com

### ASSOCIATES

**CLIFFORD M. GOVAERTS,** born Petaluma, California, December 25, 1949; admitted to bar; 1977, California. *Education:* California State University at Northridge (B.S., 1972); McGeorge School of Law (J.D., 1976); New York University (LL.M., in Taxation, 1977). Adjunct Professor, Santa Clara University, 1981-1994. *Member:* Santa Clara County and American (Member, Taxation Section) Bar Associations; State Bar of California (Member, Taxation Section). (Certified Specialist, Taxation Law, The State Bar of California Board of Legal Specialization). *PRACTICE AREAS:* Tax; Trusts and Estates; Pension Law; ERISA. *Email:* cmg@tzmm.com

**JANETTE M. HOOVER,** born Dallas, Texas, November 11, 1951; admitted to bar, 1978, California. *Education:* Long Island University (B.A., English, summa cum laude, 1973); Boalt Hall School of Law, University of California at Berkeley (J.D., 1977). Associate Editor, Ecology Law Quarterly, 1976-1977. Extern to the Honorable William T. Sweigert, U.S. District Court, Northern District of California, 1976. *Member:* State Bar of California. *PRACTICE AREAS:* Intellectual Property; Construction Law. *Email:* jmh@tzmm.com

**THOMAS E. MOORE, III,** born Houston, Texas, January 26, 1957; admitted to bar, 1984, California and U.S. District Court, Northern District of California; 1992, U.S. District Court, Central District of California. *Education:* Harvard University, Stanford University (A.B., 1979); Boalt Hall School of Law, University of California (J.D., 1984). *Member:* Palo Alto Area, Santa Clara County and American Bar Associations; State Bar of California; Association of Business Trial Lawyers of Northern California. *PRACTICE AREAS:* Breach of Fiduciary Duty; Corporations and Partnerships; Intellectual Property; Commercial Litigation. *Email:* tem@tzmm.com

**OLEG A. VIGDORCHIK,** born Kharkov, U.S.S.R., August 20, 1966; admitted to bar, 1993, California. *Education:* San Jose State University (B.S., 1986); Golden Gate University (J.D., 1991); New York University (LL.M., in Taxation, 1993). Former Agent, Internal Revenue Service. *Member:* State Bar of California. *LANGUAGES:* Russian. *PRACTICE AREAS:* Business Litigation; Corporate Tax.

**CYNTHIA M. LOE,** born Yokohama, Japan, January 26, 1955; admitted to bar, 1984, California. *Education:* University of Washington (B.A., magna cum laude, 1978); Hastings College of the Law (J.D., 1984). Phi Beta Kappa; Thurston Society. Member, Hastings Law Journal, 1982-1983. *Member:* State Bar of California. *PRACTICE AREAS:* Corporate Securities and Acquisitions; Business Transactions. *Email:* cml@tzmm.com

**KATHI A. RAWNSLEY,** born Lowell, Massachusetts, September 8, 1966; admitted to bar, 1995, California and U.S. District Court, Northern District of California. *Education:* University of Vermont (B.A., 1988); Golden Gate University (1992-1993); Santa Clara University (J.D., cum laude, 1995). *Member:* Santa Clara County Bar Association; State Bar of California. *PRACTICE AREAS:* Corporate. *Email:* kar@tzmm.com

**MICHAEL W. MARCHANT,** born Rochester, New York, July 19, 1964; admitted to bar, 1995, California. *Education:* University of Maine (B.S., 1987); University of San Francisco (J.D., 1994). Associate Survey Editor, University of San Francisco Maritime Law Journal, 1993-1994. Author: "U.S. Pacific Rim Survey," University of San Francisco Maritime Law Journal Vol. 6, Spring 1994. Judicial Extern to Judge Charles A. Legge, U.S. District Court, Northern District of California. *Member:* State Bar of California; American Bar Association (Member, International Law and Intellectual Property Sections). *PRACTICE AREAS:* Corporate; Intellectual Property; Securities.

**MICHAEL W. STEBBINS,** born San Jose, California, January 26, 1963; admitted to bar, 1988, California; U.S. District Court, Northern District of California; 1990, U.S. Court of Appeals, Ninth Circuit; U.S. District Court, Eastern District of California; 1991, U.S. District Court, Southern District of California. *Education:* Stanford University (A.B., 1985); Santa

*(This Listing Continued)*

Clara University (J.D., 1988). Phi Alpha Delta. Comments Editor, Santa Clara Law Review, 1987-1988. *Member:* Santa Clara County Bar Association; State Bar of California (Member, Intellectual Property, Litigation Sections). *LANGUAGES:* French. *PRACTICE AREAS:* Intellectual Property Litigation; General Business Litigation; Employment Litigation. *Email:* mws@tzmm.com

### SPECIAL COUNSEL

**MARTIN P. SHERMAN,** born New York, N.Y., May 2, 1940; admitted to bar, 1965, California; 1972, Pennsylvania. *Education:* University of California at Los Angeles (B.A., 1961); University of Chicago (J.D., 1964); University of Southern California (LL.M., 1969). Author: Antitrust/Intellectual Property, ALI-ABA, 1995. *Member:* State Bar of California; American Bar Association; Computer Law Association. *PRACTICE AREAS:* Intellectual Property; Antitrust; Commercial; International; Technology; Computers. *Email:* ms@tzmm.com

**RICHARD ALLAN HORNING,** born Chicago, Illinois, January 12, 1944; admitted to bar, 1970, California. *Education:* University of California (B.A., Political Science, 1966); Duke University (J.D., 1969). Author: "The Statute of Frauds in Cyberspace" in Strategic Alliances in the Information Age, John Wiley & Sons, 1996; "The Ethics of E-Mail: Is the Attorney-Client Privilege Safe in Cyberspace" in Proceedings of the 20th Annual Intellectual Property Law Institute, Intellectual Property Section, California State Bar Association, 1995; "Provisional Relief Proceedings in Technology Litigation" in Intellectual Property Litigation in Technology Cases, Prentice-Hall Trial Advocacy Institute, 1992; "Copyright Protection of Computer Software," International Conference on Computers and Law Program Materials, ICCL, 1988; "Discovery of Electronically Stored Evidence," The Computer Lawyer, Volume 3, No. 2, February, 1986; "Copyright Protection for Computer Software," in Computer Litigation, 1985: Trial Tactics and Techniques, Practicing Law Institute, 1985; "Electronically Stored Evidence: Answers to Some Recurring Questions Concerning Pretrial Discovery and Trial Usage," Washington & Lee Law Review, No. 1, 1984; "Risk Allocation in Computer Contracts," in Computer Litigation 1984: Resolving Computer Related Disputes and Protecting Proprietary Rights, Practicing Law Institute, 1984; "Elements of Copyright Protection," in American Electronics Association Legal Symposium for High Technology Industries, American Electronics Association, 1982; "Plaintiff's Discovery and Pre-Trial in a Computer Related Proprietary Rights Dispute," in Contesting Computer Disputes: Litigation and Other Remedies in Contract, Trade Secret and Copyright Cases, Law and Business, Inc., 1981; "Securing Discovery of Computer Based or Computer Generated Evidence," in Federal Discovery in Complex Civil Cases, New York Law Journal Seminars Press, 1980; "The First Amendment Right to a Public Forum," 1969 Duke Law Journal 931. Law Clerk to Judge Oliver D. Hamlin, Jr., U.S. Court of Appeals for the Ninth Circuit, 1969-1970. Chairman, Antitrust Committee, American Electronics Association Lawyer's Committee, 1983-1985. Member, Board of Directors, Computer Law Section, Bar Association of San Francisco, 1984-1985. *Member:* The Bar Association of San Francisco; Santa Clara and American (Member, Sections on Antitrust Law; Litigation) Bar Associations; The State Bar of California. *PRACTICE AREAS:* Intellectual Property; Litigation; Arbitration. *Email:* rah@tzmm.com

REPRESENTATIVE CLIENTS: Bay Networks, Inc.; Delia's Cleaners, Inc.; Designed Mobile Building Systems, Inc.; Hewlett-Packard Company; Huber, Hunt & Nichols, Inc.; HuntCor, Inc.; International Chamber of Commerce; Oak Technology Inc.; The Portola Co.; Portola Packaging, Inc.; Rosendin Electric; RSA Data Security, Inc.; SmithKline Beecham Corp.; StrataCom, Inc.; Technology Funding, Inc.; VeriSign, Inc.

---

# TOWNSEND and TOWNSEND and CREW LLP

A Limited Liability Partnership including a Professional Corporation

### 379 LYTTON AVENUE
### PALO ALTO, CALIFORNIA 94301-1431

Telephone: 415-326-2400
Telecopier: 415-326-2422
Email: inquire@townsend.com
URL: http://www.townsend.com

*San Francisco, California Office:* Two Embarcadero Center, Eighth Floor. Telephone: 415-576-0200. Facsimile: 415-576-0300.

*Denver, Colorado Office:* 1200 17th Street, Suite 2700. Telephone: 303-571-4000. Fax: 303-571-4321.

*Seattle, Washington Office:* 601 Union Street, Suite 5400. Telephone: 206-467-9600. Telecopier: 206-623-6793.

*(This Listing Continued)*

---

Patent, Trademark, Copyright and Unfair Competition Law, Intellectual Property Law. Intellectual Property, Antitrust and Commercial Litigation.

### MEMBERS OF FIRM

**KENNETH R. ALLEN,** born Salt Lake City, Utah, February 20, 1947; admitted to bar, 1975, California; registered to practice before U.S. Patent and Trademark Office. *Education:* Brigham Young University (B.S.E.E., cum laude, 1971); Massachusetts Institute of Technology (S.M., 1972); Northeastern University (J.D., 1975); Harvard University. Phi Kappa Phi; Tau Beta Pi; Eta Kappa Nu. Director, Cable Co-op of Palo Alto, 1995—. *Member:* Bar Association of San Francisco; Palo Alto Area Bar Association; The State Bar of California; American Intellectual Property Law Association; Peninsula Intellectual Property Law Association (President, 1985-1986); Institute of Electrical and Electronics Engineers. *LANGUAGES:* German. *Email:* krallen@townsend.com

**ROBERT C. COLWELL,** born Alton, Illinois, May 26, 1947; admitted to bar, 1973, California; registered to practice before U.S. Patent and Trademark Office. *Education:* University of Kansas (B.S., with highest distinction, 1969; M.S., 1970); Stanford University (J.D., 1973). Tau Beta Pi; Omicron Delta Kappa. Co-Author: "Litigating the Validity and Infringement of Software Patents," 41 Washington and Lee Law Review 1307, 1985. *Member:* The State Bar of California; American Intellectual Property Law Association; Peninsula Intellectual Property Law Association. *Email:* rccolwell@townsend.com

**DANIEL J. FURNISS,** born Jersey City, New Jersey, July 22, 1951; admitted to bar, 1976, California. *Education:* Stanford University (A.B., with honors, 1973); Boalt Hall School of Law, University of California (J.D., 1976). Co-Chair, Moot Court Board. Deputy District Attorney in charge of Consumer Fraud Division, San Mateo County District Attorneys Office, 1977-1979. Lecturer, The Rutter Group, Advanced Seminar on California Unfair Competition Law, 1990-1992. Trustee, Hillsborough School Board, 1993—. *Member:* Bar Association of San Francisco; San Mateo County and American Bar Associations; The State Bar of California. *Email:* djfurniss@townsend.com

**DAVID N. SLONE,** born Montreal, Quebec, Canada, November 26, 1946; admitted to bar, 1977, California; registered to practice before U.S. Patent and Trademark Office. *Education:* McGill University, Montreal, Quebec (B.Sc., with First Class Honors in Physics, 1967); Stanford University (Ph.D., Physics, 1974; J.D., 1977). Order of the Coif. *Member:* The State Bar of California; American Bar Association; Palo Alto Area Bar Association; American Intellectual Property Law Association; Peninsula Intellectual Property Law Association (President, 1983-1984). *Email:* dnslone@townsend.com

**JAMES F. HANN,** born Hammond, Indiana, May 21, 1948; admitted to bar, 1977, California; registered to practice before U.S. Patent and Trademark Office. *Education:* Virginia Polytechnic Institute and State University (B.S.M.E., with distinction, 1971; M.S., 1973); Hastings College of Law, University of California (J.D., 1977). Tau Beta Pi; Pi Tau Sigma. Vice President, Inventors of California, 1986-1991. Arbitrator, Bar Association of San Francisco, Attorney-Client Free Dispute Committee. *Member:* The State Bar of California; American Bar Association; American Intellectual Property Law Association. [Capt., JAGC, U.S. Army, 1977-1979] *Email:* jfhann@townsend.com

**JAMES M. HESLIN,** born San Mateo, California, October 30, 1950; admitted to bar, 1978, California; registered to practice before U.S. Patent and Trademark Office. *Education:* University of California at Santa Barbara (B.S.Ch.E., highest honors, 1973); Edinburgh University, Edinburgh, Scotland; University of California at Berkeley (J.D., 1978). *Member:* The State Bar of California; American Bar Association; American Intellectual Property Law Association; Peninsula Intellectual Property Association. *Email:* jmheslin@townsend.com

**GARY T. AKA,** born Honolulu, Hawaii, June 18, 1946; admitted to bar, 1975, California; registered to practice before U.S. Patent and Trademark Office. *Education:* University of Hawaii (B.S., 1968); State University of New York at Stony Brook (M.S., 1971); Hastings College of Law, University of California (J.D., 1974). *Member:* The State Bar of California; American Intellectual Property Law Association. *LANGUAGES:* Japanese. *Email:* gtaka@townsend.com

**WILLIAM M. SMITH,** born Toronto, Ontario, Canada, March 17, 1951; admitted to bar, 1979, California; registered to practice before U.S. Patent and Trademark Office. *Education:* University of California at San Diego (B.S., Biology, high honors, 1972); University of Southern California (M.P.A., 1979; J.D., 1979). Author: "Supreme Court Breathes New Life into the Patent Act," New Matter, Vol. 5, No. 3, 1980. *Member:* The State

*(This Listing Continued)*

**TOWNSEND and TOWNSEND and CREW LLP, Palo Alto—**Continued

Bar of California; American Intellectual Property Law Association; Licensing Executives Society (Co-Chairman, Biotechnology Transfer Committee, 1987-1989). (Also at Seattle, Washington Office). *PRACTICE AREAS:* Biotechnology Patent Prosecution, Licensing & Enforcement; Molecular Immunology. *Email:* wmsmith@townsend.com

**PAUL C. HAUGHEY,** born Toledo, Ohio, January 16, 1954; admitted to bar, 1980, California; registered to practice before U.S. Patent and Trademark Office. *Education:* University of California at Irvine (B.S.E.E., 1976); Hastings College of Law, University of California (J.D., 1980). Eta Kappa Nu. *Member:* Order of the Coif; Thurston Society. Note Editor, Hastings Law Journal, 1979-1980. *Author:* Note, "Parker v. Flook and Computer Program Patents," 30 Hastings Law Journal 1627, 1979. *Member:* Bar Association of San Francisco; The State Bar of California; American Bar Association. *PRACTICE AREAS:* Electronic Patent Prosecution, Counseling & Licensing. *Email:* pchaughey@townsend.com

**THEODORE G. BROWN, III,** born Troy, New York, October 17, 1952; admitted to bar, 1984, California; registered to practice before U.S. Patent and Trademark Office. *Education:* College of Wooster (B.A., with honors in Chemistry, 1974); Northwestern University (M.S., 1976; Ph.D., 1979); Boalt Hall School of Law, University of California (J.D., 1984). Author: "Superfund and the National Contingency Plan: How Dirty is Dirty? How Clean is Clean?" 12 Ecology Law Quarterly 89, 1974. *Member:* Bar Association of San Francisco; The State Bar of California; American Bar Association; American Chemical Society. *PRACTICE AREAS:* Intellectual Property Litigation and Counseling. *Email:* tgbrown@townsend.com

**WILLIAM J. BOHLER,** born Aurora, Illinois, February 2, 1957; admitted to bar, 1984, Illinois; 1989, California; registered to practice before U.S. Patent and Trademark Office. *Education:* Purdue University (B.S.E.E., 1979); Southern Illinois University School of Law (J.D., magna cum laude, 1984). Phi Kappa Phi. *Member:* Bar Association of San Francisco; The State Bar of California; Illinois State and American Bar Associations; American Intellectual Property Law Association; San Francisco Intellectual Property Law Association; Federal Circuit Bar Association. *PRACTICE AREAS:* Intellectual Property Litigation; Patents; Counseling. *Email:* wjbohler@townsend.com

**KAREN B. DOW,** born Washington, Pennsylvania, April 29, 1954; admitted to bar, 1979, Indiana; 1988, California; registered to practice before U.S. Patent and Trademark Office. *Education:* Bowling Green State University (B.S., Chemistry with Biology, cum laude, 1976); Indiana University (J.D., cum laude, 1979). Phi Alpha Delta. Co-author, "Proprietary Information: What Are Your Rights and Responsibilities?" Chemical Engineering Progress, 1994. Author: "Admissibility of Computer-Generated Evidence," Computer Law (Indiana Continuing Education Forum, 1984). *Member:* The State Bar of California; American Bar Associations; American Intellectual Property Law Association; San Francisco Intellectual Property Law Association; Licensing Executives Society. *PRACTICE AREAS:* Biotechnology and Chemistry Patent Prosecution; Related Technology Agreements. *Email:* kbdow@townsend.com

## OF COUNSEL

**HENRY K. WOODWARD,** born Del Rio, Texas, October 5, 1938; admitted to bar, 1963, Texas; 1972, District of Columbia; 1976, California; 1976-1982, U.S. Court of Customs and Patent Appeals; 1982, U.S. Court of Appeals for the Federal Circuit; registered to practice before U.S. Patent and Trademark Office. *Education:* University of Texas (B.S.E.E., 1961; LL.B., 1963); Southern Methodist University (M.B.A., 1970). Tau Beta Pi; Eta Kappa Nu; Phi Eta Sigma. *Member:* The State Bar of California; State Bar of Texas; San Francisco Intellectual Property Law Association; Peninsula Intellectual Property Law Association (President, 1980-1981); American Intellectual Property Law Association; Institute of Electrical and Electronic Engineers; Pacific Telecommunications Council. *PRACTICE AREAS:* Patent and Trade Secret Law; Technology Law; Electronics and Physics. *Email:* hkwoodward@townsend.com

**RENÉE A. FITTS,** born Chicago, Illinois, April 23, 1952; admitted to bar, 1991, California; registered to practice before U.S. Patent and Trademark Office. *Education:* University of Chicago (B.A., 1974); University of Colorado (Ph.D., 1980); Boalt Hall School of Law, University of California (J.D., 1991). *Member:* State Bar of California. *PRACTICE AREAS:* Patent Law. *Email:* rafitts@townsend.com

*(This Listing Continued)*

## ASSOCIATES

**JOE LIEBESCHUETZ,** born Belper, United Kingdom, November 13, 1959; admitted to bar, 1992, California; registered to practice before U.S. Patent and Trademark Office. *Education:* Cambridge University (B.A., 1982); Liverpool University (Ph.D., 1986); Indiana University (J.D., summa cum laude, 1992). Articles Editor, Indiana Law Review, 1990-1992. Author, "Statutory Control of DNA Fingerprinting in Indiana," Ind. L. Rev. Vol 25, 1991. *Member:* Bar Association of San Francisco; The State Bar of California. *PRACTICE AREAS:* Biotechnology Patents. *Email:* jliebeschuetz@townsend.com

**JOSEPH M. VILLENEUVE,** born Los Angeles, California, June 10, 1963; admitted to bar, 1992, California; registered to practice before U.S. Patent and Trademark Office. *Education:* University of California at Santa Barbara (B.S.E.E., 1985); Hastings College of the Law, University of California at San Francisco (J.D., 1992). Eta Kappa Nu Engineering Honor Society; Moot Court Board. Chancellor's Scholar. *Member:* The State Bar of California. *PRACTICE AREAS:* Electronic and Software Patents; Licensing. *Email:* jmvilleneuve@townsend.com

**WILLIAM L. SHAFFER,** born Ridgewood, New Jersey, January 21, 1966; admitted to bar, 1992, California; registered to practice before U.S. Patent and Trademark Office. *Education:* Vanderbilt University (E.E. and Computer Science, 1988); Southern Methodist University (J.D., 1992). Articles Editor, 1990-1991, Associate Comments Editor, 1991-1992, International Lawyer. *Member:* The State Bar of California; San Francisco Intellectual Property Law Association. *PRACTICE AREAS:* Electronic and Semiconductor Patent Prosecution. *Email:* wlshaffer@townsend.com

**RICHARD TAKASHI OGAWA,** born Sanger, California, October 10, 1962; admitted to bar, 1992, California; registered to practice before U.S. Patent and Trademark Office. *Education:* University of California (B.S., 1984); McGeorge School of Law (J.D., 1991). *Member:* The State Bar of California; American Bar Association. *PRACTICE AREAS:* Patent Prosecution and Licensing. *Email:* rtogawa@townsend.com

**THEODORE T. HERHOLD,** born Minneapolis, Minnesota, August 27, 1957; admitted to bar, 1986, California; 1991, Hawaii. *Education:* Stanford University (A.B., departmental honors, 1981); Hastings College of the Law, University of California (J.D., 1986). Technical Editor, Hastings Communications and Entertainment Law Journal, 1984-1985. Clerk to: Justice Mariel B. Poché, California Court of Appeal, 1985; Judge Raymond Williamson, San Francisco Superior Court, Law and Motion, 1985. Judge Pro Tem, Santa Clara Municipal Court, Small Claims Division. *Member:* The State Bar of California; Hawaii State and American Bar Associations. *LANGUAGES:* Spanish. *PRACTICE AREAS:* Commercial Litigation. *Email:* ttherhold@townsend.com

**SHAILENDRA C. BHUMRALKAR,** born Nagpur, India, March 8, 1965; admitted to bar, 1993, California; registered to practice before U.S. Patent and Trademark Office. *Education:* Stanford University (B.S., 1987); Georgetown University (J.D., 1993). National Merit Scholar. *Member:* The State Bar of California; American Bar Association; American Intellectual Property Law Association; San Francisco Intellectual Property Law Association. *LANGUAGES:* German. *PRACTICE AREAS:* Patent Law; Intellectual Property. *Email:* scbhumralkar@townsend.com

**STEPHEN Y.F. PANG,** born Evanston, Illinois, October 21, 1963; admitted to bar, 1993, California; registered to practice before U.S. Patent and Trademark Office. *Education:* Massachusetts Institute of Technology (S.B.E.E., 1985); George Washington University (J.D., 1993). *Member:* The State Bar of California; American Bar Association. *PRACTICE AREAS:* Electronics and Software Patent Prosecution. *Email:* sypang@townsend.com

**DAN H. LANG,** born New York, N.Y., October 5, 1964; admitted to bar, 1993, California; registered to practice before U.S. Patent and Trademark Office. *Education:* Case Western Reserve University (B.S.E.E., with high honors, 1986); Stanford University (M.S.E.E., 1987); Boalt Hall School of Law, University of California, Berkeley (J.D., 1993). Eta Kappa Nu; Tau Beta Pi. Senior Articles Editor, High Technology Law Journal. *Member:* Bar Association of San Francisco; The State Bar of California; American Bar Association; Institute of Electrical and Electronics Engineers. *PRACTICE AREAS:* Patent Law; Intellectual Property. *Email:* dhlang@townsend.com

**MICHAEL J. RITTER,** born Tempe, Arizona, January 6, 1965; admitted to bar, 1994, California; registered to practice before U.S. Patent and Trademark Office. *Education:* University of Texas (B.A.C.S., with honors, 1987; J.D., with honors, 1994). *Member:* The State Bar of California; American Intellectual Property Law Association; Peninsula Intellectual Property

*(This Listing Continued)*

Law Association. **PRACTICE AREAS:** Electronic and Software Patent Prosecution. **Email:** mjritter@townsend.com

**JOHN THOMAS RAFFLE,** born Aliquippa, Pennsylvania, May 23, 1968; admitted to bar, 1994, California; registered to practice before U.S. Patent and Trademark Office. *Education:* Massachusetts Institute of Technology (B.S., 1990); Duke University (J.D., 1994). Editor, Law & Contemporary Problems Journal. *Member:* The State Bar of California. **PRACTICE AREAS:** Aeronautical, Mechanical and Medical Device Patent Prosecution. **Email:** jtraffle@townsend.com

**MATTHEW B. MURPHY,** born Palo Alto, California, January 12, 1965; admitted to bar, 1994, California; registered to practice before U.S. Patent and Trademark Office. *Education:* University of California at Davis (B.S., 1988); University of San Francisco (J.D., with honors, 1994). Member, University of San Francisco Law Review. **PRACTICE AREAS:** Biotechnology, Patent Prosecution, Intellectual Property Licensing and Counseling. **Email:** mbmurphy@townsend.com

**MARK D. BARRISH,** born Lemoore, California, June 13, 1962; admitted to bar, 1994, California. *Education:* University of California, Santa Barbara (B.S.M.E., with honors, 1986); Hastings College of the Law, University of California, San Francisco (J.D., 1994). Tau Beta Ph; Pi Tau Sigma. Author, "Disclosure of Computer Reenactments During Pretrial Discovery," 16 Comm/Ent 691, 1994. Member, Licensing Executive Society. *Member:* The State Bar of California; American Intellectual Property Law Association. **LANGUAGES:** Spanish. **PRACTICE AREAS:** Medical Device, Mechanical and Electro - Mechanical Patent Prosecution. **Email:** mdbarrish@townsend.com

**MELVIN D. CHAN,** born New York, N.Y., October 2, 1965; admitted to bar, 1994, California; registered to practice before U.S. Patent and Trademark Office. *Education:* University of California, Berkeley (B.S.E.E.C.S., 1987); McGeorge School of Law (J.D., 1994). Managing Editor, The Transnational Lawyer, 1993-1994. Author, "Fortino v. Quasar Co.: Invocation of Parents' U.S. - Japan FCN Treaty Rights Gives Japanese-Owned U.S. Subsidiaries a Defense Against Title VII," 6 Transnat'l Law. 653, 1993. *Member:* The State Bar of California; American Intellectual Property Law Association. **Email:** mdchan@townsend.com

**MARGARET A. POWERS,** born Oak Park, Illinois, March 12, 1954; admitted to bar, 1994, California; registered to practice before U.S. Patent and Trademark Office. *Education:* University of Illinois (B.S., 1977); University of California, Santa Cruz (M.S., 1979; B.A., 1984); Stanford University (M.A., 1988); Hastings College of the Law, University of California, San Francisco (J.D., 1994). Alpha Lambda Delta. Illinois State Scholar. Recipient: Hastings 1066 Foundation Scholarly Journalist Achievement Award; University of California Chancellor's Award (Highest Honors). Executive Articles Editor, 1993-1994, Member, 1992-1993, Hastings International and Comparative Law Review. Stanford Graduate Fellowships. Law Extern, Honorable Cecil F. Poole, U.S. Court of Appeals, Ninth Circuit, 1993. Instructor, Chemistry, University of California, Santa Cruz, 1982 and 1983. Teaching Associate in Chemistry, University of California, Santa Cruz, 1980-1985. Co-author: "Nanosecond Laser Photolysis of Rhodopsin and Isorhodopsin," 37 Photochemistry and Photobiology 181, 1983; "Kinetics of Rhodopsin Photolysis Intermediates in Retinal Rod Disk Membranes: Temperature Dependence of Lumirhodopsin and Metarhodopsin I Kinetics," 34 Photochemistry and Photobiology 375, 1981; "Modeling of Metarhodopsin I Equilibration Kinetics," American Society for Photobiology Abstracts, 1979; *ITS40 Operator's Manual,* Finnigan Corporation, 1989. Author: published by Finnigan Corporation: *Selected Topics in Quantitation*; *Particle Beam Interface Operator's Manual,* 1991; *Electrospray Ionization System Operator's Manual,* 1991; *ITS40 (Ion Trap System) Chemical Ionization Operator's Manual,* 1990; *ITS40 Getting Started Manual,* 1990; *ITS40 Preinstallation Requirements Guide,* 1989; *Supercritical Fluid Chromatography Manual,* 1988; *BioProbe Accessory Operator's Manual,* 1988. *Member:* The State Bar of California. **PRACTICE AREAS:** Intellectual Property; Litigation; Biotechnology. **Email:** mapowers@townsend.com

**KENNETH L. JOHNSON,** born Fort Benning, Georgia, December 9, 1961; admitted to bar, 1995, California. *Education:* Georgia Institute of Technology (M.S.E.E., 1986); Georgetown University Law Center (J.D., 1994). Phi Eta Sigma. Recipient, International Academy of Trial Lawyers Student Advocacy Award. Member, GEM Fellowship. *Member:* The State Bar of California. **PRACTICE AREAS:** Patent; Trademark; Antitrust. **Email:** kljohnson@townsend.com

**STEPHEN J. AKERLEY,** born Lewiston, Maine, July 5, 1967; admitted to bar, 1992, California, U.S. District Court, Northern District of California and U.S. Court of Appeals, Ninth Circuit. *Education:* Cornell University (B.S., 1989); University of San Francisco (J.D., 1992). *Member:* The State Bar of California; American Intellectual Property Law Association; San Francisco Intellectual Property Law Association. **PRACTICE AREAS:** Intellectual Property Litigation; Commercial Litigation. **Email:** sjakerley@townsend.com

**ALICE L. WONG,** born Malaysia, March 20, 1971; admitted to bar, 1995, California; registered to practice before U.S. Patent and Trademark Office. *Education:* University of Akron (B.S.E.E., 1992); Hastings College of the Law, University of California, San Francisco (J.D., 1995). Tau Beta Pi; Eta Kappa Nu. IEEE outstanding student, Omicron Delta Kappa. *Member:* The State Bar of California. **LANGUAGES:** Mandarin, Cantonese, Malay. **PRACTICE AREAS:** Intellectual Property. **Email:** alwong@townsend.com

**MICHAEL A. GELBLUM,** born Montreal, Quebec, Canada, April 23, 1960; admitted to bar, 1994, Ontario and California. *Education:* Princeton University (B.S.E., summa cum laude, 1982); University of Toronto (M.Sc., 1984; LL.B., 1992). Phi Beta Kappa, Tau Beta Pi. *Member:* The State Bar of California. **Email:** magelblum@townsend.com

**SAM G. CAMPBELL, III,** born Melbourne, Florida, February 27, 1961; admitted to bar, 1996, Florida and California. *Education:* University of Florida (B.S., Business Administration, 1985; B.S., Computer Engineering, 1986; Electrical Engineering, cum laude, 1990; M.S., Electrical Engineering, 1991; J.D., cum laude, 1995). Eta Kappa Nu. Pro Bono Publico Certificate. *Member:* The State Bar of California; Federal Bar Association; American Intellectual Property Law Association. **PRACTICE AREAS:** Patent Prosecution. **Email:** sgcampbell@townsend.com

**BYRON W. COOPER,** born Sacramento, California, June 1, 1963; admitted to bar, 1993, California; registered to practice before U.S. Patent and Trademark Office. *Education:* United States Military Academy (B.S., 1986); University of Southern California (M.S.S.M., 1988); University of California at Los Angeles (J.D., 1993). Phi Delta Phi. *Member:* The State Bar of California; American Intellectual Property Law Association. [Capt. U.S. Army, 1981-1990]. **PRACTICE AREAS:** Intellectual Property; Patents, Trademarks and Copyrights; Commercial Litigation. **Email:** bwcooper@townsend.com

**SCOTT WILLIAM HEWETT,** born Evanston, Illinois, September 3, 1954; admitted to bar, 1996, California. *Education:* University of California, Davis (B.S.E.E., 1976); University of California School of Law, Davis (J.D., 1996). Editor, University of California Law Review. President, King Hall Intellectual Property Law Association, 1975-1976. **PRACTICE AREAS:** Patent Law. **Email:** swhewett@townsend.com

**R. TED APPLE,** admitted to bar, 1996, California. *Education:* University of California, Berkeley (B.A., Biochemistry, 1979; Ph.D., 1989); Boalt Hall School of Law, University of California, Berkeley (J.D., 1996). Postdoctroal Fellow, Genentech, Inc. South San Francisco, California, 1989-1992. Assistant Editor High Technology Law Journal, 1995. Author, "Enablement Estoppel: Should Prosecution History Estoppel Arise When Claims Are Amended to Overcome Enablement Rejections?" Santa Clara Computer and High Technology Law Journal (Winter 1996). Co-author: "20-Hydroxyescysone is Required for, and Negatively Regulates, Transcription of Drosphila Pupal Cuticle Protein Genes," Developmental Biology 146, 569-82; W.C. Darbonne, G.C. Rice, M.A. Mohler, T. Apple, C.A. Herbert, A. Valante and J.B. Baker, "Red Blood Cells Are A Sink for Interleukin 8, A Luekocyte Chemotaxin," J. Clin. Invest. 88, 1362-69, 1991. **PRACTICE AREAS:** Biotechnology Patent Prosecution. **Email:** rta@townsend.com

**CHIAHUA GEORGE YU,** born Taipei, Taiwan, February 10, 1968; admitted to bar, 1996, California. *Education:* Massachusetts Institute of Technology (B.S., 1988; M.S., 1990); Columbia University (J.D., 1996). **LANGUAGES:** Chinese (Mandarin). **PRACTICE AREAS:** Intellectual Property. **Email:** cgyu@townsend.com

**HAO-YUAN TUNG,** born Taipei, Taiwan, 1971; admitted to bar, 1996, California. *Education:* Massachusetts Institute of Technology (B.S., 1993); Stanford Law School (J.D., 1996). Tau Beta Pi; Pi Tau Sigma; Sigma Xi. Managing Editor, Stanford Journal of International Law, 1995-1996. **Email:** hytung@townsend.com

**GREGORY SCOTT BISHOP,** born Jerome, Idaho, June 23, 1962; admitted to bar, 1996, California. *Education:* Brigham Young University (B.S.E.E., 1987); Syracuse University (M.S.C.E., 1989); J. Reuben Clark Law School (J.D., 1996). **PRACTICE AREAS:** Intellectual Property. **Email:** gsbishop@townsend.com

*(This Listing Continued)*

**TOWNSEND and TOWNSEND and CREW LLP, Palo Alto**—Continued

**SHANE HORAN HUNTER,** born Edwards, California, July 11, 1967; admitted to bar, 1996, California. *Education:* GMI Engineering and Management Institute (B.S.E.E., cum laude, 1990); University of California School of the Law, Los Angeles (J.D., 1996). Tau Beta Pi; Eta Kappa Nu; Phi Alpha Delta. *PRACTICE AREAS:* Patent Law. *Email:* shhunter@townsend.com

**JAMES F. KURKOWSKI,** born 1962; admitted to bar, 1990, Maryland; 1991, District of Columbia; 1993, California; 1995, Massachusetts; registered to practice before the U.S. Patent and Trademark Office. *Education:* Tufts University (B.S.E.E., magna cum laude, 1984); University of Pennsylvania (M.S.E., 1986); University of Pennsylvania (J.D., 1990). Tau Beta Pi; Eta Kappa Nu. *PRACTICE AREAS:* Patent Law. *Email:* jfkurkowski@townsend.com

(For complete firm personnel and Biographical data, see Professional Biographies San Francisco, California).

---

## WEINBERG, ZIFF & MILLER

*Established in 1971*

**400 CAMBRIDGE AVENUE, SUITE A
PALO ALTO, CALIFORNIA 94306**

*Telephone: 415-329-0851
Fax: 415-324-2822
Email: taxlawyer@aol.com
URL: http://www.taxlawyer.com*

General Civil and Trial Practice. Business, Corporate, Taxation, Family, Personal Injury, Collections, Estate Planning, Probate, Trust Litigation, Appeals and Administration. Criminal Trials.

FIRM PROFILE: *Weinberg, Ziff & Miller was founded in 1971. The firm receives a significant portion of its work from referrals from other law firms. Each of the partners has extensive experience in his areas of concentration. Members of the firm frequently lecture and contribute articles to professional groups.*

### MEMBERS OF FIRM

**DAVID C. WEINBERG,** born Minneapolis, Minnesota, April 23, 1940; admitted to bar, 1965, Minnesota; 1969, California. *Education:* University of Minnesota (B.A., 1962; J.D., 1965). Author: "Conduct of a Custody Case," American Psychological Association Proceedings, 1985. Special Assistant Attorney General, Minnesota, 1965-1967. Assistant County Attorney, Hennepin County, Minnesota, 1968-1969. Deputy Public Defender, Santa Clara County, California, 1970-1972. Instructor: Family Law Section, American Bar Association, 1989 Family Mediation Institute, Stanford University Law School; Representing Clients in Spousal and Child Support Matters, California Continuing Education of the Bar (CEB), 1991. Guest Lecturer: Family Law-Custody, Stanford University Law School, 1983-1985; Family Law, University of Minnesota Law School, 1981; "Legal Responsibilities of the Mental Health Professional," Pacific Graduate School of Psychology, 1987-1992; "Child Custody-Role of the Expert Witness," California School of Professional Psychology, 1985-1986; "Adversary Child Custody Proceedings," Santa Clara County Family Court Services, 1987. Judge Pro Tem: San Mateo County Superior Court, 1984-1995; Santa Clara County Superior Court, 1986-1995. *Member:* Palo Alto, Santa Clara County (Member, Executive Committee, Family Law Section, 1984—), San Mateo County and American Bar Associations; State Bar of California; California Association of Certified Family Law Specialists; Northern Conference of Attorney Mediators; Academy of Family Mediators; Association of Family and Conciliation Courts. (Certified Specialist, Family Law, The State Bar of California Board of Legal Specialization). *PRACTICE AREAS:* Family Law; Tax Problems of Divorce Law; Custody Law. *Email:* 75270.35@compuserve.com

**HARVEY L. ZIFF,** born Buffalo, New York, August 24, 1942; admitted to bar, 1967, California; 1986, U.S. Supreme Court. *Education:* Wharton School of Finance, University of Pennsylvania (B.S., 1964); Stanford University (J.D., 1967); Northwestern University (LL.M., 1969). Member, Board of Editors, Stanford Law Review, 1966-1967. Faculty, Stanford University Law School Advocacy Clinic, 1994—. Special Assistant U.S. Attorney, 1968-1969. Deputy Public Defender, Santa Clara County, 1969-1970. Vice President, A. L. Schultz Jewish Community Center, 1985-1988. *Member:* Palo Alto, Santa Clara County and San Mateo County Bar Associations; State Bar of California; California Trial Lawyers Association; Million Dollar Advocates Forum. *SPECIAL AGENCIES:* Department of Motor Vehicles License Suspension Appeals. *PRACTICE AREAS:* Personal Injury; Commercial Law; Criminal Defense Law.

**MICHAEL PATIKY MILLER,** born Huntington, New York, April 16, 1944; admitted to bar, 1968, New Jersey; 1975, California; 1977, U.S. Tax Court; 1984, U.S. Supreme Court. *Education:* Rutgers University (A.B., cum laude, 1965); New York University (J.D., 1968). Author: "Creditors Rights in Proceedings Outside Estate Administration," Calif. CEB 1995; "Summary of Creditor Rights in Proceedings Outside of Formal Estate Administration," Summer, 1992, California Bar Estate Planning, Trust and Probate News; "Tax Treatment of Damage Awards and Structure & Settlements," Nov., 1991; "Joint Tenancy Agency Agreements" both articles published in The Docket, San Mateo County Bar Association. "Update on Whether to Consider Using a Funded Living Trust to Avoid Probate," 16 Estate Planning 140 (May/June, 1989); "Tax and Financial Planning For Your Children's Education," Phys. Tax & Acctg. Adv., Winter, 1988; "Estate Planning for a Client Pending Divorce," Winter, 1983 and "Estate Planning and Divorce," Summer, 1983, California Bar Estate Planning, Trust and Probate; "Survey of California Corporate Fiduciary Fees and Practices," California Bar Estate Planning & Trust News, Fall, 1985. Lecturer, "Creditor Claims," 1995, "Administration of Estates," 1981-1988, "Developments in Probate," 1986-1989, "Mathematics of Estate Planning," 1986 and "Will Drafting," 1992-1994, California Continuing Education of the Bar; "Fundamentals of Estate Administration, 1990, California Continuing Education of the Bar. Instructor, "Estate Planning," University of Santa Clara Law School, 1981. Member, California Board of Legal Specialization, 1994-1995. *Member:* Palo Alto, Santa Clara County (Member: Executive Committee, Taxation Section, 1977; 1989-1992; Estate Planning, Trust and Probate Section, 1978—; Chairman, 1982; Trustee, 1983-1984), San Mateo County (Member, Executive Committee, Probate Section, 1986—) and American (Member, Sections of: Public Contract Law and Chairman, Region VI, 1976-1979; Real Property and Probate; Taxation; Income of Estates and Trusts Committee, 1987-1989) Bar Associations; State Bar of California (Commissioner, Tax Law Advisory Commission, 1989-1992; Appointed, 1993-1995; Chairman, 1994-1995). (Certified Specialist, Taxation Law, The State Bar of California Board of Legal Specialization). *SPECIAL AGENCIES:* Internal Revenue Service Appeals Division, California State Board of Equalization, Merit Systems Protection Board, California Unemployment Insurance Appeals Board. *REPORTED CASES:* Estate of Heggstad, 16 CA4th 943 (1993). *PRACTICE AREAS:* Tax Law; Estate Planning Law; Probate and Trust Litigation.

REPRESENTATIVE CLIENTS: Hewlett-Packard Corp.; Raychem Corp.; First International Bank of Israel; Bell Industries; Fisher-Brownell; SST Systems, Inc.; Integrated Device Technologies, Inc.

---

## RANDALL M. WIDMANN

**SUITE 200, 2370 WATSON COURT
PALO ALTO, CALIFORNIA 94304**

*Telephone: 415-424-8400
Fax: 415-494-7006*

*Employment Law, Business and Real Estate Litigation.*

**RANDALL M. WIDMANN,** born Great Lakes, Illinois, June 26, 1949; admitted to bar, 1976, California. *Education:* California State University at Sacramento (B.A., 1971); University of Stockholm, Stockholm, Sweden; University of Santa Clara (J.D., cum laude, 1976). Phi Alpha Delta. Member, Santa Clara Law Review, 1975-1976. Author: Real Estate for the Student Consumer and Examinee; The Municipal Courts of Santa Clara County; "Divorce Without Marriage: The Subject Matter Jurisdiction Anomaly in California," 16 Santa Clara Law Review. Instructor, Real Estate Law and Business Law, DeAnza College, 1978-1983. Placement Director, University of Santa Clara Law School, 1975-1977. Judge Pro Tem: Santa Clara County Superior Court, 1978—; Municipal Court, 1983—. Delegate, Joint U.S./China International Trade Conference, Beijing, People's Republic of China, 1987. *Member:* Santa Clara County (Trustee, 1985-1986) and American (Member, Litigation Section) Bar Associations; The State Bar of California. *LANGUAGES:* Swedish.

REPRESENTATIVE CLIENTS: Dusty Baker; Roeder-Johnson Corp.

## WILSON MARSHALL & TAYLOR
ONE EMBARCADERO PLACE, SUITE 220
2100 GENG ROAD
PALO ALTO, CALIFORNIA 94303-3317
Telephone: 415-424-9700
Fax: 415-424-9769
Email: wmt@wmtlaw.com

*Corporate and Commercial Transactions, Intellectual Property, Securities, Mergers and Acquisitions, Real Property, International Business and Civil Litigation.*

### MEMBERS OF FIRM

**PHILIP J. WILSON,** born Long Beach, California, 1953; admitted to bar, 1983, California. *Education:* University of California at Berkeley (A.B., 1975; M.A., 1976); Harvard University (J.D., 1983). **LANGUAGES:** German, Spanish and Swedish. **PRACTICE AREAS:** Corporate Law; Commercial Transactions; Intellectual Property; Securities; Mergers and Acquisitions; International Business.

**G.E. MARSHALL IV,** born Ravenna, Ohio, 1959; admitted to bar, 1985, California. *Education:* University of California at Berkeley (A.B., with high honors, 1981); Hastings College of the Law, University of California (J.D., cum laude, 1985). Member, Thurston Society. Member, 1983-1984 and Editor, 1984-1985, Hastings Law Journal. Extern Law Clerk to the Honorable Malcolm M. Lucas, Associate Justice, California Supreme Court. **PRACTICE AREAS:** Corporate and Commercial Transactions; Corporate Law; Intellectual Property; Licensing; Real Property.

**KURT H. TAYLOR,** born Austin, Texas, July 11, 1957; admitted to bar, 1986, California. *Education:* University of California at Berkeley (B.A., 1980); Santa Clara University (J.D., 1986). Associate Editor, Santa Clara Law Review, Volume 26, 1985-1986. Founding Director and President, San Jose Chamber Orchestra. *Member:* Santa Clara County (Member, Computer Law Section) and American Bar Associations; State Bar of California (Member, Intellectual Property Section). **PRACTICE AREAS:** Intellectual Property; Commercial and Technology Litigation; Corporate Law; Licensing.

## WILSON, SONSINI, GOODRICH & ROSATI
PROFESSIONAL CORPORATION
650 PAGE MILL ROAD
PALO ALTO, CALIFORNIA 94304-1050
Telephone: 415-493-9300
Internet: postmaster@wsgr.com
Telex: 345500 wilson pla
Fax: 415-493-6811
Email: wsgr@wsgr.com
URL: http://www.wsgr.com

*General Civil and Trial Practice, Corporate, Securities, Mergers and Acquisitions, Antitrust, Domestic and International Taxation, Employee Benefits and Compensation, Estate Planning, Probate, Real Property and Intellectual Property Law.*

**FIRM PROFILE:** The Firm has developed a national practice representing emerging growth companies in the micro-electronics, interactive new media, life sciences and consumer products industries as well as investment banks, venture capital funds and other financial institutions. The Firm regularly represents more than 175 public and over 1,000 private companies, ranging from domestic start-ups to multi-national Fortune 100 companies. The Firm's practice covers a broad spectrum of corporate, litigation and intellectual property services, with substantial experience and special expertise in private and public financings, securities law compliance, mergers and acquisitions, securities and intellectual property litigation, strategic alliances and joint ventures, antitrust, patents, trade secrets, trademarks, copyright, technology licensing and software protection, venture capital fund formation, tax, and employee benefits and compensation.

**AARON J. ALTER,** born Taipei, Taiwan, May 20, 1957; admitted to bar, 1985, California. *Education:* Harvard University (A.B., magna cum laude, 1979; M.B.A., 2nd year honors, 1985; J.D., 1985); Chinese University of Hong Kong. First Marshal, Class of 1979. Recipient, Rotary International Fellowship, 1981. Director, Harvard Alumni Association, 1987-1989. *Member:* Bar Association of San Francisco; Santa Clara County and American Bar Association; State Bar of California. **LANGUAGES:** Mandarin Chinese. **PRACTICE AREAS:** Corporate Law; Securities. **Email:** aalter@wsgr.com

**DENISE M. AMANTEA,** born San Diego, California, January 7, 1951; admitted to bar, 1980, California. *Education:* University of California at San Diego (B.A., 1976); University of Santa Clara (J.D., 1979). Associate Editor, Santa Clara Law Review, 1979. Law Clerk to Justice William A. Newsom, California Court of Appeal, 1979-1980. *Member:* State Bar of California; American Bar Association. **PRACTICE AREAS:** Litigation. **Email:** damantea@wsgr.com

**AILEEN L. ARRIETA,** born Oakland, California, August 12, 1961; admitted to bar, 1987, California. *Education:* University of California at Berkeley (A.B., with high honors, 1983); Columbia University (J.D., 1987). *Member:* State Bar of California. **PRACTICE AREAS:** Litigation. **Email:** aarrieta@wsgr.com

**ALAN K. AUSTIN,** born Des Moines, Iowa, 1948; admitted to bar, 1975, California. *Education:* Harvard University (A.B., 1970); Stanford University (J.D., 1974). Order of the Coif. Senior Note Editor, Stanford Law Review, 1973-1974. Co-Author: Austin and Priest, "Risk Disclosure in Securities Filings," InSights, No. 3 at 6, 1993; Austin and Tanner, "The Private Placement Memorandum in Start-up Companies, 1994. Law Clerk to Justice William O. Douglas, U.S. Supreme Court, 1974-1975. Chairman: Securities Filings (PLI, 1986-1996); Advanced Securities Law Workshop (PLI, 1990-1991) and Introduction to Securities Filings (PLI, 1990-1991). Panelist, Understanding Securities Laws (PLI, 1992-1994); Opinions in SEC Transaction (PLI, 1990-1991); Mechanics of Underwriting (PLI, 1987); Creative Corporate Financing Techniques (PLI, 1986). Member, PLI Corporate and Securities Law Advisory Committee. *Member:* State Bar of California; American Bar Association. **PRACTICE AREAS:** Corporate Law; Securities. **Email:** aaustin@wsgr.com

**JONATHAN AXELRAD,** born New York, N.Y., March 19, 1962; admitted to bar, 1988, New York, U.S. Tax Court and U.S. Court of Federal Claims; 1990, California. *Education:* Wesleyan University (B.A., with high honors, 1984); Yale University (J.D., 1987). Claude R. Lambe Fellow. Member, Editorial Board, Journal of State Taxation. Phi Beta Kappa. Author: "How Will Treasury's Proposed Check-the-Box Regulations Affect Fund Agreements," 36 Venture Capital Journal, August 1996; "Choice of Entity: Should You Use a C Corporation, S Corporation or Limited Liability Company," Pratt's Guide to Venture Capital Sources, 1995; "Limited Liability Companies Finally Arrive for Venture Capital Firms," 34 Venture Capital Journal, November 1994; "Securities Investment Partnerships: California Taxation of Nonresident Partners," 12 Journal of State Taxation 72, Summer 1993; "Multi-tier Partnerships Can Pay General Partners for Results and Avoid Guaranteed Payments," 10 Journal of Taxation of Investments 83, Winter 1993; "California Reduces Withholding Risks for General Partners of Venture Funds," 32 Venture Capital Journal No. 10, October 1992; "Employee Partners: The Quest for Dual Status," 1 California Tax Lawyer No. 3, Fall 1991. *Member:* State Bar of California (Member Taxation Section, Committee on Pass Through Entities/Real Estate); New York State (Member, Tax Section, Committee on Partnerships) and American (Member, Taxation Section, Partnership Committee) Bar Associations. **PRACTICE AREAS:** Tax Law; Partnerships; Limited Liability Companies. **Email:** jaxelrad@wsgr.com

**MICHAEL BARCLAY,** born Los Angeles, California, June 23, 1952; admitted to bar, 1979, California; 1984, U.S. Supreme Court; registered to practice before U.S. Patent and Trademark Office. *Education:* University of California at Berkeley (B.A., 1973; M.S., 1974); University of California at Los Angeles (J.D., 1979). Phi Beta Kappa; Order of the Coif. Member, 1977-1978 and Associate Editor, 1978-1979, UCLA Law Review. Author: "Trade Secrets: How Long Should an Injunction Last?" 26 UCLA Law Review 203, 1978. *Member:* Institute of Electrical and Electronics Engineers. **PRACTICE AREAS:** Patent and Intellectual Property Litigation and Counseling. **Email:** mbarclay@wsgr.com

**HENRY V. BARRY,** born Palo Alto, California, June 20, 1949; admitted to bar, 1984, New York; 1988, California. *Education:* University of Michigan (B.A., with highest distinction, 1980); Stanford University (J.D., 1983). Phi Beta Kappa. Managing Editor, Stanford Law Review, 1983. Author: Article, "Toward a Model for Copyright Infringement," 33 Copyright L. Symp (ASCAP) 1, 1983. **Email:** hbarry@wsgr.com

**SUZANNE Y. BELL,** born Chester, Pennsylvania, June 3, 1958; admitted to bar, 1988, California. *Education:* Middlebury College (B.A., cum laude, 1980); Columbia University (M.S., 1982); Stanford Law School (J.D., with distinction, 1988). Author, "USDA Regulation of Biotechnology: Incorporating Public Participation," 7 Stanford Environmental Law Journal 6, 1987-1988. Co-Author: "Software Product Liability: Understand-

*(This Listing Continued)*

## WILSON, SONSINI, GOODRICH & ROSATI, PROFESSIONAL CORPORATION, Palo Alto—Continued

ing and Minimizing the Risks," 5 High Technology Law J., 1990; "Recent Developments in Intellectual Property Law," Annual Review of Recent Developments and Legislation of Interest to California Business Lawyers (State Bar of California, Business Law Section, 1993, 1994). *Member:* Santa Clara County (Member, Sections on: Business Law; Computer Law; Woman Lawyers) and American (Member, Sections on: Business Law; Patent, Trademark and Copyright Law; Science and Technology) Bar Associations; State Bar of California (Member, Sections on: Business Law; Intellectual Property Practice); Computer Law Association; Licensing Executives Society; American Society for Mining Metallurgical and Petroleum Engineers. *PRACTICE AREAS:* Intellectual Property. *Email:* sbell@wsgr.com

**DAVID J. BERGER,** born Boston, Massachusetts, May 19, 1959; admitted to bar, 1988, New York and U.S. District Court, Southern and Eastern Districts of New York; 1990, California. *Education:* Duke University (B.A., magna cum laude, 1982; J.D., 1987). *Member:* The Association of the Bar of the City of New York (Member, Committee on Federal Legislation); New York State and American (Member, Section on Business Law) Bar Associations; State Bar of California. *PRACTICE AREAS:* Intellectual Property; Litigation. *Email:* dberger@wsgr.com

**STEVEN L. BERSON,** born West Hartford, Connecticut, April 10, 1955; admitted to bar, 1982, New York; 1988, California; 1989, U.S. Supreme Court. *Education:* University of North Carolina (B.A., 1977); Vanderbilt University (J.D., 1981). Phi Beta Kappa. Executive Student Writing Editor, Vanderbilt Journal & Transnational Law. *Member:* American (Member, Section on: Corporations, Banking and Business Law) Bar Association. *PRACTICE AREAS:* Corporate Law; Securities. *Email:* sberson@wsgr.com

**MARK A. BERTELSEN,** born Los Angeles, California, April 14, 1944; admitted to bar, 1970, California. *Education:* University of California at Santa Barbara (B.A., with high honors, 1966); Boalt Hall School of Law, University of California at Berkeley (J.D., 1969). *Member:* State Bar of California (Member, Committee on Corporations, Business Law Section, 1983-1986); American Bar Association. *PRACTICE AREAS:* Corporate Law; Securities. *Email:* mbertelsen@wsgr.com

**JEROME F. BIRN, JR.,** born Chicago, Illinois, February 19, 1959; admitted to bar, 1984, Texas; 1985, U.S. District Court, Northern District of Texas; 1987, California. *Education:* Brown University (A.B., 1981); Harvard University (J.D., 1984). Phi Beta Kappa. Los Angeles County and American Bar Associations; State Bar of Texas; State Bar of California (Member, Litigation Section). *PRACTICE AREAS:* Litigation. *Email:* jbirn@wsgr.com

**STEVEN E. BOCHNER,** born Highland Park, Illinois, March 7, 1955; admitted to bar, 1981, California. *Education:* San Jose State University (B.A., with great distinction, 1977); Boalt Hall School of Law, University of California (J.D., 1981). Phi Kappa Phi. *Member:* State Bar of California; American Bar Association (Member, Corporation, Banking and Business Law Section). *PRACTICE AREAS:* Corporate Law; Securities. *Email:* sbochner@wsgr.com

**MARK E. BONHAM,** born Keyser, West Virginia, September 5, 1959; admitted to bar, 1988, California; 1993, Utah. *Education:* Brigham Young University (B.A., magna cum laude, 1984); Harvard Law School (J.D., 1987). *Member:* State Bar of California; Utah State Bar. *PRACTICE AREAS:* Corporate Law; Securities. *Email:* mbonham@wsgr.com

**DONALD E. BRADLEY,** born Santa Rosa, California, September 26, 1943; admitted to bar, 1968, California, U.S. Tax Court and U.S. Claims Court. *Education:* Dartmouth College (A.B., 1965); Hastings College of Law, University of California (J.D., 1968); New York University (LL.M., Taxation, 1972). Adjunct Professor, Golden Gate University School of Law and Graduate School of Taxation, 1973-1983. *Member:* State Bar of California; American (Member, Section of Taxation) and International Bar Associations. *PRACTICE AREAS:* Tax. *Email:* dbradley@wsgr.com

**TOR BRAHAM,** born New York, N.Y., September 25, 1957; admitted to bar, 1983, California. *Education:* Columbia University (B.A., 1979); New York University (J.D., 1982). Co-Chair, Software Mergers & Acquisitions Forum, 1996. Speaker: Raising, Making and Keeping Money: Financial Strategies for Successful Entrepreneurs, 1996. *Member:* State Bar of California. *PRACTICE AREAS:* Corporate Law; Securities. *Email:* tbraham@wsgr.com

**HARRY B. BREMOND,** born Austin, Texas, September 19, 1934; admitted to bar, 1963, California. *Education:* San Francisco State College (B.A., 1955; M.S., 1962); University of San Francisco (LL.B., 1962). *Member:* Bar Association of San Francisco; San Mateo County, Santa Clara County and American Bar Associations; State Bar of California; Charles Houston Bar Association. *PRACTICE AREAS:* Litigation. *Email:* hbremond@wsgr.com

**ANDREW P. BRIDGES,** born Atlanta, Georgia, September 11, 1954; admitted to bar, 1984, Georgia; 1986, California; 1987, U.S. Supreme Court. *Education:* Stanford University (A.B., with distinction, 1976); Oxford University, Oxford, England (B.A., 1980; M.A., 1985); Harvard University (J.D., cum laude, 1983). Phi Beta Kappa. Law Clerk, Honorable Marvin H. Shoob, U.S. District Court, Northern District of Georgia, 1983-1985. Author: "Private RICO Litigation Based Upon 'Fraud in the Sale of Securities,'" 18 Georgia Law Review 43, 1983. Lecturer: PLI Programs on Trademark Law and Advanced Trademark Law, 1993—; California Continuing Education of the Bar Programs on Federal Practice, 1990-1992; International Trademark Association Program on Computers and Discovery, 1995. *Member:* Bar Association of San Francisco (Co-Chair, Federal Courts Committee, 1989-1991); Atlanta, Federal and American (Sections on: Antitrust; Business Law; Litigation) Bar Associations; State Bar of Georgia; State Bar of California; International Trademark Association (Issues and Policy Committee); Hellenic Law Society of Northern California (Director, 1989-1994). *LANGUAGES:* Modern Greek, French and Italian. *PRACTICE AREAS:* Trademark Law; Advertising Law; Consumer Protection and Unfair Competition; Litigation. *Email:* abridges@wsgr.com

**ROBERT D. BROWNELL,** born Ann Arbor, Michigan, August 21, 1961; admitted to bar, 1988, California. *Education:* University of California at Berkeley (A.B., 1984); University of California at Los Angeles (J.D., 1988). *Member:* State Bar of California; American Bar Association. *PRACTICE AREAS:* Corporate Law; Securities. *Email:* rbrownell@wsgr.com

**RICHARD J. CHAR,** born Boston, Massachusetts, March 22, 1959; admitted to bar, 1984, California. *Education:* Harvard University (A.B., magna cum laude, 1981); Stanford University (J.D., 1984). *Member:* State Bar of California; American Bar Association. *PRACTICE AREAS:* Corporate Law; Securities. *Email:* rchar@wsgr.com

**PETER P. CHEN,** born Providence, Rhode Island, May 4, 1958; admitted to bar, 1983, California; registered to practice before U.S. Patent and Trademark Office. *Education:* Stanford University (B.S. with departmental honors, 1980; M.S., 1980); University of California at Davis (J.D., 1983). Executive Editor, University of California, Davis Law Review, 1982-1983. *Member:* State Bar of California; American Bar Association. *PRACTICE AREAS:* Intellectual Property Litigation; Complex Commercial Litigation. *Email:* pchen@wsgr.com

**DOUGLAS J. CLARK,** born Pittsburgh, Pennsylvania, January 26, 1963; admitted to bar, 1990, New York; 1993, California. *Education:* Allegheny College (B.A., 1985); University of Chicago (J.D., 1989). Phi Beta Kappa. Managing Editor, Legal Forum, 1989. *PRACTICE AREAS:* Litigation. *Email:* dclark@wsgr.com

**KENNETH A. CLARK,** born Atlanta, Georgia, May 7, 1958; admitted to bar, 1985, California. *Education:* Vanderbilt University (B.A., magna cum laude, 1980) Phi Beta Kappa; University of Texas (J.D., with highest honors, 1985) Chancellors. Phi Beta Kappa. Order of the Coif. Article, Editor, Texas Law Review, 1984-1985. Member, Board of Editors, Strategic Alliance Alert. Member, Board of Directors, the Parkinson's Institute. *Member:* State Bar of California. *PRACTICE AREAS:* Technology Transactions; Intellectual Property; Corporate Law. *Email:* kclark@wsgr.com

**DOUGLAS H. COLLOM,** born Palo Alto, California, September 26, 1951; admitted to bar, 1978, California. *Education:* Stanford University (B.A., with distinction, 1974); University of California at Los Angeles (J.D., 1978). Phi Beta Kappa. Member, University of California at Los Angeles Law Review, 1977-1978. *Member:* State Bar of California (Member, Committee on Corporations, Business Law Section, 1987-1990, Committee Chair, 1989-1990); American Bar Association. *PRACTICE AREAS:* Corporate Law; Securities. *Email:* dcollom@wsgr.com

**CHARLES T. C. COMPTON,** born Scarsdale, New York, October 11, 1943; admitted to bar, 1968, District of Columbia; 1969, Court of Military Appeals; 1974, California; 1988, U.S. Supreme Court. *Education:* U.S. Air Force Academy (B.S., 1965); New York University (J.D., 1968). Root-Tilden Scholar. Managing Editor, New York University Law Review, 1967-1968. Author: "Self Insurance Against Wrongful Discharge Litigation," The California Lawyer, May 1987; "Copyright Misuse and Software Licensing After Lasercomb," Twelfth Annual Computer Law Institute, 1991; "Coop-

*(This Listing Continued)*

eration, Collaboration and Coalition: A Perspective on the Types and Purposes of Technology Joint Ventures," 61 Antitrust Law Journal 861, 1993. Faculty Member, Litigation Advocacy Program, Hastings College of the Law, 1984-1990. Judge Pro Tem, Santa Clara County Superior Court, 1985—. *Member:* State Bar of California; American Bar Association (Member, Section on Antitrust Law). [Captain, USAF, JAG, 1968-1974]. *PRACTICE AREAS:* Antitrust; Litigation. *Email:* ccompton@wsgr.com

**SUSAN A. CREIGHTON,** born Alexandria, Virginia, October 4, 1959; admitted to bar, 1986, Arizona; 1988, California. *Education:* Harvard University (A.B., magna cum laude, 1981); Stanford Law School (J.D., 1984). Phi Beta Kappa; Order of the Coif. Member, Stanford Law Review, 1983-1984. Law Clerk to Justice Sandra Day O'Connor, U.S. Supreme Court, 1986-1987. Law Clerk to District Judge Pamela Ann Rymer, Central District of California, 1984-1985. *Member:* State Bar of California; State Bar of Arizona (Inactive); Association of Business Trial Lawyers. *PRACTICE AREAS:* Litigation. *Email:* screighton@wsgr.com

**FRANCIS S. CURRIE,** born New York, N.Y., April 12, 1950; admitted to bar, 1975, California. *Education:* Harvard University (B.A., 1972; J.D., 1975). *Member:* State Bar of California. *PRACTICE AREAS:* Corporate Law; Securities. *Email:* fcurrie@wsgr.com

**MICHAEL J. DANAHER,** born Frankfurt, Germany, July 28, 1953; admitted to bar, 1980, California. *Education:* Yale University (B.A., cum laude, 1975); Stanford Law School (J.D., 1980). Order of the Coif. Member, Stanford Law Review. Author: "Antitrust Law: The Clawback and Other Features of the United Kingdom Protection of Trading Interests Act, 1980," 12 Law & Policy in International Business 847, 1980; Comment, "Torture as a Tort in Violation of International Law: Filartiga v. Peña-Irala," 33 Stanford Law Review 353, 1981. Attorney-Adviser, Office of Legal Adviser, U.S. Department of State, 1980-1984. *Member:* The State Bar of California; American Bar Association; American Society of International Law; National Health Lawyers Association. *PRACTICE AREAS:* Corporate Law; Securities. *Email:* mdanaher@wsgr.com

**PAUL DAVIS,** born East Chicago, Indiana, September 10, 1951; admitted to bar, 1977, California, U.S. District Court, Northern District of California and U.S. Court of Appeals for the Federal Circuit; registered to practice before the U.S. Patent and Trademark Office. *Education:* San Jose State University (B.S., Chemistry, 1973); Santa Clara University (J.D., cum laude, 1976). President, Silicon Valley Biomedical Industry Council, 1993. *PRACTICE AREAS:* Patents; Trademarks; Copyrights. *Email:* pdavis@wsgr.com

**THOMAS C. DEFILIPPS,** born Newark, New Jersey, November 26, 1956; admitted to bar, 1981, California. *Education:* Stanford University (A.B. and B.S., 1978; J.D., 1981). Phi Beta Kappa. *Member:* State Bar of California; American Bar Association. *PRACTICE AREAS:* Corporate Law; Securities. *Email:* tdefilipps@wsgr.com

**JAMES A. DiBOISE,** born Princeton, New Jersey, January 15, 1952; admitted to bar, 1978, California. *Education:* University of Virginia (B.A., 1975); Stanford University (J.D., 1978). Member, Board of Editors, Stanford Law Review, 1977-1978. *Member:* Bar Association of San Francisco; Santa Clara County and American Bar Associations; State Bar of California. *PRACTICE AREAS:* Litigation. *Email:* jdiboise@wsgr.com

**STEPHEN C. DURANT,** born Ridgewood, New Jersey, June 9, 1956; admitted to bar, 1983, California and U.S. District Court, Central and Northern Districts of California; 1986, U.S. Court of Appeals for the Federal Circuit; registered to practice before U.S. Patent and Trademark Office. *Education:* University of Notre Dame (B.S.E.E., 1978); Cornell University (J.D., 1981). Author: "Effective Use Of Means Plus Function Elements In Patent Claims," AIPLA 1990 Basic Computer and Electronics Practice Seminar; "Patent Protection for Computer User Interfaces," The Computer Lawyer, Vol. 6, No. 5, May, 1989; "Patents in Cyberspace: Impact of Recent Federal Circuit Decisions," The Computer Lawyer, Vol. 12, No. 1, January 1995. Co-Author: "Patents and Copyrights in Computer Software Based Technology: Why Bother With Patents?" The Computer Lawyer, Volume 4, No. 2, February, 1987. *Member:* Bar Association of San Francisco (Member, Computer Law Section; Chair, 1990); State Bar of California; American Bar Association; Peninsula Intellectual Property Law Association (President, 1995-1996); American Intellectual Property Law Association (Member, Electronics and Computer Law Committee). *PRACTICE AREAS:* Intellectual Property. *Email:* sdurant@wsgr.com

**BORIS FELDMAN,** born South Bend, Indiana, August 28, 1955; admitted to bar, 1980, District of Columbia; 1987, California. *Education:* Yale University (B.A., summa cum laude, distinction in history, 1977; J.D., 1980). Phi Beta Kappa. Note and Topics Editor, Yale Law Journal, 1979-1980. Clerk, Judge Abraham D. Sofaer, Southern District of New York, 1980-1981. Special Assistant to the Legal Advisor, U.S. Department of State, 1985-1986. Lecturer: on Securities Law, Practicing Law Institute; ALI-ABA; Risk and Insurance Management Society; SEC Institute; National Investor Relations Institute. *Member:* District of Columbia Bar; State Bar of California. *PRACTICE AREAS:* Litigation; Securities Law. *Email:* bfeldman@wsgr.com

**ROBERT P. FELDMAN,** born Flushing, New York, March 28, 1951; admitted to bar, 1976, California. *Education:* State University of New York at Buffalo (B.A., 1972); Columbia University (J.D., 1975). Kent Scholar. Managing Editor, Columbia Law Review, 1974-1975. Law Clerk to Hon. Samuel P. King, U.S. District Court, District of Hawaii, 1976. Assistant U.S. Attorney and Member, Special Prosecution Unit, Northern District of California, 1979-1984. Lawyer-Delegate, Ninth Circuit Judicial Conference, 1985-1988. *Member:* State Bar of California; American Bar Association (Member, Litigation Section). *PRACTICE AREAS:* Litigation. *Email:* rfeldman@wsgr.com

**CHRIS F. FENNELL,** born Greenbrae, California, September 26, 1961; admitted to bar, 1989, California. *Education:* University of California at Berkeley (B.S., 1983); University of California, Los Angeles School of Law (J.D., 1989). Certified Public Accountant, California, 1986. *Member:* State Bar of California. *PRACTICE AREAS:* Corporate Law; Securities. *Email:* cfennell@wsgr.com

**ELIZABETH R. FLINT,** born Washington, D.C., June 20, 1960; admitted to bar, 1986, California. *Education:* Duke University (B.A., 1982); New York University School of Law (J.D., 1986). *Member:* State Bar of California; American Bar Association. *PRACTICE AREAS:* Corporate Law; Securities. *Email:* eflint@wsgr.com

**HERBERT P. FOCKLER,** born Washington, D.C., June 27, 1959; admitted to bar, 1984, California and U.S. District Court, Northern District of California. *Education:* Princeton University (A.B., 1981); Harvard University (J.D., cum laude, 1984). Sigma Xi Science Honor Society. *Member:* State Bar of California; American Bar Association (Member, Business Section). *PRACTICE AREAS:* Corporate Law; Securities. *Email:* hfockler@wsgr.com

**JOHN A. FORE,** born New York, N.Y., October 3, 1956; admitted to bar, 1984, New York; 1986, New Jersey; 1987, California. *Education:* Yale College (B.A., cum laude, 1979); New York University (J.D., with distinction, 1983). *Member:* New York State Bar Association; State Bar of California. *LANGUAGES:* German. *PRACTICE AREAS:* Corporate Law; Securities. *Email:* jfore@wsgr.com

**JOHN B. GOODRICH,** born Upland, California, August 30, 1941; admitted to bar, 1967, California. *Education:* Stanford University (B.A., 1963); University of Southern California (J.D., 1966); New York University (LL.M., in Taxation, 1970). Member, University of Southern California Law Review, 1965-1966. *Member:* Santa Clara County Bar Association; State Bar of California. *PRACTICE AREAS:* Corporate Law; Securities. *Email:* jgoodrich@wsgr.com

**DANA HAVILAND,** born Atlanta, Georgia, July 24, 1945; admitted to bar, 1975, Georgia and U.S. District Court, Northern District of Georgia; 1980, District of Columbia; 1986, California; U.S. Court of Appeals, Fifth and Ninth Circuits; U.S. District Court, Northern District of California. *Education:* Emory University and Georgia State University (A.B., 1967); Emory University (J.D., with distinction, 1975). Order of the Coif; Phi Delta Phi. Notes and Comments Editor, Emory Law Journal, 1974-1975. Law Clerk to Hon. Griffin B. Bell, U.S. Court of Appeals, Fifth Circuit, 1975-1976. Member, Panel of Arbitrators: American Arbitration Association; Asia/Pacific Center for Resolution of International Business Disputes; World Intellectual Property Organization Arbitration Centre; Korean Commercial Arbitration Board. Member, National Advisory Council, American Arbitration Association Large Complex Case Program. Chair, Intellectual Property Advisory Council, American Arbitration Association, Northern California. Member, Executive Committee, Asia/Pacific Center. Faculty, International Arbitrator Training Program for Asia/Pacific Center; Chartered Institute of Arbitrators; British Columbia International Commercial Arbitration Centre; US/Mexico. *Member:* American and Inter-Pacific Bar Associations. *LANGUAGES:* French. *PRACTICE AREAS:* Litigation; Alternative Dispute Resolution; International Arbitration; Intellectual Property; Securities; Business Law. *Email:* dhaviland@wsgr.com

**MARK A. HAYNES,** born Corpus Christi, Texas, April 10, 1955; admitted to bar, 1981, Texas; 1984, California; registered to practice before U.S. Patent and Trademark Office. *Education:* University of Texas

*(This Listing Continued)*

## WILSON, SONSINI, GOODRICH & ROSATI,
*PROFESSIONAL CORPORATION, Palo Alto—Continued*

(B.S.E.E., with highest honors, 1977); Stanford University (J.D., 1981). Tau Beta Pi; Eta Kappa Nu. Lecturer: "Software Patents," Seminar presented by California State Bar Intellectual Property Section. Author: "A Programmer's Right of Renewal and Right of Termination of Transfers and Licenses Under Copyright," Vol. 14, No. 2, New Matter, Summer 1989. Co-Author: "Patents and Copyrights in Computer Software Based Technology: Why Bother With Patents?" The Computer Lawyer, Volume 4, No. 2, February, 1987. *Member:* State Bar of California; American Bar Association; American Intellectual Property Law Association; Institute of Electrical and Electronic Engineers. **PRACTICE AREAS:** Patents; Trademarks; Copyrights. *Email:* mhaynes@wsgr.com

**ANDREW J. HIRSCH,** born Oakland, California, 1960; admitted to bar, 1987, California. *Education:* Stanford University (B.A., 1982); Fulbright Scholar, 1982-1983; Yale University (M.A., 1984); Columbia University (J.D., 1987). Harlan Fiske Stone Scholar. Associate Editor, Journal of Transnational Law, 1986-87. Contributor: *Guide to Organizing a California Corporation,* Report of the Corporations Committee, Business Law Section, State Bar of California, 1992. **PRACTICE AREAS:** Corporate; Commercial; Finance; Secured Lending. *Email:* ahirsch@wsgr.com

**IVAN H. HUMPHREYS,** born Santa Monica, California, January 11, 1957; admitted to bar, 1982, California. *Education:* University of California at Berkeley (B.A., with great distinction, 1979); Harvard University (J.D., magna cum laude, 1982). Phi Beta Kappa. Editor, Harvard Law Review, 1981-1982. Lecturer: Golden Gate University Graduate Tax School, 1986-1989; Stanford Law School, 1991—; San Jose State University Graduate School of Business, 1995—. *Member:* State Bar of California; American Bar Association (Member, Taxation Section). **PRACTICE AREAS:** Tax. *Email:* ihumphreys@wsgr.com

**GAIL CLAYTON HUSICK,** born Kansas City, Missouri, June 20, 1964; admitted to bar, 1989, California. *Education:* Rice University (B.A., magna cum laude, 1986); Harvard University (J.D., magna cum laude, 1989). Co-Author: "The Regulation of the Registration and Distribution Process Under the Securities Act of 1933," 20th Annual Securities Regulation Institute, 1993; "The Roles of the Parties in Preparing the Registration Statement," ALI-ABA, 1993. *Member:* State Bar of California. **PRACTICE AREAS:** Corporate Law; Securities; Venture Capital. *Email:* ghusick@wsgr.com

**ROBERT B. JACK,** born Alexandria, Louisiana, December 15, 1943; admitted to bar, 1969, California. *Education:* Princeton University (A.B., 1965); Stanford University (J.D., 1968). Order of the Coif. Member, Board of Editors, Stanford Law Review, 1967-1968. *Member:* State Bar of California; American Bar Association. **PRACTICE AREAS:** Corporate Law; Securities. *Email:* rjack@wsgr.com

**MEREDITH S. JACKSON,** born Boston, Massachusetts, March 16, 1960; admitted to bar, 1988, Massachusetts; 1992, California. *Education:* Princeton University (A.B., 1980); Hastings College of the Law, University of California (J.D., 1988). *Member:* State Bar of California (Vice Chair, UCC Committee); American Bar Association (Chair, UCC Committee, Subcommittee on Relation to Other Law). **PRACTICE AREAS:** Bank Financings; Public and Private Debt Securities; Structured Finance; Workouts and Debt Restructuring; Bankruptcy Planning. *Email:* mjackson@wsgr.com

**TERRY T. JOHNSON,** born New York, N.Y., May 5, 1957; admitted to bar, 1981, Colorado; 1985, California. *Education:* Stanford University (A.B., with distinction, 1978); Boalt Hall School of Law, University of California, Berkeley (J.D., 1981). Phi Beta Kappa. Associate Editor, California Law Review, 1979-1981. *Member:* State Bar of California; American Bar Association. **PRACTICE AREAS:** Litigation. *Email:* tjohnson@wsgr.com

**THOMAS CHRISTOPHER KLEIN,** born New Haven, Connecticut, October 29, 1962; admitted to bar, 1989, California, U.S. District Court, Northern District of California and U.S. Court of Appeals, Ninth Circuit; 1990, Texas and U.S. Tax Court; 1991, District of Columbia. *Education:* Swarthmore College (B.A., cum laude, 1985); University of Chicago (J.D., 1989). *Member:* State Bar of California; State Bar of Texas; American Bar Association. **PRACTICE AREAS:** Corporate Law; Securities. *Email:* tklein@wsgr.com

**JARED L. KOPEL,** born Kentfield, California, July 9, 1950; admitted to bar, 1979, New York; 1985, District of Columbia; 1986, California and U.S. District Court for the District of Columbia and Northern District of California; 1990, U.S. Court of Appeals, Ninth Circuit; 1995, U.S. Supreme Court. *Education:* Columbia College (B.A., 1972); New York University (J.D., 1976). Author: "Procedural Reforms in Securities Class Actions: Abuses and Remedies," National Center for the Public Interest; "Developments in Securities Litigation: Theories for the Defense in Securities Litigation," Practicing Law Institute, 1987. *Member:* State Bar of California; New York State Bar Association; District of Columbia Bar. **PRACTICE AREAS:** Litigation. *Email:* jkopel@wsgr.com

**MARTIN W. KORMAN,** born Philadelphia, Pennsylvania, October 10, 1963; admitted to bar, 1990, New York; 1994, California. *Education:* Stanford University (A.B., 1985); Yale University (J.D., 1989). **PRACTICE AREAS:** Corporate Law; Mergers and Acquisitions; Securities. *Email:* mkorman@wsgr.com

**PETER LABOSKEY,** born Santa Monica, California, June 30, 1950; admitted to bar, 1976, California. *Education:* Occidental College (B.A., 1972); Santa Clara University (J.D., magna cum laude, 1976). Certified Public Accountant, California, 1980. Contributing Author: "How To Plan An Estate," California Continuation of the Bar, April, 1987. *Member:* Santa Clara County Bar Association; State Bar of California. (Certified Specialist, Estate Planning, Trust and Probate Law, The State Bar of California Board of Legal Specialization). **PRACTICE AREAS:** Estate Planning. *Email:* plaboskey@wsgr.com

**MICHAEL A. LADRA,** born London, England, February 20, 1949; admitted to bar, 1975, California. *Education:* Princeton University (A.B., 1971); Hastings College of Law, University of California (J.D., 1974). *Member:* Santa Clara County and American Bar Associations; State Bar of California; San Francisco Bay Area Intellectual Property Inn of Court. **PRACTICE AREAS:** Intellectual Property. *Email:* mladra@wsgr.com

**DAVID L. LARSON,** born Mendenhall, Pennsylvania, March 24, 1956; admitted to bar, 1983, California; registered to practice before U.S. Patent and Trademark Office. *Education:* Stanford University (B.S.Ch.E., 1978); Georgetown University (J.D., 1983). Member, American Criminal Law Review, 1982-1983. *Member:* The State Bar of California; American Bar Association. **PRACTICE AREAS:** Intellectual Property Litigation. *Email:* dlarson@wsgr.com

**ROBERT P. LATTA,** born Philadelphia, Pennsylvania, January 30, 1954; admitted to bar, 1979, California and U.S. District Court, Northern District of California. *Education:* Stanford University (B.A., with high honors and distinction, 1976; J.D., 1979). Phi Beta Kappa. *Member:* State Bar of California; American Bar Association. **PRACTICE AREAS:** Corporate Law; Securities.

**DOUGLAS M. LAURICE,** born Palo Alto, California, November 14, 1946; admitted to bar, 1972, California. *Education:* Northwestern University (B.S., with highest distinction, 1968); Boalt Hall School of Law, University of California at Berkeley (J.D., 1971). Order of the Coif. Member, University of California Law Review, 1970-1971. Contributing Author: "Estate Planning for the General Practitioner," California Continuing Education of the Bar, 1979. Author: "How to Achieve Reformation of Split-Interest Charitable Trusts," Estate Planning v. 14, No. 2, March-April, 1987; "New Rules for Valuing Partial Interests Substantially Complicate Transactions," Estate Planning, Vol. 1, No. 6, November-December 1989; Co-Author: "Designing and Using Investment Guidelines," Profit Sharing, Vol. 41, No. 5, June-July 1993. *Member:* Santa Clara County and American Bar Associations; State Bar of California. **PRACTICE AREAS:** Employee Benefits; Executive Compensation; Estate Planning. *Email:* dlaurice@wsgr.com

**NINA LOCKER,** born New York, N.Y., May 24, 1958; admitted to bar, 1985, Georgia and U.S. District Court, Northern District of California; 1986, California. *Education:* Yale College (B.A., summa cum laude, 1980); Stanford University (J.D., 1984). Phi Beta Kappa. Recipient, Frank Baker Belcher Evidence Award. Member, Stanford University Law Review, 1983-1984. Law Clerk to the Hon. Anthony Kennedy, U.S. Court of Appeals, Ninth Circuit, 1984-1985. *Member:* State Bar of California. **PRACTICE AREAS:** Litigation. *Email:* nlocker@wsgr.com

**PAGE MAILLIARD,** born San Francisco, California, September 18, 1960; admitted to bar, 1987, California. *Education:* Stanford University (B.A., with highest honors, with distinction, 1982); Harvard Law School (J.D., cum laude, 1986). Phi Beta Kappa. Member, Book Review, Harvard Women's Law Journal, Spring, 1986. Co-Author: "Women's Banks and Women's Access to Credit: Competition Between Marketplace and Regulatory Solutions to Gender Discrimination," Vol. 20, No. 3, pp. 771-794, Loyola Review, April 1987. *Member:* State Bar of California. **PRACTICE AREAS:** Corporate Law; Securities. *Email:* pmailliard@wsgr.com

*(This Listing Continued)*

**HENRY P. MASSEY, JR.,** born Montclair, New Jersey, September 2, 1939; admitted to bar, 1969, California. *Education:* Cornell University (A.B., 1961; J.D., with distinction, 1968). Phi Kappa Phi. Order of the Coif. Member, Board of Editors, Cornell Law Review, 1967-1968. Member, Corporations Committee of Business Law Section, State Bar of California, 1979-1982. *Member:* American Bar Association (Member, Sections on: Corporation, Banking and Business Law; Taxation Law). *PRACTICE AREAS:* Corporate Law; Securities. *Email:* hmassey@wsgr.com

**J. CASEY MCGLYNN,** born Los Angeles, California, October 3, 1952; admitted to bar, 1978, California. *Education:* University of Santa Clara (B.S., summa cum laude, 1975; J.D., summa cum laude, 1978). Articles Editor, Santa Clara Law Review, 1977-1978. Author: "When is a Note a Security," 18 Santa Clara Law Review, 1978; "The Impact of Inflation on Taxation," 3 Santa Clara Business Review, 1975. Panelist, Recent Developments in Business Law Practice, C.E.B., 1985 through 1996. *Member:* State Bar of California; American Bar Association. *PRACTICE AREAS:* Corporate Law; Securities; Life Sciences. *Email:* cmcglynn@wsgr.com

**CHRISTOPHER D. MITCHELL,** born New York, N.Y., August 11, 1961; admitted to bar, 1986, Minnesota; 1989, California. *Education:* Haverford College (B.A., 1983); University of Minnesota (J.D., cum laude, 1986). Order of the Coif. Author: Note, "Vertical Refusals to Deal Under the Sherman Act: Products Liability and Malley-Duff Divide the Circuits," 69 Minn. L. Rev. 1355, 1985. *Member:* State Bar of California; Minnesota State and American Bar Associations. *PRACTICE AREAS:* Corporate Law. *Email:* cmitchell@wsgr.com

**ALLEN L. MORGAN,** born Decatur, Alabama, February 9, 1953; admitted to bar, 1981, California. *Education:* Dartmouth College (A.B., summa cum laude, 1976); University of Virginia (J.D., 1981); Oxford University, Oxford, England (B.A., honors, 1978; M.A., 1983). Phi Beta Kappa. *Member:* State Bar of California; American Bar Association (Member, Section on Banking and Business Law). *LANGUAGES:* Swedish. *PRACTICE AREAS:* Corporate Law; Securities. *Email:* amorgan@wsgr.com

**BRADFORD C. O'BRIEN,** born Lafayette, Indiana, January 25, 1949; admitted to bar, 1974, California. *Education:* Princeton University (A.B., magna cum laude, 1971); University of California at Los Angeles (J.D., 1974). *Member:* Santa Clara County (Member, Real Property Section) and American (Member, Section on Real Property, Probate and Trust Law) Bar Associations; State Bar of California. *PRACTICE AREAS:* Real Estate Law. *Email:* bobrien@wsgr.com

**JUDITH MAYER O'BRIEN,** born Palo Alto, California, May 6, 1950; admitted to bar, 1974, California. *Education:* Smith College (B.A., with honors, 1971); University of California at Los Angeles (J.D., 1974). Order of the Coif. *Member:* Santa Clara County and American Bar Associations; State Bar of California. *PRACTICE AREAS:* Corporate Law; Securities. *Email:* jobrien@wsgr.com

**MICHAEL J. O'DONNELL,** born Hamilton, Ohio, May 22, 1958; admitted to bar, 1983, California. *Education:* Bucknell University (B.A., summa cum laude, 1980); Harvard University (J.D., cum laude, 1983). Phi Beta Kappa. *PRACTICE AREAS:* Corporate; Securities; Venture Capital. *Email:* modonnell@wsgr.com

**MARK PARNES,** born Hollywood, California, June 5, 1957; admitted to bar, 1982, California; U.S. District Court, Northern, Eastern and Central Districts of California. *Education:* University of California at Santa Barbara (B.A., 1978); Boalt Hall School of Law, University of California (J.D., 1982). *Member:* Santa Clara County (Member, Business Litigation Section) and American (Member, Section of Litigation) Bar Associations; State Bar of California. *PRACTICE AREAS:* Litigation. *Email:* mparnes@wsgr.com

**DONNA M. PETKANICS,** born New York, N.Y., May 15, 1958; admitted to bar, 1985, California and U.S. District Court, Northern District of California. *Education:* Northwestern University (B.A., 1980), Phi Beta Kappa; Boalt Hall School of Law, University of California (J.D., 1985). Recipient, Outstanding Lawyer in Public Service Award for 1987, Bar Association of San Francisco. *Member:* Santa Clara and American Bar Associations; State Bar of California. *LANGUAGES:* German. *PRACTICE AREAS:* Corporate Law; Securities. *Email:* dpetkanics@wsgr.com

**MICHAEL S. RABSON,** born Ithaca, New York, November 3, 1953; admitted to bar, 1989, California. *Education:* Cornell University (B.S., 1975); Yale University (Ph.D., 1983; J.D., 1989). *Member:* State Bar of California; American Society for Microbiology; American Association for the Advancement of Science; American Intellectual Property Law Association; Licensing Executives Society; Association of University Technology Managers. *PRACTICE AREAS:* Technology Licensing; Intellectual Property Counseling. *Email:* mrabson@wsgr.com

**GARY L. REBACK,** born Knoxville, Tennessee, June 12, 1949; admitted to bar, 1974, Tennessee; 1975, District of Columbia; 1981, California. *Education:* Yale University (B.A., magna cum laude, 1971); Stanford University (J.D., 1974). Note Editor, Stanford Law Review, 1973-1974. Member, Board of Editors: Computer Law Strategist, 1986—; The Computer Lawyer, 1991—. *Member:* State Bar of California; The District of Columbia Bar; American Bar Association. *PRACTICE AREAS:* Intellectual Property; Antitrust. *Email:* greback@wsgr.com

**JOHN V. ROOS,** born San Francisco, California, February 14, 1955; admitted to bar, 1980, California. *Education:* Stanford University (A.B., 1977; J.D., 1980). Phi Beta Kappa; Order of the Coif. Member, Stanford University Law Review, 1979-1980. *Member:* State Bar of California. *PRACTICE AREAS:* Corporate Law; Securities. *Email:* jroos@wsgr.com

**MARIO M. ROSATI,** born Vallejo, California, June 20, 1946; admitted to bar, 1972, California. *Education:* University of California at Los Angeles (B.A., 1968); Boalt Hall School of Law, University of California at Berkeley (J.D., 1971). *Member:* State Bar of California; American Bar Association. *PRACTICE AREAS:* Corporate Law; Securities. *Email:* mrosati@wsgr.com

**RONALD M. ROTH,** born Allentown, Pennsylvania, April 14, 1954; admitted to bar, 1979, California; 1980, Pennsylvania; 1981, U.S. Tax Court. *Education:* Lehigh University (B.S., 1976); Stanford University (J.D. 1979); New York University (LL.M. in Taxation, 1980). Phi Eta Sigma; Beta Alpha Psi; Beta Gamma Sigma. Instructor, U.S. Taxation of Foreign Income and Aliens, Golden Gate University, 1982—. *Member:* Bar Association of San Francisco (Member, Tax Section); Pennsylvania (Member, Tax Section) and American (Member, Section of Taxation) Bar Associations; State Bar of California (Member, Tax Section). *PRACTICE AREAS:* Tax Law. *Email:* rroth@wsgr.com

**JEFFREY D. SAPER,** born Brooklyn, New York, April 21, 1948; admitted to bar, 1972, New York; 1979, California. *Education:* University College, New York University (B.A., summa cum laude in History, 1968); New York University School of Law (J.D., 1971). *Member:* American Bar Association (Section of Corporation, Banking and Business Law); State Bar of California. *PRACTICE AREAS:* Corporate Law; Securities. *Email:* jsaper@wsgr.com

**ELIZABETH M. SAUNDERS,** born Chicago, Illinois, November 19, 1962; admitted to bar, 1988, California and U.S. District Court, Central District of California; 1989, U.S. District Court, Northern District of California. *Education:* University of Notre Dame (B.A., with honors, 1984; J.D. magna cum laude, 1988). Note and Comment Editor, Notre Dame Law Review, 1987-1988. *Member:* State Bar of California. *PRACTICE AREAS:* Litigation. *Email:* esaunders@wsgr.com

**STEVEN M. SCHATZ,** born New York, N.Y., March 12, 1948; admitted to bar, 1973, New York and District of Columbia; 1985, California. *Education:* University of Pennsylvania (B.A., 1969); Columbia University (J.D., 1972). Notes & Comments Editor, Columbia Law Review, 1971-1972. Instructor, National Institute for Trial Advocacy. Law Clerk to Hon. Walter R. Mansfield, Judge, U.S. Court of Appeals, Second Circuit, 1972-1973. Assistant U.S. Attorney, Southern District of New York, Criminal Division, 1975-1979. Chairman, Use of Experts in Commercial Litigation, PLI, 1988. *Member:* New York State Bar Association; District of Columbia Bar; State Bar of California. *PRACTICE AREAS:* Litigation. *Email:* sschatz@wsgr.com

**ARTHUR F. SCHNEIDERMAN,** born White Plains, New York, May 21, 1942; admitted to bar, 1967, California. *Education:* Beloit College (B.A., 1964); University of Wisconsin (J.D., 1967). *Member:* Palo Alto and American Bar Associations; State Bar of California. *PRACTICE AREAS:* Corporate Law; Securities. *Email:* aschneiderman@wsgr.com

**PATRICK J. SCHULTHEIS,** born Spokane, Washington, September 3, 1964; admitted to bar, 1989, California. *Education:* Stanford University (A.B., with distinction and departmental honors, 1986); University of Chicago (J.D., 1989). *Member:* State Bar of California. *LANGUAGES:* French. *PRACTICE AREAS:* Corporate Law; Securities. *Email:* pschultheis@wsgr.com

**TIMOTHY T. SCOTT,** born San Francisco, California, June 22, 1959; admitted to bar, 1985, Illinois and U.S. District Court, Northern District of Illinois; 1986, California and U.S. District Court, Northern District of California. *Education:* Stanford University (A.B., with distinction, with highest departmental honors, 1981); University of Chicago Law School (J.D., cum

*(This Listing Continued)*

## WILSON, SONSINI, GOODRICH & ROSATI,
*PROFESSIONAL CORPORATION, Palo Alto—Continued*

laude, 1985). Order of the Coif. Associate Editor, University of Chicago Law Review, 1984-1985. *Member:* Chicago, Illinois State and American Bar Associations; State Bar of California. **PRACTICE AREAS:** Litigation. *Email:* tscott@wsgr.com

**DAVID J. SEGRE,** born Springfield, Massachusetts, March 6, 1959; admitted to bar, 1985, California and U.S. District Court, Northern District of California. *Education:* Stanford University (B.A., academic distinction, departmental honors, 1981); Harvard University (J.D., cum laude, 1985). Phi Beta Kappa. Author: "Open Market and Privately Negotiated Purchase Programs and the Market for Corporate Control," The Business Lawyer, Volume 42, Number 3, May, 1987. *Member:* State Bar of California. **PRACTICE AREAS:** Corporate Law; Securities. *Email:* dsegre@wsgr.com

**JOHN T. SHERIDAN,** born San Francisco, California, July 7, 1958; admitted to bar, 1986, California. *Education:* University of Santa Clara (B.Sc., 1980); Boalt Hall School of Law, University of California (J.D., 1986). Certified Public Accountant, California, 1983. *Member:* State Bar of California. **PRACTICE AREAS:** Corporate Law; Securities. *Email:* jsheridan@wsgr.com

**RON E. SHULMAN,** born Boston, Massachusetts, 1955; admitted to bar, 1982, New York; 1995, California. *Education:* Amherst College (B.A., 1977); Rutgers Law School (J.D., 1981). **PRACTICE AREAS:** Intellectual Property. *Email:* rshulman@wsgr.com

**KENNETH M. SIEGEL,** born Pontiac, Michigan, July 19, 1958; admitted to bar, 1985, California and U.S. District Court, Northern District of California. *Education:* Monterey Institute of International Studies (B.A., summa cum laude, 1981); Hastings College of the Law, University of California (J.D., 1985). Participant, 1983-1984 and Editor-in-Chief, 1984-1985, Hastings International and Comparative Law Review. Author: "The International Law of Compensation for Expropriation and International Debt: A Dangerous Uncertainty," 8 Hastings International and Comparative Law Review 223, 1985. Law Clerk to the Hon. Joan S. Brennan, United States Magistrate, U.S. District Court, Northern District of California, 1985-1986. *Member:* State Bar of California; American Bar Association. **PRACTICE AREAS:** Corporate Law; Securities. *Email:* ksiegel@wsgr.com

**LAURIE B. SMILAN,** born Buffalo, New York, October 30, 1959; admitted to bar, 1985, California and U.S. District Court, Central District of California; 1986, New York; 1987, U.S. District Court, Southern and Eastern Districts of New York; 1988, U.S. District Court, Eastern, Southern and Northern Districts of California and U.S. Court of Appeals, Ninth Circuit. *Education:* State University of New York at Albany (B.A., magna cum laude, 1981); University of California at Los Angeles (J.D., 1984). Editor, UCLA Law Review, 1983-1984. *Member:* State Bar of California; New York State and American Bar Associations. **PRACTICE AREAS:** Securities Litigation. *Email:* lsmilan@wsgr.com

**LARRY W. SONSINI,** born Rome, New York, February 5, 1941; admitted to bar, 1966, California. *Education:* University of California at Berkeley (A.B., 1963); Boalt Hall School of Law, University of California at Berkeley (J.D., 1966). Professor, Securities Regulation, Boalt Hall School of Law, 1984—. Legal Advisory Board to: NYSE; SEC Advisory Committee on Capital Formation and Federal Regulation of Securities; Executive Committee of University of California, San Diego, Securities Regulation Institute; Board of Advisors, Haas School of Business, University of California, Berkeley. Trustee, University of California, Berkeley. *Member:* State Bar of California; American Bar Association (Member: Committee on Federal Regulation of Securities; Subcommittee on Registration Statements). **PRACTICE AREAS:** Corporate Law; Securities; Mergers and Acquisitions. *Email:* lsonsini@wsgr.com

**TIMOTHY J. SPARKS,** born Redwood City, California, September 9, 1958; admitted to bar, 1983, California; 1984, Virginia. *Education:* University of California at Berkeley (B.S., with honors, 1980); Hastings College of the Law, University of California (J.D., 1983). *Member:* State Bar of California; American Bar Association (Member, Sections on: Taxation and Labor and Employment Law). **PRACTICE AREAS:** Employee Benefits; Executive Compensation. *Email:* tsparks@wsgr.com

**ROGER D. STERN,** born Brooklyn, New York, December 31, 1956; admitted to bar, 1989, California. *Education:* University of California at Berkeley (A.B., with honors, 1981); University of Chicago (J.D., 1989). Member, 1987-1988 and Comments Editor, 1988-1989, University of Chicago Legal Forum. Co-Author: "Designing and Using Investment Guidelines," 41 Profit-Sharing No. 5, June/July, 1993; "Guidelines Help Ensure Liability Protection," 31 Pension Management No. 4, April 1995; "SEC Simplifies Rules on Short-Swing Profits for Employee Plans," 1 High-Tech Industry, No. 2, Sept./Oct. 1996. *Member:* State Bar of California; American Bar Association (Section of Taxation). **PRACTICE AREAS:** Employee Benefits Law; Executive Compensation. *Email:* rstern@wsgr.com

**DAVID S. STEUER,** born Seattle, Washington, March 20, 1957; admitted to bar, 1983, Hawaii; 1984, District of Columbia; 1986, California. *Education:* Stanford University (A.B., with distinction and honors in History, 1979); Harvard Law School (J.D., cum laude, 1982). Phi Beta Kappa. Editor, Harvard Law Review, 1980-1982. Law Clerk to the Honorable Herbert Y.C. Choy, U.S. Court of Appeals, Ninth Circuit, 1982-1983. *Member:* State Bar of California; Hawaii State Bar Association; District of Columbia Bar; California Association of Business Trial Lawyers. **PRACTICE AREAS:** Litigation. *Email:* dsteuer@wsgr.com

**BLAIR W. STEWART, JR.,** born Los Angeles, California, October 4, 1945; admitted to bar, 1975, California. *Education:* United States Naval Academy (B.S., with distinction, 1967); Stanford University (J.D., 1975). Clerk to Chief Justice Donald R. Wright, California Supreme Court, 1975-1976. *Member:* Palo Alto, Santa Clara County and American (Member, Section of International Law and Practice) Bar Associations; State Bar of California. **PRACTICE AREAS:** Corporate Law; Securities. *Email:* bstewart@wsgr.com

**JAMES NEILSON STRAWBRIDGE,** born Baltimore, Maryland, March 30, 1961; admitted to bar, 1987, California. *Education:* Virginia Polytechnic Institute and State University (B.S., in Industrial Engineering and Operations Research, cum laude, 1984); University of Virginia (J.D., 1987). Tau Beta Pi; Omicron Delta Kappa. *Member:* State Bar of California; American Bar Association. **PRACTICE AREAS:** Corporate Law; Securities. *Email:* jstrawbridge@wsgr.com

**DEBRA S. SUMMERS,** born Dimmitt, Texas, April 11, 1950; admitted to bar, 1981, California. *Education:* University of Texas; West Texas State University (B.S., magna cum laude, 1974); University of San Francisco (J.D., magna cum laude, 1980). Phi Alpha Delta. Member, McAuliffe Honor Society. Co-Author: "Office Leasing—Drafting and Negotiating The Lease," CEB, 1996. Extern to Justice Matthew O. Tobriner, California Supreme Court, 1980. Adjunct Professor, U.C. Berkeley, Environmental Certification Program. *Member:* State Bar of California (Member: Joint Committee, Real Property and Business Law Sections on Opinions in Business and Real Property Transactions, 1993-1996; Co-Chair, Real Property Section, 1991-1995; American Bar Association (Member, Sections on: Real Property and Environmental). **PRACTICE AREAS:** Real Estate; Environmental. *Email:* dsummers@wsgr.com

**BARRY E. TAYLOR,** born Mineola, New York, March 14, 1948; admitted to bar, 1975, California. *Education:* Dickinson College (B.A., magna cum laude, 1970); University of Virginia (J.D., 1975). Phi Beta Kappa; Order of the Coif. Member, Virginia Law Review, 1973-1975. *Member:* State Bar of California; American Bar Association. **PRACTICE AREAS:** Corporate Law; Securities. *Email:* btaylor@wsgr.com

**BRUCE G. VANYO,** born Cleveland, Ohio, December 4, 1945; admitted to bar, 1974, California. *Education:* Miami University (B.S., summa cum laude, 1967); Columbia University (J.D., 1972). Managing Editor, Columbia Law Review, 1971-1972. Clerk, Judge William Timbers, U.S. Court of Appeals, Second Circuit, 1972-1973. Professor, Securities Regulation, Hastings College of the Law, 1983-1986. Chairman, Securities Litigation, Practising Law Institute (PLI), 1984—; Securities Law Update, PLI, 1993-1995. Panelist, Federal Practice Institute, CEB, 1986—; Civil Practice and Litigation in Federal and State Courts, ALI-ABA, 1987-1988; Class & Derivative Litigation in the 1990s, Prentice Hall, 1990-1994, 1996. Attorney Delegate, Ninth Circuit Judicial Conference, 1994-1997. *Member:* Bar Association of San Francisco (President, Securities Litigation Section, BASF, 1994-1995); Santa Clara County and American (Member, Committee on Securities Litigation and Corporate Counsel Committee, ABA, 1981—) Bar Associations; State Bar of California. **PRACTICE AREAS:** Securities Litigation; Intellectual Property Law. *Email:* bvanyo@wsgr.com

**ANN YVONNE WALKER,** born San Francisco, California, September 26, 1954; admitted to bar, 1979, California. *Education:* Stanford University (B.S., with distinction, 1976; J.D., 1979). Phi Beta Kappa. Director Emeritus, Friends of the Stanford String Quartet. Director, Redwood Symphony. Founding Member, Silicon Valley "Grundfest" Committee. *Member:* State Bar of California (Executive Committee, Business Law Section); Palo Alto Area Bar Association; Santa Clara County and American (Standing Committee on Professionalism; Task Force on Section 16 Developments; Vice Chair, Task Force on Lawyer Business Ethics; Federal Regulation of Secu-

*(This Listing Continued)*

rities Committee, Employee Benefits and Executive Compensation Subcommittee and Reporting Companies Subcommittee, Section of Business Law) Bar Associations. **PRACTICE AREAS:** Corporate Law; Securities. **Email:** awalker@wsgr.com

**KENNETH B. WILSON,** born Burlingame, California, October 5, 1962; admitted to bar, 1987, California. *Education:* University of California, Davis (B.S., cum laude, 1984); Boalt Hall School of Law, University of California, Berkeley (J.D., 1987). *Member:* State Bar of California (Member, Section on Litigation); American Bar Association (Member, Sections on: Intellectual Property and General Business Litigation). **PRACTICE AREAS:** Intellectual Property; Business Litigation; Internet Law. **Email:** kwilson@wsgr.com

**LLOYD WINAWER,** born Queens, New York, September 8, 1963; admitted to bar, 1990, New York; 1991, U.S. District Court, Southern and Eastern Districts of New York; 1992, California. *Education:* Brandeis University (B.A., magna cum laude, 1985, Phi Beta Kappa); New York University School of Law (J.D., 1989). Editor, New York University Moot Court Board, 1988-1989. Best Oral Advocate, University of Cincinnati, Products Liability National Moot Court Competition, 1988. *Member:* State Bar of California; American Bar Association. **PRACTICE AREAS:** Litigation. **Email:** lwinawer@wsgr.com

**NEIL JAY WOLFF,** born New Rochelle, New York, February 16, 1958; admitted to bar, 1985, California. *Education:* University of Florida (B.A., 1979); Oxford University (Lincoln College and Templeton College), Oxford, England (M.Phil. in Management Studies, 1981); University of California at Los Angeles (J.D., 1985). Phi Beta Kappa. *Member:* State Bar of California. **LANGUAGES:** Japanese. **PRACTICE AREAS:** Corporate Law; Securities. **Email:** nwolff@wsgr.com

**HOWARD S. ZEPRUN,** born Boston, Massachusetts, September 1, 1958; admitted to bar, 1983, California; 1984, U.S. District Court, Northern District of California. *Education:* University of Pennsylvania (B.S. in Engineering, 1980); The Wharton School, University of Pennsylvania (B.S., Economics, 1980); Harvard University (J.D., 1983). Tau Beta Pi; Beta Gamma Sigma. Co-Author: "Raising Capital in the U.S.: A Special Report," International Financial Law Review, May 1995. Lecturer: "U.S. Public Offerings and Periodic Reporting by Foreign Issuers," Practicing Law Institute, July 15, 1995. *Member:* Santa Clara County and American Bar Associations; State Bar of California. **PRACTICE AREAS:** Corporate Law; Securities; International Securities Offerings; Intellectual Property. **Email:** hzeprun@wsgr.com

## COUNSEL

**DOUGLAS KEITH KROHN,** born Los Angeles, California, 1954; admitted to bar, 1979, Georgia and California. *Education:* Stanford University (A.B., 1976); University of California, Los Angeles School of Law (J.D., 1979). Rotary Foundation Graduate Fellow. Graduate, Institute of International Studies, Geneva, Switzerland. **PRACTICE AREAS:** Real Estate; Commercial Law; International Law.

**THOMAS L. CRONAN, III,** born Bridgeport, Connecticut, October 1, 1959; admitted to bar, 1984, Connecticut; 1986, California and New York. *Education:* Muhlenberg College (B.S., cum laude, 1981); Fordham University (J.D., cum laude, 1984). Associate Editor, Fordham University Law Review. *Member:* Santa Clara County and American Bar Associations. **PRACTICE AREAS:** Technology Transactions; Copyright; Antitrust. **Email:** tcronan@wsgr.com

**FRANCIS W. DUBREUIL,** born Westport, Massachusetts, September 15, 1948; admitted to bar, 1974, Massachusetts, U.S. District Court, District of Massachusetts and U.S. Court of Appeals, First Circuit; 1977, U.S. Tax Court (Not admitted in California). *Education:* Boston College (B.A., summa cum laude, 1970); Harvard University (J.D., cum laude, 1974); Stanford University Graduate School of Business (M.S., 1990). Author: "Gifts and Deferred Sales of Closely Held Business Interests," ALI-ABA, September 1994; "The New Valuation Rules for Estate Planning," Federal Tax Institute of New England, Inc., April 1991. *Member:* American Bar Association (Member, Sections on: Real Property and Probate; Tax; Business). Fellow, American College of Trust and Estate Counsel. **PRACTICE AREAS:** Estate Planning; Business Planning.

**KATHLEEN BORRERO BLOCH,** born New York, N.Y., December 20, 1956; admitted to bar, 1981, California and U.S. District Court, Central District of California. *Education:* University of Southern California (B.S., magna cum laude, 1978); Stanford University (J.D., 1981). Beta Gamma Sigma. **PRACTICE AREAS:** Corporate Finance; Commercial Law. **Email:** kbloch@wsgr.com

*(This Listing Continued)*

**DAVID M. HOFFMEISTER,** born Racine, Wisconsin, October 1, 1958; admitted to bar, 1987, California, U.S. District Court, Northern District of California and U.S. Court of Appeals, Ninth Circuit; 1990, U.S. Supreme Court. *Education:* University of the Pacific (B.S., 1981); San Francisco Law School (J.D., 1987). **PRACTICE AREAS:** Life Sciences; Food and Drug Law. **Email:** dhoffmeister@wsgr.com

**RICHARD A. SHUPACK,** born Plainfield, New Jersey, July 23, 1946; admitted to bar, 1971, Maryland; 1972, District of Columbia; 1996, California. *Education:* Bowling Green State University (B.A., 1968); George Washington University (J.D., with honors, 1971). Adjunct Professor, Food and Drug Regulatory Law, Rutgers University School of Law, 1976-1992. *Member:* State Bar of California; District of Columbia Bar; Maryland State Bar Association; Food and Drug Law Institute. **PRACTICE AREAS:** Drug and Device Regulatory Law. **Email:** rshupack@wsgr.com

---

**PAUL D. ANAWALT,** born Santa Clara, California, December 16, 1967; admitted to bar, 1996, California. *Education:* University of California at Davis (B.A., Economics, with highest honors, 1990); Boalt Hall School of Law, University of California, Berkeley (J.D., 1996). Phi Beta Kappa; Order of the Coif. **LANGUAGES:** Russian. **PRACTICE AREAS:** Corporate; Securities. **Email:** panawalt@wsgr.com

**RICHARD S. ARNOLD, JR.,** born Hartford, Connecticut, May 29, 1963; admitted to bar, 1994, California. *Education:* United States Military Academy (B.S., 1985); Fuqua School of Business (M.B.A., 1994); Duke University (J.D., 1994). [CPT., Corps of Engineers, U.S. Army, 1985-1990] **Email:** rarnold@wsgr.com

**J. MICHAEL ARRINGTON,** born Orange County, California, March 13, 1970; admitted to bar, 1995, California. *Education:* Claremont McKenna College (B.A., 1992); Stanford University (J.D., 1995). **PRACTICE AREAS:** Corporate Finance. **Email:** marrington@wsgr.com

**RONALD A. BAKER,** born Los Angeles, California, August 22, 1956; admitted to bar, 1983, California. *Education:* University of California at Los Angeles (B.A., cum laude, 1979; M.B.A., 1983; J.D., 1983). Author: "Privatization of Infrastructure: The Indonesian Experience," Asia Business Law Review, April 1994. *Member:* American Bar Association (Member, Sections on: Business; International). **LANGUAGES:** Spanish and French. **PRACTICE AREAS:** Corporate; Securities; International. **Email:** rbaker@wsgr.com

**COLLEEN BAL,** born Mount Kisco, New York, January 16, 1967; admitted to bar, 1993, California. *Education:* Duke University (B.S., 1989); Harvard Law School (J.D., 1993). **PRACTICE AREAS:** Litigation. **Email:** cbal@wsgr.com

**JOHN P. BARTHOLOMAY,** born Duluth, Minnesota, December 1, 1962; admitted to bar, 1990, Massachusetts (Not admitted in California). *Education:* University of Texas at Austin (B.B.A., 1985); Boston University (J.D., cum laude, 1990). Certified Public Accountant, Texas, 1987. Note and Comment Editor, Ann. Rev. Banking Law, 1989-1990. Executive Editor, "Commentaries: Review on Books on Law and Public Policy," 1989. Author: "The Southwest Plan and FIRREA: What Have We Learned?" 9 Ann. Rev. Banking Law 501 (1990). *Member:* American Bar Association (Vice Chair, 1994-1995 and Chair, 1995-1996, Securities Committee, Young Lawyers Division). **Email:** jbartholomay@wsgr.com

**MARK B. BAUDLER,** born San Francisco, California, December 27, 1968; admitted to bar, 1996, California. *Education:* Dartmouth College (B.A., 1991); University of Chicago (J.D., 1996). **PRACTICE AREAS:** Corporate Law; Securities Law. **Email:** mbaudler@wsgr.com

**MARILYN U. BAURIEDEL,** born Oakland, California, July 17, 1942; admitted to bar, 1980, California and U.S. District Court, Northern District of California. *Education:* Mount Holyoke College (A.B., with great distinction, 1964); University of Chicago (M.Th., 1967); Santa Clara University (J.D., summa cum laude, 1980). Phi Beta Kappa. Articles Editor, Santa Clara Law Review, 1979-1980. Author: "Federal Historic Preservation Law: Uneven Standards for Our Nation's Heritage," 20 Santa Clara Law Review 189, 1980. Teaching Fellow, Stanford Law School, 1982-1983; Business Law Instructor, Foothill-DeAnza Community College District, 1986-1988, 1990. *Member:* Santa Clara County Bar Association (Member, High Technology Law Section, Executive Committee, 1996); State Bar of California; Licensing Executives Society; Computer Law Association. **PRACTICE AREAS:** Intellectual Property. **Email:** mbauriedel@wsgr.com

**JULIE ANN BELL,** born Sidney, Ohio, November 11, 1970; admitted to bar, 1996, California. *Education:* The Ohio State University (B.A., summa cum laude, 1993); Vanderbilt University (J.D., 1996). Phi Beta

*(This Listing Continued)*

**WILSON, SONSINI, GOODRICH & ROSATI,**
*PROFESSIONAL CORPORATION,* Palo Alto—*Continued*

Kappa. *PRACTICE AREAS:* Corporate Law; Securities Law. *Email:* jbell@wsgr.com

**BRADLEY A. BENBROOK,** born Springfield, Missouri, November 17, 1967; admitted to bar, 1995, California. *Education:* Stanford University (A.B., 1990); Boalt Hall School of Law, University of California (J.D., 1993). Associate Editor, California Law Review, 1992-1993. Judicial Clerk, Hon. J. L. Edmondson, U.S. Court of Appeals, Eleventh Circuit. *PRACTICE AREAS:* Corporate; Securities; Mergers and Acquisitions. *Email:* bbenbrook@wsgr.com

**STEVEN J. BENEROFE,** born New Rochelle, New York, February 8, 1964; admitted to bar, 1996, California. *Education:* Brown University (S.B., 1986); Stanford University (M.S., 1987; Ph.D., 1992); Harvard University (J.D., 1996). *PRACTICE AREAS:* Intellectual Property; Patents; Licensing. *Email:* sbenerofe@wsgr.com

**PETER H. BERGMAN,** born New York, N.Y., March 5, 1969; admitted to bar, 1994, New York; 1996, U.S. Tax Court (Not admitted in California). *Education:* Emory University (B.A., 1990); New York University (J.D., 1993); LL.M., Taxation, 1994). Law Clerk, Hon. Theodore Tannenwald, Jr., U.S. Tax Court, 1994-1996. *PRACTICE AREAS:* Taxation. *Email:* pbergman@wsgr.com

**STEVEN V. BERNARD,** born Westwood, New Jersey, March 31, 1966; admitted to bar, 1991, New Jersey and U.S. District Court, District of New Jersey; 1992, New York and U.S. District Court, Southern and Eastern Districts of New York; 1995, California. *Education:* University of Virginia (B.A., with distinction, 1988); New York University (J.D., 1991). *PRACTICE AREAS:* Corporate; Securities. *Email:* sbernard@wsgr.com

**KURT J. BERNEY,** born Phoenix, Arizona, October 4, 1961; admitted to bar, 1989, New York (Not admitted in California). *Education:* University of Arizona (B.S., Accounting, 1983); University of Texas (J.D., 1988). Beta Alpha Phi; Order of the Coif. Member: Moot Court; Mock Trial. Associate Editor, Texas Law Review. Certified Public Accountant, Arizona, 1985. *Member:* Arizona Society of Certified Public Accountants. *PRACTICE AREAS:* Mergers and Acquisitions; Securities; Banking; Corporate. *Email:* kberney@wsgr.com

**JEFFREY M. BLOOM,** born East Norwich, New York, May 20, 1966; admitted to bar, 1993, New York (Not admitted in California). *Education:* Massachusetts Institute of Technology (B.S., 1988); New York University School of Law (J.D., 1992; LL.M., Tax, 1993). *Member:* New York State Bar Association. *PRACTICE AREAS:* Taxation. *Email:* jbloom@wsgr.com

**IRA J. BLUMBERG,** born Oakland, California, April 26, 1960; admitted to bar, 1993, Virginia; 1994, District of Columbia; 1995, California. *Education:* University of Pennsylvania (B.A., magna cum laude, 1982; M.S.C.S.E., 1983); University of Virginia (J.D., 1993). Order of the Coif. *PRACTICE AREAS:* Technology Licensing. *Email:* iblumberg@wsgr.com

**LAUREN I. BORO,** born Boston, Massachusetts, February 14, 1967; admitted to bar, 1992, California. *Education:* University of California, Berkeley (B.A., with honors, 1989); New York University (J.D., 1992). *LANGUAGES:* Spanish. *PRACTICE AREAS:* Real Estate. *Email:* lboro@wsgr.com

**SUSAN BOWER,** born Long Beach, California, August 31, 1966; admitted to bar, 1994, California. *Education:* Cornell University (B.A., 1988); Stanford University (J.D., 1994). *PRACTICE AREAS:* Litigation. *Email:* sbower@wsgr.com

**CHRISTOPHER F. BOYD,** born St. Louis, Missouri, February 12, 1966; admitted to bar, 1993, California. *Education:* Princeton University (A.B., cum laude, 1987); Stanford University (J.D., 1992). Phi Beta Kappa; Order of the Coif. Law Clerk, Hon. Melvin Brunetti, U.S. Court of Appeals, Ninth Circuit, 1992-1993. *LANGUAGES:* French. *PRACTICE AREAS:* Corporate; Securities. *Email:* cboyd@wsgr.com

**JASON M. BRADY,** born Burlingame, California, November 11, 1968; admitted to bar, 1995, California. *Education:* University of California, Los Angeles (B.A., 1992); Santa Clara University (J.D., 1995). *PRACTICE AREAS:* Corporate; Securities. *Email:* jbrady@wsgr.com

**CARMINE J. BROCCOLE,** born Brooklyn, New York, February 24, 1966; admitted to bar, 1992, New York; 1994, California. *Education:* Cornell University (B.A., 1988); Stanford University (J.D., 1991). *PRACTICE AREAS:* Corporate; Securities. *Email:* cbroccole@wsgr.com

*(This Listing Continued)*

**IVAN J. BROCKMAN,** born Brooklyn, New York, October 6, 1969; admitted to bar, 1994, California. *Education:* Cornell University (B.S., Genetics and Development, with distinction, 1990); University of Pennsylvania (J.D., 1994). Alpha Epsilon Delta. National Science Foundation, Fellow, Cold Spring Harbor Laboratory, Cold Spring, New York, 1989. W. James MacIntosh Scholar, University of Pennsylvania Law School, 1991-1994. *Email:* ibrockman@wsgr.com

**GREGORY B. BROGGER,** born Santa Monica, California, August 3, 1968; (admission pending). *Education:* University of California (B.A., 1990); The Wharton School, University of Pennsylvania (M.B.A., 1996); University of Pennsylvania (J.D., 1996). Recipient, Schectman Award, Journal of International Business Law. *PRACTICE AREAS:* Mergers and Acquisitions; Venture Capital; New Ventures; Corporate. *Email:* gbrogger@wsgr.com

**THOMAS G. BROWN,** born Los Angeles, California, December 7, 1967; admitted to bar, 1994, California. *Education:* University of California at Santa Barbara (B.A., with honors, 1990); Santa Clara University (M.B.A., 1994; J.D., summa cum laude, 1994). *PRACTICE AREAS:* Employee Benefits. *Email:* tbrown@wsgr.com

**MICHELLE BROWNLEE,** born Florida, August 10, 1968; admitted to bar, 1996, California. *Education:* Dartmouth College (A.B., 1990); Columbia University (J.D., 1994). Author: Note, "Safeguarding Style: What Protection is Afforded to Visual Artists by the Copyright and Trademark Laws?" 93 Columbia Law Review 1157, 1993. Clerk, Hon. Miriam Goldman Cedarbaum, U.S. District Judge for the Southern District of New York, 1994-1995. *LANGUAGES:* French. *PRACTICE AREAS:* Trademarks; Copyright; Advertising and Promotion Law; Litigation. *Email:* mbrownlee@wsgr.com

**JASON P. BUCHA,** born West Point, New York, January 29, 1970; admitted to bar, 1995, California. *Education:* Stanford University (A.B., 1992); Duke University (LL.M., 1995; J.D., 1995). *Email:* jbucha@wsgr.com

**BRADLEY A. BUGDANOWITZ,** born Denver, Colorado, June 5, 1971; admitted to bar, 1996, California. *Education:* University of California at Santa Cruz (B.A., with honors, 1993); University of Chicago (J.D., with honors, 1996). Editor-in-Chief, The University of Chicago Law School Roundtable, 1995-1996. *PRACTICE AREAS:* Corporate; Securities. *Email:* bbugdanowitz@wsgr.com

**BRETT D. BYERS,** born Lancaster, Pennsylvania, October 7, 1963; admitted to bar, 1995, New York; 1996, California. *Education:* Cornell University (B.S., 1986); Yale University (J.D., 1994). Tau Beta Pi; Eta Kappa Nu. *PRACTICE AREAS:* Corporate Law; Venture Capital Law; Securities Law; Mergers and Acquisitions. *Email:* bbyers@wsgr.com

**GIDON M. CAINE,** born Philadelphia, Pennsylvania, August 27, 1962; admitted to bar, 1988, New Jersey; 1989, New York and District of Columbia (Not admitted in California). *Education:* University of Pennsylvania (B.A., cum laude, 1983); New York University (J.D., 1988). Member, Journal of International Law and Politics. *LANGUAGES:* Hebrew. *PRACTICE AREAS:* Litigation.

**DAVID M. CAMPBELL,** born New York, N.Y., March 9, 1967; admitted to bar, 1996, California. *Education:* Pomona College (B.A., 1992); New York University (J.D., 1996). Articles, Editor, NYU Environmental Law Journal, 1991-1992. *PRACTICE AREAS:* Corporate; Mergers and Acquisitions; Venture Capital. *Email:* dcampbell@wsgr.com

**MEGAN J. CARROLL,** born Washington, Pennsylvania, April 15, 1959; admitted to bar, 1989, California. *Education:* University of California at Santa Cruz (B.A., 1981); Hastings College of the Law, University of California (J.D., 1989). Thurston Society. Recipient, American Jurisprudence Award. Author: "Drafting Through a Crystal Ball," Outside Counsel, Winter 1995. *Member:* State Bar of California; American Bar Association (Member, Sections on: Intellectual Property Law, Business Law and Entertainment Law); California Lawyers for the Arts; Licensing Executives Society; Computer Law Association. *PRACTICE AREAS:* Intellectual Property; Licensing. *Email:* mcarroll@wsgr.com

**CHARLES C. CARY,** born Buffalo, NY, 1948; admitted to bar, 1990, New York; 1994, Colorado; registered to practice before U.S. Patent and Trademark Office (Not admitted in California). *Education:* Harvard University (B.S., 1971); State University of New York at Buffalo (J.D., 1989; B.S., 1994). Tau Beta Phi; Golden Key. *PRACTICE AREAS:* Patent. *Email:* ccary@wsgr.com

**BERNARD JAMES CASSIDY,** born Philadelphia, Pennsylvania, October 2, 1954; admitted to bar, 1989, California. *Education:* Jesuit House of

*(This Listing Continued)*

Studies, Loyola University, New Orleans (B.A., 1978); University of Toronto (M.A., 1981); Jesuit School of Theology, Berkeley (M.Div., 1984); Harvard University (J.D., 1988). Book Review and Commentary Editor, Harvard Law Review, 1987-1988; Editor, 1986-1987. Author: "Essays in Honor of Judge John T. Noonan, Jr.," 11 Journal of Law and Religion 2201, 1995; "Attorneys' Fees—Risk Multipliers: Pennsylvania v. Delaware Valley Citizens Council," 101 Harvard Law Review 290, 1987; Developments in the Law—Religion and the State," 100 Harvard Law Review 1606, 1987. Research Assistant, Professor Arthur R. Miller, 1986-1988. Law Clerk, The Hon. John T. Noonan, Jr., U.S. Court of Appeals for the Ninth Circuit, 1988-1989. *PRACTICE AREAS:* Litigation; Mergers and Acquisitions. *Email:* bcassidy@wsgr.com

**ARMANDO CASTRO,** born Los Angeles, California, December 25, 1962; admitted to bar, 1992, California. *Education:* Loyola Marymount University (B.S., 1985); Stanford University (J.D., 1992). Certified Public Accountant, California, 1989. *Member:* American Institute of Certified Public Accountants. *LANGUAGES:* Spanish. *PRACTICE AREAS:* Corporate; Securities. *Email:* acastro@wsgr.com

**JEFF CATTALINI,** born Sacramento, California, February 11, 1970; admitted to bar, 1996, California. *Education:* University of California (B.A., with honors, 1991); Boalt Hall School of Law, University of California (J.D., 1996). Recipient, American Jurisprudence Award, Business Planning. Member, California Law Review, 1994-1996. *LANGUAGES:* Italian. *PRACTICE AREAS:* Corporate; Securities. *Email:* jcattalini@wsgr.com

**MARTA CERVANTES,** born Seattle, Washington, August 7, 1963; admitted to bar, 1988, California; 1989, District of Columbia. *Education:* University of Oregon; University of Texas (B.A., 1984); Stanford University (J.D., 1988). *Member:* Santa Clara County and American Bar Associations; State Bar of California. *PRACTICE AREAS:* Litigation. *Email:* mcervantes@wsgr.com

**ALEX CHACHKES,** born Philadelphia, Pennsylvania, September 25, 1969; admitted to bar, 1996, California. *Education:* Massachusetts Institute of Technology (S.B., 1991); Columbia University (J.D., 1996). Harlan Fiske Stone Scholar. *LANGUAGES:* Japanese and French. *PRACTICE AREAS:* Intellectual Property. *Email:* achachkes@wsgr.com

**DANIEL M. CHAMBERS,** born Barstow, California, September 4, 1963; admitted to bar, 1993, California; registered to practice before U.S. Patent and Trademark Office. *Education:* University of California, Los Angeles (B.S., Biology, 1985); Southwestern University School of Law (J.D., 1992). *PRACTICE AREAS:* Intellectual Property Law; Patent Law; Technology Licensing. *Email:* dchambers@wsgr.com

**H.C. CHAN,** born Kwangtung, China, April 29, 1950; admitted to bar, 1990, California and U.S. District Court, Northern District of California ; registered to practice before U.S. Patent and Trademark Office. *Education:* Rose-Hulman Institute of Technology (B.S.E.E., 1970); Massachusetts Institute of Technology (Ph.D., 1977); University of Washington (M.B.A., 1980); University of California, Hastings College of the Law (J.D., 1989). *Member:* State Bar of California. *LANGUAGES:* Chinese. *PRACTICE AREAS:* Intellectual Property. *Email:* hchan@wsgr.com

**CARMEN I-HUA CHANG,** born Nanjing, China, January 19, 1948; admitted to bar, 1994, California and U.S. Court of Appeals, Ninth Circuit. *Education:* Sarah Lawrence College (B.A., 1970); Stanford University (M.A., 1973; J.D., with distinction, 1993). *LANGUAGES:* Chinese (Mandarin and Cantonese). *PRACTICE AREAS:* Corporate; International. *Email:* cchang@wsgr.com

**WILLIANA CHANG,** born London, England, March 11, 1969; admitted to bar, 1995, California. *Education:* University of California, Berkeley (B.A., 1991); University of Southern California (J.D., 1995). *PRACTICE AREAS:* Employee Benefits.

**WARREN CHAO,** born New York, N.Y., August 15, 1968; admitted to bar, 1994, California. *Education:* Harvard University (B.A., 1989); New York University (M.B.A., 1994; J.D., 1994). Executive Editor, Annual Survey of American Law. *Member:* Institute of Electrical and Electronic Engineers. *LANGUAGES:* Chinese (Mandarin). *PRACTICE AREAS:* Corporate; Securities. *Email:* wchao@wsgr.com

**TREVOR J. CHAPLICK,** born Syracuse, New York, February 12, 1963; admitted to bar, 1990, California; 1992, District of Columbia. *Education:* University of Virginia (B.S., 1985; J.D., 1990). Beta Gamma Sigma; Omicron Delta Kappa; Beta Alpha Psi; Raven Society. Editor-in-Chief, Virginia Tax Review, 1989-1990. Certified Public Accountant, Virginia, 1985. *Member:* Bar Association of San Francisco; District of Columbia Bar;

*(This Listing Continued)*

American Bar Association. *PRACTICE AREAS:* Corporate; Securities. *Email:* tchaplick@wsgr.com

**THEODORE C. CHEN,** born Raleigh, North Carolina, June 12, 1965; admitted to bar, 1992, New York; 1993, District of Columbia (Not admitted in California). *Education:* University of Pennsylvania (B.S., 1987; J.D., 1991). *Member:* American Bar Association. *PRACTICE AREAS:* Corporate; Securities. *Email:* tchen@wsgr.com

**HANLEY CHEW,** born New York, N.Y., September 12, 1970; admitted to bar, 1995, New York (Not admitted in California). *Education:* Harvard University (B.A., 1992); University of Pennsylvania (J.D., 1995). *LANGUAGES:* Chinese.

**ROGER J. CHIN,** born Iowa City, Iowa, August 7, 1968; admitted to bar, 1996, California. *Education:* Cornell University (A.B., 1990); Yale University (J.D., 1995); Yale Medical School (M.D., 1996). *PRACTICE AREAS:* Intellectual Property Law; Litigation. *Email:* rchin@wsgr.com

**SANDRA CHUTORIAN,** born Winnipeg, Manitoba, Canada, October 25, 1955; admitted to bar, 1987, New York; 1989, California. *Education:* University of Michigan (B.A., 1977); Columbia University School of Law (J.D., 1986). Member, Columbia Law Review, 1985-1986. *Member:* American Bar Association; New York County Bar Association; State Bar of California. *PRACTICE AREAS:* Corporate Law; Securities. *Email:* schutorian@wsgr.com

**ROBERT CLAASSEN,** born Boulder, Colorado, September 29, 1966; admitted to bar, 1993, New York (Not admitted in California). *Education:* University of Wisconsin (B.A., 1988; J.D., 1992). *PRACTICE AREAS:* Corporate; Finance. *Email:* rclaassen@wsgr.com

**TODD CLEARY,** born Urbana, Illinois, June 17, 1970; admitted to bar, 1995, California. *Education:* Johns Hopkins University (B.A., general and departmental honors, 1991); Stanford University (J.D., with distinction, 1995). Phi Beta Kappa. Article Editor, Stanford Journal of Law, Business and Finance. *PRACTICE AREAS:* Corporate; Securities. *Email:* tcleary@wsgr.com

**OLABISI L. CLINTON,** born Washington, D.C., February 28, 1966; admitted to bar, 1992, California, California Supreme Court and U.S. District Court, Northern District of California. *Education:* University of California, Los Angeles (B.A., Departmental Honors in Political Science, 1988); Harvard University (J.D., 1991). Author: "Cultural Differences and Sentencing Departures," Federal Sentencing Reporter, Vol. 5, No. 6, May/June 1993. Co-Author: with Kevin Hobgood-Brown, "Technology Transfer in Taiwan Trade and Investment Law," Oxford University Press, 1994. *Member:* International and American Bar Associations. *PRACTICE AREAS:* Corporate Law; Corporate Governance; International Law. *Email:* oclinton@wsgr.com

**ANTON THEODORE COMMISSARIS,** born Auckland, New Zealand, February 27, 1961; admitted to bar, 1985, New Zealand; 1991, United Kingdom; 1993, France (Not admitted in the United States). *Education:* University of Auckland (LL.B., Hons., 1984); University of Montpellier (Maîtrise de Droit Privé, mention Droit de l'Entreprise, 1991). *LANGUAGES:* French. *PRACTICE AREAS:* Corporate; Securities; Venture Finance; Mergers and Acquisitions. *Email:* acommissaris@wsgr.com

**GREGORY T. COX,** born Lompoc, California, April 25, 1962; admitted to bar, 1988, California; 1989, U.S. District Court, Central District of California. *Education:* Stanford University (A.B., with distinction and honors, 1984; M.B.A., 1988; J.D., with distinction, 1988). Phi Beta Kappa; Pi Sigma Alpha; Omicron Delta Epsilon. *Member:* State Bar of California; American Bar Association. *PRACTICE AREAS:* Corporate Law; Securities. *Email:* gcox@wsgr.com

**BRANDYN CRISWELL,** born Redwood City, California, November 19, 1969; admitted to bar, 1996, California. *Education:* Stanford University (B.A., 1990); Northwestern University (J.D., 1996); Kellog Graduate School of Management (M.M., 1996). Beta Gamma Sigma; Order of the Coif. *PRACTICE AREAS:* Corporate; Technology Transactions. *Email:* bcriswell@wsgr.com

**LINDA M. CUNY,** born Sacramento, California, March 6, 1968; admitted to bar, 1996, California. *Education:* Santa Clara University (B.S.C., summa cum laude, 1990); University of California School of Law at Davis (J.D., 1996). Order of the Coif. *PRACTICE AREAS:* Corporate; Securities. *Email:* lcuny@wsgr.com

**BRIAN D. DANELLA,** born Syracuse, New York, April 3, 1969; admitted to bar, 1995, New York (Not admitted in California). *Education:* Princeton University (A.B., Computer Science, 1991); Syracuse University

*(This Listing Continued)*

**WILSON, SONSINI, GOODRICH & ROSATI,**
*PROFESSIONAL CORPORATION, Palo Alto—Continued*

(J.D., magna cum laude, 1994). *PRACTICE AREAS:* Technology Licensing; Intellectual Property. *Email:* bdanella@wsgr.com

**JILL DANIELS,** born Baltimore, Maryland, March 9, 1970; admitted to bar, 1995, California. *Education:* Stanford University (A.B., with distinction, 1992); Harvard University (J.D., cum laude, 1995). Phi Beta Kappa. Recipient, American Jurisprudence Award, Sexual Harassment, 1994-1995. *Member:* American Bar Association (Member, Employment and Labor Law Section). *PRACTICE AREAS:* Employment Law. *Email:* jdaniels@wsgr.com

**LISA A. DAVIS,** born Modesto, California, May 15, 1962; admitted to bar, 1995, California. *Education:* Stanford University (A.B., with distinction, 1984); Indiana University (A.M., 1986); Harvard University (Ph.D., 1991; J.D., cum laude, 1995). Phi Beta Kappa. *LANGUAGES:* Spanish and French. *PRACTICE AREAS:* Securities Litigation; Intellectual Property.

**ROBERT G. DAY,** born Sacramento, California, November 14, 1966; admitted to bar, 1993, California. *Education:* Stanford University (A.B., 1989; J.D., 1993). Associate Editor, 1991-1992; Business Manager, 1992-1993, Stanford University Law Review. Author: "Administrative Watchdogs or Zealous Advocates? Implications For Legal Ethics in The Face of Expanded Attorney Liability," 45 Stanford Law Review, 645, 1993. *PRACTICE AREAS:* Corporate; Securities. *Email:* rday@wsgr.com

**HAROLD R. DEGRAFF,** born Mayfield, Kentucky, April 8, 1965; admitted to bar, 1996, California. *Education:* United States Military Academy (B.S., 1987); Stanford University (M.S., 1991); University of Michigan (J.D., 1995). *Email:* hdegraff@wsgr.com

**CECILIA M. DE LEON,** born Philippines, 1967; admitted to bar, 1993, California and U.S. District Court, Central and Northern Districts of California. *Education:* University of California at Los Angeles (B.A., 1989); Boalt Hall School of Law, University of California (J.D., 1993). *Email:* cdeleon@wsgr.com

**LAURA MILLER DE PETRA,** born San Diego, California, December 23, 1970; admitted to bar, 1996, California. *Education:* University of California at Los Angeles (B.A., 1993); Boalt Hall School of Law, University of California (J.D., 1996). *PRACTICE AREAS:* Corporate; Securities. *Email:* lmdepetra@wsgr.com

**STEPHEN F. DIAMOND,** born Evanston, Illinois, December 25, 1955; (admission pending). *Education:* University of California at Berkeley (B.A., 1977); University of London (M.Phil., 1989; Ph.D., 1991); Yale University (J.D., 1994). Phi Beta Kappa; MacArthur Fellow. Symposium Editor, Yale Law Journal, 1993-1994. Co-Editor, Human Rights, Labor Rights and International Trade, University of Pennsylvania, 1996. Visiting Scholar: Stanford, Harvard and University of California at San Diego. *LANGUAGES:* German and Spanish. *PRACTICE AREAS:* Mergers and Acquisitions; Start-ups; Corporate Finance. *Email:* sdiamond@wsgr.com

**MARTHA L. DIENES,** born Stanford, California, June 8, 1962; admitted to bar, 1994, California. *Education:* University of California at Davis (B.A., summa cum laude, 1991); Stanford University (J.D., 1995). Phi Beta Kappa; Phi Kappa Phi. *Member:* State Bar of California (Member, Intellectual Property Section). *PRACTICE AREAS:* Technology Licensing; Intellectual Property. *Email:* mdienes@wsgr.com

**BRET M. DIMARCO,** born San Francisco, California, May 16, 1968; admitted to bar, 1993, California. *Education:* University of Lund, Sweden; University of California at Irvine (B.A., 1990); University of Southern California (J.D., 1993). Phi Delta Phi; Kappa Sigma. *Member:* Santa Clara and Palo Alto Bar Associations; State Bar of California. *LANGUAGES:* Swedish. *PRACTICE AREAS:* Corporate; Securities. *Email:* bdimarco@wsgr.com

**VIVIAN B. DISTLER,** born Montreal, Quebec, May 7, 1965; admitted to bar, 1994, California. *Education:* Boston University (B.S., summa cum laude, 1987; B.A., magna cum laude, 1987); Boalt Hall School of Law, University of California (J.D., 1994). Member, 1992-1993 and Managing Editor, 1993-1994, California Law Review. Law Clerk: Hon. Melvin Brunetti, U.S. Court of Appeals, Ninth Circuit, 1995; Hon. Howard D. McKibben, U.S. District Court, District of Nevada, 1995-1996. *PRACTICE AREAS:* Intellectual Property; Technology Licensing. *Email:* vdistiler@wsgr.com

**ADAM R. DOLINKO,** born Chicago, Illinois, July 5, 1968; admitted to bar, 1993, California. *Education:* University of California at Los Angeles (B.A., cum laude, 1990); University of Southern California (J.D., 1993).

*(This Listing Continued)*

Senior Editor, 1992-1993 and Associate Editor, 1991-1992, Southern California Law Review. University of Southern California Law Center Merit Scholar. Douglas G. Simon Memorial Scholar. *PRACTICE AREAS:* Corporate; Securities. *Email:* adolinko@wsgr.com

**STEPHEN A. DONOVAN,** born New York, N.Y., July 2, 1967; admitted to bar, 1994, Minnesota; 1996, California. *Education:* Yale University (B.A., 1988); Columbia University (J.D., 1993). Associate Editor, Columbia Journal of Transactional Law. *LANGUAGES:* Spanish and French. *PRACTICE AREAS:* Corporate Finance. *Email:* sdonovan@wsgr.com

**STEPHEN G. DRIGGERS,** born Gainesville, Florida, October 19, 1950; admitted to bar, 1993, California. *Education:* University of Texas (B.A., 1972); Indiana University (Ph.D., English, 1981); Stanford University (J.D., 1992). Phi Beta Kappa. Member, Stanford Law Review. *PRACTICE AREAS:* Employee Benefits. *Email:* sdriggers@wsgr.com

**DAVID C. DRUMMOND,** born Fort Riley, Kansas, March 6, 1963; admitted to bar, 1989, California. *Education:* Santa Clara University (B.A., cum laude, 1985); Stanford University (J.D., cum laude, 1989). *Member:* State Bar of California. *Email:* ddrummond@wsgr.com

**CYNTHIA A. DY,** born Chapel Hill, North Carolina, December 14, 1969; admitted to bar, 1994, California. *Education:* University of North Carolina (B.A., with highest honors, 1991); Stanford University (J.D., 1994). Phi Beta Kappa. Senior Articles Editor, Stanford Journal of International Law, 1993-1994. *PRACTICE AREAS:* Litigation. *Email:* cdy@wsgr.com

**IAN B. EDVALSON,** born La Grande, Oregon, August 14, 1966; admitted to bar, 1996, California. *Education:* Brigham Young University (B.A./B.S., 1991); University of Chicago (J.D., 1995). *LANGUAGES:* Korean. *PRACTICE AREAS:* Licensing. *Email:* iedvalson@wsgr.com

**KEITH E. EGGLETON,** born Tucson, Arizona, September 17, 1965; admitted to bar, 1992, California. *Education:* California Polytechnic State University, San Luis Obispo (B.S., summa cum laude, 1987); Northwestern University (J.D., cum laude, 1990). Associate Editor, Northwestern Law Review. Clerk, Honorable Charles E. Wiggins, United States Court of Appeals, Ninth Circuit, 1990-1991. *Member:* State Bar of California; American Bar Association. *PRACTICE AREAS:* Litigation. *Email:* keggleton@wsgr.com

**NEVAN C. ELAM,** born Palo Alto, California, September 27, 1967; admitted to bar, 1993, California. *Education:* Howard University (B.A., 1989); Harvard University (J.D., 1992). *PRACTICE AREAS:* Corporate; Securities; Mergers and Acquisitions. *Email:* nealam@wsgr.com

**VERA M. ELSON,** admitted to bar, 1991, California; registered to practice before U.S. Patent and Trademark Office. *Education:* University of California, Los Angeles (B.S., Cybernetics, 1982); M.S.E.E., emphasis in integrated circuit design, 1985); University of Southern California (J.D., 1991). Intern to Chief Judge Nies, U.S. Court of Appeals, Federal Circuit, 1990. Author: "Throw a Party, Lose Your Patent Rights!" Design News, April 1995; "Reviewing Competitors' Patents: Are There Risks?" Corporate Counsel Magazine, June 1995. *Member:* State Bar of California; American Bar Association; Federal Circuit Bar. *LANGUAGES:* German and Spanish. *PRACTICE AREAS:* Intellectual Property Litigation. *Email:* velson@wsgr.com

**REBECCA L. EPSTEIN,** born Champaign, Illinois, March 30, 1968; admitted to bar, 1993, California. *Education:* Stanford University (B.A., university distinction and honors, Economics, 1990); University of Chicago; Stanford University (J.D., 1993). Phi Beta Kappa. *PRACTICE AREAS:* Securities Litigation; General Commercial Litigation. *Email:* repstein@wsgr.com

**BRIAN C. ERB,** born Albany, Oregon, March 18, 1963; admitted to bar, 1990, New York; 1994, California. *Education:* University of Oregon (B.S., 1985); Willamette University (J.D., cum laude, 1989). Phi Beta Kappa; Kappa Tau Alpha. Member, Willamette Law Review. Author: "Creative Probation Conditions: Putting the 'Unusual' Back in 'Cruel and Unusual' After Bateman," 24 Willamette Law Review 1155, 1988. *PRACTICE AREAS:* Corporate; Securities. *Email:* berb@wsgr.com

**CRAIG H. FACTOR,** born New York, N.Y., July 30, 1968; admitted to bar, 1994, New York; 1995, California. *Education:* Harvard University (A.B., cum laude, 1990); Duke University (J.D., with honors, 1993). Staff Editor, Duke Journal of Comparative and International Law. *Member:* American Bar Association; Braxton Craven Chapter Inns of Court. *PRACTICE AREAS:* Corporate; Securities; Communications. *Email:* cfactor@wsgr.com

*(This Listing Continued)*

**JANICE LEYRER FALL,** born Los Angeles, California, July 3, 1954; admitted to bar, 1984, California, U.S. Court of Appeals, Ninth Circuit and U.S. District Court, Northern and Central Districts of California. *Education:* University of California at Los Angeles (B.A., magna cum laude, 1977); Stanford University (M.A., 1980); Boalt Hall School of Law, University of California (J.D., 1984). Note and Comment Editor, California Law Review, 1983-1984. *Member:* State Bar of California. *Email:* jfall@wsgr.com

**DOROTHY L. FERNANDEZ,** born San Francisco, California, January 26, 1970; admitted to bar, 1996, California. *Education:* Stanford University (A.B., 1992); Harvard University (J.D., 1996). *PRACTICE AREAS:* Litigation. *Email:* dfernandez@wsgr.com

**ERIC J. FINSETH,** born Cambridge, Massachusetts, May 10, 1965; admitted to bar, 1994, California. *Education:* L'Institut d'Etudes Politiques de Paris, France (C.E.P., 1986); Harvard University (B.A., magna cum laude, 1988); Freie Universität, Berlin, Germany (M.A., 1991); Columbia University (J.D., 1994). *Member:* State Bar of California. *LANGUAGES:* German and French. *PRACTICE AREAS:* Corporate; Securities; Partnerships; Limited Liability Companies. *Email:* efinseth@wsgr.com

**DIANE JEAN FONG,** born Reno, Nevada, May 19, 1954; admitted to bar, 1984, California. *Education:* Stanford University (B.Sc., 1976); University of California at Los Angeles (J.D., 1984). *Member:* State Bar of California. *PRACTICE AREAS:* Estate Planning. *Email:* dfong@wsgr.com

**DEBORAH S. FOX,** born Birmingham, Alabama; admitted to bar, 1994, California. *Education:* University of California, Berkeley (B.S.B.A., 1990); Harvard Law School (J.D., 1993). *PRACTICE AREAS:* Corporate. *Email:* dfox@wsgr.com

**BRENDA R. FRANK,** born New York, N.Y., December 18, 1969; admitted to bar, 1995, New York and Florida; 1996, California. *Education:* State University of New York at Albany (B.S., 1991); New York University (J.D., 1994). *Email:* bfrank@wsgr.com

**KAREN P. FREDERICKS,** born Somerville, New Jersey, September 9, 1971; admitted to bar, 1996, New Jersey (Not admitted in California). *Education:* Wellesley College (B.A., magna cum laude, 1992); University of Pennsylvania (J.D., 1995); Stanford University (M.A., 1996). *PRACTICE AREAS:* Corporate. *Email:* kfredericks@wsgr.com

**ADELE C. FREEDMAN,** born New York, New York, August 16, 1964; admitted to bar, 1990, New York; 1995, California. *Education:* Cornell University (B.A., 1986); Fordham University (J.D., 1989). *LANGUAGES:* French. *PRACTICE AREAS:* Corporate; Securities. *Email:* afreedman@wsgr.com

**KEVIN M. GALLIGAN,** born Buffalo, New York, July 1, 1965; admitted to bar, 1995, California. *Education:* University of Colorado at Boulder (B.S., 1990; B.A., 1990; M.B.A., 1992); University of California, Boalt Hall School of Law (J.D., 1995). *Member:* State Bar of California. *PRACTICE AREAS:* Corporate Law; Securities. *Email:* kgalligan@wsgr.com

**W. H. BAIRD GARRETT,** born Wilmington, Delaware, May 26, 1961; admitted to bar, 1996, California. *Education:* Pennsylvania State University (B.A., 1983); University of Chicago (M.A., 1988); University of Virginia (J.D., 1994). *Member,* Articles Review Board, 1993-1994 and Editorial Board, 1992-1993, Virginia Law Review. Author: Note, "Toward a Restrictive View of Copyright Protection for Nonliteral Elements of Computer Programs: Recent Developments in the Federal Courts," 79 Virginia L. Rev. 2096. Clerk, Hon. Jack B. Jacobs, Delaware Court of Chancery, 1994-1995. *PRACTICE AREAS:* Technology; Licensing. *Email:* bgarrett@wsgr.com

**KONSTATIW GAVRILOV,** born New York, N.Y., July 7, 1969; (admission pending). *Education:* University of Pennsylvania (B.A., 1991); Hastings College of the Law, University of California (J.D., 1996). Order of the Coif. *LANGUAGES:* Spanish. *PRACTICE AREAS:* Corporate; Securities; Mergers and Acquisitions.

**ROGER EDWARD GEORGE,** born Washington, D.C., January 4, 1966; admitted to bar, 1992, South Carolina; 1995, District of Columbia and California. *Education:* University of Virginia (B.S., 1988; J.D., 1992). Omicron Delta Kappa; The Raven Society; Beta Alpha Psi. Certified Public Accountant, Virginia, 1991. *Member:* State Bar of California; District of Columbia Bar; South Carolina Bar; American Bar Association; American Institute of Certified Public Accountants; Virginia Society of Certified Public Accountants. *PRACTICE AREAS:* Corporate; Securities. *Email:* rgeorge@wsgr.com

*(This Listing Continued)*

**STEPHEN E. GILLETTE,** born New York, N.Y., July 7, 1969; admitted to bar, 1996, California. *Education:* University of Pennsylvania (B.A., 1991); Hastings College of the Law, University of California (J.D., 1996). Order of the Coif; Thurston Society; Blackfield Scholar. *LANGUAGES:* Spanish. *PRACTICE AREAS:* Corporate; Securities; Mergers and Acquisitions. *Email:* sgillette@wsgr.com

**SELWYN B. GOLDBERG,** born Cape Town, South Africa, November 19, 1956; admitted to bar, 1987, New York; 1991, U.S. District Court, Southern and Eastern Districts of New York; 1996, California. *Education:* University of Cape Town (B.S.E.E., 1979); Rutgers University (M.S.E.E., 1983); New York Law School (J.D., magna cum laude, 1986). *PRACTICE AREAS:* Intellectual Property Licensing; Intellectual Property Counseling; Patent. *Email:* sgoldberg@wsgr.com

**JON C. GONZALES,** born Emporia, Kansas, August 10, 1965; admitted to bar, 1992, Massachusetts; 1996, New York (Not admitted in California). *Education:* University of Texas (B.B.A., 1988; M.P.A., 1988); Stanford University (J.D., 1992). Certified Public Accountant, Texas, 1989. *Member:* New York State and American Bar Associations. *PRACTICE AREAS:* Corporate; Securities. *Email:* jgonzales@wsgr.com

**SARAH ANN GOOD,** born Chambersburg, Pennsylvania, August 15, 1964; admitted to bar, 1990, California; 1991, District of Columbia. *Education:* University of Oxford, St. Edmund Hall, England; Princeton University (A.B., 1986); University of Virginia (J.D., 1990). Raven Society. *PRACTICE AREAS:* Litigation. *Email:* sgood@wsgr.com

**MARC E. GOTTSCHALK,** born White Plains, New York, September 3, 1961; admitted to bar, 1991, New Hampshire; 1994, California and District of Columbia. *Education:* Grinnell College (B.A., 1983); Hastings College of Law, University of California (J.D., cum laude, 1991). Order of the Coif. Co-Author: "Implementation of the Clean Air Act in N.H.," National Business Institute, 1992; *New Hampshire Environmental Law Handbook,* Government Institutes, 1992. *Member:* Bar Association of San Francisco; American Bar Association. *LANGUAGES:* French. *PRACTICE AREAS:* Environmental Law. *Email:* mgottschalk@wsgr.com

**LINDA S. GRAIS,** born San Jose, California, May 23, 1956; admitted to bar, 1993, California. *Education:* Yale College (B.A., magna cum laude, 1979); Yale Medical School (M.D., 1984); Stanford Law School (J.D., 1993). Phi Beta Kappa. *LANGUAGES:* French. *PRACTICE AREAS:* Corporate; Life Sciences. *Email:* lgrais@wsgr.com

**MONICA L. GREENBERG,** born New York, N.Y., October 21, 1968; admitted to bar, 1995, New York and New Jersey (Not admitted in California). *Education:* University of Pennsylvania (B.A., 1990); Boston University (J.D., 1994). Editor, Boston University Law Review, 1993-1994. *PRACTICE AREAS:* Corporate; Securities; Life Sciences. *Email:* mgreenberg@wsgr.com

**IRWIN R. GROSS,** born Denver, Colorado, May 16, 1969; admitted to bar, 1993, California. *Education:* Stanford University (B.S., with distinction, 1990); Harvard Law School (J.D., magna cum laude, 1993). Phi Beta Kappa; Tau Beta Pi. Author: "A New Framework for Software Protection: Distinguishing between Interactive and Non-Interactive Aspects of Computer Programs," 20 Rutgers Computer & Technology Law Journal 107, 1994; "Researching Software Copyrightability: A Practical Guide," 10 Santa Clara Computer and High Technology Law Journal 70, 1994. *PRACTICE AREAS:* Intellectual Property Litigation. *Email:* igross@wsgr.com

**GEOFFREY B. HALE,** born Antibes, France, February 11, 1961; admitted to bar, 1993, California. *Education:* Middlebury College (B.A., magna cum laude, 1985); University of Virginia (M.B.A., 1993; J.D., 1993). Phi Beta Kappa. *LANGUAGES:* German and French. *PRACTICE AREAS:* Corporate; Securities. *Email:* ghale@wsgr.com

**RAMSEY HANNA,** born Beirut, Lebanon, November 11, 1968; admitted to bar, 1994, California. *Education:* Schiller University, Heidelberg, Germany (B.A., 1988); Brown University (M.A., 1990); Stanford University (J.D., 1994). Author: "Misusing Antitrust: The Search for Functional Copyright Misuse Standards," Stanford Law Review, Vol. 46, Iss. 2. *Member:* American Bar Association. *LANGUAGES:* Arabic and German. *Email:* rhanna@wsgr.com

**SARA DUVAL HARRINGTON,** born Redwood City, California, March 9, 1964; admitted to bar, 1990, New York; 1991, California. *Education:* University of California at San Diego (B.A., 1986); Cornell University (J.D., 1989). *Member:* New York State and American Bar Associations; State Bar of California. *PRACTICE AREAS:* Litigation. *Email:* sharrington@wsgr.com

*(This Listing Continued)*

**WILSON, SONSINI, GOODRICH & ROSATI,**
*PROFESSIONAL CORPORATION, Palo Alto—Continued*

**RICHARD J. HART,** born Naples, Italy, May 20, 1964; admitted to bar, 1992, New York; 1994, California. *Education:* University of Pennsylvania (B.A., 1986); New York University (J.D., 1991). **LANGUAGES:** Italian. **PRACTICE AREAS:** Corporate Law; Securities. **Email:** rhart@wsgr.com

**MICHAEL W. HAUPTMAN,** born Bronx, New York, September 28, 1971; (admission pending). *Education:* University of Virginia (B.A., with honors, 1993); New York University (J.D., 1996). Phi Beta Kappa. **PRACTICE AREAS:** Corporate; Securities. **Email:** mhauptman@wsgr.com

**MICHAEL HAYDEN,** born Sacramento, California, October 23, 1966; (admission pending). *Education:* University of California, Santa Barbara (B.A., 1990); Boalt Hall School of Law, University of California (J.D., 1996). Certified Public Accountant, California, 1992. **PRACTICE AREAS:** Corporate. **Email:** mhayden@wsgr.com

**SUSAN HEANEY,** born Reno, Nevada, December 19, 1966; admitted to bar, 1994, New York; 1995, California. *Education:* University of California-Los Angeles (B.A. in English, magna cum laude, 1989); Boalt Hall School of Law, University of California, Berkeley (J.D., 1993). Law Clerk, Honorable Robert E. Rose, Nevada Supreme Court, 1994. *Member:* Bar Association of San Francisco; American Bar Association. **PRACTICE AREAS:** Litigation. **Email:** sheaney@wsgr.com

**PETER S. HEINECKE,** born San Francisco, California, June 15, 1965; admitted to bar, 1994, California. *Education:* Princeton University (A.B., magna cum laude, 1987); University of Hong Kong; University of Chicago (M.B.A., 1994; J.D., with high honors, 1994). Order of the Coif. **PRACTICE AREAS:** Corporate Law; Securities Law. **Email:** pheinecke@wsgr.com

**JEFFREY A. HERBST,** born New York, New York, June 10, 1964; admitted to bar, 1990, California. *Education:* Brown University (Sc.B. in Computer Science, with honors, 1986); Stanford University (J.D., 1989). Sigma Xi. Associate Editor, Stanford Law Review. Law Clerk to the Honorable Glenn L. Archer, Jr., U.S. Court of Appeals for the Federal Circuit, Washington, D.C., 1989-1990. Co-Author: "Mandatory Class Action lawsuits as a Restructuring Technique," 19 Pepperdine Law Review, 1992. *Member:* State Bar of California (Standing Committee on Computer Law); American Bar Association; American Intellectual Property Law Association. **PRACTICE AREAS:** Corporate Law; Securities Law; Technology Licensing; Intellectual Property. **Email:** jherbst@wsgr.com

**MICHAEL HETHERINGTON,** born San Francisco, California, March 11, 1951; admitted to bar, 1982, California and U.S. District Court, Northern District of California; 1987, U.S. Court of Appeals, Ninth Circuit; 1988, U.S. District Court, Eastern District of California; registered to practice before U.S. Patent and Trademark Office. *Education:* Stanford University (B.A., with distinction, 1970; M.S., Eng., 1976); University of San Francisco (J.D., 1982). Phi Beta Kappa. *Member:* Palo Alto, San Mateo County and American Bar Associations; State Bar of California; American Electronics Association; Peninsula Patent Law Association. **LANGUAGES:** German. **PRACTICE AREAS:** Intellectual Property. **Email:** mhetherington@wsgr.com

**CHARLES D. HOLLAND,** born Pittsburgh, Pennsylvania, March 20, 1953; admitted to bar, 1992, California and U.S. District Court, Northern District of California; registered to practice before U.S. Patent and Trademark Office. *Education:* Carnegie Mellon University (B.S., Chem. Eng., 1975); Santa Clara University (J.D., 1992). Dean's List. Comments Editor, Santa Clara University Law Review. *Member:* State Bar of California; American Bar Association (Member, Patent and Trademark Section); San Francisco Intellectual Property Law Association; Peninsula Intellectual Property Law Association. **PRACTICE AREAS:** Patents. **Email:** cholland@wsgr.com

**BRUCE ROBERT HOPENFELD,** born Los Angeles, California, November 6, 1967; admitted to bar, 1993, California; 1994, U.S. District Court, Central District of California; registered to practice before U.S. Patent and Trademark Office. *Education:* University of California at Los Angeles (B.S.E.E., magna cum laude, 1989); University of Chicago (J.D., with honors, 1993). Eta Kappa Nu; Tau Beta Pi. Member, University of Chicago Law Review, 1991-1993. *Member:* State Bar of California. **PRACTICE AREAS:** Intellectual Property; Technology Licensing. **Email:** bhopenfeld@wsgr.com

**FRANK I. HOPPE,** born Lincoln, Nebraska, September 15, 1970; admitted to bar, 1996, California. *Education:* University of Virginia (B.A., with distinction, 1993), Echols Scholar; Boalt Hall School of Law, University of California (J.D., 1996). **PRACTICE AREAS:** Corporate; Securities. **Email:** fhoppe@wsgr.com

**JOHN MATHIAS HORAN,** born Youngstown, Ohio, December 2, 1953; admitted to bar, 1980, Illinois and U.S. District Court, Northern District of Illinois; 1987, New York; 1992, U.S. District Court, Southern and Eastern Districts of New York; 1995, California; 1996, U.S. District Court, Northern District of California. *Education:* Harvard College (A.B., 1975); University of Michigan (J.D., 1980). **PRACTICE AREAS:** Intellectual Property Litigation; Trade Secrets; Trademarks; Copyrights; Patents. **Email:** jhoran@wsgr.com

**ANNA ITOI,** born Tokkaichi, Japan, July 10, 1969; admitted to bar, 1996, California. *Education:* Stanford University (B.A., 1991); Boalt Hall School of Law, University of California (J.D., 1996). **PRACTICE AREAS:** Corporate. **Email:** aitoi@wsgr.com

**BARBARA A. IZZO,** born Evergreen Park, Illinois, July 18, 1969; admitted to bar, 1994, Illinois; 1996, California. *Education:* University of Notre Dame (B.A., summa cum laude, 1991); Harvard University (J.D, cum laude, 1994). Phi Beta Kappa. **Email:** bizzo@wsgr.com

**JAMES L. JACOBS,** born New York, N.Y., January 10, 1963; admitted to bar, 1989, New York, U.S. District Court, Southern District of New York; 1991, U.S. District Court, Northern District of California; 1992, California and U.S. District Court, Eastern District of California. *Education:* Brown University (A.B., with honors, 1985); University of Virginia School of Law (J.D., 1988). *Member:* State Bar of California; New York State and American Bar Associations. **PRACTICE AREAS:** Litigation. **Email:** jjacobs@wsgr.com

**RAJU S. JUDGE,** born London, England, October 5, 1966; admitted to bar, 1993, California. *Education:* University of California (B.A., 1989); Whittier College School of Law (J.D., 1993). *Member:* State Bar of California; American Bar Association. **LANGUAGES:** Hindi, Panjabi, Urdu and French. **PRACTICE AREAS:** Corporate; Securities; Venture Capital.

**CHRISTINE KENDRICK,** born Stanford, California, January 17, 1965; admitted to bar, 1996, California. *Education:* Stanford University (A.B., 1990); John F. Kennedy School of Government, Harvard University (M.P.P., 1993); Georgetown University Law Center (J.D., 1996). **PRACTICE AREAS:** Litigation. **Email:** ckendrick@wsgr.com

**ADIT M. KHORANA,** born Rochester, New York, November 1, 1968; admitted to bar, 1994, California; registered to practice before U.S. Patent and Trademark Office. *Education:* Washington University; Purdue University (B.S.C.E.E., 1990); Stanford University (J.D., 1994). **PRACTICE AREAS:** Technology Transactions; Strategic Alliances; Licensing; Computer; Internet; Software; Patent; Copyright. **Email:** adit@wsgr.com

**DAVID A. KILLAM,** born Reading, Massachusetts, 1967; admitted to bar, 1993, California. *Education:* Boston University (B.A., magna cum laude, 1989); Yale University (J.D., 1992). Legal Intern, Alaska Department of Justice, 1990. *Member:* State Bar of California. **Email:** dkilliam@wsgr.com

**NAN H. KIM,** born Seoul, South Korea, February 27, 1968; admitted to bar, 1993, Pennsylvania; 1994, Connecticut; 1995, New York (Not admitted in California). *Education:* Cornell University (B.S., 1990); Georgetown University (J.D., 1993). **PRACTICE AREAS:** Corporate. **Email:** nkim@wsgr.com

**STEPHEN E. KIM,** born Detroit, Michigan, September 7, 1969; admitted to bar, 1995, New York (Not admitted in California). *Education:* Johns Hopkins University (B.A., 1991); New York University (J.D., 1994). Author: "From Disclosure to Registration," Business Law Today; "Integrated Registration," Insights. **PRACTICE AREAS:** Corporate. **Email:** skim@wsgr.com

**W. BRIAN KINARD,** born Dallas, Texas, August 29, 1964; admitted to bar, 1996, California. *Education:* Texas A & M University (B.S.E.E., 1987; M.S.E.E., 1989); Harvard University (J.D., 1995). Tau Beta Pi; Eta Kappa Nu; Phi Kappa Phi. *Member:* American Intellectual Property Law Association; Institute of Electrical and Electronics Engineers. **PRACTICE AREAS:** Corporate; Securities; Venture Capital; High Technology. **Email:** bkinard@wsgr.com

**DAVID R. KING,** born San Francisco, California, December 28, 1968; admitted to bar, 1995, California. *Education:* Yale University (B.A., cum laude, 1991); University of California, Boalt Hall School of Law (J.D.,

*(This Listing Continued)*

1995). Notes and Comments Editor, California Law Review. *PRACTICE AREAS:* Corporate; Securities. *Email:* dking@wsgr.com

**CATHERINE S. KIRKMAN,** born Palo Alto, California, December 9, 1962; admitted to bar, 1990, California. *Education:* Harvard University (A.B., magna cum laude, 1986); Stanford University (J.D., with distinction, 1989). Phi Beta Kappa; Order of the Coif. *Member:* State Bar of California; Interactive Multimedia Association (Member, Legal and Policy Issues Task Group). *PRACTICE AREAS:* Intellectual Property; Multimedia. *Email:* ckirkman@wsgr.com

**CHRISTOPHER M. KOA,** born Louisville, Kentucky, August 25, 1966; admitted to bar, 1993, California and U.S. District Court, Northern and Southern Districts of California. *Education:* Carleton College (B.A., English Literature, 1988); Princeton University, Woodrow Wilson School of Public and International Affairs (M.P.A., 1992); New York University (J.D., 1992). Member, 1990-1991 and Senior Note and Comment Editor, 1991-1992, New York University Journal of International Law and Politics. Author, "The International Bank for Reconstruction and Development and Dispute Resolution: Conciliating and Arbitrating with China Through the International Centre for Settlement of Investment Disputes," 24 New York University Journal of International Law and Politics 501, 1991. Law Clerk, Hon. Edward J. Schwartz, U.S. District Court, Southern District of California, 1992-1993. *Member:* National Asian Pacific American Bar Association (Chair, Young Lawyers Committee). *LANGUAGES:* Spanish. *PRACTICE AREAS:* Corporate Law; Securities. *Email:* ckoa@wsgr.com

**ROBERT F. KORNEGAY, JR.,** born Goldsboro, North Carolina, April 8, 1965; admitted to bar, 1993, California. *Education:* Georgetown University (A.B., 1987); University of Chicago (M.B.A., 1989); University of California, Los Angeles (J.D., 1993). Comment Editor, University of California Law Review, 1992-1993. Author, "Bank Assets as Securities: A Legal and Financial Economic Analysis of the Treatment of Marketable Bank Assets Under the Securities Acts," 40 UCLA L. Rev. 799, 1993. *LANGUAGES:* French. *PRACTICE AREAS:* Corporate; Securities. *Email:* rkornegay@wsgr.com

**DAVID H. KRAMER,** born New York, N.Y., January 17, 1968; admitted to bar, 1993, California. *Education:* Dartmouth College (B.A., cum laude, 1989); Georgetown University Law Center (J.D., magna cum laude, 1993). Order of the Coif. Associate Editor, Georgetown Law Journal, 1992-1993. *PRACTICE AREAS:* Intellectual Property. *Email:* dkramer@wsgr.com

**SUSAN P. KRAUSE,** born New Haven, Connecticut, January 9, 1971; admitted to bar, 1996, California. *Education:* Harvard University (B.A., cum laude, 1993); Yale University (J.D., 1996). *PRACTICE AREAS:* Corporate; Securities. *Email:* skrause@wsgr.com

**ELIZABETH M. KURR,** born Griggsville, Illinois, August 12, 1964; admitted to bar, 1992, California. *Education:* University of Illinois (B.A., 1986); University of San Francisco (J.D., magna cum laude, 1992). Recipient, Judge Harold J. Haley Award. Editor-in-Chief and Assistant Managing Editor, University of San Francisco Law Review, 1991-1992. Certified Public Accountant, California, 1989. Author, Note, "Granting Divestiture to Private Parties as a Remedy for Anticompetitive Mergers After California v. American Stores Co.," 26 U.S.F.L. Rev. 319, 1992. *Member:* California Certified Public Accountants. *PRACTICE AREAS:* Corporate Law. *Email:* ekurr@wsgr.com

**GILBERT M. LABRUCHERIE, JR.,** born Pleasanton, California, May 14, 1971; admitted to bar, 1996, California. *Education:* University of California at Davis (A.B., with highest honors, 1993); Boalt Hall School of Law, University of California (J.D., 1996). Order of the Coif. Associate Editor, California Law Review, 1995-1996. *PRACTICE AREAS:* Corporate; Securities; Mergers and Acquisitions. *Email:* glabrucherie@wsgr.com

**JOAN E. LAMBERT,** born Philadelphia, Pennsylvania, January 13, 1965; admitted to bar, 1990, California; 1992, New York. *Education:* University of California, Berkeley (B.A., 1986); University of California at Los Angeles (J.D., 1990). *Member:* Santa Clara County and American Bar Associations; State Bar of California. *PRACTICE AREAS:* Securities and Commercial Litigation; Alternative Dispute Resolution. *Email:* jlambert@wsgr.com

**MARTHE LAROSILIERE,** born New York, N.Y., January 17, 1964; admitted to bar, 1993, New York; 1994, California, U.S. District Court, Southern and Eastern Districts of New York, U.S. District Court, Northern District of California and U.S. Court of Appeals, Ninth Circuit. *Education:* City College of the City University of New York (B.A., magna cum laude, 1986); Stanford University (J.D., 1992). *Member:* Bar Association of San Francisco; New York State and American Bar Associations; State Bar of California. *LANGUAGES:* French. *PRACTICE AREAS:* Litigation. *Email:* mlarosiliere@wsgr.com

**THOMAS G. LAWER,** born New York, N.Y., March 29, 1966; admitted to bar, 1996, California. *Education:* University of Pennsylvania, The Wharton School of Business (B.S., Econ., 1988); University of Chicago (J.D., 1995). Certified Public Accountant, California, 1988. *PRACTICE AREAS:* Executive Compensation. *Email:* tlawer@wsgr.com

**JON P. LAYMAN,** born Cornwall, New York, February 16, 1966; (admission pending). *Education:* University of Michigan (B.A., 1989); New York University (J.D., 1996). *LANGUAGES:* German. *PRACTICE AREAS:* Corporate; Securities. *Email:* jlayman@wsgr.com

**ANDREW LEIBNITZ,** born Seattle, Washington, July 22, 1970; admitted to bar, 1996, California. *Education:* Williams College (B.A., magna cum laude, 1992); New York University (J.D., 1996). Phi Beta Kappa. Member, New York University Law Review. *PRACTICE AREAS:* Litigation. *Email:* aleibnitz@wsgr.com

**MICHAEL B. LEVIN,** born Boston, Massachusetts, October 29, 1968; admitted to bar, 1994, California. *Education:* Harvard University (A.B., cum laude, 1991); University of California at Los Angeles (J.D., 1994). Order of the Coif. Editor, UCLA Law Review, 1993-1994. Extern to: Judge Harry Pregerson, U.S. Court of Appeals, Ninth Circuit, 1992; Justice Edward Panelli, California Supreme Court, 1993. Law Clerk to Judge Ronald M. Whyte, U.S. District Court, Northern District of California, 1994-1995. *PRACTICE AREAS:* Intellectual Property Litigation. *Email:* mlevin@wsgr.com

**ADAM D. LEVY,** born Boston, Massachusetts, January 5, 1962; admitted to bar, 1994, California. *Education:* Haverford College (B.A., 1983); Georgetown University Law Center (J.D., 1994). *Email:* alevy@wsgr.com

**MICHAEL J. LEVY,** born San Francisco, California, August 26, 1966; admitted to bar, 1994, California. *Education:* California Polytechnic State University (B.S., 1990); Hastings College of the Law, University of California (J.D., 1994). Author: Note, "Why Sexual Favoritism is not Sexual Discrimination," 45 Hast. L.J. 667, 1994. Law Clerk, Hon. Robert P. Aguilar, U.S. District Court, Northern District of California. *PRACTICE AREAS:* Litigation. *Email:* mlevy@wsgr.com

**JOHN R. LEWIS,** born Youngstown, Ohio, October 25, 1968; admitted to bar, 1995, California. *Education:* Boston University (B.S., 1990); University of Chicago (J.D., 1995). *Email:* rlewis@wsgr.com

**JOSHUA A. LIPP,** born Brooklyn, New York, October 13, 1967; admitted to bar, 1992, California. *Education:* Stanford University (A.B., with distinction, 1989); Boalt Hall University School of Law, Berkeley (J.D., 1992). Phi Beta Kappa. Clerk, John S. Rhoades, U.S. District Court, Southern District of California. *LANGUAGES:* Spanish. *PRACTICE AREAS:* Corporate Law; Securities Law. *Email:* jlipp@wsgr.com

**BRIDGET LOGTERMAN,** born Madison, Wisconsin, May 28, 1964; admitted to bar, 1990, Illinois; 1994, California. *Education:* University of Wisconsin-Madison (B.A., 1987); Hastings College of the Law, University of California (J.D., 1990). *Email:* blogterman@wsgr.com

**LAURIE-ANN MEI INN LOOK,** born Columbus, Ohio, September 24, 1968; admitted to bar, 1994, California; 1995, Hawaii. *Education:* Santa Clara University (B.S., 1990; M.B.A., 1994; J.D., 1994). *Member:* Santa Clara County, Hawaii State and American Bar Associations; State Bar of California. *PRACTICE AREAS:* Estate Planning. *Email:* llook@wsgr.com

**THOMAS J. LORR,** born Chicago, Illinois, October 29, 1966; admitted to bar, 1992, California; U.S. Court of Appeals, Ninth Circuit; U.S. District Court, Northern District of California. *Education:* University of Southern California (B.S., 1989); Stanford University (J.D., 1992). Certified Public Accountant, California, 1995. *PRACTICE AREAS:* Corporate. *Email:* tlorr@wsgr.com

**TIFFANY LYON,** born San Mateo County, California, October 2, 1967; admitted to bar, 1992, California. *Education:* University of California, Berkeley (B.S., 1989); Santa Clara University (J.D., 1992). Clerk to Justice Panelli, California Supreme Court. *PRACTICE AREAS:* Civil Litigation. *Email:* tlyon@wsgr.com

**JOSE F. MACIAS,** born Hollister, California, October 21, 1966; admitted to bar, 1991, California. *Education:* Stanford University (B.A., with distinction, 1988; J.D., 1991). Executive Editor, Stanford Law Review, 1990-1991. *Member:* State Bar of California; American Bar Association. *LANGUAGES:* Spanish. *PRACTICE AREAS:* Corporate Law; Securities. *Email:* jmacias@wsgr.com

*(This Listing Continued)*

**WILSON, SONSINI, GOODRICH & ROSATI,**
*PROFESSIONAL CORPORATION, Palo Alto—Continued*

**MATTHEW MACKENZIE,** born Mission Viejo, California, June 6, 1971; admitted to bar, 1996, California. *Education:* University of California at Los Angeles (B.A., 1993; J.D., 1996). **PRACTICE AREAS:** Corporate; Securities. *Email:* mmackenzie@wsgr.com

**THOMAS J. MARTIN,** born Palo Alto, California, May 2, 1962; admitted to bar, 1990, California. *Education:* Stanford University (B.A., 1984; J.D., 1990). Law Clerk to Hon. William Matthew Byrne, Jr., U.S. District Court, Central District of California, 1990-1991. **PRACTICE AREAS:** Securities; Commercial Litigation. *Email:* tmartin@wsgr.com

**NANCY D. MARTINDALE,** born Oak Park, Illinois, August 30, 1952; admitted to bar, 1983, California; 1993, Washington. *Education:* San Jose State University (B.S.B.A., with distinction, 1979); Boalt Hall School of Law, University of California, Berkeley (J.D., 1983). Beta Gamma Sigma. Law Clerk, Hon. Robert P. Alguilar, U.S. District Court, Northern District of California, 1983-1985. *Member:* Santa Clara County and American Bar Associations; State Bar of California. **PRACTICE AREAS:** Litigation. *Email:* nmartindale@wsgr.com

**TAMARA GAIL MATTISON,** born Eau Claire, Wisconsin, July 14, 1959; admitted to bar, 1990, California and U.S. Court of Appeals, Ninth Circuit; 1994, Texas. *Education:* University of Wisconsin-Eau Claire (B.B.A., summa cum laude, 1981); J.L. Kellogg Graduate School of Management (M.M., with honors, 1987); Northwestern University (J.D., 1990). Certified Public Accountant, Wisconsin, 1984. *Member:* State Bar of Texas; State Bar of California; American Bar Association. *Email:* tmattison@wsgr.com

**THOMAS E. MCKEEVER,** born San Francisco, California, October 22, 1967; admitted to bar, 1994, California. *Education:* University of California at Berkeley (A.B., 1990); Stanford University (J.D., 1994). Law Clerk, Hon. Lawrence T. Lydick, U.S. District Court, Central District of California, 1994-1995. **PRACTICE AREAS:** Litigation. *Email:* tmckeever@wsgr.com

**BRUCE M. MCNAMARA,** born New York, N.Y., August 23, 1962; admitted to bar, 1990, California. *Education:* University of California at Berkeley (A.B., 1985; M.B.A., 1990); Boalt Hall School of Law, University of California (J.D., 1990). **PRACTICE AREAS:** Corporate Law; Securities. *Email:* bmcnamara@wsgr.com,

**RUTH ANN MCNEES,** born Twin Falls, Idaho, March 23, 1964; admitted to bar, 1991, California. *Education:* Utah State University (B.A., 1986); Santa Clara University (J.D., 1991). **PRACTICE AREAS:** Securities Litigation. *Email:* rmcnees@wsgr.com

**LISA G. MECKFESSEL,** born Los Gatos, California, October 24, 1967; admitted to bar, 1994, California and Wisconsin. *Education:* Stanford University (B.A., 1989); University of Wisconsin at Madison (J.D., cum laude, 1994). Order of the Coif. Managing Editor, Wisconsin Law Review, 1993-1994. Author: "Kodak v. Image Technical Services, the taming of Matsushita and the Chicago School," Wisconsin Law Review 1633, 1993. Legal Writing Instructor, University of Wisconsin, 1993-1994. *Member:* American Bar Association. **PRACTICE AREAS:** Intellectual Property Litigation. *Email:* lmeckfessel@wsgr.com

**HEATHER MEEKER,** born Los Angeles, California, September 5, 1959; admitted to bar, 1994, California; 1995, U.S. Court of Appeals, Tenth Circuit. *Education:* Yale University (B.A., magna cum laude, 1979); Boalt Hall School of Law, University of California (J.D., 1994). Order of the Coif. Author: "Clearly Established' Law in Qualified Immunity: Analysis for Civil Rights Actions in the Tenth Circuit," 35 Washburn L.J. 79, 1995; "Issues of Property, Ethics and consent in the Transplantation of Fetal Reproductive Tissue," 9 High Tech. L.J. 185, 1994; "Multimedia and Copyright," 20 Rutgers Comp. & Tech. L.J. 375, 1994; "Fair Use and Fine Arts in the post Modern Era," 10 U. Miami Ent. & Sports L. Rev. 195, 1993. **PRACTICE AREAS:** Intellectual Property; Technology Licensing. *Email:* hmeeker@wsgr.com

**MILLICENT S. MERONEY,** born Corsicana, Texas, March 25 1964; admitted to bar, 1990, California and New York. *Education:* Yale University; Duke University (A.B., History, with distinction, 1986); University of Texas at Austin (J.D., 1989). **PRACTICE AREAS:** Labor and Employment Law; Litigation. *Email:* mmeroney@wsgr.com

**NOAH D. MESEL,** born Boston, Massachusetts, June 17, 1961; admitted to bar, 1989, California, U.S. District Court, Northern and Southern Districts of California and U.S. Court of Appeals, 9th Circuit. *Education:* Claremont Men's College (B.A., cum laude, 1983); University of Virginia (J.D., 1989). Phi Delta Phi. Member, Moot Court Board. Member, Virginia Law Review, 1988-1989. *Member:* Santa Clara County and American (Member, House of Delegates, 1988-1989) Bar Associations; State Bar of California. **PRACTICE AREAS:** Litigation. *Email:* nmesel@wsgr.com

**HAROLD J. MILSTEIN,** born Brooklyn, New York, April 19, 1957; admitted to bar, 1984, New York; 1989, California; registered to practice before U.S. Patent and Trademark Office. *Education:* Arnold and Marie Schwartz College of Pharmacy of Long Island University (B.S., Pharmacy, cum laude, 1980); Hofstra University (J.D., 1983). Registered Pharmacist, New York, 1980. *Member:* American Bar Association; International Trademark Association. *Email:* hmilstein@wsgr.com

**REBECCA A. MITCHELLS,** born Youngstown, Ohio, July 1, 1963; admitted to bar, 1991, California; 1996, U.S. Court of Appeals, Ninth Circuit; U.S. District Court, Northern and Central Districts of California. *Education:* Kent State University (B.A., summa cum laude, 1987); Northwestern University School of Law (J.D., cum laude, 1990). Phi Beta Kappa. Member, Moot Court. Note and Comment Editor, Journal of Criminal Law and Criminology. *Member:* Bar Association of San Francisco; State Bar of California. **PRACTICE AREAS:** Litigation; Unfair Trade Competition. *Email:* rmitchells@wsgr.com

**DANIEL R. MITZ,** born Washington, D.C., October 27, 1962; admitted to bar, 1989, Connecticut; 1990, New York; 1991, District of Columbia; 1995, California. *Education:* University of Michigan (A.B., 1984); New York University (J.D., 1989). **PRACTICE AREAS:** Corporate; Securities. *Email:* dmitz@wsgr.com

**ROBERT MOLL,** born Cottage Grove, Oregon, April 18, 1956; admitted to bar, 1988, California; registered to practice before U.S. Patent and Trademark Office. *Education:* San Jose State University (B.S.Ch.E., 1981; Recipient of Dow Chemical Academic Scholarship); University of Southern California (J.D., 1987). Southern California Law Review, 1986-1987. *Member:* State Bar of California (Intellectual Property Section); American Intellectual Property Association; Peninsula Intellectual Property Law Association; Licensing Executives Society. **PRACTICE AREAS:** Intellectual Property Law. *Email:* rmoll@wsgr.com

**KELLY AMES MOREHEAD,** born San Francisco, California, October 1, 1966; admitted to bar, 1994, California; 1997, Colorado. *Education:* University of California at Los Angeles (B.A., 1990); University of San Diego (J.D., magna cum laude, 1994). Phi Alpha Delta. Recipient, American Jurisprudence Awards. Comments Editor, San Diego Law Review. *Member:* State Bar of California; American Bar Association. **PRACTICE AREAS:** Corporate Law; Securities Law. *Email:* kmorehead@wsgr.com

**DIANA M. MORROW,** born Santa Monica, California, March 10, 1967; admitted to bar, 1992, California, U.S. District Court, Northern District of California and U.S. Court of Appeals, Ninth Circuit. *Education:* University of California at Los Angeles (B.A., magna cum laude, 1988); Vanderbilt University (J.D., 1992). Phi Beta Kappa; Alpha Lambda Delta; Golden Key. Member, Vanderbilt Law Review. Co-Author: "Leasehold Improvement Agreements," Chapter 40, *Guide to Office Leasing:* Drafting and Negotiating the Lease, California Continuing Education of the Bar. **PRACTICE AREAS:** Real Estate; Environmental. *Email:* dmorrow@wsgr.com

**CAINE T. MOSS,** born Malden, Massachusetts, October 4, 1971; admitted to bar, 1996, California. *Education:* Stanford University (B.A., 1993); Harvard University (J.D., 1996). **PRACTICE AREAS:** Corporate; Securities. *Email:* cmoss@wsgr.com

**MONICA MUCCHETTI,** born Baton Rouge, Louisiana, January 8, 1967; admitted to bar, 1993, California. *Education:* Yale University (B.A., 1988); University of York, York, England (M.A., 1989); Boalt Hall School of Law, University of California, Berkeley (J.D., 1992). **LANGUAGES:** Spanish. **PRACTICE AREAS:** Intellectual Property Litigation. *Email:* mmucchetti@wsgr.com

**MICHAEL J. MURPHY,** born San Jose, California, November 21, 1967; admitted to bar, 1993, California; registered to practice before U.S. Patent and Trademark Office. *Education:* Stanford University (B.S., Comp. Sys. Eng., with distinction, 1989); Stanford Law School (J.D., with distinction, 1993). Tau Beta Pi; Order of the Coif. Recipient, Stanford President's Award for Academic Excellence. **PRACTICE AREAS:** Technology Licensing; Copyrights; Patents. *Email:* mmurphy@wsgr.com

**USHA NARAYANAN,** born New Delhi, India, June 8, 1965; admitted to bar, 1996, California. *Education:* University of Maryland (B.A., B.S., 1987); University of Illinois (J.D., cum laude, 1996). Managing Editor, El-

*(This Listing Continued)*

der Law Journal. Author: Note, "Filial Responsibility Laws in the U.S. and Japan," Elder Law Journal, 1997. LANGUAGES: French and Tamil. PRACTICE AREAS: Intellectual Property Litigation. Email: unarayanan@wsgr.com

**NEIL NATHANSON,** born Detroit, Michigan, October 26, 1960; admitted to bar, 1992, California and U.S. District Court, Northern District of California; 1993, U.S. Court of Appeals, Ninth Circuit; 1995, U.S. Court of Appeals for the District of Columbia Circuit. Education: University of Michigan (B.S., 1982; M.S., 1984); Stanford University (J.D., 1992). Order of the Coif. Member, Stanford Law Review, 1991-1992. Law Clerk to the Hon. Saundra Brown Armstrong, U.S. District Court, Northern District of California, 1992-1993. PRACTICE AREAS: Intellectual Property Litigation; Antitrust. Email: nnathanson@wsgr.com

**MARNIA NICHOLS,** born California, June 28, 1964; admitted to bar, 1993, New York and California. Education: San Jose State University (B.S., 1986); Hastings College of the Law, University of California (J.D., 1992). Certified Public Accountant, 1989—. Law Clerk to the Honorable F. A. Little, Jr., U.S. District Judge, 1992-1993. Member: State Bar of California; New York State Bar Association; American Association of Attorney-Certified Public Accountants; American Institute of Certified Public Accountants. PRACTICE AREAS: Corporate. Email: mnichols@wsgr.com

**CHRISTOPHER G. NICHOLSON,** born Sacramento, California, December 4, 1969; admitted to bar, 1995, California. Education: University of California at Los Angeles (B.A., 1992); Boalt Hall School of Law, University of California (J.D., 1995). Email: cnicholson@wsgr.com

**CHRISTINA NICOLOSI,** born Daly City, California, May 2, 1970; admitted to bar, 1995, California. Education: University of California, Los Angeles (B.A., magna cum laude, 1992); University of Michigan (J.D., cum laude, 1995). Phi Beta Kappa; Golden Key. Contributing Editor and Associate Editor, Michigan Law Review, 1993-1995. Email: cnicolosi@wsgr.com

**JOHN C. NISHI,** born Tokyo, Japan, May 19, 1955; admitted to bar, 1993, Illinois and U.S. District Court, Northern District of Illinois; 1995, California, U.S. District Court, Northern District of California and U.S. Court of Appeals, Ninth Circuit. Education: Yale University (B.A., cum laude, 1977); University of Southern California (M.M., 1980); University of Chicago (J.D., 1993). Recipient, Outstanding Graduate Award, University of Southern California. Associate Articles Editor, University of Chicago Legal Forum. Member, Editorial Board, Trademark Reporter. Member: American Bar Association. PRACTICE AREAS: Trademark; Advertising Practices. Email: jnishi@wsgr.com

**DONNA KATHERINE NORMAN,** born Kenosha, Wisconsin, December 26, 1966; admitted to bar, 1993, California and District of Columbia. Education: University of Wisconsin-Madison (B.A., cum laude, 1989); Georgetown University (J.D., magna cum laude, 1992). Law Clerk, Hon. Kenneth F. Ripple, U.S. Court of Appeals, Seventh Circuit, 1992-1993. PRACTICE AREAS: Antitrust; Intellectual Property Litigation. Email: dnorman@wsgr.com

**CRAIG D. NORRIS,** born Minneapolis, Minnesota, May 19, 1967; admitted to bar, 1994, California. Education: Stanford University (A.B., 1989); Boalt Hall School of Law, University of California (J.D., 1994). Member, California Law Review, 1992-1994. PRACTICE AREAS: Securities; Corporate. Email: cnorris@wsgr.com

**BURKE F. NORTON,** born Salt Lake City, Utah, December 30, 1966; admitted to bar, 1995, California. Education: Brigham Young University (B.A., 1990); Boalt Hall School of Law, University of California, Berkeley (J.D., 1995). Member, 1993-1994 and Executive Editor, 1994-1995, University of California Law Review, 1994-1995. PRACTICE AREAS: Corporate Law; Securities. Email: bfnorton@wsgr.com

**DAVID P. O'BRIEN,** born Boston, Massachusetts, October 23, 1966; admitted to bar, 1992, Massachusetts (Not admitted in California). Education: Harvard University (B.A., cum laude, 1988); Cornell University (J.D., cum laude, 1992). Notes Editor, Cornell Journal of Law and Public Policy, 1991-1992. Member: Massachusetts Bar Association. PRACTICE AREAS: Litigation. Email: dobrien@wsgr.com

**MICHAEL OCCHIOLINI,** born Norristown, Pennsylvania, October 7, 1960; admitted to bar, 1992, California. Education: University of Chicago (B.A., cum laude, 1978); Kennedy School, Harvard University (M.P.P., 1987); Stanford University (J.D., 1992). PRACTICE AREAS: Corporate Law. Email: mocchiolini@wsgr.com

**ROBERT G. O'CONNOR,** born Santa Monica, California, February 24, 1968; admitted to bar, 1993, California. Education: University of California at Los Angeles (B.A., 1990); Loyola Law School of Los Angeles (J.D., 1993). PRACTICE AREAS: Corporate; Securities. Email: boconnor@wsgr.com

**MICHAEL OKADA,** born Berkeley, California, October 30, 1964; admitted to bar, 1989, California. Education: Columbia University (A.B., 1986); University of Southern California (J.D., 1989). Member: State Bar of California. LANGUAGES: German and Japanese. Email: mokada@wsgr.com

**JAMES C. OTTESON,** born Idaho Falls, Idaho, May 6, 1964; admitted to bar, 1992, California. Education: Brigham Young University (B.S., microbiology, 1988); Yale University (J.D., 1991). Phi Kappa Phi; Golden Key. Editor, Yale Journal on Regulation. Author: "A Constitutional Analysis of Congressional Term Limits: Improving Representative Legislation Under the Constitution," 41 DePaul Review 1, 1991. Law Clerk, Honorable Byron J. Johnson, Idaho Supreme Court, 1991-1992. LANGUAGES: Swedish. PRACTICE AREAS: Intellectual Property Law; Litigation. Email: jotteson@wsgr.com

**WILLIAM B. OWENS, JR.,** born Colorado Springs, Colorado, April 27, 1970; admitted to bar, 1995, Louisiana; 1996, California. Education: Washington & Lee University (B.A., 1992); Southern Methodist University (J.D., 1995). Phi Delta Phi. Citations Editor, Southern Methodist University Law Review, 1995. Law Clerk, Hon. Donald E. Walter, U.S. District Court, Western District of Louisiana, 1995-1996. PRACTICE AREAS: Corporate; Securities. Email: wowens@wsgr.com

**CHRISTOPHER J. OZBURN,** born 1964; admitted to bar, 1992, Texas; 1993, U.S. District Court, Northern District of Texas; 1995, California and U.S. District Court, Northern District of California. Education: Yale University (B.A., 1986); New York University (J.D., 1992). Staff Editor, 1990-1991 and Note and Article Editor, 1991-1992, New York University Journal of International Law and Politics. Co-Author: Akerly and Ozburn, "The Impact of Confirmation and Post-Confirmation Remedies: A Practical Guide," 3 Journal of Bankruptcy Law and Practice 551 (Sept./Oct. 1994). PRACTICE AREAS: Corporate; Securities. Email: cozburn@wsgr.com

**AGNES PAK,** born Seoul, Korea, October 13, 1964; admitted to bar, 1989, Illinois; 1994, Washington (Not admitted in California). Education: University of California, Berkeley (B.A., 1985); University of California, Hastings College of the Law (J.D., 1989). Phi Beta Kappa. Member, Mortar Board. Extern, California State Supreme Court, 1988-1989. Member: Chicago, King County, Illinois State and Washington State Bar Associations; Korean American Bar Association of Washington. PRACTICE AREAS: Corporate. Email: apak@wsgr.com

**MICHAEL J. PANEPUCCI,** born Detroit, Michigan, March 10, 1965; admitted to bar, 1992, Illinois, California; 1995, U.S. District Court, Northern District of Illinois and U.S. Court of Appeals, Ninth Circuit; registered to practice before U.S. Patent and Trademark Office. Education: University of Michigan (B.S.E.E., with high distinction, 1988; J.D., 1992). Tau Beta Pi. Member: American Bar Association; Peninsula Intellectual Property Law Association; San Francisco Intellectual Property Law Association; American Intellectual Property Law Association; Institute of Electrical and Electronic Engineers. PRACTICE AREAS: Intellectual Property Law; Patent, Copyright and Trade Secret Counseling. Email: mpanepucci@wsgr.com

**A. RICHARD PARK,** born Corvallis, Oregon, June 8, 1961; admitted to bar, 1996, California and U.S. District Court, Northern District of California. Education: University of California (B.S., with honors, 1983; Ph.D., 1988); Princeton University (M.S., 1984); Boalt Hall School of Law, University of California (J.D., 1996). Member: Peninsula Intellectual Property Association. PRACTICE AREAS: Intellectual Property Law; Patent Law. Email: rpark@wsgr.com

**JOHN A. PEARCE,** born Grainger, Utah, June 6, 1969; admitted to bar, 1996, California. Education: University of Utah (B.S., magna cum laude, 1992); Boalt Hall School of Law, University of California (J.D., 1996). Phi Beta Kappa. Recipient: American Jurisprudence Award, Copyright; Moot Court Advocacy Award. Associate Editor, International Tax and Business Lawyer. LANGUAGES: Spanish. PRACTICE AREAS: Litigation. Email: jpearce@wsgr.com

**SARAH PREISLER,** born Buffalo, New York, November 12, 1966; admitted to bar, 1994, California. Education: Wesleyan University; University of California (A.B., 1988); Stanford University (J.D., 1993). Phi Beta Kappa. PRACTICE AREAS: Multimedia; Intellectual Property; Corporate. Email: spreisler@wsgr.com

*(This Listing Continued)*

**WILSON, SONSINI, GOODRICH & ROSATI,**
*PROFESSIONAL CORPORATION, Palo Alto—Continued*

**DAVID PRIEBE,** born Liverpool, New York, October 16, 1960; admitted to bar, 1990, California. *Education:* State University of New York (B.A., 1981); Yale University (M.A., 1983); University of California Boalt Hall School of Law (J.D., 1990). Phi Beta Kappa. Order of the Coif. **PRACTICE AREAS:** Litigation. *Email:* dpriebe@wsgr.com

**STACEY G. PROCHASKA,** born Palo Alto, California; admitted to bar, 1990, California. *Education:* University of California, Davis (B.A., cum laude, 1986); Boalt Hall School of Law, University of California (J.D., 1990). Member, Moot Court Board. Associate Editor, Ecology Law Quarterly. Author: "Intellectual Property Rights Under NAFTA," Michigan Computer Lawyer 10, Summer 1994. Court Counsel, Supreme Court of the Republic of Palau, 1992-1993. *Member:* State Bar of California. **PRACTICE AREAS:** Technology Licensing. *Email:* sprochaska@wsgr.com

**SORAYA N. RASHID,** born Toronto, Ontario, December 5, 1968; admitted to bar, 1993, California. *Education:* San Jose State University (B.S., with great distinction, 1989); Loyola Law School; University of California at Los Angeles (J.D., 1993). Phi Kappa Phi; Order of the Coif. Recipient, American Jurisprudence Awards in Criminal Procedure, Constitutional Law I and Civil Procedure. **PRACTICE AREAS:** Intellectual Property Transactions. *Email:* srashid@wsgr.com

**AMY E. REES,** born San Diego, California, December 7, 1972; admitted to bar, 1996, California. *Education:* Stanford University (B.A., with honors, 1993); Duke University (J.D., cum laude, 1996). Member, Duke Law Journal, 1994-1996. Author: "Recent Developments Regarding the Freedom of Information Act," Duke Law Journal, April 1996. **PRACTICE AREAS:** Corporate. *Email:* arees@wsgr.com

**JULIA REIGEL,** born Boulder, Colorado, March 8, 1965; admitted to bar, 1996, California. *Education:* Colorado State University (B.S., with honors and high distinction, 1986); University of Tennessee (M.A., 1987); Stanford University (J.D., with distinction, 1996). Phi Beta Kappa; Phi Kappa Phi. **PRACTICE AREAS:** Corporate; Securities. *Email:* jreigel@wsgr.com

**ROSEMARY G. REILLY,** born Brooklyn, New York, May 13, 1967; admitted to bar, 1995, New York (Not admitted in California). *Education:* Wesleyan University (B.A., 1989); Columbia University (J.D., 1994). **PRACTICE AREAS:** Corporate; Securities. *Email:* rreilly@wsgr.com

**MARK L. REINSTRA,** born Superior, Wisconsin, August 24, 1965; admitted to bar, 1992, Illinois and U.S. District Court, Northern District of Illinois; 1994, California. *Education:* University of Wisconsin (B.S.I.E., 1988); Stanford University (J.D., 1992). *Member:* American Bar Association. **PRACTICE AREAS:** Corporate. *Email:* mreinstra@wsgr.com

**SUSAN PASQUINELLI REINSTRA,** born Evergreen Park, Illinois, October 6, 1967; admitted to bar, 1992, Illinois and U.S. District Court, Northern District of Illinois; 1994, California. *Education:* University of Notre Dame (B.A., summa cum laude, 1989); Stanford University (J.D., with distinction, 1992). Phi Beta Kappa. *Member:* State Bar of California; American Bar Association. **PRACTICE AREAS:** Real Estate. *Email:* sreinstra@wsgr.com

**GENE RHOUGH,** born Anaheim, California, December 30, 1971; admitted to bar, 1996, California. *Education:* Massachusetts Institute of Technology (S.B.E.E., 1993); Harvard University (J.D., cum laude, 1996). Phi Beta Kappa; Sigma Xi; Eta Kappa Nu. Editor, Harvard Journal of Law and Technology, 1993-1995. **PRACTICE AREAS:** Intellectual Property. *Email:* grhough@wsgr.com

**KENT R. RICHARDSON,** born Regina, Canada, June 14, 1966; admitted to bar, 1993, California; registered to practice before U.S. Patent and Trademark Office. *Education:* University of Alberta (B.S., in Computer Engineering, 1989; LL.B., 1993). Phi Delta Phi. Recipient: Bereskin & Parr Prize in Intellectual Property; Dean's Research Award; NSERC Research Award. Author: "Reverse Engineering Integrated Circuits, "8 Canadian Computer Law Reporter 115, 1991. *Member:* Santa Clara County Bar Association (Member, High Technology Law Section); State Bar of California; Peninsula Intellectual Property Law Association; American Intellectual Property Law Association. *Email:* krichardson@wsgr.com

**ERIK F. RIEGLER,** born Washington, D.C., November 27, 1967; admitted to bar, 1995, California. *Education:* University of California (B.A., 1989); London School of Economics (M.S., 1991); Boalt Hall School of Law, University of California (J.D., 1995). Order of the Coif. Law Clerk, Hon. Alicemarie H. Stotler, U.S. District Court, Central District of California, 1995-1996. *LANGUAGES:* Spanish and German. **PRACTICE AREAS:** Corporate; Securities. *Email:* eriegler@wsgr.com

**MICHELE E. ROSE,** born Houma, Louisiana, June 6, 1965; admitted to bar, 1991, California. *Education:* University of California at Berkeley (A.B., 1987); Loyola University of Los Angeles (J.D., 1991). Law Clerk, Hon. Richard A. Paez, U.S. District Court, Central District of California, 1995-1996. **PRACTICE AREAS:** Securities Litigation; Commercial Litigation; Antitrust. *Email:* mrose@wsgr.com

**ERIC JON ROSENZWEIG,** born New York, November 19, 1965; admitted to bar, 1996, California. *Education:* Harvard University (B.A., 1989); University of California, Haas School of Business (M.B.A., 1995); University of California, Boalt Hall School of Law (J.D., 1995). Recipient: American Jurisprudence Awards in Contracts, Corporations II, Commercial Transactions; Thelan Marrin Prize; Moot Court Board Award for Excellence in Written Advocacy. Order of the Coif. **PRACTICE AREAS:** Corporate; Securities. *Email:* crosenzweig@wsgr.com

**DEBRA B. ROSLER,** born Livingston, New Jersey, October 20, 1967; admitted to bar, 1994, California. *Education:* Yale University (B.A., summa cum laude, with distinction, 1989); Stanford University (J.D., 1994). Executive Editor, Stanford Law Review, 1993-1994. Author: "The European Union's Proposed Directive for the Legal Protection of Databases: A New Threat to the Free Flow of Information," 10 Boalt Hall High Tech Law Journal 105, 1995. **PRACTICE AREAS:** Corporate; Securities. *Email:* drosler@wsgr.com

**JEREMY ROSSEN,** born Ann Arbor, Michigan, January 1, 1971; admitted to bar, 1996, California. *Education:* University of Pennsylvania (B.A., 1993; J.D., 1996). **PRACTICE AREAS:** Corporate. *Email:* jrossen@wsgr.com

**ROSEANN MARIE ROTANDARO,** born Scranton, Pennsylvania, March 12, 1955; admitted to bar, 1996, Alaska and U.S. District Court, District of Alaska (Not admitted in California). *Education:* East Stroudsburg University (B.A., 1977); University of Alaska (M.A., 1989); Stanford University (J.D., 1995). Editor, Stanford Law Review. Recipient, Hilmer Oehlmann, Jr. Award for Excellence in Research and Legal Writing. Peace Corps Volunteer, 1977-1979. *Member:* Alaska and American Bar Associations. **PRACTICE AREAS:** Securities; Commercial Litigation; Intellectual Property. *Email:* rrotandaro@wsgr.com

**ALISANDE M. ROZYNKO,** born Tacoma, Washington, March 29, 1959; admitted to bar, 1991, California. *Education:* University of California at Berkeley (B.A., magna cum laude, 1984); Hastings College of the Law, University of California (J.D., 1991). Phi Beta Kappa. *Email:* arozynko@wsgr.com

**RACHEL L. RUSKIN,** born Durham, North Carolina, February 27, 1967; admitted to bar, 1996, California. *Education:* Goucher College (B.A., 1989); Columbia University (J.D., 1995). Phi Beta Kappa; Harlan Fiske Stone Scholar. **PRACTICE AREAS:** Multimedia Law; Technology Licensing. *Email:* rruskin@wsgr.com

**CHRISTOPHER K. SADEGHIAN,** born Palo Alto, California, May 19, 1966; admitted to bar, 1991, California. *Education:* University of California at Berkeley (B.A., 1988); Santa Clara University (J.D., 1991). Senior Comments Editor, Santa Clara Law Review. *Member:* State Bar of California. **PRACTICE AREAS:** Corporate Law; Securities. *Email:* csadeghian@wsgr.com

**IGNACIO E. SALCEDA,** born San Diego, California, October 25, 1967; admitted to bar, 1993, California. *Education:* Harvard University (A.B., 1989); Stanford University (J.D., 1992). Executive Editor, Stanford Law Review, 1991-1992. *LANGUAGES:* Spanish. **PRACTICE AREAS:** Litigation. *Email:* isalceda@wsgr.com

**ROBERT D. SANCHEZ,** born Santa Clara, California, September 8, 1965; admitted to bar, 1992, New York; 1996, California. *Education:* University of California at Berkeley (A.B., 1988); Stanford University (J.D., 1991). **PRACTICE AREAS:** Corporate Law; Securities Law. *Email:* rsanchez@wsgr.com

**LESLIE S. SANTOS,** born New York, N.Y., June 30, 1961; admitted to bar, 1993, California; registered to practice before U.S. Patent and Trademark Office. *Education:* Yale University (B.A., 1983); Harvard University (M.S., 1987; J.D., cum laude, 1993). *Member:* U.S. Patent and Trademark Office Bar. **PRACTICE AREAS:** Corporate. *Email:* lsantos@wsgr.com

**VAHE H. SARRAFIAN,** born Tehran, Iran, January 30, 1967; admitted to bar, 1993, California. *Education:* University of California at Riverside (B.A., 1989); University of California at Davis (J.D., 1992). Delta Sigma Pi.

*(This Listing Continued)*

Recipient: Wall Street Journal Student Achievement Award; American Jurisprudence Award in Trial Practice. *Member:* State Bar of California; American Bar Association. *LANGUAGES:* Armenian. *PRACTICE AREAS:* Corporate; Securities; Business Litigation; Employment; Communications Law. *Email:* vsarrafian@wsgr.com

**DAVID J. SAUL,** born Greenbrae, California, February 23, 1965; admitted to bar, 1991, California, U.S. District Court, Northern District of California and U.S. Court of Appeals, Ninth Circuit. *Education:* University of California at Berkeley (B.A., with distinction and high honors, 1987); University of Chicago (J.D., 1991). *Member:* State Bar of California; American Bar Association. *LANGUAGES:* German. *Email:* dsaul@wsgr.com

**THOMAS I. SAVAGE,** born Huntington, West Virginia, January 15, 1969; admitted to bar, 1995, Illinois (Not admitted in California). *Education:* Harvard University (B.A., with honors, 1991); University of Chicago (J.D., with honors, 1995). Bradley Scholarship, 1994-1995. Officer, International Law Society, 1993-1994. Author: "The Bid Rigging Case of Saitama Prefecture," Law in Japan, Spring 1995. *LANGUAGES:* Japanese. *Email:* tsavage@wsgr.com

**RICHARD J. SCHACHTILI,** born Sacramento, California, February 15, 1968; admitted to bar, 1992, California. *Education:* University of California at Los Angeles (B.A., 1989); Hastings College of the Law, University of California (J.D., 1992). *PRACTICE AREAS:* Estate Planning. *Email:* rschachtili@wsgr.com

**VALERIE SCHULTHIES,** born Pocatello, Idaho; admitted to bar, 1994, California; 1995, Utah. *Education:* Brigham Young University (B.A., 1977); University of Southern California (A.M., 1988); Stanford University (J.D., 1994). *PRACTICE AREAS:* Corporate; Securities. *Email:* vschulthies@wsgr.com

**PETER M. SCHWAB,** born Chicago, Illinois, November 8, 1957; admitted to bar, 1983, California. *Education:* University of Illinois (B.S., 1980); University of San Francisco (J.D., 1983). Certified Public Accountant, Illinois, 1980. *Member:* Alameda County Bar Association; State Bar of California. *PRACTICE AREAS:* Real Estate. *Email:* pschwab@wsgr.com

**JOANNE RENÉE SCULLY,** born Loma Linda, California, November 22, 1949; admitted to bar, 1992, California. *Education:* University of California (B.A., 1988); Harvard University (J.D., 1992). Phi Beta Kappa. *PRACTICE AREAS:* Litigation. *Email:* jscully@wsgr.com

**KAIVAN M. SHAKIB,** born New York, N.Y., February 11, 1967; admitted to bar, 1992, New Jersey; 1993, New York; 1995, District of Columbia (Not admitted in California). *Education:* Columbia College (A.B., 1989); University of California at Los Angeles (J.D., 1992). Associate Editor, UCLA Law Review. Legal Research and Writing Teaching Assistant, University of California, 1990-1991. Intern, Securities and Exchange Commission, Enforcement Division, 1991. *Member:* American Bar Association. *PRACTICE AREAS:* General Corporate; Securities; International Law. *Email:* kshakib@wsgr.com

**BEHROOZ SHARIATI,** born Tehran, Iran, August 3, 1961; admitted to bar, 1994, California; registered to practice before U.S. Patent and Trademark Office. *Education:* North Carolina State University (B.S., Computer Science, 1983); Western State University (J.D., magna cum laude, 1994). Salutatorian. Editorial Staff Member, 1991-1992 and Managing Editor, 1992-1994, Consumer Law Journal. Co-Author: "Accumulation of Information in Private Databases: Consumers Beware," Consumer Law Journal, 1991. *Member:* American Bar Association (Member, Sections on: Intellectual Property and Technology Law Sections); State Bar of California (Member, Sections on: Litigation and Intellectual Property); Computer Law Association. *LANGUAGES:* Farsi. *PRACTICE AREAS:* Intellectual Property; Patent Prosecution and Litigation.

**STEPHANIE SHARRON,** born New Orleans, Louisiana, February 7, 1964; admitted to bar, 1992, California. *Education:* University of California at Los Angeles (B.S., 1987); Cornell University (J.D., 1992). Managing Editor, Cornell Law Review, 1991-1992. *PRACTICE AREAS:* Intellectual Property; Technology Licensing; Computer Law; Life Sciences. *Email:* ssharron@wsgr.com

**CRAIG A. SHELBURNE,** born Washington, D.C., November 22, 1968; admitted to bar, 1994, Texas; 1996, California. *Education:* Duke University (B.A., cum laude, 1991); University of California at Los Angeles (J.D., 1994). *PRACTICE AREAS:* Mergers and Acquisitions; Venture Capital; Corporate Securities. *Email:* cshelburne@wsgr.com

**LAURA LEWIS SHELBURNE,** born Shreveport, Louisiana, October 8, 1967; admitted to bar, 1994, Texas; 1996, California. *Education:* Stanford University (B.A., 1989); University of California, Los Angeles (J.D., 1994).

*(This Listing Continued)*

Chief Justice, UCLA Moot Court Honors Program. Distinguished Advocate, UCLA Moot Court Honors Program. Articles Editor, Entertainment Law Review. *PRACTICE AREAS:* Corporate; Securities; Financial Services; Real Estate. *Email:* lshelburne@wsgr.com

**SUNGBO SHIM,** born Seoul, South Korea, July 19, 1963; admitted to bar, 1994, California. *Education:* Wesleyan University (B.A., magna cum laude, 1986); Stanford University (J.D., 1994). Phi Beta Kappa. Member, Stanford Journal of International Law, 1991-1994. *Member:* State Bar of California. *LANGUAGES:* Korean, Chinese and Japanese. *PRACTICE AREAS:* Business Law; International Law; Corporate Law. *Email:* sshim@wsgr.com

**VICTOR SIM,** born Seoul, Korea, February 10, 1966; admitted to bar, 1995, Texas; 1996, California. *Education:* Georgetown University (B.S.F.S., 1984); Emory University (J.D., with distinction, 1995). Recipient, American Jurisprudence Awards. Author: "Sherman v. Citibank: The Decision to Retard, Impede and Burden National Banks," 5 Journal of International Banking Law 191, 1996. *PRACTICE AREAS:* Corporate. *Email:* vsim@wsgr.com

**S. DAWN SMITH,** born Huntsville, Alabama, December 28, 1963; admitted to bar, 1996, California. *Education:* United States Naval Academy (B.S., 1986); Providence College (M.B.A., 1993); Stanford University (J.D., 1996). [With U.S. Navy, O-3, 1986-1993]. *PRACTICE AREAS:* Corporate; Securities. *Email:* sdsmith@wsgr.com

**ELLEN SOLOMON-GONZALES,** born Queens, New York, April 11, 1968; admitted to bar, 1993, Massachusetts and U.S. District Court, District of Massachusetts; 1996, U.S. Court of Appeals, First Circuit (Not admitted in California). *Education:* University of Pennsylvania (B.A., magna cum laude, 1990); Harvard University (J.D., cum laude, 1993). Phi Beta Kappa. Recipient: Kara Laczynski Scholarship; Ralph G. Treen Memorial Scholarship; Leroy E. Dettman Scholarship. *Member:* Boston, Massachusetts and American Bar Associations. *LANGUAGES:* Spanish. *PRACTICE AREAS:* Litigation. *Email:* egonzaleswsgr.com

**NOGA DEVECSERI SPIRA,** born Vancouver, British Columbia, November 23, 1969; admitted to bar, 1994, Israel; 1996, California. *Education:* Hebrew University of Jerusalem Law School (LL.B., 1993). *LANGUAGES:* Hebrew. *PRACTICE AREAS:* Corporate; Securities. *Email:* nspira@wsgr.com

**SUSAN L. STAPLETON,** born Chicago, Illinois, September 28, 1965; admitted to bar, 1994, California. *Education:* University of Illinois (B.S., 1987; M.S., 1988); Hastings College of the Law, University of California (J.D., 1994). Thurston Society. Member, Hastings International and Comparative Law Review. *PRACTICE AREAS:* Corporate; Securities. *Email:* sstapleton@wsgr.com

**RICHARD G. STEELE,** born Libertyville, Illinois, March 18, 1969; admitted to bar, 1996, California and U.S. Court of Appeals, Tenth Circuit. *Education:* University of California at San Diego (B.A., cum laude, 1991); Hastings College of the Law, University of California (J.D., summa cum laude, 1995). Order of the Coif. Member, Thurston Society. Recipient: Roger J. Traynor Student Writing Award; American Jurisprudence Awards in Trial Advocacy, Torts, Moot Court, Property, Legal Writing and Research. Member, Hastings Law Journal, 1993-1995. Author: Note, "Rethinking the After-Acquired Evidence Defense in Title VII Disparate Treatment Cases," 46 Hastings Law Journal 217, 1995. Law Clerk to the Honorable David M. Ebel, U.S. Court of Appeals, Tenth Circuit, 1995-1996. *PRACTICE AREAS:* Corporate; Securities. *Email:* rsteele@wsgr.com

**VADIM D. STEPANCHENKO,** born Moscow, Russia, October 21, 1961; admitted to bar, 1993, California. *Education:* Moscow Foreign Language University (B.A., 1984); Yale University (M.A., 1988); Columbia University (J.D., 1993). Co-Author: "1994-1995 Legislative, Regulatory, and Case Law Developments: Two Years in Review," Employee Stock Ownership Plans 1996 Yearbook, Warren, Gorham & Lamont. *Member:* State Bar of California. *LANGUAGES:* Russian, Italian and Spanish. *PRACTICE AREAS:* Corporate; Securities. *Email:* vstepanchenko@wsgr.com

**THOMAS N. STEPHENS,** born Pasadena, California, August 7, 1952; admitted to bar, 1995, California. *Education:* California State University, Los Angeles (B.A., 1992); Boalt Hall School of Law, University of California (J.D., 1995). *PRACTICE AREAS:* Corporate; Securities. *Email:* tstephens@wsgr.com

**TIMOTHY J. STEVENS,** born Sacramento, California, October 19, 1966; admitted to bar, 1991, California. *Education:* University of Oregon

*(This Listing Continued)*

## WILSON, SONSINI, GOODRICH & ROSATI,
*PROFESSIONAL CORPORATION, Palo Alto—Continued*

(B.S., summa cum laude, 1988); University of California at Davis (J.D., 1991). Order of the Coif; Beta Gamma Sigma. Most Outstanding Senior in Finance and Accounting. Member, Golden Key National Honor Society. *Member:* State Bar of California. **PRACTICE AREAS:** Corporate Law; Securities. *Email:* tstevens@wsgr.com

**RODNEY G. STRICKLAND, JR.,** born Charleston, West Virginia, July 3, 1967; admitted to bar, 1992, California. *Education:* University of Notre Dame (B.A., 1989); Santa Clara University (J.D., summa cum laude, 1992). **PRACTICE AREAS:** Litigation. *Email:* rstrickland@wsgr.com

**BETSEY SUE,** born New Hartford, New York, July 25, 1967; admitted to bar, 1992, Massachusetts; 1996, California. *Education:* Boston College (B.A., magna cum laude, 1988); New York University School of Law (J.D., 1991). **PRACTICE AREAS:** Corporate. *Email:* bsue@wsgr.com

**J. ROBERT SUFFOLETTA, JR.,** born Valparaiso, Indiana, January 15, 1961; admitted to bar, 1990, California. *Education:* Indiana University (B.S., with honors, 1982; M.B.A., 1983); University of Notre Dame (J.D., 1990). Author: Note, "Who Should Pay When Federally Insured Pension Funds Go Broke? A Strategy For Recovering From The Wrongdoers," 65 Notre Dame L. Rev. 308, 1990; Comment, "The Reasonable Approach to Excessive Force Cases Under Section 1983," 64 Notre Dame L. Rev. 136, 1989. **PRACTICE AREAS:** Corporate Law; Securities. *Email:* rsuffoletta@wsgr.com

**MATTHEW B. SWARTZ,** born Ithaca, New York, January 31, 1968; admitted to bar, 1996, California. *Education:* University of California, Berkeley (B.A., 1990); University of California, Hastings College of the Law (J.D., 1995). Articles Editor, International and Comparative Law Review. **PRACTICE AREAS:** Securities; Corporate; Technology Licensing; Multimedia Licensing. *Email:* mswartz@wsgr.com

**AHMED E. TAHA,** born Columbia, Missouri, July 22, 1967; admitted to bar, 1996, California. *Education:* University of Pennsylvania (B.A., 1988); The Wharton School, University of Pennsylvania (B.S., 1988); Stanford University (J.D., 1996; Ph.D., 1996). Beta Gamma Sigma. **PRACTICE AREAS:** Litigation. *Email:* ataha@wsgr.com

**YOICHIRO TAKU,** born Osaka, Japan, February 27, 1968; admitted to bar, 1994, California. *Education:* University of Minnesota (B.A., summa cum laude, 1990); University of Chicago (J.D., 1993). Phi Beta Kappa. **LANGUAGES:** Japanese. **PRACTICE AREAS:** Corporate. *Email:* ytaku@wsgr.com

**TOMER TAL,** born Minneapolis, Minnesota; admitted to bar, 1996, California. *Education:* San Diego State University (B.S., 1991); Santa Clara University (J.D., 1995; M.B.A., 1995). **PRACTICE AREAS:** Corporate Law; Securities Law. *Email:* ttal@wsgr.com

**ROBERT M. TARKOFF,** born Oakland, California, December 31, 1968; admitted to bar, 1995, California. *Education:* Amherst College (B.A., magna cum laude, 1991); Harvard University (J.D., cum laude, 1995). **PRACTICE AREAS:** Corporate Law; Securities Law. *Email:* rtarkoff@wsgr.com

**ROMY S. TAUBMAN,** born Guam, July 30, 1963; admitted to bar, 1993, California and U.S. District Court, Central and Northern Districts of California. *Education:* Stanford University (B.A., with distinction, 1989); University of California at Los Angeles (J.D., 1993). Order of the Coif. **PRACTICE AREAS:** Corporate; Securities. *Email:* rtaubman@wsgr.com

**BRUCE A. TELKAMP,** born Los Angeles, California, July 8, 1967; admitted to bar, 1994, California. *Education:* University of California, Los Angeles (B.A., cum laude, 1990); Hastings College of the Law, University of California (J.D., cum laude, 1994). Member, Hastings Moot Court Board, 1993-1994. Executive Editor, Hastings International and Comparative Law Review, 1993-1994. **PRACTICE AREAS:** Litigation. *Email:* btelkamp@wsgr.com

**SUSAN STUERMER THOMAS,** born Miami, Florida, 1942; admitted to bar, 1979, California. *Education:* Newcomb College, Tulane University (B.A., with honors, 1965); Hastings College of Law, University of California (J.D., 1979). Member, Thurston Honor Society. Associate Managing Editor, Hastings Law Journal, 1978-1979. Managing Editor, California Real Property Journal, 1990-1992. *Member:* Bar Association of San Francisco; State Bar of California (Member, Real Property Law Section); American Bar Association (Member, Real Property, Probate and Law Section). **PRACTICE AREAS:** Real Estate Law. *Email:* sthomas@wsgr.com

*(This Listing Continued)*

CAA1624B

**RICHARD H. THOMPSON,** born Hartford, Connecticut, January 20, 1952; admitted to bar, 1995, New York (Not admitted in California). *Education:* Stanford University (A.B., 1975); University of Virginia (Ph.D., 1990); Boalt Hall School of Law, University of California (J.D., 1994). **PRACTICE AREAS:** Corporate; Securities. *Email:* rthompson@wsgr.com

**SUSAN TIEN,** born West Chester, Pennsylvania, June 30, 1971; admitted to bar, 1996, California. *Education:* Radcliffe College (A.B., 1993); University of Pennsylvania (J.D., 1996). Phi Beta Kappa. **PRACTICE AREAS:** Litigation. *Email:* stien@wsgr.com

**PAUL R. TOBIAS,** born Austin, Texas, October 30, 1964; admitted to bar, 1991, Texas (Not admitted in California). *Education:* University of Texas (B.A., with special honors, 1987; J.D., 1990). *Member:* Travis County Bar Association (Member, Business and Tax Section); State Bar of Texas (Member, Business Law Section). **PRACTICE AREAS:** Corporate Law; Securities Law. *Email:* ptobias@wsgr.com

**TRACY L. TOSH,** born Beaver, Pennsylvania, March 16, 1971; admitted to bar, 1996, California. *Education:* Vanderbilt University (B.A., 1993); University of Michigan (J.D., 1996). **PRACTICE AREAS:** Litigation; Securities Litigation; Intellectual Property Litigation. *Email:* ttosh@wsgr.com

**JENNIFER TSAY,** born St. Louis, Missouri, May 25, 1966; admitted to bar, 1992, California. *Education:* Stanford University (B.A., 1987); Harvard University (J.D., 1992). **PRACTICE AREAS:** General Corporate. *Email:* jtsay@wsgr.com

**DANIEL W. TURBOW,** born Anaheim, California, June 27, 1969; admitted to bar, 1994, California. *Education:* Stanford University (A.B., 1991); Georgetown University Law Center (J.D., cum laude, 1994). *Member:* State Bar of California. **PRACTICE AREAS:** Litigation. *Email:* dturbow@wsgr.com

**DIANE E. TURRIFF,** born Mountain View, California, November 15, 1963; admitted to bar, 1990, California. *Education:* California Polytechnic State University (B.S., 1985); Hastings College of the Law, University of California (J.D., magna cum laude, 1990). Order of the Coif. Member, Thurston Society. Article and Note Editor, Hastings Law Journal, 1989-1990. Instructor, University of California, Hastings College of the Law, August 1995. *Member:* State Bar of California; American Bar Association (Member, Litigation Section). **PRACTICE AREAS:** Trademarks; Advertising Practices; Litigation. *Email:* dturriff@wsgr.com

**DAVID M. URSO,** born Philadelphia, Pennsylvania, May 26, 1964; admitted to bar, 1996, California. *Education:* Reed College (B.A., 1989); Harvard University (J.D., 1995). Author: "Molecular Evidence for the Expression on Nicotinic Acetycholine Receptor a Chain in Mouse Thymus," 148 J. Immunology 3105, 1992; "Molecular Analysis of the Intra-Thymic Maintenance of Acetylcholine Receptor," 681 Annals of the N.Y. Academy of Science, 73-84, 1993. **PRACTICE AREAS:** Corporate Law; Intellectual Property. *Email:* durso@wsgr.com

**JAN-MARC VAN DER SCHEE,** born Rotterdam, The Netherlands, March 12, 1968; admitted to bar, 1995, New York; 1996, California. *Education:* Erasmus University School of Law, The Netherlands (J.D., 1991); New York University School of Law (M.C.J., 1994). **LANGUAGES:** Dutch, German, Italian and French. *Email:* jvanderschee@wsgr.com

**ALICIA J. VASQUEZ,** born Fontana, California, June 5, 1962; admitted to bar, 1988, California; 1990, U.S. District Court, Northern District of California. *Education:* University of California at San Diego (B.A., 1984); Hastings College of Law, University of California (J.D., 1988). Phi Delta Phi. Member, Thurston Honor Society. Member, Hastings International and Comparative Law Review, 1986-1987. Recipient, American Jurisprudence Award in Real Property. *Member:* Santa Clara County Bar Association; State Bar of California. **PRACTICE AREAS:** Employment Law; Litigation. *Email:* avasquez@wsgr.com

**DANIEL F. VAUGHN,** born San Francisco, California, March 31, 1968; admitted to bar, 1995, Texas (Not admitted in California). *Education:* Washington State University (B.A., 1991); University of Virginia (J.D., 1995). Phi Kappa Phi; Phi Alpha Theta. **PRACTICE AREAS:** Corporate; Securities.

**ISSAC J. VAUGHN,** born San Francisco, California, December 12, 1962; admitted to bar, 1991, California. *Education:* Santa Clara University (B.S., 1984); Hastings College of the Law (1988-1989); University of Michigan Law School (J.D., 1991). Member, Board of Regents, Santa Clara University, 1992—. **PRACTICE AREAS:** Corporate. *Email:* ivaughn@wsgr.com

*(This Listing Continued)*

**JASON B. WACHA,** born Los Angeles, California, January 19, 1963; admitted to bar, 1992, California. *Education:* Stanford University (A.B., 1986); University of California School of Law, Davis (J.D., 1992). Editor, University of California Law Review. *PRACTICE AREAS:* Corporate; Securities. *Email:* jwacha@wsgr.com

**DON M. WADE,** born Brooklyn, New York, June 26, 1968; admitted to bar, 1994, New York and U.S. District Court, Western District of New York; 1996, California. *Education:* Cornell University (B.A., 1990); University of California, Los Angeles School of Law (J.D., 1993). Member, Moot Court. *Member:* New York State, National and American Bar Associations; Rochester Black Bar Association (Vice President, 1994-1996); Charles Houston Bar Association. *PRACTICE AREAS:* Intellectual Property; Technology Transactions; Corporate. *Email:* dwade@wsgr.com

**VICTORIA M. WALTER,** born Auburn, New York, January 31, 1965; admitted to bar, 1996, New York and U.S. District Court, Southern and Eastern Districts of New York (Not admitted in California). *Education:* Columbia University (B.A., magna cum laude, 1990); Cornell University (J.D., 1994). Phi Beta Kappa. *PRACTICE AREAS:* Litigation. *Email:* vwalter@wsgr.com

**DAVID C. WANG,** born Champaign, Illinois, December 17, 1970; admitted to bar, 1996, California. *Education:* University of California (B.S., Electrical Engineering and Computer Science, 1993); Cornell University (J.D., cum laude, 1996). *PRACTICE AREAS:* Intellectual Property Litigation. *Email:* dwang@wsgr.com

**SHIRLEY C. WANG,** born Taipei, Taiwan, May 5, 1971; (admission pending). *Education:* University of Washington (B.A., magna cum laude, 1992); New York University (J.D., 1996). Phi Beta Kappa.

**DAVID J. WEITZ,** born Queens, New York, April 16, 1965; admitted to bar, 1992, California; registered to practice before the U.S. Patent and Trademark Office. *Education:* Massachusetts Institute of Technology (B.S. in Chemistry, 1987); University of California, Berkeley (M.S. in Bio-Organic Chemistry, 1989; J.D., 1992). Articles Editor, High Technology Law Journal, 1991-1992. Author: "The Biological Deposit Requirement: A Means of Assuring Adequate Disclosure," High Technology Law Journal (Boalt Hall), 8:2 (1993). Co-Author: "Synthesis of Sugar Aldehydes by Ozonolysis of Oximes," J. Org. Chem., 1989, 54, 4957; "A Combined Microbial/Chemical Synthesis of (+)-(R)-Methyloxirane Having High Enantiomeric Excess," J. Orig. Chem., 1987, 52, 4042. *Member:* State Bar of California; American Bar Association; M.I.T. Club of Northern California (Vice President, Entrepreneurship); American Chemical Society; American Intellectual Property Law Association; San Francisco Patent and Trademark Law Association. *Email:* dweitz@wsgr.com

**MARTIN WELLINGTON,** born Cleveland, Ohio, December 2, 1963; admitted to bar, 1996, California. *Education:* University of California (B.A., 1986); Columbia University (M.A., 1988); Harvard University (J.D., 1996). *PRACTICE AREAS:* Corporate Law; Securities Law. *Email:* mwellington@wsgr.com

**SHANNON D. WHISENANT,** born Provo, Utah, September 1, 1967; admitted to bar, 1993, Massachusetts; 1996, California. *Education:* University of Utah (B.A., 1988); Brigham Young University (J.D., cum laude, 1992). *PRACTICE AREAS:* Corporate; Securities; Venture Capital. *Email:* swhisenant@wsgr.com

**JOHN L. G. WHITTLE,** born Richmond, Virginia, April 4, 1968; (admission pending). *Education:* University of Virginia (B.A., 1990); Cornell University (J.D., magna cum laude, 1995). Order of the Coif. Customs Aide, U.S. Customs Service, 1990. Law Clerk, Chief Judge Jackson L. Kiser, U.S. District Court, Western District of Virginia. *PRACTICE AREAS:* Corporate; Securities. *Email:* jwhittle@wsgr.com

**DON S. WILLIAMS,** born El Centro, California, December 19, 1966; admitted to bar, 1993, California. *Education:* Stanford University (A.B., 1989); Harvard University (J.D., 1993). Phi Beta Kappa. Recipient: Firestone Medal for Excellence in Research. *LANGUAGES:* Spanish. *PRACTICE AREAS:* Corporate. *Email:* dwilliams@wsgr.com

**GEORGE A. WILLMAN,** born Baltimore, Maryland, August 3, 1966; admitted to bar, 1996, California. *Education:* Stanford University (B.S., 1989); University of California at Berkeley (M.B.A., 1993); Georgetown University Law Center (J.D., cum laude, 1996). Beta Gamma Sigma. Senior Editor, Law and Policy in International Business, 1995-1996. Intern to: Judge Wilkes C. Robinson, U.S. Court of Federal Claims, 1995; Judge Wilson Cowen, U.S. Court of Appeals for the Federal Circuit, 1996. *LANGUAGES:* German. *PRACTICE AREAS:* Intellectual Property; Patents; Technology Licensing. *Email:* gwillman@wsgr.com

**RICHARD L. WOODWORTH,** born Detroit, Michigan, November 14, 1967; admitted to bar, 1994, California. *Education:* Stanford University (B.A., 1989); Georgetown University Law Center (J.D., cum laude, 1994). Recipient, Olin Prize in Law and Economics, Stanford Law School. Associate Editor, American Criminal Law Review. *PRACTICE AREAS:* Antitrust; Litigation; Intellectual Property. *Email:* rwoodworth@wsgr.com

**ERIC W. WRIGHT,** born Moses Lake, Washington, May 16, 1963; admitted to bar, 1990, New York; 1994, California. *Education:* Stanford University (A.B., 1985); New York University (J.D., 1988). Staff Member, 1986-1987 and Managing Editor, 1987-1988, Journal of International Law and Politics. *PRACTICE AREAS:* Corporate; Securities. *Email:* ewright@wsgr.com

**JAMES C. YOON,** born Boston, Massachusetts, August 6, 1967; admitted to bar, 1995, California. *Education:* GMI Engineering & Management Institute (E.E., 1990); Stanford University (J.D., 1993). Tau Beta Pi; Eta Kappa Nu. Sohey Scholar. Associate Editor, 1991-1992 and Article Editor, 1992-1993, Stanford Law Review. Member, Stanford Journal of International Law, 1990-1992. Law Clerk, Hon. Alan C. Kay, Chief Judge, U.S. District Court, District of Hawaii. *Email:* jyoon@wsgr.com

**CHRISTOPHER J. YOUNGER,** born Quincy, Illinois, November 28, 1966; admitted to bar, 1994, California. *Education:* Miami University (B.Phil., summa cum laude, 1989); Harvard University (J.D., cum laude, 1993). Editor, Volume 105 and Managing Editor, Volume 106, Harvard Law Review. Clerk, Honorable Jesse E. Eschbach, Senior Judge, U.S. Court of Appeals, Seventh Circuit, 1993-1994. *PRACTICE AREAS:* Corporate. *Email:* cyounger@wsgr.com

**STACEY A. ZARTLER,** born Lake Jackson, Texas, October 4, 1966; admitted to bar, 1992, California and U.S. District Court, Northern District of California; 1993, U.S. Court of Appeals, Ninth Circuit; 1995, U.S. Court of Appeals for the District of Columbia Circuit. *Education:* Stanford University (B.A., 1989); University of Santa Clara (J.D., 1992). *PRACTICE AREAS:* Labor and Employment Law. *Email:* szartler@wsgr.com

**LIOR ZOREA,** born Haifa, Israel, November 13, 1970; admitted to bar, 1996, New York (Not admitted in California). *Education:* Yale University (B.A., cum laude, 1990); Michigan University (J.D., 1995). Phi Delta Phi. *Member:* Association of the Bar of the City of New York; New York State Bar Association. *PRACTICE AREAS:* Mergers and Acquisitions; Securities; General Corporate. *Email:* lzorea@wsgr.com

REPRESENTATIVE CLIENTS: Alex. Brown & Sons; Apple Computer; Atmel Corp.; Autodesk Inc.; Baan Company N.V.; Boomtown Inc.; Borland International; Broderbund Software; CBT Group PLC; Cell Genesys; Cirrus Logic Inc.; Convex Computer Corp.; Cypress Semiconductor; Dell Computer; Electronic Power Research Institute; Electronics for Imaging; Fremont General Corp.; Gartner Group; Global Village Communications; Goldman, Sachs & Co.; Gymboree Corp.; Hasbro Inc.; Hewlett-Packard; Kleiner Perkins Caufield & Byers; Lam Research Corp.; LSI Logic Corp.; Mayfield Fund; Merisel, Inc.; Microage; Micron Technology; Montgomery Securities; Morgan Stanley & Co.; Netscape Communications Corp.; Novell Inc.; Octel Communications; Packard Bell; PeopleSoft Inc; Pete's Brewing Co.; Pixar Animation Studios; Robertson, Stephens & Co.; Seagate Technology; Sequoia Capital; Sequoia Therapeutics; Silicon Graphics; Silicon Valley Group; Solectron Corp.; Stormedia, Inc.; Sun Microsystems; Sybase Inc.; Synopsys Inc.; The 3DO Company; The Santa Cruz Operation; Ventritex Inc.; Vivus Inc.; Xilinx, Inc.

## WISE & SHEPARD, LLP
*3030 HANSEN WAY, SUITE 100*
**PALO ALTO, CALIFORNIA 94304**
*Telephone: 415-856-1200*
*Telecopier: 415-856-1344*

*Business and Litigation Law, representing Corporations and Individuals in Domestic and International Matters; including practice in Corporate Transactions, Financing/Securities, Taxation, Court Trials, Arbitration/Mediation, Environment, Employment/Labor, Employee Benefits, Real Estate, Technology Agreements/Intellectual Property, Mergers and Acquisitions/Strategic Alliances, Estate Planning and Domestic and European Community Competition Issues.*

### PARTNERS

**LISA B. ARMANDO,** born San Jose, California, October 30, 1959; admitted to bar, 1984, California. *Education:* University of California at Davis (B.S., with honors, 1981); Santa Clara University School of Law (J.D., 1984). *Member:* Palo Alto, Santa Clara County and American Bar Associations; State Bar of California. *Email:* ArmandoL@hws.com

**THOMAS L. BARTON,** born Burlington, Vermont, May 25, 1942; admitted to bar, 1973, California. *Education:* Yale University (B.A., 1964);

*(This Listing Continued)*

**WISE & SHEPARD, LLP, Palo Alto—Continued**

Stanford Business School (M.B.A., 1971); Northwestern University (J.D., 1967). *Member:* Palo Alto, Santa Clara County and American Bar Associations; The State Bar of California. *PRACTICE AREAS:* Bio-Pharmaceutical Companies; Business Financing and Transactions. *Email:* BartonT@hws.com

**M. SCOTT DONAHEY,** born Boca Raton, Florida, August 14, 1945; admitted to bar, 1978, California; 1989, Arizona; 1990, Illinois. *Education:* Stanford University (B.A., with distinction, 1967); Johns Hopkins University (M.A., 1968); University of Santa Clara (J.D., summa cum laude, 1978). *Member:* State Bar of California (Chairperson, Section on Antitrust and Trade Regulation, 1986-1987); American (Vice Chair: International Law Section, International Arbitration Committee) and International Bar Associations; Union Internationale des Advocats (Member: International Arbitration Committee); Licensing Executives Society International (Vice Chair, Alternative Dispute Resolution Committee). *PRACTICE AREAS:* Commercial Arbitration and Mediation (International and Domestic); Intellectual Property; Patent Litigation; General Commercial Litigation. *Email:* DonaheyS@hws.com

**DAVID R. FOLEY,** born New York City, June 22, 1946; admitted to bar, 1974, New York; 1976, District of Columbia; 1995, California. *Education:* Harvard University (A.B., magna cum laude, 1968); Columbia University (J.D., 1973). Member, Commercial Section of the Law Committee, American Arbitration Association, 1983. Co-Author: "Using Arbitration in Business Disputes," Matthew Bender, 1984. *Member:* The Association of the Bar of the City of New York; American Bar Association. *Email:* FoleyD@hws.com

**AMY L. GILSON,** born Washington, D.C., June 24, 1960; admitted to bar, 1985, California; U.S. District Court, Northern District of California. *Education:* University of California at Berkeley (A.B., 1982); University of Santa Clara (J.D., 1985). Founder and Research Editor, Santa Clara Computer and High Technology Law Journal, 1984-1985. *Member:* State Bar of California; American Bar Association. *Email:* GilsonA@hws.com

**DAVID W. HERBST,** born Pomona, California, June 17, 1952; admitted to bar, 1977, California; 1979, U.S. Tax Court. *Education:* Pomona College (B.A., magna cum laude, 1974); Stanford University (J.D., 1977). Phi Beta Kappa. *Member:* Palo Alto, Santa Clara County and American Bar Associations; The State Bar of California. *PRACTICE AREAS:* Income Taxation; Employee Benefits; Executive Compensation. *Email:* HerbstD@hws.com

**JERROLD F. PETRUZZELLI,** born San Francisco, California, November 5, 1952; admitted to bar, 1977, California; 1990, Washington. *Education:* Yale University (A.B., summa cum laude, 1974); University of Chicago (J.D., 1977). Phi Beta Kappa. *Member:* State Bar of California; State Bar of Washington; American Bar Association. *LANGUAGES:* French and Italian.

**EDWARD L. QUEVEDO,** born Glendale, California, January 13, 1957; admitted to bar, 1990, California. *Education:* University of California (B.A., cum laude, 1979); University of California Boalt Hall School of Law (J.D. 1984). *Member:* State Bar of California (Member, Sections on: Environmental Law and Litigation); American Bar Association (Member, Sections on: Environmental Law and Science and Technology); American Society of Civil Engineers.

**JAMES M. SMITH,** born Walnut Creek, California, March 16, 1963; admitted to bar, 1988, California and U.S. District Court, Northern District of California; 1990, U.S. District Court, Southern District of California; 1991, U.S. District Court, Central District of California; U.S. District Court, Northern District of Illinois, U.S. Court of Appeals, Ninth and Federal Circuits. *Education:* University of California at Berkeley (B.A., high distinction, 1985); Boalt Hall School of Law, University of California at Berkeley (J.D., 1988). Phi Beta Kappa. *Member:* Santa Clara County, San Francisco County and American (Member, Intellectual Property Law and Litigation Sections) Bar Associations; State Bar of California (Member, Intellectual Property Law Section). *PRACTICE AREAS:* Intellectual Property Litigation; General Commercial Litigation; Unfair Advertising Counselling.

**PRISCILLA WHEELER,** born Dallas, Texas, July 11, 1945; admitted to bar, 1975, California. *Education:* North Texas University (B.A., 1967); Harvard University; Hastings College of the Law, University of California (J.D., 1975). Member, Moot Court Board, National Moot Court Team, 1974-1975. *Member:* State Bar of California; American Bar Association (Former Member and Contributing Editor, The Developing Labor Law, Committee on Development of the Law under the National Labor Relations Act; Section of Labor and Employment Law).

*ASSOCIATES*

**SANJIV S. DHAWAN,** born New Delhi, India, September 9, 1963; admitted to bar, 1990, California; 1991, U.S. Court of Appeals, Ninth Circuit. *Education:* University of California at Berkeley (B.S., 1986); University of California, Davis, School of Law (J.D., 1990). *Member:* State Bar of California; American Bar Association. *PRACTICE AREAS:* Securities Law; Corporate Law. *Email:* DhawanS@hws.com

**TIMOTHY R. FULKERSON,** born San Francisco, California, March 8, 1963; admitted to bar, 1994, California. *Education:* University of California, Los Angeles (B.A., 1986); University of the Pacific (J.D., 1994). Assistant Comment Editor, Comment Staff Writer, Legislative Staff Writer, Pacific Law Journal. *Member:* State Bar of California. *Email:* FulkersT@hws.com

**JOSEPH D. HERNANDEZ,** admitted to bar, 1992, California and U.S. District Court, Northern District of California. *Education:* Santa Clara University (B.A., 1989; J.D., 1992). Research Editor, Santa Clara Computer and High Technology Law Journal, 1991-1992. *Member:* State Bar of California; American Bar Association (Member, Entertainment and Sports Forum Committee, Intellectual Property Law Section); National Hispanic Bar Association; Sports Lawyers Association. *PRACTICE AREAS:* Corporate Transactions; Intellectual Property; Sports Representation. *Email:* HernandJ@hws.com

**MICHELLE E. LENTZNER,** born Chicago, Illinois, May 26, 1966; admitted to bar, 1991, California. *Education:* University of California, Berkeley (B.A., with distinction, 1988); Hastings College of the Law, University of California (J.D., 1991). Recipient, 1066 Foundation Scholar Journalist Prize, 1991. Executive Articles Editor, Hastings Communications and Entertainment Law Journal, COMM/ENT, 1990-1991. *Member:* Santa Clara County and American Bar Associations; State Bar of California. *Email:* LentzneM@hws.com

**DANIEL H. KERN,** born Los Angeles, California, May 6, 1958; admitted to bar, 1987, California and U.S. District Court, Central District of California; registered to practice before U.S. Patent and Trademark Office. *Education:* Stanford University (B.S.M.E., 1981); Loyola University of Los Angeles (J.D., 1986). Recipient, American Jurisprudence Award in Property. *Member:* Palo Alto and Santa Clara County Bar Associations; State Bar of California (Member, Intellectual Property Section). *Email:* KernDan@hws.com

**MICHAEL G. MCCLORY,** born Torrance, California, December 24, 1963; admitted to bar, 1989, Indiana; 1990, U.S. District Court, Northern District of Indiana; 1991, U.S. District Court, Northern and Central Districts of California; 1993, Illinois. *Education:* University of Notre Dame (B.A., 1986; J.D., 1989); University of Southern California Law Center. *Member:* American Bar Association (Section of Labor and Employment Law, Equal Employment Opportunity Committee); State Bar of California. *PRACTICE AREAS:* Labor and Employment Law; Business Litigation.

**DEBORAH L. LIVORNESE,** born New York, N.Y., March 23, 1959; admitted to bar, 1984, California. *Education:* University of Pennsylvania (B.A., 1981); Hastings College of the Law, University of California (J.D., cum laude, 1984). Order of the Coif. Hastings Law Journal. *Member:* State Bar of California. *PRACTICE AREAS:* Environmental. *Email:* LivorneD@hws.com

**TINA M. SINGH,** born New Delhi, India, June 8, 1963; admitted to bar, 1988, California; 1990, District of Columbia. *Education:* McGill University (B.A., 1985); University of California at Berkeley, Boalt Hall School of Law; University of California, Davis, (J.D., 1988). Associate Editor, International Tax and Business Lawyer, 1986-1988. Editor, Davis Law Review, 1988. Court Law Clerk, U.S. Court of Appeals, Ninth Circuit, 1988-1989. *Member:* State Bar of California; The District of Columbia Bar; American Bar Association. *Email:* SinghT@hws.com

**ALISON E. SPONG,** born St. Louis, Missouri, June 4, 1965; admitted to bar, 1989, California. *Education:* University of Illinois (B.S., with highest honors, Accountancy, 1986); Harvard University (J.D., 1989). Beta Alpha Psi; Bronze Tablet. Editor-in-Chief, Harvard Environmental Law Review, 1988-1989. *Member:* Bar Association of San Francisco; State Bar of California (Environmental Law Section); Barristers Club of San Francisco (Chair, Environmental and Real Estate Committee, 1993). *PRACTICE AREAS:* Environmental Law.

**JOI C. TRUE,** born Chicago, Illinois, September 12, 1969; admitted to bar, 1993, California and U.S. District Court, Central District of California.

*(This Listing Continued)*

*Education:* University of California at Berkeley (B.A., cum laude, Economics and Rhetoric, 1990); Boalt Hall School of Law, University of California at Berkeley (J.D., 1993). *Member:* Los Angeles County Bar Association; State Bar of California; Women Lawyers of Los Angeles.

**CHRISTOPHER L. WANGER,** born Oakland, California, December 11, 1964; admitted to bar, 1993, California. *Education:* Dartmouth College (B.A., 1987); Hastings College of the Law, University of California (J.D., 1992). *Member:* State Bar of California.

**SUSAN F. WEGNER,** born Rochester, New York, March 8, 1966; admitted to bar, 1992, California; 1993, U.S. Court of Appeals, Ninth Circuit and U.S. District Court, Northern District of California. *Education:* University of Pennsylvania (B.A., 1988); Washington College of Law, The American University (J.D., summa cum laude, 1992). Senior Articles Editor, The Administrative Law Journal, American University. *Member:* State Bar of California; The District of Columbia Bar; American Bar Association (Environmental Law Section). **PRACTICE AREAS:** Environmental. *Email:* WegnerS@hws.com

COUNSEL

**NEAL M. WILLIAMS,** born Dallas, Texas, 1947; admitted to bar, 1982, California. *Education:* Georgia Institute of Technology (B.E.E. 1969); Stanford University (M.S.E.E., 1970); University of Santa Clara (J.D., 1982). Phi Eta Sigma; Eta Kappa Nu; Tau Beta Pi; Phi Kappa Phi; Omicron Delta Kappa. *Member:* Santa Clara County and American Bar Associations; State Bar of California. *Email:* WilliamsN@hws.com

REPRESENTATIVE CLIENTS: Allergan, Inc.; Amdahl Corp.; Ametek, Inc.; Bayside Capital Co.; BIOS; Candle Corporation; Care Wise; City of San Jose; Claremont Systems; Clarity; Computer Resources Group; Cornish & Carey; Dax & Co; Diva; FAO Schwartz; Graphisoft; Insight Development Corp.; Island Software, Inc.; Libbey Owens Ford; M/A-COM, Inc.; Macrovision Corp.; Neurex; OmniTel, Inc.; Oryx Technology; Otsuka America, Inc.; Paragon Vision Sciences; Pilkington Visioncare, Inc.; Pilkington Barnes Hind; Quantum Corporation; Rebis; Roche Bioscience; Silicon Valley Group; Sola International, Inc.; Sola Optical U.S.A.; Scitor Corporation; Sun Microsystems, Inc.; Synergy Semiconductor; Syntex U.S.A., Inc.; Systems Plus; Switchsoft; Tera Systems; Wells Fargo Bank, N.A.; Varian Associates, Inc.; Videonics, Inc.; Verifone; Xytec Int'l Industries, Inc.

## KATHRYN S. WUNSCH AND ASSOCIATED COUNSEL

LAW CHAMBERS
701 WELCH ROAD, SUITE 3320
**PALO ALTO, CALIFORNIA 94304**
Telephone: 415-833-1880
Fax: 415-833-1888

*Corporate, Business and Real Property Transactions, Real Property Assessment Appeals, Contracts, Probate, Trusts and Estates.*

FIRM PROFILE: *The firm's mission is to provide clients with high quality legal services producing results consistent with the client's objectives and agreed budget. Cases are staffed through association with counsel whose skills and experience levels are appropriate to the requirements of the case.*

**KATHRYN S. WUNSCH,** admitted to bar, 1977, California and U.S. District Court, Northern District of California. *Education:* Indiana University (A.B.); Stanford University and Indiana University (J.D., summa cum laude, 1977). Phi Beta Kappa; Psi Chi. Articles Editor, Indiana Law Review, 1976. *Member:* San Mateo County and American Bar Associations; State Bar of California (Member, Sections on: Business Law; Probate, Trust and Real Property).

## ZEVNIK HORTON GUIBORD & McGOVERN, P.C.

5 PALO ALTO SQUARE
3000 EL CAMINO REAL
**PALO ALTO, CALIFORNIA 94306**
Telephone: 415-842-5900
Facsimile: 415-855-9226

*Washington, D.C. Office:* Ninth Floor, 1299 Pennsylvania Avenue, N.W. Telephone: 202-824-0950. Fax: 202-824-0955.
*Chicago, Illinois Office:* Thirty Third Floor, 77 West Wacker Drive. Telephone: 312-977-2500. Telefax: 312-977-2560.
*Los Angeles, California Office:* 333 South Grand Avenue, Twenty First Floor. Telephone: 213-437-5200. Telefax: 213-437-5222.

*(This Listing Continued)*

*New York, N.Y. Office:* 745 Fifth Avenue, Twenty-Fifth Floor. Telephone: 212-935-2735. Telefax: 212-935-0614.
*London, England Office:* 4 Kings Bench Walk, Temple, London EC4Y 7DL. Telephone: 071-353-0478. Facsimile: 071-583-3549.
*Norfolk, Virginia Office:* Main Street Tower, 300 East Main Street, 13th Floor. Telephone: 757-624-3480. Fax: 757-624-3479.

*Commercial Litigation, Environmental Law, Insurance Coverage, Toxic Tort Litigation, International Law, Practice before State and Federal Courts and Administrative Tribunals.*

**PAUL ANTON ZEVNIK,** born Ashland, Wisconsin, November 2, 1950; admitted to bar, 1977, California; 1978, District of Columbia, U.S. District Court for the District of Columbia, U.S. Court of Appeals for the District of Columbia Circuit and U.S. District Court, Northern District of California; 1980, U.S. Court of Appeals, Ninth Circuit and U.S. Tax Court; 1981, U.S. Supreme Court and U.S. Claims Court; 1984, U.S. Court of Appeals for the Federal Circuit; 1985, Pennsylvania. *Education:* Harvard University (A.B., magna cum laude, 1972; A.M., 1972; J.D., cum laude, 1976). Author: "Federal Product Liability Legislation," American Bar Association, 1986; "When an Underlying Carrier Goes Broke: Recent Trends in 'Drop Down' Coverage," Coverage, ABA Committee on Insurance Coverage Litigation, Vol. 1, 1989. Faculty, Management of Mass Tort Litigation, Practising Law Institute, 1983. Fellow, Joint Center for Urban Studies, Harvard University and Massachusetts Institute of Technology, 1976. *Member:* The District of Columbia Bar; State Bar of California; Pennsylvania and Federal Communications Bar Associations. **PRACTICE AREAS:** Insurance Coverage; Environmental Law; Toxic Tort Litigation.

**MICHEL YVES HORTON,** born Washington, D.C., October 22, 1951; admitted to bar, 1984, California and District of Columbia. *Education:* Virginia Commonwealth University (B.S., cum laude, 1978); College of William & Mary (J.D., 1981). Kappa Tau Alpha. Author: "Bad Faith Insurance Litigation and Insurance Broker Liability," Practising Law Institute, Vol. 231; "The Impact of Antitrust and RICO Treble Damage Theories on the Insurance Industry," ABA National Institute, 1986; "The Status of the Unlimited Duty to Defend Under Pre-1966 CGL Policies," ABA National Institute, 1986; "When an Underlying Carrier Goes Broke: Recent Trends in 'Drop Down' Coverage," Coverage, Vol. 1, 1989, ABA Committee on Insurance Coverage Litigation. *Member:* The District of Columbia Bar; State Bar of California. **PRACTICE AREAS:** Insurance Coverage; Commercial Litigation.

**BARBARA B. GUIBORD,** born White Plains, New York, June 14, 1951; admitted to bar, 1977, New York; 1979, U.S. District Court, Western District of New York; 1983, U.S. District Court, Northern District of Illinois and Illinois (Not admitted in California). *Education:* Connecticut College (B.A., cum laude, 1973); Fordham University (J.D., 1976). Writing and Research Editor, Fordham University Urban Law Journal, Vol. IV, 1975-1976. Author: Note, "The New Equal Protection: Substantive Due Process Resurrected Under a New Name?" 3 Fordham Law Journal 311, 1975. Adjunct Professor of Environmental Law, Rachel Carson College of Environmental Studies, State University of New York at Buffalo, September, 1983 to December, 1983. Presenter: "The New Hazardous Solid Waste Amendments of 1984," Hofstra Law School Environmental Symposium, 1985; "Title III SARA: Community Right to Know," Ibidem, 1987; "Lender Liability Under Environmental Law," Continuing Legal Education Satellite Network, Inc., Springfield, Illinois, 1988 and 1989; "Environmental Auditing," Ibidem, 1988; "Siting Issues Surrounding Medical Waste Treatment and Disposal Facilities," Environmental Symposium sponsored by Katten, Muchin & Zavis, Chicago, 1990; "Environmental Aspects of Doing a Deal," American Bar Association, 1990; "Managing Risk--Anticipating Liability---Structuring the Deal," Continuing Legal Education Satellite Network, Inc., Springfield, Illinois, 1990. Associate General Counsel, New York State Department of Environmental Conservation, 1980-1983. *Member:* Chicago, Erie County (Chairperson, Environmental Law Committee, 1979-1980), Illinois State, New York State (Member, Environmental Law Section) and American (Member, Committee on Land and Natural Resources, 1988-1992) Bar Associations. **LANGUAGES:** French. **PRACTICE AREAS:** Environmental Law; Insurance Coverage.

**PATRICK MICHAEL McGOVERN,** born Yeovil, Somerset, England, June 9, 1955; admitted to bar, 1982, England and Wales (Solicitor of the Supreme Court); 1986, New York; 1987, U.S. District Court, Southern District of New York; 1991, U.S. District Court, Eastern District of New York (Not admitted in California). *Education:* University of Sheffield, England (LL.B., with Honors, 1976; M.A., 1978); College of Law, Guildford, England (Solicitors Final Qualifying Exam, 1979). *Member:* Law Society of

*(This Listing Continued)*

CAA1627B

## ZEVNIK HORTON GUIBORD & McGOVERN, P.C., Palo Alto—Continued

England and Wales. *LANGUAGES:* French. *PRACTICE AREAS:* International Law; Insurance Coverage; Commercial Litigation.

**JOSEPH G. HOMSY,** born New York, N.Y., February 27, 1945; admitted to bar, 1978, New York and U.S. District Court, Southern District of New York; 1988, Illinois (Not admitted in California). *Education:* University of Pennsylvania (B.A., 1966); New England School of Law (J.D., 1977). Author: "The Scope of Private Cost-Recovery Actions under CERCLA §107 (a) (4) (B) And Allocation Among Potentially Responsible Parties," *Hazardous Waste Litigation,* Practicing Law Institute, 1988; "Environmental Reporting Required by the Securities and Exchange Commission," BNA Environment Report, 1991. *Member:* American Bar Association (Member, Sections on: Environmental Law; Litigation); American Association of Corporate Counsel; Environmental Law Institute (Associate Representative, 1984-1987). [Capt., USAF, 1967-1971]. *PRACTICE AREAS:* Environmental Law.

**JOHN W. ROBERTS,** admitted to bar, 1982, Illinois (Not admitted in California). *Education:* Lake Forest College (B.A., 1979); Harvard University (J.D., cum laude, 1982). Phi Beta Kappa. *REPORTED CASES:* Monsanto Company in Hines v. Vulcan, 658 F.Supp. 651 (N.D. Ill. 1988); Inland Steel Company in Inland Steel v. Koppers Company, 498 N.E.2d 1247 (Ind. App. 1986). *PRACTICE AREAS:* Commercial Litigation; Compensation and Liability; Environmental; Construction.

**JOHN K. CROSSMAN,** born Miami, Florida, June 28, 1962; admitted to bar, 1987, Connecticut and New York; 1988, U.S. District Court, Southern and Eastern District of New York; 1993, U.S. Court of Appeals, Second Circuit (Not admitted in California). *Education:* Tufts University (B.S., cum laude, 1984); Boston University (J.D., 1987). *Member:* Association of the Bar of the City of New York (Computer Law Committee); American Bar Association; New York Patent, Trademark and Copyright Law Association.

**JONATHAN L. OSBORNE,** born Ft. Thomas, Kentucky, July 4, 1961; admitted to bar, 1986, Kentucky and U.S. District Court, Eastern and Western Districts of Kentucky; 1996, District of Columbia (Not admitted in California). *Education:* Georgetown College (B.A., 1983); University of Louisville (J.D., 1986). Member and Vice-President, Moot Court Board, 1985-1986. *Member:* Kentucky and American Bar Associations; The Association of Trial Lawyers of America. *PRACTICE AREAS:* Insurance Coverage; Commercial Litigation.

---

**MICHAEL C. DONOVAN,** born Washington, D.C., October 21, 1952; admitted to bar, 1978, Ohio; 1979, U.S. District Court, Southern District of Ohio; 1982, U.S. District Court, Northern District of Ohio; 1986, U.S. Court of Appeals for the District of Columbia Circuit; 1988, Colorado; 1991, California. *Education:* Northeastern University (B.S., magna cum laude, 1974); University of Notre Dame (J.D., 1978). *PRACTICE AREAS:* Complex Civil and Criminal Environmental Litigation; Toxic Tort Litigation.

**STEVEN H. DOTO,** born Camden, New Jersey, October 13, 1961; admitted to bar, 1986, New Jersey and Pennsylvania; U.S. District Court, Eastern District of Pennsylvania; 1995, U.S. District Court, Northern District of California; 1996, District of Columbia (Not admitted in California). *Education:* Franklin & Marshall College (B.A., 1983); Rutgers University (J.D., with honors, 1986). Recipient, New Jersey State Criminal Justice Writing Competition Award. Author: "The Conviction Proneness of Death-Qualified Juries," Criminal Justice Writing Competition, 1986. *Member:* Pennsylvania (Member, Litigation Section), New Jersey State and American (Member: Litigation Section; Young Lawyers Division) Bar Associations. *PRACTICE AREAS:* Environmental; Complex Litigation; Commercial Litigation; Insurance Coverage Litigation.

**CECELIA C. FUSICH,** born Oakland, California, April 2, 1960; admitted to bar, 1989, California. *Education:* University of California at Los Angeles (B.A., magna cum laude, 1982); Boalt Hall School of Law, University of California (J.D., 1986). Phi Beta Kappa. *PRACTICE AREAS:* Environmental Law.

**JOHN C. MEYER,** born New York, N.Y., June 12, 1960; admitted to bar, 1992, California. *Education:* University of California at Berkeley (B.A., 1989); McGeorge School of Law, University of the Pacific (J.D., cum laude, 1992). *PRACTICE AREAS:* Litigation; Complex Civil Environmental Litigation.

*(This Listing Continued)*

---

**ESTEBAN L. OYENQUE,** born Akron, Ohio, December 5, 1966; admitted to bar, 1993, Nebraska (Not admitted in California). *Education:* Dartmouth College (A.B., 1989); University of Michigan (J.D., 1992). *Member:* American Bar Association (Vice-Chair, Special Committee on Environmental Techniques). *LANGUAGES:* Spanish. *PRACTICE AREAS:* Complex Environmental Litigation; Environmental Insurance Litigation.

---

## BREON, O'DONNELL, MILLER, BROWN & DANNIS

2550 VIA TEJON
SUITE 3A
PALOS VERDES ESTATES, CALIFORNIA 90274
Telephone: 310-373-6857
FAX: 310-373-6808

*San Francisco, California Office:* 19th Floor, 71 Stevenson Street. Telephone: 415-543-4111. Fax: 415-543-4384.

*Salinas, California Office:* Suite H120, 17842 Moro Road, Suite F120, 93907. Telephone: 408-663-0470.

*Labor, Employment Relations and Education Law and Related Litigation on Behalf of Public and Private Sector Employers, Business, Property, Construction Litigation.*

**DAVID G. MILLER,** born Los Angeles, California, March 8, 1940; admitted to bar, 1968, California, Ohio and U.S. District Court, Central District of California; 1972, U.S. Court of Appeals, Ninth Circuit; 1975, U.S. District Court, Eastern District of California. *Education:* Antioch College (B.A., 1964); California Western School of Law (J.D., 1967). Member, Appellate Moot Court Team (State and National Competitions). Author: "Some Modest Proposals for Collective Bargaining in Professional Sports," Los Angeles Bar Bulletin, March, 1973. Lecturer, Labor Law, Mid Valley College of Law, 1972-1973. (Resident). *PRACTICE AREAS:* Labor Law; Employment Law; Education Law.

### ASSOCIATES

**JOAN BIRDT,** born Los Angeles, California, July 13, 1939; admitted to bar, 1975, California. *Education:* University of California at Los Angeles (B.A., 1961); University of West Los Angeles (J.D., 1975). (Resident).

**SUE ANN SALMON EVANS,** born Anaheim, California, April 2, 1964; admitted to bar, 1990, California. *Education:* University of California at Santa Barbara (B.A., 1986); Loyola Marymount University (J.D., 1990). (Resident).

**JANET L. MUELLER,** admitted to bar, 1992, California. *Education:* University of California, Berkeley (B.A., 1987); University of California School of Law, Davis (J.D., 1992). (Resident).

**IVETTE PEÑA,** born Caguas, Puerto Rico, December 5, 1965; admitted to bar, 1991, California. *Education:* Brown University (B.A., 1987); Harvard University (J.D., 1990). (Resident).

(For complete biographical data on all personnel, see Professional Biographies at San Francisco)

---

## JACK I. ESENSTEN

**PALOS VERDES ESTATES, CALIFORNIA**

(See Rolling Hills Estates)

*Domestic Relations, Personal Injury and General Practice.*

## McKERNAN, LANAM, BAKKE, BENSON & BODNEY

*Established in 1947*

732 FIR STREET
P.O. BOX 550
**PARADISE, CALIFORNIA 95967**
Telephone: 916-877-4961
Fax: 916-877-8163
Email: mlbbbchico@aol.com

*Chico, California Office:* 445 Normal Avenue, P.O. Box 3496. Telephone: 916-891-0247. Fax: 916-891-1704.

*General Civil Practice. Trusts, Probate, Real Estate, Estate Planning, Personal Injury, Professional Malpractice, Insurance and Corporate Law and Trials.*

(For Complete Biographical Data on all Personnel, see Professional Biographies at Chico)

---

## GERARD G. ADAMS

1122 EAST GREEN STREET
**PASADENA, CALIFORNIA 91106**
Telephone: 818-795-4544
Fax: 818-796-2554

*Business Transactional Law, with an emphasis on Real Estate and Taxation.*

**GERARD G. ADAMS,** admitted to bar, 1972, California. *Education:* California State University, Northridge (B.S., 1966); University of San Fernando Valley (J.D., 1971). **PRACTICE AREAS:** Business Law; Estate Planning Law; Real Estate Law.

---

## ADAMS & HAWEKOTTE

350 WEST COLORADO BOULEVARD, SUITE 310
**PASADENA, CALIFORNIA 91105**
Telephone: 818-583-8000; 213-684-0920
Facsimile: 818-449-1576

*International and Domestic Business Transactions, Taxation, Business Organizations, Exempt Organizations, Pension and Profit Sharing, Estate Planning, Probate and Conservatorships.*

**ROGER ADAMS,** born Glendale, California, 1938; admitted to bar, 1970, New York; 1972, California; 1991, U.S. Tax Court. *Education:* University of Southern California (A.B., 1960; J.D., 1969). Phi Beta Kappa. Member, Southern California Law Review, 1968-1969. Member, Tax Executives Institute, 1975-1986. *Member:* Pasadena (Member, Probate and Tax Law Sections) and Los Angeles County (Member, Taxation Section) Bar Associations; State Bar of California. [With U.S. Navy, 1961-1965]. **PRACTICE AREAS:** International and Domestic Business Transactions; Taxation; Corporate Law; Exempt Organizations; Pension and Profit Sharing Plans; Probate; Estate Planning; Conservatorships.

**ANGELA HAWEKOTTE,** born Whittier, California, 1953; admitted to bar, 1980, California; 1988, U.S. Tax Court. *Education:* Mount St. Mary's College (B.A., 1975); University College of Wales, United Kingdom (Diploma in International Law & Relations, 1980); Loyola Law School (J.D., 1979). Phi Alpha Delta, Vice Justice, 1978-1979. Member, Loyola International and Comparative Law Journal. Associate Justice, Scott Moot Court Honors Board, 1978-1979. Rotary International Foundation Graduate Fellow, 1979-1980. Certified Public Accountant, California, 1985. *Member:* Pasadena (Member, Probate and Tax Law Sections; Member, Board of Directors: Treasurer, 1992-1993 and 1995-1996; Trustee, 1993-1995) and Los Angeles County (Member, Taxation and Business Law Sections) Bar Associations; State Bar of California (Member, Sections on: Taxation and Estate Planning; Trust and Probate Law); California Society of Certified Public Accountants. **LANGUAGES:** French. **PRACTICE AREAS:** Tax Controversies; Tax Audits; International and Domestic Business Transactions; Taxation; Corporate Law; Probate; Estate Planning; Conservatorships.

---

## EUGENE S. ALKANA

*Established in 1975*

SUITE 310, 131 NORTH EL MOLINO AVENUE
**PASADENA, CALIFORNIA 91101**
Telephone: 818-796-8170
Telecopier: 818-795-6138

*General Civil Practice. Equine Law and Syndications. Litigation. Business, Commercial, Real Estate, Construction, Collections, Non-Profit Organizations.*

**EUGENE S. ALKANA,** born Los Angeles, California, September 3, 1949; admitted to bar, 1974, California. *Education:* New Mexico Military Institute; University of Southern California (B.S., cum laude, 1971); University of San Diego (J.D., 1974). Beta Gamma Sigma; Phi Alpha Delta. Part Time Lecturer, Contracts and Real Property, University of West Los Angeles, 1986-1992. Instructor, Los Angeles Community Colleges, 1989—. Judge Pro Tem, Los Angeles County Superior Court, 1986—. *Member:* Pasadena and Los Angeles County Bar Associations; State Bar of California; American Horse Council; California Thoroughbred Breeders Association.

REPRESENTATIVE CLIENTS: Beckett Ranch; Circle H Ranch; West Coast Farms; Kerr Stock Farm; Malibu Valley Farm; Bloodstock Services, Inc.; Abba Rubber International; Scott-Caudill Lumber Co.; Economy Office Furniture; Continental Conveyance Corp; Chemtech Chemical Co.; Trv-Wood Products; Skeptics Society.

---

## ANDERSON & SALISBURY

*A PROFESSIONAL CORPORATION*

*Established in 1957*

SUITE 310, 350 WEST COLORADO BOULEVARD
**PASADENA, CALIFORNIA 91105**
Telephone: 818-449-4812; 213-684-0920
Telecopier: 818-449-1576

*Family Law.*

**LEE W. SALISBURY,** born Oakland, California, September 14, 1951; admitted to bar, 1976, California; 1978, U.S. District Court, Central District of California; 1992, U.S. Court of Appeals, Ninth Circuit. *Education:* Stanford University (B.A., 1973); University of Southern California (J.D., 1976). *Member:* Pasadena (President, 1994-1995) and Los Angeles County (Member, Family Law Section) Bar Associations; State Bar of California (Member, Family Law Section). (Certified Specialist, Family Law, The State Bar of California Board of Legal Specialization). **PRACTICE AREAS:** Family Law.

---

**WESLEY ANN HOGE HUBANKS,** born Los Angeles, California, March 7, 1940; admitted to bar, 1984, California and U.S. District Court, Central District of California. *Education:* University of California at Los Angeles (B.A. with honors, 1962); Loyola University of Los Angeles (J.D., cum laude, 1984). Member, St. Thomas More Honor Society. *Member:* Pasadena and Los Angeles County Bar Associations; State Bar of California (Member, Family Law Section). **PRACTICE AREAS:** Family Law.

---

## ANGLEA & BANNON

*A PROFESSIONAL CORPORATION*

SUITE 711, 199 SOUTH LOS ROBLES AVENUE
**PASADENA, CALIFORNIA 91101-2460**
Telephone: 818-584-8800
Fax: 818-584-8807

*Estate Planning, Probate and Trust Law, General Tax Matters, General Business Matters, Real Estate and Environmental Law; Fiduciary and Tax Litigation.*

**ROBERT D. BANNON,** born Los Angeles, California, September 19, 1926; admitted to bar, 1953, California. *Education:* University of California at Los Angeles; University of California at Berkeley (A.B., 1949); University of Southern California (J.D., 1952). Phi Delta Phi. Co-Author: "Life Insurance Funding," Business Buy Sell Agreements (CEB, 1992); "Estate Freezing," 41 Major Tax Planning 15-1 (Matthew Bender, 1989). *Member:* Los Angeles County (Member: Board of Trustees, 1983-1984; Taxation Section; Chair, Estate and Gift Tax Committee, 1988-1989; Chair, Probate

*(This Listing Continued)*

*ANGLEA & BANNON, A PROFESSIONAL CORPORATION,
Pasadena—Continued*

and Trust Section, 1984-1985; Vice Chairman, Arbitration Committee, 1979-1981) and American (Co-Chairman, Subcommittee on Preparation of Model Clauses, Domestic Relations Tax Problems Committee, Tax Section, 1976-1978) Bar Associations; State Bar of California (Member Sections on: Estate Planning, Trust & Probate and Taxation); Lawyers Club of Los Angeles (Member, Board of Governors, 1975-1983; President, 1981-1982). Fellow, American College of Trust and Estate Counsel (Chair, Environmental Law Committee). (Certified Specialist, Probate, Estate Planning and Trust Law, The State Bar of California Board of Legal Specialization). *PRACTICE AREAS:* Estate Planning; Federal Estate and Gift Tax; Generation Skipping Tax; Family Wealth Transfer.

**ALEXANDRA LABOUTIN BANNON,** born Casablanca, Morocco, July 23, 1949; admitted to bar, 1979, California. *Education:* San Francisco State University (B.A., 1972; M.A., 1975); University of California, Berkeley, Boalt Hall School of Law (J.D., 1979). Author: "Environmental Issues in Trust Administration," California Trust Administration (Ch. 16), (CEB 1996). *Member:* Los Angeles County (Member: Executive Committee, Trusts and Estates Section, 1991-1995; Executive Committee, Tax Section, 1991-1992, 1994-1995; Chair, Tax Section, Estate and Gift Tax Committee, 1991-1992) and American (Co-Chair, Fiduciary Environmental Problems Committee, 1995—) Bar Association; State Bar of California (Member, Executive Committee, Estate Planning, Trust and Probate Section, 1994-1995). (Certified Specialist, Estate Planning, Trust and Probate Law, The State Bar of California Board of Legal Specialization). *LANGUAGES:* Russian. *PRACTICE AREAS:* Probate Administration; Contested Trusts and Estates; Environmental Liability; Environmental Tax.

**ELIZABETH T. PIERSON,** born Detroit, Michigan, September 12, 1963; admitted to bar, 1988, California; 1992, U.S. Tax Court. *Education:* Duke University (A.B., 1985); Emmanuel College, Cambridge, England; University of Southern California (J.D., 1988). Member, Major Tax Planning/Computer Law Journal, University of Southern California, 1986-1987. *Member:* Pasadena, Los Angeles County (Member, Sections on: Taxation, Trusts and Estates), Orange County (Member, Estate Planning, Probate and Trust Section) and American (Member, Sections on: Taxation, Real Property, Probate and Trust Law) Bar Associations; State Bar of California. (Certified Specialist, Probate, Estate Planning and Trust Law, State Bar of California Board of Legal Specialization). *PRACTICE AREAS:* Federal Estate and Gift Tax; Trust Administration; Probate Administration; Estate Planning.

**JOANN JACKSON KALAMA,** born Durango, Colorado, May 27, 1947; admitted to bar, 1991, California. *Education:* Brigham Young University (B.S., 1969); University of California at Los Angeles (J.D., 1991). *Member:* Pasadena and Los Angeles County Bar Associations; State Bar of California; National Academy of Elder Law Attorneys; Fiduciary Roundtable of San Gabriel Valley (President, 1993-1994). *PRACTICE AREAS:* Probate Administration; Trust Administration; Estate Planning; Estate Planning for the Elderly; Guardianship and Conservatorship.

*OF COUNSEL*

**MARTHA BURROUGHS HOGAN,** born Salamanca, New York, June 25, 1929; admitted to bar, 1981, California; 1982, U.S. Tax Court. *Education:* Mount Holyoke College (A.B., 1951); San Francisco State College; University of California at Los Angeles (J.D., 1981). Order of the Coif. Ford Foundation Fellow. Member, 1979-1981 and Managing Editor, 1980-1981, UCLA-Alaska Law Review. Member, Estate Planning Council of San Gabriel Valley. *Member:* Pasadena, Los Angeles County and American (Member, Sections on: Real Property, Probate and Trust Law) Bar Associations; State Bar of California. *PRACTICE AREAS:* Estate Planning; Federal Estate and Gift Tax; Generation Skipping Tax; Family Wealth Transfer.

## *MARGALO ASHLEY-FARRAND*

*215 N. MARENGO AVENUE, THIRD FLOOR*
**PASADENA, CALIFORNIA 91101**
*Telephone: 818-792-4700*
*Facsimile: 818-356-7414*

*Family Law, Mediation, Family Trusts and Wills, Probate, Small Business, Bankruptcy.*

**MARGALO ASHLEY-FARRAND,** born New York, N.Y., July 26, 1944; admitted to bar, 1981, District of Columbia and Maryland; 1983,

*(This Listing Continued)*

CAA1630B

California. *Education:* New York University (B.A., cum laude, 1978); Southwestern University (J.D., 1980). Judge Pro Tem, Los Angeles Superior and Municipal Courts, 1989-1995. Mediator, Los Angeles Municipal/Superior Court Settlement Officer Program, 1989-1995. Private Mediation, 1985-1995. Democratic Nominee, 59th Assembly District, 1994. *Member:* State Bar of California (Family Law Section); California Women Lawyers; Women Lawyers of Los Angeles (Member, Family Law Section, Legislative Committee). (Certified Specialist, Family Law, The State Bar of California Board of Legal Specialization). *PRACTICE AREAS:* Family Law; Mediation; Family Trusts and Wills; Probate; Small Business; Bankruptcy.

## *NAIRIE A. BALIAN*

*225 SOUTH LAKE AVENUE, 9TH FLOOR*
**PASADENA, CALIFORNIA 91101**
*Telephone: 818-564-2630*
*FAX: 818-564-2633*
*Modem: 818-564-2634*
*Email: nabalian@aol.com*

*Civil Litigation, Insurance Coverage, Construction Defect, Business, Personal Injury with an emphasis on Vehicular, Products Liability and Premises Liability, Family Law including: Dissolutions, Spousal Support, Prenuptials, Custody and Cohabitation Agreements.*

**NAIRIE A. BALIAN,** born Beirut, Lebanon, August 8, 1963; admitted to bar, 1987, California and U.S. District Court, Central District of California. *Education:* Allegheny College (B.A., 1983); University of La Verne (J.D., 1987). Recipient, American Jurisprudence Award in Contracts. Member, Moot Court. Member, La Verne Law Journal, 1985-1986. *Member:* Beverly Hills and American Bar Associations; State Bar of California; Los Angeles Trial Lawyers Association; California Trial Lawyers Association; Los Angeles Women Lawyers Association; Armenian Bar Association; The Association of Trial Lawyers of America. *LANGUAGES:* Armenian, Arabic, French, Russian.

## *BARABAN & TESKE*

*Established in 1985*

*WALNUT PLAZA, SUITE 250*
*215 NORTH MARENGO AVENUE*
**PASADENA, CALIFORNIA 91101-1569**
*Telephone: 818-440-9882*
*Fax: 818-440-9393*

*Insurance Defense, Civil Litigation, General Liability, Product Liability, Personal Injury, Construction, Insurance Law.*

*MEMBERS OF FIRM*

**JEFFREY H. BARABAN,** born Kansas City, Missouri, November 19, 1946; admitted to bar, 1978, California. *Education:* Memphis State University (B.A., 1969); California State University, Los Angeles (M.B.A., 1972); University of West Los Angeles (J.D., 1978). *Member:* State Bar of California; American Bar Association; American Board of Trial Advocates; The Association of Trial Lawyers of America; Association of Southern California Defense Counsel; Los Angeles Trial Lawyers Association (Member, Defense Section); Defense Research Institute. *REPORTED CASES:* Brown v. Presley of Southern California, 213 Cal. App. 3d 612; 261 Cal. Rptr. 779; Hughes v. Southern California Rapid Transit Dist., 173 Cal. App. 3d 512; 219 Cal. Rptr. 82. *PRACTICE AREAS:* General Liability; Products Liability; Personal Injury; Insurance.

**CHRISTOPHER S. TESKE,** born Rockford, Illinois, September 16, 1954; admitted to bar, 1980, New Jersey; 1985, California. *Education:* University of Notre Dame (B.A., 1976); University of Virginia (J.D., 1979). *Member:* State Bar of California; American Bar Association. *REPORTED CASES:* McDonald v. John P. Scripps Newspaper, 210 Cal. App. 3d 100; 257 Cal. Rptr. 473. *PRACTICE AREAS:* Civil Litigation; General Liability; Products Liability; Personal Injury; Construction Law.

*ASSOCIATES*

**EDWARD R. NEVILLE,** born New York, N.Y., June 15, 1951; admitted to bar, 1988, California. *Education:* Georgetown University (A.B., 1973); Georgia State University (M.B.A., 1979); Southwestern University (J.D., 1987). *Member:* State Bar of California. *PRACTICE AREAS:* Civil Litigation.

**WILLIAM C. HOWISON,** born Los Angeles, California, December 27, 1951; admitted to bar, 1978, California. *Education:* Pacific Lutheran Uni-

*(This Listing Continued)*

versity (B.A., 1975); University of LaVerne (J.D., 1978). *Member:* State Bar of California. *PRACTICE AREAS:* Civil Litigation; Construction Law.

**DIANE M. CORWIN,** born San Francisco, California, November 5, 1956; admitted to bar, 1983, California. *Education:* University of California, Santa Barbara (B.A., 1978); Pepperdine University (J.D., 1983). *Member:* Los Angeles County Bar Association; State Bar of California. *PRACTICE AREAS:* Civil Litigation.

**ROBIN L. HAULMAN,** born Upland, California, March 24, 1953; admitted to bar, 1992, California. *Education:* Chaffey Junior College (A.A., 1989); Western State University (B.S.L., 1991; J.D., 1992). *Member:* State Bar of California. *PRACTICE AREAS:* Civil Litigation.

**JAMES R. KULA,** born Ferndale, Michigan, September 26, 1946; admitted to bar, 1974, California and U.S. District Court, Central District of California; 1988, U.S. District Court, Eastern District of California. *Education:* University of Michigan (B.A., 1967); George Washington University (J.D., 1973). *Member:* State Bar of California. *PRACTICE AREAS:* Civil Litigation; Construction Law.

**KELLI G. HAWLEY,** born Santa Ana, California, July 4, 1960; admitted to bar, 1985, California and U.S. District Court, Central District of California. *Education:* University of Redlands (B.A., 1982); University of San Diego (J.D., 1985). *Member:* State Bar of California. *PRACTICE AREAS:* Civil Litigation; Construction Law.

**DAVID S. SCHLUETER,** born Danville, Illinois, July 22, 1957; admitted to bar, 1983, California. *Education:* University of Illinois (B.A., 1979); Santa Clara University (J.D., 1982). *Member:* Los Angeles County and American Bar Associations; State Bar of California; Association of Southern California Defense Counsel. *REPORTED CASES:* Richardson v. GAB Business Services, Inc., (1984) 161 Cal. App. 3d 519, 579 Cal. Rptr. 519. *PRACTICE AREAS:* Civil Litigation; Construction Law.

---

## BARKER & RICHARDSON

*PASADENA, CALIFORNIA*

(See Richardson & Harman)

---

## BARKER & ROMNEY

*A PROFESSIONAL CORPORATION*
*301 EAST COLORADO BOULEVARD*
*SUITE 200*
**PASADENA, CALIFORNIA 91101-1977**
*Telephone: 818-578-1970; 213-617-3112*
*Facsimile: 818-578-0768*

*Construction, Construction Defect, Business, Real Estate, Land Use, Environmental Law, Eminent Domain, General Civil Litigation, Community Association Law, Insurance Law and Appellate Law.*

**LEE BARKER** (1943-1996).

**DAVID T. ROMNEY,** born Santa Paula, California, September 5, 1944; admitted to bar, 1973, California and U.S. District Court, Central and Eastern Districts of California; 1986, U.S. Court of Appeals, Ninth Circuit. *Education:* University of California at Berkeley (B.A., 1966); University of Colorado at Boulder (J.D., 1969). Author: "California Unfair Business Practices Law--A Plaintiffs Lottery," ABA Business Torts Newsletter, February 1993; "Bidding and Awarding Public Contracts," League of California Cities, Monterey, California, 1979. Guest Lecturer, "Construction Defect Litigation," Institute of Real Estate Management, Chicago, 1996. Assistant City Attorney, City of Ventura, California, 1974-1977. City Attorney, City of Woodland, California, 1977-1985. President, Sacramento Government Attorneys Association, 1980. Member, Los Angeles Bar Association, 1987-1994. *Member:* State Bar of California (Member, Litigation Section); American Bar Association (Member, Litigation Section). *REPORTED CASES:* Bowers v. San Buenaventura (1977, 2d Dist) 75 Ca3d 65; Kimura v. Roberts (1979, 3rd Dist) 89 Ca3d 871. *PRACTICE AREAS:* Business Litigation; Construction Defect Litigation; Community Association Law; Real Estate; Eminent Domain; Land Use; Partnership; Corporate Dissolutions and Appeals.

*(This Listing Continued)*

**TIMOTHY M. HOWETT,** born Ely, England, November 17, 1961; admitted to bar, 1989, California and U.S. District Court, Central District of California; 1990, U.S. District Court, Southern, Eastern and Northern Districts of California and U.S. Court of Appeals, Ninth Circuit. *Education:* London School of Economics, London, England; Claremont McKenna College (B.A., 1983); Loyola Law School of Los Angeles (J.D., 1988). Phi Alpha Delta. *Member:* Pasadena, Los Angeles County (Member: Sections on Real Estate and Construction Law) and American Bar Associations (Member, Natural Resources, Energy and Environment Law Section; Forum on the Construction Industry); State Bar of California (Member: Sections on Real Estate and Litigation); Association of Business Trial Lawyers. *PRACTICE AREAS:* Complex Civil Litigation; Construction; Community Association Law; Real Estate Law; Environmental Law; Land Use.

**BLAINE JAY WANKE,** born Milwaukee, Wisconsin, October 15, 1955; admitted to bar, 1991, California; 1992, U.S. District Court, Central District of California. *Education:* California Polytechnic State University (B.S., cum laude, 1977); University of Southern California (M.B.A., 1979); McGeorge School of Law (J.D., with great distinction, 1991). Order of the Coif. *Member:* Pasadena, Los Angeles County and American Bar Associations; State Bar of California. *PRACTICE AREAS:* Construction Defect Litigation; Business Litigation; General Business; Community Association Law.

**CHERYL A. ORR,** born Methuen, Massachusetts, July 10, 1962; admitted to bar, 1987, California; 1988, U.S. District Court, Central District of California; 1991, U.S. Court of Appeals, Ninth Circuit; 1993, U.S. District Court, Southern, Eastern and Northern Districts of California. *Education:* Bates College (B.A., cum laude, 1984); University of Pennsylvania (J.D., 1987). Phi Beta Kappa. *Member:* Pasadena, Los Angeles County (Member: Litigation Section; Appellate Courts Committee) and American (Member, Litigation Section) Bar Associations; State Bar of California. *REPORTED CASES:* National Union Fire Insurance v. Keating, 995 F.2d, 154 (9th Cir. 1993); Aetna Cas. & Insurance Co. v. Titan Corp., 22 Cal.App 4th 457 (1994); ACL Technologies v. Northbrook Property & Casualty Insurance, 17 Cal.App 4th 1773 (1994). *PRACTICE AREAS:* Construction Defect; General Business; Insurance Coverage; Appellate Litigation.

REFERENCES: City National Bank; First LA Bank.

---

## JOEL R. BENNETT

*225 SOUTH LAKE AVENUE*
*NINTH FLOOR*
**PASADENA, CALIFORNIA 91101**
*Telephone: 818-683-3031*
*Fax: 818-795-6321*
*Email: joel__bennett@earthlink.net*

*Civil Litigation and Jury Trials in all State and Federal Courts, Antitrust, Unfair Competition, Trade Regulation, Trade Secrets, Breach of Contract, Unfair Trade Practices, Health Care Litigation, Telecommunications Antitrust, Intellectual Property, Trademark, Copyright, Patent.*

**JOEL R. BENNETT,** born New York, N.Y., November 19, 1940; admitted to bar, 1964, Arizona; 1968, California and U.S. Supreme Court. *Education:* University of Arizona (B.A., 1961; J.D., 1964). Author: "Litigation as an Integral Part of A Scheme to Create or Maintain an Illegal Monopoly," 26 Mercer Law Review 479, 1975. Law Clerk to U.S. District Judge, C.A. Muecke, Phoenix, Arizona, 1964-1966. Trial Attorney, Antitrust Division, Department of Justice, 1966-1969. *Member:* Los Angeles County, Pasadena, Federal Communications and American Bar Associations; State Bar of California; Association of Business Trial Lawyers; American Intellectual Property Law Association; National Health Lawyers Association; California Society of Health Care Lawyers. *PRACTICE AREAS:* Antitrust and Trade Regulation; Breach of Contract; Health Care; Intellectual Property; Unfair Competition.

## BENSINGER, GRAYSON & RITT

A Partnership

65 NORTH RAYMOND AVENUE, SUITE 320
**PASADENA, CALIFORNIA 91103**
Telephone: 818-685-2550
Fax: 818-685-2562
Email: bgrdjr@aol.com

*Criminal Defense in State and Federal Courts, General Civil and Appellate Practice in all State and Federal Courts. Business Litigation, Entertainment Law, Employment Discrimination, Sexual Harassment, and Mediation of Family, Divorce and Community Disputes.*

FIRM PROFILE: *Bensinger, Grayson & Ritt is a small law partnership consisting of six attorneys (four partners and two attorneys of counsel) and a support staff. The firm had its genesis in mid-1995 when Kerry Bensinger, Pegine Grayson and Jay Ritt realized their vision of creating an aggressive, efficient and technologically advanced law office that would offer clients a wide range of high quality legal services, comparable to those available at larger firms, while maintaining the responsive and personal relationships with clients that are only possible with a smaller office case load.*

**KERRY R. BENSINGER,** born Santa Monica, California, October 28, 1960; admitted to bar, 1987, California; U.S. District Court, Central District of California; U.S. Court of Appeals, Ninth Circuit. *Education:* Yale University (B.A., 1982); University of Southern California (J.D.., 1987). Hale Moot Court Honors Program, Winner, Best Oral Advocate Award; Miller Johnson Equal Justice Award; Judge Barry Russell Federal Bar Association Award for Excellence in Field of Federal Practice. Author: "From Public Charity To Social Justice: The Role Of The Court In California's General Relief Program, 21 Loyola of Los Angeles Law Review, Vol. 11, December 1987. Co-Author: "Bribery" chapter in West's California Criminal Law. Attorney, Quinn, Kully and Morrow Law Firm, 1991-1995. Deputy Federal Public Defenders, 1988-1991. Extern to the Honorable, David V. Kenyon, United States Federal District Court Judge, 1986. *Member:* Los Angeles County (Member, Pro Bono Council, Law Enforcement and Justice Committee and Judicial Election Evaluation Committee) Bar Association; State Bar of California. **LANGUAGES:** Spanish. **REPORTED CASES:** United States v. Tabacca, 924 F 2d 906 (9th Cir. 1991). **PRACTICE AREAS:** Criminal and Civil Litigation.

**PEGINE E. GRAYSON,** born Northampton, Massachusetts, December 8, 1961; admitted to bar, 1987, California and U.S. District Court, Central District of California and U.S. Court of Appeals, Ninth Circuit; 1989, District of Columbia. *Education:* Middlebury College (B.A., magna cum laude, 1983); University of Southern California (J.D., 1987). Phi Beta Kappa; Order of the Coif. Member, Hale Moot Court Honors Program. Recipient: American Jurisprudence Award, Contracts, Civil Procedure; Miller-Johnson Equal Justice Award for Demonstrated Commitment to Social Justice. Board Member, American Civil Liberties Union, 1990-1991. Member: Los Angeles City Mayor's Advisory Committee on Child Care, 1989-1992; Los Angeles County Child Care Resource Committee, 1989-1992. *Member:* The District of Columbia Bar; Los Angeles County (Member, Individual Rights Section, Executive Committee Member, 1989-1991) and American Bar Associations; Academy of Family Mediators; Southern California Mediation Association; Public Interest Law Foundation (Board of Directors, 1992-1994). **LANGUAGES:** Spanish. **PRACTICE AREAS:** Employment Discrimination; Sexual Harassment; Family and Divorce Mediation.

**D. JAY RITT,** born Frankfurt, West Germany, April 14, 1963; admitted to bar, 1988, California and U.S. District Court, Central District of California and U.S. Court of Appeals, Ninth Circuit. *Education:* University of California at Berkeley (B.A., cum laude, with distinction in General Scholarship, 1985); Boalt Hall School of Law, University of California (J.D., 1988). Member, California Law Review, 1986-1988. Co-Author: "Bribery" chapter in West's California Criminal Law. Special Master, State of California, 1990. Attorney, Quinn, Kully and Morrow Law Firm, 1988-1995. *Member:* Los Angeles County and Federal Bar Associations; State Bar of California; Legal Aid Foundation (President and Member, Associates Committee, 1991-1993). **PRACTICE AREAS:** Civil Litigation; Criminal Litigation; Employment Discrimination; Sexual Harassment. *Email:* bgrdjr@aol.com

**KAREN M. GEE,** born Boston, Massachusetts, January 31, 1960; admitted to bar, 1987, California and U.S. District Court, Central District of California. *Education:* Yale University (B.S., 1981); Boalt Hall School of Law, University of California at Berkeley (J.D., 1987). Deputy Public Defender, Los Angeles County (1987-1995). Extern to the Honorable Robert Takasugi, United States Federal District Court Judge, 1986. Legal Assis-

*(This Listing Continued)*

tant, Morrison & Foerster (1982-1984). *Member:* Pasadena (Member, Criminal Law Section) and Los Angeles County (LACBA) Bar Associations; State Bar of California; Southern California Chinese Lawyers' Association (SCCLA). **PRACTICE AREAS:** Criminal and Civil Litigation; Entertainment Law.

*OF COUNSEL*

**MARILYN M. SMITH,** born Gardena, California, September 3, 1951; admitted to bar, 1976, California; 1977, U.S. District Court, Central District of California; 1985, U.S. District Court, Eastern District of California; 1991, U.S. Court of Appeals, Ninth Circuit. *Education:* University of Southern California (B.A., magna cum laude, 1973); University of California at Los Angeles (J.D., 1976). Phi Beta Kappa. Member, Order of Barristers. Moot Court Honors Program. Clerk to U.S. Magistrate Vennetta Tassopulos, 1975. Deputy District Attorney, 1977-1980. Author: "Personal Injury litigation in the United States" (with B. Weissman and P. Senuty), International Litigation Practitioners Forum, Vol. 1, Issue 4, Sept. 1990. *Member:* Pasadena, Glendale and Los Angeles County (Member, Intellectual Property Section) Bar Associations; California Copyright Conference; The State Bar of California (Member, Sections on: Litigation and Intellectual Property); Association of Southern California Defense Counsel; American Board of Trial Advocates. **PRACTICE AREAS:** Intellectual Property Law; Civil Litigation; Insurance.

**CAROL A. KLAUSCHIE,** born Omaha, Nebraska, December 3, 1957; admitted to bar, 1985, California; U.S. District Court, Central District of California; U.S. Court of Appeals, Ninth Circuit. *Education:* University of California at Santa Barbara (B.A., with honors, 1980); Loyola Law School (J.D., 1985). Deputy Federal Public Defender, Central District of California (1987-1991); Deputy Public Defender, Los Angeles County (1986-1987); Extern to the Honorable Alfred T. Goodwin, United States Court of Appeals for the Ninth Circuit, 1985. *Member:* California Attorneys For Criminal Justice; Women's Lawyers Association of Los Angeles. **PRACTICE AREAS:** Criminal Defense; Civil Rights.

## FREDERICK B. BENSON

200 SOUTH LOS ROBLES AVENUE, SUITE 500
**PASADENA, CALIFORNIA 91101**
Telephone: 818-577-8808
Fax: 818-577-8887

*Immigration and Naturalization, Probate and Estate Planning.*

**FREDERICK B. BENSON,** born Lancaster, Pennsylvania, April 2, 1949; admitted to bar, 1975, California; 1976, Pennsylvania and U.S. District Court, Central District of California; 1980, U.S. District Court, Eastern District of Pennsylvania; 1981, U.S. Court of Appeals, Third and Ninth Circuits. *Education:* Franklin & Marshall College (B.A., 1971); University of Delaware; University of California at Los Angeles School of Law (J.D., 1975). Phi Alpha Theta; Pi Gamma Mu. Lecturer: Immigration Services of Santa Rosa, 1983-1987; Immigration Legal Assistance Project, Los Angeles County Bar Association, 1986-1995. Speaker: "How to Become a United States Citizen," Law Day Symposium sponsored by Southern California Chinese Lawyers Association, 1980; Representing Naturalization Clients," Lawyers Club of Los Angeles County, 1981; "The Naturalization Process," Seminar sponsored by International Daily News, 1982; "Adjustment of Status to Permanent Residence," Los Angeles County Bar Association Immigration Section Winter Retreat, 1989. General Attorney (Nationality), Immigration and Naturalization Service, Los Angeles, California, 1976-1980. Pro Bono Attorney for Indigents represented by Los Angeles County Bar Association/American Immigration Lawyers Association Haitian Legal Assistance Project, 1983-1984. I *Member:* Los Angeles County Bar Association (Member, Immigration Section); State Bar of California (Member, Estate Planning, Trust and Probate Section); American Immigration Lawyers Association. (Certified Specialist, Immigration and Nationality Law, the State Bar of California Board of Legal Specialization).

## BIGELOW, MOORE & TYRE
Established in 1984
EASTON HOUSE
540 SOUTH MARENGO AVENUE
**PASADENA, CALIFORNIA 91101**
Telephone: 213-681-0174; 818-792-6806
Telecopier: 818-792-1402

*Corporate, Tax, General and Business Litigation, Entertainment, Real Estate, Appellate Practice, Health Care, First Amendment, Administrative Law, Probate and Estate Planning.*

FIRM PROFILE: Bigelow, Moore & Tyre is a full service business firm concentrating its practice in the areas of general business transactions and litigation (including corporate and partnership formation & dissolution), real estate transactions, federal and state taxation (including tax Litigation and tax planning), entertainment law, Probate and estate planning, trust law, health care law, employment law and administrative law. The Firm routinely handles complicated litigation matters in all trial and appellate courts, both state and federal, in the southern half of California. All of the Firm's attorneys are members of the Pasadena Bar Association Lawyer Referral Service; and are actively involved in community and civic affairs. Originally, formed in February 1984 in Sherman Oaks, CA as "Bigelow & Moore", the Firm relocated to Pasadena, CA in January 1985. Since June 1989, the Firm's offices have been located in a two story 1905 Craftsman house, converted for use as an office.

### MEMBERS OF THE FIRM

**FRANKLIN T. BIGELOW, JR.,** born Lawrence, Massachusetts, September 17, 1949; admitted to bar, 1978, California; 1979, U.S. District Court, Central District of California and U.S. Court of Appeals, Ninth Circuit; 1983, U.S. Supreme Court. *Education:* Pomona College (B.A, 1972); Universite de la Sorbonne Nouvelle; Loyola University of Los Angeles (J.D., 1978). Member, 1976-1978 and President, 1977-1978, Jessup International Law Honors Moot Court Board. Co-Founder and Executive Editor, Loyola International and Comparative Law Annual, 1977-1978. Member, Loyola Law Review, 1976-1977. *Member:* Pasadena (Member, Sections on: Real Estate and Litigation), Los Angeles County (Member, Sections on: Litigation, Real Property, Business and Corporations Law) and American (Member, Sections on: Business Law, Entertainment and Sports Industries, International Law and Practice) Bar Associations; State Bar of California. **REPORTED CASES:** White Dragon Productions v. Performance Guarantees, Inc., 196 Cal. App. 3d 163 (1987). **PRACTICE AREAS:** Corporate Law; Entertainment Law; Business Litigation; Real Estate Law; Appellate Practice.

**JOSEPH F. MOORE,** born New York, N.Y., September, 7, 1948; admitted to bar, 1975, California; 1978, U.S. Tax Court; 1979, U.S. Court of Appeals, Ninth Circuit and U.S. District Court, Central District of California. *Education:* Pomona College (B.A., 1971); Suffolk University Law School (J.D., 1975); University of San Diego (LL.M., 1984). *Member:* Pasadena, Los Angeles County and American (Member, Taxation Section) Bar Associations; State Bar of California. (Certified Specialist in Taxation Law, The State Bar of California Board of Legal Specialization). **REPORTED CASES:** Williams v. Commissioner, T.C. Memo 1989-439; 935 F.2d 1066 (9th Cir. 1991); Cole v. Commissioner, 863 F.2d 34 (9th Cir. 1988); Naftel v. Commissioner, 85 T.C. 527 (1985); Allen v. Crocker National Bank et al., 733 F.2d 642 (9th Cir. 1984). **PRACTICE AREAS:** Federal and State Taxation; Real Estate Law; Corporate Law.

**JAMES S. TYRE,** born Los Angeles, California, April 14, 1953; admitted to bar, 1978, California; 1979, U.S. District Court, Central District of California and U.S. Court of Appeals, 9th Circuit; 1981, U.S. District Court, Southern District of California; 1982, U.S. Supreme Court. *Education:* Dartmouth College (A.B., cum laude, 1975); Loyola University of Los Angeles (J.D., cum laude, 1978). Member: St. Thomas More Law Honor Society; Jessup Moot Court Honors Board, 1976-1978 and Loyola Law Review, 1976-1977. Articles Editor, Loyola of Los Angeles International and Comparative Law Annual, 1977-1978. *Member:* Pasadena, Century City, Beverly Hills, Los Angeles County and American (Member, Antitrust Law, Law Practice Management, General Practice, Health Law, Individual Rights & Responsibilities and Litigation Sections) Bar Associations; State Bar of California (Member, Committee to Confer with California Medical Association, 1989-1991); National Health Lawyers Association; California Society for Healthcare Attorneys; Association of Business Trial Lawyers. **REPORTED CASES:** Nahrstedt v. Lakeside Village Condominium Assn., 8 Cal. 4th 361 (1994) (briefed and argued as Amicus Curiae); Miller v. Nestande, 192 Cal. App. 3d 191 (1987); Day v. Rosenthal, 170 Cal. App. 3d 1125 (1985); Santa Clarita Water Co. v. Lyons, 161 Cal. App. 3d 450

*(This Listing Continued)*

(1984); Maple Properties v. Harris, 158 Cal. App. 3d 997 (1984); Moskowitz v. Superior Court, 137 Cal. App. 3d 313 (1982). **PRACTICE AREAS:** Corporate Law; Business Litigation; Health Care Law; First Amendment; Real Estate Law; Appellate Practice.

### ASSOCIATES

**ANNE REID OPPERMANN,** born Seattle, Washington, July 25, 1958; admitted to bar, 1986, California; 1993, U.S. District Court, Central District of California and U.S. Tax Court. *Education:* Seattle Pacific University; Occidental College (A.B., 1980); McGeorge School of the Law, University of the Pacific (J.D., with honors, 1986). *Member:* Los Angeles County, Pasadena and American Bar Associations; State Bar of California. **LANGUAGES:** Russian and French. **PRACTICE AREAS:** General Litigation; Business Litigation; Corporate Law; Non-Profit Organizations; Charitable Giving.

### OF COUNSEL

**TIMOTHY D. HUMMEL,** born Pasadena, California, July 24, 1949; admitted to bar, 1979, California and U.S. District Court, Central District of California; 1993, U.S. Tax Court. *Education:* Pomona College (B.A., 1971); California State University, Los Angeles; Valley University School (J.D., 1978). *Member:* Los Angeles County (Member, Probate, Trust Law and Taxation Sections), Pasadena (Member Sections on: Probate, Estate Planning and Trust Law, Co-Chair, 1988-1991; Taxation; Real Property) and American Bar Associations; State Bar of California. (Certified Specialist, Probate, Estate Planning and Trust Law, The State Bar of California Board of Legal Specialization). **PRACTICE AREAS:** Estate Planning Law; Fiduciary Income Tax; Estate and Gift Tax; Probate and Trust; Conservatorship, Guardianship Administration; Probate Litigation.

REFERENCE: Citizens Bank.

---

## BISNO & SAMBERG
201 SOUTH LAKE AVENUE, SUITE 702
**PASADENA, CALIFORNIA 91101-3015**
Telephone: 818-585-8899
Fax: 818-585-1899

FIRM PROFILE: Bisno & Samberg's commercial litigation practice encompasses debtor/creditor litigation, related bankruptcy matters, banking and business litigation matters. The firm's tort litigation practice includes wrongful death, medical malpractice, premises liability and products liability matters. The firm serves international clients and is approved by universities and government courts in Europe to provide on site training and supervision to European law school graduates.

### MEMBERS OF FIRM

**JOHN M. SAMBERG,** admitted to bar, 1984, California. *Education:* University of California at Los Angeles (B.A., 1981); Southwestern University School of Law (J.D., magna cum laude, 1984). Recipient, Seven American Jurisprudence Awards; Two National Moot Court Championships. Court Appointed Arbitrator. *Member:* Los Angeles County Bar Association; State Bar of California.

**PETER BISNO,** admitted to bar, 1979, California; 1980, U.S. Tax Court. *Education:* Occidental College (B.A., 1973); Whittier College (J.D., 1978). Court Arbitrator, Los Angeles County Superior Court. *Member:* Los Angeles County Bar Association; State Bar of California.

### ASSOCIATE

**DENNETTE A. MULVANEY,** admitted to bar, 1988, California and U.S. District Court, Central, Northern and Eastern Districts of California; 1989, Arizona. *Education:* University of Arizona (B.S., 1983; J.D., 1986). *Member:* Los Angeles County Bar Association; State Bar of California; State Bar of Arizona; Los Angeles Bankruptcy Forum; Financial Lawyers Conference.

### OF COUNSEL

**SCOTT C. TIPS,** admitted to bar, 1980, California. *Education:* University of California at Los Angeles (A.B., magna cum laude, 1976) Universite de Paris I, Paris, France; Boalt Hall School of Law, University of California at Berkeley (J.D., 1980). Associate Editor, 1978-1979 and Managing Editor, 1979-1980, California Law Review.

REPRESENTATIVE CLIENTS: CenFed Bank; Wilshire Credit Corporation; Imperial Thrift & Loan; Credit Managers Association of California; Reliance Insurance Company; State of California; FDIC; Robinson Knife Manufacturing Co., Inc.; Inter/Media Advertising.

## LAW OFFICES OF NORMAN F. BOXLEY

*Established in 1992*

**1100 EAST GREEN STREET
PASADENA, CALIFORNIA 91106-2513**
Telephone: 818-395-7891
Facsimile: 818-395-7808

*General Civil Trial and Appellate litigation representing Insurance Companies and their insureds, defense of fraud claims, defense of product manufacturers in product liability litigation, defense of building and homeowners, construction contractors, Design Professionals, Architects, Engineers and Land Surveyors in construction and construction defect matters involving property damage to structures, claims of delay and faulty construction management or defective construction and defective design as well as personal injury allegedly caused by claimed defects in construction or design.*

**NORMAN F. BOXLEY,** born Pasadena, California, June 3, 1946; admitted to bar, 1975, California and U.S. District Court, Central, Northern and Eastern Districts of California; 1986, U.S. Supreme Court. *Education:* California State University at San Francisco (B.A., 1972); Hastings College of Law, University of California (J.D., 1975). *Member:* American Bar Association; State Bar of California; Defense Research Institute; Association of Southern California Defense Counsel; Lawyer Pilots Bar Association. [1st Lt., U.S. Army, 1966-1967]. *PRACTICE AREAS:* Fraudulent Claims Defense; Product Liability; Construction Defect Claims; General Insurance Defense.

---

## BOYLE, OLSON & ROBINSON

*Established in 1927*

**170 SOUTH EUCLID AVENUE
PASADENA, CALIFORNIA 91101-2484**
Telephone: 818-796-7181; 792-6191
Fax: 818-796-8652

*General Civil and Trial Practice in all State and Federal Courts. Corporation, Probate, Estate Planning, Family, Construction, State and Federal Tax Law.*

### MEMBERS OF FIRM

**JAMES B. BOYLE, JR.,** born Pasadena, California, August 18, 1930; admitted to bar, 1955, California. *Education:* Stanford University (A.B., 1952; LL.B., 1954). Phi Delta Phi. *Member:* Pasadena (President, 1977-1978), Los Angeles County and American Bar Associations; State Bar of California (Member, Sections on: Estate Planning, Trust and Probate Law; Business Law). *PRACTICE AREAS:* General Business Law; Family Law; Construction Law; Estate Planning.

**A. WILLIAM OLSON,** born Portland, Oregon, July 3, 1922; admitted to bar, 1951, California; 1971, U.S. Supreme Court. *Education:* University of Washington and University of California at Los Angeles (B.A., 1947); University of Southern California (J.D., 1950). Phi Alpha Delta. Deputy Assistant Attorney General, 1971-1972 and Assistant Attorney General, 1972-1973, Internal Security Division, Department of Justice. *Member:* Pasadena (President, 1978-1979), Los Angeles County and American Bar Associations; State Bar of California (Member, Sections on: Estate Planning, Trust and Probate Law; Business Law). *PRACTICE AREAS:* Estate Planning; Probate and Trust Law; General Business Law.

**EDWARD O. ROBINSON,** born Pasadena, California, April 18, 1939; admitted to bar, 1964, California. *Education:* Princeton University and University of Southern California (B.S., 1960); University of Southern California (J.D., 1963). *Member:* Pasadena and Los Angeles County Bar Associations; State Bar of California (Member, Estate Planning, Trust and Probate Law Section). *PRACTICE AREAS:* Probate and Trust Law; Estate Planning.

**STEPHEN J. MILLER,** born Marlborough, Massachusetts, April 16, 1960; admitted to bar, 1986, California. *Education:* University of California at Los Angeles (B.A., cum laude, 1983); University of Southern California (J.D., cum laude, 1986). Staff Member, 1984-1985 and Note Editor, 1985-1986, Southern California Law Review. *Member:* Pasadena and Los Angeles County Bar Associations; State Bar of California. *PRACTICE AREAS:* Business Litigation; Corporate Law; Real Property Law; Family Law; Partnership Law.

**ANN SIMMONS BOUTIN,** born Hollywood, California, August 22, 1961; admitted to bar, 1987, California. *Education:* University of California

*(This Listing Continued)*

---

at Davis (B.S., 1983); McGeorge School of Law, University of the Pacific (J.D., with distinction, 1987). Phi Delta Phi. Member, Traynor Society. Recipient, American Jurisprudence Award in Secured Transactions. Author: "International Mortgage Co. v. John P. Butler Accountancy Corp.: Third Party Liability-Accountants Beware," Pacific Law Journal, Vol. 18, April, 1987. *Member:* Pasadena, Los Angeles County and American Bar Associations; State Bar of California (Member, Estate Planning, Trust and Probate Law Section). *PRACTICE AREAS:* Estate Planning and Probate Law.

**JAMES B. BOYLE** (1927-1991).

**J. KENNETH CAMERON** (1975-1984).

**JOHN R. ATWILL, JR.** (1948-1985).

**J. DEAN BARRICK** (1927-1978).

REPRESENTATIVE CLIENTS: Alhambra Foundry Co., Ltd.; California Hydroforming Co.; Citizens Business Bank of Pasadena; Crown City Grinding Co.; Eel River Sales Co.; Jobson, Jordan, Harrison & Schulz, Inc.; J. Harold Mitchell Co. (Landscape & Irrigation Supplies); Imperial Valley Lumber Co.; Neff Instrument Corp.; San Rafael Investment Corp.; Ben F. Smith Inc. (Concrete Contractors); Trail Chemical Corp.; Costa Macaroni Mfg. Co.; Perini Building Co.; Merchant Magazine; Detoy Foundation; Murray Foundation; Zimmerman Foundation.

REFERENCES: Sanwa Bank of California, (Pasadena, Calif., Main Office); Bank of America National Trust & Savings Assn. (Pasadena, Calif., Main Office); Citizens Business Bank (Pasadena, Calif., Main Office).

---

## DARRELL G. BROOKE

**30 NORTH RAYMOND, SUITE 713
PASADENA, CALIFORNIA 91103-3930**
Telephone: 818-795-7400
Fax: 818-795-7496

*Estate Planning, Tax, Probate and Business Law.*

**DARRELL G. BROOKE,** born Pittsburgh, Pennsylvania, February 15, 1957; admitted to bar, 1985, California. *Education:* University of Southern California (B.S., 1981); Southwestern University (J.D., 1984). Instructor: "Probate Practice I"; "Advanced Probate Practice"; "Post-Death Estate Administration"; "Wills and Trusts Seminar," Paralegal Program, University of Southern California, California 1984-1990. Registered Contract Advisor, Sports Seminars, Inc. *Member:* State Bar of California (Member, Probate Committee, Estate Planning, Probate and Trust Section); American Bar Association (Real Property, Probate and Trust Section: Lifetime and Testamentary Charitable Gift Planning Committee and Lifetime Transfer: Transfer Tax Issues Committee). Old Pasadena Business & Professional Association (President, 1995—). [U.S. Army, 1975-1978]. (Also Of Counsel to Hart & Watters, Los Angeles). *PRACTICE AREAS:* Estate Planning; Tax; Probate; Business Law.

---

## BUNN AND BUNN

*Established in 1965*

**410 CORPORATE CENTER BUILDING
225 SOUTH LAKE AVENUE
PASADENA, CALIFORNIA 91101**
Telephone: 818-792-9421
Telecopier: 818-796-6839

*Estate Planning, Trust and Probate Administration and Litigation.*

**WILEY D. BUNN,** born Los Angeles, California, July 22, 1929; admitted to bar, 1953, California and U.S. District Court, Central District of California. *Education:* University of Southern California (A.B., 1950; LL.B., 1953). Phi Beta Kappa. *Member:* Pasadena and Los Angeles County Bar Associations; State Bar of California. (Certified Specialist, Estate Planning, Trust and Probate Law, The State Bar of California Board of Legal Specialization). *PRACTICE AREAS:* Estate Planning; Trust; Probate Law.

**DAVID G. BUNN,** born Pasadena, California, June 24, 1959; admitted to bar, 1985, California. *Education:* Westmont College (B.A., 1981); Pepperdine University (J.D., 1985). Adjunct Professor of Law, University of West Los Angeles School of Law, 1992—. *Member:* Pasadena and Los Angeles County Bar Associations; State Bar of California. (Certified Specialist, Estate Planning, Trust and Probate Law, The State Bar of California Board of Legal Specialization). *PRACTICE AREAS:* Estate Planning; Probate and Trust Administration and Litigation.

REFERENCE: Sanwa Bank, Pasadena, California.

## WILLIAM R. BURKITT
716 MUTUAL SAVINGS BUILDING
301 EAST COLORADO BOULEVARD
**PASADENA, CALIFORNIA 91101**
Telephone: 818-304-0395
Telecopier: 818-304-0032

*Family Law including Custody.*

**WILLIAM R. BURKITT,** born Santa Monica, California, August 14, 1941; admitted to bar, 1967, California. *Education:* University of Southern California (B.S., 1963; J.D., 1966). Phi Delta Phi (Magister, 1965-1966). Senior Law Clerk, Judge A. Andrew Hauk, Senior Chief Judge, U.S. District Court, Central District of California, 1966-1967. *Member:* Pasadena and Los Angeles County (Member, Family Law Section) Bar Associations; The State Bar of California (Member: Standing Committee on Child Custody and Visitation, 1982-1983; University of Southern California Law Center Alumni Association Board of Directors, 1985-1988).

---

## BURNS, AMMIRATO, PALUMBO, MILAM & BARONIAN

*A PROFESSIONAL LAW CORPORATION*
Established in 1989

65 NORTH RAYMOND AVENUE, 2ND FLOOR
**PASADENA, CALIFORNIA 91103-3919**
Telephone: 818-796-5053; 213-258-8282
Fax: 818-792-3078

**Long Beach, California Office:** One World Trade Center, Suite 1200.
Telephone: 310-436-8338; 714-952-1047. Fax: 310-432-6049.

*General Civil and Trial Practice in all Courts. Insurance Defense, Products Liability, Toxic Torts, Construction Litigation, Medical Malpractice, Personal Injury, Tort, Subrogation and Wrongful Termination.*

FIRM PROFILE: *Burns, Ammirato, Palumbo, Milam & Baronian is a firm of experienced civil litigators, with offices in Pasadena and Long Beach, which represents clients in all courts in California.*

*One attorney is responsible for the case from start to finish, and the firm is committed to lean staffing to minimize costs.*

*The firm handles general liability matters, including automobile, construction defect, premises liability, products liability, wrongful death claims, and business litigation, as well as environmental law, insurance coverage analysis, real estate litigation, professional malpractice, sexual assault and abuse cases, wrongful termination, and suspicious claims litigation. The firm also handles appellate practice, through our appellate department.*

*Burns, Ammirato, Palumbo, Milam & Baronian lawyers have more than 30 years experience in arbitration and mediation matters.*

*Both plaintiff and defense lawyers frequently seek out Burns, Ammirato, Palumbo, Milam & Baronian to conduct settlement conferences on high exposure matters such as intentional torts, auto, road design, premises liability, and medical malpractice.*

**MICHAEL A. BURNS,** born San Francisco, California, October 21, 1939; admitted to bar, 1970, California. *Education:* St. Joseph's College (B.S., 1961); Southwestern University (J.D., 1970). Arbitrator, Los Angeles County Panel of Arbitrators, 1980—. *Member:* Los Angeles County and American Bar Associations; State Bar of California; Southern California Defense Counsel; American Board of Trial Advocates; International Association of Defense Counsel. *PRACTICE AREAS:* Insurance Defense Law; Products Liability Law; Construction Law.

**VINCENT A. AMMIRATO,** born Somerville, New Jersey, December 6, 1942; admitted to bar, 1972, California and U.S. District Court, Central and Southern Districts of California; 1975, U.S. Supreme Court. *Education:* California State University at Long Beach (B.A., 1968); University of San Diego (J.D., 1971). Phi Alpha Delta. Deputy City Prosecutor, City of Long Beach, 1972. *Member:* Long Beach and Los Angeles County Bar Associations; The State Bar of California; Italian-American Lawyers of Los Angeles; National Order of Barristers; American Board of Trial Advocates. [With USA, active duty, 1966-1968]. Resident, Long Bch. *PRACTICE AREAS:* Products Liability; Construction Accident; General Trial Work.

**BRUCE PALUMBO,** born Los Angeles, California, April 23, 1947; admitted to bar, 1972, California. *Education:* University of California at Santa Barbara (B.A., 1969); Loyola University of Los Angeles (J.D., 1972).

*(This Listing Continued)*

*Member:* Los Angeles County and American Bar Associations; State Bar of California; Southern California Defense Counsel. **REPORTED CASES:** Imperial Cas. and Indem. Co. v. Sogomonian (Cal App. 2 Dist. 1988), 198 Cal App 3d 169. *PRACTICE AREAS:* Products Liability Law; Insurance Defense Law; Toxic Torts; Construction Defects; Construction Coverage.

**JEFFREY L. MILAM,** born Santa Monica, California, December 18, 1950; admitted to bar, 1976, California. *Education:* Amherst College (B.A., cum laude, 1973); University of Santa Clara (J.D., cum laude, 1976). *Member:* Los Angeles County and American Bar Associations; State Bar of California; Association of Southern California Defense Counsel. *PRACTICE AREAS:* Products Liability Law.

**ROBERT H. BARONIAN,** born Los Angeles, California, October 11, 1953; admitted to bar, 1978, California; 1981, U.S. District Court, Central District of California. *Education:* California State University at Northridge (B.A., cum laude, 1975); Whittier College School of Law (J.D., 1978). Member, Whittier Law Review, 1977-1978. *Member:* Los Angeles County (Member, Trial Lawyers Section) and American Bar Associations; State Bar of California. *PRACTICE AREAS:* Products Liability Law; Toxic Torts.

---

**NORMAND A. AYOTTE,** born Los Angeles, California, October 28, 1957; admitted to bar, 1987, California. *Education:* University of Southern California (B.A., 1980); Loyola Law School (J.D., 1987). *Member:* Pasadena, Los Angeles County and American Bar Associations; State Bar of California; Association of Southern California Defense Counsel. *PRACTICE AREAS:* Premises Liability.

**COLLEEN CLARK,** born Deer Park, California, January 11, 1954; admitted to bar, 1981, California and U.S. District Court, Central District of California; 1982, U.S. Court of Appeals, Ninth Circuit. *Education:* Humboldt State University (B.A., 1977); Southwestern University (J.D., 1980). *Member:* State Bar of California; Pasadena Young Lawyers Association (Treasurer, 1982-1983; President, 1983-1984); Association of Southern California Defense Counsel. *PRACTICE AREAS:* Construction Defect; Corporate.

**VALERIE JULIEN-PETO,** born Niagara Falls, New York, November 17, 1961; admitted to bar, 1990, California; 1991, U.S. District Court, Central District of California and U.S. Court of Appeals, Ninth Circuit. *Education:* Universidad de Sevilla; DePauw University (B.A., 1983); Southwestern University School of Law (J.D., 1990). *Member:* Order of the Barristers; Moot Court Honors Program. Recipient, Best Brief, Florida Bar, 1989. Judicial Extern for the Hon. Arthur L. Alarcon, Ninth Circuit, U.S. Court of Appeals. *Member:* Los Angeles County and American Bar Associations; State Bar of California. *LANGUAGES:* Spanish. **REPORTED CASES:** Ramirez v. MacAdam (Cal. App. 2 Dist. 1993) 13 Cal. App. 4th 1638. *PRACTICE AREAS:* General Civil Litigation; Appellate Law.

**SUSAN E. LUHRING,** born San Francisco, California, January 26, 1960; admitted to bar, 1985, California; 1986, U.S. District Court, Southern District of California. *Education:* University of California at Los Angeles (B.A., cum laude, 1981); University of San Diego (J.D., 1985). *Member:* San Diego County, Los Angeles County and American Bar Associations; State Bar of California; San Diego Defense Lawyers Association; Association of Southern California Defense Counsel. *PRACTICE AREAS:* General Civil Litigation.

**GRACE C. MORI,** born Bern, Switzerland, August 5, 1968; admitted to bar, 1993, California and U.S District Court, Central District of California. *Education:* University of California at Riverside (B.S., 1989); Southwestern University School of Law (J.D., 1993). *Member:* State Bar of California. Resident, Long Bch. *PRACTICE AREAS:* General Civil Litigation.

**MICHAEL P. VICENCIA,** born Bellflower, California, April 28, 1964; admitted to bar, 1990, California and U.S. District Court, Southern, Central, Northern and Eastern Districts of California. *Education:* California State University, Fullerton (B.A., 1987); McGeorge School of Law, University of the Pacific (J.D., 1990). Order of Barristers. *Member:* Los Angeles County Bar Association; State Bar of California. Resident, LOng Bch. *PRACTICE AREAS:* Civil Defense.

**MICHAEL E. WENZEL,** born Minneapolis, Minnesota, May 25, 1945; admitted to bar, 1975, California and U.S. District Court, Central and Southern Districts of California. *Education:* College of St. Thomas (B.A., 1967); Pepperdine University (J.D., 1973). Phi Alpha Delta. Assistant L.A. Claims Manager. *Member:* Los Angeles County and Orange County Bar Associations; The State Bar of California; Association of Southern California Defense Counsel. [Capt., U.S. Marine Corps, 1967-1970]. Resident,

*(This Listing Continued)*

## BURNS, AMMIRATO, PALUMBO, MILAM & BARONIAN, A PROFESSIONAL LAW CORPORATION, Pasadena—Continued

Long Bch. **PRACTICE AREAS:** General Trial; Premises; Malpractice; Construction; Insurance Defense.

REPRESENTATIVE CLIENTS: Ohio Casualty Co.; Crawford & Co.; Anheuser Busch Companies, Inc.; Economy Fire & Casualty; Prudential LMI; Maryland Casualty; Nationwide Mutual Insurance Co.; CIGNA; City of Pasadena; The Hartford Ins. Co.; Emerson Electric; Sears, Roebuck & Co.; National American Ins. Co.; Sedgewick, James & Co.
REFERENCE: First Los Angeles Bank.

## BURTON & NORRIS

35 SOUTH RAYMOND AVENUE, FOURTH FLOOR
**PASADENA, CALIFORNIA 91105**
Telephone: 818-449-8300
Fax: 818-449-4417

*Trial and Appellate Litigation in all State and Federal Courts including Civil Rights, Commercial, Securities, Intellectual Property, Professional Responsibility and Personal Injury. Medical Malpractice and Criminal Law.*

**JOHN C. BURTON,** born Pasadena, California, February 20, 1953; admitted to bar, 1979, California. *Education:* University of California at Los Angeles (B.A., 1976); Hastings College of the Law, University of California (J.D., 1978). Adjunct Professor of Law, Torts, University of West Los Angeles, 1981-1989. Extern, California Supreme Court Justice Stanley Mosk, 1978. Board of Directors, Police Misconduct Lawyers Referral Service, 1988—. *Member:* State Bar of California. **REPORTED CASES:** Montiel v. City of Los Angeles, 2 F.3d 335 (9th Cir. 1993); Greenstreet v. County of San Bernardino, 41 F.3d 1306 (9th Cir. 1994).

**DONALD G. NORRIS,** born Palo Alto, California, January 20, 1953; admitted to bar, 1979, California. *Education:* University of California at Los Angeles (B.A., 1976); Stanford University (J.D., 1979). Articles Editor, Stanford Journal of International Law, 1977-1979. Law Clerk to Judge Lawrence T. Lydick, U.S. District Court, Central District of California, 1979-1980. Member, Board of Directors of Justicia, Spanish-Speaking Lawyer Referral Service, 1982-1985. *Member:* Los Angeles County Bar Association; The State Bar of California; Association of Business Trial Lawyers. **LANGUAGES:** Spanish.

**VICTORIA E. KING,** born San Antonio, Texas, October 11, 1950; admitted to bar, 1992, California. *Education:* Fordham University (B.A., 1988); University of California at Los Angeles (J.D., 1991). *Member:* Beverly Hills and American Bar Associations; State Bar of California; Black Women Lawyers.

REFERENCE: Bank of America (Pasadena).

## JOSEPH D. BUSSONE

Established in 1986

225 SOUTH LAKE AVENUE, NINTH FLOOR
**PASADENA, CALIFORNIA 91101-3021**
Telephone: 818-583-9135
Fax: 818-583-9137
Email: bussone@msn.com
URL: http://www.bussone.com

*General Civil and Trial Practice in State and Federal Courts. Personal Injury, Professional Negligence, Construction, Employment, Business, Real Estate and Criminal Law.*

**JOSEPH D. BUSSONE,** born Joliet, Illinois, February 3, 1954; admitted to bar, 1983, California; 1984, U.S. District Court, Central District of California. *Education:* Loyola University of Chicago (B.A., 1976; M.B.A, 1979); Southwestern University School of Law (J.D., 1982). *Member:* Los Angeles County and American Bar Associations; State Bar of California; California Trial Lawyers Association; The Association of Trial Lawyers of America.

## CAIRNS, DOYLE, LANS, NICHOLAS & SONI

A LAW CORPORATION

NINTH FLOOR
225 SOUTH LAKE AVENUE
**PASADENA, CALIFORNIA 91101**
Telephone: 818-683-3111
Telecopier: 818-683-4999

*General Civil and Trial Practice in all State and Federal Courts. Banking, Bankruptcy, Corporation, Business, Insurance, Negligence, Malpractice, Real Property, Construction, Motor Transport, Employment Law, Fraud and Toxic Torts.*

**JOHN D. CAIRNS,** born Los Angeles, California, September 2, 1942; admitted to bar, 1972, California, U.S. Court of Appeals, Ninth Circuit and U.S. Supreme Court. *Education:* University of Southern California (B.A., 1969); Notre Dame Law Program in England and University of San Diego (J.D., 1972). Recipient: First place award, University of San Diego Appellant Moot Court Competition, 1971. Arbitrator, Los Angeles Superior Court, 1980—. Judge Pro Tempore, Los Angeles and Pasadena Municipal Court, 1988—. Mediator, Los Angeles Superior Court, 1988—. *Member:* Pasadena (Member, Litigation Section), Los Angeles (Member, Litigation and Environmental Sections) and American (Member, Litigation Section) Bar Associations; State Bar of California; Association of Southern California Defense Counsel; Defense Research Institute; Professional Liability Underwriting Society. **PRACTICE AREAS:** Insurance Defense; General Civil Litigation; Malpractice; Toxic Torts.

**JOHN C. DOYLE,** born Los Angeles, California, September 5, 1953; admitted to bar, 1978, California; 1979, U.S. District Court, Central District of California; 1994, U.S. Supreme Court. *Education:* Santa Clara University (B.A., 1975; J.D., 1978). Articles Editor, Santa Clara Law Review, 1977-1978. Author: "Contribution and Indemnity Collide with Comparative Negligence—The New Doctrine of Equitable Indemnity," 18 Santa Clara Law Review 779, 1978; republished, California Reporter Advance Sheets, 152 Cal. Rptr. No. 5. Law Clerk to Hon. Francis C. Whelan, U.S. District Court, Central District of California, 1978-1979. Member, Children's Hospital of Los Angeles Institutional Review Board, 1983-1989. Arbitrator, Los Angeles Superior Court Judicial Arbitration Panel, 1986—. Judge ProTempore, Los Angeles Superior Court, 1993—. *Member:* Los Angeles County and Pasadena Bar Associations; State Bar of California; Association of Southern California Defense Counsel; Defense Research Institute. **PRACTICE AREAS:** Insurance Law; Insurance Defense; Construction and General Civil Litigation.

**STEPHEN M. LANS,** born New York, N.Y., August 5, 1952; admitted to bar, 1978, California; 1979, U.S. District Court, Southern and Central Districts of California and U.S. Court of Appeals, Ninth Circuit. *Education:* Pomona College (B.A., magna cum laude, 1974); Columbia University (J.D., 1978). Associate Editor, Human Rights Law Review, 1977-1978. *Member:* Pasadena, Los Angeles County and American Bar Associations; State Bar of California; Association of Business Trial Lawyers. **LANGUAGES:** Spanish. **PRACTICE AREAS:** General Commercial Litigation; Banking Law; Bankruptcy.

**FRANCISCO J. NICHOLAS,** born Los Angeles, California, April 27, 1955; admitted to bar, 1983, California and U.S. District Court, Central District of California. *Education:* University of California at Los Angeles; University of California at Santa Barbara (B.A., 1978); Loyola University (J.D., 1982). Member, Joseph Scott Moot Court Honors Program. Arbitrator, Los Angeles Superior Court, 1992—. *Member:* Los Angeles County and American Bar Associations; State Bar of California; Association of Business Trial Lawyers. **PRACTICE AREAS:** General Civil and Business Litigation; Employment Litigation; Insurance Defense.

**ROHINI SONI** (1956-1994).

REPRESENTATIVE CLIENTS: Alliance General Insurance Company; Allstate Insurance Companies; Amelco Corp.; Burger King Corporation; California Insurance Guarantee Association; California United Bank; CASC Corporation; CIGNA Insurance Companies; City of Pasadena; Cumis Insurance Society, Inc.; Employers Mutual Insurance Company; Erie Insurance; ESIS, Inc.; Forest Lawn Memorial Park Association; Industrial Indemnity; Manufacturers Bank; National Union Fire Insurance Company; Queen City Bank; State Farm Fire and Casualty Company; Olympia Industrial, Inc.; State Farm Mutual Automobile Company; Tokio Marine Insurance; Topa Insurance.

## ELIZABETH SPEDDING CALCIANO

*Established in 1982*

301 EAST COLORADO BOULEVARD
SUITE 626
**PASADENA, CALIFORNIA 91101**
Telephone: 818-792-2173
Fax: Available Upon Request

*Real Property, Business, Estate Planning and Probate Law.*

**ELIZABETH SPEDDING CALCIANO,** born Des Moines, Iowa, July 28, 1939; admitted to bar, 1977, California. *Education:* Radcliffe College (A.B., cum laude, 1961); Stanford University (M.A., 1962); Boalt Hall School of Law, University of California (J.D., 1977). Member, 1975-1977 and Treasurer, 1976-1977, Moot Court Board. *Member:* Pasadena (Member, Sections on: Real Property; Probate), Los Angeles County (Member, Real Property Section Executive Committee, 1988—; Co-Chair, Crocker Symposium, 1993; Chairman, General Real Property Subsection, 1981-1982, 1984-1985) and American Bar Associations; State Bar of California; San Gabriel Valley Estate Planning Council (Member, Board of Directors, 1988-1990; Secretary, 1993-1994; President, 1995-1996).

REPRESENTATIVE CLIENTS: Crawford Stores, Inc.; Pacific Clinics.
REFERENCE: Citizens Commercial Trust & Savings Bank.

## CARTER, CARLSON & ELLERMAN, LLP

SUITE 320, 301 EAST COLORADO BOULEVARD
**PASADENA, CALIFORNIA 91101**
Telephone: 818-796-6161
Telecopier: 818-796-0593

*Real Estate and Business Law and Litigation.*

### MEMBERS OF FIRM

**ROBERT E. CARTER,** born Oakland, California, May 18, 1931; admitted to bar, 1960, California. *Education:* University of Southern California (A.B., 1953; J.D., 1959). Order of the Coif; Phi Delta Phi. Member, Southern California Law Review, 1958-1959. *Member:* Pasadena (Trustee, 1985-1987; Vice-President, 1988-1989; President, 1990-1991), Los Angeles County (Chairman, 1986-1987, Real Property Section) and American Bar Associations; State Bar of California. [LTJG, USN, 1955-1958]. *PRACTICE AREAS:* Real Estate Law; Business Law.

**SCOTT W. CARLSON,** born Honolulu, Hawaii, July 29, 1957; admitted to bar, 1982, California. *Education:* University of California at Los Angeles (B.A., Economics, 1979; J.D., 1982). Phi Beta Kappa. Member, UCLA Moot Court Honors Program. *Member:* Pasadena (Treasurer, 1994; Section Leader, Real Estate Section) and Los Angeles County Bar Associations; State Bar of California. *PRACTICE AREAS:* Real Estate Law; Business Law; Litigation; Creditors' Rights Law.

**JANA ELLERMAN,** born Lubbock, Texas, October 10, 1957; admitted to bar, 1986, California. *Education:* Principia College (B.A., 1979); Loyola Law School (J.D., cum laude, 1986). *Member:* Loyola of Los Angeles Law Review, 1985; Saint Thomas More Law Honor Society. *Member:* Pasadena and Los Angeles County Bar Associations; State Bar of California. *PRACTICE AREAS:* Real Estate Law; Business Law; Litigation.

### OF COUNSEL

**ROBERT M. PETERSON,** born Pasadena, California, February 27, 1934; admitted to bar, 1960, California, U.S. District Court, Central District of California and U.S. Court of Appeals, 9th Circuit. *Education:* Pacific Union College (B.A., 1956); University of Southern California (J.D., 1959). Phi Alpha Delta; Order of the Coif. Associate Editor, University of Southern California Law Review, 1958-1959. *Member:* Pasadena Bar Association; State Bar of California. *PRACTICE AREAS:* Business Law; Real Property Law.

REPRESENTATIVE CLIENTS: Pasadena/San Maria Association of Realtors; CenFed Bank; Wells Fargo Bank Trust Department.
REFERENCE: Citizens Business Bank, Pasadena.

## DAVID C. CASHION

790 EAST COLORADO BOULEVARD, NINTH FLOOR
**PASADENA, CALIFORNIA 91101-2113**
Telephone: 818-796-9606
Facsimile: 818-792-5035

*Family, Personal Injury, Business, Probate and Commercial Law. General Civil and Trial Practice.*

**DAVID C. CASHION,** born Los Angeles, California, December 12, 1935; admitted to bar, 1962, California. *Education:* University of Southern California (A.B., 1957; J.D., 1960). Phi Delta Phi. Judge Pro Tem: Pasadena Municipal Court, 1975—; Los Angeles Municipal Court, 1981—. *Member:* Los Angeles County (Member, Family Law Section; Arbitrator, 1985—) and Pasadena (Secretary, 1972) Bar Associations; State Bar of California.

REFERENCE: Community Bank (Pasadena).

## JAY D. CHRISTENSEN AND ASSOCIATES

*Established in 1985*

225 SOUTH LAKE, NINTH FLOOR
**PASADENA, CALIFORNIA 91101**
Telephone: 818-568-2900
Fax: 818-568-1566

*General Healthcare Law, Managed Health Care Arrangements, Peer Review Issues, Related Litigation.*

FIRM PROFILE: *Jay D. Christensen and Associates is a specialty healthcare law firm. Our practice is limited entirely to representing hospitals, medical staff organizations, health maintenance organizations, independent physician associations, management services organizations, outpatient surgical clinics, professional practice entities and other healthcare providers and related entities. Our practice concentrates on licensure and operational issues; medical staff and related issues and litigation; managed healthcare contracting, organizations and arrangements; healthcare corporate and organizational issues; and related contracting, operational and litigation matters.*

*The firm's founding member, Jay D. Christensen, has been a general healthcare and hospital law practitioner in California for most of the past nineteen years. Mr. Christensen's general health law practice includes a variety of issues ranging from licensure and confidentiality issues to appellate practice in medical staff and anti-trust matters. He represents numerous hospitals, medical staff organizations, independent physician associations and practitioner professional entities.*

*The firm also has well established relationships with specialists and specialty firms for additional support in such areas as litigation, corporate law and securities and tax.*

**JAY D. CHRISTENSEN, P.C.,** born Logan, Utah, May 5, 1946; admitted to bar, 1975, California. *Education:* Brigham Young University (B.S.; M.S., cum laude, in Economics, 1970); University of Utah (J.D., cum laude, 1975). Phi Kappa Phi; Omicron Delta Epsilon. Member, University of Utah Law Review, 1974-1975. Author: "A Means of Scrutiny Limit to the State Action Exemption from the Antitrust Law," Utah Law Review, 1975. *Member:* American Bar Association (Member, Health Care Committee and Subcommittee Past Chairman, Antitrust Section, 1982-1987); State Bar of California; National Health Lawyers Association; American Academy of Healthcare Attorneys.

### OF COUNSEL

**STEPHEN G. AUER,** born Jackson, Michigan, September 15, 1947; admitted to bar, 1977, California and U.S. District Court, Southern District of California; 1981, U.S. District Court, Central District of California. *Education:* University of Dayton (B.S., in Economics and Political Science, 1969); University of San Diego (J.D., 1976). Recipient, Distinguished Trial Advocacy Award, American Board of Trial Advocates, 1975. Deputy District Attorney, District Attorneys Office, Los Angeles County, 1978-1981. Associate, Jenkins and Perry, San Diego, 1981-1982. Sole Practice, San Diego, 1982-1984. Judge Pro Tem, Santa Monica Superior Court and Municipal Court, 1987. *Member:* Los Angeles County Bar Association; State Bar of California; National Association of College and University Attorneys. [Lt., Naval Aviator, U.S. Navy, 1970-1971]

**GAIL M. BETZ,** born St. Louis, Missouri, August 20, 1951; admitted to bar, 1985, California. *Education:* University of Missouri (B.A., 1973); St. Louis University (B.S., magna cum laude, 1977); Loyola Marymount University (J.D., 1984). Registered Nurse, California, 1978. *Member:* State Bar

*(This Listing Continued)*

## JAY D. CHRISTENSEN AND ASSOCIATES, Pasadena—Continued

of California. *PRACTICE AREAS:* Health Care Law; Medical Malpractice Litigation.

REPRESENTATIVE CLIENTS: Catholic Healthcare West; Tenent Hospitals, Inc.; Charter Medical Corporation; USC Physician; Saint Joseph Medical Center (Burbank); St. John's Regional Medical Center (Oxnard); Mercy Healthcare Bakersfield; Granada Hills Community Hospital; St. Mary's Medical Center (Long Beach); USC University Hospital; Doctors Medical Center (Modesto); JFK Memorial Hospital (Indio); West Side District Hospital (Taft); Northridge Hospital Medical Staff; Kaweah Delta District Hospital-Medical Staff; Pacific Alliance Medical Center; Las Encinas Hospital; Blue Cross of California; Medical Management Associates; Advanced Medical Management; AV Medical Group (Lancaster); Oakview Medical Group IPA; Alta Medical Group; California Neuro Services; Comprehensive Hospital Physicians; California Primary Care Medical Group; Family/Seniors Medical Group; Marian IPA; Good Samaritan Medical Practice Association; HealthCare Partners Medical Group; East County Physicians Medical Group (San Diego); Viva Health Plan.

## CHRISTIE, PARKER & HALE, LLP

FIFTH FLOOR, WELLS FARGO BANK BUILDING
350 WEST COLORADO BOULEVARD
P.O. BOX 7068
**PASADENA, CALIFORNIA 91109-7068**
*Telephone:* 818-795-9900
*Los Angeles:* 213-681-1800
*Cable Address:* "Patlaw"
*Telex:* ITT 4995129 (CPH PSD)
*Telecopier:* 818-577-8800

*Irvine, California Office:* Suite 1440, 5 Park Plaza. Telephone: 714-476-0757.

*Patent, Trademark and Copyright Law. Unfair Competition, Trade Secrets, Computer Law, Biotechnology, Licensing, Antitrust and Complex Business Litigation.*

*FIRM PROFILE: Christie, Parker and Hale, LLP, has for over fifty years specialized in intellectual property law and the handling of a broad range of patent, trademark, copyright, trade secret, litigation and related licensing and antitrust matters. The firm prepares and prosecutes domestic and foreign patent and trademark applications, and has established a network of carefully selected associates in all foreign countries. Integral to the firm's practice is the resolution and litigation of disputes involving prosecution, and defense of infringement of the full range of intellectual property rights. Technical expertise of the firm's lawyers covers a broad range of the electrical, chemical and mechanical arts, including in-depth experience in the field of computer science.*

### MEMBERS OF FIRM

**JAMES B. CHRISTIE** (1904-1959).

**ROBERT L. PARKER** (1920-1980).

**D. BRUCE PROUT,** born Glendale, California, June 26, 1934; admitted to bar, 1963, California and U.S. District Court, Central and Northern Districts of California; 1983, U.S. Court of Appeals for the Federal Circuit; registered to practice before U.S. Patent and Trademark Office. *Education:* University of Southern California (B.S.E.E., 1957; J.D., 1962). Eta Kappa Nu; Tau Beta Pi; Phi Alpha Delta. *Member:* Los Angeles County (Secretary, 1981-1982 and Chairman, 1982-1983, Law Office Management Section), Pasadena and American Bar Associations; The State Bar of California (Member, Executive Committee Law Office Management Section, 1981-1984); American Intellectual Property Law Association; International Patent and Trademark Association. *PRACTICE AREAS:* Domestic and International Patents; Copyrights and Trademarks; Computer Technology.

**HAYDEN A. CARNEY,** born Toledo, Ohio, June 6, 1936; admitted to bar, 1964, California; registered to practice before U.S. Patent and Trademark Office. *Education:* Webb Institute of Naval Architecture (B.S.N.A. and M.E., 1958); University of Toledo and University of Southern California (LL.B., 1964). Phi Alpha Delta. California State Bar Designee to Board of Directors, California Crime Technological Research Foundation, 1972-1976. Member, Society of Naval Architects and Marine Engineers. Member, Advisory Board, U.S. Patent Quarterly 2nd, 1988—. *Member:* Pasadena, Los Angeles County and American Bar Associations; The State Bar of California. *PRACTICE AREAS:* Intellectual Property Licensing and Taxation; Domestic and International Patent and Trademark Prosecution; Mechanical and Physical Technologies.

**RICHARD J. WARD, JR.,** born Chicago, Illinois, May 10, 1936; admitted to bar, 1965, California; U.S. Court of Appeals, Ninth and Seventh Circuits; U.S. District Court, Central, Northern and Southern Districts of California; U.S. District Court, Southern District of New York; registered to practice before U.S. Patent and Trademark Office. *Education:* St. Louis University (B.S.E.E., 1958); University of Southern California (J.D., 1964). Phi Delta Phi; Pi Mu Epsilon; Alpha Sigma Nu. Lawyer Delegate, Ninth Circuit Judicial Conference, 1990-1992. *Member:* Pasadena, Los Angeles County and American Bar Associations; The State Bar of California; Los Angeles Intellectual Property Law Association; American Intellectual Property Law Association. *PRACTICE AREAS:* Patent, Trademark and Copyright Litigation and Prosecution; Unfair Competition Litigation.

**RUSSELL R. PALMER, JR.,** born Los Angeles, California, September 30, 1927; admitted to bar, 1965, California; registered to practice before U.S. Patent and Trademark Office. *Education:* University of California at Berkeley (B.S., 1951); Stanford University (LL.B., 1964). *Member:* Pasadena, Los Angeles County and American Bar Associations; The State Bar of California. *PRACTICE AREAS:* Patents; Trademarks; Copyrights.

**LEROY T. RAHN,** born Emmaus, Pennsylvania, March 20, 1935; admitted to bar, 1963, New York; 1967, California; registered to practice before U.S. Patent and Trademark Office. *Education:* University of Southern California (B.S.E.E., 1958); New York University (LL.B., 1963). Phi Delta Phi; Eta Kappa Nu; Tau Beta Pi. Author: "Construction in New York of Bequests of Interests Subject to an Ambiguously Expressed Condition of Survivorship," New York University Intramural Law Review, Vol. 18, March 1963, No. 3. Former Member, Patent Staff: Bell Telephone, Murray Hill, New Jersey; Siemens AG, Munich, Germany. *Member:* Pasadena, Los Angeles County and American Bar Associations; The State Bar of California; American Intellectual Property Law Association; Los Angeles Intellectual Property Law Association (President, 1983-1984). *LANGUAGES:* German. *PRACTICE AREAS:* Intellectual Property Law.

**RICHARD D. SEIBEL,** born Gary, Indiana, December 5, 1930; admitted to bar, 1961, Colorado; 1963, California; registered to practice before U.S. Patent and Trademark Office. *Education:* Stanford University (B.S., 1952; M.S., in Metallurgical Engineering, 1953); University of Denver (J.D., 1961). Sigma Xi. *Member:* Pasadena, Los Angeles County and American Bar Associations; The State Bar of California; American Intellectual Property Law Association; American Society for Metals. *PRACTICE AREAS:* Patent and Trademark Prosecution; Material Science.

**RODERICK G. DORMAN,** born White Plains, New York, December 17, 1950; admitted to bar, 1976, Florida and U.S. District Court, Southern District of Florida; 1977, Texas, U.S. District Court, Southern District of Texas and U.S. Court of Appeals, 5th, 9th and Federal Circuits; 1978, District of Columbia; 1980, California and U.S. District Court, Central District of California. *Education:* Princeton University (A.B., cum laude, 1973); University of Miami (J.D., 1976). Author: "The Case for Compensation: Why Compensatory Components are Required for Effective Antitrust Enforcement," Vol. 68, No. 6 Georgetown Law Journal, August, 1980. Trial Attorney, Antitrust Division, United States Department of Justice, 1979-1980. *Member:* Los Angeles County and American Bar Associations; State Bar of California; State Bar of Texas; The Florida Bar; The District of Columbia Bar. *PRACTICE AREAS:* Antitrust Litigation; Business Law; Torts Litigation; Contracts Litigation; Patent, Trademark, Copyright and Unfair Competition Litigation.

**WALTER G. MAXWELL,** born Los Angeles, California, February 17, 1939; admitted to bar, 1969, California; registered to practice before U.S. Patent and Trademark Office. *Education:* University of California at Los Angeles (B.S., 1962); University of Southern California (J.D., 1968). *Member:* Pasadena and Los Angeles County Bar Associations; The State Bar of California. *PRACTICE AREAS:* Patents; Trademarks; Copyrights.

**JOHN P. GRINNELL,** born South Amboy, New Jersey, September 25, 1935; admitted to bar, 1968, New York; 1971, California; registered to practice before U.S. Patent and Trademark Office. *Education:* Johns Hopkins University (B.E.S., 1957); Washington University (M.S., 1962); Fordham University (J.D., 1967). *Member:* Los Angeles County, Pasadena (President, 1987-1988) and American Bar Associations; The State Bar of California; Los Angeles Intellectual Property Law Association. *PRACTICE AREAS:* Patents; Trademarks; Copyrights.

**WILLIAM P. CHRISTIE,** born Cleveland, Ohio, May 24, 1941; admitted to bar, 1978, California; registered to practice before U.S. Patent and Trademark Office. *Education:* University of New Mexico (B.S.Ch.E., 1964); U.S. Navy Nuclear Engineering School (1966); Western State University (J.D., 1977). Sigma Tau. Recipient, Am. Jur. Award, Criminal Law. *Member:* Orange County (Chairman, Business and Corporate Section, 1986), Federal (Treasurer, Orange County Section, 1988-1989; Board of Directors, 1989-1990) and American Bar Associations; The State Bar of California;

*(This Listing Continued)*

Los Angeles Intellectual Property Law Association; Orange County Patent Law Association. [Lt., USN, 1964-1969]. (Resident, Irvine Office). *PRACTICE AREAS:* Patents; Trademarks; Copyrights.

**DAVID A. DILLARD,** born Gardena, California, March 27, 1952; admitted to bar, 1981, California; registered to practice before U.S. Patent and Trademark Office. *Education:* California State Polytechnic University (B.S. in Chemistry, 1974; M.S. in Chemistry, 1979); Western State University (J.D., 1981). *Member:* Los Angeles County, Pasadena, American and Federal Circuit Bar Associations; The State Bar of California; Los Angeles Intellectual Property Law Association (President, 1993-1994; Board Member, 1988-1995); American Chemical Society. *PRACTICE AREAS:* Patent, Trademark, Copyright and Unfair Competition Litigation.

**THOMAS J. DALY,** born Chicago, Illinois, August 10, 1957; admitted to bar, 1985, California and U.S. District Court, Central District of California; 1987, U.S. Court of Appeals, Ninth Circuit; 1988, U.S. Court of Appeals for the Federal Circuit; registered to practice before the U.S. Patent and Trademark Office. *Education:* University of Illinois at Champaign-Urbana (B.S., with distinction in Chemical Engineering, 1979); Loyola Law School (J.D., magna cum laude, 1985). Alpha Sigma Nu. Member, St. Thomas More Law Honor Society. Articles Editor, Loyola of Los Angeles Law Review, 1984-1985. Professional Engineer, California, 1983. Author: "Anti-Monopoly, Inc. v. General Mills Fun Group, Inc.: Ending the Monopoly on Monopoly," Loyola of Los Angeles Law Review, Vol. 17, No. 4, 1984. *Member:* Pasadena and American Bar Associations; State Bar of California; Los Angeles Intellectual Property Law Association (Board Member, 1989—). *PRACTICE AREAS:* Patent, Trademark, Copyright and Unfair Competition Litigation.

**VINCENT G. GIOIA,** born Brooklyn, New York, February 5, 1935; admitted to bar, 1960, Virginia and District of Columbia; 1979, Pennsylvania; 1990, California; registered to practice before U.S. Patent and Trademark Office. *Education:* Colorado School of Mines (Met.E., 1956); George Washington University (J.D., 1960). Phi Alpha Delta. Author: "Plant Variety Protection in the U.S.," I.P.P.S. Bulletin, 1991; "Licensing Plant Variety Protection Under UPOV and Under U.S. Law," C.I.O.P.O.R.A. Symposium, 1993; "Revised Rose Name Registration System," *Acta Horticulturae,* 1983; "Plant Variety Protection," *New Matter,* Fall 1990. Patent Counsel, Reactive Metals, Inc., 1965-1968. Patent Counsel, Allegheny Ludlum Industries, 1968-1979. Secretary and General Counsel, Allegheny Ludlum Steel Corp., 1980-1985. President, World Federation of Rose Societies, 1985-1988. President, American Rose Society, 1982-1985. Chairman, 1982-1985 and Trustee, 1979-1988, American Rose Foundation. Member, C.I.O.P.O.R.A., an International Association of Plant Breeders. Member, International Association of Plant Propagators. *Member:* State Bar of California; Federal, Federal Circuit and American (Plant Variety Protection Subcommittee) Bar Associations; American Intellectual Property Law Association (Plant Variety Protection Subcommittee); Association of Corporate Patent Counsel; Licensing Executive Society. (Resident, Irvine Office). *PRACTICE AREAS:* Patents; Trademarks; Copyrights; Licensing; Plant Variety Protection Litigation.

**WILLIAM J. O'BRIEN,** born New York, N.Y., September 29, 1958; admitted to bar, 1981, California and U.S. District Court, Eastern District of California; 1982, U.S. District Court, Central District of California and U.S. Tax Court; 1992, U.S. District Court, Northern District of California and U.S Court of Appeals, Ninth Circuit. *Education:* University of California at Davis (A.B., 1978); University of California at Berkeley (J.D., 1981). Phi Beta Kappa. Member, Moot Court Board. Judge Pro Tem, Los Angeles Municipal Court, 1987—. Arbitrator, Los Angeles County Superior Court, 1989—. *Member:* Pasadena, Glendale, Los Angeles County (Member, Sections on: Intellectual Property; Litigation; Entertainment; Client Relations Committee), Federal and American (Member, Sections on: Litigation; Patent, Trademark and Copyright Law) Bar Associations; State Bar of California (Member, Sections on: Litigation; Intellectual Property); Los Angeles Intellectual Property Law Association; California Trial Lawyers Association. *PRACTICE AREAS:* Intellectual Property Litigation; Business Law Litigation.

**THEODORE A. PIANKO,** born Denville, New Jersey, September 5, 1955; admitted to bar, 1978, Michigan; 1979, Illinois; 1980, California. *Education:* State University of New York-Binghamton (B.A., with honors, 1975); University of Michigan (J.D., cum laude, 1978). Staff Member, Michigan Journal of Law Reform, 1976-1978. *Member:* Illinois State and American Bar Associations; State Bar of Michigan; State Bar of California. *PRACTICE AREAS:* Litigation; Bankruptcy Litigation.

**EDWARD R. SCHWARTZ,** born New York, N.Y., August 13, 1947; admitted to bar, 1982, Massachusetts; 1983, District of Columbia; 1988, California; U.S. Court of Appeals, First, and Ninth Circuits; U.S. Court of Appeals, District of Columbia Circuit; U.S. District Court, District of Massachusetts; U.S. District Court, Southern, Central, Eastern and Northern Districts of California; registered to practice before U.S. Patent and Trademark Office. *Education:* Tufts University (B.A., 1969); Adelphi University (M.A., 1972); Boston University (C.A.G.S., 1974); Suffolk University (J.D., 1982). *PRACTICE AREAS:* Patent; Trademark; Copyright and Unfair Competition; Litigation and Prosecution.

**JOHN D. CARPENTER,** born Kansas City, Missouri, October 23, 1961; admitted to bar, 1989, California, U.S. District Court, Central District of California and U.S. Court of Appeals, Ninth Circuit; 1990, U.S. Court of Appeals for the Federal Circuit; registered to practice before the U.S. Patent and Trademark Office. *Education:* University of Southern California (B.S., chem., 1984; J.D., 1989); Northwestern University (M.S., chem., 1985). Phi Lambda Upsilon. Finalist, Hale Moot Court, 1988. Recipient, Judge Barry Russell Award, Los Angeles Chapter Federal Bar Association, 1989. *Member:* Los Angeles and American Bar Association; State Bar of California; Los Angeles Intellectual Property Law Association; American Chemical Society. *PRACTICE AREAS:* Patents; Trademarks; Copyrights.

*ASSOCIATES*

**DAVID A. PLUMLEY,** born Los Angeles, California, August 28, 1960; admitted to bar, 1991, California and U.S. District Court, Central District of California; registered to practice before U.S. Patent and Trademark Office. *Education:* University of California, Santa Barbara (B.S., Chemical Engineering, with honors, 1982); Loyola Law School (J.D., 1991). Tau Beta Pi; Phi Delta Phi. *Member:* State Bar of California; Los Angeles Intellectual Property Law Association; American Institute of Chemical Engineers. *PRACTICE AREAS:* Patents; Trademarks; Copyrights.

**WESLEY W. MONROE,** born Santa Monica, California, January 21, 1966; admitted to bar, 1990, California; 1991, U.S. District Court, Central District of California; 1994, U.S. Court of Appeals, Federal Circuit; registered to practice before U.S. Patent and Trademark Office. *Education:* University of California at Los Angeles (B.S., in Mathematics/Computer Science, 1987); Loyola Law School (J.D., 1990). *Member:* Pasadena, Los Angeles County and American Bar Associations; State Bar of California; Los Angeles Intellectual Property Law Association. *PRACTICE AREAS:* Intellectual Property Law; Computer Law.

**GRANT T. LANGTON,** born Long Beach, California, July 9, 1960; admitted to bar, 1992, California; registered to practice before U.S. Patent and Trademark Office. *Education:* California Polytechnic University (B.S.Ch.E., chemical engineering, magna cum laude, 1987); Loyola Law School (J.D., 1992). *PRACTICE AREAS:* Patents; Trademarks; Copyrights.

**SYED A. HASAN,** born Culver City, California, August 13, 1968; admitted to bar, 1993, California. *Education:* University of California at Los Angeles (B.S.E.E., 1990); University of Southern California (J.D., 1993). Tau Beta Pi. Member, Hale Moot Court Honors Society. Judicial Clerk Extern, U.S. District Court, Central District of California, 1992. *PRACTICE AREAS:* Patents; Trademarks; Copyrights.

**R. DABNEY EASTHAM,** born San Juan, Puerto Rico, August 27, 1954; admitted to bar, 1984, California, U.S. District Court, Central District of California and U.S. Court of Appeals, Ninth and Federal Circuits; 1987, U.S. District Court, Eastern and Southern Districts of California; 1988, U.S. District Court, Northern District of California; registered to practice before U.S. Patent and Trademark Office. *Education:* College of William and Mary (B.S., with highest honors, 1976); New York University (J.D., 1984). Phi Beta Kappa; Phi Eta Sigma. Editor and Member, New York University Moot Court Board. Co-Author: "Trademark Families," Trademark World, April 1990; creator and prior editor of California Intellectual Property Handbook, Matthew Bender (1991). Instructor, Naval Nuclear Power School, Orlando, Florida. *Member:* The State Bar of California; Pasadena Tournament of Roses Association; American Alpine Club. [Lt. U.S. Navy, 1976-1981]. *PRACTICE AREAS:* Intellectual Property Litigation; Patent Prosecution.

**CONSTANTINE MARANTIDIS,** born Pireaus, Greece, May 17, 1960; admitted to bar, 1994, California; registered to practice before U.S. Patent and Trademark Office. *Education:* Embry-Riddle Aeronautical University (B.S., cum laude in Aeronautical Engineering and Aircraft Engineering Technology, 1984); Columbia University (M.S., 1988); Loyola Marymount University (J.D., 1994). *Member:* American Bar Association (Member, Sections on: Intellectual Property Law, Science and Technology, Forum Committee on Air and Space Law). *PRACTICE AREAS:* Patents; Trademarks; Copyrights.

*(This Listing Continued)*

**CHRISTIE, PARKER & HALE, LLP,** Pasadena—
*Continued*

**JOHN W. ELDREDGE,** born Wiesbaden, Germany, April 4, 1949; admitted to bar, 1992, California; registered to practice before U.S. Patent and Trademark Office. *Education:* Bates College (B.S., Physics, cum laude; B.S. Chemistry, cum laude, 1974); Massachusetts Institute of Technology (postgraduate studies in Material Science and Physical Chemistry); University of Florida, Gainesville (M.B.A., 1979); University of San Diego (J.D., cum laude, 1992). (Resident, Irvine Office). *PRACTICE AREAS:* Patent; Trademark; Copyright; Unfair Competition.

**YAR R. CHAIKOVSKY,** born Los Angeles, California, September 27, 1969; admitted to bar, 1994, California; 1984, U.S. Court of Appeals, Ninth and Federal Circuits; 1994, U.S. District Court, Central District of California; registered to practice before U.S. Patent and Trademark Office. *Education:* University of Southern California (B.S., magna cum laude, Computer Science, 1991); University of California at Los Angeles (J.D., 1994). Phi Kappa Phi; Wheat Scholarship; Murrey Fellowship. *Member:* State Bar of California; Los Angeles Intellectual Property Association. *PRACTICE AREAS:* Patents; Trademarks; Copyrights.

**MARILYN R. KHORSANDI,** born Clearwater, Florida, October 5, 1952; admitted to bar, 1994, California. *Education:* University of Central Florida (B.S., magna cum laude, 1973; M.S., 1976); Georgetown University Law Center (J.D., 1994). Student Member, American Inns of Court, William Bryant Inn, 1993-1994. Author: Note, "Does Your Client Have a Profit Motive? An Analysis of Tax Court Criteria Used to Evaluate a Taxpayer's Profit Motive Under Section 183," 47 Tax Law, 291, Fall 1993.

**CRAIG A. GELFOUND,** born North Hollywood, California, February 24, 1960; admitted to bar, 1995, California. *Education:* San Diego State University (B.S.E.E., 1983); Southwestern University School of Law (J.D., 1994). Member, Southwestern University Law Review, 1992-1994. Recipient, American Jurisprudence Awards. *PRACTICE AREAS:* Patents; Trademarks; Copyrights.

**GREGORY S. LAMPERT,** born Minster, Ohio, April 4, 1964; admitted to bar, 1990, California; 1992, Ohio; registered to practice before U.S. Patent and Trademark Office; U.S. District Courts, Central District of California and Southern District of Ohio; U.S. Court of Appeals, Sixth Circuit. *Education:* Ohio State University (B.S.I.S.E., 1987); University of Dayton (J.D., 1990). Member, University of Dayton Law Review. *Member:* Ohio State and American Bar Associations; State Bar of California; Los Angeles Intellectual Property Law Association; Cincinnati Intellectual Property Law Association (Secretary 1994). *PRACTICE AREAS:* Intellectual Property.

**JEFFREY A. FEHERVARI,** born Inglewood, California, November 6, 1970; admitted to bar, 1995, California; U.S. Court of Appeals, Ninth Circuit; U.S. District Court, Central and Northern Districts of California. *Education:* Yale University (B.S.E.E.S., B.S., Economics, 1992); University of Virginia (J.D., 1995). Beta Theta Pi; Order of the Coif. Editorial Board, University of Virginia Law Review. *Member:* State Bar of California; American Bar Association; Los Angeles Intellectual Property Law Association.

**STEVEN P. SKABRAT,** born Minneapolis, Minnesota, July 9, 1962; admitted to bar, 1993, Minnesota; registered to practice before U.S. Patent and Trademark Office (Not admitted in California). *Education:* University of Minnesota (B.S.C.S., 1984); William Mitchell College of Law (J.D., magna cum laude, 1993). *Member:* Minnesota State Bar Association (Member, Computer Law Section). *PRACTICE AREAS:* Patents; Copyrights; Computer Law. *Email:* sps@cph.com

**DANIEL M. CAVANAGH,** born Berkeley, California, February 25, 1965; admitted to bar, 1996, California. *Education:* Harvey Mudd College (B.S., 1987); University of Southern California (J.D., 1996). Order of the Coif. *PRACTICE AREAS:* Patent; Trademark; Copyright. *Email:* dmc@cph.com

**MARK C. SCARSI,** born Syracuse, New York, December 23, 1964; admitted to bar, 1996, California. *Education:* Syracuse University (B.S., Computer Science, 1987; M.S., Computer Science, 1993); Georgetown University (J.D., 1996). Order of the Coif. *PRACTICE AREAS:* Patent; Trademark; Copyright. *Email:* mcs@cph.com

**KENYON S. JENCKES,** born Fort Dix, New Jersey, July 29, 1970; admitted to bar, 1996, California. *Education:* Pennsylvania State University (B.S., 1992); University of Southern California (J.D., 1996). University Scholars Program, Pennsylvania State University. *PRACTICE AREAS:* Patent; Trademark; Copyright. *Email:* ksj@cph.com

*(This Listing Continued)*

**GARY J. NELSON,** born Seattle, Washington, June 3, 1959; admitted to bar, 1996, California. *Education:* Pacific Lutheran University (B.S., Chemistry, B.A., Economics, 1982); University of Southern California (M.F.A., 1986); Georgetown University (J.D., 1996). Author: "Sufficiency of Copyright Protection in the Video Electronic Game Industry," Law & Policy in International Business, Vol. 27 No. 3. *PRACTICE AREAS:* Patent; Trademark; Copyright. *Email:* gjn@cph.com

*OF COUNSEL*

**R. WILLIAM JOHNSTON,** born Fort Worth, Texas, July 28, 1924; admitted to bar, 1953, Texas; 1954, California; registered to practice before U.S. Patent and Trademark Office. *Education:* Rice University (B.S. in Chem. Eng., 1947); South Texas College of Law (LL.B., 1953). *Member:* Pasadena, Los Angeles County and American Bar Associations; The State Bar of California; American Intellectual Property Law Association. *PRACTICE AREAS:* Patents; Trademarks; Copyrights.

**PAUL W. FISH,** born Ligonier, Pennsylvania, April 12, 1933; admitted to bar, 1965, District of Columbia; 1966, New York; 1967, Michigan; 1976, Wisconsin; 1983, Illinois; 1993, Pennsylvania; registered to practice before U.S. Patent and Trademark Office (Not admitted in California). *Education:* Catholic University of America (B.E.E., 1959; M.E.E., 1961); George Washington University (LL.B., 1965). Recipient, IEEE Student Achievement Award. Member: Advisory Counsel, United States Court of Federal Claims; Board of Regents, Catholic University of America. *Member:* The District of Columbia Bar; Illinois State, New York State and Pennsylvania Bar Associations; State Bar of Michigan; State Bar of Wisconsin. *PRACTICE AREAS:* Patent, Trademark and Copyright Law; Computer Law; Lease Law; Corporate Law.

**MARC MORRIS,** born Brooklyn, New York, April 6, 1953; admitted to bar, 1979, Massachusetts; 1981, Colorado; U.S. District Courts, Massachusetts, Colorado, Northern District of California; U.S. Court of Appeals, First and Tenth Circuits; registered to practice before U.S. Patent and Trademark Office; 1996, California. *Education:* Beloit College (B.S., Biology, 1975); New England School of Law (J.D., cum laude, 1979); Boston University (LL.M., 1980). *Member:* Colorado and American (Member, Tax and Intellectual Property Sections) Bar Associations. *PRACTICE AREAS:* Intellectual Property Litigation; Securities Litigation.

**CARL KUSTIN, JR.,** born Chicago, Illinois, January 29, 1936; admitted to bar, 1962, Illinois; 1973, California; registered to practice before U.S. Patent and Trademark Office. *Education:* Illinois Institute of Technology (B.S. in Ch.E., 1958); Northwestern University (J.D., 1961). Phi Delta Phi. Author: "Enforcing U.S. Patents & Trademarks in the Courts of the United States," Journal of Japanese Institute of International Business Law, March and April, 1983. Lecturer on Patents, Trademarks and Copyrights, West Coast University, 1977-1978. Lecturer on Trying a Case Before the International Trade Commission, California State Bar Association, 1982. Lecturer on Enforcing U.S. Patents and Trademarks in U.S. Courts, Japanese Institute of International Business Law, 1983. Former Counsel, Southern California Section, American Chemical Society. Hearing Officer, Illinois Pollution Control Board, 1971-1972. *Member:* The State Bar of California; Los Angeles Intellectual Property Law Association (Chairman, Chem. Prac. Committee, 1974-1975); American Arbitration Association. *PRACTICE AREAS:* Patent, Trademark, Copyright and Unfair Competition Litigation.

**JEFFREY P. WALL,** born Iowa City, Iowa, August 12, 1960; admitted to bar, 1993, California; registered to practice before U.S. Patent and Trademark Office; U.S. Court of Appeals, Federal and Ninth Circuits and U.S. District Court, Central District of California. *Education:* University of Iowa (B.S., with highest distinction, 1982; M.D., with honors, 1986); University of California at Los Angeles (J.D., 1993). *PRACTICE AREAS:* Patents; Trademarks; Copyrights.

REFERENCE: Wells Fargo Bank, Pasadena, California.

---

## JAMES DEXTER CLARK
*1 SOUTH ORANGE GROVE BOULEVARD,*
*SUITE 11*
**PASADENA, CALIFORNIA 91105**
Telephone: 818-583-4798
Fax: 818-583-4984

*Municipal Law, Eminent Domain, Economic Development and Redevelopment.*

*(This Listing Continued)*

**JAMES DEXTER CLARK,** born Chicago, Illinois, November 27, 1941; admitted to bar, 1971, California; 1975, U.S. Supreme Court; 1977, U.S. Court of Appeals, Ninth Circuit. *Education:* Yale University (B.A., 1963); University of California at Los Angeles; University of Southern California (J.D., 1970). Phi Delta Phi. Listed in Who's Who in American Law (Marquis). Author: "Property Taxation of Foreign Goods and Enterprises— A Study in Inconsistency," 4 Pepperdine Law Review 39, 1976; "The New Appellate Attorney," San Fernando Valley Bar Journal, Vol. 4, 1981. Visiting Lecturer, University of Southern California Master of Business Tax Program, 1978. Lecturer, Administrative Law, California Continuing Education of the Bar, 1980. Deputy County Counsel for the County of Los Angeles, 1972-1980. Special Counsel: Pasadena Community Development Commission, 1984—; Victorville Redevelopment Agency, 1981—; Victorville Redevelopment Agency, 1981—; Ontario Redevelopment Agency, 1988—; Commerce Redevelopment Agency, 1991—. *Member:* Los Angeles County and American (Member, Urban Law Section) Bar Associations; State Bar of California. [Major, USMCR, 1963-1966]. **REPORTED CASES:** Michelin Tire Corp. vs. Wages (1976) 423 U.S.276 (Amicus); Zee Toys vs. County of Los Angeles (1978) Cal.App. 3d 763, 149 Cal. Rptr. 750 Affirmed 449 U.S. 1119; Mandel vs. Hutchison (C.A. Cal. 1974) 494 F.2d 364; Craig Corp. vs. County of Los Angles (1975) 51 Cal.App. 3d 909, etc. **TRANSACTIONS:** Plaza Las Fuentes Mix-Use Development, Pasadena, California; Museum of Contemporary Art, Los Angeles, California. **PRACTICE AREAS:** Municipal Law; Economic Development; Redevelopment.

REPRESENTATIVE CLIENTS: Pasadena Community Development Commission; Barstow Redevelopment Agency; Victorville Redevelopment Agency.

## LAW OFFICES OF
## ARLAN A. COHEN

**1100 EAST GREEN STREET, 2ND FLOOR**
**PASADENA, CALIFORNIA 91106**
Telephone: 818-449-0404
Fax: 818-449-1673

*Medical Malpractice, Wrongful Death Litigation and Birth Injuries.*

**ARLAN A. COHEN,** born Holyoke, Massachusetts, October 19, 1943; admitted to bar, 1990, California. *Education:* Columbia University (B.A., summa cum laude, 1964); Cornell Medical School (M.D., 1968); Harvard University (J.D., magna cum laude, 1990). Phi Beta Kappa. Licensed Medical Doctor: California, 1975—; New York, 1969; Rhode Island, 1971; North Carolina, 1979. Instructor, Legal Methods, Harvard Law School, 1989. Commander, Public Health Service, 1969-1971. Member: Los Angeles County and California Medical Associations, 1975-1987 and 1990-1992. *Member:* Los Angeles County Bar Association; State Bar of California; Los Angeles Trial Lawyers Association; California Trial Lawyers Association; The Association of Trial Lawyers of America. **PRACTICE AREAS:** Medical Malpractice, Wrongful Death; Litigation.

## COLLINS, COLLINS, MUIR & TRAVER

Established in 1964

Successor to Collins & Collins

**SUITE 300, 265 NORTH EUCLID**
**PASADENA, CALIFORNIA 91101**
Telephone: 818-793-1163
FAX: 818-793-5982

*Newport Beach, California Office:* 333 Bayside Drive, 92660. Telephone: 714-723-6284. Fax: 714-723-7701.

*Casualty, Products Liability, Construction, Malpractice Insurance, Employment Termination, Sexual Abuse, and Personal Injury Law. General Trial Practice.*

FIRM PROFILE: *The firm of Collins, Collins, Muir and Traver is the successor to Collins & Collins established in 1964. The firm has 30 years of trial practice in the Southern California area.*

*The practice emphasizes casualty defense, with focus on product liability, construction, architects and engineers, malpractice, public entity liability, automobile liability and insurance matters involving personal injury and property damage.*

*The firm has extensive experience in dealing with a wide variety of clients, as many of our cases require communication with adjusters, investigators, risk managers, claims representatives, in-house counsel, self insured parties, as well as expert witnesses of all disciplines.*

### MEMBERS OF FIRM

**JAMES E. COLLINS** (1910-1987).

**JOHN J. COLLINS,** born Los Angeles, California, 1936; admitted to bar, 1962, California; U.S. District Court, Central District of California, U.S. Court of Appeals, Ninth Circuit and U.S. Supreme Court. *Education:* University of Santa Clara (B.A. in English, 1958); Loyola University of Los Angeles (LL.B., 1961). Listed in *The Best Lawyers America,* 1987, 1989-1990, 1991-1992, 1993-1994 and 1995-1996 Editions. American Board of Trial Advocates, California Trial Lawyer of the Year, 1991. Deputy County Counsel, Los Angeles County, 1962-1964. Member: Collins & Collins, 1964-1985; Collins, Collins, Muir & Traver, 1985—. *Member:* Pasadena (President, 1989), Los Angeles County (Member: Board of Trustees, 1991-1994; Executive Committee, Litigation Section, 1992-1995), Orange County and American (Member: Committee of Product Liability and Consumer Law; Committee on Tort and Insurance Practice) Bar Associations; State Bar of California (Member, Board of Governors, 1996—) ; Defense Research Institute; International Association of Defense Counsel; Association of Southern California Defense Counsel (President, 1982-1984); California Defense Counsel (Board of Directors, 1985—; President, 1993); American Board of Trial Advocates (Rank of Diplomat; President, Los Angeles Chapter, 1989; Member, National Board of Directors, 1984-1993 and 1995; Chairman, Cal-Abota, 1990). Fellow, American College of Trial Lawyers; International Academy of Trial Lawyers. **PRACTICE AREAS:** General Trial Practice; Public Liability; Insurance Bad Faith; Products Liability; Construction Litigation; Wrongful Termination; Sexual Abuse; Professional Malpractice.

**SAMUEL J. MUIR,** born 1954; admitted to bar, 1979, California and U.S. District Court, Central District of California. *Education:* Azusa Pacific University (B.A., 1976); Loyola Law School (J.D., 1979). Volunteer to the Los Angeles Bar Association Pro Bono Counsel. Member: Schell & Delamer, 1979-1980; Gaethals & Swanson, 19801-981; Manthel & Muir, 1981-1984; Collins, Collins, Muir & Traver, 1984—. Member: Consulting Engineers and Land Surveyors of California and Pasadena Chapter of American Institute of Architects. *Member:* Pasadena (Secretary, Board of Directors, 1991-1992; Trustee, 1992-1993; Vice-President, 1993-1994; President-Elect, 1994-1995; President, 1995-1996 ), Los Angeles County (Delegate to the 1982 & 1992 California State Bar Convention) and American Bar Associations; State Bar of California; Association of Southern California Defense Counsel (Board of Directors, 1991—); Defense Research Institute; International Association of Defense Counsel. **PRACTICE AREAS:** Construction Law; Architects and Engineers Professional Liability; Trial Practice; Products Liability.

**ROBERT J. TRAVER,** born 1948; admitted to bar, 1974, California and U.S. District Court, Central District of California. *Education:* Loyola University of Los Angeles (B.A., 1971; J.D., 1974). Phi Delta Phi. Panel Member, Superior Court CRASH Settlement and JSOP Programs; Judge Pro Tem, Los Angeles Municipal Court. *Member:* Pasadena, Los Angeles County and American Bar Associations; State Bar of California; Association of Southern California Defense Counsel. **PRACTICE AREAS:** General Liability; Public Liability; Malpractice; Premises Liability; Construction Law.

**FRANK J. D'ORO,** born 1953; admitted to bar, 1978, California and U.S. District Court, Central District of California. *Education:* Hope College (B.A., 1975); Pepperdine University (J.D., 1978). Member, Pepperdine University Law Review, 1977-1978. Court Appointed Arbitrator Los Angeles County; Settlement Officer, Glendale Superior Court; Judge Pro Tem, Los Angeles Municipal Court. *Member:* Pasadena and Los Angeles County Bar Associations; State Bar of California; Association of Southern California Defense Counsel. **PRACTICE AREAS:** General Liability; Public Liability; Premises Liability.

**BRIAN K. STEWART,** born 1961; admitted to bar, 1986, California; 1987, Illinois. *Education:* Western Illinois University (B.A. in Political Science, 1983); John Marshall Law School (J.D., 1986). Pi Sigma Alpha; Delta Theta Phi. President, Securities and Exchange Law Association. *Member:* State Bar of California; Los Angeles County, Pasadena and American Bar Associations; Association of Southern California Defense Counsel; American Institute of Architects (Affiliate Member, Los Angeles Chapter); Pasadena Young Lawyers (President, 1990-1991; Vice-President, 1989-1990). **PRACTICE AREAS:** Architects and Engineers Professional Liability; Trial Practice; Public Entity Liability; Product Liability; Premises Liability.

*(This Listing Continued)*

**COLLINS, COLLINS, MUIR & TRAVER,** Pasadena—
*Continued*

### ASSOCIATES

**PAUL L. RUPARD,** born 1935; admitted to bar, 1967, California and U.S. District Court, Central District of California; 1987, U.S. District Court, Southern District of California; U.S. Court of Federal Claims. *Education:* Kansas City, Kansas Junior College (Assoc. Engr., 1957); University of Kansas; University of California Extension; Southwestern University School of Law (LL.B., cum laude, 1966). *Member:* Los Angeles County and American (Member, Sections on: Tort; Insurance Law) Bar Associations; American Board of Trial Advocates (Associate Member); Association of Southern California Defense Counsel. **PRACTICE AREAS:** General Liability; Construction Law; Architects and Engineers Professional Liability.

**ROBERT H. STELLWAGEN, JR.,** born 1964; admitted to bar, 1990, California; 1991, U.S. District Court, Central District of California. *Education:* University of California, San Diego (B.A., cum laude, 1986); Hastings College of the Law, University of California (J.D., 1990). *Member:* Pasadena, Los Angeles County and American Bar Associations; State Bar of California; Association of Southern California Defense Counsel. **PRACTICE AREAS:** Architects and Engineers Professional Liability; Premises Liability; Products Liability; Public Liability.

**TOMAS A. GUTERRES,** born 1965; admitted to bar, 1991, California; 1992, U.S. District Court, Central District of California. *Education:* Boston University (B.A., 1987); Loyola Law School (J.D., 1990). Contributing Author: Immigration Act of 1990: Handbook, Clark Boardman, 1991. *Member:* Pasadena, Beverly Hills and Los Angeles County Bar Associations; Association of Southern California Defense Counsel; Japanese and Chinese American Bar Association. **LANGUAGES:** Spanish, Japanese, Portuguese. **PRACTICE AREAS:** Architects and Engineers Professional Liability; Construction Law; Products Liability; Premises Liability; Public Liability.

**CHRISTINE E. DRAGE,** born Pasadena, California, September 25, 1968; admitted to bar, 1993, California; 1994, U.S. District Court, Central District of California. *Education:* University of San Diego (B.A., 1990); Brigham Young University (J.D., 1993). Member, Moot Court. Chair, Board of Trial Advocates, 1992-1993. *Member:* State Bar of California; Association of Southern California Defense Counsel. **PRACTICE AREAS:** Construction Defect; Architects and Engineers Professional Liability; Products Liability; Personal Injury Defense.

**PETER L. STACY,** born 1970; admitted to bar, 1995, California; U.S. District Court, Central District of California; U.S. Court of Appeals, Ninth Circuit. *Education:* Occidental College (A.B., 1992); American University, Washington College of Law (J.D., 1995). *Member:* Pasadena Bar Association; Southern California Defense Counsel. **PRACTICE AREAS:** Public Entity Defense; General Liability; Construction Law.

**STEPHEN W. OLSON,** born 1956; admitted to bar, 1995, California; U.S. District Court, Central District of California. *Education:* University of Southern California (B.S., Civil Engineer, 1979); Loyola Marymount University (J.D., 1995). Staff Writer, "USC Engineer" magazine. Licensed Civil Engineer. *Member:* Los Angeles County, Pasadena County and American Bar Associations; State Bar of California; Southern California Defense Council; ABOTA Inns of Court. **PRACTICE AREAS:** Architects and Engineers Liability; Construction Law.

---

## COOPER, KARDARAS & SCHARF L.L.P.

*141 EAST WALNUT STREET*
**PASADENA, CALIFORNIA 91103**
*Telephone: 818-795-0814*
*Telefax: 818-795-3839*

*New York, N.Y. Office:* 40 Wall Street, 32nd Floor. Telephone: 212-785-5050. Telefax: 212-785-5055.

*Civil Litigation and Appellate Practice in all State and Federal Courts. Attorney Fee Dispute Resolution and Litigation Management, Insurance and Reinsurance Coverage, Insurance Bad Faith Litigation, Subrogation, Business, Commercial, Partnership, Personal Injury, Toxic Tort, Environmental, Products Liability, Professional, Marine and Property Litigation, General Business, Corporate and Commercial Law, Homeowner Association Law and Litigation, Construction Defect Litigation, Real Estate and Real Estate Finance, Federal and State Taxation and Tax Controversies, Estate Planning and Probate Law.*

*(This Listing Continued)*

CAA1642B

### PARTNERS

**BRAND L. COOPER,** born Los Angeles, California, October 8, 1949; admitted to bar, 1975, California, U.S. District Court, Southern and Central Districts of California and U.S. Court of Appeals, Ninth Circuit. *Education:* University of Southern California (B.S., 1971); Loyola University (J.D., magna cum laude, 1975). Member, Loyola University Law Review, 1974-1975. Author: "Civil Conspiracy and Interference with Contractual Relations," 8 Loyola Law Review 312. *Member:* State Bar of California.

**WILLIAM P. KARDARAS,** born New Haven, Connecticut, January 14, 1930; admitted to bar, 1961, New York; 1965, U.S. District Court, Southern and Eastern Districts of New York; 1966, U.S. Court of Appeals, Second Circuit; 1974, U.S. Supreme Court; 1982, U.S. Court of Appeals, First Circuit; 1991, U.S. Court of Appeals, Ninth Circuit; 1992, U.S. District Court, Northern District of California. *Education:* University of Connecticut (B.S., 1957); New York Law School (LL.B., 1961). *Member:* Maritime Law Association of the United States. (Resident, New York Office).

**JEFFREY D. SCHARF,** born Los Angeles, California, December 30, 1955; admitted to bar, 1982, California; 1983, U.S. District Court, Southern and Central Districts of California, and U.S. Court of Appeals, Ninth Circuit. *Education:* University of California at Santa Barbara (B.A., with honor, 1978); Moore Hall School of Law, University of San Diego (J.D., 1982). Extern, Civil and Criminal, United States Attorney's Office. *Member:* State Bar of California.

**LOUISE A. KELLEHER,** born Hackensack, New Jersey, December 15, 1955; admitted to bar, 1987, New York, Connecticut and U.S. District Court, Southern District of New York; 1990, U.S. District Court, Eastern District of New York; 1991, U.S. Supreme Court and U.S. Court of Appeals, Ninth Circuit; 1992, U.S. District Court, Northern District of California. *Education:* Seton Hall University (B.A., 1978); St. John's University (J.D., 1986). Co-Chair, Defendants' Release Committee, Dupont Plaza Fire Litigation MDL-721. *Member:* American Bar Association; The Association of Trial Lawyers of America; Maritime Law Association of the United States. (Resident, New York Office).

**GERALD G. KNAPTON,** born Providence, Rhode Island, October 2, 1940; admitted to bar, 1977, California; 1978, U.S. District Court, Central District of California and U.S. Court of Appeals, Ninth Circuit; 1979, U.S. District Court, Northern and Southern Districts of California; 1981, U.S. District Court, Eastern District of California. *Education:* Brown University; University of California, Berkeley (B.A., with highest honors, 1973); University of California, Los Angeles (J.D., 1976). Phi Beta Kappa. Law Clerk, Office of the Attorney General, State of California, Antitrust Division, 1975-1976. *Member:* Pasadena Bar Association; State Bar of California.

**PAUL H. LUSBY,** born Baltimore, Maryland, September 8, 1955; admitted to bar, 1982, California; 1983, U.S. Tax Court; 1986, U.S. Claims Court and U.S. Court of Appeals for the Federal Circuit. *Education:* University of Virginia (B.A., with high distinction, 1977; J.D., 1982). Phi Delta Phi. Member, Editorial Board, Virginia Tax Review, 1980-1982. Author: "Loan Swaps: On the Road to Proper Federal Tax Treatment," U.S. League Legal Bulletin, July, 1988. *Member:* Los Angeles County and American Bar Associations; The State Bar of California (Member, Sections on: Business Law; Real Property and Probate Law; Taxation Law).

**LINDA A. CHALISON,** born Sacramento, California, January 5, 1950; admitted to bar, 1975, California; 1981, U.S. District Court, Central District of California; 1989, U.S. Court of Appeals, Ninth Circuit. *Education:* University of California at Los Angeles; University of California at Riverside (B.A., 1972); Southwestern University (J.D., 1975). *Member:* State Bar of California.

**BRUCE E. NEHLSEN,** born Chicago, Illinois, February 24, 1947; admitted to bar, 1979, California and U.S. District Court, District of California. *Education:* Mt. San Antonio College (A.A., 1971); University of California at Riverside (B.A., 1973); University of San Diego (Comparative Law Institute Certificate, 1977); University of La Verne (J.D., 1978). Instructor: Business Law, Legal Assisting and Paralegal Studies, Pasadena City College, 1979—. *Member:* State Bar of California.

*(This Listing Continued)*

## PROFESSIONAL BIOGRAPHIES

### ASSOCIATES

Alan C. Arnall
Edward C. Wilde
Michael S. Overing
Lori S. Evenchick
  (Resident, New York Office)
James B. Sanborn
Joseph P. Fogel
Mark M. Senior
Michael A. Branconier

Robert G. Ricco
  (Resident, New York Office)
Edward E. Dollar
Michael T. Ohira
Victor E. Aguilera
Frederick Harold Alschuler
James C. Potepan
Keith A. Turner
Thomas V. O'Hagan

Thomas M. O'Leary

### OF COUNSEL

Daniel C. David
Alison Kotlarz Katz

William Gwire (Also Practicing Individually, San Francisco, California)

REPRESENTATIVE CLIENTS: American International Adjustment Company; American International Insurance Company of Puerto Rico; American International Underwriters; Bank of America N.T. & S.A.; Cal Accountants Mutual Company; Canadian Insurance Company; CenFed Financial Corporation; CenFed Bank, a Federal Savings Bank; Chubb Group of Insurance Companies; CIGNA/INA; Coast Federal Bank, FSB; Commercial Union Insurance Companies; Continental Insurance; Crum & Forster Managers Corporation; Farmers Insurance Group of Companies; Fireman's Fund Insurance Company; Great American Insurance Company; Home Savings of America, FSB; H.F. Ahmanson & Co.; Hartford Insurance Company; INAPRO; Industrial Indemnity Insurance Company; Maryland Casualty Insurance Company; Nationwide Insurance Company; New York Marine & General Insurance Company; North Atlantic Casualty and Surety Company; Ohio Casualty Insurance Company; Oregon Mutual Insurance Company; Pomona Federal Savings & Loan Association; Royal Insurance Companies; Safeco Insurance Company; State Farm Insurance Companies; The Aetna Insurance Companies; The Home Insurance Companies; The London Agency; Transamerica Insurance Group; United Pacific/Reliance Group of Insurance Companies; Yasuda Fire & Marine Insurance Company of America; American Freight System, Incorporated; Eastman West Interiors; G.I. Trucking Company, Inc.; United States Bankruptcy Court.

---

## D'ALESSANDRO & RITCHIE
### A PROFESSIONAL CORPORATION

Established in 1990

**3521 EAST YORKSHIRE ROAD, SUITE 1000**
**PASADENA, CALIFORNIA 91107-5432**
Telephone: 818-683-8800
Facsimile: 818-683-8900

*San Jose, California Office:* 1731 Technology Drive, Suite 710, 95110. Telephone: 408-441-1100. Fax: 408-441-8400.

*Patents, Trademarks, Copyrights, Intellectual Property.*

(For complete biographical data on all personnel, see Professional Biographies at San Jose, California)

---

## DEAR & KELLEY

Established in 1992

**225 SOUTH LAKE AVENUE, SUITE 510**
**PASADENA, CALIFORNIA 91101**
Telephone: 818-568-2500
Fax: 818-405-0786

Corporate, Commercial Gaming and Real Estate Transactions, Business Litigation and Bankruptcy.

FIRM PROFILE: Dear and Kelley specializes its practice in business and transactional matters for the real estate, gaming, construction and health care industries with emphasis on trial and appellate advocacy in state and federal courts for these specialized industries.

*(This Listing Continued)*

---

### MEMBERS OF FIRM

**RICHARD D. DEAR,** born Los Angeles, California, December 22, 1931; admitted to bar, 1962, California; 1970, U.S. Supreme Court. *Education:* Los Angeles City College (A.A., 1954); University of Southern California (B.S., 1956; J.D., 1962). Licensed Real Estate Broker, California. Senior Partner and Member, Litigation Department, Department Chair, Combined Corporate and Real Estate Departments and Member, Management Committee of Musick, Peeler & Garrett, 1962-1992. *Member:* Los Angeles County, Pasadena and American Bar Associations; State Bar of California; Lawyer-Pilots Bar Association. *PRACTICE AREAS:* Corporate Formation; Partnership; Partnership Dissolutions; Limited Partnerships; Nonprofit Corporations; Joint Ventures; Subdivisions; Real Estate; Zoning, Planning and Land Use; Construction Law; Civil Litigation.

**THOMAS J. KELLEY,** born Los Angeles, California, December 9, 1936; admitted to bar, 1966, California; 1970, U.S. Supreme Court. *Education:* University of Santa Clara (B.S., 1958); Loyola University of Los Angeles (J.D., 1966). Member, 1969-1971 and Secretary, 1970-1971, Board of Governors, Loyola Law School Alumni Association. President, Santa Clara University Alumni Association, 1981-1982. Judge Pro Tempore: Los Angeles Municipal Court, 1970-1981; Los Angeles Superior Court, 1980—. Hearing Officer, State Bar Courts, 1976-1982. *Member:* Los Angeles County (Member, Trial Lawyer Section) and American (Member, Litigation Section) Bar Associations; State Bar of California; Association of Southern California Defense Counsel; Association of Business Trial Lawyers; Lawyer-Pilots Bar Association. [Maj., U.S. Marine Corps Reserve, Retired]. *PRACTICE AREAS:* Bankruptcy; Civil Litigation; Business Litigation.

### OF COUNSEL

**JOHN L. HUNTER,** born Redwood City, California, November 6, 1959; admitted to bar, 1985, California and U.S. District Court, Central District of California. *Education:* University of California at Berkeley (B.S., 1981); Loyola Law School of Los Angeles (J.D., cum laude, 1985). Phi Alpha Delta. Member, St. Thomas More Law Honor Society. *Member:* Pasadena, Los Angeles County and American Bar Associations; State Bar of California; American Board of Trial Advocates Inns of Court; Association of Southern California Defense Counsel.

---

## LAW OFFICE OF
## LOWELL JOHN DOSCH

**301 N. LAKE AVENUE, 10TH FLOOR**
**PASADENA, CALIFORNIA 91101-4107**
Telephone: 818-577-1663
Fax: 818-793-5900

Civil Litigation in all State and Federal Courts, Insurance Defense, Construction Industry Law, Probate Litigation, Business Law, Commercial Litigation.

**LOWELL JOHN DOSCH,** born Aberdeen, South Dakota, September 7, 1945; admitted to bar, 1972, California; 1976, U.S. District Court, Central District of California; 1981, U.S. Supreme Court and U.S. Court of Appeals, 9th Circuit. *Education:* University of Southern California (A.B., 1964; M.B.A., 1980; J.D., 1971). Member, Glendale Rotary. *Member:* Los Angeles County and American Bar Associations; State Bar of California. [Capt. U.S. Navy Judge Advocate Generals Corp, Ret.]

REPRESENTATIVE CLIENTS: Moffa Electrical Services, Inc.; Evilsizer Construction, Inc.; Marks Engineering and Grading Inc.; Absolut Construction; GTE.

---

## THOMAS H. DOWNEY

**PASADENA CORPORATE CENTER, BOX 29**
**225 SOUTH LAKE AVENUE, SUITE 410**
**PASADENA, CALIFORNIA 91101-3005**
Telephone: 818-577-9970
Fax: 818-796-6839

General Practice, Estate Planning including Wills and Trusts, Probate. Civil Litigation.

**THOMAS H. DOWNEY,** born Los Angeles, California, November 28, 1947; admitted to bar, 1973, California. *Education:* Williams College (B.A., 1969); University of Southern California (J.D., 1972). Phi Delta Phi. *Member:* Los Angeles County Bar Association (Member, Probate Section); State Bar of California; Pasadena Probate Bar Association.

## THEODORE C. ECKERMAN

350 WEST COLORADO BOULEVARD
SUITE 310
**PASADENA, CALIFORNIA 91105**
Telephone: 818-792-2144
Los Angeles: 213-681-2880
Fax: 818-795-6982

*Family, Business and Real Estate Law.*

**THEODORE C. ECKERMAN,** born Los Angeles, California, May 3, 1926; admitted to bar, 1954, California and U.S. District Court, Southern District of California. *Education:* University of Southern California (B.S., 1950; J.D., 1954). Phi Alpha Delta. Mediator and Judge Pro Tem, Superior Court, 1989. *Member:* Pasadena, Los Angeles County (Member, Family Law Executive Committee, 1992-1994) and American Bar Associations; State Bar of California (Member, State Bar Family Law Executive Committee, 1983-1986; Chairman, Family Law Legislation Committee, 1981-1983). Fellow, American Academy of Matrimonial Lawyers. (Certified Specialist, Family Law, The State Bar of California Board of Legal Specialization).

REFERENCE: First Interstate Bank (Pasadena Main Office).

## THOMAS H. EDWARDS

301 NORTH LAKE AVENUE, SEVENTH FLOOR
**PASADENA, CALIFORNIA 91101**
Telephone: 818-440-5211
Fax: 818-577-8597
Email: THEDWA@ix.netcom.com

*Business, Construction, Employment and Labor Litigation, Antitrust and Trade Regulation, Insurance Law, Trial Practice in all State and Federal Courts.*

**THOMAS H. EDWARDS,** born Kansas City, Missouri, May 31, 1947; admitted to bar, 1975, Georgia; 1980, California. *Education:* University of Texas (B.A., with honors, 1970; J.D., with high honors, 1975). Member, Chancellors. Order of the Coif. Author: Note, "Nonrecognition of Insurance Proceeds Under Section 337 of the Internal Revenue Code," 52 Texas Law Review 164 (1973). Judge Pro Tem, Los Angeles Municipal Court. *Member:* Los Angeles County and American (Member, Sections on: Antitrust Law; Litigation; Labor and Employment Law) Bar Associations; State Bar of California.

## FAIRSHTER & ASSOCIATES

Established in 1988

225 S. LAKE AVENUE, 9TH FLOOR
**PASADENA, CALIFORNIA 91101**
Telephone: 818-568-1200
Fax: 818-568-8930

*Corporate, Business, Bankruptcy, Entertainment, Media, International Transactions, Finance and Real Estate Law.*

FIRM PROFILE: We at FAIRSHTER & ASSOCIATES believe that a bigger law firm is not a better law firm. In this new age of business competition, you need strong lawyers to represent your interests.

We are a creative, innovative, and resourceful law firm. Our basic approach in representing you is to be attentive, timely, thorough, relentless, and tough. The hallmark of FAIRSHTER & ASSOCIATES is aggressive, cost effective legal representation.

FAIRSHTER & ASSOCIATES is sensitive to marketplace demands and client needs. Today's lawyers need to be accountable for their activities. We are willing to tie our fees to our performance. That is why, in addition to the traditional hourly fee schedule, FAIRSHTER & ASSOCIATES has instituted alternative pricing methodologies for its services. This is done to give you representation which can be budgeted for at a definable and predictable cost.

We have the expertise to design and implement media management strategies for you. FAIRSHTER & ASSOCIATES focuses not only on representing your interests in the courtroom and boardroom, but also to the "court of public opinion" when appropriate. In implementing a "media package," we have made appearances on ABC, CBS, NBC, CNN and COURTtv. We understand the need for discretion in your matters as well. We have also developed strategies on how to minimize public attention when such is desired.

FAIRSHTER & ASSOCIATES represents clients for both transactional and
*(This Listing Continued)*

litigation needs. Because of today's competitive environment, we approach every matter with the same aggressive posture. We understand how to make deals happen. We know how to successfully present a case at trial, and negotiate a settlement when it is appropriate. We understand that it is unacceptable representation to allow our clients to be simply worn down or out-maneuvered. We believe in achieving the maximum results for our clients.

**MATTHEW J. FAIRSHTER,** born Port Angeles, Washington, October 11, 1961; admitted to bar, 1987, California and U.S. District Court, Southern District of California; 1988, U.S. District Court, Central District of California; 1993, U.S. Court of Appeals, Ninth Circuit. *Education:* University of California at San Diego (B.A., 1984); University of San Diego (J.D., 1987). Award, The Academy of T.V. Arts and Sciences, Live Coverage of an Unscheduled News Event, L.A. Riots Live Coverage: The Beating of Reginald Denny (News 13) KCOP, L.A. Area Emmy Awards, 1992. Who's Who in American Colleges and Universities, 1982-1983. Provost's Honors List, 1984. Editor, Journal of Contemporary Legal Issues, 1986-1987. Author: "New Theories of Escrow Holder Liability," Escrow Update, Vol. 8, No. 5, September 1988. *Member:* Los Angeles County (Member, Sections on: Business; Real Property; International Law; Science and Technology Law) and American (Member, Sections on: Business; Real Property; International Law; Science and Technology; Member, Committee on Loan Practice and Lender Liability) Bar Associations; The State Bar of California. **LANGUAGES:** German, Spanish. **PRACTICE AREAS:** Business Law; Corporate Law.

*OF COUNSEL*

**NAIRIE A. BALIAN,** born Beirut, Lebanon, August 8, 1963; admitted to bar, 1987, California and U.S. District Court, Central District of California. *Education:* Allegheny College (B.A., 1983); University of La Verne (J.D., 1986). Recipient, American Jurisprudence Award in Contracts. Member, Moot Court. Member, La Verne Law Journal, 1985-1986. *Member:* Beverly Hills and American Bar Associations; State Bar of California; Los Angeles Trial Lawyers Association; California Trial Lawyers Association; Los Angeles Women Lawyers Association; Armenian Bar Association; The Association of Trial Lawyers of America. **LANGUAGES:** Armenian, Arabic, French, Russian. **PRACTICE AREAS:** Family Law; Insurance Law.

REPRESENTATIVE CLIENTS: Paul Davis Systems; Los Angeles New Service; Ventana Financial Services Group; Prico, Inc.; Chateau Mortgage Corp.; Newsreel Video Services; ABC Liovin Drilling, Inc.; Real Property Investment Services, Inc.; USCAN Free Trade Zones, Inc.
REFERENCE: Wells Fargo Bank.

## RICHARD I. FEINBERG

A LAW CORPORATION

301 EAST COLORADO BOULEVARD, SUITE 800
**PASADENA, CALIFORNIA 91101**
Telephone: 818-304-0805
FAX: 818-449-0946

*Medical Malpractice and Personal Injury Law.*

**RICHARD I. FEINBERG,** born Springfield, Massachusetts, April 18, 1938; admitted to bar, 1967, California and U.S. District Court, Northern District of California; 1973, U.S. District Court, Central District of California. *Education:* Swarthmore College (B.A., 1959); Jefferson Medical College (M.D., 1963); University of Southern California (J.D., 1967). Doctor of Medicine, California, 1964. Lecturer in Law, University of Southern California School of Law, 1975—. *Member:* Pasadena, Beverly Hills, Los Angeles County (Member, Medical-Legal Relations Committee, 1971-1977) and American Bar Associations; Los Angeles Trial Lawyers Association; California Trial Lawyers Association; Associate, American Board of Trial Advocates. Fellow, American College of Legal Medicine. [Capt., Medical Corps, U.S. Air Force Reserve, 1967-1972]. (Also of Counsel, Gary Logan, Las Vegas, NV).

## EDWARD L. FINE
350 WEST COLORADO BOULEVARD
SUITE 200
**PASADENA, CALIFORNIA 91105**
Telephone: 818-792-5177
Fax: 818-568-0930

*Bankruptcy.*

**EDWARD L. FINE,** born Chicago, Illinois, January 31, 1934; admitted to bar, 1975, California and U.S. District Court, Central District of California. *Education:* Indiana University (B.S., 1956); Whittier College (J.D., 1974). Member, Los Angeles Bankruptcy Forum, 1975-1995. *Member:* Los Angeles County Bar Association (Member, Bankruptcy Section, 1975-1995); State Bar of California. [U.S. Army, 1956-1960]. *PRACTICE AREAS:* Bankruptcy.

## LAW OFFICES OF
## JOHN L. FLOWERS, P.C.
225 SOUTH LAKE AVENUE, THIRD FLOOR
**PASADENA, CALIFORNIA 91105**
Telephone: 818-432-5494
Fax: 818-432-5401

*Civil Litigation, Trusts, Business and Estate Planning.*

**JOHN L. FLOWERS,** born San Bernardino, California, March 26, 1941; admitted to bar, 1966, California; 1969, U.S. District Court, Southern District of California; 1970, U.S. District Court, Central District of California; 1979, U.S. Court of Appeals, Ninth Circuit; 1982, U.S. Supreme Court; 1994, Washington. *Education:* University of Redlands; University of Southern California (B.S.L., 1965; J.D., 1966). Phi Delta Phi; Order of the Coif. Recipient, American Jurisprudence Award in Contracts. Member, Editorial Board, Southern California Law Review, 1965-1966. Author: "Federal Rules of Civil Procedure: Attacking the Party Problem," 38 So. Cal. L. Rev. 80, 1965; "Legal Aspects of Direct Mail Fund Raising," Direct Mail Fund Raising Handbook, 1975. Instructor of Business Law, San Bernardino Valley College, 1966-1967. Deputy District Attorney, Napa County, California, 1968-1969. Trial Attorney, U.S. Immigration and Naturalization Service, 1987-1988. *Member:* Pasadena, Los Angeles County and American Bar Associations; State Bar of California. (Also Of Counsel to Darling, Hall & Rae at Los Angeles). *REPORTED CASES:* Springs Industries, Inc. v. Kris Knit, Inc. (9th Circuit 1989) 880 F.2d 1129. *PRACTICE AREAS:* Civil Litigation; Trust Planning; Business Planning; Estate Planning; Trust and Estate Litigation.

## FOSS & ROBERTS
Established in 1993
NINTH FLOOR
225 SOUTH LAKE AVENUE
**PASADENA, CALIFORNIA 91101**
Telephone: 818-683-4925
Facsimile: 818-683-3986

*Financial Institutions, Creditor Rights, Bankruptcy, Real Estate, Workouts, Insolvency, Commercial Law.*

### MEMBERS OF FIRM

**LINDA JUDD FOSS,** born Ceder Rapids, Iowa, March 18, 1949; admitted to bar, 1973, California; 1975, U.S. District Court, Central and Southern Districts of California; 1990, U.S. District Court, Northern and Eastern Districts of California. *Education:* Middle Tennessee State University (B.S., 1970); University of California at Berkeley, Boalt Hall (J.D., 1973). *PRACTICE AREAS:* Financial Institutions; Creditor Rights; Bankruptcy; Real Estate.

**PATRICK M. ROBERTS,** born San Diego, California, July 31, 1957; admitted to bar, 1982, California and U.S. District Court, Central District of California; 1983, U.S. District Court, Southern and Northern Districts Of California. *Education:* University of California at Los Angeles (B.A., cum laude, 1979); Hastings College of Law, University of California (J.D., 1982). Associate Articles Editor, Hastings Communications and Entertainment Law Quarterly, 1981-1982. *PRACTICE AREAS:* Litigation (Financial Institutions); Workouts; Insolvency.

*(This Listing Continued)*

*OF COUNSEL*

**HOWARD W. FOSS,** born New Bedford, Massachusetts, June 3, 1946; admitted to bar, 1973, California. *Education:* Harvard University (B.A., cum laude, 1968); University of California at Berkeley, Boalt Hall (J.D., 1973). Associate Editor, California Law Review. Instructor: Whittier Law School, 1979—. *Member:* Los Angeles County Bar Association (Member, Commercial Law Committee).

REPRESENTATIVE CLIENTS: Chase Manhattan; Sanwa Bank California; Wells Fargo Bank; Community Bank; Bank of Westminister; First Credit Bank; Imperial Thrift & Loan; Fidelity National Title Insurance Company.

## FRANSCELL, STRICKLAND, ROBERTS & LAWRENCE
A PROFESSIONAL CORPORATION
Established in 1992
PENTHOUSE, 225 SOUTH LAKE AVENUE
**PASADENA, CALIFORNIA 91101-3005**
Telephone: 818-304-7830; 213-684-7830
Fax: 818-795-7460

*Santa Ana, California Office:* Suite 800, 401 Civic Center Drive West. Telephone: 714-543-6511. Fax: 714-543-6711.
*Riverside, California Office:* Suite 670, 3801 University Avenue. Telephone: 909-686-1000. Fax: 909-686-2565.

*Police Misconduct Liability Defense, Civil Rights Defense, Employment Defense, Municipal and Administrative Law, Legal Malpractice, Medical Malpractice, General Civil and Criminal Trial and Appellate Practice and Litigation.*

FIRM PROFILE: *The firm's decision to locate its three offices in Pasadena, Santa Ana and Riverside was borne out of a desire to be accessible to clients primarily located in Los Angeles, Riverside, San Bernardino, Orange and San Diego Counties. The three locations also place FSRL attorneys in close proximity to the various Southern California courts, thereby generating significant cost savings for many clients.*

*Franscell, Strickland, Roberts & Lawrence understands the practice of law is always changing. To continue to provide the legal services clients want, the firm is dedicated to remaining adaptable to the changes of the 1990s and to actively promoting the early and efficient resolution of all litigation.*

**GEORGE J. FRANSCELL,** born Los Angeles, California, March 31, 1933; admitted to bar, 1959, California; 1971, U.S. Supreme Court; U.S. District Court, Northern, Central, Southern and Eastern Districts of California. *Education:* Loyola University (B.A., 1955); University of California at Los Angeles (J.D., 1958). National Lecturer and Consultant, Proactive Civil Liability, Officer Involved Shootings, SWAT, Internal Affairs and Police Discipline, International Association of Chiefs of Police. Seminar Leader, Police Management and Legal Problems, Americans for Effective Law Enforcement (A.E.L.E.), California Polytechnic University, Pomona. Consultant, A.E.L.E. Defense Center. Instructor, Police Executive Level, P.O.S.T. Former Principal Assistant City Attorney, City of Los Angeles, Liability Division. Legal Advisor, Los Angeles Police Commission and Los Angeles Police Department. Member, Model Policy Committee, International Association of Chiefs of Police. *Member:* Los Angeles County and American (Member, Insurance, Negligence and Compensation Law Section) Bar Associations; State Bar of California; California Trial Lawyers Association; American Board of Trial Advocates; Association of Southern California Defense Counsel; The Association of Trial Lawyers of America; International Association of Chiefs of Police; NSSC Lawyers Advisory Council; California Peace Officers Association; National Advisory Board for Law Enforcement Liability Insurance; National Institute of Municipal Law Officers (Member, Tort Liability of Local Governments and Officials Section). *PRACTICE AREAS:* Police Misconduct Liability Defense; Civil Rights; Municipal and Administrative Law; Medical Malpractice Legal; General Civil; Criminal Trial; Title VII Discrimination; Americans with Disabilities Act; Sexual Harassment; Appellate Practice; Administrative Law; Litigation.

**TRACY STRICKLAND,** born Gary, Indiana, March 16, 1954; admitted to bar, 1979, California and U.S. District Court, Central, Northern, Southern and Eastern Districts of California. *Education:* University of Notre Dame (B.A., 1976); Pepperdine University Law School (J.D., 1979). Recipient, American Jurisprudence Award in Community Property. *Member:* State Bar of California. (Resident, Santa Ana Office). *PRACTICE AREAS:* Police Misconduct Liability Defense; Civil Rights; Municipal and Adminis-

*(This Listing Continued)*

**FRANSCELL, STRICKLAND, ROBERTS & LAWRENCE,**
*A PROFESSIONAL CORPORATION, Pasadena—Continued*

trative Law; Medical Legal; General Civil; Criminal Trial; Appellate Practice; Administrative Law; Litigation.

**BARBARA E. ROBERTS,** born Jackson, Mississippi, March 30, 1948; admitted to bar, 1979, California; 1984, U.S. District Court, Central District of California; 1985, U.S. Supreme Court; 1987, U.S. Court of Appeals, Ninth Circuit; 1990, U.S. District Court, Southern District of California; 1991, U.S. District Court, Eastern District of California. *Education:* University of California at Santa Barbara; West Los Angeles College; California State University at Los Angeles (B.S., cum laude, 1977); Loyola Marymount University (J.D., cum laude, 1979). Recipient, American Jurisprudence Award in Torts. Author: "California Arrest, Search and Seizure," Campus Press, 1979; "Legal Issues in the Use of Force," Police Chief, Jan. 1992; "Internal Affairs and the First Amendment," Police Chief, May 1992; "The Changing Nature of Relevancy," Federal Litigation Guide, Matthew Bender, 1990. Adjunct Professor, Criminal Justice, California State University, 1979-1988. Probation Monitor, 1985—. Referee Pro Tem, 1984-1989, State Bar Court. Member: California Attorneys for Criminal Justice, 1979-1986; Criminal Court Bar Association, 1981-1986. Los Angeles Women Lawyers. *Member:* State Bar of California; International Association of Chiefs of Police (Member, Legal Officers Section). [With USNR, 1974-1979]. (Resident, Riverside Office). *PRACTICE AREAS:* Police Misconduct Liability Defense; Civil Rights; Municipal and Administrative Law; Medical Malpractice Legal; General Civil; Criminal Trial; Appellate Practice; Administrative Law; Litigation.

**DAVID D. LAWRENCE,** born Evansville, Indiana, March 25, 1954; admitted to bar, 1980, Arizona and U.S. District Court, District of Arizona; 1986, California, U.S. District Court, Central, Northern, Southern and Eastern Districts of California, U.S. Court of Appeals, Ninth Circuit and U.S. Supreme Court. *Education:* Indiana University (B.S., with high distinction), Beta Gamma Sigma; University of Arizona (J.D., 1980). Member, Moot Court Board. Attorney, Pima County Attorney's Office, Tucson Arizona, 1980-1985. *Member:* State Bar of Arizona; State Bar of California. *PRACTICE AREAS:* Police Misconduct Liability Defense; Civil Rights; Title VII Discrimination; Americans with Disabilities Act; Municipal and Administrative Law; Medical Legal; General Civil; Criminal Trial; Appellate Practice; Administrative Law; Litigation.

**CAROL ANN ROHR,** born Berkeley, California, November 22, 1943; admitted to bar, 1979, California and U.S. District Court, Central District of California. *Education:* University of Southern California (B.A., 1965); Western State University (J.D., 1979). Recipient, American Jurisprudence Award in Contracts. *Member:* State Bar of California (Member, Litigation Section); Southern California Defense Counsel; International Association of Chiefs of Police. *PRACTICE AREAS:* Police Misconduct Liability Defense; Civil Rights; Municipal and Administrative Law; Medical Malpractice Legal; General Civil; Criminal Trial; Appellate Practice; Administrative Law; Litigation.

**SCOTT D. MACLATCHIE,** born Santa Monica, California, September 9, 1957; admitted to bar, 1984, California; 1985, Nebraska. *Education:* University of Southern California (B.S., cum laude, 1979); Loyola Marymount University (J.D., 1984). Phi Alpha Delta (Marshall, 1982-1983). Associate Justice, Scott Moot Court Honors Board, 1983-1984. *Member:* Los Angeles County and American Bar Associations. *PRACTICE AREAS:* Police Misconduct Liability Defense; Civil Rights; Municipal and Administrative Law; Medical Legal; General Civil; Criminal Trial; Appellate Practice; Administrative Law; Litigation.

**S. FRANK HARRELL,** born Norfolk, Virginia, July 24, 1960; admitted to bar, 1986, Virginia, U.S. District Court, Eastern District of Virginia and U.S. Court of Appeals, Fourth Circuit; 1988, California and U.S. District Court, Northern, Eastern, Central and Southern Districts of California. *Education:* University of North Carolina (B.A., 1982) Duke University (J.D., 1985). Phi Beta Kappa. Author: "Objections at Trial," Federal Litigation Guide, Matthew Bender, 1992. *Member:* Virginia and American Bar Associations; Virginia State Bar; State Bar of California. (Resident, Santa Ana Office). *PRACTICE AREAS:* Police Misconduct Liability Defense; Civil Rights; Municipal and Administrative Law; General Civil; Criminal Trial; Appellate Practice; Administrative Law; Litigation.

**DONALD C. MCFARLANE,** born Toronto, Canada, November 18, 1964; admitted to bar, 1993, California and U.S. District Court, Central District of California. *Education:* California State University, Long Beach (B.A., 1986); Whittier College School of Law (J.D., 1992). Recipient, American Jurisprudence Award in Advanced Legal Skills. *Member:* Orange County Bar Association; State Bar of California. (Resident, Santa Ana Office). *PRACTICE AREAS:* Police Misconduct Liability Defense; Civil Rights; Municipal Administrative Law; Sexual Harassment Defense; Civil Practice; Criminal Trial; Appellate Practice; Litigation.

**LIBBY WONG,** born Los Angeles, California, June 21, 1968; admitted to bar, 1994, California. *Education:* University of California at Los Angeles (B.A., cum laude, 1991); University of Southern California (J.D., 1994). Golden Key. Member, UCLA College Honors Program. *Member:* Los Angeles County (Member, Sections on: Litigation; Employment Law; Business Law) and American Bar Associations. *LANGUAGES:* Mandarin Chinese. *PRACTICE AREAS:* Police Misconduct Liability Defense; Civil Rights; Municipal and Administrative Law; Sexual Harassment; Civil Practice; Appellate Practice; Litigation.

**CINDY S. LEE,** born Seoul, Korea, April 16, 1968; admitted to bar, 1993, California; 1994, U.S. District Court, Central District of California. *Education:* University of California at San Diego (B.A. Political Science, 1990); Loyola University of Los Angeles (J.D., 1993). Judicial Extern, Hon. J. Spencer Letts, 1992. Extern, Western Law Center for Disability Rights, 1993. *Member:* Los Angeles County, Pasadena County, Korean American and American Bar Associations; State Bar of California (Probation Monitor, 1994-1996). *LANGUAGES:* Korean. *PRACTICE AREAS:* Municipal and Administrative Law; Civil Rights; Police Misconduct; Police Liability Defense; Appellate Practice; Employment Discrimination; Sexual Harassment.

**MARTIN J. DE VRIES,** born Evergreen Park, Illinois, August 21, 1960; admitted to bar, 1990, California; U.S. District Court, Central District of California; U.S. Court of Appeals, Ninth Circuit. *Education:* Dordt College (B.A., 1982); Valparaiso University (J.D., 1989). Delta Theta Phi. *Member:* San Bernardino County Bar Association; State Bar of California; Defense Research Institute; American Inns of Court. (Resident, Riverside Office). *PRACTICE AREAS:* Police Misconduct Defense; Labor and Employment; Products Liability.

**ANN MARIE SANDERS,** born Detroit, Michigan, September 30, 1969; admitted to bar, 1995, California. *Education:* University of Michigan (B.A., 1990); Southwestern University School of Law (J.D., 1995). *Member:* State Bar of California; Women Lawyers Association of Los Angeles.

**PRISCILLA F. SLOCUM,** born Morrison, Illinois, February 11, 1946; admitted to bar, 1992, California and U.S. District Court, Central District of California. *Education:* University of California at Los Angeles (B.S., summa cum laude, 1977; M.A., 1980; Ph.D., 1986); Loyola Law School (J.D., 1992). Phi Beta Kappa. Recipient: American Jurisprudence Award, Appellate Advocacy; Jean Nidetch Award; California Attorney General Research Fellowship; UCLA Chancellors Fellowship. Author: "The Impact of the Exclusionary Rule on the California Criminal Justice System," California Department of Justice. Legal Studies Coordinator, Nova College, Fort Lauderdale, Florida, 1987-1989. Member: American Political Science Association, 1980-1986; Law and Society Association, 1980-1986. *Member:* Los Angeles, Beverly Hills and Federal Bar Associations. *PRACTICE AREAS:* Civil Rights Defense; Appellate Practice.

**GARTH MATTHEW DROZIN,** born Albany, New York, December 10, 1953; admitted to bar, 1987, California, U.S. District Court, Central District of California and U.S. Court of Appeals for the Federal Circuit; 1993, District of Columbia and Massachusetts. *Education:* State University of New York (B.A., 1975); Universidad de Salamanca, Spain (Certificado Sobresaliente, 1976); North Texas State University (M.M., 1977); Cornell University (D.M.A./A.B.D., 1981); Internationales Musikinstitut Darmstadt, Germany; Southwestern University School of Law (J.D., 1987). Fulbright Scholar. Recipient: American Jurisprudence Awards in Property, Business Organizations and Pre-trial Lawyering Skills; Tom Bradley Scholarship; Farmers Insurance Group Scholarship. Member, Law Review, 1985-1986. Author: "On the Record," *Los Angeles Daily Journal,* Verdicts and Settlements Supplement, September 22, 1995, reprinted from original article titled, "Court Reporters and Technology: An Attorney's View," *Journal of Court Reporting,* Vol. 52, No. 9, July 1991, also reprinted as, "Court Reporters: Still in Style After all These Years," *North Carolina Lawyers Weekly,* July 29, 1991 and *Maine Lawyers Review,* May, 1994; "Criminal Burden of Proof: Do We Need a Bright-Line Standard?" *Lawyers World,* Vol. 2, No. 3 May/June 1996. Judge Pro Tem: Los Angeles Municipal Court, 1988—; Ventura Municipal Court, 1993—. Mandatory Early Settlement Conference Officer, Ventura Superior Court, 1993—; "CRASH" Settlement Officer, Los Angeles Superior Court in Glendale, 1992-1993. Arbitrator, Ventura Superior and Municipal Courts, 1993—. Arbitrator and Mediator, Los Angeles Superior Court, 1993—. Fulbright Senior Professor, Brazil, 1983. Member, Sports Hall of Fame, State University of New York,

*(This Listing Continued)*

Plattsburgh, 1994. *LANGUAGES:* Portuguese, Spanish, German, Italian. *PRACTICE AREAS:* Governmental Entity Defense; Civil Litigation; Products Liability; Construction Defect; Fraud.

REPRESENTATIVE CLIENTS: Red Lion Inns; Southern California Joint Powers Insurance Authority; Universal Health Services, Inc.; Representing the following Public Entities: Anaheim; Arcadia; Beverly Hills; Board of Regents, University of California; Chino; Claremont; Colton; Corona; County of Los Angeles; County of Orange; County of San Bernardino; Culver City; Downey; El Monte; Fontana; Hawthorne; Hemet; Indio; LaVerne; Livermore; Manhattan Beach; Monrovia; Montebello; Ontario; Orange; Pasadena; Placentia; Pleasanton; Pomona; Redondo Beach; Rialto; Riverside; San Bernardino; Santa Barbara City and County; Torrance; Upland; West Covina.

## FREEBURG, JUDY & NETTELS
600 SOUTH LAKE AVENUE
**PASADENA, CALIFORNIA 91106**
Telephone: 818-585-4150
FAX: 818-585-0718

*Santa Ana, California Office:* Xerox Centre. 1851 East First Street, Suite 120. 92705-4017. Telephone: 714-569-0950. Facsimile: 714-569-0955.

*General Civil Trial and Appellate Practice. Casualty, Malpractice, Products Liability, Insurance and Environmental Law. Personal Defense.*

FIRM PROFILE: *Freeburg, Judy & Nettels, established in 1991, practices primarily in the area of civil litigation. This includes all aspects of insurance defense with an emphasis upon personal injury, medical malpractice, insurance fraud, premises and product liability. The firm also handles issues relating to environmental and toxic matters, municipal liability, family law, employment discrimination and wrongful termination.*

**STEVEN J. FREEBURG,** born Evanston, Illinois, December 15, 1944; admitted to bar, 1971, California. *Education:* Claremont Men's College (B.A., 1967); Loyola University of Los Angeles (J.D., 1970). Phi Delta Phi. Member, St. Thomas More Society. *Member:* Los Angeles County Bar Association; State Bar of California; Association of Southern California Defense Counsel; American Board of Trial Advocates. *PRACTICE AREAS:* Products Liability; Insurance; Personal Injury Defense; Wrongful Termination; Employment Discrimination; Insurance Bad Faith.

**J. LAWRENCE JUDY,** born Sacramento, California, November 20, 1945; admitted to bar, 1972, California; 1973, U.S. District Court, Central District of California; 1974, U.S. District Court, Northern District of California; 1980, U.S. Supreme Court. *Education:* United States Naval Academy, Foothill College (A.A., 1965); Claremont Men's College (B.A., 1967); Loyola University of Los Angeles (J.D., 1972). *Member:* Pasadena Bar Association; State Bar of California; Association of Southern California Defense Counsel; International Association of Defense Counsel; Defense Research Institute. *PRACTICE AREAS:* Products Liability; Insurance; Environmental and Toxic Torts; Personal Injury Defense.

**CHARLES F. NETTELS,** born Los Angeles, California, March 7, 1956; admitted to bar, 1981, California. *Education:* California State University at Humboldt (B.A., magna cum laude, 1978); Loyola University of Los Angeles (J.D., 1981). *Member:* State Bar of California; Association of Southern California Defense Counsel. *PRACTICE AREAS:* Insurance Fraud; Automobile; Products Liability; Premises Liability.

### ASSOCIATES

**INGALL W. BULL, JR.,** born Los Angeles, California, July 27, 1927; admitted to bar, 1951, California. *Education:* Loyola University and Stanford University (A.B., 1948); Stanford University (LL.B., 1950). Phi Beta Kappa; Delta Theta Phi. Member, Executive Council, Los Angeles Junior Bar Association, 1954-1956. *Member:* Los Angeles County and American Bar Associations; State Bar of California (Member, Committee on Civil Practice and Procedure, 1970-1973); American Board of Trial Advocates (Treasurer, 1977-1989; President, Los Angeles Chapter, 1977-1978); Association of Southern California Defense Counsel. *PRACTICE AREAS:* Dental Malpractice; Products Liability; Insurance; Personal Injury Defense.

**RICHARD B. CASTLE,** born Rutherford, New Jersey, March 13, 1930; admitted to bar, 1956, California. *Education:* University of California at Los Angeles (A.B., 1952; LL.B., 1955). *Member:* Los Angeles County and American Bar Associations; State Bar of California; Association of Southern California Defense Counsel. *PRACTICE AREAS:* Malpractice; Products Liability; Insurance; Personal Injury Defense.

**CYNTHIA B. SCHALDENBRAND,** born Broadstairs, Kent, England, December 30, 1951; admitted to bar, 1977, California. *Education:* University

*(This Listing Continued)*

sity of California at Irvine (B.A., 1974); Pepperdine University (J.D., 1977). Professor, Alan Hancock Community College, 1977-1982. Chairman, North Santa Barbara County Youth Services, 1978-1980. *Member:* North Santa Barbara County (Vice President, 1981) and Orange County Bar Associations; Orange County Chapter, California Trial Lawyers Association. (Resident, Santa Ana Office). *LANGUAGES:* Spanish. *PRACTICE AREAS:* Insurance Defense; Premises Liability; Security Liability; Real Estate Litigation; Contract Litigation; Employee Discrimination; Wrongful Termination.

**ROBERT S. BRODY,** born Philadelphia, Pennsylvania, January 13, 1959; admitted to bar, 1984, California and U.S. District Court, Central and Southern Districts of California. *Education:* Rutgers University (B.A., cum laude, 1980); University of California, Davis (J.D., 1983). Recipient: University of California Regents Fellowship, 1983. Mediator, Los Angeles County Bar Dispute Resolution Services. Arbitrator, Superior and Municipal Courts of Los Angeles, Riverside, San Bernadino and Ventura Counties. *Member:* Pasadena, Los Angeles County and American Bar Associations; State Bar of California. *PRACTICE AREAS:* Premises Liability; Products Liability; Construction Defect Litigation; Personal Injury; Arbitration.

**HOLLY A. McNULTY,** born Indiana, October 17, 1964; admitted to bar, 1990, California. *Education:* Miami University (B.S., 1987); Pepperdine University (J.D., 1990). *Member:* Los Angeles County and American Bar Associations; State Bar of California. *PRACTICE AREAS:* Personal Injury Defense; Suspected Fraudulent Claims; Family Law; Subrogation.

**KAREN S. FREEBURG,** born Artesia, California, September 4, 1946; admitted to bar, 1972, California. *Education:* Pitzer College (B.A., 1968); Loyola University of Los Angeles (J.D., 1971). *Member:* Pasadena Bar Association; State Bar of California; Association of Southern California Defense Counsel. *PRACTICE AREAS:* Products Liability; Personal Injury Defense.

**JENNIFER D. HELSEL,** born Los Angeles, California, May 13, 1957; admitted to bar, 1988, California. *Education:* California State University at Northridge (B.A., 1981); Southwestern University (J.D., cum laude, 1988). Member, National Trial Advocacy Team. Member, Southwestern University Law Review, 1987-1988. *Member:* Pasadena Bar Association; State Bar of California. *PRACTICE AREAS:* Malpractice; Employment; Personal Injury Defense.

**WILLIAM R. FRANCIS,** born Glendale, California, April 12, 1942; admitted to bar, 1971, California; 1972, U.S. District Court, Southern and Central Districts of California; 1984, U.S. Court of Appeals, Ninth Circuit. *Education:* Whittier College (B.A., 1964); Loyola Marymount University (J.D., 1971). Phi Alpha Delta. Co-Author: "Gathering Evidence Abroad," Los Angeles Lawyers, Los Angeles County Bar Association, December, 1983. Attorney, Legal Department, Bank of America, 1975-1985. Member, Whittier College Board of Trustees and Alumni Board of Governors. *Member:* Pasadena Bar Association; State Bar of California; Southern California Defense Counsel. *PRACTICE AREAS:* Business Law; Commercial Law; Banking Litigation; Insurance; Personal Injury; Real Estate; Tort Litigation.

**FRED W. BRANDT,** born Chicago, Illinois, April 11, 1933; admitted to bar, 1964, California. *Education:* Pomona College and Stanford University (B.A., 1955); Stanford University and Southwestern University (LL.B., 1964). Deputy County Counsel, Los Angeles, 1964-1966. *Member:* Los Angeles County and American Bar Associations; The State Bar of California; American Board of Trial Advocates; Association of Southern California Defense Counsel. [Capt., J.A.G.A.R., Retired]

**CARLA CROCHET,** born Wenatchee, Washington, January 18, 1963; admitted to bar, 1995, Hawaii; U.S. District Court, District of Hawaii; 1996, California. *Education:* California State University, Dominguez Hills (B.S., 1989); University of California, Davis (J.D., 1994). Phi Delta Phi; Delta Mu Delta. Member, Law Review. *Member:* Hawaii State and American Bar Associations; State Bar of California. *PRACTICE AREAS:* Toxic Exposure; Business Litigation; Premises Liability Litigation.

## JAMES A. GALLO
SUITE ONE
THE BRYAN COURT
427 SOUTH MARENGO AVENUE
**PASADENA, CALIFORNIA 91101**
Telephone: 818-304-0909
Facsimile: 818-304-0071

*Civil Litigation in all State and Federal Courts. Real Estate, Criminal Defense and Business Litigation.*

**JAMES A. GALLO,** born Los Angeles, California, February 6, 1950; admitted to bar, 1977, California and U.S. District Court, Central District of California. *Education:* Loyola Marymount University (B.A., 1972; J.D., 1976). Phi Sigma Kappa. Arbitrator, Los Angeles Superior Court Arbitration Panel. Judge Pro Tem, Los Angeles Municipal Court, 1982—. Licensed Real Estate Broker, California, 1983. *Member:* Los Angeles County (Member, Real Property, Trial Lawyers Section) and American Bar Associations.

## GARRETT & TULLY
A PROFESSIONAL CORPORATION
35 HUGUS ALLEY, SUITE 300
**PASADENA, CALIFORNIA 91103**
Telephone: 818-577-9500
Telecopier: 818-577-0813

*Westlake Village, California Office:* 660 Hampshire Road, Suite 204. 91361. Telephone: 805-446-4141. Telecopier: 805-446-4135.

*Professional Liability, Legal Malpractice, Accountant Malpractice, Business and Real Estate Litigation in all State and Federal Courts.*

*FIRM PROFILE: Garrett & Tully was formed in 1991 by Robert Garrett and Stephen J. Tully out of their desire to build a small firm emphasizing economic efficiency and responsiveness to clients' needs. In this quest, Garrett & Tully has developed a sophisticated litigation practice emphasizing real estate and professional liability matters, in addition to a variety of other subject matter areas. Garrett & Tully's attorneys combine experience with good business sense in an effort to better serve the needs of the firm's clients.*

**STEPHEN J. TULLY,** born Seattle, Washington, September 4, 1956; admitted to bar, 1983, California; 1985, New York; 1989, District of Columbia. *Education:* California State University at Northridge (B.A., magna cum laude, 1978); Southwestern University School of Law (J.D., 1983). Honors Moot Court. *Member:* Los Angeles County and American (Member, Sections on: Litigation; Real Property, Probate and Trust Law; Tort and Insurance Practice; General Practice) Bar Associations; State Bar of California. (Resident, Westlake Village Office). **PRACTICE AREAS:** Business Litigation; Real Estate Litigation; Professional Liability.

**ROBERT GARRETT,** born Chicago, Illinois, April 30, 1950; admitted to bar, 1975, California; 1992, U.S. Supreme Court. *Education:* University of Southern California (A.B., cum laude, 1972); University of California at Los Angeles (J.D., 1975). *Member:* Beverly Hills, Los Angeles County and American (Member, Section of Litigation) Bar Associations; State Bar of California; Association of Southern California Defense Counsel; Association of Business Trial Lawyers. **PRACTICE AREAS:** Business Litigation; Real Estate Litigation; Professional Liability.

**STEPHEN C. CHUCK,** born Fresno, California, October 30, 1960; admitted to bar, 1985, California and U.S. District Court, Central District of California. *Education:* California State University at Fresno (B.S., cum laude, 1982); University of California at Davis (J.D., 1985). Phi Delta Phi. *Member:* Los Angeles County and American Bar Associations; State Bar of California. **PRACTICE AREAS:** Business Litigation; Real Estate Litigation; Professional Liability.

**EFREN A. COMPEÁN,** born Whittier, California, April 28, 1959; admitted to bar, 1985, California and U.S. District Court, Central District of California. *Education:* University of California at Los Angeles (B.A., 1982; J.D., 1985). *Member,* Chicano Law Review, 1984. *Member:* Los Angeles County Bar Association; The State Bar of California (Member: Litigation Section). **PRACTICE AREAS:** Litigation; Business Law; Commercial Law; Professional Liability.

**KEVIN S. LACEY,** born San Gabriel, California, October 19, 1956; admitted to bar, 1989, California. *Education:* California State University at Los Angeles (B.A., 1979); Southwestern University (J.D., 1988). Member,

*(This Listing Continued)*

Moot Court Honors Program, 1986-1988. Recipient, American Jurisprudence Awards. *Member:* The State Bar of California. **PRACTICE AREAS:** Business Litigation; Real Estate Litigation; Professional Liability.

**PETER B. LANGBORD,** born Los Angeles, California, February 27, 1962; admitted to bar, 1989, California; 1991, U.S. District Court, Central District of California. *Education:* California State University at Northridge (B.A., 1986); Pepperdine University (J.D., 1989). Alternative Dispute Resolution Symposium Editor and Associate Editor, Pepperdine Law Review, 1988-1989. Contributing Author: "California Supreme Court Survey," 16 Pepperdine Law Review 176-180, 218-220, 492-495. Co-Author: "Monetary Sanctions Under California Law: Are They Insurable?" Los Angeles Lawyer, December 26, 1988. *Member:* State Bar of California; Association of Southern California Defense Counsel. **PRACTICE AREAS:** Litigation; Professional Liability.

**KELLI M. WEHN,** born Ontario, California, September 18, 1960; admitted to bar, 1990, California; 1991, U.S. District Court, Central District of California and U.S. Court of Appeals, 9th Circuit. *Education:* University of California at Los Angeles (B.A., 1986); Southwestern University (J.D., 1990). Member, Moot Court Honors Program. Best Oralist Team, National Tax Moot Court Competition, 1990. *Member:* State Bar of California. **PRACTICE AREAS:** Business Litigation; Real Estate Litigation; Professional Liability.

**DANIEL DAVID KOPMAN,** born Los Angeles, California, April 17, 1958; admitted to bar, 1992, California. *Education:* University of California (B.S., 1985); Loyola Law School (J.D., 1992). Certified Public Accountant, California, 1987. *Member:* State Bar of California; American Institute of Certified Public Accounts; California Society of CPA's. **PRACTICE AREAS:** Business Litigation; Real Estate Litigation; Professional Liability.

**CHRISTOPHER G. PIETY,** born Chicago, Illinois, May 27, 1966; admitted to bar, 1994, California. *Education:* Millikin University (in History and Spanish, 1984-1986); University of California at Santa Barbara (B.A., in Slavic Languages and Literatures, 1989); Golden Gate University (J.D., 1994). Alpha Lambda Delta; Phi Sigma; Alpha Tau Omega. Representative, Student Bar Association, 1991. Member, Appellate Advocacy Team, American Bar Association Competition, 1994. *Member:* State Bar of California. (Resident, Westlake Village Office). **PRACTICE AREAS:** Professional Liability; Commercial Litigation; Real Estate Litigation.

### OF COUNSEL

**JAMES A. MOSS,** born Los Angeles, California, April 1, 1952; admitted to bar, 1978, California. *Education:* University of California at Los Angeles (B.A., cum laude, 1974); University of Southern California (J.D., 1978); New York University (LL.M., 1982). Phi Alpha Delta. Recipient, American Jurisprudence Award in Bankruptcy. *Member:* Los Angeles County and American (Member, Section of Taxation) Bar Associations; State Bar of California. **PRACTICE AREAS:** Business Litigation; Real Estate Litigation; Professional Liability.

### LEGAL SUPPORT PERSONNEL

**DAVID M. WERNEBURG** (Business Manager).

REFERENCE: 1st Business Bank, Los Angeles.

## GIBSON AND RIVERA
55 SOUTH LAKE AVENUE, SUITE 550
**PASADENA, CALIFORNIA 91101**
Telephone: 818-405-1122
Facsimile: 818-405-8966

*General Business Litigation, including Real Estate, Unfair Business Practices, Employer-Employee Relations, Plaintiff and Defendant Personal Injury, Wrongful Death, Premises Liability Law and Probate Litigation.*

### MEMBERS OF FIRM

**JAMES L. GIBSON,** born Pasadena, California, October 16, 1940; admitted to bar, 1967, California, Alaska and U.S. District Court, Central District of California; 1971, U.S. Supreme Court; 1976, U.S. District Court, Southern District of California; 1986, U.S. District Court, Eastern District of California. *Education:* Point Loma College (B.A., 1963); University of Southern California (J.D., 1966). Phi Alpha Delta. Lecturer, Recent Developments in Civil Procedure, California Continuing Education of the Bar, 1982. *Member:* Pasadena and Los Angeles County (Member, Civil Litigation Section) Bar Associations; State Bar of California; Los Angeles Trial Lawyers Association. **PRACTICE AREAS:** Employer-Employee Law; Personal Injury; Probate Litigation; Medical Malpractice.

*(This Listing Continued)*

**CLARK W. RIVERA,** born Pasadena, California, August 22, 1952; admitted to bar, 1981, California. *Education:* University of California at Santa Barbara (B.A., 1974; M.A., 1975); University of Michigan; University of California School of Law, Los Angeles (J.D., 1981). *Member:* Pasadena and Los Angeles County Bar Associations; State Bar of California. **PRACTICE AREAS:** General Business Litigation; Employer-Employee Law; Wrongful Termination; Probate Litigation; Real Estate Litigation; Personal Injury.

## THE LAW OFFICES OF NED GOOD

Established in 1952

70 SOUTH LAKE AVENUE
**PASADENA, CALIFORNIA 91101**
Telephone: 818-440-0000
Telecopier: 818-449-0214

*Practice Restricted to Plaintiff Personal Injury, Aviation and Malpractice Law in all State and Federal Courts.*

*FIRM PROFILE: The Law Offices of Ned Good handles only plaintiff personal injury and death cases.*

*Our firm has won unprecedented amounts in verdicts and we have established records for the highest awards in wrongful death and personal injury cases in California, Hawaii and South Dakota.*

*Every client is important to us and gets our full attention and best efforts regardless of whether they are rich or poor, famous or not, and regardless of their background. The names of our clients and the settlements we obtain for them are kept confidential to preserve their right of privacy.*

**NED GOOD,** born Chicago, Illinois, June 6, 1928; admitted to bar, 1951, California; 1952, Florida; 1953, Korea; 1954, Illinois; U.S. Court of Appeals, District of Columbia Circuit. *Education:* University of Southern California (B.S., 1949; LL.B., 1951). Author: "Counsel for Parties Litigant May Use Recording Devices to Record Judicial Proceedings," Los Angeles County Bar Bulletin, December, 1965; "Use of Long Interrogatories in Aviation Cases," Journal of Air Law & Commerce, Summer, 1970 and California Trial Lawyers Association Journal, Winter, 1970-1971; "Damages for Loss of Consortium," California Trial Lawyers Association Journal, Fall 1973; "Organizing a Trial," The Advocate, Dec., 1974; "Voir Dire," The Advocate, Dec., 1974; "Electronic Note Taking in Court; Better Service to the Client," California Trial Lawyers Association Journal, Spring, 1974; "Using Medical Records," The Advocate, July, 1975; "How to Organize a File," The Advocate, August, 1975; "Right to Have Plaintiff's Attorney Present During Psychiatric Examination," The Advocate, Feb., 1975; "Checklist—From Master Calendar to Jury Selection," The Advocate, June, 1975; "Using Jury Instruction," The Advocate, Sept., 1975; "Cross Examination and How Not To," The Advocate, Nov., 1976; "Briefing Medical Records," Orange County Trial Lawyers Bulletin, March, 1977; "Summarizing Depositions," Orange County Trial Lawyers Bulletin, April, 1977; "Direct Examination," Arizona Bar Association Annual Convention, 1977; "The Price and Rewards of Success," The Advocate, July, 1978; "Admissibility of Video Tape & Still Photos Showing Plaintiff's Injuries," The Advocate, August, 1978; "The Brain Damaged at Deposition," The Advocate, December, 1979; "Experiences of a Volunteer Settlement Judge," The Advocate, April, 1979; "Answering Defendants' Interrogatories," The Advocate, June, 1979; "Witness Credibility Wins or Loses Cases," The Advocate, October, 1979; "Grief & Sorrow," The Advocate, April, 1982; "Failure to Require Separate Verdicts Results in Denial of Right to Jury Trial," The Advocate, May, 1982; "Telephone/Video-Taped Depositions," The Advocate, January, 1984; "Steps in Handling A New Case," The San Diego Trial Bar News, September, 1987; "Summarizing Depositions," The Advocate, May 1987; "Effective Written Advocacy and Oral Argument," Trial Bar News, March, 1996; "Effective Written Advocacy and Oral Argument," The Advocate, Feb., 1996. Recipient: Ted Horn Award, 1983 and 1996; Los Angeles Trial Lawyers Association Presidential Award, 1984. Associate Aviation Editor, American Trial Lawyers Association Law Journal, 1957—. Editor, Lawyers Round Table, 1963. Associate Editor, California Trial Lawyers Journal, 1965—. Lecturer: University of Southern California, 1969; Loyola University of Los Angeles, 1969; Hastings College of Law, University of California, 1971 and 1973. Lecturer on Personal Injury, Aviation and Trial Practices and Procedures, Southern Methodist University Law School, Aviation Symposium, 1970. Lecturer, Aviation, American Bar Association, Washington, D.C., 1994. Member of Faculty, 1975— and Professor, Civil Procedure, 1976—, University of Southern California Law School. Judge Protem, Los Angeles Superior Court, 1962. Member: Attorney Liaison Committee, Los Angeles Superior Court, 1969-1975; Legislative Liaison Committee of Aircraft Owners and Pilots Association for California, 1971—. Member: Inner Circle Advocates, awarded Trial Lawyer of the Year, 1976 by Los Angeles Trial Lawyers Association; American Board of Professional Liability Attorneys, 1983. *Member:* Los Angeles County (Member: Nominating Committee, 1973—; Trial Lawyers Section, 1973), Illinois State and American Bar Associations; The Florida Bar; State Bar of California (Member: Committee on Rules of Court Procedure, 1966-1975; Basic Protection Plan Committee, 1971-1975; Civil Trial Procedures Reform Committee, 1971-1975); Plaintiff Trial Lawyers Association of Los Angeles County (President, 1963); California Trial Lawyers Association (President, 1969-1970; Chairman, Aviation Committee, 1966-1968 and 1973); The Association of Trial Lawyers of America (California Vice President, 1959-1960; Secretary, Aviation Section, 1966; Member, Judicial Workshop Committee, 1971-1975 and National Institute Seminar Program Committee, 1971-1975); Western Regional Conference of The Association of Trial Lawyers of America; Lawyer-Pilots Bar Association; International Academy of Trial Lawyers; Inner Circle of Advocates. **REPORTED CASES:** Rodriguez v. McDonnell Douglas - damages; Newing v. Cheatham - aviation; Solis v. So. Cal. RTD - experts; Canavin v. PSA - prejudgment interests, taxes, jury verdicts; Nevels v. Yeager - bystander rule; Eli v. Travelers - WCAB carrier has no priority; Fagerquist v. Western Sun - noneconomic damages. **PRACTICE AREAS:** Aviation; Personal Injury; Product Liability; Wrongful Death.

### ASSOCIATES

**MARK WEST,** born White Plains, N.Y., October 20, 1960; admitted to bar, 1993, California. *Education:* Northeastern University; New Hampshire College (B.S., cum laude, 1982); Southwestern University (J.D., 1993). Asbestos Handler, State of New York; U.S.E.P.A. Asbestos Handler, 1988; U.S.E.P.A. Asbestos Abatement Designated Person; U.S.E.P.A. Asbestos Abatement Contractor/Supervisor; U.S.E.P.A. Asbestos Abatement Building Inspector, 1989. *Member:* American Bar Association; California and Los Angeles Trial Lawyers Association; American Trial Lawyers Association. **PRACTICE AREAS:** Personal Injury; Product Liability; Wrongful Death.

**CARY S. MACY,** born Hollywood, Florida, January 31, 1961; admitted to bar, 1988, California; U.S. District Court, Central District of California. *Education:* Indiana State University (B.S., English and Political Science, 1983); Pepperdine University School of Law (J.D., 1987). Parmista Academic Fraternity. *Member:* Los Angeles County Bar Association; State Bar of California; Association of Trial Lawyers of America. **PRACTICE AREAS:** Personal Injury; Wrongful Death.

**B. ERIC NELSON,** born Yonkers, New York, July 7, 1948; admitted to bar, 1980, California; 1981, U.S. Court of Appeals, Ninth Circuit; 1985, U.S District Court, Central and Southern Districts of California; 1986, U.S. District Court, Northern and Eastern Districts of California. *Education:* University of California, Los Angeles (B.A., Political Science, 1970); Southwestern University (J.D., 1980). Certified Divemaster and Member, Professional Association of Diving Instructors (PADI), 1993. NAUI Certified Advanced/Rescue Diver, 1991. Instructor, Community First Aid/CPR, American Red Cross. *Member:* Los Angeles County Bar Association; State Bar of California. [U.S. Navy, Active Duty, 1971-1974]. **REPORTED CASES:** Rao v. Campo, 223 Cal.App.3d 1557, 285 Cal.Rptr. 691 (Cal.App. 2 Dist., Sept. 12, 1992) (NO. B053573); Wise v. Superior Court (Myers), 222 Cal. App. 3d 1008, 272 Cal.Rprtr. 222 (Cal.App. 2 Dist., Aug. 7, 1990) (NO. B046438); Paul v. Drost, 186 Cal. App.3d 1407, 231 Cal.Reptr. 361 (Cal.App. 2 Dist., Nov. 7, 1986) (NO. B016575); Freshman, Mulvaney, Comsky, Kahan & Deutsch v. Superior Court (Kreuger) 173 Cal.App.3d 223, 218 Cal.Rptr. 533 (Cal.App. 2 Dist., Sept. 26, 1985) (NO. CIV. B010554); Hollywood Refrigeration Sales Co., Inc. v. Superior Court (Von Lavrinoff) 164 Cal.App. 3d 754, 210 Cal.Rptr. 619 (Cal.App. 2 Dist., Feb. 15, 1985) (NO. CIV. B007351); Danner v. Himmelfarb, 858 F.2d 515, 57 USLW 2264, Fed. Sec. L. Rep. P 94,034, 13 Fed.R.Serv.3d 292 (9th Cir. Cal., Sept. 28, 1988) (NO. 87-6021). **PRACTICE AREAS:** Personal Injury; Wrongful Death.

REFERENCE: Union Bank, Pasadena, California.

## FREDERICK GOTHA

SUITE 823, 80 SOUTH LAKE AVENUE
**PASADENA, CALIFORNIA 91101**
Telephone: 818-796-1849
Telecopier: 818-405-0952

*Patent, Trademark and Unfair Competition Law.*

**FREDERICK GOTHA,** born Chicago, Illinois, April 30, 1935; admitted to bar, 1967, California, U.S. District Court, Northern District of California and U.S. Court of Appeals, Ninth Circuit; 1972, U.S. Supreme Court; 1975, U.S. District Court, Central District of California; 1985, New York; registered to practice before U.S. Patent and Trademark Office. *Education:* Purdue University (B.S.A.E., 1957); University of Southern California (M.B.A., 1982); University of San Francisco (J.D., 1966). Beta Gamma Sigma. *Member:* Pasadena, Los Angeles County and New York State Bar Associations; The State Bar of California (Member: Patent, Trademark and Copyright Section; Litigation and Business Law Sections); Los Angeles Patent Law Association.

---

## GRAY & HIRREL

SUITE 600
301 EAST COLORADO BOULEVARD
**PASADENA, CALIFORNIA 91101**
Telephone: 818-795-3344
Los Angeles: 213-681-0665
Telecopier: 818-796-2683

*Probate and Estate Planning, Trusts and Taxation.*

### MEMBERS OF FIRM

**LAWRENCE S. GRAY, JR.,** born Los Angeles, California, March 30, 1928; admitted to bar, 1954, California. *Education:* Pomona College (B.A., 1949); University of Southern California (LL.B., 1954). (Retired).

**RICHARD J. HIRREL,** born Boston, Massachusetts, March 14, 1951; admitted to bar, 1980, California. *Education:* University of Southern California (B.A., 1974); University of San Fernando Valley (J.D., cum laude, 1979). Member, San Fernando Valley Law Review, 1978-1979. *Member:* Pasadena (Treasurer, 1983-1984) and Los Angeles County Bar Associations; State Bar of California. *PRACTICE AREAS:* Estate Planning; Probate Law; Trusts Law; Taxation Law.

REFERENCE: Citizens Commercial Trust & Savings Bank (Pasadena Main Office).

---

## GRONEMEIER & BARKER

55 SOUTH LAKE AVENUE, SUITE 220
P.O. BOX 90670
**PASADENA, CALIFORNIA 91109-0670**
Telephone: 818-568-4600
Los Angeles, California: 213-681-0702
Fax: 818-449-7560

*Commercial, Business, Labor, Employment Discrimination, Real Estate, Land Use, Banking, Civil Rights and Public Law. Civil Litigation.*

### MEMBERS OF FIRM

**DALE L. GRONEMEIER,** born Normal, Illinois, February 16, 1939; admitted to bar, 1975, California. *Education:* Illinois State University (B.S., 1960); Northwestern University (M.A., 1961); University of California at Berkeley; University of Illinois (J.D., 1975). Order of the Coif. Business Editor, University of Illinois Law Forum, 1974-1975. *Member:* Los Angeles County Bar Association; The State Bar of California. *PRACTICE AREAS:* Employment Discrimination Law; Business Law; Civil Rights Law.

**NEIL J. BARKER,** born Los Angeles, California, February 23, 1952; admitted to bar, 1977, California. *Education:* University of California at Davis (A.B., cum laude, 1974); Boalt Hall School of Law, University of California (J.D., 1977). Managing Editor, Ecology Law Quarterly, 1976-1977. Law Clerk, Hon. Edward J. Schwartz, Chief Judge, U.S. District Court for the Southern District of California, 1977-1978. *Member:* Los Angeles County Bar Association; The State Bar of California. *PRACTICE AREAS:* Banking Law; Real Estate; Unfair Competition Law; Business Litigation.

*(This Listing Continued)*

---

### ASSOCIATES

**ELLEN R. HURLEY,** born Washington, D.C., September 2, 1954; admitted to bar, 1988, California. *Education:* University of Maryland (B.A., 1977); George Washington University (M.A.S.S., 1981); Loyola Marymount University (J.D., 1988). Author: "The Medicare As Secondary Payer Program: New Cost Containment Measures Present Questions Of Fairness," 22 Clearing House Review 2, 1988. *Member:* State Bar of California; American Bar Association. *PRACTICE AREAS:* General Business Litigation.

---

## GUTIERREZ & PRECIADO

200 SOUTH LOS ROBLES
SUITE 210
**PASADENA, CALIFORNIA 91105**
Telephone: 818-449-2300
Facsimile: 818-449-2330
Email: apreciado@gutierrez-preciado.com
URL: http://www.primenet.com/~crh4

*Police Liability Defense, Civil Rights Defense, Employer Liability, Appellate Practice, Civil Litigation, Insurance Defense and Local Government Liability.*

### MEMBERS OF FIRM

**ARTHUR C. PRECIADO,** born Mexico City, Mexico, January 16, 1954; admitted to bar, 1983, California; 1984, U.S. District Court, Central District of California and U.S. Court of Appeals, Ninth Circuit. *Education:* California State University at Los Angeles (B.A., 1976); Hastings College of Law, University of California (J.D., 1981). Phi Alpha Delta. Member, Association of Deputy District Attorneys, 1985. Arbitrator, Superior and Municipal Courts, California. *Member:* Los Angeles County (Member, Judicial Evaluations Committee) and American Bar Associations; State Bar of California; Mexican-American Bar Association; Lawyers Club of Los Angeles; Los Angeles County Bar Inn of Court. *LANGUAGES:* Spanish. *PRACTICE AREAS:* Civil Litigation; Police Liability Defense; Employer Liability; Local Government Liability; Civil Rights Defense; Insurance Defense.

**NOHEMI GUTIERREZ FERGUSON,** born Aguascalientes, Aguascalientes, Mexico, October 18, 1960; admitted to bar, 1986, California and U.S. District Court, Central District of California; 1988, U.S. District Court, Southern and Northern Districts of California. *Education:* Claremont McKenna College (B.A., cum laude, 1982); University of California at Los Angeles School of Law (J.D., 1986). Graduate Student Fellowship; Virginia K. Wilson Fellowship. *Member:* Los Angeles County and American Bar Associations; State Bar of California. *LANGUAGES:* Spanish, French. *PRACTICE AREAS:* Civil Litigation; Police Liability Defense; Employer Liability; Local Government Liability; Civil Rights Defense.

**CALVIN R. HOUSE,** born St. Johnsbury, Vermont, September 14, 1951; admitted to bar, 1977, New York; 1988, California. *Education:* Columbia University (B.A., 1973; J.D., 1976). Harlan Fiske Stone Scholar. Author: "Malpractice Liability to Non-Clients," Orange County Lawyer, August 1994; "Prior Restraints on Campaign Speech in California," 14 W. St. U.L. Rev. 409 (1987); "Preclusion by State Judgement in Cases Involving Exclusive Federal Jurisdiction, 13 W. St. U.L. Rev. 435 (1986); "Good Faith Rejections and Specific Performance in Publishing Contracts: Safeguarding the Author's Reasonable Expectations," 51 Brooklyn L. Rev. 95 (1984). Instructor: Cardozo Law School, 1982-1984. Assistant Professor, Western State University College of Law, 1984-1988. Adjunct Professor, Western State University College of Law, 1993—. *Member:* State Bar of California. *REPORTED CASES:* Independent Investor Protective League v. Time, Inc., 66 A.D.2d 391, 412 N.Y.S.2d 898 (1979), rev'd, 50 N.Y. 2d 259, 406 N.E.2d 486, 428 N.Y.S.2d 671 (1980); Services Employees International Union v. Fair Political Practices Commission, 747 F.Supp. 580 (E.D. Cal. 1990), aff'd 955 F.2d 1312 (9th Cir.), cert. denied, 112 S. Ct. 3056, 3057 (1992); Shawmut Bank, N.A. v. Kress Associations, 33 F.3d 1477 (9th Cir. 1994); Tetra Pak, Inc. v. State Board of Equalization, 234 Cal. App. 3d 1751, 286 Cal. Rptr. 529 (1992); Union Bank v. Superior Court, 31 Cal. App. 4th 573, 37 Cal. Rptr. 2d 653 (1995). *PRACTICE AREAS:* Business Litigation; Appellate Practice; Employer Liability; Local Government Liability.

### ASSOCIATES

**GABRIELLE HARNER BRUMBACH,** born Los Angeles, California, June 10, 1967; admitted to bar, 1994, California and U.S. District Court, Central District of California. *Education:* University of California at Los Angeles (B.A., 1989); Southwestern University School of Law (J.D., 1994);

*(This Listing Continued)*

Heidelberg University, Heidelberg, Germany. Extern to the Hon. Kathleen P. March, Bankruptcy Judge, U.S. Bankruptcy Count, Central District of California, 1993. *Member:* Los Angeles County (Member, Sections on: Labor and Employment; Government Lawyers; Bankruptcy and Commercial Litigation) Bar Association; State Bar of California (Member, Labor and Employment Section); Los Angeles County Bar Barristers (Member, Education Committee). *LANGUAGES:* German. *PRACTICE AREAS:* Civil Rights Defense; Local Government Liability; Employer Liability.

**ELISABETH F. SHEH,** born The Hague, The Netherlands, April 13, 1968; admitted to bar, 1994, California. *Education:* University of California at San Diego (B.A., cum laude and highest distinction, 1991); Loyola University Law School (J.D., 1994). *Member:* Los Angeles Bar Association (Member, Entertainment and Labor Law Sections). *PRACTICE AREAS:* Civil Rights Defense; Local Government Liability; Employer Liability.

**BRIAN P. WALTER,** born Los Angeles, California, September 30, 1969; admitted to bar, 1994, California; 1995. U.S. District Court, Central District of California. *Education:* University of California at Los Angeles (B.A., Economics, 1993); Loyola University Law School (J.D., 1993). *Member:* Los Angeles County and American Bar Associations. *PRACTICE AREAS:* Civil Rights Defense; Local Government Liability; Employer Liability.

**CLIFTON A. BAKER,** born Houston, Texas, April 15, 1964; admitted to bar, 1994, California and U.S. District Court, Central District of California. *Education:* Sam Houston State University (B.F.A., cum laude, 1986); Southwestern University School of Law (J.D., 1994). American Jurisprudence Award in Legal Research and Writing. Member, Law Review, 1992-1994. Extern to Hon. Robert Stone, Magistrate Judge, U.S. District Court, Central District of California. *PRACTICE AREAS:* Civil Rights Defense; Employer Liability; Local Government Liability.

*OF COUNSEL*

**LINDA L. STREETER,** born Burbank, California, December 25, 1957; admitted to bar, 1982, California and U.S. Court of Appeals, Ninth Circuit; 1983, U.S. District Court, Central District of California; 1985, U.S. District Court, Southern District of California. *Education:* University of California at Los Angeles (B.S., 1979); Loyola School of Law (J.D., 1982). Scott Moot Court Honors Program. *Member:* Los Angeles County Bar Association; State Bar of California; Barristers; California Young Lawyers Association.

REPRESENTATIVE CLIENTS: Los Angeles County; City Fibers, Inc.; Paragon Insulation; Cesta Punta Deportes, S.A. de C.V.; J.B. Hunt Transport, Inc.; Team Construction.

---

# WILLIAM W. HAEFLIGER

SUITE 512
201 SOUTH LAKE AVENUE
**PASADENA, CALIFORNIA 91101**
Telephone: 818-449-0467
Los Angeles: 213-684-2707

*Intellectual Property, Patent, Trademark, Copyright and Unfair Competition Law.*

**WILLIAM W. HAEFLIGER,** born Evanston, Illinois, January 17, 1925; admitted to bar, 1956, California; registered to practice before U.S. Patent and Trademark Office. *Education:* California Institute of Technology (B.S., 1950); Loyola University of Los Angeles (LL.B., 1955). Tau Beta Pi; Phi Alpha Delta. *Member:* Los Angeles County and American (Member, Patent, Trademark and Copyright Law Section) Bar Associations; State Bar of California; American Intellectual Property Law Association. [U.S. Army, 1943-1945].

REFERENCE: Union Bank (Pasadena Main Office).

# HAHN & HAHN

A Partnership including Professional Corporations
Established in 1899

NINTH FLOOR
301 EAST COLORADO BOULEVARD
**PASADENA, CALIFORNIA 91101**
Telephone: 818-796-9123
Los Angeles: 213-681-6948
Orange Co.: 714-971-5590
Cable Address: "Hahnlaw"
Telecopier: 818-449-7357

*General Civil and Trial and Appellate Practice in Federal and State Courts, Corporation, Real Estate, Estate Planning, Probate, Family, Federal and State Tax Law, Employment Law.*

FIRM PROFILE: *Hahn & Hahn is a general civil practice law firm of twenty-four attorneys, located in Pasadena, California. Founded in 1899, the firm is one of the oldest law firms in California, and is the largest and most well-respected general practice firm in the San Gabriel Valley. For nearly one hundred years we have provided our clients with quality legal services in a prompt, efficient and professional manner.*

*Hahn & Hahn's practice is comprised of three main components: business, litigation and trust/estate planning. The firm's business attorneys perform services in all of the principal substantive areas of commercial law, including corporate counseling, mergers and acquisitions, tax advice, municipal law, real property transactions and land use, securities, employment relations and general contract law. Our litigation lawyers handle cases before all state and federal courts and administrative agencies, both at the trial and appellate levels, relating to such matters as breach of contract, securities, real property disputes, environmental matters, construction problems, eminent domain, redevelopment, personal injury, wrongful death, wrongful employment termination, trademark infringement, marital dissolution, tax litigation, collections and general business disputes. The lawyers practicing in the trust/estate planning field establish trusts of all types, draft wills and durable powers of attorney, probate estates, handle will contests, litigate in the estate, trust and conservatorship fields and advise clients on estate and gift tax issues.*

*Our existing business base is distributed over many diverse clients. The firm represents both large and small businesses, as well as many public institutions and individuals. Our services are carefully planned to meet the needs and resources of each client.*

MEMBERS OF FIRM

**DAVID K. ROBINSON, (P.C.),** born Cleveland, Ohio, May 30, 1918; admitted to bar, 1947, California. *Education:* Princeton University (A.B., 1940); Harvard University and Stanford University (J.D., 1946). Special Agent, F.B.I., 1942-45. *Member:* Pasadena, Los Angeles County and American (Member, Board of Governors, 1989-1991; Member, House of Delegates, 1984-1993; Chairman, Lawyers Professional Liability Committee, 1979-1982; Member, Sections on: Litigation; Business Law; Torts and Insurance Practice) Bar Associations; The State Bar of California (Member, Board of Governors, 1969-1972; President, 1971-1972); American College of Mortgage Attorneys; American Board of Trial Advocates; Chancery Club. Fellow, American College of Trial Lawyers. *PRACTICE AREAS:* Civil Litigation; Savings and Loan; Condemnation; Redevelopment.

**LOREN H. RUSSELL, (P.C.),** born Riverside, California, April 5, 1925; admitted to bar, 1952, California. *Education:* Naval Academy (B.S., 1946); Stanford University (LL.B., 1952). Phi Delta Phi; Order of the Coif. *Member:* The State Bar of California. [Lieut., USN, 1946-49, 1952-1953]. *PRACTICE AREAS:* Corporations; Business; Securities.

**LEONARD M. MARANGI, (P.C.),** born Los Angeles, California, January 26, 1929; admitted to bar, 1957, California. *Education:* University of California at Los Angeles (A.B., 1950); University of Southern California (J.D., 1956). Order of the Coif. Associate Editor, Southern California Law Review, 1955-1956. *Member:* Pasadena (President, 1982), Los Angeles County and American Bar Associations; The State Bar of California (Member, 1971-1974 and Chairman, 1973-1974, Family Law Committee); Chancery Club (President, 1993-1994). Fellow: American College of Trial Lawyers; American Academy of Matrimonial Lawyers. [Lieut. (j.g.), USN, 1950-1953]. (Certified Specialist, Family Law, The State Bar of California Board of Legal Specialization). *PRACTICE AREAS:* Civil Litigation; Family; Real Property; Business.

**WILLIAM S. JOHNSTONE, JR., (P.C.),** born Glendale, California, January 27, 1931; admitted to bar, 1958, California. *Education:* University

*(This Listing Continued)*

*HAHN & HAHN, Pasadena—Continued*

of Southern California (A.B., 1952; J.D., 1957). Blue Key; Phi Delta Phi. Member, Board of Editors, Southern California Law Review, 1955-1957. President: University of Southern California Student Bar Association, 1956-1957; University of Southern California Law Alumni Association, 1972-1973. Listed, Best Lawyers in America, Trusts and Estates, 1995-1996. Co-Author: "California Conservatorships and Guardianships," California Continuing Education of the Bar, 1990. *Member:* Pasadena (President, 1977), Los Angeles County and American Bar Associations; The State Bar of California (Chairman, 1978-1979, Advisor, 1979-1983, Estate Planning, Trust and Probate Law Section); Chancery Club. Fellow, American College of Trust and Estate Counsel. Academician, The International Academy of Estate and Trust Law (President, 1980-1982). [LTJG, USNR, 1952-1954]. (Certified Specialist, Taxation Law, Probate, Estate Planning and Trust Law, The State Bar of California Board of Legal Specialization). *PRACTICE AREAS:* Estate Planning; Probate; Estate and Gift Tax Litigation.

*GEORGE R. BAFFA, (P.C.),* born East Paterson, New Jersey, August 11, 1937; admitted to bar, 1963, California; 1970, U.S. Supreme Court. *Education:* University of Southern California (B.A., 1959; J.D., 1962). Order of the Coif. Member, Board of Editors, 1960-1962 and Associate Managing Editor, 1961-1962, Southern California Law Review. President, University of Southern California Law Alumni Association, 1986-1987. Special Assistant to the General Counsel, Department of Health, Education and Welfare, 1969-1970. Deputy Director of the President's Cabinet Committee on Education, 1969-1970. Member, Chancery Club. *Member:* Pasadena, Los Angeles County and American Bar Associations; The State Bar of California. *PRACTICE AREAS:* Corporations; Business.

*DON MIKE ANTHONY, (P.C.),* born Los Angeles, California, August 12, 1938; admitted to bar, 1964, California; 1970, U.S. Supreme Court. *Education:* Occidental College (B.A., 1960); University of California at Los Angeles (LL.B., 1963). Order of the Coif. Member, Board of Editors, UCLA Law Review, 1961-1963; Associate Editor, 1962-1963. *Member:* Pasadena (President, 1992-1993), Los Angeles County (Chair, Committee on State Bar, 1993—; Member: Trial Lawyers Section; Executive Committee, Family Law Section, 1981-1984) and American (Member: Family Law Section; Litigation Section; Commission on Evaluation of Disciplinary Enforcement, 1989-1992; Standing Committee on Professional Discipline, 1992-1995) Bar Associations; The State Bar of California (Member, State Bar Court Executive Committee, 1980-1984; Review Department, 1980-1983; Board of Governors, 1984-1987; Vice-President, 1987; Chair, Committee on Discipline, 1986-1987; Member, Client Security Fund Commission, 1989-1993; Member, California Judicial Council Juvenile and Family Law Advisory Committee, 1993—); Los Angeles County Bar Foundation (Director, 1992—; Secretary, 1995—); Chancery Club; American Board of Trial Advocates; Association of Business Trial Lawyers. Fellow: American Academy of Matrimonial Lawyers; International Academy of Matrimonial Lawyers. (Certified Specialist, Family Law, The State Bar of California Board of Legal Specialization). *PRACTICE AREAS:* Civil Litigation.

*ROBERT W. ANDERSON,* born Norcatur, Kansas, August 9, 1925; admitted to bar, 1949, California. *Education:* University of Colorado (J.D., 1948). *Member:* Pasadena, Los Angeles County and American Bar Associations; The State Bar of California. *PRACTICE AREAS:* Estate Planning; Probate; Estate Planning; Taxation (Gift and Income).

*WILLIAM K. HENLEY, (P.C.),* born Santa Monica, California, November 11, 1944; admitted to bar, 1970, California. *Education:* Stanford University (A.B., 1966); Hastings College of Law, University of California (J.D., 1969). *Member:* Pasadena, Los Angeles County and American Bar Associations; The State Bar of California. *PRACTICE AREAS:* Business Litigation; General Civil Litigation; Employment Litigation.

*CLARK R. BYAM, (P.C.),* born Westfield, New Jersey, December 28, 1943; admitted to bar, 1972, California. *Education:* Wesleyan University (B.A., 1966); Hastings College of Law, University of California (J.D., 1972). Member, Thurston Society. Recipient, American Jurisprudence Award. Author: "Practical Tips for Handling and Settling Will Contests," Estate Planning Trust and Probate News, Winter 1992. *Member:* Pasadena, Los Angeles County and American Bar Associations; The State Bar of California (Member, 1988-1991; Advisor, 1991-1994, Executive Committee of Estate Planning, Trust and Probate Law Section). Fellow, American College of Trust and Estate Counsel (Member, Professional Standards Committee). [Lt. (jg), USNR, 1967-1969]. *PRACTICE AREAS:* Probate and Trust Litigation; Estate Planning; Employee Benefits.

*RICHARD L. HALL, (P.C.),* born Miami, Florida, July 10, 1938; admitted to bar, 1973, California; 1992, U.S. Supreme Court. *Education:* University of Santa Clara (B.S.C., 1960); Loyola University of Los Angeles (J.D., cum laude, 1973). Beta Gamma Sigma. *Member:* Pasadena, Los Angeles County (Member, Real Property Section) and American Bar Associations; The State Bar of California (Member: Investigation Department, 1980-1984; Probation Monitor, 1984-1990. Referee of State Bar Court Hearing Department, 1984-1990). *PRACTICE AREAS:* Real Property; Civil Litigation.

*SUSAN T. HOUSE, (P.C.),* born Kingston, Pennsylvania, July 28, 1950; admitted to bar, 1975, California. *Education:* Wellesley College (A.B., 1971); University of California at Los Angeles (J.D., 1975). Phi Beta Kappa. Co-Author: "California Conservatorships and Guardianships," California Continuing Education of the Bar, 1990. Editor, California Trusts and Estates Quarterly. *Member:* Pasadena, Los Angeles County and American Bar Associations; The State Bar of California (Member, Executive Committee of Estate Planning, Trust and Probate Law Section). Fellow, American College of Trust and Estate Counsel (California State Chair); The International Academy of Estate and Trust Law. (Certified Specialist, Estate Planning, Trust and Probate Law, The State Bar of California Board of Legal Specialization). *PRACTICE AREAS:* Estate Planning; Conservatorships; Probate; Trusts.

*DIANNE H. BUKATA,* born East Orange, New Jersey, November 14, 1945; admitted to bar, 1978, California. *Education:* Simmons College (B.S., 1967); University of Southern California (J.D., 1978). Order of the Coif. Member, University of Southern California Law Review, 1976-1978. *Member:* Pasadena, Los Angeles County and American Bar Associations; The State Bar of California (Referee, State Bar Court, 1982-1984). *PRACTICE AREAS:* Estate Planning; Probate.

*GENE E. GREGG, JR. (P.C.),* born Berkeley, California, July 14, 1952; admitted to bar, 1979, California. *Education:* Occidental College (A.B., 1974); McGeorge School of Law, University of the Pacific (J.D., 1979). John D. Stauffer Fellow, 1978-1979. *Member:* Pasadena, Los Angeles County and American (Member, Sections on: Corporation, Banking and Business Law; Labor and Employment Law) Bar Associations; The State Bar of California (Member, Section on Business Law). *PRACTICE AREAS:* Corporations; Business; Employment Law.

*R. SCOTT JENKINS, (P.C.),* born Pasadena, California, July 6, 1953; admitted to bar, 1979, California. *Education:* University of California at Berkeley (A.B., with honors, 1975); University of Southern California (J.D., 1979). Member, Board of Editors, 1977-1978 and Executive Managing Editor, 1978-1979, Southern California Law Review. *Member:* Pasadena, Los Angeles County (Member, Sections on: Business; Real Property; Antitrust) and American Bar Associations; The State Bar of California. *PRACTICE AREAS:* Business; Corporations; Real Property.

*CHARLES J. GREAVES, (P.C.),* born Freeport, New York, December 14, 1955; admitted to bar, 1981, California. *Education:* University of Southern California (A.B., magna cum laude, 1978); Boston College (J.D., cum laude, 1981). Administrative Editor, Boston College Uniform Commercial Code Reporter-Digest, 1980-1981. Author: "The Decline and Fall Of Trial by Jury in Trust Litigation," Los Angeles Lawyer, November, 1988; "Secondary Liability For Vehicular Negligence," Los Angeles Lawyer, October 1989. *Member:* Pasadena, Los Angeles County and American (Member, Litigation Section) Bar Associations; The State Bar of California (Referee, State Bar Court Hearing Department, 1987-1990; Member, Fee Arbitration Department, 1990—); Association of Business Trial Lawyers; Association of Trial Lawyers of America; Consumers Attorneys of California. *PRACTICE AREAS:* Civil Litigation.

*DALE R. PELCH,* born San Bernardino, California, June 30, 1957; admitted to bar, 1983, California. *Education:* University of California at Irvine (B.A., 1979); Loyola Law School; Loyola Marymount University (J.D., cum laude, 1983). Member, St. Thomas More Law Honor Society. *Member:* Pasadena, Los Angeles County (Member, Real Property, Environmental Law and Litigation Sections) and American Bar Associations; The State Bar of California; Association of Business Trial Lawyers. *PRACTICE AREAS:* Civil Litigation; Real Property; Environmental Law.

*WILLIAM S. GARR, (P.C.),* born Pasadena, California, June 17, 1959; admitted to bar, 1985, California; 1990, U.S. Supreme Court. *Education:* University of Southern California (B.A., with honors, 1981; J.D., 1984). Phi Beta Kappa. Hale Moot Court Honors Program, 1982-1983. Law Clerk to the Honorable Allen E. Broussard, Associate Justice, California Supreme Court, 1983. Judge Pro Tem, Pasadena Municipal Court, Los Angeles County, 1990—. Hearing Officer, Use of Force and Disciplinary Review Boards, Pasadena Police Department, 1995—. Panelist, "Rule 11, RICO and Professionalism" mid-year meeting, American Bar Association, 1990. *Member:* Pasadena, Los Angeles County and American Bar Associations;

*(This Listing Continued)*

The State Bar of California; Association of Business Trial Lawyers; American Judicature Society; American Inns of Court Foundation (President, U.S.C. Legion Lex Chapter VIII, 1994-1996). *LANGUAGES:* Spanish. *PRACTICE AREAS:* Federal and State Court Civil Trial Litigation; Appellate Practice.

**KARL I. SWAIDAN,** born Beirut, Lebanon, May 13, 1958; admitted to bar, 1983, California. *Education:* University of Southern California (B.S., summa cum laude, 1980; M.B.T., with honors, 1983; J.D., 1983). Phi Beta Kappa; Order of the Coif. Certified Public Accountant, California, 1986. *Member:* Pasadena, Beverly Hills, Los Angeles and American Bar Associations; The State Bar of California; California Society of Certified Public Accountants; American Institute of Certified Public Accountants. *PRACTICE AREAS:* Estate Planning; Probate; Taxation.

**SANDRA K. MURPHY,** born Carroll, Iowa, March 17, 1951; admitted to bar, 1989, California. *Education:* University of Iowa (B.S.N., with distinction, 1977; J.D., with high distinction, 1988). Order of the Coif. Recipient, American Jurisprudence Awards. Registered Nurse, Iowa, 1978. *Member:* Los Angeles County and American Bar Associations. *PRACTICE AREAS:* Estate Planning; Probate; Taxation.

**LAURA V. FARBER,** born Buenos Aires, Argentina, October 29, 1965; admitted to bar, 1990, California. *Education:* University of California at Los Angeles (B.A., cum laude, with highest honors, 1987) Mortar Board; Georgetown University (J.D., cum laude, 1990). *Member:* Los Angeles County (Barristers: President, 1996-1997; President-Elect, 1995-1996; Vice President, 1994-1995; Member: Barristers Executive Committee, 1992-1994; Barristers Education Committee, 1991—; Barristers Strategic Planning Committee, 1992—; Chair, Barristers Bench and Bar Committee, 1992—; Chair, Bias in the Legal Profession Committee, 1994-1995); Inns of Court, Board of Trustees, 1995—; Executive Committee, 1995—; Pasadena and American (Member, Litigation and Young Lawyers Section; Assistant Editor, Affiliate Newsletter, 1995-1996) Bar Associations; State Bar of California (Member, Litigation Section); Women Lawyers Association of Los Angeles; Mexican-American Bar Association. *LANGUAGES:* Spanish. *PRACTICE AREAS:* Civil Litigation.

**TALI SHADDOW,** born Afula, Israel, November 8, 1965; admitted to bar, 1992, California. *Education:* University of California, Los Angeles (B.A., 1988); Loyola University of Los Angeles (J.D., 1992). Member, St. Thomas More Law Honor Society. Author, Religious Ritual Exemptions, 24 Loyola Los Angeles Law Review, 1367. *Member:* Pasadena and Los Angeles County Bar Associations; State Bar of California. *LANGUAGES:* Hebrew. *REPORTED CASES:* Western Union v. First Data, 20 Cal.App.4, 1530. *PRACTICE AREAS:* Civil Litigation.

OF COUNSEL

**STANLEY L. HAHN, (P.C.),** born Pasadena, California, May 11, 1910; admitted to bar, 1934, California. *Education:* Pomona College (A.B., 1931); Harvard University (LL.B., 1934). *Member:* Pasadena, Los Angeles County and American Bar Associations; The State Bar of California. [Lieut., USNR, 1943-46]. *PRACTICE AREAS:* Estate Planning; Probate Law.

**GEORGE E. ZILLGITT,** born 1921; admitted to bar, 1949, California. *Education:* Stanford University (B.A., 1946; LL.B., 1949); University of Southern California (LL.M., 1963). *Member:* Pasadena and Los Angeles County Bar Associations; State Bar of California.

**EMRYS J. ROSS,** born Caldwell, Idaho, December 20, 1912; admitted to bar, 1936, California. *Education:* University of Southern California (B.S., in B.A., 1934; J.D., 1936). Phi Alpha Delta. *Member:* Los Angeles County and American Bar Associations; State Bar of California.

REPRESENTATIVE CLIENTS: Avon Products, Inc.; Becton Dickinson & Co.; California Institute of Technology; Chemical Trust Co. of California; Citizens Bank of Pasadena; City of Glendale; City of Long Beach; City of Pasadena; Cornet Stores; Dean Witter Realty; DSL Service Corp.; First Mortgage Corporation; Glendale Redevelopment Agency; Great Western Bank; Huntington Memorial Hospital; Justice Brothers Automotive Chemicals; Keeler Dilbeck Realtors; Lane-Stanton-Vance Lumber Company; Long Beach Redevelopment Agency; Los Angeles County Employees Retirement Association; Monrovia Nursery Co.; The New Otani Hotel and Garden; Pasadena Redevelopment Agency; Pasadena Tournament of Roses Assn.; Osaka Gas America, Inc.; The Ralph M. Parsons Co.; Robert Loud Ford; Symes Cadillac, Inc.; Waltco Engineering Co.; Wells Fargo Bank; Wesco Financial Corp.; Winston Tire Co.
REFERENCES: Citizens Bank of Pasadena; Bank of America National Trust & Savings Assn., Pasadena Branch; Sanwa Bank California; Wells Fargo Bank.

# HAMILTON & CUMARE

301 NORTH LAKE AVENUE, SUITE 320
PASADENA, CALIFORNIA 91101
Telephone: 818-585-2765
Fax: 818-585-2764

*Employment Discrimination, Trade Secrets, Traditional Labor Law and Client Counseling (Management), Age Discrimination, Civil Rights Defense, Americans with Disabilities Act, Wrongful Termination Defense, Sexual Harassment, Affirmative Action, Collective Bargaining, Employer Rights, Employment Contracts, Labor Relations, Personnel Policies, Title VII Discrimination, Wage and Hour Law and Whistleblower Litigation.*

FIRM PROFILE: Hamilton & Cumare was founded for the express purpose of providing employers with high quality, sophisticated, labor and employment-related legal services at reasonable rates. The firm has extensive experience acting as conflicts counsel in employment litigation matters.

**ROSA M. C. CUMARE,** born Caracas, Venezuela, December 6, 1949; admitted to bar, 1985, California and U.S. District Court, Central, Northern and Southern Districts of California and U.S. Court of Appeals, Ninth Circuit;. *Education:* University of Southern California (B.A., magna cum laude, 1971; J.D., 1985); Harvard University (M.A., 1973; Ph.D., 1977). Phi Beta Kappa; Phi Kappa Phi; Order of the Coif. Member, Southern California Law Review, 1983-1984. Associate, Munger, Tolles & Olson, 1985-1992. *Member:* Pasadena Bar Association (Secretary, 1994-1995; Chairman, Litigation Section, 1994—); State Bar of California. *LANGUAGES:* Dutch. *PRACTICE AREAS:* Employer Personnel Counseling; Employment Discrimination; Sexual Harassment; Wage and Hour Law; OSHA.

**DAVID J. HAMILTON,** born Neenah, Wisconsin, April 3, 1953; admitted to bar, 1980, Arizona, U.S. District Court of Arizona, Ninth Circuit; and U.S. Tax Court; 1984, U.S. Supreme Court; 1985, California and U.S. District Courts, Central, Eastern, Northern and Southern Districts of California. *Education:* Brigham Young University (1971-1972); Idaho State University (B.M.E., with high honors, 1975); University of Southern California (J.D., 1980). Staff, Southern California Law Review, 1979-1980. Author: Dichter and Hamilton, "Latest Case Law Developments in Employment Law Practice and Procedure," National Employment Law Institute (1991); Contributor, Pepe & Dunham, Avoiding and Defending Wrongful Discharge Claims (Callaghan, 1988); Baird, Walters, Hamilton, et. al, "Recent Developments in Public Employee Labor Relations," 16 The Urban Lawyer 777 (1984); Hamilton, "NLRB Proscription on Granting Benefits During Election Campaigns," 1981, Arizona State Law Journal 723 (1981). Associate: O'Melveny & Myers, 1985-1988; Morgan, Lewis & Bockius, 1989-1991. *Member:* Los Angeles County and American Bar Associations; State Bar of Arizona; State Bar of California; Defense Research Institute. *PRACTICE AREAS:* Employment Representation; Management Labor Law; Airline Labor Law; Trade Secrets; Wrongful Termination Defense; Employment Discrimination; Sexual Harassment.

# HAMMOND, ZUETEL & CAHILL

SUITE 540, 180 SOUTH LAKE AVENUE
PASADENA, CALIFORNIA 91101
Telephone: 818-449-5144; 213-684-2898
FAX: 213-684-1275

*General Civil and Trial Practice. Medical Malpractice, Personal Injury.*

MEMBERS OF FIRM

**KENNETH R. ZUETEL, JR.,** born Los Angeles, California, April 5, 1954; admitted to bar, 1978, California. *Education:* San Diego State University (B.A., with high honors, 1974); University of San Diego School of Law (J.D., 1978). Phi Beta Kappa; Phi Kappa Phi. Member and Lead Articles Editor, University of San Diego Law Review, 1977-1978. Author: "Ethical Considerations in Preparing Witnesses for Depositions and Trials," CEB 1984, 1986 and 1987; "California Civil Procedure," Chaps. 22-24, CEB, 1992. Consultant-Editor, "Handling Expert Witnesses Under the 1986 Civil Discovery Act," CEB Action Guide, 1987. Consultant-Author, Bancroft-Whitney, California Civil Practice and Procedure. Lecturer, Continuing Education of the Bar, 1982—. Judge Pro Temp: Los Angeles Municipal Court, 1983—; Los Angeles Superior Court, 1989—. Superior Court Arbitrator, 1982—. Disciplinary and State Bar Examiner, 1985-1986. *Member:* Pasadena and Los Angeles County (Member: Executive Committee, 1990—; Conference of Delegates, 1986—; Chair, 1995; Superior Courts Committee, 1985-1989; Barristers Executive Committee, 1984-1989; Chairperson Trial Attorney's Project, 1983-1984) Bar Associations; State

*(This Listing Continued)*

## HAMMOND, ZUETEL & CAHILL, Pasadena—Continued

Bar of California (Member, Advisory Committee of the Continuing Education of the Bar, 1985-1988). *PRACTICE AREAS:* Medical Malpractice; Business Litigation.

**RICHARD F. CAHILL,** born Columbus, Nebraska, June 18, 1953; admitted to bar, 1978, California. *Education:* University of California, Los Angeles (B.A., summa cum laude, 1975); Notre Dame Law School (J.D., 1978). Phi Beta Kappa. *Member:* Pasadena and Los Angeles County Bar Associations; The State Bar of California; Association of Southern California Defense Counsel. *PRACTICE AREAS:* Medical Malpractice.

### ASSOCIATES

**CYNTHIA L.K. STEELE,** born Toledo, Ohio, June 13, 1963; admitted to bar, 1992, California; 1994, U.S. District Court, Central District of California. *Education:* University of Toledo (B.S.N., cum laude, 1985); University of Arizona (J.D., 1992). Phi Delta Phi. Co-Author: "California Legislative Update," SCAHRM Forum, April, 1993. Civil Practice Internship, Office of the Attorney General, Insurance Defense Division, Tucson, State of Arizona, 1992. Judicial Clerk-Extern, Honorable Alfredo C. Marquez, United States District Court, District of Arizona, 1991. Registered Nurse: Ohio, 1985; Texas, 1989; Arizona, 1985; California, 1992. *Member:* Los Angeles County Bar Association; State Bar of California; The American Association of Nurse Attorneys. *PRACTICE AREAS:* Professional Liability; Medical Malpractice Defense.

**VICTORIA K. TORIGIAN,** born North Hollywood, California, January 13, 1965; admitted to bar, 1993, California and U.S. District Court, Central District of California. *Education:* Pepperdine University (B.S., 1986); Southwestern University School of Law (J.D., 1993). *Member:* Los Angeles County Bar Association. *PRACTICE AREAS:* Professional Liability; Medical Malpractice.

### OF COUNSEL

**JOHN C. CUSHMAN,** born Oakland, California, March 10, 1933; admitted to bar, 1962, California. *Education:* Occidental College (B.A., 1955); Boalt Hall School of Law, University of California (J.D., 1961). Phi Delta Phi. *Member:* Pasadena (Treasurer, 1968; President, 1985), Los Angeles County and American Bar Associations; The State Bar of California. *PRACTICE AREAS:* Probate Law; Estate Planning Law; Trust Law.

**P. THEODORE HAMMOND,** born Los Angeles, California, May 2, 1947; admitted to bar, 1972, California. *Education:* DePauw University; University of Southern California (B.S., cum laude, 1969; J.D., 1972). Delegate, State Bar Conference of Delegates, 1975— and Chair, Pasadena Delegation, 1983-1987. Los Angeles County Special Master, 1983—. *Member:* Pasadena (Treasurer, 1982; Trustee, 1991—) and Los Angeles County (Member, Healthcare Law Section) Bar Associations; The State Bar of California; Pasadena Barristers Association (President, 1974-1975). *PRACTICE AREAS:* Medical Malpractice; Personal Injury Law; Health Care Law.

COUNSEL FOR: CIGNA Healthplans of California; INA/Ross-Loos Medical Group, Inc.; American Psychiatric Association; R.L.I. Insurance Co.; Farmers Insurance Group; Truck Insurance Exchange; Cal-Air Inc.; Bay Buick-GMC Truck; Connecticut General Insurance Co.
REFERENCES: Bank of American National Trust & Savings Assn. (Green Lake Office).

---

## RICHARD C. HARDING
35 S. RAYMOND AVENUE
SUITE 400
PASADENA, CALIFORNIA 91105-1971
*Telephone: 818-304-0320*
*Fax: 818-578-0768*

General Civil Practice in State and Federal Courts. Appeals and Business Transactional Law, Personal Injury Law.

**RICHARD C. HARDING,** born Los Angeles, California, January 20, 1947; admitted to bar, 1973, California; 1986, U.S. Court of Appeals, Ninth Circuit; 1990, U.S. Supreme Court. *Education:* Georgetown University (B.A., 1968); Loyola University of Los Angeles (J.D., 1972); University of California, Los Angeles (M.B.A., 1976). Assistant Law Clerk to the Honorable A. Andrew Hauk, U.S. District Court Judge, Central District of California, 1969-1972. *Member:* Los Angeles County Bar Association; State Bar of California.

---

## HOSP, GILBERT & ASSOCIATES
*A LAW CORPORATION*
Established in 1984
301 NORTH LAKE AVENUE, SUITE 720
PASADENA, CALIFORNIA 91101
*Telephone: 818-792-2400*
*Telecopier: 818-356-9656*
*Email: 105323.2551@compuserve.com*
*URL: http://websites.earthlink.net/~hosp-gilbert/*

General Civil and Trial Practice in all State and Federal Courts. Banking, Commercial Creditors Rights and Bankruptcy Law, Corporation, Business, Insurance Defense, Automobile Liability, Bad Faith, Construction, Earth Movement, Environmental, ERISA Litigation, Equal Opportunity Law, Insurance Coverage, Insurance Fraud, Premises Liability, Product Liability, Professional Liability, Real Property, Landlord-Tenant Relations, Unlawful Detainer, Subrogation, Wrongful Termination.

*FIRM PROFILE:* Originally formed in 1984, the law corporation of Hosp, Gilbert & Associates offer advice and expertise on business, corporate, labor and employment matters. Our clients include major insurance companies, corporations, businesses and financial institutions.

**F. PHILLIP HOSP,** born Wichita Falls, Texas, August 22, 1944; admitted to bar, 1970, California and U.S. District Court, Central District of California; 1975, U.S. Court of Appeals, Ninth Circuit; 1990, U.S. Supreme Court. *Education:* University of Southern California (B.A., 1966); Loyola University of Los Angeles (J.D., 1969). Phi Delta Phi. Judge Pro Tem, Los Angeles Superior Court, 1980-1983. Settlement Officer, Pasadena Superior Court, 1989-1996. Arbitrator, Los Angeles Superior Court Arbitration Panel, 1989-1995. Mediator, Los Angeles Superior Court, 1993-1996. *Member:* Pasadena, Los Angeles County and American Bar Associations; State Bar of California; Association of Business Trial Lawyers; Association of Southern California Defense Counsel; Defense Research Institute. *PRACTICE AREAS:* Banking; Commercial Transactions and Litigation; Tort Litigation Emphasizing Construction; Premises Liability, Products, Auto and Common Carriers.

**WARREN L. GILBERT,** born Hertfordshire, England, February 11, 1951; admitted to bar, 1980, California; 1981, U.S. District Court, Central District of California; 1986, U.S. Supreme Court and U.S. Court of Appeals, Ninth Circuit. *Education:* University of California at Los Angeles (A.B., 1973); Southwestern University School of Law (J.D., 1979). Arbitrator, Los Angeles County Superior Court, 1986—. Judge pro tem of the L.A. Superior Court, 1992; Settlement Officer of the L.A. Superior Court, 1991. *Member:* Pasadena, Los Angeles County (Member, Litigation Section) and American Bar Associations; State Bar of California; Association of Southern California Defense Counsel. *REPORTED CASES:* Hughes v. SCRTD (1985) 173 CA 3d 512, 219CR82. *PRACTICE AREAS:* Tort Defense Law; Products Liability; Premises Liability; Automotive Defects; Construction Defects.

**MARVIN G. FISCHLER,** born Los Angeles, California, June 17, 1957; admitted to bar, 1982, California; 1983, U.S. District Court, Central District of California and U.S. Court of Appeals, Ninth Circuit. *Education:* Claremont McKenna College, formerly Claremont Men's College (B.A., 1979); McGeorge School of Law, University of the Pacific (J.D., 1982). Phi Alpha Phi; Order of the Coif. Arbitrator, Los Angeles Superior Court Arbitration Panel, 1989—. Judge Pro Tem, Los Angeles Superior Court and Los Angeles, South Bay and Pomona Municipal Courts, 1990—. Panel Mediator, Los Angeles Superior Court, 1994—. *Member:* Pasadena and Los Angeles County Bar Associations; State Bar of California; Association of Southern California Defense Counsel; Financial Lawyers Association. *PRACTICE AREAS:* Tort Defense; Emphasizing Construction Defects and Soils Matters; Auto; Bankruptcy; Commercial and Banking Litigation.

**ANDREA E.L. ROSS,** born South Pasadena, California, May 23, 1969; admitted to bar, 1995, California. *Education:* University of California at Davis (A.B., 1991); University of Southern California (J.D., 1995). *Member:* Los Angeles and Pasadena Bar Association. *PRACTICE AREAS:* Tort Defense; Emphasizing Auto; Products Liability; Premises Liability; Construction Defects.

REPRESENTATIVE CLIENTS: Allstate Ins. Cos.; American Golf Corp.; Aris Ins. Services; Bank of America; Bolton/RGV Insurance Brokers; California Ins. Guarantee Assoc.; Carl Warren & Co., Insurance Adjusters; Cigna Ins. Co.; Crum & Forster; Deans & Homer; Employers Mutual Ins. Co.; Esis Inc.; Fireman's Fund Ins. Co.; Gallagher Bassett Services, Inc.; International Church of the Four Square Gospel; MacFrugal's; Maguire Thomas Partners; McLarens Toplis Claims Service; National Casualty Ins. Co.; National Surety Ins. Co.; Pic

*(This Listing Continued)*

## PROFESSIONAL BIOGRAPHIES

## CALIFORNIA—PASADENA

'N' Save; One Central Bank; Reliable Brokers, Inc.; Reliance; The Rule Co. Ins. Brokers; Safeway Ins. Co.; Sanwa Bank of California; Scottsdale Ins. Co.; Solid Waste Insurance Managers; Sphere Drake Ins. Co.; State Farm Fire and Casualty Co.; Transamerica Insurance Group; Vik Bros. Ins. Group.
REFERENCE: 1st Business Bank, LA.

## LAW OFFICES OF
## EDMUND C. HOY

A PROFESSIONAL CORPORATION
SUITE 806, UNION BANK BUILDING
201 SOUTH LAKE AVENUE
**PASADENA, CALIFORNIA 91101**
Telephone: 818-792-9945

*Business Litigation, Bankruptcy, Probate, Estate Planning, Tax Planning, Landlord, Tenant Disputes, Civil Trial, Criminal Defense, Trademark, Family Law, Real Estate, Personal Injury.*

**EDMUND C. HOY,** born Greenwood, Mississippi, February 21, 1942; admitted to bar, 1976, California; 1977, U.S. District Court, Central District of California; 1980, U.S. Tax Court; 1993, U.S. Court of Appeals, Ninth Circuit. *Education:* Virginia Military Institute (B.A., History, 1964); University of West Los Angeles (J.D., 1975). *Member,* FOOTPRINTERS International, University Club (Pasadena). *Member:* Pasadena Bar Association. *LANGUAGES:* Chinese, Mandarin; Cantonese.

## HUNT, ORTMANN, BLASCO, PALFFY & ROSSELL, INC.

A PROFESSIONAL LAW CORPORATION
*Established in 1990*

301 NORTH LAKE AVENUE, SUITE 700
**PASADENA, CALIFORNIA 91101**
Telephone: 818-440-5200
Fax: 818-796-0107
Email: hunt-ortmann@hobpr.com
URL: http://www.hobpr.com

*Construction, Real Estate, Business and Commercial Litigation, Real Estate Finance, Estate Planning, Corporate, Environmental and Business Law.*

*FIRM PROFILE: Although our law firm was started on March 1, 1990, our expertise in the area of construction law goes back to the very roots of construction law in California in the early 1900s. Our senior founding partner, Gordon Hunt, began his career in 1960 under the tutelage of Glenn Behymer, the preeminent construction lawyer in California whose practice dated back to around 1908. Even though our firm is one of the foremost authorities on construction law and litigation in the state, we also offer services in many other areas of law related to real estate and business. Some of these include land development, environmental, geotechnical, corporate and partnership law. At Hunt, Ortmann, Blasco, Palffy & Rossell, we strongly believe in supporting our community. In this effort, we support a variety of civic organizations benefiting Pasadena and greater Los Angeles. For example, some of our lawyers have been members of or involved with Pasadena Tournament of Roses Association, Pasadena's Recreation and Parks Commission, Christmas in April, and Rebuild L.A. The firm itself financially supports Kidspace in Pasadena, and we've also established nonprofit, tax-exempt foundations for local elementary schools.*

**GORDON HUNT, (A PROFESSIONAL CORPORATION),** born Los Angeles, California, October 26, 1934; admitted to bar, 1960, California. *Education:* University of California at Los Angeles (B.A., 1956); University of Southern California (J.D., 1959). Author: *Construction Surety & Bonding Handbook,* PESI, 1990. Chief Consultant and Author: Chapter 2, "California Mechanic's Liens and Other Remedies," 2nd Ed., 1988; "Mechanics Liens, Stop Notices and Bond Rights for Private Work," Associated General Contractors of California, 1988; "Calculating and Proving Damages in the Construction Industry:" "The Architects Contract and Liability;" "Breach by Contractor;" "Documents in Construction Litigation;" "Breach of Construction Contract by Owner;" "Claims for Extras, Interpretation of Plans and Specifications by the Courts," all published in "Second Annual Real Property Practice Institute: Construction Law," CEB, February 1985; "Construction Disputes Regarding Building Plans and Specifications," IX Real Prop. Rptr. 141, Cal. CEB October, 1986. Co-Author: "California Construction Law," John Wiley & Sons, Inc., 1991; "California Construction Lending & The Law," 1985, 1986; "Construction Disputes," CEB,

*(This Listing Continued)*

April/May 1982; "The Law of Scheduling," Associated General Contractors of California, February 1988; "State and Local Developments In Construction Protests," ABA Public Contract Law Section, May 1988; "Construction Project Disputes," Advanced Real Property Series, CEB, October/November 1987; "Handling Mechanics' Liens and Related Remedies (Private Works)," CEB, Summer 1987; "Strict Liability in the Construction Industry," VI Real Prop. Law Rptr. 153, Cal. CEB November, 1983; "Public Works: Bidding Disputes, The Contract With the Public Body, Performance Disputes, Clauses on California State and Local Projects and Federal Clauses Under the Miller Act," 16 Bev. Hills Bar J. 3, Summer 1982. Law Clerk, Appellate Department, Superior Court for Los Angeles County, 1959-1960. Co-Chairman, Continuing Education of the Bar Committee of Los Angeles County Bar Association, 1969-1971. Delegate to State Bar of California Convention, 1964-1969. Arbitrator, Los Angeles Superior Court, State of California. Arbitrator and Mediator, American Arbitration Association. *Member:* Los Angeles County (Chairman, Real Property Section, 1975-1976) and American Bar Associations; State Bar of California Associated General Contractors of California (Chairman, Legal Advisory Committee, 1985). *PRACTICE AREAS:* Construction; Real Estate.

**DALE A. ORTMANN,** born Van Nuys, California, February 17, 1955; admitted to bar, 1980, California. *Education:* California State Polytechnic University (B.A., magna cum laude, 1976); Loyola University (J.D., 1980). *Member:* Los Angeles County and American Bar Associations; State Bar of California. *PRACTICE AREAS:* Construction; Real Estate.

**RICHARD E. BLASCO,** born Upland, California, August 8, 1955; admitted to bar, 1980, California. *Education:* University of Southern California (B.A., 1977); Southwestern University (J.D., 1980). Recipient, American Jurisprudence Book Award in Corporations and Partnership Taxation Law. Associate General Counsel, Building Industry Credit Association, 1990—. *Member:* Pasadena and Los Angeles County (Member, Real Property Law Section) Bar Associations. *PRACTICE AREAS:* Business Law; Transactions.

**THOMAS PALFFY,** born Cluj, Romania, June 30, 1956; admitted to bar, 1982, California; 1983, U.S. District Court, Eastern, Northern Southern and Central Districts of California and U.S. Supreme Court. *Education:* University of Southern California (B.A., 1978); Southwestern University (J.D., 1981). *Member:* Pasadena, Los Angeles County Bar Association; State Bar of California; American Trial Lawyers Association. *PRACTICE AREAS:* Construction; Real Estate.

**CRAIG N. ROSSELL,** born Los Angeles, California, November 11, 1951; admitted to bar, 1981, California; 1995, Utah. *Education:* Brigham Young University (B.A., 1975); University of California at Los Angeles (M.A., 1976); Western State University (J.D., 1981). *Member:* Pasadena, Los Angeles County and American Bar Associations; State Bar of California (Member, Executive Committee, Real Estate Litigation Subsection, 1984-1986); Utah State Bar. *LANGUAGES:* French. *PRACTICE AREAS:* Construction; Real Estate.

**RONALD E. WHITE,** born Monterey Park, California, January 14, 1956; admitted to bar, 1985, California; 1994, Arizona; 1995, Utah. *Education:* Brigham Young University (B.A., in International Relations, 1981; J.D., 1984). *Member:* State Bar of California; State Bar of Arizona; Utah State Bar; American Bar Association. *LANGUAGES:* Japanese. *PRACTICE AREAS:* Construction; Real Estate.

---

**LAURENCE P. LUBKA,** born Hartford, Connecticut, October 23, 1954; admitted to bar, 1980, Ohio; 1982, California; 1993, U.S. Claims Court; 1994, U.S. Court of Appeals for the Federal Circuit. *Education:* Columbia University (B.A., 1976); George Washington University (J.D., with honors, 1980). Author: "Public Contracting in California," Federal Publications, 1992-1995; "Bonds, Mechanics' Liens & Stop Notices in California," Federal Publications, 1992-1995; "Issues in Federal Government Environmental Contracting," 1992 Guide to Defense Cleanup, Pasha Publications; "Payment Bond and Stop Notice Changes," "Pay When Paid: Is There a Check in the Mail?" "What are My Rights Under the "Force Majeure" Clause?," Dodge Construction News Greensheet Construction Link, 1994. Instructor, "Corporations," Northrop University Law School, 1983. *Member:* Los Angeles County (Member, Real Property Section) and American (Member, Sections on: Public Contracts Law; Franchise Law) Bar Associations; State Bar of California. Fellow, National Contract Management Association. *PRACTICE AREAS:* Government Contracts; Construction; Franchise.

**KEVIN J. BRODY,** born Los Angeles, California, March 26, 1959; admitted to bar, 1985, California; 1986, U.S. District Court, Central District

*(This Listing Continued)*

CAA1655B

### HUNT, ORTMANN, BLASCO, PALFFY & ROSSELL, INC.
*A PROFESSIONAL LAW CORPORATION, Pasadena—Continued*

of California. *Education:* University of California at Berkeley and Santa Cruz (B.A., with college and departmental honors, 1982); University of Tours, France; Cornell Law School (J.D., 1985). Senior Editor, Cornell International Law Journal, 1984-1985. Author: "An Argument for Pre-Award Attachment in International Arbitration Under The New York Convention," 18 Cornell International Law Journal 99, 1985. Member, Board of Directors of Altadena Heritage Association, 1995—. *Member:* Century City (Co-Chair, Business Law Section, 1992-1994; Board of Governors, 1995), Los Angeles County and American Bar Associations; State Bar of California. *LANGUAGES:* French. *PRACTICE AREAS:* General Business Law; Real Estate Law.

**ERIC C. SMITH,** born San Jose, California, April 20, 1960; admitted to bar, 1986, California; 1988, U.S. District Court, Central District of California. *Education:* University of Southern California (B.S. in Public Affairs, 1982); Western State University College of Law at Fullerton (J.D., 1986). *Member:* Los Angeles County and American Bar Associations; State Bar of California. *PRACTICE AREAS:* Construction; Real Estate.

**OMEL A. NIEVES,** born San Juan, Puerto Rico, January 16, 1961; admitted to bar, 1988, California, U.S. District Court, Central and Eastern Districts of California and U.S. Court of Appeals, Ninth Circuit. *Education:* Santa Barbara City College (A.A., 1981); California State University at Fresno (B.A., 1983); University of California at Davis (J.D., 1987). *Member:* Pasadena, Los Angeles County and American Bar Associations; State Bar of California; Hispanic National Bar Association. *LANGUAGES:* Spanish.

**JEROME D. MEIER,** born Milwaukee, Wisconsin, July 14, 1939; admitted to bar, 1971, California. *Education:* Brigham Young University; Southwestern University (J.D., 1971). Member, Board of Education, Pasadena Unified School District, 1975-1979. Member, J. Reuben Clark Law Society. *Member:* Los Angeles County Bar Association; State Bar of California. *PRACTICE AREAS:* Construction; Real Estate; Torts.

**JOHN D. DARLING,** born Austin, Texas, June 28, 1963; admitted to bar, 1991, California, U.S. District Court, Central and Eastern Districts of California and U.S. Court of Appeals, Ninth Circuit; 1994, Minnesota. *Education:* University of New Mexico (B.A., 1987, Deans List); McGeorge School of Law, University of the Pacific (J.D., 1991). President, Latino Law Students Association, McGeorge School of Law. Finalist, Moot Court Oral Advocate Competition, McGeorge School of Law. Co-Author: "The Constitutionality of Mechanics' Lien Law," *Los Angeles Lawyer,* January 1994. *Member:* State Bar of California; Minnesota State Bar Association. *PRACTICE AREAS:* Construction Law; Real Estate Litigation.

**ERIC BROWN,** born St. Louis, Missouri, September 23, 1968; admitted to bar, 1994, California. *Education:* Washington University (B.A., English and American Literature, Psychology, 1989); Boalt Hall School of Law, University of California (J.D., 1992). Recipient, Prosser Award, Law and Literature, 1992. Associate Editor, Ecology Law Quarterly, 1990. Member, 1991 and Executive Editor, 1991-1992, Industrial Relations Law Journal. Editor in Chief, Boalt Hall Cross-Examiner, 1991-1992. *Member:* State Bar of California. *PRACTICE AREAS:* Construction Litigation; Real Estate Litigation.

*OF COUNSEL*

**F. GLENN NICHOLS,** born Los Angeles, California, October 22, 1948; admitted to bar, 1976, California. *Education:* San Diego State University (B.S., Civil Engineering, 1971); University of San Diego (J.D., 1976). Member, University of San Diego Law Review, 1975-1976. Author: "Debt Limitations & the Bona-Fide Long Term Lease with an Option to Purchase: Another Look at Lord Coke," 9 Urban Lawyer 403, 1977. Member, Appellate Moot Court Board, 1975-1976. Student Instructor, Legal Research and Writing, University of San Diego School of Law, 1975-1976. *Member:* Los Angeles County (Member, Real Property Section) and American (Member, Real Property Law Section) Bar Associations; State Bar of California. *PRACTICE AREAS:* Construction; Real Estate; Municipal Law.

REPRESENTATIVE CLIENTS: Modern Wholesale Electric, Inc.; Ralph M. Parsons Company; Skidmore Contracting Corporation; Glendale Memorial Hospital; Salick Health Care, Inc.; Control Air Conditioning; Charles Pankow Builders, Ltd.; Ray Wilson Company; Sachs Electric; Southern California Gas Company; Standard Pacific; Whirlpool Corporation; Baskin-Robbins; Advanced Structures Inc.; IT Corporation; City of Hope; Parr Lumber Company; The Converse Professional Group; Air Conditioning Company, Inc.; Lewis Homes of California; Building Industry Credit Association; Metropolitan Water District; Kiewit Diversified Group, Inc.

CAA1656B

### SANDRA McMAHAN IRWIN
PENTHOUSE SUITE 930
150 SOUTH LOS ROBLES AVENUE
**PASADENA, CALIFORNIA 91101-2437**
Telephone: 818-577-1065
Telecopier: 818-577-5219

*Corporate, General Business and Real Estate Law and related Litigation, Estate Planning, Probate including Surrogates Court Practice and Other Law of Reproduction.*

**SANDRA MCMAHAN IRWIN,** born San Diego, California, October 31, 1946; admitted to bar, 1980, California; U.S. District Court, Central District of California and U.S. Supreme Court. *Education:* Vassar College (A.B., 1968); University of San Diego (J.D., cum laude, 1979). Recipient, American Jurisprudence Awards: Contracts; Torts. Articles Editor, San Diego Law Review, 1978-1979. Co-Author: "Offering, Selling and Issuing Securities," *Organizing Corporations in California,* Second Edition, California Continuing Education of the Bar, 1983; "Federal Securities Laws - Public Finance," *Municipal Bond Law - Basic and Recent Developments,* Practicing Law Institute Course Handbook Series Number 200, 1982; "Federal Securities Laws: Role of Underwriters' Counsel." *Tax-Exempt Financings of Public Power Projects,* New York Law Journal Seminar Press, 1981. Author: "One Tier Beyond Ramapo: Open Space Zoning and the Urban Reserve," 15 San Diego Law Review 1211, 1978. *Member:* Los Angeles County, Pasadena and American Bar Associations; The State Bar of California. *REPORTED CASES:* Hecht v. Superior Court (1993) 16 Cal.App 4th 836; Kane v. Superior Court (1995) 37 Cal. App. 4th 1577.

### REX W. JACOBS
350 WEST COLORADO BOULEVARD, SUITE 400
**PASADENA, CALIFORNIA 91105-1894**
Telephone: 818-440-1111
Fax: 818-440-9456

*Plaintiffs Personal Injury, Construction Accidents, Auto Accidents, Products Liability and Premises Liability.*

**REX W. JACOBS,** born Los Angeles, California, August 17, 1948; admitted to bar, 1973, California; 1974, U.S. District Court, Central District of California; 1977, U.S. Court of Appeals, Ninth Circuit and U.S. Supreme CourT; 1993, Colorado. *Education:* University of California at Santa Barbara (B.A., with honors, 1970); Washington College of Law (J.D., 1973). Arbitrator, Los Angeles County Superior Court, 1981—. Judge Pro Tem, Los Angeles Municipal Court, 1979. *Member:* Los Angeles County and American Bar Associations; State Bar of California; Los Angeles Trial Lawyers Association; The Association of Trial Lawyers of America; California Trial Lawyers Association. (Also Associated with John Scott Matthew, Los Angeles (Sherman Oaks), California). *PRACTICE AREAS:* Personal Injury; Construction Injuries.

### KAJAN MATHER AND BARISH
*A PROFESSIONAL CORPORATION*
**PASADENA, CALIFORNIA**
(See Beverly Hills)

*Civil and Criminal Tax Controversy and Tax Litigation.*

### GARY W. KEARNEY
Established in 1978
SUITE 410, 225 SOUTH LAKE AVENUE
**PASADENA, CALIFORNIA 91101-3005**
Telephone: 818-796-9621
Telecopier: 818-796-6839

*Family Law, Dissolutions, Adoptions and Custody.*

FIRM PROFILE: *The firm limits its practice to all aspects of family law in order to provide its clients with quality legal representation at a reasonable cost. The firm offers two attorneys who have been certified as family law specialists by the State Bar of California along with a knowledgeable support staff. The firm has engaged in complicated litigation concerning business evaluation,*

*(This Listing Continued)*

*profit sharing plans, qualified domestic relations orders, support collections, domestic/international custody and efficient resolution of basic cases.*

**GARY W. KEARNEY,** born Philadelphia, Pennsylvania, October 26, 1947; admitted to bar, 1976, California. *Education:* California Polytechnic State University (B.S.M.E., 1971); University of LaVerne (J.D., 1976). Mediator, Los Angeles County Superior Court, 1989. Judge Pro Tem, Los Angeles Superior Court, 1990—. *Member:* Pasadena, Los Angeles County (Member, Family Law Section) and American (Member, Family Law Section) Bar Associations; State Bar of California; Association of Certified Family Law Specialists (Member and Director). (Certified Specialist, Family Law, The State Bar of California Board of Legal Specialization.). *PRACTICE AREAS:* Family Law.

### ASSOCIATE

**RONALD K. ZIFF,** born Los Angeles, California, October 18, 1953; admitted to bar, 1980, California. *Education:* West Los Angeles College; Sonoma State University; Golden West University (B.S., in Law, 1978; J.D., 1980). Licensed Real Estate Agent, California, 1975. *Member:* Pasadena and Los Angeles County (Member, Family Law Section) Bar Associations; State Bar of California; Association of Certified Family Law Specialists (Member). (Certified Specialist, Family Law, The State Bar of California Board of Legal Specialization). *LANGUAGES:* Spanish. *PRACTICE AREAS:* Family Law; Domestic Relations.

REFERENCE: Bank of America (Lake-Green Branch, Pasadena).

---

## J. STEVEN KENNEDY

**225 SOUTH LAKE AVENUE, SUITE 300**
**PASADENA, CALIFORNIA 91101-3005**
Telephone: 818-432-5440
Fax: 818-432-5401

*General Civil Trial Practice, Real Estate, Business, Probate and Estate, Personal Injury, Commercial Litigation and Family Law.*

**J. STEVEN KENNEDY,** born Ventura, California, January 21, 1949; admitted to bar, 1978, California. *Education:* University of Texas at Austin (B.A., magna cum laude, 1974); University of Illinois at Urbana-Champaign (M.A., 1975); University of California at Los Angeles (J.D., 1978). Phi Beta Kappa. *Member:* State Bar of California. *PRACTICE AREAS:* Civil Litigation; General Business and Real Estate Law; Probate Law.

---

## ALEXANDER W. KIRKPATRICK

**225 SOUTH LAKE AVENUE, 9TH FLOOR**
**PASADENA, CALIFORNIA 91101**
Telephone: 818-796-2965; 800-554-2965
Fax: 818-796-9039

*General Civil Litigation in all State and Federal Courts, Business Litigation, Commercial Litigation, Real Estate, Healthcare and Appellate.*

**ALEXANDER W. KIRKPATRICK,** born Pittsburg, Pennsylvania, October 14, 1946; admitted to bar, 1974, California; U.S. District Court, Central District of California; 1980, U.S. Court of Appeals, Ninth Circuit; 1984, U.S. District Court, Eastern District of California; 1991, Texas; U.S. District Court, Eastern Di strict of Texas; U.S. Court of Appeals, Fifth Circuit; 1993, U.S. Tax Court. *Education:* Northwestern University (B.A., 1971); University of Los Angeles, California School of Law (J.D., 1974). *Member:* Los Angeles County Bar Association.

---

## KOLTS AND NAWA

**THE WALNUT PLAZA, SUITE 195**
**215 NORTH MARENGO AVENUE**
**PASADENA, CALIFORNIA 91101**
Telephone: 818-584-6968
FAX: 818-584-5718

*Products Liability, Wrongful Termination, Medical Device Defense, Probate Law and Business Litigation, Construction Litigation, ERISA Litigation and General Civil Litigation.*

*(This Listing Continued)*

### MEMBERS OF FIRM

**RAYMOND G. KOLTS,** born Los Angeles, California, June 20, 1940; admitted to bar, 1967, California and U.S. District Court, Northern District of California; 1968, U.S. District Court, Central District of California. *Education:* California State University of Los Angeles; Loyola University of Los Angeles (J.D., 1967). Arbitrator, Los Angeles Superior Court Arbitration Panel, Judicial Arbitration for Civil Cases, 1978—. Arbitrator, Los Angeles Superior Court, 1980—. Member, Panel of Arbitrators, American Arbitration Association. Lecturer, Medical-Legal Institute, 1983-1990. *Member:* The State Bar of California (Director, Law Practice Management Section, 1985-1987); American Bar Association (Member, Sections on: Insurance, Negligence and Compensation Law) Bar Associations; Southern California Defense Counsel; American Board of Trial Advocates. *PRACTICE AREAS:* Products Liability Defense Law; Insurance Defense Law; General Civil Litigation; Wrongful Termination; Arbitration.

**GARY C. NAWA,** born Corpus Christi, Texas, October 14, 1947; admitted to bar, 1975, California. *Education:* University of California at Santa Cruz and California State University at Los Angeles (B.A., 1972); Southwestern University School of Law (J.D., with honors, 1975). *Member:* Los Angeles County Bar Association; The State Bar of California; Association of Southern California Defense Counsel. *PRACTICE AREAS:* Construction Litigation; ERISA Litigation; Arbitration.

### ASSOCIATES

**LYNN M. JOHNSON,** born Pittsburgh, Pennsylvania, May 18, 1950; admitted to bar, 1988, California. *Education:* California State University at Los Angeles (B.A., 1973; M.A., 1982); Loyola University (J.D., cum laude, 1988). *Member:* Los Angeles County Bar Association; State Bar of California. *PRACTICE AREAS:* Civil Litigation; Wrongful Termination.

**LINDA M. TOUTANT,** born Covina, California, May 10, 1962; admitted to bar, 1988, Texas; 1991, District of Columbia; 1992, California. *Education:* University of California at San Diego (B.A., 1984); University of Notre Dame (J.D., 1988). Hearings Examiner, Railroad Commission of Texas, 1990-1991. *Member:* State Bar of Texas; District of Columbia Bar; State Bar of California. *PRACTICE AREAS:* Construction; Wrongful Termination.

**FRANCIS T. KALINSKI, II,** born Hawthorne, California, September 22, 1958; admitted to bar, 1994, California, U.S. District Court, Southern District of California and U.S. Court of Appeals, Ninth Circuit. *Education:* University of California at San Diego (B.S., 1989); California Western School of Law (J.D., 1994). *Member:* State Bar of California. [Sergeant, U.S. Army, 1978-1982]. *PRACTICE AREAS:* Medical Technology Litigation; Construction Defect Litigation.

**DIANE L. DARVEY,** born Los Angeles, California, January 31, 1947; admitted to bar, 1989, California. *Education:* University of California School of Pharmacy, San Francisco (Pharm.D., 1970); Loyola Law School (J.D., 1989). Registered Pharmacist, California, 1970. Author, "Sex Discrimination in the Workplace," Pharmacy Management Advisor, March and April, 1994. *Member:* Los Angeles County and American Bar Associations; State Bar of California; American Society for Pharmacy Law; American Pharmaceutical Association; American Society of Hospital Pharmacists; Regulatory Affairs Professionals Society; California Society of Hospital Pharmacists. *PRACTICE AREAS:* Employment Discrimination and Wrongful Termination; Drug Products and Medical Device Litigation.

**MICHAEL A. J. NANGANO,** born Los Angeles, California, March 15, 1960; admitted to bar, 1988, California. *Education:* Marquette University (1978-1979); University of Southern California (B.A., 1983); Loyola Law School, Los Angeles (J.D., 1986). Phi Alpha Delta. *Member:* American Bar Association; The State Bar of California; Association of Southern California Defense Counsel; The ABOTA Inns of Court. *LANGUAGES:* Latin. *PRACTICE AREAS:* Products Liability; Premises; Construction Defect; Business Litigation; Medical Malpractice.

### OF COUNSEL

**KATHLENE LANDGRAF KOLTS,** born Dearborn, Michigan, July 25, 1952; admitted to bar, 1986, California and U.S. District Court, Northern and Central Districts of California. *Education:* Western Michigan University (B.S., cum laude, 1974); Santa Clara University (J.D., cum laude, 1985). *Member:* Los Angeles County and American Bar Associations; The State Bar of California; Southern California Defense Counsel. *PRACTICE AREAS:* Wrongful Termination; Medical Device Litigation.

## LAGERLOF, SENECAL, BRADLEY & SWIFT, LLP

Established in 1908

301 NORTH LAKE AVENUE, 10TH FLOOR
**PASADENA, CALIFORNIA 91101-4108**
Telephone: 818-793-9400
FAX: 818-793-5900

*General Civil, Trial and Appellate Practice in all State and Federal Courts and Administrative Agencies. Corporation, Antitrust, Labor, Tax, Real Estate, Probate, Trust, Estate Planning, Water, Natural Resources and Municipal Law.*

### MEMBERS OF FIRM

**JOSEPH J. BURRIS** (1913-1980).

**STANLEY C. LAGERLOF** (Retired).

**H. MELVIN SWIFT, JR.,** born Los Angeles, California, December 11, 1924; admitted to bar, 1950, California; 1961, U.S. Tax Court; 1964, U.S. Supreme Court. *Education:* University of Redlands and Stanford University (A.B., 1948); Stanford University (LL.B., 1949). Phi Alpha Delta. Member, Board of Editors, Stanford Law Review, 1947-1948. President, Stanford Club of Los Angeles, 1959-1960. President, Stanford Alumni Association, 1963-1964. Chairman, Stanford Athletic Board, 1966-1967. Member, Board of Trustees, Stanford University, 1973-1976. *Member:* Los Angeles County and American (Member, Sections on: Litigation; Natural Resources Law; Real Property, Probate and Trust Law) Bar Associations; State Bar of California. [Ensign, U.S. Naval Reserve, 1943-1946]

**H. JESS SENECAL,** born Pittsburgh, Pennsylvania, July 15, 1930; admitted to bar, 1956, California. *Education:* University of Redlands (A.B., cum laude, 1952); University of Southern California and University of California at Los Angeles (J.D., 1955). Phi Delta Phi. President, University of Redlands Alumni Association, 1970-1971. Member, 1970-1971, 1977—and Chairman, 1981-1984, Board of Trustees, University of Redlands. *Member:* Pasadena, Los Angeles County and American Bar Associations; State Bar of California.

**JACK T. SWAFFORD,** born Alhambra, California, July 26, 1922; admitted to bar, 1953, California; 1972, U.S. Supreme Court. *Education:* Pasadena Junior College and University of Southern California (B.S., 1948); University of Southern California (J.D., 1952). Order of the Coif; Phi Alpha Delta. Member, Board of Editors, 1950-1952, and Assistant Editor-in-Chief, 1951-1952, University of Southern California Law Review. Research Attorney to the Honorable Douglas L. Edmonds, Justice, Supreme Court of California, 1952-1954. *Member:* Pasadena and American (Member, Sections on: Antitrust; Judicial Administration; Litigation) Bar Associations; State Bar of California.

**JOHN F. BRADLEY,** born Los Angeles, California, March 14, 1931; admitted to bar, 1957, California; 1964, U.S. Tax Court; 1973, U.S. Supreme Court. *Education:* University of Southern California (B.S., summa cum laude, 1952); Stanford University (J.D., 1957). Order of the Coif; Phi Alpha Delta; Phi Kappa Phi; Beta Gamma Sigma; Phi Eta Sigma. Member, Board of Editors, Stanford Law Review, 1956-57. Research Attorney to the Honorable Homer R. Spence, Justice, Supreme Court of California, 1957-58. President, Stanford Law Society of Southern California, 1968-1969. President, Wilshire Estate Planning Council, 1972-1973. President, Stanford Club of Los Angeles County, 1974-1975. *Member:* Wilshire (Member, Board of Governors, 1974—; President, 1981-1982), Pasadena, and Los Angeles County Bar Associations; State Bar of California. [First Lieut., U.S. Air Force Reserve, 1952-1954]

**TIMOTHY J. GOSNEY,** born San Diego, California, January 20, 1945; admitted to bar, 1974, California. *Education:* University of California at Santa Barbara (B.A., 1966); California Western School of Law (J.D., 1974). Member, 1972-1974 and Head Notes and Comments Editor, 1973-1974, California Western Law Review. Disciplinary Examiner, State Bar of California, 1975-1979. *Member:* Wilshire (Member, Board of Governors, 1979—; President, 1985-1986), Pasadena, Los Angeles County and American Bar Associations; State Bar of California. [1st Lt., U.S. Army Reserve, 1967-1970].

**WILLIAM F. KRUSE,** born Los Angeles, California, January 4, 1955; admitted to bar, 1979, California; 1981, U.S. Tax Court. *Education:* University of Southern California (B.S., magna cum laude, 1976; M.B.A., 1979; J.D., 1979). Beta Gamma Sigma. Advocacy Vice-Chairman, Moot Court Honors Program Executive Board, 1978-1979. Member, United Way Region V Allocations Committee, 1982—. *Member:* Pasadena and Los Angeles County Bar Associations; State Bar of California.

**THOMAS S. BUNN, III,** born Pasadena, California, February 13, 1955; admitted to bar, 1979, California. *Education:* Princeton University (A.B., 1976); University of Southern California (J.D., 1979). Phi Delta Phi; Order of the Coif. Member, 1977-1978 and Notes Editor, 1978-1979, Southern California Law Review. *Member:* Los Angeles County and American (Member, Sections on: Corporation, Banking and Business Law; Family Law; Litigation) Bar Associations; State Bar of California.

**ANDREW D. TURNER,** born Fort Bragg, California, October 8, 1954; admitted to bar, 1985, California. *Education:* University of California at Santa Cruz (B.A., 1978); University of Southern California (J.D., 1985). Staff Member, Major Tax Planning and Computer/Law Journals, 1983-1984. *Member:* Pasadena and Los Angeles County Bar Associations; State Bar of California.

**REBECCA J. THYNE,** born Los Angeles, California, July 28, 1943; admitted to bar, 1986, California. *Education:* University of California at Los Angeles (B.A., 1965); Loyola Marymount University (J.D., 1986). *Member:* Pasadena, Los Angeles County and American Bar Associations; State Bar of California.

### ASSOCIATES

**JAMES D. CIAMPA,** born Long Beach, California, July 23, 1965; admitted to bar, 1992, California. *Education:* California State University, Long Beach (B.S., with great distinction, 1988); Santa Clara University (J.D., 1992). Phi Delta Phi; Beta Gamma Sigma. Business Editor, Santa Clara Law Review, 1991-1992. *Member:* Los Angeles County Bar Association; State Bar of California.

**ROBERT W. RENKEN,** born Pasadena, California, July 27, 1965; admitted to bar, 1992, California. *Education:* University of the Pacific (B.S., 1987); Loyola Marymount University (J.D., 1992). *Member:* Pasadena and Los Angeles County Bar Associations (Member, Section on Taxation); State Bar of California.

REPRESENTATIVE CLIENTS: Anchor Glass Container Corporation; Beauchamp Distributing Company; Gallo Glass Company; Metric Construction Co., Inc.; North American Chemical Company; Orthopaedic Hospital; Palmdale Water District; Public Water Agencies Group; Rhone-Poulenc Rorer, Inc.; John Stauffer Charitable Trust; Venture Port District; Walnut Valley Water District.
REFER TO: Citizens Business Bank, Pasadena, California.

## LARR & POTEET

A Partnership including a Professional Corporation

285 NORTH HILL AVENUE
SUITE 200
**PASADENA, CALIFORNIA 91106**
Telephone: 818-796-5588
Telecopier: 818-796-7635

*General Business, Litigation, Real Property Law, Commercial Law, Products Liability, FIRREA, Title Insurance Litigation, Title Insurance Claims, Insurance Law.*

*FIRM PROFILE: Founded by William R. Larr in 1983, the firm of Larr & Poteet provides legal services in the areas of real estate, insurance and general business litigation with an emphasis in title insurance law. The firm is dedicated to providing its clients with the highest quality legal representation at competitive rates.*

### MEMBERS OF FIRM

**WILLIAM RAY LARR, (P.C.),** born Whittier, California, September 28, 1948; admitted to bar, 1974, California. *Education:* University of California at Berkeley (A.B., 1970); University of Colorado (J.D., 1973). Lecturer, Continuing Education of the Bar. *Member:* Pasadena and Los Angeles County (Lecturer, Real Property Section) Bar Associations; State Bar of California; California Land Title Association. [2nd Lt., U.S. Army Reserves, 1970-1976]. **REPORTED CASES:** Kaufman v. Gross 23 Cal 3d 750 (1979); Allstate v. Lotito 116 CA 3d 998 (1981); Battle v. Kessler 149 CA 3d 853 (1983); Prichard v. Reitz 178 CA 3d 465 (1986); 1119 Delaware v. Continental Land Title Insurance Company 16 CA 4th 992 (1991); Soman Properties, Inc. v. Rikuo Corporation 24 CA 4th 471 (1994). **PRACTICE AREAS:** Real Property Litigation; Insurance Coverage Litigation; Insurance Arbitration; Title Insurance Litigation; General Insurance Law; Product Liability Litigation; Toxic Waste Litigation; General Business Litigation.

*(This Listing Continued)*

**LAWRENCE JAY POTEET,** born Long Beach, California, March 19, 1953; admitted to bar, 1978, California. *Education:* Long Beach City College (A.A., 1972); Long Beach State University (B.S., summa cum laude, 1974); University of California at Los Angeles (M.B.A., 1978; J.D., 1978). Phi Kappa Phi; Beta Gamma Sigma. UCLA Moot Court Honors Program. Settlement Conference Officer, Los Angeles County Superior Court. *Member:* Pasadena and Los Angeles County (Member, Real Property Section) Bar Associations; State Bar of California (Member, Real Estate and Litigation Sections). **SPECIAL AGENCIES:** FDIC. **REPORTED CASES:** Harris v. Northwestern National Ins. Co. (1992); 6 CA 4th 1061; Stagen v. Stewart-West Coast Title Co. (1983) 149 CA 3d 114. **PRACTICE AREAS:** Commercial and Real Property Litigation; Title Insurance Law and Litigation; FIRREA; General Insurance Law; General Business Litigation.

## ASSOCIATES

**LIZA B. DUCKWORTH,** born Kansas City, Missouri, June 8, 1956; admitted to bar, 1985, California; 1986, U.S. District Court, Central District of California. *Education:* Pepperdine University; California State University at Northridge (B.A., magna cum laude, 1978); Loyola Marymount University (J.D., 1985). Member, International Law Journal, Loyola University, 1983-1984. *Member:* Los Angeles County and American Bar Associations; State Bar of California (Member, Litigation Section). **PRACTICE AREAS:** Commercial Litigation; Real Property Litigation; General Business Litigation; Insurance Law.

---

# LAUGHLIN, FALBO, LEVY & MORESI LLP

A Partnership including Professional Corporations

200 SOUTH LOS ROBLES, SUITE 500
**PASADENA, CALIFORNIA 91101**
Telephone: 818-568-9700
Fax: 818-568-3905
Email: lflm@lflm.com
URL: http://lflm.com

*San Francisco, California Office:* Two Embarcadero Center, Fifth Floor. Telephone: 415-781-6676. Fax: 415-781-6823.
*Sacramento, California Office:* 106 K Street - Second Floor. Telephone: 916-441-6045. Fax: 916-441-7067.
*Redding, California Office:* 930 Executive Way, Second Floor. Telephone: 916-222-0268. Fax: 916-222-5705.
*Walnut Creek, California Office:* 100 Pringle Avenue, Suite 630. Telephone: 510-210-0210. Fax: 510-210-0105.
*Irvine, California Office:* 3 Park Plaza, Suite 1400, P.O. Box 17659. Telephone: 714-251-0120. Fax: 714-251-0125.
*San Jose, California Office:* 1570 The Alameda, Suite 100. Telephone: 408-286-8801. Fax: 408-286-1935.

*General Civil and Trial Practice. Workers' Compensation Defense (State and Federal), Labor Relations and Employment Discrimination.*

**JAMES C. HESTER,** born New York, New York, April 27, 1945; admitted to bar, 1971, California. *Education:* University of California at Berkeley (A.B., 1967); Hastings College of Law, University of California (J.D., 1970). Member, Planning Commission, City of Sierra Madre, California, 1985—. *Member:* Los Angeles County Bar Association. **PRACTICE AREAS:** Workers' Compensation. *Email:* jhester@lflm.com

**JERILYN COHEN,** born Van Nuys, California, August 4, 1956; admitted to bar, 1980, California. *Education:* University of California at Los Angeles (B.A., cum laude, 1977); Southwestern University School of Law (J.D., 1980) American Graduate School of International Management, 1981. Instructor, Southwestern University, Torts. **LANGUAGES:** French, Spanish, Italian. **PRACTICE AREAS:** Workers' Compensation. *Email:* jcohen@lflm.com

**MATTHEW J. KING,** born Boston, Massachusetts, April 21, 1952; admitted to bar, 1978, Massachusetts; 1992, California. *Education:* College of the Holy Cross (B.A., 1974); Suffolk University (J.D., 1978). **PRACTICE AREAS:** Workers' Compensation. *Email:* mking@lflm.com

**MARK J. EPSTEIN,** born Odessa, Ukraine, February 8, 1955; admitted to bar, 1992, California. *Education:* Institute of Technology (B.S., 1977); Pepperdine University (M.B.A., 1985); Southwestern University (J.D., 1992). **PRACTICE AREAS:** Workers' Compensation. *Email:* mepstein@lflm.com

*(This Listing Continued)*

**AMY G. RIVERA,** born Summit, New Jersey, August 9, 1958; admitted to bar, 1993, California. *Education:* Catholic University of American (B.S.N., 1980); Whittier College School of Law (J.D., 1992). Recipient, American Jurisprudence Award for Advanced Legal Writing. Registered Nurse, California, 1980. [U.S. Air Force, 1980-1984, Capt.]. **PRACTICE AREAS:** Workers' Compensation. *Email:* arivera@lflm.com

**JOHN C. CALLISTER,** born Glendale, California, April 28, 1953; admitted to bar, 1980, California. *Education:* Occidental College (B.A., 1975); Southwestern University (J.D., 1980). **PRACTICE AREAS:** Workers' Compensation Defense. *Email:* jcallist@lflm.com

Unless Otherwise Indicated All Partners and Associates are Members of the State Bar of California.

REPRESENTATIVE CLIENTS: AC Transit; Aetna Casualty & Surety Co.; Alameda County Schools; Allianz Insurance Co.; Alta Bates Hospital; American Hardware Mutual; American International Adjustment Co.; American International Underwriters; American Protective Services; Argonaut Insurance; Bank of America; California Casualty Insurance Co.; City of Anaheim; Continental Co.; Continental Loss Adjusting Service; Crawford and Co.; Eagle Marine Insurance Co.; Eagle Pacific Ins. Co.; Electric Mutual; Employers Insurance of Wausau; Fireman's Fund; Fremont Indemnity; GAB Business Services; Gates, McDonald & Co.; General Electric Co.; Hartford Accident & Indemnity; Hewlett-Packard; Industrial Indemnity Co.; Insurance Company of the West; Liberty Mutual Insurance; Majestic Insurance Company; McKesson Corp.; MHG Adjusting Co.; Regents of the University of California; Royal Globe Group; Safeway Stores; San Francisco Newspaper Agency; Sequoia Hospital; Standard Oil Co.; Todd Shipyards Corp.; TOSCO; United Airlines, Inc.; U.S. Sprint Communications; USX; Wells Fargo Bank; Zenith National Insurance; Zurich-American Insurance.

(For complete biographical data on other personnel, see professional biographies at San Francisco, Sacramento, Redding, Walnut Creek, Irvine and San Jose)

---

# LIGHTFOOT & NORTHUP

A PROFESSIONAL CORPORATION

151 SOUTH EL MOLINO AVENUE, SUITE 303
**PASADENA, CALIFORNIA 91101-2510**
Telephone: 818-577-1382; 213-684-3066
Telecopier: 818-577-1459
Email: l-n@ix.netcom.com

*Oceanside, California Office:* 1351 Harbor Boulevard North, Suite B, 92054. Telephone: 619-439-4647.

*Business, Commercial, Corporate Law, Litigation, Sales and Use Tax Law, Real Estate, Probate and Estate Planning.*

**STEPHEN K. LIGHTFOOT,** born Pasadena, California, April 3, 1943; admitted to bar, 1973, California; U.S. District Court, Northern and Central Districts of California. *Education:* Pasadena City College; Glendale University (B.S., 1968); Glendale University College of Law (J.D., 1973). California State Board of Equalization, 1965-1973. *Member:* Pasadena and American (Member, Sections of: Business; Law Office Economics) Bar Associations; State Bar of California. [U.S. Air Force, 1960-1964]. **PRACTICE AREAS:** Corporate Law; Business Law; Probate Law; Estate Planning; Sales and Use Tax.

**ROBERT W. NORTHUP, JR.,** born Princeton, New Jersey, January 19, 1958; admitted to bar, 1985, California and U.S. District Court, Central District of California; 1986, U.S. District Court, Northern and Southern Districts of California. *Education:* Lafayette College (B.A., 1980); University of San Diego (J.D., 1984). *Member:* Pasadena Bar Association; State Bar of California. **PRACTICE AREAS:** Business Litigation; Construction Litigation.

REFERENCE: Citizens Bank, Pasadena, California.

---

# JAMES S. LINK

215 N. MARENGO, 3RD FLOOR
**PASADENA, CALIFORNIA 91101-1504**
Telephone: 818-793-9570
Fax: 818-356-7414

*Appellate Practice in State and Federal Courts, Insurance Coverage and Litigation.*

**JAMES S. LINK,** born Gilroy, California, August 19, 1954; admitted to bar, 1980, California; U.S. Court of Appeals, Ninth Circuit; U.S. District Court, Central and Northern Districts of California; U.S. Supreme Court. *Education:* University of San Francisco (B.A., 1976); Southwestern University (J.D., 1980). Recipient, American Jurisprudence Award in Insurance

*(This Listing Continued)*

### JAMES S. LINK, Pasadena—Continued

Law. *Member:* Los Angeles County (Member, Appellate Courts Committee) Bar Association; State Bar of California; Association of Southern California Defense Counsel. **REPORTED CASES:** Alliance Insurance Co. v. Colella (9th Cir. 1993) 995 F.2d 944; Coleman v. Gulf Insurance Group (1986) 41 Cal.3d 782 (amicus counsel); Doctors Co. v. Superior Court (1989) 39 Cal.3d 39 (amicus counsel); Griffin v. State Farm Mutual Auto Insurance Co. (1991) 230 Cal.3d 59; Robinson v. Superior Court (1984) 158 Cal.App.3d 98; Rogers v. Hirschi (1983) 141 Cal.App.3d 847; State Farm Fire & Casualty v. Superior Court (1989) 216 Cal.App.3d 1222; Turcon Constuction, Inc. v. Norton-Villiers, Ltd. (1983) 139 Cal.App.3d 280; Briggs v. City of Rolling Hills Estates (1995) 40 Cal. App. 4th 637. **PRACTICE AREAS:** Appellate Practice (40%); Insurance Coverage (40%); Litigation (20%).

---

## EDWARD D. MACFARLANE
*Established in 1978*

**2 NORTH LAKE AVENUE, SUITE 860**
**PASADENA, CALIFORNIA 91101**
Telephone: 818-585-3570
Fax: 818-585-3568

*Real Estate and Business. General Civil Practice, Commercial Leasing, Condominium and Homeowners Association, Construction, Foreclosure, Litigation.*

**EDWARD D. MACFARLANE,** born Pasadena, California, November 21, 1947; admitted to bar, 1973, California and U.S. District Court, Central District of California; 1975, U.S. Court of Appeals, Ninth Circuit. *Education:* Loyola University of Los Angeles (B.B.A., 1969); Loyola University School of Law (J.D., 1973). Phi Delta Phi. Judge Pro Tem, Pasadena Municipal Court, 1983—. Licensed Real Estate Broker, California, 1978. *Member:* State Bar of California, Pasadena Bar Association.

---

## MARQUEZ & TEPERSON, P.C.

**301 NORTH LAKE AVENUE, 8TH FLOOR**
**PASADENA, CALIFORNIA 91101**
Telephone: 818-793-0133
Fax: 818-793-1116

*General Civil Litigation and Appellate Practice in State and Federal Courts and Arbitration Tribunals, General Insurance, Casualty, Products Liability, Legal Malpractice and Labor and Employment.*

FIRM PROFILE: *Marquez & Teperson is a minority owned law firm founded by two trial attorneys with considerable experience in the defense of casualty matters. The firm offers quality legal services in all of the practice areas described above throughout Kern County, Orange County, Los Angeles County, Ventura County and San Diego County.*

*Marquez & Teperson is responsive to the client's need for timely communication, cost effectiveness and prompt evaluation and analysis.*

**ROBERT B. MARQUEZ,** born Los Angeles, California, March 3, 1959; admitted to bar, 1987, California, U.S. District Court, Central District of California and U.S. Court of Appeals, Ninth Circuit. *Education:* Occidental College (B.A., 1981); University of San Francisco School of Law (J.D., 1985). Judge Pro Tem, Los Angeles County Municipal Court. *Member:* Los Angeles County and Mexican American Bar Associations; State Bar of California. **LANGUAGES:** Spanish. **PRACTICE AREAS:** Civil Litigation; Insurance; Employment and Labor Law.

**JONATHAN B. TEPERSON,** born Louisville, Kentucky, August 24, 1965; admitted to bar, 1991, California, U.S. District Court, Central District of California and U.S. Court of Appeals, Ninth Circuit. *Education:* University of California at Santa Barbara (B.A., 1987); Hastings College of the Law, University of California (J.D., 1991). *Member:* Los Angeles County and American Bar Associations; State Bar of California. **PRACTICE AREAS:** Civil Litigation; Casualty; Employment.

---

## MARTIN & HUDSON
**350 WEST COLORADO BOULEVARD, SUITE 320**
**PASADENA, CALIFORNIA 91105**
Telephone: 818-793-8500
Telecopier: 818-793-8779

*Taxation, Civil Tax Litigation, Estate and Trust Planning, Corporation and Real Estate Law.*

### MEMBERS OF FIRM

**ROBERT B. MARTIN, JR.,** born 1944; admitted to bar, 1970, California. *Education:* University of Southern California; Kent State University (A.B., 1966); University of Southern California (J.D., 1969). Order of the Coif. Comment Editor, Southern California Law Review, 1968-1969. Author: "Coping with the Tax Shelter Registration and Compliance Requirements, New Law and Regs," 62 Journal of Taxation 2, January, 1985; "Tax Shelter Accounting Under the New Law: An Analysis of a Dramatically Changed Area," 61 Journal of Taxation 170, September 1984; "At-Risk Rule—Sections 465 and 46(c) (8)," BNA Tax Management Portfolio No. 455, 1984; "Tax Shelters: 1984 Style," 36 U.S.C. Tax Institute 600, 1984; "Leasing Thoroughbred Broodmares: A Newly Developing Tax Shelter," 58 Journal of Taxation 152, March, 1983; "An Analysis of the Impact of the New Tax Legislation on the Use of Tax Shelters," 57 Journal of Taxation 288, November, 1982; "Living With the At-Risk Rules," 34 U.S.C. Tax Institute 1-1, 1982; "Five Easy Questions: How to Win the Tax Shelter Partnership Fee Game," The Digest of Financial Planning Ideas, September, 1982; "The Impact of the Tax Court's Straddle Opinion on Tax Shelters," The Financial Planner, May, 1982; "Tax Advantages of a Deferred Minimum Annual Royalty Provision in Oil and Gas Leases," 30 Oil & Gas Tax Quarterly 241, December, 1981; "The Martin Guide: Tax Shelters and the New Act," September, 1981; "Planning for the R&D Tax Shelter: An Analysis of the Essential Tax Elements," 53 Journal of Taxation 204, October, 1980; "When are Advance Payments of Rent Deductible?," 50 Journal of Taxation 360, June 1979; "How T-bill Spreads can be Used for Hedging and Tax Deferral," 48 Journal of Taxation 102, February, 1978; "The Trouble with Revenue Procedure 74-17," 60 American Bar Association Journal 1281, 1974; "Broker-Dealer Manipulation of the Over-the-Counter Market-Toward a Reasonable Basis for Quotation," 25 Business Lawyer 1463, 1970; Comment, "The Outsider and the Unfair Labor Practice," 41 Southern California Law Review 876, 1968. Lecturer: U.S.C. Tax Institute, 1982, 1984; California CPA Foundation, 1979-1983; California State University at Los Angeles, 1979-1982. *Member:* Los Angeles County and American (Member, Sections on: Corporation, Banking and Business Law; Taxation) Bar Associations; State Bar of California. (Certified Specialist, Taxation Law, The State Bar of California Board of Legal Specialization). **PRACTICE AREAS:** Taxation; Civil Tax Litigation; Estate and Trust Planning; Corporation and Real Estate Law.

**BOYD D. HUDSON,** born 1951; admitted to bar, 1979, California. *Education:* Claremont Mens College (B.A., cum laude, 1973); University of California at Los Angeles (M.B.A., 1978; J.D., 1978). Beta Gamma Sigma; Phi Alpha Delta. Certified Public Accountant, California, 1980. Instructor: Accounting, Glendale Community College, 1981-1986; Whittier College of Law, 1985-1987. Speaker: "Financing Development, Operations of Hotels and Casinos," Practicing Law Institute Course, July, 1989; "Tax Planning for Pass-Through Entities," California State Bar Taxation Section Course, July, 1992. Member, Board of Trustees, Claremont McKenna College, 1989-1992. President, Claremont McKenna College Alumni Association, 1987-1988. *Member:* Pasadena Bar Association (Co-Chairman, Taxation Section, 1991—); State Bar of California; American Institute of Certified Public Accountants; American Association of Attorney-Certified Public Accountants, Inc. **PRACTICE AREAS:** Taxation; Civil Tax Litigation; Estate and Trust Planning; Corporation and Real Estate Law.

---

## W. MICHAEL MAYOCK

**THE BRALEY BUILDING**
**FOURTH FLOOR, 35 SOUTH RAYMOND AVENUE**
**PASADENA, CALIFORNIA 91105**
Telephone: 818-405-1465; 310-552-1465
FAX: 818-578-0768

*Criminal Trial and Appellate Practice in all State and Federal Courts.*

**W. MICHAEL MAYOCK,** born Yuba City, California, April 27, 1944; admitted to bar, 1972, California and U.S. District Court, Central District of California; 1973, U.S. Court of Appeals, Ninth Circuit; 1977, U.S. Court of Appeals, Fifth Circuit; 1979, U.S. Supreme Court; 1990, U.S. Court of

*(This Listing Continued)*

Appeals, Eighth Circuit; 1991, U.S. District Court, District of Arizona; 1992, U.S. Court of Appeals, Eleventh Circuit; 1995, U.S. Court of Appeals, Sixth Circuit. *Education:* University of Southern California (B.A., 1967); Loyola University of Los Angeles (J.D., 1972). Blue Key; Phi Delta Phi. Member, St. Thomas More Law Honor Society. Articles Editor, Loyola of Los Angeles Law Review, 1971-1972. Author: "Redefining Federal Largess Through State Minimum Grant Regulations: Dandridge v. Williams," 4 Loyola Law Review, 1971; "Recent Decision - SEC v. Lake Havasu Estates," 5 Loyola Law Review, 1972. Instructor, Civil Procedure, Glendale College of Law, 1974-1976. Law Clerk to Honorable David W. Williams, Judge, U.S. District Court, Central District of California, 1972. Assistant U.S. Attorney, Central District of California, Criminal Division, 1973-1976. *Member:* Century City (Judge Pro Tem Program, 1979-1986), Los Angeles County (Member: Jail Study Committee, 1974-1976; Los Angeles Delegation, State Bar Conference of Delegates, 1979-1980, 1982-1984; Amicus Briefs, Committee, 1981—; Judicial Evaluation Committee, 1982-1988; Judiciary Committee, 1982-1990) and American Bar Associations; State Bar of California (Hearing Examiner, 1976-1977); First Amendment Lawyers Association; California Attorneys for Criminal Justice; National Association of Criminal Defense Lawyers.

REFERENCE: Union Bank.

## McCLAUGHERTY & ASSOCIATES

*301 NORTH LAKE AVENUE*
*SUITE 800*
**PASADENA, CALIFORNIA 91101**
Telephone: 818-449-7522
FAX: 818-583-9187

*Ontario, California Office:* 3350 Shelby Street, Suite 200, 91764. Telephone: 909-944-2505.

*Insurance Defense, General Civil Trial in all State and Federal Court.*

**JAY S. MCCLAUGHERTY,** born Los Angeles, California, March 1, 1952; admitted to bar, 1981, California and U.S. District Court, Southern, Central and Eastern Districts of California; 1983, U.S. District Court, Eastern District of California; 1989, U.S. District Court, Central District of California. *Education:* Pacific Lutheran University (B.A., magna cum laude, 1974); University of San Diego (J.D., 1979). Co-Chairman of Seminars for Southern California Defense Counsel, 1995 and 1996; Seminar Lecturer, Topic, Arbitrations, Las Vegas Seminar, Los Angeles Trial Lawyers, 1992; Seminar Moderator: Topic, Taking & Defending Expert Depositions, Southern California Defense Counsel Seminar, May 1995; Topic, Claims and Defense Perspectives on Handling a Litigated File, Southern California Defense Counsel Seminar, July 1995. Appointed to Board of Directors, Southern California Defense Counsel, 1997. Judge Pro Tem, Los Angeles Municipal Court. Settlement Officer, Los Angeles County Superior Court. Mediator, Los Angeles Superior Court. *Member:* State Bar of California (Member, Litigation and Law Practice Management Sections); Association of Southern California Defense Counsel; Defense Research Institute. **LANGUAGES:** Norwegian. **REPORTED CASES:** Valdez v. Smith (1985) 166 Cal. App. 3d 723; Holmes v. Roth (1992) 11 Cal. App. 4th 931. **PRACTICE AREAS:** High Exposure Personal Injury; Insurance Defense.

### ASSOCIATES

**ROBERT E. HENKE,** born Alliance, Ohio, August 23, 1963; admitted to bar, 1990, California; 1991, U.S. District Court, Central District of California. *Education:* The Ohio State University (B.A., 1985; J.D., 1990). Order of the Coif. Staff Member (1988-1989) and Managing Editor, 1989-1990, Ohio State Law Journal. Author: "Ohio's View of the Pollution Exclusion Clause: Is There Still Ambiguity?" 50 Ohio State Law Journal 983, 1989. *Member:* State Bar of California; Association of Southern California Defense Counsel; Defense Research Institute. **PRACTICE AREAS:** Insurance Defense.

**JEFFREY B. SMITH,** born Santa Monica, California, December 19, 1965; admitted to bar, 1991, California. *Education:* University of Southern California (A.B. in Sociology, 1988); McGeorge School of Law, University of the Pacific (J.D., 1991). *Member:* American Bar Association. **PRACTICE AREAS:** Insurance Defense Litigation.

**ANASTASIA SWIATEK HOYT,** born Pomona, California, April 15, 1964; admitted to bar, 1992, California and U.S. District Court, Central District of California. *Education:* University of Southern California at Los Angeles (B.A., 1985); Pepperdine University (J.D., 1992). Phi Alpha Delta. Recipient, American Jurisprudence Awards in Insurance Law and Family Law. Literary Editor and Staff Member, Pepperdine Law Review, 1990-1992. *Member:* San Fernando Valley and American Bar Associations; State Bar of California. **PRACTICE AREAS:** Insurance Defense.

## McKINLEY & CAPELOTO

*Established in 1987*

*201 SOUTH LAKE AVENUE, SUITE 606*
**PASADENA, CALIFORNIA 91101**
Telephone: 818-793-7788
Fax: 818-793-1013
Email: capeloto@aol.com

*Financial Institutions, Creditor Rights, Bankruptcy, Real Estate, Workouts, Commercial Law, Civil Litigation, Elder Law, Construction Law.*

*FIRM PROFILE: The law offices of McKinley & Capeloto are located in the financial district of Pasadena, California. The firm's primary client base is composed of financial institutions and its practice emphasizes loan and lease collections and workouts for both consumer and commercial indebtedness, bankruptcy matters including relief from the automatic stay, reorganizations and nondischargeability actions, real and personal property secured transactions, foreclosures, receiverships, fraud, negotiable instruments, embezzlement and other operational problems, responses to subpoenas, unlawful detainer matters, as well as defense matters. The Firm also has an Elder Law Department devoted to meeting the needs of the elderly.*

*The firm presently represents over 100 financial institutions throughout California.*

**J. SHELDON CAPELOTO,** born Seattle, Washington, September 12, 1951; admitted to bar, 1979, California, U.S. District Court, Northern District of California and U.S. Court of Appeals, Ninth Circuit; 1980, U.S. District Court, Central, Southern and Eastern Districts of California. *Education:* University of California at Berkeley (A.B., with honors, 1973); Golden Gate University School of Law (J.D., 1979). *Member:* Pasadena and Los Angeles County (Member, Commercial Litigation Section) Bar Associations ; State Bar of California; Financial Lawyers Conference; California Bankruptcy Forum; American Bankruptcy Institute; Italian American Lawyer's Association (Board of Governors); Loan Service Managers Association; California Trustee's Association. **REPORTED CASES:** In re Byron L. Kinney, Cite as 51 B.R. 840 (Bkrptcy. 1985); In re Delores Elizabeth Glasper, a/k/a Mrs. Wilford Glasper, Cite as 28 B.R. 6 (Bkrptcy. App. 1983); In re Kelley 199 B.R. 698 (9th Cir Bap 1996). **PRACTICE AREAS:** Bankruptcy; Creditor Rights; Financial Institutions; Real Estate.

**ROBERT D. MCKINLEY,** born Albuquerque, New Mexico, June 23, 1948; admitted to bar, 1979, California and U.S. District Court, Northern District of California; 1980, U.S. District Court, Central, Eastern and Southern Districts of California. *Education:* United States Air Force Academy (B.S., 1970); Southwestern University School of Law (J.D., summa cum laude, 1978). Recipient: American Jurisprudence Book Awards for Contracts, Torts, Real Property, Remedies and Scholastic Achievement, 1977-1978; American Association of Trial Advocates Award for Excellence, 1978. Chairman, Moot Court Board of Governors, 1977-1978. First Place, Regional Finals, National Moot Court Competition. *Member:* Los Angeles County Bar Association (Founding Member, Executive Committee on Pre-Judgment Remedies Section, 1985); State Bar of California; Financial Lawyers Conference; Los Angeles Bankruptcy Forum; National Academy of Elder Law Attorneys. **PRACTICE AREAS:** Creditor Rights; Commercial Litigation; Loan Workouts; Transaction Documentation; Elder Law. **Email:** capeloto@aol.com

**JAMES R. SELTH,** born Adelaide, Australia, May 7, 1958; admitted to bar, 1986, California, U.S. Court of Appeals, Ninth Circuit and U.S. District Court, Central District of California; 1989, U.S. District Court, Eastern, Northern and Southern Districts of California; 1995, U.S. District Court, District of Arizona. *Education:* University of California, Riverside (B.A., 1978); Western State University College of Law (J.D., cum laude, 1985). Recipient, American Jurisprudence Awards: Contracts; Criminal Law; Trusts. Moot Court. Law Review. Assistant Vice President and Branch Manager, California Federal Savings & Loan Association, Pasadena, California. Deputy District Attorney, Orange County. Treasurer, San Bernardino County 4-H Sponsoring Committee, 1984—. *Member:* Pasadena Bar Association; State Bar of California; Financial Lawyers Conference; Los Angeles Bankruptcy Forum. **PRACTICE AREAS:** Banking Litigation; Bankruptcy; Receiverships; Foreclosure; Pre-Judgment Remedies; Post Judgment Enforcement.

*(This Listing Continued)*

McKINLEY & CAPELOTO, Pasadena—Continued

### ASSOCIATES

MAXWELL L. JOUANICOT, born Oakland, California, April 23, 1948; admitted to bar, 1980, California; 1981, U.S. District Court, Central District of California; 1982, U.S. Court of Appeals, Ninth Circuit. *Education:* California State University, Dominguez Hills (B.A., 1976); Whittier College School of Law (J.D., 1979). Associate General Counsel, California Credit Union League, 1982-1984. *Member:* State Bar of California. [Capt., U.S. Army Infantry, 1967-1971]. *PRACTICE AREAS:* Litigation; Regulatory; Transactional; Personnel; Credit Union.

DANIELLE D. CYR, born Fall River, Massachusetts, May 6, 1963; admitted to bar, 1996, California; U.S. District Court, Central District of California. *Education:* Tufts University (B.A., 1985); Southwestern University School of Law (J.D., 1995). Instructor: Divorce Clinic, Los Angeles Free Clinic. *Member:* Century City, Beverly Hills and Los Angeles County Bar Associations; State Bar of California; Financial Lawyers Conference; Los Angeles Bankruptcy Forum; The Lawyers Club of Los Angeles County; Womens Lawyers Association of Los Angeles. *LANGUAGES:* French. *PRACTICE AREAS:* Litigation; Bankruptcy.

DAVID BRIAN LALLY, born Long Island, N.Y., November 26, 1958; admitted to bar, 1989, California, U.S. District Court, Northern, Central, Eastern and Southern Districts of California. *Education:* California State University at Long Beach (B.S., magna cum laude, 1986); California Western School of Law (J.D., 1989); McGeorge School of Law (Advanced Degree in International Law, 1989). Moot Court Board. Member, Los Angeles, Inland Empire and Orange County Bankruptcy Forums. *Member:* Orange County, Los Angeles County and American Bar Associations; State Bar of California. *LANGUAGES:* French. *PRACTICE AREAS:* Creditors' Rights; Bankruptcy; Foreclosure.

### OF COUNSEL

CRISTOPHER RAHTZ, born Joplin, Missouri, May 18, 1945; admitted to bar, 1974, New York, U.S. District Court, Southern and Eastern Districts of New York and U.S. Co urt of Appeals, Second Circuit; 1976, California, U.S. District Court, Central and Eastern Districts of California and U.S. Court of Appeals, Ninth Circuit. *Education:* Colgate University (B.A., 1967); Brooklyn Law School (J.D., cum laude, 1973). Research Editor, Brooklyn Law Review, 1972-1973. Recipient: American Jurisprudence Awards for Conflict of Laws, Wills, Trusts, Estate and Gift Taxation; West Publishing Company and Edward K. Thompson Award for Academic Excellence, 1973. Author: "Trusteeship Imposition," 38 Brooklyn Law Review 1139, 1972. *Member:* Los Angeles County Bar Association; State Bar of California. *PRACTICE AREAS:* Commercial Litigation; Transaction Documentation; Creditor Rights'; Loan Workouts; Employment Law.

REPRESENTATIVE CLIENTS: Wells Fargo Bank; Mercantile National Bank; California Federal Bank; Imperial Bank; Fannie Mae; Imperial Thrift & Loan; California Korea Bank; Coast Federal Bank; Wilshire State Bank; Upland Bank; Hanmi Bank; First Credit Bank; First State Bank; Golden Security Thrift & Loan; Charter Pacific Bank; Account Finding; Capital Finance; GMAC Commercial Mortgage; 1st Business Bank; Sanwa Bank California; Quaker City Federal Savings; AMRE, Inc.; Novus Financial Services, Inc.; Kern Federal Credit Union.

---

## KEVIN MEENAN
790 EAST COLORADO BOULEVARD
NINTH FLOOR PENTHOUSE
**PASADENA, CALIFORNIA 91101-2105**
Telephone: 818-398-0000
FAX: 818-585-0999
Email: 73313.1624@compuserve.com

*Civil Trial Practice in all State and Federal Courts. Tort Litigation, Injury and Death, Negligence, Product Liability, Professional Negligence, Premises, Carriers and Insurance.*

KEVIN MEENAN, born Waterbury, Connecticut, March 17, 1952; admitted to bar, 1978, California. *Education:* University of Connecticut (B.A., 1974); Richmond College, London, England; University of San Diego (J.D., 1978); Trial Technique Institute, Chicago. Phi Alpha Theta. Member, Moot Court. Phillip C. Jessup International Law Competition. Lead Articles Editor, San Diego Law Review, 1977-1978. Author: "Cultural Resources Preservation and Underwater Archaeology: Some Notes on the Current Legal Framework and a Model Underwater Antiquities Statute," 15 San Diego Law Review 623-662, 1978. Civil Intern, Research Assistant, California Court of Appeal, Fourth Appellate District, Division One, 1977.

*(This Listing Continued)*

CAA1662B

*Member:* Pasadena, Los Angeles County and American Bar Associations; State Bar of California; Consumer Attorneys of California; Consumer Attorneys Association of Los Angeles; The Association of Trial Lawyers of America.

---

## RICHARD F. MILLER
*A PROFESSIONAL CORPORATION*

SUITE 511, 199 SOUTH LOS ROBLES AVENUE
**PASADENA, CALIFORNIA 91101**
Telephone: 818-584-1400; 213-681-5400
Telecopier: 818-584-1447

*Probate, Estate Planning, Trust and Conservatorship Law.*

RICHARD F. MILLER, born Los Angeles, California, May 9, 1937; admitted to bar, 1964, California; 1969, U.S. Supreme Court. *Education:* Stanford University (A.B., with distinction, 1959; LL.B., 1963). Phi Delta Phi; Phi Beta Kappa. *Member:* Pasadena, Los Angeles County (Member, Trust and Probate Law Section) and American (Member, Real Property, Probate and Trust Law Section) Bar Associations; The State Bar of California (Member, Probate and Estate Planning Section). (Certified Specialist, Estate Planning, Trust and Probate Law, The State Bar of California Board of Legal Specialization) (Of Counsel to Jones, Bell, Simpson, Abbott, Fleming and Taylor, Los Angeles).

REFERENCE: Wells Fargo Bank.

---

## MILLIKAN AND THOMAS
Established in 1954

SECOND FLOOR, 704 MIRA MONTE PLACE
**PASADENA, CALIFORNIA 91101**
Telephone: 818-304-7065
Telecopier: 818-796-4738

*General Civil and Trial Practice in all State and Federal Courts. Corporate, Taxation, Construction, Government Contracts, Real Estate, Family, Estate Planning and Probate Law.*

C. E. BRAD MILLIKAN, JR. (1925-1982).

LANE J. THOMAS, born Los Angeles, California, March 7, 1951; admitted to bar, 1976, California; 1977, U.S. District Court, Central District of California. *Education:* University of California at Santa Barbara (B.A., with honors, 1973); Loyola University of Los Angeles (J.D., 1976). Judge Pro Tem: Los Angeles Superior Court 1989; Pasadena Municipal Court 1990—. *Member:* Pasadena and Los Angeles County (Member, Sections on Family Law; Real Property) Bar Associations; State Bar of California. *PRACTICE AREAS:* Business Litigation; Family Law; Real Property Law; Probate; Estate Planning.

GREGORY F. MILLIKAN, born Los Angeles, California, May 10, 1948; admitted to bar, 1977, Hawaii; 1982, California, U.S. Supreme Court, U.S. Tax Court and U.S. District Court, Central District of California. *Education:* Occidental College (B.S., with honors, 1970); University of California at Los Angeles (J.D., 1977). Order of the Coif. Member, University of California at Los Angeles Law Review, 1976-1977. *Member:* Los Angeles County (Member, Bioethics Committee, 1988-1992) and Hawaii State Bar Associations; State Bar of California; Christian Legal Society. *PRACTICE AREAS:* Real Property Law; Estate Planning Law; Business Law; Tax Law.

### ASSOCIATES

CATHARINE KARL MILLIKAN, born Pasadena, California, December 23, 1956; admitted to bar, 1995, California. *Education:* University of Southern California (B.A., 1990); Southwestern University School of Law (J.D., 1995). *Member:* Pasadena and Los Angeles County Bar Associations; State Bar of California. *PRACTICE AREAS:* Probate; Estate Planning; Business Law; Real Property Law.

REPRESENTATIVE CLIENTS: Samuelson Brothers (Land Developers); Quick Dispense Inc. (Institutional Foods); Denluck/Switzer/Associates, Inc. (Civil Engineers); Highland Auto & Truck Supply; Star Milling Co.; Architects Pacifica Ltd. (Architects); Rayson Group (Real Property Development); Fuller Theological Seminary (Campus Development); Diamond Pacific Products Company, Inc.
REFERENCE: Wells Fargo Bank, Pasadena.

## DONALD D. MON

750 EAST GREEN STREET, SUITE 303
**PASADENA, CALIFORNIA 91101-2545**
*Telephone: 818-793-9173*
*Telecopier: 818-793-9690*

*Patent and Trademark Law.*

**DONALD D. MON,** born Long Beach, California, September 6, 1921; admitted to bar, 1951, California; registered to practice before U.S. Patent and Trademark Office. *Education:* California Institute of Technology (B.S., 1947); Stanford University (J.D., 1950). Delta Theta Phi. *Member:* Los Angeles County and Pasadena (Treasurer, 1964) Bar Associations; The State Bar of California.

---

## MONTGOMERY AND MONTGOMERY

*Established in 1955*

SUITE 303, 151 SOUTH EL MOLINO AVENUE
**PASADENA, CALIFORNIA 91101**
*Telephone: 818-577-1387; 213-684-3065*

*Real Property, Civil Litigation, Estates and Trusts, Corporations, Business Transactions and Competition.*

### MEMBERS OF FIRM

**EDWARD R. P. MONTGOMERY,** born Long Beach, California, June 16, 1922; admitted to bar, 1951, California, U.S. District Court, Northern District of California and U.S. Court of Appeals, 9th Circuit; U.S. District Court, Central and Eastern Districts of California. *Education:* Pasadena Junior College (A.A., 1942); University of California at Berkeley (A.B., 1947); University of California, Boalt Hall (LL.B., 1950). *Member:* Pasadena (Chairman, Committee on Continuing Education of the Bar, 1963-1966; Secretary, 1966-1967), Los Angeles County and American Bar Associations; State Bar of California. *PRACTICE AREAS:* Real Property; Estates and Trusts; Corporations; Civil Litigation.

**CRANSTON P. MONTGOMERY,** born Long Beach, California, June 16, 1922; admitted to bar, 1951, California, U.S. District Court, Northern District of California and U.S. Court of Appeals, Ninth Circuit. *Education:* Pasadena City College (A.A., 1947); University of California at Berkeley (A.B., 1947); University of California, Boalt Hall (LL.B., 1950). *Member:* Pasadena, Los Angeles County and American (Member: Section on: International Law) Bar Associations; State Bar of California. *PRACTICE AREAS:* Government Contracts; Competition; Employee Relations.

---

## GEORGE E. MOORE

*A PROFESSIONAL LAW CORPORATION*

WELLS FARGO BUILDING
350 WEST COLORADO BOULEVARD
SUITE 400
**PASADENA, CALIFORNIA 91105-1894**
*Telephone: 818-440-1111*
*Fax: 818-440-9456*

*Plaintiff Personal Injury, Medical Negligence, Automobile, Products, Attorney Negligence, Premises Liability.*

**GEORGE E. MOORE,** born Long Beach, California, March 31, 1936; admitted to bar, 1965, California. *Education:* University of Southern California (B.S.C., 1957); Loyola University of Los Angeles (LL.B., 1964). Phi Alpha Delta. Author: "Negligent Diagnosis of Eye Disease," American Jurisprudence: Proof of Facts, Second Series, 1981. *Member:* Pasadena and American Bar Associations; The State Bar of California; Los Angeles Trial Lawyers Association (Member, Board of Governors, 1975-1978); American Board of Trial Advocates (Advocate; Member, National Board of Directors, 1994-1996); International Academy of Trial Lawyers. Fellow, American College of Trial Lawyers. [Colonel, U.S. Marine Corps Reserve]. *PRACTICE AREAS:* Personal Injury; Medical Malpractice.

---

## JOSEPH E. MUETH
## A LAW CORPORATION

*Established in 1974*

225 SOUTH LAKE AVENUE, EIGHTH FLOOR
**PASADENA, CALIFORNIA 91101-1599**
*Telephone: 818-584-0396*
*Fax: 818-584-6862*

*Patent, Trademark and Copyright Law. Trials and Appellate Practice in all Courts.*

**JOSEPH E. MUETH,** born St. Louis, Missouri, August 9, 1935; admitted to bar, 1960, Missouri; 1964, California and U.S. District Court, Central District of California; 1966, U.S. Supreme Court; 1972, U.S. Court of Appeals, Ninth Circuit; 1980, U.S. District Court, Northern District of California; 1983, U.S. Court of Appeals for Federal Circuit; registered to practice before U.S. Patent and Trademark Office. *Education:* University of Dayton (B.Ch.E., 1957); Georgetown University (LL.B., 1960; LL.M., 1961). Author, "Patent, Trademark and Copyright Law," Published by American Legal Publications, New York, 1974. Assistant Professor of Law, University of California, Hastings College of Law, 1972-1975. *Member:* State Bar of California; American Bar Association; American Patent Law Association. (Also Of Counsel, Sheldon & Mak). *REPORTED CASES:* Rex Chainbelt, Inc. v. Harco Products, Inc., U.S. Court of Appeals, 9th Cir. (1975); Herbert v. Diagnostic Products Corp., No. 85 Civ. 0856 (June 1986); Young Engineers, Inc. v. USITC; Hunting Hall of Fame Foundation v. Safari Club International, No. CIV 86-020 TUC ACM (May 1987); IMS Limited v. International Medical Systems, Inc, No. 84 CV 4126 (September 1986). *PRACTICE AREAS:* Patent, Trademark and Copyright Law; Trial Law; Appellate Practice; Food and Drugs.

REFERENCE: Bank of America, 333 South Hope Street, Los Angeles, California.

---

## MURRAY, BRADSHAW & BUDZYN

*A LAW CORPORATION*

*Established in 1969*

THE WALNUT PLAZA
3RD FLOOR, 215 NORTH MARENGO AVENUE
**PASADENA, CALIFORNIA 91101**
*Telephone: 818-584-9860*
*FAX: 818-568-3967*

*Pension, Profit Sharing, Employment, Labor and Corporate Tax Law, ERISA and Business Litigation.*

*FIRM PROFILE: The Firm has specialized in the design of all types of employee benefit plans for over 25 years. These plans include all forms of retirement benefits, deferred compensation, and executive incentive programs.*

*The Firm handles all aspects of labor and employment law, including labor-management relations, and consults on a wide range of federal and state laws and regulations in these areas. The Firm represents clients in administrative proceedings before such agencies as the National Labor Relations Board, Equal Employment Opportunity Commission, and California Department of Fair Employment and Housing. In addition, the Firm has developed considerable expertise in the wrongful discharge field and has litigated numerous wrongful discharge cases.*

*The Firm also developed a consulting team consisting of lawyers and administrators who identify issues involving ERISA welfare and pension plans.*

*The Team can also provide the client's in-house staff with forms, checklists, calendars, training materials and procedures for minimizing legal exposure and practical operational problems.*

*Murray, Bradshaw & Budzyn has serviced its clients for many years in general business law, including formation of all types of business entities, due diligence, financing, leasing, sales, mergers and acquisitions. The Firm's background and expertise enables it to provide comprehensive financial and legal guidance in commercial transactions and to assist clients in identifying and assessing business risks.*

*Not only is the Firm experienced in the courtroom, it is well-versed in the arbitration system, and in the art of negotiated settlement.*

**VERNON EDWARD MURRAY,** born Detroit, Michigan, June 18, 1943; admitted to bar, 1969, California and U.S. District Court, Central and Southern Districts of California. *Education:* University of Southern

*(This Listing Continued)*

## MURRAY, BRADSHAW & BUDZYN, A LAW CORPORATION, Pasadena—Continued

California (B.A., magna cum laude, 1965; J.D., 1968); Wharton School of Business, University of Pennsylvania, Certified Employee Benefit Specialist Degree, 1980. Chairman, Significant Issues Committee, Western Pension Conference, 1981-1982. Member, Western Pension Conference, 1972—. *Member:* Pasadena, Los Angeles County (Member: Tax Section and Employee Benefits Sub-Section, 1975—; Special Pension Plan Committee, 1976-1979) and American (Member: Committee on Employee Benefits, Section on Taxation, 1980—; Committee on Administration, Section of Real Property, Probate and Trust Law, 1975—) Bar Associations; State Bar of California. *PRACTICE AREAS:* Pension; Profit Sharing; ERISA; Business Litigation; General Corporate Transactions.

**MICHAEL J. BUDZYN,** born Santa Monica, California, March 15, 1950; admitted to bar, 1975, California; 1976, U.S. District Court, Central District of California. *Education:* University of Southern California (B.A., magna cum laude, 1972); University of California at Los Angeles (J.D., 1975); Wharton School of Business University of Pennsylvania, Certified Employee Benefit Specialist Degree, 1981. Phi Beta Kappa. Member, 1973-1974, Executive Editor, 1974-1975, UCLA-Alaska Law Review. Author: "Workmen's Compensation: Are All Remote Site Recreational Accidents Compensable?" 3 UCLA-Alaska Law Review 255, 1974. Member, Western Pension Conference, 1979—. *Member:* Pasadena, Los Angeles County (Member, Taxation Section and Employee Benefits Sub-Section, 1980—; Chairman, Pension Plan Committee, 1980—) and American Bar Associations; State Bar of California. *PRACTICE AREAS:* Pension; Profit Sharing; ERISA; General Corporate.

**DAVID S. BRADSHAW,** born Reno, Nevada, January 4, 1945; admitted to bar, 1970, California; 1975, U.S. Supreme Court; 1981, District of Columbia; 1983, New York. *Education:* Occidental College (B.A., summa cum laude, 1966); Stanford University (J.D., 1969). Phi Beta Kappa; Order of the Coif. Member, Board of Editors, Stanford Law Review, 1968-1969. Co-author: "Advising California Employers," California Continuing Education of The Bar, 1981. *Member:* State Bar of California.

REPRESENTATIVE CLIENTS: Los Angeles County Medical Assn.; California Medical Association; Magma Power Co.; Milliman & Robertson, Inc.; National Associates, Inc.; Crown, Inc.; The Hollywood Reporter, Inc.; John Breuner Company; See's Candies; Ross Stores; The Good Guys!; J.C. Penney Co.; Nordstrom, Inc.; Saks Fifth Avenue; Marshall's Stores; First Los Angeles Bank; City National Bank; FEDCO; California Manufacturers' Association.

## MYERS & D'ANGELO

A Partnership of Professional Corporations

*301 NORTH LAKE AVENUE, SUITE 800*
**PASADENA, CALIFORNIA 91101**
*Telephone: 818-792-0007; 213-380-2830*
*FAX: 818-792-0037*

General Civil and Appellate Practice. Corporation, Taxation and Real Estate Law. Litigation. Estate Planning, Trust and Probate Law.

### MEMBERS OF FIRM

**R. CHANDLER MYERS, (P.C.),** born Los Angeles, California, January 9, 1933; admitted to bar, 1959, California. *Education:* Stanford University (A.B., 1954; J.D., 1958); Awarded LL.D., by Whittier College, 1988. Phi Alpha Delta; Delta Sigma Rho. Member, National Panel of Arbitrators, American Arbitration Association, 1964—. President, Stanford Club of Los Angeles County, 1968-1969. President, Stanford Law Society of Southern California, 1970-1971. Judge Pro Tempore, Municipal Court, Los Angeles Judicial District, 1971-1981. Member, Board of Visitors, Stanford Law School, 1970-1973. Member, 1973— and Chairman, 1981-1987, Board of Trustees, Whittier College. Member, 1981-1988 and Chairman, 1985-1988, Board of Trustees, Flintridge Preparatory School. Member, Board of Visitors, Whittier College School of Law, 1988—. Member, Board of Directors, Western Justice Center Foundation, 1993—. President, Los Angeles Child Guidance Clinic, 1977-1979. *Member:* Wilshire (President, 1979-1980), Los Angeles County (Member, Board of Trustees, 1979-1981) and American Bar Associations; State Bar of California. *PRACTICE AREAS:* Business Litigation; Estate Planning; Probate; Arbitration; Commercial; Construction.

**ROBERT W. D'ANGELO, (P.C.),** born Buffalo, New York, November 10, 1932; admitted to bar, 1960, California. *Education:* Loyola University (B.B.A., 1954); University of California at Los Angeles (J.D., 1960). Alpha Sigma Nu. Phi Delta Phi. Adjunct Professor of Law, Taxation, Whittier

*(This Listing Continued)*

College School of Law, 1981-1982. *Member:* Wilshire (Member, Board of Governors, 1974-1983), Los Angeles County (Member, Attorney-Client Fee Dispute Committee and Taxation Section) and American (Member, Taxation Section) Bar Associations; The State Bar of California; American Institute of Certified Public Accountants; California Society of Certified Public Accountants; American Association of Attorney-Certified Public Accountants; California Associations of Attorney-Certified Public Accountants (President, 1980). (Certified Specialist, Taxation Law, The State Bar of California Board of Legal Specialization). *PRACTICE AREAS:* Taxation; Real Estate; Estate Planning; Trust and Probate.

## NOUSKAJIAN & CRANERT

**PASADENA, CALIFORNIA**

(See Pasadena)

*General Civil Trial and Appellate Practice in all State and Federal Courts, Products Liability, Negligence, Public Entities, Common Carrier, Insurance, Wills and Trusts.*

## KATHLEEN M. O'CONNOR

*301 NORTH LAKE AVENUE, SUITE 800*
**PASADENA, CALIFORNIA 91101-4108**
*Telephone: 818-304-2951; 304-2953*
*Fax: 818-583-9187*

*Family Law including Dissolutions, establishment of Child and Spousal Support, Enforcement of Support, Child Custody, Visitation and Adoption.*

**KATHLEEN M. O'CONNOR,** born Chicago, Illinois, April 9, 1947; admitted to bar, 1975, Illinois; 1977, Wisconsin; 1980, California. *Education:* Clarke College (B.A., 1969); DePaul University (J.D., 1975). Phi Alpha Delta. Deputy District Attorney, Los Angeles County, 1981. *Member:* Los Angeles County and Pasadena Bar Associations; State Bar of California. *PRACTICE AREAS:* Family Law.

## OHASHI & PRIVER

*215 NORTH MARENGO AVENUE*
*SUITE 225*
**PASADENA, CALIFORNIA 91101**
*Telephone: 818-584-1107*
*Facsimile: 818-356-7414*

El Segundo, California Office: 222 N. Sepulveda Boulevard. 20th Floor. 90245. Telephone: 310-364-5215. Fax: 310-364-5217.

*Business and Corporate Law. Real Estate, Federal and State Securities, Commercial and Tax Litigation.*

**MARK S. PRIVER,** born Los Angeles, California, October 15, 1955; admitted to bar, 1982, California; 1983 U.S. District Court, Central District of California, U.S. Tax Court and U.S. Court of Appeals Ninth Circuit. *Education:* University of California at Santa Cruz (B.A., 1977); Whittier College (J.D., cum laude, 1982). Trial Attorney, District Counsel, I.R.S., 1982-1986. Judge Pro Tempore, Los Angeles Municipal Court, 1991—. *Member:* Pasadena, Los Angeles County and American Bar Associations. *PRACTICE AREAS:* Business Litigation; Commercial Litigation; Tax Litigation.

**JOHN E. OHASHI,** born Tokyo, Japan, May 13, 1955; admitted to bar, 1981, California; 1982, U.S. Tax Court. *Education:* University of California at Los Angeles (B.A., 1978); University of California at Davis (J.D., 1981). General Securities Principal, NASD, 1985. *Member:* State Bar of California; National Association of Securities Dealers (Member, Board of Arbitration). *REPORTED CASES:* Reid vs. Moskovitz 208 Cal. App. 3d 29 (1989). *PRACTICE AREAS:* Business Law; Corporate Law; Real Estate; Employment Law; Federal and State Securities.

REPRESENTATIVE CLIENTS: Bellsouth Communication Systems, Inc.; CST Entertainment Imaging, Inc.; Chong Hing Goldsmith, Inc.; Cole Moving & Storage, Inc.; Couriers International; Intervalve; Marvel Jewelers, Inc.; Nationwide Mutual Insurance Co.; Tahiti Tuna S.A.; Thai Airways International Limited; Western Paving Contractors, Inc.; Yamaha Corporation of America.

## JAMES M. ORENDORFF
*25 EAST UNION STREET*
*PASADENA, CALIFORNIA 91103*
*Telephone: 818-449-8200*
*FAX: 818-449-8370*

*General Business and Transaction Practice. Business, Corporate, Real Property, Real Estate Development, Finance, Trusts and Wills.*

**JAMES M. ORENDORFF,** born Monterey Park, California, October 24, 1938; admitted to bar, 1964, California and U.S. District Court, Central District of California; 1966, U.S. Court of Appeals, Ninth Circuit; 1969, U.S. Supreme Court. *Education:* Fresno State College (B.S., 1960); Boalt Hall School of Law, University of California (J.D., 1963). Chairman, Pasadena Bar Association Business Law Committee, 1989. Member, Board of Directors, 1989— and President 1992-1995, Pasadena Lawyer Referral Service. Judge Pro Tempore, Superior Court and Municipal Court, 1988—. Arbitrator and Mediator, Los Angeles County. Settlement Officer, Pasadena Superior Court Crash Settlement Officer Program, 1989—. President and Director, Pasadena Law Foundation, 1995—. *Member:* Los Angeles, Pasadena and American Bar Associations; State Bar of California.

## OVERLANDER, LEWIS & RUSSELL
*Established in 1976*

*65 NORTH RAYMOND AVENUE, SUITE 210*
*PASADENA, CALIFORNIA 91103*
*Telephone: 818-304-0500*
*Fax: 818-304-9750*

*Business and Commercial Litigation. Personal Injury, Insurance Defense, Commercial and Tort Law, Civil Rights, Police Misconduct Defense, Public Entity Defense. General Civil Trial Practice.*

*FIRM PROFILE: Overlander, Lewis & Russell is a civil litigation firm which was established in 1976.*

*We handle all case assignments from inception through trial and appeal, both in State and Federal courts. The firm's practice involves representation of insured and self-insured public sector entities, corporate entities, and individuals. The majority of our cases are in Los Angeles, Ventura, and Orange Counties, but we frequently handle matters in other counties throughout Southern and Central California, as well as the Federal courts with jurisdiction over the same area.*

*Our practice emphasizes business litigation, public entity defense, civil rights matters, police misconduct matters, and personal injury defense.*

**THOMAS F. OVERLANDER,** born Bronx, New York, April 5, 1941; admitted to bar, 1973, California, U.S. District Court, Central District of California and U.S. Court of Appeals, Ninth Circuit. *Education:* City College of New York (B.A., 1964); Southwestern University School of Law (J.D., with honors, 1973). Delta Theta Phi (President, 1971-1972). Southwestern University Law Review, Staff Member, 1971-1972, Managing Editor, 1972-1973. Judge Pro-Tem, Los Angeles Municipal Court, 1981—. Arbitrator, Los Angeles Superior Court, 1979—. *Member:* Glendale, South Bay, Los Angeles County and American Bar Associations; State Bar of California; Association of Southern California Defense Counsel. **PRACTICE AREAS:** Personal Injury Law; Insurance Defense Law; Commercial Law; Torts; General Civil Trial Practice.

**EDWIN A. LEWIS,** born Los Angeles, California, March 13, 1957; admitted to bar, 1981, California, U.S. District Court, Central, Northern, Eastern and Southern Districts of California and U.S. Court of Appeals, Ninth Circuit. *Education:* University of California at Berkeley (B.A., 1978); University of California at Los Angeles School of Law (J.D., 1981). *Member:* Los Angeles County and National Bar Associations; State Bar of California. **PRACTICE AREAS:** Personal Injury Law; Insurance Defense Law; Commercial Law; Torts; General Civil Trial Practice; Civil Rights Law.

**RICHARD L. RUSSELL, JR.,** born Santa Barbara, California, September 7, 1956; admitted to bar, 1985, California and U.S. District Court, Central District of California; 1986, U.S. District Court, Northern, Eastern and Southern Districts of California. *Education:* University of California at Berkeley (B.A., 1979); Boston University (J.D., 1982). Lecturer, "Foreclosures of Deeds and Trust and Related Bankruptcy Proceedings," Professional Education Systems, Inc., 1981. Judge Pro Tem, Los Angeles Municipal Court, 1982. *Member:* Los Angeles County and American Bar Associations; State Bar of California; National Bar Association; Association of Business Trial Lawyers. **PRACTICE AREAS:** Business and Commercial Litigation; Real Property Litigation; Lender Liability; Wrongful Termination.

**CRAIG J. MILLER,** born Chicago, Illinois, May 6, 1963; admitted to bar, 1988, California; U.S. District Court, Central, Northern, Eastern and Southern Districts of California. *Education:* University of Michigan (B.B.A., with honors, 1985); Santa Clara University (J.D., magna cum laude, 1988). Member, Santa Clara University Law Review. Former Deputy District Attorney, Los Angeles County. *Member:* State Bar of California. **PRACTICE AREAS:** Personal Injury Law; Insurance Defense Law; Commercial Law; Torts; General Civil Trial Practice; Civil Rights Law.

**SHERRI LYNETTE WOODS,** born San Francisco, California, March 28, 1960; admitted to bar, 1986, California and U.S. District Court, Northern District of California; 1987, U.S. District Court, Central District of California. *Education:* San Francisco State University (B.A., 1982); Hastings College of Law, University of California (J.D., 1985). *Member:* State Bar of California. **PRACTICE AREAS:** Personal Injury Law; Insurance Defense Law; Commercial Law; Torts; General Civil Trial Practice; Civil Rights Law.

REPRESENTATIVE CLIENTS: ASCIP-Alliance of Schools for Cooperative Ins.; Federal Deposit Insurance Corp.; Nissan North America, Inc.; Price Waterhouse; Union Bank; Wells Fargo Bank; Cities of Inglewood, Los Angeles, Glendale, Redondo Beach, Manhattan Beach, Huntington Park and Compton; Compton, Monrovia, Downey, Lynwood, Montebello, Tustin Unified School Districts; Cerritos, Compton, Glendale, Pasadena and Citrus Community College.

## LLOYD C. OWNBEY, JR.
*180 SOUTH LAKE AVENUE, SUITE 510*
*PASADENA, CALIFORNIA 91101-2683*
*Telephone: 818-440-5960*
*Fax: 818-585-9669*

*Labor and Employment Law, Public and Private Sectors.*

**LLOYD C. OWNBEY, JR.,** born South Gate, California, December 2, 1932; admitted to bar, 1961, California, U.S. District Court, Central District of California and U.S. Court of Appeals, Ninth Circuit. *Education:* University of Southern California (B.A., 1954; J.D., 1960). Phi Delta Phi. Clerk to Hon. A. Curtis Smith, Appellate Department, Los Angeles Superior Court, 1961. Author: "The Civil Remedies for Disklegging," Southern California Law Review, 1961; "The Constitutional Copyright System: Some Suggestions for Congressional Consideration," Southern California Law Review, 1962; "Reflections on Professional Responsibility, A Positive Approach," Phi Delta Delta, 1963; Chapter, "Documents of Title," California Commercial Law II, California C.E.B., 1965; "The Positive Law Ethic," Southern California Law Review, 1965. Instructor: Labor Relations in the Public Sector, University of California at Riverside, 1977; Labor Law and Employee Relations, Advanced Professional Program, University of Southern California, 1980, 1981, 1984. Chairman, Y.M.C.A. of San Marino/Pasadena, 1993-1995. President, San Marino Rotary, 1988-1989. Employer Trustee, Southern California Health and Welfare Taft-Hartley Trust, 1970-1977. Employer Co-Chair, Industrywide Collective Bargaining Grievance Panel, 1973-1978. *Member:* Los Angeles County (Member: Labor Law Section; Executive Committee, Corporate Law Section, 1970-1977; Treasurer, 1975-1976 and Secretary, 1976-1977, Corporate Law Section), Pasadena and American Bar Associations; State Bar of California; Trojan Barristers (President, 1965). [U.S. Navy, Lieutenant (JG), 1955-1957]

## CAROL A. PETERS
*221 EAST WALNUT STREET, SUITE 136*
*PASADENA, CALIFORNIA 91101-1554*
*Telephone: 818-793-9383*
*Fax: 818-793-3552*

*Probate, Estate Planning, Bio-Ethics, Conservatorship and Related Litigation.*

**CAROL A. PETERS,** born Pittsburgh, Pennsylvania, May 27, 1941; admitted to bar, 1977, California. *Education:* Pomona College (B.A., 1962); Whittier College School of Law (J.D.). Instructor, In-service Training Programs for Caregiver Groups: Jet Propulsion Lab; Senior Care Network's Caregivers Group; St. Joseph's "I Can Cope;" Kaiser Family Practice Doctors Section; Southern California Head Injury Foundation. Employee: Los Angeles County Department of Public Social Services, 1964-1975; Welfare Benefits and Medi-Cal Benefits Administration. "Elder Law" Attorney,

*(This Listing Continued)*

*CAROL A. PETERS, Pasadena—Continued*

1983—. Member, Elder Abuse Task Force of the Greater San Gabriel Valley. Member, Bio Ethics Committee, Chairman, "Who Should Decide" Subcommittee and Participant/Speaker, Informed Medical Consent Task Force, Huntington Memorial Hospital. Member, 1976-1978 and Chairman, Los Angeles League Local Study of Police Brutality, League of Women Voters. *Member:* Pasadena (Member: Sections on: Probate; Civil Litigation; Real Property; Member, Legal Assistance to Seniors Committee) and Los Angeles County Bar Associations; State Bar of California. **PRACTICE AREAS:** Elder Law; Probate; Estate Planning, Wills, Trusts; Bioethics; Conservatorship and Related Litigation.

## MICHAEL E. PLOTKIN

Established in 1977

**150 SOUTH LOS ROBLES AVENUE**
**SUITE 910**
**PASADENA, CALIFORNIA 91101**
*Telephone: 818-568-8088*
*FAX: 818-793-9622*

*Business Litigation. Bankruptcy, Personal Injury and Criminal Law.*

**MICHAEL E. PLOTKIN,** born Brooklyn, New York, October 6, 1946; admitted to bar, 1977, California and U.S. District Court, Central District of California; 1984, U.S. District Court, Northern and Southern Districts of California; 1991, U.S. Court of Appeals, Ninth Circuit. *Education:* Northeastern University (B.A., 1969); Glendale College of Law (J.D., 1977). *Member:* State Bar of California. [Colonel, U.S. Army, 1969—]

REPRESENTATIVE CLIENTS: Clarke & Lewis, Inc.; Butterfield Farms, Inc.; Synergy Construction Corp.; Omega Entertainment, Inc.; Mines Avenue Textile, Inc.; Westbrooke Enterprises, Inc.

## CHAD T-W PRATT

Established in 1991

**221 EAST WALNUT STREET, SUITE 245**
**PASADENA, CALIFORNIA 91101**
*Telephone: 818-441-CHAD*
*Fax: 818-577-4561*

Los Angeles, California Office: 4929 Wilshire Boulevard, Suite 300, 90010. Telephones: 213-936-9002. Fax: 213-938-6069.

*Civil Trial and Appellate Practice in State and Federal Courts. Landlord and Tenant Law, Uninhabitability, Labor Law, Family Law, Personal Injury, Premises Liability and Torts Law.*

**CHAD T-W PRATT,** born Los Angeles, California, November 23, 1963; admitted to bar, 1990, California. *Education:* Durham University, Durham, England; Santa Clara University (B.A., Honors in History, 1986); Loyola Law School of Los Angeles (J.D., 1989). Phi Alpha Theta. Member, Federalist Society, 1989—. *Member:* Pasadena, Beverly Hills, Los Angeles County (Member, Small Firm Section) and American Bar Associations; State Bar of California; Consumer Attorneys Association of Los Angeles.

## ROBERT C. PROCTOR, JR.

A PROFESSIONAL CORPORATION

**553 SOUTH MARENGO AVENUE**
**PASADENA, CALIFORNIA 91101-3114**
*Telephone: 818-356-9720; 213-681-2601*
*FAX: 818-356-0251*

*Personal Injury and Products Liability. Trial Practice in all State Courts. Third Party Cases, Medical Malpractice and Americans Disability Act.*

**ROBERT C. PROCTOR, JR.,** born Los Angeles, California, December 24, 1936; admitted to bar, 1962, California and U.S. District Court, Southern District of California. *Education:* California State University at Long Beach (B.S., 1958); University of California at Los Angeles (LL.B., 1961). Phi Alpha Delta (Vice-President, 1960-1961). Member, Selective Service Board, 1970-1971. *Member:* Pasadena, San Gabriel Valley (President, 1979) and Los Angeles County Bar Associations; State Bar of California (Vice-Chairman, Workers Compensation Section, 1987-1988; Chairman, 1989-

*(This Listing Continued)*

CAA1666B

1990); Los Angeles Trial Lawyers Association; California Trial Lawyers Association. (Certified as a Civil Trial Advocate by the National Board of Trial Advocacy).

## PUMILIA & ADAMEC

**199 SOUTH LOS ROBLES AVENUE, SUITE 711**
**PASADENA, CALIFORNIA 91101-2460**
*Telephone: 818-584-9600*
*Fax: 818-584-9699*
*Email: VSRR59B@PRODIGY.COM*

*Business Transactions, Corporations, Partnerships, Contracts and Real Estate, Business and Commercial Litigation.*

### MEMBERS OF FIRM

**RICHARD B. PUMILIA,** born Fountain Hill, Pennsylvania, July 23, 1958; admitted to bar, 1984, Iowa; 1986, California. *Education:* Washington and Jefferson College (B.A., magna cum laude, 1980); Rutgers University (J.D., with honors, 1984). Editor, Rutgers Computer and Technology Law Journal, 1982-1984. *Member:* Los Angeles County Bar Association; The State Bar of California. **PRACTICE AREAS:** Corporate Law.

**JUSTENE M. ADAMEC,** born New York, N.Y., August 26, 1961; admitted to bar, 1988, California. *Education:* State University of New York at Buffalo (B.A., magna cum laude, 1982); Southwestern University (J.D., cum laude, 1988). Editor-in-Chief, Southwestern University Law Review, 1987-1988. Author: "Premium Rebating: An Unnecessary Evil," 39 Federation of Insurance & Corporate Counsel Quarterly 1, 1988; "Defining the Limited Public Forum in California: Women's Internal League for Peace and Freedom v. City of Fresno," 17 Sw. U.L. Law Review 287, 1987. Co-author, "First English Evangelical Lutheran Church of Glendale v. Los Angeles and Nollan v. California Coastal Commission: Has a Revolution Occured?" The ACMA Abstract, September 1987. *Member:* The State Bar of California. **PRACTICE AREAS:** Litigation.

## MARGARET ANN REDMOND

**SUITE 726, 301 EAST COLORADO BOULEVARD**
**PASADENA, CALIFORNIA 91101**
*Telephone: 818-584-9050*
*FAX: 818-584-6463*
*Email: 73411.230@compuserve.com*

*Immigration and Nationality Law, General Civil Practice.*

**MARGARET ANN REDMOND,** born Melrose, Iowa, September 21, 1937; admitted to bar, 1976, California; 1977, U.S. District Court, Central District of California. *Education:* Ottumwa Heights College and Marycrest College (B.A., Chemistry, magna cum laude, 1959); Glendale University (J.D., 1976). Kappa Gamma Pi. Materials Note Editor, Glendale Law Review, 1975-1976. Speaker: Pasadena Lawyer Referral "Immigration Law" cable video program "Access to Justice" series. *Member:* State Bar of California; Pasadena Bar Association; American Immigration Lawyers Association (Member, Southern California Chapter). (Certified Specialist, Immigration and Nationality Law, The State Bar of California Board of Legal Specialization).

## REED & BROWN

A LAW CORPORATION

**35 NORTH LAKE AVENUE, SUITE 960**
**PASADENA, CALIFORNIA 91101**
*Telephone: 818-449-4521; 213-684-2202*
*Facsimile: 818-449-7453*

*Real Estate; General Business and Corporate Law; Estate Planning and Probate Law; Civil Litigation.*

FIRM PROFILE: *The firm of Reed & Brown was established January 1, 1991. Despite its recent formation, its two principals, Stephen W. Reed and Mark C. Brown, have practiced in the Pasadena, California area for 26 and 19 years, respectively. The firm is committed to providing high quality legal representation by experienced attorneys with the convenience, accessibility and cost-effectiveness of a suburban law firm.*

*The primary areas of practice are real estate, probate, trust and estate planning, and general business and corporate law. In the area of real estate, its activities include legal advice in connection with the sale or exchange of industrial, commercial or residential properties, sophisticated financing*

*(This Listing Continued)*

arrangements for such acquisitions, tax deferred exchanges and real property development agreements. It is also involved on a regular basis with the creation and administration of condominium developments, leasing of commercial and industrial buildings and issues involving land use controls, such as zoning, conditional use permit and variance matters. Legal representation is regularly provided in the areas of escrow transactions, title matters and in real property security interests, just to name a few.

STEPHEN W. REED, born San Diego, California, January 31, 1944; admitted to bar, 1970, California, California Supreme Court, U.S. District Court, Central and Eastern Districts of California; U.S. Court of Appeals, Ninth Circuit and U.S. Supreme Court. *Education:* Point Loma College (B.A., magna cum laude, 1965); London University, London, England (Diploma in Law, 1967, with a mark of distinction); University of Southern California (J.D., 1969). Phi Alpha Delta (Justice, Ross Chapter, 1968-1969). *Member:* Pasadena, Los Angeles County (Member, Executive Committee, Real Estate Section, 1986-1993) and American Bar Associations; State Bar of California. *PRACTICE AREAS:* Commercial Real Estate; General Business and Corporate Law. *Email:* rejoicsail@aol.com

MARK C. BROWN, born Los Angeles, California, May 6, 1952; admitted to bar, 1977, California; U.S. District Court, Central District of California. *Education:* University of California at Los Angeles (B.A., magna cum laude, 1974); Loyola Marymount University (J.D., 1977). Phi Beta Kappa. *Member:* Los Angeles County and Pasadena Bar Associations; The State Bar of California (Member, Probate and Trust Law Section). *PRACTICE AREAS:* Estate Planning and Probate; Real Estate; General Corporate and Business Law.

---

MICHAEL J. COPPESS, born Pomona, California, March 1, 1957; admitted to bar, 1984, California; California Supreme Court; U.S. District Court, Central District of California; U.S. Court of Appeals, Ninth Circuit. *Education:* Loyola Marymount University (B.A., 1979); University of San Diego (J.D., 19 84). Member, San Diego Law Review, 1982-1984. Law Clerk to the Honorable A. Andrew Hauk, Senior Judge and Chief Judge Emeritus, U.S. District Court, Central District of California, 1984-1985. Attorney, Bureau of Competition, Federal Trade Commission, 1985-1986. Planning Commissioner, City of Pasadena. f *Member:* Pasadena and Los Angeles County Bar Associations; The State Bar of California. *PRACTICE AREAS:* Civil Litigation; Real Estate; General Corporate Law. *Email:* mcpsdna@aol.com

ROBERT L. TOMS, JR., born Upland, California, May 17, 1958; admitted to bar, 1985, California; 1986, U.S. District Court, Central District of California; U.S. Court of Appeals, Ninth Circuit. *Education:* Claremont Men's College (B.A., 1981); Duke University Law School (J.D., 1984). *Member:* Los Angeles County and American Bar Associations; State Bar of California; Christian Legal Society. *PRACTICE AREAS:* Business Litigation; Real Estate Transactions.

ROBERT R. BOWNE, II, born Van Nuys, California, August 2, 1968; admitted to bar, 1995, California; U.S. District Court, Central District of California; U.S. Court of Appeals, Ninth Circuit. *Education:* University of California, Los Angeles (B.A., 1991); Pepperdine University (J.D., cum laude, 1995). Recipient, Dean's Merit Scholar, Pepperdine Law School, 1992-1995. Extern, Associate Justice Armond Arobian, California Supreme Court, 1994. *Member:* Pasadena; Los Angeles County and American Bar Associations; State Bar of California; Christian Legal Society. *PRACTICE AREAS:* General Business; Corporate Law; Real Estate; Non-Profits/Tax; Estate Planning/Probate. *Email:* bbowne@ix.netcom.com

### OF COUNSEL

E. J. CALDECOTT, born Schenectady, New York, September 15, 1922; admitted to bar, 1949, U.S. District Court, Central District of California and U.S. Court of Appeals, Ninth Circuit; 1957, U.S. Supreme Court. *Education:* University of California at Los Angeles (A.B., 1943); University of Southern California (LL.B., 1948). Phi Delta Phi. Order of the Coif. Lecturer, Trade Regulations, University of Southern California, 1952-1953. Member, 1960 and Trustee, 1984-1989, International Council of Shopping Centers. Member: Los Angeles County and American Bar Associations; State Bar of California. [Capt., U.S. Army, 1943-1946]. *PRACTICE AREAS:* Shopping Center Law.

## LAW OFFICES OF
## RICHARD R. REYES
Established in 1988
1100 EAST GREEN STREET
PASADENA, CALIFORNIA 91106
Telephone: 818-792-5672

*Personal Injury, Products Liability, Wrongful Death, Contract Litigation. General Civil Litigation.*

RICHARD R. REYES, born Los Angeles, California, March 15, 1954; admitted to bar, 1982, California; 1983, U.S. District Court, Central District of California and U.S. Court of Appeals, Ninth Circuit. *Education:* University of Southern California (B.A., 1976); University of Strasbourg, France (Graduate Study); Western State University (J.D., 1981). Honors Moot Court. *Member:* State Bar of California (Member, Executive Committee, Law Practice Management Section, 1991-1994); Consumer Attorneys Association of Los Angeles; Consumer Attorneys of California; The Association of Trial Lawyers of America. *LANGUAGES:* Spanish.

## RICHARDSON & HARMAN
215 NORTH MARENGO AVENUE, THIRD FLOOR
PASADENA, CALIFORNIA 91101
Telephone: 818-449-5577; 909-861-7244
Facsimile: 818-356-7414
Email: KGRESQ@AOL.COM

*Civil Litigation, General Business Law, Condominium and Construction Law.*

*FIRM PROFILE:* Mr. Richardson & Mr. Harman specialize in business, construction and real estate litigation and representation of homeowners associations. The firm's members have become known for their litigation of negligent construction cases but also specialize in contract disputes, mechanics lien practice, real estate litigation, commercial unlawful detainer and foreclosures.

*The firm is a Member of The Community Associations Institute and The California Association of Community Managers.*

### MEMBERS OF FIRM

KELLY G. RICHARDSON, born Torrance, California, April 8, 1958; admitted to bar, 1983, California; U.S. Court of Appeals, Ninth Circuit; 1984, U.S. District Court, Southern, Central and Northern Districts of California. *Education:* University of California at Riverside (B.A., 1980); University of Southern California (J.D., 1983). Phi Alpha Delta. Member, Computer Law Journal and Major Tax Planning Institute, 1981-1982. Settlement Officer, Glendale Superior Court, 1995. *Member:* Los Angeles County and Pasadena Bar Associations; State Bar of California (Member, Litigation Section); Association of Business Trial Lawyers; Christian Legal Society. *PRACTICE AREAS:* Civil Litigation; General Business Law; Condominium Law; Construction Law.

STEVEN G. HARMAN, born Maywood, California, December 29, 1955; admitted to bar, 1983, California; U.S. Court of Appeals, Ninth Circuit; U.S. District Court, Central and Southern Districts of California. *Education:* University of California, Los Angeles (B.A., 1977); University of Southern California (M.B.A., 1983; J.D., 1983). Notes Editor, Southern California Law Review, 1982-1983. Author: "Alleviating Hardship Arising From Inflation and Court Congestion: Toward the Use of the Conditional Specific Performance Decree," 56 Southern California Law Review 795, 1983. Judge Pro Tem, Los Angeles Municipal Courts, 1995—. *Member:* Orange County and Los Angeles County Bar Associations; State Bar of California. *PRACTICE AREAS:* Civil Litigation; General Business Law; Real Estate.

## ROBERT L. RISLEY
790 EAST COLORADO BOULEVARD, 9TH FLOOR
PASADENA, CALIFORNIA 91101
Telephone: 818-397-2745
Fax: 818-397-2746
Email: 102763.3005@compuserve.com

*General Practice.*

ROBERT L. RISLEY, born Los Angeles, California, January 26, 1934; admitted to bar, 1964, California. *Education:* Occidental College (B.A., 1956); University of California at Los Angeles (LL.B., 1963). Phi Delta Phi (President, 1960). Author: "Death with Dignity," published September,

*(This Listing Continued)*

ROBERT L. RISLEY, Pasadena—Continued

1989; "A Humane and Dignified Death - A New Law Permitting Physician Aid-In-Dying," published August, 1987. Founder and President, Americans Against Human Suffering, 1986—. President, Board of Directors, San Fernando Valley Neighborhood Legal Services, 1969. *Member:* Los Angeles County and American Bar Associations; State Bar of California; Association of Business Trial Lawyers; International Academy of Estate and Trust Law. [Lt. Col., USAF, Retired]. **PRACTICE AREAS:** Litigation; Real Estate Law; Medical Malpractice Defense Law.

---

## RIVKIN, RADLER & KREMER

A Partnership including Professional Corporations

*123 SOUTH MARENGO AVENUE, SUITE 400*
**PASADENA, CALIFORNIA 91101**
*Telephone: 818-795-1800*
*Fax: 818-795-2255*
*URL: http://www.rivkinradler.com*

*Uniondale, New York Office:* EAB Plaza. Telephone: 516-357-3000. Cable Address: "Atlaw." Telex: 645-074. Telecopier: 516-357-3333.

*Chicago, Illinois Office:* Suite 4300, 30 North LaSalle Street. Telephone: 312-782-5680. Telecopier: 312-782-3112.

*New York, New York Office:* 275 Madison Avenue. Telephone: 212-455-9555. Telecopier: 212-687-9044.

*Santa Rosa, California Office:* 100 B Street, Suite 300, P.O. Box 14609. Telephone: 707-576-8033. Telecopier: 707-576-7955.

*Newark, New Jersey Office:* One Gateway Center, Suite 1226. Telephone: 201-622-0900. Fax: 201-622-7878.

*General Civil Practice. Trials and Appeals in all Courts. Insurance Coverage Litigation, Toxic Torts, Professional Malpractice, Products Liability, RICO, Antitrust, Legislative and Administrative, Environmental, Corporate, Securities, Bankruptcy and Creditors Rights, Finance, Real Estate, Banking and Taxation, Trusts and Estates, Labor and Patent Infringement.*

### MEMBERS OF FIRM

**MICHAEL R. BROWN,** born New York, N.Y., April 27, 1951; admitted to bar, 1975, California, U.S. District Court, Southern District of California; 1976, U.S. Court of Appeals, Ninth Circuit, U.S. District Court, Central District of California; 1981, New York and U.S. District Court, Northern District of California; 1992, U.S. Supreme Court. *Education:* Queens College of the City University of New York (B.A., 1972); California Western University (J.D., 1975). **PRACTICE AREAS:** Commercial Litigation; Employment Litigation; Insurance Litigation; Fee Litigation; Entertainment Litigation. *Email:* michael.brown@rivkin.com

**GEORGE W. WILLIAMS, JR.,** born Atlanta, Georgia, May 5, 1940; admitted to bar, 1966, Georgia, U.S. District Court, Southern and Northern Districts of Georgia; and U.S. Court of Appeals, Fifth Circuit and Eleventh Circuit; 1980, California; 1988, U.S. District Court, Central District of California; 1991, U.S. District Court, Eastern District of California and U.S. Court of Appeals, Ninth Circuit. *Education:* Georgia Institute of Technology; University of Georgia (B.B.A., 1963; J.D., 1966). Phi Delta Phi. Secretary, Anti-Trust Section, State Bar of Georgia, 1967-1968. [Capt., U.S. Army, 1962-1964.]. **PRACTICE AREAS:** Commercial and Insurance Litigation; Employment Law; Business; Real Estate Transactions. *Email:* george.williams@rivkin.com

### ASSOCIATES

**DAVID VENDLER,** born Ithaca, New York, December 30, 1960; admitted to bar, 1988, Massachusetts; 1990, California, U.S. District Court, Central, Southern and Northern Districts of California and U.S. Court of Appeals, First Circuit. *Education:* Harvard University (A.B., 1984); University of San Francisco School of Law (J.D., 1988). **PRACTICE AREAS:** Litigation. *Email:* david.vendler@rivkin.com

**THOMAS C. BRIGHT,** born Savannah, Georgia, July 21, 1965; admitted to bar, 1994, California; 1995, U.S. District Court, Central, Southern and Northern Districts of California. *Education:* Vanderbilt University (B.A., 1988), Sigma Alpha Epsilon; Pepperdine University School of Law (J.D., 1992). **PRACTICE AREAS:** Litigation; Entertainment Law; Employment Law; Insurance Litigation; Commercial Litigation. *Email:* thomas.bright@rivkin.com

**MARTIN C. BOBAK,** born New Haven, Connecticut, February, 3, 1958; admitted to bar, 1983, California and U.S. District Court, Northern, Eastern, Central and Southern Districts of California; 1993, Colorado. *Education:* University of California at Irvine (B.S., 1980); University of the Pacific, McGeorge School of Law, University of the Pacific (J.D., 1983). *Member:* The State Bar of California. **PRACTICE AREAS:** General Civil Litigation; Commercial Litigation; Product Liability Litigation; Premises Liability; Real Estate Litigation.

**RICHARD L. KELLNER,** born Queens, New York, June 14, 1961; admitted to bar, 1987, New York, U.S. Court of Appeals, Second Circuit and U.S. District Court, Southern and Eastern Districts of New York; 1994, California; 1996, U.S. District Court, Central District of California. *Education:* University of Pennsylvania (B.A., 1983); Albany Law School of Union University (J.D., 1986). Order of the Barristers. National Appellate Advocacy Competition, National Finals, Best Appellate Advocate, 1985. Assistant District Attorney, Bronx District Attorneys Office, Appeals Bureau, 1986-1991. **PRACTICE AREAS:** Commercial and Real Estate Litigation; Appellate Litigation; Employment Litigation.

(For Biographical data on other Personnel see Professional Biographies at Uniondale, New York, Chicago, Illinois, New York, New York, Santa Rosa, California and Newark, New Jersey)

---

## LARRY M. ROBERTS

*Established in 1991*

*292 SOUTH VINEDO AVENUE*
**PASADENA, CALIFORNIA 91107**
*Telephone: 818-585-8683*
*Fax: 818-585-1774*

*Los Angeles, California Office:* 3415 South Sepulveda Boulevard, Suite 1120. Telephone: 310-391-6800. Fax: 310-391-1725.

*Civil Rights, Labor Law, International Law and Business Law. General Civil Litigation.*

**LARRY M. ROBERTS,** born Sacramento, California, July 23, 1957; admitted to bar, 1982, California. *Education:* University of California at Riverside (B.A., 1979); Universite Paul Valery III, Montpellier, France; Loyola Law School (J.D., 1982); Cambridge University, Cambridge, England (LL.M., International Law, with honors, 1983). Phi Alpha Delta. *Member:* Pasadena, Los Angeles County and American Bar Associations; State Bar of California. **LANGUAGES:** French. **PRACTICE AREAS:** Contract Law; International Law; Wrongful Discharge Law.

REPRESENTATIVE CLIENTS: North American Imaging; West Coast Imaging; Software Systems Design; Pasadena Wine Bar; Martec Pacific Inc.; State of the Arts Foundation.

---

## RUSSELL, HANCOCK & JEFFRIES

*Established in 1939*

*200 SOUTH LOS ROBLES, SUITE 530*
**PASADENA, CALIFORNIA 91101**
*Telephone: 818-795-4700*
*FAX: 818-795-4790*

*General Civil and Trial Practice in all State and Federal Courts. Employment, Public Utility, Transportation, Interstate Commerce and Corporation Law.*

*FIRM PROFILE: Russell, Hancock & Jeffries specializes in transportation, employment and general business matters. The firm principally represents transportation entities such as interstate and intrastate motor and air freight carries, surface freight forwarders, property brokers, ocean freight forwarders, non-vessel operating common carriers (NVOCC's), warehouses and distribution companies. We also represent shippers in a variety of industries.*

*Our representation includes administrative, litigation, transactional and advisory work arising under state and federal transportation, safety and labor regulatory schemes, as well as probate and trust work.*

### MEMBERS OF FIRM

**THEODORE W. RUSSELL** (Retired).

**ROBERT W. HANCOCK,** born Elyria, Ohio, November 23, 1930; admitted to bar, 1963, California, U.S. District Court, Central District of California and U.S. Court of Appeals, 9th Circuit; 1979, U.S. Court of Appeals for the District of Columbia Circuit; 1980, U.S. District Court, Southern and Eastern Districts of California. *Education:* Northwestern University (B.S., 1952); University of Southern California (LL.B., 1962). Order of the Coif. *Member:* Los Angeles County Bar Association; The State Bar of California; Transportation Lawyers Association. **REPORTED CASES:** Liptak v. Diane Apartments, Inc., 109 Cal. App. 3d 762; 167 Cal. Rptr. 440

*(This Listing Continued)*

(1980). *PRACTICE AREAS:* Commercial Litigation; Land Subsidence Litigation; Probate.

**JOHN C. RUSSELL,** born Los Angeles, California, March 28, 1947; admitted to bar, 1978, California and U.S. District Court, Eastern District of California; 1979, U.S. District Court, Central and Southern Districts of California and U.S. Court of Appeals, 9th Circuit; 1982, U.S. District Court, Northern District of California; 1991, U.S. Supreme Court. *Education:* California State University at Los Angeles (B.A., 1970); California Western School of Law (J.D., 1978). *Member:* Pasadena Bar Association; The State Bar of California; Transportation Lawyers Association; Association of Transportation Practitioners; National Trucking Industrial Relations Association; Conference of California Public Utilities Counsel. *PRACTICE AREAS:* Commercial Litigation; Transportation Law; Employment Law.

**KATHLEEN C. JEFFRIES,** born Inglewood, California, May 26, 1959; admitted to bar, 1983, California, U.S. District Court, Central District of California and U.S. Court of Appeals, Ninth Circuit; 1986, U.S. Court of Appeals for the District of Columbia Circuit; 1989, U.S. District Court, Southern District of California; 1993, U.S. District Court, Eastern District of California. *Education:* California State University at Long Beach (B.A., 1980); University of California at Los Angeles (J.D., 1983). Member: Order of the Barristers; Mortar Board. *Member:* Pasadena and Federal Bar Associations; State Bar of California; Transportation Lawyers Association; National Freight Claim and Security Council; Women Lawyers Association of Los Angeles. *PRACTICE AREAS:* Freight Claim Litigation; Interstate Commerce Commission Proceedings; Safety Related Criminal Defense.

**DANIEL K. GASTON,** born Chicago, Illinois, August 25, 1951; admitted to bar, 1984, California and U.S. District Court, Central District of California. *Education:* University of California at Santa Barbara (B.A., 1973); Southwestern University School of Law (J.D., 1983). Recipient, American Jurisprudence Award in Administrative Law. *Member:* Pasadena Bar Association; State Bar of California; Conference of California Public Utilities Counsel; Association of Transportation Practitioners. *PRACTICE AREAS:* Administrative Law; Transportation Law; Commercial Law.

REFERENCE: First Interstate Bank of California, Pasadena Main Office (Los Robles Ave. and Cordova).

---

## SALZ & SALZ

*150 SOUTH LOS ROBLES, SUITE 910*
**PASADENA, CALIFORNIA 91101**
Telephone: 818-793-2800
Facsimile: 818-793-9622

*Family Law, Civil Litigation, Personal Injury and Criminal Law.*

### MEMBERS OF FIRM

**FRANK SALZ,** born Czechoslovakia, February 11, 1936; admitted to bar, 1971, Connecticut; 1974, California. *Education:* Massachusetts Institute of Technology (B.S., 1957; M.S., 1958); University of Connecticut (J.D., 1971). Member, Association of Certified Family Law Specialists. Judge Pro Tem, Los Angeles Superior and Municipal Court, 1992—. Family Law Mediator, 1988—. *Member:* Pasadena, Los Angeles County, Hartford County, Connecticut and American Bar Associations; State Bar of California. (Certified Specialist, Family Law, The State Bar of California Board of Legal Specialization). *PRACTICE AREAS:* Family Law; Personal Injury.

**CONSTANCE E. SALZ,** born Portland, Oregon, November 27, 1955; admitted to bar, 1983, California. *Education:* California State University at Los Angeles (B.S., 1980); Southwestern University (J.D., 1983). Member, Association of Certified Family Law Specialists. Judge Pro Tem, Los Angeles Superior Court, 1990—. Family Law Mediator, 1990—. *Member:* Los Angeles County, Pasadena and American Bar Associations; State Bar of California. (Certified Specialist, Family Law, The State Bar of California Board of Legal Specialization). *PRACTICE AREAS:* Family Law; Criminal; Probate.

---

**BRIAN ALAN BAKER,** born Camden, New Jersey, March 15, 1957; admitted to bar, 1984, California; 1989, U.S. Supreme Court. *Education:* Virginia Commonwealth University (B.A., 1980); California Western School of Law (J.D., 1983). Judge Pro Tem, Los Angeles Superior and Municipal Court, 1992—. Family Law Mediator, 1994—. *Member:* Pasadena, Los Angeles County and American Bar Associations; State Bar of California; The Association of Trial Lawyers of America; The Order of Barristers.

*(This Listing Continued)*

(Certified Specialist, Family Law, The State Bar of California Board of Legal Specialization). *PRACTICE AREAS:* Family Law; Civil Litigation; Real Estate; Business.

**MARIANA A. HEVIA,** born Miami, Florida, April 26, 1962; admitted to bar, 1989, California. *Education:* University of California at Los Angeles (B.A., 1985); California Western School of Law (J.D., 1988). Phi Alpha Delta. Judge Pro Tem, Los Angeles Municipal Court, 1995—. *Member:* Los Angeles County and American Bar Associations; State Bar of California. *PRACTICE AREAS:* Family Law.

---

## IRA M. SALZMAN

*Established in 1988*

*600 SOUTH LAKE AVENUE, SUITE 410*
**PASADENA, CALIFORNIA 91106**
Telephone: 818-578-0043
Fax: 818-578-0503

*General Civil Litigation in all State and Federal Courts with emphasis on the Defense of Professional Negligence, Personal Injury and Public Safety Employees, General Wrongful Termination, Criminal Defense in State and Federal Courts.*

FIRM PROFILE: *My practice has been devoted exclusively to litigation with emphasis on defense of public safety, employees and the defense of complex criminal matters in Federal and State Courts.*

*I have lectured extensively on civil and criminal liability issues before numerous law enforcement agencies and have discussed high profile litigation cases before numerous attorney groups.*

**IRA M. SALZMAN,** born Los Angeles, California, November 27, 1952; admitted to bar, 1978, California; 1979, U.S. District Court, Central District of California; 1993, U.S. Court of Appeals, Ninth Circuit; 1995, U.S. District Court, Northern District of California. *Education:* University of California, Berkeley (A.B., 1974); Southwestern University School of Law (J.D., 1978). Author: "The Solos Guide to Handling Protracted Litigation," Law Practice Management Section, State Bar of California, Vol. 6, No. 4, Dec. 1994; "Sixth Amendment Right To Jury Trial vs. External Influences on Juror Decisions," 26 University of West Los Angeles Law Review, 1995; "Managing the Internal Affairs and Criminal Investigation," Los Angeles Police Protective League "Thin Blue Line," Aug. 1995. Instructor, Civil Procedure and Torts, Waterson College, Pasadena, CA, 1990-1991. Deputy District Attorney Grade III, Los Angeles County, CA, 1979-1984. Associate: Schell & Delamer, Los Angeles, CA, 1984-1986; Murchison & Cumming, Los Angeles, CA, 1986-1988. Arbitrator, Los Angeles Superior and Municipal Courts on the Personal Injury and Medical Malpractice Panels, Central, Glendale, Burbank, Alhambra and Pasadena Districts, 1991—. *Member:* Pasadena, Los Angeles County and American Bar Associations; State Bar of California (Arbitrator, Attorney Fee Disputes, 1991—); California Public Defenders Association; California Peace Officers Association; Association of Federal Criminal Defense Lawyers; National Association of Criminal Defense Lawyers. *PRACTICE AREAS:* Criminal Defense; Public Entity Employee; Defense; Wrongful Termination.

---

## RICKARD SANTWIER

*35 SOUTH RAYMOND AVENUE*
*SUITE 301*
**PASADENA, CALIFORNIA 91105**
Telephone: 818-449-6504; 213-681-4425
FAX: 213-681-4436

*Criminal and Juvenile Defense in all State and Federal Courts.*

**RICKARD SANTWIER,** born Hollywood, California, June 23, 1942; admitted to bar, 1970, California and U.S. District Court, Central District of California. *Education:* University of San Francisco (B.A., History, 1965); University of San Diego School of Law (J.D., 1969). Moot Court Board. Recipient: Jerry Giesler Trial Attorney of the Year, Criminal Courts Bar Association, 1993. Los Angeles County Deputy Defender, 1969-1984. *Member:* Pasadena (President-elect, 1996—; Vice President, 1995-1996; Trustee, 1993-1995) and Los Angeles County (Co-Chair Indigent Criminal Defense Appointments, 1993-1995) Bar Associations; State Bar of California (Member, Executive Committee, Criminal Law Section, 1996-1997); California Attorneys for Criminal Justice (Board of Governors, 1990-1996; Executive Board, 1995-1996); Criminal Courts Bar Association (President, 1995); California Public Defenders Association; National Association of Criminal Defense Lawyers. (Certified Specialist, Criminal Law, The State

*(This Listing Continued)*

RICKARD SANTWIER, Pasadena—Continued

Bar of California Board of Legal Specialization). *REPORTED CASES:* Joe Z. v. Superior Court, 3Cal 3rd 797, 1970; Carlos v. Superior Ct. 35 Cal 3rd 131, 1983.

## STEVEN A. SCHNEIDER
### 301 NORTH LAKE AVENUE, EIGHTH FLOOR
### PASADENA, CALIFORNIA 91101
*Telephone: 818-886-4946*
*Fax: 818-583-9187*

*General Civil Trial and Appellate Practice in all State and Federal Courts, with emphasis in General Business and Commercial Litigation, including Construction Law and Insurance Law.*

**STEVEN A. SCHNEIDER,** born Brooklyn, New York, May 17, 1945; admitted to bar, 1978, California; 1979, U.S. District Court, Central District of California; 1981, U.S. Court of Appeals, Ninth Circuit and U.S. District Court, Southern, Eastern and Northern Districts of California. *Education:* Occidental College (B.A., summa cum laude, 1963); Harvard University (M.A., English, 1968; Ph.D., 1973); University of Southern California (J.D., 1978). Phi Beta Kappa. Hale Moot Court Program. Recipient: Woodrow Wilson Fellowship; Danforth Graduate Fellowship; Honorary Harvard Graduate Prize Fellowship. Finalist, Marshall Fellowship. Nominee, Rhodes Scholar. Author: "Remedies For Discovery Abuse: A Practical View," California Continuing Education of the Bar, 1985, revised and updated, 1988; "Your Liability Insurance Policy: How to Use A Valuable Asset," and "Mediation: Some Basic Questions and Answers," Associated Builders and Contractors Merit News, 1996; "Case Closed: When Is a Settlement Agreement Enforceable?" The Los Angeles Daily Journal, May, 1996. Consultant, "California Construction Disputes," 1992 and "Mechanic's Liens," 1993, California Continuing Education of the Bar. Lecturer: "Compelling, Enforcing and Opposing Discovery in State Court," 1985, 1988, 1991, "Summary Judgments," 1987 and "Written Discovery," 1989, California Continuing Education of the Bar; "How to Litigate Efficiently and Effectively," Credit Managers Association, 1994; "Credit Management and Debt Collection: How to Make More and Spend Less," Associated Builders and Contractors of Southern California and Roofers' Association of Southern California, 1996. Instructor and Consultant, California Continuing Education of the Bar Seminars, 1985, 1987, 1988 and 1991. Instructor, Torts, Los Angeles Valley College, Paralegal Program, 1996. Judge Pro Tem, Los Angeles County Municipal Court, 1989. Prosecutor, State Bar of California, 1980. Member, Arbitration Panel, Contractor's State Licensing Board/Arbitration and Mediation International, 1996. Member, Legal Advisory Committee, 1987-1988, Associated General Contractors of California, 1987-1988. Member and Chairman, Legal Rights and Strategies Committee, 1996. Associated Builders and Contractors of Southern California. *Member:* State Bar of California.

## CHARLES T. SCHOFIELD
### 200 S. LOS ROBLES AVENUE, SUITE 500
### PASADENA, CALIFORNIA 91101
*Telephone: 818-578-0708*
*FAX: 818-578-0244*

*Trust, Wills, Probate, Estate Planning, Tax, Corporate Law, Business and Commercial.*

**CHARLES T. SCHOFIELD,** born Salt Lake City, Utah; admitted to bar, 1978, California and U.S. Supreme Court; 1981, U.S. District Court, District of California, U.S. Court of Appeals, (9th Circuit; 1983, U.S. Tax Court, U.S. Court of Claims. *Education:* California State University at Los Angeles (B.A., 1974); University of San Diego (J.D., 1977). Research and Editing: Revokable Trusts, 1st Ed., 1983, 2nd. Ed., 1991 & Irrevokable Trusts, 1st Ed., 1984, 2nd Ed., 1992, published by Sheppard McGraw Hill. Lecturer, Estate Planning & Retirement Planning for Jet Propultion Laboratory (JPL), JC Penney, New York Life and California Federal Savings & Loan, 1980—. Vice President, Booster Club Rowland High School, 1995—. Boys Scouts of America, San Gabriel Valley Council (Troop Committee Chairman). Rowland United School District (Budget Planning Committee, 1994—; Curriculum Committee, 1993). *Member:* State Bar of California.

CAA1670B

## KARL W. SCHOTH & ASSOCIATES
### 1122 EAST GREEN STREET
### PASADENA, CALIFORNIA 91106
*Telephone: 818-395-7514*
*Facsimile: 818-796-2554*
*Email: kschoth@earthlink.net*

*Personal Injury, Specializing in medical malpractice and elder abuse law.*

**KARL W. SCHOTH,** born Mettman, Germany, February 8, 1955; admitted to bar, 1984, California and U.S. District Court, Central District of California; 1987, U.S. Court of Appeals, Ninth Circuit; 1994, U.S. Supreme Court; 1995, U.S. District Court, Southern District of California. *Education:* University of British Columbia; Southwestern University (J.D., S.C.A.L.E. Graduate, 1983). Member, Southwestern University Law Review, 1982-1983. Court Approved Counsel to represent catastrophic injury cases of dependents of Los Angeles City Juvenile Court. Arbitrator and Mediator, Los Angeles Supreme Court. *Member:* Pasadena and Los Angeles County Bar Associations; State Bar of California; Consumer Attorneys Association of Los Angeles; Consumer Attorneys Association of California. *REPORTED CASES:* Allstate v. Fibus, et al (9th Circ. 1988) 855 F.2d 660; Prieto v. State Farm (1991) 225 Cal.App. 3d 1188. *PRACTICE AREAS:* Personal Injury Law; Medical Malpractice; Elder Abuse; Arbitrator; Mediator.

### ASSOCIATES

**LADAN ALAVI,** born Philadelphia, Pennsylvania, July 24, 1967; admitted to bar, 1993, California and U.S. District Court, Central District of California; 1995, U.S. Court of Appeals, Ninth Circuit. *Education:* University of California at San Diego; Southwestern University School of La w (J.D., 1993). Member, Moot Court Honors Program, Board of Governors. *Member:* Los Angeles County and American Bar Associations; State Bar of California; Consumer Lawyers Association of Los Angeles; Women Lawyers' Association of Los Angeles. *LANGUAGES:* Farsi; Spanish. *PRACTICE AREAS:* Personal Injury Law; Medical Malpractice; Elder Abuse.

## LAW OFFICE OF
## FREDERICK C. SHALLER
### WALNUT PLAZA
### 215 NORTH MARENGO AVENUE, SECOND FLOOR
### PASADENA, CALIFORNIA 91101
*Telephone: 818-796-9669*
*Facsimile: 818-304-1399*

*Medical Malpractice, Products Liability, Personal Injury.*

**FREDERICK C. SHALLER,** born Eureka, California, May 29, 1953; admitted to bar, 1979, California. *Education:* University of Southern California (B.A., 1976); Loyola University of Los Angeles (J.D., 1979). *Member:* Los Angeles County and American Bar Associations; State Bar of California; Los Angeles Trial Lawyers Association; California Trial Lawyers Association. *PRACTICE AREAS:* Personal Injury Law; Medical Malpractice Law; Torts.

## SHELDON & MAK
### 9TH FLOOR, 225 SOUTH LAKE AVENUE
### PASADENA, CALIFORNIA 91101-3005
*Telephone: 818-796-4000*
*Fax: 818-795-6321*
*URL: http://www.usip.com*

San Bernardino, California Office: Suite 503, 290 North D Street, 92401. Telephone: 909-889-3649. Fax: 909-889-9865.
Upland, California Office: Suite 210, 222 North Mountain Avenue, 91786. Telephone: 909-946-3939.

*Patent, Trademark and Copyright Law. Antitrust and Unfair Competition, Trade Secrets, Customs Law and related causes in all State and Federal Courts.*

*FIRM PROFILE: Sheldon & Mak was founded in 1983 by Jeffrey G. Sheldon. Its practice centers on intellectual property and industrial property law. Sheldon & Mak also provides services in corporate and business, customs and international trade law.*

*Most of the attorneys associated with Sheldon & Mak have a technical background and training. The firm's attorneys are licensed to practice in California*

*(This Listing Continued)*

and before the Courts of the United States. Most are registered to practice before the United States Patent and Trademark Office. They regularly attend specialist conferences and training courses to maintain their expertise. Their substantive expertise often alleviates the need for outside experts.

### MEMBERS OF FIRM

**JEFFREY G. SHELDON,** admitted to bar, 1975, California and District of Columbia; 1984, U.S. Court of Appeals for the Federal Circuit; registered to practice before U.S. Patent and Trademark Office. *Education:* Carnegie Mellon University (B.S., 1969); Univ. of Strathclyde, Glasgow, Scotland (M.Sc., 1971); Marshall Scholar; Loyola University of Los Angeles (J.D., magna cum laude, 1975). Tau Beta Pi. Author: "How To Write A Patent Application," Practising Law Institute. Columnist, Los Angeles Daily Journal. Adjunct Professor, Intellectual Property: LaVerne College of Law, 1984-1989; Southwestern University, 1989-1991; Advanced Patent Law, Loyola, 1992—. *Member:* American Bar Association (Intellectual Property Section, Committee Chair); The State Bar of California (Chairman, Intellectual Property Law Section, 1989); Los Angeles Intellectual Property Patent Law Association (President, 1994-1995, Director, 1989-1996, President); American Intellectual Property Law Association (Committee Chair). *Email:* JEFF@USIP.COM

**DANTON K. MAK,** admitted to bar, 1984, California; registered to practice before U.S. Patent and Trademark Office. *Education:* University of Washington (B.S.Ch.E., 1976); University of California at Los Angeles (J.D., 1984). Member, Editorial Board, Copyright World, 1989-1990. **LANGUAGES:** Chinese, Mandarin and Cantonese. *Email:* DANTON@USIP.COM

**DENTON L. ANDERSON,** admitted to bar, 1976, California; U.S. Court of Appeals, Ninth Circuit; U.S. Court of Appeals for the Federal Circuit; registered to practice before U.S. Patent and Trademark Office. *Education:* University of Minnesota (B.Ch.E., cum laude, 1968); South Bay University (J.D., Valedictorian, 1976). Los Angeles County Bar Association. *Member:* San Bernardino County (Director), Western San Bernardino County (Past President) and Federal Bar Associations; Los Angeles Patent Law Association; American Inns of Court (Counselor). *Email:* DENTON@USIP.COM

**SURJIT P. SINGH SONI,** admitted to bar, 1987, California; 1990, U.S. Court of Appeals, Ninth, Tenth, Eleventh and Federal Circuits; U.S. District Court, Northern and Central Districts of California. *Education:* University of Toronto (B.Sc., 1974); University of Miami (J.D., cum laude, 1984). Recipient: Society of Wig and Robe; Moot Court Award; Award of Distinction. *Member:* Pasadena (Director, 1987-1988); Los Angeles County (Executive Committee Member and Programs Director, Litigation Section), Federal (Executive Committee) and American Bar Associations; State Bar of California (Member, State Bar Advisory Committee, Trial Practice to the Continuing Education of the Bar; Executive Committee Member and Co-Editor: "New Matter" Official Newsletter, Intellectual Property Section, 1989-1992); Pasadena Young Lawyers Association (President, 1987-1988); Licensing Executives Society; Los Angeles Complex Litigation Inn of Court (Founder, President, 1993-1995, Master of the Bench). **LANGUAGES:** Hindi and Punjabi. *Email:* SURJIT@USIP.COM

**ROBERT J. ROSE,** admitted to bar, 1975, Arizona; 1978, California. *Education:* University of Arizona (B.S., 1971; J.D., with high distinction, 1975). Order of the Coif. Associate Editor, Arizona Law Review, 1974-1975. Co-Author: "Pricing Practices," Matthew Bender, 1986. Adjunct Professor, University of LaVerne College of Law, 1992-1997. Trial Attorney, Antitrust Division, U.S. Department of Justice, 1975-1980. Special Assistant U.S. Attorney, Central District of California, Los Angeles, 1979. Arbitrator, Los Angeles Superior Court, East District, 1990-1997. Member, Board of Arbitrators, National Association of Securities Dealers, 1990-1994. Special Master, State Bar of California, 1991-1997. Panelist, Civil Actions for Copyright Infringement, World Intellectual Property Organization & Russian Federation Symposium on the Enforcement of Copyright, Moscow, Russia, 1994. *Member:* Los Angeles County, Pasadena and American (Member, Antitrust and Intellectual Property Sections) Bar Associations; State Bar of California (Treasurer and Member, Executive Committee, Antitrust and Trade Regulation and Intellectual Property Sections); State Bar of Arizona. *Email:* RJR@USIP.COM

**WILLIAM J. BRUTOCAO,** admitted to bar, 1977, California and U.S. District Court, Northern District of California; 1981, U.S. District Court, Central District of California. *Education:* Cornell University (B.A., 1972); Hastings College of the Law, University of California (J.D., 1977). *Member:* Pasadena, San Francisco and Los Angeles County (Member, Vice-Chair Arbitration Committee, 1984-1987) Bar Associations; State Bar of California. *Email:* WJB@USIP.COM

*(This Listing Continued)*

### OF COUNSEL

**SOL L. GOLDSTEIN,** admitted to bar, 1955, Illinois; 1962, U.S. District Court, Seventh Circuit; 1974, Ohio; 1982, U.S. Court of Appeals for the Federal Circuit; registered to practice before U.S. Patent and Trademark Office (Not admitted in California). *Education:* Illinois Institute of Technology (B.S., Ch.Eng., 1949); Loyola University (J.D., 1954). Author: "A Study of Compulsory Licensing," Journal of the Licensing Executive Society, Les Nouvelles, June, 1977; "Alternate Dispute Resolution Under 35 U.S.C. 294," Illinois Bar Journal, March 1984. *Member:* American Bar Association (Member: Patent Contracts Committee, 1979-1980; International Patent Treaties and Law Committee, 1981-1982; Patent Trademark and Copyright Law Section); American Intellectual Property Law Association. [With U.S. Navy, 1944-1946] *Email:* SOL@USIP.COM

**JOSEPH E. MUETH,** born St. Louis, Missouri, August 9, 1935; admitted to bar, 1960, Missouri; 1964, California and U.S. District Court, Central District of California; U.S. Supreme Court; U.S. Court of Appeals, Ninth Circuit; U.S. District Court, Northern District of California; U.S. Court of Appeals for Federal Circuit; registered to practice before U.S. Patent and Trademark Office. *Education:* University of Dayton (B.Ch.E., 1957); Georgetown University (LL.B., 1960; LL.M., 1961). (Also practicing individually).

### ASSOCIATES

**ERIN MCKEOWN JOYCE,** admitted to bar, 1990, California; 1991, U.S. District Court, Central District of California; 1993, U.S. District Court, Southern District of California and U.S. Court of Appeals, Ninth Circuit; 1995, U.S. Court of Appeals, Tenth and Federal Circuits. *Education:* University of California at Los Angeles (B.A., cum laude, 1987); Southwestern University School of Law (J.D., magna cum laude, 1990). Delta Theta Phi. Author: "False Claim Could Mean Treble Damages", LA Daily Journal, July 1991; "Consumer Standing under the Lanham Act Still an open Question in 9th Circuit," L.A. Daily Journal, December, 1994; "Parallels Between Trade Dress and Design Patent Protection," CEB Business Law Journal, July 1995. Editorial Consultant, Matthew Bender's, *California Intellectual Property Handbook* 1992-1993. ABA/IP Young Lawyers Committee, 1993-1995; State Bar Committee on Rules and Procedures of Court, 1994—; Chair, Los Angeles County Bar Association Barristers Education Committee, 1993-1996; Barristers Executive Committee, 1992-1996; Los Angeles County Bar Association Litigation Section Executive Committee, 1994-1996; Delegate, State Bar Conference of Delegates, 1992, 1994, 1995. *Email:* ERIN@USIP.COM

**STEPHEN R. SECCOMBE,** admitted to bar, 1983, California and U.S. District Court, Central and Southern Districts of California; registered to practice before U.S. Patent and Trademark Office. *Education:* University of California at Los Angeles (B.S., 1961); San Fernando Valley College of Law (J.D., 1982). *Member:* San Bernardino County and Riverside County Bar Associations; State Bar of California (Member, Intellectual Property Law Section); Christian Legal Society. (Resident, San Bernadino Office). *Email:* SMSRS@e2.empirenet.com

**DOUGLAS H. MORSEBURG,** born Syracuse, New York, March 8, 1950; admitted to bar, 1986, California; 1987, U.S. District Court, Central District of California; 1989, U.S. District Court, Eastern District of California. *Education:* Stanford University (B.A., 1974); Hastings College of the Law (J.D., 1986). Member, Hastings International and Comparative Law Review, 1984-1985. Associate Technical Editor, COMM/ENT, Hastings Communications and Entertainment Law Review, 1985-1986. *Member:* Los Angeles County Bar Association; State Bar of California. *Email:* DOUG@USIP.COM

**ANTHONY G. VELLA,** born Rockford, Illinois, March 11, 1955; admitted to bar, 1991, Illinois and U.S. District Court, Northern District of Illinois; 1993, U.S. Court of Appeals for the Federal Circuit; 1994, U.S. District Court, Western District of Michigan (Not admitted in California). *Education:* Northern Illinois University (B.S., 1978; J.D., magna cum laude, 1991); Cardinal Stritch College (M.S., 1987). Member, Northern Illinois University Law Review, 1990-1991. Recipient: American Jurisprudence Awards; Keck, Mahin and Cate Antitrust Prize. *Member:* Chicago, Illinois State and American (Litigation) Bar Associations; American Intellectual Property Association; Association of Trial Lawyers of America. *Email:* TONY@USIP.COM

**YINGCHAO XIAO,** born Xi'an, P.R.C., November 12, 1952; admitted to bar, 1993, Pennsylvania; 1994, District of Columbia; The Court of International Trade (Not admitted in California). *Education:* Xian Foreign Languages Institute, Xi'an, P.R.C. (B.A.); Cornell Law School (J.D., 1991). *Member:* Pennsylvania Bar Association; The District of Columbia Bar.

*(This Listing Continued)*

SHELDON & MAK, Pasadena—Continued

LANGUAGES: Mandarin Chinese. Email: YINGCHAO@USIP.COM

EDWARD A. BROWN, born Mt. Clemens, Michigan, May 28, 1959; admitted to bar, 1992, Pennsylvania; registered to practice before U.S. Patent and Trademark Office (Not admitted in California). Education: University of Illinois (B.S.Met.E., 1983, Alpha Sigma Mu); Michigan Technological University (M.S.Met.E., 1986); American University (J.D., 1992). Member: American Bar Association; American Intellectual Property Law Association. Email: ED@USIP.COM

DAVID FARAH, admitted to bar, 1993, California; registered to practice before U.S. Patent and Trademark Office. Education: University of Michigan (B.S., with honors, Chem. and Bio., 1980; J.D., 1992); Ferris State University (O.D., with high distinction, 1984); Wayne State University (M.D., 1988). Alpha Omega Alpha. Licenses: Medicine: Michigan, 1989, California, 1993 ; Optometry, Michigan, 1984. PRACTICE AREAS: Patent, Trademark and Copyright. Email: DAVIDF@USIP.COM

LEE HSU, born Shanghai, China, April 22, 1968; admitted to bar, 1994, California; registered to practice before U.S. Patent and Trademark Office. Education: University of California, Los Angeles (B.S.E.E., cum laude, 1990); Southwestern University School of Law (J.D., 1994). Southwestern Law Review. Author, "Reverse Engineering Under The Semiconductor Chip Protection Act - Complications for Standard of Infringement," Albany Law Journal of Science and Technology, Volume 5.2, 1996. Member: American Institute of Aeronautics and Astronautics. LANGUAGES: Chinese (Mandarin). Email: LEE@USIP.COM

REPRESENTATIVE CLIENTS: TRW; Raychem; Southern California Edison; Beckman; Sierracin; Quantum; Parsons; Learning Tree International; Sunburst Products; ARCO; Applied Materials; Cal Spas; Metropolitan Water District; Paramount Pictures Corporation; Columbia Pictures Industries, Inc.; TriStar Pictures, Inc.; Twentieth Century Fox Film Corp; Universal Film Exchanges, Inc.; MGM, Inc.; Orion Pictures Distribution Corp.; Warner Bros.; Buena Vista Distribution Co., Inc.; Miramax Film Corp.
REFERENCE: Citizens Bank (Pasadena, California).

## MICHAEL L. SLOAN
596 NORTH LAKE AVENUE, SUITE 204
PASADENA, CALIFORNIA 91101
Telephone: 818-584-9343
Fax: 818-584-9349

Employment Law including Sexual Harassment, Gender, Age & Race Discrimination, Workers Compensation, Civil Litigation, Business, Personal Injury.

MICHAEL L. SLOAN, born Los Angeles, California, September 14, 1959; admitted to bar, 1987, California. Education: Loyola Marymount University (B.A., 1981; J.D., 1984). Phi Alpha Theta; Phi Alpha Delta. Member: State Bar of California. PRACTICE AREAS: Litigation (40%, 25); Labor and Employment (40%, 25); Workers Compensation (20%, 100).

## SOLDWEDEL, PALERMO, BARBARO & CHINEN

A Partnership including Professional Corporations

Established in 1891

Formerly Rinehart, Merriam, Parker & Berg

SUITE 700, 301 EAST COLORADO BOULEVARD
PASADENA, CALIFORNIA 91101
Telephone: 818-793-5196
Los Angeles: 213-681-7226
FAX: 818-793-3602

Probate, Estate Planning, General Civil and Trial Practice. Federal and State Tax Law. Corporation Law. Family Law. Real Property Law.

FIRM PROFILE: Soldwedel, Palermo, Barbaro & Chinen is Pasadena's oldest law firm tracing its roots to Judge J. Howard Merriam's General Civil Law Practice which began on April 15, 1891.

J. H. MERRIAM (1862-1934).

JAY D. RINEHART (1891-1964).

RALPH T. MERRIAM (1891-1968).

RONALD D. KINCAID (1941-1980).

(This Listing Continued)

*PARTNERS*

PETER R. PALERMO, (PROFESSIONAL CORPORATION), born Somerville, Massachusetts, June 30, 1937; admitted to bar, 1964, California and U.S. District Court, Central District of California; 1967, U.S. Tax Court; 1977, U.S. Supreme Court. Education: Occidental College (A.B., 1959); University of San Diego (J.D., 1962). Estate Tax Attorney, I.R.S., 1963-1965. Judge Pro-Tem, Municipal Court, 1975—. Member: Pasadena (Trustee, 1986-1989) and Los Angeles County Bar Associations; The State Bar of California (Member: Family Law Section; Probate and Trust Section; Tax Section). PRACTICE AREAS: Primary and Ancillary Probate Law; Trust Law; Estate Planning.

PHILIP BARBARO, JR., born Glendale, California, June 4, 1955; admitted to bar, 1980, California; 1981, U.S. Court of Appeals, Ninth Circuit and U.S. District Court, Central District of California. Education: University of California at Irvine (B.S., 1977); Western State University (J.D., 1980). Instructor, Business Law and Legal Aspects of Real Estate, Pasadena City College, 1986—. President, Pasadena Young Lawyers Association, 1984-1985. Member: Pasadena (Treasurer, 1986-1987) and Los Angeles County Bar Associations; State Bar of California; Italian-American Bar Association. PRACTICE AREAS: Real Estate Property Law; Civil Practice; Litigation.

RICHARD L. CHINEN, born Tokyo, Japan, May 31, 1958; admitted to bar, 1982, California and U.S. District Court, Central District of California. Education: University of Hawaii (B.A., 1979); Southwestern University School of Law (J.D., 1982). Professor, Family Law, Simon Greenleaf School of Law, 1992. Member: Pasadena (Treasurer, 1994-1995) and Los Angeles County (Member, Family Law Section, 1983—) Bar Associations; State Bar of California; Pasadena Lawyer Referral and Information Service (Vice-President, 1992-1995). LANGUAGES: Japanese (verbal). PRACTICE AREAS: Family Law; Personal Injury; Estate Planning; Bankruptcy; Business Litigation.

*OF COUNSEL*

J. HAROLD BERG, (PROFESSIONAL CORPORATION), born Oakland, California, December 14, 1916; admitted to bar, 1940, California; 1976, U.S. Supreme Court. Education: University of California (A.B., 1937; J.D., 1940). Order of the Coif. Member: Pasadena (President, 1964) and Los Angeles County Bar Associations; The State Bar of California (Member, Probate and Trust Section); American Judicature Society. [Major, Army of the U.S., 1941-1945]. PRACTICE AREAS: Trust Administration Law; Corporate Law; Probate Law.

FRED W. SOLDWEDEL, (PROFESSIONAL CORPORATION), born Pekin, Illinois, October 15, 1931; admitted to bar, 1958, California; 1961, Illinois; 1967, U.S. Supreme Court. Education: Northwestern University (B.S., 1953); Stanford University (LL.B., 1958); University of Southern California (LL.M., 1962). Phi Delta Phi. Member: Pasadena Bar Association (President, 1984); The State Bar of California; San Gabriel Valley Estate Planning Council (President, 1984). [Captain, U.S. Naval Reserve, 1953-1983]. PRACTICE AREAS: Estate Planning Law; Primary and Ancillary Probate Law; Non-Profit Organizations Law.

HARVEY M. PARKER (Retired).

REPRESENTATIVE CLIENTS: Southern California Presbyterian Homes; Clearman's Restaurants; Monte Vista Grove Homes; Citizens Business Bank; Northern Trust of California; Bank of America; Wells Fargo Bank; Sanwa Bank.
REFERENCES: Bank of America National Trust & Savings Assn. (Pasadena Main Office); Sanwa Bank California (Pasadena Office); Citizens Business Bank; Wells Fargo Bank.

## MARK A. SPRAIC
150 EAST COLORADO BOULEVARD, SUITE 201
PASADENA, CALIFORNIA 91105
Telephone: 818-792-9333
Facsimile: 818-449-6299

Civil Litigation, General Business including Mergers and Acquisitions, Partnerships, Creditors Rights, Corporate and Real Estate.

MARK A. SPRAIC, born Los Angeles, California, March 17, 1946; admitted to bar, 1972, California. Education: University of Southern California (B.A., 1968); Boalt Hall School of Law, University of California (J.D., 1971). Member: Los Angeles County (Member, Sections on: Litigation, Real Estate and International Law) and Federal Bar Associations; State Bar of California (Member, Sections on: Litigation; International Law).

(This Listing Continued)

REPRESENTATIVE CLIENTS: Allison Systems, Inc.; Beverly Enterprises; Dye Designs International; Kobayashi & Company; LASO Foundation; Tamayo Restaurant; Telacu; Herman Weissker, Inc.
REFERENCE: Tokai Bank, Pasadena.

## STONE & DOYLE
527 SOUTH LAKE, SUITE 103
PASADENA, CALIFORNIA 91101
Telephone: 818-449-1196
Telecopier: 818-795-6402

*Practice Limited to Estate Planning, Probate and Trust Administration, Corporation, Business and Tax Law, Business Litigation.*

**WILLARD J. STONE** (Retired).

**MICHAEL C. DOYLE,** born Miami, Florida, November 29, 1942; admitted to bar, 1969, Ohio and Georgia; 1971, Wisconsin; 1975, California. *Education:* University of Cincinnati (B.B.A., 1964); Salmon P. Chase College (J.D., 1969). Phi Alpha Delta. Member, Order of the Curia. President, Student Bar Association, 1969. House Counsel, Alexander Grant & Co. (CPA's) and National Director of Tax Services, 1973-1974. *Member:* Pasadena, Ohio State and American (Member, Taxation Section) Bar Associations; State Bar of Georgia; State Bar of Wisconsin; The State Bar of California; Estate Planning Council of San Gabriel Valley. **PRACTICE AREAS:** Corporate; Tax Planning; Probate.

**PAULA G. WALUCH,** born Oakland, California, August 2, 1950; admitted to bar, 1975, California. *Education:* University of California at Berkeley (B.A., 1972); Golden Gate University (J.D., 1975). *Member:* Los Angeles County Bar Association; The State Bar of California. **PRACTICE AREAS:** Corporate; Tax Planning; Probate.

REFERENCES: Wells Fargo Bank, N.A.; Sanwa Bank; Security Pacific National Bank (Trust Department); Citizens Commercial Trust & Savings Bank, Pasadena, California.

## LAW OFFICES OF
## JOHN J. STUMREITER
225 SOUTH LAKE AVENUE, NINTH FLOOR
PASADENA, CALIFORNIA 91101
Telephone: 818-304-0300
Fax: 818-795-6321

*General Practice with emphasis on Litigation and Bankruptcy.*

**JOHN J. STUMREITER,** born Madison, Wisconsin, March 2, 1945; admitted to bar, 1973, California; 1976, U.S. Court of Appeals, Ninth Circuit; 1988, U.S. Supreme Court. *Education:* Yale University (B.A., cum laude, 1967); Harvard Law School (J.D., cum laude, 1972; LL.M., 1973). *Member:* Pasadena, Los Angeles County (Member, Sections on: Litigation; Commercial Law and Bankruptcy) and American Bar Associations; State Bar of California. [U.S. Marine Corps, 1968-1970]

## ALAN R. TALT
Established in 1956
SUITE 710, 790 EAST COLORADO BOULEVARD
PASADENA, CALIFORNIA 91101
Telephone: 818-356-0853
Telecopier: 818-356-0731

*Estate Planning, Trust, Probate, Business and Real Property Law.*

**ALAN R. TALT,** born Stockton, California, June 17, 1929; admitted to bar, 1955, California. *Education:* University of California at Berkeley (A.B., 1951; J.D., 1954). Assistant to Revising Editor, Williston Casebook on Contract Law, Sixth Edition, 1954. Law Clerk to Honorable William Denman, Chief Judge, U.S. Court of Appeals, Ninth Circuit, 1954-1955. Director, University of California School of Law Alumni Association, 1966-1968. *Member:* The State Bar of California (Member, Taxation Section; Chairman, Committee #14, 1969-1970; Member: Committee #2, 1970-1971, Disciplinary; Law Corporation Rules Committee, 1972-1978; Southern California Chairman, 1976-1978; Referee, State Bar Court, 1979-1980; Member, Subcommittee to Propose Legislation, Inheritance and Gift Tax Committee, 1979-1981).

REFERENCE: U.S. Trust Company California.

## LAW OFFICES OF
## WILLIAM V. TARKANIAN
150 SOUTH LOS ROBLES AVENUE, SUITE 860
PASADENA, CALIFORNIA 91101
Telephone: 818-683-9373
Fax: 818-683-9787

*General Civil Trial in all State and Federal Courts. Family Law, Bankruptcy including Creditors, Debtors, Chapter 7, Chapter 11, Personal Injury.*

**WILLIAM V. TARKANIAN,** born 1963; admitted to bar, 1989, California; 1990, U.S. District Court, Central District of California. *Education:* Claremont McKenna College (B.A., 1986); Arizona State University (J.D., 1989). Legal Extern, U.S. District Judge Robert Takasugi, Summer, 1988. *Member:* Pasadena and American Bar Associations; State Bar of California.

## TAYLOR KUPFER SUMMERS & RHODES
Established in 1930
301 EAST COLORADO BOULEVARD, SUITE 407
PASADENA, CALIFORNIA 91101-1911
Telephone: 818-304-0953
Fax: 818-795-6375

*General Civil and Trial Practice in all State and Federal Courts. Estate Planning, Probate, Trust, Taxation, Business, Corporation, Securities and Real Estate Law.*

### MEMBERS OF FIRM

**STANLEY A. BARKER** (1920-1965).

**OWEN E. KUPFER** (1908-1991).

**EDWIN W. TAYLOR** (Retired).

**KENNETH O. RHODES** (Retired).

**JOHN D. TAYLOR,** born Long Beach, California, January 10, 1933; admitted to bar, 1960, California. *Education:* University of California at Berkeley (B.S., 1954); University of California at Berkeley (Boalt Hall) (J.D., 1959). Phi Beta Kappa; Order of the Coif; Phi Delta Phi; Beta Gamma Sigma. Associate Editor, California Law Review, 1958-1959. *Member:* Pasadena, Los Angeles County (Member: Committee of Continuing Education of the Bar, 1964-1968; Ethics Committee, 1966-1969; Membership-Admissions Committee, 1967-1968; Committee, Prepaid Legal Services, 1968-1972; Chairman, Probate and Trust Law Section, 1974-1975; Member, Board of Trustees, 1972-1974, 1975-1979; President, 1978-1979) and American Bar Associations; The State Bar of California (Member, Executive Committee, Conference of Delegates, 1979-1980); Legal Aid Foundation of Los Angeles (President, 1973-1974); Los Angeles County Bar Foundation (President, 1985-1986); Chancery Club (President, 1988-1989). Fellow: American College of Trust and Estate Counsel; American Bar Foundation. **PRACTICE AREAS:** Estate Planning; Probate; Trusts; Taxation.

**ROBERT C. SUMMERS,** born Los Angeles, California, November 21, 1931; admitted to bar, 1959, California. *Education:* University of Southern California (B.S., 1956; J.D., 1958). Delta Theta Phi. Member, Board of Editors, Southern California Law Review, 1957-1958. Deputy City Attorney, Los Angeles, 1959-1965. *Member:* Pasadena, Los Angeles County (Member, Committee of Continuing Education of the Bar, 1966-1969; Chairman, Credit Union Committee, 1977-1979; Member, Judiciary Committee, 1978-1980) and American Bar Associations; The State Bar of California (Member, Local Administrative Disciplinary Committee, 1969-1971). **PRACTICE AREAS:** Civil Trial; Estate Planning; Probate; General Practice.

**STEPHEN F. PETERS,** born Pasadena, California, June 15, 1940; admitted to bar, 1967, California. *Education:* Pomona College (B.A., 1961); University of California at Los Angeles (LL.B., 1966). Phi Delta Phi. Lecturer and Author, Continuing Education of the Bar, 1984-1995. *Member:* Los Angeles County (Member: Ethics Committee, 1974-1978; Executive Committee of Probate Section, 1974-1981 and 1988-1992; Clients' Security Fund Committee, 1972-1978; Chairperson, 1976-1978) and American Bar Associations; The State Bar of California (Chairperson, Client Security Fund, Southern District Committee, 1972-1976; Administrative Committee, Formal Proceeding Panel No. 3, 1973-1976). (Certified Specialist, Es-

*(This Listing Continued)*

**TAYLOR KUPFER SUMMERS & RHODES,** Pasadena—
*Continued*

tate Planning, Trust and Probate Law, The State Bar of California Board of Legal Specialization). **PRACTICE AREAS:** Estate Planning; Estate Taxes; Probate; Estate Litigation; Trust Litigation.

REFERENCE: CenFed Bank (Pasadena).

---

## THON, BECK, VANNI, PHILLIPI & NUTT

A PROFESSIONAL CORPORATION

Established in 1982

1100 EAST GREEN STREET
**PASADENA, CALIFORNIA 91106-2506**
Telephone: 818-795-8333
Fax: 818-449-9933

*Civil Trial and Appellate Practice. Personal Injury, Products Liability, Medical Malpractice and Maritime Law.*

FIRM PROFILE: *Record Jury Verdicts: Macias v. Drewry (1992), San Bernardino County record jury Verdict for the wrongful death of a child, $2,000,000.00; Proctor v. Newberg, (1994), California record verdict for loss of consortium non-paralyzed spouse, $750,000.00, total verdict $6,896,264.00.*

**WILLIAM M. THON,** born Long Beach, California, August 16, 1938; admitted to bar, 1969, California. *Education:* Pasadena City College (A.A., 1958); University of California at Los Angeles; Southwestern University; Whittier College/Beverly School of Law (LL.B., cum laude, 1968). *Member:* Pasadena Bar Association; The State Bar of California; The Association of Trial Lawyers of America; Consumer Attorneys Association of Los Angeles; Consumer Attorneys of California; Cowboy Lawyers Association (President, 1992-1993). **PRACTICE AREAS:** Personal Injury Law; Malpractice; Maritime Law.

**THOMAS P. BECK,** born Upland, California, September 8, 1951; admitted to bar, 1978, California. *Education:* Loyola University (B.B.A., 1973); Loyola Law School, Los Angeles (J.D., 1977). Lecturer: Major Insurance Carriers, "Effective Claim Adjusting Practice;" Lorman Education Services, "Auto Insurance and Accident Litigation;" Consumer Attorneys Association of Los Angeles, "Effective Use of Demonstrative Evidence;" State Bar of California, "Managing the Medium to Small Law Firm." *Member:* Pasadena (President, 1997), Los Angeles County (Member, Board of Directors and Trustee, 1996-1997) and Irish American Bar Associations; The State Bar of California; Consumer Attorneys Association of Los Angeles; Consumer Attorneys of California; American Board of Trial Advocates; Cowboy Lawyers Association. **PRACTICE AREAS:** Personal Injury Law.

**GREGORY R. VANNI,** born Los Angeles, California, October 9, 1953; admitted to bar, 1982, California. *Education:* Pasadena City College (A.A., 1976); California State Polytechnic University (B.A., magna cum laude, 1978); Loyola Law School, Los Angeles (J.D., 1982). Judge Pro Tem, Santa Anita Municipal Court, 1992—. *Member:* Pasadena Bar Association; The State Bar of California; Consumer Attorneys of California; Consumer Attorneys Association of Los Angeles; The Association of Trial Lawyers of America. **PRACTICE AREAS:** Personal Injury Law; Medical Malpractice.

**STEVEN V. PHILLIPI,** born Los Angeles, California, September 2, 1958; admitted to bar, 1983, California. *Education:* University of California at Los Angeles (A.B., cum laude, 1980); Loyola Law School, Los Angeles (J.D., cum laude, 1983). Lecturer, Continuing Education of the Bar, California. *Member:* Pasadena Bar Association; The State Bar of California; Consumer Attorneys of California; Consumer Attorneys Association of Los Angeles; Association of Trial Lawyers of America. **PRACTICE AREAS:** Personal Injury Law; Malpractice; Maritime Law.

**BRIAN C. NUTT,** born Pasadena, California, December 12, 1958; admitted to bar, 1983, California, U.S. District Court, Central District of California and U.S. Supreme Court. *Education:* University of Southern California (B.A., 1980); University of Santa Clara; Loyola Law School, Los Angeles (J.D., 1983). *Member:* Pasadena and American Bar Associations; The State Bar of California; Consumer Attorneys Association of Los Angeles; Consumer Attorneys of California; Association of Trial Lawyers of America. *LANGUAGES:* Spanish. **PRACTICE AREAS:** Personal Injury Law; Products Liability; Malpractice.

*(This Listing Continued)*

CAA1674B

---

**DAVID M. PHILLIPS,** born Logansport, Indiana, April 17, 1962; admitted to bar, 1990, California; 1991, U.S. District Court, Central District of California and U.S. Court of Appeals, Ninth Circuit. *Education:* Occidental College (B.A., 1984); Loyola Law School (J.D., 1990). Recipient, American Jurisprudence Award. Author: "Adjusters Must Decide Peril Loss," Insurance Journal, April 1994. *Member:* Pasadena County, Los Angeles County and American Bar Associations; State Bar of California; Consumer Attorneys Association of Los Angeles; Consumer Attorneys of California; Association of Trial Lawyers of America. *LANGUAGES:* Spanish. **PRACTICE AREAS:** Personal Injury; Products Liability.

### OF COUNSEL

**ANTHONY DE LOS REYES,** born New York, New York, July 21, 1942; admitted to bar, 1969, California, U.S. District Court, Central District of California and U.S. Court of Appeals, Ninth Circuit; 1975, U.S. Supreme Court. *Education:* University of Southern California and Los Angeles Pierce College (A.A., 1964); Whittier College School of Law (J.D., 1968). Member, Board of Police Commissioners, City of Los Angeles, 1991-1993, Board of Civil Service Commissioners, City of Los Angeles, 1983-1991; President, 1984-1985 and 1989-1990. Delegate, State Bar Convention, 1985. Judge Pro Tem, Los Angeles Municipal Court. Lecturer, Continuing Education of the Bar, 1977—. Arbitrator, American Arbitration Association, Los Angeles Superior Court. *Member:* Los Angeles County, Mexican American and American Bar Associations; Consumer Attorneys Association of Los Angeles; Consumer Attorneys of California; Association of Trial Lawyers of America. **PRACTICE AREAS:** Personal Injury Law; Products Liability; Medical Malpractice Law.

REFERENCE: Citizens Business Bank (Pasadena/Catalina Office).

---

## THROCKMORTON, BECKSTROM, OAKES & TOMASSIAN, LLP

CORPORATE CENTER PASADENA
225 SOUTH LAKE AVENUE, SUITE 500
**PASADENA, CALIFORNIA 91101-3005**
Telephone: 818-568-2500; 213-681-2321
Fax: 818-405-0786

*Irvine, California Office:* Suite 350, 19800 MacArthur Boulevard 92715.
Telephone: 714-955-2280. Fax: 714-467-8081.

*Construction (claims and defects), Real Estate, Insurance, Business, Commercial and Medical Legal Law. General Civil Litigation, Defense of Religious Institutions. All aspects of Trial and Appellate Work.*

### MEMBERS OF FIRM

**A. ROBERT THROCKMORTON,** born Los Angeles, California, July 14, 1933; admitted to bar, 1961, California; 1962, U.S. Claims Court. *Education:* Brigham Young University (B.A., 1958); University of Southern California (J.D., 1961). *Member:* Los Angeles County and Orange County Bar Associations; State Bar of California. (Resident, Irvine Office).

**SPENCER S. BECKSTROM,** born Cedar City, Utah, March 20, 1935; admitted to bar, 1964, California. *Education:* University of Utah (LL.B., 1963). *Member:* Los Angeles County and American (Member, Section on Corporation, Banking and Business Law) Bar Associations; State Bar of California.

**GEORGE A. OAKES,** born Los Angeles, California, February 12, 1937; admitted to bar, 1968, California. *Education:* California State University at Los Angeles (B.S., 1964); University of Southern California (J.D., 1968). Phi Alpha Delta. Retired Deputy District Attorney, Los Angeles County. *Member:* Pasadena, Orange County, Los Angeles County and American (Member, Construction Section) Bar Associations; State Bar of California; Southern California General Contractor's Association. *LANGUAGES:* Portuguese.

**SERGE TOMASSIAN,** born Marseille, France, July 3, 1956; admitted to bar, 1984, California and U.S. District Court, Eastern and Central Districts of California. *Education:* University of Southern California (B.A., 1979); Institute of International and Comparative Law, Paris, France (Certificate, 1981); McGeorge School of Law, University of the Pacific (J.D., 1983). Phi Beta Kappa; Phi Delta Phi; Pi Sigma Alpha. Member, Blackstonians. Recipient, American Jurisprudence Award for Agency. Vice-President, Executive Committee, International Moot Court Honors Board,

*(This Listing Continued)*

1983. Member of the Orange County Bar Association, Chair of Legislative Committee, 1993-1995. Judge Pro Tem and Arbitrator for Orange County Superior and Municipal Courts. Arbitrator with the American Arbitration Association and Member of the Association of General Contractors of California; Building Industry of America, Orange County Chapter; Legal Advisory Committee. *Member:* Orange County Bar Association (Chair of Construction Law, 1995; Member Sections on: Business and International Law); State Bar of California. (Resident, Irvine Office). *LANGUAGES:* French.

*DAVID ALAN HUFFAKER,* born Burbank, California, April 15, 1960; admitted to bar, 1985, California; 1986, U.S. District Court, Central District of California. *Education:* Brigham Young University (B.S., 1982; J.D., 1985). Phi Delta Phi. *Member:* Los Angeles County and American Bar Associations; State Bar of California; California Young Lawyers Association.

*ROBERT S. THROCKMORTON,* born Inglewood, California, October 10, 1967; admitted to bar, 1995, California. *Education:* Brigham Young University (B.A., 1992; J.D., 1995). *Member:* Orange County Bar Association; State Bar of California. *LANGUAGES:* Spanish. *PRACTICE AREAS:* Civil Litigation; Construction Law; Partnership Law; Elder Law.

References Available Upon Request.

---

## SCOTT C. TURNER

301 NORTH LAKE AVENUE
SUITE 700
**PASADENA, CALIFORNIA 91101**
Telephone: 818-440-1822
FAX: 818-440-9409

Carmel, California Office: P.O. Box 1671, 93921. Telephone: 408-626-5626. FAX: 408-626-5634.

*Insurance Claims and Litigation regarding Insurance Coverage of Construction Disputes.*

*SCOTT C. TURNER,* born Los Angeles, California, December 6, 1948; admitted to bar, 1978, California. *Education:* University of California at Los Angeles (B.A., cum laude, 1973); University of Southern California (J.D., 1978). Author: *Insurance Coverage of Construction Disputes,* Shepard's/McGraw-Hill, 1992; *"The Contractual Liability Exclusion and Contractual Liability Coverage,"* in The Fundamentals of Insurance Coverage, John Wiley & Sons, 1996, Chapter 17; "The Care, Custody or Control Exclusion," The Risk Report, April, 1995. "Contractual Liability Coverage for Defense Claims," Construction Risk Management Newsletter, May, 1993. *"Recession Strategy: Getting Insurers To Pay Your Fee!,"* 2 California Construction Law Reporter 28, 1992; *"The Necessity of Pursuing Insurance Coverage,"* 1 California Construction Law Reporter 42, 1991. Lecturer: Construction Superconference, New York City, April, 1992 and April, 1994, San Francisco, December, 1992; Annual Construction Insurance Conference, Nashville, November, 1993; CEB Seminar, Construction and Mechanic's Lien Law, 1987; Building Industry Credit Association, June 1993; Western Council of Construction Consumers, September, 1995; Los Angeles County Bar Association, Construction Law Subsection, November, 1991, January, 1993 and June 4, 1994; Orange County Bar Association, Construction Section, November, 1991 and December, 1992, Sacramento County Bar Association, Construction Section, January, 1993. *Member:* Los Angeles County and American Bar Associations; State Bar of California.

---

## TYSON & IPSWITCH

A Partnership of Professional Corporations

Established in 1912

SUITE 526
301 EAST COLORADO BOULEVARD
**PASADENA, CALIFORNIA 91101**
Telephone: 818-792-1156; 213-681-6894
Telecopier: 818-792-9230

*Criminal and Civil Trial Practice. Probate, Trusts and Conservatorships.*

*RICHARD P. B. TYSON, (INC.),* born Tacoma, Washington, May 23, 1919; admitted to bar, 1950, California; 1951, U.S. District Court, Southern District of California; 1972, U.S. Supreme Court. *Education:* University of Southern California (A.B., 1943); Southwestern University, Los Angeles, California (J.D., 1949). President, Pasadena Bar Association, 1975. *Member:*

*(This Listing Continued)*

ber: Pasadena Bar Association; State Bar of California (Chairman, Criminal Law and Procedure Committee, 1967-1968). *PRACTICE AREAS:* Criminal Defense.

*CANDIS TYSON IPSWITCH, (INC.),* born Pasadena, California, April 2, 1945; admitted to bar, 1976, California. *Education:* Pomona College (B.A., 1967); Claremont Graduate School (M.A., 1970); University of Southern California (J.D., 1976). *Member:* Pasadena (Trustee, 1983-1986) and Los Angeles County (Member, Probate Section) Bar Associations; State Bar of California (Member, Probate Section). (Certified Specialist, Estate Planning, Trust and Probate Law, The California Board of Legal Specialization). *PRACTICE AREAS:* Probate Litigation; Probate; Trusts; Conservatorship; Estate Planning.

REFERENCE: Citizens Commercial Trust & Savings Bank of Pasadena.

---

## LAW OFFICES OF
## JEANNETTE E. VALDIVIA

Established in 1992

301 EAST COLORADO BOULEVARD
SUITE 200
**PASADENA, CALIFORNIA 91101-1977**
Telephone: 818-395-0395
Facsimile: 818-395-0396

*Product Liability, Warranty, Insurance, Employer and Business Litigation. Health Management.*

*JEANNETTE E. VALDIVIA,* born Madera, California, August 4, 1951; admitted to bar, 1980, California and U.S. District Court, Northern and Central Districts of California; U.S. Court of Appeals, Ninth Circuit. *Education:* University of California at Irvine (B.A., 1973); University of California at Los Angeles (M.S.W., 1975); Loyola University of Los Angeles (J.D. 1978). Arbitrator, Los Angeles Superior Court, 1989—. *Member:* Los Angeles County and American Bar Association; State Bar of California; Mexican-American Bar Associations; Los Angeles Women Lawyers Association. *LANGUAGES:* Spanish. *PRACTICE AREAS:* Warranty; Product Liability; Employer; Business and Insurance Litigation.

### OF COUNSEL

*ANTOINETTE M. MARINO,* born Niagara Falls, New York, June 20, 1953; admitted to bar, 1984, California; 1992, New York, U.S. Court of Appeals, Ninth Circuit, U.S. District Court, Central, Southern and Northern Districts of California. *Education:* State University of New York at Buffalo (B.A., magna cum laude, 1978); Southwestern University School of Law (J.D., 1981). Phi Beta Kappa. *Member:* State Bar of California (Member, Health Care Sub-Committee, 1990-1992; Health Insurance Committee, 1990-1994); American Bar Association; Association of Southern Defense Counsel. *PRACTICE AREAS:* Insurance Law; Professional Liability; Health Management Care Contracting; Medical Malpractice.

REPRESENTATIVE CLIENTS: Chrysler Corp.; Toyota Motor Sales, U.S.A.; Toyota Motor Corp.; Toyota Motor Co. Ins.; Nissan North America, Inc.; Mojave Medical Group; Choice Medical Group; Valley Medical Association; Cardiothoracic Surgical Associates; St. Mary Desert Valley Hospital; Nutrition and Management Services; Lancaster Madza; Jeep/Eagle, Mitsubishi; Clutter Motors, Inc.

---

## JUDITH JORDAN WELLS

201 SOUTH LAKE AVENUE, SUITE 606
**PASADENA, CALIFORNIA 91101**
Telephone: 818-304-9444
Fax: 818-304-9753

*Family Law including Custody, Dissolution, Cohabitation Agreements, Paternity, Support and Adoption.*

*JUDITH JORDAN WELLS,* born San Francisco, California, November 24, 1943; admitted to bar, 1979, California; 1980, U.S. District Court, Central District of California. *Education:* University of California; San Fernando Valley College of Law (J.D., 1979). *Member:* Los Angeles County Bar Association (Member, Family Law Section); State Bar of California (Member, Family Law Section). (Certified Specialist, Family Law, The State Bar of California Board of Legal Specialization). *PRACTICE AREAS:* Family Law.

## ARNOLD F. WILLIAMS
PASADENA, CALIFORNIA
(See Los Angeles)

*Wills, Trusts and Estate Planning, Probate, Charitable Tax Planning and Elder Law.*

---

## WILLSEY LAW OFFICES
OWNED BY A PROFESSIONAL CORPORATION

553 S. MARENGO AVENUE
**PASADENA, CALIFORNIA 91101**
Telephone: 818-577-1086
Fax: 818-304-2959

*General Civil Practice. Taxation Law, Family Law including Dissolutions, Paternity, Cohabitation, Spousal Support, Prenuptials and District Attorney Enforcement, Real Estate, Bankruptcy.*

**BURKE W. WILLSEY,** born Middle Branch Township, Michigan, June 10, 1933; admitted to bar, 1962, District of Columbia; 1976, California. *Education:* Michigan State University (B.A., 1959); Duke University (LL.B., 1962). Phi Delta Phi. Member, Board of Editors, Duke Law Journal, 1961-1962. Attorney-Advisor, Office of Tax Legislative Counsel, U.S. Treasury Department, 1969-1972. Assistant to Commissioner, Internal Revenue Service, 1973-1975. Co-Chairman and Coordinator ALI/ABA Taxation of Mineral Resources Seminar, 1979-1984. Speaker, Southwest Legal Foundation Oil and Gas Tax Seminars, U.S.C. Tax Institute, 1982. Chairman, Special Committee on Intergovernmental Relations of Internal Revenue Service, 1981-1982. *Member:* Los Angeles County (Member: Tax Section; Executive Committee, 1981-1982) and American (Member, Committees on Natural Resources, Administrative Practice, 1974-1984, Taxation Section) Bar Associations; The District of Columbia Bar; The State Bar of California. *PRACTICE AREAS:* Taxation; General Civil; Corporate; Natural Resources.

**DANIEL P. WILLSEY (A PROFESSIONAL CORPORATION),** born Durham, North Carolina, July 9, 1960; admitted to bar, 1989, California; 1990, U.S. District Court, Central and Eastern Districts of California and U.S. Court of Appeals, Ninth Circuit. *Education:* University of California at Irvine (B.A., 1983); Pepperdine University (J.D., 1989). Recipient, American Jurisprudence Award in Real Estate Financing Transactions. *Member:* Los Angeles County Bar Association (Member, Family Law Section); State Bar of California. *PRACTICE AREAS:* Family Law; Bankruptcy; Real Estate.

REFERENCE: Sanwa Bank.

---

## WITTER AND HARPOLE
WELLS FARGO BUILDING
350 W. COLORADO BOULEVARD, SUITE 400
**PASADENA, CALIFORNIA 91105**
Telephone: 213-624-1311, 818-440-1111
FAX: 213-620-0430
Email: 102444.2117@compuserve.com

*Newport Beach, California Office:* Suite 1050, 610 Newport Center Drive. Telephone: 714-644-7600. Fax: 714-759-1014.

*Federal and State Tax. Estate Planning, Tax Litigation, Trust and Probate Law.*

### MEMBERS OF FIRM

**MYRON E. HARPOLE,** born Superior, Montana, January 1, 1927; admitted to bar, 1950, California; 1953, U.S. Tax Court; 1960, U.S. Supreme Court and U.S. Court of Military Appeals. *Education:* University of California at Berkeley (B.A., 1947); Harvard University (J.D., 1949); University of Southern California (LL.M., 1957). Phi Alpha Delta. Arbitrator, American Arbitration Association. *Member:* Los Angeles County, Orange County, American (Member, Sections on: Taxation; Real Property, Probate and Trust Law) and International Bar Associations; The State Bar of California; Chancery Club. [Col., U.S.M.C.R]. *PRACTICE AREAS:* Federal and State Tax; Estate Planning; Tax Litigation; Trust and Probate Law; Arbitrator.

**GEORGE G. WITTER** (1895-1978).

*(This Listing Continued)*

CAA1676B

---

*EUGENE HARPOLE* (1896-1987).

**DEBRA M. OLSEN,** born Van Nuys, California, September 27, 1954; admitted to bar, 1979, California and U.S. Tax Court. *Education:* University of California at Davis (B.A., 1976); Western State University (J.D., cum laude, 1979); University of Florida at Gainesville (LL.M., 1980). *Member:* State Bar of California; American Bar Association (Member, Sections on: Taxation; Real Property, Probate and Trust Law). (Resident, Newport Beach Office). *PRACTICE AREAS:* Federal and State Tax; Estate Planning; Tax Litigation; Trust and Probate Law.

### OF COUNSEL

**JAMES D. HARRIS, (A PROFESSIONAL CORPORATION),** born Denver, Colorado, March 25, 1919; admitted to bar, 1948, California; 1955, U.S. Supreme Court. *Education:* University of Kansas (B.S., 1940); Stanford University (LL.B., 1948). Phi Delta Phi. Member, 1963— and Vice Chairman, 1967-1970, Advisory Board, International and Comparative Law Center, The Southwestern Legal Foundation. *Member:* Los Angeles County (Chairman, Committee on International Transactions, 1962-1963), American and International Bar Associations; State Bar of California. [Col., U.S.M.C.R., active duty, 1941-1946]. *PRACTICE AREAS:* Federal and State Tax; Estate Planning; Tax Litigation; Trust and Probate Law.

REFERENCE: Union Bank (Newport Beach, Calif.).

---

## ZEUTZIUS & LaBRAN
Established in 1976

SUITE 823, 80 SOUTH LAKE AVENUE
**PASADENA, CALIFORNIA 91101**
Telephone: 818-795-4276; 213-681-2426
FAX: 818-405-0952

*General Civil and Trial Practice in State and Federal Courts. Criminal, Personal Injury, Corporate, Real Property, Business, Commercial, Collections, Contract and Family Law. Trials and Appeals. Probate and Estate Planning.*

FIRM PROFILE: Zeutzius & LaBran has been a partnership for over 19 years, and is one of the oldest firms in Pasadena. It is dedicated to providing quality representation to small firms and organizations, other law firms, and individuals. We can handle all aspects of litigation from the complaint through enforcement and collections. We can provide further assistance to our clients by helping them stay out of court through well structured organizations and agreements.

### MEMBERS OF FIRM

**WILLIAM J. ZEUTZIUS,** born Washington, D.C., November 29, 1934; admitted to bar, 1961, California and U.S. District Court, Southern District of California; 1971, U.S. Supreme Court; 1977, U.S. Court of Appeals, Ninth Circuit; 1980, U.S. Court of Appeals, Fifth Circuit. *Education:* Loyola University of Los Angeles (B.S., 1956); Southwestern University (J.D., 1960). Phi Alpha Delta. Deputy District Attorney, Los Angeles County, 1961-1964. *Member:* Pasadena, Los Angeles County and American Bar Associations; State Bar of California. *PRACTICE AREAS:* Criminal Law; Torts; Probate Law.

**RONALD M. LABRAN,** born New York, N.Y., May 31, 1936; admitted to bar, 1965, Virginia; 1974, California; 1976, U.S. Supreme Court. *Education:* University of Pennsylvania (B.S., Economics, 1958); George Washington University (J.D., 1963). *Member:* Pasadena, Los Angeles County and American (Member, Sections on: Business Law; Public Contract Law) Bar Associations; State Bar of California; Virginia State Bar. [Major, USMCR (Ret.)]. *PRACTICE AREAS:* Business Law; Commercial Law; Litigation; Family Law; Collections.

### ASSOCIATES

**WILLIAM J. ZEUTZIUS, JR.,** born Pasadena, California, January 23, 1963; admitted to bar, 1991, California and U.S. District Court, Central District of California. *Education:* California State University at Northridge (B.S., finance, 1987); Southwestern University (J.D., 1990). *Member:* State Bar of California. *PRACTICE AREAS:* Estate Planning; Business Transactions; Commercial Collections.

REPRESENTATIVE CLIENTS: Advanced Construction Technologies, Inc.; Rassac Heating & Ventilation; Winterbottom Brothers, Inc.; Mt. Wilson Institute; Golden Star Technology, Inc.; Allied Waste Industries; Southwestern University School of Law; Hastings College of Law.
REFERENCE: Citizens Commercial Trust and Savings Bank.

## GEORGE, GALLO & SULLIVAN
A LAW CORPORATION

**PASO ROBLES, CALIFORNIA**

(See San Luis Obispo)

*Probate, Estate Planning and Trust Administration, Business and Corporate Transactions, Taxation, Real Property and Construction, Civil Litigation.*

---

## JAMES H. KNECHT
A PROFESSIONAL CORPORATION

1224 SPRING STREET
P.O. BOX 2280
**PASO ROBLES, CALIFORNIA 93447**
Telephone: 805-238-1224
Fax: 805-238-1302

*Federal and State Taxation, Estate Planning, Probate, Trust, Real Property and Corporation Law.*

**JAMES H. KNECHT,** born Los Angeles, California, August 5, 1925; admitted to bar, 1957, California and U.S. District Court, Southern District of California; 1959, U.S. Tax Court. *Education:* University of California at Los Angeles (B.S., 1947); University of Southern California (LL.B., 1957). Associate Editor, Southern California Law Review, 1956-1957. *Member:* San Luis Obispo County and American (Member, Taxation Section; Chairman, Committee on State and Local Taxes, 1975-1977; Member: Real Property, Probate and Trust Law Section; Business Law Section) Bar Associations; State Bar of California. Life Fellow, American Bar Foundation.

REFERENCE: Bank of Santa Maria (Templeton).

---

## STEPHEN B. SEFTON

530 TENTH STREET
P.O. BOX 2962
**PASO ROBLES, CALIFORNIA 93447**
Telephone: 805-238-7178
FAX: 805-238-7254
Email: asefton@tcsn.net

*Real Property, Corporate Law, Partnerships, Business Transactions, Probate and Trusts, Commercial Collections and Construction Law.*

**STEPHEN B. SEFTON,** born Peoria, Illinois, 1948; admitted to bar, 1978, California. *Education:* California Polytechnic State University (B.S., 1970); San Joaquin College of Law (J.D., 1978). Arbitrator and Judge Pro-Tem, 1990—. *Member:* San Luis Obispo County and American Bar Associations; State Bar of California; American Trial Lawyers Association. **PRACTICE AREAS:** Real Estate; General Corporation and Partnerships; Trusts and Estates; Probate; Wills; Litigation; Collections.

REPRESENTATIVE CLIENTS: Citizens Bank; Los Padres Savings; Secondwind, Inc.; Laguna Terrace Apartments; Martin Media and Martin Outdoor Advertising; Paso Robles Chamber of Commerce; Real Property Management; Mark IV Property Management; Action Prof. Collection Agency; No. Co. Engineering; Goldenwest Dev.; All Lines Corp.; C&D Towing; Nunno Corp.; River Road Ready Mix, Inc.; Hometown Nursery; P.R. Mobile Home Pk. Hilltop Estates HOA.

---

## SANDERS, DODSON, RIVES & COX

2211 RAILROAD AVENUE
**PITTSBURG, CALIFORNIA 94565**
Telephone: 510-432-3511; 228-7300
Fax: 510-432-3516

*Personal Injury, Products Liability, Construction Defects, Eminent Domain, Wills, Probate, Tax, Estate Planning and Living Trusts.*

### MEMBERS OF FIRM

**RICHARD D. SANDERS** (Retired).

**RONALD P. RIVES,** born Tulsa, Oklahoma, October 24, 1948; admitted to bar, 1974, California. *Education:* San Jose State University (B.A., 1970); University of California at Davis (J.D., 1973). City Council Member, 1980-1985 and Mayor, 1982, 1984, City of Pittsburg. *Member:* Contra Costa Bar Association; State Bar of California; Alameda-Contra Costa

*(This Listing Continued)*

Trial Lawyers Association; California Trial Lawyers Association. **PRACTICE AREAS:** Personal Injury; Medical Malpractice; Products Liability.

---

**SCOTT E. JENNY,** born El Paso, Texas, November 18, 1962; admitted to bar, 1993, California and U.S. District Court, Northern District of California. *Education:* San Francisco State University (B.S., 1989); McGeorge School of Law, University of the Pacific (J.D., 1993). Recipient, American Jurisprudence Award, Complex Civil Litigation. Member, Traynor Honor Society. *Member:* Contra Costa County Bar Association; State Bar of California. **PRACTICE AREAS:** Eminent Domain; Inverse Condemnation; Real Estate Condemnation.

**RICHARD S. LITTORNO,** born Concord, California, May 19, 1954; admitted to bar, 1984, California; U.S. District Court, Northern District of California; 1985, U.S. Tax Court. *Education:* Saint Mary's College (B.A., 1976); Hasting College of the Law, University of California (J.D., 1979); Golden Gate University (LL.M., Tax, 1986). Member, City Council, City of Clayton. *Member:* State Bar of California. **PRACTICE AREAS:** Estate Planning; Probate; Taxation; General Business.

### OF COUNSEL

**JAMES E. COX,** born St. Louis, Missouri, September 6, 1920; admitted to bar, 1951, California; 1969, U.S. Claims Court; 1970, Hawaii; 1971, Nevada; 1972, U.S. District Court, Southern District of Texas and District of Columbia. *Education:* Stanford University (A.B., 1947; LL.B., 1950). Phi Delta Phi. Lecturer, Eminent Domain Law, Continuing Education of the Bar, 1960, 1966 and 1972. Deputy District Attorney, Alameda County, 1950-1953. Special Counsel, California Boxing Investigation, 1955-1956. Appointed Special Prosecutor, 1959. *Member:* Contra Costa County (President, 1961) and American Bar Associations; The State Bar of California. Fellow, American College of Trial Lawyers. [With USMCR, 1942-1946]. **REPORTED CASES:** Standard Oil Co. v. Oil, Chemical Etc. Intl. Union (1972) 23 Cal. App. 3d 585; People ex rel. Dept. Pub. Wks. v. Hunt (1969) 2 Cal. App. 3d 158; City of Pleasant Hill v. First Baptist Church (1969) 1 Cal. App. 3rd 384; County of Contra Costa v. Nulty (1965) 237 Cal. App. 2d 593; County of Alameda v. Meadowlark Dairy Corp. (1964) 227 Cal. App. 2d 80; Contra Costa County Flood Control & Water Conserv. Dist. v. Armstrong (1961) 193 Cal. App. 2d 206; Peak v. Richmond Elementary Sch. Dist. (1958) 161 Cal. App. 2d 366. **PRACTICE AREAS:** Condemnation Law; Eminent Domain; Inverse Condemnation; Real Estate Condemnation.

**STANLEY K. DODSON,** born Martinez, California, July 5, 1934; admitted to bar, 1960, California and U.S. District Court, Northern District of California. *Education:* University of California (A.B., 1956); Boalt Hall School of Law, University of California (J.D., 1959). Phi Delta Phi. Deputy District Attorney, Contra Costa County, 1960-1964. *Member:* Mt. Diablo (President, 1969), Contra Costa County (President, 1975) and Ame ican Bar Associations; State Bar of California (Court Referee, 1982-1988); Alameda-Contra Costa Trial Lawyers Association; Association of Trial Lawyers of America. **PRACTICE AREAS:** Personal Injury.

**DAN L. GARRETT, JR.,** born San Antonio, Texas, May 5, 1920; admitted to bar, 1949, California, U.S. District Court, Northern and Eastern Districts of California and U.S. Court of Appeals, Ninth Circuit. *Education:* University of Denver; University of Oklahoma; Hastings College of Law, University of California (LL.B., 1948). Member: Order of the Coif; Thurston Society (Founding Member). *Member:* Contra Costa County Bar Association; The State Bar of California. [With U.S. Army Air Corps, 1942-1946]. **REPORTED CASES:** Pool v. City of Oakland (1986) 42 Cal. 3d 1051; Dimarco v. Dimarco (1963) 60 Cal. 2d 387; Keating v. Superior Court (1955) 45 Cal. 2d 440; Murray v. Superior Court (1955) 44 Cal. 2d 611; Carroll v. Superior Court (1954) 42 Cal. 2d 874; Hofmann Co. v. E. I. Du Pont de Nemours & Co. (1988) 202 Cal. App. 3d 390; People v. Synanon Foundation, Inc. (1979) 88 Cal. App. 3d 304; Bedford v. Bechtell Corp. (1959) 172 Cal. App. 2d 401; Menefee v. Codman (1958) 155 Cal. App. 2d 396; Foster v. Keating (1953) 120 Cal. App. 2d 435; Ho Gate Wah v. Fong Wan (1953) 118 Cal. App. 2d 159; Kalmus v. Kalmus (1951) 103 Cal. App. 2d 405; Estate of Dougherty (1951) 102 Cal. App. 2d 785; Zellmer v. Acme Brewing Co. (9th Cir. 1950) 184 F. 2d 940. **PRACTICE AREAS:** Civil Appeals; Eminent Domain; Inverse Condemnation; Land Use Law.

## PHILLIP B. BERRY
*496 MAIN STREET*
**PLACERVILLE, CALIFORNIA 95667**
*Telephone: 916-622-2186*
*Fax: 916-622-2188*

*Probate, Estate Planning, Taxation and Related Litigation.*

**PHILLIP B. BERRY,** born Placerville, California, March 21, 1939; admitted to bar, 1964, California, U.S. Court of Appeals, Ninth Circuit and U.S. District Court, Northern District of California; 1967, U.S. District Court, Eastern District of California; 1987, U.S. Tax Court. *Education:* California State University at San Jose (B.A., 1960); Boalt Hall School of Law, University of California (J.D., 1963). Member, Board of Trustees, El Dorado County Law Library, 1981-1990. *Member:* El Dorado County (President, 1967) and Sacramento County Bar Associations; State Bar of California. (Certified Specialist, Estate Planning, Trust and Probate Law, The State Bar of California Board of Legal Specialization).

---

## COMBELLACK & DRISCOLL
*Established in 1956*
*263 MAIN STREET*
*P.O. BOX 1065*
**PLACERVILLE, CALIFORNIA 95667**
*Telephone: 916-622-2992*
*Fax: 916-622-1506*

*General Civil, Criminal and Trial Practice. Real Property, Construction, Probate, Estate Planning, Business, Personal Injury, Family, Juvenile, Collection, Government, Personnel and Commercial Law.*

**DAVID W. COMBELLACK,** born Placerville, California, July 25, 1949; admitted to bar, 1975, California. *Education:* University of California at Davis (B.A., 1971); McGeorge School of Law, University of the Pacific (J.D., 1975). Director, Marshall Hospital Board, 1981-1991; President, 1984-1987. *Member:* El Dorado County Bar Association (President, 1978); State Bar of California. **PRACTICE AREAS:** Civil Trial; Real Property; Probate; Estate Planning; Business; Collection.

**JOHN W. DRISCOLL,** born Glendale, California, November 14, 1944; admitted to bar, 1970, California. *Education:* University of Oregon and University of California at Los Angeles (A.B., 1966); University of San Diego (J.D., magna cum laude, 1969). Managing Editor, San Diego Law Review, 1968-1969. Deputy District Attorney, San Bernardino County, 1970. Deputy Public Defender, El Dorado County, 1970-1971. Assistant District Attorney, El Dorado County, 1972-1974. *Member:* El Dorado County Bar Association; State Bar of California. **PRACTICE AREAS:** Trial; Real Property; Business; Government; Personnel.

### ASSOCIATES

**ANDREW W. GEORGE,** born New Bedford, Massachusetts, October 17, 1963; admitted to bar, 1995, California. *Education:* University of Massachusetts at Dartmouth (B.S., 1986); University of Pacific McGeorge School of Law (J.D., with great distinction, 1995). Order of the Coif, Traynor Honor Society. Extern to the Honorable Christopher M. Klein, U.S. Bankruptcy Judge, Eastern District of California. *Member:* El Dorado County Bar Association; State Bar of California.

REPRESENTATIVE CLIENTS: Bill Vierra Associates, Inc.; City of Placerville; D&S Tire Exchange; The Deerwood Corp.; El Dorado County Civil Service Commission; El Dorado Disposal, Inc,.; El Dorado Pediatric Medical Group; El Dorado Savings Bank; First American Title Insurance Co.; Sam Gordon; Inter-County Title Co.; Kensco Plumbing & Electric; Michigan California Lumber Co.; Mountain Orthopedic Medical Specialties; The Mountain Retreat Co.; Pacific Window Films, Inc.; Placer County Civil Service Commission; Harold Prescott, Civil Engineer; Reliant Industries; SKI Air Conditioning, Inc.; Southern California Edison; Stancil's Toyota, Inc.; Gene Thorne and Associates, Inc., Civil Engineers and Land Surveyors; Wunschel & Small, Inc.; Placerville Travel, Inc.; Founders Title Co.; Murray, Downs & Associates, A.I.A.

---

## LAURIE, MALONEY & WHEATLEY
*Established in 1988*
*345 PLACERVILLE DRIVE*
**PLACERVILLE, CALIFORNIA 95667**
*Telephone: 916-622-7769*

Cameron Park (El Dorado County), California Office: 3420 Coach Lane, Suite 15. Telephone: 916-677-0245. Fax: 916-677-4802.

*(This Listing Continued)*

CAA1678B

---

Folsom (Sacramento County), California Office: 1004 River Rock Drive, Suite 245. Telephone: 916-988-3857.

*Land Use, Business, Real Estate, Banking, Estate Planning, Municipal, Employment and Construction Law, Personal Injury and Civil Litigation.*

(For Biographical data on all Personnel, see Professional Biographies at Cameron Park, California)

---

## OLSON, GOYETTE & ADAMS
*Established in 1977*
*THE JUDGE THOMPSON HOUSE*
*3062 CEDAR RAVINE*
**PLACERVILLE, CALIFORNIA 95667**
*Telephone: 916-622-6872*
*Fax: 916-622-4445*

*Civil and Trial Practice. Personal Injury, Probate, Real Property and Family Law, Labor and Employment and Criminal Law.*

### MEMBERS OF FIRM

**JOHN R. OLSON,** born Marengo, Iowa, June 12, 1947; admitted to bar, 1977, California. *Education:* University of Iowa (B.A., 1969); University of the Pacific, McGeorge School of the Law (J.D., 1977). Member, Traynor Society. Recipient, American Jurisprudence Award in Family Law. *Member:* El Dorado County Bar Association (President, 1980); State Bar of California. [With U.S. Air Force, 1969-1973]. **PRACTICE AREAS:** Real Estate; Personal Injury; Probate and Estate Planning; Family Law; Civil Litigation.

**PAUL Q. GOYETTE,** born Sacramento, California, November 24, 1960; admitted to bar, 1988, California. *Education:* Humboldt State University (B.S., 1983); University of San Diego School of Law (J.D., 1988). Phi Delta Phi. *Member:* Los Angeles County and El Dorado County Bar Associations. **PRACTICE AREAS:** Labor and Employment Law; Trials; Personal Injury; Criminal.

**STUART D. ADAMS,** born Boulder, Colorado, December 31, 1963; admitted to bar, 1989, California. *Education:* Washington & Lee University (B.A., 1985); University of San Diego (J.D., 1989). *Member:* Los Angeles County and Sacramento County Bar Associations. **PRACTICE AREAS:** Labor and Employment; Criminal Defense; Civil Litigation.

REPRESENTATIVE CLIENTS: Lumberman's Underwriting Alliance; Western Surety Co.; Mother Lode Realty; Pony Express Realty; El Dorado Irrigation District Employees Assn.; The Mountain Democrat Newspaper; Bozarth Logging Company; Sinclair Equipment Company, Inc.; Western Foothill Mortgage, Inc.; Western Trading Company, Inc.; Pacific Jetting International, Inc.; Davies & Assoc.; Logging Co.; Marie Callendars Restaurant-South Lake Tahoe, CA; City of Placerville Police Officers Assn.; Tahoe Tropicana Motel-South Lake Tahoe, CA; Kyburz Lodge; Volcano Telephone Co,; U.P.E. Local #1, El Dorado County Professional Firefighters Assn.; Calaveras County Deputy Sheriff's Assn.; CSLB Consultants; El Dorado Hills; Associated Fire Fighters; Cameron Park Fire Fighters; El Dorado County Employees Assn.; United Public Employees Local #1; Alpine County Employees Assoc.; Glenn County DSA; Glen County Employees; Mendocino County Employees; Sutter County Employees Assoc.; Butte County Sheriff's Assn.; City of Marysville Police Officers Assn.; Sacramento County Alliance of Law Enforcement; Yuba County Deputy Sheriffs Assan.; Yolo County Correctional Officers Assn.; California Correctional Supervisors Organization; Ponce-Nicasio Broadcasting, Inc.; El Dorado Irrigation District Employees Assn.

---

## MICHAEL A. TARLTON
*THE JUDGE THOMPSON HOUSE*
*3062 CEDAR RAVINE*
*P.O. BOX 227*
**PLACERVILLE, CALIFORNIA 95667**
*Telephone: 916-622-6870*
*FAX: 916-622-4445*

*Criminal, Personal Injury and Trial Practice.*

**MICHAEL A. TARLTON,** born Long Beach, California, December 28, 1938; admitted to bar, 1966, California. *Education:* San Diego State College (B.S., 1962); University of California, Berkeley, School of Law (Boalt Hall), LL.B., 1965). *Member:* El Dorado County Bar Association; State Bar of California (Member, Criminal Law Section); California Attorneys for Criminal Justice; Criminal Defense Lawyers of Sacramento. Panel Attorney for Legal Defense Fund for Peace Officers Research Association of California

*(This Listing Continued)*

(PORAC). (Certified Specialist, Criminal Law, The State Bar of California Board of Legal Specialization). *PRACTICE AREAS:* Criminal Trial Litigation; Major Felonies and Misdemeanors.

---

## TUSTIN & HARRISON
Established in 1980

THE JUDGE THOMPSON HOUSE
3062 CEDAR RAVINE
**PLACERVILLE, CALIFORNIA 95667**
Telephone: 916-626-4300
Fax: 916-622-4445

*General Civil and Trial Practice, Real Property, Estate Planning, Probate, Business, Municipal and Family Law.*

### MEMBERS OF FIRM

**KAREN K. TUSTIN,** born Bremerton, Washington, December 9, 1942; admitted to bar, 1970, California. *Education:* Stanford University (B.A., 1964; LL.B., 1968). Phi Beta Kappa; Order of the Coif. Member, Stanford Law Review, 1967-1968. City Attorney, Placerville, 1987-1989. Member, Placerville City Council, 1977-1987; 1990-1994. Mayor, Placerville, 1982-1984. *Member:* El Dorado County Bar Association; State Bar of California. *PRACTICE AREAS:* Estate Planning; Probate; Business; Real Property; Municipal.

**ELIZABETH L. HARRISON,** born San Bruno, California, January 6, 1957; admitted to bar, 1991, California. *Education:* California State College at San Bernardino (B.A., 1980); University of the Pacific, McGeorge School of Law (J.D., 1991). *Member:* El Dorado County and American Bar Associations; State Bar of California. (Certified Specialist, Family Law, The State Bar of California Board of Legal Specialization). *PRACTICE AREAS:* Child Custody; Interstate Child Custody; Divorce; Divorce Mediation; Post Divorce; Marital Property Distribution and Settlements; Paternity.

### OF COUNSEL
**J. MARK NIELSEN**

---

## ATKINSON, ANDELSON, LOYA, RUUD & ROMO
A PROFESSIONAL CORPORATION

THE ATRIUM
5776 STONERIDGE MALL ROAD
SUITE 200
**PLEASANTON, CALIFORNIA 94588**
Telephone: 510-227-9200
Telecopier: 510-227-9202
Email: AALRR@KINCYB.COM
Email: Info@aalrr.com
URL: http://aalrr.com

Cerritos, California Office: 13304 East Alondra Boulevard. Telephone: 310-404-4444; 714-826-5480. Telecopier: 310-404-8905.

San Bernardino, California Office: 348 West Hospitality Lane, Suite 202. Telephone: 909-888-4165. Telecopier: 909-884-4118.

*Labor Relations representing Management. School and Construction Law. Civil Litigation.*

(For Biographical data on all Personnel, see Professional Biographies at Cerritos, California)

---

## CASTLEMAN, McFALONE & O'BLENNIS
5870 STONERIDGE MALL ROAD, SUITE 207
**PLEASANTON, CALIFORNIA 94588**
Telephone: 510-463-2221
Fax: 510-463-0328
Email: castlelaw.com@counsel.com

*General Civil and Trial Practice in State and Federal Courts. Insurance Defense Litigation, Personal Injury, Defense of Public Entities, Title Insurance, Construction Litigation, Business Litigation, Estate Planning and Estate Taxation, Probate, Corporate, Securities, Business, Real Property, Landslide and Subsidence, Administrative, Municipal and Taxation Law, Tax Litigation, Bankruptcy, Creditors, Defense of Employment Discrimination Cases.*

(This Listing Continued)

*FIRM PROFILE: We believe that our clients are best served when we can assist them in anticipating legal problems. To that end, we practice preventive law by gaining a knowledge of our clients' needs, and by educating and counseling our clients on current developments in the law which may affect them.*

*When disputes do arise, our goal is to avoid costly litigation where possible. Thus, we encourage the use of arbitration and other out-of-court methods of resolving disputes. However, when necessary, we will aggressively represent our clients in the courtroom, using our skills, experience and resources.*

### MEMBERS OF FIRM

**M. LORIN CASTLEMAN,** born Riverside, California, April 15, 1939; admitted to bar, 1968, California; 1978, U.S. Tax Court. *Education:* University of California, Berkeley (B.A., 1964); Syracuse University (J.D., 1967). Phi Alpha Delta. *Member:* Alameda County, Eastern Alameda County, American (Member, Sections of: Corporation, Banking and Business Law; Taxation) and International Bar Associations; State Bar of California. (Certified Specialist, Taxation Law, The State Bar of California Board of Legal Specialization). *REPORTED CASES:* Ramirez v. Redevelopment Agency, 4 Cal. App. 3d 397 (1990). *PRACTICE AREAS:* Taxation Law; Corporate Law; Real Property Law; Business Litigation; Estate Planning; Charitable Entities; Trusts.

**RAYMOND B. McFALONE,** born Toronto, Canada, April 2, 1954; admitted to bar, 1982, California. *Education:* San Jose State University (B.A., 1977); Western State University (J.D., 1981). *Member:* Alameda and Eastern Alameda County Bar Associations; State Bar of California. *PRACTICE AREAS:* Construction Law; Insurance Defense Law; Real Estate Law; Probate; Personal Injury; Business Litigation; Labor Law.

**M. KATHLEEN O'BLENNIS,** born East St. Louis, Illinois, May 20, 1951; admitted to bar, 1976, Missouri; 1984, New Jersey; 1989, California and U.S. Tax Court. *Education:* St. Louis University (A.B., 1972; J.D., 1976). *Member:* Eastern Alameda County (Past President) and Alameda County Bar Associations; State Bar of California; State Bar of Missouri. *REPORTED CASES:* Evans v. Paye, 32 Cal. App. 4th 265, 37 Cal. Rptr. 2d 915 (1995). *PRACTICE AREAS:* Estate Planning Law; Tax Law; Business Transaction and Business Litigation. *Email:* koxblenn@counsel.com

### ASSOCIATES

**BARBARA JANE SAVERY,** born Oakland, California, October 27, 1946; admitted to bar, 1988, California. *Education:* Stanford University (B.A., 1968; B.A., 1970); University of California at Berkeley; Golden Gate University (J.D., 1988). Articles Editor, Law Review, 1987-1988; Writer Law Review, 1986-1987. Author: "Eminent Domain by Regulation: Developing a Unified Field Theory for the Regulatory Taking," Golden Gate University Law Review, Vol. 17, No. 2 Summer, 1987. Fulbright Fellowship to Brazil, 1971-1972. *Member:* Eastern Alameda County and Alameda County (Member, Real Estate Subsection, 1993—) Bar Associations; State Bar of California (Member Subsections: Real Property, 1990—; Common Interest Law, 1992). *LANGUAGES:* Portuguese and German. *PRACTICE AREAS:* Common Interest Community Law; Real Property Law.

**TERRENCE P. MURPHEY,** born Chicago, Illinois, April 11, 1954; admitted to bar, 1991, California. *Education:* Michigan State University (B.S., with honors, 1976); Hastings College of the Law University of California (J.D., 1990). Member, 1988-1989, and Associate Articles Editor, 1989-1990, Hastings Journal of Communications and Entertainment Law, COMM/ENT. *Member:* Alameda County and Eastern Alameda County Bar Associations; State Bar of California. *REPORTED CASES:* Evans v. Paye, 32 Cal. App. 4th 265, 37 Cal. Rptr. 2d 915 (1995). *PRACTICE AREAS:* Civil Litigation; Business Law; Administrative Law; Personal Injury; Taxation Law; Business Litigation; Enforcing Judgments.

**CATHERINE A. NAUMANN,** born San Antonio, Texas, April 16, 1964; admitted to bar, 1990, California; 1994, Texas. *Education:* Mills College (B.A., 1986); Tulane University of Louisiana (J.D., 1990). Phi Delta Phi. *Member:* Bar Association of San Francisco; Eastern Alameda County Bar Association; The State Bar of California; State Bar of Texas; American Bar Association. *PRACTICE AREAS:* Trademarks; Copyrights; Insurance; Business Transaction and Litigation; Tax Law; Civil and Insurance Litigation.

REPRESENTATIVE CLIENTS: Mervyn's; Spring Air Mattress Co., Inc.; Seaway Semiconductor; Taitec Instruments USA, Inc.; Blue Leaf Design, Inc.; Family Care, Inc.; Lombard Plaza Partners, LP; Brookwater Design; Crown Business System; Gaton Moving & Storage; Golden Gate Air Freight, Inc.; Foundation Republic Financial Services, Inc.; Hacienda Appraisal Services; Horizon U.S.A. Data Services, Inc.; OHM Corporation; Olympia Restoration; Park Place Appraisal Service; St. Rose Hospital; United Management Corporation; Western Pioneer Insurance Company; Corrie Development Corporation.
REFERENCE: Wells Fargo Bank (Hayward Main).

## CLAPP, MORONEY, BELLAGAMBA, DAVIS AND VUCINICH

6140 STONERIDGE MALL ROAD
SUITE 545
**PLEASANTON, CALIFORNIA 94588**
Telephone: 510-734-0990
Fax: 510-734-0888

*Menlo Park, California Office:* 4400 Bohannon Drive, Suite 100. Telephone: 415-327-1300. Fax: 415-327-3707.

*San Francisco, California Office:* One Sansome Street, Suite 1900. Telephone: 415-398-6045. Fax: 425-327-3707

General Insurance Law and Civil Trial Practice. Casualty Insurance (Automobile and Fire), Aviation, Professional Liability, Medical and Legal Malpractice Law. Real Estate and Insurance Liability (Agent Errors and Omissions), Construction Litigation, Environmental and Toxic Tort, Products Liability Law, Employment Discrimination, Wrongful Termination, Discrimination Law (Sex and Housing) Insurance Coverage, Declaratory Relief and Bad Faith Litigation.

### MEMBER OF FIRM

**ROBERT A. BELLAGAMBA,** born San Francisco, California, June 24, 1947; admitted to bar, 1973, California. *Education:* University of California at Davis (B.A., 1969); University of San Francisco (J.D., 1973). Member: McAuliffe Law Honor Society; Faculty, Hastings Civil College of Advocacy, 1982. *Member:* San Mateo County, Santa Clara County and American Bar Associations; State Bar of California; Association of Defense Counsel (Member, Board of Directors, 1989-1990); Defense Research and Trial Lawyers Association; International Association of Insurance Counsel.

**CHRISTOPHER J. BEEMAN,** born Chicago, Illinois, July 29, 1960; admitted to bar, 1985, California. *Education:* University of Notre Dame (B.A., magna cum laude, 1982); University of Santa Clara (J.D., 1985). *Member:* State Bar of California.

**FRANK J. PERRETTA,** born New York, November 30, 1961; admitted to bar, 1986, California. *Education:* University of California at Davis (B.A., with honors, 1983); University of Santa Clara (J.D., 1986). Omicron Delta Epsilon (President, 1982-1983). *Member:* Santa Clara County Bar Association; State Bar of California.

**MARK T. GUERRA,** born Los Angeles, California, June 11, 1958; admitted to bar, 1983, California. *Education:* University of California at Los Angeles (B.A., 1980); University of San Francisco (J.D., 1983).

### ASSOCIATES

| | |
|---|---|
| Virginia L. Vasquez | James E. Hart, III |
| Andrew S. Miller | Sandra Kay Bean |
| John F. Doyle | Adrienne E. Dennis |
| Mark L. Dawson | James William Doran |

REPRESENTATIVE CLIENTS: Central Mutual Insurance Co.; CIGNA; California Casualty Indemnity Exchange; Farmers Insurance Group; American States Insurance Co.; Interstate National Corp.; State Farm Mutual Automobile Insurance Co.; The Travelers Insurance Co.; Continental National American Group; Kemper Group; Insurance Company of the West; Crawford & Co.; Albertsons, Inc.; American Hardware Mutual; Chubb Group; Grain Dealers Mutual; Republic Claims Services; U-Haul International; Underwriters Adjusting Co.; Argonaut Ins., Co.; Firemens Fund Insurance Co.; State Farm Fire & Casualty Co.; Wausau Ins. Co.; Black & Bland Ins. Adj.; Allianz Insurance Co.; American Star Insurance Co.; Grange Insurance; Gulf Insurance Group; Hartford Insurance Group; Industrial Indemnity; Liberty Mutual Insurance; Orion Group; Residence Mutual; Truck Insurance Exchange; Universal Underwriters Insurance Co.; Western Mutual Insurance Co.; Walgreens.

(For complete biographical data on all personnel, see Professional Biographies at Menlo Park, California)

## BURKE M. CRITCHFIELD

5510 SUNOL BOULEVARD, SUITE 5
**PLEASANTON, CALIFORNIA 94566**
Telephone: 510-484-3344
FAX: 510-484-3606

Real Estate, Business, Estate Planning and Probate Law.

**BURKE M. CRITCHFIELD,** born Deadwood, South Dakota, June 28, 1930; admitted to bar, 1961, California. *Education:* George Washington University (A.A., 1951); Macalester College (B.A., 1952); University of

*(This Listing Continued)*

South Dakota (J.D., 1960). President, Western Bar Conference, 1992-1993. *Member:* Alameda County (Member, Board of Directors, 1973-1977; President, 1979), Southern Alameda County, Livermore-Amador Valley (President, 1972-1973) and American (Delegate, 1985-1987, 1994—; Member, Standing Committee on Discipline, 1986-1992) Bar Associations; The State Bar of California (Member, Board of Governors, 1982-1985; President, 1984-1985); Alameda-Contra Costa Trial Lawyers Association (Member, Board of Governors, 1971-1977); Alameda County Law Library (Member, Board of Trustees, 1963—; President, 1970-1972, 1979; Chairman, Building Committee, 1995—). [Special Agent, Counter Intelligence Corp., U.S. Army, 1953-1957]

## EFREMSKY & NAGEL

Established in 1992

5776 STONERIDGE MALL ROAD, SUITE 360
**PLEASANTON, CALIFORNIA 94588**
Telephone: 510-463-0505
Fax: 510-463-8064

Civil Litigation, Creditor's Rights, Bankruptcy and Commercial Law.

**ROGER L. EFREMSKY,** born Castro Valley, California, April 3, 1956; admitted to bar, 1983, California and U.S. District Court, Northern and Eastern Districts of California. *Education:* Menlo College (B.S., magna cum laude, 1978); University of Santa Clara (J.D., 1983); University of Capetown School of Law, Republic of South Africa; Hastings School of Law Advocacy Program (1989). *Member:* Alameda County, Santa Clara County and American Bar Associations; State Bar of California. **PRACTICE AREAS:** Civil Litigation; Creditor's Rights; Bankruptcy; Commercial Law.

**AUSTIN P. NAGEL,** born Berkeley, California, June 20, 1957; admitted to bar, 1985, California and U.S. District Court, Northern and Eastern Districts of California. *Education:* University of California at Berkeley (B.A., 1980); Golden Gate University (J.D., 1983). *Member:* Alameda County Bar Association; State Bar of California. **PRACTICE AREAS:** Civil Litigation; Creditor's Rights; Bankruptcy; Commercial Law.

REPRESENTATIVE CLIENTS: Ford Motor Credit Co.; Toyota Motor Credit Corp.; David Burchard, Chapter 13 Standing Trustee, San Francisco Region; U.S. Rentals; Nations Bank; Primus Automotive Financial Services; Waste Management Co.

## GEOFFREY C. ETNIRE

Established in 1981

4900 HOPYARD ROAD, SUITE 260
**PLEASANTON, CALIFORNIA 94588**
Telephone: 510-734-9950
Fax: 510-734-9170
Email: etnire@ricochet.net

Real Estate Transactions, Development and Land Use Issues.

**GEOFFREY C. ETNIRE,** born Akron, Ohio, April 8, 1948; admitted to bar, 1974, California and U.S. Court of Appeals, Ninth Circuit. *Education:* University of Pennsylvania (B.S. in Economics, summa cum laude, 1970); University of London, London, England; Stanford University (J.D., 1973). Director, Mission Valley Bancorp, 1985-1989. President, Pleasanton Chamber of Commerce, 1987. President, Valley Volunteer Center, 1991. *Member:* East Alameda County, Alameda County and Contra Costa County Bar Associations; State Bar of California (Member, Sections on: Real Property; Real Property Taxation).

REPRESENTATIVE CLIENTS: Colliers Parrish Commercial Real Estate; RMC-Lone Star.
REFERENCE: Bank of America.

## HALLGRIMSON McNICHOLS McCANN LLP

Established in 1991

5000 HOPYARD ROAD, SUITE 400
**PLEASANTON, CALIFORNIA 94588**
Telephone: 510-460-3700
Fax: 510-460-0969

*San Jose, California Office:* 40 S. Market Street, Suite 700. Telephone: 408-275-6600. Facsimile: 408-275-0315. E-Mail: HMMSJ@aol.com

*(This Listing Continued)*

Civil Trial Practice, Corporate and Business Law, Real Property, Land Use and Development, Environmental Law, Insurance Law, Tort Litigation, Construction Litigation, Employment Law, Estate Planning, Federal and State Taxation, Probate and Entertainment Law.

FIRM PROFILE: The attorneys at Hallgrimson McNichols McCann have been a part of the Northern California legal community for more than 25 years. With offices in downtown San Jose and in Pleasanton, Hallgrimson McNichols McCann is strategically available to service the major growth corridors of Santa Clara, Alameda, Contra Costa and San Joaquin Counties.

### MEMBERS OF FIRM

**STEPHEN L. R. MCNICHOLS, JR.,** born Denver, Colorado, June 5, 1943; admitted to bar, 1968, Colorado; 1969, California. *Education:* Pomona College (B.A., 1965); Boalt Hall School of Law, University of California (J.D., 1968). Author: "Extra-Record Evidence in CEQA Actions," Contra Costa Lawyer, July 1995. Listed: Who's Who in American Law; Who's Who in California. Instructor: NAtional Institute for Trial Advocacy; University of Phoenix. Former Deputy District Attorney, San Luis Obispo County. Chief of Consumer Fraud Division, Former Planning Commissioner and Chairman, City of Morro Bay. Judge Pro Tem, Superior and Municipal Courts. Court Appointed Commissioner, Mediator, Arbitrator and Discovery Referee. *Member:* Contra Costa County, Alameda County (Former Director), Southern Alameda County (Former Director), Colorado and American (Member, Litigation Section) Bar Associations; State Bar of California (Former Member, Committee on Administration of Justice); Consumer Attorney of California; The Association of Trial Lawyers of America; Danville-Sycamore Valley Rotary Club (Former Director); American Arbitration Association (Member, Panel on Commercial Arbitration). *PRACTICE AREAS:* Business; Commercial; Real Estate; Tort Litigation; Dispute Resolution.

**STEVEN L. HALLGRIMSON,** born San Francisco, California, March 4, 1942; admitted to bar, 1969, California. *Education:* Claremont Men's College (B.A., 1964); Boalt Hall School of Law, University of California (J.D., 1968). Certified Public Accountant, California, 1971. President, Santa Clara County Law Library Trustees, 1975—. *Member:* Santa Clara County Bar Association (Treasurer, 1974; Trustee, 1974); The State Bar of California; California Society of Certified Public Accountants. *PRACTICE AREAS:* Business and Real Estate Transactions.

**WILLIAM D. MCCANN,** born Los Angeles, California, January 9, 1947; admitted to bar, 1972, California; registered to practice before U.S. Patent and Trademark Office. *Education:* University of California at Berkeley (A.B., with honors, 1968); Hastings College of the Law, University of California (J.D., 1971). Phi Alpha Delta. Director, San Ramon Valley YMCA, 1987—. *Member:* Bar Association of San Francisco, Contra Costa County and Alameda County Bar Associations; State Bar of California; American Immigration Lawyers Association; California Trial Lawyers Association. *LANGUAGES:* Spanish and French. *PRACTICE AREAS:* Civil Litigation; Personal Injury; International Law.

**KEVIN W. WHEELWRIGHT,** born Ogden, Utah, October 4, 1951; admitted to bar, 1976, California. *Education:* Weber State College (B.S., 1973); University of San Francisco (J.D., 1976). Staff Member, San Francisco Law Review, 1975-1976. Co-Author: "Dissolution," in Advising California Partnerships, California C.E.B. 1988. Officer/Director: Member, City of San Ramon Task Force Re: EMF TransMission, 1991,1993; American Cancer Society, Contra Costa County Unit, 1987-1989; San Ramon Valley Education Foundation, 1985-1988; Pleasanton Rotary, 1995—; CATV Channel 30, 1995—. *Member:* Eastern Alameda County (Officer/-Director, 1995—), Alameda County and Contra Costa County Bar Associations; State Bar of California. *PRACTICE AREAS:* Employment and Real Estate Litigation; General Business.

**NICKOLAS P. TOOLIATOS, II,** born San Francisco, California, December 19, 1957; admitted to bar, 1983, California; 1984, U.S. Tax Court. *Education:* University of Santa Clara (B.S., cum laude, 1980; J.D., 1983). Distinguished Military Graduate. Senior Tax Associate, Touche, Ross & Co., 1983-1985. Who's Who in American Law, 1991. Director, 1990-1993; Past President, 1992, Tri-Valley Business and Estate Planning Council. *Member:* Alameda County and Santa Clara County Bar Associations; State Bar of California; Reserve Officers Association of the U.S. [Major, Infantry, USAR, 1980—]. (Certified Specialist, Estate Planning, Trust and Probate Law, The State Bar of California Board of Legal Specialization). *PRACTICE AREAS:* Business Transactions; Tax; Probate; Estate Planning.

**PHILLIP G. VERMONT,** born Oakland, California, September 1, 1961; admitted to bar, 1987, California. *Education:* University of California

*(This Listing Continued)*

at Davis (B.A., 1983); Santa Clara University (J.D., 1987). *LANGUAGES:* French. *PRACTICE AREAS:* Products Liability; Personal Injury Litigation; Real Estate Litigation; Business Litigation; Insurance Bad Faith.

**MICHAEL E. KYLE,** born Cincinnati, Ohio, April 22, 1942; admitted to bar, 1971, California. *Education:* University of California, Davis (B.A., 1966); Davis School of Law (J.D., 1969). *Member:* Alameda County (Member, Board of Directors, 1993-1994; Member, Executive Committee, Trial Practice Section; Member, East Bay Bench Book Committee, 1994) and Eastern Alameda County (Member, Board of Directors; President, 1981; Eastern Alameda County Bar Association Representative, Alameda County Court Judicial Liaison Committee) Bar Associations; State Bar of California; Dublin Rotary Club (President, 1982-1983); Alameda Contra Costa Diabetes Association (Member, Board of Directors, 1987-1988); Alameda County 100 Club; Tri-Valley Business and Estate Planning Council. *PRACTICE AREAS:* Civil Litigation; Construction Law; Business and Real Estate Transactions; Public Entities; Estate Planning. *Email:* Michael_E_Kyle@msn.com

**PHIL SASSO,** born Waukesha, Wisconsin, February 6, 1956; admitted to bar, 1984, Wisconsin and California. *Education:* University of Wisconsin (B.B.A., 1979; J.D., 1984). Licensed Certified Public Accountant, 1982. *Member:* State Bar of California (Member, Real Property Law Section). *PRACTICE AREAS:* Real Estate Acquisitions and Sales; Leasing; Development; Land Use. *Email:* pdsasso@pacbell.com

### ASSOCIATES

**SHANNON WALLER,** born Cleveland, Ohio, April 18, 1969; admitted to bar, 1994, California. *Education:* University of California at Santa Barbara (B.A., 1991); Hastings College of the Law, University of California (J.D., 1994). *PRACTICE AREAS:* Corporate Law; Employment Law.

**LESLIE A. BAXTER,** born Fresno, California, 1957; admitted to bar, 1990, California. *Education:* University of California at Berkeley (B.A., 1982); California State University (M.P.A., 1984); Hastings College of the Law, University of California (J.D., 1990). Member, Constitutional Law Quarterly, Hastings College of the Law, 1988-1989. Teaching Assistant, Legal Writing and Research, 1989-1990. Judicial Extern: Associate Justice David N. Eagleson, California Supreme Court, 1988; U.S. Senior Judge, Honorable Joseph T. Sneed, Ninth U.S. Circuit Court of Appeals, 1990. *Member:* State Bar of California. *PRACTICE AREAS:* Real Estate; Land Use; Environmental Law.

**JAMES R. MOORE,** born Evansville, Indiana, May 21, 1940; admitted to bar, 1969, California; 1973, U.S. Tax Court; 1983, Hawaii; U.S. District Court, Northern, Central and Southern Districts of California; U.S. District Court, District of Hawaii; U.S. Court of Appeals, Ninth Circuit; U.S. Claims Court. *Education:* California State College at Los Angeles (A.B., 1965); Boalt Hall School of Law, University of California (J.D., 1968). *Member:* Bar Association of San Francisco; State Bar of California; Hawaii State and American Bar Associations; San Francisco Trial Lawyers Association; California Trial Lawyers Association. *PRACTICE AREAS:* Civil Litigation.

REPRESENTATIVE CLIENTS: American Honda; Amp Printing, Inc.; Associated Process Controls; Bradshaw, Inc.-North; Brentwood Holding Co.; Cal Cap Realty; California Pie Co., Inc.; Castlewood Country Club; Classified Records; Combee Construction Company, Inc.; Community First National Bank; Christy Concrete; Danville-San Ramon Medical Center; Drivex, Inc.; East Bay BMW, Inc.; Etch Tech, Inc.; Gold Star Technology; HG Automotive; Lani Construction, Inc.; Kaufman & Broad (Northern California Division); Kleinfelder & Assoc.; The Lexington Insurance Co.; Livermore Area Recreation and Park District; Merrill-Lynch-Hubbard, Inc.; Music Quest Studios; Odd Fellows Home of California; R.J. Builders; San Ramon Valley Orthopedic Group; San Ramon Valley Imaging Assoc., Inc.; Stoneson Development Corp.; State Farm Insurance Co.; Tritek Construction; Ximage Corp.

## J. MICHAEL HOSTERMAN
*555 PETERS AVENUE, SUITE 115*
**PLEASANTON, CALIFORNIA 94566**
Telephone: 510-426-8000
Fax: 510-426-8001

*Personal Injury, Products Liability, Wrongful Death, Insurance and Civil Litigation.*

**J. MICHAEL HOSTERMAN,** born Kansas City, Missouri, 1951; admitted to bar, 1977, California. *Education:* University of California, Los Angeles; University of California, Berkeley (B.A., 1973); University of Santa Clara (J.D., cum laude, 1977). Real Estate Broker, California,

*(This Listing Continued)*

### J. MICHAEL HOSTERMAN, Pleasanton—Continued

1982—. Member, 1980-1994 and President, 1990-1991, San Jose-West Valley Rotary; Pleasanton Rotary, 1994—. *Member:* Eastern Alameda County Bar Association; State Bar of California.

## JG, P.C., BUSINESS & CORPORATE LAW

*5000 HOPYARD ROAD, SUITE 400*
**PLEASANTON, CALIFORNIA 94588**
Telephone: 510-463-9600
Facsimile: 510-463-9644
Email: GHTD08A@PRODIGY.COM

Business. Business Transactions and Formations. Corporations. Mergers and Acquisitions, Corporate, Partnership and Limited Liability Company Law. Business Contracts and Leases. Intellectual Property and Unfair Competition. Computers and Software.

FIRM PROFILE: *General Counsel for Start-ups and Emerging Growth Companies; Providing Businesses and Their Principals with Quality, Cost-effective Legal Representation and Superior Personal Service.*

**JAMES H. GULSETH,** born Devils Lake, North Dakota; admitted to bar, 1974, California; U.S. District Court, Northern District of California; U.S. Court of Appeals, Ninth Circuit. *Education:* University of California, Berkeley (A.B., 1971); University of California, Hastings College of Law (J.D., 1974). Phi Eta Sigma; Alpha Zeta. Licensed Real Estate Broker, California, 1981—. Member: Tri-Valley Business & Estate Planning Counsel; Pleasanton Partnerships in Education; Pleasanton Chamber of Commerce; President, Rotary Club of Pleasanton, 1994-1995. *Member:* Alameda County and Eastern Alameda County (Director, 1989-1993, President, 1992; Member, 1988-1995, Chairman, 1991, Lawyer Referral Service Governing Committee); State Bar of California (Member, Corporations, Business Transactions, Securities, Tax and Intellectual Property Sections). *REPORTED CASES:* PACKER TRANSPORATION CO. v. USA, 596 F. 2d 891.; PLATTS v. SACRAMENTO NORTHERN RAILWAY, 1988, Court of Appeal, First District, 253 Cal.Rptr 269; 205 Cal.App.3rd 1025. *PRACTICE AREAS:* Business Law; Corporations; Mergers and Acquisitions; Partnerships; Intellectual Property.

### LEGAL SUPPORT PERSONNEL

**JENNIFER GRAY,** born Chico, California. *Education:* University of California at Davis. (Paralegal).

REPRESENTATIVE CLIENTS: Aegis Fire Systems Technology, Inc.; AGTEK Development Co., Inc.; Alcosta Pharmacy Associates, Inc.; American Speedy Printing Centers-Golden Gate; Cal Tech Controls, Inc.; CGC/Encore, Inc.; CN Networks, Inc.; Daily Mortgage Facts, Inc.; Health Sonics Corporation; Infomatrix; Integrated Printing Systems, Inc.; Kelly International, Ltd.; Livermore Valley Tennis Club, Ltd.; Materials Data, Inc.; Neighborhood Brewing Company, Inc.; Northstar Communications, Inc.; NSD, Inc.; Oasis Solutions, Inc.; Quality Partners; Topcon America Corporation; Topcon Laser Systems, Inc.; Touche', Inc.
REFERENCE: Wells Fargo Bank.

## JAMES J. PHILLIPS

*A PROFESSIONAL CORPORATION*
*4900 HOPYARD ROAD, SUITE 260*
**PLEASANTON, CALIFORNIA 94588**
Telephone: 510-463-1980
Fax: 510-463-8656

Hayward, California Office: 1331 B Street, Suite 4. Telephone: 510-886-2120.

*Estate Planning, Trust and Probate Law.*

**JAMES J. PHILLIPS,** born Oakland, California, April 16, 1954; admitted to bar, 1980, California and U.S. Court of Appeals, Ninth Circuit. *Education:* University of California at Davis (B.S., magna cum laude, 1976); Hastings College of Law (J.D., 1980); Golden Gate University School of Law (LL.M. in Taxation, 1988). First Place, David E. Snodgrass Moot Court Competition, 1979. Author of estate planning articles for the California Continuing Education of the Bar. *Member:* Eastern Alameda County (President, 1990) and Alameda County Bar Associations; State Bar of California (Member, Executive Committee, Section on Estate Planning, Trust and Probate Law, 1991-1992). (Certified Specialist, Estate Planning, Trust and Probate Law, The State Bar of California Board of Legal Specialization).

REFERENCES: Community First National Bank; Wells Fargo Bank; Com Core Realty; Hometown Brokers.

## RIFKIND & FUERCH

*A PROFESSIONAL CORPORATION*
**PLEASANTON, CALIFORNIA**
(See Hayward)

*General Civil and Trial Practice. Insurance, Insurance Defense, Real Estate, Transportation Law, Fire Insurance, Products Liability, Automobile, Professional Liability, Landslide and Subsidence, Construction, Business, Municipal and Education Law.*

## LAW OFFICES OF JAMES G. SCHWARTZ

*SUITE 401, 7901 STONERIDGE DRIVE*
**PLEASANTON, CALIFORNIA 94588**
Telephone: 510-463-1073
Fax: 510-463-2937

*Creditors Bankruptcy Rights, Business, Commercial Finance and Real Estate and Commercial Business Litigation. Estate Planning and Probate Law, Collections.*

**JAMES G. SCHWARTZ,** born Oakland, California, August 3, 1948; admitted to bar, 1976, California and U.S. District Court, Northern District of California; 1980, U.S. District Court, Eastern District of California; 1982, U.S. District Court, Central District of California; 1983, U.S. District Court, Southern District of California. *Education:* California State University at San Jose (B.S., 1971); University of the Pacific, McGeorge School of Law (J.D., 1975). Phi Alpha Delta. Judge Pro Tempore, Alameda County, 1977—. U.S. Bankruptcy Trustee, 1990—. *Member:* Livermore-Amador Valley, Alameda County and American Bar Associations; State Bar of California; National Association of Retail Collection Attorneys; National Association of Chapter Thirteen Trustees; American Bankruptcy Institute; Bay Area Bankruptcy Forum. *PRACTICE AREAS:* Creditor's Rights Law; Bankruptcy Law; Litigation; Collections; Business and Real Estate.

### ASSOCIATES

**EDWARD RUSSELL,** born Honolulu, Hawaii, January 16, 1959; admitted to bar, 1989, Washington; 1992, California. *Education:* University of Washington (B.A., Econ. 1981; B.A., Journalism, 1981); University of Puget Sound (J.D., 1984). *Member:* Alameda, Contra Costa County and Washington State Bar Associations; State Bar of California; National Association of Retail Collection Attorneys; National Association of Chapter Thirteen Trustees. *PRACTICE AREAS:* Creditor's Rights and Collection.

**JAMES R. LANGFORD, III,** born Santa Monica, California, April 10, 1954; admitted to bar, 1981, California. *Education:* Stanford University (B.A., 1976); University of California at Los Angeles (J.D., 1980). *Member:* Contra Costa, Alameda and Eastern Alameda County and American (Member, Section on Litigation) Bar Associations; State Bar of California. *PRACTICE AREAS:* Commercial Real Estate; Civil Litigation; Landlord-Tenant Law; Commercial Leasing; Real Estate Brokers and Agents Liability.

REPRESENTATIVE CLIENTS: Sears Roebuck and Co.; Chrysler Credit Corp.; World Savings; Beneficial Mortgage Corp.; Sam Clar Office Furniture; Gilbert-Clarke Stationers; McMahan's Furniture; Lawrence Livermore Laboratory Recreation Association; RMA Partners L.P.; National Dollar Store; Federal Financial Systems, Inc.; Global Financial Services, Inc.; VW Credit, Inc.

## DORIS HALE SLATER

*SUITE 501, 7901 STONERIDGE DRIVE*
**PLEASANTON, CALIFORNIA 94588**
Telephone: 510-463-1818
Fax: 510-847-3079

*General Civil and Trial Practice. Family, Business, Real Estate, Bankruptcy, Personal Injury, Estate Planning and Probate Law.*

**DORIS HALE SLATER,** born Germany, March 19, 1946; admitted to bar, 1979, California and U.S. District Court, Northern District of California; 1981, U.S. District Court, Eastern District of California; 1991, U.S.

*(This Listing Continued)*

Supreme Court. *Education:* Hayward State University (B.A., 1967; M.A., 1974); University of Santa Clara (J.D., 1979). *Member:* Alameda County (Director, 1988-1991), Livermore-Amador Valley (President, 1986-1987) and American Bar Associations; State Bar of California; California Trial Lawyers; California Women Lawyers (Member, Board of Governors, 1990-1993; Treasurer, 1992-1993); Alameda-Contra Costa Trial Lawyers Association. (Certified Specialist, Family Law, California Board of Specialization). *LANGUAGES:* German.

## STALEY, JOBSON & WETHERELL

A PROFESSIONAL CORPORATION

5776 STONERIDGE MALL ROAD, SUITE 310
PLEASANTON, CALIFORNIA 94588

Telephone: 510-463-0750
Fax: 510-463-0407

*Practice limited to Family Law and related areas.*

**JOHN F. STALEY,** born Sidney, Ohio, September 26, 1943; admitted to bar, 1972, California. *Education:* California State University at Fresno (B.A., 1965); Hastings College of Law, University of California (J.D., 1972). Livermore City Council, 1975-1982. Recipient, California Association of Certified Family Specialists, 4th Annual Hall of Fame Award, 1994. Listed in: Who's Who in California; Who's Who in American Law. Seminars given in: Litigating Pre-Nuptial Agreements and Family Law Office Organization; Negotiating Settlement Agreements. Judge Pro Tem, Superior Court, 1977—. Director, Xscribe Corp. (NASDAQ-XSCR). *Member:* Alameda County, Eastern Alameda County and American Bar Associations; State Bar of California; California Association of Certified Family Law Specialists (Founding Member, 1980; President, 1989); Fellow, American Academy of Matrimonial Lawyers. (Certified Specialist, Family Law, The State Bar of California Board of Legal Specialization). *REPORTED CASES:* Prevailing counsel establishing copyright as community property (Irmo Worth, 195 Cal. App. 3d 768). *PRACTICE AREAS:* Family Law.

**BRUCE JOBSON,** born San Francisco, California, June 13, 1946; admitted to bar, 1972, California. *Education:* University of Santa Clara (B.A., with honors in Economics, 1968); Boalt Hall School of Law, University of California, Berkeley (J.D., 1971); Northern California Mediation Center: Divorce Mediation and Conflict Resolution Training (1995). Judge Pro Tem in Family Law Departments of Alameda and Contra Costa County Superior Courts. *Member:* Alameda County (Member, Family Law Section; Member, Board of Directors, 1996—), Eastern Alameda County (Chairman, Family Law Section), Contra Costa County (Member, Family Law Section) and American (Member, Family Law Section) Bar Associations; State Bar of California (Member, Family Law Section; Member, Alternative Dispute Resolution Standing Committee); California Association of Certified Family Law Specialists. (Certified Specialist, Family Law, The State Bar of California Board of Legal Specialization). *PRACTICE AREAS:* Family Law; Litigation; Mediation; Private Judging.

**JOAN M. WETHERELL,** born Brooklyn, New York, August 13, 1946; admitted to bar, 1979, California. *Education:* Boston State College; California State University at Hayward (B.A., 1971); Golden Gate University (J.D., 1977). Judge Pro Tem, Family Law, Contra Costa County. Board Member, Southern Alameda County Domestic Violence Law Project, 1987-1993. *Member:* Contra Costa County, Alameda County and American Bar Associations; State Bar of California; California Women Lawyers; Women Lawyers of Alameda County; Association of Certified Family Law Specialists; Alameda County Family Law Association (Board Member, 1990—); Family Law Inter-County Council (Founding Member, Chair, 1995). (Certified Specialist, Family Law, The State Bar of California Board of Legal Specialization). *PRACTICE AREAS:* Family Law; Deferred Compensation (Family Law).

## ROBERT H. POWSNER

11315 SHORELINE
P.O. BOX 1327
POINT REYES STATION, CALIFORNIA 94956

Telephone: 415-663-1035
Telefax: 415-663-1450

*General Business, Entertainment; Litigation.*

**ROBERT H. POWSNER,** born New Haven, Connecticut, October 5, 1929; admitted to bar, 1953, California and U.S. District Court, Northern

*(This Listing Continued)*

and Central District of California; 1966, U.S. Supreme Court. *Education:* Stanford University (B.A., with great distinction, 1951; J.D., 1953). Member, Board of Editors and Revising Editor, Stanford Law Review, 1951-1953. Appointed Special Master, U.S. District Court, Securities Litigation, 1976. Chairman of Board, Pacifica Foundation, 1973-1975; Board of Fund for Psycho Neuroimmunology. *Member:* Bar Association of San Francisco (Member, Sections on: Litigation; Business; Entertainment); State Bar of California; American Bar Association. *PRACTICE AREAS:* General Business Representation; Litigation; Entertainment.

## ALLARD, SHELTON & O'CONNOR

POMONA, CALIFORNIA

(See Claremont)

General Civil and Trial Practice in all State and Federal Courts. Corporation, Non-Profit Organizations, Municipal, Real Estate, Taxation, Family Law, Estate Planning, Trust and Probate Law.

## COVINGTON & CROWE

POMONA, CALIFORNIA

(See Ontario)

General Civil and Trial Practice. Corporations, Municipal, Real Estate, Estate Planning, Trust, Probate, Family, Labor Law, Criminal Defense, Bankruptcy, Creditor's Rights and Water Rights Law.

## FURNESS, MIDDLEBROOK, KAISER & HIGGINS

A PROFESSIONAL CORPORATION

POMONA, CALIFORNIA

(See San Bernardino)

General Civil and Trial Practice. Personal Injury, Insurance and Government Law, Workers Compensation Subrogation, General Business and Construction Law.

## JONES, MAHONEY, BRAYTON & SOLL

POMONA, CALIFORNIA

(See Claremont)

General Civil and Trial Practice in State and Federal Courts. Business, Construction, Corporation, Insurance, Civil Litigation, Estate Planning, Probate, Taxation, Real Property and Family Law.

## KINKLE, RODIGER AND SPRIGGS

PROFESSIONAL CORPORATION

POMONA, CALIFORNIA

(See Riverside)

General Trial Practice. Negligence, Malpractice, Products Liability, Construction and Insurance Law.

## LAMB, MORRIS & LOBELLO, LLP

POMONA, CALIFORNIA

(See San Dimas)

Business, Corporate, Probate, Wills and Trusts, Real Property, Civil Litigation (State and Federal), Water Law and Employment Law.

## WELEBIR & McCUNE
A PROFESSIONAL LAW CORPORATION

**POMONA, CALIFORNIA**

(See Redlands)

*Practice limited to Catastrophic Personal Injury and Wrongful Death, Products Liability, Aviation, Railroad and Toxic Torts. Class Actions related to Defective Products and Mass Torts.*

---

## YOUNG, HENRIE, HUMPHRIES & MASON

Established in 1946

HOME SAVINGS OF AMERICA BUILDING
100 WEST SECOND STREET, SUITE 210
**POMONA, CALIFORNIA 91766**
Telephone: 909-629-2521
Telecopier: 909-629-3108

*General Civil and Trial Practice, Business and Corporate Law, Estate Planning, Probate, Trusts, Real Estate and Personal Injury.*

**BERT W. HUMPHRIES, JR.,** born Orlando, Florida, October 18, 1940; admitted to bar, 1965, California. *Education:* Stetson University (A.B., 1962); University of California at Los Angeles (J.D., 1965). Member, Board of Trustees, Pomona Valley Bar Association, 1971-1974. Phi Alpha Delta. Director, Pomona Valley Estate Planning Council, 1984-1985. *Member:* Eastern Bar Association of Los Angeles County; Los Angeles County Bar Association; The State Bar of California; Pomona Valley Estate Plan Council. *PRACTICE AREAS:* General Civil Practice; Business Law; Corporate Law; Estate Planning; Probate; Trusts; Real Estate.

**BARRY S. MASON,** born Upland, California, December 28, 1940; admitted to bar, 1966, California. *Education:* Pomona College (B.A., 1963); University of California at Los Angeles (J.D., 1966). Phi Delta Phi. Member, Board of Editors, University of California at Los Angeles Law Review, 1964-1966. Author: "Residence Deemed Alternative Jurisdictional Basis to Domicile in Serviceman's Divorce Action," 12 University of California at Los Angeles Law Review 586, 1965; "Defamation of Public Officials-Free Speech and the New Constitutional Standard," 12 University of California at Los Angeles Law Review 1420, 1965. *Member:* Eastern Bar Association of Los Angeles County; Los Angeles County Bar Association; The State Bar of California. *PRACTICE AREAS:* General Civil and Trial Practice; Business Law; Corporate Law; Estate Planning; Probate; Trusts; Real Estate; Personal Injury.

### OF COUNSEL

**RICHARD T. YOUNG,** born Seattle, Washington, May 18, 1911; admitted to bar, 1936, Washington; 1945, California. *Education:* University of Washington (A.B., 1933; J.D., 1936). Order of the Coif; Phi Delta Phi. Member, Board of Editors, Washington Law Review, 1935-1936. President, Pomona Valley Bar Association, 1952-1953. Instructor, University of La Verne College Law Center, 1974-1977. *Member:* Eastern Bar Association of Los Angeles County; Los Angeles (Member, Board of Trustees, 1954-1956), Washington State and American Bar Associations; The State Bar of California; International Academy of Estate and Trust Law. Fellow, American College of Trust and Estate Counsel. (Retired).

**HOMER H. HENRIE,** born Xenia, Ohio, August 31, 1909; admitted to bar, 1936, Ohio; 1947, California. *Education:* The Ohio State University (B.S., 1931); The Ohio State University and George Washington University (LL.B., 1935). Probate Judge, Greene County, Xenia, Ohio, 1938-1941. *Member:* Eastern Bar Association of Los Angeles County; The State Bar of California; American Bar Association. (Retired).

### ASSOCIATES

**RANDAL P. HANNAH,** born Fontana, California, October 19, 1962; admitted to bar, 1988, California. *Education:* University of Santa Clara (B.S.C., 1984); University of Santa Clara School of Law (J.D., 1987). *Member:* Eastern Bar Association of Los Angeles County (Trustee); Los Angeles County Bar Association; State Bar of California. *PRACTICE AREAS:* General Civil and Trial Practice; Business Law; Corporate Law; Real Estate; Personal Injury.

*(This Listing Continued)*

CAA1684B

---

REPRESENTATIVE CLIENTS: Herzig Corp.; Prime Papers, Inc.; Lemco Engineering, Inc.; Intermedics Southern California, Inc.; Graziano's Pizza Restaurant, Inc.; Scott Engineering; Braswell Management, Inc.; Delbert Blinn Co., Inc.; Xar Industries, Inc.; LaVerne Nursery, Inc.
REFERENCES: Home Savings of America, Pomona; Citizen Business Bank, Pomona.

---

## WILLIAMS WOOLLEY COGSWELL NAKAZAWA & RUSSELL

237 E. HUENEME ROAD, SUITE A
**PORT HUENEME, CALIFORNIA 93041**
Telephone: 805-488-8560
Fax: 805-488-7896
Email: wwlaw@msn.com

Long Beach, California Office: 111 West Ocean Boulevard, Suite 2000, 90802-4614. Telephone: 310-495-6000. Telecopier: 310-435-1359; 310-435-6812. Telex: ITT: 4933872; WU: 984929.

Rancho Santa Fe, California Office: P.O. Box 9120, 16236 San Dieguito Road, Building 3, Suite 3-15, 92067. Telephone: 619-497-0284. Fax: 619-759-9938.

*Commercial Transactions and Litigation, Maritime Law, Transportation and International Law, Environmental Law, Immigration Law, Personal Injury and Product Liability Litigation.*

(For Complete Biographical Data on all Personnel, see Professional Biographies at Long Beach)

---

## DAVID H. ELLISON
PROFESSIONAL CORPORATION

171 DURAZNO WAY
**PORTOLA VALLEY, CALIFORNIA 94028**
Telephone: 415-325-5300
Fax: 415-323-7647
Email: dhellison@aol.com

*General Civil and Trial Practice in all Federal and State Courts. Corporation Securities, Unfair Competition, Trade Secrets and Technology and Computer Law.*

**DAVID H. ELLISON,** born Salem, Oregon, August 10, 1937; admitted to bar, 1966, California; 1967, U.S. Court of International Trade. *Education:* Stanford University (A.B., in Economics/History, 1959; J.D., 1965). Author: "Expert Witnesses in Computer Litigation," University of Southern California Computer Law Institute Seminar on Computer Litigation, 1980. Panelist: "Contesting Computer Disputes: Litigation and Other Remedies in Contract, Trade Secret and Copyright Cases," Law and Business, Inc., 1982; "Making the Most of Your Expert Witnesses," American Bar Association National Institute, 1981; "Computer Law Institute Seminar on Computer Litigation," University of Southern California Law Center, 1980. *Member:* The Bar Association of San Francisco; Palo Alto and American (Member, Sections on: Antitrust Law; Litigation; Corporation, Banking and Business Law) Bar Associations; The State Bar of California (Member, Sections on: Litigation; Corporations). [LCDR, USN and USNR, 1959-1970]

---

## PETERS, FULLER, RUSH, FARNSWORTH & HABIB

**QUINCY, CALIFORNIA**

(See Chico)

*General Civil and Trial Practice in all State and Federal Courts. Insurance Defense, Real Property. Estate Planning and Administration, Business and Commercial Law, Workers Compensation.*

---

## ZETTERBERG & KING

P.O. BOX 3926
**QUINCY, CALIFORNIA 95971-3926**
Telephone: 916-283-0325
Fax: 916-283-5205

Claremont, California Office: 319 Harvard Avenue. Telephone: 909-621-2971. Fax: 909-625-5781.

*(This Listing Continued)*

*General Civil and Trial Practice in all State and Federal Courts. Wills, Probate, Trusts and Estate Planning Law, Civil Litigation, Family Law.*

**ALICE M. KING,** born Takoma Park, Maryland, April 5, 1934; admitted to bar, 1989, California. *Education:* University of California at Riverside (B.A., 1956; M.A., 1965); Claremont Graduate School (Ph.D., 1975); University of California School of Law, Los Angeles (J.D., 1988). Phi Beta Kappa. Author: Comment, "The Mono Lake Problem and the Public Trust Solution," UCLA Journal of Environmental Law and Policy, Vol. 7, 1987, Vol. 1. *Member:* Plumas County (President, 1995-1996) and American Bar Associations; State Bar of California; Mathematical Association of America. (Resident). *PRACTICE AREAS:* Family Law; Estate Planning; Probate; Civil Litigation.

**STEPHEN I. ZETTERBERG** (Claremont, California Office).

---

## LAW OFFICE OF
## NEIL JON BLOOMFIELD
### RANCHO BERNARDO, CALIFORNIA
(See San Rafael)

*Civil Litigation, Real Estate, Family Law, Taxation, Probate, Estate and Trust and Personal Injury Law. Bankruptcy.*

---

## BERDING & WEIL
### 2200 SUNRISE BOULEVARD, SUITE 220
### RANCHO CORDOVA, CALIFORNIA 95670
Telephone: 916-851-1910
FAX: 916-851-1914

*Alamo, California Office:* 3240 Stone Valley Road West, 94507. Telephone: 510-838-2090. Fax: 510-820-5592.
*Santa Clara, California Office:* 3600 Pruneridge Avenue, Suite 130. 95051. Telephone: 408-556-0220. Fax: 408-556-0224.
*Fresno, California Office:* 516 West Shaw Avenue, Suite 200. Telephone: 209-221-2556. Fax: 209-221-2558.

*Construction Litigation and Community Association Law. Non-Profit Corporation Law. Appellate Practice.*

(For complete biographical data on all personnel, see Professional Biographies at Alamo, California)

---

## FARMER & MURPHY
### 2701 PROSPECT PARK DRIVE, SUITE 110
### RANCHO CORDOVA, CALIFORNIA 95670
Telephone: 916-853-2420
Fax: 916-853-2424
Email: farmur@aol.com

Mailing Address: P.O. Box 276226, Sacramento, CA 95287-6226

*Civil Trial and Appellate Practice in all State and Federal Courts. Consultation and Litigation regarding Insurance Coverage, Claims Handling, Insurance "Bad Faith" and Environmental Coverage Issues; Business and Governmental Entity Self Insurance Law; Complex Litigation.*

### MEMBERS OF FIRM

**CRAIG E. FARMER,** born Palo Alto, California, March 30, 1948; admitted to bar, 1974, California and U.S. District Court, Eastern District of California; 1987, U.S. District Court, Central District of California; 1988, U.S. District Court, Northern District of California; 1995, U.S. District Court, Western District of Michigan. *Education:* University of California at Santa Barbara (B.A., cum laude, 1970); Hastings College of the Law, University of California (J.D., 1974). Author: "The Right to Jury Trial in Insurance Coverage Declaratory Relief Actions: An Historical Perspective," Pacific Law Journal, Vol. 13, No. 31, April, 1982. Lecturer: Sacramento Court Judges Insurance Seminar, January 1994. Associate Member, California Association of Joint Powers Authorities. *Member:* Sacramento County and American Bar Associations; Association of Defense Counsel of Northern California; Defense Research Institute.

**GEORGE E. MURPHY,** born Oak Park, Illinois, June 10, 1950; admitted to bar, 1980, California; 1982, U.S. Court of Appeals, Ninth Circuit and U.S. District Court, Eastern District of California; 1983, U.S. Supreme Court; 1985, U.S. District Court, Northern District of California; 1992, U.S. District Court, Central District of California. *Education:* University of

*(This Listing Continued)*

---

California at Santa Barbara (B.A., 1975); Golden Gate University (J.D., 1979). Legal Research Assistant, Superior Court Judges, Sacramento County, California, 1979-1980. Law Clerk Intern to Chief Justice Robert Boochever, Alaska Supreme Court, 1979. Judicial Attorney for Justice Frances Newell Carr of the Court of Appeal, Third Appellate District, 1980-1982. Associate Member, Risk & Insurance Management Society Inc., Sacramento Valley Chapter. *Member:* Sacramento County Bar Association; Association of Defense Counsel of Northern California.

**DOUGLAS R. ALLISTON,** born Park Ridge, Illinois, April 3, 1961; admitted to bar, 1988, California and U.S. District Court, Eastern District of California; 1989, U.S. District Court, Northern District of California; 1990, U.S. Court of Appeals, Ninth Circuit. *Education:* Oklahoma Christian College (B.A., summa cum laude, 1984); McGeorge School of Law, University of the Pacific (J.D., with distinction, 1988). *Member:* Association of Defense Counsel of Northern California.

**BLANE A. SMITH,** born Kirkland, Washington, January 25, 1955; admitted to bar, 1980, California. *Education:* Western Washington State University (B.A., 1977); McGeorge School of Law, University of the Pacific (J.D., 1980). Staff Writer and Associate Editor, Pacific Law Journal, 1979-1980. Author: "The California Legislature Steers the Antitrust Cart Right Off the Illinois Brick Road," Vol. 11, Pacific Law Journal, 1979. Instructor, NBI Bad Faith and Coverage Seminar. *Member:* Sacramento County and American Bar Associations; Association of Defense Counsel; Practicing Law Institute.

### ASSOCIATES

**FRANK J. TORRANO,** born San Francisco, California, August 8, 1963; admitted to bar, 1993, California, U.S. Court of Appeals, Ninth Circuit and U.S. District Court, Eastern District of California; 1995, U.S. District Court, Western District of Michigan. *Education:* San Francisco State University (B.A., 1985; M.A., 1988); University of San Francisco (J.D., magna cum laude, 1993). Technical Editor, University of San Francisco Law Review, 1992-1993. Judicial Extern to the Honorable Armand Arabian, Supreme Court of California, 1992. Member, McAuliffe Honor Society. Co-Author: "Mesangial Cell Activation by Bacterial Endotoxin," American Journal of Pathology 371 (1991); "Interleukin 1," 152 Journal of Cellular Physiology 223 (1992). Author: "An Intrastructural and Immunocytochemical Analysis of Myofibrils and Atrial Natriuretic Peptide Granules During Cardiac Hypertrophy," (1987).

**GERALD C. HICKS,** born Phoenix, Arizona, October 2, 1956; admitted to bar, 1990, California and U.S. District Court, Eastern District of California. *Education:* California State University, Sacramento (B.A. History and Communication, 1980); McGeorge School of Law, University of Pacific (J.D., with great distinction, 1990). Phi Delta Phi. Assistant Editor, Pacific Law Journal, 1989-1990. *Member:* Order of the Coif; Traynor Honor Society, Recipient of Charles D. Driscoll Labor Law Award. *Member:* Sacramento County Bar Association; Anthony Kennedy Inn of Court; Mensa Society.

REPRESENTATIVE CLIENTS: Aetna Casualty & Surety Company; Allstate Insurance Co.; American States Insurance Company; CalFarm Insurance Company; California Casualty; Central Mutual Insurance Company; Coregis Insurance; Financial Pacific Insurance Company; Fireman's Fund Insurance Company; Hanover; Liberty Mutual; Maryland Insurance Group; Nationwide Insurance Company; Northland Insurance Companies; St. Paul Insurance Companies; Self-Insured Risk Pools; Northern California Regional Liability Excess Fund Joint Powers Authority; Southern California Regional Liability Excess Fund Joint Powers Authority; State Wide Association of Community Colleges Joint Powers Authority.

---

## HERRIG & VOGT
### 2724 KILGORE ROAD
### RANCHO CORDOVA, CALIFORNIA 95670
Telephone: 916-631-7000
Telecopier: 916-631-7717

*Kennewick, Washington Office:* 3104 West Kennewick Avenue, Suite D. Telephone: 509-943-6691. Fax: 509-783-8808.
*Redmond, Washington Office:* 7981 168th Avenue, N.E. Telephone: 206-3129. Fax: 206-556-0595.
*Los Angeles, California Office:* 100 Wilshire Boulevard, #950, Santa Monica. Telephone: 310-260-5088. Fax: 310-260-5089.

*Civil and Trial Practice relating to Construction, Public Contract, Fidelity and Surety, Environmental Remediation, International Contracting, Corporate and General Civil Trial Matters.*

*(This Listing Continued)*

## HERRIG & VOGT, Rancho Cordova—Continued

### MEMBERS OF FIRM

**JOHN R. HERRIG,** born Bronxville, New York, November 1, 1942; admitted to bar, 1978, Washington; 1982, U.S. District Court, Western District of Washington and U.S. Court of Appeals, Ninth Circuit; 1983, U.S. District Court, Eastern District of Washington; 1984, U.S. Claims Court and U.S. Court of Appeals for the Federal Circuit; 1987, California and U.S. District Court, Southern, Eastern, Central and Northern Districts of California; 1992, U.S. Supreme Court; 1995, U.S. District Court, District of Montana. *Education:* Georgia Institute of Technology (B.S., 1968); Pepperdine University (J.D., 1976). Member: Panel of Arbitrators, California Public Works; Legal Advisory Committee, California AGC; Panel of Construction Arbitrators, American Arbitration Association, California and Washington; AGC of California and Inland Empire (Washington). *Member:* State Bar of California; Washington State and American Bar Associations; Pacific Northwest Steel Fabricators Association. *PRACTICE AREAS:* Construction; Contract Law.

**GEORGE F. VOGT, JR.,** born Cherry Hill, New Jersey, October 8, 1956; admitted to bar, 1982, California; U.S. District Court, Northern, Eastern, Central and Southern Districts of California. *Education:* Loyola University (B.A., 1979; J.D., 1982). Judge Pro Tem, Sacramento County. *Member:* Sacramento County (Member, Construction Section) and American (Member, Litigation Section on Construction Litigation; Construction Forum) Bar Association; State Bar of California. (Resident). *PRACTICE AREAS:* Construction; Contract Law; Civil Law.

### ASSOCIATES

**C. PATRICK STOLL,** born Trieste, Italy, November 24, 1948; admitted to bar, 1993, California. *Education:* U.S. Air Force Academy (B.S., 1970); McGeorge School of Law (J.D., 1993). Traynor Honor Society. [Capt., U.S. Air Force, 1966-1975]. (Resident, Rancho Cordova, California Office). *PRACTICE AREAS:* Construction Law; Business Litigation; Contract Law; Personal Injury; Domestic Relations.

**HAZEL BERGTHOLDT,** born Chico, California, February 17, 1968; admitted to bar, 1993, Washington; 1994, California. *Education:* University of British Columbia (B.A., 1990); Gonzaga University (J.D., 1993); McGeorge School of Law (L.L.M., in Transactional Business, 1994). (Resident). *LANGUAGES:* German.

**HEIDI SUSAN HART,** born Montreal, Canada, March 27, 1961; admitted to bar, 1986, California and U.S. District Court, Central District of California; 1994, U.S. Court of Appeals, 9th Circuit; 1996, U.S. District Court, Eastern District of California. *Education:* University of California at Los Angeles (B.A., magna cum laude, 1983); Loyola Marymount University (J.D., cum laude, 1986). Phi Beta Kappa. Recipient, American Jurisprudence Award, Criminal. Member, St. Thomas More Society. *Member:* Los Angeles County Bar Association; State Bar of California; Association of Southern California Defense Counsel. (Resident, Los Angeles, California Office). *PRACTICE AREAS:* Construction Industry Transactions and Litigation; Business Litigation.

**DAVID D. HILTON,** born Delta, Utah, June 8, 1957; admitted to bar, 1994, Nevada, Washington and U.S. District Court, Eastern District of Washington; 1995, U.S. District Court, District of Montana. *Education:* University of Nevada, Las Vegas (B.A., 1986); Gonzaga University School of Law (J.D., 1992). Arbitrator, Spokane Housing Rehabilitation, Washington, Construction Supervision, 1980-1986. *Member:* Spokane County, Clark County and Washington State Bar Associations; State Bar of Nevada. (Resident, Kennewick, Washington Office). *PRACTICE AREAS:* Construction Law; Property Law.

### LEGAL SUPPORT PERSONNEL

### CONSTRUCTION ANALYST

**GREGG T. GOTTGETREU,** born New London, Wisconsin, June 29, 1948. *Education:* University of Wisconsin (B.S.M.E., 1971). Member: American Welding Society, 1971-1975; American Society of Mechanical Engineers, 1970-1975. *PRACTICE AREAS:* Construction; Claims Preparation and Analysis; Engineering Evaluation; Litigation Support.

CAA1686B

## ALLARD, SHELTON & O'CONNOR
### RANCHO CUCAMONGA, CALIFORNIA
(See Claremont)

General Civil and Trial Practice in all State and Federal Courts. Corporation, Non-Profit Organizations, Municipal, Real Estate, Taxation, Family Law, Estate Planning, Trust and Probate Law.

## COVINGTON & CROWE
### RANCHO CUCAMONGA, CALIFORNIA
(See Ontario)

General Civil and Trial Practice. Corporations, Municipal, Real Estate, Estate Planning, Trust, Probate, Family, Labor Law, Criminal Defense, Bankruptcy, Creditor's Rights and Water Rights Law.

## FURNESS, MIDDLEBROOK, KAISER & HIGGINS
*A PROFESSIONAL CORPORATION*
### RANCHO CUCAMONGA, CALIFORNIA
(See San Bernardino)

General Civil and Trial Practice. Personal Injury, Insurance and Government Law, Workers Compensation Subrogation, General Business and Construction Law.

## GENSON, EVEN, CRANDALL & WADE
*A PROFESSIONAL CORPORATION*
9483 HAVEN AVENUE, SUITE 102
### RANCHO CUCAMONGA, CALIFORNIA 91730
Telephone: 909-390-4811
FAX: 909-390-1907

*Irvine, California Office:* 7700 Irvine Center Drive, #700. Telephone: 714-753-1000. FAX: 714-753-1039.
*Woodland Hills, California Office:* 21031 Ventura Boulevard, Suite 801. Telephone: 818-999-4811. FAX: 818-999-1782.
*San Diego, California Office:* 9988 Hibert Street, Suite 300. Telephone: 619-635-6300. FAX: 619-635-6306.

Trial practice in State and Federal Courts: Employment Practices Liability, Third Party Violent Crime/Premises Security, Product Liability, Warranty Litigation, Insurance Coverage, Insurance Bad Faith, Insurance Fraud, HMO/Managed Care Defense, Medical Malpractice, Directors and Officers Liability, Professional Malpractice, Construction Defect, Government Liability, Premises Liability, Transportation Liability, Vehicle Liability, Environmental Liability, Recreational Sports and Leisure Activities Liability, Appellate Practice, Business Litigation (Class Action, Fraud, Misrepresentation, Breach of Contract, etc.).

(For complete Biographical data on all personnel, see Professional Biographies at Woodland Hills, California).

## HILLSINGER AND COSTANZO
*PROFESSIONAL CORPORATION*
Established in 1973

10737 LAUREL STREET
SUITE 110 - MAIN FLOOR
### RANCHO CUCAMONGA, CALIFORNIA 91730
Telephone: 909-483-6200
Telecopier: 909-483-6277

*Los Angeles, California Office:* 12th Floor, 3055 Wilshire Boulevard. Telephone: 310-388-9441. Telecopier: 310-388-1592.
*Orange, California Office:* 701 South Parker Street, Suite 6000. Telephone: 714-542-6241. Telecopier: 714-667-6806.
*Santa Barbara, California Office:* 220 East Figueroa Street. Telephone: 805-966-3986. Telecopier: 805-965-3798.

*(This Listing Continued)*

*General Civil and Appellate Trial Practice in all State and Federal Courts. Insurance, Corporation, Commercial, Business, Medical and Professional Malpractice, Product Liability, Aviation, Asbestos, Toxic Tort, Bad Faith, Insurance Coverage, Declaratory Relief, Wrongful Termination, Vehicular, Property Damage, General Liability Cases.*

(For personnel and biographical data, see Biographical Card, Los Angeles, California).

## KEGEL, TOBIN & TRUCE

A PROFESSIONAL CORPORATION

Established in 1966

10737 LAUREL STREET, SUITE 240
P.O. BOX 3329
**RANCHO CUCAMONGA, CALIFORNIA 91729-3329**
Telephone: 909-466-5555
Facsimile: 909-466-5562
Email: comp-law@ktt.com

*Los Angeles, California Office:* 3580 Wilshire Boulevard, 10th Floor, P.O. Box 76907. Telephone: 213-380-3880. FAX: 213-383-8346.
*Ventura, California Office:* 5450 Ralston Street, Suite 204, P.O. Box 7779. Telephone: 805-644-2216. Facsimile: 805-644-8625.
*San Diego, California Office:* 2535 Kettner Boulevard, Suite 2A1. Telephone: 619-696-0906.
*Long Beach, California Office:* 330 Golden Shore Drive, Suite 150. Telephone: 310-437-1108. Facsimile: 310-437-3742.
*Van Nuys, California Office:* 14545 Friar Street, Suite 104. Telephone: 818-947-0300. Facsimile: 818-947-0303.

*Workers' Compensation, Longshore and Harborworkers, Public Employment, Retirement Law. Insurance Law, Third Party Subrogation.*

(For complete biographical data on all personnel, see Professional Biographies at Los Angeles, California)

## MANNERINO & BRIGUGLIO

Established in 1947

9333 BASELINE ROAD, SUITE 110
**RANCHO CUCAMONGA, CALIFORNIA 91730-1311**
Telephone: 909-980-1100
Telecopier: 909-941-8610

*Practice Limited to Business Litigation, Personal Injury, Corporate, Real Estate, Bankruptcy, Probate, Family and Criminal Defense.*

### MEMBERS OF FIRM

**JOHN D. MANNERINO,** born Upland, California, November 16, 1949; admitted to bar, 1974, California. *Education:* University of California at Los Angeles (B.A., cum laude, 1971); Loyola University of Los Angeles (J.D., cum laude, 1974). Member, St. Thomas More Society. *Member:* San Bernardino County and Western San Bernardino County (Secretary, 1977-1978; President, 1979-1980) Bar Associations; The State Bar of California. *PRACTICE AREAS:* Personal Injury Law; Business Litigation; Corporate Law.

**SALVATORE BRIGUGLIO,** born Jersey City, New Jersey, August 19, 1952; admitted to bar, 1979, California; 1983, U.S. Court of Appeals, Ninth Circuit; 1985, U.S. District Court, Central District of California. *Education:* Rutgers University (B.A., 1974); University of San Fernando Valley (J.D., 1978). Delta Theta Phi. *Member:* San Bernardino and Western San Bernardino County (Member, Board of Directors, 1986; Secretary, 1989) Bar Associations; The State Bar of California; West End Trial Lawyers Association (Treasurer, 1986; Member, Board of Directors, 1989); California Public Defenders Association; California Attorneys for Criminal Justice. *PRACTICE AREAS:* Civil Litigation; Bankruptcy; Personal Injury Law; Criminal Defense.

### ASSOCIATES

**MITCHELL I ROTH,** born Queens, New York, December 20, 1961; admitted to bar, 1987, New Jersey; New York; 1991, California. *Education:* Rutgers University (B.A., 1983; J.D., 1987). Phi Sigma Iota; Phi Betta Kappa. *LANGUAGES:* English and Spanish. *PRACTICE AREAS:* Litigation; Family Law; Criminal; Bankruptcy.

REPRESENTATIVE CLIENTS: Maclin Markets, Inc.; Resin Technology Inc.; Citrus Motors Ontario, Inc.; Leiserv, Inc., a Brunswick Company; Applied Cam Engineering; Security Investment Co.; Crowell Industries; Stephen Daniels

*(This Listing Continued)*

Commercial Brokerage; California State Bank; Swan Pools; Mercy Ambulance; Sun Country Bank; Upland Bank; Rancho Cucamonga Chamber of Commerce.
REFERENCES: First Trust Bank, Upland Office; California State Bank, Ontario Office; Rancho Cucamonga Chamber of Commerce, Rancho Cucamonga, California.

## MARKMAN, ARCZYNSKI, HANSON, CURLEY & SLOUGH

A PROFESSIONAL CORPORATION

Established in 1978

9113 FOOTHILL BOULEVARD, SUITE 200
**RANCHO CUCAMONGA, CALIFORNIA 91730**
Telephone: 909-381-0218; 909-980-2742
Email: MARCZYNSKI@AOL.COM

*Brea, California Office:* Second Floor, Number One Civic Center Circle, P.O. Box 1059. Telephone: 714-990-0901; 213-691-3811.

*Municipal, Redevelopment, Water Rights, Real Property, Condemnation, School and Corporation Law. Civil Litigation.*

**MARSHA G. SLOUGH,** born 1958; admitted to bar, 1987, California and U.S. District Court, Central District of California. *Education:* Ottawa University (B.A., 1980); Whittier College School of Law (J.D., 1986). *Member:* San Bernardino County and American Bar Associations; State Bar of California; Association of Southern California Defense Counsel. (Resident). *PRACTICE AREAS:* Municipal Litigation; Personal Injury Litigation.

**PAMELA P. KING,** born Arcata, California, June 8, 1950; admitted to bar, 1977, California; 1990, U.S. District Court, District of California. *Education:* University of Redlands (B.A., 1972); McGeorge School of Law, University of the Pacific (J.D., 1977). *Member:* San Bernardino Bar Association; The State Bar of California. (Resident). *PRACTICE AREAS:* Municipal Litigation; Personal Injury Litigation.

**DAREN E. HENGESBACH,** born Thousand Oaks, California, April 8, 1966; admitted to bar, 1993, California and U.S. District Court, Central District of California. *Education:* Claremont McKenna College (B.A., 1988); McGeorge School of Law, University of the Pacific (J.D., 1993). *Member:* State Bar of California. (Resident). *PRACTICE AREAS:* Municipal Litigation; Personal Injury Litigation.

REPRESENTATIVE CLIENTS: City of Brea; City of Buena Park; City of Diamond Bar; City of Hesperia; City of La Mirada; City of Rancho Cucamonga; City of Irwindale.
GENERAL COUNSEL FOR: Brea Redevelopment Agency; Buena Park Redevelopment Agency; Irwindale Housing Authority; Hesperia Redevelopment Agency; Irwindale Community Redevelopment Agency; La Mirada Redevelopment Agency; Rancho Cucamonga Redevelopment Agency; Stanton Redevelopment Agency; Upland Redevelopment Agency.
REFERENCE: Southern California Bank (Brea Branch).

(For personnel and biographical data, see professional biographies at Brea, California)

## REISS & JOHNSON

10535 FOOTHILL BOULEVARD, SUITE 410
**RANCHO CUCAMONGA, CALIFORNIA 91730**
Telephone: 909-483-0515
Fax: 909-980-7945

*General Civil and Trial Practice in all State and Federal Courts. Product Liability, Governmental Torts, Construction, Motor Carrier, Personal Injury, Criminal and Family Law.*

**JAMES V. REISS,** born Upland, California, November 19, 1961; admitted to bar, 1987, California and U.S. District Court, Central and Southern Districts of California. *Education:* Loyola Marymount University (B.A., 1983); University of Puget Sound (J.D., 1986). Member, Constitutional Rights Foundation. *Member:* Los Angeles County and San Bernardino County Bar Associations; State Bar of California; California Trial Lawyers Association; Association of Southern California Defense Counsel. *PRACTICE AREAS:* Civil Litigation; Criminal Litigation.

**STEPHAN J. JOHNSON,** born Albuquerque, New Mexico, April 21, 1954; admitted to bar, 1987, California; 1991, U.S. District Court, Central District of California. *Education:* San Jose State University (B.A., 1976) University of California at Riverside (M.A., 1978); Western State Univer-

*(This Listing Continued)*

REISS & JOHNSON, Rancho Cucamonga—Continued

sity (J.D., 1986). *Member:* Desert and Riverside County Bar Associations; State Bar of California; Association of Southern California Defense Counsel. *PRACTICE AREAS:* Civil Litigation; Criminal Litigation.

REPRESENTATIVE CLIENTS: Mark Christopher Chevrolet; Crawford & Company; Western Waste Industries; Associated Claims; Donco Carriers; Contract Freighters, Inc.; Fedco, Inc.; Houston General Insurance Company; Camco Manufacturing, Inc.; Bear Automotive; Hartman Enterprises; Forecast Corporation; Sunbeam-Oster Company; Allegiance Insurance Company; Boral Industries; City of Rancho Cucamonga; TGI Friday's; Comco Management Company; Colen and Lee; The Lineal Group; Superior Metal Truss Company; St. Joseph Health Systems; City of West Covina.

## WELEBIR & McCUNE

A PROFESSIONAL LAW CORPORATION

**RANCHO CUCAMONGA, CALIFORNIA**

(See Redlands)

*Practice limited to Catastrophic Personal Injury and Wrongful Death, Products Liability, Aviation, Railroad and Toxic Torts. Class Actions related to Defective Products and Mass Torts.*

## BEST BEST & KRIEGER LLP

A California Limited Liability Partnership including Professional Corporations

Established in 1985

HOPE SQUARE PROFESSIONAL CENTRE
39700 BOB HOPE DRIVE, SUITE 312
P.O. BOX 1555

**RANCHO MIRAGE, CALIFORNIA 92270**
*Telephone: 619-568-2611*
*Fax: 619-341-7039*

*Riverside, California Office:* 400 Mission Square, 3750 University Avenue, P.O. Box 1028. Telephone: 909-686-1450. Fax: 909-686-3083; 909-682-4612.

*Ontario, California Office:* 800 North Haven, Suite 120. Telephone: 909-989-8584. Fax: 909-944-1441.

*San Diego, California Office:* 402 West Broadway, 13th Floor. Telephone: 619-525-1300. Fax: 619-233-6118.

*Victorville, California Office:* High Desert Corporate Pointe Building, 14350 Civic Drive, Suite 270. Telephone: 619-245-4127. Fax: 619-245-6437.

*General Civil and Trial Practice. Corporation, Water Rights, Probate, Trusts and Estate Planning. Labor, Real Estate and Municipal Law.*

### RESIDENT PARTNERS

D. Martin Nethery, (P.C.)
David J. Erwin, (P.C.)
Michael J. Andelson, (P.C.)
Douglas S. Phillips, (P.C.)
Basil T. Chapman
Marc E. Empey
Brian M. Lewis
Matt H. Morris
Robert W. Hargreaves
Daniel E. Olivier
Michael D. Harris, (P.C.)
Martin A. Mueller
Jason D. Dabareiner

### RESIDENT ASSOCIATES

Mary E. Gilstrap
Barbara R. Baron
Helene P. Dreyer
Jacqueline E. Bailey
Ana Maria Z. Fredgren
Jeffrey S. Flashman
Sandy A. Jacobson
G. Henry Welles

REPRESENTATIVE CLIENTS: City of Palm Desert; City of Indio; City of Desert Hot Springs; County of Riverside; David Freedman & Co.; California Redi-Date; Westinghouse Desert Communities; City of Needles; City of Cathedral City; Mount San Jacinto Winter Park Authority; Towne Realty, Inc.; Browning-Ferris Industries; Desert Crossing Shopping Center; Baldi Bros.; Palm Desert Bank; Fairway Outdoor Advertising; City of Palm Desert; Morris Communications; Valley Independent Bank; Safeco; Sanifill, Inc.; Republic Industries; Chemical Bank; The Club at Morningside.
SPECIAL COUNSEL TO: Aqua Caliente Band of Cahuilla Indians.

(For Complete Personnel and Biographical Data, see Professional Biographies at Riverside, California)

CAA1688B

## ANTHONY C. CARONNA, P.C.

71-650 SAHARA ROAD, SUITE 2
**RANCHO MIRAGE, CALIFORNIA 92270**
*Telephone: 619-773-4849*
*Fax: 619-773-0849*

*Coachella, California Office:* 1623 6th Street, 92236. Telephone: 619-398-0001. Fax: 619-398-0281.

*Practice limited to General Civil and Trial Practice in all State and Federal Courts. Aviation, Insurance, Malpractice, Personal Injury, Products Liability, Negligence, Workers' Compensation.*

*FIRM PROFILE: The law firm is a well rounded firm that insists on hands on relationships between the firm and its clients. The bilingual firm is staffed with several associates and paralegals which allow the firm to run smoothly. The firm is listed in the Martindale-Hubbell International Law Directory and welcomes international business.*

**ANTHONY C CARONNA,** born Pasadena, California, January 31, 1960; admitted to bar, 1988, California. *Education:* University of Southern California (B.S., 1984); Whittier School of Law (J.D., 1987). Moot Court. Member, Law Review. *Member:* Desert and Riverside Bar Associations.

LEGAL SUPPORT PERSONNEL

**Dora Hotz** (Office Manager)

## SIMON A. HOUSMAN

69730 HIGHWAY 111, SUITE 207
**RANCHO MIRAGE, CALIFORNIA 92270**
*Telephone: 619-328-7995*
*Fax: 619-324-8823*

*Civil Litigation, Real Estate and Creditors Remedies in Bankruptcy.*

**SIMON A. HOUSMAN,** born East Orange, New Jersey, May 7, 1953; admitted to bar, 1981, California; 1982, U.S. Tax Court; 1983, New Jersey; 1985, New York. *Education:* Rutgers University at New Brunswick (B.A., 1977); Southwestern University School of Law (J.D., 1981). Editor, Desert Bar Association Bulletin, (A Monthly Newspaper). Instructor: Principles of Real Estate and Indian Law, College of the Desert, 1990-1991; Real Property Law, Chapman University, 1994, 1995. Member, City of Palm Springs Economic Development Commission, 1992-1994. Member, Palm Springs Airport Commission, 1995—. *Member:* Desert, Riverside County, New York State, New Jersey State and American (Member, Litigation Section) Bar Associations; State Bar of California.

## LAW OFFICES OF
## GUY MANNING

71-650 SAHARA ROAD, SUITE 2
**RANCHO MIRAGE, CALIFORNIA 92270**
*Telephone: 619-568-5474*
*Fax: 619-773-0849*

*Coachella, California Office:* 1623 6th Street, 92236. Telephone: 619-398-0001. Fax: 619-773-0849.

*Criminal Defense Trial Practice, Juvenile Criminal Defense, Personal Injury, Wrongful Death, Professional Liability Law.*

**GUY MANNING,** born Los Angeles, California, December 21, 1960; admitted to bar, 1988, California. *Education:* University of Nevada, Las Vegas (B.S., 1983); University of La Verne at San Fernando Valley College of Law (J.D., 1987). Moot Court Honors, Justice Traynor Competition. *Member:* Los Angeles County and Desert Bar Associations; State Bar of California; California Trial Lawyers Association. Association of Trial Lawyers of America; California Public Defenders Association.

## SELZER, EALY, HEMPHILL & BLASDEL, LLP

69844 HIGHWAY 111
SUITE K
**RANCHO MIRAGE, CALIFORNIA 92270**
Telephone: 619-202-1290
Fax: 619-202-1299

*Real Estate, Business Transactions, Environmental Law, Homeowners Associations, Estate Planning, Trusts and Wills, Civil Litigation.*

### MEMBERS OF FIRM

**PAUL T. SELZER,** born St. Louis, Missouri, August 7, 1940; admitted to bar, 1966, California. *Education:* Marquette University (A.B., 1962); Stanford University (J.D., 1965). Phi Alpha Delta. *Member:* Desert (President, 1971, 1972-1973), Riverside County and American Bar Associations; State Bar of California. **PRACTICE AREAS:** Real Estate Law; Governmental Affairs Law; Environmental Law.

**W. CURT EALY,** born Dunsmuir, California, April 30, 1944; admitted to bar, 1973, California. *Education:* University of the Pacific (B.A., 1966); California State University (M.B.A., 1968); University of California at Davis (J.D., 1973). *Member:* Riverside County and American Bar Associations; State Bar of California. **PRACTICE AREAS:** Real Estate Law.

**EMILY P. HEMPHILL,** born Detroit, Michigan, February 10, 1954; admitted to bar, 1992, California. *Education:* University of Michigan (B.A., 1975); McGeorge School of Law, University of the Pacific (J.D., 1992). Order of the Coif. Member, Traynor Society. Recipient, American Jurisprudence Awards in Constitutional Law, Evidence and Decedents Estate and Trusts. Author: Article, "The European Court of Justice," The Transnational Lawyer. *Member:* Riverside County Bar Association; State Bar of California. **PRACTICE AREAS:** Business; Real Estate; Estate Planning.

**DIANE C. BLASDEL,** born Whittier, California, September 1, 1962; admitted to bar, 1991, California. *Education:* California State University at Fullerton (B.S., 1983); McGeorge School of Law (J.D., 1991). Recipient, American Jurisprudence Award, Administrative Law, 1991. *Member:* Riverside County and American Bar Associations; State Bar of California. **PRACTICE AREAS:** Civil Litigation; Real Estate Litigation; Probate.

---

## C. SAMUEL BLICK

Established in 1984
P.O. BOX 9477
**RANCHO SANTA FE, CALIFORNIA 92067**
Telephone: 619-755-9794
Fax: 619-755-6335
Email: sblick@aol.com

*San Diego, California Office:* 12625 High Bluff Drive, Suite 203, 92130.
Telephone: 619-755-9794. E-Mail: sblick@aol.com

*Real Estate, Land Use and Government Law.*

**C. SAMUEL BLICK,** born Long Beach, California, January 25, 1947; admitted to bar, 1971, California. *Education:* Wayne State University (B.A., 1967); University of San Diego (J.D., 1970). Phi Delta Phi. Recipient, John Lewis King Scholar. Author: "Awards of Private Clubs to City Officials," National Institute of Municipal Officers Municipal Reporter, Fall, 1971. Author and Lecturer, "Exactions and Dedications," May 4, 1984 and May 17, 1985; "Subdivision Map Act Law," November 30, 1984, University of California at San Diego. Assistant City Attorney, Chula Vista, 1971-1973. City Attorney: Escondido, 1973-1976; Del Mar, 1976. *Member:* San Diego County and American Bar Associations; State Bar of California; National Institute of Municipal Law Officers.

REPRESENTATIVE CLIENTS: Atlantic Richfield Company, Texaco Marketing and Refining, Inc., Ernest W. Hahn Company, Hunt Properties, Inc., National Convenience Stores, Inc. (Stop-N-Go, Inc), Clifford Robertson and Associates, McDonald's Corporation, Foodmarker, Inc., Jack-in-the-Box, Inc., Shell Oil Company, Marriott Corporation, Van Law Foods, Inc.

---

## BURKHARDT & LARSON

A Partnership of Professional Corporations

6002 EL TORDO
P.O. BOX 1369
**RANCHO SANTA FE, CALIFORNIA 92067**
Telephone: 619-756-3743
Fax: 619-756-9805

*General Civil Trial Practice. Real Estate, Real Property Development, Commercial Litigation, Eminent Domain, Taxation, Estate Planning and Probate Law.*

FIRM PROFILE: *The firm provides top quality representation in most areas of real estate and business law. Although small, it competes favorably with large firms while providing personalized service on a cost-effective basis.*

**PHILIP BURKHARDT,** born Los Angeles, California, September 25, 1948; admitted to bar, 1975, California. *Education:* Loyola University of Los Angeles; St. John's College (B.A., 1970); University of San Diego (J.D., 1975). *Member:* San Diego County (Chairman, Civil Procedure and Evidence Sub-committee, 1982-1985) and North County (President, 1997; Board of Directors, 1994—) Bar Associations; State Bar of California. **REPORTED CASES:** Rancho Santa Fe Pharmacy, Inc. v. Seyfert, 219 Cal. App. 3d 875 (1990). **PRACTICE AREAS:** Real Estate Law; Business Litigation.

**CARL A. LARSON,** born San Diego, California, May 21, 1959; admitted to bar, 1988, California. *Education:* University of California at Los Angeles (B.A., 1981); Institute of Japanese Studies, 1986; University of California at Davis (J.D., 1987); University of San Diego School of Law (LL.M., Taxation, 1994). Member, University of California, San Diego, Planned Giving Committee. *Member:* San Diego County Bar Association; State Bar of California (Member, Estate Planning Section). **REPORTED CASES:** Heacock v. Ivorette-Texas, Inc. (1993), 20 Cal. App. 4th. 1665. **PRACTICE AREAS:** Taxation; Estate Planning; Civil Litigation.

### LEGAL SUPPORT PERSONNEL

**SHERRI L. WOOD,** born Phoenix, Arizona, April 22, 1953. *Education:* Pepperdine University; Palomar College (A.A., 1976); University of San Diego, Certificate of Completion, Lawyer's Assistant Program (with honors, 1980). California Certified Legal Secretary status, 1989. Member, Legal Secretaries, Incorporated 1980—; Northern San Diego County Legal Secretaries Association 1980—. *Member:* Northern San Diego County Legal Secretaries Association (President 1985-1987); Member, Board of Governors, 1987-1989, 1990-1993; Legal Secretaries, Incorporated Member of Continuing Education Council 1986-1988, 1990-1994; Civil Litigation Section Chair, 1987-1988. (Paralegal/Office Manager). **PRACTICE AREAS:** Office Management and General Paralegal Duties.

REFERENCES: Rancho Santa Fe National Bank; Union Bank.

---

## COOMBER LAW FIRM

16909 VIA DE SANTA FE, SUITE 200
P.O. BOX 7299
**RANCHO SANTA FE, CALIFORNIA 92067-7299**
Telephone: 619-759-3939
Facsimile: 619-759-3930
Email: scoomber@aol.com

*Los Angeles, California Office:* 601 S. Figueroa St., 41st Floor, 90017-5704.
Telephone: 213-622-2200. Fax: 213-243-0000.

*Business Transactions and Business Litigation.*

**SKIP R. COOMBER, III,** born January 7, 1961; admitted to bar, 1990, California. *Education:* University of California at Irvine (B.A., 1984); Loyola Law School (J.D., 1987). President, Associated Students, University of California at Irvine, 1983-1984; President, Student Bar Association, Loyola Law School, 1986-1987. *Member:* Los Angeles County Bar Association. The State Bar of California. **PRACTICE AREAS:** Business Law.

## COWLEY & CHIDESTER

6050 EL TORDO
P.O. BOX 2329
**RANCHO SANTA FE, CALIFORNIA 92067**
Telephone: 619-756-4410
Fax: 619-756-4386

*Domestic and International Estate Planning; Trust, Will and Probate Law; Charitable Giving and Nonprofit Organizations.*

FIRM PROFILE: *Cowley & Chidester was formed in 1991 by James M. Cowley and Steven J. Chidester, both formerly of Latham & Watkins. The firm has extensive experience in all aspects of sophisticated domestic and international estate planning, including charitable giving and estate and trust administration. The firm's practice also emphasizes the representation of tax-exempt organizations, including private foundations, museums, universities, churches, trade associations, social clubs, and sporting event organizers, with regard to tax, corporate, and other legal matters.*

### MEMBERS

**JAMES M. COWLEY,** born Billings, Montana, May 23, 1940; admitted to bar, 1966, California. *Education:* Brigham Young University (B.S., 1962); University of Chicago (J.D., 1965). Order of the Coif. Articles Editor, University of Chicago Law Review, 1964-1965. Author: "Challenges Arising in Postmortem Administration of Wills and Trusts That Fund Charitable Remainder Trusts," Estate Planning, 1995 at 107 (UCLA-CEB); "Coping With Partnership Interests in Estate Planning and Post-Mortem Administration," USC Law Center Probate and Trust Conference, 1996. *Member:* San Diego County and American (Member, Exempt Organizations and Estate and Gift Tax Committees, Section of Taxation, 1970—, and Real Property, Probate and Trust Law Section, 1970—) Bar Associations; State Bar of California; American College of Trust and Estate Counsel. *PRACTICE AREAS:* Estate Planning; Estate and Trust Administration; Charitable Giving; Nonprofit Organizations.

**STEVEN J. CHIDESTER,** born Provo, Utah, May 9, 1957; admitted to bar, 1987, California. *Education:* Brigham Young University (B.A., cum laude, 1982; J.D., magna cum laude, 1985). Order of the Coif. Lead Articles Editor, Brigham Young University Law Review, 1984-1985. Law Clerk to Judge Gilbert S. Merritt, U.S. Court of Appeals, Sixth Circuit, 1985-1986. *Member:* San Diego County; Northern San Diego County and American Bar Associations; State Bar of California. *PRACTICE AREAS:* Estate Planning; Estate and Trust Administration; Charitable Giving; Nonprofit Organizations; Executive Compensation. *Email:* schidester@cclaw.com

**ELLEN L. VAN HOFTEN,** born New York, N.Y., July 25, 1942; admitted to bar, 1983, California; 1985, Hawaii; 1986 District of Columbia. *Education:* Stanford University (A.B., with great distinction, 1964; M.A., 1965); University of San Diego (J.D., magna cum laude, 1982). Phi Beta Kappa. Member, San Diego Law Review, 1980-1982. Author: "Drafting Irrevocable Life Insurance Trusts: the 'Whys' and 'What Ifs'," American Bar Association Section of Real Property, Probate and Trust Law, 7th Annual CLE Meeting, 1996; "Planning for Flexibility with Intentionally Defective Grantor Trusts," 9 The Practical Tax Lawyer 31, 1995; "Challenges Arising in Postmortem Administration of Wills and Trusts That Fund Charitable Remainder Trusts," Estate Planning, 1995 at 107 (UCLA-CEB); "Materials Related to Estate Tax Returns—Privileged Communications," California Estate Planning Trust and Probate News, 1984; "Surrogate Motherhood in California: Legislative Proposals," 18 San Diego Law Review 341, 1981. Adjunct Professor, Wills and Trusts, University of Hawaii, 1986. Foreign Legal Consultant, Braun, Moriya, Hoashi & Kubota, Tokyo, Japan, 1988-1992. *Member:* San Diego County (Member, Estate Planning, Trust and Probate Law Section), Hawaii State and American (Member, Sections on: Real Property, Probate and Trust Law; Chair, Committee on Income Taxation of Trusts and Estates, 1995-1996; Taxation) Bar Associations; State Bar of California. *PRACTICE AREAS:* Estate Planning; Estate and Trust Administration; Charitable Giving. *Email:* evanhoften@cclaw.com

### ASSOCIATES

**KRISTINA A. HANCOCK,** born Santa Barbara, January 17, 1953; admitted to bar, 1990, California. *Education:* Loma Linda University (A.S., 1974); University of San Diego (J.D., summa cum laude, 1987). Member, San Diego Law Review, 1986-1987. Law Clerk to the Honorable Rudi M. Brewster, U.S. District Court, Southern District of California, 1987-1988. *Member:* State Bar of California. *PRACTICE AREAS:* Nonprofit Organizations; Estate Planning; Estate and Trust Administration; Charitable Giving.

*(This Listing Continued)*

**NANCY G. HENDERSON,** born Brooklyn, New York, April 6, 1960; admitted to bar, 1991, California. *Education:* Duke University (A.B., magna cum laude, 1981); Boalt Hall School of Law, University of California (J.D., 1991). Phi Beta Kappa; Order of the Coif. Lecturer, University of California, San Diego, Extended Studies, Fall, 1994; Spring, 1995. Author: "Drafting the Dispositive Provisions of Wills and Trusts," ABA Section of Real Property, Probate and Trust Law, 7th Annual CLE Meeting, 1996; "A Survey of Charitable Giving Techniques, From the Simple to the Sophisticated," USC Law Center Probate and Trust Conference, 1995; "Doing Well by Doing Good: Using Deferred Charitable Giving Techniques to Generate Current Income Tax Benefits," California Tax Lawyer, Fall 1995; "Reducing Income, Gift and Estate Taxes with Conservation and Scenic Easements," California Tax Lawyer, Spring 1995; "Coping With Partnership Interests in Estate Planning and Post-Mortem Administration," USC Law Center Probate and Trust Conference, 1996. *Member:* San Diego County (Member, Sections on: Taxation, Estate and Probate) and American (Member, Sections on: Taxation, Estate and Probate) Bar Associations; State Bar of California (Member, Sections on: Taxation, Estate and Probate; Editor, Tax Reporter; Chair, Young Tax Lawyers Committee of Taxation Section, 1995; Member, Executive Committee, Taxation Section, 1996—); Childrens Hospital Foundation (Member, Estates and Trust Committee, 1995—); Easter Seal Society (Member, Board of Directors, 1991-1994). *PRACTICE AREAS:* Estate Planning; Charitable Giving; Taxation; Nonprofit Organizations. *Email:* nhenders@counsel.com

### OF COUNSEL

**LYNN P. HART,** born Schenectady, New York, September 12, 1954; admitted to bar, 1979, California and U.S. District Court, Southern District of California. *Education:* Westmont College (B.A., cum laude, 1976); Boalt Hall School of Law, University of California (J.D., 1979). Law Clerk to Hon. Edward J. Schwartz, Chief Judge, U.S. District Court, Southern District of California, 1979-1980. Lecturer, Estate Planning Course, Stanford Law School, 1987-1988; 1989-1991. Author: "A Survey of Charitable Giving Techniques, From the Simple to the Sophisticated," USC Law Center Probate and Trust Conference 1995; "Planning for GRATS, GRUTS, and QPRTs in a Community Property Jurisdiction," Structured Value Transfers, ACTEC Program Materials, 1993; "Advanced Issues in Disclaimer Planning: Sharpening an Old Tool," 82 University of Miami Philip E. Heckerling Institute on Estate Planning 1400, 1994. *Member:* The State Bar of California (Member, Executive Committee, 1987-1990; Assistant Editor, Estate Planning and Probate News, 1987-1989); American Bar Association (Member, Real Property, Probate and Trust Law Section; Liaison, National Conference on Commissioners on Uniform Laws Drafting Committee to Amend Uniform Disclaimer of Property Interests Act, 1994-1995; Assistant Secretary, 1993-1994; Chair: Post-Mortem Tax Problems Committee, 1989-1992; Disclaimer Task Force, 1988-1989); American College of Trust and Estate Counsel (Member: California Membership Committee; National Nominating Committee 1995, Charitable Planning and Exempt Organizations Committee, 1995—; UCLA-CEB Estate Planning Institute Advisory Committee, 1992—). *PRACTICE AREAS:* Estate Planning; Estate and Trust Administration; Charitable Giving.

## FLYNN, SHERIDAN & TABB

6125 EL TORDO
P.O. BOX 690
**RANCHO SANTA FE, CALIFORNIA 92067**
Telephone: 619-759-7000
Facsimile: 619-756-1575

*Boston, Massachusetts Office:* One Boston Place, 18th Floor. Telephone: 617-720-2700. Facsimile: 617-720-2709.

*Civil Litigation, Commercial Litigation, Personal Injury, Products Liability, Medical Malpractice and Environmental Litigation.*

(For complete biographical data on all personnel, see Professional Biographies at Boston, Massachusetts)

## ERIC O. FREEBERG

P.O. BOX BOX 9440
**RANCHO SANTA FE, CALIFORNIA 92067-4440**
Telephone: 619-756-6632
Fax: 619-756-3506

*Commercial Transactions. General Real Estate, Real Property Secured Transactions, Business, Mediation and Arbitration.*

*(This Listing Continued)*

***ERIC O. FREEBERG,*** born Los Angeles, California, December 14, 1951; admitted to bar, 1979, California and U.S. District Court, Southern District of California; 1980, U.S. Court of Appeals, Ninth Circuit; 1987, U.S. Supreme Court. *Education:* University of California at Santa Cruz (A.B., with honors, 1974); University of California at Berkeley, Boalt Hall (J.D., 1979). Listed in, The Best Lawyers in America, 1993—. Member, Industrial Relations Law Journal. Chairman: Real Property Section, 1985, Real Property Legislation Sub-Committee, 1983 and Member, Commercial-/Industrial Council, 1986-1992, Building Industrial Association. Partner, Luce Forward Hamilton & Scripps, 1979-1992. *Member:* San Diego County Bar Association; San Diego Trial Lawyers Association; The Association of Trial Lawyers of America. **PRACTICE AREAS:** Business Mediation; Arbitration; Commercial Transactions; General Real Estate Law; Real Property Secured Transactions.

---

## *CHARLES S. LiMANDRI*

Established in 1987

BUILDING 3
16236 SAN DIEGUITO ROAD, SUITE 3-15
P.O. BOX 9120
**RANCHO SANTA FE, CALIFORNIA 92067**
Telephone: 619-759-9930
Fax: 619-759-9938

*Plaintiff's Personal Injury. Defense Maritime, Insurance, Construction and Business Litigation, Public Contracts, Claims and Disputes.*

**CHARLES S. LIMANDRI,** born San Diego, California, August 19, 1955; admitted to bar, 1983, California; 1984, District of Columbia. *Education:* University of San Diego (B.A., magna cum laude, 1977); University of Wales, Aberystwyth, Wales, U.K. (Diploma in International Law and Relations, 1980); Georgetown University (J.D., 1983). Recipient, Outstanding Senior Man, Franklin Award. Listed in: Who's Who in American Law; Who's Who in California; Who's Who in the World, 1991-1992. Rotary International Graduate Fellow, University of Wales. Member, Thomas More Society. President, University of San Diego National Alumni Association. Member, Board of Directors, Head Injury Activity Center. *Member:* San Diego County, Los Angeles County and American Bar Associations; State Bar of California; District of Columbia Bar; The Association of Trial Lawyers of America; National Italian-American Bar Association; San Diego Trial Lawyers Association; Million Dollar Advocates Circle. **PRACTICE AREAS:** Admiralty Maritime Law; Business Law; Construction Law; Environmental Law; Insurance Defense; Medical Malpractice; Personal Injury.

### ASSOCIATES

**HUGH K. SWIFT,** born Los Angeles, California, August 1, 1959; admitted to bar, 1985, California; U.S. District Court, Central and Southern Districts of California. *Education:* University of San Diego (B.B.A., 1981); California Western School of Law (J.D., 1985). *Member:* San Diego County (Member, Alternative Dispute Resolution Section) and American Bar Associations; State Bar of California (Member, Management Law Section); San Diego Defense Lawyers.

**LAWRENCE G. CAMPITIELLO,** born Astoria, New York, September 28, 1958; admitted to bar, 1983, California and U.S. District Court, Central District of California; 1984, U.S. District Court, Southern, Eastern and Northern Districts of California; U.S. Court of Appeals, Ninth Circuit. *Education:* Loyola Marymount University (B.A., cum laude, 1980; J.D., 1983). Law Clerk to the Hon. Calvin K. Ashland, U.S. Bankruptcy Court, Central District of California, 1983-1984. *Member:* San Diego County Bar Association (Member, Bankruptcy Law Section); San Diego Bankruptcy Forum; State Bar of California. **PRACTICE AREAS:** Commercial Litigation; Real Property Law; Bankruptcy Litigation.

REPRESENTATIVE CLIENTS: The Standard Steamship Owners Protection and Indemnity Association, Ltd. (London); Caribbean Marine Service Co., Inc. (San Diego); Century National Insurance.
REFERENCE: Wells Fargo Bank.

---

## *WILLIAMS WOOLLEY COGSWELL NAKAZAWA & RUSSELL*

16236 SAN DIEGUITO ROAD
BUILDING 3, SUITE 3-15
**RANCHO SANTA FE, CALIFORNIA 92067**
Telephone: 619-497-0284
Fax: 619-759-9938
Email: wwlaw@msn.com

*Long Beach, California Office:* 111 West Ocean Boulevard, Suite 2000, 90802-4614. Telephone: 310-495-6000. Telecopier: 310-435-1359.

*Port Hueneme, California Office:* 237 E. Hueneme Road, Suite A, 93041. Telephone: 805-488-8560. Fax: 805-488-7896.

*Commercial Transactions and Litigation, Maritime Law, Transportation and International Law, Environmental Law, Immigration Law, Personal Injury and Product Liability Litigation.*

(For complete Biographical Data on all Personnel, see Professional Biographies at Long Beach)

---

## *FRANCHISE LAW TEAM*

Established in 1985

30021 TOMAS, SUITE 260
**RANCHO SANTA MARGARITA, CALIFORNIA 92688**
Telephone: 714-459-7474
Fax: 714-459-7772
Email: 70702.725@compuserve.com

*Domestic and International Franchising, Licensing and Distribution Law.*

**ROBIN DAY GLENN,** born Bronxville, New York, April 15, 1947; admitted to bar, 1975, California and U.S. District Court, Northern District of California; 1984, U.S. District Court, Central District of California. *Education:* New College (B.A., 1972); University of California at Davis (J.D., 1975); Georgetown University (LL.M., in International and Comparative Law, 1983). California Chapter Author: American Bar Association Forum on Franchising Monograph on Covenants Against Competition in Franchise Agreements, 1992. Author: "Franchises: Adapting to the New Disclosure Requirements," California Business Law Reporter, April, 1994; "Subfranchising," Franchise Law Journal, Winter, 1994; "Franchise Practice in California; Selected Litigation and Operational Issues," California Business Law Practitioner, Summer, 1991; "A Model Franchise Agreement," California Business Law Practitioner, Spring, 1991; "Exporting the California Franchise to the EC," California International Law Practitioner, Winter, 1990-1991; "When Do You Have To Amend?" Franchise Law Journal, Fall, 1990; "Representing California Franchisors," California Business Law Practitioner, Summer, 1990; "Applicability of Business Opportunity Laws to Franchisors," Franchise Law Journal, Summer, 1989; "Financing of U.S. Exports of Telecommunications Equipment," International Law Institute, 1981; "Legal Issues Affecting Licensing of Television Programs in the European Economic Community from the Perspective of the U.S. Exporter," International Law Institute, 1982; "Section 605: Will it Fulfill the Obligation of the U.S. to Implement the Brussels Satellite Convention?" International Law Institute, 1983; "Standard of Care in Administering Nontraditional Psychotherapy," University of California at Davis Law Review, 1974. Contributing Editor, Franchises, California Business Law Reporter, 1991—. Research Fellow, International Law Institute, Washington, D.C. 1981-1983. Member, Board of Directors, Center for International Commercial Arbitration, 1989-1991. Member, Executive Board, Women in World Trade, 1986-1989. Recipient, Fourth National Prize, Nathan Burkan Memorial Competition, 1984. Member, Council of Franchise Suppliers ("CFS") of the International Franchise Association ("IFA"), 1989—; Host, Orange County Second Tuesday Chapter, 1993—; Member, Membership Committee, IFA, 1994—. *Member:* American (Member: International Law Section, 1981—; Forum on Franchising, 1984—) and International Bar Associations; State Bar of California (Member, Executive Board, 1987-1990 and Treasurer, 1988-1989, International Law Section; Franchise Law Committee, Business Law Section, 1989-1992). **LANGUAGES:** French.

REPRESENTATIVE CLIENTS: Anthony's International Franchise Corp.; Clean Comedians, Inc.; Koo Koo Roo, Inc.; Las Vegas Discount Golf & Tennis; O.P.E.N. Cleaning Systems; Realty World Corp.; Scrub-O-Sphere, Inc.
REFERENCE: Bank of America, Rancho Santa Margarita Branch.

CAA1691B

## DENNIS K. COWAN
**RED BLUFF, CALIFORNIA**
(See Redding)

*Debtor and Creditor, Bankruptcy, Reorganizations, Collections and Commercial Law, Real Property, Business, and Corporation Law and Related Litigation in Federal Courts.*

---

## McCARTHY & RUBRIGHT, LLP
Established in 1976
100 RIO STREET
P.O. BOX 190
**RED BLUFF, CALIFORNIA 96080**
Telephone: 916-527-0213
Fax: 916-527-7641

*General Civil Trial and Appellate Practice in all Courts. Corporation, Partnership, Business and Commercial Law, Construction, Real Property, Land Use, Agricultural and Environmental, Insurance Law, Estate Planning, Probate and Trust Law.*

### MEMBERS OF FIRM

**STEVEN B. MCCARTHY,** born Oakland, California, December 30, 1948; admitted to bar, 1975, California; 1981, U.S. Supreme Court. *Education:* University of California at Davis (B.S.B.A., 1971); San Francisco Law School (J.D., 1975). Recipient, American Jurisprudence Award. Member: Moot Court Board; Hastings College of the Law, University of California Center for Trial and Appellate Advocacy, 1984. *Member:* Tehama County Bar Association (President, 1986-1988); State Bar of California (Member, Sections on Business and Litigation); International Association of Defense Counsel.

**SCOTT E. RUBRIGHT,** born Akron, Ohio, July 21, 1959; admitted to bar, 1984, Colorado; 1986, California; 1992, Wyoming; 1993, U.S. Claims Court and U.S. Supreme Court. *Education:* University of Akron (B.A., cum laude, 1981); University of Denver (J.D., 1984); National Institute for Trial Advocacy, National Session, 1992. Real Estate Broker: California, 1986; Colorado, 1993. *Member:* Tehama County and American (Member, Sections on: Real Property, Probate & Trust Law; Corporate, Banking and Business Law; Forum Committee on Construction Law and Environmental Law) Bar Associations; State Bar of California (Member, Sections on: Real Property, Business, Estate Planning/Probate and Environmental Law); Defense Research Institute; Fidelity and Surety Association of Northern California. **PRACTICE AREAS:** Real Estate; Land Use; Construction Law; Business Law; Corporate Law; Insurance; Surety Law; Estate Planning; Probate.

**DAVID J. MURRAY,** born Richland, Washington, June 3, 1955; admitted to bar, 1992, California. *Education:* Chico State College (B.A., 1980); Western State University (J.D., with honors, 1991). Recipient: Best Brief, Moot Court; American Jurisprudence Awards: Uniform Commercial Code and Trusts. Listed in Who's Who in American Universities and Colleges. Associate Editor, Western State Law Review. Author: "New York Times v. N.A.S.A.: Troubled Skies Ahead for the Freedom of Information Act," Western State University Law Review, Vol.19, No.1, Fall 1991. *Member:* Butte County, Tehama County and American Bar Associations; State Bar of California; American Society of Clinical Pathologists.

### OF COUNSEL

**ROBERT E. MCCARTHY,** born San Francisco, California, February 16, 1920; admitted to bar, 1950, California. *Education:* University of California at Berkeley (A.B., 1941); Boalt Hall School of Law, University of California (J.D., 1949). Member, Presidential Transition Team, 1980-1981. Consultant, Office of Policy Development, The White House, 1981. Chairman, Board of Directors, Legal Services Corporation, Washington D.C., 1983-1984. Trustee, Pacific Legal Foundation, 1987—. Member, Board of Visitors, Pepperdine University School of Law, 1988—. *Member:* State Bar of California. [With USN, 1942-1946]. **PRACTICE AREAS:** Fidelity and Surety; Construction Law.

REPRESENTATIVE CLIENTS: Alsco, Inc.; Burns Brothers, Inc.; Helser Chevrolet, Inc.; Northwestern Resources, Inc.; Parish Properties; Petro, Inc.; Q-97 FM; Red Bluff Ford; Redding Toyota; Tehama County Bank; Lake California Property Owners Association, Inc.; Rancho Tehama Association; Red Bluff Bull Sale; Tehama County Cattlemen's Association; Cal-Farm Insurance; Cigna Insurance; Chubb Group; Fremont Indemnity; Globe Life Insurance; Industrial Indemnity Co.; Maryland Casualty Co.

---

## McGLYNN & McGLYNN
A Partnership including a Professional Corporation
Established in 1966
737 WASHINGTON STREET
P.O. BOX 1110
**RED BLUFF, CALIFORNIA 96080**
Telephone: 916-527-1117
Fax: 916-527-1414

*General Civil and Trial Practice. Criminal, Negligence, Probate, Estate Planning, Corporation, Contract, Real Property and Family Law.*

FIRM PROFILE: McGlynn and McGlynn provides a general practice, serving Tehama and adjacent counties, by offering a wide range of legal services. The firm has a fully staffed office, a Probate Paralegal, and handles all forms of civil and criminal litigation.

### MEMBERS OF FIRM

**THOMAS J. MCGLYNN, (P.C.),** born Red Bluff, California, May 14, 1938; admitted to bar, 1964, California. *Education:* University of Santa Clara (B.A., 1960); LL.B., magna cum laude, 1963). Deputy District Attorney, Tehama County, 1967-1971. *Member:* Tehama County Bar Association (President, 1978); The State Bar of California.

**MATTHEW C. MCGLYNN,** born San Jose, California, September 6, 1961; admitted to bar, 1986, California. *Education:* University of Santa Clara (B.A., 1983; J.D., summa cum laude, 1986). *Member:* Tehama County Bar Association (President, 1991-1993); The State Bar of California.

REFERENCES: Bank of America National Trust & Savings Assn., Red Bluff, California; Tehama County Bank, Red Bluff, California.

---

## PETERS, FULLER, RUSH, FARNSWORTH & HABIB
**RED BLUFF, CALIFORNIA**
(See Chico)

*General Civil and Trial Practice in all State and Federal Courts. Insurance Defense, Real Property. Estate Planning and Administration, Business and Commercial Law, Workers Compensation.*

---

## DONALD B. WEBSTER
Established in 1964
416 PINE STREET
P.O. BOX 870
**RED BLUFF, CALIFORNIA 96080**
Telephone: 916-527-0114

*General Civil and Trial Practice in all State Courts. Probate, Real Property, Business and Family Law.*

**DONALD B. WEBSTER,** born Fond du Lac, Wisconsin, October 28, 1924; admitted to bar, 1950, California. *Education:* Stanford University (A.B., 1947; J.D., 1949). Phi Beta Kappa. *Member:* Tehama County (President, 1963-1964) and American Bar Associations; The State Bar of California (Member, Continuing Education of the Bar Committee, 1966-1969). [With USMCR, 1943-1946; Capt., USMCR (Retired) 1951-1952]

REPRESENTATIVE CLIENTS: Northern California Title Co.; Mid Valley Bank; Tehama County Public Conservator.
REFERENCES: Bank of America National Trust & Savings Assn.; Mid Valley Bank.

---

## BANDELL • SWANSON
Established in 1980
1330 WEST STREET
P.O. DRAWER 994410
**REDDING, CALIFORNIA 96099-4410**
Telephone: 916-243-8150
Fax: 916-243-1745

*Civil Trial Practice, Real Estate, Land Use Planning, Corporation, Education, Employer/Employee Relations, Administrative and General Business.*

(This Listing Continued)

## MEMBERS OF FIRM

**LEONARD J. BANDELL,** born Pittsburgh, Pennsylvania, May 30, 1949; admitted to bar, 1975, California. *Education:* University of Pittsburgh (B.A., 1972); Golden Gate University (J.D., M.S., Taxation, 1975). *Member:* Shasta-Trinity County Bar Association; State Bar of California (Member, Real Property Law Section). **PRACTICE AREAS:** Litigation; Real Estate; Land Use Planning; Corporation and Business Law.

**L. ALAN SWANSON,** born Champaign, Illinois, October 6, 1951; admitted to bar, 1977, California. *Education:* De Anza College (A.A., magna cum laude, 1971); University of California at Berkeley (B.A., 1973); University of Santa Clara (J.D., cum laude, 1977). Judicial Extern for Judge William Ingram, U.S. District Court, Northern District, 1977. *Member:* Shasta-Trinity County Bar Association; State Bar of California. **PRACTICE AREAS:** Education; Employer/Employee Relations; Administrative Law.

REPRESENTATIVE CLIENTS: The Bank of California; Wheelabrator Shasta Energy Co.; Santa Ana Valley Irrigation Co.; Shasta County Office of Education; Siskiyou County Superintendent of Schools; Trinity County Office of Education; City of Shasta Lake; Weaverville Community Services District; Coldwell Banker C& C Properties; Redding Realty, Inc.; Fidelity National Title Insurance Company of California; Schmitt Trucking and Logging Co.; Schmitt Remediation; Shasta County Tax Assessment Appeals Board; Moss Lumber Co., Inc.; Jaxon Enterprises; Crystal Creek Aggregate.

---

## DUGAN BARR & ASSOCIATES

1824 COURT STREET
P.O. BOX 994390
**REDDING, CALIFORNIA 96099-1648**
Telephone: 916-243-8008
Fax: 916-243-1648
URL: http://www.CA-Lawyer.com/

*General Civil and Trial Practice, Business Litigation, Personal Injury, Negligence, Insurance, Aviation, Products Liability, Professional Liability, Elder Abuse and Public Entity Liability.*

**DUGAN BARR,** born Yreka, California, April 3, 1942; admitted to bar, 1967, California. *Education:* Reed College (B.A., 1964); University of Chicago (J.D., 1967). Diplomate, American Board of Trial Advocates (President, Sacramento Valley Chapter, 1991). *Member:* Shasta-Trinity County Bar Association (President, 1971); State Bar of California; California Trial Lawyers Association; The Association of Trial Lawyers of America; American Board of Professional Liability Attorneys. Fellow: American College of Trial Lawyers; International Academy of Trial Lawyers. Board Certified, Civil Trial Advocate, American Board of Trial Advocates. **PRACTICE AREAS:** Trials; Personal Injury; Professional Negligence; Products Liability; Highway Design and Maintenance. *Email:* dugan@CA-Lawyer.com

### ASSOCIATES

**DAVID L. CASE,** born Columbus, Ohio, May 22, 1947; admitted to bar, 1973, California and U.S. District Court, Northern District of California; 1984, U.S. Supreme Court. *Education:* Columbia Union College (B.A., 1969); Hastings College of the Law, University of California (J.D., 1973). Member, Panel of Arbitrators, American Arbitration Association. *Member:* Bar Association of San Francisco; Shasta-Trinity and American Bar Associations; State Bar of California; Association of Defense Counsel of Northern California. **PRACTICE AREAS:** Mediation; Trial.

**DOUGLAS MUDFORD,** born Texarkana, Arkansas, June 11, 1945; admitted to bar, 1991, California. *Education:* California State University at Humboldt (B.A., 1970); Cal Northern School of Law (J.D., 1991). *Member:* Shasta-Trinity County Bar Association; State Bar of California; California Trial Lawyers Association. **PRACTICE AREAS:** Personal Injury; Products Liability; Business Litigation; Labor Law; ADA. *Email:* doug@CA-Lawyer.com

REPRESENTATIVE CLIENTS: City of Redding; Mid Valley Bank; Scott Valley Bank; 3M; Enloe Hospital.
REFERENCES: Scott Valley Bank, Redding Branch; Mid Valley Bank, Redding Branch.

---

## RICHARD N. BATES

SUITE B, 1300 WEST STREET
**REDDING, CALIFORNIA 96001**
Telephone: 916-244-6442
Fax: 916-244-0216

*General Civil Trial Practice. Corporation, Business, Real Estate, Estate Planning and Probate Law.*

**RICHARD N. BATES,** born Los Angeles, California, January 26, 1940; admitted to bar, 1969, California. *Education:* Stanford University; Brigham Young University (B.S., 1965); University of California at Los Angeles (J.D., 1968). Member, Board of Directors, United Way of Shasta County. *Member:* Shasta-Trinity County (Probate Law Committee, Chairman, 1996) and American (Litigation Section: Chairman-Elect, 1996-1997, Committee on Intellectual Properties Litigation, 1976-1977; Division Director, Substantive Areas of Litigation, 1977-1979; Chairman, Committee on Individual and Small Firm Practice, 1979-1981; Member, Section of Corporation, Banking and Business Law) Bar Associations; The State Bar of California (Examiner, 1971-1973; Member: Local Administrative Committee, 1973-1976; Investigation Panel for State Bar District 7, 1976-1978; Referee, State Bar Court, 1978-1988).

---

## BORTON, PETRINI & CONRON

280 HEMSTED DRIVE, SUITE 100
**REDDING, CALIFORNIA 96002**
Telephone: 916-222-1530
Fax: 916-222-4498
Email: bpcred@bpclaw.com

*Bakersfield, California Office:* The Borton, Petrini & Conron Building, 1600 Truxtun Avenue, P.O. Box 2026. Telephone: 805-322-3051. Fax: 805-322-4628. Email: bpcbak@bpclaw.com.
*San Luis Obispo, California Office:* 1114 Marsh Street. Telephone: 805-541-4340. Fax: 805-541-4558. Email: bpcslo@bpclaw.com.
*Visalia, California Office:* 206 South Mooney Boulevard, P.O. Box 1028. Telephone: 209-627-5600. Fax: 209-627-4309. Email: bpcvis@bpclaw.com.
*Fresno, California Office:* T. W. Patterson Building, 2014 Tulare Street, Suite 830. Telephone: 209-268-0117. Fax: 209-237-7995. Email: bpcfrs@bpclaw.com.
*Sacramento, California Office:* 2233 Watt Avenue, Suite 290. Telephone: 916-484-3555. Fax: 916-484-3550. Email: bpcsac@bpclaw.com.
*Santa Barbara, California Office:* 211 East Victoria Street, Suite D. Telephone: 805-564-2404. Fax: 805-564-2176. Email: bpcsb@bpclaw.com
*Los Angeles, California Office:* 707 Wilshire Boulevard, Suite 5100. Telephone: 213-624-2869. Fax: 213-489-3930. Email: bpcla@bpclaw.com.
*San Diego, California Office:* John Burnham Building, 610 West Ash Street, 9th Floor. Telephone: 619-232-2424. Fax: 619-531-0794. Email: bpcsd@bpclaw.com.
*Newport Beach, California Office:* 4675 MacArthur Court, Suite 1150. Telephone: 714-752-2333. Fax: 714-752-2854. Email: bpcnb@bpclaw.com.
*Modesto, California Office:* The Turner Building, 900 "H" Street, Suite D. Telephone: 209-576-1701. Fax: 209-527-9753. Email: bpcmod@bpclaw.com.
*San Francisco, California Office:* 111 Pine Street, Suite 730. Telephone: 415-981-4415. Fax: 415-391-5538. Email: bpcsf@bpclaw.com.
*San Bernardino, California Office:* 290 North "D" Street, Suite 500. Telephone: 909-381-0527. Fax: 909-381-0658. Email: bpcsbdo@bpclaw.com.
*San Jose, California Office:* 2 North Second Street. Telephone: 408-298-3997. Fax: 408-298-3365. Email: bpcsj@bpclaw.com.
*Ventura, California Office:* 1000 Hill Road, Suite 310. Telephone: 805-650-9994. Fax: 805-650-7125. Email: bpcvta@bpclaw.com.
*Santa Rosa, California Office:* 50 Santa Rosa Avenue, Suite 300. Telephone: 707-527-9477. Fax: 707-527-9488. Email: bpcsr@bpclaw.com.

*Commercial/Real Estate Litigation, Insurance Law, General Civil Trial and Appellate Practice in State and Federal Courts, Personal Injury and Casualty Defense Litigation, Insurance Bad Faith and Coverage, Labor and Employment, Toxic Torts, Real Estate, Land Use Planning, Zoning, Municipal, Professional Errors and Omissions, Healthcare Provider Malpractice Defense, Products Liability, Oil and Gas, Water, Natural Resources, Environmental, Public Entity, Administrative, Agricultural, Banking, Contracts, Corporations,*

*(This Listing Continued)*

## BORTON, PETRINI & CONRON, Redding—Continued

Partnerships, Taxation, Creditor's Remedies, Bankruptcy, Probate, Estate Planning, Family Law.

FIRM PROFILE: Founded by Fred E. Borton in 1899, the firm offers high quality legal services in all of the practice areas described above through its California network of sixteen regional offices. Our mission is to handle each file as if we were the client. We are responsive to the clients' need for communication, cost effectiveness and prompt evaluation.

### MEMBERS OF FIRM

**RANDALL L. HARR**, born Marysville, California, January 26, 1955; admitted to bar, 1982, California. *Education:* University of California at Davis (A.B., 1978); University of the Pacific, McGeorge School of Law (J.D., 1982). Traynor Society. *Member:* Shasta/Trinity County Bar Association; The State Bar of California; Shasta Claims Association (Member, 1990—, Board Member, 1992—); Cal Davis Alumni Association; National Rifle Association; Association of Defense Counsel, Northern California. **PRACTICE AREAS:** Construction Defect; Crop Loss; Premises Liability; Real Estate Malpractice; Attorney Malpractice; Dental Malpractice; Physical Therapist Malpractice; Medical Malpractice; Real Property Boundary Disputes; International Tort Defense; Group Home, Foster Care and Developmentally disabled related claims; Products Liability.

**KENNETH B. ARTHOFER**, born Newport Beach, California, August 9, 1963; admitted to bar, 1989, California and U.S. District Court, Northern District of California; 1990, U.S. Court of Appeals, Ninth Circuit. *Education:* California State University at Long Beach (B.A., 1986); Pepperdine University (J.D., 1989). Assistant Research Editor, Dunaway, "The Law of Distressed Real Estate," Clark Boardman Company, Ltd., New York, 1987-1988. Judge Pro Tem, Skasta County Municipal Court, 1995—. *Member:* Shasta-Trinity County Bar Associations; The State Bar of California; Association of Defense Counsel, Northern California. **PRACTICE AREAS:** Real Estate; Business; Corporate Transactions; Insurance Defense; Civil Litigation.

### ASSOCIATE

**ALFRED W. MONDORF**, born Pasadena, California, June 7, 1949; admitted to bar, 1986, California. *Education:* University of Redlands (B.A., 1971); California State University at Los Angeles (M.A., 1976); Glendale College of Law (J.D., 1986). *Member:* Shasta-Trinity County Bar Association; Shasta Claims Association. State Bar of California. **PRACTICE AREAS:** Insurance Defense.

(For a Complete Listing of Personnel and Representative Clients, please refer to our Bakersfield listing).

## ARNOLD DAVID BREYER

Established in 1974

1721 COURT STREET
**REDDING, CALIFORNIA 96001**
Telephone: 916-244-3690
Fax: 916-244-0923

Mount Shasta, California Office: 112 Siskiyou Avenue, P.O. Box 201.
Telephone: 916-926-3134. Fax: 916-926-8607.

Practice Limited to Personal Injury and Family Law.

(For complete biographical data, see Professional Biography at Mount Shasta, California)

## BRICKWOOD & KEY

1135 PINE STREET, SUITE 210
**REDDING, CALIFORNIA 96001**
Telephone: 916-245-1877
Fax: 916-245-1879

FIRM PROFILE: An experienced Litigation and Trial Practice firm emphasizing Insurance Defense, Governmental Entity Defense and Employment Litigation serving Shasta, Tehama, Siskiyou, Butte and Trinity Counties. Also Licensed in Oregon.

### MEMBERS OF FIRM

**GARY C. BRICKWOOD**, born Redding, California, February 12, 1952; admitted to bar, 1980, California. *Education:* University of California at Berkeley (A.B., 1974); McGeorge School of Law (J.D., 1980). Deputy District Attorney, San Mateo County, 1981-1985. *Member:* State Bar of Cali-

*(This Listing Continued)*

CAA1694B

fornia. **PRACTICE AREAS:** Civil Litigation; Insurance; Business; Employment.

**RODNEY J. KEY**, born Oxnard, California, March 30, 1958; admitted to bar, 1986, California; 1992, Oregon. *Education:* University of the Pacific (B.A., 1980; M.A., 1982); McGeorge School of Law (J.D., 1986). *Member:* State Bar of California; Oregon State Bar. **PRACTICE AREAS:** Trials; Civil Litigation; Insurance Defense; Business and Commercial Litigation; Products Liability.

REPRESENTATIVE CLIENTS: City of Redding, Shasta County; Pepsi of Northern California; State Farm Insurance; Farmers Insurance Exchange.

## STEPHEN S. CARLTON

1716 COURT STREET
**REDDING, CALIFORNIA 96001**
Telephone: 916-244-3778
Fax: 916-241-6167

Practice Limited to Criminal Defense in State and Federal Courts.

**STEPHEN S. CARLTON**, born San Francisco, California, September 2, 1942; admitted to bar, 1969, California; 1973, U.S. Court of Appeals, Ninth Circuit. *Education:* Santa Clara University (B.S., 1965; J.D., 1968). *Member:* State Bar of California; California Attorneys for Criminal Justice. **PRACTICE AREAS:** Criminal Law (100%).

## CARR, KENNEDY, PETERSON & FROST

A LAW CORPORATION

Established in 1880

420 REDCLIFF DRIVE
P.O. BOX 492396
**REDDING, CALIFORNIA 96049**
Telephone: 916-222-2100
Fax: 916-222-0504

General Civil and Trial Practice in all State and Federal Courts. Real Estate, Taxation, Corporation, Commercial, Construction, Negligence, Products Liability, Water Rights, Estate Planning, Probate and Insurance Law.

**FRANCIS CARR** (1875-1944).

**LAWRENCE J. KENNEDY, SR.** (1883-1975).

**LAURENCE J. KENNEDY, JR.** (1918-1986).

**LAURENCE W. CARR** (1912-1991).

**R. RUSS PETERSON**, born Cedarville, California, February 19, 1939; admitted to bar, 1966, California. *Education:* University of California at Berkeley (B.S., 1961); Willamette University; Boalt Hall School of Law, University of California (J.D., 1965). Trustee, Redding School District, 1981-1985. Member, California Alumni Council, 1982-1985. Referee, State Bar Court, 1982. *Member:* Shasta-Trinity County Bar Association; The State Bar of California (Member, Sections on: Litigation; Real Property Law; Business Law). **PRACTICE AREAS:** Commercial and Real Estate Litigation; Personal Injury; Construction Law; Business and Real Estate Transactions.

**DANIEL S. FROST**, born Ely, Nevada, January 2, 1940; admitted to bar, 1967, California. *Education:* San Jose State College (B.A., 1964); University of Oregon; Boalt Hall School of Law, University of California (J.D., 1967). Associate Editor, California Law Review, 1966-1967. Author: "Labor's Antitrust Exemption," California Law Review, Volume 55, 1967. Member, California Water Commission, 1976-1982. *Member:* Shasta-Trinity County Bar Association; The State Bar of California (Member, Sections on: Litigation; Real Property Law; Business Law); National Association of Railroad Trial Counsel. **PRACTICE AREAS:** Commercial and Real Estate Litigation; Environmental Litigation; Personal Injury; Corporate Litigation; Natural Resources Litigation.

**ROBERT M. HARDING**, born Covina, California, September 18, 1955; admitted to bar, 1981, California. *Education:* University of California at Berkeley (A.B. Economics, 1977); University of San Diego (J.D., 1981). *Member:* Shasta-Trinity County and American Bar Associations; The State Bar of California (Member, Sections on: Litigation, Real Property Law; Business Law). **PRACTICE AREAS:** Personal Injury; Commercial and Real Estate Litigation; Construction Litigation.

*(This Listing Continued)*

**EVAN L. DELGADO,** born Redding, California, May 5, 1959; admitted to bar, 1984, Alaska; 1987, California. *Education:* University of California at Berkeley (B.A., 1981); University of California at Davis (J.D., 1984); University of Miami Graduate Program (LL.M., in Taxation, 1988). Co-Author: "Hydroelectric Power, The Federal Power Act and State Water Laws: Is Federal Preemption Water Over The Dam?" 17 University of California at Davis Law Review 1179, 1984. Extern, Alaska Supreme Court, 1984. *Member:* State Bar of California (Member, Sections on: Taxation; Estate Planning, Trust and Probate Law); American Bar Association. (Certified Specialist, Taxation Law and Estate Planning, Trust and Probate Law, The State Bar of California Board of Legal Specialization). *PRACTICE AREAS:* Tax Law; Estate Planning and Administration; Business Transactions; Business Law.

**STEPHEN H. BAKER,** born Sacramento, California, December 29, 1959; admitted to bar, 1987, California. *Education:* University of Oregon (B.S., 1982); University of the Pacific, McGeorge School of Law (J.D., 1986); University of Salzburg Austria (International Legal Studies, 1984. Phi Delta Phi. *Member:* Shasta-Trinity County Bar Association; Association of Defense Counsel of Northern California, The State Bar of California. *PRACTICE AREAS:* Insurance Personal Injury; Tort Law; Real Estate Litigation; Construction Litigation.

**MICHAEL P. ASHBY,** born Walnut Creek, California, April 12, 1959; admitted to bar, 1984, California; 1986, U.S. Tax Court. *Education:* University of the Pacific (B.A., magna cum laude, 1981); University of Southern California (J.D., 1984); Golden Gate University (M.S., Taxation, 1989). Phi Kappa Phi. *Member:* Shasta-Trinity County, Los Angeles County and American Bar Associations; State Bar of California. (Certified Specialist, Taxation Law, The State Bar of California Board of Legal Specialization). *TRANSACTIONS:* Knowl-Wood Restaurants, 1989; Tam's Stationers, 1990; Malcolm Smith Racing, 1990; Hansen Beverage Company, 1992; Encinitas Town Center, 1993. *PRACTICE AREAS:* Corporations; Partnerships; Real Estate; Taxation.

**RANDALL C. NELSON,** born Canoga Park, California, March 17, 1961; admitted to bar, 1988, California and U.S. District Court, Northern District of California. 1990, U.S. District Court, Eastern District of California. 1993, U.S. District Court, Central District of California. *Education:* University of California at Irvine (B.A., 1983); Santa Clara University (J.D., 1988). American Inns of Court. San Joaquin Inn. *Member:* Shasta-Trinity County Bar Association; Fresno County and American Bar Associations; The State Bar of California. *PRACTICE AREAS:* Civil Litigation; Construction; Commercial; Personal Injury.

**ROBERT A. WEST,** born Mesa, Arizona, February 21, 1965; admitted to bar, 1992, California. *Education:* Arizona State University (B.S., 1987); Pepperdine University (J.D., 1991); University of San Diego (LL.M. Taxation). *PRACTICE AREAS:* Taxation; Estate Planning; Transactional.

REPRESENTATIVE CLIENTS: Allstate Insurance Co.; Avco Financial Services; Champion International Corp.; Chicago Title Insurance Co.; CH2M Hill California, Inc.; C.I.T. Corp.; The Coca-Cola Co.; Croman Corp.; Design Professional Insurance Co.; Dresser Industries; Economic Development Corp. of Shasta Co.; Fidelity National Title Insurance Company of California; Fruit Growers Supply Co.; ITT Rayonier, Inc.; Wm. D. Johnson Co., Inc.; KIXE-TV; Klamath Medical Service Bureau; Louisiana-Pacific Corp.; Mack Financial Corp.; McConnell Foundation; Minnesota Mining & Manufacturing; Moseman Construction Co.; Norcal Electric Supply, Inc.; Northbrook Insurance Co.; Northern Calif. Educational Television Assn., Inc.; Oregon Champion Metal Co.; Pace Engineering; Pacific Power and Light Co.; Redding Air Service, Inc.; Roseburg Lumber Co.; Stewart Title Insurance Co.; Stimpel-Wielbelhaus Associates; Wisconsin-California Forest Products; W. M. Beaty & Associates, Inc.; United Grocers.

---

## FREDRICK E. CLEMENT
280 HEMSTED DRIVE, SUITE C
**REDDING, CALIFORNIA 96002**
Telephone: 916-224-7700
Fax: 916-224-2284

*Business, Real Estate and General Civil Litigation; Corporations.*

**FREDRICK E. CLEMENT,** born San Luis Obispo, California, January 13, 1960; admitted to bar, 1987, California. *Education:* Westmont College (B.A., cum laude, 1982); Hastings College of the Law, University of California (J.D., cum laude, 1987). *Member:* Shasta Trinity Counties Bar Association; State Bar of California.

---

## DENNIS K. COWAN
280 HEMSTED DRIVE, SUITE B
P.O. BOX 992090
**REDDING, CALIFORNIA 96099-2090**
Telephone: 916-221-7300
Fax: 916-221-7389
Email: dennisk@snowcrest.net

*Debtor and Creditor, Bankruptcy, Reorganizations, Collections and Commercial Law, Real Property, Business, and Corporation Law and Related Litigation in Federal Courts.*

**DENNIS K. COWAN,** born Kansas City, Missouri, January 20, 1940; admitted to bar, 1965, California. *Education:* Yale University (B.A., 1961); Stanford University (J.D., 1964). Phi Alpha Delta. *Member:* Shasta-Trinity County Bar Association (President, 1978); State Bar of California; American Bankruptcy Institute.

---

## HALKIDES & MORGAN
A PROFESSIONAL CORPORATION
833 MISTLETOE LANE
P.O. DRAWER 492170
**REDDING, CALIFORNIA 96049-2170**
Telephone: 916-221-8150
Fax: 916-221-7963
Email: gdh@halkides-morgan.com
URL: http://www.halkides-morgan.com

*General Civil and Trial Practice. Insurance, Products Liability, Medical and Legal Malpractice and Public Entity Defense Law.*

**G. DENNIS HALKIDES,** born Los Angeles, California, June 13, 1943; admitted to bar, 1969, California; 1983, Oregon; 1983, U.S. Supreme Court. *Education:* California State University, Humboldt (B.A., 1966); Willamette University (J.D., 1969). Phi Delta Phi. Member, Shasta, Tehama and Siskiyou Counties Judicial Arbitration Panels, 1979—. *Member:* Shasta-Trinity County and American Bar Associations; State Bar of California; Oregon State Bar; International Association of Defense Counsel; Northern California Association of Defense Counsel (Member, Board of Directors, 1978-1985; Liaison Committee between ADC & Bay Area representatives of Casualty Claims Association & Pacific Coast Claims Association, 1989; Membership Chairman, 1980-1985); Defense Research Institute; American Trial Lawyers Association (ATLA); Mediator, American Arbitration Association; The American Board of Trial Advocates (Diplomate, ABOTA). *Email:* gdh@halkides-morgan.com

**ARTHUR L. MORGAN, JR.,** born Portland, Oregon, July 21, 1951; admitted to bar, 1977, California; 1983, Oregon; U.S. Supreme Court. *Education:* Glendale University (B.S., 1975; LL.B., 1977). Judge Pro Tem, Municipal Court, 1981-1983. Member, Judicial Arbitration Panels, Shasta and Tehama Counties, 1981-1983. *Member:* Shasta-Trinity County and American Bar Associations; State Bar of California; Oregon State Bar; Northern California Association of Defense Counsel (Member, Board of Directors, 1985-1986; Membership Chairman, 1986); Defense Research Institute; The Association of Trial Lawyers of America; The American Board of Trial Advocates (Advocate, ABOTA).

**WILLIAM D. AYRES,** born Moses Lake, Washington, July 20, 1955; admitted to bar, 1981, California; U.S. District Court, Southern, Eastern and Northern Districts of California. *Education:* Arizona State University (B.S., 1978); University of San Diego (J.D., 1981). Appellate Moot Court Board and National Trial Advocate Team; Judge Pro Tem Municipal Court Shasta County, 1995-1996. *Member:* Shasta-Trinity Counties and San Diego County Bar Associations; State Bar of California; San Diego Barrister's; San Diego Trial Lawyers' Association; Northern California Association of Defense Counsel.

**JOHN P. KELLEY,** born San Gabriel, November 26,1968; admitted to bar, 1993, California; U.S. District Court, Eastern and Central Districts of California. *Education:* University of the Pacific (B.A., cum laude, 1989); McGeorge School of Law (J.D., 1993). *Member:* Shasta-Trinity Counties Bar Association; State Bar of California.

**MARY CATHERINE PEARL,** born Dallas, Texas, December 19, 1945; admitted to bar, 1993, California and U.S. Court of Appeals, Ninth Circuit; U.S. District Court, Eastern, Southern, Central and Northern Districts of California. *Education:* California State University at Chico (B.A., 1974); Santa Barbara College (J.D., 1993). Contributor: Cappello & Komoroske,

*(This Listing Continued)*

**HALKIDES & MORGAN,** A PROFESSIONAL CORPORATION,
Redding—Continued

Lender Liability, Butterworth, 1994; "Exercise of Undue Control Over a Borrower," 15 Am.Jur. Proof of Facts III 695, 1992. Member: Santa Barbara City Human Relations Committee, 1983; San Luis Obispo City Human Relations Commission, 1979-1981. *Member:* Santa Barbara County and Shasta-Trinity Counties Bar Associations; California State Bar (Member, Labor & Employment Law Section, 1994); Santa Barbara Women Lawyers.

REPRESENTATIVE CLIENTS: Albertson's Food Store; American Hardware Mutual Insurance Co.; Anheuser-Busch, Inc.; AVCO Financial Insurance Group; Cessna Aircraft Co.; Chubb-Pacific Insurance Group; City of Dunsmuir; City of Red Bluff; County of Shasta; Design Professionals Insurance Co.; Farmers Insurance Group; Fremont Indemnity Co.; Gallagher Bassett Insurance Service; Great American Insurance Co.; Holiday Markets, Inc.; International Harvester; Lawyers Mutual Insurance Co.; Mission Insurance Co.; National Automobile Insurance Company; National Can Corp.; National Chiropractic Insurance Co.; National General Insurance Company; National Insurance Co.; Norelco, Inc.; Northern California Schools Insurance Group; Novastar International; Safeco Insurance Co.; Safeway Stores, Inc.; Shasta General Hospital; Simpson Timber Co.; Standard Oil Company of California; State Farm Mutual Insurance Co.; Stuyvesant Insurance Co.; The Times-Mirror Co.; Transamerica Insurance Group; Travelers Insurance Co.; The Truck Insurance Exchange; Universal Underwriters; Zurich American Insurance Co.
REFERENCE: Tri Counties Bank.

## LAUGHLIN, FALBO, LEVY & MORESI LLP

A Partnership including Professional Corporations

**930 EXECUTIVE WAY, SECOND FLOOR**
**REDDING, CALIFORNIA 96002**
Telephone: 916-222-0268
Fax: 916-222-5705
Email: lflm@lflm.com
URL: http://lflm.com

*San Francisco, California Office:* Two Embarcadero Center, Fifth Floor. Telephone: 415-781-6676. Fax: 415-781-6823.

*Sacramento, California Office:* 106 K Street - Second Floor. Telephone: 916-441-6045. Fax: 916-441-7067.

*Pasadena, California Office:* 200 South Los Robles, Suite 500. Telephone: 818-586-9700. Fax: 818-568-3905.

*Walnut Creek, California Office:* 100 Pringle Avenue, Suite 630. Telephone: 510-210-0210. Fax: 510-210-0105.

*Irvine, California Office:* 3 Park Plaza, Suite 1400, P.O. Box 17659. Telephone: 714-251-0120. Fax: 714-251-0125.

*San Jose, California Office:* 1570 The Alameda, Suite 100. Telephone: 408-286-8801. Fax: 408-286-1935.

*General Civil and Trial Practice. Workers' Compensation Defense.*

**HENRY M. SLOWIK,** born Bronx, New York, April 22, 1952; admitted to bar, 1985, California. *Education:* Bates College (B.A., 1974); Hastings College of the Law, University of California (J.D., 1985). Author: "California's Going and Coming Rule in Workers' Compensation: A New Model for Consistency," Vol. 36, No. 6, p. 969, 36 Hastings Law Journal 969. Extern to Honorable M. H. Patel, U.S. District Court, Northern District of California, Summer, 1984. **PRACTICE AREAS:** Workers' Compensation. **Email:** hslowik@lflm.com

**ROY D. WOOLFSTEAD,** born Ft. Belvoir, Virginia, March 6, 1951; admitted to bar, 1976, California. *Education:* Arizona University; Northern Arizona University (B.S., 1973); Western State University (LL.B., 1976). (Certified Specialist, Workers Compensation Law, The State Bar of California Board of Legal Specialization). **PRACTICE AREAS:** Workers' Compensation. **Email:** rwoolfst@lflm.com

**BRIGHAM P. JONES,** born Glendale, California, October 13, 1943; admitted to bar, 1975, California. *Education:* Brigham Young University (A.B., 1967); Humphreys College of Law (J.D., 1975). Deputy District Attorney, Butte County, California, 1977-1983. *Member:* Butte County Bar Association; Association of Defense Counsel of Northern California. **PRACTICE AREAS:** Workers' Compensation; Insurance Defense; Subrogation. **Email:** bjones@lflm.com

*(This Listing Continued)*

CAA1696B

**JOHN S. FALBO,** born Larkspur, California, October 26, 1965; admitted to bar, 1992, California. *Education:* California State University, Sacramento (B.A., 1988); McGeorge School of Law (J.D., 1992). **PRACTICE AREAS:** Workers' Compensation. **Email:** jfalbo@lflm.com

**DAVID V. HUSCHER,** born Orange, California, February 27, 1959; admitted to bar, 1985, California; 1987, Federated States of Micronesia and Kosrae State Bar. *Education:* University of California at Los Angeles (B.S., cum laude, 1981); Honors Fellow, London School of Economics (1982); McGeorge School of Law, University of the Pacific (J.D., 1985). Author: "Recent Changes in International Banking and Trade," Comparative Law Journal, 1985. *Member:* Shasta-Trinity Bar Association; State Bar of California. **LANGUAGES:** Korean. **PRACTICE AREAS:** Workers' Compensation; Insurance Defense; Labor Relations; Subrogation. **Email:** dhuscher@lflm.com

All Partners and Associates are Members of the State Bar of California.

REPRESENTATIVE CLIENTS: AC Transit; Aetna Casualty & Surety Co.; Alameda County Schools; Allianz Insurance Co.; Alta Bates Hospital; American Hardware Mutual; American International Adjustment Co.; American International Underwriters; American Protective Services; Argonaut Insurance; Bank of America; California Casualty Insurance Co.; City of Anaheim; Continental Co.; Continental Loss Adjusting Service; Crawford and Co.; Eagle Marine Insurance Co.; Eagle Pacific Ins. Co.; Electric Mutual; Employers Insurance of Wausau; Fireman's Fund; Fremont Indemnity; GAB Business Services; Gates, McDonald & Co.; General Electric Co.; Hartford Accident & Indemnity; Hewlett-Packard; Industrial Indemnity Co.; Insurance Company of the West; Liberty Mutual Insurance; Majestic Insurance Co.; McKesson Corp.; MHG Adjusting Co.; Regents of the University of California; Royal Globe Group; Safeway Stores; San Francisco Newspaper Agency; Sequoia Hospital; Standard Oil Co.; Todd Shipyards Corp.; TOSCO; United Airlines, Inc.; U.S. Sprint Communications; USX; Wells Fargo Bank; Zenith National Insurance; Zurich-American Insurance.

(For biographical data on other personnel, see professional biographies at San Francisco, Sacramento, Walnut Creek, Irvine, San Jose and Pasadena)

## MAIRE, MANSELL & BEASLEY

A LAW CORPORATION

**2851 PARK MARINA DRIVE**
**SUITE 300**
**P.O. DRAWER 994607**
**REDDING, CALIFORNIA 96099-4607**
Telephone: 916-246-6050
Fax: 916-246-6060
Email: MAIREMB@AOL.COM

*Insurance Defense and Civil Trial Practice, including Automobile, General and Products Liability, Casualty and Surety Law, Professional Errors and Omissions, Defense of Public Entities, Real Estate Litigation, Construction Litigation and General Litigation.*

**WAYNE H. MAIRE,** born Glendale, California, December 27, 1953; admitted to bar, 1979, California; U.S. District Court, Northern and Eastern Districts of California. *Education:* Brigham Young University (B.A., 1976); University of Santa Clara (J.D., 1979). Arbitrator, Shasta Superior Court Panel. *Member:* Shasta-Trinity County Bar Association; State Bar of California; Association of Defense Counsel of Northern California (Member, Board of Directors, 1988-1991); Defense Research Institute.

**PATRICK R. BEASLEY,** born Pasadena, California, December 7, 1943; admitted to bar, 1975, California; U.S. District Court, Northern and Eastern Districts of California. *Education:* University of California at Berkeley (B.A., 1969); University of the Pacific, McGeorge School of Law (J.D., 1974). Member, Upper Division Honor Students Society. Recipient, McGraw Hill Book Award. Arbitrator, Shasta and Tehama Counties Superior Court Panel. Judge Pro Tem, Shasta County Municipal Court. *Member:* Shasta-Trinity County (Past President, 1983) and Federal Bar Associations; State Bar of California (Past Member, Committee on the Administration of Justice); California Trial Lawyers Association; Association of Defense Counsel of Northern California.

**ADAM M. PRESSMAN,** born Los Angeles, California, July 26, 1965; admitted to bar, 1991, California and U.S. District Court, Central District of California; 1992, U.S. District Court, Eastern District of California. *Education:* Reed College (B.A., 1987); McGeorge School of Law (J.D., with distinction, 1991). Associate Comment Editor, Pacific Law Journal. Author: Comment, "Examining Lender Liability Actions After Foley: Are Tort Damages Still Possible?" 22 Pacific Law Journal 123. *Member:* State Bar of California; Shasta-Trinity Bar Association.

*(This Listing Continued)*

**LINDA M. CARPENTER,** born San Diego, California, September 27, 1950; admitted to bar, 1979, California; U.S. District Court, Northern and Eastern Districts of California. *Education:* University of California at Davis (B.A., 1972); Lincoln University (J.D., 1979). Staff Member, Editorial Board, Lincoln University Law Review, 1977. Arbitrator: Shasta and Tehama Counties Superior Court Panel; Shasta County Municipal Court Panel. Judge Pro Tem, Shasta County Municipal Court. Commissioner, City of Redding Planning Commission. *Member:* Shasta-Trinity County Bar Association (Past Secretary-Treasurer, 1988-1989); State Bar of California.

**DAVID S. PERRINE,** born Westminster, California, June 18, 1965; admitted to bar, 1992, California; U.S. District Court, Northern and Eastern Districts of California. *Education:* University of California at Davis (B.A., 1987); Golden Gate University (J.D., 1992). Recipient, Distinguished Moot Court Litigator Award. Judge Pro Tem, Shasta County Municipal Court. *Member:* Shasta-Trinity Bar Association; State Bar of California; California Trial Lawyers Association. *PRACTICE AREAS:* Personal Injury; Wrongful Death; Negligence Actions; Products Liability; Professional Liability.

**CYNTHIA L. COOPER,** born Tyler, Texas, December 29, 1963; admitted to bar, 1993, California; U.S. District Court, Northern and Eastern Districts of California. *Education:* Texas A & M University (B.S., 1987); Western State University (J.D., 1992). *Member:* Shasta-Trinity Bar Association; State Bar of California; Women's Lawyer Association.

**ERIC R. MAIRE,** born September 23, 1965; admitted to bar, 1995, California; U.S. District Court, Northern and Eastern Districts of California. *Education:* California State University at Chico (B.A., 1990); Western State University (J.D., 1994). Member, Moot Court. Recipient: Moot Court Award with Recognition for Best Oral Argument in Competition and Honors, Legal Writing and Research. *Member:* Shasta-Trinity Bar Association; State Bar of California.

REPRESENTATIVE CLIENTS: AKROS Enterprises, Inc.; Allen-Bradley, Inc.; American States Insurance Co.; Automobile Club of Southern California; California Hospitals Affiliated Insurance Services, Inc.; California Hospital Insurance Corporation; California State Automobile Association; C.N.A.; Crawford & Co.; CIGNA Companies; Clarendon National Ins. Co.; Design Professionals; Employers Reinsurance Co.; Equitable Ins. Co.; Fremont Indemnity; Geico Insurance; Grange Insurance Assoc.; Great American Ins. Co.; Grocers Ins. Group; Hanover Ins. Co.; Holiday Harbors; International Surplus Adjusting Serv.; John Glenn Adjusting; John Hancock Ins. Co.; Lakeview Marina; Leland A. Wolf & Assoc.; Martin Boyer Co.; National Car Rental; Nationwide Insurance Co.; Oroville Hospital; Orange Coast Adjusters; Self Insured Management Services; Sentry Insurance Co.; Ship Western Express; Skyway Recreational Products; Underwriter Adjusting Co.; Unigard Ins. Co.; United Employers'; United Grocers Ins. Co.; Wal-Mart; Wausau.

---

## RICHARD L. MONTARBO
280 HEMSTED DRIVE, SUITE 110
**REDDING, CALIFORNIA 96002**
Telephone: 916-221-6193
Fax: 916-221-6196

*Workers Compensation. Insurance Defense. General Civil and Business Practice. Subrogation and Personal Injury.*

**RICHARD L. MONTARBO,** born San Jose, California, January 26, 1960; admitted to bar, 1987, Hawaii; 1989, California. *Education:* California State University at Sacramento (B.S., 1983); McGeorge School of Law, University of the Pacific (J.D., 1987). Moot Court Finalist. Member, Moot Court Executive Committee. *Member:* Shasta County Bar Association. [With U.S. Navy, active duty, 1987-1988]. (Certified Specialist, Workers' Compensation, The State Bar of California Board of Legal Specialization).

### ASSOCIATE

**THOMAS E. SUNDQUIST,** born Castro Valley, California, June 4, 1956; admitted to bar, 1994, California and U.S. District Court, Eastern District of California. *Education:* California State University at Chico (B.S., 1978; M.P.A.,1988); McGeorge School of Law, University of the Pacific (J.D., with distinction, 1994). Traynor Honor Society. Recipient, American Jurisprudence Award. *PRACTICE AREAS:* Workers Compensation; Insurance Defense; Civil Practice; Business Law; Subrogation; Personal Injury.

**CHERRY L. CHALLE,** born Napa, California, May 31, 1962; admitted to bar, 1991, California; U.S. District Court, Eastern District of California. *Education:* University of California at Los Angeles (B.A., 1985); California Western School of Law (J.D., 1991). Phi Alpha Delta. *Member:* Shasta-Trinity Counties (Past President) Bar Association. *LANGUAGES:*

*(This Listing Continued)*

---

Spanish. *PRACTICE AREAS:* Insurance Defense; Employer Liability; Subrogation.

REPRESENTATIVE CLIENTS: Applied Risk Management; California Compensation Insurance Co.; Care America; GAB Business Services; Glenn County Joint Powers Authority; ITT Hartford/Specialty Risk Services, Inc. Reliance Insurance; Risk Management, Inc.; Shasta County Risk Management; Superior National Insurance Co.; Transamerica Insurance Group; Tri Valley Growers; Unicare Insurance; Zenith Insurance Co.

---

## *MOSS & ENOCHIAN*
A LAW CORPORATION
2701 PARK MARINA DRIVE
P.O. DRAWER 994608
**REDDING, CALIFORNIA 96099-4608**
Telephone: 916-225-8990
Fax: 916-241-5734

*General Civil Trial Practice. Insurance, Products Liability, Professional Liability, Municipal, Real Estate and Accident and Health Insurance Law.*

**STEVEN R. ENOCHIAN,** born Berkeley, California, January 19, 1947; admitted to bar, 1974, California; 1979, U.S. Supreme Court. *Education:* University of California at Berkeley (B.S., 1969); Golden Gate University (J.D., 1974). Phi Alpha Delta. Member, Panel of Arbitrators, American Arbitration Association. *Member:* Shasta-Trinity County and American Bar Associations; State Bar of California; Northern California Association of Defense Counsel (Director, 1987—); American Board of Trial Advocates (Associate); Association of Insurance Counsel. [1st Lt., U.S. Army, 1969-1971]

**LARRY B. MOSS,** born Santa Monica, California, November 13, 1945; admitted to bar, 1971, California; 1978, U.S. Claims Court. *Education:* University of California at Los Angeles (B.A., 1967); Loyola University of Los Angeles (J.D., 1970). Phi Alpha Delta. Student Teaching Fellow, Loyola University of Los Angeles, School of Law, 1969-1970. *Member:* Shasta-Trinity County and American Bar Associations; State Bar of California; Association of Defense Counsel; National Association of Railroad Trial Counsel; American Board of Trial Advocates (Associate Member). [Lt., USAF, Ret.]

**TODD E. SLAUGHTER,** born Yokosuka, Japan, July 22, 1953; admitted to bar, 1979, California. *Education:* University of California at Berkeley (B.A., 1976); McGeorge School of Law, University of the Pacific (J.D., 1979). *Member:* Shasta-Trinity County (President, 1986) and American Bar Associations; State Bar of California; Northern California Association of Defense Counsel.

**STEWART C. ALTEMUS,** born Pittsburgh, Pennsylvania, October 16, 1953; admitted to bar, 1981, California. *Education:* University of California at San Diego (B.A., 1977); Hastings College of the Law, University of California (J.D., 1980). *Member:* Shasta-Trinity County and American Bar Associations; State Bar of California; Northern California Association of Defense Counsel.

**JOHN S. KENNY,** born San Francisco, California, February 18, 1941; admitted to bar, 1966, California; 1980, U.S. Supreme Court. *Education:* University of San Francisco (B.A, 1963); Hastings College of the Law, University of California (LL.B., 1966). Deputy City Attorney, San Francisco, 1970-1978. County Counsel, Shasta County, 1978-1986. *Member:* Shasta-Trinity Bar Association; State Bar of California (Member, Public Law Section). [Capt. U.S. Army, 1967-1969]

**ROBERT A. SPANO,** born Peoria, Illinois, September 27, 1956; admitted to bar, 1981, California. *Education:* Augustana College (B.A., 1978); McGeorge School of Law, University of the Pacific (J.D., 1981). *Member:* Federal Bar Association; State Bar of California. [Capt., USMC, 1981-1985]

---

**SANDRA L. JOHNSON,** born Aurora, Illinois, July 14, 1958; admitted to bar, 1988, California. *Education:* University of Dubuque (B.A., 1980); Gonzaga University Law School (J.D., 1987). Recipient, American Jurisprudence Award in Estate Planning. *Member:* State Bar of California.

**MARK D. NORCROSS,** born Chicago, Illinois, July 10, 1956; admitted to bar, 1987, California. *Education:* Tulane University (B.A., with honors, 1979); Golden Gate University (J.D., 1987). *Member:* Bar Association of San Francisco; American Bar Association.

*(This Listing Continued)*

## MOSS & ENOCHIAN, A LAW CORPORATION, Redding—Continued

**ERIC A. OMSTEAD,** born Lodi, California, September 1, 1956; admitted to bar, 1986, California. *Education:* California State University at Chico (B.A., 1979); Hasting College of the Law, University of California (J.D., 1986). *Member:* Sacramento County Bar Association; The State Bar of California.

**DARRYL L. WAGNER,** born Sonoma, California, July 5, 1966; admitted to bar, 1992, California. *Education:* University of California at Davis (B.A., 1989); University of the Pacific, McGeorge School of Law (J.D., 1992). *Member:* Sacramento County Bar Association (Member, Labor and Employment Law Section); State Bar of California.

**MONICA M. BALAVAGE,** born Pekin, Illinois, March 15, 1952; admitted to bar, 1977, California and U.S. District Court, Eastern District of California; 1984, U.S. Supreme Court. *Education:* Illinois State University (B.S., 1973); McGeorge School of Law, University of the Pacific (J.D., 1977). Arbitrator, Shasta County, 1991—. *Member:* Shasta-Trinity Counties Bar Association (Vice-President, 1994; Secretary-Treasurer, 1995; Chairman, Minimum Continuing Legal Education Committee, 1993); State Bar of California.

**GUSTAVO L. MARTINEZ,** born Santa Barbara, California, March 31, 1968; admitted to bar, 1994, California. *Education:* California State University at Chico (B.A., 1990); Santa Clara University (J.D., 1994). Phi Delta Phi. Deans List, California State University at Chico, 1986-1990. Environmental Law Society, 1992-1994. **LANGUAGES:** Spanish.

**GARY E. HASLERUD,** born Appleton, Wisconsin, October 10, 1968; admitted to bar, 1995, Texas and California. *Education:* Pacific Lutheran University (B.B.A., 1991); St. Mary's University School of Law (J.D., 1995). Member, Mock Trial Regional Team. Atla Mock Trial Quarter Finalist, State Mock Trial Quarter Finalist, St. Mary's National Mock Trial Semi Finalist. Walker Moot Court.

**MONIQUE GRANDAW,** born Hayward, California, June 6, 1965; admitted to bar, 1992, California. *Education:* University of California at Irvine (B.S., 1987); Southwestern University (J.D., 1992).

REPRESENTATIVE CLIENTS: Acceptance Insurance Co.; Aetna Life & Casualty Insurance Co.; AIG Claims Services; Allstate Insurance Co.; American International Companies; American Modern Home Insurance Co.; American Motorists Insurance Co.; American States Insurance Co.; American Trust Insurance Co.; Anderson-Cottonwood Disposal; Associated Aviation Underwriters; Baxter International; Burney Forest Products; Cal-Farm Insurance Co.; California Insurance Group; California State Automobile Association; Caronia Corporation; Catholic Health Corporation; Catholic Healthcare West; Cigna Insurance Co.; City of Shasta Lake; Colonial Penn Insurance Co.; Commercial Union Insurance Companies; Corroon & Black; County of Lassen; County of Modoc; County of Shasta; County of Trinity; Crum & Forster Insurance Co.; Empire Insurance Co.; Employers Reinsurance; E&O Professionals; Financial Pacific Insurance Co.; Four Rails, Inc.; Fremont Indemnity Co.; Gillig Corporation; Golden Eagle Insurance Co.; Grange Insurance Association; Hanover Insurance Co.; Harnischfeger Corporation; Herrick Pacific Corp.; H.F.I.C. Management Co., Inc.; Horace Mann Companies; Houston General Insurance Co.; Industrial Indemnity Insurance Co.; Insurance Company of British Columbia; Jackson National Life Insurance Co.; Jefferson Insurance Group; Kemper Group; KMS Research, Inc.; Lawyer's Mutual Insurance Co.; Lumbermen's Mutual Casualty Co.; Maryland Casualty Co.; Modoc County Medical Center; Morgan Emultech, Inc.; National American Insurance Co.; National Chiropractic Mutual Insurance Co.; Nautilus Insurance Co.; Northland Insurance Co.; Ohio Casualty Co.; Patients Hospital; Preferred Risk Group; Professional Liability Insurance Co.; Progressive Casualty Insurance Co.; Prudential Property & Casualty Ins. Co.; Raley's; Reliance Insurance Co.; Rooney & Anderson; Safeco Insurance Co.; Scottsdale Insurance Co.; Sentry Insurance Co.; Sequoia Insurance Co.; Shasta Mosquito Abatement District; Shasta Union High School District; St. Elizabeth Community Hospital; State Farm Fire & Casualty Co.; State Farm Mutual Automobile Ins. Co.; The Doctor's Company; Tenet Healthcare Corp.; TIG Insurance Co.; Transmission Agency of Northern California; Transport Indemnity Co.; Trinity County General Hospital; TRW, Inc.; Viking Insurance Co.; Western Indemnity Insurance Co.; Zurich-American Insurance Co.

## DOUGLAS H. NEWLAN
434 REDCLIFF DRIVE, SUITE B
P.O. BOX 491736
**REDDING, CALIFORNIA 96049-1736**
Telephone: 916-221-0184
Fax: 916-221-8744

*General Civil and Trial Practice, Insurance Defense and Business Litigation.*

**DOUGLAS H. NEWLAN,** born Morris Plains, New Jersey, December 17, 1931; admitted to bar, 1962, California; 1984, Oregon. *Education:* University of California at Los Angeles (A.B., 1957); Loyola University of Los Angeles (LL.B., 1961). *Member:* Shasta-Trinity County (President, 1980), Sacramento County, Siskiyou County and American (Member, Litigation Section) Bar Associations; State Bar of California; Northern California Association of Defense Counsel (Director, 1974-1975); Oregon Trial Lawyers Association; American Board of Trial Advocates; California Trial Lawyers Association (Member, Board of Governors, 1980-1981); The Association of Trial Lawyers of America. Member of California Trial Lawyers Association, with recognized experience as a Trial Lawyer and recognized experience in the fields of Product Liability, Professional Negligence and General Personal Injury.

## NISSON & PINCIN
1737 YUBA STREET
P.O. BOX 991966
**REDDING, CALIFORNIA 96099**
Telephone: 916-246-4201
FAX: 916-246-1426

*Insurance Defense, Business Litigation, Personal Injury.*

### MEMBERS OF FIRM

**TIMOTHY J. NISSON,** born Ft. Lewis, Washington, November 20, 1956; admitted to bar, 1982, California. *Education:* University of California at Davis (A.B., with honors, 1978); University of San Francisco (J.D., cum laude, 1982). Member, McAuliffe Honor Society. *Member:* Shasta-Trinity County Bar Association; State Bar of California; Association of Defense Counsel. **PRACTICE AREAS:** Complex Civil Litigation.

**JAMES W. PINCIN,** born McCloud, California, August 11, 1961; admitted to bar, 1986, California. *Education:* University of California at Davis (A.B., 1983); McGeorge School of Law, University of the Pacific (J.D., 1986). *Member:* Shasta-Trinity County Bar Association; State Bar of California; Association of Defense Counsel. **PRACTICE AREAS:** Complex Civil Litigation.

REPRESENTATIVE CLIENTS: 20th Century Insurance; 21st Century Insurance; AIM Insurance; ARDI Exchange; Allied Insurance; CIGNA Insurance; COREGIS Group; CUNA Mutual Insurance Group; Chubb Group of Insurance; Citation; City of Redding; Colonial Penn; Constitution Insurance; Countrywide Service Corporation; Fireman's Fund Insurance; Fraternal Insurance; Hartford; Holiday Markets; Houston General; Insurance Company of the West; Interstate Insurance; K Mart Corporation; Liberty Insurance Services; Liberty Mutual Insurance; Royal; Shopko; Simpson Paper Co.; State Farm Insurance; TIG Insurance; Transamerica Insurance; Travelers; Unigard Insurance; Wausau Insurance.

## REESE, SMALLEY, WISEMAN & SCHWEITZER
1265 WILLIS STREET
P.O. DRAWER 994647
**REDDING, CALIFORNIA 96099-4647**
Telephone: 916-241-1611
Fax: 916-241-5106

*General Business, Civil Litigation, Real Estate, Personal Injury, Land Development, Probate, Estate Planning and Taxation.*

**JOHN W. REESE, JR.,** born Elko, Nevada, December 28, 1942; admitted to bar, 1969, California. *Education:* Brigham Young University (A.B., 1965); University of California at Los Angeles (J.D., 1968). *Member:* Shasta-Trinity County and American Bar Associations; State Bar of California. **PRACTICE AREAS:** Real Estate Law; Estate Planning; Probate Law; General Business Law.

**LAWRENCE R. SMALLEY,** born Willits, California, December 30, 1951; admitted to bar, 1978, California; 1982, U.S. Tax Court. *Education:* University of Nevada (B.S., 1974); University of Santa Clara (M.B.A.; J.D., cum laude, 1978). Certified Public Accountant, California, 1981. *Member:* Shasta-Trinity County Bar Association; State Bar of California. **PRACTICE AREAS:** Taxation Law; Estate Planning Law; Probate Law; Trust Law; General Corporate Practice.

**KENT I. WISEMAN,** born Payson, Utah, October 5, 1944; admitted to bar, 1979, California. *Education:* Brigham Young University (B.A., 1972); Lincoln University (J.D., 1977). *Member:* Shasta-Trinity County Bar Association; State Bar of California. **PRACTICE AREAS:** Civil Litigation; Collection Law; General Business Law.

**HOWARD L. SCHWEITZER,** born Miami, Florida, April 20, 1941; admitted to bar, 1967, Florida; 1969, California. *Education:* University of

*(This Listing Continued)*

North Carolina (B.S., 1963); University of Miami (J.D., 1967); New York University (LL.M. in Taxation, 1968). Digest Editor, University of Miami Law Review, 1966-1967. Certified Public Accountant, Florida, 1964. Teaching Fellow, New York University Law School, 1967-1968. Member, Board of Trustees, 1989-1995 and President, 1991-1992, Junction School District. *Member:* Shasta-Trinity County and American Bar Associations; State Bar of California. *PRACTICE AREAS:* Taxation; Real Estate Law; General Business Practice.

**VICTOR R. RICHARDSON,** born La Mesa, California, October 14, 1951; admitted to bar, 1979, California. *Education:* Grossmont College and Utah State University (B.S., 1976); Western State University (J.D., 1978). *Member:* Shasta-Trinity County and American Bar Associations; State Bar of California; Northern California Association of Defense Counsel; California Trial Lawyers Association. [With US Marines, 1969-1971]. *PRACTICE AREAS:* Civil Litigation; Tort Law; Business Litigation.

**RALPH T. COLLINS, III,** born Brooklyn, New York, November 26, 1961; admitted to bar, 1989, California. *Education:* Brigham Young University (B.A., 1986); McGeorge School of Law, University of the Pacific (J.D., 1989). Staff Writer, Pacific Law Journal, 1988. Finalist, National Moot Court Best Brief, 1988. *Member:* State Bar of California; American Bar Association. *PRACTICE AREAS:* Civil Litigation; Appellate Practice.

**MICHAEL R. MCCABE,** born Eureka, California, April 15, 1960; admitted to bar, 1985, California and U.S. District Court, Southern, Central and Eastern Districts of California. *Education:* Shasta College (A.A., 1980); University of California at Davis (B.A., 1982); California Western School of Law (J.D., magna cum laude, 1985). Staff Member, 1983-1984 and Managing/Book Review Editor, 1984-1985, California Western Law Review. Associate Member, California State Senate Commission on Corporate Governance, Shareholders Rights and Securities Transactions, 1989-1991. Co-Author: "Civil RICO in Shareholder Suits Involving Defense Contractors," Civil RICO Practice: Causes of Action, Wiley Law Publications, 1991. *Member:* Shasta-Trinity and American Bar Associations; State Bar of California. *PRACTICE AREAS:* Civil Litigation; Business Litigation; Securities Consumer Litigation; Class Actions.

REPRESENTATIVE CLIENTS: Holiday Markets; Lassen Canyon Nursery, Inc.; J.F. Shea, Co.; Roy E. Ladd, Inc.; Simpson Paper Co.; Redding Bank of Commerce; Cascade Logging, Inc.; Letro Products, Inc.; Droscher Equipment; Gerlinger Foundry & Machine Works; Redding French Bakery; Shasta Livestock Auction Yard; Redding Roofing Supply, Inc.; Boone's Wholesale, Inc..

## REINER & SIMPSON
*2851 PARK MARINA DRIVE, SUITE 200*
**REDDING, CALIFORNIA 96001**
Telephone: 916-241-1905
Fax: 916-241-0622

*Personal Injury, Products Liability, Medical Malpractice and Wrongful Death.*

**RUSSELL REINER,** born Springfield, Minnesota, January 18, 1951; admitted to bar, 1978, California; U.S. District Court, District of Montana; U.S. District Court, District of Colorado; U.S. District Court, District of Minnesota. *Education:* Moorhead State University; University of Arizona (B.A., 1973); Western State University (J.D., 1978). Author: "Jeep CJ-5 Roll-over," Million Dollar Arguments, 1989. *Member:* Shasta-Trinity County Bar Association; State Bar of California; Consumer Attorneys of California; The Association of Trial Lawyers of America; Million Dollar Advocates; Institute for Injury Reduction; Safety Attorneys Federation. *PRACTICE AREAS:* Personal Injury; Wrongful Death; Product Liability; Medical Malpractice.

**ROBERT G. SIMPSON,** born Durant, Oklahoma, August 5, 1948; admitted to bar, 1975, California and U.S. District Court, Eastern District of California. *Education:* University of California at Davis (A.B., 1971); Hastings College of Law, University of California (J.D., 1975). *Member:* Shasta-Trinity County and American Bar Associations; State Bar of California; American Trial Lawyers Association; Consumer Attorneys of California. *PRACTICE AREAS:* Personal Injury; Wrongful Death; Negligence Actions; Products Liability; Medical Malpractice; Professional Liability.

### ASSOCIATES

**DARYL E. KENNEDY,** born San Jose, California, November 15, 1957; admitted to bar, 1986, California. *Education:* University of California at Berkeley (A.B., with honors, 1981); Hastings College of the Law, University of California (J.D., cum laude, 1986). Member, Thurston Society. Recipient: American Jurisprudence Award. *Member:* Shasta-Trinity County

*(This Listing Continued)*

Bar Association; State Bar of California; Consumer Attorneys of California. *PRACTICE AREAS:* Product Liability; Medical Malpractice; Wrongful Death; Personal Injury; Negligence Actions.

## SINCLAIR & HILL, A LAW CORPORATION
*100 EAST CYPRESS, SUITE 200*
**REDDING, CALIFORNIA 96002**
Telephone: 916-226-9700
FAX: 916-226-9481

Mailing Address: P.O. Box 992710, Redding, CA 96099-2710

*General Civil and Trial Practice, Insurance, Medical Malpractice, Personal Injury, Business Litigation, Negligence.,*

**CRAIG A. SINCLAIR,** born Alturas, California, October 2, 1944; admitted to bar, 1973, California; 1979, U.S. District Court, Eastern District of California; 1981, U.S. District Court, Northern District of California. *Education:* University of California at Berkeley (B.S., 1967); McGeorge College of the Law, University of the Pacific (J.D., 1973). *Member:* Shasta-Trinity Counties Bar Association; State Bar of California; American Board of Trial Advocates; American Academy of Healthcare Attorneys; California Society for Healthcare Attorneys; Northern California Association of Defense Counsel. *PRACTICE AREAS:* Trials; Hospital and Professional Negligence; Personal Injury; Business Litigation; Environmental Law.

**LARRY L. HILL,** born Chico, California, April 16, 1941; admitted to bar, 1977, California and U.S. District Court, Eastern District of California. *Education:* California State University at Chico (B.S., Business Administration, 1968); Lincoln University (J.D., 1975). *Member:* Shasta-Trinity County and American Bar Associations; State Bar of California; The Association of Trial Lawyers of America; Defense Research Institute; American Board of Trial Advocates; Northern California Association of Defense Counsel. *PRACTICE AREAS:* Trials; Personal Injury; Hospital and Professional Negligence; Business Litigation; Products Liability; Governmental Entity Litigation.

---

**MICHAEL R. DEEMS,** born Lincoln, Nebraska, November 15, 1953; admitted to bar, 1985, California; 1986, U.S. District Court, Northern District of California; 1989, U.S. Court of Appeals, Ninth Circuit. *Education:* California Lutheran College (B.A., Mathematics, 1976); University of San Francisco (J.D., 1985). *Member:* Shasta-Trinity Counties and American Bar Associations; The State Bar of California; Northern California Association of Defense Counsel. *PRACTICE AREAS:* Trials; Personal Injury Defense; Hospital and Professional Negligence; Products Liability; Insurance Coverage.

**J. MICHAEL FAVOR,** born Montgomery, Alabama, August 30, 1939; admitted to bar, 1979, California and U.S. District Court, Northern District of California; 1990, U.S. District Court, Central District of California; 1991, U.S. District Court, Eastern District of California and U.S. District Court, Central District of Texas; 1993, U.S. Court of Appeals, Ninth Circuit. *Education:* University of Alabama; United States Naval Academy (B.S., with distinction, 1963); University of San Diego (J.D., with distinction, 1970). Phi Alpha Delta. *Member:* Shasta-Trinity County Bar Association; State Bar of California. [U.S. Marine Corps, 1963-1965; Col., U.S. Marine Corps Reserve, 1968—]. *LANGUAGES:* German and French. *PRACTICE AREAS:* Personal Injury; Products Liability; Business Litigation.

**TODD ALAN JUCHAU,** born Napa, California, February 17, 1965; admitted to bar, 1994, California; 1996, U.S. District Court, Eastern District of California. *Education:* California State University (B.S., 1994; M.B.A., 1994); University of Pacific, McGeorge School of Law (J.D., 1994). *Member:* Shasta-Trinity Counties, Sacramento County and American Bar Associations; State Bar of California. *PRACTICE AREAS:* Personal Injury; Hospital and Professional Negligence; Business Litigation; Insurance Defense; Government Entity Litigation.

**ROBIN L. NICKEL,** born Redding, California, March 21, 1969; admitted to bar, 1995, California and U.S. District Court, Southern District of California; 1996, U.S. District Court, Eastern District of California. *Education:* California State University at Chico (B.A., Political Science, 1992); California Western School of Law (J.D., 1994). Recipient: American Jurisprudence Award in Trial Practice. *Member:* Shasta-Trinity Counties, San

*(This Listing Continued)*

**SINCLAIR & HILL, A LAW CORPORATION,** Redding—
*Continued*

Diego County and American Bar Associations; State Bar of California. *PRACTICE AREAS:* Trials; Personal Injury Defense; Hospital and Professional Negligence; Products Liability.

## LAW OFFICES OF HARRISON SMITH

1267 WILLIS STREET
**REDDING, CALIFORNIA 96001**
Telephone: 916-246-1222; 241-3510; 241-6359
FAX: 916-246-1941
Email: hrharrisonsmith72123.2224@compuserve.com

**Shasta, California Office:** Shurtleff Alley, P.O. Box 367, 96087. Telephone: 916-241-3510; 241-6359. FAX: 916-246-1941.

General, Civil, Trial and Appellate Practice. Corporation, Domestic Relations, Probate, Real Estate, Mining, Natural Resources, Water Rights and Private International Law. Commissioners for Affidavits for British Columbia.

**HERBERT RICHARD HARRISON SMITH,** born Vancouver, British Columbia, Canada, November 29, 1945; admitted to bar, 1971, British Columbia, Canada; 1972, California; U.S. Supreme Court, U.S. Court of Appeals, Ninth Circuit, U.S. District Court, Northern and Eastern Districts of California, Supreme Court of British Columbia, Federal Court of Canada and Supreme Court of Canada. *Education:* University of California (A.B., 1967); University of British Columbia (LL.B., 1970). Editor, University of British Columbia Law Review, 1970. *Member:* Shasta-Trinity County Bar Association (President, 1981); State Bar of California; Canadian Bar Association; Law Society of British Columbia. *PRACTICE AREAS:* Business Law; Government; Trusts and Estates; General Practice.

**HERBERT STUART HARRISON SMITH,** born Vancouver, British Columbia, Canada, June 17, 1919; admitted to bar, 1952, British Columbia; 1972, California; U.S. Supreme Court, U.S. Court of Appeals, Ninth Circuit, U.S. District Court, Northern and Eastern Districts of California, Supreme Court of British Columbia, Federal Court of Canada and Supreme Court of Canada. *Education:* University of California at Berkeley (A.B., with honors, 1948); University of British Columbia (LL.B., 1951). *Member:* Shasta-Trinity County Bar Association (Director, 1974; 1985); State Bar of California; Canadian Bar Association; Law Society of British Columbia. Life Fellow, Foundation for Legal Research Canada. (Resident, Shasta Office). *PRACTICE AREAS:* Mining Law; Business Law; Private International Law; General Practice.

## TOCHER & O'CONNOR

1901 PARK MARINA DRIVE
**REDDING, CALIFORNIA 96001**
Telephone: 916-244-2525
Fax: 916-244-4941

*Personal Injury Law.*

### MEMBERS OF FIRM

**G. NEIL TOCHER,** born Santa Rosa, California, October 1, 1926; admitted to bar, 1952, Washington; 1955, California. *Education:* Santa Rosa Junior College (A.A., 1949); Hastings College of Law, University of California (LL.B., 1952). *Member:* Shasta-Trinity Bar Association; State Bar of California; California Trial Attorneys Association. *PRACTICE AREAS:* Personal Injury; Wrongful Death; Negligence Actions.

**FRANK O'CONNOR,** born San Diego, California; admitted to bar, 1969, California; U.S. District Court, Northern District of California. *Education:* University of California at Berkeley (B.A. in English, 1965); Hastings College of Law, University of California (J.D., 1968). Instructor: Various Police Courses and Boy Scout Classes. Public Defender, Shasta County, 1981-1995. *Member:* State Bar of California. [U.S. Marine Corporation, 1969-1973; Staff Judge Advocate and Military Judge]. *PRACTICE AREAS:* Personal Injury; Criminal Law.

### LEGAL SUPPORT PERSONNEL

**SHIRLEY SMOOT** (Legal Assistant).

## WELLS, SMALL, SELKE & GRAHAM

*A LAW CORPORATION*
*Established in 1970*

292 HEMSTED DRIVE
P.O. BOX 991828
**REDDING, CALIFORNIA 96099-1828**
Telephone: 916-223-1800
Fax: 916-223-1809

Civil Litigation, Insurance and Employment Litigation, Corporation, Real Estate, Water, Business, Creditor Bankruptcy/Collection, Banking Law, Estate Planning and Probate, Environmental, Municipal and Land Use Law.

**J.M. WELLS, JR.,** born Portland, Oregon, November 15, 1940; admitted to bar, 1966, California. *Education:* Stanford University (B.A., 1962); Hastings College of the Law, University of California (J.D., 1965). *Member:* Shasta-Trinity County Bar Association; State Bar of California. *PRACTICE AREAS:* Business Law; Real Estate Law; Corporation Law; Estate Planning Law; Probate Law.

**STEVEN A. SMALL,** born Sonoma, California, September 22, 1948; admitted to bar, 1974, California. *Education:* University of California at Berkeley (A.B., 1970); Hastings College of the Law, University of California (J.D., 1974). *Member:* Shasta-Trinity County Bar Association; State Bar of California. (Certified Specialist, Estate Planning, Trust and Probate Law, The State Bar of California Board of Legal Specialization). *PRACTICE AREAS:* Estate Planning; Estate Probate Law; Business Law.

**LEO J. GRAHAM,** born Chico, California, December 17, 1950; admitted to bar, 1976, California. *Education:* University of California at Berkeley (A.B., 1973); University of Santa Clara (J.D., 1976). *Member:* Shasta-Trinity County Bar Association; State Bar of California. *PRACTICE AREAS:* Business, Real Estate and Employment Litigation; Construction Law and Litigation; Banking Law; Creditor Bankruptcy.

**DONALD A. SELKE, JR.,** born Austin, Texas, July 12, 1947; admitted to bar, 1983, California. *Education:* Ball State University (B.S., 1970; M.A.E., 1976); McGeorge School of Law, University of the Pacific (J.D., 1983). *Member:* Shasta-Trinity County Bar Association; State Bar of California. *PRACTICE AREAS:* Civil Litigation; Employment Law; Real Estate Law; Commercial Landlord and Tenant Law.

**BARTLEY S. FLEHARTY,** born Prineville, Oregon, February 25, 1955; admitted to bar, 1989, California. *Education:* Shasta Junior College (A.A., 1975); California State University at Chico (B.A., 1977; M.A., 1980); California Northern School of Law (J.D., magna cum laude, 1989). Planner, 1979-1989 and Senior Planner, 1984-1989, Tehama County. *Member:* State Bar of California. *PRACTICE AREAS:* Real Estate Law; Environmental Law; Land Use Law; Contract Law.

**FREDERICK J. WEIL,** born Warren, Ohio, April 10, 1958; admitted to bar, 1982, Arizona, U.S. Tax Court and U.S. Court of Appeals, Ninth Circuit; 1984, California; 1985, U.S. District Court, Central District of California. *Education:* University of Madrid; University of Southern California (A.B., magna cum laude, 1979); University of Arizona (J.D., 1982); University of San Diego (LL.M in Taxation, 1984). Co-Author: "Guide to Organizing and Operating a Limited Liability Company in California," State Bar Business Law Section, 1995. *Member:* State Bar of Arizona (Member, Partnerships Committee of Business Law Section); State Bar of California. (Certified Specialist, Taxation Law, The State Bar of California Board of Legal Specialization). *PRACTICE AREAS:* Tax Law; Business Law; Corporation Law; Health Care Law.

REPRESENTATIVE CLIENTS: North Valley Bank; Citizens Utilities; California Teachers Association; Evanhoe, Kellogg & Company; Great Western Bank; Bank of California; Transamerica Financial Services; Burney Water District; Grenada Irrigation District; Sharrah Dunlap Sawyer Irish Engineers, Inc.; Seco Manufacturing; Northern Medical Group; LaQuinta Inns; Pepsi-Cola Bottling Company of Northern California; Canteca Foods, Inc.; Calaveras Cement; Woodmont Managements, Inc.; Chicago Title Company; MD Imaging, Inc.; Orange County Cardiology Medical Corporation; Shasta Emergency Medical Group, Inc.

## WISE, WIEZOREK, TIMMONS & WISE

*A PROFESSIONAL CORPORATION*

**443 REDCLIFF DRIVE, SUITE 230**
**REDDING, CALIFORNIA**
Telephone: 916-221-7632
Fax: 916-221-8832

*Long Beach, California Office:* 3700 Santa Fe Avenue, Suite 300, P.O. Box 2190. Telephone: 213-834-5028. Fax: 213-834-8018.

*General Civil and Trial Practice in State and Federal Courts. Corporation, International Business, Insurance, Real Property, Immigration, Estate Planning, Probate and Tax Law.*

(For complete biographical data on all personnel. See Professional Biographies at Long Beach, California)

---

## DILL & SHOWLER

*Established in 1961*

**411 BROOKSIDE AVENUE**
**REDLANDS, CALIFORNIA 92373**
Telephone: 909-793-2377
Fax: 909-798-6557

*General Civil and Trial Practice. Construction, Negligence, Insurance, Probate, Estate Planning, Real Estate, Corporate and Business Law.*

### MEMBERS OF FIRM

**FRED H. DILL,** born Redlands, California, September 20, 1934; admitted to bar, 1959, California; 1965, U.S. Supreme Court. *Education:* University of California at Los Angeles and Riverside City College; University of Southern California (LL.B., 1958). Phi Delta Phi. Deputy District Attorney, San Bernardino County, 1959-1961. Chairman, San Bernardino County Air Pollution Control District Hearing Board, 1966-1972. Real Estate Broker, 1979. Superior Court Judge Pro Tem, 1991—. *Member:* American Bar Association; State Bar of California. **PRACTICE AREAS:** Construction; Negligence; Real Estate; Corporate Law; Business Law.

**SCOTT SHOWLER,** born Glendale, California, April 3, 1946; admitted to bar, 1972, California. *Education:* California State College at San Bernardino (B.A., 1968); Hastings College of Law, University of California (J.D., 1971). Superior Court Judge Pro Tem, 1991—. *Member:* San Bernardino County Bar Association (Member, Board of Directors, 1987-1991; Probate Committee); State Bar of California. **PRACTICE AREAS:** Real Estate Law; Construction Litigation; Business Litigation; Probate.

REPRESENTATIVE CLIENTS: Arnott Poultry; Homestead Supplies, Inc.; Riverside County Lumber Co.; Imperial Valley Lumber, Inc.; Kruger McGrew Construction; Amber Steel; Poma Automated Fueling; Bonadiman-McCain, Inc.; Burton's Ready Mix; Davis & Graeber Insurance; Green Valley Escrow Service; Soren, McAdam, Bartells; Kivett-Teeters Coldwell Banker; J. Murrey Construction; Redlands Centennial Bank.
REFERENCE: Redlands Centennial Bank.

---

## ELLIOT, LAMB, LEIBL & SNYDER

*Established in 1988*

**101 EAST REDLANDS BOULEVARD, SUITE 285**
**REDLANDS, CALIFORNIA 92373**
Telephone: 909-792-8861
Fax: 909-798-6997

*Encino, California Office:* Suite 301, 16501 Ventura Boulevard, 91436. Telephone: 818-380-0123; 310-553-5767. Fax: 818-380-0124.
*Orange County Office:* 333 South Anita Drive, Suite 660, Orange, California, 92668. Telephone: 714-978-6255. Facsimile: 714-978-9087.

*Civil Litigation. Insurance Defense and Medical Malpractice Defense.*

FIRM PROFILE: *Our law firm which specializes in the defense of professional malpractice actions against health care providers. Our cases include all types of medical malpractice, including claims involving psychiatric care, birth injuries, disputes concerning medical staff privileges and representation of physicians before the Medical Board of California. We are active in both the state and federal courts, which matters pending throughout the counties of Los Angeles, Riverside, San Bernardino and Orange. We deal primarily with complex, high damage potential cases, involving claims of brain damage, paralysis and wrongful death allegedly due to medical negligence.*

**MICHAEL V. LAMB,** born Fairfield, Iowa, December 23, 1952; admitted to bar, 1979, California; 1985, U.S. District Court, Central District of

*(This Listing Continued)*

California. *Education:* University of Michigan (B.A., 1975); Rutgers University; Pepperdine University (J.D., 1978). *Member:* Los Angeles County and American Bar Associations; State Bar of California. **PRACTICE AREAS:** Insurance Defense; Medical Malpractice Defense.

**MICHAEL R. SNYDER,** born Downey, California, July 10, 1958; admitted to bar, 1984, California; U.S. District Court, Central District of California. *Education:* California State University at Long Beach (B.A., 1980); Western State University (J.D., 1983). *Member:* State Bar of California; American Bar Association. **PRACTICE AREAS:** Insurance Defense; Medical Malpractice Defense.

**LOREN S. LEIBL,** born Pasadena, California, July 11, 1953; admitted to bar, 1983, California and U.S. District Court, Central District of California; U.S. Court of Appeals, Ninth Circuit. *Education:* California State University at Long Beach (B.A., 1979); Southwestern University (J.D., 1983). Recipient: American Jurisprudence Award in Torts; Southwestern University Award in Torts and Legal Communication Skills. *Member:* Los Angeles County and American Bar Associations; State Bar of California. **PRACTICE AREAS:** Insurance Defense; Medical Malpractice Defense.

**D. SCOTT ELLIOT,** born Cleveland, Ohio, September 3, 1952; admitted to bar, 1977, California; 1979, U.S. District Court, Central District of California; U.S. Court of Appeals, Ninth Circuit. *Education:* California State University at Northridge (B.A., cum laude, 1974); Southwestern University (J.D., 1977). Recipient, American Jurisprudence Award in Constitutional Law. *Member:* State Bar of California; Association of Southern California Defense Counsel. **PRACTICE AREAS:** Insurance Defense; Medical Malpractice Defense.

**REBECCA J. HOGUE,** born Huntington Park, California, July 20, 1954; admitted to bar, 1984, California and U.S. District Court, Central District of California. *Education:* University of California at Irvine (B.A., 1976); Western State University (J.D., cum laude, 1983). Member, Western State University Law Review, 1982-1983. Recipient: Corpus Juris Secundum Award; American Jurisprudence Awards in Torts, Evidence, Criminal Law and Community Property. *Member:* State Bar of California. **PRACTICE AREAS:** Insurance Defense; Medical Malpractice Defense.

---

**BRYAN R. REID,** born Whittier, California, August 17, 1964; admitted to bar, 1991, California; U.S. District Court, Central District of California. *Education:* California State University at Fullerton (B.A. in Communications, 1988); Southwestern University (J.D., 1991). *Member:* San Bernardino County and Riverside County Bar Associations; State Bar of California. **PRACTICE AREAS:** Insurance Defense; Medical Malpractice Defense.

**RICHARD AKEMON,** born Long Beach, California, May 16, 1940; admitted to bar, 1972, California; 1973, U.S. District Court, District of California. *Education:* University of Southern California; Western State University (B.S., cum laude, 1971; J.D., 1972). Judge Pro Tem, Long Beach Municipal Court, 1977-1979. *Member:* State Bar of California. **PRACTICE AREAS:** Insurance Defense; Medical Malpractice Defense.

**DOUGLAS K. MANN,** born Harvey, Illinois, January 1, 1965; admitted to bar, 1992, California. *Education:* California State Polytechnic University (B.S.I.E., 1988); Rutgers University (J.D., 1991). *Member:* State Bar of California. **PRACTICE AREAS:** Insurance Defense; Medical Malpractice Defense.

**WILLIAM R. MOFFITT,** born Whittier, California, March 13, 1953; admitted to bar, 1995, California and U.S. District Court, Central District of California. *Education:* University of California at Los Angeles (B.S., magna cum laude, 1976); Southwestern University (J.D., cum laude, 1995). Phi Beta Kappa. *Member:* Los Angeles, Riverside and San Bernardino County Bar Associations. **PRACTICE AREAS:** Insurance Defense; Medical Malpractice Defense.

**JEFFREY ALAN WALKER,** born Alhambra, California, December 27, 1970; admitted to bar, 1993, California. *Education:* University of California, Riverside (B.S., 1992); Southwestern University Law School (J.D., 1995). President, 1994-1995 and Secretary, 1993-1994, Student Bar Association. *Member:* State Bar of California; American Bar Association (Member, Intellectual Property). **PRACTICE AREAS:** Medical Malpractice; Insurance Defense.

REPRESENTATIVE CLIENTS: The Doctors Co.; Southern California Physicians Insurance Exchange; Fremont Indemnity Co.; National Auto & Casualty Insurance Co.

(For Complete Biographical data on all Personnel, see Professional at Encino, California)

## C L FARRELL

P.O. BOX 1470
**REDLANDS, CALIFORNIA 92373-1470**
Telephone: 909-307-2677
Fax: 909-307-2680

*Probate, Conservatorship, Guardianships, General Civil Trial Practice.*

**C L FARRELL,** born San Diego, California, December 21, 1955; admitted to bar, 1988, California and U.S. District Court, Northern, Southern and Central Districts of California; U.S. Tax Court; U.S. Claims Court; U.S. Court of Appeals, Ninth Circuit; 1993, U.S. Supreme Court. *Education:* San Francisco State University (B.A., 1979); Golden Gate University (J.D., 1982). Recipient, Matthew Bender Scholarship. Arbitrator and Judge Tempore, San Bernardino County Superior and Municipal Courts, 1994—. *Member:* State Bar of California (Member, Estate Planning, Trust and Probate Section); American Bar Association (Member, Real Property, Probate and Trust Law Section).

---

## HARTNELL, HORSPOOL & FOX

A PROFESSIONAL CORPORATION

*Established in 1975*

25757 REDLANDS BOULEVARD
**REDLANDS, CALIFORNIA 92373-8453**
Telephone: 909-796-6881
Fax: 909-796-4196

*Yucaipa, California Office:* 34544 Yucaipa Boulevard. Telephone: 909-790-6288. Fax: 909-790-6398.

*Probate, Estate Planning, Trust Administration, Conservatorships, Guardianships Personal Injury and Negligence Law, Real Property and Business Transaction, Corporate and Selected Civil Litigation.*

**BRYAN C. HARTNELL,** born Walla Walla, Washington, July 1, 1949; admitted to bar, 1975, California; 1976, U.S. District Court, Central District of California. *Education:* Pacific Union College (B.A., 1971); McGeorge School of Law, University of the Pacific (J.D., 1975). Member: Rotary International, San Bernadino Crossroads (President, 1984-1985); Loma Linda Chamber of Commerce (Board of Directors, 1991—). *Member:* San Bernardino County (Director, 1991—, President, 1995-1996; Member, Probate Section, Medical-Legal Committee; Bench and Bar Committee, 1993—; Chair, 1994-1995) and Los Angeles County Bar Associations; State Bar of California (Member, Estate Planning, Trust and Probate Law Section; Delegate, Conference of Delegates, 1992 —). (Certified Specialist, Estate Planning, Trust and Probate Law, The State Bar of California Board of Legal Specialization). **PRACTICE AREAS:** Probate; Conservatorships; Estate Planning.

**J. DAVID HORSPOOL,** born Riverside, California, January 29, 1950; admitted to bar, 1981, California; 1982, U.S. District Court, Central District of California and U.S. Tax Court;1985, U.S. Court of Appeals, Ninth Circuit; 1987, U.S. District Court, Northern District of California and U.S. Supreme Court. *Education:* Riverside City College (A.A., 1970); Brigham Young University (B.S., 1974; M.A., 1980; J.D., cum laude, 1980). Instructor, Corporations, California Southern Law School, 1982-1984. Member: City Council of Moreno Valley, 1984-1990; Rotary International, Moreno Valley Noon (President, 1993-1994. *Member:* San Bernardino County (Chairman, Probate Section, 1992-1994) and Los Angeles County Bar Associations; State Bar of California. (Certified Specialist, Estate Planning, Trust and Probate Law, The State Bar of California Board of Legal Specialization). **LANGUAGES:** Portuguese. **SPECIAL AGENCIES:** Administrative Hearing Officer; County of San Bernardino Board of Supervisors. **PRACTICE AREAS:** Probate; Trust Administration; Conservatorships; Business Transactions; Real Property.

**WALTER MOORE,** born Los Angeles, California, June 3, 1957; admitted to bar, 1989, California. *Education:* Western State University (J.D., 1989). Member: Rotary International, San Bernardino Crossroads (Director, Sargeant at Arms, 1995—); Neumark Ensemble (Vice-Chair, 1995-1997). *Member:* Christian Counseling Service (Budget & Finance, 1996—). *Member:* Bernardino County (Member, Probate Section; Lawyer Referral Committee, 1995—) and Los Angeles County Bar Associations; State Bar of California. **PRACTICE AREAS:** Probate; Conservatorships; Estate Planning; Family Law.

*(This Listing Continued)*

---

**DONALD R. FERGESON,** born Riverside, California, February 25, 1956; admitted to bar, 1993, California. *Education:* San Bernardino Valley College (A.A., 1984); Citrus Belt Law School (B.S.L., 1990); California Southern Law School (J.D., 1992). *Member:* San Bernardino County (Member, Medical Legal Committee; Tel-Law Committee) and Los Angeles County Bar Associations; State Bar of California; Inns of Court. **PRACTICE AREAS:** Personal Injury; Civil Probate and Trust Litigation.

*OF COUNSEL*

**JERE L. FOX,** born Takoma Park, Maryland, November 27, 1951; admitted to bar, 1977, California, U.S. District Court, Northern, Central and Southern Districts of California, U.S. Court of Appeals, Ninth Circuit and U.S. Supreme Court. *Education:* Loma Linda University (B.A., cum laude, 1973); Pepperdine University (J.D., cum laude, 1977). Staff Member, Pepperdine Law Review, 1976-1977. Instructor, Business Organization, California Southern Law School, Paralegal Program. *Member:* Riverside County, San Bernardino County (Member, Probate Section), San Angeles County and American Bar Associations; The State Bar of California. (Also Practicing Individually in Riverside). **PRACTICE AREAS:** Probate Litigation and Will Contests; Conservatorship Litigation; Trust Litigation; Real Property Law.

REPRESENTATIVE CLIENTS: Loma Linda University Medical Center; University Realty; Conservatorship & Resources for the Elderly (CARE); Burger King (Franchisee).
REFERENCE: Redlands Federal Bank (Loma Linda); Redlands Centennial Bank (Redlands).

---

## McPETERS McALEARNEY SHIMOFF & HATT

A PROFESSIONAL CORPORATION

615 BROOKSIDE AVENUE, SUITE B
P.O. BOX 2084
**REDLANDS, CALIFORNIA 92373**
Telephone: 909-792-8919
Fax: 909-792-6234

*San Bernardino, California Office:* 330 North D Street, Suite 320, P.O. Box 6182. Telephone: 909-884-7747. Fax: 909-885-0848.

*Taxation, Business, Pension Plans, Estate Planning, Trusts and Probate Law.*

(For Complete Biographical Data on all Personnel, see Professional Biographies at San Bernardino, California)

---

## MIRAU, EDWARDS, CANNON, HARTER & LEWIN

A PROFESSIONAL CORPORATION

222 EAST OLIVE AVENUE, SUITE 1
**REDLANDS, CALIFORNIA 92373**
Telephone: 909-793-0200
Fax: 909-792-2359

*San Bernardino, California Office:* 599 North "E" Street, Suite 205. Telephone 909-888-0200. Fax: 909-384-0203.

*Business Law, Real Estate, Taxation, Partnerships, Corporations, Commercial Law, Wills and Trusts, and Health Care Law.*

**FIRM PROFILE:** *The firm has a sophisticated practice in taxation and transactional law and has two of the four Certified Taxation Law specialists and one of the seven Estate Planning, Trust and Probate Law specialists in San Bernardino County.*

(For Complete Biographical Data on all Personnel, see Professional Biographies at San Bernardino).

---

## JOHN E. ROTH

**REDLANDS, CALIFORNIA**

(See San Bernardino)

*General Criminal Trial Practice, Criminal Defense, Administrative Law.*

## WELEBIR & McCUNE
### A PROFESSIONAL LAW CORPORATION
*Established in 1973*
**2068 ORANGE TREE LANE, SUITE 215**
**REDLANDS, CALIFORNIA 92374**
Telephone: 909-335-0444
Fax: 909-335-0452
Email: WM__Law@MSN.COM

*Mailing Address:* P.O. Box 10488, San Bernardino, California 92423

Practice limited to Catastrophic Personal Injury and Wrongful Death, Products Liability, Aviation, Railroad and Toxic Torts. Class Actions related to Defective Products and Mass Torts.

FIRM PROFILE: Douglas Welebir began an exclusively plaintiffs personal injury practice in 1970 and formed the predecessor of this firm in 1973. The firm continues in its commitment to the vigorous and ethical representation of the severely and catastrophically injured; with emphasis on injuries and deaths caused by defective products. Member: International Society of Primerus Law Firms. The Firm has been consistently successful in obtaining seven figure results for its catastrophically injured clients through trial and settlements. The firm opens its arms to the International Community, including Canada and has represented clients from several countries. The firm is listed in The Martindale-Hubbell Bar Register of Preeminent Lawyers.

**DOUGLAS F. WELEBIR,** born Washington, D.C., February 9, 1943; admitted to bar, 1966, California and U.S. District Court, Central District of California; 1967, District of Columbia, U.S. Claims Court and U.S. Tax Court; 1971, U.S. Supreme Court. *Education:* La Sierra College (A.B., cum laude, 1962); University of Southern California (J.D., 1965). Delta Theta Phi. Legal Research Assistant to Justice Kerrigan of the California Court of Appeals, 4th District, Div. 2, 1966. Deputy Public Defender of San Bernardino County, 1967. Mayor, City of Loma Linda, 1970-1974. *Member:* San Bernardino County (Member, Medical Legal Committee, 1973-1978; Chairman, 1978; Chairman, Judicial Evaluation Committee, 1988 and 1989) and American (Member, Sections on: Torts and Insurance Practice; Litigation) Bar Associations; State Bar of California; The District of Columbia Bar; Consumer Attorneys of California (Member, Board of Governors, San Bernardino-Riverside-Pomona Chapter, 1977-1979); World Association of Lawyers; The Association of Trial Lawyers of America; American Board of Trial Advocates; Attorneys Information Exchange Group; Union International Des Avocates. *LANGUAGES:* Spanish. *PRACTICE AREAS:* Products Liability Law; Personal Injury Law; Toxic Tort Litigation; Product Defect Class Action. *Email:* DFW__WMLAW@MSN.COM

**RICHARD D. McCUNE, JR.,** born Glendale, California, June 20, 1959; admitted to bar, 1987, California and U.S. District Court, Central District of California. *Education:* Loma Linda University (B.S., 1982); University of Southern California (J.D., 1987). *Member:* San Bernardino County, Riverside County and American Bar Associations; State Bar of California; Consumer Attorneys of California; Association of Trial Lawyers of America; Attorneys Information Exchange Group. *PRACTICE AREAS:* Products Liability; Personal Injury. *Email:* RDM__WMLAW@MSN.COM

---

**GEORGE S. THEIOS,** born San Francisco, California, June 25, 1948; admitted to bar, 1981, California and U.S. District Court, Central District of California. *Education:* University of California at San Diego (B.A., 1971); Western State University College of Law (J.D., 1980). Member, National Association of Counsel for Children. *Member:* San Bernardino County Bar Association; State Bar of California; The Association of Trial Lawyers of America; Consumer Attorneys of California. *PRACTICE AREAS:* Personal Injury Law; Products Liability.

**JACQUELINE CAREY-WILSON,** born Lakewood, California, January 4, 1964; admitted to bar, 1995, California and U.S. District Court, Central District of California; 1996, Colorado; 1997, District of Columbia. *Education:* California State University, Fullerton (B.A., with Honors, 1989); Southwestern University School of Law (J.D., 1995). *Member:* San Bernardino, Riverside County and American Bar Associations; State Bar of California; Consumer Attorneys of California; Association of Trial Lawyers of American. *PRACTICE AREAS:* Products Liability; Personal Injury.

*OF COUNSEL*

**ARTHUR W. KELLY, JR.** (Retired).

*(This Listing Continued)*

---

*LEGAL SUPPORT PERSONNEL*

**RENEE VARGAS,** born Glendale, California, April 11, 1963. *Education:* Walla Walla College (A.S., 1983); California State University (Paralegal, 1989; B.A., 1997). Pi Sigma Alpha. Member, Editorial Review Board, James Publishing, Inc. *Member:* Association of Trial Lawyers of America (Paralegal Associate); Inland Counties Association of Paralegals (Member, Board of Directors, 1995—). *PRACTICE AREAS:* Litigation. *Email:* RCDV__WMLAW@MSN.COM

**DEBORAH MARSH,** born Santa Clara, California, March 21, 1965. *Education:* California State University (Paralegal, 1989); Crafton Hills College (A.A., 1993). *Member:* Association of Trial Lawyers of America (Paralegal Associate). *PRACTICE AREAS:* Litigation. *Email:* DJM__WMLAW@MSN.COM

REFERENCE: Redlands Centennial Bank.

---

## GUAY P. WILSON
**14 NORTH EIGHTH STREET**
**P.O. BOX 166**
**REDLANDS, CALIFORNIA 92373**
Telephone: 909-793-2044
Fax: 909-793-9614

*General Civil Practice. Probate, Estate Planning and Real Estate Law.*

**GUAY P. WILSON,** born Loma Linda, California, October 12, 1935; admitted to bar, 1961, California and U.S. Court of Military Appeals. *Education:* McGill University, Montreal, Quebec (B.A., 1957); University of California at Los Angeles (LL.B., 1960). *Member:* San Bernardino County and American Bar Associations; The State Bar of California. *PRACTICE AREAS:* Probate Law; Estate Planning Law; Real Estate Law.

**PAUL B. WILSON** (1906-1974).

REFERENCES: Bank of America National Trust & Savings Assn.; Redlands Federal Bank (Redlands Branch).

---

## ZIPRICK, SCHILT, HEINRICH & CRAMER
**707 BROOKSIDE AVENUE**
**REDLANDS, CALIFORNIA 92373-5101**
Telephone: 909-824-4305
Telecopier: 909-478-4305

*Healthcare and Hospital Law, Corporate, Non-Profit Organizations, Medical Malpractice, University Law, Real Estate, Labor (Management).*

*MEMBERS OF FIRM*

**ROBERT H. ZIPRICK,** born Glendale, California, May 24, 1951; admitted to bar, 1976, California and U.S. Court of Appeals, 9th Circuit and U.S. District Court, Central District of California. *Education:* Loma Linda University (B.A., 1973); University of San Diego (J.D., 1976). Lecturer, Government Relations, Loma Linda University, College of Arts and Sciences, 1982. Member, San Bernardino County Youth Commission, 1971-1973. Deputy City Attorney, City of Redlands and City of Rialto, 1976-1977. *Member:* State Bar of California; American Bar Association; American Academy of Hospital Attorneys; National Health Lawyers Association.

**WILLIAM F. ZIPRICK,** born Glendale, California, May 29, 1956; admitted to bar, 1980, California; 1986, U.S. Tax Court. *Education:* Pacific Union College (B.S., magna cum laude, 1977); University of California at Los Angeles (J.D., 1980). Member: Order of the Coif. Lecturer, Loma Linda University School of Medicine, 1986—. *Member:* The State Bar of California; American Bar Association; American Academy of Hospital Attorneys; National Health Lawyers Association; California Society of Healthcare Attorneys.

**E. NATHAN SCHILT,** born Baghdad, Iraq, June 9, 1948; admitted to bar, 1973, California. *Education:* Union College (B.A., magna cum laude, 1970); University of California at Los Angeles (J.D., 1973). Chief Deputy District Attorney, San Bernardino County, 1984-1988. *Member:* State Bar of California.

**KERRY L. HEINRICH,** born Lemmon, South Dakota, February 14, 1958; admitted to bar, 1983, Washington; 1984, California. *Education:* Walla Walla College (B.A., magna cum laude, 1980); University of Oregon (J.D., 1983). *Member:* Washington State Bar Association; State Bar of Cali-

*(This Listing Continued)*

## ZIPRICK, SCHILT, HEINRICH & CRAMER, Redlands—Continued

fornia; American Academy of Hospital Attorneys; National Health Lawyers Association; California Society of Healthcare Attorneys.

**KATHLEEN M. CRAMER,** born Savanna, Illinois, November 14, 1953; admitted to bar, 1982, California; U.S. Court of Appeals, Ninth Circuit and U.S. District Court, Central District of California. *Education:* California State University at Fullerton (B.A., 1975); Loyola Marymount University; Western State University at Fullerton (J.D., 1981). *Member:* Federal and American Bar Associations; State Bar of California; American Academy of Hospital Attorneys; National Health Lawyers Association.

### ASSOCIATE

**BRIAN E. WHITLEY,** born Covina, California, 1966; admitted to bar, 1991, California. *Education:* Loma Linda University (B.B.A., summa cum laude, 1988); University of Southern California (J.D., 1991). Certified Public Accountant, Illinois, 1991. Editor: Computer/Law Journal, 1990-1991; Major Tax Planning, 1990-1991. Author: "Joint Ventures in the Semiconductor Industry," 10 Computer/Law Journal 581. *Member:* State Bar of California.

REPRESENTATIVE CLIENTS: Loma Linda University Medical Center; Southeastern California Conference of Seventh-day Adventists; Loma Linda University Behavioral Medicine Center.

---

## LAW OFFICES OF ARTHUR W. FRANCIS, JR.

A PROFESSIONAL CORPORATION

Established in 1982

2522 ARTESIA BOULEVARD
**REDONDO BEACH, CALIFORNIA 90278**
Telephone: 310-316-1988
Fax: 310-318-5894

Insurance Defense, ERISA, Coverage and Bad Faith Matters; General Liability; Personal Injury; Casualty; Life, Disability, Health and Accident; Errors and Omissions; Construction Accident; and Workman's Compensation.

*FIRM PROFILE: The firm handles a wide range of cases from common slip and falls to complex matters in both state and federal courts. The firm has extensive experience in errors and omissions litigation, insurance coverage, bad faith actions, life, disability, health and accident, and personal injury.*

**ARTHUR W. FRANCIS, JR.,** born Cleveland, Ohio, May 30, 1941; admitted to bar, 1971, California, U.S. District Court, Central District of California; 1974, U.S. Court of Appeals, Ninth Circuit; 1976, U.S. District Court, Southern and Eastern Districts of California, U.S. Supreme Court and U.S. Tax Court; 1984, U.S. District Court, Northern District of California. *Education:* California State College at Los Angeles (B.S., 1965); University of Southern California (J.D., 1970). Phi Delta Phi. Author: "How to Handle A Legal Malpractice Lawsuit," Los Angeles Lawyer Magazine, June 1989. *Member:* Los Angeles County, South Bay Bar and American Bar Associations; State Bar of California; Association of Southern California Defense Counsel; Los Angeles Business Trial Lawyers Association; Defense Research Institute, Inc.; International Association of Insurance Counsel; Consumer Attorneys Association of Los Angeles. (Also Of Counsel to The Law Offices of James J. Regan, Redondo Beach, California). *PRACTICE AREAS:* Insurance Defense; ERISA; Bad Faith; Life and Health Insurance; Disability Law; Accident Law.

### OF COUNSEL

**TERRY CHEVILLAT,** born Los Angeles, California, April 16, 1945; admitted to bar, 1971, California; 1987, U.S. District Court, Central District of California; 1991, U.S. Court of Appeals, Eleventh Circuit; 1994, U.S. Court of Appeals, Ninth Circuit. *Education:* University of Southern California (B.A., cum laude, 1967; J.D., 1970). Co-Author: "How to Handle a Legal Malpractice Lawsuit," Los Angeles Lawyer Magazine, June, 1989. *Member:* Los Angeles County and American Bar Associations; State Bar of California; Consumer Attorneys Association of Los Angeles. *PRACTICE AREAS:* Insurance Defense; ERISA; Bad Faith; Life and Health Insurance; Disability Law; Accident Law.

REPRESENTATIVE CLIENTS: The Centennial Life Insurance Company; Central Benefit Systems; Employers Reinsurance Company.

---

## HRUSKA & LESSER

Established in 1974

1 PEARL STREET
**REDONDO BEACH, CALIFORNIA 90277**
Telephone: 310-374-4808
Fax: 310-372-7715
URL: http://www.divelaw.com

*Boca Raton, Florida Office:* 21 South East Fifth Street. Telephone: 407-338-2110. Fax: 407-338-0894.

*Honolulu, Hawaii Office:* 2400 PRI Tower, Grovesnor Center, 733 Bishop Street. Telephone: 808-526-2641. Fax: 808-531-8628.

Civil Practice in State and Federal Courts specializing in the defense of Recreational and Commercial Diving Claims, Related Products Liability Actions, Insurance Litigation and Admiralty Law.

*FIRM PROFILE: Hruska & Lesser was founded in 1974 by Richard A. Lesser. The Firm now represents recreational and commercial diving instructors, companies and agencies and manufacturers of diving equipment all over the United States including the U.S. Virgin Islands and Guam. The firm is composed of avid scuba divers, diving professionals and individuals with commercial diving backgrounds who are intimately familiar with safe diving practices, technical diving, diving medicine and diving equipment.*

### MEMBERS OF FIRM

**MARK A. HRUSKA,** born Pittsburgh, Pennsylvania, June 25, 1950; admitted to bar, 1975, Pennsylvania; 1986, Florida; 1991, U.S. District Court, District of Hawaii. *Education:* University of Pittsburgh (B.A., summa cum laude, 1972; J.D., 1975). Phi Eta Sigma. Recipient: Bancroft Whitney Award for Excellence Corporate Law; Honors Moot Court Oral Argument. Former Director, Western Pennsylvania Trial Lawyers Association, 1983-1985. Lecturer, Risk Management for Diving Professionals, Diving Equipment Manufacturers Association Conventions, 1990-1992. Featured Attorney, Court TV, Beugnot v. Aquanaut Diving, 1992. *Member:* Pennsylvania Bar Associations; The Florida Bar. (Resident Boca Raton, Florida). *PRACTICE AREAS:* Personal Injury; Wrongful Death; Products Liability Defense.

**RICHARD A. LESSER,** born Hawthorne, California, December 22, 1946; admitted to bar, 1974, California; 1992, Hawaii; 1993, Texas. *Education:* California State University at Long Beach (A.B., 1969); University of Southern California (J.D., 1973). Author: "Risk Management for the Diving Instructor," Dive Industry News, Third Quarter, 1990. Lecturer, "Risk Management for Diving Professionals," DEMA Conventions, 1990-1996. *Member:* State Bar of Texas; State Bar of California; Hawaii State Bar Association; Association of Diving Contractors; Underwater Hyperbaric Medical Society. *PRACTICE AREAS:* Defense of Recreational Accidents.

**WILLIAM J. TURBEVILLE, II,** born Ashland, Wisconsin, April 4, 1957; admitted to bar, 1984, Florida; 1985, U.S. District Court, Middle and Southern Districts of Florida, U.S. Court of Appeals, Eleventh Circuit and U.S. Supreme Court; 1992, Hawaii and U.S. District Court, District of Hawaii. *Education:* Florida Atlantic University (B.A., with honors, 1978; M.A., 1981); University of Florida (J.D., with honors, 1984). Order of the Coif. Senior Articles Editor, University of Florida Law Review, 1983-1984. Author: Comment, "Establishment Clause Standing Clarified," 35 University of Florida Law Review 188, 1983; Note, "American Ocean Policy Adrift: An Exclusive Economic Zone as an Alternative to the Law of the Sea Treaty," 35 University of Florida Law Review 492, 1983; "Nonregulatory Techniques for Growth Management: Locking in the Players: in Growth Management Innovations, FAU & FIU Joint Center for Environmental and Urban Problems, Monograph, 88-1 (1988); "Liability Considerations of Nitrox Diving," The Undersea Journal (Fourth Quarter, 1992); Legal Risks of Technical Diving: How to Protect Yourself," Aqua Corps Journal, Vol. 3 No. 1 (Winter 1992). Law Clerk to the Honorable Paul H. Roney, U.S. Court of Appeals for the Eleventh Circuit, 1984-1985. *Member:* The Florida Bar; Hawaii State Bar Association. (Resident Boca Raton, Florida). *PRACTICE AREAS:* Personal Injury; Wrongful Death; Product Liability Defense; Environmental Law.

**JEANA SCIARAPPA SCHOTT,** born Weymouth, Massachusetts, July 21, 1957; admitted to bar, 1992, California; 1993, U.S. District Court, Central District of California; 1996, U.S. District Court, District of Hawaii. *Education:* Northeastern University (B.S., with honors, 1980); Western State University (J.D., awarded honors, 1992);. Author: Co-Author, Risk Management Seminar for Diving Professionals, Presenter DEMA (Diving Equipment Manufacturer Association) 1987; "Stepping Out of Bounds," Diving Training Magazine Legal Brief, January 1992; "Diving Industry

*(This Listing Continued)*

Insurance, Softening the Crunch with Quality Control and Prudent Claims Management," Undersea Journal, Third Quarter 1986; "Defensive Teaching a Must," 1988-1993 PADI Instructor Manual reprinted from the PADI Journal, First Quarter 1986; "The PADI Trademark, How They Can Be A Benefit to Your Business," The Undersea Journal, Third Quarter 1985, reprinted in the PADI Instructor Training Manual; "An Examination of Diving Litigation," The Undersea Journal, Fourth Quarter 1985. 1982 PADI Scuba Instructor Certification, Underwater Careers International. Secretary, Student Bar Association, Western State University, 1992. Course Director, Professional Association of Diving Instructors, 1984—. Medic First Aid Instructor Trainer. President, 1991-1995 and Senior Claims Manager, 1989-1991 Watersports Claims Management, Ltd. Quality Assurance Director/Training and Education International PADI, Inc., Santa Ana, California, 1984-1989. Member, International PADI Inc. 1982. *Member:* Orange County Bar Association; State Bar of California; Orange County Trial Lawyers Association; Orange County Bar Association College of Trial Advocacy.

**HILLARY S. MEISELS,** born Los Angeles, California, April 18; admitted to bar, 1993, California and U.S District Court, Central District of California; 1996, U.S. District Court, District of Hawaii. *Education:* University of California at Los Angeles (B.A., 1988); Southwestern University (J.D., cum laude, 1993). Dean's Merit Scholar. Recipient: American Jurisprudence Award, Evidence. Moot Court Honors. President, Student Bar Association, 1991-1992. Member, Editorial Board, Los Angeles Lawyer, 1994—. *Member:* Los Angeles County Bar Association; State Bar of California. *PRACTICE AREAS:* Corporate Law; Defense of Recreational Accidents; Music Law.

REPRESENTATIVE CLIENTS: Loyds Underwriters; K&K Insurance Group; AIG Insurance Group; Body Glove International; International PADI, Inc.; Diving Systems International (Kirby Morgan Commercial Equipment); Uwatec Switzerland; Sea Quest, Inc.; Dacor Corporation; St. Paul Insurance; Transamerica Insurance Group; Terra Nova Insurance; Uni International Japan; U.S. Divers Company, Inc.; IANTD Instructors/Divemasters; IDEA Instructors/Divemasters; T.D.I.; Aqua-Lung Group; Cardlogix; Elan, Inc.; Forté, Inc.

---

## LAW OFFICES OF
## JAMES J. REGAN

*Established in 1979*

2522 ARTESIA BOULEVARD
**REDONDO BEACH, CALIFORNIA 90278-3258**
Telephone: 310-372-1988; 316-1988 After Hours Answering
Fax: 310-318-5894

*Civil Litigation, Insurance Defense, Corporate, Real Estate, Family Law, Probate, Personal Injury Law, Immigration and Nationality, Alternate Dispute Resolution.*

**JAMES J. REGAN,** born Pasadena, California, May 10, 1945; admitted to bar, 1978, California and U.S. District Court, Central District of California. *Education:* California Polytechnic State University (B.S.M.E., 1968); Pepperdine University (M.B.A., 1972); Southwestern University (J.D., 1976). Metallurgical Engineer, Aluminum Ind., 1968-1973. Manager, Injection Molding Operation, 1973-1977. Corporate Attorney, Aerospace Ind., 1977-1979. President, Int'l. Technology, Inc., 1979-1981. *Member:* South Bay Bar (Bar President, 1994; Chairman, Lawyer's Referral Service Committee, 1988; Board Member, 1988-1995; Officer, 1990-1994) and American Bar Associations; American Society of Metals; Los Angeles Trial Lawyers Association. *PRACTICE AREAS:* Civil Litigation; Personal Injury; Real Property; Corporate; Contracts; Insurance Defense; Family Law; Probate; Alternate Dispute Resolution.

### ASSOCIATES

**GENE A. WILKER,** born Owatonna, Minnesota, March 5, 1945; admitted to bar, 1980, California. *Education:* University of Southern California (B.S., 1975); Loyola Law School ( J.D., 1979). *Member:* South Bay and American Bar Associations. [U.S. Marine Corps, 1963-1966]. *PRACTICE AREAS:* Civil Litigation.

**MICHELE L. WONG,** born Hawthorne, California, March 18, 1968; admitted to bar, 1993, California; 1996, U.S. District Court, Central District of California. *Education:* University of California, Irvine (B.A., cum laude, 1990); Loyola Law School (J.D., 1993). *Member:* Los Angeles County, South Bay and American Bar Associations; American Immigration Lawyers Association; Southern California Chinese Lawyers Association. *LANGUAGES:* Cantonese, Spanish and French. *PRACTICE AREAS:* Immigration; Nationality.

*(This Listing Continued)*

---

**MICHAEL S. BRAUN,** born Hastings, Nebraska, October 15, 1962; admitted to bar, 1988, Nebraska and U.S. District Court, District of Nebraska; 1991, California and U.S. District Court, Central District of California. *Education:* University of Nebraska (B.S., 1984; J.D., 1988). *PRACTICE AREAS:* Personal Injury; Civil Litigation.

### OF COUNSEL

**ARTHUR W. FRANCIS, JR. (A PROFESSIONAL CORPORATION),** born Cleveland, Ohio, May 30, 1941; admitted to bar, 1971, California, U.S. District Court, Central District of California; 1974, U.S. Court of Appeals, Ninth Circuit; 1976, U.S. District Court, Southern and Northern Districts of California, U.S. Supreme Court and U.S. Tax Court; 1984, U.S. District Court, Eastern District of California. *Education:* California State College at Los Angeles (B.S., 1965); University of Southern California (J.D., 1970). Phi Delta Phi. Author: "How to Handle A Legal Malpractice Lawsuit," Los Angeles Lawyer Magazine, June 1989. *Member:* Los Angeles County, South Bay Bar and American Bar Associations; Association of Southern California Defense Counsel; Los Angeles Business Trial Lawyers Association; Defense Research Institute, Inc.; International Association of Insurance Counsel. (Also Practicing Individually in Redondo Beach).

**FRANK DANIEL RORIE,** born Titusville, Pennsylvania, July 19, 1945; admitted to bar, 1980, California; 1981, U.S. District Court, Central District of California and U.S. Court of Appeals, Ninth Circuit. *Education:* University of Arkansas (B.S.I.E., 1968); Pepperdine University (M.B.A., 1973); Southwestern University (J.D., 1978); University of San Diego (1983-1984). *Member:* South Bay and American Bar Associations. [U.S.A.F., 1968-1973, Capt.]. *PRACTICE AREAS:* Criminal Defense.

**FRANK A. HILLSINGER** (1927-1993).

REPRESENTATIVE CLIENTS: Centennial Life Insurance Co.; Fremont Indemnity Co.; C&G Mercury Plastics; JSW Plastics Machinery; Gable Plastics; AEON Manufacturing; SE-GI Products Inc.; RAKAR Plastics; Capitol Truck EQPT Inc.; Parnelli Jones, Inc.; The Japan Steel Co. Ltd.

---

## KEVIN G. WOOD

*A PROFESSIONAL LAW CORPORATION*

*Established in 1976*

229 AVENUE I, 2ND FLOOR
**REDONDO BEACH, CALIFORNIA 90277**
Telephone: 310-540-4552
Fax: 310-540-8480

*General Civil Litigation, Personal Injury, Family Law including Dissolutions, Custody, Spousal Support, Cohabitation and Prenuptials, Real Estate, Business Law, Probate, Conservatorships, Commercial Litigation, Contracts.*

**KEVIN G. WOOD,** born Long Beach, California, May 18, 1936; admitted to bar, 1975, California; 1976, U.S. District Court, Central District of California and U.S. Court of Appeals, Ninth Circuit. *Education:* University of California at Berkeley (B.A., Physics, 1964); California State University (M.A., Physics, 1968); Loyola University (J.D., 1975). *Member:* South Bay, Los Angeles County and American Bar Associations; State Bar of California; Los Angeles Trial Lawyers Association. [Sgt., USMC, 1955-1960]. *LANGUAGES:* French and German.

---

## AARON, RIECHERT, CARPOL & RIFFLE, A P.C.

*Established in 1987*

SUITE 400, 900 VETERANS BOULEVARD
**REDWOOD CITY, CALIFORNIA 94063**
Telephone: 415-368-4662
Fax: 415-367-8531

*General Civil and Trial Practice in all Courts. Real Property, Business, Corporate, Credit Unions, Probate, Conservatorship, Trust, Estate Planning, Family, Municipal and Personal Injury Law.*

**PETER G. RIECHERT,** born Milwaukee, Wisconsin, June 18, 1950; admitted to bar, 1975, California. *Education:* University of Wisconsin (B.A., with distinction, 1972); Stanford University (J.D., 1975). Phi Kappa Phi. *Member:* San Mateo County Bar Association (Director, 1988-1990; Secretary, 1991; Treasurer, 1992; Vice President, 1993; President, 1994); The State Bar of California; San Mateo County Barristers Club (President,

*(This Listing Continued)*

CAA1705B

## AARON, RIECHERT, CARPOL & RIFFLE, A P.C.,
Redwood City—Continued

1986). *PRACTICE AREAS:* Business Law; Corporate Law; Real Estate Law; Credit Unions and Related Litigation.

**STEVEN J. CARPOL,** born San Francisco, California, September 4, 1950; admitted to bar, 1975, California. *Education:* University of California at Davis and University of California at Santa Barbara (B.A., 1972); McGeorge School of the Law (J.D., 1975); Golden Gate University (M.S. in Taxation, 1988). Life Member, Traynor Honor Society. Recipient, American Jurisprudence Award, Criminal Law, 1973. Assistant City Attorney: Pacifica, 1980-1983; Half Moon Bay, 1983-1987. Assistant Town Attorney: Woodside, 1986-1987; Foster City, 1983-1987; Belmont, 1983-1987. Member, Board of Directors, Barristers Club of San Mateo County, 1979-1985. *Member:* San Mateo County Bar Association (Chairman, Family Law Section, 1983); State Bar of California. *PRACTICE AREAS:* Real Estate Law; Corporate Law; Tax Law; Estate Planning Law; Business Law; Litigation.

**CHARLES M. RIFFLE,** born San Francisco, California, April 16, 1947; admitted to bar, 1972, California. *Education:* University of San Francisco (B.A., 1969; J.D., cum laude, 1972). Member, McAuliffe Law Honor Society. Book Review Editor, University of San Francisco Law Review, 1971-1972. Author: "Representing The Conservatee In A Contested Probate Conservatorship Proceeding," Estate Planning, Trust & Probate News, Summer 1993. *Member:* San Mateo County (Chairman, Family Law Section, 1988 and Estate Planning and Probate Section, 1990-1992; Director, 1994-1996) and American Bar Associations; The State Bar of California; Legal Aid Society of San Mateo County (President, 1983-1985). [Lt., USAR, 1972]. (Certified Specialist, Estate Planning, Trust and Probate Law, The State Bar of California Board of Legal Specialization). *PRACTICE AREAS:* Estate Planning and Probate; Family Law; Business Law.

**SCOTT C. ABRAMS,** born Lawton-Ft. Sill, Oklahoma, May 29, 1967; admitted to bar, 1993, California and U.S. District Court, Northern District of California. *Education:* University of California at Los Angeles (B.A., cum laude, 1990); University of San Francisco (J.D., 1993). *Member:* State Bar of California; Legal Aid Society of San Mateo County.

REPRESENTATIVE CLIENTS: Westbay Steel, Inc.; US First Federal Credit Union; Valley Credit Union; Vivion Chemical Co., Inc.; Elite Realty; Redwood Associates Realty; Louis F. Gamba Investments; Dumas Properties, Inc.; The O'Brien Corporation, Photolabs International; Terminal Mfg. Co., Inc.; Brian Kangas, Foulk; Service Mortgage Corp.; A.S.I.; Golden Gate Properties; Treadways, Inc. dba Sanitorio Tire; National Network Exchange, Inc.
REFERENCES: Wells Fargo Bank (Redwood City); Bay Area Bank; Say Hey, Inc. (Helena Brewers).

---

## PAUL J. BARULICH

A PROFESSIONAL CORPORATION

Established in 1989

WESTSHORE OFFICE PARK
250A TWIN DOLPHIN DRIVE
**REDWOOD CITY, CALIFORNIA 94065**
Telephone: 415-595-0444
Fax: 415-595-3976
Email: barulich@pacbell.net

*Estate Planning, Probate and Trust, Business, Corporate, Real Property and Taxation.*

**PAUL J. BARULICH,** born San Francisco, California, March 31, 1957; admitted to bar, 1985, California, U.S. District Court, Northern District of California and U.S. Tax Court. *Education:* University of California at Berkeley (A.B., 1981); Golden Gate University (J.D., 1984). *Member:* Bar Association of San Francisco (Member, Sections on: Real Property; Taxation; Member: Committees on: Barristers Taxation; Estate Planning); San Mateo County (Chair, Probate and Estate Planning Section, 1995) and American Bar Associations; State Bar of California (Member: Real Estate Taxation Subsection; Estate Planning Committee; Member, Sections on: Taxation; Real Property Law). (Certified Specialist, Estate Planning, Trust and Probate Law, The State Bar of California Board of Legal Specialization). *PRACTICE AREAS:* Probate; Estate Planning; Trusts; Business Law; Corporate Law; Taxation.

CAA1706B

---

## ROBERT A. BOLAND

702 MARSHALL STREET, SUITE 270
**REDWOOD CITY, CALIFORNIA 94063**
Telephone: 415-363-5799
Fax: 415-367-1086

*Business Law, Real Estate, Probate and Estate Planning.*

**ROBERT A. BOLAND,** born San Mateo, California, August 8, 1960; admitted to bar, 1986, California. *Education:* University of Santa Clara (B.S.C. in Accounting, 1982; M.B.A., 1986; J.D., 1986). *Member:* Santa Clara County, San Mateo County and American Bar Associations; State Bar of California. *PRACTICE AREAS:* Business Law; Real Estate; Probate; Estate Planning.

---

## BRANSON, FITZGERALD & HOWARD

A PROFESSIONAL CORPORATION
SUITE 400, 643 BAIR ISLAND ROAD
**REDWOOD CITY, CALIFORNIA 94063**
Telephone: 415-365-7710
Fax: 415-364-LAWS

*Insurance, Professional Liability, Civil Litigation. Construction, Products Liability, Insurance Defense, Medical and Other Professional Liability, Landslide and Subsidence, Personal Injury, Wrongful Death, Real Estate, Probate and Business Law. General, Civil and Trial Practice.*

**THOMAS A. BRANSON,** born San Mateo, California, September 24, 1939; admitted to bar, 1964, California. *Education:* University of Santa Clara (B.A., 1961); Hastings College of Law, University of California (LL.B., 1964); Awarded LL.D., New York University, 1965. Order of the Coif. Arbitrator, San Mateo County, 1979—. Judge Pro Tem, San Mateo County, 1985—. *Member:* San Mateo County Bar Association; State Bar of California; Association of Defense Counsel; International Association of Insurance Counsel; American Board of Trial Advocates; International Society of Barristers.

**DERMOT J. FITZGERALD,** born Dublin, Ireland, June 13, 1934; admitted to bar, 1958, Ireland; 1967, California. *Education:* University College, Dublin (B.A., 1955; B.C.L., 1958); King's Inn, Dublin (B.L., 1958). Special Master, San Mateo County Superior Court, 1986-1989. (Inactive).

**JOSEPH C. HOWARD, JR.,** born Portland, Oregon, December 23, 1943; admitted to bar, 1972, California. *Education:* Seattle University (B.C.S., 1966); University of San Francisco (J.D., 1971). Arbitrator, San Mateo County, 1979—. Judge Pro Tem, San Mateo County, 1985—. *Member:* San Mateo County and American Bar Associations; State Bar of California; Association of Defense Counsel. [Capt., U.S. Army, active duty, 1966-1968]

**FRED R. BRINKOP,** born St. Louis, Missouri, December 13, 1942; admitted to bar, 1967, California. *Education:* Washington University (A.B., 1964); Stanford University (LL.B., 1967). *Member:* San Mateo County Bar Association (Chairman, Public Affairs Committee, 1971-1972); State Bar of California.

**HENRY D. ROME,** born San Francisco, California, December 8, 1945; admitted to bar, 1971, California and U.S. Court of Military Appeals. *Education:* University of San Francisco (B.A., 1967); Hastings College of Law, University of California (J.D., 1970). Deputy District Attorney, San Diego County, 1974-1976. Arbitrator, San Mateo County, 1979—. Judge Pro Tem, San Mateo County, 1985—. *Member:* San Mateo County and American Bar Associations; State Bar of California; Association of Defense Counsel; Defense Research Institute. [Capt., Judge Advocate, USMC, active duty, 1971-1974]

**KRISTI L. CURTIS,** born Phoenix, Arizona, November 22, 1955; admitted to bar, 1981, California. *Education:* California State University, Humboldt; California State University at San Diego (A.B., 1978); University of Santa Clara (J.D., 1981). Member, Moot Court Honors Board. *Member:* San Mateo County and Santa Clara County Bar Associations; State Bar of California; Association of Defense Counsel.

**GLENN D. MARTIN,** born Brooklyn, New York, May 10, 1956; admitted to bar, 1981, California. *Education:* State University of New York at Albany (B.A., 1978); University of San Francisco (J.D., 1981); Southwestern University. Arbitrator, San Mateo County, 1987—. *Member:* San Mateo County and American Bar Associations; State Bar of California; Association of Defense Counsel.

*(This Listing Continued)*

**DAVID L. STRONG,** born San Francisco, California, June 12, 1955; admitted to bar, 1982, California. *Education:* University of California at Davis (B.A., 1977); University of Santa Clara (J.D., 1981). *Member:* San Mateo County Bar Association; State Bar of California; Association of Defense Counsel.

**HARRY A. GRIFFITH, III,** born Redwood City, California, January 15, 1959; admitted to bar, 1984, California. *Education:* California State University at San Jose (B.A., summa cum laude, 1981); University of San Francisco (J.D., magna cum laude, 1984). Member, McAuliffe Honor Society. *Member:* San Mateo County and American Bar Associations; State Bar of California. **LANGUAGES:** Spanish.

**CAROL P. SMITH,** born Riverside, California, August 22, 1962; admitted to bar, 1987, California and U.S. District Court, Northern District of California. *Education:* Stanford University (B.A., 1984); Santa Clara University (J.D., 1987). *Member:* San Mateo County and American Bar Associations; State Bar of California. **LANGUAGES:** French.

**DAVID S. SECREST,** born Rochester, New York, November 9, 1955; admitted to bar, 1989, California and U.S. District Court, Northern District of California. *Education:* Denison University (B.A., 1978); University of San Francisco (J.D., 1988). *Member:* San Mateo County and American Bar Association; State Bar of California (Member, Employment Law Section); Association of Trial Lawyers of America.

**JUDITH FRIEDERICI,** born Akron, Ohio, March 30, 1944; admitted to bar, 1986, California; U.S. Court of Appeals, Ninth Circuit; U.S. District Court, Northern and Eastern Districts of California. *Education:* University of Denver (B.F.A., 1966); University of San Francisco (J.D., 1986). Recipient, American Jurisprudence Award in Criminal Procedure. *Member:* Queen's Bench (Member, Scholarship Committee; Chair, 1992-1995). **PRACTICE AREAS:** General Litigation; Environmental/Toxic Tort Law; Insurance Coverage Law.

**SHAWN M. RIDLEY,** born Jersey City, New Jersey, October 4, 1963; admitted to bar, 1989, California and U.S. District Court, Northern District of California; 1990, U.S. District Court, Eastern District of California. *Education:* University of Notre Dame (B.A., 1986); Santa Clara University (J.D., 1989). *Member:* San Mateo County and American Bar Associations.

**JOHN R. CAMPO,** born Phoenix, Arizona, May 6, 1966; admitted to bar, 1991, California and U.S. District Court, District of California. *Education:* Santa Clara University (B.S., 1988; J.D., 1991). Phi Alpha Delta. Member, Honors Moot Court Board.

**JOHN H. PODESTA,** born La Jolla, California, August 18, 1961; admitted to bar, 1991, California, U.S. District Court, Northern District of California and U.S. Court of Appeals, Ninth Circuit. *Education:* University of California at Berkeley (A.B., 1983); University of San Francisco (J.D., 1991). *Member:* State Bar of California. **PRACTICE AREAS:** Insurance Coverage; Bad Faith.

**SONDRA E. KIRWAN,** born Palo Alto, California, December 14, 1964; admitted to bar, 1991, California. *Education:* San Jose State University (B.S., 1987); Santa Clara University (J.D., 1991). Phi Alpha Delta. *Member:* State Bar of California.

**ELIZABETH J. VON EMSTER,** born Cincinnati, Ohio, March 16, 1967; admitted to bar, 1992, California. *Education:* University of California at Berkeley (B.A., with honors, 1989); Hastings College of Law, University of California at San Francisco (J.D., with honors, 1992). Member, Moot Court Board. Recipient, American Jurisprudence Award in Torts. *Member:* State Bar of California.

### OF COUNSEL

**DWIGHT S. HALDAN,** born Lakeport, California, December 24, 1950; admitted to bar, 1976, California. *Education:* University of California at Santa Barbara (B.A., 1973); Hastings College of Law, University of California (J.D., 1976). Arbitrator, San Mateo County, 1979—. Judge Pro Tem, San Mateo County, 1985—. *Member:* San Mateo County Bar Association; State Bar of California; Association of Defense Counsel.

REPRESENTATIVE CLIENTS: American International Adjustment Company, Inc.; Agricultural Excess & Surplus Insurance Co.; AIG Group; American International Adjusting Company, Inc.; American Sentinel; American Star Insurance Co.; Argonaut Insurance Co.; The Atlantic Cos.; Chubb Group; Civil Service Employees Insurance Co.; Commercial Union; Consolidated American Insurance Co.; Crum & Forster Group; Fireman's Fund Insurance Co.; Foremost Insurance Co.; Gay & Taylor, Inc.; George Hills Company, Inc.; Great American West; Hartford Insurance Co.; Industrial Indemnity; Industrial Underwriters; International Insurance; International Surplus Lines Insurance Co.; Kemper Insurance Co.; Lexington Insurance Co.; National Union Insurance Co.; New Hampshire Insurance Co.; Omega Claims; Pacific Bell; Pacific Gas & Electric Co.; Royal Insurance Co.; St. Paul Insurance Co.; Shand, Morahan & Com-

*(This Listing Continued)*

pany, Inc.; Seibels, Bruce & Co.; Western States; Western World; United States Fidelity & Guaranty Co.; Yasuda Fire & Marine Insurance Co.; Cities of Redwood City, San Bruno, San Carlos, South San Francisco, Half Moon Bay, Menlo Park, Belmont, Millbrae, Atherton, Pacifica, Foster City, Palo Alto and the Association of Bay Area Governments PLAN.
REFERENCE: Union Bank.

## BROWN & BROWN

*Established in 1987*

BRADFORD PROFESSIONAL OFFICE CENTER
*399 BRADFORD STREET, SUITE 200*
**REDWOOD CITY, CALIFORNIA 94063**
Telephone: 415-369-4499
Fax: 415-369-3753

*Civil Litigation and Administrative Law. Construction, Products Liability, Health Care and Licensing, Insurance Defense, Medical and Other Professional Liability, Landslide and Subsidence, Personal Injury, Wrongful Death, Wrongful Termination Law and Alternate Dispute Resolution.*

### MEMBERS OF FIRM

**JEFFREY O. BROWN,** born Kansas City, Missouri, January 5, 1942; admitted to bar, 1972, California; 1975, U.S. Supreme Court. *Education:* Spring Hill College (B.S., 1963); University of Denver (J.D., 1971). Faculty Workshop Leader, Center for Civil Trial and Appellate Advocacy, Hastings College of the Law, University of California, 1982. Arbitrator and Special Master, San Mateo County Superior Court, 1979—. *Member:* San Mateo, Santa Clara County and American Bar Associations; The State Bar of California; Northern California Association of Defense Counsel; Defense Research Institute (Vice Chairman, Construction Law Committee, 1986—); International Association of Defense Counsel. **PRACTICE AREAS:** Products Liability; Medical and Professional Liability; Construction Litigation; Alternate Dispute Resolution.

**SHERIDAN H. BROWN,** born Tucson, Arizona, July 30, 1947; admitted to bar, 1972, California, U.S. District Court, Northern District of California and U.S. Court of Appeals, Ninth Circuit. *Education:* Raymond College (B.A., 1968); University of Denver (J.D., 1971). Member, University of Denver Law Review, 1970-1971. Member, Queen's Bench. Arbitrator, San Mateo County Superior Court, 1987—. Member, Panel of Arbitrators, American Arbitration Association. *Member:* San Mateo County and American Bar Associations; The State Bar of California; Northern California Association of Defense Counsel; Defense Research Institute. **PRACTICE AREAS:** Construction Litigation; Health Care Providers and Licensing Law; Administrative Law; Personal Injury Law.

---

**CLAUDIA J. GORHAM,** born Omaha, Nebraska, April 19, 1962; admitted to bar, 1990, California. *Education:* University of Missouri (A.B., cum laude, 1984); University of California, Hastings College of the Law (J.D., 1989). Phi Beta Kappa. Associate Editor, COMM/ENT. *Member:* Bar Association of San Francisco; The State Bar of California; American Bar Association.

REPRESENTATIVE CLIENTS: Albert D. Seeno Construction Co.; Allianz Insurance Co.; Bay HealthCare Corp.; Bucyrus-Erie Co.; Campania Management Co.; City of San Mateo; The Coe Manufacturing Co.; First Healthcare Corp.; Grove Worldwide; Gulf Insurance Group; Harnischfeger Industries, Inc.; HFIC Management Co., Inc. (subsidiary of National Medical Enterprises, Inc.); The Hillhaven Corp.; Marsh & McLennan Claims Management Services; Medmarc Insurance Co.; Morgan Equipment Co.; National Crane Co.; San Francisco Community Convalescent Hospital; Scotchman Industries, Inc.; State Farm Fire and Casualty Co.; Youmans Convalescent Hospitals, Inc.

## CARR, McCLELLAN, INGERSOLL, THOMPSON & HORN

*PROFESSIONAL CORPORATION*

**REDWOOD CITY, CALIFORNIA**

(See Burlingame)

*General Civil and Trial Practice. Corporation, Hospital and Health Care, Labor and Employment, Bankruptcy, Creditors Rights, Commercial, International Business, Tax, Real Estate, Estate Planning and Probate Law.*

CAA1707B

## CODDINGTON, HICKS & DANFORTH

A PROFESSIONAL CORPORATION

Established in 1977

SUITE 300, 555 TWIN DOLPHIN DRIVE
PARAGON CENTER, REDWOOD SHORES
**REDWOOD CITY, CALIFORNIA 94065**
Telephone: 415-592-5400
Facsimile: 415-592-5027

*Insurance, Aviation, Business, Tort and Products Liability Law. General Civil and Trial Practice in all State and Federal Courts.*

**CLINTON H. CODDINGTON,** born Honolulu, Hawaii, July 8, 1939; admitted to bar, 1969, California; 1974, U.S. Supreme Court. *Education:* United States Military Academy (B.S., with distinction, 1961); University of California at Berkeley (J.D., 1968). Phi Alpha Delta. Member, National Panel of Arbitrators, American Arbitration Association. *Member:* Bar Association of San Francisco; San Mateo, Santa Clara and American (Vice Chairman, Tort and Insurance Practice Section, Committee on Aviation and Space Law, 1985-1986) Bar Associations; State Bar of California; Association of Defense Counsel; Defense Research Institute; International Association of Insurance Counsel; Lawyer-Pilots Bar Association; American Board of Trial Advocates. [Capt., U.S. Army, 1961-1965]

**RANDOLPH S. HICKS,** born Oakland, California, April 17, 1953; admitted to bar, 1978, California. *Education:* University of California at Berkeley (A.B., 1975); University of Santa Clara (J.D., summa cum laude, 1978). Research Editor, University of Santa Clara Law Review, 1977-1978. Author: "The Arena— Defendant's Choice of Forum," SMU Journal of Air Law and Commerce, 1981. *Member:* Santa Clara County Bar Association; State Bar of California; Association of Defense Counsel.

**LEE J. DANFORTH,** born Los Angeles, California, June 10, 1949; admitted to bar, 1976, California; 1977, Alaska. *Education:* California Lutheran College (B.A., cum laude, 1971); University of the Pacific (J.D., 1976). Broker, California Department of Real Estate, 1981-1985. *Member:* San Mateo, Alaska and American Bar Associations; State Bar of California; Association of Defense Counsel.

**DAVID M. KING,** born Los Angeles, California, April 2, 1954; admitted to bar, 1980, California. *Education:* University of California (B.A., summa cum laude, 1977); University of Santa Clara (J.D., summa cum laude, 1980). *Member:* State Bar of California.

**RICHARD G. GROTCH,** born San Francisco, California, January 25, 1961; admitted to bar, 1987, California, U.S. District Court, Northern, Eastern and Central Districts of California and U.S. Court of Appeals, Ninth Circuit. *Education:* University of California (A.B., with high honors, 1983); Hastings College of the Law; University of San Francisco. McAuliffe Honor Society. Executive Publishing Editor COMM/ENT: Hastings Journal of Communications and Entertainment Law, 1985-1986. *Member:* Bar Association of San Francisco.

---

**EDWARD A. HEINLEIN,** born DeKalb County, Missouri, December 10, 1939; admitted to bar, 1979, California. *Education:* Yale University; Stanford University (B.A., 1975); University of Santa Clara (J.D., 1979). *Member:* State Bar of California.

**DAVID W. WESSEL,** born St. Louis, Missouri, January 3, 1953; admitted to bar, 1984, Wisconsin; 1985, California. *Education:* Concordia College (A.A., 1973); University of Wisconsin (B.A., cum laude, 1975; J.D., 1984). *Member:* Bar Association of San Francisco (Member, Bankruptcy Section); State Bar of Wisconsin; State Bar of California; American Bar Association.

**R. WARDELL LOVELAND,** born Hartford, Connecticut, August 17, 1959; admitted to bar, 1987, California. *Education:* Princeton University (A.B., 1981); Boston College Law School (J.D., 1986). *Member:* Bar Association of San Francisco; State Bar of California; American Bar Association.

**PAMELA ANN SMITH,** born Andrews, Texas, June 3, 1965; admitted to bar, 1990, California and U.S. District Court, Northern District of California. *Education:* University of California at Berkeley (A.B., 1987); Santa Clara University (J.D., 1990). *Member:* Santa Clara County Bar Association; State Bar of California; California Women Lawyers Association.

**PETER L. CANDY,** born Los Angeles, California, October 7, 1964; admitted to bar, 1990, California, U.S. District Court, Northern District of

*(This Listing Continued)*

California and U.S. Court of Appeals, Ninth Circuit. *Education:* University of the Pacific (B.A., 1986); Santa Clara University (J.D., 1990).

**DAVID K. LEVINE,** born Fargo, North Dakota, December 28, 1966; admitted to bar, 1992, California. *Education:* Stanford University (B.A., 1989); Boston University (J.D., 1992). Member, National Moot Court. Editor, Probate Law Journal.

### OF COUNSEL

**WILLIAM G. TUCKER,** born Panama Canal Zone, November 9, 1928; admitted to bar, 1957, California. *Education:* Loyola University (B.S., 1953); Loyola University School of Law (J.D., 1956). Alpha Sigma Nu; Phi Alpha Delta. Adjunct Professor, Loyola University School of Law, 1958—. National Panel of Arbitrators, American Arbitration Association. *Member:* Los Angeles County Bar Association; American Board of Trial Advocates. Fellow, American College of Trial Advocates. [First Marine Air Wing, U.S. Marine Corps, 1946-1950]

**ARNOLD I BENNIGSON,** born Spokane, Washington, January 16, 1942; admitted to bar, 1972, California. *Education:* University of Idaho (B.S., 1963); Hastings College of Law (J.D., 1972). Author: "Products Liability-Manufacturers Beware," Harvard Business Review, May, 1975. *Member:* Santa Clara County Bar Associations; State Bar of California; Lawyer-Pilots Bar Association. [Lt. U.S. Navy, active flight duty, 1963-1968]

REPRESENTATIVE CLIENTS: United States Aviation Underwriters, Inc.; California State Automobile Association, Inter-Insurance Bureau; Unigard Insurance Group; Insurance Company of North America; Bell Helicopter Textron; Mendes & Mount; Industrial Indemnity; Aetna, Cravens, Dargan Co.; Great American Insurance Co.; John D. Ryan & Co.; The Boeing Co.; Boeing Commercial Airplane Co.; Piper Aircraft Co.; Pan American World Airways, Inc.; AeroUnion Corp.; Aetna Casualty & Surety Co.; Allstate Ins. Grp.; Aviation Office of American, Inc.; Avenco Ins. Co.; The Bendix Corp.; The Taubman Co.; Teledyne Continental Motors; Traveler's Ins. Co.; Underwriters at Lloyd's; United States Aircraft Ins. Grp.; Kaiser Air, Inc.; USAir, Inc.; Delta Air Lines, Inc.; United Airlines, Inc.; General Electric Co.; Hartzell Propeller Inc.; Amerijet International, Inc.; Lockheed Corporation; Electric Mutual Liability Insurance Co.; State Farm Fire & Casualty Co.; Farmers Insurance Co.
REFERENCE: Bank of America (A.P. Giannini Branch, San Mateo).

---

## RICHARD L. ENKELIS

1771 WOODSIDE ROAD
**REDWOOD CITY, CALIFORNIA 94061-3436**
Telephone: 415-367-1771
Fax: 415-367-8711
Email: RENKELIS@DEBTCOLLECTOR.COM

*Commercial and Retail Collections, Enforcement of Judgments and Mechanics Lien.*

**RICHARD L. ENKELIS,** born Portland, Oregon, October 3, 1943; admitted to bar, 1969, California and U.S. District Court, Central District of California; 1971, U.S. District Court, Northern District of California; 1975, U.S. District Court, Eastern and Southern Districts of California; 1978, U.S. Court of Appeals, 9th Circuit. *Education:* University of Michigan (B.A., 1965); University of Southern California (J.D., 1968). Author: CEB Civil Litigation Reporter, "Practice Under the New Enforcement of Judgments Law, Part I and Part II." CEB Action Guide, "Enforcing Civil Money Judgments." *Member:* Bar Association of San Francisco; Palo Alto Area Bar Association; San Mateo and Santa Clara County Bar Associations; State Bar of California; Commercial Law League of America. **PRACTICE AREAS:** Commercial Collections; Retail Collections; Mechanics Liens.

---

## ENTERPRISE LAW GROUP, INC.

**REDWOOD CITY, CALIFORNIA**

(See Menlo Park)

## FISHER & PHILLIPS

A Partnership including Professional Corporations and Associations

SUITE 345
THREE LAGOON DRIVE
**REDWOOD CITY, CALIFORNIA 94065**
Telephone: 415-592-6160
Telecopier: 415-592-6385

*Atlanta, Georgia Office:* 1500 Resurgens Plaza, 945 East Paces Ferry Road, N.E., 30326. Telephone: 404-231-1400. Telecopier: 404-240-4249. Telex: 54-2331.

*Fort Lauderdale, Florida Office:* Suite 2300 NationsBank Tower, One Financial Plaza, 33394. Telephone: 954-525-4800. Telecopier: 954-525-8739.

*Newport Beach, California Office:* 4675 MacArthur Court, Suite 550, 92660. Telephone: 714-851-2424. Telecopier: 714-851-0152.

*New Orleans, Louisiana Office:* 3710 Place St. Charles, 201 St. Charles Avenue, 70170. Telephone: 504-522-3303. Telecopier: 504-529-3850.

*FIRM PROFILE: Fisher & Phillips, a national law firm founded in 1943, practices labor and employment law exclusively, representing management. The firm offers preventive advice and litigation defense in such areas as airline and railway law, alternative dispute resolution, business immigration, collective bargaining and arbitration, reductions in force, compensation, disability, employment discrimination, leave statutes, labor/employee relations, mergers, acquisitions, and closings, non-compete and confidentiality agreements, OSHA, pensions and benefits, personnel policies, privacy/workplace monitoring, security, sexual harassment, training, wage-hour, whistleblower claims, and wrongful discharge litigation.*

### RESIDENT MEMBERS

**NED A. FINE,** born Washington, D.C., October 11, 1940; admitted to bar, 1971, California. *Education:* Tufts University (B.A., 1962); Boalt Hall School of Law, University of California (J.D., 1970). Order of the Coif. Research Editor, 1969-1970 and Member, Board of Editors, 1968-1970, California Law Review. *Member:* State Bar of California; American Bar Association (Member, Labor and Employment Law Section). [Capt., USAF, 1962-1967]. *PRACTICE AREAS:* Labor (Management) Laws; Employment Law; Wrongful Discharge Law.

**JOHN D. MCLACHLAN,** born Los Angeles, California, August 26, 1943; admitted to bar, 1981, California. *Education:* Gonzaga University (B.A., 1965); University of Washington (M.A., 1967); University of the Pacific (J.D., 1981). *Member:* Bar Association of San Francisco; State Bar of California; American Bar Association. [Capt., USNR, active duty, 1966-1970 Underwater Demolition Team TWELVE]. *PRACTICE AREAS:* Labor (Management) Laws; Employment Law; Wrongful Discharge Law.

**LYNN D. LIEBER,** born Chicago, Illinois, July 16, 1962; admitted to bar, 1987, California. *Education:* University of the Pacific (B.A., 1984); University of Santa Clara (J.D., 1987). *Member:* Bar Association of San Francisco; State Bar of California; American Bar Association.

### RESIDENT ASSOCIATES

**DONALD E. COPE,** born Tulsa, Oklahoma, November 23, 1950; admitted to bar, 1993, California. *Education:* University of Tulsa (B.S., 1973); McGeorge School of Law, University of the Pacific (J.D., with great distinction, 1993). Order of the Coif; Traynor Society. Legislation Editor, Pacific Law Journal. Registered Professional Engineer, Oklahoma.

**JOHN PHILLIP BOGGS,** born Merced, California, August 24, 1966; admitted to bar, 1994, California. *Education:* Brigham Young University (B.A., 1991); McGeorge School of Law, University of the Pacific (J.D., with great distinction, 1994). Order of the Coif; Traynor Society. Primary Editor, The Transnational Lawyer. *LANGUAGES:* Spanish and Portuguese.

**MARTHA V. HOWTON,** born Carmel, California, February 15, 1971; admitted to bar, 1995, California. *Education:* Yale University (B.A., 1992); University of California, Hastings College of the Law (J.D., 1995). Phi Alpha Delta. Notes Editor, Hastings International and Comparative Law Review, 1994-1995.

**C. TREVOR SKARDA,** born Arcadia, California, December 29, 1969; admitted to bar, 1996, California. *Education:* University of Oregon (B.S., Economics, 1993); McGeorge School of Law, University of the Pacific (J.D., with great distinction, 1996). Order of the Coif; Traynor Society.

REPRESENTATIVE CLIENTS: Airborne Freight Corp.; Marie Callender Pie Shops, Inc.; Centex Cement; Circuit City Stores, Inc.; Consolidated Freightways, Inc.; Cypress Lawn Cemetery Assoc.; Equifax, Inc.; Fleming Cos.; General Chemical Corp.; GS Roofing Products Co.; Homestake Mining Co.; Hyatt

*(This Listing Continued)*

Corp.; Industrial Tectonics Bearings Corp; The Ink Co.; LensCrafters, Inc.; The Limited, Inc.; Lincoln Property Co.; MarkAir; California Motor Car Dealers Association; National Association of Convenience Stores; Nestle Beverage Co.; Nikko, Inc. (USA); Operational Energy Corp.; Payless ShoeSource; Rand Mining Co.; Rollins, Inc./Orkin; Sherman, Clay & Co.; Siemens Energy & Automation, Inc.; Souplantation; Southwest Airlines Co.; Tempnet; Textron, Inc.; Treasure Chest Advertising Co.; WMX Technologies, Inc.; Willamette Industries, Inc.; Wheelabrator Technologies Inc.; Yellow Freight Systems, Inc.; Zurn Nepco.

## RICHARD D. GIVENS

702 MARSHALL STREET
**REDWOOD CITY, CALIFORNIA 94063**
Telephone: 415-365-6144

*General Civil Trial Practice, Real Estate, Environmental Law and Sports Law.*

**RICHARD D. GIVENS,** born Yosemite, California, July 4, 1939; admitted to bar, 1966, California. *Education:* Stanford University (B.A., 1962); Hastings College of Law, University of California (LL.B., 1965). Phi Delta Phi. General Counsel, Boise Cascade Building Co., 1969-1973. Member, Panel of Arbitrators, American Arbitration Association. *Member:* Bar Association of San Francisco; San Mateo County and American (Member, Section of Real Property, Probate and Trust Law) Bar Associations; State Bar of California. *PRACTICE AREAS:* Litigation; Real Estate; Environmental Law; Sports Law.

REPRESENTATIVE CLIENTS: National Football League Management Council; Boise Cascade; The Rynes Co.; Daon Corp.; Cork Harbour Co.; The Ryness Co.; Paradise Pines Mobile Home Estates, Inc.; McDonalds, Inc.; J. Walter Thompson; General Foods Co.

## LAW OFFICES OF
## THOMAS R. HOGAN

**REDWOOD CITY, CALIFORNIA**

(See San Jose)

*Civil Trial Practice, State and Federal Courts. Business Litigation, Construction Law, Copyright, Trademark Disputes, Professional Malpractice Defense, Alternative Dispute Resolution.*

## LAW OFFICE OF
## CHRISTOPHER R. INAMA

399 BRADFORD STREET #102
**REDWOOD CITY, CALIFORNIA 94063**
Telephone: 415-365-7850
Fax: 415-365-4206
Email: crinama@ix.netcom.com

*General Civil, Criminal and Appellate Practice. Civil Litigation, Insurance (Subrogation, Defense), Family Law, Administrative and Extraordinary-Writ Cases.*

**CHRISTOPHER R. INAMA,** born 1952; admitted to bar, 1977, California. *Education:* University of California (B.A., 1974); Hastings College of the Law, University of California (J.D., 1977); California State University (M.A., in Economics, 1996). Sigma Pi (Life Member). College Professor, Graduate and Undergraduate Courses on Business Law and Macro and Micro-Economics, University of Phoenix, 1996—. In House Security, Burns International Security Services, Inc., 1974-1980. Law Clerk, Legal Research and Drafting Pleadings, Rapaport & Lewis, 1976-1977. Candidate for State Assembly in 1990 and 1996, State Senate in 1992. San Mateo County Chair, Libertarian Party of California, 1990-1992. *Member:* San Mateo County Bar Association; State Bar of California; California Public Defenders Association; Native Sons of the Golden West, Redwood Parlor No. 66 (President, 1990—); American Mensa, Ltd.; National Association of Scholars; Hastings and UCSB Alumni Associations; Hastings Old Boys Rugby Football Club; East Palo Alto United Homeowners' Association. [1st Class Petty Officer, U.S. Coast Guard Reserve, 1987—]. *PRACTICE AREAS:* Appellate Law (60%, 25); Criminal Law (10%, 10); Insurance Subrogation Law (10%, 5); Civil Trial (10%, 5); Family Law (10%, 5).

## JACKSON, MITTLESTEADT, MILLER & DUGONI

An Association including a Professional Corporation

*250 A TWIN DOLPHIN DRIVE*
*REDWOOD CITY, CALIFORNIA 94065*
Telephone: 415-595-0444
Fax: 415-595-3976

Mailing Address: P.O. Box 1367, San Carlos, 94070-1367

*General Practice. Civil Litigation, Contract, Family, Corporation, Probate, Wills and Estate Planning, Personal Injury, Immigration, Business, Real Property, Commercial and Construction.*

**TRAVIS M. JACKSON,** born Harrisburg, Arkansas, June 17, 1930; admitted to bar, 1961, California; 1971, U.S. Claims Court. *Education:* Wheaton College (A.B., 1956); Boalt Hall School of Law, University of California (J.D., 1960). *Member:* San Mateo County Bar Association (Director, 1974-1975); State Bar of California. **PRACTICE AREAS:** Estate Planning Law; Business Law.

**CAROL L. MITTLESTEADT,** born Berwyn, Illinois, November 8, 1953; admitted to bar, 1978, Tennessee; 1980, California. *Education:* Vanderbilt University (B.S., summa cum laude, 1975); University of Tennessee (J.D., 1977). Phi Beta Kappa. Instructor, Research and Writing III, University of Tennessee Law School, 1977. *Member:* San Mateo County Bar Association (President, 1995; Director, 1989-1996); State Bar of California; California Women Lawyers; San Mateo County Trial Lawyers Association. **REPORTED CASES:** Collins v. Smithson (1979) 585 S.W. 2d 598. **PRACTICE AREAS:** Business Litigation.

**CAMERON MILLER,** born Redwood City, California, May 30, 1953; admitted to bar, 1978, California. *Education:* University of California at Davis (B.A.,1975); Hastings College of Law, University of California (J.D., 1978). Order of the Coif; Phi Delta Phi. Member, Thurston Society. *Member:* San Mateo County (Director, 1992—; President, 1996) Bar Association; State Bar of California. **PRACTICE AREAS:** Civil Litigation; Business Law; Real Estate.

**LISA M. DUGONI, (P.C.),** born Nashua, New Hampshire, March 27, 1954; admitted to bar, 1980, California. *Education:* University of New Hampshire (B.A., cum laude, 1976); New England School of Law (J.D., 1979). Author: "Drafting An Agreement For The Purchased Sale of Medical or Dental Practices," California Business Law Practitioner, The State Bar of California, Winter, 1989; "Rightful vs. Wrongful Termination of The Dental Staff," California Dental Association Journal, California Dental Association, August, 1990. *Member:* San Mateo County (Chair, Family Law Section, 1989) and American (Member, Sections on: Family Law; Business Law) Bar Associations; State Bar of California (Member, Sections on: Family Law; Labor and Employment; Business Law). **REPORTED CASES:** In Re Marriage of Birnbaum, 211 Cal App 3d 1508 (1989). **PRACTICE AREAS:** Family Law; Business Law.

### OF COUNSEL

**ROGER D. BOLGARD,** born St. Louis, Missouri, March 9, 1939; admitted to bar, 1976, California. *Education:* Princeton University (A.B., 1961); Lincoln University at San Jose (J.D., 1976). Member, Panel of Arbitrators: American Arbitration Association; Arbitration and Mediation Association, Inc.; Asia/Pacific Center for the Resolution of International Business Disputes. *Member:* San Mateo County and Monterey County Bar Associations; State Bar of California (Member, International Law Section). (Also of Counsel to Bohnen, Rosenthal & Dusenbury in Monterey). **PRACTICE AREAS:** Business Law; Construction Law; Partnership; Corporations Law; Business Litigation; Estate Planning Law.

---

## RICHARD F. KELLY

*FIRST INTERSTATE BANK BUILDING*
*702 MARSHALL STREET, SUITE 400*
*REDWOOD CITY, CALIFORNIA 94063-1829*
Telephone: 415-365-3338
Fax: 415-368-7191

*General Civil and Trial Practice in all State and Federal Courts. Personal Injury, Insurance, Premises Liability, Landlord Tenant Law, Creditors Rights and Business Litigation, Estate Planning and Family Law.*

**RICHARD F. KELLY,** born New York, N.Y., February 24, 1944; admitted to bar, 1978, California, U.S. District Court, Northern District of

*(This Listing Continued)*

---

California, U.S. Court of Military Appeals and U.S. Tax Court; 1981, U.S. Supreme Court; 1990, U.S. District Court, Eastern District of California. *Education:* San Jose State University (B.S., 1967); LaSalle University (LL.B., 1976); San Francisco Law School (J.D., 1978). Member, St. Thomas More Law Honor Society. Judge Pro-Tem, Municipal and Superior Courts, San Mateo County, 1987—. Instructor: Cañada College, Redwood City, California, Hotel and Travel Law, 1980-1982. Member, Panel of Arbitrators, American Arbitration Association. *Member:* San Mateo County and American (Member, Litigation Section) Bar Associations; State Bar of California; San Mateo County Trial Lawyers Association; The Association of Trial Lawyers of America; San Francisco Irish-American Bar Association. **REPORTED CASES:** California Casualty Indemnity Exchange vs. Pettis 193 Cal. App. 3d 1597, 239 Cal Rptr. 205; In Re the Requested Extradition of James Joseph Smyth, 863 F. Supp. 1137. **PRACTICE AREAS:** Landlord-Tenant Law; Civil Trials; Personal Injury; Creditor's Rights.

REPRESENTATIVE CLIENTS: Hyatt Hotel Corp.; Fairmont Hotel Corp.; Park Lane Hotels; Mark Hopkins Intercontinental Hotels; Continental Construction & Supply Corp.; Chemoil Holding Co.
REFERENCE: First Interstate Bank of California.

---

## LITIGATION SOLUTIONS LAW GROUP LLP

*1775 WOODSIDE ROAD*
*REDWOOD CITY, CALIFORNIA 94061*
Telephone: 415-364-9110
Fax: 415-366-8995

### PARTNERS

**JOHN SKELTON,** born Stockton, California, September 15, 1948; admitted to bar, 1975, California. *Education:* University of California at Berkeley, School of Criminology (A.B., with honors, 1971); University of San Francisco (J.D., 1975). *Member:* San Mateo County and American (Member, Sections on: Litigation; Tort and Insurance Practice) Bar Associations; The State Bar of California; Association of Defense Counsel; Defense Research Institute.

**RICHARD J. ROMANSKI,** born Waterbury, Connecticut, January 16, 1942; admitted to bar, 1966, Virginia and Connecticut; 1970, California. *Education:* Fairfield University (B.S., 1963); Defense Language Institute (Arabic, 1968); University of Virginia (LL.B., 1966). Special Agent, Federal Bureau of Investigation, 1966-1969. *Member:* San Mateo County, Connecticut and Virginia Bar Associations; The State Bar of California.

### ASSOCIATES

**STEPHEN H. SCHMID,** born Sacramento, California, January 9, 1951; admitted to bar, 1977, California. *Education:* University of Santa Clara (B.S., 1973); McGeorge School of Law, University of the Pacific (J.D., 1977). *Member:* Santa Clara County Bar Association; The State Bar of California.

**JACQUELINE A. WILLSON,** born San Mateo, California, October 27, 1951; admitted to bar, 1978, California. *Education:* University of California at Berkeley (A.B., 1973); University of San Francisco (J.D., with honors, 1978). *Member:* San Mateo County Bar Association; State Bar of California.

**ANTHONY M. SANTANA,** born San Francisco, California, April 18, 1957; admitted to bar, 1985, California. *Education:* University of San Francisco (B.A., 1979); Golden Gate University (J.D., 1984). Member, Board of Directors, San Francisco Police Officers Association, 1986-1988. *Member:* San Mateo County Bar Association; State Bar of California; California Trial Lawyers Association.

**THOMAS J. BURNS,** born Sacramento, California, August 6, 1957; admitted to bar, 1983, California. *Education:* University of Santa Clara (B.S., 1979; J.D., 1982). *Member:* Stanislaus County Bar Association; State Bar of California; California Reserve Peace Officers Association.

**WILLIAM F. FITZGERALD,** born San Francisco, California, June 3, 1957; admitted to bar, 1983, California and U.S. District Court, Northern District of California; 1987, U.S. District Court, Eastern District of California; 1988, U.S. Court of Appeals, Ninth Circuit. *Education:* University of California at Davis (A.B., 1979); University of San Francisco (J.D., 1983). Phi Delta Phi. Recipient, California State Graduate Fellowship Award, 1981 and 1982. Digest Editor, Northern District of California, Federal Digest, 1990—. *Member:* Santa Clara County Bar Association; The State Bar of California.

*(This Listing Continued)*

**NANCY A. BRIGHTON,** born Los Angeles, California, July 4, 1955; admitted to bar, 1982, Florida; 1983, California. *Education:* Johns Hopkins University; Hampshire College (B.A.,1978); University of San Francisco School of Law (J.D., cum laude, 1981). *Member:* Santa Clara County and American Bar Associations; The State Bar of California; The Florida Bar.

**JOSEPH R. POLVERARI, JR.,** born Santa Rosa, California, September 30, 1967; admitted to bar, 1992, California and U.S. District Court, Northern District of California. *Education:* University of California at Santa Barbara; Santa Clara University (B.S., 1989; J.D., 1992); Institute of International Law and Comparative Study. *Member:* Bar Association of San Francisco; State Bar of California.

**ELIZABETH E. LAMPSON,** born San Francisco, California, September 15, 1967; admitted to bar, 1993, California. *Education:* University of California, Berkeley (B.A., 1989); Southwestern University School of Law (J.D., 1993). *Member:* San Mateo County Bar Association; State Bar of California.

*OF COUNSEL*

**JOSEPH R. POLVERARI, SR.,** born Santa Rosa, California, April 27, 1943; admitted to bar, 1974, California. *Education:* Sonoma State College (B.A., 1971); University of Santa Clara (J.D., cum laude, 1974). *Member:* Santa Clara County Bar Association; The State Bar of California; Association of Defense Counsel.

---

## LOW, BALL & LYNCH

*A PROFESSIONAL CORPORATION*

10 TWIN DOLPHIN, SUITE B-500
**REDWOOD CITY, CALIFORNIA 94065**
Telephone: 415-591-8822
Fax: 415-591-8884

*San Francisco, California Office:* 601 California Street, Suite 2100, 94108. Telephone: 415-981-6630.

*Monterey, California Office:* 10 Ragsdale Drive, Suite 175, 93940. Telephone: 408-655-8822.

*General Civil and Trial Practice. Insurance, Environmental Law, Land Use, Real Estate, Corporate, Professional Malpractice, Products Liability, Securities, Commercial Litigation and Appellate Practice.*

| | |
|---|---|
| Raymond Coates | David L. Blinn |
| Chester G. Moore, III | Janet Kulig |
| James D. Miller | Thomas E. Mulvihill |
| William H. Holsinger | Jennifer Elizabeth Acheson |

| | |
|---|---|
| John R. Baumann | Joseph M. Fenech |
| Michael E. Sandgren | |

(For complete biographical data see Professional Biographies at San Francisco, California).

---

## MEDLEN & CARROLL, LLP

702 MARSHALL STREET, SUITE 600
**REDWOOD CITY, CALIFORNIA 94063**
Telephone: 415-299-8120
Facsimile: 415-299-8127

*San Francisco, California Office:* 220 Montgomery St., Suite 2200. Telephone: 415-705-8410. Facsimile: 415-397-8338.

*Cambridge, Massachusetts Office:* Five Cambridge Center, Second Floor. Telephone: 617-354-5455. Facsimile: 617-354-8132.

*Toledo, Ohio Office:* One Seagate, Suite 960. Telephone: 419-247-1010. Facsimile: 419-247-1011.

*Patent, Trademark and Copyright Law, Trade Secrets, Unfair Competition, Technology Licensing and Evaluation and related Trial and Appellate Litigation in State and Federal Courts, and Alternative Dispute Resolution (ADR).*

*ASSOCIATES*

**KAMRIN T. MACKNIGHT,** born San Jose, California, November 10, 1959; admitted to bar, 1993, California and U.S. District Courts, Northern and Central Districts of California. *Education:* Brigham Young University (B.S., 1981); San Jose State University (M.S., 1984); University of California (Ph.D., 1990); Santa Clara University School of Law (J.D., 1993). Editor in Chief, Santa Clara Computer and High Technology Law Journal.

*(This Listing Continued)*

Author: "Scientific Aspects of HLA Typing" in Disputed Paternity Proceedings, Matthew Bender, Inc. (in press), 1994; "Polymerase Chain Reaction (PCR): The Second Generation of DNA Analysis Methods Takes The Stand," 9 Santa Clara Comp & High Tech. L.J. 287 (1993). *Member:* Peninsula Intellectual Property Law Association; San Francisco Intellectual Property Law Association; American Intellectual Property Law Association; American Society for Microbiology; Northern California Local Section of the Society for Industrial Microbiology; New York Academy of Sciences. *LANGUAGES:* Russian, French and German. *PRACTICE AREAS:* Biotechnology; Biochemistry; Microbiology; Immunology; Molecular Biology Patents. *Email:* ktmack@ix.netcom.com

**DIANE E. INGOLIA,** born New Orleans, Louisiana, October 12, 1958; admitted to bar, 1994, California. *Education:* University of New Orleans (B.S., 1980); Baylor College of Medicine (Ph.D., 1987); Santa Clara University Law School (J.D., cum laude, 1994). Predoctoral Fellow, Robert A. Welch Foundation, 1984-1987. Postdoctoral Fellow, Stanford Medical School, 1987-1991. *Member:* State Bar of California; American Intellectual Property Law Association; San Francisco Intellectual Property Law Association. *PRACTICE AREAS:* Biotechnology; Molecular Biology; Biochemistry; Immunology; Biotechnology Patents; Transgenic Plants and Animals and Related Litigation. *Email:* dingolia@ix.netcom.com

**CHRISTOPHER JOHN SMITH,** born Harbor City, California, May 17, 1965; admitted to bar, 1994, California and U.S. District Court, Northern District of California; registered to practice before U.S. Patent and Trademark Office. *Education:* University of California, Irvine (B.S., 1987); University of California, San Francisco (Pharm.D., 1991); Hastings College of the Law, University of California, San Francisco (J.D., 1994). Regents Scholar. Registered Pharmacist, 1992. Redwood City Attorney. *Member:* State Bar of California; San Francisco Intellectual Property Law Association; Peninsula Intellectual Property Law Association. *PRACTICE AREAS:* Chemical; Pharmaceutical; Biotechnology Patents; Intellectual Property Litigation; Medical Device.

---

## NOLAN & ARMSTRONG

**REDWOOD CITY, CALIFORNIA**

(See Palo Alto)

*Criminal and Business Crimes Law. Trials and Appeals, Trade Secret and Juvenile Law.*

---

## OWEN & MELBYE

*A PROFESSIONAL CORPORATION*

Established in 1962

700 JEFFERSON STREET
**REDWOOD CITY, CALIFORNIA 94063**
Telephone: 415-364-6500
Fax: 415-365-7036

*Tahoe City, California Office:* P.O. Box 1524. Telephone: 916-546-2473.

*General Civil and Trial Practice in all State and Federal Courts. Aviation, Products, Insurance Defense Law, and Insurance Coverage Analysis.*

**WILLIAM H. OWEN,** born San Francisco, California, December 5, 1931; admitted to bar, 1959, California. *Education:* University of California (B.S., 1953); Stanford University (J.D., 1958). *Member:* San Mateo County, Santa Clara County and American Bar Associations; The State Bar of California; Association of Defense Counsel (Member, Board of Governors, 1972-1973); Santa Clara County Trial Lawyers Association (President, 1974); Defense Research Institute. Pilot; Commercial, Multi Engine, Instrument and Glider Ratings. *PRACTICE AREAS:* Airplane Crash Litigation; Insurance Defense; Products Liability.

**RICHARD B. MELBYE,** born Berkeley, California, December 8, 1933; admitted to bar, 1959, California. *Education:* University of California at Berkeley (A.B., 1955); Boalt Hall, University of California (J.D., 1958). *Member:* San Mateo County and Santa Clara County Bar Associations; The State Bar of California; Lawyers Club of San Francisco; Association of Defense Counsel (Member, Board of Governors, 1974-1975); California Trial Lawyers Association; Defense Research Institute. *PRACTICE AREAS:* Accident and Personal Injury; Bad Faith Law; Defense of Legal and Medical Malpractice; Products Liability Law; Wrongful Discharge Law.

*(This Listing Continued)*

**OWEN & MELBYE**, A PROFESSIONAL CORPORATION,
Redwood City—Continued

**NORMAN J. ROGER**, born San Francisco, California, August 29, 1949; admitted to bar, 1974, California. *Education:* Georgetown University (B.S.F.S., 1971); University of San Francisco (J.D., magna cum laude, 1974). *Member:* The State Bar of California; San Mateo County and American Bar Associations; Association of Defense Counsel. *LANGUAGES:* French. *PRACTICE AREAS:* Insurance Coverage; Bad Faith Law; Insurance Defense.

**EDMUND M. SCOTT**, born Palo Alto, California, November 7, 1948; admitted to bar, 1981, California. *Education:* University of San Francisco (B.A., 1970); San Francisco University (M.A., 1975); Golden Gate University (J.D., 1980). *Member:* The State Bar of California. *PRACTICE AREAS:* Accident and Personal Injury; Defense of Legal and Medical Malpractice; Environmental Insurance Litigation; Insurance Defense Law; Products Liability Law; Wrongful Termination-Employment at Will.

**PAMELA J. HELMER**, born Los Angeles, California, November 2, 1955; admitted to bar, 1984, California. *Education:* California State University at San Diego (B.A., 1977); Wayne State University (J.D., 1984). Phi Beta Kappa; Phi Kappa Phi. *Member:* San Mateo County and American Bar Associations; The State Bar of California; Association of Defense Counsel; California Women Lawyers. *LANGUAGES:* Spanish. *PRACTICE AREAS:* Construction Defect Litigation; Construction Law.

**JOHN S. POSTHAUER**, born St. Louis, Missouri, March 9, 1956; admitted to bar, 1984, California. *Education:* Stanford University (B.A., 1980); University of California at Los Angeles (J.D., 1983). *Member:* San Mateo County Bar Association; The State Bar of California; Association of Defense Counsel of Northern California. *PRACTICE AREAS:* Accident and Personal Injury; Construction Accidents; Environmental Insurance Litigation; Insurance Defense Law; Products Liability Law.

**PAUL R. MANGIANTINI**, born Palo Alto, October 7, 1961; admitted to bar, 1988, California. *Education:* University of California at Los Angeles (B.A., 1983); Santa Clara University (J.D., 1987). *Member:* San Mateo County Bar Association; State Bar of California; Association of Defense Counsel of Northern California. *PRACTICE AREAS:* Accident and Personal Injury; Airplane Crash Litigation; Insurance Defense Law; Products Liability.

---

**ALBERT P. BLAKE, JR.**, born Milton, Florida, July 6, 1963; admitted to bar, 1990, California. *Education:* California Polytechnic State University (B.S., 1986); Santa Clara University (J.D., 1989). Business Editor, Vol. V, Santa Clara Computer and High Technology Law Journal, 1988-1989. *Member:* San Mateo County and Santa Clara Bar Associations; Association of Defense Counsel. *LANGUAGES:* Italian. *PRACTICE AREAS:* Construction Defect Litigation; Construction Law.

**DAWN M. PATTERSON**, born Chicago, Illinois, March 29, 1960; admitted to bar, 1987, Illinois; 1990, California. *Education:* Loyola University of Chicago (B.A., 1982; J.D., 1985). *Member:* Santa Clara, San Mateo County and American Bar Associations; State Bar of California. *PRACTICE AREAS:* Insurance Defense Law; Insurance Coverage Law; Construction Law.

**CONOR A. MEYERS**, born Santa Rosa, California, September 11, 1964; admitted to bar, 1992, California. *Education:* University of California, Davis (A.B., 1987); University of Notre Dame (J.D., 1991). Phi Delta Phi. *Member:* San Mateo County Bar Association; State Bar of California. *PRACTICE AREAS:* Construction Defect Litigation.

**MARY P. DERNER**, born Philadelphia, Pennsylvania, September 28, 1963; admitted to bar, 1989, California, U.S. Court of Appeals, Ninth Circuit and U.S. District Court, Northern District of California. *Education:* University of California at Santa Barbara (B.A., with highest honors, distinction in major, 1985); Hastings College of the Law, University of California (J.D., cum laude, 1989). Phi Beta Kappa; Alpha Lambda Delta. *Member:* Mortar Board; Moot Court Board; Thurston Society. Recipient, Moot Court Brief Award, 1988. *Member:* San Mateo County Bar Association; The State Bar of California. *PRACTICE AREAS:* Insurance Coverage; General Civil Litigation.

REPRESENTATIVE CLIENTS: Aetna Cravens Dargan Co.; American Home Assurance Co.; American International Adjustment Co., Inc.; American Warranty Corp.; Associated Aviation Underwriters; Avco Lycoming; Beech Aircraft Corp.; The Central Cos.; CIGNA; Crump Aviation Underwriters; Hartford Insurance Company; Interstate National Corp.; K & K Claims Service; Kemper Insurance Cos.; Landmark Insurance Co.; Mutual Service Insurance Co.;

*(This Listing Continued)*

N.S.A.A.; National Union Insurance Co.; New Hampshire Insurance Group; The Orion Group; Piper Aircraft Corp.; The PMA Group; PPG; Puritan Insurance Co.; Royal Insurance Co.; State Farm Fire & Casualty Co.; Squaw Valley Ski Corp.; State Farm Mutual Insurance Cos.; Superior National Insurance Company; Teledyne Corporation; Teledyne Continental Motors; Underwriters at Lloyds; Unigard; United States Aviation Insurance Group; United States Fidelity & Guaranty Co.; Utica Mutual Insurance Co.; Volkswagon Insurance Co.; Wilshire Insurance Co.; Zurich American Insurance Cos.

---

## JAMES D. PALMER, JR.

Established in 1960

**1771 WOODSIDE ROAD
REDWOOD CITY, CALIFORNIA 94061**
Telephone: 415-367-1771
FAX: 415-367-8711
Email: JDPalmerjr@aol.com

*Estate Planning, Special Needs Trusts, Estate and Trust Administration, Federal and State Taxation, Probate, Charitable Organizations.*

**JAMES D. PALMER, JR.**, born San Bernardino, California, December 24, 1935; admitted to bar, 1960, California. *Education:* Stanford University (A.B., 1957; LL.B., 1959). *Member:* San Mateo County and American (Member: Real Property, Probate and Trust Law Section; Vice-Chair, Special Needs Trusts Section, 1992—) Bar Associations; State Bar of California (Member, Estate Planning, Trust and Probate Law Section). *PRACTICE AREAS:* Probate; Estate Planning; Special Needs Trusts; Trust Administration; Federal Taxation; State Taxation.

REFERENCE: CoMerica Bank, University Division (Menlo Park).

---

## ROPERS, MAJESKI, KOHN & BENTLEY

A PROFESSIONAL CORPORATION

**1001 MARSHALL STREET
REDWOOD CITY, CALIFORNIA 94063**
Telephone: 415-364-8200
Fax: 415-367-0997

*San Jose, California Office:* 80 North 1st Street. Telephone: 408-287-6262. Fax: 408-297-6819.
*San Francisco, California Office:* 670 Howard Street. Telephone: 415-543-4800. Fax: 415-512-1574.
*Santa Rosa, California Office:* Fountaingrove Center, Suite 300, 3558 Round Barn Boulevard. Telephone: 707-524-4200. Fax: 707-523-4610.
*Los Angeles, California Office:* 550 South Hope Street, Suite 1900. Telephone: 213-312-2000. Fax: 213-312-2001.
*Sacramento, California Office:* 1000 G Street, Suite 400. Telephone: 916-556-3100. Fax: 916-442-7121.

*Arbitration and Mediation, Appellate Services, Banking and Financial Institutions Services, Bankruptcy, Commercial Litigation, Construction Litigation, Employment Law, Environmental Compliance and Litigation, Estate Planning, Trusts Probate and Elder Law, Fidelity and Surety Law, Health Care Law, Insurance Coverage and Litigation, Insurance Regulatory and Reinsurance, Intellectual Property Protection and Litigation, Products Litigation, Professional Malpractice Litigation, Real Estate Law, Trials and Antitrust.*

**HAROLD ROPERS** (1905-1966).

**JOHN M. RUBENS** (1936-1993).

**EUGENE J. MAJESKI**, born Chicago, Illinois, December 24, 1916; admitted to bar, 1940, Illinois; 1946, California. *Education:* De Paul University (B.S., 1937; J.D., 1940). Included in Best Lawyers in America, 1984. Instructor, De Paul University, 1937-1940. *Member:* San Mateo County Bar Association (President, 1964); The State Bar of California; International Association of Insurance Counsel; National Association of Railroad Trial Counsel; Federation of Insurance Counsel (Vice-President); Association of Defense Counsel. Fellow: International Academy of Trial Lawyers; American College of Trial Lawyers; American Board of Trial Advocates (Treasurer, 1984-1986; Chairman, Board of Directors, 1987; President, San Francisco Chapter, 1987-1988). Diplomate: American Board of Trial Advocates; California Trial Lawyer of the Year, 1989; American Bar Association Litigation Section Trial Lawyers Hall of Fame Award, 1995. *PRACTICE AREAS:* Civil Litigation.

**JOHN M. BENTLEY**, born San Francisco, California, June 29, 1929; admitted to bar, 1955, California. *Education:* University of San Francisco (LL.B., 1955). Phi Alpha Delta. *Member:* San Mateo County, San Francisco County and American Bar Associations; The State Bar of California;

*(This Listing Continued)*

Association of Defense Counsel; American Board of Trial Advocates; International Association of Insurance Counsel; Federation of Insurance Counsel; American Board of Professional Liability Attorneys. Fellow: International Academy of Trial Lawyers; American College of Trial Lawyers. **PRACTICE AREAS:** Professional Liability Law; Bad Faith Law; Environmental Coverage; General Trial Work.

**MICHAEL J. BRADY,** born Midland, Texas, September 15, 1941; admitted to bar, 1967, California. *Education:* Stanford University (B.A., 1964); Harvard University (LL.B., 1967). Phi Beta Kappa. Author: "Summary of California Appellate Decisions," Ropers, Majeski, Kohn, Bentley, Wagner & Kane, 1980—; "The Revolution in California Tort Law," For The Defense, March, 1991; "Ethics in Insurance Defense Context: Isn't Cumis Counsel Unnecessary?" Defense Counsel Journal, April, 1991; "Insurance Coverage Concerns in California Continuous Property Loss Cases After Prudential--LMI," Santa Clara Law Review, 1991; "Emotional Distress: Minor Issue Muddies the Duty to Defend," Defense Counsel Journal, April, 1990; "Insurance Coverage for Sexual Molestation of a Minor," Defense Counsel Journal, April, 1989; "The California Supreme Court Restricts Bad Faith Liability," For the Defense, November, 1988; "Welcome News From California: Lessening the Conflict Between Insurer and Insured," For the Defense, December, 1987; "The California Supreme Court Restricts Bad Faith Litigation," *For the Defense*, November 1988; "Emotional Distress: Minor Issue Muddies The Duty To Defend," *Defense Counsel Journal*, April 1990; "Insurance Coverage for Sexual Molestation of a Minor," *Defense Counsel Journal*, April 1990; "The Revolution in California Tort Law," *For The Defense*, March 1991; "Ethics in Insurance Defense Context: Isn't Cumis Counsel Unnecessary?" *Defense Counsel Journal*, April 1991; "Insurance Coverage Concerns in California Continuous Property Loss Cases After Prudential--LMI," 31 Santa Clara Law Review No. 4, Vol. 31 1991; "Insurer's Right to Reimbursement: Neglected but Valuable Remedy," *Defense Counsel Journal*, October 1992; "Demise of the Stipulated Judgment as Basis for Bad Faith Actions," *Defense Counsel Journal*, January 1993; "The Judicial Arbitration System: Its Promise and its Shortcomings," *For The Defense*, August 1993; "Death of the Handshake," *Claims Magazine*, September 1994 and *Defense Counsel Journal*, Vol. 61, No. 4, October 1994; "Trigger of Coverage in Environmental Cases," Federation of Insurance & Corporate Counsel, *Quarterly*, Vol. 45, No. 1, Fall 1994; "Insurance Coverage Issues Arising from Workplace Tort Claims," *Defense Research Journal*, July 1995; "Liability and Obligation of an Owner of Contaminated Land," *For the Defense*, August 1995; "New Perspectives on Damages for Breach of the Duty to Defend," Federation of Insurance & Corporate Counsel, *Quarterly*, Vol. 45, No. 4, Summer, 1995; "An Improved Tool for Environmental Subrogation," *Claims*, December 1995; "The Legacy of the Lucas Court: A Return to Judicial Self-Restraint and an Appreciation for the Costs of Expansive Litigation," *Underwriters' Report*, February 1996, *For the defense*, May 1996, *Lloyd's List Insurance Day*, May 1996; "Lost or Damaged Computer Data: 'Property Damage' or Intangible Information Under a Commercial Liability Policy?" Federation of Insurance & Corporate Counsel, *Quarterly*, Vol. 46, No. 1, Fall 1995; "Liability of an Insurer When Settlement or Claims-Handling Practices Adversely Affect Financial Interests of the Insured," Federation of Insurance & Corporate Counsel, *Quarterly*, Vol. 46, No. 2, Winter 1996; "The Impaired Property Exclusion: Finding a Path Through the Morass," *Defense Counsel Journal*, Vol. 64, No. 3, July, 1996. Lawyer Representative, Ninth Circuit Judicial Conference, 1982-1983. *Member:* San Mateo County Bar Association (President, 1985); The State Bar of California (Vice-Chairman, State Bar Committee on Appellate Courts, 1982-1983); California Academy of Appellate Lawyers; Association of Defense Counsel of Northern California (Secretary/Treasurer, 1989; Vice President, 1990; Chairman, Amicus Curiae Committee, 1990; President, 1992); International Association of Insurance Counsel (Secretary, Casualty Insurance Commission, 1990); Defense Research Institute. **PRACTICE AREAS:** Appellate Law; Insurance Coverage and Reinsurance; Bad Faith.

**FRANK J. PAGLIARO, JR.,** born New York, N.Y., August 10, 1940; admitted to bar, 1967, New York; 1970, California. *Education:* University of Vermont (A.B., 1963); University of Virginia (LL.B., 1966); Hague Academy of International Law (World Court), The Hague, Netherlands. Phi Alpha Delta. Vice President and General Counsel, Contel Construction Co., 1966-1970. Assistant District Attorney, San Francisco, 1971-1973. Member, Bureau of Justice Statistics Advisory Board, U.S. Department of Justice, 1982-1985. Burlingame City Council, 1983-1995. *Member:* San Mateo County, NewYork State and American Bar Associations; The State Bar of California; Association of Defense Counsel; International Association Defense Counsel; Union International Des Advocats; Inter-American Bar Association. **PRACTICE AREAS:** Construction Litigation; Products Liability Law; Fidelity and Surety Law.

*(This Listing Continued)*

**JOHN S. SIMONSON,** born Olympia, Washington, May 24, 1947; admitted to bar, 1973, California. *Education:* Gonzaga University (B.B.A., cum laude, 1969); Hastings College of the Law (J.D., 1973). *Member:* San Mateo County Bar Association; The State Bar of California; Association of Defense Counsel; American Board of Trial Advocates; National Board of Trial Advocacy. **PRACTICE AREAS:** Professional Liability; Insurance Bad Faith; Governmental Entity Liability; Civil Litigation.

**STEPHEN A. SCOTT,** born Ogallala, Nebraska, September 14, 1950; admitted to bar, 1975, California. *Education:* Stanford University (B.A., 1972); University of Santa Clara (J.D., 1975). *Member:* Santa Clara County Bar Association; The State Bar of California. **PRACTICE AREAS:** Insurance Bad Faith Defense Law; Medical Malpractice; Products Liability Law.

**DANIEL E. ALBERTI,** born San Francisco, California, February 1, 1949; admitted to bar, 1976, California. *Education:* University of Santa Clara (B.S.C., 1971); University of the Pacific (J.D., 1975). Assistant District Attorney, San Francisco District Attorney's Office, 1976-1981. Faculty Member, Business Litigation, Hastings Center for Trial and Appellate Advocacy, Hastings College of the Law, University of California, 1982, 1985. *Member:* Bar Association of San Francisco; The State Bar of California; Association of Defense Counsel. **PRACTICE AREAS:** Employment and Commercial Litigation; White Collar Criminal Defense; Complex Business Litigation including Intellectual Property Litigation.

**MARK G. BONINO,** born Los Angeles, California, April 14, 1951; admitted to bar, 1976, California. *Education:* University of California at Davis (A.B., 1973); University of Santa Clara (J.D., 1976). Phi Alpha Delta. *Member:* San Mateo County Bar Association; The State Bar of California; Association of Defense Counsel. **PRACTICE AREAS:** Appellate Law; Bad Faith Litigation; Insurance Coverage.

**RICHARD K. WILSON,** born Vallejo, California, August 6, 1949; admitted to bar, 1976, California. *Education:* University of California at Berkeley (B.S., 1972); Hastings College of the Law, University of California (J.D., 1976). Member, Hastings Law Journal, 1974-1975. Deputy District Attorney, Solano County, 1977-1978. *Member:* San Mateo County Bar Association; The State Bar of California; Association of Defense Counsel. **PRACTICE AREAS:** Environmental Insurance Coverage; Reinsurance.

**STEPHEN M. HAYES,** born St. Louis, Missouri, November 30, 1952; admitted to bar, 1978, California. *Education:* University of California at Berkeley (B.A., 1975); Hastings College of the Law, University of California (J.D., 1978). Phi Delta Phi. *Member:* San Mateo County Bar Association; The State Bar of California; Association of Defense Counsel; International Association of Defense Counsel; National Board of Trial Advocacy; American Board of Trial Advocates. **PRACTICE AREAS:** Complex Commercial and Tort Litigation.

**KATHERINE S. CLARK,** born Ottawa, Canada, December 29, 1953; admitted to bar, 1980, California. *Education:* University of California at Berkeley (A.B., with high honors, 1975); Hastings College of the Law, University of California (J.D., 1980). Phi Delta Phi (President, 1979-1980). Managing Editor and Member, 1979-1980, Constitutional Law Quarterly. Member, Joint Advisory Committee to CEB, 1986-1988. *Member:* San Mateo County Bar Association (Board Member, 1986-1988); The State Bar of California; California Women Lawyers. **PRACTICE AREAS:** Civil Litigation; Employment Law; Real Estate; Construction; Personal Injury; Products Liability; Governmental Tort Liability.

**LAWRENCE M. GUSLANI,** born San Mateo, California, August 16, 1957; admitted to bar, 1982, California. *Education:* University of California at Berkeley (B.S., 1979); University of Santa Clara (J.D., 1982). *Member:* San Mateo County Bar Association; The State Bar of California; Association of Defense Counsel - Northern California. **PRACTICE AREAS:** Insurance Coverage Law; Bad Faith Litigation; Appellate Law.

**TED J. HANNIG,** born Redwood City, California, September 13, 1958; admitted to bar, 1983, California. *Education:* California Polytechnic State University (B.S., 1980); Tokyo University, Japan; University of Santa Clara (M.B.A. and J.D., 1983). Research Editor and Computer Law Symposium Editor, University of Santa Clara Law Review, 1982-1983. Member, Board of Governors, School of Law, Santa Clara University, 1981. Author: "Public Trust Doctrine Expansion and Integration, A Proposed Balancing Test," 23 Santa Clara Law Review, 1983; "Is there a Programmer in the House?: The Emerging Tort of Computer Malpractice," San Francisco Barrister, September, 1985; "Joint Tenancy in Real Estate," Redwood City Today, October 1985; "Mechanics Liens," Redwood City Today, November 1985; "The Reagan Tax Proposal," December 1985; "Year End Planning," Redwood City Today, January/February 1986; "How does small claims court work?" Redwood City Today, April 1986. Founder and Director, Santa Clara Com-

*(This Listing Continued)*

CAA1713B

**ROPERS, MAJESKI, KOHN & BENTLEY, A PROFESSIONAL CORPORATION, Redwood City—Continued**

puter and High Technology Law Conference, 1982, 1983, 1984. Member, San Jose High Technology Committee, 1983-1984. Participant, Hastings College Center for Trial and Appellate Advocacy, 1986. Co Vice President, Northern California Fidelity and Surety Claims Association, 1988-1989. *Member:* San Mateo County Bar Association (Chair, Real Estate Section, 1992; Bench and Bar Committee, 1991; Alternative Dispute Resolution Committee, 1991; Board of Directors, 1988-1990); The State Bar of California (Member, Sections on: Business Lawn and Real Property). *PRACTICE AREAS:* Commercial Law; Corporate Law; Real Estate Law; Commercial Litigation.

**THEODORE C. ZAYNER,** born Chicago, Illinois, October 26, 1956; admitted to bar, 1983, California. *Education:* Stanford University (A.B., 1978); Hastings College of the Law, University of California (J.D., 1983). Judge Pro Tem and Judicial Arbitrator, Santa Clara County Superior Court; Judicial Arbitrator, San Mateo County Superior Court. *Member:* Santa Clara County and American Bar Associations; The State Bar of California; Association of Defense Counsel; Santa Clara County Medical Association (Public Service Committee, 1988-1991). *PRACTICE AREAS:* Environmental Coverage; Civil Litigation. *Email:* tzayner@ropers.com

**DAVID J. MICLEAN,** born Redwood City, California, October 20, 1959; admitted to bar, 1984, California. *Education:* University of California at Los Angeles (B.A., 1981); Loyola Marymount University (J.D., 1984). Recipient, American Jurisprudence Award in Labor Law and Professional Responsibility. *Member:* San Mateo County Bar Association; The State Bar of California; The Association of Defense Counsel. *PRACTICE AREAS:* Commercial Litigation; General Civil Litigation.

**PAMELA E. COGAN,** born Cambridge, Massachusetts, February 1, 1956; admitted to bar, 1982, California and U.S. District Court, Eastern, Northern and Central Districts of California; U.S. Court of Appeals, Ninth Circuit. *Education:* University of Massachusetts (B.A., cum laude, 1977); McGeorge School of Law, University of the Pacific (J.D., cum laude, 1982). Order of the Coif. Member, Comment Staff, Pacific Law Journal, 1980-1981. Author: "Negligent Infliction of Emotional Distress: New Horizons after Molien v. Kaiser Foundation Hospitals," 13 Pacific Law Journal 179, 1981. *Member:* San Mateo County Bar Association; Association of Defense Counsel. *LANGUAGES:* French. *PRACTICE AREAS:* Insurance Law; Civil Litigation.

**DAVID A. LEVY,** born Fort Monmouth, New Jersey, August 16, 1952; admitted to bar, 1977, California and U.S. District Court, Northern District of California; 1979, U.S. Court of Appeals, Ninth Circuit; 1987, U.S. District Court, Eastern District of California. *Education:* University of California at Davis (A.B., 1974); Hastings College of the Law, University of California (J.D., 1977). Member: Moot Court Board; National Moot Court Competition. Judge Pro Tem: San Mateo County Municipal Court, 1982—; San Mateo County Superior Court, 1984—. Certified as a Civil Advocate, National Board of Trial Advocacy. *PRACTICE AREAS:* Healthcare and Professional Liability; General Civil Litigation.

**COLIN R. CAMPBELL,** born Oakland, California, January 30, 1948; admitted to bar, 1976, California; 1980, U.S. Claims Court; 1981, U.S. Supreme Court; 1988, U.S. Court of Appeals, Ninth Circuit; registered to practice before U.S. Patent and Trademark Office. *Education:* University of California at Berkeley (B.S., 1969); University of California at Davis; University of Santa Clara (J.D., 1976). Licensed Mechanical Engineer, California, 1974. Licensed Nuclear Engineer, California, 1977. *Member:* San Mateo County and Marin County Bar Associations; State Bar of California; Association of Defense Counsel. *PRACTICE AREAS:* Environmental Litigation; Insurance Coverage; Construction Defect Litigation; Products Liability Litigation.

**BRAD W. BLOCKER,** born Baton Rouge, Louisiana, January 29, 1960; admitted to bar, 1986, California, U.S. District Court, Northern and Central District of California and U.S. Court of Appeals, Ninth Circuit. *Education:* University of California at Los Angeles (B.A., cum laude in Political Science and History, 1982); Tulane University (J.D., cum laude, 1986). Phi Alpha Delta. *Member:* San Mateo County Bar Association; State Bar of California; Association of Defense Counsel of Northern California. *PRACTICE AREAS:* Civil Trials and Arbitration; Commercial Litigation; Professional Liability; Environmental Litigation; Construction; Products Liability; Securities; Employment; Fidelity and Surety; General Civil Litigation.

**MARC D. ROSATI,** born Walnut Creek, California, May 17, 1954; admitted to bar, 1986, California and U.S. District Court, Northern District of California. *Education:* University of California, Berkeley (B.A., 1977); McGeorge School of Law, University of the Pacific (J.D., 1985). *Member:* The State Bar of California. *PRACTICE AREAS:* Business Law; Business Litigation; Real Property Law.

**THOMAS H. CLARKE, JR.,** born Oakland, California, October 26, 1945; admitted to bar, 1971, California and U.S. Court of Appeals, Ninth Circuit; 1975, U.S. Supreme Court; 1978, District of Columbia. *Education:* University of California at Berkeley (A.B., 1967); Boalt Hall School of Law, University of California, Berkeley (J.D., 1970); George Washington University (M.S., 1980). Phi Beta Kappa. *Member:* State Bar of California; The District of Columbia Bar. *PRACTICE AREAS:* Environmental Law; Administrative Law; Toxic Torts; Real Estate; Civil Litigation; Business Law.

**ROBERT P. ANDRIS, II,** born Santa Monica, California, June 18, 1962; admitted to bar, 1987, California and U.S. District Court, Northern, Southern, Central and Eastern Districts of California; U.S. Court of Appeals, Ninth Circuit. *Education:* San Jose State University (B.A., 1984); Santa Clara University (J.D., 1987). Comments Editor, Santa Clara Computer and High Technology Law Journal, 1986-1987. Co-author: "Insurance Coverage Concerns In California Continuous Loss Cases After Prudential-LMI," Santa Clara Law Review, 1991, Volume 31, number 4, p. 851; "Demise Of The Stipulated Judgment As Basis For Bad Faith Actions," International Association of Defense Counsel Journal 1993, Volume 60, number 1, p. 59. *PRACTICE AREAS:* Insurance Coverage and Bad Faith Litigation; Civil Appellate Law.

**TODD A. ROBERTS,** born Cambridge, Ohio, March 29, 1961; admitted to bar, 1987, California, U.S. District Court, Northern, Eastern, Central and Southern Districts of California and District of Arizona and U.S. Court of Appeals, Ninth Circuit. *Education:* University of Oregon (B.S., 1983); University of California at Davis (J.D., 1987). Member, Moot Court Board. *Member:* San Mateo County Bar Association; Association of Defense Counsel. *PRACTICE AREAS:* Insurance Coverage Law; Litigation; Appellate Practice.

**MICHAEL ROPERS,** born San Francisco, California, August 26, 1934; admitted to bar, 1962, California. *Education:* Stanford University (A.B. in Econ., 1956); Hastings College of Law, University of California (LL.B., 1961). *Member:* Bar Association of San Francisco; The State Bar of California; Defense Research Institute, Inc.; Association of Defense Counsel; American Board of Trial Advocates; Trial Attorneys of America; International Association of Defense Counsel; national Board of Trial Advocacy. (Resident). *PRACTICE AREAS:* Professional Liability; General Civil Litigation.

**DAVID M. MCLAUGHLIN,** born Palo Alto, California, May 11, 1961; admitted to bar, 1987, California and U.S. District Court, Northern District of California; 1988, U.S. District Court, Eastern District of California; 1996, U.S. District Court, Central District of California and District of Arizona. *Education:* University of California at Los Angeles (B.A., 1983); Santa Clara University (J.D., 1987). Member, Moot Court Honors Board. *Member:* San Mateo County Bar Association. *PRACTICE AREAS:* Commercial Litigation; Employment Litigation; Personal Injury Litigation.

**WILLIAM R. GARRETT,** born Arcadia, California, December 8, 1959; admitted to bar, 1987, California, U.S. District Court, Northern, Eastern, Central and Southern Districts of California and U.S. Court of Appeals, Ninth Circuit. *Education:* Stanford University (A.B., 1982); University of San Francisco (J.D., 1987). Recipient, American Jurisprudence Award in Real Estate Investment and Development. *Member:* San Mateo County Bar Association (Member, Sections on: Real Estate; Business; Litigation); State Bar of California (Member, Sections on: Real Estate; Business Law; Litigation). *PRACTICE AREAS:* Business Litigation; Construction Defect Litigation; Real Estate Litigation; Environmental Coverage Litigation; Personal Injury Matters.

**RAYMOND A. GREENE III,** born San Mateo, California, May 13, 1960; admitted to bar, 1987, California; U.S. District Court, Northern and Eastern Districts of California. *Education:* University of California at Berkeley (B.A., 1982); Georgetown University; University of San Francisco (J.D., 1987). Phi Delta Phi. Lecturer, Street Law Program, University of San Francisco, 1986. Special Assistant Deputy District Attorney, San Francisco County, 1991. *Member:* San Mateo County Bar Association; Association of Defense Counsel; San Francisco Inns of Court. *PRACTICE AREAS:* Personal Injury Law; Insurance Coverage Law; Intellectual Property Law; Construction Law; Products Liability Law; Employment Law.

*(This Listing Continued)*

# PROFESSIONAL BIOGRAPHIES
CALIFORNIA—REDWOOD CITY

**ROBERT G. ITTIG,** born San Francisco, California, December 17, 1959; admitted to bar, 1986, California and U.S. District Court, Northern District of California. *Education:* Gonzaga University; University of California at Santa Barbara (B.A., 1982); University of California at San Francisco (J.D., 1985). *Member:* Bar Association of San Francisco; State Bar of California; American Bar Association; San Francisco Trial Lawyers Association; California Trial Lawyers Association; The Association of Trial Lawyers of America. *PRACTICE AREAS:* General Civil Law; Trial Practice.

**V. RAYMOND SWOPE, III,** born Hampton, Virginia, May 22, 1952; admitted to bar, 1988, California, U.S. District Court, Northern District of California and U.S. Court of Appeals, Ninth Circuit. *Education:* Drake University (B.A., 1975; J.D., 1987). Order of the Barristers. *Member:* Midwest Regional Moot Court Team; National Civil Rights Moot Court Team. Recipient, C. Edwin Moore Appellate Advocacy Award. *Member:* San Mateo County Bar Association; State Bar of California; American Bar Association (Member, Litigation Section). *PRACTICE AREAS:* General Civil Litigation and Professional Liability; Environmental Law.

**RALPH TORTORELLA III,** born Poughkeepsie, New York, September 25, 1963; admitted to bar, 1989, California and U.S. District Court, Northern District of California; 1990, U.S. District Court, Eastern District of California and U.S. Court of Appeals, Ninth Circuit. *Education:* Union College (B.A., 1985); Santa Clara University (J.D., 1988). *Member:* San Mateo Bar Association; The State Bar of California; Association of Defense Counsel. *PRACTICE AREAS:* Insurance Coverage; Bad Faith Litigation; Appellate and Reinsurance.

**FRANCOIS G. LAUGIER,** born Avignon, France, July 22, 1963; admitted to bar, 1985, France; 1990, California and U.S. District Court, Northern District of California. *Education:* Université de Montpellier, Montpellier, France (Maitrise En Droit Prive, 1984); University of San Diego (LL.M., 1988). *Member:* The State Bar of California; American Bar Association; Union Internationale des Avocats; French Bar. *LANGUAGES:* French and Spanish. *PRACTICE AREAS:* French & EEC Law; Domestic and International Business Law.

**SUSAN H. HANDELMAN,** born Tucson, Arizona, June 6, 1946; admitted to bar, 1989, California, U.S. Court of Appeals, Ninth Circuit and U.S. Supreme Court. *Education:* Washington State University (B.A., cum laude, 1985); Golden Gate University (J.D., with honors, 1989). Recipient: American Jurisprudence Awards in Writing and Research and Trial Advocacy. Author: Articles, "When Will the Artful Pleading Doctrine Support Removal of a State Claim to Federal Court?" 18 Golden Gate L.R. 177; "Insurer's Right to Reimbursement..," 59 Defense Counsel Journal, 547; "Insurance Coverage Issues - Workplace Tort Claims," 62 Defense Counsel Journal, 354. *LANGUAGES:* Spanish. *PRACTICE AREAS:* Appellate Practice; Insurance Coverage Law.

**KEVIN G. MCCURDY,** born Evanston, Illinois, May 22, 1958; admitted to bar, 1984, California and U.S. District Court, Northern District of California. *Education:* Stanford University (B.A., with distinction, 1980); Boalt Hall School of Law, University of California (J.D., 1984). *Member:* Bar Association of San Francisco; State Bar of California; American Bar Association. *PRACTICE AREAS:* Insurance Coverage Litigation.

**STEPHEN P. ELLINGSON,** born Escanaba, Michigan, October 25, 1962; admitted to bar, 1988, California and U.S. Court of Appeals, Ninth Circuit; U.S≡ District Court, Northern, Eastern Central and Southern Districts of California. *Education:* University of California at Berkeley (B.A., 1984); Hastings College of Law, University of California (J.D., 1988). *Member:* State Bar of California; Federal Bar Association. *PRACTICE AREAS:* Complex Litigation; Insurance Bad Faith Litigation; Intellectual Property Disputes Litigation.

## OF COUNSEL

**RON W. FIELDS,** born Scott County, Virginia, January 29, 1919; admitted to bar, 1952, California. *Education:* Lincoln Memorial University (B.A., 1942); San Francisco Law School (LL.B., 1952). City Councilman, Redwood City, California, 1958-1964. *Member:* Bar Association of San Francisco; The State Bar of California; American Bar Association (Member, Fidelity and Surety Committee, Section of Insurance, Negligence and Compensation Law, 1971—). International Association of Insurance Counsel; The Association of Defense Counsel (Northern California); Lawyers Club of San Francisco.

**WALTER C. KOHN,** born Chicago, Illinois, June 9, 1925; admitted to bar, 1954, California. *Education:* Northwestern University (B.S., 1949); Hastings College of the Law, University of California (LL.B., 1953). Phi Alpha Delta. *Member:* San Mateo County Bar Association; The State Bar of California; American Board of Trial Advocates; Association of Defense

*(This Listing Continued)*

Counsel; Federation of Insurance Counsel; Lawyer-Pilots Bar Association; Society of Air Safety Investigators. *PRACTICE AREAS:* Aircraft Litigation; Products Liability Law; Business Transaction Litigation.

**CHI-HUNG A. CHAN,** born Taipei, Taiwan, September 14, 1947; admitted to bar, 1982, California. *Education:* St. John's University (B.A., 1971); University of Pittsburgh (M.B.A., 1972); DePaul University; University of Santa Clara (J.D., 1981). Director, Hong Kong Association of Northern California, 1989-1993. Chairman, Board of Directors, Kai Ming Head Start, Inc., 1983-1990. Director, Notre Dame High School, Belmont, 1989-1993. Director, San Francisco Shanghai Sister City Business School Committee, 1989-1993. Director, Palo Alto Go Club, 1991-1993. Director, Asian Neighborhood Arts Commission, 1989—. Member, Hong Kong Law Society (Registered Foreign Lawyer). Overseas Representative Shanghai Foreign Service Company, 1995—. *Member:* State Bar of California; Asian American Bar Association. *LANGUAGES:* Chinese (Mandarin, Cantonese, Taiwanese) and Japanese. *PRACTICE AREAS:* Contracts; International Matters; Real Estate; Immigration.

**JAMES H. MCKIBBEN,** born Paso Robles, California, April 25, 1938; admitted to bar, 1964, California. *Education:* Stanford University (A.B., with distinction, 1960; J.D., 1963). Phi Beta Kappa. *Member:* San Mateo County Bar Association (President, 1975); The State Bar of California; Association of Defense Counsel; American Board of Trial Advocates. *PRACTICE AREAS:* Construction Defect Litigation; Complex Litigation; Litigation.

---

**MICHAEL E. PITTS,** born Santa Barbara, California, January 30, 1948; admitted to bar, 1982, California and U.S. District Court, Northern District of California; 1983, U.S. Tax Court. *Education:* University of California at Santa Barbara (B.A., with honors, 1971); Golden Gate University (J.D., 1980; LL.M. in Taxation, 1981). Phi Alpha Delta. Staff Member, Golden Gate University Law Review, 1979-1980. *Member:* San Mateo County Bar Association; Peninsula Estate Planning Council.

**LINDA J. DVORAK,** born San Francisco, California, December 10, 1942; admitted to bar, 1982, California. *Education:* Oregon State University (B.S., 1964); University of Santa Clara (J.D., 1982). *Member:* San Mateo County Bar Association (Member, Sections on: Estate Planning and Probate); State Bar of California. (Certified Specialist, Probate, Estate Planning and Trust Law, The State Bar of California Board of Legal Specialization). *PRACTICE AREAS:* Estate Planning Law; Probate Law; Trust Administration Law.

**PETER C. SUHR,** born San Francisco, California, March 28, 1957; admitted to bar, 1986, California; U.S. District Court, Northern, Eastern and Central Districts of California; U.S. Court of Appeals, Ninth Circuit. *Education:* Thomas Aquinas College (B.A., 1979); Santa Clara University (J.D., 1986; M.B.A., 1986). *Member:* San Mateo County Bar Association; State Bar of California. *PRACTICE AREAS:* First and Third Party Insurance Coverage and Coverage Litigation; Environmental and Business Litigation.

**ALLISON LINDLEY DOBBROW,** born Montebello, California, July 7, 1960; admitted to bar, 1989, California. *Education:* University of Colorado at Boulder; University of Santa Clara (B.S., 1982; J.D., 1988). *Member:* State Bar of California.

**JUSTICE C. MCPHERSON,** born Garden Grove, California, October 23, 1963; admitted to bar, 1989, California, U.S. District Court, Northern District of California and U.S. Court of Appeals, Ninth Circuit; 1990, U.S. District Court, Eastern District of California. *Education:* University of California, Davis (B.A., 1985); University of San Diego (J.D., 1988). *Member:* San Mateo County Bar Association; Association of Defense Counsel. *PRACTICE AREAS:* Insurance Bad Faith; Insurance Coverage; Appellate Practice; Insurance Agent Malpractice.

**JOANNA R. REICHEL,** born San Francisco, California, April, 28, 1947; admitted to bar, 1986, California and U.S. District Court, Northern, Southern, Central and Eastern Districts of California. *Education:* University of San Francisco (B.S.B.A., cum laude, 1977); Golden Gate University (J.D., 1984); Insurance Institute of America (A.R.M., 1986). *Member:* San Mateo County (Member, Sections on: Litigation; Insurance) and American (Member: Sections on Litigation and Tort and Insurance; Air and Space Law Division) Bar Associations; State Bar of California. *LANGUAGES:* Spanish and Portuguese.

**KATHRYN C. CURRY,** born Alexandria, Virginia, February 14, 1965; admitted to bar, 1991, California and U.S. District Court, Northern District of California. *Education:* University of California, Berkeley (B.S., 1987); Santa Clara University (J.D., summa cum laude, 1991). Alpha Sigma

*(This Listing Continued)*

CAA1715B

**ROPERS, MAJESKI, KOHN & BENTLEY, A PROFESSIONAL CORPORATION, Redwood City—Continued**

Nu; Phi Delta Phi; (Secretary, Stephen J. Field Inn, 1990-1991). *Member:* State Bar of California. **PRACTICE AREAS:** Appeals; Insurance Litigation and Coverage.

**RICHARD FISHER,** born San Francisco, California, July 8, 1964; admitted to bar, 1991, California and U.S. District Court, Northern, Southern, Eastern and Central Districts of California; 1991, U.S. Court of Appeals, Ninth Circuit. *Education:* San Jose State University (B.S., 1987); Santa Clara University (J.D., 1991). Member, Moot Court Honors Board. *Member:* State Bar of California. **PRACTICE AREAS:** Civil Litigation; Insurance Law; Environmental Law.

**LAURA L. REIDENBACH,** born Sacramento, California, July 9, 1960; admitted to bar, 1992, California. *Education:* Santa Clara University (B.S., Math, 1982; J.D., 1991). Chartered Property Casualty Underwriter, 1988. *Member:* State Bar of California. **PRACTICE AREAS:** Insurance Coverage and Appellate Matters.

**BRIAN R. DAVIS,** born Sacramento, California, December 30, 1962; admitted to bar, 1992, California, U.S. District Court, Northern, Eastern, Central and Southern Districts of California and U.S. Court of Appeals, Ninth Circuit. *Education:* California State University at Chico (B.A., 1986); Lincoln University (J.D., 1992). *Member:* Federal Bar Association. **PRACTICE AREAS:** Insurance Contract, Bad Faith and Agency.

**KIMBERLY A. DONOVAN,** born San Francisco, California, February 2, 1961; admitted to bar, 1992, California and U.S. District Court, Northern District of California. *Education:* Santa Clara University (B.S., 1983); Pepperdine University (J.D., cum laude, 1992). Phi Alpha Delta. Recipient, American Jurisprudence Awards in Civil Procedure and Family Law.

**ROBERT P. SORAN,** born San Luis Obispo, California, June 10, 1966; admitted to bar, 1993, California and U.S. District Court, Northern and Central Districts of California. *Education:* California State University, Stanislaus (B.A., cum laude, 1990); Santa Clara University (J.D., 1993). *Member:* San Mateo County Bar Association; State Bar of California. **PRACTICE AREAS:** Civil Litigation; Environmental Law; Compliance and Litigation; Toxic Torts Litigation; Personal Injury Litigation; Trademark and Copyright.

**KELLY FRANKS,** born Honolulu, Hawaii, February 8, 1969; admitted to bar, 1993, California. *Education:* University of Texas (B.B.A., 1990); Hastings College of the Law, University of California, San Francisco (J.D., 1993). Judicial Extern, Hon. Care West Anderson, presiding Justice of the California Court of Appeal, 1992. *Member:* State Bar of California. **PRACTICE AREAS:** Insurance and Bad Faith Litigation; General Commercial and Intellectual Property Litigation; Appellate Practice.

**ANTHONY JOSEPH HOGLUND,** born San Jose, California, November 17, 1967; admitted to bar, 1993, California and U.S. District Court, Northern District of California. *Education:* University of California, Santa Barbara (B.A., with honors, 1990); University of San Francisco (J.D., 1993). *Member:* San Mateo County Bar Association; State Bar of California. **LANGUAGES:** Spanish. **PRACTICE AREAS:** Civil Litigation; Construction Law; Employment Law; Personal Injury Litigation; Insurance Bad Faith.

**HANS STEPHEN STEINHOFFER,** born Sacramento, California, August 6, 1965; admitted to bar, 1994, California; U.S. District Court, Northern, Central and Eastern Districts of California; U.S. Court of Appeals, Ninth Circuit. *Education:* Stanford University (A.B., 1987); Georgetown University (J.D., cum laude, 1991). *Member:* State Bar of California. **PRACTICE AREAS:** Appellate; Litigation.

**KEVIN HUNSAKER,** born Portland, Oregon, March 22, 1965; admitted to bar, 1994, California, U.S. District Court, Northern, Central and Eastern Districts of California and U.S. Court of Appeals, 9th Circuit. *Education:* University of California (B.A., Economics, 1988); Golden Gate University (J.D., highest honors, 1994). Associate Editor, Golden Gate University Law Review. Recipient, American Jurisprudence Awards in Torts, Criminal Procedure, Corporations, Appellate Advocacy, Remedies. Author, "U.S. v. James Daniel Good Property," Golden Gate Law Review, 1993. **PRACTICE AREAS:** Appellate; Litigation and Insurance Coverage.

**IDA SAMAWI SKIKOS,** born San Francisco, California, August 18, 1964; admitted to bar, 1991, California. *Education:* University of California at Los Angeles (B.A., 1986); University of Santa Clara (J.D., 1991). *Member:* State Bar of California. **PRACTICE AREAS:** Civil Litigation; Appellate; Insurance Coverage.

**JENNIFER C. COATES,** born Redwood City, California, January 20, 1968; admitted to bar, 1994, California. *Education:* University of California, Davis (B.A., with honors, 1990); Hastings College of the Law, University of California (J.D., 1994). Prytanean Honor Society; Psi Chi; Pi Sigma Alpha; Phi Delta Phi. Recipient, Outstanding Senior Award. **PRACTICE AREAS:** Litigation; Employment Law; Public Entity Defense.

**BRUCE M. MACKAY,** born Detroit, Michigan, July 27, 1952; admitted to bar, 1994, California. *Education:* University of Maryland (B.A., 1979); Brigham Young University (J.D., 1994). Managing Editor: Journal of Public Law; ICLA Edition, Law Review. Recipient, John S. Welch Award for Outstanding Legal Writing, 1994. **LANGUAGES:** Russian, German and Spanish. **PRACTICE AREAS:** Appellate; Bad Faith Insurance Defense; Environmental.

**STACY ANN SMITH,** born Los Angeles, California, February 12, 1964; admitted to bar, 1991, California, U.S. District Court, Northern District of California and U.S. Court of Appeals, 9th Circuit. *Education:* University of Pennsylvania (B.S., 1985); University of San Diego (J.D., 1991). *Member:* Bar Association of San Francisco. (Resident). **LANGUAGES:** French, Danish.

**MICHAEL DAVID MOREHEAD,** born Orange, California, June 4, 1967; admitted to bar, 1994, California. *Education:* University of California, Los Angeles (B.A., 1990); University of San Diego (J.D., cum laude, 1994). Phi Alpha Delta. Member, University of San Diego Law Review. **PRACTICE AREAS:** Insurance Coverage; Insurance Bad Faith Defense.

**MARK CASPER,** born Washington, D.C., August 29, 1967; admitted to bar, 1994, California; 1995, Colorado. *Education:* Santa Clara University (B.S., 1989; M.B.A., 1994; J.D., 1994). **PRACTICE AREAS:** Business Litigation; Transactional Work; Real Estate.

**BRIDGET C. HOPKINS IVANOV,** born Kittery, Maine, June 10, 1968; admitted to bar, 1995, California. *Education:* Santa Clara University (B.A., 1990); Golden Gate University (J.D., 1994). **PRACTICE AREAS:** Environmental Coverage Litigation.

**ROXANNE R. RAPSON,** born San Jose, California, December 18, 1957; admitted to bar, 1990, California and U.S. District Court, Northern District of California; 1991, U.S. District Court, Central District of California; 1993, U.S. District Court, Eastern District of California. *Education:* University of California at Berkeley (B.A., 1981); San Jose State University (M.P.H., 1986); Santa Clara University (J.D., 1990). Rotary Scholarship. Emery Scholarship. Author, "Recovering Stigma Damages Resulting from Actual or Threatened Contamination of Real Property," California Environmental Law and Regulation Reporter, April 1995. Guest Speaker, Federal Publications, 1993—. *Member:* Santa Clara County (Environmental Law Section) and San Mateo County Bar Associations; State Bar of California. **PRACTICE AREAS:** Environmental (Regulatory and Litigation).

**ROBERT S. MCLAY,** born Redding, California, June 12, 1963; admitted to bar, 1995, California and U.S. District Court, Northern, Eastern, Southern and Central Districts of California. *Education:* Westmont College (B.A., 1985); Ventura College (J.D., 1995). **PRACTICE AREAS:** Insurance Defense; Insurance Bad Faith.

**TERRY ANASTASSIOU,** born New York, N.Y., June 29, 1956; admitted to bar, 1992, California. *Education:* Michigan Technological University; George Washington University (B.A., 1983); Syracuse University; Santa Clara University (J.D., 1991). *Member:* State Bar of California. **PRACTICE AREAS:** Insurance Defense; Appellate Practice; Law and Motion; Alternative Dispute Resolution.

**DENNIS ALAN DUCHENE,** born Kankakee, Illinois, November 9, 1961; admitted to bar, 1995, California; U.S. District Court, Eastern and Northern Districts of California; U.S. Court of Appeals, Ninth Circuit. *Education:* University of Illinois (A.A.E., 1983); University of San Diego (J.D., 1995). Member, USD Appellate Moot Court Board. Recipient, Harold A. Shertz Award, 1995. Author, "The Third Package of Liberalization in the European Air Transport Sector," 23 Transp. L.J. 119, 1995. *Member:* State Bar of California; American Bar Association. **PRACTICE AREAS:** Civil Litigation; Insurance Defense; Environmental.

**ROGER B. FREDERICKSON,** born Montebello, California, March 18, 1965; admitted to bar, 1992, California and U.S. District Court, Central District of California. *Education:* University of California, Los Angeles (B.A., 1987); Pepperdine University (J.D., 1992). **PRACTICE AREAS:** Civil Litigation.

**NEDA NAVABPOUR,** born December 14, 1967; admitted to bar, 1992, California and U.S. District Court, Northern, Eastern and Central Districts

*(This Listing Continued)*

of California; U.S. Court of Appeals, Ninth Circuit. *Education:* Santa Clara University (B.A., 1989; J.D., 1992).

**H. ANN LIROFF,** born Philadelphia, Pennsylvania, July 30, 1952; admitted to bar, 1978, Pennsylvania; 1984, California and U.S. District Court, Northern District of California. *Education:* University of Pennsylvania; Wellesley College (B.A., with distinction, 1974); Simmons College (M.L.S., 1975); Villanova University (J.D., 1978); Catholic University of America. Judge, Moot Court. Member: National Association of Remodeling Industry, San Francisco Branch, 1989—; Associated General Contractors of Northern California, 1984-1988; Associated Building Contractors, Inc., 1985-1988; Peninsula Builders Exchange, 1989—. *Member:* Bar Association of San Francisco (Member, Labor Law, Litigation and Construction Sections); San Mateo (Member, Labor and Construction Sections) and American (Member, Construction, Litigation and Labor Law Sections) Bar Associations; State Bar of California. *PRACTICE AREAS:* General Commercial Litigation and Transactional Fields.

**TARA JANE WALSH,** born Palo Alto, California, September 2, 1969; admitted to bar, 1994, California. *Education:* University of Southern California (B.A., 1991); Fordham University (J.D., 1994). *PRACTICE AREAS:* Insurance Litigation.

**DENISE A. COLE,** born St. Mary's, Pennsylvania, April 4, 1970; admitted to bar, 1995, California. *Education:* State University of New York at Plattsburgh (B.A., 1992); Boalt Hall School of Law, University of California, Berkeley (J.D., summa cum laude, 1995). Phi Alpha Theta; Sigma Delta Pi. Recipient: Eugene P. Link Award for Academic Excellence; Inez Mulholland Boissevain Award for Excellence in writing. *PRACTICE AREAS:* Appellate Law; Insurance Defense Litigation.

**MICHAEL R. SOLOMON,** born St. Petersburg, Florida, May 12, 1959; admitted to bar, 1993, California. *Education:* University of New Mexico (B.A., 1982); Bowling Green State University (M.A., 1984); University of San Francisco School of Law (J.D., 1992). *PRACTICE AREAS:* Medical Malpractice; Public Entity; General Civil Litigation.

REPRESENTATIVE CLIENTS: Aetna Life & Casualty Co.; Aetna Casualty & Surety Co.; Alamo Rent A Car, Inc.; Alta Bates Corp.; American International Group; Avemco; Bank of America; Bank of California; Bedford Properties, Inc.; Black Mountain Spring Water Co.; Cadence Design Systems Inc.; California Casualty; California Micro Devices; California State Automobile Assn.; Chubb Group; CIGNA; Continental Insurance Cos.; Continental National Assurance; County of San Mateo; Employers Reinsurance; Farmers Insurance Group; Fireman's Fund American Insurance Co.; First American Title Insurance, Co.; First Interstate Bank; Granite Construction Co.; Grinnell Corp.; Hallmark Cards, Inc.; Hartford Insurance Co.; Holiday Inn Corp.; Home Insurance; Industrial Indemnity; Intel Corp.; Kelly Moore Paint Co.; Kinetic Systems, Inc.; Certain Lloyd's Underwriters; Lucky Stores; Mansville Trust; Metropolitan Life & Casualty; Montgomery Ward; Nationwide Insurance Co.; North American Van Lines, Inc.; Orion Group; Prudential Property & Casualty; Reliance Insurance Cos.; Royal Globe Insurance Cos.; San Mateo Co.; Santa Clara County; Santa Cruz County; Service Corporation International (SCI); Shand Morahan & Co.; Signetic Corp.; Southern Pacific Transportation Co.; Stanford University Hospital; State Farm Insurance Cos.; TeleVideo Systems, Inc.; Transport Insurance Co.; Truck Insurance Exchange; The Travelers; USAA; Volvo Corporation of America; Watkins Johnson; Westinghouse; White Consolidated Industries; Zimpro.

(For Data on all Firm Personnel, see Professional Biographies at San Jose, San Francisco, Sacramento, Santa Rosa and Los Angeles, California).

---

## M. GERALD SCHWARTZBACH

*601 BREWSTER AVENUE*
*P.O. BOX 3389*
*REDWOOD CITY, CALIFORNIA 94103*
*Telephone: 415-367-6811*
*Fax: 415-368-0367*

*Civil Trial, Criminal Trial and Appellate Practice in State and Federal Courts.*

**M. GERALD SCHWARTZBACH,** born Wilkes-Barre, Pennsylvania, October 6, 1944; admitted to bar, 1970, Michigan and U.S. District Court, Eastern District of Michigan; 1974, California and U.S. District Court, Northern District of California; 1980, U.S. Court of Appeals, Ninth Circuit; 1982, U.S. Supreme Court. *Education:* Washington & Jefferson College (B.A., 1966); George Washington University (J.D., 1969). Recipient, Skip Glenn Outstanding Lawyer Award, California Attorneys for Criminal Justice. *Member:* Bar Association of San Francisco (Chair, Criminal Justice Section, 1988-1991; Member, Criminal Justice Advisory Council, 1988-1992); State Bar of California; California Attorneys for Criminal Justice (Member, Board of Governors, 1986-1993); National Association of Criminal Defense Lawyers; Northern California Criminal Trial Lawyers Association (Member, Board of Governors, 1989—); National Lawyers Guild; State Bar of Michigan (inactive).

*(This Listing Continued)*

---

## SMITH & BENTLEY

*777 MARSHALL STREET*
*REDWOOD CITY, CALIFORNIA 94063*
*Telephone: 415-568-2820*
*Fax: 415-568-2823*

*General Civil and Trial Practice, Personal Injury Litigation, General Business Litigation and Criminal Defense Litigation.*

### MEMBERS OF FIRM

**CHARLES J. SMITH,** born Elgin, Illinois, October 22, 1951; admitted to bar, 1976, California and U.S. District Court, Northern District of California. *Education:* Lehigh University (B.A., 1973); University of Santa Clara (J.D., 1976). Deputy District Attorney, San Mateo County, 1978-1987. *Member:* San Mateo County and Santa Clara County Bar Associations; State Bar of California; American Board of Trial Advocates. *PRACTICE AREAS:* Criminal Law; Civil Litigation.

**JOSHUA M. BENTLEY,** born San Francisco, California, February 27, 1965; admitted to bar, 1991, California. *Education:* University of California at Santa Barbara (B.A., 1988); University of Santa Clara (J.D., 1991). Phi Alpha Delta. Deputy District Attorney, 1991-1993. *Member:* San Mateo County and American Bar Associations; State Bar of California. *PRACTICE AREAS:* Criminal Law; Civil Litigation.

**JIM HARTNETT,** born San Mateo, California, July 11, 1950; admitted to bar, 1978, California; 1982, U.S. District Court, Northern and Central Districts of California; U.S. Court of Appeals, Ninth Circuit. *Education:* Sophia University, International Division, Tokyo (B.A., 1975); Santa Clara Law School (J.D., 1978). Author: "How to Reduce Risks In International Contracts (Kokusai Keiyaku No Risku Keigin Saku)," Practical Manual For Risk Management, R.M. Jitsumu Manualu, 1983. Mayor, City of Redwood, 1995-1996. President, Redwood City/San Mateo County Chamber of Commerce, 1995. Former Chair, County of San Mateo Business Development Commission. Commissioner, Redwood City Planning Commission, 1994-1995. Vice-President, American Chamber of Commerce in Japan, 1981. *Member:* Santa Clara County and San Mateo County Bar Associations; State Bar of California. [U.S. Naval Security Group, Active Duty, 1970-1972]. *PRACTICE AREAS:* International Law; Business Law; Real Estate Law; Litigation.

### OF COUNSEL

**LEE W. CLARK,** born Boise, Idaho, February 9, 1957; admitted to bar, 1994, California; 1995, U.S. District Court, Northern District of California. *Education:* University of Portland (B.A. magna cum laude, 1991); Santa Clara University (J.D., 1994). Judicial Extern, to the Honorable Magistrate Joan S. Brennan, U.S. District Court, Northern District of California. *Member:* San Mateo County and American Bar Associations; State Bar of California; California Public Defenders Association. *PRACTICE AREAS:* Criminal Law; Civil Litigation.

REPRESENTATIVE CLIENTS: Furnished Upon Request.

---

## LAW OFFICES OF
## JAMES A. THOMPSON

*600 ALLERTON STREET, SECOND FLOOR*
*REDWOOD CITY, CALIFORNIA 94063*
*Telephone: 415-365-7333*
*Fax: 415-365-7735*

*General Civil and Trial Practice. Wills, Trusts, Probate and Personal Injury.*

**JAMES A. THOMPSON,** born Santa Rosa, California, February 16, 1943; admitted to bar, 1971, California; 1978, U.S. Supreme Court. *Education:* University of California at Berkeley (A.B., 1965); Hastings College of Law, University of California (J.D., 1970). *Member:* San Mateo County and American Bar Associations; State Bar of California; California State Trial Lawyers Association; San Mateo County Trial Lawyers Association. *LANGUAGES:* Spanish and French. *PRACTICE AREAS:* Civil Litigation (25%, 30); Real Estate Law (20%, 5); Probate Law (25%, 15); Wills Law (25%, 30); Family Law (5%, 5).

*(This Listing Continued)*

*LAW OFFICES OF JAMES A. THOMPSON, Redwood City—Continued*

ASSOCIATE

**MAURICE J. CREEGAN,** born 1963; admitted to bar, 1993, California. *Education:* University of California (B.S.); University of Santa Clara (J.D., 1993). *Member:* State Bar of California. **LANGUAGES:** Spanish. **PRACTICE AREAS:** General Practice (35%).

## WAGSTAFFE & WAGSTAFFE

333 BRADFORD STREET
P.O. BOX 5009
**REDWOOD CITY, CALIFORNIA 94063**
Telephone: 415-366-9593

*General Civil and Trial Practice. Probate, Real Property, Business, Corporation and Hospital Law.*

MEMBERS OF FIRM

**GERARD WAGSTAFFE,** born Victoria, British Columbia, Canada, August 20, 1917; admitted to bar, 1940, California. *Education:* University of Santa Clara (A.B., 1938; J.D., 1940). District Counsel, Sequoia Hospital District, 1949—. *Member:* San Mateo County Bar Association; The State Bar of California. **PRACTICE AREAS:** Probate Law; Real Property Law; Business Law; Corporation Law; Hospital Law.

**DENNIS G. WAGSTAFFE,** born Redwood City, California, April 13, 1954; admitted to bar, 1978, California and U.S. District Court, Northern District of California; 1979, U.S. Court of Military Appeals. *Education:* University of Southern California (A.B., 1975); Hastings College of Law, University of California (J.D., 1978). *Member:* San Mateo County Bar Association; The State Bar of California. [Capt., Judge Advocate, U.S. Air Force, 1979-1982]. **PRACTICE AREAS:** Probate Law; Real Property Law; Business Law; Corporation Law; Hospital Law.

REFERENCES: Bank of America N.T.&S.A.; Wells Fargo Bank.

## WEINBERG, ZIFF & MILLER

**REDWOOD CITY, CALIFORNIA**

(See Palo Alto)

*General Civil and Trial Practice. Business, Corporate, Taxation, Family, Personal Injury, Collections, Estate Planning, Probate and Trust Litigation, Appeals and Administration, and Criminal Trials.*

## WINTERS, KRUG & DELBON

**REDWOOD CITY, CALIFORNIA**

(See Burlingame)

*General Civil and Trial Practice, including Insurance Law, General and Product Liability, Aviation Law, Construction Law, Environmental and Toxic Tort Claims.*

## NORRIS & NORRIS

Established in 1950
3260 BLUME DRIVE, SUITE 400
**RICHMOND, CALIFORNIA 94806**
Telephone: 510-222-2100
Facsimile: 510-222-5992

Walnut Creek, California Office: 500 Ygnacio Valley Road, Suite 400, 94596. Telephone: 510-934-8181. Facsimile: 510-934-3665.

*Business, Commercial and Real Estate Litigation and Transactions, Class Action Defense and Complex Litigation, Government Approvals, Environmental, Solid Waste, Health Care Law, Cable Television, Property Taxation, Sales and Use Taxation, Employment, Discrimination, Wrongful Termination, Workplace Harassment, Land Use, Probate, Trust and Estate Planning.*

FIRM PROFILE: *Norris & Norris was founded in 1950 by the Honorable Allen L. Norris, now a retired Municipal Court judge. It is the largest law firm in West Contra Costa County and counts many major local institutions among its clients. The firm endeavors to provide the information and risk analysis necessary for the clients to direct services in its most economical and beneficial manner.*

MEMBERS OF FIRM

**RICHARD E. NORRIS,** born Berkeley, California, June 20, 1952; admitted to bar, 1977, California. *Education:* University of California at Los Angeles (B.A., cum laude, 1974); Hastings College of the Law, University of California, San Francisco (J.D., 1977). Chairman, Board of Directors, Richmond Chamber of Commerce, 1989—. Member and President, Board of Directors, Richmond Art Center, 1989—. Member, Board of Directors, Opportunity West, 1996—. (Managing Partner). **PRACTICE AREAS:** Business Transactions; Corporate Law; Discretionary Government Approvals; Environmental Law; Solid Waste Law.

**DOUGLAS C. STRAUS,** born Berkeley, California, September 29, 1955; admitted to bar, 1980, California. *Education:* Northwestern University (B.S., with highest distinction, 1977); Boalt Hall School of Law, University of California (J.D., 1980). Winner, 1980 McBaine Moot Court Competition. President, Rotary Club of Richmond, 1994-1995. Member, Board of Directors, Richmond Unified Education Fund, 1983— (Vice President, 1984-1988; Treasurer, 1988-1992). **PRACTICE AREAS:** Business; Real Estate and Contract Litigation.

**CY EPSTEIN,** born Cleveland, Ohio, September 25, 1936; admitted to bar, 1977, California. *Education:* University of California at Santa Barbara (B.A., summa cum laude, 1960); Yale University (M.A., 1965); University of California, San Francisco (J.D., 1977). Note Editor, Hastings International and Comparative Law Review. Licensed Real Estate Broker, California. Instructor: California Community College; Real Estate Law, Contra Costa College; Department of Real Estate Continuing Education Program. Visiting Lecturer, Legal Writing and Research Program, Hastings College of the Law, 1985. Member, 1987—, and Chair, 1987-1988, Contra Costa County Human Relations Commission. Assistant City Attorney, City of El Cerrito, 1978-1980. Judge Pro Tempore, Contra Costa Municipal Court, Bay Judicial District. *Member:* National Lawyers Guild. **PRACTICE AREAS:** Real Property Transactions; Litigation and Condemnation Law.

**COLIN J. COFFEY,** born Walnut Creek, California, July 24, 1959; admitted to bar, 1983, California. *Education:* University of California at Berkeley (B.A., with great distinction, 1980); Hastings College of the Law, University of California (J.D., 1983). Phi Beta Kappa. Editor, Hastings International Law Review. Author: "Foreign Investment in Cable Television," Hastings International Law Review, Vol. 6, December 1983). *Member:* Contra Costa Bar Association (Board of Directors); California Society of Healthcare Attorneys; American Society of Healthcare Attorneys; National Health Lawyers Association. **PRACTICE AREAS:** Health Care Law; Government Approvals Law.

**EDWARD L. SHAFFER,** born Boston, Massachusetts, October 10, 1951; admitted to bar, 1986, California. *Education:* Boston University (B.A., cum laude, 1973); Rutgers University (Masters, City and Regional Planning, 1975); Hastings College of the Law, University of California (J.D., 1986). Order of the Coif; Thurston Society; Moot Court Board. Co-Author: "California Environmental Law and Land Use Practice (Chapters 60, 61)", Matthew Bender, 1989; "Understanding Development Regulations", Solano Press, 1994. Eight years experience as a professional planner. Author and Lecturer on Land Use and Environmental Law. On Editorial Board and Case Commentator for Matthew Bender's monthly " California Environmental Law Reporter", 1991—. **PRACTICE AREAS:** Land Use and Environmental Regulation; Development Permitting; Local Government Law; Real Estate Law.

**SHARON MOODY IVERSEN,** born Alameda, California, January 19, 1941; admitted to bar, 1987, California. *Education:* University of California, Los Angeles (B.S., Nursing, 1964); University of California, San Francisco (M.S., 1971); John F. Kennedy University (J.D., 1987). Registered Nurse, 1964—. *Member:* California Society of Health Law Attorneys; American Academy of Hospital Attorneys; National Health Lawyers Association; Women Health Care Executives. **PRACTICE AREAS:** Health Care Law; General Business Law.

ASSOCIATES

**LEONARD H. WATKINS,** born New York, N.Y., March 8, 1959; admitted to bar, 1987, California, U.S. District Court, Northern, Central and Eastern Districts of California and U.S. Court of Appeals, Ninth Circuit. *Education:* United States Merchant Marine Academy (B.S., 1980); University of San Francisco (J.D., cum laude, 1987). Member, McAuliffe Law Honor Society. Recipient, American Jurisprudence Awards in Corporations, Evidence, Criminal Law and Procedure. Extern to the Hon. Joseph Grodin, California Supreme Court, 1986. Author: "The Supreme Court In-

*(This Listing Continued)*

terprets Interstate Banking Under the Bank Holding Company Act of 1956," 20 University of San Francisco Law Review, No. 4. *Member:* State Bar of California; American Bar Association. **PRACTICE AREAS:** Commercial Litigation; Lender Liability; Real Estate; Banking Law.

**NOËL M. CAUGHMAN,** born San Francisco, California, November 29, 1966; admitted to bar, 1991, California. *Education:* University of California (B.S., 1988); Hastings College of the Law, University of California (J.D., 1991). **LANGUAGES:** German. **PRACTICE AREAS:** Employment Discrimination; Sexual Harassment. *Email:* norncaughman@mcimail.com

**GEORGE A. HARRIS, III,** born Richmond, California, May 17, 1963; admitted to bar, 1995, California. *Education:* University of Michigan (B.B.A., 1992); George Washington University (J.D., 1995).

**MICHAEL A. SWEET,** born San Francisco, California, September 2, 1969; admitted to bar, 1996, California. *Education:* Brandeis University (B.A., cum laude, 1991); University of California (J.D., 1996). *Member:* State Bar of California. *Email:* normsweet@mcimail.com

REPRESENTATIVE CLIENTS: NationsCredit; Household Finance Corp.; The Mechanics Bank of Richmond; Citibank; Richmond Sanitary Service; Solano Garbage Co.; Mt. Diablo Medical Center; Brookside Hospital; American Vanpac Carriers; ARCO; Potrero Hills Landfill, Inc.; City of Oakland; The Martin Group; Cost Plus, Inc.; Ladbroke; Box USA; Security Pacific Real Estate.

---

## WATSON, HOFFE & HASS

3700 BARRETT AVENUE
P.O. BOX 5001
RICHMOND, CALIFORNIA 94805-2297
Telephone: 510-237-3700
Facsimile: 510-237-3714

*General, Civil and Trial Practice in all State and Federal Courts. Corporate, Banking, Family, Probate, Estate Planning, Real Estate, Construction, Environmental and Commercial Law.*

### MEMBERS OF FIRM

**FRANCIS A. WATSON, JR.,** born San Jose, California, December 21, 1929; admitted to bar, 1953, California. *Education:* Stanford University (A.B., 1950); University of California at Berkeley (LL.B., 1953). Phi Delta Phi. Instructor, San Francisco Law School, 1954-1956. Listed in: The Best Lawyers in America by Steven Naifed and Gregory White (1990). *Member:* Bar Association of San Francisco; Contra Costa County, Marin County and American Bar Associations; The State Bar of California; Association of Trial Lawyers of America; Northern California Golf Association (Past-President). **REPORTED CASES:** Estates of Propst (1990) 50 C.3d 448; Bouquet v. Bouquet (1976) 16 C.3d 583; In re Marriage of Van Sickle (1977) 68 C.A.3d 728; McMillan v. American General Finance Corp. (1976) 60 C.A. 3d 175; Estate of Barbikas (1959) 171 C.A.2d 452. **PRACTICE AREAS:** Family Law; Business; Commercial Litigation; Probate; Estate Planning.

**R. BRUCE HOFFE,** born Oakland, California, May 1, 1927; admitted to bar, 1954, California. *Education:* University of California at Berkeley (A.B., 1950); LL.B., 1953). Phi Delta Phi. Instructor, San Francisco Law School, 1960-1961. Past President, Richmond Chamber of Commerce. *Member:* Contra Costa and Marin County Bar Associations (President, 1977); The State Bar of California. **REPORTED CASES:** Nelson v. Orosco (1981) 117 CA.3d 73; Trans Container Services v. Security Forwarders, Inc. (1985) 752 F2d 483; United States of America to the Use of Wayne Bailey dba Wayne Bailey Trucking v. Elmer J. Freethy, individually and dba Elmer J. Freethy Co. (1972) 469 F2d 1348. **PRACTICE AREAS:** Commercial Litigation; Real Property; Corporate; Construction Law.

**PETER A. HASS,** born Palo Alto, California, June 18, 1960; admitted to bar, 1987, California. *Education:* University of California at Santa Cruz (B.A., 1982); University of San Francisco (J.D., 1986). Member, Board of Directors, Richmond Chamber of Commerce, 1990—. (Past President, 1995); President, Board of Directors, Richmond Art Center. *Member:* Contra Costa and Marin County Bar Associations; The State Bar of California. **PRACTICE AREAS:** Real Estate; Banking; Civil Litigation; Commercial Litigation; Construction Law.

**JOSEPH E. B. GAUDET** (1936-1983).

### ASSOCIATES

**JEAN M. SCHULZ,** born Waukesha, Wisconsin, February 9, 1962; admitted to bar, 1991, California. *Education:* Marquette University (B.A., 1984); Pepperdine University School of Law (J.D., 1990). *Member:* Contra Costa, Marin and Alameda County Bar Associations; State Bar of California; Contra Costa County Bar Committee. **PRACTICE AREAS:** Family Law; Civil Litigation.

*(This Listing Continued)*

**DAVID L. HALLIKAINEN,** born Berkeley, California, June 15, 1955; admitted to bar, 1995, California. *Education:* John F. Kennedy University (J.D., 1995). *Member:* Contra Costa and Marin County Bar Associations; State Bar of California. **PRACTICE AREAS:** Family Law; Civil Litigation.

REPRESENTATIVE CLIENTS: The Mechanics Bank of Richmond; Chevron U.S.A., Inc.; Chevron Chemical Co.; General Chemical Corp.; El Cerrito Mill & Lumber Co.; McNevin Cadillac; City of Richmond; Dublin Honda; Bartels-Realtors, Inc.; Farmers Insurance Group; Smith Bros. Motors, Inc.; Mira Vista Golf & Country Club, Inc.; Contra Costa Community College District; Nations-Bank of Texas, N.A..
REFERENCE: The Mechanics Bank of Richmond.

---

## WHITING & RUBENSTEIN

Established in 1981

3260 BLUME DRIVE, SUITE 110
RICHMOND, CALIFORNIA 94806
Telephone: 510-222-6000
Fax: 510-222-6001

*Walnut Creek, California Office:* 1220 Oakland Boulevard, Suite 200. 94596.

*General Civil and Trial Practice in all State and Federal Courts including Real Property, Family, Commercial, Corporate, and Business Law.*

### MEMBERS OF FIRM

**WILLIAM F. WHITING,** born Richmond, California, October 17, 1940; admitted to bar, 1965, California; 1966, U.S. Court of Military Appeals; 1979, U.S. Supreme Court. *Education:* Stanford University (A.B., 1962); Boalt Hall, University of California (J.D., 1965). Phi Delta Phi. Author: "Compulsory License in Copyright Law Revision," 53 California Law Review, 1520, 1965. *Member:* Contra Costa County and American Bar Associations; State Bar of California; Alameda-Contra Costa Trial Lawyers Association (President, 1983); Fellow, American Academy of Matrimonial Lawyers. [Capt., U.S. Marine Corps, JAGC, 1965-1968]. (Certified Specialist, Family Law, The State Bar of California Board of Legal Specialization). **REPORTED CASES:** Valley Bank of Nevada v. Superior Court (1975) 15 Cal. 3d 652; Burger v. Superior Court (1984) 151 CA 3d 1013. **PRACTICE AREAS:** Family Law; Civil Litigation.

**RONALD A. RUBENSTEIN,** born Stockton, California, August 28, 1944; admitted to bar, 1970, California; U.S. District Court, Northern District of California; 1978, U.S. Supreme Court. *Education:* University of California at Santa Barbara (A.B., 1966); Boalt Hall School of Law, University of California (J.D., 1969). Instructor, Business Law, Contra Costa College, 1972. *Member:* Contra Costa County Bar Association; State Bar of California. **REPORTED CASES:** Bouquet v. Bouquet (1976) 16C3 583; In re Marriage of Van Sickle (1977) 68 CA3 728. **PRACTICE AREAS:** Civil Litigation; Commercial Law; Corporate Law; Business Law.

### ASSOCIATES

**ANDREW ROSS,** born Brooklyn, New York, February 12, 1946; admitted to bar, 1972, New York and U.S. District Court, Eastern and Southern Districts of New York; 1978, California; 1986, U.S. District Court, Eastern and Northern Districts of California. *Education:* St. Lawrence University (B.A., 1967); Brooklyn Law School (J.D., 1971). Member, Brooklyn Law Review, 1970-1971. Judge Pro Tem, Santa Clara County Municipal Court, 1980-1984. *Member:* Bar Association of San Francisco; Santa Clara County, Los Angeles County and New York State Bar Associations; State Bar of California. (Certified Specialist, Family Law, The State Bar of California Board of Legal Specialization). **PRACTICE AREAS:** Family Law; Civil Litigation.

**R. ANN FALLON,** born Pittsburgh, Pennsylvania, June 12, 1942; admitted to bar, 1984, California; U.S. District Court, Northern District of California. *Education:* Fordham University (B.A., magna cum laude, 1970); Boalt Hall School of Law, University of California at (J.D., 1983). *Member:* Contra Costa Bar Association (Member, Board of Directors, Family Law Section, 1988-1991); State Bar of California (Member, Property Committee North, Family Section, 1993-1994; Legislative Liaison for 1995 and 1996). **PRACTICE AREAS:** Family Law; Family Law Pensions.

**JON A. JOHNSEN,** born Petaluma, California, November 14, 1946; admitted to bar, 1975, California and U.S. District Court, Northern District of California. *Education:* University of California at Berkeley (B.S., 1969); Hastings College of the Law (J.D., 1975). *Member:* Contra Costa County (Member, Attorney Reference Panel Committee, 1978-1986; Family Law Section Board, 1987-1988); State Bar of California (Member, Fam-

*(This Listing Continued)*

CAA1719B

*WHITING & RUBENSTEIN, Richmond—Continued*

ily Law Subcommittee on Custody and Visitation, 1980-1986). **PRACTICE AREAS:** Family Law.

**DAVID D. BUNN,** born Los Angeles, California, August 22, 1964; admitted to bar, 1989, California and U.S. District Court, Northern District of California. *Education:* University of California at Berkeley (A.B., 1986); Columbia University (J.D., 1989). Harlan F. Stone Moot Court Semi-Finalist. Staff Member, Journal of Law and Social Problems. *Member:* Contra Costa County and American Bar Associations; State Bar of California. **LANGUAGES:** Spanish. **REPORTED CASES:** In Re Marriage of Moschetta, 25 Cal.App. 4th 1218 (1994). **PRACTICE AREAS:** Family Law; Civil Litigation.

**GRETCHEN B. BARBER,** born San Mateo, California, October 2, 1966; admitted to bar, 1995, California. *Education:* Wellesley College (B.A., cum laude, 1988); University of California, Boalt Hall School of Law (J.D., 1995). *Member:* State Bar of California. **PRACTICE AREAS:** Family Law.

---

## AKLUFI AND WYSOCKI

3403 TENTH STREET, SUITE 610
**RIVERSIDE, CALIFORNIA 92501**
*Telephone: 909-682-5480*
*Telecopier: 909-682-2619*

*General Civil, Trial and Appellate Practice in State and Federal Courts, Water Law, Municipal, Eminent Domain, Corporation, Real Property, Zoning, Public Agency, Business, Contract and Construction Law.*

### MEMBERS OF FIRM

**JOSEPH S. AKLUFI,** born Kassel, Germany, October 5, 1947; admitted to bar, 1976, California; 1982, U.S. Supreme Court. *Education:* University of California at Riverside (B.A., 1973); Syracuse University (M.P.A., 1975; J.D., 1975). Member, Moot Court Board. Visiting Instructor, University of California at Riverside, 1982. Co-author: "A Summary of Rules of Liability in Water Damage Cases," California State Bar Journal, November, 1980. Member: Board of Directors of Tel Law, Inc., 1979-1984; Superior Court Arbitration Panel, 1981-1987. *Member:* Riverside County Bar Associations; The State Bar of California (President, Barristers, 1979-1980).

**DAVID L. WYSOCKI,** born Grand Rapids, Michigan, February 7, 1952; admitted to bar, 1978, California; 1979, U.S. District Court, Central District of California and U.S. Court of Appeals, Ninth Circuit; 1982, U.S. Supreme Court. *Education:* California State University at Long Beach (B.A., cum laude, 1974); Southwestern University (J.D., 1977). Author: "AB3303: The Proposed California Limited Partnership Act," California Real Property Law Section, Real Property News, Fall, 1980. Instructor, Citrus Belt Law School, 1982-1987. Legal Research Assistant to The Honorable Arthur L. Alarcon, 1976-1977. Judicial Research Attorney to the Honorable Dan Kaufmann, the Honorable Raymond Roberts and the Honorable Richard American, 1978-1979. Member, Board of Directors, Tel-Law, Inc., 1980-1981; Vice President, General Counsel, and Member, Board of Directors, Inland Empire Make-A-Wish Foundation, Inc., 1985-1987. *Member:* Riverside County (Member, Fee Arbitration Committee, 1982—; Committee Chairman, 1991—) Bar Association; The State Bar of California (Member, State Bar Committee on Mandatory Fee Arbitration, 1992-1994). **REPORTED CASES:** Wong v. Davidian, 206 Cal. App. 3d 264 (1988); Koehrer v. Superior Court, 181 Cal. App. 3d 1155 (1986); Guinn v. Dotson, 23 Cal. App. 4th 262 (1994); Schaefer Dixon Associates v. Santa Ana Watershed Project Authority, 48 Cal. App. 4th 524 (1996).

### ASSOCIATE

**DANIEL R. AKLUFI,** born Plainfield, New Jersey, July 30, 1968; admitted to bar, 1994, California; U.S. District Court, Southern District of California; 1996, U.S. District Court, Central District of California. *Education:* University of California-San Diego (B.A., 1991); California Western School of Law (J.D., 1994). *Member:* Riverside County Bar Association; State Bar of California.

REPRESENTATIVE CLIENTS: Santa Ana Watershed Project Authority; Idyllwild Fire District; Idyllwild Water District; City of Beaumont; Arrowbear Park County Water District; City of Hemet; Kretschmar & Smith, Inc.; Riverside Construction Co.; Tilden-Coil Constructors, Inc.; Eastern Municipal Water District; Elsinore Valley Municipal Water District; Western Riverside County Regional Wastewater Authority; Joshua Basin Water District.

---

## ANDERSON, McPHARLIN & CONNERS

A Partnership including Professional Corporations
3750 UNIVERSITY AVENUE, SUITE 225
**RIVERSIDE, CALIFORNIA 92501-3313**
*Telephone: 909-787-1900*
*Telecopier: 908-787-6749*

*Los Angeles, California Office:* One Wilshire Building, Nineteenth Floor. 624 South Grand Avenue. Telephone: 213-688--0080. Telecopier: 213-622-7594.

*General Civil and Trial Practice in all State and Federal Courts. Fidelity and Surety, Environmental Litigation (Hazardous Waste, Toxic Torts), Products Liability, Property Insurance, Title Insurance, Maritime, Fire Insurance, Commercial and General Liability Insurance Defense, Insurance Coverage, Bad Faith Litigation, Business Torts, Architects' and Engineers' Errors and Omissions, Construction Litigation, Commercial Litigation, Banking, Labor and Professional Malpractice Law.*

(For Complete Biographical Data on all Personnel, see Professional Biographies at Los Angeles, California)

---

## BEST BEST & KRIEGER LLP

A California Limited Liability Partnership including Professional
Corporations
Established in 1891
400 MISSION SQUARE
3750 UNIVERSITY AVENUE
P.O. BOX 1028
**RIVERSIDE, CALIFORNIA 92502**
*Telephone: 909-686-1450*
*Fax: 909-686-3083; 909-682-4612*

*Rancho Mirage, California Office:* Hope Square Professional Centre, 39700 Bob Hope Drive, Suite 312, P.O. Box 1555. Telephone: 619-568-2611. Fax: 619-340-6698; 619-341-7039.
*Ontario, California Office:* 800 North Haven, Suite 120. Telephone: 909-989-8584. Fax: 909-944-1441.
*San Diego, California Office:* 402 West Broadway, 13th Floor. Telephone: 619-525-1300. Fax: 619-233-6118.
*Victorville, California Office:* High Desert Corporate Pointe Building, 14350 Civic Drive, Suite 270. Telephone: 619-245-4127. Fax: 619-245-6437.

*General Civil and Trial Practice. Corporation, Water Rights, Probate, Trusts and Estate Planning, Labor, Real Estate, Municipal, Public Finance, Health Care and Indian Land Law.*

### MEMBERS OF FIRM

**RAYMOND BEST** (1868-1957).

**JAMES H. KRIEGER** (1913-1975).

**EUGENE BEST** (1893-1981).

**ARTHUR L. LITTLEWORTH, (P.C.),** born Anderson, California, May 2, 1923; admitted to bar, 1951, California. *Education:* Yale University (B.A., 1944; LL.B., 1950); Stanford University (M.A., 1947). President, Riverside Unified School District Board of Education, 1962-1973. Member, Commission on Educational Innovation and Planning, California, 1972-1975. President, Riverside Press Council, 1973-1975. Member of Governor's Commission to Review California Water Rights Law, 1977-1978. Appointed in 1987 by U.S. Supreme Court as Special Master in *Kansas v. Colorado.* Co-Author: *California Water* published 1995. *Member:* Riverside County (President, 1971-1972) and American Bar Associations; The State Bar of California. **PRACTICE AREAS:** Water Law; Environmental.

**GLEN E. STEPHENS, (P.C.),** born Salt Lake City, Utah, August 17, 1927; admitted to bar, 1953, California. *Education:* University of Utah (B.S., 1949); Stanford University (J.D., 1952). Member, Board of Editors, Stanford Law Review, 1950-52. *Member:* Riverside County and American Bar Associations; The State Bar of California; National Association of Bond Lawyers. **PRACTICE AREAS:** Public Finance and Securities Law.

**WILLIAM R. DEWOLFE, (P.C.),** born Bangor, Maine, October 1, 1935; admitted to bar, 1962, California. *Education:* University of Paris and University of California at Riverside (B.A., 1958); University of California at Berkeley (LL.B., 1961). Phi Delta Phi; Phi Beta Kappa. Member, Board of Editors, California Law Review, 1960-1961. Research Associate, California District Court of Appeal, Second District, Third Division, 1961-62.

*(This Listing Continued)*

Attorney and Counsellor of the U.S. Supreme Court. Member, Board of Directors of "Settlement Now". Member, Panel of Neutrals, American Arbitration Association. *Member:* Riverside County and American Bar Associations; The State Bar of California; Association of Business Trial Lawyers. *PRACTICE AREAS:* Real Property Litigation; Business Litigation; Probate and Trust Litigation; Title Insurance Litigation.

**CHRISTOPHER L. CARPENTER, (P.C.),** born Washington, D.C., September 24, 1940; admitted to bar, 1966, District of Columbia; 1968, California. *Education:* Pomona College (B.A., 1962); Yale University (LL.B., 1965). Phi Delta Phi. *Member:* Riverside County and American Bar Associations; The State Bar of California. Fellow, American College of Trust and Estate Planning Counsel. Fellow, College of Law Practice Management. (Managing Partner). *PRACTICE AREAS:* Estate Planning; Probate; Health Care.

**RICHARD T. ANDERSON, (P.C.),** born Scottsbluff, Nebraska, February 1, 1936; admitted to bar, 1963, Wyoming; 1964, Iowa; 1970, California. *Education:* University of Wyoming (B.S., 1959; LL.B., 1962). *Member:* Riverside County and American Bar Associations; The State Bar of California; Wyoming State Bar. *PRACTICE AREAS:* Municipal Finance Law; Natural Resources Law; Public Law.

**JOHN D. WAHLIN, (P.C.),** born Chicago, Illinois, June 10, 1946; admitted to bar, 1971, Wisconsin; 1972, California. *Education:* Augustana College (A.B., 1968); University of Wisconsin (J.D., 1971). Phi Beta Kappa; Order of the Coif. Member, Board of Editors, Wisconsin Law Review, 1969-1971. *Member:* Riverside County and American Bar Associations; The State Bar of California. *PRACTICE AREAS:* Employee Benefits Law; Taxation Law. *Email:* bbkjdw@pe.net

**MICHAEL D. HARRIS, (P.C.),** born Henderson, North Carolina, February 22, 1936; admitted to bar, 1973, California. *Education:* Louisburg College (A.S., 1966); North Carolina State University (B.S., 1968); University of North Carolina (J.D., 1973). Xi Sigma Pi; Gamma Sigma Delta; Phi Alpha Delta. *Member:* Riverside County and American Bar Associations; The State Bar of California. (Rancho Mirage Office). *PRACTICE AREAS:* Real Estate; Indian Land Law; Indian Financing Law.

**JOHN E. BROWN, (P.C.),** born Blissfield, Michigan, January 18, 1949; admitted to bar, 1975, California. *Education:* Claremont Men's College (B.A., magna cum laude, 1971); Occidental College (M.A., 1972); Boalt Hall School of Law, University of California (J.D., 1975). Public Affairs Fellow, CORO Foundation, Los Angeles, California, 1971-1972. *Member:* Riverside County and American Bar Associations; The State Bar of California; National Association of Bond Lawyers. (Also at San Diego Office). *PRACTICE AREAS:* School Law; Public Finance Law; Public Law; Redevelopment Law.

**MICHAEL T. RIDDELL, (P.C.),** born San Bernardino, California, May 3, 1951; admitted to bar, 1976, California. *Education:* University of Notre Dame (B.A., summa cum laude, 1973; J.D., 1976). Phi Beta Kappa. Roger Kiley Fellow. Associate Editor, Notre Dame Law Review, 1975-1976. *Member:* Riverside County Bar Association; The State Bar of California. *PRACTICE AREAS:* Public Law; Water Law; Land Use; Contract Law.

**MEREDITH A. JURY, (P.C.),** born Kansas City, Missouri, April 11, 1947; admitted to bar, 1976, California. *Education:* University of Colorado at Boulder (B.A., cum laude, 1969); University of Wisconsin-Madison (M.A., 1971; M.S., 1972); University of Wisconsin-Madison and University of California at Los Angeles (J.D., 1976). Phi Beta Kappa. President-elect, Inland Empire Bankruptcy Forum, 1993-1994. *Member:* Riverside County, San Bernardino County (Board Member, 1992-1993), Los Angeles County and American Bar Associations; The State Bar of California. (Ontario Office). *PRACTICE AREAS:* Business Litigation Law; Land Use and Natural Resources Law; Real Property Litigation; Bankruptcy Litigation Law.

**MICHAEL GRANT, (P.C.),** born Fairfield, Iowa, December 14, 1945; admitted to bar, 1977, California. *Education:* Brigham Young University (B.A., magna cum laude, 1970); Hastings College of the Law, University of California (J.D., 1977). Phi Kappa Phi; Order of the Coif. Member, Hastings Constitutional Law Quarterly, 1976-1977. *Member:* Riverside County and American Bar Associations; The State Bar of California. [U.S. Navy, 1970-1974; CDR, USNR, Ret.]. *PRACTICE AREAS:* Real Estate Law; Zoning and Subdivision Law; Real Estate Finance Law.

**FRANCIS J. BAUM, (P.C.),** born Hawthorne, California, February 1, 1949; admitted to bar, 1978, California. *Education:* University of California at Santa Barbara (B.S., with high honors, 1971); University of California at Los Angeles (M.J., 1973); University of California at Los Angeles School of Law (J.D., 1977). Phi Beta Kappa. *Member:* Riverside County and American Bar Associations; The State Bar of California; California Redevelop-

*(This Listing Continued)*

ment Association; California Association of Bond Lawyers; National Association of Bond Lawyers. *PRACTICE AREAS:* Public Finance Law.

**ANNE T. THOMAS, (P.C.),** born Norfolk, Virginia, September 22, 1936; admitted to bar, 1978, California. *Education:* Duke University (B.A., 1958); University of California at Los Angeles (J.D., 1978). Phi Beta Kappa. President, United Way of Riverside, 1983. Chair, Board of Trustees, Riverside Community Hospital, 1989-1992. Member, Advisory Council of the University of California Water Resources Center, 1990—. Contributing Editor (Water) CEB-Land Use & Environment Forum, 1994—. *Member:* Riverside County and American Bar Associations; The State Bar of California. *PRACTICE AREAS:* Water Rights Law; Environmental Land Use Law; Environmental Law; Hazardous Waste; Zoning Law.

**D. MARTIN NETHERY, (P.C.),** born Fort Sill, Oklahoma, March 27, 1948; admitted to bar, 1975, California; 1986, U.S. Supreme Court. *Education:* University of California at Los Angeles (A.B., 1972); University of Southern California (J.D., 1975). President, 1995, and Member, Board of Trustees, 1989—, Family YMCA and Youth Center. Member, Board of Trustees, College of the Desert Foundation, 1994—. *Member:* Desert (President, 1991-1992; Member, Board of Trustees, 1986-1993; Chairman, Attorney/Client Fee Arbitration Committee, 1987-1991), Riverside County and American Bar Associations; The State Bar of California. (Rancho Mirage Office). *PRACTICE AREAS:* General Business; Real Estate; Securities; Construction Litigation.

**GEORGE M. REYES,** born Riverside, California, August 15, 1953; admitted to bar, 1978, California. *Education:* Harvard College (B.A., cum laude, 1975); University of California at Davis (J.D., 1978). *Member:* Riverside County and American Bar Associations; The State Bar of California. *PRACTICE AREAS:* Mergers and Acquisitions; Private Financing; General Business Law; Tax Law; Estate Planning Law. *Email:* bbkgmr@pe.net

**WILLIAM W. FLOYD, JR.,** born San Bernardino, California, August 5, 1950; admitted to bar, 1979, California. *Education:* California State University at San Diego (B.A., 1972); McGeorge College of the Law, University of the Pacific (J.D., 1979). *Member:* Riverside County and American (Member, Labor Law Section) Bar Associations; The State Bar of California (Member, Labor and Employment Law Section). *PRACTICE AREAS:* Labor Law; Employment Law; Management Law.

**GREGORY L. HARDKE,** born Benton Harbor, Michigan, February 16, 1949; admitted to bar, 1976, California. *Education:* Michigan State University (B.S., cum laude, 1971); Hastings College of the Law, University of California (J.D., 1976). *Member:* Riverside County and American Bar Associations; The State Bar of California. *PRACTICE AREAS:* Real Estate Law.

**KENDALL H. MACVEY,** born Washington, D.C., October 13, 1948; admitted to bar, 1973, California. *Education:* Occidental College (B.A., magna cum laude, 1970); University of California at Los Angeles (J.D., 1973). Phi Beta Kappa. Author: "What Is Left of Municipal Antitrust Liability?" *Competition*, Spring, 1990; "The Unfair Competition Act," chapter in *California Antitrust Law* (State Bar 1992); " A Beginner's Guide to the Federal Clean Air Act," League of California Cities 1992 Conference. Co-Interviewer, "Interviews of Judges of the United States District Court for the Central District of California," *Daily Journal Report*, January 1989. Instructor, Eminent Domain, 1989-1990, Air Quality Law, 1991, University of Riverside California Extension. Member, Riverside Superior Court Policy Committee on the Trial Court Delay Reduction Act, 1987. Member, Federal Court Clerk Liaison Committee, U.S. District Court, Central District of California, 1995—. *Member:* Riverside County, Los Angeles County (Member, Executive Committee, 1987— and Chair, 1994-1995, Antitrust Section; Member, Executive Committee, Condemnation and Land Valuation Section, 1988-1991) and American Bar Associations; The State Bar of California (Member, Executive Committee, Antitrust and Trade Regulation Section, 1987-1990; Ex-Officio Member, 1990-1991; Chair, Unfair Competition Committee, 1989-1991); Los Angeles Complex Litigation Inn of Court. *PRACTICE AREAS:* Litigation; Antitrust/Unfair Competition; Eminent Domain; Air Quality Law.

**CLARK H. ALSOP,** born Salinas, California, January 19, 1947; admitted to bar, 1974, California. *Education:* Claremont Men's College (B.A., 1969); University of California at Berkeley (M.B.A., 1971); University of Santa Clara (J.D., 1974). Author: "A Lawful Hold-Up," Law Enforcement Journal, March, 1974; "San Jose Gets Proposal for Alarm Ordinance," The Police Chief, September, 1974. Deputy County Counsel, San Bernardino County, 1975-1985. Legal Counsel, California Association of Local Agency Formation Commissions, 1981—. City Attorney, Fontana, 1989—. City Attorney, Big Bear Lake, 1996—. *Member:* San Bernardino County, River-

*(This Listing Continued)*

## BEST BEST & KRIEGER LLP, Riverside—*Continued*

side County and American (Member, Section of Urban, State and Local Government Law) Bar Associations; State Bar of California (Member, Section of Public Law); Greater Inland Empire Municipal Law Association (Treasurer, 1985—); American Planning Association. *PRACTICE AREAS:* Municipal Law; Land Use and Environmental.

**DAVID J. ERWIN,** (P.C.), born Oklahoma City, Oklahoma, October 6, 1934; admitted to bar, 1958, Oklahoma; 1962, California; 1973, U.S. Supreme Court. *Education:* University of Oklahoma (B.A., 1957; LL.B., 1958). Phi Alpha Delta. City Attorney: Indio, 1964-1996; Palm Desert, 1973—; City of Rancho Mirage, 1983-1985; Indian Wells, 1969-1979; Cathedral City, 1993—. *Member:* Desert (Secretary, 1969; Vice-President, 1970; President, 1971-1972), Riverside County, Oklahoma and American Bar Associations; State Bar of California (Member, Sections on: Estate Planning and Trusts; Probate Law; Public Law). (Rancho Mirage Office).

**MICHAEL J. ANDELSON,** (P.C.), born Los Angeles, California, January 20, 1947; admitted to bar, 1972, California. *Education:* California State University at San Jose (B.S., 1968); Hastings College of the Law, University of California (J.D., 1971). Author: California Education of the Bar Civil Discovery Practice, Chapter on "Interrogatories," 1988. Deputy District Attorney, Riverside County, 1972-1974. *Member:* Desert (Chairman, Mandatory Fee Dispute Committee, 1981—; Treasurer, 1981; Secretary, 1982-1983; Vice President, 1983-1984; President, 1984-1985 ), Riverside County, Federal and American Bar Associations; State Bar of California (Chair, Committee to Confer with the California Medical Association, 1987-1988). (Rancho Mirage Office). *PRACTICE AREAS:* Business Law; Real Estate Law; Public Law; Litigation. *Email:* mandelson@counsel.com

**DOUGLAS S. PHILLIPS,** (P.C.), born Hagerstown, Maryland, June 11, 1951; admitted to bar, 1977, California; 1983, U.S. Supreme Court. *Education:* Syracuse University (B.A., cum laude, 1973); Syracuse University College of Law (J.D., 1976). Deputy City Attorney: City of Indio, 1979—; Palm Desert, 1979—. Assistant City Attorney City of Rancho Mirage, 1983-1985. Deputy City Attorney, Coachella, 1984-1988. City Attorney, City of Coachella, 1988-1990. *Member:* Desert and American Bar Associations; State Bar of California. (Rancho Mirage Office). *PRACTICE AREAS:* Civil Litigation; Environmental; Land Use; Public Law; Litigation.

**GREGORY K. WILKINSON,** born Los Angeles, California, October 19, 1947; admitted to bar, 1972, California; 1980, U.S. Supreme Court. *Education:* Claremont McKenna College (B.A., cum laude, 1969); Boalt Hall School of Law, University of California (J.D., 1972). Law Clerk to Justice Stephen K. Tamura, California Court of Appeal, 1972-1973. Author: "Role of Legislation in Land Use Planning For Developing Countries" U.N. FAO, 1985; "Delta Protection or Delta Ripoff: An Analysis of the California Delta Protection Act," Los Angeles Bar Journal, 1976. Lecturer, Environmental Law, Boalt Hall School of Law, 1978-1979. Deputy Attorney General, State of California, 1973-1982. Chief, Land and Water Law, United Nations Food and Agriculture Organization, Rome, Italy, 1982-1986. *Member:* The State Bar of California. *PRACTICE AREAS:* Water Rights Law; Water Quality Law; Endangered Species Law; Environmental Law. *Email:* gwilki02@counsel.com

**WYNNE S. FURTH,** born Berkeley, California, July 8, 1947; admitted to bar, 1973, California. *Education:* Stanford University (B.A., 1968); Harvard University (J.D., 1971). City Attorney: La Verne, California, 1975-1988; Claremont, 1978—. Trustee: Webb Schools of California, 1984-1986; Vivian Webb School, 1979-1984. Visiting Lecturer, Pitzer College, 1990. *Member:* Western San Bernardino County (Director, 1992-1994) and Los Angeles County Bar Associations; The State Bar of California (Member, Committee on Administration of Justice, 1980-1982); National Association of College and University Attorneys. (Ontario Office). *PRACTICE AREAS:* Land Use Law; Environmental Law; Public Law; Estate Planning.

**GENE TANAKA,** born Chicago, Illinois, June 5, 1956; admitted to bar, 1981, California. *Education:* Columbia University (B.A., 1978; J.D., 1981). Writing and Research Editor, Columbia Journal of Transnational Law, 1980-1981. Instructor, Course on Hazardous Materials Litigation, University of California Riverside Extension, 1992, 1994, 1995, 1996. Instructor/Assistant Team Leader, National Institute of Trial Advocacy, Rocky Mountain Region, 1992, 1994. Member, Advisory Committee on Hazardous Materials Management Certificate Program, University of California Riverside Extension, 1991-1995. *Member:* Riverside County Bar Association; State Bar of California; Japanese-American Bar Association of Southern California (Board of Governors, 1984-1985).

*(This Listing Continued)*

**BASIL T. CHAPMAN,** born Jersey City, New Jersey, August 7, 1947; admitted to bar, 1981, California. *Education:* Rutgers University, Newark (B.A., highest honors, 1976); California Western School of Law (J.D., magna cum laude, 1981). Phi Alpha Delta. Recipient, American Jurisprudence Awards: Civil Procedure; Conflicts of Law; Administrative Law; Family Law; Remedies; Property. Notes and Comments Editor, California Western Law Review, 1980-1981. Author: "Keener v. Municipal Court: Should A Discretionary Reduction Require a Mandatory Dismissal," 16 California Western Law Review 556, 1981. Judge Pro Tempore, Palm Springs Municipal Court. *Member:* Desert (Member, Judicial Evaluation Committee, Indio Superior Court Settlement Panel), Riverside County and American Bar Associations; The State Bar of California. (Rancho Mirage Office) (Certified Specialist, Family Law, The State Bar of California Board of Legal Specialization). *PRACTICE AREAS:* Litigation; Family Law.

**VICTOR L. WOLF,** born San Bernardino, California, July 29, 1958; admitted to bar, 1983, California. *Education:* Stanford University (A.B., 1980); Hastings College of the Law, University of California (J.D., 1983). *Member:* Riverside County and American Bar Associations; State Bar of California. *PRACTICE AREAS:* General Business Litigation; Real Property Law; Title Insurance Litigation.

**DANIEL E. OLIVIER,** born San Francisco, California, June 14, 1958; admitted to bar, 1983, California. *Education:* University of California at Santa Barbara; University of California at Berkeley (A.B., cum laude, 1980); McGeorge School of Law, University of the Pacific (J.D., 1983). Phi Delta Phi. *Member:* Desert, Riverside County and American Bar Associations; State Bar of California. (Rancho Mirage Office). *PRACTICE AREAS:* Real Estate Law; Redevelopment Law; Endangered Species.

**HOWARD B. GOLDS,** born Los Angeles, California, December 6, 1958; admitted to bar, 1983, California. *Education:* University of California at Riverside (B.A., with honors, 1980); University of Southern California (J.D., 1983). Staff Member, Southern California Law Review, 1981-1982. *Member:* Riverside County and American Bar Associations; The State Bar of California. *PRACTICE AREAS:* Public Resources; General Business; Litigation.

**STEPHEN P. DEITSCH,** born New York, N.Y., April 3, 1948; admitted to bar, 1974, New Jersey; 1979, California. *Education:* Brandeis University (B.A., cum laude, 1969); University of Pennsylvania (M.C.P., 1974; J.D., 1974). Law Clerk to Honorable Arthur C. Dwyer, Judge, Superior Court of New Jersey, 1974-1975. Attorney, Department of Law and Public Safety, Division of Law, State of New Jersey, 1975-1979; Pacific District Office of Special Counsel, U.S. Department of Energy, 1979-1981. *Member:* Los Angeles County, San Bernardino County and New Jersey State Bar Associations; State Bar of California. (Ontario Office). *PRACTICE AREAS:* Municipal Law; Redevelopment Law; Environmental Law; Real Estate Law; Land Use Law.

**MARC E. EMPEY,** born Palm Springs, California, April 10, 1957; admitted to bar, 1984, California. *Education:* University of California at Los Angeles (B.A., cum laude, 1979); Hastings College of the Law, University of California (J.D., 1984). Member, Moot Court Board. Adjunct Professor, University of California, Riverside, 1987—. *Member:* Riverside County and American Bar Associations; The State Bar of California. (Rancho Mirage Office). *PRACTICE AREAS:* Business Law; Securities Law; Health Care Law.

**JOHN R. ROTTSCHAEFER,** born Los Angeles, California, May 17, 1950; admitted to bar, 1984, California. *Education:* University of California at Riverside (A.B., with honors, 1981); Boalt Hall School of Law, University of California (J.D., 1984). Phi Beta Kappa. *Member:* Riverside County and American Bar Associations; The State Bar of California; National Association of Bond Lawyers. *PRACTICE AREAS:* Public Finance Law.

**MARTIN A. MUELLER,** born Oceanside, California, December 23, 1956; admitted to bar, 1984, California. *Education:* University of California at Santa Barbara (B.A., 1980); Hastings College of the Law, University of California (J.D., 1984). *Member:* Desert, Riverside County and American Bar Associations; The State Bar of California. (Rancho Mirage Office). *PRACTICE AREAS:* Business Litigation; Probate and Estate Litigation; Bankruptcy.

**J. MICHAEL SUMMEROUR,** born Dalton, Georgia, September 29, 1956; admitted to bar, 1984, California. *Education:* University of California at Santa Cruz (B.A., 1979); Loyola Law School at Los Angeles (J.D., 1984). *Member:* Riverside County and American Bar Associations; The State Bar of California. *PRACTICE AREAS:* Litigation.

*(This Listing Continued)*

**SCOTT C. SMITH,** born Salt Lake City, Utah, November 16, 1958; admitted to bar, 1985, California. *Education:* Utah State University (B.A., 1982); Brigham Young University (J.D., cum laude, 1985). Member, Brigham Young University Law Review, 1984-1985. Author: "The Crime Control Act of 1968 and Cordless Telephones: State v. Howard," 1984 B.Y.-U.L. Rev. 695. *Member:* San Diego County and American (Member, Section on Urban, State and Local Government Law) Bar Associations; The State Bar of California (Member, Section on Public Law); American Planning Association. (San Diego Office). *LANGUAGES:* Spanish.

**BRIAN M. LEWIS,** born Indio, California, March 9, 1957; admitted to bar, 1983, Colorado; 1986, California. *Education:* University of Southern California (B.S., 1979); University of Denver (J.D., 1983); New York University (LL.M. in Taxation, 1986). Certified Public Accountant, Colorado, 1983. *Member:* Riverside County, Colorado and American Bar Associations; The State Bar of California. (Rancho Mirage Office). *PRACTICE AREAS:* Tax; Estates; Business Law.

**JACK B. CLARKE, JR.,** born Sacramento, California, October 23, 1956; admitted to bar, 1985, California. *Education:* University of California at Riverside (B.S., 1980); McGeorge School of the Law, University of the Pacific (J.D., with distinction, 1985). Member, The Order of Barristers. Recipient, U.S. Law Week Award. *Member:* Riverside County, American and National Bar Associations; State Bar of California. *PRACTICE AREAS:* Litigation.

**BRADLEY E. NEUFELD,** born Loma Linda, California, December 5, 1960; admitted to bar, 1986, California. *Education:* University of California at Riverside (B.S., with honors, 1982); University of California at Los Angeles (J.D., 1986). *Member:* San Bernardino, Riverside County and American (Member, Labor Law Section) Bar Associations; The State Bar of California (Member, Labor and Employment Law Section). *PRACTICE AREAS:* Labor and Employment (Management) Law.

**PETER M. BARMACK,** born Mineola, New York, July 9, 1950; admitted to bar, 1981, California and U.S. Tax Court. *Education:* University of California at Riverside (A.B., 1972; M.A., 1975); University of La Verne (J.D., 1981). Instructor, Corporate Taxation, Partnership Taxation and Estate and Gift Taxation, University of California, Riverside, 1981—. Member, National Tax Association, Tax Institute of America, 1976—. Member, Board of Directors, Building Industry Association, 1989—. *Member:* Western San Bernardino County (Member, Board of Directors, 1984-1985), San Bernardino County and American Bar Associations; The State Bar of California. (Ontario Office). *PRACTICE AREAS:* Business Law; Real Estate Law; Taxation Law.

**MATT H. MORRIS,** born Seattle, Washington, December 21, 1960; admitted to bar, 1987, California. *Education:* Weber State College; Brigham Young University (B.A., 1984; J.D., 1987). *Member:* Desert, Riverside County and American Bar Associations; The State Bar of California. (Rancho Mirage Office). *LANGUAGES:* Spanish.

**JEFFREY V. DUNN,** born Salt Lake City, Utah, February 25, 1957; admitted to bar, 1987, California. *Education:* Brigham Young University (B.S., 1983; J.D., 1987). *Member:* Riverside County and American Bar Associations; The State Bar of California. *LANGUAGES:* Spanish. *PRACTICE AREAS:* Litigation. *Email:* jdunnn04@counsel.com

**STEVEN C. DEBAUN,** born Wilmington, Delaware, August 24, 1962; admitted to bar, 1987, California. *Education:* University of California at Berkeley (B.A., 1984); University of California at Los Angeles (J.D., 1987). Editorial Board Member, University of California Law Review, 1986-1987. *Member:* Riverside County and American Bar Associations; The State Bar of California. *PRACTICE AREAS:* Transportation Law; Municipal Law; Land Use/Environmental Law.

**ERIC L. GARNER,** born Lexington, Kentucky, August 9, 1962; admitted to bar, 1987, California. *Education:* Earlham College (A.B., with honors, 1984); University of Michigan (J.D., 1987). Co-Author: *California Water,* 1995; Article, "The Colorado River in the Twenty-First Century," Arizona State Law Journal, Vol. 27, No. 2, Summer 1995. Author: "Coping With Shortages: Allocating Water in the 1990's and Beyond," ABA Natural Resources and Environment Magazine, Spring, 1991; Article, "Institutional Reforms in California Groundwater Law," Pacific Law Journal, Vol. 25, No. 3, April 1994. *Member:* Riverside County and American (Member, Natural Resources Section) Bar Associations; The State Bar of California. *PRACTICE AREAS:* Environmental Law; Water Law.

**DENNIS M. COTA,** born Santa Maria, California, June 9, 1958; admitted to bar, 1987, California. *Education:* University of California at Los Angeles (B.S., 1983); University of California at Davis (J.D., 1986). Chairman, Trial Practice Honors Board, 1985-1986. *Member:* The State Bar of California; American Bar Association. (Ontario Office).

**PATRICK H.W.F. PEARCE,** born Elm Park, Essex, England, March 26, 1964; admitted to bar, 1986, United Kingdom and Commonwealth; 1988, California. *Education:* De Montfort University, Leicester, England (LL.B., Hon., 1985). Council of Legal Education, London, England, Gray's Inn, London, 1986—. *Member:* Los Angeles, Orange County, Riverside County and American Bar Associations; The State Bar of California; Gray's Inn of Court London. *PRACTICE AREAS:* Employment Litigation; Insurance Coverage Analysis and Litigation; Commercial Transactions.

**ROBERT W. HARGREAVES,** born Montebello, California, May 17, 1951; admitted to bar, 1988, California. *Education:* University of California at Berkeley (B.A., with great distinction in general scholarship, 1974); Boalt Hall School of Law, University of California (J.D., 1988). *Member:* Desert and Riverside County Bar Associations; The State Bar of California. (Rancho Mirage Office). *LANGUAGES:* Spanish. *REPORTED CASES:* Evans v. City of San Jose (1992) 3 Cal. App. 4th 728; City of Needles v. Griswold, 6 Cal. App. 4th 1881. *PRACTICE AREAS:* Public Law; Land Use Law; Land Use Litigation; Indian Law.

**C. MICHAEL COWETT,** born Los Angeles, California, January 24, 1946; admitted to bar, 1972, California. *Education:* University of California at Berkeley (A.B., 1968); University of California at Davis (J.D., 1972). Recipient, American Jurisprudence in Torts. Associate Editor, 1971-1972, University of California at Davis Law Review. *Member:* State Bar of California (Member, Executive Committee, Public Law Section). (San Diego Office). *PRACTICE AREAS:* Public Agency; Water Law.

**BRUCE W. BEACH,** born Memphis, Tennessee, June 1, 1945; admitted to bar, 1974, California. *Education:* Miami University of Ohio (B.A., 1967); California Western University Law School (J.D., 1973); Southern Methodist University (LL.M. in Government Regulation of Trade, 1974). Deputy County Counsel, Office of San Diego County Counsel, 1976-1987. Member, International Right of Way Association, 1978—. Member, State Bar of California Condemnation Committee, 1986-1988. [LTJG, USNR, 1967-1968]. (San Diego Office). *PRACTICE AREAS:* Condemnation Law; Land Use Law; Public Agency.

**ARLENE PRATER,** born Brooklyn, New York, August 21, 1947; admitted to bar, 1975, California. *Education:* University of Wisconsin (B.A., 1970); University of San Diego (J.D., 1975). Deputy County Counsel, Office of San Diego County Counsel, 1977-1988. (San Diego Office). *PRACTICE AREAS:* Employment Law; Labor Law; Public Agency; Education Law.

**JASON D. DABAREINER,** born Burlington, Wisconsin, January 29, 1963; admitted to bar, 1989, California and Wisconsin. *Education:* Ripon College; University of Minnesota (B.A., 1987); University of Wisconsin (J.D., cum laude, 1989). Wisconsin Land Title Association Scholarship. *Member:* Desert and American Bar Associations; The State Bar of California; State Bar of Wisconsin. (Rancho Mirage Office). *PRACTICE AREAS:* Real Estate Law; Business Law.

**MARK A. EASTER,** born Philadelphia, Pennsylvania, June 27, 1964; admitted to bar, 1989, California. *Education:* University of La Verne (B.A., magna cum laude, departmental honors in History/Political Science, 1986); University of California at Davis (J.D., 1989). Member, Riverside County Fee Arbitration Committee. *Member:* Riverside County Bar Association; The State Bar of California. *PRACTICE AREAS:* Business Litigation; Real Estate Litigation; Eminent Domain Litigation.

**MICHELLE OUELLETTE,** born Redlands, California, July 19, 1958; admitted to bar, 1989, California. *Education:* Kenyon College; University of California at Santa Cruz (B.A., with honors, Environmental Studies, 1980); University of Southern California (J.D., 1989). Staff Member, Journal of Law and the Environment, 1988-1989. Co-Author: "Institutional Reforms in Groundwater Law," 25 Pacific Law Journal 1021, 1994; "The Colorado River in the Twenty-First Century," 27 Arizona State University Law Journal 469 (1995). Contributing Author, *California Water Law,* 1995. *Member:* Riverside County (Director) and American (Member, Natural Resources Law Section) Bar Associations; The State Bar of California. *PRACTICE AREAS:* Environmental Law; Water Law; Natural Resources Law; Litigation.

*(This Listing Continued)*

## BEST BEST & KRIEGER LLP, Riverside—Continued

### ASSOCIATES

**WILLIAM D. DAHLING, JR.,** born Detroit, Michigan, August 24, 1956; admitted to bar, 1983, Michigan; 1987, California. *Education:* Williams College (B.A., cum laude, 1978); University of Michigan Law School (J.D., 1983). *Member:* Riverside County and American Bar Associations; State Bar of Michigan; The State Bar of California; American Judicature Society. **PRACTICE AREAS:** Estate Planning Law; Probate and Conservatorships.

**KIRK W. SMITH,** born Pomona, California, March 15, 1959; admitted to bar, 1986, California; 1989, District of Columbia. *Education:* Claremont McKenna College (B.A., 1981); University of Copenhagen, Copenhagen, Denmark; Georgetown University Law Center (J.D., 1984); University of Stockholm, Stockholm, Sweden (G.D., 1985). Phi Delta Phi. *Member:* Los Angeles County (Member, Sections on: Real Property; International Practice), Orange County (Member, Section on International Law), Riverside County (Member, Section on Real Property) and American (Member, Sections on: Real Property, Probate and Trust Law; International Practice) Bar Associations; The State Bar of California. **LANGUAGES:** Swedish. **PRACTICE AREAS:** Real Estate Finance; Leasing; Redevelopment; Business Transactions; International Trade Law.

**KYLE A. SNOW,** born Sacramento, California, October 23, 1962; admitted to bar, 1989, California. *Education:* Weber State College (B.A., magna cum laude, 1986); University of Washington (J.D., 1989). Phi Kappa Phi; Phi Sigma Alpha; Phi Sigma Iota. Recipient, American Jurisprudence Award, Insurance Law. *Member:* Riverside County and American Bar Associations; The State Bar of California; National Association of Bond Lawyers; Government Finance Officers Association. **LANGUAGES:** Spanish. **PRACTICE AREAS:** Public Finance Law.

**BERNIE L. WILLIAMSON,** born Omaha, Nebraska, July 17, 1958; admitted to bar, 1990, California. *Education:* University of Nebraska at Omaha (B.S., 1981; B.S., 1983); University of California at Los Angeles (J.D., 1989). Author: "Federal Family & Medical Leave Act of 1993" and "State Family Leave Law Amended", RCBA Bar Bulletin. President, Riverside Employer Advisory Council. *Member:* Riverside County and American (Member, Labor Law Section) Bar Associations; The State Bar of California (Member, Labor Law Section); African-American Attorneys of the Inland Empire. **PRACTICE AREAS:** Labor Law.

**KEVIN K. RANDOLPH,** born Los Angeles, California, May 23, 1958; admitted to bar, 1990, California. *Education:* California State University, Pomona (B.S., magna cum laude, 1982); Loyola Law School (J.D., cum laude, 1990). Phi Kappa Phi. Order of the Coif. Adjunct Professor, University of California. *Member:* Riverside County, San Bernardino County and American Bar Associations; The State Bar of California. (Ontario Office). **PRACTICE AREAS:** Public Agency Law; Redevelopment Law; Water Rights Law. *Email:* bbkkkr@pe.net

**MARY E. GILSTRAP,** born Burbank, California, September 18, 1961; admitted to bar, 1990, California. *Education:* California State University at Long Beach (B.A., in Journalism, 1985); University of Minnesota (J.D., 1990). *Member:* Desert and Federal Bar Associations; The State Bar of California (Member, Litigation Section); California Women Lawyers. (Rancho Mirage Office). **PRACTICE AREAS:** Appellate; Securities Fraud; General Business Litigation; Public Law Litigation.

**CYNTHIA M. GERMANO,** born Covina, California, April 20, 1965; admitted to bar, 1990, California. *Education:* Whittier College (B.A, in Political Science and Religion, magna cum laude, 1987); Loyola Law School (J.D., 1990). Recipient, Fritz Burns Three Year Full Scholarship. Author: "Do You Promise to Love, Honor and Equitably Divide Your Celebrity Status Upon Divorce?: A Look at the Development and Application of New York's Equitable Distribution Statute," 9 Loy. L.A. Ent. L.J. 153, 1989. *Member:* The State Bar of California. **PRACTICE AREAS:** Civil Litigation Law.

**KIM A. BYRENS,** born Long Beach, California, June 20, 1965; admitted to bar, 1990, California. *Education:* University of California at Irvine (B.A., 1987); University of San Diego (J.D., 1990). Comments Editor, San Diego Law Review, 1989-1990. *Member:* The State Bar of California; National Association of Bond Lawyers; California Association of Bond Lawyers. **PRACTICE AREAS:** Municipal Securities Law.

**JAMES B. GILPIN,** born Riverton, Wyoming, February 4, 1963; admitted to bar, 1990, California. *Education:* University of Wyoming (B.S., 1985; J.D., 1990). Order of the Coif. Casenote Editor, Land and Water Law Review, 1989-1990. Author: Casenote, "Foreclosure of Sweat Equity: Should a Hard Day's Work Be Worth an Honest Dollar," Vol. XXIV No. 2 Land and Water L. Rev. 515. Co-Author: Comment, "The New Wyoming Statutory Close Corporation Supplement: Should Your Corporation Elect Statutory Close Corporation Status?" Vol. XXV No. 2 Land and Water L. Rev. 589. Member, Inland Empire Bankruptcy Forum. *Member:* San Diego County Bar Association; The State Bar of California. (San Diego Office). **PRACTICE AREAS:** Eminent Domain; Land Use; Wrongful Termination Defense; Civil Litigation.

**G. HENRY WELLES,** born Boston, Massachusetts, January 28, 1963; admitted to bar, 1991, California. *Education:* Bucknell University (B.A., 1985); Washington University (J.D., 1991). *Member:* Desert and American Bar Associations; The State Bar of California. (Rancho Mirage Office). **PRACTICE AREAS:** Business Litigation; Probate and Estate Litigation; Real Estate Litigation.

**DINA O. HARRIS,** born La Mirada, California, June 6, 1967; admitted to bar, 1992, California. *Education:* Brigham Young University (B.S., 1988; M.Ed., 1991; J.D., 1991). *Member:* Riverside County Bar Association; The State Bar of California; California Council of School Attorneys. **PRACTICE AREAS:** School Law; Public Law; Environmental Law.

**BARBARA R. BARON,** born Chicago, Illinois, February 17, 1952; admitted to bar, 1977, California. *Education:* University of California at San Diego (B.A., with high honors, 1973); University of California, Hastings College of the Law (J.D., 1977). *Member:* Desert Bar Association; The State Bar of California. (Rancho Mirage Office). **PRACTICE AREAS:** Labor and Employment Litigation and Advice; Discrimination and Wrongful Termination Defense; Sexual Harassment Defense; Business Litigation; Public Labor and Employment Law and Litigation; Management Labor Relations Law; Pre-Termination Counseling for Business and Employers.

**RICHARD T. EGGER,** born Ann Arbor, Michigan, October 23, 1967; admitted to bar, 1992, California. *Education:* University of California at Riverside (B.A., cum laude, 1989); University of California at Davis (J.D., 1992). Senior Research Editor, University of California, Davis Law Review, 1991-1992. *Member:* San Bernardino County and American (Member, Litigation Section) Bar Associations; California Bankruptcy Forum. (Ontario Office). **PRACTICE AREAS:** Business Litigation; Probate Litigation; Bankruptcy Litigation.

**DEAN DERLETH,** born Harbor City, California, August 29, 1965; admitted to bar, 1992, California. *Education:* University of California at Irvine (B.A., cum laude, 1987); McGeorge School of Law, University of the Pacific (J.D., with distinction, 1992). Order of the Coif. Member, Traynor Honor Society. Recipient, American Jurisprudence Awards. Listed in Who's Who Among American Universities and Colleges. *Member:* Riverside County Bar Association; The State Bar of California (Member, Sections on: Environmental Law; Public Law). **PRACTICE AREAS:** Public Law; School Law; Environmental Law.

**HELENE P. DREYER,** born Detroit, Michigan, August 13, 1965; admitted to bar, 1992, California. *Education:* University of Michigan (B.A..Ed., 1987); University of Texas School of Law (J.D., 1992). *Member:* Desert, Riverside County and American Bar Associations; The State Bar of California. (Rancho Mirage Office). **PRACTICE AREAS:** Litigation; Family Law.

**SONIA RUBIO CARVALHO,** born West Covina, California, September 28, 1967; admitted to bar, 1992, California. *Education:* University of California at Irvine (B.A., cum laude, 1989); University of California at Los Angeles (J.D., 1992). Phi Beta Kappa. Member, Moot Court. Co-Editor-in-Chief, Chicano-Latino Law Review, 1991-1992. *Member:* Los Angeles County and American Bar Associations; The State Bar of California; Mexican-American Bar Association. (Ontario Office). **PRACTICE AREAS:** Municipal Law; Redevelopment Law; Land Use Law.

**PATRICIA BYARS CISNEROS,** born San Bernardino, California, March 16, 1964; admitted to bar, 1993, California. *Education:* University of California at Los Angeles (B.A., 1986); Georgetown University (M.A., 1989); University of Southern California (J.D., 1993). **PRACTICE AREAS:** Public Law (Municipal).

**JULIANN ANDERSON,** born Glendale, California, October 29, 1964; admitted to bar, 1990, California. *Education:* Stanford University (A.B., 1986); Harvard University (J.D., 1990). *Member:* Riverside County Bar Association. **PRACTICE AREAS:** Public Law; Public Law Litigation; Land Use.

**SUSAN DUMOUCHEL WILSON,** born Webster, Massachusetts, September 9, 1966; admitted to bar, 1991, California. *Education:* Yale Univer-

*(This Listing Continued)*

sity (B.A., 1988); Tulane Law School (J.D., 1991). *Member:* Riverside County Bar Association; State Bar of California. *PRACTICE AREAS:* Litigation.

**JACQUELINE E. BAILEY,** born Van Nuys, California, May 12, 1965; admitted to bar, 1993, California. *Education:* California State University at Northridge (B.A., cum laude, 1990); McGeorge School of Law, University of the Pacific (J.D., with distinction, 1993). Member, Traynor Honor Society. Recipient, American Jurisprudence Award in Professional Responsibility. Member, Trial Advocacy Competition Team, 1992-1993. Editor, The Transnational Lawyer, 1992-1993. Author: "Title VII Protections do not Extend to Americans Working Overseas," The Transnational Lawyer, Vol. 5, No. 1, Spring 1992. *Member:* Desert, Riverside County and American Bar Associations. (Rancho Mirage Office). *PRACTICE AREAS:* Civil Litigation.

**DAVID CABRAL,** born San Diego, California, March 8, 1963; admitted to bar, 1994, California. *Education:* Wheaton College (B.A., 1987); University of Notre Dame (J.D., 1994). Member, National Appellate Moot Court Team. Recipient, Harold S. Weber Award for Excellence in Oral Advocacy. (San Diego Office).

**DAVID J. HANCOCK,** born American Fork, Utah, December 19, 1966; admitted to bar, 1994, California. *Education:* Brigham Young University (B.A., 1991; J.D., 1994).

**MARC T. RASICH,** born Montebello, California, November 18, 1968; admitted to bar, 1994, California. *Education:* University of San Diego (B.A., 1991); University of Utah (J.D., 1994). Leary Scholar. Member, University of Utah Law Review, 1991-1994. *PRACTICE AREAS:* Litigation.

**PHILIP M. SAVAGE, IV,** born San Bernardino, California, June 9, 1967; admitted to bar, 1994, California. *Education:* Stanford University (B.A., 1989); Loyola Law School of Los Angeles (J.D., 1994). Assistant Chief Articles Editor, Loyola of Los Angeles Law Review, 1993-1994. *PRACTICE AREAS:* Estate Planning; Trust Administration; Business Transactions; Healthcare.

**ANA MARIA Z. FREDGREN,** born New Orleans, Louisiana, January 26, 1968; admitted to bar, 1995, California. *Education:* University of Southern California (B.S., magna cum laude, 1989); Cornell Law School (J.D., 1994). President, Latino-American Law Students Association. (Rancho Mirage Office). *LANGUAGES:* Spanish. *PRACTICE AREAS:* General Business Transactional.

**KAREN M. LEWIS,** born Sacramento, California, March 4, 1959; admitted to bar, 1995, California. *Education:* Glendale University College of Law (B.S., 1993; J.D., 1994). (Ontario Office). *PRACTICE AREAS:* Litigation; Bankruptcy; Public Law.

**HAYLEY ELIZABETH PETERSON,** born Milwaukee, Wisconsin, August 22, 1970; admitted to bar, 1995, Wisconsin and California. *Education:* University of Arizona (B.A., cum laude, 1992); University of Wisconsin-Madison (J.D., cum laude, 1995). Order of the Coif. (San Diego Office). *LANGUAGES:* Spanish. *PRACTICE AREAS:* Public Law; Litigation.

**MICHAEL J. SCHAEFER,** born Aberdeen, South Dakota, March 4, 1970; admitted to bar, 1995, California. *Education:* University of New Mexico (B.B.A., with distinction, 1992); University of California at Davis (J.D., 1995). Articles Editor, U.C. Davis Law Review, 1994-1995. *Member:* Riverside County Bar Association; State Bar of California. *PRACTICE AREAS:* Litigation.

**ZACHARY R. WALTON,** born Walnut Creek, California, January 23, 1970; admitted to bar, 1995, California. *Education:* University of California (B.A., 1992); Vanderbilt School of Law (J.D., 1995). *PRACTICE AREAS:* Natural Resources; Water; Endangered Species; Public Law.

**SANDY A. JACOBSON,** born Bloomer, Wisconsin, February 13, 1970; admitted to bar, 1995, California. *Education:* University of California at Los Angeles (B.A., 1992); Loyola Law School (J.D., 1995). (Rancho Mirage Office). *PRACTICE AREAS:* Public Law.

**JEFFREY S. FLASHMAN,** born Atlanta, Georgia, February 21, 1965; admitted to bar, 1992, California. *Education:* Wesleyan University (B.A., 1987); University of California at Davis; Boalt Hall School of Law, University of California (J.D., 1992). Recipient: American Jurisprudence Award in Criminal Law, 1990; Prosser Prize in Criminal Procedure, 1991. *Member:* State Bar of California. (Rancho Mirage Office).

**JEFFREY T. MELCHING,** born San Jose, California, June 15, 1969; admitted to bar, 1995, California. *Education:* University of California at Los Angeles (B.A., 1992); King Hall School of Law, University of Califor-

*(This Listing Continued)*

nia at Davis (J.D., 1995). (Ontario Office). *PRACTICE AREAS:* Litigation; Bankruptcy.

**SCOTT D. HOWIE,** born March 2, 1962; admitted to bar, 1995, California. *Education:* Pomona College (B.A., 1992); Boalt Hall School of Law, University of California (J.D., 1995). *PRACTICE AREAS:* Business.

**MARGUERITE S. STRAND,** born Milwaukee, Wisconsin, May 25, 1949; admitted to bar, 1989, California. *Education:* Macalester College (B.A., 1971); University of Chicago (M.A., 1974); University of San Diego (J.D., 1989). *Member:* San Diego County and American Bar Associations; State Bar of California; California Women Lawyers. (San Diego Office). *PRACTICE AREAS:* Public Law; Environmental; Water.

**ROGER K. CRAWFORD,** born San Pedro, California, February 19, 1965; admitted to bar, 1993, California. *Education:* Brigham Young University (B.A., 1989); Loyola Law School (J.D., 1993). Field Attorney, National Labor Relations Board, Region 21, 1993-1995. *LANGUAGES:* Spanish. *PRACTICE AREAS:* Labor and Employment.

**KEITH L. HIGGINS,** born Iowa City, Iowa, February 25, 1944; admitted to bar, 1986, California. *Education:* Augustana College (B.A., 1966); Citrus Belt Law School (J.D., Valedictorian, 1986). Deputy City Attorney: Victorville, 1987—; Barstow, 1987. *Member:* San Bernardino County Bar Association; State Bar of California. [With USAF, 1966-1978]. (Victorville Office). *PRACTICE AREAS:* Municipal; Civil Litigation; Business; Corporate; Personal Injury.

**JOHN R. PERRY,** born Roanoke, Virginia, October 21, 1966; admitted to bar, 1995, California. *Education:* University of Virginia (B.A., 1990; J.D., 1995). *PRACTICE AREAS:* Business Transactions; Mergers and Acquisitions.

**SHAWN HAGERTY,** born Greeley, Colorado, December 31, 1968; admitted to bar, 1995, Wisconsin; 1996, California. *Education:* College of William and Mary (B.A., cum laude, 1991); University of Wisconsin (J.D., cum laude, 1995). Member, International Right of Way Association. (San Diego Office). *PRACTICE AREAS:* Eminent Domain; Litigation.

**MITCHELL L. NORTON,** born Los Angeles, California, December 20, 1965; admitted to bar, 1993, California; 1994, U.S. District Court, Central and Eastern Districts of California and U.S. Court of Appeals, Ninth Circuit. *Education:* University of California at Los Angeles (B.A., summa cum laude, 1988); Georgetown University (J.D., 1993). Phi Eta Sigma; Phi Beta Kappa. Managing Editor, American Criminal Law Review, 1992-1993. Co-Author, "Government Contract Fraud," 29 American Criminal Law Review 429, 1992. *Member:* Los Angeles County, Federal and American Bar Associations; State Bar of California (Litigation Section). *LANGUAGES:* Spanish. *PRACTICE AREAS:* Litigation.

**PEDRO C. DALLARDA,** born Buenos Aires, Argentina, November 16, 1965; admitted to bar, 1992, Ohio; 1995, California; 1996, District of Columbia. *Education:* Georgetown University (B.S.F.S., magna cum laude, 1989; J.D., 1992). *Member:* American Bar Association (International Law Section, 1992-1994). [Argentine Navy, Lieutenant, 1982-1984]. *LANGUAGES:* Spanish, Italian, French. *PRACTICE AREAS:* Business Litigation; Employment Law.

**KRISTI LYNN GUDOSKI,** born Plainfield, New Jersey, September 22, 1971; admitted to bar, 1996, California. *Education:* Colgate University (B.A., 1993); University of Southern California (J.D., 1996). Recipient, Miller Johnson Equal Justice Award. President, 1994-1995 and Executive Board Member, 1995—, Public Interest Law Foundation. *PRACTICE AREAS:* Litigation.

**CARYN LEIGH CRAIG,** born Wilmington, Delaware; admitted to bar, 1996, California. *Education:* University of California, Los Angeles (B.A., 1992); Hastings College of the Law, University of California (J.D., 1996). (San Diego Office).

**KEVIN COLLINS,** born San Bernardino, California, March 30, 1970; admitted to bar, 1996, California. *Education:* University of the Redlands (B.A., 1992); McGeorge School of Law, University of the Pacific (J.D., highest honors, 1996). Member, Traynor Honor Society. Moot Court Top Oralist. *PRACTICE AREAS:* Litigation.

**JAMES P. MORRIS,** born San Bernardino, California, May 23, 1968; admitted to bar, 1996, California. *Education:* Dartmouth College (B.A., 1990); University of California at Los Angeles (M.A., Urban Planning, 1996; J.D., 1996). *PRACTICE AREAS:* Public Law; Environmental Law; Water Law; Land Use Law.

**DWIGHT M. MONTGOMERY,** born Seoul, South Korea, October 26, 1958; admitted to bar, 1989, California; 1990, U.S. Tax Court. *Education:*

*(This Listing Continued)*

## BEST BEST & KRIEGER LLP, Riverside—Continued

University of Michigan (B.S., 1985; J.D., 1989); University of Toledo. Attorney, Office of Chief Counsel, Internal Revenue Service, Department of Treasury, 1991-1996. *Member:* Los Angeles County, Riverside County and American Bar Associations; State Bar of California. **LANGUAGES:** German.

### OF COUNSEL

**JOHN C. TOBIN,** born Sacramento, California, February 16, 1952; admitted to bar, 1980, Kentucky; 1991, U.S. District Court, Central District of California; 1993, California. *Education:* University of Kentucky (B.A., Honors Program, 1974); University of Louisville (J.D., 1980). Delta Theta Phi. Member, Journal of Law and Education. Author: "Now You See 'Em, Now You Don't: Appearances & Protection Under the Soldiers & Sailors' Act," The Barrister, Penn Trial Lawyers Association, Summer, 1991. *Member:* Riverside County, Orange County, Louisville and Kentucky Bar Associations; State Bar of California; Inland Empire Bankruptcy Forum (Director, 1994-1997); Orange County Bankruptcy Forum. [Lieutenant Colonel, U.S. Army, JAGC Corp., 1980-1983; Reserve, 1983—]. **PRACTICE AREAS:** Bankruptcy; Financial Litigation.

**DONALD F. ZIMMER,** born Newark, New Jersey, June 19, 1933; admitted to bar, 1963, California. *Education:* Riverside City College (A.A., 1959); University of Southern California (B.S.L., 1962; J.D., 1963). Phi Alpha Delta. Member, Board of Editors, Southern California Law Review, 1962-1963. Master Member, Leo A. Deegan Inn of Court. *Member:* Riverside County and American Bar Associations; The State Bar of California. [Pilot, USAF, 1952-1957]. **PRACTICE AREAS:** General Civil Law; Trial Law; Appellate Practice; Real Estate Law; Municipal Law; Corporate Law; Business Law; Estate Planning Law; Probate Law.

**HENRY R. KRAFT, (P.C.),** born Los Angeles, California, April 27, 1946; admitted to bar, 1972, California. *Education:* San Fernando Valley State College (B.A., 1968); University of Southern California (J.D., 1972). Phi Alpha Delta; Pi Sigma Alpha; Phi Alpha Theta. Deputy Public Defender, 1972-1978. Victorville Assistant City Attorney, 1978-1979. Acting Needles City Attorney, 1981-1982. Barstow City Attorney, 1980—. Victorville City Attorney, 1987—. *Member:* High Desert Bar Association (Secretary, 1980; Vice President, 1981; President, 1982), San Bernardino County (Member: Client Relations Committee, 1983; Fee Dispute Committee, 1983—), Los Angeles County and American Bar Associations; State Bar of California; California Trial Lawyers Association; League of California Cities (Legal Advocacy Committee, Executive Committee, 1992); California Society for Health Care Attorneys. (Victorville Office). **PRACTICE AREAS:** Municipal Law; Business Litigation; Personal Injury.

REPRESENTATIVE CLIENTS: ARCO; Cities of Palm Desert, Corona, Fontana, Claremont, Azusa and Santa Maria; County of Riverside; Desert Water Agency; Eisenhower Medical Center; First American Title Insurance Co.; Hunter Engineering Co.; The Irvine Company; Kaiser Steel Resources; La Quinta Country Club; Loma Linda Orthopedic Medical Group, Inc.; Nevada Power Co.; Pitzer College; Press Enterprise Co.; Redevelopment Agencies of Corona, Riverside, Rancho Cucamonga, Westminster and Indio; Texaco, Inc.; Del Webb Corporation; Riverside Community Hospital; San Bernardino and Orange Local Agency Formation Commission; Metropolitan Water District of Southern California; Pomona and Riverside Unified School Districts; Rancho Las Flores Limited Partnership; Valley Health System; Antelope Valley - East Kern Water Agency; State Water Contractors; Western Municipal Water District; Crestline - Lake Arrowhead Water Agency; Running Springs Water Agency; Anheuser - Busch; Friant Water Users Assn.; Newhall Land and Farming Co.; Motel 6; Riverside Community College District; Union Bank; Stone & Youngberg; Paine Webber, Inc.; Chilton & O'Connor, Inc.; Housing Authority of the County of Kern; Gage Canal Co.; Rancon Financial Corp.; Commonwealth Land Title Insurance Co.; Regents of University of California; Santa Ynez River Water Conservation District ID#1; Castroville Agricultural Water Coalition; California Water Service Co.; California Artichoke, Inc.; Riverside Medical Clinic, Inc.; Coachmen Industries, Inc.; Southeastern California Association of Seventh-Day Adventists; Metropolitan Life Insurance Co.; Richmond American Homes of California; City Azusa; City of Santa Maria; Unocal Land & Development Company; Continental-Lawyers Title Insurance Corporation; The Mills Corporation.

CAA1726B

## BONNE, BRIDGES, MUELLER, O'KEEFE & NICHOLS

*PROFESSIONAL CORPORATION*

3403 TENTH STREET, SUITE 800
P.O. BOX 747
**RIVERSIDE, CALIFORNIA 92501-0747**
Telephone: 909-788-1944
Fax: 909-782-4666

*Los Angeles, California Office:* 3699 Wilshire Boulevard, 10th Floor, 90010-2719. Telephone: 213-480-1900. Fax: 213-738-5888.
*Santa Ana, California Office:* 1750 East Fourth Street, Suite 450, P.O. Box 22018, 92702-2018. Telephone: 714-835-1157. Fax: 714-480-2585.
*Santa Barbara, California Office:* 801 Garden Street, Suite 300, 93101-5502. Telephone: 805-965-2992. Fax: 805-962-6509.
*San Luis Obispo, California Office:* 1060 Palm Street, 93401-3221. Telephone: 805-541-8350. Fax: 805-541-6817.

*General Insurance Defense, Professional Malpractice, Products Liability Claims, Drug and Medical Device Claims, Environmental and Toxic Tort Claims, Insurance and Wrongful Termination, Professional Administrative Hearing Counsel.*

(For complete biographical data on all personnel and list of representative clients, see Professional Biographies at Los Angeles, California)

## LAW OFFICES OF TERRY BRIDGES

Established in 1986

MISSION SQUARE PLAZA
3750 UNIVERSITY AVENUE, SUITE 240
**RIVERSIDE, CALIFORNIA 92501-3313**
Telephone: 909-682-2760
Facsimile: 909-682-8626

*Civil Trial Practice.*

**TERRY BRIDGES,** born Riverside, California, October 10, 1940; admitted to bar, 1966, California and U.S. District Court, Central District of California; 1981, U.S. Court of Appeals, Ninth Circuit. *Education:* Santa Clara University (B.A., 1962); University of Southern California (LL.B., 1965). Author: "Advice from Outside," California Lawyer, October 1985; "Careful Evaluation of Your Cases Is the Key to Successful Lawyering," California Lawyer, February, 1991; "More Effective Case Analysis," The Idaho Trial Lawyer, Summer, 1991; "Evaluating Your Cases," Bench & Bar of Minnesota, April 1994. "Court-ordered Mini-Trial With--A Participant's Perspective," California Litigation, May, 1996. Faculty: Hastings College of Trial Advocacy, Hastings College of Law, 1978-1990; Riverside County Bar Association Civil Litigation Seminar, 1985-1993. Guest Lecturer: le Centre de Formation Professionnelle des Avocats de Paris, Paris, France, 1991; University of California at Riverside, International Lawyers Conference, 1994, 1995. Member, Riverside Charter Review Commission, 1980-1981. Chair, 1992-1993, Riverside-San Bernardino Federal Court Project. Member, University of Santa Clara Law School Board of Visitors, 1993—. Member, Riverside Community Hospital Bio-Ethics Committee, 1985-1992. Chair, Scripps College Association of Families, 1986-1987. Listed in "The Best Lawyers in America," 1993-1994 and 1994-1995 and 1995-1996. Founding Member and Master, Leo A. Deegan Inns of Court. *Member:* Riverside County (President, 1987-1988; Chair, Courts and Calendar Committee, 1979-1981; Chair, Judicial Evaluation Committee, 1990—; Member, Alternative Dispute Resolution Committee, 1994-1996; Member, Board of Directors, Alternative Dispute Services, Inc.), Los Angeles County and American (Member, Litigation Section) Bar Associations; State Bar of California; Association of Business 5rial Lawyers. **PRACTICE AREAS:** Civil Litigation.

### ASSOCIATE

**ALAN J. LEAHY,** born Arcadia, California, May 14, 1967; admitted to bar, 1994, California and U.S. District Court, Northern District of California. *Education:* University of California at Los Angeles (B.A., 1990); Santa Clara University (J.D., 1994). *Member:* Riverside County and American Bar Associations; State Bar of California. **PRACTICE AREAS:** Civil Litigation.

*LEGAL SUPPORT PERSONNEL*
*(This Listing Continued)*

*PARAPROFESSIONAL*

**Mechelle Winsor**

REPRESENTATIVE CLIENTS: California Portland Cement; Denny's Inc.; El Pollo Loco, Inc.; Flagstar Companies, Inc.; Flagstar Corporation; The Press-Enterprise; Stewart/Walker Co.; The Vons Companies, Inc.; Winchell's Donut House Operating Co.

---

## BUTTERWICK, BRIGHT & O'LAUGHLIN, INC.

*A PROFESSIONAL LAW CORPORATION*

Established in 1953

4000 TENTH STREET
P.O. BOX 1229
**RIVERSIDE, CALIFORNIA 92502**
Telephone: 909-686-3092
Telefax: 909-684-5743

*Civil Litigation, Commercial Law, Collection, Financial Institutions Law, Debtor-Creditor Relations, Insolvency and Bankruptcy Law, Business, Torts, Probate, Estate Planning, Real Property, Family Law, Homeowner Association Law.*

**J. D. BUTTERWICK,** born Devils Lake, North Dakota, August 7, 1923; admitted to bar, 1948, North Dakota; 1952, California. *Education:* University of North Dakota (Ph.B., 1948; J.D., 1948). Phi Delta Phi; Scabbard and Blade. Assistant State's Attorney, Benson County, North Dakota, 1948-1951. Deputy City Attorney, Los Angeles, California, 1957-1959. *Member:* Riverside County Bar Association (President, 1976-1977); The State Bar of California. *PRACTICE AREAS:* Homeowners Association Law; Real Property Law; Corporate Law.

**MICHAEL T. BRIGHT,** born Long Beach, California, March 27, 1942; admitted to bar, 1968, California. *Education:* University of New Mexico and Humboldt State College (A.B., 1964); California Western University (J.D., 1967). Phi Delta Phi. *Member:* Riverside County Bar Association (Treasurer, 1973-1974); The State Bar of California; Riverside County Barristers (President, 1972). *PRACTICE AREAS:* Family Law; Estate Planning Law; Probate Law.

**JOHN F. O'LAUGHLIN,** born Chicago, Illinois, December 31, 1953; admitted to bar, 1982, California. *Education:* San Diego State University (B.A., 1977); University of San Diego (J.D., magna cum laude, 1981). *Member:* Riverside County Bar Association; The State Bar of California. *PRACTICE AREAS:* Civil Litigation; Construction Law; Commercial Law.

**ROBERT J. MITCHELL,** born Ft. Campbell, Kentucky, November 11, 1952; admitted to bar, 1989, California. *Education:* University of California at Riverside (B.A., with honors, 1974; M.A., Political Science, 1975; Ph.D. Political Science, 1980); Loyola University Law School of Los Angeles (J.D., 1989). Author: "Peace in the Fields: A Study of the 1975 California Agricultural Labor Relations Act." Instructor: American Politics, University of California, Riverside, Political Science Department, 1981; Constitutional Law, 1980-1985, Business Law, 1989, and Personal Injury, 1990, University of California, Riverside, Extension, 1980-1985; American Politics, Chaffey Community College, 1983; Constitutional Law, University of California, San Diego, 1982-1984; Business Law, California State University, San Bernardino, 1990. *Member:* Riverside County Bar Association; State Bar of California. *PRACTICE AREAS:* Business Litigation; Real Property Law; Personal Injury Law.

REPRESENTATIVE CLIENTS: Empire Nissan, Inc.; Romero Motors Corp.; Canyon Lake Property Owners Assn.; Rockledge Gardens Condominium Assn.; Laguna Lido, Inc.; Riverside Acoustics, Inc.; Butler Advertising; Continental Dataforms; American Danatron Corp.; Powell Pipe & Supply Co.; California Custom Design, Inc; RED-E-Kamp; Certified Restoration Services; Braemar Homeowners Assoc.; FPC Graphics; Corona Aluminum Co.; Proclaim Construction, Inc.; No-View Development, Inc.; Diversified Construction Equip., Inc.; Vine-Life Christian Fellowship, Inc.; Life Church of God in Christ. REFERENCE: Riverside National Bank.

---

## CALDWELL & KENNEDY

*A PROFESSIONAL CORPORATION*

**RIVERSIDE, CALIFORNIA**

(See Victorville)

*Corporate, Real Property, Business, Commercial Transactions, Construction Disputes, Civil Litigation, Family Law, Estate Planning, Wills and Trusts, Personal Injury Law. Criminal Law and Special Appearances in Local, State and Federal Courts.*

---

## THE CARLOS LAW FIRM

*A PROFESSIONAL CORPORATION.*

2000 MARKET STREET
**RIVERSIDE, CALIFORNIA 92501**
Telephone: 909-686-2310
Fax: 909-686-2640

General Practice.

**MARY JO CARLOS,** born Riverside, California, April 11, 1951; admitted to bar, 1983, California. *Education:* University of San Diego (B.A., 1972); University of Santa Clara (J.D., 1982). *Member:* Riverside County Bar Association; State Bar of California. *LANGUAGES:* Spanish. *PRACTICE AREAS:* Workers Compensation Law; Personal Injury Defense.

**WILFRED J. SCHNEIDER, JR.,** born Whittier, California, April 17, 1951; admitted to bar, 1979, California; 1982, U.S. District Court, Central District of California and U.S. Court of Appeals, Ninth Circuit. *Education:* Rio Hondo College (A.A., 1972); University of California (B.A., 1974); Southwestern University (J.D., 1978). Member, Panel of Arbitrators: Riverside County Superior Court, San Bernardino County Superior Court; American Arbitration Association. *Member:* San Bernardino County and American Bar Associations; State Bar of California; Association of Southern California Defense Counsel.

**DONALD F. CASH,** born Atlanta, Georgia, May 7, 1951; admitted to bar, 1979, California; 1981, Georgia. *Education:* University of Georgia; University of Redlands (B.A., 1973); University of LaVerne (J.D., 1979). *Member:* San Bernardino County (Member, Workers Compensation and Insurance Section) and American Bar Associations; State Bar of California; State Bar of Georgia. *PRACTICE AREAS:* Personal Injury; Insurance Defense.

**MARILEE M. REYNOLDS,** born Chicago, Illinois, August 30, 1942; admitted to bar, 1986, California and U.S. District Court, Central District of California; 1991, U.S. Supreme Court. *Education:* California State University, Fullerton (B.A., 1982); Western State University (J.D., 1985). *Member:* State Bar of California. *PRACTICE AREAS:* Personal Injury.

REPRESENTATIVE CLIENTS: CIGNA; Insurance Company of North America.

---

## CHANDLER & ASSOCIATES

3800 ORANGE STREET, SUITE 270
**RIVERSIDE, CALIFORNIA 92501**
Telephone: 909-276-3022
Fax: 909-782-0230

*General Civil Litigation, Family Law, Landlord and Tenant, Consumer Contracts, Lemon Law.*

**ROBERT C. CHANDLER, (P.L.C.),** born Seoul, Korea, October 22, 1956; admitted to bar, 1988, California; 1989, New Mexico; U.S. District Court, Central District of New Mexico. *Education:* Suffolk University (B.S.B.A., 1980); New Hampshire College (M.B.A., 1982); Loyola Law School (J.D., 1988). *Member:* Riverside and San Bernardino County Bar Associations; State Bar of California. *PRACTICE AREAS:* General Civil Litigation (Contracts) (60%, 140); Family Law (40%, 65).

**STEVEN M. MATULIS,** born Parma, Ohio, July 8, 1966; admitted to bar, 1994, California; 1995, U.S. District Court, Central District of California. *Education:* University of California at Los Angeles (B.A., Economics-/International Area Studies, 1988); University of California, Hasting College of the Law (J.D., 1994). Phi Beta Kappa. *Member:* Riverside, San Bernadino County and American Bar Associations; State Bar of California. *PRACTICE AREAS:* Civil Litigation (70%, 140); Business Litigation (20%, 20); Family Law.

*(This Listing Continued)*

## CHANDLER & ASSOCIATES, Riverside—Continued

**MICKEY WALKER,** born Gallatin, Tennessee, May 29, 1954; admitted to bar, 1995, California; 1996, U.S. District Court, Central District of California. *Education:* Volunteer State Community College (A.S., 1973); California Southern Law School (J.D., 1995). *Member:* Los Angeles and Riverside County Bar Associations; State Bar of California. **PRACTICE AREAS:** Contract Disputes (50%, 80); Warranty & Lemon Law (30%, 40); Real Property/ Unlawful Detainer (10%, 15); Family Law (10%, 15).

---

## CUMMINGS & KEMP
A PROFESSIONAL CORPORATION

3877 TWELFTH STREET, SUITE 200
**RIVERSIDE, CALIFORNIA 92501**
Telephone: 909-781-1929
Fax: 909-788-9040

Santa Ana, California Office: 1851 East First Street, Suite 1000. Telephone: 714-835-8858. Fax: 714-835-1342.

General Civil Trial and Appellate Practice in State and Federal Courts. Insurance, Corporation, Negligence, Malpractice, Construction, Products Liability and Public Entity Defense Law.

FIRM PROFILE: *Cummings & Kemp was established in 1982 as a law firm specializing in the defense of claims for money damages against our clients, which have generally been submitted to us through an insurance carrier. The founding partners, Thomas Cummings and Clive Kemp, have been involved in defense litigation for their entire careers.*

*Mr. Cummings and Mr. Kemp both belong to the American Board of Trial Advocates, a national organization composed of trial attorneys from both the plaintiffs' attorneys' bar and the defense attorneys' bar who have handled at least 20 jury trials to a conclusion in a court of general jurisdiction, which is a prerequisite for consideration for membership in that organization.*

REPRESENTATIVE CLIENTS: Farmers Insurance Group of Cos.; State Farm Fire & Casualty Co.; INA/AETNA Insurance; Westfield Insurance; City of Garden Grove; Regents of the University of California; Peck/Jones Contractor.
REFERENCES: Peck/Jones Contractor, Los Angeles, California; Wells Fargo Bank, Santa Ana, California; Regents of the University of California; City of Garden Grove.

(For Complete Biographical Data on all Personnel, see Professional Biographies at Santa Ana, California)

---

## DICKMAN & HOLT
3638 UNIVERSITY AVENUE
SUITE 212
**RIVERSIDE, CALIFORNIA 92501-3349**
Telephone: 909-683-3693
Facsimile: 909-683-3670
Email: DICKHOLT@viasub.net

General Civil and Trial Practice in all State and Federal Courts. Construction Law, Landslide and Subsidence, Design Professionals, Product Liability, Premises Liability, Government Liability, Transportation Accidents, Errors and Omissions, Business and Commercial Litigation, Real Estate Litigation and Insurance.

### MEMBERS OF FIRM

**JOHN G. DICKMAN,** born Modesto, California, August 31, 1959; admitted to bar, 1986, California; 1987, New York; 1988, District of Columbia; U.S. District Court, Eastern, Southern, Central and Northern Districts of California; U.S. Court of Appeals, Ninth Circuit. *Education:* University of California at Berkeley (B.A., 1981); Northern Illinois University (M.B.A., 1983); McGeorge School of Law, University of the Pacific (J.D., 1986). Phi Alpha Delta; Order of the Barristers. *Member:* Riverside County Bar Association; New York State Bar Association; State Bar of California; District of Columbia Bar.

**MONTESSA D. HOLT,** born Stuttgart, Germany, December 10, 1958; admitted to bar, 1987, California; 1988, U.S. District Court, Eastern, Southern, Central and Northern Districts of California and U.S. Court of Appeals, Ninth Circuit. *Education:* California State University at Fullerton (B.A., 1982; M.A., 1983); McGeorge School of Law, University of the Pa-

*(This Listing Continued)*

cific (J.D., 1986). Recipient, American Jurisprudence Award in Creditors Rights and Debtors Remedies. *Member:* Riverside County Bar Association; State Bar of California.

REFERENCE: Wells Fargo Bank, Riverside, California.

---

## ERICKSEN, ARBUTHNOT, KILDUFF, DAY & LINDSTROM, INC.
Established in 1950

1770 IOWA AVENUE, SUITE 210
**RIVERSIDE, CALIFORNIA 92507-2403**
Telephone: 909-682-3246
Fax: 909-682-4013

Oakland, California Office: 530 Water Street, Port Building, Suite 720. Telephone: 510-832-7770. Fax: 510-832-0102.
San Francisco, California Office: 260 California Street, Suite 1100. Telephone: 415-362-7126. Fax: 415-362-6401.
Sacramento, California Office: 100 Howe Avenue, Suite 240N. Telephone: 916-483-5181. Fax: 916-483-7558.
Fresno, California Office: 2440 West Shaw Avenue, Suite 101. Telephone: 209-449-2600. Fax: 209-449-2603.
San Jose, California Office: 152 North Third Street, Suite 700. Telephone: 408-286-0880. Fax: 408-286-0337.
Walnut Creek, California Office: 2700 Ygnacio Valley Road, Suite 280. Telephone: 510-947-1702. Fax: 510-947-4921.
Los Angeles, California Office: 835 Wilshire Boulevard, Suite 500. Telephone: 213-489-4411. Fax: 213-489-4332.

General Civil Practice in all State and Federal Courts. Medical Malpractice, Corporate, Probate and Insurance Law.

FIRM PROFILE: *Ericksen, Arbuthnot, Kilduff, Day & Lindstrom is a statewide, civil litigation and insurance defense firm founded in 1950. This multiple office approach ensures uniform procedures and capabilities for both out-of-state and California-based clients. Experienced attorneys, backed by a well-trained paralegal staff, handle cases involving liability defense and insurance coverage and general civil litigation.*

**E. AURORA HUGHES,** born Douglas, Arizona, July 25, 1954; admitted to bar, 1979, California; 1980, U.S. District Court, Central District of California. *Education:* University of Arizona (B.S., 1975); Southwestern University (J.D., 1979). Phi Alpha Delta. Member, Southwestern University Law Review, 1978-1979. *Member:* Los Angeles County Bar Association (Member, Bridging the Gap Committee, 1989-1992; Delegate, State Bar Conference of Delegates, 1989-1992). **PRACTICE AREAS:** Class Action Defense; Complex Tort Litigation; Products Liability Defense; Malpractice Defense.

**ANNE WALKER,** born Escondido, California, May 25, 1960; admitted to bar, 1989, California, U.S. District Court, Central District of California and U.S. Court of Appeals, Ninth Circuit. *Education:* Mary Washington College (B.A., 1981); Pepperdine University (J.D., 1987). *Member:* Riverside County Bar Association. **PRACTICE AREAS:** Insurance Defense; Construction Defect; Employment Discrimination.

(For biographical data on other personnel, see Professional Biographies at other office locations).

---

## FIORE, WALKER, RACOBS & POWERS
A PROFESSIONAL LAW CORPORATION

6670 ALESSANDRO, SUITE B
**RIVERSIDE, CALIFORNIA 92506**
Telephone: 909-789-8100
Fax: 909-789-8105

Irvine, California Office: Koll Center Irvine. 18400 Von Karman, Suite 600. 92612-1514. Telephone: 714-955-0560. Fax: 714-955-2894.
Palm Desert, California Office: 74-361 Highway III, Suite 1. Telephone: 619-776-6511. Fax: 619-776-6517.

Community Association, Real Property, Civil Litigation, Construction and Business.

FIRM PROFILE: *Fiore, Walker, Racobs & Powers, A Professional Law Corporation, has been in existence since August, 1972, and has established the practice of law in the fields of community association law, real property and civil litigation.*

*(This Listing Continued)*

## PROFESSIONAL BIOGRAPHIES

CALIFORNIA—RIVERSIDE

*Our mission is to: Provide quality legal services to our clients; set a positive example for the legal profession; contribute to the continuing success of community associations through education, legislation and legal services.*

**PETER E. RACOBS,** born Lucerne Valley, California, November 4, 1957; admitted to bar, 1983, California. *Education:* University of California at Riverside (B.A., 1979); University of California at Davis (J.D., 1983).

---

**MICHAEL J. WHITE,** born North Hornell, New York, May 9, 1957; admitted to bar, 1986, California; 1989, U.S. District Court, Central District of California. *Education:* University of California at Los Angeles (B.A., 1979; M.A., 1982); McGeorge School of Law, University of the Pacific (J.D., 1986).

**ERIN A. MALONEY,** born Sunnyvale, California, November 14, 1965; admitted to bar, 1991, California. *Education:* University of California, Los Angeles (B.A.,1988); Loyola Law School (J.D., 1991).

**DENNIS M. BURKE,** born Los Angeles, California, November 5, 1967; admitted to bar, 1994, California. *Education:* University of California at Los Angeles (B.A., 1989); University of California at Davis (J.D., 1994).

(For Complete Biographical Data on all Personnel see Professional Biographies at Irvine, California)

---

## FRANSCELL, STRICKLAND, ROBERTS & LAWRENCE

A PROFESSIONAL CORPORATION

Established in 1992

SUITE 670, 3801 UNIVERSITY AVENUE
P.O. BOX 12008
RIVERSIDE, CALIFORNIA 92502-2208
Telephone: 909-686-1000
Fax: 909-686-2565

*Pasadena, California Office:* Penthouse, 225 South Lake Avenue. Telephone: 818-304-7830. Fax: 818-795-7460.
*Santa Ana, California Office:* Suite 800, 401 Civic Center Drive West. Telephone: 714-543-6511. Fax: 714-543-6711.

*Police Misconduct Liability Defense, Civil Rights Defense, Employment Defense, Municipal and Administrative Law, General Civil and Criminal Trial and Appellate Practice, Administrative Law and Litigation.*

*FIRM PROFILE: The firm's decision to locate its three offices in Pasadena, Santa Ana and Riverside was borne out of a desire to be accessible to clients primarily located in Los Angeles, Riverside, San Bernardino, Orange and San Diego Counties. The three locations also place FSRL attorneys in close proximity to the various Southern California courts, thereby generating significant cost savings for many clients.*

*Franscell, Strickland, Roberts & Lawrence understands the practice of law is always changing. To continue to provide the legal services clients want, the firm is dedicated to remaining adaptable to the changes of the 1990s and to actively promoting the early and efficient resolution of all litigation.*

(For complete biographical data on all personnel, see Professional Biographies at Pasadena, California)

---

## FURNESS, MIDDLEBROOK, KAISER & HIGGINS

A PROFESSIONAL CORPORATION

RIVERSIDE, CALIFORNIA

(See San Bernardino)

*General Civil and Trial Practice. Personal Injury, Insurance and Government Law, Workers Compensation Subrogation, General Business and Construction Law.*

---

## DONALD J. GARY, JR., P.C.

3700 SIXTH STREET AT MAIN, SECOND FLOOR
P.O. BOX 664
RIVERSIDE, CALIFORNIA 92502-0664
Telephone: 909-786-0100
Facsimile: 909-683-8458

*Los Angeles, California Office:* 445 South Figueroa Street, Twenty Sixth Floor, 90017. Telephone: 213-439-5385.

*Federal and State Taxation, Probate and Estate Planning, General Business, Corporation, Partnerships, Limited Liability Company.*

**HARRY M. HALSTEAD** (1918-1995).

**DONALD J. GARY, JR.,** born Baltimore, Maryland, February 25, 1956; admitted to bar, 1992, California, U.S. Court of Appeals, Ninth Circuit and U.S. Tax Court. *Education:* University of Baltimore (B.S., 1979); Southwestern University School of Law (J.D., magna cum laude, 1992). Delta Theta Phi. Research Editor, Southwestern University School of Law Review, 1992. Certified Public Accountant, Maryland, 1980. Author: "Lenders Under CERCLA; What is the Risk in the Aftermath of Fleet Factors?" Southwestern U. L.Rev. Vol. 21, No. 4, 1992. *Member:* Los Angeles County and American Bar Associations; State Bar of California (Member, Sections on: Business Law, Estate Planning, Trust and Probate; Taxation). (Also Of Counsel to Feldman & Shaffery).

---

## GILBERT, KELLY, CROWLEY & JENNETT

3801 UNIVERSITY AVENUE, SUITE 700
RIVERSIDE, CALIFORNIA 92501
Telephone: 909-276-4000
Fax: 909-276-4100

*Los Angeles, California Office:* 1200 Wilshire Boulevard. Telephone: 213-580-7000. Fax: 213-580-7100.
*Orange County Office:* Suite 310 Nexus Financial Center, 721 South Parker Street, Orange, California. Telephone: 714-541-5000. Fax: 714-541-0670.
*San Diego, California Office:* 501 West Broadway, Suite 1260 Koll Center. Telephone: 619-687-3000. Fax: 619-687-3100.

*General Civil and Trial Practice in all State and Federal Courts. Appellate Practice. Corporation and Insurance Law.*

### RESIDENT PARTNERS

**MICHAEL B. DONNER,** born Pasadena, California, January 21, 1947; admitted to bar, 1983, California and U.S. District Court, Central and Southern Districts of California. *Education:* California State University at Fullerton (B.A., 1974); Southwestern University School of Law (J.D., 1983). *Member:* Los Angeles County, Riverside County and American (Litigation Section) Bar Associations; State Bar of California; Association of Southern California Defense Counsel (Past Co-Chair, Industry Liaison and Amicus Committees); American Inns of Court. **PRACTICE AREAS:** Construction Defect; Environmental Litigation; Products Liability Litigation.

**EDWARD A. FERNANDEZ,** born Washington, D.C., September 26, 1957; admitted to bar, 1983, California. *Education:* University of California at San Diego (B.A., 1979); University of San Diego Law School (J.D., 1982). Contributions Editor, En Banc, 1981-1982. Arbitrator, Riverside County Consolidated Superior/Municipal Courts, San Bernardino Superior Court. *Member:* Beverly Hills (Chairman, Small Law Firm/Sole Practitioner's Committee, 1984-1985), Century City, Los Angeles County, Riverside County (Litigation Section) and American Bar Associations; State Bar of California; Association of Southern California Defense Counsel; Southern California Insurance Professionals. **PRACTICE AREAS:** Construction Defect; Premises Liability Litigation.

**ANDREW C. HUBERT,** born Minneapolis, Minnesota, February 21, 1959; admitted to bar, 1985, California; 1987, U.S. District Court, Central District of California. *Education:* Claremont Men's College (B.A., 1981); Southwestern University (J.D., 1984). Phi Alpha Delta. Member, Moot Court. *Member:* Los Angeles County, Riverside County and American Bar Associations; State Bar of California; Association of Southern California Defense Counsel; The Association of Trial Lawyers of America. *LANGUAGES:* French, Hungarian.

*(This Listing Continued)*

## GILBERT, KELLY, CROWLEY & JENNETT, Riverside—Continued

### RESIDENT ASSOCIATES

**JEFFREY W. ABEL,** born Panorama City, California, October 31, 1966; admitted to bar, 1996, California. *Education:* California Polytechnic State University (B.S., 1990); University of La Verne (J.D., 1996). *Member:* State Bar of California.

**MICHELE ASSAEL-SHAFIA,** born Montebello, California, January 26, 1970; admitted to bar, 1995, California. *Education:* California Polytechnic State University at Pomona (B.S., 1991); University of La Verne (J.D., 1995). Delta Theta Phi. *Member:* State Bar of California.

**KIRK A. LAUBY,** born Burbank, California, November 26, 1949; admitted to bar, 1978, California. *Education:* University of California at Los Angeles (B.A., 1974); Southwestern University (J.D., 1978). *Member:* Los Angeles County, Riverside County and American Bar Associations; State Bar of California. *PRACTICE AREAS:* Products Liability; Construction Defect; Contract Litigation; Bad Faith; Energy Litigation.

**JAMES F. LINDSAY,** born Springfield, Illinois, November 27, 1949; admitted to bar, 1989, California and U.S. District Court, Central District of California. *Education:* Marquette University (B.S., Business Administration, 1971); Southwestern University School of Law (J.D., 1989). Recipient, George A. Yanase Scholarship, 1988-1989. *Member:* Riverside County and American Bar Associations; State Bar of California; Association of Southern California Defense Counsel. *PRACTICE AREAS:* Construction Defect Litigation.

**PEGGY E. MARKSON,** born Los Angeles, California, September 4, 1954; admitted to bar, 1986, California. *Education:* University of California at San Diego; California State University at Fullerton (B.A., 1976); Western State University (J.D., 1985). *Member:* Orange County (Member, Insurance Law Section) and American Bar Associations; State Bar of California. *PRACTICE AREAS:* Insurance Coverage.

**RODGER A. MAYNES,** born Los Angeles, California, September 20, 1946; admitted to bar, 1985, California; 1986, U.S. District Court, Central District of California and U.S. Court of Appeals, Ninth Circuit. *Education:* California State University at Long Beach (B.S., 1969); University of La Verne (J.D., 1984). Instructor: Contracts, 1986-1987; Criminal Law, 1987; Evidence, 1988; Procedure, 1989, University of La Verne. Recipient, American Jurisprudence Award in Torts *Member:* San Bernardino County Bar Association; The State Bar of California; The Association of Trial Lawyers of America; Association of Southern California Defense Counsel.

**GERALDINE J. PUTNAM,** born Providence, Rhode Island, November 20, 1946; admitted to bar, 1988, California. *Education:* California Polytechnic State University (B.A., 1969); University of La Verne (J.D., 1984). Staff Editor, University of La Verne Law Review. *Member:* Riverside and San Bernardino Bar Associations; State Bar of California; Southern California Defense Counsel. *PRACTICE AREAS:* Personal Injury Defense.

**ROBERT S. RODDICK,** born Loma Linda, California, November 29, 1949; admitted to bar, 1977, California; 1982, U.S. District Court, Central District of California. *Education:* University of Southern California (B.A., magna cum laude, 1971); Loyola University of Los Angeles (J.D., 1976). President, Political Science Association, University of Southern California. Arbitrator: San Bernardino Courts, 1985; Riverside Superior Courts, 1989. *Member:* San Bernardino County Bar Association; State Bar of California; Association of Southern California Defense Counsel; The Defense Research and Trial Lawyers Association. [With Army National Guard, 1971-1977]. *PRACTICE AREAS:* Insurance Defense.

**FRANK A. ROMEU, JR.,** born New Orleans, Louisiana, April 11, 1961; admitted to bar, 1987, Louisiana; 1988, California. *Education:* University of New Orleans; Southeastern Louisiana University (B.S., 1983); Louisiana State University and A. and M. College (J.D., 1987). *Member:* Riverside County and Louisiana State Bar Associations; State Bar of California.

**STEPHANIE J. YAMASHITA,** born Los Angeles, California, September 30, 1954; admitted to bar, 1987, California and U.S. District Court, Central District of California. *Education:* University of Southern California (B.S.Ch.E., 1983); Southwestern University (J.D., 1987). Phi Alpha Delta. Arbitrator, Los Angeles County Superior and Municipal Courts. *Member:* Los Angeles County and American Bar Associations; State Bar of California; American Institute of Chemical Engineers; American Inns of Court (ABOTA Chapter, Los Angeles); Women's Environmental Council (Founding Member and Incoming President of Los Angeles/Orange County Chapter); Association of Southern California Defense Counsel. *PRACTICE AREAS:* Environmental Litigation; Products Liability Litigation.

(For complete biographical data on all personnel, see Professional Biographies at Los Angeles, California)

---

## GRAVES, SUZANNE M.
### RIVERSIDE, CALIFORNIA
(See Upland)

*Estate Planning, Probate, Civil Litigation, Business Planning.*

---

## GRESHAM, VARNER, SAVAGE, NOLAN & TILDEN

3750 UNIVERSITY AVENUE, SUITE 610 (92501)
P.O. BOX 1148
**RIVERSIDE, CALIFORNIA 92502**
Telephone: 909-274-7777
Fax: 909-274-7770
Email: info@gvsnt.com

*San Bernardino, California Office:* 600 North Arrowhead Avenue, Suite 300. Telephone: 909-884-2171. Fax: 909-888-2120.

*General Civil and Trial Practice. Business Law, Corporate Law, Real Estate, Land Use, Administrative Law, Mining, Natural Resources, Environmental Law, Water Law, Probate, Estate Planning, Labor and Employment Law, Taxation, Natural Resources, Health Care and Hospital Law.*

### MEMBERS

**BRUCE D. VARNER,** born Los Angeles, California, November 12, 1936; admitted to bar, 1963, California. *Education:* University of California at Santa Barbara (B.A., 1958); University of California, Hastings College of Law (J.D., 1962). Delta Theta Phi; Order of the Coif; Thurston Honor Society. Editor-in-Chief, Hastings Law Journal, 1961-1962. Treasurer, Board of Directors, San Bernardino Legal Aid Society, 1967-1968. Member and Chairman, Board of Directors, San Bernardino Economic Development Council, 1983-1989. Member, Board of Directors, Arrowhead Health Care System (San Bernardino Community Hospital), 1984-1993. Member, Board of Directors, Inland Empire Economic Council, 1986-1990. Member: Board of Directors, Santee Dairies, Inc., 1986—; Board of Directors, Monday Morning Group, 1992—; Board of Directors, Silver Eagle Club, 1993—; University of California, Riverside Foundation Board of Trustees, 1995—; Advisory Board, California State University-San Bernardino, 1987—; Board of Directors, Stater Bros. Markets, 1985—; Board of Directors, National Orange Show, 1987—; Inland Commercial Division Board, Security Pacific National Bank, 1988-1992. Member, Inland Empire Advisory Board, Bank of America National Savings and Trust Association, 1992—. Deputy, San Bernardino County Sheriff, Specialized Services Bureau, 1993—. *Member:* San Bernardino County (Treasurer, Board of Directors, 1967-1968) and American Bar Associations; The State Bar of California; State Bar of Montana. (Also at San Bernardino). *PRACTICE AREAS:* Financing; Business Law; Corporate Law; Real Estate Law.

**STEPHAN G. SALESON,** born East Lansing, Michigan, June 3, 1949; admitted to bar, 1976, California and U.S. District Court, Central and Southern Districts of California. *Education:* Michigan State University (B.A., 1973); Pepperdine University (J.D., 1976). Lecturer, Trial and Appellate Advocacy, Hastings Law Center, 1983-1991. Instructor, Los Angeles County Bar Association Trial Attorney Project, 1991-1994. Deputy District Attorney, San Bernardino County, 1977-1980. *Member:* Riverside County, San Bernardino County and American Bar Associations; The State Bar of California; The Association of Trial Lawyers of America. [With USMC, 1969-1971]. *PRACTICE AREAS:* State and Federal Civil Litigation; Labor and Employment Law; OSHA Law.

**CRAIG O. DOBLER,** born Spokane, Washington, May 9, 1956; admitted to bar, 1981, Washington and U.S. District Court, Eastern District of Washington; 1989, California and U.S. District Court, Central District of California. *Education:* University of Washington (B.A., cum laude, 1978); Gonzaga University School of Law (J.D., cum laude, 1981); New York University School of Law (LL.M., Taxation, 1982). Adjunct Professor, Gon-

*(This Listing Continued)*

zaga University School of Law, 1982-1984. *Member:* Riverside County (Chairman, Tax Section) and Washington State Bar Associations.

### RESIDENT ASSOCIATES

**MICHAEL O. WOLF,** born Ames, Iowa, February 12, 1942; admitted to bar, 1976, California. *Education:* Iowa State University; Santa Ana College; Long Beach State College (B.S., Accounting, 1965); Pepperdine University (J.D., 1974). *Member:* Riverside County (Member, Tax Section) and American (Member, Tax Section) Bar Associations; The State Bar of California (Member, Tax Section). [With U.S. Army, 1965-1967]. **PRACTICE AREAS:** Tax and ERISA Law.

**BRENDAN W. BRANDT,** born Vandenberg AFB, California, February 4, 1964; admitted to bar, 1990, California and U.S. District Court, Central District of California. *Education:* University of California at Los Angeles (B.A., 1986); University of San Diego (J.D., 1990). *Member:* The State Bar of California; American Bar Association.

**ELIZABETH ASHLEY BIANCO,** born Riverside, California, May 2, 1967; admitted to bar, 1992, California. *Education:* California State University; University of Utah (B.A., summa cum laude, 1989); Pepperdine University (J.D., 1992). Phi Kappa Phi. Member, Golden Key National Honor Society. General Contractor, California, 1987—. *Member:* Riverside County and San Bernardino County Bar Associations; The State Bar of California.

(For complete biographical data on all personnel, see Professional Biographies at San Bernardino, California)

---

## HAIGHT, BROWN & BONESTEEL

A Partnership including Professional Corporations

Established in 1937

**3750 UNIVERSITY AVENUE, SUITE 650**
**RIVERSIDE, CALIFORNIA 92501**
Telephone: 909-341-8300
FAX: 909-341-8309

*Santa Monica, California Office:* 1620 26th Street, Suite 4000 North, P.O. Box 680. Telephone: 310-449-6000. Fax: 310-829-5117. Telex: 705837.

*Santa Ana, California Office:* Suite 900, 5 Hutton Centre Drive. Telephone: 714-754-1100. Telecopier: 714-754-0826.

*San Francisco, California Office:* 201 Sansome Street, Suite 300. Telephone: 415-986-7700. Fax: 415-986-6954.

*General Civil and Trial Practice in all State and Federal Courts. Municipality, Construction, Landowner/Operator and Products. Corporation. Commercial. Tax. Real Estate. Probate. Estate Planning, Business and Labor Law.*

*FIRM PROFILE: Today's complex society seems ever-changing. Rapidly advancing technologies spawn everything from new medical devices that help us live longer to electronics that enhance our business lives. This same society is also litigious, creating an increasing number of complex disputes, claims and lawsuits.*

*Haight, Brown & Bonesteel distinguishes itself by having more top-level litigators than most firms in the country and the specialized resources and sophistication needed to handle complex issues both successfully and cost efficiently. Our broad and deep experience in virtually all phases of civil litigation enables us to analyze every option - from arbitration to jury trial - based on client goals.*

*During the firm's early years in the 1930's, 1940's and 1950's, its foundation was insurance defense. But as the theories of liability expanded throughout California, and later throughout the nation, the firm rapidly developed expertise in product liability and business matters, as well as other specialized areas of litigation.*

*The practice of litigation remains the firm's major focus, with an average of more than 50 cases tried to conclusion each year. Litigation activities are conducted in a variety of areas. One of these is environmental law and toxic tort litigation, where the firm is deeply involved in the defense of numerous substances alleged to be environmentally or personally harmful. In its corporate product litigation practice, the firm represents and has successfully defended matters for the manufacturers of a wide variety of products, including automobiles, farm equipment, construction equipment, and household appliances. Haight, Brown & Bonesteel is also well represented in the fields of pharmaceutical products and medical devices, acting as local, regional and national counsel for some to the nation's largest manufacturers. The firm is also well known for its expertise in the defense of attorneys, accountants, architects, engineers, and other professionals involved in errors and omissions cases. Additional fully staffed litigation practice areas include commercial and real estate litigation,*

(This Listing Continued)

*insurance coverage and bad faith litigation, and insurance defense.*

*As support services to its clients, the firm has a fully staffed Appellate Department, a Business Transactions Group, and an Internal Investigation Unit. Once a very small firm, it now has more than 150 attorneys and a total staff of more then 350. All the growth has been from within, without the benefit of merger or acquisition. Throughout the firm's history, as the practice has grown in size and scope, Haight, Brown & Bonesteel has remained focused by its strength in litigation.*

### RESIDENT MEMBERS

**MARK S. LESTER,** born Los Angeles, California, June 19, 1960; admitted to bar, 1985, California; 1986, U.S. District Court, Central District of California; U.S. District Court, Southern District of California. *Education:* University of California at San Diego (B.A., 1982); University of San Diego School of Law (J.D., 1985). Member, University of San Diego Law Review, 1984-1985. *Member:* Los Angeles County and American Bar Associations; The State Bar of California; Association of Southern California Defense Counsel; Defense Research Institute. **PRACTICE AREAS:** Land Owners Liability; Construction and Contractors Liability; Product Liability; Municipality Defense; Common Carrier and Transportation Claims.

### RESIDENT ASSOCIATES

**KEVIN M. OSTERBERG,** born Joliet, Illinois, February 21, 1956; admitted to bar, 1988, California and U.S. District Court, Central, Southern and Eastern Districts of California. *Education:* New Jersey Institute of Technology; William Paterson College of New Jersey (B.S., 1978); Southwestern University School of Law (J.D., 1988). Police Officer, City of Pasadena, California, 1980-1986. *Member:* Los Angeles County and American Bar Associations; The State Bar of California; Association of Southern California Defense Counsel. **PRACTICE AREAS:** General Civil Liability; Premises Liability Law; Defense of Public Entities; Public Entity Liability.

**MICHAEL S. KELLY,** born Williamsport, Indiana, September 6, 1966; admitted to bar, 1991, California. *Education:* University of California at Los Angeles (B.A., 1988); University of Notre Dame (J.D., 1991). *Member:* Orange County and Riverside County Bar Associations. (Also in Santa Monica Office). **PRACTICE AREAS:** General Liability; Medical Malpractice; Products Liability.

(For complete biographical data on other personnel, see Professional Biographies at Santa Monica, San Francisco and Santa Ana, California)

---

## STEVEN L. HARMON

**THE LORING BUILDING**
**3685 MAIN STREET, SUITE 250**
**RIVERSIDE, CALIFORNIA 92501**
Telephone: 909-787-6800
Fax: 909-787-6700

*Criminal Trial Practice.*

**STEVEN L. HARMON,** born Upland, California, October 23, 1947; admitted to bar, 1972, California; 1973, U.S. District Court, Central District of California; 1981, U.S. District Court, Southern District of California. *Education:* University of California at Los Angeles (B.A., 1969); Loyola University of Los Angeles School of Law (J.D., 1972). Faculty: National Criminal Defense College, Macon, Georgia 1993—. Listed in the 1991-1992 and 1993-1994 edition of "The Best Lawyers in America". Faculty Member, Criminal Defense Advocacy Institute, San Diego, 1992—. Master, Leo A. Deegan Inns of Court. Coach, Riverside County Mock Trial, 1987—. *Member:* Riverside County Bar Association (Treasurer, 1980; Secretary, 1992-1993; Vice President, 1993-1994; President-Elect, 1994-1995; President, 1995-1996); State Bar of California; California Attorneys for Criminal Justice; National Association of Criminal Defense Lawyers.

---

## HEITING & IRWIN

**3845 MARKET STREET, THIRD FLOOR**
**RIVERSIDE, CALIFORNIA 92501**
Telephone: 909-682-6400
Fax: 909-682-4072

*Civil Trial Practice, Personal Injury, Wrongful Death, Medical Malpractice, Professional Liability, Workers Compensation, Estate Planning and Probate, Business, Corporate, Family Law, Dispute Resolution.*

(This Listing Continued)

## HEITING & IRWIN, Riverside—Continued

**JAMES O. HEITING,** born Chicago, Illinois, April 21, 1949; admitted to bar, 1976, California; 1977, U.S. Supreme Court and U.S. District Court, Central District of California; 1982, U.S. District Court, Southern District of California. *Education:* Riverside University (B.S., 1971); Western State University (J.D., 1975). Speaker/Lecturer: Continuing Legal Education, 1990—. Judge Pro Tem. Mediator, Court of Appeals, 1991—. *Member:* Riverside County (President, 1996) and American Bar Associations; State Bar of California; California Trial Lawyers Association; American Society of Law and Medicine; Leo A. Deegan Inn of Court (Founding and Board Member, 1992—). *REPORTED CASES:* Fellers v. Fellers; Soto v. Royal Globe. *PRACTICE AREAS:* Medical Malpractice; Personal Injury Law; Legal Malpractice; Professional Negligence; Civil Litigation.

**RICHARD H. IRWIN,** born San Antonio, Texas, June 30, 1955; admitted to bar, 1980, California and U.S. District Court, Central District of California. *Education:* University of California at Los Angeles (B.A., 1977); Southwestern University School of Law (J.D., 1980). *Member:* Riverside County Bar Association; State Bar of California; California Applicants Attorneys Association. (Certified Specialist, Workers' Compensation Law, The State Bar of California Board of Legal Specialization). *PRACTICE AREAS:* Workers Compensation.

### ASSOCIATES

**REBECCA S. REED,** born Arcadia, California, June 18, 1962; admitted to bar, 1992, California and U.S. District Court, Southern District of California; 1993, U.S. District Court, Central and Northern Districts of California. *Education:* California Southern, Riverside (J.D., 1992). Member, Leo A. Deegan Inn of Court, 1994—. *Member:* Riverside County Bar Association (Member, Sections on: Probate and Estate Planning; Fee Arbitration Committee, 1994—); State Bar of California. *PRACTICE AREAS:* Civil Litigation; Personal Injury; Medical Malpractice; Guardianships.

**MATTHEW G. MARKHAM,** born Lynwood, California, November 1, 1950; admitted to bar, 1983, California; 1984, U.S. District Court, Southern and Central Districts of California. *Education:* University of California at Berkeley (B.A., 1973); Southwestern University (J.D., 1983). *Member:* San Diego County and Riverside County Bar Associations; State Bar of California. *REPORTED CASES:* Brose v. Union Tribune 183 CA 3d. 1986; Thai v. Stang 214 CA 3d. 1989. *PRACTICE AREAS:* Civil Litigation; Family Law.

**SCOT THOMAS MOGA,** born California; admitted to bar, 1996, California; U.S. District Court, Central District of California. *Education:* University of San Diego (B.B.A., Accounting, 1990); University of La Verne (J.D., 1996). Phi Kappa Theta (Treasurer/Secretary/National Convention Delegate; Delta Theta Phi (Board Member, 1994-1995). Recipient, American Jurisprudence Awards, Property, 1993; Torts, 1992. Certified Law Clerk, California State Bar, 1993-1996. Board of Editors, 1995-1996 and Staff Writer, 1993-1994, Journal of Juvenile Law, Law Review. Author, Parental Rights Under The Individuals with Disabilities Education Act, IDEA 15 J.Juv.L 178, 1994. *Member:* San Bernardine, Riverside County Bar Associations; State Bar of California. *PRACTICE AREAS:* Family Law; Workers' Compensation; Civil Litigation.

**SHERI B. CRUZ,** born Hartford, Connecticut, January 17, 1966; admitted to bar, 1994, California and U.S. District Court, Central and Southern Districts of California. *Education:* Western State University (B.S., 1992; J.D., 1994). Moot Court. Leo A. Deegan Inns of Court, 1995—. *Member:* Riverside County Bar Association (Member, Probate Section). *PRACTICE AREAS:* Business; Real Estate; Probate; Estate Planning; Guardianship/Conservatorship.

---

## HOWARD, MOSS, LOVEDER, STRICKROTH & WALKER

A Partnership including Professional Corporations

*6700 INDIANA AVENUE, SUITE 160*
**RIVERSIDE, CALIFORNIA 92506-4200**
Telephone: 909-341-8353
Telecopier: 909-275-9637

*Santa Ana, California Office:* 2677 North Main Street, Suite 800. Telephone: 714-542-6300. Telecopier: 714-542-6987.

*(This Listing Continued)*

---

*General, Civil and Trial Practice in all State and Federal Courts. Personal Injury Defense, Business Litigation, Insurance Law, Construction Defect Litigation, Products Liability, Governmental Entity, Wrongful Termination, Appellate Practice.*

(For complete biographical data on all Personnel, See Professional Biographies at Santa Ana, California.)

---

## IVES, KIRWAN & DIBBLE

A PROFESSIONAL CORPORATION

**RIVERSIDE, CALIFORNIA**

(See Palm Springs)

---

## KINKLE, RODIGER AND SPRIGGS

PROFESSIONAL CORPORATION

*3333 14TH STREET*
**RIVERSIDE, CALIFORNIA 92501**
Telephone: 909-683-2410; 800-235-2039
Fax: 909-683-7759

*Los Angeles, California Office:* 600 North Grand Avenue. Telephone: 213-629-1261. Fax: 213-629-8382.

*Santa Ana, California Office:* 837 North Ross Street. Telephone: 714-835-9011. Fax: 714-667-7806.

*San Diego, California Office:* Suite 900 Driver Insurance Center, 1620 Fifth Avenue, P.O. Box 127900. Telephone: 619-233-4566. Fax: 619-233-8554.

*Santa Barbara, California Office:* 125 East De La Guerra Street. Telephone: 805-966-4700. Fax: 805-966-4120.

*General Trial Practice. Negligence, Malpractice, Products Liability, Construction and Insurance Law.*

**EVERETT L. SPRIGGS,** born Safford, Arizona, July 30, 1930; admitted to bar, 1960, California. *Education:* Arizona State University (B.S., 1955); University of Arizona (J.D., 1958). Deputy City Attorney, City of Los Angeles, 1960. *Member:* Los Angeles County Bar Association; The State Bar of California; American Board of Trial Advocates. (Managing Attorney).

**BRUCE E. DISENHOUSE,** born New York, N.Y., July 22, 1952; admitted to bar, 1977, California. *Education:* Colgate University (A.B., cum laude, 1974); McGeorge School of Law (J.D., cum laude, 1977). *Member:* State Bar of California.

**CLAUDIA L. REYNOLDS,** born Tucson, Arizona, November 14, 1956; admitted to bar, 1982, California. *Education:* University of California at Riverside (A.B., 1978); Southwestern University School of Law (J.D., 1981). *Member:* State Bar of California.

**SCOTT B. SPRIGGS,** born Fullerton, California, December 20, 1960; admitted to bar, 1985, California. *Education:* University of Southern California (B.S., 1981); Southwestern University (J.D., 1984). *Member:* State Bar of California.

**TOBY J. ELDER,** born Long Beach, California, February 14, 1952; admitted to bar, 1978, California. *Education:* California State University (B.A., 1975); Pepperdine University (J.D., 1978). Phi Alpha Delta. *Member:* San Diego County Bar Association; State Bar of California; Association of Southern California Defense Counsel.

**THOMAS P. SCHLAX,** born Chicago, Illinois, May 5, 1949; admitted to bar, 1994, California. *Education:* Unites States Naval Academy (B.S., 1971); University of San Diego (J.D., 1994). *Member:* State Bar of California.

**MARC S. HURD,** born Santa Monica, California, May 17, 1962; admitted to bar, 1987, California. *Education:* University of California at Los Angeles (B.A., cum laude, 1984); Hastings College of the Law, University of California (J.D., 1987). Phi Delta Phi (Magister, 1986-1987). *Member:* The State Bar of California.

**BURTON M. SELMAN,** born Chicago, Illinois, December 22, 1942; admitted to bar, 1966, California; 1969, New York. *Education:* University of Illinois; Reed College (B.A., 1963); Harvard University (J.D., cum laude, 1966); Stanford University (M.A., Economics, 1968); American University

*(This Listing Continued)*

of the Caribbean (M.A., 1986). *Member:* State Bar of California. *LANGUAGES:* Spanish.

**MICHAEL D. SHAFER,** born Beloit, Wisconsin, June 27, 1958; admitted to bar, 1987, California. *Education:* University of California at Los Angeles (B.A., 1981); Western State University (J.D., 1986). *Member:* State Bar of California; Southern California Defense Counsel.

(For complete biographical data on personnel at Los Angeles, Santa Ana, San Diego and Santa Barbara, California, see Professional Biographies at those locations)

## KISTLER, McCARTY & PEARCY

3890 TENTH STREET, 3RD FLOOR
P.O. BOX 1583
**RIVERSIDE, CALIFORNIA 92502-1583**
Telephone: 909-686-1583
Fax: 909-686-1619

*General Practice.*

**HARLAN B. KISTLER,** born Columbus, Ohio, 1960; admitted to bar, 1989, California. *Education:* University of Iowa (B.A., 1982; J.D., 1988). NCAA All American Wrestler, University of Iowa. Editor, Iowa Law Review, 1987-1988. *PRACTICE AREAS:* Tort; Personal Injury Litigation; Wrongful Death (Plaintiff and Defense); Construction Law; Commercial Collections; Business and Commercial Litigation; Civil Litigation; Business Law.

**ROBERT A. MCCARTY, JR.,** born California, 1967; admitted to bar, 1993, California. *Education:* Menlo College (B.S., 1989); Whittier College School of Law (J.D), 1993). *PRACTICE AREAS:* Family Law; D.A. Child Support Actions; Parental Kidnapping; Jurisdictional Issues; Adoptions.

**BRIAN C. PEARCY,** born California, 1961; admitted to bar, 1991, California. *Education:* University of California (B.S., 1984); Los Angeles Police Academy (P.O.S.T., 1987); University of the Pacific, McGeorge School of Law (J.D., 1991). *PRACTICE AREAS:* Civil Litigation; Business and Commercial Litigation; Real Estate Law; Business Law; Trade Secrets; Administrative Law; Police Officer Rights; A.D.A. Law.

REPRESENTATIVE CLIENTS: Montgomery Ward & Co., Inc.; Southern California Water Co.; Fireman's Fund Insurance Co.; Bear Valley Electric Services; Livacich Produce Co.; Bud Childs Trucking Co.

## KNOBBE, MARTENS, OLSON & BEAR, LLP

A Limited Liability Partnership including Professional Corporations
Established in 1962

3801 UNIVERSITY AVENUE, SUITE 710
**RIVERSIDE, CALIFORNIA 92501**
Telephone: 909-781-9231
Fax: 909-781-4507

*Newport Beach, California Office:* 620 Newport Center Drive, 16th Floor. Telephone: 714-760-0404. Fax: 714-760-9502.

*San Diego, California Office:* 501 West Broadway, Suite 1400. Telephone: 619-235-8550. Fax: 619-235-0176.

*Intellectual Property Law including Patent, Trademark, Copyright, Unfair Competition, Trade Secret, Licensing, Computer Law, Antitrust Law, and related litigation.*

**WILLIAM B. BUNKER,** born Las Vegas, Nevada, 1951; admitted to bar, 1978, California; registered to practice before U.S. Patent and Trademark Office. *Education:* California State Polytechnic University (B.S., in Aerospace Eng., with honors, 1975) Tau Beta Pi; Brigham Young University (J.D., cum laude, 1978). Author: "Drafting Representations and Warranties in Contracts Involving Intellectual Property," California Business Law Practitioner, Vol. VII, No. 4, Fall, 1992. *Member:* Orange County, Riverside County, San Bernardino County and San Diego County Bar Associations. *Email:* wbunker@kmob.com

**WILLIAM H. NIEMAN,** born St. Louis, Missouri, 1942; admitted to bar, 1980, California; registered to practice before U.S. Patent and Trademark Office. *Education:* Washington University (B.S.E.E., 1964) Eta Kappa Nu; Arizona State University (M.B.A., 1970); University of San Diego (J.D., cum laude, 1980). Author: "Officer & Director Liability for Patent Infringement: Managing the Risks," Issues & Solutions Vol. 3, No. 1, April, 1990. *Member:* Orange County, Riverside County and San Bernardino County Bar Associations; Los Angeles Patent Law Association; San Diego County Patent Law Association; American Intellectual Property Law Association. *Email:* wnieman@kmob.com

**MICHAEL H. TRENHOLM,** born Seattle, Washington, 1964; admitted to bar, 1992, California; registered to practice before U.S. Patent and Trademark Office. *Education:* University of California at Los Angeles (B.S.E.E., 1987); McGeorge School of Law, University of the Pacific (J.D., with distinction, 1992). Order of the Coif. *Member:* Riverside County and San Bernardino County Bar Associations. *Email:* mtrenholm@kmob.com

**FRED C. HERNANDEZ,** born Fullerton, California, March 12, 1967; admitted to bar, 1995, California; registered to practice before U.S. Patent and Trademark Office. *Education:* California Polytechnic State University (B.S.A.E., 1990); University of California, Los Angeles (J.D., 1995). *Member:* Riverside County Bar Association.

REPRESENTATIVE CLIENTS: Air Quality Products, Inc.; Idyllwild; Bird Products Corporation, Palm Springs; Chiuminatta Concrete Concepts, Riverside; Cox Hobbies, Inc., Corona; Endar Corporation, Corona; Galasso's Bakery, Mira Loma; G.S. Aerospace Technology, Inc., Ontario; ICEE-USA, Ontario; International Permalite, Inc., Ontario; JTL Medical Corp, Riverside; Joytech International, Riverside; Loma Linda University Medical Center, Loma Linda; Minka Lighting, Corona; Opto 22, Temecula; Pan International, Rancho Cucamonga; San Bernardino County, San Bernardino; Strong Box, Inc., Ontario; Telos Medical Corporation, Upland; Tolco, Corona.
REFERENCE: Tolco, Corona; United Can Co., La Mirada; Hunter Engineering, Loma Linda University.

(For other Personnel and Biographical data, see Professional Biographies at Newport Beach and San Diego)

## LA FOLLETTE, JOHNSON, DE HAAS, FESLER & AMES

A PROFESSIONAL CORPORATION
Established in 1965

3403 TENTH STREET, SUITE 820
**RIVERSIDE, CALIFORNIA 92501**
Telephone: 909-275-9192
Fax: 909-275-9249

*Los Angeles, California Office:* 865 South Figueroa Street, Suite 3100. Telephone: 213-426-3600. Fax: 213-426-3650.

*San Francisco, California Office:* 50 California Street, Suite 3350. Telephone: 415-433-7610. Telecopier: 415-392-7541.

*Santa Ana, California Office:* 2677 North Main Street, Suite 901. Telephone: 714-558-7008. Telecopier: 714-972-0379.

*Civil Litigation, Employment Law, Medical Malpractice, Professional Liability, Insurance Defense Coverage and Bad Faith, Construction Law and Product Liability.*

*FIRM PROFILE: La Follette, Johnson, De Haas, Fesler & Ames recently celebrated its 30th year of dedicated legal service to the insurance industry, medical and professional community. Founded in 1965, the firm has grown steadily over the last quarter century to a position of leadership and innovation in the industry. With over 70 attorneys and an entire complement of highly qualified support personnel, the firm fully staffs offices in Los Angeles, Orange County, the Inland Empire and San Francisco. The firm is thus positioned to serve clients' needs throughout the State of California.*

REPRESENTATIVE CLIENTS: Ohio Casualty Insurance Co.; AETNA Casualty Insurance Co.; Twentieth Century Insurance Co.; Kaiser Foundation Health Plan; Cooperative of America Physicians (CAP); Crawford & Company; Interinsurance Exchange of Automobile Club of Southern California.
REFERENCES: Union Bank (4th & Figueroa Branch, Los Angeles); California Federal Savings and Loan (Vermont & Beverly Branch, Los Angeles).

(For complete biographical data on all personnel, see Professional Biographies at Los Angeles, California)

## LORENZ ALHADEFF CANNON & ROSE

THE ORLEANS BUILDING
3638 UNIVERSITY AVENUE, SUITE 256
**RIVERSIDE, CALIFORNIA 92501**
Telephone: 909-369-3281
Facsimile: 909-683-4307

*San Diego, California Office:* 550 West "C" Street, Nineteenth Floor, 92101-3540. Telephone: 619-231-8700. Facsimile: 619-231-8323.

*Temecula, California Office:* The Tower Plaza, 27555 Ynez Road, Suite 203 92591-4677. Telephone: 909-699-9088. Facsimile: 909-699-9878.

*(This Listing Continued)*

CALIFORNIA—RIVERSIDE

**LORENZ ALHADEFF CANNON & ROSE,** Riverside—
*Continued*

*Lafayette, California Office:* Lafayette Terrace, 3697 Mount Diablo Boulevard, Suite 100, 94549. Telephone: 510-283-1599. Facsimile: 510-283-5847.

*General Civil and Trial Practice in all State and Federal Courts, Administrative Law, Antitrust, Banking, Bankruptcy, Reorganization and Creditors Rights, Business, Construction, Corporations, Environmental, International Business and Litigation, Public Finance, Real Estate Litigation, Real Estate Transactions, Federal and State Securities and Trade Regulation, White Collar Crime, Estate Planning, Probate, Criminal.*

(For complete biographical data on all personnel, see Professional Biographies at San Diego, California)

---

## THE LAW OFFICES OF
## GERALD R. LUNDBERG

RIVERSIDE, CALIFORNIA

(See Victorville)

*State and Federal Litigation, Real Estate, Estate Planning, Probate, Trust Administration, Corporate Law, Creditor and Debtor Bankruptcy, Business Law, Collection, Construction Law, Family Law, Subpoenas, Unlawful Detainer, Employment and Labor Law.*

---

## ROBERT A. McCARTY

A PROFESSIONAL CORPORATION

4545 ALLSTATE DRIVE
RIVERSIDE, CALIFORNIA 92501
Telephone: 909-781-2180
Fax: 909-781-6110

*Real Estate, Estate Planning, Probate, Business and Mediation.*

**ROBERT A. McCARTY,** born Riverside, California, November 11, 1936; admitted to bar, 1964, California. *Education:* University of California at Berkeley (B.A., 1959); Hastings College of Law, University of California (LL.B., 1963). Phi Delta Phi. President, Citizens University Committee, University of California, Riverside, 1981-1983. Vice President, Inland Counties Legal Services, 1977-1978. Member, Board of Trustees, University of California at Riverside, Foundation, 1981—. Mediator, 4th District Court of Appeals. Member, Board of Directors, Dispute Resolution Service, Inc., 1995—. *Member:* Riverside County Bar Association (Treasurer, 1979-1980); State Bar of California; Riverside County Estate Planning Council (Member, Board of Directors, 1993-1994).

REPRESENTATIVE CLIENT: Bank of America; Dutton Motor Company New Car Dealers Assoc.
REFERENCE: Bank of America

---

## THOMAS L. MILLER

A PROFESSIONAL LAW CORPORATION

Established in 1978

3891 ELEVENTH STREET
P.O. BOX 949
RIVERSIDE, CALIFORNIA 92502
Telephone: 909-683-7263
Fax: 909-683-3805

*Real Estate, Construction, Business. Corporate, Transactional and Trial Practice in State and Federal Courts.*

**THOMAS L. MILLER,** born Donalsonville, Georgia, June 12, 1947; admitted to bar, 1978, California and U.S. District Court, Central District of California; 1981, U.S. Court of Appeals, Ninth Circuit; 1984, U.S. Supreme Court; 1985, U.S. District Court, Southern District of California. *Education:* Riverside City College (A.A., 1972); Western State University (B.S.L., 1975; J.D., 1977). Member, 1978-1984 and Chairman, 1983-1984, Board of Zoning Adjustment, City of Riverside. Member, 1986-1991 and Chairman, 1988-1989, Planning Commission, City of Riverside. Member, Airport Commission, City of Riverside, (Chairman, 1992-1996). *Member:* Riverside County and American Bar Associations; State Bar of California.

*(This Listing Continued)*

CAA1734B

---

MARTINDALE-HUBBELL LAW DIRECTORY 1997

*PRACTICE AREAS:* Real Estate Law; Construction Law; Business Law; Corporate Law.

**JOHN B. LIGHTFELDT,** born Sioux City, Iowa, June 19, 1958; admitted to bar, 1992, California. *Education:* Western State University (B.S.L., 1990; J.D., 1991). *Member:* State Bar of California. **PRACTICE AREAS:** Business Litigation; Real Estate Law.

REPRESENTATIVE CLIENTS: First American Title Insurance Co.; City of Hemet; Riverside Community Hospital Foundation; DeAnza National Bank; Historic Mission Inn Corporation; O.H. Kruse Grain & Milling, Inc.; Lorcin Engineering, Inc.; U.S. Truck Driving Schools, Inc.; Enterprise Steel, Inc.; Preferred Framing, Inc.; Eagle Plumbing, Inc.; Barr Lumber Co.; Bowlus-Pacific Construction Co.;
REFERENCES: Riverside National Bank; De Anza National Bank.

---

## JOSEPH PETER MYERS

Established in 1968

4048 TENTH STREET
RIVERSIDE, CALIFORNIA 92501
Telephone: 909-684-4330
Fax: 909-686-6686
Email: myerslaw@aol.com

*Civil and Criminal Trial Practice. Personal Injury, Workers Compensation and Medical Malpractice Law.*

**JOSEPH PETER MYERS,** born Hollywood, California, November 1, 1940; admitted to bar, 1968, California; 1971, U.S. Supreme Court. *Education:* Pomona College (A.B., 1961); University of Southern California (J.D., 1967); University of California at Riverside (M.A., 1990). Sigma Xi; Phi Alpha Delta. Member, Legion Lex, University of Southern California. Articles Editor, Southern California Law Review, 1966-1967. Author: "The Allocation of Financial Responsibility for Mental Illness or Defect," 39 Southern California Law Review, 574, 1966. Co-Author with S. Passamaneck: "Aspects of Land Use and Commercial Regulation in Medieval Rabbinic Sources," 16 Revue Internationale des Droits de l'Antiquite, 31, 1969, Brussels. Lecturer in Law, Southern California Law Center, 1968-1970. Visiting Instructor, University of Redlands, 1978-1979. Member, 1983-1992 and Vice President, 1989-1992, Board of Education, Riverside Unified School District. Chairman, Riverside City and County Library Commission, 1985-1990. Host, Business and The Law, Southern California Consortium For Public Television, 1989—. *Member:* Riverside County and American Bar Associations; The State Bar of California; California Trial Lawyers Association (Member, Board of Governors, Inland Chapter, 1974-1980); California Applicants' Attorneys Association; California Attorneys for Criminal Justice.

---

## O'FLAHERTY & BELGUM

3880 LEMON STREET
SUITE 450
RIVERSIDE, CALIFORNIA 92501-3301
Telephone: 909-341-0049
Fax: 909-341-3919
Email: oandb@law.com
URL: http://www.oandb-law/oandb

*Glendale, California Office:* 1000 North Central, Suite 300, 91202-2957. Telephone: 818-242-9229. Fax: 818-242-9114.
*Long Beach, California Office:* 100 Oceangate, Suite 500, 90802-4312. Telephone: 310-437-0090. Fax: 310-437-5550.
*Orange County, California Office:* 222 South Harbor Boulevard, Suite 600, Anaheim, CA 92805-3701. Telephone: 714-533-3373. Fax: 714-533-2607.
*Ventura, California Office:* 840 County Square Drive, Suite 200, 93003-5406. Telephone: 805-650-2600. Fax: 805-650-2658.

*General Civil, Trial and Appellate Practice in State and Federal Courts. Medical and Dental Malpractice, Products Liability, General Insurance Law, Insurance Coverage, Wrongful Termination, Workers' Compensation, Business and Environmental Litigation.*

(For Complete Biographical Data on all Personnel, see Professional Biographies at Glendale).

## GERALD D. POLIS
A PROFESSIONAL CORPORATION
Established in 1976
THE LORING BUILDING
3685 MAIN STREET, SUITE 250
RIVERSIDE, CALIFORNIA 92501
Telephone: 909-684-0131
Fax: 909-684-2808

*Practice Limited to Criminal Defense in all Courts.*

**GERALD D. POLIS,** born Charleston, South Carolina, January 11, 1941; admitted to bar, 1965, South Carolina; 1969, California. *Education:* College of Charleston (B.S., 1962); University of South Carolina (LL.B., 1965). Co-Author: "Chapter 10-Pleas and Case Settlement," California Criminal Law-Procedure and Practice, California Continuing Education of the Bar, 1986. Deputy District Attorney, Riverside County, 1969-1971. Commissioner, City of Riverside Community Relations Commission, 1979-1980. Listed, "The Best Lawyers in America," 1991-1992, 1993-1994 and 1995-1996 editions. Judge Pro Tempore: Riverside Municipal Court, 1973—; Superior Court, 1978—. *Member:* Riverside County Bar Association (Treasurer, 1975-1977; Vice-President, 1979-1980); South Carolina State Bar (Member, Criminal Law Section); The State Bar of California; California Attorney's for Criminal Justice; California Public Defenders Association; National Association of Criminal Defense Lawyers. [Capt., USAF, JAG, 1965-1969]. (Certified Specialist, Criminal Law, The State Bar of California Board of Legal Specialization).

REFERENCE: Wells Fargo Bank.

---

## REDWINE AND SHERRILL
Established in 1958
1950 MARKET STREET
RIVERSIDE, CALIFORNIA 92501
Telephone: 909-684-2520
Facsimile: 909-684-9583

*Santa Ana, California Office:* 13611 Winthrope Street. 92705. Telephone: 714-832-2256. Fax: 714-832-1719.

*General Civil, Trial and Appellate Practice in State and Federal Courts. Water Rights Law, Municipal, Eminent Domain, Corporation, Real Property, Business, Zoning, Probate Law, Contract, Intentional Tort and Defamation, Federal and State Taxation.*

*FIRM PROFILE: Redwine and Sherrill's strength as an excellent general-purposes civil law firm is augmented by seasoned expertise in a number of complex legal arenas, including matters involving Eminent Domain, Water Law, Real Estate Taxation, Business Law, public agency law and others. During fifty years of legal service to a diverse clientele, Redwine and Sherrill has earned a reputation as a leader in these areas of specialization.*

*Representing both plaintiffs and defendants, the firm has amassed significant experience and professional respect as the result of its participation in landmark cases that made or changed the law in areas of importance such as apportionment of the water of the Colorado River, interpretation of the California Coastal Act, rules of liability of public agencies in flooding cases and public domain. The firm retains a respected presence by serving on committees of statewide water and sanitation associations.*

*Redwine and Sherrill has earned a reputation for responsiveness and sensitivity to the concerns of the client. The firm's policy is to avoid unnecessary litigation if possible and failing that, to hold down costs of litigation when possible. When litigation is required or unavoidable, the firm excels in court representation in all areas of litigation in Federal and State courts.*

**EARL REDWINE** (1894-1967).

### OF COUNSEL

**MAURICE C. SHERRILL,** born Troutman, North Carolina, July 30, 1922; admitted to bar, 1950, California; 1960, U.S. Supreme Court. *Education:* Riverside College (A.A., 1942); University of Southern California (B.S., 1950; J.D., 1949). Phi Delta Phi. Deputy County Counsel, 1951; Public Defender, 1952-1956, Riverside County. *Member:* Riverside County and Los Angeles County Bar Associations; The State Bar of California. *PRACTICE AREAS:* Water Law; Water District Administration Law.

*(This Listing Continued)*

### MEMBERS OF FIRM

**JUSTIN M. MCCARTHY,** born Cleveland, Ohio, May 31, 1926; admitted to bar, 1954, California and U.S. Supreme Court; 1962, U.S. District Court, Central and Southern Districts of California and U.S. Court of Appeals, Ninth Circuit. *Education:* Loyola University at Los Angeles (B.S., 1950; LL.B., 1953). Deputy County Counsel, Riverside County, 1956-1959. Assistant City Attorney, City of Riverside, 1961-1962. *Member:* Riverside County, Los Angeles County and American (Chairman, Urban, State and Local Government Law Condemnation Section, 1987-1988) Bar Associations; The State Bar of California (Member, Committee on Condemnation, 1976-1977; 1983); American Board of Trial Advocates (Diplomate). [Capt., USCGR (Retired)]. *PRACTICE AREAS:* Eminent Domain Law; Commercial Litigation; General Civil Trials.

**GERALD D. SHOAF,** born Altadena, California, September 20, 1941; admitted to bar, 1967, California. *Education:* Riverside City College; San Diego State College (B.A., 1964); University of California at Los Angeles (J.D., 1967). Co-author: with Joseph S. Aklufi, "A Summary of Rules of Liability in Water Damage Cases," California State Bar Journal, November, 1980. Lecturer, C.E.B., Flooding, 1982-1984. President: Riverside Barristers, 1973-1974; Inland Counties Legal Services, 1975-1978. City Attorney, Norco, 1976-1978. *Member:* Riverside County, Los Angeles County and American Bar Associations; The State Bar of California. *PRACTICE AREAS:* Water Law; Water District Administration Law; Inverse Condemnation Law.

**GARY E. REDDISH,** born Los Angeles, California, December 6, 1935; admitted to bar, 1973, California; 1978, U.S. Tax Court. *Education:* University of California at Los Angeles (B.S., 1965); Loyola University of Los Angeles (J.D., 1972). Certified Public Accountant, California, 1970. Revenue Agent and Appellate Appeals Officer, Internal Revenue Service. *Member:* Los Angeles County and American (Member, Taxation Section) Bar Associations; The State Bar of California (President, Riverside Estate Planning Council, 1983-1984; Chairman, Riverside County Bar Tax Section, 1984-1985; 1986-1987). *PRACTICE AREAS:* Federal and State Taxation Law; Corporate Law; Litigation.

**GERALD W. EAGANS,** born San Francisco, California, October 17, 1954; admitted to bar, 1980, California. *Education:* University of the Pacific (B.A., 1975); University of Santa Clara (J.D., 1980); New York University (LL.M. in Taxation, 1981). Recipient, American Jurisprudence Award in Trusts. *Member:* Riverside County and American Bar Associations; The State Bar of California. *PRACTICE AREAS:* Federal and State Taxation Law; Contract Law; Real Property Law; Corporation Law.

**GILBERT J. GRANITO,** born Santa Fe, New Mexico, July 12, 1941; admitted to bar, 1974, California and U.S. District Court, Central District of California; 1976, U.S. Tax Court. *Education:* Woodbury University (B.B.A., 1962); Pepperdine University (J.D., 1973). Lecturer, Real Estate Law/Taxation, University of California at Riverside, 1976. Revenue Agent and Appellate Conferee, Internal Revenue Service 1962-1975. *Member:* Orange County (Chairman, Tax Section), Los Angeles County and Riverside County Bar Associations; State Bar of California. (Also at Santa Ana). *PRACTICE AREAS:* Water Law; Water District Administration Law; State and Federal Tax Litigation; Administrative Appeals.

**THOMAS E. BRUYNEEL,** born Los Angeles, California, March 3, 1942; admitted to bar, 1970, California; U.S. Court of Appeals, Ninth Circuit; U.S. District Court, Northern, Central and Southern Districts of California. *Education:* San Diego State University (A.B., 1964); Hastings College of the Law (J.D., 1969). Instructor, Civil Procedure, Lone Mountain College, 1978-1981. *Member:* Riverside County, Los Angeles County and Orange County Bar Associations; State Bar of California; World Affairs Council. *PRACTICE AREAS:* Civil Trials; Appellate Practice (State and Federal) Law; Water Law; Business Law; Eminent Domain.

**STEVEN B. ABBOTT,** born Covina, California, August 16, 1961; admitted to bar, 1986, California; 1987, U.S. Court of Appeals, Ninth Circuit and U.S. District Court, Central District of California; 1989, U.S. District Court, Southern District of California; 1992, U.S. Supreme Court. *Education:* University of California at Davis (B.A., with highest honors, 1983); University of California at Los Angeles (J.D., 1986). Phi Kappa Phi; Pi Sigma Alpha. *Member:* Riverside County Bar Association; State Bar of California. *PRACTICE AREAS:* Water Law; Eminent Domain Law.

**JEFFRY F. FERRE,** born San Bernardino, California, May 4, 1963; admitted to bar, 1988, California; U.S. District Court, Central District of California. *Education:* University of Redlands (B.A., 1985); University of the Pacific, McGeorge School of Law (J.D., 1988). Phi Alpha Delta. *Member:* Riverside County and American Bar Associations; State Bar of Califor-

*(This Listing Continued)*

REDWINE AND SHERRILL, Riverside—Continued

nia. *PRACTICE AREAS:* Public and Governmental Law; Contract Law; Real Property Law.

### ASSOCIATES

**ROBERT T. ANDERSEN, JR.,** born Los Angeles, California, March 2, 1950; admitted to bar, 1979, California, U.S. Court of Appeals, Ninth Circuit and U.S. District Court, Northern, Eastern, Central and Southern Districts of California; 1981, U.S. Claims Court; 1982, U.S. Tax Court; 1987, U.S. Supreme Court. *Education:* University of California at Los Angeles (B.A., 1971; M.P.A., 1972); Talbot Theological Seminary (M.A., 1977); University of the Pacific, McGeorge School of the Law (J.D., 1979). Instructor, Business Law, California Baptist College, 1980, 1985, 1986, 1987. *Member:* Riverside County Bar Association; State Bar of California. *PRACTICE AREAS:* Business; Litigation; Probate; Public Law; Eminent Domain.

**SCOTT RICHARD HEIL,** born Mobile, Alabama, June 19, 1963; admitted to bar, 1992, California. *Education:* University of Southern California (B.S., 1986); University of California-Berkeley (M.B.A., 1992); Hastings College of the Law, University of California (J.D., 1992). Recipient, Outstanding Oral Argument Award. Member, David E. Snodgrass Moot Court Competition. *Member:* Riverside County Bar Association; State Bar of California. *PRACTICE AREAS:* General Civil Trial Law; Contract Law; Real Property Law.

**ANDREW P. BYRNE,** born Los Angeles, California, September 4, 1967; admitted to bar, 1994, California. *Education:* U.S. Marine Corps Officer Candidate School, Quantico, Virginia (Summer, 1987) University of California, Los Angeles (B.A., English, 1989); Cambridge University, England (Summer, 1988); Santa Clara University School of Law (J.D., 1994). Member, Editorial Staff, Environmental Law Bulletin. Qualified Whitewater Rafting Guide. U.S. Probation Officer, Los Angeles, California 1995-1996. *Member:* Riverside and San Bernardino County Bar Associations. *PRACTICE AREAS:* Water Law; Civil Litigation.

**SETH C. THOMPSON,** born New York, N.Y., June 6, 1966; admitted to bar, 1995, California. *Education:* University of California-Berkeley (B.A., Economics, 1989); University of California-Los Angeles (J.D., 1995). *Member:* Riverside and Los Angeles County Bar Associations. *LANGUAGES:* Spanish. *PRACTICE AREAS:* Water Law; Civil Litigation.

REPRESENTATIVE CLIENTS: Coachella Valley Water District; Eastern Municipal Water District; West San Bernardino County Water District; Twentynine Palms Water District; Beaumont-Cherry Valley Water Districts; Rincon Del Diablo Municipal Water District; Teledyne, Inc.; Hahn Devcorp; County of San Bernardino; Triego Farms; Circle K Corp.; Commonwealth Land Title Insurance Co.; Fidelity National Title Insurance Co.; Bourns, Inc.; Avco Financial Service; S. W. Plastics, Inc.; North American Science Associates; Metropolitan Automotive Warehouse; Temtex Products of California; Aetna Casualty and Surety Co.; Harbor Ins. Co.

## REID & HELLYER
### A PROFESSIONAL CORPORATION
3880 LEMON, 5TH FLOOR
P.O. BOX 1300
**RIVERSIDE, CALIFORNIA 92502-3834**
Telephone: 909-682-1771
Telecopier: 909-686-2415
Email: rhlaw@rhlaw.com

General Civil and Trial Practice in all State and Federal Courts. Administrative, Bankruptcy, Commercial, Communications, Constitutional, Construction, Corporate, Environmental, Ethics and Professional Responsibility, Estate Planning, Eminent Domain and Water Rights Law, Government, High Technology, Insurance, Intellectual Property, Labor and Employment Law, Litigation, Malpractice, Military, Personal Injury, Probate, Real Property, Torts, Zoning and Municipal.

**DONALD F. POWELL,** born Vancouver, Washington, November 25, 1939; admitted to bar, 1966, California. *Education:* Menlo College (A.A., 1959); University of California at Berkeley (A.B., 1962); Hastings College of Law, University of California (LL.B., 1965). Order of the Coif; Phi Delta Phi. Member, Thurston Society. Member, Board of Editors, Hastings Law Journal, 1964-1965. *Member:* Riverside County Bar Association; National Association of Railroad Trial Counsel. *PRACTICE AREAS:* Business Litigation; Real Estate Litigation; Condemnation Law. *Email:* rhlaw@rhlaw.com

*(This Listing Continued)*

**DAVID G. MOORE,** born Washington, D.C., June 28, 1938; admitted to bar, 1965, California. *Education:* University of California at Berkeley (B.S., 1961); Hastings College of Law, University of California (LL.B., 1964). Listed in "The Best Lawyers in America," 1996-1997. Mediator, Fourth District Court of Appeals. *Member:* Riverside County Bar Association (President, 1984-1985); Leo A. Deegan Inn of Court (President, 1994-1996); Settlement Now (President, 1995-1996). *PRACTICE AREAS:* Business and Real Estate Litigation; Tort Defense; Water Law; Legal and Medical Malpractice Defense; General Civil Litigation. *Email:* rhlaw@rhlaw.com

**JAMES J. MANNING, JR.,** born Los Angeles, California, April 10, 1949; admitted to bar, 1976, California. *Education:* Marquette University and University of California at Riverside (B.A., 1971); La Verne College (J.D., 1976). Member, Board of Editors, La Verne College Law Review, 1975-1976. *Member:* Riverside County and San Bernardino County Bar Associations. *PRACTICE AREAS:* Real Estate Law; Title Insurance Litigation; Construction Law; Newspaper Law. *Email:* rhlaw@rhlaw.com

**DIANE S. BREWER,** born Ventura, California, October 8, 1940; admitted to bar, 1978, California. *Education:* Sacramento State College (B.A., 1962); University of San Diego (J.D., cum laude, 1978). Recipient: Grant Richardson Award in Juvenile Law; American Jurisprudence Awards in Conflict of Laws, Creditors Rights and Criminal Procedure. *Member:* Riverside County Bar Association; Riverside County Estate Planning Council. *PRACTICE AREAS:* Probate Law; Estate Planning Law. *Email:* rhlaw@rhlaw.com

**RICHARD D. ROTH,** born Columbus, Ohio, November 6, 1950; admitted to bar, 1974, Georgia; 1975, U.S. Court of Military Appeals; 1980, California. *Education:* Miami University (B.A., 1972); Emory University (J.D., 1974). Phi Delta Phi. Author: "Hiring Practices in the 1990's - Employment Under Pressure," 1990, American Somerset, Inc. Attorney, National Labor Relations Board, 1979-1981. *Member:* Riverside County Bar Association. [Capt., JAGD, USAF, 1975-1979; Col., USAFR, 1979— ]. *PRACTICE AREAS:* Labor Relations Law; Employment Law; Business Litigation. *Email:* rhlaw@rhlaw.com

**DAN G. MCKINNEY,** born San Jose, California, June 21, 1956; admitted to bar, 1981, California. *Education:* George Mason University (B.A., 1978); McGeorge School of Law, University of the Pacific (J.D., cum laude, 1981). Phi Delta Phi; Order of the Coif. Member, Traynor Society. Recipient, American Jurisprudence Award in Corporations. *Member:* Riverside County Bar Association (President, 1994-1995). *PRACTICE AREAS:* Real Estate Litigation; Land Use Law; Condemnation Law. *Email:* rhlaw@rhlaw.com

**CHARLES T. SCHULTZ,** born Minneapolis, Minnesota, August 3, 1954; admitted to bar, 1983, California. *Education:* University of California at Riverside (B.A., 1975); University of the Pacific (J.D., 1983). Member, Moot Court. Consultant, California State Legislature, 1975-1982. *Member:* Riverside County Bar Association. *PRACTICE AREAS:* Land Use Law; Development Law; Government Law. *Email:* rhlaw@rhlaw.com

**MICHAEL J. GILLIGAN,** born Riverside, California, November 4, 1948; admitted to bar, 1984, California and U.S. District Court, Southern District of California. *Education:* California State University at San Bernardino (B.A., 1978); University of San Diego (J.D., cum laude, 1984). *Member:* Riverside County and San Diego County Bar Associations; Bankruptcy Forum; American Bankruptcy Institute; California Trustees Association. [S. Sgt., USAF, 1966-1970]. *PRACTICE AREAS:* Bankruptcy Title Law; Real Estate Law; General Civil Litigation. *Email:* rhlaw@rhlaw.com

**MICHAEL G. KERBS,** born Great Bend, Kansas, May 27, 1963; admitted to bar, 1987, California. *Education:* University of San Diego (B.A., 1984; J.D., magna cum laude, 1987). Recipient, American Jurisprudence Award in Sales. Member, San Diego Law Review, 1986-1987. *Member:* Riverside County Bar Association. *PRACTICE AREAS:* Corporate Partnership Real Estate Law; Litigation. *Email:* rhlaw@rhlaw.com

**DEBRA BARTLE GERVAIS,** born San Gabriel, California, December 14, 1956; admitted to bar, 1984, California and U.S. District Court, Northern and Central Districts of California. *Education:* University of California at Berkeley (B.A., 1980); Santa Clara University (J.D., 1984). Editor: *Ideas in the Workplace,* written by Professor Howard Anawalt, 1988. *Member:* San Bernardino County Bar Association. *LANGUAGES:* Spanish. *PRACTICE AREAS:* Construction Law; Real Estate Litigation; Intellectual Property. *Email:* rhlaw@rhlaw.com

**DAVID M. DIVER,** born Montgomery, Alabama, October 13, 1951; admitted to bar, 1976, California; 1977, U.S. Court of Military Appeals. *Education:* The Citadel (B.A., with high honors, 1973); University of San

*(This Listing Continued)*

Diego (J.D., 1976); George Washington University (LL.M., in Labor Law, with high honors, 1987). [Maj. JAG USAF, 1976-1990; Lt. Col. USAFR]. *PRACTICE AREAS:* Labor Relations Law; Employment Law; Business Litigation. *Email:* rhlaw@rhlaw.com

*STEVEN G. LEE,* born Mt. Pleasant, Utah, July 31, 1960; admitted to bar, 1988, California; U.S. District Court, Central District of California. *Education:* Snow College (A.A., 1982); Brigham Young University (B.A., magna cum laude, 1984; J.D., 1988). Hinckley Scholar. Editor, Journal of Public Law, 1987-1988. *Member:* Riverside Bar Association. *PRACTICE AREAS:* Business Law; Real Estate Law; Commercial Litigation. *Email:* rhlaw@rhlaw.com

*DENNIS KOTTMEIER,* born Washington, D.C., March 30, 1944; admitted to bar, 1969, California; 1970, U.S. District Court, Central District of California. *Education:* University of Redlands (B.A., cum laude, 1966); Hastings College of the Law, University of California (J.D., 1969). Instructor, Criminal Law and Evidence, Crafton College. District Attorney, San Bernardino County, 1981-1995. Member, Board of Directors, California District Attorney Association, 1984-1986 and 1988-1990. *Member:* San Bernardino County Bar Association. *PRACTICE AREAS:* State and Local Government; Police Excessive Force Defense; Fair Political Practices; Environmental Crimes Defense; Zoning and Land Use Law. *Email:* rhlaw@rhlaw.com

*OF COUNSEL*

*GERALD J. GEERLINGS,* born Gardena, California, April 22, 1928; admitted to bar, 1955, California. *Education:* University of California at Los Angeles (B.S., 1951); University of California at Los Angeles School of Law (LL.B., 1954). County Counsel, Riverside County, Retired, June 1990. *PRACTICE AREAS:* Land Use Law; Development Law; Government Law. *Email:* rhlaw@rhlaw.com

All Attorneys are Members of The State Bar of California and the American Bar Association.

REPRESENTATIVE CLIENTS: Atchison, Topeka & Santa Fe Railway; Bear Valley Mutual Water Co.; Blue Banner Co., Inc.; Chicago Title Insurance Co.; J. D. Diffenbaugh, Inc.; First American Title Co.; Gateway Title Company; Great Western Bank; Matich Corp.; Montgomery Ward & Co.; Rohr, Inc.; Sweetheart Cup; Tandy Corp.

## ROBERTS & MORGAN
*Established in 1973*
CITRUS PARK
*1650 IOWA AVENUE, SUITE 200*
**RIVERSIDE, CALIFORNIA 92507**
*Telephone: 909-682-2881*
*FAX: 909-682-2928*
*Email: akcrjo@SoCa.com*

*General Civil and Trial Practice; Insurance Coverage Analysis and Litigation; Insurance Broker and Agent Litigation; Municipal Law; Police Misconduct Defense; Construction Defect Litigation; Subrogation; Products Liability Litigation; Uninsured Motorist Law; Medical and Legal Malpractice Defense; Appellate Practice.*

*ROGER W. ROBERTS* (1917-1986).

*ROBERT W. ENGLE* (1923-1985).

*BRUCE MORGAN,* born Minnesota, August 26, 1932; admitted to bar, 1965, California and U.S. District Court, District of California. *Education:* Arizona State University (B.S., 1954); Southwestern University (J.D., 1965). *Member:* Riverside County, Los Angeles County and American Bar Associations; The State Bar of California; American Board of Trial Advocates (Member, National Executive Committee, 1979-1982; President, Riverside/San Bernardino Chapter, 1981); California Trial Lawyers Association; International Association of Defense Counsel; Association of Southern California Defense Counsel.

*JOHN M. PORTER,* born California, August 7, 1947; admitted to bar, 1974, California; U.S. District Court, District of California; 1981, U.S. Court of Appeals, Ninth Circuit. *Education:* San Diego State University (B.A., 1969); University of San Diego (J.D., 1974). Phi Alpha Delta. Assistant City Attorney, Lake Elsinore, 1975-1980. City Attorney, Lake Elsinore, 1981-1984. *Member:* Los Angeles County, Riverside County and American (Charter Member, Litigation Section) Bar Associations; The State Bar of California (Charter Member, Litigation Section); Association of Southern California Defense Counsel; American Board of Trial Advocates. *Email:* PDWK66A@PRODIGY.COM

*(This Listing Continued)*

*JAMES C. PACKER,* born California, March 2, 1951; admitted to bar, 1977, California. *Education:* University of Redlands; University of California at Santa Barbara (B.A., 1973); California Western School of Law (J.D., 1977). Member, International Law Journal, 1976-1977. *Member:* Riverside County, San Bernardino County and American Bar Associations; The State Bar of California; Association of Southern California Defense Counsel; American Board of Trial Advocates.

*ARTHUR K. CUNNINGHAM,* born Massachusetts, October 17, 1953; admitted to bar, 1981, California and U.S. District Court, District of California. *Education:* University of California at Irvine (B.S., 1975); Western State University (J.D., 1980). Recipient, American Jurisprudence Awards in Contracts and Conflict of Laws. *Member:* Riverside County and American Bar Associations; The State Bar of California; Association of Southern California Defense Counsel. *Email:* akcrjc@SoCa.com

*DOUGLAS McCARTHY,* born Carbondale, Pennsylvania, August 19, 1946; admitted to bar, 1978, California; 1979, Nevada, U.S. District Court, District of Nevada and U.S. District Court, District of California. *Education:* Columbia University (B.A., 1968); University of California at Los Angeles (J.D., 1978). Deputy District Attorney, Clark County, Nevada, 1980-1984. *Member:* Riverside County Bar Association; State Bar of California; State Bar of Nevada. [Capt. USAF, 1969-1975] *Email:* tracker@pacbell.net

*FIONA G. LUKE,* born San Francisco, California, October 1, 1961; admitted to bar, 1989, California; 1990, U.S. District Court, Central District of California. *Education:* California State University at Los Angeles (B.A., 1983); Loyola Law School, Los Angeles (J.D., 1986). Member, Asian-/American Law Students Association, 1983-1986. *Member:* San Bernardino County and Riverside County Bar Associations; State Bar of California; Association of Southern California Defense Counsel.

*AARON HANCOCK,* born San Francisco, California, January 27, 1967; admitted to bar, 1992, California; 1994, U.S. District Court, Central District of California; 1996, U.S. Court of Appeals, Ninth Circuit. *Education:* University of California at Berkeley (B.A., English, 1989; B.A., History, 1989); University of California at Davis (J.D., 1992). *Member:* Riverside County Bar Association; State Bar of California.

*CYRIL C. STANFIELD, III,* born Tulsa, Oklahoma, February 4, 1948; admitted to bar, 1979, California and U.S. District Court, Central District of California. *Education:* University of Tulsa (B.S., 1971); Citrus Belt Law School (J.D., 1979). *Member:* Riverside County and American Bar Associations; State Bar of California; Association of Southern California Defense Counsel. [Lt. Col., U.S.A.F., 1971-1979; Lt.Col., U.S.A.F.R., 1979—]. *LANGUAGES:* German.

*MATTHEW J. MARNELL,* born November 7, 1955; admitted to bar, 1982, California. *Education:* Loyola Marymount University (B.A., 1978; J.D., 1982). *Member:* Riverside County Bar Association; The State Bar of California; Association of Southern California Defense Counsel.

*CYRUS J. LEMMON,* born Denver, Colorado, July 28, 1942; admitted to bar, 1970, Colorado; U.S. District Court, District of Colorado; U.S Court of Appeals, Tenth Circuit; 1973, California; 1978, U.S. Court of Appeals, Ninth Circuit; 1980, U.S. Supreme Court. *Education:* University of San Francisco; University of Colorado (B.A., 1965; J.D., 1970). Judge Pro-Tem, San Bernardino Municipal Court, 1978—. Arbitrator, San Bernardino Superior Court, 1980—. *Member:* San Bernardino County, Colorado and American Bar Associations; The State Bar of California; American Board Institute International Association of Defense Counsel; Trial Lawyers Association; Association of Southern California Defense Counsel. *Email:* jacklemmon@prodigy.com

REPRESENTATIVE CLIENTS: Farmers Insurance Group; Ohio Casualty Insurance Group; City of Riverside; County of Riverside; City of Corona; Automobile Club of Southern California; Aetna Casualty & Surety Co. (Personal & Commercial Lines); Liberty Mutual Insurance Co.; Foremost Insurance Co.; Risk Enterprise Management; City of Banning; California Fair Service Authority; Crawford & Co.; Carl Warraen & Co.; Reliance Insurance Co.; Utica Mutual Insurance Co.; Hertz Claim Management Corp.

## PETER W. SCALISI
*3890 ELEVENTH STREET, SUITE 115*
**RIVERSIDE, CALIFORNIA 92501-3524**
*Telephone: 909-686-9914*
*Fax: 909-686-8401*

*Criminal Trial, Grand Jury, White Collar Crime and Appellate Practice in all State and Federal Courts.*

*FIRM PROFILE: Well Over 100 jury trials in state and federal court to verdict, including death penalty, white collar, major narcotics, vehicular manslaughter and child molestation cases.*

*(This Listing Continued)*

**PETER W. SCALISI,** Riverside—Continued

**PETER W. SCALISI,** born Los Angeles, California, September 17, 1954; admitted to bar, 1979, California; 1980, U.S. District Court, Central District of California; U.S. Court of Appeals, Ninth Circuit; 1981, U.S. District Court, Southern District of California; 1984, U.S. Supreme Court; 1992, U.S. District Court, District of Arizona; 1996, U.S. District Court, Northern District of California. *Education:* Claremont Mens College (B.A., cum laude, 1976); Southwestern University Law School (J.D., 1979). Deputy District Attorney, County of Riverside, 1980-1985. Deputy Public Defender, County of Orange, 1985. Partner, Law Offices of Michael R. McDonnell, Inc., La Habra, California, 1985-1993. (Practice limited to criminal defense in all state and federal courts). Co-Chairperson and Founding Member, Federal Criminal Defense Panel, U.S. District Court, Central District of California, Riverside Division. Management Committee, Criminal Defense Panel, Riverside Courts. Adjunct Professor of Criminal Law, Riverside City College, 1981-1984. Adjunct Professor of Criminal Justice, Graduate Division, California State University at Long Beach, California, 1985. *Member:* Riverside County and Federal Bar Associations; State Bar of California; California Attorneys for Criminal Justice; National Association of Criminal Defense Lawyers. (Certified Specialist, Criminal Law, The State Bar of California Board of Legal Specialization). **PRACTICE AREAS:** Criminal Law.

## SCHELL & DELAMER, LLP
### RIVERSIDE, CALIFORNIA
(See Los Angeles)

*Products Liability, Premise Liability and Security Issues, Insurance Coverage and Bad Faith, Public Entity and Government Liability, Automobile and Transportation, Truck and Heavy Equipment, Restaurant and Club Liability, Medical and Dental Malpractice, Wrongful Termination and Employers Liability, Defamation and Invasion of Privacy, Environmental (including EMF and RFI Exposure and Toxic Torts), Construction Defect and Land Subsidence, Business and Commercial Law, Professional Liability, Pharmaceutical Liability.*

## THE LAW OFFICES OF
## WILLIAM J. SIMON
4333 ORANGE STREET, SUITE 2
### RIVERSIDE, CALIFORNIA 92501
Telephone: 909-686-1561
Fax: 909-686-4859

*Bankruptcy and Insolvency Law.*

**WILLIAM J. SIMON,** born Boston, Massachusetts, August 7, 1943; admitted to bar, 1976, California and U.S. District Court, Central District of California; 1982, U.S. Tax Court; 1987, U.S. Court of Appeals, Ninth Circuit. *Education:* San Bernardino Valley College (A.A., 1966); California State University at Los Angeles; Western State University (B.S.L., 1974; J.D., 1976). Member, U.S. Trustee Panel, 1982-1988, and Member, Board of Directors, 1980—, Inland Counties Legal Services. President, San Bernardino County Legal Aid Society, 1981-1987. Member, Financial Lawyers Conference, 1984—. *Member:* San Bernardino County and American (Member, Section on Legal Economics) Bar Associations; State Bar of California (Member, Section on Legal Economics); Commercial Law League of America; Bankruptcy Study Group (Los Angeles); Orange County Bankruptcy Forum. **PRACTICE AREAS:** Bankruptcy Law; Insolvency Law.

## SINGER & SILVERGLEID, INC.
*Established in 1985*

3750 UNIVERSITY AVENUE, SUITE 550
### RIVERSIDE, CALIFORNIA 92501
Telephone: 909-784-3800
Facsimile: 909-781-4083

*Municipal Law, Civil Litigation. Eminent Domain, Real Estate, Probate and Business Law.*

**M. NEAL SINGER,** born Denver, Colorado, 1937; admitted to bar, 1963, California; 1964, Colorado. *Education:* University of Colorado at Boulder (B.S., 1959); University of Denver (J.D., 1962). Editor in Chief,

*(This Listing Continued)*

Denver Law Journal, 1962. Author: "Municipal Corporations-Eminent Domain," Dicta (now Denver Law Journal), Vol. 38, No. 4, July-August, 1960; "Colorado's Maximum Recovery for Wrongful Death v. the Constitution," Dicta, Vol. 38, No. 4, July-August, 1961. Deputy and Assistant City Attorney, 1965-1972, Riverside, California. Town Attorney, Apple Valley, 1988—. *Member:* Riverside County Bar Association. **PRACTICE AREAS:** Municipal; Eminent Domain; Civil Litigation.

**NAOMI SILVERGLEID,** born New York, N.Y., 1943; admitted to bar, 1977, California. *Education:* University of Rochester (B.A., with high honors, 1964); University of Santa Clara (J.D., cum laude, 1977). Town Attorney, Yucca Valley. *Member:* Riverside County Bar Association. **PRACTICE AREAS:** Business and Real Estate Transactions; Estate Planning; Municipal.

**PATRICK J. SAMPSON,** born Los Angeles, California, 1937; admitted to bar, 1963, California. *Education:* University of California at Los Angeles (A.B., 1959; LL.B., 1962). Adjunct Professor, University of Laverne, College of Law, 1980-1988. City Attorney, Pomona, 1973-1989. President, Orange County City Attorney Association, 1984. *Member:* Los Angeles County Bar Association (Chair, Governmental Law Section, 1986); Eastern Bar Association of Los Angeles County (President, 1988-1989). [Lt. Col. U.S. Air Force, California Air National Guard, Retired]. **PRACTICE AREAS:** Municipal.

All Attorneys are Members of the California State Bar.

REPRESENTATIVE CLIENTS: City of Moreno Valley; Town of Apple Valley; Town of Yucca Valley; Metropolitan Water District; Allbann Industries.

## STUTZ, GALLAGHER, ARTIANO, SHINOFF
## & HOLTZ, A PROFESSIONAL
## CORPORATION
43537 RIDGE PARK DRIVE, SUITE 206
### RIVERSIDE, CALIFORNIA 92590
Telephone: 909-699-1231
Fax: 909-699-1261

*San Diego, California Office:* 15th Floor, First National Bank Building, 401 West "A" Street. Telephone: 619-232-3122. Fax: 619-232-3264.

*General Civil Trial Practice with Special Emphasis in Product Liability, Employment, Environmental, Professional Liability, Construction Defect Litigation, Public Entity, Commercial Litigation, Insurance Coverage, Defense of the Hospitality Industry and Medical Providers.*

FIRM PROFILE: *Stutz, Gallagher, Artiano, Shinoff & Holtz has served as litigation counsel representing the interests of individuals, corporations of all sizes, including major national and international companies, major insurance companies, school districts, municipalities and the State of California. The firm practices throughout Southern California.*

(For Complete Biographical Data on all Personnel, see Professional Biographies at San Diego)

## SWARNER & FITZGERALD
A Partnership including Professional Corporations
*Established in 1946*

3403 TENTH STREET, SUITE 700
P.O. BOX 827
### RIVERSIDE, CALIFORNIA 92502
Telephone: 909-683-4242
Telecopier: 909-683-4518
Email: attyonline@attorneys-on-line.com
URL: http://www.attyonline@attorney_on_line.com

*General Civil Trial and Appellate Practice, Business Litigation, Corporate, Estate Planning, Wills/Trusts, Probate, Family, Real Estate, Commercial, Negligence, Tort.*

### MEMBERS OF FIRM

**LEWIS F. JACOBSEN, (A PROFESSIONAL CORPORATION),** born Redlands, California, June 22, 1926; admitted to bar, 1954, California; U.S. District Court, Central and Southern Districts of California; U.S. Supreme Court. *Education:* University of California at Los Angeles (A.B., highest honors in Political Science, 1950); Stanford University (J.D., 1953). Phi Beta Kappa. Member, Board of Editors, Stanford Law Review, 1952-1953. Assistant County Counsel, County of Riverside, California, 1954-

*(This Listing Continued)*

1956. *Member:* Riverside County and American Bar Associations; The State Bar of California. **PRACTICE AREAS:** Real Property Law; Commercial; Corporate; Secured Transactions; Appellate Practice.

**EDWARD L. MACKEY, (A PROFESSIONAL CORPORATION),** born Riverside, California, September 19, 1933; admitted to bar, 1959, California, U.S. District Court, Northern and Central Districts of California and U.S. Court of Appeals, Ninth Circuit; U.S. Supreme Court. *Education:* Stanford University (B.A., 1955; LL.B., 1959). Phi Delta Phi. *Member:* Riverside County and American Bar Associations; The State Bar of California. **PRACTICE AREAS:** Corporations; Real Property; Trusts; Civil Litigation.

**DAVID B. BOWKER,** born Chicago, Illinois, October 6, 1954; admitted to bar, 1977, California; U.S. District Court, Central and Southern Districts of California; 1993, U.S. Tax Court. *Education:* University of California at Riverside (B.A., highest honors in Classics, 1974); University of California at Los Angeles (J.D., 1977). Phi Beta Kappa. *Member:* Riverside County and American Bar Associations; The State Bar of California. **PRACTICE AREAS:** Probate; Conservatorship; Wills and Trusts; Estate Planning.

**THOMAS D. ALLERT,** born Riverside, California, October 4, 1952; admitted to bar, 1978, California; U.S. District Court, Central District of California. *Education:* University of California at Riverside (B.A., 1974); Western State University (J.D., 1978). Recipient, American Jurisprudence Award in Torts. *Member:* Riverside County and American Bar Associations; The State Bar of California; Leo A. Deegan Inn of Court. (Certified Specialist, Family Law, The State Bar of California Board of Legal Specialization). **PRACTICE AREAS:** Marital Dissolutions.

REPRESENTATIVE CLIENTS: Edgemont Community Services District, Agri-Empire, Inc.; Bank of America; Public Administrator of Riverside County; Public Guardian of Riverside County; Sterling Motors.
REFERENCES: Bank of America (Riverside Office); Bank of California (Riverside Office).

---

# THOMAS, MORT, PROSSER & KNUDSEN, LLP

Established in 1982

3403 TENTH STREET, SUITE 300
P.O. BOX 1609
**RIVERSIDE, CALIFORNIA 92502**
Telephone: 909-788-0100
Facsimile: 909-788-5785

*Business, Corporate, Securities, Real Estate, Public Finance, Redevelopment, Environmental Law, Products Liability, Toxic Torts, Health Care, Land Use and Zoning. Appellate and Trial Practice in all State and Federal Courts.*

## MEMBERS OF FIRM

**WILLIAM E. THOMAS,** born Riverside, California, September 25, 1948; admitted to bar, 1973, California. *Education:* University of California at Santa Barbara (B.A., 1970); Hastings College of Law, University of California (J.D., 1973); New York University (LL.M. in Corporate and Securities Law, 1976). Phi Beta Kappa. Co-Author - Hannan and Thomas, "The Importance of Economic Reality and Risk in Defining Federal Securities," 25 Hastings Law Journal 219, 1974. Lecturer and Member, Advisory Council, University of California at Riverside Graduate School of Management, 1988—. Attorney, U.S. Securities and Exchange Commission, 1974-1975. *Member:* Riverside County Bar Association; The State Bar of California. Fellow, New York University Securities Institute, 1976. **PRACTICE AREAS:** Business Law; Health Care; Corporate Law; Municipal Finance; Real Estate; Securities.

**PETER J. MORT,** born Guilford, Connecticut, August 7, 1947; admitted to bar, 1978, Connecticut; 1982, California; 1990, U.S. Supreme Court. *Education:* University of California at Riverside (B.A., 1974); University of Connecticut (J.D., 1978). President, Master Leo A. Deegan Inn of Court. Mediator, Division Two Fourth District Court of Appeal. Director, Dispute Resolution Corporation. Arbitrator, Riverside Superior Court. *Member:* Riverside County and American Bar Associations; State Bar of California. [Captain, U.S. Army, 1966-1974]. **PRACTICE AREAS:** Business; Commercial; Real Estate; Construction Defect Litigation.

**DEBORAH C. PROSSER,** born Frankfurt, Germany, July 15, 1950; admitted to bar, 1980, New Jersey; 1981, New York; 1983, California. *Education:* Hobart & William Smith Colleges; Franklin & Marshall College (B.A., 1973); Rutgers School of Law-Newark (J.D., 1980). *Member:* Riverside County, Los Angeles and American Bar Associations; State Bar of California. **LANGUAGES:** French. **PRACTICE AREAS:** Environmental; Civil Trial and Toxic Torts; Products Liability; Construction.

**CURTIS E. KNUDSEN,** born Rosholt, South Dakota, February 26, 1953; admitted to bar, 1978, South Dakota; 1979, Colorado; 1989, California. *Education:* Northern State University (B.S., magna cum laude, 1975); University of South Dakota (J.D., 1978). *Member:* Riverside County, Colorado and American (Member, Sections on: Real Property, Probate and Trust Law; Corporation, Banking and Business Law) Bar Associations; State Bar of California. **PRACTICE AREAS:** Real Estate; Lending; Lease Law.

**ANDREW D. BROOKS,** born San Diego, California, August 14, 1961; admitted to bar, 1986, California; 1987, U.S. Tax Court. *Education:* University of California at Berkeley (A.B., 1983); University of Southern California (J.D., 1986). *Member:* Riverside County Bar Association; State Bar of California. **PRACTICE AREAS:** Business Law; Corporate Law; Municipal Finance; Securities; Tax Exempt Organizations.

**JOHN W. VINEYARD,** born San Bernardino, California, October 24, 1961; admitted to bar, 1989, California. *Education:* Northeast Louisiana University (B.A., cum laude, 1985); University of California at Davis (J.D., 1989). Phi Kappa Phi; Phi Alpha Delta (Justice, 1988-1989). Instructor, University of California, Riverside, Extension. *Member:* Riverside County (Chief Financial Officer, 1996) and American Bar Associations; State Bar of California (Member, Committee on Rules and Procedures of Court, 1995); Riverside County Barristers (President, 1993-1994). **PRACTICE AREAS:** Business; Real Estate; Toxic Tort Litigation.

**DONNA M. BAKER,** born February 13, 1957; admitted to bar, 1989, California. *Education:* Loyola Marymount University (B.S., magna cum laude, 1978); University of California, Los Angeles (M.B.A., J.D., 1989). Chief Comment Editor, UCLA Law Review, 1989. *Member:* Riverside County Bar Association; State Bar of California. **PRACTICE AREAS:** Commercial Litigation.

## ASSOCIATES

**MICHAEL A. DESJARDINS,** born Fargo, North Dakota, February 9, 1961; admitted to bar, 1986, Wisconsin; U.S. District Court, Eastern District of Wisconsin; 1990, California, U.S. District Court, Southern District of California and U.S. Court of Military Appeals. *Education:* University of Minnesota (B.A., with distinction, 1983); Marquette University (J.D., 1986). Member, Marquette University Law Review, 1985-1986. *Member:* Riverside County, San Diego County and American Bar Associations. [JAGC, USNR, 1986-1990, Lt.]. **LANGUAGES:** Spanish.

**WARREN D. KELLY,** born Cheyenne, Wyoming, August 14, 1962; admitted to bar, 1993, California and U.S. District Court, Central, Southern, Northern and Eastern Districts of California. *Education:* California Polytechnic State University (B.S., Mechanical Engineering, 1985); Hastings College of Law, University of California (J.D., 1993). Member, Hastings Constitutional Law Quarterly, University of California, Hastings College of the Law, 1991-1993. *Member:* Riverside County Bar Association; State Bar of California.

**IRENA LEIGH NORTON,** born Santa Clara, California, February 7, 1969; admitted to bar, 1993, California; 1994, U.S. District Court, Central, Southern, Northern and Eastern Districts of California. *Education:* University of California, Irvine (B.A.,1990); Georgetown University (J.D., 1993). Pi Sigma Alpha. Staff Member, The Tax Lawyer, 1991-1993. *Member:* Riverside County Bar Association; State Bar of California.

**KEVIN J. REISCH,** born San Bernardino, California, March 2, 1970; admitted to bar, 1995, California. *Education:* University of Notre Dame (B.A., with high honors, 1992); University of California, Hastings College of the Law (J.D., 1995). Member, Hastings Constitution Law Quarterly, 1993-1995. *Member:* Riverside County Bar Association; State Bar of California; Riverside County Barristers.

**ERIC M. STRONG,** born Redlands, California, October 10, 1967; admitted to bar, 1995, California; 1996, U.S. District Court, Eastern District of California. *Education:* United States Military Academy, West Point, New York (B.S., 1989); Golden Gate University School of Law (J.D., 1995). Editor, Golden Gate University Law Review, 1994-1995. *Member:* San Joaquin County and American Bar Associations; State Bar of California; Association of Trial Lawyers of America. [Capt., U.S.A.R.; 1st. LT., U.S. Army Active Duty, 1989-1992]

REPRESENTATIVE CLIENTS: Bird Medical Technologies, Inc.; Capital Co.; Children's Comprehensive Services, Inc.; Coachella Valley Recreation and Park District; E.L. Yeager Construction Co. Inc.; Fritts Ford; General Electric Company; HARSCO Corporation; Hemet Community Medical Group; Kemper Real Estate Management Company; Koll Management Services; KPC Global

*(This Listing Continued)*

**THOMAS, MORT, PROSSER & KNUDSEN, LLP,**
*Riverside—Continued*

Care: Lee & Associates Commercial Real Estate Services; Los Angeles Daily Journal Corporation; Miller's Outpost; Mission Hills Resort; Modular Metal Fabricators, Inc.; Provident Savings Bank; Riverside Community Hospital; Riverside County Transportation Commission; Riverside Community Ventures Corp.; Roverside National Bank; Southwest Pet Products, Inc.; SMA Equipment Company, Inc.; Stericycle, Inc.; Sullivan Dental Products; Tavaglione Construction; Valley Bank; Victorville Public Development Corporation; Wells Fargo Bank.

---

## *THOMPSON & COLEGATE*

Established in 1915
3610 FOURTEENTH STREET
P.O. BOX 1299
**RIVERSIDE, CALIFORNIA 92502**
Telephone: 909-682-5550
Fax: 909-781-4012

Palm Desert, California Office: 74-303 Highway III, Suite 2-B, 92260.
Telephone: 619-773-1998. Fax: 619-773-9078.

*General Civil and Trial Practice, Personal Injury Defense, Business Litigation, Construction, Medical Malpractice, Products Liability, Corporate, Estate Planning, Wills and Trusts, Probate, Insurance, Real Estate, Commercial, Education, Employment Law and Appellate Practice, Media-First Amendment Law and Bankruptcy.*

**H. L. THOMPSON** (1885-1962).

**ROY W. COLEGATE** (1906-1960).

**LEIGHTON B. TEGLAND,** born Windom, Minnesota, March 9, 1947; admitted to bar, 1972, California; 1984, U.S. Supreme Court; 1990, U.S. District Court, Southern District of California. *Education:* U.S. International University (B.A., 1969); University of Southern California (J.D., 1972). Phi Alpha Delta. *Member:* Riverside County and Desert Bar Associations; The State Bar of California; Desert Bar Association; Association of Southern California Defense Counsel (Director, 1991-1992); Riverside County Barristers Association (President, 1975-1976); Defense Research Institute. Advocate, American Board of Trial Advocates (President, Riverside-San Bernadino Chapter, 1992). (Resident, Palm Desert Office). *PRACTICE AREAS:* Personal Injury Defense; Medical Malpractice Law.

**DON G. GRANT,** born Glasgow, Scotland, February 20, 1945; admitted to bar, 1972, California and U.S. District Court, Southern and Central Districts of California; 1979, U.S. Supreme Court. *Education:* University of California at Los Angeles (B.A., 1968); California Western School of Law and U.S. International University (J.D., 1972). *Member:* Riverside County Bar Association; State Bar of California; Association of Southern California Defense Counsel (Director, 1982-1986). Advocate: American Board of Trial Advocates (President, Riverside/San Bernardino Chapter, 1984). *PRACTICE AREAS:* Personal Injury Defense; Medical Malpractice Law.

**J. E. HOLMES, III,** born Canton, Ohio, April 18, 1942; admitted to bar, 1968, California, U.S. District Court, Central, Northern and Eastern Districts of California and U.S. Court of Military Appeals; 1970, U.S. Tax Court, U.S. Claims Court, U.S. Court of Appeals, Ninth Circuit and U.S. Supreme Court; 1992, U.S. Army Court Military Review. *Education:* Claremont Men's College (A.B., 1964); Hastings College of the Law, University of California (J.D., 1967). Phi Alpha Delta; Phi Delta Theta. White House Military Social Aide, 1968-1970. Chairman, Disaster Relief and Emergency Preparedness Committee. Settlement Mediator, State of California Court of Appeals, Fourth District. Arbitrator and Settlement Mediator, Riverside County Superior Courts. *Member:* Riverside County and San Bernardino County Bar Associations; State Bar of California; Association of Southern California Defense Counsel; Riverside County Barristers; American Board of Trial Advocates (President, 1990 and Member, Executive Committee, 1988-1991 and 1993—, Riverside/San Bernardino Chapter; Director, State of California Chapter, 1990; Director, National Board of Directors, 1993—). [Capt., U.S. Army, JA, 1968-1974; Col. JA Senior Military Judge, Trial Judiciary, U.S. Army Reserve, 1992—]. *PRACTICE AREAS:* Products Liability; Personal Injury Defense; Public Entity Defense; Construction Law; General Litigation.

**ROBERT B. SWORTWOOD,** born Chicago, Illinois, August 20, 1946; admitted to bar, 1978, California. *Education:* Grinnell College (B.A., 1968); University of Iowa (J.D., 1978); Golden Gate University (M.B.A., Taxation, 1987). Marine White House Social Aide to President Nixon, 1973-1974. Director, Riverside County Estate Planning Council. *Member:* Riverside County Bar Association; State Bar of California. [Capt., U.S. Marine Corps, 1969-1975]. *PRACTICE AREAS:* Estate Planning; Will Contests; Trust Litigation; Probate; Commercial Litigation; Business Litigation; Education.

**JOHN W. MARSHALL,** born Brooklyn, New York, October 20, 1946; admitted to bar, 1978, California; U.S. District Court, Central District of California; U.S. Supreme Court. *Education:* St. Francis College (B.A., in Economics, 1967); Fordham University (M.A., in Economics, 1968); Pepperdine University (J.D., 1978). Omicron Delta Epsilon. Member, Pepperdine University Law Review, 1977-1978. *Member:* Riverside County Bar Association; The State Bar of California; Riverside County Barristers (Past President); Association of Southern California Defense Counsel (President, 1996; Member, Board of Directors, 1986-1996); American Board of Trial Advocates. [Lt., U.S. Navy, 1968-1972]. *PRACTICE AREAS:* Personal Injury Defense; Construction Law; Commercial and Business Litigation; Insurance Coverage and Bad Faith Litigation; Public Entity Defense.

**JOHN A. BOYD,** born Corona, California, July 26, 1954; admitted to bar, 1979, California, U.S. District Court, Southern and Central Districts of California and U.S. Supreme Court. *Education:* San Diego State University (B.S., in Marketing, 1976); Pepperdine University (J.D., cum laude, 1979). Business Editor, Pepperdine University Law Review, 1977-1979. Author: Casenote, "Trimble v. Gordon: An Unstated Reversal of Labine v. Vincent?" 5 Pepperdine Law Review. *Member:* Riverside County Bar Association; The State Bar of California; Riverside County Barristers (Vice President, 1985). *PRACTICE AREAS:* Business Litigation; Construction Law; Real Estate; Bankruptcy.

**GEOFFREY H. HOPPER,** born Jackson, Mississippi, January 21, 1957; admitted to bar, 1982, California and U.S. District Court, Southern District of California; 1983, U.S. District Court, Central District of California; 1984, U.S. Court of Appeals, Ninth Circuit; U.S. Supreme Court. *Education:* University of California at Riverside (B.A., 1979); California Western School of Law (J.D., 1982). California Western School of Law Best Oralist, 1981. Member, Advocacy Honors Board, 1981-1982. President, Tel-Law, Inc., 1986. *Member:* Riverside County (Treasurer, 1991; Member, Board of Directors, 1989-1996; Vice President, 1992; President, 1994; President, Dispute Resolution Services, 1996) and Los Angeles County Bar Associations; State Bar of California; Southern California Defense Counsel; Riverside County Barristers (President, 1990); Leo A. Deegan Inn of Court. *PRACTICE AREAS:* Employment and Construction Law; Business Litigation.

**MICHAEL J. MARLATT,** born Los Angeles, California, January 15, 1957; admitted to bar, 1984, California and U.S. District Court, Central District of California; U.S. Court of Appeals, Ninth Circuit. *Education:* University of Southern California; California Pomona Polytechnic University (B.S., 1981); Pepperdine University School of Law (J.D., 1984). Phi Alpha Delta. Member, Dalsimer Moot Court Competition. Recipient, NASA Achievement Award, Pathology Department, USC School of Medicine. Vice President, Student Bar Association, 1983-1984. Listed in Who's Who in American Law, 1995-1996 Edition. Judge Pro Tem, Riverside Municipal Court, 1989—. Lecturer: California Trial Lawyers Association, 1991; University of Amsterdam Law School, 1994. *Member:* Riverside County Bar Association; The State Bar of California; Southern California Defense Counsel (Member, Board of Directors); Southern California Association of Healthcare Managers. *PRACTICE AREAS:* Personal Injury Defense; Medical Malpractice Law; Public Entity Law.

---

**JOAN F. ETTINGER,** born Minneapolis, Minnesota, January 27, 1959; admitted to bar, 1986, California; U.S. Supreme Court; U.S. Court of Appeals, Ninth Circuit and U.S. District Court, Central, Southern and Eastern Districts of California. *Education:* Arizona State University (B.S., summa cum laude, 1982); Western State University (J.D., cum laude, 1985). Member, Western State University Law Review, 1984-1985. *Member:* Riverside County Bar Association; State Bar of California; Association of Southern California Defense Counsel. *PRACTICE AREAS:* Personal Injury Defense; Medical Malpractice Law; Appellate Practice.

**DAVID J. PORRAS,** born El Paso, Texas, June 23, 1952; admitted to bar, 1988, California and U.S. District Court, Central District of California. *Education:* Loyola University of Los Angeles (B.A., 1975); Western State University (J.D., 1987). *Member:* Riverside County Bar Association; State Bar of California. *PRACTICE AREAS:* Personal Injury Defense; Medical Malpractice Law; Insurance Coverage; Product Liability Defense.

**J. ALAN PLOTT,** born Murfreesboro, Tennessee, December 13, 1952; admitted to bar, 1988, California; 1989, U.S. District Court, Central Dis-

*(This Listing Continued)*

trict of California. *Education:* Glendale Community College (A.A., 1973); Arizona State University (B.S., 1975); Northrop University (J.D., 1983). *Member:* Riverside County Bar Association; State Bar of California; Association of Southern California Defense Counsel. (Resident, Palm Desert Office). *PRACTICE AREAS:* Personal Injury Defense; Medical Malpractice Law; Products Liability.

**MAXINE M. MORISAKI-PRICE,** born Los Angeles, California, April 4, 1951; admitted to bar, 1988, California, U.S. Court of Appeals, Ninth Circuit and U.S. District Court, Central and Southern Districts of California. *Education:* California State University at Los Angeles (B.A., Dean's List, 1972; M.A., Alumni Scholarship Award, 1983); Loyola Law School of Los Angeles (J.D., 1986). Phi Alpha Delta. *Member:* Riverside County Bar Association (Member, Judicial Evaluations Committee); State Bar of California; Association of Southern California Defense Counsel; Leo A. Deegan Inn of Court. *PRACTICE AREAS:* Personal Injury Defense; Medical Malpractice Law.

**LISA VICTORIA TODD,** born Honolulu, Hawaii, October 1, 1962; admitted to bar, 1987, California; 1993, Colorado; U.S. District Court, Central District of California. *Education:* Schiller International University, Heidelberg, Germany (Dean's List, 1982); Loyola Marymount University (B.A., Political Science, 1984, Pi Gamma Mu, Social Science Honor Society); University of Santa Clara (J.D., 1987). *Member:* Riverside County Bar Association; State Bar of California; Association of Southern California Defense Counsel; Leo A. Deegan Inn of Court. *PRACTICE AREAS:* Personal Injury Defense; Medical Malpractice Law.

**PATRICIA L. RICH,** born Pittsburgh, Pennsylvania, August 31, 1961; admitted to bar, 1989, California. *Education:* Cypress Community College (A.S., 1981); California State University at Long Beach (B.S., 1985); Western State University (J.D., cum laude, 1989). Author: "When Technology and the Law Collide— Look and Feel Copyright Evolves," Western State University Law Review, Vol. 16, No. 1 (Fall 1988). *Member:* State Bar of California. *PRACTICE AREAS:* Personal Injury Defense; Products Liability.

**DIANE M. WIESMANN,** born Los Angeles, California, January 18, 1961; admitted to bar, 1986, California. *Education:* University of Arizona (B.A., 1983; J.D., 1986). Phi Delta Phi (Vice Magister, 1985-1986). Listed in Who's Who Among American Law Students, 1986. Member, California District Attorneys Association, 1986-1989. *Member:* Riverside County and American (Representative, Law Student Division, 1983-1986) Bar Associations; State Bar of California; Southern California Defense Counsel. *PRACTICE AREAS:* Personal Injury Defense; Medical Malpractice Law.

**DULCE L. PENA,** born Cuba, March 25, 1957; admitted to bar, 1990, California. *Education:* Loma Linda University (B.A., 1981; M.A., 1987); Pepperdine University (J.D., 1990). Member, Board of Trustees, La Sierra University. President Elect, La Sierra University Alumni Association. Member, School of Business Advisory Council. *Member:* Riverside County Bar Association (Member: Women's Law Section, Steering Committee; Alternatives to Domestic Violence Fund Raising Committee); State Bar of California. *PRACTICE AREAS:* Civil and Employment Litigation.

**DONALD R. LEE,** born Key West, Florida, April 18, 1960; admitted to bar, 1989, California; 1992, U.S. District Court, Southern, Central, Northern and Eastern Districts of California. *Education:* Hyles-Anderson College (B.S., 1986); California Western School of Law (J.D., 1989). Member, Advocacy Honors Board, 1987-1989. *Member:* Riverside County Bar Association; State Bar of California; Association of Southern California Defense Counsel; Riverside County Barristers. *PRACTICE AREAS:* Products Liability; Lemon Law; Public Entity; General Civil.

**GARY T. MONTGOMERY,** born San Bernardino, California, January 10, 1967; admitted to bar, 1993, California and U.S. District Court, Central District of California. *Education:* Princeton University (A.B., 1989); Pepperdine University (J.D., 1993). Recipient: Steven J. Hirsch 1917 Scholarship; Class of 1926 Scholarship. *Member:* Los Angeles County and Riverside County Bar Associations; State Bar of California. *PRACTICE AREAS:* Personal Injury Defense; Insurance Defense.

**JEFFREY T. GWYNN,** born Inglewood, California, January 2, 1966; admitted to bar, 1995, California. *Education:* Loyola Marymount University (B.S., 1989); Boston University (J.D., 1995). Member, Boston University Public Interest Law Journal, 1995. *Member:* Riverside County Bar Association; State Bar of California. *PRACTICE AREAS:* Insurance Defense.

**RONALD V. LARSON,** born Los Angeles, California, July 21, 1968; admitted to bar, 1995, California. *Education:* California State University at Fullerton (B.A., 1992); University of California at Davis (J.D., 1995). *Member:* State Bar of California. *PRACTICE AREAS:* Labor and Employment; Business Litigation; Products Liability; Insurance Defense.

*(This Listing Continued)*

**KIMBERLY ANN WHITE,** born Palo Alto, California, September 13, 1968; admitted to bar, 1995, California. *Education:* Santa Clara University (B.S., 1991); McGeorge School of Law (J.D., 1995). National Moot Court Oral Competition Finalist. *PRACTICE AREAS:* Public Entity; Civil Rights; Employment.

COUNSEL FOR: Amerisure; Auto Club of Southern California Inter-Insurance Exchange; Carl Warren & Company; Chrysler Motor Corporation; Crawford & Company (Alamo Rent-A-Car); Crosby Insurance Company; The Doctor's Company; E&O Professionals; Farmers Insurance Group of Companies; Fireman's Fund; Fleetwood Enterprises; Healthcare Professional Liability; Professional Risk Management; Scottsdale Insurance Company; Sisters of Charity; State Farm Insurance Company; Tristar Risk Services; Ward-THG; CM Engineering Associates, Inc.; DePuy Inc.; Dyncorp; E.L. Yeager Construction; First American Title; J.F. Davidson Associates, Inc.; March Federal Credit Union; Moreno Valley Unified School District; Norwest Financial; Provident Savings Bank; County of Riverside; Riverside County Schools Credit Union; Riverside County Federal Credit Union; Wilbur-Ellis Company.

---

## VAN HULLE & PREVOST

### RIVERSIDE, CALIFORNIA

(See San Bernardino)

*General Civil Trial Practice in all Courts. Appellate Practice. Insurance, Malpractice and Products Liability Law.*

---

## WELEBIR & McCUNE

A PROFESSIONAL LAW CORPORATION

### RIVERSIDE, CALIFORNIA

(See Redlands)

*Practice limited to Catastrophic Personal Injury and Wrongful Death, Products Liability, Aviation, Railroad and Toxic Torts. Class Actions related to Defective Products and Mass Torts.*

---

## WILSON, BORROR, DUNN & DAVIS

### RIVERSIDE, CALIFORNIA

(See San Bernardino)

*General Civil and Trial Practice in all State Courts. Appellate Practice, Corporation, Insurance, Real Estate, Probate, Negligence, Personal Injury, Malpractice and Products Liability Law.*

---

## OWEN & BABIKIAN, P.C.

550 SILVER SPUR ROAD, SUITE 310
ROLLING HILLS, CALIFORNIA 90274
Telephone: 310-541-5655
Fax: 310-541-7643

*General Civil Litigation.*

**TIMOTHY R. OWEN,** born Syracuse, New York, March 8, 1956; admitted to bar, 1982, New York; 1983, U.S. District Court, Northern District of New York; 1987, California; 1990, U.S. District Court, Southern and Central Districts of California; 1992, U.S. Court of Appeals, Ninth Circuit. *Education:* Colgate University (B.A., 1978); Vermont Law School (J.D., 1981). *Member:* State Bar of California; American Bar Association. *PRACTICE AREAS:* Business Law; Litigation; Product Liability; Professional Liability; Insurance Coverage.

**ERIN BABIKIAN,** born Syracuse, New York, March 17, 1958; admitted to bar, 1983, California; 1986, New York. *Education:* Syracuse University (B.S., 1979); Pepperdine University (J.D., 1983). Phi Delta Phi. *Member,* Law Review. *Member:* Los Angeles County Bar Association; State Bar of California. *PRACTICE AREAS:* Litigation.

---

**MICHAEL A. LLOYD,** born Washington, D.C.; admitted to bar, 1992, California and U.S. District Court, Central District of California. *Education:* Stanford University (A.B., cum laude, 1975); Concordia College (B.M., summa cum laude, 1983); U.C.L.A. School of Law (J.D., 1992).

*(This Listing Continued)*

**OWEN & BABIKIAN, P.C., Rolling Hills—Continued**

Editor, UCLA, Law Review. Extern, The Honorable Robert M. Takasugi, U.S. District Court for the Central District of California. *Member:* Los Angeles County and Beverly Hill Bar Associations; State Bar of California. *PRACTICE AREAS:* Civil Litigation.

**MARY PUCELIK,** born Portland, Oregon, June 25, 1964; admitted to bar, 1992, California; 1993, Oregon. *Education:* Barnard College; Columbia University (B.A., 1986); Lewis and Clark College (J.D., 1992). Associate Editor, Law Review. *Member:* State Bar of California. *PRACTICE AREAS:* Civil Litigation.

*OF COUNSEL*

**RAFAEL BERNARDINO, JR.,** born Bellflower, California, November 4, 1959; admitted to bar, 1984, California; U.S. District Court, Central, Northern, Southern and Eastern Districts of California and U.S. Court of Appeals, Ninth Circuit. *Education:* University of Southern California (A.B., summa cum laude, 1981; J.D., 1984). Delta Sigma Rho; Tau Kappa Alpha. Editor: California Environmental Law and Regulatory Reporter, 1991; The Computer Law Journal, 1983-1984. Member, Southern California Law Review, Articles Editor, Major Tax Planning and Notes Editor, The Computer Law Journal, 1983-1984. Law Clerk, Hon. Manual L. Real, Chief Judge, U.S. District Court, Central District of California, 1985. Attorney/Advisor, Office of Intelligence Policy and Review, U.S. Department of Justice, 1988. *Member:* American Bar Association; State Bar of California; Association of Trial Lawyers of America.

---

## JACK I. ESENSTEN

*Established in 1955*

SUITE 207, 4030 PALOS VERDES DRIVE NORTH
**ROLLING HILLS ESTATES, CALIFORNIA 90274-2584**
*Telephone: 310-377-5557*
*Telecopier: 310-544-5036*

*Domestic Relations, Personal Injury and General Practice.*

**JACK I. ESENSTEN,** born St. Paul, Minnesota, November 19, 1927; admitted to bar, 1955, California. *Education:* University of Minnesota; University of Southern California (B.S., 1950); Southwestern University School of Law (J.D., 1955). *Member:* South Bay (President, 1977), Los Angeles County (Member, Executive Committee, Family Law Section) and American Bar Associations; State Bar of California (Member, Peer Review Committee on Legal Specialization, 1986-1987); Los Angeles Trial Lawyers Association; California Trial Lawyers Association; The Association of Trial Lawyers of America. (Certified Specialist, Family Law, The State Bar of California Board of Legal Specialization). *PRACTICE AREAS:* Domestic Relations; Personal Injury; General Practice.

**JULIE A. MILLIGAN,** born Palo Alto, California, January 16, 1961; admitted to bar, 1986, California. *Education:* University of California at Los Angeles (B.A., 1982); University of the Pacific; McGeorge School of Law (J.D., 1986). *Member:* South Bay and Los Angeles County Bar Associations; State Bar of California. (Certified Specialist, Family Law, The State Bar of California Board of Legal Specialization). *PRACTICE AREAS:* Family Law; Personal Injury; General Litigation.

---

## LAW OFFICES OF
## IVAN K. STEVENSON

501 DEEP VALLEY DRIVE, SUITE 315
**ROLLING HILLS ESTATES, CALIFORNIA 90274**
*Telephone: 310-541-9344*

Santa Ana, California Office: 1851 E. First Street, Suite 900, 92705.
Telephone: 714-564-2522.

*General Civil and Trial Practice in all State and Federal Courts. Personal Injury, Products Liability, Health Care, Professional Liability, Insurance, Military and Veterans Law, Governmental Entity Law.*

**IVAN K. STEVENSON,** born Quonset Point Naval Air Station, Rhode Island, October 4, 1949; admitted to bar, 1974, California and U.S. District Court, Central District of California; 1975, U.S. Court of Military Appeals; 1975, U.S. Supreme Court and U.S. District Court of the Northern Marianas. *Education:* University of California at Los Angeles (B.A., 1971); Southwestern University School of Law (J.D., 1974). Delegate, State Bar

*(This Listing Continued)*

CAA1742B

---

Convention, 1989. *Member:* Los Angeles County (Vice Chairman, Attorney Client Relations Committee, 1985-1992), Orange County and American Bar Associations; State Bar of California; Judge Advocates Association; U.S. Naval Institute; South California Defense Counsel Association. [Lt. Cmdr., JAGC, USNR, 1971—]

**JEFFREY L. BOYLE,** born Santa Barbara, California, September 3, 1959; admitted to bar, 1987, California. *Education:* Santa Barbara City College (A.A., 1981); University of California at Los Angeles (B.A., 1984); Western State University (J.D., 1987). *Member:* Orange County and American Bar Associations; State Bar of California.

REPRESENTATIVE CLIENTS: Lincoln Insurance Group; Amoco Oil Co.; Bituminous Insurance Co.; Prudential Insurance Company of Canada; Home Insurance Company of Canada; Capistrano Unified School District; City of Seal Beach; City of Garden Grove; Piaggio, S.P.A.; GRE Albany-Atlas Group; City of San Juan Capistrano; Bramalea California Inc.; Adamsons Ltd.; Maxson Young and Associates; Tayson Insurance Administrators; Saskatchewan Government Insurance; Boats U.S.; Santa Ana Unified School District; HAFA ADAI Properties.

---

## SUSAN A. COLLIER

419 OAK STREET
**ROSEVILLE, CALIFORNIA 95678**
*Telephone: 916-784-2444*
*Fax: 916-784-3926*

*Personal Injury, Products Liability, Employment Law, Professional Malpractice.*

**SUSAN A. COLLIER,** born Baltimore, Maryland, December 11, 1953; admitted to bar, 1985, California. *Education:* University of California at Davis (B.A., 1981); McGeorge School of Law, University of the Pacific (J.D., 1984). Order of the Coif. Member: Traynor Honor Society; Moot Court Honors Board, 1983-1984. Recipient, American Jurisprudence Awards in Civil Procedure and Administrative Law. Assistant Editor, Pacific Law Journal, 1983-1984. Author: "Reporting Child Abuse: When Moral Obligations Fail," 15 Pacific Law Journal, 1984. Speaker, National Employment Lawyers Association, 1987. *Member:* Sacramento County, Placer County and American Bar Associations; The State Bar of California; The Association of Trial Lawyers of America; Women Lawyers of Sacramento County; Capitol City Trial Lawyers Association; Consumer Attorneys of California.

---

## DUDUGJIAN & MAXEY

*A LAW CORPORATION*

13 SIERRAGATE PLAZA, BUILDING B
**ROSEVILLE, CALIFORNIA 95678**
*Telephone: 916-786-7272*
*Facsimile: 916-786-7306*
*Email: newerlaw@msn.com*
*URL: http://pages.prodigy.com/newestlaw*

*Corporate Law, Real Estate, Contract Law, Tax Law, Tax Planning, Bankruptcy, Franchise Law, Family Law, Estate Planning, Business Litigation and Litigation Support.*

**ROBERT P. DUDUGJIAN,** born Akron, Ohio, April 22, 1947; admitted to bar, 1976, California and U.S. District Court, Eastern District of California; 1977, U.S. Tax Court. *Education:* University of California at Los Angeles (M.S., 1971; M.B.A., 1972); McGeorge School of Law. Instructor, Law for Engineers, California State University, 1982-1984. *Member:* Placer and Sacramento County Bar Associations; The State Bar of California. *REPORTED CASES:* Hatch vs. Collins, 225 Ca3d 1104 (1980). *PRACTICE AREAS:* Business Dissolutions; Investor Fraud; Civil Litigation; Transactional Corporate; Tax; Estate Planning. *Email:* newerlaw@msn.com

**JOHN D. MAXEY,** born Vallejo, California, January 25, 1953; admitted to bar, 1985, California; 1996, U.S. Tax Court; U.S. District Court, District of California. *Education:* California State University at Chico (B.S., 1975); California State University at Sacramento (M.B.A., 1979); University of the Pacific, McGeorge School of the Law (J.D., 1984). Certified Public Accountant, California, 1982. Member, American Institute Certified Public Accountants. *Member:* American Bar Association; The State Bar of California. *PRACTICE AREAS:* Tax Litigation; Bankruptcy; Tax Work; Estate Planning. *Email:* newerlaw@msn.com

*(This Listing Continued)*

**EDWARD A. SMITH,** born Antioch, California, March 11, 1962; admitted to bar, 1989, California. *Education:* University of California at Davis (B.A., 1984); McGeorge School of Law, University of the Pacific (J.D., 1988). Pi Sigma Alpha. Associate Staff Writer, Owens California Forms and Procedure, 1986. *Member:* Yuba-Sutter Bar Association; State Bar of California. **PRACTICE AREAS:** Civil Litigation; Probate; Conservatorship; Elder Law. *Email:* newerlaw@msn.com

### LEGAL SUPPORT PERSONNEL

**SANDRA F. KNELL,** born San Mateo, California, May 17, 1948. *Education:* Washington University (1969); University of Missouri-Columbia (1966). (Office Manager). **PRACTICE AREAS:** Client Relations; Financial Management.

**JOANN F. GILLMAN,** born Sacramento, California, September 19, 1966. *Education:* Lincoln Paralegal School (Paralegal Certificate, 1989). (Paralegal). **PRACTICE AREAS:** Drafting Legal Documents and Research. *Email:* NEWERLAW@MSN.COM

## GIBSON & GIBSON, INC.

*A LAW CORPORATION*

Established in 1953

100 ESTATES DRIVE
P.O. BOX 639
**ROSEVILLE, CALIFORNIA 95661-0639**
Telephone: 916-782-4402
Fax: 916-782-4582

*General Civil and Trial Practice. Business, Corporate, Real Property, Estate Planning, Probate Law and Elder Law.*

**HOWARD G. GIBSON** (1921-1986).

**GUY R. GIBSON,** born Sacramento, California, June 6, 1952; admitted to bar, 1977, California and U.S. District Court, Eastern District of California. *Education:* University of California at Davis (B.A., 1974); McGeorge School of Law, University of the Pacific (J.D., 1977). Member, Traynor Honor Society. Member, Roseville City School District, Board of Education, 1981-1990. *Member:* Placer County Bar Association (President, 1989); State Bar of California. (Certified Specialist, Probate, Estate Planning and Trust Law, The State Bar of California Board of Legal Specialization). **PRACTICE AREAS:** Probate; Estate Planning and Trust Law; Real Property.

REPRESENTATIVE CLIENTS: Dawson Oil Co.; Kirk Doyle Real Estate Co.; Dry Mix Products Co.; First Commercial Bank; Hewlett-Packard Co.; John Morier Construction, Inc.; Project Go, Inc.; Roseville Chamber of Commerce; John L. Sullivan Chevrolet; Sunrise Pools, Inc.; Wade Associates; Paul Wagner Big & Tall Clothing.

## JONES & STEPHENS

2130 PROFESSIONAL DRIVE, SUITE 250
**ROSEVILLE, CALIFORNIA 95661**
Telephone: 916-786-0950; 800-304-5044
Fax: 916-786-6703

*Workers' Compensation, Personal Injury, Construction, Real Estate, Insurance, Dissolution of Marriage, Probate, Wills and Trusts.*

**W. RAY JONES,** born Shrewsbury, G.B., February 18, 1940; admitted to bar, 1971, California. *Education:* Sacramento State College (B.A., 1964); McGeorge School of Law. *Member:* Sacramento County Bar Association; California Trial Lawyers Association; The Association of Trial Lawyers Association. **PRACTICE AREAS:** Personal Injury; Construction; Real Estate; Insurance.

**ALISA J. STEPHENS,** born Woodland, California, April 25, 1952; admitted to bar, 1977, California. *Education:* University of the Pacific (B.A., 1974); University of California (J.D., 1977). *Member:* Sacramento County and Placer County Bar Associations; State Bar of California; Women Lawyers of Placer County; California Trial Lawyers Association. **LANGUAGES:** Spanish. **PRACTICE AREAS:** Personal Injury Plaintiff; Dissolution of Marriage; Probate, Wills and Trusts.

*(This Listing Continued)*

### ASSOCIATES

**MICHAEL D. TRAINER,** born Bozeman, Montana, September 12, 1954; admitted to bar, 1993, California; 1994, U.S. District Court, Eastern District of California; 1995, U.S. District Court, Northern District of California. *Education:* San Jose State University; McGeorge School of Law (J.D., 1992). **PRACTICE AREAS:** Workers Compensation; Personal Injury; Criminal Defense; General Litigation.

**THOMAS L. WALSH,** born San Francisco, California, July 16, 1936; admitted to bar, 1970, California. *Education:* University of California at Berkeley (A.B., 1963); University of San Francisco (J.D., 1969). Phi Delta Phi. *Member:* Bar Association of San Francisco; Sacramento (Lecturer, Continuing Education of the Bar, 1985) and American Bar Associations; The State Bar of California; California Trial Lawyers Association; American Judicature Society; The Association of Trial Lawyers of America; Northern California Association of Defense Counsel; Southern California Association of Defense Counsel; Defense Research Institute. **PRACTICE AREAS:** Personal Injury; Commercial Torts; Environmental Law.

**RALPH W. MANN,** born Anaheim, California, April 14, 1966; admitted to bar, 1996, California. *Education:* McGeorge School of Law (J.D., 1994); University of San Diego School of Law (LL.M., 1995). **PRACTICE AREAS:** Workers Compensation; Personal Injury; General Civil; Criminal Law Defense.

## LIEBMAN & REINER

*A PROFESSIONAL LAW CORPORATION*

3017 DOUGLAS BOULEVARD, SUITE 300
**ROSEVILLE, CALIFORNIA 95661**
Telephone: 916-852-0777
Fax: 916-852-8077

*Los Angeles, California Office:* 3255 Wilshire Boulevard, 12th Floor. Telephone: 213-387-0777. Fax: 213-383-6754.
*San Francisco, California Office:* 100 First Street, Suite 2250. Telephone: 415-227-0777. Fax: 415-227-0537.
*San Diego, California Office:* 225 Broadway, Suite 1500. Telephone: 619-232-0777. Fax: 619-238-5442.
*San Jose, California Office:* 95 South Market Street, Suite 300. Telephone: 408-993-0777. Fax: 408-993-0789.

*General Liability, Defense, Products Liability, Workers Compensation Defense, Insurance and Subrogation Law, Insurance Coverage and Bad Faith, Professional Liability. Trial Practice. Appellate Practice. Environmental and Industrial Disease Law.*

FIRM PROFILE: Liebman & Reiner is a prominent California defense Firm, serving the insurance industry, self insureds, public entities and the business community. With offices in 5 cities, the firm is able to respond to the needs of our clients throughout the State of California.

**JAMES M. O'BRIEN,** born Santa Monica, California, December 19, 1952; admitted to bar, 1978, California. *Education:* California State University at Northridge (B.S., 1975); Southwestern University (J.D., 1978). *Member:* The State Bar of California; American Bar Association. **PRACTICE AREAS:** Personal Injury Defense Law; Insurance Law; Subrogation Law; Wrongful Discharge Law.

**BRUCE S. BAKER,** born January 11, 1955; admitted to bar, 1986, California and U.S. District Court, Eastern District of California. *Education:* Florida International University (B.A., 1979); McGeorge School of Law, University of the Pacific (J.D., 1986).

(For Complete Biographical Data on all Personnel, See Professional Biographies at Los Angeles, Santa Ana, San Francisco, San Diego and San Jose, California)

## ROBBINS & LIVINGSTON

3300 DOUGLAS BOULEVARD, SUITE 365
**ROSEVILLE, CALIFORNIA 95661**
Telephone: 916-773-4700
Facsimile: 916-773-4747
Email: plazolaw@aol.com

*The Firm specializes in Land Use, Planning and Zoning matters, Environmental and Natural Resource issues, Energy and Utility matters and Real Estate.*

*(This Listing Continued)*

## ROBBINS & LIVINGSTON, Roseville—Continued

### MEMBERS OF FIRM

**STEPHEN ROBBINS,** born Seattle, Washington, April 13, 1942; admitted to bar, 1973, District of Columbia, U.S. District Court, District of Columbia, U.S. Court of Appeals, District of Columbia Circuit and U.S. Court of Appeals, Third Circuit; 1975, California; 1982, U.S. District Court, Eastern and Northern Districts of California; 1983, U.S. District Court, Central District of California; 1994, Supreme Court of the Republic of Palau. *Education:* London School of Economics and Political Science, University of London; University of California at Los Angeles (A.B., 1964); Yale University (J.D., 1971). *Member:* District of Columbia Bar; State Bar of California; American Bar Association (Member, Sections on: Urban, State and Local Government Law - Land Use, Planning and Zoning Committee; Real Property, Probate and Trust Law; Natural Resources, Energy and Environmental Law; Forum Committee on Affordable Housing and Community Development); The Urban Land Institute (Associate); The National Institute of Municipal Law Officers (Associate); The American Planning Association (Member: Planning and Law Division; International Division); the International Urban Development Association. [Staff Sgt., U.S. Army, 1966-1968]. **LANGUAGES:** Spanish, French. **REPORTED CASES:** State of Koror v. Blanco et al 4 ROP Intrm. 310 (Sup. Ct. Palau). **TRANSACTIONS:** North Central Roseville Specific Plan ($250,000,000 land use plan, master development agreement and related financing plan and assessment districts; Southeast Roseville Specific Plan ($200,000,000 land use plan, master development agreement and related financing plan and landscaping/lighting district); Northwest El Dorado Hills Specific Plan ($100,100,100 land use plan, master development agreement landscaping/-lighting district). **PRACTICE AREAS:** Zoning, Planning and Land Use; Environmental Law.

**J. CLEVE LIVINGSTON,** born Los Angeles, California, May 24, 1947; admitted to bar, 1975, California; 1984, Massachusetts, U.S. Court of Appeals, First Circuit and U.S. District Court, District of Massachusetts. *Education:* Harvard University (A.B., cum laude, 1969); Antioch School of Law (J.D., 1975); Kennedy School of Government, Harvard University (M.P.A., 1982). General Counsel, California Department of Housing and Community Development, 1978-1979. Author: "Growth Controls, State Housing Regulations, and the New Federal Program Requirements," Can We Afford Local Growth Controls?, Institute of Government Affairs, University of California at Davis, 1977. Co-Author: *The California Housing Element Manual,* California Department of Housing and Community Development, 1978; *The Fair Share Planning Manual,* California Department of Housing and Community Development, 1978; *Underground Petroleum Storage Tanks: Local Regulation of a Groundwater Hazard,* Conservation Law Foundation, 1984; *Fueling the Conservation Power Plant,* Conservation Law Foundation, 1992. *Member:* Sacramento County and Massachusetts Bar Associations; State Bar of California.

REPRESENTATIVE CLIENTS: Ahmanson Developments, Inc.; Balcor Property Management Inc.; The Coker-Ewing Companies; Morrison Homes of Northern California; Grove Investment Company, Inc.; Trammell Crow Residential; Richland Properties; Rancho Murieta Community Services District; Lone Tree Partnership; California Environmental Associates; National Land Company; Dahlawi California, Inc.; Cresleigh Homes; S.H. Cowell Foundation.

---

## LARRY P. SINCLAIR
### 2390 PROFESSIONAL DRIVE
### ROSEVILLE, CALIFORNIA 95661
Telephone: 916-783-3290
Fax: 916-783-5232

*Domestic and Family Law Trial and Appellate Practice. Premarital Transactional Planning. Child Custody. Child Support.*

**LARRY P. SINCLAIR,** born Berkeley, California, November 5, 1947; admitted to bar, 1972, California and U.S. District Court, Central District of California. *Education:* University of California at Davis (B.A., in Math, 1969); University of Santa Clara (J.D., magna cum laude, 1972). Deputy District Attorney, Ventura County, California, 1972-1975. Member, Board of Trustees, Placer County Law Library, 1977-1992. Director, Placer County Legal Aid Society, 1976-1983. President and Director, Roseville Host Lions Club, 1983-1984. *Member:* Placer County Bar Association (President, 1980); State Bar of California (Member, Family Law Section). (Certified Specialist, Family Law, The State Bar of California Board of Legal Specialization). **PRACTICE AREAS:** Domestic and Family Law.

---

## SINCLAIR, WILSON & BEDORE
### 2390 PROFESSIONAL DRIVE
### ROSEVILLE, CALIFORNIA 95661
Telephone: 916-783-5281
Fax: 916-783-5232

*General Civil Trial and Appellate Practice, Personal Injury, Real Estate, Business, Estate Planning, Trust, Probate, Tax, Employment, Discrimination, Insurance and Criminal Defense.*

**FLOYD H. BOWERS** (1896-1969).

**ROBERT F. SINCLAIR,** born Auburn, California, May 31, 1952; admitted to bar, 1977, California and U.S. District Court, Central District of California. *Education:* University of California at Davis (B.S. in Genetics, 1974); University of Santa Clara (J.D., magna cum laude, 1977). Law Clerk to Hon. William P. Clark, Jr., Associate Justice, California Supreme Court, 1977. Staff Attorney, Court of Appeal, Third Appellate District, 1978. Chairperson and Member, Board of Directors, Placer County Lawyer Referral Service, 1982-1990. California Governor's Local Judicial Nominees Evaluation Committee, 1984-1987. Member, Board of Directors, Alta California Regional Center, 1985-1990. Delegate, Placer County, California Bar Association Conference of Delegates, 1981-1983. Member and President, 1993-1994, Rotary Club of Roseville. *Member:* Placer County Bar Association (President, 1983); State Bar of California (Member: Real Property Law Section; Litigation Section); Women Lawyers of Placer County. **PRACTICE AREAS:** Real Estate Transactions and Litigation.

**RANDALL R. WILSON,** born Sacramento, California, April 2, 1956; admitted to bar, 1982, California and U.S. District Court, Eastern District of California; 1983, Nevada. *Education:* University of the Pacific (B.S., in Business Administration, 1978); McGeorge School of Law, University of the Pacific (J.D., 1981; LL.M. in Taxation, 1985). Certified Public Accountant, California, 1985. Secretary and Director, Rotary Club of Roseville; Rotary Club of Roseville Foundation. Founding Director, Eureka Schools Foundation. *Member:* Placer County, Bar Association; State Bar of California (Member, Litigation, Estate Planning, Trust and Probate Sections); State Bar of Nevada. (Certified Specialist, Estate Planning, Trust and Probate Law, The State Bar of California Board of Legal Specialization). **PRACTICE AREAS:** Estate Planning Law; Taxation Law; Business Planning Law.

**JESS C. BEDORE, III,** born San Francisco, California, January 26, 1949; admitted to bar, 1976, California; 1977, U.S. District Court, Eastern District of California. *Education:* California State University at Sacramento (B.A., in Government, 1972); Lincoln University Law School (J.D., 1976). Outstanding Brief in Appellate Advocacy. Member, Moot Court. Senior Deputy District Attorney, Placer County, California, 1981-1990. Assistant Public Defender, Placer County, California, 1981. Civil Trial Attorney, Law Offices of Leo M. O'Connor, Inc. Sacramento, California, 1978-1980. Assistant Public Defender, Sacramento County, California, 1976-1978. *Member:* Placer County Bar Association; State Bar of California (Member, Litigation Section); California Trial Lawyers Association; Capital City Trial Lawyers Association; Association of Trial Lawyers of America. (Certified Specialist, Criminal Law, The State Bar of California Board of Legal Specialization). **REPORTED CASES:** People v. Silverbrand (1990) 220 Cal. App. 3d 1621; People v. Moten (1989) 210 Cal. App. 3d 765; People v. Disandra (1987) 193 Cal. App. 3d 1354; People v. Dominquez (1989) 201 Cal. App. 3d 345; People v. Riffey (1985) 171 Cal. App. 3d 419. **PRACTICE AREAS:** Plaintiff's Personal Injury; Criminal Defense Law.

**LAWRENCE T. RING,** born Hattiesburg, Mississippi, March 14, 1958; admitted to bar, 1984, California and U.S. District Court, Eastern District of California. *Education:* University of California at Davis (B.A., with honors, 1981; J.D., 1984). Court Appointed Arbitrator, Sacramento, El Dorado, Placer and Nevada Counties, 1990—. *Member:* Sacramento County and Placer County Bar Associations; State Bar of California (Member, Environmental Law Section); Association of Trial Attorneys of America. **PRACTICE AREAS:** Real Estate; Personal Injury-Plaintiff; Business Transactional; Contract; Employment; Insurance.

### OF COUNSEL

*Larry P. Sinclair* (Certified Specialist, Family Law, The State Bar of California Board of Legal Specialization)

*F. Larry Sinclair*

REPRESENTATIVE CLIENTS: Chicago Title Co.; City of Colfax; Coldwell Banker Residential Real Estate Services; Diablo Manufacturing, Inc.; Fibreform Wood Products, Inc.; Fred Festersen & Associates Real Estate and

*(This Listing Continued)*

Insurance; Fuller-Jeffrey Broadcasting Corporation; Kenco Engineering, Inc.; Latham Ventures; Neighborly Pest Management; Pacer Title Co.; Roseville Termite and Pest Control; Sierra Industrial Park, Inc.; Sierra Wes Drywall, Inc.; Thelen Construction Company; Ticor Title Insurance Co.; Transamerica Title Insurance Co.

## WILLIAM J. SWEENEY
*100 ESTATES DRIVE*
**ROSEVILLE, CALIFORNIA 95678-2310**
*Telephone: 916-786-2011*
*Fax: 916-782-4582*
*Email: wsweeney@pacbell.net*

*Civil Practice, Construction, Engineering and Architectural Law Malpractice, Mechanics Liens, Personal Injury, Business, Corporation, Estate Planning, Trusts and Probate Law.*

**WILLIAM J. SWEENEY,** born South Gate, California, March 28, 1946; admitted to bar, 1972, California and U.S. District Court, Eastern District of California; 1986, U.S. Supreme Court. *Education:* Loyola University (B.A., 1968; J.D., 1971). Phi Delta Phi. Judge Pro Tem: Placer County Municipal Court, 1981—; Placer County Superior Court, 1985—. Arbitrator: Placer County Superior Court, 1983—; Placer County Municipal Court, 1985—. *Member:* Placer County Bar Association (President, 1990); State Bar of California (Delegate, Conference of Delegates, 1987—). **PRACTICE AREAS:** Construction Law; Personal Injury; Probate Law.

## LAW OFFICES OF
## WILLIAM H. CURTISS
*7 HILLGIRT DRIVE*
*P.O. BOX 1743*
**ROSS, CALIFORNIA 94957**
*Telephone: 415-454-0756*
*Fax: 415-454-0434*
*Email: wcurtiss@msn.com*

*General Civil Trial Practice, Business Litigation, Entertainment Law and Employment Law.*

**WILLIAM H. CURTISS,** born Toledo, Ohio, January 21, 1948; admitted to bar, 1976, California and U.S. District Court, Northern District of California; 1992, U.S. District Court, Eastern District of California. *Education:* Stanford University (B.A., 1970); University of Pennsylvania (J.D., 1975). Instructor: "Sharpening Your Basic Trial Skills", California Continuing Education of the Bar, 1989 and 1991. Faculty: College of Advocacy, Hastings College of Law, University of California, 1992; Trial Skills Workshop, California Continuing Education of the Bar, 1993; Advocacy Skills Workshop, Stanford Law School, 1994, 1995, 1996 and 1997. Lecturer, lead instructor and founder of MCLE program "Taking Depositions Workshop" May/June, 1990 and "Deposition Skills Workshop, November/December, 1992, sponsored by California Continuing Education of the Bar and the State Bar Litigation Section. *Member:* Los Angeles County Bar Association; State Bar of California.

# SERVICES, SUPPLIERS, CONSULTANTS SECTION

---

CALIFORNIA
A — R

The Services, Suppliers, Consultants Section presents information in our new three-tiered format on over 200 major categories of businesses and professionals serving the legal community. Each volume index is listed alphabetically by category then within each category alphabetically by state, city and service name. Whether you are looking for a court reporter in your own jurisdiction or an expert witness in another state, the Services, Suppliers, Consultants Section is your direct link to legal support services.

# Guess where many law firms look first for the best job candidates.

More and more, prospective employers are performing online searches to find candidates who meet specific needs. And they're searching where the best candidates are easiest to find — in the LEXIS®-NEXIS® CAREER library.

Whether you're looking for a summer job or a permanent position, in private practice or in the government sector, putting your resume in the Martindale-Hubbell® and LEXIS® Student Directory (RESUME file) is equivalent to sending your resume to hundreds of law firms throughout the country — in a matter of seconds. The Martindale-Hubbell and LEXIS Student Directory is easy to use — and best of all, it's FREE. All you have to do is input key information about yourself. You select the information you wish to provide, and can update or delete your personal listing any time. It's accessible only by potential employers (not other students). It's a great tool for employers who want the perfect candidate.

The LEXIS-NEXIS CAREER library contains not only the RESUME file, but also a rich collection of job prospecting tools designed to assist you in conducting a personalized career exploration. The CAREER library offers a variety of directories for your reference, including the Martindale-Hubbell® Law Directory, the LEXIS Employer Directory, Judicial Clerkship Directory, Public Interest Directory, Federal Staff Directory, Judicial Staff Directory, Congressional Staff Directory, and much more. When it comes to your future, only the best will do: the LEXIS-NEXIS CAREER library.

It's your time. It's your money. It's your grades. It's your future. For additional information, contact your LEXIS representative, or call **1-800-45-LEXIS**.

LEXIS·NEXIS®
A member of the Reed Elsevier plc group

LEXIS, NEXIS and Martindale-Hubbell are registered trademarks of Reed Elsevier Properties Inc., used under license.
The INFORMATION ARRAY logo is a trademark of Reed Elsevier Properties Inc., used under license.
©1996 LEXIS-NEXIS, a division of Reed Elsevier Inc. All rights reserved.

# SERVICES, SUPPLIERS, CONSULTANTS
## *List of Categories*

Abstractors
Accident Investigation & Reconstruction Services
Accident Investigation, Safety-Training-Environmental
Accountants
Actuaries
Admiralty & Maritime Expert & Consultant
Advertising & Public Relations Firms
Alternate Dispute Resolution
  (See Arbitration & Mediation)
Americans With Disabilities Act (ADA)
Ancillary Financial/Trust Services
Appellate Consultant
Appraisal & Valuation Services
Appraisal Services
Appraisal Services - Coin, Currency & Bullion
Appraisal Services - Health Care Property
Appraisal Services - Insurance
Appraisal Services - Jewelry & Gems
Appraisal Services - Machinery & Equipment
Appraisal Services - Mines & Quarries
Appraisal Services - Personal Property
Arbitration & Mediation - Prof. Assns for Arbitrators & Prac
Arbitration & Mediation Services
Asset Locators
Asset Management
Association Management
Attorney - Lobbyist
Attorney - World Nations League Corporate Code
Attorney Referral Services
Attorney Services
Auctioneers & Appraisers Of Autographs, Rare Books
Audio/Video Services
Autographs, Rare Books
  (See Process Servers)
Automobile & Office Equipment Leasing
Autopsy Service
Aviation Medicine
Aviation-Investigation

Bail Bonds
Bank Associations & Societies
Banking - On Line Internet Access
Bankruptcy Assets/Purchase of
Banks & Trust Companies
Bar Associations
Bar Associations - World Nations League Corporate Code
Bonds - Surety & Fidelity
Briefs
  (See Legal Brief Printers)
Building Evaluation - Due Diligence
Building/Home Inspection
Business & Financial Information Providers
Business & Trade Organizations
Business Valuations

Captioning
Career Services
Case Management Systems
CD-ROM Products
Civil Rights Under Color of Law
Class Action Notice
Closed Captioning
Coins and Currency
Collection Agencies
Collection/Commercial Attorneys
Computer - Programming & Consulting
Computer Animation, Graphics & Simulation
Computer Consultants

Computer Conversion & Migration
Computer Evidence Investigation
Computer Systems Integration
Conference/Seminar Center
Conferencing
Construction Accidents, Safety
Construction Consultants
Construction Consultants-Construction Defects
Construction Consultants-Structural Damage
Continuing Legal Education
Copier Services
Copyright Search Services
Corporate Services Companies
Corporation Companies
Court Recording Systems
Court Reporter - Adwell
Court Reporters
Credit Bureaus
Criminal Background Checks
Criminal Records Research

Debugging
Demonstrative Evidence
Discovery And Document Reproduction Services
DNA Forensic Testing
Document Delivery Systems
  (See Process Servers)
Document Filing/Retrieval
Document Imaging
Document Management Services
Document Research, Retrieval & Delivery
Document Scanning
Document Searches/Retrieval

Economic And Statistic Consulting Services
Economic And Statistical Consulting Services - Automobiles
Educational Consultant
Elder Care
Electronic Billing
Electronic Packaging & Production
Employment Agencies - Permanent/Temporary
Employment Screening
Engineering & Scientific Consulting Services
Engineering - Metallurgy/Reconstruction/Forensic Consulting
Engineers/Engineering - Architectural
Environmental & Ecological Services
Environmental Consultants
Environmental Consultants - Geology
Environmental Engineering & Remediation Services
Environmental-Statistical Consultant
Equine - Appraisers & Consultants
Escrow Services
Estate Planning & Personal Benefits
Examiners Of Questioned Documents (Handwriting Experts)
Expert Witness
    Accident Reconstruction
    Accidents/Fires/Product Liability
    Accounting
        Auditing
        Business Damages
        Financial Issues
        Malpractice
    Accoustics
        Sound, Noise & Vibration
    Admiralty
    Agri-Horticultural
    Alcohol
    Animal Behavior

# LIST OF CATEGORIES

*Expert Witness (Continued)*
- Appraisal Services
- Aquatics
- Architects
- Audio-Tape Analysis/Authentication/Voice ID
- Automobile
    - Forensic
        - Occupant Biomechanics
- Banking
    - Finance
        - Trading, Financial & Derivative Instruments
        - Trusts & Investments
- Bicycle Litigation
- Biomedical Engineering
- Burglar & Fire Alarm
- Child Abuse
- Coatings/Paint
- Commercial Law/Banking/UCC
- Compensation
- Computer & Business Information Systems
- Computer Forensics/Data Recovery
- Computer Programming & Consulting
- Computer Science/Intellectual Property
- Computer Technology Industry
- Concrete Surface Prep. & Adhesive Applications
- Construction
    - Architecture/Landscape
    - Defects
    - Residential
    - Scaffolding
    - Underground
        - Underground Tanks
- Cooling Towers
- Crime Prevention
- Criminalistics & Firearms
- Damage Valuation
- Day Care Centers
- Dog Behavior/Dog Bites
- Drugs
- Economics/Economists
    - Agricultural/Environmental
    - Damages
    - Financial Valuation
    - Litigation
    - Statistics
- Electronic Countermeasures
- Elevators
- Elevators & Escalators
- Employee/Employment
    - Discrimination
    - Negligence Hiring/Retention
    - OSHA Regulations/Procedures
    - Practices
    - Standards of Conduct
    - Whistle Blower Protection
    - Wrongful Termination/Harassment
- Employment Practices
- Engineers/Engineering
    - Acoustics
    - Agricultural/Mechanical
    - Architecture
    - Automotive
    - Civil/Mechanical/Structural
    - Electrical
    - Forensic Engineering
    - Mechanical/Machine Design
    - Metallurgical Corrosion
    - Petroleum
    - Safety
    - Scientific
- Environmental Consultant
- Fire
    - Explosion
    - Protection, Investigation
    - Reconstruction
    - Wildland/Urban Interface
- Floor Covering/Non Carpet
- Forensic Animation
- Forensic Chemist
    - Toxicologist/Criminalist
- Forensic Vocational/Medical Consultant
- Franchising
- Gas Engineering
- Gasoline Station: Accid; Bus Prac; UST Leaks
- Glass
- Hair & Fiber/Related Materials
- Handwriting
- Highway Design
- Horses (Equine)
- Hospitality & Hotel Management
- Hostage Negotiation & Critical Incident Mgt.
- Human Factors & Safety
- Human Factors/Personal Injury
- Insurance
    - Agency Conduct
    - Bad Faith
    - Casualty/Professional Liability
    - Corporate Conduct
    - Life, Disability & Medical Expense
    - Marine
    - Risk Management Consulting
- Intellectual Property/Infringement Damages
- Law Enforcement
- Lead Based Paint
- Legal Fees
- Letters of Credit
- Libel/Linguistic Analysis
- Liquor Liability
- Magazine Publishing
- Marine
    - Insurance
- Martial Arts
    - Hand to Hand
- Mechanical Failure/Auto & Industrial
- Medical
    - (See Medical Expert Witness)
- Medical Facility Management
- Medical Instrument & Product Injury
- Medicare Fraud & Abuse
- Metallurgy/Failure Analysis
- Meteorology/Climatology
- Mining
- Mortality/Longevity Analysis
- Motorcycle/ATV Accident/Invest/Reconstruction
- Occupational Safety
- Oil & Gas
- Packaging
- Patent Law
- Pesticide Products
- Photographic Analysis
    - Environmental Site Assessment
- Playground Equipment Accidents
- Police Dogs
- Police/Security
    - Dogs
    - Hotel/Resort/Casino
    - Malpractice
    - Negligence
        - (See also Security; Expert Witness)
    - Negligence/Security Misconduct
    - Police Misconduct
    - Use of Force
- Premises Security & Liability
    - (See also Expert Witness - Slip, Trip and Fall)
- Public Utilities
- Real Estate
    - Appraisal & Valuation
    - Finance
- Roofing & Waterproofing

# SERVICES, SUPPLIERS, CONSULTANTS — LIST OF CATEGORIES

**Expert Witness (Continued)**
- Safety
- Secured Transactions
- Securities Law
- Securities/Litigation Support
- Securities/Portfolio Analysis & Review
- Sexual Harassment/Sexual Assault
- Slip, Trip and Fall
  (See also Expert Witness - Premises Security & Liability)
- Sports, Leisure, Recreation
- Stylistics/Linguistics
- Telecommunications
- Tire Identification
- Toxicology
- Trademark Evaluations
- Transportation
  - Aviation
  - Aviation/Aircraft/Airports
  - Railroads
  - Tire & Wheel
  - Traffic Engineering & Safety
- Tree & Landscape Consultants
- Underground Tanks
- Video
  - Consumer/Pro./ Programming/Hardware/Dist.
- Weather & Climate
- Windows & Doors
- Wood Science & Technology

Expert Witness Referral Services

Facilities Management
Failure Analysis/Testing Services
Family Business Consultants
Fax Filing Of Court Documents
Filing & Searching Services
Financial Insts - Dir/Officers/Atty
Financial Investigations/Forensic Accounting
Fire Investigators
Fire Loss Experts
Foreign Embassy Services
Forensic Documentation - Demonstrative Evidence
Forensic Engineers
Forensic Financial Analysis
Forensic Medicine
Forensic Psychiatry
Forensic Services

Genealogical Services
Geology
Government - Foreign Government Incorporating Offices
Government - Foreign Government Philatelic Bureaus
Government Regulatory Research Specialists
Graphics Design & Production
Groupware

Handwriting Experts
Hedonic Damages/Loss of Enjoyment of Life
Heir Tracers
Heir/Probate Research
Horses
  (See Equine)
Hotel/Apartment Consultants & Experts
Hotel/Restaurant Consultants & Experts

Imaging Services
Importer Associations
Incorporating Companies - Overseas Corporations
Incorporation Services
Information Brokers
Information Clearing House
Insurance
Insurance - Corporate Owned Life Insurance
Insurance - Health
Insurance - Intellectual Property
Insurance - Professional Liability

Insurance - Property/Casualty
Insurance - Risk Management Consulting
Intellectual Property Document Services
International Personal Tax Consultant
International Trade Consultants
Internet On Line Stock Exchange
Internet Services
Interpreters
  (See also Interpreters & Translators; Translation Services)
Interpreters & Translators
  (See also Translation Services)
Investigative Consultants
Investigators
Investment Clubs

Japanese Matters - Expert/Consultant
Jury Consultants
Jury Verdict Reporting Services

Labor Relations, Products & Services
Laboratories - Parentage Testing
Laboratories - Testing & Analytical
Law Books - New/Used
Law Office Automation Services
Lawyer Search & Placement Consultants
Legal Advertising
Legal Associations
Legal Auditors
Legal Brief Printers
Legal Copying
Legal Information Brokers
Legal Office Supplies
Legal Publications
Legal Research
Legal Research/Appellate Practice
Legal Research/Brief Preparation
Legal Software
Legal Support Personnel - Temporary & Permanent
Letters of Credit
Library Cataloging
Library Management Services
Lie Detectors
  (See Polygraph)
Life Care Planning
Litigation Consulting
Litigation Support - Detecting Deception
Litigation Support Services
Lobbyist

Mail Room Services
Malpractice Prevention Consultants
Management Consultants
Marine Consultants
Marketing
Medical Case Review & Preparation/Trial Consulting
Medical Expert Testimony
Medical Expert Witness
- Asbestos Related Diseases
- Breast Implants
- Cardiology
- Cardiology, Internal Medicine & Geriatric
- Chiropractic Medicine
- Dental
  - Prosthodontics/Dental Implants
  - TMJ
- Devices
- Emergency Medicine/Malpractice
- Epilepsy/Seizure Disorder
- Family Practice
- Foot Surgery/Care
- Forensic Odontology
- Gastroenterology
- Gynecology
- Hand Surgery & Impairments
- Head Injury

## LIST OF CATEGORIES

*Medical Expert Witness - Head Injury (Continued)*
        Forensic Neuropsychology
        Forensic Psychiatry
    Internal Medicine
    Medical Case Review
        Malpractice & Personal Injury
    Medical Information Specialist
    Neonatology/Pediatrics
    Nephrology
    Neurology
        Neurosurgery
        Neurosurgery & Acupuncture
    Ophthalmology
    Pathology
    Pediatrics
    Pharmacy
    Physiatry
        EMG
    Physical Medicine & Rehabilitation
    Podiatry
    Product Injury
    Psychiatry
     (See also Medical Expert Witness - Neurology)
        Forensic
        Neuropsychiatry
        Psychopharmacology
    Psychology
        Forensic
        Neuropsychology
        Trauma
    Radiology
        MRI/Musculoskeletal Imaging
    Rehabilitation
        Catastrophic Injuries/Life Care Planning
    Respiratory Therapist
    Snakes, Spiders & Poisonous Plants
    Surgery
        Cardiovascular Thoracic
        Orthopedic
        Orthopedic/Sports Medicine
        Pedicle
        Plastic Reconstructive/Burns
        Vascular
    Toxicology
    Urology
    Vocational Rehabilitation
Medical Expert Witness Referral Services
Medical Illustrators
Medical Malpractice Consulting/Personal Injury
Medical Records
Medical Services
Messenger Services
Meteorology
Microfilming Services

Network - CD-ROM
News Services On Line Internet Access
Nursing Consultants

Office Management Services
Offshore Financial Services
On-Line Public Records Service
Online Network/Internet Provider

Pain Management
Paralegal Services
Parliamentarian
Patent Copyright & Trademark Agents
Patent Searching Services
Patent/Trademark Illustrators
Personal Injury
  (See Medical Malpractice)
Personnel Consultants
Photographs, Video & Map Analysis

Photography
Photography - Aerial
Polygraph Examination Services
Printing & Reprographics
Process Servers & Document Delivery Services
Process Servers & Document Retrieval
Product Defect Library - Searches/Analysis/Research
Product Safety
Project Attorney Services
Property Management
Psychological Injury - File Review & Analysis
Public Adjusters
Purchases & Buying of Judgements
Purchases of Structured Settlements & Annuities

Real Estate Consultants
Real Estate Reporting
Record Services
Research & Support Services
Restaurant Consultants & Experts

Secretarial Services
Securities Litigation Consulting Services
Security Consultants
Security Equipment
Security; Expert Witness
  (See also Expert Witness - Police/Security)
Signage & Sitewear Products
Skip Tracers
Sports Accidents/Serious Slips & Falls
Stock & Bond Brokers Associations
Stock & Bond Brokers Internet Access
Stock Exchanges - Direct Internet Access
Storage/Record Services
Strategic Planning
Subpoena Preparation Services
Surveys & Opinion Research

Technical Publications - Electrical Handbooks
Technical Service Companies
Television
  (See Video)
Temporary Attorney Services
Time Billing Software/Systems
Title Abstract Companies
Title Insurance
Toxicology
Trademark Investigation
Trademark Search Services
Traffic Engineering - Consulting & Forensic Services
Transcription Services
Translation Services
  (See also Interpreters; Interpreters & Translators)
Transportation Engineering - Consulting & Forensic Services
Trial Consultants
Trial Presentation Systems
Trust & Fiduciary Services
Trust Companies
TV News Research

UCC Search Services

Video Production, Editing & Graphics
Video Tape Services
Video Teleconferencing
Video Trial Presentations
Video, Computer, Audio Equipment for Court/Trials
Violence in the Workplace
Vocational Evaluations/Life Care Planning
Vocational Expert - Psychologist

Web Design - Internet Consulting
White Collar Criminal/Fraud Investigation
Witness Preparation & Assessment
World Nations League Corporate Code - Practitioners

# Services, Suppliers, Consultants In This Volume

## ACCIDENT INVESTIGATION & RECONSTRUCTION SERVICES
**CALIFORNIA**
LOS ANGELES .................................................... FIRE & ACCIDENT RECONSTRUCTION
TRAFFIC RECON

## ADMIRALTY & MARITIME EXPERT & CONSULTANT
**CALIFORNIA**
RANCHO SANTA MARGARITA .............................. MAREX

## APPRAISAL SERVICES - PERSONAL PROPERTY
**CALIFORNIA**
LOS ANGELES .................................................... STUART H. SALSBURY

## ASSET LOCATORS
**CALIFORNIA**
LOS ANGELES .................................................... NATIONAL LAWYERS LOCATE SERVICE, INC.

## ATTORNEY SERVICES
**CALIFORNIA**
FRESNO ............................................................ APPLEBY & COMPANY, INC.
ARVAL LEGAL SERVICES

LOS ANGELES .................................................... RICHARD GERSTENBERG, P.I.
MICRO QUICK
PROMPT LEGAL SERVICES
WADE'S ATTORNEY SERVICE

OAKLAND ......................................................... WESTERN ATTORNEY SERVICES

PALO ALTO ...................................................... WESTERN ATTORNEY SERVICES

## AUDIO/VIDEO SERVICES
**CALIFORNIA**
LOS ANGELES .................................................... DECISIONQUEST

## AUTOMOBILE & OFFICE EQUIPMENT LEASING
**CALIFORNIA**
LOS ANGELES .................................................... TRANS LEASING INTERNATIONAL

## BUSINESS VALUATIONS
**CALIFORNIA**
LOS ANGELES .................................................... HOULIHAN LOKEY HOWARD & ZUKIN
HOULIHAN VALUATION ADVISORS
KLARIS, THOMSON & SCHROEDER, INC.
SANLI PASTORE & HILL, INC.

## CASE MANAGEMENT SYSTEMS
**CALIFORNIA**
LOS ANGELES .................................................... THE POSEIDON GROUP

## CD-ROM PRODUCTS
**CALIFORNIA**
LOS ANGELES .................................................... DQ² EXHIBIT BANK

## COLLECTION AGENCIES
### CALIFORNIA
FRESNO .................................................... ACCURATE ATTORNEY SERVICES

## COMPUTER ANIMATION, GRAPHICS & SIMULATION
### CALIFORNIA
LOS ANGELES ............................................. DECISIONQUEST
                                                            INDATA CORPORATION

## COMPUTER EVIDENCE INVESTIGATION
### CALIFORNIA
LOS ANGELES ............................................. ONTRACK DATA RECOVERY, INC.

## CONFERENCING
### CALIFORNIA
FRESNO .................................................... NETWORKMCI CONFERENCING

LOS ANGELES ............................................. COMPRESSION LABS, INC.
                                                            CONFERENCECALLSERVICE
                                                            INTERCALL
                                                            NETWORKMCI CONFERENCING
                                                            POLYCOM, INC.
                                                            U.S. ROBOTICS

RIVERSIDE ................................................ NETWORKMCI CONFERENCING

## CONSTRUCTION CONSULTANTS
### CALIFORNIA
LOS ANGELES ............................................. COOPERS & LYBRAND, L.L.P.
                                                            JAX KNEPPERS ASSOCIATES, INC.
                                                            JERRY L. POLLAK, A.I.A., A.I.C.P.
                                                              ARCHITECT
                                                            THE SOLENDER GROUP, INC.
                                                            SPEXWEST
                                                            WAGNER . HOHNS . INGLIS . INC.

NEWPORT BEACH ......................................... HILL INTERNATIONAL, INC.

## CONSTRUCTION CONSULTANTS-CONSTRUCTION DEFECTS
### CALIFORNIA
LOS ANGELES ............................................. PRINGLE & ASSOCIATES STRUCTURAL
                                                            INSPECTION CONSULTANTS

## COPIER SERVICES
### CALIFORNIA
LOS ANGELES ............................................. MICRO QUICK

## CORPORATION COMPANIES
### CALIFORNIA
LOS ANGELES ............................................. CSC THE UNITED STATES CORPORATION
                                                            COMPANY

## COURT REPORTERS
### CALIFORNIA
BAKERSFIELD ............................................. KERNS & GRADILLAS

BERKELEY ................................................. TRAHAN REPORTING SERVICES

BEVERLY HILLS .......................................... ABBOTT & ASSOCIATES
                                                            ABRAMS, MAH & KAHN

# Alderson Reporting Company

**Worldwide Court Reporting & Litigation Support**

## Our record is undeniable.

**For over 60 years we have been official reporters to…**
- U.S. Presidents
- U.S. Supreme Court Justices
- Members of Congress
- Special Presidential Commissions

**Our other major clients include…**
- International Trade Agencies
- Business Thinktank Organizations
- Academic Institutions and,
- **THE TOUGHEST LITIGATORS AROUND THE WORLD.**

Through our strategic alliance with Arthur Andersen, we also serve legal counsel representing many major corporations.

You can count on our accuracy in every detail. With our on-line tracking databases, we can answer any of your questions at any hour of the day.

**We work to exceed your expectations with our services and…
We guarantee your satisfaction.**

   1-800-FOR-DEPO (367-3376)
   Fax: 1-800-367-3310
   CompuServe: 71064, 1256
   Internet: Alderson@Imssys.com

## 1-800-FOR-DEPO

Some of Alderson's services which help centralize your litigation with one source:

### CENTRALIZED CASE MANAGEMENT

Centralized tracking and retrieval of transcripts taken anywhere in the world, standardized transcript formatting, coordination between parties for document access and retrieval of transcripts, case-specific word lists, single source electronic billing.

### CYBER-REPORTING

Computer connectivity during deposition, telecommunications anywhere at anytime, on-line technical support, standardization of any disk format or media to your specifications, scheduling and transcript delivery via Internet, America OnLine, CompuServe, Counsel Connect.

### COMPREHENSIVE SUPPORT SERVICES

All security clearances, CaseView, VideoZX, Discovery ZX, compressed transcripts, master indexing by phrase or word, video/transcript syncing, document scanning, deposition suites anywhere, interpreters and translators.

# SERVICES, SUPPLIERS, CONSULTANTS

# COURT REPORTERS—CALIFORNIA

|  |  |
|---|---|
|  | CALIFORNIA DEPOSITION REPORTERS |
|  | INTERIM COURT REPORTING |
| CARLSBAD | CALIFORNIA DEPOSITION REPORTERS |
|  | INTERIM COURT REPORTING |
| CHICO | SWITZER & ASSOCIATES |
| COSTA MESA | PAULSON REPORTING SERVICE |
| COVINA | CALIFORNIA DEPOSITION REPORTERS |
| CRESCENT CITY | ALTRNET |
| EL CENTRO | ATWOOD JENNINGS & ASSOCIATES |
| ESCONDIDO | PAULSON REPORTING SERVICE |
| EUREKA | ALTRNET |
|  | BRUNNELL DEPOSITIONS |
| FAIRFIELD | DEMICHELLE DEPOSITION REPORTERS |
|  | LANGSTAFF REPORTING SERVICE |
| FORT BRAGG | ADAIR, POTSWALD & HENNESSEY |
| FRESNO | ALTRNET |
|  | CENTRAL VALLEY REPORTERS |
|  | RAY EGGEBRAATEN CSR, INC. |
| HAYWARD | BAY AREA COURT REPORTERS |
| IRVINE | A.A. NICHOLS, INC. |
|  | ABRAMS, MAH & KAHN |
|  | HAHN AND BOWERSOCK |
|  | IMHOF & ASSOCIATES |
|  | INTERIM COURT REPORTING |
|  | SHERR COURT REPORTERS |
| LA JOLLA | A.A. NICHOLS, INC. |
|  | INTERIM COURT REPORTING |
| LAKEPORT | ADAIR, POTSWALD & HENNESSEY |
| LONG BEACH | ABRAMS, MAH & KAHN |
|  | HAHN AND BOWERSOCK |
|  | INTERIM COURT REPORTING |
| LOS ANGELES | A.A. NICHOLS, INC. |
|  | ABA REPORTERS |
|  | ABBOTT & ASSOCIATES |
|  | ABBOTT LEGAL VIDEO SERVICES |
|  | ABRAMS, MAH & KAHN |
|  | ACCUTRAN REPORTING SERVICES |
|  | A. EDELIST DEPOSITION SERVICE, INC. |
|  | ALDERSON REPORTING COMPANY, INC. |
|  | ALTRNET |
|  | ASSOCIATED REPORTERS OF NEVADA |
|  | AT LAW LITIGATION SUPPORT |
|  | BOB MCCANN & ASSOCIATES |
|  | BUTTERFIELD & BUTTERFIELD |
|  | CALIFORNIA DEPOSITION REPORTERS |
|  | CERTIFIED REPORTING COMPANY |
|  | CHAIT MEDIA INC. |

## COURT REPORTERS — Continued
### CALIFORNIA — Continued
#### LOS ANGELES — Continued

CHICAGO REPORTING COMPANY
DOYLE REPORTING, INC.
DRAGON DEPOSITION SERVICE
EATON COURT REPORTING SERVICES
ESQUIRE COMMUNICATIONS, LTD.
  (ESQ.COM)
GILLESPIE REPORTING AND DOCUMENT
  MANAGEMENT, INC.
HAHN AND BOWERSOCK
HARRY A. CANNON, INC.
HUDGINS MCHALE
IMHOF & ASSOCIATES
INTERIM COURT REPORTING
JONNELL AGNEW & ASSOCIATES
KERNS & GRADILLAS
KILLION COURT REPORTERS
LACEY SHORTHAND REPORTING CORPORATION
  AND LACEY VIDEO SERVICES
LYON REPORTING, INC.
MAXENE WEINBERG AGENCY
MCCORKLE COURT REPORTERS, INC.
MILLER & COMPANY REPORTERS
PARKER REPORTING, INC.
PAULSON REPORTING SERVICE
PETERSON & ASSOCIATES
PRATTON & ASSOCIATES
SAN JOSE DEPOSITION REPORTERS, INC.
SHERR COURT REPORTERS
VENTURA COUNTY REPORTING SERVICE
WESTSIDE DEPOSITION REPORTERS
WOMACK REPORTING SERVICE

MENLO PARK ............................................. BELL & MYERS

MERCED ................................................. ASSOCIATED REPORTERS
CENTRAL CALIFORNIA REPORTERS

MODESTO ................................................ AL CALA & ASSOCIATES
FAINTER & SMITH
MAY & PALERMO

MONTEREY .............................................. BELL & MYERS
MONTEREY PENINSULA COURT REPORTERS
  INC.

NAPA .................................................... DEMICHELLE DEPOSITION REPORTERS
GOLDEN GATE REPORTERS

NEVADA CITY ........................................... ALPINE REPORTING

NEWPORT BEACH ........................................ ABRAMS, MAH & KAHN
CALIFORNIA DEPOSITION REPORTERS
INTERIM COURT REPORTING
MAXENE WEINBERG AGENCY
SHERR COURT REPORTERS

OAKLAND ............................................... ABA REPORTERS
ALTRNET
BEHMKE REPORTING & VIDEO SERVICES
COMBS & GREENLEY
DIABLO VALLEY REPORTING SERVICES

# SERVICES, SUPPLIERS, CONSULTANTS

## DOCUMENT IMAGING—CALIFORNIA

GOLDEN GATE REPORTERS
HARRY A. CANNON, INC.
INTERIM COURT REPORTING
JACK LONDON COURT REPORTERS
ROTH * KELTY * RHUDY
VIGNATI REPORTING

ONTARIO .................................................. CALIFORNIA DEPOSITION REPORTERS

PALM SPRINGS ............................................ ALL-IN-ONE DEPOSITION REPORTING
    SERVICE
CALIFORNIA DEPOSITION REPORTERS
J. GREENUP & ASSOCIATES

PALO ALTO ............................................... ALDERSON REPORTING COMPANY, INC.
BEHMKE REPORTING & VIDEO SERVICES
BELL & MYERS
GOLDEN GATE REPORTERS
HARRY A. CANNON, INC.
INTERIM COURT REPORTING
OBUJEN & MCCUTCHEON
ROTH * KELTY * RHUDY
SAN JOSE DEPOSITION REPORTERS, INC.

PASADENA ................................................ ALBRIGHT & ASSOCIATES
CALIFORNIA DEPOSITION REPORTERS
INTERIM COURT REPORTING

RED BLUFF ............................................... RED BLUFF REPORTERS

REDDING .................................................. J.V. KILLINGSWORTH & ASSOCIATES

REDWOOD CITY ............................................ ROTH * KELTY * RHUDY

RIVERSIDE ................................................ ABRAMS, MAH & KAHN
CALIFORNIA DEPOSITION REPORTERS
IMHOF & ASSOCIATES
PAULSON REPORTING SERVICE

## DEMONSTRATIVE EVIDENCE

### CALIFORNIA
LOS ANGELES ............................................. DECISIONQUEST
ELEVENTH HOUR FORENSIC PHOTOGRAPHY
INDATA CORPORATION

## DISCOVERY AND DOCUMENT REPRODUCTION SERVICES

### CALIFORNIA
LOS ANGELES ............................................. CALIFORNIA LEGAL SUPPORT SERVICES
    INC.

## DOCUMENT FILING/RETRIEVAL

### CALIFORNIA
LOS ANGELES ............................................. COMPEX
CSC THE UNITED STATES CORPORATION
    COMPANY
DOCU-SEARCH CALIFORNIA
PARASEC
SUPER BUREAU, INC.

## DOCUMENT IMAGING

### CALIFORNIA
LOS ANGELES ............................................. DECISIONQUEST

## DOCUMENT MANAGEMENT SERVICES

### CALIFORNIA

LOS ANGELES ............................................. GILLESPIE REPORTING AND DOCUMENT
MANAGEMENT, INC.

PALM SPRINGS ............................................. ALL-IN-ONE DEPOSITION REPORTING
SERVICE

## DOCUMENT RESEARCH, RETRIEVAL & DELIVERY

### CALIFORNIA

LOS ANGELES ............................................. RESEARCH INFORMATION SERVICES, INC.

## ECONOMIC AND STATISTIC CONSULTING SERVICES

### CALIFORNIA

LOS ANGELES ............................................. ANALYSIS GROUP ECONOMICS
CHARLES RIVER ASSOCIATES INCORPORATED
MICRONOMICS, INC.
NATIONAL ECONOMIC RESEARCH
ASSOCIATES, INC.

## ECONOMIC AND STATISTICAL CONSULTING SERVICES - AUTOMOBILES

### CALIFORNIA

LOS ANGELES ............................................. THE FONTANA GROUP, INC.

## ELECTRONIC PACKAGING & PRODUCTION

### CALIFORNIA

LOS ANGELES ............................................. STEINBERG & ASSOCIATES

## ENVIRONMENTAL ENGINEERING & REMEDIATION SERVICES

### CALIFORNIA

LOS ANGELES ............................................. DAMES & MOORE
TERRA VAC, INC.

NEWPORT BEACH ............................................. INNOVATIVE CONSULTANTS INCORPORATED

## EQUINE - APPRAISERS & CONSULTANTS

### CALIFORNIA

LOS ANGELES ............................................. FMV APPRAISAL COMPANY
JILL MCEWAN

## ESCROW SERVICES

### CALIFORNIA

LOS ANGELES ............................................. COMMERCE ESCROW COMPANY

## EXAMINERS OF QUESTIONED DOCUMENTS (HANDWRITING EXPERTS)

### CALIFORNIA

LOS ANGELES ............................................. JAMES A. BLACK
BROOKES & CHUNG
MARTA CHAUSEE, M.S.

## EXPERT WITNESS

### *ACCIDENT RECONSTRUCTION*

#### CALIFORNIA

LOS ANGELES ............................................. ERROR ANALYSIS, INC.

### *ADMIRALTY*

#### CALIFORNIA

RANCHO SANTA MARGARITA ............................................. MAREX

## AGRI-HORTICULTURAL

**CALIFORNIA**
LOS ANGELES .................................................... KLAUS RADTKE, PH.D.

## AUDIO-TAPE ANALYSIS/AUTHENTICATION/VOICE ID

**CALIFORNIA**
LOS ANGELES .................................................... FORENSIC AUDIO LAB

## BANKING

**CALIFORNIA**
LOS ANGELES .................................................... JRB ASSOCIATES
MCS ASSOCIATES

## BIOMEDICAL ENGINEERING

**CALIFORNIA**
LOS ANGELES .................................................... BIOMEDICAL CONSULTING SERVICES

## COATINGS/PAINT

**CALIFORNIA**
LOS ANGELES .................................................... CCC CONSOLIDATED CONSULTANTS CO.

## COMMERCIAL LAW/BANKING/UCC

**CALIFORNIA**
LOS ANGELES .................................................... UNIFORM COMMERCIAL CODE CONSULTANTS

## COMPUTER & BUSINESS INFORMATION SYSTEMS

**CALIFORNIA**
LOS ANGELES .................................................... COMPUTOMATA INTERNATIONAL CORPORATION

## CONSTRUCTION

**CALIFORNIA**
LAFAYETTE ...................................................... THE HAIST CORPORATION

LOS ANGELES .................................................... JAX KNEPPERS ASSOCIATES, INC.
JERRY L. POLLAK, A.I.A., A.I.C.P.
  ARCHITECT
THE SOLENDER GROUP, INC.
WAGNER . HOHNS . INGLIS . INC.

NEWPORT BEACH ............................................... CONSTRUCTION CONSULTING SERVICES

PASADENA ...................................................... FORENSISGROUP

RICHMOND ..................................................... INTERACTIVE RESOURCES

## CRIME PREVENTION

**CALIFORNIA**
LOS ANGELES .................................................... SECURITY MANAGEMENT SERVICES, INC.

## CRIMINALISTICS & FIREARMS

**CALIFORNIA**
LOS ANGELES .................................................... CCC CONSOLIDATED CONSULTANTS CO.

## EMPLOYEE/EMPLOYMENT DISCRIMINATION

**CALIFORNIA**
LOS ANGELES .................................................... BARRINGTON PSYCHIATRIC CENTER
JAY M. FINKELMAN, PH.D., C.P.E.
FRIEDLAND ASSOCIATES, INC.
BRIAN H. KLEINER, PH.D

PASADENA ...................................................... G. GOVINE STEELE CONSULTING

## EXPERT WITNESS—EMPLOYEE/EMPLOYMENT — Continued

### OSHA REGULATIONS/PROCEDURES

**CALIFORNIA**
LOS ANGELES .................................................... CCC CONSOLIDATED CONSULTANTS CO.

### WRONGFUL TERMINATION/HARASSMENT

**CALIFORNIA**
LOS ANGELES .................................................... JAY M. FINKELMAN, PH.D., C.P.E.
BRIAN H. KLEINER, PH.D

### ENGINEERS/ENGINEERING

**CALIFORNIA**
LOS ANGELES .................................................... B.E.S.T., INC.
CCC CONSOLIDATED CONSULTANTS CO.

### ELECTRICAL

**CALIFORNIA**
LOS ANGELES .................................................... YBI

### FORENSIC ENGINEERING

**CALIFORNIA**
LOS ANGELES .................................................... CCC CONSOLIDATED CONSULTANTS CO.
PRINGLE & ASSOCIATES STRUCTURAL
INSPECTION CONSULTANTS

### MECHANICAL/MACHINE DESIGN

**CALIFORNIA**
LOS ANGELES .................................................... ERIK K. ANTONSSON, PH.D., P.E.

### SAFETY

**CALIFORNIA**
ENCINITAS ....................................................... SAFETY FACTOR ASSOCIATES, INC.

## FIRE

### PROTECTION, INVESTIGATION

**CALIFORNIA**
LOS ANGELES .................................................... O'ROURKE & COMPANY

### WILDLAND/URBAN INTERFACE

**CALIFORNIA**
LOS ANGELES .................................................... KLAUS RADTKE, PH.D.

### HUMAN FACTORS & SAFETY

**CALIFORNIA**
LOS ANGELES .................................................... JILL A. STRAWBRIDGE, PH.D.

### INSURANCE

**CALIFORNIA**
LOS ANGELES .................................................... TOLE CONSULTING SERVICE

### BAD FAITH

**CALIFORNIA**
LOS ANGELES .................................................... JIM SCHRATZ AND ASSOCIATES
CLINTON E. MILLER, J.D., BCFE

### RISK MANAGEMENT CONSULTING

**CALIFORNIA**
LOS ANGELES .................................................... STONE & WEBSTER MANAGEMENT
CONSULTANTS, INC.

## SERVICES, SUPPLIERS, CONSULTANTS
## EXPERT WITNESS - SECURED—CALIFORNIA

### LEAD BASED PAINT
**CALIFORNIA**
LOS ANGELES ............................................. CCC CONSOLIDATED CONSULTANTS CO.

### LETTERS OF CREDIT
**CALIFORNIA**
LOS ANGELES ............................................. UNIFORM COMMERCIAL CODE CONSULTANTS

### MAGAZINE PUBLISHING
**CALIFORNIA**
LOS ANGELES ............................................. BAY SHERMAN & CRAIG

### MARINE
**CALIFORNIA**
RANCHO SANTA MARGARITA ............................. MAREX

### MARTIAL ARTS
#### HAND TO HAND
**CALIFORNIA**
LOS ANGELES ............................................. CCC CONSOLIDATED CONSULTANTS CO.

### MEDICAL INSTRUMENT & PRODUCT INJURY
**CALIFORNIA**
LOS ANGELES ............................................. CCC CONSOLIDATED CONSULTANTS CO.

### METEOROLOGY/CLIMATOLOGY
**CALIFORNIA**
COVINA .................................................. ALLIED WEATHER CONSULTANTS

OAKLAND ................................................ CLIMATOLOGICAL CONSULTING CORPORATION

### POLICE/SECURITY
#### USE OF FORCE
**CALIFORNIA**
LOS ANGELES ............................................. CCC CONSOLIDATED CONSULTANTS CO.

### PREMISES SECURITY & LIABILITY
**CALIFORNIA**
LOS ANGELES ............................................. CCC CONSOLIDATED CONSULTANTS CO.

### REAL ESTATE
**CALIFORNIA**
LOS ANGELES ............................................. CAMDAN & ASSOCIATES
SAMUEL K. FRESHMAN
MARK S. MALAN, MAI
MCS ASSOCIATES

#### FINANCE
**CALIFORNIA**
LOS ANGELES ............................................. WHIPPLE H. MANNING

### ROOFING & WATERPROOFING
**CALIFORNIA**
LOS ANGELES ............................................. RJ CONSULTANTS INTERNATIONAL, INC.
ROBERT D. BYRD & ASSOCIATES, INC.

### SECURED TRANSACTIONS
**CALIFORNIA**
LOS ANGELES ............................................. UNIFORM COMMERCIAL CODE CONSULTANTS

## EXPERT WITNESS — Continued

### SLIP, TRIP AND FALL

**CALIFORNIA**
LOS ANGELES ............................................. CCC CONSOLIDATED CONSULTANTS CO.

### TRANSPORTATION

#### AVIATION

**CALIFORNIA**
LOS ANGELES ............................................. JACOBY AND ASSOCIATES

#### TRAFFIC ENGINEERING & SAFETY

**CALIFORNIA**
LOS ANGELES ............................................. WILLIAM KUNZMAN, P.E.

### WOOD SCIENCE & TECHNOLOGY

**CALIFORNIA**
LOS ANGELES ............................................. PHILIP MASON OPSAL, INC.

## EXPERT WITNESS REFERRAL SERVICES

**CALIFORNIA**
LOS ANGELES ............................................. TASA

## FAX FILING OF COURT DOCUMENTS

**CALIFORNIA**
LOS ANGELES ............................................. FAX & FILE LEGAL SERVICES, INC.

## FIRE INVESTIGATORS

**CALIFORNIA**
LOS ANGELES ............................................. KLAUS RADTKE, PH.D.

## FORENSIC PSYCHIATRY

**CALIFORNIA**
LOS ANGELES ............................................. ALFRED COODLEY, M.D., PH.D.

## FORENSIC SERVICES

**CALIFORNIA**
LOS ANGELES ............................................. VOLLMER-GRAY ENGINEERING LABORATORIES

## GROUPWARE

**CALIFORNIA**
LOS ANGELES ............................................. TRAX SOFTWORKS, INC.

## HEDONIC DAMAGES/LOSS OF ENJOYMENT OF LIFE

**CALIFORNIA**
LOS ANGELES ............................................. ECONOMIC CONSULTANTS & ASSOCIATES

## HEIR TRACERS

**CALIFORNIA**
LOS ANGELES ............................................. AMERICAN RESEARCH BUREAU, INC.
FRASER & FRASER
HOERNER BANK

## INCORPORATION SERVICES

**CALIFORNIA**
LOS ANGELES ............................................. CSC THE UNITED STATES CORPORATION COMPANY

## INFORMATION BROKERS

### CALIFORNIA
LOS ANGELES .............................................. SUPER BUREAU, INC.

## INTERPRETERS & TRANSLATORS

### CALIFORNIA
MENLO PARK ............................................ JAPANESE LINGUISTIC SERVICE

## INVESTIGATORS

### CALIFORNIA
LOS ANGELES .............................................. ALPINE INVESTIGATION SERVICES
                     BARNES & ASSOCIATES PROFESSIONAL SERVICES, INC.
                     CALIFORNIA ATTORNEYS INVESTIGATORS
                     NICK HARRIS DETECTIVES, INC.
                     JOHN T. LYNCH INTERNATIONAL
                     LARRY MALMBERG INVESTIGATIONS
                     STARSIDE PROTECTION
                     SYLNIC INVESTIGATIONS

NEWPORT BEACH .......................................... GLOBAL INVESTIGATIONS & V.I.P. SECURITY SERVICES
                     VENEZIA INVESTIGATIVE SERVICES

## JURY CONSULTANTS

### CALIFORNIA
LOS ANGELES .............................................. DECISIONQUEST
                     JURY RESEARCH INSTITUTE

## LAWYER SEARCH & PLACEMENT CONSULTANTS

### CALIFORNIA
LOS ANGELES .............................................. BARRY GOLDBERG & ASSOCIATES, INC.
                     DOUG SEARS & ASSOCIATES

## LEGAL PUBLICATIONS

### CALIFORNIA
LOS ANGELES .............................................. NILS PUBLISHING COMPANY

## LEGAL RESEARCH

### CALIFORNIA
LOS ANGELES .............................................. THE POSEIDON GROUP

## LEGAL SOFTWARE

### CALIFORNIA
LOS ANGELES .............................................. OPTICIMAGE SOFTWARE CORPORATION

## LEGAL SUPPORT PERSONNEL - TEMPORARY & PERMANENT

### CALIFORNIA
LOS ANGELES .............................................. THE AFFILIATES

## LIFE CARE PLANNING

### CALIFORNIA
BAKERSFIELD ............................................ COMPREHENSIVE CARE SYSTEMS (CCS)

PASADENA ............................................... LINC CASE MANAGEMENT AND MEDICAL/LEGAL CONSULTING SERVICES

## LITIGATION CONSULTING

### CALIFORNIA
LOS ANGELES .............................................. DECISIONQUEST

## LITIGATION SUPPORT SERVICES

### CALIFORNIA
LOS ALTOS .............................................. THE CHATHAM GROUP

LOS ANGELES .......................................... COMPEX
OSTROVE, KRANTZ & OSTROVE, A P.C.
THE POSEIDON GROUP
REGENT PACIFIC

## MANAGEMENT CONSULTANTS

### CALIFORNIA
LOS ANGELES .......................................... ALTMAN WEIL PENSA, INC.

## MARINE CONSULTANTS

### CALIFORNIA
RANCHO SANTA MARGARITA ........................... MAREX

## MEDICAL CASE REVIEW & PREPARATION/TRIAL CONSULTING

### CALIFORNIA
LOS ANGELES .......................................... CCC CONSOLIDATED CONSULTANTS CO.
LAKE ELSINORE FAMILY MEDICAL CLINIC INC.
MEDICALLY SPEAKING - MEDICAL LEGAL CONSULTANTS

OAKLAND .............................................. SHERYL R. PICCO, RN, BSN

PASADENA ............................................. GSG ASSOCIATES, INC.
LINC CASE MANAGEMENT AND MEDICAL/LEGAL CONSULTING SERVICES

## MEDICAL EXPERT TESTIMONY

### CALIFORNIA
LOS ANGELES .......................................... DR. STEVEN E. LERNER & ASSOCIATES

## MEDICAL EXPERT WITNESS

### CALIFORNIA
BERKELEY ............................................. AMERICAN MEDICAL FORENSIC SPECIALISTS, INC.

LOS ANGELES .......................................... CCC CONSOLIDATED CONSULTANTS CO.
DR. STEVEN E. LERNER & ASSOCIATES
JASON I. GREEN, M.D., F.A.C.S.
RICHARD N. SHAW, MD, FACP, FACR

### *DENTAL*

#### CALIFORNIA
BEVERLY HILLS ........................................ TOM K. KALILI, D.M.D.

LOS ANGELES .......................................... CCC CONSOLIDATED CONSULTANTS CO.

### *PROSTHODONTICS/DENTAL IMPLANTS*

#### CALIFORNIA
LOS ANGELES .......................................... CCC CONSOLIDATED CONSULTANTS CO.

### *TMJ*

#### CALIFORNIA
LOS ANGELES .......................................... CCC CONSOLIDATED CONSULTANTS CO.

**SERVICES, SUPPLIERS, CONSULTANTS**     **MEDICAL MALPRACTICE CONSULTING—CALIFORNIA**

### *DEVICES*

**CALIFORNIA**
- LOS ANGELES .................................................. CCC CONSOLIDATED CONSULTANTS CO.
- NEWPORT BEACH ........................................... N.N. SALMAN, PH.D.

### *MEDICAL CASE REVIEW*
#### *MALPRACTICE & PERSONAL INJURY*

**CALIFORNIA**
- BERKELEY ..................................................... AMERICAN MEDICAL FORENSIC SPECIALISTS, INC.
- LOS ANGELES .................................................. ELLIOT D. FELMAN, M.D.

### *NEUROLOGY*
#### *NEUROSURGERY & ACUPUNCTURE*

**CALIFORNIA**
- LOS ANGELES .................................................. LORNE S. LABEL, M.D.

### *OPHTHALMOLOGY*

**CALIFORNIA**
- BEVERLY HILLS ............................................... CHARLES ARONBERG, M.D.
  ANDREW I. CASTER, M.D., F.A.C.S.

### *PSYCHIATRY*

**CALIFORNIA**
- BEVERLY HILLS ............................................... CAROLE LIEBERMAN, M.D., M.P.H.
- LOS ANGELES .................................................. PSYBAR, P.L.C.®

#### *FORENSIC*

**CALIFORNIA**
- LOS ANGELES .................................................. BARRINGTON PSYCHIATRIC CENTER

### *PSYCHOLOGY*

**CALIFORNIA**
- LOS ANGELES .................................................. PSYBAR, P.L.C.®

#### *FORENSIC*

**CALIFORNIA**
- LOS ANGELES .................................................. BARRINGTON PSYCHIATRIC CENTER

#### *NEUROPSYCHOLOGY*

**CALIFORNIA**
- IRVINE .......................................................... ROBERT J. SBORDONE, PH.D.

### *SURGERY*
#### *ORTHOPEDIC*

**CALIFORNIA**
- IRVINE .......................................................... ROBERT ANTHONY BAIRD, M.D.
- LOS ANGELES .................................................. MICHAEL D. ROSCO, M.D.

## MEDICAL EXPERT WITNESS REFERRAL SERVICES

**CALIFORNIA**
- LOS ANGELES .................................................. CCC CONSOLIDATED CONSULTANTS CO.

## MEDICAL MALPRACTICE CONSULTING/PERSONAL INJURY

**CALIFORNIA**
- HACIENDA HEIGHTS ........................................ MED-LINK

## MEDICAL MALPRACTICE CONSULTING/PERSONAL INJURY — Continued
### CALIFORNIA — Continued

LOS ANGELES .............................................. CCC CONSOLIDATED CONSULTANTS CO.

## MEDICAL RECORDS
### CALIFORNIA
LOS ANGELES .............................................. COMPEX

## MESSENGER SERVICES
### CALIFORNIA
LOS ANGELES .............................................. MICRO QUICK

## MICROFILMING SERVICES
### CALIFORNIA
LOS ANGELES .............................................. COMPEX

## NURSING CONSULTANTS
### CALIFORNIA
BAKERSFIELD ............................................. COMPREHENSIVE CARE SYSTEMS (CCS)

LOS ANGELES .............................................. CCC CONSOLIDATED CONSULTANTS CO.

## PARALEGAL SERVICES
### CALIFORNIA
LOS ANGELES .............................................. AT LAW LITIGATION SUPPORT
                                                          CAMILLE M. CADOO, CLA

## PHOTOGRAPHY
### CALIFORNIA
LOS ANGELES .............................................. ELEVENTH HOUR FORENSIC PHOTOGRAPHY

## PROCESS SERVERS & DOCUMENT DELIVERY SERVICES
### CALIFORNIA
ANAHEIM .................................................. PROMPT LEGAL SERVICES

FRESNO ................................................... ACCURATE ATTORNEY SERVICES

LOS ANGELES .............................................. AARONS & ASSOCIATES
                                                          ABC PROCESS SERVING BUREAU, INC.
                                                          BEACH CITIES ATTORNEY SERVICE
                                                          CALIFORNIA LEGAL SUPPORT SERVICES
                                                             INC.
                                                          D.L.S., INC. (DEMOVSKY LAWYER
                                                             SERVICE)
                                                          MICRO QUICK
                                                          PROMPT LEGAL SERVICES
                                                          SYLNIC INVESTIGATIONS
                                                          WADE'S ATTORNEY SERVICE

MONTEREY ................................................ SAYLER LEGAL SERVICE

OAKLAND ................................................. CALIFORNIA LEGAL SUPPORT SERVICES
                                                           INC.

## PRODUCT SAFETY
### CALIFORNIA
ENCINITAS ............................................... SAFETY FACTOR ASSOCIATES, INC.

LOS ANGELES .............................................. CCC CONSOLIDATED CONSULTANTS CO.

# When a Detail Has To Be Right

CLSS has offices throughout California, each fully bonded and insured. Our staff of experienced professionals are committed to seeing every detail of your assignment completed on time, every time and in a manner that reflects our professionalism...and yours.

- Professional Registered Bonded and Certified Process Servers
- Skip Tracing/Locate/Investigative Services
- Litigation Search and Status
- Experienced State and Federal Court Service Specialists
- Fax Filing Service - All Courts
- City, County, State and Federal Agency Filings and Research
- Public Records Research and Retrieval
- Litigation Support Service
- Registered Professional Photocopiers
- Subpoena Preparation
- On/Off Site Document Reproduction
- Complete Micrographic and Optical Scan Production Service

All principals are members of the California Association of Photocopiers and Process Servers and the National Association of Professional Process Servers.

Representative clients consist of major law firms, in-house corporate counsel, financial institutions, insurance carriers and governmental agencies. References furnished upon request.

**CLSS**

Nationwide Service Center
**800-899-2577**
Fax: 800-998-2577

| | |
|---|---|
| LOS ANGELES OFFICE | 213-383-5822 |
| OAKLAND OFFICE | 510-839-2605 |
| SAN FRANCISCO OFFICE | 415-882-2270 |
| SAN JOSE OFFICE | 408-491-8770 |

**CALIFORNIA LEGAL SUPPORT SERVICES INC.**

*See our individual listing under Los Angeles, Oakland, San Jose and San Francisco.*

**Major Credit Cards Accepted**

---

LEGAL SUPPORT SERVICES

# EACH TIME
# EVERY TIME
# ON TIME

*How you handle details can mean the difference between winning and losing.*

*At CLSS, we like to think of ourselves as the...*

<u>WINNING ADVANTAGE.</u>

# Martindale-Hubbell is Now Available in Four Formats—the Internet, Print, CD-ROM, and Online

**Now, you can access the Martindale-Hubbell® database in the format that is most convenient for your research needs.**

Avail yourself to data on over 900,000 lawyers and law firms via the multi-volume print directory. Engage in electronic access via the CD-ROM which is updated quarterly and available in MS-DOS® and new Windows® format as well as local area network versions. Take advantage of sophisticated search technology via the LEXIS®-NEXIS® services.

These electronic media enable you to perform complex searches that are difficult or impossible via traditional research methods. In seconds you can combine search criteria to create extraordinarily precise searches. Identify a law firm in Aspen, Colorado that practices real estate law and whose clients include condominium associations ... locate a Japanese-speaking corporate business lawyer in San Francisco. The search strategies are endless.

## Announcing the Availability of the Martindale-Hubbell Database on the Internet—www.martindale.com

The **Martindale-Hubbell Law Directory** is now accessible via the **Martindale-Hubbell Lawyer Locator**™ on the Internet at http://www.martindale.com to an estimated user base of tens of millions, extending well beyond the legal community to encompass libraries, government, small and large corporations, service and supplier firms, and consumers.

No matter what your information requirements or your technology orientation, Martindale-Hubbell provides you with the data you need in the format you prefer.

Please contact our Customer Relations Department at 1-800-526-4902 for more information on the full range of Martindale-Hubbell services.

**MARTINDALE-HUBBELL®**
A Member of the Reed Elsevier plc group

121 Chanlon Road • New Providence, NJ 07974
1-800-526-4902
Email: info@martindale.com
http://www.martindale.com

MARTINDALE-HUBBELL, LEXIS and NEXIS are registered trademarks of Reed Elsevier Properties Inc., used under license.
MS-DOS and Windows are registered trademarks of the Microsoft Corporation.

## PSYCHOLOGICAL INJURY - FILE REVIEW & ANALYSIS
### CALIFORNIA
LOS ANGELES .......................................... BARRINGTON PSYCHIATRIC CENTER

## SPORTS ACCIDENTS/SERIOUS SLIPS & FALLS
### CALIFORNIA
LOS ANGELES .......................................... DISCOVERY SYSTEMS, INC.

## SUBPOENA PREPARATION SERVICES
### CALIFORNIA
LOS ANGELES .......................................... COMPEX

## SURVEYS & OPINION RESEARCH
### CALIFORNIA
LOS ANGELES .......................................... COGAN RESEARCH GROUP

## TITLE ABSTRACT COMPANIES
### CALIFORNIA
LOS ANGELES .......................................... TITLE COURT SERVICE, INC.

## TRANSLATION SERVICES
### CALIFORNIA
BERKELEY ............................................... BERKELEY SCIENTIFIC TRANSLATION SERVICE, INC.

MENLO PARK .......................................... AD-EX WORLDWIDE
JAPANESE LINGUISTIC SERVICE

## TRIAL PRESENTATION SYSTEMS
### CALIFORNIA
LOS ANGELES .......................................... INDATA CORPORATION

## VIDEO TAPE SERVICES
### CALIFORNIA
BEVERLY HILLS ....................................... AAA LEGAL VIDEO SERVICES

FRESNO .................................................. RAY EGGEBRAATEN CSR, INC.

LOS ANGELES .......................................... ABBOTT LEGAL VIDEO SERVICES
CHAIT MEDIA INC.
CHARLES HELLER & COMPANY
LACEY SHORTHAND REPORTING CORPORATION AND LACEY VIDEO SERVICES

## VIDEO TRIAL PRESENTATIONS
### CALIFORNIA
LOS ANGELES .......................................... DECISIONQUEST

OAKLAND ............................................... VIDEO SOLUTIONS

## VIDEO, COMPUTER, AUDIO EQUIPMENT FOR COURT/TRIALS
### CALIFORNIA
LOS ANGELES .......................................... DECISIONQUEST

## VOCATIONAL EVALUATIONS/LIFE CARE PLANNING
### CALIFORNIA
LOS ANGELES .......................................... CRAWFORD DISABILITY MANAGEMENT SERVICES

## WITNESS PREPARATION & ASSESSMENT
### CALIFORNIA
LOS ANGELES .............................................. DECISIONQUEST

# SERVICES, SUPPLIERS, CONSULTANTS

# CALIFORNIA—BAKERSFIELD

## ANAHEIM, 266,406, *Orange Co.*

### PROCESS SERVERS & DOCUMENT DELIVERY SERVICES

"We Serve You by Serving Others"
Established 1975

10573 West Pico Boulevard • Suite 344
Los Angeles, California 90064
Toll Free: (800) 838-9044
Telephone: (310) 838-9000 • Facsimile: (310) 838-0855

*Registered, Certified, Bonded & Insured*

**Prompt Legal Services** is a full litigation services company. Located near Beverly Hills, we specialize in very fast, efficient and courteous process service. Our firm is known for hard to serves, celebrity, and other special circumstance services. We are fully computerized and are on-line with databases nationwide.

Counties:
LOS ANGELES
Orange / Riverside
San Bernardino / San Diego
Santa Barbara / Ventura

Serving throughout California, United States and International

— *24 HOUR SERVICE* —

- ◆ **SPECIALIZATIONS:**
  - Rush Service
  - Multiple Attempts at no extra charge
  - Skip Tracing
  - Surveillance
  - County, State & Federal Courts
  - Writs of Execution
  - Small Claims Specialist

- ◆ **LITIGATION SERVICES AVAILABLE UPON REQUEST**
  - Public Record Retrieval
  - Post Office Checking
  - Database Searches
  - Real Property Searches
  - Document Retrieval, Filing & Research
  - DMV & Credit Research
  - Subpoena Preparation
  - Witness Statements
  - Summons & Complaints

Member: *(CAPPS) California Association of Photocopiers & Process Servers*
*(NAPPS) National Association of Professional Process Servers*
*(APSA) Arizona Process Servers Association*
*(FAPPS) Florida Association of Professional Process Servers*
*(TPPS) Texas Professional Process Servers Association*
*(OAPS) Oregon Association of Professional Process Servers*
*(NJPSA) New Jersey Process Servers Association*
*Chamber of Commerce*

Standard Service
Los Angeles County  $35
All Other Counties  $45

## BAKERSFIELD, * 174,820, *Kern Co.*

### COURT REPORTERS

**KERNS & GRADILLAS**
Certified Court Reporters

1430 Truxtun Avenue, Suite 777
Bakersfield, CA 93301

Telephone: (805) 832-1611
(800) 875-5071
Facsimile: (805) 633-0102

DEPOSITIONS * HEARINGS * ARBITRATIONS

A Full-Service Court Reporting Agency
with over 100 CSR's Nationwide

| BEVERLY HILLS | SAN FRANCISCO |
| BURLINGAME | SANTA BARBARA |
| VENTURA | COSTA MESA |
| RIVERSIDE | SAN DIEGO |
| NEW YORK | LONDON |

- - - - - - - - - - - -

Real Time
Remote Real Time
CaseView/LiveNote
Exhibit Imaging
Video Services

COMPLIMENTARY
* Condensed Transcripts
* Full-Text Word Indexing
* Archiving
* Deposition Suites
* Parking
* Private Meeting Rooms

WMBE Certified

Member:
National Court Reporters Association
California Court Reporters Association
Los Angeles General Court Reporters Association
Society for the Technological Advancement of Reporting
California Notary Association

### LIFE CARE PLANNING

**Comprehensive Care Systems (CCS)**
Suite 310
1412 17th St.
Bakersfield, CA 93301
Phone:(805)328-2138

*See Nursing Consultants*

## BAKERSFIELD (Continued)
### NURSING CONSULTANTS

### COMPREHENSIVE CARE SYSTEMS (CCS)
1412-17th Street, Suite 310
Bakersfield, California 93301
(805)328-2138

Life Care Planning
Medical Case Management
Medical Rehabilitation Consulting Services

Nancy Nusbaum (Proprietor), R.N., C.R.R.N., C.C.M.
Graduate — Rehabilitation Training Institute with
Certification in Life Care Planning and Workers' Compensation Law

CCS is comprised of a team of Registered Nurses with backgrounds in virtually all facets of nursing including acute, and traumatic neurological and head injury; orthopedic, burn injury, hazardous material-induced illness/injury and chronic pain management. Strong background in rural/agriculture-related injury/illness.

CCS offers a diverse range of services to address injury and disease management issues to include:

- Initial evaluation with appropriate follow-up
- Medical record review, analysis and summary
- Establishment of a comprehensive Treatment Care Plan
- Transport to and attendance at surgery/medial/therapy appointments
- Onsite review and file assistance
- Life Care Planning (Catastrophic cost projections for setting of financial reserves)
- Coordination of specialist care and Independent Medical Examinations
- Round the-clock availability for patient concerns
- Medical translation services including Spanish, Punjabi, Tagalog
- Customized report presentation
- 90-Day Workers' Compensation Benefit Review
- Job Analysis
- Expert Witness

With CCS you can expect:
Quick Response • Flexibility, Personalized Care

805-328-2138

---

## BERKELEY, 102,724, Alameda Co.

### COURT REPORTERS

### TRAHAN REPORTING SERVICES
918 Parker St., 2nd Floor
Berkeley, CA 94710
(510) 549-3193     (800) 773-3193     Fax (510) 549-1418

Professionals Serving Professionals

Serving Entire Bay Area          Over 17 Years Experience

- COMPLIMENTARY DEPOSITION SUITES
- COMPUTERIZED TRANSCRIPTS
- CENTRALLY LOCATED
- ASCII DISKETTES/CONDENSED FORMAT AVAILABLE
- REAL-TIME TRANSLATION

### MEDICAL EXPERT WITNESS

**American Medical Forensic Specialists, Inc.**
Suite 302
2991 Shattuck Ave.
Berkeley, CA 94705
Phone: (800) 275-8903

*See Medical Expert Witness - Medical Case Review - Malpractice & Personal Injury*

---

The **Martindale-Hubbell Law Directory** is now available online...exclusively through the LEXIS®-NEXIS® services.

---

Now it's easy to find lawyers practicing a specific area of law! Simply consult the
**Martindale-Hubbell Law Directory
Areas of Practice Index.**

## MEDICAL CASE REVIEW

### Specializing in: Malpractice & Personal Injury

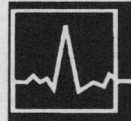
American Medical Forensic Specialists, Inc.
Physicians providing physicians

1-800-275-8903
2991 Shattuck Avenue
Suite 302
Berkeley, CA. 94705
email: bgustin@amfs.com
URL: http://www.amfs.com

**American Medical Forensic Specialists, Inc.** is recognized as a leader in the field of medical malpractice case review and expert witness testimony. AMFS is the only forensic consulting group staffed exclusively by board-certified physicians.

**American Medical Forensic Specialists'** in-house physicians provide attorneys incisive, initial in-depth medical record review to determine case merit, rapidly and for a low flat fee.

**AMFS'** physician managed consortium of over 2000 reputable medical experts in 170 medical specialties, provide medical malpractice and personal injury case evaluation and testimony for **both** plaintiff and defendant, nationwide.

*No one is more qualified to evaluate the abilities of a physician expert than an expert physician.*

**AMFS** in-house physicians are uniquely prepared to consult, recommend and arrange for medical analysis and testimony for the duration of the case.

**AMFS** experience, resources and large proprietary data base enables us to match medical experts to each case based *specifically on your case needs.*

• Each doctor has been screened for superior education, training and technical competence. Many are medical school faculty members with publications in their areas of expertise. All are outstanding practitioners and highly regarded in the medical community.

• **AMFS** represents a panel of board-certified specialists who provide more credible testimony because they are not 'professional witnesses'.

Having reviewed more than 3,000 cases, "...of the cases in which AMFS participates, its experts are on the winning side more than 90% of the time..." – California Lawyer, May 1996.

---

Fast ... Easy ... Flexible...
**The Martindale-Hubbell Law Directory on CD-ROM** gives you instant access through multiple search criteria to information on over 900,000 lawyers and law firms. For more details and a FREE demonstration disc, call **1-800-323-3288.**

## TRANSLATION SERVICES

### Berkeley Scientific Translation Service, Inc.

*

EXPERT PATENT TRANSLATIONS FROM AND INTO ALL MAJOR EUROPEAN AND ASIAN LANGUAGES SINCE 1974

Phone: 1-800-488-9884
FAX: 1-510-548-4666

2161 Shattuck Avenue
Suite 315
Berkeley, California 94704

*

We have translated thousands of patents and supporting technical documents from and into all major languages.

We are specialists in Japanese patent translations.

Next time you have a PCT filing abroad, ask us for a quote for translations into any of the world's major languages.

Our translators are full-time professionals. Many have advanced degrees in the sciences or technology. All are qualified native speakers of the target language!

You will receive our price quote by return fax. usually within an hour of your request.

Fast normal turnaround time-about 5 working days for a normal sized patent.

RUSH SERVICE is available if you are pressed by a deadline. Let us know what you need!

---

To update your listing
in the **Martindale-Hubbell Law Directory**
call **1-800-MARTIND(ALE).**

# CALIFORNIA—BEVERLY HILLS

**BEVERLY HILLS, 31,971,** *Los Angeles Co.*

## COURT REPORTERS

The Court Reporting Firm
For The 90's

714 West Olympic Boulevard
Suite 1112
Los Angeles, California 90015
800-266-2268
213-749-1234

**ORANGE COUNTY OFFICE**

16462 Grimaud Lane
Huntington Beach, California 92649
800-266-2268

FAX: 213-749-0644

COMPLIMENTARY CONFERENCE ROOMS
IN-HOUSE VIDEO SERVICES
ASCII DISKS
DISCOVERY Z-X LITIGATION DISKS
COMPRESSED TRANSCRIPTS
KEYWORD INDEXING
REALTIME REPORTING
ARCHIVING OF ALL DEPOSITIONS
DAILY AND EXPEDITED TRANSCRIPTS
DEPOSITIONS, ARBITRATIONS & HEARINGS
FREE TRANSPORTATION TO AND FROM MAJOR AIRPORTS
SUBPOENA SERVICE

SERVING LOS ANGELES, ORANGE,
VENTURA, SAN DIEGO, RIVERSIDE AND
SAN BERNARDINO COUNTIES

---

Need an extra copy of the **Martindale-Hubbell Law Directory?** Or of a specific volume?
Call Martindale-Hubbell Customer Service at
**1-800-526-4902**

---

## ABRAMS, MAH & KAHN
Court Reporting Service

4101 Birch Street
Suite 130
Newport Beach, California 92660
Los Angeles, California Telephone: 213-848-8686
Newport Beach, California Telephone: 714-261-8686
FAX: 714-261-6688
800-622-0226

Serving all of:
• Los Angeles •
• Orange County •
• San Diego •
• Riverside •
• San Bernardino •

Realtime
Condensed Transcripts
Complimentary Conference Rooms
Computer-aided Transcription
Video Taping and Interpreters
• Two-week Delivery •
Daily Copy Available

Experienced in:
• Multi-party Complex Litigation •
and
• Technical Testimony •

---

Now you can find the lawyer even if you don't
know where he or she practices -
with the **Martindale-Hubbell Law
Directory Alphabetical Index.**

---

The **Martindale-Hubbell Law Directory** is now
available online...exclusively
through the LEXIS®-NEXIS® services.

SERVICES, SUPPLIERS, CONSULTANTS                                                  CALIFORNIA—BEVERLY HILLS

## California DEPOSITION REPORTERS

**COURT REPORTERS (800) 242-1996**

DON'T WORRY!
WE HAVE YOUR
DEPOSITIONS COVERED
in every County in California.

Conference Rooms
& Court Reporters
Nationwide & Abroad

**1-800-242-1996**

*FREE services include:*

★ Complimentary conference rooms in all of our offices
★ Senior Account Executives throughout Southern California servicing your law firm's special needs
★ Airport, shuttle & hotel information provided to traveling attorneys
★ Condensed transcripts with keyword indexing
★ Direct billing of insurance carriers
★ Interpreters and video operators scheduled upon request

*Other services include:*

★ Conference rooms & court reporters nationwide & abroad
★ Two-week turnaround on transcripts
★ ASCII/CAT-LINKS/DISCOVERY ZX
★ Real-Time
★ Professionally bound transcripts with exhibit management
★ Aviation, technical, construction and medical specialists
★ CD imaging & video imaging
★ Video conferencing

ORANGE COUNTY           COVINA
(714) 548-2435          (818) 915-1996

ONTARIO                 SAN BERNARDINO
(909) 391-1579          (909) 888-8992

LOS ANGELES             PALM SPRINGS
(213) 387-9630          (619) 323-9908

SAN DIEGO
(619) 233-1996

---

## INTERIM COURT REPORTING

Nationwide Court Reporting Services
Main Office
3530 Wilshire Boulevard, Suite 1700
Los Angeles, CA 90010
1-800-722-1235
Fax: 213-389-8514

Realtime Transcription, CaseView, LiveNote
Daily and Expedited Service
Videotape Depositions and Videosync Timestamping
Computer Aided Transcription and Litigation Support
ASCII, Discovery ZX and CATLinks Diskettes
Telecommunication Capabilities
Condensed Transcripts with Keyword Indexes
Interpreters
Document Depository
Conference Rooms Available

Experienced, Qualified Court Reporters
Skilled in technical, medical, patent and environmental testimony

---

Now it's easy to find lawyers practicing a specific area of law! Simply consult the
**Martindale-Hubbell Law Directory
Areas of Practice Index.**

---

Fast ... Easy ... Flexible...
**The Martindale-Hubbell Law Directory on CD-ROM** gives you instant access through multiple search criteria to information on over 900,000 lawyers and law firms. For more details and a FREE demonstration disc, call **1-800-323-3288**.

---

To update your listing
in the **Martindale-Hubbell Law Directory**
call **1-800-MARTIND(ALE)**.

CAA5S

## BEVERLY HILLS (Continued)
## MEDICAL EXPERT WITNESS

### DENTAL

**TOM K. KALILI, D.M.D.**
416 NORTH BEDFORD DRIVE, SUITE 102-A
BEVERLY HILLS, CA 90210-4308
Ph: (310) 273-9485
Fx: (310) 273-2138

Legal Positions of Interest: Defense and/or plaintiff work for any injuries which relate to: dental, oral and/or TMJ as a result of Workmen Compensation, Automobile accident, Biting on foreign objects, Sports Injuries, Assault and battery claims and Victims of Violent Crimes.

Education: Dr. Kalili received his doctorate degree from Boston University. He continued his research endeavor at Harvard and went on to treat emergency patients at the US Coast Guard in San Francisco as an Honorary Captain. Presently he is in his eighth year as a lecturer and researcher at UCLA School of Dentistry, Department of Biomaterials Science, and is in private practice in Beverly Hills, CA 90210 for the past eight years.

Area of Expertise: Dr. Kalili's areas of expertise are in stress and strain analysis of anatomical orofacial structures. There, his research has addressed stresses and strains associated with load capacity of bone and teeth. His research has been with the materials involved in dentistry, to include porcelain and dental fractures, which he has presented and published articles with Dr. Angelo Caputo, Professor and Chairman of the UCLA School of Dentistry, Department of Biomaterials Science. In addition, his expertise lies in facial pain and temporomandibular joint (TMJ) dysfuntion, of which a three-year TMJ research study with Dr. Gratt, Professor and Chairman of the UCLA Radiology Department, was recently presented at the International and American Dental Research Meeting held in Singapore. Additionally, his paper has been accepted for publication in the Compendium, one of the largest and most renown dental research journals in the country.

Affiliations: Qualified Medical Examiner (QME); Los Angeles Police Department Academy of Martial Arts Advisory Panel, Medical Consultant; Member: American Orthodontic Society; The Compendium Journal; World Fighting Federation Ringside Doctor; Ultimate Fighting Championship Ringside Doctor; Academy of Sports Dentistry; Academy for International Medical Studies; International Platform Association, Mid-America.

Researchship/publications: Researcher/Lecturer: UCLA School of Dentistry, Author: American Dental Association (ADA) Update, Practical Periodontics & Aesthetic Dentistry, International Federation of Dental Education Associations; National University of Singapore Symposium 1996, American Association Dental Research and International Association Dental Research; Canada, Mexico, Chicago.

Need an extra copy of the **Martindale-Hubbell Law Directory**? Or of a specific volume? Call Martindale-Hubbell Customer Service at 1-800-526-4902

## Ophthalmology

**CHARLES ARONBERG, M.D.**
465 North Roxbury Drive
Beverly Hills, CA 90210
Telephone: (310) 271-7000
Fax: (310) 271-7003

OPHTHALMOLOGY
MEDICAL-LEGAL CONSULTANT

Specialty Board Diplomas (Certified)
Diplomate, American Board of Ophthalmology
    American Board of Quality Assurance and Utilization Review
    American Board of Disability Evaluation Consultants

Offices:
Medical Board of California (formerly Board of Medical Quality Assurance), President, Division of Allied Health Professions
Chief of Ophthalmology: Cedars-Sinai Medical Center
    Century City Hospital
    Beverly Hills Medical Center
    Westside Hospital
Director, California Medical Review, Inc.
President:    Cedars-Sinai Medical Group
    Los Angeles Preferred Medical Group
Los Angeles County Hospitals Commission
University of California Ophthalmology Faculty
Team Ophthalmologist: Los Angeles Lakers; Raiders; Kings
Ophthalmology Consultant: Los Angeles Dodgers; UCLA Athletic Teams

Medical Societies:  American, California, Los Angeles County Medical Associations
    Fellow, American Academy of Ophthalmology
    American Society of Cataract and Refractive Surgery
    Association for Research in Vision and Ophthalmology
    American Society for Laser Medicine and Surgery
    American Board of Eye Surgery

Services Offered:
Consultation, record review, research, case analysis and evaluation, report preparation, deposition and trial testimony in cases of trauma, surgery, diseases of adults and children, vision loss, disability evaluation and rehabilitation, emotional effects, toxicology, pharmaceutical and chemical injury, glasses and contact lenses, lasers.

More than 20 years of experience. Preliminary inquiry at no charge.

Now you can find the lawyer even if you don't know where he or she practices - with the **Martindale-Hubbell Law Directory Alphabetical Index.**

# SERVICES, SUPPLIERS, CONSULTANTS
## CALIFORNIA—BEVERLY HILLS

## ANDREW I. CASTER, M.D., F.A.C.S.
Diseases and Surgery of the Eyes and Eyelids

9033 Wilshire Boulevard, Suite 402
Beverly Hills, California 90211
(310) 839-4111
Fax (310) 839-0950

3831 Hughes Avenue, Suite 705
Culver City, California 90232
(310) 839-4111
Fax (310) 839-0950
E-mail: ACaster@aol.com

AREAS OF MEDICAL-LEGAL EXPERTISE:

Ophthalmology; diseases, surgery, and trauma of the eyes and eyelids; ophthalmic product liability; medical malpractice; personal injury; extensive trial experience as an expert witness for both plaintiff and defense; Refractive surgery (radial keratotomy, excimer laser surgery): over 3,000 surgeries performed.

EDUCATION:

Harvard College, Cambridge, Massachusetts
(B.A., 1976—Phi Beta Kappa honors)

Harvard Medical School, Boston, Massachusetts
(M.D., 1980)

Resident in Ophthalmology, UCLA Jules Stein Eye Institute
(Completed 1984)

ACADEMIC APPOINTMENTS:

Clinical Instructor in Ophthalmology,
UCLA Jules Stein Eye Institute

Past Chief of Ophthalmology, Brotman Medical Center

CERTIFICATIONS:

Board Certified, American Board of Ophthalmology
Fellow, American College of Surgeons
Fellow, American Academy of Ophthalmology

PROFESSIONAL MEMBERSHIPS:

American Society of Cataract and Refractive Surgeons
American Academy of Ophthalmology
American Medical Association

References Available Upon Request

---

The **Martindale-Hubbell Law Directory** is now available online...exclusively through the LEXIS®-NEXIS® services.

## PSYCHIATRY

**Carole Lieberman, M.D., M.P.H.**
247 S. Beverly Drive, Suite 202
Beverly Hills, CA 90212

310/278/5433
310/456-2458 - fax

Degrees/Licenses: M.D., M.P.H. (Masters in Public Health), Diplomate, American Board of Psychiatry and Neurology, Clinical Faculty of Psychiatry at UCLA.

Board certified psychiatrist experienced in expert witness testimony, psych-legal consultations and evaluations. All psychiatric-legal issues, including: criminal behavior, sexual harassment, wrongful termination, entertainment law, media-incited behavior, divorce, custody, psychiatric malpractice, sports injuries, violence, personal injury, workers' compensation. Special experience in high profile and celebrity cases. Emmy-Award winning media consultant. Media specialties include effects of media on society and media violence. Detailed c.v., references and fee schedule available upon request. Also reachable at 310/456-2458.

## VIDEO TAPE SERVICES

### AAA LEGAL VIDEO SERVICES
A FULL SERVICE VIDEO COMPANY NOW SERVING
THE LEGAL PROFESSION 24 HOURS A DAY!

**Certified Professional Operators**

**Affiliated with the California Court Reporters Association**

**Serving All of California, the United States and the World**

Depositions            Satellite/Telephonic
Expert Witness         Conferencing
Computer Graphics      Copying & Editing
            Competitively Priced

Los Angeles • Orange • Riverside
San Bernardino • Ventura • San Diego

**Client List 1996:** Alschuler, Grossman & Pines; Breidenbach, Swainston, Crispo & Way; Christensen White; Coudert Bros.; Cox, Castle & Nicholson; Gibson, Dunn & Crutcher; Haight, Brown & Bonsteel; Irell & Manella; Jeffer, Mangels, Butler & Marmaro; Jones, Day, Reavis & Pogue; Kinsella, Boesch, Fujikawa & Towle; Latham & Watkins; Manatt Phelps & Phillips; Millbank, Tweed, Hadley & McCloy; Musick, Peeler & Garrett; Paul, Hastings, Janofsky & Walker; Rosenfeld, Meyer & Susman; Sidley & Austin; Skadden, Arps, Slate, Megher & Flom; Thelen, Marrin, Johnson & Bridges.

(310) 271-2340
(213) 380-5400    (714) 821-5400    (818) 503-5400
Fax (310) 274-3350
Headquarters: 301 N. Alpine Dr. Beverly Hills, CA. 90210

# CARLSBAD, 63,126, *San Diego Co.*

## COURT REPORTERS

**COURT REPORTERS (800) 242-1996**

**DON'T WORRY!
WE HAVE YOUR
DEPOSITIONS COVERED**
in every County in California.

| | |
|---|---|
| Carlsbad Pacific Center | Conference Rooms |
| 701 Palomar Airport Road | & Court Reporters |
| Third Floor | Nationwide & Abroad |
| Carlsbad, CA 92009 | |
| | 1-800-242-1996 |

*FREE services include:*

★ Complimentary conference rooms in all of our offices

★ Senior Account Executives throughout Southern California servicing your law firms special needs

★ Airport, shuttle & hotel information provided to traveling attorneys

★ Condensed transcripts with keyword indexing

★ Direct billing of insurance carriers

★ Interpreters and video operators scheduled upon request

*Other services include:*

★ Conference rooms & court reporters nationwide & abroad

★ Two-week turnaround on transcripts

★ ASCII/CAT-LINKS/DISCOVERY ZX

★ Real-Time

★ Professionally bound transcripts with exhibit management

★ Aviation, technical, construction and medical specialists

★ CD imaging & video imaging

★ Video conferencing

| | |
|---|---|
| **ORANGE COUNTY** | **COVINA** |
| (714) 548-2435 | (818) 915-1996 |
| | |
| **RIVERSIDE** | **SAN BERNARDINO** |
| (909) 888-8992 | (909) 888-8992 |
| | |
| **LOS ANGELES** | **PALM SPRINGS** |
| (213) 387-9630 | (619) 323-9908 |

**SAN DIEGO**
(619) 233-1996

---

## INTERIM COURT REPORTING

**Nationwide Court Reporting Services
Main Office**
3530 Wilshire Boulevard, Suite 1700
Los Angeles, CA 90010
1-800-722-1235
Fax: 213-389-8514

Realtime Transcription, CaseView, LiveNote
Daily and Expedited Service
Videotape Depositions and Videosync Timestamping
Computer Aided Transcription and Litigation Support
ASCII, Discovery ZX and CATLinks Diskettes
Telecommunication Capabilities
Condensed Transcripts with Keyword Indexes
Interpreters
Document Depository
Conference Rooms Available

Experienced, Qualified Court Reporters
Skilled in technical, medical, patent and environmental testimony

---

Now it's easy to find lawyers practicing a specific
area of law! Simply consult the
**Martindale-Hubbell Law Directory
Areas of Practice Index.**

---

Fast ... Easy ... Flexible...
**The Martindale-Hubbell Law Directory on
CD-ROM** gives you instant access through
multiple search criteria to information on over
900,000 lawyers and law firms. For more details and a
FREE demonstration disc, call **1-800-323-3288**.

---

To update your listing
in the **Martindale-Hubbell Law Directory**
call **1-800-MARTIND(ALE)**.

## CHICO, 40,079, *Butte Co.*

### COURT REPORTERS

### SWITZER & ASSOCIATES
DEPOSITION, COURT AND GENERAL REPORTING

Serving Northern California and Surrounding Counties
Since 1989

*Switzer & Associates is proud to have been chosen as the Deponet Quality Assurance Network representative for Chico and the surrounding vicinity.*

686 Rio Lindo Avenue
Chico, California 95926

TOLL FREE: 800-200-DEPO (3376)
FAX: 916-342-3388

Advanced Technology and Old Fashioned Service
with a Can Do Attitude

We Go the Extra Mile to Meet Our Clients' Needs

### Services Include:

Complimentary Conference Rooms in Chico & Oroville

Telephone Conference Facilities

Condensed Transcripts

Concordance Index

Daily & Expedited Transcripts on Request

ASCII Disks

Professional Videographers

Interpreters Scheduled on Request

Fax & Photocopy Service

Direct Billing of Insurance Carriers on Request

Multi-County Coverage

No Milage Charge Within 75 Miles

### Member:
California Court Reporters Association
National Shorthand Reporters Association
Northern California Court Reporters Association

916-342-0199

---

## COSTA MESA, 96,357, *Orange Co.*

### COURT REPORTERS

### PAULSON REPORTING SERVICE

Serving California with offices in:
- Los Angles
- Orange County
- San Diego
- Escondido
- Temecula

Full-service Court Reporting Nationwide

Call Toll Free
(800) 300-1214

In Orange County
575 Anton Boulevard, Suite 230
Costa Mesa, CA 92626
Tel: (714) 668-0166
Fax: (714) 668-0261

Paulson Reporting Service has provided quality, cost-effective court reporting services for two decades. We work with all the latest technologies and offer:

- ASCIIs, Discovery ZX, CAT-Links
- Bates Stamping, Prefixing and Indexing
- Case Management
- Complete Litigation Support
- Compressed Transcripts & Master Word Index
- Document Imaging
- Interpreters
- Medical & Technical Reporting
- On-site Depositories
- RealTime, Instant Rough Drafts, LiveNote
- Time Stamping
- Videographers & Video Synchronization

For out-of-town legal professionals

- Airport transportation
- Continental breakfast
- Hotel reservations
- Refreshments anytime you like
- Spacious conference suites

Member:
National Shorthand Reporters Association
California Court Reporters Association

---

Need an extra copy of the **Martindale-Hubbell Law Directory?** Or of a specific volume?
Call Martindale-Hubbell Customer Service at
**1-800-526-4902**

COVINA, 43,207, *Los Angeles Co.*

## COURT REPORTERS

**COURT REPORTERS (800) 242-1996**

DON'T WORRY!
WE HAVE YOUR
DEPOSITIONS COVERED
in every County in California.

Corporate Office:
Eastland Securities Bldg.
599 S. Barranca Ave.
Penthouse
Covina, CA 91723

Conference Rooms
& Court Reporters
Nationwide & Abroad

1-800-242-1996

*FREE services include:*

★ Complimentary conference rooms in all of our offices
★ Senior Account Executives throughout Southern California servicing your law firm's special needs
★ Airport, shuttle & hotel information provided to traveling attorneys
★ Condensed transcripts with keyword indexing
★ Direct billing of insurance carriers
★ Interpreters and video operators scheduled upon request

*Other services include:*

★ Conference rooms & court reporters nationwide & abroad
★ Two-week turnaround on transcripts
★ ASCII/CAT-LINKS/DISCOVERY ZX
★ Real-Time
★ Professionally bound transcripts with exhibit management
★ Aviation, technical, construction and medical specialists
★ CD imaging & video imaging
★ Video conferencing

**ORANGE COUNTY**
(714) 548-2435

**COVINA**
(818) 915-1996

**ONTARIO**
(909) 391-1579

**SAN BERNARDINO**
(909) 888-8992

**LOS ANGELES**
(213) 387-9630

**PALM SPRINGS**
(619) 323-9908

**SAN DIEGO**
(619) 233-1996

## EXPERT WITNESS

### METEOROLOGY/CLIMATOLOGY

**Allied Weather Consultants**
P.O. Box 4584
Covina, CA 91723
(818) 332-8411
(800) 933-6278

Erwin K. Kauper
Certified Consulting Meteorologist
Reg. Engineer, State of California

Mr. Kauper has a BA degree in Physics-Meteorology, University of California, Los Angeles, with post-graduate courses at UCLA and Loyola-Marymount University. He served as a Weather Officer in the U.S. Air Force, as an Aviation Forecaster for the National Weather Service in Los Angeles, and as Head of the Meteorology Unit at the Los Angeles County Air Pollution Control District. He held the position of Senior Meteorologist/Research Meteorologist at Meteorology Research, Inc. in Altadena, CA. A self-employed consulting meteorologist since 1975, he specializes in forensic meteorology, accident investigation, weather-observer training and private-client weather forecasting.

He has specialized in air pollution meteorology, with wide-ranging experience with local wind flow and turbulence conditions in all parts of the U.S., including Alaska and Hawaii.

His clients have included the Los Angeles City Department of Water and Power, for which he performed meteorological analyses and courtroom testimony of precipitation records for periods of heavy rain and mud slides in mountainous terrain.

He has been involved in aircraft accident investigations, reconstructing the pertinent weather conditions involved. These included wind shear, icing and fog formation in Alaska and the lower forty-eight states.

Member:

American Meteorological Society
National Council of Industrial Meteorologists
Air and Waste Management Association

Licenses/Certifications:

Registered California Control Systems Engineer
Certified Consulting Meteorologist #54,
American Meteorological Society, Boston, MA

---

Now you can find the lawyer even if you don't know where he or she practices - with the **Martindale-Hubbell Law Directory Alphabetical Index.**

## CRESCENT CITY, * 4,380, Del Norte Co.

### COURT REPORTERS

THE *court reporting network for all of California*

1080 Mason Mall, Suite 4-A
Crescent City, CA 95531

Online     http://www.altr.com
Phone    800.961.1116

When it comes to managing complex litigation or scheduling depos in distant locations, many law firms recognize the advantages of a **single-contact resource for California and national reporting services.** A clear focus on leading-edge technology, the expertise of professionals, as well as a California-wide presence is now at your disposal and local control with the ALTRNET.

*Private, complimentary deposition suites are available in thirteen California offices:*

- ■ **Crescent City**
- ☐ Eureka
- ☐ Fresno
- ☐ Los Angeles
- ☐ Oakland
- ☐ San Diego
- ☐ San Francisco
- ☐ San Jose
- ☐ San Luis Obispo
- ☐ Santa Barbara
- ☐ Santa Maria
- ☐ Stockton
- ☐ Ventura

*One call* can arrange Certified Shorthand Reporting services in remote locations as well as prompt transmission of transcripts to your local ALTRNET office where they are printed to your specifications and delivered. Transcripts can be converted locally to disk or formatted to the litigation support software program of your choice. Transcripts can be telecommunicated instantly from one city to another, making it possible to review testimony minutes later.

The ALTRNET imparts our unique style of technical know-how for depositions taken across California and *assures continuity of quality and service* from distant locations -- without added travel expenses or surprise charges.

*One call gets it all.*     800 . 961 . 1116.

## EL CENTRO, * 31,384, Imperial Co.

### COURT REPORTERS

**ATWOOD JENNINGS & ASSOCIATES**

*COURT REPORTERS*

Covering Imperial, San Diego, Riverside and Yuma Counties

P.O. Box 1849
El Centro, California 92244

(760) 352-6488
Fax (760) 353-9516

President: Janie Jennings

This company was founded by Eldon M. Atwood, California CSR No. 17 in 1947. We have proudly provided service to the Imperial Valley and all surrounding areas with dedicated, hard-working reporters for 50 years. We're a company you can count on.

Services Include:

- ●Daily/Expedited Copy
- ●Deposition Pick-up & Delivery
- ●References Available Upon Request
- ●ASCII Diskettes
- ●Depositions, Arbitrations, Hearings, Trials
- ●Computer Aided Transcription
- ●Condensed Transcripts With Keyword Index
- ●Medical, Technical, Environmental, Agricultural

Member:
National Court Reporters Association

---

The **Martindale-Hubbell Law Directory** is now available online...exclusively through the LEXIS®-NEXIS® services.

## ENCINITAS, 55,386, *San Diego Co.*

### EXPERT WITNESS

#### ENGINEERS/ENGINEERING

#### Specializing in: Safety

### *Safety Factor Associates, Inc.*
#### A California Corporation

Dr. Michael V. Frank is founder and President of Safety Factor Associates, Inc., a company dedicated to the reliability and safety technologies. During a 26 year career, he has authored over 50 technical publications and has made numerous presentations in both national and international forums. Forensic specialties include: 1) Product Defects, Hazards, Risk and Safety; 2) Industrial and Commercial Risk, Safety, Hazards and Accidents; 3) Reliability Engineering of Products, Systems and Facilities; 4) Human Reliability in Industrial Situations; 5) Risk Evaluation and Management; 6) Statistical Analysis of Data; 7) Safety and Risk Comparisons. He brings a system of risk perspective to litigative cases derived from studies involving the risk of high tech, complex engineered systems in the aerospace and nuclear power industries.

Past forensic assignments include the following: Helicopter; Medical Devices; Beer Kegs; Bicycles; Hand Trucks; Plastic Steam Iron; Ordnance Explosion; Mining Train Accident; Truck Explosion; Coffee Manufacturing Machine; Fertilizer Sacks; School Gate; Coffee Cup; Cart and Casters; Street Drain Cover; Milling Machine; Chairs; Leg Press Equipment; Doors; Glass Bottles; Plastic Pipes.

Among recent non-forensic achievements are 1) risk assessment of the Space Shuttle including consideration of fire, explosion, and equipment hazards for NASA; 2) risk assessment of launch vehicles that carry nuclear materials for the Interagency Nuclear Safety Review Panel, which is chartered to evaluate the safety of nuclear payload space launches for the President of the United States; 3) review of fire, earthquake, wind, flood, and other risks to nuclear power plants for the United States Nuclear Regulatory Commission.

4401 Manchester Avenue, Suite 106, Encinitas, CA 92024
Phone: (619) 436-9132   Fax: (619) 436-4132
E-mail: sfainc@worldnet.att.net

### PRODUCT SAFETY

#### Safety Factor Associates, Inc.
Suite 106
4401 Manchester Ave.
Encinitas, CA 92024
Phone: (619) 436-9132
Fax: (619) 436-4132

*See Expert Witness - Engineers/Engineering - Safety*

---

## ESCONDIDO, 108,635, *San Diego Co.*

### COURT REPORTERS

### PAULSON REPORTING SERVICE

Serving California with offices in:
- Los Angles
- Orange County
- San Diego
- Escondido
- Temecula

**Full-service Court Reporting Nationwide**

**Call Toll Free**
(800) 300-1214

**In Escondido**
270 West Second Avenue, Suite C
Escondido, CA 92025
Tel: (619) 738-8620
Fax: (619) 738-8622

Paulson Reporting Service has provided quality, cost-effective court reporting services for two decades. We work with all the latest technologies and offer:

- ASCIIs, Discovery ZX, CAT-Links
- Bates Stamping, Prefixing and Indexing
- Case Management
- Complete Litigation Support
- Compressed Transcripts & Master Word Index
- Document Imaging
- Interpreters
- Medical & Technical Reporting
- On-site Depositories
- RealTime, Instant Rough Drafts, LiveNote
- Time Stamping
- Videographers & Video Synchronization

**For out-of-town legal professionals**

- Airport transportation
- Continental breakfast
- Hotel reservations
- Refreshments anytime you like
- Spacious conference suites

**Member:**
National Shorthand Reporters Association
California Court Reporters Association

---

Now it's easy to find lawyers practicing a specific area of law! Simply consult the
**Martindale-Hubbell Law Directory
Areas of Practice Index.**

EUREKA, * 27,025, *Humboldt Co.*

## COURT REPORTERS

# ALTRNET
### Advanced Legal Technology Reporters Network

THE *court reporting network for all of California*

730 Fifth Street, Suite K
Eureka, CA 95501

Online    http://www.altr.com
Phone    800.961.1116

When it comes to managing complex litigation or scheduling depos in distant locations, many law firms recognize the advantages of a **single-contact resource for California and national reporting services**. A clear focus on leading-edge technology, the expertise of professionals, as well as a California-wide presence is now at your disposal and local control with the ALTRNET.

*Private, complimentary deposition suites are available in thirteen California offices:*

- ☐ Crescent City
- ■ **Eureka**
- ☐ Fresno
- ☐ Los Angeles
- ☐ Oakland
- ☐ San Diego
- ☐ San Francisco
- ☐ San Jose
- ☐ San Luis Obispo
- ☐ Santa Barbara
- ☐ Santa Maria
- ☐ Stockton
- ☐ Ventura

*One call* can arrange Certified Shorthand Reporting services in remote locations as well as prompt transmission of transcripts to your local ALTRNET office where they are printed to your specifications and delivered. Transcripts can be converted locally to disk or formatted to the litigation support software program of your choice. Transcripts can be telecommunicated instantly from one city to another, making it possible to review testimony minutes later.

The ALTRNET imparts our unique style of technical know-how for depositions taken across California and *assures continuity of quality and service* from distant locations -- without added travel expenses or surprise charges.

        *One call gets it all.*      800 . 961 . 1116.

---

## BRUNNELL DEPOSITIONS
P.O. Box 955
Arcata, CA 95521

*Located Near Arcata McKinleyville Airport*

Telephone: (707) 822-6554
Fax: (707) 826-1216

### Services Available:

- ♦ ASCII Diskettes
- ♦ Computer Aided Transcription
- ♦ Conference Rooms
- ♦ Daily/Expedited Copy
- ♦ Depositions, Arbitrations, Hearings, Trials
- ♦ Deposition Pick-Up & Delivery
- ♦ Litigation Support Services
- ♦ Medical, Technical, Environmental, Agricultural
- ♦ Real Time Transcription
- ♦ Teleconferencing Services
- ♦ Video Tape Services

### Member
California Court Reporters Association
NCRA

*Serving Eureka County Since 1981*

---

Fast ... Easy ... Flexible...
**The Martindale-Hubbell Law Directory on CD-ROM** gives you instant access through multiple search criteria to information on over 900,000 lawyers and law firms. For more details and a FREE demonstration disc, call **1-800-323-3288**.

---

To update your listing
in the **Martindale-Hubbell Law Directory**
call **1-800-MARTIND(ALE)**.

**FAIRFIELD, * 77,211,** *Solano Co.*

## COURT REPORTERS

### DeMICHELLE DEPOSITION REPORTERS

SERVING NORTHERN CALIFORNIA AS
WELL AS NATIONWIDE SINCE 1975

"In Deposition Reporting you require
dependability, availability and stability, as
well as quick turnaround. Anything else is
just not acceptable!"

- Real-Time Translation
- Computer Aided Transcription
- Litigation Support
- ASCII Diskettes
- WP Diskettes
- 10-Day Delivery
- Expedited & Daily Copy
- Page Condensing
- Concordance Reports
- Deposition Suites
- Videotape Services
- Interpreters
- Subpoena Services
- Key-Word Indexing
- Free Mileage
- Across from Courthouse

### DEPOSITION SUITES

**Napa**
1001 Second Street
Suite 311
Napa, CA 94559
(707) 226-6000
Fax: (707) 226-6786

**Fairfield**
609 Jefferson Street
Suite F
Fairfield, CA 94533
(707) 425-6000
Fax: (707) 425-6019

Three Conference Rooms Directly Across the Street
From the Napa & Fairfield Courthouses

Copy Machine • Fax Machine • Refreshments
Peking Restaurant and PJ's Cafe located in Building.

---

Need an extra copy of the **Martindale-Hubbell Law Directory?** Or of a specific volume?
Call Martindale-Hubbell Customer Service at
1-800-526-4902

---

### LANGSTAFF REPORTING SERVICE
Certified Court Reporters

Kathy Langstaff, RPR, CSR No. 3433

601 Madison Street, Suite D
Fairfield, California 94533

TOLL-FREE NATIONWIDE: 1-800-429-5055
Telephone: 707-427-5055
Fax: 707-427-5057

Conveniently Located near the Major
Northern California Metropolitan Areas
including
San Francisco, The East Bay, Sacramento,
Santa Rosa, and Stockton
One hour or less driving time.

Conveniently located
near the Solano County Hall of Justice
and
Serving Solano, Napa, Contra Costa, Yolo
and Sonoma Counties and the North Bay
and Sacramento Regions

SPACIOUS COMPLIMENTARY CONFERENCE ROOMS

Computerized Transcription
Videotaped Depositions
Condensed Transcripts
Realtime Reporting
Daily and Expedited Copy
Litigation Support Diskettes
Full-Text and Customized Concordance
On-site Photocopying including Color Copies

Members
National Court Reporters Association
California Court Reporters Association
Northern California Court Reporters Association

---

Now you can find the lawyer even if you don't
know where he or she practices -
with the **Martindale-Hubbell Law
Directory Alphabetical Index.**

**SERVICES, SUPPLIERS, CONSULTANTS**  **CALIFORNIA—FRESNO**

## FORT BRAGG, 6,078, *Mendocino Co.*

### COURT REPORTERS

#### ADAIR, POTSWALD & HENNESSEY
Certified Shorthand Reporters
Certified Legal Video Specialist

**LAKE, MENDOCINO, SONOMA & HUMBOLDT COUNTIES**

| UKIAH | LAKEPORT |
|---|---|
| 212 W. Perkins St. | 55 First St. |
| P.O. Box 761 | P.O. Box 397 |
| Ukiah, California 95482 | Lakeport, California 95453 |
| | |
| FORT BRAGG | SANTA ROSA |
| | |
| 100 Manzanita St. | 131A Stony Ci. |
| Fort Bragg, California 95437 | Santa Rosa, California 95401 |

**CALL TOLL FREE 24 HOURS**

1-800-747-DEPO    FAX: (707) 462-4517

Courtesy Deposition Suites

Photocopy and Video Service

Complimentary Condensed Copy and Disk

Daily Copy or Expedite

Medical and Expert Testimony

Subpoena Service

Realtime

---

The **Martindale-Hubbell Law Directory** is now
available online...exclusively
through the LEXIS®-NEXIS® services.

## FRESNO, * 354,202, *Fresno Co.*

### ATTORNEY SERVICES

#### Appleby & Company, Inc.
Attorney Support Services

Appleby & Company, Inc., is one of California's oldest and most respected investigation companies. We have provided our services to insurance companies and attorneys throughout the state for 38 years.

We have offices in Fresno and Bakersfield, California and offer the following services:

(1) **Photo Copy Services**

(2) **Document Imaging to CD-ROM**

(3) **Field Investigations**

(4) **Pre-deposition Witness Interview & Evaluation**

(5) **35mm Photography**

(6) **Video Taping**

(7) **Video Surveillance**

It is our goal that Appleby & Co., Inc., will be included in your list of approved vendors, and we can be of service to your firm.

**2828 N. Wishon Avenue, Fresno, California 93704**
(209) 222-8402 : Fax (209) 222-5043

**1701 Westwind Drive, Suite 202, Bakersfield, California 93301**
(805) 324-6045 : Fax (805) 324-6047

---

Now it's easy to find lawyers practicing a specific
area of law! Simply consult the
**Martindale-Hubbell Law Directory
Areas of Practice Index.**

---

Fast ... Easy ... Flexible...
**The Martindale-Hubbell Law Directory on
CD-ROM** gives you instant access through
multiple search criteria to information on over
900,000 lawyers and law firms. For more details and a
FREE demonstration disc, call **1-800-323-3288**.

CALIFORNIA—FRESNO                    MARTINDALE-HUBBELL LAW DIRECTORY 1997

## FRESNO (Continued)
Attorney Services (Continued)

### ARVAL LEGAL SERVICES
*"Over 19 Years of Service to Attorneys"*

Lemore Office:
P.O. Box 667
Leemore, CA 93245
Tel: 209-924-7606
Fax: 209-924-8378

Fresno Office:
P.O. Box 1792
Fresno, CA 93721
TOLL-FREE: 800-994-1404
Fax: 209-268-1615

Visalia Office:
P.O. Box 2870
Visalia, CA 93279
Tel: 209-738-1404
Fax: 209-738-1407

For over 19 years, Arval Legal Services have provided the legal communities of Kings, Tulare and Fresno counties with **FULL ATTORNEY SUPPORT**. All of our branch offices are located either directly across from or near the courthouse. We serve all forms of legal documentation for process for all courts - County, State and Federal jurisdictions. Call us today.

Litigation Support Services Include:
- Post Office Checks
- Document Retrieval, Filing
- Court Searchings
- On-Site Document Reproduction
- Flat Rate - Unlimited Attempts
- Skip Tracing
- Rush Service Available
- Surveillance
- Subpoenas Prepared By Phone
- Messenger & Delivery Services Available
- Writs of Execution

Memberships:
California Association of Photocopiers & Process Servers (CAPPS)
National Association of Professional Process Servers (NAPPS)

*"We Specialize In Everything We Do - We Really Do !"*

## COLLECTION AGENCIES

**Accurate Attorney Services**
Suite 206
2115 Kern
Fresno, CA 93721
Phone: (209) 485-1453
Fax: (209) 485-2356

*See Process Servers & Document Delivery Services*

## CONFERENCING

**Fast. Convenient. Flexible.**

**General Description:**

networkMCI® is a complete portfolio of communications and information services solutions that gives you the competitive advantage in today's rapidly changing business environment.

Competing successfully in today's business requires you to work smarter. One way to do this is by improving how your firm communicates. If you can exchange information faster and more effectively with clients and colleagues, your company will be more productive, more responsive and ultimately, more profitable.

At the heart of networkMCI Conferencing is our global operations centers located in North America, Europe and Asia-Pacific. It allows you to communicate with anyone, almost anywhere in the world. We provide four core services: Audioconferencing, Document Conferencing, Videoconferencing and Tele-Management Services.

**Audioconferencing Services:**

Audioconferencing gives you the flexibility to hold meetings any time you need to, no matter where you are. With audioconferencing we can:

- Record and transcribe your call
- Conduct a survey during your conference in which participants respond using their telephone keypads
- Provide language interpretation
- Fax information to all conference participants before your call

**Document Conferencing Services:**

With Document Conferencing, you and remote clients or colleagues can review documents using your personal computers. Document Conferencing allows you to:

- Edit and review documents with distant colleagues right from your PC
- Communicate with the aid of clear, full-color visuals
- Share almost any document in your PC
- Work in real time

**Videoconferencing Services:**

Videoconferencing enables you to bring a group of people together for a face-to-face meeting. You can quickly hold an impromptu meeting with others in different offices and save thousands of dollars on travel costs. Videoconferencing lets you:

- Meet face-to-face right from your office
- Speed decision-making and company responsiveness

(This Listing Continued)

# SERVICES, SUPPLIERS, CONSULTANTS

## CALIFORNIA—FRESNO

### NETWORKMCI CONFERENCING℠ (Continued)

- Save time and travel costs

**Tele-Management Services:**

Tele-Management Services are convenient and flexible electronic management tools that can help you better coordinate your upcoming conferences as well as your daily business operations. With Tele-Management you can:

- Plan conferences and other events in a variety of ways
- You can simultaneously distribute announcements or invitations to unlimited destinations in minutes
- Provide automated response tracking to better forecast attendance for events
- Tape and broadcast the event for those who could not attend

HOW DO YOU MAINTAIN YOUR COMPETITIVE EDGE IN TODAY'S BUSINESS ENVIRONMENT? NETWORKMCI, THAT'S HOW.

**networkMCI Conferencing**
1-800-475-5000

8750 W. Bryn Mawr, #900
Chicago, IL 60631

---

To update your listing
in the **Martindale-Hubbell Law Directory**
call 1-800-MARTIND(ALE).

---

Need an extra copy of the **Martindale-Hubbell Law Directory?** Or of a specific volume?
Call Martindale-Hubbell Customer Service at
1-800-526-4902

---

Now you can find the lawyer even if you don't know where he or she practices -
with the **Martindale-Hubbell Law Directory Alphabetical Index.**

## COURT REPORTERS

*Advanced Legal Technology Reporters Network*

THE *court reporting network for all of California*

1810 Van Ness Avenue
Fresno, CA 93721

Online    *http://www.altr.com*
Phone    800.961.1116

When it comes to managing complex litigation or scheduling depos in distant locations, many law firms recognize the advantages of a **single-contact resource for California and national reporting services**. A clear focus on leading-edge technology, the expertise of professionals, as well as a California-wide presence is now at your disposal and local control with the ALTRNET.

*Private, complimentary deposition suites are available in thirteen California offices:*

- ☐ Crescent City
- ☐ Eureka
- ■ **Fresno**
- ☐ Los Angeles
- ☐ Oakland
- ☐ San Diego
- ☐ San Francisco
- ☐ San Jose
- ☐ San Luis Obispo
- ☐ Santa Barbara
- ☐ Santa Maria
- ☐ Stockton
- ☐ Ventura

*One call* can arrange Certified Shorthand Reporting services in remote locations as well as prompt transmission of transcripts to your local ALTRNET office where they are printed to your specifications and delivered. Transcripts can be converted locally to disk or formatted to the litigation support software program of your choice. Transcripts can be telecommunicated instantly from one city to another, making it possible to review testimony minutes later.

The ALTRNET imparts our unique style of technical know-how for depositions taken across California and *assures continuity of quality and service* from distant locations -- without added travel expenses or surprise charges.

*One call gets it all.*      800 . 961 . 1116.

CALIFORNIA—FRESNO  MARTINDALE-HUBBELL LAW DIRECTORY 1997

## FRESNO (Continued)
### Court Reporters (Continued)

**Central Valley Reporters**
Certified Shorthand Reporters

1285 West Shaw Avenue, Suite 101
Fresno, California 93711
Telephone: 209-224-5511
Toll-Free inside California: 1-800-248-6611
Fax: 209-224-1813

Complimentary Conference Rooms
Computer-assisted Transcription
All Litigation Support
Real-Time and CaseView available upon request
Videography

Serving Fresno, Madera, Merced,
Hanford and Visalia

Reference: Local Bench and Bar

Members
California Court Reporters Association
National Shorthand Reporters Association

DepoNet® The reliable source for Quality-Assured legal support services worldwide.

1-800-DEPONET

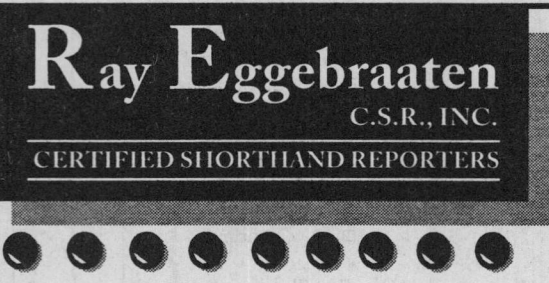

*Registered Professional Reporters*
*Depositions and General Reporting*
*Specializing in Quality Service*

*Deposition suites available at no charge*
*Daily copy on request   All litigation support*

WE OFFER COMPUTER ASSISTED TRANSCRIPTION BY *TurboCat*

**Ray Eggebraaten CSR, Inc.**
Certified Shorthand Reporters
1810 Van Ness Avenue, 93721
Telephone 209-441-1681
800-225-1681
FAX: 209-441-1809

COMPLIMENTARY CONFERENCE ROOMS
Photocopy Machine Available
Videotaping
All Litigation Support
(Discovery ZX and CATLinks)

Reference: Local Bench and Bar

Members
California Court Reporters Association
National Court Reporters Association
National Network Reporting Company

*SEE OUR AD ON PAGE CAA18S*

---

The **Martindale-Hubbell Law Directory** is now available online...exclusively through the LEXIS®-NEXIS® services.

---

Now it's easy to find lawyers practicing a specific area of law!  Simply consult the **Martindale-Hubbell Law Directory Areas of Practice Index.**

---

Fast ... Easy ... Flexible...
**The Martindale-Hubbell Law Directory on CD-ROM** gives you instant access through multiple search criteria to information on over 900,000 lawyers and law firms.  For more details and a FREE demonstration disc, call **1-800-323-3288**.

# SERVICES, SUPPLIERS, CONSULTANTS — CALIFORNIA—FRESNO

## PROCESS SERVERS & DOCUMENT DELIVERY SERVICES

### ACCURATE ATTORNEY SERVICES

2115 Kern, Suite 206
Fresno, CA 93721

| Telephone | Fax |
|---|---|
| (209) 485-1453 | (209) 485-2356 |

Brad Jacobson, *Owner*

Brad Jacobson is a paralegal and has worked as a registered process server for 12 years. Brad is also a fiduciary partner with Steven R. Hrdlicks and Associates, which is involved with 25% of civil litigation in Fresno. He has personally served over 75 thousand documents and has contacts within the United States and abroad. Brad specializes in collections, garnishments and writs of execution; having served more writs of execution than any other process server in Fresno County.

List of Services

* County, State & Federal Courts
* Court Filing
* Database & Real Property Searches
* Paralegal Services
* Post Office Checks
* Radio/Cell Phone Equipped
  ~ All Servers Have Cell Phones
* Rush Service Available
* Writs of Execution

*SERVING FRESNO AND MADERA COUNTIES*

Memberships
CAPPS
PSI

*BONDED & INSURED*

To update your listing
in the **Martindale-Hubbell Law Directory**
call 1-800-MARTIND(ALE).

## VIDEO TAPE SERVICES

**Ray Eggebraaten CSR, Inc.**
Certified Shorthand Reporters
1810 Van Ness Avenue, 93721
Telephone 209-441-1681
800-225-1681
FAX: 209-441-1809

COMPLIMENTARY CONFERENCE ROOMS
Photocopy Machine Available
Videotaping
All Litigation Support
(Discovery ZX and CATLinks)

Reference: Local Bench and Bar

Members
California Court Reporters Association
National Court Reporters Association
National Network Reporting Company

Need an extra copy of the **Martindale-Hubbell Law Directory**? Or of a specific volume?
Call Martindale-Hubbell Customer Service at
**1-800-526-4902**

Now you can find the lawyer even if you don't know where he or she practices -
with the **Martindale-Hubbell Law Directory Alphabetical Index.**

The **Martindale-Hubbell Law Directory** is now available online...exclusively
through the LEXIS®-NEXIS® services.

## HACIENDA HEIGHTS, 35,969, *Los Angeles Co.*

### MEDICAL MALPRACTICE CONSULTING/PERSONAL INJURY

#### MED-LINK
A Medical Resource for
The Legal Community
818-333-5110

**MED-LINK** is a Legal Nurse Consulting Network owned & operated by an R.N. who has over 28 years combined clinical and surgical experience. Our primary role as consultants is to analyze, evaluate and render informed opinions on medical-legal issues. We can offer you support in the following areas:

- Personal Injury
- Workers Compensation
- Risk Management
- Fraud Investigation
- Medical Malpractice
- Forensic Analysis
- Product Liability
- Insurance

- COST EFFECTIVE
- RESOURCEFUL
- KNOWLEDGEABLE

**Services Offered:**

- Screening of Medical Records for Merit
- Review and Analysis of Medical Records
- Organization of Medical Records
- Compile Chronologies for Summary of Medical Records
- Research Medical & Nursing Issues Pertinent to Case
- Glossary of Medical Terms Relative to Records
- Identification of Deviation from Standards of Care
- Analysis of Discrepancies, (non) Compliance
- Objective and Confidential Opinions
- Observation of Independent Medical Exams
- Analysis of Depositions
- Preparation of Questions for Deposition and Trial
- Referral of Expert Witnesses

**MED-LINK BALANCES THE SCALES !**
818-333-5110 • • • FAX 968-0064

---

Now it's easy to find lawyers practicing a specific area of law! Simply consult the
**Martindale-Hubbell Law Directory Areas of Practice Index.**

## HAYWARD, 111,498, *Alameda Co.*

### COURT REPORTERS

#### BAY AREA COURT REPORTERS

21573 Foothill Boulevard, Suite 212
Hayward, California 94541

41 Sutter Street, Suite 1222
San Francisco, California 94104

From Northern California 800 339-DEPO
PHONE 510-889-9400
FAX 510-889-9401

**SERVING THE ENTIRE SAN FRANCISCO BAY AREA**

CERTIFIED SHORTHAND REPORTERS
NOTARIES PUBLIC

—

**DEPOSITIONS • ARBITRATIONS • HEARINGS
CONFERENCES • MEETINGS**

—

Realtime Transcription
Condensed Transcripts
Telecommunications
Computer Diskettes
Same Day and Next Day Delivery
Conference Room and Videotape Arrangements
Specializing in Technical and Medical Testimony

---

Fast ... Easy ... Flexible...
**The Martindale-Hubbell Law Directory on CD-ROM** gives you instant access through multiple search criteria to information on over 900,000 lawyers and law firms. For more details and a FREE demonstration disc, call **1-800-323-3288**.

---

To update your listing
in the **Martindale-Hubbell Law Directory**
call **1-800-MARTIND(ALE)**.

SERVICES, SUPPLIERS, CONSULTANTS                                    CALIFORNIA—IRVINE

IRVINE, 110,330, *Orange Co.*

## COURT REPORTERS

**A.A. NICHOLS, INC.**
CERTIFIED COURT REPORTERS
SINCE 1976

*THE WAVE OF THE FUTURE*

Certified Court Reporters
Certified Legal Videographers

TOLL FREE: 1-800-227-0577

ALL OF ORANGE COUNTY
NEWPORT BEACH, IRVINE, MISSION VIEJO,
SAN CLEMENTE, DANA POINT, LAGUNA
FAX 602-998-7228

REGISTERED PROFESSIONAL REPORTERS
CALIFORNIA CERTIFIED REPORTERS

**A Full Service Reporting and
Video Production Company**

Serving the Bar for over 21 years

Experts in Complex Litigation

Medical and Technical Deposition Specialists

Interpreters & Translators

Daily and Expedited Transcripts on Request

Large Deluxe Conference Rooms

Convenient Locations with Easy-Parking

Videotape and Teleconferencing Facilities

Videotape/Laserdisc presentations

Transcript/Video Synchronization

Certified Legal Video Specialists

Adjacent to Luxury Hotels

Prompt Out-of-State Delivery


Complimentary Condensed Transcripts & Concordances
State of the Art Computer-Aided Transcriptions
Video and Litigation Support Formats
Realtime Translation

**MANY OFFICE LOCATIONS THROUGHOUT
CALIFORNIA & ARIZONA**
including San Diego, Del Mar, San Francisco,
Laguna, La Jolla, Newport Beach, Palm Springs, Sacramento,
Irvine, Orange County, Los Angeles, Phoenix, Tucson,
Scottsdale and All Surrounding Areas

**ADDITIONAL DEPOSITION SUITES AT SAN DIEGO, PHOENIX,
SAN FRANCISCO, ORANGE COUNTY
AND LOS ANGELES AIRPORTS**

Member of:
National Court Reporters Association
California Court Reporters Association

(This Listing Continued)

A.A. NICHOLS, INC. (Continued)

Arizona Court Reporters Association
Michigan Court Reporters Association

**ABRAMS, MAH & KAHN**
REPORTING SERVICE

4101 Birch Street • Suite 130
Newport Beach • California 92660

• Serving Los Angeles, Riverside,
  San Bernardino, San Diego
  and Orange Counties
• Complimentary Conference Rooms
• Litigation Support
• Realtime
• Two-week Delivery
• Condensed Transcripts and
  Master Keyword Index

714 • 261 • 8686
213 • 848 • 8686
800 • 622 • 0226


Need an extra copy of the **Martindale-Hubbell
Law Directory**? Or of a specific volume?
Call Martindale-Hubbell Customer Service at
1-800-526-4902

CAA21S

# IRVINE (Continued)
## Court Reporters (Continued)

### ABRAMS, MAH & KAHN
Court Reporting Service

4101 Birch Street
Suite 130
Newport Beach, California 92660
Telephone: 714-261-8686
Los Angeles, California Telephone: 213-848-8686
FAX: 714-261-6688
800-622-0226

Serving all of:
- Orange County -
- San Diego -
- Riverside -
- Los Angeles -
- San Bernardino -

Realtime
Condensed Transcripts
Complimentary Conference Rooms
Computer-aided Transcription
Video Taping and Interpreters
- Two-week Delivery -
Daily Copy Available

Experienced in:
- Multi-party Complex Litigation -
and
- Technical Testimony -

*SEE OUR AD ON PAGE CAA21S*

---

Now you can find the lawyer even if you don't know where he or she practices - with the **Martindale-Hubbell Law Directory Alphabetical Index.**

The **Martindale-Hubbell Law Directory** is now available online...exclusively through the LEXIS®-NEXIS® services.

---

### HAHN AND BOWERSOCK
3187 REDHILL, SUITE 115
COSTA MESA, CALIFORNIA 92626
800 660-3187
FAX 714 662-1398

A Full-Service Court Reporting Company
Serving all of California and Nationwide
With Cost-Effective Services

24-hour Deposition Setting Service

Offices and Complimentary Conference Rooms in The Following Counties: San Diego, Orange, Los Angeles, San Bernardino, Riverside, Ventura and San Francisco

Leaders In Technology Including Real-Time/Instant Transcript, Text Browsing, Video/Real-Time Synchronization, Document Imaging And Scanning, CD-ROM Archiving. Certified Real-Time Writers On Staff Depositions Modemed or Faxed Anywhere In The United States

Real-Time/Instant Transcript With Every Deposition

In-House Video

LiveNote Browsing

Specializing In Large Case/Complex Litigation

With Complimentary Conference Rooms For Any Size Gathering In Any Location In The Nation

DAILY and REAL-TIME TRANSCRIPTS

Complimentary Condensed Transcripts

Interpreters

Litigation Support: ASCII disks, Discovery ZX, Catlinks

Document Management/Document Depository

Customized Billing Summaries

Customized Case Management Reports

Rate Proposals and Company Brochure Upon Request

*SEE OUR AD ON PAGE CAA23S*

---

Now it's easy to find lawyers practicing a specific area of law! Simply consult the **Martindale-Hubbell Law Directory Areas of Practice Index.**

SERVICES, SUPPLIERS, CONSULTANTS · CALIFORNIA—IRVINE

# Two Ways To Get Your Transcripts.

## Sooner.

At Hahn & Bowersock, we believe your deposition transcripts are too important to trust to a delivery service with an attitude.

Instead, we offer Real Time Instant Transcript free with every copy order.

Here's how it works. Our real time court reporter uses a laptop computer as well as a steno machine.

During the proceeding, you see each word on the monitor as it's being transcribed.

When the deposition ends,

## Or Later.

the data is then copied onto a computer diskette.

You can then leave the deposition with an unedited transcript on a diskette. And begin case preparation sooner rather than later.

For more facts on the fastest way to take delivery of your transcripts, without any delays, give us a call. Offices in Costa Mesa, Long Beach, Los Angeles, Ontario, San Francisco, San Diego. **(800) 660-3187.**

*Cost-effective court and deposition reporting through cutting-edge technology.*

CAA23S

# IRVINE (Continued)
## Court Reporters (Continued)

### Imhof & Associates
**Full Service Court Reporting**

- Guaranteed 10-Day Turnaround
- Daily or Expedited Transcripts
- Computerized Transcription
- Realtime Court Reporting - CaseView & LiveNote
- Condensed Transcripts and ASCII Disks Free of Charge
- Keyword Indexing
- Interpreters Available
- Conference Rooms
- Transcripts Archived
- In-house Videographers

1-800-939-DEPO
3376

7720 Painter Avenue
Suite A
Whittier, CA 90602
(310) 907-4455
Fax (310) 907-4453

19732 Larkridge Drive
Yorba Linda, CA 92686
(714) 693-1213
WWW.Imhof.com
VImhof@aol.com

*Serving Los Angeles, Orange, Riverside and San Bernardino Counties*

---

### INTERIM COURT REPORTING

**Nationwide Court Reporting Services**
**Main Office**
3530 Wilshire Boulevard, Suite 1700
Los Angeles, CA 90010
1-800-722-1235
Fax: 213-389-8514

Realtime Transcription, CaseView, LiveNote
Daily and Expedited Service
Videotape Depositions and Videosync Timestamping
Computer Aided Transcription and Litigation Support
ASCII, Discovery ZX and CATLinks Diskettes
Telecommunication Capabilities
Condensed Transcripts with Keyword Indexes
Interpreters
Document Depository
Conference Rooms Available

Experienced, Qualified Court Reporters
Skilled in technical, medical, patent and environmental testimony

***SEE OUR AD ON PAGE CAA25S***

---

## SHERR COURT REPORTERS
### A FULL-SERVICE REPORTING AGENCY

**THE REALTIME SPECIALISTS**

Conference rooms in
San Diego; Carlsbad; Orange County, including Irvine, Newport Beach, Huntington Beach, and El Toro; Los Angeles; Woodland Hills; Riverside; San Bernardino and Las Vegas

Serving all of Southern California

San Diego headquarters one block from Amtrak,
10 minutes from airport

We handle all **accommodation details**,
including **free shuttle** service to and from San Diego's Lindbergh Field and discounted accommodations at Wyndham Plaza Hotel adjacent to our complimentary conference rooms and next door to the new courthouse.

(619) 231-1600

State-of-the-art Reporting Technology & Services
♦
Complex & Expert Litigation
♦
Realtime/Text Browsing
♦
Laptops Available
♦
Paralegal Reports/Case Notes
♦
Catlinks, Discovery ZX, ASCIIs
♦
Compressed Transcripts with Indices
♦
Immediate Rough Drafts, Transcript Modeming
♦
Daily Copy
♦
Interpreters and Video Technicians
♦
Facsimile & Copy Service
♦
Local Subpoena Service

**SHERR COURT REPORTERS**
**THE REALTIME SPECIALISTS**
**Emerald Plaza**
**402 West Broadway**
**Fourth Floor**
**San Diego, CA 92101**
(619) 231-1600, Fax (619) 595-4822
SherrReporters@compuserve.com

SERVICES, SUPPLIERS, CONSULTANTS                                              CALIFORNIA—IRVINE

## More than capable. Capable of anything.

Experienced and highly skilled court reporters who show up when you need them and do the job right. That's what you can expect from **Interim® Court Reporting**, the nation's largest, most technologically advanced court reporting firm in the nation.

As an **Interim® Legal Services** company, we are part of the nation's largest network of legal support services. By using us, we can schedule all your court reporting needs whenever and wherever you desire. And, because we're nationwide you can expect the same consistent service here, there and everywhere.

- Centralized Scheduling
- Deposition Suites
- Real-Time Reporting
- Videotaped Deposition Services
- CaseView/LiveNote
- ASCII and Other Electronic Media Formats
- Condensed Transcripts
- Case Management
- Deposition Summarization

**Interim®**
COURT REPORTING

| Los Angeles | San Diego | San Francisco |
|---|---|---|
| (800) 685-6600 | (619) 235-2400 | (415) 362-6666 |

© Copyright 1996, Interim Services Inc.

CAA25S

## IRVINE (Continued)

### MEDICAL EXPERT WITNESS

#### PSYCHOLOGY

#### Specializing in: Neuropsychology

### Robert J. Sbordone, Ph.D.

| | |
|---|---|
| Specialties | Neuropsychology |
| | Head Trauma |
| | Post-Concussion Syndrome |
| | Post-Traumatic Stress Disorder |
| | Recovery following Brain Trauma |
| Address | 7700 Irvine Center Drive |
| | Suite 750 |
| | Irvine, CA 92718 |
| Telephone | (714) 753-7711 |
| Fax | (714) 753-7708 |
| E-Mail | BOBNEURPSY@AOL.COM |

BACKGROUND:

Dr. Sbordone is internationally recognized for his expertise in clinical neuropsychology, head trauma, post-concussion syndromes, post-traumatic stress disorders, cognitive rehabilitation and recovery of cognitive functioning following brain injury. He received his doctorate from U.C.L.A. and was a National Institute of Health Postdoctoral Fellow at the U.C.L.A. Neuropsychiatric and Brain Research Institutes. He has been awarded a Diplomate in Clinical Neuropsychology from both the American Board of Professional Psychology and the American Board of Professional Neuropsychology. He is also a Diplomate of the American Board of Assessment Psychology. He is a Fellow of the National Academy of Neuropsychology and the American College of Professional Neuropsychology. He has received numerous awards for his contributions to neuropsychology. He has authored a total of over 95 books, book chapters, and publications, including Neuropsychology for the Attorney; Disorders of Executive Functions: Civil and Criminal law Applications (with Harold V. Hall, Ph.D.); The Ecological Validity of Neuropsychological Testing (with Charles Long, Ph.D.), and Forensic Neuropsychology (in preparation, with Arnold Purisch, Ph.D. and Lawrence Cohen, Esq.).

Dr. Sbordone maintains a private practice in Irvine, California, and is a Clinical Assistant Professor in the Departments of Neurosurgery, Physical Medicine and Rehabilitation at the University of California at Irvine College of Medicine. He is a member of numerous professional societies and has also consulted to many of the leading head trauma programs in the United States. He has served on the Editorial Advisory board of the International Journal of Clinical Neuropsychology, Journal of Head Trauma Rehabilitation, The Journal of Head Injury, JMA Bulletin, and Neurlaw.

---

#### SURGERY

#### Specializing in: Orthopedic

### ROBERT ANTHONY BAIRD, M.D.

OFFICE: 16300 Sand Canyon Avenue, Suite 511, Irvine, CA 92618, Phone: (714) 727-3636, Fax: (714) 727-9515

MEDICAL LICENSURE: California, 1972 (G23472)

EDUCATION: Graduate: State University of New York, Downstate Medical Center, Degree: M.D., 1971
Postgraduate training completed at the University of California, San Diego ● 1971-72 -Straight Surgical Internship, ● 1972-73 -General Surgery Residency, ● 1973-77 -Orthopaedic Surgery Residency.
Board Certification: American Board of Orthopaedic Surgery

APPOINTMENTS:

| | |
|---|---|
| 1977 - 1979 | Chief, Division of Orthopaedic Surgery Kern Medical Center, Bakersfield, California |
| 1977 - 1981 | Clinical Instructor in Surgery, Orthopaedics University of California, San Diego |
| 1979 - 1984 | Assistant Professor in Residence, Department of Surgery, University of California, Irvine |
| 1979 - 1987 | Staff Physician, Section of Orthopaedic Surgery Long Beach Veterans Administration Hospital, Long Beach, CA |
| 1981 - 1983 | Acting Chief, Division of Orthopaedic Surgery University of California, Irvine |
| 1984 - 1986 | Chief, Orthopaedic Surgery Section Long Beach Veterans Administration Medical Center |
| 1985 - 1986 | Co-Director, STAMP Program Long Beach Veterans Administration Medical Center |
| 1984 - 1994 | Associate Adjunct Professor Department of Surgery, University of California, Irvine |
| 1989 - 1991 | Chairman, Department of Orthopaedic Surgery Irvine Medical Center, Irvine, California |
| 1991 - 1993 | Chief of Staff, Irvine Medical Center |
| 1994 - present | Qualified Medical Evaluator, State of California |
| 1994 - present | Associate Clinical Professor, Department of Orthopaedic Surgery, University of California, Irvine |

SOCIETY MEMBERSHIPS: ● Orthopaedic Research Society ● American Academy of Orthopaedic Surgeons ● Orange County Medical Association ● California Medical Association ● Western Orthopaedic Association ● American Spinal Injury Association

Full C.V. available upon request which will include an extensive list of committee service, presentation, publications, abstracts and brief communications, grant support and scientific exhibits.

---

Fast ... Easy ... Flexible...
**The Martindale-Hubbell Law Directory on CD-ROM** gives you instant access through multiple search criteria to information on over 900,000 lawyers and law firms. For more details and a FREE demonstration disc, call **1-800-323-3288**.

SERVICES, SUPPLIERS, CONSULTANTS — CALIFORNIA—LA JOLLA

LA JOLLA, *San Diego Co.*

### COURT REPORTERS

### THE WAVE OF THE FUTURE

Certified Court Reporters
Certified Legal Videographers

TOLL FREE: 1-800-227-0577

7825 Fay Avenue
Suite 200
La Jolla, California 92037
FAX: 602-998-7228

REGISTERED PROFESSIONAL REPORTERS
CALIFORNIA CERTIFIED REPORTERS

A Full Service Reporting and
Video Production Company

Serving the Bar for over 21 years
Experts in Complex Litigation
Medical and Technical Deposition Specialists
Interpreters & Translators

Daily and Expedited Transcripts on Request
Large Deluxe Conference Rooms
Convenient Locations with Easy-Parking
Videotape and Teleconferencing Facilities
Videotape/Laserdisc presentations
Transcript/Video Synchronization
Certified Legal Video Specialists
Adjacent to Luxury Hotels

Prompt Out-of-State Delivery

Complimentary Condensed Transcripts & Concordances
State of the Art Computer-Aided Transcriptions
Video and Litigation Support Formats
Realtime Translation

**MANY OFFICE LOCATIONS THROUGHOUT
CALIFORNIA & ARIZONA**
including San Diego, Del Mar, San Francisco, La Jolla,
Laguna, Newport Beach, Palm Springs, Sacramento,
Irvine, Orange County, Los Angeles, Phoenix, Tucson,
Scottsdale and All Surrounding Areas

**ADDITIONAL DEPOSITION SUITES AT SAN DIEGO, PHOENIX,
SAN FRANCISCO, ORANGE COUNTY
AND LOS ANGELES AIRPORTS**

Member of:
National Court Reporters Association
California Court Reporters Association
Arizona Court Reporters Association
Michigan Court Reporters Association

### INTERIM COURT REPORTING

Nationwide Court Reporting Services
Main Office
3530 Wilshire Boulevard, Suite 1700
Los Angeles, CA 90010
1-800-722-1235
Fax: 213-389-8514

Realtime Transcription, CaseView, LiveNote
Daily and Expedited Service
Videotape Depositions and Videosync Timestamping
Computer Aided Transcription and Litigation Support
ASCII, Discovery ZX and CATLinks Diskettes
Telecommunication Capabilities
Condensed Transcripts with Keyword Indexes
Interpreters
Document Depository
Conference Rooms Available

Experienced, Qualified Court Reporters
Skilled in technical, medical, patent and environmental testimony

---

To update your listing
in the **Martindale-Hubbell Law Directory**
call 1-800-MARTIND(ALE).

---

Need an extra copy of the **Martindale-Hubbell
Law Directory**? Or of a specific volume?
Call Martindale-Hubbell Customer Service at
**1-800-526-4902**

---

Now you can find the lawyer even if you don't
know where he or she practices -
with the **Martindale-Hubbell Law
Directory Alphabetical Index.**

# LAFAYETTE, 23,501, *Contra Costa Co.*

## EXPERT WITNESS

### CONSTRUCTION

WHITNEY S. HAIST
Expert Witness
Construction Issues

### THE HAIST CORPORATION
General Contractor No. 472347
925 Village Center, Suite One
Lafayette, Ca. 94549
510-283-2070

---

Specializing in construction issues: cost estimating, design, installation, technical specifications, code compliance and industry standards, investigation and repair.

---

*Expert Witness Services:*
- Inspections and reporting of construction defects and/or failures; conformance to the Uniform Building Code and standard construction practice.
- Preparation and review of cost estimates to repair or correct defects or failures.
- Inspections and certification of work in progress.
- Construction method analysis.
- Destructive and nondestructive investigation.
- Project management.

*Professional Qualifications and Background:*
- Uniform Building Code - ICBO Certified Inspector No. 89996
- California Licensed General Contractor since 1976 - B1 Lic. No. 472347
- California State University, Chico - B.A., Economics - 1968

Whitney S. Haist is recognized by attorneys and insurance companies for his thorough understanding of construction processes, methods, procedures and materials and as a highly credible expert witness in litigation. Mr. Haist is the President of The Haist Corporation.

The Haist Corporation, established in 1976, enjoys an excellent reputation as a fine homebuilder and light commercial contractor throughout the San Francisco East Bay. It has developed numerous small tracts and custom new homes as well as repair, remodel and renovation of existing single family residences.

---

The **Martindale-Hubbell Law Directory** is now available online...exclusively through the LEXIS®-NEXIS® services.

---

# LAKEPORT, * 4,390, *Lake Co.*

## COURT REPORTERS

### ADAIR, POTSWALD & HENNESSEY
Certified Shorthand Reporters
Certified Legal Video Specialist

### LAKE, MENDOCINO, SONOMA & HUMBOLDT COUNTIES

| UKIAH | LAKEPORT |
|---|---|
| 212 W. Perkins St. | 55 First St. |
| P.O. Box 761 | P.O. Box 397 |
| Ukiah, California 95482 | Lakeport, California 95453 |
| | |
| FORT BRAGG | SANTA ROSA |
| | |
| 100 Manzanita St. | 131A Stony Ci. |
| Fort Bragg, California 95437 | Santa Rosa, California 95401 |

**CALL TOLL FREE 24 HOURS**

1-800-747-DEPO    FAX: (707) 462-4517

Courtesy Deposition Suites

Photocopy and Video Service

Complimentary Condensed Copy and Disk

Daily Copy or Expedite

Medical and Expert Testimony

Subpoena Service

Realtime

---

Now it's easy to find lawyers practicing a specific area of law! Simply consult the
**Martindale-Hubbell Law Directory**
**Areas of Practice Index.**

SERVICES, SUPPLIERS, CONSULTANTS

**LONG BEACH, 429,433,** *Los Angeles Co.*

## COURT REPORTERS

- Serving Los Angeles, Riverside, San Bernardino, San Diego and Orange Counties
- Complimentary Conference Rooms
- Litigation Support
- Realtime
- Two-week Delivery
- Condensed Transcripts and Master Keyword Index

714 • 261 • 8686
213 • 848 • 8686
800 • 622 • 0226

Fast ... Easy ... Flexible...
**The Martindale-Hubbell Law Directory on CD-ROM** gives you instant access through multiple search criteria to information on over 900,000 lawyers and law firms. For more details and a FREE demonstration disc, call **1-800-323-3288**.

To update your listing
in the **Martindale-Hubbell Law Directory**
call **1-800-MARTIND(ALE)**.

CALIFORNIA—LONG BEACH

**ABRAMS, MAH & KAHN**
Court Reporting Service

4101 Birch Street
Suite 130
Newport Beach, California 92660
Los Angeles, California Telephone: 213-848-8686
Newport Beach, California Telephone: 714-261-8686
FAX: 714-261-6688
800-622-0226

Serving all of:
• Los Angeles •
• Orange County •
• San Diego •
• Riverside •
• San Bernardino •

Realtime
Condensed Transcripts
Complimentary Conference Rooms
Computer-aided Transcription
Video Taping and Interpreters
• Two-week Delivery •
Daily Copy Available

Experienced in:
• Multi-party Complex Litigation •
and
• Technical Testimony •

*SEE OUR AD ON PAGE CAA29S*

Need an extra copy of the **Martindale-Hubbell Law Directory?** Or of a specific volume? Call Martindale-Hubbell Customer Service at **1-800-526-4902**

Now you can find the lawyer even if you don't know where he or she practices - with the **Martindale-Hubbell Law Directory Alphabetical Index.**

CAA29S

## CALIFORNIA—LONG BEACH

### LONG BEACH (Continued)
Court Reporters (Continued)

### HAHN AND BOWERSOCK
3780 KILROY AIRPORT WAY, SUITE 200
LONG BEACH, CALIFORNIA 90806
800 660-3187
FAX 714 662-1398

A Full-Service Court Reporting Company
Serving all of California and Nationwide
With Cost-Effective Services

24-hour Deposition Setting Service

Offices and Complimentary Conference Rooms in The Following
Counties: San Diego, Orange, Los Angeles, San Bernardino,
Riverside, Ventura and San Francisco

Leaders In Technology Including Real-Time/Instant Transcript, Text
Browsing, Video/Real-Time Synchronization, Document Imaging And
Scanning, CD-ROM Archiving. Certified Real-Time Writers On Staff
Depositions Modemed or Faxed Anywhere In The United States

Real-Time/Instant Transcript With Every Deposition

In-House Video

LiveNote Browsing

Specializing In Large Case/Complex Litigation

With Complimentary Conference Rooms For Any Size Gathering
In Any Location In The Nation

DAILY and REAL-TIME TRANSCRIPTS

Complimentary Condensed Transcripts

Interpreters

Litigation Support: ASCII disks, Discovery ZX, Catlinks

Document Management/Document Depository

Customized Billing Summaries

Customized Case Management Reports

Rate Proposals and Company Brochure Upon Request

---

The **Martindale-Hubbell Law Directory** is now
available online...exclusively
through the LEXIS®-NEXIS® services.

## MARTINDALE-HUBBELL LAW DIRECTORY 1997

### INTERIM COURT REPORTING

Nationwide Court Reporting Services
Main Office
3530 Wilshire Boulevard, Suite 1700
Los Angeles, CA 90010
1-800-722-1235
Fax: 213-389-8514

Realtime Transcription, CaseView, LiveNote
Daily and Expedited Service
Videotape Depositions and Videosync Timestamping
Computer Aided Transcription and Litigation Support
ASCII, Discovery ZX and CATLinks Diskettes
Telecommunication Capabilities
Condensed Transcripts with Keyword Indexes
Interpreters
Document Depository
Conference Rooms Available

Experienced, Qualified Court Reporters
Skilled in technical, medical, patent and environmental testimony

### LOS ALTOS, 26,303, *Santa Clara Co.*

### LITIGATION SUPPORT SERVICES

### THE CHATHAM GROUP
Technology Litigation Support Services

101 First Street, Suite 477
Los Altos, California 94022
Telephone: 415-948-1243
Fax: 415-949-0534
E-mail: CHATHAM@INTERRAMP.COM
chatham001@aol.com

Consulting, expert witnesses and case management, specializing in matters relating to computers, electronics, semiconductors, telecommunications, communications and office automation. The Group is composed of senior scientists, engineers, technologists and managers in high technology industry and academics.

Members of The Chatham Group have supported litigation involving intellectual property, contract disputes, insurance claims, regulatory issues, mergers and acquisitions, bankruptcy and others.

The Chatham Group can provide expert technical, scientific, management and marketing expertise and services in the following areas:

- Technology counseling and seminars
- Expert witness testimony and consulting
- Technology evaluation
- Market research studies and reports
- Discovery and deposition support
- Trial aids
- Case analysis and strategy evaluation
- Patent searches and evaluation
- Claims and damages assessment
- Witness search and investigation
- Registered Patent Agents

LOS ANGELES, * 3,485,398, *Los Angeles Co.*

## ACCIDENT INVESTIGATION & RECONSTRUCTION SERVICES

### FIRE & ACCIDENT RECONSTRUCTION
21465 EAST FORT BOWIE DRIVE
WALNUT, CA 91789
(909) 598-8919
Fax: (909) 598-5666

### WHAT DOES YOUR LOSS INVOLVE?

Complete and comprehensive independent technical evaluations of the causes of fires and accidents.

FIRE CAUSE AND ORIGIN
AUTO COLLISION
PERSONAL INJURY
INDUSTRIAL ACCIDENTS
CONSTRUCTION PROBLEMS
PRODUCT FAILURE
PROPERTY DAMAGE

1. EXAMINATIONS - On-site field examinations; desk reviews and research, laboratory and empirical testing; documentation and verification of physical evidence; codes, specifications, standards; photography and graphics.

2. ANALYSIS - Evaluation of gathered information and the application of engineering principles and scientific data as it relates to the causes of accidents, fires and various losses; necessary specialists sought for consultation. Preparation of the report including probable cause and origin.

3. EXPERT WITNESS - Provides one who can clearly represent unbiased findings before laymen and court believably and with integrity; one who's advanced degree from a major university, professional experience, published papers and technical on-going education qualifies him in all courts of law.

CONTACT:
John A. Caudron, M.S.S., B.C.F.E.
Ref. Best's Directory of Recommended Insurance Attorneys (Expert Service Section)

Professional society memberships include: Institute of Forensic Experts; The American Board of Forensic Examiners; American Society of Safety Engineers; National Fire Protection Association; American Society of Civil Engineers; American Society for Metals; Firearms Research and Identification Association (President); and National Association of Professional Accident Reconstruction Specialists.

---

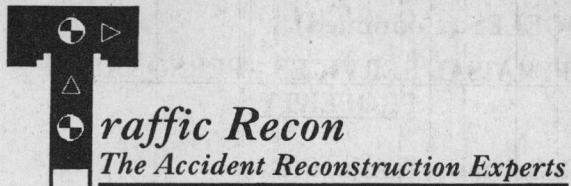

*Traffic Recon*
*The Accident Reconstruction Experts*

*4464 Bella Vista Drive*
*Moorpark, CA 93021*
*Voice: (800) 481-9300*
*Fax: (805) 529-8100*
*E-mail: trecon11@themall.net*
*trecon11@aol.com*
*Website: http://205.216.138.50/biz/trafficrecon*

TRAFFIC RECON offers full service accident reconstruction investigation. Reports written by TRAFFIC RECON are comprehensive and conclusively establish whether a collision occurred, occurred as alleged, or was simply staged. TRAFFIC RECON reports can also address liability in cases involving disputed right of way and other "rules of the road" violations. A TRAFFIC RECON report provides you with the information necessary to speak with a complete understanding of the collision sequence. This understanding flows from reports written in plain English and not confused by the addition of technical terms or endless pages of unnecessary information.

Accident Reconstruction investigation includes matters involving suspected fraud and *low impact* or g force analysis. Written reports based solely on the photographs and statements will be returned to you within 14 days from the date that the assignment is received by TRAFFIC RECON. Our low impact or g force reports, successfully merge damage analysis *and* g force analysis in one report. This eliminates the time and expense of having damage and forces analyzed in separate reports. All of our g force analysis reports contain references comparing the collision forces to events routinely experienced by people in everyday circumstances. Such real life comparisons allow you to bring the type of forces experienced during low speed impacts into perspective. Examples of like forces used in the reports are determined by ongoing in house testing.

TRAFFIC RECON experts can respond quickly to conduct on site inspection and investigation of vehicles and collision locations.

TRAFFIC RECON has a history of providing honest, realistic opinions of how a traffic collision occurred. We look forward to providing you with honest answers to the often complicated questions of did it happen, if so-- how, and who is at fault.

---

Now it's easy to find lawyers practicing a specific area of law! Simply consult the
**Martindale-Hubbell Law Directory**
**Areas of Practice Index.**

## LOS ANGELES (Continued)
### APPRAISAL SERVICES - PERSONAL PROPERTY

**Stuart H. Salsbury, A.A.A., G.G.**
*Appraisal Services*

Telephone: (213) 874-6781
Facsimile: (213) 851-6755
E-mail: salsbury@earthlink.net

Specializing in the appraisal of period, contemporary and vintage furnishings, fine art and antiques, jewelry and other valued personal property.

Formerly, head of the Appraisal Department, Sotheby Parke Bernet and Consulting Fine Arts Editor and Columnist, <u>Architectural Digest.</u>

Appraisals authored for insurance and tax purposes, dissolution of marriage, probate, litigation, considered purchase or sale, and personal reference; after damage and loss reports.

Extensive insurance claim and litigation experience.

Recognized expert witness.

Serving Los Angeles, Southern California and the West since 1972.

Curriculum vitae, fee schedule and professional references upon request.

---

Fast ... Easy ... Flexible...
**The Martindale-Hubbell Law Directory on CD-ROM** gives you instant access through multiple search criteria to information on over 900,000 lawyers and law firms. For more details and a FREE demonstration disc, call **1-800-323-3288**.

---

To update your listing
in the **Martindale-Hubbell Law Directory**
call **1-800-MARTIND(ALE)**.

---

## ASSET LOCATORS

### NATIONAL LAWYERS LOCATE SERVICE, INC.

*"PROFESSIONAL PRIVATE INVESTIGATIONS"*

<u>Searches Available:</u>

- Subject & Employment Locates
- Bank Accounts
- Complete Asset Searches
- Criminal Background
- DMV
- Decedent Trees
- Real Property
- Many Other Searches Available

*Ask About our No Find/No Fee Searches*

1-800-962-1099

---

Need an extra copy of the **Martindale-Hubbell Law Directory**? Or of a specific volume?
Call Martindale-Hubbell Customer Service at
**1-800-526-4902**

---

Now you can find the lawyer even if you don't know where he or she practices -
with the **Martindale-Hubbell Law Directory Alphabetical Index.**

---

The **Martindale-Hubbell Law Directory** is now available online...exclusively
through the LEXIS®-NEXIS® services.

## ATTORNEY SERVICES

### RICHARD GERSTENBERG, P.I.

660 North Enid Avenue
Covina, CA 91722

Telephone/Fax: (818) 332-4740
24 Hour Pager: (800) 325-3071

Richard Gerstenberg
*President*

- Male and Female Investigators
- Written Reports Provided
- Nationwide Contacts
- Nationwide & Worldwide Travel
- Process Service
- Polygraph/Lie Detection
- Specializing in Homicide/Criminal Investigations
- Court Qualified Expert Witness In: Criminal Homicide
- Accident Recreation/Reconstruction
- Undercover/Surveillance, Video Still/Evidential Photography
- Skip Tracing, Missing Persons
- Due Diligence, Court Research
- Litigation Support Services
- Attorney Services
- Debugging
- Child Custody, Kidnapping, Family, Marital, Spousal, Divorce
- Record/Asset/DMV/UCC Searches
- Trademark/Copyright Infringement
- Pre-Employment, Background Checks

Member
CALI

---

*Micro Quick*
(800) 655-FAST
(3278)

A Litigation, Photocopy & Messenger Service

- volume copying specialist
- court indexing & research
- court filings & fax filings
- subpoena preparation & service
- complete messenger service
- access to complete DMV files
- licensed process servers
- photocopying anywhere in Southern California

CD ROM document storage and retrieval
(no software needed)

Medical and legal on-site copying
x-ray duplication

Serving All of Southern California

*Micro Quick*
It's our image you can count on!
visit us at www.microquick.com

Bonded    Certified    Insured

---

Fast ... Easy ... Flexible...
**The Martindale-Hubbell Law Directory on CD-ROM** gives you instant access through multiple search criteria to information on over 900,000 lawyers and law firms. For more details and a FREE demonstration disc, call **1-800-323-3288**.

---

To update your listing
in the **Martindale-Hubbell Law Directory**
call **1-800-MARTIND(ALE)**.

CALIFORNIA—LOS ANGELES  MARTINDALE-HUBBELL LAW DIRECTORY 1997

## LOS ANGELES (Continued)
### Attorney Services (Continued)

**"We Serve You by Serving Others"**
Established 1975

10573 West Pico Boulevard • Suite 344
Los Angeles, California 90064
Toll Free: (800) 838-9044
Telephone: (310) 838-9000 • Facsimile: (310) 838-0855

*Registered, Certified, Bonded & Insured*

**Prompt Legal Services** is a full litigation services company. Located near Beverly Hills, we specialize in very fast, efficient and courteous process service. Our firm is known for hard to serves, celebrity, and other special circumstance services. We are fully computerized and are on-line with databases nationwide.

Counties:
LOS ANGELES
Orange / Riverside
San Bernardino / San Diego
Santa Barbara / Ventura

Serving throughout California, United States and International

— *24 HOUR SERVICE* —

- **SPECIALIZATIONS:**
  - Rush Service
  - Multiple Attempts at no extra charge
  - Skip Tracing
  - Surveillance
  - County, State & Federal Courts
  - Writs of Execution
  - Small Claims Specialist

- **LITIGATION SERVICES AVAILABLE UPON REQUEST**
  - Public Record Retrieval
  - Post Office Checking
  - Database Searches
  - Real Property Searches
  - Document Retrieval, Filing & Research
  - DMV & Credit Research
  - Subpoena Preparation
  - Witness Statements
  - Summons & Complaints

Member: *(CAPPS) California Association of Photocopiers & Process Servers*
*(NAPPS) National Association of Professional Process Servers*
*(APSA) Arizona Process Servers Association*
*(FAPPS) Florida Association of Professional Process Servers*
*(TPPS) Texas Professional Process Servers Association*
*(OAPS) Oregon Association of Professional Process Servers*
*(NJPSA) New Jersey Process Servers Association*
*Chamber of Commerce*

Standard Service
Los Angeles County  $35
All Other Counties  $45

---

**Wade's Attorney Service**
a legal support service company

*From Big Cities...*

*...To Rural Communities*

*Our Network Is Your Network*

- Process Service
- Difficult Serves
- Skip Trace/Locates
- Stand-by/Stakeouts
- Court Filing
- Court Research
- Court Indexing
- Court Retrieval
- Public Records Search
- Statewide Forwarding
- Nationwide Forwarding

5410 Wilshire Blvd.
Suite 237
Los Angeles, CA 90036
(213) 933-4448
FAX: (213) 1474

**SEE OUR AD ON PAGE CAA35S**

---

Need an extra copy of the **Martindale-Hubbell Law Directory**? Or of a specific volume? Call Martindale-Hubbell Customer Service at
1-800-526-4902

---

Now you can find the lawyer even if you don't know where he or she practices - with the **Martindale-Hubbell Law Directory Alphabetical Index.**

*From Big Cities...*

*...To Rural Communities*

## Our Network Is **Your** Network

• Process Service • Difficult Serves • Skip Trace/Locates • Stand-by/Stakeouts • Court Filing • Court Research
Court Indexing • Court Retrieval • Public Records Search • Statewide Forwarding • Nationwide Forwarding

# Wade's Attorney Service
a legal support service company

5410 Wilshire Blvd., Suite 237 • Los Angeles, CA 90036

## (213) 933-4448
FAX: (213) 933-1474

CALIFORNIA—LOS ANGELES             MARTINDALE-HUBBELL LAW DIRECTORY 1997

## LOS ANGELES (Continued)
### AUDIO/VIDEO SERVICES

### DECISIONQUEST
2050 West 190th Street, Suite 205, Torrance, CA 90504
(310) 618-9600; Fax: (310) 618-1122

e-mail address: dqi@aol.com
www address: http://www.decisionquest.com
Principal Contact: Michael E. Cobo

Los Angeles, Houston, Chicago, New York, Boston,
Washington and Atlanta

DecisionQuest utilizes the most advanced technology and equipment available. All elements of design and production are completed in DecisionQuest facilities to ensure confidentiality and value to our clients. We have invested heavily in the latest technologies that allow us to deliver the best quality at the lowest cost.

DecisionQuest uses digital technology for deposition editing, video presentations and other trial presentations.

We can provide both CD-ROM based computer presentation systems or laser disc based presentations for your case. CD-ROM based computer presentations may include scanned documents, photographs, graphics or video elements, which can be manipulated, highlighted, colorized and interactively presented to the jury.

*Call us to find out why, contrary to popular belief, not all exhibits should be presented on TV monitors.*

Knowledge  |  Control  |  Persuasion  |  Winning℠

---

The **Martindale-Hubbell Law Directory** is now
available online...exclusively
through the LEXIS®-NEXIS® services.

---

Now it's easy to find lawyers practicing a specific
area of law! Simply consult the
**Martindale-Hubbell Law Directory
Areas of Practice Index.**

## AUTOMOBILE & OFFICE EQUIPMENT LEASING

### Trans Leasing International®
3000 Dundee Road
Northbrook, Illinois 60062
Switchboard: 800-323-1180
Fax: 847-272-2174

Founded in 1972, Trans Leasing International, Inc. is a leading provider of capital equipment leasing services. Our leasing services are focused primarily on three types of equipment: general office equipment, healthcare equipment, and automobiles (through the LeaseCard Auto Group).

Trans Leasing's competitive advantage is clearly demonstrated by our LeaseCard® program. With credit references alone, the LeaseCard program allows attorneys to acquire up to $100,000 in pre-approved credit for equipment and automobile lease financing. Our commitment to service is further exemplified by features such as prompt credit decisions, single-page documentation, and responsive, efficient and innovative lease financing programs. For more information on the LeaseCard program, please contact John Dondey, Director of Legal Leasing Services at 800-535-2756.

**LeaseCard Legal Funding Group**
777 Yamato Road
Boca Raton, Florida 33431
800-535-2756

**LeaseCard Auto Group**
1039 E. North Corporate Circle, P.O. Box 388
Grayslake, Illinois 60030
800-854-2000

---

Fast ... Easy ... Flexible...
**The Martindale-Hubbell Law Directory on
CD-ROM** gives you instant access through
multiple search criteria to information on over
900,000 lawyers and law firms. For more details and a
FREE demonstration disc, call **1-800-323-3288**.

## SERVICES, SUPPLIERS, CONSULTANTS

## CALIFORNIA—LOS ANGELES

### BUSINESS VALUATIONS

### HOULIHAN LOKEY HOWARD & ZUKIN
1930 Century Park West
Los Angeles, CA 90067
(310) 788-5300
FAX: (310) 553-2173

Houlihan Lokey Howard & Zukin provides a wide variety of specialty investment banking services to more than 5,000 clients, from Wall Street to Main Street. With more than $100 billion in transaction experience in the last five years, Houlihan Lokey's specialties include:

Business & Securities Valuation
ESOP Advisory Services
Solvency Analysis
Fairness Opinions
Dispute Analysis and Litigation Support
Expert Witness Testimony
Estate and Gift Tax Valuations
Valuation of Intangible Assets
Financial Restructuring
Corporate Finance
Mergers, Acquisitions and Divestitures
Merchant Banking
Corporate Finance Issues
Information Services
Mergerstat

Our resources include more than 125 financial professionals with a variety of advanced degrees, licenses and industry designations. With extensive experience in accounting, commercial banking, engineering and corporate law, an appropriate Houlihan Lokey team is always available to serve your needs.

Houlihan Lokey is a national firm with offices in Los Angeles, New York, Chicago, San Francisco, Minneapolis, Washington, D.C., Dallas and Toronto. To find out more about Houlihan Lokey's value-added services, please call Scott Beiser at (310) 788-5300.

---

To update your listing
in the **Martindale-Hubbell Law Directory**
call 1-800-MARTIND(ALE).

---

### HOULIHAN VALUATION ADVISORS®

#### VALUATION & CAPITAL CONSULTANTS

A national firm specializing in valuation
and financial opinion services.

- FAIRNESS & SOLVENCY OPINIONS
- ESTATE & GIFT TAXES
- CORPORATIONS & PARTNERSHIPS
- ESOPs
- LBOs
- MERGERS AND ACQUISITIONS
- DIVESTITURES
- RECAPITALIZATIONS
- EQUITY ALLOCATION / SECURITY PRICING
- DUE DILIGENCE
- EXPERT WITNESS TESTIMONY
- INTANGIBLE ASSETS

*HVA's professional staff includes Ph.D.s, CFAs, ASAs, CPAs, and financial analysts with a breadth of industry and project experience that add value to even the most demanding assignments. Our clients and their legal counsel attest to our reputation for thorough, well-documented results.*

**For more information contact
Richard Houlihan at 714-668-0272**
E-mail: rahoulihan@aol.com
World Wide Web: www.houlihan.com

- Los Angeles        (310) 859-8300
                     (800) 977-8999
- Orange County      (714) 668-0272
- San Francisco      (415) 392-0888
- Las Vegas          (702) 385-1675
- Salt Lake City     (801) 322-3300
- Denver             (303) 295-8923
- Kansas City        (913) 385-1800
- Chicago            (312) 759-1303
- Indianapolis       (317) 264-1005
- Atlanta            (770) 951-4820
- Washington, D.C.   (301) 940-8900

---

Need an extra copy of the **Martindale-Hubbell Law Directory**? Or of a specific volume?
Call Martindale-Hubbell Customer Service at
**1-800-526-4902**

CALIFORNIA—LOS ANGELES                MARTINDALE-HUBBELL LAW DIRECTORY 1997

## LOS ANGELES (Continued)
### Business Valuations (Continued)

### Klaris, Thomson & Schroeder, Inc.
*Valuation and Consulting Professionals*

| Los Angeles | St. Louis | Chicago |
|---|---|---|
| (310) 597-0821 | (314) 739-1000 | (708) 577-0802 |

| Tampa | Philadelphia |
|---|---|
| (813) 978-1804 | (215) 339-1996 |

**Full Service Valuation Firm Specializing In:**

- Litigation Support
- Expert Testimony
- Closely Held Companies
- Family Limited Partnership Interests
- Machinery and Equipment
- Transfer Pricing Studies
- Fairness Opinions
- Solvency Opinions

**Klaris, Thomson & Schroeder, Inc.** is a full service valuation company that is built on the 65 years of experience of its three founders. Our philosophy is simple: To offer superior quality and impeccable service at competitive fees.

Our staff brings experience, professionalism and innovation to assist you and/or your client in solving or defending any valuation issues.

For a free quote call us at (800) KTS-1631, or write to:

6102 Costa Del Rey
Long Beach, CA 90803

E-Mail
kts@htc.net

---

# SANLI PASTORE & HILL

**Business Valuations and Financial Analysis**
*The Measure of Value™*

Headquarters:
1990 S. Bundy Drive, Suite 800
Los Angeles, CA 90025
Telephone: (310) 837-6678
Facsimile: (310) 837-6260

San Francisco:
44 Montgomery Street, Suite 500
San Francisco, CA 94104
Telephone: (415) 955-2699
Facsimile: (415) 397-6309

San Diego:
5355 Mira Sorrento Place, Suite 100
San Diego, CA 92121
Telephone: (619) 597-7505
Facsimile: (619) 597-7450

*Services Offered*

Business Valuations
Strategic Litigation Consulting
Estate & Gift Tax Valuations
Corporate Finance
Eminent Domain Valuations

Economic Research & Consulting
Merger & Acquisition Advisory Services
Industry, Market and

(This Listing Continued)

---

**SANLI PASTORE & HILL, INC. (Continued)**

Reorganization & Bankruptcy Valuations
Advisory Services
Financial Analysis
Expert Witness Testimony
Competition Studies
Intangible & Intellectual Asset Valuations
Real Estate & Machinery and Equipment

The professionals of SANLI PASTORE & HILL, INC. ("SP&H") combine expertise in valuations, accounting, corporate finance, litigation consulting, economic research and analysis, and international business to provide litigation consulting services to law firms, attorneys, government agencies, privately-held companies, and public corporations.

Staff members have advanced degrees in business administration, finance, economics and statistics. Professional designations held by SP&H professionals include Accredited Senior Appraiser (ASA), Chartered Financial Analyst (CFA), Member Appraisal Institute (MAI), Certified Public Accountant (CPA) and Certified Management Accountant (CMA). Mr. Nevin Sanli, President, is listed in *Who's Who Worldwide*, *Who's Who in Finance and Industry* and *Who's Who in America*.

SP&H provides expert witness testimony in complicated business litigation such as calculation of lost business value and economic damages for breach of contract, anti-trust violations, eminent domain, copyright and patent infringement and other business litigation. Our technical capabilities cover valuation analysis; financial analysis and forecasting; accounting reconstruction for valuations; industry, market and competition studies; statistics and econometrics; damage calculations; and strategic advice for discovery, interrogatories, depositions and cross-examinations of opposing economic expert witnesses.

*Principals:* Mr. Nevin Sanli, ASA, President
Mr. Thomas E. Pastore, ASA, CFA, CPA, Chief Executive Officer

*Academic Affiliates:* Dr. Johnston, Dr. Newcomb, and many others.

*Branch Offices:* San Diego, CA and San Francisco, CA

*Affiliate Offices:* In the United States: New York, New York; Washington, D.C.; Chicago, Illinois; Boston, Massachusetts; Houston, Texas.

International: London, United Kingdom; Paris, France; Geneva, Switzerland; Brussels, Belgium; Munich, Germany; Istanbul, Turkey; Moscow, Russia.

*Representative Clients:* O'Melveny & Myers; McDonough, Holland & Allen; Stradling, Yocca, Carlson & Rauth; Haight, Brown & Bonesteel; Richman, Lawrence, Mann, Greene & Chizever; Jeffer, Mangels, Marmaro & Butler; The Busch Firm; Demetriou, Del Guercio, Springer & Moyer; Goldfarb & Lipman; The State of California Department of Transportation; The Federal Deposit Insurance Corporation; The Government of Nepal; City Redevelopment Agencies; Wells Fargo Bank; Unified School Districts; privately-held middle market companies.

**SEE OUR AD ON PAGE CAA39S**

---

Now you can find the lawyer even if you don't know where he or she practices - with the **Martindale-Hubbell Law Directory Alphabetical Index.**

SERVICES, SUPPLIERS, CONSULTANTS  CALIFORNIA—LOS ANGELES

# Specialists in Business Valuations

- Business & Securities Valuations
- Estate & Gift Tax Valuations
- Family Limited Partnership Discounts
- Expert Witness Testimony & Litigation Support
- Goodwill Valuations
- Bankruptcy, Insolvency & Fairness Opinions
- Valuations for Financing
- Valuations for Mergers & Acquisitions
- Customized Industry, Market & Competition Research

*At Sanli Pastore & Hill, Inc., expert staff provide the highest level of due diligence and research to produce quality and timely results for you and your clients.*

SANLI PASTORE & HILL

*Main Office:*
1990 S. Bundy Drive, Suite 800
Los Angeles, California 90025
310/837-6678

*San Francisco Office:*
44 Montgomery Street, Suite 500
San Francisco, California 94104
415/955-2699

*San Diego Office:*
5355 Mira Sorrento Place, Suite 100
San Diego, California 92121
619/597-7505

E-mail: sphvalue@ix.netcom.com

CALIFORNIA—LOS ANGELES  MARTINDALE-HUBBELL LAW DIRECTORY 1997

## LOS ANGELES (Continued)
### CASE MANAGEMENT SYSTEMS

The **Martindale-Hubbell Law Directory** is now available online...exclusively through the LEXIS®-NEXIS® services.

---

Now it's easy to find lawyers practicing a specific area of law! Simply consult the **Martindale-Hubbell Law Directory Areas of Practice Index.**

Fast ... Easy ... Flexible...
The **Martindale-Hubbell Law Directory on CD-ROM** gives you instant access through multiple search criteria to information on over 900,000 lawyers and law firms. For more details and a FREE demonstration disc, call **1-800-323-3288**.

---

To update your listing in the **Martindale-Hubbell Law Directory** call **1-800-MARTIND(ALE)**.

---

# GRYPHON®: the complete litigation case and practice management software system for Microsoft® Windows™.

Information and working demonstration copy of GRYPHON are available on the world-wide web, or by calling 1-800-547-9746.

www.poseidon.com

*The future of the practice of law.*

As featured in the
*Microsoft*® Access
Solutions Portfolio™

Copyright © 1996 The Poseidon Group

CAA40S

# SERVICES, SUPPLIERS, CONSULTANTS

# CALIFORNIA—LOS ANGELES

### FIRST-OF-ITS-KIND SOFTWARE PROGRAM INTEGRATES TIME AND BILLING INTO LITIGATION CASE MANAGEMENT SYSTEM
#### Innovative Technology Designed For Small Law Firms and Corporate Legal Departments

SANTA BARBARA, CA — The Poseidon Group announces that it has developed a first-of-its-kind software program which integrates time and billing into a litigation case management system for use with Windows-based systems. The final release of GRYPHON™ Litigation Case & Management Software for Microsoft® Windows™ combines practice management, case management and time and billing tracking features into one program. The GRYPHON Litigation Case & Practice Management Software was one of the six Windows business solutions demonstrated by Microsoft Corporation at the 1995 Access Advisor Developer's Conference and Exposition. It was the only law office application to be selected in Microsoft's *Solutions in Action Portfolio*. GRYPHON combines critical practice management features through the use of *Integrated Decision Assistance*™ (IDA), which leads the user from one task to the next in a logical sequence. Produced by a litigation attorney and a software developer, the program is designed for small law firms and corporate litigation departments to save attorney and administrative time by facilitating information management.

GRYPHON creates "slips" for a lawyer's phone calls, documents, contacts, deadlines, appointments and billing entries, and links these through IDA. For example, preparing a motion with GRYPHON becomes a sequence of easy steps. It allows a secretary or attorney to create the motion, profile the document for tracking and retrieval, calendar the hearing date, and bill for the attorney's time, all in less time than it used to take to type the motion alone. By the time a lawyer first reads a draft of the motion, it has been logged, billed and calendared. Later, because the software keeps track of unserved documents, a secretary can create a proof of service with just a few clicks of the mouse.

The software is network ready and works with any version of Windows, including Windows NT and Windows 95.

GRYPHON features a 30-day, money-back guarantee and 60 days of free technical support. It only requires a license for timekeepers (lawyers) on the system, allowing unlimited use by secretaries and paralegals. The Sole Practitioner license sells for $995 and the Small Office Pack (2-3 lawyers) for $1,695. Additional timekeeper licenses are available at any time for $495 and site licenses are available for firms with more than 10 attorneys.

The Poseidon Group offers a free, working demonstration program. To order the demo or to obtain further information, please call 1-800-547-9746, or visit our web site @ www.poseidon.com.

## THE POSEIDON GROUP

For more information:
Scott M. Moore, Director of Customer Service
The Poseidon Group, 800/547-9746
Email to scott@poseidon.com

*SEE OUR AD ON PAGE CAA40S*

---

## CD-ROM PRODUCTS

2050 West 190th Street, Suite 205, Torrance, CA 90504
(800) 826-5353; Fax: (310) 618-0736
Principal Contact: Michael E. Cobo

e-mail address: dqi@aol.com
www address: http://www.decisionquest.com

The DQ2™ Exhibit Bank offers over 2,000 jury tested exhibits. You simply decide which charts are most appropriate for your case. The data and graphics in any exhibit design you choose will be customized by artists at DQ². Once you approve the exhibit design DQ² delivers it to you on an exhibit board, overhead transparency or 8.5" x 11" color copy, within 24 hours.

The DQ² library is arranged by the following case types:

| | |
|---|---|
| Antitrust | Labor/Employment |
| Banking/Lender Liability | Personal Injury |
| Contracts | Product Liability |
| Construction | Professional Malpractice |
| Insurance | Securities |
| Intellectual Property | Toxic Tort |

Choose from a wide selection of charts:

| | |
|---|---|
| Bar Charts | Line Charts |
| Chronologies | Maps |
| Damage Charts | Medical Illustrations |
| Document Charts | Organization Charts |
| Flow Charts | Pie Charts |
| Illustrations | Text Charts |

**"Trial Tested - Jury Proven"**

---

Need an extra copy of the **Martindale-Hubbell Law Directory?** Or of a specific volume?
Call Martindale-Hubbell Customer Service at
**1-800-526-4902**

---

Now you can find the lawyer even if you don't know where he or she practices - with the **Martindale-Hubbell Law Directory Alphabetical Index.**

## LOS ANGELES (Continued)
### COMPUTER ANIMATION, GRAPHICS & SIMULATION

### DECISIONQUEST
2050 West 190th Street, Suite 205, Torrance, CA 90504
(310) 618-9600; Fax: (310) 618-1122
Principal Contact: Michael E. Cobo

e-mail address: dqi@aol.com
www address: http://www.decisionquest.com

Los Angeles, Houston, Chicago, New York, Boston,
Washington and Atlanta

The professional staff at DecisionQuest is trained in the psychology of visual perception. We can assist you in developing a visual strategy for communicating persuasively to judges, jurors, arbitrators, mediation panels, public and private decision makers, regulatory groups or any other trier of fact. We have designed graphics for trials and other proceedings in urban and rural venues all over the country. Whether your case calls for 2-D or 3-D animation, we have the ability to make the proper recommendation, develop a cost-effective solution and produce a high quality animation for your case.

*Call us to find out how jurors perceive "slick" exhibits.*

Knowledge | Control | Persuasion | Winning℠

---

The **Martindale-Hubbell Law Directory** is now available online...exclusively through the LEXIS®-NEXIS® services.

---

Now it's easy to find lawyers practicing a specific area of law! Simply consult the **Martindale-Hubbell Law Directory Areas of Practice Index.**

---

**inData Corporation**
402 W. Broadway
#1850
San Diego, CA 92101

Prove it...

With compelling computer animation.

**Animation: A Tool for Settlement and Trial**

Working with you and your experts, inData produces compelling computer animations ordinary people can understand. Computer animation communicates hours of technical testimony in a few moments.
• Evidence is simplified
• Images are persuasive
Technically accurate presentations give you a decisive tool in settlement negotiations.

As your animation experts, we will work with your team to create an unimpeachable animation presentation. For added impact at trial, inData can further enhance your presentation using TrialDirector™, a powerful tool for exhibit display.

inData's computer animation is serious visual communication; used successfully in all areas of law:
• Criminal • Patent • Personal Injury • Medical
• Construction • Product Liability • Environmental

inData is a full service company, dedicated to excellence in computer animation, exhibit presentation, and trial support. Over the past few years, we've been involved with many high profile cases.
• The Exxon Valdez Case • The Keating S&L case
• The Oklahoma City bombing case

While not costly, make no mistake, when your case demands the best presentation solution, we're the ones to call.

Additional inData Services include:
• **3D Computer Modeling**
• **Audio Visual Services**
• **Comprehensive Product Line Animation Packages**
• **Computer Generated Graphics**
• **Equipment Rental and Installation**
• **Scanning Services**
• **Software Development**
• **Trial Presentation Systems**
• **Trial Presentation Consulting**
• **Video Editing and Production**

inData invites you to experience our trial services and the power of computer animation. For a free case evaluation call... **1-800-828-8292** or visit our web site http://www.indatacorp.com

SERVICES, SUPPLIERS, CONSULTANTS					CALIFORNIA—LOS ANGELES

## COMPUTER EVIDENCE INVESTIGATION

**Ontrack Data Recovery, Inc.**
6321 Bury Drive
Eden Prairie, MN 55346
Tel: 1-800-872-2599 • Fax: (612) 937-5750
E-mail: rshimanski@ontrack.com • Internet: www.ontrack.com
Contact: Computer Evidence Services

**Areas of Expertise:** Ontrack provides access to computer data evidence including deleted, damaged or altered files. Services include:
- **Data Seizure** — *Ensures that all data is seized without possibility of destroying valuable evidence through hidden programs or "bombs".*
- **Data Duplication** — *Duplication process includes all aspects of the media, including recoverable deleted files. Allows for original media to be preserved for evidentiary purposes.*
- **Data Recovery** — *Restoration of data that has been corrupted or lost due to mechanical failure ("crashed"), user "error", intentional deletion or natural disaster.*
- **Data Analysis** — *Searching for key documents, file alteration/deletion history, "computer forensics", to facilitate pre-trial discovery or investigation.*
- **Expert Services** — *Providing the expertise you need to make your case easily understood.*

**Experience:** Ontrack's engineers have over 500 years of combined computer technology experience and have completed tens of thousands of successful recoveries. Ontrack engineers have courtroom experience as expert witnesses, representing law enforcement in criminal prosecutions, and both plaintiffs and defendants in civil matters.

**Education:** After completing technical and formal degrees, Ontrack engineers must undergo rigorous training in Ontrack proprietary technology before they are able to become expert witnesses.

**Awards:** Recipient of the Department of Defense James S. Cogswell Outstanding Industrial Security Achievement Award.

**Certifications:** Certified software developers for Microsoft, Novell and Apple.

**Operating Structures:** Experience with virtually every operating system. All computer media types serviced.

**Representative Clients:** Federal, state and local law enforcement agencies, major corporations, military agencies, educational and financial institutions.

**Facilities:**
- Worldwide locations
- Secured facilities include a Class 100 Clean Room
- Personnel trained to handle sensitive material

**References:** Available upon request.

©1996 Ontrack Data Recovery, Inc.

---

Fast ... Easy ... Flexible...
**The Martindale-Hubbell Law Directory on CD-ROM** gives you instant access through multiple search criteria to information on over 900,000 lawyers and law firms. For more details and a FREE demonstration disc, call **1-800-323-3288**.

To update your listing
in the **Martindale-Hubbell Law Directory**
call **1-800-MARTIND(ALE)**.

Need an extra copy of the **Martindale-Hubbell Law Directory?** Or of a specific volume?
Call Martindale-Hubbell Customer Service at
**1-800-526-4902**

Now you can find the lawyer even if you don't know where he or she practices -
with the **Martindale-Hubbell Law Directory Alphabetical Index.**

The **Martindale-Hubbell Law Directory** is now available online...exclusively
through the LEXIS®-NEXIS® services.

CAA43S

# LOS ANGELES (Continued)

## CONFERENCING

### Compression Labs, Inc.

350 East Plumeria Drive
San Jose, CA 95134

408-428-6791
Fax: 408-922-5429
http://www.clix.com

Compression Labs, Inc. (CLI) is the world's principal provider of end-to-end, television quality videoconferencing solutions, with customers in business, education, government and healthcare markets.

Now in its twenty-fifth year, CLI is uniquely positioned to meet the needs of the changing videoconferencing marketplace. Our mission is to provide effortless videoconferencing in addition to:

- Focusing on making videoconferencing solutions as easy to implement as its products are easy to use. The company is doing this through its own technologies, combined with the simultaneous adherence to emerging standards, the development of open architectures, and the forming of strategic partnerships with leading telecommunications companies including AT&T, Pacific Bell, WilTel, and Norstan Communications.

- CLI is committed to providing enhanced services that remove the complexities of videoconferencing. Implementation is a key component in this strategy. In the area of group teleconferencing, for example, CLI's ServiceLink Network Ordering program manages the complete installation of a customer's digital communications network — from project management to filing out the proper forms. In the desktop arena, Lucent Technologies now provides comprehensive worldwide installation and service to both CLI desktop and room system videoconferencing customers.

- CLI will continue to pioneer solutions that address the full spectrum of application needs — from large group videoconferencing, including classrooms, to small group and desktop applications — and from economical low bandwidth to the highest bandwidth communications.

*Behind these commitments lies the world's most extensive experience and broadest range of expertise in developing, deploying, and supporting videoconferencing technologies, solutions, and standards.*

---

Now it's easy to find lawyers practicing a specific area of law! Simply consult the **Martindale-Hubbell Law Directory Areas of Practice Index.**

- Convenient - on demand calls set up in minutes.
- Fast, flexible billing, including court, case and matter number.
- Professional operators dedicated to the legal community.
- Best value in teleconferencing.
- 100% satisfaction guaranteed.

### For complete information call
# 800-272-5663

*Where lawyers put their best ideas on the line.*

---

Fast ... Easy ... Flexible...
**The Martindale-Hubbell Law Directory on CD-ROM** gives you instant access through multiple search criteria to information on over 900,000 lawyers and law firms. For more details and a FREE demonstration disc, call 1-800-323-3288.

---

To update your listing
in the **Martindale-Hubbell Law Directory**
call **1-800-MARTIND(ALE).**

networkMCI Conferencing. It's about making work easier and more productive

with just a phone and a computer. It's about going to a meeting without having

to travel. It's about turning your office into the world's largest conference room.

networkMCI Conferencing℠ can help anyone, anytime, anywhere, make better use of their time. MCI Audioconferencing instantly brings as few as 3 or as many as 1,000 people together for the same meeting, 24 hours a day. Our Videoconferencing lets people from around the world meet face-to-face without ever leaving their offices. With our Document Conferencing, employees in distant offices can edit and review the same document at the same time. How, you may wonder, can one company provide all this? Call 1-800-475-3555 or http://www.mci.com to find out.

©MCI Telecommunications Corporation, 1996

## LOS ANGELES (Continued)
### Conferencing (Continued)

### CONFERENCECALLSERVICE
*WHERE LAWYERS PUT THEIR BEST IDEAS ON THE LINE*

ConferenceCallService is a worldwide teleconferencing provider offering high quality, reliable connections at affordable rates. In addition to standard teleconferencing services, ConferenceCallService offers many special features and services tailor made for the legal community. Our experience with the legal profession makes us uniquely qualified to handle calls from several to several hundred participants. ConferenceCallService, to enhance your teleconferencing experience, also provides the latest in teleconferencing equipment.

**Standard Services:**

- Operator Dialed Conference
- 800 Dial-In Conference
- Regular Dial-In Conference
- Tape Recording
- Transcription Services
- Polling and Q&A Conferences

**Special Services:**

- *Conference Mail℠* - A digital recording of your conference, accessible 24 hours a day.
- *Show and Tell℠* - Document/Computer Conferencing that allows the sharing of documents between multiple locations. All you need is a PC and a modem.
- *Simulfax℠* Broadcast Fax - Faxes can be sent to multiple locations at the same time.
- *Customized Billing* - Invoices that include court and matter number for easy reference and client billing.

*The
ConferenceCallService
100% Performance Pledge*

At ConferenceCallService,
we are responsible for the quality
of your conference call.

We pride ourselves on superior
client service, and guarantee it 100%.

Anything less than your complete
satisfaction is unacceptable to us.

If our service does not meet your
highest expectations, we'll make it right.

ConferenceCallService
(800) 272-5663

**SEE OUR AD ON PAGE CAA44S**

---

### Intercall/InView

8420 West Bryn Mawr-Suite 400
Chicago, Illinois 60631
(312) 399-1528 Fax:(312)399-1588
E-mail: elochner@itchold.com
24 Hr. Reservations: 1-800-374-2441

#### InterCall

Preparing and conducting successful conferences is time consuming and costly. When you want high return on your investment, high participation is essential.

InterCall has focused on the interactive technology for today's corporate executives. We have invested in the technology and systems necessary to provide reliability, consistency, and quality.

*InterCall is committed to the future of each company it serves by offering the following:*

- **Program Recruiting**-Intercall will customize a recruitment strategy that offers personal and individual contact

- **Program Registration**-Monitor the enrollment of your upcoming live meeting or conference call with Intercall's weekly update of registered participants. Now a single report tells you who's on the list and how many.

- **Program Confirmation**-Our staff will confirm each participant's registration prior to your live meeting or audioteleconference call.

- **Fulfillment Services**-Intercall mailing service can get the materials to your participants prior to and during your program.

#### InView

*We make video bridging as easy as a telephone call.*

The future is in video conferencing, and InterCall has been there and back again. The proof is in its streamlined InView Multipoint Videoconferencing service, which allows customers to set-up video conferences the same day they call-not tomorrow.

Customers simply call InView's Reservation Center anytime, 24-hours-a-day, 7 days-a-week, and their video conference becomes a priority. They get the conference extension options they need, full-service technical support, and integrated video and audio bridging on the same call. It's the advantage of being there with time to spare.

- Local dedicated Account Manager
- Dial-in/<u>Dial-out</u> Service (InView will set up the call for you)
- ASAP/Ad-hoc conferences with set-ups at a moments notice
- Same day site certification (including ASAP conference with non-certified sites)
- 24 hr.- 7 days/wk. reservations with same day conferencing
- Live operator assistance at no charge

*(This Listing Continued)*

# SERVICES, SUPPLIERS, CONSULTANTS

## INTERCALL (Continued)

- Proactive technical support and help desk (full monitoring of connections for entire call)
- No cancellation fees
- Automatic call extension or 10 minute end time notification
- Echo free audio bridging add ons
- Fax confirmation to each site
- Cascading
- Per minute/Per site billing
- Centralized, Decentralized and Department Billing or Custom Billing Options

- Reservations 1-800-603-9402
- International Reservations 706-645-6865
- www.inview.net

**Fast. Convenient. Flexible.**

**General Description:**

networkMCI® is a complete portfolio of communications and information services solutions that gives you the competitive advantage in today's rapidly changing business environment.

Competing successfully in today's business requires you to work smarter. One way to do this is by improving how your firm communicates. If you can exchange information faster and more effectively with clients and colleagues, your company will be more productive, more responsive and ultimately, more profitable.

At the heart of networkMCI Conferencing is our global operations centers located in North America, Europe and Asia-Pacific. It allows you to communicate with anyone, almost anywhere in the world. We provide four core services: Audioconferencing, Document Conferencing, Videoconferencing and Tele-Management Services.

**Audioconferencing Services:**

Audioconferencing gives you the flexibility to hold meetings any time you need to, no matter where you are. With audioconferencing we can:

- Record and transcribe your call
- Conduct a survey during your conference in which participants respond using their telephone keypads
- Provide language interpretation
- Fax information to all conference participants before your call

**Document Conferencing Services:**

With Document Conferencing, you and remote clients or colleagues can review documents using your personal computers. Document Conferencing allows you to:

- Edit and review documents with distant colleagues right from your PC
- Communicate with the aid of clear, full-color visuals
- Share almost any document in your PC
- Work in real time

**Videoconferencing Services:**

Videoconferencing enables you to bring a group of people together for

(This Listing Continued)

## CALIFORNIA—LOS ANGELES

### NETWORKMCI CONFERENCING℠ (Continued)

a face-to-face meeting. You can quickly hold an impromptu meeting with others in different offices and save thousands of dollars on travel costs. Videoconferencing lets you:

- Meet face-to-face right from your office
- Speed decision-making and company responsiveness
- Save time and travel costs

**Tele-Management Services:**

Tele-Management Services are convenient and flexible electronic management tools that can help you better coordinate your upcoming conferences as well as your daily business operations. With Tele-Management you can:

- Plan conferences and other events in a variety of ways
- You can simultaneously distribute announcements or invitations to unlimited destinations in minutes
- Provide automated response tracking to better forecast attendance for events
- Tape and broadcast the event for those who could not attend

HOW DO YOU MAINTAIN YOUR COMPETITIVE EDGE IN TODAY'S BUSINESS ENVIRONMENT? NETWORKMCI, THAT'S HOW.

networkMCI Conferencing
1-800-475-5000

8750 W. Bryn Mawr, #900
Chicago, IL 60631

***SEE OUR AD ON PAGE CAA45S***

---

Need an extra copy of the **Martindale-Hubbell Law Directory**? Or of a specific volume? Call Martindale-Hubbell Customer Service at 1-800-526-4902

---

Now you can find the lawyer even if you don't know where he or she practices - with the **Martindale-Hubbell Law Directory Alphabetical Index.**

## LOS ANGELES (Continued)
### Conferencing (Continued)

### POLYCOM, INC.
2584 Junction Ave.
San Jose, California 95134-1902
Telephone: (408) 526-9000
Facsimile: (408) 526-9100

Polycom develops, manufactures and markets audioconferencing and dataconferencing products that facilitate meetings at a distance. Polycom has established itself as the leading worldwide provider of audioconferencing equipment with products such as SoundStation, SoundStation Premier and SoundPoint.

At $299 SoundPoint is Polycom's most affordable, high-quality audioconferencing solution for the office. SoundPoint uses a single hypercardioid microphone and full-duplex, two-way communications to make sure your words get heard. You can also connect the SoundPoint PC to a personal computer, opening a new horizon of high-quality, full-duplex audio for internet telephony and computer-based videoconferencing.

SoundStation is the most recognized and respected conference phone in the industry. At $499, SoundStation is excellent for executive office suites and small-to medium-sized conference rooms. It is also being used, with great success in the legal profession by judges and attorneys through the CourtCall program, allowing courtroom appearances via conference phone.

The new SoundStation Premier delivers the absolute best sound quality available at any price. Exclusive liquid crystal display. intelligent mic mixing, high-fidelity speaker and the industry's first infrared wireless remote make the feature-rich SoundStation Premier the right choice for superior audiocenferencing in even your largest conference room.

Polycom's innovative ShowStation document conferencing projector enables real-time exchange of data and other images over ordinary phone lines via the rapidly emerging T.120 dataconferencing protocol standard. ShowStation is a cost-effective, easy-to-use, high-resolution dataconferencing solution that enables groups in multiple locations to simultaneously view, edit. and annotate paper or electronic documents and data in a lights-on environment. Polycom sells its products through its direct sales force and an extensive network of resellers and OEMs.

For more information, call 1-800-POLYCOM (765-9266) or visit the Polycom home page at http://www.polycom.com. Polycom®, the Polycom logo design, and SoundStation® are registered trademarks and ShowStation™, SoundStation Premier™, and SoundPoint™ are trademarks of Polycom, Inc. in the U.S. and various countries. © 1997 Polycom, Inc. All rights reserved.

---

The **Martindale-Hubbell Law Directory** is now available online...exclusively through the LEXIS®-NEXIS® services.

## U.S. ROBOTICS

ConferenceLink™ conference speakerphones

When you are on an important call with a client, you need to sound your best. That's why we've designed the ConferenceLink family of conference speakerphones to outperform the ordinary office phone you currently use for conference calls. Finally, you can conduct hands-free conference calls that are both **Professional** and **Productive**, while reducing expenses with less time and travel.

Whether you need to negotiate a contract, take a deposition, or hold a strategy meeting, ConferenceLink speakerphones ensure the high quality communication that your clients expect. Full duplex technology lets you and your client talk and listen at the same time without clipped sentences, missed words, or one-way conversation. 360° coverage picks up all voices in the room.

Whether you're looking for a conference speakerphone for your office, large or small conference room or boardroom, there's a ConferenceLink to fit your needs. The CS1000 is designed for conference rooms and larger offices. The CS1050 can also plug into your PC for full duplex audio with videoconferencing and Internet voice calls. The CS1070-1 is specifically designed to connect directly into a Siemens ROLM PBX system and can also plug into your PC. The CS850 comes in a convenient desktop size, ideal for offices and small conference rooms.

ConferenceLink speakerphones are affordable and it only takes a phone call to locate a dealer near you, just call 1-88-4PERFORM (1-888-473-7367).

U.S. Robotics
7770 North Frontage Road
Skokie, IL 60613

---

Now it's easy to find lawyers practicing a specific area of law! Simply consult the
**Martindale-Hubbell Law Directory Areas of Practice Index.**

---

Fast ... Easy ... Flexible...
**The Martindale-Hubbell Law Directory on CD-ROM** gives you instant access through multiple search criteria to information on over 900,000 lawyers and law firms. For more details and a FREE demonstration disc, call **1-800-323-3288**.

## CONSTRUCTION CONSULTANTS

**Coopers & Lybrand L.L.P.**

a professional services firm

1751 Pinnacle Drive
McLean, Virginia 22102
(800) 527-7686

Responsiveness and credibility are essential ingredients in successful technical support of construction litigation. When construction litigators need dependable help and need it fast, they also want the confidence of getting the best. In this environment, attorneys, sureties, contractors, owners, design professionals and other parties in construction disputes often turn to Coopers & Lybrand for our deeply specialized knowledge and know how in resolving such disputes. Coopers & Lybrand is an industry leader in the use of business, financial and project management skills, along with state-of-the-art technology, in the prevention and resolution of complex construction claim issues. We assist counsel and clients with the entire dispute resolution process, from project control and preemptive services through litigation and settlement.

With our National Construction Litigation Practice based in McLean, Virginia and our network of experienced colleagues in major cities throughout the country, we are ready to work with counsel and clients wherever necessary and at every stage of the construction claims and dispute resolution process. Our group members' diverse technical training, construction industry experience, and analytical skills allow us to respond quickly and effectively to help win a wide spectrum of construction disputes. Our experience is built on working full time with counsel and clients to help successfully resolve construction disputes quickly and cost-effectively. Our experts have extensive hands-on experience in the issues surrounding a construction dispute. These areas include:

- Contract defaults
- Changed work
- Defective specifications
- Breach of contract
- Contract administration
- Troubled loans
- Cost allocation/allowability
- Lost profits
- CPM schedules analysis
- Delay and disruption
- Acceleration
- Loss of productivity
- Contract termination
- Projected/future costs
- Home office costs
- Structural failure

**Jax Kneppers Associates, Inc.**
**Construction Consultants**
(800) 833-4371
jaxknepper@aol.com

2950 Buskirk Ave., Suite 180
Walnut Creek, CA 94596
Tel: (510) 933-3914
Fax: (510) 933-9370

575 Anton Blvd., Suite 300
Costa Mesa, CA 92626
Tel: (714) 432-6343
Fax: (714) 432-6344

JKA's professional standard and successful record are built upon the practical experience and analytical training of its team members. Our practice offers design, construction management, and litigation related services. Internationally educated and familiar with both state and national requirements/standards, the JKA team is an indispensable resource for clients.

### SERVICES

- Defective Construction Claims
- Delay Impact Analysis
- Schedule Analysis
- Construction Cost Analysis and Estimates
- Value Engineering
- Cost to Reconstruct/Reproduce (Eminent Domain)
- Insurance Losses
- Standard of Care Analysis for Architects, Engineers, and Contractors
- Project Management
- Construction Document Preparation
- Trial Exhibits and Graphics
- Expert Witness Testimony
- National and International Experience

### DEGREES AND LICENSES

- Structural and Civil Engineers
- Architects
- Certified Professional Estimators
- Project/Construction Managers
- General Contractors
- ICBO Certified Inspectors

Our engineers, architects, estimators, construction managers, and claims analysts will provide the client, the jury, and the judge with a clear, concise, and total picture of all the issues involved. The JKA professional standard ensures a complete case analysis.

---

**Jerry L. Pollak, A.I.A., A.I.C.P.**
**Architect**
14209 Chandler Blvd.
Sherman Oaks, Ca 91401
Phone: (818) 909-3757
Fax: (818) 997-7999

*See Expert Witness - Construction*

# CALIFORNIA—LOS ANGELES
## MARTINDALE-HUBBELL LAW DIRECTORY 1997

### LOS ANGELES (Continued)
#### Construction Consultants (Continued)

**The Solender Group, Inc.**
11022 Santa Monica Blvd., #220
Los Angeles, CA 90025
Phone: (800) 954-8485
Fax: (310) 445-5160

*See Expert Witness - Construction*

---

**SPEXWEST**
P.O. Box 3861
Laguna Hills, CA 92653

The REAL Construction Experts

You'll want us on YOUR Side

ARCHITECTURAL & ENGINEERING
CONTRACT DOCUMENT ERRORS
CONSTRUCTION DEFECTS
INSPECTIONS & ANALYSIS
RECONSTRUCTION CONSULTING

RESIDENTIAL
COMMERCIAL
INDUSTRIAL

Phone: 714-832-2222
Fax: 714-832-2222

spexwest@earthlink.net

*SEE OUR AD ON PAGE CAA50S*

---

## SPEXWEST

**The REAL Construction Experts**
You'll Want Us On YOUR Side

ARCHITECTURAL & ENGINEERING
CONTRACT DOCUMENT ERRORS
CONSTRUCTION DEFECTS
INSPECTION & ANALYSIS
RECONSTRUCTION CONSULTING

**RESIDENTIAL
COMMERCIAL
INDUSTRIAL**

Phone: 714-832-2222
Fax: 714-832-2222

spexwest@earthlink.net

---

To update your listing
in the **Martindale-Hubbell Law Directory**
call **1-800-MARTIND(ALE)**.

---

**WAGNER · HOHNS · INGLIS · INC.**
*Construction Consultants*
100 High Street
P.O. Box 460
Mount Holly, NJ 08060-0460

Telephone:  609-261-0100
Fax:        609-261-8584
e-mail:     whi@corsa.com
internet:   http://www.corsa.com/whi/

- Alternate Dispute Resolution Consulting
- Expert Witness Testimony
- Delay/Acceleration/Out of Sequence Analysis
- Defective Design/Construction Evaluation
- Change Order Computation
- Construction Audits
- Inspection Reports

WHI has been serving the construction industry, the financial community and the legal profession for over 25 years. WHI combines a broad range of professional talent with the capability to quickly assemble additional specialized personnel based on a client's particular requirements.

WHI can assist clients in negotiations of all kinds of disputes, serve as arbitrators/mediators in dispute resolution, function as a

*(This Listing Continued)*

# SERVICES, SUPPLIERS, CONSULTANTS

# CALIFORNIA—LOS ANGELES

**WAGNER • HOHNS • INGLIS • INC. (Continued)**

partnering facilitator and bring innovative solutions to contemporary construction problems.

WHI's full-time staff of civil, mechanical, structural, electrical and industrial engineers, architects, construction managers, scheduling consultants, construction cost specialists, and support personnel, allows **WHI** to provide professional expertise in all construction areas by providing solutions to construction related problems.

Since its founding, **WHI** has become one of the recognized leaders in resolving and mitigating construction disputes. **WHI** has served thousands of clients on cases representing billions of dollars worth of construction.

Other offices are located in:

600 South Lake Avenue, Suite 500
Pasadena, CA 91106-6245
818-578-0817 • FAX 818-578-0254
e-mail: whi-pas@ix.netcom.com

1800 Sutter Street, Suite 260
Concord, CA 94520-2500
510-609-1570 • FAX 510-609-1580
e-mail: whi-con@ix.netcom.com

3280 Northdale Boulevard, Suite 309A
Tampa, FL 33624-1841
813-962-1618 • 813-963-1229
e-mail: whi-fla@ix.netcom.com

600 West Jackson Boulevard, Suite 701
Chicago, IL 60661-5612
312-627-9500 • FAX 312-627-9660
e-mail: whi-chi@ix.netcom.com

---

Need an extra copy of the **Martindale-Hubbell Law Directory?** Or of a specific volume? Call Martindale-Hubbell Customer Service at
**1-800-526-4902**

## CONSTRUCTION CONSULTANTS- CONSTRUCTION DEFECTS

### Pringle & Associates
### STRUCTURAL INSPECTION CONSULTANTS
### 800-598-1970

*Serving Architects, Law Firms, Structural Engineers, and other professionals. SIC has earned a solid reputation for handling delicate cases with the utmost concern for accuracy and confidentiality.*

*Successfully providing Licensed Special/Deputy Inspections for projects throughout California has given our field teams the knowledge and ability to get your special project done right, assuring minimum intrusion to your project site and it's occupants.*

- Non Destructive Examinations
- Forensic Investigations
- Legal Support
- Crack Mapping
- As-Built Structural Plans
- Photographic Documentation

*Principal Structural Inspector*
Ronald "Sandy" Pringle

*Licenses*
Special/Deputy Inspector
    City of Los Angeles - County of Los Angeles - City of Long Beach - Orange County - City of Burbank - City of Manhattan Beach - City of Irvine - City of Newport Beach - City of Pasadena
Concrete Field Testing Technician
ICBO Certified Special Instructor
ACIA Registered Construction Inspector
Licensed California Contractor

*Memberships*
Seismic Special/Deputy Inspector Association (SSDIA)
Structural Engineers Association of Southern California (SEAOSC)
State of California, Office of Emergency Services (OES)
Joint Committee Residential Repair & Retrofit
CA Building Officials (CALBO) & Special Inspection Liaison
State of California Seismic Safety Commission (SSC)
International Conference of Building Officials (ICBO)
American Society for Testing Materials (ASTM)
American Construction Inspectors Association (ACIA)
American Concrete Institute (ACI)
American Society for Nondestructive Testing (ASNT)
American Welding Society (AWS)

*From nail spacing to shear transfers, our field proven Forensic Investigators are remarkably skilled at ferreting out construction errors and omissions from the approved plans. In many cases we may be able to help you identify your potential litigants with just a preliminary site survey. At SIC we give you the data you need when you need it.*

*Call today for a FREE consultation, company information packet, and to find out why "high profile" professionals and institutions like UCLA regularly call on us for support.*

    office - 310-798-6868
    fax - 310-376-5294
    email - sandyp@beachnet.com
    http://www.beachnet.com/~sandyp/index.htm

# CALIFORNIA—LOS ANGELES
## MARTINDALE-HUBBELL LAW DIRECTORY 1997

### LOS ANGELES (Continued)

## COPIER SERVICES

*Micro Quick*
(800) 655-FAST
(3278)

Serving All of Southern California

- volume copying specialist
- mobile photocopying at any location
- immediate same day copying service
- clear copies from poor original (guaranteed)

CD ROM document storage and retrieval
(no software needed)

ADDITIONAL SERVICES:
messenger service
subpoena preparation & service
court filings & fax filings
court indexing & research
licensed process servers
x-ray duplication

*Micro Quick*
It's our image you can count on!

visit us at www.microquick.com

Bonded  Certified  Insured

## CORPORATION COMPANIES

5670 Wilshire Boulevard, Suite 750
Los Angeles, CA 90036
Toll Free: 800-458-0700
Phone: 213-954-3854
Fax: 213-954-0871
E-Mail: info@cscinfo.com
Website Address: http://www.cscinfo.com

Serving the legal, corporate and financial communities since 1899, **CSC The United States Corporation Company**® is one of the nation's leading providers of public records document filing and retrieval. We also offer a complete suite of Windows-based software solutions designed to improve legal workload management including: **CSC DIRECT**™ for on-line corporate filing services and research, **UCCXPRESS**™ for automated UCC filings, **PowerTXT** for intelligent document assembly and **Secretariat** for corporate secretary management. Through our nationwide network of 29 offices and affiliates in 160 countries worldwide, we offer a complete selection of public records filing, corporate services, search and registered agent services.

---

Now you can find the lawyer even if you don't know where he or she practices - with the **Martindale-Hubbell Law Directory Alphabetical Index.**

---

The **Martindale-Hubbell Law Directory** is now available online...exclusively through the LEXIS®-NEXIS® services.

---

Now it's easy to find lawyers practicing a specific area of law! Simply consult the **Martindale-Hubbell Law Directory Areas of Practice Index.**

---

Fast ... Easy ... Flexible...
**The Martindale-Hubbell Law Directory on CD-ROM** gives you instant access through multiple search criteria to information on over 900,000 lawyers and law firms. For more details and a FREE demonstration disc, call **1-800-323-3288**.

---

To update your listing in the **Martindale-Hubbell Law Directory** call **1-800-MARTIND(ALE)**.

SERVICES, SUPPLIERS, CONSULTANTS                             CALIFORNIA—LOS ANGELES

## COURT REPORTERS

**A.A. NICHOLS, INC.**
CERTIFIED COURT REPORTERS
SINCE 1976

### THE WAVE OF THE FUTURE

Certified Court Reporters
Certified Legal Videographers

**TOLL FREE: 1-800-227-0577**

GATEWAY TOWERS
1801 Avenue of the Stars
Suite 640
Los Angeles, California 90067
**(Adjacent to Beverly Hills)**
FAX: 602-998-7228

REGISTERED PROFESSIONAL REPORTERS
CALIFORNIA CERTIFIED REPORTERS

**A Full Service Reporting and
Video Production Company**

Serving the Bar for over 21 years
Experts in Complex Litigation
Medical and Technical Deposition Specialists
Interpreters & Translators
Daily and Expedited Transcripts on Request
Large Deluxe Conference Rooms
Convenient Locations with Easy-Parking
Videotape and Teleconferencing Facilities
Videotape/Laserdisc presentations
Transcript/Video Synchronization
Certified Legal Video Specialists
Adjacent to Luxury Hotels
Prompt Out-of-State Delivery

Complimentary Condensed Transcripts & Concordances
State of the Art Computer-Aided Transcriptions
Video and Litigation Support Formats
Realtime Translation

**MANY OFFICE LOCATIONS THROUGHOUT
CALIFORNIA & ARIZONA**
including San Diego, Del Mar, San Francisco,
La Jolla, Newport Beach, Palm Springs, Sacramento,
Irvine, Orange County, Los Angeles, Phoenix, Tucson,
Scottsdale and All Surrounding Areas

**ADDITIONAL DEPOSITION SUITES AT SAN DIEGO, PHOENIX,
SAN FRANCISCO, ORANGE COUNTY
AND LOS ANGELES AIRPORTS**

Member of:
National Court Reporters Association
California Court Reporters Association
Arizona Court Reporters Association
Michigan Court Reporters Association

***SEE OUR AD ON PAGE CAA54S***

## ABA Reporters

Telephone: 800-434-TEXT
415-391-2999
Fax: 415-391-0753
www.abacomm.com

**"THE EXPERTS IN TECHNICAL REPORTING"** ℠

San Francisco * Marin * Alameda * Solano
Santa Clara * Sonoma * Napa * San Mateo
Contra Costa * Sacramento Counties

- Conference Rooms
- Depositions
- Real Time
- Captioning
- Condensed Transcripts
- Master Word Indexing
- Video - National Certified Legal Video Specialists
- Deposition Summary Services
- Large Staff of Experienced Reporters
- Medical/Expert Witness
- Arbitrations/Hearings
- ASCII/AMICUS/CAT-Links/Discovery ZX/LiveNote
- Document Production

SERVING ALL OF NORTHERN CALIFORNIA

Members:
- National Court Reporters Association
- California Court Reporters Association
- Bay Area General Reporters

**ABA REPORTERS**
A Division of
Linda L. Chavez, CSR, Inc.

Telephone: 415-391-2999
Fax: 415-391-0753

115 Sansome Street, Suite 1050
San Francisco, CA 94104

State-Certified Shorthand Reporters

AbA Reporters is widely respected for its expertise in transcribing legal, medical, and other formal proceedings with a court-reporting staff that offers over 100 years of combined professional service. We proudly uphold the highest standards for accuracy and stylistic consistency, and especially appreciate and emphasize the client's need for a dependably punctual product.

AbA is a continuously diversifying company, consistently striving to remain on the cutting edge with the latest technologies to more effectively meet our clients' ever-growing needs. Whether it be the need for flexible and mobile services - - including videographic and open or closed captioning - - or simply the accurate sequential marking of exhibits, AbA Reporters delivers experienced reporting capacities and quality transcripts - - on time, every time.

***SEE OUR AD ON PAGE CAA59S***

**A Full Service Reporting and Video Production Company**

**A.A. NICHOLS, INC.**
CERTIFIED COURT REPORTERS
SINCE 1976

*THE WAVE OF THE FUTURE*

**LOS ANGELES**
Century City / Beverly Hills
Gateway Towers
Suite 640
1801 Avenue of the Stars
Los Angeles, CA 90067

**SAN DIEGO**
Downtown
110 West "C" Street
Suite 1300
San Diego, CA 92101

**LA JOLLA**
Downtown
Suite 200
7825 Fay Avenue
La Jolla, CA 92037

**SCOTTSDALE**
Mercado Del Lago
Suite 207
8300 North Hayden Road
Scottsdale, AZ 85258

### Serving all of Arizona & California

*A Full Service Reporting & Video Production Company*
*Specializing in Medical & Technical Depositions*

**CENTRAL SCHEDULING**
**Toll Free 1-800-227-0577**
**Fax 1-602-998-7228**

**MEDICAL/TECHNICAL/SCIENTIFIC REPORTERS**

Malpractice • Engineering • Aviation • Mechanical
Accident Reconstruction • Banking • Corporate
Construction • Maritime • General Litigation

### In-House Certified Legal Videographers

- State-of-the-Art Computer Transcriptions
- Realtime Translations
- Multiple Audio/Visual and Litigation Support Formats
- Teleconferencing Facilities
- 24-hour/Weekends/Holiday Service
- Condensed Transcripts & Concordances Full Text Listing Indexes
- Large Deluxe Conference Facilities
- Convenient Locations

**Other Office, Private Club & Airport Locations Include:**

**PHOENIX, TUCSON, LA JOLLA, LOS ANGELES, NEWPORT BEACH, IRVINE, SAN DIEGO, SACRAMENTO, SAN FRANCISCO, ORANGE COUNTY, SCOTTSDALE & MAJOR METROPOLITAN AREAS THROUGHOUT ARIZONA AND CALIFORNIA**

## 1-800-227-0577

# LEGAL EASE.

Since 1981, Maxene Weinberg Agency has proven that Court and Deposition Reporting firms *are not* created equal. Our experience and reputation make your job a lot *easier*.

Our select staff of highly trained Certified Court and Deposition Reporters use the latest state-of-the-art equipment and techniques for timely and accurate transcripts.

Maxene Weinberg Agency also offers the most advanced **Real-Time Services** in the industry to attorneys who want to have *instant access* to all of their deposition testimony. We simply connect our computer to yours (or we can provide you with one of our laptops).

Please feel free to contact me to schedule an appointment. We can put the "*ease*" back into *your* "legalese".

*Prompt. Experienced. Professional. Dedicated To Better Service.*
**REALTIME & CIR COURT REPORTERS • INSTANT TRANSCRIPTS
IMPAQT CODING • MAXCAM℠ VIDEO TAPING SERVICES
CONDENSED TRANSCRIPTS • KEYWORD INDEXES • DISCOVERY ZX
CAT LINKS • ASCII's • COMPLIMENTARY CONFERENCE SUITES**

**Call Toll-Free: 800-640-1949**
or visit us at http://www.interim.com/legal

## MAXENE WEINBERG AGENCY
AN Interim LEGAL SERVICES℠ COMPANY

CERTIFIED COURT & DEPOSITION REPORTERS

**Five Convenient Locations:**

| **Los Angeles** | **Mission Viejo** | **Newport Beach** | **San Diego** | **San Bernardino** |
|---|---|---|---|---|
| *Close to LAX and downtown.* | *Within 75 miles of San Diego.* | *Easy access from John Wayne Airport and close to Irvine and Costa Mesa.* | *Convenient downtown location just minutes from the airport.* | *Serving Pomona, Riverside and the entire Inland Empire.* |

KARYN ABBOTT
CSR 5272/RPR

# ABBOTT & ASSOCIATES

**CERTIFIED SHORTHAND REPORTERS AND LEGAL VIDEO SERVICES**

## (800) 266-2268

714 W. OLYMPIC BLVD., STE. 1112
LOS ANGELES, CALIFORNIA 90015

**FAX (213) 749-0644**

**COMPLIMENTARY CONFERENCE ROOM**

**FREE AIRPORT TRANSPORTATION**

ORANGE COUNTY OFFICE
16462 GRIMAUD LANE
HUNTINGTON BEACH, CA 92649

**SERVING LOS ANGELES, ORANGE, RIVERSIDE, SAN DIEGO, SAN BERNARDINO, VENTURA COUNTIES**

ASCII, DISCOVERY & CATLINKS DISKS, CONDENSED TRANSCRIPTS, KEYWORD INDEXES, IN-HOUSE VIDEO AND INTERPRETING SERVICES, DOCUMENT COPYING, REALTIME REPORTING, DAILY AND EXPEDITED DELIVERY, SERVICE OF SUBPOENAS

DEPOSITIONS, HEARINGS, ARBITRATIONS, AND COURT APPEARANCES

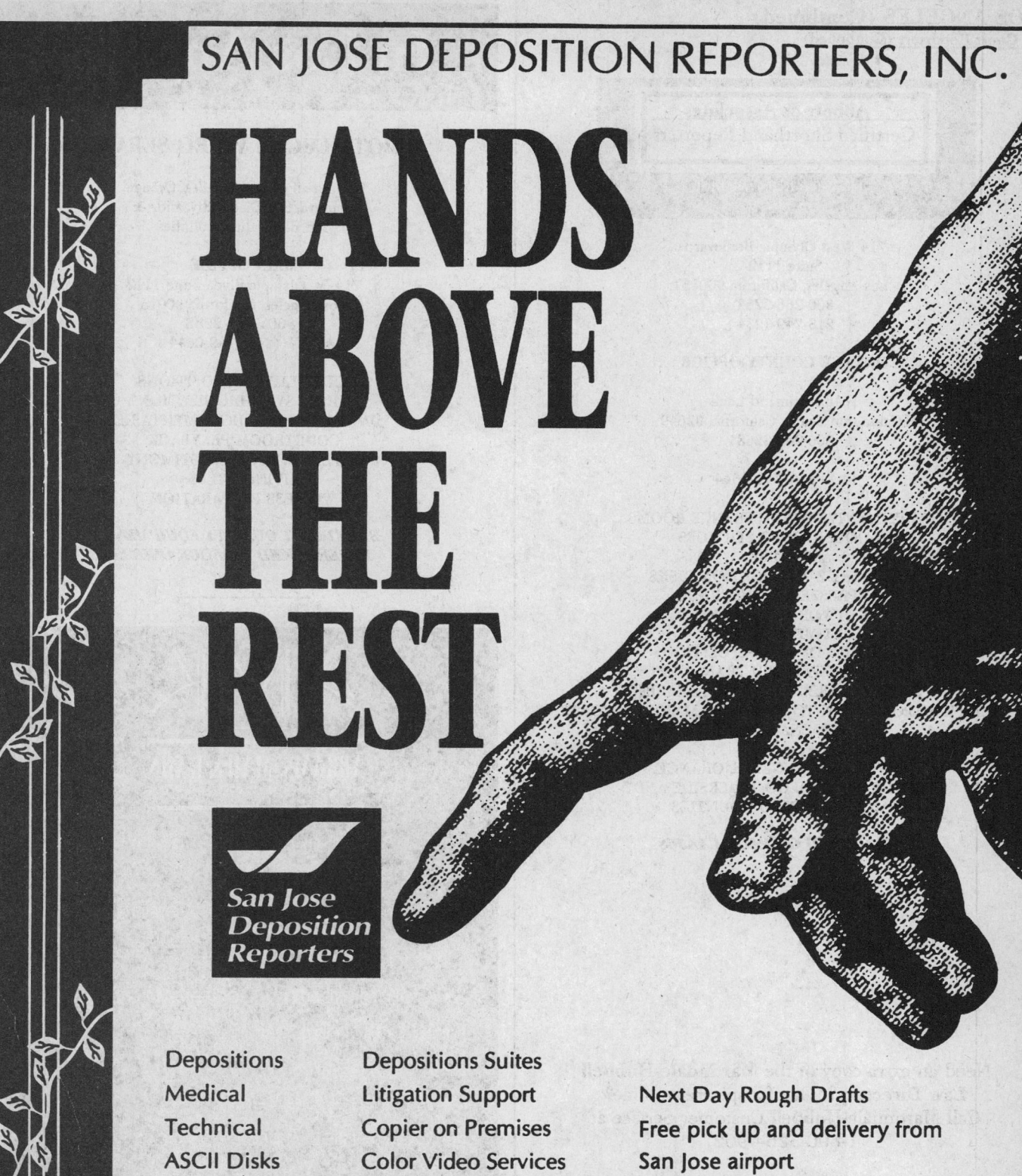

# CALIFORNIA—LOS ANGELES
## MARTINDALE-HUBBELL LAW DIRECTORY 1997

### LOS ANGELES (Continued)
#### Court Reporters (Continued)

**Abbott & Associates**
**Certified Shorthand Reporters**

The Court Reporting Firm
For The 90's

714 West Olympic Boulevard
Suite 1112
Los Angeles, California 90015
800-266-2268
213-749-1234

**ORANGE COUNTY OFFICE**

16462 Grimaud Lane
Huntington Beach, California 92649
800-266-2268

FAX: 213-749-0644

COMPLIMENTARY CONFERENCE ROOMS
IN-HOUSE VIDEO SERVICES
ASCII DISKS
DISCOVERY Z-X LITIGATION DISKS
COMPRESSED TRANSCRIPTS
KEYWORD INDEXING
REALTIME REPORTING
ARCHIVING OF ALL DEPOSITIONS
DAILY AND EXPEDITED TRANSCRIPTS
DEPOSITIONS, ARBITRATIONS & HEARINGS
FREE TRANSPORTATION TO AND FROM MAJOR AIRPORTS
SUBPOENA SERVICE

SERVING LOS ANGELES, ORANGE,
VENTURA, SAN DIEGO, RIVERSIDE AND
SAN BERNARDINO COUNTIES

*SEE OUR AD ON PAGE CAA56S*

---

Need an extra copy of the **Martindale-Hubbell Law Directory**? Or of a specific volume?
Call Martindale-Hubbell Customer Service at
1-800-526-4902

---

## In Los Angeles

### ABBOTT LEGAL VIDEO SERVICES

Serving all of Los Angeles, Orange,
Ventura, San Diego, Riverside &
San Bernardino Counties

**MAIN OFFICE**
714 W. Olympic Blvd., Suite 1112
Los Angeles, California 90015
(800) 266-2268
FAX: (213) 749-0644

VIDEOTAPED DEPOSITIONS
VIDEO SYNCHRONIZATION
DAY IN THE LIFE DOCUMENTARIES
COURTROOM PLAYBACK
EXPERT WITNESS TESTIMONY
LIVING WILLS
WITNESS PREPARATION

*BROADCAST-QUALITY EQUIPMENT*
*EXPERIENCED VIDEOGRAPHERS*

---

**ABRAMS, MAH & KAHN**
REPORTING SERVICE

4101 Birch Street • Suite 130
Newport Beach • California 92660

- Serving Los Angeles, Riverside, San Bernardino, San Diego and Orange Counties
- Complimentary Conference Rooms
- Litigation Support
- Realtime
- Two-week Delivery
- Condensed Transcripts and Master Keyword Index

714 • 261 • 8686
213 • 848 • 8686
800 • 622 • 0226

CAA58S

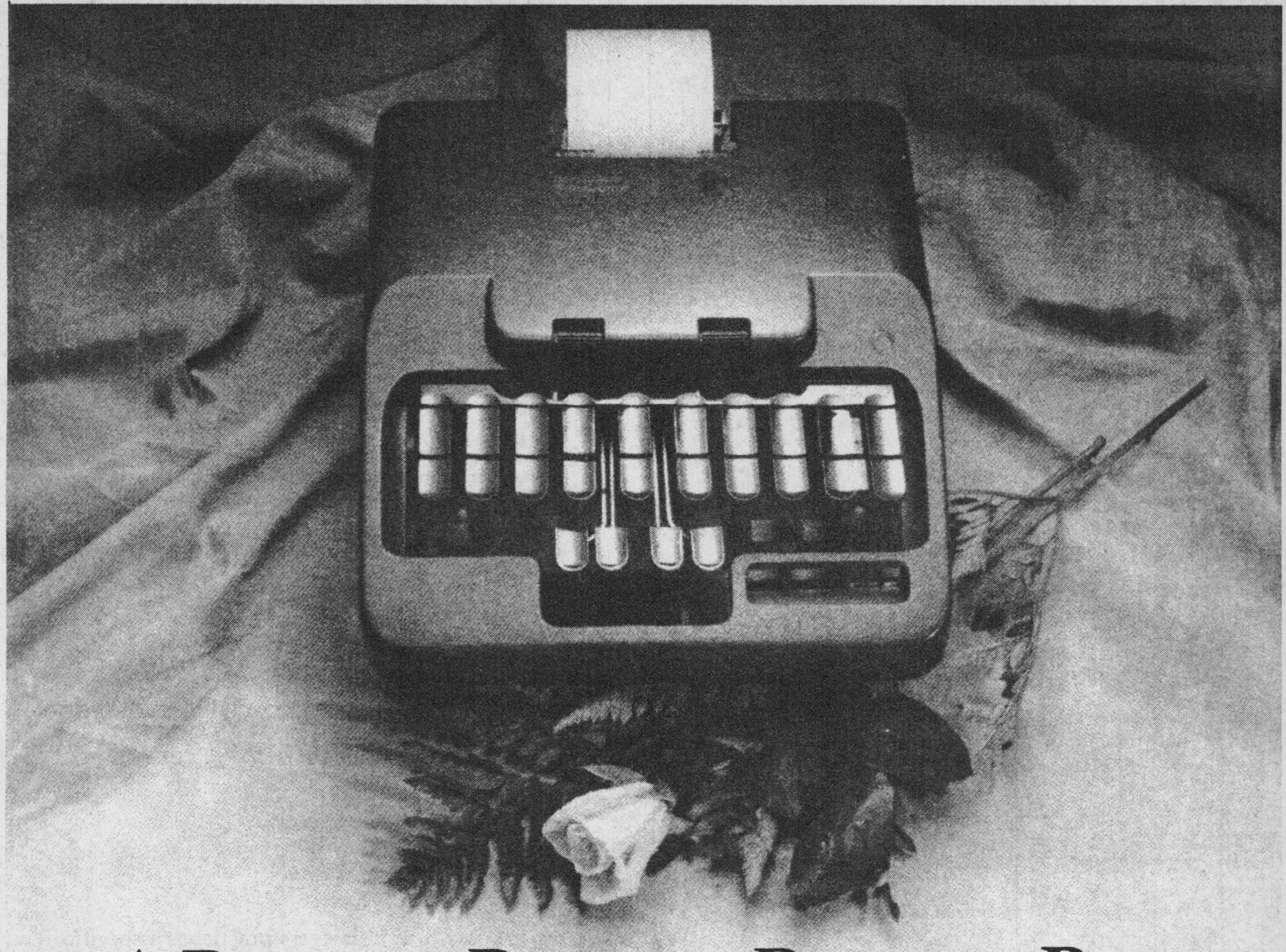

# A Rose is a Rose is a Rose is a Rose
### (AND NOT A "ROWS" OR A "RUSE" OR A "NOSE")

During the deposition, you asked how the witness "derived the information". In the transcript, your question shouldn't turn into how the witness "arrived at the station," "enjoyed her vacation" or "survived her immolation".

Responsible court reporting and quality control are interchangeable—you can't have one without the other.

So when you receive our transcript, you won't see homonyms or unintentional rhymes.
What was said is what you'll get, pure and simple.

Our product IS our reputation. When you receive it, you'll see that "everything is coming up roses" when the botanist speaks, and that "everything is coming up noses" when the witness is an ear, nose and throat man.

## WE WOULDN'T HAVE IT ANY OTHER WAY.

**ABA REPORTERS**
*A Division of Linda L. Chavez, CSR, Inc.*
115 Sansome Street, Suite 1050
San Francisco, CA 94104 • (415) 391-2999
800-434-TEXT

## LOS ANGELES (Continued)
### Court Reporters (Continued)

**ABRAMS, MAH & KAHN**
Court Reporting Service

4101 Birch Street
Suite 130
Newport Beach, California 92660
Los Angeles, California Telephone: 213-848-8686
Newport Beach, California Telephone: 714-261-8686
FAX: 714-261-6688
800-622-0226

Serving all of:
• Los Angeles •
• Orange County •
• San Diego •
• Riverside •
• San Bernardino •

Realtime
Condensed Transcripts
Complimentary Conference Rooms
Computer-aided Transcription
Video Taping and Interpreters
• Two-week Delivery •
Daily Copy Available

Experienced in:
• Multi-party Complex Litigation •
and
• Technical Testimony •

*SEE OUR AD ON PAGE CAA58S*

---

Now you can find the lawyer even if you don't know where he or she practices - with the **Martindale-Hubbell Law Directory Alphabetical Index.**

---

The **Martindale-Hubbell Law Directory** is now available online...exclusively through the LEXIS®-NEXIS® services.

---

## ACCUTRAN REPORTING SERVICES
Certified Shorthand Reporters

SERVING
LOS ANGELES AND ORANGE COUNTIES
***
HUNTINGTON BEACH, CALIFORNIA
714/374-3137
FAX 714/374-3139
***
PASADENA, CALIFORNIA
818/577-5995
FAX 818/577-5997
***
SANTA MONICA, CALIFORNIA
310/917-2211
***
800/562-5567
***
Depositions, Arbitrations, Trials
Specializing in Rush and Daily Transcript Delivery
ASCII, Discovery ZX & CatLinks Computer Disks
Condensed Transcripts, Videotape, Real Time
Deposition Suites Throughout Los Angeles
***
Member
National Court Reporters Association
California Court Reporters Association
***

WE ARE COMMITTED TO COMPLETE CLIENT SATISFACTION

REFERENCES AVAILABLE UPON REQUEST

---

Now it's easy to find lawyers practicing a specific area of law! Simply consult the **Martindale-Hubbell Law Directory Areas of Practice Index.**

---

Fast ... Easy ... Flexible...
**The Martindale-Hubbell Law Directory on CD-ROM** gives you instant access through multiple search criteria to information on over 900,000 lawyers and law firms. For more details and a FREE demonstration disc, call 1-800-323-3288.

SERVICES, SUPPLIERS, CONSULTANTS — CALIFORNIA—LOS ANGELES

# Deposition in the Bay Area?

Leave the details up to...

## Harry A. Cannon, Inc.

### Full Service Court Reporting & Associated Support

- Conference rooms seating up to 40 persons available at no charge.
- Daily & expedited copy/Real-Time
- ASCII & Discovery ZX, Imaging in VZN
- Compressed transcipts
- Video capabilities
- Medical & Business Records per Evidence Code
- Professional photocopying

*Serving the California Legal Community for over 45 years*

**HARRY A. CANNON, INC.**
Certified Reporters and Notaries
550 California Street
Sacramento Street Tower, Suite 600
San Francisco, CA 94104

**(415) 391-7421 • Fax (415) 391-4978**

CALIFORNIA—LOS ANGELES  MARTINDALE-HUBBELL LAW DIRECTORY 1997

## LOS ANGELES (Continued)
Court Reporters (Continued)

### A. EDELIST DEPOSITION SERVICE, INC.

**CALIFORNIA STATE LICENSED CERTIFIED SHORTHAND REPORTERS**
SERVING SOUTHERN CALIFORNIA SINCE 1979

15300 VENTURA BOULEVARD, SUITE 216
SHERMAN OAKS, CALIFORNIA 91403

**COMPLIMENTARY CONFERENCE ROOMS - STATEWIDE**

**REPORTER AVAILABILITY - STATEWIDE**

(818) 788-3376     (800) 936-3375 (STATEWIDE)
(818) 788-3376 (FAX)

---

**REPORTER EXPERTISE:**

\*\*\*WORKERS' COMPENSATION     PERSONAL INJURY\*\*\*
\*\*\*ARBITRATIONS\*\*\*
\*\*\*BUSINESS LITIGATION     LEGAL & MEDICAL MALPRACTICE\*\*\*
\*\*\*LABOR\*\*\*
\*\*\*ENTERTAINMENT     FAMILY LAW\*\*\*
\*\*\*WRONGFUL TERMINATION     AVIATION\*\*\*

---

**PRODUCTS AND SERVICES:**

\*\*REALTIME     \*\*FIRST PASS

\*\*ASCII DISKS     \*\*DISCOVERY ZX

\*\*FULL KEYWORD INDEXES

\*\*CONDENSED TRANSCRIPTS

\*\*VOLUME CALENDARING

\*\*VOLUME BILLINGS     \*\*EXHIBIT HANDLING

\*\*VIDEOTAPING     \*\*TELECOMMUNICATIONS

---

ALLEN H. EDELIST
CALIFORNIA CSR #4140
NATIONAL REGISTERED REPORTER #024376

**MEMBER**
LOS ANGELES GENERAL SHORTHAND REPORTERS ASSOCIATION
CALIFORNIA COURT REPORTERS ASSOCIATION
NATIONAL COURT REPORTERS ASSOCIATION

BOARD OF TRUSTEES: UNIVERSITY OF WEST LOS ANGELES SCHOOL OF LAW

BANK REFERENCE: FIRST LOS ANGELES BANK - CENTURY CITY BRANCH

---

### ALDERSON REPORTING COMPANY, INC.
Worldwide Court Reporting & Litigation Support

*Our record is undeniable.*

For over 60 years we have been the official reporters to . . .
• U.S. Presidents
• U.S. Supreme Court Justices
• Special Presidential Commissions

Our other major clients include:
• International Trade Agencies
• Business Thinktank Organizations
• Academic Institutions,
• and THE TOUGHEST LITIGATORS AROUND THE WORLD.

Through our strategic alliance with Arthur Anderson, we also serve legal counsel representing many major corporations.

You can count on our accuracy in every detail. With our on-line tracking databases, we can answer any of your questions at any hour of the day.

Some of Alderson's Services which help centralize your litigation with one source:

**Centralized Case Management:**
Centralized tracking and retrieval of transcripts and exhibits taken anywhere in the world, standardized transcript formatting, coordination between parties for document access and retrieval of transcripts, case specific word lists, single source electronic billing.

**CyberReporting:**
Computer connectivity during deposition, telecommunications anywhere at anytime, on-line technical support, standardization of any disk format or media to your specifications, Internet, America OnLine, CompuServe, Counsel Connect.

**Comprehensive Support Services:**
All security clearances, CaseView, VideoZX, Discovery ZX, compressed transcripts, master indexing by phrase or word, video/transcript syncing, document scanning, deposition suites anywhere, interpreters & translators.

We work to exceed your expectations with our services.

We guarantee your satisfaction.

1-800-FOR-DEPO (367-3376)
FAX: 1-800-367-3310
CompuServe: 71064,1256
Internet: Alderson@Imssys.com

1-800-FOR-DEPO

# MILLER & COMPANY
## REPORTERS

5757 Wilshire Boulevard, Suite 720
Los Angeles, California 90036
Telephone: 213-933-7144
Fax: 213-938-9731
(800) 48-SMART

100 Bush Street, Suite 1850
San Francisco, California 94104
Telephone: 415-956-6405
Fax: 415-956-2141

- RealTime - CaseView Reporting
- ASCIIs and Discovery ZX
- Videotape Depositions
- Daily Copy a Specialty
- Deposition Suites Available
- Indexed Min-U-Scripts

*Althea L. Miller, Principal, CSR No. 3353*

*Debra V. Helgeson, Principal, CSR No. 3189*

Members: National Court Reporters Association; California Court Reporters Association; Los Angeles General Shorthand Reporters Association (Member, Board of Directors, 1982-1985); Bay Area General Reporters Association.

Miller & Company Reporters Reports in the Areas of: Medical and Legal Malpractice, Aviation, Business, Computer Matters, Products Liability, Securities Fraud, First-Party Sworn Statements, Arbitrations, Stockholder Proceedings, Insurance Hearings and Personal Injury.

**SMART PEOPLE USE THE BEST®**
References Furnished Upon Request.

CALIFORNIA—LOS ANGELES | MARTINDALE-HUBBELL LAW DIRECTORY 1997

## LOS ANGELES (Continued)
Court Reporters (Continued)

THE *court reporting network for all of California*

11862 LaGrange Street
Los Angeles, CA 90025

Online  *http://www.altr.com*
Phone  800.961.1116

When it comes to managing complex litigation or scheduling depos in distant locations, many law firms recognize the advantages of a **single-contact resource for California and national reporting services.** A clear focus on leading-edge technology, the expertise of professionals, as well as a California-wide presence is now at your disposal and local control with the ALTRNET.

*Private, complimentary deposition suites are available in thirteen California offices:*

- ☐ Crescent City
- ☐ Eureka
- ☐ Fresno
- ■ **Los Angeles**
- ☐ Oakland
- ☐ San Diego
- ☐ San Francisco
- ☐ San Jose
- ☐ San Luis Obispo
- ☐ Santa Barbara
- ☐ Santa Maria
- ☐ Stockton
- ☐ Ventura

*One call* can arrange Certified Shorthand Reporting services in remote locations as well as prompt transmission of transcripts to your local ALTRNET office where they are printed to your specifications and delivered. Transcripts can be converted locally to disk or formatted to the litigation support software program of your choice. Transcripts can be telecommunicated instantly from one city to another, making it possible to review testimony minutes later.

The ALTRNET imparts our unique style of technical know-how for depositions taken across California and *assures continuity of quality and service* from distant locations -- without added travel expenses or surprise charges.

*One call gets it all.*    800 . 961 . 1116

## ASSOCIATED REPORTERS OF NEVADA

ASSOCIATED REPORTERS HAS BEEN
SERVING THE LAS VEGAS AREA
FOR OVER 20 YEARS

Barbara Seaton
*Owner*

1-800-845-3376

720 S. Fourth Street, Suite 202
Las Vegas, Nevada 89101
(702) 382-8778
Fax: (702) 382-2050

ONE OF THE LARGEST AGENCIES IN NEVADA

ALL REFERRALS GIVEN PROMPT, COURTEOUS SERVICE

NATIONAL DEPOSITION COVERAGE
AND COORDINATION

MINUSCRIPT

EXPEDITED AND DAILY COPY

DELIVERY IN 10 WORKING DAYS

• EXPERIENCED PROFESSIONAL REPORTERS
AND SUPPORT STAFF •
Certificates of Merit & Proficiency
Outstanding Accuracy & Reliability
Medical & Technical Experience
Certified in Nevada & California

• TECHNOLOGICALLY ADVANCED •
Real Time with Case View
Discovery ZX, ASCII
Videotaping by CLVS, Document Scanning
Videoconferencing

• CUSTOMER SERVICE •
Location Map with Accommodation/Restaurant Listings
Complimentary Deposition Suite
Subpoena Services
Interpreters

• MEMBER •
NCRA, National Court Reporters Association
NVCRA, Nevada Court Reporters Association
CCRA, California Court Reporters Association
STAR, Society of Technological Advancement of Reporting

SERVICES, SUPPLIERS, CONSULTANTS  CALIFORNIA—LOS ANGELES

# If depositions bring you to town, Let us show you around

Throughout Southern California we offer out-of-town legal professionals all kinds of extra services and facilities to make your job a joy. These include:

- Airport transportation
- Continental breakfast
- Guide to our five cities
- Hotel reservations
- Refreshments anytime you like
- Spacious conference suites

Getting down to the business at hand, we've been providing superior reporting service for two decades now. You can always count on:

- ASCIIs, Discovery ZX, CAT-Links
- Bates Stamping, Prefixing and Indexing
- Case Management
- Complete Litigation Support
- Compressed Transcripts & Master Word Index
- Document Imaging
- Interpreters
- On-site Depositories
- RealTime, Instant Rough Drafts, LiveNote
- Superior service overall
- Time Stamping
- Videographers & Video Synchronization

We're a very special firm and we specialize in RealTime reporting and Master Case management. Our staff of experienced reporters are highly skilled and equipped with all the latest technologies.

Next time you're taking depositions in Southern California, put some joy in your job. We're available to serve you from our offices in Los Angeles, Orange County, Temecula, Escondido and San Diego.

**Call Toll Free 1-800-300-1214**

## PAULSON REPORTING SERVICE

CAA65S

## LOS ANGELES (Continued)
Court Reporters (Continued)

**AT LAW LITIGATION SUPPORT**
**WESTSIDE DEPOSITION**
**REPORTERS**

1-800-493-7874

2049 Century Park East-Suite 1100
Los Angeles, California 90067

10841 Paramount Boulevard-Suite 205
Downey, California 90401
(310) 552-8052  FAX (310) 552-0704

A Full Service Agency
Serving all of Southern California
Spacious Conference Suites
Realtime Reporitng
Complimentary condensed transcript/ASCII/WP disk
CAT-Links and Discovery ZX Dealer
Videographers-Interperters
On-Site Teleconference Suite

Temporary Paralegal And Support Personnel
Document Production, Preparation, and Staffing
Microfilming-Document Management
Computerized Litigation Support
Deposition and Trial Transcript Summarization

Member of: National And California
Court Reporters Association

---

To update your listing
in the **Martindale-Hubbell Law Directory**
call 1-800-MARTIND(ALE).

---

Need an extra copy of the **Martindale-Hubbell Law Directory**? Or of a specific volume?
Call Martindale-Hubbell Customer Service at
1-800-526-4902

---

**BOB McCANN & ASSOCIATES**
Certified Court Reporters
15350 Sherman Way, Suite 101
Van Nuys, California 91406
Telephone: 818-780-0604
Facsimile: 818-780-0446
E-Mail: 103036.53@compuserve.com
Web Page: http://ourworld.compuserve.com/homepages/bma

A FULL SERVICE REPORTING
AGENCY SERVING LOS ANGELES, ORANGE, VENTURA,
RIVERSIDE AND SAN BERNARDINO COUNTIES

—

COMPLIMENTARY DEPOSITION SUITES
LOCATED IN MID SAN FERNANDO VALLEY
CLOSE TO BURBANK AIRPORT
WITH FREE PARKING

—

INTERPRETING

—

VIDEO

—

FREE ASCII DISKS

—

FREE CONDENSED TRANSCRIPTS

—

FREE ALL-WORD-INDEXING

—

BOB McCANN
CSR 1776

Member
National Court Reporters Association
California Court Reporters Association
Los Angeles General Shorthand Reporters Association

---

Now you can find the lawyer even if you don't
know where he or she practices -
with the **Martindale-Hubbell Law
Directory Alphabetical Index.**

---

The **Martindale-Hubbell Law Directory** is now
available online...exclusively
through the LEXIS®-NEXIS® services.

# More than capable. Capable of anything.

Experienced and highly skilled court reporters who show up when you need them and do the job right. That's what you can expect from **Interim® Court Reporting**, the nation's largest, most technologically advanced court reporting firm in the nation.

As an **Interim® Legal Services** company, we are part of the nation's largest network of legal support services. By using us, we can schedule all your court reporting needs whenever and wherever you desire. And, because we're nationwide you can expect the same consistent service here, there and everywhere.

- Centralized Scheduling
- Deposition Suites
- Real-Time Reporting
- Videotaped Deposition Services
- CaseView/LiveNote
- ASCII and Other Electronic Media Formats
- Condensed Transcripts
- Case Management
- Deposition Summarization

**Interim® COURT REPORTING**

| Los Angeles | San Diego | San Francisco |
|---|---|---|
| (800) 685-6600 | (619) 235-2400 | (415) 362-6666 |

## LOS ANGELES (Continued)
### Court Reporters (Continued)

## BUTTERFIELD & BUTTERFIELD

General Court Reporting Services
P.O. Box 15
Las Vegas, Nevada 89125-0015

Telephone: 702-382-7861
Fax: 702-382-5193
Cellular: 702-596-2846

Stella Butterfield, CCR #7, RPR

"A Professional Serving Professionals"

*Services include:*

★ Deposition Suite Available ★

★ Short Notice Availability ★

★ Condensed Transcripts ★

★ Daily Copy ★

★ Keyword Indexing ★

★ Expedited Delivery ★

★ Video Available ★

★ 24 Hour Services ★

★ ASCII Disk Conversion ★

Serving Rural Counties of Nevada

Experienced in *all* phases of reporting since 1955

Member
National Court Reporters Association
Past President, Nevada Court Reporters Association
Past Secretary/Treasurer, Nevada CCR Board

Issue Notice or Commission to Read: "Before Stella Butterfield or any other officer duly qualified to administer oaths."

---

Now it's easy to find lawyers practicing a specific area of law! Simply consult the
**Martindale-Hubbell Law Directory
Areas of Practice Index.**

---

COURT REPORTERS (800) 242-1996

DON'T WORRY!
WE HAVE YOUR
DEPOSITIONS COVERED
in every County in California.

| | |
|---|---|
| Downtown Los Angeles<br>Broadway Plaza<br>700 S. Flower St.<br>Eleventh Floor<br>Los Angeles, CA 90017 | Conference Rooms<br>& Court Reporters<br>Nationwide & Abroad<br><br>1-800-242-1996 |

*FREE services include:*

★ Complimentary conference rooms in all of our offices

★ Senior Account Executives throughout Southern California servicing your law firm's special needs

★ Airport, shuttle & hotel information provided to traveling attorneys

★ Condensed transcripts with keyword indexing

★ Direct billing of insurance carriers

★ Interpreters and video operators scheduled upon request

*Other services include:*

★ Conference rooms & court reporters nationwide & abroad

★ Two-week turnaround on transcripts

★ ASCII/CAT-LINKS/DISCOVERY ZX

★ Real-Time

★ Professionally bound transcripts with exhibit management

★ Aviation, technical, construction and medical specialists

★ CD imaging & video imaging

★ Video conferencing

| | |
|---|---|
| **ORANGE COUNTY**<br>(714) 548-2435 | **COVINA**<br>(818) 915-1996 |
| **ONTARIO**<br>(909) 391-1579 | **SAN BERNARDINO**<br>(909) 888-8992 |
| **LOS ANGELES**<br>(213) 387-9630 | **PALM SPRINGS**<br>(619) 323-9908 |

**SAN DIEGO**
(619) 233-1996

*SEE OUR AD ON PAGE CAA70S*

# SERVICES, SUPPLIERS, CONSULTANTS

FOR CHICAGO DEPOSITIONS
## Certified Reporting Company
11 East Adams Street
Suite 1108
Chicago, Illinois 60603-5603

24-HOUR PHONES: 312-922-1666
and 800-682-5201
MOBILE PHONE: 312-607-1374
FAX: 312-922-1696

A well-established court reporting firm serving Chicago, O'Hare Airport, the suburban areas and the National and International markets for more than 30 years.

ONLY EXPERIENCED CERTIFIED AND
RPR SHORTHAND REPORTERS
REALTIME REPORTERS UPON REQUEST

TECHNICAL, MALPRACTICE, PRODUCT LIABILITY
AND PATENT DEPOSITIONS

COMPUTER-AIDED TRANSCRIPTION

DAILY AND EXPEDITED DELIVERY ON TRANSCRIPTS

MIN-U-SCRIPT® CONDENSED TRANSCRIPTS
AND MASTER INDEXES AVAILABLE

COMPLETE LITIGATION SUPPORT AVAILABLE

ASCII AND DISCOVERY ZX DISKETTES AVAILABLE
COMPATIBLE WITH ANY DOS-BASED SYSTEM

KEY WORD INDEXING AND PROXIMITY SEARCH

COMPLIMENTARY DEPOSITION SUITES AVAILABLE

VIDEO DEPOSITIONS
BY CERTIFIED TECHNICIANS/ATTORNEY
INCLUDING "DAY IN THE LIFE" RECORD AND
ACCIDENT SCENE VIDEOS

SUBPOENA SERVICES AVAILABLE

MEMBER OF:
NATIONAL COURT REPORTERS ASSOCIATION
ILLINOIS STATE REPORTERS ASSOCIATION
CHICAGO METROPOLITAN REPORTERS ASSOCIATION

References upon request.

---

Fast ... Easy ... Flexible...
**The Martindale-Hubbell Law Directory on CD-ROM** gives you instant access through multiple search criteria to information on over 900,000 lawyers and law firms. For more details and a FREE demonstration disc, call 1-800-323-3288.

---

# CALIFORNIA—LOS ANGELES

## CHAIT MEDIA INC.
Certified Legal Video Specialists
Serving New York, Connecticut & New Jersey
212-877-9200
800-713-9769 (24 hrs.)

When in NEW YORK, do as New Yorkers do — Call CHAIT MEDIA!

**CHAIT MEDIA** provides high quality video production services to the legal community. Video depositions are conducted by a Certified Legal Video Specialist according to National Court Reporters Association (NCRA) protocol. Our video experience includes the production of nationally acclaimed videos for corporations and other organizations for over 20 years.

Our services to the legal community include::

- **Video Depositions**
- **Full-Service, Experienced Court Reporters**
- **Video Editing and Duplication**
- **Courtroom Playback**
- **Day-in-the-Life Videos**
- **Videotaping or Photographing Inventory**
- **Animation (Film or Computer)**

Our Certified Legal Video Specialists are skilled professionals. At each deposition we provide:
- Log of Objections & of Exhibits with time indications
- Audiotape recording for the court reporter
- Professional lighting and/or backdrop

241 Central Park West, NY, NY 10024 ▪ 212-877-9200
Call anytime — 24 hrs. a day, 7 days a week ▪ 800-713-9769

---

To update your listing
in the **Martindale-Hubbell Law Directory**
call 1-800-MARTIND(ALE).

---

Need an extra copy of the **Martindale-Hubbell Law Directory**? Or of a specific volume?
Call Martindale-Hubbell Customer Service at
1-800-526-4902

## LOS ANGELES (Continued)
### Court Reporters (Continued)

Now you can find the lawyer even if you don't know where he or she practices - with the **Martindale-Hubbell Law Directory Alphabetical Index.**

The **Martindale-Hubbell Law Directory** is now available online...exclusively through the LEXIS®-NEXIS® services.

### Chicago Reporting Company
*Highly Qualified Certified Shorthand Reporters*
An Interim Legal Services Company

100 North La Salle Street
Chicago, Illinois 60602-2402
Telephone: (312) 553-0733
Fax: (312) 553-0735

The firm of Chicago Reporting Company (State of Illinois Certified Shorthand Reporters) has over 50 years of collective experience. We have and are now serving many law firms both large and small in Chicago, O'Hare and Suburban Areas.

Professional Services Offered:
☐ Deposition Suites
☐ Videotaped Depositions
☐ ASCII & Discovery ZX
☐ Real-Time Reporting
☐ CaseView
☐ Min-U-Script
☐ Telecommunications of Transcripts
☐ Reproduction Facilities

*We provide personalized, professional handling of your litigation needs at competitive, local rates.*

Now it's easy to find lawyers practicing a specific area of law! Simply consult the **Martindale-Hubbell Law Directory Areas of Practice Index.**

Fast ... Easy ... Flexible...
The **Martindale-Hubbell Law Directory on CD-ROM** gives you instant access through multiple search criteria to information on over 900,000 lawyers and law firms. For more details and a FREE demonstration disc, call **1-800-323-3288**.

### Doyle Reporting, Inc.
369 Lexington Avenue
New York, New York 10017
(212) 867-8220
(800) 63-DOYLE
(212) 286-1853 FAX
www.doyle-reporting.com
info@doyle-reporting.com

- Website Scheduling and Delivery
- 24-Hour Service
- Worldwide Coverage
- RealTime with Browsing
- Litigation Support
- Videography
- Mid-town Conference Room
- Tape Transcription
- Process Serving
- Translation Services

Doyle Reporting offers worldwide service, as well as being the oldest and largest court reporting firm in the New York area, having been in business for 40 years! Of that time, Charice and Walter Shapiro have personally been at the helm for the past 25 years, and are both working court reporters!

We supply instantaneous transcription with the browsing feature, condensed transcripts and litigation support in any format, in any time frame, in any location! We offer simultaneous delivery in many locations using modems. You can also download an encrypted transcript from our website at http//www.doyle-reporting.com

For your convenience we provide conference facilities across the United States, videography, translations and process serving. Volume discounts are offered for multiple depositions.

When you use Doyle Reporting your account representative is on call 24 hours a day, seven days a week via pager for emergency spot coverage or to answer any questions! It's our blend of "new-fangled" technology and good, old-fashioned family service that has kept our clients happy for decades!

To update your listing
in the **Martindale-Hubbell Law Directory**
call **1-800-MARTIND(ALE)**.

### DRAGON DEPOSITION SERVICE
626 Wilshire Boulevard, Suite 330
Los Angeles, California 90017
Telephone: 213-622-5122
800-624-8862
FAX: 213-622-5542

OVER 45 YEARS OF PERSONALIZED SERVICE
TO THE LEGAL COMMUNITY

MEDICAL, EXPERT AND TECHNICAL TESTIMONY

ASCII DISKS, AND ALL FORMS OF LITIGATION SUPPORT

**CONDENSED TRANSCRIPT FORMAT AVAILABLE**

COMPLIMENTARY DEPOSITION SUITE

**PROMPT DELIVERY AND REASONABLE RATES**

Member of:
National Association of Shorthand Reporters
California Court Reporters Association
Los Angeles General Court Reporters

---

Need an extra copy of the **Martindale-Hubbell Law Directory?** Or of a specific volume?
Call Martindale-Hubbell Customer Service at
**1-800-526-4902**

---

Now you can find the lawyer even if you don't know where he or she practices -
with the **Martindale-Hubbell Law Directory Alphabetical Index.**

---

The **Martindale-Hubbell Law Directory** is now available online...exclusively
through the LEXIS®-NEXIS® services.

CALIFORNIA—LOS ANGELES  MARTINDALE-HUBBELL LAW DIRECTORY 1997

## LOS ANGELES (Continued)
### Court Reporters (Continued)

*Guarding The Record Since 1966*

### EATON COURT REPORTING SERVICES
Professional Court Reporting Services
Two Oliver Street, 11th Floor
Boston, MA 02109

**800-235-6860** (US & Canada)

617-338-7333 (Voice/TDD)
617-338-7330 (Facsimile)

*When Words Matter*

**Reporting Services:**
Depositions/Arbitrations/Hearings
Conferences/Seminars/Workshops
Conference Rooms Available
Video Services
Realtime/Instant Translation/CART
Expedited/Daily Copy/CaseView

**Medical/Technical Specialties:**
Environmental
Biotechnical
Intellectual Property

**Litigation Support Services:**
ASCII Diskettes
CAT-Links/Discovery ZX
Exhibit Scanning
Compressed Transcripts
 (Condensed)
Word Indexing/
 Master Indexing

Providing Communication access pursuant to the Americans with Disabilities Act using Realtime reporting services for deaf and hard-of-hearing persons in personal, work, educational and legal environments.

*Nancy L. Eaton, RPR, RMR, RDR*
*Registered Professional Reporter*
*Registered Merit Reporter*
*& Registered Diplomate Reporter*

*Guarding the Record since 1966*

Member of National Court Reporters Association
Member of Massachusetts Shorthand Reporters Association
Former Official Reporter - US District Court of Massachusetts
Former Official Reporter - Massachusetts Superior Court

800-235-6860

## ESQUIRE COMMUNICATIONS LTD. (ESQ.COM)*
6222 Wilshire Boulevard, Suite 204
Los Angeles, CA 90048

Sarnoff Deposition Service
800.640.2461

Pelletier & Jones
800.800.2207

Coleman, Haas, Martin & Schwab
800.497.1235

Nevill & Swinehart
800.748.6336

Over 250 Certified Court Reporters in Southern California

Depositions, Arbitrations, Hearings and Trials

Our **Complimentary** Services and Products Include:

- Nationwide Setting - ESQ.COM offices across the country, Member of National Network Reporting Company (NNRC)
- Spacious Deposition Suites in All Offices
- Compressed Format Transcripts
- Word Indexes
- ASCII, Discovery ZX, CAT-Links Disks
- Realtime Reporting
- Transcript Archival
- Litigation Support Software and Training

We Also Provide:

- In-house Legal Video Services
- Private Courtrooms in Our Los Angeles Office
- Document Depositories
- Imaging and Coding Services
- Interactive Realtime Reporting

Sarnoff Deposition Service/ESQ.COM
213.938.2461   FAX: 213.931.3016

Coleman, Haas, Martin & Schwab/ESQ.COM
213.480.1234   FAX: 213.480.0381

Pelletier & Jones/ESQ.COM
213.380.5077   FAX: 213.736.6739

Nevill & Swinehart/ESQ.COM
818.584.9944   FAX: 818.577.5170

* NASDAQ: ESQS

Now it's easy to find lawyers practicing a specific area of law!  Simply consult the
**Martindale-Hubbell Law Directory**
**Areas of Practice Index.**

# SERVICES, SUPPLIERS, CONSULTANTS

# CALIFORNIA—LOS ANGELES

## Gillespie Reporting and Document Management, Inc.
### (800) 211-0577

| Indiana Business Center | (800) 211-0577 |
| 6820 Indiana Ave., Ste. 140 | (909) 682-5686 |
| Riverside, CA 92506 | Fax (909) 682-4990 |

For quality deposition reporting and document management in the Southern California area or nationwide. For all of your litigation support needs, call GRDM.

*Our Reporting Services include:*

- Free conference rooms and document review suites
- Free Min-U-Script™ condensed transcripts with keyword indexing
- Free ASCII diskettes
- Insurance carrier direct billing
- Cat-Links, Discovery ZX™, Summation diskettes
- Real-Time reporting
- Interpreters available
- Coordination of your video depositions
- Experienced Certified Shorthand Reporters

*Our Document Management Services include:*

- Photocopying and blueprint service
- Management of complex litigation documents
- CD imaging and video imaging available
- Exhibit book development and management
- Storing and organizing your documents
- Computerized indexing of documents as needed
- Color copying of photographs in house
- Scanning of documents in PICT, TIFF, GIF, JPEG, or EPS formats

GRDM Specializes in complex litigation-
Medical Malpractice, Hearings, Corporate Board and Constituency Meetings, Construction Defects, Technical, Scientific, Environmental, and Antitrust Litigation, City, County, and State Hearings and Boards

*SEE OUR AD ON PAGE CAA74S*

---

Fast ... Easy ... Flexible...
**The Martindale-Hubbell Law Directory on CD-ROM** gives you instant access through multiple search criteria to information on over 900,000 lawyers and law firms. For more details and a FREE demonstration disc, call **1-800-323-3288**.

---

## HAHN AND BOWERSOCK
11601 WILSHIRE BOULEVARD, 5TH FLOOR
LOS ANGELES, CALIFORNIA 90025
800 660-3187
FAX 714 662-1398

A Full-Service Court Reporting Company
Serving all of California and Nationwide
With Cost-Effective Services

24-hour Deposition Setting Service

Offices and Complimentary Conference Rooms in The Following Counties: San Diego, Orange, Los Angeles, San Bernardino, Riverside, Ventura and San Francisco

Leaders In Technology Including Real-Time/Instant Transcript, Text Browsing, Video/Real-Time Synchronization, Document Imaging And Scanning, CD-ROM Archiving. Certified Real-Time Writers On Staff Depositions Modemed or Faxed Anywhere In The United States

Real-Time/Instant Transcript With Every Deposition

In-House Video

LiveNote Browsing

Specializing In Large Case/Complex Litigation

With Complimentary Conference Rooms For Any Size Gathering In Any Location In The Nation

DAILY and REAL-TIME TRANSCRIPTS

Complimentary Condensed Transcripts

Interpreters

Litigation Support: ASCII disks, Discovery ZX, Catlinks

Document Management/Document Depository

Customized Billing Summaries

Customized Case Management Reports

Rate Proposals and Company Brochure Upon Request

---

To update your listing
in the **Martindale-Hubbell Law Directory**
call **1-800-MARTIND(ALE)**.

## LOS ANGELES (Continued)
### Court Reporters (Continued)

**For Quality Court Reporting and Document Management**
Call (800) 211-0577

- Medical Testimony
- Hearings, Boards
- Expert Testimony
- Real-Time Reporting
- Video Taping
- Complex Litigation
- Document Depository
- Document Indexing
- Color Photocopying
- Depo Exihibit Books
- CD-ROM Imaging
- Databasing

— Serving The Inland Empire —
Riverside and San Bernardino Counties
and the Southern California Area

---

### Harry A. Cannon, Inc.
Certified Reporters and Notaries
Sacramento Street Tower #600
550 California Street
San Francisco, California 94104
415-391-7421
FAX: 415-391-4978

Reporting depositions in San Francisco,
the Peninsula, East Bay and Marin since 1945.
Imaging/"inVzn" ZX Discovery, ASCII Diskettes
Real-Time "Case View"

Deposition Suites seating up to Forty

Members of State & National Associations,
Reporters Cooperative, Inc.

C.S.R. Certificate No. 68

**SEE OUR AD ON PAGE CAA61S**

---

### HUDGINS MCHALE
■ *ComputerScripts* ■
*Serving the Legal Profession Since 1962*

**Certified Court Reporters**

**10 DAY TRANSCRIPT DELIVERY**

- Full Service Reporting Agency Offering the latest in Technological Support.
- Our People Make The Difference.
- We Go That Extra Mile For You.
- We'll Go Anywhere, Any Time.
- Conference Rooms Available All Locations.

Offices:

Los Angeles
San Francisco
Newport Beach
Palm Springs
San Diego

*WHEN YOU NEED A COURT REPORTER, CALL THE BEST!*

**800-4400-CSR**

---

### Imhof & Associates
Full Service Court Reporting

- Guaranteed 10-Day Turnaround
- Daily or Expedited Transcripts
- Computerized Transcription
- Realtime Court Reporting - CaseView & LiveNote
- Condensed Transcripts and ASCII Disks Free of Charge
- Keyword Indexing
- Interpreters Available
- Conference Rooms
- Transcripts Archived
- In-house Videographers

**1-800-939-DEPO**
3376

| | |
|---|---|
| 7720 Painter Avenue<br>Suite A<br>Whittier, CA 90602<br>(310) 907-4455<br>Fax (310) 907-4453 | 19732 Larkridge Drive<br>Yorba Linda, CA 92686<br>(714) 693-1213<br>WWW.Imhof.com<br>VImhof@aol.com |

*Serving Los Angeles, Orange, Riverside and San Bernardino Counties*

## INTERIM COURT REPORTING

Nationwide Court Reporting Services
Main Office
3530 Wilshire Boulevard, Suite 1700
Los Angeles, CA 90010
1-800-722-1235
Fax: 213-389-8514

Realtime Transcription, CaseView, LiveNote
Daily and Expedited Service
Videotape Depositions and Videosync Timestamping
Computer Aided Transcription and Litigation Support
ASCII, Discovery ZX and CATLinks Diskettes
Telecommunication Capabilities
Condensed Transcripts with Keyword Indexes
Interpreters
Document Depository
Conference Rooms Available

Experienced, Qualified Court Reporters
Skilled in technical, medical, patent and environmental testimony

***SEE OUR AD ON PAGE CAA67S***

---

Need an extra copy of the **Martindale-Hubbell Law Directory?** Or of a specific volume? Call Martindale-Hubbell Customer Service at
1-800-526-4902

---

Now you can find the lawyer even if you don't know where he or she practices - with the **Martindale-Hubbell Law Directory Alphabetical Index.**

---

The **Martindale-Hubbell Law Directory** is now available online...exclusively through the LEXIS®-NEXIS® services.

---

### *Jonnell Agnew & Associates*
Certified Court Reporters • Legal Video Specialists

*Full Time Technical Reporting Staff* offers prompt, reliable and accurate service. We specialize in expert witness testimony, personal injury, intellectual properties, medical malpractice, toxic tort and environmental law.

*Fully Computerized Text Processing* featuring Realtime plus Key word indexing with word concordance, instant and condensed transcripts, ASCII, Discovery$^{zx}$ and CaseView.

*Truly Comprehensive Reporting Services* with an emphasis on daily copy expedites, bound and indexed exhibits, interpreters, depositions, arbitrations and hearings.

*State-of-the-Art Conference Room* which is equipped with computerized text processing and videotaping equipment. This spacious, comfortable room provides seating for 20.

*Videotape Services and Leading-Edge Technology Expedite Research Time* through the use of a synchronized videotape with reporter's transcript.

Welcome to Jonnell Agnew & Associates. The following is a list of our services to help you become familiar with our firm.

- Reporting Depositions, Arbitrations, Hearings and Court Proceedings.
- Our reporters bring fresh bagels with cream cheese or cookies.
- We have Timestamping on reporter transcripts for video depositions which expedite the edit and search process.
- We offer Legal Video Specialists with broadcast quality equipment for videotaped depositions.
- Exhibits are indexed and tabbed.
- Same-day ASCII.
- Seven-day turnaround.
- Realtime Reporting with CaseView/Live Notes hookup including free training.
- Condensed transcripts with word indexing.
- 25-Line, 10-Pitch transcript format.
- Transcription of audiotapes.
- 24-hour emergency pager number (818) 932-7629.
- Document repository.
- Conference rooms throughout Southern California/Pasadena Conference Room seats 20.
- 25 Professional, Experienced reporters holding valid California Shorthand Reporter licenses held in good standing with the State of California.
- WILL BEAT THE PRICES YOU ARE CURRENTLY PAYING FOR COURT REPORTING AND VIDEO SERVICES.

We look forward to a mutually beneficial relationship while providing you with the highest degree of professionalism. Give us a call today to set up your next deposition!

744 E. Walnut Street • Pasadena, California 91101
(818) 568-9854 • (800) 524-DEPO • Fax: (818) 568-9987

## LOS ANGELES (Continued)
Court Reporters (Continued)

### KERNS & GRADILLAS
CERTIFIED COURT REPORTERS

Serving all of California • Just 15 minutes from LAX

**DEPOSITIONS • ARBITRATIONS
HEARINGS**

Litigation Support Specialists
Real-time
CaseView/LiveNote™
Condensed Transcripts
Imaging
In-House Video
Complimentary Deposition Suites
"DiscoveryVideo ZX"
WMBE Certified

For information call
(310) 556-1136 • (800) 729-1136
FAX (310) 247-1136

9320 WILSHIRE BOULEVARD
SUITE 100
BEVERLY HILLS, CA 90212

BEVERLY HILLS • SAN FRANCISCO • BURLINGAME
BAKERSFIELD • SANTA BARBARA • VENTURA
COSTA MESA • SAN DIEGO • NEW YORK • LONDON

---

Now it's easy to find lawyers practicing a specific area of law! Simply consult the **Martindale-Hubbell Law Directory Areas of Practice Index.**

---

Fast ... Easy ... Flexible...
**The Martindale-Hubbell Law Directory on CD-ROM** gives you instant access through multiple search criteria to information on over 900,000 lawyers and law firms. For more details and a FREE demonstration disc, call **1-800-323-3288.**

---

### KERNS & GRADILLAS
Certified Court Reporters

9320 Wilshire Boulevard, Suite 100
Beverly Hills, CA 90212-3221

Telephone: (310) 556-1136
(800) 729-1136
Facsimile: (310) 247-1136

Serving all of California including Los Angeles, Orange County, Bakersfield, San Francisco and San Diego counties plus all surrounding areas. Additional offices in New York and London.

| | |
|---|---|
| COSTA MESA<br>(800) 729-1136 | SAN DIEGO<br>(800) 875-5085 |
| BAKERSFIELD<br>(800) 875-5071 | SAN FRANCISCO<br>(800) 556-1136 |
| SANTA BARBARA<br>(800) 729-1136 | BURLINGAME<br>(800) 556-1136 |
| VENTURA<br>(800) 729-1136 | RIVERSIDE<br>(800) 729-1136 |

NEW YORK
(800) 729-1136

DEPOSITIONS • HEARINGS • ARBITRATIONS

A Full-Service Court Reporting Agency
with over 100 CSR's Nationwide

Expert and Medical Testimony, Business Law,
Asbestos, Construction, Toxic Torts, Civil RICO

* Condensed Transcripts
* Full-Text Word Indexing
* Archiving
* Diskettes
* Real Time
* Remote Real Time
* CaseView/LiveNote
* Imaging
* In-house Video
* DiscoveryVideo ZX

COMPLIMENTARY DEPOSITION SUITES
IN ALL LOCATIONS

WMBE Certified

Member:
National Court Reporters Association
California Court Reporters Association
Los Angeles General Court Reporters Association
Society for the Technological Advancement of Reporting
California Notary Association

***SEE OUR AD ON PAGE CAA76S***

## KILLION COURT REPORTERS
11862 La Grange Avenue
Los Angeles, California 90025
Telephone: 310-820-2060
Fax: 310-820-3575
(800) 823-6060
E-mail: depo@primenet.com
Internet: http://northcoast.com/reporter/la

730 Fifth Street, Suite K
Eureka, California 95501
Telephone: 707-443-7067
Fax: 707-443-4776
(800) 600-7067
E-mail: reporter@northcoast.com
Internet: http://northcoast.com/reporter

* Extremely experienced court reporters

* Efficient and courteous support staff

* Full computer-aided litigation support

   -Real-Time reporting with immediate unedited ASCII

   -ASCII/CAT-Links/DISCOVERY ZX

   -Condensed transcripts with keyword indexing

* Last-minute reporter availability

* Regular transcript delivery in two weeks

* Daily or expedited delivery upon request

* Special bid rates and flexible billing arrangements

* Complimentary conference rooms

* Certified interpreters and videographers scheduled upon request

**KILLION COURT REPORTERS SPECIALTIES:** Intellectual Property, Medical and Legal Malpractice, Environmental, Entertainment, Labor, Business, Real Estate, Expert Testimony, Stockholder Proceedings, Arbitrations and Hearings.

---

To update your listing
in the **Martindale-Hubbell Law Directory**
call 1-800-MARTIND(ALE).

---

## Lacey Shorthand Reporting Corporation
## and
## Lacey Video Services

FULL-SERVICE COURT REPORTING AND VIDEO BY CERTIFIED PROFESSIONAL REPORTERS AND CERTIFIED LEGAL VIDEO SPECIALISTS.

ESTABLISHED 1965

Large staff, catered conference rooms locally & nationwide, DWQ's, litigation support, ASCII, compressed transcripts. Environmental, medical, technical specialists. Daily copy, telecommunications, imaging, OCR. Interpreters. LiveNote. CaseView. Discovery.

CORPORATE HEADQUARTERS:

695 So. Harvard Blvd., Los Angeles, CA 90005
L.A. (213) 386-1108 • Orange County (714) 978-6046
FAX (213) 387-6124

1-800-90-LACEY
(1-800-905-2239)
E-mail • lacey_depos@laceycorp.com

LOCAL SERVICE AREA:
All of California
NATIONAL SERVICE AREA:
All States
INTERNATIONAL SERVICE AREA:
Europe, Asia, Canada, Middle East, South America

MEMBER
National Court Reporters Association
California Court Reporters Association
Los Angeles Court Reporters Association
Baron Users Group
Discovery Users Group
Continuum Users Group
Society for the Technical Advancement of Reporting
Reporters Cooperative Inc.

• Visa & MasterCard Accepted •

---

Need an extra copy of the **Martindale-Hubbell Law Directory**? Or of a specific volume?
Call Martindale-Hubbell Customer Service at
1-800-526-4902

## LOS ANGELES (Continued)
Court Reporters (Continued)

### LYON REPORTING, INC.
Certified Court Reporters

Suite 100, 5899 New Peachtree Road
Atlanta, GA 30340

1-800-767-2030

FAX 1-800-298-4277

Mailing Address: P.O. Box 81124
Atlanta, GA 30366

"Sandi Lyon - Who's Who in Executives & Professionals"

**DEPOSITIONS - GENERAL REPORTING:**
— Fully Computerized
— Medical and Technical Expertise
— Near All Major Hospitals
— Condensed/Compressed Transcripts
— Realtime and Daily Copy
— Keyword Indexing
— CaseView
— ASCII Diskettes
— CAT-Links
— Discovery ZX
— Videotaping In-House
— Videotape Editing
— Document Imaging
— Conference Rooms Available
— Airport Conference Room Available
— Nationwide Reporter Referral Service
— Statewide Notaries Public
— Visa and MasterCard Accepted

**STATE CERTIFICATIONS:**
— Georgia
— California
— Colorado
— Michigan

**NATIONAL ACCREDITATIONS:**
— Registered Professional Reporters
— Registered Merit Reporters
— Registered Diplomate Reporter

**MEMBERSHIPS:**
— National Court Reporters Association
— Georgia Shorthand Reporters Association
— Georgia Certified Court Reporters Association
— California Court Reporters Association
— Colorado Court Reporters Association
— Michigan Association of Professional Court Reporters
— Board of Court Reporting, State of Georgia, 1986-1990
— Member Set Depo Referral Service

1-800-767-2030

Serving the Legal Profession since 1974

*SEE OUR LISTINGS IN LOS ANGELES,
SAN FRANCISCO & WASHINGTON, DC*

---

A NATION-WIDE COURT REPORTING COMPANY

CALL TOLL-FREE
1 800 640-1949

*REALTIME & CIR COURT REPORTERS*

**Experts in Large, Multi-Party Complex Litigation,
Medical & Technical Testimony**

On-Site Instant Real-Time Transcripts * ASCII Disks
Condensed Transcripts * Keyword Indexes * Impaqt Coding
Text Browsing * Video/Real-Time Synchronization
Document Imaging and Scanning * CD-ROM Archiving
Nation-Wide On-line Deposition Services
Discovery ZX * Catlinks * Interpreters
Complimentary Conference Suites

24 Hour/7 Days a Week Scheduling
Free Airport and Hotel Information Provided

Company Brochure and Rate Proposals Upon Request

FAST 10 DAY DELIVERY & EXPEDITING SERVICES

**Convenient Locations:**
Los Angeles * (Close to LAX)
Newport Beach * (Minutes from John Wayne Airport)
Mission Viejo * (Within 75 miles of San Diego)
San Diego * (Located Downtown)
San Bernardino * (Serving the Inland Empire)

**Corporate Headquarters:**
27281 Las Ramblas * Suite 160
Mission Viejo, CA 92691
714 582-2503 * Fax 714 582-8569

*SEE OUR AD ON PAGE CAA55S*

---

Now you can find the lawyer even if you don't
know where he or she practices -
with the **Martindale-Hubbell Law
Directory Alphabetical Index.**

SERVICES, SUPPLIERS, CONSULTANTS                                         CALIFORNIA—LOS ANGELES

## MC CORKLE COURT REPORTERS, INC.

1-800-622-6755
200 North La Salle Street
Suite 300
Chicago, Illinois 60601
312-263-0052
Fax: 312-263-7494

THE AGENCY TO TURN TO FOR QUALIFIED SERVICE.

THE LARGEST COURT REPORTING AGENCY IN CHICAGO, with over 40 years experience, serving a distinguished clientele all over the United States and overseas, directly and through network affiliates.

Mc Corkle Reporting has many contracts, including the Illinois State Medical Insurance Society (insuring 80 percent of the doctors in Cook County), and Commonwealth Edison.

* 24-Hour Phone Service
* Evening, Saturday and Sunday Service Available
* 65 In-house Reporters
* 25 Suburban Reporters
* Reporters Specializing in Conventions and Meetings
* Real Time Transcripts
* Litigation Support
    * All types of Diskettes
    * Min-U-Scripts (Condensed Transcript)
        Includes Word Index - Master Word Index Available
* Archiving and Immediate Retrieval of Transcripts
* VIDEO DEPOSITIONS (CLVS Approved In-House Videographers)
    * Depositions
    * Courtroom Playback
    * Professional Editing Facilities (Immediate Service)
    * Duplication
    * On-site or Off-site Deposition Capabilities
        (Three Conference Rooms Available)
* City-to-City Videoconferencing

---

The **Martindale-Hubbell Law Directory** is now
available online...exclusively
through the LEXIS®-NEXIS® services.

## MILLER & COMPANY
### REPORTERS

5757 Wilshire Boulevard, Suite 720    100 Bush Street, Suite 1850
Los Angeles, California 90036          San Francisco, California 94104
Telephone: 213-933-7144                Telephone: 415-956-6405
Fax: 213-938-9731                      Fax: 415-956-2141
(800) 48-SMART

♦ RealTime - CaseView Reporting
♦ ASCIIs and Discovery ZX
♦ Videotape Depositions
♦ Daily Copy a Specialty
♦ Deposition Suites Available
♦ Indexed Min-U-Scripts

*Althea L. Miller, Principal, CSR No. 3353*

*Debra V. Helgeson, Principal, CSR No. 3189*

Members: National Court Reporters Association; California Court Reporters Association; Los Angeles General Shorthand Reporters Association (Member, Board of Directors, 1982-1985); Bay Area General Reporters Association.

Miller & Company Reporters Reports in the Areas of: Medical and Legal Malpractice, Aviation, Business, Computer Matters, Products Liability, Securities Fraud, First-Party Sworn Statements, Arbitrations, Stockholder Proceedings, Insurance Hearings, and Personal Injury.

SMART PEOPLE USE THE BEST®
References Furnished Upon Request.

***SEE OUR AD ON PAGE CAA63S***

---

Now it's easy to find lawyers practicing a specific
area of law! Simply consult the
**Martindale-Hubbell Law Directory
Areas of Practice Index.**

---

Fast ... Easy ... Flexible...
**The Martindale-Hubbell Law Directory on
CD-ROM** gives you instant access through
multiple search criteria to information on over
900,000 lawyers and law firms. For more details and a
FREE demonstration disc, call **1-800-323-3288.**

CAA79S

# CALIFORNIA—LOS ANGELES
# MARTINDALE-HUBBELL LAW DIRECTORY 1997

## LOS ANGELES (Continued)
### Court Reporters (Continued)

### PARKER REPORTING, INC.
LITIGATION SUPPORT SERVICES

*ONE CALL SERVICE!*

- ☐ Nationwide Service
- ☐ 20 Minutes From LAX
- ☐ Complimentary Airport Shuttle
- ☐ Convenient Location Beverly Hills & LA
- ☐ Conference Rooms
- ☐ 10-12 Day Delivery. Guaranteed!
- ☐ Real-Time
- ☐ Videographers
- ☐ Interpreters Scheduled At No Charge
- ☐ *FREE:*
  - Condensed Transcripts
  - Key Word Indexing
  - ASCII Disks
  - Document Archival

Visit Our WEB Site

    Request A Competitive Quote
&  Order Your Next Court Reporter
    Receive Your Transcript Through The Internet
    Review Latest Technological Advances

www.ParkerReporting.com

Get To Know Us!

213.782.1333 ■ 213.782.0733 FAX

800.277.2468

516 S. San Vicente Boulevard • Los Angeles, CA 90048

---

To update your listing
in the **Martindale-Hubbell Law Directory**
call **1-800-MARTIND(ALE)**.

## PAULSON REPORTING SERVICE

Serving California with offices in:
- Los Angles
- Orange County
- San Diego
- Escondido
- Temecula

Full-service Court Reporting Nationwide

**Call Toll Free**
(800) 300-1214

**In Los Angeles**
5959 West Century Boulevard, Suite 1204
Los Angeles, CA 90045
Tel: (310) 342-5600
Fax: (310) 342-5608

Paulson Reporting Service has provided quality, cost-effective court reporting services for two decades. We work with all the latest technologies and offer:

- ASCIIs, Discovery ZX, CAT-Links
- Bates Stamping, Prefixing and Indexing
- Case Management
- Complete Litigation Support
- Compressed Transcripts & Master Word Index
- Document Imaging
- Interpreters
- Medical & Technical Reporting
- On-site Depositories
- RealTime, Instant Rough Drafts, LiveNote
- Time Stamping
- Videographers & Video Synchronization

**For out-of-town legal professionals**

- Airport transportation
- Continental breakfast
- Hotel reservations
- Refreshments anytime you like
- Spacious conference suites

Member:
National Shorthand Reporters Association
California Court Reporters Association

*SEE OUR AD ON PAGE CAA65S*

---

Need an extra copy of the **Martindale-Hubbell Law Directory**? Or of a specific volume?
Call Martindale-Hubbell Customer Service at
**1-800-526-4902**

# SERVICES, SUPPLIERS, CONSULTANTS

# CALIFORNIA—LOS ANGELES

## PETERSON & ASSOCIATES
### COURT REPORTING, INC.

DEPOSITIONS, ARBITRATIONS,
COMPUTERIZED TRANSCRIPTS, ASCII DISKS,
CONDENSED TRANSCRIPTS/WORD INDEX

REPORTERS WILL TRAVEL TO ORANGE COUNTY,
LOS ANGELES, RIVERSIDE, IMPERIAL COUNTY,
SAN FRANCISCO

**WE ARE COMMITTED TO SERVICE**

7851 MISSION CENTER COURT, SUITE 120
SAN DIEGO, CA 92108

TELEPHONE (619) 260-1069  FAX 688-1733
(800) 649-6355

---

## PRATTON & ASSOCIATES
### COURT REPORTERS

**1-800-916-DEPO**

**CALIFORNIA AND ARIZONA CSRs**

6033 West Century Blvd.        1800 Century Park East
Suite 400                      Suite 600
Los Angeles, California 90045  Los Angeles, California 90067
                               (Adjacent to Beverly Hills)

2929 North Central
Suite 1500
Phoenix, Arizona 85012

(See our map in the Phoenix section)

- EXPERTS IN COMPLEX LITIGATION
- MEDICAL AND TECHNICAL DEPOSITION SPECIALISTS
- CONFERENCE ROOMS AVAILABLE AT ALL MAJOR AIRPORTS
- VIDEOCONFERENCING AVAILABLE AT 42 LOCATIONS
- INSTANT AND SAME-DAY TRANSCRIPTS ON REQUEST
- VIDEOTAPE AND INTERPRETERS
- FREE ASCII DISKS
- REAL-TIME REPORTING

**Many office locations throughout California
including San Francisco, LaJolla, San Diego,
Orange County, Irvine and all surrounding areas.**

MEMBERS OF:
National Court Reporters Association
California Court Reporters Association
Arizona Court Reporters Association
Ohio Court Reporters Association

---

## SAN JOSE DEPOSITION REPORTERS, INC.
### CALL TOLL FREE 1-800-827-DEPO

Kathrine A. Giocondi, CSR, CP, CM
CSR #2104
3002 Calle de Las Flores
San Jose, California 95148
**Telephone: 408-270-7985**
FAX: 408-270-5291

Quality, Excellence, Experience, and Perfection - San Jose Deposition Reporters represents a comprehensive, state of the art, court reporting service specializing in daily copy, technical and medical terminology, dedicated to providing professional support and solutions.

- We provide PC diskettes of testimony same day
- We provide a key word retrieval system for clients
- Free Deposition Summary via Case View
- Color Video Depositions
- We are able to provide INSTANT TRANSCRIPT with Real-Time
- We provide Discovery ZX
- We service Santa Clara, Santa Cruz, San Mateo, Alameda, San Francisco and Monterey Counties
- We provide compressed transcript & word list - Free
- We provide color legal videotape depositions - Free
- We have conference rooms available
- We have exhibit reproduction facilities on premises
- We are minutes away from San Jose Airport

*Member:*
- National Shorthand Reporters Association
- California Shorthand Reporters Association
- Northern California Chamber of Commerce
- Certified in California and Washington
- Baron Users Group

- Hearings
- Arbitrations
- Medical
- Technical
- Daily Copy
- Copier on Premises
- Litigation Support

*OVER 20 YEARS OF EXPERIENCE AND RELIABILITY
IN SANTA CLARA COUNTY*

*SEE OUR AD ON PAGE CAA57S*

---

Now you can find the lawyer even if you don't
know where he or she practices -
with the **Martindale-Hubbell Law
Directory Alphabetical Index.**

## LOS ANGELES (Continued)
### Court Reporters (Continued)

**THE REALTIME SPECIALISTS**

Conference rooms in
San Diego; Carlsbad; Orange County, including Irvine, Newport Beach, Huntington Beach, and El Toro; Los Angeles; Woodland Hills; Riverside; San Bernardino and Las Vegas

Serving all of Southern California

San Diego headquarters one block from Amtrak,
10 minutes from airport

We handle all **accommodation details**,
including **free shuttle** service to and from San Diego's Lindbergh Field and discounted accommodations at Wyndham Plaza Hotel adjacent to our complimentary conference rooms and next door to the new courthouse.

(619) 231-1600

State-of-the-art Reporting Technology & Services
♦
Complex & Expert Litigation
♦
Realtime/Text Browsing
♦
Laptops Available
♦
Paralegal Reports/Case Notes
♦
Catlinks, Discovery ZX, ASCIIs
♦
Compressed Transcripts with Indices
♦
Immediate Rough Drafts, Transcript Modeming
♦
Daily Copy
♦
Interpreters and Video Technicians
♦
Facsimile & Copy Service
♦
Local Subpoena Service

**SHERR COURT REPORTERS
THE REALTIME SPECIALISTS
Emerald Plaza
402 West Broadway
Fourth Floor
San Diego, CA 92101
(619) 231-1600, Fax (619) 595-4822
SherrReporters@compuserve.com**

---

### Ventura County Reporting Service
Certified Shorthand Reporters
1-800-933-1760
- One Block From Courthouse
- Condensed Transcripts
- ASCII, Discovery ZX Disks
- Real Time Reporting
- Videotaping/Synchronization
- Complimentary Conference Rooms
- CD-ROM Imaging

1190 South Victoria Avenue, Suite 202 • Ventura, California 93003
• 805-654-8092   FAX 805-654-8094

---

### WESTSIDE DEPOSITION REPORTERS
800-493-7874
2049 Century Park East – Suite 1100
Los Angeles, California 90067
10841 Paramount Boulevard – Suite 205
Downey, California 90401
(310) 552-8052   FAX (310) 552-0704

\* \* \*

A Full Service Agency
Serving all of Southern California
Spacious Conference Suites
Realtime Reporting
Complimentary condensed transcript/ASCII/wp disk
CAT-Links and Discovery ZX Dealer
Videographers - Interpreters
On-Site Teleconference Suite

Temporary Paralegal and Support Personnel
Document Production, Preparation, and Staffing
Microfilming – Document Management
Computerized Litigation Support
Deposition and Trial Transcript Summarization

Member of: National and California
Court Reporters Association

---

The **Martindale-Hubbell Law Directory** is now
available online...exclusively
through the LEXIS®-NEXIS® services.

---

Now it's easy to find lawyers practicing a specific
area of law! Simply consult the
**Martindale-Hubbell Law Directory
Areas of Practice Index.**

SERVICES, SUPPLIERS, CONSULTANTS | CALIFORNIA—LOS ANGELES

## Womack Reporting Service

801 Travis Street, Suite 2020
Houston, TX 77002

Telephone: 713-227-3443
FAX: 713-227-6385
1-800-327-9662

Established 1973

Wallie Womack, owner

Our staff of trained specialists provides prompt, accurate and professional service.

Certified Shorthand Reporters
Experts in all phases of court reporting

Condensed Transcripts with Concordance
Daily and Expedited Delivery
Discovery ZX, ASCII, CAT-Links
Translation Services
Video Services
Conference Rooms

References furnished upon request

Member of:
National Court Reporters Association
Texas Court Reporters Association
Houston Court Reporters Association

---

Fast ... Easy ... Flexible...
**The Martindale-Hubbell Law Directory on CD-ROM** gives you instant access through multiple search criteria to information on over 900,000 lawyers and law firms. For more details and a FREE demonstration disc, call **1-800-323-3288**.

---

To update your listing
in the **Martindale-Hubbell Law Directory**
call **1-800-MARTIND(ALE)**.

---

## DEMONSTRATIVE EVIDENCE

### DecisionQuest
2050 West 190th Street, Suite 205, Torrance, CA 90504
(310) 618-9600; Fax: (310) 618-1122
Principal Contact: Michael E. Cobo

e-mail address: dqi@aol.com
www address: http://www.decisionquest.com

Los Angeles, Houston, Chicago, New York, Boston,
Washington and Atlanta

The professional staff at DecisionQuest is trained in the psychology of visual perception. Having extensively studied judges, juries and other decision makers, we are aware of the preference for visual presentations in the courtroom and other situations. Actual juror interviews confirm that a critical element in developing the most persuasive case presentation is the visual material that will support your case themes, strategies, facts and expert testimony.

We can assist you in developing a visual strategy for communicating persuasively to judges, jurors, arbitrators, mediation panels, public and private decision makers, regulatory groups or any other trier of fact.

A key element of this strategy is the recommendation of the most effective presentation medium and technology to be used in your particular case. The advice we give is based upon what we know about how jurors understand and process visual information, what we learn from case-specific jury research, the latest information on the design of meaningful and persuasive visual information, the needs of your expert witnesses and the demands and constraints of the physical location of your courtroom or hearing facility.

*Call us to find out how to animate a static exhibit board.*

Knowledge | Control | Persuasion | Winning℠

---

### Eleventh Hour Forensic Photography
P.O. Box 1776
Duarte, California 91010
Phone: 818-358-5715

*See Photography*

---

### inData Corporation
402 W. Broadway, #1850
San Diego, CA 92101
Phone: (800) 828-8292

*See Computer Animation, Graphics & Simulation*

CAA83S

LOS ANGELES (Continued)

Need an extra copy of the **Martindale-Hubbell Law Directory?** Or of a specific volume? Call Martindale-Hubbell Customer Service at 1-800-526-4902

---

Now you can find the lawyer even if you don't know where he or she practices - with the **Martindale-Hubbell Law Directory Alphabetical Index.**

---

The **Martindale-Hubbell Law Directory** is now available online...exclusively through the LEXIS®-NEXIS® services.

---

Now it's easy to find lawyers practicing a specific area of law! Simply consult the **Martindale-Hubbell Law Directory Areas of Practice Index.**

---

### DISCOVERY AND DOCUMENT REPRODUCTION SERVICES

CALIFORNIA LEGAL SUPPORT SERVICES INC.

## CALIFORNIA LEGAL SUPPORT SERVICES, INC.
# 800-899-2577
### FAX: 800-998-2577
NATIONWIDE SERVICE CENTER

LOS ANGELES OFFICE
2808 West Temple Street
Suite 203
Los Angeles, CA 90026
Telephone: 213-383-5822
FAX: 213-383-1686

**Patricia D. Karotkin**
**Managing Partner**

| | |
|---|---|
| LOS ANGELES OFFICE | 213-383-5822 |
| OAKLAND OFFICE | 510-839-2605 |
| SAN FRANCISCO OFFICE | 415-882-2270 |
| SAN JOSE OFFICE | 408-491-9770 |

CLSS has offices throughout California, each fully bonded and insured. Our staff of experienced professionals are committed to seeing every detail of your assignment completed on time, every time and in a manner that reflects our professionalism...and yours.

- Professional Registered Bonded and Certified Process Servers
- Skip Tracing/Locate/Investigative Services
- Litigation Search and Status
- Experienced State and Federal Court Service Specialists
- Fax Filing Service - All Courts
- City, County, State and Federal Agency Filings and Research
- Public Records Research and Retrieval
- Litigation Support Service
- Registered Professional Photocopiers
- Subpoena Preparation
- On/Off Site Document Reproduction
- Complete Micrographic and Optical Scan Production Service

Representative clients consist of major law firms, in-house legal departments, financial institutions, insurance carriers and governmental agencies. References furnished upon request.

California Association of Photocopiers and Process Servers
National Association of Professional Process Servers

*Major Credit Cards Accepted*

*Continuous listing in M-H Law Directory Since 1981*

## DOCUMENT FILING/RETRIEVAL

**COMPEX**
841 Apollo St.
El Segundo, CA 90245
Phone: (800) 426-6739
Fax: (800) 479-3365

*See Litigation Support Services*

---

**CSC The United States Corporation Company**
Suite 750
5670 Wilshire Blvd.
Los Angeles, CA 90036
Phone: (213) 954-3854
Fax: (213) 954-0871

*See Corporation Companies*

---

Fast ... Easy ... Flexible...
**The Martindale-Hubbell Law Directory on CD-ROM** gives you instant access through multiple search criteria to information on over 900,000 lawyers and law firms. For more details and a FREE demonstration disc, call **1-800-323-3288**.

To update your listing
in the **Martindale-Hubbell Law Directory**
call **1-800-MARTIND(ALE)**.

Need an extra copy of the **Martindale-Hubbell Law Directory**? Or of a specific volume?
Call Martindale-Hubbell Customer Service at
**1-800-526-4902**

---

# Docu-Search
## CALIFORNIA

TELEPHONE (TOLL FREE) 1-800-466-9450
FAX (TOLL FREE) 1-888-466-9459

PUBLIC RECORDS INVESTIGATION
♦
DOCUMENT & DATA RETRIEVAL

UCC SEARCHES & FILING

REAL PROPERTY/MORTGAGE INFORMATION
DETERMINE OR VERIFY REAL PROPERTY OWNERSHIP,
LAST OWNER, SHORT TITLE, LIENS AGAINST, ETC.

TAX LIEN & JUDGEMENT SEARCHING

BANKRUPTCY COURT SEARCHING

DISTRICT/FEDERAL COURT SEARCHING

STATE LEVEL LITIGATION SEARCHING

FEDERAL ARCHIVES RETRIEVAL

SECRETARY OF STATE SEARCHING
UCC, TAX LIENS, JUDGEMENTS

DUE DILIGENCE

PROBATE SEARCHING

PARTNERSHIP INFORMATION

OTHER DOCUMENT SERVICES AVAILABLE

MEMBER: NATIONAL PUBLIC RECORDS RESEARCH
ASSOCIATION (*NATIONWIDE CONTACTS!*)

SERVING: LOS ANGELES COUNTY & ALL OF CALIFORNIA

MAILING ADDRESS:
14252 CULVER DRIVE
SUITE #A802
IRVINE, CA 92604

---

Now you can find the lawyer even if you don't know where he or she practices -
with the **Martindale-Hubbell Law Directory Alphabetical Index.**

# WE CAN DO A LOT MORE THAN FETCH DOCUMENTS

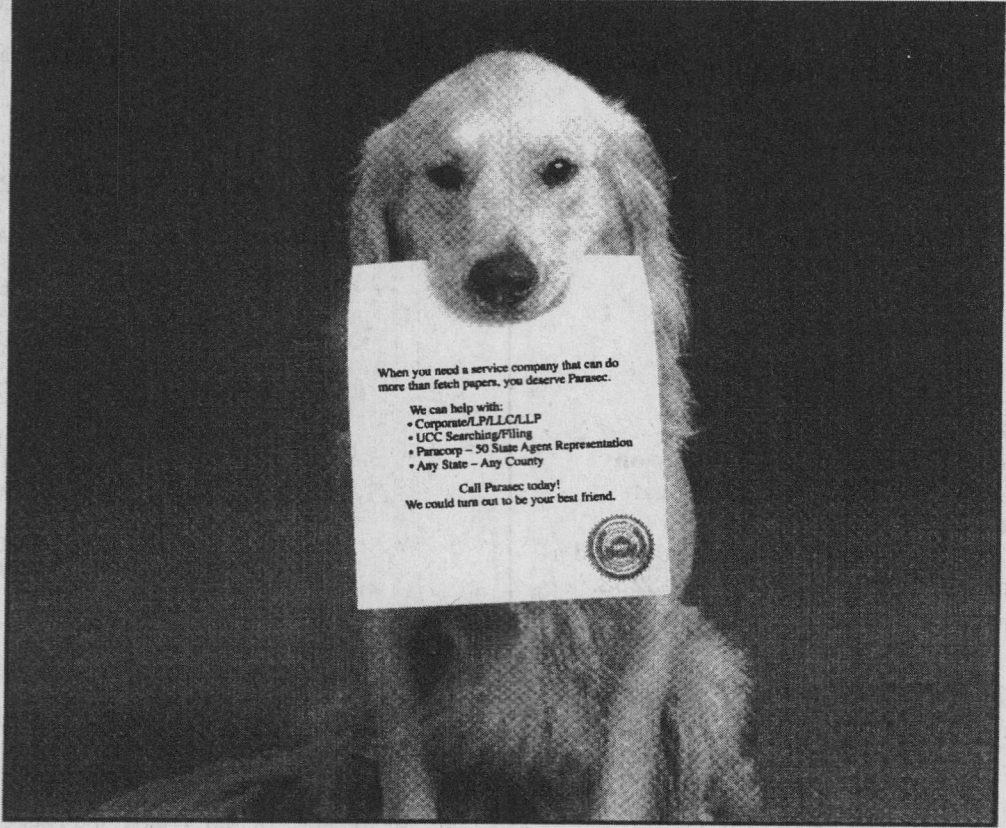

**P**arasec may even turn out to be your best friend. Since 1977, we've built our reputation on filing, researching and retrieval of County, State and Federal documents in all fifty states. And look at all the other services Parasec provides:

- On-time delivery of sensitive documents
- Business entity filing and retrieval
- Statutory agent representative (50 states)
- Litigation research and retrieval
- On-line data resources
- Branches in: Los Angeles, San Diego and Nevada.

## PARASEC

The Original Document Retriever
800.533.7272 EXT28

# SERVICES, SUPPLIERS, CONSULTANTS — CALIFORNIA–LOS ANGELES

## PARASEC
*Search, Filing & Retrieval Services in All 50 States*

We provide:

Corporate/Legal Filings and Document Retrieval

Limited Partnership Filing and Document Retrieval

Limited Liability Partnership Filing and Document Retrieval

Uniform Commercial Code Filing and Document Retrieval

Litigation Document Services

County Filing and Document Retrieval

50 State Agent Representation

800.533.7272

**Sacramento, CA**
Toll Free 800-533-7272
FAX 800-603-5868
- Corporate Headquarters
- Nationwide Filing/Retriever
- Sacramento County Recorder
- **Paracorp** - 50 state agents representation

**Los Angeles, CA**
Toll Free 800-672-7273
FAX 213-975-1526
- LA County Recorder
- Orange County Recorder
- UCC, Tax Liens, Judgments, Suits
- Consulates

**San Diego, CA**
Toll Free 888-372-7273
FAX 888-572-7273
- Same Day Incorp./Qualification
- San Diego County Recorder
- Draft & File Artifacts
- Good Standings
- Apostille

**Carson City, NV**
Toll Free 888-972-7273
FAX 702-883-0340
- Nevada State Filing & Retrieval
- Carson County Recorder
- Douglas County Recorder
- State Wide Services

E-mail Address: parasec@rcip.com
WEB SITE: HTTP://www.parasec.com

Parasec maintains a nationwide network of correspondents.

*SEE OUR AD ON PAGE CAA86S*

---

The **Martindale-Hubbell Law Directory** is now available online...exclusively through the LEXIS®-NEXIS® services.

## SUPER BUREAU, INC.

**COURIER:** 28633 SOUTHWESTERN AVE., #202
RANCHO PALOS VERDES, CA 90275-0817

**MAIL:** P.O. BOX 6400
SAN PEDRO, CA 90734-6400

**TELEPHONE:** (310) 548-2830   TOLL-FREE (800) 541-6821
**FAX:** (800) 423-8915
**E-MAIL:** 3119776@mcimail.com

**CONTACT:** Ned Fleming, President
**ADDITIONAL CONTACT(S):** Marla Cude, Information Specialist

**FOUNDED:** 1984

**SERVICES:**

| | |
|---|---|
| UCC FILINGS: | No |
| UCC SEARCHES: | Yes |
| FED COURT SEARCHES: | Yes |
| COUNTY COURT SEARCHES: | Yes |
| COUNTY RECORDER SEARCHES: | Yes |
| LAND TITLE REC. SEARCHES: | No |
| UCC MICROFILM ONSITE: | No |
| ONLINE/DATABASE ONSITE: | Yes |
| DMV: | Yes |
| CORPORATE DOC. PREP: | No |
| INCORPORATING SERVICES: | No |
| CORPORATE FILINGS: | No |
| CORPORATE DOC. RETRIEVAL: | Yes |
| CORPORATE STATUS REPORTS: | Yes |
| REGISTERED AGENT SERVICES: | No |

**OTHER:** CALL OUR OFFICE

**NARRATIVE:**

We provide information support services to subscribers via E-mail and fax. Our coverage is nationwide and also includes some foreign resources. We use many NPRRA offices as resources. In addition to UCC records, corporate, criminal, skip-tracing, credit, news retrieval, document retrieval and other services are available.

**AFFILIATIONS/ BRANCHES:**
DATA LINE CREDIT, HUNTINGTON BEACH, CA;
LITIGATION ALLIES, DALLAS, TX; KEY SOURCE, SYRACUSE, NY

---

Now it's easy to find lawyers practicing a specific area of law! Simply consult the
**Martindale-Hubbell Law Directory Areas of Practice Index.**

## LOS ANGELES (Continued)
### DOCUMENT IMAGING

### DECISIONQUEST
2050 West 190th Street, Suite 205, Torrance, CA 90504
(310) 618-9600; Fax: (310) 618-1122
Principal Contact: Michael E. Cobo

e-mail address: dqi@aol.com
www address: http://www.decisionquest.com

Los Angeles, Houston, Chicago, New York, Boston,
Washington and Atlanta

DecisionQuest utilizes the most advanced technology and equipment available anywhere today. Similarly, all elements of design and production are completed in DecisionQuest facilities to ensure both confidentiality and value to our clients. We have invested heavily in the latest technologies that will allow us to deliver the best quality at the lowest cost to our clients.

We can provide both CD-ROM based computer presentation systems or laser disc based presentations for your case. CD-ROM based computer presentations may include scanned documents, photographs, graphics or video elements, which can be manipulated, highlighted, colorized and interactively presented to the jury.

*Call us to find out why dark backgrounds work well on exhibits.*

Knowledge | Control | Persuasion | Winning℠

---

Fast ... Easy ... Flexible...
**The Martindale-Hubbell Law Directory on CD-ROM** gives you instant access through multiple search criteria to information on over 900,000 lawyers and law firms. For more details and a FREE demonstration disc, call 1-800-323-3288.

To update your listing
in the **Martindale-Hubbell Law Directory**
call 1-800-MARTIND(ALE).

## DOCUMENT MANAGEMENT SERVICES

**Gillespie Reporting and
Document Management, Inc.**
(800) 211-0577

| | |
|---|---|
| Indiana Business Center | (800) 211-0577 |
| 6820 Indiana Ave., Ste. 140 | (909) 682-5686 |
| Riverside, CA 92506 | Fax (909) 682-4990 |

For quality deposition reporting and document management in the Southern California area or nationwide. For all of your litigation support needs, call GRDM.

*Our Reporting Services include:*

- Free conference rooms and document review suites
- Free Min-U-Script™ condensed transcripts with keyword indexing
- Free ASCII diskettes
- Insurance carrier direct billing
- Cat-Links, Discovery ZX™, Summation diskettes
- Real-Time reporting
- Interpreters available
- Coordination of your video depositions
- Experienced Certified Shorthand Reporters

*Our Document Management Services include:*

- Photocopying and blueprint service
- Management of complex litigation documents
- CD imaging and video imaging available
- Exhibit book development and management
- Storing and organizing your documents
- Computerized indexing of documents as needed
- Color copying of photographs in house
- Scanning of documents in PICT, TIFF, GIF, JPEG, or EPS formats

GRDM Specializes in complex litigation-
Medical Malpractice, Hearings, Corporate Board and Constituency Meetings, Construction Defects, Technical, Scientific, Environmental, and Antitrust Litigation, City, County, and State Hearings and Boards

---

Need an extra copy of the **Martindale-Hubbell Law Directory**? Or of a specific volume?
Call Martindale-Hubbell Customer Service at
1-800-526-4902

SERVICES, SUPPLIERS, CONSULTANTS

CALIFORNIA—LOS ANGELES

## DOCUMENT RESEARCH, RETRIEVAL & DELIVERY

205 South Broadway, Suite 1023
Los Angeles, CA 90012
(800) 766-3320 (212) 680-7813
e-mail: ris@ris4info.com

*"We guarantee it."*

RIS is a leading national document research, retrieval and delivery firm whose offices have expanded coast to coast. RIS offices are always located downtown in major cities, only blocks from the courts and other important information sources. Through our branch offices and correspondent network, we are capable of obtaining documents and information from every federal, state and local court in the country and all government agencies, at a moments notice.

The California office is located downtown in Los Angeles, across the street from the County, State and Federal Courts and Agencies. We can provide a turnaround time of just a few hours. We also perform research and retrieval services throughout the states of Nevada, Oregon, Washington, Alaska and Hawaii.

Local Retrieval:

Federal Courts & Agencies in California.
Federal Record Centers in San Bruno (Northern CA) & Laguna Niguel (Southern CA).
California Superior, Appeals and Supreme Courts.
All of California's 58 County Courts.
All of California's 58 Registrar-Recorder's Offices.
California Secretary of State.
California Department of Corporations.
California Department of Insurance.
California Legislative History.

National Local Retrieval:   All Federal Government Agencies in Washington, DC and in all 50 states.
Court Records
Corporate Records           U.S. Supreme Court
Decisions                   All State Supreme Courts
Dockets                     All U.S. District Courts
Bankruptcy Records          All U.S. Bankruptcy Courts
Judgments                   Food & Drug Commission
Petitions                   Library of Congress
Tax Liens                   Patent & Trademark Office
UCC Searches                Secretary of State
Orders                      Securities & Exchange Commission
CASE WATCHES                Senate / White House

We will meet your deadline
and deliver your documents
on time, everytime, or
you pay nothing.

*"We guarantee it."*

## ECONOMIC AND STATISTIC CONSULTING SERVICES

# ANALYSIS GROUP ECONOMICS

*An Analysis Group Company*

601 South Figueroa Street, Suite 1300
Los Angeles, CA 90017

Telephone (213) 896-4500
Facsimile (213) 623-4112
http://www.ag-inc.com

Analysis Group Economics provides economic research, consulting, and expert testimony services for a variety of complex business litigation and regulatory matters. Analysis Group Economics' staff has expertise in numerous areas, including:

- Antitrust
- Banking & Insurance
- Employment & Compensation
- Energy
- Environmental Economics
- General Business Litigation
- Health Care Economics
- Intellectual Property
- Real Estate & Construction
- Securities & Derivatives
- Taxation
- Telecommunications

The firm provides assistance with day-to-day litigation requirements, including preparation of economic and statistical studies, review of case filings and discovery, selection of expert witnesses, and critique of the arguments of opposing experts.

Staff members hold advanced degrees in economics, finance, marketing, accounting, law, statistics, and management, with extensive experience in numerous industries. Analysis Group Economics also maintains relationships with scholars in economics, business and finance who complement our full-time professional staff and serve as experts.

Analysis Group Economics offices are located in Los Angeles, San Francisco, Cambridge, MA and Washington, D.C.

*Senior staff:* Bruce E. Stangle, Michael F. Koehn, Martha S. Samuelson, Michael J. Doane, Mark H. Egland, Paul E. Greenberg, John C. Jarosz, Robert A. Sherwin, Marc Vellrath, Martha S. Amram, Laura G. Boothman, Roy J. Epstein, Elizabeth A. Evans, Stanley I. Ornstein, Brett L. Reed, Ronald D. Rudkin, Richard M. Starfield, Michael A. Williams, Almudena Arcelus, Patrick G. Goshtigian, Susan E. Hoag, Terry Lloyd and Alyssa A. Lutz.

*Academic experts:* Dennis J. Aigner, Arnold I. Barnett, Robert J. Barro, William J. Baumol, Ernst R. Berndt, John Y. Campbell, Ronald C. Curhan, Patricia M. Danzon, Robert J. Dolan, James R. Emshoff, Paul J. Feldstein, Stanley N. Finkelstein, Michael C. Jensen, John M. Lacey, Paul W. MacAvoy, R. Preston McAfee, Burton G. Malkiel, Kevin J. Murphy, Joseph P. Newhouse, Sharon M. Oster, Robert S. Pindyck, Eduardo S. Schwartz, David S. Sibley, Roman L. Weil, Karen H. Wruck and Richard J. Zeckhauser.

*Representative clients:* Baker & Botts; Fulbright & Jaworski; Gibson, Dunn & Crutcher; Goodwin, Procter & Hoar; Hale and Dorr; Heller, Ehrman, White & McAuliffe; Jenner & Block; Jones, Day, Reavis & Pogue; LeBoeuf, Lamb, Greene & MacRae; McKool Smith; Nutter, McClennen & Fish; Pillsbury, Madison & Sutro; Shearman & Sterling; Sheppard, Mullin, Richter & Hampton; Sidley & Austin; Skadden, Arps, Slate,

(This Listing Continued)

# CALIFORNIA—LOS ANGELES

## LOS ANGELES (Continued)
### Economic And Statistic Consulting Services (Continued)
#### ANALYSIS GROUP ECONOMICS (Continued)

Meagher & Flom; Stroock & Stroock & Lavan; Sullivan & Cromwell; Vinson & Elkins.

---

## Charles River Associates Incorporated
200 Clarendon Street
Boston, MA 02116-5092
Telephone: (617) 425-3000, FAX: (617) 425-3132

Suite 750 North
1001 Pennsylvania Avenue, N.W.
Washington, D.C. 20004-2505
(202) 662-3800
FAX: (202) 662-3910

Suite 370
285 Hamilton Avenue
Palo Alto, CA 94301-2539
(415) 617-9700
FAX: (415) 325-2488

CRA provides analysis, support, and testimony involving the use of economics in such areas as:

| | |
|---|---|
| Antitrust analysis | International trade |
| Asset valuations | Intellectual property |
| Bankruptcies | Mergers and acquisitions |
| Commodity futures markets | Natural resource damages |
| Contract disputes | Regulatory proceedings |
| Damages calculations | Securities manipulation |
| Environmental analysis | Sports economics |
| Healthcare | Tax and transfer price issues |
| | Telecommunications |

CRA also assists clients with business strategy, market assessment, and technology assessment in such industries as chemicals, coal, consumer products, industrial components, minerals and metals, oil and gas, pharmaceuticals, healthcare, and transportation. Senior staff have extensive experience testifying before courts, regulatory agencies, and other legal bodies.

Selected Senior Staff: James C. Burrows, President; Jagdish C. Agarwal; Gregory K. Bell; Stanley M. Besen; Daniel Brand; Steven R. Brenner; William B. Burnett; George C. Eads; Myron J. Feld; Franklin M. Fisher; Joen E. Greenwood; William R. Hughes; Stephen H. Kalos; Firoze E. Katrak; Michael A. Kemp; Robert J. Larner; Arnold J. Lowenstein; Christopher Maxwell; Bridger M. Mitchell; W. David Montgomery; Monica G. Noether; Thomas R. Overstreet, Jr.; Richard S. Ruback; Steven C. Salop; Robert M. Spann; Philip K. Verleger, Jr.; Ronald M. Whitfield; Louis L. Wilde; John R. Woodbury; Deloris R. Wright.

Outside Senior Consultants: A. Denny Ellerman; Kenneth G. Elzinga; Richard P. Felak; Carl Kaysen; W. Carl Kester; Paul Milgrom; Rowland T. Moriarty; James L. Sweeney.

---

## MICRONOMICS, INC.
25th Floor
400 South Hope Street
Los Angeles, California 90071
Telephone: (213) 629-2655
Fax: (213) 688-8899

1201 New York Ave., N.W.
Suite 530
Washington, D.C. 20005
Telephone: (202) 408-0272
Fax: (202) 408-0273

300 Capitol Mall, Suite 1460
Sacramento, California 95814
Telephone: (916) 449-2860
Fax: (916) 449-2870

Micronomics provides economic research and consulting services, including competitive analysis, statistical analysis, damage studies, and expert testimony in the following areas: antitrust, banking and financial services, energy, entertainment, intellectual property, patents, regulation, securities, telecommunications and valuation.

Officers: Dr. Jeffrey J. Leitzinger; Roy Weinstein, M.A.

Consultant to the Firm: Dr. Thomas W. Hazlett

Senior Staff: Danielle Caluwaerts; John Culbertson, Ph.D.; Lynette Hilton, Ph.D.; Charles R. Mahla, Ph.D.; Barry Pulliam, M.A.; Gale Richards, M.B.A.; Roger Ridlehoover, M.A.; Lisa Skylar; Robert A. Skylar, M.A.; Atanu Saha, Ph.D.; Bruce Sloan, M.B.A.

References furnished upon request.

---

Now you can find the lawyer even if you don't know where he or she practices - with the **Martindale-Hubbell Law Directory Alphabetical Index.**

---

The **Martindale-Hubbell Law Directory** is now available online...exclusively through the LEXIS®-NEXIS® services.

**SERVICES, SUPPLIERS, CONSULTANTS**  **CALIFORNIA—LOS ANGELES**

## NATIONAL ECONOMIC RESEARCH ASSOCIATES, INC.
*Consulting Economists*

555 South Flower Street
Los Angeles, California 90071
Tel. 213.628.0131   Fax. 213.628.9368

NERA provides economic consulting, expert testimony, research and litigation support services in

| | |
|---|---|
| Antitrust | Securities |
| Utility Regulation | Telecommunications |
| Energy and Environmental | Health Care |
| Employment Discrimination | Intellectual Property |
| Sports Economics | Banking and Finance |

Our senior staff has extensive experience testifying before courts, administrative agencies and legislative bodies.

**Senior Officers:** Sumanth Addanki, Bruce J. Ambrose, Kent P. Anderson, Mark P. Berkman, Paul S. Brandon, Gary J. Dorman, Frederick C. Dunbar, Gregory M. Duncan, Joseph K. Eckert, David S. Evans, Rodney Frame, Dermot Glynn, Kenneth Gordon, Judith H. Greenman, Louis A. Guth, David Harrison, Jr., Sally S. Hunt, Vinita M. Juneja, Edward P. Kahn, Howard P. Kitt, Michael W. Klass, John H. Landon, Jeff D. Makholm, Peter Max, Marcia K. Mayer, Thomas R. McCarthy, Linda McLaughlin, Eugene T. Meehan, Todd A. Morrison, Albert L. Nichols, Hethie Parmesano, Lewis J. Perl, Richard T. Rapp, Bernard J. Reddy, Michael B. Rosenzweig, Richard P. Rozek, Steven Schwartz, John G. Sepple, Marion B. Stewart, Timothy J. Tardiff, William E. Taylor, Stephen E. Usher, Christopher A. Vellturo.

**Special Consultants:** Eugene P. Ericksen, Kenneth A. Froot, Victor P. Goldberg, Paul A. Griffin, Bruce Grundy, Jerome E. Hass, Jules Joskow, Paul L. Joskow, Alfred E. Kahn, Robert B. Lamb, Bruce C. Netschert, Robert H. Porter, Michael A. Salinger, Richard L. Schmalensee, Bernard Shull, Michael L. Tennican, Anthony M. Yezer.

**Representative Clients:** Baker & Botts; Gibson, Dunn & Crutcher; Heller Ehrman White & McAuliffe; Howrey & Simon; Hunton & Williams; Jones, Day, Reavis & Pogue; Kaye, Scholer, Fierman, Hays & Handler; Mayer, Brown & Platt; Morgan & Finnegan; Morgan, Lewis & Bockius; Morrison & Foerster; Rosenman & Colin; Vinson & Elkins; Weil, Gotshal & Manges; Williams & Connolly; Wilmer, Cutler & Pickering.

**Additional Offices in:** White Plains, NY; Washington, D.C.; Cambridge, MA; San Francisco, CA; New York, NY; Philadelphia, PA; Ithaca, NY; Seattle, WA; London, England; Madrid, Spain.

A MARSH & MCLENNAN COMPANY

---

Now it's easy to find lawyers practicing a specific area of law! Simply consult the
**Martindale-Hubbell Law Directory Areas of Practice Index.**

## ECONOMIC AND STATISTICAL CONSULTING SERVICES - AUTOMOBILES

**The Fontana Group, Inc.**
Ernest H. Manuel, Jr. PhD
President
3507 N. Campbell Ave., Ste. 111
Tucson, AZ 85719

Tel: (520) 325-9800
Fax: (520) 325-9847

**Specialties:** Marketing and economic impact studies in automotive retailing; Largest specialist with state and federal litigation experience (since 1973) in terminations, relocations, new dealerships, allocation systems, business valuations and economic damages; All linemakes; US and Canada. Outstanding references.

**Degrees/licenses:** PhD, DBA, MBA.

---

Fast ... Easy ... Flexible...
**The Martindale-Hubbell Law Directory on CD-ROM** gives you instant access through multiple search criteria to information on over 900,000 lawyers and law firms. For more details and a FREE demonstration disc, call **1-800-323-3288**.

---

To update your listing
in the **Martindale-Hubbell Law Directory**
call **1-800-MARTIND(ALE)**.

---

Need an extra copy of the **Martindale-Hubbell Law Directory**? Or of a specific volume? Call Martindale-Hubbell Customer Service at
**1-800-526-4902**

## LOS ANGELES (Continued)
### ELECTRONIC PACKAGING & PRODUCTION

**STEINBERG & ASSOCIATES**
3410 Ridgeford Drive
Westlake Village, CA 91361
Phone & Fax: 818-889-3636

Dave S. Steinberg
President

**PREVENTING THERMAL, VIBRATION AND SHOCK FAILURES IN ELECTRONICS**

Dave S. Steinberg is an internationally recognized authority on the mechanical packaging, design and analysis of electronic equipment for improved reliability during operation in severe thermal, vibration and shock environments. He is the author of two popular textbooks COOLING TECHNIQUES FOR ELECTRONIC EQUIPMENT and VIBRATION ANALYSIS FOR ELECTRONIC EQUIPMENT, published by John Wiley & Sons. His company, STEINBERG & ASSOCIATES, provides seminars and consulting services that will increase the operating life and reduce the operating costs of sophisticated electronic systems required to operate in harsh environments. Don't wait until your electronic equipment fails. Help is available for solving problems and improving the designs of existing hardware, or with the design of new equipment. Training help is also available to bring your engineers up to speed very quickly in the latest state of technology in the rapidly changing electronics industry.

**SEMINARS AND CONSULTING SERVICES AVAILABLE ON ELECTRONICS DESIGN, EVALUATION, PHYSICS OF FAILURE AND FATIGUE LIFE ANALYSIS**

1. Natural and Forced Convection Air and Liquid Cooling
2. Vibration, Shock and Acoustic Dynamic Response in Printed Circuit Boards (PCBs)
3. Preventing Vibration and Shock Failures in Surface Mounted and Through Hole Mounted Components on PCBs
4. Preventing Thermal Cycling Failures in Surface Mounted and Through Hole Components on PCBs
5. Vibration and Shock Isolation Design, Evaluation and Analysis
6. Combining Fatigue Due to Vibration and Thermal Cycling
7. Desired Circuit Board Resonant Frequency for Different Types of Surface Mounted and Through Hole Components
8. Estimating the PCB Transmissibility Q From the Resonant Frequency and the Input Acceleration G level
9. Mounting High Power Types Of Electronic Components on PCBs
10. Effective Cooling of Large Racks and Cabinets Without Fans

---

Now you can find the lawyer even if you don't know where he or she practices -
with the **Martindale-Hubbell Law Directory Alphabetical Index.**

## ENVIRONMENTAL ENGINEERING & REMEDIATION SERVICES

**DAMES & MOORE**

ENVIRONMENTAL SERVICES FOR LAW FIRMS

*CERCLA/RCRA Support*
·
*Insurance Claims Support*
·
*Expert Witnessess*
·
*Due Diligence Support*
·
*Environmental Compliance Support*

OFFICES WORLDWIDE
301-652-2215
909-980-4000

---

The **Martindale-Hubbell Law Directory** is now available online...exclusively
through the LEXIS®-NEXIS® services.

---

Now it's easy to find lawyers practicing a specific area of law! Simply consult the
**Martindale-Hubbell Law Directory Areas of Practice Index.**

SERVICES, SUPPLIERS, CONSULTANTS  CALIFORNIA—LOS ANGELES

# DAMES & MOORE

Dames & Moore is a professional services company with more than a half century of experience providing comprehensive environmental and other specialized consulting and engineering services.

With offices in principal cities worldwide, the company has successfully completed hundreds of litigation support projects, and has a proven track record of helping attorneys achieve positive case resolutions. It assists with the development of case strategies, identifies technical issues, develops supportive evidence, prepares declarations, provides expert testimony, selects and manages the work of outside expert witness, assists in deposition and cross-examination of opposing experts, provides case management and administrative support during discovery, and prepares video/graphic evidence for trial.

- Full Range of Technical Experts - from A to Z (Atmospheric Scientists to Zoologists)
- Assistance in Remedial Cost Recovery Claims
- PRP Allocation Studies and Contaminant Source Investigations
- RI/FS and RFI/CA Support
- Timing of Releases, Forensics, Age Dating, and Modeling
- Historic Standards of Practice
- File Management and GIS Data Management
- Video and Graphic Computer-simulation Services

Dames & Moore also supports real estate transactions and environmental regulatory compliance activities under CERCLA, RCRA, TSCA, CAAA, SARA Title III, SDWA, OSHA, and CWA.

- Planning
- Due Diligence, Phase I and II Site Assessments
- Regulatory Compliance Audits
- Regulatory Analysis
- Permitting Assistance
- Negotiations
- Geophysical, Soil-Gas, Asbestos, Radon, and Wetlands Surveys
- Air, Surface-water, and Ground-water Modeling
- Risk Assessment
- Waste Minimization
- NEPA Environmental Assessments and Impact Statements
- Public Involvement
- Reporting

For additional information about Dames & Moore's services, please contact:

William D. Webb, Senior Vice President and Manager, Eastern North America Division - 704-522-0330

Glenn D. Martin, Senior Vice President and Manager, Central Division - 847-228-0707

Kevin J. Freeman, Senior Vice President and Manager, Western North America Division - 206-728-0744

*SEE OUR AD ON PAGE CAA92S*

---

**Terra Vac, Inc.**
Established in 1984
17821 Mitchell Avenue
Irvine, California 92614-6003
Phone: (714) 252-8900
Fax: (714) 252-8901

San Leandro, California Office:
1651 Alvarado Street
(tel) 510-351-8900
(fax) 510-222-1445

Seattle, Washington Office:
10740 Meridian Avenue North, Suite 202
(tel) 206-362-8128
(fax) 206-362-9528

Darien, Illinois Office:
8404-H South Wilmette Avenue
(tel) 630-971-2200
(fax) 630-971-2205

Temperance, Michigan Office:
3200 West Temperance Road
(tel) 313-847-4444
(fax) 313-847-0424

Windsor, New Jersey Office:
92 North Main Street, Building 15
(tel) 609-371-0070
(fax) 609-371-9446

Westford, Massachusetts Office:
2 Park Drive, Suite 5
(tel) 508-392-9310
(fax) 508-392-9315

Marietta, Georgia Office:
1555 Williams Drive, Suite 102
(tel) 770-421-8008
(fax) 770-421-8188

San Juan, Puerto Rico Office:
356 Fortaleza Street
(tel) 787-723-9171
(fax) 787-725-8750

Tokyo, Japan Office:
Mita NN Building 11F, 1-23 Shiba 4-Chome, Minato-ku
(tel) 81-3-5446-1656
(fax) 81-3-5446-1658

Castleford, England Office:
Whitwood Enterprise Park, Unit A7
(tel) 44-1977-556637
(fax) 44-1977-57587

Terra Vac is a soil and groundwater remediation engineering company. Since 1984 Terra Vac has been designing, installing, and operating remediation systems on properties that are impacted with hazardous materials. For four years, we have been offering our remediation services on a "Fixed-fee-to-closure" basis. Terra Vac can provide your clients with an A++ rated performance bond on fixed-fee-to-closure work.

CALIFORNIA—LOS ANGELES                    MARTINDALE-HUBBELL LAW DIRECTORY 1997

## LOS ANGELES (Continued)
### EQUINE - APPRAISERS & CONSULTANTS

### FMV Appraisal Company
(Fair Market Value)

Fred V. McClendon, AAA, ASA, CCRA
President
MBA Harvard University

**ONLY US CERTIFIED EQUINE APPRAISER IN:**
Appraisers Association of America
American Society of Appraisers
Equine Appraisal/Consultant Services

**EQUINE "BUSINESS VERSUS HOBBY" CONSULTANTS**
(Equine Data Base reference IRS Appellate Division)
P.O. Drawer #330
Hampton, Tennessee 37658
(423) 772-3343 • FAX 1 (423) 772-3122

**CALL/FAX - today - World-wide!**

FMV APPRAISAL COMPANY Regional Offices as below:

TENNESSEE -   (Main Office), P.O. Drawer #330, Hampton, TN 37658
              PH 423-772-3343, FX 423-772-3122

CALIFORNIA -  (Regional Office), Paul Dayton, Mgr.
              22525 Pacific Coast Hwy.,
              Ste. #101, Malibu, CA 90265
              PH 310-456-5511, FX 310-456-7177

**IRS! IRS!**
- Program legitimacy aids/Audits/Conference "preps"/Litigation Support/Appellate aid/ IRS Program "buffers"/Donations Validated/

**INSURANCE**
- FMV (Fair Market Value) aid at Policy Inception/Claims help/FMV Uninsured losses/ Feasibility Analyses/Placement aid/

**IN COURTS**
- Divorce/Estate Probate/Contract disputes/ Transport losses/Vet malpractice/Injuries/ Diminished use Validations/Damages Values

**QUALIFICATIONS/CLIENT DATA**

Member many Breed Registries, LIFE Member AQHA, AHC (Amer. Horse Council), Certified Sr. Appraiser, Equines, Appraisers Assoc. of America, American Society of Appraisers, Member Intl. Bd. of Examiners, ibid., author of AHC's "Business Quarterly" on Equine Appraisal, author many articles Equine publications. Educated BBA @ Baylor Univ., MBA from Harvard Business School, additional work Harvard Law School, post-grad work in Banking @ Colo. Univ. and Denver Univ. Clients include US Marshals Service, US Customs, IRS, FBI, Canadian Govt., Ins./Adj./Law/CPA firms/Veterinarians, Banks, corporate CEO's, IRC Tax Donor and Donee Entities, SBA, many Equine Investment Groups, private Stables, etc.

*"When Only the Best is Acceptable"*

CAA94S

---

## EXPERT EQUINE RESEARCH

Legal Consultant – Technical Investigation

### JILL McEWAN

12750-75 Torrey Bluff Drive
San Diego, California
92130
619-259-6796
407-694-2105 (Florida)
312-222-1012 (Illinois)

**DEGREES & LICENSES:** ABEA-All Breeds Equine Appraiser, Accredited: Equine Appraisal Institute International; Winning, Licensed Thoroughbred Racehorse Trainer-Santa Anita; British Horse Society HORSEMASTER-Accredited by the Maryland Department of Education in Riding Instruction & Pre-Vet; Graduate Degree in ABA Accredited Para-legal University of San Diego; B.A.

**SPECIALTIES:** HORSES: Provide equine education to assist case substantiation; horse valuations; horse behavior; horse breeding; horse jumping; horse performance; horse racing; horse showing; horse training; riding instruction; stable management; horse fencing; horse insurance fraud; leather; all aspects.

HORSE ACCIDENTS: accident investigation, accident prevention, accident reconstruction, accident scene analysis; fair market valuations; livestock marketing; all equine related activities.

ONE OF THE HANDFUL OF WOMEN IN THE ENTIRE WORLD TO WIN A RACE AT SANTA ANITA RACETRACK

**SPECIALIZING IN THOROUGHBREDS**
**NATIONAL AND INTERNATIONAL CASEWORK**
**EXPERIENCED TESTIFYING**

---

Fast ... Easy ... Flexible...
**The Martindale-Hubbell Law Directory on CD-ROM** gives you instant access through multiple search criteria to information on over 900,000 lawyers and law firms. For more details and a FREE demonstration disc, call **1-800-323-3288**.

---

To update your listing
in the **Martindale-Hubbell Law Directory**
call **1-800-MARTIND(ALE).**

## ESCROW SERVICES

### COMMERCE ESCROW COMPANY
1545 WILSHIRE BOULEVARD, SUITE 600
LOS ANGELES, CALIFORNIA 90017
TELEPHONE: 213/484-0855
FAX: 213/484-0417

COMMERCE ESCROW COMPANY WAS FOUNDED IN 1980 BY PRESIDENT PHILIP R. GRAF AND EXECUTIVE VICE PRESIDENT MARK R. MINSKY. COMMERCE ESCROW COMPANY PROVIDES ALL FORMS OF ESCROW SERVICES INCLUDING THOSE RELATING TO COMMERCIAL PROPERTIES, INDUSTRIAL FACILITIES, DEVELOPER SITE ACQUISITIONS, BUSINESS OPPORTUNITY ESCROWS, STOCK TRANSFERS AND EXCHANGE ESCROWS. COMMERCE ESCROW COMPANY MEETS ALL BONDING REQUIREMENTS PURSUANT TO THE CALIFORNIA DEPARTMENT OF CORPORATIONS REGULATORY BODY.

PRESIDENT AND MANAGER: PHILIP R. GRAF
EXECUTIVE VICE PRESIDENT AND MANAGER:
MARK R. MINSKY
OFFICE MANAGER AND SENIOR ESCROW OFFICER:
LAREEN "LARI" KUNZE

SENIOR ESCROW OFFICERS:
LILY BACHOR
MARY LEBLANC

ESCROW OFFICERS:
SHIRLEY BODENHEIMER
PHYLLIS CHAMBERS
JULIA MOSS DAVIS
TINA DEBOW
TRACY HUGHES
JB JENNINGS
GWEN KINNARD
JENNY MA
BRIDGET SNYDER

---

Need an extra copy of the **Martindale-Hubbell Law Directory?** Or of a specific volume?
Call Martindale-Hubbell Customer Service at
**1-800-526-4902**

---

Now you can find the lawyer even if you don't know where he or she practices -
with the **Martindale-Hubbell Law Directory Alphabetical Index.**

## EXAMINERS OF QUESTIONED DOCUMENTS (HANDWRITING EXPERTS)

### JAMES A. BLACK
Examiner of Questioned Documents
24331 Muirlands Boulevard,
Suite 4-152
Lake Forest, California 92630
(714) 380-1733
Telecopier: (714) 380-0187

Since 1981, experienced in all aspects of Document Examination including wills, real estate cases, medical records, signatures, typewriting, photocopiers and obliterations.

The only fully-equipped private document laboratory in Orange County, including a typewriter reference library, microscopes, an Electrostatic Detection Apparatus (ESDA), a VSC, specialized cameras, and a library of over 100 volumes of books on documentary subjects.

Participant In The Crime Laboratory Proficiency Testing Program.

Author of numerous monographs published in the forensic science literature.

Testimonial experience in numerous superior courts as well as Federal Court. Case load for 1995 was 379 cases and 15 trials.

Membership in the Questioned Documents Section of the American Academy of Forensic Sciences, the International Association for Identification and former chairman of the Questioned Documents Subcommittee of the Forensic Sciences Committee of the American Society of Testing and Materials.

Retainers include six Orange County police departments, and selected cases prosecuted by the California Department of Justice and the Federal Department of Justice.

Guest Lecturer for the Department of Criminal Justice at the California State University at Long Beach and have lectured at the Forensic Evidence Seminar of the California Association of Public Defenders.

---

### Brookes & Chung
Document Examiners & Handwriting Experts

S E Asia
66 32 433924

US enquiries: 213 225 8288
213 486 0245
Fax: 213 486 8367

Fax and Phone: 011 441 273 473003

Reports on **suspect signatures** and **dubious documents** including all forms of property deeds; agreements, contracts, cheques and money orders; invoices, bills, delivery notes, receipts, account- & log-books, share certificates & bonds; wills, powers of attorney, etc., etc.

For fifteen years the firm has undertaken the forensic examination of Oriental & Western handwritten scripts for authentication purposes. Additionally reports are produced on alterations; printing processes; computer and fax documents; the comparative dating of documents, etc. Clients are in China, Europe, Hong Kong, Queensland, Taiwan, Thailand, Vietnam.

## LOS ANGELES (Continued)
**Examiners Of Questioned Documents (Handwriting Experts) (Continued)**

# MARTA CHAUSÉE, M.S.

*FORENSIC DOCUMENT EXAMINER*
*COURT QUALIFIED EXPERT WITNESS*

Handwriting Identification

Questioned Ink, Typewriting, Paper Stock

Altered/Manipulated Documents and Photographs

**(714) 460-0114**

*WILL TRAVEL TO YOUR LOCATION*

For over twenty years, Marta Chausée, M.S., has prepared hundreds of reports on questioned documents for attorneys, business concerns and private individuals. She has been retained by the Office of the United States Attorney, the Small Business Administration and the Association of Los Angeles Deputy Sheriffs. She has testified in Superior Courts in Los Angeles, California and Orlando, Florida and in the Circuit Court of Cook County in Chicago, Illinois.

In 1982, she appeared on CNN, discussing historical signatures. In Orlando, Florida, in 1986, she appeared on WCPX, discussing historic forgeries and famous fraudulent documents. She has appeared as a guest lecturer to civic organizations in Orlando and Chicago.

Marta Chausée earned her Master of Science Degree from Benedictine University in 1995 and her Bachelor of Arts Degree from UCLA in 1975.

Concurrently, she completed two years of formal training in document examination, handwriting identification and identification of questioned typewriting, ink and paper stock under the private tutelage of forensic document examiner, Henry Silver. She assisted Mr. Silver for two years, after which time she began her private practice as an independent document examiner. Mr. Silver practiced in the Southern California area for over fifty years, until the time of his death in 1985.

Ms. Chausée maintains a professional library and laboratory equipment in her office. She has continued her professional education at symposiums in California, Illinois, Massachusetts, Michigan, Texas, and Wisconsin held by the Association of Forensic Document Examiners and the Independent Association of Questioned Document Examiners.

Topics have included credit card fraud, computer-generated documents, altered faxes and photos, manufacture of paper stock, innovations in laboratory photographic equipment, the effects of neurological damage, blindness a/o DID on writing, and the changing role of the expert witness at the threshold of the twenty-first century.

---

## EXPERT WITNESS

### ACCIDENT RECONSTRUCTION

**ERROR ANALYSIS, INC.**
*Human Factors, Engineering & Safety Consultants*
Corporate Office: 5811 Amaya Drive, Suite 205
La Mesa, CA 91942-4156
Greater LA Area . . . . . . . . . . . . . . . . . . (909) 279-6152
San Diego County . . . . . . . . . . . . . . . (619) 464-4427
SF Bay Area . . . . . . . . . . . . . . . . . . . . (415) 861-1852
Rocky Mountain Regional Office . . . . (303) 843-6365
South East Regional Office . . . . . . . . (919) 828-2443

**Error Analysis, Inc.**, founded in 1988, is a firm dedicated to research and consulting in the fields of human factors, engineering and safety. We are an extensive group of experts providing consulting and expert witness services to attorneys, the insurance industry and businesses throughout the country.

- Slips, Trips and Falls
- Premise and Product Design
- Motor Vehicle Collisions including Motorcycles, Bicycles and Forklifts
- Accident/Injury Reconstruction (All Types)
- Accident Kinematics/Biomechanics
- Industrial and Recreational Equipment Design
- Motor Vehicle Related Products
- Effectiveness of Warnings, Labels and Instructions
- Visibility and Lighting
- Perception and Reaction
- Pedestrians
- Safety Management, Training and Instruction
- Negligent Supervision
- Human Error
- Behavioral Expectations
- Risk Perception
- Reasonable Conduct
- Memory, Attention and Impairments
- Safety Codes and Standards
- Industry Customs and Practices
- Architectural and Construction Standards of Care

**Expert Qualifications**
Our staff consists of skilled professionals, qualified with solid expertise in virtually all segments of human factors, engineering and safety, including:
- Numerous respected scientists and professors from universities throughout the country
- Renowned authors of human factors, engineering and safety publications
- Highly experienced design professionals
- Courtroom experienced experts

"Your Expert Source..." Error Analysis, Inc. will provide you with the credible experts necessary for a strong case.

## SERVICES, SUPPLIERS, CONSULTANTS

### AGRI-HORTICULTURAL

**Klaus Radtke, Ph.D.**
1462 Lachman Ln.
Pacific Palisades, CA 90272
Phone: (310) 459-9453
Fax: (310) 459-6187

*See Expert Witness - Fire - Wildland/Urban Interface*

### AUDIO-TAPE ANALYSIS/AUTHENTICATION/VOICE ID

**FORENSIC AUDIO LAB**
*"THE MOST COMPREHENSIVE & STATE-OF-THE-ART AUDIO LAB"*

**ANTHONY J. PELLICANO**
President

9200 Sunset Boulevard, #322
Los Angeles, CA 90069

(310) 859-8755
1-800-FOR-N-SIC

- Authentication Of Questioned Tape Recordings
- Examinations To Determine Illegal Alterations & Deletions
- Enhancement of Noise-Ridden Recordings
- Certified Transcripts of Cleansed Recordings
- Verification Of Recorded Content, Including Voice Identification or Elimination

Anthony J. Pellicano is a qualified forensic audio expert who has testified in the capacity of, and has been appointed as, an expert in the Federal and State courts across the nation for the past 25 years. He has been retained by the District and United States Attorney's Offices as well as other law enforcement agencies, and private and public defense attorneys throughout the country.

Mr. Pellicano owns Forensic Audio Lab in Los Angeles, a state-of-the-art laboratory that is the most comprehensive in the field. He has been involved in many notable cases, including the forensic analysis of the "18-Minute Gap". More recently, he provided forensic analysis in the criminal trials of John DeLorean and Marion Barry, and testified in the successful defense in the civil case against the rock band Judas Priest.

Mr. Pellicano is on referrals lists of many related organizations such as the National Forensic Center and the National Association of Criminal Defense Lawyers. He is the Chairman of the Tape Authentication & Analysis Committee at the National Forensic Center and belongs to the International Association of Identification. He is a published co-author (<u>Audio Recordings as Evidence</u>, Lawyers Cooperative Publishing) and a guest speaker.

### BANKING

John R. Britt
**JRB ASSOCIATES**
24208 Heritage Lane
Newhall, California 91321-3536
(805) 255-0090
FAX (805) 255-0091

AREAS OF EXPERTISE:

Lender Liability             Operations
Insider Transactions         Bank Fraud and Security
Credit Policy and Procedure  Branch Administration
Loan Review and Analysis     Code of Conduct
Board of Directors           Personnel

QUALIFICATIONS:

Thirty eight years banking and financial services experience, with fifteen years at the executive management and President and CEO levels.

Deposition and trial experience since 1989. Over 250 consulting cases, including complex lender liability, check fraud, and FDIC officer and director negligence actions.

Board Certified Forensic Examiner and Diplomate, American Board of Forensic Examiners.

EDUCATION:

Claremont McKenna College: BA Business Administration/Economics.
University of Washington: Graduate, Pacific Coast Banking School.
University of Southern California: Graduate, Managerial Policy Institute.

PROFESSIONAL:

Past President, Robert Morris Associates (So. Calif. Chapter)
California Bankers Association
National Forensic Center
American Board of Forensic Examiners
Forensic Consultants Association of Orange County
The Economic Roundtable

---

Now it's easy to find lawyers practicing a specific area of law! Simply consult the
**Martindale-Hubbell Law Directory
Areas of Practice Index.**

## LOS ANGELES (Continued)
### Expert Witness—Banking (Continued)

### MCS Associates

18300 Von Karman, Suite 1100
Irvine, CA 92715
(714) 263-8700   Fax: (714) 553-0168
E-Mail: mcs@earthlink.net

Contact: Norman Katz - (Managing Partner)

MCS Associates is a nationally recognized consulting group that specializes in the banking, financial services and real estate industries. Established in 1973, MCS has provided consulting services to more than 1000 banks, thrift institutions, mortgage banks, insurance companies, regulatory agencies as well as real-estate and financial service organizations throughout the U.S.

Expert witness and litigation consulting assignments are an important focus of MCS Associates' services. Our clients include some of the nation's leading law firms, working on behalf of financial institutions, insurance companies, directors and officers, regulatory agencies, borrowers, depositors, developers and investors. MCS consultants are familiar with the issues, practices and standards of financial institutions of all sizes and have expertise in a wide range of real estate activities.

The firm has key strategic alliances in banking, insurance, securities brokerage and real estate matters, and takes great pride in identifying exactly the right experts for each assignment. Our experts/litigation consultants are experienced senior bankers, lenders, consultants, economists, real estate analysts/developers, accountants, appraisers and former regulators who combine specialized hands-on expertise with substantial litigation/expert witness experience.

Expert areas include:

- Banking Transactions
- Banking Operations & Administration
- Bank & S&L Lending - All Types (Policies, Procedures, Customs & Practice)
- Loan Underwriting/Admin.
- Commercial & Corporate Lending
- Real Estate/Mortgage Lending
- Construction Loans
- Mortgage Banking
- Insurance Coverage, Broker/Agent Standards, Industry Practice
- Wrongful Termination/Compensation Disputes
- Real Estate Appraisal
- Real Estate Development/Feasibility
- Real Estate Transactions/Practices
- Real Estate Brokerage
- Securities, Trusts & Investments
- Valuations/Damages Assessment
- Forensic Accounting

---

Fast ... Easy ... Flexible...
**The Martindale-Hubbell Law Directory on CD-ROM** gives you instant access through multiple search criteria to information on over 900,000 lawyers and law firms. For more details and a FREE demonstration disc, call **1-800-323-3288**.

## BIOMEDICAL ENGINEERING

### JEROME T. ANDERSON, CCE
### BIOMEDICAL CONSULTING SERVICES
19700 Fairchild Road, Suite 100
Irvine, CA 92612

Phone: (714) 756-1412
Fax: (714) 756-2740
E-mail: biocons@ix.netcom.com

**Specialties:** Medical device and equipment incident investigations, hospital equipment maintenance, medical equipment planning and medical technology risk management.

**Background:** Jerome T. Anderson has in excess of 30 years experience in clinical applications, maintenance and research in medical devices and systems. His background includes clinical engineering experience in hospitals, surgical research, aerospace medicine, hyperbaric therapy, clinical and research laboratory equipment, and medical equipment planning for health facility construction. Mr. Anderson is a Certified Biomedical Equipment Technician and is also certified as a Clinical Engineer. He has authored numerous articles on application, maintenance and management of medical instrumentation.

Prior to establishing Biomedical Consulting Services, Mr. Anderson was the Director of Biomedical Engineering for a major Southern California hospital, Regional Manager for a shared hospital biomedical engineering service and established biomedical equipment maintenance services for several hospitals and businesses. His specialty areas include surgery, cardiovascular, neonatology, laboratory and general medical instrumentation.

**Services Offered:** Independent medical device incident investigations for hospitals, insurance carriers and attorneys
Failure analysis
Functional testing
Product improvement consultation
Litigation support
Expert witness testimony
Opinions on proper application, standard of care, and maintenance of medical equipment

**Affiliations:** American College of Clinical Engineering
American Society for Healthcare Engineering
American Society for Healthcare Risk Management
Association for Advancement of Medical Instrumentation
National Fire Protection Association

## COATINGS/PAINT

**CONSOLIDATED CONSULTANTS CO.**
739 Twin Oaks Ave.
Chula Vista, CA 91910-5924
Phone: (800) 683-9847
Fax (619) 422-8101
E-Mail steve_vr@msn.com
Internet Home Page: http://www.FreeReferral.com

(This Listing Continued)

# SERVICES, SUPPLIERS, CONSULTANTS

## CCC CONSOLIDATED CONSULTANTS CO. (Continued)

### PAINT COATINGS SCIENTIST/CONSULTANT

- DURABILITY
- TOXICITY
- COLOR MATCHING/DETERMINATION
- APPLICATION
- SUBSTRATES
- DRYING RATE/TIME
- DEFECTS
- FAILURES
- WORKMANSHIP
- CURE RATE
- CHEMICAL ANALYSIS
- WARRANTY EVALUATION

### EDUCATION

JURIS DOCTORATE, 1982, Western State University College of Law, Fullerton, California

MASTERS BUSINESS ADMINISTRATION, 1976, University of California, Riverside

BACHELORS OF SCIENCE, CHEMISTRY, 1973, University of California, Riverside

### POSITIONS HELD

- 1990-present **Coatings Scientist and Consultant, Expert Witness**
  Formulation, batchmaking software representative, colormatching software representative, environmental regulatory advisor, Investigative 3rd party fault finder for coatings failure determination, 3rd party certification of testing procedures, including adequacy of testing equipment and instruments, ASTM testing on concrete and concrete coatings. OSHA safety programs implementation, both physical and chemical. Lead paint abatement seminars, training sessions, and determination of extent of containment and degree of abatement.

- 1982-1990: **Technical Sales, Technical Director, Operations Manager, Environmental and Safety Officer for Architectural/Industrial Maintenance coatings manufacturer.** Solved application problems of distributors and contractors. Provided environmental/safety regulatory assistance to customers and sister companies. Implemented forklift program using CalOSHA standards for training and documentation.

- 1980-1982: **Paint Consultant**
  Custom paint and adhesive formulations for several companies.

- 1978-1979: **Lab Manager**
  Coil Coatings

- 1977: **Assistant Technical Director**
  Coil and Can Coatings, Wood Coatings, General Industrial Coatings

- 1963-1976: **Chief Chemist**
  Coil and General Industrial Coatings

---

# CALIFORNIA—LOS ANGELES

## COMMERCIAL LAW/BANKING/UCC

### UNIFORM COMMERCIAL CODE CONSULTANTS

Rob LeVine
82 Loyola Street
Ventura, CA 93003
805-650-3472

My specialty within the Uniform Commercial Code involves two processes. First, retrieving all UCC provisions throughout the Code in its totality, which bear on any phase of the matter under consideration. Second, aligning the facts of the case with a logical progression of statutory language and commercial policies selected from these provisions which support the advocated result.

The first process recognizes that commercial transactions are integrated, and often involve a majority of the UCC articles in their execution. A typical sale of goods for example, could involve the sale (Art.2), shipment (7), payment (3), bank processing (4) or a letter of credit (5). If the transaction is secured, Article 9 would come into play, while electronic funds transfers would activate 4A. Critical (and most often overlooked), Article 1 applies to all transactions under the Code.

The second process recognizes that within the large number of transactions activated there exists tremendous flexibility to shape, structure and control litigation or transactions

The combination of the volume of the first process, with the logic and policy of the second process presents an extremely powerful arsenal by which to achieve the desired result.

I graduated from the University of Chicago Law School in 1974; taught the Uniform Commercial Code at the University of Miami Law School for six and one half years, and wrote The Uniform Commercial Code: A Operational Translation. Information about the book as well as copies of articles published in the Los Angeles Daily Journal during the past year can be obtained at no cost at LawInfo.Com on the Internet.

---

To update your listing
in the **Martindale-Hubbell Law Directory**
call **1-800-MARTIND(ALE)**.

---

Need an extra copy of the **Martindale-Hubbell Law Directory**? Or of a specific volume?
Call Martindale-Hubbell Customer Service at
**1-800-526-4902**

## LOS ANGELES (Continued)
Expert Witness (Continued)

### COMPUTER & BUSINESS INFORMATION SYSTEMS

### Computomata International Corporation

25 years consulting experience in the U.S., Latin America, Europe and the Far East. Our consultants have advanced academic degrees and many years experience in information system management, software systems, research and education, and day-to-day application of computing and communications technology. Our top experts have national and international reputation, and are authors of many journal publications and textbooks.

- **Technical and cost/benefit assessment.** Evaluation of litigation case strategy from a technical and cost/benefit standpoint. Identification of strengths and weaknesses, and of approaches by the opposition.

- **Investigation/forensic analysis.** Analysis of chronology of events leading to a current situation and direction, and of cause and effect.

- **Depositions.** Support to counsel and witnesses.

- **Expert Witness.** Acting as expert witnesses, or identifying other experts in the field.

- **Theft of intellectual property.** Identification of originality and uniqueness of software products. Comparison of competing products.

- **Copyright infringement.** Comparison between original product and allegedly copied version (functionality, design, implementation, and feel/look)

- **Protection of computing resources.** Evaluation of exposure, and of data integrity, security, and fraud prevention features.

**TECHNICAL EXPERTISE INCLUDES:**

- Data Base Systems
- Multimedia Systems
- Software Engineering
- Application Development
- Client/Server Systems
- Heterogenous Systems
- PC Software
- Storage and Retrieval Technology
- Data Protection and Security
- System Connectivity
- Voice and Data Networks
- Network Protection and Security
- System Metrics and Tuning
- Computer Operations

Computomata International Corporation
500 S. Sepulveda Boulevard, Suite 606
Los Angeles, California 90049
Tel. (310) 471-0224
Fax. (310) 471-5534

### CONSTRUCTION

### Jax Kneppers Associates, Inc.
Suite 180
2950 Buskirk Ave.
Walnut Creek, CA 94596
Phone: (800) 833-4371
Fax: (510) 933-9370

*See Construction Consultants*

---

### JERRY L. POLLAK, A.I.A., A.I.C.P.
### ARCHITECT
CONSTRUCTION CONSULTANT

14209 Chandler Boulevard
SHERMAN OAKS, CA 91401
(818) 909-3757 • FAX (818) 997-7999

Licensed Architect (CA,NV); 40 Years Experience as Architect in Commercial, Residential, Industrial, Urban Design and Planning.

- Providing Litigation Support Services
- Extensive Deposition, Arbitration and Court Experience
- Expert Testimony and Witness Preparation on Technical Aspects of Architectural and Construction Industry Practices
- Construction (Methodology, Defect Analysis, Building Codes, Cost Estimates)
- Safety (Accidents, Hazards and Failures)

---

Now you can find the lawyer even if you don't know where he or she practices - with the **Martindale-Hubbell Law Directory Alphabetical Index.**

---

The **Martindale-Hubbell Law Directory** is now available online...exclusively through the LEXIS®-NEXIS® services.

---

Now it's easy to find lawyers practicing a specific area of law! Simply consult the **Martindale-Hubbell Law Directory Areas of Practice Index.**

# SERVICES, SUPPLIERS, CONSULTANTS

# CALIFORNIA—LOS ANGELES

## THE SOLENDER GROUP, INC.
### CONSTRUCTION DEFECT EXPERTS

**EXPERT WITNESS**

**LITIGATION SUPPORT**

*PRINCIPAL HAS OVER
40 YEARS EXPERIENCE
(OVER 16,000 HOURS AS AN EXPERT WITNESS)*

**INCLUDING NEVADA & CALIFORNIA
TRIAL EXPERIENCE**

— — —

**RESIDENTIAL/COMMERCIAL/INDUSTRIAL
DEFENSE/PLAINTIFF TESTIMONY IN GENERAL
TYPE V AND CLASS A STRUCTURES
PLANS, SPECIFICATIONS, CONSTRUCTION DEVIATIONS
AND DEFECTS ANALYSIS • SAFETY STANDARDS
DAMAGE CALCULATIONS • CLAIMS AND REPORTS
DEVELOPMENT**

Defense / Plaintiff, testimony ranging from construction costs, quality analysis and survey, including complete cost breakdown procedures from both plans and completed structures. Standard industry practices. Safety standards. Plans and specifications deviations analysis. Construction defects investigations. Destructive testing. Analysis of waterproofing systems and design remediation. CPM scheduling and delays. Damages calculations. Foundation, slope and retaining wall failure. Grading, compaction, backfilling and waterproofing. Real estate development entitlement processing.

— — —

**OUR HIGHLY TRAINED TEAM OFFERS THE FOLLOWING
CERTIFIED SERVICES:**

- ALA Architectural
- Civil Engineering
- Structural Engineering
- Soils Engineering
- Acoustical Engineering
- Plumbing Engineering
- Heating & A/C Engineering
- General Contracting
- Geological Engineering

**CV UPON REQUEST
11022 SANTA MONICA BLVD. #220
LOS ANGELES, CALIFORNIA, 90025
PHONE (310) 445-5166 — (800) 954-8485
FAX (310) 445-5160**

---

## Wagner • Hohns • Inglis • Inc.
100 High St.
P.O. Box 460
Mount Holly, NJ 08060-0460
Phone: (609) 261-0100
Fax: (609) 261-8584

*See Construction Consultants*

---

## CRIME PREVENTION

### SECURITY MANAGEMENT SERVICES, INC.
CRIME PREVENTION EXPERT

28170 Avenue Crocker, Suite 100
Valencia, CA 91355

1-800-494-3066

Tel: (805) 269-4417
Fax: (805) 269-5665

Mark Gleckman, MS, CPO
Crime Prevention Specialist

E-Mail: 103642.3564@CompuServe.com

Web Site: www.SecurityManagementSvcs.com

---

- Professional credentials have been developed through 28 years of security management experience. Mark holds a Master of Science degree in Security Administration and has earned the State of California "Crime Prevention Certificate of Merit."

- Crime Prevention Consultant specializing in physical security assessments and employee security awareness training in personal safety, robbery prevention and workplace violence.

- Specialist Areas: Banking and Financial Services, City and County Government, Commercial Property, Educational Institutions, Food Services Establishment, Healthcare Services, Lodging, Personal, Residential, Retail, Security Design.

- Featured as a security expert on the NBC news and the nationally syndicated television show "Save Our Streets." Mark has written numerous articles on crime prevention that have been published throughout the United States.

- Mark has written a Credit Union Security Program Manual that is being marketed and distributed by the Credit Union Executives Society (CUES).

- Featured as a personal safety expert in the personal safety video "Protect Yourself" distributed by Kelly News & Entertainment.

- Instructs an 8 hour crime prevention class at the Los Angeles Police Academy.

- Has Worked with Cal/OSHA investigating Workplace Violence occurrences.

- Professional Affiliations: Los Angeles Police Departments; San Fernando Police Department; Los Angeles County Sheriff's Department; Moorpark Police Department; Cal/OSHA; The California Crime Prevention Officers Association.

## LOS ANGELES (Continued)
Expert Witness (Continued)

### CRIMINALISTICS & FIREARMS

**CONSOLIDATED CONSULTANTS CO.**
739 Twin Oaks Ave.
Chula Vista, CA 91910-5924
Phone (800) 683-9847
Fax (619) 422-8101
E-Mail steve_vr@msn.com
Internet Home Page: http://www.FreeReferral.com

#### FIREARMS CONSULTANT
#### LEGAL EXPERT WITNESS

- Firearms Business Marketing – Retail and Wholesale Customer Relations
- Hunting and Shooting Range Incidences
- Safety Classes
- Governmental Agency Relationships (A.T.F. and Department of Justice)
- Gunshop Etiquette Repairs
- Customizing, Manufacture, Alteration, Assembly-Disassembly
- Distribution and Appraisals of Pistols, Rifles, Shotguns
- Blackpowder Weapons, Airguns & all the Accessories connected with these Weapons and their Applications.
- Ballistics, Cartridges, Re-loading
- Use and Manufacture of Ammunition.

**SUMMARY**
Long Term, Multifaceted, in Depth, Experience Based Knowledge of Firearm's Safety and Firing Mechanisms—their Design and Testing.

In depth knowledge of Shop Set Up, Tool Layout, Safety and Use of Equipment

This expert is devoted full time to win your case, plaintiff or defendant, with fees being a secondary consideration. When retaining his services you will receive prompt, timely, courteous service along with an unprecedented 40 years experience in the Firearms Trade with a world wide reputation second to none. This expert is a university science graduate and published author that can deliver convincing, straight forward, articulate, irrefutable testimony based on a reputable, wide range of Firearms Trade Experiences. He is a certified Expert Witness in California with Trial, Deposition, and Attorney Advisory Experience spanning the last 5 years.

---

### EMPLOYEE/EMPLOYMENT

Specializing in: Discrimination

**Barrington Psychiatric Center**
Suite 320
1990 S. Bundy Dr.
Los Angeles, CA 90025
Phone: (310) 826-3235
Fax: (310) 447-0840

*See Medical Expert Witness - Psychiatry - Forensic*

---

Fast ... Easy ... Flexible...
**The Martindale-Hubbell Law Directory on CD-ROM** gives you instant access through multiple search criteria to information on over 900,000 lawyers and law firms. For more details and a FREE demonstration disc, call **1-800-323-3288**.

---

To update your listing
in the **Martindale-Hubbell Law Directory**
call **1-800-MARTIND(ALE)**.

---

Need an extra copy of the **Martindale-Hubbell Law Directory**? Or of a specific volume?
Call Martindale-Hubbell Customer Service at
**1-800-526-4902**

# SERVICES, SUPPLIERS, CONSULTANTS
## CALIFORNIA—LOS ANGELES

### Jay M. Finkelman, Ph.D., C.P.E.
2675 Nottingham Ave.
Los Angeles, CA 90027
Tel: (213) 666-0900
Fax: (213) 666-0330

Industrial Psychologist, Forensic Psychologist, Employment Expert
Licensed Psychologist - State of California - State of New York

Over 25 years experience as expert witness/litigation consultant testifying regarding employment matters. Retained as an employment expert, pursuant to litigation, in over 100 matters. Unique combination of academic, consulting and line management credentials.

Featured speaker at the Defense Research Institute: "How to Properly Manage a Sex Harassment Investigation". (3-1-96)

*SPECIALIZING IN BUT NOT LIMITED TO:*

- Employment Discrimination (Age, Sex, Race, Disability)
- Wrongful Termination
- Sexual Harassment
- Negligent Hiring/Retention
- ADA Compliance
- Adverse Impact
- Statistical Analysis of Employment Data
- Performance Appraisal
- Conflict of Interest
- Human Factors/Ergonomics

Formerly: Dean of Students and Professor of Industrial Psychology, The Bernard M. Baruch School of Business, The City University of New York; Doctoral Faculty in Business (Organizational Behavior), The Graduate Center, The City University of New York.

Currently: Vice President, Metro Markets Division and Regional Manager, Los Angeles & Orange Counties, Kelly Temporary Services. (Kelly Tel: 213/782-8008   Fax: 213/782-8039)

Education: Ph.D. (Industrial/Organizational Psychology) New York University * M.B.A. (Industrial Psychology) The City College - Bernard M. Baruch School of Business, The City University of New York * B.A. (Psychology/Communications) Brooklyn College, C.U.N.Y.

Professional Associations: American Psychological Association, Division 14 Industrial Psychology, Division 21 Engineering Psychology * Human Factors and Ergonomics Society * American College of Forensic Examiners.

Licenses/Certification
Diplomate, American Board of Professional Psychology - Diplomate, American Board of Forensic Psychology - Fellow, American Board of Forensic Psychology - Diplomate, American Board of Forensic Examiners - Professional Ergonomist, Board of Certification in Professional Ergonomics - Certified Personnel Consultant, National Association of Personnel Consultants - Certified Employment Specialist, California Association of Personnel Consultants - Licensed Psychologist, State of California, State of New York - National Register of Health Service Providers in Psychology

---

### FRIEDLAND ASSOCIATES
Litigation expertise in employment discrimination

David L. Friedland, Ph.D.
Friedland Associates, Inc.
2080 Century Park East, Suite 1403
Los Angeles, CA 90067

Phone: (310) 553-6195
Fax: (310) 553-7557
Email: fried@primenet.com

Friedman Associates is a consulting firm with other twenty years experience in providing personnel assessment and organizational consulting services. Clients include both public and private sector organizations. Services include the following areas:

○ *Employee Selection Procedures:* Development and validation of employee selection procedures for use in hiring and promotion of employees.

○ *Job Analysis:* Performance of job analyses for a variety of applications, including: employee selection and promotion, training design and analysis, performance appraisal, and identification of essential job functions for compliance with the Americans With Disabilities Act.

○ *Litigation Support and Expert Services:* Friedland Associates assists clients with EEO compliance reviews and litigation. We are often consulted as an expert by legal counsel for both defendants and plaintiffs in employment discrimination lawsuits concerning employee recruitment, hiring, and promotion, and sexual harassment. We have assisted in more than thirty cases in both state and federal courts, including both class action and individual matters.

○ *Organizational Consulting:* We conduct organizational interventions addressing workplace issues such as employee skill and ability deficits, absenteeism, turnover, functional illiteracy, executive coaching, organizational climate surveys, team building, and conflict resolution.

**David Friedland, Ph.D.:** (California Psychologist license PSY6249) Director, Consulting Services, Friedland Associates, Inc. Twenty years in human resources consulting with both private and public sectors. Specialties include: personnel testing and validation; statistics, personnel assessment; EEO and litigation consulting; performance appraisal; layoff systems; absenteeism, turnover, and workplace illiteracy. Member, American Psychological Association; Society for Industrial-Organizational Psychology; Personnel Testing Council, Southern California; International Personnel Mgt. Assoc.

---

### Brian H. Kleiner, Ph.D
800 N. State College Blvd.
Fullerton, CA 92634
Phone: (714) 528-5700
Fax: (714) 528-7300

*See Expert Witness - Employee/Employment - Wrongful Termination/Harassment*

---

Specializing in: OSHA Regulations/Procedures

### CCC Consolidated Consultants Co.
739 Twin Oaks Ave.
Chula Vista, CA 91910-5924
Phone: (800) 683-9847
Fax: (619) 422-8101

*See Expert Witness - Coatings/Paint*

CALIFORNIA—LOS ANGELES

MARTINDALE-HUBBELL LAW DIRECTORY 1997

## LOS ANGELES (Continued)
Expert Witness—Employee/Employment (Continued)

### Specializing in: Wrongful Termination/Harassment

**Jay M. Finkelman, Ph.D., C.P.E.**
2675 Nottingham Ave.
Los Angeles, CA 90027
Phone: (213) 666-0900
Fax: (213) 666-0330

*See Expert Witness - Employee/Employment - Discrimination*

---

**Brian H. Kleiner, Ph.D**
Professor of Human Resource Management
Department of Management
School of Business Administration and Economics
California State University, Fullerton
800 N. State College Boulevard
Fullerton, California 92634
Telephone: (714) 528-5700/528-5015/773-3834
Fax: (714) 528-7300

#### SPECIALTIES
- WRONGFUL TERMINATION
- SEXUAL HARASSMENT
- NEGLIGENT HIRING
- RACE DISCRIMINATION
- AGE DISCRIMINATION
- SEX DISCRIMINATION
- DISABILITY DISCRIMINATION
- ADA
- COMPENSATION
- ACADEMIC GRIEVANCES
- OSHA

#### DEGREES
Ph.D. in Management, U.C.L.A., 1977
Master of Business Administration., U.C.L.A., 1973
B.S. in Business Administration,
Drexel University, 1969

#### CONSULTATION
Over 25 years experience as a consultant to over 100 organizations around the world concerning how to improve human resource management policies and practices.

#### PUBLICATIONS
Have published over 435 articles in a wide variety of academic and professional journals.

#### HONORS
In 1996 a program was hosted in my honor at CSUF in recognition of my accomplishments as a teacher scholar.

In 1996 taught the first graduate course on managing human resources ever to be televised for the public in the United States.

In 1995 taught the first graduate course on human behavior in organizations ever to be televised for the public in the United States.

Selected in 1994 to develop a peer review of faculty program to be implemented throughout the California State University system.

Nominee for the 1993 Bradford Outstanding Educator in the United States Award.

*(This Listing Continued)*

---

**BRIAN H. KLEINER, PH.D (Continued)**

Finalist for the 1992 Annual Outstanding Faculty Award, School Business Administration and Economics, California State University, Fullerton.

Recipient of the 1986, 1987, 1988, 1989, 1990 School Business and Economics' Meritorious Performance and Professional Promise Award.

From 1988 to present have taught classes on wrongful termination, sexual harassment and employment discrimination for the general public through University Extended Education at California State University, Fullerton, helping members from hundreds of organizations.

Selected for the following: Who's Who in Finance and Industry, Who's Who in California, Personalities of America, Community Leaders of America, and Who's Who in the World.

#### REFERENCES
Extensive recent references of satisfied law offices available upon request.

### ENGINEERS/ENGINEERING

Specializing in: PERSONALIZED SERVICE

**Ronald H. Berger, B.S. M.S., Mt.E.**
**B.E.S.T., Inc.**
24 Verde Vista Drive
Thousand Oaks, CA 91360-2645
(805) 493-4684 – (805) 493-5135 FAX
(800) 788-5605

Member No. 6319 American Board of Forensic Examiners

**COURT QUALIFIED EXPERT WITNESS and
CONSULTING ENGINEERS for
AUTOMOTIVE, PROPERTY,
GENERAL LIABILITY and
CATASTROPHE
CLAIMS and LITIGATION**

- Slip and Fall, Handicap/ADA, Construction, OSHA and Catastrophic Evaluation
- Accident Reconstruction, Biomechanical and Engineering Reports
- CADD-Computer Aided Design and Drafting Services up to "E" size Drawings
- Safety, Product Failure, Geotechnical and Environmental Evaluations
- Mechanical, Electrical Design and Failure
- Fire Cause and Origin

Initial Case Evaluation
Pre-Litigation
Trial and Mediation Testimony

**PLAINTIFF, DEFENSE and INSURANCE COMPANIES**

# SERVICES, SUPPLIERS, CONSULTANTS

# CALIFORNIA—LOS ANGELES

## CCC Consolidated Consultants Co.
739 Twin Oaks Ave.
Chula Vista, CA 91910-5924
Phone: (800) 683-9847
Fax: (619) 422-8101

*See Expert Witness Referral Services*

## Specializing in: Electrical

### YBI
880 West First Street, Suite #203
Los Angeles, CA 90012
Tel: (213) 620-0272
Fax: (213) 617-0558

**Yale Barkan**
Electrical Engineer

Over 40 years experience including forensic investigations, testifying in depositions, arbitration hearings and trials.

*Specializing in but not limited to:*

- Construction Defects
- Product Defects Liability
- Electrical Shock/Electrocution
- Industrial Explosions
- Building & Safety Code Violations
- Consumer, Industrial, and Military Products Defense
- Electrical Fire Cause and Origin
- Failure Analysis & Product Defects Analysis on:
    Computers
    Transformers
    DC & AC Motors
    Timers
    Industrial Process Control Systems
    Controllers
    Relays
    Analog & Digital Circuits
    Elevator Motion Controls
    Microwave/Toaster Ovens
    Hair Dryers
    Treadmill Exercise Machines

### Degrees
M.S.E.E. in Electrical Engineering, UC Berkeley
B.S.E.E. in Electrical Engineering, UC Berkeley

## Specializing in: Forensic Engineering

### CONSOLIDATED CONSULTANTS CO.
739 Twin Oaks Ave.
Chula Vista, CA 91910-5924
Phone (800) 683-9847
Fax (619) 422-8101
E-mail steve_vr@msn.com
Internet Home Page: http://www.FreeReferral.com

### FORENSIC MECHANICAL ENGINEER

### SERVICES

- Forensic Engineering Investigations; Expert Testimony in Product Liability and Equipment Failures
- Reconstruction of Industrial and Domestic Accidents Involving Personal Injuries
- Defects Analysis of Consumer Products and Building Materials
- Safety and Hazards Evaluation for Compliance with Regulations
- Supervision of Mechanical, Physical and Engineering Laboratory Tests with Interpretation of Results

### CASE SUBJECTS

| | |
|---|---|
| Appliances | Medical Apparatus |
| Arson Fires | Playground Equipment |
| Beds, Hospital | Patents |
| Bicycles | Plastic, Parts |
| Building Codes | Plumbing Failures |
| Carts, Shopping | Power Tools |
| Chairs, Collapsed | Rubber Hoses |
| Cigarettes Lighters | Sharpness |
| Containers | Shelves & Cabinets |
| Conveyor Belts | Shoes & Boots |
| Fences & Gates | Slips & Falls |
| Flammability | Sprinklers |
| Flooring | Traction/Friction |
| Garage Doors | Toys & Sports |
| Garments | Water Heaters |
| Glass & Glazing | Weather & Wind |
| Infant Car Seats | Wheel Chairs |
| Ladders | Window Screens |

### EXPERIENCE

Registered Professional Engineer in CA & NJ. B.Sc. (Engineering) University of London; M.S. (Mechanical Engineering) NJ Institute of Technology. Career experience includes over 20 yrs. as Product Evaluation Manager and Group Vice President of Calif. Division of United States Testing Co.; plus 10 years in research, design and sales engineer functions with major chemical, electrical and air conditioning corporations in NJ & NY.

Ongoing full-time consulting practice. Is qualified as an expert witness in seven regions, California Superior Court; has testified in Federal Courts in CA, NJ, DE, and TX. He holds active memberships in NSPE, ASME, ASSE, ASTM, ANSI, NFPA, ICBO. Granted several patents.

# LOS ANGELES (Continued)
Expert Witness—Engineers/Engineering—Forensic Engineering (Continued)

**Pringle & Associates**
**Structural Inspection Consultants**
1300 Aviation Blvd.
Redondo Beach, CA 90278
Phone: (800) 598-1970
Fax: (310) 376-5294

*See Construction Consultants - Construction Defects*

## Specializing in: Mechanical/Machine Design

**Erik K. Antonsson, Ph.D., P.E.**
Professor of Mechanical Engineering
California Institute of Technology
1200 E. California Blvd.
Mail Code: 104-44, Pasadena, CA 91125
818/395-3790 - 818/568-2719 FAX

**Specialties:** Machine design, product and process design, mechanical engineering, CAD, computer simulation, manufacturing.
Expert witness practice limited to patent infringement, trade secret and other intellectual property matters.

**Current Position:** Associate Professor of Mechanical Engineering, Division of Engineering and Applied Science, California Institute of Technology (Caltech).

**Consulting/Expert Witness Experience:** 10 patent and trade secret matters including technical analysis, model construction, photography, literature search, litigation preparation and support, reports, affidavits and declarations, depositions and court appearances.

**Professional Registration:** Registered Professional Engineer, California, M-26563.

**Professional Experience:** 16 years consulting experience in the design, analysis and manufacture of mechanical products and equipment. Associate Technical Editor, ASME Journal of Mechanical Design (1989-1993). Associate Professor (1990-), Assistant Professor (1984-1990) of Mechanical Engineering, California Institute of Technology. Assistant Professor of Orthopaedics (Bioengineering), Harvard University Medical School (1984). Assistant Professor Mechanical Engineering, University of Utah (1983).

**Education:** Ph.D. (1982) and M.S. (1978), Mechanical Engineering, M.I.T.; B.S. with distinction (1976), Mechanical Engineering, Cornell University.

**Honors and Awards:** Richard P. Feynman Prize for Excellence in Teaching (1995).
Presidential Young Investigator Award, National Science Foundation (1986-91).

**Publications:** 68 scientific/technical publications, 2 patents.

**Memberships:** American Society of Mechanical Engineers (ASME), Society of Manufacturing Engineers (SME), Institute of Electrical and Electronics Engineers (IEEE).

---

# FIRE

## Specializing in: Protection, Investigation

**O'ROURKE & Company**
P.O. Box 751
Glendale, California 91209
818-246-2293
(facsimile) 818-246-9366

Gerald W. O'Rourke, P.E.

Registered Engineer in 12 States. Registered as Fire Protection Engineer and Mechanical Engineer.

Member: NFPA, SFPE, NSPE, ICBO, IFCI, BOCA, SBCCI, AIA, SMPS

Graduate and Registered Engineer with more than 25 years experience in the design and evaluation of fire protection systems in facilities ranging from commercial to specialized industrial and institutional functions. Assignments included design and project management responsibilities. Active in the preparation of fire protection standards and code materials. Litigation support work includes both plaintiff and defense, investigation, deposition and trial testimony. Cases have been in both state and federal courts.

Specialty areas include the design and analysis of automatic sprinkler, fire pump and water supply systems, fire alarm and detection systems, specialized suppression systems including foam, carbon dioxide, halon and dry chemical.

Code Compliance as related to building and fire codes and issues.

Fire spread and computer modeling of fire growth.

---

Now you can find the lawyer even if you don't know where he or she practices - with the **Martindale-Hubbell Law Directory Alphabetical Index.**

The **Martindale-Hubbell Law Directory** is now available online...exclusively through the LEXIS®-NEXIS® services.

# SERVICES, SUPPLIERS, CONSULTANTS  CALIFORNIA—LOS ANGELES

## Specializing in: Wildland/Urban Interface

### Klaus Radtke, Ph.D.
(Pres. Geo Safety, Inc.; National Foundation for Environmental Safety).

1462 Lachman Lane
Pacific Palisades, CA 90272
Tel: (310) 459-9453   Fax: (310) 459-6187
E-Mail: Geo2@ix.netcom.com

Wildland Resource Scientist with 28 years of practical field experience in fire science and vegetation management/arboriculture/forestry. Expert witness and investigator in the country's biggest wildland fire and property loss cases: 1991 Oakland (Tunnel) Fire, 1993 Malibu Fire.

**Degrees/Lic:** Ph.D. (1981) UC Berkeley: Wildland Resource Sciences; MS (1977) HSU: Natural Resource Mgmt.; BS (1968) HSU: Forest Engin.; RPF (Reg. Prof. Forester); CCA (Community College Teaching, Supervisorial, Administrative Credentials).

**Specialties:** *Fire Behavior (Urban-Wildland). Fire Risk-Hazard-Structural Loss Assmt.; Wildland Fire Fuels Assmt.; Fire Spread Modeling & Fire Prediction; 'Fire-safe' Landscp. & Fuel Modification; Fire Ecology. Postfire Watershed Rehabilitation.
*Botany (Forensic)/Horticulture/Aboriculture Urban Forestry.
*Research & Investigation.
*Insurance Claims, Hazard Assessment.

**Honors:** Radtke's fire research recognized by County of L.A. as top priority for funding as part of the L.A. Co. Fire Dept. 1978 post-Prop. 13 Mgmt. Audit.
Natl. recognized wildland/urban interface fire authority.

**Publications:** Author & editor of US Forest Service & County Fire Depts. state of the art fire safety books such as *A Homeowner's Guide to Fire & Watershed Mgmt.*; *Living More Safely at the Chaparral-Urban Interface*, *Living in the Chaparral of California: An Integrated Approach to Public Safety*, <u>Urban Forestry: Los Angeles County 1911-1977</u> (with wildland fire maps), etc.

---

Now it's easy to find lawyers practicing a specific area of law!  Simply consult the
**Martindale-Hubbell Law Directory
Areas of Practice Index.**

## HUMAN FACTORS & SAFETY

### Jill A. Strawbridge, Ph.D.
Human Factors Expert
4850 Parkglen Avenue
Los Angeles, CA 90043-1012
Tel: 310-559-4377
Fax: 213-293-9370

**Degrees:** Ph.D. Human Factors, Industrial & Systems Engineering (minor in Gerentology, minor in Industrial & Organizational Psychology); M.A. Human Factors & Applied/Experimental Psychology; B.A. Psychology

**Specialties:**
- Product design & liability: design induced error & Products Defects
- Consumer products and design criteria
- Labels & Warnings
- Hazards and safety
- Human errors & behavioral expectations
- Gerentology: design implications and design criteria
- Accident prevention and safety
- Reasonable conduct
- Perception and human performance
- Multimedia software design
- User Interface design
- Toys
- Automotive & highway safety

The application of theories and models of human behavior to the design of products and systems with which humans interact. The principals of perception, cognition, behavior and learning theory applied to consumer products and man-machine systems design and analysis.

Specialization in gerentological design and accident analysis. Specialization in warnings and safety. Specialization in consumer product design and user interface design.

Authored numerous articles on consumer product design criteria and the ramifications of poor design.

**Forensic Summary**
Investigation of accidents or failures of:
- Warning procedures and notification for children & adults
- Child safety design: products and systems
- In-store guard rail design
- Pedestrian/automotive accident as a function of faulty warning procedures
- Tow truck design deficiency resulting in limb severing
- Automobile and truck accidents
- Older adult driving accidents and visual conspicuity issues
- Older adult falls
- Machine safety and injury
- Railroad crossing accidents

---

Fast ... Easy ... Flexible...
**The Martindale-Hubbell Law Directory on CD-ROM** gives you instant access through multiple search criteria to information on over 900,000 lawyers and law firms. For more details and a FREE demonstration disc, call **1-800-323-3288**.

## LOS ANGELES (Continued)
### Expert Witness (Continued)

### INSURANCE

## TOLE CONSULTING SERVICE

985 South Clarence Street
Anaheim, California 92806

Phone: 714-778-1592
Fax: 714-778-6313

In-depth knowledge of:

- Good/Bad faith issues
- Standards of care for insurance companies, agents, brokers and surplus lines brokers
- Property/casualty insurance
- California insurance code and ethics, environmental laws and other state laws
- Coverages including business interruption, earthquakes, liability, high catastrophy insurance liability, products liability, punitive, wrongful death and workers compensation

*Mary Tole, Insurance Expert With 25 Years Experience*

- Licensed Liability, Property and Surety Broker, State of California
- Insurance Instructor
- Member of Anaheim Chamber of Commerce and its legislative committee
- Member of Insurance Education Association

---

To update your listing
in the **Martindale-Hubbell Law Directory**
call 1-800-MARTIND(ALE).

---

### Specializing in: Bad Faith

## Jim Schratz and Associates
LITIGATION MANAGERS

664 Wild Oak Drive
Santa Rosa, CA 95407

Telephone: 707-538-8540
Facsimile: 707-539-5808

**Jim Schratz, President**

**Jim Schratz** is an experienced insurance executive with extensive knowledge of claims handling procedures. During his fourteen year career in the insurance industry, he rose from Associate General Counsel to Vice President. In his current practice he advises insurance carriers and insureds on numerous industry related topics including proper claims handling procedures and policies.

- Supervised extra-contractual cases throughout the United States.
- Qualified as expert witness in state and federal court.
- Directed nationwide automobile and general liability anti-fraud program with special emphasis on assuring proper claims handling in light of high potential for extra-contractual exposure.
- Formerly responsible for case management of all cases with a potential exposure of $3 million or more worldwide.
- Profiled on the front page of The Wall Street Journal, and appeared on NBC's Today Show and ABC's Business World.
- Published more than twenty articles on proper claims handling, litigation management and related topics.
- Law school professor who has lectured throughout the United States, in Canada and England.
- Delivered paper to the 1995 National convention of Risk Managers on the extra-contractual liability for mismanagement of legal fees.
- Member of the California Bar since 1976.

---

## Clinton E. Miller, J.D., BCFE

Author of:
*How Insurance Companies Settle Cases*

30 Years Experience
Testified Approximately 350 Times
Qualified Trial Insurance Expert
Civil/Criminal Cases
Nationwide

- Coverage Disputes
- Customs and Practices in the Claims Industry
- Good Faith/Bad Faith Issues

(408) 279-1034   Fax: (408) 279-3562

***SEE OUR AD ON PAGE CAA109S***

SERVICES, SUPPLIERS, CONSULTANTS | CALIFORNIA—LOS ANGELES

---

## Insurance Bad Faith Expert

### Clinton E. Miller, J.D., BCFE

Author of:
*How Insurance Companies Settle Cases*

30 Years Experience
Testified Approximately 350 Times
Qualified Trial Insurance Expert
Civil/Criminal Cases
Nationwide

o Coverage Disputes
o Customs/Practices in the Claims Industry
o Good Faith/Bad Faith Issues

(408) 279-1034    Fax: (408) 279-3562

---

**Specializing in: Risk Management Consulting**

### STONE & WEBSTER MANAGEMENT CONSULTANTS, INC.
One Penn Plaza 250 West 34 Street, New York, NY 10119
212 - 290-7032

**EXPERT TESTIMONY FOR TRIAL PREPARATION:**

Contract and Policy Standards

Best Practices in Risk Management

Claims Standards and Litigation Management

Broker and Insurance Company Performance Standards

**CONSULTING STAFF**

William J. Gombocz, JD

Michael A. Colin, CPCU, ARM, ARP

Stephen R. Geller

Alice M. Rushforth

---

### LEAD BASED PAINT

**CCC Consolidated Consultants Co.**
739 Twin Oaks Ave.
Chula Vista, CA 91910-5924
Phone: (800) 683-9847
Fax: (619) 422-8101

*See Expert Witness - Coatings/Paint*

### LETTERS OF CREDIT

**Uniform Commercial Code Consultants**
82 Loyola St.
Ventura, CA 93003
Phone: (805) 650-3472

*See Expert Witness - Commercial Law/Banking/UCC*

### MAGAZINE PUBLISHING

**Bay Sherman & Craig**
(Certified Public Accountants)
11845 West Olympic Boulevard, Suite 845
Los Angeles, California 90064
Phone - (310) 477-1400
Facsimile - (310) 479-0720

Our consulting group has over thirty years of experience in all aspects of the business of magazine publishing. We furnish expert operational and advisory assistance on consumer and trade magazines and newsletters.

SCOPE OF SERVICES

Expert Witness Testimony

Litigation Consulting

Assistance in preparation for depositions, trials and settlement negotiations

Operations and Systems

Valuations

Printing and Production Cost Reviews

### MARTIAL ARTS

**Specializing in: Hand to Hand**

**CCC Consolidated Consultants Co.**
739 Twin Oaks Ave.
Chula Vista, CA 91910-5924
Phone: (800) 683-9847
Fax: (619) 422-8101

*See Expert Witness - Criminalistics & Firearms*

### MEDICAL INSTRUMENT & PRODUCT INJURY

**CCC Consolidated Consultants Co.**
739 Twin Oaks Ave.
Chula Vista, CA 91910-5924
Phone: (800) 683-9847
Fax: (619) 422-8101

*See Medical Expert Witness - Devices*

## LOS ANGELES (Continued)
### Expert Witness (Continued)

### POLICE/SECURITY

#### Specializing in: Use of Force

**CCC Consolidated Consultants Co.**
739 Twin Oaks Ave.
Chula Vista, CA 91910-5924
Phone: (800) 683-9847
Fax: (619) 422-8101

*See Expert Witness - Criminalistics & Firearms*

#### PREMISES SECURITY & LIABILITY

**CCC Consolidated Consultants Co.**
739 Twin Oaks Ave.
Chula Vista, CA 91910-5924
Phone: (800) 683-9847
Fax: (619) 422-8101

*See Expert Witness - Engineers/Engineering - Forensic Engineering*

---

Need an extra copy of the **Martindale-Hubbell Law Directory**? Or of a specific volume? Call Martindale-Hubbell Customer Service at
**1-800-526-4902**

---

Now you can find the lawyer even if you don't know where he or she practices - with the **Martindale-Hubbell Law Directory Alphabetical Index.**

---

### REAL ESTATE

## CAMDAN & ASSOCIATES
and
Valuation Counselors

Join forces to bring you their combined expertise and skill for all your business and real estate appraisal and consulting needs.

---

#### CAMDAN & ASSOCIATES

Camdan & Associates provides a unique combination of legal and financial skills, making it one of the most respected valuation companies in the country today.

MICHAEL J. CAMRAS is a Certified General Real Estate Appraiser as well as a Licensed Attorney at Law in the State of California. He has served as an expert witness for over 25 years.

ROBERT L. DANIELS is a Licensed Certified Public Accountant in the State of California and a Member of the California Society of Certified Public Accountants.

---

#### Valuation Counselors

Valuation Counselors brings expertise in tangible and intangible asset valuation and has served its clients for over 25 years. Key Staff include:

SALLY HAFT, MAI, a member of the Appraisal Institute, has appraised an array of real estate.

TODD KALTMAN, CFA, is a Chartered Financial Analyst and senior member of the American Society of Appraisers in Business Valuation.

JON STUEHLING is a senior member of the American Society of Appraisers in Machinery and Equipment.

---

Tangible and Intangible Asset Values
Real Estate Acquisition & Disposal
Purchase Price Allocation
Mergers & Acquisitions
Shareholder Disputes
Marriage Dissolution
Leveraged Buy-Outs
Estate Planning
Condemnation
Tax Disputes
Bankruptcy
Litigation
ESOPs

**For Further Information Contact:**
Michael J. Camras, Camdan & Associates
11500 W. Olympic Boulevard, Suite 640, Los Angeles, CA 90064
Tel. 310-477-3450   Fax (310) 477-4440

## SERVICES, SUPPLIERS, CONSULTANTS

## CALIFORNIA—LOS ANGELES

### SAMUEL K. FRESHMAN
6151 W. CENTURY BLVD., STE. 300
LOS ANGELES, CA 90045

**REAL ESTATE EXPERT**

- ATTORNEY/REALTOR/DEVELOPER/MANAGER

- FORMER ADJUNCT PROFESSOR, USC GRADUATE SCHOOL OF BUSINESS/LECTURER STANFORD, USC, UCLA LAW SCHOOLS.

- 38 YRS REAL ESTATE TRADE PRACTICE.

- QUALIFIED IN LEGAL MALPRACTICE, LEASE INTERPRETATION, TITLE INSURANCE, AND ALL MATTERS RELATING TO REAL ESTATE TRANSACTIONS, BROKERAGE, E&O, FIDUCIARY DUTY, SYNDICATION, FINANCE, DUE DILIGENCE.

- 25 YEARS EXPERT WITNESS EXPERIENCE OVER THIRTY CASES.

- 21 PUBLISHED ARTICLES AND BOOKS.

- FORMER VICE CHAIRPERSON ABA SUB COMMITTEE ON REAL ESTATE TRADE PRACTICE AND SUBCOMMITTEE ON REAL ESTATE OPTIONS.

- ARBITRATOR, BANKER, TITLE COMPANY PRESIDENT

SAMUEL K. FRESHMAN (310) 410-2300, EXT. 306
FAX: 310/410-2919

---

The **Martindale-Hubbell Law Directory** is now available online...exclusively through the LEXIS®-NEXIS® services.

---

Now it's easy to find lawyers practicing a specific area of law! Simply consult the
**Martindale-Hubbell Law Directory
Areas of Practice Index.**

---

### MARK S. MALAN, MAI
REAL ESTATE APPRAISAL AND CONSULTING
- LEASE ANALYSIS -

110 W. Ocean Boulevard
Suite 426, Long Beach, CA 90802
PO Box 14885, Long Beach, CA 90803

(310) 983-6700    FAX (310) 983-1622

**AFFILIATIONS & LICENSES**
Appraisal Institute Member-MAI
Certified Appraiser: CA, AZ, OR, TX, WA
California General Contractors License
National Retail Federation

**COLLEGE INSTRUCTOR**
Cypress College       California State University, Dominquez Hills
Fullerton College     Appraisal Institute (Faculty Training)

**EDUCATION**
MBA - Finance (Real Estate emphasis)   BA - International Marketing
Specific Appraisal Institute and College Real Estate Courses Below:

Real Estate Appraisal Principles, Basic Valuation Procedures, Capitalization A & B, Case Studies, Report Writing, Standards of Professional Practice & USPAP, Appraising Apartments Seminar, Capitalization Seminar, Real Estate Practice, Real Estate Appraisal (Residential), Real Estate Finance, Real Estate Valuation, Marshall & Swift - Cost Estimating, Litigation Seminar, Appraisal Regulations of Federal Banking, Comprehensive Exam Seminar, International Financial Seminar, London, England, Subdivision Seminar, OREA and Evaluations Workshop, Survey Seminar, Relocation Appraising, Market Analysis, Understanding Limited Appraisals, International Valuation & Investing, Hotel/Motel Appraisal.

**NON VALUATION EXPERIENCE**
Investments, Syndications, Real Estate Sales, Energy Usage Analysis and Studies Development (Commercial/Industrial/Multi-family), Small Business Consultation, Real Property Management, Lease Audits.

---

Fast ... Easy ... Flexible...
**The Martindale-Hubbell Law Directory on CD-ROM** gives you instant access through multiple search criteria to information on over 900,000 lawyers and law firms. For more details and a FREE demonstration disc, call **1-800-323-3288**.

---

To update your listing
in the **Martindale-Hubbell Law Directory**
call **1-800-MARTIND(ALE)**.

## LOS ANGELES (Continued)
### Expert Witness—Real Estate (Continued)

## MCS Associates

18300 Von Karman, Suite 1100
Irvine, CA 92715
(714) 263-8700   Fax: (714) 553-0168
E-Mail: mcs@earthlink.net

Contact: Norman Katz - (Managing Partner)

MCS Associates is a nationally recognized consulting group that specializes in the banking, financial services and real estate industries. Established in 1973, MCS has provided consulting services to more than 1000 banks, thrift institutions, mortgage banks, insurance companies, regulatory agencies as well as real-estate and financial service organizations throughout the U.S.

Expert witness and litigation consulting assignments are an important focus of MCS Associates' services. Our clients include some of the nation's leading law firms, working on behalf of financial institutions, insurance companies, directors and officers, regulatory agencies, borrowers, depositors, developers and investors. MCS consultants are familiar with the issues, practices and standards of financial institutions of all sizes and have expertise in a wide range of real estate activities.

The firm has key strategic alliances in banking, insurance, securities brokerage and real estate matters, and takes great pride in identifying exactly the right experts for each assignment. Our experts/litigation consultants are experienced senior bankers, lenders, consultants, economists, real estate analysts/developers, accountants, appraisers and former regulators who combine specialized hands-on expertise with substantial litigation/expert witness experience.

Expert areas include:

- Banking Transactions
- Banking Operations & Administration
- Bank & S&L Lending - All Types (Policies, Procedures, Customs & Practice)
- Loan Underwriting/Admin.
- Commercial & Corporate Lending
- Real Estate/Mortgage Lending
- Construction Loans
- Mortgage Banking
- Insurance Coverage, Broker/Agent Standards, Industry Practice
- Wrongful Termination/Compensation Disputes
- Real Estate Appraisal
- Real Estate Development/Feasibility
- Real Estate Transactions/Practices
- Real Estate Brokerage
- Securities, Trusts & Investments
- Valuations/Damages Assessment
- Forensic Accounting

---

Need an extra copy of the **Martindale-Hubbell Law Directory**? Or of a specific volume?
Call Martindale-Hubbell Customer Service at
**1-800-526-4902**

---

### Specializing in: Finance

## Whipple H. Manning
5009 Alta Canyada Road
La Canada, CA. 91011
Phone (818) 790-1697 Fax (818) 952-9539

### AREAS OF EXPERTISE

Issues involving: financial institutions' policies, procedures and practices, loan underwriting, loan structure, loan documentation, loan closing, construction lending, property standards, valuation, standards of care for officers and directors, forensic analysis of loan transactions for possible fraud, required levels of due diligence in the loan origination process and measurement against established standards, lender's attitudes in dealing with toxic contamination and lender's responsibilities to borrowers, among others.

Assistance in pre-trial preparation including discovery, analysis of documentation and explanation of pertinent findings. Participated in over 20 cases in the past 4 years.

### PROFESSIONAL EXPERIENCE

- **Consultant:** Expert Witness, litigation support and real estate / real estate finance consulting for various law firms, financial institutions, real estate developers and individuals. Specific assignments have included: analysis of financial institution's real estate lending policies, procedures and practices and testing against industry standards; availability and cost of financing; valuation analysis; toxic contamination issues relative to lenders; loan structure analysis including determination as to intent regarding participation / joint venture or conventional financing; lender's policies and responsibilities to borrowers / purchasers regarding loan modifications and assumptions; and, analysis of a particular institution's lending practices and due diligence from loan officers to board members in regard to specific loan transactions.

- **Prior Experience**
Twenty-seven plus years experience in mortgage lending, asset management, secondary marketing and related activities. Seventeen years with a national life insurance company and ten years in charge of all income property lending for two surviving savings and loans.

### PARTIAL LISTING OF SPEAKING ENGAGEMENTS

California Mortgage Bankers' Convention
- Monterey, California - 1982
California Mortgage Bankers' Income Property Seminar
- Los Angeles, California - 1983
Hospitality Industry Investment Conference
- New York, New York - 1984
International Council of Shopping Centers - Maui, Hawaii - 1985
Crittenden Seminar - Washington, D.C. - 1986
National Mortgage Bankers' Convention - Chicago, Illinois - 1986

### PRIOR PROFESSIONAL ORGANIZATIONS

National Association of Industrial and Office Parks
International Council of Shopping Centers
Urban Land Institute
California Mortgage Bankers
California Business Properties Association - Director
Chicago Title - Los Angeles Advisory Board

## Roofing & Waterproofing

### RJ CONSULTANTS INTERNATIONAL, INC.
23441 GOLDEN SPRINGS RD., #147
DIAMOND BAR, CA 91765
TELE/FAX (909) 861-5928

Incorporated in 1984, RJ Consultants has provided Expert Witness/Testimony in over 150 lawsuits, on behalf of both defendant and plaintiff (60%, 40%), with an impressive success rate. Our clients include: attorneys, insurance carriers, homeowner's associations, developers, property managers, contractors at all levels, building and home owners.

Our President, Dr. Robert Vorlick, with over 22 years within the industry, is one of two Ph.D.'s within the field of *Technology & Ecological Environmental Sciences*, with a Major in Construction Technology, within the State of California. He is also the *only* Board Certified Forensic Examiner - Construction Forensics (American College of Forensic Examiners), specializing in water invasion, in the Western States. As an international author & lecturer, Dr. Vorlick is recognized throughout the U.S., Asia and parts of Europe and is the owner of one of the largest privately-owned research libraries in the U.S. As the President of RJ Consultants, Dr. Vorlick is the primary signatory of all Expert Witness/Testimony Reports and is solely responsible for all depositions, mediations, arbitrations and court proceedings. He remains active in the preparation of new construction & remedial specification development and inspections.

Dr. Vorlick is a member of: American Arbitration Association, American College of Forensic Examiners, American Institute of Architects, American Institute of Plant Engineers, Construction Specifications Institute.

Our expertise is within the field of:

- ✓ Roofing (built-up, single ply, polyurethane, shingles, shake, tile, metal, elastomeric & cold process)
- ✓ Waterproofing (above & below grade)
- ✓ Deck Coatings & Membranes
- ✓ Sealants (including glazing, fire & expansion joints)
- ✓ Concrete sealing & restoration
- ✓ Metal (all metal related to water repulsion & exclusion)
- ✓ Thermal Barriers (roof, wall, ceiling & refrigerator)

If you require an *honest* evaluation of possible construction defects, restoration or replacement, please feel free to contact us at any time.

---

Now you can find the lawyer even if you don't know where he or she practices - with the **Martindale-Hubbell Law Directory Alphabetical Index.**

---

### ROBERT D. BYRD & ASSOCIATES, INC.
P.O. Box 2905
Big Bear Lake, CA 92315-2905
Phone: (909) 866-5777
Fax: (909) 866-5946

*Robert D. Byrd*

Contractor's License C-39; BS; GS.
Expert witness for sheet metal, waterproofing & roofing.
15 years experience for plaintiff & defense.

#### BACKGROUND

A construction expert specializing in waterproofing, sheet metal and roofing. Byrd's background includes both hands-on and management experience in Class "A" and residential construction. His roofing experience began by working at his father's roofing company throughout high school and college. He later managed the roof engineering department at a major roofing manufacturer and is the past president of a successful multi-million dollar waterproofing and roofing corporation. Byrd has spent the last fifteen years in construction litigation as a plaintiff and defense expert. A background that includes teaching speech and international lecturing complements his construction experience to provide the best settlement conference and jury presentation available.

#### MEMBERSHIPS IN PROFESSIONAL SOCIETIES

Specifications Institute; National Roofing Contractors Assn.; Roof Consultants Institute; Western Roofing Contractors Assn.; ASTM.

Call for recent trial results, curriculum vitae and other information.

## Secured Transactions

### Uniform Commercial Code Consultants
82 Loyola St.
Ventura, CA 93003
Phone: (805) 650-3472

*See Expert Witness - Commercial Law/Banking/UCC*

## Slip, Trip and Fall

### CCC Consolidated Consultants Co.
739 Twin Oaks Ave.
Chula Vista, CA 91910-5924
Phone: (800) 683-9847
Fax: (619) 422-8101

*See Expert Witness - Engineers/Engineering - Forensic Engineering*

# LOS ANGELES (Continued)
Expert Witness (Continued)

## TRANSPORTATION

### Specializing in: Aviation

### JACOBY AND ASSOCIATES
Richard Downing Jacoby, Esq.
28112 Edelweiss Court
Laguna Niguel, CA 92677
(714) 831-6980 (24hr message center)

Prior Experience with U.S. Department of Transportation, California State Legislature, Federal Aviation Administration, Boeing Aircraft Co., McDonnel Douglas, United, Northwest Orient, Delta, Aveaco Airlines, Thompson Express Travel, A.L.P.A., Teamsters, E.E.O.C., Garden Grove City College, F.A.P.A. **Expertise in Pilot wrongful termination.** Expertise as witness in air transportation litigation cases, in nearly all aspects of flight operations and related federal air regulations. Expertise in Department of Transportation legal filings for airline licenses. Federal Aviation Administration operations specifications manuals. Both defense and prosecution experience.

#### BACKGROUND (Past 33 years)

**Jacoby and Associates (since 1968) - Administrative Aviation Law**
**Emery Worldwide Airlines (since 1991) - DC 8 Captain**
Alta Financial Corporation - Of Counsel/Real Estate
Evergreen International Airline - DC8; 747 Pilot
Northwest Orient Airline - 747 Pilot Training
Piedmont Airline - 727 Flight Engineer
British American Airline - DC8 Captain, Founder
Flying Tiger Airline - DC8 Pilot Training
Golden West Airline (FAR 121) - SD-3 Captain
Van Nuys Aviation - General Manager, FAR 141, 135 Chief Instructor
Edwin G. Davies, Esq. and Associates - Of Counsel/Estate Planning

#### Education

Law Degree - La Salle University
Brokers License - California Department of Real Estate
Teaching Credential - University of California at Los Angeles
**Ph.D. - Psychology of Religion**
M.A. - Comparative Religion
B.A. - Philosophy/Theology

#### F.A.A. Certification

Airline Transport Pilot - ASMEL, DC-3, SD-3, DC-8
Flight Engineer - Turbojet 727
Certified Flight Instructor - Airplane Single and Multi Engine Land and Instrument
Certified Ground Instructor - Advanced and Instrument

#### Professional Organizations

Air Line Pilots Association International
American Bar Association
Administrative Bar (Transportation)

Minimum Retainer: 10 hours at $500 per hour.

---

### Specializing in: Traffic Engineering & Safety

### William Kunzman, P.E.
1111 Town & Country Road, Suite 34
Orange, CA 92668
(714) 973-8383
FAX (714) 973-8821
Visit Web Page: http://www.traffic-engineer.com

William Kunzman has worked professionally in traffic engineering and transportation planning since 1968 in both the public and private sectors. He is an Expert Witness in Traffic Engineering involving highway accidents.

#### TECHNICAL EXPERTISE

Traffic engineer expert regarding motor vehicle accidents (automobile, truck, bus, pedestrian, bicycle, motorcycle).

Knowledge of governmental agency procedures, design, geometrics, signs, traffic controls, parking, and maintenance.

#### EDUCATION

Undergraduate Work: Bachelor of Science Degree (1967), University of California at Los Angeles, School of Engineering (September, 1963 to June, 1967)

Graduate Work: One Year (10 classes) Certificate in Traffic Engineering (1968), Yale University, Bureau of Higway Traffic (September, 1967 to June, 1968)

Guest Lecturer: University of California at Irvine (1975)

Class Instructor: California State University at Fullerton (1976)

#### REGISTRATION

Registered Professional Traffic Engineer in the State of California, TE0056 since 1975.

#### WORK EXPERIENCE

1. Federal Highway Administration, Office of Policy Planning (1969-1972) Worked in Oregon, Illinois, Pennsylvania, and Washington, D.C. Prepared Highway Needs Study which was presented to Congress
2. County of Riverside, Assistant Traffic Engineer (1972-1973)
3. Lampman Associates, Traffic Engineer Associate (1973-1974)
4. City of Irvine, Transportation Planning Engineer (1974-1975)
5. Weston Pringle and Associates, Traffic Engineer Associate (1975-1976)
6. Self Employment (1976 to Present)

#### HONORS AND AWARDS

1. Received fellowship and living stipend to attend Yale University from the Insurance Institute of Highway Safety
2. Elected Class President of Yale University Bureau of Highway Traffic
3. Recipient of the 1978 Institute of Transportation Engineers Past Presidents' Award (This is most prestigious award given by Institute of Transportation Engineers)
4. Recipient of the 1979 Institute of Transportation Engineers, Southern California Section, Young Traffic Engineer of the Year Award

#### MEMBER OF FOUR PROFESSIONAL SOCIETIES

1. Institute of Transportation Engineers - ITE (joined in 1967)
2. American Society of Civil Engineers (joined in 1971)
3. Yale University Bureau of Highway Traffic Alumni Association (joined in 1972)
4. Forensic Consultants Association of Orange County (joined in 1995)

Traffic engineer expert witness, motor vehicle accidents (automobile, truck, pedestrian, bicycle, motorcycle). Dozens of cases; both defense and plaintiff. Largest settlement $2,000,000 in case against CalTrans. Knowledge of governmental agency procedures, design, geometrics, signs, traffic controls, parking, and maintenance. Six publications in traffic engineering.

SERVICES, SUPPLIERS, CONSULTANTS

## WOOD SCIENCE & TECHNOLOGY

### PHILIP MASON OPSAL, INC.

Post Office Box 64591
Tucson, Arizona 85728
Telephone: (520) 797-1256
FAX:    (520) 797-0986
ALSO:   (800) 659-1256

**PHILIP MASON OPSAL**

**Education**

Bachelor of Science-University of Minnesota In Wood Science-Emphasis on Wood Preservation and Wood Deterioration; Master of Science-University of Minnesota In Wood Chemistry-Minor in Industrial Engineering

**Experience**

Professor of Wood Science-Colorado State University; Founder and President-Firm of Consulting Wood Scientists (JASON ASSOCIATES, INC.); Vice President, Utilities Services (LOADMASTER SYSTEMS, INC.) Wood Scientist-Consultant (PHILIP MASON OPSAL, INC.)

Since 1961, When Opsal served as the expert in case in Denver Federal Court, he has been consulted in over 600 potential litigations and has been recognized as an expert in courts of law in sixteen states.

Opsal has been consulted on wood used as utility poles, crossarms/braces, ladders, tool handles, plywood composition board, furniture and other wood and wood products used in construction of all types such as trusses and wood preservation and wood deterioration matters. Clients have been equally Plaintiffs and Defendants.

**Member**

American Institute of Timber Construction
American Society for Testing & Materials
American Wood-Preservers' Association
Forest Products Society
Society of Forensic Engineers & Scientists
Society of Wood Science and Technology

---

The **Martindale-Hubbell Law Directory** is now available online...exclusively through the LEXIS®-NEXIS® services.

---

CALIFORNIA—LOS ANGELES

## EXPERT WITNESS REFERRAL SERVICES

**TECHNICAL ADVISORY SERVICE FOR ATTORNEYS**
Headquarters: 1166 DeKalb Pike, Blue Bell, PA 19422-1853
U.S. and Canada: 800-523-2319   Fax: 800-329-8272
United Kingdom: 0800-89-1292
E-mail: experts@tasanet.com

**LOS ANGELES ATTORNEYS CALL TASA
WHEN ONLY AN EXPERT WILL DO®.**

North America's Largest And Most Experienced Expert Referral Service® is the leading source of Experts, Consultants, and ADR Specialists for attorneys, insurance firms, corporations, and government agencies.

No other Expert source can match our combination of:

- More than 24,000 outstanding experts
- More than 6,500 categories of expertise
- More than 200,000 clients
- More than 35 years' experience
- Competitive fees
- Efficiency and personalized service

**TASA SAVES YOU TIME AND MONEY**

One call to TASA puts you in touch with experienced advisors who will assist you promptly and tailor referrals to your requirements, *free of charge*.

Often, we complete referrals during that initial call, making further searching unnecessary.

For cases of all sizes...
for plaintiff or defense...
for cases that make headlines and
for thousands that do not...
at the eleventh-hour or early in the case...
**TASA WILL MEET YOUR EXPERT NEEDS.**

Some areas of expertise available through TASA:

**AGRICULTURE:** chemicals, machinery, explosions, crops, feed, forestry.

**AUTOMOTIVE/TRANSPORTATION:** accident reconstruction, seat belts, vehicle/road design, trucks, railroads, aviation.

**BUSINESS/FINANCE/ECONOMICS:** banking, securities, insurance, economic valuation, appraisals, real estate.

**CONSTRUCTION/ARCHITECTURE:** building design, maintenance, structural integrity, HVAC, plumbing; bridges.

**CRIMINOLOGY/POLICE PROCEDURES:** document examination, fingerprinting, ballistics, prisons, tape analysis.

**ELECTRICITY/ELECTRONICS:** safety, wiring, power lines, communication equipment, computers, appliances.

**ELEVATORS/LIFTS:** cranes, controls, design and safety.

**ENVIRONMENT:** water, air & noise pollution; hazardous waste, asbestos, ecology.

**FALLS:** lighting, surfaces, ladders, scaffolding.

**FIRES:** explosions, arson, flammable clothing.

**MACHINERY:** design, safety; industrial, agricultural, and home devices.

(This Listing Continued)

CAA115S

## CALIFORNIA—LOS ANGELES

### LOS ANGELES (Continued)
#### Expert Witness Referral Services (Continued)

**TASA (Continued)**

**MARITIME:** seamanship, cargo handling, ship/boat design, accident reconstruction.

**MEDICAL/HEALTH CARE:** issues relating to medical personnel, institutions, equipment, and procedures.

**MATERIALS:** metals, polymers, glass, wood, textiles.

**INTELLECTUAL PROPERTY:** patents/copyrights/trademarks.

**PERSONNEL/LABOR:** wages & hours, discrimination, workplace safety, ADA issues.

**PHARMACEUTICALS/TOXICOLOGY:** drugs, food poisoning, labels & warnings, cosmetics, coatings.

**SPORTS/RECREATION:** equipment, supervision, facilities.

Call for a FREE CONSULTATION.
And ask for a complimentary copy of
TASA's Directory of Expertise.

**800-523-2319**

### FAX FILING OF COURT DOCUMENTS

---

## FILE YOUR COURT DOCUMENTS ELECTRONICALLY IN ALL THESE CALIFORNIA COUNTIES.*

*To set up an account at no charge, telephone our office in one of the following counties —*

| | | | |
|---|---|---|---|
| Alameda (Oakland) | (510) 835-3100 | Riverside | (213) 617-1212 |
| Alameda (Hayward) | (510) 786-9550 | Sacramento | (916) 446-7666 |
| Contra Costa | (510) 228-3191 | San Bernardino | (213) 617-1212 |
| Los Angeles | (213) 617-1212 | San Francisco | (415) 563-7440 |
| Marin | (415) 491-0606 | San Mateo | (415) 365-8707 |
| Orange | (213) 617-1212 | Santa Clara | (408) 287-2093 |
| Placer | (916) 823-7815 | Solano | (707) 425-8828 |

Sonoma (707) 524-6999

FAX &FILE™ is fast, reliable and economical. Just fax your document to the appropriate branch, where it's received on plain paper fax machines. Our paralegals check it for deficiencies and assemble it in compliance with local rules. Then we file the document, advance any filing fee, and fax you a conformed copy. We also retrieve court documents and obtain judges' signatures.

**CALIFORNIA'S FIRST, LARGEST, MOST EXPERIENCED FAX FILING NETWORK.**

*Other branches opening soon. Call (415) 491-0606 for update.*

---

### FAX & FILE LEGAL SERVICES, INC.
Corporate Office
24 Professional Center Parkway, Suite 200
San Rafael, CA 94903
Tel: (415) 491-0606   FAX: (415) 491-0434

CALIFORNIA'S OLDEST, LARGEST AND MOST EXPERIENCED
FAX FILING NETWORK

**NEED TO FILE A DOCUMENT IN A CALIFORNIA COURT?** We can do it for you in several counties! Call our branch in the county where you want to file and we'll set up an account for you at no charge. Then simply FAX your court document to that branch where it's received on plain paper laser fax machines. Next, our paralegals look it over for completeness and compliance with local rules. Shortly thereafter, we go to court and file the document, advancing any filing fee required. After filing, we fax you a confirmation. It's that easy! We can also:

- Retrieve Court Documents
- Obtain Judge's Signatures
- Do Court Research
- Access Public Records

#### BRANCH OFFICES

| County | Telephone | County | Telephone |
|---|---|---|---|
| Alameda (Oakland) | (510) 835-3100 | Sacramento | (916) 446-7666 |
| Alameda (Hayward) | (510) 786-9550 | San Bernardino | (213) 617-1212 |
| Contra Costa | (510) 228-3191 | San Francisco | (415) 563-7440 |
| Los Angeles | (213) 617-1212 | San Mateo | (415) 365-8707 |
| Marin | (415) 491-0606 | Santa Clara | (408) 287-2093 |
| Orange | (213) 617-1212 | Santa Cruz | (408) 469-3056 |
| Placer | (916) 823-7815 | Solano | (707) 425-8828 |
| Riverside | (213) 617-1212 | Sonoma | (707) 524-6999 |

Please check out our Website at faxfile.com for
more complete information and the latest updates.

FILE YOUR COURT DOCUMENTS ELECTRONICALLY.
IT'S FAST, RELIABLE AND ECONOMICAL.

*SEE OUR AD ON PAGE CAA116S*

### FIRE INVESTIGATORS

**Klaus Radtke, Ph.D.**
1462 Lachman Ln.
Pacific Palisades, CA 90272
Phone: (310) 459-9453
Fax: (310) 459-6187

*See Expert Witness - Fire - Wildland/Urban Interface*

**SERVICES, SUPPLIERS, CONSULTANTS**  |  **CALIFORNIA—LOS ANGELES**

## FORENSIC PSYCHIATRY

### ALFRED COODLEY, M.D., Ph.D.
10921 Wilshire Boulevard #614
Los Angeles, CA 90024
310-208-4411

M.D., Univ. of California at San Francisco Sch. of Medicine
Sch. of Military Neuropsychiatry & Electroencephalography, Mason Gen. Hosp. 1st Lt. to Major, Medical Corps, Last duty as Chief of Neurology & Asst. chief Neuropsychiatry, Letterman Gen. Hosp., San Francisco
Senior resident and U.S. Public Health Service Fellow in psychiatry, Cincinnati General Hospital
Diplomate, American Board of Psychiatry
Associate Clinical Professor of Psychiatry, UCLA Sch. of Medicine
Clin. Prof. Emeritus of Psychiatry, USC Sch. of Medicine

Psychiatric Consultant:
  U.S. Public Health Service 49-68
  L.A. Co. Juvenile Hall 49-71
  Psychiatric Section, L.A. Co. Superior Court 50-57
  L.A. Co. Probation Department 50-71
  State of Calif. Parole Clinic 62-92
  Allergy & Immunology Clinic & Family Medicine Dept., UCLA Sch. of Medicine 62-82
  Criminal Division, L.A. Co. Superior Court 71-
  Forensic Inpatient & Outpatient Mental Health Units, Central Jail, L.A. County 79-89
  Federal Public Defender & L.A. Unified School District & L.A. City Pension Dept. 81-
Life Fellow, American Psychiatric Association & Amer. Orthopsychiatric Assn.

Member:  Amer. Psychosomatic Society 51-
    So. Calif. Psychoanalytic Institute & Society Ph.D. in Psychoanalysis 55-
    American & International Psychoanalytic Association 58-

Councilor: So. Calif. Psychiatric Society 62-65
Executive Councilor: American Psychoanalytic Association 70-78
Contributing Editor: Annual Survey of Psychoanalysis 61, 63-64
Associate Editor: The Psychoanalytic Forum 66-70
Editorial Board: Journal of American College of Forensic Psychiatry 83-
Training & Supervising Analyst, So. Calif. Psychoanalytic Institute 72-
IME & QME, St. of Calif. Workers' Compensation Appeals Board, 77-95
Appointed by L.A. Co. Counsel to evaluate all County Jails & by Sonoma Co. and San Jose Co. to evaluate said jails 76-79, 82-83
Appointed by L.A. City Attorney to evaluate all city jails 82
Member, American Academy of Psychiatry & Law 84-
Faculty Executive Committee, UCLA Sch. of Medicine, 92-94
92 Publication in psychiatry, psychoanalysis, psychosomatic medicine, and forensic psychiatry

---

Now it's easy to find lawyers practicing a specific
area of law! Simply consult the
**Martindale-Hubbell Law Directory
Areas of Practice Index.**

## FORENSIC SERVICES

### VOLLMER-GRAY ENGINEERING LABORATORIES

(310) 437-6468
FAX (310) 432-1805

1403 W. Gaylord Street
Long Beach, CA 90813

*Vollmer-Gray Engineering Laboratories employs 14 full-time staff engineers in a 10,000 square foot laboratory and evidence storage facility. Our clients, therefore, benefit from the experience and education of the entire staff. Please call any of the following staff members:*

**Metallurgical and Material Failure Analysis**
Gerald F. Zamiski, Ph.D., P.E.
Paul S. Guthorn, M.S.M.E., P.E.

**Vehicular Accident Reconstruction**
Cory L. Gray, M.S.M.E., P.E.
Reuben P. Vollmer, B.S.M.E., P.E.
Kenneth L. Pearl, B.S.M.E.
Leonard Lacaze, Jr., B.S.M.E., P.E.
Jon B. Landerville, M.S.M.E., P.E.
Steven H. Anderson, B.S.M.E.

**Traffic Engineering**
Robert F. Douglas, B.S.C.E., P.E.

**Safety Engineering & Premises Liability**
Ned Wolfe, P.E.
Taryn L. Johnson, M.S.S.E., Cert. in Safety Mgmt.
Richard C. Warner, B.S.M.E., P.E.

**Industrial Machine Safety**
Ned Wolfe
Ian L. Morrison, M.E., P.E.
Richard C. Warner

**Vehicle or Mechanical Failure Analysis**
Reuben P. Vollmer
Ned Wolfe
Paul S. Guthorn
Leonard Lacaze, Jr.
William J. Kluge, Jr., B.S.M.E., P.E.
Ian L. Morrison

**Tire Failure Analysis**
Kenneth L. Pearl

**Fire Analysis**
Gerald F. Zamiski
Paul S. Guthorn
William J. Kluge, Jr.

## LOS ANGELES (Continued)
### GROUPWARE

TeamTalk™
5840 Uplander Way
Culver City, CA 90230-6620
800-367-8729, 310-649-5800
Fax: 310-649-6200
info@traxsoft.com
www.traxsoft.com/traxsoft/

Now your entire organization can discuss important topics, clients, rulings, and corporate issues without a complex implementation and administrative burden. TeamTalk is a group discussion application that facilitates communication within organizations. It is very easy to install and requires very little administration or training.

TeamTalk organizes information and documents by topic in a hierarchical structure. The information in public topics is always available to all TeamTalk members to review or respond to. Private topics can be created, as well; this information is only available to the members of the individual private topics. Once entered into TeamTalk, the members don't need to worry about organizing the data or saving individual comments; TeamTalk manages the information for them. They can, however, put comments on hold as a reminder to accomplish a task or research something before responding.

Any member can easily create a new public or private topic and build the member list in a few minutes. TeamTalk includes OLE 2.0 support, so members can include documents, spreadsheets, graphics, and audio and video files in comment. This allows other member to review the objects in the context of the conversation. TeamTalk includes a powerful search facility. A customizable sticker bar is available, for including small graphics in comments that convey the tone.

TeamTalk will run on most networks. It supports Windows, Windows NT, and OS/2 clients. Because files and individual preferences are stored on the network, TeamTalk consumes no space on the individual workstations.

---

Fast ... Easy ... Flexible...
**The Martindale-Hubbell Law Directory on CD-ROM** gives you instant access through multiple search criteria to information on over 900,000 lawyers and law firms. For more details and a FREE demonstration disc, call **1-800-323-3288**.

## HEDONIC DAMAGES/LOSS OF ENJOYMENT OF LIFE

### Economic Consultants & Associates
### Forensic Economics

Stephen T. Riley, Ph.D.
Forensic Economist

2102 Business Center Drive, Suite 130
Irvine, CA 92715

(310) 246-9993
Fax (619) 729-7027

Dr. Riley has over thirteen years experience as an expert in the field of Forensic Economics. He has provided expert testimony for both plaintiff and defense attorneys. He has over twenty years of teaching experience at the college and university level and is the author of several articles on Forensic Economics including "The Economic Consultant in Forensic Economics", "Economics of Hedonic Damages", "Investment Approach and Loss of Enjoyment of Life to Parents in the Death of a Child", and "Lets Move Hedonic Damages Into the Courtroom and See What's Happening," Although Dr. Riley's Primary focus is on P/I, W/D, business litigation, wrongful termination, and legal/medical malpractice, he has taken a special interest in the research and quantification of the loss of enjoyment of life (hedonic damages). He has lectured at conventions and conducted seminars for attorneys on the topic of hedonic damages.

Although Dr. Riley's consulting practice is located in California, he has consulted for attorneys in Arizona, Nevada, Maryland, Colorado, New York, Wyoming and New Mexico.

**Representative Cases Involving Loss of Enjoyment of Life (Hedonic Damages)**
(California Superior Court Cases)

Medical Malpractice (Death of a Child): Lopex vs. Cox, M.D...hedonic damages $5.0 million. Case settled.

Personal Injury (Employed Related): Kunard vs. American Recreational Properties, et al. Hedonic damages $959,000. Set for arbitration.

Personal Injury (Automobile Accident): Kinloch vs. Kramer Motors...loss of enjoyment of life $763,000. Case settled.

Wrongful Death of a Child: Ripley vs. EDS...hedonic damages $685,000. Case pending.

Defective Home: Christophier vs. Placer Savings and Loan Association...hedonic damages $1.0 million (physical and psychological trauma to owners of home). Case settled.

Wrongful Termination: Coleman vs. Loan Mills, Inc...total damages (hedonic damages) $1.2 million. Case settled.

Personal Injury (Burn Victim): Qi Zhao vs. So. Calif. Pipe...loss of enjoyment of life $1.1 million. Jury verdict for plaintiff.

Medical Malpractice: Patterson vs. Kaiser...hedonic damages $1.6 million (husband and wife). Case pending.

Wrongful Termination: Clemens vs. Sea World...hedonic damages $457,000. Verdict for defense.

Wrongful Death: Zamaripa vs. Isley...hedonic damages $1.3 million (wife of the deceased). Case settled.

Personal Injury/Wrongful Termination: Curtis vs. U. Soe Nyun...loss of enjoyment of life $813,000. Case pending.

Wrongful Death of an Adult and Unborn Child: Vargas vs. County of Los Angeles...hedonic damages $804,000 (husband and father of the child). Case pending.

Personal Injury (Automobile Accident): Daly vs. Dayton...loss of enjoyment of life $391,000. Trial pending.

# SERVICES, SUPPLIERS, CONSULTANTS

## HEIR TRACERS

# LOCATING HEIRS
# IDENTIFYING HEIRS
# PROVING RELATIONSHIP
*U.S. and Foreign Countries*

# DOCUMENTATION AND FAMILY CHARTS
*professionally prepared and certified for accuracy*

# AMERICAN RESEARCH BUREAU
*Salt Lake City Research Center*

## PHONE 1-800-628-7221
## FAX 1-800-446-2626

---

**American Research Bureau, Inc.**
Accredited Professional Genealogists
Expert Genealogical Witnesses

TELEPHONE 1-800-628-7221
FAX 1-800-446-2626

Missing and Unknown Heirs Located
Documentation for Court Submission
Heirship Certified for Completeness and Accuracy

Prompt and Efficient - No Cost to the Estate

U.S. and Foreign Research
International Network of Affiliates and Correspondents

*"A simple solution to complex heirship problems"*

QUALITY - ESTABLISHED 1935 - INTEGRITY

References Available

**SEE OUR AD ON PAGE CAA119S**

---

# CALIFORNIA—LOS ANGELES

## FRASER & FRASER

GENEALOGISTS
AND INTERNATIONAL PROBATE RESEARCHERS

Lost Kin?

Take the easy step towards finding them

When no Will exists, we prepare a family tree to discover all possible claimants. When people named in a Will or Trust have disappeared, we are expert in tracing them.

We have behind us over 50 years' experience and a full-time staff of specialist researchers. We have at our fingertips the latest computer systems which enable us to access some of the world's largest databases. With our network of international offices we are able to carry out research throughout Europe, Scandinavia and Commonwealth countries.

The partners, Simon and Nathan Fraser, together with their own staff, travel extensively to carry out research worldwide, with offices in London, Rome, Paris and Warsaw.

If you would like more information please write for explanatory brochure.

**Messrs. Fraser & Fraser
Manfield House
376 Strand
London WC2R 0LR England
Telephone: 44 171 240 0788
Fax: 44 171 836 9975**

Member
The Association of Genealogist and Record Agents

---

To update your listing
in the **Martindale-Hubbell Law Directory**
call **1-800-MARTIND(ALE)**.

---

Need an extra copy of the **Martindale-Hubbell Law Directory**? Or of a specific volume?
Call Martindale-Hubbell Customer Service at
**1-800-526-4902**

## LOS ANGELES (Continued)
### Heir Tracers (Continued)

# HOERNER BANK
### AKTIENGESELLSCHAFT

**TRACING MISSING HEIRS WORLDWIDE**

- THE OLDEST ESTABLISHED AND ONE OF THE WORLD'S LARGEST PROBATE RESEARCH FIRMS

- SERVICES RENDERED TO PROBATE COURTS, PERSONAL REPRESENTATIVES OF ESTATES, FIDUCIARIES, HEIRS AND BENEFICIARIES, OTHERS INTERESTED

- CONTINGENCY OR FEE BASIS

- HIGHLY QUALIFIED AND EXPERIENCED STAFF

- SERVICES INCLUDE SEARCH FOR UNKNOWN OR MISSING HEIRS, OWNERS OF ABANDONED PROPERTY, COLLECTIONS OF COMPLETE PROOF OF HEIRSHIP DOCUMENTATION

- TRANSLATION FROM GERMAN, FRENCH, SPANISH, CZECH, POLISH, RUSSIAN, BALTIC, SERBO-CROATIAN AND OTHER LANGUAGES, CORRESPONDENCE IN ENGLISH, FRENCH OR GERMAN

- REAL ESTATE SALES, COLLECTION OF BANK ACCOUNTS, TRANSFER OR SALE OF STOCKS AND BONDS

- HELP MAKING PREPARATIONS FOR COURT COMMISSIONS, EXECUTION OF AFFIDAVITS INCLUDING AFFIDAVITS OF DILIGENT SEARCH, EFFECTING DISTRIBUTIONS AND COLLECTING RECEIPTS

- ALL OTHER TRADITIONAL BANKING BUSINESS

- SUBJECT TO SUPERVISION BY THE FEDERAL SUPERINTENDENT OF BANKS

**CHALLENGE OUR EFFICIENCY**

D-74072 Heilbronn, Oststrasse 77
Germany
Tel. (0) 7131 / 9322-0
Fax (0) 7131 / 9322-93

## INCORPORATION SERVICES

### CSC The United States Corporation Company
Suite 750
5670 Wilshire Blvd.
Los Angeles, CA 90036
Phone: (213) 954-3854
Fax: (213) 954-0871

*See Corporation Companies*

---

## INFORMATION BROKERS

### Super Bureau, Inc.
P.O. Box 6400
San Pedro, CA 90734-6400
Phone: (800) 541-6821
Fax: (800) 423-8915

*See Document Filing/Retrieval*

---

Now you can find the lawyer even if you don't know where he or she practices - with the **Martindale-Hubbell Law Directory Alphabetical Index.**

---

The **Martindale-Hubbell Law Directory** is now available online...exclusively through the LEXIS®-NEXIS® services.

---

Now it's easy to find lawyers practicing a specific area of law! Simply consult the **Martindale-Hubbell Law Directory Areas of Practice Index.**

---

Fast ... Easy ... Flexible...
**The Martindale-Hubbell Law Directory on CD-ROM** gives you instant access through multiple search criteria to information on over 900,000 lawyers and law firms. For more details and a FREE demonstration disc, call **1-800-323-3288**.

SERVICES, SUPPLIERS, CONSULTANTS | CALIFORNIA—LOS ANGELES

## INVESTIGATORS

### Alpine Investigation Services
19 E. Willamette Avenue
Colorado Springs, Colorado 80903-1131
Telephone: (719) 520-5252
Facsimile: (719) 520-0015
Pager: (719) 389-3341
Sky Pager: (800) 539-1264
TOLL FREE: 1-800-520-5250
24 Hour Service
Answering Service after normal business hours

Investigator with extensive experience in criminal and civil investigations based on prior police career and education.

Services are not limited to the state of Colorado and extend nation and world wide.

The owner, Ralph J. Sanchez, Jr., has an extensive police background in all facets of police duties and procedures and has developed contacts worldwide.

He is an expert in police policies and has been recognized in District and County Courts as an expert witness in police matters.

His testimony has been upheld by the Colorado Court of Appeals on numerous cases.

Mr. Sanchez has the ability to analyze police investigations, due to his experience, and is recognized by the courts for his credibility.

Alpine Investigation Services specializes in homicide and death investigations, skip tracing, juvenile investigations, custody matters, adoptions, surveillance (day or night), personal injury, traffic investigations, marital, premarital background checks, asset checks, and wildlife criminal investigations.

This investigation service is utilized by major companies involving workers compensation investigations, insurance claims, fraud, internal thefts.

Mr. Sanchez has invested in extensive equipment and has become an expert in photographic and video documentations.

Male and female agents involved in this business have an extensive background in preparing arrest, search warrants, nontestimonial warrants, wire tapping and understand what can be done and their limitations.

Alpine Investigation Services guarantees all work and stands behind our clients and offer a professional approach to all cases. This investigative firm is insured and references are available upon request.

---

To update your listing
in the **Martindale-Hubbell Law Directory**
call **1-800-MARTIND(ALE)**.

---

## BARNES & ASSOCIATES
### PROFESSIONAL SERVICES INC.

*Est. 1966*
6300 Wilshire Boulevard
Suite 700
Los Angeles, CA 90048-5209
Tel: 213 782-3500
Fax: 213 782-1007

507 N. Sam Houston Parkway East
Suite 610
Houston, TX 77060-4077
Tel: 713 820-0694
Fax: 713 931-9312

| | |
|---|---|
| Environmental matters | Toxic torts |
| Due diligence | Employment issues |
| Corporate internal | White collar crime |
| Professional liability | Expert witness evaluation |
| Securities and corporate fraud | Product liability |
| Asset location | Litigation support |
| Jury profiles | Unfair competition |
| Locating and interviewing witnesses | Copyright/patent/trademark infringement |

**Experience:** Over 25 years of providing ethical, complex fact-finding and unique intelligence gathering to corporate and legal clients throughout the nation; offices in Los Angeles, California and Houston, Texas.

**Staff:** Includes attorneys, MBAs, former government enforcement agents, journalists, career investigators and business people fully licensed to work in numerous states.

**Resources:** Hundreds of database sources for efficient and cost-effective research; in-house public record collection dating back to the 1940's on CD-ROM and microfiche.

James E. Barnes, Esq.
President

---

Need an extra copy of the **Martindale-Hubbell Law Directory**? Or of a specific volume?
Call Martindale-Hubbell Customer Service at
**1-800-526-4902**

# CALIFORNIA—LOS ANGELES
MARTINDALE-HUBBELL LAW DIRECTORY 1997

## LOS ANGELES (Continued)
### Investigators (Continued)

### California Attorneys Investigators

## NICK HARRIS DETECTIVES, INC.

Founded 1906 • 91st Year
**Established before the FBI!**

**THE WORLD'S MOST DISTINGUISHED
AND RESPECTED PROFESSIONAL
PRIVATE INVESTIGATORS**

Under the direction of Milo A. Speriglio
Internationally renowned Master Detective

*First Choice of the Legal Profession Throughout the World*
• REASONABLE FEES
• IMMEDIATE SERVICE & REPORTS
*Over One Million Successful Assignments*

**SPECIALIST FOR EVERY
INVESTIGATIVE SERVICE:**

| | | |
|---|---|---|
| Accident Investigations | Estate Matters | Litigation History |
| Actionable Torts | Expert Witnesses | Missing Persons |
| Activity Checks | Extortion | Negligence |
| Alimony Matters | Family Law | Parental Kidnapping |
| Antitrust | Forgery | Patent Matters |
| Arson | Franchise Contract | Personal Injury |
| Asset & Financial | Violations | Photography |
| Searches | Fraud | Polygraph |
| Background | Handwriting | Product Counterfeiting |
| Investigations | Comparison | and Liability |
| Bad Faith | Heirs Located | Questioned Documents |
| Blackmail | Hidden Assets | Record Searching |
| Breach of Contract | Uncovered | Sexual Harassment |
| Burglary | Hijacking | Skip Tracing |
| Clandestine Bugs/ | Homicide | Slander |
| Wiretaps Detected | Hostile Takeovers | Statement Taking |
| Commercial Matters | Illegal Search | Surveillance |
| Criminal Defense | and Seizure | Trademark Matters |
| Criminal Records | Impeach Witnesses | Undercover |
| Data Base Searches | and Defendants | Unfair Competition |
| Drug Matters | Infringement | & Trade Practice |
| Eavesdropping | Labor Matters | White Collar Crimes |
| Detection | Liability | Will Contest |
| Embezzlement | Libel | Wiretap Detection |
| Employee Theft | Litigation History | |

***ANY CASE! ANYWHERE!***

$1,000,000 LIABILITY INSURANCE

**FREE PHONE CONSULTATION & FEE QUOTE**

818-343-6611      310-273-6101

1-800-NICK HARRIS

FAX 818-343-5725

VISIT US AT iMALL: www.NICKHARRISDETECTIVES.COM

Los Angeles County
Nick Harris Building, 16917 Enadia Way, Van Nuys CA 91406

---

# JOHN T. LYNCH INTERNATIONAL

OUTSTANDING SERVICE
EST. 1953
LICENSED, BONDED, LIABILITY INSURED
WORLD CLASS, WORLDWIDE INVESTIGATIONS
NETWORK OF FORMER FBI AGENTS
IMMEDIATE SERVICE, REASONABLE FEES
COMPLETE INVESTIGATIONS SERVICES
PROCESS SERVICE WORLDWIDE
ACCIDENTS
BACKGROUNDS
BODYGUARDS
BURGLARY
CIVIL & CRIMINAL
FINANCIAL
FIRE
INSURANCE INVESTIGATIONS
MALPRACTICE
PRODUCT LIABILITY
SKIP TRACING
STRIKE PROTECTION
SUDDEN DISASTERS
VIDEO SURVEILLANCE
UNDERCOVER AGENTS
WORKERS' COMPENSATION
ANYWHERE ANY TIME
TEL. (213) 624-4301
FAX (213) 624-7187

---

Now you can find the lawyer even if you don't
know where he or she practices -
with the **Martindale-Hubbell Law
Directory Alphabetical Index.**

---

The **Martindale-Hubbell Law Directory** is now
available online...exclusively
through the LEXIS®-NEXIS® services.

**SERVICES, SUPPLIERS, CONSULTANTS**     **CALIFORNIA—LOS ANGELES**

# IF IT HAPPENS HERE ...

## We're Watching For You ...

### STARSIDE PROTECTION

**SECURITY AND INVESTIGATIVE SERVICES**

**Toll-Free 1-888-4STARSIDE**

**OVER 38 YEARS EXPERIENCE — CONFIDENTIAL FREE CONSULTATION**

CAA123S

## LOS ANGELES (Continued)
Investigators (Continued)

# LARRY MALMBERG INVESTIGATIONS

638 North "D" Street
San Bernardino, CA 92401
PHONE: 909-383-8565
FAX: 909-383-8566
TOLL-FREE: 800-655-4549

California:  License PI 15211
 License PPO 12446

We at **Larry Malmberg Investigations** have over 25 years of experience in law enforcement and investigations. All of our staff has either a prior law enforcement or insurance claims background. Our agency is known to "**go the extra mile**", whether it be to Hong Kong, New Zealand, Mexico or right here in the U.S., we'll follow your case wherever it goes.

**Larry Malmberg**, president, is a lifelong resident of San Bernardino County and is a retired 20 year veteran of the San Bernardino County Sheriffs Department.

### ATTORNEY SERVICES AVAILABLE:

- ✓ Male/Female Investigators
- ✓ 24 Hours — 7 Day/Week
- ✓ Written Reports Given
- ✓ National & International Contacts
- ✓ Polygraph Services Available
- ✓ Undercover Assignments Accepted
- ✓ Missing Persons Found & Witnesses Located
- ✓ Due Diligence
- ✓ Debugging, Eavesdrop Detection
- ✓ (Counter)surveillance
- ✓ Spousal Investigations
- ✓ Personal/Corporate Protection
- ✓ Pre-Employment Checks
- ✓ Hard-To-Serve Process
- ✓ Corporate/Trade Secrets
- ✓ Sub Rosa
- ✓ Asset Checks
- ✓ Insurance/Municipal Defense
- ✓ Statements & Declarations
- ✓ Computer Links to Numerous Databases
- ✓ Public & Non Public Records Research & Retrieval

*— We Go The Extra Mile For Our Clients —*

---

Now it's easy to find lawyers practicing a specific area of law! Simply consult the **Martindale-Hubbell Law Directory Areas of Practice Index.**

---

# ★ STARSIDE PROTECTION

Telephone: (818) 549-4800
Fax: (818) 549-4808
**Toll Free: (888) 4STARSIDE**

Corporate Headquarters:
1101 E. Broadway
Suite 102
Glendale, CA  91205

E-Mail:
starside@earthlink.net

### Investigative Services

- Civil/Criminal Investigations
- Undercover/Surveillance, Video, Still/Evidential Photography
- Accident Recreation/Reconstruction Investigation/Traffic Accidents
- Debugging, Electronic Counter-Measures, Counter-Intelligence, Eavesdropping, Counter-surveillance
- Child Custody, Kidnapping, Family, Marital, Spousal, Divorce
- Skip Tracing, Missing Persons
- Process Service
- Male & Female Investigators
- Availability-24 Hours/7 Days/Week
- Written Reports Provided via modem, E-mail, Fax
- Contacts (worldwide)
- Worldwide Travel

### Data Research
- Record/Asset/DMV/UCC Searches
- Attorney Services

### Security
- Security (Armed/Unarmed) Bodyguard, Executive Protection
- Corporate/Industrial Security Consulting
- Large Event Security/Consultation
- Corporate Pilots Available Rotar/Fixed Wing

**MEMBER**
CAI
NAIS
PORAC
CALI (California Association of Licensed Investigators)

***SEE OUR AD ON PAGE CAA123S***

---

Fast ... Easy ... Flexible...
**The Martindale-Hubbell Law Directory on CD-ROM** gives you instant access through multiple search criteria to information on over 900,000 lawyers and law firms. For more details and a FREE demonstration disc, call **1-800-323-3288**.

SERVICES, SUPPLIERS, CONSULTANTS
CALIFORNIA—LOS ANGELES

To update your listing
in the **Martindale-Hubbell Law Directory**
call 1-800-MARTIND(ALE).

Need an extra copy of the **Martindale-Hubbell Law Directory?** Or of a specific volume?
Call Martindale-Hubbell Customer Service at
1-800-526-4902

**A Proven Investigative
Resource for the Legal
&
Business Community**

Sylnic Investigations is a fully licensed and insured private investigation agency founded with the purpose of providing quality and confidential investigative services to the legal community at competitive rates.

Sylnic investigators are skilled in using only those methods necessary to quickly and thoroughly complete an assignment without needless expense to the client. They take considerable pride in having developed a high degree of expertise in support of the following practice areas:

- General Civil Litigation
- Insurance Defense
- Medical Malpractice Defense
- Personal Injury – Product Liability
- Bad Faith Insurance Fraud
- Copyright, Trademark
- Criminal Defense
- Employment Matters
- Entertainment Law

Sylnic is capable of delivering a host of additional investigative services for clients in the legal sector. For further information regarding Sylnic Investigations please contact:

Nick Roberts, Director
SYLNIC INVESTIGATIONS
*Lic. #11410*

106 West 4th St., #310
Santa Ana, CA 92701
(714) 667 3460

1278 Glenneyre St., #115
Laguna Beach, CA 92651
(714) 449 4815

Facsimile:
(714) 499 5455

Internet:
www.sylnic.com

REPRESENTATIVE CLIENTS: Donahue, Gallagher, Wood & Woods- Oakland, CA ~ Ford, Walker, Haggarty & Behar- Long Beach, CA ~ Bishop, Payne, Williams & Werley- Fort Worth, TX ~ Cairns, Doyle, Lans, Nicholas & Soni- Pasadena, CA ~ Kirsch & Mitchell- Los Angeles, CA ~ Higgs, Fletcher & Mack- San Diego, CA ~ Hall, Dickler, Kent, Friedman & Wood- Los Angeles, CA ~ Hosp, Gilbert & Associates- Pasadena, CA

*SEE OUR AD ON PAGE CAA125S*

Now you can find the lawyer even if you don't know where he or she practices - with the **Martindale-Hubbell Law Directory Alphabetical Index.**

# LOS ANGELES (Continued)
## JURY CONSULTANTS

### DecisionQuest
2050 West 190th Street, Suite 205, Torrance, CA 90504
(310) 618-9600; Fax: (310) 618-1122
Principal Contact: Dr. Allan H. Colman

e-mail address: dqi@aol.com
www address: http://www.decisionquest.com

Los Angeles, Houston, Chicago, New York, Boston,
Washington and Atlanta

DecisionQuest is recognized by top civil and criminal trial lawyers as the most experienced and knowledgeable group of trial consultants and producers of courtroom exhibits in the country.

Our professionals have consulted on thousands of cases all over the United States. We are expert in strategy and theme development; witness evaluation and preparation; the design and production of demonstrative exhibits; jury profiling and selection; and business presentation strategies. We are retained by major corporations and leading law firms because **we are creative, experienced, responsive and fast.**

When you retain DecisionQuest, you retain a highly trained and experienced consulting team. You work with consultants who understand your objectives and who are expert at working with trial lawyers to develop an effective case presentation.

Our strategic Research Options include:

| | |
|---|---|
| Venue Evaluation/Selection | Motion Practice |
| Risk Assessment/Evaluation | Discovery |
| Case Structure | Damage Evaluation/Control |
| Opening/Closing Statements | Witness Preparation/Discovery |
| Verdict Forms/Instructions | Theme Development |
| Jury Profiling | Jury Selection/Voir Dire |
| Strategy/Tactics | Bad Fact/Bad Documents |
| Trial Monitoring/Evaluation | Post-Trial Assessment |
| Demonstrative Evidence Preparation/Evaluation | |

*Call us to find out a common and dangerously wrong conclusion lawyers often make after conducting jury research.*

Knowledge | Control | Persuasion | Winning℠

---

The **Martindale-Hubbell Law Directory** is now available online...exclusively through the LEXIS®-NEXIS® services.

---

## JURY RESEARCH INSTITUTE

Jury Research Institute can help you develop, pre-test and implement winning trial strategies. Our communications specialists know what it takes to help you refine your case strategy, enhance your settlement position and improve your success at trial.

Attorneys who use litigation research have made JRI one of the most recognized trial consulting firms in the nation. Most of our business comes from repeat clients and referrals. We have provided assistance on some of the most significant litigation in the country, serving litigators from Anchorage, Alaska to Tampa, Florida. In doing so we have earned an exceptional reputation for the quality of our work, the results our litigators have obtained, and our ability to contain costs. We would be happy to provide a list of references from your trial jurisdiction.

JRI provides a full range of services: focus groups, mock trials, community surveys, jury selection assistance, post-trial interviews, settlement evaluations and witness preparation. We have experience in state and federal courts throughout the country on a broad range of cases including contracts, insurance coverage and bad faith, personal injury, product liability, toxic tort, wrongful termination, antitrust, intellectual property, and professional negligence.

The directors of Jury Research Institute, Drs. Joseph A. Rice, Susan E. Jones and Ellen L. Leggett, have been nationally recognized experts on juror behavior for over a decade. They are *directly involved* in all JRI consultations.

Call or write:

Dr. Ellen L. Leggett
Dr. Joseph A. Rice
Dr. Susan E. Jones
**JURY RESEARCH INSTITUTE**
225 South Lake Ave.,
Suite 300
Pasadena, CA 91101

1-800-233-5879

---

Now it's easy to find lawyers practicing a specific area of law! Simply consult the
**Martindale-Hubbell Law Directory
Areas of Practice Index.**

---

Fast ... Easy ... Flexible...
**The Martindale-Hubbell Law Directory on CD-ROM** gives you instant access through multiple search criteria to information on over 900,000 lawyers and law firms. For more details and a FREE demonstration disc, call **1-800-323-3288**.

SERVICES, SUPPLIERS, CONSULTANTS

CALIFORNIA—LOS ANGELES

## LAWYER SEARCH & PLACEMENT CONSULTANTS

### BARRY GOLDBERG & ASSOCIATES, INC.
Legal Search Consultants

2049 Century Park East
Suite 1100
Los Angeles, CA 90067
Telephone: (310) 277-5800
FAX: (310) 277-7944

Barry Goldberg & Associates is celebrating it's 13th Anniversary. With six highly qualified experienced consultants, we are one of the largest full-service legal search firms in the country. We specialize in exclusive and non-exclusive retained and contingent searches solely for attorneys at all levels of experience. Our clients are prestigious international, national, regional and local law firms. Although our firm emphasizes California, we work actively with the nation's top law firms. In 1993, we added specialists who practice nationally in Intellectual Property and Environmental Law.

**MERGERS AND ACQUISITIONS, PRACTICE GROUPS AND PARTNERS**
• Barry Goldberg

**PARTNERS AND ASSOCIATES - CALIFORNIA AND NATIONWIDE**
- Carl Reece
- Deanna Gerber
- Sherry Glaser
- Greg Malin

*We work our heads off for you!*

---

To update your listing
in the **Martindale-Hubbell Law Directory**
call **1-800-MARTIND(ALE)**.

---

Need an extra copy of the **Martindale-Hubbell Law Directory**? Or of a specific volume?
Call Martindale-Hubbell Customer Service at
**1-800-526-4902**

6339-1 Argyle Forest Boulevard
Jacksonville, Florida 32244
(800) 553-5361
(904) 573-6919  Fax (904) 573-6942

Doug Sears & Associates is among the largest and strongest national search firms based in the Southeast. We have built our strength by developing long term relationships with hundreds of the nation's finest law firms. We take the time to understand their needs and goals, surpassing their expectations and earning their trust. We conduct both retained and contingency searches, coordinate mergers of law firms and the acquisitions of stand alone departments for client firms nationally and internationally.

For candidates, our commitment is to present your credentials in a timely, professional manner to all qualified options in your discipline. In addition, we offer a complete roster of consulting services to candidates and firms directed toward building a stronger career path and more productive law firm in the 21st century.

Doug Sears & Associates' recruiters provide loyalty, trust, integrity and the strongest work ethic in the industry. This makes Doug Sears & Associates leaders in your profession.

---

Now you can find the lawyer even if you don't
know where he or she practices -
with the **Martindale-Hubbell Law
Directory Alphabetical Index.**

---

The **Martindale-Hubbell Law Directory** is now
available online...exclusively
through the LEXIS®-NEXIS® services.

CAA127S

## LOS ANGELES (Continued)
### LEGAL PUBLICATIONS

When the question is compliance, the answer is INSource

**INSource Services**

For fast answers to compliance questions, you need information that's expertly selected, properly organized and consistently indexed. Intelligent information that responds to your questions with immediate, precise answers. The kind of information you'll find only on INSource CD-ROM services.

*It's a fact:* Different states use different terms to discuss the same regulatory concepts. INSource indexing-consistently applied to every section of statute and regulation-is critical to your research success. Using INSource index terms in searches, you retrieve on-target information from every state. You answer your questions quickly and confidently.

Whether you're interested in just one or all 50 states, there's an INSource CD-ROM service that fits. And INSource can be installed on a laptop, a single PC or your network-INSource works wherever you do.

*INSource Insurance*
The only CD-ROM service that delivers complete statutory and regulatory information for 54 U.S. jurisdictions. Updated every month.

*INSource Healthcare*
The only information service that delivers both the State and Federal Laws and Regulations affecting American healthcare businesses. Updated every month.

*INSource In-Time*
Time-lease version of INSource Insurance and INSource Healthcare-meeting the needs of legal professionals with comprehensive compliance information.

INSource services are designed for compliance... delivering answers, eliminating confusion.

For more information and FREE TRIAL, call
1-800-423-5910

INSource is a product of
*NILS Publishing Company*

P.O. Box 2507 • Chatsworth, CA 91313-2507
An ABC, Inc. Company

---

## LEGAL RESEARCH

**FIRST-OF-ITS-KIND SOFTWARE PROGRAM INTEGRATES TIME AND BILLING INTO LITIGATION CASE MANAGEMENT SYSTEM**

Innovative Technology Designed For Small Law Firms and Corporate Legal Departments

**SANTA BARBARA, CA** — The Poseidon Group announces that it has developed a first-of-its-kind software program which integrates time and billing into a litigation case management system for use with Windows-based systems. The final release of GRYPHON™ Litigation Case & Management Software for Microsoft® Windows™ combines practice management, case management and time and billing tracking features into one program. The GRYPHON Litigation Case & Practice Management Software was one of the six Windows business solutions demonstrated by Microsoft Corporation at the 1995 Access Advisor Developer's Conference and Exposition. It was the only law office application to be selected in Microsoft's *Solutions in Action Portfolio*. GRYPHON combines critical practice management features through the use of *Integrated Decision Assistance*™ (IDA), which leads the user from one task to the next in a logical sequence. Produced by a litigation attorney and a software developer, the program is designed for small law firms and corporate litigation departments to save attorney and administrative time by facilitating information management.

GRYPHON creates "slips" for a lawyer's phone calls, documents, contacts, deadlines, appointments and billing entries, and links these through IDA. For example, preparing a motion with GRYPHON becomes a sequence of easy steps. It allows a secretary or attorney to create the motion, profile the document for tracking and retrieval, calendar the hearing date, and bill for the attorney's time, all in less time than it used to take to type the motion alone. By the time a lawyer first reads a draft of the motion, it has been logged, billed and calendared. Later, because the software keeps track of unserved documents, a secretary can create a proof of service with just a few clicks of the mouse.

The software is network ready and works with any version of Windows, including Windows NT and Windows 95.

GRYPHON features a 30-day, money-back guarantee and 60 days of free technical support. It only requires a license for timekeepers (lawyers) on the system, allowing unlimited use by secretaries and paralegals. The Sole Practitioner license sells for $995 and the Small Office Pack (2-3 lawyers) for $1,695. Additional timekeeper licenses are available at any time for $495 and site licenses are available for firms with more than 10 attorneys.

The Poseidon Group offers a free, working demonstration program. To order the demo or to obtain further information, please call 1-800-547-9746, or visit our web site @ www.poseidon.com.

## THE POSEIDON GROUP

For more information:
Scott M. Moore, Director of Customer Service
The Poseidon Group, 800/547-9746
Email to scott@poseidon.com

## LEGAL SOFTWARE

## Corporation

**OPTICIMAGE SOFTWARE INTRODUCES *legalimage*™**
**LITIGATION SUPPORT SOFTWARE**
New Software for Court Reporters and Litigators Provides
Paper-Free Documentation and Review

MARLTON, NJ — September 18, 1996 — OpticImage Software Corporation, a wholly owned subsidiary of OpticImage, Inc., a Delaware corporation, recently unveiled a new generation of litigation support software designed specifically for court litigators and reporters. The new software, *legalimage*™, allows the marriage of transcripts and exhibits, and provides an unprecedented array of litigation support features.

*legalimage* software's extensive search capabilities will greatly reduce the time it takes to review a transcript and to prepare for trial. It can search entire depositions and annotations of all exhibits in seconds. The software provides wide-ranging search options, using various rules of logic, such as Boolean, Within, Phrase, Group, Fuzzy, Phonic, and Stemming. *legalimage's* ability to support color exhibits and photos, for example, is another differentiating factor that will have special significance for attorneys trying medical malpractice, product liability, toxic waste cases, etc. Competitive systems can support only black and white line art and gray scale photos. *legalimage* features optical character recognition (OCR) capability as well.

*legalimage* software is available for single users, multi-users, and on wide-area networks. Users on a network can actually work on the same case concurrently, sharing their notes without any need for photocopying, memo writing or paper shuffling. Both transcripts and exhibits can be annotated by the person(s) working on the case. *legalimage* users also have the capability to electronically send deposition transcripts with exhibits across the country over our secure "firewall" website.

*legalimage* software is compatible with all of the most popular operating systems, including Windows 95, Windows 3.x, Windows for WORKGROUPS, Windows NT and Novell Netware. To run *legalimage*, attorneys need an IBM PC or compatible 486 or greater, with a minimum of 8 megs of RAM.

To request additional information, please call OpticImage Software Corporation at 1-888-64-IMAGE or visit our website at http://www.opticimage.com.

**OPTICIMAGE SOFTWARE CORPORATION**
5 Greentree Centre
Suite 215
Marlton, NJ 08053

---

## LEGAL SUPPORT PERSONNEL - TEMPORARY & PERMANENT

### The Affiliates

601 West Fifth Street, Suite 630, Los Angeles, CA 90071
*Telephone (213) 624-8335* • *FAX (213) 624-8449*

1901 Avenue of the Stars, Suite 350, Los Angeles, CA 90067
*Telephone (310) 557-2334* • *FAX (310) 557-3553*

18300 Von Karman Avenue, Suite 430, Irvine, CA 92715
*Telephone (714) 752-2334* • *FAX (714) 752-1908*

Throughout our history, *The Affiliates* has been committed to maintaining the highest possible standards in all aspects of staffing for the legal community, including law firms and corporate legal departments. As legal staffing specialists, consultants at *The Affiliates* have considerable prior experience within law firms and corporate legal departments. Our experience ensures that you will always be presented with legal support professionals who are precisely matched to your full-time or temporary staffing needs.

For reliable legal support, you can count on *The Affiliates*. We recruit only experienced personnel, test them and match them to your special environment, all for one purpose - your guaranteed satisfaction!

*The Affiliates* provides comprehensive legal support staffing, such as:

| | |
|---|---|
| Executive Director | Paralegals |
| Director of Administration | Case Clerks |
| Office Manager | Legal Secretaries |
| Human Resources Director | Word Processing |
| Paralegal Coordinator | Records Clerk |
| Automated Litigation Support Teams | |

*Plus, all other professional legal support positions*

*Located in major cities such as Arlington VA, Century City CA, Chicago IL, Cleveland OH, Irvine CA, Los Angeles CA, Palo Alto CA, San Francisco CA, Seattle WA, Washington DC*

**SEE OUR AD ON PAGE CAA130S**

# CALIFORNIA—LOS ANGELES
MARTINDALE-HUBBELL LAW DIRECTORY 1997

## YOU ARE A PERFECTIONIST IN EVERYTHING YOU DO...

*That's Why You Call The Affiliates For Your Specialized Legal Staffing Support*

As legal staffing specialists, *The Affiliates* understands your unique legal support needs. Consultants at *The Affiliates* have considerable prior experience within law firms and corporate legal departments. Our experience ensures that you will always be presented with legal support professionals who are precisely matched to your full-time or temporary staffing needs. Guaranteed!

*The Affiliates* provides comprehensive legal support staffing, such as:

| | |
|---|---|
| Executive Director | Case Clerks |
| Director of Administration | Legal Secretaries |
| Office Manager | Automated Litigation |
| Human Resources Director | Support Teams |
| Paralegal Coordinator | Word Processing |
| Paralegals | |

*Plus, all other professional legal support positions*

### Call Today –

| | |
|---|---|
| Los Angeles, CA | (213) 624-8335 |
| Irvine, CA | (714) 752-2334 |
| Century City, CA | (310) 557-2334 |

## THE AFFILIATES®
The Legal Staffing Division of Robert Half International Inc.

© 1996 The Affiliates An Equal Opportunity Employer

---

## LITIGATION CONSULTING

### DECISIONQUEST
2050 West 190th Street, Suite 205, Torrance, CA 90504
(310) 618-9600; Fax: (310) 618-1122
Principal Contact: Dr. Allan H. Colman

e-mail address: dqi@aol.com
www address: http://www.decisionquest.com

Los Angeles, Houston, Chicago, New York, Boston,
Washington and Atlanta

The people at DecisionQuest invented trial consulting in the early 70's and have experience in thousands of cases. We have been retained by hundreds of lawyers over the years to provide all of the services that are traditionally associated with trial or jury consulting. These include:

| | |
|---|---|
| Drafting of opening statements | Juror profiles/jury selection |
| Testimony before regulatory agencies | Change of venue studies |
| Witness preparation | Focus groups |
| Preparation for arbitration/mediation | Post-trial interviews |
| Trial monitoring with surrogate jurors | Trial simulations |
| Development and testing of visual exhibits | |

Our experience in this field allows us to feature new and creative methods and solutions designed to address your objectives. We pride ourselves on being responsive and flexible in applying our expertise to your specific concerns while carefully observing the highest research standards. You get the significant advantage of having the most experienced and capable trial consultants available to you in one group, working as a team.

*Call us to find out what defense attorneys often overestimate and why they end up settling winnable cases.*

Knowledge | Control | Persuasion | Winning℠

---

Now it's easy to find lawyers practicing a specific area of law! Simply consult the
**Martindale-Hubbell Law Directory Areas of Practice Index.**

CAA130S

SERVICES, SUPPLIERS, CONSULTANTS — CALIFORNIA—LOS ANGELES

## LITIGATION SUPPORT SERVICES

### COMPEX
### Legal Services, Inc.

- Record Retrieval
- Subpoena Preparation
- Litigation Copying
- Microfilming
- Micro Graphics
- Deposition Reporting
- Repository Services
- Exhibit Boards
- On or Off-Site Prodution
- Complex Case Management
- Research-Indexing
- Binding-Paginating
- Office Services Program

Let **COMPEX** Simplify
YOUR LIFE
Call 1-800-4COMPEX

OFFICES
Corporate Headquarters:
841 Apollo Street
El Segundo, CA 90245

| CALIFORNIA | | TEXAS | OHIO |
|---|---|---|---|
| Bakersfield | Sacramento | Austin | Cincinnati |
| Century City | San Bruno | Dallas | Cleveland |
| Colton | San Diego | Houston | |
| Irvine | San Francisco | Irving | NEVADA |
| Los Angeles | Ventura | San Antonio | Las Vegas |
| | | Tyler | |

---

Fast ... Easy ... Flexible...
**The Martindale-Hubbell Law Directory on CD-ROM** gives you instant access through multiple search criteria to information on over 900,000 lawyers and law firms. For more details and a FREE demonstration disc, call **1-800-323-3288**.

---

To update your listing
in the **Martindale-Hubbell Law Directory**
call **1-800-MARTIND(ALE)**.

---

### COMPEX
National Headquarters
841 Apollo Street
El Segundo, CA 90245
(800) 4 Compex
(310) 726-0000
Fax (800) 479-3365

For nearly a quarter of a century COMPEX has provided outstanding value in support activities serving the legal and insurance communities. Our expert staff is well trained in the art of providing personalized service and innovative solutions in managing document processing while controlling your costs.

**COMPEX services include:**

- **Record Retrieval & Subpoena Preparation**

    COMPEX experts provide all services required to complete any document request whether by authorization or subpoena.

- **Document Copying**

    COMPEX provides day and night copying and support services both on and off site. COMPEX is the foremost expert in large scale document productions.

- **Litigation Support Services**

    COMPEX many years of experience enable us to provide innovative programs that can manage your complex litigation while controlling costs. COMPEX has vast experience with product liability, toxic tort, construction defect and asbestos litigation.

- **Document Imaging**

    COMPEX offers full service microfilming and imaging. As well as the ability to provide you with microfilm and/or microfiche we can transfer your documents to various storage media such as optical disk, CD-ROM and magnetic tape.

- **Office Services Management**

    COMPEX provides firms with equipment, personnel, and supplies tailored to your Facilities Management requirements. COMPEX packages are designed to meet the reprographic, faxing and mail room needs of our clientele, creating a positive impact on their bottom line.

- **Deposition Reporting**

    COMPEX quality reporting services utilizing the most advanced technology at competitive rates.

By utilizing the experience and technological capabilities of **COMPEX**, all your document needs can be met. Let **COMPEX** simplify your life.

**COMPEX** serves its clients from 11 California offices in Los Angeles, Orange County, San Fernando Valley, San Diego, Kern County, Inland Empire, San Francisco, Sacramento and Ventura County. In Texas **COMPEX** has offices located in Austin, Dallas, Houston, San Antonio and Tyler. **COMPEX** also has offices in Cincinnati and Cleveland, Ohio and Compex's newest office in Las Vegas.

*SEE OUR AD ON PAGE CAA131S*

## LOS ANGELES (Continued)
### Litigation Support Services (Continued)

### Ostrove, Krantz & Ostrove, A P.C.
Litigation Support Services
5757 Wilshire Boulevard
Suite 535
Los Angeles, California 90036-3600

Contact: David Ostrove, Attorney-CPA

Telephone: 213 939-3400
Fax: 213 939-3500

David Ostrove, Attorney-CPA Professor of Law and Accounting, Certified Specialist, Taxation Law, Author and Lecturer, Expert Witness services to the legal community for more than 35 years. Together with his associates, Mr. Ostrove has analyzed, advised and testified with regard to many types of complex, litigated cases, including accounting and auditing, business valuations, breach of fiduciary duty, tax cases, analysis of books, records and financial statements, estate and gift tax issues, real estate transactions, purchases and sales of businesses, calculation of damages, reasonable value of legal and other services rendered, international accounting, fiduciary accounting, probate and trust accounting, investigation and analysis of damage claims, accountant's malpractice, lawyer's malpractice.

Consultations, case analysis and evaluation. References sent upon request.

Frequently, your needs are best satisfied by a team approach, involving specialists with different avenues of expertise in many fields. Once we determine the scope of the problem, we will complete your assignment individually or together, as your situation demands.

---

### The Poseidon Group
Suite 1-138
1187 Coast Village Rd.
Santa Barbara, CA 93101
Phone: (800) 547-9746

*See Case Management Systems*

---

Need an extra copy of the **Martindale-Hubbell Law Directory**? Or of a specific volume?
Call Martindale-Hubbell Customer Service at
1-800-526-4902

---

10600 North DeAnza Boulevard
Cupertino, California 95014
Telephone: (408) 973-0616
Fax: (408) 973-8251

745 Fifth Avenue, Suite 1409
New York, New York 01051
Telephone: (212) 035-6760
Fax: (212) 935-6766

Regent Pacific is a leading international turnaround management and financial advisory firm. The firm provides a broad spectrum of hands-on management and advisory services to underperforming and operationally- and financially-troubled companies and stakeholders worldwide. Regent Pacific's range of services include turnaround strategy and implementation, crisis management, solutions to enhance corporate and operational restructuring, business situation analysis and litigation support.

Regent Pacific is comprised of senior-level executives with extensive operational experience in general management, finance and administration, marketing and sales, engineering, and operations. Each full-time professional has a proven track record of exceptional performance as a Regent Pacific team member and an average of 27 years per team member in general management experience. The distinguished strength of Regent Pacific is its ability to staff all executive functions with individuals expert in meeting the demanding performance requirements of our client companies and their stakeholders.

Specific litigation support services include:

- Financial analysis
- Fiduciary obligations
- Prudence of decisions
- Business reorganization and restructuring
- Bankruptcy/insolvency
- Fraudulent conveyance
- Business valuation
- Mergers and acquisitions
- Intellectual property
- Lender liability
- Payment terms and conditions
- Errors and omissions
- Expert witness testimony
- Business interruption and loss of income calculations
- Forensic analysis and exhibit preparation

In over twenty years of service to clients, Regent Pacific has built, and continues to enhance, its reputation for professional excellence, integrity, discretion, and exceptional results.

---

Now you can find the lawyer even if you don't
know where he or she practices -
with the **Martindale-Hubbell Law
Directory Alphabetical Index.**

## MANAGEMENT CONSULTANTS

### ALTMAN WEIL PENSA, INC.
Management and Technology Consultants
to the Legal Profession

Headquarters:
Two Campus Boulevard, Suite 200
Newtown Square, PA 19073
610-359-9900
Fax: 610-359-0467
Internet: altmanweil.com

Altman Weil Pensa, Inc., specializes in providing management, technology and marketing consulting services exclusively to legal organizations. The firm serves law firms and corporate law departments of all sizes and areas of practice throughout North America and abroad from its headquarters in suburban Philadelphia, its regional offices in the New York and Chicago metropolitan areas, and its international affiliate in London.

Altman Weil Pensa offers a broad range of consulting services in strategic planning, process engineering, bench marking, organizational development, profitability analysis and planning, micro-economic forecasting, marketing planning, compensation systems, law firm mergers and acquisitions, attorney and staff training, human resources management, quality management programs, financial management, client surveys, and automation technology.

Altman Weil Pensa is a major source of economic information about the legal profession. Its annual *Survey of Law Firm Economics* is widely recognized as the premier bench marking survey on law firm financial performance. Other specialized law firm surveys and the corporate *Law Department Compensation Bench marking Survey* and *Law Department Functions and Expenditures Survey* provide the foundation for the firm's information-based consultancies.

The firm also publishes a growing array of management resources. It's leading *Report to Legal Management* newsletter is now complemented by *Bottom-Line Management for Law Firms*, *Law Office Technology Solutions*, and *In-House Law Practice and Management*. It's five volume *Altman Weil Pensa Archive Series* and the now classic reference manual *How to Manage Your Law Office* are authored by Altman Weil Pensa's corps of law practice management consultants.

---

The **Martindale-Hubbell Law Directory** is now available online...exclusively through the LEXIS®-NEXIS® services.

## MEDICAL CASE REVIEW & PREPARATION/TRIAL CONSULTING

### CONSOLIDATED CONSULTANTS CO.
739 Twin Oaks Ave.
Chula Vista, CA 91910-5924
Phone: (800) 683-9847
Fax (619) 422-8101
E-Mail steve_vr@msn.com
Internet Home Page: http://www.FreeReferral.com

Retaining Legal Nurse Consultants (LNC) makes good sense because they save you time and money. Trained to review the entire medical record from a legal perspective, LNC's work in a cost-effective manner with clients to maximize the case value, or alternatively, assist in defending the case through mitigation or obliteration of the damage issues and award.

LNC's at CCc are founding members of the American Association of Legal Nurse Consultants (1989). They are well qualified and experienced in the assistance they provide the legal community in the areas of:

- Bad Faith
- Bodily Injury
- Criminal
- Elder Abuse
- Employment
- Medical Malpractice
- Products Liability
- Toxic Torts
- Worker's Compensation

Possessing a strong clinical background, resourcefulness, and an understanding of tort law, LNC's can:

- Organize, review and analyze medical records
- Prepare chronologies, summaries and specific focus
- Assess etiology and evaluate injuries and/or conditions
- Identify, locate evaluate and confer with expert witnesses
- Research Medical Literature
- Define and delineate standards of care and deviations
- Provide depositions and trial support
- Identify missing and/or relevant medical providers

Skilled in bill review procedures, LNC's apply their medical expertise to identify:

- Suspected Fraud
- Duplication of Services
- Treatment Lapse or Overlap
- Non-compensable Charges
- Inappropriate or Unreasonable Care
- Treatment for Non-injury Related Conditions

LNC's also reduce the billings in accordance with:

- Documentation Principles
- "Usual and Customary" Percentiles
- CPT Coding Protocol
- Duration and/or Intensity of Treatments Guidelines

# LOS ANGELES (Continued)
### Medical Case Review & Preparation/Trial Consulting (Continued)

## Lake Elsinore Family Medical Clinic, Inc.
17037 Lake Shore Drive
Lake Elsinore, CA 92530

Telephone: (909) 674-6971
Fax: (909) 674-6368

**Bradley C. Grant**

### Degrees and Licenses
DO; MEd; MPH; FACGP; QME; AME; IME
3 yrs. law school

### Specialties
Board Certified Family Practice
Quality Assurance/Utilization Review
Additionology
Sports Medicine
Geriatrics
Medical Management
Board Eligible
Emergency Medicine
Public Health
Occupational Medicine

---

Now it's easy to find lawyers practicing a specific area of law! Simply consult the **Martindale-Hubbell Law Directory Areas of Practice Index.**

---

Fast ... Easy ... Flexible...
**The Martindale-Hubbell Law Directory on CD-ROM** gives you instant access through multiple search criteria to information on over 900,000 lawyers and law firms. For more details and a FREE demonstration disc, call **1-800-323-3288.**

---

# MEDICALLY SPEAKING
# MEDICAL LEGAL CONSULTANTS

1-800-633-7754

Medically Speaking is filling a void in the litigation and insurance industry, by performing cost effective medical record review and analysis of the entire medical record. Objective summaries and opinions are provided in layperson terms. We paginate and highlight the records, so there are no futile searches attempting to locate important information. Issues, damages and discrepancies are identified, as are issues of compliance, liability, comparative negligence, pre-existing conditions, and deviations from the Standards of Care.

Medically Speaking performs the majority of the medical record discovery work for you! With the applicable information extracted from the medical records, you are prepared to make informed decisions on how a case should be handled.

Medically Speaking is making a difference as many firms have already found out. Let us help you take a big step towards protecting your interests, processing more cases faster, reducing litigation costs and putting you in control.

**LIST OF SERVICES**
- Medical Record Organization
- Medical and dental review
- Screening for merit
- Objective chronological summaries in layperson terms
- Confidential opinions
- Medical terms and procedures defined
- Identification of issues, discrepancies, beneficial and detrimental aspects, compliance pre-existing conditions, etc.
- Identification of liability and damages
- Identification of missing records
- Rapid information retrieval
- Questions for deposition and trial
- Expert witness referral
- Medical literature searches
- Demonstrative exhibits
- Medical bill audits
- Deposition review
- Medical transcription
- Medical record copy service
- Other medical litigation support services available

1-800-633-7754

## MEDICAL EXPERT TESTIMONY

### Dr. Steven E. Lerner & Associates
185 Riviera Dr.
San Rafael, CA 94901-1525
Phone: (800) 952-7563

*See Medical Expert Witness*

SERVICES, SUPPLIERS, CONSULTANTS
CALIFORNIA—LOS ANGELES

## MEDICAL EXPERT WITNESS

### CCC Consolidated Consultants Co.
739 Twin Oaks Ave.
Chula Vista, CA 91910-5924
Phone: (800) 683-9847
Fax: (619) 422-8101

*See Expert Witness Referral Services*

---

To update your listing
in the **Martindale-Hubbell Law Directory**
call 1-800-MARTIND(ALE).

---

Need an extra copy of the **Martindale-Hubbell Law Directory**? Or of a specific volume?
Call Martindale-Hubbell Customer Service at
1-800-526-4902

---

Now you can find the lawyer even if you don't know where he or she practices -
with the **Martindale-Hubbell Law Directory Alphabetical Index.**

---

The **Martindale-Hubbell Law Directory** is now available online...exclusively
through the LEXIS®-NEXIS® services.

---

### DR. STEVEN E. LERNER & ASSOCIATES
MEDICAL EXPERT TESTIMONY
(800) 952-7563

Dr. Steven E. Lerner & Associates is a multidisciplinary group of MD's, DDS's, DPM's, OD's, OTR's, PharmD's, PhD's, RN's and RPT's who are available for case evaluations, written reports and expert testimony. All physician specialists are board-certified medical school faculty members or caliber. The majority of specialists are both clinicians and researchers with publications in their areas of expertise.

Within 90 minutes of your conversation with Dr. Lerner we will send by facsimile the proposed specialist's curriculum vitae and retainer agreement for review. Professional services are billed on an hourly basis. Upon completion of record review the specialist will provide an oral opinion. If requested the specialist will then prepare and sign a written report and be available for testimony. Since 1975 our specialists have provided services to plaintiff and defendant's counsel. Currently our group covers over 100 specialty areas including:

| | | |
|---|---|---|
| Addiction Medicine | Interventional Radiology | Ped Infectious Diseases |
| Addiction Psychiatry | Liver Transplantation | Pediatric Immunology |
| Allergy | Mammography | Pediatric Nephrology |
| Anesthesiology | Medical Genetics | Pediatric Neurology |
| Blood Banking | Medical Licensure | Pediatric Oncology |
| Cardiology | Neonatology | Ped. Orthopaedic Surgery |
| Cardiovascular Surgery | Nephrology | Pediatric Otolaryngology |
| Colorectal Surgery | Neurology | Pediatric Urology |
| Cornea Surgery | Neurosurgery | Pharmacology |
| Critical Care | Nursing | Pharmacy |
| Cytology | Obstetrics | Physical Therapy |
| Dentistry | Occupational Medicine | Psychopharmacology |
| Dermatopathology | Occupational Therapy | Plastic Surgery |
| Dermatological Surgery | Oncology | Podiatric Surgery |
| Dysmorphology | Ophthalmology | Psychiatry |
| Emergency Medicine | Optometry | Pulmonary Medicine |
| Endocrinology | Oral Implantology | Quality Assurance |
| Family Practice | Orthodontics | Radiation Oncology |
| Gastroenterology | Orthopaedic Surgery | Radiology |
| General Surgery | Otolaryngology | Reconstructive Surgery |
| Geriatric Medicine | Pain Management | Rheumatology |
| Gynecologic Oncology | Ped. Anesthesiology | Surgical Critical Care |
| Hand Surgery | Pediatrics | Thoracic Surgery |
| Hematology | Pediatric Cardiology | Toxicology |
| Immunology | Ped. Critical Care | Trauma Surgery |
| Infectious Diseases | Ped. Endocrinology | Urology |
| Internal Medicine | Ped. Gastroenterology | Vascular Surgery |

Call now for a Free Consultation,
Specialist Curriculum Vitae and Fee Schedule
Based on an Hourly Rate.

### DR. STEVEN E. LERNER & ASSOCIATES
(800) 952-7563

| | | | |
|---|---|---|---|
| Chicago | (773) 631-3900 | San Francisco | (415) 861-8787 |
| Denver | (303) 713-1943 | San Rafael | (415) 453-6900 |
| Honolulu | (808) 947-8400 | Washington, D.C. | (202) 628-8697 |
| Houston | (713) 799-1010 | | |

Visit our web site at:
http://www.drlerner.com

## LOS ANGELES (Continued)
### Medical Expert Witness (Continued)

### JASON I. GREEN, M.D., F.A.C.S.
General Surgery
Quality Assurance

**Plaintiff/Defense Case Evaluation
Deposition and Trial Testimony**

Areas of Special Expertise:

Breast Surgery: inappropriate evaluation and missed diagnosis of breast cancer.

Abdominal Surgery: gall bladder, appendectomy, colon, hernia surgery. Minimally Invasive Surgery (MIS) with special emphasis on laparoscopic cholecystectomy.

Quality Assurance Issues: providing patients proper care in an increasingly cost conscious and managed care medical environment. Evaluation in all specialties of medicine.

CERTIFICATES:
American College of Medical Quality, Distinguished Fellow
American Board of Forensic Examiners, Fellow
American Board of Surgery, Diplomate
American College of Surgeons, Fellow
American Board of Quality Assurance & Utilization Review, Diplomate
UCLA, School of Public Health (Health Care Administration), Certified

LICENSE: CA (G-7140)

MEMBERSHIPS:
American Medical Association
American College of Physician Executives
American College of Medical Quality

Curriculum Vitae on Request

No charge for initial telephone consultation

**JASON I. GREEN, M.D., F.A.C.S.
3341 TARECO DRIVE
LOS ANGELES, CA 90068**

TEL: (213) 969-0681
FAX: (213) 969-0683

---

Now it's easy to find lawyers practicing a specific area of law! Simply consult the
**Martindale-Hubbell Law Directory
Areas of Practice Index.**

---

### RICHARD N. SHAW, MD, FACP, FACR
16133 Ventura Bl., # 400
Encino, CA 91436
Tel: 818-986-1357
Fax: 818-986-9370

MEDICAL CONSULTING/EXPERT WITNESS

EDUCATION: BA Zoology UCLA 1966
MD St. Louis School of Medicine 1970

Certifications/Licenses:
1976 Certified in Internal Medicine
1978 Certified in Rheumatology

Honors/Awards:
Humanitarian Award 1989, Lupus Foundation of America

Specialties: Rheumatology, soft tissue rheumatism; systemic lupus; internal medicine. Worker's comp QME, AME, IME.

Membership, Professional Societies:
LACMA, Arthritis Foundation, Lupus Foundation, LA Society of Internal Medicine, LA Rheumatology Society, California Society of Industrial Medicine & Surgery.

## DENTAL

### CCC Consolidated Consultants Co.
739 Twin Oaks Ave.
Chula Vista, CA 91910-5924
Phone: (800) 683-9847
Fax: (619) 422-8101

*See Medical Expert Witness - Dental/TMJ*

**Specializing in: Prosthodontics/Dental Implants**

### CCC Consolidated Consultants Co.
739 Twin Oaks Ave.
Chula Vista, CA 91910-5924
Phone: (800) 683-9847
Fax: (619) 422-8101

*See Medical Expert Witness - Dental/TMJ*

---

Fast ... Easy ... Flexible...
**The Martindale-Hubbell Law Directory on CD-ROM** gives you instant access through multiple search criteria to information on over 900,000 lawyers and law firms. For more details and a FREE demonstration disc, call **1-800-323-3288**.

# SERVICES, SUPPLIERS, CONSULTANTS  CALIFORNIA—LOS ANGELES

### Specializing in: TMJ

**CONSOLIDATED CONSULTANTS CO.**
739 Twin Oaks Ave.
Chula Vista, CA 91910-5924
Phone (800) 683-9847
Fax (619) 422-8101
E-Mail steve_vr@msn.com
Internet Home Page: http://www.FreeReferral.com

**BOARD CERTIFIED DENTIST (PROSHODONTIST)**

- DENTAL & FACIAL PROSTHETICS
- RADIATION/XEROSTOMIA MANAGEMENT
- DENTAL RECONSTRUCTION
- TEMPORO MANDIBULAR JOINT (TMJ) DISORDERS
- HEAD & NECK CANCER MANAGEMENT
- CROWN & BRIDGE PROBLEMS
- OCCLUSAL (BITE) PROBLEMS
- DENTAL IMPLANT RECONSTRUCTION
- PROSTHODONTICS (FIXED, REMOVABLE)

**EDUCATION**

| | |
|---|---|
| 1967-68 | College of William & Mary, Williamsburg, VA |
| 1968-71 | Utica College of Syracuse University, BS Biology |
| 1971-75 | State University of New York at Buffalo (DDS) |
| 1977-79 | Wadsworth/Veterans Administration Hospital Certificate in Prosthodontics |
| 1979-80 | University of California, Los Angeles, Certificate in Maxillovacial Prosthodontics |
| 1986-96 | Numerous continuing education courses, particularly in Implant Prosthodontics (Corevent, Branemark, Denar, ITI, IMZ) and forensic dentistry |

**LICENSES**

California & Virginia (Active)
NY (Inactive)

**PRESENT POSITIONS**

| | |
|---|---|
| 1980-present | Private practice limited to fixed, removable & Maxillofacial Prosthodontics |
| 1980-86 | Clinical assistant professor in restorative dentistry. Advanced Prosthodontics section, UCLA-School of Dentistry |
| 1990-present | Lecturer - Maxillofacial Prosthodontics, Southern California - School of Dentistry |

### DEVICES

**CONSOLIDATED CONSULTANTS CO.**
739 Twin Oaks Ave.
Chula Vista, CA 91910-5924
Phone (800) 683-9847
Fax (619) 422-8101
E-Mail steve_vr@msn.com
Internet Home Page: http://www.FreeReferral.com

**MEDICAL DEVICE DESIGN & FAILURE ANALYSIS**

| | |
|---|---|
| *510 K Submissions* | *Marketing Communications* |
| *Advertising* | *Marketing Research* |
| *Component Sourcing* | *Material Selection* |
| *Computer Aided Design* | *Mold Design* |
| *Concept Development* | *Organic Chemistry* |
| *Contract Assembly* | *Package Design* |
| *Contract Packaging* | *Project Management* |
| *Decorating & Finishing* | *Polymer Finishing* |
| *Detailed Part Design* | *Prototype Development* |
| *Engineering* | *Printing* |
| *Graphic Design* | *Public Relations* |
| *Injection Molding* | *Spin Casting* |
| *Labeling* | *Thermoforming* |

**EXPERIENCE:**

30+ years experience in all phases of medical device, toy & consumer product design & engineering project management. Responsible for product design, development & analysis, from original product conception through high volume manufacturing including liaison with governmental regulatory agencies.

Have intimate knowledge & experience with prototype models, computer aided plastic part design, failure & hazard analysis, high volume plastic extrusion & injection molding, labeling & packaging of medical, toy & consumer products.

Have up-to-date knowledge of FDA requirements for Good Manufacturing Procedures. Have developed, licensed character, Col. Snootz®, & full line of toys and games.

- OVER 21 PATENTS ISSUED
- FORMER MEMBER OF AMMI MEDICAL DEVICE STANDARDS COMMITTEES

---

To update your listing
in the **Martindale-Hubbell Law Directory**
call **1-800-MARTIND(ALE)**.

## LOS ANGELES (Continued)
Medical Expert Witness (Continued)

### MEDICAL CASE REVIEW

### Specializing in: Malpractice & Personal Injury

### ELLIOT D. FELMAN, M.D.
*Diplomate of the American Board of Family Practice*

2428 Santa Monica Boulevard
Suite 302
Santa Monica, CA 90404

(310) 453-0033
Fax (310) 453-2114

*Medical Case Review*

*Evaluation of Standard of Care*

*Evaluation of Malpractice*

*Personal Injury Cases*

*Deposition and Testimony*

*Family, General or Internal Medicine Practices*

*Plaintiff and Defense*

**Professional Activity:**

Board certified family physician in California and Colorado, in private practice in the Los Angeles area since 1970
Clinical Faculty at the UCLA Medical School
Qualified Expert Reviewer for the Medical Board of California

**Education:**

M.D., Hahnemann Medical College, 1969
B.A., University of Pennsylvania, 1965

**Certification and Boards:**

Recertified, American Board of Family Practice, 1984, 1991
Diplomate, American Board of Family Practice, 1977
Member, American Academy of Family Practice

Curriculum Vitae Available Upon Request

---

Need an extra copy of the **Martindale-Hubbell Law Directory?** Or of a specific volume?
Call Martindale-Hubbell Customer Service at
**1-800-526-4902**

### NEUROLOGY

### Specializing in: Neurosurgery & Acupuncture

### Lorne S. Label, M.D.
California Neurological Specialists
2100 Lynn Road, #230
Thousand Oaks, CA 91360
Tel: 805-497-4500
Fax: 805-495-1717

<u>Degrees/Licenses:</u> M.D.; Board Certified; Fellow, American Academy of Neurology

<u>Specialties:</u> Neurological field (Adult & Child), with particular attention to trauma causing brain, muscle, nerve or spinal disorder. Head trauma, seizures, encephalitis, behavioral disorders, dementia, all neuromuscular abnormalities, carpal tunnel syndrome. Medical acupuncture. Medical malpractice. Tests of higher cerebral function (EEG, Evoked Responses), EMG.

<u>Birthdate:</u> Aug. 1, 1952. <u>Birthplace:</u> Montreal, Canada.

<u>Education:</u> McGill University, 1969-1970; University of Texas at Austin, B.A. Psychology with High Honors, 1973; University of Texas Medical Branch, Galveston, TX, M.D., 1978; University of Michigan Medical Center, Neurology, 1982. Neuromuscular fellowship, USC, 1983.

<u>Certifications/Licenses:</u> Diplomate, American Board of Psychiatry & Neurology, 1984; Fellow, American Academy of Neurology; Diplomate, American Academy of Pain Management, 1990; CA Medical License; Worker's Compensation, IME, QME, AME.

<u>Previous Positions/Appointments:</u> Clinical Associate Professor of Neurology, UCLA; California Medical Association, Hospital Surveyor, appointed 1994; Board of Directors, Executive Committee Member at several hospitals.

<u>Honors/Awards:</u> Who's Who of American Professionals, 1994; Phi Beta Kappa.

<u>Number of Publications:</u> 24 including book chapters; lectures; medical editor for Matthew Bender Publications.

<u>Membership in Professional Societies:</u> Medical Quality Review Center, Medical Board of California, appointed by Lou Deukmejian; Board of Directors, Ventura County Medical Society; Board of Governors, UCP; Muscular Dystrophy Association of Los Angeles; American Headache Society.

<u>Consulting/Expert Witness Experience, Civil & Criminal:</u> Depositions, record review and court testimony, plaintiff and defense, since 1984.

### PSYCHIATRY

### PsyBar, P.L.C.®
5749 Nicollet Ave. S.
Minneapolis, MN 55419-2414
Phone: (612) 866-1000

*See Medical Expert Witness - Psychology*

### Specializing in: Forensic

## BARRINGTON PSYCHIATRIC CENTER
1990 South Bundy Drive
Suite 320
Los Angeles, California 90025
(310) 826-3235
Fax: (310) 447-0840

"Our goal is to match the right expert to the case."

Established in 1972 and built upon a tradition of thoroughness and professionalism, **Barrington Psychiatric Center** has provided expertise for a range of litigation issues involving emotional distress claims (**sexual harassment, wrongful termination, employment discrimination, personal injury, malpractice, Americans with Disability Act claims, Post Traumatic Stress Disorder**) and has successfully supported clients in establishing strong cases for settlement or trial. These services include:

**CASE PLANNING**

**RECORD REVIEW**

**"BEHIND THE SCENES" CASE PREPARATION**

**PSYCHIATRIC AND PSYCHOLOGICAL EVALUATION**

**NEUROPSYCHOLOGICAL TESTING**

**EXPERT WITNESS TESTIMONY**

**Barrington Psychiatric Center** was founded and is directed by Raymond Friedman, M.D., Ph.D. who has recruited and trained a skilled, highly professional staff of psychiatrists, psychologist and neuropsychologists.

Dr. Friedman is a 1966 honors graduate of the University of Southern California School of Medicine. In addition to his medical degree, he received his Ph.D. at the Southern California Psychoanalytic Institute in 1978. Dr. Friedman is Board Certified in Psychiatry by the American Board of Psychiatry and Neurology, and is Certified in Psychoanalysis by the American Psychoanalytic Association. Dr. Friedman is recognized for his contributions and teaching on subjects ranging from Post Traumatic Stress Disorder to the psychotherapeutic process. His latest book is entitled <u>Clinical Intersubjectivity</u> and was published by Jason Aronson Inc in 1995. He is a training and supervising analyst at the Southern California Psychoanalytic Institute and is a nationally and internationally recognized expert.

---

Now you can find the lawyer even if you don't know where he or she practices - with the **Martindale-Hubbell Law Directory Alphabetical Index.**

---

## PSYCHOLOGY

## PsyBar, P.L.C.®

PROVIDING PSYCHOLOGICAL AND PSYCHIATRIC CONSULTATION NATIONWIDE

5749 Nicollet Avenue South
Minneapolis, MN 55419-2414

voice: (612) 866-1000
e-mail: Psybar@aol.com
http://www.psybar.com

♦ Psychological Experts ♦ Psychiatric Experts ♦
♦ Expert Witnesses ♦ Trial Strategy ♦ Consultation ♦
♦ Jury Selection Assistance ♦

**PsyBar, P.L.C.** is a national professional services company offering psychological and psychiatric experts to law firms, courts, corporations, insurance companies, and government agencies. We provide consultation, expert witnesses, voir dire and jury selection assistance, trial strategy, and challenges to psychological and psychiatric testimony. We can serve as a consultant to your case or assist in locating the appropriate experts. PsyBar's mission of raising the forensic standards of psychological and psychiatric experts is carried through both our consultation and expert research practices.

**Forensic Consultation**
PsyBar psychologists and psychiatrists can analyze the strengths and weaknesses of your case, brief you on the relevant scientific research literature, prepare deposition questions, observe depositions, prepare witnesses, critique exhibits and communication styles, and help you to challenge expert testimony. Our jury consultants can assist you with voir dire and jury selection, provide community surveys, focus groups, shadow juries, and assist with communication strategies.

**Expert Research**
We are experts on the credentials and competencies of psychological and psychiatric experts. Our experts are a network of nearly four hundred doctoral-level professionals, psychologists, psychiatrists, and statisticians throughout the country who have made significant contributions to their scientific and professional communities.
When you engage us to recommend an expert for you, you get the value of discussing your case with a psychological credentials expert. We can advise you as to which specialty credentials are appropriate and quickly find experts of stature.

### Specializing in: Forensic

**Barrington Psychiatric Center**
Suite 320
1990 S. Bundy Dr.
Los Angeles, CA 90025
Phone: (310) 826-3235
Fax: (310) 447-0840

*See Medical Expert Witness - Psychiatry - Forensic*

# CALIFORNIA—LOS ANGELES

## LOS ANGELES (Continued)
### Medical Expert Witness (Continued)

### SURGERY

#### Specializing in: Orthopedic

## MICHAEL D. ROSCO, M.D.
### Board Certified orthopedic surgeon

Announces
His Availability for Evaluations
and
Expert Witness Testimony

Dr. Rosco has practiced medicine for 35 years, and has over 20 years of experience in forensic matters. He is familiar with all types of personal injury cases including, but not limited to: automobile collisions, premises liability, work related injuries, medical malpractice, Jones Act, Longshore Act, FELA, and diving deaths, for plaintiff and defense. Dr. Rosco will treat patients on a lien basis. He has testified in over 240 trials and conducted in excess of 10,000 medical legal examinations, evaluations, and medical record reviews.

Call Toll Free 800-636-9100

No charge to attorney for preliminary evaluations.

Reports completed promptly in less than two weeks.

Offices in:
VENTURA   SACRAMENTO   LOS ANGELES   SANTA BARBARA

EDUCATION:
- 1952-1956  University of Vermont, B.A. Degree
- 1956-1960  Albany Medical College, M.D. Degree
- 1960-1961  E.J. Meyer Memorial Hospital, Buffalo, N.Y., Rotating Internship
- 1961-1963  V.A. Hospital, Buffalo, N.Y., Resident, General Surgery
- 1965-1968  University of Louisville Hospitals, Resident, Orthopedic Surgery

MILITARY SERVICE:
Commissioned First Lieutenant, Medical Corps, Captain in 1963

STATE LICENSE:
California, 1965-Present  G10737

CERTIFICATION:
American Board of Orthopedic Surgery, 1970
NAUI Certified Diving Physician, May 1971
Agreed Medical Examiner, 1980-Present
Independent Medical Examiner, 1982-Present
Qualified Medical Examiner, 1990-Present

FIELD OF REHABILITATION:
Consultant, Amputee Clinic Veterans' Administration, 1968-1990
Rehabilitation Director, Pasadena Community Hospital, 1974-1978
Rehabilitation Director, Lake View Medical Center, 1982-1984
Examiner, American Board for Certification Orthotics and Prosthetics, 1974-1976

FIELD OF WORKERS' COMPENSATION:
Medical Advisor, Argonaut Insurance Companies, 1981-1982
Medical Advisor, St. Paul Insurance Companies, 1986-1989
LACMA Section of Industrial Medicine and Surgery-President, 1985

(This Listing Continued)

## MICHAEL D. ROSCO, M.D. (Continued)

COMMUNITY SERVICE:
Board of Directors, Santa Barbara Grand Opera Society
Board of Directors, Boys and Girls Club
Crippled Children's Screening Clinics, 1970-Present
4 Gallon Blood Donor

Mailing Address:
VENTURA OFFICE
953 E. Main Street • Ventura, CA 93001
(805)643-9022 • (800)635-9100
FAX (805)643-9025
E-Mail: mrosco@mem.p.o.com

## MEDICAL EXPERT WITNESS REFERRAL SERVICES

## CONSOLIDATED CONSULTANTS CO.
739 Twin Oaks Ave.
Chula Vista, CA 91910-5924
Phone (800) 683-9847
Fax (619) 422-8101
E-Mail steve_vr@msn.com
Internet Home Page: http://www.FreeReferral.com

### FREE CONSULTANT & EXPERT WITNESS REFERRAL

- *MEDICAL*
- *TECHNICAL*

**Experts listed meet specific requirements prior to being with us:**

- Experts must demonstrate professional competence in their areas of specialty
- Experts must demonstrate litigation experience
- Experts must provide references from previous clients
- Experts must be available for plaintiff or defense cases equally
- Expert must charge their regular rate to the client

Experts employs CCc as a marketing & service support company. CCc is therefore able to provide free Expert Witness referral from a broad selection of quality professionals

| TECHNICAL | MEDICAL |
|---|---|
| ACCIDENT RECONSTRUCTION | ALLERGISTS |
| • Cars - Trucks, Light Duty - Sport Utility Vehicles | ANESTHESIOLOGISTS |
| | CARDIOLOGISTS |
| • Busses - Motorcycles - Motorhomes | DENTISTS |
| | ECONOMIC LOSS |
| • Heavy Trucks | HOSPITAL ADMIN. |
| ADA | INTERNISTS |
| AGRONOMY | LEGAL NURSE |
| ANIMAL BITES | CONSULTANTS |
| AQUATIC ACCIDENTS | NEUROLOGISTS |
| BANKING & FINANCE | NEUROPSYCHOLOGISTS |
| BIOMECHANICS | NURSE-MIDWIVES |

(This Listing Continued)

## SERVICES, SUPPLIERS, CONSULTANTS

**CCC CONSOLIDATED CONSULTANTS CO. (Continued)**

COMPUTER TECHNOLOGY
CONSTRUCTION DEFECTS
ELEVATORS & ESCALATORS
FIRE INVESTIGATION
FIRE & LIFE SAFETY
ECONOMICS
ENGINEERING
HOTEL, BAR & CASINO
HUMAN FACTORS
PREMISES & PRODUCTS LIABILITY
REAL ESTATE
RAILROAD ACCIDENTS
SECURITY
OB/GYN
ORTHOTICS & PROSTHETICS
PATHOLOGISTS
PHARMACOLOGISTS
PSYCHIATRISTS
PSYCHOLOGISTS
PODIATRISTS
PROSTHODONDISTS
SURGEONS
TOXICOLOGISTS
VOIRE DIRE

*Please call or visit us on the internet for complete list!*

### MEDICAL MALPRACTICE CONSULTING/PERSONAL INJURY

**CCC Consolidated Consultants Co.**
739 Twin Oaks Ave.
Chula Vista, CA 91910-5924
Phone: (800) 683-9847
Fax: (619) 422-8101

*See Medical Case Review & Preparation/Trial Consulting*

### MEDICAL RECORDS

**COMPEX**
841 Apollo St.
El Segundo, CA 90245
Phone: (800) 426-6739
Fax: (800) 479-3365

*See Litigation Support Services*

---

The **Martindale-Hubbell Law Directory** is now available online...exclusively through the LEXIS®-NEXIS® services.

---

Now it's easy to find lawyers practicing a specific area of law! Simply consult the **Martindale-Hubbell Law Directory Areas of Practice Index.**

## CALIFORNIA—LOS ANGELES

### MESSENGER SERVICES

*Micro Quick*
(800) 655-FAST
(3278)

Serving All of Southern California

- pick up and delivery for same day service
- serving any location in southern California
- rush court filing
- third party billing available

CD ROM document storage and retrieval
(no software needed)

ADDITIONAL SERVICES:
large volume copying & management specialists
subpoena preparation & service
court filings & fax filings
court indexing & research
licensed process servers

*Micro Quick*
It's our image you can count on!

visit us at www.microquick.com

Bonded          Certified          Insured

### MICROFILMING SERVICES

**COMPEX**
841 Apollo St.
El Segundo, CA 90245
Phone: (800) 426-6739
Fax: (800) 479-3365

*See Litigation Support Services*

### NURSING CONSULTANTS

**CCC Consolidated Consultants Co.**
739 Twin Oaks Ave.
Chula Vista, CA 91910-5924
Phone: (800) 683-9847
Fax: (619) 422-8101

*See Medical Case Review & Preparation/Trial Consulting*

---

Fast ... Easy ... Flexible...
The **Martindale-Hubbell Law Directory on CD-ROM** gives you instant access through multiple search criteria to information on over 900,000 lawyers and law firms. For more details and a FREE demonstration disc, call **1-800-323-3288**.

## LOS ANGELES (Continued)

### PARALEGAL SERVICES

### AT LAW LITIGATION SUPPORT

800-493-7874
2049 Century Park East — Suite 1100
Los Angeles, California 90067
10841 Paramount Boulevard — Suite 205
Downey, California 90401
(310) 552-8052  FAX (310) 552-0704

\* \* \*

A Full Service Agency
Serving all of Southern California
Spacious Conference Suites
Realtime Reporting
Complimentary condensed transcript/ASCII/wp disk
CAT-Links and Discovery ZX Dealer
Videographers - Interpreters
On-Site Teleconference Suite

Temporary Paralegal and Support Personnel
Document Production, Preparation, and Staffing
Microfilming — Document Management
Computerized Litigation Support
Deposition and Trial Transcript Summarization

Member of:  National and California
Court Reporters Association

---

### CAMILLE M. CADOO, CLA
*Independent Certified Legal Assistant*

5763 Bloomfield Street
Simi Valley, California 93063

Phone: 805-583-2588 (M-F)
Phone: 818-755-4848 (M-W)
Facsimile: 805-583-4582

*Specializing in Probate, Adoptions & Real Estate*

*In Practice Since 1981*

Practices Probate from A to Z including Form 706, detailed accountings. Acts as Administrator of Decedent's Estates and Conservator of Person and Estate; bondable. Familiar with probate policy and procedure in all countries in California; also, Arizona and Nevada.

Educated — University of California at Berkeley; certificated from NALA. Completes 25-40 hours per year in CEB courses. Member of Ventura Bar Association and Los Angeles County Bar Association. Former Escrow Officer.

*Recommendations Available Upon Request*

---

### PHOTOGRAPHY

### ELEVENTH HOUR FORENSIC PHOTOGRAPHY

Mailing Address:
P.O. Box 1776
Duarte, California 91010

Bill Courtice
Director

818-358-5715

For over 25 years, the director of Eleventh Hour Forensic Photography has been producing demonstrative evidence, including exhibit size mounted photographs, charts, document enlargements and videos to enhance the persuasive appeal of your case. We go on location to shoot your photos today for presentation tomorrow. Although we are based in the Los Angeles area, upon appointment, we can travel to more distant locations to create the images you need to win your case. Our expertise includes aerial stills and videos, with exceptional clarity. Video editing service to your exact specifications is also available. Video-assisted witness preparation is available as well. We also shoot "in house" product liability photos. We travel to your office or courthouse to make black and white document enlargements "while you wait" within our service area. Our services are reasonably priced, and we have a list of references upon request. For more information, call Bill Courtice at (818) 358-5715.

---

To update your listing
in the **Martindale-Hubbell Law Directory**
call **1-800-MARTIND(ALE)**.

---

Need an extra copy of the **Martindale-Hubbell Law Directory**?  Or of a specific volume?
Call Martindale-Hubbell Customer Service at
**1-800-526-4902**

**SERVICES, SUPPLIERS, CONSULTANTS**           **CALIFORNIA—LOS ANGELES**

## PROCESS SERVERS & DOCUMENT DELIVERY SERVICES

- **Service of Process - National & International**
  Subpoenas/Summonses/Complaints/Notices
- **Court - Agency Filing Service**
  Filing/Research/Retrieval    Public Records Procurement
- **Investigative Services**
  Skiptracing & Locating    Service of Witnesses & Parties
- **Out of State - Foreign Commissions & Petitions**
  Preparation/Noticing/Filing    All Jurisdictions
- **Discovery Facilitation - Litigation Support**
  Subpoena Preparation & Noticing    Subpoena Service
  Service of Subpoena & Fees When Required
- **On & Off Site Document Production**
  CD - Optical Scan Imaging & Micrographic Services
  Electronic Case Management, Repository, & On-Line Service
- **Document & File Archival Storage Systems**
  Analysis/Design/Implementation & Management
  CD-Rom & On-Line Systems    Office & Remote Access
- **Court Reporting & Deposition Service**
  Real Time/Instant/Daily/Expedited    Video Depositions
  Deposition Suites    National Coverage

We manage your *Discovery* needs from *Service of Process* through taking the *Deposition* and *Production of Documents.* Don't waste time following up with process servers and others all over the country when one phone call can do it all!

NATIONWIDE SERVICE CENTER
**(800) 998-8849**
FAX: (800) 888-8564

REFERENCES UPON REQUEST      FOUNDING MEMBER: NAPPS

---

Now you can find the lawyer even if you don't know where he or she practices - with the **Martindale-Hubbell Law Directory Alphabetical Index.**

---

- **Service of Process - National & International**
  Subpoenas/Summonses/Complaints/Notices
- **Court - Agency Filing Service**
  Filing/Research/Retrieval    Public Records Procurement
- **Investigative Services**
  Skiptracing & Locating    Service of Witness & Parties
- **Out of State - Foreign Commissions & Petitions**
  Preparation/Noticing/Filing    All Jurisdictions
- **Discovery Facilitation - Litigation Support**
  Subpoena Preparation & Noticing    Subpoena Service
  Service of Subpoena & Fee's When Required
- **On & Off Site Document Production**
  CD - Optical Scan Imaging & Micrographic Services
  Electronic Case Management, Repository, & On-Line Service
- **Document & File Archival Storage Systems**
  Analysis/Design/Implementation & Management
  CD-ROM & On-Line Systems    Office & Remote Access
- **Court Reporting & Deposition Service**
  Real Time/Instant/Daily/Expedited    Video Depositions
  Deposition Suites    Nationwide Coverage

We manage your *Discovery* needs from *Service of Process* through taking the *Deposition* and *Production of Documents.* Don't waste time following up on process servers and others all over the country when one phone call can do it all!

NATIONWIDE SERVICE CENTER
**(800) 998-8849**
FAX: (800) 888-8564

REFERENCES UPON REQUEST      FOUNDING MEMBER: NAPPS

*SEE OUR AD ON PAGE CAA143S*

---

**ABC Process Serving Bureau, Inc.**
150 Nassau Street
New York, New York 10038
1-800-524-3254
Telephone: 212-732-6490    FAX: 212-267-2843

> Process Serving
> Court Filings - Record Searches
> Serving Manhattan - Brooklyn - Queens
> Bronx - Staten Island
> ALL COURTS
>
> Secretary of State
> Nassau-Suffolk-Westchester
>
> NATIONWIDE & INTERNATIONAL SERVICE

Member:
National Association of Professional Process Servers
New York State Professional Process Serving Agencies

License 697794

*SEE OUR AD ON PAGE CAA146S*

# LOS ANGELES (Continued)
## Process Servers & Document Delivery Services (Continued)

### BEACH CITIES ATTORNEY SERVICE
P.O. Box 14061
Torrance, CA 90503-8061

Telephone
(310) 787-8686

Fax
(310) 787-8393

Mr Pat Woodman • Owner

Pat Woodman established *Beach Cities Attorney Service* in July of 1995. He has 14 years experience as a certified process server of California. *Beach Cities Attorney Service* specializes in Skip Tracing and also offers other investigative services. *Beach Cities Attorney Service* serves all of Los Angeles and Orange counties, and is a member of the California Association of Photocopiers & Process Servers (CAPPS).

List of Services
- ✓ Public Records Retrieval
- ✓ Post Office Checks
- ✓ Document Retrieval, Filing & Research
- ✓ Database & Real Property Searches
- ✓ Skip Tracing
- ✓ Specializing in Rush Service
- ✓ Litigation Support Services
- ✓ Attorney Services
- ✓ County, State & Federal Courts
- ✓ Messenger Services
- ✓ Delivery Services

---

The **Martindale-Hubbell Law Directory** is now available online...exclusively through the LEXIS®-NEXIS® services.

---

## CALIFORNIA LEGAL SUPPORT SERVICES, INC.
### 800-899-2577
### FAX: 800-998-2577
NATIONWIDE SERVICE CENTER

LOS ANGELES OFFICE
2808 West Temple Street
Suite 203
Los Angeles, CA 90026
Telephone: 213-383-5822
FAX: 213-383-1686

**Patricia D. Karotkin**
**Managing Partner**

| | |
|---|---|
| LOS ANGELES OFFICE | 213-383-5822 |
| OAKLAND OFFICE | 510-839-2605 |
| SAN FRANCISCO OFFICE | 415-882-2270 |
| SAN JOSE OFFICE | 408-491-9770 |

CLSS has offices throughout California, each fully bonded and insured. Our staff of experienced professionals are committed to seeing every detail of your assignment completed on time, every time and in a manner that reflects our professionalism...and yours.

- Professional Registered Bonded and Certified Process Servers
- Skip Tracing/Locate/Investigative Services
- Litigation Search and Status
- Experienced State and Federal Court Service Specialists
- Fax Filing Service - All Courts
- City, County, State and Federal Agency Filings and Research
- Public Records Research and Retrieval
- Litigation Support Service
- Registered Professional Photocopiers
- Subpoena Preparation
- On/Off Site Document Reproduction
- Complete Micrographic and Optical Scan Production Service

Representative clients consist of major law firms, in-house legal departments, financial institutions, insurance carriers and governmental agencies. References furnished upon request.

California Association of Photocopiers and Process Servers
National Association of Professional Process Servers

***Major Credit Cards Accepted***

*Continuous listing in M-H Law Directory Since 1981*

SERVICES, SUPPLIERS, CONSULTANTS — CALIFORNIA—LOS ANGELES

# PROMPT LEGAL SERVICES

*"We Serve You by Serving Others"*
**Established 1975**

**David C. Hassman** — All-American Process Servers
10573 West Pico Boulevard • Suite 344 • Los Angeles, CA 90064

*Counties:*
LOS ANGELES • Orange • Riverside
San Bernadino • San Diego • Santa Barbara • Ventura

*Serving throughout California, United States and International*

— 24 HOUR SERVICE —

**✱ SPECIALIZATIONS:**
- Process Serving/Rush Service
- Multiple Attempts at no extra charge
- Skip Tracing
- Surveillance
- County, State & Federal Courts
- Writs of Execution
- Small Claims Specialist

**✱ LITIGATION SERVICES AVAILABLE UPON REQUEST**
- Public Record Retrieval
- Post Office Checking
- Database Searches
- Real Property Searches
- Document Retrieval, Filing & Research
- DMV & Credit Research
- Subpoena Preparation
- Witness Statements
- Summons & Complaints

★ Los Angeles

Member: *(CAPPS) California Association of Photocopiers & Process Servers*
*(NAPPS) National Association of Professional Process Servers*
*(APSA) Arizona Process Servers Association*
*(FAPPS) Florida Association of Professional Process Servers*
*(TPPS) Texas Professional Process Servers Association*
*(OAPS) Oregon Association of Professional Process Servers*
*(NJPSA) New Jersey Process Servers Association*
*Chamber of Commerce*

★ San Diego

Tel: (310) 838-9000    **800-838-9044**    Fax: (310) 838-0855

## LOS ANGELES (Continued)
### Process Servers & Document Delivery Services (Continued)

### PROCESS SERVERS & DOCUMENT DELIVERY SERVICES

**ABC Process Serving Bureau, Inc.**

150 Nassau Street
New York, New York 10038
1-800-524-3254    212-732-6490
Fax 212-267-2843

*Process Serving • Court Filings • Record Searches*

*Same Day Service Available*

*Serving Manhattan — Brooklyn — Queens
Bronx — Staten Island*

ALL COURTS

*Nassau Suffolk-Westchester
Secretary of State - Albany*

**NATIONWIDE & INTERNATIONAL SERVICE**

Member:
National Association of Professional Process Servers
New York State Professional Process Serving Agencies
License 697794

---

**D.L.S., Inc. (Demovsky Lawyer Service)**
401 Broadway, Suite 510
New York, New York 10013
Telephone: 212-925-1220
Fax: 212-941-0235

ALAN DEMOVSKY
President

**D.L.S., Inc. (Albany Office)**
4 Central Avenue
Albany, New York 12210
Telephone: 518-449-8411
Fax: 518-449-2467

**D.L.S. (Bayonne Office)**
For Retrieval at Bayonne Archives
Telephone: 201-823-2290
Fax: 201-823-8603

**D.L.S., Inc. (WESTCHESTER/ROCKLAND OFFICE)**
FAX: 914-637-7809
MAIN TOLL-FREE # 800-443-1058

---

## PROMPT LEGAL SERVICES

"We Serve You by Serving Others"
Established 1975

10573 West Pico Boulevard • Suite 344
Los Angeles, California 90064
Toll Free: (800) 838-9044
Telephone: (310) 838-9000 • Facsimile: (310) 838-0855

*Registered, Certified, Bonded & Insured*

**Prompt Legal Services** is a full litigation services company. Located near Beverly Hills, we specialize in very fast, efficient and courteous process service. Our firm is known for hard to serves, celebrity, and other special circumstance services. We are fully computerized and are on-line with databases nationwide.

Counties:
LOS ANGELES
Orange / Riverside
San Bernardino / San Diego
Santa Barbara / Ventura

Serving throughout California, United States and International

**— 24 HOUR SERVICE —**

- **SPECIALIZATIONS:**
  - Rush Service
  - Multiple Attempts at no extra charge
  - Skip Tracing
  - Surveillance
  - County, State & Federal Courts
  - Writs of Execution
  - Small Claims Specialist

- **LITIGATION SERVICES AVAILABLE UPON REQUEST**
  - Public Record Retrieval
  - Post Office Checking
  - Database Searches
  - Real Property Searches
  - Document Retrieval, Filing & Research
  - DMV & Credit Research
  - Subpoena Preparation
  - Witness Statements
  - Summons & Complaints

Member:  (CAPPS) California Association of Photocopiers & Process Servers
(NAPPS) National Association of Professional Process Servers
(APSA) Arizona Process Servers Association
(FAPPS) Florida Association of Professional Process Servers
(TPPS) Texas Professional Process Servers Association
(OAPS) Oregon Association of Professional Process Servers
(NJPSA) New Jersey Process Servers Association
*Chamber of Commerce*

Standard Service
Los Angeles County  $35
All Other Counties  $45

**SEE OUR AD ON PAGE CAA145S**

SERVICES, SUPPLIERS, CONSULTANTS | CALIFORNIA—LOS ANGELES

## *From Big Cities...*

## *...To Rural Communities*

## *Our Network Is Your Network*

• Process Service • Difficult Serves • Skip Trace/Locates • Stand-by/Stakeouts • Court Filing • Court Research
Court Indexing • Court Retrieval • Public Records Search • Statewide Forwarding • Nationwide Forwarding

# Wade's Attorney Service

a legal support service company

5410 Wilshire Blvd., Suite 237 • Los Angeles, CA 90036

# (213) 933-4448

FAX: (213) 933-1474

CALIFORNIA—LOS ANGELES   MARTINDALE-HUBBELL LAW DIRECTORY 1997

## LOS ANGELES (Continued)
**Process Servers & Document Delivery Services (Continued)**

### Sylnic Investigations
1278 Glenneyre St., #115
Laguna Beach, CA 92651
Phone: (714) 449-4815
Fax: (714) 499-5455

*See Investigators*

---

Now it's easy to find lawyers practicing a specific area of law! Simply consult the **Martindale-Hubbell Law Directory Areas of Practice Index.**

### Wade's Attorney Service
a legal support service company

*From Big Cities...*

*...To Rural Communities*

*Our Network Is Your Network*

- Process Service
- Difficult Serves
- Skip Trace/Locates
- Stand-by/Stakeouts
- Court Filing
- Court Research
- Court Indexing
- Court Retrieval
- Public Records Search
- Statewide Forwarding
- Nationwide Forwarding

5410 Wilshire Blvd.
Suite 237
Los Angeles, CA 90036
(213) 933-4448
FAX: (213) 1474

***SEE OUR AD ON PAGE CAA147S***

---

# WHEN SPEED AND ACCURACY MATTER MOST

- Volume Copying Specialists
- Court Indexing & Research
- Court/Fax Filings
- Access to Complete DMV Files
- Complete Messenger Service
- Subpoena Preparation and Service
- Photocopying
- Process Serving

**CD ROM document storage and retrieval**
(no software needed)

## MICRO QUICK
*IT'S OUR IMAGE YOU CAN COUNT ON!*

**Nationwide Toll-Free Number**  **(800) 655-FAST** *(3278)*  **Serving all of Southern California**

Visit our Website at WWW.MICROQUICK.COM

**BONDED**   **CERTIFIED**   **INSURED**

SERVICES, SUPPLIERS, CONSULTANTS | CALIFORNIA—LOS ANGELES

## PRODUCT SAFETY

**CCC Consolidated Consultants Co.**
739 Twin Oaks Ave.
Chula Vista, CA 91910-5924
Phone: (800) 683-9847
Fax: (619) 422-8101

*See Medical Expert Witness - Devices*

## PSYCHOLOGICAL INJURY - FILE REVIEW & ANALYSIS

**Barrington Psychiatric Center**
Suite 320
1990 S. Bundy Dr.
Los Angeles, CA 90025
Phone: (310) 826-3235
Fax: (310) 447-0840

*See Medical Expert Witness - Psychiatry - Forensic*

---

Fast ... Easy ... Flexible...
**The Martindale-Hubbell Law Directory on CD-ROM** gives you instant access through multiple search criteria to information on over 900,000 lawyers and law firms. For more details and a FREE demonstration disc, call **1-800-323-3288.**

---

To update your listing
in the **Martindale-Hubbell Law Directory**
call 1-800-MARTIND(ALE).

---

Need an extra copy of the **Martindale-Hubbell Law Directory**? Or of a specific volume?
Call Martindale-Hubbell Customer Service at
**1-800-526-4902**

## SPORTS ACCIDENTS/SERIOUS SLIPS & FALLS

**DISCOVERY SYSTEMS, INC.**
Expert Engineering and Discovery Consultants
Ray E. Omholt, President
800-762-2848

**EXPERTISE**
- Engineering & Physics
- Wood Floors & Finishes
- Sport Surfaces & Equipt.
- All Slips, Trips and Falls
- Sight Perception Factors
- Bodies in Motion Factors
- Building and Safety Codes
- Product Liability Evaluations
- Human Factors in Accidents
- Technical Discovery Assistance
- Ptf & Defense Liability Strategies

**EDUCATION**
- B.A. Science Major, Lehigh University
- B.S. Civil Engineering, Lehigh University

**PUBLICATIONS**
- 48 Sport Courts & Surfaces Related Patents
- Series of Articles for "The Legal Intelligencer"

**EXPERIENCE**
- Over 200 Cases Successfully Concluded to Date
- Recognized in Federal, State and County Courts
- Natl. Expert Engineering & Discovery Consultant
- Litigation-Specific Software Applications Designer
- Pres. of Sport Surfacing Mfg. Companies, 30 Yrs.
- National Sport Surfacing Engineering Consultant

**ASSOCIATIONS**
- Bldg. Officials & Code Admin. Intnatl. (BOCA)
- Member American Concrete Institute (ACI)
- National Expert Witness Training (SEAK)

**DISCOVERY SYSTEMS, INC.**
248 Los Angeles Ave., San Anselmo, CA 94960
800-762-2848

## SUBPOENA PREPARATION SERVICES

**COMPEX**
841 Apollo St.
El Segundo, CA 90245
Phone: (800) 426-6739
Fax: (800) 479-3365

*See Litigation Support Services*

# LOS ANGELES (Continued)
## SURVEYS & OPINION RESEARCH

### Cogan Research Group

*Specializing in these services:*

- Designing and conducting consumer, business and industrial market surveys for use in litigation.
- Reviewing survey research conducted by others.
- Serving as an expert witness and consulting.

*Types of Legal Issues Addressed in Surveys:*

- Trademark/Trade Dress/Trade Name Likelihood of Confusion, Secondary Meaning, Genericness, Dilution
- Design Patent
- Unfair Competition
- Misleading Advertising

*About Dr. Sandra R. Cogan:*

- Over 25 years of market research experience.
- Doctorate in Business Administration (DBA) from USC; MBA and BS from UCLA.
- Has taught marketing and marketing research classes at Loyola Marymount University, California State University-Dominguez Hills, Pepperdine University, and UCLA Extension.
- Case experience in trademark, design patent, unfair competition, antitrust, defamation of character, and misleading advertising.
- Conducts a course entitled "Survey Research for Trademark Cases" which is approved by the State Bar of California for one unit of MCLE credit.
- Past President of the Southern California Chapter of the American Marketing Association (1991-92).
- Associate member of the International Trademark Association.
- Associate member of the Intellectual Property Section of the State Bar of California.

*Contact: Dr. Sandra R. Cogan     (310) 316-4289*

**Cogan Research Group**
3528 Torrance Boulevard, Suite 219
Torrance, California 90503
Fax (310) 316-4939

---

Now you can find the lawyer even if you don't know where he or she practices -
with the **Martindale-Hubbell Law Directory Alphabetical Index.**

---

## TITLE ABSTRACT COMPANIES

### TITLE COURT SERVICE, INC.

(213) 626-8753

(213) 626-0147 Fax

Serving the State of California Since 1978

- COURTHOUSE RECORD RESEARCH/VERIFICATION
- LAND TITLE RESEARCH
- BANKRUPTCY DOCUMENT RETREIVAL
- BANKRUPTCY FILING LISTS
- BUILDING PERMIT RETREIVAL
- PENDING LITIGATION RESEARCH
- LIMITED PARTNERSHIP/LIMITED LIABILITY COMPANY/UCC RESEARCH
- MISCELLANEOUS RECORDATION/FILING

TWELVE OFFICES IN THE POPULATION CENTERS OF CALIFORNIA

CENTRAL DISPATCH ADDRESS:

Southern CA: 205 S. Broadway, Suite 302, Los Angeles, CA 90012

Northern CA: 1305 Franklin, Suite 501, Oakland, CA 94612

MEMBER:
NATIONAL PUBLIC RECORDS RESEARCH ASSOCIATION

---

The **Martindale-Hubbell Law Directory** is now available online...exclusively through the LEXIS®-NEXIS® services.

---

Now it's easy to find lawyers practicing a specific area of law! Simply consult the
**Martindale-Hubbell Law Directory Areas of Practice Index.**

## TRIAL PRESENTATION SYSTEMS

**inData Corporation**
402 W. Broadway
#1850
San Diego, CA 92101

We can help you win your case!
**Proven Trial Presentation System:**
inData has grown to be one of the country's leading electronic trial presentation specialists. Over the past few years, we've been involved with many successful high profile cases.
- The Exxon Valdez Cases
- The Keating S&L Cases
- The Oklahoma City bombing cases

While not costly, make no mistake, when your case demands the presentation solution we are the ones to call.

**Experienced Trial Presentation Consultants:**
There's a lot of electronic solutions out there. Don't waste valuable time and financial resources building and supporting a complicated system that might not meet all of your needs. Our experts can tackle all technical issues of an automated system while showing you how to effectively use electronic trial presentations including:
- Optimal courtroom design
- Use of equipment
- Computer based presentation expertise
- Witness Preparation

Our courtroom specialist have worked with leading attorneys on some of the most well know cases in the country. Let them prove their value to you. Call today.

**Equipment Rental and Installation:**
Adding audio visual capabilities to a courtroom is a easy as calling inData. Over the years, our development staff and trial consultants have perfected a system that makes courtroom installation hassle free.
- Monitors
- Hardware integration
- Jury display systems
- Cabling
- Projection systems

We are the most complete automated legal support bureau.
inData Services include:
- Animation Services
- Audio Visual Services
- Barcoding
- Trial Presentation Consulting
- Equipment Rental and Installation
- Scanning Services
  - Microfilm to CD conversion
  - CD to Paper "blow-backs"
- Software Development
- Trial Presentation Systems

Need more information?
Call us toll free 1-800-828-8292 or visit our web site
http://www.indatacorp.com

---

Fast ... Easy ... Flexible...
The **Martindale-Hubbell Law Directory** on **CD-ROM** gives you instant access through multiple search criteria to information on over 900,000 lawyers and law firms. For more details and a FREE demonstration disc, call **1-800-323-3288**.

---

To update your listing
in the **Martindale-Hubbell Law Directory**
call **1-800-MARTIND(ALE)**.

---

Need an extra copy of the **Martindale-Hubbell Law Directory?** Or of a specific volume?
Call Martindale-Hubbell Customer Service at
**1-800-526-4902**

---

Now you can find the lawyer even if you don't know where he or she practices -
with the **Martindale-Hubbell Law Directory Alphabetical Index.**

---

The **Martindale-Hubbell Law Directory** is now available online...exclusively
through the LEXIS®-NEXIS® services.

## VIDEO TAPE SERVICES

### In Los Angeles

### ABBOTT LEGAL VIDEO SERVICES

Serving all of Los Angeles, Orange,
Ventura, San Diego, Riverside &
San Bernardino Counties

**MAIN OFFICE**
714 W. Olympic Blvd., Suite 1112
Los Angeles, California 90015
(800) 266-2268
FAX: (213) 749-0644

VIDEOTAPED DEPOSITIONS
VIDEO SYNCHRONIZATION
DAY IN THE LIFE DOCUMENTARIES
COURTROOM PLAYBACK
EXPERT WITNESS TESTIMONY
LIVING WILLS
WITNESS PREPARATION

*BROADCAST-QUALITY EQUIPMENT
EXPERIENCED VIDEOGRAPHERS*

*SEE OUR AD ON PAGE CAA153S*

---

### Chait Media Inc.
241 Central Park W.
New York, NY 10024
Phone: 212-877-9200
Phone: 800-713-9769

*See Court Reporters*

---

Now it's easy to find lawyers practicing a specific area of law! Simply consult the **Martindale-Hubbell Law Directory Areas of Practice Index.**

---

### Charles Heller & Company
N.C.R.A. Certified
Legal Video Specialists

Los Angeles
San Francisco
Seattle

Services:

Depositions
Videotaped Wills
Day-in-the-life Documentaries
Inventories
Construction Inspections
Property Damage Documentation
Medical Examinations
Courtroom Playback
Legal Photography
Seminars/Symposiums

Members:

National Court Reporters Association
California Court Reporters Association
Washington Shorthand Reporters Association
Los Angeles General Shorthand Reporters Association
State Bar of California - Litigation Section
Reporters Network

Dedicated to serving the legal community with professionalism and high production standards, **Charles Heller & Co.** offers you the security of legal video production done by professionals trained and certified by the N.C.R.A. Reliable, responsible, flexible and conscientious, **Charles Heller & Co.** gives you the freedom to pursue your depositions, inspections or documentations with video operators who are familiar with the laws relevant to your undertakings, giving you the maximum benefits video can offer you.

Qualified * Experienced * Professional

For more information call:

1-800-841-5888

Serving the Pacific Rim since 1989

---

### Lacey Shorthand Reporting Corporation and Lacey Video Services

695 S. Harvard Blvd.
Los Angeles, CA 90005
Phone: (800) 905-2239
Fax: (213) 387-6124

*See Court Reporters*

---

Fast ... Easy ... Flexible...
**The Martindale-Hubbell Law Directory on CD-ROM** gives you instant access through multiple search criteria to information on over 900,000 lawyers and law firms. For more details and a FREE demonstration disc, call **1-800-323-3288.**

# ABBOTT & ASSOCIATES

CERTIFIED SHORTHAND REPORTERS AND LEGAL VIDEO SERVICES

## (800) 266-2268

714 W. OLYMPIC BLVD., STE. 1112
LOS ANGELES, CALIFORNIA 90015

FAX (213) 749-0644

**COMPLIMENTARY CONFERENCE ROOM**

**FREE AIRPORT TRANSPORTATION**

ORANGE COUNTY OFFICE
16462 GRIMAUD LANE
HUNTINGTON BEACH, CA 92649

**KARYN ABBOTT
CSR 5272/RPR**

**SERVING LOS ANGELES, ORANGE, RIVERSIDE, SAN DIEGO, SAN BERNARDINO, VENTURA COUNTIES**

ASCII, DISCOVERY & CATLINKS DISKS, CONDENSED TRANSCRIPTS, KEYWORD INDEXES, IN-HOUSE VIDEO AND INTERPRETING SERVICES, DOCUMENT COPYING, REALTIME REPORTING, DAILY AND EXPEDITED DELIVERY, SERVICE OF SUBPOENAS

DEPOSITIONS, HEARINGS, ARBITRATIONS, AND COURT APPEARANCES

# CALIFORNIA—LOS ANGELES

## LOS ANGELES (Continued)
### VIDEO TRIAL PRESENTATIONS

### DECISIONQUEST
2050 West 190th Street, Suite 205, Torrance, CA 90504
(310) 618-9600; Fax: (310) 618-1122
Principal Contact: Michael E. Cobo

e-mail address: dqi@aol.com
www address: http://www.decisionquest.com

Los Angeles, Houston, Chicago, New York, Boston,
Washington and Atlanta

DecisionQuest utilizes the most advanced technology and equipment available anywhere today. Similarly, all elements of design and production are completed in DecisionQuest facilities to ensure both confidentiality and value to our clients. Whether your case calls for 2-D or 3-D animation, we have the ability to make the proper recommendation, develop a cost effective solution and produce a high quality animation for your case.

DecisionQuest has invested heavily in the latest technologies that allow us to deliver the best quality at the lowest cost to our clients. Any video presentation can be shot and edited in our state-of-the-art digital editing facility. Virtually any video format can be accommodated.

*Call us to find out why, contrary to popular belief, not all exhibits should be presented on TV monitors.*

Knowledge | Control | Persuasion | Winning℠

---

To update your listing
in the **Martindale-Hubbell Law Directory**
call 1-800-MARTIND(ALE).

Need an extra copy of the **Martindale-Hubbell Law Directory?** Or of a specific volume?
Call Martindale-Hubbell Customer Service at
1-800-526-4902

---

## MARTINDALE-HUBBELL LAW DIRECTORY 1997

### VIDEO, COMPUTER, AUDIO EQUIPMENT FOR COURT/TRIALS

### DECISIONQUEST
2050 West 190th Street, Suite 205, Torrance, CA 90504
(310) 618-9600; Fax: (310) 618-1122
Principal Contact: Michael E. Cobo

e-mail address: dqi@aol.com
www address: http://www.decisionquest.com

Los Angeles, Houston, Chicago, New York, Boston,
Washington and Atlanta

From exhibit boards to sophisticated CD-ROM presentations, DecisionQuest is on the cutting edge of courtroom presentation technology.

We work closely with you to determine the most effective medium for demonstrative exhibits. We examine the courtroom space, pay attention to the attorney's comfort level with technology and analyze which form of presentation will be most persuasive for your case.

Our services include:

| | |
|---|---|
| Exhibit Strategy and Design | Computer Animation |
| Video Production | Video/Audio Editing |
| Laser Disc Technology | Bar Coding |
| ELMO Projection System | InVzn Courtroom Presentation System |
| Equipment Rentals | High Resolution Video, Laser & Computer Playback Installations |

*Call us to find out which type of exhibits we do not recommend presenting on TV monitors.*

Knowledge | Control | Persuasion | Winning℠

---

Now you can find the lawyer even if you don't
know where he or she practices -
with the **Martindale-Hubbell Law
Directory Alphabetical Index.**

# SERVICES, SUPPLIERS, CONSULTANTS — CALIFORNIA–LOS ANGELES

## VOCATIONAL EVALUATIONS/LIFE CARE PLANNING

### Crawford Disability Management Services

Certified vocational and R.N. medical-legal consultants providing comprehensive litigation support services for personal injury, divorce and medical malpractice.

**Services:**

Medical
- life care plans
- expert witness testimony
- medical consultation
- medical records review
- case management services

Vocational
- employability evaluations
- loss of wage earning capacity
- expert witness testimony
- labor market analysis
- ADA consultation

Jeanine Metildi, M.A., CRC, CCM, CDMS
Certified Rehabilitation Counselor

Cynthia Ward, M.ED., CRC, CCM, CDMS
Certified Rehabilitation Counselor

Peggy Zannotti, R.N., CCM, CDMS
Certified Case Manager

Oonagh Burke, R.N., MCR, CRC, CCM
Certified Case Manager

Ruth Arnush, M.E.D., CDMS
Certified Rehabilitation Specialist

10805 Holder Street, #220 • Cypress, CA 90630
400 Corporate Pointe, 6th Floor • Culver City, CA 90230
(714) 236-7975
(310) 430-9262
(213) 975-0091

Servicing Southern California

---

The **Martindale-Hubbell Law Directory** is now available online...exclusively through the LEXIS®-NEXIS® services.

## WITNESS PREPARATION & ASSESSMENT

### DecisionQuest
2050 West 190th Street, Suite 205, Torrance, CA 90504
(310) 618-9600; Fax: (310) 618-1122
Principal Contact: Dr. Allan H. Colman

e-mail address: dqi@aol.com
www address: http://www.decisionquest.com

Los Angeles, Houston, Chicago, New York, Boston, Washington and Atlanta

Sometimes a witness the attorney feels most comfortable and confident about actually does the worst when testifying. The rapport established by an attorney with a witness can lead to direct testimony that appears rehearsed and nonspontaneous. It can make the cross examination appear much more powerful.

DecisionQuest helps clients evaluate and choose expert witnesses. In addition, the professionals at DecisionQuest work to prepare witnesses for trial so they can testify with credibility and comprehensibility.

*Call us to find out the one critical question attorneys most often fail to ask their witnesses.*

Knowledge | Control | Persuasion | Winning℠

---

Now it's easy to find lawyers practicing a specific area of law! Simply consult the
**Martindale-Hubbell Law Directory Areas of Practice Index.**

---

Fast ... Easy ... Flexible...
**The Martindale-Hubbell Law Directory on CD-ROM** gives you instant access through multiple search criteria to information on over 900,000 lawyers and law firms. For more details and a FREE demonstration disc, call **1-800-323-3288**.

MENLO PARK, 28,040, *San Mateo Co.*

## COURT REPORTERS

### BELL & MYERS

CERTIFIED SHORTHAND REPORTER, INC.

| | |
|---|---|
| 1083 LINCOLN AVENUE | 2465 EAST BAYSHORE ROAD |
| SAN JOSE, CA 95125 | SUITE 301 |
| (408) 287-7500 | PALO ALTO, CA 94303 |
| FAX (408) 294-1211 | (415) 328-7500 |

1-800-293-DEPO

A PROFESSIONAL STAFF OF CERTIFIED REPORTERS
IN-HOUSE VIDEOGRAPHER

SERVING THE ENTIRE BAY AREA
ALAMEDA, CONTRA COSTA, FRESNO, MONTEREY, SACRAMENTO,
SAN BENITO, SAN FRANCISCO, SAN MATEO, SANTA CLARA &
SANTA CRUZ COUNTIES

COMPLIMENTARY CONFERENCE ROOMS AVAILABLE
COMPLETE LITIGATION SUPPORT

| | |
|---|---|
| *AMICUS | *ARBITRATIONS/HEARINGS/MEETINGS |
| *ASCII | *AVIATION |
| *CAT LINKS | *BUSINESS LITIGATION |
| *CONDENSED TRANSCRIPTS | *COMPUTER ELECTRONICS |
| *DISCOVERY ZX | *EXPERT TESTIMONY |
| *REALTIME REPORTING | *MEDICAL/TECHNICAL |
| *WORD PERFECT DISKS | *PATENT |
| *EXPEDITED TRANSCRIPTS | *REAL ESTATE |

*WORKERS COMPENSATION

*WRITTEN INTERROGATORIES

CLOSE TO SAN FRANCISCO & SAN JOSE AIRPORTS
WE CONFIRM ALL DEPOSITIONS THE DAY BEFORE
LAST MINUTE SETTINGS WELCOMED

CALL BELL & MYERS
TO PROVIDE THE LITIGATION SERVICES YOU NEED

1-800-293-DEPO

*SEE OUR AD ON PAGE CAA157S*

---

To update your listing
in the **Martindale-Hubbell Law Directory**
call 1-800-MARTIND(ALE).

Need an extra copy of the **Martindale-Hubbell Law Directory**? Or of a specific volume?
Call Martindale-Hubbell Customer Service at
**1-800-526-4902**

Now you can find the lawyer even if you don't
know where he or she practices -
with the **Martindale-Hubbell Law
Directory Alphabetical Index.**

The **Martindale-Hubbell Law Directory** is now
available online...exclusively
through the LEXIS®-NEXIS® services.

Now it's easy to find lawyers practicing a specific
area of law! Simply consult the
**Martindale-Hubbell Law Directory
Areas of Practice Index.**

SERVICES, SUPPLIERS, CONSULTANTS      CALIFORNIA—MENLO PARK

# Bell & Myers
## CERTIFIED SHORTHAND REPORTER, INC.

# Color Video Depositions

**Professional Staff**
**Serving The Entire Bay Area**

- Complimentary Condensed Transcripts
- Ascii/Amicus Disks
- Discovery ZX
- Realtime

- Expert Testimony
- Arbitrations
- Hearings
- Complimentary Conference Suites

**(408) 287 - 7500**

1083 Lincoln Avenue
San Jose, CA 95125
FAX (408) 294-1211

**(415) 328 - 7500**

2465 East Bayshore Road
Suite 301
Palo Alto, CA 94303

**(800) 293 - 3376**

## MENLO PARK (Continued)
### INTERPRETERS & TRANSLATORS

**Japanese Linguistic Service**
Specialists in Legal Translation and Interpreting since 1977

- Proven expertise and capacity to handle large technical translation projects supporting international litigation
- Deposition and trial interpreting
- Patent translation into and from Japanese
- In-house professionals with technical and legal backgrounds
- Outstanding references in the professional community

We offer expert support at all stages of the legal process.

Call us today at (415) 321-9832 for a confidential discussion of your special requirements.

135 Willow Road
Menlo Park, CA 94025
(415) 321-9832
FAX: (415) 329-9864

---

Fast ... Easy ... Flexible...
**The Martindale-Hubbell Law Directory on CD-ROM** gives you instant access through multiple search criteria to information on over 900,000 lawyers and law firms. For more details and a FREE demonstration disc, call 1-800-323-3288.

To update your listing in the **Martindale-Hubbell Law Directory** call **1-800-MARTIND(ALE)**.

---

Need an extra copy of the **Martindale-Hubbell Law Directory**? Or of a specific volume? Call Martindale-Hubbell Customer Service at **1-800-526-4902**

## TRANSLATION SERVICES

### AD-EX® WORLDWIDE

*TRANSLATORS FOR
SCIENCE, INDUSTRY, MEDICINE, LAW, COMMERCE
SINCE 1957*

- Expert translations from/into the world's major languages
- In the major fields of science, technology, industry, medicine, law, commerce
- By teams of subject-specialized translators and editors working into the translators' native languages
- Extensive reference library: thousands of multilingual dictionaries plus customized computer-based glossaries compiled over decades
- Translations prepared on computers: DOS, Windows, Macintosh environments with laser printouts and free copies on diskette
- Desktop publishing - available in a variety of options
- Accept jobs or projects large, medium and small
- Prompt service nationwide, worldwide - 24 hours a day, every day of the year
- Delivery worldwide (at our expense) via fax, modem, e-mail, messenger and/or air courier
- Based in California's dynamic Silicon Valley (close to Stanford University) - high-technology world capital
- Our past and present clientele includes hundreds of the nation's and world's leading industrial enterprises, research institutions and law firms
- Quality work at affordable prices (references provided on request)
- Prompt price and delivery-time quotations/estimates via fax and/or e-mail
- Major credit cards accepted: American Express, Visa, MasterCard, Discover

If it needs to be done right, call:
**AD-EX WORLDWIDE**
525 Middlefield Road - Suite 150
Menlo Park, California 94025-3458, USA
Telephone: (800) 223-7753 and (415) 854-6732
Fax: (415) 325-8428 and (415) 325-7409
76620.3521@compuserve.com
ADEXTRAN@aol.com

Corporate Member of the American Translators Association (ATA)

---

Now you can find the lawyer even if you don't know where he or she practices - with the **Martindale-Hubbell Law Directory Alphabetical Index.**

# SERVICES, SUPPLIERS, CONSULTANTS

## CALIFORNIA—MERCED

### Japanese Linguistic Service
Specialists in Legal Translation and Interpreting since 1977

- Proven expertise and capacity to handle large technical translation projects supporting international litigation
- Deposition and trial interpreting
- Patent translation into and from Japanese
- In-house professionals with technical and legal backgrounds
- Outstanding references in the professional community

We offer expert support at all stages of the legal process.

Call us today at (415) 321-9832 for a confidential discussion of your special requirements.

135 Willow Road
Menlo Park, CA 94025
(415) 321-9832
FAX: (415) 329-9864

## MERCED, * 56,216, *Merced Co.*

### COURT REPORTERS

**DEPOSITIONS * HEARINGS**

*SERVING MERCED - LOS BANOS - MODESTO - FRESNO*

COMPUTERIZED LITIGATION SUPPORT

CONDENSED TRANSCRIPTS * WORD INDEXING

ASCII * SUMMATION * AMICUS * CAT-LINKS

COMPLIMENTARY DEPOSITION SUITES

EXPEDITED AND DAILY COPY DELIVERY

MULTI-COPY DISCOUNT

MEMBERS CCRA, NCRA

**ASSOCIATED REPORTERS**
*Certified Shorthand Reporters*

728 West 19th Street
Merced, CA 95340

(800) 847-1518 * (209) 384-0165 * FAX (209) 384-8842

---

### CENTRAL CALIFORNIA REPORTERS
Certified Shorthand and Video Reporters

Main Bookkeeping and Calendaring
1801 H Street, Ste B-5
Modesto, Ca. 95353
FAX (209) 532-9362

Toll Free 1 (888) 532-5273

Providing only Experienced Certified Shorthand Reporters for General and Special Reporting Services for the Central California Region

▸ Depositions, Video Taping, Hearings
▸ Computerized; IBM Compatible
▸ Expert testimony
▸ Expedited and Daily Transcripts
▸ Condensed Transcripts
▸ E-mail; Exhibit scanning to ascii
▸ FAX Filing; Process Referrals
▸ State and Nationwide Referrals
▸ Conference Rooms
▸ Competitive Pricing

Covering Counties of: Alameda; Amador; Claveras; Contra Costa; El Dorado; Fresno; Kings; Lake; Madera; Mariposa; Mendocino; Merced; Monterrey; Napa; Placer; Sacramento; San Joaquin; Solano; Sonoma; Stanislaus; Tuolumne and Yolo

Member

National Shorthand Reporters Association
California Court Reporters Association

---

The **Martindale-Hubbell Law Directory** is now available online...exclusively through the LEXIS®-NEXIS® services.

---

Now it's easy to find lawyers practicing a specific area of law! Simply consult the
**Martindale-Hubbell Law Directory
Areas of Practice Index.**

**MODESTO, \* 164,730, *Stanislaus Co.***

## COURT REPORTERS

### Al Cala & Associates
Over 43 years of Shorthand Reporting Service

P.O. Box 1930
1601 I Street, Suite 410
Modesto, California 95353
Telephone: 209-521-5316
Fax: 209-521-9898

Al Cala - CSR
Elisa Cala - CSR, RPR
Jordan Cala - Office Mgr.

Depositions - Statements - Medical - Technical
Computer-Aided Transcription
Key Word Indexing
Litigation Support
Videotape Service
Condensed Transcript
ASCII - DISCOVERY ZX - CATLINKS - AMICUS
Deposition Suites Available
Photocopy Service
Airport Pick-up Service

Member
National Shorthand Reporters Association
California Court Reporters Association

---

### Fainter & Smith
**Certified Shorthand Reporters**

928 - 12th Street, Suite 303
Modesto, California 95354
Telephone: 209-521-1034
Fax: 209-521-2210
Toll-Free: 888-465-8426

★ Computer-Aided Transcription - Realtime

★ Keyword Indexing

★ Condensed Transcripts

★ ASCII Diskettes

★ Complimentary Deposition Suites

★ Serving Stanislaus, San Joaquin, Merced, Tuolumne Counties

Member
National Shorthand Reporters Association
California Court Reporters Association

Established 1975

---

### MAY & PALERMO
318 McHENRY AVENUE, SUITE B
MODESTO, CALIFORNIA 95354
1-800-644-DEPO
Telephone: (209) 577-4451
FAX: (209) 577-4453

GAYLE MAY-BARKER, CSR, RPR
JULIE RISHWAIN PALERMO CSR, RPR

Depositions - Hearings - Medical - Technical
Real-Time Translation
Daily Copy Service
Medical/Legal Transcription
**CATLINKS - AMICUS**
**CONDENSED - WORD INDEXING**
Complimentary Conference Rooms
Videotape Services Available
Airport Pick-up Service
Interpreters Available
Photocopy Service

MEMBER
NATIONAL COURT REPORTERS ASSOCIATION
SOCIETY for the TECHNOLOGICAL ADVANCEMENT OF REPORTING
AMERICAN NETWORK/DEPO-NET
CALIFORNIA COURT REPORTERS ASSOCIATION

SERVING: Stanislaus, San Joaquin, Merced & Tuolumne Counties

DepoNet® The reliable source for Quality-Assured legal support services worldwide.

**1-800-DEPONET**

---

Fast ... Easy ... Flexible...
**The Martindale-Hubbell Law Directory on CD-ROM** gives you instant access through multiple search criteria to information on over 900,000 lawyers and law firms. For more details and a FREE demonstration disc, call **1-800-323-3288**.

---

To update your listing
in the **Martindale-Hubbell Law Directory**
call **1-800-MARTIND(ALE)**.

SERVICES, SUPPLIERS, CONSULTANTS                               CALIFORNIA—MONTEREY

## MONTEREY, 31,954, *Monterey Co.*

### COURT REPORTERS

### BELL & MYERS

CERTIFIED SHORTHAND REPORTER, INC.

| | |
|---|---|
| 1083 LINCOLN AVENUE | 2465 EAST BAYSHORE ROAD |
| SAN JOSE, CA 95125 | SUITE 301 |
| (408) 287-7500 | PALO ALTO, CA 94303 |
| FAX (408) 294-1211 | (415) 328-7500 |

1-800-293-DEPO

A PROFESSIONAL STAFF OF CERTIFIED REPORTERS
IN-HOUSE VIDEOGRAPHER

SERVING THE ENTIRE BAY AREA
ALAMEDA, CONTRA COSTA, FRESNO, MONTEREY, SACRAMENTO,
SAN BENITO, SAN FRANCISCO, SAN MATEO, SANTA CLARA &
SANTA CRUZ COUNTIES

COMPLIMENTARY CONFERENCE ROOMS AVAILABLE
COMPLETE LITIGATION SUPPORT

| | |
|---|---|
| *AMICUS | *ARBITRATIONS/HEARINGS/MEETINGS |
| *ASCII | *AVIATION |
| *CAT LINKS | *BUSINESS LITIGATION |
| *CONDENSED TRANSCRIPTS | *COMPUTER ELECTRONICS |
| *DISCOVERY ZX | *EXPERT TESTIMONY |
| *REALTIME REPORTING | *MEDICAL/TECHNICAL |
| *WORD PERFECT DISKS | *PATENT |
| *EXPEDITED TRANSCRIPTS | *REAL ESTATE |

*WORKERS COMPENSATION

*WRITTEN INTERROGATORIES

CLOSE TO SAN FRANCISCO & SAN JOSE AIRPORTS
WE CONFIRM ALL DEPOSITIONS THE DAY BEFORE
LAST MINUTE SETTINGS WELCOMED

CALL BELL & MYERS
TO PROVIDE THE LITIGATION SERVICES YOU NEED

1-800-293-DEPO

---

## MONTEREY PENINSULA COURT REPORTERS, INC.
P.O. BOX 2681
MONTEREY CA 93942-2681

| FREE IN USA | FAX |
|---|---|
| (800) 542-6727 | (408) 655-2258 |

E-mail
mpcr@redshift.com

DEPOSITIONS • HEARINGS • ARBITRATIONS

★ FULL LITIGATION SUPPORT & VIDEOTAPE SERVICES
★ DISCOVERY ZX DEALER
★ REAL TIME REPORTING
★ CONDENSED TRANSCRIPTS AND WORD INDEX
★ PROFESSIONAL REPORTING SERVICES
   WITH A *CAN DO* ATTITUDE

Near Monterey Airport • Convenient Parking
• Complimentary Conference Rooms
in Monterey & Salinas

### PROCESS SERVERS & DOCUMENT DELIVERY SERVICES

210 Capitol Street
Suite Number Eight
Salinas, California 93901
(408) 757-2551  FAX (408) 757-2363

Sayler Legal Service is a full service agency serving all of **West Central California**. We also offer same day court filings, notary services, and messenger deliveries. Please call us today.

### LITIGATION SUPPORT SPECIALISTS

- Service of Process
- Portable Photocopying
- Subpoena Preparation
- Court Filing & Records Search
- Courier Service
- Daily Overnight Courier Service Available
- Secretary of State Service
- Skip Tracing Services

Member: *California Association of Photocopiers & Process Servers*

CALIFORNIA—NAPA

NAPA, * 61,842, *Napa Co.*

## COURT REPORTERS

### DeMICHELLE DEPOSITION REPORTERS

SERVING NORTHERN CALIFORNIA AS
WELL AS NATIONWIDE SINCE 1975

"In Deposition Reporting you require
dependability, availability and stability, as
well as quick turnaround. Anything else is
just not acceptable!"

- Real-Time Translation
- Computer Aided Transcription
- Litigation Support
- ASCII Diskettes
- WP Diskettes
- 10-Day Delivery
- Expedited & Daily Copy
- Page Condensing
- Concordance Reports
- Deposition Suites
- Videotape Services
- Interpreters
- Subpoena Services
- Key-Word Indexing
- Free Mileage
- Across from Courthouse

#### DEPOSITION SUITES

| Napa | Fairfield |
|---|---|
| 1001 Second Street | 609 Jefferson Street |
| Suite 311 | Suite F |
| Napa, CA 94559 | Fairfield, CA 94533 |
| (707) 226-6000 | (707) 425-6000 |
| Fax: (707) 226-6786 | Fax: (707) 425-6019 |

Three Conference Rooms Directly Across the Street
From the Napa & Fairfield Courthouses

Copy Machine • Fax Machine • Refreshments
Peking Restaurant and PJ's Cafe located in Building.

---

Need an extra copy of the **Martindale-Hubbell Law Directory?** Or of a specific volume?
Call Martindale-Hubbell Customer Service at
**1-800-526-4902**

---

MARTINDALE-HUBBELL LAW DIRECTORY 1997

## GOLDEN GATE REPORTERS

*CERTIFIED PROFESSIONALS REPORTING SINCE 1974*
COVERING ALL OF NORTHERN CALIFORNIA
1-800-442-4611
All 50 States • Puerto Rico • Canada
FAX: (415) 491-4635
Local No.: (415) 491-4611

Main Office:
35 MITCHELL BOULEVARD, SUITE 8
SAN RAFAEL, CA 94903-2010

*Complimentary Deposition Suites:*
San Francisco. Alameda, Marin and Sonoma Counties;
and San Francisco/Oakland Airports

Principals:
JILL P. PERKINS, CSR NO. 4760
JOLINE C. STONE, CSR NO. 4202
• Depositions/Statements/Hearings
• Medical/Technical Specialists
• Condensed Transcripts • Concordances
• ASCII Disks • CaseView • LiveNote
Video Proceedings • Realtime • Imaging
• Notice Depositions: "Before any Deposition Officer"

Member California Court Reporters Association
National Shorthand Reporters Association
San Rafael Chamber of Commerce

## NEVADA CITY, * 2,855, *Nevada Co.*

## COURT REPORTERS

### ALPINE REPORTING

408 Broad Street
P.O. Box 2014
Nevada City, CA 95959-1941
(916) 265-8616
(800) 900-8616
Fax (916) 265-9228

Largest reporting firm in Nevada County

Court, Depositions, Hearings and Arbitrations

Serving Nevada, Placer, Butte, Sierra and
Sacramento Counties.

Have machine, will travel

Convenient to courthouse (2 blocks)

Complimentary Deposition Suite
Free ASCII disks
Videotaped depositions
Nevada County Airpark transportation

---

SERVICES, SUPPLIERS, CONSULTANTS

NEWPORT BEACH, 66,643, *Orange Co.*

## CONSTRUCTION CONSULTANTS

# Hill International, Inc.

Construction Claims Consultants

4695 MacArthur Court, Suite 1450
Newport Beach, California 92660
Telephone: (714) 474-6280
Contact: Neil F. Katz, Senior Vice President

One Levitt Parkway
Willingboro, NJ 08046
Telephone: (609) 871-5800
Contact: Vincent O. Manuele, Vice President

Other Offices:

- San Diego, CA
- Los Angeles, CA
- Washington, D.C.

Claims Analysis and Technical Evaluation
Cost/Damages Evaluation
Delay/Disruption Analysis
Defective Construction/Design Forensics
Litigation & ADR Support
Expert Witness Testimony
Claims Avoidance Consulting

Hill International, Inc. is a multi-faceted international consulting firm focusing on the management and resolution of engineering and construction claims.

As a leader in claims management, Hill International has participated in the resolution of more than 5,000 complex claims with a total value in excess of $30 billion. Through this experience, Hill has developed a unique perspective on risk management and related expertise in claim prevention.

Hill can help clients evaluate project risk from the outset and develop procedures which will minimize potential liability and promote the expeditious and equitable resolution of claims.

---

Now you can find the lawyer even if you don't know where he or she practices - with the **Martindale-Hubbell Law Directory Alphabetical Index.**

---

CALIFORNIA—NEWPORT BEACH

The **Martindale-Hubbell Law Directory** is now available online...exclusively through the LEXIS®-NEXIS® services.

---

Now it's easy to find lawyers practicing a specific area of law! Simply consult the **Martindale-Hubbell Law Directory Areas of Practice Index.**

---

Fast ... Easy ... Flexible...
**The Martindale-Hubbell Law Directory on CD-ROM** gives you instant access through multiple search criteria to information on over 900,000 lawyers and law firms. For more details and a FREE demonstration disc, call **1-800-323-3288**.

---

To update your listing in the **Martindale-Hubbell Law Directory** call **1-800-MARTIND(ALE)**.

---

Need an extra copy of the **Martindale-Hubbell Law Directory**? Or of a specific volume? Call Martindale-Hubbell Customer Service at 1-800-526-4902

## NEWPORT BEACH (Continued)
## COURT REPORTERS

**AMK**
ABRAMS, MAH & KAHN
REPORTING SERVICE

4101 Birch Street • Suite 130
Newport Beach • California 92660

- Serving Los Angeles, Riverside, San Bernardino, San Diego and Orange Counties
- Complimentary Conference Rooms
- Litigation Support
- Realtime
- Two-week Delivery
- Condensed Transcripts and Master Keyword Index

714 • 261 • 8686
213 • 848 • 8686
800 • 622 • 0226

---

Now you can find the lawyer even if you don't know where he or she practices - with the **Martindale-Hubbell Law Directory Alphabetical Index.**

---

The **Martindale-Hubbell Law Directory** is now available online...exclusively through the LEXIS®-NEXIS® services.

CAA164S

---

### ABRAMS, MAH & KAHN
Court Reporting Service
4101 Birch Street
Suite 130
Newport Beach, California 92660
Telephone: 714-261-8686
Los Angeles, California Telephone: 213-848-8686
FAX: 714-261-6688
800-622-0226

Serving all of:
• Orange County •
• San Diego •
• Riverside •
• Los Angeles •
• San Bernardino •

Realtime
Condensed Transcripts
Complimentary Conference Rooms
Computer-aided Transcription
Video Taping and Interpreters
• Two-week Delivery •
Daily Copy Available

Experienced in:
• Multi-party Complex Litigation •
and
• Technical Testimony •

*SEE OUR AD ON PAGE CAA164S*

---

Now it's easy to find lawyers practicing a specific area of law! Simply consult the
**Martindale-Hubbell Law Directory Areas of Practice Index.**

---

Fast ... Easy ... Flexible...
**The Martindale-Hubbell Law Directory on CD-ROM** gives you instant access through multiple search criteria to information on over 900,000 lawyers and law firms. For more details and a FREE demonstration disc, call **1-800-323-3288**.

SERVICES, SUPPLIERS, CONSULTANTS  CALIFORNIA—NEWPORT BEACH

# LEGAL EASE.

Since 1981, Maxene Weinberg Agency has proven that Court and Deposition Reporting firms *are not* created equal. Our experience and reputation make your job a lot *easier*.

Our select staff of highly trained Certified Court and Deposition Reporters use the latest state-of-the-art equipment and techniques for timely and accurate transcripts.

Maxene Weinberg Agency also offers the most advanced **Real-Time Services** in the industry to attorneys who want to have *instant access* to all of their deposition testimony. We simply connect our computer to yours (or we can provide you with one of our laptops).

Please feel free to contact me to schedule an appointment. We can put the "*ease*" back into *your* "legalese".

*Prompt. Experienced. Professional. Dedicated To Better Service.*
**REALTIME & CIR COURT REPORTERS • INSTANT TRANSCRIPTS
IMPAQT CODING • MAXCAM℠ VIDEO TAPING SERVICES
CONDENSED TRANSCRIPTS • KEYWORD INDEXES • DISCOVERY ZX
CAT LINKS • ASCII's • COMPLIMENTARY CONFERENCE SUITES
Call Toll-Free: 800-640-1949**
or visit us at http://www.interim.com/legal

# MAXENE WEINBERG AGENCY
AN INTERIM LEGAL SERVICES₅ COMPANY

CERTIFIED COURT & DEPOSITION REPORTERS

## Five Convenient Locations:

**Los Angeles**
*Close to LAX and downtown.*

**Mission Viejo**
*Within 75 miles of San Diego.*

**Newport Beach**
*Easy access from John Wayne Airport and close to Irvine and Costa Mesa.*

**San Diego**
*Convenient downtown location just minutes from the airport.*

**San Bernardino**
*Serving Pomona, Riverside and the entire Inland Empire.*

## NEWPORT BEACH (Continued)
Court Reporters (Continued)

**COURT REPORTERS (800) 242-1996**

DON'T WORRY!
WE HAVE YOUR
DEPOSITIONS COVERED
in every County in California.

Newport Beach
Newport Center
620 Newport Center Dr.
Eleventh Floor
Newport Beach, CA 92660

Conference Rooms
& Court Reporters
Nationwide & Abroad

1-800-242-1996

*FREE services include:*

★ Complimentary conference rooms in all of our offices
★ Senior Account Executives throughout Southern California servicing your law firms special needs
★ Airport, shuttle & hotel information provided to traveling attorneys
★ Condensed transcripts with keyword indexing
★ Direct billing of insurance carriers
★ Interpreters and video operators scheduled upon request

*Other services include:*

★ Conference rooms & court reporters nationwide & abroad
★ Two-week turnaround on transcripts
★ ASCII/CAT-LINKS/DISCOVERY ZX
★ Real-Time
★ Professionally bound transcripts with exhibit management
★ Aviation, technical, construction and medical specialists
★ CD imaging & video imaging
★ Video conferencing

ORANGE COUNTY
(714) 548-2435

COVINA
(818) 915-1996

RIVERSIDE
(909) 888-8992

SAN BERNARDINO
(909) 888-8992

LOS ANGELES
(213) 387-9630

PALM SPRINGS
(619) 323-9908

SAN DIEGO
(619) 233-1996

## INTERIM COURT REPORTING

Nationwide Court Reporting Services
Main Office
3530 Wilshire Boulevard, Suite 1700
Los Angeles, CA 90010
1-800-722-1235
Fax: 213-389-8514

Realtime Transcription, CaseView, LiveNote
Daily and Expedited Service
Videotape Depositions and Videosync Timestamping
Computer Aided Transcription and Litigation Support
ASCII, Discovery ZX and CATLinks Diskettes
Telecommunication Capabilities
Condensed Transcripts with Keyword Indexes
Interpreters
Document Depository
Conference Rooms Available

Experienced, Qualified Court Reporters
Skilled in technical, medical, patent and environmental testimony

---

To update your listing
in the **Martindale-Hubbell Law Directory**
call **1-800-MARTIND(ALE)**.

---

Need an extra copy of the **Martindale-Hubbell Law Directory**? Or of a specific volume?
Call Martindale-Hubbell Customer Service at
**1-800-526-4902**

---

Now you can find the lawyer even if you don't
know where he or she practices -
with the **Martindale-Hubbell Law
Directory Alphabetical Index.**

| SERVICES, SUPPLIERS, CONSULTANTS | CALIFORNIA—NEWPORT BEACH |

## MAXENE WEINBERG AGENCY
AN [Esquire] LEGAL SERVICES... COMPANY

**A NATION-WIDE COURT REPORTING COMPANY**

**CALL TOLL-FREE**
1 800 640-1949

*REALTIME & CIR COURT REPORTERS*

**Experts in Large, Multi-Party Complex Litigation,
Medical & Technical Testimony**

On-Site Instant Real-Time Transcripts * ASCII Disks
Condensed Transcripts * Keyword Indexes * Impaqt Coding
Text Browsing * Video/Real-Time Synchronization
Document Imaging and Scanning * CD-ROM Archiving
Nation-Wide On-line Deposition Services
Discovery ZX * Catlinks * Interpreters
Complimentary Conference Suites

24 Hour/7 Days a Week Scheduling
Free Airport and Hotel Information Provided

Company Brochure and Rate Proposals Upon Request

FAST 10 DAY DELIVERY & EXPEDITING SERVICES

**Convenient Locations:**
Los Angeles * (Close to LAX)
Newport Beach * (Minutes from John Wayne Airport)
Mission Viejo * (Within 75 miles of San Diego)
San Diego * (Located Downtown)
San Bernardino * (Serving the Inland Empire)

**Corporate Headquarters:**
27281 Las Ramblas * Suite 160
Mission Viejo, CA 92691
714 582-2503 * Fax 714 582-8569

***SEE OUR AD ON PAGE CAA165S***

---

The **Martindale-Hubbell Law Directory** is now
available online...exclusively
through the LEXIS®-NEXIS® services.

---

## SHERR COURT REPORTERS
A FULL-SERVICE REPORTING AGENCY

**THE REALTIME SPECIALISTS**

Conference rooms in
San Diego; Carlsbad; Orange County, including Irvine, Newport
Beach, Huntington Beach, and El Toro; Los Angeles; Woodland
Hills; Riverside; San Bernardino and Las Vegas

Serving all of Southern California

San Diego headquarters one block from Amtrak,
10 minutes from airport

We handle all **accommodation details**,
including **free shuttle** service to and from San Diego's Lindbergh Field
and discounted accommodations at Wyndham Plaza Hotel
adjacent to our complimentary conference rooms
and next door to the new courthouse.

(619) 231-1600

State-of-the-art Reporting Technology & Services
♦
Complex & Expert Litigation
♦
Realtime/Text Browsing
♦
Laptops Available
♦
Paralegal Reports/Case Notes
♦
Catlinks, Discovery ZX, ASCIIs
♦
Compressed Transcripts with Indices
♦
Immediate Rough Drafts, Transcript Modeming
♦
Daily Copy
♦
Interpreters and Video Technicians
♦
Facsimile & Copy Service
♦
Local Subpoena Service

**SHERR COURT REPORTERS
THE REALTIME SPECIALISTS**
Emerald Plaza
402 West Broadway
Fourth Floor
San Diego, CA 92101
(619) 231-1600, Fax (619) 595-4822
SherrReporters@compuserve.com

# NEWPORT BEACH (Continued)

## ENVIRONMENTAL ENGINEERING & REMEDIATION SERVICES

### INNOVATIVE CONSULTANTS INCORPORATED

Environmental Consultants
*Since 1972*
3740 Campus Drive, Suite 200
Newport Beach, California 92660
(213) 724-0234   (714) 756-8750
Fax (714) 261-8419

**Environmental Scientists and Engineers**
*Working Exclusively for the Private Sector*

A professional consulting engineering firm providing comprehensive services in the disciplines of environmental engineering and water resources, dedicated to developing workable solutions, and compliance with local, state and federal regulations.

Environmental and water resources services include:

- Compliance Audits
- Site Investigation
- Permitting and Compliance Liaison
- Environmental Sampling and Monitoring
- Wastewater Treatment
- Zero Discharge Systems
- EPA Compliance Orders
- Expert Testimony and Litigation Support
- EPA Pretreatment Requirements
- NPDES Storm Water Compliance
- RCRA Hazardous Waste
- Upstream Minimization and Control
- Resource Recovery
- Water Resources
- Water Reclamation and Wastewater Reuse
- Engineering Design and Specifications
- Process Development
- Corporate Environmental Strategies

Professional Engineers Licensed In:

- State of California
- State of Arizona
- State of Nevada
- State of Oregon
- State of Utah
- State of Colorado
- State of New Mexico
- State of Wisconsin
- State of New York
- Commonwealth of Massachusetts
- Commonwealth of Pennsylvania

*For Further Information, Contact:*
*Robert C. Thomas, P.E.*

---

## EXPERT WITNESS

### CONSTRUCTION

### George Hedley

## Construction Consulting Services

5010 Campus Drive #101
Newport Beach, California 92660
(714) 851-2240
Fax (714) 851-2240

Mr. Hedley, owner & president of a top 10 general contractor in Southern California provides personal and "hands-on" construction consulting services that produce positive litigation results. Mr. Hedley's overall and detailed knowledge of the construction operation from field supervision to cost estimating, contract to completion; and quality control to defect investigation qualifies him as the premier expert in his field. His broad experience enables him to testify in a professional manner; assist his client with case management and strategy; and coordinate, select and work with the right experts required for you case.

**Advisory Board Member**
American Arbitration Association
Construction Complex Cases

**Speaker To**
Associated General Contractors
Associated Builders & Contractors
American Subcontractors Association
American Society of Professional Estimators
National Association of Home Builders

**Past President**
Associated Builders and Contractors
Southern California Builders Association
Orange County Builders Association

**General Contractor on:**
500 major projects
10,000 subcontracts executed
15 million square feet built
Projects valued at over $500 million

| | | |
|---|---|---|
| Commercial | Industrial | Retail |
| Office | Warehouse | Shopping Centers |
| Public Works | Mini-Storage | Tenant Improvements |
| Tilt-Up Concrete | Carpentry | Site Improvements |
| Condominiums | Homes | Apartments |

**Services**

| | | |
|---|---|---|
| Defects | Contracts | Claims |
| Disputes | Field Inspections | Plans & Specifications |
| Standards | Procedures | Scheduling |
| Estimating | Costs | Change Orders |
| Repairs | Injuries | Project Management |
| Safety | Accidents | Field Operations |

# INVESTIGATORS

## GLOBAL INVESTIGATIONS & V.I.P. SECURITY SERVICES

3535 E. Pacific Coast Highway
Suite 356
Newport Beach, California 92625

Phone: (714) 525-3956 * (310) 559-1880

Global Investigations & V.I.P. Security Services is a highly specialized investigative & security firm with over 21 years of experience worldwide. Attorneys, corporations, and V.I.P.'s have utilized & greatly benefited from our coterie of global resources.

### INVESTIGATIVE SERVICES

* THEFT OF PROPRIETARY INFORMATION/CORPORATE ESPIONAGE

* UNSOLVED CRIME INVESTIGATIONS

* FRAUD INVESTIGATIONS

* UNDERCOVER OPERATIONS

* GLOBAL ASSIST SEARCH & RECOVERY - COMPLETE BANK SEARCH - BROKERAGE ACCOUNT SEARCH - WIRE TRANSFER INQUIRY - CREDIT CARD TRANSACTION

* INTERNATIONAL KIDNAPPING

* SKIP-TRACING / MISSING PERSONS

* COMPETITIVE INTELLIGENCE - DOSSIERS

* ELECTRONIC EVIDENCE; DATA SEIZURE, DATA DUPLICATION, DATA RECOVERY, DATA ANALYSIS, MEDIA CONVERSION, EXPERT SERVICES

* SURVEILLANCE

* POLYGRAPH EXAMINATIONS

* ELECTRONIC COUNTERMEASURES, PROVIDES EAVESDROPPING DETECTION FOR TELEPHONE - INDUSTRIAL - RESIDENTIAL - VEHICLE.

### SECURITY SERVICES

* **Security seminars for the 90's.** Topics include: Awareness training & attack survival skills * Carjacking defense exercises * Survival training for rape, kidnapping, street & ATM robberies * Residential burglaries, home invasion, & automobile theft countermeasures * Presence of mind & self defense * Training includes certification in the lawful use of pepper-spray & electronic stun-guns. Group & corporate rate discounts.

* Armed fixed post and escort services, for VIP'S & corporations

Investigative License No. PI 11743 - Security License No. PPO 9827

---

## VENEZIA INVESTIGATIVE SERVICES

3535 East Coast Highway
Newport Beach, California 92625
24 hours: 800-568-9380
Office: 714-833-0505
Fax: 714-833-0511

PROVIDING INVESTIGATIVE SERVICES NATIONWIDE
PROVIDING LOCAL SERVICE TO THE GREATER LOS ANGELES, ORANGE COUNTY AND SOUTHERN CALIFORNIA AREA

Venezia Investigative Services provides to the private sector the same level of service which has historically only been available to government and law enforcement agencies.

### PUT THE PROFESSIONALS TO WORK FOR YOU.

White Collar Crime
Computer Fraud
Insurance Fraud
Asset Searches
Civil Litigation Support
Criminal Litigation Support
Individual Background Profiles

Skip-Tracing
Identification and Location of Missing Persons
Corporation Status Reports
Competitive Intelligence Gathering
Eavesdropping Detection
Surveillance
Wiretap Detection

### COMPANY PROFILE:

Venezia Investigative Service (VIS) provides nationwide investigative service with the objective of furnishing detailed, accurate and timely information while adhering to the highest ethical standard of the industry. VIS specialists routinely consult with law firms, corporations, financial institutions and insurance companies.

### RESOURCES:

Our organization consists of veteran ranking officers from the N.Y.P.D. and Special Agents of the F.B.I. as well as professionals in the business community specializing in the fields of accounting, computer and communications technologies. This alliance of law enforcement and technological expertise offers an unparalleled wealth of fact finding and information gathering sources.

### POLICY:

All information gathered, along with our clients identity, will remain confidential unless we are authorized by our client in writing that such information be released.

### OWNER PROFILE:

Robert Venezia, President, founded VIS after a distinguished twelve year career as a New York City Police Sergeant. As president of the firm, he analyzes, coordinates and directs all investigations.

During Mr. Venezia's career with the N.Y.P.D., he supervised and coordinated the efforts of entire neighborhood units, addressing a wide range of criminal activities. Mr Venezia served as an instructor at the Police Academy and as a trainer for divisions of newly appointed Police Officers.

Based on his efforts, Mr. Venezia was awarded the Medal for Valor, the New York City Police Department's highest award. He has also received numerous citations and commendations for the successful apprehension of armed and dangerous suspects, as well as many life saving rescue efforts. Mr. Venezia is currently an active member of the New York City Police Department's prestigious Honor Legion and the Emerald Society.

California Investigative License No. PI16757

CALIFORNIA—NEWPORT BEACH         MARTINDALE-HUBBELL LAW DIRECTORY 1997

## NEWPORT BEACH (Continued)
### MEDICAL EXPERT WITNESS
#### DEVICES

1830 - 16th Street
R313
Newport Beach CA 92663
Telephone: (714) 722-7679
Facsimile: (714) 722-7679

Are you involved in a Medical Device Failure Case?

Dr. Salman will assist you in determining if the device was manufactured and marketed in compliance with the FDA Regulations, Good Manufacturing Practices (GMP's), and other applicable standards and guidelines.

### N. N. SALMAN, PH.D.

15 years experience in medical devices, FDA Regulations, manufacturing standards, Plaintiff/Defense. Available for Deposition and Trials.

#### CREDENTIALS AND EXPERIENCES

- Ph.D Biomedical Engineering
- FDA Senior Scientist for five years
- Expert Witness on Medical Devices for last eleven years
- Assistant Editor for the Journal of Applied Biomaterials, since 1987
- Published over twenty articles and abstracts on medical devices
- Consultant to medical devices industry, providing regulatory and technical assistance on orthopaedic, dental cardiovascular, neurology, gastroenterology, ophthalmic-urology, general and plastic surgery, general hospital and personal use, and physical medicine devices and instrumentations

#### INVENTIONS

- Self-Guiding Interlocking Fracture Fixation Nail U.S. Patent No. 4,913137, 1990
- Fracture Alignment Device, U.S. Patent No. 5003969, 1991
- Biodegradable Toothbrush, U.S. Patent No. 5213426, 1993

#### PROFESSIONAL SOCIETIES

- Orthopaedic Research Society
- Biomaterials Society
- IEEE Society

#### PARTIAL LIST OF CASES IN WHICH DR. SALMAN RENDERED SERVICES

1. Dorothy Reeves v. Acromed Corp.
   (USDC 91-4689 New Orleans)
2. Larry Weather v. Acromed Corp.
   (USDC 592-0120 BR)
3. Rosci v. Acromed Corp., Philadelphia, PA
4. Nita Reiter v. Zimmer Inco, New York, NY
   (91 Civ. 8599 (LMM))
5. Vaughn v. Acromed Corp., CA
6. George Norman v. Advanced Spine Fixation Inc., SC
7. A number of Breast Implant Cases

(This Listing Continued)

---

N.N. SALMAN, PH.D. (Continued)

8. Klesener v. Cox, etal., NC

A FULL CURRICULUM VITAE IS AVAILABLE UPON REQUEST

### OAKLAND, * 372,242, *Alameda Co.*

#### ATTORNEY SERVICES

### WESTERN ATTORNEY SERVICES
75 Columbia Square
San Francisco, CA 94103-4015
Nationwide 1-800-696-3558

**We Make It Simple**

LEGAL EXPERIENCE
PROMPT TURNAROUND
24 HOUR AVAILABILITY
EXTENDED SERVICE NETWORK
REGISTERED AND CERTIFIED
DOOR-TO-DOOR SERVICE
STAKEOUT

**Western Attorney Services**

SERVICE OF PROCESS
RECORDS RETRIEVAL
DOCUMENT COPY
SKIP TRACE
DECLARATION OF DUE DILIGENCE
DECLARATION OF HAND DELIVERY
PROOF OF SERVICE INCLUDED
SERVICES TAILORED TO YOUR NEEDS

**Summons and Complaint through Writ of Execution**

Highly Trained Staff
24 Hour Service
**Call Western Attorney Services:**
1-800-696-3558
(415) 487-4140
Fax: (415) 864-6238
Email: WestAttny@aol.com
Website: http://members.aol.com/westattny/

Member of California Association of Photocopiers and Process Servers

**WESTERN ATTORNEY SERVICES
SERVICE YOU CAN DEPEND ON**

---

Now it's easy to find lawyers practicing a specific area of law! Simply consult the
**Martindale-Hubbell Law Directory
Areas of Practice Index.**

# SERVICES, SUPPLIERS, CONSULTANTS
## CALIFORNIA—OAKLAND

## COURT REPORTERS

### ABA Reporters
Telephone: 800-434-TEXT
415-391-2999
Fax: 415-391-0753
www.abacomm.com

**"THE EXPERTS IN TECHNICAL REPORTING"** ℠

San Francisco * Marin * Alameda * Solano
Santa Clara * Sonoma * Napa * San Mateo
Contra Costa * Sacramento Counties

- Conference Rooms
- Depositions
- Real Time
- Captioning
- Condensed Transcripts
- Master Word Indexing
- Video - National Certified Legal Video Specialists
- Deposition Summary Services
- Large Staff of Experienced Reporters
- Medical/Expert Witness
- Arbitrations/Hearings
- ASCII/AMICUS/CAT-Links/Discovery ZX/LiveNote
- Document Production

**SERVING ALL OF NORTHERN CALIFORNIA**

Members:
- National Court Reporters Association
- California Court Reporters Association
- Bay Area General Reporters

**ABA REPORTERS**
A Division of
Linda L. Chavez, CSR, Inc.

Telephone: 415-391-2999
Fax: 415-391-0753

115 Sansome Street, Suite 1050
San Francisco, CA 94104

State-Certified Shorthand Reporters

AbA Reporters is widely respected for its expertise in transcribing legal, medical, and other formal proceedings with a court-reporting staff that offers over 100 years of combined professional service. We proudly uphold the highest standards for accuracy and stylistic consistency, and especially appreciate and emphasize the client's need for a dependably punctual product.

AbA is a continuously diversifying company, consistently striving to remain on the cutting edge with the latest technologies to more effectively meet our clients' ever-growing needs. Whether it be the need for flexible and mobile services - - including videographic and open or closed captioning - - or simply the accurate sequential marking of exhibits, AbA Reporters delivers experienced reporting capacities and quality transcripts - - on time, every time.

### ALTRNET
#### Advanced Legal Technology Reporters Network

THE *court reporting network for all of California*

2101 Webster Street, Suite 1500
Oakland, CA 94612-3061

Online  http://www.altr.com
Phone  800.961.1116

When it comes to managing complex litigation or scheduling depos in distant locations, many law firms recognize the advantages of a **single-contact resource for California and national reporting services**. A clear focus on leading-edge technology, the expertise of professionals, as well as a California-wide presence is now at your disposal and local control with the ALTRNET.

*Private, complimentary deposition suites are available in thirteen California offices:*

- ☐ Crescent City
- ☐ Eureka
- ☐ Fresno
- ☐ Los Angeles
- ■ Oakland
- ☐ San Diego
- ☐ San Francisco
- ☐ San Jose
- ☐ San Luis Obispo
- ☐ Santa Barbara
- ☐ Santa Maria
- ☐ Stockton
- ☐ Ventura

*One call* can arrange Certified Shorthand Reporting services in remote locations as well as prompt transmission of transcripts to your local ALTRNET office where they are printed to your specifications and delivered. Transcripts can be converted locally to disk or formatted to the litigation support software program of your choice. Transcripts can be telecommunicated instantly from one city to another, making it possible to review testimony minutes later.

The ALTRNET imparts our unique style of technical know-how for depositions taken across California and *assures continuity of quality and service* from distant locations -- without added travel expenses or surprise charges.

*One call gets it all.*   800 . 961 . 1116.

---

Fast ... Easy ... Flexible...
**The Martindale-Hubbell Law Directory on CD-ROM** gives you instant access through multiple search criteria to information on over 900,000 lawyers and law firms. For more details and a FREE demonstration disc, call **1-800-323-3288**.

CAA171S

# OAKLAND (Continued)
## Court Reporters (Continued)

### BEHMKE REPORTING & VIDEO SERVICES

CERTIFIED SHORTHAND REPORTERS
& LEGAL VIDEO SPECIALISTS
SERVING SAN FRANCISCO
AND THE GREATER BAY AREA

1-800-335-3376

DOWNTOWN SAN FRANCISCO:
353 SACRAMENTO STREET, SUITE 600
SAN FRANCISCO, CALIFORNIA 94111
TELEPHONE: 415-693-0636

NEAR SFO:
1320 ADOBE DRIVE
PACIFICA, CALIFORNIA 94044
TELEPHONE: 415-359-3201

DOWNTOWN SAN MATEO:
177 BOVET ROAD, SUITE 600
SAN MATEO, CALIFORNIA 94402
TELEPHONE: 415-359-3201

DOWNTOWN SAN JOSE:
95 S. MARKET STREET, SUITE 300
SAN JOSE, CALIFORNIA 95133
TELEPHONE: 408-294-5370

DOWNTOWN SACRAMENTO:
400 CAPITOL MALL, 9TH FLOOR
SACRAMENTO, CALIFORNIA 95814
TELEPHONE: 800-335-3376

HTTP://WWW.BEHMKE.COM/BEHMKE/
e-mail: depos@behmke.com
facsimile: 415-359-3293

COMPLIMENTARY CONFERENCE ROOMS
COMPUTERIZED TRANSCRIPTION
ASCII, AMICUS, SUMMATION, WP DISKS
MIN-U-SCRIPT/MASTER WORD INDEX
REAL-TIME SPECIALISTS
LIVENOTE SERVICE PROVIDER
BROADCAST QUALITY VIDEO (IN-HOUSE)
DISCOVERY VIDEO ZX & DISCOVERY ZX
VIDEO/ASCII/TRANSCRIPT COORDINATION
DOCUMENT IMAGING/SCANNING
DOCUMENTS TO CD-ROM
EXPEDITED, DAILY & SAME-DAY COPY
TECHNICAL/MEDICAL/EXPERT
ARBITRATIONS/HEARINGS
PERMANENT ARCHIVING

Licenses

California CSR
New Jersey CSR
Registered Professional Reporters
Certified Real-Time Reporters

(This Listing Continued)

---

### BEHMKE REPORTING & VIDEO SERVICES (Continued)

Members

National Court Reporters Association
California Court Reporters Association
Deposition Reporters Association of California
Certified Shorthand Reporters Association of New Jersey
Bay Area General Reporters Association

*SEE OUR AD ON PAGE CAA173S*

---

THE LEADER IN DISCOVERY TECHNOLOGY

*Certified Deposition Reporters*
*Complex Litigation Specialists*

2101 Webster Street, Suite 1500
Oakland, CA 94612-3061

| | |
|---|---|
| Online | http://www.comgre.com |
| Phone | 800.869.9132 |
|  | 510.273.8877 |
| Fax | 510.273.8535 |

The outcome of your successful depositions is rooted in the fundamental knowledge of our people. Not only will Combs & Greenley professionals take the time to fully understand your firm's particular needs -- we will efficiently manage the many ancillary factors that contribute to achieving your case objectives.

**Combs & Greenley is the technological leader in deposition reporting services in Northern California. We offer a total-service program for litigation support and conveniently arrange depositions across California and the United States.**

Combs & Greenley specializes in state-of-the-art litigation management tools, including:

- Expert RealTime Deposition Reporters
- Certified Legal Video Specialists
- Synchronized Transcript/Video
- Complete Litigation Support
- Legal Videoconferencing
- Free Deposition Suites
- On-line Scheduling

The convenience and security of trained client support specialists and private, *complimentary deposition suites* are available in each of our *four offices:*

- San Francisco
- **Oakland**
- San Jose
- Stockton

SERVICES, SUPPLIERS, CONSULTANTS   CALIFORNIA—OAKLAND

# ALWAYS THE SAME QUALITY & PERSONALIZED SERVICE!

*Certified Shorthand Reporters & Legal Video Specialists*

## 1-800-335-3376

*Serving San Francisco & The Greater Bay Area*

- Conference Rooms
- Computerized Transcription
- ASCII, Amicus, Summation, WP Disks
- Min-U-Script/Master Word Index
- Real-Time Specialists
- Livenote Service Provider
- Broadcast Quality Video (In-House)
- DiscoveryVideo$^{zx}$ & Discovery$^{zx}$
- Video/ASCII/Transcript Coordination
- Document Imaging/Scanning
- Expedited, Daily & Same-Day Copy
- Technical/Medical/Expert
- Arbitrations/Hearings
- Permanent Archiving

## BEHMKE REPORTING & VIDEO SERVICES

HTTP://WWW.BEHMKE.COM/BEHMKE/

**1320 Adobe Drive**
Pacifica, Ca 94044
Telephone • 415.359.3201
Facsimile • 415.359.3293

**353 Sacramento Street • Suite 600**
San Francisco, California 94111
415.693.0636

**400 Capitol Mall • 9th Floor**
Sacramento, California 95814
800.335.3376

**177 Bovet Road • Suite 600**
San Mateo, California 94402
415.359.3201

**95 S. Market Street • Suite 300**
San Jose, California 95133
408.294.5370

CAA173S

# ROTH * KELTY * RHUDY

### CERTIFIED SHORTHAND REPORTERS

### YOUR BAY AREA DEPOSITION CONNECTION

### FULL SERVICE REPORTING AGENCY

*DEPOSITION SUITE AVAILABLE
*TOTALLY COMPUTERIZED
*VIDEOTAPE SERVICES
*LITIGATION SUPPORT

## 1-800-694-5558
## 415-368-1881
## FAX 415-368-7924

**KATHY KELTY**
CSR 5064

**KAREN RHUDY**
CSR 4027

**SERVICES, SUPPLIERS, CONSULTANTS**  **CALIFORNIA—OAKLAND**

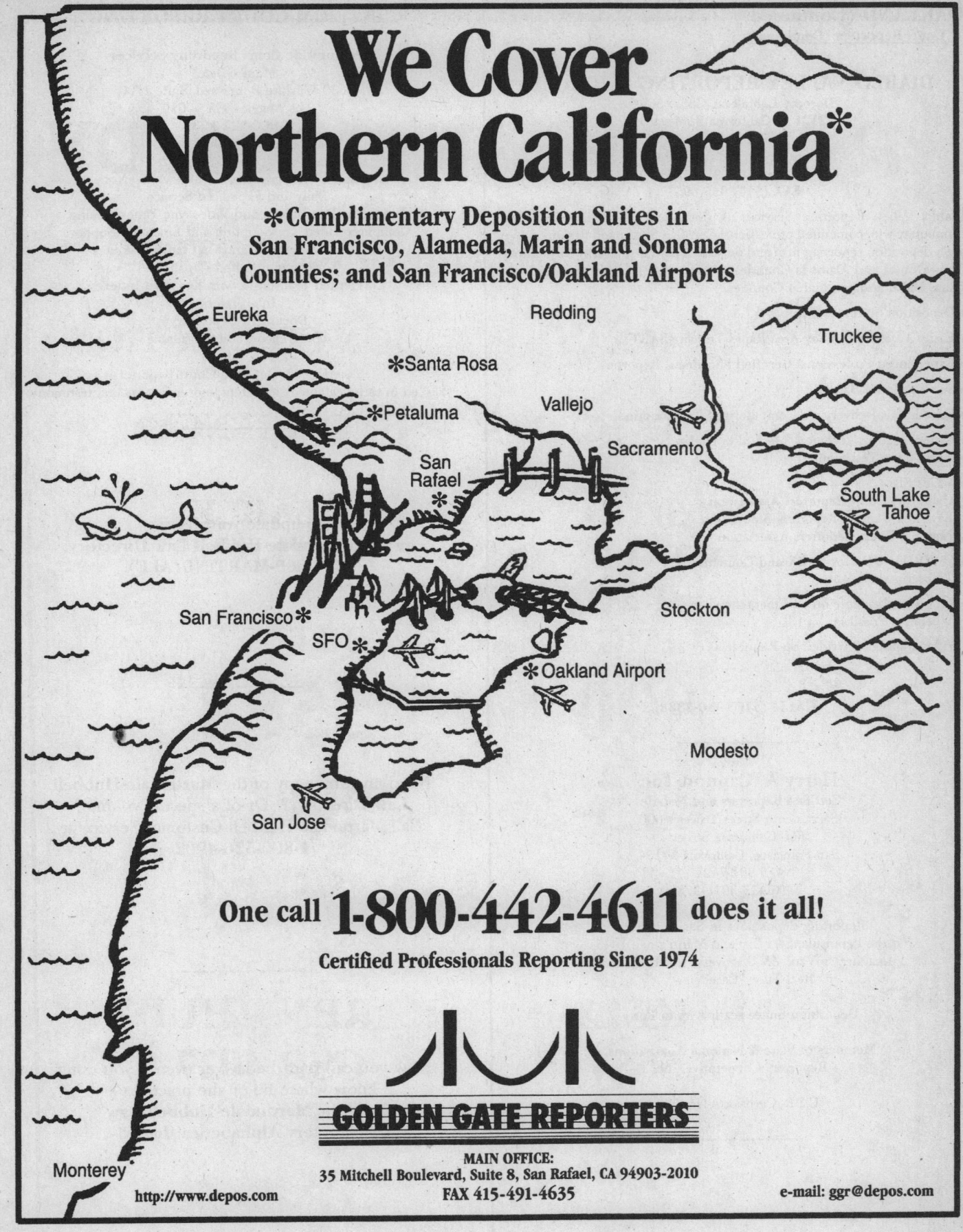

CAA175S

## OAKLAND (Continued)
### Court Reporters (Continued)

## DIABLO VALLEY REPORTING SERVICES

Dorothy L. Malone, CSR #5094
2121 N. California Boulevard
Suite 310
Walnut Creek, California 94596
Phone (510) 930-7388
FAX (510) 935-6957

Diablo Valley Reporting Services is dedicated to serving the legal community with committed professional Certified Shorthand Reporters. We are a deposition reporting firm and our client base is primarily throughout Contra Costa and Alameda Counties. We also cover San Francisco, Santa Clara, Marin and San Mateo Counties.

- Deposition Suites Available
- Easily Accessible to Bay Area Rapid Transit (BART)
- Experienced Professional Certified Shorthand Reporters
- Serving Entire Bay Area
- Expeditious Delivery via Computerized Transcription
- Experienced in Technical, Medical & Highly Specialized Testimony
- MEMBER:
  California Court Reporters Association
  Bay Area General Reporters Association
  National Court Reporters Association
- ASCII Disks, Discovery ZX and Condensed Transcripts Available
- Reporters Available on an Emergency Basis Whenever Possible
- Videographers Provided on Request

CALL: (510) 930-7388

---

### Harry A. Cannon, Inc.
Certified Reporters and Notaries
Sacramento Street Tower #600
550 California Street
San Francisco, California 94104
415-391-7421
FAX: 415-391-4978

Reporting depositions in San Francisco,
the Peninsula, East Bay and Marin since 1945.
Imaging/"inVzn" ZX Discovery, ASCII Diskettes
Real-Time "Case View"

Deposition Suites seating up to Forty

Members of State & National Associations,
Reporters Cooperative, Inc.

C.S.R. Certificate No. 68

---

## INTERIM COURT REPORTING

Nationwide Court Reporting Services
Main Office
3530 Wilshire Boulevard, Suite 1700
Los Angeles, CA 90010
1-800-722-1235
Fax: 213-389-8514

Realtime Transcription, CaseView, LiveNote
Daily and Expedited Service
Videotape Depositions and Videosync Timestamping
Computer Aided Transcription and Litigation Support
ASCII, Discovery ZX and CATLinks Diskettes
Telecommunication Capabilities
Condensed Transcripts with Keyword Indexes
Interpreters
Document Depository
Conference Rooms Available

Experienced, Qualified Court Reporters
Skilled in technical, medical, patent and environmental testimony

---

To update your listing
in the **Martindale-Hubbell Law Directory**
call **1-800-MARTIND(ALE)**.

---

Need an extra copy of the **Martindale-Hubbell Law Directory**? Or of a specific volume?
Call Martindale-Hubbell Customer Service at
**1-800-526-4902**

---

Now you can find the lawyer even if you don't
know where he or she practices -
with the **Martindale-Hubbell Law
Directory Alphabetical Index.**

**SERVICES, SUPPLIERS, CONSULTANTS**

**CALIFORNIA—OAKLAND**

## JACK LONDON COURT REPORTERS
*A COMPLETE & UNIQUE DEPOSITION SERVICE*

HQ OAKLAND CITY CENTER
1300 CLAY STREET, SUITE 600
OAKLAND, CA 94612

**1-800-LAW-DEPO**
1-800-529-3376

FAX 510-763-9004

*Fresh Donuts and Coffee in the Morning!
Lunch is on Us!*

*COMPLIMENTARY JLCR CONFERENCE ROOMS:*

HQ OAKLAND CITY CENTER
1300 CLAY STREET
SUITE 600
OAKLAND, CA 94606
510-464-8000

HQ SAN FRANCISCO DOWNTOWN
44 MONTGOMERY STREET
SUITE 1900
SAN FRANCISCO, CA 94104
415-781-5000

HQ OAKLAND LAKE MERRITT
2101 WEBSTER STREET
SUITE 1500
OAKLAND, CA 94612
510-446-7700

HQ SAN FRANCISCO AIRPORT
1250 BAYHILL DRIVE
SUITE 200
SAN BRUNO, CA 94066
415-794-2600

HQ EMERYVILLE
2000 POWELL STREET
SUITE 1200
EMERYVILLE, CA 94608
510-596-1700

HQ SAN JOSE
2055 GATEWAY PLACE
SUITE 400
SAN JOSE, CA 95110
408-451-3900

HQ NEWARK
39899 BALENTINE DRIVE
SUITE 200
NEWARK, CA 94560
510-683-3970

*CALL 1-800-LAW-DEPO (529-3376)
FOR OTHER HQ BUSINESS
CENTER LOCATIONS*

WATERFRONT PLAZA HOTEL
JACK LONDON SQUARE
TEN WASHINGTON STREET
OAKLAND, CA 94607
510-729-3638

EXECUTIVE INN
EMBARCADERO COVE
1755 EMBARCADERO
OAKLAND, CA 94606
510-536-6633

SHENANIGAN'S
30 JACK LONDON SQUARE
OAKLAND, CA 94607
510-839-8333

MARRIOTT HOTEL
OAKLAND CONVENTION CENTER
OAKLAND, CA 94612
510-839-7505

1200 LAKESHORE, INC.
*OVERLOOKING LAKE MERRITT
ACROSS FROM OAKLAND COURTHOUSE*
1200 LAKESHORE AVENUE
OAKLAND, CA 94606
510-834-1200

PRESERVATION PARK
CONFERENCE CENTER
1233 PRESERVATION PARK WAY
OAKLAND, CA 94612
510-874-7580

ALAMEDA COUNTY LAW LIBRARY
*ACROSS FROM OAKLAND COURTHOUSE*
125 TWELFTH STREET
OAKLAND, CA 94607
510-272-6480
FAX: 510-208-4836

Please call **1-800-LAW-DEPO**, 529-3376 for an information package that includes our pamphlet on the complimentary "LUNCH IS ON US!" old-time tradition in unique deposition conference room settings, our "GETTING REACQUAINTED WITH OAKLAND," Jack London Square, Old Town, and the City Center material, our standard price list in a legal-sized folder with our file name of deposition reporting. **1-800-LAW-DEPO**, 529-3376.

## ROTH * KELTY * RHUDY
702 MARSHALL STREET
SUITE 413
REDWOOD CITY, CALIFORNIA 94063

415-368-1881
FAX 415-368-7924
1-800-694-5558

CERTIFIED SHORTHAND REPORTERS

YOUR BAY AREA DEPOSITION CONNECTION
COURT PROCEEDINGS
REPORTING DEPOSITIONS
ARBITRATIONS
BOARD MEETINGS
HEARINGS
DEPOSITION SUITE AVAILABLE
TOTALLY COMPUTERIZED
VIDEOTAPE SERVICES
LITIGATION SUPPORT
RECORDS SERVICE
REAL-TIME REPORTING
CONDENSED TRANSCRIPTS
KEY WORD/PHRASE INDEXING
DISCOVERY ZX
ASCII
FAX SERVICES

KATHY KELTY, CSR 5064    KAREN RHUDY, CSR 4027

***SEE OUR AD ON PAGE CAA174S***

---

The **Martindale-Hubbell Law Directory** is now available online...exclusively through the LEXIS®-NEXIS® services.

---

Now it's easy to find lawyers practicing a specific area of law! Simply consult the **Martindale-Hubbell Law Directory Areas of Practice Index.**

CALIFORNIA—OAKLAND

MARTINDALE-HUBBELL LAW DIRECTORY 1997

## OAKLAND (Continued)
### Court Reporters (Continued)

# VIGNATI REPORTING
### Certified Shorthand Reporters

*"Serving the Entire Bay Area Since 1978"*

1537 Fourth Street, Suite 215
San Rafael, CA 94901

Phone: 415-456-4640
Fax: 415-456-3107

Services Include:

- Daily/Expedited Copy
- Conference Rooms available
- Process Service
- ASCII Diskettes
- Depositions, Arbitrations, Hearings, Trials
- Computer Aided Transcription
- Discovery ZX
- Video Tape Services
- Teleconferencing Services
- Condensed Transcripts With Keyword Index
- Litigation Support Services
- Realtime Transcription
- Transcription Services Available
- Medical/Technical/Expert
- Environmental and Agricultural

Member of:

National Court Reporters Association
California Court Reporters Association
Bay Area General Reporters Association
Deposition Reporters Association

---

Fast ... Easy ... Flexible...
**The Martindale-Hubbell Law Directory on CD-ROM** gives you instant access through multiple search criteria to information on over 900,000 lawyers and law firms. For more details and a FREE demonstration disc, call **1-800-323-3288**.

## EXPERT WITNESS

### METEOROLOGY/CLIMATOLOGY

# CLIMATOLOGICAL CONSULTING CORPORATION

1216 Babel Lane
Concord, California 94518
(510) 676-2228

Robert N. Swanson, C.C.M.
*Specializing in Forensic Meteorology*

Mr. Robert N. Swanson, C.C.M., represents Climatological Consulting Corporation of Asheville, North Carolina as an Associate in Concord, California.

Mr. Swanson has a B.S. degree in Chemistry and Mathematics from Wisconsin State University (1953), a B.S. equivalent in Meteorology from the University of Washington (1954), an M.S. in Meteorology from the University of Michigan (1958), and participated in post graduate courses at the Universities of Michigan and Utah.

He served as a weather officer in the U.S. Air Force, 1953-57.

He held posts as a Research Meteorologist and a Staff Scientist in New Mexico and Utah, and was Director of Meteorology for Pacific Gas and Electric Company in San Francisco 1984-93.

His specialties include Near Ground Level Turbulence, Atmospheric Hazards and Wind Energy. He is widely published on these topics.

He is President of the National Council of Industrial Meteorologists and is a Fellow in the American Meteorology Society.

He is an experienced Expert Witness in Meteorology and Climatology. As an Associate of Climatological Consulting Corporation, he has available to him the combined specialized expertise of the nationwide team of Associates, all Certified Consulting Meteorologists. (See display ad under Asheville, North Carolina.)

The Associates collectively have varied and special expertise in specific aspects of Meteorology and serve as members of a team to assist each other to provide a broader combined capability to serve clients effectively than is ordinarily available from a single expert.

---

To update your listing
in the **Martindale-Hubbell Law Directory**
call **1-800-MARTIND(ALE)**.

# SERVICES, SUPPLIERS, CONSULTANTS — CALIFORNIA—OAKLAND

## MEDICAL CASE REVIEW & PREPARATION/TRIAL CONSULTING

### SHERYL R. PICCO, RN, BSN
Legal Nurse Consultant
704 Tonstad Place
Pleasant Hill, CA 94523

510 687-5657

My consulting services are a liaison between the legal and health care communities. With medical records review and analysis, I simplify the complicated health care system. Summaries and reports are presented in a readable, chronological form without medical jargon. Relevant issues, discrepancies, and inconsistencies are noted and easy to find.

Law firms, insurance companies, government offices and risk management departments will process cases easier, faster and more cost effectively with my expertise. I have 23 years of nursing experience to offer your firm including 22 years in Emergency, Trauma and Pre-hospital Care.

**SERVICES OFFERED** include:

- Initial screening for merit
- Organization of medical records, including pagination and table of contents
- Medical record summaries in format of choice
- Brief opinion reports
- Comprehensive review and analysis of medical records, including pre-existing conditions
- Identification of deviation and adherence to related Standards of Care
- Literature Searches
- Deposition assistance
- Identification of missing documents
- Expert witness referral
- Expert witness, emergency dept., trauma issues

510-687-5657

---

Need an extra copy of the **Martindale-Hubbell Law Directory**? Or of a specific volume? Call Martindale-Hubbell Customer Service at
**1-800-526-4902**

---

Now you can find the lawyer even if you don't know where he or she practices - with the **Martindale-Hubbell Law Directory Alphabetical Index.**

## PROCESS SERVERS & DOCUMENT DELIVERY SERVICES

## CALIFORNIA LEGAL SUPPORT SERVICES, INC.
## 800-899-2577
FAX: 800-998-2577
NATIONWIDE SERVICE CENTER

OAKLAND OFFICE
449 15th Street
Suite 101
Oakland, CA 94612
Telephone: 510-839-2605
FAX: 510-268-1929

Elaine J. Erdman, Operations

| | |
|---|---|
| LOS ANGELES OFFICE | 213-383-5822 |
| OAKLAND OFFICE | 510-839-2605 |
| SAN FRANCISCO OFFICE | 415-882-2270 |
| SAN JOSE OFFICE | 408-491-9770 |

**CLSS has offices throughout California, each fully bonded and insured. Our staff of experienced professionals are committed to seeing every detail of your assignment completed on time, every time and in a manner that reflects our professionalism...and yours.**

- Professional Registered Bonded and Certified Process Servers
- Skip Tracing/Locate/Investigative Services
- Litigation Search and Status
- Experienced State and Federal Court Service Specialists
- Fax Filing Service - All Courts
- City, County, State and Federal Agency Filings and Research
- Public Records Research and Retrieval
- Litigation Support Service
- Registered Professional Photocopiers
- Subpoena Preparation
- On/Off Site Document Reproduction
- Complete Micrographic and Optical Scan Production Service

Representative clients consist of major law firms, in-house legal departments, financial institutions, insurance carriers and governmental agencies. References furnished upon request.

California Association of Photocopiers and Process Servers
National Association of Professional Process Servers

*Major Credit Cards Accepted*

*Continuous listing in M-H Law Directory Since 1981*

CALIFORNIA—OAKLAND

OAKLAND (Continued)

**VIDEO TRIAL PRESENTATIONS**

*Certified Legal Video Specialists*

2101 Webster Street, Suite 1500
Oakland, CA 94612-3061

| | |
|---|---|
| Online | http://www.vidsol.com |
| Phone | 800.551.3376 |
| Fax | 415.546.6403 |

Video Solutions' certified videographers and our skilled operations support team meet every complex technical objective. We provide a full-service legal video program, including:

- Laserdisc & CD-ROM Instant Access Presentation
- Courtroom Video Presentation
- Videotape Editing
- Videotape Duplication
- Computer-generated Graphics
- Animations
- Video Equipment Rentals
- Video Depositions
- Video Depositions with Timecode Synchronization
- Multi-camera Depositions
- Day-in-the-Life Documentaries
- Site Inspections
- Accident Re-creations
- Video Settlement Brochures
- Photos from Video
- Litigation Training Videos
- Custom Training Videos
- Video Consultation

The convenience and security of trained client support specialists and private, *complimentary deposition suites* are available in each of our *four offices:*

- San Francisco
- ■ Oakland
- San Jose
- Stockton

The **Martindale-Hubbell Law Directory** is now available online...exclusively through the LEXIS®-NEXIS® services.

---

Now it's easy to find lawyers practicing a specific area of law! Simply consult the **Martindale-Hubbell Law Directory Areas of Practice Index.**

---

Fast ... Easy ... Flexible...
**The Martindale-Hubbell Law Directory on CD-ROM** gives you instant access through multiple search criteria to information on over 900,000 lawyers and law firms. For more details and a FREE demonstration disc, call 1-800-323-3288.

---

To update your listing
in the **Martindale-Hubbell Law Directory**
call **1-800-MARTIND(ALE)**.

---

Need an extra copy of the **Martindale-Hubbell Law Directory?** Or of a specific volume?
Call Martindale-Hubbell Customer Service at
**1-800-526-4902**

---

Now you can find the lawyer even if you don't know where he or she practices - with the **Martindale-Hubbell Law Directory Alphabetical Index.**

# California Deposition Reporters

• Complimentary Conference Rooms • Interpreters • Video Operators • Condensed Transcripts & Keyword Index •

*When Every Word Counts...*

## (800) 242-1996

Serving all of Southern California since 1978

| | |
|---|---|
| **CARLSBAD** (619) 233-5533 | **IRVINE** (714) 548-2435 |
| **LOS ANGELES** (213) 387-9630 | **ONTARIO** (909) 888-8992 |
| **PALM SPRINGS** (619) 233-1996 | **RIVERSIDE** (909) 888-8992 |
| **SAN BERNARDINO** (909) 888-8992 | **SAN DIEGO** (619) 233-5533 |

**WOODLAND HILLS** (213) 387-9630

**CORPORATE OFFICE**
Eastland Securities Building
599 South Barranca Avenue
Penthouse
Covina, CA 91723
(818) 915-1996
FAX (818) 915-0197

**COURT REPORTERS & CONFERENCE ROOMS**
Nationwide & Abroad

*Offering deposition services and modern technology for all your court reporting needs.*

## QUALITY!
## SERVICE!
## TIME!

California Deposition Reporters, Inc.

RealTime • Exhibit Imaging • Custodian of Records • ASCII Disks • Discovery ZX • Video Conferencing •

*Side banners:* Day Scheduling • Discovery ZX • Cat-Links • Same Day • Videographers • IBM Disks • WMBE Certified • CAT-Links • Expedited Services • Daily Copy

CaseView • Account Managers • Traveling Attorney Services • Document Storage • Litigation Support Software • Video Operators • Interpreters

CAA181S

CALIFORNIA—ONTARIO                                              MARTINDALE-HUBBELL LAW DIRECTORY 1997

ONTARIO, 133,179, *San Bernardino Co.*

## COURT REPORTERS

**COURT REPORTERS (800) 242-1996**

DON'T WORRY!
WE HAVE YOUR
DEPOSITIONS COVERED
in every County in California.

Ontario Airport Center
337 N. Vineyard Ave.
Fourth Floor
Ontario, CA 91764

Conference Rooms
& Court Reporters
Nationwide & Abroad

1-800-242-1996

*FREE services include:*

★ Complimentary conference rooms in all of our offices
★ Senior Account Executives throughout Southern California servicing your law firm's special needs
★ Airport, shuttle & hotel information provided to traveling attorneys
★ Condensed transcripts with keyword indexing
★ Direct billing of insurance carriers
★ Interpreters and video operators scheduled upon request

*Other services include:*

★ Conference rooms & court reporters nationwide & abroad
★ Two-week turnaround on transcripts
★ ASCII/CAT-LINKS/DISCOVERY ZX
★ Real-Time
★ Professionally bound transcripts with exhibit management
★ Aviation, technical, construction and medical specialists
★ CD imaging & video imaging
★ Video conferencing

ORANGE COUNTY
(714) 548-2435

COVINA
(818) 915-1996

ONTARIO
(909) 391-1579

SAN BERNARDINO
(909) 888-8992

LOS ANGELES
(213) 387-9630

PALM SPRINGS
(619) 323-9908

SAN DIEGO
(619) 233-1996

*SEE OUR AD ON PAGE CAA181S*

PALM SPRINGS, 40,181, *Riverside Co.*

## COURT REPORTERS

# ALL-IN-ONE
### DEPOSITION REPORTING SERVICE OF PALM SPRINGS

*An Affiliate of*
*Yates & Associates*
*Certified Court and Deposition Reporters*

**Court Reporting Services**

*Depositions, Arbitrations & Hearings Specializing in:*
Medical Malpractice ● Personal Injury ● Construction Defect
Aviation Worker's Compensation ● Business Litigation ● Real Time Available

**Complimentary Court Reporting Service**

Conference rooms ● ASCII's and compressed transcripts (with copy order) ● Travel (*to any location*) ● Video and interpreting arrangements ● Assistance with hotel accommodations ● Direct billing to insurance carriers

**Mobile Copy Service**

*High quality document reproduction*
Medical, employment, school, insurance and business records.
On-site microfilming ● X-ray duplication ● Blueprints and oversized drawings ● Preparation and service of records subpoenas

**Document Depository**

Case management ● Paralegal services ● Comfortable viewing facilities
Document preparation — Bates stamping, letter coding, indexing
On-site blueprint copier and microfilming

Main Office
73-255 El Paseo, Suite 15, Palm Desert, CA 92260
(800)669-1866 / (619)341-4431
Fax (800)569-9338 / (619)568-9338
e-mail Alln1depo@aol.com

Members of Depo*Link*, LLC

The **Martindale-Hubbell Law Directory** is now available online...exclusively
through the LEXIS®-NEXIS® services.

# SERVICES, SUPPLIERS, CONSULTANTS

# CALIFORNIA—PALM SPRINGS

*When Every Word Counts...*

**(800) 242-1996**

Offering deposition services and modern technology for all your court reporting needs.

*Corporate Office*
599 S. Barranca Avenue
Penthouse
Covina, CA 91723
(818) 915-1996
FAX (818) 915-0197

---

Now it's easy to find lawyers practicing a specific area of law! Simply consult the **Martindale-Hubbell Law Directory Areas of Practice Index.**

---

Fast ... Easy ... Flexible...
**The Martindale-Hubbell Law Directory on CD-ROM** gives you instant access through multiple search criteria to information on over 900,000 lawyers and law firms. For more details and a FREE demonstration disc, call **1-800-323-3288.**

COURT REPORTERS (800) 242-1996

**DON'T WORRY!
WE HAVE YOUR
DEPOSITIONS COVERED**
in every County in California.

Wells Fargo Bank Building
2601 Tahquitz Canyon
Suite 202
Palm Springs, CA 92262

Conference Rooms
& Court Reporters
Nationwide & Abroad

1-800-242-1996

*FREE services include:*

★ Complimentary conference rooms in all of our offices
★ Senior Account Executives throughout Southern California servicing your law firm's special needs
★ Airport, shuttle & hotel information provided to traveling attorneys
★ Condensed transcripts with keyword indexing
★ Direct billing of insurance carriers
★ Interpreters and video operators scheduled upon request

*Other services include:*

★ Conference rooms & court reporters nationwide & abroad
★ Two-week turnaround on transcripts
★ ASCII/CAT-LINKS/DISCOVERY ZX
★ Real-Time
★ Professionally bound transcripts with exhibit management
★ Aviation, technical, construction and medical specialists
★ CD imaging & video imaging
★ Video conferencing

| | |
|---|---|
| ORANGE COUNTY<br>(714) 548-2435 | COVINA<br>(818) 915-1996 |
| ONTARIO<br>(909) 391-1579 | SAN BERNARDINO<br>(909) 888-8992 |
| LOS ANGELES<br>(213) 387-9630 | PALM SPRINGS<br>(619) 323-9908 |

SAN DIEGO
(619) 233-1996

*SEE OUR AD ON PAGE CAA183S*

CALIFORNIA—PALM SPRINGS MARTINDALE-HUBBELL LAW DIRECTORY 1997

PALM SPRINGS (Continued)
Court Reporters (Continued)

# J. GREENUP & ASSOCIATES
## Certified Shorthand Reporters

PALM SPRINGS/PALM DESERT
ALSO:

INDIO • BLYTHE
ORANGE COUNTY

Telephone: 619-345-5545
FAX: 619-345-2766

DEPOSITION SPECIALISTS
Since 1975

• Medical Malpractice • Technical Material •
• Construction Defect • Antitrust •
• Scientific • Securities & Exchange •
• Deposition Suites •
• Daily & Expedited Delivery •
• Exhibit Imaging •
• Exhibit Repository •
• ASCI •
• Telecommunications •
• Litigation Support •
• Videotaping •

41-750 Adams Street
Palm Desert, CA 92201

619-345-5545

## DOCUMENT MANAGEMENT SERVICES

### All-In-One Deposition Reporting Services
Suite 15
73-255 El Paseo
Palm Desert, CA 92260
Phone: (800) 669-1866
Fax: (800) 569-9338

*See Court Reporters*

To update your listing
in the **Martindale-Hubbell Law Directory**
call 1-800-MARTIND(ALE).

PALO ALTO, 55,900, *Santa Clara Co.*

## ATTORNEY SERVICES

### WESTERN ATTORNEY SERVICES
75 Columbia Square
San Francisco, CA 94103-4015
Nationwide 1-800-696-3558

**We Make It Simple**

LEGAL EXPERIENCE
PROMPT TURNAROUND
24 HOUR AVAILABILITY
EXTENDED SERVICE NETWORK
REGISTERED AND CERTIFIED
DOOR-TO-DOOR SERVICE
STAKEOUT

**Western Attorney Services**

SERVICE OF PROCESS
RECORDS RETRIEVAL
DOCUMENT COPY
SKIP TRACE
DECLARATION OF DUE DILIGENCE
DECLARATION OF HAND DELIVERY
PROOF OF SERVICE INCLUDED
SERVICES TAILORED TO YOUR NEEDS

**Summons and Complaint through Writ of Execution**

Highly Trained Staff
24 Hour Service
**Call Western Attorney Services:**
1-800-696-3558
(415) 487-4140
Fax: (415) 864-6238
Email: WestAttny@aol.com
Website: http://members.aol.com/westattny/

Member of California Association of Photocopiers and Process Servers

**WESTERN ATTORNEY SERVICES
SERVICE YOU CAN DEPEND ON**

Need an extra copy of the **Martindale-Hubbell Law Directory**? Or of a specific volume?
Call Martindale-Hubbell Customer Service at
1-800-526-4902

**SERVICES, SUPPLIERS, CONSULTANTS**　　　　　　　　　　　　　　　　　　　　　　　　　**CALIFORNIA—PALO ALTO**

## COURT REPORTERS

**ALDERSON REPORTING COMPANY, INC.**
Worldwide Court Reporting & Litigation Support

*Our record is undeniable.*

For over 60 years we have been the official reporters to . . .
- U.S. Presidents
- U.S. Supreme Court Justices
- Special Presidential Commissions

Our other major clients include:
- International Trade Agencies
- Business Thinktank Organizations
- Academic Institutions,
- and THE TOUGHEST LITIGATORS AROUND THE WORLD.

Through our strategic alliance with Arthur Anderson, we also serve legal counsel representing many major corporations.

You can count on our accuracy in every detail. With our on-line tracking databases, we can answer any of your questions at any hour of the day.

Some of Alderson's Services which help centralize your litigation with one source:

**Centralized Case Management:**
Centralized tracking and retrieval of transcripts and exhibits taken anywhere in the world, standardized transcript formatting, coordination between parties for document access and retrieval of transcripts, case specific word lists, single source electronic billing.

**CyberReporting:**
Computer connectivity during deposition, telecommunications anywhere at anytime, on-line technical support, standardization of any disk format or media to your specifications, Internet, America OnLine, CompuServe, Counsel Connect.

**Comprehensive Support Services:**
All security clearances, CaseView, VideoZX, Discovery ZX, compressed transcripts, master indexing by phrase or word, video/transcript syncing, document scanning, deposition suites anywhere, interpreters & translators.

We work to exceed your expectations with our services.

We guarantee your satisfaction.

1-800-FOR-DEPO (367-3376)
FAX: 1-800-367-3310
CompuServe: 71064,1256
Internet: Alderson@lmssys.com

1-800-FOR-DEPO

---

## BEHMKE REPORTING & VIDEO SERVICES

CERTIFIED SHORTHAND REPORTERS
& LEGAL VIDEO SPECIALISTS
SERVING SAN FRANCISCO
AND THE GREATER BAY AREA

1-800-335-3376

DOWNTOWN SAN FRANCISCO:
353 SACRAMENTO STREET, SUITE 600
SAN FRANCISCO, CALIFORNIA 94111
TELEPHONE: 415-693-0636

NEAR SFO:
1320 ADOBE DRIVE
PACIFICA, CALIFORNIA 94044
TELEPHONE: 415-359-3201

DOWNTOWN SAN MATEO:
177 BOVET ROAD, SUITE 600
SAN MATEO, CALIFORNIA 94402
TELEPHONE: 415-359-3201

DOWNTOWN SAN JOSE:
95 S. MARKET STREET, SUITE 300
SAN JOSE, CALIFORNIA 95133
TELEPHONE: 408-294-5370

DOWNTOWN SACRAMENTO:
400 CAPITOL MALL, 9TH FLOOR
SACRAMENTO, CALIFORNIA 95814
TELEPHONE: 800-335-3376

HTTP://WWW.BEHMKE.COM/BEHMKE/
e-mail: depos@behmke.com
facsimile: 415-359-3293

COMPLIMENTARY CONFERENCE ROOMS
COMPUTERIZED TRANSCRIPTION
ASCII, AMICUS, SUMMATION, WP DISKS
MIN-U-SCRIPT/MASTER WORD INDEX
REAL-TIME SPECIALISTS
LIVENOTE SERVICE PROVIDER
BROADCAST QUALITY VIDEO (IN-HOUSE)
DISCOVERY VIDEO ZX & DISCOVERY ZX
VIDEO/ASCII/TRANSCRIPT COORDINATION
DOCUMENT IMAGING/SCANNING
DOCUMENTS TO CD-ROM
EXPEDITED, DAILY & SAME-DAY COPY
TECHNICAL/MEDICAL/EXPERT
ARBITRATIONS/HEARINGS
PERMANENT ARCHIVING

Licenses

California CSR
New Jersey CSR
Registered Professional Reporters
Certified Real-Time Reporters

Members

National Court Reporters Association
California Court Reporters Association
Deposition Reporters Association of California
Certified Shorthand Reporters Association of New Jersey
Bay Area General Reporters Association

## PALO ALTO (Continued)
### Court Reporters (Continued)

## BELL & MYERS

CERTIFIED SHORTHAND REPORTER, INC.

| | |
|---|---|
| 1083 LINCOLN AVENUE | 2465 EAST BAYSHORE ROAD |
| SAN JOSE, CA 95125 | SUITE 301 |
| (408) 287-7500 | PALO ALTO, CA 94303 |
| FAX (408) 294-1211 | (415) 328-7500 |

1-800-293-DEPO

A PROFESSIONAL STAFF OF CERTIFIED REPORTERS
IN-HOUSE VIDEOGRAPHER

SERVING THE ENTIRE BAY AREA
ALAMEDA, CONTRA COSTA, FRESNO, MONTEREY, SACRAMENTO,
SAN BENITO, SAN FRANCISCO, SAN MATEO, SANTA CLARA &
SANTA CRUZ COUNTIES

COMPLIMENTARY CONFERENCE ROOMS AVAILABLE
COMPLETE LITIGATION SUPPORT

| | |
|---|---|
| *AMICUS | *ARBITRATIONS/HEARINGS/MEETINGS |
| *ASCII | *AVIATION |
| *CAT LINKS | *BUSINESS LITIGATION |
| *CONDENSED TRANSCRIPTS | *COMPUTER ELECTRONICS |
| *DISCOVERY ZX | *EXPERT TESTIMONY |
| *REALTIME REPORTING | *MEDICAL/TECHNICAL |
| *WORD PERFECT DISKS | *PATENT |
| *EXPEDITED TRANSCRIPTS | *REAL ESTATE |

*WORKERS COMPENSATION

*WRITTEN INTERROGATORIES

CLOSE TO SAN FRANCISCO & SAN JOSE AIRPORTS
WE CONFIRM ALL DEPOSITIONS THE DAY BEFORE
LAST MINUTE SETTINGS WELCOMED

CALL BELL & MYERS
TO PROVIDE THE LITIGATION SERVICES YOU NEED

1-800-293-DEPO

---

## GOLDEN GATE REPORTERS

*CERTIFIED PROFESSIONALS REPORTING SINCE 1974*

COVERING ALL OF NORTHERN CALIFORNIA

1-800-442-4611
All 50 States • Puerto Rico • Canada
FAX: (415) 491-4635
Local No.: (415) 491-4611

Main Office:
35 MITCHELL BOULEVARD, SUITE 8
SAN RAFAEL, CA 94903-2010

*Complimentary Deposition Suites:*
San Francisco, Alameda, Marin and Sonoma Counties;
and San Francisco/Oakland Airports

Principals:
JILL P. PERKINS, CSR NO. 4760
JOLINE C. STONE, CSR NO. 4202
• Depositions/Statements/Hearings
• Medical/Technical Specialists
• Condensed Transcripts • Concordances
• ASCII Disks • CaseView • LiveNote
Video Proceedings • Realtime • Imaging
• Notice Depositions: "Before any Deposition Officer"

Member California Court Reporters Association
National Shorthand Reporters Association
San Rafael Chamber of Commerce

---

### Harry A. Cannon, Inc.
Certified Reporters and Notaries
Sacramento Street Tower #600
550 California Street
San Francisco, California 94104
415-391-7421
FAX: 415-391-4978

Reporting depositions in San Francisco,
the Peninsula, East Bay and Marin since 1945.
Imaging/"inVzn" ZX Discovery, ASCII Diskettes
Real-Time "Case View"

Deposition Suites seating up to Forty

Members of State & National Associations,
Reporters Cooperative, Inc.

C.S.R. Certificate No. 68

---

The **Martindale-Hubbell Law Directory** is now
available online...exclusively
through the LEXIS®-NEXIS® services.

**SERVICES, SUPPLIERS, CONSULTANTS**  **CALIFORNIA—PALO ALTO**

# More than capable. Capable of anything.

Experienced and highly skilled court reporters who show up when you need them and do the job right. That's what you can expect from **Interim® Court Reporting**, the nation's largest, most technologically advanced court reporting firm in the nation.

As an **Interim® Legal Services** company, we are part of the nation's largest network of legal support services. By using us, we can schedule all your court reporting needs whenever and wherever you desire. And, because we're nationwide you can expect the same consistent service here, there and everywhere.

- Centralized Scheduling
- Deposition Suites
- Real-Time Reporting
- Videotaped Deposition Services
- CaseView/LiveNote
- ASCII and Other Electronic Media Formats
- Condensed Transcripts
- Case Management
- Deposition Summarization

**Interim® COURT REPORTING**

| Los Angeles | San Diego | San Francisco |
| --- | --- | --- |
| (800) 685-6600 | (619) 235-2400 | (415) 362-6666 |

CAA187S

## PALO ALTO (Continued)
Court Reporters (Continued)

### INTERIM COURT REPORTING

Nationwide Court Reporting Services
Main Office
3530 Wilshire Boulevard, Suite 1700
Los Angeles, CA 90010
1-800-722-1235
Fax: 213-389-8514

Realtime Transcription, CaseView, LiveNote
Daily and Expedited Service
Videotape Depositions and Videosync Timestamping
Computer Aided Transcription and Litigation Support
ASCII, Discovery ZX and CATLinks Diskettes
Telecommunication Capabilities
Condensed Transcripts with Keyword Indexes
Interpreters
Document Depository
Conference Rooms Available

Experienced, Qualified Court Reporters
Skilled in technical, medical, patent and environmental testimony

*SEE OUR AD ON PAGE CAA187S*

---

### OBUJEN & McCUTCHEON
Certified Shorthand Reporters

2555 Park Boulevard
Palo Alto, California 94306

Telephone: (415) 326-9920
Fax: (415) 326-6211

DEPOSITIONS

Computer Transcripts
Litigation Support
Experienced Reporters in
Medical and Technical Testimony
Deposition Suites

Serving Santa Clara County
(In the Heart of Silicon Valley),
San Mateo County and San
Francisco County since 1958

Member
National Court Reporters Assn.
California Court Reporters Assn.

---

Now it's easy to find lawyers practicing a specific area of law! Simply consult the
**Martindale-Hubbell Law Directory
Areas of Practice Index.**

---

### ROTH * KELTY * RHUDY
702 MARSHALL STREET
SUITE 413
REDWOOD CITY, CALIFORNIA 94063

415-368-1881
FAX 415-368-7924
1-800-694-5558

CERTIFIED SHORTHAND REPORTERS

YOUR BAY AREA DEPOSITION CONNECTION
COURT PROCEEDINGS
REPORTING DEPOSITIONS
ARBITRATIONS
BOARD MEETINGS
HEARINGS
DEPOSITION SUITE AVAILABLE
TOTALLY COMPUTERIZED
VIDEOTAPE SERVICES
LITIGATION SUPPORT
RECORDS SERVICE
REAL-TIME REPORTING
CONDENSED TRANSCRIPTS
KEY WORD/PHRASE INDEXING
DISCOVERY ZX
ASCII
FAX SERVICES

KATHY KELTY, CSR 5064    KAREN RHUDY, CSR 4027

---

Fast ... Easy ... Flexible...
**The Martindale-Hubbell Law Directory on CD-ROM** gives you instant access through multiple search criteria to information on over 900,000 lawyers and law firms. For more details and a FREE demonstration disc, call **1-800-323-3288**.

---

To update your listing
in the **Martindale-Hubbell Law Directory**
call **1-800-MARTIND(ALE)**.

## SERVICES, SUPPLIERS, CONSULTANTS

### SAN JOSE DEPOSITION REPORTERS, INC.
CALL TOLL FREE 1-800-827-DEPO

Kathrine A. Giocondi, CSR, CP, CM
CSR #2104
3002 Calle de Las Flores
San Jose, California 95148
Telephone: 408-270-7985
FAX: 408-270-5291

*Quality, Excellence, Experience, and Perfection - San Jose Deposition Reporters represents a comprehensive, state of the art, court reporting service specializing in daily copy, technical and medical terminology, dedicated to providing professional support and solutions.*

- We provide Realtime Instant transcript conference room facilities
- We provide PC diskettes of testimony same day
- We provide a key word retrieval system for clients
- Free Deposition Summary via Case View
- Color Video Depositions
- We are able to provide INSTANT TRANSCRIPT with Real-Time
- We provide Discovery ZX
- We provide multiple computer systems (Premier Power and Stenocat)
- We service Santa Clara, Santa Cruz, San Mateo, Alameda and San Francisco Counties
- We provide compressed transcript & word list
- We provide color legal videotape depositions
- We have conference rooms available
- We have exhibit reproduction facilities on premises
- We are minutes away from San Jose Airport

*Member:*
- National Shorthand Reporters Association
- California Shorthand Reporters Association
- Northern California Chamber of Commerce
- Certified in California and Washington
- Baron Users Group

- ASCII Disks
- AMICUS
- Hearings
- Arbitrations
- Medical
- Technical
- Daily Copy
- Copier on Premises
- Litigation Support
- Overnite/Expedite

*Over 20 Years of Experience and Reliability in Santa Clara County*

SAN JOSE DEPOSITION REPORTERS, INC.
CALL TOLL FREE 1-800-827-DEPO

---

Need an extra copy of the **Martindale-Hubbell Law Directory?** Or of a specific volume?
Call Martindale-Hubbell Customer Service at
**1-800-526-4902**

---

## CALIFORNIA—PASADENA

PASADENA, 131,591, *Los Angeles Co.*

### COURT REPORTERS

### ALBRIGHT & ASSOCIATES
CERTIFIED SHORTHAND REPORTERS

3579 East Foothill Boulevard
Pasadena, California 91107-3119

Phone: 818-355-6123
Fax: 818-355-5528

74217.1344@compuserve.com

Vicki Albright-Howard, CSR, RMR
*President*

\*\*\*

*SERVING ALL OF SOUTHERN CALIFORNIA
WITH QUALIFIED, PROFESSIONAL REPORTERS*

Depositions * Arbitrations * Hearings
General * Medical * Technical

\*\*\*

Conference Rooms Available

Travel/Hotel Information

RealTime Reporting to Better Serve You

Complimentary ASCII, Mini Transcript and Keyword Indexing

Large-Print Transcripts Available

Interpreters, Videographers and Other Special Needs Scheduled Upon Request

Fast Turnaround Time on Transcripts

All Your Deposition Needs Scheduled at No Additional Charge

---

Now you can find the lawyer even if you don't know where he or she practices -
with the **Martindale-Hubbell Law Directory Alphabetical Index.**

## PASADENA (Continued)
Court Reporters (Continued)

**COURT REPORTERS (800) 242-1996**

**DON'T WORRY!
WE HAVE YOUR
DEPOSITIONS COVERED
in every County in California.**

**Conference Rooms
& Court Reporters
Nationwide & Abroad**

**1-800-242-1996**

*FREE services include:*

★ Complimentary conference rooms in all of our offices
★ Senior Account Executives throughout Southern California servicing your law firm's special needs
★ Airport, shuttle & hotel information provided to traveling attorneys
★ Condensed transcripts with keyword indexing
★ Direct billing of insurance carriers
★ Interpreters and video operators scheduled upon request

*Other services include:*

★ Conference rooms & court reporters nationwide & abroad
★ Two-week turnaround on transcripts
★ ASCII/CAT-LINKS/DISCOVERY ZX
★ Real-Time
★ Professionally bound transcripts with exhibit management
★ Aviation, technical, construction and medical specialists
★ CD imaging & video imaging
★ Video conferencing

ORANGE COUNTY
(714) 548-2435

COVINA
(818) 915-1996

ONTARIO
(909) 391-1579

SAN BERNARDINO
(909) 888-8992

LOS ANGELES
(213) 387-9630

PALM SPRINGS
(619) 323-9908

SAN DIEGO
(619) 233-1996

---

## INTERIM COURT REPORTING

Nationwide Court Reporting Services
Main Office
3530 Wilshire Boulevard, Suite 1700
Los Angeles, CA 90010
1-800-722-1235
Fax: 213-389-8514

Realtime Transcription, CaseView, LiveNote
Daily and Expedited Service
Videotape Depositions and Videosync Timestamping
Computer Aided Transcription and Litigation Support
ASCII, Discovery ZX and CATLinks Diskettes
Telecommunication Capabilities
Condensed Transcripts with Keyword Indexes
Interpreters
Document Depository
Conference Rooms Available

Experienced, Qualified Court Reporters
Skilled in technical, medical, patent and environmental testimony

---

The **Martindale-Hubbell Law Directory** is now
available online...exclusively
through the LEXIS®-NEXIS® services.

---

Now it's easy to find lawyers practicing a specific
area of law! Simply consult the
**Martindale-Hubbell Law Directory
Areas of Practice Index.**

---

Fast ... Easy ... Flexible...
**The Martindale-Hubbell Law Directory on
CD-ROM** gives you instant access through
multiple search criteria to information on over
900,000 lawyers and law firms. For more details and a
FREE demonstration disc, call **1-800-323-3288**.

SERVICES, SUPPLIERS, CONSULTANTS — CALIFORNIA–PASADENA

# EXPERT WITNESS

## CONSTRUCTION

### ForensisGroup

Contact: Mercy Steenwyk, Director
711 E. Walnut Street, Ste. 409
Pasadena, CA 91101
TEL: (800) 555-5422  (818) 795-5000
FAX: (818) 795-1950
EMAIL: forensis@earthlink.net
WEBSITE: http://www.lawinfo.com/biz/forensisgroup

**Degrees/Licenses:** Various credentials and licenses in major disciplines of engineering, architecture, construction, safety, environmental, appraisal: PE, SE, PhD, Dsc, REA, CIH, GC, CSP, ASA.

**Specialties:**
Full spectrum of Consulting & Expert Testimony Services in:

- Engineering (all disciplines)
  civil, structural, mechanical, geotechnical, electrical, safety, chemical, fire protection, metallurgical, petroleum, traffic

- Construction & Architecture
  defects, liabilities, cost estimates, earthquake damage assessment, building code compliance, subsidence, design, landscaping, interior design, industry standard, others
- Product Liability
- Accident Reconstruction
- Safety
- Real Estate
- Appraisal
- Environmental
- Automotive & Traffic
- Fires & Explosions
- Slip, Trip & Fall
- Economics

- Other Technical & Scientific Disciplines

A highly credentialed multidisciplined group. Excellent track record. Experts average 35 years of professional experience.

## EMPLOYEE/EMPLOYMENT

### Specializing in: Discrimination

### G. GOVINE STEELE CONSULTING

Expertise in Employment Discrimination
260 N. Mar Vista
Suite No. 2
Pasadena, CA 91106
Phone: (818) 564-0502
FAX: (818) 564-8702
Additional phone: (800) 564-0501

**SPECIALTIES**

Gender discrimination and sexual harassment; race discrimination; age discrimination; wrongful termination; research and evaluation of

(This Listing Continued)

### G. GOVINE STEELE CONSULTING (Continued)

policies/practices/procedures/forms/handbooks/systems; communications; training and research analysis; school desegregation and deposition preparation.

**FORMAL EDUCATION AND CREDENTIALS**

Ed.D. and M.A. from Columbia University in Higher and Adult Education Administration and Research; M.A. and B.S. from New York University in Business Education; State of California Lifetime Community College Teaching Credential.

**PARTIAL CLIENT LIST**

Walt Disney Imagineering; California State University, Los Angeles; Hollywood Records; City of Pasadena; Flagstar Foods (Denny's Restaurants); Walt Disney Pictures and Television; Luce, Forward, Hamilton & Scripps; Littler, Mendelson, Fastiff, Tichy and Mathiason; San Diego County Prosecutors Office; Prindle, Decker & Amaro.

**HONORS/AWARDS**

Board member, California Women's Law Center, Women at Work and African-American Cultural Institute. Pasadena Commission on the Status of Women, award, Outstanding Contributions to Women; Pasadena City College and the California Humanities Project, award - Women of the Year; Business and Professional Woman, award - Outstanding Businesswoman of the Year; Graduate, Leadership California Program. Interviews include: Tom Brokaw's Nightly News on NBC as expert on race relations in the City of Pasadena; Los Angeles Times as expert on gender and race relations. Talk show host and producer, EBONY '96, live, weekly, one-hour call-in on National Public Radio, KPCC, 89.3, focusing on issues of particular interest to the African-American Community, for example, workplace and community diversity.

**PUBLICATIONS**

Over 200 articles as columnist for The Pasadena Journal and contributing writer for Business Life Magazine. Topics include workplace issues, for example, cultural diversity, sexual harassment, sexual discrimination, race discrimination and race relations.

**EXPERIENCE**

Broad experience as a litigation consultant and expert witness on behalf of both plaintiff and defendant, Superior and Federal courts. Conduct research and training for private and public sector employers in workplace diversity issues: gender, race, age; human resource policies and practices and communications.

---

To update your listing
in the **Martindale-Hubbell Law Directory**
call 1-800-MARTIND(ALE).

## PASADENA (Continued)
### LIFE CARE PLANNING

**LINC CASE MANAGEMENT AND MEDICAL/LEGAL CONSULTING SERVICES**

424 NORTH LAKE AVE.
SUITE 200
PASADENA, CA 91101
PHONE: (818) 585-4100
FAX: (818) 585-4115

*LINC CASE MANAGEMENT AND MEDICAL/LEGAL CONSULTING SERVICES OFFERS A COMPLETE, COST EFFECTIVE MEANS OF ASSISTING THE ATTORNEY WITH MEDICAL LITIGATION CASES.*

WE SPECIALIZE IN:

- Medical Record Review
- Medical Record Summarization (i.e. chronology)
- Case Merit Review and Analysis
- Appropriate Expert Identification and Retention
- Disability Evaluation
- Life Care Plan Construction
- "Day in the Life" Video Documentation
- Expert Witness Testimony

OUR DIAGNOSTIC SPECIALTIES FOR ADULT/PEDIATRIC CATEGORIES INCLUDE:

- Amputations
- Brain Injury
- Burns
- Chronic Pain Syndrome
- Immunology Syndrome
- Orthopedic Injuries
- Toxic Exposure
- Spinal Cord Injury
- Vascular Syndromes

JAN ROUGHAN, PRINCIPLE
BSN, PHN, RN, CRRN, CDDN, CDMS, CCM
LIFE CARE PLANNING SPECIALIST

---

Need an extra copy of the **Martindale-Hubbell Law Directory?** Or of a specific volume? Call Martindale-Hubbell Customer Service at
**1-800-526-4902**

---

Now you can find the lawyer even if you don't know where he or she practices - with the **Martindale-Hubbell Law Directory Alphabetical Index.**

---

## MEDICAL CASE REVIEW & PREPARATION/TRIAL CONSULTING

*Professional Medical Review*
*Legal Nurse Consulting*
*Customized Medical Management*

2275 Huntington Drive
Number 910
San Marino, CA 91108

Telephone: (818) 585-1808
Fax: (818) 585-9070

GSG Associates, Inc., nurse owned and operated, is highly qualified to provide Workers' Compensation Legal Nurse Consulting. Our services include but are not limited to the following:

**Identifying:**

- Strengths and weaknesses in both applicant and defense medicals
- Work restrictions not appropriate or consistent with injury
- Apportionment issues
- Defense against PD rating
- Correlation of subjective/objective findings with the diagnosis
- Pre-existing injuries or illnesses
- Inconsistencies between and within doctor's reports
- Medical evidence that contradicts statements made to AMEs and others
- Medically defensible issues

**Liens:** Hospital or provider bills;

- Tests, procedures and meds inappropriate or unrelated to the industrial injury
- Excessive, unnecessary, unreasonable or unjustified treatments
- Double billings
- Attend trial as expert witness on lien issues

**Our Registered Nurses also:**

- Review Sub-Rosa films from a medical perspective and write medical questions to be addressed to the evaluating doctor regarding our findings
- Conduct and integrate medical literature research and include citations into our case reports
- Draft "ghost" letters to QMEs, treating doctors or others guiding their focus on the medical issues at hand in the case, as opposed to sending generic letters receiving generic responses
- Formulate medical deposition questions for deposing of doctors and claimants
- Confer with physicians in specialized fields when appropriate

We also offer medical management services for workers' compensation.

## Linc Case Management and Medical/Legal Consulting Services
Suite 200
424 North Lake Ave.
Pasadena, CA 91101
Phone: (818) 585-4100
Fax: (818) 585-4115

*See Life Care Planning*

## RANCHO SANTA MARGARITA, 11,390, *Orange*

### ADMIRALTY & MARITIME EXPERT & CONSULTANT

**MAREX**
Marine Expertise

Captain Mitchell Stoller

30021 Tomas Street, Suite 300
Rancho Santa Margarita, CA 92688

Phone: (714) 858-5475, (714) 459-2125
Fax: (714) 858-5336
E Mail: MarexCo@aol.com

*BECAUSE YOUR EXPERT HAS TO BE BETTER*

Captain Mitchell Stoller has extensive deep sea experience and a safety record so remarkable that oil companies and coastal states alike have sought him out for his safety knowledge, particularly in the wake of the Exxon Valdez disaster. Having mastered the most difficult aspects of shiphandling and vessel operations, Captain Stoller has been qualified in both state and federal court cases on topics ranging from jet skis to supertankers in both international and inland waterways.

**QUALIFICATIONS:**

**EXPERIENCE:**

| | |
|---|---|
| 1992 to present: | Expert witness, marine consultant |
| 1988 to 1992: | Los Angeles Harbor Pilot (Piloted vessels of any size, any gross tons) |
| 1984 to 1988: | Sailed as Master (Vessels of any size, any gross tons, any ocean) |
| 1979 to 1984: | Chief Mate |
| 1977 to 1979: | Second Mate |
| 1975 to 1977: | Third Mate |

**EDUCATION:**

| | |
|---|---|
| 1983-1985 | Completed advanced casework in ship handling, Marine firefighting, Inert gas, Crude oil washing, and Offshore storage treatment vessels. |
| 1975 | California Maritime Academy, Vallejo, California Valedictorian, Best Conduct Award, Seamanship Award |

*(This Listing Continued)*

---

**MAREX (Continued)**
**CONSULTANT TO:**

ARCO Marine Co.; Baker & Hostetler; Cappiello, Hofmann, & Katz, P.C.; Dewey Ballantine; Lindsey, Hart, Neil, & Weigler, LLP.; McCutchen, Doyle, Brown, & Enerson; Pillsbury, Madison & Sutro; Preston, Thorgrimson, Shidler, Gates & Ellis; Rutter & Montagna; Schneider, Kleinick, Weitz, Damashek & Shoot; Williams, Wooley, Cogswell, Nakazawa & Russell; West Coast Shipping Company

**AFFILIATIONS:**

Navigation Safety Advisory Counsel, Appointed by Secretary of the U.S. Department of Transportation in 1994
Council of American Master Mariners

### EXPERT WITNESS

#### ADMIRALTY

**Marex**
Suite 300
30021 Tomas St.
Rancho Santa Margarita, CA 92688
Phone: (714) 858-5475
Fax: (714) 858-5336

*See Admiralty & Maritime Expert & Consultant*

---

The **Martindale-Hubbell Law Directory** is now available online...exclusively through the LEXIS®-NEXIS® services.

---

Now it's easy to find lawyers practicing a specific area of law! Simply consult the **Martindale-Hubbell Law Directory Areas of Practice Index.**

## RANCHO SANTA MARGARITA (Continued)
### Expert Witness (Continued)

### MARINE

**MAREX**
Marine Expertise

Captain Mitchell Stoller

30021 Tomas Street, Suite 300
Rancho Santa Margarita, CA 92688

Phone:  (714) 858-5475, (714) 459-2125
Fax:  (714) 858-5336
E Mail:  MarexCo@aol.com

*BECAUSE YOUR EXPERT HAS TO BE BETTER*

Captain Mitchell Stoller has extensive deep sea experience and a safety record so remarkable that oil companies and coastal states alike have sought him out for his safety knowledge, particularly in the wake of the Exxon Valdez disaster. Having mastered the most difficult aspects of shiphandling and vessel operations, Captain Stoller has been qualified in both state and federal court cases on topics ranging from jet skis to supertankers in both international and inland waterways.

**QUALIFICATIONS:**

**EXPERIENCE:**

| | |
|---|---|
| 1992 to present: | Expert witness, marine consultant |
| 1988 to 1992: | Los Angeles Harbor Pilot (Piloted vessels of any size, any gross tons) |
| 1984 to 1988: | Sailed as Master (Vessels of any size, any gross tons, any ocean) |
| 1979 to 1984: | Chief Mate |
| 1977 to 1979: | Second Mate |
| 1975 to 1977: | Third Mate |

**EDUCATION:**

| | |
|---|---|
| 1983-1985 | Completed advanced casework in ship handling, Marine firefighting, Inert gas, Crude oil washing, and Offshore storage treatment vessels. |
| 1975 | California Maritime Academy, Vallejo, California Valedictorian, Best Conduct Award, Seamanship Award |

**CONSULTANT TO:**

ARCO Marine Co.; Baker & Hostetler; Cappiello, Hofmann, & Katz, P.C.; Dewey Ballantine; Lindsey, Hart, Neil, & Weigler, LLP.; McCutchen, Doyle, Brown, & Enerson; Pillsbury, Madison & Sutro; Preston, Thorgrimson, Shidler, Gates & Ellis; Rutter & Montagna; Schneider, Kleinick, Weitz, Damashek & Shoot; Williams, Wooley, Cogswell, Nakazawa & Russell; West Coast Shipping Company

(This Listing Continued)

---

MAREX (Continued)
AFFILIATIONS:

Navigation Safety Advisory Counsel, Appointed by Secretary of the U.S. Department of Transportation in 1994
Council of American Master Mariners

### MARINE CONSULTANTS

**Marex**
Suite 300
30021 Tomas St.
Rancho Santa Margarita, CA 92688
Phone: (714) 858-5475
Fax: (714) 858-5336

*See Expert Witness - Marine*

### RED BLUFF, * 12,363, *Tehama Co.*

### COURT REPORTERS

**RED BLUFF REPORTERS**
Certified Shorthand Reporters
P.O. Box 1327
633 Washington Street, Room 22
Red Bluff, California 96080
916-527-8012

\# Computer-aided transcription
\# ASCII Disks
\# Realtime Reporting
\# Daily copy available
\# Conference Rooms
\# Compressed/condensed transcripts
\# Word indexes included with every transcript

Depositions - Statements
Arbitrations

Member
National Court Reporters Association
California Court Reporters Association
North State Court Reporters Association

---

Fast ... Easy ... Flexible...
**The Martindale-Hubbell Law Directory on CD-ROM** gives you instant access through multiple search criteria to information on over 900,000 lawyers and law firms. For more details and a FREE demonstration disc, call **1-800-323-3288**.

# SERVICES, SUPPLIERS, CONSULTANTS

# CALIFORNIA—REDWOOD CITY

**REDDING, * 66,462, Shasta Co.**

## COURT REPORTERS

### J.V. KILLINGSWORTH & ASSOCIATES
**Certified Shorthand Reporters**

1422 Oregon Street
Redding, California 96001
800-994-0447 or 916-241-2224
FAX: 916-241-5992

A full staff of Certified Shorthand
Reporters serving Northern California

- Complimentary deposition suites
- All in-town transportation provided
- Conveniently located by Courthouse, ample free parking
- Certified Reporters on standby and will travel
- Complimentary ASCII disks and Word Indexing
- Full litigation support formats
- Condensed transcripts available
- Daily, expedited and Realtime services available
- Professional color videotaping
- Teleconferencing capability
- Prompt Delivery Guaranteed

DepoNet® The reliable source for Quality-Assured
legal support services worldwide.

---

To update your listing
in the **Martindale-Hubbell Law Directory**
call 1-800-MARTIND(ALE).

---

Need an extra copy of the **Martindale-Hubbell Law Directory**? Or of a specific volume?
Call Martindale-Hubbell Customer Service at
1-800-526-4902

**REDWOOD CITY, * 66,072, San Mateo Co.**

## COURT REPORTERS

### ROTH * KELTY * RHUDY
702 MARSHALL STREET
SUITE 413
REDWOOD CITY, CALIFORNIA 94063

415-368-1881
FAX 415-368-7924
1-800-694-5558

CERTIFIED SHORTHAND REPORTERS

YOUR BAY AREA DEPOSITION CONNECTION
COURT PROCEEDINGS
REPORTING DEPOSITIONS
ARBITRATIONS
BOARD MEETINGS
HEARINGS
DEPOSITION SUITE AVAILABLE
TOTALLY COMPUTERIZED
VIDEOTAPE SERVICES
LITIGATION SUPPORT
RECORDS SERVICE
REAL-TIME REPORTING
CONDENSED TRANSCRIPTS
KEY WORD/PHRASE INDEXING
DISCOVERY ZX
ASCII
FAX SERVICES

KATHY KELTY, CSR 5064   KAREN RHUDY, CSR 4027

---

Now you can find the lawyer even if you don't
know where he or she practices -
with the **Martindale-Hubbell Law
Directory Alphabetical Index.**

# RICHMOND, 87,425, *Contra Costa Co.*

## EXPERT WITNESS

### CONSTRUCTION

## INTERACTIVE RESOURCES

Architects and Engineers
117 Park Place
Richmond, CA 94801
Telephone: 510/236-7435
Facsimile: 510/232-5325
email: tkb@intres.com

Thomas K. Butt, FAIA
John E. Clinton, SE AIA
Sharon M. Waterman, AIA

Full-service architecture and engineering firm with mainstream practice

- 15 years of litigation consulting experience
- Licensed architects, engineers, and contractors
- Nation-wide practice
- Members of AIA, NCARB, ASTM, AAA, ICBO, RCI, CSI, ACI, ASCE, ACFE, etc.
- Plaintiff and defense expert experience
- Experience with largest construction litigation cases in California history
- Lead expert for consultant teams in complex cases
- Graphic capabilities for trial exhibits
- Architect and engineer negligence evaluation
- All building systems and components
- Foundations and structural systems
- Roofing, waterproofing and moisture problems
- Walls, windows and doors

# RIVERSIDE, * 226,505, *Riverside Co.*

## CONFERENCING

### networkMCI Conferencing℠

**Fast. Convenient. Flexible.**

**General Description:**

networkMCI® is a complete portfolio of communications and information services solutions that gives you the competitive advantage in today's rapidly changing business environment.

Competing successfully in today's business requires you to work smarter. One way to do this is by improving how your firm communicates. If you can exchange information faster and more effectively with clients and colleagues, your company will be more productive, more responsive and ultimately, more profitable.

At the heart of networkMCI Conferencing is our global operations centers located in North America, Europe and Asia-Pacific. It allows you to communicate with anyone, almost anywhere in the world. We provide four core services: Audioconferencing, Document Conferencing, Videoconferencing and Tele-Management Services.

*(This Listing Continued)*

---

**NETWORKMCI CONFERENCING** (Continued)

**Audioconferencing Services:**

Audioconferencing gives you the flexibility to hold meetings any time you need to, no matter where you are. With audioconferencing we can:

- Record and transcribe your call
- Conduct a survey during your conference in which participants respond using their telephone keypads
- Provide language interpretation
- Fax information to all conference participants before your call

**Document Conferencing Services:**

With Document Conferencing, you and remote clients or colleagues can review documents using your personal computers. Document Conferencing allows you to:

- Edit and review documents with distant colleagues right from your PC
- Communicate with the aid of clear, full-color visuals
- Share almost any document in your PC
- Work in real time

**Videoconferencing Services:**

Videoconferencing enables you to bring a group of people together for a face-to-face meeting. You can quickly hold an impromptu meeting with others in different offices and save thousands of dollars on travel costs. Videoconferencing lets you:

- Meet face-to-face right from your office
- Speed decision-making and company responsiveness
- Save time and travel costs

**Tele-Management Services:**

Tele-Management Services are convenient and flexible electronic management tools that can help you better coordinate your upcoming conferences as well as your daily business operations. With Tele-Management you can:

- Plan conferences and other events in a variety of ways
- You can simultaneously distribute announcements or invitations to unlimited destinations in minutes
- Provide automated response tracking to better forecast attendance for events
- Tape and broadcast the event for those who could not attend

HOW DO YOU MAINTAIN YOUR COMPETITIVE EDGE IN TODAY'S BUSINESS ENVIRONMENT? NETWORKMCI, THAT'S HOW.

networkMCI Conferencing
1-800-475-5000

8750 W. Bryn Mawr, #900
Chicago, IL 60631

# IMHOF & ASSOCIATES

Certified Court Reporters & Videographers

7720 Painter Avenue, Suite A • Whittier, CA 90602
19732 Larkridge Drive • Yorbe Linda, CA 92886

- Guaranteed 10-Day Turnaround
- Daily or Expedited Transcripts
- Computerized Transcription
- Realtime Court Reporting — CaseView & LiveNote
- Condensed Transcripts and ASCII Disks Free of Charge
- Keyword Indexing • Interpreters Available
- In-House Videographers
- Conference Rooms • Transcripts Archived

## 1-800-939-DEPO(3376)
(310) 907-4455 • (714) 693-1213
FAX: (310) 907-4453